P9-DBR-907

# Who'sWho in America®

REFERENCE BOOK
Use in Reference
Dept. Only

REFERENCE BOOK
Use in Reference
Dept. Only

# Who'sWho in America®

## 2007

# 61st Edition
# Volume 2 ✦ M-Z

## Geographic Index ✦ Professional Index

890 Mountain Avenue, Suite 4
New Providence, NJ 07974 U.S.A.
www.marquiswhoswho.com

# Who's Who in America®
## Marquis Who's Who®

| | | | |
|---|---|---|---|
| Chief Executive Officer | Gene M. McGovern | President | James A. Finkelstein |
| Chief Financial Officer | William Hyer | | |
| Chief Technology Officer | Ariel Spivakovsky | | |
| Senior Managing Director | Fred Marks | | |
| Senior Managing Director, Special Projects | Jon Gelberg | | |
| Director, Editorial & Product Development | Robert Docherty | | |
| Director, Marketing & Reference Sales | Michael Noerr | | |

**Editorial**

| | |
|---|---|
| Managing Editor | Karen Chassie |
| Senior Editors | Alison Perruso |
| | Sara Randazzo |
| Editors | Janine Fechter |
| | LeighAnne Helfmann |
| | Deanna Richmond |
| | Alison Rush |

**Research**

| | |
|---|---|
| Senior Managing Editor | Kerry Nugent Morrison |
| Senior Research Editors | Patricia Delli Santi |
| | Todd Kineavy |
| Research Editors | Laura Franklin |
| | Vanessa Karis |
| | Rachel Moloshok |
| | Todd Neale |
| | Geoffrey Schmidt |
| | Bill Schoener |
| | Kate Spirito |

**Editorial Services**

| | |
|---|---|
| Production Manager | Paul Zema |
| Production Associate | David Lubanski |
| Freelance Manager | Mary SanGiovanni |
| Editorial Services Assistant | Ann Chavis |
| Mail Processing Manager | Kara A. Seitz |
| Mail Processing Staff | Hattie Walker |

**Marketing**

| | |
|---|---|
| Creative Services Manager | Rose Butkiewicz |
| Production Manager | Jeanne Danzig |
| Associate Marketing Manager | Anna McMahon |

**Information Technology**

| | |
|---|---|
| Director of Infrastructure | Rob Heller |
| Software Engineer Manager | Ben Loh |
| Composition Programmer | Tom Haggerty |
| Database Programmer | Latha Shankar |
| Web Architect | Anup Nair |
| Systems Engineers | Knight Hui |
| | Ben McCullough |

Published by Marquis Who's Who LLC. Copyright ©2006 by Marquis Who's Who LLC. All rights reserved.

No part of this publication may be reproduced, stored in a retrieval system, or transmitted, in any form or by any means—including, but not limited to, electronic, mechanical, photocopying, recording, or otherwise—or used for any commercial purpose whatsoever without the prior written permission of the publisher and, if publisher deems necessary, execution of a formal license agreement with publisher.

For information, contact:
  Marquis Who's Who
  890 Mountain Avenue, Suite 4
  New Providence, New Jersey 07974
  1-908-673-1001
  www.marquiswhoswho.com

WHO'S WHO IN AMERICA is a registered trademark of Marquis Who's Who LLC.

| | | |
|---|---|---|
| International Standard Book Number | 0-8379-7006-7 | (Set, Classic Edition) |
| | 0-8379-6999-9 | (Volume 2, Classic Edition) |
| | 0-8379-7005-9 | (Set, Deluxe Edition) |
| | 0-8379-7003-2 | (Volume 2, Deluxe Edition) |
| International Standard Serial Number | 0083-9396 | |

No payment is either solicited or accepted for the inclusion of entries in this publication. Marquis Who's Who has used its best efforts in collecting and preparing material for inclusion in this publication, but does not warrant that the information herein is complete or accurate, and does not assume, and hereby disclaims, any liability to any person for any loss or damage caused by errors or omissions in this publication, whether such errors or omissions result from negligence, accident, or any other cause.

Manufactured in the United States of America.

# Table of Contents

Received
DEC 2006
Acquisitions
C. U. Library

Campbell University Library
Buies Creek, NC 27506

# Preface

[Library stamp: Received DEC 2006 Acquisitions C.U. Library]

**"W**HO'S WHO IN AMERICA *shall endeavor to list those individuals who are of current national reference interest and inquiry either because of meritorious achievement or because of the position they hold."*

**Albert Nelson Marquis**
Founder, 1899

Marquis Who's Who is proud to present the 2007 Edition of *Who's Who in America.* This edition features over 100,000 profiles of prominent individuals representing virtually every major field of endeavor. This edition also honors a group of "difference makers", men and women who have made profound contributions to America and the World.

In 1899, our first year of publication, Marquis biographees numbered 8,602. While the number of individuals profiled in *Who's Who in America* has grown substantially, our selection standards remain stringent. Fewer than one in 2,900 Americans are included in the 2007 edition of *Who's Who in America.*

While the vast majority of the individuals profiled on the following pages are American, *Who's Who in America* also includes the biographies of select individuals from around the world whose lives have had considerable impact and influence in America.

On the pages that follow, you will find Olympic champions, Nobel and Pulitzer Prize winners, university presidents, accomplished artists, renowned entertainers, entrepreneurs, and leaders representing hundreds of industries. Our 2007 Edition includes some long-established biographees like Barbara Walters, Lee Iacocca, and Jack Nicklaus, as well as many intriguing first-time listees. *Who's Who in America* also includes the profiles of thousands of remarkable achievers who, despite extraordinary accomplishments in everything from breakthrough medical research to cutting-edge technological innovations, have not as yet become household names.

Our profiles provide you with critical biographical information, including educational background, family history, work history, civic activity, memberships, honors, and awards. In many cases, hobbies and special interests are also listed.

## One Principle Governs Selection

As in all Marquis Who's Who biographical volumes, the individuals profiled in *Who's Who in America* are selected on the basis of current reference value. Factors such as position, noteworthy accomplishments, visibility, and prominence in a field are all taken into account. An individual's desire to be listed is not sufficient reason for inclusion. Similarly, wealth and social position are not relevant criteria. Of course, Marquis Who's Who has never charged a fee for publishing a biography, nor is purchase of the book ever a factor in the selection of biographees. Final decisions concerning inclusion or exclusion are made following extensive discussion, evaluation, and deliberation.

Biographical information is gathered in a variety of manners. In most cases, we invite our biographees to submit their biographical details. In many cases, though, the information is collected independently by our research and editorial staffs, which use a wide assortment of tools to gather the most complete, accurate, and up-to-date information available. Sketches researched by Marquis Who's Who are followed by an asterisk (*).

## Responding to Your Reference Needs

As a complement to the biographical profiles, the Geographic and Professional Indexes featured in Volume 2 make *Who's Who in America* an even more productive research tool. Through these indexes, users can identify and locate individuals in any of thirty-eight professional categories, as well as by country, state, or city. Each entry contains name and occupation description.

The Geographic Index lists names in the United States under state and city designations, as well as biographees in American territories. Canadian listings include provinces and cities. Names in Mexico and other countries appear by city. Biographees whose addresses are not published in their sketches are found under Address Unpublished.

The Professional Index includes categories ranging alphabetically from Agriculture to Social Science. Within each area, the names appear under geographic subheadings. Names without published addresses appear at the end of each professional area listing under Address Unpublished. If the occupation does not fall within one of the specified areas, the name is listed under Unclassified.

Some biographees have professions encompassing more than one area; each of these appears under the field best suited to the biographee's occupation. Thus, while most bankers are listed under Finance: Banking Services, investment bankers are found in Finance: Investment Services. A biographee with two or more diverse occupations is found under the area that best fits his or her professional profile.

## Our Challenge

While the Marquis Who's Who editors exercise the utmost care in preparing each biographical sketch for publication, it is inevitable in a publication involving so many profiles that occasional errors will appear. Users of this publication are urged to notify the publisher of any issues so that adjustments can be made, which will not only be reflected in all subsequent editions of the book but which can now be immediately displayed via Marquis Who's Who on the Web.

We sincerely hope that this volume will be an indispensable reference tool for you. We are always looking for ways to better serve you and welcome your ideas for improvements. In addition, we continue to welcome your Marquis Who's Who nominations. Feel free to submit these via our Web site (www.marquiswhoswho.com) or by e-mail and postal mail.

## Our Utmost Thanks

Without the cooperation and assistance of those profiled on the pages that follow, *Who's Who in America* would not be possible. We would like to specifically thank our biographees for reviewing and editing their profiles. As a consequence, *Who's Who in America* remains the unchallenged leader in the field of biographical reference works. For this we are truly grateful.

Campbell University Library
Buies Creek, NC 27506

# Key to Information

[1] **GIBSON, OSCAR JULIUS,** [2] physician, medical educator; [3] b. Syracuse, N.Y., Aug. 31, 1937; [4] s. Paul Oliver and Elizabeth H. (Thrun) G.; [5] m. Judith S. Gonzalez, Apr. 28, 1968; [6] children: Richard Gary, Matthew Cary, Samuel Perry. [7] BA magna cum laude, U. Pa., 1960; MD, Harvard U., 1964. [8] Diplomate Am. Bd. Internal Medicine, Am. Bd. Preventive Medicine. [9] Intern Barnes Hosp., St. Louis, 1964-65, resident, 1965-66; clin. assoc. Nat. Heart Inst., NIH, Bethesda, Md., 1966-68; chief resident medicine U. Okla. Hosps., 1968-69; asst. prof. cmty. health Okla. Med. Ctr., 1969-70, assoc. prof., 1970-74, prof., chmn. dept., 1974-80; dean Coll. Medicine U. Okla. , 1978-82; v.p. med. staff affairs Bapt. Med. Ctr., Oklahoma City, 1982-86, exec. v.p., 1986-88, chmn., 1988-95, chmn, CEO, 1995—; [10] mem. governing bd. Ambulatory Health Care Consortium, Inc., 1979-80; mem. Okla. Bd. Medicolegal Examiners, 1985—; mem. Okla. Bd. of Med. Ethics, 1994—. [11] Contrb. articles to profl. jours. [12] Bd. dirs., v.p. Okla. Arthritis Found., 1982—; trustee N. Ctrl. Mental Health Ctr., 1985—. [13] Served U.S. Army, 1955-56. [14] Recipient R.T. Chadwick award Overlook Hosp., 1968; Am. Heart Assn. grantee, 1985-86, 88, 1995-96. [15] Fellow Assn. Tchrs. Preventive Medicine; mem. AAAS, AMA, Am. Fedn. Clin. Rsch., Assn. Med. Colls., Masons, Shriners, Sigma Xi. [16] Republican. [17] Roman Catholic. [18] Avocations: swimming, weight lifting, travelling. [19] Home: 6060 N Ridge Ave Oklahoma City OK 73126 [20] Office: Bapt Med Ctr 1986 Cuba Hwy Oklahoma City OK 73120*

## KEY

| | |
|---|---|
| [1] | Name |
| [2] | Occupation |
| [3] | Vital statistics |
| [4] | Parents |
| [5] | Marriage |
| [6] | Children |
| [7] | Education |
| [8] | Professional certifications |
| [9] | Career |
| [10] | Career-related |
| [11] | Writings and creative works |
| [12] | Civic and political activities |
| [13] | Military |
| [14] | Awards and fellowships |
| [15] | Professional and association memberships, clubs and lodges |
| [16] | Political affiliation |
| [17] | Religion |
| [18] | Avocations |
| [19] | Home address |
| [20] | Office address |
| [*] | Researched by Marquis Who's Who |

# Table of Abbreviations

The following abbreviations and symbols are frequently used in this book.

*An asterisk following a sketch indicates that it was researched by the Marquis Who's Who editorial staff and has not been verified by the biographee.*

## A

**A** Associate (used with academic degrees only)

**AA, A.A.** Associate in Arts, Associate of Arts

**AAAL** American Academy of Arts and Letters

**AAAS** American Association for the Advancement of Science

**AACD** American Association for Counseling and Development

**AACN** American Association of Critical Care Nurses

**AAHA** American Academy of Health Administrators

**AAHP** American Association of Hospital Planners

**AAHPERD** American Alliance for Health, Physical Education, Recreation, and Dance

**AAS** Associate of Applied Science

**AASL** American Association of School Librarians

**AASPA** American Association of School Personnel Administrators

**AAU** Amateur Athletic Union

**AAUP** American Association of University Professors

**AAUW** American Association of University Women

**AB, A.B.** Arts, Bachelor of

**AB** Alberta

**ABA** American Bar Association

**ABC** American Broadcasting Company

**AC** Air Corps

**acad.** academy, academic

**acct.** accountant

**acctg.** accounting

**ACDA** Arms Control and Disarmament Agency

**ACHA** American College of Hospital Administrators

**ACLS** Advanced Cardiac Life Support

**ACLU** American Civil Liberties Union

**ACOG** American College of Ob-Gyn

**ACP** American College of Physicians

**ACS** American College of Surgeons

**ADA** American Dental Association

**a.d.c.** aide-de-camp

**adj.** adjunct, adjutant

**adj. gen.** adjutant general

**adm.** admiral

**adminstr.** administrator

**adminstrn.** administration

**adminstrv.** administrative

**ADN** Associate's Degree in Nursing

**ADP** Automatic Data Processing

**adv.** advocate, advisory

**advt.** advertising

**AE, A.E.** Agricultural Engineer

**A.E. and P.** Ambassador Extraordinary and Plenipotentiary

**AEC** Atomic Energy Commission

**aero.** aeronautical, aeronautic

**aerodyn.** aerodynamic

**AFB** Air Force Base

**AFL-CIO** American Federation of Labor and Congress of Industrial Organizations

**AFTRA** American Federation of TV and Radio Artists

**AFSCME** American Federation of State, County and Municipal Employees

**agr.** agriculture

**agrl.** agricultural

**agt.** agent

**AGVA** American Guild of Variety Artists

**agy.** agency

**A&I** Agricultural and Industrial

**AIA** American Institute of Architects

**AIAA** American Institute of Aeronautics and Astronautics

**AIChE** American Institute of Chemical Engineers

**AICPA** American Institute of Certified Public Accountants

**AID** Agency for International Development

**AIDS** Acquired Immune Deficiency Syndrome

**AIEE** American Institute of Electrical Engineers

**AIM** American Institute of Management

**AIME** American Institute of Mining, Metallurgy, and Petroleum Engineers

**AK** Alaska

**AL** Alabama

**Ala.** Alabama

**ALA** American Library Association

**alt.** alternate

**Alta.** Alberta

**A&M** Agricultural and Mechanical

**AM, A.M.** Arts, Master of

**Am.** American, America

**AMA** American Medical Association

**amb.** ambassador

**A.M.E.** African Methodist Episcopal

**Amtrak** National Railroad Passenger Corporation

**AMVETS** American Veterans of World War II, Korea, Vietnam

**ANA** American Nurses Association

**anat.** anatomical

**ANCC** American Nurses Credentialing Center

**ann.** annual

**ANTA** American National Theatre and Academy

**anthrop.** anthropological

**AP** Associated Press

**APA** American Psychological Association

**APGA** American Personnel Guidance Association

**APHA** American Public Health Association

**APO** Army Post Office

**apptd.** appointed

**Apr.** April

**apt.** apartment

**AR** Arkansas

**ARC** American Red Cross

**arch.** architect

**archeol.** archeological

**archtl.** architectural

**Ariz.** Arizona

**Ark.** Arkansas

**ArtsD, ArtsD.** Arts, Doctor of

**arty.** artillery

**AS** American Samoa

**AS** Associate in Science

**ASCAP** American Society of Composers, Authors and Publishers

**ASCD** Association for Supervision and Curriculum Development

**ASCE** American Society of Civil Engineers

**ASHRAE** American Society of Heating, Refrigeration, and Air Conditioning Engineers

**ASME** American Society of Mechanical Engineers

**ASNSA** American Society for Nursing Service Administrators

**ASPA** American Society for Public Administration

**ASPCA** American Society for the Prevention of Cruelty to Animals

**assn.** association

**assoc.** associate

**asst.** assistant

**ASTD** American Society for Training and Development

**ASTM** American Society for Testing and Materials

**astron.** astronomical

**astrophys.** astrophysical

**ATLA** Association of Trial Lawyers of America

**ATSC** Air Technical Service Command

**AT&T** American Telephone & Telegraph Company

**atty.** attorney

**Aug.** August

**AUS** Army of the United States

**aux.** auxiliary

**Ave.** Avenue

**AVMA** American Veterinary Medical Association

**AZ** Arizona

**AWHONN** Association of Women's Health Obstetric and Neonatal Nurses

## B

**B.** Bachelor

**b.** born

**BA, B.A.** Bachelor of Arts

**BAgr, B.Agr.** Bachelor of Agriculture

**Balt.** Baltimore

**Bapt.** Baptist

**BArch, B.Arch.** Bachelor of Architecture

viii

**BAS, B.A.S.** Bachelor of Agricultural Science

**BBA, B.B.A.** Bachelor of Business Administration

**BBB** Better Business Bureau

**BBC** British Broadcasting Corporation

**BC, B.C.** British Columbia

**BCE, B.C.E.** Bachelor of Civil Engineering

**BChir, B.Chir.** Bachelor of Surgery

**BCL, B.C.L.** Bachelor of Civil Law

**BCLS** Basic Cardiac Life Support

**BCS, B.C.S.** Bachelor of Commercial Science

**BD, B.D.** Bachelor of Divinity

**bd.** board

**BE, B.E.** Bachelor of Education

**BEE, B.E.E.** Bachelor of Electrical Engineering

**BFA, B.F.A.** Bachelor of Fine Arts

**bibl.** biblical

**bibliog.** bibliographical

**biog.** biographical

**biol.** biological

**BJ, B.J.** Bachelor of Journalism

**Bklyn.** Brooklyn

**BL, B.L.** Bachelor of Letters

**bldg.** building

**BLS, B.L.S.** Bachelor of Library Science

**BLS** Basic Life Support

**Blvd.** Boulevard

**BMI** Broadcast Music, Inc.

**BMW** Bavarian Motor Works (Bayerische Motoren Werke)

**bn.** battalion

**B.&O.R.R.** Baltimore & Ohio Railroad

**bot.** botanical

**BPE, B.P.E.** Bachelor of Physical Education

**BPhil, B.Phil.** Bachelor of Philosophy

**br.** branch

**BRE, B.R.E.** Bachelor of Religious Education

**brig. gen.** brigadier general

**Brit.** British, Brittanica

**Bros.** Brothers

**BS, B.S.** Bachelor of Science

**BSA, B.S.A.** Bachelor of Agricultural Science

**BSBA** Bachelor of Science in Business Administration

**BSChemE** Bachelor of Science in Chemical Engineering

**BSD, B.S.D.** Bachelor of Didactic Science

**BSEE** Bachelor of Science in Electrical Engineering

**BSN** Bachelor of Science in Nursing

**BST, B.S.T.** Bachelor of Sacred Theology

**BTh, B.Th.** Bachelor of Theology

**bull.** bulletin

**bur.** bureau

**bus.** business

**B.W.I.** British West Indies

# C

**CA** California

**CAA** Civil Aeronautics Administration

**CAB** Civil Aeronautics Board

**CAD-CAM** Computer Aided Design–Computer Aided Model

**Calif.** California

**C.Am.** Central America

**Can.** Canada, Canadian

**CAP** Civil Air Patrol

**capt.** captain

**cardiol.** cardiological

**cardiovasc.** cardiovascular

**CARE** Cooperative American Relief Everywhere

**Cath.** Catholic

**cav.** cavalry

**CBC** Canadian Broadcasting Company

**CBI** China, Burma, India Theatre of Operations

**CBS** Columbia Broadcasting Company

**C.C.** Community College

**CCC** Commodity Credit Corporation

**CCNY** City College of New York

**CCRN** Critical Care Registered Nurse

**CCU** Cardiac Care Unit

**CD** Civil Defense

**CE, C.E.** Corps of Engineers, Civil Engineer

**CEN** Certified Emergency Nurse

**CENTO** Central Treaty Organization

**CEO** chief executive officer

**CERN** European Organization of Nuclear Research

**cert.** certificate, certification, certified

**CETA** Comprehensive Employment Training Act

**CFA** Chartered Financial Analyst

**CFL** Canadian Football League

**CFO** chief financial officer

**CFP** Certified Financial Planner

**ch.** church

**ChD, Ch.D.** Doctor of Chemistry

**chem.** chemical

**ChemE, Chem.E.** Chemical Engineer

**ChFC** Chartered Financial Consultant

**Chgo.** Chicago

**chirurg.** chirurgical

**chmn.** chairman

**chpt.** chapter

**CIA** Central Intelligence Agency

**Cin.** Cincinnati

**cir.** circle, circuit

**CLE** Continuing Legal Education

**Cleve.** Cleveland

**climatol.** climatological

**clin.** clinical

**clk.** clerk

**C.L.U.** Chartered Life Underwriter

**CM, C.M.** Master in Surgery

**CM** Northern Mariana Islands

**CMA** Certified Medical Assistant

**cmty.** community

**CNA** Certified Nurse's Aide

**CNOR** Certified Nurse (Operating Room)

**C.&N.W.Ry.** Chicago & North Western Railway

**CO** Colorado

**Co.** Company

**COF** Catholic Order of Foresters

**C. of C.** Chamber of Commerce

**col.** colonel

**coll.** college

**Colo.** Colorado

**com.** committee

**comd.** commanded

**comdg.** commanding

**comdr.** commander

**comdt.** commandant

**comm.** communications

**commd.** commissioned

**comml.** commercial

**commn.** commission

**commr.** commissioner

**compt.** comptroller

**condr.** conductor

**Conf.** Conference

**Congl.** Congregational, Congressional

**Conglist.** Congregationalist

**Conn.** Connecticut

**cons.** consultant, consulting

**consol.** consolidated

**constl.** constitutional

**constn.** constitution

**constrn.** construction

**contbd.** contributed

**contbg.** contributing

**contbn.** contribution

**contbr.** contributor

**contr.** controller

**Conv.** Convention

**COO** chief operating officer

**coop.** cooperative

**coord.** coordinator

**CORDS** Civil Operations and Revolutionary Development Support

**CORE** Congress of Racial Equality

**corp.** corporation, corporate

**corr.** correspondent, corresponding, correspondence

**C.&O.Ry.** Chesapeake & Ohio Railway

**coun.** council

**CPA** Certified Public Accountant

**CPCU** Chartered Property and Casualty Underwriter

**CPH, C.P.H.** Certificate of Public Health

**cpl.** corporal

**CPR** Cardio-Pulmonary Resuscitation

**C.P.Ry.** Canadian Pacific Railway

**CRT** Cathode Ray Terminal

**C.S.** Christian Science

**CSB, C.S.B.** Bachelor of Christian Science

**C.S.C.** Civil Service Commission

**CT** Connecticut

**ct.** court

**ctr.** center

**ctrl.** central

**CWS** Chemical Warfare Service

**C.Z.** Canal Zone

# D

**D.** Doctor

**d.** daughter

**DAgr, D.Agr.** Doctor of Agriculture

**DAR** Daughters of the American Revolution

**dau.** daughter

**DAV** Disabled American Veterans

**DC, D.C.** District of Columbia

**DCL, D.C.L.** Doctor of Civil Law

**DCS, D.C.S.** Doctor of Commercial Science

**DD, D.D.** Doctor of Divinity

**DDS, D.D.S.** Doctor of Dental Surgery

**DE** Delaware

Dec.  December
dec.  deceased
def.  defense
Del.  Delaware
del.  delegate, delegation
Dem.  Democrat, Democratic
DEng, D.Eng.  Doctor of Engineering
denom.  denomination, denominational
dep.  deputy
dept.  department
dermatol.  dermatological
desc.  descendant
devel.  development, developmental
DFA, D.F.A.  Doctor of Fine Arts
D.F.C.  Distinguished Flying Cross
DHL, D.H.L.  Doctor of Hebrew Literature
dir.  director
dist.  district
distbg.  distributing
distbn.  distribution
distbr.  distributor
disting.  distinguished
div.  division, divinity, divorce
divsn.  division
DLitt, D.Litt.  Doctor of Literature
DMD, D.M.D.  Doctor of Dental Medicine
DMS, D.M.S.  Doctor of Medical Science
DO, D.O.  Doctor of Osteopathy
docs.  documents
DON  Director of Nursing
DPH, D.P.H.  Diploma in Public Health
DPhil, D.Phil.  Doctor of Philosophy
D.R.  Daughters of the Revolution
Dr.  Drive, Doctor
DRE, D.R.E.  Doctor of Religious Education
DrPH, Dr.P.H.  Doctor of Public Health,
  Doctor of Public Hygiene
D.S.C.  Distinguished Service Cross
DSc, D.Sc.  Doctor of Science
DSChemE  Doctor of Science in Chemical
  Engineering
D.S.M.  Distinguished Service Medal
DST, D.S.T.  Doctor of Sacred Theology
DTM, D.T.M.  Doctor of Tropical Medicine
DVM, D.V.M.  Doctor of Veterinary
  Medicine
DVS, D.V.S.  Doctor of Veterinary Surgery

## E

E, E.  East
ea.  eastern
E. and P.  Extraordinary and Plenipotentiary
Eccles.  Ecclesiastical
ecol.  ecological
econ.  economic
ECOSOC  Economic and Social Council (of
  the UN)
ED, E.D.  Doctor of Engineering
ed.  educated
EdB, Ed.B.  Bachelor of Education
EdD, Ed.D.  Doctor of Education
edit.  edition
editl.  editorial
EdM, Ed.M.  Master of Education
edn.  education
ednl.  educational
EDP  Electronic Data Processing
EdS, Ed.S.  Specialist in Education

EE, E.E.  Electrical Engineer
E.E. and M.P.  Envoy Extraordinary and
  Minister Plenipotentiary
EEC  European Economic Community
EEG  Electroencephalogram
EEO  Equal Employment Opportunity
EEOC  Equal Employment Opportunity
  Commission
E.Ger.  German Democratic Republic
EKG  Electrocardiogram
elec.  electrical
electrochem.  electrochemical
electrophys.  electrophysical
elem.  elementary
EM, E.M.  Engineer of Mines
EMT  Emergency Medical Technician
ency.  encyclopedia
Eng.  England
engr.  engineer
engring.  engineering
entomol.  entomological
environ.  environmental
EPA  Environmental Protection Agency
epidemiol.  epidemiological
Episc.  Episcopalian
ERA  Equal Rights Amendment
ERDA  Energy Research and Development
  Administration
ESEA  Elementary and Secondary Education
  Act
ESL  English as Second Language
ESPN  Entertainment and Sports
  Programming Network
ESSA  Environmental Science Services
  Administration
ethnol.  ethnological
ETO  European Theatre of Operations
Evang.  Evangelical
exam.  examination, examining
Exch.  Exchange
exec.  executive
exhbn.  exhibition
expdn.  expedition
expn.  exposition
expt.  experiment
exptl.  experimental
Expy.  Expressway
Ext.  Extension

## F

F.A.  Field Artillery
FAA  Federal Aviation Administration
FAO  Food and Agriculture Organization (of
  the UN)
FBA  Federal Bar Association
FBI  Federal Bureau of Investigation
FCA  Farm Credit Administration
FCC  Federal Communications Commission
FCDA  Federal Civil Defense Administration
FDA  Food and Drug Administration
FDIA  Federal Deposit Insurance
  Administration
FDIC  Federal Deposit Insurance Corporation
FE, F.E.  Forest Engineer
FEA  Federal Energy Administration
Feb.  February
fed.  federal
fedn.  federation

FERC  Federal Energy Regulatory
  Commission
fgn.  foreign
FHA  Federal Housing Administration
fin.  financial, finance
FL  Florida
Fl.  Floor
Fla.  Florida
FMC  Federal Maritime Commission
FNP  Family Nurse Practitioner
FOA  Foreign Operations Administration
found.  foundation
FPC  Federal Power Commission
FPO  Fleet Post Office
frat.  fraternity
FRS  Federal Reserve System
FSA  Federal Security Agency
Ft.  Fort
FTC  Federal Trade Commission
Fwy.  Freeway

## G

G-1 (or other number)  Division of General
  Staff
GA, Ga.  Georgia
GAO  General Accounting Office
gastroent.  gastroenterological
GATE  Gifted and Talented Educators
GATT  General Agreement on Tariffs and
  Trade
GE  General Electric Company
gen.  general
geneal.  genealogical
geod.  geodetic
geog.  geographic, geographical
geol.  geological
geophys.  geophysical
geriat.  geriatrics
gerontol.  gerontological
G.H.Q.  General Headquarters
GM  General Motors Corporation
GMAC  General Motors Acceptance
  Corporation
G.N.Ry.  Great Northern Railway
gov.  governor
govt.  government
govtl.  governmental
GPO  Government Printing Office
grad.  graduate, graduated
GSA  General Services Administration
Gt.  Great
GTE  General Telephone and
  Electric Company
GU  Guam
gynecol.  gynecological

## H

HBO  Home Box Office
hdqs.  headquarters
HEW  Department of Health, Education and
  Welfare
HHD, H.H.D.  Doctor of Humanities
HHFA  Housing and Home Finance Agency
HHS  Department of Health and Human
  Services
HI  Hawaii
hist.  historical, historic

**HM, H.M.** Master of Humanities
**HMO** Health Maintenance Organization
**homeo.** homeopathic
**hon.** honorary, honorable
**Ho. of Dels.** House of Delegates
**Ho. of Reps.** House of Representatives
**hort.** horticultural
**hosp.** hospital
**HS, H.S.** High School
**HUD** Department of Housing and Urban Development
**Hwy.** Highway
**hydrog.** hydrographic

# I

**IA** Iowa
**IAEA** International Atomic Energy Agency
**IATSE** International Alliance of Theatrical and Stage Employees and Moving Picture Operators of the United States and Canada
**IBM** International Business Machines Corporation
**IBRD** International Bank for Reconstruction and Development
**ICA** International Cooperation Administration
**ICC** Interstate Commerce Commission
**ICCE** International Council for Computers in Education
**ICU** Intensive Care Unit
**ID** Idaho
**IEEE** Institute of Electrical and Electronics Engineers
**IFC** International Finance Corporation
**IGY** International Geophysical Year
**IL** Illinois
**Ill.** Illinois
**illus.** illustrated
**ILO** International Labor Organization
**IMF** International Monetary Fund
**IN** Indiana
**Inc.** Incorporated
**Ind.** Indiana
**ind.** independent
**Indpls.** Indianapolis
**indsl.** industrial
**inf.** infantry
**info.** information
**ins.** insurance
**Insp.** inspector
**insp. gen.** inspector general
**inst.** institute
**instl.** institutional
**instn.** institution
**instr.** instructor
**instrn.** instruction
**instrnl.** instructional
**internat.** international
**intro.** introduction
**IRE** Institute of Radio Engineers
**IRS** Internal Revenue Service
**ITT** International Telephone & Telegraph Corporation

# J

**JAG** Judge Advocate General
**JAGC** Judge Advocate General Corps
**Jan.** January

**Jaycees** Junior Chamber of Commerce
**JB, J.B.** Jurum Baccalaureus
**JCB, J.C.B.** Juris Canoni Baccalaureus
**JCD, J.C.D.** Juris Canonici Doctor, Juris Civilis Doctor
**JCL, J.C.L.** Juris Canonici Licentiatus
**JD, J.D.** Juris Doctor
**jg.** junior grade
**jour.** journal
**jr.** junior
**JSD, J.S.D.** Juris Scientiae Doctor
**JUD, J.U.D.** Juris Utriusque Doctor
**jud.** judicial

# K

**Kans.** Kansas
**K.C.** Knights of Columbus
**K.P.** Knights of Pythias
**KS** Kansas
**K.T.** Knight Templar
**KY, Ky.** Kentucky

# L

**LA, La.** Louisiana
**L.A.** Los Angeles
**lab.** laboratory
**L.Am.** Latin America
**lang.** language
**laryngol.** laryngological
**LB** Labrador
**LDS** Latter Day Saints
**LDS Church** Church of Jesus Christ of Latter Day Saints
**lectr.** lecturer
**legis.** legislation, legislative
**LHD, L.H.D.** Doctor of Humane Letters
**LI, L.I.** Long Island
**libr.** librarian, library
**lic.** licensed, license
**L.I.R.R.** Long Island Railroad
**lit.** literature
**litig.** litigation
**LittB, Litt.B.** Bachelor of Letters
**LittD, Litt.D.** Doctor of Letters
**LLB, LL.B.** Bachelor of Laws
**LLD, L.L.D.** Doctor of Laws
**LLM, L.L.M.** Master of Laws
**Ln.** Lane
**L.&N.R.R.** Louisville & Nashville Railroad
**LPGA** Ladies Professional Golf Association
**LPN** Licensed Practical Nurse
**LS, L.S.** Library Science (in degree)
**lt.** lieutenant
**Ltd.** Limited
**Luth.** Lutheran
**LWV** League of Women Voters

# M

**M.** Master
**m.** married
**MA, M.A.** Master of Arts
**MA** Massachusetts
**MADD** Mothers Against Drunk Driving
**mag.** magazine
**MAgr, M.Agr.** Master of Agriculture
**maj.** major
**Man.** Manitoba

**Mar.** March
**MArch, M.Arch.** Master in Architecture
**Mass.** Massachusetts
**math.** mathematics, mathematical
**MATS** Military Air Transport Service
**MB, M.B.** Bachelor of Medicine
**MB** Manitoba
**MBA, M.B.A.** Master of Business Administration
**MBS** Mutual Broadcasting System
**M.C.** Medical Corps
**MCE, M.C.E.** Master of Civil Engineering
**mcht.** merchant
**mcpl.** municipal
**MCS, M.C.S.** Master of Commercial Science
**MD, M.D.** Doctor of Medicine
**MD, Md.** Maryland
**MDiv** Master of Divinity
**MDip, M.Dip.** Master in Diplomacy
**mdse.** merchandise
**MDV, M.D.V.** Doctor of Veterinary Medicine
**ME, M.E.** Mechanical Engineer
**ME** Maine
**M.E.Ch.** Methodist Episcopal Church
**mech.** mechanical
**MEd., M.Ed.** Master of Education
**med.** medical
**MEE, M.E.E.** Master of Electrical Engineering
**mem.** member
**meml.** memorial
**merc.** mercantile
**met.** metropolitan
**metall.** metallurgical
**MetE, Met.E.** Metallurgical Engineer
**meteorol.** meteorological
**Meth.** Methodist
**Mex.** Mexico
**MF, M.F.** Master of Forestry
**MFA, M.F.A.** Master of Fine Arts
**mfg.** manufacturing
**mfr.** manufacturer
**mgmt.** management
**mgr.** manager
**MHA, M.H.A.** Master of Hospital Administration
**M.I.** Military Intelligence
**MI** Michigan
**Mich.** Michigan
**micros.** microscopic, microscopical
**mid.** middle
**mil.** military
**Milw.** Milwaukee
**Min.** Minister
**mineral.** mineralogical
**Minn.** Minnesota
**MIS** Management Information Systems
**Miss.** Mississippi
**MIT** Massachusetts Institute of Technology
**mktg.** marketing
**ML, M.L.** Master of Laws
**MLA** Modern Language Association
**M.L.D.** Magister Legnum Diplomatic
**MLitt, M.Litt.** Master of Literature, Master of Letters
**MLS, M.L.S.** Master of Library Science
**MME, M.M.E.** Master of Mechanical Engineering

MN  Minnesota
mng.  managing
MO, Mo.  Missouri
moblzn.  mobilization
Mont.  Montana
MP  Northern Mariana Islands
M.P.  Member of Parliament
MPA  Master of Public Administration
MPE, M.P.E.  Master of Physical Education
MPH, M.P.H.  Master of Public Health
MPhil, M.Phil.  Master of Philosophy
MPL, M.P.L.  Master of Patent Law
Mpls.  Minneapolis
MRE, M.R.E.  Master of Religious Education
MRI  Magnetic Resonance Imaging
MS, M.S.  Master of Science
MS, Ms.  Mississippi
MSc, M.Sc.  Master of Science
MSChemE  Master of Science in Chemical
  Engineering
MSEE  Master of Science in Electrical
  Engineering
MSF, M.S.F.  Master of Science of Forestry
MSN  Master of Science in Nursing
MST, M.S.T.  Master of Sacred Theology
MSW, M.S.W.  Master of Social Work
MT  Montana
Mt.  Mount
MTO  Mediterranean Theatre of Operation
MTV  Music Television
mus.  museum, musical
MusB, Mus.B.  Bachelor of Music
MusD, Mus.D.  Doctor of Music
MusM, Mus.M.  Master of Music
mut.  mutual
MVP  Most Valuable Player
mycol.  mycological

# N

N, N.  North
NAACOG  Nurses Association of the
  American College of Obstetricians and
  Gynecologists
NAACP  National Association for the
  Advancement of Colored People
NACA  National Advisory Committee for
  Aeronautics
NACDL  National Association of Criminal
  Defense Lawyers
NACU  National Association of Colleges and
  Universities
NAD  National Academy of Design
NAE  National Academy of Engineering,
  National Association of Educators
NAESP  National Association of Elementary
  School Principals
NAFE  National Association of Female
  Executives
N.Am.  North America
NAM  National Association of Manufacturers
NAMH  National Association for Mental
  Health
NAPA  National Association of Performing
  Artists
NARAS  National Academy of Recording
  Arts and Sciences
NAREB  National Association of Real Estate

Boards
NARS  National Archives and Record Service
NAS  National Academy of Sciences
NASA  National Aeronautics and Space
  Administration
NASP  National Association of School
  Psychologists
NASW  National Association of Social
  Workers
nat.  national
NATAS  National Academy of Television
  Arts and Sciences
NATO  North Atlantic Treaty Organization
NATOUSA  North African Theatre of
  Operations, United States Army
nav.  navigation
NB  New Brunswick
NBA  National Basketball Association
NBC  National Broadcasting Company
NC, N.C.  North Carolina
NCAA  National College Athletic Association
NCCJ  National Conference of Christians
  and Jews
ND, N.D.  North Dakota
NDEA  National Defense Education Act
NE  Nebraska
NE, N.E.  Northeast
NEA  National Education Association
Nebr.  Nebraska
NEH  National Endowment for Humanities
neurol.  neurological
Nev.  Nevada
NF  Newfoundland
NFL  National Football League
Nfld.  Newfoundland
NG  National Guard
NH, N.H.  New Hampshire
NHL  National Hockey League
NIH  National Institutes of Health
NIMH  National Institute of Mental Health
NJ, N.J.  New Jersey
NLRB  National Labor Relations Board
NM  New Mexico
N.Mex.  New Mexico
No.  Northern
NOAA  National Oceanographic and
  Atmospheric Administration
NORAD  North America Air Defense
Nov.  November
NOW  National Organization for Women
N.P.Ry.  Northern Pacific Railway
nr.  near
NRA  National Rifle Association
NRC  National Research Council
NS, N.S.  Nova Scotia
NSC  National Security Council
NSF  National Science Foundation
NSTA  National Science Teachers
  Association
NSW  New South Wales
N.T.  New Testament
NT  Northwest Territories
nuc.  nuclear
numis.  numismatic
NV  Nevada
NW, N.W.  Northwest
N.W.T.  Northwest Territories
NY, N.Y.  New York

N.Y.C.  New York City
NYU  New York University
N.Z.  New Zealand

# O

OAS  Organization of American States
ob-gyn  obstetrics-gynecology
obs.  observatory
obstet.  obstetrical
occupl.  occupational
oceanog.  oceanographic
Oct.  October
OD, O.D.  Doctor of Optometry
OECD  Organization for Economic
  Cooperation and Development
OEEC  Organization of European Economic
  Cooperation
OEO  Office of Economic Opportunity
ofcl.  official
OH  Ohio
OK  Oklahoma
Okla.  Oklahoma
ON  Ontario
Ont.  Ontario
oper.  operating
ophthal.  ophthalmological
ops.  operations
OR  Oregon
orch.  orchestra
Oreg.  Oregon
orgn.  organization
orgnl.  organizational
ornithol.  ornithological
orthop.  orthopedic
OSHA  Occupational Safety and Health
  Administration
OSRD  Office of Scientific Research and
  Development
OSS  Office of Strategic Services
osteo.  osteopathic
otol.  otological
otolaryn.  otolaryngological

# P

PA, Pa.  Pennsylvania
P.A.  Professional Association
paleontol.  paleontological
path.  pathological
PBS  Public Broadcasting System
P.C.  Professional Corporation
PE  Prince Edward Island
pediat.  pediatrics
P.E.I.  Prince Edward Island
PEN  Poets, Playwrights, Editors, Essayists
  and Novelists (international association)
penol.  penological
P.E.O.  women's organization (full name not
  disclosed)
pers.  personnel
pfc.  private first class
PGA  Professional Golfers' Association of
  America
PHA  Public Housing Administration
pharm.  pharmaceutical
PharmD, Pharm.D.  Doctor of Pharmacy
PharmM, Pharm.M.  Master of Pharmacy
PhB, Ph.B.  Bachelor of Philosophy

**PhD, Ph.D.** Doctor of Philosophy
**PhDChemE** Doctor of Science in Chemical Engineering
**PhM, Ph.M.** Master of Philosophy
**Phila.** Philadelphia
**philharm.** philharmonic
**philol.** philological
**philos.** philosophical
**photog.** photographic
**phys.** physical
**physiol.** physiological
**Pitts.** Pittsburgh
**Pk.** Park
**Pky.** Parkway
**Pl.** Place
**P.&L.E.R.R.** Pittsburgh & Lake Erie Railroad
**Plz.** Plaza
**PNP** Pediatric Nurse Practitioner
**P.O.** Post Office
**PO Box** Post Office Box
**polit.** political
**poly.** polytechnic, polytechnical
**PQ** Province of Quebec
**PR, P.R.** Puerto Rico
**prep.** preparatory
**pres.** president
**Presbyn.** Presbyterian
**presdl.** presidential
**prin.** principal
**procs.** proceedings
**prod.** produced (play production)
**prodn.** production
**prodr.** producer
**prof.** professor
**profl.** professional
**prog.** progressive
**propr.** proprietor
**pros. atty.** prosecuting attorney
**pro tem.** pro tempore
**PSRO** Professional Services Review Organization
**psychiat.** psychiatric
**psychol.** psychological
**PTA** Parent-Teachers Association
**ptnr.** partner
**PTO** Pacific Theatre of Operations, Parent Teacher Organization
**pub.** publisher, publishing, published
**pub.** public
**publ.** publication
**pvt.** private

## Q

**quar.** quarterly
**qm.** quartermaster
**Q.M.C.** Quartermaster Corps
**Que.** Quebec

## R

**radiol.** radiological
**RAF** Royal Air Force
**RCA** Radio Corporation of America
**RCAF** Royal Canadian Air Force
**RD** Rural Delivery
**Rd.** Road
**R&D** Research & Development

**REA** Rural Electrification Administration
**rec.** recording
**ref.** reformed
**regt.** regiment
**regtl.** regimental
**rehab.** rehabilitation
**rels.** relations
**Rep.** Republican
**rep.** representative
**Res.** Reserve
**ret.** retired
**Rev.** Reverend
**rev.** review, revised
**RFC** Reconstruction Finance Corporation
**RFD** Rural Free Delivery
**rhinol.** rhinological
**RI, R.I.** Rhode Island
**RISD** Rhode Island School of Design
**Rlwy.** Railway
**Rm.** Room
**RN, R.N.** Registered Nurse
**roentgenol.** roentgenological
**ROTC** Reserve Officers Training Corps
**RR** Rural Route
**R.R.** Railroad
**rsch.** research
**rschr.** researcher
**Rt.** Route

## S

**S, S.** South
**s.** son
**SAC** Strategic Air Command
**SAG** Screen Actors Guild
**SALT** Strategic Arms Limitation Talks
**S.Am.** South America
**san.** sanitary
**SAR** Sons of the American Revolution
**Sask.** Saskatchewan
**savs.** savings
**SB, S.B.** Bachelor of Science
**SBA** Small Business Administration
**SC, S.C.** South Carolina
**SCAP** Supreme Command Allies Pacific
**ScB, Sc.B.** Bachelor of Science
**SCD, S.C.D.** Doctor of Commercial Science
**ScD, Sc.D.** Doctor of Science
**sch.** school
**sci.** science, scientific
**SCLC** Southern Christian Leadership Conference
**SCV** Sons of Confederate Veterans
**SD, S.D.** South Dakota
**SE, S.E.** Southeast
**SEATO** Southeast Asia Treaty Organization
**SEC** Securities and Exchange Commission
**sec.** secretary
**sect.** section
**seismol.** seismological
**sem.** seminary
**Sept.** September
**s.g.** senior grade
**sgt.** sergeant
**SHAEF** Supreme Headquarters Allied Expeditionary Forces
**SHAPE** Supreme Headquarters Allied Powers in Europe
**S.I.** Staten Island

**S.J.** Society of Jesus (Jesuit)
**SJD** Scientiae Juridicae Doctor
**SK** Saskatchewan
**SM, S.M.** Master of Science
**SNP** Society of Nursing Professionals
**So.** Southern
**soc.** society
**sociol.** sociological
**S.P.Co.** Southern Pacific Company
**spkr.** speaker
**spl.** special
**splty.** specialty
**Sq.** Square
**S.R.** Sons of the Revolution
**sr.** senior
**S S** Steamship
**SSS** Selective Service System
**St.** Saint, Street
**sta.** station
**stats.** statistics
**statis.** statistical
**STB, S.T.B.** Bachelor of Sacred Theology
**stblzn.** stabilization
**STD, S.T.D.** Doctor of Sacred Theology
**std.** standard
**Ste.** Suite
**subs.** subsidiary
**SUNY** State University of New York
**supr.** supervisor
**supt.** superintendent
**surg.** surgical
**svc.** service
**SW, S.W.** Southwest
**sys.** system

## T

**TAPPI** Technical Association of the Pulp and Paper Industry
**tb.** tuberculosis
**tchg.** teaching
**tchr.** teacher
**tech.** technical, technology
**technol.** technological
**tel.** telephone
**Tel. & Tel.** Telephone & Telegraph
**telecom.** telecommunications
**temp.** temporary
**Tenn.** Tennessee
**Ter.** Territory
**Ter.** Terrace
**TESOL** Teachers of English to Speakers of Other Languages
**Tex.** Texas
**ThD, Th.D.** Doctor of Theology
**theol.** theological
**ThM, Th.M.** Master of Theology
**TN** Tennessee
**tng.** training
**topog.** topographical
**trans.** transaction, transferred
**transl.** translation, translated
**transp.** transportation
**treas.** treasurer
**TT** Trust Territory
**TV** television
**TVA** Tennessee Valley Authority
**TWA** Trans World Airlines
**twp.** township

**TX** Texas
**typog.** typographical

# U

**U., univ.** University
**UAW** United Auto Workers
**UCLA** University of California at Los Angeles
**UDC** United Daughters of the Confederacy
**U.K.** United Kingdom
**UN** United Nations
**UNESCO** United Nations Educational, Scientific and Cultural Organization
**UNICEF** United Nations International Children's Emergency Fund
**UNRRA** United Nations Relief and Rehabilitation Administration
**UPI** United Press International
**U.P.R.R.** United Pacific Railroad
**urol.** urological
**U.S.** United States
**U.S.A.** United States of America
**USAAF** United States Army Air Force
**USAF** United States Air Force
**USAFR** United States Air Force Reserve
**USAR** United States Army Reserve
**USCG** United States Coast Guard
**USCGR** United States Coast Guard Reserve
**USES** United States Employment Service
**USIA** United States Information Agency
**USMC** United States Marine Corps
**USMCR** United States Marine Corps Reserve

**USN** United States Navy
**USNG** United States National Guard
**USNR** United States Naval Reserve
**USO** United Service Organizations
**USPHS** United States Public Health Service
**USS** United States Ship
**USSR** Union of the Soviet Socialist Republics
**USTA** United States Tennis Association
**USV** United States Volunteers
**UT** Utah

# V

**VA** Veterans Administration
**VA, Va.** Virginia
**vet.** veteran, veterinary
**VFW** Veterans of Foreign Wars
**VI, V.I.** Virgin Islands
**vice pres.** vice president
**vis.** visiting
**VISTA** Volunteers in Service to America
**VITA** Volunteers in Technical Assistance
**vocat.** vocational
**vol.** volunteer, volume
**v.p.** vice president
**vs.** versus
**VT, Vt.** Vermont

# W

**W, W.** West
**WA** Washington (state)
**WAC** Women's Army Corps
**Wash.** Washington (state)

**WATS** Wide Area Telecommunications Service
**WAVES** Women's Reserve, US Naval Reserve
**WCTU** Women's Christian Temperance Union
**we.** western
**W. Ger.** Germany, Federal Republic of
**WHO** World Health Organization
**WI** Wisconsin
**W.I.** West Indies
**Wis.** Wisconsin
**WSB** Wage Stabilization Board
**WV** West Virginia
**W.Va.** West Virginia
**WWI** World War I
**WWII** World War II
**WY** Wyoming
**Wyo.** Wyoming

# X Y

**YMCA** Young Men's Christian Association
**YMHA** Young Men's Hebrew Association
**YM & YWHA** Young Men's and Young Women's Hebrew Association
**yr.** year
**YT** Yukon Territory
**YWCA** Young Women's Christian Association

# Z

**zool.** zoological

# Alphabetical Practices

Names are arranged alphabetically according to the surnames, and under identical surnames according to the first given name. If both surname and first given name are identical, names are arranged alphabetically according to the second given name.

Surnames beginning with De, Des, Du, however capitalized or spaced, are recorded with the prefix preceding the surname and arranged alphabetically under the letter D.

Surnames beginning with Mac and Mc are arranged alphabetically under M.

Surnames beginning with Saint or St. appear after names that begin Sains, and are arranged according to the second part of the name, e.g., St. Clair before Saint Dennis.

Surnames beginning with Van, Von, or von are arranged alphabetically under the letter V.

Compound surnames are arranged according to the first member of the compound.

Many hyphenated Arabic names begin Al-, El-, or al-. These names are alphabetized according to each biographee's designation of last name. Thus Al-Bahar, Neta may be listed either under Al- or under Bahar, depending on the preference of the listee.

Also, Arabic names have a variety of possible spellings when transposed to English. Spelling of these names is always based on the practice of the biographee. Some biographees use a Western form of word order, while others prefer the Arabic word sequence.

Similarly, Asian names may have no comma between family and given names, but some biographees have chosen to add the comma. In each case, punctuation follows the preference of the biographee.

Parentheses used in connection with a name indicate which part of the full name is usually omitted in common usage. Hence, Chambers, E(lizabeth) Anne indicates that the first name, Elizabeth, is generally recorded as an initial. In such a case, the parentheses are ignored in alphabetizing and the name would be arranged as Chambers, Elizabeth Anne.

However, if the entire first name appears in parentheses, for example, Chambers, (Elizabeth) Anne, the first name is not commonly used, and the alphabetizing is therefore arranged as though the name were Chambers, Anne.

If the entire middle name is in parentheses, it is still used in alphabetical sorting. Hence, Belamy, Katherine (Lucille) would sort as Belamy, Katherine Lucille. The same occurs if the entire last name is in parentheses, e.g., (Brandenberg), Howard Keith would sort as Brandenberg, Howard Keith.

For visual clarification:

Smith, H(enry) George: Sorts as Smith, Henry George
Smith, (Henry) George: Sorts as Smith, George
Smith, Henry (George): Sorts as Smith, Henry George
(Smith), Henry George: Sorts as Smith, Henry George

## Biographies M-Z

**MA, CHUNG-PEI MICHELLE,** astronomer, educator; BS, PhD, MIT, 1993. From asst. prof. to assoc. prof. physics and astronomy U. Pa., Phila., 1996—2001; assoc. prof. astronomy U. Calif., Berkeley, 2001—. Contbr. articles to profl. jours. Recipient Annie J. Cannon award, 1997, 1st prize Taiwan Nat. Violin Competition, 1983, Cottrell Scholars award Rsch. Corp., 1999, Lindback award for Disting. Tchg., U. Pa., 1999; Alfred P. Sloan fellow, 1999; Sherman Fairchild fellow, 1993. Mem. Phi Beta Kappa. Achievements include research in the formation and evolution of galaxies and large scale structure in the Universe; performed numerical simulations of the clustering of dark matter in various cosmological models of structure formation from the Early Universe until the present day; computation of the temperature variations imprinted on the cosmic microwave background radiation which provides a snapshot of the infant Universe. Office: U Calif Berkeley Dept Astronomy 601 Campbell Hall Berkeley CA 94720

**MA, C-M (CHARLIE),** physicist, educator; b. Heilongjiang, China, Aug. 28, 1956; s. Defu Ma and Haibo Zhang; m. Lili Chen, Jan. 1, 1983; children: Caroline, Glenn. PhD, U. London, 1992. Diplomate Am. Bd. Radiology. Prof., dir. radiology physics Fox Chase Cancer Ctr., Phila., 2001 —; assoc. prof. Stanford U., Calif., 2000— 01; asst. prof., 1996—99; rsch. assoc. NRC, Ottawa, Ont., Canada, 1993—95; postdoctoral fellow Inst. Cancer Rsch./Royal Marsden Hosp., Sutton, Surrey, England, 1992—93. Mem. adv. bd. Physics Med. Biology Internat., 2002—. Grantee R01 (two cycles), NIH, 1999—; Idea grantee, U.S. Army Breast Cancer Rsch. Program, 1998—2001. Fellow: Inst. Physics, Am. Assn. Physicists in Medicine (computer com. 1996—2001, pub. edn. 1996—2001, radiation therapy com. 2000—03, pres. Del. chpt. 2004, Med. Physics Travel award 2000); mem.: Am. Coll. Med. Physics, Med. Dosimetry (adv. editor 2005—), Phys. Med. Biology (internat. adv. bd. 2002—), Am. Soc. Therapeutic Radiology and Oncology (Best Paper in Basic Sci. 1999), European Soc. Therapeutic Radiology and Oncology, Can. Orgn. Med. Physicists (Best Poster award 1999). Achievements include development of clinical implementation of Monte Carlo techniques for radiotherapy dose calculation; research in energy and intensity-modulated electron therapy (MERT) for radiation therapy; development of laser-accelerated proton (ion) beams for radiation therapy. Office: Fox Chase Cancer Center Radiology Oncology Dept 333 Cottman Ave Philadelphia PA 19111 Office Phone: 215-728-2996. Business E-Mail: charlie.ma@fccc.edu.

**MA, HE-PING,** physiologist; s. Hong-Xun Ma and Shu-Zhen Ni; m. You Liang, Mar. 21, 2003; m. Weiying Gao, Feb. 2, 1989 (div. July 28, 1998); children: Thomas, Joshua. MD, Harbin Med. U., China, 1987. Asst. prof. Emory U., Atlanta, 2003—05; assoc. prof. U. of Ala., Birmingham, 2005—. Grantee, NIH. Mem.: Am. Physiol. Soc. Office: U Ala 1530 3d Avenue S Birmingham AL 35294 Office Phone: 205-823-3327. Home Fax: 205-934-1147. Personal E-mail: hepingma@uab.edu. E-mail: heping_ma@yahoo.com.

**MA, JUN,** researcher; b. Jinan, China, Oct. 16, 1966; s. Enqi Ma and Xiuzhi Zhou; m. Yalan Li; 1 child, Alyssa. PhD, CUNY, 2004. Rsch. assoc. Jinan Inst. Botany, 1990—97; postdoctoral assoc. Biotech Ctr. Rutgers U., New Brunswick, NJ, 2004—. Contbr. articles to profl. jours. Mem. Am. Soc. Pharmacognosy (travel grantee 2002). Home: 1 Redcliffe Ave Apt 1B Highland Park NJ 08904 Office: Biotech Ctr Rutgers U 59 Dudley Rd New Brunswick NJ 08901 Office Phone: 732-932-8165 ext 229. Home Fax: 732-993-0174; Office Fax: 732-932-6535. Personal E-mail: junmalehman@yahoo.com. Business E-Mail: jun@rci.rutgers.edu.

**MA, JUN,** environmental consultant; Investigative journalist South China Morning Post, 1993—2000; cons., sr. rschr. Sinosphere Corp., Beijing; environ. cons. Bo Xin Consulting Co., Beijing. World fellow Yale U., New Haven. Author: China's Water Crisis, 1999. Named one of 100 Most Influential People, Time Mag., 2006.*

**MA, KOUGEN,** engineering educator, researcher; b. Jianhu, Jiangsu Province, China, Feb. 24, 1965; arrived in US, 2001; s. Guoxian Ma and Guilan Xu; m. Yang Tian, Aug. 28, 1992; 1 child, Zhengyuan. PhD, Nanjing U. Aeronautics and Astronautics, China, 1992. Assoc. prof. Nanjing U. Aeronautics and Astronautics, China, 1992—99; sr. scientist German Aerospace Ctr., Braunschweig, 1999—2001; assoc. rschr. U. Hawaii, Honolulu, 2001—. Recipient 2nd award Advancement of Sci. and Tech., China Aviation Industry, 1995, 3d award Advancement of Sci. and Tech., 1996, 1998, 1st award Advancement of Sci. and Tech., Jiangsu Province, 1995, 4th award Advancement of Sci. and Tech., 1996, Outstanding Young Core Faculty, 1996, 3d award Advancement of Sci. and Tech., Ministry of Edn., China, 1998, 1st in Advancement of Sci. and Tech., Nanjing U. Aeronautics and Astronautics, 1998, 3d prize article in natural sci., Nanjing Mcpl. Govt., 1999. Office: Univ of Hawaii Dept ME Holmes 302 2540 Dole St Honolulu HI 96822 Personal E-mail: kougen@wiliki.eng.hawaii.edu.

**MA, L. EVE ARMENTROUT,** television producer, educator; b. Dec. 28, 1943; d. Edward Goodwin and Lucy McIver (Watson) Ballard; m. David Parker Armentrout, 1966 (div. 1969); 1 child, Lucy Ann; m. Jeong-Huei Ma, Jan. 1970 (div. 1986); children: William Marshall, Edward Benjamin. Student, Middlebury Coll., 1961-63; BA, San Francisco State Coll., 1968; postgrad. in Chinese, Stanford U., 1971, MA, Calif. State U., Hayward, 1972; PhD in Chinese History, U. Calif., Davis, 1977; JD, U. Calif., Hastings, 1993. Bar: Calif., 1994. Tchg. asst. history dept. U. Calif., Davis, 1973-76; rsch. assoc. anthropology dept., 1977-79; asst. prof. history dept., 1980, 1982; rsch. assoc. applied behavioral scis. dept., 1982-83; asst. prof. Mills Coll., Calif., 1988-90; pvt. practice law, 1999—; asst. prof. Calif. State U., Hayward, 1986—88; prodr. Palomino Prodns. Cons. Golden Gate Nat. Rec. Area, San Francisco, 1979-80, Oakland (Calif.) Mus., 1981, ARC Assocs., Inc., Oakland, 1981-82, James R. Moore Atty. at Law, San Francisco, 1982, Pacific Ocean divsn. U.S. Army Corps. Engrs. Hawaii, 1983-86, Japan Engr., dist. U.S. Army Corps Engrs. Camp Zama, Japan, 1986-89. Author: (with others) Chinese of Oakland, 1982, sole author: Revolutionaries, Monarchists and Chinatowns, 1990, Hometown Chinatown, 2000; editor, contbr.: Farms, Firms and Runways: U.S. Military Bases, 2001; editor, contbr.: One Day, One Dollar, 1984, Chung-Hsi Liao-way T'ai (newsletter), 1986; contbr. articles to scholary volumes and jours.; prodr., host (TV series): Languages of Sound and Movement; prodr., dir. (TV series) Roots and Branches, others; prodr. DVDs. Mem. hist. and interpretive rev. com. Calif. Dept. Pks. and Recreation Multicultural Ctr., 1982-84; mem. design rev. com. Calif. State Railroad Mus., 1982-83; vol. tchr. pub. and pvt. schs., San Francisco Bay Area, 1973-86; local Girl Scout leader, 1976-79; local Cub and Boy Scout leader, 1985-98; other neighborhood assn., Richmond, Calif., 1974-87; bd. dirs. Chinese/Chinese-Am. History Assn., El Cerrito, Calif., 1979-86, Chinese Hist. Soc. of Am., 1983-90, Oakland Asian Culture Ctr., 1993-97, Celebrating Culture and Cmty., 1996-03; commr. Arts and Cultural Com. Contra Costa City, 1998-2004. Nat. Def. Fgn. Lang. fellow Stanford U., 1971, Am.-East Asian Rels. fellow U. Calif., Davis, 1972-73, Kellogg Found. grantee, 1977-79, Calif. Coun. Humanities grantee, 1981, 83-84, 98. Mem. Chinese Hist. Soc. Am. (bd. dirs. 1983-90), Assn. for Asian Studies, Am. Hist. Assn., Calif. Bar Assn., Contra Costa City Bar Assn., Inst. for Hist. Study, Ind. Scholars Asia, U. Calif-Berkeley Inst., East Asian Studies. Democrat. Address: 1355 Arlington Blvd El Cerrito CA 94530-2514 also: Palomino Prodns calle Carmen 6 11403 Jarez Spain Office Phone: 510-236-3257. Personal E-mail: palopro2004@yahoo.com.

**MA, LILI,** engineering educator; d. Qiang Ma and Yongqin Li. BS in Elec. Engring., Harbin U. Sci. and Tech., China, 1995; MS in Elec. Engring., Harbin U. Sci. and Tech., 1998; PhD in Elec. Engring., Utah State U., Logan, 2004. Engr. R&D, Hawei Electric Co. Ltd., Shenzhen, China, 1998—99; adj. lectr. dept. elec. and computer engring. Utah State U., Logan, Utah, 2004; software engr. Integrated Quality, Inc, Columbus, Ohio, 2005; postdoctoral rsch. assoc. dept. aerospace and ocean engring. Va. Tech, Blacksburg, 2005—. Finalist Robin Reward, Utah State U., 2003-2004. Mem.: AIAA, IEEE, Sigma Xi. Avocation: hiking. Office: Virginia Tech Aerospace and Ocean Engring Blacksburg VA 24061 Office Phone: 540-231-2019. Office Fax: 540-231-9632. Personal E-mail: lilima99@gmail.com. Business E-Mail: lma05@vt.edu.

**MA, MARY (MARY MA XUEZHENG),** computer company executive; married; 1 child. BA, Capital Normal U., Beijing, 1976. Bureaucrat, Chinese Academy of Sciences' Internat. Corp. bureau China State Coun., 1978—90; with Lenovo Group, 1990—, sr. v.p., CFO Beijing & Purchase NY, 1997—. Bd. dirs. SOHU.com. Named one of most powerful women, Forbes mag., 2005, 50 Most Powerful Women in Global Bus., Fortune mag., 2005. Office: Lenovo Group Haidan District No 6 Chuang Ye Road Beijing 100085 China Office Phone: 86-10-58868888.*

**MA, PATRICK C.,** oncologist, researcher; arrived in U.S., 1996; s. Hon-Ching Ma and Sook-Wah Lam; m. Liane L. Lee, Feb. 3, 1990; 1 child, Charissa T. BSc, U. Hong Kong, 1986; MSc, U. Toronto, Ont., Can., 1989, MD, 1994. Bd. cert. diplomate internal medicine and med. oncology ABIM. Instr. U. Chgo., 2003—05, asst. prof., 2005, Case Western Res. U., Cleve., 2005—. Contbr. articles to profl. jours. Recipient Lung Cancer Treatment award, Am. Cancer Soc., LUNGevity Found., 2004, K08 Career Devel. award, NIH/Nat. Cancer Inst., 2005—, Rsch. award, Ohio Cancer Rsch. Assocs., 2006—; Instl. Rsch. Grant award, Am. Cancer Soc., 2003, 2006. Mem.: Case Comprehensive Cancer Ctr., Am. Soc. Clin. Oncology (Young Investigator award 2002), Am. Assn. for Cancer Rsch. (Translational Lung Cancer Rsch. fellowship 2003—06). Office: Case Western Res U 10900 Euclid Ave Cleveland OH 44106 Office Fax: 216-368-1166. Business E-Mail: pcm9@case.edu.

**MA, SHIJUN,** engineering educator; b. Jixian, China, Sept. 29, 1932; s. Jintang and Xirong (Zhang) M.; m. Yuerui Tong, Feb. 14, 1958; children: Min Tong, Da Ma, Nian Ma. Student, Huazhong U. Sci. and Tech., China, 1957. Asst. lectr. HUST, Wuhan, China, 1957—61; lectr. Sichuan Forestry Inst., Xichang, China, 1962—71; lectr. assoc. prof. Southwest Jiotong U., Emei, China, 1975-89; engr. Xichang Machinery Factory, China, 1972-74; prof. Southwest Jiotong U., Chengdu, China, 1990—. Vis. scholar Howard U., Washington, 1987-88. Contbr. articles to profl. jours. Recipient Sichuan Province Sci. and Tech. award Sicuhan Province, Chengdu, 1989, Thesis award The Railway Ministry, Beijing, 1985, Govt. Spl. Allowance award The State Coun., Beijing, 1993, Nat. Sci. and Tech. award, Sci. and Tech. Ministry, Beijing, 1999. Mem. (sr.) CMES. Avocations: swimming, chinese chess. Office: Sch Mech Engring SW Jiaotong U Chengdu 610031 China Home: 6101 Emmett Guards Ct Fairfax Station VA 22039 Personal E-mail: shijun_ma@yahoo.com.

**MA, VU,** chemist; BA, Immaculata U., Malvern, Pa., 1997. Rsch. assoc. Pharmacopiea, Princeton, NJ, 1997—99; sr. assoc. scientist Amgen, Thousand Oaks, Calif., 1999—. Achievements include patents for Vanilloid receptor ligands and their use in treatments.

**MA, XIAOLIANG,** research scientist; b. Fuzhou, Fujian, China, Mar. 18, 1957; s. Hongxiang Ma and Xuan Lin; m. Xiuna Jiang; children: Ruilong, Toby. B in Engring. Sci., Zhejiang U., Hangzhou, China, 1982; M in Engring. Sci., China Coal Rsch. Inst., Beijing, 1987; D in Engring. Sci., Kyushu U., Fukuoka, Japan, 1995. Asst. engr. China Coal Rsch. Inst., Beijing, 1982—84, engr., 1987—91; vis. rschr. Nat. Inst. for Resources and Environment, Tsukuba, Ibaraki, Japan, 1991—92; rsch. assoc. dept. materials sci. and engring. Pa. State U., University Park, 1995—97, rsch. assoc. Energy Inst., 1998—2002, group leader Energy Inst., 2000—, sr. rsch. assoc., 2003—. Contbr. chapters to books, articles to profl. jours.; reviewer: profl. jours. Mem.: Am. Chem. Soc. (reviewer 1996—, mem. divsn. fuel chemistry 1995—, mem. divsn. petroleum chemistry 1995—). Avocation: photography. Office: The Energy Inst 209 Academic Projects Building University Park PA 16802-2308 Office Fax: 814-863-7432. Business E-Mail: mxx2@psu.edu.

**MA, XIAOMIN,** communications educator; s. Deying Wang and Yongzhong Ma; m. Ziping Hu, Mar. 15, 1991; 1 child, Siqi. PhD, Beijing U. Posts & Telecom, 1999. Asst. prof. Petroleum U. China, Dongying, 1989—95, assoc. prof., 1995—99; sr. rschr. Huawei Comm. Tech. Corp., Beijing, 1999—2000; postdoctoral rsch. assoc. Duke U., Durham, NC, 2000—03; asst. prof. Oral Roberts U., Tulsa, 2003—. Cons. Motorola, Chgo., 2000—02. Contbr. articles to profl. jours. Mem. tech. program com. IEEE Wireless Comm. Conf., Maui, Hawaii, 2005. Named Scholar of the Yr., Oral Roberts U., 2004—05; recipient Excellent Tchg. award Signal & Sys. course, Petroleum U. China, 1995; grantee Analysis of MAC layer protocols for Inter-vehicle comm., Oral Roberts U., 2005—06, Application of computational intelligence to modern code, Chinese Nature Sci. Found., 1997—2000, Auditing theory for communication networks, Motorola, 2000-2002. Mem.: IEEE (corr.). Achievements include patents pending for Methods and Systems for Improving Utilization of Traffic Channel in a Mobile Communications Network, Xiaomin Ma, Yun Liu, and K. S. Trivedi, filed by Patent Office of Duke University in Jan. 2002. Office: Oral Roberts University 7777 S Lewis Ave Tulsa OK 74171 Office Fax: 918-495-7648. E-mail: xma@oru.edu.

**MA, YEWEI,** research scientist; parents Jiaquan Ma and Yaqing Chen; m. Tong Xuefei, May 25, 2000; 1 child, Lucy. PhD, CAMS and PUMC, Beijing, 2003. Scientist U. Tex. Med. Br., Galveston, 2004—. Contbr. scientific papers to profl. pubis. Mem.: Am. Heart Assn. Achievements include research in medicine.

**MA, YINGYU,** research scientist; b. Chuma, China, Aug. 19, 1973; d. Xiaonian Ma and Shuirong Wang; m. Qing Ma. MD, Beijing Med. U., 1998; PhD, Northwestern U., Chgo., 2004. Postdoctoral fellow Roswell Pk. Cancer Inst., Buffalo, 2004—. Contbr. scientific papers to profl. jours. Recipient Achievements in Clin. Rsch. of Dermatology First prize, Bejing Med. U., 1997—98; grantee, Northwestern U. Grad. Sch., 2002—03; scholar, 1999—2004; Scholarship for Excellent Students, Bejing Med. U., 1994—95. Home: 175 North St #308 Buffalo NY 14201 Office: Roswell Park Cancer Inst Elm & Carlton Sts Buffalo NY 14263 Office Phone: 716-845-1257. Office Fax: 716-845-1258. Personal E-mail: yingyuma@yahoo.com. Business E-Mail: yingyu.ma@roswellpark.org.

**MA, YO-YO,** cellist; b. Paris, Oct. 7, 1955; m. Jill; children: Nicholas, Emily. Studied with Janos Scholz; studied with Leonard Rose, Juilliard Sch. Music, N.Y.C., 1962; AB, Harvard U., 1976, MusD (hon.), 1991. Peace amb. UN, 2006—. Debut at age 9, Carnegie Hall, N.Y.C.; appeared with Pablo Casals, Isaac Stern, Leonard Bernstein, Emanuel Ax, Jaime Laredo, performs throughout world with maj. orchs.; rec. artist Sony Classical; recs. include Portrait of Yo-Yo Ma, Japanese Melodies, Anything Goes (with Stephanie Grapelli), Hush (with Bobby McFerrin), Yo-Yo Ma at Tanglewood, The New York Album, Cello Suites Inspired By Bach, Great Cello Concertos, Made in America, Portrait of Cello Works, Premieres, Simply Baroque, Simply Baroque 2, Solo, Soul of The Tango, Tavener-Protecting Veil/Wake Up, Vivaldi's Cello, 2004. Recipient Avery Fisher prize, 1978, Sonning Music prize, 2006; 14-time Grammy award winning artist. Office: ICM Artists 40 W 57th St Fl 16 New York NY 10019*

**MA, ZHENKUI,** remote sensing applications scientist, consultant; b. Shenyang, Liaoning, China, Nov. 4, 1955; arrived in U.S., 1983; s. Deshan Ma and Shuxuan Zhang; m. Shufang Zhao; children: Bin, Jeanne. BS, Beijing Forestry Coll., 1982; MS, U. Mich., 1985, PhD, 1990. Sr. specialist Weyerhaeuser, Federal Way, Wash., 1996—2002, info. tech. cons., 2002—. Internat. cons. UN, Beijing, 1994—96. Mem.: Am. Soc. for Photogrammetry and Remote Sensing (bd. dirs. Seattle 2001, Puget Sound region). Achievements include research in mapping large geographic areas biodiversity protection. Home: 21745 113th Place SE Kent WA 98031 Office: Weyerhaeuser 33405 Eighth Ave South Federal Way WA 98003 Office Phone: 253-924-4772. Personal E-mail: zhenkui_ma@yahoo.com. Business E-Mail: zhenkui.ma@weyerhaeuser.com.

**MA, ZHENQIANG,** education educator; m. Shaoqin Gong, 1995; children: Alice L., David L. BS in Applied Physics, Tsinghua U., Beijing, 1991, BEE, 1991; MSEE, U. Mich., Ann Arbor, 1997, MS in Nuc. Sci., 1997, PhD, 2001. Faculty Tsinghua U., Beijing, 1991—94; rsch. asst. U. Mich., Ann Arbor, 1995—2001; R&D engr. Conexant Sys., Newport Beach, Calif., 2001—02, Jazz Semiconductor, Inc., Newport Beach, 2002; asst. prof. U. Wis., Madison, 2002—. Tech rev. rsch. panel MIT, Cambridge, 2004—; reviewer, presenter in field. Contbr. articles to profl. jours. Named Excellent Grad., Tsinghua U., 1991, Best Student Mentor, 1993; recipient 5.4 Youth medal, 1992, 12.9 award, 1992, Collaborative Disting. Publ. award, NASA, 2002, Best Student Paper award, ISDRS, 2005, SiRF, 2006; fellow, Ohio State U., 1994—95; scholar Grad. Student Rsch. scholar, U. Mich., Ann Arbor, 1995—2002; Rackham Travel fellow, 1996, 1998, Excellent Student scholar, Tsinghua U., 1987—91. Mem.: IEEE (exec. com. 2006—, session chmn. 2004, tech. program co-chmn. 2006), Electrochem. Soc., IEEE Comm. Soc., IEEE Lasers and Electro-Optics Soc., IEEE Microwave Theory and Techniques Soc., IEEE Electron Devices Soc. Achievements include design of heat transfer counter-balanced power devices; development of first model for recombination enhanced impurity diffusion process, first PIN-SiGe HBT integration; discovery of recombinantion enhanced impurity diffusion process in SiGe heterojuntion bipolar transistors, unconditionally stable common-base SiGe HBTs; relation between Kirk effect and Early effect at high bias in bipolar transistors; correlation between doping profile and power gain of SiGe HBTs, analytical expression for parasitic effects on power gain degradation; power gain relation between common-source and common-gate configurations, photoconductivity on decomposed Si linked by carbon nanotube network; invention of Integration of SiGe HBT and SiGe MODFET on SOI; patents for novel power devices for cell phone and other portable wireless devices; patents pending for Si-based common-base power amplifier, methods of fabricating one-side and/or double-side integrated thin-film transistors on single-crystal Semiconductors via layer transfer; process and device for enhanced resolution and readout speed in image sensing; solid-state high frequency high power device; fastest thin film transistor; first to report radiation effects on power SiGe HBTs and power MOSFETs; explore common-base configuration of SiGe power HBTs; State-of-the-art SiGe power HBTs; Analytical and graphical, full-frequency-range power gain relation between common-emitter and common-base configurations; First SiGe/Si power MODFETs; Up-scaling rule for high power semiconductor devices; research in new ballast resistor implemntaion rules in power semiconductor devices; relation between maximum oscillation frequency and device structure; first thin film transistors on tranferred strained single-crystal Si; Ge profile impact on power gain of SiGe HBTs; SiGe power HBTs at L-, S-, C-, X-, Ku- and K-bands; metal film texture control method using ion beam, FET-disciplined power bipolar transistors; SiGe power HBT base region optimization method, current gain enhancement using Ge under high base doping concentrations. Avocations: swimming, travel, ping pong/table tennis, home improvement, multimedia entertainment. Office: Univ Wis 1415 Engineering Dr 3445EH Madison WI 53706 Office Phone: 608-261-1095. Office Fax: 608-261-1095. Business E-Mail: mazq@engr.wisc.edu.

**MAACK, THOMAS,** physiology professor; MD, U. Sao Paulo, Brazil, 1961, D in Nephrology, 1980. Prof. physiology Weill Med. Sch. of Cornell U., N.Y.C., 1974—. Contbr. over 100 articles to profl. jours. Fellow: Am. Heart Assn.; mem.: Brazilian Acad. Scis. (life). Home: 402 E 90 St New York NY 10128 Office: Weill Med Coll of Cornell Univ 1300 York Ave New York NY 10021 Office Phone: 212-746-6343.

**MAAR, ROSINA,** medical products executive; BS, Ga. Inst. Tech., 1984; MD, Morehouse Sch. Medicine, 1988. Cert. internal medicine Ga. Med. Intern and resident in internal medicine Emory U. Sch. Medicine, Atlanta, 1991; physics lab. instr. Ga. Inst. Tech., Atlanta, 1981-84; rsch. asst. Emory U., Atlanta, 1985-86; med. evaluator maternal and infant project Grady Meml. Hosp., Atlanta, 1987-88; contract physician Wesley Woods Geriatric Hosp., Atlanta, 1989-90; contract physician, program dir. Piedmont Hosp./Spinal Shepard Ctr., Atlanta, 1989-91; med. dir. Cellcor, Inc., Atlanta, 1991-92, corp. med. dir. Newton, Mass., 1992-93; med. scientist med./regulatory svcs. Quintiles, Inc., Research Triangle Park, N.C., 1993-94, dir. med. svcs., 1994-95, v.p. clin. ops. 1995—, sr. v.p. strategic mgmt., until 1999; COO Clinicor, Inc., Austin, Tex., 1999—; venture prtnr. A.M. Pappas & Associates, 2000—. Contbr. articles and abstracts to med. jours. Mem.: AMA, ACP, Am. Bd. Internal Medicine (diplomat). Office: AM Pappas and Associates PO Box 110287 7030 Kit Creek Rd Durham NC 27709

**MAARBJERG, MARY PENZOLD,** retired office equipment company executive; b. Oct. 2, 1943; d. Edmund Theodore and Lucy Adelaide (Singleton) Penzold; m. John Peder Maarbjerg, Oct. 20, 1966; 1 child, Martin Peder. AB, Hollins Coll., 1965; MBA, Wharton Sch., Pa., 1969. Cons. bus. and fin., Stamford, Conn., 1977-78; corp. staff analyst Pitney Bowes, Inc., Stamford, 1978-80, mgr. pension and benefit fin., 1980-81, dir. investor rels., 1981-85; v.p. planning and devel. Pitney Bowes Credit Corp., Norwalk, Conn., 1985-86, treas., v.p. planning, 1986-94; v.p. mktg. devel. and mng. dir. Asia Pacific Bowes Fin. Svcs., 1994-95, v.p. ops. and mng. dir., 1995-97; v.p. corp. svcs. Pitney Bowes, Inc., Stamford, 1997-99, v.p. real estate and adminstrn., 1999-2001, v.p. adminstrn. and process integration, 2001—05. Bd. dirs. Stanford Dental Ctr., 2003—; mem. cmty. bd. U. Conn., Stamford, 2003—; bd. dirs. Person-to-Person, 2004—, treas., 2005—. Mem. adv. com. City of Stamford Mcpl. Employees Retirement Fund, 1980-85; mem. fin. adv. com. YWCA, Stamford, 1982-86; bd. dirs. Stamford Symphony, 1995-95, Vis. Nurses Assn., 1984-86, Am. Recorder Soc., 1986-98, Am. Classical Orch., 1999-2002; bd. dirs. Stamford Partnership, chmn., 1998—2003. Bd. dirs., treas. Amherst Early Music, 2000—. Fellow Royal Statis. Soc.; mem. Fin. Execs. Inst., Phi Beta Kappa. E-mail: mmaar@optonline.net.

**MAAS, COREY,** plastic surgeon; BS in Bio., Fla. St. Univ., Tallahassee, 1982; MD with hon., Univ. Fla. Coll. Med. Gainesville, Fla., 1986. Cert. Nat. Bd. Med. Examiners, 1987, Miss., 1987, Calif., 1991, Fla., 1996, Am. Bd. Otolaryngology, 1992, Am. Bd. Facial Plastic and Reconstructive Surgery, 1996. Gen. surg. intern St. Louis Univ. Med. Clinic, 1986—87, otolaryngology-head neck surgery resident, 1987—90, chief resident,

1990—91; fell. facial plastic and reconstructive surgery divsn. UC San Francisco Med. Clinic, 1991—92; private practice plastic surgeon San Francisco. Clin. instr., divsn. plastic surgery UC, San Francisco, 1991, assoc. clin. prof., 1992—; dir., facial plastic surgery tng. fell. Am. Acad. Facial Plastic and Reconstructive Surgery, 2000. Recipient Gold Key Scholastic Leadership honor, FSU, 1982, Sir Harold Delf Gilles Rsch. award, Am. Acad. Facial and Plastic Surgery, 1992, Nat. Cmty. Svc. award, 1994. Office: The Maas Clinic 2400 Clay St San Francisco CA 94115 Office Fax: 415-567-7011.*

**MAAS, DUANE HARRIS,** distilling company executive; b. Tilleda, Wis., Aug. 26, 1927; s. John William and Adela (Giessel) M.; m. Sonja Johnson, Mar. 11, 1950; children: Jon Kermit, Duane Arthur, Thomas Ervin. BS, U. Wis., 1951. With Shell Chem. Corp., 1951-59; plant mgr. Fleischmann Distilling Corp., Owensboro, Ky., 1959-63, Plainfield, Ill., 1963-65; asst. to v.p. Barton Distilling Co., Chgo., 1965-68, exec. asst. to pres., 1968, v.p. adminstrn., 1968; v.p., gen. mgr. Barton Brands, Inc., Chgo., 1968— 72; pres. Leaf Confectionery div. W.R. Grace, Chgo., 1972-74; v.p., gen. mgr. Romano Bros., Chgo., 1974-79; v.p., sec.-treas. Marketing Directions Inc., Chgo., 1974-77; pres. Associated Wine Producers, Inc., 1979-80; exec. v.p., chief exec. officer Mohawk Liqueur, Detroit, 1980-86; v.p. McKesson Wine & Spirits Group of N.Y., Detroit, 1982-86; pres. Mgmt. Cons. Services Co., Chgo., 1986—, U.S. Distilled Products Co., Princeton, Minn., 1996-99, Am. Distilled Products Corp., 2001—. Chmn. Qingdao Johnson Distiller Co. Ltd., Qingdao, China, 1996-99; past pres. Bart on Distilling (Sn.), Ltd.; past mng. dir. Barton Distilling (Scotland), Ltd.; past dir. Barton Distillers Europe, Barton Internat., Ltd. Sec.-treas. Plainfield Twp. Park Dist., 1967-70; chmn. Plainfield Planning and Zoning Commn., 1965-70. Served with USAAF, 1945-47. Mem.: Wis. Alumni Assn. Lutheran. Home and Office: N28W22312 Foxwood Ln Waukesha WI 53186 Office Phone: 262-617-6151. E-mail: dhm@mcservices.com.

**MAAS, JANE BROWN,** advertising executive; b. Jersey City; d. Charles E and Margaret (Beck) Brown; m. Michael Maas, Aug. 30, 1957; children: Katherine, Jennifer. BA, Bucknell U., 1953; postgrad., U. Dijon, France, 1954; MA, Cornell U., 1955; LittD, Ramapo Coll., 1986, St. John's U., 1988. Assoc. producer Name That Tune TV Program, N.Y.C., 1957—64; v.p. Ogilvy and Mather Inc., N.Y.C., 1964—76; sr. v.p. Wells, Rich, Greene, Inc., N.Y.C., 1976—82; pres. Muller Jordan Weiss Inc., N.Y.C., 1982—89, Earle Palmer Brown Cos., N.Y.C., 1989—92, chmn., 1992—94, chmn. emeritus, 1994—. Co-author: (book) How to Advertise, 1975, Better Brochures, 1981, Adventures of a Advertising Woman, 1986, The New How to Advertise, 1992, Christmas in Wales: A Homecoming, 1994. Bd govs comt Scholastic Achievement, 1985—92; active Girl Scouts US, NY, 1970—76; mem adv bd William E Simon Grad Sch Bus, Univ Rochester, 1989—2005; pub dir AIA, 1993—95; trustee Bucknell Univ, Lewisburg, 1976—86, Fordham Univ, NY, 1983—91. Named Woman of the Yr, NY Advert, 1986; recipient Matrix Award, Women in Communications, 1980. Mem.: AIA (hon.), Am Assn. Advt. Agys. (bd govs), Am Archtl. Found (regent 1993—2000), Phi Beta Kappa. Avocations: creative writing, jogging. Home: 3 Meadow Way Westhampton Beach NY 11978 Office Phone: 631-288-5881. Personal E-mail: janemaas@att.net.

**MAAS, JOE (MELVIN JOSEPH MAAS),** retired federal agency administrator; b. Washington, Feb. 29, 1940; s. Melvin Joseph and Katherine (Endress) M.; m. Constance Mary Haile, June 13, 1965; children: Christine, Michael, Kevin. BS, U. Md., 1965; postgrad., Stanford U., 1972—73. Dir. career edn. U.S. Dept. Labor, Washington, 1969-73; dep. dir. pers. SBA, Washington, 1973-76; dir. pers., 1976-82, asst. adminstr., 1982-95; founder, prin. Advancement Power, 2003—. Sr. v.p. Crave Entertainment Group, Inc., 2000 Bd. dirs., treas. Snowden Mill Assn., Silver Spring, Md., 1994-2002, pres. 2002-04; Wash. rep. Ind. Charities Am., 1995-96; bd. dirs. Amen Found., 1998—, Pres. Amen Found., 2003-05; chmn. Internat. Pers. Assn., 1982. With USMCR, 1957-64. Mem. Fed. Exec. Adminsts. Assn., Sr. Exec. Assn., Pub. Employee Roundtable (bd. dirs. 1994—, chmn. Pub. Svc. Excellence awards 1996-98, treas. 1998-2002), Coun. Former Fed. Execs. (pres., bd. dirs. 1995-2005), Nat. Assn. Ret. Fed. Employees (chpt. pres. 1996-98, v.p. 1998-2000, state tng. officer 1997-01), Volkswagen Club (pres. Washington chpt. 1988-95). Roman Catholic. Home: 2213 Aventurine Way Silver Spring MD 20904-5253 Personal E-mail: jm73bug@aol.com.

**MAAS, WERNER KARL,** microbiology educator; b. Kaiserslautern, Germany, Apr. 27, 1921; came to U.S., 1936, naturalized, 1945; s. Albert and Esther (Meyer) M.; m. Renata Diringer, Oct. 15, 1960; children— Peter, Andrew, Helen. AB, Harvard U., 1943; PhD, Columbia U., 1948. Postdoctoral fellow Calif. Inst. Tech., Pasadena, 1946-48; commd. officer USPHS, Tb Research Lab., Cornell U. Sch., N.Y.C., 1948-54; asst. prof. pharmacology NYU, 1954-57, assoc. prof. microbiology, 1957-63, prof., 1963-94, prof. emeritus, 1994—, chmn. dept. basic med. scis., 1974-81. Consultant USPHS, 1962—94. Mem.: Am. Soc. Microbiology, Genetics Soc. Am., Am. Soc. Biol. Chemists. Home: 86 Villard Ave Hastings On Hudson NY 10706-1821 Office: 550 1st Ave New York NY 10016-6402 Office Phone: 212-263-5322. E-mail: maasw01@endeavor.med.nyu.edu.

**MAATHAI, WANGARI,** environmentalist, consultant; b. Nyeri, Kenya, Africa, Apr. 1, 1940; children: Waweru, Wanjira, Muta. BSc, Mt. St. Scholastica, Atchison, Kans., 1964; MS in Biol. Scis., U. Pitts., 1966; PhD in Anatomy, U. Nairobi, Kenya, 1971; LLD (hon.), Williams Coll., 1990; DSc (hon.), Hobart & William Smith Coll., 1994; DAgr (hon.), U. Norway, 1997; LLD (hon.), Yale U., 2004. Lectr. U. Nairobi, 1971-82, chair, dept. veterinary anatomy, 1976, assoc. prof., dept. veterinary anatomy, 1977; ran for presidency Kenya, 1997; founder Green Belt Movement, Nairobi, 1977, coord., 1984—2002; mem. Parliament, Tetu Constituency Republic of Kenya, 2002—, asst. min. of environ., natural resources & wildlife, 2003—. Bd. dir. UN Sec. Generals Adv. Bd. on Disarmament; mem. UN Commn. on Global Governance; founding mem. GROOTS Internat., 1985; endowed chair in gender and women's studies named "Fuller-Maathai", Conn. Coll., 2002; Montgomery Fellow, Dartmouth Coll., 2001; Dorothy McCluskey vis. fellow for conservation, Yale U., 2002. Author: The Green Belt Movement, 1985, The Green Belt Movement: Sharing the Approach and the Experience, 1988, The Green Belt Movement: Sharing the Approach, 1992; featured in many publs. Bd. dir. Kenya Red Cross Soc., 1973-80, Jane Goodall Inst., Women and Environment Develop. Orgn., World Learning for Internat. Develop., Green Cross Internat., Worldwide Network of Women in Environ. Work; bd. dir., chmn. Environ. Liaison Ctr. Internat., Kenya, 1974-84, Nat. Coun. Women, Kenya, 1976-87, chair 1981-87; active Friends of Kenyatta Nat. Hosp., Kenya, 1975; launched Kenya Jubilee 2000 coalition, 1998; mem. adv. bd. Democracy Coalition Project; mem. Earth Charter Commn.; mem. selection com., Sasakawa Environ. prize, UN Environ. Program., Kenya. Recipient Women of Yr. award, 1983, Right Livelihood, 1984, Better World Soc. award, 1986, Windstar award for the Environment, 1988, Women of the World, 1989, Offeramus medal, 1990, Goldman Environ. prize, 1991, Africa prize for Leadership The Hunger Project, 1991, medal City of Edinburgh, Scotland, 1993, Jane Adams Leadership award, 1993, Golden Ark award, 1994, Juliet hollister award, 2001, Nobel Prize for Peace, 2004; co-recipient with Green Belt Movement Excellance award, Kenyen Cty. Council, 2004, 2001, Outstanding Vision and Commitment award, 2002, WANGO Environ. award, 2003, Sophie prize, 2004, Petra Kelly prize for Environment, 2004, J. Sterling Morton award, Conservation Scientist award, 2004, Arbor Day Found.; named to Global 500 Roll of Honor UN Environ. Program, 1990, 100 Heroines of the World, Internat. Women's Hall of Fame, 1995; elected by Earth Times as one of 100 persons in the World who have made a difference in the environ. arena, 1997; named one of 100 Most Influential People in World, Time Mag., 2005, one of most powerful women, Forbes mag., 2005. Mem. Club of Rome, Sasakawa Environ. Prize. Achievements include her work as a leader of the Green Belt Movement which has planted more than 30 million trees across Africa; awarded Nobel Peace Prize for her contribution to sustainable development, democracy, human rights, environmental conservation, peace and also for campaigning for broader women's rights; first East

and Central African women to earn a PhD; first female chair and assoc. prof. of the Dept. of Veterinary Anatomy at the U. Nairobi; first female African to be awarded the Nobel Peace Prize. Office: care Green Belt Movement PO Box 67545 Nairobi Kenya*

**MAATMAN, GERALD LEONARD,** insurance company executive; b. Chgo., Mar. 11, 1930; s. Leonard Raymond and Cora Mae (Van Der Laag) M.; children: Gerald L. Jr., Mary Ellen; m. Bernice Catherine Brummer, June 3, 1971. BS, Ill. Inst. Tech., 1951. Asst. chief engineer Ill. Inspection & Rating Bur., Chgo., 1951-58; prof., dept. chmn. Ill. Inst. Tech., Chgo., 1959-65; v.p. engring. Kemper Group, Chgo., 1966-68, pres. Nat. Loss Control Svc. Corp., 1969-74, v.p. corp. planning Long Grove, Ill., 1974-79, sr. v.p. info. svcs. group, 1979-85, exec. v.p. ins. ops., 1985-87; pres. Kemper Nat. Ins. Co., Long Grove, Ill., 1987-92, CEO, 1989-95, also bd. dirs., chmn. bd. dirs., 1991-95. Bd. dirs. Underwriters Labs., 1991-2002. Lt. (j.g.) USCGR, 1952-54. Mem. Knollwood Golf Club, Springs Club, Tau Beta Pi. Republican.

**MAATSCH, DEBORAH JOAN,** manufacturing executive; b. Lincoln, Nebr., Mar. 26, 1950; d. Leon F. Forst and Jarolyn J. Hoffman Forst Conrad; m. Gordon F. Maatsch, Mar. 14, 1969; children: Jason, Diana. BS, U. Nebr., Lincoln, 1976; MBA, U. Phoenix, 1997. Accredited tax advisor; IRS enrolled agt. Acct., supr. US Civil Svc., Heidelberg, Germany, 1971—73; paralegal Mattson Rickets Davies et al, Lincoln, Nebr., 1976—87; tax cons., 1981—; paralegal Wade Ash Woods & Hill, P.C., 1986—94; sr. trust adminstr. Investment Trust Co., 1994—96; compliance officer Nelson, Benson and Zellmer, Inc., 1995—96; pres. DGJD Inc., 1993—; contr. Arena Devel., Inc., 1996—2000; pres. Boyd Industries, Inc., 2001—. Mem. Park County Sr. Wellness Team, 1999—; mem. bus. adv. bd. Ponderosa HS, 1994-98. Contbr. articles to profl. jour. Event chmn., vol. Jefferson Cmty. Ctr., 1999—; bd. dirs. JCCA, 2001-03, pres., 2002-03; bd. dirs. Kids Roundup, 2002—; coord. Jefferson Hist. Preservation Fund; mem. Women's C. of C. Mem. Doane Coll. Alumni Assn. (dir. 1989-93), Nebr. Alumni Assn. Avocations: travel, outdoor activities, horses. Office: DGJD Inc PO Box 267 Jefferson CO 80456-0267 also: Boyd Industries Inc PO Box 315 Boyd TX 76023 E-mail: dgjdmaatsch@aol.com.

**MAAZEL, LORIN,** conductor, composer, violinist, music director; b. Neuilly, France, Mar. 6, 1930; s. Lincoln and Marie (Varencove) M.; m. Dietlinde Turban, 1986; 3 children; 4 children from previous marriages. Studies with Vladimir Bakaleinikoff; student, U. Pitts., Mus. D. (hon.), 1968; H.H.D., Beaver Coll., 1973. Debut as condr., 1938; condr. Am. symphony orchs., 1939—; violin recitalist; European debut, 1953; festivals include Bayreuth, Salzburg, Edinburgh; tours include S.Am., Australia, USSR, Japan, Korea, People's Republic China; artistic dir. Deutsche Opera Berlin, 1965-71; assoc. prin. condr. New Philharm. Orch., London, 1970-72; dir. Cleve. Orch., 1972-82, condr. emeritus, 1982-86; dir. Vienna State Opera, 1982-84; music dir. Pitts. Symphony Orch., 1988-96, Orchestre Nat. de France, 1988-90, Bavarian Radio Symphony Orch., Munich, 1993-2001; music dir. NY Philharmonic, 2002-. Decorated officer Legion d'Honneur 1981; Finnish Commdr. of the Lion; Portuguese Commdr.; Comdr. Cross of Merit, Germany. Achievements include 500 opera and concert performances with 150 orchestras; raised millions of dollars for benefit of UNESCO, World Wide Fund for Nature, the Red Cross, and UN High Commisioner for Refugees. Avocations: tennis, swimming, collecting American paintings and Oriental art. Office: NY Philharmonic Avery Fisher Hall 10 Lincoln Center Plaza New York NY 10023-6990*

**MABASA, TERESA ALBAR,** social welfare association administrator; b. Roxas City, Capiz, The Philippines, Oct. 2, 1935; d. Catalino Martelino Mabasa and Antonia Andrada Albar. BE, U. The Philippines, Diliman, Quezon City, 1956; MA in Social Work, St. Louis U., 1968; PhD in Orgn. & Devel. and Planning Inst., S.E. Asia Interdisciplinary Devel., Antipolo, The Philippines, 1981. Registered social worker. Acad. dean La. Salette U., Santiago City, The Philippines, 1982-85; prin. Devel. Ctr. of Nazareth, Aklan, The Philippines, 1988-91; ministry coord. for social svcs. Daus. of Charity of St. Vincent de Paul, Paranaque, The Philippines, 1991-94, asst. visitatrix, 1994-97, CEO, 1997—2003. Program dir. CARITAS Manila, 1978-81; cons. planning Manila Archdiocese, 1996-97. Vol. Nat. Movement Free Election, Indonesia and The Philippines, co-chair Parañaque chpt., 1996-2004; mem. Konsyensyang Pilipino, 1996-2004. Recipient Most Outstanding Adminstr. in Western Visayas Region award Dept. of Edn., Iloilo, 1987, Most Outstanding Profl. Social Worker award Profl. Regulation Com., Manila, 2000; scholar U. The Philippines, 1952. Mem. AMRSP (bd. dirs. 1999-2003), Philippine Assn. Social Workers Inc. (life, pres. Iloilo chpt. 1987-88, cons. 1998-99) Roman Catholic. Avocations: reading, swimming, museums, plays. Home and Office: Daus of Charity St Vincent 8486 E Service Rd Km 18S NCR Paranaque 1700 MM Philippines Fax: 63.2.838.8987. Office Phone: 632-838-3961, 838-39-61 to 63.

**MABE, WALTER LEE,** music educator; b. Reidsville, N.C., Mar. 19, 1958; s. Morris and Ruth Mabe; m. DeLee Mabe; 1 child, Zach Micah. B in Music Edn., U. N.C., 1980, MusM, 1987. Lic. tchr. N.C. Tchr. Guildford County Sch., Greensboro, NC, 1980—81, Lexington (N.C.) City Sch., 1981—. Dir. music 1st Meth. Ch., Lexington, 1994—. Named Tchr. of Yr., Lexington City Sch., 1997, 2005. Mem.: Am. Choral Dirs. Assn. (N.C. h.s. rep. 1998—2000), N.C. Music Educators Assn. (chmn. 2000—02, Music Tchr. of Yr. 2005). Home: 309 W 2nd Ave Lexington NC 27292

**MABEE, CARLETON,** historian, educator; b. Shanghai, Dec. 25, 1914; s. Fred Carleton and Miriam (Bentley) M.; m. Norma Dierking, Dec. 20, 1945; children: Timothy 1., Susan (Mrs. Paul Newhouse). AB, Bates Coll., 1936; MA (Perkins scholar), Columbia U., 1938, PhD, 1942. With Civilian Pub. Svc., 1941-45; instr. history Swarthmore (Pa.) Coll., 1944; tutor Olivet (Mich.) Coll., 1947-49; asst. prof. liberal studies Clarkson Coll. Tech., Potsdam, NY, 1949-51, asso. prof., 1951-55; prof., 1955-61; dir. social studies divsn. Delta Coll., University Center, Mich., 1961-64; prof., chmn. dept. humanities and social scis. Rose Poly. Inst., Terre Haute, Ind., 1964-65; prof. history State U. Coll. at New Paltz, NY, 1965-80, prof. emeritus NY, 1980—. Participant in projects for Am. Friends Svc. Com., 1941-47, 53, 63; Fulbright prof. Keio U., Tokyo, 1953-54 Author: The American Leonardo, A Life of Samuel F.B. Morse, 1943, The Seaway Story, 1961, Black Freedom: The Nonviolent Abolitionists from 1830 through the Civil War, 1970, Black Education in New York State: From Colonial to Modern Times, 1979, (with Susan Mabee Newhouse) Sojourner Truth: Slave, Prophet, Legend, 1993, Listen to the Whistle: An Ancedotal History of the Wallkill Valley Railroad in Ulster and Orange Counties, N.Y., 1995; editor: (with James A. Fletcher) A Quaker Speaks from the Black Experience: The Life and Selected Writings of Barrington Dunbar, 1979, Bridging the Hudson: The Poughkeepsie Railroad Bridge and its Connecting Rail Lines, a Many-Faceted History, 2001, Gardiner and Lake Minnewaska, 2003; contbr. articles to profl. jours. Trustee Young-Morse Hist. Site, Poughkeepsie, N.Y., 1991-2002; ofcl. town historian, Gardiner, N.Y. Recipient Pulitzer prize in biography, 1944, Bergstein award for excellence in tchg. Delta Coll., 1963, Anisfield-Wolf award race rels., 1971, Gustavus Myers award for outstanding book on human rights, 1994; rsch. grantee Rsch. Found. SUNY, 1965, 67, 68, 80, Am. Philos. Soc., 1970, Nat. Inst. Edn., 1973-76, NSF, 1982-83. Mem. N.Y. State Hist. Assn., Phi Beta Kappa, Delta Sigma Rho. Methodist. Home: 2121 Route 44-55 Gardiner NY 12525-5808

**MABEY, RALPH R.,** lawyer; b. Salt Lake City, May 20, 1944; s. Rendell Noel and Rachel (Wilson) M.; m. Sylvia States, June 5, 1968; children: Kathryn, Rachel, Elizabeth, Emily, Sara. BA, U. Utah, 1969; JD, Columbia U., 1972. Bar: Utah 1972, U.S. Dist. Ct. Utah 1972, U.S. Ct. Appeals (10th cir.) 1976, N.Y. 1985, U.S. Supreme Ct. 1988, U.S. Ct. Appeals (4th cir.) 1988, U.S. Ct. Appeals (3d cir.) 1993. Law clk. Atty. Gen., Salt Lake City, 1970, U.S. Dist. Ct., Salt Lake City, 1972-73; ptnr. Irvine, Smith & Mabey, Salt Lake City, 1973-79; U.S. bankruptcy judge U.S. Ct., Salt Lake City, 1979-83; ptnr. LeBoeuf, Lamb, Greene & MacRae LLP, Salt Lake City and

NYC, 1983—2005, Mabey & Murray LC, Salt Lake City, 2005—06; sr. of counsel Stutman Treister & Glatt, LA, 2006—. Sr. lectr. Brigham Young U. Sch. Law, Provo, Utah, 1983-2005, U. Utah Coll. Law, Salt Lake City, 1983-85, adj. prof., 2006—. Mng. editor Norton Bankruptcy Law Adviser, 1983-85. With USAR, 1968-74. Mem. ABA (bus. bankruptcy com., select adv. com. on bus. reorgns.), Nat. Bankruptcy Conf., Am. Law Inst., Am. Bankruptcy Inst., Am. Coll. Bankruptcy. Republican. Mem. Lds Ch. Avocations: running, fly fishing. E-mail: rmabey@stutman.com.

**MABILANGAN, FELIPE HUGO, JR.,** diplomat; b. Manila, Feb. 15, 1936; s. Felipe and Felisa (Hugo) M.; m. Ada Ledesma, Dec. 8, 1943; children: Jose Antonio, Anne Marie, Lisa. BA, Balliol Coll., U. Oxford, Eng., 1959; MA, Balliol Coll., U. Oxford, 1964; diploma in internat. rels., U. Geneva, 1965. Fgn. svc. officer Philippines Ministry Fgn. Affairs, 1962-75, dir. gen., 1975-79, permanent del. to UNESCO, 1980—88, amb. to France and Portugal, 1979—88; amb. to People's Republic of China, 1990-94; permanent rep. of The Philippines to the UN, NYC, 1994—2001; sr. fgn. affairs adviser Dept. Fgn. Affairs, Republic of the Philippines, Manila, 2004—. Mem. adv. com. on adminstrv. and budgetary questions UN, 2001—03. Decorated Order of Diplomatic Merit Republic of Korea; Nat. Order of Merit France; recipient Outstanding Young Men award for govt. svc. Manila Jaycees, 1975, Gawad Mabini award Pres. of Philippines; Carnegie fellow U. Geneva, 1964-65. Mem. Manila Polo Club, Racing Club France (Paris). Office: 117 Gamboa St Legaspi Village Makati Philippines

**MABRY, CYNTHIA CALLANDS,** secondary school educator; b. Lynchburg, Va., Oct. 2, 1956; d. Frank James and Jeannette Irvine Callands; m. Bruce Dolese Mabry, July 19, 1980; 1 child, Brandon Dolese. BA, Lynchburg Coll., Va., 1979. Tchr. Lynchburg City Schs., 1989—. Vol. Share Va., Lynchburg, 2000—06; pres. Fifth St. Bapt. Ch. Task Force, 2006; dir. Fifth St. Bapt. Ch. Vacation Bible Sch., 2000—06; mem. Fifth St. Bapt. Ch. Mass Choir, 1988—2006; asst. treas. Fifth St. Bapt. Ch. Edn. Ministry, 2004—06; pres. His Chosen Sounds, 1998—2006. Mem.: NEA (life), Va. Edn. Assn. (life), Lynchburg Edn. Assn. (life), Delta Sigma Theta (life). Home: 227 Lansing Avenue Lynchburg VA 24503 Office: Heritage High School 2030 Wardsferry Road Lynchburg VA 24502 Office Phone: 434-582-1147. Home Fax: 434-582-1137; Office Fax: 434-582-1137. Personal E-mail: mabrycc@yahoo.com. E-mail: mabrycc@lcsedu.net.

**MABRY, DONALD JOSEPH,** retired academic administrator, history professor; b. Atlanta, Apr. 21, 1941; s. Jerry Leon and Eunice Leigh (Harris) M.; m. Susan Strong Johnston, July 28, 1962 (div. Oct. 1986); children: Scott, Mark; m. Paula Ann Crockett, Dec. 18, 1992. BA, Kenyon Coll., Gambier, Ohio, 1963; MEd, Bowling Green State U., 1964; PhD, Syracuse U., 1970. Instr. St. Johns River CC, Palatka, Fla., 1964—67; rsch. asst. fin. aid Syracuse U., NY, 1967—68, teaching fellow in history, 1968—69, Maxwell fellow, 1969—70, vis. lectr. dept. history, 1969—70; asst. to chancellor U. Kans., Lawrence, 1978—79; from. asst. prof. to prof. dept. history Miss. State U., Mississippi State, 1970—, asst. to pres., 1979—81, assoc. dean for budget and rsch., 1991—2001; now dir., assoc. dean Biol. Physical Sciences Rsch. Inst., Mississippi State, Miss.; ret. Sr. fellow, Ctr. for Internat. Security and Strategic Studies Miss. State U., 1981—91. Author: Mexico's Accion Nacional, 1973, The Mexican University and the State, 1982, (with others) Neighbors--Mexico and the United States, 1981; editor: The Latin American Narcotics Trade and U.S. National Security, 1989; contbr. articles to profl. jours. Mem. Am. Coun. on Edn. (exec. com. Coun. of Fellows 1980-83), South Ea. Coun. on Latin Am. Studies, Hist. Text Archive (founding editor) Avocation: computer telecommunications. Home: 206 Hiwassee Dr Starkville MS 39759-2105 Office Phone: 662-325-3604.

**MABRY, PHILIP T.,** political scientist, consultant; b. Spartanburg, SC, Feb. 29, 1940; s. Roy T. and Eleanor Eva (Waddell) Mabry; m. Mary E. Byars, July 3, 1961 (div. Mar. 1980); children: Tammy Kay Waldrop, Phyllis Dianne Gibbons, Sonya Kowalski; m. Amy D. Mabry, June 18. Founder Ams. for Human Rights, Greenville, SC, 1975—79; pres. Western Rsch. Cons., Euless, Tex., 1982—; dir. Western Rsch., Euless, Tex., 2000—. Cons. U.S. Dept. State, Washington, 1982—87. Contbr. news articles, interviews on Iran/Contra and Iran hostage af. Polit. activist Rep. Party, Washington, 1962—. Recipient Cert. of Appreciation, Nat. Rep. Party, 2001, Cert. of Membership, Acad. Polit. Sci., 2001, Republican Commn. Accomplishment award, Nat. Rep. Senatorial Com., D.C., 2003, U.S. Congl. Order Merit award, Nat. Rep. Congl. Com., D.C., 2005. Mem.: Acad. Polit. Sci. Republican. Avocations: golf, coin collecting/numismatics, reading, history. Home: 125 Wanda Way Apt 119 Hurst TX 76053

**MAC, BERNIE,** actor, comedian; b. Chgo., Oct. 5, 1958; m. Rhonda McCullough, 1977; 1 child. Became profl. comedian, 1977. Actor: (films) Mo' Money, 1992, Who's the Man?, 1993, House Party 3, 1994, The Walking Dead, 1995, Friday, 1995, Get on the Bus, 1996, Don't Be a Menace to South Central While Drinking Your Juice in the Hood, 1996, How to Be a Player, 1997, Booty Call, 1997, The Players Club, 1998, Life, 1999, The Original Kings of Comedy, 2000, What's the Worst That Could Happen?, 2001, Ocean's Eleven, 2001, Head of State, 2003, Charlie's Angels: Full Throttle, 2003, Bad Santa, 2003, Mr. 3000, 2004, Ocean's Twelve, 2004, (voice) Lil' Pimp, 2005, Guess Who, 2005; (TV series) Moesha, 1996; actor, prodr.: The Bernie Mac Show, 2001— (Image award NAACP, 2003, 2004). Recipient Outstanding Actor in a Comedy Series, NAACP Image Awards, 2006. Office: The Bernie Mac Show Attn Fox Broadcasting Publicity Dept PO Box 900 Beverly Hills CA 90213-0900*

**MACADAM, STEPHEN E.,** wholesale distribution executive; BS, Univ. Ky.; MS, Boston Coll.; MBA, Harvard Univ. Cons. positions through prin. McKinsey & Co., Charlotte, NC. 1988—98; sr. v.p. containerboard & packaging Georgia-Pacific Corp., 1998—2000; exec. v.p. pulp & paperboard Georgia-Pacific, 2000—01; pres., CEO Consolidated Container Co., 2001—05; dir. BlueLinx Holdings, Atlanta, 2004—, CEO, 2005—. Office: BlueLinx Holdings 4300 Wildwood Pkwy Atlanta GA 30339*

**MACAGNO, EDUARDO R.,** biology professor, dean; b. Argentina, 1943; arrived in US, 1956; married; 2 children. PhD, Columbia Univ., 1968. Faculty Columbia Univ., 1973—93, assoc. v.p. rsch., grad. edn., dean grad. sch. arts and sci., 1993—2000; founding dean, divsn. biology, Richard C. Atkinson prof. biology Univ. Calif. San Diego, 2001—. Rev. panel NIH, NRC. Co-editor: Jour. Neurobiology. Named one of 50 Most Important Hispanics in Govt., Edn., Hispanic Engineer and Info. Tech. mag., 2005; recipient Javits Investigator award, NIH. Office: Dean - Biological Sci-0376 UCSD 9500 Gilman Dr La Jolla CA 92093-0376 Office Phone: 858-534-4281. Office Fax: 858-534-7314. Business E-Mail: dean@biology.ucsd.edu, emacagno@ucsd.edu.*

**MACAL, ZDENEK,** conductor, music director; b. Jan. 8, 1936; Student, Janacek Music Acad. Music dir. Milw. Symphony Orch., 1986-96; chief condr. Cologne Radio Orch., 1970-74; former chief condr. Prague Symphony, Hannover Radio Orch., Sydney Symphony Orch.; music dir. N.J. Symphony, Newark, 1993—2002, music dir. emeritus, 2002—; music dir. Czech Philharm. Orch., 2003—. Office: NJ Symphony 2 Central Ave Newark NJ 07102-3119*

**MACALISTER, ROBERT STUART,** retired oil industry executive; b. LA, May 22, 1924; s. Robert Stuart and Iris Grace (Doman) MacAlister; m. Catherine Vera Willby, Nov. 15, 1947 (dec. 1994); children: Rodney James, Sara Marjorie; m. Grace V. LeClerc, Dec. 2, 1995. Student, Brighton Coll., Sussex, Eng., 1945; BSME, Calif. Inst. Tech., 1947. Registered profl. engr., Tex. Petroleum engr. Shell Oil Co., 1947—56; mgmt. trainee Royal Dutch Shell, The Hague, Netherlands, 1956—57; with exec. staff, mgr. Shell Oil Co., U.S.A., 1957—60; v.p., ops. mgr. Occidental Petroleum Corp., Tripoli, Libya, 1968—71, mng. dir. various subs. London, 1971—76; mng. dir. Occidental Internat. Oil, Inc., London, 1976—78; chmn. bd. Can. Occidental Petroleum Ltd., Calgary, Alta., 1978—81; mng. dir. Australian

Occidental Petroleum Ltd., Sydney, 1982—83, Hamilton Bros. Oil & Gas Ltd., London, 1983—86. Exe. U.K. Offshore Operators, London, 1972—78, London, 1983—86. Cubmaster Boy Scouts Am., Larchmont, NY, 1964—65, scoutmaster Houston, 1965—68. Sgt. U.S. Army, 1944—45, ETO. Mem.: Can. Petroleum Assn. (bd. govs. 1978—81), Soc. Petroleum Engrs., Am. Assn. Petroleum Geologists, Caltech Torchbearer, Las Posas Country Club, Gold Coast Srs. Republican. Episcopalian. Avocations: carpentry, crafts, watercolor painting, golf, gardening. Home and Office: 78 Lopaco Ct Camarillo CA 93010-8846

**MACALLASTER, ARCHIE,** investment company executive; Grad., U.S. Naval Acad., 1953. Pres. Pitfield MacKay (now MacAllaster Pitfield MacKay), 1984—; CEO MacAllaster Pitfield MacKay, N.Y., chmn. Trustee emeritus St. Lawrence U.; trustee Clark Fedn. Mem.: The Clark Found. Office: MacAllaster Pitfield MacKay 30 Broad St New York NY 10004 Office Phone: 212-422-9250.

**MACALPINE, MICHELLE LEWIS,** neuroscientist; b. Colorado Springs, Colo., Dec. 19, 1954; d. Arthur and Erma Lewis; m. J. David MacAlpine; children: Kira, Caylan. BA, Colo. State U., 1983; PhD, U. Tex.-Dallas, Richardson, 1998. Owner Lariat, Ft. Collins, Colo., 1983-87, Brain Tng., Plano, Tex., 1995—; trainer Lectra, Richardson, 1987-89. Author: Word Master, 1996, Treating Developmental Delays and Autistic Spectrum Disorders, 1997, 2d edit., 1998, Brain Training: New Hope for Children with Developmental Delays, 2004, Sensory Processing Disorders, 2006. Mem.: Mensa. Democrat. Achievements include obtaining of 100% recovery rate in group of autistic children by promoting their cognitive development. Office: Brain Tng 2301 Ohio Dr #130 Plano TX 75093 Office Phone: 972-964-8510. E-mail: braintrain@aol.com.

**MACALUSO, CHRISTIE A.,** bishop; b. June 12, 1945; M in Sacred Theology, St. Mary's Seminary, Balt.; MA in philosophy, Trinity U., Hartford; MA in psychology, NYU; Doctoral Studies, New Sch. for Social Rsch. N.Y.C. Ordained priest Roman Cath. Ch., 1971. Priest Archiodecese of Hartford, Conn., 1971, consecrated aux. bishop Conn., 1997, aux. bishop Conn., 1997, consecrated bishop Conn., 1997—. Office: 134 Farmington Ave Hartford CT 06105-3723

**MACALUSO, FRANK AUGUSTUS,** oil industry executive, bank executive; b. Cheyenne, Wyo., May 27, 1931; s. Frank R. and Thelma Elizabeth (Speight) M.; m. Margaret Ann Lynch, Oct. 14, 1950; children: Anne Marie Macaluso Foust, Elizabeth Mary Macaluso Nance, Margaret Mary Macaluso Walters, Teresa Marie Macaluso Fleming, Frank A. Jr. BA, Regis Coll., 1950. Asst. cashier Merchants Bank, Gallup, N.Mex., 1950—52, Citizens Bank, Aztec, N.Mex., 1952—56; v.p. 1st Nat. Bank, Farmington, N.Mex., 1957—59; founder, chmn., CEO Macaluso Oil Co., Farmington, 1959—2000; dir. Four Corners Savs. Bank, Farmington, 1969—85; organizer, chmn. bd. dirs. Sunwest Bank, Farmington, 1974—97; dir. Sunwest Fin. Svcs., Albuquerque, 1988—92. Chmn. Amigo Petroleum Co., Albuquerque, 1988—; chmn. Texaco Wholesale Coun., 1994; pres., dir. Star Makers Acceptance Corp., 1994-97; founder, dir., chmn. bd. Four Corners Cmty. Bank, Farmington, N.Mex., 2000—. Mem. Gov's. Bus. Adv. Coun., N.Mex. State Bd. Fin., Santa Fe, 1972-80, 91-95, N.Mex. Energy Conversation Comm., N.Mex. 1st, Albuquerque, 1986—; bd. dirs. U. N.Mex. Found., Albuquerque, 1988-98. Named Boss of Yr. by Jaycees, 1971, Top 100 Powerbrokers N.Mex. Bus. Weekly, 2000. Mem. N.Mex. Petroleum Marketers Assn. (pres. 1974-75), N.Mex. Amigos, San Juan Country Club (pres. 1980-82), Farmington C. of C., KC, Elks. Democrat. Roman Catholic. Avocation: golf. Office: PO Box 90 2501 E Main St Farmington NM 87401-7723 E-mail: fmacaluso@amigopetroleum.com.

**MACAN, WILLIAM ALEXANDER, IV,** lawyer; b. Boston, Nov. 21, 1942; s. William A. and Carol (Whitten) M.; m. Jane Mitchell Ahern, Sept. 3, 1965; children: Sandi, Andrew. BS, Haverford Coll., 1964; LLB, U. Pa., 1967. Bar: Pa. 1968, U.S. Tax Ct. 1970, N.Y. 1999. Law clk. to judge U.S. Tax Ct., Washington, 1967-69; assoc. firm Morgan, Lewis & Bockius LLP, Phila., 1969-76, ptnr., 1976-2000, Allen & Overy LLP, N.Y.C., 2000—, of counsel, 2004—. Lectr. legal instns., seminars. Author publs. on tax-oriented equipment leasing, other tax subjects. Mem. ABA. Presbyterian. Office: Allen & Overy 1221 Ave of the Americas New York NY 10020 Office Phone: 212-610-6413. Business E-Mail: william.macan@newyork.allenovery.com.

**MACARIN-MARA, LYNN,** psychotherapist, consultant; b. Queens, N.Y., Feb. 27, 1948; d. David and Grace Macarin; m. Marvin Weingast, Sept. 2, 2000; 1 child, Leah Mara. MA, NYU, 1972; MSW, Hunter Sch. Social Work, 1980. Cert. psychoanalytic psychotherapy, hypnotherapy and hypnoanalysis. With Greenwich Inst. Psychotherapy and Psychoanalysis, 1984-87; pvt. practice, 1987—; pres. Face to Face Psychotherapy Svcs., Metuchen, N.J., 1987—; dir. family and children svcs. Ednl. Alliance, Inc., N.Y.C., 1990-95. Adj. prof. SUNY, Staten Island, N.Y., 1972-73, New Sch. for Social Rsch., N.Y.C., 1980-81. Contbr. articles to profl. jours. Chairperson membership com. Temple Emanu-El, Edison, N.J., 1998-2001. Mem. N.J. Soc. for Clin. Social Work (newsletter editor 1997-99). Democrat. Jewish. Avocations: travel, dance, writing, painting. Office: Face to Face Psychotherapy Svcs 2 Blair Ave Metuchen NJ 08840

**MACARIO, ALBERTO JUAN LORENZO,** physician; b. Naschel, Argentina, Dec. 1, 1935; came to the U.S., 1974, naturalized, 1980; s. Alberto Carlos and Maria Elena (Gir)udi) M.; m. Everly Conway, Mar. 16, 1963; children: Alex, Everly. MD, Nat. U. Buenos Aires, 1961. Intern Ramos Mejia Hosp., Buenos Aires, 1958—60, resident, 1960, Rivadavia Hosp., Buenos Aires, 1961—62, physician-hematologist, 1962—64; fellow NRC Argentina, Buenos Aires, 1964—69; head dept. radioactive isotopes Inst. Hematol. Investigations Nat. Acad. Medicine, Buenos Aires, 1967—69; Eleanor Roosevelt fellow Internat. Union Against Cancer Dept. Tumor Biology Karolinska Inst., Stockholm, 1969—71; mem. sci. staff Lab, Cell Biology NRC Italy, Rome, 1971—73; head lab. immunology Internat. Agy Rsch. on Cancer, WHO, Lyons, France, 1973—74; rsch. scientist Brown U., Providence, 1974—76; rsch. scientist divsn. labs. and rsch. N.Y. State Dept. Health, Albany, 1976—79, chief hematology clin. lab. ctr., 1979—81; dir. clin. and exptl. immunology sect. Lab. Medicine Inst., 1981—83, rsch. physician, 1981—83; rsch. physician Wadsworth Ctr. N.Y. State Dept. Health, 1981—2006; rschr. U. Md. Biotechnology Inst., Balt., 2006—. Prof. dept. biomed. scis. Sch. Pub. Health, SUNY, Albany, 1985—, mem. senate, 1989-94; adj. prof. pathology and lab. medicine Albany Med. Coll., 1991-2004; mem. structural and cell biology program Albany Univs. and Colls.; grant reviewer for nat. and internat. agys.; manuscript reviewer for sci. jours. Editor multivolume treatise Monoclonal Antibodies Against Bacteria and treatise Gene Probes for Bacteria; contbr. chpts. to books and encys. and articles to profl. jours. Recipient Diploma de Honor prize Nat. U. Buenos Aires, 1961, Bernardino Rivadavia prize Nat. Acad. Medicine Argentina, 1967, Ciencia e Investigation prize Argentinian Soc. Advancement Sci., 1967; Ford Found.-NAS travel fellow, 1968, Eleanor Roosevelt fellow, 1969. Mem. Internat. Soc. Microbial Ecology, Cell Stress Soc. Internat., Scandinavian Soc. Immunology, Italian Assn. Immunologists, French Soc. Immunology, Am. Assn. Immunologists, Am. Soc. Microbiology (sect. editor Manual of Clin. Lab. Immunology 4th and 5th edits. 1989-97), Am. Soc. Investigative Pathology, Assn. Internat. Union Against Cancer. Achievements include patents in field; discovered primary myeloperoxydase deficiency in leucocytes, and oscillations of antibody affinity during maturation of immune responses; developed method for immunologic identification of bacteria (archaea) that produce methane gas; discovered antigenic diversity of these microbes in natural and manufactured ecosystems; described structural topography of methanogenic archaea and population dynamics in granular microbial consortia; found novel multicellular forms of archaea; isolated for the first time ABC-transporter genes and the genes in the hsp70(dnaK) locus from an archaebacterium (archaeon); devised and constructed the first integration vector for genetically engineering a methanogen useful for waste bioconversion; discovered a uni-celled organism with the main four chaperoning systems in its cytosol; found two new chaperonins in archaea;

developed concept of sick chaperone or chaperonopathy as a factor contributing to the aging process and disease; discovered that archaeal hsp70 (dnaK) genes belong to various evolutionary lineages. Office: Ctr Marine Biotech Columbus Ctr 701 E Pratt St Baltimore MD 21202 Office Phone: 518-474-2781. Business E-Mail: macario@wadsworth.org, macario@umbi.umd.edu. *I am capable of walking alone, but with my wife by me, I fly. We can both ascend toward the sky and together we reach the stars. Separately, alone, who knows, we might never have been able to rise above the mountains, perhaps not even the hills, we have conquered, flapping our wings in unison.*

**MACARTHUR, DIANA TAYLOR,** advanced technology executive; b. Santa Fe, July 7, 1933; widowed; children: Elizabeth Tschursin, Alexander Tschursin. BA, Vassar Coll., 1955. Cons. economist Checchi & Co., 1957-61; v.p., dir. Thomas J. Deegan Co., 1961-62; dep. chief West Africa Peace Corps, 1963, reg. program officer for North Africa, Near East, South Asia, 1964, dir. divsn. pvt. and internat. orgns., 1965-66; pvt. cons., 1966-74; program mgr. Aerospace Divsn. Gen Elec. Co., 1974-76; pres. Consumer Dynamics, 1977-80; v.p., dir. Dynamac Internat. Inc., 1980-88, chmn., pres., CEO, 1988—; chmn., CEO Rsch. Analysis and Mgmt. Corp., 1988-92. Pres. Fgn. Traders, Inc., 1980—86. Trustee Menninger Found., Topeka, 1972-04, Santa Fe Inst., 2005-; bd. dirs. Sci. and Tech. Corp. U. N.Mex.; bd. visitors Menninger-Baylor Coll. Medicine, Meth. Hosp. Found., 2004-06; Lady Bird Johnson Wildflower Ctr., 1985-; mem. Pres.'s Com. of Adv. on Sci. and Tech., 1994-01; citizens adv. bd. to the Pres. Coun. on Youth Opportunity, 1966-70; served on CSIS Strengthening of Amer. Com., 1992, Nat. Benefits from Nat. Lab. Com., 1993, Sr. Policy on Nat. Challenges, 1996, Geopolitics of Energy Com., 2000; mem. The Chancellor's Adv. Coun. U. Sys. of Md.; bd. visitors U. Md. Biotech. Inst.; adv. com. Ctr. Strategic & Internat. Studies; bd. dirs. Atlantic Coun. USA; bus. adv. coun. Ctr. for China-U.S. Coop., U. Denver. Mem. Coun. on Competitiveness, Business-Higher Edn. Forum (mem. exec. com.), Tech. Coun. Md. (mem. exec. com.), Los Alamos Nat. Lab. Found. (mem. exec. com.), Nat. Hispanic Cultural Ctr. Found., The Santa Fe Opera, Phi Beta Kappa. Office: Dynamac Internat Inc 2275 Research Blvd Rockville MD 20850-3268 E-mail: dmacarthur@dynamac.com.

**MACARTHUR, JOHN RODERICK C. G. (RICK MACARTHUR),** magazine publisher, journalist; b. N.Y.C., June 4, 1956; s. J. Roderick and Christiane (L'Etendart) MacA. BA, Columbia Coll., 1978. Reporter Wall Street Jour., Chgo., summer 1977, Washington Star, 1978, Bergen Record, Hackensack, N.J., 1978-79. Chgo. Sun Times, 1979-82; asst. fgn. editor UPI, N.Y.C., 1982; pres., pub. Harper's Mag., N.Y.C., 1983—. Author: Second Front: Censorship and Propaganda in the Gulf War, 1992, The Selling of "Free Trade": NAFTA, Washington, and the Subversion of Democracy, 1999. Bd. dirs. Com. to Protect Journalists, Overseas Press Club, Death Penalty Info. Ctr. Fellow N.Y. Inst. Humanities; mem. Econ. Club of N.Y. Office: Harper's Mag 666 Broadway Fl 11 New York NY 10012-2394*

**MACASKILL, LLOYD EDWIN,** systems analyst, consultant; b. Detroit, Jan. 24, 1944; s. Angus Duncan MacAskill and Catherine Mary MacLeod; m. Diane Elizabeth Axelson, Aug. 15, 1970; children: Meredith Lynn, Heather Elizabeth. BA, Alma Coll., 1966; BS, U. Wis., 1974; MS, U. Tenn., 1978. Programmer Berkeley Sci. Labs., Bethesda, Md., 1968—71; sys. programmer Johns Hopkins Sch. Medicine, Balt., 1978—80; project mgr. U. Md. Hosp., Balt., 1980—82; sys. analyst King Faisal Specialist Hosp., Riyadh, Saudi Arabia, 1982, Georgetown U. Med. Ctr., Washington, 1984, US Dept. of Navy, Washington, 1988—92, US Dept. Vets. Affairs, Silver Spring, Md., 1992—97, McKesson HBOC, Washington, 1997—99; sys. cons. Online Med. Networks, Springfield, Va., 1985—88; sr. sys. cons. Clin. Informatics Assocs., Carmel, Ind., 2005. Scout, lobbyist Am. Discovery Trail; author, publicist Gt. Ea. Trail. Recipient President's Call to Svc. award, President's Coun. Svc. and Civic Participation, 2004. Mem.: Am. Med. Informatics Assn., W.Va. Scenic Trails Assn., Keystone Trails Assn., Am. Discovery Trail Soc., Am. Hiking Soc., Appalachian Trail Conservancy (registrar 1995), Potomac Appalachian Trail Club (trail mgr. 1993—2004, svc. awards 1991—2004). Episcopalian. Avocation: hiking trail development. Home: 1407 Grady Ave Apt D Charlottesville VA 22903-2260 Office: U Va Career Ctr Immunology Rsch PO Box 801386 Charlottesville VA 22908 Personal E-mail: lloydmaca@aol.com.

**MACAULAY, DAVID ALEXANDER,** author, illustrator; b. Burton-on-Trent, Eng., Dec. 2, 1946; s. James and Joan (Lowe) M.; m. Janice Elizabeth Michel, 1970 (div.); 1 child, Elizabeth Alexandra; m. Ruth Marris, 1978 (div.); 1 child, Charlotte Valerie; m. Ruth Ellen Murray, 1997. BArch, R.I. Sch. Design, 1969. Instr. interior design R.I. Sch. Design, Providence, 1969-73, instr. two-dimensional design, 1974-76, adj. faculty dept. illustration, 1977-79; tchr. art Central Falls (R.I.) Pub. Schs., 1969-70, Newton, Mass., 1972-74; designer Morris Nathanson Design, 1969-72. Author, illustrator: Cathedral: The Story of Its Construction, 1973 (Caldecott Honor book 1973), City, 1974, Pyramid, 1975 (Christopher medal 1975), Underground, 1976, Castle, 1977 (Caldecott Honor book 1977), Great Moments in Architecture, 1978, Motel of the Mysteries, 1979, Unbuilding, 1980, Mill, 1983, Baaa, 1985, Why the Chicken Crossed the Road, 1987, The Way Things Work: From Levers to Lasers, Cars to Computers- A Visual Guide to the World of Machines, 1988, Black and White, 1990 (Caldecott medal 1991), Ship, 1993, Shortcut, 1995, Rome Antics, 1997, The New Way Things Work, 1998, Angelo, 2002; illustrator: Help! Let Me Out!, 1982, Electricity, 1983, The Amazing Brain, 1984, David Macaulay, 1997, Building Big, 2000, Angelo, 2002; cons., presenter various TV projects. Recipient Wash. Children's Book Guild award, 1977, AIA medal, 1978, Bradford Washburn meda. Boston Mus. Sci., 1993, Charles Frankel prize NEH, 1995, Chevalier of Order of Arts and Letters, France, 1995, MacArthur Fellow, John D. and Catherine T. MacArthur Found., 2006.*

**MACAULAY, LAWRENCE A.,** former Canadian government official member of Parliament; b. St. Peters Bay, Sept. 2, 1946; s. Archibald and Bernadette Mae Aulay; m. Frances Elaine O'Connell, Aug. 16, 1972; children: Carolyn, Rita, Lynn. Mem. House of Commons 1988—, apptd. assoc. critic for fisheries and oceans, 1989, apptd. critic for srs. and assoc. critic for fisheries, 1990; sec. of state for Can., 1993—96, min. labour, solicitor gen. of Can. Ottawa, 1998—2002. Mem. standing com. on forestry and fisheries, caucus com. on health and social devel.; acclaimed chair Atlantic Caucus, 1992. Roman Catholic. Office: House of Commons 556 Confederation Bldg Ottawa ON Canada K1A OA6

**MACAULAY, SUSAN JANE,** lawyer, law educator; b. Oceanport, NJ, Feb. 18, 1952; d. Gordon Livingston and Mary Forrest Macaulay; children: Lauren Mei, Anna Haiqiong. MusB, Oberlin Conservatory Music, 1974; JD, Loyola U., Chgo., 1984; LLM, Chgo.-Kent Coll. Law, 1990; M in Liberal Arts, U. Chgo., 1995. Bar: Ill. 1984, U.S. Dist. Ct. (no. dist.) Ill. 1984. Regional counsel Burroughs Corp., Lombard, Ill., 1984—86; atty. Borg-Warner Acceptance Corp., Chgo., 1986—88; assoc. gen. counsel Heller Fin., Inc., Chgo., 1986—94; gen. counsel ArcVentures, Inc., Chgo., 1994—95, Lamb Ptnr., Chgo., 2006—; v.p., corp. counsel Caremark Internat., Inc., Northbrook, Ill., 1995—96; sr. assoc. Skadden Arps Slate Meagher & Flom, Chgo., 1996—2001; ptnr Gardner Carton & Douglas LLP, Chgo., 2001—06; gen. counsel Lamb Ptnrs., 2006—. Adj. prof. law Chgo.-Kent Coll. Law, 1992—. Contbr. chapters to books, articles to profl. jours. Bd. dirs. The Thereplay Inst., Skokie, Ill., 1995. Named Ill. Leading Lawyer, The Law Bull./Ill. Superlawyers Chgo. Mag., 2004, 2005, Ill. Superlawyer, Chgo. Mag., 2004. Mem.: ABA, Chgo. Bar Assn., Families with Children from China. Avocations: classical music, local symphony orchestra member, writing. Office: Lamb Ptnrs 900 N Michigan Ste 1900 Chicago IL 60606 Office Fax: 312-915-3053. Business E-Mail: macaulay@lambllc.com.

**MACAULAY, WILLIAM EDWARD,** financial executive; b. NYC, Sept. 2, 1945; s. John H. and Ella M. (Cook) M.; m. Linda L. Rodger, June 17, 1967; children: Elizabeth R., Anne R. BBA cum laude, CCNY, 1966; MBA, U. Pa., 1968. Asst. v.p. Dominick & Dominick, N.Y.C., 1968—71; v.p. Midlantic Bank, Newark, 1972—73, Oppenheimer Mgmt. Corp., N.Y.C., 1973—75, exec. v.p., 1976—79; dir. corp. fin. Oppenheimer & Co., Inc., N.Y.C.,

1979—81, ptnr., 1976-81; gen. ptnr. Meridien Capital Co., Greenwich, Conn., 1981-92. Pres., CEO, dir. First Res. Corp., Greenwich, 1982—; chmn. Dresser Rand, Olean, NY; bd. dirs. Weatherford Inc., Dresser Inc., Dallas, So. Cross Holdings, Brisbane, Australia. Mem.: Indian Harbor Yacht Club. Presbyterian. Office: First Reserve Corp One Lafayette Pl Greenwich CT 06830-7165

**MACAULEY, KAREN ELIZABETH,** nursing administrator, emergency nurse practitioner; b. Sayre, Pa., Mar. 12, 1965; d. Barry and Joie Rake; 1 child, Kelli Susan. BSN, Pa. State U., 1987, MEd, 1993. Cert. prehospital RN Pa. Emergency Med. Svcs. Coun.; RN pA., cert. critical care nurse, Am. Assn. Critical Care Nurses, emergency nurse, Emergency Nurses Assn. Staff nurse M.S. Hershey (Pa.) Med. Ctr., 1987—96, trauma program coord. Luther Hosp., Eau Claire, Wis., 1996—2001, Thomas Jefferson U. Hosp., Phila., 2001—04; trauma prevention and outreach dir. St. Christopher's Hosp. for Children, Phila., 2004—. Pres. Pa. State U. Nursing, 2001—. Bd. dirs. Pa. State U. Coll. Health and Human Devel.; vol. Hosts for Hosps., Pa., 2001. Recipient Family Fun Vol. award, Family Fun Mag., 2005. Mem.: Am. Trauma Soc. (pres. to chair trauma nurse coun. 2000—, bd. dirs.), Soc. Trauma Nurses, Pa. State U. Alumni Assn. (life). Home: 503 Fitzwater St Philadelphia PA 19147 Office: St Christopher's Hosp for Children Erie Ave at Front St Philadelphia PA 19134 Office Phone: 215-427-5581. E-mail: karenm@psualum.com.

**MACAVERY, TRISTAN ALEXANDER (TRISTAN BLACK WOLF),** small business owner, writer, actor; b. Petersburg, Va., Aug. 16, 1958; s. Carroll Alden and Mildred Harriet (Lcon) Peabody. BA, Sam Houston State U., 1979. Edit. assoc Internat. Fire Svc. Tng. Assn., Stillwater, Okla., 1983—84; pub. Aegis Unicorne, Davis, Calif., 1985—92; exec. assoc. Okla. Ctr. Integrated Design and Mfg., Stillwater, 1993—95; Houston bur. chief Tex. Triangle newspaper, 1995; actor, writer, dir., prodr. ADV Films, Houston, 1996—99; owner Intangible Plastics, Midlothian, Va., 1999—. Spkr. numerous Japanese anime convs., 1996—; founding mem. Third Coast Comedy, Houston. Voice actor: Neon Genesis Evangelion, 1996—2001; author: Divine Intervention, 2001, Lion Dance, 2002, Tea for Twenty, 2003, Remnant Stew, 2004; editor: Chronoscope, 2004; author: over 100 articles and short stories. Democrat. Native Am. Shaman. Avocations: piano, voice. Home: 5218 Hunt Master Dr Apt B Midlothian VA 23112-2714 also: PO Box 4208 Midlothian VA 23112-0004 Personal E-mail: frightfully_clever@msn.com. Business E-Mail: tristan@intangibleplastics.com.

**MACAVINTA-TENAZAS, GEMORSITA,** physician; b. Numancia, Aklan, Phillippines, Dec. 18, 1938; arrived in U.S., 1967; d. Dominador Zalazar and Georgina Estrada (Tabanera) Macavinta; m. Salvador Torrefiel Tenazas Jr., Apr. 18, 1963; children: Alan, Alex, Albert, Alfred. BA, Far Ea. U., Manila, 1959, MD, 1964. Diplomate Am. Bd. Family Practice. Intern North Gen. Hosp., Manila, 1963-64; pvt. practice Manila, 1965-67; extern Chinese Gen. Hosp., Manila, 1965-67; with St. Joseph Med. Ctr., Burbank, Calif., 1967-69; chief cytotechnologist Cancer Screening Svcs., North Hollywood, Calif., 1969-73; resident in family practice medicine Health Scis. Ctr., Tex. Tech. U., Lubbock, 1974-75; staff physician VA Outpatient Clinic, L.A., 1975—. Recipient physician recognition awards AMA, 1973-85, 92-94; named Mrs. Aklan, 1986, Disting. Alumna, Aklan Acad., Philippines, 1991, Most Outstanding Parent award Builders Lions Club, 1995, Citizen of Yr. Builders Lions Club, 1996, Outstanding Physician Club Filipino, 1996, one of 10 Outstanding Women of Nation, Uliran, 1997. Fellow Am. Acad. Family Physicians (bd. govs. 2003-05); mem. Philippine-Am. Assn. Family Physicians (bd. govs. 1996, 2003—, sec. 1998, outstanding leader award 2000, sec. 1998-2002, Mrs. Philippine Am. 2000), Am. Assn. Family Physicians, Calif. Acad. Family Physicians, Filipino Asian-Pacific VA Employees Soc. (pres. L.A. chpt. 1988—), Assn. Philippine Physicians in Am. (bd. govs. 2004—, named Mrs. Mindanao 2002), Aklanons of Am. (pres. 1988—, bd. govs. 1998-2000, 04-06, bd. dirs. 2004-06, 1st Mrs. Aklan 1986-89), Far Ea. U. Med. Alumni Assn. (life mem., assc. sec. 1988—). Roman Catholic. Avocations: dance, singing, sewing, piano playing, gardening. Office: VA Outpatient Clinic 425 S Hill St Los Angeles CA 90013-1110 Office Phone: 213-253-2677. Business E-Mail: tenazas@med.va.gov.

**MACAVOY, THOMAS COLEMAN,** manufacturing executive, educator; b. Jamaica, NY, Apr. 24, 1928; s. Joseph V. and Edna M. Mac A.; m. Margaret M. Walsh, Dec. 27, 1952; children: Moira Mac Avoy Brown, Ellen Mac Avoy Jennings, Christopher, Neil. BS in Chemistry, Queens Coll., 1950; MS in Chemistry, St. John's U., 1952, DSc (hon.), 1973; PhD in Chemistry, U. Pa., 1952. Chemist, Charles Pfizer & Co., Bklyn., 1957-60; mgr. electronics rsch. Corning Glass Works, NY, 1960-64, dir. phys. rsch., 1964-66, v.p. electronic products divsn., 1966-69, v.p. tech. products divsn., 1969-71, pres., 1971-83, vice-chmn., 1983-87; prof. mgmt. grad. sch. U. Va., 1988—. Patentee in field; contbr. articles to tech. jours. Trustee Corning Mus. Glass; past pres. Boy Scouts Am. With USN, 1946; with USAF, 1952-53. Recipient Silver Antelope award Boy Scouts Am., 1976, Silver Beaver award, 1975, Silver Buffalo award, 1982, Bronze Wolf award, 1988. Roman Catholic. Personal E-mail: tmacavoy@aol.com. E-mail: tcm2m@virginia.edu.

**MACBAIN, LOUISE T. BLOUIN,** publishing executive; b. Can., 1958; m. David Stewart (div.); m. John H. McBain (div.); 3 children. Grad., Harvard U. With various investment banking firms, 1977—87; co-founder, CEO ops. Hebdo Mag Group (now Trader Classified Media), Montreal, Canada, 1987—2000; CEO Phillips, de Pury & Luxembourg, 2002; chmn. LTB Holdings, 2003—; owner Art & Auction Mag., 2003—, Art Knowledge Corp., 2004—, Spoon mag., Paris, 2004—. Chmn. Louise T Blouin Found.; bd. trustees Solomon R. Guggenheim Found.; bd. dir. Bard Ctr., NYC; hon mem. Chmn's Coun., Whitney Mus.; mem. internat. coun. Tate Mus., London; mem. internat. coun. Les Arts Decoratifs, Paris; internat. chmn. Byrd Hoffman Watermill Ctr. Office: Art & Auction Mag 9th Fl 11 E 36th St New York NY 10016 also: LTB USA Inc Ste 302 111 Eighth Ave New York NY 10011

**MACBAIN, WILLIAM HALLEY,** minister, theology studies educator, academic administrator; b. Cambridge, Ont., Can., Aug. 12, 1916; s. George Alexander and Grace Ann (Wilkins) MacB.; m. Mary Ann Munday, Aug. 20, 1941; children: Grace Elizabeth MacBain Silvester, Constance Marilyn MacBain Parker. Licentiate in Theology, Toronto Baptist Sem., Ont., 1939; DD (hon.), Cen. Bapt. Sem., Toronto, 1962. Ordained to ministry Bapt. Ch., 1940. Pastor, founder Temple Bapt. Ch., Sarnia, Ont., 1937-64; pastor Forward Bapt. Ch., Toronto, 1964-73; dir., gen. sec. Fellowship Fgn. Missions, Toronto, 1973-81; chancellor Cen. Bapt. Sem., 1981-93, Heritage Bapt. Bible Coll. and Theol. Sem., Cambridge, Ont., Canada, 1993—. Pastor emeritus Forward Bapt. Ch., Toronto, 1994—; chmn. Can. Bd. Greater Europe Mission, 1963-73. Mem. Fellowship Evang. Bapt. Chs. in Can. (pres. 1953-54, 83-84) Conservative. Home: 1540 Kipling Ave Apt 903 Etobicoke ON Canada M9R 4C6 Office: Heritage Bapt Bible Coll and Theol Sem 175 Holiday Inn Dr Cambridge ON Canada N3C 3T2

**MACBENN, JOSEPH VERNON,** director; b. Youngstown, Ohio, Aug. 31, 1979; s. Joseph Edison and Darlene MacBenn; m. Melissa Strouble, July 8, 2006. B in Music Edn., Mt. Union Coll., Alliance, Ohio, 2001; MEd, Ohio No. U., 2005. Tchg. lic. Ohio. Orch. dir. Lima (Ohio) City Schs., 2001—. Mem.: Am. String Tchrs. Assn., Internat. Trumpet Guild, Ohio Music Edn. Assn., Kappa Kappa Psi, Mu Phi Epsilon. Avocations: music, aquariums, travel. Home: 5097 Shields Rd Canfield OH 44406 Office: Lima Sr High Orch 1 Spartan Way Lima OH 45801 Office Phone: 419-996-3466. Personal E-mail: orchestrajoe@hotmail.com. Business E-Mail: jmacbenn@hotmail.com.

**MACBETH, ANGUS,** lawyer; b. LA, May 9, 1942; BA, Yale U., 1964, LLB, 1969. Bar: NY 1970, DC 1981. Law clk. to Hon. Harold R. Tyler, Jr. US Dist. Ct. (so. dist.) NY, 1969-70, asst. US atty. criminal divsn., 1975-77; chief pollution control sect. Land and Natural Resources Divsn., US Dept. Justice, 1977-79, dep. asst. atty. gen., 1979-81; ptnr. environ. law Sidley Austin LLC,

Washington; and mem. exec. com. Sidley Austin, Washington. Adj. prof. law NY Law Sch., 1985—; spl. counsel Wartime Relocation and Internment Civilians Commn., 1981-83. Mem. DC Bar (steering com. energy and natural resources divsn. 1982-84), NY State Bar Assn., Phi Beta Kappa. Office: Sidley Austin LLC 1501 K St NW Washington DC 20005 Office Phone: 202-736-8271.

**MACCALLUM, DAVID HOPPER,** investment banker; b. Long Branch, N.J., Oct. 13, 1937; s. Frank Hopper and Helen Douty (McLean) MacC.; m. Tonin Mersch, Oct. 18, 1961 (div. Feb. 1972); m. Lee Neill, Nov. 18, 1978; children: Alexandra, Neill, John. AB, Brown U., 1959; MBA, NYU, 1963. Cert. fin. analyst. Ptnr. Faulkner Dawkins & Sullivan, NYC, 1968-78; 1st v.p. Paine Webber, NYC, 1978-83; gen. ptnr., head health care rsch. Hambrecht & Quist, NYC, 1983—85, joined investment banking group, 1985, head, health care investment banking practice NYC, 1987—90, co-head, Investment Banking, 1990—94; mng. dir., global head of life sciences UBS Securities, 1994—98; exec. v.p., head Health Care group ING Barings Furman Selz LLC, 1998—99; global head health care investment banking, Salomon Smith Barney Citigroup, 1999—2001; mng. ptnr. Outer Islands Capital. Bd. dirs. MannKind Corp., 2004—, Peninsula Pharmaceuticals Inc., 2004—, Zymogenetics Inc., Seattle, 2005—, Vital Signs, Inc. Mem. N.Y. Soc. Security Analysts. Democrat. Episcopalian. Avocations: tennis, running, squash.

**MACCARIO, MAURICE MALCOLM,** oral and maxillofacial surgeon, consultant; b. Newark, Jan. 17, 1942; s. Melchiorre Malcolm and Susan (Bocchino) M.; m. Rosemarie Agnes Nocera; children: Lenora, Marcus. BA, Villanova U., 1964; DDMedicine, Fairleigh Dickinson U., 1968. Diplomate Am. Bd. Oral and Maxillo Facial Surgery. Intern Bklyn. Jewish Hosp., 1969; resident Bklyn. Vets. Hosp., 1970; chief resident Bklyn. Cumberland Med. Ctr., 1971; sr. registrar North Staffordshire Royal Infirmary, Eng., 1971-72; tchr. oral surgery Bklyn. Hosp., 1972-82; pvt. practice, Oakland, N.J., 1972—; mem. staff Valley Hosp., Ridgewood, N.J., 1971—, dir. oral surgery, 1980—87, chief and dir. oral surgery, 1999—. Cons. St. Joseph Hosp., Paterson, N.J., 1971—. Contbr. articles to profl. jours. V.p. Oakland (N.J.) Rep. Club., 1986-88. Fellow Am. Assn. Oral and Maxillofacial Surgeons, Oral Surgery Soc. N.J., Am. Mensa Soc. Roman Catholic. Avocation: private pilot. Home: 160 Long Hill Rd Oakland NJ 07436-3113 Office: 180 Ramapo Valley Rd Oakland NJ 07436-2524 Address: 103 St Martin Dr Palm Beach Gardens FL

**MACCARTHY, JOHN L.,** lawyer; b. St. Louis, Dec. 26, 1959; BA magna cum laude, Williams Coll., 1982; JD, Stanford U., 1985. Bar: Ill. 1985, U.S. Dist. Ct. Ill. (no. dist.) 1985. Assoc. to ptnr. Winston & Strawn LLP, Chgo., 1985—; sr. v.p., gen. counsel Nuvren Investments LLC, 2006—. Bd. dirs. Met. Family Svcs., Renaissance Soc. U. Chgo., Nature Conservancy Chgo. Mem.: Phi Beta Kappa, Order of Coif. Office: Winston & Strawn LLP 333 W Wacker Dr Chicago IL 60601-9703 Office Phone: 312-917-7955. Office Fax: 312-558-5700. E-mail: jmaccarthy@winston.com, john.maccarthy@nuvcen.com.

**MACCARTHY, TALBOT LELAND,** civic volunteer; b. St. Louis, Jan. 28, 1936; d. Austin Porter Leland and Dorothy (Lund) Follansbee; m. John Peters MacCarthy, June 21, 1958; children: John Leland MacCarthy, Talbot MacCarthy Payne. BA, Vassar Coll., 1958. Sec., treas. Station List Pub. Co., St. Louis, 1975-85, pres., 1985-90. Hon. trustee Robert E. Lee Meml. Assn., Arts and Edn. Coun. Greater St. Louis, pres., 1978-80, emerita; past vestry mem. St. Michael and St. George Ch., 1997-00; past trustee St. Louis Art Mus., St. Louis Merc. Libr. Assn., Family & Children's Svc. Greater St. Louis, Health and Welfare Coun., Greater St. Louis, Jr. Kindergarten St. Louis Page Park YMCA, Scholarship Found. St. Louis, Friends St. Louis Art Mus. Bd., Ch. St. Michael and St. George Sch. Bd., Mid-Am. Arts Alliance; chmn. Mo. Arts Coun., 1980-85; past chmn. Vol. Action Ctr. Greater St. Louis; past vice chmn. bd. dirs. Mary Inst.; past pres. Jr. League St. Louis; mem. Nat. Coun. Arts, 1985-91; past mem. nat. coun. for Sch. of Art Washington U.; bd. dirs. Sheldon Art Galleries, trustee Seabury-Western Theol. Sem. Recipient Woman of Achievement citation St. Louis Globe Democrat, 1979, Mo. Citizens for Arts/Arts Advocacy award, 1987, Mo. Arts Award, 1993, Honor medal, Mary Inst. and Country Day Sch., 2005. Mem. Vassar Club St. Louis (past pres.), Mary Inst. Alumnae Assn. (past pres.), Colonial Dames Am., Garden Club St. Louis, Belvedere Club (Charlevoix, Mich.; former mem. bd. dirs.). Republican. Episcopalian. Avocations: tennis, visual arts, performing arts.

**MACCARTHY, TERENCE FRANCIS,** lawyer; b. Chgo., Feb. 5, 1934; s. Frank E. and Catherine (McIntyre) MacC.; m. Marian Fulton, Nov. 25, 1961; children— Daniel Fulton, Sean Patrick, Terence Fulton, Megan Catherine BA in Philosophy, St. Joseph's Coll., 1955; JD, DePaul U., 1960. Bar: Ill. 1960, U.S. Dist. Ct. (no. dist.) Ill. 1961, U.S. Ct. Appeals (7th cir.) 1961, U.S. Supreme Ct. 1966. Assoc. prof. law Chase Coll. Law, Cin., 1960-61; law clk. to chief judge U.S. Dist. Ct., 1961-66; spl. asst. atty. gen. Ill., 1965-67; exec. dir. Fed. Defender Program, U.S. Dist. Ct. (no. dist.) Ill., Chgo., 1966—. Mem. nat. adv. com. on criminal rules; 7th cir. criminal jury instrn. com.; chmn. Nat. Defender Com.; chmn. bd. regents Nat. Coll. Criminal Def.; faculty Fed. Jud. Ctr., Nat. Coll. Criminal Def., Nat. Inst. Trial Advocacy, U. Va. Trial Advocacy Inst., Harvard Law Sch. Trial Advocacy Program, Western Trial Advocacy Inst., Northwestern U., U. Ill. Defender Trial Advocacy course, Nat. Criminal Def. Coll., Loyola U. Trial Advocacy Program; lectr. in field Contbr. articles on criminal law to profl. jours. Bd. dirs. U.S. Served as 1st lt. USMC, 1955-57 Recipient Nat. Legal Aid and Defender Assn./ABA Reginald Heber Smith award, 1986, Alumni Merit award St. Joseph Coll., 1970, Cert. of Distinction USO, 1977, Harrison Tweed Spl. Merit award Am. Law Inst./ABA, 1987, Bill of Rights award Ga. chpt. ACLU, 1986, William J. Brennan award U. Va., 1989, Alumni Svc. award DePaul U. Coll. Law, 1994, Ann. Significant Contbns. award Calif. Attys. for Criminal Justice, Defender of the Century Fed. Defenders Assn., Inns of Ct. and Ct. of Appeals (7th cir.) Professionalism award; named to Outstanding Young Men of Am., 1970. Mem. ABA (past chmn. criminal justice sect., ho. of dels., bd. govs., Charles English award criminal justice sect.), Ill. Bar Assn., Chgo. Bar Assn., 7th Cir. Bar Assn., Nat. Assn. Criminal Def. Lawyers (Disting. Svc. award 1993), Nat. Legal Aid and Defender Assn., Nat. Coll. Criminal Def. (chair), Union League of Chgo. (pres.). Democrat. Roman Catholic. Office: US Dist Ct No Dist Ill 55 E Monroe St Ste 2800 Chicago IL 60603-5802

**MACCHIA, DAVID ALAN,** management consultant; s. Edmund Joseph and Anna Alice Macchia; m. Robin Cynthia Haley, Mar. 8, 1997; children: Spencer David, Ava Haley. Pres. Donahue-Macchia Ins. Agy., Inc., Braintree, Mass., 1985—2000; pres., CEO Wealth2k, Inc., Hingham, Mass., 2000—. Cons. PaineWebber, N.Y.C., 1987-89, Aviva Life Ins. Co., North Quincy, Mass., 1988—2001, Nat. Life, Montpelier, Vt., 1998—2000, Keyport Life Ins. Co., Boston, 1999—2000, ING U.S., DesMoines. Author: (seminar selling program) The Alternative Plan, (video series) Generations. Mem.: Soc. Cert. Sr. Advisors. Achievements include design of unique utilization of a life insurance policy. Office: Wealth2k Inc 50 Derby St Hingham MA 02043 Office Phone: 781-740-9777. E-mail: dmacchia@wealth2k.com.

**MACCHIAROLA, FRANK JOSEPH,** academic administrator, educator; b. NYC, Apr. 7, 1941; s. Joseph John and Lucy (Bernardo) M.; m. Mary Teresa Collins, June 13, 1970; children: Joseph John, Michael Collins, Frank Joseph. BA, St. Francis Coll., 1962, L.H.D. (hon.), 1981; LL.B., Columbia U., 1965, PhD, 1970; L.H.D. (hon.), Coll. S.I., 1983; LL.D. (hon.), Dominican Coll., 1983, Manhattan Coll., 1983, St. Joseph's Coll., Molloy Coll., 1999. From fellow to prof. polit. sci. CUNY, 1964-83, v.p., 1977-78; asst. v.p Columbia U., N.Y.C., 1973-74; dep. dir. N.Y. State Emergency Fin. Control Bd. for N.Y.C., 1976-77; chancellor of schs. N.Y.C. Public Sch. System, 1978-83; pres., chief exec. officer N.Y.C. Partnership, Inc., 1983-87; pres. Acad. of Polit. Sci., 1987-91; prof. bus. Columbia U., N.Y.C., 1987-91; dean Benjamin N. Cardozo Sch. of Law, Yeshiva U., N.Y.C., 1991-96; of counsel Tannenbaum, Helpern, Syracuse and Hirschtritt, N.Y.C., 1996—. St. Francis Coll., NY, 1996—. Bd. dirs Jeffries Group Inc.; trustee Manville Personal Injury Settlement Trust. Decorated cavalieri Order of Merit Italy; recipient

---

cert. of merit Dirigible Soc. Am., 1976 Democrat. Roman Catholic. Office: 900 3rd Ave New York NY 10022-4728 also: 180 Remsen St Brooklyn NY 11201-4305 Office Phone: 718-489-5345. E-mail: fmacchia@stfranciscollege.edu.

**MACCINI, LOUIS JOHN,** economist, educator; b. Cambridge, Mass., Aug. 3, 1942; s. Joseph and Jennie (Leccacorvi) M.; m. Carol Monterisi, June 25, 1965; children: Michael S., Sharon L. BS in Economics, Boston Coll., 1965; PhD in Economics, Northwestern U., 1970. From asst. prof. to assoc. prof. economics The Johns Hopkins U., Balt., 1969-86, prof., 1986—, chair, 1992—. Ad hoc com. mem. graduate fin. aid, Johns Hopkins U., editorial bd., public interest investment adv. com., law sch. com., med. sch. com., and other coms.; mem. recruiting chair dept. grad. student advisor dept., and other depts. Referee Am. Econ. Review, Jour. Econ. Dynamics and Control, Oxford Econ. Papers, and others; contbr. articles to profl. jours. Grantee NSF. Mem. Am. Econ. Assn., The Econometric Soc., Nat. Bur. Econ. Inventory Rsch. Office: Johns Hopkins U 3400 N Charles St Baltimore MD 21218-2680 Office Phone: 410-516-7607. E-mail: maccini@jhu.edu.

**MACCLEAN, WALTER LEE,** dentist; b. Sheridan, Wyo., July 10, 1935; s. Edward Satterlee and Eleanor Elizabeth (Weir) Mac.; m. Nancy Lee Strale, Sept. 4, 1965 (div. 1975); children: David Satterlee, Carrie Lynn. BS with honors, U. Wyo., 1957, postgrad., 1958; DMD, U. Oreg., Portland, 1962. Mil. dental adv. Korean Mil: Adv. Group, Wonju, 1962-63; chief dental svc. Dugway Chem. Testing Ctr., Utah, 1965-68; pvt. dental practice Cheyenne, Wyo., 1968-70; assoc. prof. Sheridan Coll., Wyo., 1970-76; staff dentist VA Hosp. Med. Ctr., Ft. Meade, S.D., 1976-93; ret., 1993. Cons., lectr. Health Edn. Program Svc., Ft. Meade, 1984-93. With U.S. Army, 1962-68. Mem. ADA. Seventh-Day Adventist. also: Highbourne House 13 15 Marylebone High St London W1M 3PE England Home: 1898 Fort Rd Sheridan WY 82801

**MACCOBY, ELEANOR EMMONS,** psychology professor; b. Tacoma, May 15, 1917; d. Harry Eugene and Viva May (Johnson) Emmons; m. Nathan Maccoby, Sept. 16, 1938 (dec. Apr. 1992); children: Janice Carmichael, Sarah Maccoby Blunt, Mark. BS, U. Wash., 1939; MA, U. Mich., 1949, PhD, 1950. Study dir. div. program surveys USDA, Washington, 1942-46; study dir. Survey Rsch. Ctr. U. Mich., Ann Arbor, 1946-48; lectr., rsch. assoc. dept. social rels. Harvard U., Cambridge, Mass., 1950-58; from assoc. to full prof. Stanford (Calif.) U., 1958-87, Barbara Kimball Browning prof., 1979, chmn. dept. psychology, 1973-76, prof. emeritus, 1987—. Author: (with R. Sears and H. Levin) Patterns of Child-Rearing, 1957, (with Carol Jacklin) Psychology of Sex Differences, 1974, Social Development, 1980, (with R.H. Mnookin) Dividing the Child: Social and Legal Dilemmas of Custody, 1992, (with Buchanan and Dombusch) Adolescents after Divorce, 1996, The Two Sexes: Growing Up Apart, Coming Together, 1998; editor: (with Newcomb and Hartley) Readings in Social Psychology, 1957, The Development of Sex Differences, 1966. Recipient Gores award for Excellence in Tchg., Stanford U., 1981, Disting. Contbn. to Ednl. Research award Am. Ednl. Rsch. Assn., 1984, Lectureship award Soc. for Devel. and Behavioral Pediats., 2002. Fellow APA (pres. Divsn. 7, 1971-72, G. Stanley Hall award 1982), Soc. for Rsch. in Child Devel. (pres. 1981-83, mem. governing coun. 1963-66, Disting. Sci. Contbn. award 1987), Am. Psychol. Soc. (Disting. Sci. Contbns. award 1988); mem. NAS, Am. Acad. Arts and Scis., Inst. Medicine, Western Psychol. Assn. (pres. 1974-75, Lifetime Achievement award 2004), Inst. for Rsch. on Women and Gender, Social Sci. Rsch. Coun. (chmn. 1984-85), Consortium of Social Sci. Assns. (pres. 1997-98), Am. Psychol. Found. (Life Achievement award 1996). Democrat. Office: Stanford U Dept Psychology Stanford CA 94305-2130 Personal E-mail: Maccoby@psych.stanford.edu.

**MACCOMBIE, BRUCE FRANKLIN,** composer, college administrator; b. Providence, Dec. 5, 1943; s. Franklin S. and Florence (Corbishley) MacC.; m. Frances Holliday, Sept. 4, 1965 (div. 1970); m. Turi Gundersen, Mar. 10, 1979; 1 child, Juliana. BA, U. Mass., 1967, M of Music, 1968, DFA (hon.), 1986; PhD in Music, U. Iowa, 1971. Assoc. prof. Yale U., New Haven, 1975-80; v.p., dir. publications G. Schirmer Mus. Publs., N.Y.C., 1980-85; assoc. dean, Amherst Coll. Humanities and Fine Arts U. Mass.; dean, provost The Juilliard Sch., N.Y.C., 1986-92; dean Coll. Fine Arts Boston U., 1992, prof., 2002—; dir. Jazz at Lincoln Ctr., N.Y.C., 2001. Composer numerous musical works. Recipient Goddard Lieberson award Am. Acad. Arts and Letters, N.Y.C., 1979; Sutherland Dows fellowship, Martha Baird Rockefeller Fund for Music grant. Mem. Coll. Music Soc., Charles Ives Soc. (bd. dirs.). Office: Boston U Dept Music 855 Commonwealth Ave Boston MA 02215-1303 E-mail: maccombie@hfa.umass.edu.*

**MAC CORMAC, EARL RONALD,** retired education educator; b. N.Y.C., Apr. 26, 1935; s. Earl Copeland and Katherine Kissel MacC.; m. Nancy Hamilton, Aug. 23, 1958; children: Ann F., Susan H. B Engring., Yale U., 1955, MA, 1959, PhD, 1961, Karlsruke U., Germany, 2003. Adminstrv. asst. Hazen Found., New Haven, 1958-61; Charles A. Dana Prof. of Philosophy Davidson (N.C.) Coll., 1961-86; Fulbright Prof. U. Madras, India, 1985-86; sci. advisor to gov. Gov.'s Office, Raleigh, NC, 1986-92; pres. N.C. Quality Leadership Found., Raleigh, 1992-94; v.p., cons. prof. of radiology Duke U. med. Ctr., Durham, NC, 1994—. Adj. prof. indsl. engring. N.C. State U., Raleigh 1986-92; exec. dir. N.C. Bd. Sci. and Technology, Raleigh, 1986-92; mem. kuratorium Wissenschaftszentrum, North-Rhine Westphalia, 1991—; nat. Fulbright selection com. mem. Inst. of Internat. Edn., N.Y., 1984-87. Author: (books) Metaphor and Myth in Science and Religion, 1976, A Cognitive Theory of Metaphor, 1985, Myths of Science and Technology, 1986; co-author: Decision Analysis Applied to Electrical Rate Design, 1985; co-editor: (book) Fractals in Brain, Fractals in Mind, 1995; editl. bd. John Benjamins Pubs., 1998—. Bd. dirs. Alt. Energy Corp., N.C., 1989-92; adv. bd. N.C. Solar Ctr., Raleigh. Named Outstanding Engring. Student, ASME, 1955; recipient Jefferson award for Tchg., McConnell Found., Davidson, 1971. Mem. N.C. Soc. for Electron Microscopy and Microbeam Analysis (hon.), Tau Beta Pi, Sigma Xi. Presbyterian. Avocations: tennis, golf. Home: 4413 Keswick Dr Raleigh NC 27609-6325 E-mail: ermnhm@earthlink.net.

**MACCORMACK, CHARLES FREDERICK,** international relief organization executive; b. Oct. 27, 1941; married; two children. AB, Middlebury Coll., 1963, EdD (hon.), 1982; MIA, Columbia U., 1965, PhD, 1974. Staff assoc. internat. div. First Nat. City Bank, Caracas, Venezuela, 1964; instr. latin-Am. politics U. N.H., Durham, 1967; asst. to dean Internat. Fellows Program Columbia U., N.Y.C., 1967-68; rsch. fellow fgn. policy studies Brookings Instn., Washington, 1969-70; dir. internat. career tng. program Experiment Internat. Living, Brattleboro, Vt., 1970-74; v.p. programs Save the Children Fedn./Community Devel. Found., Westport, Conn., 1974-77; pres. World Learning (formerly The Experiment Internat. Living/Sch. for Internat. Tng.), Brattleboro, 1977—92; pres., CEO Save the Children Fedn., Inc., Westport, Conn., 1993—. Bd. dirs Arthur D. Little Mgmt. Edn. Inst., Ptnrs. Internat. Edn. and Tng., Am. Forum for Global Edn., Landmark Coll., Save the Children Fedn., Inc., 1993- Mng. editor Jour. Internat. Affairs. Mem. founding com. U., 1971-72, Vt. Commn. Edn. and the Econ. Future, 1982, coun. advisors Peace Corps Future Team, 1987, Coun. Fgn. Rels., N.Y.C., global awareness adv. bd. Wheaton Coll., Norton, Mass.; mem. exec. coun., chair devel. assistance com., co-chair com. refugee svcs. Am. Coun. Voluntary Internat. Action. Universidad Cen. de Venezuela Fulbright fellow, Caracas, Venezuela, 1965-66, Universidad Nacional Autonoma de Mexico NSF fellow, Mexico City, 1968-69, Edward John Noble Leadership fellow, 1963-65; Gould scholar, Middlebury scholar, Travelli scholar, 1959-63. Office: Save the Children Fedn Inc 54 Wilton Rd Westport CT 06880

**MACCORMACK, JEAN F.,** academic administrator; d. George and Helen MacCormack. BA, Emmanuel Coll., Boston, 1969; MEd, U. Mass., Amherst, 1978, EdD, 1979. Assoc. dean Coll. of Edn. U. Mass, Boston, 1984—87, acting dean Coll. of Edn., 1984—85, assoc. chancellor, 1987—88, vice chancellor arts and fin., 1988—95, interim chancellor, 1995—96, dep. chancellor and vice chancellor arts and fin., 1996—99, chancellor Dartmouth, 1999—. Mem. South Coast Econ. Devel. Partnership, 1999, Joint CEO Group, 2000, Racial and Ethnic Access and Fairness Adv. Bd., 2001; chair

---

South Coast Edn. Compact, 2000; mem. vis. com. U. So. Maine New Eng. Assoc. of Sch. and Coll., 2000—01; ex-officio mem. U. Mass. Dartmouth Libr. Archive Campaign, 2001; bd. mem. South Coast Health Sys., Inc., 2002; mem. marine sci. com. Fall River CEO Group, 2003, mem. med. device com., 03, mem. south coast edn. com., 03; mem. Regional Competitiveness Coun., 2003. Vice chair bd. govs. New Bedford Oceanarium, 1999, chair edn and rsch. com., 1999, trustee, chair edn. com., 2000; trustee Artworks! at Dover St., 2000, mem. edn. com., 2000, mem. pers. com., 2000; trustee Global Learning Charter Sch., 2000; bd. mem. Greater New Bedford Workforce Investment Bd., 2000, mem. legis. affairs and pub. info. com., 2000, mem. youth coun., 2000; mem. New Bedford Econ. Devel. Coun., 2000; corporator Child and Family Svcs., Inc., 2002; incorporator Home Aged People in Fall river, 2003; corporator Narragansett Fin. Corp. Citizens - Union Savs. Bank, 2003; mem. pres.'s coun. New Bedford Symphony Orch., 2003; mem. leadership coun. New Bedford Whaling Mus. Mem.: YMCA of Southeastern Mass., WHALE, Am. Assn. of State Coll. and U., U. Mass. Dartmouth Libr. Assoc. E-mail: jmaccormack@umassd.edu.

**MACCRACKEN, THOMAS GREGG,** musicologist; b. Norwalk, Connecticut, May 15, 1951; s. Constable and Eleanor (Dickson) MacCracken; m. Alexandra Jane (Moore-Robinson), May 28, 1988. BA, Yale Univ., 1973; PhD, Univ. of Chgo., 1985. Asst. prof. of music U. of Va., Charlottesville, 1986—90. Trustee Kinhaven Music Sch., Weston, Vt., 1974—80, 1993—98. Co-editor: (musical score) Mathurin Forestier Opera Omnia; musician: (CD recording) Pour 2 Clavecins; contbr. articles to profl. journals. Rsch. fellow, Smithsonian Instn., 1991—93. Mem.: Am. Musical Instrument Soc. (editor 1996—2006), Am. Musicological Soc., Am. Recorder Soc. Early Music Am. (bd. mem. 1990—94), Southeastern His. Keyboard Soc. (rev. editor 1991—96), Viola da Gamba Soc. of Am. (editl. bd. 1996). Presbyterian. Home: 12108 Vale Rd Oakton VA 22124

**MACCRATE, ROBERT,** lawyer; b. Bklyn., July 18, 1921; s. John and Flora (MacNicholl) MacC.; m. Constance Trapp, May 4, 1946; children: Christopher Robert, Barbara Constance MacCrate Gatti, Thomas John. BA, Haverford Coll., 1943, LLD (hon.), 1987; LLB, Harvard U., 1948; LLD (hon.), Union U., 1986, Dickinson Sch. Law, 1987, William Mitchell Coll. Law, 1994, Quinnipiac Coll. Law, 1995, CUNY, 2001, U.S.C., 2003. Bar: N.Y. 1949, U.S. Supreme Ct. 1955, D.C. 1965. Assoc. Sullivan & Cromwell, N.Y.C., 1948-51, 51-55, ptnr., 1956-59, 62-91, ret., 1991—96, sr. counsel, 1997—; law sec. N.Y. Appelate Divsn. Presiding Justice David W. Peck, 1951; counsel N.Y. Gov. Nelson A. Rockefeller, 1959-62; spl. counsel U.S. Army for Investigation Mylai incident, 1969-70; counsel N.Y. State Ct. on Judiciary, 1971; mem. jud. selection com. for fed. judgeships Senator Jacob K. Javits, 1972-80; mem. jud. nominating com. N.Y. 2d Jud. Dept., 1975-82. Trustee Lawyers Com. for Civil Rights Under Law, 1976—; chmn. emeritus Fund for Modern Cts., 1978—; cons. N.Y. Profl. Edn. Project, 1994-96. Co-author: Appellate Justice in New York, 1982, Legal Education and Professional Development--an Educational Continuum, 1992, Preserving the Core Values of the American Legal Profession, 2000; contbr. articles to profl. jours. Bd. mgrs. Haverford Coll., 1971-85, emeritus 1986—. Lt. USNR, 1943-46. Recipient Justice System Improvement award Coun. for Ct. Excellence, 1988, Gold medal Nat. Inst. Social Scis., 1989. Fellow Am. Bar Found. (chmn. N.Y. state 1973-80, bd. dirs. 1989—; sec. 1992-94, v.p. 1994-96, pres. 1996-98); mem. ABA (pres. 1987-88, del. 1972-78, 89—, N.Y. State del. 1979-81, bd. govs. 1981-84, 86-89, chair task force law schs. and the profession 1989-92, chair spl. adv. com. internat. activities 1988-89, 2d cir. mem. standing com. on fed. judiciary 1984-86, mem. common. on opportunities in profession 1993-96, mem. coun. sect. individual rights and responsibilities 1997-2000, medal 2002), N.Y. State Bar Assn. (pres. 1972-73, del. 1972—, chair com. law governing firm structure and operation 1999-2002, medal 1999), Assn. Bar City of N.Y. (v.p. 1969-71, chmn. exec. com. 1968-69, chmn. election com. 1977-80, chmn. 2d century com. 1989-92), Bar Assn. Nassau County, D.C. Bar Assn., N.Y. County Lawyers Assn. (Disting. Svc. award 1991), Nat. Bar Assn., Am. Coll. Trial Lawyers, Am. Soc. Internat. Law (exec. coun. 1975-80), Union Internationale des Avocats, Acad. Polit. Sci. (bd. dirs. 1975-94), Am. Judicature Soc. (pres. 1979-81, bd. dirs. and mem. exec. com. 1974-83, Justice award 1989), Practising Law Inst. (trustee and mem. exec. com. 1972-95, emeritus trustee 1995—, Seligson award 1995), Am. Law Inst. (coun. 1975—, ALI-ABA com. on continuing profl. edn. 1994-97, chair subcom. on future 1994-97), N.Y. Bar Found. (pres. 1976-91), Phi Beta Kappa. Home: 40 The Terrace Plandome NY 11030-1349 Office: Sullivan & Cromwell Rm 2421 125 Broad St New York NY 10004-2498 Office Phone: 212-558-3614.

**MACDIARMID, ALAN GRAHAM,** metallurgist, educator; b. Masterton, New Zealand, Apr. 14, 1927; married, 1954; 4 children. BSc, U. New Zealand, 1948, MSc, 1950; MS, U. Wis., 1952, PhD in Chemistry, 1953, Cambridge U., 1955. Asst. lectr. in chemistry St. Andrews U., 1955; from instr. to assoc. prof. U. Pa., Phila., 1955-64, Sloan fellowship, 1959-63, prof. chemistry, 1964—, Blanchard prof. chemistry, 1998—. Vis. prof. Kyoto Univ., Japan. Recipient Frederic Stanley Kipping award, 1970, Marshall award, 1982, Doolittle award, 1982, Chemical Pioneer award, 1984, Royal Soc. of Chem. Centenary Medal, Francis J. Clamer medal, Franklin Inst., 1993, Nobel Prize in Chemistry, 2000. Mem.: Royal Soc. Chemistry, Am. Chem. Soc. Achievements include preparation and characterization of organosilicon compounds; preparation and characterization of derivatives of sulfur nitrides and quasi one-dimensional semiconducting and metallic covalent polymers such as polyacetylene and its derivatives. Office: U Pa Dept Chemistry Rm 343 231 S 34th St Philadelphia PA 19104-6323*

**MACDONALD, ALAN HUGH,** academic administrator; b. Ottawa, Ont., Can., Mar. 3, 1943; s. Vincent C. and Hilda C. MacDonald; children: Eric Paul Henry, Nigel Alan Christopher. BA, Dalhousie U., Halifax N.S., 1963; BLS, U. Toronto, Ont., 1964. With Dalhousie U., 1964-78, law libr., 1965-67, 69-71, asst. univ. libr., 1972-78, health sci. libr., 1972-78, lectr. Sch. Libr. Svcs., 1969-78; with U. Calgary, Canada, 1979—2003, sr. advisor Info. Resources, 1999—2003, asst. to provost, 1999—2003, adj. prof. faculty comm. and culture, 2000—03, dir. Info Svcs., 1988—99, dir. librs., 1979-92, univ. orator, 1989—2003; dir. U. Calgary Press, 1984—90. Chair editl. bd. U. Calgary Press, 2001—03; libr. emeritus 2003—; libr. N.S. Barristers Soc., 1969—74; mem. adv. bd. Nat. Libr. Can., 1972—76, Health Scis. Resource Ctr., Can. Inst. Sci. and Tech. Info., 1977—79; mem. Coun. of Prairie Univ. Librs., 1979—92, 1997—98, chair, 1984—85, 1989, 91; Bassam lectr. U. Toronto Faculty Info. Studies, 1990; Lorne MacRae lectr. Libr. Assn. Alta., 1996; mem. steering com. Alta. Libr. Knowledge Network, 1999—2002; steering com. Can. Digital Libr. Rsch. Initiative, 1999—2000. Mem. editl. bd. America: History and Life (ABC-CLIO), 1985-93. Pres. TELED Cmty. Media Access Orgn., Halifax, N.S., 1972—74; mem. Minister's Com. on Univ. Affairs, Alta., 1979—83; bd. dirs. Alta. Found. for Can. Music Ctr., 1985—92, Can. Inst. for Hist. Microreprodn., 1990—98, pres., 1996—97; bd. dirs. Calgary Learning Ctr., 1997—2004, vice-chair, 2000—04. Coun. Libr. Resources fellow, 1975; exec. fellow Univ. Microfilms Internat., 1986; recipient Disting. Acad. Librarian award Can. Assn. of Coll. and Univ. Libraries, 1988, U. Toronto Faculty of Info. Studies Alumni Jubilee award, 1999. Mem.: Order of U. Calgary, Calgary Cmty. Network Assn. (bd. dirs. 1994—99, chair 1996—99), Can. Assn. Rsch. Librs. (bd. dirs. 1981—86, v.p. 1985—86, Disting. Svc. award to rsch. librarianship 2003), Can. Assn. Info. Sci. (pres. 1979—80), Foothills Libr. Assn., Atlantic Provinces Libr. Assn. (pres. 1977—78, Libr. Assn. (treas. 1977—79, pres. 1980—81, Award for Outstanding Svc. to Librarianship 1997), Australian Libr. and Info. Assn. (assoc.), Can. Health Libr. Assn. (life; treas. 1977—79), Libr. Assn. Alta. (life; v.p. 1988—89, Pres.' award 1992), AeroSpace Mus. Assn. Calgary (bd. dirs. 2002—, exec. dir. 2003—04, sec. 2004—). E-mail: ahmacdon@ucalgary.ca.

**MACDONALD, ALAN S.,** diversified financial services company executive; BS, Drexel U.; MS, London Sch. Econs.; PhD in Economics. Cambridge U., Eng. Economist UN Econ. Commn. for Europe, Geneva; fin. mgmt. assoc. GM, Wilmington, Del.; co-head global markets Citigroup, head corp. and investment banking U.S. and Can., head corp. banking in emerging markets, head info. bus. group, head Banco de Investimento Crefisul, head Banco Internacional de Colombia; vice chmn., head global relationship banking Citibank and Citicorp, 2000—04; COO global banking Citigroup, 2004—. Bd. dirs. Liberty Brokerage Co. Trustee NY Philharm. Orch., Hosp. for Spl. Surgery, NY. Mem.: NY Partnership (mem. high tech. com.), Am. Bankers Assn. (bd. dirs.), Am. Inst. Contemporary German Studies (trustee), Conf. Bd., Nat. Policy Assn. (trustee, mem. exec. com. new Am. realities com.), Econ. Club NY. Office: Citigroup Inc 399 Park Ave New York NY 10043

**MACDONALD, BRUCE E.,** career military officer, lawyer; b. Cinn., 1956; BA, Coll. Holy Cross, 1978; JD, Calif. We. Sch. Law, 1987. Bar: Calif., U.S. Dist. Ct. (so. dist.) Calif. Advanced through grades to rear adm. USN; main propulsion asst., navigator USS Hepburn, 1979; intermediate combat sys. team training and advanced multi-threat team course dir. Fleet Combat Training Ctr.; sr. def. counsel, trial counsel, med. care recovery act claims officer Naval Legal Svc. Office, San Diego, 1987—90; command judge advocate USS Independence, 1990—92; chief, operational law divsn. UN Command, Combined Forces Command, U.S. Forces, Seoul, Republic of Korea, 1992—94; chief operational law divsn., staff judge advocate U.S. Naval Forces, Seoul, Republic of Korea, 1992—94; exec. officer Naval Legal Svc. Office N.W., 1994—96; officer in charge Trial Svc. West Detachment Bremerton, 1996—97; fleet judge advocate Yokosuka, Japan, 1997—99; comdr. Naval Legal Svc. Office N.W., 1999—2002; spl. counsel to chief of naval ops., 2002—04; dep. judge advocate gen., comdr. Naval League Svc. Command, 2004—06; judge advocate gen. USN, 2006—. Decorated Legion of Merit with two gold stars, Def. Meritorious Svc. Medal, Navy Meritorious Svc. Medal with gold star, Navy Commendation Medal with gold star, Navy Achievement Medal with gold star. Office: USN 1200 Navy Pentagon Washington DC 20350*

**MACDONALD, DAVID ROBERT,** lawyer, pension fund administrator; b. Chgo., Nov. 1, 1930; s. James Wear and Frances Esther (Wine) M.; m. Verna Joy Odell, Feb. 17, 1962; children: Martha, Emily, David, Rachel, Rebecca. BS, Cornell U., 1952; JD, U. Mich., 1955. Bar: Ill. 1955, Mich. 1955, D.C. 1983. Practiced in Chgo., 1957-74; mem. firm Kirkland, Ellis, Hodson, Chaffetz & Masters, Chgo., 1957-62, ptnr., 1962, Baker & McKenzie, Chgo., 1962-74, 77-81; asst. sec. of Treasury for enforcement, ops. and tariff affairs Dept. Treasury, Washington, 1974-76; undersec. of Navy, 1976-77; dep. U.S. Trade Rep., 1981-83; ptnr. Baker & McKenzie, Chgo., 1983-96. Bd. dirs. Mestek, Inc. (N.Y. Stock Exch.). Pres. David R. Macdonald Found., 1996—. Mem. ABA, D.C. Bar Assn., Chgo. Assn. Commerce and Industry (bd. dirs. 1977-81), Order of Coif, Econ. Club (Chgo.), Cosmos Club (Washington), Grolier Club (N.Y.C.). Home: 6605 Radnor Rd Bethesda MD 20817-6324 Office: 815 Connecticut Ave NW Washington DC 20006-4004

**MACDONALD, DONALD ARTHUR, JR.,** physician, surgeon; b. Englewood, NJ, May 9, 1955; s. Donald Arthur and Ruth Moran M.; m. Florence Twombly Childs, June 14, 1980; children: Donald, Alexandra, Margaret, Ian. BA with highest honors, Williams Coll., 1977; MD, Dartmouth U., 1980. Diplomate Am. Bd. Ophthalmology. Intern Mary Imogene Bassett Hosp., Cooperstown, NY, 1980-81; resident Manhattan Eye Ear & Throat Hosp., N.Y.C., 1981-84; attending physician, 1985—; fellow N.Y. Eye Ear & Throat Hosp., 1984-85; attending physician Riverview Med. Ctr., Red Bank, N.J., 1985—, chief dept. ophthalmology, 1995-97. Trustee Rumson (NJ) Country Day Sch., 1990-96, Monmouth County Vol. Ctr., 1996-98, Horizons Program, Rumson, 1996-98; trustee, bd. dirs. ALS Assn. Greater NY chpt.; bd. dirs. Burden Ctr. for the Aging, 2000-03. Mem. Lions, Rumson Country Club (commodore 1996-2003), Seabright Lawn Tennis and Cricket Club, St. Andrews Soc. N.Y., N.Y. Yacht Club, Monmouth Beach Club. Roman Catholic. Office: 21 Gilbert St N Tinton Falls NJ 07701-4913 Office Phone: 732-741-1902. E-mail: Drdonaldmadonald@mac.com.

**MACDONALD, DONALD PAUL,** lawyer; b. Newport, RI, Apr. 19, 1931; s. Bertram I. and Pauline E. (Toomey) MacD.; widowed; children: Theresa Carroll, Sheila Joan, D. Patrick. BA, Providence Coll., 1952; LLB, Georgetown U., 1956, LLM, 1963. Assoc. then ptnr. Smith & Pepper, Washington, 1957-61; asst. U.S. atty. Dept. Justice, Denver, 1962-67; ptnr. Carroll & MacDonald, Denver, 1967-72, Hornbein & MacDonald, Denver, 1972—. Dir. Legal Ctr., Denver, 1986—, pres., 1989—; dir. Qualife Wellness Com., Denver, 1994-2000; trustee, fellow Coll. Labor and Employment Lawyers, 1995—, labor and employment law sect. mem. coun., 1985—, vice pres. 1995-96, pres. 1999, dir. Denver Children Advocacy Ctr., 2000-. With U.S. Army, 1952-54. Recipient Cath. Lawyers Guild St. Thomas More award, 1983. Fellow Am. Bar Found.; Internat. Soc. Barristers; mem. ABA (mem. labor and employment sect., bd. govs. 1974-84), Denver Bar Assn. (pres. 1981-82), Univ. Club. Roman Catholic. E-mail: dpmacdonald@netzero.com.

**MACDONALD, DONALD STOVEL,** public policy advisor; b. Ottawa, Ont., Can., Mar. 1, 1932; s. Donald Angus and Marjorie (Stovel) M.; m. Ruth Hutchison, Mar. 4, 1961 (dec.); children: Leigh, Nikki, Althea, Sonja; m. Adrian Merchant Lang, Sept. 10, 1988; stepchildren: Maria (dec.), Timothy, Gregory, Andrew, Elisabeth, Amanda, Adrian. Student, Ashbury Coll., Ottawa; BA, U. Toronto, Ont., 1951; LLB, Osgoode Hall Law Sch., 1955; LLM, Harvard, 1956; diploma internat. law, Cambridge U., 1957; LLD, St. Lawrence U.; U.N.B. Saint John, 1990, U. Toronto, 2000, Carleton U., 2003; DEng, Colo. Sch. Mines. Bar: Called to Ont. bar 1955. Assoc. McCarthy & McCarthy, Toronto, 1957-62; M.P. for Toronto-Rosedale, 1962; reelected, 1963, 65, 68, 72, 74; parliamentary sec. to Min. of Justice, 1963-65, to Min. of Finance, 1965, to Sec. of State for External Affairs, 1966-68, to Min. of Industry, 1968; pres. Privy Coun. and Govt. House Leader, 1968-70; min. of nat. def., 1970-72; min. energy, mines and resources, 1972-75; min. of fin 1975 77; ptnr. firm McCarthy & McCarthy, Toronto, 1977-88; high commr. for Can. to U.K., 1988-91; counsel McCarthy Tetrault, Toronto, 1991-2000; co-chmn. Trudeau Ctr., U. Toronto, 2006—. Sr. advisor UBS Bunting Warburg, Toronto, 2000-02; sr. advisor pub. policy Lang Michener Barristers and Solicitors, 2002—; spl. lectr. U. Toronto Law Sch., 1978-82, 86-88; chmn. Royal Commn. on Econ. Union and Devel. Prospects for Can., 1982-85; chmn. adv. com. competition Ont. Electricity Sys., 1995-96; chmn. Inst. for Rsch. on Pub. Policy, Montreal, 1991-97, Siemens Can. Inc., 1991-04, Atlantic Coun. of Can., 1998-02; bd. dirs. The Clan Donald Lands Trust, Skye, Scotland, Century Mining Corp., Boise Cascade Corp., 1995-04; chmn., trustee IPC US REIT, 2001—; trustee Clean Power Operating Trust, 2001—; chmn. Vector Wind Energy, 2005—; trustee Energy Savs. Income Fund, 2005—; co-chmn. Trudeau Ctr. U. Toronto, 2006—; mem. adv. coun. Ctr. Am. Studies U. Western Ont., 2006-. Named Freeman of the City of London, 1990, hon. fellow Trinity Hall, Cambridge U., 1994, Companion of the Order of Can., 1994. Mem. Queen's Privy Coun. Can., Delta Kappa Epsilon. Liberal. Baptist. Office: Lang Michener Toronto Office Box 747 ste 2500 BCE place 181 Bay st Toronto ON Canada m5j 2t7 Office Phone: 416-307-4241. Business E-Mail: dmacdonald@langmichener.ca.

**MACDONALD, DUNCAN,** broadcaster, writer, communications consultant; b. Beaumont, Tex. d. William Whyte MacDonald and Martha (Schalies) Hammond. Grad. high sch., Houston. Supr. women's and religious programming DuMont TV Network, N.Y.C., 1950-53; prodr. Home show NBC-TV, N.Y.C., 1954; broadcaster Yankee Network, Boston, 1955-59, Sta. WQXR, N.Y.C., 1960-62; monthly article writer House Beautiful, N.Y.C., 1966-67, exec. asst. to editor, 1967-70; pres. The Media Group, Edgartown, Mass., 1967—; exec. dir. Nat. Friends Pub. Broadcasting, N.Y.C., 1970-72; administrv. aide Dukes County Commrs., Edgartown, 1976-82; features editor Martha's Vineyard (Mass.) Times, 1983-88. Mem. White House Conf. Nutrition, Washington, 1969. Author: Rain, Hail & Baked Beans, 1958; home editor Yankee Mag., 1956-63; food editor Old Farmer's Almanac, 1957-65. Founder, pres. Com. for the Ams., N.Y.C., 1963-67; trustee Nat. Coun. Women, N.Y.C., 1962-72, Am. Youth Hostels, N.Y.C., 1968-73, Am. Friends Scottish Opera, N.Y.C., 1982-87, pres., 1986-87; trustee Caledonian Found., Inc., Sarasota, Fla., 1987—, pres., treas. Recipient UN Children's Fund award UNICEF, 1957, citation Pres.'s Com. on Aid to Physically Handicapped, 1957, citation OAS, 1970; recordings and writings in Duncan MacDonald Collection U. Wyo., Coun. Scottish Clans & Assns. nat. award, 2001. Fellow Soc. Antiquaries of Scotland; mem. Am. Women in Radio and TV (pres.

N.Y.C. chpt.), Overseas Press Club, Clan Donald USA, Broadcast Pioneers, Sarasota Opera Guild, Caledonian Found. Inc. (trustee Sarasota, Fla. 1987-, pres., treas. 2000, exec. v.p., treas. 2001-), Scottish Soc. Martha's Vineyard (co-founder 1986), Scottish Coalition (co-founder 1997-). Baptist. Achievements include Called a key figure in the establishment of Tartan Day as a national observance. Address: PO Box 1242 Edgartown MA 02539-1242

**MACDONALD, FLORA ISABEL,** Canadian government official; b. North Sydney, N.S., Can., June 3, 1926; d. George Frederick and Mary Isabel (Royle) MacD. Attended Empire Bus. Coll.; grad., Nat. Def. Coll., 1972; DHL (hon.), Mt. St. Vincent U., 1979, various univs., Can., U.S. and U.K. Exec. dir. Progressive Conservative Party Hdqs., Ottawa, Ont., Canada, 1957—66; adminstrv. officer, tutor dept. polit. studies Queen's U., 1966—72; mem. Can. Parliament for Kingston and Islands, Ont., 1972—88; Progressive Conservative spokesman for Indian affairs and no. devel. Can. Parliament, 1972; for housing and urban devel., 1974; chmn. Progressive Conservative Caucus Com. on Fed.-Provincial Rels., 1976; sec. of state for external affairs, 1979—80; min. employment and immigration, 1984—86; min. comms., 1986—89; chairperson Internat. Devel. Rsch. Ctr., 1992—97; spl. adv. Commonwealth of Learning, 1990—91. Vis. fellow Ctr. for Can. Studies, U. Edinburgh, 1989; host T.V. series North South Vision T.V., 1990-94. Bd. dirs. Carnegie Commn. Re-preventing Deadly Conflict, 1994-99, Friends of the Nat. Libr., Shashtri Indo-Can. Adv. Coun., pres., 1996-2004; program advisor CARE Can., 1995-2005, Helpage Internat., London, 1996-2001; chmn. Partnership Africa-Can., 2001-04, Ottawa, Can., Future Generations, 2001—; Franklin, W.va.; co-chair Can Coord. Com. UN Yr. of Older Persons, 1999; hon. pres. Assn. Can. Clubs, World Federalists, Can., 2000-04; patron Commonwealth Human Rights Initiative. Decorated Companion Order of Can., Order of Ont. Mem. Nat. Mus. Scotland (hon. patron Can.), UN (Eminent Persons to study Trans-Nat. Corps. in South Africa 1989). Mem. United Ch. of Canada. Office: Ste 1103 350 Queen Elizabeth Driveway Ottawa ON Canada K1S 3N1 E-mail: flora@intranet.ca.

**MACDONALD, GORDON RHODES,** retired urologist, military officer; b. Washington, Dec. 28, 1943; s. Gordon Rhodes and Sally Steele MacDonald; m. Marie Teresa Sweeney, July 2, 1966. MD, George Wash. U., Washington, D.C., 1968. Medical Board Certification Am. Bd. of Urology, 1978. Surg. intern Cleve. Clinic, Ohio, 1968—69; med. dept. head USS Capricornus and USS El Paso, Norfolk, Va., 1969—70; gen. med. officer Nat. Naval Med. Ctr., Bethesda, Md., 1970—72, resident in urology, 1972—76; head urology dept. Naval Hosp., Charleston, SC, 1976—83, Naval Regional Med. Ctr., Portsmouth, Va., 1983—90, Fleet Hosp. Five, Jubail, Saudi Arabia, 1990—91, Naval Hosp. Roosevelt Roads, Ceiba, PR, 1991—99. Chmn. urology residency program Naval Regional Med. Ctr., Portsmouth, Va., 1983—90. Capt. USN, 1969—99. Mem.: Am. Urol. Assn. Home: 340 Harbour Dr #73 Humacao PR 00791-6217

**MACDONALD, HUGH IAN,** economics professor, public policy professor, retired academic administrator; b. Toronto, Ont., Can., June 27, 1929; s. Hugh and Winnifred (Mitchell) M.; m. Dorothy Marion Vernon, June 4, 1960; 5 children. B.Com., U. Toronto, 1952; MA, Oxford U., Eng., 1954, B.Phil., 1955; LLD (hon.), U. Toronto, 1974; D Univ. (hon.), Open U., U.K., 1998; DLitt (hon.), Open U., Sri Lanka, 1999, Open U., Hyderabad, India, 2001. Lectr. U. Toronto, 1955-62, asst. prof., 1962-65; dean of men U. Toronto (Univ. Coll.), 1956-65; chief economist Govt. Ontario, 1965-67, dep. treas., 1967, dep. treas., dep. minister econs., 1968, dep. treas., dep. minister econs. and intergovtl. affairs, 1972; pres. York U., Toronto, Ont., Canada, 1974-84, dir. MPA program Schulich Sch. Bus., prof. econ. and pub. policy, pres. emeritus, 1984—; dir. York Internat., 1984-94. Past pres. World Univ. Svc. Can.; past chmn. Hockey Can. Named Officer, Order of Can., 1977; recipient Can. Centennial medal, 1967, Queen's Silver Jubilee medal, 1977, Commemorative medal, 125th Anniversary Can. Confedn., 1992, Vanier medal for distinction in pub. svc. and excellence in pub. adminstrn., 2000, Queen's Golden Jubilee medal, 2002, Senator Boorsma medal recognition pub. adminstrn., Southeastern Conf. Pub. Adminstrn. US, 2006; Rhodes scholar, 1952. Fellow: The Commonwealth of Learning (past chmn.). Office: York U Schulich Sch Bus Rm N207 Seymour Schulich Bldg 4700 Keele St Toronto ON Canada M3J 1P3 Office Phone: 416-736-5632. Office Fax: 416-736-5643. Business E-Mail: yorkmpa@yorku.ca.

**MACDONALD, J. RANDALL,** information technology executive, human resources specialist; B in Polit. Sci., St. Francis Coll., M in Indsl. Rels. Human resources position Ingersoll-Rand Co., Sterling Drug Inc.; various human resources positions including exec. v.p. human resouces IBM, 2000—. Bd. dirs. Covance (formerly Corning Pharm. Svcs.); mem. Cornell U. Ctr. for Advanced Human Resources Study, chmn. exec. bd. Bd. trustees St. Francis Coll., Pa. Fellow: Nat. Acad. Human Resources (bd. dirs. 2000—); mem.: Labor Policy Assn. (vice chmn. human resouces), Pers. Roundtable, Cowdrick Group. Office: IBM 1133 Westchester Ave White Plains NY 10604 Office Phone: 800-426-4968.

**MACDONALD, JAMES ROSS,** physicist, researcher; b. Savannah, Ga., Feb. 27, 1923; s. John Elwood and Antonina Jones (Hansell) Macdonald; m. Margaret Milward Taylor, Aug. 3, 1946; children: Antonina Hansell, James Ross IV, William Taylor. BA, Williams Coll., 1944; SB, MIT, 1944, SM, 1947; PhD, Oxford U., Eng., 1950, DSc, 1967. Staff Digital Computer Lab., MIT, 1946-47; physicist Armour Rsch. Found., Chgo., 1950-52; assoc. physicist Argonne Nat. Lab., 1952-53; with Tex. Instruments Inc., Dallas, 1953-74 v.p. corp. rsch. and engring. 1969-73, v.p. corp. R & D, 1973-74; cons., 1974—; dir. Simmonds Precision Products Inc., 1979-83; William Rand Kenan Jr. prof. physics U.N.C., Chapel Hill, 1974-91, prof. emeritus, 1991—. Adj. prof. biophysics U. Tex. Med. Sch., Dallas, 1954—74; mem. solid state scis. panel NRC, 1965—73; mem. adv. com. sci. edn. NSF, 1971—73; mem. vis. com. physics MIT, 1971—74; mem. external adv. com. Engring. Exptl. Sta. Ga. Inst. Tech., 1976—79. Editor, co-author: Impedance Spectroscopy-Theory, Experiment, and Applications, 2005, 2d edit., 2005; mem. editl. bd. Jour. Applied Physics, 1984—86; contbr. articles to profl. jours. Bd. dirs. League Ednl. Advancement Dallas, 1965—70; mem. Dallas Radio Commn., 1967—71; mem. sci. adv. coun. Callier Hearing and Speech Ctr., Dallas, 1971—74; mem. adv. com. Weber Rsch. Inst., 1985—90. Rhodes scholar, Oxford U., 1948—50. Fellow: AAAS, IEEE (editor Transactions Profl. Group Audio 1961—66, editor Transactions Audio and Electroacoustics 1966—73, award 1962, 1974, Edison Gold medal 1986), Am. Phys. Soc. (mem. com. edn. 1973—75, mem. com. applicaitons physics 1975—78, George E. Pake prize 1985); mem.: NAS (chmn. numerical data adv. bd. 1970—74, mem. motor vehicle emissions 1971—74, chmn. com. motor vehicle emissions 1973—74, mem. com. satellite power sys. 1979—81, mem. com. sci., engring., and pub. policy 1981—83, mem. commmn. phys. scis., math. and applications 1985—88, mem. report rev. com. 1990—97), NAE (mem. coun. 1971—74, mem. exec. com. assembly engring. 1975—78), Audio Engring. Soc., Electrochemical Soc., Am. Inst. Physics (mem. governing bd. 1975—78), Sigma Xi, Phi Beta Kappa, Tau Beta Pi. Achievements include patents in field. Office: U NC Dept Physics and Astronomy Chapel Hill NC 27517-7549 Business E-Mail: macd@email.unc.edu.

**MACDONALD, JOHN,** marketing executive; V.p. mktg. Chrysler Corp., Auburn Hills, Mich., 1996-98, v.p. sales and svc., 1997-99; sr. v.p. sales and svc. DaimlerChrysler Corp., Auburn Hills, 1999—. Office: DaimlerChrysler Corp 1000 Chrysler Dr Auburn Hills MI 48326-2766

**MACDONALD, JOHN STEPHEN,** oncologist, educator; b. Bklyn., June 2, 1943; s. John Stephen and Margaret (Martin) M.; m. Mary Suzanne Stock, July 11, 1964; children: Margaret Wilson, John Stephen, Kathleen Lenore, Frederick Stock. AB, Dartmouth Coll., 1965, BMS, 1967; MD, Harvard U., 1969. Diplomate Am. Bd. Internal Medicine (mem. med. oncology com. 1989-93, chmn. med. oncology self edn. process com. 1993-95). Intern and resident in medicine Beth Israel Hosp., Boston, 1969-71; clin. assoc. immunology and med. oncology Nat. Cancer Inst., Bethesda, Md., 1971-74, assoc. dir. cancer therapy evaluation program, div. cancer treatment, 1979-82,

med. oncologist Washington Clin., 1982-84; instr., asst. prof., then assoc. prof. medicine Georgetown U., Washington, 1974-79, clin. assoc. prof., 1979-84, George Washington U., 1980-84; prof. medicine, chief div. hematology-oncology U. Ky., Lexington, 1984-89, assoc. dir. Markey Cancer Center, 1984-89; prof. medicine, chief sect. med. oncology, dir. cancer ctr. Temple U., Phila., 1989-97; dir. gastrointestinal oncology St. Vincent's Comprehensive Cancer Ctr., N.Y.C., 1997—; nat. dir. physician orgns. Salick Health Care, Inc., L.A., 1997-98, exec. v.p. med. affairs, 1998—, chief med. officer, 1999—. Chmn. gastrointestinal cancer com. S.W. Oncology Group, 1985—. Editor-in-chief: Cancer Treatment Reports, 1979-82; co-editor: Gastrointestinal Oncology, 1992; mem. editorial bd. Jour. Clin. Oncology, 1988-91; contbr. more than 250 articles to med. jours. Bd. mgmt. YMCA, 1979-84; bd. dirs. CYO, 1979-84. Served with USPHS, 1971-74. Jr. faculty clin. fellow Am. Cancer Soc., 1974-76 Fellow ACP; mem. Am. Fedn. Clin. Research, Am. Soc. Clin. Oncology, Am. Assn. for Cancer Research, Am. Cancer Soc. (bd. dirs. Phila. chpt. 1994—). Roman Catholic. Office: St Vincent's Comprehensive Cancer Ctr 325 W 15th St New York NY 10011-5903 Home: PO Box 32 Castine ME 04421-0032

**MACDONALD, JOHN THOMAS,** school system administrator; b. Utica, N.Y., Nov. 21, 1932; s. Gerald Clement and Mildred (Hayes) MacD.; m. Marcia Sprague Gallup; children: Terrence (dec.), Anthony, Elizabeth Michele, Elise, Denise. BS, Northeastern U., 1958, EdM, 1960; PhD, U. Conn., 1970. Cert. elem. and secondary sch. tchr., prin., supt., Mass., Conn. Supervising prin. Noank, Ft. Hill. and Poquonnock Elem. Schs., Groton, Conn., 1962-66, Robert E. Fitch Jr. H.S., Groton, 1966-70; rsch. asst. Ednl. Resources and Devel. Ctr. U. Conn., Storrs, 1969-70; supt. Wallingford (Conn.) Pub. Schs., 1970-73, Walpole (Mass.) Pub. Schs., 1973-78, Dartmouth (Mass.) Pub. Schs., 1978-86; commr. edn. State Dept. Edn., Concord, NH, 1986-90; asst. sec. for elem. and secondary edn. U.S. Dept. Edn., Washington, 1990-93; dir. state leadership ctr. Coun. of Chief State Sch. Officers, Washington, 1993-99, sr. advisor, 2000-01; prof. of ednl. policy and leadership Neag Sch. Edn., U. Conn., 2001—; dir. NE Ctr. for Ednl. Policy and Leadership. Mem. Postsecondary Edn. Commn., Concord, 1986-90, Coun. for Tchr. Edn., Concord, 1986-90, Profl. Stds. Bd., Concord, 1986-90, trustee Univ. System of N.H., Durham, 1986-90; mem. Surgeon Gen's Task Force, 1990-93; mem. White House Conf. on Indian Edn., 1990-93; mem. Interagy. Com. on Sch. Health, 1990-93, others; mem. dean's adv. coun. U. Conn., 1999—, Coll. Arts and Scis., Northeastern U., 1999—; mem. adv. coun. Va. Edn. Policy Inst., Va. Commonwealth U., 2000—; mem. adv. bd. ERIC, Washington, 1998—. Contbr. articles to profl. jours. Co-chmn. Emergency Sch.-Aide Proposals, U.S. Office Edn., 1973—75; mem. adv. com. external program rev. CDC, 1992—; mem. nat. adv. bd. ERIC Clearinghouse, 1999—; mem. Mass. Adv. Commn. for Ednl. TV, 1983—86, N.H. Task Force on Child Abuse, 1987—90; mem. Nat. Adv. Coun. Northeastern U., 1990—; mem. Galaxy Classroom Nat. Adv. Coun. Galaxy Inst. for Edn., 1992—; mem. sch. health policy initiative Ctr. for Population & Family Health Columbia U., 1992—; mem. Packard roundtable to children Ctr. for Health Policy George Washington U., 1992—; mem. adv. bd. Va. Commonwealth Policy Inst., 1999—; mem. Dean's adv. coun. Neag Sch. Edn. U. Conn., 1999—, Coll. Arts & Scis. Northeastern U., 1999—. Recipient Sears Ph.D. Condit award, 1958, Alumni award Northwestern U., 1973, Recognition award Coun. of Chief State Sch. Officers, 1990. Fellow Phi Delta Kappa, Phi Alpha Theta; mem. N.H. Sch. Bldg. Authority, Mass. Assn. Sch. Supts. (pres. 1985-86). Office: U Conn Neag Sch Edn Dept Ednl Leadership 249 Glenbrook Rd Box U-2093 Storrs Mansfield CT 06269-2064 Business E-Mail: John.MacDonald@uconn.edu. E-mail: macmarjack@aol.com.

**MACDONALD, JOSEPH LESTER,** retired metal products executive; b. Waltham, Mass., June 7, 1931; s. Ronald Francis MacDonald and Nellie Catheran Fontaine; 1 child from previous marriage, James Paul stepchildren: Kimberlee, Kristan, Kevin, Kellie. Grad., Sch. Dental Tech., Boston, 1949. Owner, pres. M&M Alloys Casting Inc., Naples, Maine, 1951—81; v.p. sales & mktg. Boroloy Industries Inc., Post Falls, Idaho, 1984—85; pres. Rocky Mountain Casting Inc., Eagle, Colo., 1985—87; ret., 1987. Instr. mktg. & sales Small Bus. Pers. Seminar, Spokane, Wash., 1987. Represented in permanent collections Smithsonian Inst., Sheire Crump & Lowe, Boston. Bd. dirs. Bridgton (Maine) C. of C. With U.S. Army, 1948—51. Named Best Aluminum Shell Caster, Precision Metal Mag., 1980. Mem.: Soc. Mfg. Engrs. (sr.), Lions (pres. Bridgton 1975—76). Independent. Avocations: hunting, fishing, art, photography, gardening. Home: 7100 Ulmerton Rd #200 Largo FL 33771-5142 E-Mail: scottsman3@verizon.net.

**MACDONALD, KAREN CRANE,** occupational therapist, geriatrics services professional; b. Denville, N.J., Feb. 24, 1955; d. Robert William and Jeanette Wilcox (Crane) M.; m. Geno Piacentini, Oct. 22, 1993. BS, Quinnipiac U., 1977; MS, U. Bridgeport, 1982; PhD, NYU, 1998. Cert. occupl. therapist. Occupational therapy, coord. of spl. care unit Jewish Home for the Elderly, Conn., 1987-92, N.Y. Inst., N.Y.C., 1984-86; pvt. practice Fairfield County, Conn., 1977-88; occupl. therapist Rehab. Assocs., Fairfield, Conn., 1993-96; instr. Housatonic Cmty. Coll., Conn. Instr. NYU, 1985—89, Quinnipiac Coll., 1986—92, Housatonic CC, Bridgeport, Conn., 2002; lectr., cons. in field. Contbr. articles to profl. jours. Youth leader, deacon Union Meml. Ch., Stamford, Conn., 1980-88; deacon Southport Congl. Ch., 1992-94; chair consumer com. Alzheimer's Coalition of Conn., 1991-92. Teaching fellow NYU, 1983-86. Mem. AAAS, P.E.O., World Fedn. Occupl. Therapy, Am. Occupl. Therapy Assn. (scholar 1985, coun.), Conn. Occupl. Therapy Assn. (gerontology liaison 1980-83), Am. Bd. Disability Analysts, NY Acad. Scis., Grange, Pi Lambda Theta. Avocations: poetry writing, quilting. Home: 198 Glenbrook Rd Bridgeport CT 06610-1149

**MACDONALD, KEN CRAIG,** geophysicist; b. San Francisco, Oct. 14, 1947; m. Rachel Haymon, 1984. BS in Engring. Geoscis., U. Calif., Berkeley, 1970; PhD in Marine Geophysics, MIT/Woods Hole, 1975. Cecil H. and Ida Green postdoctoral scholar Scripps Instn. of Oceanography, 1975-76, asst. rsch. geophysicist, lectr., 1976-80; assoc. prof. U. Calif., Santa Barbara, 1980-83, prof., 1983—. Chief scientist on over 30 deep sea expeditions; ALVIN diver on over 40 dives to the mid-ocean ridge. Assoc. editor Jour. of Geophys. Rsch., 1979-82, Earth and Planetary Sci. Letters, 1978-88; mem. editorial bd. Marine Sci. Revs., 1986—; editor Marine Geophys. Rschs., 1986-90; contbr. over 100 articles to profl. jours. Mem. ALVIN Rev. Com., 1979-82; mem. Ocean Sci. Bd. of NAS, 1980-83, Lithosphere Panel Advanced Ocean Drilling Project, 1983-85, Ocean Scis. Panel, NSF, 1984-86, COSOD II planning com.; mem. various RIDGE coms., RIDGE steering com., 1987-90; mem. NSF Ocean Scis. Strategic Plan for Rsch. and Edn. Com., 1993-94, U.S. Geodynamics Comm., 1997—. Regents scholar U. Calif., Berkeley, 1966-70, Mineral Tech. scholar 1967-70, Cecil H. and Ida Green scholar Inst. Geophysics and Planetary Physics/U. Calif., San Diego, 1975-76; NSF Grad. fellow, 1970-73, World Innovation Found. fellow, 2005; recipient AAAS Newcomb-Cleveland prize, 1980, Robert L. and Bettie P. Cody prize and medal Scripps Instn. Oceanography, 1994; named U. Hawaii SOEST Disting. lectr., 1990, ISI Highly Cited Rschr., 2004. Fellow Am. Geophys. Union, Geol. Soc.; mem. Phi Beta Kappa, Sigma Psi. Avocations: windsurfing, fly fishing. Office: U Calif Santa Barbara Dept Geol Sci Santa Barbara CA 93106 Office Phone: 805-893-4005. Business E-Mail: macdonald@geol.ucsb.edu.

**MACDONALD, KENNETH R., JR.,** author, artist; b. N.Y.C., Apr. 14, 1944; s. Kenneth and Wilma Christine (Lange) M. Bd., Lehigh U., 1967; MA, W.Va. U., 1970, PhD, 1976. Instr. W.Va. U., Morgantown, 1980-81. Author: The Destiny of Man, 1978, The Gods, 1993, The Palace of Time: The Proof of God and Immortality, 1999, Henry Lange: Master Painter, 2001; exhbns. include Art's Alive (fifty Vt. artists) Festival of Fine Art, Burlington, 2003; commd. portraits KMacD Art, 2003—. Home and Studio: PO Box 1027 Middlebury VT 05753-5027

**MACDONALD, KIRK STEWART,** lawyer; b. Glendale, Calif., Oct. 24, 1948; s. Bruce Mace and Phyllis Jeanne MacDonald. BSCE, U. So. Calif., 1970; JD, Western State U., 1982. Bar: Calif. 1982, U.S. Dist. Ct. (cen. dist.) Calif. 1982, U.S. Ct. Appeals (9th cir.) 1982, U.S. Dist. Ct. (no. dist.) Calif.

1984, U.S. Dist. Ct. (so. dist.) Calif. 1985, U.S. Dist. Ct. (ea. dist.) Calif. 1987. Dist. engr. Pacific Clay Products, Corona, Calif., 1971-76, Nat. Clay Pipe Inst., La Mirada, Calif., 1976-82; ptnr. Gill and Baldwin, Glendale, Calif., 1982—. Mem. ABA, L.A. County Bar Assn., Water Environ. Assn., Calif. Water Environ. Assn. Avocations: travel, woodworking. Office: Gill & Baldwin Ste 405 130 N Brand Blvd Glendale CA 91203-2646 E-mail: kirk@gillandbaldwin.com.

MACDONALD, LAURIE, film company executive; m. Walter Parkes, 1983; 2 children. BA in English Lit., Sonoma State U., Calif. Documentary and news prodr. K-RON, NBC affiliate, San Francisco; creative exec. Columbia Pictures, 1984—85, v.p. prodn., 1985—88; head Aerial Pictures, 1988—94; exec. prodr. Amblin Entertainment, 1994; co-head motion pictures divsn. DreamWorks Pictures, 1994—. Prodr.: (films) Hayseed, 1997, Men in Black, 1997 (nominated Golden Globe best musical or comedy), Men in Black II, 2002, The Ring, 2002, The Terminal, 2004, Lemony Snicket's A Series of Unfortunate Events, 2004, The Ring Two, 2005, The Island, 2005, Just Like Heaven, 2005, The Legend of Zorro, 2005; (TV series) SFO; exec. prodr.: (films) How to Make an American Quilt, 1995, The Trigger Effect, 1996, Twister, 1996, The Mask of Zorro, 1998, Gladiator, 2000, The Time Machine, 2002, The Tuxedo, 2002, Catch Me If You Can, 2002. Named one of 100 Most Powerful Women in Hollywood, Hollywood Reporter, 2003, 2005, 50 Most Powerful People in Hollywood, Premiere mag., 2004—05; recipient Women in Hollywood Icon award, Premiere Mag., 1999. Office: DreamWorks SKG 100 Flower St Glendale CA 91201 Office Phone: 818-733-7000. Office Fax: 818-695-7574.*

MACDONALD, LELAND LLOYD, lawyer; b. Marfa, Tex., July 19, 1931; s. John Edward and Nannye Myrtle (Barnett) M.; m. Juanice L. Koen, Nov. 22, 1958; children: David Allen, Kathryn Ann. BBA, Baylor U., 1952, LLB, 1957. Bar: Tex. 1957, U.S. Dist. Ct. (we. dist.) Tex. 1960, U.S. Ct. Appeals (5th cir.). Title analyst Shell Oil Co., Midland, Tex., 1957—60; pvt. practice Midland, 1960—64; ptnr. Kerr, Fitz-Gerald & Kerr, Midland, 1964—73, Turpin, Smith, Dyer, Saxe & MacDonald, Midland, 1973—2003; pvt. practice, 2004—. Mem. admissions com. Tex. State Bar, 1978—80, grievance com., 1976—78. Author: The Alamo Generation, 2004, Seven Sketches of Valor, 2006. Past chmn. adv. bd. Salvation Army, 1962—82. Lt. USAF, 1952—54. Fellow: Tex. Bar Found. (life); mem.: Midland County Bar Assn. (pres. 1973—74), Baylor Law Alumni Assn. (bd. dirs. 1980—86), Tex. Assn. Def. Counsel, Tex. State Bar Assn., Midland County Jr. Bar Assn. (pres. 1964—65), The Alamo Soc., Midland Jaycees (v.p. 1960), Green Tree Country Club (bd. dirs. 1983—85), Rotary (pres. 1972—73), Free Masons Lodge (writer). Baptist. Home: 1515 Community Ln Midland TX 79701-4011 Office: Ste 1310 500 W Texas Midland TX 79701-4289 Office Phone: 432-684-9990.

MACDONALD, PATRICIA LYNN, gifted and talented educator; d. Harold Allen and Sally Anne Davis; m. James Allan Macdonald, Aug. 14, 1982; children: Michael James, Lindsay Marie. BA in Elem. Edn., U. No. Colo., 1980, MA in Spl. Edn., 2000, EdS in Ednl. Leadership and Policy Studies. Lic. educator Colo., prin. Colo. Elem. tchr. Bennett (Colo.) Sch. Dist. 29J, 1980—83, Aurora (Colo.) Pub. Schs. 1983—90, Cherry Creek Schs. Englewood, Colo., 1990—97, gifted/talented resource tchr., 1997—. Co-author: The Power of Words, 2004. Rep. adv. com. Cherry Creek Gifted/Talented Bd. Dirs., Englewood, 1997—. Named Outstanding Math. Educator of the Yr., Colo. Coun. Tchrs. Math., 2001. Mem.: ASCD, Nat. Assn. Gifted Children, Colo. Acad. Edns. Gifted, Talented and Creative, Nat. Coun. Tchrs. Math., Colo. Assn. Gifted and Talented (educator liaison 2005—, bd. dirs., named Educator of Yr. 2003), Delta Kappa Gamma. Avocations: antiques, gardening. Home: 9205 S Madras Ct Highlands Ranch CO 80130 Office: Cherry Creek Schs 6100 S Fulton St Englewood CO 80111 Personal E-mail: patlynmac@comcast.net.

MACDONALD, PAUL EDWARD, electrical engineer; b. Syracuse, N.Y., Nov. 2, 1954; s. Cornelius J. and Virginia F. (Vassallo) MacD.; m. Linda Marie Fredrick, Aug. 20, 1983; children: Maeghen Leigh, Charles Fredrick. B Archtl. Engring., Pa. State U., 1977. Registered profl. engr., Va., Md., D.C., Conn., W.Va., Del., Ill. Engring. in tng. Syska & Hennessy, Washington, 1977-78, jr. engr., 1978-79, project engr., 1979-80, Meta Engrs. P.C., Washington, 1980-82, dir. elec. engring., 1982-88, chief elec. engring., 1988-91, v.p., chief elec. engring., 1991-99, pres., 1999—. Den leader Cub Scouts, Boy Scouts Am., Alexandria, Va., 1994-99, asst. scoutmaster Troop 993, Alexandria, 1999—; mem. consortium for the advancement of bldg. scis. Pa. State U., 1995—. Mem. NSPE, Nat. Soc. Archtl. Engrs., D.C. Soc. Profl. Engrs. (pres. 1991-92, bd. dirs. 1986-2001, Outstanding Svc. award 1987, 88, Bus. Adv. Coun. 2003, named Businessman of Yr., 2002), Sierra Club (life), Appalachian Trail Conf. Roman Catholic. Avocations: woodworking, making stringed musical instruments, playing guitar, banjo and dulcimer, hiking. Home: 8801 Lukens Ln Alexandria VA 22309-4105 Office: Meta Engrs PC 1515 Wilson Blvd Arlington VA 22209 E-mail: pmacdonald@metaengineers.com.

MACDONALD, PETER J., lawyer; b. 1957; BA, Northwestern Univ., 1980; JD cum laude, Boston Univ., 1984. Bar: Mass. 1985, NY 2001. Ptnr., vice chmn. Litigation dept, mem. exec. com. Wilmer Cutler Pickering Hale & Dorr, Boston. Former adj. prof. Northeastern Univ. Sch. Law. Editor: Boston Univ. Law Rev.; contr. articles to profl. jours. Mem.: ABA, Boston Bar Assn. Office: Wilmer Cutler Pickering Hale & Dorr 60 State St Boston MA 02109 Office Phone: 617-526-6123. Office Fax: 617-526-5000. Business E-Mail: peter.macdonald@wilmerhale.com.

MACDONALD, PRISCILLA ANN, history professor; b. Knoxville, Tenn., Dec. 7, 1949; d. Elmer Franklin and Mae Helen Lee; m. Robert Eugene MacDonald (div.); children: Brock Glyn, Heather Mae, Megan Lee. AA in Bus. Adminstrn., Lourdes Coll., 2002, BA in Hist., 2004; MA in Hist., U. Toledo, 2006. Life lab Lourdes Coll., Sylvania, Ohio, 1999—2003, active Upward Bound program, 2003—04; all hosts svc. U. Toledo, 2004—05, tchg. asst., 2005—06, ind. instr., 2006—. Editl. com. Lourdes Coll., 2005—; presenter in field. Vol. Rotaract Lourdes Coll., 1999—2004, Habitat for Humanity, Lourdes Coll., 2000—04, Pine Ridge Indian Reservation, SD, 2000—05. Named Student of Yr., TRIO Lourdes Coll., 2004; recipient Student Life award, Lourdes Coll., 2000. Mem.: Orgn. Am. Historians, Am. Soc. for Ethnohistory, Western Hist. Assn., Am. Hist. Assn., Phi Alpha Theta (sec. 2004—05). Democrat. Avocations: writing, crafts, sewing, movies. Personal E-mail: cilla202@sbcglobal.net.

MACDONALD, PURIFICACION O., statistician, researcher; m. Warren MacDonald, Oct. 28, 1942; children: Mark W., Michelle O. Steiner, Melissa A. PhD in Agrl. Econs./Econometrics, Pa. State U., 1972. Sr. planning analyst Pa. State U., University Park, 1980—95; prin. statistician U.S. Postal Svc., 1998—2001; math. statistician Bur. Transp. Stats. U.S. Dept. Transp., Washington, 2001—. Rsch. statistician Md. Dept. of Edn., Balt., 1995—98. Advisor for racial/ethnic diversity Pa. State U., University Park, 1990—95. East West Ctr. Rsch. U. S. Govt., 1963—65, Ford Found. fellow, 1967—69. Mem.: Am. Statis. Assn. Achievements include research in multivariate analyses. Avocations: travel, gardening, music, cooking. Office: US Dept Transp Bur Transp Stats 400 7th Street SW Washington DC 20590

MACDONALD, ROBERT ALAN, language educator; b. Salamanca, N.Y., Mar. 25, 1927; s. Guy E. and Hildur V. (Helene) MacD. BA, U. Buffalo, 1948; MA, U. Wis., 1949, PhD, 1958. Asst. prof. U. Richmond, Va., 1955-61, assoc. prof., 1961-67, prof. Spanish, 1967-95, prof. emeritus, 1995; ofcl. project reviewer NEH, Washington, 1977-95; mem. Social Sci. and Humanities Rsch. Coun., Ottawa, Ont., Canada, 1981-95. Author: Espéculo, texto jurídico atribuido a Alfonso X, 1990, Alfonso X, Libro de las Tahurerías, 1995, Alfonso X, Libro de los Adelantados Mayores, 2000; editor Bull. of Fgn. Lang. Assn. Va., 1964-67, 72-86; contr. articles to profl. jours. With U.S. Army, 1946-47, 51-53. A.L. Markham traveling fellow U. Wis., 1958-59, Am. Coun. Learned Socs. fellow, 1976; fellow, grantee U. Richmond, 1958-94;

named Cultural Laureate of Va., 1977; recipient Disting. Svc. award Fgn. Lang. Assn. Va., 1981. Mem. Acad. Am. Rsch. Historians on Medieval Spain, Am. Assn. Spanish and Portuguese (past pres. state chpt.), AAUP (past pres. local chpt.), Am. Coun. on Tchg. Fgn. Langs., Medieval Acad. Am. MLA, Torch Club (Richmond).

MACDONALD, ROBERT RIGG, JR., retired museum director; b. Pitts., May 11, 1942; s. Robert Rigg and Ruth (Johnson) M.; m. Catherine Ronan, Nov. 27, 1965; children: Matthew, Robert, Catherine. BA, U. Notre Dame, 1964, MA, 1965, U. Pa., 1970. Asst. curator Smithsonian Instn., Washington, 1965; curator Mercer Mus., Doylestown, Pa., 1966-70; dir. New Haven Colony Hist. Soc., 1970-74, La. State Mus., New Orleans, 1974-85; dir., CEO Mus. of City of N.Y., 1985—2002; ret., 2002. Adj. prof. mus. studies NYU, 1989—; mem. Commn. Mus. for a New Century; bd. dirs. SC Aquarium.; trustee SC Aquarium, 2004-; mem. adv. bd. Riley Inst., Coll. Charleston, 2004-; vice chair Internat. Coms. Mus. of City, Internat. Coun. Mus., 2005-. Editor: Editor: New Haven Colony Furniture, 1973, Louisiana Images 1880-1920, 1975, Louisiana Black Heritage, 1977 Louisiana Portraitures, 1979, Louisiana Legal Heritage, 1981, The Sun King: Louis XIV and the New World, On Being Homeless, A Community of Many Worlds: Arab American New Society, 2002; organizer (children's art, photographs) The Day Our World Changed: Children's Art of 9/11, The City Resilient: Photographs by Joel Meyerowitz. Decorated chevalier de l'Ordre des Arts et des Lettres (France), cruz de Caballero de la Orden de Isabel La Catolica (Spain); assoc. fellow Berkeley Coll., Yale U., 1978; Hagley fellow U. Del., 1970-71; Univ. scholar U. Notre Dame, 1964-65 Mem.: Mus. City N.Y. (dir. emeritus 2002—), Am. Assn. Mus. (pres. 1985—88, chmn. ethics task force 1988—91, Disting. Svc. award 2003), Am. Assn. State and Local History (coun.), Century Assn. Roman Catholic. Home: 602 Island Walk East Mount Pleasant SC 29464 Office Phone: 843-670-7440. Personal E-mail: robertrm2@aol.com.

MACDONALD, RONALD FRANCIS, diversified financial services company executive; b. Detroit, July 23, 1946; s. Alfred and Marianne Dorothy (Paddock) MacDonald; m. Harriet Pratt Higgins, Dec. 18, 1982 (div. 1997); children: John Higgins, Peter Brewer. BS, U. Detroit, 1968; MBA, Mich. State U., 1970. V.p. No. Trust Co., Chgo., 1970—84, Bankers Trust Co., NYC, 1984—89; mng. dir. CapMAC Holdings, Inc., NYC, 1989—97, MBIA Ins. Corp., Armonk, NY, 1998—2000, Chubb Fin. Solutions Inc., NYC, 2001—02; pres. Hartwell Cons. Co., NYC, 2002—. Mem.: Ins. Industry Planning Forum, NY Athletic Club, Royal Oak Soc. Roman Catholic. Avocations: skiing, running, art history, reading. Home: # 5-E 64 E 94th St New York NY 10128-0773 E-mail: go2ron68@cs.com.

MACDONALD, SALLY POLK BOWERS, retired addictions therapist; b. Memphis, Tenn., Feb. 23, 1930; d. Joel Polk and Sara Louise (Nee Zearing) Bowers; m. Lemuel Coover Shattuck, Jr. (div.); children: L. C. Shattuck III, Mark Bowers Shattuck, Melissa Polk Shattuck; m. Robert Donald Macdonald, Mar. 1, 1960; 1 child, Heather Stuart Macdonald LaMarre. BA, U. Ariz., Tucson, 1950. Lic. Alcohol and Drug Abuse Counselor State of Tenn. Adminstr. Clare Found., Santa Monica, Calif., 1978—88; counselor Wilder Youth Devel. Ctr., Somerville, Tenn., 1981—90; alcohol and drug abuse therapist Profl. Care Svcs., Inc., Somerville, 1983—2006; ret., 2006. Contbr. articles various profl. jours. Founding mem. Memphis Alcohol and Drug Coun., Memphis, 1984—86, Fayette County Animal Rescue, Somerville, Tenn., 1996—98; thriftshop chmn. Women's Symphony Assn., Ojai, Calif., 1967—69; precinct com. GOP, Tucson, 1952. Mem.: AOPA, Clare Found. (bd. mem. 1977—80), Assn. Preservation Tenn. Antiquities, Fayette County Hist. Soc. Republican. Episcopal. Avocations: birdwatching, painting, interior decorating, dog rescue. Home and Office: 612 S Somerville St Somerville TN 38068-1837

MACDONALD, SCOTT, real estate company executive; Realtor Gladstone and Assocs., Washington, BartonAschman, Evanston, Ill.; pres., CEO Plaza Properties Am.; exec. v.p., COO Hahn Co.; CEO CenterAmerica Property Trust; pres. New Plan Excel Realty Trust, N.Y., 2002—, COO, 2002—.

MACDONALD, SUSAN PRIEST, media specialist, writer; b. Lakeland, Fla., Sept. 24, 1958; d. Thomas Mitchell and Betty Jo Priest; m. Randall Malcolm MacDonald, Nov. 24, 1984; 1 child, Sarah Elizabeth. AA, South Fla. Jr. Coll., Avon Park, 1978; BA, Fla. State U., 1980, MS in Libr. Sci., 1984. Cert. educator Fla. Media specialist Canal Point (Fla.) Elem. Sch., 1980—81; libr. assoc. I Del-Trail Br., Palm Beach County Libr. Sys., Delray Beach, Fla., 1981—82, libr. assoc. II West Atlantic Ave. Br., 1982—83; media specialist North Heights Elem. Sch., Rome, Ga., 1985—86, Jesse Keen Elem. Sch., Lakeland, 1986—98; sch. libr. media specialist Lawton Chiles Mid. Acad., Lakeland, 1998—. Author: Successful Keyword Searching: Initiating Research on Popular Topics Using Electronic Databases, 2001; prodr.: (TV documentary) Our Town: Lakeland, 2002. Mem. Asheville (N.C.) Sch. Parents Assn., 2002—; adult vol. Campfire, Lakeland, 1986—88. Mem.: ALA, Polk Ednl. Media Assn. (legis. contact 1996—97, v.p. 2001—03, pres. 2003—05, 2d v.p. 2005—), Fla. Assn. for Media in Edn., Fla. So. Coll. Women's Club, Phi Theta Kappa, Delta Kappa Gamma. Avocations: bicycling, reading, geocaching. Home: PO Box 2501 Lakeland FL 33806-2501 Office: Lawton Chiles Mid Acad 400 N Florida Ave Lakeland FL 33801-4804 Office Phone: 863-499-2742.

MACDONALD, THOMAS COOK, JR., lawyer, mediator; b. Atlanta, Oct. 11, 1929; s. Thomas Cook and Mary (Morgan) MacD.; m. Gay Anne Everiss, June 30, 1956; children: Margaret Anne, Thomas William. BS with high honors, U. Fla., 1951, LLB with high honors, 1953. Bar: Fla. 1953. Practice law, Tampa, Fla., 1953—; mem. firm Shackleford, Farrior, Stallings & Evans, 1953-97; mem. Cook & MacDonald, Tampa, 1997—2002; pvt. practice law Tampa, 2003—. Spl. counsel Gov. of Fla., 1963, U. Fla., 1972-98; del. 5th cir. Jud. Conf., 1970-81; mem. adv. com. U.S. Ct. Appeals (5th cir.), 1975-78, (11th cir.), 1988-93; mem. Fla. Jud. Qualifications Commn., 1983-88, vice chmn., 1987, chmn., 1988, gen. counsel, 1997—; mem. jud. nominating com. Fla. Supreme Ct., 1995-99. Mem. Fla. Student Scholarship and Loan Commn., 1963-67; bd. dirs. Univ. Cmty. Hosp., Tampa, 1968-78, Fla. West Coast Sports Assn., 1965-80, Hall of Fame Bowl (now Outback Bowl) Assn., 1989-93, Jim Walter Corp., 1979-87; mem. Hillsborough County Pub. Edn. Study Commn., 1965; lic. lay eucharistic min. Episcopal Ch., 1961—; chancellor Episcopal Diocese of S.W. Fla., 1990-93, 2000—, ch. atty. for ecclesiastical ct., 1998-2000; bd. dirs. U. Fla. Found., 1978-86, Shands Tchg. Hosp., U. Fla., 1981-95; counsel Tampa Sports Authority, 1983-94. Recipient George Carr award FBA, 1991, Herbert Goldburg award Hillsborough County Bar Assn., 1995. Fellow Am. Coll. Trial Lawyers (chmn. state com. 1990-91), Am. Bar Found., Fla. Bar (chmn. com. profl. ethics 1966-70, bd. govs. 1970-74, bar mem. Supreme Ct. com. on stds. conduct governing judges 1976, Presdl. award of merit 1995); mem. ABA (com. on ethics and profl. responsibility 1970-76), Am. Law Inst. (life), 11th Cir. Hist. Soc. (trustee 1982-95, pres. 1989-95), U. Fla. Nat. Alumni Assn. (pres. 1973), Phi Kappa Phi, Phi Delta Phi, Fla. Blue Key, Kappa Alpha. Episcopalian. Home: 1904 S Holly Ln Tampa FL 33629-7004 Office Phone: 813-254-9871. Personal E-mail: TCMacdonald@msn.com.

MACDONALD, TIMOTHY LEE, chemistry professor; b. Long Beach, Calif., Mar. 12, 1948; m. Deborah L. Patrick; children: Kate, Alice. BS with honors, UCLA, 1971; PhD, Columbia U., 1975. Asst. prof. chemistry Vanderbilt U., Nashville, 1977-82; assoc. prof. chemistry U. Va., Charlottesville, 1982-89, prof. chemistry, 1989—, chmn. chemistry, 1997—. Contbr. articles to profl. publs.; patentee in field. Office: U Va Dept Chemistry Mccormick Rd Charlottesville VA 22904-0001

MACDONALD, GARY EDWARD, corporate board member, foundation trustee; b. Chgo., July 3, 1936; s. Thomas William and Lorna Lee (McDougall) MacD.; children: Gary Edward, Michael Scott; m. Charlene Gehm, June 15, 1992. BS in Engring., UCLA, 1958; MBA with distinction, Harvard U., 1962. Cons. McKinsey & Co., L.A., 1963-68, ptnr., 1968-69; chmn. bd., chief

exec. officer Mark Controls Corp. (formerly Clayton Mark & Co.), Evanston, Ill., 1969-87; gen. dir. N.Y.C. Ballet, 1993-94; chmn. Gov. Task Force on Human Svcs. Reform State of Ill., 1993-97; chmn. Ill. Rep. Party, 2002. Sr. advisor and asst. campaign mgr. George Bush for Pres., Washington, 1988; chmn. Ill. Rep. Party, 2002; chmn. Bulgarian-Am. Enterprise Fund, Chgo. and Sophia, Bulgaria, 1991-93, bd. dirs., 1991—; apptd. to U.S. Commn. on Effectiveness of UN, 1992-93; bd. dirs. United Parcel Svc. Am., Inc., Atlanta; adv. dir. Saratoga Ptnrs., N.Y.; instr. UCLA, 1969. Author: Make a Difference: How One Man Helped Solve America's Poverty Problem, 2000; contbr. articles to Harvard Bus. Rev., Wall St. Jour., N.Y. Times, Chgo. Tribune, other publs., chpts. to books. Trustee Annie E. Casey Found., UCLA Found., 1973-79, W.T. Grant Found., 1992-94, Russell Sage Found., 1981-91, chair, 1987-90; apptd. by Pres. Bush as pub. del., alt. rep., U.S. Del. UN 44th Gen. Assembly, 1989-90; commr. Sec. Labor's Commn. on Workforce Quality and Productivity, Washington, 1988-89; chmn. Ill. Rep. Party, 2002. Lt. USN, 1958-61. Mem. Coun. Fgn. Rels., Author's Guild, Harvard Club, Kappa Sigma. Episcopalian. Home: 505 N Lake Shore Dr Apt 3611 Chicago IL 60611-3406

MACDOUGALL, HARTLAND MOLSON, retired bank executive; b. Montreal, Que., Can., Jan. 28, 1931; s. Hartland Campbell and Dorothy (Molson) MacD.; m. Eve Gordon, Oct. 29, 1954; children: Cynthia, Wendy, Keith, Willa, Tania. Student, LeRosey, Switzerland, 1947-48, McGill U., 1949-53, Advanced Mgmt. Program, Harvard U., 1976. With Bank Montreal, various locations, 1953-84, dir., 1974, vice chmn., 1981; chmn., dir. Royal Trustco Ltd., Toronto, 1984-93. Dep. chmn. London Ins. Group, Inc., London Life Ins. Co., 1985-97; chmn., dir. Robert T. Jones Jr. Can. Scholarship Found. Founding chmn. Heritage Can., St. Michael's Hosp. Found., The Japan Soc.; past chmn. Can.-Japan Bus. Coun.; gov., past pres. Coun. Can. Unity; dir. Friends of the Youth Awards Inc., U.S.; past pres. Royal Agrl. Winter Fair; mem. Internat. Coun. Music Ctr. L.A., Can. Sports Hall of Fame; bd. govs. Can. Olympic Found.; sen. Stratford Shakespearean Found.; former chmn. The Duke of Edinburgh Awards Internat. Coun.; v.p., dir. The Macdonald Stewart Found. Decorated Order of Can., comdr. Royal Victorian Order, Order of the Rising Sun, Gold and Silver Star (Japan); recipient Gabrielle Leger medal, 1978. Avocations: golf, gardening, tennis, farming. Home: 16978 Shaws Creek Rd Belfountain ON Canada L7V OE8 Office: BCE Place 181 Bay St Ste 300 PO Box 771 Toronto ON Canada M5J 2T3

MACDOUGALL, JOHN DUNCAN, thoracic surgeon; b. Indpls., Mar. 4, 1925; s. Duncan Campbell and Beulah Stewart (Ward) MacDougall; m. Inga Margaretha Tranberg, Oct. 6, 1951 (div. 1980); children: Duncan Campbell, Stewart Andrew, Eric Matthew, Victoria Suzanne MacDougall Oehmen; m. Barbara Lee Mayse, Nov. 1, 1980; children: Katherine Jane, James William. BS, Ind. U., 1948; MD, Ind. U., Indpl., 1951. Diplomate Am. Bd. Surgery, Am. Bd. Thoracic Surgery. Pvt. practice, Indpls., 1957-93; pres. med. staff St. Francis Hosp., Beech Grove, Ind., 1975, pres. adv. bd., 1993-95, mem. governing bd. trustees, 2003—, chmn. governing bd. trustees, 1995—2003. Chmn. bd. dirs. Med. Assurance Ind., Indpls., 1987—2000, med. cons., 1993—. Mem. Ind. Gov.'s Task Force Organ Transplantation, Indpls., 1986—89; bd. dirs. Ind. Med. History Mus., 1989—2000; active Ind. Hist. Soc., Indpls. Mus. Art; pres. Ind. Med. Polit. Action Com., Indpls., 1992—98; mem. exec. com. dean's coun. Ind. U. Sch. Medicine, Indpls., 1988—; mem. adv. com., 1989—96, pres. dean's coun., 1992—95; pres. English Speaking Union, 1987—2001. With U.S. Army, 1943—46, ETO. Decorated Bronze Star. Fellow: ACS; mem.: AMA (del., chmn. Ind. delegation 1994—2003), Nat. Med. Vets. Assn. (bd. dirs. 1992—2004), Orgn. State Med. Assn. Pres. (pres. 1994—95), Indpls. Med. Soc. (pres. 1978—79), Ind. State Med. Assn. (pres. 1987—88), Purdue U. Pres.'s Coun., Ind. U. Sch. Medicine J. O. Ritchery Soc., Ind. U. Arbutus Soc., Univ. Club Indpls., Meridian Hills Country Club, Contemporary Club, Indpls. Lit. Club, Masons (33d degree), Am. Legion (comdr. Paul Coble Post #25 1999—2007), Soc. Ind. Pioneers. Republican. Episcopalian. Avocations: woodworking, golf, fishing. Home: 7202 Dean Rd Indianapolis IN 46240-3628 Office: ProAssurance Profl Liability Group Castle Creek VI 5975 Castle Creek Pky North Dr Ste 300 Indianapolis IN 46250 Office Phone: 317-558-2536.

MACDOUGALL, PETER, retired lawyer; b. Boston, Sept. 22, 1937; s. Duncan Peck and Hildegard (Moebius) MacD. AB, Harvard U., 1958, LLB, 1963. Assoc. Ropes & Gray, Boston, 1964-73, ptnr., 1973-97, ret., 1997—. Sheldon fellow Harvard U., 1963-64. Mem.: Harvard (Boston). Avocations: concert and opera going, gardening, reading, travel. Home: 1720 Washington St Key West FL 33040-4916 also: 542 River Rd Westport MA 02790-5161 E-mail: pmacdougall@earthlink.net.

MACDOUGALL, VICKI LAWRENCE, law educator, writer; d. Clyde W. and Mary Ellen Lawrence; children: Katherine Erin, Emily Dyan. BA with distinction, U. Okla., Norman, 1974; JD with distinction, Okla. City U., 1976. Bar: Okla. 1977, Calif. 1977. Jud. clerkship to judge Dwain D. Box Okla. Ct. Civil Appeals, Oklahoma City, 1977—78; prof. law Okla. City U. Sch. Law, 1978—. Law rev. faculty advisor Okla. City U. Law Rev., 2004—. Author: (book) Products Liability Law in Oklahoma, Products Liability Law; contbr. articles to profl. jours. Mem. PTA, Oklahoma City, 1994—2006. Mem.: Calif. Bar Assn., Okla. Bar Assn. (mem. 1977—2006), Phi Beta Kappa. Democrat. Methodist. Avocations: swimming, gardening, reading, crocheting. Office: Oklahoma City University School of Law 2501 N Blackwelder Oklahoma City OK 73106 Office Phone: 405-208-5187. E-mail: vmacdougall@okcu.edu.

MACDOUGALL, WILLIAM LOWELL, magazine editor; b. Des Moines, July 24, 1931; s. David Gregory and Elizabeth Jeanette (Dugan) MacD. AB, Willamette U., Salem, Oreg., 1952; M.J. in Journalism (Pulitzer scholar 1953-54), Columbia U., 1953. Reporter Washington Star, 1958-62; corr. Los Angeles Times, 1962-63; asso. editor, then London corr. U.S. News & World Report, 1964-68, asst. mng. editor Washington, 1978-86; mng. editor Artsreview mag. NEA, 1987; pres. Mid-Atlantic Media Co., Arlington, Va., 1989—. Author: American Revolutionary: A Biography of General Alexander McDougall, 1977. Served with USAF, 1954-57. Recipient George Washington medal Freedoms Found., 1978, citation U.S. Bicentennial Commn., 1976 Methodist. Office: Mid-Atlantic Media Co 5000 37th St N Arlington VA 22207-1823

MACDOWELL, ANDIE (ROSE ANDERSON MACDOWELL), actress; b. Gaffney, S.C., Apr. 21, 1958; m. Paul Qualley, 1986 (div. 1999); children: Justin, Rainey, Sarah Margaret; m. Rhett DeCamp Hartzog, Nov. 10, 2001 (div. Oct. 2004). LittD (hon.), Lander U., Greenwood, 2001. Spokesmodel L'Oreal cosmetics and haircare. Films include: Greystoke, 1984, St. Elmo's Fire, 1985, Sex, Lies and Videotape, 1989, Green Card, 1990, Hudson Hawk, 1991, The Object of Beauty, 1991, The Player, 1992, Ruby, 1992, Groundhog Day, 1993, Luck, Trust and Ketchup, 1994, Short Cuts, 1993, Four Weddings and a Funeral, 1994, Bad Girls, 1994, Unstrung Heroes, 1995, Michael, 1996, Multiplicity, 1996, The End of Violence, 1997, Town and Country, 1998, Shadrack, 1998, The Scalper, 1998, The Muse, 1999, Muppets From Space, 1999, Just the Ticket, 1999, Harrison's Flowers, 2000, Town & Country, 2001, Crush, 2001, Ginostra, 2002, The Last Sign, 2005, Beauty Shop, 2005, Tara Road, 2005, (voice) Barnyard: The Original Party Animals, 2006; TV movies include The Secret of the Sahara, 1987, Women and Men: Stories of Seduction, 1990, Women and Men 2: In Love There Are No Rules, 1991, On the Edge, 2000, Dinner With Friends, 2001, Jo, 2002, Riding the Bus with My Sister, 2005; prodr. Just the Ticket, 1999; TV guest appearances include Spenser: For Hire, 1985, Clive Anderson All Talk, 1996, Muppets Tonight!, 1997, The Practice, 2003.*

MAC DOWELL, SAMUEL WALLACE, retired physics professor; b. Camaragibe, Brazil, Mar. 24, 1929; came to U.S., 1963; s. Samuel Wallace and Maria Anita (Amazonas) Mac D.; m. Myriam Ramos Da Silva, Feb. 2, 1953; children: Ana Myriam, Samuel Wallace, Maria Dolores. BSc in Engring., U. Pernambuco, Brazil, 1951; PhD in Math. Physics, Birmingham (Eng.) U., 1958. Rsch. assoc. Princeton (N.J.) U., 1959-60; assoc. prof. Centro Brasileiro De Fisicas Pesquisas, Rio de Janeiro, 1960-63; fellow Inst.

for Advanced Study, Princeton, 1963-65; assoc. prof. Yale U., New Haven, 1965-67, prof., 1968—2004, prof. emeritus, 2004—. Fellow Am. Phys. Soc.; mem. Brazilian Acad. Scis. Roman Catholic. Office: Yale U Sloane Physics Lab PO Box 208120 New Haven CT 06520-8120 Office Phone: 203-432-6921.

**MACDUFF, ILONE MARGARET,** music educator; b. Berwyn, Ill., Jan. 30, 1938; d. Albert Kenneth Hinckle and Dorothy Lydia Ardina Lange; m. James Donald Macduff, Jr., Apr. 2, 1959; children: Gordon Scott, James Alexander, Charles Colin. MusB, U. Idaho, 1976. Internat. rep. Boy Scouts Am., 1983—93; mem. Thurston County (Wash.) Hist. Commrs., 1984—98; active Boy Scouts Am., Tumwater, Wash., 1968—93, dist. Cub Scout program chmn., 1973—75, mem. coun. Pow Wow staff, 1973—76; founder Cub Scout Day Camp, Tumwater Area Coun., 1973; chmn. Coun. Scout-O-Rama, 1979, 1980, 1981; mem. coun. Eagle bd. Boy Scouts Am., 1985—90; dir. monthly musicales State Captial Mus., 1970—74. Recipient Single and Double awards, Nat. Fedn. Music Clubs, 1969, 1977, Silver Beaver award, Boy Scouts Am., 1981, Disting. Commr. award, 1981, Lamb award, 1987. Mem.: Am. Coll. Musicians, Olympia Music Tchrs. Assn. (pres. 2003—04, student recitals chair 2005), Music Tchrs. Nat. Assn. (Olympia chpt. voice auditions chair 2001, 2004), Gordon Setter Club Am. (chmn. nat. dog show 2003), Puget Sound Gordon Setter Club (treas. 1998—2000, show chmn. 2003—04). Lutheran. Avocation: photography. Home: 8524 Delphi Rd SW Olympia WA 98512 Personal E-mail: delphimuse@msn.com.

**MACE, JERILEE MARIE,** performing arts association administrator; BA in Speech Comm. and Mgmt. magna cum l, Simpson Coll., 1991. Mem. adminstrv. staff Des Moines Metro Opera, 1976, dir. mktg., exec. dir., 1988—. Developer OPERA Iowa, Des Moines Metro Opera; cons. various opera cos. On-site evaluator NEA; grad., bd. dirs. Greater Des Moines Leadership Inst : founding mem. Warren County Leadership Coun. Named Iowa Arts Orgn. of Yr., 2000, Employee of Yr., Indianola C. of C., 2004; recipient Outstanding Achiever award, Ft. Dodge C. of C., 1994, Best Kept Secret award for bus. excellence, Greater Des Moines Partnership 2001, Women of Influence award, Des Moines Bus. Record, 2001; fellow exec., OPERA Am., 1993. Office: Des Moines Metro Opera 106 W Boston Ave Indianola IA 50125-1836 E-mail: jerimace@aol.com.

**MACE, JOHN WELDON,** pediatrician; b. Buena Vista, Va., July 9, 1938; s. John Henry and Gladys Elizabeth (Edwards) M.; m. Janice Mace, Jan. 28, 1962; children: Karin E., John E., James E. BA, Columbia Union Coll., 1960; MD, Loma Linda U., 1964. Diplomate: Am. Bd. Pediatrics, Sub-bd. Pediatric Endocrinology. Intern U.S. Naval Hosp., San Diego, 1964-65, resident in pediatrics, 1966-68; fellow in endocrinology and metabolism U. Colo., 1970-72; asst. prof. pediatrics Loma Linda (Calif.) U. Med. Ctr., 1972-75, prof., chmn. dept., 1975—2003. Med. dir. Loma Linda U. Children's Hosp., 1990-92, physician-in-chief, 1992—2003. Contbr. articles to profl. jours. Treas. Found. for Med. Care San Bernandino County, 1979-80, pres., 1980-82; mem. Congl. Adv. Bd., 1984-87; pres. So. Calif. affiliate Am. Diabetes Assn., 1985-86, dir., 1987-89; chmn. adv. bd. State Calif. Children's Svcs., 1986—; bd. dirs. So. Calif. Children's Cancer Svcs., 1993-94, Loma Linda Ronald McDonald House, 1991—2003, Aetna Health Plans of Calif., 1993-95; bd. dirs. Loma Linda U. Health Care, 1995—2003. Named Alumnist of Yr., Loma Linda U. Sch. Medicine, 1994; named one of Best Doctors in Am., 1998, America's Top Pediatricians, 2006; recipient Shirley N. Pettis award, 2002, Contrbn. to Medicine award, San Bernardino County Med. Soc., 2003. Mem. AAAS, Nat. Y. Acad. Sci., Calif. Med. Soc. (adv. panel genetic diseases State Calif., 1975—, chmn. acad. practice forum 1997—), Western Soc. Pediatric Rsch., Lawson Wilkens Pediatric Endocrine Soc., Assn. Med. Pediatric Dept. Chmn., Am. Acad. Pediatrics, Sigma Xi, Alpha Omega Alpha. Office: Loma Linda Univ Med Ctr 25590 Prospect Ave Apt 27c Loma Linda CA 92354-3150 Office Phone: 909-558-4130. Business E-Mail: jmace@ahs.llumc.edu.

**MACE, MICHAEL R.,** academic administrator, real estate development consultant, mortgage executive; b. Billings, Mont., Oct. 4, 1951; s. Robert E. and Ruth (Fox) M.; m. Karen Marie Lawrenz, June 10, 1974; children: Ann Michelle, Joseph Michael. BBA, Mont. State U., 1975. V.p. Mace Realty & Ins., Billings, 1974-84; pres. Mut. Montago Group, Billings, 1984—; pvt. practice cons. Billings and Seattle, 1986—; pres. Mut. Trade Services, Billings and Seattle, 1988—; chief ops. exec., chmn. D&M Industries; interim pres. Rocky Mountain Coll., Billings, 2005—06, pres., 2006—. Developer in field, Billings, 1983—; mortgage banker Mut. Montago Group, 1984—; cons. in field. Mem. Nat. Assn. Realtors, Rotary. Avocations: music, fishing. Office: Rockey Moauntain Coll 1511 Poly Dr Billings MT 59102 also: 735 Grand Ave Billings MT 59101-5823 Office Phone: 406-657-1026. E-mail: president@rocky.edu.*

**MACEDO DE LA CONCHA, RAFAEL,** former Mexican government official; b. Mexico City, May 6, 1950; Grad., Heroic Mil. Coll.; law degree, U. Nacional Autónoma Mex., Mexico City; Dr Degree (hon.), Nat. Inst. Criminal Sci., Mex., 2003. With Mexican Army, advanced through grades to brig. gen.; legal, fiduciary and asst. dir. Nat. Bank of the Army, Air Force and Navy; judge, 1st magistrate Supreme Mil. Ct.; legal coun. fed. exec. br. Govt. of Mex., asst. chief legal counsel Presdl. staff, atty. gen. mil. justice, legal counsel Secretariat Nat. Def., atty. gen., 2000—05; prof. various subjects including Mexican positive law, polit., econ. and social problems of Mex., constl. law U. Nacional Autónoma Mex., Lat. Am. U., dir. law program. Rep. of Govt. of Mex. and Secretariat of Nat. Def. regarding arms and drug trafficking U.S. Dept. of State; rep. Secretariat of Nat. Def. before the Int. Secretariat Com.; pres. drug abuse control commn. CICAD, 2002—03; chair, 5th mtg. mins. or justice mins. or atty. gen. Ams. REMJA, Washington, 2004. Decorated great cross Order of Isabella the Cath. Spain, Army 5th, 4th, 3d, 2d and 1st class medals, Army Spl. Class medal; recipient Mil. Tchg. award, Mexican Army, 1992, Melchor Ocampo, Nat. Acad., A.C., Blue Ribbon Gown and Eight-Cornered Academic Cap for univ. excell. w., Benito Juarez knight's badge for profl. dignity, Jose Vasconcelos honor award for academic merits, Fed. Dist. award, Mex. Mil. Legion of Honor, 2000. Mem.: Mex. Nat. Legion of Honor.

**MACER, GEORGE ARMEN, JR.,** orthopedic hand surgeon; b. Pasadena, Calif., Oct. 17, 1948; s. George A. and Nevart Akullian M.; m. Celeste Angelle Lyons, Mar. 26, 1983; children: Christiana Marilu, Marina Lynn, Emily Sue. BA, U. So. Calif., 1971, MD, 1976. Diplomate Am. Bd. Med. Examiners; diplomate in orthop. surgery and hand surgery Am. Bd. Orthop. Surgery. Intern Meml. Hosp. Med. Ctr., Long Beach, Calif., 1976; resident Orthop. Hosp./U. So. Calif., 1977-81; pvt. practice Long Beach, 1983—; vol. clin. faculty orthops. U. So. Calif., L.A., 1983-89, 90—; cons. hand surgery svc. Rancho Los Amigos Hosp. Downey, 1990—. Cons. Harbor UCLA Med. Ctr., Torrance, 1983—; asst. clin. prof. U. Calif. Irvine, 2004-. Joseph Boyes hand fellow, 1982. Mem. AMA, Calif. Med. Assn., Los Angeles County Med. Assn., Calif. Orthop. Assn., Western Orthop. Assn., Am. Soc. for Surgery of Hand, Am. Acad. Orthop. Surgery, So. Calif. Soc. Surgery of Hand (pres. 2004-06). Republican. Avocations: boating, skiing, scuba diving, carpentry. Office: 3550 Linden Ave Ste 2 Long Beach CA 90807-4577 Office Phone: 562-424-2600. E-mail: macer4337@aol.com.

**MACER-STORY, EUGENIA ANN,** writer; b. Mpls., Jan. 20, 1945; d. Dan Johnstone and Eugenia Loretta (Andrews) Macer; divorced; 1 child, Ezra Arthur Story. BS in Comms., Northwestern U., Evanston, Ill., 1965; MFA, Columbia U., N.Y.C., 1968. Writing instr. Polyarts, Boston, 1970-72; theater instr. Joy of Movement, Boston, 1972-75; artistic dir. Magik Mirror, Salem, Mass., 1975-76, Magick Mirror Comm.—. Author: Congratulations: The UFO Reality, 1978, Angels of Time, 1982, Project Midas, 1986, 2d edit., 2004, Dr. Fu Man Chu Meets the Lonesome Cowboy: Sorcery and the UFO Experience, 1991, 3d edit., 1994, Gypsy Fair, 1991, The Strawberry Man, 1991, Sea Condor/Dusty Sun, 1994, Awakening to the Light-After the Longest Night, 1995, Battles with Dragons: Certain Tales of Political Yoga, 1993, 2d edit., 1994, Legacy of Daedulus, 1995, The Dark Frontier, 1997, Troll and Other Interdimensional Invasions, 1999, Congratulations: The UFO

Reality, 2000, Vanishing Questions, 2000, Carrying Thunder, 2002, Crossing Jungle River, 1998, Doing Business in the Adirondacks; True Tales of the Bizarre and Supernatural, 2003, The Merry Piper's Hollow Hills, 2003, Struck By Green Lightning aka Project Midas, 2004, reissued 2006; (poetry) Theatre Cosmos, 2005; (novels) The Sin of Love, 2006, OM/NADA, 2006; (plays) Fetching the Tree, Archaeological Politics, 1986, Strange Inquiries, Divine Appliance, 1989, The Zig Zag Wall, 1990, The Only Qualified Huntress, 1990, Telephone Taps Written Up for Tabloids, 1991, Wars with Pigeons, 1992, Conquest of the Asteroids, 1993, Commander Galacticon, 1993, Meister Hemmelin, 1994, Six Way Time Play, 1994, Radish, 1996, Setting Up for the World Trade Centaur, 1996, Mister Shooting Star, 1998, Wild Dog Casino, 1999, Magic Mirror Space Installation at 515 Greenwich Street, 1999-2001, The Old Gaffer From Boise (at Gallery 113), 2000, The Redecoration According to Currier (at Gallery 113), 2001; (plays) Ars Chronicon Sylvestre, 2002, Swords of the Equinox, 2003, New Life Expo, New Yorker Hotel, NYC, 2003, Sayeed/Sayeeda, NYC, 2003, New Day, 2004, New Life Expo, 2005, Theatre For The New City, NYC, 2005, Honky Tonk Tornado Warnings, 2005, The Liberation of Little Lulu, Martin Luther King Detained in Limbo, 2006, Eternal Flowers of Ghost Mountain, Lower East Side Festival of Arts, 2006 others; editor Yankee Oracle Gazette, 1999; personal appearance as profl. clairvoyant (TV documentary) Haunted Houses, 1996, UFO Desk, Sta. WBAI radio shows, 1996-2001, Star People Confs., 1998—; exhbn. paintings Barcelona, Spain, 1999, 2000, 02, Magick Mirror Comm. Installation, 1999-2001, 515 Greenwich Gallery, So-Ho, N.Y., 1999, City Art Gallery, Stockholm, 2000, 04, Gam'Art Diffusion, Port Frejus, France, 2003, Kelikian Gallery, Beirut, 2002-03, Holland Art Fair, The Hague, 2003, BCN Art-Directe Gallery, Barcelona, Spain, 2003, Times Square Fashion Dist., Magick Mirror Space Fashion Ctr., 2003-06, Europ'art Expo, Geneva, 2006; author numerous poems; contbr. articles to profl. jours. and mags. Slubert fellow, 1968. Mem. Am. Soc. Dowsers, Dramatists Guild (spkr., interviewer on radio shows and internet confs.). Theosophical Soc. Democrat. Avocations: swimming, outdoor activities, hiking. Office: Magick Mirror Comm PO Box 741 New York NY 10116-0741 Office Phone: 212-727-0002. Personal E-mail: e.macer-story@att.net. E-mail: magickmirr@aol.com.

**MACEWAN, BONNIE,** librarian, dean; b. Memphis, Sept. 10, 1950; m. Thomas Manig. BA, Whitter Coll., 1972; M, U. Denver, 1978. Humanities libr. Ctl. Mo. State Coll., Warrensboro, 1978—84; art, archaeology and music libr. U. Mo., Columbia, 1984—91; asst. dean scholarly comm. Pa. State U., University Park, 1991—98, dean collections and scholarly comm., co-dir. digital scholarly pub., 1998—2003; dean liblrs. Auburn U., Ala., 2006—. Mem.: ALA (vice chair, chair-elect collection mgmt. and develop. sect. 2001—02). Office: Auburn U Librs 231 Mell St Auburn University AL 36849 Office Phone: 334-844-1715. E-mail: macewbj@auburn.edu.*

**MACEWAN, NIGEL SAVAGE,** retired merchant banker; b. Balt., Mar. 21, 1933; s. Nigel Savage and Ellen (Wharton) MacE.; children: Alison, Nigel, Pamela, Elizabeth; m. Judith Sperry, Sept. 2, 1995. BA, Yale U., 1955; MBA, Harvard U., 1959. Assoc. Morgan Stanley & Co., N.Y.C., 1959-62, White, Weld & Co., N.Y.C., 1962-63; v.p. R.S. Dickson & Co., Charlotte, NC, 1963-68; chmn. Fin. Cons. Internat. Ltd., Brussels, 1965-68; successively gen. ptnr., exec. v.p., pres., dir. White, Weld & Co., N.Y.C., 1968-78; sr. v.p., dir. Merrill Lynch, Pierce, Fenner & Smith, N.Y.C., 1978-87; chmn. Merrill Lynch Capital Ptnrs., N.Y.C., 1985-87; pres., CEO Kleinwort Benson, N.Am. Inc., N.Y.C., 1987-93, also bd. dirs.; ret., 1993. Chmn. Kleinwort Benson North Am., Inc., Kleinworth Benson Holdings, Inc., Alex Brown Kleinwort Benson Realty Advs.; bd. dirs. Kleinwort Benson Group plc, Kleinwort Benson Ltd., 1987-93, Kleinworth Benson Australian Income Fund, 1992-99; adj. prof. bus. adminstrn. NYU, 1973-75. Pres. Tokeneke Tax Dist., Darien, 1978-80, later treas.; bd. dirs. Islesboro (Maine) Health Ctr., 1994-2005, Sailors Mus. and Lighthouse, Islesboro, 1993-2000; trustee coun. Island Inst., 1997-02; adv. coun. Islesboro Island Trust, 1997-, Conservation Law Found., 1998-2006. Served with USN, 1955-57. Mem. Securities Industry Assn. (chmn. N.Y. group 1975-76), N.Y. Yacht Club, Yale Club N.Y., Harvard Club of Fairfield County, Conn., Wee Burn Country Club, Tokeneke Club, Tarrantine Club (pres.) (Dark Harbor, Maine), Cruising Club Am. Republican. Episcopalian, Home: 153 Oenoke Ln New Canaan CT 06840-4518 Personal E-mail: nsmace@msn.com.

**MACEY, JONATHAN R.,** law educator; b. 1955; BA, Harvard U., 1977; JD, Yale U., 1982; PhD (hon.), Stockholm Sch. Econs., 1996. Bar: Ga. 1986. Law clk. to Hon. Henry J. Friendly U.S. Ct. Appeals (2nd cir.), NYC, 1982-83; asst. prof. Emory U., 1983-86, assoc. prof., 1986-87; vis. assoc. prof. U. Va., 1986-87; prof. Cornell U., 1987-90; vis. prof. U. Chgo., fall 1989, prof., 1990-92; J. Dupratt White prof. law Cornell U., Ithaca, NY, 1993—2004; dir. John M. Olin program in law and econs. Cornell U. Law Sch., Ithaca, 1992—2004; vis. prof. Harvard U., 1999, Yale U., 2003—05; Sam Harris prof. corp. law, fin. and securities regulation Yale U. Law Sch., 2004—. Vis. prof. Harvard U., 1999, Bocconi, Milan, 2000. Recipient Paul M. Bator prize Federalist Soc. for Law and Pub. Policy, 1995, D.P. Jacobs prize. Mem. ABA (bus. assn. and corp. gov.), Am. Law Inst., Assn. Am. Law Schs. (com. corp. law), NY Stock Exchange (legal adv. bd.), Nat. Assn. Securties Dealers (economic adv. bd.). Office: Yale U Law Sch 127 Wall St New Haven CT 06511 Office Phone: 203-432-7913. Business E-Mail: jonathan.macey@yale.edu.

**MACEY, WILLIAM BLACKMORE,** oil industry executive; b. Buffalo, Aug. 1, 1920; s. Richard Charles and Doris (Bourne) M.; m. Jean Olive Mullins, Oct. 6, 1945; 1 dau., Barbara Jean. BS in Petroleum Engring, N.Mex. Sch. Mines, 1942; D.Engring. (hon.), N.Mex. Inst. Mining and Tech., 1984. Dist. engr. N.Mex. Oil Conservation Commn., 1946-48; dist. supt. Am. Republics Corp., 1948-52; chief engr. N.Mex. Oil Conservation Commn., 1952-54, state geologist, dir., 1954-56; v.p. Internat. Oil & Gas Corp. (and predegossor co., developers mineral properties), Denver, 1956-60, then pres., 1960-67; pres. Nielson Enterprises Inc., oil and gas prodn. and pipelines, livestock ranching, 1967-74; v.p., dir. Y-Tex Corp. (mfr. livestock identification tags), 1972-73; pres. GEN Oil Inc. (oil and gas prodn.), 1972-75, Col. Cody Inn (real estate and golf course devel.), 1970-73; dir. Macey & Mershon Oil, Inc., 1974-93; dir. Juniper Oil and Gas Corp., Denver, 1981-83, Ruidoso (N.Mex.) State Bank Holding Co., 1987—; pres. The Macey Corp., Denver, 1985—99. Chmn. Pres.'s N.Mex. Inst. Mines and Tech., 1980-82; mem. adv. bd. Am. Heart Assn., 1997-2002; mem. Pres.'s U. Ariz. Found. Served from 2d lt. to capt. USAAF, 1942-45. Mem.: N.Mex. Oil and Gas Assn. (exec. com. 1949—52, 1960—61), Popejoy & Pres.'s Club (U. N.Mex.), N.Mex. Jockey Club (bd. dirs. 1985—88, 1991—93, pres. 1993), Ruidoso, Tucson Country Club, Altolakes Golf and Country Club, Skyline Country Club (Tucson) (dir., treas. 1980—82, pres. 1982—83), Garden of the Gods. Episcopalian. also: 10153 Masters Dr NE Albuquerque NM 87111-5894 Office: PO Box 2210 Denver CO 80201-2210

**MACFARLAND, MIRIAM KATHERINE (MIMI MACFARLAND),** computer engineer, consultant, writer, educator; b. Trenton, NJ, June 21, 1949; d. James and Merrianne (Collins) MacF.; children: Bridget Lorraine McFarland, Chloe Merrianne Griffin. Attended: Rutgers U., 1976-78, U. Pa., 1981-83, Oxford U., Eng., 1988; B in Liberal studies with distinction, U. Okla., 2000; MFA, L.I. Univ., 2002. Programmer analyst R&D Computer Sci. Corp., Naval Air Devel. Ctr., Warminster, Pa., 1977-81; programmer analyst NASA Ames Rsch. Ctr., Moffett Field, Calif., 1978; staff writer Aydin Controls, Inc., Ft. Washington, Pa., 1981-82; writer Banc Tec, Inc., Oklahoma City and Dallas, 1983-95; cons. engr. MCI Comm. Internat., Rye Brook, NY, 1984-86, Western Union Internat., N.Y., 1984, RCA Global Comm., Ft. Lee, NJ, 1985; cons. engr., writer Siemens Med. Sys., Iselin, NJ, 1988-98; adj. asst. prof. English and writing Southampton Coll. L.I. Univ., 2000—02; instr. English Cameron U., Lawton, Okla., 2004—05; tech. writer Harris Corp., Norman, Okla., 2005, El Paso Exploration and Prodn., Houston, 2005—. Guest spkr. U. Ctrl. Okla., Edmond, 1994, Americorp Patch project, Okla. City, 1995; mem. dean's student adv. com. U. Okla., 1999-2000. Author stories, plays, journalism, numerous lit. rev.; CONTACT II, Hightimes Mag., The Bloomsbury Rev.; Another Chgo. Mag.; Renovated Lighthouse; author:

32 books, numerous poems; contbr. articles to books and profl. jours. L.I. U. fellow in writing. Grad. Acad. Performance award, 2000—02. Mem.: MLA, U.S. Landing Ship Tank Assn., Associated Writing Programs, Southampton Coll. Alumni Assn., Phi Kappa Phi. Home and Office: PO Box 722808 Norman OK 73070-9137 Office Phone: 405-364-5000. Business E-Mail: mkm@mimimacfarland.com. E-mail: mimimacfarland@sbcglobal.net.

**MACFARLANE, ALASTAIR IAIN ROBERT,** manufacturing executive; b. Sydney, Australia, Mar. 7, 1940; arrived in U.S., 1978; s. Alexander Dunlop and Margaret Elizabeth (Swan) M.; m. Madge McCleary, Sept. 24, 1966; children: Douglas, Dennis, Robert, Jeffrey. B in Econs. with honors, U. Sydney, 1961; MBA, U. Hawaii, 1964; postgrad., Columbia U., 1984; AMP, Harvard U., 1977. Comml. cadet B.H.P. Ltd., Australia, 1958-62; product mgr. H.J. Heinz Co., Pitts., 1965-66, gen. mgr. new products divsn. Melbourne, Australia, 1967-72; ptnr., dir., gen. mgr. Singleton, Palmer & Strauss McAllan Pty. Ltd., Sydney, 1972-73; dir., gen. mgr. successor co. Doyle Dane Bernbach Internat. Inc., Sydney, 1973-77, group sr. v.p. N.Y.C., 1978-84; pres., CEO PowerBase Systems, Inc., 1984-85, Productivity Software Internat. L.P., N.Y.C., 1985-86; divsn. pres., pub. Whittle Comm. L.P., Knoxville, Tenn., 1987-88; chmn., CEO Phyton Techs. Inc., Knoxville, 1988-94; pres., CEO Knox Internat. Corp., Knoxville, 1988-94; chmn., CEO Mich. Bulb Co., Grand Rapids, 1988-94; dir. Univ. of Sydney USA Found., 1994—; chmn., CEO Creative Pub. Internat., Inc., Minnetonka, Minn., 1997-99; sr. v.p. Pleasant Co., Middleton, Wis., 2000-2001; CEO Centric Strategies Internat., Inc., Mpls., 2001—02; sr. v.p. The Middleton Doll Co., Waukesha, Wis., 2002—04; CEO Lee Middleton Original Dolls, Inc., Columbus, Ohio, 2002—04; pres Biz Coaching & Assocs., LLC, Madison, Wis., 2004—. Chmn., CEO Lansinoh, Labs., Inc., Oak Ridge, Tenn., 1994—96; lectr. Monash U., Melbourne, 1970—71; int. mgmt. cons., Melbourne, 1970—72; dir. World Future Soc., Madison, Wis., 2004—, Hilton Oceanfront Resort Hotel, Hilton Head Island, SC. Contbr. articles to profl. jours. V.p. Waverley Dist. Cricket Club, 1975-77. East-West Ctr. fellow, 1962-64; Australian Commonwealth scholar, Australian Steel Industry scholar, 1958-61. Fellow Australian Inst. Mgmt. (assoc.); mem. Australian Soc. Accts. (assoc.), Harvard Club N.Y.C., Blackhawk Country Club (Madison). Home: 6219 S Highlands Ave Madison WI 53705 Office Phone: 608-238-7844. E-mail: iainmacfarlane@action-international.com.

**MACFARLANE, CATHY M.,** federal agency administrator; BS, Manhattanville Coll.; MA, Georgetown U. Counter-intelligence specialist FBI, 1980; with Nat. Inst. Justice U.S. Dept. Justice; dir. bus. devel. Jones Day, Dallas and Washington; assoc. Cassidy & Assocs.; v.p. Devillier Comm.; founder Marcom 21; exec. v.p. Direct Impact Co.; dir. pub. rels. FTC, 2001—04; asst. sec. pub. affairs U.S. Dept. Housing and Urban Devel., Washington, 2004—. Vis. scholar East China Inst. Politics and Law, Shanghai, 1987—88. Office: Dept Housing and Urban Devel Mail Code W 451 Seventh St SW Rm 10130 Washington DC 20410 Office Phone: 202-708-0980. Office Fax: 202-708-3106. E-mail: cathy_macfarlane@hud.gov.

**MACFARLANE, JOHN ALEXANDER,** retired federal agency administrator; b. Winnipeg, Man., Can., Sept. 6, 1916; s. John MacKay and Annie Catherine (Smith) MacF.; m. Gladys Valda Church, Dec. 20, 1941; children: John Lane, Elizabeth Ann, Janet Christine. BA with honours, U. Man., Winnipeg, 1939. With stats. br. Wartime Prices and Trade Bd., Ottawa, Ont., Canada. 1940-46; supr. stats. dept. Cn. Mortgage and Housing Corp., Ottawa, 1946-65, asst. dir. econs. and stats. div., 1965-69, asst. dir. secretariat div., 1969-73; ret., 1978; treas. Caribbean and N.Am. area coun. World Alliance Ref. Chs., 1984—2002. Treas. Ottawa Valley Cricket Coun., 1946-70, 73-80, pres., 1970-73, 83-88; moderator Presbytery of Ottawa, Presbyn. Ch. Can., 1994-96, rep. elder, 1961-97. Recipient Long Svc. medal Boy Scouts Assn., 1945, Centennial medal Govt. of Can., 1967, spl. achievement award for amateur sport Govt. of Ont., 1991. Mem. Def. Cricket Club (sec.-treas. 1944-46, pres. 1951-76, 78-92). Address: New Edinburgh Square 420 Mackay St Ste 207 Ottawa ON Canada K1M 204 Personal E-mail: jamacf@sympatico.ca. I have touched many people as the years have passed; if I have helped one for the better I shall rest content.

**MACFARLANE, JOHN CHARLES,** utilities executive; b. Hallock, Minn., Nov. 8, 1939; s. Ernest Edward and Mary Bell (Yates) MacF.; m. Eunice Darlene Axvig, Apr. 13, 1963; children: Charles, James, William. BSEE, U. N.D., 1961. Staff engr. Otter Tail Power Co., Fergus Falls, Mn., 1961-64, div. engr. Jamestown, N.D., 1964-71, div. mgr. Langdon, N.D., 1972-78, v.p. planning and control Fergus Falls, 1978-80, exec. v.p., 1981-82, pres. and chief exec. officer, 1982—, also bd. dirs., now chmn. Bd. dirs. Wells Fargo, Fergus Falls, Pioneer Mut. Ins. Co. Pres. Langdon City Commn., 1974-78; chmn. Fergus Falls Port Authority, 1985-86; bd. dirs. Minn. Assn. Commerce and Industry, Minn. Safety Coun., Edison Electric Inst., Village Family Svcs., Fargo; bd. dirs. U. N.D. Energy Rsch. Adv. Coun. Served with U.S. Army, 1962-64. Mem. Am. Mgmt. Assn., IEEE (chmn. Red River chpt.), N.D. Alumni Assn., Fergus Falls C. of C. Lodges: Rotary, Masons. Republican. Presbyterian.

**MACFARLANE, MALCOLM HARRIS,** physicist, educator; b. Brechin, Scotland, May 22, 1933; came to U.S., 1956; s. Malcolm P. and Mary (Harris) M.; m. Eleanor Carman, May 30, 1957; children: Douglas, Kenneth, Sheila, Christine. MA, U. Edinburgh, Scotland, 1955; PhD, U. Rochester, 1960. Research asso. Argonne (Ill.) Nat. Lab., 1959-60; asst. prof. physics U. Rochester, 1960-61; vis. physicist Argonne Nat. Lab., 1961-68. sr physicist, 1968-80; prof. physics U. Chgo., 1968-80, Ind. U., Bloomington, 1980—2003, prof. emeritus, 2003—. Vis. fellow All Souls Coll. Oxford (Eng.) U., 1966-67; mem, much u sc11i adv. comt. Dept. Energy-NSF, 1983-87; cons. Ency. Brit. Contbr. articles of theoretical nuclear physics to profl. jours. Guggenheim fellow physics, 1966-67; Alexander von Humboldt Found. sr. scientist award, 1985. Fellow Am. Phys. Soc.; mem. Nuclear Physics sect. Am. Phys. Soc. (mem. exec. com. 1969-71) Home: 1008 S Meadowbrook Dr Bloomington IN 47401-4217 Office: Dept Physics Indiana U Bloomington IN 47405 Office Phone: 812-855-3709. E-mail: macfarla@indiana.edu.

**MACGINITIE, WALTER HAROLD,** psychologist, educator; b. Carmel, Calif., Aug. 14, 1928; s. George Eber and Nettie Lorene (Murray) MacG.; m. Ruth Olive Kilpatrick, Sept. 2, 1950; children: Mary Catherine, Laura Anne. BA, UCLA, 1949; A.M., Stanford U., 1950; PhD, Columbia U., 1960. Tchr. Long Beach (Calif.) Unified Sch. Dist., 1950, 1955-56; mem. faculty Columbia U. Tchrs. Coll., 1959-80, prof. psychology and edn., 1970-80; Lansdowne scholar, prof. edn. U. Victoria, B.C., Canada, 1980-84. Research assoc. Lexington Sch. Deaf, N.Y.C., 1963-69; mem. sci. adv. bd. Ctr. for Study of Reading, 1977-80, chmn. 1979-80. Co-author: Gates-MacGinitie Reading Tests, 1965, 78, 89, 2000, Psychological Foundations of Education, 1968; Editor: Assessment Problems in Reading, 1972; co-editor: Verbal Behavior of the Deaf Child, 1969. Life mem. Calif. PTA. Served with USAF, 1950-54. Fellow APA, AAAS, Am. Psychol. Soc., Nat. Conf. on Rsch. on Language and Literacy, N.Y. Acad. Scis.; mem. Internat. Reading Assn. (pres. 1976-77, Spl. Svc. award 1981), Reading Hall of Fame (pres. 1989-90). Home and Office: PO Box 1789 Friday Harbor WA 98250-1789

**MACGOWAN, SANDRA FIRELLI,** publishing executive, consultant; b. Phila., Nov. 9, 1951; d. William Firelli and Barbara (Gimbel) Kapalcik. BS in Biology, BA in English, Pa. State U., 1973, MA in English Lit., 1978. Cert. supervisory analyst N.Y. Stock Exch. Editor McGraw-Hill Pub. Co., N.Y.C., 1979-81; sr. acquisitions editor Harcourt Brace Jovanovich, Inc., N.Y.C., 1981-82; sr. editor The Coll. Bd., N.Y.C., 1982-88; v.p., head editorial CS First Boston Corp., N.Y.C., 1988-94; v.p. supervisory analyst internat. rsch. SBC Warburg, N.Y.C., 1994-96; v.p., supervisory analyst internat. rsch. Arnhold and S. Bleichroeder, N.Y.C. (formerly Arnhold and S. Bleichroeder Inc.), N.Y.C., 2003—; mgr. Rsch. Dept. 2003—. Part time assoc. prof. pub. NYU Sch. Continuing Edn., N.Y.C., 1985—. Author: 50 College Admission Directors Speak to Parents,

1988. Democrat. Avocations: art, reading, travel. Office: Natexis Bleichroeder Fl 44 1345 Avenue Of The Americas New York NY 10105-4300 Office Phone: 212-698-3219. Business E-Mail: sandra.macgowan@natexisblr.us.

**MACGRAW, ALI,** actress; b. Pound Ridge, N.Y., Apr. 1, 1939; m. Robert Evans, 1970 (div.); 1 child, Joshua; m. Steve McQueen, 1973 (div.). Student, Wellesley Coll. Former editorial asst. Harper's Bazaar Mag.; former asst. to photographer Melvin Sokolsky. Actress in films including Goodbye, Columbus, 1969, Love Story, 1971, The Getaway, 1973, Convoy, 1978, Players, 1979, Just Tell Me What You Want, 1979, Natural Causes, 1994, Glam, 2001; TV mini-series The Winds of War, 1983, China Rose, 1983, Dynasty, 1985, Falcon Crest; TV movies Survive the Savage Sea, 1992, Gunsmoke, The Hollywood Fashion Machine, 1995; the Long Ride, 1993; Broadway plays Festen, 2006; author: (autobiography) Moving Pictures, 1991. Address: PO Box 284 Tesuque NM 87574-0284*

**MACGREGOR, DAVID BRUCE,** lawyer; b. Miami Beach, Fla., Feb. 21, 1953; s. Bruce Herbert and Mary Don (Doty) MacG.; m. Carol Louise Edler, Aug. 21, 1976; children: Meredith Elder, Christine Elder, Scott Elder. BA magna cum laude, Bucknell U., 1975; JD magna cum laude, Georgetown U., 1978. Bar: Pa. 1978, US Dist. Ct. (ea. dist.) Pa., US Ct. Appeals (4th cir.). Law clk. to presiding justice US Ct. Appeals (4th cir.), Richmond, Va., 1978-79; assoc. Morgan, Lewis & Bockius LLP, Phila., 1979-85, ptnr., mem. firm energy practice group, 1985–2005; shareholder Post & Schell PC, Phila., 2005—. Mem. ABA, Pa. Bar Assn., Phila. Bar Assn. Republican. Presbyterian. Avocation: golf. Office: Post & Schell PC Four Penn Ctr 1600 JFK Blvd Philadelphia PA 19103-2808 Office Phone: 215-587-1197. Fax: 215-963-5001. Business E-Mail: dmacgregor@postschell.com.

**MACGREGOR, GEORGE LESCHER, JR.,** freelance/self-employed writer, brokerage house executive; b. Dallas, Sept. 15, 1936; s. George Lescher and Jean (Edge) MacG.; divorced; children: George Lescher III (dec.), Michael Fordtran. BBA, U. Tex., 1958. Asst. cashier First Nat. Bank in Dallas, 1960-64, asst. v.p., 1964-68; v.p. Nat. Bank of Commerce of Dallas, 1968-70, sr. v.p., 1970-73, exec. v.p., 1973-74; pres., chief exec. officer Mountain Banks Ltd., Colorado Springs, 1974-77; chief exec. officer Highfield Fin. (U.S.A.) Ltd., 1978-83; chmn. bd., chief exec. officer, dir. Dominion Nat. Bank, Denver, 1981-84; chmn. bd., chief exec. officer Royal Dominion Ltd., Denver; chmn. bd., chief exec. officer, dir. Market Bank of Denver, 1983-84; vice chmn., dir. Bank of Aurora, Denver, 1983-84; chmn., pres., chief exec. officer Alamosa Bancorp. of Colo., Denver, 1983-84; pres., chief exec. officer Am. Interstate Bancorp., 1984-88; pres. Banco Inc., 1984-89; sr. mng. ptnr. Scotland Co., Denver, London, 1988-91; free-lance writer, 1992—. Served with M.C. AUS, 1958-60. Mem. Am. Mil. Inst. Ranking (hon.), Young Pres.'s Orgn., Coon Creek Club, Broadmoore Golf Club, Oxford Club, Phi Gamma Delta. Anglican Catholic. Home and Office: 1736 Blake St Denver CO 80202-1226 Home Fax: 303-292-9794. Personal E-mail: twotatertotts@aol.com.

**MACH, JAN ELLEN WALKENHORST,** literature educator, editor; b. Madison, Nebr. d. Dale Edward and Mary Moyer Walkenhorst; m. Daniel Blount (div.); 1 child, Byron K. Rupp; m. Robert Mach, 2006. BS in English Edn., U. Nebr.-Lincoln, 1974. Cert. tchr. Tex., 1982, Nebr., 2001, coll. bd. cert. 1995. Pres. Papillion (Nebr.) Edn. Assn., 1976—79; tchr. english Papillion (Nebr.) Pub. Schs., 1974—80, Richardson (Tex.) Ind. Sch. District, 1982—2000, Lincoln (Nebr.) Pub. Schs., 2001—04; instr. writing, asst. acad. counselor, tchr. theory of knowledge U. Nebr., Lincoln, 2004—. Mem. core team successful strategies, English Dept. chair, site-based facilitator, tchr. cadre; mem. project to convert curriculum to software Baylor U., 1994; rater statewide writing assessment Nebr., 2003. Editor: McGraw-Hill, 2000—, DC Health. Mem.: Nat. Assn. Acad. Advisors for Athletics. Avocations: reading, politics, travel. Office: Univ Nebr Athletic Dept 1 Memorial Stadium Lincoln NE 68588 Home: 1561 Rokeby Rd Pleasant Dale NE 68423 Office Phone: 402-472-9985. Personal E-mail: janwalk1952@aol.com. Business E-Mail: jwalkenhorst@huskers.com.

**MACHADO, EDUARDO OSCAR,** playwright; b. Guanabacoa, Cuba, June 11, 1953; came to U.S., 1961; s. Othon Eduardo and Gilda Luz (Hernandez) M.; m. Harriett Marilyn Bradlin, June 19, 1972. Ind. playwright, N.Y.C., 1981—. Playwright Rosario and the Gypsies, 1981, The Modern Ladies of Guanabacoa, 1983, Broken Eggs, 1984, Fabiola, 1985, When It's Over, 1987, Why to Refuse, 1987, Once Removed, 1988, Wishing You Well, 1988, Revotillo, 1988, A Burning Beach, 1988, Don Juan in N.Y.C., 1988, The Cook, 2005. Playwriting fellow Nat. Endowment for the Arts, 1981, 83, 85, Rockefeller Found., 1984. Mem. New Dramatists. Roman Catholic. Mailing: c/o Hartford Stage 50 Church St Hartford CT 06103

**MACHADO-ECHEZURIA, MARIANELLA PERPETUA,** composer, writer, educator; b. Caracas, Venezuela, Aug. 4, 1959; arrived in U.S., 1981; d. German Machado and Isabel C. Echezuria de Ruiz. MusB, Ind. U., 1984, MusM, 1986; MusD, U. Cin., 1993, MMA, 1996, PhD in Hispanic Lit., 1998. Rsch. asst. Romulo Coll., Caracas, Venezuela, 1987—88, Biblioteca Nacionel, Caracas, 1988—89; grad. tchg. asst. U. Cin., 1989—97; asst. prof. arts U. Catolica Andres Bello, Caracas, 1998—2003; asst. prof. Spanish Ea. Ky. U., Richmond, Ky., 2003—. Libr. music Cin. (Ohio) Symphony Orch., 1993—94; spkr. in field. Composer: (works) Obertura, 1987, Distonia, 1988, Las Semanas Tienen Sabados, 1988, Parafernalia, 1988, Psalm 32:10, 1990, Finneytown Suite, 1995; contbr. articles to profl. jours. Fellow, Taft Found., 1997—98; scholar, Ministry Edn., Caracas, Venezuela, 1974—80, Found. Gran Mariscal de Ayacucho, 1981—85, U. Cin., 1989—93, 1994—97; U. Rsch. Coun. fellow, 1991. Mem.: ASCAP (scholar 1993), Nat. Capital Lang. Resource Ctr., Multimedia Ednl. Resource Learning and On-line Tchg., Queen Am., Am. Composers Forum, Am. Music Ctr. Office: Eastern Ky Univ Lancaster Ave Richmond KY 40475 Home: 303 Timothy Way Apt 4 Richmond KY 40475-2724

**MACHASKEE, ALEX,** newspaper publishing company executive; b. Warren, Ohio; m. Carol Machaskee. BA in Mktg., Cleve. State U., 1972, LHD (hon.), 1995, U. Akron, 1998. Sports reporter The Warren (Ohio) Tribune; asst. to pub., promo dir. to dir. labor rels. & pers. to v.p., gen. mgr. The Plain Dealer, Cleve., 1985—90, pres., pub., 1990—. V.p. Mus. Arts Assn. (Cleve. Orch.); chmn. bd. United Way, 2000; mem. bd. governance, fin. and adminstrn. com. Cleve. Found.; bd. dirs. Univ. Cir. Inc., Greater Cleve. Partnership, St. Vladimir's Orthodox Theol. Sem., Crime Stoppers of Cuyahoga County, Urban League Greater Cleve.; chmn. bd. dirs. United Way Svcs., 2002—03; bd. trustees Cleve. Mus. Art; nat. bd. dirs. IOCC. Named to N.E. Ohio Bus. Hall of Fame, 2001. Mem.: Am. Soc. Newspaper Editors, Newspaper Assn. Am. Office: Plain Dealer Pub Co 1801 Superior Ave E Cleveland OH 44114-2198 Business E-Mail: publisher@plaind.com.

**MACHEN, JAMES BERNARD,** academic administrator; m. Chris; children: Maggie, Michael, Lee. DDS, St. Louis U., 1968; MS, U. Iowa, 1972, PhD in Edn. Psychology, 1974. Prof., assoc. dean U N.C., 1983-89; pres. Am. Assn. Dental Schs., 1987; dean U. Mich. Sch. Dentistry, 1989-95; provost, exec. v.p. acad. affairs U Mich., 1995-97; pres. U. Utah, 1998—2003, U. Fla., Gainesville, 2004—. Mem. Inst. Medicine Com. in Future Dental Edn. Nat. Acad. Scis., 1993-95. Office: U Fla Office of the Pres 226 Tigert Hall PO Box 113150 Gainesville FL 32611-3150*

**MACHER, FRANK E.,** automotive executive; b. Detroit, Mar. 1, 1941; BSME, GMI Engring & Mgmt. Inst., Flint, Mich., 1963; MBA, Mich. State U., 1975. Various positions Ford Motor Co., Saline, Mich., mfg. engr. mgr., 1971, prodn. mgr., 1972, mfg. mgr., 1973, mgr. plastics, paint and vinyl div. Saline Plastics and Instrumentation Plant, 1975—, v.p., gen. mgr., Automotive Components Divsn.; pres., CEO ITT Automotive, 1997—99; CEO, chmn. Federal-Mogul, 2001—04; pres., CEO Collins & Aikman, 2005—. Bd. dir. Dacoma Intern., Tenneco Automotive. Bd. trustees Kettering U., Flint, Mich. Office: Collins & Aikman 250 Stephenson Hwy Troy MI 48083*

---

**MACHINA, MARK JOSEPH,** economist; b. Detroit, Oct. 27, 1954; BA in Econs., Mich. State U., East Lansing, 1975, BA in Math., 1975; PhD in Econs., MIT, Boston, 1979. Asst. prof. econs. U. Calif., San Diego, 1979—84, assoc. prof. econs., 1984—88, prof. econs., 1988—. Vis. prof. econs. Duke U., Durham, NC, 1996; jr. rsch. officer Cambridge U., 1980—81; vis. asst. prof. econs. Princeton (N.J.) U., 1981—82; instr. People's U. China, Beijing, 1987, 90, 91, 93; Kaiser vis. prof. econs. Stanford (Calif.) U., 1999. Assoc. editor: Jour. Econ. Theory, 1983—91, Econometrica, 1984—91, Quarterly Jour. Econs., 1985—91, Jour. Econ. Perspectives, 1987—90, Jour. Econ. Surveys, 1987—91; co-editor: Theory and Decision, 1986—, Jour. Math. Econs., 1999—; founding co-editor: Jour. Risk and Uncertainty, 1988—90; contbr. articles to profl. jours. Trustee U. Calif. San Diego Found., 2001—04. Fellow, Ctr. for Advanced Study in the Behavioral Scis., 1987—88; grantee, NSF, 1983—86, 1992—95, 1998—2001; Grad. fellow, 1975—78, Vis. fellow, Australian Nat. U., Canberra, 1983, Rsch. fellow, Alfred P. Sloan Found., 1984—86, Erskine fellow, U. Canterbury, Christchurch, New Zealand, 1994. Fellow: Econometric Soc., Am. Acad. Arts and Scis.; mem.: Phi Beta Kappa. Office: Univ Calif San Diego 9500 Gilman Dr La Jolla CA 92093-0508 Office Phone: 858-534-2391. Business E-Mail: mmachina@ucsd.edu.

**MACHKOUR, NADIA,** optical engineer, researcher; m. Nadia Deshayes, Mar. 2, 2001. M, ENSEEIHT, Touluse, France, ENSEM, Casablanca; PhD with honors, Blaise Pascal U., Clermont Ferrand, France, 2003. Rschr. NIST, Gaithersburg, Md., 2003—. Achievements include research in metrology.

**MACHLE, EDWARD JOHNSTONE,** religious studies educator, philosopher; b. Canton, China, Sept. 29, 1918; s. Edward Charles and Jean (Mawson) M.; m. Neva Hull, Aug. 29, 1942; children—Stewart, Douglas, Kathi; m. Mary Lou Reynolds, Dec. 15, 1970; 1 adopted child, Michelle; stepchildren—Rebecca, Richard, Robin. Student, Pacific Lutheran Jr. Coll., 1937; BA, Whitworth Coll., 1939; B.D., San Francisco Theol. Sem., 1942, MA, 1944; PhD, Columbia U., 1952. Ordained to ministry Presbyn. Ch., 1942; minister Concrete, Wash., 1942-43; asst. minister San Francisco, 1943-44, Mineola, N.Y., 1944-46; instr. Columbia, 1944-47; asst. prof. U. Colo., 1947-53, assoc. prof., 1953-63, prof., 1963-80, emeritus, 1981—, chmn. dept., 1951-52, 56-58, 66-69. Vis. lectr. U. Alta., summer 1960, Iliff Sch. Theology, 1962, Evergreen State, 1981, Peninsula Coll., 1985-86; in-parish research dir. San Francisco Theol. Sem.; dir. music St. Andrew Presbyn. Ch., Boulder, Colo., 1961-70; guest lectr. ch. music U. Colo. Mus. Sch., 1950-65; disting. faculty fellow Sheldon Jackson Coll., 1986-88 Author: Nature and Heaven in the Xunzi, 1993. Mem. Am. Phil. Assn., Soc. Asian and Comparative Philosophy, Acad. Religion. Presbyterian. Home: 11 Silver Canyon Place The Woodlands TX 77381 E-mail: machle@wt.net. Faith is largely willingness to learn of what can destroy us. Idolatry feeds on our fear of having faith. Research methods spring from the soil of our cultured idolatries. Thus, to learn, faith must at times be a traitor to "learning.".

**MACHLOWITZ, DAVID STEVEN,** lawyer; b. Phila., Jan. 23, 1954; s. Roy Alan and Eleanore Machlowitz; m. Sheryl Lynn Steinberg, June 30, 1985; children: Jennifer, Amanda. BA, Princeton U., 1974; JD, Yale U., 1977. Bar: Pa. 1977, U.S. Dist. Ct. (ea. dist.) Pa. 1977, N.Y. 1981, U.S. Dist. Ct. (so. and ea. dists.) N.Y. 1981, U.S. Ct. Appeals (2d cir.) 1981. Assoc. Ballard, Spahr, Andrews & Ingersoll, Phila., 1977-80, Christy & Viener, NYC, 1981-85, Morrison, Cohen & Singer, NYC, 1985-87; asst. gen. counsel Gen. Instrument Corp., NYC, 1994—99; gen. counsel Siemens Med. Solutions, Iselin, NJ, 1992—98; assoc. gen. coun. Siemens Corp., Iselin, 1993-98, dep. gen. counsel NYC, 1999—2000; sr. v.p. gen. counsel Merck-Medco Managed Care, LLC (now Medco Health Solutions), 2000—, sec., 2002—. Contbr. articles to profl. jours. including ABA Jour., 1981—. Mem. N.Y. Corp. Counsel Assn. (bd. dirs., pres.), N.J. Corp. Counsel Assn. (bd. dirs., pres.). Avocations: history, film, books, basketball. Office: Medco Health Solutions Inc 100 Parsons Pond Dr Franklin Lakes NJ 07417

**MACHOVEC, FRANK J.,** psychologist; b. Balt., May 16, 1930; s. James Joseph and Theresa Ann MacH.; m. Evelyn Mary Stultz, May 5, 1951; 1 child, Frank. BA, U. Md., 1964; MA, Loyola U., Balt., 1965; PhD, Fielding Inst., 1979. Diplomate Am. Bd. Psychol. Hypnosis, Am. Bd. Med. Psychotherapy; lic. clin. psychologist. Asst. dir. New Sch. Psychotherapy, Washington, 1970-71; chief psychologist Victoria Hosp., Winnipeg, Man., Canada, 1973-75, Alta. Mental Health, Lethbridge, Canada, 1975-77; psychologist Alaska Psychol. Inst., Anchorage, 1977-79, State Hosp. South, Blackfoot, Idaho, 1979-81; dir. psychol. svcs. South Va. Mental Health Inst., Danville, 1981-86; dir. quality assurance Va. Dept. Mental Health, 1986-90; supr. psychology Va. Juvenile Corrections, 1991-95, ret., 1995. Author: Hypnosis Complications, 1986, Expert Witness Survival Manual, 1987, Humor Theories, History, 1988, Interview and Interrogation, 1989, Cults and Personality, 1989, Becoming Street Smart, 1994, Spiritual Intelligence, 2003, Light from the East, 2005, Private Investigative and Security Services, 2006; contbr. numerous articles to profl. jours. Staff sgt. USMC, 1950-52. Avocations: writing, travel, teaching. E-mail: fmacho@adelphia.net.

**MACHOVER, CARL,** computer graphics designer, consultant, computer engineer; b. Bklyn., Mar. 26, 1927; s. John Herman and Rose (Alter) M.; m. Wilma Doris Simon, June 18, 1950; children: Tod, Julie, Linda. BEE, Rensselaer Poly. Inst., 1951; postgrad., NYU, 1953-56. Mgr. applied engring. Norden div. United A/C Corp., 1951-59; mgr. sales Skiatron Electronics & TV, N.Y.C., 1959-60; v.p. mktg., dir. Info. Displays, Inc., Mount Kisco, NY, 1960-73, v.p., gen. mgr., 1973-76. Pres. Machover Assocs. Corp., White Plains, NY, 1976—. Adj. prof. Rensselaer Poly. Inst.; mem. RPI H&SS adv. bd. Bradford EIMC Indsl. Adv. Bd.; pres. bd. Art & Sci. Collaborations, Inc., 1994-2004. Author: Gyro Primer, 1957, Basics of Gyroscopes, 1958; mem. editl. bd., new products editor IEEE Computer Graphics and Applications; mem. editl. bd. Computers and Graphics; editor C4 Handbook, 1989, 2d edit., 1995, The CAD/CAM Handbook, 1996; co-editor Computer Graphics Rev.; co-exec. prodr. The Story of Computer Graphics, 1999; contbr. articles to profl. jours. Mem. adv. bd. Pratt Ctr. for Computer Graphics in Design. With USNR, 1945-46. Named to Computer Graphics Hall of Fame, Fine Arts Mus. of L.I., Hempstead, N.Y., 1988; recipient Frank Oppenheimer award, Am. Soc. Engring. Edn., 1971, Orthagonal award, N.C. State U., 1988, Vanguard award, Nat. Computer Graphics Assn., 1993, Industry Lifetime Achievement award, CAD Soc., 2003. Fellow Soc. for Info. Display (pres. 1968-70), Eurographics Assn.; mem. IEEE, Assn. for Computing Machinery, Am. Inst. Design and Drafting, Soc. Mfg. Engrs., Nat. Computer Graphics Assn. (bd. dir., pres. 1989-90), Computer Graphics Pioneer, Art and Sci. Collaborators Inc. (pres. 1995—), Sigma Xi, Tau Beta Pi, Eta Kappa Nu. Home: 152 Longview Ave White Plains NY 10605-2314 Office: Machover Assocs Corp PO Box 308 152A Longview Ave White Plains NY 10605-2314 Office Phone: 914-949-3777. Personal E-mail: cmachover@aol.com.

**MACIAS, E. JAMES,** utilities executive; BA in Mech. Engring., Calif. Polytech State U., 1976; grad, Harvard U., 1998. Sr. v.p. Pacific Gas & Elec., 1987—2000; sr. v.p. power and indsl. mktg. Calpine Corp., 2001—02, exec. v.p., CEO power and indsl. mktg. v.p., 2002—. Office: Calpine 50 W San Fernanco St 5th Fl San Jose CA 95113

**MACIAS, EDWARD S.,** chemistry professor, dean, academic administrator; b. Milw., Feb. 21, 1944; s. Arturo C. Macias and Minette (Schwenger) Wiederhold; m. Paula Wiederhold, June 17, 1967; children: Matthew Edward, Julia Katherine. AB, Colgate U., 1966; PhD, MIT, 1970. From asst. prof. to Barbara and David Thomas Disting. prof. Arts and Scis. Washington U., St. Louis, 1970—2005, Barbara and David Thomas Disting. prof. Arts and Scis., 2005—, exec. vice chancellor and dean Faculty Arts and Scis., 1995—. Cons. Meteorology Rsch., Inc., Altadona, Calif., 1978-81, Salt River Project, Phoenix, 1980-83, Santa Fe Rsch., Bloomington, Minn., 1985-88, AeroVironment, Inc., Monrovia, Calif., 1986-88. Author: Nuclear and Radiochemistry, 1981; editor: Atmospheric Aerosol, 1981; contbr. numerous articles to profl. jours. Bd. dirs. Mark Twain Summer Inst., St. Louis, 1984-87, 88-90, The Coll. Sch., St. Louis, 1984-88, Colgate U., 1997—. Grantee NSF, EPA, Electric Power Rsch. Inst., So. Calif. Edison Co., Dept. Energy, AEC. Mem.

---

Am. Chem. Soc., Am. Assn. Aerosol Rsch. (editorial bd.), Am. Phys. Soc., AAAS. Home: 6907 Waterman Ave Saint Louis MO 63130-4333 Office: Washington U Campus Box 1094 One Brookings Dr Saint Louis MO 63130 Office Phone: 314-935-6800.

**MACIEJEWSKI, NORA JEAN,** elementary school educator; b. Milw., Sept. 6, 1948; d. Norbert Anthony and Julia Marie Datka; m. Lee Thomas Maciejewski, Aug. 22, 1970; children: Laura Hofland, Anne, David. BSc, U. Wisc., 1970. Tchr. St. John's Sch., Waunakee, Wis., 1970—71, 1972—73, Glen Hill Sch. and Pheasant Ridge Sch., Glendale Heights, Ill., 1973—79, Queen Bee Sch. and Glen Hill Sch. Dist. 16, Glendale Heights, 1979—. Mem.: Ill. Edn. Assn., Nat. Edn. Assn., Ill. Tchr. Assn., Internat. Reading Assn., Ill. Reading Coun. Roman Catholic. Home: 2 S 524 Danbury Dr Glen Ellyn IL 60137 Office Phone: 630-260-6141.

**MACILVAINE, CHALMERS ACHESON,** retired financial executive, former association executive; b. Bklyn., Oct. 25, 1921; s. James Andrew and Helen Marguerite (Acheson) MacI.; m. Elizabeth Jean Babcock, Mar. 26, 1943; children: Judith Anne, Joseph Chad, Martha Elizabeth. AB, Stanford U., 1943. With Kaiser Steel Corp., 1946-73, asst. controller, 1953-62, treas., 1962-70, v.p., 1970-70, v.p. finance and planning, 1970-73; also v.p., dir. subsidiaries; v.p. project financing group Bank of Am., San Francisco, 1973-74, sr. v.p., dep. head Asia div., 1977-78; sr. v.p.-fin. Peabody Coal Co., St. Louis, 1978-80; sr. v.p., dir. Stifel, Nicolaus & Co., St. Louis, 1980-83; pres. Assn. Soc. of St. Louis, 1983-85. Pres. Financial Internat. Fin. Corp., 1973-74 Served to lt. (j.g.) USNR, 1943-46. Mem. Phi Beta Kappa, Sigma Chi. Clubs: Tokyo Lawn Tennis, Burns Club of St. Louis. Home: PO Box 99 Friendship ME 04547-0099

**MACINNES, SALLY ACKERMAN,** computer education educator; b. Columbus, Ind., Nov. 12, 1946; d. Louis L. and Josephine K. Ackerman; m. James C. MacInnes, June 13, 1981; children: Todd Keenan, Jennifer Mangel, Christopher Keenan, Daniel Keenan. BA, U. Iowa, Iowa City, 1968; MS, No. Ill. U., Dekalb, 1989; postgrad., Nat. Coll. Edn., Evanston, Ill., DePaul U., Chgo., St. Xavier Coll. Cert. tchr. Computer lab. asst. York High Sch., Elmhurst, Ill.; tchr. 2nd grade Cossitt Sch., LaGrange, Ill.; library-media coord. Unit Sch. 205, Elmhurst; tchr. computer edn. Dist. 93, Hillside, Ill. Home: 915 Saylor Ave Elmhurst IL 60126-4762

**MACINNIS, FRANK T.,** construction executive, securities trader, holding company executive; b. Camrose, Alta., Can., Nov. 10, 1946; came to U.S., 1978; s. H. Frank and Adele M. (Irving) MacI.; m. Beverley J. McAndrews, Nov. 3, 1977; children: Christopher, Katrina, Lauren, Robbie. BA, Univ. Alta., Edmonton, 1968, LLB, 1971. Assoc. Liden, Ackroyd & Co., Edmonton, 1971-75; gen. counsel Banister-Price Internat., Tehran, Iran, 1975-77; dir. Banister-Price Overseas, London, 1977-78; exec. v.p. H.C. Price Co., Bartlesville, Okla., 1978-80; chmn., chief exec. officer H.C. Price Constrn. Co., Dallas, 1980-84; pres. Spie Group, Inc., Dallas, 1986—94; v.p., CFO Comstock Group, Inc., Danbury, Conn., 1986—90, chmn., pres., CEO, 1990—94; pres. EMCOR Group Inc., Norwalk, Conn., 1994—97, chmn., CEO, 1997—. Mem. exec. com. Spie Batignolles, Paris, 1985-94; bd. dirs. The Williams Companies, ITT Industries, Inc. Served to lt. Royal Can. Navy, 1964-68; bd. dirs. Greater New York Chapter of the March of Dimes. Roman Catholic. Avocations: sports, coin collecting/numismatics, music. Office: EMCOR Croup Inc 301 Merritt Seven Corporate Park 6th Fl Norwalk CT 06851-1060 Office Phone: 203-849-7800. Office Fax: 203-849-7900.*

**MACINTOSH, JAY W.,** lawyer, realtor, actress; b. Gainesville, Ga., Mar. 30, 1937; d. Jesse Dickson Jewell and Anna Louise Dorough Jewell; m. Darrell William MacIntyre, Aug. 17, 1957 (div. Dec. 1972); children: Trascey Lee, Craig Dickson, Blake William; m. Felice Steven Orlandella, Aug. 7, 2005. Student, U. Wis., 1955—57; BFA Speech and Drama, U. Ga., 1961, MA Drama, 1962; JD, Whittier Law Sch., Costa Mesa, Calif., 1999. Bar: Calif. 2000, U.S. Dist. Ct. (cen. dist.) Calif. 2000, U.S. Ct. Appeals (9th cir.) 2000. Real estate broker Merrill Lynch Realty, 1976—85, MacIntosh Realtors, 1985—; jud. extern Calif. Ctrl. Dist., 1998, U.S. Bankruptcy Ct.; pvt. practice L.A., 2000—. Prof., head dept. speech and drama Brenau U., Gainesville, Ga., 1962—65; prof., chmn. divsn. humanities Gainesville Coll., 1966—68. Actor: (films) My Science Project, Sgt. Pepper's Lonely Hearts Club Band, The Quest, Like It Is, Hostages, J.W. Coop, Joni, Time Step, Wild Rovers, After Arthur Minsky Died; (TV films) Liz: The Elizabeth Taylor Story, Murder of Innocence, Beverly Hills Madame, Mark, I Love You, Pomeroy's People, The Blue Knight, Incident on a Dark Street, Studs Lonigan, Ishy, The Last of His Tribe, Auto Da Fe, The Haunting of Seacliff Inn, Secret Sins of the Father, Hollywood Wives, Senior Year, The Healers, Pollyanna, Centennial, Elvis and the Beauty Queen, Where Have All The People Gone; (TV series) Picket Fences, Eight is Enough, Cannon, Barnaby Jones, Simon & Simon, The Waltons, many others. Mem.: ABA, Nat. Assn. Realtors, Calif. Assn. Realtors, Greater L.A. Assn. Realtors, Fed. Bar Assn., Consumer Attys. Calif., Consumer Attys. Assn. L.A., Women Lawyers Assn. L.A., Century City Bar Assn., Beverly Hills Bar Assn., L.A. County Bar Assn., Acad. TV Arts and Scis. (blue ribbon panels), Women in Film (bd. dirs.), Actors Studio (chmn. membership com.), Phi Kappa Phi, Phi Beta Kappa. Democrat. Episcopalian. Avocations: hiking, swimming, theater, reading, skiing. Office: Ste 500 1925 Century Park East Los Angeles CA 90067 Office Phone: 310-789-2034.

**MACINTYRE, MALCOLM SCOTT,** retired secondary education educator; b. N.Y.C., Feb. 17, 1924; s. Malcolm and Robina Dunlop (Scott) M.; m. Anita Arden Schlosser, June 25, 1955; children: Robina Anne, Samuel Scott. BS, U.S. Mcht. Marine Acad., 1944; BA, Hobart Coll., 1950; MA, Colombia U., 1961. Officer Mcht. Marine, 1947-53; tchr. Andrew Warde H.S., Fairfield, Conn., 1953-82; retired, 1982. Lt. USN, 1944-46. Mem. Coun. Am. Master Mariners. Republican. Avocation: yachting. Home: 489 Black Rock Tpke Redding CT 06896-1628

**MACIUSZKO, KATHLEEN LYNN,** librarian, educator; b. Nogales, Ariz., Apr. 8, 1947; d. Thomas and Stephanie (Horowski) Mart; m. Jerzy Janusz Maciuszko, Dec. 11, 1976; 1 child, Christina Aleksandra. BA, Ea. Mich. U., 1969; MLS, Kent State U., 1974; PhD, Case Western Res. U., 1987. Reference libr. Baldwin-Wallace Coll. Libr., Berea, Ohio, 1974-77, dir. Conservatory of Music Libr., 1977-85; dir. bus. info. svcs. Harcourt Brace Jovanovich, Inc., Cleve., 1985-89; staff asst. to exec. dir. Cuyahoga County Pub. Libr., Cleve., 1989-90; dir. Cleve. Area Met. Library System, Beachwood, Ohio, 1990; media specialist Cleve. Pub. Schs., 1991-93, Berea (Ohio) City Sch. Dist., 1993—. Author: OCLC: A Decade of Development, 1967-77, 1984; contbr. articles to profl. jours. Named Plenum Pub. scholar, 1986. Mem. Spl. Librs. Assn. (pres. Cleve. chpt. 1989-90, v.p. 1988-89, editor newsletter 1988-89), Baldwin-Wallace Coll. Faculty Women's Club (pres. 1975), Avocation: music. Office: Midpark HS 7000 Paula Dr Middleburg Heights OH 44130

**MACK, ALAN WAYNE,** interior designer; b. Cleve., Oct. 30, 1947; s. Edmund B. and Florence I. (Oleksa) M. BS in Interior Design, Case Western Res. U., 1969. Designer interior design dept. Halle's, Cleve., 1969, 71-73; designer Nahan Co., New Orleans, 1973-75, Hemenway's Contract Design, New Orleans, 1975-76; ptnr. Hewlett-Mack Design Assocs., New Orleans, 1976-85; prin., dir. interior design HLM Design, Inc., 1985—2001; prin., founding ptnr. Proteus Group, Chgo., 2001—. Mem. adv. com. interior design dept. Delgado Jr. Coll., New Orlean s; mktg./merchandising adv. coun. St. Mary's Dominican Coll., New Orleans; mem. friends devel. coun. U. Iowa Mus. Art. 1986-91, chair, 1990-91; chmn. adv. com. interior design program Iowa State U., 1991-96; mem. design review com., City of Iowa City, 1992-93. Co-author: audiovisual presentation Nat. Home Improvement COun. Conf., 1981. Bd. dirs. Johnson County United Way, 1991-96. Served with U.S. Army, 1969-71. Mem. ASID (profl. mem., presdl. citation 1980, treas. La. dist. chpt. 1984), Vis. Nurses Assn. (bd. dirs. 1991-96), Found. for Interior Design Edn. Rsch. (standards com. 1972-76, bd. visitors 1977-80, accreditation com. 1981-95, trustee 1996-99, chmn. bd. dirs. 1998, pres. 1999). Home: 3800 N Lake Shore Dr Ste 2G Chicago IL 60613-3313 Office Phone: 312-337-7800. Business E-Mail: amack@proteusgroup.net.

**MACK, ARTHUR NEAL,** emergency medicine and family practice physician; b. Abiline, Tex., Dec. 3, 1955; s. Alonzo Vandeveer and Mary Elizabeth (Milner) M.; m. Teresa Ann Wehrheim, Nov. 29, 1987; children: Aaron Matthew, Andrew Nathan, Abram Daniel, Hannah Michele, Abby Lynn. BS in Biology, Graceland Coll., 1978; MD, U. Ill., 1983. Pvt. practice family medicine Richland Meml. Hosp., Olney, Ill., 1986-90; dir. emergency svcs. Harrisburg (Ill.) Med. Ctr., 1990-91; staff emergency physician St. Mary's Med. Ctr., Evansville, Ind., 1991-94; assoc. dir. Family Practice Residency, Evansville, 1995-96; dir. St. Mary's Med. Ctr., Evansville, 1996-98; clin. asst. prof. of family medicine Ind. U., Evansville, 1995-98; preceptor of family nurse practitioners U. So. Ind., Evansville, 1996-98; dir. TPI Ctr. for Med. Studies, 1996—2001. Compiler: contbr. articles to profl. jours. Mem. Am. Acad. of Family Physicians (grad. nat. inst. for program dir. devel. 1996), Ind. Acad. of Family Physicians. Avocations: medicine, writing. Office: 119 Oakfield Dr Brandon FL 33594 Home: 1704 Coyote Crossing Olney IL 62450 E-mail: anmack55@aol.com.

**MACK, CONNIE,** congressman; b. Cape Coral, Fla., Aug. 12, 1967; s. Connie Mack III and Priscilla Mack; m. Ann Mack; children: Addison, Connie Mack V. BS, U. Fla., 1993. Mem. Fla. Ho. of Reps., 2000—03, US Congress from 14th Fla. dist., 2005—; mem. budget com., internat. relations com., transp. and infrastructure com. Republican. Office: US House Reps 317 Cannon House Office Bldg Washington DC 20515-0914 Office Phone: 202-225-2536. Office Fax: 202-225-0439.

**MACK, CONNIE, III, (CORNELIUS MCGILLICUDDY III),** former senator; b. Phila., Oct. 29, 1940; s. Cornelius and Susan (Sheppard) McGillicuddy; children: Debra Lynn, Cornelius Harvey. Degree in bus., U. Fla., 1966. Mktg. Cape Coral Bank, Cape Coral, Fla., 1966-68, sr. v.p., dir., 1971-75; v.p. bus. devel. First Nat. Bank, Ft. Myers, 1968-71; pres., dir. Fla. Nat. Bank, Cape Coral, 1975-82; mem. U.S. Ho. of Reps. from 13th Dist. Fla., Washington, 1983-89; U.S. Senator from Fla Washington, 1989-2001; sr. policy advisor Shaw Pittman LLP, Washington, 2001—05; King & Spalding LLP, Washington, 2005—, co-chmn. govt. rels. group, 2005—. Chmn. joint econ. com., 1997-2001; past com. on fin., com. on banking, housing and urban affairs; bd. dirs Moody's Corp, Mutual Am. Life. Ins., Genzyme Corp., Darden Restaurants; chmn. bd., H. Lee Moffit Cancer Ctr.& Rsch. Inst. Tampa, 2001. Bd. dirs., chmn. Palmer Drug Abuse Program, Cape Coral; bd. dirs. Cape Coral Hosp. Republican. Roman Catholic. Office: King & Spalding LLP 1700 Penn Ave Washington DC 20006 Business E-Mail: cmack@kslaw.com.

**MACK, DENNIS WAYNE,** lawyer; b. Chgo., Sept. 11, 1943; s. Walter Andrew and Betty Jane (Klimek) M. BA, Yale U., 1965; JD, Harvard U., 1969. Bar: (NY) 1970. Assoc. firm Curtis Mallet-Prevost Colt & Mosle, N.Y.C. and Paris, 1969-78; sec., gen. counsel Dominion Textile (USA) Inc., N.Y.C., 1978-91, v.p., 1986-91; pvt. practice N.Y.C., 1991—; gen. counsel Knoa Corp., 2000—02. Alt. rep. Internat. Lesbian and Gay Assn. at ECOSOC of UN, 1994. Mem. dept. fin. Presbytery N.Y., 1978-83. Mem. ABA, N.Y. State Bar Assn., Bar Assn. City N.Y. (spl. com. on AIDS and the law 1996-2001). Home: 180 Riverside Dr New York NY 10024-1021

**MACK, EARLE IRVING,** former ambassador, former real estate company executive; b. N.Y.C., July 11, 1939; s. H. Bertram and Ruth (Kaufman) M.; m. Carol L. Dickey, July 26, 1990; children: Andrew, Beatrice, BS, Drexel U., 1959; postgrad., Fordham Law Sch., 1960-61; LHD (hon.), Yeshiva U., 1992; D in Bus. Administrn. (hon.), Drexel U., 2006. Sr. ptnr. The Mack Co., Fort Lee, 1964—2005; owner, breeder thoroughbred horses Fla., Ky., NJ, NY, Md., Can., Calif., 1964—; US amb. to Finland US Dept. State, Helsinki, 2004—05. Mem. adv. bd. N.Y. State Bus. Venture Partnership, 1988-98; mem. transition team for Gov. George Pataki, 1994-95; chmn., CEO, N.Y. State Coun. Arts, 1996-99, chmn. emeritus, 1999-. Prodr., co-dir. film The Children of Theater Street, 1977 (Acad. Award Feature Documentary nomination). Bd. dirs. Benjamin N. Cardozo Sch. of Law, N.Y.C., 1980-2004, chmn. exec. com., 1990, vice chmn. bd. dirs., 1991, chmn. bd. dirs., 1992-2004, chmn. emeritus, 2004; bd. dirs. N.Y.C. Ballet, 1988-2004; chmn. N.Y. State Racing Commn., 1983-89, The New 42d St., Inc., 1990-92; bd. dirs. Dance Theatre of Harlem, N.Y.C., 1987, co-chmn. bd., 1988-89; trustee N.Y. Racing Assn., Inc., 1990-2004; trustee, exec. com. Yeshiva U., 1992-2004. 1st lt. USAR, 1960—68. Recipient Can. Sovereign award Horse of Yr., 1993, Can. Sovereign award for best 3 yr. old horse, 1994, Ellis Island Medal of Honor, 1997; named One of Drexel 100, Drexel U., 1992, Commencement Spkr., 2006. Mem. Nat. Realty Com. (bd. dirs., exec. com. 1986-88), Urban Land Inst., Union League Club, Univ. Club, Reading Room Club. Avocations: skiing, swimming, jogging, boating. Office: 2115 Linwood Ave Ste 110 Fort Lee NJ 07024

**MACK, GREGORY JOHN,** financial executive and consultant; b. Buffalo, Oct. 11, 1954; m. Rosemary Lynn Testa, Aug. 17, 1979; children: Lindsey Marie, Stephanie Kaitlyn. BS in Polit. Sci., SUNY, Buffalo, 1978. Cert. tchr., N.Y. Police officer Town of Amherst, N.Y., 1978-81; fin. cons., regional v.p. Cigna Individual Fin. Advisors, Amherst, 1981-94; dir. new bus. devel. Manulife Fin., U.S., Williamsville, N.Y., 1997—. Host radio show Fin. Forum, Sta. WXBX; speaker in field. Host daily radio show Fin. Forum, Sta. WWWS. Mem. Buffalo Life Underwriters Assn., Buffalo C. of C., Gen. Agts. and Mgrs. Assn. (Agt. of Yr. award 1987-92), Cigna's President's Club (life, pres. 1990-91), Cigna's Honor Table (pres. 1987-89), Cigna's Gold Ky (chmn. 1988), Cigna's Excalibur (life). Republican. Roman Catholic. Avocations. hockey, golf, tennis, baseball, skiing. Home: 241 Halston Pky East Amherst NY 14051-1856 Office: Manulife Fin 6225 Sheridan Dr Ste 203 Williamsville NY 14221-4800

**MACK, INA LEAH,** secondary school educator, pre-school administrator; b. Macon, Mo., Jan. 10, 1959; d. David Neil and Ina Bernadine Milburn; m. Gary Ray Mack, Sept. 3, 1988; children: Brittany, Cameron, Delaney. BA in Edn., Ariz. State U., 1982; MA in Edn., No. Ariz. U., 2005. Tchr. Antelope High Sch., Wellton, Ariz., 1983—86, Mt. View High Sch., Tucson, 1987—90, Snowflake High Sch., 1990—95, Northland Pioneer Coll., Holbrook, 1991—, Blue Ridge High Sch., Lakeside, 1995—. Advisor Family, Career, Cmty. Leaders Am., Lakeside, 1990—; coach various schs., 1983—93. Vol. Hope Ho., Show Low, Ariz., 2003—05. Mem.: Ariz. Family and Consumer Scis. Edn. Assn., Nat. Assn. Edn. Young Children, Ariz. Career & Tech. Edn. Assn. Republican. Baptist. Avocations: camping, motorcycling, water-skiing, scrapbooks. Home: PO Box 1973 Lakeside AZ 85929 Office: Blue Ridge High Sch 1200 W White Mountain Rd Lakeside AZ 85929

**MACK, JAMES CURTIS, II,** cultural organization administrator; b. LA, Dec. 22, 1944; s. James Curtis and Ahli Christina (Youngren) M.; m. Tamara Jo Kriner, Jan. 23, 1988; children: James Curtis III, Robert Lee, Edward Albert. BA cum laude, U. So. Calif., 1967, M in Pub. Adminstrn., 1969, MA, 1976. Asst. to regional dir. VA, Los Angeles, 1973-79; exec. dir. Citizens for the Republic, Santa Monica, Calif., 1979-85; assoc. oceans and atmosphere U.S. Dept. Commerce, Washington, 1985-88; pres. Los Angeles World Affairs Coun., 1988—. Adj. prof. Pepperdine U. Grad. Sch. Pub. Policy, 1999—; bd. dirs. Brentwood Bank of Calif. Mem. Pres.'s Commn. on White House Fellowships, 1984-85; mem. exec. adv. bd. European Union Ctr. Calif. Col. USAFR, 1969-99. Mem. Coun. Fgn. Rels., Nat. Space Club (bd. dirs. 1987-88). Republican. Episcopalian. Avocation: philatelist. Home: 4921 Fulton Ave Sherman Oaks CA 91423 Office: LA World Affairs Coun 345 S Figueroa St Ste 313 Los Angeles CA 90071-1002 Office Phone: 213-628-2333. Business E-Mail: jcmack@lawac.org.

**MACK, JOHN J.,** diversified financial services company executive; b. Mooresville, NC, Nov. 17, 1944; s. Charles and Alice (Azouri) Mack; m. Christy King; children: John, Stephen, Jenna. BA, Duke U., 1968. Municipal bond trader and salesman Smith Barney; mem. bond dept. Morgan Stanley & Co., 1972, v.p., 1976—77, principal, 1977, mng. dir., 1979, head Worldwide Taxable Fixed Income Divsn., 1985—92; mem. bd. dirs. Morgan Stanley Group, NYC, 1987-97, chmn. operating com., 1992-97, pres., 1993-97; pres., COO Morgan Stanley Dean Witter & Co., NYC, 1997—2001; pres., CEO Credit Suisse First Boston, LLC, 2001—04; co-CEO Credit Suisse Group, NYC, 2003—04; chmn. Pequot Capital Mgmt. Inc., Westport, Conn., 2005; chmn., CEO Morgan Stanley, NYC, 2005—. Bd. dirs. Catalyst, Inc., Celiant Corp., Cousins Properties Inc.; bd. dir. NYSE, bd. exec., 2003—04; mem. internat. adv. panel Monetary Authority, Singapore; mem. chmn. adv. com. Nat. Assn. Securities Dealers (NASD); past mem. Beijing's Advisory Coun.; past dir. CICC (first investment bank in China), India Bus. Sch.; past bd. visitors Fuqua Sch. Bus., Duke U. Serves numerous positions of leadership for bus., civic and philanthropic org.; chmn. bd. trustees NY Presbyn. Hosp., U. Hosp. Columbia, Cornell; mem. bd. trustees Duke U.; trustee Doris Duke Charitable Found.; vice chmn. NYC2012; co-founder CJ Mack Found. Recipient Thomas F. Keller Disting. Leadership award, Fuqua Sch. Bus., Duke U., 1998. Office: Morgan Stanley 1585 Broadway New York NY 10036*

**MACK, JUDITH COLE SCHRIM,** retired political scientist; b. Cin., Aug. 9, 1938; d. James Douglass and Cathleen (Cole) Schrim; m. Thomas H. Mack, Jan. 3, 1968; children: Robert Michael, Cathleen Cole. AB with high distinction, U. Ky., 1960; AM, Radcliffe Grad. Sch., 1962; MPhil, Columbia U., 1988, postgrad., 1986—. Tchr. Lexington (Ky.) Sch., 1962-63; instr. Russian Emory U., Atlanta, 1963-64, Kent (Ohio) State U., 1964-65; instr. Hunter Coll., N.Y.C., 1988-90; adj. lectr. Barnard Coll., NYC, 1991—92; instr. Douglass Coll. Rutgers U., New Brunswick, NJ, 1992—93; ret., 1993. Rsch. asst. sociology dept. U. Ky., 1961; rsch. asst. Russian and E. European Studies Ctr. UCLA, 1965—67, rsch. asst. Security Studies Ctr., 1967—68; adj. lectr. Hunter Coll., N.Y.C., 1988; presenter in field. Chmn. state pub. affairs com. N.J. Jr. Leagues, 1979—80; bd. dirs. Children's Aide Adoption Soc., Hackensack, NJ, 1979—90, v.p., 1985—90; bd. dirs. Assn. Children N.J., Newark, 1982—2003, v.p., 1983—88, chair spl. events, 1999; trustee Divsn. Youth and Family Svcs., Trenton, NJ, 1982—91, v.p., 1983—88; others; trustee Dumbarton Ho., Washington; active Millburn-ShortHills County Rep. Com., 1994—2003, corr. sec., 1994—96, chmn., 1996—98. Woodrow Wilson fellow, Radcliffe Coll., 1960—61, Nat. Def. fellow, 1961—62. Mem.: Mortar Bd., Nat. Soc. Colonial Dames Am. (N.J. treas. 1995—2001), Phi Sigma Iota, Phi Beta Kappa. Episcopalian. Avocations: bridge, cooking, ballet, theater, movies. Home: 657 Del Parque Dr Unit C Santa Barbara CA 93103 E-mail: jsmack22@att.net.

**MACK, JULIA COOPER,** retired judge; b. Fayetteville, NC, July 17, 1920; d. Dallas L. and Emily (McKay) Perry; m. Jerry S. Cooper, July 30, 1943; 1 dau., Cheryl; m. Clifford S. Mack, Nov. 21, 1957. BS, Hampton Inst., 1940; LLB, Howard U., 1951; JD (hon.), U. DC 1999. Bar: DC 1952. Legal couns. OPS, Washington, 1952-53; atty.-advisor office gen. counsel Gen. Svcs. Adminstrn., Washington, 1953-54; trial appellate atty. criminal div. Dept. Justice, Washington, 1954-68; civil rights atty. Office Gen. Counsel, Equal Employment Opportunity Commn., Washington, 1968-75; assoc. judge Ct. Appeals, Washington, 1975-89; sr. judge DC Ct. of Appeals, Washington, 1989—2001. Mem. Am., Fed., Washington, Nat. Bar Assns., Nat. Assn. Women Judges. Home: 1610 Varnum St NW Washington DC 20011-4206

**MACK, MARK PHILIP,** chemical company executive; b. Buffalo, Jan. 14, 1950; s. Stanley Joseph and Florence M. Mack; m. Jean Ann Merrick, June 2, 1984; 1 child, Hannah Elizabeth. BS in Chemistry, Buffalo State Coll., 1971; PhD in Chemistry, SUNY, Buffalo, 1976. Rsch. assoc. Duke U., Durham, NC, 1975-77; rsch. chemist Conoco Inc., Ponca City, Okla., 1977-80, group supr., 1980-81; group leader Conoco/DuPont, Ponca City, 1982-85; sr. supr. DuPont Polymer Products, Wilmington, Del., 1985-89; rsch. mgr. OxyChem, Houston, 1989-90; dir. tech. Occidental Chem. Corp., Houston, 1990-95; Lyondell Petrochem. Co., Houston, 1995-97, v.p. licensing, 1996-97; dir. R&D Equistar Chems., LP, 1997-99, dir. catalyst R&D, analytical chemistry and polymer sci., 1999—2002; chief scientist Lyondell/Equistar, Cin., 2002—. *Invented polymer technology that speeds crude oil transportation through pipelines by reducing turbulence or drag. Material was named "CDR" or "Conoco Drag Reducer" and introduced in 1979 at Pump Station #1, in the Alyeska Pipeline, Prudhoe Bay, Alaska. Brought Nissan process technology to North America in the 80's and modified it to produce plastic containers and flexible packing with step-out performance called "ALATHON" polyethylene. Discovered a class of unique polymerization catalysts at EQUISTAR to produce new polymers and plastic called "STAR" SSC. Patentee in field; contbr. articles to profl. jours.* Recipient Linus Pauling award, SUNY-Buffalo, 1971, Outstanding Student in Chemistry award, Western N.Y. Sect. Am. Chem. Soc., 1971, Conoco Patent award, 1983, Equistar/Lyondell Inventor award, 2001, St. Labre Indian Sch. Ednl. Assn. award, 2002, Operational Excellence award, 2004; grantee Samuel B. Silbert fellowship, SUNY-Buffalo, 1974—75. Mem. AAAS, Am. Chem. Soc., Soc. Plastics Engrs., N.Y. Acad. Sci., Am. Mgmt. Assn., Product Devel. and Mgmt. Assn., Sigma Xi. Home: 8483 Beckett Pointe Dr West Chester OH 45069-6440 Office Phone: 513-530-4096. Office Fax: 513-530-4267. Business E-Mail: mark.mack@equistarchem.com.

**MACK, SARA ROHRBACH,** librarian, educator; b. Topton, Pa., Nov. 20, 1921; d. Jonathan H. and Alda S. (Heffner) Rohrbach; m. George Mack, June 26, 1943 (wid. Jan. 1949); 1 child, Carol Mack Foy. BS, Kutztown State Tchrs. Coll., 1943; MS in Libr. Sci., Columbia U., 1955; postgrad., Temple U. and U. Pa. Elem. (Pa.) Chiffont (Pa.) Pub. Sch., 1943-45; libr. Mt. Penn Jr.-Sr. High Sch., Reading, Pa., 1949-58; prof. libr. sci. Kutztown (Pa.) State Coll., 1958-82, dept. chmn., 1977-82; retired, 1982. Adj. prof. Drexel U., Phila., 1968; bd. dirs. Friends of the Reading-Berks Pub. Librs., pres., 1983-84, exec. bd., 1985—. Compiler: Inspirational Readings for Elementary Grades, 1964; contbr. articles to profl. jours, book reviewer; contbg. author: American Reference Books Annual, Along the Saucony. Trustee Kutztown U. Coun., 1983-2001, chair, 1993-95; com. chmn. Kutztown Area Hist. Soc., 1983-93, 2002-05; ch. libr. Trinity Luth. Ch., Topton, 1966-05; del. to Pa. Govs. Conf. on Librs., 1990; mem. Berks Authors Bibliography Com., 1992-98. Recipient Superior Tchg. award Kutztown State Coll., 1962, Alumni Citation, 1980, 88, Award of Merit, Pa. Libr. Assn., 1969, Outstanding Libr. Contbn. award Loisa Gonser Cmty. Libr., 2002. Mem. ALA (com. mem. 1945), Pa. Libr. Assn., Pa. Sch. Librs. Assn. (pres. 1963-65, exec. bd. 1977-80 Named Outtanding Contbr. to Sch. Libr. Programs, 1981), Ch. and Synagogue Libr. Assn. (speaker and book reviewer), Pa. Citizens for Better Librs., Emeriti Faculty Kutztown U. (coord. 1989—), Phila. Children's Reading Roundtable, Am. Assn. Univ. Women, Delta Kappa Gamma. Home: 105 Dries Rd 34 Reading PA 19605

**MACK, STAN,** cartoonist; b. Bklyn., May 13, 1936; s. Frank and Pearl (Kamaiko) M.; m. Gail Kredensek, Dec. 7, 1965 (div. July 1987); children: Kenneth, Peter. BFA, R.I. Sch. Design, 1958. Art dir. Book Week N.Y. Herald Tribune, N.Y.C., 1964-66, Book and Edn. div. Book Rev. and Sunday Mag. N.Y. Times, N.Y.C., 1967-71; advt./editorial illustrator N.Y.C., 1965—; Stan Mack's Real Life Funnies The Village Voice, N.Y.C., 1975—; Stan Mack's Out-Takes Adweek Mag., N.Y.C., 1981-92; co-creator non-fiction graphic books for young adults, author, illustrator Real Life Funny History Books, N.Y.C., 1992—. Author, illustrator: The ABC of Bumptious Beasts, 1966, Potato Talk, 1969, One Dancing Drum, 1971, 10 Bears in my Bed, 1974, Where's My Cheese?, 1977, (with Janet Bode) Death is Hard to Live With, 1993, Stan Mack's Real Life American Revolution: The Sweep of History Told in Colorful Detail, 1994, Story of the Jews: A 4,000-Year Adventure, 1998, Janet & Me: An Illustrated Story of Love and Loss, 2004; writer, artist two animated shorts for children's program Electric Co. Pub. TV, 1979. With U.S. Army, 1959-61. Recipient Soc. of Illustrators award, 1967, Jr. Literary Guild award, Aiga Children's Book Coun. Showcase award. Mem. The Graphic Artists Guild. Office: The Village Voice 36 Cooper Sq New York NY 10003-7149 also: c/o David Black Literary Agy 156 Fifth Ave New York NY 10001

**MACK, THOMAS RUSSELL,** foundation administrator, management consultant; b. Independence, Iowa, May 22, 1955; s. Russell John and A. Catherine M.; children: Christopher E., Stephen A. BA, Morningside Coll., 1978; MBA, U.S.D., 1988. CEO, dir. Whitestone Found. Rsch., Inc. Sioux City, Iowa, 1981—; tax splst. Commerce Clearing House, 1991-95; v.p.; controller Grand Prairie Cos., 1996-98; pres. Greenway-Infinity Internat., Inc., 1998—. Staff instr. Upper Iowa U., 1989-90; vis. prof. Mont. Coll. Mineral Sci. & Tech., 1988-89, auditor, examiner Iowa Dept. Revenue. Bd. dirs. The Exodus Counseling Ctr., Lombard, Ill., 1998—, Iowa Bapt. Mission Inc, West Des Moines, 1998—, Shepherd Ministries, Milo, Iowa, 1981—. Home: 1513 S Rustin St Sioux City IA 51106-2240

**MACK, TOM,** retired professional football player; b. Cleve., Nov. 1, 1943; Guard L.A. Rams, 1966—78. Named to Pro Football Hall of Fame, 1999. Achievements include Rams No. 1 draft pick, 1966; player 4 NFC championship games; player 3 NFL Pro Bowls; 8 AFC-NFC Pro Balls; All-Pro 1970, 71, 73, 84; All-NFL, 1969; All-NFC, 1970, 71, 72, 73, 74, 75, 77, 78; All-Am., Mich., 1965; playing in 184 consecutive games; never missed a game in 13-season career. Office: Pro Football Hall of Fame 212 George Halas Dr NW Canton OH 44708

**MACK, WILLIAM L.,** real estate investment company executive; m. Phyllis Mack. BS, NYU; grad. Wharton Sch., U. Pa., 1961. Past pres., sr. mng. ptnr. The Mack Orgn.; sr. mng. ptnr. The Mack Co.; bd. dirs. Mack-Cali Realty Corp., 1997—, chmn., 2000—; founder, sr. ptnr. Apollo Real Estate Advisors LP, 1993—. Bd. dirs. Bear Stearns Companies Inc., 1997—2004, Wyndham Internat. Inc. Bd. trustees Solomon R. Guggenheim Mus., NYC; vice chmn. North Shore LI Jewish Health Sys.; trustee U. Pa., bd. overseers The Wharton Sch., endowed $10 million for the William and Phyllis Mack Ctr. for Technol. Innovation, 2001. Office: Mack-Cali Realty Corp 11 Commerce Dr Cranford NJ 07016

**MACKALL, CRYSTAL L.,** medical researcher; BS/MD, Northeastern Ohio Universities Coll. Medicine, 1984. Medicine/pediatrics resident, Akron, Ohio; clin. assoc. Pediatric Oncology Br. Nat. Cancer Inst., 1989—92, postdoctoral sci. training Exptl. Immunology Br., 1990—96, rschr. Pediatric Oncology Br., 1996—, now also chief Pediatrics Oncoolgy Br., chief Immunology Sect. Office: Pediatric Oncology Br Ctr Cancer Rsch 10 CRC 1W 3940 Bethesda MD 20892-1104 Office Fax: 301-451-7052. Business E-Mail: cm35c@nih.gov.

**MACKALL, HENRY CLINTON,** lawyer; b. Ft. Lauderdale, Fla., Apr. 6, 1927; s. Douglass Sorrel and Mildred (Parker) M.; m. Mary Margaret Sullivan, June 21, 1952 (dec. Dec. 23, 2002); children: Caroline Clark, Nancy Sorrel, Lucy Parker BA, U. Va., 1950, LLB, 1952. Bar: Va. 1951. Ptnr. Mackall, Mackall & Gibb, P.C. and predecessors, Fairfax, Va., 1952—. Asst. commr. accounts Fairfax County (Va.), 1963-2006; spl. commr. in chancery for audit functions for Cir. Ct. Fairfax County, 1976-2006; substitute judge Fairfax County Ct., Juvenile and Domestic Rels. Ct. Fairfax County, 1964-69 Trustee Fairfax Hosp. Assn., 1966-75; with Va. State Bar Client Security Fund Bd., 1976-88, chmn., 1977-78; past bd. dirs. F&M Bank, No. Va. Served with AUS, 1945-46 Fellow Am. Coll. Trusts & Estate Counsel, Am. Coll. Real Estate Lawyers, Va. Law Found.; mem. ABA, Va. Bar Assn. (regional v.p. 1963-64), Fairfax County Bar Assn. (pres. 1966-67), Hist. Soc. Fairfax County (pres. 1970-72), Jamestowne Soc. (gov. 1995-97), River Bend Country Club (Gt. Falls, Va., pres. 1967-68), Georgetown Assembly Washington Democrat. Episcopalian. Home: 1032 Towlston Rd Mc Lean VA 22102-1111 Office: 4031 Chain Bridge Rd Fairfax VA 22030-4103 Office Phone: 703-273-0320. E-mail: mackmarhen@aol.com, mackgibb@aol.com.

**MACKALL, LAIDLER BOWIE,** retired lawyer; b. Washington, Aug. 8, 1916; s. Laidler and Evelyn M. (Bowie) M.; m. Nancy M. Taylor, Aug. 28, 1942; children: Nancy Taylor Mackall Lurton (dec.), Christie Beall Mackall Connard, Susan Somervell Mackall Smythe, Bruce Bowie Mackall McConihe; m. Prudence Robertson Colbert, July 26, 1978. AB, Princeton U., 1938; postgrad., Georgetown U., 1938-40, JD, 1947. Bar: D.C. 1947, Interstate Commerce Commn. 1951, U.S. Supreme Ct. 1958. Law clk. to chief judge of predecessor to D.C. Ct. Appeals, 1946-47; assoc. Minor, Gatley & Drury, Washington, 1947-49, Steptoe & Johnson, Washington, 1949-51, ptnr., 1952-86, of counsel, 1986-98; ret., 1998. BAP examiner D.C. ct. appeals com. on admissions to D.C. Bar, 1974-78, D.C. Circuit Jud. Conf., 1983, 85, 86; bd. mgrs. Nat. Conf. Bar Examiners, 1974-77 Served to colo. USAAF, 1940-46, 51. Decorated Silver Star, 2 D.F.C.s, 5 Air medals, 3 Presdl. unit citations. Fellow Am. Coll. Trial Lawyers (emeritus); mem. ABA (past vice chmn. standing com. aviation ins. law), D.C. Bar, Bar Assn. D.C. (past chmn. com. on negligence, motor vehicle and compensation law), Barristers Club (v.p. 1964), Chevy Chase Country Club, Met. Club (Washington), Hawk's Nest Golf Club of Fla. Episcopalian. Home (Summer): 3809 Village Park Dr Chevy Chase MD 20815-5746 Home: 151 Passage Island Vero Beach FL 32963-4265 E-mail: lbmackall@webtv.net.

**MACKAY, A. D. DAVID,** food products executive; b. Hamilton, New Zealand, Aug. 16, 1955; m. Michelle Mackay; 2 children. B of Bus., Charles Stuart U., Australia. Group product mgr. Kellogg Australia, 1985—87; category dir. ready-to-eat cereals corp. hdqs. Kellogg, Battle Creek, Mich., 1987—91; mng. dir. Sara Lee Bakery, Australia, 1992—98; mng. dir. Kellogg Australia Kellogg, Battle Creek, 1998, mng. dir UK and Republic of Ireland, 1998—2000, pres Kellogg USA, 2000—03, exec. v.p. Kellogg Co., 2000—03, pres., COO Kellogg Co., 2003—. Bd. dir. Fortune Brands Inc., 2006—. Mem.: Kellogg Co. (bd. dirs. 2005—), Grocery Mfrs. of Am. (mem. industry affairs coun.), Australian Food Coun. (former dir., bd. dirs.), Grocery Mfrs. of Australian (former dir., bd. dirs.). Office: Kellogg PO Box 3599 1 Kellogg Sq Battle Creek MI 49016-3599

**MACKAY, CAROL HANBERY,** literature educator; b. San Francisco, Calif., July 1, 1944; d. John William and Shirley Virginia Hanbery; m. Kirk Richard Hampton, July 1, 1979; m. Hugh Trent MacKay, Aug. 28, 1966 (div. Jan. 15, 1972). BA in English, Stanford U., Calif., 1966, MA in English Edn., 1967; PhD in English, U. Calif., LA, 1979. Tchr. English Sir Francis Drake H.S., San Anselmo, Calif., 1967—74; fellow U. Calif., L.A., 1974—78; from asst. prof. to prof. English U. Tex., Austin, Tex., 1979—2002, prof. English, 2002—. Mem. exec. com. Dickens Project, Santa Cruz, Calif., 2002—04. Author: Soliloquy in 19th-c. Fiction, 1987, Creative Negativity, 2001; editor: Dramatic Dickens, 1989; author: The Two Thackerays, 1988; assoc. editor: Thackeray Newsletter, 1984—89. Named to Acad. Disting. Tchrs., U. Tex., 2003; fellow, U. Calif., 1978—79. Mem.: AAUW, MLA, N.E. Victorian Studies Assn., Phi Beta Kappa (bd. dirs. 2004—). Democrat. Avocations: swimming, yoga, feldenkrais. Home: 100 Laurel Ln Austin TX 78705 Office: Univ Texas English Dept B5000 1 University Station Austin TX 78712 Office Phone: 512-471-4991. Business E-mail: mackay@mail.utexas.edu.

**MACKAY, CHARLES ROBERT,** federal official, consultant; b. Waterbury, Conn., Nov. 26, 1937; s. Charles Anselm and Marie Carmella MacKay; m. Maria Giovanna Pillon, Mar. 28, 1967; children: Daniel Brian, Lawrence Frank. STL, St. Mary's Sem. and U., Balt., 1961; MA, U. Notre Dame, South Bend, Ind., 1961; PhD, Urban U., Rome, 1966. Dean Keystone Coll., LaPlume, Pa., 1969—73; exec. dir. Pub. Com. for the Humanities, Lewisburg, Pa., 1973—74; vis. faculty U. Pa., Phila., 1974—75; sr. policy analyst and acting staff dir. President's Biomed. Rsch. Panel, Washington, 1975—76; dep. dir. comm. control of Huntington's disease NIH, Bethesda, Md., 1976—78, dep. dir. office protection from rsch. risks, 1978—90, project clearance officer, 1990—; adj. faculty Georgetown U. Sch. of Medicine, Washington, 1995—. Cons. Uniformed Svcs. U. of Health Scis., Bethesda, 1981—, Nat. Inst. of Neurol. Disorders and Stroke, Bethesda, 1990—, GeneLogic, Inc., Gaithersburg, 1995—, Nat. Inst. of Stds. and Tech., Gaithersburg, 1997—, Nat. Inst. Child Health and Human Devel., Bethesda, 2001—; inaugural keynote spkr. plenary address Internat. Dimensions of Bioethics, 1988; invited lectr. Dimensions of Bioethics, 1988; invited lectr. Holroyd Lectr., 1989; Regents lectr. U. Calif., Berkeley, 1988—89; mem. adv.

bd. Partnership for Human Rsch. Protection, Washington, 2000—03; adj. faculty Montgomery Coll., Rockville, Md., 2004. Prodr.: (videotape series) Protecting Human Subjects (CINE Golden Eagle award, 1989); contbr. articles to profl. jours. (Nellie Westerman prize Rsch. in Ethics, 1975). Recipient Outstanding Svc. awards, U.S. Dept. Health and Human Svcs., 1975—2003; fellow Biomedical Ethics, NEH, 1974—75. Office: NIH 9000 Rockville Pike Bethesda MD 20892-7974

**MACKAY, DONALD ROY,** plastic surgeon, educator; b. Johannesburg, Apr. 19, 1953; arrived in U.S., 1988; s. David James and Joan Adelaide Mackay; m. Susan Jane Ash, Dec. 9, 1978; children: Duncan, Andrew, Calum. DDS, U. Witwatersrand, 1976, MB, BChir, 1980. Diplomate Am. Bd. Plastic Surgery. Pvt. practice dentistry, London, 1976; resident surgery and plastic surgery U. Witwatersrand Tchg. Hosp., Johannesburg, 1981—86; plastic surgeon U. Witwatersrand Tchg. Hosps., Johannesburg, 1986—88; clin. head divsn. plastic surgery, asst. prof. U. Witwatersrand, Johannesburg, 1990—91; asst. prof. surgery divsn. plastic surgery Pa. State Coll. Medicine, Hershey, 1989—90, asst. prof. dept. surgery and pediat., 1991—93, asst. prof. surgery and pediat., 1993—95; resident plastic surgery Pa. State Coll. Medicine, Milton S. Hershey Med. Ctr., 1995—98, assoc. prof. surgery and pediat., chief divsn. plastic surgery, 1998—2003, William P. Graham III prof. plastic surgery, 2003—. Presenter in field; sec. Am. Plastic and Reconstructive Surgeons South Africa, Johannesburg, 1990—91; pres. Fedn. Cleft Palate Clinics Pa., 1997—99; senator Pa. State U. Faculty Senate, State College, 1995—96. Contbr. articles to profl. jours. Recipient Cmty. Svc. award, March of Dimes, 1995. Fellow: ACS, Am. Acad. Pediat., Royal Coll. Surgery; mem.: Am. Soc. Aesthetic Plastic Surgery, Northeastern Soc. Plastic Surgeons, Internat. Soc. Aesthetic Plastic Surgeons, Am. Soc. Maxillofacial Surgeons, Am. Cleft Palate/Craniofacial Assn., Am. Soc. Plastic Surgeons, Am. Assn. Plastic Surgeons, Am. Acad. Plastic Surgery (chmn.), Plastic Surgery Rsch. Coun., Robert H. Ivy Soc. (pres.). Democrat. Avocations: sculpting, bagpipes, sailboarding, squash, travel. Office: Pa State Univ Coll Medicine 500 University Dr Hershey PA 17033

**MACKAY, HAROLD HUGH,** lawyer; b. Regina, Sask., Can., Aug. 1, 1940; s. John Royden and Grace Madeliene (Irwin) MacK.; m. Jean Elizabeth Hutchison, Dec. 27, 1963; children: Carol, Donald. BA, U. Sask., 1960; LLB, Dalhousie U., Halifax, N.S., 1963; LLD (hon.), U. Regina, 2002. Bar: Sask. 1964, Queen's Counsel 1981. Assoc. MacPherson Leslie & Tyerman LLP, Regina, 1963-69, ptnr., 1969—2004, mng. ptnr., 1989-96, chmn., 1997—2003, of counsel, 2005—. Bd. dirs. The Mosaic Co., The Toronto-Dominion Bank; chmn. task force Future of the Can. Fin. Svcs. Sector, 1997-98; Clifford Clark vis. economist Dept. of Fin., Govt. of Can., 2002-04. Recipient Officer Order of Can., 2002. Mem. Internat. Bar Assn., Can. Bar Assn., Law Soc. Sask. Mem. United Ch. Office: 1500 1874 Scarth St Regina SK Canada S4P 4E9 Office Phone: 306-347-8417.

**MACKAY, LEO SIDNEY, JR.,** healthcare company executive, former federal agency administrator; b. San Antonio, Tex., Aug. 15, 1961; s. Leo Sidney Sr. and Barbara Jean (Hodge) MacK.; m. Heather Lee Deebel, Jan. 9, 1993; children: Sarah Bley, Josiah Edward Earl. BS, U.S. Naval Acad., 1983; M Pub. Policy, J.F. Kennedy Sch. Govt., 1991; PhD, Harvard U., 1993. Commd. ensign USN, 1983, advanced through grades to lt. comdr., 1993; flight student Naval Aviation Tng. Comd., Pensacola, Fla., 1983-85; F-14 fighter pilot U.S. Navy, Virginia Beach, Va., 1985-89; grad./doctoral student Harvard U., Cambridge, Mass., 1989-92; instr. history dept. U.S. Naval Acad., Annapolis, Md., 1992-93; mil. asst. to sec. US Dept. Def., Washington, 1993-95; dir. market devel. Lockheed Martin Corp., Bethesda, Md., 1995-97; v.p. bus. devel. and strategic planning Bell Helicopter Textron, Inc., Ft. Worth, 1997—2001; dep. sec. U.S. Dept. Vets Affairs, Washington, 2001—03; COO, ACS State Healthcare Solutions Affiliated Computer Services, Inc., Atlanta, 2003—. Chair Advisory Com. on Minority Health US Dept. Health & Human Services, 2005—. Contbr. articles to profl. jours.; article reviewer Internat. Security Jour., Cambridge, Mass., 1991-94. Pres. congregation St. Martin's Luth. Ch., Annapolis, 1996-97. Kennedy fellow J.F. Kennedy Sch. Govt., Cambridge, 1989-90, guest fellow Brookings Inst., Washington, 1992-93, Internat. Affairs fellow Coun. Fgn. Rels., 1995-96; MacArthur scholar MacArthur Found., Cambridge, 1991-92. Mem. Internat. Inst. Strategic Studies, U.S. Naval Inst., Coun. Fgn. Rels., Arlington C. of C. (bd. dirs.), U.S. Naval Acad. Alumni Assn. (nat. trustee 1995-98), Army and Navy Club. Republican. Lutheran. Avocations: reading, golf.

**MACKAY, NEIL DUNCAN,** plastics company executive, consultant; b. Chelsea, Mass., Nov. 5, 1931; s. Allan Foster and Helen May (Smith) MacKay; m. Marcia Ann McCarthy, Aug. 22, 1953 (dec. 1979); children: Duncan, Jerry, Alan, Neil, Bonnie; m. Beverly J. Burke, May 31, 1991. BSBA, Northeastern U., Boston, 1954. Gen. mgr. Plastic Molding Corp., Newtown, Conn., 1954-67; market specialist Chem. div. Uniroyal, N.Y.C., 1967-70; project mgr. Colt Ind. Korean Project, N.Y.C., 1970-76; pres. Automatic Injection Molding Corp., Berkeley Heights, NJ, 1976-87, Diamond Mgmt. Cons., Inc., Winchester, NH, 1988—. Bd. dir. Frazier & Son, Inc., Lor-Tech Plastics, Inc. Author: Korean Plastics, 1973. Mem. Rep. Nat. Com., Washington, 1986—92. Recipient Outstanding Performance award, Ministry Nat. Def. Republic of Korea, 1974. Mem.: Plastic Pioneers Assn., Soc. Plastics Engrs. (sec. 1963—70, treas. 1983—86), Am. Profl. Cape.'s Assn., Scottish-Am. Cultural Soc., Am. Yacht Club, Stuyvesant Yacht Club, St. Andrews Soc. N.Y. Republican. Presbyterian. Avocation: sailing. Home: 19 Lovely Ln Winchester NH 03470-2916

**MACKAY, RAYMOND ARTHUR,** chemist; b. N.Y.C., Oct. 30, 1939; s. Theodore Henry and Helen Marie (Cusack) M.; m. Mary Dilberian, Aug. 13, 1966; 1 child, Chelsea Christine; children by previous marriage: Brett, Edward. BS in Chemistry, Rensselaer Poly. Inst., 1961; PhD in Chemistry, SUNY-Stony Brook, 1966. Rsch. assoc. Brookhaven Nat. Lab., Upton, N.Y., 1966-67; prof. Drexel U., Phila., 1969-83; chief chem. div. Chem. Research and Devel. Ctr., Aberdeen Proving Ground, Md., 1983-91; prof. chemistry, dir. ctr. advanced materials processing Clarkson U., Potsdam, N.Y., 1991—99, on leave as dir. Rsch. and Tech., U.S Army Edgewood Chem. Biol. Ctr., 199-2003; dir., mem. sr. exec. sci U.S Army, 2003—. Contbr. articles to profl. jours. Served to capt. U.S. Army, 1967-69. Grantee U.S. Army, Dept. Energy, Army Rsch. Office, NSF, Acad. Applied Scis., 1972-83, 95—, NATO, 1982-86, NYSSTF, 1991—. Mem. Am. Chem. Soc., Internat. Assn. Colloid and Interface Scientists (past. pres.), Sigma Xi. Office: US Army Chemical Biological Ctr Aberdeen Providing Ground Aberdeen Proving Ground MD 21010 Office Phone: 410-436-3250. Business E-Mail: raymond.mackay@us.army.mil.

**MACKAY, TRUDY FRANCES CHARLENE,** genetics professor; b. Moncton, NB, Can., Sept. 10, 1952; d. Charles Edward Mackay and Jean McGregor Somerville; m. Robert Rene Henri Anholt, July 10, 1990. BSc, Dalhousie U., Halifax, NS, Can., 1974; MSc, Dalhousie U., 1976; PhD, U. Edinburgh, Scotland, 1979. Lectr. U. Edinburgh, 1980—87; prof. genetics NC State U., Raleigh, 1987—. Recipient medal, Genetics Soc. Am., 2004; fellow AAAS, 2003, Am. Acad. Arts and Scis., 2005, Royal Soc., 2006. Office: NC State U Dept Genetics Box 7614 Raleigh NC 27695 Office Phone: 919-515-5810. E-mail: trudy_mackay@ncsu.edu.

**MACKAY, WILLIAM ANDREW,** judge; b. Halifax, N.S., Can., Mar. 20, 1929; s. Robert Alexander and Mary Kathleen (Junkin) MacK.; m. Alexa Eaton Wright, July 7, 1951; 1 dau., Margaret Kathleen. BA, Dalhousie U., 1950, LLB, 1953, LLM, 1954, Harvard U., 1970; LLD (hon.), Meml. U. Nfld.; LLD, St Francis Xavier U., N.S., Dalhousie U. Bar: N.S.; Named queen's counsel. Egn. service officer Dept. External Affairs, Ottawa, Ont., Canada, 1954-57; asst. sec. Royal Com., Ottawa, 1955-57; successively asst. prof., assoc. prof. law, dean Faculty of law Dalhousie U. (Halifax), N.S., Canada, 1957-69, v.p. N.S., 1969-80, pres., vice-chancellor N.S., 1980-86; ombudsman N.S., Canada, 1986-88; judge trial divsn. Fed. Ct. Can., Ottawa, 1988—2004, dep. judge trial divsn., 2004—. Chmn. Assn. Atlantic Univs., Halifax, 1981-83; v.p. Assn. Univs. and Colls. Can., 1982-83, pres., 1983-85; pres. Conf. Gov. Bodies Legal Profession Can., 1968-69, Assn. Can.

Law Tchrs., 1964-65 Chmn. N.S. Human Rights Com., Halifax, 1967-86; chmn. N.S. Commns. on Salary and Allowances of Elected Provincial Ofcls., 1974, 78, 81, 83, 84, 85; chmn. N.S. Task Force on AIDS, 1987-88. Mem. Can. Bar Assn. Home: 601 6369 Coburg Rd Halifax NS Canada B3H 4J7 Office: Fed Ct Ottawa ON Canada K1A 0H9 E-mail: andrewmackay@earthlink.ca.

**MACKEN, DANIEL LOOS,** cardiologist, educator; b. Rochester, N.Y., May 7, 1933; s. Daniel Edward and Mary Frances (Loos) Macken; m. Maria Luisa Medina de Palma, Nov. 16, 1979; children: Daniel Edward, Mary Frances Loos. BA, Holy Cross Coll., Worcester, Mass., 1955; post grad., Yale U., 1956-57; MD, U. Mass, Boston, 1960. Diplomate Am. Bd. Cardiovascular Disease. Resident Roosevelt and Columbia-Presbyn. Hosp., N.Y.C., 1960—63; fellow Am. Heart Assn., 1964—65; dir. coronary care unit Walter Reed Gen. Hosp., Washington, 1968; staff rsch. physician Walter Reed Army Inst. Rsch., Washington, 1970; instr. Columbia U., N.Y.C., 1966—78. Vis. lectr. U. Saigon, Vietnam, 1969; pres. Medica Found., Inc., N.Y.C., 1971—; bd. dirs. Medica Endowment Fund. Contbr. chapters to books, articles to profl. jours.; student editor: Jour. History Medicine and Allied Scis., 1956—57. Lt. col. M.C. U.S Army, 1967—70, Vietnam. Decorated Bronze Star, Vietnam Cross. Fellow: N.Y. Acade. Medicine, Royal Soc. Medicine, Am. Coll. Cardiology, Harvey Soc.; mem.: AMA, Am. Heart Assn., Assn. Mil. Surgeons U.S., Met. Gov. Island Officers Club. Roman Catholic. Office: Columbia-Presbyn Med Ctr 161 Ft Washington Ave New York NY 10032-3713 Office Phone: 212-751-4343.

**MACKENBACH, FREDERICK W.,** welding products manufacturing company executive; b. St. Marys, Ohio, Mar. 10, 1931; s. Frederick Jacob and Mabel (Tangeman) M.; m. Jo Ann Dietrich, Oct. 21, 1953; children: John Frederick, David Dietrich. BS in Econs., Wharton Sch. Fin. & Commerce, 1953. Various sales engr. positions The Lincoln Electric Co., Indpls., Ft. Wayne, L.A., 1956-64, asst. dist. mgr. L.A., 1973-76, dist. mgr., 1976-88; pres. Lincoln Electric Mexicana, 1988-91, Lincoln Electric Latin Am., 1991-92; pres., COO The Lincoln Electric Co., Cleve., 1992-96, ret., 1996. Mem. Com. on Fgn. Rels. Mayor City of Palos Verdes Estates (Calif.) City Coun., 1999-2005. With U.S Army 1953-55. Mem.: Am. Welding Soc., Econ. Round Table in L.A. Office: Lincoln Electric Co 732 Via Somonte Palos Verdes Estates CA 90274-1629 Personal E-mail: mackenbach@aol.com.

**MACKENSEN, GEORG BURKHARD,** anesthesiologist, educator; b. Munich, Aug. 1, 1965; s. Gerhard and Karin Mackensen; m. Jutta Friederike von Stieglitz; 1 child, Aya Luise. MD, U. Hamburg, Germany, 1994; PhD, Technische U. Munich, Germany, 2004. Diplomate Am. Bd. Anesthesiology, 1994. Resident Dept. Medicine Westfaelische Wilhelmsuniversitaet, Muenster, Germany, 1994—95; resident anesthesiology Klinikum rechts der Isar Technische U. Muenchen, Munich, 1995—97, assoc. anesthesiology Klinikum rechts der Isar, 2000—02, asst. anesthesiology Klinikum rechts der Isar, 2000—04; post-doctoral fellow Dept. Anesthesiology Med. Ctr. Duke U., Durham, NC, 1997—2000, assoc. prof. Dept. Anesthesiology Med. Ctr., 2004—. Contbr. articles to profl. jours. Mem. Am. Soc. of Anesthesiologists (Resident Rsch. Essay Contest 1st prize 2000). Office: Duke University Medical Center Erwin Rd Durham NC 27710 Office Phone: 919-684-4449.

**MACKENZIE, CHARLES SHERRARD,** academic administrator; b. Quincy, Mass., Aug. 21, 1924; s. Charles Sherrard and Dorothy MacKenzie; m. Florence Evelyn Phelps Meyer, Aug. 28, 1964 (dec. 1981); 1 child, Robert Walter Meyer; m. Lavonne Rudolph Gaiser, Mar. 30, 1985. Student, Boston U., 1942-43; BA, Gordon Coll., 1946; M.Div., Princeton Theol. Sem., 1949, ThD, 1955, PhD, 1957; LHD, Grove City Coll., 1997; postgrad., U. Paris, 1953. Ordained to ministry Congl. Christian Ch., 1949. Pastor Carversville (Pa.) Christian Ch., 1948-51; fellow faculty Princeton Theol. Sem., 1949-51, 53-54, Princeton U., 1954-64; pastor First Presbyn. Ch., Avenel, NJ, 1954-64, Broadway Presbyn. Ch., Columbia U., N.Y.C., 1964-67, First Presbyn. Ch., Stanford U., San Mateo, Calif., 1967-71; pres. Grove City (Pa.) Coll., 1971-91, chancellor, 1991-92; advisor to pres., prof. philosphy Reformed Seminary, Orlando, Fla., 1992—; sr. min. Eastminster Presbyn. Ch., Wichita, Kans., 1993. Bd. dirs. Covenant Life Ins. Co., CS Lewis Inst.; cons. Oxford Project, 1992—; Provident Mutual Ins. Co.; lectr. Oxford U., 1965, U. Hamburg, 1968, Columbia U., 1964-67, Stanford U., 1967-71, U. Pitts., 1990-93; adv. Provident Mutual Ins. Co. Author: The Anguish and Joy of Pascal, 1973, Freedom, Equality, Justice, 1980, The Trinity and Culture, 1985. Bd. dirs. Knox Fellowship, Frontline, Orlando; mem. Human Relations Commn., San Mateo, 1968-70; mem. Indsl. Devel. Council, Grove City, 1972-75. Served with USAF, 1951-53. Mem. Presbyn. Coll. Union, Am. Assn. Pres.'s Ind. Colls. and Univs. (dir., pres.), Nat. Assn. Ind. Colls. and Univs. (mem. secretarial 1985-91), Freedoms Found. (nat. jury), Soc. Christian Philosphers, Duquesne Club (Pitts.), Univ. Club Boston, Citrus Club (Orlando), Evangelical initiative Notre Dame U., Rockford Inst. Main St. com. (De Toqueville award 1998). Republican. Address: 1231 Reformation Dr Oviedo FL 32765-7197

**MACKENZIE, DONALD MURRAY,** health facility administrator; b. Toronto, Ont., Can., June 5, 1947; s. Donald Alexander and June Cameron MacKenzie; m. Marilyn Adele McNaughton, Jan. 3, 1970; children: Jennifer, Katherine, Kenneth. BA in Econs., U. Toronto, 1968, MA in Polit. Sci., 1970, D Health Adminstr., 1974. Exec. asst. Mt. Sinai Hosp., Toronto, 1974-76, successively asst. exec. dir., assoc. exec. dir., v.p., 1974-89; pres. North York Gen. Hosp., Toronto, 1989—2002; asst. prof. U. Toronto, 1989—; internat. healthcare cons., 2002—. Chair Cardiac Care Network Ont., 2001-2002; bd. dirs. Neuchâtel Jr. Coll., The Seeing Eye; trustee R. Alan Hay Awards. Editor: History of Canadian Hospitals, 1972; contbr. articles to profl. jours. Bd. dirs. Cancer Care Ont., 1989-99. Mem. Can. Coll. Health Svc. Execs. (cert., various coms.), Can. Cancer Soc. (hon. life, pres. Ont. div. 1989-91, award of merit 1988), Ont. Hosp. Assn. (chmn. 1999-2000), York Club, Toronto Bd. Trade, Parkview Golf Club (bd. dirs.). Anglican. Avocations: golf, tennis, canoe tripping. E-mail: mmackenzie55@hotmail.com.

**MACKENZIE, GEORGE ALLAN,** medical products executive; s. George Adam and Annette Louise MacKenzie; m. Valerie Ann Marchand, June 30, 1971; children from previous marriage: Richard Michael, Barbara Wynne. Student, Jamaica Coll., Kingston, 1944-48. Commd. flying officer Canadian Air Force, 1951, advanced through grades to lt. gen., 1978; comdr. Canadian Forces Air Command, Winnipeg, Man., 1978-80, resigned, 1980; exec. v.p., COO Gendis Inc., 1980-89, pres., COO, 1989-99, pres., CEO, 1999—2002; bd. dirs. Sony of Can. Ltd., Willowdale, Ont., Canada; pres., CEO CANUSA MedExpress Ltd., 2003—. Mem. regional adv. bd. Carleton U. Decorated comdr. Order of Mil. Merit, Order St. Johns, Can. Decoration, Knight of St. Lazarus of Jerusalem. Mem. United Services Inst. Can. (hon. v.p.), Can. Corps Commissionaires (gov.), Police Chiefs Rsch. Found. (co-chmn.), Manitoba Club, Royal Mil. Inst. Manitoba. Home: 383 Christie Rd Winnipeg MB Canada R2N 4A5 Office Phone: 204-941-0675. Personal E-mail: gallanmac@hotmail.com.

**MAC KENZIE, JAMES DONALD,** clergyman; b. Detroit, Nov. 17, 1924; s. James and Ida Catherine (Conklin) M.; m. Elsie Joan Kerr, May 7, 1960; children: Janet Eileen, Kayly Kathleen, Christy Carol, Kenneth Kerr. Student, Moody Bible Inst., 1946-49, Union Theol. Sem., 1952. Ordained to ministry Presbyn. Ch., 1953. Pastor Calvary Ch., Swan Quarter, NC, Edenton (N.C.) Presbyn. Ch., 1952-60, Kirkwood Ch., Kannapolis, 1960-64, Barbecue and Olivia Ch., Olivia, 1964-71, Horse Elk Ch., Robbins, 1971-92, Horseshoe Presbyn. Ch., Carbonton, 1971—. Co-founder, Rehoboth Gospel Fellowship Chicago, 1949. tchr. North Moore High School, 1977-87.; instr. Sandhills Comm Coll. 1986. Columnist The Chowan Herald, Edenton, N.C., 1952-60, The Robbins (N.C.) Record, 1971-86, The Pilot, Southern Pines, N.C., 1987—. Historian Fayetteville Presbytery, 1975—; chmn. hist. com., 1983—, moderator, 1978. Founder Conf. on Celtic Studies, Campbell Coll. (now Campbell U.), Buies Creek, N.C., 1972—; councillor Conf. on Scottish Studies (Can.), 1968-75; co-founder Rehoboth Gospel Fellowship, Chgo., 1949. With AUS, 1943-45, ETO. Decorated Purple Heart, Bronze Star, Combat Inf. Badge; recipient Disting. Citizen award, Robbins, 1983, Disting. Pastor award, 1988, Scottish

Heritage Ctr. award St. Andrews Presbyn. Coll., Laurinburg, N.C., 1999. Mem. N.C. Presbyn. Hist. Soc. (pres. 1972-74, Author's award 1970, 75, Cert. Merit 1975), Harnett Hist. Soc. (pres. 1968-71, Distinguished Service award 1970, Scottish Heritage award 1999), Illuis Uillean Pipers Soc., Gaelic Soc. of Inverness, An Comunn Gaidhelach (life). Author: Colorful Heritage, 1970; editor: The Uilleann Piper, 1974—; contbr. articles to profl. jours. Home: 1364 Spanish Dr Asheboro NC 27205-2222 Office Phone: 336-672-3415.

**MACKENZIE, JOHN,** retired oil industry executive; b. 1919; BS, N.Y. U., 1948. Accountant S.Am. Devel. Co., N.Y.C., 1938-41; financial comptroller French Oil Ind. Agy.-Groupment D'Achat des Carburants, N.Y., 1946-53; v.p., treas. George Hall Corp., 1954-56; treas. Am. Petrofina, Inc., 1956-61, sec., 1961-64, v.p., sec., 1964-68, sr. v.p., 1968-84; ret., 1984. Decorated comdr. Order of Crown (Belgium) Address: 3861 Frio Way Frisco TX 75034-8469

**MACKENZIE, NANCI,** gas company executive; m. Len Mackenzie, 1988. Co-founder (with Sue Palmer) Lucky Lady Oil Co., 1976—82; founder, pres. USGT/Aquila (formerly U.S. Gas Transp. before sale to Aquila), Dallas, 1986—2001; pres. Aquila Dallas Marketing LP. Recipient Entrepreneur of the Yr, 1998. Mem.: Nat. Assn. Women's Bus. Owners, Am. Gas Assn. Office: Aquila Inc 20 W Ninth St Kansas City MO 64105

**MACKENZIE, RONALD ALEXANDER,** anesthesiologist; b. Detroit, Mar. 31, 1938; s. James and Elizabeth Mackenzie; m. Nancy Lee Vogan, Aug. 25, 1962; children: Margaret, James. BS, Alma Coll., 1961; DO, Kansas City Coll., 1967. Diplomate Am. Bd. Anesthesiology. Resident in anesthesiology Detroit Osteo. Hosp., 1970-72, Cleve. Clinic, 1972-73, Mayo Clinic, Rochester, Minn., 1973-74, cons. in anesthesia, 1974—87, vice-chmn. anesthesiology, 1988—99, chmn. GYN/ENT anesthesia, 1998—99; pres. ceo Am. Soc. Anesthesiologists. Vice-chmn. dept. anesthesiology Mayo Clinic, 1988-98. Pres. Minn. Orch., Rochester, 1987-89. Fellow Am. Coll. Anesthesiologists; mem. Am. Soc. Anesthesiologists (bd. dirs. 1983-87, sec. 1991-97, 1st v.p. 1998, pres.-elect 1999), Sigma Xi. Avocations: sailing, photography. Office: Mayo Clinic 200 1st St SW Rochester MN 55905-0002

**MACKERODT, FRED,** public relations specialist; b. Bklyn., Sept. 17, 1938; s. Leroy and Margaret (Murphy) M.; m. Christy Woods, June 7, 1987. Student, NYU, 1958-59. Freelance writer, photographer, N.Y.C. and Barcelona, Spain, 1968-73; editor Cars Mag., Popular Publs. Inc., N.Y.C., 1973-76; pres. Fred Mackerodt, Inc. (pub. relations and publicity), N.Y.C., 1976—, Stone House Farm, Inc., 2001—. Contbr. articles to popular mags.; contbg. editor, sci. and tech.: Popular Mechanics, 1987—. Spl. dep. sheriff Indian River County, Fla., 1994—2001. Mem. Aviation and Space Writers Am., Internat. Motor Press Assn., Publicity Club N.Y., Wings Club, N.Y. Zool. Soc. (aquarium field assoc. 1971—) Home: 940 Craigville Rd Chester NY 10918 Address: Apt 612 205 W 86th St New York NY 10024-3362 E-mail: fmackerodt@fredmackerodt.com.

**MACKERRAS, SIR CHARLES (ALAN MACLAURIN),** conductor; b. Schenectady, N.Y., Nov. 17, 1925; s. Alan Patrick and Catherine Mackerras; m. Helena Judith Wilkins, 1947; 2 children. Student, Sydney Conservatorium Music, Australia, 1938-42; student with Vaclav Talich, Prague Acad. Music, 1947-48; DMus (hon.), U. Hull, 1990, U. Nottingham, 1991, U. Brno, Czech Republic, 1994, York U., Eng., 1994, Griffith U., Brisbane, Australia, 1994, Oxford U., Eng., 1997, Prague Acad. Music, 1999, Napier U., Scotland, 2000, U. Sydney, 2003, U. Melbourne, 2003, Janácek Acad. Music, Brno, 2004, U. London, 2005, Cardiff U., 2006, Royal Welsh Coll. Music and Drama, 2006, Royal No. Coll. Music London, Trinity Coll. Music London, St. Peter's Coll. Prin. oboist Sydney (Australia) Symphony Orch., 1943-46; staff condr. English Nat. Opera (formerly Sadler's Wells Opera), London, 1948-54, musical dir., 1970-77; prin. condr. BBC Concert Orch., 1954-56; first condr. Hamburg Opera, 1966-69; chief guest condr. BBC Symphony Orch., 1976-79; chief condr. Sydney Symphony Orch., Australian Broadcasting Commn., 1982-85; prin. guest condr. Royal Liverpool Philharm. Orch., 1986-88, Scottish Chamber Orch., 1992-95, condr. laureate, 1995—; music dir. Orch. of St. Luke's, 1998-2001, music dir. emeritus, 2001—; pres. Trinity Coll. Music, London, 2000. Freelance condr. with most Brit. and many continental orchs., c concert tours, Russia, South Africa, N. Am., Australia, 1957—66, U.S. coast-to-coast, 1983; prin. guest condr. San Francisco Opera, 1993—96, prin. guest condr. emeritus, 1996—; prin. guest condr. Royal Philharm. Orch., 1993—96, Czech Philharm. Orch., 1997—2003, Philharmonia Orch., 2002—; mus. dir. Welsh Nat. Opera, 1987—92, condr. emeritus, 1993—; appearances at internat. festivals and opera houses, frequent radio and TV broadcasts; condr. comml. recordings, notably Handel, Mozart operas and symphonies, Janácek, Brahms, Beethoven, Dvorák, Mahler and Schubert. Published ballet arrangements Pineapple Poll (Sullivan), Lady and the Fool (Verdi), reconstrn. Sullivan's Lost Cello Concerto, contbr. appendices to book Charles Mackerras: A Musicians' Musician, by Nancy Phelan, articles to Opera Mag., other jours. Decorated comdr. Order of Brit. Empire, Knight Bachelor, Companion Order of Australia, Companion of Honor; recipient Evening Std. award for opera, 1977, Janacek medal, 1978, Gramophone Record of Yr. award, 1977, 1980, 1999, Grammy award for best opera recording, 1981, Gramophone Best Opera Recording award, 1983, 1984, 1994, 1999, prix. Fondation Jacques Ibert, 1983, Record of Yr. award, Stereo Rev., 1983, Medal of Merit, Czech Republic, 1996, Chocs de l'Année award, 1998, Edison award, Preis der Deutschen Schallplattenkritik, Prix Caecilia, 1999, Conducting award, Royal Philharm. Soc., 1999, Chopin prize and lifetime achievement award, Cannes Classical awards at Midem, 2000, award, Assn. Brit. Orchs., 2001, Disting. Musician award, Inc. Soc. Musicians, 2002, Gold medal, Royal Philharmonic Soc., 2005, Listeners' award, BBC Radio 3, 2005, Queen's medal for Music, 2005. Office: Askonas Holt Ltd Lonsdale Chambers 27 Chancery Ln London WC2A 1PF England Office Phone: 44 0207 400 1710.

**MACKESEY, DANIEL R.,** lawyer; b. Ithaca, NY, July 14, 1954; m. Jennifer Mackesey; 2 children. BA in Anthropology (cum laude), Cornell U., 1977; JD, U. of Va. Sch. Law, 1980. Bar: DC 1980, Va. 1980, admitted to practice: All Va. State Cts. Assoc. David & Hagner, 1982—85; v.p., sr. counsel Artery Organization, Inc., 1985—88, sr. v.p., gen. counsel, 1988—92; counsel Piper & Marbury, Washington, 1992—96; founding ptnr. Jefferson Law Firm, PLC, McLean, Va., 1996—2001; mng. mem. Womble Carlyle Sandridge & Rice PLLC, Tyson Corner, Va., 2001—, mem. firm mgmt. com. (ex-officio), chair firm. leadership com., mem. recruiting com., mem. professionalism com. Recipient NCAA Top Five award. Mem.: Va. State Bar (mem. real property sect., mem. corp. counsel sect.), ABA (mem. law practice mgmt. sect.). Office: Womble Carlyle Sandridge & Rice PLLC 8065 Leesburg Pike 4th Fl Vienna VA 22182-2738 Office Phone: 703-790-4682. Office Fax: 703-918-2242. Business E-Mail: dmackesey@wcsr.com.

**MACKEY, JEFFREY ALLEN,** priest; b. Kingston, NY, July 12, 1952; s. Allen William and Vivian Mathilda (Hornbeck) M.; m. Martha LaVonne Webster, Dec. 18, 1971; children: Guy Linwood, Kenyon Paul, Geoffrey Joel. BS, Nyack Coll., 1974; D of Sacred Lit., Ridgedale Theol. Sem., 1975; MDiv, Macon Baptist Sem., Ga., 1976; D Ministry, Mansfield Div., 1985, Grad. Theol. Found., 1990; cert. of theol. studies, Gen. Theol. Sem., 1993; postgrad., Grad. Theol. Found. 1991—, U. of the South; DHL, St. Paul Theol. Sem., 2000; DLitt, Evangel U., 2003; DD, Grad. Theol. Found. 2005. Ordained to ministry Congl. Christian Ch., 1974; ordained priest Episcopal Ch., 1993. Min. music Neversink Valley Bapt. Ch., Huguenot, NY, 1969-70; pastor Ponckhockie Congl. Ch., Kingston, 1971-74, The Alliance Ch., Andover, 1974-76; acad. dean Macon (Ga.) Bible Inst., 1976-78; min. Oak Grove Gospel Tabernacle, Williamsport, Pa., 1977-80, 69th St. Alliance Ch., Phila., 1980-83; sr. min. Vestavia Alliance Ch., Birmingham, Ala., 1983-87, Hope Alliance Ch., New Hartford, NY, 1987-91; assoc. rector Grace Ch., Utica, NY, 1991-96, vicar Waterville, NY, 1995-96; rector Trinity Episcopal Ch., DeRidder, La., 1996-97; vicar Polk Meml. Episcopal Ch., Leesville, La., 1996-97; rector St. Mark the Evangelist Ch., North Bellmore, NY, 1997-99; registrar/Bible faculty Nyack Coll., Manhattan Campus, N.Y.C., 1999-2000, assoc. dean for acad. affairs, 2000-2001, acad. dean, 2001—03, asst. v.p., dean Coll. Arts and Scis., 2003—05; v.p., acad. dean Trinity Sch. Ministry, 2005—. Adj. prof. Cranmer Theol. Ho., Shreveport, La., 1997, Nyack Coll., 1998—99; asst. priest St. John's Episcopal Ch., Kingston, NY, 2000—02; interim rector St. John's Ch., Kingston, 2002—03, St. Gregory's, Woodstock, NY, 2003—04. Author: A Worship Manifesto, 1986, Indicatives and Imperatives, 1987, Christ's Centripetal Cross, 1990; co-author: Where Love and People Are, 1990, Prophet of Justice, Prophet of Life: Essays on William Stringfellow, 1997, A Diary of Three Decades: Grace Church, Utica, N.Y., 1963-96, 1999, and Jesus Everything: Conversations with A.B. Simpson, 2000, A Heart for the Future, 2004, Hidden Mirth, 2005; co-editor: Korea Witness, 2006; contbr. numerous articles to profl. jours. Mem. Alcohol and Drug Abuse Prevention Treatment Program, Birmingham, 1987—88; chaplain N. Bellmore Vol. Fire Dept., 1998—99; trustee Cathedral of St. John the Divine, N.Y.C., 2002—. Mem. Fellowship Christian Sch. Adminstrs., Evang. Theol. Soc., Am. Assn. Sch. Adminstrs., Am. Guild Organists, Anglican Assn. of Biblical Scholars, Order of Preachers (Anglican), Inst. for Advanced Theology, Soc. Biblical Lit. Avocations: piano, collecting art and statues, hymn writing, walking, auto restoration. Office Phone: 724-266-3838. Personal E-mail: parsonsmanor@verizon.net. Business E-Mail: jmackey@tesm.edu.

**MACKEY, JOHN P.,** food products executive; s. Bill and Margaret Mackey; m. Deborah Morin. Student, Trinity Coll., San Antonio, Tex., U. of Texas, Austin. Owner Safer Way Natural Foods, Austin, 1978—80; co-founder, chmn., CEO Whole Foods Market Inc., Austin, 1980—, pres., 2001—04. Named Overall Nat. Entrepreneur of Yr., Ernst & Young, 2003. Achievements include hiking entire Applachian Trail (2168 miles), 2002. Avocations: yoga, meditation, scuba diving. Office: Whole Foods Market Inc 550 Bowie St Austin TX 78703-4677*

**MACKEY, MARGARET EMMIE,** library media specialist; b. Lancaster, S.C., Aug. 2, 1947; d. Furman Robert and Margaret Edna (Stogner) M. BA, Winthrop Coll., 1968, MEd, 1980; MAT, U. S.C., 1975. Tchr. English, social studies Alexander Graham Jr. H.S., Charlotte, NC, 1968—69; grad. tchg. asst. U. S.C., Columbia, 1969—71; tchr. English, chemistry Andrew Jackson H.S., Kershaw, SC, 1971—82; libr. media specialist Heath Springs Elem. Sch., SC, 1968—86, Andrew Jackson H.S., 1986—2006; ret., 2006. Mem. ALA, S.C. Assn. Sch. Librs. (treas. 1989-91), Lancaster County Librs. Assn. (pres. 1991-93), Libr. Media Specialist Network (pres. 1987-88), Assn. Sch. Librs., Young Adult Libr. Svcs. Assn. Presbyterian. Avocations: reading, computers, travel.

**MACKEY, PAMELA ROBILLARD,** lawyer; b. Harlingen, Tex., July 16, 1956; d. Gregory Leo and Rosanne Elizabeth (Niland) Robillard; m. Craig W. Mackey, Dec. 30, 1983. BS in Journalism, U. Colo., 1981; JD, George Wash. U., 1985. Bar: Colo. 1985, U.S. Dist. Ct. Colo. 1985. Assoc. Davis, Graham & Stubbs, Denver, 1985-87, Haddon, Morgan & Foreman, P.C., Denver, 1987—, shareholder, 1997—. Pub. defender Colo., 1989-94. Exec. editor George Wash. Law Review, 1984-85. Mem. ABA, Colo. Bar Assn., Denver Bar Assn., Colo. Women's Bar Assn. (bd. dirs. 1988-96; pres. 1995-96), Colo. Criminal Def. Bar (newsletter editor 1988—). Democrat. Roman Catholic. Avocations: skiing, golf. Office: Haddon Morgan Mueller Jordan Mackey & Foreman PC 150 E Tenth Ave Denver CO 80203 Office Phone: 303-831-7364. E-mail: pmackey@hmflaw.com.

**MACKEY, PATRICIA ELAINE,** university librarian; b. Balt., July 29, 1941; d. Timothy and Hazel Mozelle (Davis) M. BA in Anthropology, CUNY, 1978; MLS, Columbia U., 1981. Asst. prof. I, European Exch. Sys., Mainz-Kastel, Germany, 1966-68; interlibr. loan asst. Poly. U., Bklyn., 1968-72, Rockefeller U., N.Y.C., 1972-73, sr. libr. asst., 1974-80, libr., 1981-91, univ. libr., 1991—. Mem. various libr. coms., N.Y.C., 1991—. Chair pub. svc. scholars program Hunter Coll. CUNY, 1992—; trustee Met. N.Y. Libr. Coun., 2000—, also 1st v.p. Named to, Hunter Coll. Hall of Fame, 2002. Mem.: ALA, Assn. Coll. and Rsch. Librs., N.Y. State Libr. Assn., Hunter Coll. Alumni Assn. (bd. dirs. 1998—, 2d v.p. 1998—2002). Democrat. Roman Catholic. Avocations: reading, chess, gardening. Office: Rockefeller U Libr RU Box 263 1230 York Ave New York NY 10021-6307 Office Phone: 212-327-8909. Business E-Mail: rmackey@mail.rockefeller.edu.

**MACK-HARVIN, DIONNE,** library director; MA in Africana Studies, SUNY, Albany, 1995, MLS in Sci., 1996. Libr. Queens Coll., NY, 1996; libr. Crown Heights Libr. Bklyn. Pub. Libr., NY, 1996, asst. branch libr. NY, branch mgr. NY, regional libr. NY, dir. Ctrl. Libr. NY, chief of staff NY, 2005—06, interim dir. NY, 2006—. Office: Bklyn Pub Libr Ctrl Libr Grand Army Plaza Brooklyn NY 11238 E-mail: d.mack@brooklynpubliclibrary.org.*

**MACKICHAN, MARGARET ANNA,** artist, art educator; b. Charleston, W.Va., Feb. 27, 1948; d. Kenneth Allen and Lois Alma (Deyton) MacK.; 1 child, Jemma Moccasin. BFA, U. Nebr., 1970; MA, U. N.Mex., 1974, MFA, 1977. Assoc. VISTA, Ky., 1966-67; photographer Ky., 1968—87, Rosebud (S.D.) Reservation, 1987-92; founding dir. Great Plains Art Inst., Sinte Gleska U., Rosebud Reservation, SD, 1987. Curatorial intern Internat. Mus. of Photography, George Eastman House, Rochester, N.Y., 1971-72; artist-in-community Western Nebr. Art Ctr., Scottsbluff, 1978-79; instr. Nebr. Western Coll., Scottsbluff, 1978-79; vis. prof. Nebr. Wesleyan U., Lincoln, 1980-87; participant Annual Plains Indian Seminar, 1987-98. Co-author: In the Kingdom of Grass, 1992. Recipient 1st prize photography Mademoiselle Mag., 1970, Vreeland award U. Nebr., 1970, Artist grant Nebr. Arts Coun./Nebr. Com. on Humanities, 1978, Artist fellowship Mid-Am. Arts Alliance, 1983, Outstanding Svc. in Art Edn. award S.D. Gov., 2003. Fellow Ctr. for Great Plains Study; mem. Soc. for Photographic Edn., Nat. Am. Art Studies Assn., Scottish Soc. Artists. Presbyterian. Avocations: walker horses, Lakota arts, Scottish dancing, banjo, bagpipes. Home: PO Box 6 Mission SD 57555-0006 Office: Sinte Gleska University PO Box 105 Mission SD 57555-0105

**MACKIN, CHARLES PHILIP, JR.,** lawyer; b. Boston, Dec. 13, 1947; s. Charles Philip and Mary Patricia (Sparkes) M.; m. Deborah Ann Huey, Oct. 18, 1980; children: Emily K., Claire E.S. BA, St. Anselm Coll., 1969; JD, Loyola U., New Orleans, 1972; MGA, U. Pa., 1987; grad., U.S. Army War Coll., 1990. Bar: Pa. 1972, U.S. Ct. Mil. Appeals 1973, U.S. Ct. Appeals (D.C. cir.) 1977, U.S. Supreme Ct. 1977, U.S. Ct. Appeals (3rd cir.) 1985. Asst. dist. atty., Coudersport, Pa., 1978-81; sr. dep. atty. gen. Office of Atty. Gen. of Pa., Harrisburg, 1982-86, chief dep. atty. gen., 1986-89; dep. chief counsel for investigations Dept. Auditor Gen. of Pa., Harrisburg, 1989-91, dep. auditor gen., 1991-96. Capt. USMC, 1972-77. Mem. Pa. Bar Assn., Army Navy Club (Washington). Office: 3344 Trindle Rd Camp Hill PA 17011-4432 Office Phone: 717-214-3700.

**MACKIN, JEANNE ANN,** journalist, educator; b. Waterloo, N.Y., June 9, 1948; d. Richard J. and Helen (Campfield) M.; m. Stephen Poleskie. BA in English, Ithaca Coll., 1970; MFA in Creative Writing, Bennington Coll., 1986. Columnist Ithaca (N.Y.) Times, 1974—; sci. writer Cornell U., Ithaca, 1979—; writing instr. Ithaca Coll., 1991—; MFA faculty mem. Goddard Coll., 2001—; cons. Strong Mus., Rochester, 1994; cons., auditor N.Y. State Coun. on Arts, N.Y.C., 1984—; writing tchr. State Coun. on Arts, Hawaii, 1992; spkr. in field. Author: The Frenchwoman, 1989, The Queen's War, 1991, Dreams of Empire, 1996, The Sweet By and By, 2001, The Cornell Book of Herbs, 1993; editor: Book of Love, 1998. Recipient Excellence in Newswriting award Coun. for Advancement and Support of Edn., 1986, Writing Scholarship award Wesleyan U., 1989; rsch. fellow Am. Antiquarian Soc., 1999. Mem. Author's Guild. Home: PO Box 849 Ithaca NY 14851-0849

**MACKINNEY, ARCHIE ALLEN,** physician; b. St. Paul, Aug. 16, 1929; s. Archie Allen and Doris (Hoops) MacK.; m. Shirley Schaefer, Apr. 9, 1955; children— Julianne, Theodore, John. BA, Wheaton Coll., Ill., 1951; MD, U. Rochester, 1955. Intern, resident in medicine U. Wis. Hosp., 1955-59; clin. assoc. NIH, 1959-61; clin. investigator VA, 1961-64; asst. prof. medicine U.

---

Wis., Madison, 1964-68, assoc. prof., 1968-74, prof., 1974-98, med. alumni prof., 1987. Mentor class of '03 U. Wis. Med. Sch.; chief hematology VA Hosp., Madison, 1964-98, chief nuclear medicine, 1964-73, 78-79 Author (editor): Pathophysiology of Blood, 1984, Hematology for Students, 2002; contbr. articles to profl. jours. Trustee Intervarsity Christian Fellowship, 1985-88. Served with USPHS, 1959-61. Danforth assoc., 1962 Mem. Am. Soc. Hematology, Am. Fedn. Clin. Research, Central Soc. Clin. Research. Republican. Baptist. Home: 190 N Prospect Ave Madison WI 53705-4071 Office: 2500 Overlook Ter Madison WI 53705-2254

**MACKINNON, CATHARINE ALICE,** lawyer, educator, writer; d. George E. and Elizabeth V. (Davis) MacKinnon. BA in Govt. magna cum laude with distinction, Smith Coll., 1969; JD, Yale U., 1977, PhD in Polit. Sci., 1987. Vis. prof. Harvard U., Stanford U., others, Osgoode Hall, York U., Canada, U. Basel, Switzerland; prof. law U. Mich., Ann Arbor, 1990—, Elizabeth A. Long Prof. Law. Long term vis. prof. U. Chgo., 1997—; co-dir. LAW Project Equality Now, 2001—; fellow Ctr. for Advanced Study, 2005-06. Author: Sexual Harassment of Working Women, 1979, Feminism Unmodified, 1987, Toward a Feminist Theory of the State, 1989, Only Words, 1993, Sex Equality, 2001, Women's Lives, Men's Laws, 2005, Are Women Human? and other international dialogues, 2006; co-author: In Harm's Way, 1997, Directions in Sexual Harassment Law, 2003. Mem.: AAAS (assoc.). Office: U Mich Law Sch 625 S State St Ann Arbor MI 48109-1215 Office Phone: 734-647-3595. Office Fax: 734-764-8309. E-mail: camtwo@umich.edu.

**MACKINNON, JAMES GORDON,** economist, educator; b. Charlottetown, P.E.I., Can., Jan. 4, 1951; s. James William and Marion Elizabeth MacKinnon; m. Susan Gentleman, Nov. 23, 1985. BA with honors, York U., 1971; MA, Princeton U., 1974, PhD, 1975. Asst. prof. Queen's U., Kingston, Ont., Canada, 1975—78, assoc. prof., 1978—82, prof., 1982—, Sir Edward Peacock prof. econometrics, 1991—. Mem. editl. bd. Can. Jour. Econs., 1984—87, assoc. editor Jour. Applied Econometrics, 1989—91, Jour. Econometrics, 1991—, software rev. editor Jour. Applied Econometrics, 1991—. Fellow: Royal Soc. Can., Econometric Soc.; mem.: Can. Econs. Assn. (pres.-elect 2000—01, pres. 2001—02, past pres. 2002—03). Office: Queen's U Dept Econs Kingston ON Canada K7L 3N6 Office Phone: 613-533-2293. Business E-Mail: jgm@econ.queensu.ca.

**MACKINNON, JOHN ALEXANDER,** lawyer; b. Glen Ridge, NJ, Feb. 5, 1949; s. John and Carol McNeir (Cox) M.; m. Anne Rider Patterson, Aug. 19, 1972; children: Lindsay Rider, John William. BA, Williams Coll., 1971; JD, U. Va., Charlottesville, 1974. Assoc. Brown & Wood, NYC, 1974-82, ptnr., 1983-2001; ptnr. securities law Sidley Austin Brown & Wood LLP, NYC, 2001—06, Sidley Austin LLC, NYC, 2006—. Adv. bd. Mutual Fund Dir. Forum. Trustee, Tuxedo Park Libr., NY, 1982-89; mem. chmn., bd. zoning appeals, Tuxedo Park, 1987-89. Mem. ABA, Assn. of the Bar of NYC, The Tuxedo Club. Office: 212-839-5300.

**MACKINNON, KEVIN SCOTT,** lawyer; b. San Jose, Calif., June 29, 1958; s. Hector Neil and Margie Lou (Riggs) MacK.; m. Hanna T. Piech, Sept. 1, 1984. BA, U. Calif., Santa Barbara, 1980; JD, U. Santa Clara, 1983. Assoc. Fisher & Hurst, Chgo., 1983-84, Isham, Lincoln & Beale, Chgo., 1984-86, Schiff, Hardin & Waite, Chgo., 1986; sr. corp. counsel, staff dir. McDonald's Corp.; ptnr. Katten Muchin Zavis Rosenman, Chgo. Mem.: ABA, Lawyers for Creative Arts (v.p.), Internat. Franchise Assn., Chgo. Bar Assn., Internat. Trademark Assn. Office: Katten Muchin Zavis Rosenman 525 W Monroe St Chicago IL 60661 Office Phone: 312-902-5285. Office Fax: 312-577-4504. E-mail: kevin.mackinnon@kmzr.com.

**MACKINNON, MALCOLM D(AVID),** retired insurance company executive; b. Guelph, Ont., Can., Mar. 9, 1931; came to U.S., 1955; s. A.L. and Jean (Butchart) MacK.; m. Betty Campbell, June 18, 1955; children: Sandra, Katherine, Donald. BA, U. Toronto, 1953. CLU; chartered fin. analyst. With Prudential Ins. Co., 1954-94, v.p. Newark, 1979-81, sr. v.p., 1981—94; ret., 1994. Commentator pub. radio. Trustee Kean Coll., Union, N.J., 1990-93, Millburn Free Pub. Libr., 1996-2005, pres., 1997-2000; chmn. Milburn Short Hills chpt. ARC, 1992-94. Fellow Soc. Actuaries; mem. Canoe Brook Country Club (Summit, N.J.). Home: 23 Grosvenor Rd Short Hills NJ 07078-1639

**MACKINNON, REBECCA,** media consultant, researcher; Grad. magna cum laude, Harvard U. Taiwan stringer Newsweek mag., 1991—92; bur. asst. CNN, Beijing, 1992—93, assoc. prodr., 1993—96, prodr., correspondent, 1997—98, bur. chief, 1998—2001, Tokyo, 2001—03; media cons., 2004—; fellow Shorenstein Ctr. on the Press Harvard U., 2004; rsch. fellow Berkman Ctr. for Internet and Society Harvard Law Sch., 2004—; co-founder Global Voices Online. Office: Harvard Law Sch Baker House 1587 Massachusetts Ave Cambridge MA 02138 Office Phone: 617-495-7547. Office Fax: 617-812-7950. E-mail: rmackinnon@cyber.law.harvard.edu.*

**MACKINNON, RODERICK,** neuroscientist, educator; b. Burlington, Mass., 1956; married. BA, Brandeis U., 1978; MD, Tufts U., 1982, PhD (hon.), 2002. Postdoctoral fellow Beth Israel Hosp., Harvard U., 1985—86, Brandeis U., 1986—89; from asst. to prof. dept. neurobiology Harvard Med. Sch., 1989—96; John D. Rockefeller Jr. prof. lab. molecular neurobiology and biophysics Rockefeller U., 1996—. Recipient W. Alden Spencer award, Young Investigator award, Biophysical Soc., 1995, Newcomb Cleveland prize, AAAS, 1998, Albert Lasker Basic Med. Rsch. award, 1999, Lewis S. Rosentiel award, 2000, Gairdner Found. Internat. award, 2001, Nobel prize for chemistry, 2003; grantee, Howard Hughes Med. Inst. Chevy Chase, Md., 1997—. Mem.: NAS, Alpha Omega Med. Honor Soc. Avocation: trout fishing. Office: Rockefeller Univ 1230 York Ave New York NY 10021 also: Howard Hughes Med Inst 4000 Jones Bridge Rd Chevy Chase MD 20815-6789*

**MACKINNON, ROGER ALAN,** psychiatrist, educator; b. Feb. 13, 1927; Student, Princeton U., 1944-46; MD, Columbia U., 1950, cert. in psycoanalytic medicine, 1957. Diplomate Am. Bd. Psychiatry and Neurology. Intern E.W. Sparrow Hosp., Lansing, Mich., 1950-51; resident in psychiatry N.Y. State Psychiat. Inst., N.Y.C., 1951-52, 52-54; chief psychiatry Vanderbilt Clinic, Presbyn. Hosp., N.Y.C., 1959-77; prof. clin. psychiatry Coll. Physicians & Surgeons, Columbia U., N.Y.C., 1986-97, prof. emeritus, 1997—; tng., supervising analyst Columbia U. Psychoanalytic Ctr., 1970—, asst. dir. for selection, 1981-91, dir., 1991-97; attending psychiatrist Presbyn. Hosp., N.Y.C., 1977—; N.Y. State Psychiatric Inst., N.Y.C., 1972—. Asst. examiner Am. Bd. Psychiatry and Neurology, 1960-70; cons., lectr. in field. Co-author textbook: The Psychiatric Interview, 1971, The Psychiatric Evaluation, 1986; contbr. articles to profl. jours., chpts. to books. Lt. USNR, 1952-54. Fellow Am. Psychiat. Assn. (life), N.Y. Acad. Medicine; mem. Am. Psychoanalytic Assn., Assn. Psychoanalytic Medicine (George E. Daniels Merit award 1995), N.Y. Psychoanalytic Soc. (pres. 1987-88), N.Y. Psychiat. Inst. (Centennial award 1996). Avocations: woodworking, boating, hiking. Home: 11 Edgewood St Tenafly NJ 07670-2909 Office: 11 E 87th St New York NY 10128-0527 Office Phone: 212-289-0511.

**MACKINNON, STEPHEN R.,** Asian studies administrator, educator; b. Columbus, Nebr., Dec. 2, 1940; s. Cyrus Leland and Helen (Wigglesworth) MacK.; m. Janice Carolyn Rachie, July 15, 1967 (dec. Sept. 1999); children: Rebecca, Cyrus R. BA, Yale U., 1963, MA, 1964; PhD, U. Calif., Davis, 1971. Acting instr. Chinese U. Hong Kong, 1968-69; dir. Asian Studies, prof. history Ariz. State U., Tempe, 1971—; vis. assoc. Chinese Acad. Social Sci., Beijing, 1979-81, 85. Mem. U.S. State Dept. Selection Bd., Washington, 1991, Nat. Com. on U.S.-China Rels., N.Y.C., 1991—; cons. PBS film documentary "Dragon and Eagle." Author: Power/Politics China, 1980; co-author: Agnes Smedley, 1988, China Reporting, 1987; co-editor: Chinese Women Revolution, 1976 (ALA notable book 1976), Scars of War, 2001; lectr. on China to local orgns. and TV, 1981—. Commr. Phoenix Sister Cities, 1986-91; bd. dirs. Com. on Fgn. Rels., Phoenix, 1988—; bd. dirs. Marshall

---

Fund Ariz., 1995—. Rsch. fellow Am. Coun. Learned Socs., Hong Kong, 1978, Fulbright Found., India, 1977-78; rsch. sr. Com. on Scholarly Com. People's Republic China, Washington-Beijing, 1992, Pacific Cultural Found., 1999, Am. Inst. Indian Studies, 2003, Fulbright-Hays ACLS, China, 2005—. Mem. Assn. Asian Studies (bd. dirs. 1990-91), Am. Hist. Assn. (program com. 1990-91). Avocations: tennis, hiking, jazz. Office: Ariz State U Dept History Tempe AZ 85287-4302 Office Phone: 480-965-6692. E-mail: stephen.mackinnon@asu.edu.

**MACKINTOSH, FREDERICK ROY,** oncologist; b. Miami, Fla., Oct. 4, 1943; s. John Harris and Mary Carlotta (King) MacK.; m. Judith Jane Parnell, Oct. 12, 1961 (div. Aug. 1977); children: Lisa Lynn, Wendy Sue; m. Claudia Lizanne Flournoy, Jan. 7, 1984; 1 child, Gregory Warren. BS, MIT, 1964, PhD, 1968; MD, U. Miami, 1976. Intern then resident in gen. medicine Stanford (Calif.) U., 1976-78, fellow in oncology, 1978-81; asst. prof. med. U. Nev., Reno, 1981-85, assoc. prof., 1985-92, prof. medicine, 1992—. Contbr. articles to profl. jours. Fellow ACP; mem. Am. Soc. Clin. Oncology, Am. Cancer Soc. (pres. Nev. chpt. 1987-89, Washoe chpt. 1988-90), No. Nev. Cancer Coun. (bd. dirs. 1981-92), No. Calif. Cancer Program (bd. dirs. alt. 1983-87, bd. dirs. 1987-91). Avocations: bicycling, sporting clays. Office: Med Sch Assocs North Ste 302 1500 E 2nd St Reno NV 89502 Office Phone: 775-784-7500. E-mail: roy.mackintosh@va.gov.

**MACKLEM, MICHAEL KIRKPATRICK,** publisher; b. Toronto, Ont., Can., July 12, 1928; s. Anne Woodburne Hardy, Dec. 30, 1950; children— Timothy Street, Nicholas Hardy. BA, U. Toronto, 1950; AM (Charles Scribner fellow), Princeton U., 1952, PhD (Porter Ogden Jacobus fellow, Royal Soc. Can. fellow), 1954. Instr., English Yale U., New Haven, 1954-55; staff editor Ency. Canadiana, 1955-58; asst. to dir. Humanities Research Council of Can., 1958-60; gen. mgr. Oberon Press, Ottawa, Ont., 1966-85. Pres. Michael, Hardy, Ltd., Ottawa, 1972— Author: The Anatomy of the World: Relations Between Natural and Moral Law from Donne to Pope, 1958, God Have Mercy: The Life of John Fisher of Rochester, 1967, Cinderella, 1969, Voyages to New France 1615-1618, 1970, Voyages to New France 1599-1603, 1971, The Sleeping Beauty, 1973, Jacques the Woodcutter, 1977, Liberty and the Holy City, 1978, The Oberon Reader, 1991, The Oberon Poetry Collection, 1992. Can. Council fellow, 1964-65 Home: 555 Maple Ln Ottawa ON Canada K1M 0N7 Office: Oberon Press 205-145 Spruce St Ottawa ON Canada K1R 6PI E-mail: oberon@sympatico.ca.

**MACKLIN, CROFFORD JOHNSON, JR.,** lawyer; b. Columbus, Ohio, Sept. 10, 1947; S. Crofford Johnson, Sr. and Dorothy Ann (Stevens) M.; m. Mary Carole Ward, July 5, 1969; children: Carrie E., David J. BA, Ohio State U., 1969; BA summa cum laude, U. West Fla., 1974; JD cum laude, Ohio State U., 1976. Bar: Ohio 1977, U.S. Tax Ct. 1978. Acct. Touche Ross, Columbus, 1976-77; assoc. Smith & Schnacke, Dayton, 1977-81; ptnr. Porter, Wright, Morris & Arthur, Dayton, 1983-88; shareholder Smith & Schnacke, 1988-89; ptnr. Thompson, Hine LLP, 1989—, practice group leader pers. and succession planning, 2001—; sole practice Dayton, 1981-82. Adj. faculty Franklin U., 1977; adj. prof. U. Dayton Law Sch., 1981. Contbr. articles to profl. jours. Bd. dirs. Great Lakes Nat. Bank Ohio, 1997, Easter Seals, 1984-86. Served to capt. USMCR, 1969-74. Fellow Am. Coll. Trust and Estate Counsel; mem. ABA, Dayton Bar Assn. (chmn. probate com. 1981-83), Dayton Trust & Estate Planning (pres. 1983-84), Ohio Bar Assn. Presbyterian. Home: 7276 Wetherington Dr West Chester OH 45069 Office: Thompson Hine LLP 2000 Courthouse Pla NE PO Box 8801 Dayton OH 45401-8801 Office Phone: 937-443-6730.

**MACKLIN, PHILIP ALAN,** retired physics professor; b. Richmond Hill, N.Y., Apr. 13, 1925; s. Egbert Chalmer and Margaret Griswold (Collins) M.; m. Cora Baldwin Galindo, Sept. 5, 1953 (dec. Feb. 2005); children: Susan, Steven, Peter. BS cum laude, Yale U., 1944; MA, Columbia U., 1949, PhD, 1956. Physicist Carbide & Carbon Chems. Corp., Oak Ridge, 1946-47; research scientist AEC, Columbia U., 1949-51; instr. physics Middlebury Coll., Vt., 1951-54, acting chmn. dept., 1953-54; mem. faculty Miami U., Oxford, Ohio, 1954—, prof. physics, 1961-93, chmn. dept., 1972-85, prof. emeritus, 1993—; ret., 1993. Research scientist Armco Steel Co., summers 1955-56; vis. prof. U. N.Mex., summers 1957-68, Boston U., fall 1985-86; physicist Los Alamos Sci. Labs., summers 1960-62; participant NSF summer insts., 1970-71; vis. scientist MIT, 1985-86 Author publs. in field; patentee in field. Vestryman Holy Trinity Episcopal Ch., Oxford, 1959-61, 67, 71-73, 75-77, mem. fin. com., chmn. blood assurance program, 1980—, lector, 1989— With USN, 1944-46. Mem. AAAS, LWV of Oxford (treas. 1986-88, dir. governance 1997—), Am. Phys. soc., Forum Physics and Soc., Kiwanis (bd. dirs. 1996-97), Torch Club of Butler County (pres. 1982-83, 96-97, mem. editl. adv. com. The Torch), 1809 Club (pres. 1964-65), Campus Ministry Ctr. (trustee 1994-2002), Union of Concerned Scientists, Ctr. for Voting and Democracy (charter), Membership Assn. Miami U. Art Mus. (exec. com. 1999-2002), Phi Beta Kappa (pres. Iota of Ohio chpt. 1988-89), Sigma Xi, Sigma Pi Sigma, Omicron Delta Kappa. Democrat. Home: 211 Oakhill Dr Oxford OH 45056-2710 Office: Culler Hall Miami Univ Oxford OH 45056 Office Phone: 513-529-5625. E-mail: macklipa@muohio.edu.

**MACKLIN, RUTH,** bioethics educator; b. Newark, Mar. 27, 1938; d. Hyman and Frieda (Yaruss) Chimacoff; m. Martin Macklin, Sept. 1, 1957 (div. June 1969); children: Meryl, Shelley Macklin Taylor. BA with distinction, Cornell U., 1958; MA in Philosophy, Case Western Res. U., 1966, PhD in Philosophy, 1968. Instr. in philosophy Case Western Res. U., Cleve., 1967—68, asst. prof., 1968—71, assoc. prof., 1971—76; assoc. for behavioral studies The Hastings Ctr., Hastings-on-Hudson, NY, 1976—80; vis. assoc. prof. Albert Einstein Coll. Medicine, Bronx, NY, 1977—78, assoc. prof., 1978—84, prof. dept. epidemiology and social medicine, 1984—. Cons. NIH, 1986—; advisor WHO, Geneva, 1989—; mem. White House Adv. Com. on Human Radiation Experiments, Washington 1994; chair ethical rev. com. UNAIDS, Geneva, 1996—2000. Author: Man, Mind and Morality, 1982, Mortal Choices, 1987, Enemies of Patients, 1993, Surrogates and Other Mothers, 1994, Against Relativism, 1999, Double Standards in Medical Research, 2004; contbr. articles to ethics, law and med. jours. Fellow: APHA, Am. Soc. Law, Medicine and Ethics, Inst. Medicine NAS, The Hastings Ctr., Am. Philosophys. Assn. (life); mem.: Am. Soc. Bioethics and Humanities (bd. dirs. 1997—99), Internat. Assn. Bioethics (bd. dirs., pres. 1999—2001). Democrat. Office: A Einstein Coll Medicine Dept Epidemiology Population Health 1300 Morris Park Ave Bronx NY 10461-1926 E-mail: macklin@aecom.yu.edu.

**MACKLIS, ROGER MILTON,** physician, educator, researcher; Stamford, Conn., Mar. 12, 1956; m. Carol Clark, July 25, 1987; children: Andrew Clark, Paul Clark. BS, MS, Yale U., 1978; MD, Harvard U., 1983. Diplomate Am Bd Radiation Oncology. Instr. Harvard Med. Sch., Boston, 1988-89, asst. prof. radiation oncology, 1989-93; dep. div. chief Children's Hosp., Boston, 1990-93; chmn. dept. radiation oncology Cleve. Clinic Found., 1993—. Biomedical consult, Boston, 1989—; assoc prof hist med Case Western Res Univ, 1995—; prof. medicine Cleve. Clin. Lerner Coll. of Medicine, 2004—. Author: (book) Manual of Introductory Clinical Medicine, 1984; contbr. articles to profl jours. Recipient Resident Research Award, ASTRO, 1988, Jr Faculty Research Award, Am Cancer Soc, 1990. Mem.: Soc Chairs of Acad Radiation Oncology Programs (treas, vpres, pres), Am Soc Therapeutic Radiology and Oncology, Am Soc Clin Oncology (Young Investigator Award 1987), Radiation Research Soc. Achievements include research in research on new approaches to cancer treatment involving radioactively labeled molecules and novel technologies for minimizing medical errors in oncology. Office: Cleve Clinic Found Dept Radiation Oncology 9500 Euclid Ave Cleveland OH 44195-0001 Office Phone: 216-444-5576. Business E-Mail: macklir@ccf.org.

**MACKNIGHT, CAROL BERNIER,** educational association administrator; b. Quincy, Mass., Apr. 12, 1938; d. Harold Nelson and Marguerite (Norris) Bernier; m. William J. MacKnight, Aug. 19, 1967. BS, Ithaca Coll., N.Y., 1960; MM, Manhattan Sch. Mus., N.Y.C., 1961; Dipl., Fontainebleau Sch.

Music/Art, France, 1968; EdD, U. Mass., 1973. Asst. to supt. Falmouth (Mass.) pub. schs., 1975-76; dir. bus., mgmt., engring. prog. Sch. Bus. Adminstrn. U. Mass., Amherst, 1976-79, assoc. dir. continuing edn., 1979-82, dir. Office Instructional Tech., 1982—93. Trustee New Eng. Regional Computer Program, Inc., 1986—92; bd. dirs. Info. Sys. and Bus. Exch., 1992—93; keynote spkr. Australian Soc. for Computers in Learning In Tertiary Edn. Conf., Adelaide, 1996; conf. chair Transforming Practice with Tech., 2002. Editor: Jour. Computing in Higher Edn., 1988—, Jour. Info. Sys. for Mgrs., 1992—93; mem. editl. rev. bd.: Jour. of Computer-Based Instrn., 1988—2002, author/editor: computer progs.; contbr. articles to profl. jours. Grantee, CDC, 1986, Regents of Boston, 1988; Lilly Fellow Mentor, 1991—92. Mem. ACM, Assn. for Computing Machinery, Educom, Soc. Applied Learning Techs. (bd. dirs. 2003—), New England Regional Computer Program. Avocations: music, photography, tennis, hiking, skiing. Office: Norris Consulting and Pub PO Box 2593 Amherst MA 01004 Business E-Mail: cmacknight@oit.umass.edu.

**MACKNIGHT, WILLIAM JOHN,** chemist, educator; b. NYC, May 5, 1936; s. William John and Margaret Ann (Stuart) M.; m. Carol Marie Bernier, Aug. 19, 1967 BS, Rochester U., 1958; MA, Princeton U., 1963, PhD, 1964. Rsch. assoc. Princeton U., 1964-65; asst. prof. chemistry U. Mass., Amherst, 1965-69, assoc. prof. chemistry, 1969-74, prof. chemistry, 1974-76, dept. head polymer sci., 1976-85, prof. polymer sci. and engring., 1985-88, 95-96, head dept. polymer sci. and engring., 1988-95, disting. univ. prof., 1996-98, Wilmer D. Barret disting. prof., 1998-99, Wilmer D. Barret Disting. prof. emeritus, 1999—. Mem. sci. and tech. adv. bd. Alcoa, Pitts., 1984-86, Diversitech Gen., Akron, Ohio, 1985-89; mem. panel for materials sci. Nat. Bur. Standards, Washington, 1983-89. Author: Polymeric Sulfur and Related Polymers, 1965; Introduction to Polymer Viscoelasticity, 3d edit., 2005. Served to lt. USN, 1958-61 Recipient Ford prize in high polymer physics Am. Phys. Soc., 1984, award for disting. svc. in the advancement of polymer sci. Japan Soc. for Polymer Sci., 1998; Guggenheim fellow, 1985 Fellow: AAAS, Am. Phys. Soc. (exec. com. 1975—76); mem.: Am. Chem. Soc. (award in polymer chemistry 1997, Herman F. Mark award, polymers chemistry divsn. 2002, Flory award, polymer chemistry divsn. 2006), Nat. Acad. Engring., Cosmos Club. Avocations: music, sports. Home: 127 Sunset Ave Amherst MA 01002-2019 Office: U Mass Polymer Sci & Engring Cntr Conte Bldg Amherst MA 01003 Office Phone: 413-577-1412. Business E-Mail: wmacknight@polysci.umass.edu.

**MACKOWIAK, PHILP ARTHUR,** medical educator, epidemiologist; b. Richmond, Va., Sept. 15, 1945; s. Stephen Casimir and Grace Marie Mackowiak; m. Connie Lyn Gooch, Feb. 28, 1947; children: Stephanie Lee, Rebecca Lyn. BS, Bucknell U., Lewisburg, Pa., 1966; MD, U. Md. Sch. Medicine, Balt., 1970; MBA, Johns Hopkins U., Balt., 2003. Lic. med. dr. Nat. Bd. Med. Examiners, 1972, cert. internal medicine Am. Bd. Internal Medicine, 1972, infectious diseases Subspecialty Bd. of Am. Bd. Internal Medicine, 1972. Med. resident U. Md. Sch. Medicine, Balt., 1970—72; epidemic intelligence officer Centers Disease Control, Atlanta, 1972—74; infectious diseases fellow U. Tex. Southwestern Med. Sch., Dallas, 1974—75, instr. to prof. medicine, 1975—88; chief med. care clin. ctr. Va Md. Healthcare Ctr., Balt., 1988—; prof. and vice chmn. dept. medicine U. Md. Sch. Medicine, Baltimore, Md., 1988—. Epidemiologist La. Dept. Health, New Orleans, 1972—74; instr. La. State U., New Orleans, 1972—74, John Peter Smith Hosp., Fort Worth, Tex., 1974—88; cons. Un Relief Ops., N.Y.C., 1974, Consumer Reports On Health, Ortho Pharmaceuticals, Bridgewater, NJ, 1988, Govt. Of Kuwait, 1992, Waverly Press, Balt., 1994, Beckton Dickinson Diagnostic Instrument Systems, 1996—96, Bayer Corp., West Haven, Conn., 1997—97, Neuroleptic Malignant Syndrome Info. Svc., 2000—; editl. bd. alumni bull. U. Md. Sch. Medicine, Balt., 1993—; editl. bd. Infectious Diseases Practice (Jour.), Boston, 1996—2002; editor Am. Jour. Med. Sci., Hagerstown, Md., 1999—2005; guest editor med. jour. Med Chi, Balt., 1999—99; sect. editor Current Treatment Options In Infectious Diseases (Jour.), 2002—02; editl. bd. Infectious Jour. Medicine, Netherlands, 2002—; editor Transactions Am. Clin. And Climatol. Assn., 2005—. Author: Post Mortem. Solving History's Great Medical Mysteries; editor: Symposium Marking Four Millennia Of Antipyretic Therapy; author and editor: Fever. Basic Mechanisms And Management (2 Editions); contbr. chapters to books, articles to profl. jours. Lt. comdr. CDC USPH, 1972—74. Named Top Doc, Balt. Mag., 2002; recipient Alexander D. Langmuir award, Ctr. Disease Control, 1974, Governor's Salute To Excellence, State Of Md., 1991, faculty awards, U. Md. Sch. Medicine, 1993—2003, 2006; fellow, Infectious Diseases Soc. Am., 1986, ACP, 1989. Fellow: ACP (gov. md. chpt. 2002—06, chpt. excellence awards 2002, 2003, 2004, 2005), Infectious Diseases Soc. Am. (editor Clin. Infectious Diseases (jour.) 1994—, publications com. 1994—98); mem.: Balt. Monthly Med. Reunion (sec. 2003—06), Am. Clin. And Climatol. Assn. (recorder 2005—06), Assn. Profs. Medicine, Assn. Va. Chiefs of Medicine (coun. mem. 1998—2002), Amercian Soc. Microbiology, Alpha Omega Alpha. Office: Va Md Health Care Sys Med Svc 111 10 N Greene St Baltimore MD 21201 Office Phone: 410-605-7199. Home Fax: 410-605-7849; Office Fax: 410-605-7849. Business E-Mail: philip.mackowiak@med.va.gov.

**MACKOWSKI, JOHN JOSEPH,** retired insurance company executive; b. Westport, Mass., Feb. 1, 1926; s. John J. and Victoria K. (Skript) Mieczkowski; m. Ruth Williams, Feb. 3, 1951; children: Martha, John Matthew, Daniel, Joan. AB, Duke U., 1948; student, Harvard Advanced Mgmt. Program, 1970, 71. With Ins. Co. of N.Am., Boston, Phila., Chgo., 1948-51; with Atlantic Mut. Ins. Co., N.Y.C., 1951-88, chmn., CEO, to 1988. Bd. dirs. Transatlantic Holdings, Inc. 1st lt. USMCR, 1943-46. Mem. Sawgrass Club (Ponte Vedra Beach, Fla.), Acoaxet Country Club (Westport Harbor, Mass.), Spindle Rock Yacht Club, Sigma Chi, Beta Lambda. Episcopalian. Home: 19 Village Walk Cir Ponte Vedra Beach FL 32082-3500 also: 19 Village Walk Cir Ponte Vedra FL 32082-3543 E-Mail: jmackowski@aol.com.

**MACKS, RYAN JEFFREY,** psychologist; b. Silver Spring, Md., June 14, 1977; s. Marshall Jay and Nancy Howe Macks. PhD, U. of Va., 2004. Staff psychologist Cin. Children's Hosp. Med. Ctr., Cin., 2004—. Vol. staff mem. Save The Animals Found. (S.T.A.F.), Cin., 2004—06. Libertarian. Home: 3827 Paxton Ave Apt 1011 Cincinnati OH 45209 Personal E-Mail: littlekingryan@hotmail.com.

**MACKWELL, STEPHEN JOSEPH,** geophysicist, educator; b. Christchurch, New Zealand, June 5, 1956; arrived in U.S., 1984; s. Alan Gordon Mackwell and Mary Veronica (Carter) Francis; m. Kathleen Garland, March 27, 2004. BSc in Physics and Math., U. Canterbury, Christchurch, New Zealand, 1978, MSc in Physics, 1979; diploma of edn., Christchurch Tchrs. Coll., New Zealand, 1979; PhD in Geophysics, Australian Nat. U., Canberra, 1985. Postdoctoral assoc. Cornell U., Ithaca, NY, 1984-86, rsch. fellow, 1984—87; asst. prof. Pa. State U., University Park, 1987—92, assoc. prof., 1992—98; prof. exptl. geophysics Bayerisches Geoinst., Germany, 1998—2000, dir., 2000—02, Lunar and Planetary Inst., Houston, 2002—. Program dir. for geophysics, divsn. of earth sci.. NSF, Washington, 1993-94, expert cons., 1995; panelist proposal rev. NASA, Houston, 1994-95; expert rev. Geoscis. Rsch. program, Dept. Energy, 1993; mem. rev. panel Planetary Geology and Geophysics program, NASA, 1994-96, 2002-, group chief, 1996-98, 2004, panel chief, 2005—. Assoc. editor Jour. Geophys. Rsch. - Solid Earth, 1992—97, mem. editl. bd. Physics of the Earth and Planetary Interiors, 1992—98, Tectonophysics, 2002; editor: (Solid Earth) Geophys. Rsch. Letters, 2000—01; editor-in-chief Geophys. Rsch. Letters, 2002—05; contbr. articles to profl. jours. Recipient Stipendiat der Alexander von Humboldt-Stiftung, Bayreuth, Germany, 1996; grantee, NSF, 1988—98, NASA, 1993—98. Fellow: Mineral. Soc. Am.; mem.: AAAS, Am. Geophys. Union (mem. meetings program com. 1988—91, mem. mineral acquisition and distbn. subcom. 1989—90, mem. phys. properties of Earth materials com., tectonophysics section 1989—91, mem. mineral physics com. 1990—92, mem. 75th anniversary com. 1992—94, mem. meetings com. 1992—96, mem. mineral and rock physics com. 2000—03, mineral physics

editor for EOS trans. 1990—92, editor-in-chief, frontiers in mineral physics 1988). Office: Lunar & Planetary Inst USRA Ctr Advanced Space Studies 3600 Bay Area Blvd Houston TX 77058

**MACLACHLAN, DOUGLAS LEE,** marketing educator; b. Hollywood, Calif., Aug. 27, 1940; s. Alexander D. and Patricia E. (Culver) MacL.; m. Natalie Bowditch Knauth, July 23, 1966; children: Heather Bowditch, Trevor Douglas. AB in Physics, U. Calif., Berkeley, 1962, MBA, 1965, MA in Stats., 1970, PhD in Bus. Adminstrn., 1971; student, Hastings Sch. Law, 1965—66. Instr. bus. adminstrn. U. Calif., Berkeley, 1969-70; v.p. Hartec Corp., Newport Beach, Calif., 1965-70; acting asst. prof. U. Wash., Seattle, 1970-71, asst. prof., 1971-74, assoc. prof., 1974-78, chair dept. mktg. and internat. bus., 1978—86, 1993—94, 2006—, Affiliate Program Disting. prof. mktg. and internat. bus., 1986-88, Nordstrom prof. retail mktg., 1988-89, Ford Motor Co. prof. mktg., 1989-90, assoc. dean Sch. Bus., 1995-99, prof. mktg., 1999—, faculty dir. Internat. Alliances, 2003—06. Vis. prof. bus. adminstrn. U. Calif., Berkeley, 1974; vis. prof. Institut Europeen des Affaires, Fontainebleau, France, 1982—83, Cath. U. Leuven, Belgium, 1991—92, Koc U., Istanbul, 2001; dir. Univ. Book Store, 1985—2002, 2004—. Contbr. articles to profl. jours.; mem. editl. bd.: Jour. Mktg. Rsch., 1975-81. Mem. Am. Mktg. Assn. (dir. Puget Sound chpt. 1975-77, 90-91, pres. 1978-79), Informs, Am. Statis. Assn., Assn. Consumer Rsch., Clan MacLachlan Soc. (pres. n.w. br. 1995—), Alpha Kappa Psi, Kappa Delta Rho, Beta Gamma Sigma. Home: 16305 Inglewood Rd NE Kenmore WA 98028-3908 Office: U Washington Box 353200 Seattle WA 98195-3200 Office Phone: 206-543-4369. E-mail: macnat01@hotmail.com.

**MACLACHLAN, KYLE,** actor; b. Yakima, WA, Feb. 22, 1960; m. Desiree Gruber, 2002. BFA, U. Wash., Seattle, 1981. Actor: (films) Dune, 1984, Blue Velvet, 1986, The Hidden, 1987, Don't Tell Her It's Me, 1990, The Doors, 1991, Twin Peaks: Fire Walk with Me, 1992, Where the Day Takes You, 1992, Rich in Love, 1993, The Trial, 1993, The Flintstones, 1994, Showgirls, 1995, The Trigger Effect, 1996, Mad Dog Time, 1996, One Night Stand, 1997, Hamlet, 1999, Perfume, 2001, Me Without You, 2001, Miranda, 2002, Northfork, 2003, Touch of Pink, 2004; TV series Twin Peaks, 1990-91 (Golden Globe award, 1991), Sex and the City, 2000; TV movies: Against the Wall, 1994, Roswell, 1994, Moonshine Highway, 1996, Thunder Point, 1996, Route 9, 1998, The Spring, 2000; dir. (TV series) Tales from the Crypt, 1989; TV guest appearance Miami Vice, 1988. Address: Industry Entertainment Ste 300 955 S Carrillo Dr Los Angeles CA 90048 also: ICM 8942 Wilshire Blvd Beverly Hills CA 90211

**MACLACHLAN, PATRICIA,** author; b. Cheyenne, Wyo., Mar. 3, 1938; d. Philo and Madonna (Moss) Pritzkau; m. Robert MacLachlan, Apr. 14, 1962; children: John, Jamie, Emily. BA, U. Conn., 1962. Tchr. English Bennett Jr. High Sch., Manchester, Conn., 1963-79. Vis. lectr. Smith Coll., Northampton, Mass., 1986. Author: The Sick Day, 1979, Arthur, for the Very First Time, 1980 (Golden Kite award Soc. Children's Book Writers 1980), Moon, Stars, Frogs, and Friends, 1980, Through Grandpa's Eyes, 1980, Cassie Binegar, 1982, Mama One, Mama Two, 1982, Tomorrow's Wizard, 1982, Seven Kisses in a Row, 1983, Unclaimed Treasures, 1984 (Boston Globe/Horn Book award 1984), Sarah, Plain and Tall, 1985 (Golden Kite award 1985, Scott O'Dell Historical Fiction award 1985, John Newbery medal 1986, Jefferson Cup award Va. Libr. Assn. 1986, Christopher award 1986, Garden State Children's Book award N.J. Libr. Assn. 1988), The Facts and Fictions of Minna Pratt, 1988 (Parent's Choice award Parent's Choice Found. 1988), Three Names, 1991, Journey, 1991, All the Places to Love, 1993, Baby, 1993, Skylark, 1994, What You Know First, 1995, Caleb's Story, 2001, More Perfect Than The Moon, 2004, Who Loves Me?, 2005; author (screenplays): Sarah Plain and Tall, 1988, Skylark, 1992, Journey, 1992. Bd. dirs. Children's Aid Family Svc. Agency, 1970-80. Recipient numerous awards for children's fiction. Office: Curtis Brown Ltd c/o Marilyn Marlow 10 Astor Pl Fl 3D New York NY 10003-6935

**MACLAINE, SHIRLEY,** actress; b. Richmond, Va., Apr. 24, 1934; d. Ira O. and Kathlyn (MacLean) Beatty; m. Steve Parker, Sept. 17, 1954 (div. 1982); 1 child, Stephanie Sachiko. Broadway appearances include Me and Juliet, 1953, Pajama Game, 1954, films appearances The Trouble With Harry, 1954, Artists and Models, 1954, Around the World in 80 Days, 1955-56, Hot Spell, 1957, The Matchmaker, 1957, The Sheepman, 1957, Some Came Running, 1958 (Fgn. Press award 1959), Ask Any Girl, 1959 (Silver Bear award as best actress Internat. Berlin Film Festival), Career, 1959, Can-Can, 1959, The Apartment, 1959 (Best Actress prize Venice Film Festival), Children's Hour, 1960, The Apartment, 1960, Two for the Seesaw, 1962, Irma La Douce, 1963, What A Way to Go, The Yellow Rolls Royce, 1964, John Goldfarb Please Come Home, 1965, Gambit and Woman Times Seven, 1967, The Bliss of Mrs. Blossom, Sweet Charity, 1969, Two Mules for Sister Sara, 1969, Desperate Characters, 1971, The Possession of Joel Delaney, 1972, The Other Half of the Sky: A China Memoir, 1975, The Turning Point, 1977, Being There, 1979, A Change of Seasons, 1980, Loving Couples, 1980, Terms of Endearment, 1983 (Acad. award 1984, Golden Globe-Best Actress), Cannonball Run II, 1984, Madame Sousatzka, 1988 (Best Actress Venice Film Festival, Golden Globe-Best Actress), Steel Magnolias, 1989, Waiting For the Light, 1990, Postcards From the Edge, 1990, Defending Your Life, 1991, Used People, 1992, Wrestling Ernest Hemingway, 1993, Guarding Tess, 1994, Evening Star, 1995, Mrs. Winterbourne, 1996, Carolina, 2003, Bewitched, 2005, In Her Shoes, 2005, Rumor Has It..., 2005; TV appearances Shirley's World, 1971-72, Shirley MacLean: If They Could See Me Now, 1974-75, Gypsy in My Soul, 1975-76, Where Do We Go From Here?, 1976-77, Shirley MacLaine at the Lido, 1979, Shirley MacLaine...Every Little Movement, 1980 (Emmy award 1980), TV movie appearances Out On A Limb, 1987, The West Side Waltz, 1995, Joan of Arc, 1999, These Old Broads, 2001, Hell on Heels: The Battle of Mary Kay, 2002, TV mini-series Salem Witch Trials, 2002; (directorial debut) Bruno, 2000; co-dir. documentary: China The Other Half of the Sky; star U.S. tour stage musical Out There Tonight, 1990; author: Don't Fall Off the Mountain, 1970, The New Celebrity Cookbook, 1973, You Can Get There From Here, 1975, Out on a Limb, 1983, Dancing in the Light, 1985, It's All in the Playing, 1987, Going Within: A Guide for Inner Transformation, 1989, Dance While You Can, 1991; editor: McGovern: The Man and His Beliefs, 1972, My Lucky Stars, 1995, The Camino, 2000, Out On A Leash: Exploring The Nature of Reality and Love, 2003. Address: C/O ICM 8942 Wilshire Blvd Beverly Hills CA 90211-1934*

**MACLAREN, ROY,** retired Canadian government official; b. Vancouver, B.C., Can., Oct. 26, 1934; s. Wilbur and Anne (Graham) MacLaren; m. Alethea Mitchell, June 25, 1959; children: Ian, Vanessa, Malcolm. BA, U. B.C., 1955; MA, U. Cambridge, Eng., 1957; postgrad., Harvard U., 1974; MDiv, U. Toronto, 1991, DCL (hon.), 1996; DHL (hon.), U. N. Ala.; LLD (hon.), U. N.B., U. P.E.I. Fgn. svc. officer Can. Diplomatic Svc., 1957-69; dir. corporate pub. affairs Massey-Ferguson Ltd., Toronto, Ont., 1969-74; chmn., CEO Ogilvy & Mather, Toronto, 1974-76; chmn. C.B. Media Ltd., 1976-93; mem. Parliament of Can., 1979-84, 88-96, parliamentary sec. to min. of energy, mines and resources, 1980-82, min. of state (fin.), 1983-84, min. of nat. revenue, 1984, min. of internat. trade, 1993-96; high commr. for Can. to U.K. of Gt. Britain and No. Ireland, 1996-2000; ret., 2000. Bd. dirs. Std. Life, Brascan, Patheon, Algoma Ctrl. Author: (book) Canadians in Russia: 1918-19, 1976, Canadians on the Nile, 1882-1898, 1978, Canadians Behind Enemy Lines, 1939-1945, 1981, Honourable Mentions, 1986, African Exploits: The Diaries of William Stairs, 1998, Commission High, 2006; contbr. articles to profl. jours. Commr. Trilateral Commn.; chmn. Can. Inst. Internat. Affairs, Can.-India Bus. Coun.; com. mem. Internat. Inst. Strategic Studies, Ditchley Found. Hon. col. 7th Toronto Rgt. Royal Can. Arty. Mem.: Pratt's (London), White's (London), Rideau Club (Ottawa), Toronto Club, Royal Can. Yacht Club. Address: 425 Russell Hill Rd Toronto ON Canada M5P 2S4

**MACLAREN, WILLIAM GEORGE, JR.,** engineering executive; b. Chgo., May 6, 1928; s. William George Sr. and Dorothy Pauline (Costello) MacL.; m. Marie Lorraine Logan, Sept. 15, 1951 (div. Dec. 1977); children: Vanessa Ann MacLaren-Wray, Jon. Mark, Scott William; m. Mary Patricia Loftus, Dec. 22, 1977 (div. Oct. 1995); m. Brigitte Hildegard Krakau, Apr. 19,

1997. BS in Indsl. Engring., U. Pitts., 1951; MS in Indsl. Engring., Syracuse U., N.Y., 1958; PhD in Indsl. Mgmt., Columbia Pacific U., 1989. Commd. 2nd lt. USAF, 1951, advanced through grades to major gen., 1974; comdr. 5BW Minot AFB, ND, 1972-74; chief of staff 15 AF, 1975; comdr. Pacific Comm. Area, 1975-78; vice comdr. Air Force Comm. Command, 1978-79; dir. Command Control and Comm. Hdqs. USAF, 1979-81; dir. Comm. and Info. Sys. NATO, 1981-84; ret. USAF, 1984; v.p. Gia, Inc., Arlington, Va., 1984-90, 1993-95; gen. NATO/NATO Air Command and Control Mgmt. Agy., Brussels, 1990-93; v.p. BEI, Inc., Alexandria, Va., 1995—. Contbr. articles to profl. jours. Regional bd. dirs. Boy Scout Am., Minot, N.D., 1972-74. Named Disting. Engring. Alumnus U. Pitts., 1986. Mem. AIAA, Inst. Indsl. Engrs., Air Force Assn., Armed Forces Comm. and Electronics Assn. (regional v.p. 1975-78, Gold medal 1983), Am. Def. Preparedness Assn., Order of Daedalians (chpt. pres. 1976-78, merit award 1979), Rotary. Republican. Avocations: golf, long distance bicycling, private flying. Office: SAIC 1800 Diagonal Rd Ste 430 Alexandria VA 22314-2840 Home: 91 Clark Ct Dover DE 19901 Office Phone: 302-229-5223. E-mail: wilmack@aol.com.

**MACLAUGHLIN, FRANCIS JOSEPH,** lawyer; b. Davenport, Iowa, Oct. 5, 1933; s. Francis Joseph and Sylvia (Boone) MacL.; m. Joan Elizabeth Pfeiffer, Oct. 17, 1959; children: Lisa Ann, Christine Ann, Francis Joseph BA, Yale U., 1955; JD, U. Mich., 1958. Bar: Ill. 1958, Calif. 1963. Assoc. Graham, Califf, Harper & Benson, Moline, Ill., 1958-59, Lillick, McHose & Charles, Los Angeles, 1963-70, ptnr. L.A., 1970-90, White and Case, 1990—. Lt. USN, 1959-63 Mem. ABA, Calif. Bar Assn., Los Angeles County Bar Assn., Maritime Law Assn. U.S. Republican. Office: White & Case 633 W 5th St Ste 1900 Los Angeles CA 90071-2087 Office Phone: 213-553-7900. Personal E-mail: rusty1933@charter.net.

**MACLAY, DONALD MERLE,** retired lawyer; b. Belleville, Pa., Feb. 16, 1934; s. Robert Barr and Grace Virginia (Royer) M.; m. Nancy Margaret Hixenbaugh, Sept. 13, 1958; children: Susan Jo (dec.), Timothy Dean. AB magna cum laude, Grove City Coll., 1956; LLB, U. Pa., 1961. Bar: D.C. 1968, Pa. 1970. Commd. fgn. svc. officer U.S. Dept. State, 1961; assigned Am. embassy, Cotonou, Dahomey (Benin), 1962-64, Am. Consulate Gen., Frankfurt, Fed. Republic Germany, 1964-66, U.S. Dept. State, Washington, 1966-69; dir. courses of study Am. Law Inst.-ABA Com. on Continuing Profl. Edn., Phila., 1969-87, dep. exec. dir., 1987-99, ret., 1999. Served with U.S. Army, 1956-58. Mem.: Am. Law Inst. Democrat. Presbyterian. Home: 936 Church Rd Springfield PA 19064-3935

**MACLEAN, BARBARA HUTMACHER,** retired journalist, writer; b. Toledo, Dec. 16, 1926; d. Norman Eugene and Betty Lucille Price; div. 1971; m. E. Fraser MacLean, Aug. 30, 1977; children: Beth, Jessica, Cary, David, Clay. Student, Rockford Coll., 1945, Western Mich. Coll., 1946. Reporter News-Leader, Richmond, Va., 1962; editor-writer News-Chronicle, Thousand Oaks, Calif., 1963-70, Star-Free Press, Ventura, Calif., 1971-75, Daily Dispatch, East London, South Africa, 1974-78, Wenatchee (Wash.) World, 1980-92, ret., 1992. Exchange journalist The Examiner, Huddersfield, Eng., 1983, China Daily, Beijing, 1988, The Times, Windhoek, Namibia, 1991. Author: In Black and White: Voices of Apartheid, 1980 (Eng.), 1983, I Can't Do What? Voices of Pathfinding Women, 1997, Strike A Woman, Strike A Rock: Fighting for Freedom in South Africa, 2004. Named Woman of Achievement AAUW, 1997; recipient Nat. Headliners award, 1968, 1st Social Issues Reporting award Soc. of Profl. Journalists, 1989. Home: 50 Harborview Dr #3 Port Townsend WA 98368 Personal E-mail: barbhm@olympus.net.

**MACLEAN, CALVIN A.,** theater educator, department chairman, theater director; b. Cin., Ohio, May 31, 1953; BA in History, U. Mich., Ann Arbor, 1975, MA in Theatre, 1977; MFA in Theatre Directing, U. Mass., Amherst, Mass., 1980. Vis. asst. prof. So. Ill. U., Carbondale, Ill., 1981—84; artistic dir. The Commons Theatre, Chgo., 1986—88; prof. Denison U., Granville, Ohio, 1990—91; head directing Ill. State U., Normal, Ill., 1991—2006; head Dept. Theatre U. Tenn., Knoxville, Tenn., 2006—. Artistic dir. Ill. Shakespeare Festival, Normal, 1995—2006, Clarence Brown Theatre, Knoxville, 2006—. Mem.: Univ. Resident Theatre Assn. (bd. dirs.). Office: Dept Theater Univ Tenn 206 McClong Tower Knoxville TN 37996

**MACLEAN, DOUG,** professional sports team executive; b. Summerside, P.E.I., Can., Apr. 12, 1954; m. Jill MacLean; 2 children. Student, P.E.I.; M in Ednl. Psychology, We. Ont. Asst. coach London Knights of OHL, 1984-85, St. Louis Blues, 1986-87, 87-88, Washington Capitals, 1988-89, 89-90, Detroit Red Wings, 1990-91, asst. gen. mgr., 1992-93, 93-94; gen. mgr. Adirondack, Red Wing orgn., 1992-93, 93-94; dir. player devel., scout Fla. Panthers, 1994-95, head coach, 1995-98; gen. mgr Columbus Blue Jackets, 1998—, pres., 1998—, head coach, 2003—04. Office: 200 W Nationwide Blvd Ste Level Columbus OH 43215-2563*

**MACLEAN, JOHN,** professional hockey coach, former professional hockey player; b. Oshawa, Ont. Can., Nov. 20, 1964; m. Adrienne MacLean; children: John Carter, Kyle Christopher. Hockey player NJ Devils, 1983-97, San Jose Sharks, 1997-98, NY Rangers, 1998—2000, Dallas Stars, 2000—02; asst. coach NJ Devils, 2002—. Named to Meml. Cup All-Star team, 1982-83; played in NHL All-Star game, 1989, 91. Achievements include mem. Stanley Cup Champion, NJ Devils, 1995. Office: NJ Devils 50 Rt 120 N PO Box 504 East Rutherford NJ 07073-0504*

**MACLEAN, JOHN RONALD,** lawyer; b. Pueblo, Colo., Jan. 19, 1938; s. John Ronald and Mary Victoria (Curlin) MacL.; m. Carol Jean Turner, Aug. 18, 1962; children: Leslie Carol, John Ronald. Student, U. Okla., 1956; BS. U.S. Mil. Acad., 1961; JD, Vanderbilt U., 1967. Bar: Tex. 1967; cert. in personal injury trial law Tex. Bd. Legal Splzn. Practicing atty. Turner & MacLean, Cleburne, Tex., 1967-68; county atty. Johnson County, Tex., 1968-76; dist. atty. 18th Jud. Dist. Tex., 1976-84; dist. judge 249th Jud. Dist. Tex., 1984-91; pvt. practice MacLean & Boulware, 1992—. Pres. Johnson County United Fund, 1976 With U.S. Army, 1961—64. Fellow Tex. Bar Found.; mem. Tex. Bar Assn., Johnson County Bar Assn. (pres. 1969), Am. Bd. Trial Advocates (past nat. dir.). Tex. Trial Lawyers Assn., Vanderbilt U. Law Sch. Bar Assn. (past pres.), Elks. Democrat. Methodist. Home: 1216 W Westhill Dr Cleburne TX 76033-6021 Office: 11 N Main St Cleburne TX 76033-5543 Office Phone: 817-645-3700.

**MAC LEAN, LLOYD DOUGLAS,** surgeon; b. Calgary, Alta., Can., June 15, 1924; s. Fred Hugh and Azilda MacL.; m. Eleanor Colle, June 30, 1954; children: Hugh, Charles, Ian, James, Martha. B.Sc. (Viscount Bennett scholar), U. Alta., 1947, MD (Viscount Bennett scholar), 1949; PhD, U. Minn., 1957. Resident U. Minn. Hosp., Mpls., 1950-56; instr. dept. surgery U. Minn., Mpls., 1956-58, asst. prof. surgery, 1958-59, asso. prof., 1959-62; prof. McGill U., Montreal, Que., Canada, 1962—, chmn. dept. surgery, 1968-73, 77-82, 87-88. Surgeon-in-chief Ancker Hosp., St. Paul, 1957-62 Royal Victoria Hosp., Montreal, 1962-88; Edward Archibald prof. surgery McGill U., 1988-93, prof. surgery 1993—. Contbr. numerous articles on surgery, shock, host resistance and transplantation to profl. jours. Decorated officer Order Can. Fellow Royal Soc. Can.; mem. ACS (pres. 1993-94), Am. Surg. Assn. (pres. 1993), Ctrl. Surg. Assn. (pres. 1982-83), Am. Physiol. Soc., Am. Assn. Thoracic and Cardiovasc. Surgery, Soc. Surgery of Alimentary Tract. Home: # 1402-80 Berlioz Montreal PQ Canada H3E 1N9 Personal E-mail: lloydm@citenet.net.

**MACLEAN, RHONDA,** information technology executive; m. Lynn Maclean. Various positions to sr. mgr. computer and comm. security The Boeing Co., 1982—96; dir. corp. info. security Nations Bank (now Bank of Am.), 1996; sr. v.p. Bank of Am., 1998—. Tech. adv. Pres. Nat. Security Telecom. Adv. Com. Fin. Services Risk Assessing, 1997; private sector coord. for fin. services industry public/private partnership on critical infostructure protection and homeland security Dept. of Treasury, 2002—. Mem. bd. adv. U. NC, Charlotte Coll. of Info. Tech. Named Women of Vision, Information Security mag., 2003, one of the 50 Most Powerful People in Networking, Networking

World mag., 2003. Mem.: Fin. Services Info. Security Analysis Ctr. (FS/ISAC) (adv. to bd. dirs.), Internat. Inst. Info. Integrity (vice chmn. mem. Adv. Com.), Banking Industry Tech. Secretariat (elected mem. of Security Laboratory Governance Bd.).

**MACLEAN, STEVE(N) G.,** astronaut; b. Ottawa, Ont., Can., Dec. 14, 1954; m. Nadine Wielgopolski; 3 children. BS in Physics with honors, York U., Toronto, Ont., 1977, PhD, 1983; DSc (hon.), Royal Military Coll., Saint-Jean, Quebec, York U., Toronto, Acadia U. Worked in sports adminstrn. & pub. rels. York U., Toronto, 1974—76; mem. Can. Nat. Gymnastics Team, 1976—77; astronaut Can. Space Agy., 1983—88, program mgr., Advanced Space Vision Sys., 1987—93, astronaut advisor to strategic technolgies in automation and robotics program, 1988—91, program mgr. orbiter space vision sys., chief sci. advisor for Internat. Space, 1993—94; acting dir.-gen. Can. Astronaut Program, 1994—96; astronaut NASA, Johnson Space Ctr., Houston, 1996—. Adj. instr. York U., Toronto, 1980—83; adj. prof. Internat. Aerospace Studies U. Toronto, 1993; payload specialist, Space Shuttle Columbia Mission STS-52, 1992; crew mem. Space Shuttle Atlantis (STS-115), 2006. Achievements include research in electro-optics, laser-induced fluorescence of particles and crystals and multi-photon laser spectroscopy; second Canadian to walk in space; first Canadian to operate Canadarm2. Avocations: hiking, canoeing, flying, parachuting, gymnastics. Office: Astronaut Office/CB NASA Johnson Space Ctr Houston TX 77058*

**MACLEISH, RODERICK, JR.,** lawyer; b. Boston, Oct. 31, 1952; AB with gen. honors, Vassar Coll., 1975; JD cum laude, Boston U., 1978. Bar: Mass. 1979, US Court Appeals, 1st Cir., US Court Appeals, 11th Cir., US Dist. Ct. for the Dist. Mass. Law clerk to Hon. Joseph L. Tauro US Dist. Ct. Mass., 1978-79; shareholder, atty. Greenberg Traurig, LLP, Boston. Lectr. and guest spkr. in the field. Editor Boston U. Law Rev., 1977-78; contbr.articles to profl. publs. Mem. civil justice adv. bd. US Dist. Ct., 1995; bd. dir. Cotting Sch., Lexington, Mass., 1990—; Internat. Assn. for the Right to Effective Treatment, 1988—92, Greater Boston Legal Svcs., 1988—90; founder, chmn. bd. dirs. The Mass. 9/11 Fund, Inc., 2002; mem. adv. com. Alliance for the Mental Ill of Mass. Inc., 1988—90. Named one of Top 10 Litigators, Nat. Law Jour., 2003; recipient Award for Outstanding Advocacy in a successful 10-yr. pro bono litigation effort on behalf of Bridgewater State Hospital Clients, Alliance for the Mentally Ill of Mass., 1988, Civil Rights award, Mass. Coalition of Families and Advocates for the Retarded, 1997. Fellow: Mass. Bar Found. Office: Greenberg Traurig LLP One International Pl Boston MA 02110 Office Phone: 617-310-6000. Office Fax: 617-310-6001. Business E-Mail: macleishr@gtlaw.com.

**MACLELLAN, STEVE,** diversified financial services company executive; Chief exec. pvt. client svcs. J.P. Morgan Chase & Co. Office: JP Morgan Chase & Co 270 Park Ave New York NY 10017-2070*

**MACLENNAN, BERYCE WINIFRED,** psychologist; b. Aberdeen, Scotland, Mar. 14, 1920; came to U.S., 1949, naturalized, 1965; d. William and Beatrice (MaCrae) Mellis; m. John Duncan MacLennan, Nov. 29, 1944. BSc with honors, London Sch. Econs., 1947; PhD, London U., 1960. Diplomate Am. Bd. Clin. Psychology, cert. group therapist, trauma specialist. Group psychotherapist, youth specialist cons., N.Y.C. and Washington, 1949-63; dir. Ctr. for Prevention Juvenile Delinquency and New Careers, Washington, 1963-66; sect. chief NIMH, Mental Health Study Ctr., Adelphi, Md., 1967-70, chief, 1971-74; regional adminstr. Mass. Dept. Mental Health, Springfield, 1974-75; sr. mental health adv. GAO, Washington, 1976-90; pvt. practice, specialist psychotherapy Bethesda, Md., 1990—. Clin. prof. George Washington U., 1970—; group therapy cons. D.C. Mental Health Svcs., 1993-2002, Washington Assessement and Therapy Svcs., 1992-2006; lectr. Montgomery C.C., 1988-91, Washington Sch. Psychiatry Geropsychiatric Program, 1997—; mem. tech. adv. com. Prince George's County Mental Health Assn., 1968-84; cons. Washington Bus. Group on Health, 1990-91, KOBA, 1991; leader Trauma Psychotherapy Groups, 2002-03, Hebrew Home Rsch. Inst. Elder Housing Socialization and Memory Improvement Groups, 2000-02. Mem. NIMH Prevention Intervention Rsch. Task Force, 1990-91, Montgomery County Victims Assistance Programs, 1990-95; v.p. Compliance, Federally Employed Women, 1979-81; pres. Glenecho chpt. Older Women's League, 1993-94; mem. Montgomery County Disaster Outreach Team, 2004—. Fellow APA, Am. Orthopsychiat. Assn.; disting. fellow Am. Group Psychotherapy Assn.; mem. Washington Mushroom Club. Democrat. Office Phone: 301-320-4151.

**MACLENNAN, DAVID HERMAN,** research scientist, educator; b. Swan River, Man., Can., July 3, 1937; s. Douglas Henry and Sigridur (Sigurdson) MacL.; m. Linda Carol Vass, Aug. 18, 1965; children: Jessica Lynn (dec.), Jeremy Douglas, Jonathan David. BSA, U. Man., 1959; MS, Purdue U., 1961, PhD, 1963; DSc (hon.), U. Man., 2001. Postdoctoral fellow Inst. Enzyme Research, U. Wis., Madison, 1963-64; asst. prof. U. Wis., Madison, 1964-68; assoc. prof. U. Toronto, 1969-74, prof., 1974-93, J.W. Billes prof. med. rsch. 1987—, Univ. prof., 1993—, acting chmn., 1978-80, chmn., 1980-90; prin. investigator Can. Genetic Diseases Network of Ctrs. of Excellence, 1991—. Med. adv. bd. Muscular Dystrophy Assn. Can., 1976-87; scientists' rev. panel Med. Rsch. Coun. Can., 1988-90; chmn. molecular biology and pathology grants com. Heart and Stroke Found. Can., 1995-99; rsch. rev. panel U. Ottawa Heart Inst., 1991-95; med. rev. panel Gairdner Found., 1999-2001, med. adv. bd., 2001—; cons. Merck, Sharp and Dohme, West Point, Pa., 1992-98. Assoc. editor Can. Jour. Biochemistry, 1972-76; mem. editl. bd. Jour. Biol. Chemistry, 1975-80, 82-87; contbr. articles on muscle membrane biochemistry to profl. jours. Decorated Officer Order of Can.; recipient Gairdner Found. Internat. award, 1991; Can. Med. Rsch. Coun. scholar, 1969-71, I.W. Killam Meml. scholar, 1977-78; recipient I.W. Killam Meml. prize Health Scis., 1997, Jonas Salk award Ont. March of Dimes, 1998, Salute to the City award, City of Toronto, 2002, Rick Gallop award Heart and Stroke Found. Ont., 2002. Fellow Royal Soc. Can., Royal Soc. London (Glaxo-Wellcome prize 2000), NAS (fgn. assoc.); mem. Can. Biochem. Soc. (Ayerst award 1974), Am. Soc. Biol. Chemists, Biophys. Soc. (Nat. Lectr. award 1990), Japanese Biochem. Soc. (hon.). Home: 293 Lytton Blvd Toronto ON Canada M5N 1R7 Office: U Toronto-Banting & Best Med Rsch 112 College St Toronto ON Canada M5G 1L6 E-mail: david.maclennan@utoronto.ca.

**MACLEOD, ANGUS,** retired internist; b. Romford, Essex, Eng., Apr. 24, 1943; came to U.S., 1967; s. Malcolm Macleod and Jean (Littlefair) McKean; m. Gwynne Louise Grellner, May 23, 1969 (div. Aug. 1987); children: Kenneth, Anne, Stephen. MB, ChB, Glasgow U., 1967. Diplomate Am. Bd. Internal Medicine. Intern Luth. Hosp., St. Louis, 1967—68; resident in internal medicine St. Louis U., 1969, 1971—73, fellow in cardiology, 1973—74; physician Grandel Med. Group, St. Louis, 1974—2000, ret., 2000. Instr., then asst. prof. medicine St. Louis U.; chmn. dept. medicine Lutheran Hosp., St. Louis; pres. Grandel Med. Group, St. Louis. Capt. U.S. Army, 1969-71. Decorated Bronze Star. Fellow: ACP; mem.: St. Louis Met. Med. Soc., Mo. State Med. Soc. E-mail: corvus1745@yahoo.com.

**MACLEOD, DONALD WILLIAM,** secondary school educator; b. Stornoway, Scotland, Oct. 3, 1935; s. Angus and Mary (MacArthur) MacL.; m. Theresa Plaskon, Aug. 25, 1973; children: Heather Anne, Robert Angus. BS, Fairleigh Dickinson U., 1964; MA, Seton Hall U., 1968, Kean U., 1977. Tchr. English and pub. speaking Hawthorne (N.J.) H.S., 1964-97, head soccer coach, 1977-79, asst. soccer coach, 1988-94, tchr. English and pub. spkg., 1995-98. Adj. prof. comms. Ramapo Coll. of N.J., Mahwah, N.J., 1981-84; tchr. English Englewood (N.J.) Adult H.S., 1987-94; adj. prof. English Ramapo Coll. N.J., 1998. With U.S. Army, 1958-60. Mem. NEA, N.J. Edn. Assn., Hawthorne Tchrs. Assn. (past v.p.). Presbyterian. Avocations: soccer, Gaelic and Scottish, bagpipes, jogging.

**MACLEOD, GORDON KENNETH,** internist, educator; b. Boston, Jan. 30, 1929; s. Gordon Kenneth and Margaret J. MacL.; m. Janet B., Aug. 17, 1957; children: Gordon K. III, Alexander B. AB, Blackburn Coll., 1954; MD, U. Cin., 1960. Indsl. engr. Procter & Gamble Co., Cin., 1954-56; intern Boston City Hosp., 1960-61; resident, clin. fellow Mass. Gen. Hosp., Boston, 1961-64; rsch. fellow Harvard U., 1962-64; sr. resident, sr. physician Boston VA Hosp., 1964-66; asst. clin. prof. medicine Yale U., 1966-69, assoc. clin. prof. medicine and pub. health, 1969-71; dir. HMO Svc., HEW, 1971-73; prof. emeritus health svcs. adminstrn. Grad. Sch. Pub. Health, U. Pitts., 1974—, chmn. dept., 1974-83, assoc. clin. prof. medicine, 1976-86, clin. prof. medicine, 1986—; pres. senate U. Pitts., 1997-98. Sec. health, State of Pa., 1979; academic dean Semester at Sea, 1999, interim dir. MD/MPH program, 2000—; mem. staff West Penn Hosp.; mem. nat. adv. coun. divsn. rsch. resources NIH, 1983-87; bd. dirs. Inst. Rsch., Edn. and Tng., 2004—; cons. Shadyside Hosp.; cons. in field. Editor: (with Mark Perlman) Health Care Capital: Competition and Control, 1978; contbr. articles to profl. jours. Served with U.S. Army, 1948-49. Ford Found. travel grantee, 1973 Fellow ACP; mem. Allegheny County Med. Soc., AMA (editl. bd. jour. 1986-94), Am. Pub. Health Assn., Med. Adminstrs. Conf., Pa. Pub. Health Assn., Pa. State Med. Soc. (pres.), Pitts. Acad. Medicine. Office: 130 Desoto St Pittsburgh PA 15213-2535 Business E-Mail: gmacleod@pitt.edu. *My first job was an industrial engineer with later training in internal medicine; it uniquely prepared me for an academic career in health management with intervals as a government executive at federal and state levels. My most challenging assignments were in initiating the federal Health Maintenance Organization program nationally, in managing the health aspects of the nuclear accident at Three Mile Island, and in training young persons for careers in internal medicine and health management.*

**MACLEOD, JAMES L.,** minister, finance company executive, art gallery owner; b. Oakdale, La., Apr. 27, 1937; s. William Lasater and Sara Louise (Macaulay) MacLeod. BA, Washington and Lee U., 1959; MA, BD, Emory U., 1968; D, Miss. State U., 1972. Ordained to ministry Presbyn. Ch., 1963. Minister U.S.-So. Presbyn. Ch., 1963—85, minister assoc. reform synod, 1985—; educator Ga. State Schs., 1972—91; pres. Brunswick Fin., Ga., 1991—, Brunswick Gallery, 1993—; min. First Assoc. Reformed Presbyn. Ch., Augusta, Ga., 1988—99. Author: (book) Great Dr. Waddel, 1985, A Season of Grace, 1974, Presbyterian Tradition in the South, 1978. Councilman City of Brunswick, 1994—, mayor pro tem, 1996—; mem. Sec. Disc. Washington, 1970. Scholar, NEH, 1986. Fellow: Soc. Antiquaries Scotland; mem.: NEA, Ga. Assn. Edn., Fulbright Alumni Assn., Pinnacle Club, Phi Delta Kappa. Democrat. Home: 508 Walker Road Augusta GA 30901

**MACLEOD, JOHN AMEND,** lawyer; b. Manila, June 5, 1942; s. Anthony Macaulay and Dorothy Lillian (Amend); m. Ann Klee; children: Kerry, Jack. BBA, U. Notre Dame, 1963, JD, 1969. Bar: D.C. 1969, U.S. Supreme Ct. 1980. Assoc. Jones, Day, Reavis & Pogue, Washington, 1969-73, ptnr., 1974-79, Crowell & Moring LLP, Washington, 1979—. Mem. mgmt. com., 1979-82, 83-86, 91-94, 99-2000, 2000-06, chmn.firm, 1984-85, 93-94., 2000-06, chmn. emeritus, 2006. Editor-in-chief Notre Dame Law Rev., 1968-69; contbr. articles to profl. jours. Trustee Energy Mineral and Law Found., 1979—2002; bd. dirs. St. Francis Ctr., 1982—91, Notre Dame Law Assn., 1981—86, C&M Internat., 1991—94, 1999—; bd. dirs. C&M Capitolink, 2004—06. Served to lt. U.S. Army, 1963—65. Recipient disting. mining lawyer award Nat. Mining Assn., 1995, forest industry victory of yr. award Am. Forest and Paper Assn., 1994. Mem. ABA, D.C. Bar Assn., Ptnrs. Leadership Forum, Metro. Club (Washington). Home: 4040 Swartz Rd Maurertown VA 22644-2320 Office: Crowell & Moring LLP 1001 Pennsylvania Ave NW Washington DC 20004-2595

**MACLEOD, LINDA ANN,** secondary school educator; b. Kans. City, Dec. 30, 1946; d. William Glennon Price and Victoria Murdza; children: Angela Renee, Sara Kristen. BA in Art Edn., U. Mo., 1969, MA in Secondary Edn., 1983, degree in Edn., 1988. Tchr. art Consolidated Sch. Dist. 2, Raytown, Mo., 1980—. Torchbearer Olympics, 2002. Recipient Nat. Merit award, Knights Pythias, 2003. Mem.: Raytown (Mo.) Cmty. Tchrs. Assn. (sec. 1986—87), Mo. State Tchrs. Assn., Kans. City (Mo.) Ski Club (trip capt. 1986—). Roman Catholic. Avocations: tennis, art, skiing, volleyball. Office: Raytown South Sr High Sch 8211 Sterling Ave Raytown MO 64138-2690

**MACLEOD, MARY FRANCES,** mathematics educator; b. NYC, Feb. 22, 1965; d. Michael James and Margaret Mary Murray; m. Todd Cameron MacLeod, July 23, 1994; children: Meghan Nicole, Todd Cameron MacLeod, Jr., Jenna Mary. BEd, Marymount Coll., Tarrytown, NY, 1983—87; MS in Math. Edn., SUNY, New Paltz, NY, 1988—92. Cert. tchr. NY, 1992. Math tchr. NY Mil. Acad., Cornwall, 1987, Cornwall Ctrl. Sch. Dist., 1992—. Mem.: Nat. Coun. Tchrs. Math. Roman Catholic. Home: 27 Rose Hill Pk Cornwall NY 12518 Office: Cornwall Ctrl HS 10 Dragon Dr New Windsor NY 12553 Business E-Mail: mmacleod@ccsd.ouboces.org.

**MACLEOD, ROBERT ANGUS,** microbiology educator, researcher; b. Athabasca, Alta., Can., July 13, 1921; s. Norman John and Eleonora Pauline Bertha (Westerhoff) MacL.; m. Patricia Rosemarie Robertson, Sept. 1, 1948; children— Douglas John, Alexander Robert, Kathleen Mary, David Gordon, Michael Norman, Susan Joan BA with honors in Chemistry, U. B.C., Vancouver, Can., 1943, MA in Chemistry and Biology, 1945; PhD in Biochemistry, U. Wis., Madison, 1949. Asst. prof. Queen's U., Kingston, Ont., Canada, 1949-52; sr. biochemist Fisheries Research Bd. Can., Vancouver, B.C., 1952-60; assoc. prof. to prof., chmn. dept. microbiology Macdonald Coll., McGill U., Ste. Anne de Bellevue, Que., Canada, 1960-86, prof. emeritus, 1986—. Cons. Def. Research Bd., Ottawa, Ont., 1965—75; assoc. editor Can. Jour. Microbiology, Ottawa, 1965—70. Author tech. papers. Recipient Harrison prize, Royal Soc. Can., 1960. Fellow: Royal Soc. Can.; mem.: Am. Soc. Microbiology (hon.), Can. Soc. Microbiologists (hon.; pres. 1976—77, award 1973). Avocations: swimming, fishing. Home: 10 Slate St Stittsville ON Canada K2S 1Y5 E-mail: ramacl@sympatico.ca.

**MACLEOD, WILLIAM BENTLEY,** economics professor, law professor; b. Iserlohn, Germany, 1954; came to U.S., 1995; m. Raisa Nones (div.); children: Raisa, Gabriela; m. Janet Marion Currie, May 18, 1997; children: Joana, Daniel. BA magna cum laude, Queen's U., Kingston, Ont., Can., 1975, MSc in Math., 1979; PhD in Econs., U. B.C., Vancouver, Can., 1984. From asst. prof. to assoc. prof. Queen's U., 1982-90; assoc. prof. U. Montreal, 1990-92, prof. econs., 1992-96, Boston Coll., 1996-97; prof. econs. and law U. So. Calif., LA, 1997—2000, dir. Ctr. for Law, Econs. and Orgn., 1997—2006, chair jr. recruiting, 2000—03; program dir., personnel and behavioral econs. IZA, Bonn, Germany, 2003; prof. econs. and pub. policy Columbia U., NY, 2005—, chair jr. recruiting, 2005—06. Cons. Ind. Power Producers Ont., Toronto, 1990-92, Human Resources Can., Ottawa, Ont., 1993-95; Harold Innis Meml. lectr., 1996; vis. prof. econs. and law Calif. Inst. Tech., 2002, Princeton U., 2003-04; bd. dirs. We. Econs. Assn. Assoc. editor: Jour. Econ. Behavior and Orgn., 2002—; editor: Jour. Labor Econs., 2003—; contbr. articles to profl. jours. NSF grantee, 1997-2003, 2006. Fellow Econometric Soc.; mem. AAAS, Am. Econs. Assn., Soc. Labor Economists (H. Gregg Lewis prize 2002), Assn. for Comparative Systems, Econ. Sci. Assn., Am. Law and Econs. Assn., Western Econs. Assn. (bd. dirs. 2003—). Office: Columbia U Dept Econ MC3308 420 W 118th St New York NY 10028-3308

**MACLIN, ALAN HALL,** lawyer; b. DuQuoin, Ill., Dec. 22, 1949; s. John E. and Nora (Hall) M.; m. Joan Davidson (div. Dec. 1981); children: Molly, Tess, Anne; m. Jeanne Sittlow, Nov. 17, 1984. BA magna cum laude, Vanderbilt U., 1971; JD, U. Chgo., 1974. Bar: Minn. 1974, U.S. Dist. Ct. Minn. 1974, U.S. Ct. Appeals (8th cir.) 1974, U.S. Ct. Appeals (5th cir.) 1975. U.S. Supreme Ct. 1978. Asst. atty. gen. Minn. Atty. Gen., St. Paul, 1974-80; chief anti-trust divsn. Briggs & Morgan, St. Paul, 1980—; mem. adv. bd., 1993-96. Mem. Minn. State Bar Assn. (treas. anti-trust sect. 1978-80, 96-98, chair 1998—), Ramsey County Bar Assn. (sec. jud. com. 1980-82), Phi Beta Kappa. Unitarian Universalist. Office Phone: 612-977-8400. Personal E-mail: amaclin@briggs.com.

**MACLIN, AMY,** editor; Staff editor NY Times Syndication Sales Corp. Contbr. US Weekly, 2000; author: (article) State of Grace, 2004; contbr. (chapters to books) Diverse Issues – Diverse Answers: Reading, Writing, & Thinking About Social Issues, 2006. Office: NY Times Syndication Sales Corp 14th Fl 122 E 42nd St New York NY 10168 Office Phone: 212-499-3411. Office Fax: 212-499-3382. E-mail: maclin@nytimes.com.*

**MACLIN, ERNEST,** medical products executive; b. N.Y.C., Jan. 25, 1931; s. Samuel and Dora (Sonsky) M.; m. Edith Samuel, Feb. 18, 1956; children: Alan David, Deborah Ellen, Julie Anne. BME, CCNY, 1952, M Engring., 1969. Registered profl. engr., N.Y., N.J. Engr. Reeves Instrument Corp., N.Y.C., 1952-54, Adrian Wilson Assocs., Nagoya, Japan, 1956-57, Ford Instrument Co., L.I., NY, 1957-58, Technicon, Tarrytown, NY, 1968-69; engr. unit head Kearfott divsn. Singer Corp., Little Falls, NJ, 1958-68; v.p. R & D. Electro-Nucleonics Inc., Fairfield, NJ, 1969-90; pres. The Product Devel. Group, Paramus, NJ, 1990—. Bd. dirs. Nat. Com. for Clin. Lab. Stds., Villanova, Pa., 1981-87. Contbr. articles to profl. jours.; patentee various instruments. Capt. USAF, 1954-57; mem. USAFR ret. Fellow ASME; mem. Am. Assn. Clin. Chemistry. Jewish. Home and Office: 659 Rutgers Pl Paramus NJ 07652-4207 Office Phone: 201-261-4180. Personal E-mail: eqmchai@aol.com.

**MACLIN, SAMUEL TODD,** diversified financial services company executive; With Chem. NY Corpn., Chem. Banking Corpn., Chase Manhattan Corpn.; exec. v.p. J.P. Morgan Chase & Co., chmn., CEO Tex. Region and head mid. market banking, head comml. banking, 2004—. Office: JP Morgan Chase & Co 270 Park Ave New York NY 10017-2070*

**MAC LOW, MORDECAI-MARK,** astrophysicist; b. N.Y.C., Mar. 9, 1963; s. Jackson Mac Low and Iris Lezak. BA, Princeton U., 1983; PhD, U. Colo., 1989. Rsch. asst. U. Colo., Boulder, 1983-88; NRC fellow NASA Ames Rsch. Ctr., Moffett Field, Calif., 1989-90; rsch. assoc. U. Calif., Berkeley, 1991-92, U. Chgo., 1992-95; sci. Max-Planck-Inst. für Astronomie, Heidelberg, Germany, 1995-99; asst. curator of astrophysics Am. Mus. Natural History, N.Y.C., 1999—2002, assoc. curator astrophysics, 2002—, chair dept. astrophysics, 2005—. Adj. asst. prof. Columbia U., 1999—2002, adj. assoc. prof., 2003—; mem. grant rev. panels NSF and NASA, chair panels; mem. adv. com. tchr. renewal for urban sci. tchg. program Am. Mus. Natural History and CUNY; mem. several conf. sci. organizing coms.; spkr. in field; reviewer in field. Contbr. articles to popular mags. and profl. jours. Grantee, NSF, 1999—, NASA, 1999—. Mem. Am. Astron. Soc. (com. on employment 2001-04), Am. Phys. Soc., Internat. Astron. Union. Office: Am Mus Natural History Dept Astrophysics CPW & 79th St New York NY 10024-5192 Business E-Mail: mordecai@amnh.org.

**MACLUCKIE, MICHELLE LYNN,** educational consultant; d. Steven Kurtz and Carol Hummel; m. William MacLuckie, Mar. 1, 1990; children: Katherine N., William C. EdB, Kurtztown U., 1993; M in Spl. Edn., Pa. State U., 1998. Cert. elem. edn. Pa., 1993, edn. mentally and physically handicapped Pa., 1993, supr. spl. edn. Pa., 2002. Elem. learning support tchr. Twin Valley Sch. Dist., Elverson, Pa., 1993—96, mid. sch. life skills support tchr., 1996—98, mid. sch. learning support tchr., 1998—2000; h.s. learning support tchr. Chester County Intermediate Unit, Downingtown, Pa., 2000—05, ednl. cons., 2005—. Presenter Pa. Coun. for Exceptional Children, 2002—03. Vol. wish granter Make-a-Wish Found., Blue Bell, Pa., 2004—06; Sunday sch. coord./tchr. New Hanover Evang. Luth. Ch., Gilbertsville, Pa., 2000—05. Recipient Outstanding Spl. Edn. Maj. award, Pa. State U., 1998, Outstanding Svc. award, Chester County Intermediate Unit, 2002. Mem.: ASCD, Coun. For Exceptional Children (professionally recognized spl. educator). Office Phone: 484-237-5033. Personal E-mail: mmacluckie@msn.com.

**MACMAHON, THOMAS P.,** healthcare company executive; B in mktg., St. Peter's Coll., NJ; MBA, Fairleigh Dickinson U., 1975. Joined Roche Bio-Med. Labs. as mktg. rsch. analyst, 1969; v.p. pub. affairs and planning Hoffman-La Roche Inc., Nutley, NJ, 1982—83, v.p. and gen. mgr. diagnostics systems unit, 1983—86, pres. Roche Diagnostics Group, 1988—96, mem. exec. com., 1988—96, sr. v.p., 1993—96; vice chmn. Lab. Corp. Am. Holdings, Burlington, NC, 1995—96, chmn., 1996—, CEO, pres., 1997—. Named to The Pinnacle (highest award), Fairleigh Dickinson U., 2001. Office: Lab Corp Am Holdings 358 S Main St Burlington NC 27215*

**MACMANUS, SUSAN ANN,** political science professor, researcher; b. Tampa, Fla., Aug. 22, 1947; d. Harold Cameron and Elizabeth (Riegler) MacM. BA cum laude, Fla. State U., 1968, PhD, 1975; MA, U. Mich., 1969. Instr. Valencia C.C., Orlando, Fla., 1969-73; rsch. asst. Fla. State U., 1973-75; asst. prof. U. Houston, 1975-79, assoc. prof., 1979-85, dir. MPA program, 1983-85; rsch. assoc. Ctr. Pub. Policy, 1982-85; prof., dir. PhD progam Cleve. State U., 1985-87; prof. pub. adminstrn. and polit. sci. U. South Fla., Tampa, 1987—, chair dept. govt. and internat. affairs, 1987-93, disting. univ. prof., 1999. Vis. prof. U. Okla., Norman, 1981—; field rsch. assoc. Brookings Inst., Washington, 1977—82, Princeton (N.J.) U., 1979—, Cleve. State U., 1982—83, Westat, Inc., Washington, 1983—; summer field rsch. assoc. Columbia U., N.Y.C., 1979, Nat. Acad. Pub. Adminstrn., Washington, 1980. Author: Revenue Patterns in U.S. Cities and Suburbs: A Comparative Analysis, 1978, Reapportionment and Representation in Florida: A Historical Collection, 1991, Doing Business with Government: Federal, State, Local and Foreign Government Purchasing Practices for Every Business and Public Institution, 1992, Federal Aid to Houston, 1993, Young v. Old: Generational Combat in the 21st Century, 1996, Targeting Senior Voters, 2000; co-author (with others): Governing A Changing America, 1984; co-author: (with Francis T. Borkowski) Visions for the Future: Creating New Institutional Relationships Among Academia, Business, Government, and Community, 1989; co-author: (with Elizabeth R. MacManus) Citrus, Sawmills, Critters & Crackers: Life in Early Lutz and Central Pasco County, 1998, The Lutz Depot, 2000; editor: Mapping Florida's Political Landscape: The Changing Art and Politics of Reapportionment and Redistricting, 2002; co-editor (with Thomas R. Dye): Politics in States and Communities, 11th edit., 2003; co-editor: (with Dano Moreno and Kevin Hill) Florida's Politics: Ten Media Markets, One Powerful State, 2004; writer: manuals in field, mem. editl. bd.: various jours; contbr. articles to profl. jours., chapters to books. Bd. dirs. Houston Area Women's Ctr., 1977, past pres., v.p. fin., treas.; mem. LWV, Gov.'s Coun. Econ. Advisers, 1988-90, Harris County (Tex.) Women's Polit. Caucus, Houston; bd. dirs. USF Rsch. Found., Inc.; chair Fla. Elections Commn., 1999-2003; mem. Fla. Gov.'s Coun. Econ. Advisers, 2000—. Recipient U. Houston Coll. Social Scis. Tchg. Excellence award, 1977, Herbert J. Simon award for best article in 3d vol., Internat. Jour. Pub. Adminstrn., 1981, Theodore & Venette Askounes-Ashford Disting Scholar award U. South Fla., 1991, Disting. Rsch. Scholar award, 1991, Tchg. Excellence award, 1999; Ford Found. fellow, 1967-68; grantee Valencia C.C. Faculty, 1972, U. Houston, 1976-77, 79, 83; Fulbright Rsch. scholar, Korea, 1989; Choice mag. award, 1996; named Disting. Univ. Prof., 1999; rsch. fellow Fla. Inst. of Govt., 2000—. Mem. Am. Polit. Sci. Assn. (program com. 1983-84, chair sect. intergovtl. rels., award 1989; mem. exec. com. 1994—, pres.-elect sec. urban politics 1994-95, pres. sect. urban politics 1995-96), So. Polit. Sci. Assn. (v.p. 1990-91, pres.-elect 1992-93, pres. 1993-94, V.O. key award com. 1983-84, best paper on women and politics 1988, Diane Blair award 2001), Midwest Polit. Sci. Assn., Western Polit. Sci. Assn., Southwestern Polit. Sci. Assn. (local arrangements com. 1982-83, profession com. 1977-80), ASPA (convention com. Houston chpt. 1983, bd. mem. Suncoast chpt., pres.-elect 1991, Lilly award 1992), Policy Studies Orgn. (mem. editl. bd. jour. 1981—, exec. coun. 1983-85), Women's Caucus Polit. Sci. (portfolio pre-decision rev. coun. (Houston) coun. 1981, fin.-budget com. 1980-81), Fla. Polit. Sci. Assn. (pres. 1997-98, Manning Dauer Disting. Fla. Polit. Sci. award 2001), Acad. Polit. Sci., Mycpl. Fin. Officers Assn., Phi Kappa Phi (Artist/Scholar award U. South Fla. 1997), Phi Beta Kappa, Pi Sigma Alpha (mem. exec. coun. 1994-96, 2002), Pi Alpha Alpha. Methodist. Home: 2506 Collier Pky Land O Lakes FL 34639-5228 Office: U South Fla Dept Polit Sci Tampa FL 33620 E-mail: samacmanus@aol.com.

**MACMASTER, DANIEL MILLER,** retired museum official; b. Chgo., Feb. 11, 1913; s. Daniel Howard and Charlotte Louise (Miller) MacM.; m. Sylvia Jane Hill, Feb. 22, 1935; children— Daniel Miller, Jane Irene (Mrs. Robert W. Lightell). Student, Lakeside Press Tng. Sch., 1930-31, U. Chgo., 1931-x. L.H.D., Lincoln Coll., 1970; D.H.L., DePaul U., 1978. Mem. staff Mus. Sci. and Industry, Chgo., 1933—, acting dir., 1950, dir., 1951-72, pres., 1968-78, pres. emeritus, 1978—, life trustee, 1968—. Gen. mgr. Chgo. R.R. Fair, 1948-49 Author: (with others) Exploring the Mysteries of Physics and Chemistry, 1938; book reviewer; contbr. to newspapers, mags., encys. Mem. Homewood (Ill.) Bd. Edn., 1945-49, pres., 1948-49; mem. U. Ill. Citizen' Adv. Com., 1945—; sec. Higher Edn. Commn. Ill., 1955-59; dir. Hyde Park Bank and Trust Co., 1965-86; U.S. State Dept. Specialist to Ireland, Germany, Sweden, 1963; dir. Floating Seminar to Greece, 1960; guest mus. cons. Fed. Republic Germany, 1961, Iran, 1973, 74, 76, Hong Kong, 1978, 89, 90, 91, Singapore, Chili and Peru, 1978, Poland, Czechoslovakia and Hungary, 1979, Mexico, 1980, 81, Saudi Arabia, 1981, 82, 84, Columbia, Ecuador and Bolivia, 1983, Taiwan 1986-90, 92, 94; mem. Nat. 4-H Svc. Com.; hon. dir. Chgo. Chamber Orch. Soc., pres., 1969-70; bd. dirs. Sears Roebuck Found., 1970-73, Internat. Coll. Surgeons Hall of Fame; mem. Lincoln Acad. Ill.; hon. trustee U. Chgo. Cancer Rsch. Found.; life trustee Adler Planetarium; dir. emeritus Monmouth Coll.; bd. govs. Chgo. Heart Assn., vice chmn., 1972-73; founder Scottish Heritage Libr., 1999. Decorated Golden Cross Royal Order Phoenix Greece; Officer's Cross Polonia Restituta Poland; Grand Badge of Honor Austria; Grand Badge of Honor of Burgenland Austria; Golden Badge of Honor Vienna; Officer's Cross 1st class Order of Merit Germany; Officer Order of Merit Luxembourg; Order Cultural Merit Poland; Royal Swedish Order North Star; recipient Patriotic Civilian Service award U.S. Army, St. Andrews Soc. Citizen of Yr. award, 1978 Fellow Assn. Sci. and Tech. Centers; mem. Kappa Sigma. Clubs: Tavern, Quadrangle, Commercial. Home: 19715 Governors Hwy Flossmoor IL 60422-1794

**MACMASTER, ROBERT ELLSWORTH,** historian, educator; b. Winthrop, Mass., Oct. 10, 1919; s. Joseph Oscar and Ruby (Slocomb) MacM.; m. Ann Elizabeth Lynch, Apr. 28, 1942; children— Angus Michael, Martha Ann, David Joseph. AB, Harvard, 1941, A.M., 1948, PhD, 1952. Mem. faculty MIT, 1952-90, prof. history and lit., 1967-90, prof. emeritus, 1990—, chmn. history faculty, 1970-72. Author: Danilevsky: A Russian Totalitarian Philosopher, 1967; contbr. articles on L.N. Tolstoi to publs. Served with AUS, 1941-46. Mem. Am. Assn. Advancement Slavic Studies. Home: 461 Main St Hingham MA 02043-4701 Office: MIT Dept History Cambridge MA 02139

**MACMEEKEN, JOHN PEEBLES,** foundation executive, educator; b Aug. 15, 1924; s. John West and Esther (Strong) M.; m. Mary Swanberg, Nov. 26, 1949; children: Carol B. Macmeeken Luther, John W., Susan G. Student, U. Calif., Berkeley, 1941-43, U. Ill., 1943-44; JD, Harvard U., 1948. Bar: Calif. 1948. Assoc. Chickering & Gregory, San Francisco, 1948-60, ptnr., 1960-82, Pettit & Martin, San Francisco, 1982-93; v.p. Zynk Indsl. Corp., 1995-98; pres. Found. for Books to China, 1993—, SOAR Bus. Inst., 1998—. Bd. dirs. Lanark West Corp.; pres. Clinton U., San Francisco, 1995-97; lectr. law Fudan U., Shanghai, China, East China Normal U., Shanghai, Nanking U., China, Zhongshan U., Guangzhou; sec. Twan Co. LLC, Sian Tien Dao Yuan. Sgt. U.S. Army, 1943-45. Mem. Nat. Com. on US-China Rels., Calif. Bar Assn. Outlook Club Calif. Republican. Congregationalist. Home: 5708 Glenbrook Dr Oakland CA 94618-1724 Office Phone: 510-428-2145. Personal E-mail: jmacmeeken@aol.com.

**MACMILLAN, HOKE,** former state attorney general; m. Becky Klemt; children: Ryan Klemt, Christopher Klemt. BA, U. Wyo., 1967, JD, 1970. Bar: Wyo., Colo., Nebr., U.S. Ct. Appeals (10th cir.), U.S. Ct. Mil. Appeals, U.S. Supreme Ct. Capt. U.S. Army JAG, 1970—74; mem. Pence and Millett, Laramie, Wyo., 1974—2001, sr. ptnr., 1982—2001; atty. gen. State of Wyo., 2001—02. Fellow: Am. Bar Found.; mem.: Albany County Bar Assn., Nebr. State Bar, Wyo. State Bar (pres. 1996—97). Home: 42210 N Long Cove Way Anthem AZ 85086-1247

**MACMILLAN, ROBERT SMITH,** electronics engineer; b. LA, Aug. 28, 1924; s. Andrew James and Moneta (Smith) M.; m. Barbara Morison, Aug. 18, 1962; 1 child, Robert G. BS in Physics, Calif. Inst. Tech., 1948, MS in Elec. Engring., 1949, PhD in Elec. Engring./Physics cum laude, 1954. Rsch. engr. Jet Propulsion Lab., Calif. Inst. Tech., Pasadena, 1951-55, asst. prof. elec. engring., 1955-58; assoc. prof. elec. engring. U. So. Calif., L.A., 1958-70; mem. sr. tech. staff Litton Sys., Inc., Van Nuys, Calif., 1969-79; dir. sys. engring. Litton Data Command Sys., Agoura Hills, Calif., 1979-89; pres. The Macmillan Group, La Canada Flintridge, Calif., 1989—. Treas., v.p. Video Color Corp., Inglewood, 1965-66; cons. fgn. tech. div. USAF, Wright-Patterson AFB, Ohio, 1957-74, Space Tech. Labs., Glendale, Calif., 1956-60, Space Gen. Corp., El Monte, Calif., 1960-63. With Air Corps U.S. Army, 1943—46. Recipient Nat. Patriot's medal, Nat. Rifle Assn., 2002, Rep. Senatorial medal of freedom, 2004. Mem.: IEEE, Am. Phys. Soc., Am. Inst. Physics, Eta Kappa Nu, Tau Beta Pi, Sigma Xi. Republican. Presbyterian. Achievements include research in ionospheric, radio-wave, propagation; very low frequency radio-transmitting antennas; optical coherence and statistical optics. Home: 350 Starlight Crest Dr La Canada Flintridge CA 91011-2839 Office: The Macmillan Group 350 Starlight Crest Dr La Canada Flintridge CA 91011-2839 Office Fax: 818-952-1735. Personal E-mail: rsmacmillan08@aol.com.

**MACMILLAN, SHANNON ANN,** professional soccer player; b. Syosset, N.Y., Oct. 7, 1974; Student in social work, U. Portland. Profl. soccer player San Diego Spirit, 2001—03. Mem. U.S. Nat. Women's Soccer Team, 1993—, including silver medal World Univ. Games team, 1993, gold medal U.S. Olympic Team, 96; mem. U.S. Women's Under-20 Nat. Team, 1993—94, including championship Internat. Women's Tournament, France, 1993; mem. LaJolla (Calif.) Nomads club soccer team, winning state club championship, 1991, 92, Japanese Women's Profl. League, 1996, 97. Named 1995 Soccer Am. Player of Yr., Female Athlete of Yr., 1993, 1995, U. Portland, World Cup Champion, 1999; named to San Diego Union Tribune All-Acad. team; recipient Mo. Athletic Club award, 1995, Hermann award, U. Portland, 1995, Bill Hayward award, 1995, Silver medal, Sydney Olympic Games, 2000. Office: US Soccer Fedn 1801-1811 S Prairie Ave Chicago IL 60616

**MACMILLAN, STEPHEN P.,** health products executive; b. July 19, 1963; married; 2 children. BA in econ., Davidson Coll.; grad. advanced mgmt. program, Harvard Bus. Sch. Various mktg. positions Procter & Gamble; with over the counter div. McNeil Consumer and Specialty Pharm. Johnson & Johnson Corp., mktg. dir. J&J/Merck over-the-counter franchise worldwide England; mgr. dir. Johnson & Johnson MSD (Merck), England, 1995; v.p., mktg. and profl. sales McNeil Consumer and Splty. Pharm. Johnson & Johnson Corp., 1997; pres. Johnson & Johnson-Merck Consumer Pharmaceuticals; sector v.p. global splty. ops. Pharmacia & Upjohn, 1999—2003; COO Stryker Corp., 2004—05, pres., 2005—, CEO, 2005—. Office: Stryker Corp 2725 Fairfield Rd Kalamazoo MI 49002

**MACMILLAN, WHITNEY,** retired food products and import/export company executive; married; 2 children. BA, Yale Univ., 1951; D (hon.), Mont.State Univ., Bozeman, 2002. With Cargill, Wayzata, Minn., 1951—95, chmn., CEO, 1977—95, chmn. emeritus, 1995. Bd. dirs. Deluxe Corp., Minn.; exec. fellow, tchr. Univ. St. Thomas Grad. Sch. Bus., Minn. Named one of 400 Richest Americans, Forbes Mag., 2005; recipient Outstanding Alumni award, Blake Sch., 1997, 400 Richest Americans, Forbes Mag., 2006. Mem.: Care Internat., Trilateral Commn., Coun. Fgn. Affairs.*

**MACMILLEN, RICHARD EDWARD,** biological sciences educator, researcher; b. Upland, Calif., Apr. 19, 1932; s. Hesper Nichols and Ruth Henrietta (Golder) MacM.; m. Ann Gray, June 12, 1953 (div. 1975); children: Jennifer Kathleen, Douglas Michael; m. Barbara Jean Morgan, Oct. 23, 1980; 1 child, Ian Richard. BA, Pomona Coll., 1954; MS, U. Mich., 1956; PhD, UCLA, 1961. From instr. to assoc. prof. Pomona Coll., Claremont, Calif., 1960-68, Wig Disting. prof., 1965; assoc. prof., then prof. U. Calif., Irvine,

1968—, chair dept. population and environ. biology, 1972-74, chair dept. ecology and evolutionary biology, 1984-90, prof. emeritus, 1993—. Award panel NSF, Washington, 1976-80; coord. U. Calif. Multi-Campus Supercourse in Environ. Biology, White Mountain Rsch. Sta., 1996-97, tchg. participant, 1998—; rev. panel, EPA Star grad. fellowship program, 2002, 04; budget com., Jackson County Fire Dist. 5, 2001—; Alumni Admissions vol., Pomona Coll., 2001—; vol. morphologist U.S. Fish and Wildlife Svc. Forensics Lab., 2004—. Contbr. numerous articles to profl. jours. Chair sci. adv. bd. Endangered Habitats League, 1991-93. Recipient Rsch. award NSF, 1961-83; Fulbright-Hays Advanced Rsch. fellow Monash U., Australia, 1966-67. Fellow AAAS; mem. Am. Soc. Mammalogists (life), Ecol. Soc. Am. (cert. sr. ecologist), Am. Ornithologists Union (life), Cooper Ornithol. Soc. (life, bd. dirs. 1982-84). Democrat. Avocations: fly fishing, camping, hiking, nature photography. Home: 705 Foss Rd Talent OR 97540-9758 Business E-Mail: bidmac@jeffnet.org. *As world human populations continue to increase, our natural world continues to degrade. It is incumbent upon all of us to accept the responsibility of stewarding our land and its biota as precious and renewable resources.*

**MACMURREN, HAROLD HENRY, JR.,** psychologist, lawyer; b. Jersey City, Sept. 18, 1942; s. Harold Sr. and Evelyn (Almone) MacM.; m. Margaret Bartro, Nov. 21, 1970. BA, William Paterson Coll., Wayne, N.J., 1965; MA, Jersey City Coll., 1973; EdD, St. Johns U., N.Y.C., 1985; JD, Rutgers U., 1989. Cert. secondary tchr., N.J.; Bar: N.J. 1989. Instr. Wanaque (N.J.) Bd. Edn., 1965-66, cons. psychologist, 1983-84; instr. Elmwood Park (N.J.) Bd. Edn., 1967-70; coll. faculty mem., psychologist Assoc. Clinic, Jersey City, 1971-72; cons. psychologist Rockaway (N.J.) Bd. Edn., 1972-83; intern lawyer Environ. Law Clinic, Newark, 1988-89; cons. psychologist Pequannock (N.J.) Bd. Edn., 1984—; pvt. practice law, 2000—. Coord. child study team Sandyston Walpack Sch. Sys.; adj. prof. William Paterson U.; spkr., writer in field. Mem. ABA, NEA, N.J. Edn. Assn., N.J. Psychologists Assn., N.J. Bar Assn., Sierra Club, Phi Delta Kappa. Avocations: reading, travel, skiing, hiking. Home: 4 Systema Pl Sussex NJ 07461-2833 Office: PO Box 2510 22 Wantage Ave Branchville NJ 07890 Office Phone: 973-948-3500. E-mail: macmurrenesq@earthlink.net.

**MACMURREN, MARGARET PATRICIA,** secondary school educator, consultant; b. Newark, Nov. 4, 1947; d. Kenneth F. and Doris E. (Lounsberry) Bartro; m. Harold MacMurren, Nov. 21, 1970. BA, Paterson State U., 1969; MA, William Paterson Coll., 1976; postgrad., Jersey City State Coll., 1976—. Tchr. Byram (N.J.) Twp. Schs., 1969-77; learning cons., child study team coord. Andover Regional Schs., Newton, N.J., 1977—. Mem.: NEA, Andover Regional Edn. Assn. (pres. 1986-87), Sussex County Assn. Learning Cons. (pres. 1982—83, 1993—94, sec.-treas. 1991—92, v.p. 1992—93), N.J. Learning Assn. Avocations: skiing, dance, weightlifting, travel, reading. Home: 4 Systema Pl Sussex NJ 07461-2833 Office: Andover Regional Schs 707 Limecrest Rd Newton NJ 07860-8801 Office Phone: 973-940-1234 246. Business E-Mail: haroldm@nac.net.

**MACNAUGHTON, ANGUS ATHOLE,** finance company executive; b. Montreal, July 15, 1931; s. Athole Austin and Emily Kidder (MacLean) MacN.; children: Gillian Heather, Angus Andrew. Student, Lakefield Coll. Sch., 1941-47, McGill U., 1949-54. Auditor Coopers & Lybrand, Montreal, 1949-55; acct. Genstar Ltd., Montreal, 1955, asst. treas., 1956-61, treas., 1961-64, v.p., 1964-70, exec. v.p., 1970-73, pres., 1973-74, vice chmn., chief exec. officer, 1976-81, chmn. or pres., chief exec. officer, 1981-86; chmn. Genstar Investment Corp., 1987—. Bd. dirs. Barrick Gold Corp., Genstar Investment Corp., Varian Semicondr. Assocs., Inc., San Ramon Med. Ctr.; past pres. Montreal chpt. Tax Execs. Inst. Bd. govs. Lakefield Coll. Sch.; past chmn. San Francisco Bay Area coun. Boy Scouts Am.; bd. dirs. San Francisco Opera; trustee World Affairs Coun. of No. Calif. Mem. Pacific Union Club, Villa Taverna (San Francisco), Mt. Royal Club (Montreal), Toronto Club. Office: 4 Embarcadero Ctr Ste 1900 San Francisco CA 94111-4191

**MACNAUGHTON, NEIL SCOT,** nursing educator; b. Marshalltown, Iowa, Jan. 2, 1958; s. Hillis Allen and Eunice Kruse MacNaughton; m. Lise Kathryn Morris, June 11, 1983; children: Andrew, Hannah. BSN, Graceland Coll., Lamoni, Iowa, 1980; MA, U. Iowa, Iowa City, 1990, PhD, 2006. RN Iowa Nurse mgr. VA Med. Ctr., Iowa City, 1994—2000; staff nurse Mercy Hosp., 2000—04; instr. U. Iowa, 2002—03; asst. prof. St. Ambrose U., Davenport, 2004—. Mem.: Sigma Theta Tau (pres. elect Gamma chpt. 1994—96, pres. Gamma chpt. 1996—98). Office: Health Scis Coll Edn St Ambrose U 518 Locust St Davenport IA 52803-2898

**MACNEIL, IAN RODERICK,** lawyer, educator; b. N.Y.C., June 20, 1929; s. Robert Lister and Kathleen Gertrude (Metcalf) Macneil; m. Nancy Carol Wilson, Mar. 29, 1952; children: Roderick, Jennifer, Duncan (dec.), Andrew. BA magna cum laude, U. Vt., 1950; LLB magna cum laude, Harvard U., 1955. Bar: N.H. 1956-02. Law clk. Hon. Peter Woodbury, 1955-56; assoc. Sulloway Hollis Godfrey & Soden, Concord, NH, 1956-59; mem. faculty Cornell U. Law Sch., Ithaca, NY, 1959-72, 74-80, Ingersoll prof. Law, 1976-80; Wigmore prof. law Northwestern U. Sch. Law, Chgo., 1980-99, prof. emeritus, 1999—. Vis. prof. U. East Africa, 1965-67, Duke U., 1971-72; prof. law, mem. Inst. Advanced Studies, U. Va., 1972-74; vis. fellow Centre for Socio-legal Studies and Wolfson Coll., Oxford U., 1979; hon. vis. fellow faculty law U. Edinburgh, 1979, 87; Rosenthal lectr. Northwestern U. Sch. Law, 1979; Braucher vis. prof. Harvard U., 1988-89. Author: Bankruptcy Law in East Africa, 1966, Contracts: Exchange Transactions and Relations, 3d edit., with Paul J. Gudel, 2001. The New Social Contract, 1980, American Arbitration Law: Reformation Nationalization Internationalization, 1992; co-author: Federal Arbitration Law, 1994. Served with U.S. Army, 1951-53. Guggenheim fellow, 1978-79. Fellow Soc. Antiquaries (Scotland), Am. Acad. Arts and Scis.; mem. Scottish Soc. No. Studies, The Scottish Medievalists, Standing Coun. Scottish Chiefs. Home: 95/6 Grange Loan Edinburgh EH9 2ED Scotland

**MACNEIL, ROBERT BRECKENRIDGE WARE,** retired journalist, writer; b. Montreal, Que., Can., Jan. 19, 1931; came to U.S., 1963; s. Robert A.S. and Margaret Virginia (Oxner) MacN.; m. Rosemarie Anne Copland, 1956 (div. 1964); children: Catherine Anne, Ian B.; m. Jane J. Doherty, May 29, 1965 (div. 1983); children: Alison N., William H.; m. Donna P. Richards, Oct. 20, 1984. Student, Dalhousie U., 1949-51; BA, Carleton U., 1955; LHD (hon.), William Paterson Coll., 1977, Beaver Coll., Bates Coll., 1979, Lawrence U., 1980, Bucknell U., 1982, George Washington U., Kings Coll., Trinity Coll., U. Maine, 1983, Brown U., 1984, Colby Coll., Carleton Coll., U. S.C., 1985, Franklin and Marshall Coll., 1987, Nazareth Coll., Washington Coll., 1988, Kenyon Coll., 1990, U. Western Ont., 1992, U. Miami, Clark U., 1994, U. L.I., 1995, Columbia U., 1995, Princeton U., 1995, The Cooper Union, 1996, U. Toronto, 1997, Mt. Allison U., 1998; LHD (hon.), Dalhousie U., 2000. Radio actor CBC, Halifax, N.S., Canada, 1950-52, radio/TV announcer, 1954-55; announcer Sta.-CJCH, Halifax, 1951-52; announcer, news writer Sta. CFRA, Ottawa, Ont., Canada, 1953-54; sub-editor to filing editor Reuters News Agy., London, 1955-60; news corr. NBC, London, 1960-63, Washington, 1963-65, N.Y.C., 1965-67; corr. Panorama program BBC, London, 1967-71, 73-75; sr. corr. Nat. Public Affairs Center for TV, Washington, 1971-73; exec. editor, co-anchor MacNeil/Lehrer Report, Sta. -WNET-TV, N.Y.C., 1975—, MacNeil/Lehrer News Hour, PBS, 1983-95, ret., 1995. Author: The People Machine, The Influence of Television on American Politics, 1968, The Right Place at the Right Time, 1982, Wordstruck, 1989, Burden of Desire, 1992, The Voyage, 1995, Breaking News, 1998, Looking For my Country, 2003; co-author: The Story of English, 1986, Do You Speak American?, 2005; editor The Way We Were 1963, 1988. Trustee Freedom Forum Newseum. Decorated Officer Order of Can., 1998; inductee TV Acad. Hall of Fame, 1999; recipient Lifetime Achievement award Overseas Press Club, 1995, Broadcaster of Yr. Internat. Radio and TV Soc., 1991, Paul White award Radio TV News Dirs. Assn., 1990, Medal of Honor U. Mo. Sch. Journalism, 1980; Catto fellow The Aspen Inst. Fellow

AAAS, The MacDowell Colony (chmn. 1993); mem. AFTRA, Assn. Radio and TV News Analysts, Writers Guild Am., Century Club (NYC). Office: c/o MacNeil-Lehrer Prodns 2700 S Quincy St Ste 240 Arlington VA 22206-2226 E-mail: wordstruck2@cs.com.

**MACNEILL, FREDERICK DOUGLAS,** artist; b. Boston, Sept. 28, 1929; s. Frederick Douglas and Agnes (Thompson) MacN.; m. Anita Concetta Venti, Sept. 1, 1961; children: John, Paul. Student, Vesper George Sch. of Art, 1952-54, Arthur Safford, Alphonse Shelton. One man shows include Guild Boston Artists, 1980, 82; exhibited in group shows at Springfield (Mass.) Mus. Fine Art, 1965, Hobe Sound Gallery, Miller Gallery, Cin., Guild Boston Artists, 1982, Hobe Sound N. Gallery (formerly Payson Waldron Gallery), Portland, Maine, 1982, Nat. Wildlife Art Mus, Jackson, Wyo., 1994, Mus. of SW, Midland, Tex., 1992, Gibbs Mus. Art, Charleston, SC, Mystic Maritime Gallery and Mus., Mystic, Conn., 1995; represented in numerous and pvt. collections; painting included in Crucifixion in American Art; also book cover. Recipient Marion Quimby award Ogunquit Art Assn., 1975, Elliot Liskin award Rockport Art Assn., 1984, John Chetcutti, 1985, Silver medal of honor, 1985, Guild of Boston Artists award, 1988, Arts for the Pk. Top 100 award, 1991, 92, 94, 2004, others. Mem. Am. Artists Profl. League, Allied Artists Am., Acad. Artists of Am., Guild Boston Artists, Concord Art Assn., North Shore Art Assn. (Gloucester Coop. Bank award 2005, Gift Cert. award 2006, Alden Bryan Meml. award 2006), Rockport Art Assn. (Helen Van Wyk Gold medal, 2000, Marguerite Pearson Gold medal, 2002, Virginia Karl Meml. award 2004, Maurice E. Goldberg Meml. award 2005, Popular Vote award 2006), Salmagundi Club (NYC, Martin Hannon Meml. award). Home: 23 Dana Rd Concord MA 01742-3408

**MACNEILL, JAMES WILLIAM,** environmental energy and management consultant; b. Sask., Can., Apr. 22, 1928; s. Leslie William and Helga Ingeborg (Nohlgren) MacN.; m. Phyllis Beryl Ferguson, Nov. 30, 1953; children: Catherine Anne, Robin Lynne. BA, U. Sask., 1949, BE Mech., 1958, LLD (hon.), 1988; Diplome, U. Stockholm, 1951; DSc (hon.), McGill U., 1992; D of Environ. Studies (hon.), U. Waterloo, 1993; LHD (hon.), Lakehead U., 1994. Spl. adv. on constl. rev. Privy Council Office, Govt. Can., Ottawa, Ont., 1970-73; asst. sec. Can. Ministry of State for Urban Affairs, Ottawa, 1970-73, permanent sec., 1973-76; Can. AEP, Can. commr.-gen. UN Human Settlements Conf., Vancouver, B.C., 1975-78; dir. environ. directorate OECD, Paris, 1978-84; sec. gen. World Commn. Environment and Devel., Geneva, 1984-87; sr. fellow Inst. Research Pub. Policy, Ottawa, 1987-93; pres. J.W. MacNeill and Assocs., 1987-98; chmn. Internat. Inst. for Sustainable Devel., 1994-99. Spl. advisor to adminstrn. UN Devel. Program, 1994-97; chmn. ind. insp. panel World Bank, 1997-2002; mem. adv. panel BP Caspian Devel., 2003--. Author: Environmental Management, 1971, Beyond Interdependence, 1991. Apptd. officer Order of Can., 1995. Recipient Saskatchewan Achievement award, 1984, Silver medal City of Paris, 1983, Climate Inst. award, 1991, Swedish WASA award, 1991, Lifetime Achievement award Govt. of Can., 1994, Candlelight award UN, 2002, Elizabeth Haub award for internat. environ. diplomacy, 2005. Mem. Assn. Profl. Engrs. Ont., Assn. Profl. Engrs. Sask. Personal E-mail: jwmacneill@hotmail.com.

**MACOMBER, DEBBIE,** writer; m. Wayne Macomber. Author: Morning Comes Softly, 1993 (Waldenbooks Bestselling Non-Series Debut Romance, finalist, Romance Writers of Am. Member's Golden Choice award, Colo. Romance WRiters Keeper award, 1996), Trouble With Angels, 1994 (Waldenbooks Trend Book award), One Night, 1994, Someday Soon, 1995, Sooner or Later, 1996, Mrs. Miracle, 1996, This Matter of Marriage, 1997, Three Brides, No Groom, 1997, Lonesome Cowboy, 1998, Texas Two-Step, 1998, Caroline's Child, 1998, Dr. Texas, 1998, Nell's Cowboy, 1998, Lone Star Baby, 1998, Montana, 1998, Can This Be Christmas, 1998, Shirley, Goodness & Mercy, 1999, Moon Over Water, 1999, Promise Texas, 1999, A Season of Angels, 1999, The Touched by Angels, 1999, Dakota Born, 2000, Return to Promise, 2000, Thursdays at Eight, 2001 (one of Amazon.com's Top 10 Women's Fiction titles of 2001), Buffalo Valley, 2001, Always Dakota, 2001, 16 Lighthouse Road, 2001 (finalist, Dorothy Parker award of excellence for best contemporary romance novel), 204 Rosewood Lane, 2002, Between Friends, 2002, The Christmas Basket, 2002 (RITA award, Romance Writers of America), 311 Pelican Court, 2003, Those Christmas Angels, 2003, Changing Habits, 2003, The Snow Bride, 2003, 44 Cranberry Point, 2004 (Quills award for romance, 2005), The Shop on Blossom Street, 2004 (Named one of best romances of 2004, Oakland Press, Publishers Weekly paperback bestseller, 2005), When Christmas Comes, 2004, A Good Yarn, 2005, 50 Harbor Street, 2005 (Publishers Weekly paperback bestseller), There's Something About Christmas, 2005, Savannah's Garden, 2006, numerous others. Named a Tennessee Colonel for humanitarian svc., Gov. State of Tenn., 1994; named Favorite Top 10 Author, Affaire de Coeur Mag., 1995; recipient Regional Svc. award, Romance Writers of Am., 1989, Career Achievement award for contemporary romance, Romantic Times, 1992—93, Woman of Distinction award, Soroptimist Internat., 1996—97. Avocation: knitting. Mailing: c/o Author Mail Mira Books eHarlequin PO Box 5190 Buffalo NY 14240-5190*

**MACOPIYO, LABAN ADERO,** geographer, researcher, ecologist; b. Kisumu, Nyanza, Kenya, June 23, 1969; arrived in U.S., 2002; s. Stephen Opiyo Omolo and Rachel Adero Opiyo; m. Beldinah Rachel Ochola, May 16, 2001; 1 child, Serabi Akinyi Opiyo. BSc in Geography, U. Nairobi, 1993, MSc in Geography, 2000; student in Rangeland Ecology, Tex. A&M U., 2002—. Geog. info. sys. analyst Internat. Livestock Rsch. Inst., Nairobi, Kenya, 1998—2000; geog. info. sys. analyst and scientist Internat. Ctr. Insect Physiology and Ecology, Nairobi, 2000—02; rsch. asst. Tex. A&M U., College Station, Tex., 2002—. Mem. Geog. Info. Tech. Cmty. USAID, Washington, 2002—. Scholar, Swiss Agy. Devel. and Cooperation, 1994, U.S. AID, 2002—05; Jim Ellis fellowship, Global Livestock Collaborative Rsch. Support Program, 2003. Mem.: AAAS, African Students Assn. (v.p. 2003—04), Geo-info. Soc. Kenya (treas. 2000—01), Environ. Info. Sys. Program in Sub-Saharan Africa, Assn. Am. Geographers, Phi Kappa Phi. Office: Texas A&M University 2126 TAMU Animal Industries Building College Station TX 77843 Office Phone: 979-458-3215. Business E-Mail: lmacopiyo@cnrit.tamu.edu.

**MACOVSKI, ALBERT,** electrical engineer, educator; b. NYC, May 2, 1929; s. Philip and Rose (Winogr) Macovski; m. Adelaide Paris, Aug. 5, 1950; children: Michael, Nancy. BEE, City Coll. N.Y., 1950; MEE, Poly. Inst. Bklyn., 1953; PhD, Stanford U., 1968. Mem. tech. staff RCA Labs., Princeton, NJ, 1950—57; asst. prof., then assoc. prof. Poly. Inst. Bklyn., 1957—60; staff scientist Stanford Rsch. Inst., Menlo Park, Calif., 1960—71; fellow U. Calif. Med. Center San Francisco, 1971—72; prof. elec. engring. and radiology Stanford U., 1972—; endowed chair, Canon USA prof. engring., 1991—. Dir. Magnetic Resonance Sys. Rsch. Lab.; cons. to industry. Author. Recipient award for color TV cirs., Inst. Radio Engrs., 1958; spl. fellow, NIH, 1971. Fellow: IEEE (Zworykin award 1973), Internat. Soc. Magnetic Resonance in Medicine (trustee 1991—94, gold medal 1997), Optical Soc. Am., Am. Inst. Med. Biol. Engring.; mem.: NAE, Am. Assn. Physicists in Medicine, Nat. Acad. Medicine, Eta Kappa Nu, Sigma Xi. Jewish. Achievements include patents in field. Office: Stanford Univ Dept Elec Engring Stanford CA 94305 Home: 620 Sand Hill Rd Apt 407B Palo Alto CA 94304 Office Business E-Mail: macovski@stanford.edu.

**MACPHERSON, DANIEL CRAIG,** music educator; b. Columbo, Sri Lanka, Sept. 30, 1958; s. Neil Macpherson and Mary Pat Fox; m. Susan Marie Mancuso, Sept. 19, 1957; children: Katherine Esther, Brian Daniel. BA in Music Performance/Edn., SUNY, Fredonia, 1981; MusM, Youngstown State U., 1982; permanent N.Y. State elem. classroom cert., Nazareth Coll., 1993. Cert. elem. tchr. N.Y. Tchr./band dir. Brockport Sch. Dist., NY, 1982—84; Greece Sch. Dist., NY, 1984—. Bd. dirs, mem. in charge of edn. The Commn. Project, Rochester, NY, 1999—2006. Mem.: Music Educator's Nat. Conf., Internat. Trombone Assn. (corr.), N.Y. State Sch. Music Assoc. (assoc.). Home: 92 Colonial Village Rd Rochester NY 14625 Office: Kirk Road Elem

Sch 299 Kirk Rd Rochester NY Office Phone: 585-966-4300. Personal E-mail: dcm921@aol.com. Business E-Mail: dan.macpherson@greeceschools.k12.ny.us.

**MACPHERSON, ELLE,** model; b. Sydney, Australia, Mar. 29, 1964; m. Gilles Bensimon, May 24, 1986 (div.) Appeared on covers of Sports Illustrated swimsuit edit., 1986, 87, 88, 94, Elle, Cosmopolitan, Self; film appearances include Husbands and Wives, 1992, Sirens, 1994, If Lucy Fell, 1996, Jane Eyre, 1996, The Mirror Has Two Faces, 1996, The Edge, 1997, Batman and Robin, 1997, Beautopia, 1998, With Friends Like These, 1998, South Kensington, 2001; TV mini-series, A Girl Thing, 2001; TV appearance in Friends, 1999-2000.

**MACPHERSON, GRANT,** chef; Chef The Regent, The Ritz Carlton, Four Seasons; exec. chef Datai Hotel, Raffles Hotel, Bellagio, Las Vegas, Wynn Macau, Wynn Las Vegas. Team capt. Singapore Nat. Team; participant St. Moritz Gourmet Festival, Cape Gourmet, South Africa, Lanesborough, London, Crystal Cruises Alaskan Food and Wine Sailing, James Beard House, NYC, Labortario Del Galileo, Washington, The Masters, Sydney, Australia, Consentino Winery Anniversary Celebration, Napa, Calif.; chef's coun. Chef's for Humanity, 2005—. Featured in Cuisine Scene, Bon Appétit mag., Ansett Chefs, Foie Gras, Art Culinaire. Nominee Premier's award. Canada; recipient Gold medal, Culinary Olympics, 1992. Office: Country Club Wynn Las Vagas 3131 Las Vegas Blvd S Las Vegas NV 89109 Office Phone: 702-770-7000.*

**MACPHERSON, ROBERT DUNCAN,** mathematician, educator; b. Lakewood, Ohio, May 25, 1944; s. Herbert G. and Jeanette (Wolfenden) MacP. BA, Swarthmore Coll., 1966; MA, PhD, Harvard U., 1970; DSc (hon.), Brown U., 1994, U. Lille, France, 1993. Instr. Brown U.: Providence, 1970-72, asst. prof., 1972-74, assoc. prof., 1974-77, prof., 1977-85, Florence Pirce Grant prof., 1985-87; prof. MIT, Cambridge, Mass., 1987-94, Inst. Advanced Study, 1994—. Mem. Inst. des Hautes Etudes Sci., Paris, France, 1974-75, 76-77, 80-81, Steklov Math Inst., Moscow, USSR, 1980; vis. prof. U. Rome, 1985, 2000, U. Chgo., 1991, Max-Planck Inst. for Math, 1992; chmn. NRC Bd. Math. Scis., 1997-2000; mem. sci. adv. com. Math Sci. Rsch. Inst., 2004-. Co-author: Stratified Morse Theory, 1988, Nilpotent Orbits, 1989; contbr. numerous articles to profl. jours. Chmn. Former Soviet Union Aid Fund, 1991-96. Mem.: NAS (Math award 1992), Nat. Orgn. of Gay and Lesbian Sci. and Tech. Profs., Soc. for Applied and Indsl. Math., Am. Math. Soc. (Steele prize 2002), Am. Philos. Soc., Am. Acad. Arts and Scis., Moscow Math. Soc. (hon.), Phi Beta Kappa. Home: 14 Haslet Ave Princeton NJ 08540-4913 Office: Inst for Advanced Study Princeton NJ 08540 Office Phone: 609-921-8100. Business E-Mail: rdm@ias.edu.

**MACQUEEN, CHERIE K.,** interior designer, retired newscaster, sportscaster; b. Kansas City, Mo., Mar. 20, 1952; d. Ira Raymond and Peggy Estelle (Turner) Milks. AA in Liberal Arts, L.A. Valley Coll., 1982; BS in Liberal Studies, Excelsior Coll., Albany, N.Y., 1993; grad., Barbizon Sch. Modeling, 1996; postgrad., Calif. State U., San Bernardino, 1998—; cert. in Interior Design, U. Calif., Riverside, 2002. Lic. radio-TV operator. Personnel specialist U.S. Army, Honolulu, 1973-75, administrv. specialist San Francisco, 1975-77, broadcast journalist Vicenza, Italy, 1977-80; radio traffic specialist Armed Forces Radio and TV, L.A., 1980-84, radio prodn. specialist, 1984-86, supr. broadcast support specialist Sun Valley, 1986-90, broadcast support mgr, 1990-91, internal rifo. mgr., 1991-94, news and sports specialist, 1994-99; owner The Keilani Co., Highland, Calif., 2003—, Ladysmythe Handcrafts, Highland, 2003—. Mem.: DAV (life), Am. Soc. Interior Designers (bd. dirs. Inland/Palm Springs chpt. 2003—04, allied mem. Pasadena chpt. 2004—), Pacific Pioneer Broadcasters, Women in Mil. Svc. for Am. (charter), Armed Forces Broadcasters Assn. (v.p. L.A. chpt. 1991—93). Avocations: crafts, crocheting. Home: PO Box 276 Highland CA 92346-0276

**MACQUEEN, ROBERT MOFFAT,** solar physicist; b. Memphis, Mar. 28, 1938; s. Marion Leigh and Grace (Gilfillan) MacQ.; m. Caroline Gibbs, June 25, 1960 (div. Dec. 1997); children: Andrew, Marjorie; m. Marsha Anne Sime, Mar. 9, 1998. BS, Rhodes Coll., 1960; PhD, Johns Hopkins U., 1968. Asst. prof. physics Rhodes Coll., 1961-63; instr. physics and astronomy Goucher Coll., Towson, Md., 1964-66; sr. research scientist Nat. Ctr. for Atmospheric Research, Boulder, Colo., 1967-90, dir. High Altitude Obs., 1979-86, asst. dir., 1986-87, assoc. dir., 1987-89; prof. physics Rhodes Coll., Memphis, 1990—; prin. investigator NASA Apollo program, 1971-75, NASA Skylab program, 1970-76, NASA Solar Maximum Mission, 1976-79, NASA/ESA Internat. Solar Polar Mission, 1978-83; affiliate scientist NCAR, 1994—. Lectr. U. Colo., 1968-79, adj. prof., 1979-90; mem. com. on space astronomy Nat. Acad. Scis., 1973-76, mem. com. on space physics, 1977-79; mem. Space Sci. Bd., 1983-86 Recipient Exceptional Sci. Achievement medal NASA, 1974 Fellow Optical Soc. Am.; mem. Am. Astron. Soc. (chmn. solar physics div. 1976-78), Assn. Univ. Research Astronomy (dir.-at-large 1984-93, chmn. bd. 1989-92), Am. Assn. Physics Tchrs., Sigma Xi. E-mail: rmac@rhodes.edu.*

**MAC RAE, ALFRED URQUHART,** physicist, electrical engineer; b. NYC, Apr. 14, 1932; s. Farquhar and Eliza J. (Urquhart) Mac R.; m. Peggy M. Hazard, May 13, 1967; children: Susan, Pamela. BS in Physics, Syracuse U., 1954, PhD in Physics, 1960. Dir. integrated circuit devel. Bell Labs., Murray Hill, NJ, 1979-83, dir. satellite communications systems Homdel, NJ, 1983-95; pres. Mac Tech., Berkeley Heights, NJ, 1995—. Sr. rsch. fellow Potomac Inst. New Zealand; chair NASA Internat. Technology Studies, 1997-98; mem. adv. com. to bd. trustees N.J. Inst. Tech., 1981-85. Bd. editor: Vacuum Sci. and Tech., 1965-67, Rev. Sci. Instruments, 1969-71; contbr. articles to jours.; patentee in field. Bd. dirs. Summit Area ARC, 1996-2004, chmn., 2001-02. Fellow IEEE (mem., chmn. numerous coms. 1969—, Third Millennium medal 2000), Am. Phys. Soc., Nat. Acad. Engring. (mem. Bohmische Phys. Soc., IEEE Electron Devices Soc. (pres. 1986-87, chmn. field awards coun. 1989-93, Ebers award 1994, Disting. Svcs. award 1996). Office: 72 Sherbrook Dr Berkeley Heights NJ 07922-2346 Personal E-mail: a.macrae@ieee.org.

**MACRAE, CAMERON FARQUHAR, III,** lawyer; b. NYC, Mar. 21, 1942; s. Cameron F. and Jane B. (Miller) MacR.; m. Ann Wooster Bedell, Nov. 30, 1974; children: Catherine Fairfax, Ann Cameron. AB, Princeton U., 1963; LLB, Yale U., 1966. Bar: N.Y. 1966, D.C. 1967, U.S. Dist. Ct. (so. dist.) N.Y. 1975. Atty.-advisor Office of Gen. Counsel to Sec. Air Force, Washington, 1966-69; assoc. Davis, Polk & Wardell, N.Y.C., 1970-72; dep. supt. and counsel N.Y. State Banking Dept., N.Y.C., 1972-74; sr. ptnr. LeBeouf, Lamb, Greene & MacRae, LLP, N.Y.C., 1975—2004, sr. of counsel, 2005—. Dir. Nat. Integrity Life Ins. Co., 2000—. Note and comment editor Yale Law Jour., 1965-66. Trustee, sec. St. Andrew's Dune Ch., 1982—; hon. chmn. Clear Pool Inc., 1990-94. Capt. USAF res., 1966-69. Mem. Assn. of Bar of City of N.Y. (past mem. securities regulation com., banking law com.), D.C. Bar Assn., Union Club (N.Y.C.), Meadow Club (v.p., bd. govs.), Bathing Corp. Southampton, Shinnecock Hills Golf Club (Southampton), Cottage Club (Princeton, N.J.), Jupiter Island Club. Independent. Episcopalian. Office: LeBeouf Lamb Greene & MacRae LLP 125 W 55th St New York NY 10019-5369 Office Phone: 212-424-8080. E-mail: cfmacrae@llgm.com

**MACRAE, ELIZABETH (ELIZABETH MACRAE HALSEY),** counselor, actor; b. Columbia, S.C., Feb. 22, 1936; d. James and Dorothy (Hendon) MacRae; m. Charles Day Halsey, Jr., 1969; m. Nedrick Young, 1965 (dec. 1968); children: Benjamin Young(dec.), Beryl MacRae Young(dec.). Student, Herbert Berghof Studio, N.Y.C., 1956—58, Arts Students League, 1958, U. So. Calif., L.A., 1965, Marymount Manhattan Coll., N.Y.C., 1989—91, Breakthrough at Gracie Sq. Hosp., 1990—91. Cert. Alcoholism and Alcohol Abuse, Credentialed Alcoholism Counselor 1992 Interm Acres, Carmel, NY, 1990; counselor chem. dependency Breakthrough at Gracie Sq. Hosp., 1990; adult counselor Manhattan Bowery Corp., 1991—93; program dir., counselor alcoholism outpatient clinic Freedom Inst., 1993—98. Actor: (plays) off Broadway, 1956, New. Eng. Stock, 1957, 1963, (as Elizabeth

MacRae): (films) Everything's Ducky, 1961, Love in a Goldfish Bowl, 1961, The Incredible Mr. Limpet, 1964, The Wild Westerners, 1962, For Love or Money, 1963; (TV series) Route 66, 1969, 1972, 1974; (films) The Conversation, 1974; (TV series) Naked City, 1960, 77 Sunset Strip, 1961, Harrigan and Son, 1961, Surfside 6, 1961, Maverick, 1961, Asphalt Jungle, 1961, Dr. Kildare, 1962, Hawaiian Eye, 1962, Stoney Burke, 1962, Death Valley Days, 1962, Sam Benedict, 1962, Gunsmoke, 1961—64, The Untouchables, 1962, Burke's Law, 1963, Rawhide, 1963, The Virginian, 1964, The Fugitive, 1964, I Dream of Jeannie, 1965, Gomer Pyle, USMC, 1966—68, Andy Griffith, 1967, Bonanza, 1968, Judd for the Defense, 1969, Rheingold Theatre - England, 1969, Kojak, 1974, Petrocelli, 1974, Mannix, 1974, Rhoda, 1976, Barnaby Jones, 1976, General Hospital, 1969, 1971; (TV films), 1974; (TV series) Days of Our Lives, 1976—77, All My Children, 1978, Guiding Light, 1980, Another World, 1980, 1989, Search for Tomorrow,: (live TV) The Verdict is Yours, 1958—59, Ellery Queen, 1960, Ninotshka, 1960. Vol. Help Line, NYC, 1982. Recipient Disting. Counselor award, Freedom Inst., 2003. Mem.: AFTRA, SAG, Nat. Assn. Alcoholism and Drug Abuse Counselors, Actors Equity, Acad. Motion Picture Arts and Scis., Nat. Soc. Colonial Dames Am. (N.C. chpt.). Achievements include representation in Elizabeth MacRae Archive at Wilson Libr. U. N.C., Chapel Hill. Home: 1405 Raeford Rd Fayetteville NC 28305 Office Phone: 910-485-5061. E-mail: chalsey@nc.rr.com.

**MACRAE HALSEY, ELIZABETH See MACRAE, ELIZABETH**

**MACRI, THEODORE WILLIAM,** book publisher; b. NYC; s. Francis Carl and Emma Julia (Fantini) M.; m. Joan Michele Damato; children: Alicia, Theodore William AB, Villanova U.; MA, NYU. With Doubleday & Co. Inc., N.Y.C., dir. domestic rights, 1978-82, editorial group dir., 1982-83, asst. to pres., 1983; v.p., pub. R.R. Bowker Co., 1983-85; v.p., dir. subs. rights Contemporary Books, Inc., 1985-90; v.p. Carol Pub. Group, Inc., N.Y.C., 1990-94; pres. Ted Macri Assocs., 1994—. Bd. dirs. CUNY Ctr. for Pub., Nat. Book Awards Mem. N.Y. County Republican Com.; mem. men's com. Mus. Natural History, N.Y.C. Served to lt. (j.g.) USNR. Named Disting. Alumnus Villanova U. Mem. Assn. Am. Pubs. (edn. com.), Am. Bookseller's Assn. Clubs: N.Y. Athletic (N.Y.C.). Republican. Roman Catholic. Office: 180 Central Park S Ste 441 New York NY 10019-1562 Personal E-mail: papatwm@aol.com.

**MACRIS, MICHAEL,** lawyer; b. Jackson Heights, NY, July 12, 1949; Student, Cornell U.; BA with distinction, Stanford U., 1971; JD, Columbia U., 1974. Bar: N.Y. 1975, Conn. 1976. Mem. Cahill Gordon & Reindel LLP, N.Y.C. Bd. editors Columbia Law Rev., 1973-74; co-editor ERISA & Benefits Law Jour., 1992-99. Harlan Fiske Stone scholar. Fellow: Am. Coll. Employee Benefits Counsel (charter); mem.: ABA (group vice chmn. employee benefit plans and compensation arrangements, real property, probate and trust law sect.), Phi Beta Kappa. Office: Cahill Gordon & Reindel LLP 80 Pine St Fl 19 New York NY 10005-1790 Office Phone: 212-701-3409. E-mail: mmacris@cahill.com.

**MACRURY, KING,** management consultant; b. Manchester, NH, Oct. 14, 1915; s. Colin H. and Lauretta C. (Shea) MacR.; 1 son, Colin C. AB, Rollins Coll., 1938; postgrad., St. Anselms Coll., L.I. Coll. Medicine, Princeton. Asst. personnel dir. Lily-Tulip Cup Corp., 1939; asst. dir. market research Ward Baking Co., 1940-41; staff mem. Nat. Indsl. Conf. Bd., 1941-43; cons. indsl. relations and orgn. planning McKinsey & Co., 1946-48; internal cons. Oxford Paper Co., 1949-50; installer, dir. indsl. relations Champion Internat. Co., 1950-51; pvt. practice Rye, NH, 1951—. Lectr. Indsl. Rsch. Inst., 1962-68, Mgmt. Center, Cambridge, 1968-71, Dun & Bradstreet, 1979—; extension div. U. N.H., 1968—; extension program U. Maine,* 1978—; also U. Bridgeport, extension program U. Conn.; coordinator mgmt. edn. extension div. U. Conn., 1964-68, Philippine Council Mgmt., 1969—, Econ. Devel. Found. Philippines, 1969—, Am. Metal Stamping Assn., 1969—; condr. mgmt. seminars for Asian Assn. Mgmt. Orgns. C.I.O.S., 1972; Mem. Indsl. Devel. Commn. Andover, 1957-58; manpower com. U.S. Dept. Labor Bus. Adv. Council, 1958-61. Author: Developing Your People Potential; Contbr. numerous articles in field to profl. jours. Served to lt. USNR, 1943-46. Mem. N.H. Dental Soc. (hon.), Smaller Bus. Assn. N.E., Res. Officers Assn. Office: Box 988 York Beach ME 03910 Office Phone: 207-351-1019. Business E-Mail: king@kingmacrury.com. *As individuals or as corporations, we derive our vitality from the responsiveness of those to whom we are bound in interest or effort. So it becomes, necessarily, our primary goal to inspire and to nurture this elemental source of strength.*

**MACSAI, JOHN,** architect; b. Budapest, Hungary, May 20, 1926; came to U.S., 1947, naturalized, 1954; s. Ferenc and Margit (Rosenfeld) Lusztig; m. Geraldine Marcus, May 7, 1950; children: Pamela, Aaron, Marian, Gwen. Baccalaureate summa cum laude, Kolcsey Gimnasium, Budapest, 1944; student, Atelier Art Sch., Budapest, 1941-43, Poly. U., 1945-47; BArch magna cum laude, Miami U., Oxford, Ohio, 1949. Archtl. designer Skidmore, Owings & Merrill, Chgo., Pace Assos., Chgo., Raymond Loewy Assos., Chgo., 1949-55; ptnr. Hausner & Macsai, Chgo., 1955-71, Campbell & Macsai, Chgo., 1971-74; prin. John Macsai & Assocs. Architects, Inc., Chgo., 1975-90, O'Donnell Wicklund Pigozzi & Peterson, Chgo., 1991-2000, ret., 2000. Prof. architecture U. Ill., Chgo., 1970-76, prof. emeritus, 1997—. Author: High Rise Apartment Buildings: A Design Primer, 1972, Housing, 1976, Housing, 2d edit., 1982, Housing, Russian edit., 1980, Housing, Mexican edit., 1984; co-author: Designing Environments for the Aged, 1977, Housing for a Maturing Population, 1983, (ency.) Highrise Apartment Buildings, 1988, East European Modernism, 1996; contbr. articles to profl. jours.; prin. works include Nat. Opinion Rsch. Ctr., U.Chgo., 1967, High Energy Physics Bldg., 1968, Social Svcs. Ctr., 1970, Harbor House, 1965, Malibu East, 1972, Waterford apt. bldg., 1976, U. Chgo. faculty townhouses, 1986, Fairfield Ct. housing for the elderly, 1989, Evanston Pl. apt. bldg and city garage, 1991, 2960 N. Lake Shore Dr. Housing for the Elderly, 1991; staff arch. Tel Tanninim Archaeol. Project, Israel, 1996—2000, Elike Archaeol. Project, Greece, 2001; exhibitions include Gallery 1756, Chgo., 1991—2005, Chgo. Cultural Ctr., 2000, Cliffdwellers Club, 2002; author: (monthly article) Evanston Round Table. Fellow AIA (13 design award citations Chgo. chpt.). Jewish. Home: 1501 Hinman Ave Apt 3B Evanston IL 60201-4675 Office Phone: 847-328-5748. Business E-Mail: jgmacsai@uic.edu.

**MACTAGGART, TERRENCE JOSEPH,** professor, former university chancellor; b. Buffalo, Sept. 20, 1946; s. Joseph Carol and Genieve Mary (Quinn) MacT. BA in English and Philosophy, Canisius Coll., Buffalo, 1967; MA in Lit., St. Louis U., 1971, PhD in Lit., 1976; MBA, St. Cloud (Minn.) State U., 1986. Prof. Blackburn Coll., Carlinville, Ill., 1973-74; dir. Webster U., St. Louis, 1974-77; acting dean U. Alaska, Fairbanks, 1977-79; dean St. Cloud State U., Minn., 1979-83; v.p. Met. State U., St. Paul, 1983-86; vice chancellor Minn. State U. System, St. Paul, 1986-87, chancellor, 1991-95, U. Wis., Superior, 1987-91; prof. English Minn. State U., St. Paul, 1991-95; chancellor U. Maine Sys., Bangor, 1996—2001, interim chancellor, 2006—; prof. Univ. of Maine, 2002—. Fulbright Scholar in Thailand, 1996. Editor: Cost Effective Assessment of Prior Learning, 1983; contbr. articles on higher edn. to profl. jours. Sgt. U.S. Army, 1969-71, Viet Nam. NDEA fellow, 1968-72. Mem. Phi Beta Kappa. Avocations: cross country skiing, sailing. Office: U Maine Sys 16 Central St Bangor ME 04401-5106*

**MACTAS, MARK V.,** diversified financial services company executive; BA in math and Econ., Lehigh Univ., Bethlehem, Penn. Former internat. consul, later mng. dir. global health and welfare bus. Towers Perrin, 1977, former v.p., former pres., chmn., CEO, 2001—. Office: Towers Perrin One Stamford Plaza Stamford CT 06901*

**MACTAVISH, CRAIG,** professional hockey coach, former professional hockey player; b. London, Ont., Can., Aug. 15, 1958; m. Debbie MacTavish; children: Nathan, Sean, Brianna. Center Boston Bruins, 1980-85, Edmonton Oilers, 1985-94, NY Rangers, 1994, Phila. Flyers, 1994-96, St. Louis Blues, 1996-97; asst. coach NY Rangers, 1997—99, Edmonton Oilers, 1999—2000,

head coach, 2000—. Achievements include being a member of Stanely Cup Champion Edmonton Oilers, 1987, 1988, 1990, NY Rangers, 1994. Office: Edmonton Oilers Rexall Place 11230-110 St Edmonton AB Canada T5G 3H7*

**MACTAVISH, SUSANNE HANNA,** library and information scientist; b. Atlanta, Jan. 6, 1947; d. Albert Kenneth and Mary Ann Hanna; m. Nelson Thomas Henderson, May 4, 1974 (div. Sept. 3, 1993); children: Russell Evan Henderson, Andrea Renee Henderson; m. Douglas Stewart MacTavish, Aug. 1, 1998; 1 child, Ian Steward. BA, DePauw U., Greencastle, Ind., 1969; MS in Lib. Sci., Case Western Res. U., Cleve., 1970. Libr. Denver Pub. Libr., 1970—72; info. officer, libr. US CIA, 1972—81; mgr. libr. svcs. Gen. Electric Co., Gaithersburg, Md., 1981—93; project lead Lockheed Martin, Falls Church, Va., 1993—2001, ethics officer Gaithersburg, 2001—. Mem.: ALA (life), Internat. Orgn. for Standardization/Internat. Electrotechnial Commn. Joint Tech. Com., Libr. Adminstrn. and Mgmt. Assn. (pres. 1990—91, councilor 2005—), Ethics Officer Assn. (assoc.), Beta Phi Mu, Delta Zeta (v.p. 1968—69). Methodist. Home: 1500 S Quincy St Arlington VA 22204 Office Phone: 301-240-6465.

**MACTIER, ANN DICKINSON,** state agency administrator; b. Ravenna, Nebr., June 29, 1922; d. Robert Smith and Carrie (Clark) Dickinson; m. James Allan Mactier, Feb. 26, 1944; children: James Allan II, Judith Ann, Robert Dickinson. BS, Northwestern U., 1944; BA, U. Nebr., Omaha, 1963, MA, 1969; EdD (hon.), U. Nebr., 2005. Owner, mgr. Ponca Hills Riding Acad., Omaha, 1966-73; cmty. coord. Coll. Fine Arts. U. Nebr., Omaha, 1974-75; mem. Nebr. State Bd. Edn., 1966—, v.p., 2001—. Mem. Omaha Jr. League, 1944—57; mem. exec. com. Riverfront Devel. Corp., Omaha, 1973—79; founder, pres. Florence Arts Coun., Omaha, 1975 —79; mem. Omaha Pub. Schs. Bd. Edn., 1983—98; mem. steering com. Coun. Urban Bds. Edn., 1996—98; bd. dirs. Coun. Great City Schs., 1984—89. Home: 3811 N Post Rd Omaha NE 68112-1209 Office Phone: 402-453-4580. E-mail: mactier@starband.net.

**MACUR, PATRICIA ALICE,** systems analyst, application developer; b. Chgo. d. Alexander J. and Alice Mary (Styburski) Mackiewicz; m. George J. Macur; children: Alexander, Cindy Macur Conti. BS, SUNY, 1978; MS, Thomas J. Watson Sch. of Engring., 1984. System control analyst IBM Corp., Endicott, N.Y., 1977; programmer trainee intelligent systems NCR, Ithaca, N.Y., 1978-79, assoc. programmer software integration, 1980, assoc. programmer I gen. purpose systems, 1980-81, programmer, analyst terminal software div., 1981-84; applications analyst material mgmt. systems Eastman Kodak Co., Rochester, N.Y., 1984-86, applications analyst planning and control systems, 1986-88; sr. programmer, analyst mfg. systems Ingersoll-Rand Systems, Athens, Pa., 1989-91; sr. assoc. programmer copics packing applications system IBM, Atlanta, 1991-94, customer svc. rep. S.E. region, 1991-94; fin. analyst People Soft/Oracle Fins., Atlanta, 1995; sr. sys. analyst PPL, 1996—. Avocation: horseback riding. Office: 945 E Paces Ferry Rd NW Box 18616 Atlanta GA 31126-0616 E-mail: macur@plantation-ppl.com.

**MACURDY, JOHN EDWARD,** bass; b. Detroit, Mar. 18, 1929; s. Blanchard Archibald and Dorathea Rosalie (Radtke) Macurdy; m. Justine May Votypka, Apr. 12, 1958; children: Allison Anne, John Blanchard. Student, Wayne State U., 1947; student of Avery Crew, Detroit, 1946. Mem. N.Y.C. Opera, 1959-62, Met. Opera, 1962—. Appeared in U.S., Europe, including San Francisco Opera, La Scala; performances include world premieres Mourning Becomes Electra, Met. Opera, 1967, opening night Anthony and Cleopatra, Met. Opera, 1966, Wuthering Heights, Santa Fe Opera, 1958, Six Characters in Search of an Author, N.Y.C. Opera, 1959, Griffalkin, Tanglewood Festival, 1957; Am. premieres Capriccio, Santa Fe Opera, 1958, Murder in the Cathedral, Empire State Music Festival, Bear Mountain Park, N.Y., 1959, Inspector General, N.Y.C. Opera, 1960; appeared with numerous orchs.; film Don Giovanni, 1979; participant 40th Anniversary Sud-Deutsche Rundfunk, 100th Anniversary Gala Met. Opera, 1983. Served with USAF, 1950-54. Recipient medal for artistic merit during Mich. Week City of Detroit, 1969, Arts Achievement award Wayne State U., 2003; inducted into Acad. Vocal Hall of Fame, 1985. Mem.: Bohemian Club of San Francisco. Presbyterian. Office: 73 Tall Oaks Ct Stamford CT 06903-1515

**MAC WATTERS, VIRGINIA ELIZABETH,** singer, music educator, actress; b. Phila. d. Frederick-Kennedy and Idoleein (Hallowell) Mac W.; m. Paul Abée, June 10, 1960. Grad., Phila. Normal Sch. for Tchrs., 1933; student, Curtis Inst. Music, Phila. 1936. With New Opera Co., N.Y.C., 1941-42; artist-in-residence Ind. U. Sch. Music, 1957-58; assoc. prof. U. Ind. Sch. Music, 1958-68, prof. voice, 1968-82, prof. emeritus, 1982—. Singer: leading roles Broadway mus. Rosalinda, 1942-44, Mr. Strauss Goes to Boston, 1945, leading opera roles New Opera Co., N.Y.C., 1941-42, San Francisco, 1944, N.Y.C. Ctr., 1946-51; leading soprano for reopening of Royal Opera House, Covent Garden, London, 1947-48, Guatemala, El Salvador, Cen. Am., 1948-49; debut at Met. Opera, N.Y.C., 1952; TV spls. on NBC include Menotti's Old Maid and the Thief, 1949, Would-be Gentleman (R. Strauss), 1955; leading singer with Met. Opera Co. on coast to coast tour of Die Fledermaus, 1951-52, Met. Opera debut, N.Y.C., 1952, leading soprano Cen. City Opera Festival, Colo., 1952-56; performed with symphony orchs. in U.S., Can., S.Am.; concert recitalist U.S., Can., 1950-62; opened N.Y. Empire State Music Festival in Ariadne auf Naxos (Strauss), 1959; soloist Mozart Festival, Ann Arbor, Mich. Recipient Mile award Album Familiar Music, 1949, Ind U. Disting. Tchg. award, 1979; named One of 10 Outstanding Women of the Yr.; Zeckwer Hahn Phila. Mus. Acad. scholar, 1941-42; MacWatters chair donated by New Auer Grand Concert Hall, U. Ind. Sch. Music. Mem. Nat. Fedn. of Music Clubs, Nat. Soc. Arts and Letters, Nat. Soc. Lit. and Arts, Soc. Am. Musicians, Nat. Assn. Tchrs. of Singing, Internat. Platform Assn., Sigma Alpha Iota. Clubs: Matinee Musical (hon. mem. Phila., Indpls. chpts.). Achievements include having only original recorded version of Zerbinetta aria from Ariadne auf Naxos (Strauss). Home: 3800 Arlington Rd Bloomington IN 47404-1347 Office: Ind U Sch Music Bloomington IN 47405

**MACWILLIAMS, KENNETH EDWARD,** investment banker; b. Newburyport, Mass., Aug. 21, 1936; s. Harold Freeman and Helen (Melia) MacW.; children: Robert Hovey, James Stuart; m. Natalya V. Fedorova, Aug. 29, 2004. BA, Harvard U., 1958, MBA, 1962. V.p. Morgan Guaranty Trust Co., N.Y.C., 1962-71; sr. assoc. Goldman Sachs & Co., N.Y.C., 1971-74; mng. dir., domestic merchant banking group Manfacturers Hanover Trust Co., N.Y.C., 1975-82; chmn., chief exec. officer Prudential Capital Corp. subs. Prudential Ins. Co. Am., Newark, 1982-90; pres. Prudential Equity Mgmt. Assn. subs. Prudential Ins. Co. Am., Newark, 1990-92; founder, pres. Woodrow Wilson Assocs., N.Y.C., 1993—. Personal E-mail: macwilliams@earthlink.net.

**MACWILLIAMS, MICHAEL BROUGHTON,** lawyer; b. Balt., Oct. 11, 1966; s. Roger W. and Bette Burk (Broughton) MacW. BSME, Va. Tech. U., 1989; JD, U. Balt., 1994. Tech. rep. ARCO Chem. Co., Chgo., 1989-91; assoc. Goodell, DeVries, Leecy & Gray, Balt., 1994—2001, Venable LLP, Balt., 2001—03, ptnr., comml., intellectual property litig., 2003—. Editor-in-chief Balt. Law Rev. Mem. Md. State Bar Assn. (tech. task force 1997—). Avocation: sailboat racing. Office: Venable LLP 1800 Mercantile Bank & Trust Bldg 2 Hopkins Plz Baltimore MD 21201 Office Phone: 410-244-7514. Office Fax: 410-244-7742. Business E-Mail: mbmacwilliams@venable.com.

**MACY, WILLIAM H.,** actor; b. Miami, Mar. 13, 1950; m. Felicity Huffman, 1997; children: Sofia Grace, Georgia Grace. Founding mem. St. Nicholas Theater, Chgo., Atlantic Theatre Co., NYC. Actor: (TV series) The Awakening Land, 1978, Kate & Allie, 1984, Spenser: For Hire, 1985, The Equalizer, 1985, L.A. Law, 1986, Law & Order, 1990, Civil Wars, 1991, Bakersfield P.D., 1993, Frasier, 1993, ER, 1994, Superman, 1996, King of the Hill, 1997, The Lionhearts, 1998, Hercules, 1998, Sports Night, 1998, Batman Beyond, 1999, Out of Order, 2003; writer: thirtysomething, 1987; writer, actor Above Suspicion, 1995; dir., actor: Lip Service, 1988; actor: (TV films) The Cradle

Will Fall, 1983, The Boy Who Loved Trolls, 1984, The Dining Room, 1984, The Murder of Mary Phagan, 1988, In the Line of Duty: Siege at Marion, 1992, A Private Matter, 1992, The Water Engine, 1992, The Heart of Justice, 1993, Texan, 1994, The Writing on the Wall, 1994, In the Shadow of Evil, 1995, Andersonville, 1996, The Night of the Headless Horseman, 1999, It's a Very Merry Muppet Christmas Movie, 2002, Reversible Errors, 2004; writer, actor: The Con, 1998; A Slight Case of Murder, 1999; Door to Door, 2002 (Screen Actors Guild award best actor, 2003, Emmy award best actor in a TV movie, 2003, Emmy award best writing TV movie, 2003); actor, writer, actor: (TV films) The Wool Cap, 2004; writer Every Woman's Dream, 1996; Just a Walk in the Park, 2002; actor: (films) Foolin' Around, 1980, Somewhere in Time, 1980, Without a Trace, 1983, The Last Dragon, 1985, Radio Days, 1987, House of Games, 1987, Things Change, 1988, Homicide, 1991, Shadows and Fog, 1992, Benny & Joon, 1993, Searching for Bobby Fischer, 1993, Twenty Bucks, 1993, Being Human, 1993, The Client, 1994, Oleanna, 1994, Murder in the First, 1995, Roommates, 1995, Tall Tale, 1995, Evolver, 1995, Mr. Holland's Opus, 1995, Down Periscope, 1996, Fargo, 1996, Hit Me, 1996, Ghosts of Mississippi, 1996, Colin Fitz, 1996, Air Force One, 1997, Boogie Nights, 1997, Wag the Dog, 1997, Jerry and Tom, 1998, Pleasantville, 1998, Psycho, 1998, The Secret of NIMH 2: Timmy to the Rescue, 1998, A Civil Action, 1998, Happy, Texas, 1999, Mystery Men, 1999, Magnolia, 1999, Panic, 2000, State and Main, 2000, Jurassic Park III, 2001, Focus, 2001, Welcome to Collinwood, 2002, The Cooler, 2003, Seabiscuit, 2003, Cellular, 2004, Sahara, 2005, Edmond, 2005, Thank You for Smoking, 2006, (voice) Doogal, 2006, Bobby, 2006, (voice) Everyone's Hero, 2006; exec. prodr.: Transamerica, 2005. Spokesperson United Cerebral Palsy. Office: Creative Artist Agency 9830 Wilshire Blvd Beverly Hills CA 90212*

**MACZULSKI, MARGARET LOUISE,** event marketing professional, meeting manager; b. Detroit, Apr. 01; d. Bohdan Alexander and Olga Louise (Martinuick) Maczulski. BS, Mich. State U.; cert. E-Commerce Mgmt., DePaul U., 2000. Cert. meeting mgr. Mgr. meetings Nat. Assn. Realtors, Mktg. Inst., Chgo., 1977-82, mgr. mktg., 1982-83; regional sales mgr. Fairmont Hotels, Chgo., 1982; dir., mgr. trade shows and confs. Capital Cities Am. Broadcasting Co./Pub. Div., Wheaton, Ill., 1983-85; mgr. meeting and conf. planning Soc. Human Resource Mgmt., Alexandria, Va., 1985-90; mgr. meeting and conv. planning Kraft Foods, Glenview, Ill., 1990-95; cons. meetings and spl. events Chgo., 1996-98; sr. mgr. meeting and travel svcs. Coll. Am. Pathologists, Northfield, Ill., 1998-2000; conv. mgr. Common, A User Group, 2001—02, cons. spl. events, 2002—. Mem. Meeting Planners Internat., Greater Washington Soc. Assn. Execs. (past chmn. site inspection com.), Soc. Corporate Meeting Planners, Am. Soc. Assn. Execs., Mich. State U. Alumni Assn. (treas. D.C. chpt. 1987-90), Soc. for Corp. Mtg. Planners, Assn. Forum, Profl. Conf. Mgmt. Assn. Republican. Roman Catholic. Avocations: piano, swimming, skiing. Home: 16830 W Serranda Dr Libertyville IL 60048 Personal E-mail: gwenraz@hotmail.com.

**MADA, SRIPAL REDDY,** pharmacologist, researcher; b. Warangal, India, June 3, 1973; s. Madhusudhan Reddy and Bharathi Reddy Mada; m. Pramathi Reddy Pannala, Dec. 20, 2000; children: Sahil Reddy, Sahith Reddy. MPharm, Andhra U., India, 2000; PhD, Kakatiya U., India, 2003. Computer applications specialist Kein Informatics, India, 1998; cert. Yoga instr. Kakatiya U., India, 2002. Lectr. Kakatiya U., Warangal, Ap, India, 2002; rsch. scientist Ranbaxy Rsch. Labs., Gurgaon, Haryana, India, 2003—04; postdoctoral fellow Temple U. Sch. of Medicine, Phila., 2004—06; rsch. assoc. U. Pitts. Sch. Pharmacy, 2006—. Registered pharmacist AP Pharmacy Coun., Hyderabad, Ap, India, 1997—2004; rsch. assoc. NIH, OPRU, 2006—. Presenter: in field; contbr. numerous articles to profl. jours. Sr. Rsch. fellow, Coun. of Sci. Indsl. Rsch., 2 ys, Jr. Rsch. fellow, U. Grants Commn., 2 Ys, Rsch. grants, Suresh Kare Indigo Found., 3 Ys, Postdoctoral fellow, NIH, 2004. Mem.: AAAS, Am. Assn. Lab. Animal Sci., Am. Soc. Hematology, Am. Assn. Pharm. Scientists, Indian Assn. Cancer Rsch. (life), Indian Pharmacol. Soc. (life), Indian Soc. Pharmacognosy (life), Indian Pharm. Assn. (life). Achievements include research in Cancer - Telomerase and Ageing; Diabetes - Animal Models; Hypolipidemics - Animal Models; Rheumatoid Arthritis - Animal Models; Pregnancy Drug Metabolism; Human Hepatocytes. Avocations: travel, music, reading, science. Home: 536 Chatham Park Dr Apt 2A Pittsburgh PA 15220 Office: U Pitts Sch Pharmacy 718 Salk Hall Pittsburgh PA 15261 Personal E-mail: srmada@yahoo.com.

**MADACH, MICHELLE GAYLE,** school psychologist; b. Naperville, Ill., Feb. 1, 1978; d. Michael Joseph Madach and Bonnie Lynn Owens. BS in Psychology and Music, Bradley U., Peoria, Ill., 2000; Specialist in Sch. Psychology, Western Ill. U., 2003. Cert. type 73 sch. svc. pers., sch. psychologist. Grad. asst. Western Ill. U., Macomb, Ill., 2000—02; sch. psychology intern Peoria Pub. Sch. Dist. 180, 2002—03; sch. psychologist Round Lake Area Sch. Dist. 116, Round Lake, Ill., 2003—, presenter in svc., 2005—. Flutist/webmaster Arlington Hts. Cmty. Concert Band, 2003—. Mem.: Ill. Sch. Psychologists Assn., Nat. Assn. for Sch. Psychologists, Sigma Alpha Iota (v.p. membership 1996—, Sword of Honor Scholastic award 2000). Avocations: music, photography, puzzles, exercise.

**MADAN, DEEPAK S.,** engineering executive; s. S. M. and K. S. Madan; m. A. P. Madan; 1 child, N. S. B Technology/Metall. Engr., Indian Inst. Technology, Kanpur, India, 1982; MS Materials Engr., Rensselaer Polytechnic Inst., 1986, PhD Materials Engr., 1988. Rsch. fellow Rensselaer Polytechnic Inst., Troy, NY, 1982-87; sr. materials engr. Elkem Metals Co., Pitts., 1987-95; exec. v.p. F.W. Winter, Inc. & Co., Camden, NJ, 1995—. Patentee in field; contbr. articles to profl. jours. Mem.: Am. Powder Metallurgy Inst., Am. Soc. Metals. Avocations: photography, travel, computers. Office: FW Winter Inc & Co Delaware Ave and Elm St Camden NJ 08102 Office Phone: 610-517-1060.

**MADARA, JAMES LEE,** dean, pathologist, educator, epitheliologist; b. Altoona, Pa., Sept. 16, 1950; s. Daniel Rodman and Margaret Jane (Hauser) M.; m. Victoria Mollenkopf, May 14, 1975; children: J. Maxwell, Alexis Lindsy. BA, Juniata Coll., 1971; MD, Hahnemann Med., 1975. Cert. anatomic and clin. pathology. Intern Deaconess Hosp., Boston, 1975—76, resident in pathology, 1976—78; fellow in internal medicine Harvard Med. Ctr., Boston, 1978—80; instr. pathology Harvard Med. Sch., Boston, 1980-81, asst. prof. pathology, 1981-85, assoc. prof. pathology, 1985-91, prof. pathology, 1993-97; assoc. prof. of health scis. and tech. Harvard-M.I.T., Boston, 1986-91; Timmie prof., chmn. dept. pathology & lab. medicine Emory U. Sch. Medicine, Atlanta, 1997—2002; dean, v.p. for medical affairs Pritzker Sch. of Med. and Div. of Biological Sciences, U. of Chicago, Chicago, Ill., 2002—, Sara and Harold Lincoln Thompson disting. svc. prof. Assoc. editor Gastroenterology, 1986-91; mem. editl. bd. Jour. Clin. Investigation, 1987—; editor-in-chief Am. Jour. Pathology, 2000; contbr. over 160 articles to profl. jours. Grantee NIH, 1980—. Mem. Am. Soc. for Clin. Investigation (elected), Am. Soc. for Cell Biology, Am. Gastroenterological Assn. (rsch. coun. 1988-90, Ross Rsch. scholar award 1982), Am. Physiol. Soc., Am. Assn. Pathology (Parke/Davis award 1990), Am. Am. Physicians. Achievements include description of functional sequellae of neutrophil-epithelial cell interactions; recognition that tight junctions between epithelial cells are regulated under physiological conditions. Office: Biological Sci U Chicago 5812 S Ellis St Chicago IL 60637 Office Fax: 773-702-1897. E-mail: jmadara@bsd.uchicago.edu.*

**MADDALONI, MARTIN J.,** retired labor union administrator; BA, George Meany Ctr. Nat. Labor Coll., 2004. Bus. mgr. Steamfitters Local 420; v.p., Phila. internat. rep. United Assn. Journeyman and Apprentices Plumbing and Pipe Fitting Industry U.S. and Can., Wash., DC, 1988—97, gen. pres., 1997—2004. V.p. AFL-CIO, 1995. Office: United Assn 901 Massachusetts Ave NW Washington DC 20001-4307 also: 1717 K St NW Ste 207 Washington DC 20036 Office Phone: 202-628-5823.*

**MADDEN, DARRYL JAY,** federal agency administrator; b. Balt., July 16, 1963; BS, U. Balt., 1986. Operating mgr. Equifax, Atlanta, 1986—91; spl. asst. to mayor Office of the Mayor, Balt., 1991—98; dir. comm. City of Washington, 1998—2004; chief ops. officer The Trident Group, Inc., Balt., 2004—. Office: The Trident Group Inc PO Box 75535 Washington DC 20056

**MADDEN, DAVID,** author; b. Knoxville, Tenn., July 25, 1933; s. James Helvy and Emile (Merritt) M.; m. Roberta Margaret Young, Sept. 6, 1956; 1 son, Blake Dana. BS, U. Tenn., 1957; MA, San Francisco State Coll., 1958; postgrad., Yale Drama Sch., 1959-60. Faculty Appalachian State Tchrs. Coll., Boone, NC, 1957-58, Centre Coll., Danville, Ky., 1960-62, U. Louisville, 1962-64, Kenyon Coll., Gambier, O., 1964-66, Ohio U., Athens, 1966-68; writer-in-residence La. State U., Baton Rouge, 1968-92, dir. creative writing program, 1992-94, dir. U.S. Civil War Ctr., 1992-99, Donald and Velvia Crumbley prof. creative writing, 1999—. Alumni prof. La. State U., 1994. Author: (novels) Cassandra Singing, 1969, Bijou, 1974, The Suicide's Wife, 1978, Pleasure Dome, 1979, On the Big Wind, 1980, Sharpshooter: A Novel of the Civil War, 1996, (stories) The Shadow Knows (Nat. Coun. on Arts selection), 1970, The New Orleans of Possibilities (lit. criticism) Wright Morris, 1964, Poetic Image in Six Genres, 1969, James M. Cain, 1970, A Primer of the Novel, 1980, Writers' Revisions, 1981, Cain's Craft, 1985, Revising Fiction, 1988, Rediscoveries II, 1988; asst. editor: The Kenyon Rev., 1964-66; editor: Remembering James Agee, 1974; co-editor: (with P. Bach) Classics of Civil War Fiction, 1991, Beyond the Battlefield, 2000, The Legacy of Robert Penn Warren, 2000, Thomas Wolfe's Civil War, 2004, Losses of the Sultana, 2004, Touching the Web of Southern Novelists, 2006, Primer of the Novel, 2006. Served with AUS, 1953-55. Recipient Rockefeller grant in fiction, 1969; John Golden fellow in playwriting, 1959; recipient Robert Penn Warren award for excellence in fiction. Mem. Authors League, Associated Writing Programs (bd. dirs.). Democrat. Office: La State U Dept English Baton Rouge LA 70803-0001 Office Phone: 225-344-3630. Business E-Mail: dmadden@lsu.edu.

**MADDEN, EDWARD HARRY,** philosopher, retired educator; b. Gary, Ind., May 18, 1925; s. Harry Albert and Amelia Dorothy (Schepper) M.; m. Marian Sue Canaday, Sept. 15, 1946; children: Kerry Arthur, Dennis William. AB, Oberlin Coll., 1946, A.M., 1947; PhD, U. Iowa, 1950. Prof. philosophy U. Conn., 1950-59, San Jose State Coll., 1959-64, SUNY, Buffalo, 1964-80, prof. emeritus, 1980, U. Ky., 1982-95, ret., 1995. Vis. prof. Brown U., 1954-55, Amherst Coll., 1962, U. Toronto, 1967, Am. U. Beirut, Lebanon, 1969-70; sr. research fellow Linacre Coll., Oxford U., 1978, Inst. Advanced Study, Princeton, 1980-81, The John Dewey Summer Inst., 2002. Author: Philosophical Problems of Psychology, 1962, Chauncey Wright and the Foundations of Pragmatism, 1963, Evil and the Concept of God, 1968, Civil Disobedience and Moral Law, 1968, The Structure of Scientific Thought, 1960, Causal Powers, 1975, Causing, Perceiving and Believing, 1975, Freedom and Grace, 1982; co-author, editor: Theories of Scientific Method, 1960, Philosophical Perspectives on Punishment, 1968, The Idea of God, 1968; gen. editor: Harvard U. Press Source Books in History Sci.; mem. editl. bd.: The Works of William James, Thoreau Quar., History of Philosophy Quar., Philosophy of Sci., 1960-76; mem. adv. bd.: A Critical Edition of the Correspondence of William James (Am. Coun. Learned Socs.). Served with USNR, 1943-45. Recipient Am. Philos. Soc. research grant, 1961, Fulbright-Hays award, 1969-70, Herbert W. Schneider award Soc. for Advancement Am. Philosophy, 1991. Fellow Asa Mahan Soc.; mem. C.S. Peirce Soc. (pres. 1962-63, sec.-treas., editl. bd. Transactions of Soc.), Am. Coun. Learned Socs. (selection com.), Am. Philos. Assn. (co-chmn. com. publs. 1960-77), Phi Kappa Phi. Home: 4 Sanctuary Cir White River Junction VT 05001-2960

**MADDEN, GLENDA GAIL,** sales professional; b. Norman, Okla., Aug. 30, 1949; d. John Samuel Jr. and Z. June (Pence) M. BA in Polit. Sci., Okla. Coll. Liberal Arts & Scis., 1970. Account clk. U. Okla. Press, Norman, 1977-78, advt. asst., 1978-80, asst. supr., 1980-81, sales mgr. 1981-98, asst. dir. mktg., 1998—. Avocations: home renovation, antiques, reading, genealogy.

**MADDEN, JAMES D.,** forensic engineer; b. Jersey City; s. Louis A. and Ann Madden. BSChemE, U. S.C., 1963, ME, 1966. Lic. profl. engr., Ohio; cert. diplomate forensic engr. Process engr. Monsanto Co., Alvin, Tex., 1966-67; process and project engr. Union Carbide Corp., Houston, 1967-70; systems engr. M.W. Kellogg Co., Houston, 1970-73, prin. systems engr., 1974-77; sr. process engr. Litwin Co., Houston, 1973-74; sr. project engr. Davy Powergas, Houston, 1977-78, supervising project engr., 1978-79; mgr. equipment engring. DM Internat., Houston, 1979-80, project engring. mgr., 1980-83; owner, forensic engr. Madden Accident Analysis and Forensic Engring., Parma, Parma Heights and Brecksville, Ohio, 1983—. NSF rsch. grantee, 1963; NASA fellow, 1963-65; named to Outstanding Young Men Am., 1973. Mem. ASME, NSPE, AIChE, Soc. Automotive Engrs., Nat. Fire Protection Assn., Inst. Transp. Engrs., Am. Soc. Agrl. Engrs., Bldg. Ofcls. and Code Adminstrs. Internat., Nat. Acad. Forensic Engrs., Sigma Xi, Sigma Pi Sigma, Tau Beta Pi, Omicron Delta Kappa. Office: 10175 Brecksville Rd Cleveland OH 44141-3205

**MADDEN, JANICE FANNING,** economics professor; b. Fall River, Mass., Jan. 30, 1947; d. Richard and Concorde Roseanne (Thibault) Fanning; m. Paul Charles Madden, June 6, 1969; children: Patrick, Erin. BA, U. Denver, 1969; MA, Duke U., 1971, PhD, 1972. Prof. regional sci., sociology and real estate U. Pa., Phila., 1972—; economist Nat. Commn. on Employment and Unemployment Stats., Washington, 1978; cons. Abt Assn., Cambridge, Mass., 1979-81, U.S. Dept. Justice, Washington, 1984-88, EEOC, Washington, 1979-91; dir. women's studies U. Pa., 1988—91, 2002—04, Robert C. Daniels Found. chair in urban studies Phila., 1990—2000, vice provost grad. edn., 1991—99. Bd. dirs. Econsult Corp., Phila.; co-dir. Temple-Penn Phila. Econ. Monitoring Project, 1987—91; dir. MGA Program, 2000—02. Author: The Economics of Sex Discrimination, 1973, Post-Industrial Philadelphia: Structural Changes in the Metropolitan Economy, 1990, Work, Wages and Poverty: Income Distribution in Post-Industrial Philadelphia, 1991, Changes in Income Inequality within U.S. Metropolitan Areas, 2000, Mommies and Daddies in the Fast Track, 2004; contbr. articles to profl. jours. Adv. coun. mem. Office Employment and Tng., Phila., 1981—84; commr. Fellowship Commn., Phila., 1981—82; bd. dirs. Career Alternatives for Women, Jenkintown, Pa., 1979—82, Friends Select Sch., 1991—2000, 2002—. Vis. scholar, U. Indonesia, 1991, Fed. Res. Bank Phila., 1999—2000, 2005; Rsch. grantee, Manpower Devel., 1971—72, William Penn Found., 1988—91, W.E. Upjohn Found., 1993—95, NSF, 1993—95, Brookings Inst., 1998—2000, HUD, 2004—05, James B. Duke fellow, Duke U., 1966—71, Boettcher scholar, U. Denver, 1965—69. Mem.: Regional Sci. Assn., Am. Econs. Assn. Home: 2031 Spruce St Philadelphia PA 19103-5623 Office: U Pa 3718 Locust Walk Philadelphia PA 19104-6209 Office Phone: 215-898-6739. Business E-Mail: madden@ssc.upenn.edu.

**MADDEN, JOHN,** sportscaster, retired professional football coach; b. Austin, Minn., Apr. 10, 1936; s. Earl and Mary O'Flaherty M.; m. Virginia Madden; children: Mike, Joe. BS, Calif. Poly. U., 1959, MA, 1961. Player Phila. Eagles (NFL team), 1959; asst. coach Hancock Jr. Coll., Santa Maria, Calif., 1960-62, head coach, 1962-64; defensive coordinator Calif. State U., San Diego, 1964-66; linebacker coach Oakland Raiders, Am. Football League (now Am. Football Conf. Nat. Football League), 1967-69, head coach, 1969-79; head coach NFL Pro Bowl team Am. Football Conf., 1971, 73, 74, 75; head coach 6 Western div. Am. Football Conf. championship teams, Super Bowl champions, 1976; sports commentator, football analyst CBS Sports, 1979-93; appears in TV and radio commls.; sports commentator, football analyst Fox Sports, 1994—2002, Monday Night Football (ABC), 2002—06, NBC Sunday Night Football, 2006—. Author: Hey, Wait a Minute, I Wrote a Book!, 1984; One Knee Equals Two Feet (and Everything Else You Wanted To Know About Football), 1987, One Size Doesn't Fit All, 1993; co-author (with Dave Anderson) All Madden: Hey, I'm Talking Pro Football, 1996, (with Peter Kaminsky) John Madden's Ultimate Tailgating, 1998, (with Bill Gutman) John Madden's Heroes of Football, 2006; developer (software) John Madden Football, 1988, John Madden Football II, 1993. Named Coach of

Year Am. Football League, 1969, Sports Personality of the Yr., Am. Sportscasters Assn., 1985; recipient Emmy awards for sports broadcasting, 1982, 83, 85, 86, 87, 88, Pete Rozelle Radio-Television award, 2002; elected to Pro Football Hall of Fame, 2006 Office: c/o NBC Sports 30 Rockefeller Plaza New York NY 10014

**MADDEN, JOHN J.,** lawyer; b. NYC, May 27, 1946; s. John L. and Bertha M.; m. Mary A. O'Neill, June 19, 1976; children: Elisabeth, Samuel. BA, U. Pa., 1968; JD cum laude, Fordham U. 1975. Bar: NY 1976, US Dist. Ct. (So. Dist.) NY 1976; avocat a la cour de Paris 1994. From assoc. to ptnr. Shearman & Sterling LLP, NYC, 1975—83, ptnr., 1983—, co-head mergers and acquisitions group, 1987—91, head mergers and acquisitions group, 1995—2001, mng. ptnr. European Offices Paris, 1991-95, co-mng. ptnr., 2004—. Articles editor Law Review, Fordham Law Sch. Trustee St. David's Sch., N.Y.C. 1981-91 Served to 1st lt., Infantry platoon leader, 101st Airbourne Divsn. U.S. Army, 1969—71, Vietnam. Mem. ABA, N.Y. Bar Assn., Assn. Bar City of N.Y., Internat. Bar Assn., Cercle de l'Union Interalliee (Paris), World Policy Inst. (bd. advisors 2004—) Office: Shearman & Sterling LLP 599 Lexington Ave New York NY 10022-6069 Office Fax: 646-848-7055. Business E-Mail: jmadden@shearman.com.

**MADDEN, JOSEPH DANIEL,** trade association executive; b. Bayside, N.Y., Dec. 25, 1921; s. Thomas A. and Margaret (McFadden) M.; m. Eileen M. MacDonnell, Sept. 8, 1951; children: Joseph Daniel Jr., Maureen A. BS, Fordham U., 1951; MBA, N.Y. U., 1956. Credit investigator Dun & Bradstreet, N.Y.C. 1947-48; credit mgr. Devoe & Raynolds Co., N.Y.C., 1948-50, Admiral Corp., N.Y.C., 1950-51; nat. credit mgr. Standard Toch Chems., Inc., S.I., N.Y., 1951-52; with chems. and plastics div. Union Carbide Corp., Midland, Mich., 1952-62; mgr. Detroit sales office, 1958-60; sr. staff adminstr. Soc. Plastics Industry, Washington, 1962-69; exec. v.p. Drug, Chem. and Assoc. Techs. Assn., Robbinsville, NJ, 1969-88, cons. assn. mgmt., 1988—. With U.S. Army, 1942-43. Mem. AARP (pres. local chpt.), Am. Soc. Assn. Execs. (cert.), N.Y. Soc. Assn. Execs. (past bd. dirs., Exec. of Yr. award 1988), Soc. Friendly Sons of St. Patrick, Kiwanis (past pres. Bayside, sec.), Am. Legion, Toastmasters Internat. (past pres. local club). Home: 211-37 18th Ave Bayside NY 11360-1529 Personal E-mail: jdmadden21@verizon.net.

**MADDEN, M. STUART,** lawyer, educator; b. Washington, Dec. 1, 1948; s. Murdaugh Stuart and Louise (Kenney) M. BA, U. Pa., 1971; MA, London Sch. Econs., 1972; JD, Georgetown U., 1976. Bar: DC 1976. Assoc. Reed, Smith, Shaw & McClay, Washington, 1976-78, Weil, Gotshal & Manges, Washington, 1978-80, Santarelli & Gimer, Washington, 1980-83; ptnr. Santarelli & Bond, Washington, 1983-85; prof. law Pace U. Sch. Law, White Plains, NY, 1956—, Disting. prof. law, 1986—. Co-editor Jour. Products and Toxics Liability, 1984—95; Author: Madden and Owen on Products Liability, 3d edit, 2000, (with Boston) Law of Environmental and Toxic Torts, 2005; editor: Exploring Tort Law, 2005; contbr. articles to profl. jours. Mem. ABA, Am. Law Inst. Office: Pace U Sch Law 78 N Broadway White Plains NY 10603-3710 Office Phone: 914-422-4237. Business E-Mail: smadden@law.pace.edu.

**MADDEN, MARTIN GERARD,** former state legislator; b. Washington, May 24, 1949; s. Anthony M. and Catherine W. Madden; m. Julia Gatewood Spangler, July 29, 1988; children: Donald Gerard, Thomas Martin, Christina Lynne, Marguerite Allen Spangler. BA in Econs., Iona Coll., 1971. Mem. Md. Ho. of Dels., Annapolis, 1991-94, Md. Senate, Annapolis, 1995—2002; senate minority leader State of Md. Gen. Assembly, Annapolis, 1999—2001, mem. Senate Budget and Taxation com. Mem. Budget and Tax com.; co-chmn. joint com. on welfare reform. Chmn. Critical Area Commn. for Atlantic and Chesapeake Bays, 2003—. Republican. Roman Catholic. Avocation: folk art collector. Office: 1804 West St Annapolis MD 21401 Personal E-mail: themaddens@hotmail.com.

**MADDEN, MICHAEL DANIEL,** finance company executive; b. Buffalo, Feb. 16, 1949; s. Daniel Francis and Miriam (Catron) M.; m. Mary Madden, May 1, 1976; children: Daniel, Kristina, Megan, Michael. BA in Econs. magna cum laude, Le Moyne Coll., 1971; MBA with distinction, U. Pa., 1973. Assoc. Kidder, Peabody & Co., NYC, 1971-79, v.p., 1977-80, mng. dir., 1980-85, global head investment banking, 1985-88; head investment banking Lehman Bros., NYC, 1989—93; exec. mng. dir. Global Capital Markets Kidder, Peabody Co., NYC, 1993-94; vice chmn., chief origination officer Paine Webber Inc., NYC, 1995-96; chmn., CEO Hanover Capital LLC, NYC, 1996—; ptnr. Beacon Group, NYC; sr. ptnr. Questor Mgmt., NYC, 1999—2005; mng. ptnr. Black Eagle Ptnrs., NYC, 2005—. Bd. dirs. Geologistics Corp., Transonic Sys. Inc., Chef Solutions Inc., Pinn Oak Mining, Freeport Properties, Inc. Bd. dirs. Cath. TV Ctr., NYC, 1981-85, Canisius Prep. Sch., Buffalo, 1992—; mem. Bd. dirs. Solutions Inc., Syracuse, NY, 1987—. Mem. Am. Petroleum Inst., MBA Assn., Univ. Club, The Creek, Longboat Key Club. Republican. Roman Catholic. Avocations: boxing, hunting, tennis, coin collecting/numismatics, fishing. Office: Black Eagle Ptnrs 1285 6th Ave New York NY 10019 Office Phone: 212-554-4600. Business E-Mail: mmadden@blackeaglepartners.com.

**MADDEN, MICKEY,** musician; b. Austin, Tex., May 13, 1979; Bassist Kara's Flowers (name changed to Maroon 5, 2001), 1994—; signed to Reprise Records, 1997—99, Octone Records, 2001—. Musician (as Kara's Flowers): (albums) Fourth World, 1997; musician: (as Maroon 5) Songs About Jane, 2002, 1.22.03.Acoustic, 2004, Live Friday the 13th, 2005, (songs) Harder to Breathe, 2003, This Love, 2004 (MTV Video Music award for Best New Artist, 2004, Grammy award, Best Group Pop Performance, 2006), She Will Be Loved, 2004, Shiver, 2005, contbr. to Spider-Man 2 soundtrack, 2004. Recipient World Music award for Best New Group, 2004, MTV Europe award for Best New Act, 2004, Grammy award for Best New Artist (with Maroon 5), 2005. Address: Maroon 5 PO Box 884564 San Francisco CA 94188 Office: Octone Records Rm 500 560 Broadway New York NY 10012 Office Phone: 646-613-0200. E-mail: maroon5@maroon5.com.*

**MADDEN, MURDAUGH STUART,** lawyer; b. Morgantown, W.Va., Feb. 26, 1922; s. Joseph Warren and Margaret (Liddell) M.; m. Constance Viens McKenna, May 12, 1999; children by previous marriage: Liddell Louise, Murdaugh Stuart Jr., Michael Mann. Student, Oberlin Coll., 1939-40; BA, George Washington U., 1942; JD, Harvard U., 1948. Bar: D.C. 1948, Va. 1948, U.S. Supreme Ct. 1953. Asst. counsel Bur. Aero., Washington, 1948-50; sole practice Washington, 1950-61, 71—; sr. ptnr. Shaw, Pittman, Potts, Trowbridge & Madden, Washington, 1961-71. Sr. counsel Humane Soc. U.S., Atlantic Devel. Co. and related corps. Author: (with Sherman L. Cohn) The Legal Status and Problems of the American Abroad, 1966. Trustee Inst. for Study Nat. Behavior, Princeton, N.J., Friends of India Com., Washington; pres. World Fedn. for Protection Animals, The Netherlands; v.p. World Soc. forProtection Animals, London. With USAAF, 1942-45, ETO. Mem. ABA (past chmn. internat. and comparative law com. internat. transp., chmn. subcom. on charitable orgns. internat. bar 1985—), D.C. Bar Assn., (past dir., past chmn. com. bar ethics), Va. Bar Assn., The Barristers, Am. Soc. Internat. Law, Harvard Law Sch. Assn., Oberlin Alumni Assn., Metropolitan Club, Harvard Club N.Y., Internat. Lawn Tennis Club U.S., Chevy Chase Club, Phi Sigma Kappa. Episcopalian. Home: 2530 Queen Annes Ln NW Washington DC 20037-2148 Office: 2100 L St NW Washington DC 20037-1525

**MADDEN, PALMER BROWN,** lawyer; b. Milw., Sept. 19, 1945; m. Susan L. Paulus; Mar. 31, 1984. BA, Stanford U., 1968; JD, U. Calif., Berkeley, 1973. Bar: Calif. 1973, U.S. Dist. Ct. (no. dist.) Calif. 1973, U.S. Supreme Ct. 1982. Ptnr. McCutchen, Doyle Brown & Enersen, Walnut Creek, 1985-98; prin ADR Svcs., Alamo, Calif., 1999—. Pres. State Bar Bd. Govs., 2000-01. Chair bd. govs. Continuing Edn. of the Bar, 1997; judge pro tem Contra Costa Superior Ct., 1991-98; pres. Contra Costa Coun., 1995, Kennedy-King Found., 1994; bd. dirs. Episcopal Homes Found., 2001-05, Bay Area Legal

Aid, 2005—. Mem. Contra Costa County Bar Assn. (pres. 1996-97). Democrat. Episcopalian. Office: ADR Svcs 3000 Danville Blvd # 543 Alamo CA 94507 Office Phone: 925-838-8593. Business E-Mail: pbm@netvista.net.

**MADDEN, PAUL ROBERT,** lawyer, director; b. St. Paul, Nov. 13, 1926; s. Ray Joseph and Margaret (Meyer) Madden; m. Rosemary R. Sorel, Aug. 7, 1974; children: Margaret Jane, James Patrick, Derek R. Sorel, Lisa T. Schoutsen. Student, St. Thomas Coll., 1944; AB, U. Minn., 1948; JD, Georgetown U., 1951. Bar: Ariz. 1957, Minn. 1951, D.C. 1951. Assoc. Hamilton & Hamilton, Washington, 1951-55; legal asst. to commr. SEC, Washington, 1955-56; assoc. Lewis and Roca, Phoenix, 1957-59, ptnr., 1959-90, Beus, Gilbert & Morrill, Phoenix, 1991-94, Chapman and Cutler, Phoenix, 1994-97; of counsel Gallagher & Kennedy, Phoenix, 1997—. Mem. nat. bd. visitors U. Ariz. Law Sch., Embry Riddle Aero. U., Prescott, 2002—; hon. life mem., mem. adv. bd. Cath. Cmty. Found., Cath. Social Svcs. No. Ariz., 2002—; bd. dirs. Ind. Devel. Authority of City of Prescott, 2002—. Found. Jr. Achievement Ctr. Ariz., Phoenix, Yavapai Symphony Assocs., Prescott, 2004—; Prescott People Who Care, 2001—; past bd. dirs., past chmn. Mesa Air Group, Inc., Camelback Charitable Trust, Found. for Sr. Living; bd. dirs., pres. Ariz. Club, Phoenix, 1990—93; past bd. dirs., vice chmn. Ctrl. Ariz. chpt. ARC; past bd. dirs., past pres. Jr. Achievement Ctrl. Ariz., Inc.; past bd. dirs. The Samaritan Found., Phoenix, St. Joseph the Worker, Phoenix; former mem. bd. dirs. Hidden Valley Homeowners Assn., Prescott, 2002—04; nat. co-chmn. Youth for Eisenhower, 1951—52; sec. Minn. Fedn. Coll. Rep. Clubs, 1947—48; chmn. 4th dist. Minn. Young Rep. Club, 1948; mem. Ariz. Rep. Com., 1960—62; past bd. dirs., sec. Yavapai Coll. Dist. Governing Bd., Prescott, Ariz. With USNR, 1946—48. Mem.: ABA, Ariz. Bar Assn., Maricopa County Bar Assn., Yavapai County Bar Assn., The Barristers Club (Washington), Phi Delta Phi. Home: 1565 Range Rd Prescott AZ 86303 Office: Gallagher & Kennedy PA 101 E Gurley Ste 214 Prescott AZ 86301 Office Phone: 928-445-5800. E-mail: prm@gknet.com.

**MADDEN, RICHARD BLAINE,** forest products executive; b. Short Hills, NJ, Apr. 27, 1929; s. James L. and Irma (Twining) M.; m. Joan Fairbairn, May 24, 1958; children: John Richard, Lynne Marie, Kathryn Ann, Andrew Twining. BS, Princeton U., 1951; JD, U. Mich., 1956; MBA, NYU, 1959; PhD (hon.), St. Scholastica Coll., 1994. Bar: Mich. 1956, N.Y. 1958. Gen. asst. treas.'s dept. Socony Mobil Oil Corp., N.Y.C., 1956-57, spl. asst., 1958-59, fin. rep., 1960; asst. to pres. Mobil Chem. Co.; also dir. Mobil Chems. Ltd. of Eng., 1960-63; exec. v.p., gen. mgr. Kordite Corp.; also v.p. Mobil Plastics, 1963-66; v.p. Mobil Chem. Co., N.Y.C., 1966-68, group v.p., 1968-70; asst. treas. Mobil Oil Corp., 1970-71; chmn. Mobil Oil Estates Ltd., 1970-71; pres., chief exec. Potlatch Corp., San Francisco, 1971-77, chmn. chief exec. officer, 1977-94; ret., 1994. Former bd. dirs. URS Corp., Potlatch Corp., PG&E Corp., CNF Inc., Del Monte Corp., AMFAC Inc., Bank Calif. N.A. and BankCal Tri-State Corp.; from lectr. to adj. assoc. prof. fin. NYU, 1960-63; bd. dirs., chmn., Knight Grand Cross Magistral Grace in Obedience Order of Malta, Western Assn.; bd. govs., chmn. audit com., mem. adminstrv. compensation and labor rels. com. San Francisco Symphony. Bd. dirs. Smith-Kettlewell Eye Rsch. Inst., trustee emeritus, former chmn. Am. Enterprise Inst.; former mem. bd. Nat. Park Found.; hon. trustee Com. for Econ. Devel. Lt. (j.g.) USNR, 1951-54. Mem. N.Y. Bar Assn., Mich. Bar Assn. Clubs: Bohemian (San Francisco); Lagunitas (Ross, Calif.); Metropolitan (Washington). Roman Catholic. Office Phone: 415-461-0683.

**MADDEN, ROBERT EDWARD,** surgeon, educator; b. Oak Park, Ill., Sept. 16, 1925; s. Joseph Edward and Gertrude Celelia (McGowan) M.; m. Susan Ann Hale, May 24, 1958; children: Robert Joseph, Lisa Marie, Karen Louise, Kevin Francis. BS in Medicine, U. Ill., Chgo., 1950, MS in Biochemistry, 1952, MD, 1952. Diplomate Am. Bd. Surgery, Bd. Thoracic Surgery. Assoc. in surgery U. Ill. Coll. Medicine, Chgo., 1957-58; sr. surgeon Nat. Cancer Inst., Bethesda, Md., 1959-60; asst. prof. surgery N.Y. Med. Coll., N.Y.C., 1961-66, assoc. prof., 1966-71, prof. Valahlla, 1971—. Mem. N.Y. State Health Rsch. Coun., Albany, 1976—; med. coord. N.Y. State Dept. Health, 1998—. Author: (with Lippincott) Problems In General Surgery, 1988; editor: Gastrointestinal Bleeding, 1987; editor-in-chief N.Y. Med. Quarterly, 1979-90; contbr. articles to profl. jours. With U.S. Army, 1943-46. Recipient Borden Undergrad. Rsch. award Borden Corp., 1952; postdoctoral fellow Am. Cancer Soc., 1958-59. Fellow ACS (com. on cancer 1993-97); mem. Am. Soc. for Vascular Surgery, Soc. Internat. Chirurgie, Am. Assn. Cancer Edn. (pres. 1979), N.Y. Cancer Soc. (pres. 1975-76), N.Y. State Cancer Programs Assn. (pres. 1975-76), Knights of Holy Sepulchre, Knights of the Order of Malta, Pi Gamma Mu. Republican. Roman Catholic. Home: 6 Crows Nest Rd Bronxville NY 10708-4802 Office: NY Med Coll Munger Pavilion Valhalla NY 10595 Office Phone: 914-493-7615. E-mail: remadden@bellatlantic.net.

**MADDEN, TERESA DARLEEN,** insurance agency owner; b. Dallas, Aug. 4, 1960; d. Tommy Joe Frederick Dodd and Mary Helen (Sterner) Smith; m. Kim Ashley Madden, June 2, 1989. Student, Tex. Tech U., 1978-81. Cert. ins. counselor, 1985, risk mgr., 2006. With personal lines svc. Charles R. Ervin Ins., Midland, Tex., 1981, Bryant Scalf Ins., Richardson, Tex., 1981-82; with comml. ins. svc. Street & Assocs. Inc., Dallas, 1982-84; with comml. ins. sales/svc. Hotchkiss Ins., Dallas, 1984-85; mgr. sales Abbott-Rose Ins. Agy., Dallas, 1985-89; owner Glenn-Madden & Assocs. Ins., Dallas, 1990—. Bd. dirs. Ind. Ins. Agents of Dallas, 2004—06, exec. bd., 2006. Methodist. Office: Glenn Madden & Assocs Inc 13601 Preston Rd Ste 106E Dallas TX 75240-4906 Business E-Mail: dmadden@glenn-maddeninsurance.com.

**MADDEN, THOMAS A.,** finance educator; BBA, Ind. U. of Pa.; MBA, U. Pitts. CPA, Mich. Audit mgr. Coopers & Lybrand, 1975; various positions including v.p. corp. devel., v.p. fin., asst. corp. contr. Rockwell Internat., 1981—97; sr. v.p. Meritor Automotive, Inc., 1997—2000; sr. v.p., CFO ArvinMeritor, Inc., Troy, Mich., 2000—01; exec. v.p. CFO Ingram Micro Inc., Santa Ana, Calif., 2001—05. lectr. acctg. U. Calif. Irvine Paul Merage Sch. Bus., 2005—. Bd. dirs. Mindspeeded Technologies, Inc. Office: U Calif Irvine Paul Merage Sch Bus Irvine CA 92697-3125*

**MADDEN, THOMAS JAMES,** lawyer, educator; b. Trenton, NJ, Sept. 13, 1941; m. Irene Lyons. BEE, Villanova U., 1964; JD with honors, Cath. U., 1968. Bar: N.J. 1968, D.C. 1968, U.S. Patent Office 1968. Atty. adv. Naval Air Sys. Command, 1968—69; dep. gen. counsel Dept. Justice Law Enforcement Assistance Adminstrn., 1970—71, gen. counsel, 1972—79; dir. Nat. Adv. Commn. on Criminal Justice Stds. and Goals, 1971—73; adv. U.S. Office Mgmt. and Budget on Fed. Assistance Programs, Washington, 1979—80; gen. counsel Dept. Justice Office Justice Assistance Rsch. and Stats., 1980; from assoc. to ptnr. Kay Scholer, Fierman, Hays and Handler, Washington, 1980—84; ptnr., gen. counsel, intellectual property litig. Venable, LLP (formerly Venable, Baetjer, Howard & Civiletti), Washington, 1984—. Adj. prof. contract law Am. U., 1980-85; gen. counsel Nat. Coun. Juvenile and Family Ct. Judges; adv. panel on streamlining and codifying fed. acquisition laws Dept. Def., 1991-93; mem. Procurement Round Table, 1998—, vice chmn., 2002—. Contbr. articles to profl. jours. Pres. U.S. Ct. Fed. Claims Bar Assn., 1999-2000. Recipient Louis Brownlow award Am. Soc. for Pub. Adminstrn., 1982, Disting. Svc. award Dept. Justice Law Enforcement Assistance Adminstrn., 1973, Wilson Cowen award U.S. Ct. Fed. Claims, 1998. Fellow Am. Bar Found.; mem. ABA (chmn. pub. contract law sect. 1988-89, pres. fellows of pub. contract law sect. 1992-93), D.C. Bar Assn., Fed. Bar Assn. (pres. D.C. chpt. 1982-83). Office: Venable LLP 575 7th St N W Washington DC 20004 Office Phone: 202-344-4803. Business E-Mail: tmadden@venable.com.

**MADDEN, WALES HENDRIX, JR.,** lawyer; b. Amarillo, Tex., Sept. 1, 1927; s. Wales Hendrix and Kathryn (Nash) Madden; m. Alma Faye Cowden, Nov. 8, 1952; children: Wales Hendrix III, Straughn. BA, U. Tex., 1950, LLB, 1952. Bar: Tex. 1952. Pvt. practice, Amarillo. Mem. Tex. Constl. Revision Commn., 1973. Mem. Tex. Coll. and Univ. Sys. Coord. Bd., 1964—69, Amarillo Area Found.; Cal Farley's Boys Ranch, Pres.'s Export Coun., 1981, Select Com. Higher Edn., 1985, 1987; chmn. SWST regional panel Pres.'s Commn. White Ho. Fellowships, 1989—90; chmn. Tex. Water Devel. Bd., 2002; mem. Gov.'s Com. Ad Valorem Taxes, 1996; bd. regents Amarillo

Coll., 1958—59, U. Tex., 1959—65; trustee Trinity U., San Antonio; chmn. bd. Internat. Food and Agrl. Devel., 1990—94. With USNR. Named Outstanding Man of Amarillo, 1972, Disting. Alumnus, U. Tex., 1979, U. Tex. Law Sch., 1986. Mem.: ABA, State Jr. Bar Tex. (pres. 1956), State Bar Tex. (Outstanding 50 Year Lawyer award 2003), Amarillo Bar Assn. (pres. 1956), Friar Soc., Amarillo C. of C. (pres. 1968), Tex. Philos. Soc., Sigma Alpha, Phi Eta Sigma, Phi Delta Theta, Phi Alpha Delta. Presbyterian. Avocation: mountain climbing. Home and Office: PO Box 15288 Amarillo TX 79105-5288 Office Phone: 806-374-2422.

**MADDEN-LUNSFORD, KERRY ELIZABETH,** writer; b. Daytona Beach, Fla., Nov. 22, 1961; d. Joseph Anthony Madden and Mary Janis Baker; m. Alfred Kiffen Lunsford, Sept. 12, 1986; children: Flannery, Lucy, Norah. Student, U. Manchester, Eng., 1983; BA, U. Tenn., 1984, MFA, 1986. Voice and diction tchr. U. Tenn., Knox, 1984-86; English and drama tchr. Ningbo (China) U., 1986-87; ESL, speech and writing tchr. L.A. Unified Sch. Dist./Garfield Adult Sch., East Los Angeles, Calif., 1989-95; creative writing tchr. Vol.-Teen Moms, East Los Angeles, 1992—; guest playwright-in-schs. Audrey Skarball-Kenis, L.A., 1998—. Tchr. Sewanee (Tenn.) Young Writers Conf., summers 1997—. Author: (play) Blood and Marriage, 1993, (novel) Offsides, 1996, (children's book)Gentle's Holler, 2005, also essays and short stories. Vol. TeenMoms, 1992—; vol. creative writing tchr. L.A. elem. schs., 1994—. Mem. Am. PEN West, Authors Guild. Mailing: c/o Viking Publicity 375 Hudson St New York NY 10014 E-mail: kiffnkerry@aol.com.

**MADDIN, ROBERT,** metallurgist, educator; b. Hartford, Conn., Oct 20, 1918; s. Isadore I. and Mae (Jacobs) Levine; married, July 8, 1945; children: Leslie, Jill. BS in Metall. Engring., Purdue U., 1942; DEng., Yale U., 1948. Registered profl. engr., Pa. Asst., assoc. prof. Johns Hopkins U., Balt. 1949-55; prof. U. Pa., phila., 1955-73, univ. prof., 1973-83; vis. prof. Harvard U., Cambridge, Mass., 1983-87, curator, 1987—; vis. prof. Oxford (Eng.) U., 1970, vis. fellow Wolfson Coll., 1987. Vis. prof. U. Birmingham, Eng. 1953-54; vis. scholar Hebrew U., Jerusalem, 1976; hon. prof. Beijing Sci. and Engring. U., 1986; hon. mem. Japan Metals. Editor-in-chief Math., Sci., and Engring, 1965-82; contbr. more than 250 publs. to profl. jours. 1st Lt. USAF, 1942-45. Disting. Sr. Sci. fellow A. von Humboldt Found., Germany, 1989-90, Disting. Alumnus Purdue U., 1974; recipient Pomerance award Archaeol. Inst. Am., 1994, medal of merit U. Pa. Fellow Am. Soc. Metallurgists, TMS. Avocation: history early metallurgy. Personal E-mail: robertmaddin@comcast.net.

**MADDOCK, JAY E.,** medical educator; b. Syracuse, N.Y., June 27, 1973; PhD, U. R.I., 1999. Jr. rschr. Cancer Rsch. Ctr. Hawaii, Honolulu, 1999—2000; asst. rschr. U. Hawaii, Honolulu, 2000—04, assoc. prof., 2004—, grad. chair pub. health, 2004—, assoc. chmn. Pub. Health, 2005—06, chmn. pub. health, 2006—. Mem. Hawaii Bd. Health, 2004—; dir. Asia-Pacific Ctr. for Pub. Health and Population Rsch. Mem.: APA, Soc. Behavioral Medicine. Office: Univ Hawaii 1960 East-West Rd Honolulu HI 96822

**MADDOCK, JEROME TORRENCE,** library and information scientist; b. Darby, Pa., Feb. 7, 1940; s. Richard Cotton and Isobel Louise (Mezger) M.; m. Karen Rhueama Weygand, Oct. 2, 1965. BS in Biology, Muhlenberg Coll. 1961; MS in Info. Sci., Drexel U., 1968. Editl. assoc. Biol. Abstracts, Phila., 1962—63; mgr. rsch. info. Merck & Co., West Point, Pa., 1963—72; sr. cons. Auerbach Assocs., Inc., Phila., 1972—79; mgr. libr. and info. svcs. Solar Energy Rsch. Inst., Golden, Colo., 1979—88; mgr. info. svcs. Transp. Rsch. Bd., Washington, 1988—99; project mgr. IHS Enterprise Solutions, Boulder, Colo., 1999—2001; ind. cons., 2002—; faculty online U. Phoenix, 1999—. Del. Gov.'s Conf. on Libr. and Info. Svc., Pa., 1978; mem. blue ribbon panel to select archivist of U.S., Washington, 1979; U.S. del. to ops. com. on transp. rsch. info. Orgn. for Econ. Cooperation and Devel., 1988-99. Bd. dirs. Paoli (Pa.) Pub. Libr., 1976-77, Boulder Friends of Jazz, 2003-; bd. trustees Louisville County Pub. Libr., 2002-, pres. 2004. With USAFR, 1962-68. Mem. AAAS, Am. Soc. Info. Sci. (chmn. 1974-75), Elks, Beta Phi Mu, Pi Delta Epsilon. Republican. Episcopalian. Achievements include projection of information science operations 10 years into the future. Home: 545 W Laurel Ct Louisville CO 80027-1116

**MADDOCK, LAWRENCE HILL,** retired language educator, writer; b. Ogden, Utah, July 14, 1923; s. Lawrence J. and Nellie (Hill) Maddock. Student, U. Fla., 1941-42; BA, George Peabody Coll., 1946, PhD, 1965; MA, U. So. Calif., 1949. Tchr. pub. schs., Jacksonville, Fla., 1949-52; instr. U. Fla. Gainesville, 1952-53; asst. prof. California (Pa.) State Coll., 1955-56, assoc. prof., 1956-64, N.E. La. State Coll., Monroe, 1964-67, U. West Fla., Pensacola, 1967-90. Author: The Door of Memory, 1974, revised, 2003, John Maddock: Mormon Pioneer, 1996; contbr. chpts. to books and articles to profl. jours. Mem. MLA (bibliographer 1978-93), Thomas Wolfe Soc., Mormon History Assn. Republican. Mem. Lds Ch. Home: 1012 Gerhardt Dr Pensacola FL 32503-3222

**MADDON, JOE,** professional baseball coach; b. Sept. 19, 1954; BS in Econ., Lafayette Coll., Easton, Pa., 1976. Mgr. Idaho Falls Minor League Baseball, 1981, Salem Minor League Baseball, Peoria Minor League Baseball, Midland Minor League Baseball, 1985—86; coord. Calif. Angels Arizona Instrnl. League, 1984—93; roving hitting instructor Calif. Angels, 1987—93, dir. player develop., 1994, bullpen coach, 1994, first base coach, 1995, bench coach, 1996, interim mgr., 1996, 1999, bench coach, 2000—05; mgr. Tampa Bay Devil Rays, 2005—. Office: Tampa Bay Devil Rays One Tropicana Dr Saint Petersburg FL 33705*

**MADDOW, RACHEL,** radio personality, political activist; BA, Stanford U., 1994, PhD in Pollitics, Oxford U. Host The Big Breakfast, WRSI, Northampton, Mass., 2002—04; co-host (with Chuck D. & Liz Winstead) Unfiltered, Air Am. Radio, NYC, host The Rachel Maddow Show, 2005—. Fellow AIDS Legal Referral Panel, San Francisco; grantee John Gardner Pub. Svc. Fellowship, Ludlam Health Policy Fellowship; Rhodes Scholar, 1995. Office: Air America Radio 641 Avenue Of The Americas Fl 4 New York NY 10011-2038

**MADDOX, ALVA HUGH,** retired state supreme court justice; b. Andalusia, Ala., Apr. 17, 1930; s. Christopher Columbus and Audie Lodella Maddox; m. Virginia Roberts, June 14, 1958; children: Robert Hugh, Jane Maddox. AB in Journalism, U. Ala., Tuscaloosa, 1952, JD, 1957. Bar: Ala. 1957. Law clk. to Judge Aubrey Cates, Ala. Ct. Appeals, Montgomery, 1957-58; field examiner Chief Atty.'s Office, VA, Montgomery, 1958-59; law clk. to Judge Frank M. Johnson, U.S. Dist. Ct., Montgomery, 1959-61; pvt. practice Montgomery, 1961-65; cir. judge, spl. cir. judge Montgomery Cir. Ct., 1963, asst. dist. atty., 1964; legal advisor to govs. including George C. Wallace, Lurleen B. Wallace, Albert P. Brewer, State of Ala., Montgomery, 1965-69; assoc. justice Supreme Ct. Ala., Montgomery, 1969-2001; ret., 2001. Author: Billy Boll Weevil: A Pest Becomes A Hero, 1976, Alabama Rules of Criminal Procedure, 1991, supplements, 1992—. Founder youth jud. program YMCA, Montgomery, 1979, also mem. metro. bd. dir. 2d lt. USAF, 1952-54, col. USAF Res. ret. Recipient Man of Yr. award YMCA, 1988, Disting. Program Svc. award, 1989, Srs. of Achievement award Montgomery Coun. on Aging, 1999. Mem.: ABA, Am. Inns of Ct. (former trustee), Hugh Maddox Inn of Ct. Montgomery (charter, founding mem.), Christian Legal Soc., Inst. Jud. Adminstrn., Ala. Bar Assn. (Jud. award of merit 1997), Order of Samaritan/U. Ala. Law Sch., Kiwanis. Baptist. Office: 3137 Hathaway Pl Montgomery AL 36111-1707

**MADDOX, JERRY AVEN,** retail executive; b. Atlanta, Sept. 27, 1935; s. George Ernest and Emilie Marion (Peeples) Maddox; m. Roberta Ann Eddy; children: Lamont Edward, Ryan Allen, Jolie Aven. BBA in Fin. and Acctg., Emory U., Atlanta, 1957, JD, 1964. Catalog Mgmt. Exec. Sears, Roebuck & Co., Atlanta, 1957—89; Substitute Tchr. DeKalb County Sch. System, Atlanta, 1992—2000. Author: (geneology books) Descendants of John Allen, 1997, The Peeples Family, Descendants of William Peeples, 1999, (historical fiction) Song of the Ogeechee, 2002, From Salacoa to Tahlequah, 2004. Page Congressman James C. Davis, Washington, 1951; adminstrv. bd. Dunwoody

United Meth. Ch., 1972—81; coach nat. age group U.S. Swimming, 1978—88; v.p., sec. DeKalb County Jaycees, Ga., 1964—70; life mem. Dunwoody Preservation Trust, Inc., 2004. With U.S. Marine Corps. active duty and reserves, 1957—63. Mem.: Mil. Order Stars and Bars (Lt. Comdr. Gen. William J. Hardee chpt. 2002—03, The Jackson medal 2000), St. Andrews Soc., Clan Hay/Clan Irwin, Nat. Eagle Scout Assn. (life), Ft. Delaware Soc. (life), Eddy Family Assn. (life; rec. sec. 1995—2000), Belle Meade Hunt Club (equestrian), SCV (Comdr. Maj. Charles A. Dunwoody Camp 2002—), St. David's Welch Soc. of Georgia, Phi Alpha Delta, Pi Kappa Alpha, Alpha Kappa Psi. Republican. Avocation: running. Home: 4917 Cambridge Dr Dunwoody GA 30338-5007

**MADDOX, LAUREN M.,** federal agency administrator; B, Creighton U.; M, Northwestern U. Sr. v.p. Comm. Fedn. Am. Hospitals; sr. Comm. adv. US Rep. Newt Gingrich, US Rep. J.C. Watts, Jr.; sr. comm. adv. to US Rep. Joel Hefley US Congress; commr. dir. Ho. Rep. Conf.; prin. PodestaMattoon; asst. sec. for comm. & outreach US Dept. Edn., Washington, 2006—. Office: 400 Maryland Ave SW Rm 7C115 Washington DC 20202-1510 Office Phone: 202-401-0404. Office Fax: 202-401-8607.*

**MADDOX, LYNDELL E.,** utilities company executive; BS, Wichita State U., MBA in bus. admin. Fin. analyst NCR Corp.; gas acquisitions rep. No. Natural Gas Co.; dir. supplemental supplies Peoples Natural Gas Co.; sr. v.p., operations Aquila Energy Inc.; pres., COO Brooklyn Interstate Natural Gas Corp. (formerly Brooklyn Union Gas and subsidiary of Keyspan); pres. PennUnion Energy Services (subsidiary of Pennzoil), 1995—97; pres., CEO PG&E Energy Trading, 1997; sr. v.p. PG&E Corp., San Francisco.

**MADDOX, MARK LEE,** academic administrator; b. Dresden, Tenn., Feb. 10, 1959; s. Sam R. and Bonnie L. (Brundige) M. BA in Math., Trinity U., San Antonio, 1981, MEd, 1986. Cert. math., psychology tchr., adminstr. and supervision. Computer programmer Texaco Inc., Houston, 1981-84; math. tchr. James Madison H.S., San Antonio, 1984-86, Dresden (Tenn.) H.S., 1986-89; adminstrv. asst. State Rep. Roy Herron, Dresden, Tenn., 1986-90; prin. Weakley County Vocat. Sch., Dresden, Tenn., 1989-91; supr. vocational edn. and technol. and fed. projects Weakley County Schs., Dresden, 1991-96, supr. Tech. Ctr., 1996—. Mem., Tenn. Edn. Assn., Weakley County Edn. Assn., Rotary (state rep. 1996—). Home: 245 Legens St Dresden TN 38225-4107 Office: Weakley County Ctr Adult Learning 8250 Highway 22 Dresden TN 38225-2354

**MADDOX, MARTHA LACEY GARDNER,** artist; b. Birmingham, Ala., Jan. 5, 1926; d. Searcy Preston and Willard Morris Gardner; m. Steve Wilson Maddox, Mar. 3, 1946; children: Steve Wilson Jr., James Wayne, David Worthington. B in Applied Art, Ala. Poly. Inst. (now Auburn U.), 1947. Cert. tchr. Ala., Fla. Art prof. U. Ala., Tuscaloosa, 1947, 1948; H.S. and elem. sch. tchr. Ala. Sch. Bd., Flomaton, 1949—51; tchr. Byrneville (Fla.) Elem., 1951—52. Exhibitions include Vincent Price Touring Exhbn., Golden Heritage Exhbn., Cheaha Exhbn., Old Mobile Exhbn., Dauphin Island Exhbn., Art for Art's Sake, Wiregrass Mus. Art, Outstanding Artists S.E., Met. Mus. Art, High Mus. Art, Fine Arts Mus. of the South, Birmingham Mus. Art, Ea. Shore Art Ctr., Alpha Omicron Pi scholar, 1947. Mem.: Exptl. Artists Ala., Pastel Soc. Am., United Pastelists Am., Oil Pastel Soc., Watercolor Soc. Ala., Ea. Shore Art Assn., Mobile Art Assn., Nat. Women in the Arts, Malone Painters, Panama Art Assn., Hoover Art Assn., Dothan-Wiregrass Art League. Methodist. Home and Office: 2724 Southview Terr Birmingham AL 35216 Office Phone: 205-824-6426.

**MADDOX, NADANA,** secondary school educator; m. John Maddox, Sept. 1, 1969; children: Brian D., Gregory D. BA, Southwestern Okla. State U., Weatherford, Okla., 1972; MS in Sch. Counseling, East Ctrl. U., Ada, Okla., 2002. Tchr., counselor Walters (Okla.) Pub. Schs., 1984—2004; project dir. Osage County Interlocal Coop., Hominy, Okla., 2004—. Avocations: travel, baseball, reading. Office Phone: 918-885-2667.

**MADDOX, RICHARD,** manufacturing executive; Pres. Blue Bird, Macon, Ga., 1999, CEO, 1999—2003, vice-pres., gen. mgr. school bus div. Office: Blue Bird Corporation 402 Bluebird Blvd PO Box 937 Fort Valley GA 31030-0938 Office Phone: 800-486-7122.

**MADDOX, ROBERT NOTT,** chemical engineer, educator; b. Winslow, Ark., Sept. 29, 1925; s. R.L. and Mabel (Nott) M.; m. Paula Robinson, Oct. 6, 1951 (dec. Apr. 1984); children: Deirdre O'Neil, Robert Dozier; m. Pauline Razook, Nov. 30, 1987. Student, Iowa State Coll., 1944-45; BS, U. Ark., 1948; MS, U. Okla., 1950; PhD, Okla. State U., 1955; Sc.D. (hon.), U. Ark., 1991. Registered profl. engr., Okla. Mem. faculty Sch. Chem. Engring., Okla. State U., 1950-51, 52-58, prof., head dept., 1958-77, Leonard F. Sheerar prof., 1976-86, dir. phys. properties lab., 1976-86. Design engr. process div. Black, Sivalls & Bryson, Inc., Oklahoma City, 1951-52; adminstrv. v.p., tech. dir. Fluid Properties Research, Inc., 1972-85; chem. engring. cons. Author: Gas and Liquid Sweetening, 1971, rev. ed. 1978, 83, (with J. Erbar) Gas Conditioning and Processing Vol. 3 - Computer Techniques and Applications, 1981, rev. ed. (with L. Lilly), 1988, (with A. Hines) Mass Transfer - Fundamentals and Applications, 1985; also numerous tech. papers. Served with USNR, 1944-45. Recipient award for personal achievement Chem. Engring. mag., 1988; Phillips lectr. in chem. engring. edn., Oklahoma State U., 1989; inducted into Engring. Hall of Fame, U. Ark., 1989, Okla. Higher Edn. Hall of Fame, 1996; Dr. Robert N. Maddox Professorship in Chem. Engring. established in his honor by Gas Processors Suppliers Assn. at Okla. State U., 1989, Founders award Am. Inst. of Chemical Engineers, 1994 Fellow AIChE (hmpt. pres. 1956-57, Andre Wilkins Meml. award 1981, Founder's award 1994). mem. NSPE, Okla. Soc. Profl. Engrs. (chpt. pres. 1961-62, dir. 1966-68, Engr. of Yr. 1972), Am. Inst. Mining Engrs., Soc. Petroleum Engrs., Acad. Chem. Engrs., Am. Chem. Soc. (treas. indsl. and engring. chemistry div. 1966-68, chmn. div. 1970, Stewart award 1971), Gas Processors Assn. (Hanlon award 1985, Svc. citation 1987, Meritorious Svc. award 1994), Gas Processors Suppliers Assn. (editorial adv. bd. Engring. Data Book 1972—), Sigma Xi, Omega Chi Epsilon (nat. pres. 1968-70), Tau Beta Pi, Alpha Chi Sigma, Omicron Delta Kappa, Sigma Nu (high coun. 1966-70, regent 1972-74, Hall of Honor 1988). Episcopalian (lay reader, vestryman). Clubs: Elks, Masons. Home: 1710 Davinbrook Ln Stillwater OK 74074-2339

**MADDREY, WILLIS CROCKER,** medical educator, internist, academic administrator, consultant, researcher; b. Roanoke Rapids, N.C., Mar. 29, 1939; s. Milner Crocker and Sara Jean (Willis) M.; m. Ann Marie Matt; children: Jeffrey, Gregory, Thomas. BS, Wake Forest U., 1960; MD, Johns Hopkins U., 1964. Diplomate: Am. Bd. Internal Medicine. Intern Osler Med. Service Johns Hopkins Hosp., Balt., 1964-65, asst. resident, 1965-66, 68-69, chief resident, 1969-70; fellow in liver disease Yale U., 1970-71; asst. prof. medicine Johns Hopkins U., Balt., 1971-75, assoc. prof., 1975-79, prof., 1980—82, asst. dean Sch. Medicine, 1975-79, assoc. dir. dept. medicine, 1979-82; prof., chmn. dept. medicine Jefferson Med. Coll., Phila., 1982-90; v.p. clin. affairs U. Tex. Southwestern Med. Ctr., Dallas, 1990-93, exec. v.p. clin. affairs, 1993—. Assoc. editor: Medicine, 1972-82, Hepatology, 1988-95, mem. editl. bd., 1981-84, 86-87, Gastroenterology, 1982-87, Am. Jour. Medicine, 1978-88; contbr. articles to profl. jours. Bd. dirs. Am. Liver Found., 1978-81, Dallas County Med. Soc., 1996-98; trustee Magee Rehab. Hosp., Phila., 1982-87. With USPHS, 1966-68. Mem. ACP (bd. regents 1986-92, pres. 92-93), Am. Soc. Clin. Investigation, Am. Gastroenterol. Assn., Am. Assn. Study Liver Disease (pres. 1981). Republican. Office: U Tex Southwestern Med Ctr 5323 Harry Hines Blvd Dallas TX 75390-8570

**MADDUX, GREGORY (GREGORY ALAN MADDUX),** professional baseball player; b. San Angelo, Tex., Apr. 14, 1966; Grad., H.S., Las Vegas. Baseball player Chgo. Cubs, 1986—92, 2004—06, Atlanta Braves, 1992—2003, LA Dodgers, 2006—. Named Nat. League Pitcher of Yr., Sporting News, 1993, Nat. League Innings Pitched Leader, 1991—95, Nat. League Earned Run Avg. Leader, 1993—95, 1998; named to All-Star team, 1988, 1992, 1994—98, 2000; recipient Cy Young award, Baseball Writers

Assn. Am., 1992, 1993, 1994, 1995, Gold Glove award, 1990—2002, Gold Glove Award, 2004—05. Achievements include being a mem. of World Series Championship team, 1995; becoming 13th pitcher in MLB history to throw 3,000 strikeouts, 2005. Office: LA Dodgers Dodger Stadium 1000 Elysian Park Ave Los Angeles CA 90012-1199*

**MADEIRA, FRANCIS KING CAREY,** conductor, educator; b. Jenkintown, Pa., Feb. 21, 1917; s. Percy Childs and Margaret (Carey) M.; m. Jean E. Browning, June 17, 1947. Grad., Avon Old Farms, 1934; student, Julliard Grad. Sch., 1937-43; DFA (hon.), Providence Coll., 1966; DHL, R.I. Coll., 1969; MusD (hon.), Brown U., 1976. Instr. music Brown U., 1943-46, asst. prof. music, 1946-56, assoc. music, 1956-66. Founder, condr. R.I. Philharm. Orch., 1945-78; concert pianist recitals and condr. concerts, U.S. and Europe; also guest condr. U.S. and fgn. orchs. World premiere Trilogy (JFK-MLK-RFK) (by Ron Nelson), R.I. Philharmonic Orch., 1969. Mem. music panel Maine State Arts Commn., 1987-90; bd. trustees Saco River Festival Assn., 1988-94; mem. adv. bd., trustee Portland (Maine) Symphony Orch., 1996—. Recipient Gov.'s award for excellence in arts, 1972; John F. Kennedy award for svc. to cmty., 1978, Maestro award R.I. Philharm. Orch., 1998, Millennium Reflections award R.I. Philharm. Orch., 1999, John Hazen White Sr. Leadership award R.I. Philharm. Orch., 2003, Citizen Citation award Mayor or Providence, R.I., 2003.

**MADER, CHARLES LAVERN,** chemist; b. Dewey, Okla., Aug. 8, 1930; s. George Edgar and Naomia Jane (Harer) M.; m. Emma Jean Sinclair, June 12, 1960; 1 child, Charles L. II. BS, Okla. State U., 1952, MS, 1954; PhD, Pacific Western U., 1980. Fellow Los Alamos (N.Mex.) Nat. Lab., 1955—; JIMAR sr. fellow U. Hawaii, Honolulu, 1985-94; pres. Mader Cons. Co., Honolulu, 1985—. Author: Numerical Modeling of Detonation, 1979, Numerical Modeling of Water Waves, 1988, Numerical Modeling of Explosives and Propellants, 1997, Numerical Modeling of Water, 2d edit., 2004; editor: Los Alamos Explosives Performance Data, 1982, LASL Phermex Data, vol. 1, 1980, vol. 2, 1980, vol. 3, 1981; contbr. numerous articles to profl. jours.; author 70 reports. Scoutmaster Boy Scouts Am., Los Alamos, 1971-85. Fellow Am. Inst. Chemists; mem. Am. Chem. Soc., Combustion Inst., Tsunami Soc. (editor 1985—2006), Marine Tech. Soc., Sigma Xi, Pi Mu Epsilon, Phi Lambda Upsilon. Methodist. Achievements include development and definition of field of numerical modeling of explosives and water waves. Office: Mader Consulting Co 1049 Kamehame Dr Honolulu HI 96825-2860 also: 214 Barranca Rd Los Alamos NM 87544-2410 also: PO Box 5930 Avon CO 81620-5930 Office Phone: 808-396-9855. E-mail: mccohi@aol.com.

**MADERN, LAURENE PATRICIA,** secondary school educator; b. Malden, Mass., Feb. 28, 1953; d. James A. and Constance Catherine (Downing) Lawless; m. Lenny Madern, Dec. 29, 1979; children: James L., Ashley L. BA in English and Sociology, U. Mass., 1975; postgrad., Brandeis U., 1975, Tufts U., 1977-78; MEd, Cambridge Coll., 1997; EdS, Liberty U., 2003. Cert. tchr., Mass., N.C. Tchr. St. Rose H.S., Chelsea, Mass., 1975-78, Browne Jr. High, Malden, 1978-81, Ea. Wayne H.S., 1991-97; A.G. specialist Wayne County Pub. Schs., 1997—2000; curriculum specialist Johnston County Schs., 2000—03, coord. profl. devel., 2003—. Organizer drama program Ea. Wayne H.S., Goldsboro, 1991-93, dir. prodn., 1991-94, English dept. chair, 1993-94, sr. class advisor, 1992-93, forensic team organizer, 1996-97; nat. spkr. on differentiation, nat. USA Today nat. tchg. team, 2001; ednl. accolate, dept. pub. instrn., N.C., 2001; bd.mem. NCAGT, 2001—. Bd. dirs. Goldsboro Civic Ballet, 1994—; exec. bd. dirs. Future Cath. H.S., Goldsboro, 1994—. Theater Prodn. grant Cmty. Arts Coun., Goldsboro, 1992-94; recipient Helping Hand award Miss. Ea. Wayne Pageant, Goldsboro, 1993-94; honoree N.C. Ctr. for Advancement of Tchg., 1995, Tchr. Exec. Inst., 1996-97. Roman Catholic. Avocations: soccer, education, travel. Office: Adm Annex PO Box 1336 Smithfield NC 27577 Home: 9243 Fawn Lake Dr Raleigh NC 27617-7444

**MADGETT, NAOMI LONG,** poet, editor, publisher, educator; b. Norfolk, Va., July 5, 1923; d. Clarence Marcellus and Maude Selena (Hilton) Long; m. Julian F. Witherspoon, Mar. 31, 1946 (div. Apr. 1949); 1 child, Jill Witherspoon Boyer; m. William H. Madgett, July 29, 1954 (div. Dec. 1960); m. Leonard P. Andrews, Mar. 31, 1972 (dec. May 1996). BA, Va. State Coll., 1945; MEd, Wayne State U., 1955; PhD, Internat. Inst. for Advanced Studies, 1980; LHD (hon.), Siena Heights Coll., 1991, Loyola U., 1993; DFA (hon.), Mich. State U., 1994. Reporter, copyreader Mich. Chronicle, Detroit, 1946; svc. rep. Mich. Bell Telephone Co., Detroit, 1948-54; tchr. English pub. high schs. Detroit, 1955-65, 66-68; rsch. assoc. Oakland U., Rochester, Mich., 1965-66; mem. staff Detroit Women Writers Conf. Ann. Writers Conf., 1968—; lectr. English U. Mich., 1970-71; assoc. prof. English Eastern Mich. U., Ypsilanti, 1968-73, prof., 1973-84, prof. emeritus, 1984—; editor-pub. Lotus Press, 1974—. Editor Lotus Poetry Series, Mich. State U. Press, 1993-98. Author: (poetry) Songs to a Phantom Nightingale (under name Naomi Cornelia Long), 1941, One and the Many, 1956, Star by Star, 1965, 2d edit., 70, (with Ethel Tincher and Henry B. Maloney) Success in Language and Literature B, 1967, Pink Ladies in the Afternoon, 1972, 2d edit., 90, Exits and Entrances, 1978, A Student's Guide to Creative Writing, 1980, Phantom Nightingale: Juvenilia, 1981, Octavia and other Poems (Creative Achievement award Coll. Lang. Assn.), 1988, Remembrances of Spring: Collected Early Poems, 1993, Octavia: Guthrie and Beyond, 2002, Connected Islands, 2004, Pilgrim Journey, 2006; editor: (anthology) A Milestone Sampler: 15th Anniversary Anthology, 1988, Adam of Ife: Black Women in Praise of Black Men, 1992; In Her Lifetime tribute Afrikan Poets Theatre, 1989 Participant Creative Writers in Schs. program. Recipient Esther R. Beer Poetry award Nat. Writers Club, 1957, Disting. English Tchr. of Yr. award, 1967; Josephine Nevins Keal award, 1979; Mott fellow in English, 1965, Robert Hayden Runagate award, 1985, Creative Artist award Mich. Coun. for the Arts, 1987, award Nat. Coalition 100 Black Women, 1984, award Nat. Coun. Tchrs. English Black Caucus, 1984, award Chesapeake/Virginia Beach chpt. Links, Inc., 1981, Arts Found. Mich. award, 1990, Creative Achievement award Coll. Lang. Assn., 1988; Arts Achievement award Wayne State U., 1985, The Black Scholar Award of Excellence, 1992; Am. Book award, 1993, Mich. Artist award, 1993; Creative Contbrs. award Gwendolyn Brooks Ctr. Black Lit. and Creative Writing Chgo. State U., 1993, Lifetime Achievement award Furious Flower, 1994, George Kent award, 1995, Lifetime Achievement award Gwendolyn Brooks Ctr., 2003; Naomi Long Madgett Poetry award named for her, 1993—, Alain Locke award Detroit Inst. Arts, Friends of African and African Am. Art, 2003; inducted Sumner H.S. Hall of Fame, St. Louis, 1997, Nat. Lit. Hall Fame for Writers of African Descent, Chgo. State U., 1999, Mich. Women's Hall of Fame, 2002; named Poet Laureate, City of Detroit, 2001—; Mayor's award Literary Excellence, 2005; named one of 23 Enterprising Women, Detroit Hist. Soc., 2004; Bronze Bust created by Artis Lane unveiled at Charles H. Wright Mus. African Am. History, 2005. Mem. NAACP, Coll. Lang. Assn., So. Poetry Law Ctr., Langston Hughes Soc., Charles H. Wright Mus. of African Am. History, Detroit Working Writers, Detroit Inst. Arts, Fred Hart Williams Geneal. Soc., Alpha Kappa Alpha. Congregationalist. Home: 18080 Santa Barbara Dr Detroit MI 48221-2531 Office: PO Box 21607 Detroit MI 48221-0607 Office Phone: 313-861-1280. Personal E-mail: nlmadgett@aol.com. *I have tried to set an example of excellence in the use of language, especially the language of poetry. If I can leave behind some enduring work—my own words and the words of others I have published—I will consider myself amply rewarded for my labors. The truly great people I have known have given a great deal of themselves in the service of others, have not been puffed up about their own importance, and have maintained integrity in their personal and professional lives. They have been my models.*

**MADHAPPAN-KEMPURAJ, BHUVANESHWARI,** medical researcher; d. Kolanthai and Ranganayaki Madhappan; m. Duraisamy Kempuraj, June 4, 1998; 1 child, Deepak Kempuraj. MBBS, Annamalai U., Chidambaram, India, 1998. Cert. Tamil Nadu Med. Coun. Vt. practice, Palacode, 1998—99; rschr., cons. Tufts U. Sch. Medicine, Boston, 2002—03. Mem. editl. staff. European Jour. Inflammation; contbr. over 16 articles to profl. jours. Home: 99 Florence St Apt 422 Malden MA 02148 Personal E-mail: lathakempuraj@yahoo.com.

**MADHAVAN, KUNCHI,** engineering educator; PhD, U. Miss., Oxford. Profl. engr., NJ., Pa., 2006. Prof. Christian Bros. U., Memphis, 1976—. Achievements include design of building foundations. Office: Christian Brothers U 650 East Pky South Memphis TN 38104-5581

**MADHAVAN, MAHENDRAKUMAR,** structural engineer, researcher; s. Madhavan Periyasamy Konar and Mathialagu Madhavan. BEng, Anna U., Channai, India, 1998; MEng, Nat. U. Singapore, 2000; postgrad., U. Ala., 2001—. Rsch. scholar Nat. U. Singapore, 1998—2000; grad. rsch. asst. U. Ala., Birmingham, 2001—. Contbr. articles to profl. jours. Pres. Hindu Student Coun., Birmingham, Ala., 2001—05; vol. Vol. Income Tax Assistance, IRS, Birmingham, Ala., 2002—04. Mem.: ASCE, Phi Beta Delta, Tau Beta Phi. Avocations: jogging, racquetball. Office: Univ Ala Hohen 140 1075 13th St S Birmingham AL 35294 E-mail: mahendra@alumni.nus.edu.sg.

**MADHAVAN, RAJ,** electrical engineer, electronics engineer; BEE, Anna U., Madras, India, 1994; MSc in Engring., Australian Nat. U., 1997; PhD, U. Sydney, 2000. Rsch. fellow Oak Ridge (Tenn.) Nat. Lab., 2001—02; guest rschr. Nat. Inst. Standards and Tech., Gaithersburg, Md., 2002—. Contbr. articles to profl. jours., chpt. to book. Fellow, CRC Mining and Tech. Equipment, 1997; scholar, Australian Nat. U., 1995. Mem.: IEEE (Student Paper award 1998), Wash. Acad. Scis., Sigma Xi. Office: Nist 100 Bureau Dr MS 8230 Gaithersburg MD 20899 Office Phone: 301-975-2865. Office Fax: 301-990-9688. Personal E-mail: raj.madhavan@ieee.org. Business E-Mail: raj.madhavan@nist.gov.

**MADIA, WILLIAM JUUL,** chemist; b. Pitts., May 20, 1947; s. William Anthony and Joanna (VanKerchkoven) M.; m. Audrey Marie Madia, May 23, 1970; children: Joseph Anthony, Benjamin Paul, William Byron. BS in Chemistry, Ind. U. of Pa., 1969, MS in Nuclear Chemistry, 1970; PhD in Radiochemistry, Va. Polytech. Inst., 1975. With Battelle, 1975—; chemist, researcher Battelle Columbus (Ohio) div., 1975-77, assoc. sect. mgr., 1977-80, sect. mgr., 1980-83, mgr. office of nuclear waste isolation, 1983-85; pres. Battelle Project Mgmt. div., 1985-86; sr. v.p. Battelle Meml. Inst., 1988-89, 89—; pres. Battelle Tech. Internat., 1988-89, corp. sr. v.p., 1990-91, gen. mgr. environ. systems and tech. divsn., corp. sr. v.p., 1992-94; dir. Pacific Northwest Nat. Lab., 1994—99, Oak Ridge Nat. Lab., Tenn., 2000—03; pres., CEO UT- Battelle, Oak Ridge, Tenn., exec. v.p., 2003—. Mem. adv. bd. Ohio State U. Coll. Engring.; bd. dirs. Mason & Hanger. Mem. editl. bd. R&D Mag.; contbr. articles to profl. jours. Bd. dirs. Franklin U., 1987-94, Franklin County Children Svcs., 1988-94; editorial adv. bd. High Tech. Bus. 1988—; bd. dirs. Tri-City Indsl. Devel. Coun., Washington Roundtable; hon. bd. dirs. Mid-Columbia Edn. Alliance; adv. bd. Jr. Achievement Greater Tri-Cities; bd. dirs. Reading Found.; co-chair Tri-Cities Corp. Coun. Arts; mem. exec. com. Children's Ctr. Capital Campaign. With U.S. Army, 1970-72. Mem. AAAS, Indsl. Rsch. Inst. (fed. sci. and tech. com.), Midwest Rsch. Inst. (trustee), Nat. Renewable Energy Lab. (bd. govs.), Brookhaven Sci. Assocs. (bd. dirs.), U.S. Dept. Energy Lab. Ops. Bd., Washington Tech. Alliance. Roman Catholic. Office: Battelle 505 King Ave Columbus OH 43201

**MADIGAN, ELIZABETH M.,** lawyer; b. Detroit, Mar. 30, 1960; d. James Wilfred Madigan and Patricia Mary Thundow; m. Joseph V. Korth, July 15, 1989. BA in Humanities, Mich. State U., 1994; JD, U. Mich., 1998. Bar: Mich. 1998. Mng. atty. Madigan Law Firm, PLC, Okemos, Mich., 1998—. Scholar Carolyn Stell scholar, Women Lawyers Assn. of Mich.-Mid-Mich., 1998. Mem.: ABA, Women Lawyers Assn. of Mich., Ingham County Bar Assn., State Bar of Mich.

**MADIGAN, JOHN WILLIAM,** publishing executive; b. Chgo., June 7, 1937; s. Edward P. and Olive D. Madigan; m. Holly Williams, Nov. 24, 1962; children: Mark W., Griffith E., Melanie L. BBA, U. Mich., 1958, MBA, 1959. Fin. analyst Duff & Phelps, Chgo., 1960—62; audit mgr. Arthur Andersen & Co., Chgo., 1962—67; v.p. investment banking Paine, Webber, Jackson & Curtis, Chgo., 1967—69; v.p. corp. fin. Salomon Bros., Chgo., 1969—74; v.p., CFO, dir. Tribune Co., Chgo., 1975—81, exec. v.p., 1981—90; pub. Chgo. Tribune, 1990—94; pres., CEO Tribune Pub. Co., Chgo., 1991—94; pres., COO Tribune Co., Chgo., 1994—95, pres., 1994—2001, CEO, 1995—2002, chmn., 1996—2004. Bd. dir. AP, AT&T Wireless Svcs.; former dir. Morgan Stanley. Trustee Rush-Presbyn.-St. Luke's Med. Ctr., Mus. TV and Radio in N.Y., Northwestern U., Ill. Inst. Tech.; mem. bd. overseers Hoover Instn. Mem.: Chgo. Coun. on Fgn. Rels. (chmn.), Robert R. McCormick Tribune Found.*

**MADIGAN, JOSEPH EDWARD,** financial executive, director, consultant; b. Bklyn., June 26, 1932; s. James Peter and Mary (Goldman) M.; m. Catherine Cashman, July 26, 1980; children: Kerri Ann, Kimberly Ann Burquest, Elizabeth Ann Lagniss. BBA cum laude, Baruch Coll., CUNY, 1958; MBA, NYU, 1963. Adminstrv. asst. Assoc. Metals & Minerals Corp., 1961-63; fin. analyst, fgn. exch. trader, corp. portfolio trader AMAX, Inc., 1963-65; mgr. corp. portfolio, dir. cash mgmt., asst. treas. TWA, Inc., 1965-68; treas. Borden, Inc., 1968-76, v.p., treas., 1976-80; exec. v.p., chief fin. officer, dir. Wendy's Internat., Inc., Dublin, Ohio, 1980-87. Bd. dirs Frank Gates Co., Columbus Show Case Co., Scioto Properties LLC. Chmn. bd. Lexford Residential Properties, 1997-99. With USN, 1951-55. Mem. Fin. Execs. Inst., Nat. Investor Rels. Inst., Baruch Coll.-CUNY Alumni Assn., NYU Alumni Assn., Imperial Golf Club, Allendale Country Club, Beta Gamma Sigma. Republican. Roman Catholic. Home: 5555 Heron Point Dr # 2102 Naples FL 34108

**MADIGAN, LISA,** state attorney general; m. Pat Byrnes; 1 child, Rebecca. BA, Georgetown U., 1988; attended, Loyola U. Asst. dean adult, continuing edn., dir. Sr. Acad. Lifelong Learning Wrights Family Coll. Wilbur Wright Coll., with positive alts. project; litigator Sachnoff & Weaver, Ltd., Chgo.; mem. Ill. Senate, Springfield, 1998—2002, mem. senate appropriations com., edn. com., joint com. adminstrv. rules; atty. gen. State of Ill., 2002—. Former vol. tchr., South Africa. Bd. dirs. AIDS Living Rememberance Com. Named one of Top 40 Lawyers Under 40, Nat. Law Jour., 2005. Mem. Ill. Bar Assn., Women's Bar Assn. Ill., Chgo. Bar Assn. Republican. Office: Office of Atty General James R Thompson Ctr 100 W Randolph St Chicago IL 60601 Office Phone: 312-814-3000.*

**MADIHALLY, SUNDARARAJAN V.,** engineering educator; s. Venkatesh Iyengar and Janakamma R. H. PhD, Wayne State U., Detroit, 1998. Asst. prof. Okla. State U., Stillwater, Okla., 2002—. Vis. asst. prof. The State U. N.J., Piscataway, NJ. Named Student Orgn. Advisor of Yr., Okla. State U., 2005; recipient Tchr. of Yr. award, Sch. Chem. Engring., 2006, Halliburton Excellent Young Tchr. award, Coll. Engring., Architecture and Tech., 2005; scholar, India, 1986. Mem.: AIChE, Tau Beta Pi, Omega Chi Epsilon. Achievements include research in burn injury and tissue engineering. Office: Oklahoma State University 423 Engineering North Stillwater OK 74078 Business E-Mail: sundar.madihally@okstate.edu.

**MADISON, ANNE CONWAY,** public relations and marketing professional; b. Balt., Mar. 13, 1963; d. Earl Cranston Jr. and Nancy C.; 1 child, Ryan Douglas. BS in Commun., Wittenberg U., 1985. Pub. rels. specialist Springfield (Ohio) Met. Housing Authority, 1984-85; account rep. CT Corp. Sys., Washington, 1985-86; pub. rels. asst. Ryland, Columbia, Md., 1986-88, comm. coord., 1988-90, mgr. mktg. comm., 1990-92, dir. mktg. comm., 1992-94, v.p. comm., 1994—2003; v.p. mktg. and comm. ESIC, Inc., Columbia, 2003—05; v.p. corp. comm. Choice Hotels Internat., Silver Spring, Md. Bd. dirs., officer Domestic Violence Cr. of Howard County, Columbia, 1987-96; bd. dirs. Norbel Sch., Nat. Family Resiliency Ctr. Named Vol. of Yr. Domestic Violence Ctr., 1988, recipient Spirit award, 1992; named one of Top 100 Women in Md., The Daily Record, 1996. Mem. Pub. Rels. Soc. Am., Nat. Investor Rels. Inst. Republican. Roman Catholic. Office Phone: 301-592-6723. Personal E-mail: acmadison@comcast.net. Business E-Mail: anne_madison@choicehotels.com.

**MADISON, DEBORAH LEAFY,** writer, chef; b. West Hartford, Conn., June 21, 1945; d. John Herbert and Winifred (Law) Madison; m. Dan Welch, Mar. 17, 1979 (div. Nov. 1986); m. J. Patrick McFarlin, May 29, 1991. BA, U. Calif., Santa Cruz, 1968. Founding chef The Greens Restaurant, San Francisco, 1978-83, Cafe Escalera, Santa Fe, N.Mex., 1990-93; menu cons. Rancho San Miguel, Baja Sur, Mex., 1996. Cons. to various restaurants, 1986—. Author: The Greens Cookbook, 1986 (Andre Simon award 1987), The Savory Way, 1990 (Best Cookbook of Yr. Julia Childs award 1991), The Vegetarian Table: America, 1996, Vegetarian Cooking for Everyone, 1997 (James Beard Award), This Can't be Tofu, 2000, Local Flavors: Cooking and Eating from America's Farmers' Markets, 2002, Vegetarian Suppers from Deborah Madison's Kitchen, 2005; adv. editor Saveor, 1994—; contbg. author books; contbr. articles to profl. jours. Pres. Santa Fe Area Farmers Mkt., 1990—; mem. Student Nutrition Action Com., Santa Fe, 1995—. Named to Honor Roll of Am. Chefs, Food and Wine Mag., 1983; recipient Contessa Premium Foods Whos Who of Food and Beverage in Am. award, James Beard Found., 2005. Mem. Internat. Assn. Culinary Professions, The Chef's Collaborative (founder), Les Dames D'Escoffier (MFK Fisher Mid-Career award 1994). Avocations: gardening, reading.*

**MADISON, EDDIE LAWRENCE,** public relations consultant, editor, writer; b. Tulsa, Sept. 8, 1930; s. Eddie Lawrence Sr. and Laverta (Pyle) M.; m. Davetta Jayn Cooksey, Nov. 17, 1956; children: Eddie Lawrence III, Karyn Devette, David Cooksey. B in Journalism, Lincoln U., Jefferson City, Mo., 1952; MA, U. Tulsa, 1959. Editor-in-chief, gen. mgr. Okla. Eagle, Tulsa, 1954-59; assoc. editor Daily Defender, 1959-61; dep. editor Assoc. Negro Press, Chgo., 1961-63; sect. editor Chgo. Tribune, 1963-65; dir. domestic pub. affairs Paris Air Show Newsletter, U.S. Dept. Commerce; dep. dir. publs. divsn. Domestic and Internat. Bus., U.S. Dept. Commerce, Washington, 1965-69; mgr. cmty. svcs. Evening Star Broadcasting Co., Washington, 1969-78; asst. editor Bus. Am. Mag., Washington, 1978-81; press asst. Ho. of Reps., Washington, 1981-82; pub. affairs specialist U.S. Dept. HHS, Washington, 1982-92, mgr. HHS radio, 1991-92; asst. prof., chmn. dept. comm. Lincoln U., 1992-99; exec. editor, CEO, Okla. Eagle, Tulsa, 2001—; pres., CEO Three Elms & Assoc., Inc., Tulsa, 2001—. Founder Nat. Broadcast Assn. for Cmty. Affairs, Washington, 1974, 1st pres., 1974-77. Correspondent, Native Am. Times. Pres. Brightwood Civic Assn., Washington, 1969-72; mem. media adv. com. Mo. Arts Coun., 1996-99; mem. tobacco coalition and assist coms. Am. Cancer Soc., 1993-99; Hist. Preservation Commn., 1997-99; bd. dirs. Opportunities Industrialization Ctr. Washington, 1971-77, D.C. United Way, 1972-77, Boy Scouts Am., Washington, 1972-77. With U.S. Army, 1952-54; corr., Army Times, columnist, Recon Observer, Ellsworth AFB, S.D. Recipient Lifetime Achievement award, Tulsa Assn. Black Journalists, 2005. Mem. Alpha Phi Alpha (pres. Washington chpt. 1969-72, nat. dir. pub. rels. 1985-91, co-chair nat. pub. policy com. 1973, v.p. Montgomery County chpt. 1987-89, pres. Jefferson City Beta Zeta Lambda chpt. 1993, assoc. editor Sphinx mag., award of merit Ea. region 1992). Methodist. Avocations: photography, aerobics, jazz. Home: 4355 S Braden Ave Tulsa OK 74135-6337 Office: The Okla Eagle 624 E Archer St Tulsa OK 74120-1000 Address: Native Am Times 12833 E 41st St Tulsa OK 74146 also: Three Elms & Assocs PO Box 161 Tulsa OK 74101-0161 Fax: 918-852-8905. Office Phone: 918-582-7124 224. E-mail: emadsept@aol.com.

**MADISON, GEORGE W.,** lawyer; b. Jersey City, Oct. 17, 1953; BS, NYU, 1975; MBA, Columbia U., 1977, JD, 1980. Law clk. to Hon. Nathaniel R. Jones U.S. Ct. Appeals (6th cir.) Ohio, Cin., 1980-81; assoc. Shearman & Sterling, NYC, 1981-87; with Mayer, Brown & Platt, NYC, 1987-89, ptnr., 1989-96; exec. v.p., corp. sec., gen. counsel Comerica Inc., Detroit, 1997—2003; exec. v.p., gen. counsel TIAA-CREF, NYC, 2003—. Bd. visitors Law Sch. Columbia U. Recipient Invaluable Pro Bono Legal Svcs. award, NAACP, 1997, Diversity 2000 award, MCCA, 1998, Learned Hand award, Am. Jewish Com., 2003, Disting. Svc. award, Detroit Met. Bar Assn., 2003, Pres. Choice award, State Bar Mich., 2003. Mem. ABA (chmn. com. corp. gen. counsel), Am. Judicature Soc., Am. Law Inst., Am. Corp. Counsel Assn., Assn. of Bar of City of N.Y. (mem. exec. com.). Office: TIAA-CREF 730 Third Ave New York NY 10017 Office Phone: 212-916-4750. Business E-Mail: gmadison@tiaa-cref.org.

**MADISON, JACQUELINE EDWINA,** librarian; b. Darlington, S.C., July 16, 1951; d. John Brown and Lula M. (Mack) McLeod; m. Calvin Lee Madison, Aug. 18, 1975; children: Jaquenette M., Calexandria J. BS, Fayetteville State U., N.C. 1972; MLS, Emporia State U., Kans., 1991. Insp. FDA, Orlando, Fla., 1972-73; supr. appt. clk. US Army Hdqrs., Nurnberg, Germany, 1975-78; tchr. ESL Big Bend Coll., Ft. Lewis, Wash., 1980-82; libr. tech. Ft. Riley Libr., Kans., 1987-90; info. specialist Battelle Pacific N.W. Nat. Lab., Richland, Wash., 1991-97; prin. libr. Wyeth Rsch., Chazy, NY, 1997—. Mem. Wash. Com. Student Learning, Olympia, Wash., 1994—97; owner, cons. Jaqcal's, Pasco, 1995—. Author: Jaqcal's Infophone Parent/Teacher Communication Line, 1995. Bd. dirs., pres. Girl Scouts USA North Country, 1998—, chair, 2002—; mem. Friends Mid Columbia Libr., Kennewick, Wash., 1992—, Multi Cultural Affairs, Pasco; v.p. Parent Tchr. Group, 1991—. Served U.S. Army, 1974—77, Germany. Mem.: Am. Registry Outstanding Professionals, Am. Chem. Soc., Spl. Libr. Assn., AAUW (sec. 1991), NAFE, Phi Beta Kappa. Avocations: computers, reading, cooking, museums, animals. Office: Battelle Pacific NW Nat Lab PO Box 999 Richland WA 99352-0999 also: Wyeth Rsch Drug Safety Info Ctr 641 Ridge Rd Chazy NY 12921-2420

**MADISON, JAMES RAYMOND,** lawyer; b. White Plains, NY, Apr. 27, 1931; s. Raymond S. and Katherine (Sherwin) M.; m. Mary Massey, Sept. 19, 1953; children: Michael, Matthew, Molly. BS, Stanford U., 1953, LLB, 1959. Bar: Calif. 1960, U.S. Dist. Ct. (no. dist.) Calif. 1960, U.S. Ct. Appeals (9th cir.) 1960, U.S. Dist. Ct. (ctrl. dist.) Calif. 1970, U.S. Supreme Ct. 1973, U.S. Dist. Ct. (ea. dist.) Calif. 1981, U.S. Dist. Ct. (so. dist.) Calif. 1988. Assoc. Orrick, Herrington & Sutcliffe, San Francisco, 1959-67, ptnr., 1968-95; pvt. practice Menlo Park, Calif., 1996—. Trustee Antioch U., Yellow Springs, Ohio, 1980-87; bd. dirs. Planned Parenthood Alameda/San Francisco, 1984-89; pres. Calif. Dispute Resolution Coun., 2001. Lt. (j.g.) USN, 1953-56. Mem. ABA, ASCE, State Bar Calif., Bar Assn. San Francisco, San Mateo County Bar Assn., Am. Arbitration Assn. (large complex case panel arbitrators and mediators, No. Calif. regional adv. coun.), Mediation Soc., Calif. Dispute Resolution Coun., Dispute Rev. Bd. Found., Coll. Comml. Arbitrators. Democrat. Episcopalian. Avocation: soccer. Office: 750 Menlo Ave Ste 250 Menlo Park CA 94025-4758 Office Phone: 650-614-0160. E-mail: jrmcoach@aol.com.

**MADISON, JOHN MARK,** pulmonologist, educator; b. Springfield, Ill., Nov. 1, 1953; s. Thomas Alvin and Georgie Lou (Huss) Madison; m. Paula Jean Drach, Nov. 30, 1985; children: Lindsey R., Elliot C.T. BA, Carleton Coll., 1975; MD, Harvard U., 1979. Cert. internal medicine and pulmonary diseases Md. Resident in internal medicine Washington U., St. Louis, 1982; fellow in pulmonary medicine U. Calif., San Francisco, 1985, instr., 1985—87, asst. prof., 1987—90; asst. prof. medicine U. Mass. Med. Sch., Worcester, 1990—95, assoc. prof. medicine, 1995—2005, prof. medicine, 2005—, chief divsn. pulmonary allergy and critical care medicine, 2005—. Mem. editl. bd.: Am. Jour. Respiratory, Cell and Molecular Biology, 1998—2003, Chest, 2006—; contbr. articles to profl. jours. Recipient R01-HL48166, NIH, 1992—95, R01-HL54143, 1995—2006. Mem.: Am. Coll. of Chest Physicians, AM. Thoracic Soc. Avocations: skiing, travel. Home: 75 Wyndhurst Dr Holden MA 01520 Office: U Mass Med Sch 55 Lake Ave N Worcester MA 01655 Business E-Mail: mark.madison@umassmed.edu.

**MADISON, PAULA,** broadcast executive; b. NYC, 1952; m. Roosevelt Madison; 1 child, Imani. Grad., Vassar Coll., 1974. Reporter Syracuse Herald Jour., 1974—80; investigative bur. reporter Ft. Worth Star - Telegram, 1980—82; asst. city editor Dallas Times Herald, 1982; cmty. affairs dir. WFAA-TV, Dallas, 1982—84, news mgr., 1984—86; news dir. KOTV-TV, Tulsa, 1986—87; exec. news dir. KHOU-TV, Houston, 1987—89; asst. news dir. WNBC, N.Y.C., 1989—96, v.p., news dir., 1996—2000; v.p., sr. v.p.

diversity NBC, N.Y.C., 2000—02; pres., gen. mgr. KNBC, L.A., 2000—; regional gen. mgr. KNBC, KVEA, KWHY, 2002—. Bd. trustees Vassar Coll. Named Disting. African-Am. New Yorker, N.Y.C. Comptroller Alan Hevesi, Citizen of Yr., City of LA Marathon, 2004; recipient Ida B. Wells award, Nat. Assn. Black Journalists', 1998, Ellis Island medal of honor, Nat. Ethnic Coalition of Orgns., 1999, President's award, NAACP, 2001, Frederick C. Patterson award, United Negro College Fund, 2001, Diversity award, Nat. Assoc. Minority Media Execs., 2002, Woman of the Year, Los Angeles County Com. for Women, 2002, Excellence in Media Award, Calif. NOW Chap., 2003, TRISCCORT award, Tri-State Catholic Com. on Radio and TV, Asian-Pacific Am. Corp. Impact award, Org. Chinese Americans Greater Los Angeles Chap. Image award Corp. Achievement., Deborah award, Anti-Defamation League, 2003. Mem.: N.Y. Assn. Black Journalists, Nat. Assn. Black Journalists. Office: NBC 4 3000 West Alameda Ave Burbank CA 91523*

**MADISON, ROBERT PRINCE,** architect; b. Cleve., July 28, 1923; s. Robert J. and Nettie (Brown) M.; m. Leatrice L. Branch, Apr. 16, 1949; children: Jeanne Marie, Juliette Branch. Student, Howard U., 1940—43, HHD, 1987; BArch, Western Res. U., 1948; MArch, Harvard U., 1952; DFA (hon.), Cleve. State U., 2000; HHD (hon.), Kent State U., 2001; DSc (hon.), Case We. Res. U., 2004. Mem. various archtl. firms, 1948; instr. Howard U., Washington, 1952—54; chmn., CEO Robert P. Madison Internat., architects, engrs. and planners, Cleve., 1954—. Trustee Am. Automobile Assn.; vis. prof. Howard U., 1961-62; lectr. Western Res. U., 1964-65; mem. U.S. architects del. Peoples Repub. China, 1974 Prin. works include U.S. Embassy Dakar, Senegal, West Africa, 1966, State of Ohio Computer Ctr., 1988, Cuyahoga County Jail, 1990, Continental Airlines Hub Concourse, Cleve. Internat. Airport, 1991. Mem. tech. adv. com. Cleve. Bd. Edn., 1960—; mem. adv. com. Cleve. Urban Renewal, 1963—; mem. fine arts adv. com. to mayor, Cleve.; mem. archtl. adv. coun. Cornell U.; trustee Case Western Res. U., Cleve. Opera, 1990, NCCJ, 1990, Commn. on Higher Edn., 1990, Cleve. (Ohio) Orch., 1998, Cleve. (Ohio) Arts Prize, 2001; bd. dirs. Jr. Achievement Greater Cleve.; trustee Cuyahoga County Hosp. Found., 1983—, Univ. Circle Inc., Midtown Corridor Inc.; mem. Ohio Bd. Bldg. Standards, 1986, Cleveland Heights City Planning Commn., 1987. 1st lt., inf. AUS, 1943-46. Decorated Purple Heart; Fulbright fellow, 1952-53; recipient Disting. Svc. award Case Western Res. U., 1989, Disting. Archtl. Firm award Howard U., 1989, Entrepreneur of Yt. award Ernst Young, Inc., Merrill Lynch, 1991, Arch. of Yr. Nat. Tech. Assn., 1996, Martin Luther King Jr. Corp. award African-Am. Archives Aux. Western Res. Hist. Soc., 1997, Disting. Alumni award Case We. Res. U., 1997; named to Corp. Hall of Fame, Ohio Assembly of Couns., 1991, Pres. award Kent State U., 1999; named to Cleve. Bus. Hall of Fame, 2002. Fellow AIA (chpt. pres., nat. task force for creative econs. 1976, mem. jury of fellows 1983-85, mem. nat. judicial coun. 1993, Gold Medal Firm award Ohio 1994, Gold Medal award Ohio 1997, Whitney M. Young Jr. award 2002); mem. Architects Soc. Ohio, Epsilon Delta Rho, Alpha Phi Alpha, Sigma Pi Phi. Office: Robert P Madison Internat Inc 2930 Euclid Ave Cleveland OH 44115-2416 Home: 18975 Van Aken Blvd Apt 410 Shaker Heights OH 44122-3539 Office Phone: 216-861-8195. Business E-Mail: rmadison@rpmadison.com.

**MADISON, VICKI DIANNE,** retired music educator; b. Paducah, Ky., July 17, 1947; d. Warren G. Dunkerson and Vernelle Frances Phillips Dunkerson; m. David Norris Madison, June 6, 1969; 1 child, Philip Warren. MusB rank II, Murray State U., 1970. Yamaha Keyboard Lab Instr. Yamaha Corp., 2001, Orff/Schulwerk Level I Orff/Schulwerk, 2000. Music specialist k/12 Marshall County Schools, Benton, Ky., 1970—98, 1998—; adj. instr. Murray State U., Ky., 2001—; organist /pianist First Bapt. Ch. Calvert City, Ky., 1976— Mem./sect. leader Paducah Symphony Chorus, Paducah, Ky., 1999—2002. Sec. Calvert City Lions Club, Ky., 1996—97, pres., 1998—99, dir., 2003—, pres., 1998—2000, dir., 2003—; councilwoman Calvert City City Coun., Ky., 1999—2004, coun. rep., 1999—; state historian for Ky. choral directors Am. Choral Directors Assn., Okla. City. Recipient Ky. Col., Commonwealth of Ky., 1996, Lion of the Yr., Calvert City Lions Club, 1998, Ky. Elem. Music Tchr. of the Yr., Ky. Music Educators Assn., 1996, Mid. Sch. Music Tchr. of the Yr., First Dist./Ky. Music Educators Assn., 1996—97. Mem.: Music Educators Nat. Conf. Am. Choral Dirs. Assn. (historian 1996—2003, Ky. chpt.), Ky. Music Educators Assn. (elected/apptd. bd. rep. 1992—2005), Ky. Alliance Arts Edn. (treas. 2003, dir. Marshall County Arts Commn.), Ky. Cols. Democrat-Npl. Bapt. Avocation: travel. Home: 79 Camelot Dr Calvert City KY 42029

**MADIX, ROBERT JAMES,** chemical engineer, educator; b. Beach Grove, Ind., June 22, 1938; s. James L. and Marjorie A. (Strohl) M.; children: Bradley Alan, David Eric, Micella Lynn, Evan Scott. BS, U. Ill., 1961; PhD, U. Calif., 1964. NSF postdoctoral fellow Max Planck Inst., Göttingen, Fed. Republic of Germany, 1964-65; asst. prof. chem. engr. Stanford (Calif.) U., 1965-72, assoc. prof., chem. engr., 1972-77; prof. chem. engring. Stanford U. 1977—, chmn., chem. engr., 1983-87, prof. chemistry, 1981—, Charles Lee Powell prof., 1990—, Charles Lee Powell prof. emeritus, 2006. Cons. Monsanto Chem., St. Louis, 1975-84, Shell Oil Co., Houston, 1985-86; Peter Debye lectureship Cornell U., 1985; Eyring lectr. chemistry Ariz. State U., 1990; Barnett Dodge lectr. Yale U., 1996; disting. prof. lectr. U. Tex., Austin, 1980; Walter Robb Disting. lectr. Penn State U., 1996; chmn. Gordon Rsch. Conf. on Reactions on Surfaces, 1995; sr. rsch. fellow divsn. engring. and applied scis. Harvard U., 2006. Assoc. editor Catalysis Rev., 1986—, Catalysis Letters, 1992—, Rsch. on Chem. Intermediates, 1994—; contbr. articles to profl. jours. Recipient Alpha Chi Sigma award AIChemE, 1990, Paul Emmett award Catalysis Soc. N.Am., 1984, Humboldt U.S. Sr. Scientist prize, 1978; Ford Found. fellow, 1969-72. Mem. AIChE, Internat. Precious Metal Inst. (Henry J. Alber award 1997), Am. Chem. Soc. (Irving Langmuir Disting. Lectr. award 1981, Arthur Adamson award 1997, Am. Phys. Soc., Am. Vacuum Soc., Calif. Catalysis Soc.

**MADJID, A. HAMID,** retired science educator; b. Tashkent, Russia, Aug. 16, 1922; arrived in US, 1966; s. A. Madjid and Emilia (Madjid) Zabuli; m. Anni Neukomm-Madjid, Dec. 31, 1958; children: Torai, A. Hamid Jr. BA, Cornell U.; DSc, Swiss Fed. Inst. Tech. Sec., sci. adv. to pres., coord. Afghan scholarships, head indsl. planning Afghan Nat. Bank, Munich, 1948—55; sr. rsch. assoc. Swiss Fed. Inst. Tech., Zurich, 1955—66; asst. assoc. prof., dir. thermionic emission lab. co-head of sci. program Pa. State U., University Park, 1966—90; ret., 1990. Chair various com. Pa. State U., 1977—86. Contbr. articles various profl. jours. Mem. Am. European Swiss Phys. Soc. 1966—90; chair Harris Twp. Planning Commn., Pa., 1982—86; mem. State Coll. Area Sch. Dist. Curriculum Coun., 1987; dir. A.M. Zabuli Charitable Found., 1998, Renaissance Charitable Found., 1999. Mem.: AAAS, Am. Assn. of Naval Engrs., US Holocaust Meml. Mus., Heritage Found., Nat. Rifle Assn. Achievements include research in electron emission from metal, semi conductor and insulator surfaces and the transport and optical properties of such substances; patents for layer structured switching and negative resistance devices; development of methods of incorporating undergraduate students in basic scientific rsch. Avocation: growing bonsai trees. Home and Office: 326 Harris Dr State College PA 16801 Office Phone: 814-466-7127.

**MADLE, ROBERT ALBERT,** writer; b. Phila., June 2, 1920; s. Vincent Robert and Mary Virginia (Kidwell) M.; m. Billie Franklin Lindsay, Nov. 7, 1943 (dec. Dec. 1997); children: Robert, Richard, Jane, Mary Anne; m. Ana Lisseth Martinez, Feb. 28, 2002; 1 stepchild, Sarah Nicole Martinez. BS, Drexel U., 1951, MBA, 1953. Asst. to sales mgr. Masland Duraleather, Phila., 1951—53; asst. to dir. indsl. rels. Chadbourne Hosiery, Charlotte, NC, 1953—54; mgr. pers. and credit Shaw Mfg. Co., Charlotte, 1954—56; pers. rsch. specialist U.S. Army, Washington, 1956—59; rsch. psychologist, program mgr. USN, Washington, 1959—80. Sci. fiction rsch. cons. Paramount Prodns., other film cos.; rsch. cons. projects Yesterday's Tomorrows and Study on Hugo Gernsback, Smithsonian Inst.; spkr. in field Co-author: Science Fiction Fandom, 1994; contbr. articles to sci. fiction and sports mags.; condr. search svcs. rare books in field of sci. fiction and fantasy lit.; cons. editor profl. fantasy mags., including Mag. of Horror, Bizarre Mystery, Startling Mystery, Famous Sci. Fiction. With U.S. Army, 1942-46. Named

Guest of honor World Sci. Fiction Conv., Miami, 1977, U. Md. Sci. Fiction Conv., 1982, Boston Sci. Fiction Conv., 1996; rep. Am. sci. fiction Brit. Worldcon, 1957; recipient E.E. Evans Sci. Fiction Achievement award, 1974, Sam Moskowitz Achievement award, 2002 Mem.: Phila. Sci. Fiction Soc. (founder), First Fandom (pres. 1959—82, Hall of Fame 1990), Washington Sci. Fiction Assn., Sci. Fiction Writers Am. Achievements include development of survey on science fiction's predictions of atomic energy. Home: 4406 Bestor Dr Rockville MD 20853-2137 Office Phone: 301-460-4712.

**MADLOCK, YVONNE,** city health department administrator; m. Lawrence Madlock; 3 children. BS, Wellesley Coll.; MAT, Wesleyan U., Middletown, Conn.; studied, U. Tex. Sch. Pub. Health. Administr., bur. personal health svcs. Shelby Co. Divsn. Health Svcs., Memphis, 1995—. Bd. pres. Cmty. Inst. for Early Childhood; bd. dirs. W. Tenn. Area Health Edn. Ctr., Memphis Leadership Inst., Cmty. Found. of Greater Memphis, Shelby Co. Ground Water Quality Control Bd. Mem.: Nat. Assn. City and County Health Officials (bd. dirs.). Office: Shelby Co Divsn Health Svcs 814 Jefferson Ave Memphis TN 38103 Business E-Mail: HealthDirector@co.shelby.tn.us.*

**MADNI, ASAD MOHAMED,** engineering executive; b. Bombay, Sept. 8, 1947; came to U.S., 1966; s. Mohamed Taher and Sara Taher (Wadiwalla) M.; Gowhartaj Shahnawaz, Nov. 11, 1976; 1 child, Jamal Asad. Gen. cert. edn., U. Cambridge, Eng., 1964; AAS in Electronics, RCA Insts., Inc., 1968; BS in Engring., UCLA, 1969, MS in Engring., 1972; postgrad. exec. inst., Stanford U., 1984; cert. in engring. mgmt., Calif. Inst. Tech., 1987; PhD in Engring., Calif. Coast U., 1987; sr. exec. program, MIT, 1990. chartered engr. Engring. Coun., U.K. Sr. instr. Pacific States U., LA, 1969—71; sr. electronics auditor Pertec Corp., Chatsworth, Calif., 1973—75; project engr., sr. engr., program mgr., dir. advanced programs Microwave divsn. Systron Donner, Van Nuys, Calif., 1975—82, dir. engring., 1982—92; gen. mgr. Microwave and Instrument divsn. Systron Donner, Van Nuys, Calif., 1985—90; chmn., pres., CEO Systron Donner Corp., 1990—92; pres., CEO Sensors and Controls Group BEI Electronics, Inc., 1992—93, BEI Sensors & Sys. Co., 1993—2006; pres. BEI Techs. Inc., 2000—, COO, 2000—06. Vice-chmn. IEEE-MTTS, San Fernando Valley chpt., 1991-92, chmn., 1992-94; tech. advisor Test and Measurement World, Boston, 1982-90; adv. Calif. State U. Northridge, Coll. Elec. Engring. and Computer Sci.; bd. adv. UCLA Mech. and Aerospace Engring. Dept., UCLA WINMEC, UCLA Elec. Engring. Dept., chmn.; mem. adv. bd. UCLA RFID Group; chmn. adv. bd. elec. engring. dept U. So. Calif. Mem. editl. rev. bd. Microwave Sys. News and Comms. Tech., 1982—90, chmn. West coast, 1982—90, mem. editl. review bd. SENSORS Jour. 2001—, mem. tech. review com. World Automation Congress, 1996—. Named George Washington Engr. of Yr., LA Coun. of Engrs. and Scientists, 2003; recipient Joseph F. Engelberger Best Paper award, World Automation Congress, 2000, Disting. Alumni award, Calif. Coast U., 2001, Profl. Achievement award, UCLA, 2002, Alumnus of Yr. award, UCLA Sch. Engring. and Applied Sci., 2004, Dist. Engring. Achievement award, San Fernando Valley Engrs. Coun., 2004, Achievement medal, Inst. Elec. Engrs., 2005, Lifetime Achievement award, World Automation Compress and AutoSoft Jour., 2006. Fellow: AAAS, IEEE (adv. bd. MTT-S San Fernando Valley chpt. 1993—2001, tech. review com. aerospace conf. 1994—, 3d Millennium medal), AIAA (life; vice chair honors and awards L.A. sect. 2000—01; sr.), Inst. Engring. and Tech., Soc. Automotive Engrs., NY Acad. Scis., Inst. Advancement Engring., Instn. Elec. Engrs. U.K. (chartered elec. engr., Achievement medal 2005); mem.: NRA (life), MIT Soc. Sr. Execs. (life), Assn. Old Crows (life gold cert. of merit 1992), UCLA Engring. Alumni Assn. (life; mem. bd. govs.), MIT Alumni Assn. (life), UCLA Alumni Assn. (life), Calif. Rifle and Pistol Assn. (life). Home and Office: BEI Techs Inc 3281 Woodbine St Los Angeles CA 90064-4836 Personal E-mail: ammadni@yahoo.com. Personal philosophy: There is no substitute for talent and vision complemented by perseverance, dedication and integrity.

**MADONNA, (MADONNA LOUISE VERONICA CICCONE),** singer, actress, producer; b. Bay City, Mich.-Aug. 16, 1958; d Sylvio and Madonna Ciccone; m. Sean Penn, Aug. 16, 1985 (div. Sept. 14, 1989); m. Guy Ritchie, Dec. 22, 2000; 2 children. Lourdes, Rocco. Student, U. Mich., 1976-78. Dancer Alvin Ailey Dance Co., N.Y.C., 1979; CEO Maverick Records, L.A., 1992—. Albums include Madonna, 1983, Like a Virgin, 1985, True Blue, 1986, Who's That Girl (soundtrack), 1987, (with others) Vision Quest (soundtrack), 1983, You Can Dance, 1987, Like a Prayer, 1989, I'm Breathless: Music From and Inspired by the Film Dick Tracy, 1990, The Immaculate Collection, 1990, Erotica, 1992, Bedtime Stories, 1994, Something to Remember, 1995, Evita (soundtrack), 1996, Ray of Light, 1998 (Grammy award for Best Pop Album 1999), (with others) Austin Powers: The Spy Who Shagged Me (soundtrack), 1999, Music, 2000, GHV2: Greatest Hits Volume II, 2002, American Life, 2003, Confessions on a Dancefloor, 2005, I'm Going to Tell You a Secret, 2006; film appearances include A Certain Sacrifice, 1980, Vision Quest, 1985, Desperately Seeking Susan, 1985, Shanghai Surprise, 1986, Who's That Girl, 1987, Bloodhounds of Broadway, 1989, Dick Tracy, 1990, Shadows and Fog, 1992, Truth or Dare, 1991, Body of Evidence, 1992, A League of Their Own, 1992, Dangerous Game, 1993, Blue in the Face, 1995, Four Rooms, 1996, Girl 6, 1996, Evita, 1996 (Golden Globe, 1997), The Next Best Thing, 2000, Swept Away, 2002; Broadway theater debut in Speed-the-Plow, 1987, stage appearance in Up for Grabs, 2002; TV appearances include Happy Birthday Elizabeth: A Celebration of a Life, 1997, Will & Grace, 2003; author: Sex, 1992, (children's books) The English Roses, 2003, Mr. Peabody's Apples, 2003, Yakov and the Seven Thieves, 2004, Adventures of Abdi, 2004, Lotsa de Casha, 2005.*

**MADOR, JONATHAN MARK,** director, education educator; b. Lakewood, NJ, Oct. 4, 1974; s. Hurbert Phillip and Joan Carol Mador. BA, Pace U., 1993, MS, 2004. Asst. dir. student accounts and registrar svcs Pace U., 2000—04; dir. student accounts Post U. Waterbury, Conn., 2004 — Adj. prof. Post U., Waterbury, Conn., 2005—. Treas. Lake Forrest Assn., Bridgeport, Conn., 2006. Mem.: Nat. Assn. Student Pers. Adminstrs., ACA, Am. Coll. Counseling Assn., Psi Chi, Nat. Honors Soc. in Psychology (treas. 1996—97), Delta Upsilon Internat. Frat. (fundraiser, pub. rels. & spl. events chmn. 1997—98). Office: Post Univ 800 Country Club Rd Waterbury CT 06823 Office Phone: 203-596-4571. Office Fax: 203-596-4561. Personal E-mail: jonathan10474@optonline.net. Business E-Mail: jmador@post.edu.

**MADOU, MARC,** materials scientist, educator; b BSc, Rijksuniversiteit, Ghent, Belgium, 1973, MSc, 1975; PhD, Solid-State Physics Lab. Rijksuniversiteit, Ghent, Belgium, 1978. Vis. scientist SRI Internat., Menlo Park, Calif., 1979—80; sr. materials scientist Materials Rsch. Lab. SRI Internat. 1981—82; assoc. dir., founder and mgr. microsensor program Phys. Electronics Lab. SRI Internat., 1982—83; dir. Microsensor Dept. SRI Internat. 1983—89; vice chmn. and founder Teknekron Sensor Devel. Corp. 1989—93; vis. prof. La. State U., Baton Rouge, 1994—95; vis. Miller prof. U. Calif., Berkeley, 1995—96, vis. scholar, 1996—2000; prof. materials and chemistry Ohio State U., Columbus, 1997—2000; v.p. advanced tech. Nanogen Inc., San Diego, 2001—02; prof. U. Calif., Irvine, Calif. Ctr. Materials Rsch. scholar Ohio State U., Columbus, 1997—2000; dir. NSF Ctr. for Indsl. Sensors and Measurements, 1997—2000; cons. Corning-IntelliSense, Woburn, Mass., 1998—2003. Author: Fundamentals of Microfabrication, 2d edit. Achievements include patents for photolithographic and electron beam lithographic fabrication of micron and submicron three-dimensional arrays of electronically conductive polymers. Office: Univ Calif Irvine Rm 3231 4200 Engring Gateway Bldg Irvine CA 92697 E-mail: mmadou@uci.edu.

**MADOW, LEO,** psychiatrist, educator; b. Cleve., Oct. 18, 1915; s. Solomon Martin and Anna (Meyers) Madow; m. Jean Antoinette Weisman, Apr. 16, 1942 (dec.); children: Michael, Robert; m. Barbara N. Young, Dec. 26, 2000. AB, Western Res. U., 1937, MD, 1942; MA, Ohio State U., 1938. Diplomate Am. Bd. Psychiatry and Neurology. Intern Phila. Gen. Hosp., 1942-43; resident Phila. Gen. Hosp., Jefferson Hosp., Inst. Pa. Hosp., 1943-46; practice medicine specializing in psychiatry Phila., 1948—; prof., chmn. dept. neurology Med. Coll. Pa., Phila., 1958-65, prof., chmn. dept. psychiatry and neurology, 1965-70, prof., chmn. dept. psychiatry, 1970-81, clin. prof.

psychiatry Hershey Med. Ctr., 1982—; sr. cons. psychiatry Inst. Pa. Hosp., Phila., 1975—. Tng. analyst, past pres. Phila. Psychoanalytic Inst.; past pres., mem. med. staff Inst. Pa. Hosp. Author: Anger, 1972, Love, 1983, Guilt, 1989; editor: Dreams, 1970, Sensory Deprivation, 1970, Psychomimetic Drugs, 1971, Integration of Child Psychiatry with Basic Resident Program, 1975. Served to capt. U.S. Army, 1944—46. Named Outstanding Educator, Am. Med. Coll. Pa., 1972. Fellow: ACP, Am. Coll. Psychoanalysts (pres. 1989—90, Laughlin award 1990), Am. Coll. Psychiatrists, Am. Psychiat. Assn. (life), Phila. Psychiat. Soc. (past pres., Lifetime Achievement award 1991); mem.: Phila. Psychoanalytic Soc. (past pres.), Am. Neurol. Assn., Am. Psychoanalytic Assn., Phi Soc., Alpha Omega Alpha. Home and Office: 2401 Pennsylvania Ave Philadelphia PA 19130 Office Phone: 215-235-5253. Personal E-mail: leomadow@aol.com.

**MADRA, SATBIR SINGH,** materials researcher, mechanical engineer; arrived in U.S., 1995; s. Bhupinder Singh and Satwant Kaur Madra. BSME, Punjab U., 1993; MSME, San Jose State U., Calif., 1997. Lectr. San Jose State U., Calif., 1996—97; process devel. engr. R&D Watkins Johnson Co., Scotts Valley, Calif., 1997—99; sr. staff engr. Wj Comm., Inc., San Jose, 1999—2002, sr. rsch. scientist, 2002—05; sr. mgr. Semiconductor Package, 2005—06, RFID Engring., 2005—06; v.p. tech. Silitronics, Inc., San Jose, Calif. Presenter in field. Contbr. articles to profl. jours. Mem.: ASME, IEEE, Materials Rsch. Soc., Internat. Microelectronics And Packaging Soc., Pi Tau Sigma. Avocations: tennis, travel, hockey. Office: Silitronics Inc 85 Great Oaks Blvd San Jose CA 95119 Office Phone: 408-577-6302. Office Fax: 408-360-9170. Business E-Mail: satbir.madra@wj.com

**MADRAS, BERTHA KALIFON,** federal official, neuroscientist; b. Montreal, Quebec, Canada, Dec. 9, 1942; m. Peter Madras, June 21, 1964; children: Cynthia Gumbert, Claudine D. BSc, McGill U., 1963, PhD, 1967. Postdoctoral fellow Tufts U., Boston, 1966-67; postdoctoral fellow rsch. assoc. MIT, Cambridge, 1967-69, 72-74; asst. prof. U. Toronto, 1979—80, Harvard Med. Sch., Boston, 1986-90, assoc. prof., 1990-99, prof., 1999—2006, assoc. dir. pub. edn. divsn. addictions, 1998—2006; dep. dir. for demand reduction Office Nat. Drug Control Policy, Washington, 2006—. Sci. adv. com. Brookhaven Nat. Lab., Upton, N.Y., 1998—; rev. com., cons. Nat. Inst. Drug Abuse, chair B study sect., 1998-99; MDCN-5 MNPS rev. com.; cons. Ont. Mental Health Found., 1984-90, chmn. fellowships and awards com., 1988-90; chmn. radiation safety Harvard U., 1995-99, acting dir. Primate Ctr., 1998-99; chmn. faculty affairs Harvard Med. Sch.; mem. Dana Alliance for Brain Initiatives. Author: (book chpt.) Dopamine, 1984; editor: Neurosci.; mem. editl. bd. Synapse, 1991-2004; contbr. articles to profl. jours. Sci. fair judge. Recipient Rsch. grants Nat. Inst. Drug Abuse, 1992—, 94—, Sci. Edn. Partnership award grant, 1992-94, Parkinson's Disease Found., 1990-91, Nat. Inst. Neurol. Disease and Stroke, 1994, 99—, NIMH, Dana Alliance for Brain Initiatives, Merit award NIH, Sr. Scientist award. Mem. Soc. for Neuroscience, Coll. Probs. Drug Dependence. Achievements include development of a marker for Parkinson's disease and attention deficit hyperactivity disorder, a probe for cocaine binding sites in brain; developed a PET imaging SPECT for living brain; developed a PET and SPECT imaging drug to monitor Parkinsonism in brain; rsch. in how drugs work in brain; co-developer of CD-ROM on how drugs affect brain. Office: Office Nat Drug Control Policy 750 17th St NW Rm 609 Washington DC 20503*

**MADRID, MICHAEL JOHN,** director; s. Octavio and Alicia Madrid. B of Music Edn., Tex. Tech. U., 1997, M of Music Performance, 1999. Asst. choir dir. Mayde Creek HS, Houston, 1999—2000, dir. choral activities, 2000—. Mem.: Nat. Assn. Tchrs. Singing, Tex. Music Adjudicators Assn., Am. Choral Dirs. Assn., Tex. Choral Dirs. Assn., Tex. Music Educators Assn. (treas. region 23 2005—). Roman Catholic. Office: Mayde Creek High Sch 19202 Groschke Rd Houston TX 77084

**MADRID, OLGA HILDA GONZALEZ,** retired elementary school educator, school system administrator; b. San Antonio, May 4, 1928; d. Victor A. and Elvira Ardilla Gonzalez; m. Sam Madrid, Jr., June 29, 1952; children: Ninette Marie, Samuel James. Student, U. Mex., San Antonio, St. Mary's U.; BA, Our Lady of Lake U., 1956, MEd, 1963. Cert. bilingual tchr., adminstr., Tex. Sec. Lanier HS San Antonio Ind. Sch. Dist., San Antonio, 1945-52; tchr. Collins Garden Elem. Sch., Storm Elem. Sch., San Antonio Ind. Sch. Dist., San Antonio, 1963-92; tutor Dayton, Ohio, 1952-54. Bd. dir., sch. rep. San Antonio Tchr. Coun., 1970-90; chair various coms. Collins Garden Elem., 1970-92. Elected dep. precinct, senatorial and state Dem. Conv., San Antonio, 1968—; apptd. commr. Keep San Antonio Beautiful, 1985; life mem., past pres. San Antonio YWCA; bd. dir. Luth. Gen. Hosp., Nat. Conf. Christians and Jews, Cath. Family and Children's Svc., St. Luke's Luth. Hosp.; nat. bd. dir. YWCA, 1985-96, also mem. exec. com.; mem. edn. commn. Holy Rosary Parish, 1994—; mem. bus. assoc. com. Our Lady of the Lake U., 1995—. Recipient Outstanding Our Lady Lake Alumni award Our Lady Lake U., 1975, Guadalupana medal San Antonio Cath. Archdiocese, 1975, Yellow Rose Tex. citation Gov. Briscoe, 1977; Olga H. Madrid Ctr. named in her honor, YWCA San Antonio and San Antonio City Coun.; 1983; Lo Mejor De Lo Nuestro honoree San Antonio Light, 1991, honoree San Antonio Women's History Month Coalition, 1996; named Our Lady of Lake Outstanding Alumna, 1999, one of five women honored for promoting literacy and cultural hertiage with a sch. wall mural titled "Mis Palabras, Mi Poder", 2002. Mem. San Antonio Bus. and Profl. Women, Inc. (mem. exec. com.), Salute Quality Edn. (honoree 1993), Delta Kappa Gamma (Theta Beta chpt., mem. exec. com.). Avocations: reading, gardening. Home: 2726 Benrus Blvd San Antonio TX 78228-2319

**MADRID, PATRICIA A.,** state attorney general; BA in English and Philosophy, U. N.Mex., 1969, JD, 1973; cert., Nat. Jud. Coll., U. Nev., 1978. Bar: N.Mex. Dist. judge State of N.Mex., 1978—84, atty. gen., 1999—. Chmn. Western Conf. of Attys. Gen. Named Latina Atty. of Yr., Nat. Hispanic Bar Assn., 2001, N.Mex. Power Broker, N.Mex. Bus. Weekly; recipient Mary V. Orozco Abriendo Caminos award, Latina Lawyers Bar Assn., 2003, Trailblazer award, N.Mex. Commn. on the Status of Women, Las Primeras award, MANA, 2004, Woman of the Yr. in Govt. award, Capital Bus. and Professional Women of Santa Fe, 2004, Exec. Dir. award, Animal Protection of N.Mex., 2004. Democrat. Office: Atty Gens Office PO Drawer 1508 Santa Fe NM 87504-1508

**MADRY-TAYLOR, JACQUELYN YVONNE,** educational association administrator; d. Arthur Chester and Janie (Cowart) Madry; 1 child, Jana LeMadry. BA, Fisk U., 1966; MA, Ohio State U., 1969; EdD, U. Fla., 1975. Cert. Inst. for Ednl. Mgmt., Harvard U., 1981. Tchr. Spanish Terry Parker Sr. High Sch., Jacksonville, 1967-72; instr. U. Fla., Gainesville, 1972-75; asst. to v.p. for acad. affairs. Morris Brown Coll., Atlanta, 1975-76; dean for instructional svcs. No. Va. Community Coll., Annandale, Va., 1976-83; dean undergrad. studies Bridgewater (Mass.) State Coll., 1983-92, exec. asst. to acting pres., 1988, acting v.p. acad. affairs, 1988-90; dir. Acad. Leadership Acad. Am. Assn. State Coll. and Univs., Washington, 1992-94; dir. ednl. programs and svcs. United Negro Coll. Fund Hdqs., 1994-97; pres. JYM Assocs., 1999—; sr. advisor Nat. Assn. for Equal Opportunity in Higher Edn., 1997—2003. Cons. to colls., univs. and orgns.; cons. W.K. Kellog Found., 1993-97; bd. dirs. Bridgewater State Coll. Early Learning Ctr. 1984-88; evaluator U.S. Dept. State/Fgn. Svc., Washington, 1982—, U.S. Dept. Edn., 1989—; pres. JYM Assocs., 1999—. Vice chmn. No. Va. Manpower Planning Coun., Fairfax County, Va., 1981. Recipient Cert. Achievement Bridgewater State Coll. Black Alumni, 1988, Women Helping Women award Soroptimist Internat., 1983, Outstanding Young Women Am. award, 1976, 78; named Personalities of South, 1977; recipient Outstanding Tchr./Student Rels. Humanitarian award B'nai B'rith, 1972. Mem. Pub. Mem. Assn. U.S. Fgn. Svc., Soroptimist Internat., Boston Club (v.p. 1986-88), Jack and Jill of Am., Inc., Am. Assn. of Univ. Women, Phi Delta Kappa, Alpha Kappa Alpha, Links Inc. (Reston, Va. chpt.). Methodist. Avocations: playing piano, bike riding. Home and Office: 12274 Angel Wing Ct Reston VA 20191-1119 Fax: 703-716-4364. E-mail: jkemt@aol.com.

**MADSEN, AARON JEFFREY,** athletic trainer; b. Kearney, Nebr., Aug. 2, 1978; s. Kevin Dean and Christy Ann Madsen. BS in Exercise Sci. and Athletic Tng., U. Nebr., Kearney, Nebr., 2001. Cert. nurse's asst., Nebr., 1996; lic. EMT Nebr., 1998, cert. Nat. Athletic Trainer's Assn., lic. athletic trainer Nebr., cert. rehab. aid Nebr., 2000, firefighter Nebr., 2000. Athletic trainer, EMT U. Nebr., Lincoln, 2001—02, Lincoln Orthop. Phys. Therapy, PC, 2002—04; athletic trainer Concordia U., Seward, Nebr., 2004—, EMT, 2004—. Mem.: Nebr. Sch. Activities Assn., Great Plains Athletic Conf. (v.p. 2005—), Athletic Trainer's Assn., Nat. Athletic Intercollegiate Assn., Alliance Health and Fitness Profls., Am. Coll. Sports Medicine, Nebr. State Athletic Trainer's Assn., Mid. Am. Athletic Trainer's Assn., Nat. Athletic Trainer's Assn. Republican. Luth. Avocations: exercise, sports, travel, collecting husker memorabilia, yardwork. Home: 307 Lindell Ave Seward NE 68434 Office: Concordia Univ NE Sports Medicine Dept 800 North Columbia Ave Seward NE 68434

**MADSEN, ANDREW H.,** food service executive; Grad., DePauw Univ., 1978. V.p., mktg. Gen. Mills Inc.; v.p., gen. mgr. James River Corp., 1993—97; pres. Internat. Master Publishers, 1997—98; exec. v.p. mktg., Olive Garden div. Darden Restaurants Inc., Orlando, Fla., 1998—2002, sr. v.p., pres. Olive Garden div., 2002—04, pres., COO, 2004—. Mailing: Darden Restaurants Inc PO Box 593330 Orlando FL 32859-3330 Office: Darden Restaurants Inc 5900 Lake Ellenor Dr Orlando FL 32809*

**MADSEN, BARBARA A.,** state supreme court justice; b. Renton; BA, U. Wash., 1974; JD, Gonzaga U., 1977. Pub. defender King and Snohomish Counties, 1977—82; staff atty. Seattle City Atty.'s Office, 1982—84, spl. prosecutor, 1984—88; judge Seattle Mcpl. Ct., 1988—92; justice Wash. Supreme Ct., Olympia, 1993—. Chair Wash. State Gender and Justice Commn., Supreme Ct. Circulation Com., Ct. Personnel Com.; co-chair Internal Rules Com., Death Penalty Rules Com.; mem. Ct. Budget Com., Administrative Com., Reporter of Decisions Com. Active in Judges in the Classroom prog., Tacoma Public Sch. Recipient Wash. Women Lawyers Vanguard award, 1998, Wash. Women Lawyers Found. award, 2001, Presidents award, Nat. Assn. of Women Judges, 2002, Equal Justice Coalition Judicial award, 2004, Access to Justice award of distinction for public svc., 2006. Mem.: Judicature Soc., Am. Assn. of Women Judges, Am. Judges Assn. Office: Wash Supreme Ct PO Box 40929 Olympia WA 98504-0929*

**MADSEN, BRIGHAM DWAINE,** history professor; b. Magna, Utah, Oct. 21, 1914; s. Brigham and Lydia (Cushing) M.; m. Betty McAllister, Aug. 11, 1939; children—Karen Madsen Loos, David B., Linda Madsen Dunning, Steven M.; m. Lola Kastler, Dec. 1, 2001; m. Mary Harriman, June 7, 2003. BA, U. Utah, 1938; MA, U. Calif., Berkeley, 1940, PhD, 1948. Prin. Grade Sch. and Jr. High Sch., Pingree, Idaho, 1938-39; assoc. prof. history Brigham Young U., Provo, Utah, 1948-54; pres., mgr. Madsen Bros. Constrn. Co., Salt Lake City, 1954-61; prof. history Utah State U., Logan, 1961-64; asst. dir. tng. Peace Corps, Washington, 1964-65; first dir. tng. Vols. in Service to Am., Washington, 1965; dean dir. continuing edn. U. Utah, Salt Lake City, 1965-66, dep. acad. v.p., 1966-67, adminstrv. v.p., 1967-71, dir. libraries, 1971-73, prof. history, 1973-84, chmn. dept. history, 1974-75. Author: Bannock of Idaho, 1958, The Lemhi: Sacajawea's People, 1980, Corinne: Gentile Capital of Utah, 1980, The Northern Shoshoni, 1980, (with Betty M. Madsen) North to Montana: Jehus, Bullwhackers and Muleskinners on the Montana Trail, 1980; Gold Rush Sojourners in Great Salt Lake City, 1849 and 1850, 1983, The Shoshoni Frontier and the Bear River Massacre, 1985, Chief Pocatello: the "White Plume", 1986, Glory Hunter: A Biography of Patrick Edward Connor, 1990, Against the Grain: Memoirs of a Western Historian, 1998; editor: The Now Generation, 1971, Letters of Long Ago, 1973, A Forty-niner in Utah: Letters and Journal of John Hudson, 1982, B.H. Roberts: Studies of the Book of Mormon, 1985, Exploring the Great Salt Lake: The Stansbury Expedition of 1849-50, 1989, The Essential B.H. Roberts, 1999. 1st lt., inf. AUS, 1943-46. Mem. Phi Beta Kappa, Phi Kappa Phi., Phi Alpha Theta. Home: 451 Bishop Federal Ln Apt 4117 Salt Lake City UT 84115-2222 E-mail: mimih02@aros.net.

**MADSEN, DOROTHY LOUISE (MEG MADSEN),** writer; b. Rochester, N.Y. d. Charles Robert and Louise Anna Agnes Meyer; m. Frederick George Madsen, Feb. 17, 1945 (dec.) BA, Mundelein Coll., Chgo., 1978; grad., U.S. Army Command and Gen. Staff Coll., 1960. Feature writer Gannett Newspapers, Rochester Democrat & Chronicle, NY, 1937—41; pub. rels. rep. Rochester Tel. Corp., 1941—42; exec. dir. LaPorte chpt. ARC, Ind., 1964; dir. adminstrv. svcs. Bank Mktg. Assn., Chgo., 1971—74; exec. dir. Eleanor Women's Found., Chgo., 1974—84; founder Meg Madsen Assocs., Chgo., 1984—88, women's career counselor; founder Eleanor Women's Forum, Clearinghouse Internat., Eleanor Intern Program Coll. Students and Returning Women. Chief global radiotelephone and radioteletype top secret encrypted conf. ctr. war dept. gen. staff Pentagon, Washington, 1944—46; conf. aide to Pres. Harry S Truman, Washington, 1945. Lt. col. WAC, 1942-47, 67-70 Decorated Legion of Merit, Meritorious Svc. award Mem.: Res. Officers Assn. (life), Mundelein Alumnae Assn., Ret. Officers Assn. (life), Phi Sigma Tau (charter mem. Ill. Kappa chpt.). Achievements include Aide to Pres. Truman during Sigsaly encoded phone conf. with Prime Min. Winston Churchill and U.S. Joint Chiefs Staff concerning terms of German surrender, WWII, Apr. 25, 1945. Home and Office: 1030 N State St Apt 25H Chicago IL 60610-2831 E-mail: megmadsenchgo@aol.com.

**MADSEN, ELIZABETH KARLENE,** librarian; b. Swarthmore, Pa., Aug. 16, 1944; d. Roy Harding and Katharine (Walters) M. BA, Western Wash. State U., 1966; MLS, U. Hawaii, 1972, postgrad.; MA, Stanford U., 1985; postgrad., Fielding Inst., 1994—. Editor Kodiak (Alaska) Daily Mirror, 1967-68; outreach libr. Fairbanks (Alaska) North Star Borough Libr., 1972; asst. libr. A. Holmes Johnson Libr., Kodiak, 1973-74, Bothell Libr. King County, Wash., 1974-76; coll. infor. Matanuska-Susitna Coll. U. Alaska, Palmer, 1976-90; social sci. libr. U. Hawaii, Manoa, 1990-91; libr. dir. Matanuska-Susitna Coll. U. Alaska, 1992—2001; prof. emeritus U. Alaska, Anchorage, 2003—; legis. aide Alaska State Legislature, 1998; assoc. prof. Western Wash. U. Librs., 2002—. Del. Alaska Gov.'s Conf. on Librs., 1979; mem. Western Libr. Network Users Bd., 1993. Contbr. articles to profl. jours. Chmn. Alaska Collection Devel., 1985; bd. dirs. Alaska Pub. TV, Anchorage, 1978-80; Named Boss of Yr. Profl. Secs. Internat., 1993. Mem. ALA, Pacific N.W. Libr. Assn. (chmn. libr. instrn. interest group 1996—), Alaska State Libr. Assn. (chmn. Mat-Su chpt. 1976, state treas. 1979-80), Hawaii Libr. Assn., Internat. Platform Assn., Western Stanford U. Alumni Assn. Home: 35 Grand View Ln Bellingham WA 98229-2743

**MADSEN, H(ENRY) STEPHEN,** retired lawyer; b. Momence, Ill., Feb. 5, 1924; s. Frederick and Christine (Landgren) Madsen; m. Carol Ruth Olmstead, Dec. 30, 1967; children: Stephen Stewart, Christie Morgan, Kelly Ann. MBA, U Chgo., 1948; LLB, Yale U., 1951. Bar: Wash. 1951, Ohio 1953, U.S. Supreme Ct. 1975. Resch. asst. Wash. Water Power Co., Spokane, 1951; assoc. Baker, Hostetler & Paterson, Cleve., 1952-59, ptnr., 1960-88, sr. ptnr., 1989-92; ret., 1992. Danish consul for Ohio, 1973—2004. Active Bus. Advisers Cleve.; trustee Ohio Presbyn. Ret. Svcs. With AC U.S. Army, 1943—46. Decorated Knight Queen of Denmark. Fellow: ABA (life); mem.: Cleve. Bar Assn., Am. Law Inst., Am. Coll. Trial Lawyers (life), Country Club Cleve.

**MADSEN, MICHAEL,** actor; b. Chicago, Sept. 25, 1958; m. Georganne LaPierre (div.); m. Jeannine Bisignano (div.); 1 child, Christian; m. De Anna Morgan Apr. 15, 1996; 4 children. Films include: Wargames, 1983, The Natural, 1984, Racing with the Moon, 1984, The Killing Time, 1987, Shadows in the Storm, 1988, Iguana, 1988, Blood Red, 1989, Kill Me Again, 1990, The Doors, 1991, The End of Innocence, 1991, Thelma and Louise, 1991, Fatal Instinct, 1992, Inside Edge, 1992, Reservoir Dogs, 1992, Straight Talk, 1992, Almost Blue, 1992, Free Willy, 1993, A House in the Hills, 1993, Money for Nothing, 1993, Trouble Bound, 1993, Wyatt Earp, 1994, The Getaway, 1994, Dead Connection, 1994, Species, 1995, Free Willy II: The Adventure Home, 1995, The Winner, 1996, Red Line, 1996, Mullholland Falls, 1996, Man With a Gun, 1996, The Last Days of Frankie the Fly, 1996, Rough Draft, 1997, The Maker, 1997, Donnie Brasco, 1997, Catherine's

Grove, 1997, Papertrail, 1997, The Girl Gets Moe, 1997, Executive Target, 1997, The Thief and the Stripper, 1998, Supreme Sanction, 1998, The Florentine, 1998, Species II, 1998, Fait Accompli, 1998, The Thief & the Stripper, 1998, Flat Out, 1998, Ballad of the Nightingale, 1998, The Florentine, 1999, Detour, 1999, The Stray, 1999, Luck of the Draw, 2002, The Alternate, 2000, The Price of Air, 2000, Love.com, 2000, Ides of March, 2000, The Ghost, 2000, Fall, 2000, Choke, 2000, Bad Guys, 2000, Extreme Honor, 2001, Pressure Point, 2001, Outlaw, 2001, L.A.P.D.: To Protect and to Serve, 2001, Die Another Day, 2002, Welcome to America, 2002, The Real Deal, 2002, Where's Angelo, 2003, My Boss's Daughter, 2003, Kill Bill: Vol. 1, 2003, Vampires Anonymous, 2003, Hunt for the Devil, 2003, Blueberry, 2004, Kill Bill: Vol. 2, 2004, Sin City, 2005, Chasing Ghosts, 2005, (voice) The Chronicles of Narnia: The Lion, the Witch and the Wardrobe, 2005, BloodRayne, 2005; TV movies include: Special Bulletin, 1983, War and Remembrance, 1988, Montana, 1990, Baby Snatcher, 1992, Beyond the Law, 1994, Supreme Sanction, 1999, The Inspectors 2: A Shred of Evidence, 2000, Sacrifice, 2000, High Noon, 2000, 44 Minutes: The North Hollywood Shoot-Out, 2003, Frankenstein, 2004; TV series include: Our Family Honor, 1985-86, Vengeance Unlimited, 1998, Big Apple, 2001, Tilt, 2005; author: The Complete Poetic Works of Michael Madsen, Vol 1: 1995-2005. also: Creative Artists Agy Michael Manchal 9830 Wilshire Blvd Beverly Hills CA 90212-1804*

**MADSEN, PETER,** music educator, musician; b. Ames, Iowa, Dec. 1969; s. Richard William and Carole Maud Madsen; m. Carla Lee Coleman, Aug. 13, 1994; children: Christian Lee, Ashleigh Coleman. B in Music Edn., U. Mo. 1993; MusM, No. Ill. U., 1995; D of Musical Arts, U. Ill., 1998. Coord. jazz studies Adams State Coll., Alamosa, Colo., 1998—2000, U. Nebr. at Omaha, 2000—. Musician: (Quartet) Continental Trombone Quartet. Musician Christ Cmty. Ch. Orch., Omaha, 2000—06. Mem.: Music Educators Nat. Conf., Internat. Trombone Assn., Internat. Assn. for Jazz Edn. (Nebr. chpt. pres. 2005—). Achievements include performances as a trombonist all over the world including Japan, Brazil, Canada, Mexico, Europe, and throughout the United States. Avocations: jogging, hiking, camping, bicycling.

**MADSEN, ROY I., JR.,** language educator; b. LA, Jan. 12, 1940; s. Roy I and Beulah Lee Madsen; m. Linda Sue Madsen, July 10, 1966; 1 child, Laura Danielle. BA French, U of Redlands, Redlands, CA, 1961; MA French, Middlebury Coll., Middlebury, VT, 1963; PhD French, UCLA, Los Angles, Ca., 1978; studied flute with, Jean-Pierre Rampal. Cert. sec. and CC tchr., lang. devel. specialist. Tchr. French Palmer Twp. Elem. Sch., Easton, Pa., 1961—62, Santa Catalina Sch. Monterey, Calif., 1980—86; French/Latin tchr. Chatsworth HS, L.A., 1963—65; French tchg. asst. UCLA, 1965—66; asst. prof. French Oakland U, Rochester, Mich., 1970—73, Cal. State Coll., San Bernardino, Calif., 1973—76; instr. French San Bernardino C.C., Calif., 1977—78, Monterey Peninsula C.C., 1986, 1988; French/world his. tchr. Salinas HS, Salinas, Calif., 1987—2003; entrepreneur fin. svcs. AL Williams, Mapbook, Calif., Oreg., and Wash., 1978—81. Creator self-paced French program Calif. State Coll., San Bernardino; workshop dir. French Advanced Placement, 1985; group leader AIFS, 1984, 85, Elderhostel, 1987. Active ACLU, 1999—, Human Rights Watch, 1999—; sec. Alliance Francaise of Monterey County, 1980—; VP Walton Housing Homeowners Assoc., Rochester, Mich., 1970—73; flutist Orch. Soc. Westchester; mem. Dem. Party, 1972—; polit. activist to preserve civil rights, UN, global environ.; Bd. dirs. San Bernardino Symphony, Calif., 1975—76; bd. dirs. UN Assn. Monterey County, 2004—. Recipient first place in tchr. placement exam, Los Angeles City Sch., 1963. Mem.: NAACP, NEA, Calif. Lang. Tchr. Assoc., Fgn. Lang. Assoc. Monterey County (charter mem. v.p., pres.), Fgn. Lang. Assoc. North Calif., Am. Fedn. of Tchr., Am. Assoc. Tchrs. French, Am. Soc. for Eighteenth-Century Studies, So. Poverty Law Ctr. Avocations: flute, tennis. Home: 3108 Fehring Place Marina CA 93933

**MADSEN, VIRGINIA,** actress; b. Chgo., Sept. 11, 1963; m. Danny Huston, 1989 (div. 1992); 1 child. Represented by Creative Artists Agy., Beverly Hills, Calif. Actor: (films) Class, 1983, Dune, 1984, Electric Dreams, 1984, Creator, 1985, Fire with Fire, 1986, Modern Girls, 1986, Slam Dance, 1987, Zombie High, 1987, Mr. North, 1988, Hot to Trot, 1988, Heart of Dixie, 1989, The Hot Spot, 1990, Highlander II—The Quickening, 1991, Becoming Colette, 1992, Candyman, 1992, Blue Tiger, 1994, Caroline at Midnight, 1994, The Prophecy, 1995, Ghosts of Mississippi, 1996, The Rainmaker, 1997, Ambushed, 1998, Ballad of the Nightingale, 1998, The Florentine, 1998, The Haunting, 1999, After Sex, 2000, Lying in Wait, 2000, Almost Salinas, 2001, American Gun, 2002, Artworks, 2003, Tempted, 2003, Nobody Knows Anything!, 2003, Sideways, 2004 (Screen Actors Guild Award, outstanding performance by cast in motion picture, 2005), Firewall, 2006, A Prairie Home Companion, 2006; (TV films) A Matter of Principle, 1984; The Hearst and Davies Affair, 1985, Long Gone, 1987, Gotham, 1988, Third Degree Burn, 1989, Ironclads, 1991, Victim of Love, 1991, Love Kills, 1991, A Murderous Affair: The Carolyn Warmus Story, 1992, Linda, 1993, Bitter Vengeance, 1994, The Apocalypse Watch, 1997, Children of Fortune, 2000, The Inspector General, 2000, Crossfire Trail, 2001, Just Ask My Children, 2001, Tempted, 2003, Brave New Girl, 2004; (TV miniseries) Mussolini: The Untold Story, 1985; (TV series) American Dreams, 2002-03, Smith, 2006—; TV appearances include The Hitchhiker, 1987, Moonlighting, 1989, Earth 2, 1994, Star Trek: Voyager, 1998, Frasier, 1999, The Practice, 2001, (voice) Justice League, 2002, Dawson's Creek, 2003, CSI: Miami, 2003, Boomtown, 2003. Democrat.*

**MADSON, PHILIP WARD,** engineering executive, consultant; b. Atlantic, Iowa, Aug. 27, 1948; s. Philip Ward and Pearl Elaine (Thomson) M.; m. Maria Concepcion Casamitjana, Aug. 11, 1968; children: Peter Wesley, David Philip. BSChemE, Iowa State U., 1969, MSChemE, 1970. Registered profl. engr., Ohio. Process engr. Procter & Gamble, Cin., 1971-74, tech. brand mgr., 1974-76, sect. head, 1976-77, assoc. dir., 1977-79; cons. engr. Raphael Katzen Assocs., Cin., 1979-84, v.p., 1984-90, sr. v.p. tech. and mktg., 1990-92, pres., 1993-98; pres., CEO, COO Katzen Internat., Inc., Cin., 1999—. Guest lectr. Alltech's Annual Internat. Short Course, 1983—. Chmn. Police/Community Rels. Com. Kennedy Heights, 1978-84; chmn. media response team S.W. Ohio Sportsmen's Assn., 1990—; chmn. pub. rels. com. Firearms Facts Com., 1991—; founder, chmn. Kennedy Heights Concerned Citizens, Cin., 1979-85; mem. exec. bd. dirs. Kennedy Heights Community Coun., 1979-84. Recipient Spl. award Kennedy Heights Community Coun., 1984, Recognition Hamilton County Crime Prevention Assn., 1983, Ky. Col. Fellow Am. Inst. Chemists; mem. AIChE, Tech. Assn. Pulp and Paper Industry, New Uses Coun., Clean Fuels Devel. Coalition (chmn. mem. com. 1999—), Am. Chem. Soc., Internat. Inst. of Distillers (founding bd. dirs., v.p.), Internat. Exec. Svc. Corp. Avocations: music, hunting, target shooting. Home: 3749 Davenant Ave Cincinnati OH 45213-2218 Office: Katzen Internat Inc 2300 Wall St Ste K Cincinnati OH 45212-2789 E-mail: madson@katzen.com.

**MADU, LEONARD EKWUGHA,** lawyer, human rights advocate, columnist; b. Ibadan, Nigeria, Mar. 17, 1953; came to U.S., 1977; s. Luke E. and Grace (Dureke) M.; m. Jaculine Stephanie Turner, June 4, 1980; children: Christine, Oscar. BA, Marshall U., 1980; JD, U. Tenn., 1988; MA, Am. U. Rsch. assoc. Lamberts Publs., Washington, 1980-82; data specialist Govt. Employees Ins. Co., Washington, 1982-85; law intern Knoxville (Tenn.) Urban League, 1986-88; cons. Morris Brown Coll., Atlanta, 1988; staff atty. East Carolina Legal Svc., Wilson, NC, 1989-90; cons. youth devel. Nat. Crime Prevention Coun., Washington, 1990; contract compliance officer Walters State C.C., Morristown, Tenn., 1990; examiner Dept. of Human Svc., Nashville, 1990-93; human rights officer Human Rights Commn., Nashville, 1993—; pres. Panafrica, Nashville, 1994—; CEO Madu and Assoc. Internat. Bus. Cons., 1996—; with Bus. Forum & Banquet, Internat.; 1st v.p. Nashville Multicultural Partnership, Inc., 2000—. Polit. cons. Embassy of Nigeria, Washington, 1995; cons. Embassy of Sierra Leone, Washington, 1995, Healthcare Internat. Mgmt. Co., 1996-2001, Embassy of Mozambique, 2000-01, Embassy of Togo, 2001—; bd. dirs. Peace and Justice Ctr., Nashville; pres. African Conglomerates Internat., Inc. Editor: African Nations Handbook, 1994, Directory of African Universities and Colleges, 1994;

editor-in-chief Panafrican Digest, 1994, Panafrican Jour. of World Affairs, 1994; columnist Met. Times, Nashville, 1991—, The African Herald, Dallas, 1995—, U.S./African Voice, Balt., 1995—, African Sun Times, 1995—, The Nigerian and African, 1995—, The African Press, N.Y. Co-chmn. Clergy and Laity Concerned, Nashville, 1992-95; mem. curriculum and character com. Met. Sch. Bd. Nashville, 1994-97; co-coordinator The Haitian Project, 1991-94; vice-chmn. Nigerian Network Leadership awards N.Y., 1996; chmn. Internat. Women's Expo, Knoxville, 1996; co-chair Miss Nigeria Internat. Beauty Pageant, Washington, 1995, Miss Africa Internat. Beauty Pageant, Nashville, 1996, Igbo Union Chieftaincy Coronation Ceremony, Nashville, 1995; chmn. Nigerian Patriotic Front, 1997—; coord. United Nigeria Congress Party, 1997-98, Southeast U.S.; recruiter internat. students Tenn. State U., 1998-99; chmn. bd. dirs. Africa Found., Washington, 2001—2002. Recipient World Hunger Devel. Program award Marshall U., 1978-79, Hall of Nations scholar Am. U., 1980, 82, Mary Strohbel award United Way, 1994-95, Non-profit Vol. award Nat. Conf. of Christians and Jews, 1994. Mem. NAACP, U.S. Com. on Fgn. Rels., Soc. Profl. Journalists, UN Assn., Orgn. African Natonals (pres. 1994), African C. of C. (pres. 2000—). Avocations: reading, travel, soccer, ping-pong, tennis. Office: Panafrica 1016 18th Ave S Nashville TN 37212-2105

**MADUKA, CHIKEZIE,** journalist; b. Umuahia, Abia, Nigeria, Apr. 25, 1963; arrived in U.S., 1993; s. Frank Chijioke and Comfort Ehichanya Maduka; m. Ngozi Nwanyisunday Enwere, Mar. 15, 1988; children: Chikerenma, Chibuisi, Chinomnso, Chijiaku, Chiamaka. BA in Journalism, St. Petersburg State U., Russia, 1989; MA in Internat. Journalism, St. Petersburg State U., 1991, MA in Russian Lang., 1991; Rsch. cert., St. Petersburg Humanitarian U., 1993. Pres. Chyke Dimensions Inc., Landover, Md., 2000—, Chykes Gift Gallery, Landover, 2000—. Author: International Information Relations in the New Millennium: Interrelationship with the Common Heritage of Mankind, 2001. Gen. sec. Prince George's Head Start Policy Coun., Prince George's, Md., 1996, 1997—98, Judge Sylvannia Woods Sch. PTA, Glenarden, Md., 2002—. Avocations: photography, travel, reading, sports. Home: 2416 Greeley Pl Landover MD 20785

**MADURA, JAMES ANTHONY,** surgeon, educator; b. Campbell, Ohio, June 10, 1938; s. Anthony Peter and Margaret Ethel (Sebest) M.; m. Loretta Jayne Sovak, Aug. 8, 1959; children: Debra Jean, James Anthony II, Vikki Sue. BA, Cogate U., 1959; MD, Western Res. U., 1963. Diplomate Am. Bd. Surgery. Intern in surgery Ohio State U., Columbus, 1963—64, resident in surgery, 1966—71; asst. prof. surgery Ind. U., Indpls., 1971—76, assoc. prof. Surgery, 1976—80, prof. Surgery, 1980—, J.S. Battersby prof. surgery, 2001—. Dir. gen. surgery Ind. U. Sch. Medicine, Indpls., 1985—, vice-chmn., 1985—. Contbr. articles to profl. jours. Capt. U.S. Army, 1964-66, Vietnam. Fellow Am. Coll. Surgeons; mem. Cen. Surg. Assn., Western Surg. Assn., Soc. Surgery Alimentary Tract, Midwest Surg. Assn., Internat. Biliary Assn., Assn. Acad. Surgeons, The Columbia Club. Republican. Roman Catholic. Home: 9525 Copley Dr Indianapolis IN 46260-1422 Personal E-mail: jmadura1@comcast.net. Business E-Mail: jmadura@iupui.edu.

**MADURGA, GONZALO F.,** performing company executive, actor, singer; b. Havana, Cuba, Jan. 21, 1932; arrived in U.S., 1953; s. Bernabé Madurga and Matilda Barrena. MS, L.I. U., 1977; student, Tamara Daykarhanova Acting Sch., 1956. Cert. bilingual tchr., NY. Artistic dir. Counterpoint Theatre, N.Y.C., 1972-75, Operatic Concert & Theatre Artists, Inc., Miami, Fla., 1996—. Acting appearances include King of the Dark Chamber, N.Y.C., 1961, Romeo and Juliet, 1965, Macbeth, 1966, The Fantasticks, N.Y.C., 1971, Kismet, Lincoln Ctr., 1974, Sound of Music, 1975, Carmelina, N.Y.C., 1979, La Verbena de la Paloma, Queens, NY, 1985 (Best Actor, Assn. Cronistas de Espectaculos 1985), Romeo and Juliet, NYC, 1994, Coimbra, Miami, 1994 (Best Actor Assn. Críticos Cronistas de las Artes 1994), The Fantasticks, Miami, 1996, Macbeth, NY, 1997, The Merchant of Venice, 1997, NY, Drama, Death and the Maiden, Coconut Grove, Fla., 1999, Praying with the Enemy, Coconut Grove, 2000, Hamlet, Fla., 2000, Anna in the Tropics, Fla., 2000, Ala, 2002, The Man of La Mancha, NJ, The Most Happy Fella, One Life to Live, As the World Turns, America's most Wanted,others With U.S. Army, infantry, 1956-58. Mem. Actors' Equity, Screen Actors' Guild, Am. Fed. T.V. Radio Artists, Nat. Acad. T.V. & Sciences, Home and Office: Operatic Concert & Theatre Artists Inc 1315 SW 21st St Miami FL 33145 Fax: (305) 858-0365. E-mail: gonzalomadurga@msn.com.

**MADVA, STEPHEN ALAN,** lawyer; b. Pitts., July 27, 1948; s. Joseph Edward and Mary (Zulick) M.; children: Alexander, Elizabeth. BA cum laude, Yale U., 1970; JD, U. Pa., 1973. Bar: Pa. 1973, U.S. Dist. Ct. (ea. dist.) Pa. 1975, U.S. Ct. Appeals (3d cir.) 1976, U.S. Ct. Appeals (11th cir.) 1987, U.S. Supreme Ct. 1985, N.Y. 1990. Asst. defender Defender Assn. Phila., 1973—75, fed. defender, 1975—77, also bd. dirs.; assoc. Montgomery, McCracken, Walker & Rhoads, Phila., 1977—81, ptnr., 1981—, mem. mgmt. com., 1993—, chmn. litig. sect., 1993—2002, vice chmn., 2002—03, chmn. 2003—. Bd. dirs. Ferag-Ams., LLC, chmn., 2004—; bd. dirs. WRH Mktg. Ams., LLC., chmn. 2004—. Bd. dirs. Ctrl. Phila. Devel. Corp., St. Christopher's Hosp. for Children, chmn., 2004—; bd. dirs. St. Christopher's Found. for Children, Opera Co. of Phila., v.p., 2002—04, chmn., 2004—; bd. dirs. Police Athletic League, Phila. C. of C., World Affairs Coun. Fellow Internat. Soc. Barristers, Am. Coll. Trial Lawyers; mem. ABA, Internat. Assn. Def. Counsel, Pa. Bar Assn. (ho. of dels.), Phila. Bar Assn. (bd. govs. 2002-, fed. cts. com., chmn. commn. on jud. selection and retention,), Def. Rsch. Inst., Hist. Soc. Pa., Phila. C. of C. (bd. dirs.), Yale Alumni Assn. (schs. com.), Yale Rowing Assn., Union League of Phila., Sunday Breakfast Club. Democrat. Avocations: tennis, distance running, opera, classical music. Home: 523 Delancey St Philadelphia PA 19106 Office: Montgomery McCracken Walker & Rhoads LLP 123 S Broad St Fl 24 Philadelphia PA 19109-1099 Office Phone: 215-772-7600. Business E-Mail: smadva@mmwr.com.

**MADZIK, ELIZABETH MAY,** hospital administrator; b. St. Louis, Mo., Sept. 21, 1963; d. William J. and Nadine Madzik; children: Derek Embry, Nathaniel Embry. Student, St. Leo U., 2003—. Client liaison Receivables Mgmt., Arlington, Tex., 1996—99; denials mgmt. mgr. Presbyn. Hosp. Dallas, 1999—2005, privacy and compliance officer, 2005—. Dir. bd. dirs. HM Caps, Inc., 2004—. Author: Dark Passion Deaf Reflections, Book of Poetry, 2006. Exec. bd. mem. Parkway Elem. Sch. PTA, Ft. Worth, 2000—03; mem. Am. Ex-Prisoners of War, Ft. Worth, 2001. Mem.: Health Care Compliance Assn., Healthcare Fin. Mgmt. Assn., Phi Theta Kappa. Mem. Lds Ch. Avocations: reading, exercise, poetry, dance, music. Home: 1728 Wild Willow Trail Fort Worth TX 76134 Office: THR - Presbyn Hosp Dallas 8200 Walnut Hill Ln Dallas TX 75231 Personal E-mail: madzik@sbcglobal.net. Business E-Mail: elizabethmadzik@texashealth.com

**MAEDA, J. A.,** data processing executive, consultant; b. Mansfield, Ohio, Aug. 24, 1940; d. James Shunso and Doris Lucille Maeda; m. Robert Lee Hayes; 1 child, Brian Sentaro Hayes. BS in Math., Purdue U., 1962, postgrad., 1962—63, Calif. State U. Northridge, 1968—75; cert. profl. designation in tech. of computer operating systems and tech. of info. processing, UCLA, 1971. Cons. rsch. asst. computer ctr. Purdue U., West Lafayette, Ind., 1962-63; computer operator, sr. tab operator, mem. faculty Calif. State U., Northridge, 1969, programmer cons., tech. asst. II, 1969-70, supr. acad. applicatons, EDP supr. II, 1970-72, project tech. support coord. programmer II, office of the chancellor, 1972-73, tech. support supervisor, 1973-74, supr. computer ctr. support, programmer II, 1973-74, acad. coord. tech. support coord. internat., 1974-83; coord. user svcs. info. ctr., mem. tech. staff IV CADAM INC subs. Lockheed Corp., Burbank, Calif., 1983-86, coord. user svcs., tech. specialist computing dept., 1986-87; v.p., bd. dirs Rainbow Computing, Inc., Northridge, 1976-85; dir. Aki Tech/Design, Northridge, 1976—. Mgr. mktg. thaumaturge Taro Quipu Cons., Northridge, 1987—; tech. cons. Digital Computer Cons., Chatsworth, Calif., 1988; computer tech., fin. and bus. mgmt., sys. integration, 1988—90; tech. customer software support Collection Data Sys., Westlake, Calif., 1991; sr. tech. writer info mgmt. divsn. Sterling Software, 1992—2000; sr. tech. writer, quality analyst Computer Assocs. Internat., Inc., 2000—. Author, editor more than 460 user publs., tutorials, reference manuals, user guides, CD graphics/packaging; contbr. articles and photos to profl. jours. Mem.: DECUS (ednl. spl. interest group 1977—83, ednl. steering com. RSTS/E 1979—82), SHARE, IEEE, Soc. for Tech. Comm. Avocations: photography, photojournalism, vintage automobiles.

**MAEDA, JOHN,** graphics designer, artist, computer scientist; b. Seattle, 1966; m. Kris Maeda. BS, MIT, 1988, MS; PhD in Design, Tsukuba U. Inst. of Art and Design, Japan, 1992; DFA (hon.), Md. Inst. Coll. Art, 2003. Assoc. prof., design and computation MIT, E. Rudge and Nancy Allen prof. media arts and sciences, coach, physical language workshop, dir., aesthetics + computation group; co-dir. SIMPLICITY; assoc. dir. MIT Media Libr. Lectr. on the topic of work and philosophy at numerous academic, cultural, and indsl. institutions. One-man shows include Design Machines, Axis Gallery, Tokyo, 1995, Deconstructing Cyberspace, Axis Gallery Annex, Tokyo, 1995, John Maeda:Paper and Computer, Ginza Graphic Gallery, Tokyo and Dai Nippon Dojima Gallery, Osaka, 1996, one-line.com, Ginza Graphic Gallery, Tokyo, 1999, maeda@media, Calif. Inst. Arts and Crafts, San Francisco and Inst. Contemporary Art, London, Post-Digital, Cristinerose Gallery, NY, 2000, John Maeda: Towards Post Digital, NTT Inter-communication Ctr., Tokyo, 2001, NTT ICC, Tokyo, Japan, 2001, John Maeda: FooD, Cristinerose Gallery, NY, 2003, exhibited in group shows at NHK Heart Exhibitions, Bukamura Gallery, Tokyo, 1996, Organic Computation, NY Art Director's Club, 1999, Design Triennale, Cooper-Hewitt Nat. Design Mus., 2000, 010101:Art in Technological Times, San Francisco Mus. Modern Art, 2001, Workspheres, Mus. Modern Art, NY, 2001; author: Reactive Square, 1995, Flying Letters, 1996, 12 o'clocks, 1997, Tap, Type, Write, 1998, Design By Numbers, 1999, maeda@media, 2000, Creative Code, 2004. Named Best Book in Computer Science, Am. Assn. Publishers, 2000, Köln Designer of Yr., 2001; named one of 21 Most Important People for the 21st Century, Esquire, 1999, 15 Master Graphic Designers, Yahoo, 1999, 10 To Watch, ResFest, 2001, 20 Masters of Design, Fast Company Design, 2004; recipient Grand Prix, Interactive prize, Multimedia Assn. Japan, 1995, Gold prize, Tokyo Type Director's Club, 1996, Interactive prize, 1998, Japan Ministry of Culture, 1998, Gold prize, ID Magazine, 1998, NY Art Director's Club, 1998, DaimlerChrysler Design prize, 2000, Nat. Design award, Smithsonian Institution, 2001, Muriel Cooper prize, Design Mgmt. Inst., 2001, Mainichi Design prize, Japan, 2002. Address: The Media Laboratory, MIT Bldg E15 217 Massachusetts Ave Cambridge MA 02139-4307 Office: The Media Laboratory, MIT Wiesner Bldg Room E15-305 20 Ames St Cambridge MA 02139-4307 Office Phone: 617-253-3133. Fax: 617-258-5079; Office Fax: 617-258-6264. Business E-Mail: maeda@media.mit.edu.

**MAEDER, MICHAEL C.,** endocrinologist; b. Brownsville, Tex., Aug. 11, 1945; s. Charles E. and Betty L. Maeder; m. Jan Zipf; children: Michael Robert, Melissa. BA, Depauw U., Greencastle, Ind., 1967; MD, Ohio State U., Columbus, Ohio, 1971. Diplomate Am. Bd. Internal Medicine. Internal medicine resident U. Fla., Gainesville, 1971—74; fellow in endocrinology Ohio State U., Columbus, 1976—78; endocrinologist Mt. Auburn Internists Inc., 1978—95, Hyde Park Internists Inc., Cin., 1996—2006. Major U.S. Army, 1974—76. Avocations: bicycling, hiking, golf. Home: 7019 Spruce Wood Ct Cincinnati OH 45241 Office: Hyde Park Internists Inc 2727 Madison Rd #208 Cincinnati OH 45209 Office Phone: 513-321-0833. Office Fax: 513-321-6063. E-mail: mcmaeder@pol.net.

**MAEHARA, PAULETTE V.,** fundraising executive; b. Happy, Tex. married; 2 children. BA, U. Hawaii. Cert. Fund Raising Exec. (CFRE), Assn. Exec. (CAE). Exec. U. Hawaii Found., March of Dimes Birth Defects Found., Hawaii Chap.; v.p. devel. Project HOPE; exec. Am. Red Cross; CEO Epilepsy Found.; pres., CEO Assn. of Fundraising Profls. (AFP). Exec. com. Internat. Bur. for Epilepsy, Internat. Svc. Agencies, chair membership com.; bd. dirs. Nat. Health Coun.; mem. Assn. Com. of 100, US C. of C. Recipient Best Direct Mail Program award, Direct Mktg. Assn. of Am., 1994. Mem.: Am. Soc. of Assn. Execs. (bd. dirs. 2000—02, vice chair exec. bd. dirs. 2001, sec., treas. 2003, past chair Exec. Mgmt. Coun., chair 2005—). Office: Assn of Fundraising Profls 1101 King St, Ste 700 Alexandria VA 22314 Office Phone: 703-684-0410. Office Fax: 703-684-0540.*

**MAEHL, WILLIAM HARVEY,** retired historian; b. Bklyn., May 28, 1915; s. William Henry and Antoinette Rose (Salamone) M.; m. Josephine Scholl McAllister, Dec. 29, 1941; children: Madeleine, Kathleen. BSc, Northwestern U., 1937, MA, 1939; PhD, U. Chgo., 1946. Asst. prof. history St. Louis U., 1941-42, Tex. A&M U., College Sta., 1943, De Paul U., Chgo., 1944-49; historian Dept. of Def., Karlsruhe, Stuttgart, Fed. Rep. Germany, 1950-52; chief briefing office U.S. hdqrs. U.S. Hdqs. European Command, Frankfurt, Germany, 1952-53; chief historian Arty. Sch., Okla., 1954; with War Plans Office, Hdqs. No. Air Materiel Area for Europe, Burtonwood, England, 1954-55; assoc. prof. European history Nebr. Wesleyan U., Lincoln, 1955-57, prof., 1958-62, 65-68; prof. German history Auburn (Ala.) U., 1968-81, prof. emeritus, 1981—. Vis. prof. U. Nebr., 1962, U. Auckland, New Zealand, 1963-64, Midwestern U., Wichita Falls, Tex., 1965. Author: German Militarism and Socialism, 1968, History of Germany in Western Civilization, 1979, A World History Syllabus, 3 vols., 1980, August Bebel, Shadow Emperor of the German Workers, 1980, The German Socialist Party: Champion of the First Republic, 1918-33, 1986; author monographs for U.S. Army in Europe, chpts. in books, atomic, biol. and emergency war plans for No. Air Materiel Area for Europe; contbr. poetry to Question of Balance, Tears of Fire, Disting. Poets Am., Best Poems of 1995, Journey of Mind; contbr. articles to profl. jours. Grantee Nebr. Wesleyan U., 1959, Auburn U., 1969-73, 79-80, Am. Philosophical Soc., 1973-74, Deutscher Akademischer Austauschdienst, 1978. Mem.: Am. Hist. Assn., Phi Alpha Theta, Phi Kappa Phi.

**MAEHL, WILLIAM HENRY,** historian, academic administrator, consultant; b. Chicago Heights, Ill., June 13, 1930; s. William Henry and Marvel Lillian (Carlton) M.; m. Audrey Mae Ellsworth, Aug. 25, 1962; 1 child, Christine Amanda. BA, U. Minn., 1950, MA, 1951; postgrad., King's Coll., U. Durham, Eng., 1955—56; PhD, U. Chgo., 1957; LHD (hon.), Fielding Inst., 1993. Asst. prof. Montclair (N.J.) State Coll., 1957-58, Washington Coll., Chestertown, Md., 1958-59, U. Okla., Norman, 1959-64, assoc. prof., 1964-70, prof. English history, 1970-86; dean Coll. Liberal Studies, 1976-86, vice provost for continuing edn. and public service, 1979-86; pres. The Fielding Inst., Santa Barbara, Calif., 1987-93, pres. emeritus, 1993—. Prin. investigator Partner for a Nation of Lifelong Learners, Regents Coll., Albany, N.Y., 1994-97; vis. prof. U. Nebr., summer 1965; vis. fellow Wolfson Coll. Oxford (Eng.) U., spring 1975; fellow Salzburg Seminar in Am. Studies, 1976. Author: The Reform Bill of 1832, 1967, Lifelong Learning at Its Best: Innovative Practices in Adult Credit Programs, 2000; contbg. author: Encyclopedia of Education, 2d edit., 2003, Encyclopedia of Distributed Learning, 2004; editor: R.G. Gammage, Chartist Reminiscences, 1981, Continuum. Jour. of the Nat. Continuing Edn. Assn., 1980-83, also articles. Mem. Coun. Nat. Ctr. for Adult Learning, 1990—2001; bd. dirs. Alliance for Alternative Degree Programs, 1988—90; trustee Coun. for Adult and Exptl. Learning, 1990—94, Southwestern Coll., 2000—02. Fulbright fellow, 1955-56; Leverhulme Rsch. fellow, 1961-62; grantee Am. Philos. Soc., 1961-62, 67-68, 71, 76. Fellow: Assn. Grad. Liberal Studies Programs, Royal Hist. Soc.; mem.: Adult Higher Edn. Alliance. Office: PO Box 31757 Santa Fe NM 87594-1757 Personal E-mail: whmaehl05@earthlink.net.

**MAEHR, MARTIN LOUIS,** psychology professor; b. Guthrie, Okla., June 25, 1932; s. Martin J. and Regina (Meier) M.; m. Jane M. Pfeil, Aug. 9, 1959; children— Martin, Michael, Katherine BA, Concordia Coll., 1953, MA, 1959; PhD, U. Nebr., 1960. Counselor U. Nebr., Lincoln, 1959-60; asst. prof. to assoc. prof. Concordia Sr. Coll., Fort Wayne, Ind., 1960-67; assoc. prof. ednl. psychology U. Ill., Urbana, 1967-70, prof., 1970—, chmn. dept. ednl. psychology, 1970-75, assoc. dean grad. and internat. programs prof., 1975-77, research prof., dir. Inst. Research on Human Devel., prof. ednl. psychology, 1977-88, assoc. dir. Office Gerontology and Aging Studies, 1980-82; prof. edn. and psychology U. Mich., Ann Arbor, 1988—, chair combined program edn. and psychology, 1988-92. Vis. prof. U. Queensland, Australia, 1981; vis. prof., cons. to dean Faculty Edn. U. Tehran, Iran, 1973-74 Author: Sociocultural Origins of Achievement, 1974, (with Jane Maehr) Being a Parent in

Today's World, 1980, (with L.A. Braskamp) The Motivation Factor, 1986, (with Carol Midgley) Transforming School Cultures, 1996; editor: Advancement in Motivation and Achievement series; contbr. articles to profl. jours. Lutheran. Office Phone: 734-647-0627. Business E-Mail: mlmaehr@umich.edu.

**MAEKAWA, KOJI OGURA,** technology company administrator; b. Fukui, Japan, Sept. 11, 1954; s. Eiji and Toshiko M.; m. Yukiko Ogura, Nov. 30, 1995. BSChemE, Tokyo U. of Agr. & Tech., 1979; MBA, U. St. Thomas, St. Paul, 1992. Analytical engr. Analytical Lab. Sumitomo 3M, Sagamihara, Japan, 1979-81, chem. engr., Corporate Lab., 1982-87; process engr., Optical Storage Divsn. 3M, St. Paul, 1988—92, sr. process devel. engr., 1993—96; technical team leader Imation Corp. Adv. Imaging Technology, St. Paul, 1997-98, bus. devel. mgr., 1998-99, program mgr., 1998—2000; program mgr., bus. devel. mgr. PDF Solutions, San Jose, Calif., 2000—05, account gen. mgr., 2006—. Intellectual property translator (English/Japanese), language soc. Minn. Mining Mfg., 1993—; cons. Expert Magnetics Corp., Chiba, Japan, 1993—. Patentee in field. Mem. Am. Japanese Soc. Avocations: golf, gardening. Office: Ste 700 333 W San Carlos St San Jose CA 95110 Office Phone: 408-938-4409. Business E-Mail: kojim@pdf.com.

**MAELAND, ARNULF JULIUS,** research scientist; b. Aakrehamn, Norway, Apr. 21, 1933; came to U.S., 1952; s. Erling Magnus and Dagny Marie M.; m. Gunhild Olaug, June 18, 1955; children: Lynn Solveig, David Erling, Kerry Brynhild. BS, Augsburg Coll., 1955; MS, Tufts U., 1959; PhD, U. Vt., 1965. NATO postdoctoral fellow NRC Inst. Atomic Energy, Kjeller, Norway, 1965-66; NAS-NRC postdoctoral rsch. assoc. Army Materials Rsch. Ctr., Watertown, Mass., 1966-68; prof. Worcester (Mass.) Polytechnic Inst., 1968-75; adj. prof. N.J. Inst. Tech., Newark, 1981—84; sr. rsch. assoc. Allied Corp., Morristown, N.J., 1975-90; vis. sr. rsch. fellow Inst. Energy Tech., Lillestrom, Norway, 1992—. Chmn. Gordon Rsch. Confs., Kingston, R.I., 1999; advisor Internat. Sci. and Tech. Ctr., Moscow, 1998—; program evaluator Norwegian Rsch. Coun., Oslo, Norway, 1998-99; cons. Norsk Hydro, Oslo, 2000—. Editor: Hydrides for Energy Storage, 1977; contbr. articles to profl. jours. Rsch. grantee Aluminum Assn., 1969-75. Mem.: Am. Physics Soc. Lutheran. Achievements include patents in field. Avocations: stamp collecting/philately, travel, classical music. Home: 305 Cactus Hill Ct Royal Palm Beach FL 33411 Office: Inst Energy Tech Kjeller N-2027 Norway Office Phone: 476-380-6000. Personal E-mail: arnulf@ife.no. E-mail: arnulf@juno.com.

**MAES, PETRA JIMENEZ,** state supreme court justice; widowed; 4 children. BA, U. N.Mex., 1970, JD, 1973. Bar: N.Mex. 1973. Pvt. pratice law, Albuquerque, 1973-75; rep., then office mgr. No. N.Mex. Legal Svcs., 1975-81; dist. judge 1st Jud. Dist. Ct., Santa Fe, Los Alamos, 1981-98; chief judge, 1984-87, 92-95; assoc. justice N.Mex. Supreme Ct., 1998—, chief justice, 2003—04. Mem. N.Mex. Commn. on Access to Justice; mem. nat. rev. bd. U.S. Conf. Cath. Bishops. Mem.: Nat. Hispanic Bar Assn., N. Mex. Hispanic Bar Assn., N. Mex. Women's Bar Assn., N. Mex. Bar Assn. Office: Supreme Court NMex PO Box 848 Santa Fe NM 87504-0848 Office Phone: 505-827-4883.

**MAESHIRO, MITZI (MIKILANI),** literature and language educator; d. Roy Mitchell and Takako Hayes; m. Brian Morikazu Maeshiro, July 29, 1995. BA, U. of Hawaii at Hilo, 1982—83; Profl. diploma in Tchg., U. of Hawaii at Manoa, 1983—86, M in edn., 1995—2000. Hawaiian lang. specialist Kamehameha Schools, Honolulu, 1984—86, elem. sch. tchr., 1986—2003, literacy resource tchr., 2003—. Co-author: (book) Elevating Expectations: A New Take on Accountability, Achievement, and Evaluation, 2004. Mem.: ASCD (assoc.), Ka Hui Heluhelu (pres. 2001—02), Internat. Reading Assn. (assoc.), Nat. Coun. of Techers of English (assoc.). Home: 45-621 Puuluna Pl Kaneohe HI 96744-2841 Office Phone: 808-843-3332.

**MAESTRONE, FRANK EUSEBIO,** diplomat; b. Springfield, Mass., Dec. 20, 1922; s. John Battista and Margaret Carlotta (Villanova) M.; m. Jo Colwell, Jan. 20, 1951; childen: Mark, Anne. BA, Yale U., 1943; grad., Naval War Coll., 1963. With Fgn. Svc., Dept. State, 1948-84; assigned to Vienna and Salzburg, Austria, 1948, 1954, Hamburg, Germany, 1949, Khorramshahr, Iran, 1960; with NATO, Paris, 1963, dep. asst. sec. gen. Brussels, 1968—71; counselor of embassy for polit. affairs Am. Embassy, Manila, 1971-73; Dept. State adviser to pres. Naval War Coll., 1973; min.-counselor Am. Embassy, Cairo, 1974, amb. to Kuwait, 1976-79; diplomat-in-residence U. Calif., San Diego, 1979; spl. rep. of Pres., dir. U.S. Sinai Support Mission, 1980; exec. dir. World Affairs Coun., San Diego, 1984-86; adj. prof. internat. rels., amb.-in-residence U.S. Internat. U., San Diego, 1986-90. Mem. bd. San Diego World Affairs Coun., 2005. With AUS, 1943-46. Decorated chevalier du Merite Agricole (France). Mem. Internat. Inst. Strategic Studies. Office Phone: 858-457-1656. Personal E-mail: fmaestrone@prodigy.net.

**MAFFEI, GREGORY B.,** media company executive, former computer software company executive; b. NYC, May 24, 1960; s. Ralph J. and Sheila (Quinn) M. AB, Dartmouth Coll., 1982; MBA, Harvard U., 1986. Analyst Dillon, Read & Co., Inc., N.Y.C., 1982-84, assoc.; pres. Beacon Hill Cons. Co., Boston, 1984; dir. bus. devel & investments Microsoft Corp., Redmond, Wash., 1993—94, treas., 1994—96, v.p. corp. devel., 1996—97, sr. v.p., fin. & adminstrn., CFO, 1997—2000; non-exec. chmn. Expedia, Inc., Bellevue, Wash., 1999—2002; pres., CEO 360networks, Inc., Vancouver, BC, Canada, 2000—05, chmn., 2000—05; pres., CFO Oracle Corp., Redwood City, Calif., 2005; CEO elect Liberty Media Corp., Englewood, Colo., 2005—06, pres., CEO, 2006—. Bd. dir. Starbucks Corp., Seattle, 1999— Electronic Arts Inc., Redwood City, Calif., 2003—, Liberty Media Corp., Englewood, Colo., 2005—. Bd. trustee Seattle Pub. Libr. George F. Baker scholar Harvard U., 1986. Roman Catholic. Office: Liberty Media Corp 12300 Liberty Blvd Englewood CO 80112*

**MAFFEO, ALPHONSE A.,** anesthesiologist; b. 1947; MD, SUNY Syracuse, 1972. Diplomate Am. Bd. Anesthesiology. Intern Harrisburg Hosp., 1972-73; res. anesthesiology Mass Gen. Hosp., Boston, 1973-75; physician Lehigh Valley Hosp., Allentown, Pa., 1977—, chmn. anesthesiology, 1990-2001. Clin. assoc. prof., assoc. chmn. anesthesiology Pa. St. U. Hershey Med. Ctr., 1994—2001. Fellow ABA, Am. Coll. Anesthesiologists, mem. Am. Soc. Anesthesiologists. Office: Allentown Anesthes Assn Inc 1245 S Cedar Crest Blvd Ste 301 Allentown PA 18103-6258

**MAFFEO, PINO,** chef; b. 1970; Grad., Newbury Culinary Coll., 1991. Task force chef Marriott Corp., 1991—92; chef Cafe Katie, San Francisco, 1992; chef de partie Molhern and Shackern, San Francisco; chef de cuisine Inn at the Opera, San Francisco; co-exec. chef Eagle, Boston, 1996—99; chef de cuisine AZ, NYC, 1999—2002; co-exec. chef Pazo, NYC, 2002—03; exec. chef Restaurant L, Boston, 2004—. Guest appearances (TV series) The Early Show, Food Network, Simply Ming. Named Best New Chef: Up and Coming, Boston Mag., 2005; named one of Boston's Rising Stars, StarChefs.com, 2006, Boston's Best New Faces, Boston Globe Mag., 2004, Boston's Top Tastemakers, Boston Mag., 2004; recipient Best New Chef award, Food and Wine Mag., 2006. Office: Restaurant L 234 Berkeley St Boston MA 02116 Office Phone: 617-266-4680.*

**MAFFEO, VINCENT ANTHONY,** lawyer, director; b. NJ, Jan. 22, 1951; s. Michael Anthony and Marie Maffeo; m. Debra Maffeo, Dec. 16, 1972. BA summa cum laude, Bklyn. Coll., 1971; JD, Harvard U., 1974. Bar: NY 1975, Calif. 1982, Va. 1988, DC 1988, Mich. 1994. Assoc. Simpson Thacher & Bartlett, N.Y.C., NY, 1974—77; legal counsel Comms. Sys. divsn. ITT, Hartford, Conn., 1977—79; v.p., gen. counsel Bus. Comms. divsn. ITT, Des Plaines, Ill., 1979—80; asst. counsel western region ITT, 1980—83; group counsel ITT Europe, Inc., 1983—86; v.p. gen. coun. ITT Defense Inc., 1987—91; v.p., gen. coun. ITT Automotive, Inc., 1992—95; sr. v.p., gen. counsel ITT Industries, Inc., 1995—. Lt. Judge Adv. Gen. Corps. USNR,

1975. Mem.: ABA, N.Y.State Bar Assn., Calif. State Bar, Phi Beta Kappa. Office: ITT Industries Inc 4 W Red Oak Ln White Plains NY 10604-3617 Business E-Mail: vince.maffeo@itt.com

**MAFFIA, CHRISTINA,** elementary school educator, consultant; b. Astoria, N.Y.C., Dec. 3, 1953; d. Edward and Madeline Maffia; m. Joseph Dunn, Sept. 20, 1975 (div. June 1993); children: Lisa Dunn, Joseph Dunn III; life ptnr. Donna J. Crinnian. BA, Iona Coll., 1975; MS with distinction, Hofstra U., 1991; advanced cert. degree in adminstrn., SUNY, Stony Brook, 2005. Nat. bd. cert. tchr., 1999. Tchr. 4th grade N.Y.C. Bd. Edn., Cambria Hts., NY, 1994—97, Deer Park, NY, 1997—2000, 3 Village Sch. Dist., E. Setauket, NY, 2000—05, mem. profl. devel. and diversity coms., 2000—, math, sci., tech. coord., 2005—. Ednl. advisor Bronx Zoo, NY, 1993—97, Columbia U. Tchr.'s Coll., NY, 1998, Nat. Wildlife Fedn., Wash., 2002—, Suffolk County BOCES, 2002—, NY State Dept. Edn., 2004. Author articles and essays. Mem. 3 Village Civic Assn., Setauket, NY, 2001—, 3 Village Hist. Soc., Setauket, 2001—, 3 Village Sch. Dist. Grantee, Impact, N.Y.C., 1995, Western Suffolk Boces, Dix Hills, N.Y., 1997, 1998, 1999, Suffolk County Math Assn., N.Y., 1998, 1999, 2002, Newsday Future Corp., 2000, McDonald's Corp., 2002—03, Mid. Ea. Suffolk Tchrs. Ctr., 2003—04. Mem.: Kappa Delta Phi. Avocations: hiking, photography, cooking, kayaking, travel. Home: 175 Quaker Path Setauket NY 11733 Office: Arrowhead Elem Sch 62 Arrowhead Ln East Setauket NY 11733 Office Phone: 631-730-4100. Personal E-mail: cmaffia58@aol.com.

**MAFFIA, ROMA,** actress; b. Brooklyn, May 31, 1958; Actress: (films) Smithereens, 1982, Stuck on You!, 1984, Married to the Mob, 1988, American Blue Note, 1989, The Paper, 1994, Disclosure, 1994, Nick Of Time, 1995, Eraser, 1996, Kiss the Girls, 1997, Double Jeopardy, 1999, Things You Can Tell Just By Looking at Her, 2000, The New Women, 2001, I Am Sam, 2001, Treading Water, 2002, Holes, 2003; (TV movies) Internal Affairs, 1988, Her Deadly Rival, 1995, The Heidi Chronicles, 1995, Her Costly Affair, 1996, Mistrial, 1996, The Defenders: Payback, 1997, Route 9, 1998, The David Cassidy Story, 2000; (TV series) Chicago Hope, 1994-95, Profiler, 1996, Nip/Tuck, 2003-.

**MAFFITT, JAMES STRAWBRIDGE,** lawyer; b. Raleigh, NC, Oct. 29, 1942; s. James Strawbridge III and Lois (Handy) M.; children: Amy Maffitt Barkley, Margaret Maffitt Kramer; m. Frances Holten, Aug. 15, 1981. BA, Washington and Lee U., 1964, LLB, 1966. Bar: Va. 1966, Md. 1969. Assoc. Apostolou, Place & Thomas, Roanoke, Va., 1966-67; trust officer Mercantile-Safe Deposit & Trust Co., Balt., 1967-71; from assoc. to ptnr. Cable, McDaniel, Bowie & Bond, Balt., 1971-82; ptnr. Maffit & Rothschild, Balt., 1982-85, Anderson, Coe & King, Balt., 1986-90, Miles & Stockbridge, Easton, Balt., 1990—. Chmn. Acad. Art Mus., 1994—97, bd. dirs., 1993—99; trustee Grayce B. Kerr Fund, Inc., 1998—; bd. dirs. Chesapeake Coll., 2002—, Leadership Md., 2002—04, United Fund of Talbot County, 1994—98, pres., 1997—98. Fellow Md. Bar Found.; mem. ABA (ho. dels. 1986-88), Md. Bar Assn. (bd. govs. 1989-91), Va. Bar Assn., Balt. City Bar Assn. (pres. 1985-86), Wednesday Law Club, Talbot Country Club. Republican. Episcopal. Avocation: golf. Home: 6272 Country Club Dr Easton MD 21601 Office: Miles & Stockbridge 101 Bay St Easton MD 21601-2748 also: Miles & Stockbridge 10 Light St Baltimore MD 21202-1407 Office Phone: 410-820-0222. E-mail: jmaffitt@milesstockbridge.com.

**MAFFRE, MURIEL,** ballet dancer; b. Enghien, Val D'Oise, France, Mar. 19, 1966; came to U.S., 1990; d. Bernard and Monique (Berteaux) M. Diploma, Paris Opera Ballet Sch., 1981; Baccalauréat (hon.), France, 1984; BA (hon.), St. Marys Coll., 2002. Dancer Hamburg Ballet, Fed. Republic Germany, 1983-84; soloist Sarragoza Ballet, Spain; premiere danseuse Monte Carlo Ballet, Monaco, 1985-90; prin. dancer San Francisco Ballet, 1990—. Guest artist with Berlinor Staatsoper and Lines Contemporary Ballet. Recipient 1st prize Nat. Conservatory, Paris, 1983, Grand prize and Gold medal Paris Internat. Ballet Competition, 1984, Isadora Duncan award, 1990. Office: San Francisco Ballet 455 Franklin St San Francisco CA 94102-4471

**MAFFUCCI, DAVID G.,** paper company executive; b. Stamford, Conn., 1950; Degree, Sacred Heart U., 1972. Cert. CPA. Asst. contr. Bowater Inc, 1977, v.p.; treas., exec. v.p., CFO Greenville, SC, 1995—. Office: Bowater Inc 55 E Camperdown Way Greenville SC 29602

**MAGANA, JORGE CARLOS,** pediatrician; b. Merida, Yucatan, Mexico; married; 4 children. MD, U. Mexico, 1956. Diplomate Am. Bd. Pediat. Rotating intern El Paso (Tex.) Gen. Hosp., 1957-58; resident in pediat. R.E. Thomason Gen. Hosp., El Paso, 1960-61, Children's Hosp. Denver, 1961-63; pvt. practice Mexico City, 1963-64, Cleburne, Tex., 1965-68, El Paso, 1969-89; dir. pediat. R.E. Thomason Gen. Hosp., El Paso, 1969-70; chief pediat. Providence Meml. Hosp., 1971, 75, 82,83, vice chief med. staff, 1984, chief med. staff, 1985; chief pediat. Hotel Dieu Hosp., 1983-84; med. dir. Border Children's Health Ctr., 1985-89. Pediat. Arthritis Clinic, 1986—; interim pub. health physician Health Authority El Paso City-County Health & Environ. Health Dist., 1995—. Pediat. cons. El Paso County Health and Environ. Dist., 1989-95; chmn. El Paso City-County Health and Environ. Dist. Lead Task Force. V.p. bd. El Paso Guidance Ctr., 1976, pres., 1977. Mem. Am. Acad. Pediat. Southwestern Assn. Hispanic Am. Physicians, Tex. Med. Assn., El Paso Pediat. Soc. (pres. 1972), El Paso County Med. Soc. (alt. del. 1985, del. 1986-87, v.p. 1988). Office: El Paso City-County Health & Env Dis 5115 El Paso Dr El Paso TX 79905-2818

**MAGANZINI, BROTHER JOHN BERNARD,** academic administrator; b. Somerville, Mass., Nov. 11, 1947; s. Bernard Louis and Eva (Alo) M. BS, St. Friar's Coll., 1982; MS, Fordham U., 1987; postgrad., 1987—. Tchr. spl. religious edn. Kennedy Meml. Hosp. Day Program, Brighton, Mass., 1980-81; parish asst. Our Lady Queen of Peace, Hewitt, N.J., 1981; tchr. Holy Cross Sch., Bronx, N.Y., 1982, St. Anthony's Grade Sch., Washington, 1982-83; dir. religious edn. Holy Cross Parish & Sch., Bronx, 1983-84, tchr., 1984-88, dept. chmn., 1984, 1990-93, asst. prin., 1993—; tchr. East Boston (Mass.) Ctrl. Cath. Sch., 1988-90; asst. dir. Franciscan Sch. Arch St., 2003— With U.S. Army, 1967-69. Recipient John J. Duffy award Archdiocese of N.Y., 1987, Call to the Brotherhood award, Religious Bors. Conf. Mem. Cath. Edn. Assn., Am. Assn. Pastoral Counselors, Spiritual Dirs. Internat., Order of Friars Minor, Holy Name Province, 11th Armored Cavalry's Vets. Vietnam and Cambodia. Avocations: music, theater, youth work. Address: Saint Anthony Shrine 100 Arch St Boston MA 02110-1111 Office Phone: 617-542-6440. Personal E-mail: magsofm@aol.com.

**MAGAOAY, MICHAEL Y.,** state representative; b. Wailua, Hawaii, Aug. 13, 1953; m. Felimar C. Visaya; children: Chanel, Michael. BEE, U. of Hawaii, 1976. Chief elec. engr., estimator, project mgr. George S. Okano Elec. Contracting Corp., 1976—86; mgr., chief engr. of facilities and bldg. svcs. Queen's Med. Ctr., 1986—89; dir. engring. and sales Am. Techs., Inc., 1989—94; project mgr., estimator Am. Electric Co., 1994—96; sr. project engr. A-1 A-lectrican, Inc., 1997—. Chairperson St. Michael's Sch. Bd., Waialua, Hawaii, 1995—98; elected mem. C. of C. of Hononlulu Neighborhood Bd. #27, 1998, 2000, chmn., 1999—2000; pres., bd. dirs. Aloha Ke Akua HS, 1996—; mem. pastoral coun. St. Michael's Ch., 1995—98; corp. bd. mem. Cath. Charities, 1998—2003. Mem.: Engring. Alumni Assn. (treas. 1992, sec. 1993, v.p. 1994, pres. 1995, bd. dirs. 2003—), Hawaii Soc. of Hosp. Engrs. (pres. 1989), IEEE, Mililani Lions Club (1st v.p. 1994, pres. 1995, 2d v.p. 1993, 3d v.p. 1992). Democrat. Office: State Capitol Rm 418 415 S Beretania St Honolulu HI 96813 E-mail: repmagaoay@Capitol.hawaii.gov.

**MAGARGEE, W(ILLIAM) SCOTT, III,** lawyer; b. Abington, Pa., Sept. 3, 1940; m. Annette Bruno, July 6, 1963; children: Scott, Todd, Ashley. AB, Princeton U., 1962; LLB, Yale U., 1966. Bar: Pa. 1966, U.S. Dist. Ct. (ea. dist.) Pa. 1966, U.S. Tax Ct. 1973. Assoc. Dechert LLP, Phila., 1966-75, ptnr., 1975—2005, of counsel, 2006—. Bd. dirs. United Way Southeastern Pa., 1994—2005, CC Phila. Found., pres., 2000—04. Fellow Am. Coll. Employee

Benefits Counsel; mem. ABA (sect. taxation, real estate, probate, trust law, bus. law), Phila. Bar Assn., Princeton Club Phila., Princeton Univ. Alumni Coun. (chmn. 1985-87). Office: Dechert LLP Cira Ctr 2929 Arch St Philadelphia PA 19104 Office Phone: 215-994-2609.

**MAGARIEL, DALE L.,** law librarian; b. St. Louis, Dec. 4, 1951; d. David Lee and Carol Hart; m. Larry K. Magariel, Jan. 8, 1972. BS in Libr. Mgmt., Park U., 1977. Law libr. Morrison, Hecker, Curtis, Kuder & Parrish, Kansas City, Mo., 1977—81; dir. libr. svcs. Stinson Morrison Hecker LLP, Kansas City, Mo., 1983—. Office: Stinson Morrison Hecker LLP 1201 Walnut Ste 2900 Kansas City MO 64106 E-mail: dmagariel@stinsonmoheck.com.

**MAGAW, JOHN W.,** former federal agency administrator; b. Columbus, Ohio, 1935; m. Helen Mahley; 5 children. BA in Edn., Otterbein Coll., 1957. Patrolman State of Ohio, Columbus, 1958-66; joined US Secret Svc., US Dept. Treasury, Columbus, 1967, spl. agt., 1967, head protection for U.S. President and First Lady Washington, 1986—92, dir., 1992-93, Bur. Alcohol, Tobacco & Firearms, US Dept. Justice, Washington, 1993—99; spl. advisor to dir. Fed. Emergency Mgmt. Agy, Washington, 1999—2001, acting dep. dir., 2001, acting dir., 2001, acting exec. dir., Office Nat. Preparedness, 2001—02; under sec. for security U.S. Dept. Transp., Washington, 2002. Mem. Homeland Security Advisory Coun., 2006—. Bd. trustees Otterbein Coll., Westerville, Ohio. Recipient Presdl. Rank Meritorious award, 1991, 1999, Presdl. Rank Disting. award, 1995. Mem. Fed. Investigators Assn., Internat. Assn. Chiefs of Police (exec. com. adv. com. for internat. policy).*

**MAGAZINE, ALAN HARRISON,** association executive, consultant; b. Cambridge, Mass., May 16, 1944; s. Arnold Lloyd and Ruth Magazine; m. June Ann O'Donohue, June 20, 1971 (div. Feb. 1984); children: Sarah Elizabeth, David Michael; m. Cynthia Louise Cordiner, Aug. 30, 1984. BA, Monmouth Coll., 1966; MPA, Kent State U., 1968; PhD, U. Md., 1976. Sr. cons. Real Estate Rsch. Corp., Washington, 1969-72; exec. dir. Nat. Ctr. for Pub. Svc. Internships, Washington, 1972-75; nat. policy coord. Internat. City Mgmt. Assn., Washington, 1973-76; dep. asst. dir. U.S. Commn. on Fed. Paperwork, Washington, 1976-78; dir. office of intergovernmental rels. EPA, Washington, 1978-81; dir. Bus.-Higher Edn. Forum, Washington, 1981-86; pres. Coun. on Competitiveness adv. com. Congl. Tech. Policy Task Force, 1986-89; adv. bd. George Mason U. Ctr. Conflict Resolution, 1986-89; pres. Health Industry Mfgs. Assn., 1990-99; cons. in field, 1999—2001; sr. advisor Coun. on Competitiveness, 1999—2003; prin., sr. advisor New Economy Strategies, 2003—04. Bd. dir. Dickinson Coll., Clark Ctr. Pub. Policy, Congrl. Econ. Leadership Inst., Healthcare Tech. Inst. Bd. Advisors, Sunrise Techs. Internat., Inc., Eyetel Corp., PLC Med. Inc., Innotech, USA; mem. adv. bd. Brookings Inst. Ctr. Econ. Progress and Employment, 1986-89; mem. U.S. China Joint Commn. on Commerce and Trade, 1996-97 Author: Environmental Management in Local Government, 1977. Bd. dir. Met. Washington Coun. of Govts., 1972-79; mem. Fairfax County Bd. Suprs., Va., 1972-79; chmn. No. Va. Transp. Commn., 1974-75; mem. No. Va. Planning Dist. Commn., Fairfax, 1976-79; mem. Dickinson Coll. Parents Coun., 1994-98, bd. dir. Clark Ctr. for the Study of Contemporary Issues. With USAFR, 1968-71. Ford Found. fellow, 1970-71. Democrat. Jewish. Avocation: photography. Home: 28 Fillingame Way Rehoboth Beach DE 19971 Personal E-mail: amagazine@comcast.net.

**MAGAZINE, TODD,** food products executive; BA, U. Mich., 1986; MBA, Northwestern U., 1990. Media planner Jordan McGrath Advt.; mktg. mgr. Procter & Gamble Co., 1990—99; v.p. ready-to-eat cereals Quaker Foods, Chgo., 1999—2002, v.p. mktg., 2004—05, pres., 2005—; v.p. new products Gatorade, 2002—04. Office: Quaker Foods PO Box 049003 Chicago IL 60604-9003*

**MAGAZINER, ELLIOT ALBERT,** musician, conductor, educator; b. Springfield, Mass., Dec. 25, 1921; m. Sari Fromkin; 2 children. Student, Nat. Orch. Assn., 1937-40, Princeton U., 1943, Juilliard School of Music, 1946-50. Music dir., prof. music Manhattanville Coll., Purchase, NY, 1970—. Faculty Westchester Conservatory Music, Summit Music Festival, 2001. Debut: Town Hall, NYC, 1952; staff artist, concertmaster CBS-TV and Radio; Networks; condrs. Reiner, Ansermet, Beecham, Stokowski; condr., sr. violin instr. Westchester Conservatory of Music; vis. condr. Dubuque Symphony; soloist N.Y. Philharm. Symphony, Symphony of the Air, Kol Visrael, symphonies in Chgo., Ft. Myers, Dubuque, York, St. Petersburg, Lincoln Ctr., NYC, 2002; recitals in N.Y.C., Washington, Detroit, Amsterdam, Paris, Jerusalem; star of CBS-TV, The Violin. Recs.: Charles Ives Sonata #2, Charles Ives Trio (with Frank Glazer and David Weber); Vivaldi Concerto in C and Concerto in B (with orchestre Symphonique de Paris); conductor Westchester All County Festival Orch. Mem. AAUP, N.Y. TV Musicians (pres.), CBS Musicians Fund (sec.) Avocation: collecting unique and ancient instruments. Home: 220 Garth Rd Apt 2b3 Scarsdale NY 10583-3954 Office: Manhattanville Coll 2900 Purchase St Purchase NY 10577-2131 Office Phone: 914-694-2200 ext 6267.

**MAGAZINER, FRED THOMAS,** lawyer; b. Phila., July 4, 1947; s. Henry Jonas and Reba (Henken) M.; m. Phyllis Heller, June 28, 1970; children: Daniel, Andrew. BA, Columbia U., 1969, JD, 1976. Bar: Pa., U.S. Dist. Ct. (ea. dist.) Pa., U.S. Ct. Appeals (3rd cir.), U.S. Claims Ct. Law clk. to judge Max Rosenn U.S. Ct. Appeals (3rd cir.), Phila., 1976-77; assoc. Dechert, Price & Rhoads, Phila., 1977-84, ptnr., 1984—. Mem. ABA, Pa. Bar Assn., Phila. Bar Assn., Am. Law Inst. Democrat. Jewish. Home: 1021 W Cliveden St Philadelphia PA 19119-3702 Office Phone: 215-994-2587. Business E-Mail: fred.magaziner@dechert.com.

**MAGAZINER, HENRY JONAS,** architect, writer; b. Phila., Sept. 13, 1911; s. Louis and Selma (Jonas) M.; m. Reba Henken, June 19, 1938; children: Ellen Louise (Mrs. Alan I. Widiss), Fred Thomas. BArch, U. Pa., 1936. Cert. Nat. Coun. Arch. and Registration Bds. Draftsman Phila. City Planning Project, 1936-37; draftsman Louis Magaziner (Architect), Phila., 1937-39, architect, 1946-48; chief Architects' Squad, Day & Zimmermann, Inc., Burlington, Iowa, 1940-41; architect Albert Kahn (Architect), Detroit, 1942; designer Wright Aero. Corp., Wood Ridge, N.J., 1943-45; ptnr. Louis & Henry Magaziner, Phila., 1948-56; architect, planner pvt. practice, 1956-72; regional hist. architect, archtl. historian Mid-Atlantic region Nat. Pk. Svc., Phila., 1972-87; pvt. practice architecture, 1987—. Archtl. adviser Phila. Hist. Commn., 1970-75, mem. archtl. com., 1979-85, chmn. archtl. com., 1972-75. Author: The Golden Age of Ironwork, 2000. Mem. Carpenters' Co. of City and County of Phila., mem. mng. com. historic Carpenters' Hall, 2000-02; v.p. Phila. Health and Welfare Coun., 1957-61, Phila. chpt. Victorian Soc. Am., 1975; v.p. city planning Germantown Comty. Coun., 1957-62; bd. dirs. Downtown Children's (day care) Ctr., 1956-73, v.p., 1960-61; bd. dirs. Allens Ln. Art Ctr., 1945-67, Neighborhood Ctr. Phila., 1956-74, Hist. Soc. Pa., 1970-74, Chestnut Hill Hist. Soc., 1970-80, Phila. chpt. Assn. for Preservation Tech., 1991-98, Clean Air Coun., 1980-92, Center City Residents Assn., 1995-96; bd. dirs. Maxwell Mansion Mus., pres., 1964-67; trustee Stewardsom Meml. Fellowship in Arch., 1958-90. Recipient Presdl. award for Excellence in Design for the Govt., 1988, James Biddle award Preservation Alliance for Greater Phila., 1999; named to Germantown Hall of Fame, 1994. Fellow AIA (mem. com. on hist. resources, John Harbeson award 2000); mem. ASTM (mem. com. on hist. preservation stds. 1981-90), Am. Inst. Conservation, Assn. for Preservation Tech., Ea. Nat. Pk. and Monument Assn., Fellows in Am. Studies (pres. 1983-84), Nat. Trust for Hist. Preservation, Soc. Archtl. Historians (bd. dirs. 1977-80, mem. editl. bd. 58 vol. Buildings of the United States 1992-98), Bldg. Conservation Internat., Victorian Soc. Am., T-Square Atelier (mem. 1963-65), Pa. Soc. Architects, Pa. Acad. Fine Arts, Libr. Co. Phila., Sierra Club, Athenaeum of Phila., Preservation Action. Home: 2 Franklin Town Blvd Apt 2404 Philadelphia PA 19103-1237 Office Phone: 215-545-8397. *I do hope that we can pass on to future generations a prejudice-free America having a natural environment without pollution and a man-made environment with its best elements both preserved and appreciated. Achieving these objectives is an unending struggle but one certainly worth winning. God willing, I expect to continue to fight for these ends.*

**MAGDON-ISMAIL, MALIK,** computer science professor; US, 1989; s. Hamim and Fathima Magdon-Ismail; m. Fathima Zainab Muhsin, July 17, 1999; children: Zain, Deen. BS summa cum laude, Yale U., New Haven, Conn., 1992; PhD, Calif. Inst. of Tech., Pasadena, 1998. Postdoctoral rsch. scholar Calif. Inst. of Tech., Pasadena, 1998—2000; prof. computer sci. Rensselaer Poly. Inst., Troy, NY, 2000—. CEO, chief tech. officer Swooge LLC, Albany, NY, 2006—; chief tech. officer Gold Finger Mgmt. LLC, Hong Kong, 2003—. Contbr. articles to profl. jours. Recipient Wilts prize for best PhD thesis in elec. engring., Calif. Inst. of Tech., 1998, Grant Funding awards to study social comm. networks, NSF, ONR, KDD, 2003, 2004, 2005, 2006. Mem.: IEEE, Assn. for Computing Machinary, Phi Beta Kappa. Achievements include patents pending for Remote Caller ID Projection Device. Avocations: bridge, squash, badminton, tennis, travel. Office: Rensselaer Poly Inst 110 8th St Troy NY 12180 Office Phone: 518-276-4857. Office Fax: 518-276-4033. E-mail: magdon@cs.rpi.edu.

**MAGDOSKO, PAULA,** school psychologist; b. Weehawken, NJ, Mar. 21, 1958; d. Paul and Linda Magdosko. BA in Psychology, Fairleigh Dickinson U., 1981, MA in Tchg., 1994, MA in Sch. Psychology, 2002. Cert. elem. tchr. NY, NJ, sch. psychologist NJ. V.p. F.G. Distributors Inc., Teaneck, NJ, 1984—92; tchr. Paramus (NJ) Pub. Schs., 1994—2003; sch. psychologist Ridgefield Park (NJ) Pub. Schs., 2003—. Athletic scholar, Fairleigh Dickinson U., 1976—78. Mem.: NEA, APA, Ridgefield Park Edn. Assn., NJ Assn. Sch. Psychologists, NJ Edn. Assn., Nat. Assn. Sch. Psychologists. Avocations: gardening, refinishing furniture, antiques. Office: Ridgefield Park Pub Schs Office Spl Svcs 98 Central Ave Ridgefield Park NJ 07660

**MAGE, ROSE GOLDMAN,** immunologist, educator; d. Abraham and Augusta (Wagner) Goldman; m. Michael Gordon Mage, June 12, 1955; children: Dan, Gene, Anita. BS, Cornell U., Ithaca, N.Y., 1956; PhD, Columbia U., N.Y.C., 1963. Postdoctoral fellow NIAID, NIH, Bethesda, Md., 1963—65, career investigator, 1965—, sect. chief, 1988—. Adj. prof. George Washinton U., Washington, 1976—. Contbr. over 170 articles to scholarly and profl. jours. Fellow AAAS; mem. Am. Assn. Immunologists, Am. Soc. Microbiology. Office Phone: 301-496-6113. Personal E-mail: rmage@comcast.com.

**MAGEE, A. CARTER,** lawyer, educator; b. Wiesbaden, Germany, Oct. 13, 1954; s. Archibald Carter Magee and Doris Geraldine Lancaster; m. Leslie Cochran Magee, June 25, 1983; children: John Carter, Julia Parks, Caroline Lancaster. BA, Hampden-Sydney Coll., Va., 1976; JD, Washington and Lee U., Lexington, Va., 1979. Cert.: Am. Bd. Cert. (bus. bankruptcy law) 1992, bar: Va. 1980, U.S. Dist. Ct. (ea. and we. dists.) Va. 1980, U.S. Bankruptcy Ct. 1980, U.S. Ct. Appeals (4th cir.) 1981, U.S. Supreme Ct. 2003. Jud. law clk. U.S. Bankruptcy Ct. We. Divsn. Va., Roanoke, Va., 1979—81; assoc. Woods Rogers & Hazlegrove, Roanoke, 1981—85; pres., shareholder Magee, Foster, Goldstein & Sayers, PC, Roanoke, 1986—. Adj. prof. law Washington and Lee U. Sch. Law, 1992, 2006, bd. govs., mem. law coun., 2003—; lectr. in field. Contbr. articles to profl. jours. Alumni rep. North Cross Sch. Bd. Trustees, Roanoke, 1982—84; chmn. Roanoke Office on Youth, 1987—88, Roanoke City Rep. Com., 1992—96. Named Va. Super Lawyer, 2006; recipient Algernon Sydney Sullivan award, NY So. Soc., 1976. Mem.: ATLA, ABA (bus. bankruptcy law sect., comml. law sect., legal econs. sect.), Va. State Bar, Va. Trial Lawyers Assn., Va. Bar Assn. (bankruptcy sect.), Am. Bankruptcy Inst. (unsecured trade creditor com.), Roanoke Bar Assn. (pro bono cmty. svc. orgn., bankruptcy sect.), Aircraft Owners and Pilots Assn. Avocations: flying, coaching soccer, running, exercise. Home: 2528 Avenham Ave Roanoke VA 24014 Office: Magee Foster Goldstein and Sayers PC Ste 1200 310 1st St SW Roanoke VA 24011

**MAGEE, ALAN,** artist; b. Newtown, Pa., May 26, 1947; s. Richard Forrest and Rena (Cook) M.; m. Monika Gabriele Ruth Siekmann, Jan. 4, 1969. Student, Tyler Sch. of Art, 1965-66, Phila. Coll. Art, 1967-69. Contbr. articles to profl. jours.; one-person shows include Allport Assocs. Gallery, Larkspur, Calif., 1978, 81, Clark Gallery, Lincoln, Mass., 1979, Staempfli Gallery, N.Y.C., 1980, 82, 90, FIAC Grand Palais, Paris, 1983, Norton Gallery and Sch. of Art, West Palm Beach, Fla., 1983, San Jose Mus. of Art, 1983, Newport Art Mus., 1984, Farnsworth Art Mus., Rockland, Maine, 1984, Ark. Art Ctr., Columbus Mus. of Art, Ohio Chgo. Art Inst., U. Maine, 1985, Fresno Art Ctr., 1985, L.A., 1986, Schmidt-Bingham Gallery, N.Y.C., 1986, 88, 89, Allport Assocs. Gallery, San Francisco, 1986, Joan Whitney Payson Gallery at Westbrook Coll., Portland, Maine, 1990, Farnsworth Art Mus., 1991, James A. Michener Art Mus., Bucks County, Pa., 1991, Ringling Sch. Art & Design, Sarasota, Fla., 1992, Fine Arts Ctr. at Cheekwood, Nashville, 1992, Edith Caldwell Gallery, San Francisco, 1992, 93, 95, 96, 97, Edith Lambert Gallery, Santa Fe, 1995, Hollis Taggart Gallery, N.Y.C., 2000, San Francisco, 2000, Berlin Philharm. Hall, 2000, Forum Gallery, L.A., 2001, 02, Forum Gallery, N.Y., 2003, James A. Michener Art Mus., 2003; 30-Yr. Retrospective traveling exhbn. James A. Michener Art Mus., 2003, Farnsworth Art Mus., 2004, Mus. of Tex. Tech U., 2004, Frye Art Mus., 2005, Luxemburg Embassy, Berlin, 2005, Forum Gallery, NY, 2006, Goethe Inst., NY, 2006, Sardoni Art Mus., Pa., 2006; group shows include Farnsworth Art Mus., Rockland, Maine, 1985, Akron (Ohio) Mus. of Art, 1985, Maine Coast Artists, Rockport, 1985, Ark. Art Ctr, Little Rock, 1985, Smithsonian Instn., Nat. Air and Space Mus., Washington, 1985, Wunderlich & Co., N.Y.C., 1986, Light Gallery, N.Y.C., 1986, Schmidt-Bingham Gallery, N.Y.C., 1986, 88, Mus. Fine Arts, Springfield, 1986, Butler Inst. Am. Art, Youngstown, Ohio, 1987, Am. Acad. and Inst. Arts and Letters, N.Y.C., 1987, Nat. Invitational Drawing Exhbn., 1989, Staempfli Gallery, N.Y.C., 1990, Albrecht Art Mus., St. Joseph, 1990, NAD, N.Y.C., 1990, Edith Caldwell Gallery, San Francisco, 1993, 94, 95, 96, Nora Eccles Harrison Mus., Art, Logan Utah, 1992, Portland Mus. of Art, 1993, Creiger Dane Gallery, Boston, 1995, Phila. Art Mus., 1995, Forum Gallery, N.Y.C., 1996, Nat. Mus. Am. Art, Washington, 1997, Hollis Taggart Gallery, N.Y., 1998, Hackett, Feedman Gallery, San Francisco, 1998, Portland Mus. Art, 1998, Farnsworth Art Mus., 1998, Art Inst. Chgo., 1999, Katonah Mus. Art, 1999, U. Rochester, 1999, O.P. FotoGalery, Hong Kong, 1999, others; pub. collections include Farnsworth Art Mus., Rockland, Arco Collection, Lucasfilm, Bank of Japan, Mobil Oil, Janss Collection, L.A., Achenbach Collection, Palace of the Legion of Honour, San Francisco, Art Inst. Chgo., Portland (Maine) Mus. of Art, Rutgers U. Art Mus., Tapestry for Riverview Psychiat. Ctr., Maine, and others; commns. include mural U. Maine, 1997, Maine State House, 1999; author: Stones and Other Works, 1987, Alan Magee 1981-91, Archive, Monotypes, Alan Magee, 2000, 03, Alan Magee - paintings, sculpture, graphics, 2003; prin. commd. works include portrait of Senate Majority Leader George Mitchell 2003 and Alan Magee, Maine, 2002; TV: Visions of Darkness and Light, 1988. Recipient Richard and Hinda Rosenthal Found. award N.Y.C., Am. Book award, Nevelson award, 1982; The Leo Meissner prize NAD, 1990. Home: 476 Pleasant Point Rd Cushing ME 04563-3422 E-mail: info@alanmagee.com.

**MAGEE, CHARLES THOMAS,** international consultant, retired diplomat; b. Clifton Forge, Va., Mar. 6, 1932; s. Charles Thomas and Dorothy Elizabeth (McPherson) M.; m. Maideh Mazda, May 30, 1959; 1 child, Maya. BA, Harvard U., 1953. Vice consul Am. Consulate, Windsor, Can., 1961-63; polit.-mil. affairs officer Am. Emb., Paris, 1964-66; polit. officer Soviet desk Dept. State, 1966-68; adv. Russian language and area studies Garmisch, Germany, 1968—69; polit. officer Am. Embassy, Moscow, 1969—71; dep. dir. for ops. Exec. Secretariat Dept. State, Washington, 1971-72, officer-in-charge French desk, 1972-74; chief internal polit. affairs, exec. asst. to amb. Am. Embassy, Paris, 1974—77, dep. chief mission Sofia, Bulgaria, 1977-80; chief jr. officer div. Bur. Pers. Dept. State, 1980-82, fgn. svc. insp., 1982-83; cons. gen. U.S. Consulate Gen., Leningrad, USSR, 1984-86; spl. asst. to mayor City of San Francisco, 1986-87; dir. Russian lang. ops. U.S. Del. to Negotiations on Nuclear and Space Arms with USSR, Geneva, 1988-91; sr. program officer for Russia Citizens Democracy Corps, Washington, 1992—93; amb. mission to Latvia Orgn. Security and Coop. Europe, 1994-97, amb. mission to Ukraine, 1998-99, Ofcl. election observer, Ukraine, 1998, 2002, 04, 06, Russia, 2000, 03, 04, Latvia, 2002, Azerbaijan, 2005; polling supr., Bosnia and Herzegovina, 2000; head Orgn. for Security and Coop. in Europe election observation mission to Macedonia, 2000, Azer-

baijan, Moldova, Bulgaria, 2001; field rep Census Bur., 2005; cons. Acad. Arrangements Abroad, N.Y.C., 1987—, Dept. of State, 1989—, Seabourn Cruise Line, San Francisco, 1989-92, Acad. Travel Abroad, Washington, 1995; asst. prof. Dept Navy, 1959-61. Active duty USN, 1953—59, lt. comdr. USNR. Mem. Am. Fgn. Svc. Assn., Harvard Club. Home and Office: 4518 Albemarle St NW Washington DC 20016-2016 Personal E-mail: ctmagee32@aol.com.

**MAGEE, CHRISTOPHER L.,** systems engineer; PhD in Metallurgy and Materials Sci., Carnegie Inst. Tech. Exec. dir. Ford/MIT Strategic Tech. Partnership MIT, Cambridge, prof., Engring. Systems Divsn. Lectr. in field; prof. MIT. Ford Tech. fellow, 1996. Mem. NAE. Achievements include vehicle design, concepts and processes, systems engineering, application of computer-aided engineering and vehicle crashworthiness. Office: Engring Sys Div MIT Bldg E40-293 77 Massachusetts Ave Cambridge MA 02139-4307 Fax: 617-452-3760. E-mail: cmagee@MIT.edu.*

**MAGEE, DONALD EDWARD,** retired national park service administrator; b. Trenton, N.J., Sept. 24, 1937; s. Donald A. and Anna C. (Bocskowics) M.; m. Linda Kimball, June 27, 1964; children: Kevin, Bonnie Magee Burch, Gale. BS in Forestry Mgmt., U. Mass., 1964. Pk. ranger Bryce Canyon (Utah) Nat. Pk., 1966-68; area mgr. Sunset Crater Nat. Monument, Flagstaff, Ariz., 1968-73; mgmt. analyst Nat. Capital Region, Washington, 1973-80; supt. Stones River Nat. Battlefield, Murfreesboro, Tenn., 1980-89, USS Ariz. Meml., Pearl Harbor, Hawaii, 1989-95; ret., 1995. With USN, 1956-58. Recipient Excellence of Svc. award Dept. of Interior, 1991. Home: 95-457 Kaukoe St Mililani HI 96789-1865

**MAGEE, JOHN FRANCIS,** research and development company executive; b. Bangor, Maine, Dec. 3, 1926; s. John Henry and Marie (Frawley) M.; m. Dorothy Elma Hundley, Nov. 19, 1949; children: Catherine Anne, John Hundley, Andrew Stephen. AB, Bowdoin Coll., 1947; MS, U. Maine, 1952; MBA, Harvard U., 1948; LLD, Bowdoin Coll., 1996. With Arthur D. Little, Inc., Cambridge, Mass., 1950-98, v.p., 1961-72, pres., 1972-86, chief exec. officer, 1974-88, chmn., 1986-98, also dir., 1968-98. Author: Physical Distribution Systems, 1967, Industrial Logistics: Analysis and Management of Physical Supply and Distribution Systems, 1968, (with D. M. Boodman) Production Planning and Inventory Control, 1968; (with W. Capacino and W. Rosenfield) Modern Logistics Management, 1985. Trustee Emerson Hosp., Thompson Island Outward Bound Ed. Ctr., chair, 1995—2000; emeritus trustee Bowdoin Coll.; hon. trustee Woods Hole Oceanographic Instn.; chmn. trustees Bowdoin Coll., 1990—94; overseer emeritus Mus. Sci., Boston. Recipient Disting. Leadership award, MIT, 1977. Fellow: Inst. for Ops. Rsch. and Mgmt. Sci., Phi Beta Kappa (life); mem.: Am. Soc. Metals (disting. life mem.), Inst. Mgmt. Scis. (pres. 1971—72), Ops. Rsch. Soc. Am. (pres. 1966—67, Kimball medal 1978), Comml. Club (pres. 1992—94), Somerset Club (Boston), The Country Club (Brookline, Mass.), Concord (Mass.) Country Club (gov. 1971—74), Phi Kappa Psi. Personal E-mail: magjfmagee@netscape.net.

**MAGEE, KATHLEEN S.,** foundation executive; b. NJ; m. William Preston Magee, Jr.; 5 children. BSN, Coll. Misericordia, Pa.; MEd, U. Md.; MSW, Norfolk State U. Nurse, social worker; co-founder (with William P. Magee, Jr.) Operation Smile, 1982, pres., bd. dir. Featured guest Montel Williams, guest appearances Dateline NBC, CBS Sunday Morning, 48 Hours, NBC Nightly News. Bd. gov. World of Children; adv. bd. World Healing Inst.; founder, organizer World Journey of Hope, 1999. Co-recipient Common Wealth award disting. svc., 2001; named to Mad. Mission Hall of Fame, 2004; recipient Conrad N. Hilton Humanitarian prize, 1996, Servants of Peace award, 1997, Golden Plate award, Am. Acad. Achievement, 1999, Kellogg's Hannah Neil World of Children award, 1999, Lifetime Volunteer Achievement award, Operation Smile, 2005. Office: Operation Smile 6453 Tidewater Dr Norfolk VA 23509*

**MAGEE, STEPHEN PAT,** economics professor, finance professor; b. Wichita, Kans., Mar. 17, 1943; s. Lawrence Patrick and Edna Willard (Brock) M.; m. Naneska Nall, Aug. 20, 1965 (div. Dec. 1987); children: Christopher Sean Patrick, Theodore Parker; m. Frances Jean Toepperwein, July 28, 1988. BA in Econs., Tex. Tech. U., 1965, MA in Econs., 1966; PhD in Econs., MIT, 1969. Asst. prof. U. Calif., Berkeley, 1969-71; assoc. prof. U. Chgo., 1971-76; economist The White House, Washington, 1972-73; rsch. fellow Brookings Insts., Washington, 1973-74; prof. fin. and econs. U. Tex., Austin, 1976—, chmn. fin., 1980-84, McDermott prof., 1980-84, Fred H. Moore prof., 1984-92, Charles and Sarah Seay prof., 1992-94; Bayless/Enstar Corp. chairholder, 1994—. Mem. econ. adv. bd. U.S. Sec. Commerce, Washington, 1978-79, NSF, 1979; expert witness Mesa Petroleum, Avis Rent-a-Car, El Paso Natural Gas, Kodak, Proctor & Gamble, AB Dick, Exxon; acad. lectr. in 11 fgn. countries for U.S. govt., 1977-88; vis. prof. Aus. U. Chgo., 1990-91, 1997; expert effects of lawyers on U.S. economy and microeconomics and intellectual property and internat. econs. Author: International Trade (transl. to Japanese, Chinese, Korean), 1980, Black Hole Tariffs and Endogenous Policy Theory, 1989; mem. editorial bd. Rev. Econs. and Stats., 1972-79, Jour. Internat. Econs., 1977-79, Econs. and Politics, 1988-94, Rev. Internat. Econs., 1992-94; contbr. articles to scholarly pubs., fin. publs. including Fortune Mag., Wall St. Jour. Capt. U.S. Nat. Soccer Champions, 1999—2001. Grantee NSF, 1972-77; recipient Joe Beasley Teaching award U. Tex. Grad. Sch. Bus., 1979, Outstanding Career Rsch. Contbn. award, 1990, named TopCore MBA prof., 1986. Avocations: soccer, drag racing, photography. Home: 714 Post Oak St Austin TX 78704-1665 Office Phone: 512-471-5777. Business E-Mail: magee@mail.utexas.edu.

**MAGEE, THOMAS HENRY,** radiologist, educator; b. Newport, Rhode Island, Nov. 26, 1958; s. Francis Robert and Anne Louise (Moriarty) M.; m. Christina Marie (Lapolla), June 7, 1987. BA, Wesleyan Univ., 1979? AI; MD, NY. Med. Coll., 1982-86. Diplomate Am. Bd. Radiology. Staff radiologist Bethesda Naval Hosp., Md., 1991-94; asst. prof. medicine Uniformed Svc. Sch. of Med., Bethesda, Md., 1991-94, Kans. U. Sch. of Med. Kans. City, Kans., 1994—; staff radiologist Menorah Med. Pk., Overland Pk., Kans., 1994—; asst. prof. radiology U. Mo., Kans. City, Mo., 1997—2006; clin. prof. radiology U. Miami, 2006—. Pres. Rockhill Radiology, 1999; bd. examiner Am. Bd. Radiology; reviewer prof. jours. Contbr. articles to profl. jours. including Radiology, Jour. of Computer Assisted Tomography, Am. Jour. Roentgenology. Lt. comdr. USNR, 1991-94. Recipient: Jonas N. Muller Award, NY. Med. Coll., 1986. Mem. Am. Roentgen Ray Soc., Radiol. Soc. N.Am. (moderator, cert. of merit 1990); Kansas City Roentgen Ray Soc. (pres.), Internat. Skeletal Soc., Am. Bd. Radiology (bd. examiner, 2005). Avocations: stamp collecting/philately, tennis. Home: 185 Lanternback Island Dr Satellite Beach FL 32937-4704 Office: Neuroskeletal Imaging Melbourne FL Personal E-mail: tmageerad@cfl.rr.com.

**MAGEE, THOMAS HUGH,** lawyer; b. Rochester, NY, Aug. 15, 1943; s. Edward Charles and Jane Kathleen (Cranmer) M.; m. Judith Joy Stone, Oct. 2, 1982; 1 child, Michael Julian. BSME, U. Rochester, N.Y., 1965; JD, Syracuse U., 1973. Bar: N.J. 1974, U.S. Dist. Ct. N.J. 1974, U.S. Ct. Appeals (D.C. cir.) 1975, N.Y. 1981, U.S. Supreme Ct. 1978, U.S. Patent and Trademark Office. Sr. patent counsel RCA Corp., Princeton, N.J., 1973-84, GE/RCA Licensing Operation, Princeton, 1986-88; corp. counsel E.I. duPont de Nemours & Co., Wilmington, Del., 1988—. Lt. USN, 1965-70, Capt. USNR (ret.), 1991. Decorated Navy commendation medal with combat V Vietnam. Mem. Am. Intellectual Property Law Assn. (com. chair 1974—), Phila. Intellectual Property Law Assn. (com. chmn. 1984—), N.J. Patent Law Assn., Justinian hon. law soc., Phi Alpha Delta. Republican. Presbyterian. Avocations: tennis, handball, coin collecting/numismatics. Home: 721 Severn Rd Wilmington DE 19803-1724 Office: E I duPont de Nemours & Co Barley Mill Plz BMP 25-1372 Wilmington DE 19880 Office Phone: 302-892-0795. Business E-Mail: thomas.h.magee@usa.dupont.com.

**MAGEE, WILLIAM PRESTON, JR.**, plastic surgeon; b. NJ; m. Kathleen S. Magee; 5 children. BS, Mt. St. Mary's Coll., Maryland; DDS, U. Md.; MD, George Washington U. Resident gen. surgery U. Va. Med. Sch.; resident plastic surgery Ea. Va. Grad. Sch. Medicine; pvt. practice Norfolk, Va.; co-founder (with Kathleen S. Magee) Operation Smile, 1982, CEO; co-dir. Inst. Craniofacial and Plastic Surgery Children's Hosp. of King's Daughters, chmn. Plastic Surgery Dept.; assoc. prof. plastic surgery Ea. Va. Med. Sch. Contbr. chapters to books, articles to med. jours.; past appearances NBC Nightly News, Dateline NBC, Fox News, Leeza, The Rosie O'Donnell Show, Hour of Power, 48 Hours, CBS Sunday Morning, Touched by an Angel. Bd. dirs. Operation Smile; founder, organizer World Journey of Hope, 1999; bd. dirs. talksurgery.com. Co-recipient Common Wealth award disting. svc., 2001; named to Med. Mission Hall of Fame, 2003; recipient Conrad N. Hilton Humanitarian prize, 1996, Servants of Peace award, 1997, Golden Plate award, Am. Acad. Achievement, 1999, Frank Annunzio award, Christopher Columbus Fellowship Found., 2002. Mem.: Am. Soc. Plastic Surgeons (Disting. Svc. award 1998), Va. Soc. Plastic and Reconstructive Surgeons (pres. 1991—93), AMA (Pride in the Profession award 2000). Office: Operation Smile 6435 Tidewater Dr Norfolk VA 23509*

**MAGELITZ, LARRY L.**, construction company executive; CFO Dillingham Constrn. Corp., Pleasanton, Calif. Office: Dillingham Pacific Ltd PO Box 1268 Placerville CA 95667-1268

**MAGEN, JED GARY**, child psychiatrist; b. Des Moines, Iowa, May 10, 1953; s. Myron Shimon and Ruth May Magen; m. Carol Ann Barrett, June 18, 1978; children: Benjamin Barrett, Zachary Barrett, Eli Barrett, Nelly Victoria. BA, Oakland U., 1975; DO, Coll. Osteo. Med. and Surgery, Des Moines, 1978. Cert. in gen. psychiatry. Intern Botsford Gen. Hosp., Farmington Hills, Mich., 1978—79; with Ind. Health Service, Bowler, Wis., 1979—82; resident in psychiatry, fellow in child psychiatry U. Mich., 1982—86; clin. instr. psychiatry, research fellow Inst. Social Research U. Mich., 1986—88; chief resident child psychiatry U. Mich., 1984—85, dept. chief, 1985—86; asst. prof., residency tng. dir. dept psychiatry Mich. State U., East Lansing, 1988—, dir. of residency tng., 1991—, acting chmn. Dept. Psychiatry, 2003—05, chmn. Dept. Psychiatry, 2002—, assoc. prof., 2003—, chmn. Dept. Psychiatry, 2005—. Reviewer Jour. Am. Acad. Child & Adolescent Psychiatry. Served with USPHS, 1979-82. Mem. Am. Psychiat. Assn., Am. Osteo. Assn., Am. Coll. Neuropsychiatry, Am. Assn. Dirs. Psychiatry Residency Tng. (exec. bd.), Am. Assn. Med. Colls., Coun. Acad. Socs., Nat. Psychiatry Tng. Coun. Home: 2045 Belding Ct Okemos MI 48864-3657 Office: Mich State U A 222 East Fee Hall East Lansing MI 48824-1316 Business E-mail: magenj@msu.edu.

**MAGENHEIM, MARK JOSEPH**, physician, epidemiologist, educator; b. Deland, Fla., Nov. 1, 1947; s. Milton David and Dolores Ella (Raithel) M. BA cum laude, Wash. U., 1969; MPH, Yale U., 1971; MD with honors, McMaster U., 1974. Diplomate Am. Bd. Preventive Medicine, Am. Bd. Pub. Health, Am. Bd. Family Medicine. Health officer, prof. Oreg. State U., Corvallis, 1976-78; prof. cmty. health U. Sierra Leone, Freetown, West Africa, 1978-81; asst. prof. McMaster U., Hamilton, Ont., Canada, 1978-83; asst. state health officer State of Fla., Tallahassee, 1989-91; health officer, dir. County Health Dept., Sarasota, Fla., 1984—2003; med. dir. Hospice of S.W. Fla., Sarasota, 1994-99; CEO, med. dir. Suncoast Cmtys. Blood Bank, 2003—. Chair adv. com. HIV and STD prevention CDC, 1997—2000. Author, editor Clinics in Geriatric Medicine, 1986, (with others) Practice of Geriatrics, 1986; contbr. articles to profl. jours. Med. dir., instnl. rev. bd. Sarasota Meml. Hosp., 1992—. Recipient Surgeon Gen.'s medallion of excellence, USPHS, 1989, award of commendation, CDC, 1989, Leadership award, 1991—92, numerous grants. Fellow: Royal Soc. Tropical Medicine and Hygiene; mem.: Sarasota County Med. Soc. (chair pub. health com. 1987—), Fla. Soc. Preventive Medicine, Fla. Med. Assn. (Roy Baker Leadership award 2000), Fla. Pub. Health Assn., Fla. Pub. Health Leadership Inst., Pub. Health Leadership Soc. (chair 1993—95). Avocations: tennis, music, bicycling, international travel. Home: 4571 Robin Hood Trail W Sarasota FL 34232-2640 Office: Suncoast Communities Blood Bank 1760 Mound St Sarasota FL 34236 Office phone: 941-954-1600 x229. E-mail: mmagenheim@scbb.org, markomag@comcast.net.

**MAGER, ARTUR**, retired aerospace executive; b. Nieglowice, Poland, Sept. 21, 1919; arrived in U.S. 1939, naturalized, 1944; s. Herman and Ella (Kornbluh) M.; m. Phyllis R. Weisman, Aug. 19, 1942; 1 child, Ilana Gail. BS, U. Mich., 1943; MS, Case Inst. Tech., 1951; PhD in Aeros., Calif. Inst. Tech., 1953. Aero. rsch. scientist NASA Lewis Labs., Cleve., 1946-51; rsch. scientist Marquardt Corp., Van Nuys, Calif., 1954-60; dir. Nat. Engring. Sci. Co., Pasadena, Calif., 1960-61; dir. spacecraft scis. Aerospace Corp., El Segundo, Calif., 1961-64, gen. mgr. applied mechanics divsn., 1964-68, v.p. gen. mgr. engring. sci. ops., 1968-78, v.p. engring. group, 1978-82, cons., 1982—. Mem. BSD Re-entry Panel, 1961—63; mem. NASA com. missile and space vehicle aerodynamics, 1963—65; mem. adv. com. AFML, 1971—72; mem. NASA Adv. Coun., 1982—86; chmn. NASA Space Applications Adv. Com., 1982—86; mem. Aeros. and Space Engring. Bd. NRC, 1982—87; mem. Space Sta. Task Force NRC, 1983—87, mem. Shuttle Critically and Hazard Analysts Rev. Bd., 1986—88; mem. DSB NASP Task Force, 1987—88, AFSB Hypersonic Task Force, 1987—88. Contbr. articles to profl. jours. Mem. alumni fund coun. Calif. Inst. Tech., 1972—. trustee West Coast U., 1980—92; mem. devel. disabilities bd. Area X, 1976—80, chmn., 1976—78; 1st v.p. Calif. Assn. Retarded, 1983—85; pres. Exceptional Children's Found., 1970—72; bd. councilors U. So. Calif. Sch. Engring., 1976—86. Recipient Disting. Alumni award, U. Mich., 1969, Golden Rule award, Calif. Assn. Retarded, 1977, 1989. Fellow: AAAS, AIAA (chmn. L.A. sect. 1967—68, bd. dirs. 1975—77, pres. 1980—81), Inst. Advanced Engring.; mem.: Nat. Acad. Engring., Technion Soc. Sigma Xi Home and Office. 1330 Woodruff Ave Los Angeles CA 90024-5129 Personal E-mail: ap.mager1@verizon.net.

**MAGER, EZRA PASCAL**, investment company executive; b. NYC, Nov. 1, 1941; s. Harold and Naomi (Levinson) M.; m. Sarah Johnson, Mar. 25, 1964 9div.); 1 child, Emma Rachel; m. Reeva Starkman, May 14, 1972; children: Camilla Elizabeth, Michael Johanon. BA, Cornell U., 1963; MBA, Harvard, 1966. Successively sr. v.p., exec. v.p. and dir. Seiden & DeCuevas, Inc. N.Y.C., 1966-73; exec. v.p. dir. Furman Selz Mager Dietz & Birney, Inc., N.Y.C., 1973-90; vice chmn. United Auto Group, Inc., N.Y.C., 1990-96, Cross Continent Auto Retailers, Inc., N.Y.C., 1996-97, First Team Auto Corp., N.Y.C., 1997-98; CEO EPM Advisory LLC, N.Y.C., 1998—; pres. The Torrey Funds, 1998—2004. Trustee Baron de Hirsch Fund, The Textile Mus., Washington. Mem. N.Y. Soc. Security Analysts, Alpha Delta Phi. Clubs: Harvard (N.Y.C.). Democrat. Home: 141 E 72d St New York NY 10021-4315 Office: EPM Advisory LLC 509 Madison Ave Penthouse New York NY 10022 Office phone: 212-223-2333. Business E-Mail: epmager@epmadvisory.com.

**MAGER, INGRID IRINA**, artist; b. San Luis Obispo, Calif., Dec. 16, 1955; d. Hans and Irina Mager; life ptnr. Daniel Elidege Renault. BS, No. Ariz. U., 1996. Designer Carpenter & Stringham Archs., Salt Lake City, 1983—2000, Madonna Constrn. Co., San Luis Obispo, Calif., 1994—2000. Personal artist & designer Essam Khashogi Family & Estate, Lake Tahoe, Nev., 1989—90. Winner of final design for estate, Estate for Essam Khashoggi. Healer/student Heart Awakening Project, Sedona, Ariz., 1998—2002. Moller scholarship, No. Ariz. U., 1995, Art and Design scholarship, 1995. Achievements include design of Designer of spearhead project for the State of California; Designer for spearhead project for the State of California DSS/EDA. Avocations: skiing, camping, glass etching, painting, photography. E-mail: imaeger@netscape.net.

**MAGERKO, MARGARET HARDY (MAGGIE MAGERKO)**, lumber company executive; b. Pitts., Dec. 7, 1965; d. Joseph Hardy; m. Peter Magerko. Student, W.Va. U. Pres. Nemacolin Woodlands Resort & Spa,

---

1987—, 84 Lumber Co., Eighty Four, Pa., 1994—. Named one of 400 Richest Ams., Forbes mag., 2006. Office: 84 Lumber Co 1019 Route 519 Eighty Four PA 15330 Business E-Mail: magerkom@84lumber.com.

**MAGGARD, WOODROW WILSON, JR.**, management consultant; b. Quincy, Ill., Feb. 5, 1947; s. Woodrow Wilson and Claire Lorraine (Lyons) M.; m. Linda Margaret Davis, Dec. 30, 1967; children: Jared Isaac, Erin Leigh-Taylor, Solveig Kirsten, Christian Heinrich, Anica May, Kayla Margaret. BA, Brigham Young U., 1971; postgrad., Ventura Coll. Law, 1975; MPA, Consortium of Calif. State U., 1978. Cert. rev. appraiser; registered mortgage underwriter. Divsn. mgr. Sears, Roebuck & Co., Provo, Utah and Ventura, Calif., 1967-74; adminstrv. officer County of Ventura, 1974-78; founding ptnr. Maggard, Maughan, Gress and Assocs., Ventura, 1976-83; founder Intermountain Property Svcs., Ventura, 1974—; pres., CEO Ariz. Tech. Incubator, Inc., 2000—. Bd. dirs. EmisCo Internat. Corp., Phoenix, Qameleon, Inc., Scottsdale, Ariz.; v.p. econ./bus. devel. Dineh Coops., Inc., Chinle, Navaho Nation Ariz., 1978-80; dir. econ. devel. City of Scottsdale, Ariz., 1980-81; exec. dir., CEO Fairbanks (Alaska) Devel. Authority, 1981-87; co-founder Pacific Rim Inst., 1984—; founder Maggard & Maggard, Fairbanks and Orlando, 1983—; pres., co-founder So. Global Trading Co., Tex. and Orlando, 1991-98; sr. v.p. Cookies N' Cream, Inc., Tex. and Fla., 1990-91; exec. dir., CEO Reichenbach Techs, Provo, Utah, 1975—, pres., 1999—; exec. dir., CEO Ctrl. Fla. Rsch. Park, Orlando, 1988-91, Reichenbach Maegert Internat., Provo, 1997—; chmn. NETeXc, Inc., Wilmington, Del. and Provo, 1998-2000, bd. dirs. 1998—; co-founder LearnDaily.com, Provo, 1999—; pres., CEO Del. Tech. Park, Inc., Newark, 1993-98; chmn. Calif. Mission Days Food, Altaloma, Calif., 1996-99, Ariz. Mfg. Ext. Partnership, Scottsdale, 2000-02, Rural Incubator Bd. Ariz., 2000—; exec. dir., CEO Inst. Applied Composites Tech., Newark, 1993-98; instr. real estate econs./appraisal Oxnard (Calif.) Coll., 1975-78; instr. bus. Utah Tech. Coll., Provo, 1978. Contbr. articles to profl. jours. and books. Active Boy Scouts Am.; high priest Ch. of LDS; econ. dir. City of Dover, N.H., 1988; exec. dir. Dover Indsl. Devel. Authority; exec. dir. Del. Tech. Park and Inst. for Applied Composites Tech.; office of vice provost U. Del., Newark, 1993-98; bd. dirs. WMFE-TV, Fla. Hosp. Found.; bd. dirs. Next Level Found., 2002—; interim dir., Miller Bus. Innovation Ctr., Salt Lake City, 2002—. Recipient Nat. Merit award for excellence in comml. devel., 1987, Dixwell Pierce award, 1975, Alaska Environ. Enhancement award, 1983; one of Top 10 Sci. Parks in the World Cen. Fla. Rsch. Park, 1991. Mem. Nat. Assn. Seed and Venture Funds (sec.), Am. Soc. Pub. Adminstrn., Internat. Right-of-Way Assn. (internat. property mgmt. com.), Nat. Assn. Rev. Appraisers and Mortgage Underwriters (sr.), Nat. Coun. on Urban Econ. Devel., Am. Econ. Devel. Coun. (internat. com.), Nat. Bus. Incubation Assn., So. Indsl. Devel. Coun., Assn. Univ.-Related Rsch. Parks (bd. dirs.), Del. Innovation Fund (bd. dirs.), Urban Land Inst., Nat. Assn. Indsl. and Office Parks, Am. C. of C. Rschrs. Assn., Acad. Polit. Sci., United Indian Planners, Japan-Am. Soc. Cen Fla. (bd. dirs.), Inst. Internal Auditors, Am. U. Tech. Mgrs., Sci. and Tech. Coun. of the States, Soc. Profl. Composite Engrs. (charter), Suppliers Advanced Composite Materials Assn., Soc. for Advancement of Materials and Process Engring., Assn. Tech. Transfer Soc., Licensing Execs. Soc., Rotary, Phi Alpha Theta. Independent. Home: 4006 N Canyon Rd Provo UT 84604-5018 Office: 1435 N Hayden Rd Scottsdale AZ 85257-3773

**MAGGIPINTO, V. ANTHONY**, lawyer; b. Tucson, Apr. 15, 1943; s. William Vito and Elizabeth Maria (Rice) M.; m. Maria Teresa Zequeira, Aug. 31, 1976; children: Marshall Albert Nicholas, Spencer William Jonathan. AB cum laude, Southampton Coll., 1970; JD, Fordham U., 1976. Bar: Fla. 1977, N.Y. 1978, U.S. Dist. Ct. (ea. and so. dists.) N.Y. 1979, U.S. Ct. Appeals (2d cir.) 1980. Asst. to pres. Interpub. Group of Cos., N.Y.C., 1965-66; asst. dean of admission Southampton (N.Y.) Coll., 1971-73; investigative aide N.Y. State Com. on Jud. Conduct, N.Y.C., 1974-76; asst. state atty. Dade County State Atty., Miami, Fla., 1977-78; asst. dist. atty. Suffolk Dist. Atty., Hauppage, N.Y., 1978-80; asst. county atty. Suffolk County Atty., Hauppauge, 1980-84; sole practice Riverhead and St. James, N.Y., 1982—. Mem. spl. coms. on discovery, civil litigation U.S. Dist. Ct. (ea. dist.) N.Y., Bklyn., 1983-90, 95—, arbitrator, 1986—, Civil Justice Reform Act adv. group, 1990-95, chair jury task force, 1993—, commendation U.S. Dist. Ct., 1997. Mem. appeals bd. SSS, 1982—2001, vice chmn., 1986—97, chmn., 1997—2001. With submarine svc. USN, 1961—65. Recipient Disting. Alumni award L.I. U., 1990. Mem.: Southampton Coll. Alumni Assn. (exec. com. 1997—2004, pres. 2001—02), Navy League (judge adv. L.I. coun. 1992—), U.S. Naval Inst., Fla. Bar Assn., Suffolk County Bar Assn., N.Y. State Bar Assn. (exec. com. real property sect. 1997—2002), Nissequogue Golf Club (counsel 1980—2004, bd. govs.). Republican. Roman Catholic. Avocations: hiking, horseback riding. Office: 1212 Roanoke Ave Riverhead NY 11901-2740

**MAGGS, PETER BLOUNT**, lawyer, educator; b. Durham, N.C., July 24, 1936; s. Douglas Blount and Dorothy (Mackay) M.; m. Barbara Ann Widenor, Feb. 27, 1960; children: Bruce MacDowell, Gregory Eaton, Stephanie Ann, Katherine Ellen. AB, Harvard U., 1957, JD, 1961; postgrad. (exchange student), Leningrad State U., USSR, 1961-62. Bar: D.C. 1962. Research assoc. Law Sch. Harvard U., 1963-64; asst. prof. law U. Ill., 1964-67, assoc. prof., 1967-69, prof., 1969-88, William and Marie Corman prof., 1988-98, Peer & Sarah Pedersen prof., 1998—2002, acting dean, 1990, Clifford M. and Bette A. Carney chair in law, 2002—; dir. Rule of Law Program Washington, 1994. Fulbright lectr. Moscow State U., 1977; reporter Uniform Simplification of Land Transfers Act.; vis. prof. George Washington U., 1998. Author: (with others) The Mandelstam File, 1996; co-translator Civil Code of the Russian Federation, translation, 2003, Civil Code of the Republic of Armenia, translation, 1999, Intellectual Property (in Russian), 2000, Internet and Computer Law, 2001, Trademark and Unfair Competition, 2002; designer talking computers for the blind. Fulbright rsch. scholar, Yugoslavia, 1967; Fulbright disting. chair, Trento, 2002; East-West Ctr. fellow, 1972, Guggenheim fellow, 1979. Mem. ABA, D.C. Bar, Am. Assn. Advancement Slavic Studies, Assn. Am. Law Schs., Am. Law Inst. (consultative group, UCC Article 2), Internat. Acad. Comparative Law. Office: U Ill Coll Law 504 E Pennsylvania Ave Champaign IL 61820-6909 Office Phone: 217-333-6711. E-mail: p-maggs@uiuc.edu.

**MAGID, CREIGHTON (CHIP) REID**, lawyer; b. Cedar Rapids, Iowa, Dec. 11, 1961; s. Frank N. and Marilyn (Young) M. AB, Princeton U., 1984; JD, U. Mich., 1987. Bar: Iowa 1987, Minn. 1987, Mont. 1988, U.S. Dist. Ct. Minn., U.S. Dist. Ct. (no. dist.) Iowa. Ptnr., trial, regulatory, tech. group Dorsey & Whitney PLLP, Mpls., 1987—, and co-chmn., products and tech. liability litig. group. Mem. Mpls. Rowing Club (pres. 1991-95). Avocation: rowing. Office: Dorsey & Whitney Ste 1500 50 S 6th St Minneapolis MN 55402-1498 Office Phone: 612-340-5661. Office Fax: 612-340-2868. Business E-Mail: magid.chip@dorsey.com.

**MAGIELNICKI, ROBERT L.**, lawyer; b. Perth Amboy, N.J., Mar. 28, 1947; s. Leon C. and Dorothy M. (Hudanish) M.; m. Kathleen J. Urban, June 14, 1969; children: Robert Jr., Kimberly, Peter, Matthew. AB with honors, Rutgers U., 1967; JD with distinction, Cornell U., 1970. Bar: N.Y. 1971, U.S. Supreme Ct. 1974, D.C. 1990. Commd. lt. USN, 1968; assoc. Donovan Leisure Newton & Irvine, N.Y.C., 1970-71, 74-80; asst. staff judge advocate U.S. Naval Base Subic Bay, Republic of Philippines, 1971-73; asst. prof. law U.S. Naval Acad., Annapolis, Md., 1973-74; assoc. litigation and antitrust counsel Gen. Electric Co. Hdqrs., Fairfield, Conn., 1980-83, counsel, 1989-90; divsn. gen. counsel Gen. Electric Factory Automation Products, Charlottesville, Va., 1983-88; ptnr. Kutak Rock, Washington, 1990-2000, Schnader Harrison Segal & Lewis LLP, Washington, 2000—03, Sheppard Mullin Richter & Hampton LLP, Washington, 2003—. Avocations: tennis, golf, swimming, reading. Office: Sheppard Mullin Richter & Hampton LLP 11th Fl East 1300 I St NW Washington DC 20005-3314 Office Phone: 202-218-0002. E-mail: rmagielnicki@sheppardmullin.com.

**MAGILL, FRANK JOHN**, federal judge; b. Verona, N.D., June 3, 1927; s. Thomas Charles and Viola Magill; m. Mary Louise Timlin, Nov. 22, 1955; children: Frank Jr., Marguerite Connolly, R. Daniel, Mary Elizabeth, Robert,

---

John. BS in Fgn. Svc., Georgetown U., 1951, LLB, 1955; MA, Columbia U., 1952. Ptnr. Nilles, Hansen, Magill & Davies, Ltd., Fargo, ND, 1955—86; judge U.S. Ct. Appeals (8th cir.), Fargo, 1986—2000, sr. judge, 2000—. Chmn. fin. disclosure com. U.S. Jud. Conf., 1993—98. Fellow: Am. Coll. Trial Lawyers; mem.: Cass County Bar Assn. (Pres. 1970). Republican. Avocations: tennis, sailing, skiing. Home: 501 7th St S Apt 301 Fargo ND 58103-2761 Office: Quentin N Burdick US Courthouse 655 1st Ave N Ste 320 Fargo ND 58102-4932 Fax: 701 297-7255. Office Phone: 701-297-7250. E-mail: frank_magill@ca8.uscourts.gov.*

**MAGILL, JOSEPH HENRY**, chemist, educator; b. Drumnabreeze, Ireland, Dec. 16, 1928; came to U.S., 1962; s. Hugh James and Margaret (Gilliland) M.; m. Joyce Elizabeth Morrow, Dec. 17, 1956; children: Annesley Joyce, Aylmer Campbell. BSc, Queens U., Belfast, Ireland, 1952, PhD, 1956; DIC, U. London, 1957; DSc, Queens U., Belfast, 1990. Prof. dept. materials sci. and engring. U. Pitts., 1975-91, prof. dept. chem. and petroleum engring., 1980-91, adj. dept. chemistry, 1980-91, prof. emeritus, 1991—; cons. Polymer Specialty, 1991—. Liaison scientist ONR, London, 1991-93, adv. bd. Jour. Polymer Sci., 1991-93; vis. prof. U. Yamagata, Japan, 1988-89. Contbr. over 250 papers to profl. publs. Nat. Coal Bd. fellow Imperial Coll. Sci. and Tech., 1956-57; Mellon Inst. fellow, Pitts., 1962-64, 65-68; sr. rsch. fellow Sci. Rsch. Coun., U. Bristol, Eng., 1975-76; sr. awardee Alexander von Humboldt Found., U. Hamburg-Harburg, Germany, 1984-85, Max Planck Inst. Mainz, Germany, 1984-85. Fellow Am. Phys. Soc., Royal Soc. Chemistry; mem. Am. Chem. Soc.

**MAGILL, KENT B.**, lawyer; b. Kansas City, Mo., Dec. 2, 1952; m. Teresa A. Magill. BS, Kent State U., 1975; JD, U. Iowa, 1977. Bar. Mo. 1977, Kans. 1987, US Dist. Ct. Dist. Kans. Assoc. Shughart, Thomson & Kilroy, Kansas City, Mo., 1977—80, atty., 1980—89; assoc. gen. counsel, v.p. The Marley Co., Mission Woods, Kans., 1989—92; v.p., gen. counsel, sec. Layne Christensen Co., Mission Woods, Kans., 1992—2000; assoc. gen. counsel Interstate Brands Corp., 2000—02, v.p., gen. counsel, sec., 2002—, Interstate Bakeries Corp., Kansas City, Mo., 2002—. Office: Interstate Bakeries Corp 12 E Armour Blvd Kansas City MO 64111

**MAGILL, M(ARY) ELIZABETH**, law educator; b. Fargo, ND; m. Leon Francis Szeptycki; children: Alexander Magill Szeptycki, Claire Magill Szeptycki. BA in History, Yale Coll., New Haven, 1988; JD, U. Va. Sch. Law, Charlottesville, 1995. Bar: Md. 1997. Legis. asst. for energy & natural resources US Senator Kent Conrad, Washington, 1988—92; summer assoc. Covington & Burling, Washington, 1994; law clk. to Hon. J. Harvie Wilkinson III US Ct. Appeals 4th Cir., 1995—96; law clk. to Hon. Ruth Bader Ginsburg US Supreme Ct., Washington, 1996—97; assoc. prof. U. Va. Sch. Law, Charlottesville, 1997—2002, 2002—, John V. Ray rsch. prof., 2003—. Mem.: ABA (vice-chair jud. rev. subcom., assoc. reporter Adminstrv. Procedure Act Project). Office: U Va Sch Law 580 Massie Rd Charlottesville VA 22903-1789 Office Phone: 434-924-3898. E-mail: mem2a@virginia.edu.

**MAGILL, ROSALIND MAY**, psychotherapist; b. Albany, N.Y., Apr. 27, 1944; d. Fenton Elliot Sr. and Rosalind Pearl (Gross) M.; m. Theodore T. Solomon, May 18, 1970 (div. 1980). Student, N.Y. State Tech., 1963-64, Pace Coll., 1970-71; cert. in process piping design, Voorheese Tech. Inst., 1968; MEd in Counseling and Psychology, Cambridge Coll., 1994. Lic. master pipefitter, Mass., mental health counselor, Mass.; EIT; cert. alcohol counselor, Mass. Piping designer Badger Am., Inc., Cambridge, Mass., 1976-77; tchr. advanced math. Vision-in-Action, Natick, Mass., 1977-80; plumbing designer R. G. Vanderweil Assocs., Boston, 1980-81; vol. counselor alcohol/substance abuse social detox program Bergen County Hosp., Paramus, N.J., 1981-83; field engr. United Engrs. and Constructors, Phila., 1983-84; tchr. spl. edn. math. and sci. Amesbury (Mass.) High Sch., 1984-85; resident engr. Hoyle, Tanner Assocs., Londonderry, N.H., 1985-86; resident engr., constrn. mgr. dept. environ. mgmt. Commonwealth of Mass., Boston, 1986-89; clin. supvr. counselor substance abuse Positive Lifestyles, Mattapan, Mass., 1990-93; substance abuse therapist Respond Program Ctr. for Family Devel., Lowell, Mass., 1993-94; dir. Respond Program Ctr. for Family Devel., Lowell, 1994-96; substance abuse counselor The Pine St. Inn-Women's Unit, Boston, 1996-98; psychotherapist Brickett's Mill Counseling Assn., 1995—; program mgr. Project Access New Eng. Shelter Homeless Vets., 1998-2000; mem. act team Tri-City Mental Health and Retardation Ctr., Lowell, Mass. Counselor alcoholism and substance abuse Serenity House/Gift of Serenity, 1977-80; counselor substance abuse Baldpate Hosp., Georgetown, Mass., 1984.85. With USMC, 1962. N.Y. State Regent's scholar, 1962. Mem. ACA, Internat. Assn. Addictions and Offender Counselors, Women's Ordination Conf., Daus. Bilitis (pres. N.Y. chpt. 1968-70), Matachine Soc. (bd. dirs. 1968-70).

**MAGILL, SAMUEL HAYS**, academic administrator, consultant; b. Decatur, Ga., July 19, 1928; s. Orrin Rankin and Ellen Howe (Bell) M.; children: Samuel Hays Jr., Katherine Magill Walters, Suzanne Magill Weintraub. AB, U. N.C., 1950; BD, Yale U., 1953; PhD, Duke U., 1962; LHD (hon.), Stockton State Coll., 1990; EdD (hon.), Monmouth U., 2005. Ordained to ministry Congl. Christian Ch., 1953; gen. sec. Davidson Coll. YMCA, 1953-55; the student activities U. N.C., Chapel Hill, 1955-58, asst. dean student affairs, 1958-59; chaplain Dickinson Coll., 1962-63, asst. prof. religion, 1962-66, assoc. prof. religion, 1966-68, dean coll., 1963-68; pres. Council Protestant Colls. and Univs., Washington, 1968-70; exec. assoc., chief office acad. affairs Assn. Am. Colls., 1971-76; pres. Simon's Rock Early Coll., Great Barrington, Mass., 1976-79, Monmouth U., West Long Branch, NJ, 1980-93, pres. emeritus, 1993—; higher edn. cons., 1993-98; assoc. dir. gift planning U N.C., 1999—2004, major gifts officer, 2004—06. Adj. prof. Duke U., 1996. Trustee Jersey Shore Med. Ctr., 1985-93; bd. overseers N.J. Gov.'s Schs., 1986-93. Guerney Harris Kearns fellow in religion, 1960-61; Danforth Found. spl. grad. fellow 1950-61. Fellow Soc. Values in Higher Edn. (dir. 1969-81); mem. Am. Assembly Collegiate Schs. Bus. (accreditation task force 1989-90), NCAA (pres.'s commn. 1990-93), Am. Coun. Edn. (commn. leadership devel. 1982-85, commn. on minority affairs 1989-99), Harvard Inst. Ednl. Mgmt., Assn. Ind. Colls. and Univs. N.J. (dir. 1980-93, exec. com. 1983-93, chair 1987-89); Order of Golden Fleece U. N.C., Fearrington Dem. Club (co-chair 1997-98), Delta Psi. Home: 319 Burlage Creek Chapel Hill NC 27514 Personal E-Mail: smagill@nc.rr.com.

**MAGINN, JOHN LEO**, retired insurance company executive; b. Omaha, Feb. 17, 1940; s. Walter J. and Ruth C. (Sawtelle) M.; m. Carol Varnes, Aug. 3, 1963; children: Mary Kay, Karen, Colleen, Matthew. BSBA, Creighton U., 1961; MS, U. Minn., 1962. Chartered fin. analyst. Investment analyst Continental Casualty, Chgo., 1962-64, Mut. Omaha Ins. Co., 1964-68, asst. v.p., 1968-69, 2d v.p., 1969-76, v.p., asst. treas., 1976-82, exec. v.p., 1982-87, treas., 1982-2000, exec. v.p., chief ins. officer, 1987-2000; sr. advisor Summit Strategies, Inc., 2000—03; pres. Maginn Assocs. Pres. Mut. Asset Mgmt. Co.; bd. dirs. Companion Life Ins. Co., Rye, N.Y., Kirkpatrick, Pettis, Smith, Polian, Omaha. Editor, author: Managing Investment Portfolios, 1983, 2d edit., 1990. Sgt. U.S. Army, 1957-65. Mem. CFA Inst. (bd. dirs. 1991, chmn. bd. govs.), Inst. Chartered Fin. Analysts (C. Steward Sheppard award 1990). Republican. Roman Catholic. Office Phone: 402-384-8200.

**MAGINNIS, ROBERT P.**, bishop; b. Phila., Dec. 22, 1933; Student, St. Charles Borromeo Sem., Overbrook, Pa. Ordained priest Roman Cath. Ch. 1961. Titular bishop Diocese of Chimkha, 1996; auxiliary bishop Diocese of Phila., 1996—. Office: 222 N 17th St Philadelphia PA 19103

**MAGLACAS, A. MANGAY**, nursing researcher, educator; BSN, Vanderbilt U.; MPH, U. Minn.; DPH, Johns Hopkins U.; DSc (hon.), U. Ill. Former chief sci. for nursing devel. health manpower divsn. WHO, Geneva, Switzerland, 1976-89. regional nurse adviser Southeast Asia Office Delhi, India, 1972-75. Internat. health/nursing cons., 1989—; adj. prof. Coll. Nursing, U. Ill., Chgo., 1990-2000; various vis. prof. positions in several countries, 1990—. Former mem., bd. dirs. Internat. Coun. Nurses, 1989-93; fgn. assoc. NAS Inst. Medicine, 1988—. Rockefeller fellow, 1964-67; Fulbright-Smith-Mundt scholar, 1952-54; recipient Outstanding alumni award Vanderbilt U., 1986,

Internat. Pub. Health Leadership award Johns Hopkins U., 1992, Outstanding Profl. award for Nursing, Profl. Regulation Commn. of Philippines, 2000, Profl. Recognition award U. Philippines, 1989, Disting. Achievement award Philippine Nurses Assn., 1989, Outstanding Alumni award U. Philippines Sch. Nursing, 1987, Disting. Leadership award USA Commn. on Grads. of Fgn. Nursing Schs., 2002; named Woman of Yr. Am. Rsch. Inst. Bd. Internat. Rsch., 1988, named Most Outstanding Paulinian St. Paul's U., Philippines, 2002. Fellow Royal Coll. Nursing U.K. (hon.). Office: 70 Rue De La Prulay CH-1217 Meyrin Geneva Switzerland Personal E-mail: hjmaglacas@femanci.com. Business E-mail: hjm@firsteurasian.com.

**MAGLIONE, MARGARET A.,** public policy analyst, researcher; BA in Econs., Columbia U.; M in Pub. Policy, U. So. Calif. Sr. analyst UCLA Drug Abuse Rsch. Ctr., 1994—99; policy analyst RAND Corp., Santa Monica, Calif., 1999—. Mem. event com. Humane Soc. of the US, Hollywood, Calif., 2001—06; active Shambala Animal Preserve, Acton, Calif., 2002—06. Avocations: health and fitness, surfing, travel, animal welfare. Office: RAND Corp 1776 Main St Santa Monica CA 90407 Office Phone: 310-393-0411.

**MAGLOIRE, ALIX J. (MAGLOIRE),** internist; b. Port-au-Prince, Haiti, Feb. 26, 1953; arrived in U.S., 1969; s. Jean Gerard Magloire and Paulette Andrea Rigaud; m. Fanita Bryant Magloire, Dec. 31, 1986; children: Alix B. Magloire, Joshua Yves Magliore. MD, U. Mex., Villa Hermosa, 1979. Diplomate Am. Bd. Internal Medicine, lic. physician Mass., Calif. InternEl Elmhurst Hosp., Queens, NY, 1981—82; resident in internal medicine Bronx/Mt. Sinai Med. Ctr./NYU, Bronx, 1982—85; endocrinology fellow U. Calif., Davis, 1985—87; pvt. practice internal medicine; assoc. chief of medicine NCHCS VA, Oakland, Calif., 1995—. Contbr. articles to profl. jours. Vol. Drs. Without Borders; missionary Franciscan Orgn., 1996—. Recipient Jan Harschyer award, Richmond, Calif., 2002. Mem.: U. Calif.-Davis Alumni Assn., Endocrine Soc., Am. Diabetes Assn. Democrat. Avocations: painting, sculpting, prayer. Office: NCHCS Veterans Administration 2221 MLK St Oakland CA 94612

**MAGNAN, SARAH E.,** court reporter; d. Henry Joseph and Loretta Agnes Magnan; m. Tommy Bentley. AS, Champion Coll., Burlington, Vt., 1986. Court reporter State of N.H., Manchester, 1987—93, Lyon Reporting, Inc., Atlanta, 1993—. Mem.: Nat. Ct. Reporters Assn. Home: 4515 Otha Way Lilburn GA 30047 Office Phone: 770-458-5500. E-mail: slmagnan@aol.com.

**MAGNANO, SALVATORE PAUL,** retired finance company executive, treasurer; b. Portland, Conn., Jan. 10, 1934; s. Salvatore and Lucy (Dimodica) M.; m. Lois Jewel Johnson, July 16, 1955; children: Paul C., Mark J., Peter E B.Metall. Engineering., Rensselaer Poly. Inst., Troy, N.Y., 1955; MBA, Northwestern U., Chgo., 1959. Div. controller Sanders Assocs., Inc., Nashua, NH, 1962-73; v.p., controller Teledyne Mec, Palo Alto, Calif., 1973-75; div. controller Sanders Assocs., Inc., Nashua, 1975-79, grp. controller, 1979-81, grp. v.p., controller, 1981-86, v.p. fin. and treas., 1986-96; ind. fin. and adminstrv. cons., 1996—; ret. Pres. Boys and Girls Club of Greater Nashua, 1988-89, bd. dirs., 1981—, sec. bd. dirs., 2004; bd. dirs. Boys and Girls Club of Greater Nashua Charitable Found., 1991—; trustee Daniel Webster Coll., Nashua, 1993—, sec. bd. trustees, 2005, Congl. Ch. of Hollis, 2002—; founding mem. bd. dirs., treas. N.H. Prostate Cancer Coalition, 2006—. Lt. USN, 1955-57 Mem. Fin. Execs. Inst. (life mem.), Beta Gamma Sigma (award for excellence 1959), N.H. Prostate Cancer Coalition (dir., treas. 2006). E-mail: spm-ljm@charter.net.

**MAGNANTI, THOMAS L.,** management educator, engineering educator; b. Omaha, Oct. 7, 1945; s. Leo A. and Florence L. Magnanti; m. Beverly A. McVinney, June 10, 1967; 1 child, R. Randall. BS in chem. engring., Syracuse U., 1967; MS in stats., Stanford U., 1969, MS in math., 1971, PhD in ops. rsch., 1972; Doktor honoris causa, Linköping U., 1995; PhD (hon.), U. Montreal, Universite Catholique de Louvain. Asst. prof. Alfred P. Sloan Sch. Mgmt. MIT, Cambridge, Mass., 1971-75, assoc. prof., 1975-79, prof., 1979-85, George Eastman prof. of mgmt. sci., 1985—, head mgmt. sci. area, 1982-88, co-dir. Ops. Rsch. Ctr., 1986—, founding co-dir. Leaders for Mfg. Program, 1988-94, prof. dept. elec. engring. and computer sci., 1995—, founding co-dir. Sys. Design and Mgmt. Program, 1995—, founding dir. Leaders for Mfg. Program, dean Sch. Engring., 1999—; rsch. fellow; vis. prof. Ctr. for Ops. Rsch. and Econometrics Univ. Catholique de Louvain, 1976-77, 89. Vis. scientist Bell Labs., 1977, GTE Labs., 1989; vis. scholar Grad. Sch. Bus. Adminstrn., Harvard U., 1980-81; mem. corp. mfg. bd. Digital Equipment Corp., 1990; mem. editl. bd. Jour. Computational Optimization and Applications; mem. adv. bd. North Holland Handbooks in Ops. Rsch. and Mgmt. Sci.; bd. dirs. Ford Design Inst., Emptoris Inc; mem. internat. advisory bd., Linköping Univ. Author: Applied Mathematical Programming, 1977, Network Flows, 1993; editor: Jour. Ops. Rsch., 1983-87; co-editor: Math. Programming, 1981-83; assoc. editor SIAM Jour. Algebraic and Discrete Methods, 1981-83, Mgmt. Sci., 1978-81, Ops. Rsch., 1978-81, SIAM Jour. Applied Math., 1976-81, Math. Programming, 1988—; adv. editor Transp. Sci., 1985—, Mktg. Sci., Math. of Artificial Intelligence, 1987-91; contbr. numerous articles to profl. jours. Mem. NSF Sci. and Tech. Exchange Delegation to Soviet Union, 1977, NSF Rsch. Initiation Grant panels, 1985, 90; advisor NSF program on decision, risk and mgmt. sci., 1988, 89; mem. mfg. studies bd. Nat. Rsch. Coun., 1993—; mem. internat. adv. bd. Linkopeg U., Sweden; mem. pres. coun. Olin Coll.; mem. adv. bd. Harvard Bus. Sch., Stanford Sch. Engring. Recipient Gordon Billard award MIT, 1992, Irwin Sizer Award; Mgmt. Program Exch. grantee IREX, Curriculum Devel. grantee Sloan Found., 1990-94. Mem. IEEE (com. on large scale systems 1979-83), TIMS (mem. and chmn. various coms.), NAE, Am. Acad. Arts and Sciences, Ops. Rsch. Soc. Am. (pres. 1988-89, mem. and chmn. various coms., coun. mem. computer sci. tech. sect. 1983-87, co-organizer 1st doctoral consortium 1983, plenary speaker conf. on telecom. 1983, Lanchester prize 1993, Kimball medal 1994), Tau Beta Pi, Pi Mu Epsilon, Phi Kappa Phi. Achievements include research in network analysis and optimization, network design and combinatorial optimization, and applications in manufacturing, telecommunications, and transportation; development of new engineering/management programs. Home: 33 School St Hopkinton MA 01748-2003 Office: MIT Ops Rsch Ctr 77 Massachusetts Ave Cambridge MA 02139-4307

**MAGNER, JEROME ALLEN,** performing company executive; b. Bklyn., Mar. 14, 1929; s. Herman and Evelyn I. (Wolfe) M.; m. Frances Ogens, Mar. 22, 1953; children: Merrill, Steven. BBA cum laude, CCNY, 1951. Asst. to treas., chief acct. Grayson-Robinson Stores, Inc., S. Klein Dept. Stores, N.Y.C., 1951-59; contr. Food Fair Properties, N.Y.C., 1959-61; v.p., contr. Am. Leisure Corp., N.Y.C. and Providence, 1961-69; sr. v.p. fin., treas., CFO, Nat. Amusements Inc., NE Theatre Corp., Dedham, Mass., 1969—. Mem. Nat. Assn. Theatre Owners (bd. dirs.), CCNY Alumni Assn. Office: Nat Amusements Inc 200 Elm St Dedham MA 02026-4536 Business E-Mail: jmagner@nationalamusements.com.

**MAGNER, MARJORIE,** former bank executive; b. Bklyn. BS in Psychology, Brooklyn Coll., NY, 1968; MS, Purdue U., 1974; D of Mgmt. (hon.), Purdue University, 2004. Mng. dir. Chem. Tech. Divsn. Chemical Bank; from mem. staff Commercial Credit to chmn., CEO Citigroup, NYC, 1987—2003, chmn., CEO Global Consumer Group, 2003—05. Bd. dirs. Gannett Co., 2006—, The Charles Schwab Corp., 2006—, Accenture, 2006—; chmn. bd. trustees Bklyn. Coll. Found.; mem. dean's adv. coun. Krannert Sch. Mgmt. Purdue U. Bd. dirs. Welfare to Work Partnership, Dress for Success Worldwide, Port Discovery Children's Mus., Balt.; Md. Bus. Roundtable Edn. Named One of 50 Most Powerful Women in Am. Bus., Fortune mag., 2001, 2002, 2003, 2004, One of 25 Most Power Women in Banking, US Banker mag., 2003, 2004, 2005; named one of Most Powerful women, Forbes mag., 2005; recipient Am. Found. for the Blind Helen Keller Achievement award, 2001.*

**MAGNER, RACHEL HARRIS,** retired banker; b. Aug. 05; d. Garner Greer and Catherine Alice (Cloaninger) Harris; m. Fredric Michael Magner, May 14, 1972. BS in Fin., U. S.C., 1972; postgrad, UCLA, 1974, Calif. State U., 1975. Mgmt. trainee Union Bank, L.A., 1972-75, comml. loan officer, 1975-77; asst. v.p. comml. fin. Crocker Bank, L.A., 1978, v.p. comml. svcs. divsn., 1981-82, v.p., sr. account mgr. bus. banking divsn., 1982-83; v.p. and mgr. corp. banking Office of Pres. Sumitomo Bank Calif., L.A., 1983-00; ret., 2000—. Investment cons., 2000—. Home: 2200 Pine Ave Manhattan Beach CA 90266-2833

**MAGNES, HARRY ALAN,** physician; b. Orange, N.J., Dec. 3, 1948; s. Sam and Shirley (Daniels) M.; m. Patricia Bruce, Mar. 25, 1989; 1 child, Carlos Fontiveros. AB in Biology magna cum laude, Brown U., 1970; MD, Yale U., 1974; M in Med. Mgmt., Tulane U., 1998; cert. in med. mgmt., Am. Coll. Physician Execs., 1997. Diplomate Am. Bd. Internal Medicine, Am. Bd. Med. Mgmt. Intern, resident internal medicine U. Iowa Hosps. and Clinics, 1974—77; ptnr., med. dir., pres., CEO Gallatin Med. Clinic, Downey, Calif., 1997—2001; pres., CEO Gallatin Med. Corp., Downey, Calif., 1992—94; med. dir., bd. dirs. Gallatin Med. Found., Downey, Calif., 1993—2001; chief med. officer Gallatin Med. Group, 2000—01, Physician Assocs. of Greater San Gabriel Valley, Pasadena, Calif., 2001—05; CEO Lovelace Med. Group, Albuquerque, 2005—. Staff physician Downey Cmty. Hosp., 1996-99, Presbyn. Intercmty. Hosp., 1992—2001; clin. instr. Rancho Los Amigos Hosp., Downey, 1981—83; chairperson bd. dirs. Primehealth of So. Calif., 1997—99; sec.-treas. Calif. Health Network, 1998—99; project adv. bd. VA/UCLA/RAND Calif. Med. Group, IPA Governance Project, 1997—98; prin. investigator Reach Asthma Rsch. Project, 2002; bd. dirs. Calif. Health Network; bd. govs. Lovelace Clinic Found., Lovelace Med. Ctr., 2006—. Author: Rheumatic Fever in Connecticut, 1974. James Manning scholar Brown U., 1968. Mem.: Med. Group Mgmt. Assn., Am. Med. Group Assn. (policy com. 1994—98, legis. com. 1997—2000), Am. Coll. Physician Execs., Delta Omega, Sigma Xi, Phi Beta Kappa. Avocation: racquetball. Office             Phone:             505-262-3085.             Business             E-Mail: harry.magnes@lovelacesandia.com.

**MAGNESS, RHONDA ANN,** retired microbiologist; b. Stockton, Calif., Jan. 30, 1946; d. John Pershing and Dorothy Waneta (Kelley) Wetter; m. Barney LeRoy Bender, Aug. 26, 1965 (div. Jan. 1977); m. Gary D. Magness, Mar. 5, 1977; children: Jay D.(dec.), Troy D. BS, Calif. State U., Sacramento, 1977. Med. asst. C. Fred Wilcox, MD, Stockton, 1965-66; clk. typist Dept. of U.S. Army, Ft. Eustis, Va., 1967, Def. Supply Agy., New Orleans, 1967-68; med. asst. James G. Cross, MD, Lodi, Calif., 1969, Arthur A. Kemalyan, MD, Lodi, 1969-71, 72-77; med. sec. Lodi Meml. Hosp., 1972; lab. aide Calif. State U., Sacramento, 1977; phlebotomist St. Joseph's Hosp., Stockton, 1978-79; microbiologist Dameron Hosp. Assn., Stockton, 1980—2004. Active Concerned Women Am., Washington, 1987—. Mem.: San Joaquin County Med. Assts. Assn., Calif. Assn. Clin. Lab. Technologists, Nat. Audubon Soc., Nat. Geog. Soc., Jobs Daus. (chaplain 1962—63). Baptist. Avocations: birdwatching, sewing, reading. Home: 9627 Knight Ln Stockton CA 95209-1961

**MAGNUSON, JEFFERY SCOTT,** surgeon; b. Big Rapids, Mich., Feb. 22, 1966; s. Wayne Ferris and Marilyn Ruth Magnuson; m. Alicia Ann Lester, Aug. 19, 1988; children: Andrew Charles, Annette Lea. BA, U. Tex., 1988, MD, 1994. Lic. MD Ala. Asst. prof. surgery U. Ala., Birmingham, Ala., 1999—; otolaryngology head, neck surgery residency program dir, surgical oncologist U. Ala., 1999—. Contbr. articles various profl. jours. Fellow: ACS, Am. Acad. Otolaryngology Head Neck Surgery; mem.: Ala. Soc. Otolaryngology Head Neck Surgery. Avocations: gardening, camping, marathons. Office Phone: 205-934-9766. Office Fax: 205-934-3993. Business E-Mail: entdoc@uab.edu.

**MAGNUSON, KAREN M.,** editor; m. Tod Myers. City editor Sturgis (Mich.) Daily News; writer, bur. mgr. UP Internat., Ill., Iowa, Utah and Calif.; various mgmt. positions Daily News, L.A.; editor Oxnard (Calif.) Press-Courier, Calif.; mng. editor Valley Times, Pleasanton, Calif., 1994—97, Wichita (Kans.) Eagle, 1997—99, Rochester (NY) Dem. and Chronicle, 1999—2001, editor, v.p. news, 2001—. Mem.: AP Mng. Editors (vice chmn. journalism studies 2001—). Office: Rochester Dem and Chronicle 55 Exchange Blvd Rochester NY 14614-2001

**MAGNUSON, NANCY,** librarian; b. Seattle, Aug. 15, 1944; d. James Leslie and Jeanette (Thomas) M.; 2 sons, Daniel Johnson, Erik Johnson. BA in History, 1977; MLS, U. Wash., 1978. With. King County Libr. System, Seattle, 1973-80; rsch. asst. Free Libr. Phila., 1980-81; asst. libr. Haverford (Pa.) Coll., 1981-87; libr. dir. Goucher Coll., Balt., Md., 1987—. Contbr. to profl. publs. Mem. ALA (com. on status of women in librarianship, various others), Online Computer Libr. Ctr. Users Coun., Md. Libr. Assn., Congress Acad. Libr. Dirs., NOW, Women's Internat. League for Peace and Freedom, Balt. Bibliophiles, Jane Austen Soc. N.Am. Democrat. Office: Goucher Coll Julia Rogers Libr 1021 Dulaney Valley Rd Baltimore MD 21204-2753

**MAGNUSON, ROBERT G.,** former communications executive; BA in Polit. sci., U. Calif. Berkeley; M in Econ., U. Mass.; M in Journalism, Columbia U. Bus. editor L.A. Times, 1990—96, pres. Orange County Edit., 1996—97, sr. v.p., 1997—2000; pres., CEO InfoWorld Pub., San Mateo, Calif., 2000—02. Exec. bd. mem. Coll. of Letters and Sci. U. Calif. Berkeley; bd. dirs. Daily Californian Found. Bd.; corp. adv. bd. mem. Pacific Coun. on Internat. Policy. Recipient Pulitzer prize, 1993, 1995.

**MAGNUSON, ROGER JAMES,** lawyer; b. St. Paul, Jan. 25, 1945; s. Roy Gustaf and Ruth Lily (Edlund) M.; m. Elizabeth Cunningham Shaw, Sept. 11, 1982; children: James Roger, Peter Cunningham, Mary Kerstin, Sarah Ruth, Elizabeth Camilla, Anna Clara, John Edlund, Britta Kristina. BA, Stanford U., 1967; JD, Harvard U., 1971; BCL, Oxford U., 1972. Bar: Minn. 1973, U.S. Dist. Ct. Minn. 1973, U.S Ct. Appeals (8th, 9th, 10th, 11th cirs.) 1974, U.S. Supreme Ct. 1978. Chief pub. defender Hennepin County Pub. Defender's Office, Mpls., 1973; ptnr., trial group Dorsey & Whitney, Mpls., 1972—, and head, strategic litig. group. Dean Oak Brook Coll. of Law and Govt. Policy, 1995—; chancellor Magdalen Coll., 1999—. Author: Shareholder Litigation, 1981, Are Gay Rights Right, The White-Collar Crime Explosion, 1992, Informed Answers to Gay Rights Questions, 1994; Internat. Judicial Asst. in Civil Matters (1999), contbr. articles to profl. jours. Elder, Straitgate Ch., Mpls., 1980—. Fellow, Ctr. of Internat. Legal Studies, Mem. Christian Legal Soc., The Am. Soc. Writers of Legal Subjects, Mpls. Club, White Bear Yacht Club. Republican. Office: Dorsey & Whitney LLP 50 S 6th St Ste 1500 Minneapolis MN 55402-1498 Office Phone: 612-340-2738. Office Fax: 612-340-2807. Business E-Mail: magnuson.roger@dorsey.com.

**MAGOON, MAGGIE E.,** law educator, director; d. Rod A. and Carol A. (Blane) Magoon; m. Robert M. Roe, Aug. 7, 1993. BS in Psychology, Purdue U., Indpls., 1992; MA in Counseling Psychology, Ind. U., Indpls., 1993; PhD, Ind. U., Bloomington, 2002. Mental health therapist Seven Counties Svcs., Louisville, 1993—97; career counselor Right Assocs., Ft. Knox, Ky., 1997; curriculum developer Purdue U., West Lafayette, Ind., 1997—98; career counselor Ind. U., Bloomington, 1998—2001; postdoctoral fellow McGill U., Montreal, Canada, 2003—04; ct. svcs. dir./ext. educator Ohio State U., Fremont, 2005—. Author: articles in profl. jours. Recipient Group Honor award, USDA, 1999; Frieda Alice Renfro fellowship, Ind. U., 2002. Mem.: Soc. for Rsch. in Child Devel., Soc. for Rsch. in Adolescence, Nat. Assn. Ext. 4-H Agts., Ohio Ext. Agts. Assn. Office: Ohio State Univ Juvenile Ct 100 N Park Ave Ste 224 Fremont OH 43420 Office Phone: 419-334-6216. Office Fax: 419-334-6210. Business E-Mail: mmagoon@ag.osu.edu.

**MAGOR, LOUIS ROLAND,** conductor; b. Auburn, Mebr., May 16, 1945; s. John William and Eleanor Lucille (Niemann) M. B.Mus. Edn., Northwestern U., 1967, Mus.M., 1974. Choral dir. Avoca Jr. High Sch., Wilmette, Ill., 1968-70; choral dir. Niles North High Sch., Skokie, Ill., 1970-73; dir. San Francisco Symphony Chorus, 1974-82, Schola Cantorum, 1982-85, San Francisco Boys Chorus, 1985-88; artistic dir. Seattle Bach Choir, 1990—2001. Founder The Louis Magor Singers; mem. faculty San Francisco Conservatory of Music, 1976-78, San Francisco State U., 1979-80 Founder West Seattle Children's Chorus, 1990—; condr. Sing-It-Yourself Messiah, 1979-91, Calif. Symphony Chorus, 1990-92; exec. prodr. Sandy Bradley's Potluck, 1995-96; co-founder, mng. dir. Kenyon Hall, 1993—. Mem. Pi Kappa Lambda. Personal E-mail: louis@magor.com.

**MAGORIAN, JAMES,** poet, writer; b. Palisade, Nebr., Apr. 24, 1942; s. Jack and Dorothy (Gorthey) M. BS, U. Nebr., 1965; MS. Ill. State U., 1969; postgrad., Oxford U., 1972, Harvard U., 1973. Author children's books: School Daze, 1978, 17%, 1978, The Magic Pretzel, 1979, Ketchup Bottles, 1979, Imaginary Radishes, 1980, Plucked Chickens, 1980, Fimperings and Torples, 1981, The Witches' Olympics, 1983, At the City Limits, 1987, The Beautiful Music, 1988, Magic Spell #207, 1988; author numerous books of poetry, including: Ideas for a Bridal Shower, 1980, The Edge of the Forest, 1980, Spiritual Rodeo, 1980, Tap Dancing on a Tight Rope, 1981, Training at Home to Be A Locksmith, 1981, The Emily Dickinson Jogging Book, 1984, Keeper of Fire, 1984, Weighing the Sun's Light, 1985, Summer Snow, 1985, The Magician's Handbook, 1986, Squall Line, 1986, The Hideout of the Sigmund Freud Gang, 1987, Haymarket Square, 1998, Dragon Bones, 1999, Millennial Journal, 2000, Voices, 2006, (novels) America First, 1992, Hearts of Gold, 1996; contbr. poems and stories to numerous publs. Home and Office: 2626 North 49th St #402 Lincoln NE 68504

**MAGOVERN, JAMES ANTHONY,** thoracic surgeon; b. San Antonio, June 8, 1954; MD, U. Pitts., 1980. Diplomate Am. Bd. Thoracic Surgery, Am. Bd. Surgery. Intern Johns Hopkins, Balt., 1980-81, resident in surgery, 1981-82, Pa. State U. Coll. Medicine, Hershey, 1982-89; fellow in rsch. cardiothoracic surgery Milton S. Hershey Med. Ctr., 1988-87; with Allegheny Gen. Hosp., Pitts. Prof. surgery Drexel U. Sch. Med. Mem. Assn. Acad. Surgery, Am. Coll. Cardiology, Am. Coll. Surgeons, Am. Heart Assn., Soc. Thoracic Surgery, Am. Assn. Thoracic Surgery. Office: 490 E North Ave Ste 302 Pittsburgh PA 15212-4740 Business E-Mail: jmagover@wpahs.org.

**MAGOWAN, PETER ALDEN,** professional sports team executive, retail executive; b. NYC, Apr. 5, 1942; s. Robert Anderson and Doris (Merrill) Magowan; m. Jill Tarlau (dec. July 1982); children: Kimberley, Margot, Hilary; m. Deborah Johnston, Aug. 14, 1982. BA, Stanford U., 1964; MA, Oxford U., Eng., 1966; postgrad., Johns Hopkins U., 1967—68. Store mgr. Safeway Stores Inc., Washington, 1968—70, dist. mgr. Houston, 1970—71, retail ops. mgr. Phoenix, 1971—72, divsn. mgr. Tulsa, 1973—76, mgr. internat. divsn. Toronto, Ont., Canada, 1976—78, mgr. western region San Francisco, 1978—79, CEO Oakland, Calif., 1980—93, chmn. bd. dirs., 1980—98; pres., mng. gen. ptnr. San Francisco Giants, 1993—; ret. Safeway Stores Inc., 2005. Bd. dirs. Daimler Chrysler Corp, Caterpillar. Office: San Francisco Giants 24 Willie Mays Plz San Francisco CA 94107-2199 Office Phone: 415-972-1950. Business E-Mail: scasabat@sfgiants.com

**MAGRATH, C. PETER,** educational association executive; b. NYC, Apr. 23, 1933; s. Laurence Wilfrid and Giulia Maria (Dentice) M.; m. Deborah C. Howell, 1988; children: Valerie Ruth, Monette Fay. BA summa cum laude, U. N.H., 1955; PhD, Cornell U., 1962. Faculty Brown U., Providence, 1961-68, prof. polit. sci., 1967-68, assoc. dean grad. sch., 1965-66; dean Coll. Arts and Scis. U. Nebr., Lincoln, 1968-69, dean faculties Coll. Arts and Scis., 1969-72, interim chancellor, 1971-72, prof. polit. sci., 1968-72, vice-chancellor for acad. affairs, 1972; pres. SUNY, Binghamton, 1972-74, prof. polit. sci., 1972-74; pres. U. Minn., Mpls., 1974-84, U. Mo. System, 1985-91, Nat. Assn. State Univs. and Land Grant Colls., Washington, 1991—2005, sr. presdl. advisor to the Coll. Bd., 2006—. Author: The Triumph of Character, 1963, Yazoo: Law and Politics in the New Republic, The Case of Fletcher v. Peck, 1966, Constitutionalism and Politics: Conflict and Consensus, 1968, Issues and Perspectives in American Government, 1971; (with others) The American Democracy, 2d edit.; 1973; (with Robert L. Egbert) Strengthening Teacher Education, 1987; contbr. articles to profl. jours. With AUS, 1955—57. Mem. Assn. Am. Univs. (chmn. 1985-86, bd. dirs. Salzburg Sem. 2000-05), Phi Beta Kappa, Phi Kappa Phi, Pi Gamma Mu, Pi Sigma Alpha, Kappa Tau Alpha. Office: Coll Bd 1233 20th St NW Washington DC 20036-2375 Office Fax: 202-741-4743. Business E-Mail: pmagrath@collegeboard.org. *True personal success cannot be measured by public acclaim, recognition, or status. It grows out of an ability to recognize right from wrong, and to maintain principles of fairness and understanding in all human relationships - regardless of one's role in life. In my case I have tried to fulfill this ideal; I have been willing to exercise leadership by asserting my judgments and views openly and directly on the educational and human issues that came my way.*

**MAGRATH, KATHLEEN BARRY,** retired municipal official; b. Raymond, Neb., Aug. 10, 1930; d. Leo D. Barry and Eileen K. Larkin; m. Frank J. Magrath, June 6, 1953 (dec. Dec. 13, 1992); children: Maureen, Teresa, Patricia, Timothy, Cecilia, Mary Kathleen. BS in Chemistry, Mt. Marty Coll., Yankton, S.D., 1952; MPA, Nova Southeastern U., Ft. Lauderdale, Fla., 1978, D in Pub. Adminstrn., 1979. Cert. med. technologist SD, 1952. Med. technologist St. Catherine Hosp., McCook, Nebr., 1952—53; St. Joseph's Hosp., South Bend, Ind., 1953—54; adminstrv. asst. Dade County Sch. Bd., Miami, Fla., 1974—84; dir. child care ctr. Riviera Presbyn. Ch., Miami, 1980—82; mem. and vice chair Dade County Sch. Bd., Miami, 1984—86; coord. portfolio program Barry U., Miami, 1987—92, adj. prof. orgnl. comms., 1987—89. Founding mem. Greater Miami Urban League Fair Housing Group, 1966—70; mem. Dade County Cmty. Rels. Bd., Miami, 1983—90; dir. Fla. Sch. Bds. Assn., Talahassee, 1985—86; mem. Dade County Property Adjustment Bd., Miami, 1986. Contbr. book reviews to Miami Herald, 1966—68; poet:. Mem. Archdiocese of Miami Synod, 1986—89; mem. local and state bds. PTA, 1970—74; vol. Fairchild Tropical Bot. Gardens 1998—. Recipient Svc. award, Music Edn. Dade County Schs., 1985, Outstanding Svc. to Edn., Kappa Delta Pi, 1985, Recognition cert., Fla. Women's Hall of Fame, 1986, Women Helping Women cert. of Appreciation, Soroptimist Internat. of the Ams., 1991, Vol. of Yr., Homestead Mid. Sch., 2002—03. Democrat. Roman Catholic. Avocations: watercolor, drawing, volunteering, reading. Home: 7730 SW 134th St Miami FL 33156 E-mail: KBM810@aol.com.

**MAGRILL, JOE RICHARD, JR.,** religious organization administrator, minister; b. Marshall, Tex., Aug. 7, 1946; s. Joe Richard and Mary Belle (Chadwick). M. BA summa cum laude, East Tex. State U., 1967; MDiv, Princeton Theol. Sem., 1970, MTh, 1972; MLS, Rutgers U., 1971. Ordained to ministry Cumberland Presbyn. Ch., 1970. Stated supply min. Newsome (Tex.) Cumberland Presbyn. Ch., 1966-67; Christian edn. asst. United Presbyn. Ch., Carlstadt, NJ, 1967-70; order libr. Princeton (N.J.) Theol. Sem., 1969-72; head libr., prof. Memphis Theol. Sem., 1972-79; pastor Brookhaven Cumberland Presbyn. Ch., Nashville, 1987-89; asst. to stated clk. Gen. Assembly Office, Cumberland Presbyn. Ch., Memphis, 1979-83, supt. ctrl. acctg. div., 1980-87, editor The Cumberland Presbyn., 1984-87, chief exec. bd. stewardship, 1989—, mem. Gen. Assembly Coun., 1993—, chief exec. Cumberland Presbyn. Investment Loan Program, Inc., 1999—. Mem. Trinity Presbytery of Cumberland Presbyn. Ch., 1970—; sec.-treas. Hist. Found. Cumberland Presbyn. Ch., Memphis, 1974—; bd. dirs. Hist. Found. Presbyn. Ch. U.S., Montreat, N.C., 1980-83. Editor: In the Valley of the Cauca, 1981, One Family Under God, 1982, Family of Faith, 1998. Recipient achievement award Hist. Found. Cumberland Presbyn. Ch., 1980; scholar Phi Alpha Theta, 1967, Am. Theol. Libr. Assn., 1970. Democrat. Avocations: computers, historical research. Office: Cumberland Presbyn Ch 1978 Union Ave Memphis TN 38104-4134 E-mail: jrm@cumberland.org.

**MAGRILL, ROSE MARY,** library director; b. Marshall, Tex., June 8, 1939; d. Joe Richard and Mary Belle (Chadwick) M. BS, East Tex. State U., 1960, MA, 1961; MS, U. Ill., 1964, PhD, 1969. Asst. to dean women E. Tex. State U., Commerce, 1960-61, librarian II, 1961-63; teaching asst. U. Ill., Urbana, 1963-64; instr. to asst. prof. E. Tex. State U., Commerce, 1964-67; asst. prof. Ball State U., Muncie, 1969-70; asst. prof. U. Mich., Ann Arbor, 1970-81; prof. U. N. Tex., Denton, 1981-99; dir. libr. E. Tex. Bapt. U.,

Marshall, 1987-2001. Accreditation site visitor ALA, Chgo., 1975—; cons. in field. Co-author: Building Library Collections, 4th edit. 1974, Library Technical Services, 1977, Building Library Collections, 5th edit. 1979, Acquisition Management and Collection Development in Libraries, 2d edit. 1989; author: Family of Faith, 1998. Trustee Memphis Theol. Sem., 1988-98; treas. Mission Synod of Cumberland Presbyn. Ch., 1989—; mem. bd. fin. Trinity Presbytery, 1989—98; sec.-treas. Harrison County Hist. Commn., 1995—; trustee Hist. Found., 1999—; sec. Nat. Conv. Cumberland Presbyn. Women, 2000-02, chmn. bd., 2003—05, sec., 2005—. Recipient award Cumberland Presbyn. History, 1995. Mem. ALA (RTSD Resources Sect. pub. award 1978), Tex. Libr. Assn., Presbyn. Hist. Soc. of S.W. (bd. dirs. 2000—, sec. 2005—), Marshall (Tex.) Regional Med. Ctr. Aux. (treas. 2004—). Home: 203 Pitts ave Marshall TX 75672-4719

**MAGRO, CYNTHIA MARIA,** pathologist; BS, U. Man., MD, 1985. Medical diplomate, diplomate Am. Bd. Cytopathology, Am. Bd. Dermatopathology, Am. Bd. Anatomic Pathology. Intern Harvard Med. Sch., Boston, 1985—87, resident, 1987—89, fellow, 1989—91; asst. prof. U. Winnipeg, 1991—93; asst. clin. prof. pathology Harvard Med. Sch., Boston, 1995—98; assoc. clin. prof. dermatology U. Hosps., Case Western Res. U., Cleve., 1998—99; assoc. prof. pathology Thomas Jefferson U., Phila., 1999—2000; prof. Ohio State U., Columbus, 2000—, dir. dermatopathology, 2000—. Author: (textbook) The Melanocytic Proliferations: A Comprehensive Textbook of Pigmented Lesions (Am. Assn. Pubs. award for Excellence, 2001); contr. 133 publs. in field. Mem.: Am. Soc. Dermatopathology (chair elect. com. 2000—02). Achievements include research in neelanocyclic, lymphoproliferative and inflammatory disorders of the skin and malignant disorders of skin; inflammatory lung disease; interstitrol lung disease and lung transplantation. Office: Cornell U/Cornell Med Coll Joan and Sanford I Weill Divsn of Pathology Rm F-309 New York NY 10021 Business E-Mail: magro-1@medctr.osu.edu.

**MAGRUDER, JACK,** retired academic administrator; m. Sue Brimer; children: Julie Magruder Lochbaum, Kerry, Laura Magruder Mann. BS in Chemistry and Math., Truman State U., 1957; postgrad., La. State U., 1959; MA in Chemistry and Sci. Edn., U. No. Iowa, 1960; EdD in Chemistry and Sci. Edn., U. No. Colo., 1966; grad., Harvard U. Inst. Ednl. Mgmt., 1992. Asst. prof. chemistry Truman State U., Kirksville, Mo., 1966—87, head divsn. sci., 1986—89, acting dean instrn., 1989—91, v.p. acad. affairs, 1991—94, pres., 1993—2003; ret., 2003. Cons.-evaluator Higher Learning Commn. North Ctrl. Assn. Colls. and Schs.; chmn. com. on transfer and articulation Mo. Coord. Bd. for Higher Edn.; past pres. Coun. of Pub. Liberal Arts Colls., Coun. Pub. Higher Edn. for Mo. Mem.: Sci. Tchrs. Mo., Am. Chem. Soc., Sigma Beta Delta, Phi Kappa Phi, Phi Delta Kappa, Beta Gamma Sigma, Phi Beta Kappa. E-mail: wjm@truman.edu.

**MAGUAD, BEN ABRICO,** management educator; arrived in US, 2000; s. Camilo Jalipa and Ascencion Abrico Maguad; m. Narinee Petchploysri, Dec. 8, 1985; children: Melanie, Maverick. Diploma cum laude, U. Santo Tomas, Manila, 1980; PhD in Bus. and Mgmt., U. South Australia, Adelaide, 1998. Clk. Bank of Philippine Islands, Makati, 1980—81; secondary tchr. Adventist English Sch., Bangkok, 1983—88; prof. Hong Kong Adventist Coll., Kowloon, 1988—98, Caribbean Union Coll., Maracas, Trinidad and Tobago, 1998—2000, Andrews U., Berrien Springs, Mich., 2000—. Contbr. articles to profl. jours. Deacon to head deacon Bangkok Adventist Hosp. Ch., 1981—83; deacon Adventist English Ch., Bangkok, 1983—88, Pioneer Meml. Ch., Berrien Springs, Mich., 2001—; elder to head elder Bayview Ch. of Seventh-day Adventists, Hong Kong, 1988—98. Scholar, Rockefeller Found., 1981—83; Rector's grant, U. Santo Tomas, 1976—80. Mem.: Am. Soc. Quality, South East Asia Club (co-sponsor 2001—). Seventh-Day Adventist. Office: Andrews Univ 100 Old US 31 Berrien Springs MI 49104-0022 Office Phone: 269-471-3103.

**MAGUIRE, CHARLOTTE EDWARDS,** retired pediatrician; b. Richmond, Ind., Sept. 1, 1918; d. Joel Blaine and Lydia (Betscher) Edwards; m. Raymer Francis Maguire, Sept. 1, 1948 (dec.); children: Barbara, Thomas Clair II (dec.). Student, Stetson U., 1936—38, U. Wichita, 1938—39; BS, Memphis Tchrs. Coll., 1940; MD, U. Ark., 1944; LHD (hon.), Fla. State U., 2002. Intern, resident Orange Meml. Hosp., Orlando, Fla., 1944—46, med. staff., 1944—69, instr. nurses, 1947—57; resident Bellevue Hosp. and Med. Ctr., NYU, NYC, 1954—55; staff mem. Fla. Santarium and Hosp., Orlando, 1946—56, Holiday House and Hosp., Orlando, 1950—62; mem. courtesy and cons. staff West Orange Meml. Hosp., Winter Garden, Fla., 1952—67; active staff, chief dept. pediat. Mercy Hosp., Orlando, 1965—68; med. dir. childrens med. svcs., asst. sec. Fla. Dept. Health and Rehab. Svcs., 1969—71, med. dir. med. svcs. and basic care, 1975—84; med. exec. dir., med. svcs. divsn. worker's compensation Fla. Dept. Labor, Tallahassee, 1984—87; chief of staff physicians and dentists Ctrl. Fla. divsn. Children's Home Soc. Fla., 1947—56; dir. Orlando Child Health Clinic, 1949—58; pvt. practice Orlando 1946—68; asst. regional dir. HEW, 1970—72; ret., 1987. Asst. dir. health and sci. affairs Dept. Health Edn. & Welfare, Atlanta, 1971-72 Washington, 1972-75; pediat. cons. Fla. Crippled Children's Commn., 1952-70, dir., 1968-70; med. dir. Office Med. Svcs. and Basic Care, sr. physician Office of Asst. Sec. Ops., Fla. Dept. Health and Rehab. Svcs.; clin. prof. dept. pediat. U. Fla. Coll. Medicine, Gainesville, 1980-87; mem. Fla. Drug Utilization Rev., 1983-87; real estate salesperson Investors Realty, 1982-2003; bd. dirs. Stavros Econ. Ctr. Fla. State U., Tallahassee; pres.'s coun. Fla. State U., U. Fla., Gainesville; Charlotte Edwards Maguire eminent scholar chair and scholarships for qualified students, 1999. Mem. profl. adv. com. Fla. Ctr. for Clin. Svcs. at U. Fla., 1952-60; del. to Mid-century White House Conf. on Children and Youth, 1950; U.S. del. from Nat. Soc. for Crippled Children to World Congress for Welfare of Cripples Inc., London, 1957; pres. of corp., Eccleston-Callahan Hosp. for Colored Crippled Children, 1956-58; sec. Fla. chpt. Nat. Doctor's Com. for Improved Med. Svcs., 1951-52; med. adv. com. Gateway Sch. for Mentally Retarded, 1959-62; bd. dirs. Forest Park Sch. for Spl. Edn. Crippled Children, 1949-54, mem. med. adv. com., 1955-68, chmn., 1957-68; mem. Fla. Adv. Coun. for Mentally Retarded, 1965-70; dir. ctrl. Fla. poison control Orange Meml. Hosp.; mem. orgn. com., chmn. com. for admissions and selection policies Camp Challenge; participant 12th session Fed. Exec. Inst., 1971; del. White House Conf. on Aging, 1980; dir. Stavros Econ. Ctr. Fla. State U.; trustee Fla. State U. Found., 1998—, mem. campaign com. Charlotte Edwards Maguire Eminent Scholarship named in her honor Fla. State U., Charlotte Edwards Maguire MLS Med. Libr., Fla. State U. Coll. Medicine named in her honor, 2005; named Outstanding Woman in Our Cmty. AAUW, Tallahassee, 2002; recipient David M. Solomon Disting. Pub. Svc. award Am. Geriatric Soc., 2005, Torch award Fla. State U., 2005. Mem. AMA (life), Nat. Rehab. Assn., Am. Congress Phys. Medicine and Rehab., Fla. Soc. Crippled Children and Adults, Ctrl. Fla. Soc. Crippled Children and Adults (dir. 1949-58, pres. 1956-57), Am. Assn. Cleft Palate, Fla. Soc. Crippled Children (trustee 1951-57, v.p. 1956-57, profl. adv. com. 1957-68), Mental Health Assn. Orange County (charter mem.; pres. 1949-50, dir. 1947-52, chmn. exec. com. 1950-52, dir. 1963-65), Fla. Orange County Heart Assn., Am. Med. Women's Assn., Am. Acad. Med. Dirs., Fla. Med. Assn. (life, chmn. com. on mental retardation), Orange County Med. Assn., Orange Med. Soc. (life), Fla. Pediat. Soc. (pres. 1952-53), Fla. Cleft Palate Assn. (counselor-at-large, sec.), Nat. Inst. Geneal. Rsch., Nat. Geneal. Soc., Assn. Profl. Genealogists, Tallahassee Geneal. Soc., Fla. State U. Econ. Club (bd. dirs. Stavoris Ctr. for Econ. Edn.), Capital City Tiger Bay Club, Fla. Econs. Club, Francis Eppes Soc. Fla. State U., Econ. Club Fla., Governors Club. Home: 4158 Covenant Ln Tallahassee FL 32308-5765

**MAGUIRE, GREGORY,** writer; life ptnr. Andy Newman; children: Luke, Alex, Helen. PhD in English and Am. Lit., Tufts U., 1990. Fellow Bread Loaf Writers Conf., Middlebury, Vt., 1978; prof., assoc. dir. Ctr. for the Study of Children's Lit., Simmons Coll., 1979—86; co-dir., founding bd. mem. Children's Lit. New England, Inc., 1986—; artist-in-residence Isabella Stewart Gardner Mus., Boston, 1994; fellow Blue Mountain Ctr., NY, The Hambridge Ctr., Ga., 1998, The Va. Ctr. for the Creative Arts, 1999. Author: (novels) Wicked: The Life and Times of the Wicked Witch of the West, 1995 (devel. into long-running Broadway musical, Tony

award-winning Broadway play, 2003), Confessions of an Ugly Stepsister, 1999 (made into ABC/Disney movie, 2002), Mirror Mirror, 2003, Son of a Witch, 2005, (children's novels) The Dream Stealer, 1983 (named one of the Children's Books of the Yr., Child Study Children's Books Com., 1983, named a Nat. Coun. Tchrs. of English Tchr.'s Choice, 1984), Missing Sisters, 1994 (named a Parents Choice Hon. book, 1994), The Good Liar, 1996, Lost, 2001, The Hamlet Chronicles, Seven Spiders Spinning (named an ALA Notable book, 1994, Judy Lopez Meml. Award Hon. book, 1995), Six Haunted Hairdos, Five Alien Elves, Four Stupid Cupids, Three Rotten Eggs, A Couple of April Fools, Leaping Beauty: And Other Animal Fairy Tales, 2004; contbr. articles to profl. mags. including the Boston Rev., Christian Sci. Monitor, The Horn Book Mag., others. Office: William Reiss - Literary Agt John Hawkins and Assocs 71 W 23rd St Ste 1600 New York NY 10010 Address: Jennifer Suitor - Publicist HarperCollins 10 E 53rd St New York NY 10022*

**MAGUIRE, JAMES HARVEY,** physician; b. Easton, Pa., Nov. 25, 1948; s. James I. and Elizabeth C. (Updegrove) Maguire. AB, Princeton U., 1970; MD, Harvard U., 1974, MPH, 1978. Cert. internal med, infectious disease. Rsch. assoc. Harvard Sch. Pub. Health, Boston, 1978-81; instr. in medicine Harvard Med. Sch. Pub. Health, 1982-85; asst. prof. Medicine Tropical Pub. Health, Boston, 1985-92, assoc. prof. medicine, 1992-2001; physician, clin. dir. infectious disease Brigham Womens Hosp., Boston, 1992-2001; chief parasitic disease br. Ctrs. for Disease Control & Prevention, Atlanta, 2001—05; prof., dir. internat. health divsn. U. Md. Sch. Medicine, Balt., 2005—. Editor: Parasitic Diseases, 1993; sect. editor: Am. Jour. Tropical Medicine and Hygiene, 2002—. Mem.: Infectious Disease Soc. Am., Am. Soc. Tropical Medicine and Hygiene (councillor 2000—04, Ben Kean medal 2001). Avocation: tennis. Business E-Mail: jmaguire@epi.umaryland.edu.

**MAGUIRE, JOHN DAVID,** academic administrator, educator, writer; b. Montgomery, Ala., Aug. 7, 1932; s. John Henry and Clyde (Merrill) M.; m. Lillian Louise Parrish, Aug. 29, 1953; children: Catherine Merrill, Mary Elizabeth, Anne King. AB magna cum laude, Washington and Lee U., 1953, Litt.D. (hon.), 1979; Fulbright scholar, Edinburgh U., Scotland, 1953-54; B.D. summa cum laude, Yale, 1956, PhD, 1960; postdoctoral research, Yale U. and U. Tübingen, Germany, 1964-65; U. Calif., Berkeley, 1968-69, Silliman U., Philippines, 1976-77; HLD (hon.), Transylvania U., 1990. Dir. Internat. Student Ctr., New Haven, 1956-58; mem. faculty Wesleyan U. Middletown, Conn., 1960-70, asso. provost, 1967-68; vis. lectr. Pacific Sch. Religion and Grad. Theol. Union, Berkeley, 1968-69; pres. (charter) Keck Grad. Inst. Applied Life Scis., 1997-98, (hon) Claremont Grad. U., 1998-, Union Theological Seminary, 2003-; dir. nat. project Renewing Democracy through Interracial/Multicultural Comty. Bldg., 1998—; mem. adv. coun. Pacific Oaks Coll., Ga. State U., 1999-, The Advancement Project; sr. adv. Claremont Mus. Art; nat. co-dir. Inst Democratic Renewal/Project Change's joint antiracism venture, 2002-. Author: The Dance of the Pilgrim: A Christian Style of Life for Today, 1967; also numerous articles. Mem. Coun. adv. comt. US Comn. Civil Rights, 1961—70; participant White House Coun. on Civil Rights, 1966; advisor Martin Luther King Cent. Social Change, Atlanta, 1968—; permanent trustee, 1968—; 1st chmn. bd. dirs., 1968—; bd. dirs. Nassau County Health and Welfare Coun., 1971—81, pres., 1974—76; trustee United Bd. Christian Higher Ed in Asia, 1975—81, Inst. Int. Ed. 1980—86; charter trustee Tomas Rivera Policy Inst., Claremont, Calif., 1984—, vice chmn., 1987—94, treas., 1995—; with Asn. Ind. Calif. Cols. and Univs., 1985—98, chmn., 1990—92, mem. exec. com., 1992—98; with Calif. Achievement Coun., 1985—94, chmn., 1990—94; with Transylvania Univ. Bingham Trust, 1987—, Lincoln Found. and Lincoln Inst. Land Policy, Inc., 1987—94; The JL Found., 1988—; with Educ. Found. African Ams., 1991—99; bd. dirs. Asn. Am. Cols. and Univs., 1981—86, chmn., 1984—85; bd. dirs. Legal Def. and Edu. Fund NAACP, 1991—, west coast div., 1981—91, Thacher Sch., Ojai, Calif., 1982—94, vice chmn., 1986—90; with Salzburg Seminar, 1992—96; charter mem. Pacific Coun. Int. Policy, 1995—; mem. Am. Comt. US-Soviet Rels., 1981—92, Blue Ribbon Calif. Comn. Teaching Profession, 1984—86; mem. gov. coun. Aspen Inst. Wye Faculty Seminar, 1984—94; mem. Coun. Fgn. Rels., 1983—; mem. adv. bd. RAND Cent. Research Immigration Policy, 1994—97, Peter F. Drucker Found. Non-Profit Mgt, 1990—, Andrew Young Sch. Policy Ga. State Univ., 1999—, The Eureka Communities, 1998—; mem. Pres.'s Adv. Coun. Comn. on Calif. Master Plan Higher Educ., 1986—87, Los Angeles Educ. Alliance Restructuring Now, 1992—98, Calif. Bus. Higher Educ. Forum, 1992—98; leader Idyllwild Sch. Summer Poetry Festival, 1998—. Recipient Julia A. Archibald High Scholarship award Yale Div. Sch., 1956; Day fellow Yale Grad. Sch., 1956-57; Kent fellow, 1957-60; Howard Found. postdoctoral fellow Brown U. Grad. Sch., 1964-65; Fenn lectr., 7 Asian countries, 1976-77; recipient Conn. Prince Hall Masons' award outstanding contbns. human rights in Conn., 1965; E. Harris Harbison St. Tchr. prize Danforth Found., 1968 Fellow Soc. Values Higher Edn. (pres. 1974-81, bd. dirs. 1972-88); mem. Phi Beta Kappa, Omicron Delta Kappa Democrat. Office: Claremont Grad U Inst for Dem Renewal 170 E 10th St Claremont CA 91711-5909 Office Phone: 909-607-9220. Business E-Mail: john.maguire@cgu.edu.

**MAGUIRE, MARGARET LOUISE,** lawyer; b. Bklyn., Oct. 31, 1944; d. William L. and Elizabeth L. (Steinbugler) M.; 1 child, William Egginton. BA, Marymount Coll., 1965; MA, Colgate U., 1969; JD, U. Louisville, 1977. Bar: Ky. 1977, D.C. 1987. Counsel 1st Ky. Nat. Corp., Louisville, 1977-79; atty. Fed. Res. Bd., Washington, 1979-80; dep. to chmn. FDIC, Washington, 1980-86; atty., cons. The Secura Group, Washington, 1986—. Co-author: Bank Holding Companies: A Practical Guide to Bank Acquisitions and Mergers, 1970-79. Office: The Secura Group Ste 950 1921 Gallows Rd Vienna VA 22182

**MAGUIRE, MARTIE (MARTHA ELENOR ERWIN MAGUIRE),** musician; b. York, Pa., Oct. 12, 1969; d. Paul and Barbara Erwin; m. Ted Seidel, 1995 (div.); m. Gareth MaGuire, Aug. 10, 2001. Student, So. Meth. U. Performer Blue Night Express, 1984—89; fiddle player, violinist, vocalist Dixie Chicks, 1989—. Musician: (albums) Thank Heavens for Dale Evans, 1990, LIttle Ol' Cowgirl, 1992, Shouldn't a Told You That, 1993, Wide Open Spaces, 1998 (Album of Yr., Acad. Country Music, 1998, Best Country Album, Grammy Awards, 1998, Best Country Artist Clip of Yr., Billboard Awards, 1998, Maximum Vision Clif of Yr., Billboard Awards, 1998, Best Selling Album, Can. Country Music Award, 1999, Song of Yr. (Country), WB Radio Music Awards, 1999, Album of Yr., Acad. Country Music, 1999), Fly, 1999 (Best Country Album, Grammy Awards, 1999, Best Selling Album, Can. Country Music Awards, 2000, Internat. Album, British Country Music Awards, 2000, Country Album of Yr., Billboard Awards, 2000, Album of Yr., Acad. Country Music, 2000, Album of Yr., CMA, 2000), Home, 2002 (Favorite Country Album, Am. Music Awards, 2002, Best Recording Package, Grammy Awards, 2002, Best Country Album, Grammy Awards, 2002), Top of the World Tour: Live, 2003 (Grammy award for Best Country Group Vocal Performance, 2005), Taking the Long Way, 2006. Named Top New Country Artist, Billboard, 1999, Most Significant New Country Act, Country Monitor, 1998, Group of Yr., CMA, 1998, Top Vocal Group, Acad. Country Music, 1998, Internat. Rising Star, British Country Music Awards, 1999, Country Artist of Yr., Rolling Stone, 1999, Artist of Yr. (Country), WB Radio Music Awards, 1999, Favorite New Country (Country), AMA, 1999, Vocal Group of Yr., CMA, 1999, Country Artist of Yr., Billboard, 1999, 2000, Vocal Group of Yr., CMA, 2000, Entertainer of Yr., 2000, ACM, 2000, 2001, Vocal Group of Yr., 2001, Favorite Musical Group or Band, People's Choice Awards, 2001, Favorite Country Band, Am. Music Award, 2002, Vocal Group of Yr., Country Music Assn. Award, 2002, Country Duo/Group of Yr., Billboard, 2002; named one of 100 Most Influential People, Time Mag., 2006; recipient Horizon award, CMA, 1998, others. Office: Monument Sony Nashville 34 Music Sq East Nashville TN 37203*

**MAGUIRE, MILDRED MAY,** chemistry professor, researcher; b. Leetsdale, Pa., May 7, 1933; d. John and Mildred (Sklarsky) Magura. BS in Chemistry, Carnegie-Mellon U., 1955; MS in Phys. Chemistry, U. Wis., 1960;

PhD in Phys. Chemistry, Pa. State U., 1967. Devel. chemist Koppers Co., Monaca, Pa., 1955-58; rsch. chemist Am. Cyanamid Co., Stamford, Conn., 1960-63; asst. prof. chemistry Waynesburg (Pa.) Coll., 1967-70, assoc. prof., 1970-74, prof., 1974—. Leverhulme vis. prof. U. Leicester, Eng., 1980-81, 1989; cons. Pitts. Energy Tech. Ctr., summers 1978-80; faculty rsch. participant Oak Ridge Assoc. Univs., 1978-80, 82-85; U.S. del. Internat. Conf. Phys. Chemists, China, 1996, Sci. and Tech. Conf., India, 1997; vis. prof. chemistry U. Wis., Madison, 2004. Contbr. articles to sci. jours., chpt. to book. Sec. Waynesburg Women's Club, 1981-82; citizen amb. People to People Program, 1996, 97. Recipient Woman of the Yr. award AAUW, Waynesburg, 1983; Cottrell grantee Rsch. Corp. N.Y., 1970-71; Leverhulme vis. fellow U.K., 1980-81; Curie Internat. fellow AAUW, U.K., 1980-81; Robert West Superconductor Rsch. Grantee, Univ., 2001-05. Mem. AAUP, AAAS, Am. Chem. Soc.; Spectroscopy Soc. of Pitts.; Pitts. Soc. of Analytical Chemists. Avocations: gardening, painting, swimming, classical music, reading. Home: 1550 Crescent Hill Rd Waynesburg PA 15370-1654 Office: Waynesburg Coll College St Waynesburg PA 15370 Office Phone: 724-852-3265. Business E-Mail: mmaguire@waynesburg.edu.

**MAGUIRE, ROBERT FRANCIS, III,** real estate investor; b. Portland, Oreg., Apr. 18, 1935; s. Robert Francis Jr. and Jean (Shepard) M. BA, UCLA, 1960. Vice pres. Security Pacific Nat. Bank, L.A., 1960-64; chmn. Maguire Ptnrs., L.A., 1964—. Exec. bd. med. scis. UCLA. Bd. dirs. Los Angeles County Mus. Art; trustee UCLA Found., Bard Coll.; bd. dirs. St. John's Hosp., Music Ctr. Bd. Govs., Calif. Presidential Citation of Excellence, Am. Inst. Achitects; Real Estate Exec. Yr., NACORE. Mem.: California (Los Angeles); Valley (Montecito, Calif.), L.A. Country. E-mail: robert.maguire@maguirepartners.com.*

**MAGUIRE, TOBEY (TOBIAS VINCENT MAGUIRE),** actor; b. Santa Monica, Calif., June 27, 1975; s. Vincent and Wendy Maguire. Actor: (films) The Wizard, 1989, This Boy's Life, 1993, Healer, 1994, SFW, 1994, Revenge of the Red Baron, 1994, Joyride, 1996, The Ice Storm, 1997, Deconstructing Harry, 1997, Pleasantville, 1998 (Saturn Award for best performance by a younger actor, 1999), Fear and Loathing in Las Vegas, 1998, Ride with the Devil, 1999, The Cider House Rules, 1999, Wonder Boys, 2000 (Toronto Film Critics Assn. Award for best male supporting performance, 2000), Don's Plum, 2001, Spider-Man, 2002, Spider-Man 2, 2004; voice (films) Cats & Dogs, 2001; actor: (TV films) Tales from the Whoop: Hot Rod Brown Class Clown, 1990, Spoils of War, 1994, A Child's Cry for Help, 1994, Seduced by Madness: The Diane Borchardt Story, 1996, (short film) Duke of Groove, 1996 (Oscar nomination for best short film, 1996); (TV series) Great Scott!, 1992; actor, exec. prodr.: (films) Seabiscuit, 2003; (TV films) Rock of Ages, 2003; prodr.: (films) 25th Hour, 2002, Whatever We Do, 2003; guest appearences on: Blossom, 1991, Roseanne, 1991, Eerie, Indiana, 1991, Wild & Crazy Kids, 1992, Walker, Texas Ranger, 1994, Tracey Takes On, 1996. Office: c/o SFM 1122 S Robertson Blvd Los Angeles CA 90035 also: c/o Creative Artists Agency 9830 Wilshire Blvd Beverly Hills CA 90212-1825

**MAGURNO, RICHARD PETER,** lawyer; b. Suffern, N.Y., June 29, 1943; s. Eugene and Rose (Foresta) M. BS, Georgetown U., 1964; MS, U. Wis., 1965; JD, Fordham U., 1968. Bar: N.Y. 1970, Fla. 1982, U.S. Supreme Ct. 1974, U.S. Ct. Appeals (2d, 5th, 11th cirs.) 1976, U.S. Dist. Ct. (so. and ea. dists.) N.Y. 1979. Atty. Eastern Air Lines, N.Y.C., 1970-73, sr. atty., 1973-76, gen. atty., 1976-79, dir. legal Miami, Fla., 1980, v.p. legal, asst. sec., 1980-84, gen. counsel, sr. v.p. legal, sec., 1984-88; ptnr. Lord Day & Lord, Barrett Smith, 1989-94; gen. counsel, sr. v.p. legal Trans World Airlines, St. Louis, 1994-98; aviation cons., 1998-2000; gen. counsel, sr. v.p., sec. AirTran Airways, 2000—. Author: Romantic Suffern, 1773-1973, 1973. Served in Peace Corps, 1968-69. Mem. ABA, Fla. Bar Assn. Democrat. Roman Catholic.

**MAGWOOD, WILLIAM D.,** federal agency administrator; BS in Physics, Carnegie-Mellon U., BA in English; MFA, U. Pitts. Scientist Westinghouse Electric Corp., Pitts., 1984—94; with Edison Electric Inst., Washington, 1984—94; exec. sec. highly enriched uranium oversight com. Office Nuc. Energy, Sci. and Tech., Washington, assoc. dir. tech. and program planning, 1994—95, acting dir., 1996—98, dir., 1998—. Office: US Dept Energy NE-10 Office Nuc Energy Sci and Tech 1000 Independence Ave SW Washington DC 20585-1290

**MAGYAR, KIM S.,** lawyer; d. Louis George and Rita Kay Smarzinski; m. William R Magyar, Sept. 18, 1999. BS, U. Wis., 1996; JD, Marquette U., 1999. Bar: Wis. 1999, U.S. Dist. Ct. (ea. dist.) Wis. 1999, U.S. Dist. Ct. (we. dist.) Wis. 2000, Ariz. 2002, U.S. Dist. Ct. Ariz. 2002, U.S. Dist. Ct. (so. dist.) Tex. 2004, U.S. Ct. Appeals (9th cir.) 2005. Intern Wis. Supreme Ct., Justice Ann Walsh Bradley, Madison, 1999—99; asst. county counsel Kenosha County, Kenosha, Wis., 1999—2001; assoc. atty. Peterson, Johnson & Murray, SC, Milw., 2001—02; assoc. Snell & Wilmer, LLP, Phoenix, 2003—, Vice-chmn. Valley Youth Theatre, 2005—, bd. dirs. Phoenix, 2004—. Mem.: DRI (assoc.; vice-chair young lawyers' pub. svc. subcom. 2003—04, chair young lawyers' pub. svc. subcom. 2004—05, vice liaison product liability com. 2004—05, liaison product liability 2005—06). Office: Snell & Wilmer LLP One Arizona Center Phoenix AZ 85004-2202 Office Phone: 602-382-6266. Office Fax: 602-382-6070. Business E-Mail: kmagyar@swlaw.com.

**MAH, SILVIA ARMITANO,** director, educator; b. Caracas, Venezuela, Nov. 21, 1973; d. Ernesto Amadei and Shirley McDaniel Armitano; m. Edward Anthony Mah, June 27, 1998; children: Alexio Nicolas, Matteo Andreas, Sofia Alegria. PhD, U. Calif. San Diego, La Jolla, 2004. Rsch. technician Abilene Christian U. Tex. field tchg. asst. marine biology, 1996; tchg. asst. invertebrate zoology and cell biology Pepperdine U., Malibu, Calif., 1993—95, lab coord., 1996; field technician Smithsonian Instn., Washington, 1995; expdn. organizer Royal Ont. Mus., Ontario, Canada, 1997; grad. rsch. asst. U. Calif. San Diego, La Jolla, 1997—2004, head tchg. asst. structural biochemistry, 2003, teams in enging. svc. program dir., 2005—; terraclima outreach program coord. Scripps Instn. Oceanography, La Jolla, 2004—05; sci. cons. Encinitas Sch. Dist. - Mission Estancia Elem. Sch., Calif., 2004—05. Founding mem. Scripps Women in Sci. and Scripps Cmty. Outreach Program for Edn.ope) Scripps Instn. Oceanography, U. Calif. San Diego, La Jolla, 2000—02, career mentor, 2001—02; rsch. mentor U. Calif. San Diego, La Jolla, 2001—04, coord./instr. for sci. outreach, 2002—03; sci. fair judge Greater San Diego Sci. and Engring. Fair, 2004. Membersip chair Am. Women in Sci., San Diego, 2005. Recipient TA Excellence in Tchg. award, Divsn. Biol. Scis., U. Calif. San Diego, 2003, Outstanding Sr. Rschr. award, Pepperdine U., 2005; fellow Travel award, Am. Soc. for Cell Biology Minorities Affairs Com., 2001—02; scholar, U. ND Alumni Found., 1996; Summer Undergraduate Rsch. in Biology Summer fellow, Pepperdine U., 1994, Advanced Tng. in Molecular Marine Biology fellow, Office Naval Rsch., 1995, Minority Grad. Rsch. fellow, NSF, 1997—2001, Shirley Boyd Meml. Fund fellow, Scripps Instn. Oceanography, U. Calif. San Diego, 2001. Mem.: Golden Key. Office: University of California San Diego 9500 Gilman Dr La Jolla CA 92093-0403 Office Phone: 858-822-4164. Personal E-Mail: samah@ucsd.edu. Business E-Mail: samah@ucsd.edu.

**MAHADEVA, MANORANJAN,** financial executive, accountant; b. Colombo, Sri Lanka, Feb. 12, 1955; came to U.S., 1977; s. Kandiah and Rupavathy (Ponniah) M.; m. Donna Sue Martin, May 12, 1986; 1 child, Danielle. BBA, U. Tex., 1981; MBA, Tex. A&M U., 1985. Notary pub., Tex.; lic. real estate broker, Tex.; CPA, Tex.; cert. mgmt. acct. and fin. mgr. Inst. Mgmt. Accts., fraud examiner, cash mgr., internal auditor, 2003, forensic acct., profl. Acad. Healthcare Mgmt., 2006, forensic acct., 2003; accredited in bus. valuation AICPA. Asst. contr. Presbyn. Village North, Dallas, 1981-84; CFO Dallas Meml. Hosp., 1984-86; exec. dir. Associated Orthopedics & Sports Medicine, Plano, Tex., 1986-95; CFO Access Med. Supply Inc., Plano, 1988-95; mng. dir. YNM Corp., Plano, 1987-95; practice administr. Tex. Orthopaedic Assocs., Dallas, 1995-96; dir. project mgmt. Physician Reliance Network, Dallas, 1996-99; dir. valuations, bus. devel. US Oncology, Houston, 1999—2001, dirp. fin. planning 2001—03, dir. regional fin. 2003—. Chief fin. officer Access Med. Supply, Inc., 1988-96. Mem. editl. rev. bd. Jour.

Accountancy and Strategic Fin., mem. editl. rev. bd., column editor Today's CPA; mem. editl. rev. bd.: Fin. Analyst Jour. Mem. Leadership Plano Class 8, 1990-91, bd. dirs., mem. exec. bd., 1991-97, chmn. exec. bd., 1992-93; mem. Mental Health Assn. Collin County, Tex. State Bd. of Physical Therapy Examiners; bd. dirs. Nat. Assn. Cmty. Leadership, vice chair, 1995-97, chair-elect, 1997-98, chair, 1998-99; bd. dirs. Am. Heart Assn., Inst. Mgmt. Accts., 2002—, Then, 2004; bd. dirs. Internat. Students Assn.; Crisis Ctr. of Collin County; chmn. emergency svcs. Coalition of Collin County; steering com. Leadership USA, 1996-97. Recipient Nat. Disting. Leadership award, 1994; Presdl. scholar Wayne (Nebr.) State U., 1977-78; Mano Mahadeva Day proclaimed in his honor Mayor of Plano, 1999. Mem. CFA Inst., Nat. Assn. Accts. (bd. dirs. North Dallas chpt. 1985-86), Am. Hosp. Assn., Internat. Students Assn., Am. Arbitration Assn. (mem. panel of neutrals), Houston Soc. Fin. Analysts, Plano C. of C. (chmn. cmty. edn. com.), Leadership Plano Alumni Assn. (bd. dirs.), Toastmasters, Lions (past pres. Plano, Lion of Yr. award 1993), Rotary (sec., program chmn., pres. Plano 1996-97, Rotarian of Yr. award 1995, Paul Harris fellow 1998), Delta Sigma Pi, Beta Gamma Sigma. Avocations: reading, tennis, playing drums, jogging, cooking. Home: 23 Indian Summer Pl Spring TX 77381-6236 Office: US Oncology 16825 Northchase Dr Ste 1400 Houston TX 77060-6005 Office Phone: 832-601-6128.

**MAHADEVAN, KUMAR,** marine life administrator, researcher; b. Madras, Tamilnadu, India, Sept. 29, 1948; came to U.S., 1971; s. Sockalingam Ponnusamy and Pankajam (Nadar) M.; m. Linda Claire Goggin, Sept. 27, 1980; children: Andrew, Alexander, Chad, Vijayan. BS, Madras U., 1967; MS, Annamalai U., Chidambaram, India, 1971; PhD, Fla. State U., 1977. Instr. Chingleput (India) Med. Coll., 1967-68, Lakshman's Coll., Madras, 1968-69; rsch. asst. Fla. State U., Tallahassee, 1971-75; staff scientist Conservation Cons., Inc., Palmetto, Fla., 1975-78; sr. scientist Mote Marine Lab., Sarasota, Fla., 1978-79, dir. divsn., 1979—86, interim co-dir., 1984, pres., 1986—. Mem. Coun. on Ocean Affairs, Washington, 1989-91, steering com. Gulf of Mex. Program, Atlanta, 1988-96; mem. South Atlantic and Gulf States Coastal Protection Commn., 1990-93; vice chmn. NOAA Marine Rsch. Bd., Gulf of Mex., 1992-96. Contbr. articles to profl. jours. Mem. sch. adv. bd., Sarasota, 1988-89; mem. tech. adv. bd. Myakka River, Sarasota, 1987-90; legis. liason Parents Assn. of Sarasota Schs., 1988-89; bd. dirs. Jason Found. for Edn., 1991-2004, Health Care Sarasota, 1997-98; vice chmn. Fla. Ocean Alliance, 2000—; mem. Fla. Gov.'s Ocean Com., 1997-98; mem. adv. bd. Harte Inst. for Gulf of Mex. Studies, 2001—; active Sarasota Cmty. Video Archives Hall of Fame, 2005. Nat. Merit scholar Univ. Grants Commn., India, 1969-71. Fellow Explorers Club (nat.); mem. N.Am. Benthological Soc., Oceanographic Soc., World Aquaculture Soc., Deep Sea Biol. Soc. (hon.), Fla. Acad. Scis. (councillor 1975), So. Assn. Marine Labs (pres. 1990, exec. bd. 1986-91, treas. 1995—), Assn. Marine Labs Caribbean (pres. 1987-88, exec. bd. 1984—), Nat. Assn. Marine Labs. (pres. 1994-95), Sci. & Environment Coun. Sarasota (chmn. 2003—), Greater Sarasota C. of C. (dir. 2005—), Sarasota Rotary Club, Sigma Xi. Republican. Avocations: racquetball, fishing, gardening. Office: Mote Marine Lab 1600 Ken Thompson Pky Sarasota FL 34236-1096 Business E-Mail: kumar@mote.org.

**MAHADY, JOSEPH M.,** former pharmacy products company executive; Pres. Am. Home Products Corp., Madison, NJ; pres., North Am. & Global bus. Wyeth Pharmaceuticals, 1997—, sr. v.p. Office: Wyeth Pharm Five Giralda Farms Madison NJ 07940-0874 also: Wyeth Phar North Am & Global Bus 500 Arcola Rd Collegeville PA 19426 Office Phone: 484-865-5476, 973-660-5771.

**MAHAFFEY, JOHN CHRISTOPHER,** medical association executive; b. Jefferson City, Mo., July 20, 1953; s. Fred Turner and Betty Cord (Woodfill) Mahaffey; children: Michael, Katherine. BA, Western Ill. U., Macomb, 1975; MS, DePaul U., 1999. Legis. aide Congressman Harold R. Collier. Washington, 1972-73; legis. asst. Nat. Assn. Retail Druggists, Washington, 1975-76; dir. Commn. and Meetings Nat. Assn. Bds. of Pharmacy, Chgo., 1976-80; pres., CEO Assn. Forum, Chgo., 1980—2002; exec. dir. Am. Coll. Foot and Ankle Surgeons, Park Ridge, Ill., 2002—. Bd. dirs Healthcare Assocs. Credit Union, 2003—. Commr. City of Park Ridge (Ill.) Econ. Devel. Commn., 1990—94, 1996—2000; mem. exec. com. Chgo. Convention and Tourism Bur., Chgo., 1993—2002. Recipient Disting. Alumni award, Western Ill. U., Macomb, 1993. Fellow: Am. Soc. Assn. Execs. (Key award 1994); mem.: U.S. C. of C., Assn. Com. 100. Presbyn. Office: Am Coll Foot and Ankle Surgeons 8725 W Higgins Rd Chicago IL 60631 Office Phone: 773-693-9300. Business E-Mail: mahaffey@acfas.org.

**MAHAFFEY, MARCIA HIXSON,** retired educational administrator; b. Scobey, Mont. d. Edward Goodell and Olga Marie (Frederickson) Hixson; m. Donald Harry Mahaffey (div. Aug. 1976); 1 child, Marcia Anne (dec.); m. George Justin Fair, Mar. 26, 1997 (div. June 9, 2004). BA in English, U. Wash.; MA in Secondary Edn., U. Hawaii, 1967. Cert. secondary and elem. tchr., adminstr. tchr. San Lorenzo (Calif.) Sch. Dist., 1958-59, Castro Valley (Calif.) Sch. Dist., 1959-63, vice prin., 1963-67, Sequoia Union HS Dist., Redwood City, 1967-77, asst. prin., prin., 1977-91, ret., 1991. Tchr. trainer Project Impact Sequoia Union Sch. Dist., Redwood City, 1986-91; mem. supr.'s task force for dropout prevention, 1987-91, Sequoia Dist. Grading Commn. (chair subcom. staff devel. 1988) chair, Sequoia Union H. S. Dist. Grading Com., 1976-1894; mentor tchr. selection com., 1987-91; mem. Stanford Program Devel. Ctr. Com., 1987-91; chairperson gifted and talented Castro Valley Sch. Dist., 1966; mem. family svcs bd., San Leandro, Calif. Vol. Am. Cancer Soc., San Mateo, Calif., 1967, Castro Valley, 1965; chair Carlmont H.S. Site Coun., Belmont, Calif., 1977—91; active Nat. Trust for Hist. Preservation; Neighborhood Beautification project dir. Bridle Trails Cmty. Club, 1999—2001; mem. Golden Grads. scholarship com. Roosevelt HS, Seattle, 2000—, co-chair, 2004—; Sunday sch. tchr. Hope Luth. Ch., San Mateo, 1970—76. Recipient Life Mem. award Parent, Tchr., Student Assn., Belmont, 1984, Svc. award 1989, Exemplary Svc award Carlmont High Sch., 1989, 92; named Woman of the Week, Castro Valley, 1967, Outstanding Task Force Chair Adopt A Sch. Program San Mateo (Calif.) County, 1990. Mem.: DAR, AAUW, ASCD, Acad. Am. Poets, Sequoia Dist. Mgmt. Assn. (pres. 1975, treas. 1984—85), Assn. Calif. Sch. Adminstrs. (Project Leadership plaque 1985), The Heritage Found., Am. Heritage-The Soc. of Am. Historians, Smithsonian Instn., Met. Mus. Art, Libr. of Congress Assocs. (charter), Animal Welfare Advocacy, White Ho. Hist. Assn. (charter), Am. Mus. Natural History (charter), Woodrow Wilson Internat. Ctr. Scholars, Alpha Xi Delta (Order of Rose award 1997), Delta Kappa Gamma. Avocations: painting, travel, tap dancing, redecorating, poetry. *Personal philosophy: Life is short, so make haste to be kind to one another.*

**MAHAFFEY, REDGE ALLAN,** movie producer, director, writer, actor, scientist, business executive; b. Bethesda, Md., Dec. 15, 1949; s. George Newton and Lila Katherine (Drum) M.; m. Ellen Cecilia Cranston, May 30, 1973 (div. Dec. 1980); m. Patricia Jane Guy, Apr. 29, 1984 (div. Sept. 1994); children: Travis Guy, Morgan Nicole; m. Veronica Bird, Sept. 24, 1994; children: Ryan Alexander, Ramsey Blake. BS, U. Md., 1971, MS, 1973, PhD, 1976. NRC postdoctoral fellow Nat. Acad. of Scis., Washington, 1976-77; research physicist Naval Research Lab., Washington, 1977-78; sr. research physicist Sachs/Freeman Assocs., Bladensburg, Md., 1978-79, dir. research Bowie, Md., 1979-81, exec. v.p., chief scientist Largo, Md., 1981-91, 1999—, also bd. dirs. Landover, Md., 1985—; mng. ptnr. Ramsway Pictures, 1991—; pres. WHOH, Davidsonville, Md., 1999—. Instr. George Washington U., Washington, 1979-80, Prince George's Coll., 1987; pres. Capitol Contracts, Bowie, 1981-83. Author: A Higher Education, 1989, Me, Myself and I, 1992, Deadly Rivals, 1992; prod. prodr., writer Deadly Rivals, 1992, Quest of the Delta Knights, 1993; prodr., actor, writer, dir. Life 101, 1995 (hon. mention Atlantic City Film Festival 1997), First Encounter, 1997; prodr., actor, dir., writer She's Too Tall, 1998 (Best Comedy award Atlantic City Film Festival 1998); contbr. articles on lasers and particle beams to sci. jours., also short stories, essays and poems to mags.; patentee laser, x-rays and particle beams. Recipient Research Publ. award Naval Research Lab., 1978, 1st Place Novel Internat. Lit. Awards, 1988, award of merit Internat. Soc. for Advancement of Poetry, 1990. Mem. IEEE, Am. Phys. Soc., Mensa, Intertel, Nat. Writer's Club, Internat. Platform Assn., Internat. Soc. Phil. Enquiry, Writer's Assn.

Anne Arundel County, Bethesda Writer's Ctr., Inst. Noetic Scis. Clubs: Sea Dragons Martial Arts(Washington) (treas. 1984-85, instr. 1987-91). Republican. Avocations: martial arts, softball, basketball. Office: SFA Inc 2200 Defense Hwy Crofton MD 21114 Office Phone: 301-858-1244. E-mail: redge@sfa.com.

**MAHAJAN, ARVIND,** finance educator; b. Delhi, India, Nov. 24, 1951; arrived in U.S., 1974; s. Vedavrata and Shakuntala Mahajan; m. Vanita Mahajan, Jan. 16, 1983; children: Aseem K., Sia S. B of Commerce in Acctg. and Fin., U. Delhi, 1972; MBA in Fin., U. Scranton, 1975; PhD in Fin., Ga. State U., 1980. Fin. officer Raisina Press, Delhi, 1972—74; instr., rsch. asst. Ga. State U., Atlanta, 1976—79; sr. cons. Mfrs. Hanover Trust Co., N.Y.C. 1987—88; asst. prof. fin. Tex. A&M U., College Station, 1980—86, assoc. prof., 1986—92, prof., 1992—94, Lamar Savings prof. fin., 1994—, assoc. dir. acad. programs Ctr. Internat. Bus. Studies and CIBER, 1990—99. Vis. prof. Group Ecole Superieure de Commerce, Rennes, France, 2000, Johannes Kepler U., Linz, Austria, 1992—99, Group Ecole Superieure de Commerce, Dijon, France, 1991; faculty mem. Acad. Future Internat. Leaders, 1998—2000. Contbr. articles to rsch. jours. and confs. Pres. Coalition Support Pub. Schs., College Station, 2003. Avocations: travel, reading, music. Office: Tex A&M U Mays Bus Sch College Station TX 77843

**MAHAJAN, DEVINDER,** chemical engineer, chemistry professor; s. Dewan Chand and Kanta Mahajan; m. Salema Mahajan, July 18, 1981; children: Manoj D., Maneka. PhD, U. B.C, Vancouver, Canada, 1979. Scientist, group leader Brookhaven Nat. Lab., Upton, NY, 1983—; prof., co-dir. Stony Brook U., 2002—. Mem.: ACS (assoc.), AIChE (assoc.), Russian Acad. Natural Scis. Hindu. Achievements include patents for Alternative Fuels. Office: Brookhaven National Laboratory Building 815 Upton NY 11973-5000 Office Phone: 631-344-4985. Personal E-mail: devinder.mahajan@stonybrook.edu. E-mail: dmahajan@bnl.gov.

**MAHAJAN, SUBHASH,** electronic materials educator; b. Gurdaspur, India; m. Sushma Sondhi, Sept. 3, 1965; children: Sanjoy, Sunit, Ashish. BS with highest honors, Panjab U., India, 1959; BE in Metallyrgy with highest honors, Indian Inst. Sci., 1961; PhD in Materials Sci. and Engring., U. Calif., 1965. Rsch. asst. U. Calif., Berkeley, 1961-65; rsch. metallurgist U. Denver, 1965-68; Harwell fellow Atomic Energy Rsch. Establishment, Harwell, England, 1968-71; mem. tech. staff AT&T Bell Labs., Murray Hill, NJ, 1971-83, rsch. mgr., 1981-83; prof. electronic materials dept. material sci. and engring. Carnegie Mellon U., Pitts., 1983-97; prof. electronic materials Ariz. State U., Tempe, 1997—, assoc. chair, 1999, interim chair and chair dept. chem. and materials engring., 2000—06, dir. Sch. Materials, 2006—. Mem. site panel Materials Rsch. Lab., 1993; vis. prof. U. Antwerp, Belgium, 1991, Ecole UnI. Lyon, Ecully, France, 1993; lectr., spkr., patentee, cons. in field. Editor: Handbook on Semiconductors, vol. 3, 1994, Acta Materialia, 2001; editor: (with V.G. Keramidas) Electrochemical Society Symposium Volume, 1983; editor: (with L.C. Kimerling) The Concise Encyclopedia of Semiconducting Materials and Related Technologies, 1992; editor: (with D. Bloor, R.J. Brook and M.C. Flemings) The Encyclopedia of Advanced Materials, 1994; editor: (with K.H. Jurgen Buschow, Robert W.-Cahn et al) Encyclopedia of Materials: Science and Technology, 2001; coordinating editor: The Acta Materiala Jours., 2004—; contbr. more than 200 articles to profl. jours. Mem. materials rsch. adv. com. divsn. materials rsch. NSF, 1989-92. Fellow TMS, Am. Soc. Metals Internat. (trustee bd., Albert Sauveur Achievement award); mem. NAE, Materials Rsch. Soc. (editor symposium volume 1983, organizer symposium Am. Assn. Crystal Growers), Electrochem. Soc. (mem. electronics divsn. 1973-86, divisional editor 1976-86), Minerals, Metals and Materials Soc. (mem. phys. metallurgy com. 1976-83, vice chmn. mech. metallurgy com. 1978-79, mem. 1975-80, mem. electronic materials com. 1990-94, chmn. electronic, magnetic and photonic materials com. 1984-86, tech. dir. bd., John Bardeen award, The Educator award), Sigma Xi. Home: 8824 S Poplar St Tempe AZ 85284-4521 Office: Ariz State U Sch Materials Tempe AZ 85287 Office Phone: 480-727-9322. Business E-Mail: smahajan@asu.edu.

**MAHALAWICH, ANNE MARY,** retired mathematics educator; b. Norwich, Conn., Mar. 10, 1922; d. Dimitry and Emilia Pisarko; m. Nicholas Mahalawich, Nov. 24, 1945. BS, Willimantis State Tchrs. Coll., 1943, MS, 1967. Mem. RSVP, 1980—2006; mem. bd. Otis Libr.; pres. Taxpayer's Assn. Mem.: New London Retired Tchrs. (pres.), Norwich Tchrs. League (pres. 1972—73), AARP (pres.), Beta Sigma Phi (profl. Woman of Yr. 1989), Phi Beta Kappa, Delta Kappa Gamma (pres.). Ea. Orthodox. Home: 7838 Naples Heritage Dr Naples FL 34112 Personal E-mail: amahalawich@aol.com.

**MAHAN, CHARLES SAMUEL,** public health educator; b. Pitts., Nov. 4, 1938; AB, W.Va. U., 1960; MD, Northwestern U., 1964. Diplomate Am. Bd. Ob-Gyn. Intern Hennepin County Gen. Hosp., Mpls., 1964-65; med. fellow in obstetrics and gynecology U. Minn. Hosp., Mpls., 1965-68; staff physician Shands Teaching Hosp., Coll. Medicine U. Fla., Gainesville, 1974-95, dir. divsn. ambulatory svcs. women, 1974-87, assoc. prof. dept. obstetrics and gynecology, 1974-80, prof., 1980—, acting chmn. dept. obstetrics and gynecology, 1978-79; asst. and assoc. prof. dept. obstetrics and gynecology med. sch. U. Minn., Mpls., 1970-74; dir. maternal and child health State of Fla., 1982-86; dep. sec. health, state health officer Fla. Dept. Health and Rehabilitative Svcs., 1988-95; prof. dept. cmty. and family health, maternal health program U. South Fla. Coll. Pub. Health, Tampa, 1995—, dean, 1995—2002. Sr. assoc. physician ob-gyn. Pilot City Health Ctr., Mpls., 1970-74; med. dir. Red Door Venereal Disease Clinic, Mpls., 1972-74; dir. North Ctrl. Fla. Maternity and Infant Care, Family Planning, Teen-Age Pregnancy Team Projects, and WIC Program, 1974-87; assoc. dir. Tech. Assistance Health Rsch. Group, Gainesville, 1975-82; chmn. med. care evaluation com. Shands Teaching Hosp., 1976-80; mem. faculty senate U. Fla., 1976-78, 79-80, 87-88, mem. outpatient clinics com., 1978-86, mem. health policy task force, 1992—, mem. promotion and tenure com. coll. medicine, 1978-81, dir. undergrad. edn. dept. ob-gyn., 1980-85, pres. faculty, 1982-83, mem. faculty coun., 1982-85, dir. Fla. midwifery resource ctr., 1992-94, mem. nurse-midwife tng. program adv. com. coll. nursing, 1982—, mem. adv. com. HIV rsch. and edn., 1992-94; mem. State of Fla. Family Planning Coun., 1976-79; chmn. 1st ann. med. alumni sci. seminar Hennepin County Med. Ctr., Minn., 1976; mem. Alachua County Child Advocacy Coun., 1977-79; mem. adv. bd. Rape Info. and Counseling Ctr., 1977-79; mem. nat. adv. coun. maternal, fetal and infant nutrition USDA, 1978-81; chmn. health com. Alachua County Human Svcs. Planning Coun., 1980-82, acting pres. coun., 1982; mem. adv. bd. Nat. Cesarean/Support, Edn. and Concern, 1984-89; gov.'s rep. Healthy Mothers/Healthy Babies Steering Com., 1985-94; chmn. rsch. adv. com. nat. study freestanding birth ctrs. Nat. Assn. Childbearing Ctrs., 1986-88; chmn. Gov.'s Task Force AIDS, 1988-90; mem. child health initiative nat. adv. com. Robert Wood Johnson Found., 1992-94, dir. Healthy Futures: a program to imporve maternal and infant care in the South, 1987-92; mem. adv. com. to dir. Ctrs. Disease Control and Prevention, 1994-03, chair, 1995-03; mem. secy. adv. com. on Infant Mortality Health and Human Svcs., 1996-05, Bright Futures for Women Commn., 2000-05; vis. prof. various instns.; lectr. in field. Editor: Generally Funny: A Monograph of Medical Anecdotes and Cartoons, 1976; contbr. chpts. and revs. to books and articles to profl. jours. Active Nat. Found.-Mar. Dimes, 1978-88. chmn. edn. adv. com., 1978-82, 85-87; active Leadership Gainesville, 1978; mem. ob-gyn. alumni coun. med. sch. Northwestern U., 1986—; mem. Gov.'s Adv. Coun. Farmworkers Affairs, 1988-95; mem. innovation coun. Ounce Prevention Found Fla., 1994—; mem. nat. bds. Frontiers Nursing Svc., 2002-; Nat. Perinatal Info. Ctr., 2003-; chair Prematurity Prevention Fla. Task Force, 2003-, Fla. Blue Cross Blue Shield Sapphire award, 2004-. With USN, 1957-70, res. Recipient Cmty. Svc. award Gainesville Women's Health Ctr., 1976, Spl. MCH award Fla. Coun. Primary Care, 1984, Spl. Award for Mother-Infant Health, Coalition Fla. Childbirth Educators, 1984, Award for MCH Leadership, So. Health Assn., 1991, Mary E. Switzer award Am. Schs. Applied Health Professions, 1992, State of Fla. Cabinet Disting. Svc. award, 1992, Astho McCormack award, 2000, Chabon award La Maze Internat., 2004; Rsch. fellow USN, Aviation Med. Acceleration Lab., 1961. Mem. AMA, APHA (mem. coun. maternal and child health

1985-88, Martha May Eliot award 2004), Am. Coll. Ob-Gyn. (chmn. spl. interest group ambulatory reproductive health care 1978-80, chmn. dist. IV maternity mortality com. 1979-81, mem. com. health care underserved women 1988-94, chmn. 1992, chmn. nat. fetal-infant mortality rev. steering com. 1990-94), Nat. Assn. Childbearing Ctrs. (bd. dirs. 1983-05), Nat. Perinatal Assn. (bd. dirs. 1996-01), Fla. Ctr. Children and Youth, Fla. Healthy Mothers/Healthy Babies Coalition (Spl. Award for MCH Leadership 1985), Fla. Med. Assn. (mem. com. pub. health 1988-02, mem. com. AIDS 1988-96), Fla. Obstet. and Gynecol. Soc., Fla. Perinatal Assn. (bd. dirs. 1993-98), Fla. Pub. Health Assn. (chmn. maternal and child health sect. 1987-88, mem. jour. editl. bd. 1987-01), Fla. Soc. Childbirth Educators, State and Territorial Health Ofcls. (mem. exec. com. 1991—, pres. 1993-94), Jacobs Inst. Women's Health (founding mem.), W.Va. U. Alumni Assn. (life), Rotary Club Tallahassee (bd. dirs. 1989-90), Rotary Club Temple Terrace. Home: 1001 N Riverhills Dr Tampa FL 33617-4241 Office: MDC 100 Chiles Ctr U S Fla Coll Pub Heal 3111 E Fletcher Ave Tampa FL 33613 Office Phone: 813-974-8336.

**MAHAN, CLARENCE,** federal agency administrator, writer; b. Dayton, Ohio, Jan. 1, 1939; s. Clarence Mahan and Elsie (Crouch) Dlitz; m. Suky Mahan, May 27, 1962; children: Sean M., Christiane Elizabeth. BA, U. Md., 1963; MA, Am. U., 1968; MBA, Syracuse U., 1969. Dep. comptroller U.S. Army, Japan, 1974-76; dep. chief program and budget Defense Commn. Agy., Arlington, Va., 1976; aide Asst. Sec. Army, Washington, 1976-77; chief operating appropriations Dept. AF, Washington, 1979-80; dir. fin. and acctg. Dept. Energy, Washington, 1980-81, dep. comptroller, 1981-82; dir. fiscal and contracts mgmt. EPA, Washington, 1982-83, dep. comptroller, 1983-85, dir. Rsch. Program Mgmt. Office, 1985-95. Instr., lectr. in field. Author: Classic Irises and the Men and Women Who Created Them, 2006; contbr. articles to profl. jours. and hort. mags. With U.S. Army, 1959-62, Korea. Mem. Am. Iris Soc. (bd. dirs., 2d v.p. 1991-95, 1st v.p. 1995-98, pres. 1998-2001), Hist. Iris Preservation Soc. (pres. 1991-93), Soc. Japanese Irises (pres. 1989-92), Reblooming Iris Soc. (bd. dirs. 1986-94, pres. 2002-05). Democrat. Home and Office: 7311 Churchill Rd Mc Lean VA 22101-2001 Office Fax: cemahan@aol.com.

**MAHAN, DAVID JAMES,** retired academic administrator; b. St. Louis, May 29, 1934; s. John William and Eleanor (Johnson) M.; m. Jane E. Pyle, Nov. 28, 1957; children: Elizabeth Mahan-Shaw, Kathryn Goodman. BA, Okla. Baptist Coll., 1956; MA, Washington U., St. Louis, 1962, EdD, 1968. Cert. elem., secondary English tchr., Mo., cert. elem. prin., Mo., cert. supt., Mo. Adminstr., tchr. St. Louis Pub. Schs., 1958-90, supt., 1990-96; supt. in residence U. Mo., St. Louis, 1996-99. Co-author: The Faculty Team: School Organization for Results, 1971. Bd. dirs. Commerce and Growth Assn., St. Louis, 1990—, Asthma and Allergy Found. Am., St. Louis, 1990—, St. Louis Symphony Soc., 1992—, Boy Scouts Am., 1992—. Home: 5 Portland Ct Saint Louis MO 63108-1293

**MAHAN, GERALD DENNIS,** physicist, researcher; s. Thomas Finley and Julia Kay (Swails) M.; m. Sally Ann Spaugh, Feb. 20, 1965; children: Christopher Parker, Susan Thayer, Roy Finley AB, Harvard U., 1959; PhD in Physics, U. Calif.-Berkeley, 1964. Rsch. physicist GE, Schenectady, 1963-67, part-time, 1967-84; assoc. prof. physics U. Oreg., Eugene, 1967-73; prof. physics Ind. U., Bloomington, 1973-82; disting. prof., 1982-84; disting. prof. physics U. Tenn., Knoxville, 1984—2001, Penn State U., University Park. Guest prof. Niels Bohr Inst., Copenhagen, 1977-78 author: Many-Particle Physics, 1981; contbr. articles to profl. jours. Alfred Sloan fellow, 1968-70. Fellow Am. Phys. Soc.; mem. NAS, AAAS. Office: Penn State U 104 Davey Lab University Park PA 16802 Business E-Mail: gmahan@psu.edu.

**MAHAN, JAMES CAMERON,** judge; b. El Paso, Tex., Dec. 16, 1943; m. Eileen Agnes Casale, Jan. 13, 1968; 1 child, James Cameron Jr. BA, U. Charleston, 1965; JD, Vanderbilt U., 1973. Bar: Nev. 1974, U.S. Dist. Ct. Nev. 1974, U.S. Ct. Appeals (9th cir.) 1975, U.S. Tax Ct. 1980, U.S. Supreme Ct. 1980. Assoc. Lee & Beasey, Las Vegas, Nev., 1974-75; mem. firm John Peter Lee Ltd., Las Vegas, 1975-82; sr. ptnr. Mahan & Ellis, Chartered, Las Vegas, 1982-99; dist. ct. judge 8th Jud. Dist. Nev., Las Vegas, 1999—2002; U.S. dist. judge, 2002—. With USN, 1966-69. Office: 333 Las Vegas Blvd S Las Vegas NV 89101 Office Phone: 702-464-5520. E-mail: james_mahan@nvd.uscourts.gov.

**MAHAN, MARY HOYLE,** retired physical educator; b. Boston, July 19, 1939; d. Frederick John and Mary Dwyer Hoyle; m. J. Roger Mahan Jr., Mar. 21, 1970 (dec. June 1999). BS in Phys. Edn., Bridgewater State Coll., 1960; MS in Phys. Edn., U. N.C., 1963; EdD, Nova U., 1975. Tchr. phys. edn. Stoughton Jr. High Sch., Mass., 1960—62; tchr. phys. edn., coach Locust Valley Jr./Sr. High Sch., NY, 1963—65; prof. phys. edn., coach Ctrl. Conn. State U., New Britain, 1965—71, Miami-Dade C.C. North, 1971—2001, assoc. athletic dir., dept. chair, prof., 1980—2001, ret., 2001. CEO, pres. The Teaching Well, Ftr. Lauderdale, Fla., 2000—. Bd. trustees Cheshire Acad., Conn., 2000—, Bridgewater State Coll. Found., 2002—, Lake Isle Woods, Centerville, 2004—; edn. found. Villanova U., Pa., 2003—. Named Weymouth High Sch. Hall Fame, Bridgewter State Coll. Hall Fame, Fla. C.C. Activities Assn. Hall Fame; recipient 3 Outstanding Faculty awards, Miami-Dade C.C., 1985, Case Prof. of Yr., U. Tex., 1996, Endowed Tchg. Chair, Bowden award, Cheshle Acad. Mem.: Nat. Assn. Coll. Directors of Athletics, Am. Alliance Health, Phys. Edn., Recreation and Dance, Am. Coll. Sports Medicine, Delta Psi Kappa. Independent. Roman Catholic. Avocations: golf, interior decorating, travel. Home (Winter): 3750 Galt Ocean Dr #2007 Fort Lauderdale FL 33308 Home (Summer): 30 Crestview Cir Centerville MA 02632

**MAHANEY, KELLIE ROSE,** elementary school educator, consultant; b. Troy, Ohio, Mar. 28, 1970; d. John David and Jerry Wright Rose; m. Paul Mitchell Mahaney, Mar. 28, 1967; children: Karson Rose, Keegan Mitchell. MusB in Edn., Ea. Ky. U., Richmond, 1993; M in Ednl. Leadership, Wright State U., Dayton, OH, 2002. Tchr. Mechanicsburg Exempted Village Schools, Ohio, 1993—94, Akron Pub. Schools, 1994—95, Milton-Union Schools, West Milton, 1995—. Chairperson Citizens Miami East Sch., Casstown, 2006; bd. mem. Stepping Stones Co-operative Pre-Sch., Tipp City, Ohio, 2000—06. Recipient Tchr. of Yr., Milton-Union Schools, 2002; Martha Holden Jennings scholar, 2003. Mem.: Nat. Music Educators Assn. (corr.). Achievements include director of first band to qualify for state competition at Milton-Union High School; development of curriculum for the first 8th Grade drama class at Milton-Union Middle School. Home: 4100 LeFevre Rd Troy OH 45373 Office: Milton Union Schs 146 S Spring St West Milton OH 45383 Office Phone: 937-884-7930. Office Fax: 937-884-7931. E-mail: mahanaeyk@milton-union.k12.oh.us.

**MAHANEY, MICHAEL C.,** library director; BA with honors, MLS with honors, SUNY, Buffalo. Joined Buffalo & Erie County Pub. Libr., NY, 1973, with Ctrl. Libr. NY, asst. dep. dir. cmty. rels. NY, 1990, dep. dir., CEO NY, 1999—2002, dir. NY, 2002—. V.p. Explore and More, East Aurora, NY; bd. trustees NY Ctr. for Books and Reading. Mem.: ALA. Office: Buffalo & Erie County Pub Libr 1 Lafayette Sq Buffalo NY 14203 Office Phone: 716-858-8900. Office Fax: 716-858-6211.*

**MAHARIDGE, DALE DIMITRO,** journalist, educator, writer; b. Cleve., Oct. 24, 1956; s. Steve and Joan (Kopfstein) Maharidge. Student, Cleve. State U., 1974—75. Freelance reporter various publs., Cleve., 1976, Cleve. Plain Dealer, 1978—80; reporter The Gazette, Medina, Ohio, 1977—78, Sacramento Bee, 1980—91; vis. prof. Stanford U., Palo Alto, Calif., 1992—2002; asst. prof. Columbia U. Grad. Sch. Journalism, NYC, 2002—. Art colony resident Yaddo Residency, 2004. Author: Journey to Nowhere: The Saga of the New Underclass, 1985, Journey to Nowhere: The Saga of the New Underclass repub. with introduction by Bruce Springsteen, 1996, And Their Children After Them, 1989 (Pulitzer Prize for gen. nonfiction 1990), The Last Great American Hobo, 1993, The Coming White Minority: California, Multiculturalism and the Nation's Future, 1996, The Coming White Minority:

California's Eruptions and the Nation's Future, Vintage Books edit., 1999, Homeland, 2004, Denison, Iowa: Searching for the Soul of America Through the Secrets of a Midwest Town, 2005; contbr. articles to profl. jours. Grantee, Open Soc. Inst., 2006; Freedom Forum grantee, 1995, Nieman fellow, Harvard U., 1988, Pope Found. grantee, 1994. Democrat. Office Phone: 212-854-3854. Personal E-Mail: dmaharidge@yahoo.com.

**MAHATO, RAM ISHWAR,** pharmacist, educator; b. Janakpur, Nepal, Jan. 11, 1963; s. Srinarayan and Sarswati Mahato; m. Subhashini Mahto, Jan. 18, 1993; 1 child, Kalika. PhD, U. of Strathclyde, Scotland, 1992; B.S., China Pharm. U., 1989; diploma in Chinese, Beijing Lang. Inst., 1985. PhD in Pharm. Sciences U. of Strathclyde, 1992. Rsch. assoc. U. of So. Calif., Dept of Pharm. Sciences, Los Angeles, Calif., 1992—97; postdoctoral fellow Wash. U., St Louis, Mont., 1993—93; guest scholar Kyoto U., Faculty of Pharm. Sciences, Kyoto, 1994—96; sr. scientist GeneMedicine, Inc., The Woodland, 1996—99; mgr., pharm. drug devel. Copernicus, Inc., Cleve., 1999—99; rsch. asst. prof. U. of Utah, Dept of Pharmaceutics and Pharm. Chemistry, Salt Lake City, 1999—2001; asst. prof. U. of Tenn. Health Sci. Ctr., Memphis, 2001—. Ad hoc grant reviewer NIH, Bethesda, Md., 2002—04. Am. Inst. of Biol. Sciences, 2002; session chair Controlled Release Soc., 2002—. Editor: (book on nucleic acid delivery) Pharmaceutical Perspectives of Nucleic Acid-Based Therapeutics. Fellow, Goho and Uehara Foundations of Japan, 1995—96. Mem.: Assn. for the Advancement of Sci., NY Acad. of Sci., Am. Assn. of Pharm. Sciences, Am. Chem. Soc., Am. Soc. of Gene Therapy, Controlled Release Soc. (assoc.). Achievements include research in Pharmaceutical Perspectives of Oligonucleotides and Genes. Office: Univ of Tenn Dept of Pharm Sci 26 S Dunlap St Feurt Bldg RM 406 Memphis TN 38103 4909 Home Fax: (901)448-6092. Business E-Mail: rmahato@utmem.edu.

**MAHDAVI, KAMAL B.,** writer, researcher; b. Esfahan, Iran, Sept. 1, 1933; came to U.S., 1958, naturalized; s. Ebrahim B. and Ghamar (Jalilian) M. BA, U. Calif., Berkeley, 1964; MA, U Toronto, 1965; postgrad., U. Cambridge, 1965—69. Cert. coll. tchr., Calif. R&D rschr. U. Stockholm, 1969—71; freelance rschr., writer self-employed, San Francisco, San Diego, 1972—. Ind. legal rschr. San Francisco, San Diego, 1980—. Author (as K.M.B. Writer): Technological Innovation: An Efficiency Investigation, 1972; contbr. articles to profl. jours. Civil rights litigant. Avocations: swimming, chess. Office: PO Box 121164 San Diego CA 92112-1164

**MAHDAVIANI, MIRIAM,** choreographer, educator; Student, Sch. Am. Ballet, 1968. Past mem., instr. Balanchine Co. Choreographer Jacob's Pillow Dance Festival, 1986, 87, Am. Music Festival N.Y.C. Ballet, 1988. Choreographer (ballets) N.Y.C. Ballet's Am. Music Festival, 1988, Dance Preludes Dancer's Emergency Fund Benefit, N.Y.C., 1991, Images, N.Y.C., 1992, Images Maggio Danza Festival, Florence, Italy, 1994, Correlazione N.Y.C. Ballet, 1994; dancer over 40 ballets including Ballo Della Regina, Coppelia, Donizetti Variations, Jewels, Raymonda Variations, La Valse. Office: Pacific Northwest Ballet 301 Mercer St Seattle WA 98109-4600

**MAHER, BILL,** television personality, comedian, television producer; b. NYC, Jan. 20, 1956; s. Bill and Julie (Berman) M. BA in English, Cornell U., 1978. Creator, host Politically Incorrect, Comedy Central, NYC, 1993-96, Politically Incorrect, ABC, 1996—2002; host Real Time With Bill Maher, HBO, 2003—. Performances include (theatre) Seymour Glick is Alive But Sick (Steve Allen); (stand-up) The Bob Monkhouse Show, Late Night with David Letterman, The Tonight Show Anniversary Show, The Tonight Show, HBO Spl., 1989, 92, 95, 97, 2000, 03; (TV shows) Steve Allen's Music Room, Alice, Sara, Max Headroom, Hard Knocks, Newhart, Murder, She Wrote, The Midnight Hour, Say What?; (TV movies) Out of Time, Rags to Riches, Club Med; (films) D.C. Cab, Rat Boy, House II, Cannibal Women in the Avocado Jungle of Death, Pizza Man; author: (books) True Story, 1994, Does Anybody Have a Problem With That? Politically Incorrect's Greatest Hits, When You Ride Alone You Ride with bin Laden, 2002, New Rules: Polite Musings from a Timid Observer, 2005. Recipient CableACE award Nat. Acad. Cable Programming, 1990, CableACE award for best talk show series, 1995, CableACE award for best talk show host, 1995, President's award for championing free speech, LA Times Press Club, 2002. Office: Brillstein Grey Entertainment Ste 350 9150 Wilshire Blvd Beverly Hills CA 90212

**MAHER, BRENDAN ARNOLD,** retired psychology educator, editor; b. Widnes, Eng., Oct. 31, 1924; came to US, 1955; s. Thomas F. and Agnes (Power) M.; m. Winifred Barbara Brown, Aug. 27, 1952; children: Rebecca, Thomas, Nicholas, Liam, Niall. BA with honours, U. Manchester, Eng., 1950; MA, Ohio State U., 1951, PhD, 1954; student, U. Ill. Med. Sch., 1952-53; AM (hon.), Harvard, 1972; DPhil (hon.), U. Copenhagen, 1998. Diplomate Am. Bd. Examiners in Profl. Psychology. Psychologist Her Majesty's Prison, Wakefield, England, 1954-55; instr. Ohio State U., Ohio, 1955-56; asst. prof. Northwestern U., 1956-58; asso. prof. La. State U., La., 1958-60; lectr. Harvard, 1960-64; chmn. Ctr. Rsch. Personality, 1962-64; prof. U. Wis., 1964-67, 71-72; vis. fellow U. Copenhagen, 1966-67, vis. fellow and rsch. scientist, 1979, 96-98; prof. psychology Brandeis U., 1967-72; dean Brandeis U. (Grad. Sch.), 1969-71, dean faculty, 1971-72; E. C. Henderson prof. psychology Harvard U., 1983-99, E.C. Henderson rsch. prof., 1999—2004, E.C. Henderson prof. emeritus, 2004—, prof., 1972—, chmn. dept. psychology and social relations, 1973-78, chmn. dept. psychology, 1987-88, dean Grad. Sch. Arts and Scis., 1989-92; assoc. psychologist McLean Hosp., Belmont, Mass., 1968-77, psychologist, 1977-84; prof. emeritus, 2004—. Cons. in medicine Peter Bent Brigham Hosp., Boston, 1977-85; cons. in psychology Mass. Gen. Hosp., 1977 2002. Author: Principles of Psychopathology, 1966, Introduction to Research in Psychopathology, 1970, A Passage to Sword Beach, 1996; co-editor: National Research Council: Rsch. Doctorate Programs in the United States, 1995; editor Progress in Exptl. Personality Rsch., 1964-87, Jour. Cons. and Clin. Psychology, 1972-78; cons. editor Rev. Personality and Social Psychology, Clin. Psychology Rev. Served with Brit. Royal Navy, 1943-47. Recipient Zubin award for rsch. in psychopathology, 1998. Fellow AAAS, Am. Psychol. Soc.; mem. Brit. Psychol. Assn. (chartered psychologist UK), Soc. Rsch. in Psychopathology (pres. 1985-87), Phi Beta Kappa. Office: Harvard U William James Hall Cambridge MA 02138 also: Giffords Island Mahone Bay NS Canada Business E-Mail: bam@wjh.harvard.edu.

**MAHER, CHRISTINE R.,** biologist, educator; b. Norwich, NY, June 18, 1963; d. John J. and Ann K. Lucas; m. Michael J. Maher, May 21, 1983. BS Zoology, Miami U., Oxford, Ohio, 1984; MS Zoology, U. Idaho, Moscow, 1986; PhD Animal Behavior, U. Calif., Davis, 1992. Asst. prof. biology Mont. State U. Billings, 1992—97, U. So. Maine, Portland, 1997—2001, assoc. prof. biology, 2001—. Curator behavior ZooMontana, Billings, 1996—97. Recipient Emerging Tchr. and Scholar award, U. So. Maine, 2001. Mem.: Coun. for Undergrad. Rsch., Internat. Soc. for Behavioral Ecology, Animal Behavior Soc., Am. Soc. Mammalogists. Office: Univ Southern Maine Dept Biology 96 Falmouth St Portland ME 04104 Office Fax: 207-228-8116. E-mail: cmaher@usm.maine.edu.

**MAHER, DAVID WILLARD,** Internet company executive; b. Chgo., Aug. 14, 1934; s. Chauncey Carter and Martha (Peppers) M.; m. Jill Waid Armagnac, Dec. 20, 1954; children: Philip Armagnac, Julia Armagnac. BA, Harvard, 1955, LLB, 1959. Bar: N.Y. 1960, Ill. 1961, Wis. 1996, U.S. Patent Office 1961. Pvt. practice, Boston, 1960-65, ptnr., 1966-78, Reuben & Proctor, 1978-86, Isham, Lincoln and Beale, 1986-88, Sonnenschein, Nath & Rosenthal, Chgo., 1988—2003; ret., 2003; chmn. bd. dirs. Publ. Interest Registry, 2003—04, sr. v.p law and policy, 2004—. Dir. BBB Chgo. and No. Ill., 2004—; lectr. DePaul U. Sch. Law, 1973—79, Loyola U. Law Sch., Chgo., 1980—84. Vis. com. U. Chgo. Div. Sch., 1986—. 2d lt. USAF, 1955-56. Fellow Am. Bar Found. (life); mem. ABA, Am. Law Inst., Wis. State Bar, Chgo. Bar Assn.,

Chgo. Lit. Club. Roman Catholic. Home: 501 N Clinton St Apt 1503 Chicago IL 60610-8886 Office: Pub Interest Registry 1775 Wiehle Ave Ste 102A Reston VA 20190 Office Phone: 312-876-8055. Business E-Mail: dmaher@pir.org.

**MAHER, FRANCESCA MARCINIAK,** lawyer, former air transportation executive; b. Chgo., Oct. 27, 1957; BA, Loyola U., 1978, JD, 1981. Ptnr. Mayer, Brown & Platt, Chgo., 1981—84, 1987—93; v.p. law, corp. sec. UAL Corp., Elk Grove Village, Ill., 1993-97, v.p., gen. counsel, sec., 1997-98, sr. v.p., gen. counsel, sec., 1998—2003; spl. counsel Mayer, Brown, Rowe & Maw, Chgo., 2003—. Bd. dirs. YMCA Met. Chgo., Lincoln Park Zool. Soc. Mem. Ill. Humane Soc. (pres. 1996-98).

**MAHER, FRANK J.,** former communications executive; V.p., mgmt. dir. Foote, Cone & Belding, Chgo.; pres., CEO Creswell, Munsell, Fultz & Zirbel, Des Moines, 2002—03.

**MAHER, JAMES VINCENT, JR.,** physics professor, academic administrator; b. NYC, Aug. 25, 1942; s. James Vincent and Anne (Cunneen) M.; m. Angela Beth Braunstein, Aug. 13, 1966; children: Robin, James. BS in Physics, U. Notre Dame, 1964; MS in Physics, Yale U., 1965, PhD in Physics, 1969. Postdoctoral fellow Argonne (Ill.) Nat. Lab., 1968-70; asst. prof. U. Pitts., 1970-74, assoc. prof., 1974-80, prof., 1980—, fellow Ctr. for Philosophy of Sci., dept. chair physics and astronomy, 1991-94, provost and sr. vice-chancellor, 1994—. Dir. Scaife nuclear physics lab., 1979-80. Contbr. over 100 articles to profl. jours. Intellectual property task force Assn. Am. Univs., 1998—99; task force on accreditation Nat. Assn. State Univs. and Land Grant Colls., 1997—2000. Grantee Dept. Energy, NSF. Fellow AAAS, Am. Phys. Soc.; mem. Am. Crystal Growth Assn. (pres. Pitts. chpt. 1989-92, exec. com. 1988-93), Sigma Xi. Democrat. Roman Catholic. Home: 1313 Denniston Ave Pittsburgh PA 15217-1330 Office: U Pitts Office of the Provost Pittsburgh PA 15260 Office Phone: 412-624-4223. Business E-Mail: jvmaher@pitt.edu.

**MAHER, JOHN,** literature educator, writer; b. Cedar Rapids, Iowa, Apr. 25, 1945; s. Rose F. (Hopkins) Maher. BS, So. Ill. U., 1972; MA, Ariz. State U., 1976; PhD, Pacific W. U., 1992. Tchg. asst. So. Ill. U., 1972; tchr. Phoenix Union H.S. Dist., Ariz., 1976—82; Mesa Sch. Dist., 1982—97; adj. prof. Ctrl. Ariz. Coll., 1990—2002; ret., 2002. Author: Twentieth Century Campfire Culture, 1999. Chmn. Pinal County Transp. Com., 1990—2005; mem. Gov. Task Force on Transp., 2001. With U.S. Army, 1963—65. Mem.: C.A.A.R.S. Corvette Club (founder). Democrat. Roman Catholic. Avocation: Grand Canyon hiking. Home: 131 W Canyon St Apache Junction AZ 85220

**MAHER, JOHN GENE,** music educator, musician; b. Aledo, Ill., Nov. 11, 1951; s. Lewis Alexander and Ellen Irene Maher; m. Linda Kay Evans, June 3, 1978. BS, Ind. Wesleyan U. (Marion Coll.), 1975; MusM, Ball State U., 1979, ArtsD, 1986; MLS, Ind. U., 1988. Prof. music Ind. Wesleyan U., Marion, 1978—. Sub-dean Am. Guild Organists, Muncie, Ind., 1980—82, dean, 1982—83; organist Fairmount (Ind.) Friends Meeting, 1990—2005; condr. numerous workshops and master classes. Organist Marion Philharm. Orch., harpsichordist, numerous ch. and faculty recitals. Musician Marion Easter Pageant, 1979—2003, bd. dirs., 1998—2001; organist Fairmount (Ind.) Cmty. Sing, 1991—2004. Recipient Excellence in Tchg. award, Ind. Wesleyan U., 1994, 1995, 1996, 1998, 1999, 2000, Presdl. award for meritorious svc. in tchg., 1996. Achievements include development of Indiana Wesleyan University's first online music theory class. Office: Indiana Wesleyan U 4201 S Washington St Marion IN 46953 Office Phone: 765-677-2152. E-mail: john.maher@indwes.edu.

**MAHER, JONATHAN BANNON,** finance executive; b. Manhattan, NY, June 21, 1981; s. Richard Donald and Marianne Bannon Maher. BA in Bus. Adminstrn., U. San Diego, 2005. Cert. Oracle Developer, Oracle Corp., Calif., 2000; EMT NJ. Founder, CEO Host1, NYC, 1993—. Cons. Bear Stearns, NYC, 2005. Named a Master Scuba Diver, Nat. Assn. Underwater Instrs. Achievements include patents pending for structure & interface for building an information management application. Office: One Columbus Pl S 46A New York NY 10019 Office Phone: 646-496-5104. Business E-Mail: jonathan.maher@host1.com.

**MAHER, L. JAMES, III,** molecular biologist; b. Mpls., Nov. 28, 1960; s. Louis James and Elizabeth Jane (Crawford) M.; m. Laura Lee Moseng, July 2, 1983; children: Elizabeth Lillian, Christina Ailene. BS in Molecular Biology, U. Wis., 1983, PhD in Molecular Biology, 1988. Fellow U. Wis., Madison, 1983-84, rsch. asst., 1984-88; postdoctoral fellow Calif. Inst. Tech., Pasadena, 1988-91; asst. prof. molecular biology Eppley Inst., U. Nebr. Med. Ctr., Omaha, 1991-95; assoc. prof. biochem. molecular biology Mayo Clinic Coll. Medicine, Rochester, Minn., 1995-2000, prof., 2000—02, vice chmn., 2002—, assoc. dean for academic affairs, 2003—. Editorial bd. Antisense and Nuclear Acid Drug Design, 1991—, Nucleic Acids Rsch. Jour., 1988—; contbr. articles to profl. jours. Musician, Madison Symphony Orch., 1983-88, Calif. Inst. Tech. Symphony Orch., L.A., 1988-91. Gosney fellow, 1988; Am. Cancer Soc. postdoctoral fellow, 1988. Mem. AAAS, Phi Beta Kappa. Evangelical Christian Ch. Achievements include research in chemical and biochemical agents designed to artificially regulate the flow of genetic information in biological systems. Office: Mayo Clinic Coll Medicine Dept Biochem and Molec Biol 200 1st St SW Rochester MN 55905-0001 Office Phone: 507-284-9041. Business E-Mail: maher@mayo.edu.

**MAHER, LOUIS JAMES, JR.,** geologist, educator; b. Iowa City, Iowa, Dec. 18, 1933; s. Louis James and Edith Marie (Ham) M.; m. Elizabeth Jane Crawford, June 7, 1956; children: Leah James, Robert Crawford, Barbara Ruth. BA, U. Iowa, 1955, MS, 1959; PhD, U. Minn., 1961. Mem. faculty dept. geology and geophysics U. Wis.-Madison, 1962—, prof., 1970—2003, chmn. dept., 1980-84, prof. emeritus, 2003—. Contbr. articles to profl. jours. With U.S. Army, 1956—58, with counter intelligence corps U.S. Army, 1957—58, Duty Sta., La Rochelle, France. Danforth fellow, 1955-61; NSF fellow, 1959-61; NATO fellow, 1961-62 Fellow AAAS, Geol. Soc. Am.; mem. Am. Quaternary Assn., Ecol. Soc. Am., Wis. Acad. Sci., Arts and Letters, Sigma Xi. Episcopalian. Office: U Wis Dept Geology and Geoph 1215 W Dayton St Madison WI 53706-1600 Office Phone: 608-262-9595. E-mail: maher@geology.wisc.edu.

**MAHER, THOMAS GEORGE,** academic administrator, producer, media educator; b. St. Louis, Feb. 18, 1947; s. Dale Russel and Dorothy Leone M.; m. (div.). AB, St. Louis U., 1969, MA, 1971; PhD, U. So. Calif., 1985. Cert. C.C. tchr. and supr., Calif. Tchg. fellow St. Louis U., 1969-71; assoc. prof. Chaffey Coll., Rancho Cucamonga, Calif., 1974-79, media dir., 1980-84; assoc. producer Corp. for C.C. TV, Orange, Calif., 1979-80; assoc. dir. instrnl. tech. Calif. State Poly. U., Pomona, 1984-89; dir. office media svcs. U. Ill., Chgo., 1989-94; dir. office instrnl. svcs. Colo. State U., Ft. Collins, 1994—2006, interim v.p. divsn. ednl. outreach, 2002; dir. ebs and digital media, 2006—. Cons. Rsch. Comm., Ltd., Boston, 1984-94; book reviewer Focal Press, Inc., Boston, 1985-94. Writer: (TV series) Project: Universe, 1978 (Emmy award nomination 1979), The Business of Management, 1981; assoc. producer, dir., writer (TV series) Oceanus: The Marine Environment, 1979 (Emmy award 1980); exec. producer (TV program) For the People: Local Gov. Budget Making, 1992 (Cert. Merit, Chgo. Internat. Film/Video Festival 1992); producer, dir. (live nat. video teleconference, moderated by Sen. Bill Bradley) Campus Line-up with Carol Moseley Braun, 1992; instrnl. designer (interactive videodisc) Smog Check Multimedia Simulation Test, 1993 (INVISION Merit award, NewMedia Multimedia awards, 1993); prodr., dir. numerous additional refereed ednl. TV shows, 1974—. 1st lt. USAF, 1971-74. Grantee Air Force, 1967-69; Mary Clemmens scholarship St. Louis U., 1965-67, Educare scholar U. So. Calif., 1983-84; grantee numerous competitive contracts. Mem. Acad. TV Arts and Scis. (judge coll. Emmy awards, 1989), Am. Ednl. Research Assn., Assn. for Ednl. Comm. and Tech, Alpha Sigma Nu, Psi Chi. Democrat. Roman Catholic. Avocations: spy

novels, computers, running, theater, piano. Office: Colorado State Univ Mail Stop 1018 Fort Collins CO 80523-2023 Office Phone: 970-491-3315. Business E-Mail: thomas.maher@colostate.edu.

**MAHER, VIRGINIA JONES,** art historian, educator; b. Milw., Oct. 11, 1941; d. Frederick Thomas Murphy and Virginia June Harmon; m. William H. Jones, Aug. 22, 1964 (dec. Nov. 23, 1982); children: William H. Jones Jr., Michael J. Jones, Megan Jones Townsend; m. J. Thomas Maher, III, May 14, 1994. BS, U. Wis., Milw., 1964, MA in Art History, 1994, cert. art mus. studies, 1994. Tchr. French and English Custer HS, Milw., 1964; curatorial asst. Kohler Art Ctr., Sheboygan, Wis., 1993; curator fine arts commn. Cathedral of St. John, Milw., 1995—2003; instr. art history Cardinal Stritch U., Milw., 1997—99, Peninsula Art Sch., Fish Creek, Wis., 2001—06; lectr. art history Milw. Art Mus., 2004—. Guest art curator Miller Art Mus., Sturgeon Bay, Wis., 2000—06; bd. dirs. Peninsula Art Sch., chmn. acquisitions com., 2002—06; lectr. in field. Organizer Friends of Art History, Milw., 2000—03; hist. preservation Jr. League Evanston, Ill., 1980—81, lectr. art in the sch., 1978—80; mem. dean's adv. com. Inst. Visual Arts U. Wis. Milw., 2004; bd. dirs. Wis. Heritages Inc., Milw., 1996—99, Am. Heritage Soc. Milw. Art Mus., 1994—98. Named Writer of Yr. award, Metalsmith Mag., 1998; recipient Grad. of Last Decade (G.O.L.D.) award, U. Wis., Milw., 2000. Mem.: Nat. Mus. Women in Arts, Collectors' Corner Milw. Art Mus., Contemporary Art Soc. Milw. Art Mus., Womans Club Wis., Alpha Phi. Roman Catholic. Avocations: art collecting, painting, gardening. Home: 5611 Schauer Rd Sturgeon Bay WI 54235 Personal E-Mail: vmaher@itol.com.

**MAHEY, JOHN ANDREW,** retired museum director; b. DuBois, Pa., Mar. 30, 1932; s. Manasseh A. and Bernyce (Holdar) M. Student, Columbia U., 1950-52; BA, Pa. State U., 1959, MA, 1962. Asst. dir. Peale Mus., Balt., 1964-69; dir. E.B. Crocker Art Gallery, 1969-72, Cummer Gallery of Art, 1972-75, Meml. Art Gallery of U. Rochester, 1975-79; chief curator Philbrook Art Center, Tulsa, 1979-84; dir. San Antonio Mus. Art, 1984-89, Flint (Mich.) Inst. of Arts, 1989-96; ret., 1996. Contbr. articles on artists to art his. jours.; author exhbn. catalogs. Fulbright scholar, 1962 Mem. Phi Beta Kappa, Phi Alpha Theta. Home: 4645 N Progress Ave Harrisburg PA 17119 E-mail: mahey@aol.com.

**MAHINKA, STEPHEN PAUL,** lawyer; b. Hazleton, Pa., June 25, 1949; s. Stephen and Mary (Stanziola) M.; m. Nancy Marie Casper, Aug. 30, 1975; 1 child, Alexandra Kathryn. AB, Johns Hopkins U., 1971; JD, Harvard U., 1974. Bar: Pa. 1974, D.C. 1975, U.S. Dist. Ct. D.C. 1975, U.S. Ct. Appeals (D.C. cir.) 1976. Law clk. to chief justice Mass. Appeals Ct., Boston, 1974-75; assoc. Morgan, Lewis & Bockius, 1975-81, ptnr., 1981—. Chmn. Life Sci. Interdisciplinary Group; mem. Antitrust and FDA Healthcare Groups, Fin. Com. Contbr. articles to Food and Drug Law Jour., Antitrust Law Jour.; contbr. treatise chpt.: Nat. Labor Rels. Act: Law & Practice, 1995, Winning Antitrust Strategies, 2004; mem. editl. bd. Food and Drug Law Jour., 1992-95. Trustee Johns Hopkins U., Balt., 1974-79. Mem. ABA (chair com. labor exemptions, sect. antitrust law, Chgo., 1983-87), Regulatory Affairs Profls. Soc., Phi Beta Kappa. Republican. Roman Catholic. Office: Morgan Lewis & Bockius LLP 1111 Pennsylvania Ave Washington DC 20004 Office Phone: 202-739-5205. Office Fax: 202-739-3001. Business E-Mail: smahinka@morganlewis.com.

**MAHL, GEORGE FRANKLIN,** retired psychologist, educator; b. Akron, Ohio, Nov. 27, 1917; s. Floyd Alexander and Margaret (Strecker) M.; m. Martha Jane Fenn, Jan. 10, 1944; 1 dau., Barbara Jessica. A. B., Oberlin Coll., 1939, MA, 1941; PhD, Yale U., 1948; certificate, Western New Eng. Inst. Psychoanalysis, 1962. Asst. psychology Oberlin Coll., 1939-41; rsch. asst. in psychology Yale U., New Haven, 1941-42, mem. faculty, 1947—, prof. psychiatry and psychology, 1964-88, prof. emeritus, 1988—; tchr. Western New Eng. Inst. Psychoanalysis, 1961-85, pres., 1972-74; ret., 1988. Served to 1st lt. AUS, 1942-46. Fellow AAAS, APA; mem. Ea. Psychol. Assn., Western New Eng. Inst. Psychoanalysis, Western New Eng. Psychoanalytic Soc., Internat. Psychoanalytical Assn., Inst. Psychoanalytic Tng. and Rsch. (N.Y.). Home: 106 Bayard Ave North Haven CT 06473-4303

**MAHL, THOMAS CHRISTOPHER,** physician, educator; b. North Tonawanda, NY, Aug. 5, 1958; s. John Frederic and Barbara L. Mahl; m. Patricia Jeanne Giesler, July 12, 1980; children: Christopher William, Eric Thomas. BS, Oswego State U., NY, 1980; MD, U. Buffalo, NY, 1984. Diplomate internal medicine Am. Bd. Internal Medicine, 1987, gastroenterology Am. Bd. Internal Medicine, 1989. Assoc. prof. clin. medicine U. Buffalo, 1900—; chief internal medicine VA Western NY, Buffalo, 2000—. Pres. faculty coun. U. Buffalo, Sch. Medicine, 2005—06. Recipient Siegel award for med. tchg., 2005. Fellow: Am. Gastroent. Assn; mem.: Am. Assn for the Study of Liver Disease, Alpha Omega Alpha. Office: Veterans Admin - Western New York 3495 Bailey Ave Buffalo NY 14215 Office Phone: 716-862-3160. Business E-Mail: thomas.mahl@med.va.gov.

**MAHLE, CHRISTOPH ERHARD,** electrical engineer; b. Stuttgart, Germany, Mar. 7, 1938; came to U.S. 1968; s. Ernst Johannes and Else (Wurth) M.; m. Mary Heavenrich, Mar. 23, 1975; children: Lisa, Charles. Diploma engring., Swiss Fed. Inst. Polytech., Zurich, 1961, D of Sci. Tech., 1966. Rsch. asst. Swiss Fed. Inst. Tech., Zurich, Switzerland, 1961-67; with tech. staff Comsat Labs., Clarksburg, Md., 1968-71, sect. head, 1971-73, dept. mgr., 1973-81, dir., 1981-83, exec. dir., 1983-94, v.p., 1995-96; ret., 1996. Patentee in field; contbr. articles to profl. jours. Fellow IEEE. Avocations: music, mountain climbing. E-mail: chrismahle@usa.net.

**MAHLEN, TATUM L.,** voice educator; d. William U. Young and Rhonda R. Moen, Jon L. Moen (Stepfather); m. DuWayne L. Mahlen, Jr.; children: Jasa E., Sasha A., Gabriel J. MusB, U. S.D., 1998. Vocal dir. Mitchell Sch. Dist., 2000—. Choir dir. Mitchell Wesleyan Ch., 2004—. Mem.: Am. Choral Dirs. Assn. (state R&S show choir chair 2004—06). Home: 319 E 6th Mitchell SD 57301 Office: Mitchell School District 920 N Capital Mitchell SD 57301 Office Phone: 605-995-3044.

**MAHLENDORF, URSULA RENATE,** literature educator; b. Strehlen, Silesia, Germany, Oct. 24, 1929; arrived in US, 1953; Student, Oberschule an der Hamburgerstraße, Bremen, Fed. Republic Germany, 1950, U. Tübingen, Fed. Republic Germany, 1950-52, Brown U., 1953-57, MA in English Lit., 1956, PhD in German Lit., 1958; student, Bonn U., Fed. Republic Germany, 1953, London U.; grad., New Directions in Psychoanalysis, Washington, 2002. Teaching asst. Brown U., Providence, 1953-57; from acting instr. to prof. German U. Calif., Santa Barbara, 1957—93, prof. women's studies, 1988—93, assoc. dir., campus coord. edn. abroad program, 1967—69, chmn. dept. Germanic and Slavic langs. and lits., 1980-83, assoc. dean Coll. Letters and Sci., 1986-89, emeritus, 1993—. Chmn. symposium in honor of Harry Slochower, 1977; campus coord. edn. abroad program U. Calif., 1967-69, assoc. dir., 1969-72; co-chair Nietzsche symposium Dept. Germanic and Slavic Langs. and Lits., U. Calif., Santa Barbara, 1981. Author: The Wellsprings of Literary Creation, 1985; editor: (with John L. Carleton) Man for Man: A Multi-Disciplinary Workshop on Affecting Man's Social and Psychological Nature through Community Action (Charles C. Thomas), 1973, Dimensions of Social Psychiatry, 1979, (with Arthur Lerner) Life Guidance through Literature, 1992, (in German) Surviving Childhood; assoc. editor Am. Imago, Am. Jour. Social Psychiatry, Jour. Evolutionary Psychology; contbr. more than 90 articles to profl. jours. Recipient Alumni Tchg. award, 1981; rsch. grantee, U. Calif., 1974—. Fulbright fellow, 1951—52, Festschrift named in her honor, 2004. Mem. MLA, Am. Assn. for Aesthetics and Art Criticism (past pres. Calif. div.), Assn. for applied Psychoanalysis (profl. mem.), Am. Assn. Social Psychiatry (councillor 1977-81), Internat. Assn. Social Psychiatry (treas. 1978-83). Avocations: sculpting, woodcarving. Home: 1505 Portesuelo Ave Santa Barbara CA 93105-4626 Office: U Calif Dept Germanic Semitic Slavic Studies Santa Barbara CA 93106 E-mail: mahlendo@gss.ucsb.edu.

**MAHLER, HALFDAN THEODOR,** physician, health organization executive; b. Vivild, Denmark, Apr. 21, 1923; s. Magnus and Benedicte (Suadicani) M.; m. Ebba Fischer-Simonsen, Aug. 31, 1957; children: Per Bo, Finn. MD, U. Copenhagen, 1948, degree in pub. health; LLD (hon.), U. Nottingham, Eng., 1975; MD (hon.), Karolinska Inst., Stockholm, 1977; Docteur, U. Scis. Sociales de Toulouse, France, 1977; DPH (hon.), Seoul Nat. U., 1979; ScD (hon.), U. Lagos, Nigeria, 1979, Emory U., 1989; MD (hon.), Warsaw Med. Acad., 1980; LHD (hon.), U. Nat. Federico Villareal, Lima, Peru, 1980, U. Gand, Belgium, 1983, CUNY, 1989; MD (hon.), Charles U., Prague, 1982, Mahidol U., Bangkok, Thailand, 1982, Aarhus U., Denmark, 1988, U. Copenhagen, 1988, Aga Khan U., Pakistan, 1989; LHD (hon.), U. Nat. Autonoma de Nicaragua, 1983; PhD (hon.), Semmelweis U., Budapest, Hungary, 1987; LLD (hon.), McMaster U., Can., 1989; DSc (hon.), SUNY, 1990; MD (hon.), U. Newcastle Upon Tyne, 1990; LLD (hon.), U. Exeter, 1990, U. Toronto, 1990; DPH (hon.), U. Goteborg, 2005. Specialized tng. in TB; active field of internat. pub. health work; planning officer mass Tb campaign Ecuador, 1950-51; sr. officer nat. Tb program WHO, India, 1951-61, chief Tb unit, Hdqrs., Geneva, 1962-69, sec. to expert adv. panel on Tb, 1962-69, dir. project systems analysis, 1969-70, asst. dir.-gen. div. health services and div. family health, 1970-73, dir.-gen., 1973-88, dir. gen. emeritus, 1988; sec. gen. Internat. Planned Parenthood Fedn., 1989-95. Contbr. articles on epidemiology and control of Tb, polit., social, econ, and technol. priorities in health sector, application of systems analysis to health care problems to profl. jours. Decorated Grand Officier de l'Ordre Nat. du Benin, 1975, Grand Officier de l'Ordre Nat. du. Voltaique, Upper Volta, 1978, comdr. de l'Ordre du Mali, 1982, Grand Officer de l'Ordre du Merite de la Rep. du Senegal, 1982, comdr. 1st class Order White Rose (Finland), Grand Officier de l'Ordre nat. malgache, Madagascar, 1987, Grand Cross Icelandic Order of the Falcon, 1988, Grand Cordon of Order Sacred Treasure, Japan, 1988, Bourgeoisie d'Honneur, Geneva, Switzererland, 1988, Grand Croix De L'Ordre De Merite, Luxembourg, 1990, Grand Cross Ordem do Merito Medico, Brazil, 2003; recipient Jana Evangelisty Purkyne medal (Presdl. award) Prague, 1974, Comenius U. Gold medal Bratislava, 1974, Carlo Forlanini gold medal Federazione Italiana contro la Tubercolosi et le Malattie Polmonari Sociali Rome, 1975, Ernest Carlsens Found. Prize Copenhagen, 1980, Georg Barfred-Pedersen prize Copenhagen, 1982, Hagedorn medal and prize Denmark, 1986, Freedom From Want medal Roosevelt Inst., 1988, Storkors Af Dannebrogsordenen, Denmark, 1988; hon. prof. U. Nat. Mayor de San Marcos, Lima, Peru, U. Chile Faculty of Medicine, Beijing Med. Coll., Rep. of China, Shanghai Med. U.; Bartel World Affairs fellow Cornell U., 1988; U.N. Population award, 1995, Andrija Stampar award, 1995. Fellow Royal Coll. Physicians (London), Faculty Community Medicine of Royal Colls. Physicians U.K. (hon.), Indian Soc. for Malaria and other Communicable Diseases (hon.), Royal Soc. Medicine (London) (hon.), U.K.-U.S. Hewitt award 1992), London Sch. Hygiene and Tropical Medicine (hon.); mem. Med. Assn. Argentina (hon.), Latin Am. Med. Assn. (hon.), Italian Soc. Tropical Medicine (hon.), Belgium Soc. Tropical Medicine (assoc.), Societe medicale de Geneve (hon.), Union Internat. contre la Tuberculose (hon.), Soc. Francaise d'Hygiene, de Medecine sociale et de Genie sanitaire (hon.), Uganda Med. Assn. (hon. life), Coll. Physicians and Surgeons, Bangladesh Royal Coll. Gen. Practitioners (ad eundem), List of Honour of the Internat. Dental Fedn., Am. Pub. Health Assn. (hon.), Nat. Acad. Medicine Mex. (hon.), Nat. Acad. Buenos Aires (hon.), Swedish Soc. Medicine (hon.), Brit. Medal Assn. (hon. fgn. corr. 1990), Inst. Medicine (NAS U.S.A.). Home and Office: Chemin de Pont-Céard 12 CH-1290 Versoix Switzerland Office Fax: 022 755 26 10. Business E-Mail: halfdan.mahler@bluewin.ch.

**MAHLER, STEPHANIE IRENE,** retired administrative manager; b. Bennington, Vt., Jan. 29, 1952; d. Guenther Alexander and Barbara Irene (Overlock) M.; m. Kirby B. Schuller, Apr. 28, 1990. BA in Speech with honors, Allegheny Coll., 1973. Customer service rep. Albany (N.Y.) Felt Co., 1974-77; order systems analyst Miller Brewing Co., Milw., 1977-78, area mgr., 1978-80, regional adminstr., 1980-83, price promotions mgr., 1983-85, asst. brand mgr., 1985-88, mgr. mktg. projects, 1988-90; market mgr. Johnson Controls, Inc., Milw., 1990-92; sr. acct. AMEX Life Assurance Co., Milw., 1992-93; asst. to the pres. Performance Enhancement Psychol. and Phys. Therapy Svcs., Brookfield, Wis., 1994-95, mktg. dir., 1994-95; asst. to gen. mgr. SPI Comms., Brookfield, Wis., 1996, human resources adminstr., 1996-97, acct., 1996-97, systems adminstr., 1997; regional adminstr. mgr. STS Cons., Ltd., Milw., 1997-2000; ret., 2000. Mem. pres.'s club Albany Area C. of C., Albany, 1975-76; mgmt. advisor Jr. Achievement, 1973-74. Named One of Outstanding Young Women of Am., Montgomery, Ala., 1983; Presdl. scholar, 1969, Alden scholar Allegheny Coll., Meadville, Pa., 1970-73. Mem.: Phi Beta Kappa. Home: 8325 N Links Way Milwaukee WI 53217-2821

**MAHLEY, ROBERT W.,** health facility administrator; b. July 23, 1941; m. Linda Mahley; children: Stephen, Leslyn. BS, Maryville Coll., Tenn., 1963; PhD, Vanderbilt U., 1968, MD, 1970; MD (hon.), U. Gsoteborg, Sweden. Instructor biology Maryville Coll., Tenn., 1963—64; MD and PhD program Vanderbilt U., 1964—70, pathology intern, 1970—71; staff Nat. Heart, Lung, and Blood Inst., NIH, Bethesda, Md., 1971—75, head, comparative atherosclerosis and arterial metabolism sect., lab. exptl. atherosclerosis, 1975—79; dir., sr. investigator Gladstone Inst. of Cardiovascular Disease, San Francisco, 1979—; prof. pathology and medicine U. Calif., San Francisco, 1979—; pres. J. David Gladstone Inst., U. Calif., San Francisco, 1992—; sr. investigator Gladstone Inst. of Neurological Disease, San Francisco, 1998—. Contbr. articles to profl. jours. Recipient Heinrich Wieland prize, George Lyman Duff Meml. Lectureship, Am. Heart Assn. award, CIBA-GEIGY award in Biomedical Rsch., Metropolitan Life award for Medical Rsch. in Alzheimer's Disease, Nat. Cholesterol Education Program DeWitt S. Goodman award for Basic Science Achievement, Distinguished Alumnus Award, Vanderbilt U. Sch. Medicine. Fellow: Am. Acad. Arts & Sciences; mem.: NAS, Am. Soc. for Clinical Investigation, Assn. Am. Physicians, IOM. Office: J David Gladstone Inst 1650 Owens St San Francisco CA 94158 Office Phone: 415-794-2000. Office Fax: 415-355-0826. Business E-Mail: rmahley@gladstone.ucsf.edu.*

**MAHLMAN, JERRY DAVID,** retired meteorologist; b. Crawford, Nebr., Feb. 21, 1940; s. Earl Lewis and Ruth Margaret (Callendar) M.; m. Janet Kay Hilgenberg, June 10, 1962; children: Gary Martin, Julie Kay. AB, Chadron State Coll., Nebr., 1962, LHD (hon.), 2000; MS, Colo. State U., 1964, PhD, 1967. Instr. Colo. State U., Ft. Collins, 1964-67; from asst. prof. to assoc. prof. Naval Postgrad. Sch., Monterey, Calif., 1967-70; rsch. meteorologist NOAA Geophys. Fluid Dynamics Lab., Princeton, NJ, 1970-84, lab. dir., 1984-2000; lectr. with rank of prof. Princeton U., NJ, 1980—2002; sr. rsch. fellow Nat. Ctr. for Atmospheric Rsch., Boulder, Colo., 2001—. Chmn. panel on mid-atmosphere program NAS-NRC, 1982-84, mem. climate rsch. com., 1986-89, mem. panel on dynamic extended range forecasting, 1987-90; mem. U.S.-USSR Commn. on Global Ecology, 1989-92; mem. Bd. on Global Change, 1991-95, Bd. on Sustainable Devel., 1995-2000, Commn. to Review U.S. Climate Change Program Strategic Plan, 2002-03; U.S. rep. world climate rsch. program Joint Sci. Commn., 1991-96. Contbr. over 100 articles to profl. jours. Bd. dirs. Lawrence Non-Profit Housing Inc., 1978-88. Recipient Disting. Authorship award Dept. Commerce, 1980, 81, Gold medal, 1986, Disting. Svc. award Chadron State Coll., 1984, Presdl. Rank award disting. exec. 1994, Honor Alumnus award Colo. State U. 1995, Climate Protection award EPA, 2000. Fellow Am. Geophys. Union (Jule Charney lectr. 1993), Am. Meterol. Soc. (awards com. 1984, 95, chmn. 2000, chmn. upper atmosphere com. 1979, assoc. editor Jour. Atmospheric Sci. 1979-86, councilor 1991-94, Editor's award 1978, Carl-Gustaf Rossby Rsch. medal 1994, disting. lectr. 1999). Home: 460 Golden Ln Longmont CO 80501 Office: Nat Ctr for Atmospheric Rsch PO Box 300 Boulder CO 80307-3000 Office Phone: 303-497-1608. Business E-Mail: jmahlman@ncar.edu.

**MAHLUM, DALE DUANE,** state legislator, small business owner; b. Bowman, ND, June 12, 1930; s. Lloyd S. and Ragna (Paulson) M.; m. Sandra Sue Little, Dec. 21, 1956; children: Douglas, Connie, Thomas, Dee Ann, Michele. BS, U. Mont, 1956. Mgr. Super Foods, Kalispell, Mont., 1958—93; store owner Ace Hardware, Missoula, Mont., 1959-93; thoroughbred farm owner, breeder Missoula, Mont.; mem. Mont. Senate, Dist. 35, Helena, 1996—2003. Chmn. Mont. Bank Bd., Missoula, 1974—; bd. dirs. Mont. Hardware Implement, Helena, St. Patricks Hosp., Missoula; chmn. adv. bd. sch. bus U. Mont., Missoula, 1985-88. Mem. Western Mont. Fair Commn., Missoula, 1974-94. With USN, 1950-54. Mem. Mont. Thoroughbreds Breeders Assn. (pres.), Thoroughbred Owners/Breeders Assn. Republican. Lutheran. Home: 10955 Us Highway 93 N Missoula MT 59808-9227 Office: Mont Legislature PO Box 201706 Helena MT 59620-1706 Office Phone: 406-549-3115. Personal E-mail: mal51732@aol.com.

**MAHMOOD, NAFEESA F.,** physician, consultant; MD, Punjab U., Lahore, Pakistan. Lic. Nat. Bd. Med. Examiners; cert. personal trainer Am. Coun. Exercise. Faculty, staff physician U. Minn., Mpls.; cons. internal medicine Mayo Clinic Outreach, Rochester, Minn.; med. dir., CEO, pres. New You Med. Aesthetics, LLC, St. Paul. Academic faculty, staff physician U. Ill., Urbana-Champaign, adviser, preceptor, clin. instructor, Chgo.; genomics liason Mayo Clinic, spkr. women's seminars in hypertention. Contbr. articles to profl. jours. Recipient Shield Healing Skills From God award, U. Ill. dept. medicine, Outstanding Clinician for Oustanding Diagnostic Skills & Clin. Achievement award, Certificate Commendation For Outstanding Clin. Performance award, U. Ill. dept. internal medicine. Mem.: Am. Soc. Laser Medicine and Surgery, Day Spa Assn., Am. Coll. Sports Medicine, ACP, Aerobics and Fitness Assn. of Am. (assoc.), Am. Acad. Aesthetic Medicine (assoc. Mem.), Am. Acad. Anti Aging Medicine (assoc. Membership), Am. Acad. Cosmetic Surgery (assoc.) Achievements include research in angiotensin II and amiodarone induced apoptosis of type 2 alveolar epithelial cells, duet to blockade of AT1 receptors by losartan and L compound. Avocations: jogging, exercise, reading, music, baking.

**MAHMOOD, TALLAT,** oncologist, hematologist; b. Lahore, Pakistan, Apr. 9, 1968; arrived in U.S.A., 1994; d. Mahmood Ali and Furrukh Begum Khan; m. Shahid H. Khan, Jan. 29, 1993; children: Aquila, Nadir, Mohsin. MD, Aga Khan U., 1991. Diplomate Am. Bd. Internal Medicine, Oncology, and Hematology. Clin. fellow Tulane U. Med. Ctr., New Orleans, 1997—99, rsch. fellow, 1999—2000; staff physician Marquette (Mich.) Gen. Hosp., 2000—. Contbr. articles to profl. jours. Mem.: AMA, Am. Soc. Hematology, Am. Soc. Oncology. Avocations: skiing, golf. Office: Marquette General Hospital 1414 W Fair Ave Ste 332 Marquette MI 49855

**MAHMOODI, HAMID,** engineer; s. Teimoor Mahmoodi and Fatemeh Dehghan. BSEE, Iran U. Sci. and Tech., 1998; MS in Elec. and Computer Engring., U. Tehran, 2000. Design engr. IUST Electronic Rsch. Ctr., Tehran, Iran, 1998—99; grad. rsch. asst. Purdue U., West Lafayette, Ind., 2001—. Author: (tech. jour. paper) Estimation of Delay Variations Due to Random-Dopant Fluctuations in Nanoscale CMOS Circuits. Recipient Best Paper award, Internat. Conf. on Computer Design, 2004. Mem.: Toastmasters Internat., Gigascale Systems Rsch. Corp., Semiconductor Rsch. Corp., IEEE. Achievements include patents pending for Dynamic Logic Styles Using Independent Gate Control in Double-Gate SOI Technologies; First Level Supply Gating for Low Power Scan-Based Testing; research in low power, robust and high performance circuit design in nano-scaled technologies, low power and robust memory design, circuit design with nano-scaled devices. Avocations: swimming, cooking. Office Phone: 765-494-0750. Business E-Mail: mahmoodi@ecn.purdue.edu.

**MAHMOUD, ADEL A.,** medical educator, pharmaceutical executive; b. Cairo, Aug. 24, 1941; arrived in U.S.A., 1972; s. Abdel Fattah and Fathia (Osman) Mahmoud; m. Sally L. Hodder, Jan. 31, 1993. Grad., Cairo U., 1958, MD, 1963; PhD, U. London, 1971. Asst. lectr. Ain Shams U., Cairo, 1965—68; WHO fellow U. London, 1969—72; rsch. assoc., prof. Case Western Res. U., Cleve., 1973—87; physician-in-chief Univ. Hosps., Cleve., 1987—98; prof., chmn. dept. medicine Case Western Res. U., Cleve., 1987—98; pres. vaccines Merck & Co. Inc., Whitehouse Sta., NJ, 1998—. Editor: The Eosinophil in Health and Disease, 1979, Tropical and Geographical Medicine, 1990, Schistosomaisis, Tropical Medicine Sci. and Practice, Vol. 1, 2001, Biological Threats and Terrorism: Assessing the Science and Response Capabilities, 2002. Fellow: Infectious Diseases Soc. Am.; mem.: Inst. Medicine, Assn. Am. Physicians, Am. Soc. Clin. Investigations. Office: Merck & Co One Merck Dr Whitehouse Station NJ 08889

**MAHMUD, SHIREEN DIANNE,** photographer; b. Chittagong, Pakistan, Oct. 4, 1949; came to U.S., 1974; d. Mohammed Mazhurul Qudus and Mumtaz Mahal Begum; m. Abdul Wazed Mahmud, Apr. 10, 1966 (div. 1996); children: Sharmin, Anita. BA in Mass Comm., U. Hartford, 1982. Part-time med. sec., Middletown, Conn., 1979—82; freelance photographer, 1985—; typist Aetna Ins. Co., Middletown, 1991. Prodr. feature program Storer Cable Comm., Clinton, Conn., 1991-95; mem. Bridgeport Regional Bus. Coun., 1997; realtor Buyer's Capital. Literacy vol. Russell Librr., Middletown, Conn. Mem. AAUW, Nat. League Am. Pen Women, Internat. Soc. Poets (Hall of Fame award 1997), Conn. Soc. Poets, Conn. Songwriter's Assn., Internat. Platform Assn. Office Phone: 860-306-9090. E-mail: sdshireen@optonline.net.

**MAHOLIC, JULIE LYNN,** music educator, elementary school educator; b. Springfield, Ohio, Dec. 7, 1967; d. James and Nancy Maholic. B of Music Edn., Grove City Coll., 1990; MEd, Holy Family U., 1998. Elementary Education Holy Family U., 1998. Dir. elem. band Coun. Rock Sch. Dist., Newtown, Pa., 1993—. Asst. dir. dist. orch. Coun. Rock Sch. Dist., 1998—2003. Musician: Coun. Rock Cmty. Band, 2002—05, Del. Valley Coll. Wind Ensemble, 2002—04. Vol. Habitat for Humanity, Quakertown, Pa., 2002—. Mem.: Music Educators Nat. Conf., Coun. Rock Edn. Assn. (pub. rels. dir. 2001—02), Bucks County Music Educators Assn. (com. chairperson 2002—04). Avocations: bicycling, skiing. Office: Goodnoe Elementary School 298 Frost Lane Newtown PA 18940 Office Phone: 215-944-2940. Personal E-mail: jlmusic15@aol.com. Business E-mail: jmaholic@crsd.org.

**MAHOLIC, NANCY L.,** nurse; b. Bradford, Pa., Jan. 25, 1937; d. George Edward and Leona Dolores Cuthberston; m. James Andrew Maholic, Nov. 12, 1955; children: James Jr., Jeffrey, Julie. AA, Bucks County C.C., Newtown, Pa., 1980; degree, Upper Bucks Nursing Sch., Upper Black Eddy, Pa., 1981. Teller Bradford Nat. Bank, 1957—62, Springfield (Ohio) Bank, 1964—66; office mgr. Woodrow Mfg. Co., Springfield, 1968—70; coord. adjustment svcs. for the blind, dept. head Bucks county Assn. for the Blind, 1970—78; staff nurse Doylestown (Pa.) Hosp., 1981—2003; patient coord. Doylestown Women's Health, 1990—2003; pvt. duty nurse Bayada Nurses, Langhorne, Pa., 2003—. Preceptor Doylestown Hosp., 1983—2003. Youth choir dir. United Meth. Ch., Ivyland, Pa., 1970—74; parish nurse St. John's United Meth. Ch., 1999—, lay leader, 2005—. Recipient Nurse Excellence award, Doylestown Hosp., 1993. Republican. Avocations: music, reading. Home: 19 Meadow Ln Richboro PA 18954 Personal E-mail: nursecubby@aol.com.

**MAHON, ARTHUR JOSEPH,** lawyer; b. NYC, Jan. 13, 1934; s. Arthur Logan and Mary Agnes (Craine) M.; m. Myra E. Murphy, Aug. 10, 1957; children: Maura, Madonna, Arthur, Nancy. BA, Manhattan Coll., 1955; JD, NYU, 1958. Bar: NY, Fla., DC. Adj. prof. law NYU Sch. of Law, NYC, 1964-78; ptnr. Mudge, Rose, Guthrie, Alexander & Ferdon, N.Y.C., 1970-94; counsel Donovan Leisure Newton & Irvine, N.Y.C., 1994-98, McDermott, Will & Emery, 1998—. Trustee Manhattan Coll., 1982-98, Adrian and Jesse Archbold Charitable Trust, NYC, 1976-, NY Presbyn. Hosp., NYC, 1994—, Alvin Ailey Am. Dance Theatre, 1998—; mem. joint bd. NY Hosp.-Cornell Med. Ctr., NYC, 1990-98; com. on trust and estate gift plans Rockefeller U., NYC, 1984—; bd. dirs. United Way Internat., 1988-94, Alexandria, Va., chmn. planned giving and endowments com. Archdiocese, NYC, 1982-97; bd. overseers Cornell Med. Coll., NYC, 1986—, chmn., 1992-95, vice chmn., 1990-91, 96-; dir. Am. Skin Assn., NYC, 1989-00; v.p. dir. Cath. Communal Fund, Archdiocese of NY, 1997—, trustee Inner City Scholarship Fund, 1998—. Served to capt. USAF, 1958-60. Root-Tilden scholar NYU. Mem. N.Y. State Bar Assn., Bar Assn. City of N.Y., Fla. Bar Assn., D.C. Bar Assn. Home: 41 Middle Beach Rd W Madison CT 06443-3016 Office: McDermott Will & Emery 340 Madison AVe 14th Fl New York NY 10017-4613 E-mail: famg@rcn.com.

**MAHON, MALACHY THOMAS, SR.,** lawyer, educator; b. NYC, Jan. 4, 1934; s. James and Alice (Rooney) M.; m. Margaret Phyllis Kirwan, Jan. 25, 1958 (dec. 1993); children: Veronica Mahon Grover, Laura Mahon Chandonnet, Malachy. BA, Manhattan Coll., 1954; JD, Fordham U., 1960. Bar: N.Y. 1960. Law clk. to chief magistrate John M. Murtagh, N.Y.C., 1959-60; law clk. to justice Tom C. Clark U.S. Supreme Ct., 1960-61; assoc. Hale Russell & Stentzel, N.Y.C., 1961-62, Mudge Rose Guthrie & Alexander, N.Y.C., 1979-80; of counsel Farrell, Fritz, Caemmerer, Cleary, Barnosky & Armentano, Mineola, NY, 1982-83, Havens & Lombard, Flushing, NY, 1994-95; prof. Fordham U. Law Sch., 1962-68; prof. law Hofstra U. Law Sch., 1968—, founding dean, 1968-73, S.B. Wilzig disting. prof. banking, 1985—. Vis. prof. U. Tex. Law Sch., 1973-74; exec. dir., spl. N.Y. State asst. atty. gen. Meyer Investigation of State Police Murder Coverup Charges Against the NY. Attica Prison Riot Prosecutor's Office, 1975; chief counsel N.Y. Gov.'s Spl. Com. on Criminal Offenders, 1966; mem. Nassau County Bd. Ethics, 1983-96, chmn., 1989-96; chmn. merit selection com. EDNY Bankruptcy Judges, 1985-88. Staff author: Mental Illness, Due Process and the Criminal Defendant, 1968; monthly comml. law columnist: N.Y. Law Jour, 1976-78. Served with U.S. Army, 1954-56. Mem. ABA, N.Y. State Bar Assn., Assn. Bar City N.Y., Am. Law Inst. Home: 14 Duke Of Gloucester Manhasset NY 11030-3210 Office: Hofstra U Law Sch Hempstead NY 11550 Office Phone: 516-463-5868. Business E-Mail: lawmtm@hofstra.edu.

**MAHON, ROBERT,** photographer; b. Wilmington, Del., Dec. 28, 1949; s. Clifton and Mary Veronica (Figash) M.; m. Carol Joyce, Apr. 24, 1983. BA in Am. Studies, U. Del., 1971. One-man shows include Twining Gallery, N.Y.C., 1985, Mercer Coll., Trenton, N.J., 1993, Anne Reid Gallery, Princeton, 1996, N.J. State Mus., 1997, Dana Libr. Rutgers U., Newark, 1998, RVC Coll., N.J., 2001, PhilosophyBox, N.Y.C., 2004, Witherspoon Gallery, Princeton, N.J., 2005, Rittenhouse, Phila., 2006, exhibited in group shows at Whitney Mus. Am. Art, 1982, Phila. Mus. Art, 1982, 1995, Am. Ctr., Paris, 1982, Mus. Modern Art, N.Y.C., 1983, 1984—85, 1993, Kolnischer Kunstverein, 1983, Art Inst., Chgo., 1985, Twining Gallery, 1985—86, 1988, 1989, N.J. State Mus., 1990, 1997, 2002, 1999, Guggenheim Soho, 1994, Sandra Gering Gallery, N.Y.C., 1996, Newark Mus., 1997, 2002, Korn Gallery Drew U., Madison, N.J., 1999, N.Y. Pub. Libr., 1999, Guild Hall, East Hampton, N.Y., 1999, also others, Represented in permanent collections Phila. Mus. Art, Mus. Modern Art, Met. Mus. Art, N.Y. Pub. Libr., Humanities Rsch. Ctr., U. Tex., Austin, Princeton U. Libr., Princeton U. Art Mus., Harvard U. Art Mus., N.J. State Mus., Newark Mus., Montclair Art Mus., Rutgers U., Dana Libr., Zimmerli Mus., Noyes Mus., also pvt. collections, exhibitions include 100 NJ Artists Nat. Tour, 2002—03. Guggenheim grantee, 1985; RCIP Printmaking fellow, 1996. Home: PO Box Q Stockton NJ 08559-0390 E-mail: mailbox@robertmahon.net.

**MAHON, STEPHEN C.,** lawyer; b. New Rochelle, NY, 1964; BA, Vanderbuilt U., 1986, JD, 1989. Bar: NY 1989, DC 1992, Ohio 1993, US Ct. Appeals, DC Cir. 1993. Ptnr., corp. transactions & securities regulation Squire, Sanders & Dempsey, LLP, Cin., NY, mem., mgmt. com. Bd. dir. Entrepreneurship Inst. Bd. dir. Cin. Zoo & Botanical Garden. Mem.: Cin. Bar Assn. Office: Squire Sanders & Dempsey LLP 312 Walnut St Ste 3500 Cincinnati OH 45202-4036 Address: Squire Sanders & Dempsey LLP 350 Park Ave New York NY 10022-6022 Fax: 216-479-8780. Office Phone: 513-361-1230. Office Fax: 513-361-1201. Business E-Mail: smahon@ssd.com.

**MAHONE, BARBARA JEAN,** automotive executive; BS, Ohio State U., 1968; MBA, U. Mich., 1972; program for mgmt. devel., Harvard U., 1981. Sys. analyst GM, Detroit, 1968-71, sr. staff asst., 1972-74, mgr. career planning, 1975-78, dir. pers. adminstrn. Rochester, NY, 1979-81, mgr. indsl. rels. Warren, Ohio, 1982-83, dir. human resources mgmt. Chevrolet-Pontiac-Can. group, 1984-86, dir. gen. pers. and pub. affairs Inland divsn. Dayton, Ohio, 1986-88, gen. dir. pers. Indland Fisher Guide divsn. Detroit, 1989-91, gen. dir. employee benefits, 1991-93, dir. human resources truck group Pontiac, Mich., 1994—2000, exec. dir. human resources, 2001—. Chmn. Fed. Labor Rels. Authority, Washington, 1983-84, Spl. Panel on Appeals; dir. Metro Youth; mem. bd. govs. U. Mich. Alumni. Bd. dirs. ARC, Rochester, 1979-82, Urban League Rochester, 1979-82, Rochester Aea Multiple Sclerosis; mem. human resources com. YMCA, Rochester, 1980-82; mem. exec. bd. Nat. Coun. Negro Women; mem. allocations com. United Way Greater Rochester. Recipient Pub. Rels. award Nat. Assn. Bus. and Proff. Women, 1976, Mary McLeod Bethune award Nat. Coun. Negro Women, 1977, Senate resolution Mich. State Legislature, 1980; named Outstanding Woman, Mich. Chronicle, 1975, Woman of Yr., Nat. Assn. Bus. and Profl. Women, 1978, Disting. Bus. Person, U. Mich., 1978, one of 11 Mich. Women, Redbook mag., 1978. Mem. Nat. Black MBA Assn. (bd. dirs., nat. pres. Disting. Svc. award, bd. dirs., nat. pres. Outstanding MBA), Women Econ. Club (bd. dirs.), Indsl. Rels. Rsch. Assn., Internat. Assn. for Pers. Women, Engring. Soc. Detroit. Republican. Home: 2697 Melcombe Cir Unit 402 Troy MI 48084

**MAHONE, GLENN R.,** lawyer; b. Apr. 22, 1945; m. Andrea Mahone; 2 children. BS, Pa. State U., 1968; JD, Duquesne U., 1973; LLM, Yale U., 1975. Bar: Pa. 1973. With Reed Smith LLP, 1973—80, 1991—; now ptnr., mem. exec. com.; broadcast industry exec., 1980—91. Dir. Matthews Internat. Corp.; bd. mem. Allegheny County Airport Authority. Trustee Duquesne U., Westminster Coll.; chmn. Manchester Bidwell Corp. Mem.: Homer S. Brown Law Assn., Allegheny County Bar Assn., Nat. Bar Assn., ABA. Office: Reed Smith LLP 435 Sixth Ave Pittsburgh PA 15219 Office Phone: 412-288-4240. Office Fax: 412-288-3063. Business E-Mail: gmahone@reedsmith.com.

**MAHONEY, ANN DICKINSON,** fundraiser; b. Topeka, Sept. 12, 1961; d. Jacob Alan II and Ruth (Curd) Dickinson; m. Michael James Mahoney, May 29, 1993; children: James Junius Castle, Catherine Lane, Grace Dickinson, Christopher Michael Hayes. AB in History, Grinnell Coll., 1983; postgrad., McGill U., Montreal, Que., Can., 1985. Analyst, corp. fin. dept. E.F. Hutton & Co., Inc., NYC, 1983-85; pres., owner The Dark Side, NYC, 1985-87; asst. dir. individual giving Meml. Sloan-Kettering Cancer Ctr., NYC, 1987-88, dir. spl. gifts, 1988-91; assoc. dir. devel. Sch. Humanities and Scis. Stanford (Calif.) U., 1991-96; ind. fundraising cons., 1996—. Devel. asst. regional office Brandeis U., NYC, 1987. Vol. interviewer Grinnell Coll., NYC, San Francisco, 1983—; chair No. Calif. adv. bd. Nat. Found. for Tchg. Entrepreneurship, 2000-02. Mem.: Peninsula Assn. Retarded Children and Adults Aux. (bd. dirs. 1998—2002, pres. 2000), Pacific Rsch. Inst. for Pub. Policy, Nat. Soc. Fund Raising Execs., San Francisco Ballet Aux., Friends of Filoli (Woodside, Calif.), Jr. League San Francisco (com. chmn. 1996—98), Hist. Topeka Assn., Hayden Lake (Idaho) Country Club, Spokane Club, Villa Taverna (San Francisco). Republican. Episcopalian. Personal E-mail: admahone@pacbell.net.

**MAHONEY, CAROLYN RAY,** academic administrator; b. Memphis, Dec. 22, 1946; d. Stephen and Myrtle (Gray) Boone; m. Charles Augustus Mahoney, May 20, 1972; children: Cindy Rae, Megan Ruth, Carolyn Bernadette. BS, Sienna Coll., 1970; MS in Math., Ohio State U., 1972, PhD in Math., 1983. Asst. prof. math. Denison U., Granville, Ohio, 1984-87; founding faculty prof. math. Calif. State U., San Marcos, 1989—2000; dean sch. math. sci. and tech. Eiizabeth City State, Elizabeth City, NC, provost, vice chancellor academic affairs; pres. Lincoln U., Jefferson City, Mo., 2005—. Mem. Coll. Bd. Test Devel. Com., Princeton, N.J., 1986-89; advisory com. Coll. Bd. Math. Scis., 1992—; vis. asst. prof. math. Ohio State U., Columbus, 1987-89; instr. South African Program Denison U., Granville, 1987; math. campus coord. Young Scholars Program, Columbus, 1987—; cons., researcher regarding increasing the numbers and achievement of minorities and women in math. at all levels; dir. Middle Sch. Math. and Sci. San Marcos, 1992—. Contbr. articles to Jour. Combinatorial Theory, Soc. Indsl. and Applied Math. Newsletter. Active Edn. Commn. of States Task

Force on Improving Achievement of Minorities in Higher Edn., 1990. Grantee NSF, 1987, 90, 92, Math. Assn. Am., 1992, Charles A. Dana Found., 1989, Ohio Bd. Regents, 1989, Math. Scis. Edn. Bd., 1989; named to State of Ohio Women's Hall of Fame, 1989. Mem. Am. Math. Soc., Assn. for Women in Math., Math. Assn. Am., Nat. Assn. Mathematicians, Phi Kappa Phi. Office: Lincoln Univ 820 Chestnut St Jefferson City MO 65102-0029 E-mail: president@lincolnu.edu.

**MAHONEY, CATHERINE ANN,** artist, educator; b. Macon, Mo., Nov. 18, 1948; d. Joe H. and Berniece Joyce (Garnett) Dickson; m. Michael W. Mahoney, July 19, 1969; children: Karin Lynn Mahoney Broeker, Ryan Michael. BS in Edn. with honors, Truman U., Kirksville, 1969. Mo. state life cert. for tchg. art. Elem./secondary art instr. Bucklin (Mo.) R-I Schs. 1970-74; pvt. art instr. Groom (Tex.) Artist's Assn., 1974-75; substitute tchr. Gasconade R-I Schs., Hermann, Mo., 1977-89; pvt. art instr. Colorful Brushes Studio, Hermann, Mo., 1987—; elem./secondary art instr. Crosspoint Christian Schs., Union, Mo., 1994-98. Pres. City of Hermann Arts Coun., 1983-87, membership chmn., 1980-82; dir. Summertime Children's Watercolor Workshops, Colorful Brushes, Hermann, 1987—; artist-in-residence Mo. State Fair, 2005. One-woman shows at Truman U., Kirksville, 1969, Capitol City Art Guild, Jefferson City, Mo., 1983, Kolbe Gallery of Art, Hermann, 1984, Colorful Brushes Studio, Hermann, 1987-94; designer Sister Cities Emblem City of Hermann/Arolsen, Germany, 1989, 20 ft. histl. mural, Gasconade County; works published in: Best of Watercolor: Texture, 1998, The Artful Home II, 2004, Art Resource Book IV, Mo. Life Mag, 2005. Guild's Source Book of Residential Art 4, 2006. Pres. Hermann Parent-Tchr. Orgn., 1985—87; leader 4-H, Girl and Boy Scouts, Hermann, 1982—95; organist, pianist, tchr. Hermann Cath. and Bapt. Chs., 1977—97, E. Free Ch., 1997—. Named Outstanding Young Woman of Yr., Hermann Jaycees, 1984, 1st place award Mo. Artists Collection, Mo. Pub. Svc., Sedalia, Mo., 1992, 3d place award and purchase prize Watercolor USA, Springfield (Mo.) Art Mus., 1995, 1st place award Arts Rolla Art Show, 1999, 2004, 1st pl. watercolor Top 50 Exhbn., Sedalia Excellence award, Tex. Watercolor Soc. and Traveling Exhbn., 2005. Mem.: Mo. Watercolor Soc. (signature mem., bd. dirs. 1998—2006, M. Graham Mdse. award 2003), Oil Painters Am., St. Louis Artist Guild (mem. art sect., Hon. Mention 1993, 1998, 2002), Watercolor USA Honor Soc. (hon. Art Show award 1995), Okla. Watercolor Assn. (assoc. included Art Show 1989), Nat. Watercolor Soc. (assoc. included Nat. Art Show 1995). Avocations: piano, reading, embroidery, sewing, knitting. Home: 1058 Old Stonehill Hermann MO 65041 Office: Colorful Brushes Studio 126 E 4th St Hermann MO 65041-1130 Office Phone: 573-486-2444. E-mail: camahoney@ktis.net.

**MAHONEY, EILEEN HERON,** secondary school educator; b. N.Y., Sept. 18, 1942; d. Michael Francis and Nora Ita (Tierney) Heron; m. John Francis Mahoney, Oct. 21, 1967; children: Kathleen Mary, John Edward. AAS in Bus. Adminstrn. cum laude, Nassau C.C., Uniondale, N.Y., 1981; BS in Bus. Adminstrn. cum laude, N.Y. Inst. Tech., Old Westbury, 1983; MS in Computers in Edn., L.I. U., 1987. Cert. tchr. in bus. edn. (N-12), elem. edn. (N-6), social studies (7-12), N.Y.; cert. sch. dist. adminstr. and sch. bus. adminstr. Bus. tchr. Hewlett-Woodmere Pub. Schs., Hewlett, 1983—91, Hewlett-Woodmere, 1992—99, asst. prin., 1999—; exec. asst. SFM Media, N.Y.C., 1991-92. Mem. bus. adv. bd. Hewlett H.S., 1993—, site-based decision-making team, 1994-97; leader, mem. exec. bd. Coop. Ext./4-H Divsn., L.I., 1977-89; treas. Hewlett Woodmere Faculty Assn., 1996-99. Mem.: ASCD, Nat. Assn. Secondary Sch. Prin., Phi Delta Kappa. Office: George W Hewlett High School 60 Everit Ave Hewlett NY 11557-2100

**MAHONEY, GEORGE LEFEVRE,** lawyer; b. Washington, Mar. 28, 1952; s. George Francis Xavier and Elaine (LeFevre) M.; m. Lucinda Stuart, July 11, 1986. BA, U. Va., 1974, JD, 1978. Bar: N.Y. 1979, U.S. Dist. Ct. (so. and ea. dists), N.Y. 1979, U.S. Ct. Appeals (5th cir.), 1980, U.S. Ct. Appeals (2d cir.) 1981, U.S. Ct. Appeals (D.C. cir.) 1991. Assoc. Satterlee & Stephens, N.Y., 1978-82; asst. gen. counsel Dow Jones & Co., Inc., N.Y.C. and Princeton, N.J., 1982—93; corp. sec., gen. counsel Media General, Inc., Richmond, Va., 1993—, v.p., 2006—. Office: Media General 333 W Franklin St Richmond VA 23219-6100*

**MAHONEY, GEORGE R., JR.,** lawyer; b. Oct. 18, 1942; m. Linda L. Mahoney. AB, Ohio Wesleyan U.; LLB, Duke U. Gen. counsel Family Dollar Stores Inc., 1976—77, v.p., gen. counsel, sec., 1977—84, sr. v.p., gen. counsel, sec., 1984—91, exec. v.p., gen. counsel, sec., 1991—2005. Office: Family Dollar Stores Inc 10401 Monroe Rd Matthews NC 28105 Home: 1603 Forest Ridge Dr Linville NC 28646 Office Phone: 704-847-6961. Office Fax: 704-847-0189.

**MAHONEY, JAMES E.,** information technology executive; BS in Info. Sys., Boise State Univ., 1981. Joined Micron Technology, Boise, Idaho, 1981, various mgmt. positions in info. sys., v.p. info. sys., 1997—. Achievements include being involved in devel. of software applications for Fab, Probe, Assembly, Test, Sales, Shipping, Fin. and Plant ops. depts. Office: VP Info Sys Micron Tech 8000 S Federal Way Boise ID 83716-9632

**MAHONEY, JAMES R.,** federal agency administrator; b. Syracuse, NY; m. Taya Mahoney; 2 children; 6 children from previous marriage. BS in Physics, LeMoyne Coll., Syracuse; PhD in Meteorology, MIT. Faculty pub. health Harvard U.; co-founder Environ. Rsch. and Tech., Inc., 1968—84; dir. environ. industries ctr. Bechtel Group Inc., San Francisco, 1984—88; dir. Nat. Acid Precipitation Assessment Program, 1988; sr. exec. Internat. Tech. Group, LA, 1991—99; pres. Consulting and Ventures Group, 2000—01; asst. sec. of commerce for oceans and atmosphere Commerce Dept., Washington, 2002—; and dep. adminstr. NOAA, Washington, 2002—. Mem.: NAS (com. mem., co-chmn. bd. on atmospheric sci. and climate), Am. Meteorol. Soc. (pres. 1990—91). Office: Dept Commerce Oceanic and Atmospheric Rsch 1315 East-West Hwy Silver Spring MD 20910-3279

**MAHONEY, JILL ELIZABETH,** music educator; b. Phoenix, Oct. 2, 1961; d. John Richard and Janet Louise Mahoney. Student, Grand Canyon Coll., 1979—80; MusB, Ariz. State U., 1984, postgrad., 1984—89. Secondary tchg. cert. grades K-12 with music endorsement. Music tchr. Avondale (Ariz.) Elem. Sch. Dist., Ariz., 1984—85; band/instrumental music tchr. Peoria Unified Sch. Dist., Glendale, Ariz., 1985—. Honor band condr. Isaac Mid. Sch., Phoenix, 1997; honor orch. condr. Paradise Valley (Ariz.) Unified Dist., 1998. Editor: (newsletter) PEA Educator, 1989—91 (Sch. Bell award, 1991). Recipient Pride in Peoria award, 1994, Raymond S. Kellis Leadership in Tchg. award, 2002. Mem.: Ariz. Music Educators Assn. (v.p. 1997—99, condr. Elem. All State Band 2000, George C. Wilson Leadership award 1999, OM Harsell Excellence in Tchg. Music award 2006), Am. String Tchrs. Assn., Internat. Assn. Jazz Educators. Avocations: gardening, music, reading. Home: 2154 W Earll Dr Phoenix AZ 85015 Office: Marshall Ranch Elem Sch 12995 N Marshall Ranch Glendale AZ 85304

**MAHONEY, JOHN,** actor; b. Blackpool, Eng., June 20, 1940; MA in English, Western Ill. U.; student, Quincy Coll.; trained for the theater, St. Nicholas Theatre, Chgo. Stage performances include The Water Engine, 1977, The Hothouse, Taking Steps, Death of a Salesman, Orphans, 1985 (Theater World award), The House of Blue Leaves, 1986 (Tony award, Clarence Derwent award), The Subject Was Roses, 1991, The Drawer Boy, 2005; films include Mission Hill, 1982, Voyeur, 1984, Code of Silence, 1985, The Manhattan Project, 1986, Streets of Gold, 1987, Tin Men, 1987, Suspect, 1987, Moonstruck, 1987, Frantic, 1988, Betrayed, 1988, Eight Men Out, 1988, Say Anything, 1989, Love Hurts, 1990, The Russia House, 1990, Barton Fink, 1991, Article 99, 1992, In the Line of Fire, 1993, Striking Distance, 1993, Reality Bites, 1994, The Hudsucker Proxy, 1994, The American President, 1995, Mariette in Ecstasy, 1996, Primal Fear, 1996, She's the One, 1996, Antz (voice), 1998, The Iron Giant (voice), 1999, The Broken Hearts Club, 2000, Almost Salinas, 2001, Atlantis: The Lost Empire (voice), 2001, Atlantis: Milo's Return (voice), 2003; TV series: Lady Blue, 1985-86, H.E.L.P., The Human Factor, 1991, Frasier, 1993-2004; TV movies

Chicago Story, 1981, Listen to your Heart, 1983, Dance of the Phoenix., 1984, The Killing Floor, 1984, First Steps, 1985, Trapped in Silence, 1986, Favorite Son, 1988, (TNT) Dinner at Eight, 1989, (HBO) The Image, 1990, The 10 Million Dollar Getaway, 1991, The Secret Passion of Robert Clayton, 1992; TV special The House of Blue Leaves, 1987. Served AUS Recipient award SAG, 2000.

**MAHONEY, JOHN J.,** office supply company executive; BA, College of Holy Cross; MBA, Northeastern U. Ptnr. Ernst & Young; exec. v.p., CFO Staples Inc., Framingham, Mass., 1996—97, exec v.p., CFO, chief adminstrv. officer, 1997—2006, vice chmn., CFO, 2006—. Office: Staples Inc 500 Staples Dr Framingham MA 01701*

**MAHONEY, JOHN L.,** English literature educator; b. Somerville, Mass., Feb. 4, 1928; AB, Boston Coll., 1950, AM, 1952, DHL (hon.), 2003; PhD, Harvard U., 1957. From instr. English to prof. Boston Coll., 1955—94, Rattigan prof. English, 1994—2002, prof. emeritus, 2002—. Chmn. dept. English, Boston Coll., 1962-67, 69-70, dir. PhD program in English, 1970-75, 82-85, mem. ednl. policy com. Grad. Sch. Arts and Scis., 1985-87; vis. prof. English Harvard U. summer sch., 1963, 65, 67, 71, 80, 83, 86; cons. for self-study Weston Coll. Schs. of Philosophy and Theology, Boston Coll., 1965; sem. leader programs for women, Boston Coll., Newton Coll., 1976, 78, 79; mem. numerous acad. coms. and couns.; cons., mem. English adv. com. Commonwealth of Mass., 1968-70; mem. acad. coun. Coll. of Advancing Studies, Boston Coll., 1969—, univ. core curriculum devel. com., 1991-97; trustee St. John's Sem., Brighton, Mass., coun. on acad. affairs, 1980-86; sec. bd. trustees Katharine Gibbs Sch., Boston, 1982-90; mem. adv. bd. Jesuit Inst., Boston Coll., 1987—; mem. Boston Coll. Coun. the Arts, 1997—2006, mem. edn. com. religion and the arts. Author: The Whole Internal Universe: Imitation and the New Defense of Literature in British Criticism, 1660-1830, 1985, The Persistence of Tragedy: Episodes in the History of Drama, 1985, The Logic of Passion: The Literary Criticism of William Hazlitt, rev. edit., 1981, Wordsworth: A Poetic Life, 1997, Wordsworth and the Critics, 2001, Wordsworth of Rydal: Religious Experience and Religious Practice, 2003; editor, author intro. and notes: The Enlightenment and English Literature, 1980, The English Romantics: Major Poetry and Critical Theory, 1978, An Essay of Dramatic Poetry and Other Critical Writings by John Dryden, 1965, William Duff's Essay on Original Genius, 1964; contbr. Imagination and the Ways of Genius (in Approaches to Hazlitt), 1986, Teaching the Immortality Ode with Coleridge's Dejection: An Ode (in Approaches to Teaching Wordsworth's Poetry), 1986, Teaching Shelley's Skylark and the Defence of Poetry (in Approaches to Teaching Shelley's Poetry), 1990, and others; editor: (with J. Robert Barth, S.J.) Coleridge, Keats, and the Imagination: Romanticism and Adam's Dream, 1990, Seeing Into the Life of Things: Essays on Literature and Religion, 1998; mem. editl. bd. Boston Coll. Mag.; 1981-90; author articles, papers delivered at profl. confs.; reviewer for Studies in Romanticism, The Wordsworth Circle, European Romantic Rev., Nineteenth Century Contexts, So. Humanities Rev., Coll. Lit., Religion and the ARts 1650-1850; series editor Fordham U. Press Series on Religion and Lit., 1997-2005. Active Sacred Heart Parish, Lexington, Mass., del. to Lexington Coun. Chs., 1968, chmn. parish coun., 1969-72, mem. parish coun., 1995-98, 2005—, vice chmn., 1996-98, mem. religious edn. commn., 1974-79, 90-93, sem. leader Christian Youth Edn., 1969-73, lector, 1972—; mem. Archdiocese of Boston Commn. for Promotion of Parish Couns., 1969-74, Benjamin Mays Mentor Ahana program, 1993-2003. Boston Coll. Grad. Sch. fellow, 1950-52; Boston Coll. Faculty rsch. grantee, 1964, 68, 86, 92, 96, 97, 98, Mellon Found. grantee for rsch. and faculty devel., 1981-82; grantee rsch. Am. Philos. Soc., 1987; recipient Boston Coll. Campus Coun. Tchr. of Yr. award, 1966, Boston Coll. alumni award for excellence in edn., 1978, André Favat award Mass. Coun. Tchrs. English, 1988, Prof. of Yr. award Coun. for Advancement and Support of Edn. Mass., 1989, Ann. Wordsworth Meml. Lectr., Rydal Ch., 2003. Mem. AAUP (pres. Boston Coll. chpt. 1962), MLA, N.E. Soc. Eighteenth Century Studies, Wordsworth-Coleridge Assn. Am., Keats-Shelley Assn. Am., The Johnsonians, Alpha Sigma Nu, Phi Beta Kappa (Tchg. award Boston Coll. 1994). Office Phone: 617-552-3720. Business E-Mail: mahoneyj@bc.edu.

**MAHONEY, JOSEPH FRANCIS,** historian, educator; b. Jersey City, N.J., July 4, 1927; s. Daniel Joseph and Margaret Cecilia Mahoney; m. Natalie Helen Krolovich, May 9, 1953; children: Joseph, Natalie, Cecilia, Claire. AB, Duns Scotus Coll., 1949; AM, Seton Hall U., 1958; PhD, Columbia U., 1964. From instr. to prof. history dept. Seton Hall U., South Orange, NJ, 1958—99; ret., 1999. Dir. N.J. Cath. Hist. Rec. Commn. Newark, 1976—2005. Author: The Healing Touch, 1992; co-editor (with P. Wosh): Diocesan Journal of M.A. Corrigan, 1987; editor: N.J. Hist. Soc. Jour., 1969—79. Col. U.S. Army, 1952—82. Recipient Scroll of Achievement, N.J. Hist. Soc., 1981, Award of Recognition, N.J. Hist. Commn., 1978; fellow, N.J. Hist. Soc., 1970. Mem.: Orgn. Am. Historians, Am. Cath. Hist. Assn., Am. Hist. Assn. Roman Catholic. Avocations: reading, walking. Home: 639 Sayre Ln Paramus NJ 07652-1908 E-mail: franjo@verizon.net.

**MAHONEY, JULIA DELONG,** law educator; b. Boston; BA, Barnard Coll., Columbia U., 1984; JD, Yale U., 1987. Bar: NY 1988. Mem. faculty U. So. Calif. Law Sch., U. Chgo. Law Sch.; named assoc. prof. U. Va. Sch. Law, 1999, now prof., also David H. Ibbeken rsch. prof. Office: U Va Sch Law 580 Massie Rd Charlottesville VA 22903-1789 Office Phone: 434-924-3942. E-mail: jdm8t@virginia.edu.

**MAHONEY, KIMBERLY LYNNE,** event and facility executive; b. Johnson City, N.Y., Nov. 1969; d. Dewitt Duncan and Selina Faye Smith; m. Michael Mahoney, June 24, 2000. BA, U. Ky., 1992; MEd, U. Ga., 1994; PhD, Ohio State U., 2006. Facility mgmt. intern Charlotte Coliseum, NC, 1994; event coord. Charlotte Conv. Ctr., NC, 1994—95; account mgr. Show Pros Entertainment Svcs., Inc., Charlotte, NC, 1995—97, regional mgr. Greensboro, NC, 1997—98; guest services mgr. Schottenstein Ctr., Ohio State U., Columbus, 1998—2000, asst. dir. event svcs. and adminstrn., 2000—03; asst. commr. Ohio High Sch. Athletic Assn., 2003—05; instr. Univ. S.C., 2005—06, asst. prof., 2006—. Cons., trainer NFL Jacksonville Jaguars, 2002—03; lectr. Ohio State U., 2003. Office: Univ South Carolina 2012 Carolina Coliseum Columbia SC 29208 Office Phone: 803-777-4690. Business E-Mail: kmahoney@sc.edu.

**MAHONEY, MARGARET ELLERBE,** foundation executive; d. Charles Hallam and Leslie Nelson (Savage) M. BS magna cum laude, Vanderbilt U., 1946; LHD (hon.), Meharry Med. Coll., 1977, U. Fla., 1980, Med. Coll. Pa., 1982, Williams Coll., 1983, Smith Coll., 1985, Beaver Coll., 1985, Brandeis U., 1989, Marymount Coll., 1990, Mt. Sinai Sch. Medicine, 1992, Rush U., 1993, SUNY, Bklyn., 1994, N.Y. Med. Coll., 1995. Fgn. affairs officer State Dept., Washington, 1946-53; exec. assoc., assoc. sec. Carnegie Corp., N.Y.C., 1953-72; v.p. Robert Wood Johnson Found., Princeton, NJ, 1972-80; pres. Commonwealth Found., N.Y.C., 1980-94, MEM Assocs., Inc., 1995—. Spkr. in field. Contbr. articles to profl. jours. Trustee Carnegie Found. Advancement of Tchg., 1985—2001, John D. and Catherine T. MacArthur Found., 1985—2002, Smith Coll., 1988—93, Columbia U., 1991—96, Arthur Ashe Found., 1997—2005; vis. fellow Sch. Archtl. and Urban Planning, Princeton U., 1973—80; bd. dirs. Coun. on Found., 1982—88, Skillbuilders Fund, 1993—99, adv. dir., 1999—; bd. dirs. Alliance for Aging Rsch., 1986—99, Overseas Devel. Coun., 1988—2001, Nat. Found. Ctrs. for Disease Control and Prevention, Inc., 1994—2004; mem. MIT Corp., 1984—89, N.Y.C. Commn. on the Yr. 2000, 1985—87; chmn. Nat. Found. Ctrs. for Disease Control and Prevention, Inc., 1996—98; bd. govs. Am. Stock Exch., 1987—92, Am. Skin Assn., 1994—; Classroom Inc., 1996—2005, Buckminster Fuller Inst., 2005; mem. adv. bd. Office of Med. Examiner, N.Y.C., 1987—; vice chmn. N.Y.C. Mayor's Com. for Pub./Pvt. Partnerships, 1990—93; mem. vestry Parish of Trinity Ch., 1982—89, 1991—95. Recipient Frank H. Lahey Meml. award, 1984, Women's Forum award, 1989, Walsh McDermott award, 1992, Disting. Grantmaker award Coun. Founds., 1993, Edward R. Loveland award ACP, 1994, Spl. Recognition award AAMC, 1994, Merit medal Lotos Club, 1994, Terrance Keenan Leadership award in health philanthropy Grantmakers in health, 1995,

Distinction award Am. Skin Assn., 1998, Rsch. Am. award, 1999, Hon. Classmate Class of 1976 award Princeton U., 2001, Picker Inst. award, 2003. Mem. AAAS, Inst. Medicine of NAS, Am. Acad. Arts and Scis., Am. Philos. Soc., Coun. Fgn. Rels., Fin. Women's Assn. N.Y., N.Y. Acad. Medicine, N.Y. Acad. Scis., Alpha Omega Alpha. Office: MEM Assocs Inc 521 5th Ave 29th Fl New York NY 10175-0088 Office Phone: 212-297-0500.

**MAHONEY, MARGARET ELLIS,** accountant; b. Detroit, Mar. 17, 1929; d. Seth Wiley and Mildred Elizabeth (Hill) Ellis; m. Stephen Bedell Smith, Mar. 15, 1956 (div. Oct. 1962); 1 child, Laura Elizabeth; m. Patrick John Mahoney, Sept. 1, 1972 (dec.). BA, Butler U., 1953. Copywriter Hook Drugs Inc., Indpls., 1953; continuity dir. Sta. WXLW, Indpls., 1954-57; ptnr. Steve Smith and Assocs. Advt., Indpls., 1956-62; account mgr. Sive Advt., Cin., 1963-64, Associated Advt., Cin., 1964-65; copywriter SupeRX Drugs Inc., Cin., 1965-72; promotion writer U.S. News and World Report, Washington, 1974; asst. mgr. advt. Drug Fair, Alexandria, Va., 1975-82; dir. advt. Cosmetic and Fragrance Concepts Inc./DBA Cosmetic Ctrs., Beltsville, Md., 1982-89; advt., prodn. cons. Nat. Red Cross, Galladet U., Washington, 1989-94; asst. to real estate agt. Carmel, Ind., 1994-96; editl. cons., mem. svc. rep., acct. clk. Angie's List, Carmel, Ind., 1996—. Vestrywoman St. Matthews Episcopal Ch., Cin., 1969-71; vol. jr. achievement hosp. chmn. Sleepy Hollow Citizens Assn., Falls Church, Va., 1973; vol. resident assoc. program Smithsonian Instn., Washington, 1989-94; chmn. membership and pub. rels. Friends Chinn Park Regional Libr., Woodbridge, Va., 1991-94; vol. Indpls. Art Ctr. Gift Shop, 1997—, Prince William Symphony Orch., Prince William County Voter Registration Bd. Mem. Potomac Valley Aquarium Soc. (past treas., past sec., editor jour.), Am. Cichlid Assn. (nat. pub. rels. chair 1985-90), Delta Delta Delta. Avocations: swimming, reading, needlecrafts, travel, computers. Home: 9850 Greentree Dr Carmel IN 46032-9099 Office Phone: 317-803-3961. Personal E-mail: mmah317@aol.com.

**MAHONEY, MARY,** hotel executive; b. Orlando, Fla., Dec. 20, 1959; Various positions Days Inn of Am., Inc., 1980—90; founder Targa Internat., Inc, 1990—94; dir. preferred vendor mktg. Cendant Corp., dir. market devel., 1994—96, v.p. mktg., Howard Johnson, 1996-98, pres., CEO, Howard Johnson Internat. Inc., 1998—2003, sr. v.p., member relations and customer support, Fairfield Resorts, 2003—. Adv. bd. William F. Harrah Coll. Hotel Admin., UNLV. Mem. state bd. Junior Achievement, NJ; bd. dirs. Nat. Academy's Found. Travel & Tourism. Named Most Powerful Women in Travel Travel Agt. mag., 1997, 98, 99, Next Generation of Hot New Marketers list Brandweek. Mem.: Am Hotel & Lodging Assoc. Coun. Inns & Suites (audit com., fin. com.), Hospitality Industry Hall of Honor. Office: Fairfield Resorts 8669 Commodity Cir Orlando FL 32819

**MAHONEY, MAUREEN A.,** academic administrator; PhD in Human Devel. and Family Studies, Cornell U., 1977. Prof. psychology Hampshire Coll., Amherst, Mass.; dean Smith Coll., Northampton, Mass., 1996—. Office: Smith Coll Dean of the College College Hall 21 Northampton MA 01063

**MAHONEY, MAURICE JEREMIAH,** medical educator; b. Washington, Aug. 4, 1935; s. Maurice Mahoney and Julia Johnson; m. Blanche Katz, May 23, 2004; children: Tatyana Renner, Karen, Cydney, Matthew, Allison, Linnea. AB, Cornell U., 1957; MD, U. Pitts., 1962; JD, U. Conn., 1994. Bar: Conn. 1994; diplomate Med.Genetics Am. Bd. of Med. Genetics, 1982, Pediats. Am. Bd. of Pediat., 1967. Prof. of genetics Yale U., New Haven, 1970—; dir. human investigation com. Yale U. Sch. of Medicine, 2000—. Editl. bd. Am. Jour. of Med. Genetics, NYC, 1977—94, Fetal Diagnosis and Therapy, Basel, Switzerland, 1984—; Jour. of BioLaw & Bus., Denville, NJ, 1997—; bd. dirs. Am. Soc. of Human Genetics, Bethesda, Md., 1981—84, Soc. for Inherited Metabolic Disorders, Washington, 1984—87; fellow Am. Pediat. Soc., The Woodlands, Tex., 1983—, Am. Coll. of Med. Genetics, Bethesda, Md., 1991—. Editor: (medical text book) Medicine of the Fetus & Mother. Capt. U.S. Army, 1966—68, Ft. McClellan, AL USA. Fellow, AAAS, 1998—2005. Avocations: kayaking, triathlon, opera, bioethics. Home: 526 Riverdale Dr Stratford CT 06615 Office Phone: 203-785-2661. Office Fax: 203-785-7673. Personal E-mail: maurice.mahoney@yale.edu.

**MAHONEY, MICHAEL JAMES,** investment company executive; b. Spokane, Wash., July 18, 1960; s. James Lyle and Frances Edith (Castle) Mahoney; m. Ann Dickinson, May 29, 1993; children: James Junius Castle, Catherine Lane, Grace Dickinson, Christopher Michael Hayes. BA in History cum laude, Whitman Coll., 1982; MBA, Stanford U., 1991. Analyst corp. fin. dept. E.F. Hutton & Co., Inc., N.Y.C., 1982—85; assoc. cons. Bain & Co., Inc., Boston, 1985—87, cons., 1987—89; summer assoc. Goldman, Sachs & Co., N.Y.C. 1990; investment analyst G.T. Global (acquired by AIM Funds), San Francisco, 1991—93; portfolio mgr., lead mgr. G.T. Global Telecom. Fund, 1993—99; sr. portfolio mgr. AIM Funds, San Francisco, 1998—99; founding ptnr. J&M Investments, Menlo Park, Calif., 1996—; sr. analyst, portfolio mgr., dir. Dresdner RCM Global Investors, San Francisco, 1999—2000; chief strategy officer Neon Yoyo, Inc. (acquired by Interwoven, Inc.), San Francisco, 2000; dir. Interwoven, Inc., Sunnyvale, Calif., 2000—01; mng. dir., sr. portfolio mgr., bd. dirs. EGM Capital, LLC, San Francisco, 2001—, sr. mng. dir., 2004—. Guest lectr. in investments Stanford Grad. Sch. of Bus., 1994—; frequent print and TV commentator on the telecomms. industry and investing, 1993—; profiled in Investment Visionaries by Peter Tanous, 2003. Pres. Spokane County Young Reps., 1976-78; campaign mgr. Malone for U.S. Senate, Boston, 1988; bd. overseers Whitman Coll., investment com., 1990—. Recipient Pete Reid award, Whitman Coll., 1997. Mem. O'Mahony Records Soc., Ea. Wash. Geneal. Soc., Pacific Rsch. Inst. for Pub. Policy (mem. tech. adv. bd.), Stanford Alumni Assn. (life), Guardsmen, Villa Taverna (San Francisco), Spokane Club (Washington), Lincoln Club of No. Calif., Hayden Lake Country Club (Idaho), Phi Beta Kappa, Sigma Chi (com. chmn. 1979-80). Office: EGM Capital LLC Two Embarcadero Ctr Ste 1300 San Francisco CA 94111 Business E-Mail: mmahoney@egm.com.

**MAHONEY, MICHAEL ROBERT TAYLOR,** art historian, educator; b. Worcester, Mass., Jan. 24, 1935; s. Michael J. and Mary (Taylor) M. Grad., Phillips Acad., 1953; BA, Yale U., 1959; PhD, Courtauld Inst., U. London, 1965. Finley fellow Nat. Gallery Art, 1962-64; fellow Harvard Center Italian Studies, Villa I Tatti, 1963; museum curator Nat. Gallery Art, 1964-69; prof. fine arts, chmn. dept. Trinity Coll., Hartford, Conn., 1969-86, Genevieve Harlow Goodwin prof. fine arts, 1974-99. Incorporator Hartford Pub. Library, 1970-99; elector Wadsworth Atheneum, Hartford, 1974-85 Author: The Drawings of Salvator Rosa, 1977, (with Jean Cadogan) Wadsworth Atheneum Paintings II: Italy and Spain; editor: National Gallery of Art Report and Studies in the History of Art, 1968-69. Trustee Cesare Barbieri Found., Trinity Coll., 1977-99, Watkinson Libr., Trinity Coll., 1989, Somerset House Art History Found., NYC, 1985-2004; bd. govs. Hill-Stead Mus., Farmington, Conn., 1992-95; mem. adv. coun. Am. Friends of Georgian Group, 1996—.

**MAHONEY, PAUL G.,** law educator; b. St. Louis, 1959; BS, MIT, 1981; JD, Yale Law Sch., 1984. Bar: NY 1987. Law clk. to Hon. Ralph K. Winter Jr. US Ct. Appeals 2nd Cir., New Haven, 1984—85; law clk to Hon. Thurgood Marshall US Supreme Ct., Washington, 1985—86; assoc. Sullivan & Cromwell, NYC, 1986—90; assoc. prof. U. Va. Sch. Law, Charlottesville, 1990—95, prof., 1995—, Albert C. BeVier rsch. prof., 1996—, also Brokaw prof. corp. law. Vis. prof. U. Chgo. Law Sch., U. So. Calif. Law Sch., U. Toronto Faculty of Law; recipient All-Univ. Tchr. Award, U. Va., 1997. Office: U Va Sch Law 580 Massie Rd Charlottesville VA 22903-1789 Office Phone: 434-924-3996. E-mail: pgm9h@virginia.edu.

**MAHONEY, ROBERT WILLIAM,** electronic and security systems manufacturing executive; b. N.Y.C., Sept. 10, 1936; s. Francis Joseph and Margaret (Colleton) M.; m. Joan Marie Sheraton, Oct. 3, 1959; children: Linda Marie, Stephen Francis, Brian Michael. BS, Villanova U., 1958, MBA, Roosevelt U., Chgo., 1961. With sales dept. NCR, Inc., Phila., 1961-70, sales mgr., Allentown, Pa. and Atlanta, 1971-76, v.p., Dayton, Ohio, 1977-80; pres. NCR

Can. Ltd., Toronto, 1981-82; sr. v.p. Diebold, Inc., Canton, Ohio, 1983-84, pres., COO, 1984-85, pres., CEO, 1985-88, CEO, 1988-99, pres.-, 1988-2000, also bd. dirs.; Chmn. Fed. Reserve Bank Cleveland; bd. dirs. Timken Co., Sherwin-Williams Co., Cin. Bell. Bd. dirs. Timken Mercy Med. Ctr., Canton, 1983—; Northeast Ohio Council, Cleve., 1986—; Profl. Football Hall of Fame, Canton, 1987—, Stark County Devel. Bd., Canton, 1986—; Canton Symphony Orch., 1985, Jr. Achievement, Canton, 1984, Akron (Ohio) U. Econ. Devel. Bd., 1982; trustee Canton City Schs., 1986, Mount Union Coll., 1988—, Ohio Found. Ind. Colls., 1988—; mem. adv. bd. C. of C. Leadership Canton, 1987. Served with USN, 1958-61. Republican. Roman Catholic. Clubs: Firestone Country (Akron); Brookside Country (Canton). *

**MAHONEY, SHAWN PATRICK,** artist; b. Camden, NJ, Dec. 17, 1970; s. Michael Joseph and Catherine Mahoney; m. Tracy Ann Baldwin, Apr. 5, 1998; 1 child, Shawna Cheyenne. Acrylic painting, Dreaming of Capemay, digitally altered photograph, Girl Kisses, digitally altered photos, Angels at Play, series of digitally altered photos, Venus to Venus Collection, acrylic painting, Beautiful Abomination, Enigma of a Purple Beauty with Ancient Lawn Jockey, The Wall, A Fathers Wish. Office Phone: 856-742-1914. Personal E-mail: shocktherapyartbyshawn@yahoo.com.

**MAHONEY, WILLIAM FRANCIS,** editor, writer; b. Joliet, Ill., Jan. 24, 1935; s. Cletus George and Mildred Marie (Ochs) Mahoney; m. Carroll Frances Johnson, June 28, 1958; children: Erin Michele Alderfer, Kevin William, Megan Ann, Sheila Marie Startup, Nora Aileen Petchkofski. BS in Journalism, Marquette U., 1957. Reporter Ft. Wayne (Ind.) News Sentinel, 1958-59; pub. rels. mgr. Motorola, Inc., Franklin Park, Ill., 1959-66; sr. acct. exec. Young & Rubicam, Inc., Chgo., 1966-68; pub. info. dir. ABA, Chgo., 1969-71; investor rels. mgr. Chemetron Corp., Chgo., 1971-76; corp. comm. dir. Scott Paper Co., Phila., 1976-80; pub. rels. dir. Esmark Inc., Chgo., 1980-81; prin. Mahoney & Mitchell Incorp., Phila., 1981-89, Investor Rels. Ptnrs., Livingston, NJ, 1993—, prin., editl. dir. VI LLC, 2004—. Author: Investor Relations: The Professional's Guide to Financial and Marketing Communications, 1991, The Active Shareholder, 1993, The Strategy and Practice of Investor Relations, 1997; author, editor: The Investor Relations Guide, 1999, The IR Book, Capital Markets and Valuation, 2003; exec. editor Shareholder Value Mag., 2000-2003; Investor Rels. Update, 1981-99, Valuation Issues. Mem. Nat. Investor Rels. Inst., Vesper Club. Republican. Roman Catholic. Home: 716 S Brandywine St West Chester PA 19382 Personal E-mail: wfmahoney35@verizon.net. Business E-Mail: wfmahoney@vi-llc.com.

**MAHONY, EDWARD B.,** corporate financial executive; BS in Acctg., Manhattan Coll.; MBA in Fin., NYU. CPA 1977. With Price Waterhouse, Touche Ross & Co.; v.p., controller consumer products divsn. Bristol-Myers Squibb, 1978—93; v.p., chief fin. officer The Purdur Frederick Co., 1993—99; v.p. Purdue Pharma, 1993—99, exec. v.p., chief fin. officer, 1999—. Office: Purdue Pharma 1 Stamford Forum Stamford CT 06901

**MAHONY, ROGER MICHAEL,** archbishop; b. Hollywood, Calif., Feb. 27, 1936; s. Victor James and Loretta Marie (Baron) Mahony. AA, Our Lady Queen of Angels Sem., 1956; BA, St. John's Sem. Coll., 1958, BST, 1962; MSW, Cath. U. Am., 1964. Priest Roman Cath. Ch., 1962, ordained bishop, 1975, created cardinal priest, 1991. Asst. pastor St. John's Cathedral, Fresno, Calif., 1962, 1968—73, rector, 1973—80; administr. St. Genevieve's Parish, Fresno, Calif., 1964—67, pastor, 1967—68; titular bishop of Tamascani, aux. bishop of Fresno Fresno, Calif., 1975—80; chancellor Diocese of Fresno, 1970—77, vicar gen., 1975—80; bishop Diocese of Stockton, Calif., 1980—85; archbishop Archdiocese of L.A., 1985—, cardinal priest, 1991—; diocesan dir. Cath. Charities and Social Svc., Fresno, 1964—70; exec. dir. Infant of Prague Adoption Svc., Cath. Welfare Bur., Fresno, 1964—70. Faculty extension divsn. Fresno State U., 1965—67; sec. U.S. Cath. bishops ad hoc com. on farm labor Nat. Conf. Bishops, 1970—75; chmn. com. on pub. welfare and income maintenance Nat. Conf. Cath. Charities, 1969—70; administr. com. Nat. Conf. Cath. Bishops, 1976—79, 1982—85, 1987—90, 1992—95, 1998—2001, com. migration and refugees, 1976—95, chmn. com. farm labor, 1981—92, com. moral evaluation of deterrence, 1986—88, cons. com., chmn. for prolife activities, 1990—95; com. social devel. and world peace U.S. Cath. Conf., 1985—93, chmn. internat. policy sect., 1987—93; com. justice and peace Pontifical Couns., 1984—98, chmn. com. domestic policy, 1998—2001, pastoral care of migrants and itinerant people, 1986—91, social comms., 1989—. Active Mexican-Am. Coun. for Better Housing, 1968—72, Fed. Commn. Agrl. Workers, 1987—93, Urban Coalition of Fresno, Calif., 1968—72, Fresno County Econ. Opportunities Commn., Calif., 1964—65, Fresno County Alcoholic Rehab. Com., Calif., 1966—67, Fresno City Charter Rev. Com., 1968—70, Fresno Redevel. Agy., 1970—75, L.A. 2000 Com., 1985—88, Blue Ribbon Com. Affordable Housing City of L.A., L.A., 1988; mem. commn. to draft an ethics code L.A. City Govt., 1989—90; trustee St. Agnes Hosp., Fresno, 1969—73, Cath. U. Am., 1984—88, 1998—; named chaplain to Pope Paul VI, 1967; chaplain St. Vincent de Paul Soc., 1964—70; bd. dirs. West Coast Regional Office Bishops Com. for Spanish-Speaking, 1967—70; chmn. Calif. Assn. Cath. Charities Dirs., 1965—69; trustee St. Patrick's Sem., Archdiocese of San Francisco, 1974—75; bd. dirs. Fresno Cmty. Workshop, 1965—67, Rebuild L.A. 1992—95. Named Young Man of Yr., Fresno Jr. C. of C., 1967. Mem.: Canon Law Soc. Roman Catholic. Office: Archdiocese LA 3424 Wilshire Blvd Los Angeles CA 90010-2241

**MAHONY, SHEILA ANNE,** retired communications executive; b. Yonkers, N.Y., Jan. 30, 1942; d. Paul Ambrose and Grace (Sullivan) M.; m. Charles A. Riggs, July 7, 1983; stepchildren: Charles Riggs, Julia Riggs Shultis. BA, Newton Coll. Sacred Heart, Mass., 1963; JD, Fordham U., 1967. Asst. corp. counsel Law Dept. City of N.Y., N.Y.C., 1967—72; regional dir. Cable TV Info. Ctr., The Urban Inst., Washington, 1972—74, gen. counsel, 1974-75, exec. dir., 1976-77, Carnegie Commn. on Future of Pub. Broadcasting, N.Y.C., 1977-79, Cablevision Systems Corp., Woodbury, NY, 1980—95, sr. v.p. comm. and pub. affairs, 1995—99, exec. v.p. comm., govt. and pub. affairs, 1999—2004, dir., 1988—2005. Mem. exec. com. CSPAN, 2000—04. Author: Keeping PACE With the New Television, 1979. Dir. C-SPAN, Washington, 1990-2004, Found. for Minority Interests in Media, N.Y.C., 1992-2003; bd. dirs. Lustgarten Found., 2000—, Legal Aid Soc. of N.Y., 2000-2004. Office: Cablevision Systems Corp 1111 Stewart Ave Bethpage NY 11714-3581

**MAHOOD, KEN,** music educator; s. Kenneth Mahood Sr. and Helen Mahood; children: Jonathan Scott, Jason Kenneth. BS Music, The King's Coll., 1969; MusM, Manhattan Sch. Music, 1971; PhD of Music Theory, Met. Coll., 1981; PhD of Music, Concordia Coll., 1999; EdD, Am. U., 2001. Assoc. dir. music Christian Fellowship Ch., Ashburn, Va., 1981—2005; exec. dir. edn. KME Internat., Inc., Leesburg, Va., 1983—; dir. music ministries The Ch. of the Valley, Strasburg, Va., 2005—. Adj. faculty prof. No. Va. C.C. Recipient 20 yr. Achievement Award, Assn. of Music Students, 2001. Mem.: Music Educators Nat. Conf., Am. Coll. Musicians, Music Tchrs. Nat. Assn. Office: KME Internat Inc Leesburg VA 20177 Personal E-mail: drken@musikdok.com.

**MAHOOD, RAMONA MADSON,** library science educator, financial consultant; b. Brigham City, Utah, June 7, 1933; d. Stanley Johnson and Effie (Webb) Madson; m. Harry Richard Mahood, Dec. 21, 1962. BS, Utah State U., 1955; MS, U. Ill., 1959, cert. advanced study, 1971. Cert. tchr. Utah. Reference librarian Weber State U., Ogden, Utah, 1955-62; asst. prof. libr. sci. U. Memphis, 1964—. Editor: Young Adult Literature, 1980; contbr. articles on libr. sci. edn. methods and investing to various publs. Mem. ALA, Tenn. Libr. Assn., Nat. Coun. Tchrs. English, Tenn. Coun. Tchrs. English, Tenn. Assn. Sch. Libr., Phi Kappa Phi, Beta Phi Mu, Delta Kappa Gamma. Avocations: reading, music, knitting.

**MAHORNER, JAMES M.,** lawyer; b. DeLand, Fla., Jan. 28, 1932; s. James Glennon and Sue Mahorner; m. Brenda Johnson (div. May 0, 1992); children: John G., James G., Mary Christine Gore, Amy Caprice, Ted G. JD, Stetson U., DeLand, FL; BSEE, US Naval Acad., Annapolis, MD. Bar: Fla. Atty. Pvt. Practice, Fla., 1975—; gen. counsel Dept. of HRS, Fla., 1970—74; trial counsel Dept. of Agr., Fla., 1965; ptnr. Dickens, Linn, and Mahorner, Tallahassee, Fla., 1967—70, White, Phipps, Linn, Furnell and Mahorner, Tallahassee, Fla., 1965—67; atty. State Attorney's Gen. Office, Fla., 1960—65. Mem.: Mensa. Democrat-Npl. Avocations: chess, bridge, tennis. Office: 234 9th Avenue South Jacksonville Beach FL 32250 Home: PO Box 50774 Jacksonville Beach FL 32240-0774 E-mail: jgmahorner@netzero.net.

**MAHR, AARON LEE,** government agency administrator; b. Canton, Ill., Jan. 4, 1947; s. Ivan Lee and Nina Berniece Mahr; m. Nicole Adrienne Bourque, June 30, 1987; children: Jennifer Ward, David Abba, Timothy. BA, Emory U., 1969; Sr. Ofcls. in Nat. Security, Harvard U., 1991. Cert. Army Acquisitions Corps. Inventory mgmt. specialist U.S. Army Weapons Command, Rock Island, Ill., 1969-70; supply sys. analyst Frankford Arsenal, Phila., 1970-71, U.S. Army Gen. Materiel & Petroleum Ctr., New Cumberland, Pa., 1971-74; Jordan/Kuwait country desk officer U.S. Army Internat. Logistics Command, Alexandria, Va., 1974-76; Mid-East program mgr. U.S. Army Security Assistance Command, Alexandria, 1976-82; Mid-East program mgr. Office Dep. Chief Staff for Logistics Hdqs. Dept. of the Army, Pentagon, Washington, 1982-83; chief Israel and Turkey divsn. U.S. Army Security Assistance Command, Alexandria, 1983-85; dir. Internat. Coop. Programs Activity, Alexandria, 1986—2000. Diabetes hotline cons. Inst. for Peripheral Nerve Surgery, Balt., 2000—. Mem. Order of DeMolay, Delta Tau Delta. Avocations: videography, photography, travel, fishing. Home: 1228 Vista Hills Dr Lakeland FL 33813-5641 Personal E-mail: aruba4us@earthlink.net.

**MAHR, JOE,** journalist; Reporter The State Jour.-Register, Copley News Svc., Ill., 1995; statehouse reporter Copley News Svc., Ill., 1998—2000; gen. assignment/projects reporter Block News Alliance (The Blade and The Pitts. Post-Gazette), 2000—. Recipient Pulitzer Prize for investigative reporting, 2004, medal winner, Investigative Reporters and Editors, Inc., 2004. Office: The Blade 541 N Superior St Toledo OH 43660

**MAHRAUN, DANIEL ALLEN,** musician, director; b. Muscatine, Iowa, Feb. 2, 1971; s. Donald Gene and Janet Gail Mahraun. MusB in Edns., Wartburg Coll., 1993; MusM in Conducting, U. No. Iowa, 1995, MusM in Performance, 1996; PhD in Musical Arts, U. Colo., Boulder, 2003. Vocal music dir. Clear Lake Jr. HS, Iowa, 1995—97; dir. choral activities Bethany Coll., Lindsborg, Kans., 2000—. Chancel choir dir. Bethany Luth. Ch., Lindsborg, 2004—. Study grant, Evang. Luth. Ch. Am., 2002, Burmeister grant, Bethany Coll., 2003. Mem.: Herbert Howells Soc., Assn. Luth. Ch. Musicians, Coll. Music Soc., Music Educators Nat. Conf., Am. Choral Dirs. Assn., Luth. Concerned N.Am. D-Liberal. Lutheran. Avocations: hiking, art, films, theater. Office: Bethany Coll 421 N First St Lindsborg KS 67456 Office Phone: 785-227-3380 x 8334. Business E-Mail: mahraund@bethanylb.edu.

**MAHSMAN, DAVID LAWRENCE,** writer; b. Quincy, Ill., Aug. 16, 1950; s. Alvin Henry and Dorothy Marie (Schnack) M.; m. Lois Jean Mohn, July 27, 1975. BS in Journalism, So. Ill. U., 1972; MDiv, Concordia Theol. Seminary, Fort Wayne, Ind., 1983; STM, Concordia Sem., St. Louis, 1995. Staff writer Paddock Publs., Arlington Heights, Ill., 1972-73, Decatur (Ill.) Herald & Rev., 1973-76; press asst. Hon. Tom Railsback U.S. Ho. Reps., Washington, 1976-79, campaign press sec. Hon. Dan Coats Ft. Wayne, Ind., 1979-80, 82; pastor Trinity Luth. Ch., Glen Cove, NY, 1983-85; dir. news and info. Luth. Ch.-Mo. Synod, St. Louis, 1985—2005; exec. editor, contbr. Luth. Witness, St. Louis, 1985—2005; exec. editor Reporter, St. Louis, 1985—2005; asst. to exec. dir. Bd. Mission Svcs. Mo. Synod, 2005—. Mem. Inter-Luth. task force on pornography Luth. Coun. U.S.A., 1986; mem. Washington adv. coun. Mo. Synod, Office of Govt. Info., Washington, 1987-2000. Editor: Augsburg Today: This We Believe, Teach and Confess, 1997. Recipient Jacob Scher Investigative Reporting award Women in Comm., 1974, Commendation award Concordia Hist. Inst., 1988, 98, 1st Place Reporting award Evang. Press Assn., 2003. Mem. Concordia Hist. Inst. (life). Republican. Lutheran. Avocations: travel, photography. Office: Luth Ch-Mo Synod 1333 S Kirkwood Rd Saint Louis MO 63122-7226 E-mail: david.mahsman@lcms.org.

**MAI, AIMEE MARIE,** social studies educator; b. Cin., Ohio, Apr. 30, 1971; d. John Robert and Caroline Annette (Labmeier) Fuller; m. Robert Eric Mai, Apr. 5, 1997; children: Christopher Aaron, Matthew Alexander. BA with hons., No. Ky. U., Highland Heights, Ky., 1994. Cert. tchr. Ohio, 1994. Tchr. Oak Hills H.S., Cin., 1995—97, St. Margaret Mary Sch., Cin., 1997—99, Our Mother Sorrows Sch., Cin., 1999—. Republican. Roman Cath. Avocations: crossword puzzles, reading. Home: 4133 Woodchuck Dr Cincinnati OH 45251

**MAI, WILLIAM FREDERICK,** plant nematologist, educator; b. Greenwood, Del., July 23, 1916; s. William Frederick and Laurana (Owens) M.; m. Barbara Lee Morrell, June 2, 1941; children: Virginia Mai Abrams, William Howard Mai, Eliabeth Hardy Mai. BS, U. Del., 1939; PhD, Cornell U., 1945. Asst. prof. Cornell U., Ithaca, N.Y., 1946-49, assoc. prof., 1949-52, prof., 1952-81, Liberty Hyde prof. plant nematology, 1981-83, prof. emeritus, 1983—. Cons. Nat. Acad. Scis., Internat. Potato Ctr., Brands Co., AID. Author (with H.H. Lyon), Pictoral Key to Genera of Plant Parasitic Nemtodes, 1960, 5th edit. 1993, Plant Parasitic Nematodes, 1971; editor: Control of Plant Parasitic Nematodes, 1968. Coach Little League Baseball and Football, Ithaca, 1955—60; chmn. Community Orgn., 1960—65. Recipient award of distinction Internat. Plant Protection Conf., 1979; Paul Harris fellow Rotary Found., 1997. Fellow Am. Phytopath. Soc. (pres. Northeastern div. 1968-69 award of merit Northeastern div); mem. AAAS, Soc. Nematologists (pres. 1969 hon. life), Helminthological Soc. Washington, Soc. European Nematologists, Potato Assn. Am. Lodges: Rotary. Home: Apt 203 103 Bundy Rd Ithaca NY 14850 Office: Cornell U Dept Plant Pathology Ithaca NY 14853

**MAIBACH, BEN C., JR.,** consumer products company executive; b. Bay City, Mich., 1920; With Barton-Malow Co., Detroit, 1938—, v.p., dir.-in-charge field ops., 1949-53, exec. v.p., 1953-60, pres., 1960-76, chmn. bd., 1976; chmn. and dir. Barton-Malow Ent.; chmn. bd. Cloverdale Equipment Co. Trustee Barton-Malow Found, Maibach Found., 1967—; chmn Apostolic Christian Woodhaven, Detroit; bishop Apostolic Christian Ch., Mich., Ont., Fla.; bd. dirs. S.E. Mich. chpt. ARC, Rural Gospel and Med. Missions of India. Home: 29711 Wentworth St Apt 207 Livonia MI 48154-3887 also: 5525 Azure Way Sarasota FL 34242-1857

**MAIBACH, BEN C., III,** construction company executive; b. May 5, 1946; BS, Mich. State U., 1968. With Barton-Malow Corp., Oak Park, Mich., 1964—, v.p. field ops., 1964-68, systems analyst, programmer, 1968-70, project administr., 1970-72; officer mgr., purchasing agt. Barton-Malow Co., Oak Park, Mich., 1972-73, v.p., 1973-76, exec. v.p., 1976-81, pres., 1981—. Office: Barton Malow Co 26500 American Dr Southfield MI 48034*

**MAICKEL, ROGER PHILIP,** pharmacologist, educator; b. Floral Park, N.Y., Sept. 8, 1933; s. Philip Vincent and Margaret Mary (Rose) M.; m. Lois Louise Pivonka, Sept. 8, 1956; children: Nancy Ellen Maickel Ward, Carolyn Sue Maickel Anderson. BS, Manhattan Coll., 1954; postgrad., Poly. Inst. Bklyn., 1954-55; MS, Georgetown U., 1957, PhD, 1960. Biochemist Nat. Heart Inst., Bethesda, Md., 1955-65; assoc. prof. pharmacology Ind. U., 1965-69, prof., 1969—, head sect. pharmacology med. scis. program, 1971-77; prof. pharmacology and toxicology, head dept. Sch. Pharmacy and Pharmacal Scis. Purdue U., West Lafayette, Ind., 1977-83; dir. lab. animal program Purdue U., West Lafayette, 1988-98, emeritus prof., 1999—; acting v.p. product acquisition and devel. BetaMED Pharms., Inc., Indpls., 1983-84. Adv. editor: Pergamon Press, 1970-88; adv. editorial bd.: Neuropharmacology, 1974-88. Bd. dirs. TEAMS, Inc., 1981-87, Am. Coun. on Sci. and Health, 1993-2000; trustee AAALAC, 1992—. Recipient Alumni Award in medicine Manhattan Coll., 1972 Fellow: AAAS, Collegium Internat. de Neuro-Psychopharmacology, Royal Soc. Chemistry, Am. Coll. Neuropsychopharmacology, Am. Inst. Chemists (bd. dirs. 1989—92, 2001—, pres.-elect 1992—94, pres. 1994—96, chmn. 1996—98); mem.: ASTM, Soc. Toxicology, Soc. Neurosci., N.Y. Acad. Scis., Internat. Soc. Psychoneuroendocrinology, Internat. Assn. Chiefs Police, Soc. Forensic Toxicologists, Am. Soc. Clin. Pharmacology and Therapeutics, Am. Soc. Pharmacology and Exptl. Therapeutics, Am. Chem. Soc., Rho Chi, Sigma Xi. Home: 3567 Canterbury Dr Lafayette IN 47909-3714 Office Phone: 765-474-2855. Business E-Mail: maickel@pharmacy.purdue.edu. *As a human being, I hope to be able to do my best in the roles of scientist, teacher, and citizen by fulfilling the academic criteria of teaching, research, and service to the utmost degree humanly possible.*

**MAIDA, ADAM JOSEPH CARDINAL,** cardinal; b. East Vandergrift, Pa., Mar. 18, 1930; Student, St. Vincent Coll., Latrobe, Pa., St. Mary's U., Balt., Lateran U., Rome, Duquesne U. Ordained priest Roman Cath. Ch., 1956, consecrated bishop Roman Cath. Ch., 1984. Bishop, Green Bay, Wis., 1984—89; archbishop Detroit, 1990—; created cardinal, 1994—; appt. superior Cayman Islands, 2000. Home and Office: Archdiocese of Detroit 1234 Washington Blvd Detroit MI 48226-1825

**MAIDIQUE, MODESTO ALEX,** academic administrator; b. Havana, Cuba, Mar. 20, 1940; s. Modesto Maidique and Hilda Rodriguez; children: Ana Teresa, Mark Alex. BS, MIT, 1962, MS, 1964, PhD, 1970. Instr. MIT, Boston, 1976-79; v.p., gen. mgr. Analog Devices Semiconductor, Boston, 1970-76; asst. prof. Harvard U., Boston, 1976-81; assoc. prof. Stanford U., Palo Alto, Calif., 1981-84; sr. ptnr. Hambrecht and Quist Venture Ptnrs., Palo Alto, Calif., 1981-86; co-founder, dir. U. Miami (Fla.) Innovation and Entepreneurship Inst., 1984-86; pres. Fla. Internat. U., Miami, 1986—. Mem. Pres.'s Edn. Policy Adv. Com.; chmn. Beacon Coun., 1992-93. Recipient Citizenship award HEW, 1973, Teaching award Stanford U., 1983 Mem. IEEE, Assn. Cuban Engrs. Republican. Roman Catholic. Office: Fla Internat U Office of Pres Univ Park PC 528 Miami FL 33199-0001 Fax: 305-348-3660. E-mail: maidique@fiu.edu.

**MAIDMAN, RICHARD HARVEY MORTIMER,** lawyer; b. NYC, Nov. 17, 1933; s. William and Ada (Seegle) M.; m. Lynne Rochelle Lateiner, Apr. 3, 1960 (div. Sept. 1987); m. Gail Lowe Haymes, Sept. 27, 1998; children: Patrick, Mitchel, Dagny. BA, Williams Coll., 1955; JD, Yale U., 1959; postgrad., NYU Grad. Sch. Bus., 1957, NYU Grad. Sch. Law, 1960, 77. Bar: N.Y. 1961, Fla. 1961, U.S. Dist. Ct. 1962, 79, U.S. Ct. Appeals 1966, U.S. Supreme Ct. 1978. Assoc. Saxe, Bacon & O'Shea, N.Y.C., 1962-64; ptnr. Weiner, Maidman & Goldman, N.Y.C., 1964-67; pvt. practice N.Y.C. and Fla., 1968—. Of counsel Shwal, Thompson & Bloch, NYC and Geneva, 1976-87, Maidman and Mittelman, LLP, 1996—; pres. MBS Equities, Inc., 1970-88, Fashion Wear Realty Co., Inc., NYC, 1975-2004, chmn., 2003—; mng. gen. ptnr. Richard and David Maidman, NYC, 1972—; Barcelona Hotel Ltd., Miami Beach, Fla., 1975-84, New Haven Projects Co., 1987—; dir., gen counsel The Farr Companies, Washington, 1990-92; legis. counsel Theodore R. Kupferman, 17th Congl. Dist. NY, 1966-68; receiver Halloran House Hotel, NYC, 1981; prin. Manhattan Parking Sys. Group, NYC, 2000—; chmn. Townhouse Mgmt. Co., 2002—. Contbr. articles to profl. jours. Mem. ABA, N.Y. State Bar Assn., Fla. Bar Assn., Assn. of the Bar of the City of N.Y., Bankruptcy Lawyers Assn., N.Y.C. Real Estate Bd. N.Y. Home: Steamboat Landing 27 Astor Ln Sands Point NY 11050-2602 also: 9 E 79th St New York NY 10021-0123 Office: 70 E 55th St New York NY 10022-3222 Office Phone: 212-755-0500. Personal E-Mail: rhmm59@aya.yale.edu. Business E-Mail: richard@maidman.org.

**MAIDMENT, PAUL,** publishing executive; m. Lisa Martineau; 2 children. Grad., St. Catherine's Coll. Sr. editor Newsweek, 1992—95; editor FT.com, 1995—2001; exec. editor Forbes.com, 2001—, Forbes, 2001—. Author: (online publ.) A Middlesex Cricket Gazetteer, The Plain Words Glossary of Financial and Economic Terms. Office: Forbes 60 Fifth Ave New York NY 10011

**MAIDMENT, STEVE W.,** elementary school educator; b. Kansas City; s. Jimmy and Phyllis Maidment. BSE, MA, Cerl. Mo. State U., Warnensburg. Tchr. De LaSalle Edn. Ctr., Kansas City. Contbr. chapters to books. Recipient Sabbatical award, De LaSalle Edn. Ctr., 2005. Mem.: Nat. Coun. Social Studies.

**MAIDON, CAROLYN HOWSER,** director; b. Chgo., May 13, 1946; d. Lloyd Earl and Esther Lillian (Beck) Howser; m. Charles Randall Maidon, Nov. 21, 1970; children: Randall Scott, April Janel. BS in Edn., Okla. State U., 1968; MS in Edn., N.C. State U., 1984, postgrad., 1987—. Tchr. biology and English Cary (N.C.) High Sch., 1968-71; grad. instr. N.C. State U., Raleigh, 1984-85, asst. affirmative action officer, 1985-89, asst. dir. univ. undesignated program, 1989-95; dir. tchr. edn., 1995-99; coord. MentorNet N.C. State U., Raleigh, 2000—; chief, tchr. edn. sect. N.C. Dept. Pub. Instrn., 1999-2000. Home: 4204 Belnap Dr Apex NC 27502-5378 Office: NC State U PO Box 7632 Raleigh NC 27695-7632

**MAIENSCHEIN, FRED,** retired physicist; b. Belleville, Ill., Oct. 28, 1925; s. Fred and Ethel (Forsythe) M.; m. Joyce Kylander, Aug. 14, 1948; children: Jane, Jon. BS in Chem. Engring. Rose Hulman Inst. Tech., 1945; MS in Physics, Ind. U., 1948, PhD in Physics, 1949. Physicist Oak Ridge Nat. Lab., 1951-60, assoc. dir. engring. physics div., 1960-66; co-dir. Oak Ridge Electron Linear Accelerator, 1965-74, dir. engring. physics div., 1966-90, ret., 1990. Mem. com. reactor physics Nuclear Energy Div., 1962-89; mem. adv. com. radiation aspects of SST, FAA, 1969-74; mem. subcoms. Nat. Com. Radiation Protection, 1959-71. Contbr. articles profl. jours., chpts. in books. Fellow Am. Nuclear Soc.; mem. Physics Soc., AAAS, Soc. Neurosci., Tau Beta Pi. Home: 838 W Outer Dr Oak Ridge TN 37830-8402

**MAIENSCHEIN, JANE ANN,** historian, philosopher, educator; b. Oak Ridge, Tenn., Sept. 23, 1950; d. Fred Conrad and Joyce Evelyn (Kylander) M.; m. J. Richard Creath, Mar. 13, 1982. BA, Yale U., 1972; MA, Ind. U., 1975, PhD, 1978. Asst. prof. Dickinson Coll., Carlisle, Pa., 1978-80; vis. scholar Harvard U., Cambridge, Mass., 1983-84; vis. assoc. prof. Stanford (Calif.) U., 1987; asst. prof. Ariz. State U., Tempe, 1981-86, assoc. prof. philosophy, 1986-90, prof. philosophy and bioogy, 1990—. Author: Transforming Traditions, 1991, 100 Years Exploring Life, 1989, Whose View of Life, 2003; editor: Defining Biology, 1986; co-editor: Biology and the Foundations of Ethics, 1999, Biology and Epistemology, 2000. Recipient various grants NSF; fellowship Josiah Macy Jr. Found., 1974-78, Ariz. Congressional fellowship, US Congress, 1998-99. Fellow AAAS (various coms.); mem. History of Sci. Soc. (v.p. 2006—, various coms.), Internat. Soc. for History, Philosophy and Social Studies of Sci. (pres. 1989-91), Sigma Xi.

**MAIER, CHARLES STEVEN,** history professor; b. N.Y.C., Feb. 23, 1939; s. Louis and Muriel (Krailsheimer) M.; m. Pauline Alice Rubbelke, June 17, 1961; children: Andrea Nicole, Nicholas Winterer, Jessica Elizabeth Heine. AB, Harvard U., 1960, PhD, 1967; postgrad., St. Anthony's Coll., Oxford, Eng., 1960-61. Instr. history Harvard U., Cambridge, Mass., 1967-69, asst. prof., 1969-73, lectr., 1973-75 prof. history, 1981-91, Krupp Found. prof. European studies, 1991—2002, Leverett Saltonstall prof. history, 2002, dir. Ctr. for European Studies, 1994-2001; vis. prof. U Bielefeld, Germany, 1976; assoc. prof. history Duke U., Durham, NC, 1976-79, prof., 1979-81. Rsch. fellow Lehrman Inst., N.Y.C., 1975-76; mem. assoc. staff Brookings Instn., Washington, 1978-84; mem. coun. Fondation Jean Monnet pour l'Europe, Lausanne, Switzerland; mem. joint comm. on W. Europe Social Sci. Rsch. Coun. and Am. Coun. Learned Socs., 1978-84, chmn., 1979-81; mem. German Am. Acad. Coun., Bonn, Germany and Washington, 1998-2001. Author: Recasting Bourgeois Europe, 1975 (Am. Hist. Assn. George Louis Beer award 1976, Herbert Baxter Adams award 1977), In Search of Stability, 1987, The Unmasterable Past, 1988, Dissolution: The Crisis of Communism and the End of East Germany, 1997, Among Empires: American Arcendancy and its Predecesssons, 2006; editor: The Origins of the Cold War and Contemporary Europe, 1978, rev. edit., 1990, (with Dan S. White) The Thirteenth of May and the Advent of de Gaulle's Republic, 1967, (with Leon Lindberg) The Politics of Inflation and Economic Stagnation, 1985, Changing Boundaries of the Political, 1987, The Marshall Plan and Germany, 1991. Decorated comdr.'s cross Order of Merit, Germany; fellow NEH, 1977-78, German Marshall Found., 1980-81, Guggenheim Found., 1984-85; rsch. grantee MacArthur Found., 1988-89; recipient Alexander von Humboldt Found. Rsch. prize, 2003; fellow Woodrow Wilson Ctr. for Scholars, Washington, D.C., 1989. Mem. Coun. on Fgn. Rels., Am. Hist. Assn., Soc. Italian Hist. Studies, Soc. Historians of Am. Fgn. Rels., Am. Acad. Arts and Scis., Phi Beta Kappa. Home: 60 Larchwood Dr Cambridge MA 02138-4639 Office: Harvard U Ctr for European Studies Cambridge MA 02138 Office Phone: 617-495-4303. Business E-Mail: csmaier@fas.harvard.edu.

**MAIER, DONNA MARIE,** psychologist; b. Somerville, N.J., July 22, 1959; d. Donald Victor and Patricia Norma (Ledwith) Maier. BS in Biology, Youngstown State U., 1980; respecialization cert. in Clin. Psychology, U. Cin., 1992; PhD in Psychology, Rutgers U., 1986. Cert. health care qual. in psycho. Assn. State and Provincial Psycho. Bds., 1996. Grad. fellow, tchg. asst. Rutgers U., New Brunswick, NJ, 1981—86; rsch. fellow Armed Forces Radiobiology Rsch. Inst., Wash., 1986—89; psycho. intern. VA Hosp., Lexington, Ky., 1991—92; clin. psychologist Comprehensive Care N. Ky., Covington, 1992—95, Group Health Assoc., Dayton, Ohio, 1995—2003, Maier Psychol. Svcs., Cin., 2003—. Inst. Montgomery Coll., Rockville, 1988—89, U. Cin., Psycho. Dept., Cin., 1991—91, No. Ky. U., Highland Heights, 1990—91. Contbr. articles various profl. jours. Mem.; Nat. Register Health Svc. Providers in Psychology, Cin. Acad. Profl. Psychology, Feminists for Life, Amnesty Internat. Office: Maier Psychological Svcs 4301 State Rt 725 Bellbrook OH 45305 Office Phone: 937-848-9858 x25.

**MAIER, GERALD JAMES,** gas industry executive; b. Regina, Sask., Can., Sept. 22, 1928; s. John Joseph and Mary M. Student, Notre Dame Coll., Wilcox, U. Man., U. Alta., U. Western Ont.; LLD (hon.), U. Alta., 1999; LLD, U. Calgary, 2005. With petroleum and mining industries Can., U.S., Australia, U.K.; responsible for petroleum ops. Africa, United Arab Emirates, S.E. Asia; past chmn., pres., CEO TransCan. PipeLines, Calgary, Canada, 1985-99; vice-chmn. NOVA Chems. Corp., Calgary, 1998-2000. Bd. dirs. Stream-Flo Industries, Ltd., Master Flo Valve Inc., Bow Valley Energy Ltd., Vintage Petroleum, Inc.; chmn. Can. Nat. Com. for World Petroleum Congresses, 1991—94, Van Horne Inst. for Internat. Transp., 1992—2000. Chmn. bd. dirs. Notre Dame Coll. Named Hon. Col. (ret.) King's Own Calgary Rgt., Resource Man of Yr. Alta. Chamber of Resources, 1990, Officer Order of Can.; 2004; named to Can. Petroleum Hall of Fame, 1999; recipient Can. Engr.'s Gold medal Can. Coun. Profl. Engrs., 1990, Disting. Alumni award U. Alta., 1992, Mgmt. award McGill U., 1993, Centennial award Alta. Assn. Engrs., Geologists and Geophysicists, 1994, Hal Godwin award U. Calgary, 1999, Can. Bus. Leader award U. Alta., 1999, Can. Engring. Leader award U. Calgary, 2003, Alta. Centennial medal, 2005. Fellow Can. Acad. Engring.; mem. Assn. Profl. Engrs., Geologists and Geophysicists Alta. (past pres.), Can. Inst. Mining and Metallurgy (Past Pres.'s Meml. medal 1971). Avocations: golf, downhill skiing, shooting, fishing. Office: Granmar Investments Ltd 88 Massey Pl SW Calgary Canada T2V 2G8

**MAIER, HAROLD GEISTWEIT,** lawyer, educator; b. Cin., Mar. 25, 1937; s. Alfred F. and Alberta (Wilmes) M.; divorced; children: Marc L., Kurt S. BA in English Lit., U. Cin., 1959, JD, 1963; postgrad., Free U., Berlin, 1959-60; LLM, U. Mich., 1964; postgrad., U. Munich, 1964-65. Bar: Ohio 1963. Mem. law faculty Vanderbilt U., Nashville, 1965—, prof., 1970—, David Daniels Allen prof. law, 1988—, dir. Transnat. Legal Studies program, 1973-99. Faculty San Diego Internat and Comparative Law Inst., King's Coll., U. London, 1986-87, Regent's Coll., 1989, 91, 96; vis. prof. law U. Pa., 1985, U. NC, Chapel Hill, 1987; vis. Lyle T. Alverson prof. law George Washington U., Washington,DC, 1987-88; vis. Woodruff prof. internat. law U. Ga., Atlanta, 1995; prof. law LSU, Aix-en-Provence, France, 1995; vis. Straus disting. prof. law Pepperdine U., Malibu, Calif., 2000-01; cons. Office of Sec. Army, Panama Canal Treaty Negotiations, 1976; guest scholar Brookings Instn., Washington, DC, 1976-77; dir. PDS Patrons, Inc. U. Sch. Nashville, 1975-87, pres., 1978-79; counselor on internat. law Office of Legal Adviser, US Dept. State, 1983-84; Blain Sloan disting. lectr. internat. law Pace U. Sch. Law, White Plains, NY, 2001 Mem. editl. bd. Am. Jour. Internat. Law, 1984-88, Academic Coun., Inst. Transnational Arbitration, 1996—; Am. Jour. Comparative Law, 1997—, U.S. Assoc. Constitutional Law, 1997-2002, Am. Br. Internat. Law Assn., 2001—; author: (with T. Buergenthal) Public International Law in a Nutshell, 1985, 2d edit., 1989, (with T. Buergenthal, K. Doehring, J. Kokott) Grundzüge des Völkerrechts, 1987, Manual de Derecho Internacional Publico, 1994; contbr. articles to profl. jours. Recipient Luftbrucke Dankstipendium, Free U. Berlin, 1959-60; Ford internat. studies fellow U. Mich., 1964-65, Vanderbilt U. faculty fellow, 1976-77. Mem. Am. Soc. Internat. Law (exec. coun. 1974-78, 84-87, steering com. pvt. internat. law working group 2003--), Am. Soc. Comparative Law (bd. dirs. 1984-2001), Am. Law Inst., Order of Coif, Omicron Delta Kappa, Phi Alpha Delta, Tau Kappa Alpha, Pi Delta Epsilon, Nashville Symphony Guild, 2002-. Office: Vanderbilt U Law School 131 21st Ave S Nashville TN 37203 Home: 1710 Magnolia Blvd Apt 717 Nashville TN 37212-3747

**MAIER, JACK C.,** food products executive; Chmn. Frisch's Restaurants, Inc., Cin. Office: Frisch's Restaurants Inc 2800 Gilbert Ave Cincinnati OH 45206-1206

**MAIER, KAREN MARIE,** school librarian; b. Philip, S.D., Dec. 8, 1956; d. Clell and Cheryl Joan Baker; m. Gary Lee Maier, Dec. 23, 1978; children: Pamela Ann, Robert James, Crystal Lea, Jonathan Walter. A in English, Presentation Coll., Aberdeen, S.D., 1995, B in Bus. Mgmt., 1998. Libr. student asst. Presentation Coll., 1994—97, tech. svcs./circulation libr. 1998—. Libr. tech./dept. liaison Presentation Coll., 2001—, sys. libr., 1999—. Avocations: reading, knitting. Office: Presentation Coll 1500 N Main St Aberdeen SD 57401 Office Phone: 605-229-8498. E-mail: Karen.Maier@presentation.edu.

**MAIER, PAULINE,** historian, educator; b. Apr. 27, 1938; d. Irvin Louis and Charlotte (Winterer) Rubbelke; m. Charles Steven Maier, June 17, 1961; children: Andrea Nicole, Nicholas Winterer, Jessica Elizabeth Heine. AB, Radcliffe Coll., 1960; postgrad., London Sch. Econs., 1960-61; PhD in History, Harvard U., 1968; LLD (hon.), Regis Coll., 1987; DHL (hon.), Williams Coll., 1993. Asst. prof. then assoc. prof. history U. Mass., Boston, 1968-77; Robinson-Edwards prof. history U. Wis., Madison, 1977-78; prof. history MIT, Cambridge, Mass., 1978—, William R. Kenan Jr. prof. history, 1990—. Dept. head, MIT, 1979-88, mem. coun. Inst. Early Am. History, 1982-84; trustee Regis Coll., 1988-93; trustee Commonwealth Sch., 1991-96; bd. mgrs. Old South Meeting House, 1987-97, bd. advisors Internat. Ctr. Jefferson Studies, 2000-. Author: From Resistance to Revolution: Colonial Radicals and the Development of American Opposition to Britain, 1765-1766, 1972, The Old Revolutionaries: Political Lives in the Age of Samuel Adams, 1980, The American People: A History, 1986, American Scripture: Making the Declaration of Independence, 1997; co-author: Inventing America, 2002, 2d edit. 2006. Recipient Douglass Adair award Claremont Grad. Sch.-Inst. Early Am. History, 1976, Kidger award New Eng. History Tchrs. Assn., 1981; fellow Nat. Endowment Humanities, 1974-75, 88-89, Charles Warren fellow, 1974-75, Guggenheim fellow, 1990. Mem. Orgn. Am. Historians (mem. exec. bd. 1977-82), Am. Hist. Assn. (mem. nominations com. 1983-85, chmn. 1985), Soc. Am. Historians, Am. Antiquarian Soc. (mem. exec. coun. 1984-89), Colonial Soc. Mass. (mem. exec. coun. 1990-93), Mass. Hist. Soc., Am. Acad. Arts and Scis. The Hist. Soc. (bd. govs. 1998—). Home: 60 Larchwood Dr Cambridge MA 02138-4639 Office: MIT E51-279 77 Massachusetts Ave Cambridge MA 02139-4307 Office Phone: 617-253-2646. Business E-Mail: pmaier@mit.edu.

**MAIER, PETER KLAUS,** lawyer; b. Wurzburg, Germany, Nov. 20, 1929; came to U.S., 1939, naturalized, 1945; s. Bernard and Joan (Sonder) M.; m. Melanie L. Stoff, Dec. 15, 1963; children: Michele Margaret, Diana Lynn. BA cum laude, Claremont McKenna Coll., 1949; JD, U. Calif., Berkeley, 1952; LLM in Taxation, NYU, 1953. Bar: Calif. 1953, U.S. Supreme Ct. 1957; cert. specialist in taxation law, Calif. Atty. tax div. U.S. Dept Justice, Washington, 1956-59; pvt. practice tax law San Francisco, 1959-81. Prof. law Hastings Coll. Law, U. Calif., San Francisco, 1967-95; vis. prof. U. Calif. Boalt Sch. Law, Berkeley, 1988-89, Stanford U. Sch. Law, 1996-98; chmn. Maier, Siebel. Baber, Inc., San Francisco, 1981—; mng. dir. U.S. Trust Co. NA, San Francisco, 1998—; chmn. Fromm Inst. for Lifelong Learning, U. San Francisco, 1997—; pres. John B. Huntington Found., 1996—, Alfred and Hanna Fromm Found., 1974—. Author books on taxation; contbr. articles to profl. jours. Chmn. Property Resources Inc., San Jose, Calif., 1968-77; pres. Calif. Property Devel. Corp., San Francisco, 1974-81. Capt. USAF, 1953-56. Mem. San Francisco Bar Assn. (chmn. sect. taxation 1970-71), Order of Coif. Home: 2559 Clay St San Francisco CA 94115 Office: Maier Siebel & BaberInc 1 Embarcadero Ctr 20th Fl San Francisco CA 94111 E-mail: pmaier@ustrust.com.

**MAIER, ROMULUS,** journalist; b. Bucharest, Romania, May 5, 1961; arrived in U.S., 1998; s. Romulus and Victoria Maier; m. Irena Maier, July 20, 1990. BSc in Engring., Polytech. Inst., Bucharest, Romania, 1987; Grad. degree in Journalism, Superior Sch. Journalism, Bucharest, Romania, 1993; MA in Polit. Sci., U.Conn., Storrs, 2001. Reporter Romanian Reality, Bucharest, Romania, 1991—92, chief editor, 1992—93; econ. chief editor Free Romania, Bucharest, 1993—97, dep. chief editor, 1997, press corr., 1997—; grad. asst. U. Conn. T. Dodd Rsch. Ctr., Storrs, 2000—. Exec. prod. mgr. Rsch. Eqipment Factory, Bucharest, 1990—91; polit. and econ. advisor CDR Campaign 1996, Bucharest, 1995—96; vis. prof. Superior Sch. Journalism, Bucharest, 1994—95. Mem.: Internat. Orgn. Journalists, Acad. Polit. Sci., Am. Polit. Sci. Assn. Eastern Orthodox. Office: Univ Conn 541 Mansfield Rd Storrs Mansfield CT 06269 Home: 88 Thornton Rd Chestnut Hill MA 02467-3611 E-mail: irerom@msn.com.

**MAIER, RONALD VITT,** surgeon, educator; b. Wheeling, W.Va., Oct. 23, 1947; BS, U. Notre Dame, 1969; MD, Duke U., 1973. Intern Parkland Meml. Hosp., Dallas, 1973-74; resident U. Wash. Hosps., Seattle, 1974-78; rsch. assoc. Scripps Rsch. Found., La Jolla, Calif., 1978-81; surgeon-in-chief HMC, Seattle, 1993—; vice chair U. Wash., Seattle, 1994—, Jane and Donald D. Trunkey prof., 2005—. Office: Dept Surgery 359796 Harborview Med Ctr 325 9th Ave Seattle WA 98104-2499 Office Phone: 206-731-3299. Business E-Mail: ronmaier@u.washington.edu

**MAIESE, KENNETH,** neurologist, neuroscientist; b. Audubon, N.J., Dec. 5, 1958; s. Charles and Margaret (Fioretti) M. BA summa cum laude, U. Pa., 1981; MD, Cornell U., 1985. Intern N.Y. Hosp., 1985—86, resident neurology, 1986—89, asst. attending physician, 1989—94; asst. prof. Cornell U. Med. Coll., N.Y.C., 1989—94; assoc. prof. dept. neurology, anatomy and cell biology Ctr. Molecular Toxicology and Medicine Wayne State U., Detroit, 1994—99, dir. lab. molecular and cellular cerebral ischemia Ctr. Molecular Toxicology, 1994—, prof. dept. neurology, anatomy, cell biology Ctr. Molecular Toxicology, 1999—. Dir. neurol. diagnosis NY Hosp., 1991—94; chmn. nat. brain/stroke consortium Am. Heart Assn., 2000—01, exec. coun., 2001—, nat peer rev. commission, 2002—, mem. rsch. com., 2003—; mem. minority edn. tng. NIH, 2002—; mem. study sect. cell death and injury NIH/CDIN, 2003—; spl. emphasis panel cellular pathophysiology NIH, 2004—, spl. emphasis panel cellular degeneration, 2004—; mem. neurobiology study sect. Vet.'s Adminstrn., 2004—. Author: Neurology and General Medicine, 1989, Neurological and Neurosurgical ICU Medicine, 1988; editor-in-chief Current Neurovascular Rsch., 2002—; editor: Neuronal and Vascular Plasticity, 2003; assoc. editor, mem. editl. bd. Letters in Drug Design and Discovery, 2002—, Histology and Histopathology, 2002—, Jour. Histological Histopathology, 2002—; mem. editl. bd. Internat. Jour. Molecular Medicine, 2005—; contbr. articles to profl. jours. Joseph Collins scholar, 1981-85, Grupe Found. scholar, 1985; grantee NIH, 1990—, Nat. Stroke Assn., 1992-94, Alzheimer's Assn., 1994—, Am. Heart Assn., 1995—, United Cerebral Palsy Found., 1995—, Janssen Found., 1995—; recipient Young Scientist award Jours. Cerebral Blood Flow, 1991, Hoechst Investigator award, 1993, Robert G. Siekert award in stroke, 1994, Johnson and Johnson Disting. Investigator award, 1996-98, Maiese Lab. Neurosci. Tng. award & J/Janssen, 1998, Boehringer Investigator award, 1999, NIH/NIEHS award, Learn Found. award, 2002, 2003, MI Challenge award, Bugher Found. award, 2005, Am. Diabetes Assn. award, 2006; named one of Am.'s Top Physicians, 2005, 06. Mem. Am. Acad. Neurology, N.Y. Acad. Scis., Assn. for Rsch. in Nervous and Mental Diseases, Am. Neurol. Assn. (elected), Soc. Neurosci., Internat. Acad. Cardiology (sci. com. 2003-, Bugher Found. award 2005-), Am. Diabetes Assn. (Sr. Investigator award 2006). Roman Catholic. Achievements include rsch. in imidazole receptors, cerebral ischemia, nitric oxide toxicity, growth factor neuroprotection, signal cellular transduction mechanisms, metabotropic glutamate receptors, gene regulation, and gene therapy, patents in field; member of group ranked in the top percent of apoptosis research groups. Office: Wayne State U Sch Medicine 8C-1 U Health Ctr Dept Neur 4201 Saint Antoine St Detroit MI 48201-2153 Business E-Mail: kmaiese@med.wayne.edu.

**MAIKON, MARC STEVEN,** podiatrist; BA, Grinnell Coll., 1980; BS, U. Iowa, 1982; DPM, U. Osteo. Medicine, Des Moines, 1989. Cert. Am. Coun. Cert. Podiatric Physicians and Surgeons. Podiatrist, owner Family Foot Care Ctr. PLC, Cedar Rapids, Iowa, 1991—. Mem. Am. Coll. Foot Surgeons, Am. Podiatric Med. Assn., Iowa Podiatric Med. Soc., C. of C. Cedar Rapids, Rotary Internat. Office: Family Foot Ctr 3359 Center Point Rd NE Cedar Rapids IA 52402-5568 Home: 1750 Emerald Ct Robins IA 52328-9651

**MAILER, NORMAN KINGSLEY,** writer; b. Long Branch, NJ, Jan. 31, 1923; s. Issac Barnett and Fanny (Schneider) M.; m. Beatrice Silverman, 1944 (div. 1952); 1 dau., Susan; m. Adele Morales, 1954 (div. 1962); children: Danielle, Elizabeth; m. Jeanne Campbell, 1962 (div. 1963); 1 dau., Kate; m. Beverly Bentley, 1963 (div. 1980); children: Michael, Steven; m. Carol Stevens, 1980 (div. 1980); 1 dau., Maggie; m. Norris Church, 1980; 1 son, John Buffalo. SB cum laude, Harvard U., 1943; postgrad., Sorbonne, Paris, France, 1947-48. Columnist Village Voice, 1946, Commentary, 1962-63, Esquire, 1962-63; contbg. editor Dissent, 1953-69; co-founding editor Village Voice, 1955. Author: No Percentage, 1941, The Naked and the Dead, 1948, Barbary Shore, 1951, The Deer Park, 1955, The White Negro: Superficial Reflections on the Hipster, 1957, Advertisements for Myself, 1959, Deaths for the Ladies and Other Disasters, 1962, The Presidential Papers, 1963, An American Dream, 1965, Cannibals and Christians, 1966, Why Are We in Vietnam?, 1967 (Nat. Book award nomination 1967), The Short Fiction of Norman Mailer, 1967, The Bullfight, 1967, The Armies of the Night, 1968 (Pulitzer prize for non-fiction 1969, George Polk award 1969), Miami and the Siege of Chicago, 1968 (Nat. Book award for non-fiction 1968), The Idol and the Octopus, 1968, Of a Fire On The Moon, 1970, King of the Hill, 1971, The Prisoner of Sex, 1971, The Long Patrol, 1971, Existential Errands, 1972, St. George and the Godfather, 1972, Marilyn, 1973, The Faith of Graffiti, 1974, The Fight, 1975, Some Honorable Men, 1975, Genius and Lust, 1976, A Transit to Narcissus, 1978, The Executioner's Song, 1979 (Pulitzer Prize for fiction 1980, Nat. Book Critics Circle award nomination 1979, Am. Book award nomination 1980), Of a Small and Modest Malignancy, Wicked and Bristling with Dots, 1980, Of Women and Their Elegance, 1980, Pieces and Pontifications, 1982, Ancient Evenings, 1983, Tough Guys Don't Dance, 1984, The Last Night, 1984, Harlot's Ghost, 1991, How the Wimp Won the War, 1991, Oswald's Tale, 1995, Portrait of Picasso as a Young Man, 1995, The Gospel According to the Son, 1997, The Spooky Art: Thoughts on Writing, 2003; (plays) The Deer Park: A Play, 1967, Strawhead, 1985; editor: Genius and Lust: A Journey Through the Major Writings of Henry Miller, 1976; screenwriter: (films) The Executioner's Song, 1982 (Emmy award nomination outstanding adapted screenplay 1983); screenwriter, prodr., dir., actor: (films) Wild 90, 1967, Maidstone: A Mystery, 1971; screenwriter,

prodr.: (films) Beyond the Law, 1968; screenwriter, dir.: (films) Tough Guys Don't Dance, 1987; actor: (films) Ragtime, 1981. Served with AUS, 1944-46. Recipient Edward MacDowell medal MacDowell Colony, 1973, Nat. Arts Club Gold medal, 1976, Emerson-Thoreau Medal for lifetime of literary achievement, 1989, Nat. Book Found. medal for disting. contbn. to Am. letters, 2005, Legion of Honor France, 2006; Nat. Inst. and Am. Acad. grantee, 1960; Pappas fellow U. Pa., 1983. Mem. PEN Am. Ctr. (pres. 1984-86), Nat. Inst. Arts and Letters.*

**MAILLOUX, ROBERT JOSEPH,** physicist; b. Lynn, Mass., June 20, 1938; s. Joseph H. and Nora S. M.; m. Marlene Schirf, Jan. 14, 1967; children: Patrice, Julie, Denise. BS, Northeastern U., 1961; SM, Harvard U., 1962, PhD, 1965. Physicist NASA Electronics Rsch. Ctr., Cambridge, Mass., 1965—70, Air Force Cambridge Rsch. Labs., Bedford, Mass., 1970—77, Rome Air Devel. Ctr., Bedford, 1977—80, chief antennas and components divsn., electromagnetic directorate, 1990—91; sr. scientist Air Force Rsch. Lab., 1992—2004; rsch. prof. U. Mass., 2006—. Author: Phased Array Antenna Handbook; editor History of Wireless; guest editor IEEE/AP-S Transactions Spl. Issue on Phased Array Antennas, 1999; contbr. chpts. to 8 textbooks, articles to sci. jours. Served with C.E. U.S. Army, 1966-68. Recipient Air Force Marcus O'Day paper award, 1971, Engineer of Yr. award Rome Air Devel. Ctr., 1988, fellow 1988 Fellow IEEE (chmn. tech. com. 1997 phased array symposium, spl. achievement award 1969, 76, nat. lectr., assoc. editor Trans. on Antennas and Propagation 1984-92, Harry Diamond award 1991, Fred Diamond award 1997, Third Millenium medal, 2000, Disting. Achievement award 2005); mem. Antenna and Propagation Soc. (chmn. Boston chpt. 1968, nat. meetings chmn. 1977-80, adcom mem. 1977-80, v-p. 1982, pres. 1983), Internat. Sci. Radio Union (Commn. B tech. activities chmn. 1980—), Sigma Xi (pres. Hanscom chpt. 1980-81), Eta Kappa Nu, Tau Beta Pi. Achievements include 12 patents in field. Office: AFRL/SNH 31 Grenier St Hanscom Afb MA 01731-3008

**MAIMAN, MITCHELL,** oncologist, gynecologist; b. Bklyn., 1957; s. Irwin and Gloria (Pepper) Maiman; m. Judith E. Levy, 1985. MD, SUNY-Health Sci. Ctr., 1981. Diplomate Am. Bd. Obstetrics and Gynecology with subspecialty in gynecologic oncology. Resident Einstein Coll. Medicine, Bronx, 1981—85; fellow Univ. Hosp., Bklyn., 1985—87; pvt. practice oncology, gynecology S.I., NY, 1987—. V.p. women's health S.I. Univ. Hosp., chmn. dept. ob-gyn., 1999—; prof. SUNY, Bklyn. Office: 256 Mason Ave Staten Island NY 10305-3408 Office Phone: 718-226-9269. Business E-Mail: mmaiman@siuh.edu.

**MAIMON, ELAINE PLASKOW,** university chancellor; b. Phila., July 28, 1944; d. Louis J. and Gertrude (Canter) Plaskow; m. Morton A. Maimon, Sept. 30, 1967; children: Gillian Blanche, Alan Marcus. AB, U. Pa., 1966, MA, 1967, PhD, 1970. Asst. prof. Haverford (Pa.) Coll., 1971-73; lectr. Arcadia U., Glenside, Pa., 1973-75, asst. prof., dir. writing, 1975-77, assoc. prof., 1977-83, assoc. dean, 1980-84, assoc. v.p., prof. English, 1984-86; adj. assoc. prof. U. Pa., Phila., 1982-83; assoc. dean of coll. Brown U., Providence, 1986-88; dean, prof. English Queens Coll. CUNY, Flushing, NY, 1988-96; campus CEO, provost Ariz. State U. West, Phoenix, 1996—2004; v.p Ariz. State U., 1996—2004; chancellor U. Alaska, Anchorage, 2004—. Nat. bd. cons. NEH, 1977-81; mem. adv. bd. Cox Comm., 1997-2001; bd. dirs. Arrowhead Cmty. Bank. Co-author: Writing in the Arts and Sciences, 1981, A Writer's Resource, 2003; co-editor: Readings in the Arts and Sciences, 1984, Thinking, Reasoning and Writing, 1989, A Writer's Resource, 2003, 2d edit., 2007, The New McGraw Hill Handbook, 2007, Writing Intensive, 2007. Trustee Heard Mus., Phoenix, 1999—2005. Recipient Golden Heart award, Today's Ariz. Woman, 2000, Women of Distinction award, YMCA, Maricopa County, 2001, YWCA award in Edn., 2002, World award, Girl Scouts Am., Ariz. Cactus-Pine Coun., 2002, Woman of Vision award, Phoenix Bus. Jour.; Elaine Maimon award for Excellence in Writing named in her honor, Arcadia U., 1994. Mem.: MLA (exec. com., tchg. of writing divsn.), Am. Assn. Colls. and Univs. (exec. bd. 2002—), Conf. on Coll. Composition Comm. (exec. com. 1985—87), ACE Nat. Commn. Women, Nat. Coun. Tchrs. English (nominating com. 1986—87, teaching of writing divsn. 1991), Phi Beta Kappa. Office: U Alaska Anchorage 3211 Providence Dr Anchorage AK 99508-8060 Home: 2831 UAA Dr Unit B Anchorage AK 99508 Office Phone: 907-786-1437. Business E-Mail: elaine.maimon@uaa.alaska.edu.

**MAIN, DAVID C.,** lawyer; b. Des Moines, Iowa, Feb. 29, 1948; BA, DePauw Univ., 1970; MTS, Harvard Divinity Sch., 1973; JD, Georgetown Univ., 1976. Bar: DC 1977, Va., US Dist. Ct. (DC), US Ct. Appeals (DC cir.), US Supreme Ct. Staff mem. U.S. Senate Rep. Policy Com., 1974—76; health counsel to U.S. Senator Richard S. Schweiker, 1976—79; counsel U.S. Senate Subcom. on Health & Scientific Rsch., 1977—79; atty., chmn. managed care practice Gardner Carton & Douglas; atty., chmn. health care practice Crowell & Moring; ptnr., co-chmn. Healthcare practice Pillsbury Winthrop Shaw Pittman, McLean, Va. Founder & coord. Healthcare Tech. Network of Greater Washington; counsel Health Mgmt. Academy. Contbr. articles to profl. jours. Mem.: Am. Health Lawyers Assn., Md. BioScience Alliance, DC Hosp. Assn., Phi Beta Kappa. Office: Pillsbury Winthrop Shaw Pittman 1650 Tysons Blvd Mc Lean VA 22102-4859 Office Phone: 703-770-7518. Office Fax: 702-770-7901. Business E-Mail: david.main@pillsburylaw.com.

**MAIN, EDNA DEWEY (JUNE MAIN),** education educator; b. Hyannis, Mass., Sept. 1, 1940; d. Seth Bradford and Edna Wilhelmina (Wright) Dewey; m. Donald John Main, Sept. 9, 1961 (div. Dec. 1989); children: Alison Teresa Main Ronzon, Susan Christine Main Leddy, Steven Donald. Degree in merchandising, Tobe Coburn Sch., N.Y., 1960; BA in Edn., U. North Fla., Jacksonville, 1974. MA in Edn., 1979, M in Adminstrn. and Supervision, 1983; PhD in Curriculum and Instrn., U.Fla., Gainsville, 1990. Asst. buyer Abraham & Straus, Bklyn., 1960-61; asst. mdse. mgr. Interstate Dept. Stores, NYC, 1962-63; tchr. Holiday Hill Elem. Sch., Jacksonville. Fla., 1974-86; instr. summer sci. inst., 1984-92; prof. edn. Jacksonville U., 1992—, dir. masters program in integrated learning and ednl. tech. Instr. U. Fla., 1987—90, U. North Fla., 1990—92; cons. Assn. Internat. Schs. Africa, 1994—97. Co-author: (book) Developing Critical Thinking Through Science, Book I, 2001, Developing Critical Thinking Through Science, Book II, 2002. Rep. United Way, 1981—86; tchr. rep., chpt. leader White Ho. Young Astronaut Program, 1984—85; team leader NSF Shells Elem. Sci. Project. Named Fla. Prof. of the Yr., Carnegie Found., 2002, Prof. of Yr.. Jacksonville U., 2003; recipient Innovative Excellence in Tchg., Learning and Tech. award, Internat. Coll. Conf., 1999, Outstanding Alumni award. U. North Fla., 1999, Eve award for Edn., 2001, Apple Disting. Educator award, 2003—05. Mem.: Internat. Soc. Tech. Edn., Soc. Info. Tech. and Tchr. Edn., ASCD, NSTA (Sci. Tchrs. Achievement Recognition award 1983), Kappa Delta Pi, Phi Delta Kappa, Phi Kappa Phi. Episcopalian. Office: Jacksonville U 2800 University Blvd N Jacksonville FL 32211-3394 Personal e-mail: main750@bellsouth.net.

**MAIN, JAMES L.,** lawyer; b. Chgo., July 24, 1947; BS in Engring. sci., Fla. State U.; JD with honors, U. Fla., 1974; LLM in Taxation, NYU, 1978. Ptnr. Holland & Knight LLP, Jacksonville, Fla., leader private equity funds practice group, chair budget and fin. com. Mem. U. Fla. Law Review, 1973—74. Bd. dir., officer Rotary Club, Deerwood. Mem.: Jacksonville Bar Assn., ABA, Fla. Bar, Omicron Delta Kappa, Order of the Coif, Phi Kappa Phi. Office: Holland & Knight LLP 50 N Laura St Ste 3900 Jacksonville FL 32202 Office Phone: 904-798-7319. Business E-Mail: jmain@hklaw.com.

**MAIN, ROBERT GAIL,** communications educator, training services executive, television producer, film producer, retired military officer; b. Bucklin, Mo., Sept. 30, 1932; s. Raymond M. and Lenz L. (Griever) M.; m. Anita Sue Thoroughman, Jan. 31, 1955; children: Robert Bruce, David Keith, Leslie Lorraine. BS magna cum laude, U. Mo., 1954; grad. with honors, Army Commd. Gen. Staff Coll., 1967; MA magna cum laude in Comm., Stanford U., 1968; PhD, U. Md., 1978. Commd. 2d lt. U.S. Army, 1954, advanced through grades to lt. col., 1968; mem. faculty Army Commd. Gen. Staff Coll., 1968-70; chief speechwriting and info. materials divsn. U.S. Army Info. Office, 1971, chief broadcast and film divsn., 1972-73; dir. def. audiovisual activities Office of Info. for Armed Forces, 1973-76; ret., 1976; prof. instrnl. tech. Calif. State U., Chico, 1976—; dept. chair, 1993-98, prof. emeritus. Cons. in field. Author: Rogues, Saints and Ordinary People, 1988; prodr. (TV documentary) Walking Wounded, 1983, Army Info. Films, Army Radio Series, 1972-73; contbr. articles on computer based tng. and telecoms. to scientific and profl. jours. Decorated Legion of Merit, Meritorious Svc. medal, Commendation medal with oak leaf cluster, combat Inf. Badge; Vietnamese Cross of Gallantry; recipient Freedom Found. awards, 1972, 73, 74; Bronze medal Atlanta Film Festival, 1972; Best of Show award Balt. Film Festival, 1973; Creativity award Chgo. Indsl. Film Festival, 1973; Cine gold award Internat. Film Prodrs. Assn., 1974; named an Outstanding Prof. Calif. State U., 1987-88. Mem. Phi Eta Sigma, Alpha Zeta, Phi Delta Gamma, Omicron Delta Kappa, Alpha Gamma Rho. Personal E-mail: rmain75@aol.com.

**MAIN, TIMOTHY L.,** electronics company executive; b. 1957; BS, Mich. State U.; M in Internat. Mgmt., Am. Grad. Sch. Internat. Mgmt. Comml. lending officer internat. divsn. Nat. Bank Detroit; mgr. prodn. control Jabil Circuit Inc., St. Petersburg, Fla., 1987, ops. mgr., 1987-89, project mgr., 1989-91, v.p. bus. devel., 1991, sr. v.p. bus. devel., pres., 1999—, CEO, 2000—. Bd. dirs. Jabil Circuit Inc., 1999—. Office: Jabil Cir 10560 9th St N Saint Petersburg FL 33716*

**MAINE, MICHAEL ROLAND,** lawyer; b. Anderson, Ind., Feb. 22, 1940; s. Roland Dwight and Vivian Louise (Browning) M.; m. Suzanne Bauman, Aug. 25, 1962; children: Christopher Michael (dec.), Melinda Louise. AB with high distinction, DePauw U.; JD with distinction, U. Mich. Bar: Ind., D.C., U.S. Dist. Ct. (so. dist.) Ind., U.S. Ct. Appeals (7th cir.), U.S. Supreme Ct. Assoc. Baker & Daniels, Indpls., 1964-71, ptnr., 1972—2004. Contbr. articles to profl. jours. Bd. dirs. Ind. Repertory Theatre, Indianapolis, 1986—2003, Cmty. Hosp. N., 1988—91, Japan-Am. Soc. Ind. Inc., 1988—2003, Royal Palm Players, 2005—; pres. Mental Health Assn. Ind., Indpls., 1985; bd. visitors Sch. Law Ind. U., Indpls.; trustee De Pauw U., Greencastle, Ind. 1990—; bd. dirs. U.S.-China Bus. Coun. Legal Cooperation Fund, 2002—05. Capt. USAF, 1965-67. Named Sagamore of Wabash, Gov. Ind., 1986. Fellow: Indpls. Bar Found., Ind. Bar Found.; mem.: Indpls. Bar Assn. (sec. 1983, pres. 1985, extraordinary svc. award 1985), Ind. Bar Assn. (chmn. fed. judiciary com. 1986—88), Kiwanis (lt. gov. Ind. club 1972, pres. Indpls. club 1969), Masons, Kiwanis (lt. gov. Ind. club 1972, pres. Indpls. club 1969), Masons, Phi Beta Kappa, Order of Coif. Avocation: golf. Home: 13100 Joseffa Ct Placida FL 33946 Office: Baker & Daniels 300 N Meridian St Ste 2700 Indianapolis IN 46204-1782

**MAINELLA, FRAN (FRANCES P. MAINELLA),** federal agency administrator; b. Groton, Conn., 1947; BS cum laude, U. Conn.; MS cum laude in Counseling, Ctrl. Conn. State Univ.; PhD in Pub. Svc. (hon.), Ctrl. Conn. State U., 2002. H.S. phys. edn. tchr. Vernon Pub. Sch., Rockville, Conn., 1969—77; asst. ctr. dir. Tallahassee Parks and Recreation Dept., 1977—78; dir. recreation Town of Lake Park, Fla., 1978—83; exec. dir. Fla. Recreation and Park Assn., Tallahassee, 1983—89; dir. divsn. Recreation and Parks Fla. Dept. Environ. Protection, Tallahassee, 1989—2001; dir. Nat. Park Svc. US Dept. Interior, Washington, 2001—. Spkr. in field. Contbr. numerous articles to profl. publs. Co-chair Com. for Preservation of the White House, mem. adv. coun. on hist. preservation; bd. trustees John F. Kennedy Ctr. for Performing Arts; liaison White House Hist. Soc.; sec., treas. Nat. Park Found.; mem. Am. Folklife Bd.; past pres. Nat. Assn. State Park Dirs.; past bd. mem. Am. Acad. Park and Recreation Adminstr.; past mem. Fla. Commn. Ttourism; past officio bd. mem. Fla. Recreation and Park Assn.; past mem. Gov.'s Mansion adv. com.; past bd. mem. Fla. Gov.'s Coun. on Phys. Fitness and Sports; past sec., bd. dirs. Spl. Olympics; past pres. Tallahassee Soc. Assn. Execs.; past chair United Way Drive for Tallahassee Soc. Assn. Execs.; past bd. dirs. Tallahassee Leon County Convention and Visitors Bur.; bd. dirs. Ford's Theatre Soc., Wolf Trap Found. for Performing Arts. Recipient Disting. Svc. award, Nat. Assn. Recreation Resource Planners, 1996, Woman of Distinction award, Girl Scout Coun. of Apalachee Bend, 1998, Pugsley medal, Am. Acad. Park and Recreation Adminstrn., 1998, Disting. Svc. award, Nat. Assn. State Park Dirs., 1999, Senator Bob Williams award, State of Fla., 2001, Sheldon Coleman Outdoors award, 2002, Walter T. Cox Pub. Svc. Achievement award, Clemson U., 2002. Mem.: Nat. Recreation and Park Assn. (congress planning com. 1984, 1987, past chair coun. exec. dirs., pres. 1997—, Harold D. Meyer Profl. award 2000). Office: US Dept Interior Nat Park Svc 1849 C St NW Washington DC 20240

**MAINES, NATALIE LOUISE,** musician; b. Lubbock, Tex., Oct. 14, 1974; d. Lloyd and Tina M.; m. Michael Tarabay, May 9, 1997 (div. Jan. 1999); m. Adrian Pasdar, June 24, 2000; children: Jack Slade, Beckett Finn. Student, Tex. Tech.; grad., Berklee Coll. Music, Boston, 1995. Performer Dixie Chicks, 1995—. Singer: (albums) Wide Open Spaces, 1998 (Maximum Vision Clip of Yr., Billboard, 1998, Best New Country Artist Clip of Yr., Billboard, 1998, Best Country Album, Grammy Awards, 1998, Album of Yr., Acad. Country Music, 1998, Best Selling Album, Can. Country Music Awards, 1999, Song of Yr. (Country), WB Radio Music Awards, 1999, Album of Yr., ACM, 1999), Fly, 1999 (Best Country Album, Grammy Awards, 1999, Best Selling Album, Can. Country Music Awards, 2000, Internat. Album, British Country Music Awards, 2000, Country Album of Yr., Billboard, 2000, Album of Yr., ACM, 2000, Album of Yr., CMA, 2000), Home, 2002 (Favorite Country Album, Am. Music Awards, 2002, Best Recording Package, Grammy Awards, 2002, Best Country Album, Grammy Awards, 2002), Top of the World Tour: Live, 2003 (Grammy award for Best Country Group Vocal Performance, 2005), Taking the Long Way, 2006. Named Most Significant New Country Act, Country Monitor, 1998, Top New Country Artist, Billboard, 1998, Group of Yr., CMA, 1998, Top Vocal Group, Acad. Country Music, 1998, Country Artist of Yr., Rolling Stone, 1999, Top Country Artist, Billboard, 1999, Internat. Rising Star, British Country Music Awards, 1999, Artist of Yr., WB Radio Music Awards, 1999, Favorite New Artist (Country), AMA, 1999, Vocal Group of Yr., CMA, 1999, Country Artist of Yr., Billboard, 1999, Entertainer of Yr., CMA, 2000, ACM, 2000, 2001, Vocal Group of Yr., 2001, Favorite Musical Group or Band, People's Choice Award, 2002, Vocal Group of Yr., Country Music Assn. Awards, 2002, others; named one of 100 Most Influential People, Time Mag., 2006; recipient Horizon award, CMA, 1998. Office: Monument Sony Nashville 34 Music Sq East Nashville TN 37203

**MAINHART, ROBERT,** music educator; s. Robert William and Barbara Mainhart; m. Jessica Lynn Monish, Aug. 3, 2005. MusB in Music Edn., Old Dominion U., Norfolk, Va., 1996; MusM Edn., Shenandoah Conservatory, Winchester, Va., 2003. Music resource tchr. Norfolk Pub. Sch., Norfolk, Va., 1996—2001; music specialist Loudoun County Pub. Schs., Leesburg, Va., 2001—. Performing mem. and music libr. Va. Symphony Chorus, Norfolk, Va., 1996—2001; online mktg. cons. MENC: The Nat. Assn. for Music Edn., Reston, Va., 2003—05. Scholar Presdl. Scholarship, Old Dominion U., 1991-1995. Mem.: Va. Music Educators Assn. (dist. elem. rep. 2004—), Gordon Inst. for Music Learning, Orgn. of Am. Kodaly Educators, Nat. Assn. for Music Edn. (MENC), Phi Kappa Phi. Office Phone: 703-771-6720.

**MAINPRIZE, DONALD CHARLES,** minister, writer; b. Coleman, Mich., Aug. 28, 1930; s. James Raymond and Ople Belle Mainprize; m. Doris Olive Humphrey, July 27, 1952; children: Daniel Andrew, Debra Ann, Susan Lynn, Edward Raymond. Pastor's diploma, Grand Rapids Sch. Bible & Music, 1953; student, Dallas Theol. Sem., 1957; BA in Profl. Writing, U. Okla., Norman, 1960; MA in English and Am. Lit., Ctrl. Mich. U., 1967; D (hon.), Destiny Christian U., 2006. Ordained Evangel Assn. Ch. and Ministries, 2006. Pastor Dildine Comty. Ch., Ionia, Mich., 1953—56; pastor First Presbyn. Ch., Minco, Okla., 1958—60; mng. editor Scripture Press, Wheaton, Ill., 1960—64; freelance writer Houghton Lake, Mich., 1965; 5th grade tchr. Houghton Lake Elem. Sch., 1965—66; grad. asst. Ctrl. Mich. U., Mt. Pleasant, 1966—67; instr. journalism, advt., composition, 1967—68; English

tchr. Houghton Lake Schs., 1965—94. Writing cons. Writing Doctor, Roscommon, Mich., 1994—2002; supply pastor various denominations, Mich., 1965—2001. Author: Enjoy The Christian Life, 1966, 2d edit., 1971, Meditations for Teachers, 1974 (1st prize humorous poetry, Poetry Soc. Mich.), Christian Heroes of Today, 1964, Happy Anniversary, with Wife, 1975, Your Journey into Joy, 2002, (poetry) ABC's for Educators, Fragments of Faith and Failure, 2003, (poetry book) Whispers of My Heart, 2005, Cracks in the Foundation, 2006; editor: Pure Mountain Air, 1979, (student poems) STARS STARS STARS, 1977. Mem. Kiwanis, Minco, Okla., 1958—60. Mem.: Mich. Edn. Soc., Nat. Edn. Assn., Kappa Tau Alpha. Republican. Episcopalian. Achievements include first to introduce rollercoaster poems in Language Arts and the English Jour. Avocations: travel, writing, walking, reading. Home: 519 W Higgins Lake Dr Roscommon MI 48653

**MAINWARING, THOMAS LLOYD,** transportation executive, director; b. Cleve., Aug. 25, 1928; s. Hugh Trevor and Mary Beatrice (Ottman) M.; m. Gladys Fraser Mehr, June 10, 1983; children by previous marriage— Kevin, James, Eileen, Scott, Bruce BA, Albion Coll., 1950; MBA, Western Res. U., 1958. C.P.A., Ohio. Controller Cleve. Cartage Co., 1959-61, v.p., treas., 1961-64; controller Associated Truck Lines, Inc., Vandenberg Ctr., Grand Rapids, Mich., 1964-69; v.p. fin. Associated Transport, Inc., N.Y.C., 1969-70, exec. v.p. fin. and adminstrn., 1970-72; pres. Ryder Truck Lines Inc., Jacksonville, Fla., 1972-78, exec. v.p., chief operating officer, 1978-81, chief exec. officer, 1981-84; pres. Freight System div. Ryder System Inc., Miami, Fla., 1984-86; cons. trucking industry affairs Arlington, Va., 1986-88; pres., chief oper. officer H & M Internat. Transp., Inc., 1989-91, vice chmn., 1991-92; transp. cons., 1992-93; pres., gen. mgr. E.I. Kane Intermodal Transport, Inc., Balt., 1993-95, vice chmn., 1995, transp. cons., 1996—99; COO, Am. C. of C. Execs., 0200—2001; mgmt. cons., 2002—03; treas. & CFO AICHI-USA 2005 World Expn., Inc., 2003—, exec. v.p., 2006, Shanghai-USA 2010 Work Expo., Inc., 2000—. Bd. dirs. Trucking Mgmt. Inc. Mem. exec. com. United Way Jacksonville, 1981-84; trustee Albion Coll., 1977; bd. dirs. Goodwill Industries North Fla. Served with AUS, 1950-53. Mem. Am. Trucking Assn. (nat. acctg. and fin. council 1964, pres. 1971, chmn. ATA Found. 1986-88, exec. com. 1985-88), Fla. Trucking Assn. (bd. dirs. 1973, pres. 1979), Am. Mgmt. Assn. (lectr. seminars), Jacksonville Area C. of C. (bd. govs., com. of 100, v.p. internat. 1984), Cen. and So. Motor Freight Tariff Assn. (bd. dirs. 1981-84, pres. 1983, exec. com. transp. rsch. bd. 1987-89), Sigma Nu. Home: Apt 334 South 1600 S Eads St Arlington VA 22202

**MAINWARING, WILLIAM LEWIS,** publishing company executive, author; b. Portland, Oreg., Jan. 17, 1935; s. Bernard and Jeanne (Lewis) M.; m. Mary E. Bell, Aug. 18, 1962; children: Anne Marie, Julia Kathleen, Douglas Bernard. BS, U. Oreg., 1957; postgrad., Stanford U., 1957-58. With Salem (Oreg.) Capital Jour., 1958-76, editor, pub., 1962-76; pub. Oreg. Statesman, 1974-76; pres. Statesman-Jour. Co., Inc., Salem, 1974-76, Westridge Press, Ltd., 1977—, MediAmerica, Inc., Portland, 1981-96, CEO, 1988—91. Bd. dirs. MediAmerica, Inc. Author: Exploring the Oregon Coast, 1977, Exploring Oregon's Central and Southern Cascades, 1979, Exploring the Mount Hood Loop, 1992, Government, Oregon-Style, 1996, rev. edit., 1997, 99. Pres. Salem Beautification Coun., 1968, Marion-Polk County United Good Neighbors, 1970, Salem Social Svcs. Commn., 1978-79, Salem Hosp. Found., 1978-81, Marion Hist. Found., 2002-03, 2d lt. AUS, 1958; capt. Res. Ret. Mem. Salem Area C. of C. (pres. 1972-73), Oreg. Symphony Soc. Salem (pres. 1973-75), Salem City Club (pres. 1977-78), Sigma Chi. Republican. Presbyterian. Home and Office: 1090 Southridge Pl S Salem OR 97302-5947

**MAIO, HEATHER ALLEN,** environmental services administrator; d. Lyle R. Allen and Sonja Wolhart; m. Gene Maio, July 8, 1978; children: Hilary Chigro, Nicole. MPA, U. of Colo., 2005. Registered environ. health specialist. With wildlife conservation office N.Mex. Dept. of Game and Fish, 1977—79; environ. health specialist I-III Pueblo City-County Health Dept., Pueblo, Colo., 1985—94; dir. of environ. health Pueblo City-County Health, Pueblo, 1995—. Mem. Environ. Policy Adv. Com., Pueblo, 1995—99. Named Student of the Yr., U. of Colo., 2005. Mem.: Colo. Dirs. Environ. Health (chairperson, treas. 1998—99), Colo. Environ. Health Assn. (past pres., v.p. 1993—99), Pueblo County Environ. Health Assn. (bd. dirs. 1997—2004), Dirs. of Environ. Health (assoc.; treas. 2005—06). Democrat. Avocation: travel. Home: 4015 Valley Dr Pueblo CO 81008 Office: Pueblo City-County Health 131 S Main Pueblo CO 81003 Office Phone: 719-583-4321. Personal E-mail: g.maio@comcast.net. E-mail: heather.maio@co.pueblo.co.us.

**MAIOLINI, GLORIA J.,** nursing case manager, poet, writer; d. Harriet Yvonne and Matthew Boyd; 1 child, Galen R. Young Jr. AS Nursing, C.C. Allegheny County, 1994; BS in Health Arts, U. St. Frances, 2000. Health ins. assoc.; cert. case mgr., gerontol. nurse. RN FMC Carswell, Bur. Prisons, Fort Worth, Tex., 1995—95; nurse Heritage Shadyside Nursing Rehab Ctr., Pitts., 1996—99; unit mgr. St. Joseph's Nursing Rehab Ctr., Pitts., 1997—98; RN case mgr. Highmark Blue Shield, Pitts., 1998—2005, Peidmont Geriatric Hosp., Richmond, Va., 2006—. Author numerous poems. Coord. United Way, Pittsburgh, 2000—03. Recipient Editor's Choice award/Outstanding Achievement Poetry, Poetry.com, 2001, Editor's Choice award, Internat. Libr. Poetry, 2002—04, 2005, 2006, merit award, outstanding achievement award. Mem.: Acad. Cert. Case Mgr., Ams. Health Ins. Plans (Wash. DC) (health ins. assoc. designation), Internat. Soc. Poets, Broadcast Music (BMI), Internat. Songwriters Assn. Avocation: exercise. Personal E-mail: iwrktolive1@cs.com.

**MAIONE, DONNA,** fashion designer; Degree with honors, FIT. With various cos. Liz Claiborne, Macy's; prin., owner Donna Maione Studio, 1988—; ptnr. DMI, 1992—. Office: 525 7th Ave Fl 19 New York NY 10018-4901*

**MAIORIELLO, RICHARD PATRICK,** retired otolaryngologist; b. Mar. 17, 1936; s. Gesumino Theodore and Angelina (Del Rossi) M.; m. Susan Hemenway, Mar. 6, 1979; children: Gabriel, Angela, Richard. AB, U. Pa., 1960; MD, Jefferson Med. Coll., 1964; MS, Thomas Jefferson U., 1972. Diplomate Nat. Bd. Med. Examiners, Am. Bd. Otolaryngology. Commd. 2d lt. USAF, 1963, advanced through grades to col., 1977, ret., 1979; intern Keesler Hosp., 1965-67; chief flight medicine USAF Base, Bitburg, Fed. Republic Germany, 1965-68; intern in otolaryngology Thomas Jefferson Hosp., Phila., 1968-71, 72-73; dir. med. edn. Andrews AFB, 1974-78; assoc. prof. uniformed svcs. Univ. Health Scis., 1978-79; assoc. prof. Northeastern Ohio U. of Medicine, 1983—; mem. staff Aultman Hosp., 1979—; assoc. staff Timken Mercy Med. Ctr., 1981—, Union Hosp., 1988—; retired, 2001. Cons. otolaryngology to Surgeon Gen., 1977—; pres. Mid-Ohio Dressage Assn. With USNR, 1954-58. Decorated Air Force Commendation medal. Fellow ACS, Am. Soc. Head and Neck Surgery; mem. Am. Acad. Otolaryngology, Am. Acad. Facial Plastic and Reconstructive Surgery, Am. Assn. Cosmetic Surgery, Vail Cosmetic Surg. Soc., Hanoverian Soc. (exec. v.p.), US Dressage Fedn. (chmn. all-breeds coun.), Centurion Club. Republican. Roman Catholic.

**MAIR, BRUCE LOGAN,** interior designer, architectural firm executive; b. Chgo., June 5, 1951; s. William Logan and Josephine (Lee) M. BFA, Drake U., 1973; postgrad., Ind. Wesleyan U., 1990—. Mgr., head designer Reifers of Indpls., 1973-79; pres. Interiors Internat., Indpls., 1979-87; sr. designer Kasler Group, Indpls., 1987-89; dir. devel. Tillery Interiors and Imports, Greenwood, Ind., 1990, v.p. Indpls., 1990-92; owner Mair Interior Design Group, Indpls., 1992—. Pres. Tokens Inc., Indpls., 1982-88, Meg-A-Wat Enterprises Inc., Indpls., 1985-87, Luxury Ice Creams Inc., Indpls., 1986-87. Cover designer Indpls. Home and Garden mag., 1978, feature designer 1980; feature designer Builder mag., 1979; co-designer feature Indpls. At Home mag., 1979. Campaigner Anderson for Pres., 1980. Mem. Am. Soc. Interior Designers (profl., treas. local chpt. 1982-83, Press. awards 1981-82), U.S. Rowing Assn. (master 1987—), St. Joseph Hist. Neighborhood Assn., Columbia Club (rowing crew coxswain 1986—), Highland Model A Club, Tower Harbor Yacht Club (Douglas, Mich.), Royal Palm Yacht Club Ft. Myers, Alpha

Epsilon Pi. Avocations: sculling, historic preservation, model a ford restoration, fishing, farming. Office: Mair Interior Design Group 1716 Fowler St Fort Myers FL 33901 Office Phone: 239-476-9404. E-mail: BruceMairID@aol.com.

**MAISEL, SHERMAN JOSEPH,** economist, educator; b. Buffalo, July 8, 1918; s. Louis and Sophia (Beck) M.; m. Lucy Cowdin, Sept. 26, 1942; children: Lawrence C., Margaret L. AB, Harvard U., Cambridge, Mass., 1939, MPA, 1947, PhD, 1949. Mem. bd. govs. FRS, 1965-72; economist, fin. service res. officer Dept. State, 1945-46; teaching fellow Harvard U., 1947-48; asst. prof., assoc. prof., prof. bus. adminstrn. U. Calif. at Berkeley, 1948-65, 72-86; sr. economist Nat. Bur. Econ. Research-West, 1973-78; chmn., bd. dirs. Farmers Savings & Loan, 1986-88; pres. Sherman J. Maisel & Asscs. Inc., 1986—. Fellow Fund For Advancement Edn., 1952-53, Inst. Basic Math. with Application to Bus., 1959-60, Center for Advanced Study in Behavioral Scis., 1972; mem. adv. coms. to Bur. Census, FHA, State of Calif., Ford Found., Social Sci. Research Council; mem. bldg. research adv. bd. NRC. Author: Housebuilding in Transition, 1953, Fluctuations, Growth, and Forecasting, 1957, Managing the Dollar, 1973, Real Estate Investment and Finance, 1976, Risk and Capital Adequacy in Commercial Banks, 1981, Macroeconomics: Theories and Policies, 1982, Real Estate Finance, 1987, 2d edit., 1992. Bd. dirs. Berkeley Unified Sch. Dist., 1962-65. Served to capt. AUS, 1941-45. Recipient citation, U. Calif., Berkeley, 1986. Fellow Am. Fin. Assn. (pres. 1973); mem. Am. Econ. Assn. Home: 2164 Hyde St San Francisco CA 94109-1788 Office: U Calif Haas Bus Sch Berkeley CA 94720-1900

**MAISSEL, GERDA SHARON,** physician; b. Poughkeepsie, N.Y. married; 2 children. BS in Pharmacology summa cum laude, U. Conn., 1983; MD, SUNY, 1987. Diplomate Am. Bd. Phys. Medicine and Rehab. Intern Crozier Chester Med. Ctr., Chester, Pa., 1987-88; resident in phys. medicine and rehab. Thomas Jefferson U., Phila., 1988-91, instr. dept. rehab. med., 1991-94; chief divsn. phys. med. and rehab., sec. Baystate Med. Ctr., Springfield, Mass., 1994—, pres. med. staff, 2003—04, med. dir. post acute care svcs., 2004—; med. dir., chief Baystate Med. Home Care & Post Acute Medicine. Asst. prof. Tufts U. Sch. Medicine, 1994—; med. dir. Baystate Med. Assocs., Baystate Med. and Rsch. Found.; co-med. dir. short stay units Heritage Hall. Contbr. articles to profl. jours. Mem. Mass. Med. Soc. (del.), Acad. Phys. Medicine and Rehab. Office: Baystate Med Ctr Dept Rehab Medicine 759 Chestnut St Springfield MA 01199-1001 Office Phone: 413-794-5436.

**MAISSEL, LEON ISRAEL,** physicist, engineer; b. Cape Town, South Africa, May 31, 1930; came to U.S., 1956; s. Charles and Emily (Cohen) M.; m. Raina Eve Corren, Jan. 26, 1956; children: Simon, Gerda, Joseph. B.Sc., U. Cape Town, 1949, M.Sc., 1951; PhD, U. London, 1955. Staff scientist Philco Corp., Phila., 1956-60; adv. physicist IBM Corp., Poughkeepsie, NY, 1960-63, sr. engr., 1963-81, sr. tech. staff mem., 1981-93; patent writer, 1994—. Author, editor: Handbook of Thin Film Technology, 1969, An Introduction to Thin Films, 1970; contbr. articles profl. jours.; patentee in field. Recipient Outstanding Invention award IBM Corp., 1968; recipient Outstanding Contbr. award IBM Corp., 1969 Fellow IEEE; mem. Am. Vacuum Soc. (Dir. 1966-68) Lodges: B'nai B'rith. Democrat. Jewish. Home: 16 Smoke Rise Ln Wappingers Falls NY 12590-1240 Personal E-mail: maissel@att.net. *Most people, properly trained, can solve well-defined problems. The ability to deal with poorly-defined problems is much rarer and is the key to success in science.*

**MAISSEL, RAINA EVE,** lawyer; b. London, Apr. 12, 1931; came to U.S., 1956; d. Louis and Golde Pearl Corren; m. Leon Israel Maissel, Jan. 22, 1956; children: Simon Joseph, Gerda Sharon, Joseph Saul. LLB, Univ. Coll. London, 1952; pupil to Hon. S.C. Silkin, London, 1953—54. Barrister-at-law Eng., 1953; bar: N.Y. 1977, U.S. Dist. Ct. (so. dist.) N.Y. 1979, U.S. Dist. Ct. (ea. dist.) N.Y. 1979, U.S. Supreme Ct. 1982. Pvt. practice, Bournemough, England, 1954—56; rsch. assoc. Ballard, Spahr et al, Phila., 1956—58; counsel Moran, Spiegel, et al, Poughkeepsie, NY, 1977—80; pvt. practice Wappingers Falls, NY, 1980—86; assoc. Gellert & Cutler P.C., Poughkeepsie, 1986—95; of counsel Gellert & Klein, 1995—. V.p. Dutchess County Players, Poughkeepsie, 1962-64; pres. Merrywood Civic Assn., 1972-74; mem. 1st ward com. Dem. party, Poughkeepsie, 1973-74; mem. Poughkeepsie Zoning Bd. Appeals, 1982-83; commr. N.Y. State Bridge Authority, 1991-1999, vice-chmn., 1995-98. Mem. N.Y. State Bar Assn. (Tippins Family Law Task Force 1994-96). Jewish. Home and Office: 16 Smokerise Ln Wappingers Falls NY 12590-1240

**MAISTO, JOHN F.,** ambassador; b. Braddock, Pa., Aug. 28, 1938; married; 3 children. BSFS, Georgetown U., 1961; MA, San Carlos Coll., Guatemala, 1962. With BiNational Ctr., Cordoba, Argentina, 1963-66; asst. cultural affairs officer USIA, Cochabamba, Bolivia, 1966-68; with Fgn. Svc., 1968—; adminstrv. asst. Fgn. Svc. Inst. Dept. State, 1968-69; econ. and comml. officer U.S. Embassy, La Paz, Bolivia, 1969-71; internat. rels. officer Ops. Ctr., 1971-72; spl. assist. Office of Counselor, 1972-73; internat. rels. officer office Andean affairs, dir. inter-Am. affairs Dept. State, 1973-75; polit. officer U.S. Embassy, San Jose, Costa Rica, 1975-78, Manila, 1978-82; dep. dir. office Philippine affairs, bur. East Asian and Pacific affairs Dept. State, 1982-84, dir., 1984-86; dep. chief of mission and charge d'affaires Am. Embassy, Panama, 1986-89; dep. permanent U.S. rep. to OAS, 1989-92; dep. asst. sec. state for Ctrl. Am. and Panama U.S. Dept. State, 1992-93; U.S. amb. to Nicaragua, 1993-96; U.S. amb. to Venezuela, 1997—2000; fgn. policy advisor U.S. so. commd., 2000—01; spl. asst. to Pres., sr. dir. for western hemisphere affairs Nat. Security Coun., 2001—03; U.S. permanent rep. to OAS U.S. Dept. State, Washington, 2003—. Office: Harry S Truman Bldg 2201 C St NW Rm 5914 Washington DC 20520 Office Phone: 202-647-9430.*

**MAITEH, BILAL,** research engineer; PhD in Mech. Engring., NJ Inst. Tech., 2000. Sr. rschr. engr. Delphi, Troy, Mich., 2000—. Mem.: ASME (divsn. chair 2004—, LDI award 2003—04). Achievements include invention of Automotive and Virtual Reality.

**MAITLAND, GUY EDISON CLAY,** lawyer; b. London, Dec. 28, 1942; (mother Am. citizen); s. Paul and Virginia Frances (Carver) M. BA, Columbia U., 1964; JD, N.Y. Law Sch. 1968. Bar: N.Y. 1969, U.S. Dist. Ct. (so. and ea. dists.) N.Y. 1969, U.S. Ct. Appeals (2d and D.C. cirs.) 1969. Assoc. Burlingham, Underwood & Lord, N.Y.C., 1969-74; admiralty counsel Union Carbide Corp., N.Y.C., 1974-76; exec. v.p., gen. counsel, officer Liberian Svcs., Inc., N.Y.C. and Reston, Va., 1976-99; pres. Trust Co. of the Marshall Islands, Inc., 1990—; mng. ptnr. Internat. Registries, Inc., 2000—. Del. UN Conf. on Trade and Devel., Manila, 1979, Belgrade, 1983; participant London Conf. on Limitation of Maritime Liability, 1976; mem. legal com. Internat. Maritime Orgn. (UN) London, 1980—; del. UN Conf. on Law of the Sea, 1976-82, London UN Maritime Law Conf., 1984; co-founder The Admiralty-Fin. Forum, N.Y.C., 1986; mng. ptnr. Internat. Registries, Inc. Contbr. articles on maritime law, U.S. shipping policy. Mem. N.Y. Rep. State Exec. Com., 1974-76; del. Rep. Nat. Conv., Kansas City, 1976; sec. N.Y. Rep. County Com., 1976-87, vice chmn., 1988—, mem. exec. com., 1974-76; co-chmn. Citizens for Reagan, N.Y. State, 1979-80; trustee Am. Mcht. Marine Mus. Found. at U.S. Mcht. Marine Acad., King's Point, Nat. Maritime Hist. Soc., chmn., 2000-01; trustee N.Y. Maritime Coll. at Ft. Schuyler Found., Inc.; bd. dirs. Coast Guard Found.; UN Geneva Conf. on Arrest of Vessels 1999; bd. dirs. Seamen's Ch. Inst., N.Y.C., Ctr. for Seafarers Rights; mem. adv. com. Am. Maritime History Project. Named Outstanding Young Man of Am. U.S. Jaycees, 1975; hon. del. Rep. Nat. Conv., Dallas, 1984. Mem. ABA, Assn. of Bar of City of N.Y. (chmn. admiralty com. 1982-85), Maritime Law Assn. U.S. (chmn. com. on intergovtl. orgns. 1987-95), Ctr. for Seafarer's Rights Seamen's Ch. Inst. (bd. dirs. 1994—), Maritime Assn. Port of N.Y. (dir. 1984-87, 98—, pres. 1999-2001). Office: Internat Registries Inc 437 Madison Ave 32d Fl New York NY 10022-7001

**MAITOZA, COLLEEN,** professional sports team executive; Gen. mgr., co-owner Sacramento (Calif.) Sirens, 2001—. Achievements include an undefeated 2003 season in the Independent Women's Football League; the Sacramento Sirens won the 2003 Independent Women's Football League Championship against the New York Sharks.

**MAITRA, UMADAS,** biomedical researcher, educator; arrived in U.S., 1959; s. Ramadas and Radhabani Maitra. BSc, MSc, Calcutta U., 1958; PhD, U. Mich., Ann Arbor, 1963; DSc, Calcutta U., 1976. Tchg. fellow U. Mich., Ann Arbor, 1959—62; postdoctoral fellow Albert Einstein Coll., Bronx, NY, 1965—66, from asst. prof. to assoc. prof., 1967—77, prof., 1977—. Mem. biochem. study sect. NIH, Bethesda, Md., 1987—91, mem. cell devel. function study sect., 1999—2003. Contbr. articles to profl. jours. Recipient Established Investigatorship, Am. Heart Assn., 1967, Faculty Rsch. award, Am. Cancer Soc., 1972, rsch. grant, NIH, 1967—2006. Mem.: Am. Soc. Microbiology, Am. Biochemistry and Molecular Biology. Achievements include discovery of new proteins involved in translation initiation pathway. Office: Albert Einstein Coll 1300 Morris Park Ave Bronx NY 10461 Office Fax: 718-430-8527. Business E-Mail: maitra@alcom.yu.edu.

**MAIWURM, JAMES JOHN,** lawyer; b. Wooster, Ohio, Dec. 5, 1948; s. James Frederick and Virginia Anne (Jones) M.; m. Wendy S. Leeper, July 31, 1971; children: James G., Michelle K. BA, Coll. Wooster, 1971; JD, U. Mich. 1974. Bar: Ohio 1974, D.C. 1986, Md. 1987, N.Y., 1987. Ptnr. Squire, Sanders & Dempsey, Cleve. and Washington, 1974-90; ptnr., group head Crowell & Moring, Washington, 1990-98; ptnr. Squire, Sanders & Dempsey, Washington, 1998-99; chmn., CEO Kaiser Group Internat., Inc., Fairfax, Va., 1999-2000; mng. ptnr. Squire, Sanders & Dempsey LLP, Washington, 2001—03, firmwide mng. ptnr., 2003—. Bd. dirs. George Mason U. Coll. Visual and Performing Arts. Contbr. articles to profl. jours. Mem. ABA, DC Bar Assns., Leadership Washington, The Tower Club (bd. govs. 2003-). Home: 9419 Brian Jac Ln Great Falls VA 22066-2002 Office: Squire Sanders & Dempsey LLP 14th fl 8000 Towers Crescent Vienna VA 22182 Business E-Mail: jmaiwurm@ssd.com.

**MAIZE, JOHN CHRISTOPHER,** dermatologist, educator; b. Elizabeth, NJ, July 23, 1943; s. Donald Adam and Caroline Marie (Costanzo) Maize; m. Janice Lee Bentley, May 21, 1966; children: Sandra Kristine Tolly, John C. Jr., Jennifer Lee. MD, U. Mich., 1968. Cert. Am. Bd. Dermatology. Intern U. Mich., Ann Arbor, 1968—69, residency in dermatology, 1968—72; asst. prof. dermatology SUNY, Buffalo, 1972—77, assoc. prof., 1977—80, Med. U. SC, Charleston, 1980—83, prof., 1983—89, prof., chmn. dept. dermatology, 1989—2003, clin. prof., 2003—. Author: Pigmented Lesions of the Skin, 1987, Cutaneous Pathology, 1998; editor-in-chief Am. Jour. Dermatology, 1986—90. Fellow: Am. Soc. Dermapathology (pres. 1995), Am. Acad. Dermatology; mem.: Am. Bd. Dermatology (dir. 1990—99, pres. 1999), S.C. Dermatol. Assn. (pres. 2001), S.C. Med. Assn., Internat. Soc. Dermatopathology (sec. 1987—89, pres. 1989—91), Am. Dermatol. Assn. Roman Catholic. Avocations: fishing, golf, travel. Office: 266 W Coleman Blvd Unit 101 Mount Pleasant SC 29464 Office Phone: 843-388-6911. E-mail: jmaizesr@ameripath.com.

**MAIZE, MOHAMED ANIS,** physics professor; b. Abokebeir, Sharkia, Egypt, July 4, 1948; Doctorate, Purdue U., West Lafayette, Ind., 1983. Assoc. prof. St. Vincent Coll., Latrobe, Pa., 1995—2000, prof., 2000—. Dept. chairperson St. Vincent Coll., Latrobe, Pa., 1996—. Office: St Vincent Coll Dept Physics 300 Fraser Purchase Rd Latrobe PA 15650

**MAJEED, D. HADAYAI S.,** publishing executive, writer; b. Milwaukee, Wis., Jan. 14, 1955; d. Fred J. and Evelyn L. Spencer; m. Abdul H. Abdullah, Jan. 28, 1998. BA in Biology, U. Ark., 1976. Prin., owner Spencer-Majeed, Ltd., Conley, Ga., 1995—; adminstr. Baitul Salaam Network, Inc., Atlanta, 1997—. Author: Emerging Victorious: A Dialogue on Polygamy/Polygyny in America (nominated Writer of Yr., Ga. Writers, 2000). Mem. coun. Masjid Al Mu minun, Atlanta, 2002—04. Nominee Noble Peace prize, 2005; recipient Real Life is Drug Free award, State of Ga., 1997. Mem.: 1000 Peace Women 2005 (assoc.). Independent. Islam. Office Phone: 404-366-6610.

**MAJERUS, PHILIP WARREN,** physician; b. Chgo., July 10, 1936; s. Clarence Nicholas and Helen Louise (Mathis) Majerus; m. Janet Sue Brakensiek, Dec. 28, 1957; children: Suzanne, David, Juliet, Karen; m. Elaine Michelle Flansburg, 1996. BS, Notre Dame U., 1958; MD, Washington U., 1961. Resident in Medicine Mass. Gen. Hosp., Boston, 1961—63; research assoc. NIH, Bethesda, Md., 1963—66; asst. prof. biochemistry Washington U., St. Louis, 1966—75, assoc. prof. medicine, 1966—69, assoc. prof. medicine, 1969—71, prof. medicine, 1971—, dir. div. hematology, 1973—, prof. biochemistry, 1976—. Mem. editl. bd. numerous jours. and profl. mags.; contbr. articles to profl. jours. Recipient Faculty Rsch. Assoc. award, Am. Cancer Soc., 1966—75, Disting. Career award for contbns. to hemostasis, Internat. Soc. for Thrombosis and Hemostasis, 1985, Alumni Faculty award, Washington U. Sch. Medicine, 1986, The Robert J. and Claire Pasarow Found. award, 1994, Bristol-Myers Squibb prize for cardiovascular rsch. 1998, numerous others. Fellow: ACP; mem.: Inst. of Medicine of NAS, Am. Soc. Clin. Investigation (pres. 1981—82), Am. Soc. Biol. Chemists, Am. Fedn. Clin. Rsch., Am. Soc. Hematology (pres. 1991), Assn. Am. Physicians, Am. Acad. Arts and Scis., Alpha Omega Alpha, Sigma Xi. Home: 7220 Pershing Ave Saint Louis MO 63130-4248 Office: Wash Univ Sch of Med Dept Int Med Saint Louis MO 63110

**MAJESKI, SUSAN SAXER,** elementary school educator; d. Raymond Anthony and Marjorie Kelham Saxer; m. Frank Ronald Majeski, July 6, 1985. BS in Elem. Edn., Ball State U., 1973, MEd, 1976. Tchr. elem. sch. East Noble Sch. Corp., Kendallville Ind, 1973—85, Prairie Hills Elem. Sch. Dist. 144, Markham, Ill., 1985—. Mem. Dist. 144 Edn. Assn., treas., 2000—04. Named Profl. Educator of Yr., Prairie-Hills Elem. Sch. Dist. 144, 2004. Mem.: Internat. Reading Assn., Ill. Edn. Assn., Gamma Sigma Sigma (pres. 1985—87). Office: Prairie-Hills Elem Sch Dist 144 3015 W 163d St Markham IL 60426 Business E-Mail: sjsmajeski@sbcglobal.net.

**MAJESTY, MELVIN SIDNEY,** psychologist, consultant; b. New Orleans, June 6, 1928; s. Sidney Joseph and Marcella Cecilia (Kieffer) M.; m. Bettye Newanda Gordon, Dec. 18, 1955; 1 child, Diana Sue. BA, La. State U., 1949; MS, Western Res. U., 1951; PhD (USAF Inst. Tech. fellow), Case-Western Res. U., 1967. Commd. 2d lt. USAF, 1951, advanced through grades to lt. col., 1968; program mgr., asst. dir. tng. rsch. Air Force Human Resources Lab., 1967-69; dir. faculty and profl. ednl. rsch. USAF Acad., 1969-72; dir. plot tng. candidate selection program Officer Tng. Sch., Air Tng.Command, 1972-76; ret. USAF, 1976; personnel selection cons. to Calif. State Pers. Bd., Sacramento, 1976-92. Patentee listening center; founded pers. testing for ballistic missile and space systems; directed largest study of fighter pilot selection since World War II; pioneered use of phys. testing as replacement for the maximum age requirement in law enforcement jobs; developed phys. fitness tests and established psychol. screening standards for state highway patrol officer and police officers; contbr. numerous articles to profl. publs. With U.S. Army, WWII, 1944-46, Korea, Vietnam, USAF, 1951-76. Decorated Commendation medal (2), Meritorious Svc. medal (2), Am. Campaign medal, WWII Victory medal, WWII Overseas Occupation medal, Ballistic Missile badge, numerous others. Mem.: DAV, VFW, APA, Veterans for Peace, Reserve Officers Assn., Mil. Officers Assn. Am., Am. Family Assn., Am. Legion, Mil. Order Fgn. Wars, Vietnam Vets. Am., Amvets, Bible Soc., Nat. Assn. Uniformed Svc. Office: 801 Capitol Mall Sacramento CA 95814-4806

**MAJETTE, DENISE,** former congresswoman; b. Bklyn., May 18, 1955; d. Voyd and Olivia Majette; m. Rogers Mitchell Majette; 2 children. BA, Yale U., 1976; JD, Duke U., 1979. Atty. Legal Aid Soc. Winston-Salem, NC, 1981—83; law assoc. Ga. Ct. Appeals, 1984—89; ptnr. Jenkins Nelson & Welch, 1989—92; asst. atty. gen. State of Ga., 1991—92; adminstrv. law juste Ga. State Bd. Workers' Compensation, 1992; judge State Ct. of DeKalb County, 1993—2002; congresswoman 4th Dist. Ga. U.S. Ho. Reps.,

2003—05; mem. budget, edn. and workforce, and small bus. ho. coms. Grad. Leadership DeKalb, 1992; mem. Kidney Caucus; former com. mem. Miller Grove PTA; past mem. vestry Episcopal Ch. of Holy Cross; former pres. DeKalb Lawyers Assn.; mem. Childcare Com. YMCA, Decatur; mem. adv. bd. Jr. League DeKalb County; mem. Congl. Black Caucus, Congl. Caucus on India and Indian Ams.; mem. steward bd. Antioch AME Ch. Recipient Judge's Cmty. Recognition award, Black Law Students' Assn., Ga. State U. Coll. Law, 2001, You Go Girl award, Ga. Assn. Black Women Attys., 2003. Democrat. Home: PO Box 33678 Decatur GA 30033-0678

**MAJEV, HOWARD RUDOLPH,** lawyer; b. NYC, Dec. 10, 1952; s. Benny and Hela (Wolowicz) M.; m. Janet Brandt; children: Brendan Joshua, Collin Campbell. BA, Johns Hopkins U., 1973; JD, U. Md., 1976. Bar: Md. 1978, D.C. 1995. Exec. asst. to city coun. pres. City of Balt., Balt., 1976-79; assoc. Weinberg and Green, Balt., 1979-84; ptnr. Weinberg & Green, Balt., 1985-94, Piper Rudnick LLP (formerly Rudnick & Wolfe), Washington, 1994—2001, Winston & Strawn LLP, Washington, 2001—. Author: (with K.S. Koenig) How to be a Legal Eagle: A Checklist for Remodelers, 1988; dir. Lex Mundi, 1992-94. Dir. Citizens Planning and Housing Assn., Balt., 1985-95, pres., 1990-92; bd. dirs. Md. Food Bank, Inc., 1988-92, Florence Crittenton Svcs. Balt., 1986-87, Sinai Hosp. Balt., 1990-92, Levindale Hebrew Geriat. Home and Hosp., 1991; devel. coun. The Kennedy Krieger Inst., 1988-92; participant Leadership-Greater Balt. Com., 1986. Mem. ABA, D.C. Bar Assn., Md. State Bar Assn. Avocations: tennis, reading. Office: Winston & Strawn LLP 1700 K St NW Washington DC 20006 Office Phone: 202-282-5781. Business E-Mail: hmajev@winston.com.

**MAJEWSKI, KAREN MARIE,** curator; b. Chgo., Apr. 21, 1955; d. John Marion and Geraldine Majewski; m. Matthew Feazell, 2005. BA, So. Ill. U., 1977, MA, 1981; PhD, U. Mich., 1998. Lectr. N.C. State U., Raleigh, 1983—88; assoc. prof. St. Mary's Coll., Orchard Lake, Mich., 1994—2003; curator polish book collection Orchard Lake Sch., Orchard Lake, Mich., 1996—. Author: (book) Traitors and True Poles: Narrating A Polish-American Identity, 1880-1939 (Kulczycki Award for Outstanding Book in Polish Am. Studies, 2003). Mem. Hamtramck Hist. Commn., Hamtramck, 2002—03; mayor Hamtramck, 2006—; pres. City Coun., Hamtramck, 2004—05. Recipient Lednicki prize, Polish Inst. Arts and Scis Am., 2005; grantee, Am. Coun. Learned Soc., 2002. Mem.: MLA, Immigration and Ethnic History Soc., Am. Studies Assn., Am. Hist. Assn., Polish Inst. Arts and Sci. Am., Polish Am. Hist. Assn. (exec. dir. 1998—, Halicki prize 2000, Disting. Svc. award 2003, Kulczycki prize 2003). Home: 2627 Pulaski Hamtramck MI 48212-3010 Office: Alumni Meml Libr 3535 Indian Trail Orchard Lake MI 48324 Office Phone: 248-683-1743. Home Fax: 313-365-5929. Personal E-mail: kmaj@umich.edu.

**MAJOR, CLARENCE LEE,** writer, educator; b. Atlanta, Dec. 31, 1936; s. Clarence and Inez (Huff) M.; m. Pamela Ritter, May 8, 1980. BS, SUNY, Albany; PhD, Union Inst. Prof. U. Colo. Boulder, 1977-89, U. Calif., Davis, 1989—. Author: All-Night Visitors, 1969, 2d version, 1998, Dictionary of Afro-American Slang, 1970, No, 1973, Reflex and Bone Structure, 1975, rev. edit., 1996, Emergency Exit, 1979, My Amputations, 1986, Such Was the Season, 1987, Painted Turtle: Woman with Guitar, 1988, Fun and Games, 1990, Calling the Wind, 1993, Juba to Jive: A Dictionary of African American Slang, 1994, Dirty Bird Blues, 1996; poetry: Swallow the Lake, 1970 (Nat. Coun. on the Arts award 1970), Symptoms & Madness, 1971, Private Line, 1971, The Cotton Club, 1972, Inside Diameter: The France Poems, 1985, Surfaces and Masks, 1988, Some Observations of a Stranger at Zuni in the Latter Part of the Century, 1989, Parking Lots, 1992, The Garden Thrives, 1996, Configurations: New and Selected Poems, 1958-1998, 1998 (Nat. Book Award Bronze medal 1999), Clarence Major and His Art: Portraits of an African American Postmodernist, 2001, Necessary Distance, 2001, Come By Here: My Mother's Life, 2002, Waiting for Sweet Betty, 2002, Conversations with Clarence Major, 2002, One Flesh, 2003; on man shows include Kresge Mus., Mich., 2001; group shows include Schacknow Mus. Fine Art, Plantation, Fla., 2003, Paterson Mus. NJ, 2006, Exploding Head Gallery, Calif., 2003-06; contbr. articles to Washington Post Book World, L.A. Times Book Rev., N.Y. Times Book Rev. Recipient Nat. Council on Arts award, Washington, 1970; Western States Book award, Western States Found., Santa Fe, 1986; Fulbright grantee, 1981-83. Office: U Calif Dept English 281 Voorhies Hall Davis CA 95616

**MAJOR, JOHN CHARLES,** judge; s. William and Elsie M.; m. Hélène Provencher, 1959; children: Suzan, Peter, Paul, Steven. BComm. Loyola Coll., Montreal, 1953; LLB, U. Toronto, 1957, LLD (hon.), 2005, Concordia U., 2003, U. Calgary, 2005. Bar: Alta. 1958, Queen's Counsel, 1972. With Bennett, Jones & Verchere, Calgary, 1957-91, sr. ptnr., 1967; sr. counsel City of Calgary Police Svc., 1975-85; counsel McDonald Commn., 1978-82; sr. counsel Province of Alta., 1987, Alta. Ct. Appeal, 1991; justice Supreme Ct. of Can., Ottawa, Ont., Canada, 1992—. Fellow: Am. Coll. Trial Lawyers. Avocation: golf. Office: Bennett Jones LLP 4500 855-2 Str SW Calgary AB Canada T2P 4K7

**MAJOR, PATRICK WEBB, III,** principal; b. Wai, Maharastra, India, Mar. 12, 1947; s. Patrick W. Jr. and Alice (Seeland) M.; m. Daphnelynn Jantz, June 26, 1971; children: Mindy Joy, Matthew Patrick Webb. BA in BE, Columbia Internat. U., 1969; BA, Biola U., 1972; MA, Point Loma Nazarene U., 1979; postgrad., U. Calif., Irvine. Cert. secondary tchr., adminstr., Calif. Prin. Omega High Sch., Bakersfield, Calif., 1980-84; headmaster Bakersfield Christian Life Schs., 1984-86; prin. North Kern Christian Sch. Wasco, Calif 1986-88; prin., adminstr. Yucaipa (Calif.) Christian Schs., 1988-2000; prin. Christian H.S., El Cajon, Calif., 2000—03; adminstr. First Bapt. Ch. of Lakewood (Calif.) Schs., 2003—. Chmn. ACSI So. Calif. Accreditation Commn., 1998-2003. Mem. ASCD, Assn. Christian Schs. Internat. (former dist. rep., exec. bd. 1992-2001), Ctrl. Redwood League (pres. 1985-86), CIF Ctrl Sect., Internat. Fellowship Christian Sch. Adminstrs. Office Phone: 562-425-3358. Business E-Mail: administrator@fbcoles.org.

**MAJOR, RICHARD,** theater educator, actor, director; b. Portsmouth, Ohio, June 9, 1953; s. Charles Richard and Frances Major; m. Karen Elizabeth Brewster, Oct. 22, 1955; children: Will, Shannon. BA, Milligan Coll., Tenn., 1978; MFA, Mich. State U., East Lansing, 1982. Actor Nebr. Theatre Caravan, Omaha, 1982—83; guest artist U. Miss., Oxford, 1983—85; actor/dir. Barter Theatre, Abingdon, Va., 1983—89, actor, 2002—04; prof. theatre Milligan Coll., 1985—, chair performing, visual, and communicative arts, 1994—. Cons. Eyes and Ears Prodns., Tampa Bay, Fla., 1998—, numerous productions; presenter in field. Actor: Phantom, Guys & Dolls, 1776, One flew Over the Cuckoo's Nest, Around the World in 80 Days, You can't Take it With You, To Kill a Mockingbird, various plays, Twelfth Night, The Mousetrap, Ten Little Indians; dir.: The Gospel According to Jazz & Class Act, Godspell, Footloose, Man of La Mancha, Oklahoma!, Smoke on the Mountain, Shenandoah, 1940's Radio Hour, Pirates of Penzance; (plays) The Recycling Play (Outstanding Ecology award 1991), Shadowlands, Proof, On the Verge, Steel Magnolias, Under Milkwood, Story Theatre, The Night Thoreau Spent in Jail, Oedipus the King, Hamlet, Romeo and Juliet, Much Ado about Nothing, A Midsummer Night's Dream, The Rock and The Rabbi; author: (how-to book) Developing A Dynamic Drama Ministry; voiceover: Titanic; Red Jack, Blackbeard; commercials and industrial productions. Deacon Hopwood Meml. Christian Ch., Milligan College, 1993—2006; Sunday sch. tchr.; com. mem. for regional arts ann. conf. Johnson City Area Arts Coun., Tenn. 1988—2006. Grantee, Tenn. Arts Commn., 1986—, NEH, 1989, Waste Mgmt. N.Am., 1989—92, Eastman Chemical Decatur, 1989—92, Tenn. Humanities Coun., 1995, Tri-Cities Health Hero award Edn., 2000. Mem.: Actors' Equity Assn., Tenn. Theatre Assn. (assoc.; children's theatre 2005—06). Democrat. Avocations: reading, travel, special needs advocate, music, photography. Office: Milligan College PO Box 500 Milligan College TN 37682 Office Phone: 423-929-2058. Office Fax: 423-461-8789. Business E-Mail: rmajor@milligan.edu.

**MAJORAS, DEBORAH PLATT,** commissioner; m. John Majoras. BA summa cum laude, Westminster Coll.; JD, U. Va., 1989. Law clk. to Hon. Stanley S. Harris US Dist. Ct., DC; dep. asst. atty. gen. US Dept. Justice, Antitrust Div., 2000—01, prin. dep. asst. atty. gen., 2002—03; ptnr. antitrust sec., mem. tech. issues practice Jones Day, Washington, DC, 2004; chmn. FTC, Washington, DC, 2004—. Chair Internat. Competition Network's (ICN) Merger Working Group; mem. Antitrust Modernization Commn. Mem.: ABA (mem. Antitrust Law Sec.). Avocations: golf, shopping. Office: FTC 600 Pennsylvania Ave, NW Washington DC 20580 Office Phone: 202-326-2100.

**MAJORS, NELDA FAYE,** physical therapist; b. Houston, Aug. 3, 1938; d. Columbus Edward and Mary (Mills) M. Cert. in Phys. Therapy, Hermann Sch. Phys. Therapy, Houston, 1960; BS, U. Houston, 1963. Lic. phys. therapist, Tex. Staff therapist Tex. Med. Ctr. Hermann Hosp., Houston, 1960-61; phys. therapist Chelsea Orthopedic Clinic, Houston, 1961-63; dir. phys. therapy Meml. Hosp. Southwest, Houston, 1963-75; owner, pres. Nelda Majors, Inc., Houston, 1975—. Profl. adv. bd. Logos Home Health Agy., Houston, 1985-86; adv. dir. Prime Bank, Houston; sec.-treas., bd. dirs. Dominion Media Corp. Ptnr. Houston Proud Ptnr., 1986—; founder, pres. Instnl. Safety Advs. Inc., 1994—; bd. dirs. Texans for the Improvement of Long Term Care Facilities, 1995—; active St. Stephens Episcopal Ch., 2001—; trustee St. Stephen's Episc. Sch., Houston. Named All Am. Softball Pitcher, Amateur Softball Assn., 1964, All-Regional and All-State Pitcher, Tex. Amateur Softball Assn., 1954-70; named to Houston Amateur Softball Assn. Softball Hall of Fame, 1994, Houston Softball Legends Hall of Fame, 2002. Mem. Am. Phys. Therapy Assn (pvt. practice sect.), Ams. for Separation of Ch. and State, Tex. Phys. Therapy Assn., U. Houston Alumni Assn., E. Cullen Soc. (U. Houston), Rotary Club (Houston, Meml. Spring br.), Phi Kappa Phi. Clubs: U. Houston Cougar. Avocations: softball, bicycling, travel, golf, reading. Personal E-mail: nmajors370@aol.com.

**MAJTENYI, STEVEN ISTVAN,** retired civil engineer, consultant; b. Elek, Hungary, Jan. 20, 1936; came to U.S., 1962; s. Vilmos Gyorgy and Edit (Laczo) M.; m. Joan E. Zimmerman, Jan. 21, 1972; children: Vivian Claire, Juliet Eve. Student, U. Poitiers, France, 1962; MSc, Cornell U., 1965, PhD, 1969. Registered profl. engr., Ohio. Tchg. and rsch. asst. Cornell U., Ithaca, N.Y., 1964-68; soils engr. TAMS, N.Y.C., 1968-71; hwy. rsch. engr. U.S. Dept. Transp./FHWA, Washington, 1971-76; hwy. engr. The World Bank, Washington, 1976-81; sr. cons. The World Bank, U.S. Dept. Transp./FHWA, Washington, 1981-95; procurement expert UN, N.Y.C., 1995-98; civil engring. cons. Gahanna, Ohio, 1998—; ret., 2001. Speaker in field. Contbr. articles to profl. jours. Josephine de Karman scholar, 1962-64. Fellow: ASCE (life). Roman Catholic. Achievements include participation in the development of numerous technical ideas in the U.S. Government and private industry; improvement of procurement documents in numerous countries worldwide. Home: 167 Highmeadow Dr Gahanna OH 43230-1791

**MAJUMDAR, KINGSHUK,** physics professor, researcher; b. Howrah, India, Jan. 27, 1968; s. Alokenath and Bhabani Majumdar; m. Smiti Majumdar, Dec. 10, 1999; 1 child, Ritwik. PhD, U. Fla., 1998. Postdoctoral rsch. asst. U. Cin., 1999—2000; asst. prof. Berea Coll., Berea, Ky., 2000—. Contbr. articles to profl. jours. Recipient Cottrell Coll. Sci. award, Rsch. Corp., 2004—06; grantee, Berea Coll., 2000—04; Kavli Inst. Theoretical Physics scholar, U. Calif., Santa Barbara, 2005—. Mem.: Am. Phys. Soc. (reviewer Phys. Rev. A, B and Letters 2004—). Office: Berea Coll Dept Physics Berea KY 40404 Office Phone: 859-985-3299.

**MAJUMDAR, MUKUL KUMAR,** economist, educator; b. Krishnagar, India. Dec. 6, 1944; came to U.S., 1965, naturalized, 1971; s. Nirmal Kanti and Sita (Mitra) M.; m. Malabika Dutta, Aug. 8, 1969. BA in Econs. with honors 1st class, Calcutta U., India, 1966; PhD in Econs, U. Calif., Berkeley, 1970. Asst. prof. econs. Stanford U., 1969-72; lectr. London Sch. Econs., 1972-73; assoc. prof. Cornell U., 1973-77, prof., chmn. dept. econs., 1977—, Warshow prof. econs., 1983—. Ford rotating research prof. U. Calif., Berkeley, 1976-77 Coordinating editor: The Rev. Econ. Studies, 1976—; asso. editor: Jour. Math. Econs, 1974—, Jour. Econ. Theory, 1977—. Recipient Coll. de France medal, 1989; Guggenheim fellow, 1976-77. Fellow Econometric Soc. Office: Cornell U Dept Econs Uris Hall Ithaca NY 14850 Office Phone: 607-255-3640. Business E-Mail: mkm5@cornell.edu.

**MAJUMDAR, SHARANYA JYOTI,** meteorologist, educator; b. St. Albans, Eng., Aug. 22, 1971; BA in Math. with honors, U. Cambridge, 1992; PhD, U. Cambridge, Eng., 1997. Postdoctoral fellow Pa. State U., University Park, 1997—2000; asst. scientist U. of Miami Rosentiel Sch Marine and Atmospheric Sci, Divsn. Meteorology and Phys. Oceanography, 2001—02. Rsch. asst. prof. RSMAS/MPO U. of Miami, 2002—. Recipient Smith's Prize, U. of Cambridge, 1995. Fellow: Royal Meteorol. Soc. (assoc.); mem.: Am. Geophys. Union, Am. Meteorol. Soc. Office: RSMAS/MPO University of Miami 4600 Rickenbacker Causeway Miami FL 33149 Office Phone: 305-421-4779. E-mail: smajumdar@rsmas.miami.edu.

**MAK, KITTY,** lawyer; b. Hong Kong, Jan. 23, 1973; arrived in US, 1983; d. Michael and Murenda Mak; ptnr. Jennifer Stump. BA, U. Calif., Berkeley, 1995; JD, Loyola U., LA, 1999. Shareholder Law Office of Kitty Mak, West Hollywood, Calif., 2003—, Century City, Calif., 2004—. Avocation: painting. Office: 1875 Century Park E Ste 600 Century City CA 90067

**MAKADOK, STANLEY,** management consultant; b. NYC, Mar. 30, 1941; s. Jack and Pauline (Speiner) Makadok; m. Neilia A. David, Nov. 12, 1989; 1 child from previous marriage, Richard. BME, CCNY, 1962; MS in Mgmt. Sci., Rutgers U., 1964, Run nya analyst Westinghouse Electric Corp., Balt., 1964—65; project engr., cons. Am. Cyanamid Corp., Pearl River, NY, Wayne, NJ, 1965—68; v.p. bus. devel. and planning Pepsico Inc. and affiliates, Purchase, NY, Miami, Fla., 1968—75; mgr. fin. and planning cons. Coopers & Lybrand, N.Y.C., 1975—77; pres. Century Mgmt. Cons., Inc., Princeton, NJ, 1977—. Contbr. articles to profl. jours. Office: Century Mgmt Cons Inc 32 Nassau St Princeton NJ 08542-4503 Office Phone: 609-921-7070.

**MAKALOU, OUMAR,** economic advisor; b. Kita, Mali, 1934; s. Sambou and Coumba (Tounkara) M.; m. Morimoussou Koite, July 30, 1944; children: Modibo Mao, Kalle, Mamaye, Sambou, Coumba. BA in Law (Polit. Economy), Paris U., 1960, MA in Econs., 1968; PhD in Econs., U. Paris-Sorbonne, 1970. Insp. Fin. Services, Paris, 1956-60; pres. Devel. Bank, Bamako, Mali, 1961-63; state controller Office of Pres., Koulouba, Mali, 1963-68; dir. gen. Treasury Banks and Ins., Koulouba, 1968-71, Internat. Coop., Koulouba, 1971-73; chmn. bd. dirs. Cen. Bank, Bamako, Mali, 1973-77; chief of staff Office of Pres., Bamako; dep. dir. African dept. IMF, Washington, 1977-84; sr. advisor IMF Inst., Washington, 1984—; ret., 1993. Vis. prof. U. Montreal, Que., Canada, 1983; dir. gen. taxes, investments and credit Ministry of Fin., Mali, 1984—91; spl. advisor to Pres. of Mali, 1991—93; pres. Ctr. of Studies and Rsch. for Democracy, Econ. and Social Devel., 1993—2002; sr. fellow, disting. vis. prof. Sch. Pub. Policy George Mason U., 1997—2002. Author: Budget Equilibrium in Developing Countries, 1970, Privatization in Africa: A Critical Analysis, 1999. Named Grand Officer of the Cross of Merit, Fed. Republic of Germany, Officer of Merit Order of France, Officer and Knight of the Nat. Order of Mali. Fellow: Asian Inst. Mgmt. (Manila), Asian Inst. Tech. (Bangkok), mem. Soc. for Internat. Devel. (bd. dirs. 1986-90), Internat. Profl. Bankers' Assn., Nat. Economists Club (Washington). Avocations: reading, music, the arts. Office: IMF 700 19th St NW Washington DC 20431-0001 Home: 126 Swarthmore Ave Gaithersburg MD 20877-1260

**MAKAROV, IOURI,** advertising executive; b. Ukraine, Dec. 2, 1946; arrived in U.S., 1993; m. Sofia Gaisinskaja, Dec. 19, 1970; 1 child, Ganna Makarova. Journalist and mem. editl. bd. Izvestia, Moscow, 1985—93; creative supr. YAR Comm., Inc, N.Y.C., 1993—98; creative dir. and v.p. Kang & Lee Advt., 1998—. Author: He wasn't, he didn't attend, he didn't participate. (All-Russian Theatrical Union award, 1985); Mousetrap (Best of

NY, 1995); creative dir.: TV commercial; contbr. U.S. Census 2000 advertising campaign (Golden Effie, 2001); author: (plays) He Was Not, He Didn't Attend, He Didn't Participate, 1985, Front Page Picture, 1987, (films) Criminal Talent, 1988, Hostage, 1990, Deadly Game of Love, 1991. Recipient Telly award, ATRT TV Comml. Office Phone: 212-375-8150.

**MAKE, ISABEL ROSE,** multicultural studies educator, adult education educator, small business owner; b. Phila., Oct. 6, 1947; d. Aaron M. and Lillian (Simon) Rose; children: Jonathan David, Jeremy Simon. BA, George Wash. U., 1969; EdM, Temple U., 1970; EdD, W.Va. U., 1975. Cert. tchr., Pa., Mich., W.Va., Mass. Dir. learning ctr. Kirkbride Elem. Sch., Phila., 1970-71, Huron High Sch., Ann Arbor, 1971-73; learning disabilities tutor Brookline (Mass.) Pub. Schs., 1976-82; edni. cons. Newton, Mass., 1982-84; child care cons. Isabel Make Assocs., Newton, 1984-88; adj. prof. reading C.C. Denver, 1989—92; adj. prof. multicultural studies, critical thinking and creativity Metro State Coll., Denver, 1992—2002; pres. Top Hat Gourmet, 1992—2000; bus. lectr. on The Art of Corp. Giving, 1993; lectr. adult edn. South Fla. Lib. Sys., 2001—. Ednl. counselor Phila. Home for Emotionally Disturbed Girls, 1970; cons. Ann Arbor Pub. Schs., 1971; child care cons. Newton Cmty. Schs., 1985; founding mem. Denver Parenting Ctr., 1989—92; chair legis. and regulations subcom. Commonwealth of Mass., Boston, 1984-88; adj. prof. Mett. State Coll., 1992-2002, C.C. Denver, 1992-96. Founder Temple Shalom Nursery Sch., Newton, 1975; chmn. childcare task force The U. Hosp., Boston U. Med. Ctr., 1985-88; bd. dirs. Greenwood Village Arts and Humanites Coun., 1991—2001; mem. at large Colo. Consortium Community Arts Couns., 1992, Greenwood Village Arts and Humanities Coun. (chair A Space of my Own, Parent-Child Art Day), 1991—; mem. steering coun. Colo. Alliance for Arts in Edn., 1993; co-chair Teen Arts Adv. Bd., 1999-, Greenwood Village, Colo., 1999-; founding mem. Delray Cultural Roundtable, 2005—, Delray Film Festival, 2005. Democrat. Jewish. Avocations: gourmet cooking, swimming. Home and Office: 1584 Estuary Trail Delray Beach FL 33483 Office Phone: 561-243-2108.

**MAKEEV, MAXIM A.,** physicist; b. Moscow, Mar. 11, 1970; s. Alexander N. and Vera M. Makeev. MS, Moscow Engring. Physics Inst., 1993; PhD, U. Notre Dame, 1999. Rsch., tchg. asst. U. Notre Dame, Ind., 1994—99; rsch. assoc. U. So. Calif., LA, 1999—2001, 2003—05; rsch. assoc. La. State U., Baton Rouge, 2001—03; rsch. assoc. NASA Ames Rsch. Ctr., Moffett Field, Calif., 2005—. Mem.: Materials Rsch. Soc., Am. Phys. Soc. Achievements include contributions to development of methodologies for large-scale parallel simulations; research in statistical mechanics, surface science, nanoscience. Office: NASA Ames Rsch Ctr MS 229-1 Moffett Field CA 94035-1000 Business E-Mail: makeev@usc.edu, mmakeev@mail.arc.nasa.gov.

**MAKEL, LARRY A.,** lawyer; b. Vestaburg, Pa., Dec. 7, 1953; BA cum laude, Washington & Jefferson Coll., 1975; JD, W.Va. Univ., 1978; LLM, NYU, 1980. Bar: W.Va. 1978, Pa. 1978, Tex. 1981, DC. Asst. atty. gen. Commonwealth of Pa., 1978—79; ptnr., Banking, Bus. Law & Internat. Bus. Transactions practices, mem. exec. com. Patton Boggs LLP, Dallas. Former counsel & legis. liaison S.W. Chpt. Nat. Comml. Fin. Assn. Mem.: ABA (past chmn. Acquisition Fin. Subcommittee), State Bar Assn. Pa., State Bar Tex. (past vice chmn. Comml. Fin. Svc. Subcommittee), Dallas Bar Assn., Am. Coll. Comml. Fin. Attys. Office: Patton Boggs LLP Suite 3000 2001 Ross Ave Dallas TX 75201-8001 Office Phone: 214-758-1560. Office Fax: 214-758-1550. Business E-Mail: lmakel@pattonboggs.com.

**MAKEN, SONNY,** real estate company executive, real estate developer; b. India, Sept. 27, 1975; arrived in U.S., 1989; s. Mani and Pam Maken; m. Debbie Maken, Mar. 2, 2002; children: Hannah, Abigail. BS in Internat. Econs., Georgetown U., 1997. Chief legal assoc. No. Trust Inc., Chgo., 1997—99; lead subrogation specialist Grotefeld & Denenberg, LLC, Chgo., 1999—2001; pres., CEO The Maken Group, Inc., Palm Beach, Fla., 2001—. Recipient Diamond Cir. award, Coldwell Banker Real Estate Inc., 2002, Pres. Cir. award, 2003, Coldwell Baker Real Estate Inc., 2004; scholar, Gen. Mills Corp., 1995—97, United Meth. Ch., 1995—97. Mem.: CCIM (corr.), Fla. Assn. Realtors (assoc.; mem. 2001), Georgetown Alumni Interviewer Program (corr.), Georgetown Club Miami (corr.). Office: The Maken Group Inc Ste 215 6299 West Sunrise Blvd Sunrise FL 33313 also: Ste 203 2247 Palm Beach Lakes Blvd West Palm Beach FL 33409 Office Phone: 561-721-9855. Office Fax: 800-983-5007. Business E-Mail: sonnymaken@themakengroup.com.

**MAKEPEACE, MARY LOU,** foundation administrator, former mayor; 2 children. BA in Journalism, U. ND, 1962; MPA, U. Colo., Colorado Springs, 1980. Tchr. Am. Sch., Tananarive, Madagascar; asst. to Def. Attaché Am. Embassy, Prague, Czechoslavakia; adult edn. officer Ramstein AFB, Germany; case worker, adminstr. El Paso County Dept. Social Svcs., 1974-82; exec. dir. Cmty. Coun. Pikes Peak Region, 1982-84; dist. 1 rep. City Colorado Springs, 1985-97, vice mayor, 1997; mayor, 1997—2003; exec. dir. Leadership Pike's Peak, Colo. Springs, 2003—04, Gill Found. Gay and Lesbian Fund, Colo., 2004—. Exofficio mem. Econ. Devel. Coun. Bd. Dirs.; chair Econ. Devel. Com., Task Force City Svcs. to Srs., urban affairs com. Pikes Peak Area Coun. Govt's.; apptd. Colo. Space Adv. Coun.; adj. prof. U. Colo.; ex-dir. leadership Pikes Peak Mem. steering com. Imagination Celebration; sr. advisor Palmer Found., Pikes Peak Partnership; mem. Nat. League Cities Leadership Tng. Coun.; past mem. Colo. Mcpl. League Exec. Bd., 1st United Meth. Ch. Gates Found. fellow, 1992; recipient Svc. Mankind award Centennial Sertoma Club, 1985, Mary Jean Larson Cmty. Svc. award Girl Scouts Wagon Wheel Coun., 2002, Spence Vanderlin Pub. Ofcl. award Am. Pub. Power Assn., 2002, Outstanding Cmty. award Econ. Devel. Corp., 2003; named Super Woman Women's Health Ctr., 1988, Best City Councilmem. Springs Mag., 1991; honored Women in Your Life dinner Women's Found. Colo., 2002. Mem. Am. Soc. Pub. Adminstrn., Pi Alpha Alpha. Personal E-mail: maryloum@gillfoundation.org.

**MAKI, ATSUSHI,** economics professor; b. Kanagawa, Japan, Jan. 14, 1948; s. Sadao and Eiko (Yamaguchi) M.; m. Michie Yabu, Feb. 28, 1975; children: Chiori, Hisashi. BA, Keio U., Japan, 1971; MA, Keio U., 1973, PhD, 1993. Asst. prof. Keio U., Tokyo, 1973-79, assoc. prof., 1979-87, prof., 1987—. Guest rsch. officer Ministry Posts and Telecom., 1988-90; vis. scholar Harvard U., Cambridge, Mass., 1982-84, 2001, George Washington U., 2001, U. Sydney, Australia, 2002; vis. prof. Osaka U., Japan, 1989, Ecole Superieure des Scis. Econs. et Commls., France, 1994, 2005; vis. fellow Australian Nat. U., Canberra, 1990, Massey U., New Zealand, 1991, U. Western Australia, Perth, 1993, Victoria U., Wellington, New Zealand, 1997, Bur. Labor Stats., Washington, 2001. Author: Consumer Preferences and Measurement of Demand, 1983, Japanese Consumer Behavior, 1998, Applied Econometrics, 2001. Recipient award Japan Found., 1996; Abe fellow SSRC, 2001; Ministry of Edn. grant-in-aid, 1997-99, 2003-06. Mem. Am. Econ. Assn., Econometric Soc., Japanese Econ. Assn., Japan Assn. Stats., Japan Soc. Household Econs., Royal Econ. Soc. Home: 107-8 Terao Kawagoe-shi Saitama 350-1141 Japan Office: Keio U 2-15-45 Mita Minato-ku Tokyo 108-8345 Japan Business E-Mail: maki@fbc.keio.ac.jp.

**MAKI, DENNIS G.,** epidemiology educator; b. River Falls, Wis., May 8, 1940; m. Gail Dawson, 1962; children: Kimberly, Sarah, Daniel. BS in Physics with honors, U. Wis., 1962, MS in Physics, 1964, MD, 1967. Diplomate Am. Bd. Internal Medicine, Am. Bd. Infectious Diseases, Am. Bd. Critical Care Medicine. Physicist, computer programmer Lawrence Radiation Lab., AEC, Livermore, Calif., 1962; intern, asst. resident Harvard Med. unit Boston City Hosp., 1967-69, chief resident, 1972-73; with Hosp. Infections sect. Ctrs. for Disease Control, USPHS, Atlanta, 1969-71; acting chief nat. nosocomial infections study Ctr. for Disease Control, Atlanta, 1970-71; sr. resident dept. medicine Mass. Gen. Hosp., 1971-72, clin. and research fellow infectious disease unit, 1973-74; asst. prof. medicine U. Wis., Madison, 1974-78, assoc. prof., 1978-82, prof., 1982—; hosp. epidemiologist, U. Wis. Hosp. and Clinic, Madison, 1974—; Ovid O. Meyer prof. medicine U. Wis., Madison, 1975—; head sec. infectious diseases, 1979—; attending physician Ctr. for Trauma and Life Support, 1976—. Clinician, rschr., educator in field; mem. program com. Intersci. Conf. on Antimicrobial Agts.

and Chemotherapy, 1987-94; mem. Am. Bd. Critical Care Medicine, 1989-95. Sr. assoc. editor Infection Control and Hosp. Epidemiology, 1979-93; mem. editl. bd. Jour. Lab. and Clin. Investigation, 1980-86, Jour. Critical Care, 1985-96, Jour. Infectious Diseases, 1988-90, Critical Care Medicine, 1989-94, 97—, Mayo Clinic Procs., 2002—; contbr. articles to med. jours. Recipient 1st award for disting. rsch. in Antibiotic Rev., 1980, Internat. CIPI award, 1994, SHEA lectr., 1999, numerous tchg. awards and hon. lectrs. Master ACP; fellow Infectious Diseases Soc. Am. (coun. 1993-96, Critical Care Medicine, Wis. Acad. Scis., Arts and Letters; mem. Soc. Hosp. Epidemiologists Am. (pres. 1990), Ctrl. Soc. for Clin. Rsch., Am. Soc. Microbiology, Am. Fedn. Clin. Rsch., Alpha Omega Alpha (nat. bd. dirs. 1983-89). Office: U Wis Hosp and Clinics H4/574 Madison WI 53792 Fax: 608-833-0327. Personal E-mail: dgmaki@yahoo.com. Business E-Mail: dgmaki@medicine.wisc.edu.

**MAKI, JOAN OWEN,** gifted and talented educator; b. Brevard, N.C., Mar. 1, 1950; d. Coy Lee Owen and Mary Jane Phillips; m. J. F. Williamson, Mar. 20, 1969 (div. June 14, 1986); 1 child, Owen Lee Williamson; m. Bernard Maki, July 14, 1988. BA, Tift Coll., Forsyth, Ga., 1972; MA in Edn., Mercer U., Macon, Ga., 1983. Cert. in gifted edn. Ga., NC, master in reading Western Carolina U. Tchr. Ga. Pub. Schs., Roberta, Eatonton, Gray, 1978—85, Bur. Indian Affairs, Cherokee, NC, 1985—89, Macon County Schs., Franklin, NC, 1985—. Judge, trainer Odyssey of the Mind, Cullowhee, NC, 1985—. Edn. chair LWV, Franklin, NC, 1990—95. Recipient Disting. Educator award, US Dept. Edn., Omer-Disting. Svc. award, Svc. award, NC Assn. Educators, Distinguished Educator award, Disting. Svc. award, NC Assn. Educators, Excellence in Tchg. award, Cherokee Ctrl. Schs. Mem.: Macon County Assn. Educators (licentiate; pres., treas., sec. 1990—2004, Disting. Svc. Award 1998), Nat. Coun. Tchrs. English (assoc.), Assn. Curriculum and Devel. (assoc.), Phi Delta Kappa (assoc.), Kappa Delta Pi (assoc.). Conservative. Baptist. Achievements include research in diagnostic/prescriptive teaching techniques. Avocations: writing, developing educational games and materials, reading. Home: 56 Leaning Pine Rd Franklin NC 28734 Office: Macon Mid Sch 1345 Wells Grove Rd Franklin NC 28734 Personal E-mail: zjowmaki@yahoo.com. Business E-Mail: joan.maki@mcsk-12.org.

**MAKI, KAZUMI,** physicist, researcher; b. Takamatsu, Japan, Jan. 27, 1936; s. Toshio and Hideko M.; m. Masako Tanaka, Sept. 21, 1969. BS, Kyoto U., 1959, PhD, 1964. Research asso. Inst. for Math. Scis., Kyoto U., 1964; research asso. Fermi Inst., U. Chgo., 1964-65; asst. prof. physics U. Calif., San Diego, 1965-67; prof. Tohoku U., Sendai, Japan, 1967-74; vis. prof. Universite Paris-Sud, Orsay, France, 1969-70; prof. physics U. So. Calif., Los Angeles, 1974—. Vis. prof. Inst. Laue-Langevin, U. Paris-Sud, France, 1979-80, Max Planck Inst. fur Festkorper Forschung, Stuttgart, Germany, 1986-87, U. Paris-7, 1990, Hokkaido U., Sapporo, Japan, 1993, Centre de Recherche sur Tres Basses Temperatures, Grenoble, France, 1993-94, Instituto de Ciencia de Materiales, Madrid, Spain, 1994, Max Planck Inst. Phys. Complex Sys., Dresden, Germany, 2001-02. Assoc. editor Jour. Low Temperature Physics, 1969-91; contbr. articles to profl. jours. Guggenheim fellow, 1979-80, Japan Soc. Promotion of Sci. fellow, 1993; Fulbright scholar, 1964-65; recipient Nishina prize, 1972, Alexander von Humboldt award, 1986-87, John Bardeen prize, 2006. Fellow Japan Soc. Promotion of Sci., Am. Phys. Soc.; mem. AAAS, Phys. Soc. Japan. Office: U So Calif Dept Physics and Astronomy Los Angeles CA 90089-0484 Office Phone: 213-740-8405. Business E-Mail: kmaki@usc.edu.

**MAKI, ROBERT G.,** physician, oncologist; s. Robert (Sr.) Glenn and Frances Christine Maki; m. Nathalie Elizabeth Blachere, Aug. 18, 1999; 1 child, Julien Paul Elias. BA, Northwestern U., 1985; PhD, Cornell U. Grad. Sch. Med. Sciences, 1991; MD, Cornell U. Med. Coll., 1992. Diplomate Am. Bd. Internal Medicine, PA, 1992, in oncology Am. Bd. Internal Medicine, PA, 1998. Attending physician Brigham and Women's Hosp., Boston, 1995—99; instr. Harvard Med. Sch., Boston, 1995—99, Cornell U. Med. Coll., NYC, 1999—2001, asst. prof., 2001—; clin. assoc. mem. Meml. Sloan-Kettering Cancer Ctr., NYC, 1999—2001, asst. mem., 2001—. Achievements include research in clinical trials and basic science research in sarcoma medical oncology. Office: Memorial Sloan-Kettering Cancer Ctr 1275 York Ave New York NY 10021-6007 Office Phone: 212-639-5720.

**MAKINEN, MARVIN WILLIAM,** biophysicist, educator; b. Chassell, Mich., Aug. 19, 1939; s. William John and Milga Katarina (Myllyla) M.; m. Michele de Groot, July 30, 1966; children: Eric William, Stephen Matthew. AB, U. Pa., 1961; postgrad., Free U. Berlin, 1960-61; MD, U. Pa., 1968; DPhil, U. Oxford, Eng., 1976. Diplomate Am. Bd. Med. Examiners. Intern Columbia-Presbyn. Med. Ctr., N.Y.C., 1968-69; rsch. assoc. NIH, Bethesda, Md., 1969-71; vis. fellow U. Oxford, Eng., 1971-74; asst. prof. biophysics U. Chgo., 1974-80, assoc. prof., 1980-86, prof. biochemistry and molecular biology, 1986—, chmn. dept., 1988-93. Established investigator Am. Heart Assn., 1975-80; lectr. in field. Contbr. numerous articles to profl. jours. Sr. surgeon USPHS, 1969-71. John Simon Guggenheim fellow 1997-98, John E. Fogarty Sr. Internat. fellow, 1984-85, European Molecular Biology Orgn. sr. fellow, 1984-85, NIH spl. fellow, 1971-74, Berquist fellow Am. Scandinavian Found., 1970. Fellow Am. Inst. Chemists; mem. Am. Chem. Soc., Biophys. Soc., Am. Soc. Biochemistry and Molecular Biology, The Protein Soc., AAAS. Office: U Chgo Dept Biochemistry/Mol Biol 920 E 58th St Chicago IL 60637-5415 Office Phone: 773-702-1080. Business E-Mail: makinen@uchicago.edu.

**MAKINO, SHINJI,** virologist, educator; DVM, Iwate U., Morioka, Japan, 1979; PhD in Virology, U. Tokyo Inst. Med. Sci., 1984. Scientist Sealy Ctr. Vaccine Devel. U. Tex. Med. Br., Galveston, mem. Ctr. Biodefense and Emerging Infectious Disease, prof. dept. microbiol. and immunology. Contbr. articles to profl. jours., chapters to books. Achievements include discovery of the method the SARS virus uses to prevent production of a protein the immune system would normally use to defend against viruses. Office: Dept Microbiol and Immunology U Tex Med Br 301 Univ Blvd Galveston TX 77555-1019 E-mail: shmakino@utmb.edu.\*

**MAKISHI, YASUKO,** securities trader, writer; m. Kevin Shuppert, July 8, 1977. BA in Econs., U., 1981. Commodity futures trader, Shreveport, La., 1995—97; stock trader, 1998—2004; founder of marketreadings.com Fortuna Prodns., LLC, Shreveport, La., 2003—; owner Craters & Freighters of Shreveport, Shreveport, La., 2005—. Author: America 2003 Predictions: Timing the Sectors of the Economy, Fortuna Sqaure 1: Reading is Fundamental - Power to Control Your Own Destiny for an Independent Life, 2004; creator: astrology course and seminar The Fortuna System of Business and Financial Astrology, 2004. Office: Fortuna Prodns LLC 3070-A Baird Rd Shreveport LA 71118 Office Phone: 318-688-4410. Personal E-mail: makishiy@bellsouth.net. Business E-Mail: yasuko@marketreadings.com

**MAKOUS, BRUCE B.,** fundraiser, writer; b. Phila., June 24, 1953; s. Norman and Dorothy Makous; m. Barbara H. Makous, Oct. 17, 1981; children: Dyani, Kacie. BA in Lit., Oberlin Coll., 1976; MA in Cultural Adminstrn., NYU, 1986. CLU, ChFC. Gen. mgr. 78th Street Theatre Lab., N.Y.C., 1979-81; comm. cons. Price Waterhouse Nat. Offices, N.Y.C., 1981-84; dir. info. svcs. Theatre Comm. Group, N.Y.C., 1984-86; mng. dir. Attic Theatre, Detroit, 1986-89, Players Theatre Columbus, Ohio, 1989-90; founder, pres. Makous Mktg. & Fundraising, Phila., 1990-93; dir. devel. Am. Coll., Bryn Mawr, Pa., 1993-98, dir. planned giving, 1998-99; dir. major and planned gifts Drexel U., Phila., 1999-2000, asst. v.p. for major and planned giving, 2000—01; maj. gifts and planned giving officer Am. Assn. for Cancer Rsch., 2001—. Lectr. Wayne State U., Detroit, 1988-89, Am. Assn. Fundraising Profls.-Villanova (Pa.) U., 1998-2004, Am. Coll., Bryn Mawr, Pa., 2002-2004. Author: Riding the Brand, 2004, Virtually Dead, 2006; co-prodr. Back in the World, 1987 (award for best play outside N.Y. Nat. Theatre Critics Assn. 1987); assoc. editor Boulevard lit. mag., 1991— Grad. Leadership, Inc. Class of 1992, 1991-92; co. dirs. bd. dirs. Prints in Progress, Phila., 1993-95. Mgmt. for Arts Rev. scholar NYU, 1983-86. Mem. Nat. Com. on Planned Giving, Mystery Writers of Am. Democrat. Roman Catholic. Home: 7905

Cadillac Ln Philadelphia PA 19128 Office: Am Assn Cancer Rsch 615 Chestnut St Ste 1200 Philadelphia PA 19106-3483 Fax: 215-895-4966. Office Phone: 267-251-9060. E-mail: makous@aacr.org, bmakous@aol.com, bruce@brucemakous.com.

**MAKOUS, NORMAN,** retired internist, cardiologist, educator; b. Chgo., July 22, 1924; s. Lawrence Alonzo and Ruth (Luehring) M.; m. Dorothy Murl Bowlin, Sept. 25, 1948 (dec. July 25, 2003); children: David, Bruce, Catherine, Monte, Joseph, Martin, John, Virginia, Dorothy, Margaret; m. Eleanor B. Sullivan Feb. 21, 2004. BS, U. Wis., 1945, MD, 1947. Diplomate in internal medicine and cardiovascular diseases Am. Bd. Internal Medicine. Mixed intern Rsch. Hosp., Kansas City, Mo., 1947—48, resident in internal medicine, 1948—50; fellow in cardiovasc. disease U. Vt., Burlington, 1950—51; resident in internal medicine U.S. Naval Hosp., Camp Lejeune, NC, 1951—52; dir. cardiac catheterization lab. Kansas City, Mo., 1955—56; fellow in cardiovasc. disease Pa. Hosp., Phila., 1953—54, assoc. cardiologist, assoc. physician to hosp., 1960—72, cardiologist, physician to hosp., 1972—2000, cons., 2000—01; pvt. practice Kansas City and Independence, Mo., 1956—59, Phila., 1959—2001; assoc. in medicine U. Pa., Phila., 1959—71, assoc. in clin. medicine, 1971—74, clin. asst. prof. medicine, 1974—2000; clin. asst. prof. medicine Thomas Jefferson U., Phila., 1994—; ret., 2006. Physician advisor Keystone Profl. Rev. Orgn., 1986-93; mem. cons. Pa. Bur. Disability Determination, 1981-2001; cardiology cons. Phila. City Solicitor's Office, 1986-2005; mem. peer rev. panel Jour. Cardiopulmonary Rehab., 1990; mem. adv. group Greater Delaware Valley Regional Med. Program, 1971-75. Contbr. articles to med. jours., chpts. to books. Founder, acting chmn. Southeastern Pa. Regional High Blood Pressure Control Program, 1978-80; mem. interim bd. Health Sys. Agy. Southeastern Pa., 1975-77, chmn. adv. coun., 1979-80; trustee Edna B. Kynett Meml. Found., Phila., 1963—, v.p., 1994-96, pres., 1997—2004; pres. Home and Sch. Assn., Our Lady of Lourdes Parish, Phila., 1972-73, mem. parish pastoral coun., 1991-95, co-chmn., 1993-95; trustee Vis. Nurse Assn. Greater Phila., 1997-2000. Lt. USNR, 1943-45, 50-52, Res., 1952-62. Recipient Legion of Honor, Chapel of Four Chaplains, 1980, Spl. Achievement award Southeastern Pa. Regional High Blood Pressure Control Program, Fellow ACP, Am. Coll. Cardiology, Am. Soc. Internal Medicine; mem. AMA, Pa. Med. Soc. (chmn. profl. liaibility ins. appeals com. 1986-91), Phila. County Med. Soc. (standing com. Med. Econs., 1979-86, pres. Center City br. 1980-81, sec. 1990-91, chmn. membership and orgn. com. 1991-2000, Cristol award 1994), Am. Heart Assn. (fellow coun. clin. cardiology, pres. Southeastern Pa. affiliate 1988-89, bd. govs., program chmn. 1988-92, pres. Pa. affiliate 1981-82, Disting. Svc. award Pa. affiliate 1982, Disting. Achievement award Pa. affiliate, 1986, Disting. Achievement award Southeastern Pa. affiliate 1988, Vol. of Yr. award Southeastern Pa. affiliate 1988), Pa. Soc. Internal Medicine (pres. 1983-84). Avocations: tennis, cinematography. Office: 243 Freedom Blvd Coatesville PA 19320 Office Phone: 610-466-9441. Personal E-mail: drnmakous@aol.com.

**MAKOUS, WALTER LEON,** visual scientist, educator; s. Lawrence and Ruth Lorraine (Luehring) Makous; m. Marilyn Ann Carlson, Feb. 2, 1958 (div. 1973); children: Ann, James, Matthew; m. Joyce Brown Menconi, 1974 (div. 1981); m. Barbara Anne Duggins, Apr. 29, 1982. BS, U. Wis., 1958; M.Sc., Brown U., 1961, PhD, 1964. Mem. staff IBM, Yorktown Heights, NY, 1963-66; asst. prof. psychology U. Wash., 1966-69, lectr. in physiology and biophysics, 1966-69, assoc. prof. psychology, 1969-74, prof. psychology, 1974-79; prof. psychology, ophthalmology and visual sci. U. Rochester, 1979-95; prof. brain and cognitive sci., ophthalmology & visual sci., 1995—; dir. Ctr. for Visual Sci. U. Rochester, 1979-90. Northwest rep, charter mem steering comt West Coast Regional Consortium Univs in Neurosciences, 1976—79; mem coun on energy saving through more efficient lighting NAS-NRC, 1978—79, night vision coun, 1985—86; chmn ctr symp Univ Rochester, 1981—82; sensory processes panelist NSF, Washington, 1977—82, mem adv comt applied sci and research applicaitons policy, 1978—81; rev comt Presidential Young Investigator Award Program, 1984; vis scientist IBM Research, 1970—71. Editor (consult ed): Sensory Processes, 1977—79, Jour of the Optical Soc Am, 1982—86; contbr. articles to profl jours. With USNR, 1953—55. Grantee, Nat Eye Inst, 1969—, NSF, 1959—62, 1981—82. Fellow: AAAS, Optical Soc Am (mem coord vision and physiological optics comt 1983—89, coord vision and med optics comt 1983—89, publs comt 1985—89, chmn fellows and hon mems comt 1986, ed vision and color 1982—86, feature ed applied vision 1989—90), Am Psychol Soc; mem.: Am Nat Standards Inst/Human Factor & Ergonomics Soc-100 (rev comt 1992—), Human Factors and Ergonomics, Psychonomic Soc, Soc Neuroscience, Asn Research in Vision and Ophthalmology (chmn sect psycho-physics 1977). Office: U Rochester Ctr for Visual Sci Rochester NY 14627 Business E-Mail: walt@cvs.rochester.edu.

**MAKOVSKY, KENNETH DALE,** public relations executive; b. St. Louis, Oct. 3, 1940; s. Jack and Minnie (Freedman) Makovsky; m. Phyllis Ann Peck, Oct. 15, 1972; children: Evan, Matthew. BA, Washington U., St. Louis, 1962, JD, 1965. Asst. account exec. Curtis Hoxter Inc., N.Y.C., 1965—66; account exec. Ruder & Finn Inc., N.Y.C., 1966—69, Harshe-Rotman & Druck, N.Y.C., 1970—72, v.p., 1973—75, sr. v.p., 1975—79, sr. v.p., dep. gen. mgr N.Y. office, 1978—79; founder, pres. Makovsky & Co., Inc., N.Y.C., 1979—; founder, past pres. Internat. Pub. Rels. Exch.; chmn. Makovsky & Co., Inc. N.Y.C. Contbr. articles to profl. pubs. Nat. bd. govs. Am. Jewish Com. N.Y., 1999—, nat. pub. rels. com. chmn., 1981—; speechwriter 17th Dist. Congl. Campaign, N.Y.C., 1972; v.p. Am. Jewish Com. N.Y., N.Y.C., 1985—, N.Y. bd. dirs., 1978—; adv. com. S.I. Newhouse Sch. Pub. Commun., 1996—, Washington U. Nat. Arts and Sci. Coun., 1998—; bd. trustees Inst. PR, 2000—. Recipient Gold Quill IABC, 1990, Cipra award Inside Pub. Rels., 1994, PRSA's Silver Anvil, PRSA-NY's Big Apple award; named Pub. Rels. All Star, Inside Pub. Rels., 1992; co. named one of ten fastest growing pub. rels. firms in U.S., O'Dwyer Rankings, 1985, 86, 87, 89, 90, 91, one of four top pub. rels. firms in N.Y.C., Small Agy. Yr. Inside Pub. Rels., 1990, among 12 Best Managed Firms in U.S., 1993, 94, among the 12 top strategic counseling firms in U.S., 1995, one of the 8 hot bus.-to-bus. agys., 1996, one of the 8 best managed agys., 1997, one of the 12 top investor relations agys., 1997, among the 15 top tech. agys., 1997, best managed PR agy. in U.S., 1998, among 16 top investor relations agys., 1998, among 9 top bus.-to-bus., 1998, 16 nat. capabilities agys., 1998, among 12 best managed agys., 1999, one of 12 top bus.-to-bus. mktg., 1999, among 12 top investor relations agys., 1999, one of 15 top agys. in N.Y.C., 1999, among top 8 bus.-to-bus. mktg., 1999. Mem.: Inst. Pub. Rels., Arthur Page Soc., Nat. Investors Rels. Inst. Pub. Rels. Soc. Am. (Silver Anvil Award for Chem. Spltys. Mfrs. Assn. 1978, award for Am. Superconductor 1994), India House, Washington U. Alumni Club N.Y.C. (pres. 1970). Avocations: theater, movies, travel. Office: Makovsky & Co Inc 575 Lexington Ave Fl 15 New York NY 10022-6104 E-mail: kmakovsky@makovksy.com.

**MAKOWIEC, JUDITH A. NEILSON,** family nurse practitioner; b. Medford, Mass., Apr. 11, 1951; d. William Henry and Mary Josephine (McIntyre) Neilson; m. Joseph Makowiec, Apr. 28, 1984; children: Sara Lorene, Mary Elizabeth. BA, Russell Sage Coll., 1973; MS, Pace U., 1980. RN, N.Y.; cert. family nurse practitioner. Family nurse practitioner St. Francis Hosp., Roslyn, N.Y., 1980-81, St. Lukes Roosevelt Hosp., N.Y.C., 1981-82, Cumberland Neighborhood Family Care Ctr., Bklyn., Woodhull Med. and Mental Health Ctr., Bklyn., 1982-86, Berkshire Med. Ctr., Pittsfield, Mass., 1987-88, Samaritan Hosp., Troy, N.Y., 1988-95, Troy Pediatrics LLP, 1995—; assoc. prof. Russell Sage Coll., 1994—. Mem. Coalition Nurse Practitioners. Home: PO Box 157 Cropseyville NY 12052-0157

**MAKRAM, ELHAM B.,** engineering educator; d. Badie Makram and Renee Mina; m. Adly A. Girgis, July 15, 1971; children: Ric M. Girgis, Amy A. Girgis. PhD, Iowa State U., Ames, 1981. Profl. Engr., S.C., 1985. Elec. engr. Assiut U., 1969—76; sr. engr. Siemens-Allis Co., Raleigh, NC, 1981—83; asst. prof. N.C. A&T State U., Greensboro, 1983—85, Clemson U., SC, 1985—87, assoc. prof., 1987—91, prof., 1991—98, disting. prof., 1998—. Contbr. more than 100 papers to profl. jours. and pubs. Recipient Rsch. award, Clemson U., 1991, Faculty award for Women, NSF, 1992, 1994—99,

Oustanding Faculty award, Clemson U., 1994. Fellow: IEEE; mem.: Soc. Women Engrs. (Disting. Educator award 1993). Office Phone: 864-656-3378. Business E-Mail: makram@clemson.edu.

**MAKTOUF, SAMIR,** education company executive; b. Sousse, Tunisia, June 25, 1957; s. Salem Bechir and Douja (Zaabouri) M.; m. Raja Khabcheche, Apr. 3, 1995 (div. Feb. 1997); 1 child, Ameen. Grad., Tunisian Air Force Acad., pilot cert. Pilot Tunisian Air Force, Bizerta, 1979-83; sales mgr. Sorena, Tunis, Tunisia, 1983-84; pilot Aeroclub Herault, Montpellier, France, 1984-86; asst. chief flight instr. Pro-flite, Vero Beach, Fla., 1986-89; pres., owner Fla. Pilot Sch. Inc., Fort Pierce, Fla., 1990—; tchr. Indian River Cmty. Coll., Fort Pierce, Fla., 1992—. Cons. aviation degree Palm Beach Cmty. Coll., 1997-99; cons. Training Piper Aircraft Corp., Pratt & Whitney and Sikorsky Aircraft; aviation safety counsellor, FAA, 1997—. Author: Radio Communication, 1989, Economic Growth of General Aviation in South Fla., 1989. Mem. Aircraft Owner & Pilot Assn., Nat. Assn. Flight Instr. Avocations: reading, boating, travel. Home: 502 Palm Ste 17 West Palm Beach FL 33401-7045

**MAKUPSON, AMYRE PORTER,** broadcast executive; b. River Rouge, Mich., Sept. 30, 1947; d. Rudolph Hannibal and Amyre Ann (Porche) Porter; m. Walter H. Makupson, Nov. 1, 1975; children: Rudolph Porter, Amyre Nisi. BA, Fisk U., 1970; MA, Am. U., Washington, 1972. Asst. dir. news Sta. WGPR-TV, Detroit, 1975-76; dir. pub. rels. Mich. Health Maintenance Orgn., Detroit, 1976-77; mgr. pub. affairs, news anchor Sta. WKBD-TV, Southfield, Mich., 1977–2004, Children's Miracle Network Telethon, 1989—. Mem. Cu-Ette Club, Inc., Met. Detroit Teen Conf. Coalition; mem. adv. com., bd. dirs. Alzheimers Assn.; bd. dirs. com. March of Dimes, bd. dirs. Providence Hosp. Found., Sickle Cell Assn., Covenant House Mich., AAA, Home Fed. Savs. Bank, Skillman Found. Recipient 6 Emmy awards 4 Best Commentary/Best Anchor, Best Interview/Discussion Show, 26 Emmy nominations NATAS, Editl. Best Feature award AP, Media award UPI, Oakland County Bar Assn., TV Documentary award, Detroit Press Club, Bishop Gallagher award Mental Illness Rsch. Assn., Svc. award Arthritis Found. Mich., Mich. Mchts. Assn., DAV, Jr. Achievement, City of Detroit, Salvation Army, Spirit award City of Detroit, Spirit award City of Pontiac, Golden Heritage award Little Rock Bapt. Ch., 1993, Neal Shine award outstanding contbn. Nat. Soc. Fundraising Execs., Virginia Merrick award outstanding contbn. Christ Child Soc., Outstanding Achievement award Tuskegee Airmen, Best Feature Story award Mich. Assn. Broadcasters; named Media Person of the Yr., So. Christian Leadership Conf., 1994, Humanitarian of the Yr., March of Dimes, 1995, Michiganian of the Yr., Detroit News, Outstanding Woman of the Yr., GM Women's Club. Mem. Pub. Rels. Soc. Am., Am. Women in Radio and TV (Outstanding Achievement award 1981, Outstanding Woman in TV Top Mgmt. 1993, Mentor award 1993), Women in Comm., Nat. Acad. TV Arts and Scis., Detroit Press Club, Ad-Craft, Howard U. Nat. Gold Key Honor Soc. (hon.). Roman Catholic. Office: 26955 W 11 Mile Rd Southfield MI 48034-2292

**MALA, THEODORE ANTHONY,** physician, consultant; b. Santa Monica, Calif., Feb. 3, 1946; s. Ray and Galina (Liss) M.; children: Theodore S., Galina T.; 1 adopted child, Christine A. Lindholm. BA in Philosophy, DePaul U., 1972; MD, Autonomous U., Guadalajara, Mex., 1976; MPH, Harvard U. 1980. Spl. asst. for health affairs Alaska Fedn. Natives, Anchorage, 1977-78; chief health svcs. Alaska State Divsn. Corrections, Anchorage, 1978-79; assoc. prof., founder, dir. Inst. for Circumpolar Health Studies, U. Alaska, Anchorage, 1982-90; founder Siberian med. rsch. program U. Alaska, Anchorage, 1982, founder Magadan (USSR) med. rsch. program, 1988; commr. Health and Social Svcs. State of Alaska, Juneau, 1990-93; pres., CEO Ted Mala, Inc., Anchorage, 1993-97; pres., ptnr. Mexican-Siberian Trading Co., Monterrey, Mex., 1994-96; CEO, Confederated Tribes of Grand Ronde, Oreg., 1998-99; dir. tribal rels. Southcentral Found., Anchorage, 1999—, 2000—. Traditional healing dir. Southcentral Found., Anchorage, 2000—; Alaska rsch. and publs. com. Indian Health Svc., USPHS, 1987-90; advisor Nordic Coun. Meeting, WHO, Greenland, 1985; mem. Internat. Organizing Com., Circumpolar Health Congress, Iceland, 1992-93; chmn. bd. govs. Alaska Psychiat. Inst., Anchorage, 1990-93; cabinet mem. Gov. Walter J. Hickel, Juneau, 1990-93; advisor humanitarian aid to Russian Far East U.S. Dept. State, 1992-96; cons. USAID on U.S.-Russian Health Programs, 1994; apptd. adv. com. Sec. of Health and Human Svc. on Minority Health for the U.S., 2000—; mem. coun. pub. reps. NIH, 2002-05. Past columnist Tundra Times; contbr. articles to profl. jours. Trustee United Way Anchorage, 1978-79; chmn. bd. trustees Alaska Native Coll., 1993-96. Recipient Gov.'s award, 1988, Outstanding Svc. award Alaska Commr. Health, 1979, Ministry of Health citation USSR Govt., 1989, Citation award Alaska State Legislature, 1989-90, 94, Commendation award State of Alaska, 1990, Alaska State Legislature, 1994, Honor Kempton Svc. to Humanity award, 1989, citation Med. Comty. of Magadan region, USSR, 1989; Nat. Indian fellow U.S. Dept. Edn., 1979. Mem. Assn. Am. Indian Physicians (pres.), N.Y. Acad. Scis., Internat. Union for Circumpolar Health (permanent sec.-gen. 1987-90, organizing com. 8th Internat. Congress on Circumpolar Health 1987-90), Russian Acad. Polar Medicine (elected). Avocations: cross country skiing, hiking, photography, travel. Office Phone: 907-729-4955. E-mail: tmala@post.harvard.edu. *Personal philosophy: Progress in the North will come only when circumpolar countries put aside their geopolitical thinking and work together as one northern family.*

**MALACH, MONTE,** physician; b. Jersey City, Aug. 15, 1926; s. Charles and Yetta (Pascher) M.; m. Ann Elaine Glazer, June 15, 1952 (dec. June 1989); children: Barbara Sandra, Cathie Tara, Matthew David. BA, MD, U. Mich., 1949. Diplomate Am. Bd. Internal Medicine, Nat. Bd. Med. Examiners. Intern Beth Israel Hosp., Boston, 1949-50, resident, 1950-51, chief resident, 1951-52, Kings County Hosp., Bklyn., 1954-55; practice medicine specializing in internal medicine and cardiology Bklyn., 1955–2001; dir. CCU Bklyn. Hosp., 1965-91, dir. emeritus CCU, 1991—; med. dir., clin. coord. Medicare IPRO Downstate N.Y., 1990–2005; cardiology cons., 2005—. Pres. profl. staff Bklyn. Hosp., 1966-69, emen. med. bd., 1971-72; attending staff Caledonian Hosp., pres. profl. staff, 1984-85; pres. profl. staff Bklyn. Hosp.-Caledonian Hosp., 1987-89; chmn. med. bd., 1988-89; cons. Kings County Hosp.; tchg. fellow Tufts U. Med. Sch., 1951-52; instr. medicine Downstate Med. Ctr., Bklyn., 1955-59, clin. asst. prof. medicine, 1959-68, clin. assoc. prof., 1969-76, clin. prof., 1976—; clin. prof. medicine NYU Med. Ctr., 1994—; bd. dirs. Bay St. Landing One Owners Corp., 1985-87; v.p. Ocean View Condos, 1989-90, pres., 1990-95; med. dir. IPRO Medicare Rev., N.Y. State, 1990—, IPRO N.Y. State Peer Rev., 1990—. Kings County committeeman Democratic Party, 1964, 65. Served with USNR, 1944-46, to 1st lt. M.C. U.S. Army, 1952-54. Recipient 1st Prize for Crisis Mgmt. Habitat Mag., 1987. Fellow Am. Coll. Chest Physicians, ACP (master, Laureate award 2000), Am. Coll. Cardiology (task force Health Care Quality Improvement Initiative 1996—); mem. AMA (chmn. sect. coun. internal medicine 1980), N.Y. Heart Assn., Am. Soc. Internal Medicine (master, trustee 1975-79, sec.-treas. 1979—, pres. elect 1981, pres. 1982-83, chmn. investment com. 1985-93), N.Y. State Internal Medicine (pres. 1973-74, dir. 1966-84, chmn. Bklyn. chpt., v.p. 1971, award of merit 1978), Bklyn. Soc. Internal Medicine (mem. council 1965, pres. 1969-72), Med. Soc. State of N.Y. (dir. sect. internal medicine 1976, chmn. med. care ins. com. 1988-93), Federated Council for Internal Medicine (chmn. 1979-80), Med. Soc. County Kings (censor 1985-91). Office Phone: 917-522-1201. Office Fax: 917-522-1201. Personal E-mail: montemalach@hotmail.com. *There is a place for hard work, scrupulous ethics and pride of accomplishment. A great marriage and a fine close family are buffers against adversity.*

**MALACHOWSKI, NICOLE,** pilot; b. 1974; Grad., Air Force Acad., 1996. F-15E (Strike Eagle fighter jet) pilot Royal Air Force, Lakenheath, Eng., 494th Fighter Squadron; No. 3 right wing pilot Thunderbirds, US Air Force Air Demonstration Squadron, 2005—. Served in Operation Iraqi Freedom, 2005. Achievements include being the first female demonstration pilot in the 52 year history of the Thunderbirds, US military high performance jet team. Office: USAFADS 4445 Tyndall Ave Nellis Afb NV 89191

**MALACHOWSKY, CHRIS ALAN,** electrical engineer; b. Danville, Pa., May 2, 1959; s. Martin Norman and Zelda Luba (Rutenberg) M.; m. Melody Ann Connella, Oct. 10, 1981; children: Ryan David, Spencer Gordon. BSEE with high honors, U. Fla., 1980; MS in Computer Sci., Santa Clara U., 1986. Mem. tech. staff Hewlett-Packard Co., Cupertino, Calif., 1980-87; sr. mem. tech. staff Sun Microsystems Computer Corp., Mountain View, Calif., 1987-89, staff engr. 1989-90, sr. staff engr., 1991—. Instr. grad. extension program U. Calif., Berkeley, 1990—. Patentee in electronic circuit designs for computer graphics; contbr. articles to profl. publs. Avocations: woodworking, basketball, tennis, salt-water aquariums. Office: Sun Microsystems Computer Corp MS MTV 18-112 2550 Garcia Ave Mountain View CA 94043

**MALAFRONTE, DONALD,** health facility administrator; b. Bklyn., Dec. 16, 1931; s. Pasquale and Amalia (Castaldo) M.; m. Diane Freedenberg, Jan. 7, 1961 (dec. Nov. 14, 1970); children: Philip, Victor.; m. Hillary Demby, Oct. 30, 1982. BS, NYU, 1954. Reporter L.I. Daily Press, 1956-58; reporter, editor Newark Star-Ledger, 1958-65, art columnist, 1963-70; administrv. asst. to mayor of Newark, 1965-70; dir. Newark Model Cities Program, 1967-70, Newark Community Devel. Adminstrn., 1968-70; dir. urban field operations N.J. Regional Med. Program, 1970-73; pres. Urban Health Inst., Roseland, NJ, 1973—. Cons. to hosps., local govts., 1970— Author articles in field. Served with AUS, 1954-56. Recipient Joyce Kilmer fiction prize NYU, 1953 Office: Urban Health Inst 101 Eisenhower Pky Roseland NJ 07068-1028 Home: 1056 5th Ave New York NY 10028-0112 Office Phone: 973-228-9000.

**MALAKHOV, VLADIMIR,** dancer; b. Krivoy Rog, Ukraine, USSR, Jan. 7, 1968; arrived in Can., 1994; s. Anatoly and Elena Malakhov. Grad., Bolshoi Ballet Acad., Moscow, 1986. Prin. dancer Vienna State Opera, 1992-94, Nat. Ballet Can., 1994-97, guest artist, 1997-98; prin. dancer Am. Ballet Theatre, N.Y.C., 1995—; artistic dir. & principal dancer Deutsche Straatsoper, Berlin, 2002—. Guest artist Am. Ballet Theatre, 1994. Appeared in Giselle, Swan Lake, Nutcracker, Manon, Romeo and Juliette, others; performed in major opera houses worldwide. Recipient Gold medal Varna Ballet Competition, 1986, Gold medal Moscow Ballet Competition, 1986, Serge Lifar prize, 1991, Nijinsky prize, 2002, Benois Prix de la Dance, London, 2004. Address: Am Ballet Theatre 890 Broadway New York NY 10003-1211

**MALAMBRI, WILLIAM F., JR.,** music educator, consultant; b. Fairmont, NC, Dec. 28, 1944; s. William F. Malambri and Sarah S. Ciszewski; m. Rebecca Oliver Malambri, June 28, 1964; children: Maria Cecily Hedinger, William F. III, Anna Oliver. BS, U. NC, Pembroke, 1969; MusM, East Carolina U., 1975; D of Mus. Arts, U. SC, 1995. Asst. prof. music Limestone Coll., Gaffney, SC, 1975–78; prof. music, dir. bands Winthrop U., Rock Hill, SC, 1978—. Condr., clinician, cons. numerous countries. Rsch. grantee, Winthrop U., 2004, 2005. Home: 813 Eden Ter Rock Hill SC 29730 Office: Winthrop U 122 Conservatory of Music Rock Hill SC 29730 Office Fax: 803-323-2343. Business E-Mail: malambriw@winthrop.edu.

**MALAMUD, DEBORAH C.,** law educator; b. 1955; BA in Religion, magna cum laude, Wesleyan U., 1976; grad. work in Anthropology, U. Chgo., 1978—81, JD cum laude, 1986. Bar: Pa. 1987, DC 1988. Law clk. to Hon. Louis H. Pollack US Dist. Ct. Ea. Dist. Pa., Phila., 1986–87; law clk. to Hon. Harry A. Blackman US Supreme Ct., Washington, 1988—89; assoc. Bredhoff & Kaiser, DC, 1987–88, 1989—92; asst. prof. law U. Mich. Law Sch., 1992—97, prof., 1997—2003, James E. and Sarah A. Degan prof. law, 2002; NYU Sch. Law, 2003—, An-Bryce prof. law. Vis. prof. NYU, 2002, Yale U., 2002—03. Mem.: Am. Soc. Legal History, Law and Soc. Assn. Office: NYU Sch Law Vanderbilt Hall Rm 310 40 Washington Sq S New York NY 10012-1099    Office    Phone:    212-992-8902.    E-mail: deborah.malamud@nyu.edu.

**MALAMUTH, NEIL MOSHE,** psychology and communication educator; BA in Psychology summa cum laude, UCLA, 1972, MA in Psychology, 1972, PhD in Social Psychology and Personality, 1975. Lectr. dept. psychology, UCLA and postdoctoral fellow Ctr. for Behavioral Therapy, Beverly Hills, Calif., 1975-77; asst. prof. psychology U. Man., Winnipeg, Can., 1977-80, assoc. prof., 1980-82; prof. comm. and psychology, chairperson dept. comm. U. Mich., Ann Arbor, 1991-94; tchg. asst. dept. psychology UCLA, 1971-73, rsch. assoc. Ctr. for Computer-Based Behavioral Studies, 1973-75, assoc. prof., 1982-86, assoc. dir. Ctr. for Study of Women, 1986-87, prof. comm. and psychology, 1982-91, 94—, chairperson comm. studies program and speech dept., 1984-91, 94—. Vis. scholar Stanford (Calif.) U., fall 1988; mem. rev. com. on violence and stress NIMH, 1989-93; Lady Davis sr. fellow Hebrew U. Jerusalem, spring 1995; participant leadership inst. Freedom Forum, Columbia U., summer 1992; participant workshop for deans and chairpersons Annenberg Programs, Washington, winter 1993; presenter various profl. and ednl. confs., most recently Oakland (Mich.) U., 1994, Nat. Assn. for Devel. of Work with Sex Offenders, Durham (Eng.) U., 1994, Soc. for Sci. Study of Sex., Miami, Fla., 1994, Ctr. for Study of Evolution and Origins of Life, UCLA, 1994, Ctr. for Evolutionary Psychology, Santa Barbara, Calif., 1995, Tel Aviv U., 1995, Bar-Ilan U., Israel, 1995, Hebrew U. Jerusalem, 1995, NRC, Washington, 1995, Soc. Exptl. Social Psychology, Washington, 1995, Nat. Assn. for Treatment of Sexual Aggression, New Orleans, 1995, Polish Nat. Acad. Sci., Warsaw U., 1995. Co-author: An Instructor's Manual and Guide for Teaching a Course in Social Psychology, 1976, Pornography, 1993; co-editor Sites and Insights in Psychology, 1976; co-editor, contbr. chpt. to: Pornography and Sexual Aggression, 1984, Sex, Power, Conflict: Evolutionary Feminist Perspectives, 1996; contbr. chpt. to: Aggression in Children and Youth, 1984, Handbook of Research on Rape and Sexual Assault, 1984, Media Violence and Pornography: An International Perspective, 1984, The psychology of Women: Ongoing Debates, 1987, Public Communication and Behavior, Vol, 2, 1989: contbr. or co-contbr. various chptn, also numerous artiicles; mem. editl. bd. Motivation and Emotion, 1983-89, Comm. Rsch., 1986-92, Jour. Sex Rsch., 1982-99, Sexual Abuse: A Jour. and Treatment, 1995-99; assoc. editor Comm. Concepts Series, 1989-98, Jour. Rsch. in Personality, 1990-93; co-editor issue Jour. Social Issues, 1986. Recipient John Kendall award for Outstanding Contbns. to Psychology, Gustavus Coll., Minn., 1987; rsch. grantee Social Sci. and Humanities Rsch. Coun. Can., 1979-81, NIMH, 1986-89, 89-91, 91-92; named one of 7 scholars among top 100 rschrs. in 4 categories of eminence Personality and Social Psychology Bull., 1992. Fellow APA, Am. Psychol. Soc.; mem. Internat. Comm. Assn. (presenter 1994, Top 5 Conf. Paper award mass comm. divsn. 1987), Internat. Soc. for Rsch. on Aggression, Soc. for Psychol. Study of Social Issues, Soc. for Sci. Study of Sex, Phi Beta Kappa. Office: UCLA Comm Studies Program 334 Kinsey Hall Los Angeles CA 90095-0001

**MALANEY, STEPHANIE J.,** reading specialist; b. Lafayette, Ind., Feb. 7, 1949; d. George Walter Joseph and Audrey (Fisher) Schneider; m. Michael J. Malaney; children: Amanda Lynn, Kyle Patrick, Ryan Elliot. BS Elem. Edn., U. Wis., Oshkosh, 1990, MS Elem. Edn., 1992; MSE Reading, U.Wis., Oshkosh, 1997; MS Ednl. Adminstrn., U.Wis., Madison, 2004. Tchr. grades 1-3 Appleton Area Sch. Dist., Wis., 1990—92, instrnl. lead tchr. and dist. leader social studies program, 1992—97, tchr. 6th grade, 1995—98, reading specialist, 1998—. Docent Ontagami Hist. Soc. Grigmon Mansion, Appleton, 2002—, Hearthstone (Hist. Site), Appleton, 2005—. Mem.: NEA, AAUW (pres. Appleton chpt. 2004—06), Wis. Edn. Assn. (bd. dirs.), Mid East Reading Coun. (pres. 2004—06). Avocations: reading, gardening, walking, travel, history research. Home: 307 E McArthur St Appleton WI 54911 Office: Appleton Area Sch Dist 2505 W Capitol Dr Appleton WI 54914 Office Phone: 920-832-4608. Office Fax: 920-993-7078. Business E-Mail: malaneystephan@aasd.k12.wi.us.

**MALANGA, GERARD ANTHONY,** sports medicine physician, director; b. Montclair, NJ, Feb. 24, 1961; s. Lorenzo and Antoinette Malanga; m. Carrie Helen Rowe, May 6, 1989; children: Tara, Grace, Luke, John. BA in Biology cum laude, Villanova U., Pa., 1983; MD, U. Medicine and Dentistry NJ, Newark, 1987. Resident U. Medicine and Dentistry NJ, 1989—92; fellow in sports medicine Mayo Clinic, Rochester, Minn., 1992—93; sr. assoc. cons. 1993—96; dir. sports, spine and orthop. rehab. Kessler Inst. Rehab., West Orange, NJ, 1996—2004; dir. pain mgmt. Overlook Hosp., Summit, NJ,

2005—; dir. sports medicine Mountaineer Hosp., Montclair, NJ, 2005—; dir. NJ Sports Medicine Inst., Verona, 2005—. Assoc. prof. phys. medicine and rehab. U. Medicine and Dentistry NJ/NJ Med. Sch., 2003—; Rhala A. Helm MD disting. lectr. U. Tex., SW Med. Ctr., 2005. Editor: Whiplash, 2002, Musculoskeletal Physical Exam, 2005. Named Tchr. of Yr., Mayo Clinic, 1995; named one of Top Drs. in NY Metro Area, 2003—05, Best Drs. in Am., 2003—06; recipient Dean Charles Brown award, NJ Med. Sch., 1987. Fellow: Am. Coll. Sports Medicine, Am. Acad. Physicians Rehab.; mem.: N.Am. Spine Soc. (chmn. patient edn. com. 1996—), Physicians Assn. Sport, Spine and Occupl. Rehab. (disting.), Alpha Omega Alpha. Avocations: basketball, reading. Office: NJ Sports Medicine Inst 799 Bloomfield Ave Ste 304 Verona NJ 07044 E-mail: gmalanga@pol.net.

**MALANGONI, MARK ALAN,** surgeon, educator; b. East Chicago, Ind., Nov. 3, 1949; s. Roland G. and Cornelia (Marza) M.; m. Nancy Knapp, Aug. 12, 1972; children: Michael, Jonathan. AB in Zoology cum laude, Ind. U., 1971, MD, 1975. MD; diplomate Am. Bd. Surgery. Asst. prof. surgery Med. Coll. Wis., Milw., 1980-84, assoc. program dir., gen. surgery, 1981-84; assoc. prof. Surgery U. Louisville, 1984-90, chief surgery Humana Hosp., 1985-90; prof. surgery Case Western Res. U., Cleve., 1990—. Chmn. dept. surgery MetroHealth Med. Ctr., Cleve., 1990—. Merit Rev. grantee VA, Louisville, 1985-88. Fellow Am. Coll. Surgeons; mem. Cen. Surg. Assn., So. Surg. Assn., Am. Surg. Assn., Phi Beta Kappa, Alpha Omega Alpha. Office: MetroHealth Med Ctr 2500 Metrohealth Dr # 914 Cleveland OH 44109-1998

**MALANY, LE GRAND LYNN,** lawyer, engineer, bank executive; b. May 14, 1941; s. LeGrand Franklin and Marion (Jaynes) M.; m. Barbara Bumgarner, June 26, 1965; children: LeGrand Karl, Siobhan, Carleen. BS in Engring. Physics, U. Ill., 1964, JD, 1970. Registered profl. engr., Ill.; bar: Ill. 1970, U.S. Dist. Ct. (cen. dist.) Ill. 1970, Ill. Supreme Ct. 1970, U.S. Ct. Mil. Appeals 1971, U.S. Ct. Appeals (7th cir.) 1972, U.S. Dist. Ct. (so. dist.) Ill. 1974, U.S. Supreme Ct. 1975, U.S. Dist. Ct. (no. dist.) Ill. 1982; lic. real estate broker, bldg. inspector, mgmt. planner, and asbestos project designer Ill. Asst. astonomer Adler Planetarium, Chgo., 1960-63; rsch. asst. Portland Cement Rsch. Assn., Skokie, Ill., 1964; instr. dept. gen. engring. U. Ill., 1965-70; instr. Office Instrn. Resources, 1967-68; lectr. Police Tng. Inst., Urbana, Ill., 1969-70; project dir. driver control program U.S. Dept. Transp., 1971-73, project dir., author driver license examiner tng. curriculum, 1973; assoc. drivers license adminstr. State of Ill., Springfield, 1973-74, asst. auditor gen., 1977-83, asst. atty. gen., dir. policy, planning and tech., 1983-85, chief internal auditor office of atty. gen., 1985-86, spl. asst. atty. gen., 1986—, spl. asst. auditor gen. and gen. counsel office auditor gen., 1986-92, gen. counsel state comptroller Cusas II project, 1986-88; ptnr. Kabumoto and Malany, Springfield, 1986—97; emergency and disaster engr. U.S. Office of Fgn. Disaster Assistance, 2003—; chief counselor, land devel., bldg. and infrastructure engr to Minister of Urban Devel. and Housing, Kabul, Afghanistan, 2004; team engr. Darfur Sudan Disaster Response Team Office Fgn. Disaster Assistance, USAID, 2005. Commr. Williamsville-Sherman Water Commn., 1997—2003; pres. Microgeneral Ltd., 1983—; assoc. prin. Johnson & Assoc., 1990-93, Mgmt. Control Sys., Inc., 1986; chmn. bd. Flowers LaGrand Ltd., 1985—; founder, dir. Foster Bank, Chgo., 1988-90; expert U.S. Fed. Energy Adminstrn., 1974; counsel juvenile divsn. Cir. Ct., Sangamon County, Ill., 1973-75; chief counsel Ill. Dept. Motor Vehicles, Springfield, 1974; trustee Meret Ctr., Inc., 1973-75; internat. dir. constrn. Shelter Now Internat., Oshkosh, Wis., 1999—. Dem. candidate for States Atty., Sangamon County, Ill., 1980; program dist sch. renovation projects, Macedonia, 2000, Housing Renovations for Refugees, Macedonia, 1999; bd. dirs. J. Keil Braid Leadership Found., Villagrove, Colo., 1997—, Home Ownership Program for Equity, Springfield, Ill., 1998-2001, Springfield Heritage Found., 1999—; country dir. Macedonia for Shelter Now Internat., 2000—03. Recipient Midwest Intergovtl. Audit Forum Recognition award, 1981. Mem. ABA, Am. Phys. Soc., Nat. Soc. Profl. Engrs., Ill. Socs. Profl. Engrs., Ill. Farm Bur., Ill. Christmas Tree Growers Assn., Ill. Foster parents Assn., Rotary (Springfield chpt. sec. 1983-85, pres. 1986-87, trustee Rotary South Found. 1986-93), Habitat for Humanity-Sangamon County (bd. dirs. 1996-2001, dir. constrn. 1998-2000). Achievements include development statewide motorcycle driver licensing program. Home: 600 S Rose Hill Ave Springfield IL 62704-1560 Office: 631 E Adams St Springfield IL 62701-1947 Office Phone: 217-525-1132.

**MALAVE, ANDRES,** pharmacologist, educator; b. San Juan, Puerto Rico, Nov. 18, 1949; s. Andres Malave, Adela Nevarez; m. Lillian Arce, July 28, 1972; children: Jose A., Jaime E., Josue I., Jessica M. BS in Pharmacy, U. P.R., 1972; MS, Purdue U., 1981, PhD, 1983. Registered pharmacist P.R. Instr. U. P.R., San Juan, 1975—78, asst. prof., 1984—87, assoc. prof., 1988—91; prof., chmn. Nova Southeastern U., Ft. Lauderdale, Fla., 1992—2001, assoc. dean, 2001—04, dean Coll. Pharmacy, 2004—. CEO Malave Consulting Svcs., Inc., Ft. Lauderdale, 2001—04; dean coll. pharmacy U. P.R., 1987—91. Recipient Bristol Meyers/Squibb Faculty Devel. award, 1991—92; scholar, Fulbright, 2001. Mem.: Peruvian Acad. of Pharmacy, N.Y. Acad. Sci., Soc. Neurosci., Am. Assn. Coll. Pharmacy. Achievements include development of simple non-radioactive assay for estimating protein kinase C and protein phosphatase-1. Avocations: sports, racquetball, basketball, music, guitar. Home: 224 La Costa Way Weston FL 33326 Office Phone: 954-262-1304. E-mail: amalave@nova.edu, copdean@nova.edu.

**MALAWISTA, STEPHEN E.,** medical educator; s. Lawrence Malawista and Ann Marlowe Straus; m. Tobé Miller. AB, Harvard Coll., Cambridge, Mass., 1954; MD, Columbia U., 1958. Intern Yale-New Haven Med. Ctr., New Haven, 1958—60, asst. resident, medicine, 1960—63; trom epl. fellow to prof. Sch. Medicine Yale U., New Haven, 1963—75, prof. Sch. Medicine, 1975—. Chief sect. of rheumatology Sch. Medicine Yale U., 1967—88. Contbr. articles to profl. jours. Sr. asst. surgeon USPHS, 1960—62. Recipient prize, Ciba-Geigy Internat. League Against Rheumatism, 1985, Disting. Investigator award, 1994, Lifetime Achievement award; fellow, Josiah Macy Jr. Found., 1979—80, Fogarty Internat. Ctr., 1987—88, 1994—95, John Simon Guggenheim Found., 2001—02. Master: Am. Coll. Rheumatology (sec., 2d v.p., 1st v.p., pres.); fellow: AAAS, Am. Coll. Physicians, Biotech Study Ctr. NYU; mem.: Assn. Am. Physicians, Am. Soc. Cell Biology, Assn. Patient-Oriented Rsch. (life), Am. Soc. Clin. Investigation, Am. Fedn. Clin. Rsch., N.Y. Acad. Medicine (Paul Klemperer lectr. and medal 2002), Coll. Physicians and Surgeons Alumni Assn. (Gold medal 2006), Sigma Xi (life). Achievements include discovery of lyme disease. Office: Yale University Dept Int Medicine TAC S525D 300 Cedar Street New Haven CT 06520-8031 Office Phone: 203-785-2453.

**MALBON, CRAIG CURTIS,** pharmacology educator, dean; b. Providence, June 1, 1950; s. Elroy Willis and Edith Roberta (Curtis) M.; children: Lindsey Gei Sook, Hailey Sook Yee; m. Hsien-yu Wang, June 26, 1993. BA, Mass. State Coll., Worcester, 1972; PhD, Case Western Reserve U., 1976. NIH postdoctoral fellow sect. physiological chemistry Brown U., Providence, 1976-77, research assoc. physiological chemistry, 1977, asst. prof. research sect. physiological chemistry, 1978; asst. prof. pharmacology SUNY Sch. Medicine, Stony Brook, 1978-83, assoc. prof., 1983-90, prof., 1990—; leading univ. prof. Sch. Medicine SUNY, Stony Brook, 1993—, vice chmn. dept. pharmacology, 1988-89, prof. dept. pharmacology Stony Brook, 1990—, assoc. dean biomed. scis. Sch. Medicine, 1989-93, v.p. rsch., 1993-97; vice dean Univ. Hosp. and Med. Ctr. SUNY, Stony Brook, 1993—2005. Bd. dir. diabetes & metabolic diseases rsch. program NIH, Stony Brook, NY; mem. cell biology & physiology study sect., Bethesda, Md., 1981—86; bd. dir. LI High Tech. Incubator; mem. sci. adv. bd. Brookhaven Nat. Lab. DOE, 1996—2005. Mem. editl. bd. Am. Jour. Physiology, 1985—, assoc. editor, 1993-99; mem. editl. bd. Jour. Biol. Chemistry, 1988-93; contbr. articles to profl. jours. Mem. Marine Biol. Lab. Inc., Woods Hole, Mass., 1986; bd. dirs. Faculty/Student Assn., Inc., Stony Brook, 1979-82. Recipient nat. rsch. Svc. award NIH, 1976-80, career devel. award, 1981-86; rsch. award Am. Cancer Soc., 1998. Mem. Biophys. Soc., N.Y. Acad. Scis., Am. Physiol. Soc. (editl. bd. 1986, assoc. editor 1990), Am.

Soc. for Biochemistry and Molecular Biology (editl. bd. 1988), Biochem. Soc. (U.K.) (hon.), Sigma Xi. Home: PO Box 2726 East Setauket NY 11733-0852 E-mail: craig@pharm.sunysb.edu.

**MALCHESKY, PAUL S.,** medical association administrator; s. Paul P. and Lucy C. Malchesky; m. Carol H. Hoose, June 24, 1945; children: Paul R., Michael P., Christina L. Urban, Mark S. BS, St. Francis, Loretto, Pa., 1968; MS, Case Western Res., Cleve., Ohio, 1971, Cleve. State, 1977; D of Engring., Cleve. State, Cleveland, OH, 1983. Staff Cleve. Clinic Found., 1969—92; v.p. Steris Corp., Mentor, Ohio, 1992—2001, NanoScale Materials, Inc., Manhattan, Kans., 2002—04; pres. Internat. Ctr. Artificial Organs and Transplantations, Painesville, Ohio, 1994—; chief sci. officer EnviroSys, Inc., Santa Clara, Calif., 2006—; pres. Malchesky & Assocs., LLC, Painesville, Ohio. Contbr. over 300 sci. articles. Pres. Am. Soc. Artif. Organs, Boca Raton, Fla., 1999—2000, Internat. Soc. for Apheresis, Tokyo, 2001—03; chmn., bd. trustees Lakeland C.C., Kirtland, Ohio, 1990—91. Recipient Disting. Alumni, Cleve. State, 1990, Outstanding Engring. Alumnus, 1990, Elected Fellow, Amer. Inst. for Med. and Biloogical Engring., 1997; scholar NSF Traineeship, Case Western Res., 1968; Fr. Benedict English scholarship, St. Francis, 1964—68. Cath. Achievements include patents in field. Avocations: travel, gardening, boating. Office: Icaot 10 W Erie St Ste 200 Painesville OH 44077 Office Phone: 440-358-1102.

**MALCOLM, GLORIA J.,** small business owner; b. Atlanta, Apr. 16, 1956; d. George and Norella Camp; m. Ericka Monique Malcolm. B in Bus. Mgmt., DeKalb Coll., Atlanta; PhD in Edn. Leadership, Nova Southeastern U. Cert. notary pub. Team leader MS Soc., Atlanta; cons., advisor Home Testing Inst., NYCq; rep., organizer Nielsen TV, Dunedin, Fla.; mem. Alliance Corp., Memphis; assoc., advisor Joyner Hutcheson Rsch., Atlanta; owner, pres. GJM Profl. Cleaning Svc., Inc., East Point, Ga., 1988—2004; floor supr., U-scan coord. Kroger Co., Atlanta, 2005—. Bd. dirs Atlanta FCU. Active United Food Commil. Unions, Home Test Inst., MS Walk Soc., Am. Stroke Assn.; mem. svcs. Mt. Carmel Bapt. Ch., Atlanta; bd. dirs. St. Matthew's Ch. Mem.: NAFE, Bldg. Trader Assn., Am. Stroke Assn. Avocations: travel, reading, volleyball, tennis, bicycling. Home: PO Box 490365 Atlanta GA 30349

**MALCOLM, MOLLY BETH,** political organization worker, counselor; BAS in Elem. Edn. with high honors, So. Meth. U., 1976; MS in Counseling and Guidance, Tex. A&M U.-Texarkana, 1988. Lic. profl. counselor, lic. chem. dependency counselor, Tex. Tchr. pub. schs., Ark., Tex., Okla., 1977-87; elem. counselor Texarkana (Ark.) Schs., 1987-89; drug abuse prevention and counseling specialist Region VII Edn. Svc. Ctr., Kilgore, Tex., 1989-90; drug free schs. student assistance coord. Longview (Tex.) Ind. Sch. Dist., 1990-92; counseling and student svcs. coord. Texarkana (Tex.) Ind. Schs., 1992-93; owner, counselor Malcolm Cons., 1993—; field dir. Max Sandlin for Congress Campaign, 1996; dist. cmty. outreach coord. Congress Max Sandlin, Tex. 1st Dist., 1997-98; state chair Tex. Dem. Party, 1998—2003. V.p. nominations exec. com. Lyceum, 2005—. Contbr. publs. and curricula. Active Dem. Nat. Com., 1998-2003, exec. com., 2000-2003; active Presbytery of the Pines, Synod of the Sun Presbyn. Ch. USA, Pine Street Middle Sch. PTA; pres. Texarkana Ind. Sch. Dist., 1993-94, mem. adv. bd.; active Main Street Texarkana Bd.; bd.d irs. Texarkana People's Clinic; chair cmty. awareness com. Women for A&M Texarkana Bd.; deacon First Presbyn. Ch., Texarkana; advisor career devel. U. Tex. Chi Omega, 1999-2001; v.p. Lyceum Nominations Exec. Com., 2005- Named one of Rising Stars in Politics, Campaigns and Elections Mag., 2000, Pres.' award Ark. Counseling Assn., 1989, Hon. Bill Clinton Gov. Ark. Traveler award, 1989, Texarkana Alumni Achievement award Tex. A&M U., 1989, Winnsboro ISD Disting. Alumni award, 2003, Tex. Women's Polit. Caucus Blazing New Trails award, 2004. Mem. NAACP (life), Tex. Counseling Assn. (Disting. Svc. award 1993, 96), Tex. Mental Health Counselors Assn., Tex. Sch. Counselors Assn., N.E. Tex. Counseling Assn., Assn. State Dem. Chairs (co-chair resolution com. 1999-2001, exec. com., treas. exec. com. 2001-2004), Tex. Rural Cmtys. Bd., Clinton Birthplace Found. Bd., Assn. State Dem. Chairs Alumni Assn. (pres. 2005), Texarkana Mus. Sys. Bd., Texarkana Hist. Landmark Preservation Commn., Texarkana Regional Arts and Humanities Coun., Inc.(mem. AMAX adv. bd. 2004-), Tex. Dem. Women (pres. 1997-99, Mem. of Yr. 1998), Leadership Texarkana Alumi Assn. (adv. bd. 1996-99), Jr. League Texarkana, Leadership Tex. Alumnae Assn. (life, adv. bd. 1996-99), Ark. PTA (life), DAR, Tex. A&M U. at Texarkana Alumni Assn. (life, Achievement award 1989), So. Meth. U. Alumni Assn. (life), Assn. State Dem. Chairs Alumni Assn. (pres. 2005), Rotary Internat., Psi Chi (v.p. 1987-89), Delta Kappa Gamma (pres. chpt. 1988-89), Chi Omega (pres. chpt. alumni assn. 1998-99), Texarkana C. of C. (mil. affairs com.), Am. Legion. Office: Malcolm Consulting PO Box 6282 Texarkana TX 75505

**MALCOLM, STEVEN J.,** petroleum pipeline company executive; b. St. Louis, Sept. 1948; m. Gwen Malcolm; 1 child. BCE, U. Mo.-Rolla, 1970; attended, Northwestern U. With Cities Gas Co.; dir., bus. develop. Williams Nat. Gas Co., 1984—86, dir. gas mgmt., 1986—89; v.p., gas mgmt. & supply Williams Field Svcs. Co., 1993-93, sr. v.p., gen. mgr., 1994—98; pres., CEO Williams Energy Svcs. LLC, 1998—2001; pres., COO Williams Companies, Tulsa, Okla., 2001—02, pres., CEO, 2002—. Bd. mem. Tulsa Area United Way, Tulsa Community Found., Tulsa Metro Chamber, St. John Medical Ctr.; bd. of trustees U. Tulsa. Mem.: Nat. Energy Svc. Assn., Gas Processors Assn. Office: Williams 1 Williams Ctr Tulsa OK 74172*

**MALCOM, SHIRLEY MAHALEY,** science association executive; b. Birmingham, Ala., Sept. 6, 1946; m. Horace Malcom, 1975; children: Kelly A., Lindsey E. BS in Zoology, U. Wash., 1967; MA in Zoology, UCLA, 1968; PhD in Ecology, Pa. State U., 1974; LHD, Coll. St. Catherine, 1990, Knox Coll., 1993; DSc, N.J. Inst. Tech., 1991, Coll. St. Joseph, 1994, Hood Coll., 1994, Ball State U., 1996. Asst. prof. biology U.N.C., Wilmington, 1974-75; rsch. asst., staff assoc. and project dir. Office of Opportunities of AAAS, 1975-77, program head, 1979-89; program mgr. Minority Inst. Sci. Improvement Program NSF, 1977-79, mem. equal opportunities sci. and technol. com., 1983-86, chair equal opportunities sci. and technol. com., 1984-86; head directorate edn. and human resource programs AAAS, 1989—. Mem. technol. and women's empolyment panel, Commn. on Behavioral and Social Sci. and Edn., NRC, 1984-86, panel to evaluate Nat. Ctr. for Edn. Statistics, com. on nat. statistics, 1984-86; mem. adv. coun. Carnegie Forum on Edn. and Econs., 1984-88, task force tchg. profession, 1985-87; bd. dirs. Carnegie Corp., N.Y. Hon. trustee, Am. Museum Natural History; bd. dir. Howard Heinz Endowment, H. John Heinz III Ctr. for Sci., Econ. and Environment; adv. bd., Nat. Park Sys.; mem. adv. coun. Smithsonian Inst., 1990—; mem. Nat. Sci. Bd., 1994-98; mem. Pres.'s Com. for Advancement of Sci. and Tech., 1994-2001; regent, Morgan State Univ.; trustee, Calif. Inst. Tech. Named to Top 50 Black Scientists, Career Comm. Group, 2004; recipient Alumna Summa Laude Dignata award, Univ. Wash. and UW Alumni Assn., 1998, Public Welfare medal, NAS, 2003. Fellow AAAS, Am. Acad. Arts and Sci.; mem. Sci. Rsch. Soc., Sigma Xi. Office: AAAS 1200 New York Ave NW Ste 640 Washington DC 20005-3928

**MALDACENA, JUAN,** physicist, researcher; b. Buenos Aires, Sept. 10, 1968; married; 2 children. Student, U. Buenos Aires, 1985—88, Inst. Balseiro, U. Cuyo, Bariloche, Argentina, 1988—91; PhD program, Princeton U., 1992—96. Rsch. assoc. Rutgers U., 1996—97; vis. assoc. prof. Harvard U., 1997, Tomas D. Cabot assoc. prof., 1998—99, prof. physics, 1999—2001; prof. Inst. for Advanced Study, 2001—. Contbr. artilces to profl. jours. Named a Disting. Lectr. Stanford U., 2004; recipient UNESCO Husein prize for Young Scientists, 1999, Sackler prize in Physics, 2000, Xanthopoulas prize in general relativity, 2001, Pius XI medal, 2002, Edward A. Bouchet award, Am. Phys. Soc., 2004; Sloan Fellowship, 1998, Packard Fellowship in Sci. and Engring., 1998, MacArthur Fellowship, 1999. Office: Inst for Advanced Study Sch Natural Sciences 1 Einstein Dr Princeton NJ 08540 Office Phone: 609-734-8307. Office Fax: 609-951-4489. E-mail: malda@ias.edu.*

**MALDE, HAROLD EDWIN,** retired federal government geologist; b. Reedsport, Oreg., July 9, 1923; s. Emil and Bessie May (Alspaugh) M.; m. Caroline Elizabeth Rose, Dec. 21, 1954; children: Margaret Jean, Melissa Ruth. AB, Willamette U., 1947; postgrad., Harvard U., 1947-48, U. Colo., 1948-51. Geologist U.S. Geol. Survey, Denver, 1951-87, emeritus, 1987—; affiliate prof. U. Idaho, 1968—76, 1887—91. Mem. Colo. com. for Nat. Register Hist. Places, 1972-80; vol. photographer Nature Conservancy, 1987—; mem. paleoanthropology del. to Peoples Republic China, Nat. Acad. Scis., 1975, mem. various coms. for study surface mining, 1973-79; mem. oil shale environ. adv. panel US Dept. Interior, 1976-80; seasonal geologic studies Valsequillo Archeol. Nat. Sci. Found. Harvard U., Puebla, Mex., 1964-73, 2004. Contbr. numerous sci. papers to profl. lit. Served to ensign USNR, 1947-48. Recipient Meritorious Service award U.S. Dept. Interior, 1979, Oak Leaf award Nature Conservancy, 1993. Fellow Geol. Soc. Am. (Kirk Bryan award 1970, assoc. editor 1982-88), AAAS, Ariz.-Nev. Acad. Sci., Explorers Club; mem. Am. Quaternary Assn., Assn. Earth Sci. Editors. Democrat. Unitarian Universalist. Home: 842 Grant Pl Boulder CO 80302-7415 E-mail: halmalde@msn.com.

**MALDEN, KARL (MALDEN SEKULOVICH),** actor; b. Chgo., Mar. 22, 1912; s. Peter and Minnie (Sebera) Sekulovich; m. Mona Graham, Dec. 18, 1938; children— Mila, Carla. Student, Goodman Theatre, Chgo., 1935-38. Pres. Acad. of Motion Arts and Scis., 1989-92; mem. Citizens Stamp Com., U.S. Govt., Washington. Actor, 1935—; stage plays include Golden Boy, 1938, Gentle People, 1939, Key Largo, 1940, Flight to the West, 1942, Uncle Harry, 1940, All My Sons, 1949, A Streetcar Named Desire, 1950, Desire Under the Elms, 1952, Desperate Hours, 1954; in motion pictures, 1940—, films include: Boomerang, Gunfighter, 1945, Halls of Montezuma, 1950, A Streetcar Named Desire (Acad. award for best supporting actor, Oscar award, 1951), 1951, Ruby Gentry, 1952, I Confess, 1953, On the Waterfront, 1954, Baby Doll, 1956, Desperate Hours, 1957, Fear Strikes Out, 1957, The Hanging Tree, 1959, Pollyanna, 1960, One Eyed Jacks, 1961, Parrish, The Adventures of Bullwhip Griffin, 1967, Patton, 1970, Beyond the Poseidon Affair, 1978, Meteor, 1979, Sting II, 1982, Twilight Time, 1982, Billy Galvin, 1987, Nuts, 1987; TV films include: Word of Honor, 1981, Miracle on Ice, 1981, Intent to Kill, 1983, Fatal Vision, 1984 (Emmy award), My Father My Son, 1988, The Hijacking of the Achille Lauro, 1989, Call Me Anna, 1990, Absolute Strangers, 1991, Back to the Streets of San Francisco, 1992; dir.: Time Limit, 1957, Billion Dollar Brain, 1967, Hot Millions, 1968, Hotel, Cat O'Nine Tails, 1971, Wild Rovers, 1971, Summertime Killer, 1973, Nuts, 1987; star TV series Streets of San Francisco, 1972-77, Skag, 1980. Recipient Donaldson award, 1950, Critic's award, 1950, Lifetime Achievement Award, Screen Actors Guild, 2003; Barrington Station post office in L.A. renamed in his honor, 2005. Address: 1845 Mandeville Canyon Rd Los Angeles CA 90049-2222

**MALDONADO, F. CÉSAR,** priest, educator; b. Itapaya-Cochabamba, Bolivia, Jan. 6, 1962; arrived in U.S., 1998; s. Benigno Maldonado, Pastora Sanabria. Philosophy Licenciatura, Cochabamba, 1986; B. Theology, U. Catolica, 1990; M.Anthropology, FLACSO, Quito, Ecuador, 1992; postgrad., Georgetown U., Washington, 1999—. Ordained priest, Roman Cath. Ch.; entered Soc. of Jesus. Tchr. Juan XXIII H.S., Cochabamba, Bolivia, 1987—88; prof. Pontificia U. Católica, Quito, Ecuador, 1991—92; cons. Acción Cultural Loyola, Sucre, Bolivia, 1993—95; prof. U. Catolica, Colhambamba, Bolivia, 1995—97; prin. Juan XXIII H.S., Colhambamba, 1996—97; cons. Centro de Investigacion y Promoción Campesinato, Santa Cruz, Bolivia, 1997—98; prof. U. Gabriel Renê Moreno, Santa Cruz, 1997—98. Contbr. articles to profl. jours. Mem.: Spanish Masses Arlington. Roman Catholic. Avocations: sports, meditation, poetry. Mailing: 37th and O Sts NW Washington DC 20057-0001 E-mail: fcm@georgetown.edu.

**MALDONADO, KIRK FRANCIS,** lawyer; b. Omaha, Mar. 7, 1950; s. Manuel and Orpha Mae (Kovar) Maldonado. BA, U. Nebr.-Omaha, 1975; JD, Creighton U., 1978; MLT, Georgetown U., 1981. Bar: Nebr. 1978, Calif. 1982. Atty. Employee Plans and Exempt Orgns. Divsn. Office of Chief Counsel IRS, Washington, 1978—81; assoc. Gibson, Dunn & Crutcher, Newport Beach, Calif., 1982—85; prin. Stradling, Yocca, Carlson & Rauth, Newport Beach, 1985—89, Riordan & McKinzie, Costa Mesa, Calif., 1989—2001; ptnr. Bobeck Phleger & Harrison LLP, 2001—03; mem. Sherman & Howard, LLC, Denver, 2003—. Contbr. articles to profl. jours. Mem.: ABA (employee benfits com.), State Bar Calif. Office: Sherman & Howard LLC 633 17th St Ste 3000 Denver CO 80202 E-mail: kmaldonado@sah.com.

**MALDONADO-BEAR, RITA MARINITA,** economist, educator; b. Vega Alta, P.R., June 14, 1938; d. Victor and Marina (Davila) Maldonado; m. Larry Alan Bear, Mar. 29, 1975. BA, Auburn U., 1960; PhD, NYU, 1969. With Min. Wage Bd. & Econ. Devel. Adminstr., Govt. of P.R., 1969-70; asst. prof. econs. Manhattan Coll., 1970-72; assoc. prof. econs. Bklyn. Coll., 1972-75; assoc. prof. fin. & econs., undergrad/grad. divsn. Stern Sch. Bus. NYU, 1975-81, prof., 1981—2004, prof. emerita, 2004—. Vis. assoc. prof. fin. Stanford (Calif.) Grad. Bus. Sch., 1973-74; acting dir. markets, ethics & law, NYU, 1993-94; cons. Morgan Guaranty Trust Co., N.Y.C., 1972-77, Bank of Am., N.Y.C., 1982-84, Res. City Bankers, N.Y.C., 1978-87, Swedish Inst. Mgmt., Stockholm, 1982-91, Empresas Master of P.R., 1985-90. Author: Role of the Financial Sector in the Economic Development of Puerto Rico, 1970; co-author: Free Markets, Finance, Ethics and Law, 1994, The Economy of Puerto Rico: Restoring Growth, 2006; contbr. articles to profl. jours. Bd. dirs. Medallion Funding Corp., 1985-87; mem. NYU Senate and Faculty Coun., 1995-2003, chair fin. com., 1996-2000; apptd. adv. bd. dirs. equity & diversity in edntl. environs. Mid. States Commn. Higher Edn., 1991—; trustee Securities Industry Assn., N.Y. Dist. Econ. Edn. Found., 1994—; chair NSF, Nat. Vis. Com. Curriculum Devel. Project Networked Fin. Simulation, 1995—; econ. cons. Inst. Women of Color, Nat. Coun. Black Women Cmty. Svcs. Fund, 2000—; trustee Bd. Edn., Twp. Mahwah, N.J., 1991-92. P.R. Econ. Devel. Adminstrn. fellow, 1960-65, Marcus Nadler fellow, NYU, 1966-67, Phillips Lods Dissertation fellow, 1967-68. Mem. Am. Econs. Assn., Am. Fin. Assn., Metro. Econ. Assn. N.Y., Assn. Social Econs. (trustee exec. coun. 1994-96). Home: 95 Tam O Shanter Dr Mahwah NJ 07430-1526 Office: Mgmt Edn Ctr 44 W 4th St Ste 9-190 New York NY 10012-1106 Business E-Mail: rmaldona@stern-nyu.edu.

**MALDONADO-CLASS, JOAQUIN,** language educator; b. Manati, PR, Nov. 15, 1959; s. Juan Maldonado-Rodriguez and Albina Class-Santiago; m. Katherine Velez-Andujar, June 30, 1990; 1 child, Sebastian Gioachino Maldonado-Velez. BA, Universidad Central de Bayamon, PR, 1982, MA, 1993; PhD summa cum laude, U. PR, Rio Piedras, 2004. Cert. Spanish tchr. PR. Spanish tchr. Escuela Superior Catolica, Bayamon, 1986—89, Escuela Angel Sandin Martinez, Vega Baja, PR, 1989—93, Escuela Emilior R. Debado, Corozal, PR, 1993—2000; asst. prof. Spanish Truman State U., Kirksville, Mo., 2000—. Spanish instr. Universidad Interamericana, Bayamon, 1998—2000; texts author Editorial Norma, Catano, PR, 1998—2001. Author: (textbook) Sueños y Palabras 7, 2000, Sueños y Palabreas 12, 2002. Tutor Casa Hogar Sagrados Corazones, Bayamon, 1985—86; missionary Fathers of Holy Spirit, French Guyana, 1984—85; co-dir. Servidores de Jesus, Vega Baja, PR, 1987—2000. Rsch. grantee, U. PR, 1999—2000. Mem.: L.Am. Studies Assn. Roman Catholic. Office: Truman State U 100 E Normal Kirksville MO 63501 Office Phone: 660-785-4500. Business E-Mail: jmaldona@truman.edu.

**MALE, ALAN THOMAS,** engineering educator, foundation administrator; b. Birmingham, Eng., Sept. 3, 1937; came to U.S., 1968; s. Albert Leslie and Olive (Caddel) M.; m. Beryl Glover, Sept. 20, 1958; children: Andrew James, Christopher John. BSc, U. Birmingham, 1958, PhD, 1962. Registered profl. engr. Pa., Ky.; chartered engr. U.K. Lectr. U. Birmingham, 1960-67; supr. Westinghouse Astronuclear Lab., Pitts., 1968-70; from mgr. metals processing to mgr. processing rsch. Westinghouse Rsch. Labs., Pitts., 1970-83; mgr. advanced processing Westinghouse Sci. & Tech. Ctr., Pitts., 1990-91; prin., tech. mgr. Concurrent Techs. Corp., Johnstown, Pa., 1992-96; dir. Ctr. for Robotics and Mfg. Systems U. Ky., assoc. dean rsch. and grad. studies

College of Engring., 1996—2002, prof. mech. engring., 1996—. Holder 16 patents in field. Fellow Inst. Materials (award 1977), Soc. Mfg. Engrs. (life, internat. dir. 1991-99, pres. N.Am. mfg. rsch. inst. 1988-89, Frederick W. Taylor Rsch. medal 1989, internat. pres. 1997-98), ASM Internat. (life); mem. ASME, Am. Welding Soc. Republican. Methodist. Avocations: freemasonry, carpentry, fishing. Home: 3390 Mantilla Dr Lexington KY 40513-1039 Office Phone: 859-257-6262. Business E-Mail: atmale@engr.uky.edu.

**MALECHA, MARVIN JOHN,** architect, academic administrator; b. Lonsdale, Minn., June 26, 1949; s. George and Barbara Malecha; m. Cynthia Marie Miller, Aug. 8, 1970; children: Peter, Michelle. Student, St. Thomas Coll.; BArch, U. Minn.; MArch, Harvard U. Registered architect, Calif. Designer Wallace and Mundt Architects, Edina, Minn., 1969-73, Hugh Stubbins and Assocs., Cambridge, Mass., 1973-76; instr. Cambridge Urban Awareness Program, 1973-76, Boston Archtl. Ctr., 1974-76; asst. chmn., asst. prof. dept. arch. Coll. Environ. Design Calif. State Poly. U., Pomona, 1976-77, chmn., assoc. prof., 1979-82, prof., dean Coll. Environ. Design, 1982-94; dean Coll. Design N.C. State U., 1994—. Chmn. Univ. Fall Conf. com. Calif. State Poly. U., 1984; mem. steering com. Architects for Social Responsibility; mem. bd. advisors Tchrs. cert. program City Bldg. Edn. Program, planning com. So. Calif. Assn. Govts.; vis. critic UCLA, 1985, U., Minn., 1981-83, 87, U. So. Calif., 1980-87, Calif. Poly. State U., San Luis Obispo, 1979-87, Clemson U., 1988, Columbia U. 1993, U. Tenn., 1994, U. Md., 1995, Miss. State U., 1995, U. Wis., Milw., 1996, Roger Williams U., 1997; lectr. to schs. and archtl. assns.; cons. in architecture and research, Claremont, Calif., 1976—; master juror Nat. Council Archtl. Registration Bds.; mem. edn. equity com. Calif. State U. System, 1985-86; pres. Calif. Coun. Archit. Edn., 1986-88; mem. accreditation vis. team for collegiate programs in landscape architecture, 1988—; bd. dirs. Nat. Archtl. Accreditation Bd.; campus architect cons. U. Calif., Riverside, 1990-94. Author: Reconfiguration in the Study and Practice of Architecture, Form of Performance, The Fabric of Architecture, The Pomona Method; co-sgner, author internat. protocol for internat. exch. in arch. edn.; contbr. articles to profl. jours. Mem. Art and Liturgy com. Our Lady Assumption Ch., Claremont, Calif., 1982-94; mem. bldg. and real estate com. Archdiocese of Raleigh; bd. dirs. United Arts Raleigh, City Gallery Raleigh, 1995—; bd. dirs. Raleigh Am. Inst. Architects; master juror workgroup, bd. dirs. Downtown Raleigh Alliance. Recipient Ellerbe Archtl. award, 1972, Hon. Mention Mass. Housing Dept., 1976, Topaz medallion for excellence in archtl. edn., 2003, Prize for Creative Integration of Practice and Edn. in the Acad., Nat. Coun. Archtl. Registration, 2002; Rotch scholar, 1980. Fellow AIA (bd. dirs. L.A. chpt. 1982-83, chmn. state and nat. awards coms. 1983-85, chmn Monterey design conf. com., Henry Adams award 1973, mem. steering com. archs. in edn. com. 1991, chair archs. in edn. com. 1994-95, adv. bd. ArchVoices, presdl. citation L.A. chpt. 1987, mem. Calif. coun. 1994, nat. bd. dirs. 2005, Excellence in Arch. Edn. award), European Assn. for Arch. Educators (hon.), Soc. Am. Registered Archs., Assn. Collegiate Schs. Arch. (v.p. 1988-89, chair ann. meeting, pres. 1988-89, adminstrs. conf. Wash. 1985, Disting. Prof. 2002), Calif. Coun. Archtl. Edn. (pres. 1988-89), Golden Key (hon. mem. N.C. chpt.). Office: NC State U Coll Design PO Box 7701 Raleigh NC 27695-0001 Office Phone: 919-515-8300. E-mail: marvin_malecha@ncsu.edu.

**MALEFAKIS, EDWARD E.,** history professor; b. Springfield, Mass., Jan. 2, 1932; s. Emmanuel A. and Despina (Sophoulakis) M.; m. Cali Doxiadis, 1988; children from previous marriage: Michael, Laura. Ab, Bates Coll., 1953; MA, Johns Hopkins U., 1955; PhD, Columbia U., 1965. Instr. Northwestern U., 1962-63; assoc. prof., 1968-71; asst. prof. modern European history Columbia U., 1964-67, prof., 1975—. U. Mich., Ann Arbor, 1971-74. Author: Agrarian Reform and Peasant Revolution in Spain, 1970, Southern Europe in the 19th and 20th Centuries, 1992; editor: Indalecio Prieto, 1975, La guerra de España, 1936-39, 1996, Franquismo: El juicio de la historia, 2000. Recipient Herbert Baxter Adams award Am. Hist. Assn., 1971, Faculty Teaching award Northwestern U., 1971, medal of honor U. Internacional Menendez Pelayo, 1982, Orden de Mérito Civico (Spain), 1988, Nebrija prize U. Salamanca, 2000; Social Scis. Rsch. Coun. grantee, 1967, NEH grantee, 1977; Guggenheim fellow, 1974, Inst. Juan March fellow, 1991. Mem. Modern Greek Studies Assn. (exec. com. 1981-87), Soc. for Spanish and Portuguese Hist. Studies (exec. council 1969-72), Spanish Inst. N.Y.C. (bd. dirs. 1982—). Democrat. Greek Orthodox. Office: Columbia Univ 524 Fayerweather Hall New York NY 10027 Home: 2109 Broadway #1477 New York NY 10023-2106 Business E-Mail: eem1@columbia.edu.

**MALEK, FREDERIC VINCENT,** finance company executive; b. Oak Park, Ill., Dec. 22, 1936; s. Fred W. and Martha (Smicklas) M.; m. Marlene A. McArthur, Aug. 5, 1961; children: Fred W., Michelle A. BS, U.S. Mil. Acad., 1959; MBA, Harvard U., 1964; D of Humanities (hon.), St. Leo Coll., St. Petersburg, Fla., 1970. Assoc. McKinsey & Co., Inc., Washington, 1964—; comm. exec. com. Triangle Corp., Columbia, SC, 1967-69; dep. under sec. HEW, Washington, 1969-70; spl. asst. to Pres. U.S., Washington, 1970-73; dep. dir. U.S. Office of Mgmt. and Budget, Washington, 1973-75; with Marriott Corp., Washington, 1975-88, sr. v.p., 1975-77, exec. v.p. 1978-88; pres. Marriott Hotels and Resorts, 1981-88, Northwest Airlines, Mpls., 1989-90, vice chmn., 1990-91, also bd. dirs.; campaign mgr. Bush-Quayle '92, 1991-92; co-chmn. CB Richard Ellis, 1989-96; chmn. Lodging Opportunities Fund, 1991—; Thayer Capital Ptnrs., 1992—, Thayer Hotel Investors, 1994—. Chmn. 1996 Rep. Presdl. Trust, 1995-96; bd. dirs. Automated Data Processing Corp., N.W. Airlines, CB Richard Ellis; dir. with rank of amb., 1990 Econ. Summit, 1989—; adj. prof. U. S.C., 1986-89; lectr. Kennedy Sch. Govt., Harvard U., 1976 Mem. Pres.'s Commn. on White House Fellows, 1971-75, White House Domestic Coun., 1974-75, Pres.'s Commn. on Pers. Interchange, 1974-76; dep. dir. com. for Re-election of Pres., 1972; Pres.'s Commn. on Pvt. Sector Initiatives, 1982-85, dir. conv. Bush for Pres., 1988; mem. Nat. Coun. on Surface Transp. Rsch., 1993-95; nat. adv. bd. Nat. Ctr. Econ. Edn. of Children, 1980-82; mem. Pres.'s Coun. on Phys. Fitness and Sports, 1986-91. Named Bus. Statesman of Yr. Harvard Bus. Sch. Club Washington, 2000, Citizen of Yr. Boy Scouts Am. Nat. Capitol Coun., 2000, Am. Friends of Czech Republic Civil Soc. Vision award, Woodrow Wilson award for corp. citizenship, 2004; named to Washington Bus. Hall of Fame, 2005. Mem. Am.-Israel Friendship League (bd. trustees 1991—), Aspen Inst. (bd. trustees 1996—). Episcopalian. Avocations: bicycling, skiing. Office: 1455 Pennsylvania Ave NW Washington DC 20004-1008 Office Phone: 202-371-0150. Business E-Mail: fmalek@thayercapital.com.

**MALEK, M. MIKE,** medical association administrator; Diplomate Am. Bd. Surgery. Resident Hamot Med. Ctr., Duke U. Ctr., Shriners Hosp. Sys.; dir. Washington Orthop. and Knee Clinic. Lectr. Contbr. articles to profl. jours. Founder Nat. Knee Rsch. Edn. Found. Fellow Sports Medicine, U. Cin. Med. Ctr. Fellow: ACS, Soc. Knee, Internat. Arthoscopy Assn., Am. Orthop. Soc. Sports Medicine, Am. Acad. Orthop. Surgeons, Anthroscopic and Reconstructive Knee Surgery; mem.: Arthroscopy Assn. N.Am. (pres.), European Soc. Sports Traumatology, Knee Surgery and Anthroscopy, Internat. Soc. Anthroscopy, Knee Surgery, and Orthop. Sports Medicine, Am. Assn. Hip and Knee Surgeons. Office: Washington Orthop & Knee Clinic 7777 Leesburg Pike Ste 3025 Falls Church VA 22043-2403

**MALEK, MANU,** information scientist, educator; BSEE, U. Tehran, Iran; MSc in Elec. Engring. and Computer Sci., PhD in Elec. Engring. and Computer Sci., U. Calif., Berkeley. Disting. mem. tech. staff Lucent Technologies Bell Labs.; mem. faculty to industry prof. computer sci. and telecom. mgmt. Stevens Inst. Tech., Hoboken, NJ, 2001—. Adj. prof. elec. engring., computer sci. and telecom. mgmt. Stevens Inst. Tech., active in cybersecurity prog.; hon. dir. Computer Networks Forensics Lab. Shandong Acad. Scis., Jinan, China, 2005—. Contbr. articles to profl. jours.; editor network mgmt.: IEEE Transactions on Comm., 1989—92; editor: Basic Concepts for Mng. Telecom. Networks: Copper to Sand to Glass to Air, 1999, Cooperative Mgmt. of Enterprise Networks, 2000, Mng. Bus. and Svc. Networks, 2001, Active Networks and Active Network Mgmt., 2001; co-editor: Guarding Your Bus.: A Mgmt. Approach to Security, 2004; founder, editor-in-chief: Jour. Network and Systems Mgmt., 1992—. Fellow: IEEE (Third Millennium medal 2000); mem.: NY Acad. Scis., Sigma Xi, Internat. Fedn. Info. Processing, IEEE Comm. Soc. (disting. lectr.), Eta Kappa Nu. Achievements include patents in field. Office: Dept Computer Sci Stevens Inst Tech Castle Point on Hudson Hoboken NJ 07030 E-mail: mmalek@stevens.edu.*

**MALEK, MARLENE ANNE,** foundation administrator; b. Oakland, Calif., June 22, 1939; d. William and Yolanda (Stella) McArthur; m. Frederic Malek; children: Frederic William, Michelle A. Olson. Degree in Nursing, Marymount U. Pres. Friends Cancer Rsch., Washington, 2000—. Vice chmn. bd. dirs. Marymount U., Arlington, Va.; presdl. appointee bd. dirs. Kennedy Ctr., 2002—; adv. bd. Second Genesis, Bethesda, Md.; bd. dirs. Nat. Mus. Women in Arts, Vital Voices Global Partnership, Best Friends Found.; collectors com. Nat. Gallery of Art; presdl. appointment to Nat. Cancer Adv. Bd., 1991-96; bd. overseers Duke U. Cancer Ctr.; mem. Nat. Dialogue on Cancer, Episcopalian. Avocations: cross country skiing, bicycling.

**MALEK, SAMI NIMER,** oncologist, researcher, hematologist; b. Braunschweig, Germany, Oct. 12, 1965; arrived in U.S., 1992; s. Wasfi Nimer and Helga Malek; m. Lilia Sofia Badillo, May 28, 1999; children: Isabella Ashley, Julian Andrew. MD, U. Hamburg, Germany, 1991. Diplomate Am. Bd. Internal Medicine, Am. Bd. Oncology, Am. Bd. Hematology. Postdoctoral fellow Johns Hopkins U., Balt., 1992—96, mem. rsch. faculty, 1996—97, fellow in oncology, 0012—2004; resident Baylor Coll., Houston, 1997—2000, chief resident in medicine, 2000—01; rsch. fellow Columbia U., NYC, 2003—04; asst. prof. U. Mich., Ann Arbor, 2004—. Contbr. articles to profl. publs. Recipient Young Investigator award, Am. Soc. Oncology, 2004; fellow, Leukemia and Lymphoma Soc., 2004— Mem.: ASCO, ASH. Home: 4794 Polo Fields Dr Ann Arbor MI 48103 Office: U Mich 1150 W Medical Center Dr Ann Arbor MI 48109 Business E-mail: smalek@med.umich.edu.

**MALENG, NORM,** prosecutor; b. Acme, Wash., 1938; m. Judy Maleng; 1 child. BS in Econs., U. Wash., 1960, JD, 1966. Bar: Wash. State 1967, U.S. Supreme Ct. 1983, USOC Wash. 1973. Staff atty. U.S. Senate Com. on Commerce; pvt. practice Seattle; chief dep. civil divsn. King County, Seattle, prosecutor, 1978—. Chair Gov.'s Task Force on Cmty. Protection, 1989; vice chair Wash. Sentencing Guidelines Commn. Named Outstanding Pub. Ofcl. in King County, Mcpl. League, 1986. Mem. Wash. Assn. Pros. Attys. (pres.), Nat. Dist. Attys. Assn. (v.p., mem. exec. bd.), Wash. Assn. County Ofcls. (pres.). Office: W554 KC Courthouse 516 3d Ave Seattle WA 98104 Office Phone: 206-296-9067.

**MALENKA, BERTRAM JULIAN,** physicist, researcher; b. N.Y.C., June 8, 1923; s. Morris and Mollie (Wichtel) M.; m. Ruth D. Stolper, Mar. 28, 1948; children: David Jonathan, Robert Charles. AB, Columbia, 1947; MA, Harvard, 1949, PhD, 1951. Research fellow Harvard, 1951-54; asst. prof. physics Washington U., St. Louis, 1954-56; asso. prof. Tufts U., Medford, Mass., 1956-60; faculty Northeastern U., Boston, 1960—, prof. physics, 1962-93, prof. emeritus, 1993—. Mem. sci. adv. group Harvard-Mass. Inst. Tech. Cambridge Electron Accelerator, 1956— Mem. vis. com. dept. conservation Mus. Fine Arts, Boston, 1997—; mem. collections mgmt., 2004—; mem. vis. com. Art of the Ams. Dept. Mem. Am., Italian phys. socs., N.Y. Acad. Scis., Phi Beta Kappa, Sigma Xi. Achievements include research and publications on theory of nuclear forces and structure of nucleus, explanation polarization phenomena in high-energy scattering, gamma radiation, electric polarization deuteron, accelerator design. Home: 16 Rutledge Rd Belmont MA 02478-3323 Office: Northeastern Univ Dept Of Physics Boston MA 02115 E-mail: bjm11@verizon.net.

**MALENKA, ROBERT C.,** psychiatrist, educator; b. Boston, June 21, 1955; PhD in Neuroscis., MD, Stanford U., 1983. Resident in psychiatry Stanford Sch. Medicine; postdoctoral work U. Calif., San Francisco, asst. prof. psychiatry and physiology, prof. psychiatry and physiology; dir. Ctr. for Neurobiology of Addiction; assoc. dir. Ctr. for Neurobiology and Psychiatry; Pritzker prof. psychiatry and behavioral scis., dir. Pritzker Lab. Stanford U. Sch. Medicine, 1999—; lectr. in field. Scientific adv. bd. Renovis, Inc., 2000—, Merck, Inc., 2000—; Wendy and Stanley Marsh lectr., 2002. Mem. editl. bd. jours.; co-author: (textbook) Molecular Neuropharmacology: A Foundation for Clinical Neuroscience, 2001; contbr. articles to profl. jours. Mem. Nat. Adv. Coun. on Drug Abuse. Recipient Alfred P. Sloan rsch. fellowship, 1990, Young Investigator award, Nat. Alliance for Rsch. in Schizophrenia and Depression, 1990, 1992, Scholars award in neurosci., McKnight Endowment Fund for Neurosci., 1990, Investigator award in neurosci., 1997, Soc. for Neurosci. Young Investigator award, 1993, Daniel H. Efron award, Am. Coll. Neuropsychopharmacology, 1998, Dargut and Milena Kemali Found. Internat. prize in neurosci., 2000, MERIT award, NIMH, 2001—11, Basic Neuroscience Rsch. award, Collegium Internationale Neuropsychopharmacologicum, 2002. Mem.: Am. Acad. Arts & Sciences, Inst. Medicine, Soc. for Neurosci. (program com.). Office: Stanford U Sch Medicine Psychiatry and Behavioral Scis MSLS P104 Mail Code 5485 Stanford CA 94305-5485 E-mail: malenka@stanford.edu.*

**MALERNEE, JAMES KENT, JR.,** financial consultant; b. Durango, Colo., June 15, 1947; s. James Kent and Norma Virginia (Calhoon) M.; m. Charlean Ann Born, Aug. 21, 1971 (div. May 1, 1992). BS in Engring., U. Tex., Austin, 1970; PhD in Bus. Adminstrn., U. Tex., 1977; MBA, So. Meth. U., 1972. Petroleum engr. Tex. R.R. Commn., 1970-71; instr. fin. U. Tex., 1973-75; lectr. fin. U. Tulsa, 1975-76; assoc. Mgmt. Analysis Ctr., Northbrook, Ill. 1977-80, v.p., 1980-83; sr. v.p. The MAC Group, 1987-89; also dir. MAC Rsch.; mng. dir. Cornerstone Rsch., N.Y.C., 1989-2000, pres., CEO, 2000—. Lectr. mgmt. Stanford GSB, 1983; leader seminars on mergers and acquisitions and corp. strategy; guest speaker in field of strategy; speaker on damages in securities litigation P.I.I and ARA; expert witness in securities and fin., bd. dirs. RealPage. Contbr. articles to profl. jours. Named one of Outstanding Young Men Am. U.S. Jaycees, 1977. Mem. Fin. Mgmt. Assn. (v.p. 1981-82, bd. dirs. 1983-85), Assn. Corp. Growth. Home: 208 E 51st St # 123 New York NY 10022-6557 Office: Cornerstone Rsch 599 Lexington Ave New York NY 10022-6030

**MALEY, PATRICIA ANN,** preservation planner; b. Wilmington, Del., Dec. 25, 1955; d. James Alfred and Frances Louise (Fenimore) M.; m. Scott A. Stone, Dec. 7, 1991 (div. June 1994). AA, Cecil C.C., 1973; BA, U. Del., 1975, MA, 1981. Cert. secondary tchr., Del. Analyst econ. devel. City of Wilmington, 1977-78, evaluation specialist, 1978-80, planner II mayor's office, 1980-86, cons. preservation, 1986-87; dir. Belle Meade Mansion, Nashville, 1987-88; dir. planning, devel. Children's Bur. of Del., Wilmington, 1988; prin. preservation planner Environ. Mgmt. Ctr., Brandywine Conservancy, Chadds Ford, Pa., 1988-92; planning cons., 1992-95; design review and preservation commn. coord. Wilmington Dept. Planning, 1995—; code enforcement constable, 1997—. Cons. cultural resources M.A.A.R. Inc., Newark, Del., 1987, ITC Cons., Wilmington, 1985-86; mem. Planned Approach to Comty. Health, Wilmington, task force for Wilmington Enterprise Comty. Health Benchmarking Project. Contbg. photographer America's City Halls, 1984; author numerous Nat. Register nominations, 1980-86; 88—. Pres., founder Haynes Park Civic Assn., Wilmington, 1977-80; photographer Biden U.S. Senate Campaign, New Castle County, Del., 1984; sec. parish coun. Our Lady Fatima Roman Cath. Ch., 1985-86, choir dir., 1983-87; mem. com. on design & renovation of worship spaces Diocese of Wilmington; also mem. Diocesan com. on music; bd. dirs. Del. Children's Theatre; music dir. St. Elizabeth Ann Seton parish Bear, Del., 1988—, mem. long range planning com./demographics. U. Del. fellow, 1976-77. Mem.: Del. Inst. for Planning and Design (bd. dirs. 2002—, v.p. 2004), New Castle County (Del.) Bd. Realtors, Am. Planning Assn. (exec. com. Del. chpt. 1997, elected state chpt. treas. 1997—2005, elected v.p. 2005, chpt./regional conf. organizer 2006), Am. Inst. Cert. Planners (cert. planner), Nat. Trust Hist. Preservation, Del. Hist. Soc., Nat. Pastoral Musicians Assn., Pi Sigma Alpha. Democrat. Avocations: photography, singing, piano, cello. Office: City of Wilmington Dept Planning 800 N French St Fl 7 Wilmington DE 19801-3590 Office Phone: 302-576-3113. Personal E-mail: trish1225@aol.com. Business E-mail: pmaley@ci.wilmington.de.us.

**MALFA, FRANCES,** lawyer; b. Bklyn., Dec. 16, 1969; BBA, Baruch Coll., 1991; JD, Touro Coll., 1994. Bar: NJ 1994, NY 1995, US Dist. Ct. Ea. Dist. NY, NY Dist. Ct. So. Dist. NY. Ptnr. Wilson, Elser, Moskowitz, Edelman & Dicker LLP, NYC. Office: Wilson Elser Moskowitz Edelman & Dicker LLP 23rd Fl 150 E 42nd St New York NY 10017-5639 Office Phone: 212-490-3000 ext. 2296. Office Fax: 212-490-3038. Business E-mail: malfaf@wemed.com.

**MALGIERI, LEWIS JOSHUA,** psychologist, consultant; b. Syracuse, NY, Nov. 10, 1943; s. Severino Vincenzino and Maria Francesca Malgieri; life ptnr. Kathleen Anne Stevens; children: Donald Wayne Stevens, Brian Michael Stevens, Scott Matthew Stevens. BA in Psychology, SUNY, Buffalo, 1968; MA in Psychology, Roosevelt U., 1974; PhD in Clin. Psychology (hon.), New Sch. For Social Rsch., 1991; postgrad., Greystone Park Psychiat. Hosp., 1995. Cert. in biofeedback NJ Biofeedback Assn., 1981, psychologist NJ State Bd. Psychol. Examiners, 1993, NY State Bd. Psychol. Examiners, 2001, hypnotherapist Wellness Inst. Seattle, 1995, lic. FCC amateur radio operator. Psychologist NY State Assn. for Retarded Citizens, Geneva, 1974—77, Rahway State Prison, NJ, 1985—93; prin. clin. psychologist Greystone Park Psychiat. Hosp., NJ, 1993—2001; chief psychologist Oswego Hosp., NY, 2001—. With U.S. Army, 1969—71, Viet Nam. Named Grad. Asst., Roosevelt U., 1969—74; scholar Syracuse U. 1962. Mem.: APA (Med. Corps. Psychologist Honor award 2002), Ctrl. NY Psychol. Assn. Roman Catholic. Home: 103 Pineledge Rd Camillus NY 13031 Office: Oswego Hospital 74 Bunner St Oswego NY 13126 Office Phone: 315-343-8162, 315-529-3758. Personal E-mail: fermi1001@aol.com.

**MALGIERI, NICK,** food service executive, educator, chef, writer; b. Newark, Sept. 30, 1947; s. Nufre and Antoinette (LoConte) M. BA in French, Seton Hall U., 1970; AOS in Culinary Arts, Culinary Inst., Hyde Park, N.Y., 1973. Pastrycook Seehotel Meierhof, Zurich, 1973-74, Hotel de Paris, Monte Carlo, 1974, Sporting Club, Monte Carlo, 1974-76, Hotel la Reserve, Beaulieu, France, 1974; pastry chef Windows on the World, NYC, 1976-79; asst. pastry chef Hotel Waldorf Astoria, NYC, 1979; chmn. baking dept. NY Restaurant Sch., NYC, 1979-83; dir. baking program Inst. Culinary Edn., NYC, 1984—; founder, owner Total Heaven Baking Co. Exec. chef Paine Webber; pastry chef Board Room; cons. Inhilco, Inc.; guest lectr. Smithsonian Instn.; Am. spokesperson for Switzerland tourism. Author: Nick Malgieri's Perfect Pastry, 1989, Great Italian Desserts, 1990, How to Bake, 1995 (James Beard Found. Cookbook award/Best Book on Baking/Desserts of 1995), Chocolate, 1998 (IACP/Julia Child cookbook award 1998, Salon Internat. du Livre award), Cookies Unlimited, 2000, Perfect Cakes, 2002 (100 Best Books of 2002 Pub. Weekly), A Baker's Tour: Nick Malgieri's Favorite Baking Recipes from Around the World, 2005, Perfect Light Desserts, 2006; contbr. articles and recipes to newspapers and profl. jours. Named One of 10 Best Pastry Chefs in USA, Pastry Art & Design Mag., 1998, 99. Mem. Internat. Assn. Culinary Profls. Found. (former trustee), Internat. Assn. Culinary Profls. (cert. culinary profl., chmn. certification 1989-91), Amicale Culinaire de Monaco, Societe Culinaire Philanthropique N.Y., Federazione Italiana dei Cuochi, James Beard Found. (coord. competitions 1991-95), N.Y. Assn. Cooking Tchrs. (former bd. dirs., Ann. honor 2000), Bakers Dozen East (founding mem.). Home: 277 W 10th St New York NY 10014-2562 Office: Inst of Culinary Education 50 W 23d St New York NY 10010

**MALHERBE, ABRAHAM JOHANNES,** retired religious studies educator, writer; b. Pretoria, South Africa, May 15, 1930; arrived in US, 1951; s. Abraham Johannes and Cornelia Aletta (Meyer) Malherbe; m. Phyllis Melton, May 28, 1953; children: Selina, Cornelia, Abraham Johannes VII. BA, Abilene Christian U., 1954; STB, Harvard U., 1957; student, U. Utrecht, The Netherlands, 1960-61; ThD, Harvard U., 1963; LLD (hon.), Pepperdine U., 1981; LHD (hon.), Centre Coll., 1990; STD (hon.), Providence Coll., 1994; DD (hon.), U. Pretoria, 2000. Minister Ch. of Christ, Lexington, Mass., 1956-63; asst. and assoc. prof. Abilene (Tex.) Christian U., 1963-67; vis. scholar Harvard Divinity Sch., Cambridge, Mass., 1967-68; assoc. prof. Abilene Christian U., 1968-69, Dartmouth Coll., Hanover, NH, 1969-70, Yale Divinity Sch., New Haven, 1970-77, prof., 1977-81, Buckingham prof., 1981-94, assoc. dean acad. affairs, 1987-89, prof. emeritus, 1994—. Guest prof. U. Pretoria, South Africa, 1989, 98, 2005. Author: (book) Social Aspects of Early Christianity, 1983, Moral Exhortation, 1986, Paul and the Thessalonians, 1987, Ancient Epistolary Theorists, 1988, Paul and the Popular Philosophers, 1989, The Letters to the Thessalonians, 2000; cons.: Anchor Bible Dictionary, 1992; inspiration for books Greeks, Romans and Christians: Essays in Honor of Abraham J Malherbe, 1990, Early Christianity and Classical Culture: Comparative Studies in Honor of Abraham J. Malherbe, 2003; mem. editl. bd.: Bible Rev., 1986—, Novum Testamentum, 1991—, Religious Studies Rev., 1980—2002, co-founder: Restoration Quar., 1957; contbr. articles to profl. jours. Recipient Teaching Award, Abilene Christian U., 1965, 1967, Outstanding Alumni Citation, 1996, NEH award, 1973; Abraham J. Malherbe scholarship developed in his honor, Yale U. Sch. Divinity, 1997—, Abraham J. Malherbe rsch. fellowship developed in his honor, U. Tex. Dept. Classics, Austin, 2002—, Abraham J. Malherbe doctoral fellowship, Yale U. Sch. Divinity, 2004—. Mem.: Studiorum Novi Testamenti Societas, Soc. Bibl. Lit., South African New Testament Soc. (hon.). Ch. Of Christ. Home: 71 Spring Garden St Hamden CT 06517-1913 Business E-Mail: abraham.malherbe@yale.edu.

**MALHI, GURBAX SINGH,** Canadian government official; b. India; m. Devinder Brar, Mar. 16, 1976; children: Gurinder, Harinder. BA in Polit. Sci., English, History, Punjab U., India; BA in Polit. Sci., English and History. Prior com. appts. Ho. of Commons Standing Com. for Govt. Ops., Standing Com. for Procedure and Ho. Affairs, tpl. Com. on Code of Conduct for MPs and Senators, Subcom. on Bus. of Supply, Pearson Airport Subcom., Limoousine Subcom.; assoc. mem. Com. for Fgn. Affairs; with Justice, Legal Affairs, Human Rights, Industry Coms.; mem. Scrutiny of Regulations Com.; chmn. Ho. of Commons Standing Com. for Libr. of Parliament; former pres. Bramalea-Gore-Malton Fed. Liberal Assn.; elected Ho. of Commons, 1993, re-elected, 1997, 2000, 2004, apptd. parliamentary sec. to min. of nat. revenue, 2005—; mem. Standing Com. on Human Resources Devel. Founder, chair Canada-South Asia Parliamentary Friendship Group. Active Toronto Real Estate Bd., Canadian Real Estate Assn.; former dir. Malton Neighborhood Svcs., 2004; appointed parliamentary sec. to min. of human resources. Office: 8500 Torbram Rd # 44 Brampton ON L6T 5C6 Canada Office Phone: 905-790-9211. E-mail: malhig@parl.gc.ca.

**MALHOTRA, ASHOK KUMAR,** philosophy educator; b. Ferozepur, India, 1940; came to the U.S., 1963, naturalized, 1977. s. Nihal Chand and Vidya (Wanti) M.; m. Nina Judith Finestone, Oct. 24, 1966 (dec.); children: Raj Kumar, Ravi Kumar. BA, U. Rajasthan, 1961, MA, 1963; PhD, U. Hawaii, 1969. Asst. prof. SUNY, Oneonta, 1967-70, assoc. prof., 1970-80, prof., 1980—, chmn. philosophy dept., 1975-80. Vis. prof. SUNY-Buffalo, summer 1970, Kurukshetra U. and Birla Inst., Pilani, India, spring 1980; grants reviewer NEH, 1978—; bd. dirs. SUNY Press editorial, 1989-93, dir. SUNY study abroad, program to India, 1980—; cons. TV series Kung Fu: The Legend Continues., 1992. Author: Sartre's Existentialism in Nausea and Being and Nothingness, 1978, Sartre's Existentialism as Literature and Philosophy, 1995, Pathways to Philosophy: A Multidisciplinary Approach, 1996, Culture and Self, 1997, Transcreation of the Bhagavad Gita, 1998, Instant Nirvana, 1999, An Introduction to Yoga Philosophy, 2001; TV appearances include ABC World News Now, NBC News, JAIN TV, Doordarshan TV, ZEE TV (India), Natraj TV (Holland), All India Radio, NPR. Founder Ninash Found. Oneonta; established Indo-Internat. Sch., Dundlod, Rajasthan, Mahapura, Rajasthan and Kuran, Gujarat, India; founder, chmn. Yoga and Meditation Soc., SUNY, Oneonta. Recipient Excellence in Tchg. award and Disting. Tchg. Prof. award United Univ. Profession: Friend of Ednl. award City of Oneonta, 1998, Disting. Alumni award East-West Ctr., 2000, Jewel of India award 2002, Bharat Excellence award Friendship Forum of India, 2002; East-West Ctr. fellow, 1963-65, 66-67; N.Y. State Dept. Edn. grantee, 1967-69, NEH grantee, 1979. Mem. Am. Philos. Assn., Soc. Asian

and Comparative Philosophy, Assn. Asian Studies, N.Y. State Asian Studies Soc., Internat. Phenomenol. Soc., Yoga and Meditation Soc. (founder, chair). Home: 17 Center St Oneonta NY 13820-1445 Office Phone: 607-436-3220. E-mail: malhotak@oneonta.edu.

**MALHOTRA, NARESH KUMAR,** marketing educator; arrived in U.S., 1975; s. Har Narian and Satya (Kakkar) M.; m. Veena Bahl, Aug. 13, 1980; children: Ruth Veena, Paul Naresh. *Dr. Malhotra converted from Hinduism to Christianity on March 19, 1978. He is a Bible preacher, teacher, and evangelist. He has preached the Gospel in 25 countries and has been blessed to see more than 132,000 people pray to accept the Lord Jesus Christ as their personal Savior. He frequently travels overseas to share his faith in the Lord Jesus Christ. He is a Deacon and member of the First Baptist Church, Atlanta. He has been married to Veena for over 25 years and they have two children, Ruth and Paul.* BTech with honors, Indian Inst. Tech., Bombay, 1971; MBA, I.I.M., Ahmedabad, India, 1973; MS, PhD, SUNY, Buffalo, 1979. Mgmt. cons. ASCI, Hyderabad, India, 1971-73; asst. prof. Ga. Tech. Inst., Atlanta, 1979—, assoc. prof. mgmt., coord. mktg.; 1982-87, 89—, prof., 1988, Regents' prof., 1992—. Organizer several nat. and internat. mktg. mgmt. confs. Author: Marketing Research: An Applied Orientation (N.Am., European, Internat., Australia and New Zealand, Indian, Spanish, Portuguese, Chinese, Russian, French, Japanese, Bahasa Indonesia, Japanese and Hungarian edits.), Basic Marketing Research: A Decision-Making Approach; contbr. articles to profl. jours. Lay preacher of the Gospel. Recipient Outstanding Mktg. Educator, Acad. of Mktg. Sci., 2005. Fellow Acad. Mktg. Sci. (disting. program chmn. 1984-85, 85-86, v.p. programs 1988-90, chmn. bd. 1990-92, pres. 1994-96, chmn. found. 1996-98, Top Rsch. Jour., Jour. Mktg. Rsch., Jour. Acad. Mktg. Sci., Jour. Healthcare Mktg., Internat. Mktg. Rev., Outstanding Mktg. Educator award 2005), Decision Scis. Inst. (track chmn. 1984-86); mem. Am. Mktg. Assn. (track chmn. 1983-84), Am. Statis. Assn. Republican. Baptist. Achievements include globally top ranked researcher based on four independent publication rankings. Avocations: reading, writing, outdoor activities. Home: 1956 Lenox Rd NE Atlanta GA 30306-3035 Office: Ga Tech Inst Coll Mgmt Atlanta GA 30332-0520 Office Phone: 404-894-4358. Business E-Mail: naresh.malhotra@mgt.gatech.edu.

**MALHOTRA, YOGESH,** computer scientist, educator, computer engineer; b. India, Jan. 11, 1964; B Engring. distinction, U. Delhi, India, 1984; MBA Phi Kappa Phi and Beta Gamma Sigma honors, U. Nev., Las Vegas, 1993; PhD Bus. Adminstrn./Info. Sys. and Knowledge Mgmt. with honors, U. Pitts., 1998. Cert. computing profl., info. sys. security profl.; chartered engr. Exec. engr. Suzuki Maruti Udyog Ltd., Gurgaon, India, 1984—87; sys. analyst Tata Unisys Ltd., New Delhi, 1987—89; sr. sys. analyst JK Technosoft, Neepz, India, 1989; sr. cons. info. sys. Bank Am., Nev., 1990—91; prin. founder, knowledge architect @BRINT.COM, The Biztech Network, Pitts., 1994—98; founder, chmn., chief knowledge officer Brint.com L.L.C., 1998—2001; founding chmn., chief knowledge architect BRINT Inst. LLC, 2001—, Coun. ptnr., Inter-Agency Benchmarking & Best Practices Coun. US Fed. Govt., 1995—99; advisory com. Intel, Br. Telecom, Ziff Davis, Hewlett Packard, Arthur Andersen, South Korean, Vision Korea Nat. Campaign, Govt. of Netherlands, U.S. Fed. Govt, and, Govt. of Mex., 1995—2001, NSF, 2003—05, UN, Philips, Netherlands, 1996—; founder, editor-in-chief, pub. WWW Virtual Libr. on Knowledge Mgmt., 1996—2001; founder, editor-in-chief The Knowledge Mgmt. Think Tank, 1997—2001; plenary keynote presenter, spkr. Conf. Bd., Maeil Bus. TV Network and Bus. Newspaper Vision Korea Campaign (South Korea), Govt. of Mex., Silicon Valley based tech. entrepreneurs global orgn., KMWorld, others, 1998—2001; cons., advisor Govt. of Netherlands, 1998; internat. advisory bd. Knowledge Mgmt. Jour., London, 1998—; disting. faculty, advisory bd. mem. BrainTrust, San Francisco, 1998; knowledge mgmt. spl. issues editor Expert Sys. with Applications Jour. (Elsevier Science), Info. Strategy: The Executive's Jour. (CRC Press), Info. Resources Mgmt. Jour. (IRMA), Jour. of Global Info. Mgmt. (IRMA), 1998—2001; assoc. editor e-Svc. Jour. (Ind. U. Press), Bloomington, 1999—; founding mem., contbg. editor Ziff Davis Internet Commerce Standard, 1999—2000; mem. adv. bd., Most Admired Knowledge Leaders study Teleos, London, 2000; assoc. editor Info. Resources Mgmt. Jour., Hershey, Pa., 2001—03; conf. bd. Intel Corp., 2001; mem. adv. bd. on leading new economy workplaces conf. Conf. Bd., N.Y.C., 2001; cons., advisor Intel Corp., 2002, NSF, 2002, UN, 2003; cons., advisor intellectual property com. Syracuse U., 2002; founder The Knowledge Mgmt. Network, 2002—; editl. adv. bd. The Learning Orgn., 2004—05; bd. dir. Commonwealth Ctr. e-Governance, India; scif./editl. com. World Coun. of Nuc. Workers, France, 2004—; asst. prof. mgmt. infor. and decision Syracuse U., 2001—; faculty exec. edn. program Carnegie Mellon U., 1998, Northwestern U., Kellogg Grad. Sch. Mgmt., 2000; spkr. in field. Lead author and editor: Knowledge Management and Virtual Organizations, 2000 (5-Star award for Strategy Web Site for Managers by Accreditation Bd. Anbar Electronic Intelligence (UK), 1999); author: Knowledge Management and Business Model Innovation, 2001 (Computerworld 'Best Web Site' Award, 1997), BRINT.com e-learning knowledge portals; editor: (spl. issue on knowledge mgmt.) Expert Sys. with Applications Jour. (Top Nominee, Industry.Net Online Achievement Awards, 1996), Info. Strategy: The Executive's Jour. 2000 (Acad. Mgmt. 'Best Reviewer Award', 1997), Jour. of Global Info. Mgmt., 2000, Info. Resources Mgmt. Jour., 2000; contbr. refereed and invited articles and papers to profl. jours., articles refereed conf. proceedings; reviewer: info. tech. publs. and e-commerce and knowledge mgmt. books. Expert interviews analyses featured in Bus. Week, Wall St. Jour., Forbes, Fortune, Inc., CIO Mag., Info. Week, Computerworld, etc. BRINT Inst., Syracuse, NY, 1998—2006, As thought leader, advice and opinion quoted in strategy and policy documents of pre-eminent worldwide govts., corp., and instns. Recipient Top Rank cert., Am. Inst. Banking, Kaizen Quality Improvement award, Japanese Car Mfg. Co., 1984 -87, Japanese Lang. award, Largest car mfr. India, Gurgaon, 1984—87, Online Achievement award, Industry.Net, 1996, Top Two Practitioner Experts in Knowledge Mgmt., ISWorld Survey, 2000, CNET Networks Corp. Computing award, 2002; grantee, UN, 2003, SAP Univ. Alliance, 2003, Kaufman Found., 2003; Rsch. Grant, Inst. for Indsl. Competitiveness, U. Pitts., 1996, Doctoral Consortium Fellow, Acad. Mgmt., 1997, Am. Conf. Info. Sys., 1997. Mem.: Internat. Info. Sys. Security Cert. Consortium (cert.), Info. Sys. Security Assn., Inst. Ops. Rsch and Mgmt. Sci., Assn. Info. Sys., Assn. Computing Machinery, Acad. Mgmt., Inst. Cert. Computing Profls. (Cert. 1993-current), Inst. Engrs. (life Chartered Engr. 1987-current), Phi Kappa Phi, Beta Gamma Sigma. Avocations: information systems, e-business, knowledge management. Office: School of Management Syracuse University Syracuse NY 13244 Office Phone: 315-443-3571. E-mail: yogesh@syr.edu.

**MALI, PAUL,** publisher, retired management educator; b. Hartford, Conn., July 6, 1926; m. Mary S. Mali; children: Faith, Dawn. BS in Engring., U. Conn., 1953, MS, 1962, PhD in Mgmt. and Engring., 1967; postgrad., Cornell U., 1964. Cert. mgmt. cons. Inst. Mgmt. Cons. Elec. engr. Gen. Dynamics, Groton, Conn., 1953—67, dir., 1961—67; prof. mgmt. Entrepreneurial, New London, Conn., 1961—67. U. Hartford, Conn., 1967—94; minister/co-pastor Bible Student ch., New London, Conn., 1994—; prof. Swiss Inst. Tech., Hebrew U.; pub. Horizon Publs.; mentor cons. to IBM, Westinghouse, U.S. Steel, United Tech., Aetna, Hanes, Alcan Aluminum, Combustion Engring. Founding fellow Acad. Disting. Engrs. and Hall of Fame of U. Conn. Author: various profl. books, including Writing and Word Processing for Scientists and Engineers, 1981, MBO Updated, 1986, (ministerial books) Magnetic Amplifiers, 1960, The Bible as a Rising Civilization, 1998, Ten Bad Mistakes About God, 2000, Terrorism and the Permission of Evil, 2002, Biblical View on Human Cloning, others, 2002, Spirituality: The Roadmap to Heaven. Pres. Good Samaritan Fund, New London, Conn., 1994—; bd. dirs. 12 state cmty. colls., Conn., 1981—88. Mem.: Am. Mgmt. Assn., Tau Beta Pi, Beta Gamma Sigma, Phi Delta Kappa, Eta Kappa Nu. E-mail: malipnm@aol.com.

**MALICAY, MANUEL ALABAN,** physician; b. Zamboonga City, The Philippines, Aug. 13, 1947; arrived in US, 1973; s. Bernardino Macay Agan and Juliana (Alaban) Malicay; m. Lourdes V. Manzano, Jan. 12, 1974; children: Mark, Marlo, Brian, Michael, Margaret. BS, Far Eastern U., Manila, 1967, MD, 1972. Rsch. and tchg. fellow Far Eastern U., Manila, 1972-73;

intern St. Francis Hosp., Evanston, Ill., 1973-74; resident in internal medicine Vets. Hosp., Hines, Ill., 1974-76; pvt. practice Bolingbrook, Ill., 1976—; physician Hinsdale (Ill.) Hosp., 1976-97, 1976—, Good Samaritan Hosp., Downers Grove, Ill., 1977—, vice chmn. dept. medicine, 1998—2001, chmn. Clin. Quality Coun., 1999-2001; asst. prof. in medicine Rush Med. Coll., Chgo., 2004—. Chmn continuing med educ comt IPMS, 1998—; prin. clin. investigator Dynacirc Assessment Trial Analysis, 1990, The Safety and Efficacy of Cardizem SR as anti-anginal medication, 1991, Comparative Outcome Study of Metformin vs. conventional approach, 1996, Lantus GOAL AIC Clin. Trials, 2003, REACH Registry, 2004—; spkr., bureau mem. Novartis Pharm. Corp., 2003, Abbott Pharm. Editor: IPMS Today, 1989—91. Trustee Far Ea. U. Sch. Med. Alumni Found., 1993—2001, v.p., 2002—04; pres. Class of 1972 Far Ea. U. Dr. N. Reyes Med. Alumni Found.; chmn. continuing med. edn. Far Ea. U. DNR Sch. Med. Alumni Found., 2005—; co-chmn. physician adv. bd. Nat. Rep. Congl. Com., 2002—. Named Most Outstanding Silver Jubilarian, Far Eastern U. Dr N Reyes Med. Alumni Found., 1997, Physician of Yr., Nat. Rep. Congl. Com., 2003. Fellow: ACP; mem.: AMA, Far Eastern U. Med. Alumni Assn. Ill. (pres. 1991—93, co-chair conv. ann. reunion and sci. seminar 1993, Oustanding Alumnus 1995), Assn. Philippine Physicians Am. (co-chair 25th ann. conv. and sci. seminar 1996, gov. 1996—2001), Ill. Med. Soc. (del. 1990—, coun. on econs. com. 2002—), DuPage County Med. Soc. (bd. dirs. 1986—), Ill. Philippine Med. Soc. (seminar program dir. 1994, pres. 1994—96, chmn CME comt 1998—, program dir. Primary Care Update 1999, 2001, Disting Leadership Award 1996, Disting Physician Award Organized Med 1999, Disting Serv Award 2001). Avocations: tennis, dance. Home: 2 S 676th Ave Vendome Oak Brook IL 60521 Office: 402 W Boughton Rd Bolingbrook IL 60440-1872 also: 47 6th Ave La Grange IL 60525-2499 Office Phone: 630-759-3782. Personal E-mail: mmalicaymd@hotmail.com.

**MALICK, TERRENCE (DAVID WHITNEY II),** film director; b. Waco, Tex., Nov. 30, 1943; m. Jill Jakes (div. 1978); m. Michele Malick, 1985 (div. 1998); m. Alexandra Wallace, 1998. Student, Harvard U., Oxford U.; MFA, Am. Film Inst. Dir., prodr., writer (films) Badlands, 1973 (Golden Seashell award 1974); dir., writer, Lanton Mills, 1969, Days of Heaven, 1978 (Best Dir. award Cannes Film Festival 1979, nominee Golden Globe award 1979, N.Y. Film Critics Circle award 1978), The Thin Red Line, 1998 (Acad. award nomination for Best Dir., Golden Berlin Bear award 1999, Chgo. Film Critics Assn. award 1999, Golden Satellite award, 1999), The New World, 2005; prodr. (films) Endurance, 1999, The Endurance, Shackleton's Legendary Antartic Expedition, 2000, Happy Times, 2001, The Beautiful Country, 2004, Undertow, 2004; writer (films) Drive, He Said, 1971, Deadhead Miles, 1972, Pocket Money, 1972, The Gravy Train, 1974, Bear's Kiss, 2002 Office: Creative Artists Agy 9830 Wilshire Blvd Beverly Hills CA 90212*

**MALIFRANDO, FRANK,** healthcare executive, theater producer, consultant, film producer, international real estate investor, publisher; b. N.Y.C., Feb. 16, 1954; s. Frank Malifrando and Michele Michelin Kuhn. BS, Southwest U., L.A., 1986, MS in Health Scis., 2004. Cert. media comm. Boston U. 1991. CEO Spring Fed Corp., N.Y.C., 1982—88, Kalanakila Prodns., Hawaii, 1985—91, Thunder Key Inc., 1982—89; mktg. dir. Mus. Edits. West, L.A., 1988—91; dir. of devel. No. Calif. Svc. League, 1997—99; exec. dir. Keith Haring AIDS Interfaith Chapel, 1994—2000, Grace Cathedral, San Francisco; dir. devel. Life Lines Ministries, San Francisco, 1997—98; dir. of career svcs. Computer Learning Ctr., 1999—2001; project dir., designer Career Acceleration Mentor Program, 2000—01; exec. dir. fundraising arm Seton Med. Ctr., Seton Med. Ctr. Coastside, Dau. Charity Healthcare Sys., Seton Health Svcs. Found., Daly City, Calif., 2001—04, Marin Gen. Hosp., Novato Cmty. Hosp., Marin Cmty. Health Found., San Rafael, Calif., 2004—; owner Restaurant Spring Fed., NYC; personal mgr. of photographer Kenn Duncan. Dir. of programs Alma DelFina Group, San Francisco, 1995—2000; CEO Artist Alliance Against AIDS, 1996; bd. dirs. Bethany Ctr. Prodr.; Red Shoes, Kenn Duncan, 1984, (fine art reproductions) Hula Kahiko Series, 1986 (Pele Award of Excellence), Dance Cos., 1984 (Nat. Ann. Print award and Comm. Arts award, 1984); prodr., dir.: (documentaries) Poets and Painters, A Night at the Palace, 1994; Willie by Madaglia Cruz, starring Sean San Jose, 1996; In Conversation with David Henry Hwong, 1996; Awakening New Futures (behind bars), 1997; The making of an event: Charity Ball-150 Years for Daughters of Charity Seton Medical Center, 2001. Exec. dir., bd. mem. Marin Cmty. Health Found.; bd. dirs. Seton Health Svcs. Found., Bethany Ctr.; mem. adv. bd. Philanthropy Leadership Coun., Washington. Recipient Radiant Baby Gold Pin, Keith Haring Found., 1995, Canon Pastor award, Grace Cathedral, San Francisco, 1995, Pele award for excellence, Advertising Assn. of Hawaii, 1984, Cert. of Design Excellence, Print's Regional Design Annual, 1986, Black and White award, Assn. Honolulu Artist, 1987, Resolution recognition, State of Calif., 2003. Mem.: Dir.'s Coun. Devel.-Sutter Health, San Francisco C. of C., Seniors RSVP/San Francisco (adv. bd.), Brisbane C. of C., Half Moon Bay C. of C., Daly City C. of C. Achievements include creator and founder of the AIDS Interfaith Chapel in Grace Cathedral, San Francisco. Office: Marin Cmty Health Found Box 8010 San Rafael CA 94012-8080 Address: 4000 Civic Ctr Dr Ste 150 San Rafael CA 94903 Office Phone: 415-492-4735. E-mail: malifrf@sutterhealth.org.

**MALIK, HAFEEZ,** political science professor; b. Lahore, Pakistan, Mar. 17, 1930; m. Lynda P. Malik; children: Cyrus, Dean. BA, Government Coll., Lahore, Pakistan, 1949; grad. diploma in journalism, U. Punjab, Lahore, 1952; MS in Journalism, Syracuse U., 1955, MA in Polit. Sci., 1957, PhD in Polit. Sci., 1961. Asst. prof. polit. sci. Villanova (Pa.) U., 1961-63, assoc. prof., 1963-67, prof.—. Pub. rels. officer City of Lahore, 1950—53; White House corr. Nawa-i-Waqt, 1958—61, The Shabaz, 1958—61; mem. grad. com. dept. polit. sci. Villanova U., 1961—67, chmn., 1967—78; vis. prof. Fgn. Svc. Inst., Washington, 1961—63, Washington, 1966—68, Washington, 1970—87, Syracuse U., 1964, 65, Drexel U., Phila., 1968—69; mem. grad. coun. com. rsch. and publs., 1969—70; mem. grad. adv. com. liberal arts and social studies, 1964—67; mem. faculty libr. com., 1964—67; mem. undergraduate com. polit. sci., 1980—; mem. rank and tenure com., 1991—92; pres. Am. Inst. Pakistan Studies, 1972—88, Pakistan Am. Found., 1972—; exec. dir. Am. Coun. Study Islamic Scis., 1983—; cons. Soviet Acad. Scis., 1979, Dept. Def., 1980, USIA, 1986; presenter in field. News editor: Daily Magharabi Pakistan, 1948—50, tech. editor: Meteorol. and Geoastrophysical Abstracts, Am. Meteorol. Soc., 1960—63; author: Muslim Nationalism in India and Pakistan, 1963, Sir Sayyid Ahmad Khan's History of the Bijnore Rebellion, 1972; rev. edit., 1980, Sir Sayyid Ahmad Khan and Muslim Modernization in India and Pakistan, 1980, Political Profile of Sir Sayyid Ahmad Khan: A Documentary Record, 1982, Sir Sayyid Ahmad Khan's Educational Philosophy: International Security in Southwest, 1984, Domestic Determinants of Soviet Foreign Policy Towards South Asia and the Middle East, 1990, Dilemmas of National Security and Cooperation in India and Pakistan, 1993, Soviet-Pakistan Relations and Post-Soviet Dynamics, 1996, Central Asia: Its Strategic Importance and Future Prospects, 1994, U.S., Russia, China in the New World Order, 1996; editor: Iqbal: Poet-Philosopher of Pakistan, 1971, rev. edit., 1982, Soviet-American Relations with Pakistan, Iran, and Afghanistan, 1987, Jour. South Asian and Middle Eastern Studies, 1977—; mem. editl. adv. bd. Islam and the Modern Age, Islam Awr Aser-i Jadid, 1974—79; contbr. articles to profl. jours., encyclopedias, chapters to books. Grantee, Office Health, Edn. Welfare, 1974, 1978, Assn. Pakistan and Indic-Islamic Studies/Pakistan Am. Found., 1982. Office: Villanova U 416-421 SAC 800 E Lancaster Ave Villanova PA 19085-1603 Business E-Mail: hafeez.malik@villanova.edu.

**MALIK, OM,** former venture capitalist, blog website company executive, journalist; Honors Degree in Chemistry, St. Stephens' Coll., New Delhi, 1986. Position with Quick Nikkei News; sr. editor, founding mem. Forbes-.com, 1999; with Hambrecht & Quist Asia Pacific, 1999—2000; sr. writer Red Herring, 2000; co-founder Masala.com; sr. writer Business 2.0, San Francisco, 2003—06; founder Giga Omni Media, Inc., San Francisco, 2006—; exec. editor GigaOm.com, 2006—. Guest appearances Business Week TV,

BBC TV and Radio, CNNfn, CNBC and TechTV; contbr. articles to publications, including Economic Times, The Week, Wall Street Journal, Brandweek, Crains, NY Business; author: Broadbandits: Inside the $750 Billion Telecom Heist, 2003.*

**MALIK, OM PARKASH,** electrical engineering educator, researcher; b. Sargodha, Punjab, India, Apr. 20, 1932; arrived in Can., 1966; s. Arjan Dass and Kesar Bai (Ahuja) M.; m. Margareta Fagerstrom, Dec. 22, 1968; children: Ola Parkash, Mira, Maya. Nat. Diploma in Elec. Engring., Delhi Poly., India, 1952; M in Engring., Roorkee U., India, 1962; PhD, London U., 1965; D.I.C., Imperial Coll., London, 1966. Registered profl. engr., Ont., Alta. Asst. engr. Punjab State Elec. Bd., 1953-61, asst. to chief engr., 1957-59; rsch. engr. English Elec. Co., England, 1965-66; asst. prof. U. Windsor, Ont., Canada, 1966-68; assoc. prof. U. Calgary, Alta., Canada, 1968-74, prof. Alta., 1974-97, faculty prof. Alta., 1997—2000, assoc. dean student affairs, faculty engring. Alta., 1995-98, assoc. acad. dean faculty engring. Alta., 1979-90, acting dean Alta., 1981, prof. emeritus Alta., 1997—. Cons. prof. Huazhong U. Sci. and Tech., Wuhan, People's Republic China, 1996—; chief judge Can. Wide Sci. Fair, 2003. Assoc. editor Can. Elec. and Computer Engring. Jour., 1988-97, mng. editor, 1998-2003; contbr. 400 articles to profl. jours. Indsl. tng. scholar Govt. India, 1952-53, sr. indsl. tng. scholar Confedn. Brit. Industries, 1959-60; recipient Rsch. Excellence award Elec. and Computer Engring. Dept. U. Calgary, 1996, Can. Pacific Rwy. engring. medal Engring. Inst. Can., 1997, Disting. Lifetime Leadership award Faculty Engring. U. Calgary, 2001, Alberta Ingenuity Fund Rsch. Excellence award, 2002. Fellow IEEE (life, chmn. life mems. com. 2004-05, chmn. Western Can. coun. 1983-84, chmn. student activities Can. region 1979-82, chmn. life mems. com., mem. Found., Centennial medal 1984, Merit award 1986, Third Millennium medal 2000, A.G.L. McNaughton award 2001), Inst. Elec. Engrs., Can. Acad. Engring., World Innovation Found.; mem. IEEE Power Engring. Soc. (vice chair machine theory com. 2006—, machine theory subcom. 1979-2004, excitation sys. subcom. 1988—, chmn. 2004—, sys. dynamic performance com. 1988—, energy devel. and power generation com. 1990—, electric machinery com. 2002—, vice chmn. 2006—), Assn. Profl. Engrs., Geologists and Geophysicists Alta. (Vol. Svc. award 1990, Alta. Ingenuity Rsch. Excellence award), Assn. Profl. Engrs. Ont., Am. Soc. Engring. Edn., Can. Elec. Assn. (assoc., controls com 1977-92, chmn. digital control com. 1977-85, chmn. edn. com. 1983-85, mem. expert sys. com. 1989-94), Confederacion Panamericana de Ingenieria Mecanica, Electica y Ramas Afines (v.p. 1987-00, bd. dirs. region I, 1991-93), U. Calgary Retired Assn. (v.p. 2002-03, pres. 2003-04), Internat. Fed. Automatic Control (chmn. power plants and power sys. control comm. 2002-). Hindu. Home: 4 6841 Coach Hill Rd SW Calgary AB Canada T3H 3T9 Office: U Calgary Dept Elec & Computer Engring 2500 University Dr NW Calgary AB Canada T2N 1N4 Office Phone: 403-220-6178. Personal E-mail: maliko@ucalgary.ca.

**MALIK, WAHEED AHMAD,** cardiologist; s. Gohar Sultana Malik; m. Samina Ahmed Malik, Oct. 24, 1996; children: Danial Ahmed, Harris Ahmed, Waleed Ahmed. MB & BChir, Army Med. Coll., Rawalpindi, Pakistan, 1986; MD, Ednl. Commn. Fgn. Med. Grads., 1993. Diplomate Am. Bd. Internal Medicine, 2001, Am. Bd. Nuc. Cardiology, 2002. Nuc. cardiologist and dir. Advanced Cardiology Ctr., Rockville, Md., 2002—. Mem.: Am. Soc. Nuc. Cardiology. Office: Advanced Cardiology Center 11119 Rockville Pike Ste 100 Rockville MD 20852 Office Phone: 301-816-9000. Home Fax: 301-816-8616; Office Fax: 301-816-8616. Personal E-mail: waheed5@verizon.net.

**MALIN, HAROLD MARTIN, JR.,** sexologist, educator; b. Colorado Springs, Aug. 26, 1945; s. Harold M. and Harriett Anne (Heyer) M.; m. Janice Karen Atkins. BA in Chemistry and Biology, Cornell Coll., 1967; postgrad., U. Iowa Med. Sch., 1968; PhD in Human Sexuality, Inst. for Advanced Study of Human Sexuality, 1986; postgrad. med. sch., Johns Hopkins U., 1986-87; MA in Psychology/Counseling, Western Inst. for Social Rsch., 1996. Diplomate Am. Coll. Sexologists. Clin. sexologist Sexology Assocs., Inc., 1985-90; cons. clin. sexologist Johns Hopkins Hosp. Sexual Disorders Clinic Johns Hopkins U. Med. Sch., 1987-89, mgr. Johns Hopkins Hosp. Sexual Disorders Clinic, 1989-91, cons. clin. sexologist Johns Hopkins Hosp. Sexual Disorders Clinic, 1991-92, instr. clin. sexology dept. psychiatry and behavioral scis., 1992-95; assoc. prof. clin. sexology, chair clin. studies dept. Inst. for Advanced Study of Human Sexuality, 1992-96; MET intern Child and Family Inst., Sacramento, 1996-97; pres., chmn. Bd. Skolos, 1997—; pres. Planetsex, 1997—. Cons. clin. sexologist, corp. sec. Nat. Ctr. for Study and Treatment of Pathol. Gambling, Balt., 1986-95; cons. clin. sexologist Nat. Inst. for Study, Prevention and Treatment of Sexual Trauma, Balt., 1991-99, Drug and Alcohol Prevention Program, Inc., Ocean City, Md., 1991-95; cons. clin. sexologist for program devel. Nat. Ctr. on Instns. and Alternatives, Alexandria, Va. and Balt., 1991-94; sr. case mgmt. supr. Planned Parenthood Shasta-Diablo, Fairfield, Calif., 1994-96. Cons. editor Jour. of Sex and Marital Therapy; peer reviewer Jour. Sex Rsch.; contbr. articles to profl. jours. Mem. Solano County Adolescent Resource Network, Solano County Ryan White Consortium, Solano County Cmty. Health Outreach Sys., Solano Cmty. Svcs. Task Force. Mem. Am. Profl. Soc. on the Abuse of Children, Calif. Assn. Marriage and Family Therapists, Am. Bd. Sexology (bd. clin. examiners, diplomate, cert. sex therapist, cert. clin. supr., cert. sex rschr.), Assn. Sexologists, Am. Acad. Clin. Sexologists (founding, life, clin. fellow), Soc. for Sci. Study of Sexuality, World Assn. for Sexology, Harry Benjamin Internat. Gender Dysphoria Assn., Inst. for Advanced Study of Sexuality Alumni Assn. Inc. (pres., bd. dirs. 1994-98), Adolescent Perpetrators Network, Intersex Soc. of N.Am. (bd. dirs.), Calif. Coalition on Sexual Offending (bd. dirs., pres. bay area network). E-mail: mmalin@skolos.org.

**MALIN, HOWARD GERALD,** podiatrist; b. Providence, Dec. 2, 1941; s. Leon Nathan and Rena Rose (Shapiro) M. AB, U. R.I., 1964; MA, Brigham Young U., 1969; BSc, Calif. Coll. Podiatric Medicine, 1969, DPM, 1972; MSC, Pepperdine U., 1978; MD (hon.), Internat. U. Sch. Medicine, Winnipeg, Man., Can., 2001. Diplomate Am. Bd. Podiatric Pub. Health, Am. Bd. Podiatric Orthopedics, Am. Acad. of Wound Care Mgmt. Extern in podiatry VA Med. Ctr., Wadsworth, Kans., 1971-72, Marine Corps Res. Dept., San Diego, 1972; resident in podiatric medicine and surgery N.Y. Coll. Podiatric-Medicine, N.Y.C., 1972-73; resident in podiatric surgery, instr. in podiatric surgery N.Y. Coll. Podiatric Medicine, N.Y.C., 1973-74; pvt. practitioner in podiatric medicine and surgery Bklyn., 1974-77; mem. staff Prospect Hosp., Bronx, NY, 1974-77; chief podiatry service, mem. staff, cons. sports medicine David Grant U.S. Air Force Med. Ctr., Travis AFB, Calif., 1977-80; chief podiatric sect., mem. staff VA Med. Ctr., Martinsburg, W.Va., 1980—. Instr. ednl. devel. program VA Med. Ctr., Martinsburg, W.Va., 1980—; clin. prof. med. sci. Alderson-Broaddus Coll., U. Osteopathic Medicine and Health Scis.; adj. faculty Barry U. Sch. Podiatric Medicine; adj. clin. prof. Ohio Coll. Podiatric Medicine, dir. extern program; clin. asst. prof. surgery W.Va. U. Sch. Medicine. Mem. editl. rev. bd. Jour. Contemporary Podiatric Physician, 1991—. Lt. Col. USAFR, ret. Fellow Am. Soc. Podiatric Dermatology (archivist), Am. Coll. Foot Orthopedics (emeritus), Am. Coll. Podiatric Physicians, Am. Coll. Podiatric Radiology (archivist, past pres.), Am. Soc. Podiatric Medicine (asst. exec. dir. emeritus, past pres., archivist), Am. Podiatric Med. Writers Assn. (pres., archivist, historian), Am. Profl. Wound Care Assn., Royal Soc. Health, Royal Soc. Medicine, Coll. Cert. Wound Specialists; mem. Am. Acad. Podiatric Sports Medicine (assoc.), Assn. Mil. Surgeons U.S. (life), Am. Coll. Podiatric Surgery (assoc.), Phi Kappa Theta, Phi Kappa Psi. Home and Office: 2250 Bear Den Rd Ste 210 Frederick MD 21701-9408 Office Phone: 304-263-0811 3770.

**MALIN, IRVING,** language educator, critic; b. NYC, Mar. 18, 1934; s. Morris and Bertha (Silverman) M.; m. Ruth Lief, Dec. 18, 1955; 1 child, Mark. BA, Queens Coll., 1955; PhD, Stanford U., 1958. Acting instr. English Stanford U., 1955-58; instr. Ind. U., 1958-60; from instr. to prof. CCNY, 1960-72, prof., 1972—. Cons. Jewish Publ. Soc., 1964, Am. Quar., 1964, NEH, 1972, 79, 80, 81, 82, B'nai B'rith, 1974-75, Yaddo, 1975-77, Jewish Book Coun., 1976, 79, PEN, 1978-82, Princeton U. Press, 1979, Fairleigh Dickinson Press, 1980, Wayne State U. Press, 1980, Internat. Coun. Exch. of Scholars, 1980-81, Duke U. Press, 1981, Jewish Daily Forward, 1981, U.

Pitts. Press, 1981, Papers on Lang. and Lit., 1981, U. Ga. Press, 1983, UMI Rsch., 1989, Gordian Press, 1990, Ctr. for Study of Higher Edn., 1990, Mosiac, 1991, MacArthur Found., 1996, U. of S.C. Press, 1998, Purdue U. Press, Lafayette, Ind., 1999; adv. bd. James Purdy Soc.; cons. U. Tex.2005 Author: William Faulkner: An Interpretation, 1957, New American Gothic, 1962, Jews and Americans, 1965, Saul Bellow's Fiction, 1969, Nathanael West's Novels, 1972, Isaac Bashevis Singer, 1972; co-editor: Breakthrough: A Treasury of Contemporary American Jewish Literature, 1964, William Styron's The Confessions of Nat Turner: A Critical Handbook, 1970, The Achievement of William Styron, 1975, William Goyen, 1997, Into the Tunnel, 1998, Garrett's Elizabethan Trilogy, 1998; editor: Psychoanalysis and American Fiction, 1965, Saul Bellow and the Critics, 1967, Truman Capote's in Cold Blood: A Critical Handbook, 1968, Critical Views of Isaac Bashevis Singer, 1969, Contemporary American-Jewish Literature: Critical Essays, 1973, Conrad Aiken's Prose, 1982; co-editor: Underwords: Perspectives on Don DeLillo's Underworld, 2002; adv. editor: Studies in American Jewish Literature, Jour. Modern Literature, Review of Contemporary Fiction, Saul Bellow Jour., 20th Century Literature; Hollins Critic, So. Quar.; co-editor Paul Bowles, 1986, Spl. Issue of 20th Century Lit., James Dickey Spl. Issue of S.C. Rev., 1994, Pynchon and Mason and Dixon, 2000, So. Novelists on Stage and Screen So. Quar., 1995, James Dickey's Fiction Spl. Tex. Rev., 1996, Leslie Fiedler and American Culture, 1999, Torpid Smoke: The Stories of Vladimir Nabokov, 2000. Fellow Yaddo, 1963, Nat. Found. for Jewish Culture, 1963-64, Huntington Libr., 1978. Mem. MLA, AAUP, Am. Studies Assn., Am. Jewish Hist. Soc., Melville Soc., Authors League Am., Soc. Study of So. Lit., Poe Studies Assn., English Inst., Nathaniel Hawthorne Soc., N.Y. Acad. Scis., Poetry Soc. Am., Popular Culture Assn., Nat. Book Critics Circle, Sherwood Anderson Soc., Internat. Assn. Univ. Prof. English, Kafka Soc., English-Speaking Union, Multi-Ethnic Lit. U.S. Soc., Hastings Ctr., Am. Jewish Congress, Assoc. Writing Programs, Nat. Coun. Tchrs. of English, Vladimir Nabokov Soc., Phi Beta Kappa. Jewish. Home: 96-13 68th Ave Forest Hills NY 11375-5039 Office: CCNY Dept English New York NY 10031

**MALIN, ROBERT ABERNETHY,** investment company executive; b. Mt. Vernon, NY, Dec. 13, 1931; s. Patrick Murphy and Caroline Cooper (Biddle) M.; m. Gail Lassiter, Nov. 5, 1960; children: Alison Campbell, Robert Lassiter. AB, Dartmouth Coll., 1953, MBA, 1954. Asst. to comptr. Biddle Purchasing Co., N.Y.C., 1958-59; with Blyth & Co., Inc., N.Y.C., 1960-71, v.p., 1965-71, dir., 1968-71; sr. v.p., mem. exec. com., 1971-72; sr. v.p. corp. fin. Reynolds Securities Inc., N.Y.C., 1972-74, dir., 1973-74; mng. dir. First Boston Corp., N.Y.C., 1974-90; gen. ptnr. Tiedemann Investment Group, N.Y.C., 1991-96; mng. dir. SeaBridge Investment Advisors, Summit, NJ, 1997—. Mem. adv. coun. Fin. Acctg. Stds. Bd., 1973-78. Served as lt. (j.g.) USNR, 1954-57. Mem.: Securities Industry Assn. (acctg. com.), Investment Bankers Assn. Am., The Moorings Club, Morris County Club, Beacon Hill Club. Republican. Office: SeaBridge Investment Advisors 450 Springfield Ave Ste 301 Summit NJ 07901-2610 Office Phone: 908-273-5763. Personal E-mail: malinrobta@aol.com. Business E-Mail: bobmalin@seabridge.com.

**MALIN, STUART,** educator; s. Murray H. and Dorothy Malin; m. Patricia Anne Pompano, Nov. 8, 1970; 1 child, John David. MEd, Coll. NJ, Trenton, 1977. Instr. Plainfield Bd. Edn., NJ, 1968—99; cons. Stevens Inst. Tech., Hoboken, NJ, 1999—2001; adj. prof. Northampton CC, Tannersville, Pa., 2002—. Mem., pres. Bd. Edn. North Plainfield, NJ, 1993—2002; mem. Somerset County Edn. Commn., Manville, NJ, 1994—2002. Mem.: Masons (life). Achievements include Westry G. Horne Excellence in Education award. Office Phone: 570-620-2149.

**MALINA, MICHAEL,** lawyer; b. Bklyn., Mar. 20, 1936; s. William and Jean (Kutlowitz) M.; m. Anita May Oppenheim, June 22, 1958; children: Rachel Lynn, Stuart Charles, Joel Martin. AB, Harvard U., 1957, LLB, 1960. Bar: N.Y. 1961, U.S. Dist. Ct. (so. and ea. dists.) N.Y. 1962, U.S. Ct. Appeals (2d, 3d, 4th, 9th, and D.C. cirs.) 1965, U.S. Supreme Ct. 1965, U.S. Tax Ct. 1991. Assoc. Kaye, Scholer, Fierman, Hays & Handler, N.Y.C., 1960-69, ptnr., 1969—. Contbr. articles to profl. jours. Mem. ABA (antitrust sect.), N.Y. State Bar Assn. (chmn. antitrust sect. 1998-99), Assn. Bar City N.Y. (profl. ethics com. 1985-88), Phi Beta Kappa. Democrat. Jewish. Home: 12 Innes Rd Scarsdale NY 10583-7110 Office: Kaye Scholer Fierman Hays & Handler 425 Park Ave New York NY 10022-3506

**MALINDA, PAUL F.,** emergency physician; b. Balt., Dec. 21, 1961; s. Adam Frank and Diane Mary Malinda; m. Maria C. Sam, May 20, 1989; children: James, Benjamin, Ann. BS cum laude, Loyola Coll., Balt., 1983; MD, U. Md., Balt., 1987. Diplomate Am. Coll. Forensic Examiners, Am. Bd. Family Practice, Emergency Medicine. Intern, resident U. Md., Balt., 1987—90; emergency rm. physician St. Joseph's Hosp., Buckhannoy, W.Va., 1990—93, Olmsted Cmty. Hosp., Rochester, 1993—96, Annie Penn Meml. Hosp., Reidsville, NC, 1996, Wesley Long Cmty. Hosp., Greensboro, NC, 1997—2000, Moses Cone Meml. Hosp., Greensboro, 1997—2000, Alamance Regional med. Ctr., Burlington, NC, 1997—. Dir. physicians asst. program, interim emergency rm. dir. Upshur County, Buckhannon, 1992—93; adj prof US Army Command and Gen. Staff Coll. (CGSOC), 2005. Vol. Our Lady Mercy Sch., Winston-Salem, 2002—; adult leader Boy Scouts Am., Kernersville, NC, 2003—. Cpt. USAR, 1996—99, maj. USAR, 1999—2004, ltc. USAR, 2004—. Fellow: Am. Acad. Emergency Physicians (gov. 2002—), Am. Acad. Family Physicians; mem.: AMA, Am. Assn. Physician Specialists, NC Med. Soc. Avocations: travel, reading, swimming, hiking. Office: Alamance Regional Med Ctr Hoffman Mill Rd Burlington NC 27215

**MALING, GEORGE CROSWELL, JR.,** physicist; b. Boston, Feb. 24, 1931; s. George Croswell and Marjory Maling; m. Norah J. Horsfield, Dec. 29, 1960; children: Ellen P., Barbara J., Jeffrey C. AB, Bowdoin Coll., 1954; SB, MIT, 1954, SM, 1954, PhD in Physics, 1963. Rsch. asst., postdoctoral fellow MIT, 1957—65; adv. physicist IBM Corp., Poughkeepsie, NY, 1965—71, sr. physicist, 1971—92; pres. Empire State Software Sys. Ltd., 1992—93; dir. Noise Control Found., Inc., Poughkeepsie, 1975—2006; chmn. com. Sl-acoustics Am. Nat. Std. Com., 1976—79; dir. Internat. Noise Control Engring. Found., Inc., 1993—2006; mng. dir. Inst. of Noise Control Engring., 1994—2001; ret. Pres. Internat. Noise Control Engring. Found., 1999—. Editor: Noise/News, 1972—92; mng. editor: Noise/News Internat., 1993—, assoc. editor: Jour. Acoustical Soc. Am., 1976—83, editor tech. proc.; contbr. articles to profl. jours. Recipient Raleigh medal, Inst. Acoustics U.K., 1999, Dist. Noise Ctrl. Eng., INCE, 2001. Fellow: AAAS, IEEE, Audio Engring. Soc., Acoustical Soc. Am. (exec. coun. 1980—83, Silver medal in noise 1992); mem.: Nat. Acad. Engring., Internat. Inst. Noise Control Engring. (editor-in-chief 2002—, bd. dirs. 1980—86, v.p. comms. 1997—; bd. dirs.), Inst. Noise Control Engring. (bd. dirs. 1972—74, pres. 1975, award 2001). Personal E-mail: maling@alum.mit.edu.

**MALININ, THEODORE,** medical educator, researcher; b. Krasnodar, Russia, Sept. 13, 1933; arrived in US, 1949; s. Ivan M. and Olga A. (Senitzkaya) M.; m. Dorothy Rearick, Sept. 4, 1960; children: Ellen T., Alexander T., Catherine T., Michael T. BS, Concord Coll., 1955; MS, U. Va., 1958, MD, 1960; DSc (hon.), U. Scranton, 1990. Asst. prof. Georgetown U., Washington, 1964-68, assoc. prof., 1968-70; prof. surgery U. Miami, Fla., 1970-79, prof. orthopaedics, 1979—. Author: Surgery and Life, 1978; editor 3 books; contbr. over 200 articles to profl. jours. Active Nat. Rep. Com., Washington, 1964—; treas. Mannheimer Found. Surgeon USPHS, 1962—64. Recipient Order, U. Javeriana, 1992. Mem. AMA, Am. Acad. Orthop. Surgeons, Orthop. Rsch. Soc., So. Med. Assn., Am. Assn. Cancer Rsch., Am. Assn. Tissue Banks, Cell Transplantation Soc., Am. Soc. Invest. Pathology, Royal Soc. Medicine, Rotary (Disting. Rotarian 1994). Achievements include patents in field; research on latent injury in cryopreservation of cartilage, cartilage structure, and tissue banking; definition of behavior of transplanted cartilage and bone. Office: U Miami Dept Orthopaedics R-12 PO Box 16960 Miami FL 33101-6960 Office Phone: 305-243-6786. Business E-Mail: tmalinin@med.miami.edu.

**MALINOWSKI, ARTHUR ANTHONY,** lawyer, arbitrator; b. Chgo., Apr. 4, 1929; s. Ignatius and Sophie (Data) M. BS in Econs., DePaul U., 1956, JD, 1960; MS in Indsl. Rels., Loyola U., 1958; PhD, Ill. Inst. Tech., 1972; LLM in Labor Law, Chgo. Kent Coll. Law, 1981. Bar: Ill. 1960. Instr. indsl. rels. Loyola U., Chgo., 1963-69, prof. 1969-94; prof. emeritus, 1994—; mem. Ill. Office Collective Bargaining, Chgo., 1973-83. Lectr. dept. econs. Ill. Inst. Tech., Chgo., 1965-68. Mem. Ill. Bar Assn., Indsl. Rels. Rsch. Assn., Nat. Acad. Arbitrators, Knights Malta, Phi Alpha Delta, Alpha Sigma Nu, Pi Gamma Mu, Iota Sigma Epsilon, Beta Gamma Epsilon. Home: 9240 Major Ave Morton Grove IL 60053-1552 Office: Loyola U of Chgo One E Pearson Ste 460 Chicago IL 60611-2147 Office Phone: 312-915-6613.

**MALINOWSKI, DARIUSZ PIOTR,** horticulturist, educator; s. Ryszard Wojciech Malinowski and Gabriela Maria Malinowska. Degree in Horticulture, Warsaw Agrl. U., Poland, 1989; PhD in Natural Scis., Swiss Fed. Inst. Tech., Zurich, Switzerland, 1995. Asst. prof. Tex. A&M U., College Station, 2001—. Mem.: Am. Forage and Grasslands Coun. (assoc. Emerging Scientist award 1998, Merit award 2006), Am. Soc. Agronomy (assoc.). Achievements include research in discovery of chemical modifications in the rhizosphere of grasses infected with shoot-located Neotyphodium spp. fungal endophytes. Office: Texas Agricultural Experiment Station 11708 Hwy 70W Vernon TX 76385 Office Phone: 940-552-9941. Office Fax: 940-552-4657. Business E-Mail: d-malinowski@tamu.edu.

**MALINOWSKI, MARYELLEN,** photographer, artist; b. Oak Park, Ill., Oct. 10, 1961; d. Richard A. and Mary Jo (Curran) Lamz; m. Preston Malinowski; children: Nicole, Brielle, Demi. Student, Internat. Acad. Merch./Design, Chgo., 1985, Maine Photog. Workshops, Rockport, 1996, Elgin (Ill.) C.C., 1993-94. Owner Visual Elements, Dundee, Ill., 1992-94; owner, dir. The Infrared Light Gallery, St. Charles, Ill., 1994—; prin. owner Enlighten Pub., St. Charles, 2004—. Spkr. in field. Author: The Sacred Light, 1999; exhibited infrared photography in shows. Founder, bd. dirs. the Sacred Light Found. Recipient awards for photography; People's Choice award Women's Work Exhbn., Woodstock, 1995, 1st place Georgetown Internat. Fine Art Exhbn., Washington, 1997; recipient Ill. Women's Works Scholarship, 1996. Mem. Kodak Profl. Network, Luminos Printmakers Guild. Home: 6N779 IL RT 31 Saint Charles IL 60175 Office: Infrared Light Gallery PO Box 1281 Saint Charles IL 60175 Office Phone: 800-571-2730, 630-584-8068. Business E-Mail: maryellen@infraredlight.com.

**MALINOWSKI, MATTHEW J.,** lawyer; b. Lansing, Mich., Sept. 22, 1976; BA with honors, Michigan State U., 1998; JD, Emory U., 2003. Bar: Va. 2003, US Dist. Ct. (Ea. Dist.), Va. Assoc., pharm. products and toxic torts group & product liability group Spriggs & Hollingsworth, Washington, 2003—. Mem. Va. State Bar Assn. Office: Spriggs & Hollingsworth 1350 I St NW Ste 900 Washington DC 20005 Office Phone: 202-898-5800. Office Fax: 202-682-1639. Business E-Mail: mmalinowski@spriggs.com.

**MALINS, DONALD CLIVE,** biochemist, researcher; b. Lima, Peru, May 19, 1931; came to U.S., 1947; s. Richard Henry and Mabel (Madeline) M.; m. Mary Louise Leiren, 1962; children: Christopher W., Gregory S., Timothy J. BA, U. Washington, 1953; BS in Chemistry, Seattle U., 1954; PhD in Biochemistry, U. Aberdeen, 1967, DSc, 1976. Dir. environ. conservation div. Nat. Marine Fisheries Svc., Seattle, 1974-87; sr. scientific cons. U.S. Dept. Justice, Washington, 1989-91; sci. cons. NOAA, 1990-92; prin. scientist, dir. molecular epidemiology program Pacific N.W. Rsch. Inst., Seattle, 1992—2001, dir. biochem. oncology program, 2001—06, prin. scientist emeritus, 2006—; rsch. prof. dept. chemistry Seattle U., 1972-95. Affiliate prof. dept. environ. health U. Washington, 1984—, Coll. Ocean & Fishery Scis. U. Washington, 1974-91; editor-in-chief Aquatic Toxicology, 1980-95; lectr., speaker in field. Mem. editl. bd. Tech. in Cancer Rsch. and Treatment, 2001—; mem. editl. bd. Tech. in Cancer Rsch. and Treatment, 2001—; contbr. articles to profl. jours.; inventor in field. Bd. dirs. Am. Oceans Campaign, 1989-91; adv. bd. Internat. Jt. Commn., 1990-91. Recipient U.S. Dept. Commerce Gold medal, 1982. Mem. NAS, Am. Soc. Biochemistry and Molecular Biology, Am. Assn. for Cancer Rsch. Office: Pacific Northwest Rsch Inst Biochem Oncology Program 720 Broadway Seattle WA 98122-4302 Office Phone: 206-726-1200. Business E-Mail: dmalins@pnri.org.

**MALINSKY, MARCI ANN,** education educator; b. New Orleans, July 10, 1950; d. Walter Henry Tekippe and Mary Margaret Martin; m. Robert A. Malinsky, July 13, 1991; stepchildren: Matthew, Craig, Jennifer. BA in Edn., U. New Orleans, 1972; MA in Adminstrn., Coll. St. Thomas, St. Paul, 1983; PhD in Curriculum and Instrn., U. New Orleans, 2001. Tchr. Orleans Parish Sch., New Orleans, 1972—2001; asst. prof. Ark. State U., Jonesboro, Ark., 2001—05. Mem.: Nat. Sci. Tchrs. Assn., Internat. Reading Assn., Kappa Delta Pi. Roman Catholic. Avocations: reading, bridge. Home: 1607 Roleson Ln Jonesboro AR 72404 Office Phone: 870-972-3059. Personal E-mail: mmalinsky@cox-internet.com.

**MALIPIERO, VICTORIA SCHNEIDER,** vocalist; d. Donald Francis and Alice Eva (Billig) Snyder; m. Riccardo Malipiero, Dec. 21, 1988 (dec. Nov. 2003). MusB magna cum laude, Eastman Sch. Music, Rochester, NY, 1974, MusM, 1980; postgrad., U. Pisa, Italy, 1982; diploma in opera, Stuttgart Conservatory, Germany, 1984. Performer's cert. 1978. Singer: (Operas) Stuttgart State Opera, 1980—85, La Scala, 1985, 1990, 1993, Genova Opera, 1986, 1998, Holland Festival Opera, 1987, 1990, Bologna Opera, 1987, 1988, 1995, Vienna Musikverein, 1992, Paris Chatelet Theater, 1993, Frankfurt Opera, 1999—2000, Rome Opera, 2001, others; singer: (soloist) Italian RAI Radio Broadcasts, 1984—2006, Schoenberg Festival, 2003, Lake Como Festival, 2005; singer: (radio recs.) Schoenberg Lied der Waldtaube, Mahler Lieder eines fahrenden gesellen, Dallapiccola An Mathilde. Flagstad Grant, Kirsten Flagstad Found., 1979—80. Mem.: Nat. Assn. Tchrs. Singing, Coll. Music Soc., Amici Della Scala (hon.), Pi Kappa Lambda, Sigma Alpha Iota. Home: 2848 Dove Pond Dr Grapevine TX 76051 Office: Via Pusgnano SNC 22010 Cremia Italy

**MALIS, ANDREW GARY,** telecommunications company executive; b. Boston, Aug. 20, 1953; s. Irving and Nora Malis; m. Leslie Seaton, July 30, 1978; 1 child, Jonathan. ScB in Computer Sci., Brown U., 1975; ScM in Applied Math. and Computer Sci., Harvard U., 1979. Mem. tech. staff Mitre Corp., Bedford, Mass., 1975-78; divsn. engr. Bolt Beranek and Newman, Cambridge, Mass., 1979-93; cons. engr. Ascom Nexion, Acton, Mass., 1993-96; sr. cons. engr. Cascade Comm./Ascend Comm./Lucent Techs., Westford, Mass., 1996-2000; chief technologist Vivace Networks, Inc., San Jose, Calif., 2000—03, Tellabs, San Jose, 2003—. Chmn. working group Internet Engring. Task Force, Reston, Va., 1993—, ATM Forum, St. Louis, 1998-2000; mem. tech. adv. bd. Megisto Sys., Inc., Germantown, Md., 2000—; cons. Coun. Tech. Advisors, Gerson Lehrman Group, N.Y.C. 2000—; press, chmn. Multi-Protocol Label Switching Forum, Fremont, Calif., 2002-03; chmn., pres. MFA Forum, Fremont, 2003—; spkr., chmn. numerous telecom.-related confs. Contbr. articles to sci. jours., including Procs. IEEE, IEEE Comm.; author telecom. stds. documents, 1981—. Bd. dirs., past pres. Temple Emanuel, Andover, Mass., 1986—. Recipient spl. tech. achievement award Frame Relay Forum, 1994, Disting. Svc. award, 1999; Spotlight award ATM Forum, 2000. Mem. IEEE, Internet Soc., Sigma Xi. Democrat. Jewish. Achievements include patent for method and apparatus for enabling flow control over multiple networks having disparate flow control capability. Office: Tellabs 90 Rio Robles Dr San Jose CA 95134 Office Phone: 630-798-6626. Personal E-mail: amalis@gmail.com. Business E-Mail: andy.malis@tellabs.com.

**MALISHENKO, TIMOTHY PETER,** aerospace company executive; b. Reading, Eng., Nov. 4, 1944; s. John and Myra Phillys (Morris) M.; m. Jane Baxter, Mar. 17, 1968; 1 child, Andrew. BSBA, Ohio State U., 1968; MBA in Supply Chain Mgmt., Mich. State U., 1969; MS in Sys. Mgmt., U. So. Calif., 1972; postgrad., Nat. War Coll., Washington, 1986. Commd. 2d lt. USAF, 1968, advanced through grades to maj. gen., 1998, chief contracts and acquisition NATO E-3A Early Warning Sy. Brunssum, Netherlands, 1979-82,

dep. dir. R&D contracting Aero. Sys. Divsn. Wright-Patterson AFB, Ohio, 1982-84, dir. contracting, dep. aero. equipment, 1984-86, chief contract support divsn. Office Asst. Sec. Washington, 1987-88, chief, sys. and logistics contracting divsn., 1988-89, asst. dep. asst. sec. for contracting, 1989-90, dir. contracting Electronic Sys. Ctr. Hanscom AFB, Mass., 1990-93, dep. dir. contracting Hdqrs. Air Force Materiel Command Wright-Patterson AFB, Ohio, 1993-94, dir. contracting Hdqrs. Air Force Materiel Command, 1994-95; dep. asst. sec. for contracting USAF, Pentagon, Washington, 1995-97, dir. def. contract mgmt. agy., 1997—2001; v.p., contracts and pricing, integrated def. sys. Boeing Co., Seal Beach, Calif., 2001—03, corp. v.p., contracts and pricing Chgo., 2003—. Contbr. articles to profl. jours. Served to maj. gen. USAF. Decorated Def. Disting. Legion of Merit with oak leaf cluster, Def. Meritorious Svc. medal. Personal E-mail: tim@malishenko.com. Business E-Mail: timothy.p.malishenko@boeing.com.

**MALKANI, PRAKASH,** neuroradiology educator; b. New Delhi, July 16, 1956; came to the U.S., 1990; s. Kotumal D. and Parpati K. (Abichandani) M.; m. Sonia N. Jiandani, Sept. 15, 1986; children: Natasha, Alisha. Student, U. Delhi, 1973; MB, BChir, All India Inst. Med. Sci., Delhi, 1979, MD, 1983. Diplomate Am. Bd. Radiology, Am. Bd. Neuroradiology. Intern All India Inst. Med. Sci., 1978; resident in radiology N.Y. Med. Coll., 1990-93, fellow in neuroradiology, 1990-91; head dept. imaging Hinduja Hosp., Bombay, 1985-90; clin. asst. prof. Mich. State U., East Lansing, 1993—2003; pres. Advanced Diagnostic Imaging, Saginaw, Mich., 2001—02, Saginaw County Med. Soc., 2002—03. Mem. MRI adv. bd. GE Asia Pacific, Singapore, 1986-90; chmn. radiology Covenant Health Sys., 1998-2001, Berkshire Med. Ctr., 2003—. Merit scholar Bd. Secondary Edn., New Delhi, 1972. Mem. Am. Soc. Neuroradiology, Saginaw Med. Radiology (treas. 1994-98). Home: 50 Meadow Ridge Pittsfield MA 01201 Office: Advanced Berkshire Med Imaging Dept Radiology Berkshire Med Ctr 725 North St Pittsfield MA 01201 Office Phone: 413-447-2401. E-mail: pmalkani@bhsl.org.

**MALKASIAN, GEORGE DURAND, JR.,** obstetrician, educator; b. Springfield, Mass., Oct. 16, 1927; s. George Dur and Gladys Mildred (Trombley) M.; m. Mary Ellen Koch, Oct. 16, 1954; children: Linda Jeanne, Karen Diane, Martha Ellen. AB, Yale U., 1950; MD, Boston U., 1954; MS, U. Minn., 1963. Diplomate Am. Bd. Ob-Gyn. Intern Worcester (Mass.) City Hosp., 1954-55; resident in ob-gyn Mayo Grad. Sch. Hosp., Rochester, Minn., 1955-58, 60-61; mem. faculty Mayo Med. Sch., 1962—, prof. ob-gyn, 1976—, chmn. dept. ob-gyn, 1976-86. Author articles in field. Served to lt. comdr. M.C., USNR, 1958-60. Named Tchr. of Yr., Mayo Grad. Sch. Medicine, 1973, 77, Alumnus of Yr., Boston U. Sch. Med., 1990. Fellow Royal Coll. Obstetricians and Gynecologists (ad eundum); mem. ACS, Am. Coll. Ob-Gyn (pres. 1989-90), Am. Ob-Gyn Soc., Am. Radium Soc., Soc. Ob-Gyn, Assn. Profs. Ob-Gyn, N.Am. Ob-Gyn Soc., Ctrl. Assn. Ob-Gyn, Minn. Soc. Ob-Gyn, Internat. Fedn. Ob-Gyn (v.p. 1997-2000), Zumbro Valley Med. Soc. (exec. dir. 1996-2002). Home: 211 NW 2nd St #503 Rochester MN 55901 Office: Mayo Clinic 200 1st St SW Rochester MN 55905-0001

**MALKI, HEIDAR A.,** dean; arrived in U.S., 1979; s. Karim A. and Rokhsareh A. Malki; m. Layla F. Niaki, June 12, 1962; 1 child, Armeen. PhD, U. Wis., Milw., 1990. Prof. U. of Houston, 1991—2005, assoc. dean, 2004—. Adviser Mind and Vision Computing, Houston, 1992—2000. Author: (textbook) Control Systems Technology (Best Paper award, 1998). Named Alumnus of Yr., 2005; recipient Invited Paper award, Sci. Am., 1997, Rsch. in Outstanding Faculty award. Mem.: IEEE, Am. Soc. Engring. Edn. (zone chair 1997—98, Best Paper award). Office: U Houston 4800 Calhoun Rd Houston TX 77204-4020 Office Phone: 713-743-4075. Office Fax: 713-743-4032. Business E-Mail: malki@uh.edu.

**MALKIEL, BURTON GORDON,** economist, educator; b. Boston, Aug. 28, 1932; s. Sol and Celia (Gordon) Malkiel; m. Judith Ann Atherton, July 16, 1954 (dec. 1987); 1 child, Jonathan; m. Nancy Weiss, July 31, 1988. BA, Harvard, 1953, MBA, 1955; PhD, Princeton, 1964. Assoc. Smith Barney & Co., N.Y.C., 1958—60; asst. prof. dept. econs. Princeton U., 1964—66, assoc. prof., 1966—68, prof., 1968—81, Rentschler prof. econs., 1969—81, chmn. dept. econs., 1974—75, 1977—81, Chem. Bank chmn.'s prof. econs., 1988—; dean Sch. Orgn. and Mgmt., Yale U., 1981—87. Mem. Pres.'s Coun. Econ. Advisors, 1975—77; bd. dirs. Jeffrey Co., CareGain, Inc., BKF Capital, Vanguard Group. Author: The Term Structure of Interest Rates, 1966; author: (with others) Strategies and Rational Decisions in the Securities Options Market, 1969; author: The Inflation-Beater's Investment Guide, 1980, Global Bargain Hunting, 1998; author: (with others) The Index Fund Solution, 1999; author: A Random Walk Down Wall Street, 8th edit., 2003, The Random Walk Guide to Investing, 2003. 1st lt. U.S. Army, 1955—58. Mem. Am. Fin. Assn. (dir., pres. 1978). Home: 76 North Rd Princeton NJ 08540-2430 Office: Princeton U Dept Econs Princeton NJ 08544-0001 Office Phone: 609-258-6445. Business E-Mail: bmalkiel@princeton.edu.

**MALKIEL, NANCY WEISS,** dean, historian, educator; b. Newark, Feb. 14, 1944; d. William and Ruth Sylvia (Puder) Weiss; m. Burton G. Malkiel, July 31, 1988. BA summa cum laude, Smith Coll., 1965; MA, Harvard U., 1966, PhD, 1970. From asst. to assoc. prof. history Princeton (N.J.) U., 1969-82, prof., 1982—, master Dean Mathey Coll., 1982-86, dean coll., 1987—. Author (as Nancy J. Weiss): (book) Charles Francis Murphy, 1858-1924: Respectability and Responsibility in Tammany Politics, 1968; author: (with others) Blacks in America: Bibliographical Essays, 1971, The National Urban League, 1910-1940, 1974, Farewell to the Party of Lincoln: Black Politics in the Age of FDR, 1983 (Berkshire Conf. of Women Historians prize, 1984), Whitney M. Young Jr., and the Struggle for Civil Rights, 1989. Trustee Woodrow Wilson Nat. Fellowship Found., 1975—, chmn. bd. trustees, 1999—; trustee Smith Coll., Northampton, Mass., 1984—94. Fellow, Woodrow Wilson Found., 1965, Charles Warren Ctr. Studies in Am. History, 1970—77, Radcliffe Inst., 1976—77, Ctr. Advanced Study Behavioral Scis., 1986—87. Mem.: So. Hist. Assn., Orgn. Am. Historians (chmn. status women hist. profession 1972—75), Am. Hist. Assn., Phi Beta Kappa. Democrat. Jewish. Office: Princeton U Office Dean Of College Princeton NJ 08544-0001

**MALKIN, BARRY,** film editor, consultant; b. NYC, Oct. 26, 1938; s. Richard and Helen (Kandix) M.; m. Stephanie Byer; 1 child, Sacha Janine. BA, Adelphi U., 1960. Freelance film editor Sacha Prodns., Inc., N.Y.C., 1964—. Editor: (films) The Rain People, 1969, Cotton Comes to Harlem, 1970, They Might Be Giants, 1971, Who is Harry Kellerman?, 1971, Cops and Robbers, 1973, The Godfather Part 2, 1974, One Summer Love, 1976, Somebody Killed Her Husband, 1978, Last Embrace, 1979, One Trick Pony, 1980, Windows, 1980, Four Friends, 1981, Hammett, 1982, Rumble Fish, 1983, The Cotton Club, 1984 (Acad. award nominee for best film editing 1984), Peggy Sue Got Married, 1986, Gardens of Stone, 1987, Big, 1988, New York Stories ("Life Without Zoe"), 1989, The Freshman, 1990, The Godfather Part III, 1990 (Acad. award nominee for best film editing 1990), Honeymoon in Vegas, 1992, It Could Happen to You, 1994, Jack, 1996, The Rainmaker, 1997, Isn't She Great, 1999, Lucky Numbers, 2000, The Big Bounce, 2003. Mem. Acad. Motion Picture Arts and Scis., Motion Picture Editors Guild, Am. Cinema Editors. Home and office: 275 Central Park W New York NY 10024-3015 E-mail: cpwblackie@aol.com.

**MALKIN, CARY JAY,** lawyer; b. Chgo., Oct. 6, 1949; s. Arthur D. and Perle (Slavin) Malkin; m. Lisa Kimley, Oct. 27, 1976; children: Dorothy R., Victoria S., Lydia R. BA, George Washington U., 1971; JD, Northwestern U., 1974. Bar: Ill. 1974, U.S. Dist. Ct. (no. dist.) Ill. 1974, N.Y. 2001. Assoc. Mayer, Brown & Platt, Chgo., 1974—80, ptnr., 1991—2002, Mayer, Brown, Rowe & Maw LLP, Chgo., 2002—. Chmn. spl. events com. Mental Health Assn., 1984—85; mem. steering com. Endowment Campaign Latin Sch. Chgo., 1990—91, trustee, 1991—2000, nat. trustee, 2000—02, sr. trustee, 2002—; chmn. Campaign Latin Sch. Chgo., 1995—98; mem. exec. com. Friends Prentice Women's Hosp., 1991—92; bd. dirs. SOS Children's Village Ill., 1992—96; mem. M. S. Weiss fund bd. Children's Meml. Hosp., 1993—96, mem. Graziano fund bd., 1993—96; trustee Field Mus., 1999—; mem. fin. com., 2002—05, mem. investment com., 2003—05, mem. budget com., 2005—, mem. founder's coun., 1995—, chmn. founder's coun.,

1999—2003. Mem.: Std. Club, Arts Club, Saddle and Cycle Club (bd. govs. 1998—2001, 2006—), Chgo. Club, Phi Beta Kappa, Order of Coif. Home: 233 E Walton St Chicago IL 60611-1526 Office: Mayer Brown Rowe & Maw LLP 71 S Wacker Dr Chicago IL 60606

**MALKIN, EVGENI,** professional hockey player; b. Magnitogorsk, Russia, July 31, 1986; s. Vladimir and Tatiana Malkin. Center Metallurg Magnitogorsk (Russian Super League), 2003—06, Pitts. Penguins, 2006—. Mem. Team Russia, Olympic Games, Torino, Italy, 2006. Achievements include being drafted in the first round (2nd overall) in the NHL Entry Draft, 2004; being a member of silver medal Team Russia, World Junior Championships, 2006. Office: c/o Pitts Penguins 66 Mario Lemieux Pl Pittsburgh PA 15219 also: c/o IMG Hockey 520 Broadway, Ste 660 Santa Monica CA 90401*

**MALKIN, HAROLD MARSHALL,** retired medical researcher; b. San Francisco, Oct. 9, 1923; s. Charles Herman and Dorothy Levin Malkin; m. Joanne Clark (div.); m. Sonja Sandeman (div.); children: Alison, Dinah, Aaron, Miriam, Richard. AB, U. Calif., Berkeley, 1947, MA, 1949; MD, U. Chgo., Chicago, 1951. Dir. MML Diagnostic Labs, Palo Alto, Calif., 1954—72, Solano Clin. Labs, Berkeley, Calif., 1972—78, Oslerwelch Laboratories, San Leandro, Calif., 1978—86; cons. Smith Kline Laboratories, Dublin, Calif., 1986—93, Quest Diagnostic Labs, Dublin, Calif., 1993—2002; ret., 2002. Instr. Stanford U. Sch. Medicine, Palo Alto, Calif., 1954—60, intern in pathology, 1960—62. Author: (pathology book) Out of the Mist; contbr. articles to profl. jours. Sgt. U.S. Army, 1943—46, PTO. Fellow, Nat. Found. Infantile Paralysis, 1951—53, Am. Cancer Soc., 1953—54. D-Liberal. Achievements include research in Protein and Nucleic Acid Metabolism. Avocation: medical history. Home: 9 Rio Porto Court Sacramento CA 95831

**MALKIN, JOSEPH M.,** lawyer; b. NYC, Jan. 26, 1947; BA, Claremont Men's Coll., 1968; JD, Yale U., 1972. Bar: Calif. 1972, U.S. Dist. Ct. (ctrl. dist.) Calif. 1972, U.S. Dist. Ct. (no. dist.) Calif. 1972, U.S. Fed. Cts. 1972, U.S. Ct. Appeals (9th cir.) 1973, U.S. Supreme Ct. 1976. Mem. O'Melveny & Myers, San Francisco; ptnr. in charge-San Francisco Office Orrick, Herrington & Sutcliffe LLP, San Francisco, co-chmn. energy & project fin. group. Editor Yale Law Jour., 1970-72. Recipient Carter, Ledyard and Milburn prize Yale Law Sch., 1970. Mem. ABA, Bar Assn. San Francisco. Office: Orrick, Herrington & Sutcliffe LLP The Orrick Building 405 Howard St San Francisco CA 94105 Office Phone: 415-773-5505. Office Fax: 415-773-5759. Business E-Mail: jmalkin@orrick.com.

**MALKIN, MICHAEL M.,** lawyer; b. New Haven, Nov. 1, 1944; s. Eli B. and Gladys (Pollak) M.; children: Andrea, Lisa, Daniel. BA, U. N.Mex., 1966; JD, NYU, 1969. Bar: N.Y. 1970, U.S. Dist. Ct. (so. dist.) N.Y. 1971, U.S. Dist. Ct. (ea. dist.) N.Y. 1971, U.S. Ct. Appeals (2d cir.) 1972, U.S. Supreme Ct. 1984. Assoc. Weil, Lee & Bergin, N.Y.C., 1970-76, Weil, Guttman & Davis, N.Y.C., 1976-77, ptnr., 1977-82, Weil, Guttman, Davis & Malkin, N.Y.C., 1982-86, Weil, Guttman & Malkin, N.Y.C., 1986-95, Weil, Guttman & Malkin, LLP, N.Y.C., 1995—2001. Judge Giles Sutherland Rich Moot Ct. Competition, N.Y.C., 1982; arbitrator Civil Ct. of City N.Y., 1984-88. Mem. editl. bd. Trademark Reporter, 1973-75, 88-90, contbg. editor, 1974-75. Mem. N.Y. State Bar Assn., U.S. Trademark Assn., Phi Delta Phi, Alpha Epsilon Pi. Office Phone: 480-513-2859. Business E-Mail: mikemalkin@cox.net.

**MALKIN, MICHELLE,** syndicated columnist; b. Phila. married; 2 children. B. Oberlin Coll.. Ohio. Editorial writer, columnist LA Daily News, 1992—94; editorial bd. Seattle Times, 1996—99. Author: Invasion: How America Still Welcomes Terrorists, Criminals and Other Foreign Menaces to Our Shores, 2002 (NY Times bestseller), In Defense of Internment: The Case for Racial Profiling in World War II and the War on Terror, 2004 (NY Times bestseller), Unhinged: Exposing Liberals Gone Wild, 2005; syndicated columnist, commentator Fox News Channel, polit. blogger michellemalkin.com, 2004—(rated as one of the best polit. blogs in 2005, Forbes Mag. and The Week Mag.). Warren Brookes Fellow, Competitive Enterprise Inst., 1995. Avocations: fishing, piano, crocheting. Mailing: Creators Syndicate Ste 700 5777 W Century Blvd Los Angeles CA 90045 E-mail: writemalkin@gmail.com.*

**MALKIN, MOSES MONTEFIORE,** retired employee benefits administration company executive, diversified financial services company executive; b. Revere, Mass., Sept. 18, 1919; s. Irving and Annie (Helfant) M.; m. Hannah Lacob, Oct. 11, 1941. AB, U. N.C. 1941; BSME, Columbia U., 1948. Enrolled actuary; CLU. Engr. GE, Schenectady, NY, 1948-50; engr. Gen. Bronze, Inc., Jersey City, 1950-51; v.p. Malkin Warehouse, Inc., New Haven, 1951-57; pvt. practice actuary and adminstr. New Haven, 1957—72; chmn., actuary Profl. Pensions, Inc., Middletown, Conn., 1973—93; ret., 1993. Presenter pension issues at numerous confs., 1970-80. Pres., founder Milford, Conn., 1962, Milford Child Guidance Clinic, 1966; pres. Clifford Beers Child Guidance, New Haven, 1971, Jewish Family Svc., New Haven, 1973. With U.S. Army, 1941-45, ETO. Mem. Am. Acad. Actuaries (ret. mem.), Am. Soc. Pension Actuaries (ret. mem., instr. 1984), Am. Soc. CLUs (ret. mem.), Phi Beta Kappa, Tau Beta Pi. Jewish. Address: 1514 Heron Dr Sun City Center FL 33573-4707

**MALKIN, PETER LAURENCE,** lawyer, investor; b. NYC, Jan. 14, 1934; s. Samuel and Gertrude (Greenberger) Malkin; m. Isabel L. Wien, July 10, 1955. Grad. cum laude, Poly. Prep. Country Day Sch., 1951; AB summa cum laude, Harvard Coll., 1955; LLB magna cum laude, Harvard U. Law Sch., 1958. Bar: N.Y. 1958, Conn. 1976, Fla. 1977. Sr. ptnr., chmn. Wien & Malkin LLP, N.Y.C., 1958—; mng. Empire State Bldg. Assocs. L.L.C., 1961—; chmn. W & M Properties, Inc. NYC, 1965—; bd. dirs. UJ Trust Corp.; ptnr. NYC Partnership, NYC, 2001—; founding chmn. Grand Ctrl. Partnership Inc. & 34th Street Partnership, Inc.; founding dir., sec. Fashion Ctr. Bus. Improvement Dist.; dir. Realty Found. N.Y., 1981—, v.p., 1995—; mem. adv. com. Greenwich (Conn.) Japanese Sch., 1992—2005; mem. N.Y.C. Mayor's Bus. Adv. Coun., 1997—2002; gov. Real Estate Bd., NYC, 1993—2005; co-founder, hon. co-chmn. Coun. to Encourage Corp. Philanthropy, 1998—. Chmn. Met. Aircraft Noise Mitigation Commn., 1990—; vice-chmn. Harvard Law Sch. Fund, 1967-71, chmn. nat. scholarship com., 1975-76, chmn. NYC com., 1981-83; founder, bd. dirs. Urban League Southwestern Fairfield County, 1969-73, treas., 1969-71; bd. dirs., exec. com. Lincoln Ctr. for Performing Arts, 1979—; bd. dirs. Inst. Internat. Edn., 1983-89, hon. 1994—; trustee Nat. Trust for Hist. Preservation, 1988-91, adv. coun., 1997—, trustee emeritus, 2006—; founding chmn. Greenwich (Conn.) Green & Clean, Inc., 1986—, Greenwich Adopt-A-Road, 1996—, founding co-chmn., Merritt Pkwy. Conservancy, 2002—; v.p., exec. com. Brandeis Univ. Boston chpt. NAACP, 1967-69; trustee Citizens Budget Commn., NYC, 1971-91, Jewish Communal Fund, NY, 1976-81; dean's coun., Harvard U., 1987-95; chmn. capital campaign and chmn. dean's coun. Kennedy Sch. Govt., 1995—, overseers com. to visit Kennedy Sch. Govt., 1976-82, 83-89, 90—, to visit Harvard Law Sch. 1977-83; exec. com. Program for Ctr. for Jewish Studies, 1974-80; bd. overseers Harvard Coll., 1989-95, overseers com. univ resources, 1972—, exec. com., 1985—; dean's adv. com. Harvard Law Sch., 1988-90; elected dir. Harvard Alumni Assn., 1981-83; chmn. schs. and scholarship com. Harvard Coll., Greenwich, 1973-79; exec. com. Assn. Better N.Y., 1972—. Brandeis U. fellow, 1970—; named Outstanding Young Man, NYC Jaycees, 1969, Man of Yr., Hist. Soc. Greenwich, Conn., 1993, Man of Yr., Greenwich Rotary, 2005; recipient Nat. Preservation Honor award Nat. Trust Hist. Preservation, 1987, Pres. award Grad. Sch. and Univ. Ctr. CUNY, 1989, Crain's All-Star award, 1994, Nacore Disting. Man of Yr. award, 1995; Murray Hill Archl. award, 1996, PENCIL award for outstanding commitment to NYC Pub. Schs., 2003, Lincoln Ctr. Outstanding Vol. Leader award, 2004. Mem. Harvard Law Sch. Assn. NYC (trustee 1968-70, v.p. 1973-74), Assn. Bar City NY, Century Assn., Links NY, The Hasty Pudding Inst. 1770, AD Hon., Harvard Varsity Club (Cambridge), Harvard Club NYC (bd. mgrs. 1979-81), Harvard Club (Fairfield County, Conn., v.p. 1974-75, bd. dirs. 1976-80), Bailwick Club (hon. life, founding pres.), Blind Brook Club, Conn. Golf Club, Phi Beta Kappa. Office: 60 E 42d St New York NY 10165-0015 Business E-Mail: plmalkin@wienmalkinllp.com

**MALKIN, STANLEY LEE,** neurologist; b. Pitts., Pa., Nov. 11, 1942; s. Maurice and Bessie Beatrice (Serbin) M.; m. Candace N. Conard; children: Justin Ross, Keith Richard. BA with honors, U. Pa., 1964; MD, U. Pitts., 1968. Diplomate Am. Bd. Psychiatry and Neurology, Nat. Bd. Med. Examiners. Intern Montefiore Hosp., Pitts., 1968-69; resident in neurology Columbia-Presbyn. Med. Ctr., N.Y.C., 1969-72; chief neurology svc., Wright-Patterson AFB, Dayton, 1972-74; practice medicine specializing in neurology N.Y.C.; attending staff Mt. Sinai Hosp.; former dir. Neuro-Diagnostic Lab., Englewood; asst. clin. prof. neurology Mt. Sinai Sch. Medicine; founder Bergen-Passaic Tomography Ctr., Fairlawn, N.J. Neurology cons. Regent Hosp.; med. dir. Pain Suppression Labs., Inc.; med. dir. Efficient Health Systems, Inc.-N.Y.C. Healthline; founder, med. dir., exec. v.p. Hosp. Diagnostic Equipment Corp., 1987—; pres. Cancer Treatment Holdings, Inc, 1993-95, dir. 1993-94, sr. med. dir. 1995-97; founder Montvale Med. Imaging Assocs. (N.J.), N.Y. Med. Imaging, N.Y.C., Hosp. Diagnostic Equipment Corp. Co-mcpl. councl. Ft. Lee Citizens for McGovern, 1972; ptnr. Sall/Myers Med. Assocs., prin. 1995—; mem. Edgewater Rent Control Bd., 1978. Maj. M.C. USAF, 1972-74. Recipient Comdr.'s Recognition award for care of repatriated prisoners of war, 1973, award Am.'s Top Physicians, 2004-05. Fellow Royal Soc. Medicine; mem. Am. Acad. Neurology, Am. Assn. Electrodiagnostic Medicine, Am. Soc. Neuro-Imaging (charter), EEG and Clin. Neurosci. Soc., Am. Headache Soc. (rev. bd.), Nat. Headache Found., Internat. Headache Soc., Nat. Neurotrauma Soc., N.Y. Acad. Scis., NYU Bellevue Psychiat. Soc., European Fedn. Neurol. Socs. Office: 60 E 42d St Ste 2214 New York NY 10165

**MALKINE-FALVEY, FERN SYLVIE,** writer, journalist, painter; b. Bklyn., Apr. 11, 1950; d. Georges Alexandre and Sonia May Malkine; m. Peter Anthony Falvey, June 20, 1992. MS Spl. Edn., Fordham U., New York, New York, 1976; BS History/English Lit., NYU, New York, New York, 1974; AA History/English, Ulster County CC, Stone Ridge, New York, 1972. Rschr., writer Editions de la Difference, Paris, 1976—78; fgn. correspondant Paris Match, New York, NY, 1979—81; copy editor Elle Mag., Paris, 1983—85; painter, freelance journalist Woodstock, NY, 1985—89; gallery dir. Isidore Ducasse Fine Arts, Manhattan, NY, 1989—92; art cons. Pavillon des Arts Mus., Paris, 1998—99; copy editor Look Mag., New York, NY, 1978—79; curator On-line Gallery, Woodstock, NY, 2001—. Author: Georges Malkine: An Arbitrary Destiny; co-author: Georges Malkine: Le Vagabond du Surrealism; exhibitions include Tom Fletcher Gallery, Woodstock, 2001, The Art Gallery-Western New Eng. Coll., Springield, Mass., 2002— Vol. Congressman Matt McHugh, Kingston, NY, 1981, Oglala Sioux Emergency Svcs., 1987, ARC, 2001—; Congressman Hinchey, Kingston, NY, 2004. Mem.: Hist. Soc. of Woodstock. Avocations: guitar, historical post cards, designing moccasins, designing tapestries. Home: PO Box 261 Shady NY 12409 Business E-Mail: fern@hvc.rr.com.

**MALKINSON, FREDERICK DAVID,** dermatologist, educator; b. Hartford, Conn., Feb. 26, 1924; s. John Walter and Rose Malkinson; m. Una Zwick, June 15, 1979; children by previous marriage: Philip, Carol, John. Student, Loomis Inst. 1937-41; 3 yr. cert. cum laude, Harvard U., 1943, DMD, 1947, MD, 1949. Intern Harvard-Beth Israel Hosp., Boston, 1949-50; resident in dermatology U. Chgo., 1950-54, from instr. to assoc. prof. dermatology, 1954-68; prof. medicine and dermatology U. Ill., Chgo., 1968-71; chmn. dept. dermatology Rush Med. Coll. and Rush-Presbyn.-St. Luke's Med. Ctr. (now Rush U. Med. Ctr.), Chgo., 1968-92, Clark W. Finnerud, M.D. prof. dept. dermatology, 1981-95, 95—; trustee Sulzberger Inst. Dermatol. Comm. and Edn., 1976-96; pres. Sulzberger Inst. Dermatol. Communication and Edn., 1983-88, 93-96; prof. emeritus Rush U. Med. Ctr., Chgo., 2000—. Editor: Year Book of Dermatology, 1971-78; chief editor: AMA Archives of Dermatology, 1979-83; bd. editors 1976-84, Jour. AMA, 1979-83; editorial cons. World Book Medical Encyclopedia, 1991-2000; contbr. articles to profl. jours., chpts. to books. Active Evanston (Ill.) Libr. Bd., 1988-94, pres., 1993-94. With M.C. USNR, 1950-52. Grantee, U.S. Army, 1955—61, USPHS, 1962—73. Fellow AAAS; mem. Am. Acad. Dermatology (v.p. 1987-89, dir. 1964-67), Am. Dermatol. Assn., Soc. Investigative Dermatology (v.p. 1978-79, dir. 1963-68), Am. Fedn. Med. Rsch., Cen. Soc. Clin. Rsch., Radiation Rsch. Soc., Assn. Profs. of Dermatology (dir. 1982-85), Dermatology Found. (exec. com., trustee 1980-93, pres. 1983-85), Nat. Coun. on Radiation Protection and Measurements (mem. com. on cutaneous radiobiology 1986-92), Chgo. Dermatol. Soc. (pres. 1964-65, Gold Medal award 1992, established ann. lectureship, 2004), Chgo. Lit. Club (v.p. 1997-99, 2000-03, pres. 1999-2000). Office: Rush Univ Med Ctr Dept Dermatology 707 S Wood St 220 Annex Bldg Chicago IL 60612 Office Fax: 312-942-7778.

**MALKOVA, NATALIA,** physicist, mathematician, researcher; d. Michail Ivanovich Prosvirin and Vera Makarovna Prosvirina; m. Serghei Malkov, May 28, 1980; 1 child, Olga. PhD (hon.), Inst. Applied Physics Acad. Sciences of Moldova, Kishinev, 1987. Post-doctoral rschr. Materials Rsch. Inst., Pa. State U., University Park, 2001—04; rsch. assoc. U. Calif., Berkeley, 2004—. Vis. scientist Lab. Photonics and Microwave Enrging, dept. electronics Royal Inst. Tech., Stockholm, 2000—01. Recipient Associateship award, NRC, 2001, award, Swedish Inst., 2000—01; grantee, Soros Found., 1994, 1999, European Union Intergovtl. Conf., 2000. Mem.: Materials Rsch. Soc. (assoc.). Office: NASA Ames Rsch Ctr Mail Stop 229-1 Moffett Field CA 94035 Office Phone: 650-604-4874. E-mail: nmalkova@mail.arc.nasa.gov.

**MALKOVICH, JOHN,** actor; b. Christopher, Ill. Dec. 9, 1953; m. Glenne Headley, 1982 (div. 1988); m. Nicoletta Peyran, 1989; children: Amandine and Loewy. Student, Eastern Ill. U., Ill. State U. Co-founder Steppenwolf Theatre, Chgo., 1976 Made N.Y.C. theatrical debut in True West, 1982 (Obie award, Clarence Derwent award); other theatrical appearances include: Death of a Salesman, 1984, Burn This, 1987, States of Shock; dir. Balm in Gilead, 1984-85, Arms and the Man, 1985, The Caretaker, 1986, Coyote Ugly, (Chgo., Kennedy Ctr. for Performing Arts, Washington) 1985, Libra, 1994, Steppenwolf, 1994; appeared in films Places in the Heart, 1984, The Killing Fields, 1984, Eleni, 1985, Making Mr. Right, 1987, Glass Menagerie, 1987, Empire of the Sun, 1987, Miles From Home, 1988, Dangerous Liaisons, 1988, The Sheltering Sky, 1990, Queen's Logic, 1991, The Object of Beauty, 1991, Shadows and Fog, 1992, Jennifer 8, 1992, Of Mice and Men, 1992, In The Line Of Fire, 1993 (Academy award nomination best supporting actor 1993), Alive, 1993, Touchstone, 1994, Para De La Nuages, 1994, Mary Reilly, 1994, Mulholland Falls, 1996, Der Unhold, 1996, The Portrait of a Lady, 1996, Primary Colors, 1997, Con Air, 1997, The Man in the Iron Mask, 1998, Rounders, 1998, Le Temps retrouvé, 1999, The Libertine, 1999, Ladies Room, 1999, Joan of Arc, 1999, Being John Malkovich, 1999 (American Comedy Award, 2000), Shadow of the Vampire, 2000, Les Ames Forte, 2001, Knockaround Guys, 2001, Je rentre a la Maison, 2001, Ripley's Game, 2002, Hotel, 2001, The Dancer Upstairs, 2002, Johnny English, 2003, The Hitchhiker's Guide to the Galaxy, 2005, Colour Me Kubrick, 2005, Klimt, 2006; exec. prodr. The Accidental Tourist, 1988, Somewhere Else, 2000; prodr. Ghost World, 2000, The Loner, 2001, Found in the Street, 2001, The Dancer Upstairs, 2002, Ripley's Game, 2002, Johnny English, 2003, A Talking Picture, 2003, The Libertine, 2004, Kill the Poor, 2006, Art School Confidential, 2006; co-exec. prodr. The Accidental Tourist, 1988; The Dancer Upstairs, 2002; appeared in TV films Word of Honor, 1981, American Dream, 1981, Death of a Salesman, 1985 (Emmy award 1986), Heart of Darkness, 1994, RKO 281, 1999, Les Miserables, 2000, Napoleon, 2002. Office: William Morris Agency One William Morris Place Beverly Hills CA 90212*

**MALKOVICH, MARK PAUL, III,** musician, performing company executive; b. Eveleth, Minn., July 10, 1930; s. Mark II and Mary Frances (Greben) M.; m. Joan Shewring, Feb. 7, 1959; children: Mark IV, Erik, Kent, Kara. BS in Chemistry, Columbia U., 1952, MS, 1953; studied piano with Dorothy Crost Bourgin, Chgo. Mus. Coll., 1947-50; William Beller ch. Piano Dept., Columbia U., 1951-54; Adele Marcus, Juilliard Sch., 1959-62; MusD (hon.), Salve Regina, 1993; DFA, U. RI, 1994; MusD, Cath. U. Am., 1999. Pres. Chem. Gum Industries, Ltd., NYC, 1964—69. Artistic and gen. dir. Newport Music Festival, 1975—; exec. dir. Palm Beach Festival, Fla., 1984-86; guest lectr. TV and radio appearances and adjudicator at music competitions; pres.

Chopin Found. of U.S., Miami, Fla., 1985; presented N.Am. debuts of Bella Davidovich, Jean-Philippe Collard, Dmitry Sitkoveksky, Andrei Gavrilov, Mikhail Pletnev, others; founder Sports US*A*SR; negotiator/agt. for USSR leading hockey players Fetisov, Krutov, Larionov, Makarov, 1989. Recipient Individual Achievement award Bus. Vols. for the Arts, RI, 1998; named to RI Heritage Hall of Fame, 2000; named hon. citizen, Tbilisi, Republic of Ga., hon. prof. Tbilisi Conservatoire. Mem. Harvard Mus. Assn., Newport Reading Rm., Newport Hist. Soc., Spouting Rock Beach Assn., Royal Arts Found. (pres.), Clambake Club. Office: care Newport Music Festival PO Box 3300 Newport RI 02840-0992 Office Phone: 401-846-1133. Business E-Mail: staff@newportmusic.org.

**MALKOWICZ, STANLEY BRUCE,** urologist; b. Passaic, NJ; s. Stanley Jacob and Jeanne (iracki) M.; m. Denise Elaine Ewald, Sept. 22, 1985. BA, U. Vt., 1977; MD, U. Pa., Phila., 1981. Intern in surgery Hosp. U. Pa., Phila., 1981-82, resident in surgery, 1982-83, resident in urology 1983-86, chief resident in urology, 1986-87; fellow in urologic oncology U. So. Calif., LA, 1987-88, Hosp. U. Pa., Phila., 1988-90, asst. prof. surgery, 1990-95, assoc. prof., 1995—2003, prof. urology, 2003—; chief urology Phila. VA Med. Ctr. Assoc. scientist Wistar Inst. Anatomy and Biology, Phila., 1988—; Nat. Kidney Found. rsch. fellow, 1983-84; Am. Found. Urologic Disease rsch. scholar, 1988-90. Contbr. articles to profl. jours. Mem. AAAS, Am. Urologic Assn., Am. Assn. GU Surgeons, Am. Soc. Clin. Oncology, Soc. Univ. Urologists, Urodynamics Soc., Assn. Academic Surgeons, Soc. Pelvic Surgeons (treas.-sec.), Soc. Urologic Oncology, Urol. Rsch. Soc., Phila. Urol. Soc. (pres.), S.E. Pa. Am. Cancer Soc. (pres.), Sigma Xi. Presbyterian. Avocations: camping, reading, cooking. Office: Hosp U Pa Philadelphia PA 19104-4206 Office Phone: 215-662-7330.

**MALKS, BETTY F.,** social worker; d. Benjamin Fishman and Bertha Finkelstein; m. Joshua B. Malks, Aug. 28, 1988; children: Nicole S. Rosen, Brannon B. BA, U. Md., College Park, 1967; MSW, Adelphi U., L.I., N.Y., 1982. LCSW N.Y., 1982; cert. mgmt. devel. U. Calif., Berkeley, 1994. Dir. enriched housing programs Associated Y's of Greater N.Y., N.Y.C., 1983—88; social svcs. program mgr. County of Santa Clara, San Jose, Calif., 1993—97, dir. dept. aging and adult svcs., 1997—. Project dir. Faith-based Initiative for Elder Abuse Awareness in Diverse Communities, San Jose, 2006—; chair Elder and Dependent Adult Law Enforcement Protocol Task Force, San Jose, 1999—2002; founder Fin. Abuse Specialist Team, San Jose, 1999, Vets. Resource Faire, San Jose, 1999; panelist Second World Conf. on Family Violence, Prague, Czech Republic, 2003; chair Fin. Institutions Team to Combat Elder Fin. Abuse, San Jose, 2003—; chair First Aging Summit Calif. Social Work Edn. Ctr., Long Beach, Calif., 2004; panelist Internat. Assn. Gerontology Conf., Rio de Janeiro, 2005; N.Am. regional rep. Internat. Network for Prevention of Elder Abuse, 2003—. Contbr. articles to profl. jours. Congl. del. White House Conf. on Aging, 2005; bd. dirs. Jewish Cmty. Rels. Coun., San Jose, 1990—93, Coun. on Aging, San Jose, 1992—93; Women's Fund of Silicon Valley, San Jose, 2002—04; chair Sr. Citizen's Commn., San Jose, 1992—94; charter mem. Nat. Holocaust Mus., Washington, 1998—2006. Named Woman of Achievement, Women's Fund of Silicon Valley, 2001; recipient award for outstanding svc. to the disabled cmty., Internat. Assn. Workforce Profls., Am.'s Crown Communities award for creation of the FAST team, Am. City and County mag., 2001, President's award, Nat. Assn. Adult Protective Svcs., 2004. Mem.: Internat/Network for Prevention of Elder Abuse, Am. Soc. on Aging, Nat. Com. for Prevention of Elder Abuse. Avocations: exercise, travel. Office Phone: 408-975-4848. E-mail: betty.malks@ssa.sccgov.org.

**MALKUS, DAVID STARR,** mathematician; b. Chgo., June 30, 1945; s. Willem V.R. Malkus and Joanne (Gerould) Simpson; m. Evelyn R. (div.); children: Christopher, Annelise, Byron, Renata. AB, Yale U., 1968; PhD, Boston U., 1976. Mathematician U.S. Nat. Bur. Standards, Gaithersburg, Md., 1975-77; asst. prof. math. Ill. Inst. Tech., Chgo., 1977-83, assoc. prof., 1983-84; assoc. prof. mechanics U. Wis., Madison, 1984-87, prof., 1987—2002, chmn. Rheology Rsch. Ctr., 1991-94, prof. emeritus, 2002—. Chair prof. Nanjing (People's Republic China) Aero. Inst., 1986. Co-author: Concepts and Applications of Finite Element Analysis, 1989; contbr. articles to Computer Methods Applied Mech. Engring., Jour. Computational Physics. Achievements include research on finite element methods--reduced and selective integration techniques, a unification of concepts. Home: 2710 Mason St Madison WI 53705-3716 Office: U Wis Dept Engring Physics 1500 Engineering Dr Madison WI 53706-1609 Business E-Mail: malkus@engr.wisc.edu.

**MALL, WILLIAM JOHN, JR.,** aerospace transportation executive, retired military officer; b. Pitts., Jan. 13, 1933; s. William John and Margaret (Henry) M.; m. Vivian Lea Fenton; children— Michele, William, Catherine BBA, U. Pitts., 1954; MBA, George Washington U., 1966; sr. mgrs. in govt. program, Harvard U., 1980. Commd. officer USAF, 1954, advanced through grades to maj. gen., 1981; insp. gen. Mil. Airlift Command, Scott AFB, Ill., 1978, comdr. 436 wing Dover AFB, Del., 1979; DCS personnel Mil. Airlift Command, Scott AFB, Ill., 1979-81; comdr. Air Rescue Service, Scott AFB, Ill., 1981-83, 23d AF/MAC, Scott AFB, Ill., 1983-85; assigned to Hdqrs USAF, Bolling AFB, DC, 1985-86; ret.; dir. integrated logistics support div. Douglas Aircraft Co., Long Beach, Calif., 1987-89, gen. mgr. human resources, 1989-91; exec. dir. LAX Two Corp., L.A., 1991-99. Decorated Legion of Merit, Bronze Star, Air medal Mem. Airlift Assn., Daedalians, Jolly Green Pilots Assn. Avocations: tennis, sailing. Office: LAX Two Corp 200 World Way Los Angeles CA 90045-5859

**MALLACH, ALAN,** writer, consultant, city planner; b. Pitts., Oct. 15, 1944; S. Aubrey and Esther (Dingol) M. BA cum laude, Yale U., 1966. Lic. profl. planner, N.J. Evaluation coord. Community Progress, Inc., New Haven, 1965-67; dir. program devel. N.J. Dept. Community Affairs, Trenton, 1967-71; asst. dean Livingston Coll., Rutgers U., New Brunswick, N.J., 1971-73; asst. prof. Stockton State Coll., Pomona, N.J., 1974-74; research dir. N.J. Govt. Study Commn., Trenton, 1973-75; pres. Alan Mallach Assocs., Inc., Phila., 1975-80; exec. dir. Atlantic Co. Improvement Authority, Atlantic City, 1980-83; city planning and housing con. Roosevelt, N.J., 1983-90; dir. dept. housing and devel. City of Trenton, N.J., 1990-99; pvt. practice Roosevelt, N.J., 1999—; rsch. dir. Nat. Housing Inst., Montclair, NJ, 2003—. Adj. lectr. Rutgers U., Newark, 1988-90, New Brunswick, 2001-03; exec. com. Housing and Cmty. Devel. Network N.J., 1988—. Author: Inclusionary Housing Programs, 1984, Pietro Mascagni and his Operas, 2002, Bringing Buildings Back, 2006; contbr. articles to profl. jours. V.p. Bedminster Hills Housing Corp., Pluckemin, N.J., 1985-91; chmn. Roosevelt Borough Planning Bd., 1986-90; pres. Abrams Hebrew Acad., Yardley, Pa., 1984-87; mem. Roosevelt Arts Project, 1987—; commr. Delaware Valley Regional Planning Commn., 1990-99; N.J. adv. bd. Local Initiatives Support Corp., 1997-2003; sec., bd. dirs. Preservation N.J., 1999-2005; pres., bd. dirs. The Fund for Roosevelt; adv. bd. Nat. Vacant Properties Campaign. Named Citizen of Yr. N.J. Soc. Arch., 1998; recipient Environ. Quality award U.S. Environ. Protection Agy., 1997. Mem. Am. Inst. Cert. Planners (mem. Coll. Fellows), AIA, R/UDAT (task force), Am. Planning Assn. (Paul Davidoff award N.J. chpt. 1998). Office: PO Box 623 Roosevelt NJ 08555-0623 Office Phone: 609-448-5614. Personal E-mail: amallach@comcast.net.

**MALLAK, AUGUSTINE KENNETH,** monk, music educator; b. Champaign, Ill., Dec. 31, 1957; s. Bernard Andrew and Ludmilla Cora Mallak. MusM in Organ Performance, Am. Conservatory of Music, 1984. Dir. music and organist St. Procopius Abbey, Lisle, Ill., 1982—99; dir. music and liturgy St. Mary Star of Sea Ch., Chgo., 1999—2002; dir. music and organist St. Procopius Abbey, Lisle, 2003—. Instr. Benedictine U., Lisle, 1984—99, St. Mary Star of Sea Sch., Chgo., 1999—2002, Benedictine U., Lisle, 2002—. Composer: (choral music) A Child This Day is Born, A Mass for Saint Benedict, An Introit for Solemn Profession, (organ music) A Prelude on Saint Denio. Recipient Commencement Competition award, Am. Conservatory of Music, 1983. Mem.: Nat. Assn. Pastoral Musicians, Benedictine Musicians Am., Panel of Monastic Musicians, Am. Guild Organists. Roman Catholic. Avocations: food and wine connoisseur, computer desktop publishing. Home:

5601 College Rd Lisle IL 60532 Office: St Procopius Abbey 5601 College Rd Lisle IL 60532 Office Phone: 630-829-6331. Home Fax: 630-969-6426; Office Fax: 630-969-6426. E-mail: amallak@ben.edu.

**MALLAK, JAMES A.,** auto parts company executive; BS in Acctg., Mich. StateU.; MBA, Mich. State U. Numerous fin. mgmt. positions ITT Automotive, 1977—98; v.p. fin. Heavy Vehivle Systems divsn. Arvin/Meritor, 1998—99; exec. v.p., chief fin. officer Textron Automotive Corp., 1999—2001; chief fin. officer Tower Automotive Inc, Novi, Mich., 2004—. Mem. adv. bd. acctg. and fin. dept. Oakland U., Mich. Office: Tower Automotive Inc 27175 Haggarty Rd Novi MI 48377

**MALLARD, BENJAMIN FRANKLIN,** engineering educator; b. LA, July 1, 1952; s. Benjamin Franklin and Bernice Elizabeth Mallard; m. Paulett Kay Reese, Apr. 16, 1983; children: Benjamin Paul, Emily Frances. MSEE, U. So. Calif., LA, 1978; BSEE, MIT, Cambridge, 1975. Tech. staff TRW Def. and Space Sys. Group, Redondo Beach, Calif., 1975—82; engr. specialist Northrop Corp., Newbury Park, Calif., 1982—86; tech. staff Digital Radio Corp., Redondo Beach, Calif., 1986—90; rsch. asst. U. Calif., Santa Barbara, 1990—92; lectr. Calif. State U., Northridge, 1994—. Cons. Celerix Corp., Westlake Village, Calif., 1995—96, State of Calif., Northridge, 1995—2006; co-dir. NAACP Saturday Sch., Thousand Oaks, Calif., 1992—93; sec. LA Coun. of Black Profl. Engrs., 1981—82; instr. Johns Hopkins U., Ctr. for Talented Youth, Balt., 2006—. Treas. Newbury Park HS Girls Basketball Boosters Club, Calif., 2003—05; mission leader Azusa Pacific U., Calif., 2000—03; mem. of session Monte Vista Presbyn. Ch., Newbury Park, Calif., 2004—06; coach Newbury Park Youth Athletic Assn., 1990—2000. Named Disting. Educator of the Yr., 2006. Mem.: IEEE (assoc.), U. So. Calif. Engring. Alumni Assn., MIT Club So. Calif. Avocations: model railroading, travel, sports, reading. Home: 3876 Blackwood St Newbury Park CA 91320-4920 Office: Calif State Univ 18111 Nordhoff St Northridge CA 91330-8346 Office Phone: 818-677-5636. Home Fax: 805-375-3731; Office Fax: 818-677-7062. Personal E-mail: bfm7152@cs.com. Business E-Mail: bmallard@csun.edu.

**MALLARD, STEPHEN ANTHONY,** retired utilities executive; b. Jersey City, Sept. 15, 1924; s. Stephen F. and Gertrude V. (Donahue) M.; m. Winifred Anne Carey, June 7, 1947; children: Stephen Kevin, Catherine Anne, Eileen Rosemary Mallard McClenahan. M.E., Stevens Inst. Tech, Hoboken, N.J., 1948, MSE.E., 1951. Registered profl. engr. With elec. distbn., system planning and devel. Pub. Service Electric and Gas Co., Newark, 1951-77, v.p. system planning, 1977-80, sr. v.p. planning and research, 1980-88, sr. v.p. transmission systems, 1989; pvt. practice engring. Nutley, N.J., 1990—. Advisor Brookhave Nat. Lab.; cons. Manhattan Coll. Bd. dirs. Met. chpt. ARC, Fairfield, N.J., 1985—, bd. dirs. No. N.J. chpt., 1988—; bd. dirs. Essex County Grand Jury Assn., 1978-87. With USN, 1944-46, PTO. Fellow IEEE; mem. Nat. Soc. Profl. Engrs., Conf. Internationale des Grands Reseaux Electriques a Haute Tension, Eta Kappa Nu, Tau Beta Pi Roman Catholic. Home and Office: 68 High St Nutley NJ 07110-1134 Office Phone: 973-667-2350. E-mail: samallardnj@aol.com.

**MALLEIN, DARLA J.,** social studies educator; BS in Secondary Edn., Emporia State U., 1980, MS, 1994; PhD in Curriculum and Instrn., Kans. State U., 2003. Tchr. Americus Elem. Sch., 1981-83; 8-12 grade lang. arts, yearbook LeRoy H.S., 1983-87; 9-11th grade lang. arts Emporia H.S., 1987-88; 8th grade social studies Emporia Mid. Sch., 1988—2001; social studies edn. educator Emporia State U., 2001—, asst. prof. social scis. edn., 2003. Adj. faculty Emporia State U. Coll. Liberal Arts and Scis., 1998. Contbr. articles to profl. jours. Named Outstanding Young Educator Kans. Jaycees, 1996, Wal-Mar Tchr. of Yr. 1998, Kans. Tchr. of Yr. 1998, Outstanding Grad. Student in Edn., Kans. State U., 2003; grantee Emporia Middle Sch. PTO, 1992, Southeastern Kans. Edn. Found., 1995, 7 grants Southwestern Bell Excellence in Edn., 1991-95, Emporia Schs. Found., 1998, 99, Michael Jordan Found. grant, 2000. Mem. NEA (chair comms. com. 1997-99, bd. edn. liaison 1995-99, others), Kans. Coun. for the Social Studies (state bd. dirs. 1994—, pres. 2003-04, others), Nat. Coun. for the Social Studies, Phi Kappa Phi, Phi Delta Kappa. Home: 1901 Meadowlark Ln Emporia KS 66801-6125 Office Phone: 620-341-5567. E-mail: malleind@emporia.edu.

**MALLERY, DAVID,** education association executive, consultant; b. Sugar Hill, N.H., Aug. 3, 1923; s. Otto Tod and Louise Marshall Mallery; m. Judith Chappell Mallery, June 15, 1956; children: Roger, Diane Mallery Cusick. BA, Haverford (Pa.) Coll., 1945, PhD (hon.), 1995; MA, Middlebury (Vt.) Coll., 1950. Tchr. English Germantown Friends Sch., Phila., 1946-58; seminar leader Friends Coun. on Edn., Phila., 1959-94; dir. profl. devel. Nat. Assn. Ind. Schs., Washington, 1959—. Edn. cons., 1959—; tchr. Bell Tel./U. Pa. Inst. for Humanistic Studies for Execs., 1960's. Author: High School Students Speak Out, 1960's, Ferment on the Campus, 1960's. Edn. advisor Tracy S. Voorhees, Pres. Eisenhower's rep. on Cuban refugee crisis, 1959-60; founding trustee Am. Film Inst., 1967-79. Lt. (j.g.) USNR, 1943-46, WW II. Recipient Klingenstein award Columbia U. Tchrs. Coll., 1996. Avocations: films, theater, music, international networking. Home: 9006 Crefeld St Philadelphia PA 19118-3607 Office: Nat Assn Ind Schs Sugar Loaf Conf Ctr 9230 Germantown Ave Philadelphia PA 19118-2603 Office Phone: 215-242-0731.

**MALLERY, MARY SILCOX,** librarian, director; b. Utica, N.Y., Nov. 9, 1936; d. William Henry and Maybelle Ruth (Jones) Silcox; m. Richard Carruth Mallery, July 16, 1960. BLS, Simmons Coll., Boston, 1958; MLS, Drexel U., 1968; MBA, FrostBurg U., 1988. Cert. library administr., Md. Libr. U.S. Army, various posts, 1958-60; dir. Lansdale (Pa.) Pub. Library, 1960-68; extension librarian Montgomery County Library, Norristown, Pa., 1968-70; regional librarian Western Md. Pub. Libraries, Hagerstown, 1970—2000; exec. dir. Citizens for Med. Librs., 2000—. Mem. adv. bd. Regional Edn. Svc. Agy., Cumberland, Md., 1973-83, Md. State Libr. Resource Ctr. Balt., 1975-89, Md. Network Planning Coun., 1990-1997. Author: A Sign System for Libraries, 1982 (John Cotton Dana award 1982); co-designer the nat. library symbol, 1982 (Recognition cert., 1983). Mem. ALA, Md. Library Assn., Cumberland Valley Libr. Assn., Hagerstown Preservation Design Dist. Commn. Democrat. Episc. Avocations: dog training, dog shows, gardening, flower shows. Office: P O Box 267 Funkstown MD 21734

**MALLETT, CONRAD LEROY, JR.,** former state supreme court chief justice, hospital administrator; b. Detroit, Oct. 12, 1953; s. Conrad LeRoy and Claudia Gwendolyn (Jones) M.; m. Barbara Straugh, Dec. 22, 1984; children: Alex Conrad, Mio Thomas, Kristan Claudia. BA, UCLA, 1975; MPA, JD, U. So. Calif., 1979; MBA, Oakland U. Bar: Mich. 1979. Legal asst. to congressman, Detroit, 1979-80; dep. pol. div. Dem. Nat. Com., Washington, 1980-81; assoc. Miller, Canfield, Paddock & Stone, Detroit, 1981-82; legal counsel, dir. to gov. State of Mich., Lansing, 1983-84; sr. exec. asst. to Mayor City of Detroit, 1985-86; ptnr. Jaffe, Raitt, Heuer & Weiss, Detroit, 1987-90; justice Mich. Supreme Ct., Lansing, 1990—98, chief justice, 1997—98; pvt. practice Miller Canfield, Detroit, 1999; gen. counsel, chief adminstrv. officer Detroit Med. Ctr., 1999—2001, exec. v.p., chief adminstrv. officer, 2003—; COO City of Detroit, 2002; pres., gen. counsel Hawkins Food Group, 2002—03; interim pres. Sinai Grace Hosp., Detroit, 2003—. Bd. mem. Lear Corp., TechTeam Global, Inc. Mem. NAACP, Kappa Alpha Psi. Democrat. Roman Catholic. Avocations: writing, fiction. Office: Sinai-Grace Hosp 6071 W Outer Dr Detroit MI 48235-2624

**MALLETT, T. CONN,** biochemist, educator; s. Terry Conn and Kay Marlene Mallett; m. Melissa Flavia Jacobini, Feb. 29, 2000; children: Natalie Kay, Finnigan Connor. BSc, Va. Poly. Inst. and State U., Blacksburg, 1993; PhD, Wake Forest U., Winston Salem, N.C., 1999. Japan Soc. for Promotion of Sci. rsch. fellow Inst. for Protein Rsch., Osaka U., Suita, Japan, 1999—2001; asst. prof. of biochemistry Wake Forest U. Sch. of Medicine, Ctr. for Structural Biology, Winston Salem, 2001—. Dir. macromolecular x-ray diffraction lab. Ctr. for Structural Biology, Wake Forest U., Winston

Salem, 2003—. Contbr. scientific papers to profl. jours. Recipient Mechanisms involved in flavin-linked oxygen metabolism grant, NIH, 2002—06, Dissertation Enhancement award, NSF, 1998—99, Camillo Artom scholarship of biochemistry, Wake Forest U. Sch. of Medicine, 1996—99. Mem.: Am. Crystallography Assn., Am. Soc. for Biochemistry and Molecular Biology, Am. Chem. Soc., Internat. Union of Crystallography. Independent. Office: Wake Forest Univ School of Medicine Medical Center Blvd Winston Salem NC 27157 Office Phone: 336-716-8981. E-mail: conn@csb.wfu.edu.

**MALLEY, RAYMOND CHARLES,** retired foreign service official, industrial executive; b. Cambridge, Mass., Dec. 22, 1930; s. William and Evangeline (Vautour) M.; m. Rita Ann Masse, May 26, 1951 (dec. June 1989); children: Keith, Bruce, Gregory; m. Josette Lucile Vidril Murphy, Aug. 11, 1995. AA, Boston U., 1950, BS, 1952; MA Equivalent, U. Geneva, 1955; MA, PhD ABD, Fletcher Sch. Law & Diplomacy, Tufts U. and Harvard U., Mass., 1956. Economist, fin. analyst Texaco, Inc., NYC, 1957—61; fgn. svc. officer U.S. Dept. State, AID, Washington & fgn. posts, 1961—82; dir. U.S. Trade and Devel. Program, Washington, 1980; v.p. Silopress, Inc., Sioux City, Iowa, 1982—87; pres. Silopress Can., 1985—87; cons., advisor Labat-Anderson Internat., Arlington, Va., 1988—93; sr. group advisor, N.Am. and S.Am. rep. Halla Bus. Group, Seoul, Republic of Korea, NYC, Washington, 1991—. Chmn. Halla Am. Inc., 1996—2001. Mem. exec. bd. Coll. of Mgmt., L.I. U., Brookville, NY, 1994—. 2nd lt., 1st lt., capt. then maj. USAFR. Recipient Nat. Def. Svc. medal, USAFR, Korean War. Mem. Acadian Cultural Soc., Am. Fgn. Svc. Assn., Diplomatic and Consular Officers Ret., U.S. Profl. Tennis Registry, Harvard Club. Roman Catholic. Avocation: tennis. Office: Halla America Inc 6224 Lock Raven Dr Mc Lean VA 22101-3133 Office Phone: 703-893-8083. Personal E-mail: Rcmalley@aol.com.

**MALLIA, MARIANNE,** medical writer; b. Davenport, Iowa, Feb. 14, 1948; d. Norman Bramblett and Mary Jane (Hilkemeyer) Hagar; 1 child from previous marriage, Lindsay Sharyn. BA in English, U. Iowa, 1970. Cert. tchr. Tchr. tech. writing Houston Ind. Sch. Dist., 1970—76; med. writer Tex. Heart Inst., Houston, 1976—; editl. cons. Tex. Heart Inst. Jour., Houston, 1977—87, head sci. publ., 1986—, sr. med. writer, 1994—. Instr. Sch. Allied Health Sci. and Sch. Pub. Health U. Tex., 1990—94. Editor: Techniques in Cardiac Surgery, 1984; editor: (with Denton A. Cooley) Surg. Treatment of Aortic Aneurysms, 1985; editor: (essays) Reflections and Observation, Denton A. Cooley, MD, 1985; author: (handbook) Heart Owner's Handbook, 1995; bd. editors: Life Sci., 2002. Fellow: Am. Med. Writers Assn. (core curriculum cert. 1984, instr. 1985—, advanced curriculum cert. 1989, honor roll workshop leader 1992—, bd. dir., exec. com. 1996—2005, pres. 2002—03, writer and advanced core curriculum, Award Tchg. Excellence 1998); mem.: Women in Comm. (core curriculum cert. in life sci., Matrix award 1990—2000), Coun. Biology Editors, Pi Beta Phi. Avocation: classic cars. Office: Tex Heart Inst PO Box 20345 Houston TX 77225-0345 Home: 3779 Tangley St Houston TX 77005-2031 Office Phone: 832-355-6776. Business E-Mail: mmallia@heart.thi.tmc.edu.

**MALLIK, MUHAMMAD ABDUL-BARI,** soil microbiologist; b. Pabna, Bangladesh, Mar. 15, 1927; s. Monsur Ali and Ataharun-Nisa Mallik; m. Rowshan Jahan Hamida, Sept. 24, 1966; 1 child, Abds-Sami. BSc, Rajshahi (Bangladesh) Coll., 1949; MSc, Dhaka (Bangladesh) U., 1952; MS, Minn. U., 1961; PhD, Okla. U., 1964. Lectr. botany U. Karachi, Pakistan, 1956-59, asst. prof., 1964-68, 69-72; vis. scholar dept. botany Baghdad (Iraq) U., 1968-69; asst. prof. Dhaka (Bangladesh) U., 1973-74; rsch. assoc. dept. botany and microbiology u. Okla., Norman, 1974-75; assoc. rsch. assoc. prof. agrl. rsch. program Langston (Okla.) U., 1975-82, rsch. prof. agrl. rsch. program, 1982—. Author: Introduction to Fungi, 1973; contbr. articles to profl. and popular publs. Fulbright scholar Minn. U., St. Paul, 1961; rsch. grantee Pakistan Agrl. Rsch. Coun., Karachi, 1968-69, USDA, Langston, 1982—. Mem. Am. Soc. Agronomy, Internat. Allelopathy Soc., Okla. Acad. Sci., Bangladesh Bot. Soc. Democrat. Moslem. Avocation: gardening. Home: 2611 S Oxford Dr Stillwater OK 74074-2276 Office: Langston Univ Agrl Rsch Program PO Box 730 Langston OK 73050-0730

**MALLIN, JOEL,** lawyer; m. Sherry Vogel. BS, Cornell U.; LLB, Columbia U. Bar: NY 1961. Atty. Joel Mallin LLP, NYC. Chmn. Aldrich Mus., Conn. Named one of Top 200 Collectors, ARTnews Mag., 2004—. Mem.: Manhattan Theatre Club. Avocation: collector of modern & contemporary art, particularly sculpture. Office: 110 East 59th St New York NY 10022-1304 Home: 60 Pound Ridge Rd Pound Ridge NY 10576 Office Phone: 212-715-0569, 212-486-0511. E-mail: jmallin@aol.com.

**MALLIS, MELISSA MERCEDES,** research psychologist, biomedical scientist; b. Kingston, Pa., Apr. 24, 1972; d. Thomas John and Paulette Mary Mallis. BS in Physics, Villanova U., 1994; PhD in Biomed. Sci., Drexel U., 1999. Dir. Fatigue Countermeasures Group NASA Ames Rsch. Ctr., Moffett Field, Calif., 1999—2005; dir. sci. affairs Alertness Solutions, Cupertino, Calif., 2005—. Contbr. chapters to books, articles to profl.jours. Recipient NASA Turning Goals into Reality Exceptional Progress Toward Aviation Safety award, NASA, 1999, NASA Turning Goals into Reality Exceptional Progress Toward Support of MER Ops, 2004, numerous Superior Performance awards, NASA. Mem.: Sleep Rsch. Soc. (Merit award 1998, Trainee Rsch. Excellence award 1998), Human Factors and Ergonomics Soc., Associated Profl. Sleep Socs., Am. Acad. Sleep Medicine, Aerospace Human Factors Assn. (Arnold D. Tuttle award 2003, William E. Collins award 2003), Aerospace Med. Assn., World Fedn. Sleep Rsch. Socs., European Sleep Rsch. Soc. Roman Catholic. Avocations: swimming, travel, frogs. Office Phone: 650-604-3654, 408-253-1019.

**MALLO-GARRIDO, JOSEPHINE ANN,** advertising executive; b. Agana, Guam, Mar. 20, 1955; d. Benjamin Correja and Salvacion (Lacuesta) Mallo; m. John Marco Haniu Garrido, Feb. 16, 1980; children: Josiah Michael (dec.), Jordan Thaddeus. Student, U. Guam, Agana, 1972-74; BA in Journalism, Seattle U., 1976; MBA, Pepperdine U., 1982. Reporter Pacific Daily News, Agana, 1976, features editor, 1977-78, asst. city editor, 1978-79; copy editor features Honolulu Star-Bull., 1979-81; advt. copywriter Advt. Factors, Honolulu, 1981-83; communications specialist Liberty House, Honolulu, 1983-84; editor, advt. copywriter Safeway Stores Inc., Oakland, Calif., 1984-88; features writer Tracy (Calif.) Press, 1988-91; mktg. mgr. ComputerLand of Guam, Maite, 1992-93; mktg. officer Citibank, Agana, 1993-94; owner JMG Advt., 1994—. Newspaper graphics cons. Pacific Daily News, 1984. Editor/writer Foods Unltd., 1984-88, Tracy Community Hosp. Health Beat and Update, 1988-91; editor Pacific Voice, 1977-78; contbr. articles to profl. jours. Vol. Engaged Encounter, Honolulu, 1989, Trans-Pacific Yacht Race, Honolulu, 1983, United Way, Oakland, 1986; advt. coord. Easter Seals, Oakland, 1987; organist St. Patrick's Ch., Honolulu, 1980—84, Immaculate Heart of Mary Ch., Toto, Guam, 1994—; mem. adv. bd. Cath. Social Svcs., Agana, Guam, 1993—97, bd. dirs., 1997—, bd. trustees, 2002—. Recipient Cert. Achievement award Adv. Age Mag., 1985, Cert Appreciation award Am. Heart Food Festival, 1985, Best in the West award Am. Advt. Fedn., 1986, Retail Nutrition award Nat. Potato Promotion Bd., 1986, Spl. Achievement award Newspaper Spl. Sect. Mother's Day/Father's Day Coun., 1989, 90, First Place Story 2d place Calif. Newspaper Pubs., 1989, 1st place Classified Advt. Assn., 1989, 1st place appetizer Spam Food Festival, 1991. Mem. Guam C. of C. (media coord. 1993-95), Citiclub (exec. sec. 1994-95). Roman Catholic. Avocations: piano, travel, Karate (black belt).

**MALLON, FRANCIS J.,** health science association administrator; Chief exec. officer Am. Physical Therapy Assn., Alexandria, Va., 1993—. Office: Am Physical Therapy Assn 1111 N Fairfax St Alexandria VA 22314-1436 Office Phone: 703-684-2782.*

**MALLON, KELLIE JANE,** special education educator; b. Silver Spring, Md., Apr. 18, 1969; d. James A. and Barbara E. Mallon. B. St. Leo Coll. Fla., 1994; Master's degree, Nova Southeastern U., 1997. Learn. Cert. profl. tchr. Fla. Specific learning disabilities and spl. edn. tchr. Pasco County Sch. Bd., New

Port Richey, Fla., 1996—. Sec Schwettman Alternative Sch. Adv. Bd., New Port Richey, 1997—2004. Recipient After Sch. Activities grant, Pasco County Sch. Bd., 1997—98, Svc. Learning grant, Fla. Dept. of Edn. Mem.: CEC (assoc.; specific learning disability divsn. 2001—02). Roman Catholic. Avocations: reading, rescue animal advocate. Home: 6618 Crossbow Ln New Port Richey FL 34653 Office: Pasco County Sch Bd 7227 Land O' Lakes Blvd Land O Lakes FL 34638 Office Phone: 727-774-2000. Personal E-mail: kmallon@ij.net. E-mail: kmallon@pasco.k12.fl.us.

**MALLON, MEG,** professional golfer; b. Natick, Mass., Apr. 14, 1963; Student, Ohio State U., 1983-87. Prof. Golfer LPGA Tour, 1987—. Mem. Solheim Cup Team, 1992, 94, 96, 98, 2000, 2002, 2003 Named Female Player of Year, Golf Writers Assn. of Am., 1991, one of the LPGA's top 50 players and tchrs., LPGA's 50th Anniversary, 2000. Achievements include winner 18 career LPGA victories including: Mazda LPGA Championship, 1991, U.S. Women's Open, 1991, 2004. Avocations: music, sports, travel. Office: care LPGA 100 International Golf Dr Daytona Beach FL 32124-1082

**MALLON, THOMAS,** writer; b. Glen Cove, NY, Nov. 2, 1951; s. Arthur Vincent and Caroline (Moruzzi) M. AB, Brown U., 1973; AM, Harvard U., 1974, PhD, 1978. Asst. prof. English Vassar Coll., Poughkeepsie, NY, 1979-85, assoc. prof., 1985-89, lectr. in English 1989-91; lit. editor Gentlemen's Quar., N.Y.C., 1991-95, writer-at-large, 1995-99; mem. Nat. Coun. on Humanities, 2002—05; dep. chmn. NEH, 2005—. Author: Edmund Blunden, 1983, A Book of One's Own, 1984, Arts and Sciences, 1988, Stolen Words, 1989, Aurora 7, 1991, Rockets and Rodeos, 1993, Henry and Clara, 1994, Dewey Defeats Truman, 1997, Two Moons, 2000, In Fact, 2001, Mrs. Paine's Garage, 2002, Bandbox, 2004. Recipient Ingram Merrill award, 1994, Nat. Book Critics Cir. citation for excellence in reviewing, 1998, Great Lakes Book award for fiction, 1998; Rockefeller Found. fellow, 1986-87, Guggenheim fellow, 2000-2001. Mem. PEN Am., Phi Beta Kappa. Home: 801 25th St NW Washington DC 20037 Personal E-mail: TVMallon@aol.com.

**MALLORY, ARTHUR LEE,** dean, retired state official; b. Springfield, Mo., Dec. 26, 1932; s. Dillard A. and Ferrell (Claxton) M.; m. Joann Peters, June 6, 1954; children: Dennis Arthur (dec.), Christopher Lee, Stephanie Ann, Jennifer Lyn. BS, S.W. Mo. State Coll., 1954; MEd, U. Mo., 1957, EdD, 1959; HHD, S.W. Bapt. Coll., Mo., 1972. History supr. U. Mo. Lab. Sch., Columbia, 1956-57; asst. to supt. schs. Columbia, 1957-59; asst. supt. schs. Parkway Sch. Dist., St. Louis County, Mo., 1959-64; dean evening div. U. Mo., St. Louis, 1964; pres. S.W. Mo. State U., Springfield, 1964-70, dean Coll. Edn., 1991-94; commr. edn. Mo. Dept. Edn., Jefferson City, 1971-87. Dir. Internat. House, U. Mo., Columbia, 1956-59; chmn. bd. Mo. Coun. on Econ. Edn., 2000—. V.p. Ozarks coun. Boy Scouts Am., 1967, pres. Gt. Rivers coun., 1972-73, Greene County Assn. for Retarded Citizens, 1989—, pres., 1991-96; mem. north crtl. region exec. bd., 1984—; bd. dirs. Meml. Cmty. Hosp., Mid-Continent Regional Ednl. Lab., Ozark Pub. Telecoms. Inc., 1989—; chmn. bd. Mo. Coun. on Econ. Edn.; bd. regents Mo. State Univs.; trustee Pub. Sch. Retirement, William Jewell Coll., 1972-74; chmn. com. bds. So. Bapt. Conv., 1972-73, mem. com. or bds., 1981—; mem. exec. bd. Mo. Bapt. Conv., 1972-75, 77-80, 2d v.p. 1995-96, pres., 1996-97; trustee Southwestern Bapt. Theol. Sem., Fort Worth, 1995—; mem. adv. com. Young Audiences, Inc., 1986, ARC Bd., Greene County, 1986, Children's Svcs. Commn., chmn., 1986—, Edn. Commn. U.S.; bd. dirs. Ozark Pub. TV; chmn. bd. advisors Windemere Bapt. Assembly, 1992—, chmn. bd. trustees, 2000—; pres. Gt. River coun. Boy Scouts Am., 1972, 73; chmn. Mo. Coun. for Econ. Edn., 2000—. With U.S. Army, 1954-56. Recipient Disting. Service award Mo. Jr. C. of C., 1966; Distinguished Service award U Mo., 1976; Faculty/Alumni award U. Mo., 1976; Silver Beaver award Boy Scouts Am., 1983, Good Shepherd and Cross, 1986, Disting. Citizen award, 1986; hon. life mem. Mo. Congress Parents and Tchrs.; named Springfield's Outstanding Young Man of Yr., 1965; Champion of Excellence PUSH, 1978 Mem. Am. Assn. State Colls. and Univs., N. Central Assn. Colls. and Secondary Schs., Council Chief State Sch. Officers, Mo. Assn. Sch. Administrs., NEA, Mo. Tchrs. Assn. So. Baptist (deacon). Clubs: Masons (33 deg.), Rotary.

**MALLORY, BENJAMIN WADE,** music educator; s. Wade C and Doris M Mallory; m. Beverly K Hicklin, June 5, 2004; children: Rob, Drew. MusB in Edn., Troy State U., Ala., 1989. Cert. tchr. Ala., Ga., 1989. Dir. of bands Calera H.S., Calera, Ala., 1989—91, Pierce County H.S., Blackshear, Ga., 1991—93, Crisp County Schs., Cordele, Ga., 1993—2003, Sumter County Mid. Sch., Americus, Ga., 2003—. Named STAR Tchr., 1998; named to Outstanding Young Men of Am., 1989; recipient Paul Yoder Music award, Paul Yoder Found., 1989. Mem.: NEA, Ga. Assn. of Educators, Ga. Music Educators Assn.

**MALLORY, BRUCE,** academic administrator; BA in American History with hon., Allegheny Coll., Meadville, Pa., 1971, MEd in Secondary Edn. Social Studies, 1972; PhD Special Edn. Cmty. Psychology, Vanderbilt Univ., 1979. Dean Grad. Sch. U. NH, Durham, prof. edn., sr. vice provost, provost, 2003—. Vis. lectr. Univ. Milan. Co-editor Early Childhood Rsch. Quarterly Operas. Vol. Suncook Learning Ctr., 1993. Office: Office Acad Affairs Thompson Hall 207 Univ NH Durham NH 03824*

**MALLORY, CHARLES KING, III,** lawyer; b. Norfolk, Va., Nov. 16, 1936; s. Charles King Mallory Jr. and Dorothy Pratt (Williams) Swanke; m. Florence Beale Marshall; children: King, Raburn, Anne, Richard. BA, Yale U., 1958; JD, Tulane U., 1961. Bar: La. 1961, Calif. 1965, D.C. 1972. Ptnr. Monroe & Lemann, New Orleans, 1965-72; acting exec. dir. SEC, Washington, 1972; dep. asst. sec. U.S. Dept. Interior, Washington, 1973, acting asst. sec., 1974; v.p., gen. counsel Middle South Svcs., Inc. New Orleans, 1975-79; ptnr. Hunton & Williams, Washington, 1979—. Gen. counsel Com. on the Present Danger, 1977-99. Mem. Reagan-Bush Transition Team, Washington, 1980-81, Grace Commn. on Pvt. Sector Survey Cost in the Fed. Govt., Washington, 1983-84. Served to lt. USNR, 1961-65. Mem. ABA, La. Bar Assn., Calif. Bar Assn., D.C. Bar Assn., Energy Bar Assn., Nat. Assn. Bond Lawyers. Republican. Episcopalian. Office: Hunton & Williams 1900 K St NW 12th Floor Washington DC 20006-1110 E-mail: kmallory@hunton.com.

**MALLORY, FRANK LINUS,** lawyer; b. Calgary, Alta., Can., May 5, 1920; s. Frank Louis and Anna Amy (Allstrum) M.; m. Jean Ellen (Lindsey), Jan. 29, 1944; children: Susan Mallory Redmond, Ann M. Kenney, Bruce R. AB, Stanford U., 1941, LLB, 1947. Bar: Calif., 1948. Assoc. Gibson, Dunn and Crutcher, L.A., 1947-54; ptnr. L.A. and Orange County, 1955-88. Cert. specialist taxation law Calif. Bd. Legal Splty., 1973-89. Pres. town hall of L.A., 1970; Boys Republic, Chino, Calif., 1962-64; pres. Braille Inst. Am., L.A., 1988-92; Lt.(j.g.), USNR, 1942-46. Mem. ABA, Los Angeles County Bar Assn., Orange County Bar Assn., Newport Harbor Yacht Club, Big Canyon Country Club, Transpacific Yacht Club (staff commodore), Order of Coif, Phi Beta Kappa. Republican. Home: 633 Bayside Dr Newport Beach CA 92660-7213 E-mail: flmallory@cs.com.

**MALLORY, JEANNINE MAREK,** public relations and marketing professional; b. Richmond, Va., Feb. 21, 1958; d. Thomas Edward and Suzanne (Brown) Marek; m. Peter Altman Mallory, May 30, 1981. BS in Pub. Rels., U. South Fla., 1980; postgrad., Troy State U. Pub. rels. intern Tampa Bay Buccaneers franchise NFL, Tampa, Fla., 1980-81; benefits analyst The Bank of New Orleans, 1981-82; pub. rels. mgr. S.E. La. Blood Ctr., New Orleans, 1982-84; pub. rels. and mktg. dir. Orlando (Fla.) Gen. Hosp., 1984-85; state info. officer Va. Dept. Health, Richmond, 1985; pub. rels. cons., health promotions dir. Mallory Bayou, Panama City, Fla., 1987—; health promotions dir. Hosp. Corp. Am. Gulf Coast Hosp., Panama City, 1989—. Communications coord., speakers bur. coord. Am. Heart Assn. Panama City, 1990—; pub. rels. coord. Bay County Drug Free, Panama City, 1990—; pub. rels. cons. Bay Dist. Schs., Panama City, 1989—. Mem. United Way N.W. Fla., 1989—; mem. Community Image Com., 1991—; bd. dirs. Am. Heart Assn.; participant Leadership Bay, 1990-91; mem. Heart at Work Team, Save the Manatee Club. Recipient Image award Internat. Assn. Bus. Communica-

tors, 1989, Communications award Am. Heart Assn., 1990. Mem. Nat. Assn. Occupational Health, Nat. Writers Club, Fla. Pub. Rels. Assn. (bd. dirs. 1990), Bay County C. of C. Republican. Avocations: writing, tennis, reading, photography. Home: 5948 27th St N Saint Petersburg FL 33714-1400

**MALLORY, MARK L.,** mayor, former state legislator; b. Cin., Apr. 2, 1962; s. William L. Mallory. Student, Xavier U.; BS in Adminstrv. Mgmt., U. Cin. Dept. mgr. Hamilton County Pub. Libr. Graphic Prodn., Cin., 1981—95; rep. dist. 31 Ohio Ho. Reps., Columbus, 1995—98; mem. Dist. 9 Ohio State Senate, Columbus, 1998—2005, asst. minority whip, 2000—03, asst. minority leader, 2003—05; mayor City of Cin., 2005—. Bd. trustees Friar's Club; advisory coun. 4C for Children; advisory bd. Ronald McDonald House of Cin. Recipient Devel. Leadership award, Bowhay Inst. for Legis. Leadership, 1996, Myrl Shoemaker Legis. of the Year award, 1998, Excellence in Correctional Edn. award, Correctional Edn. Assn., 1999, Pub. Svc. award, Gothic Lodge 122, 2000, Legis. of the Year award, Nat. Assn. Social Workers, 2001, Wolfe award of Excellence, OH Assn. Elected Officials, 2002, Pub. Svc. award, Nat. Assn. Grad. & Profl. Students, 2003, Passport to Excellence award, Phi Delta Kappa, 2003, Andrew Carnegie award, OH Library Coun., 2003, Legis. of the Year award, OH Community Corrections Assn., 2004. Mem. NAACP, Libr. Staff Assn., Black Male Coalition, Friends of Pub. Libr., Urban League of Cin., Pub. Libr. Staff Assn., Internat. TV Assn. Achievements include being the African American to be directly elected by the people of Cincinnati, 2005. Office: Office of Mayor 801 Plum St Cincinnati OH 45202*

**MALLORY, PATRICIA JODY,** museum curator; b. De Ridder, La., Sept. 22, 1951; d. William Buford and Gwendolyn (singletary) M. BBA, La. State U., 1979. Mgr. Harpers Records, De Ridder, 1979-83; dir. pub. rels. Goldband Records, Lake Charles, La., 1983-89; mgr. Bargain Time, Baton Rouge, 1989-91, Hills Music, De Ridder, 1991-96; sales and mktg. exec. Krok Radio, De Ridder, 1996-97; mus. curator Beauregard Parish, De Ridder, 1997—. Leader blues band Blues Horizon. Drummer Goldband Studios, 1971-83, Lake Charles; drummer recs. include Blessed Rain (Blue Rain), 1987, Drenched (Blue Rain), 1989, Saturday Nights and Sunday Mornings (OFB), 1987. Active Beauregard Econ. Devel., De Ridder; mem. main street promotions com.; mem. bd. dirs. Downtown Mchts. Assn., Beauregard Assn. Retarded Citizens. Named one of Best Unsigned Drummers, Promark, 1995. Mem. Percussive Arts Soc., Daus. of Confederacy, Humane Soc., People for Ethical Treatment Animals, Nat. Geog. Soc., World Wildlife Fund, Beauregard Woman's Orgn. Avocations: music, travel. Home: 501 S Stewart St Deridder LA 70634-4955 Office Phone: 337-463-8148. E-mail: museum@beau.org.

**MALLORY, ROBERT MARK,** controller, finance company executive; b. Mattoon, Ill., Apr. 15, 1950; s. Robert Monroe and Betty Ann (Mudd) M.; m. Diana Marie Burde, Aug. 19, 1972; 1 child, Laura Elizabeth. BS in Accountancy, U. Ill., 1972; MBA, Northwestern U., 1985. CPA Ill. Staff acct. Price Waterhouse, Chgo., 1972-74, sr. acct., 1974-77, mgr., 1977-79; dir. internal audit Mark Controls Corp., Skokie, Ill., 1979-81, corp. contr., 1981-86, v.p., contr., 1986-88; contr., dir. planning Tribune Co., Chgo., 1988-91, v.p., contr., 1991—. Bd. dirs. Met. Family Svcs. Mem. AICPA (Elijah Watts Sells award 1972), Ill. CPA Soc., Fin. Execs. Internat. (bd. dirs.), Internat. Newspaper Fin. Execs. (bd. dirs.), Beta Gamma Sigma. Methodist. Home: 3312 Lakewood Ct Glenview IL 60026-2505 Office: Tribune Co 435 N Michigan Ave Chicago IL 60611-4066 Personal E-mail: mallory435@aol.com.

**MALLORY, TROY L.,** accountant; b. Sesser, Ill., July 30, 1923; s. Theodore E. and Alice (Mitchell) M.; m. Magdalene Richter, Jan. 26, 1963. Student, So. Ill. U., 1941-43, Washington and Jefferson Coll., 1943-44; BS, U. Ill., 1947, MS, 1948. Staff sr. supr. Scovell, Wellington & Co., CPAs, Chgo., 1948-58; mgr. Gray Hunter Stenn CPAs, Quincy, Ill., 1959-62, ptnr., 1962-99. Mem. fin com. United Fund, Adams County, 1961-64; bd. dirs. Woodland Home for Orphans and Friendless, 1970—2005, pres., 1981-84, 87-90. Served with 84th Inf. Divsn. AUS, 1942-45. Decorated Purple Heart, Bronze Star. Mem. AICPA, Ill. CPA Soc., Quincy C. of C. (bd. dirs. 1970-76), Rotary (bd. dirs. Quincy 1967-70, pres. 1978-79), Shriners (bd. dirs. Quincy 1982-85, pres. 1988), Royal Order Jesters (Ct. 20 dir. 1997), Railsplitters Soc. (pres. 1993). Home: 2229 Jersey St Quincy IL 62301-4341

**MALLOW, MATTHEW J.,** lawyer; b. Bklyn., 1943; AB, Brown U., 1964; JD, NYU, 1967, LLM, 1968. Bar: NY 1967. Ptnr. corp. fin. Skadden, Arps, Slate, Meagher & Flom LLP, NYC. Guest lectr. Harvard Bus. Sch. Bd. trustee Brown U., 1990—96, 1997—, treas., 1999—; represented Bard Coll. in the creation of the Bard HS Early Coll., 2001; rep. of the city council pres. to the bd. trustees Metropolitan Mus. Art, 1978—85. Mem.: Assn. Bar City NY (exec. com. 1971—75, vice-chmn., grievance com. 1976—77, chmn. securities regulation com. 2003—06). Office: Skadden Arps Slate Meagher & Flom LLP 4 Times Sq New York NY 10036 Office Phone: 212-735-3930. Office Fax: 917-777-3930. Business E-Mail: mmallow@skadden.com.

**MALLOY, DANNEL PATRICK,** mayor; m. Cathy Malloy; children: Dan, Ben, Sam. LLB, Boston Coll. Bar: Conn., Mass., N.Y., U.S. Dist. Ct. Conn., U.S. Dist. Ct. (ea. and so. dists.) N.Y. Asst. dist. atty. Bklyn., N.Y. Dist. Atty.'s Office, 1980-84; ptnr. Abate & Fox, Stamford, Conn., 1984-95; mayor City of Stamford, 1995—. Mem. bd. fin. City of Stamford, 1983-94, Stamford Bd. Edn., 1994-95; spl. master Conn. Superior Ct.; lectr. Family Law Tng. Seminar. Past bd. dirs. Teen Life Ctr., Liberation Programs, Inc., CTE; treas. Conn. Conf. Municipalities, 1997-98, v.p.; vice chair mayors and pub. schs. task force U.S. Conf. Mayors; mem. full policy steering coun. Nat. League of Cities, 1997-98, mem. task force on youth and edn; chmn. Dem. Mcpl. Ofcls. Orgn.; mem. Dem. Nat. Com., mem. exec. com.; mem. adv. bd. U.S. Conf. Mayors. Mem. ABA, ATLA, Nat. Trial Lawyers Assn., Conn. Bar Assn., Conn. Trial Lawyers Assn. Democrat. Office: 10th Fl Govt Center 888 Washington Blvd Stamford CT 06902

**MALLOY, EDWARD ALOYSIUS,** academic administrator; b. Washington, May 3, 1941; s. Edward Aloysius and Elizabeth (Clark) Malloy. BA, U. Notre Dame, 1963, MA, 1967, ThM, 1969; PhD, Vanderbilt U., 1975. Ordained to ministry Cath. Ch., 1970. Instr. U. Notre Dame, South Bend, Ind., 1974—75, asst. prof., 1975—81, assoc. prof., 1981—88, prof. theology, 1988—, assoc. provost, 1982—86, pres. elect, 1986, pres., 1987—2005, pres. emeritus, 2005—. Established chair Cath. Studies in name of Edward A. Malloy Vanderbilt U., 1997; editl. adv. bd. The Presidency mag.; bd. dir. Nat. Com. on Higher Edn. and Health of Youth; co-chmn. Nat. Inst. on Alcohol Abuse and Alcoholism; chmn. Nat. Commn. on Substance Abuse and Sports; regent U. Portland, 1985—; bd. govs., trustee Notre Dame, Australia, 1990—. Author: Culture & Commitment: The Challenge of Today's University, 1992, Notre Dame: The Unfolding Vision, 1994, Monk's Reflection: A View from the Dome, 1999, Monk's Travels People, Places & Events, 2004, Monk's Notre Dame, 2005; co-author: Colleges and Universities as Citizens, 1999. Chmn. Am. Coun. Edn.; bd. dirs. NCAA Found., 1994—; mem. Pres. Adv. Coun. on Drugs, 1989—; mem. adv. bd. AmeriCorps and Nat. Civilian Cmty. Corps, 1994—97; interim chmn. Ind. Commn. Cmty. Svc., 1994—97; mem. Boys and Girls Clubs Am., 1997—; trustee St. Thomas S. Univ., 1967—; Vanderbilt U., 1999; bd. advisors Bermadin Ctr., 2004—2005; founding dir., bd. dir. Points of Light Found.; past chmn. Campus Impact; mem. Bishopps and pres. com. Assn. Cath. Colls. and Univs., 1988—2005; bd. dir. Internat. Fedn. Cath. Univs. 1988—2005. Mem.: Nat. Assn. Ind. Colls. and Univs. (bd. dirs. 1997), The Conf. Bd., Assn. Governing Bds. of Univs. and Colls. (vice chair 1996—2004), Bus.-Higher Edn. Forum, Am. Soc. Christian Ethics, Cath. Theol. Soc. Roman Catholic. Office: Univ Notre Dame Pres Emeritus Notre Dame IN 46556 Office Phone: 574-631-6755.

**MALLOY, INA ARLENE,** secondary school educator, photographer; m. K. O. Malloy; children: Bryanne, Zachary, Elyse. MS, Quinnipiac U., 2003; BFA, Temple U., 1982. Lic. tchr. K-12 art Conn., 1982, N.J., 1982, Pa., 1982. Tchr. photography Amity H.H., Woodcridge, Conn., 1998—. Mem. Beth Ahm

Congregation, Windsor, Conn., 2003—06. Mem.: N.J. Art Edn. Assn. (life scholar 2003). Office: Amity Regional Hs 25 Newton Rd Woodbridge CT 06082 Office Phone: 203-397-4830. Business E-Mail: inamalloy_x@yahoo.com.

**MALLOY, JOHN RICHARD,** lawyer, chemicals executive; b. Boston, Nov. 26, 1932; s. Thomas Francis and Mary (Field) M.; m. Maraleta Ellerson, May 24, 1960; children: Maureen, John, Megan, Elizabeth. BA, St. John's Sem., Brighton, Mass., 1954; LLB, Boston Coll., 1957. Bar: Mass. 1957. With chief counsel's office IRS, 1961—64; atty. advisor Tax Ct. of U.S., 1964—65; legal dept. Du Pont, 1965—73, asst. comptroller taxes, 1973—75; v.p., dir. fin. Remington Arms Co., Inc., Bridgeport, Conn., 1975-78; chief counsel, energy and raw materials E. I. du Pont de Nemours and Co., Wilmington, Del., 1978-79, asst. gen. counsel legal, 1979-83, dir. pub. affairs, 1983-85, v.p. pub. affairs, 1983-85, sr. v.p. external affairs, 1985-92, sr. v.p., spl. counsel to chmn. bd., 1992-93; ret., 1993. Chmn. Jobs for Del. Grads, Wilmington, 1985-97, Del. Compensation Commn., 1988-96; trustee Med. Ctr. of Del., Christiana, 1985—, dir., 2004—, Del. Pension Fund, 1993-99; bd. dirs. Del. Cmty. Found., 1996-2000, Children's Beach House, 1993-2000; mem. Minner Commn., Del., 1993-96; chmn. Ursuline Acad., 1978-84, Del. Coun. on Transp., 1994-2001, Riverfront Devel. Corp., 2002—05; trustee Archmere Acad., 2001-05. With JAGC U.S. Army, 1958—60. Mem. ABA, Fed. Bar Assn. Democrat. Roman Catholic. Avocations: tennis, golf, skiing.

**MALLOY, MICHAEL DENNIS,** radio personality; s. Joseph Anthony Malloy and Silvia Star Dantico; m. Katherine Laurissa Bay, Feb. 23, 1997; children: Molly Bay children: Diana Lynn Spear, Jay Anthony, Wendy Shannon, Libby Colleen Machemer, Christopher Jay. Student, Toledo U., 1961—63, Jacksonville U., 1964—65, NC State U., 1969—70, Ga. State U., 1975—76. News writer CNN TV, Atlanta, 1984—86; talk show host WSB-AM Radio, Atlanta, 1987—94, WLS-AM Radio, Chgo., 1997—2000; news writer CNN-Internat., 2000—00; talk show host I. E. Am. Radio Network, Atlanta, Air Am. radio, 2005—. Actor: (plays) Various Productions; editor: (mags.) Mng. Editor; contbr. mags. Atlanta Mas.; columnist: newspaper Atlanta Gazette; contbr. mags. So. Women; author: (plays) So. Theater Conspiracy. Organizer SDS, Raleigh, NC, 1970—70, SANE, Atlanta, 1976—77; tel. counselor CONTACT, York, Pa., 1973—73; vol. Open Door Cmty., Atlanta, 1980—81, Salvation Army, Chgo., 1997—97. Named one of Top 100 Talk Show Hosts Am.a, 1999, 2000, 2003; recipient Broadcast award, B'nai B'rith, 1987, LIberty Bell Ringer award, Libertarian Party, 1988, Journalistic Integrity award, AADC, 1992, Chicago A.I.R., 2000, Best Talk Show award, NY A.I.R., 2004; scholar Acad. scholar, Ford Found., 1962. Mem.: ACLU, Am. Fedn. TV and Radio Artists, Amnesty Internat. Office: Air America Radio 641 Avenue Of The Americas Fl 4 New York NY 10011-2038 Personal E-Mail: mikedmalloy@aol.com. E-Mail: mikedmalloy@earthlink.net, mike@mikemalloy.com.

**MALLOY, MICHAEL P.,** lawyer; b. Providence, July 18, 1959; s. Judge Edward Francis and Patricia Marie Malloy; m. Jamie Marie Azzara, Aug. 20, 1983; children: Christofer, Nicholas, Michael, Cara. BA summa cum laude, Boston Coll., 1981, JD cum laude, 1984. Bar: Pa. 1984. Assoc. Drinker Biddle & Reath LLP, Phila., 1984-93, ptnr., 1993—, ptnr., head investment mgmt. group. Coach numerous childrens athletics teams. Mem. ABA, Phila. Bar Assn. (co-chair investment com.). Avocations: tennis, paddle tennis, racketball. Office: Drinker Biddle & Reath LLP One Logan Square 18th & Cherry Sts Philadelphia PA 19103-6996 Office Phone: 215-988-2978. Office Fax: 215-988-2757. Business E-Mail: michael.malloy@dbr.com.

**MALLOY, MICHAEL PATRICK,** law educator, consultant; b. Haddon Heights, N.J., Sept. 23, 1951; s. Francis Edward and Marie Grace (Nardi) Malloy; divorced; 1 child. Elizabeth; m. Susie Pieratos, Jan. 1992; children: Michael Emil, Nicholas Charles, Edward Francis, Theodora Marie, Sophia Grace. BA magna cum laude (scholar), Georgetown U., 1973, PhD, 1983; JD (scholar), U. Pa., 1976. Bar: N.J. 1976, U.S. Supreme Ct. 1991. Rsch. assoc. Inst. Internat. Law and Econ. Devel., Washington, 1976—77; atty. advisor Office Fgn. Assets Control U.S. Dept. Treasury, Washington, 1977—80, spl. asst. Office Gen. Counsel, 1985; atty. advisor Office Comptr. Currency, Washington, 1981; spl. counsel SEC, Washington, 1981—82; asst. prof. N.Y. Law Sch., N.Y.C., 1982—83; assoc. prof. Seton Hall U. Sch. Law, Newark, 1983—86, prof., assoc. dean, 1986—87; prof. Fordham U. Sch. Law, N.Y.C., 1987—96, dir. grad. studies, 1990—94; prof. U. Pacific McGeorge Law Sch., Sacramento, 1996—2002, disting. prof. schol. , 2003—, dir. Ctr. Global Bus. and Devel., 2004—. Law lectr. Morin Ctr. Banking and Fin. Law Studies Boston U. Law Sch., 1986—90, 1995—96, 2001; vis. prof. U. Salzburg, Austria, 2000, 2005—, Macao U. Sci. and Tech., 2006—; vis. prof. Suffolk U., 2001—02; cons. bank regulation and pvt. internat. law matters. Author: Corporate Law of Banks, 2 vols., 1988, Economic Sanctions and U.S. Trade, 1990, The Regulation of Banking, 1992, Banking Law and Regulation, 3 vols., 1994, Fundamentals of Banking Regulation, 1998, International Banking, 1998, Banking and Financial Services Law, 1999;: 2d edit., 2005, Hornbook on Bank Regulation, 1999, 2d edit., 2003, U.S. Economic Sanctions: Theory and Practice, 2001; contbr. articles, revs. and comments to profl. jours. Mem.: L'Association des Auditeurs et Anciens Auditeurs de l'Academie de Droit International de la Haye, Hegel Soc. Am., Assn. Am. Law Schs. (chair-elect and program chair 2001—02, chair sect. fin. insts. and consumer fin. svcs. 2002—03), Internat. Law Assn. (com. chair Am. br. 1995—97), Am. Soc. Internat. Law (exec. coun. 1986—89), Phi Beta Kappa. Office: U of Pacific McGeorge Sch Law 3200 5th Ave Sacramento CA 95817-2705 Office Phone: 916-716-7645. Personal E-Mail: malloympm@aol.com.

**MALLOY, MICHAEL TERRENCE,** journalist, reporter; b. Chgo., Feb. 26, 1936; s. Medard Valentine and Lucille (Zehrol)M.; m. Ruth Gwendolyn Lur, June 5, 1965; children: Linda Jo, Terrence. Student, Reed Coll., 1953-54, Columbia U., 1966-67; BA, U. Toronto, 2001. Police reporter City News Bur. Chgo., 1956-58; reporter, then bur. chief and chief corr. S.E. Asia UPI, Japan, Laos, India, Vietnam and Thailand, 1960-66; reporter Nat. Observer, Washington, 1968-76, mng. editor, 1976-77; reporter Asian Wall St. Jour., Manila, 1977-80, mng. editor, Hong Kong, 1980-84; mng. editor Dow Jones Can., Toronto, Ont., 1984-94; chief corr. Dow Jones India Report, 1995-97. Author: Racing Today, 1967, The Art of Retirement, 1967. With U.S. Army, 1958-60. E-Mail: mikemalloy@idirect.ca.

**MALLOY, TIMOTHY J.,** lawyer; m. Patricia A. Smid; children: Christopher J., Brigid E. Malloy Kloostra. BSEE, U. Notre Dame, Ind., 1966; JD, U. Notre Dame, Indiana. Cert.: US Patent Trademark Office (Patent Atty.), bar: Ill., US Ct. Appeals (7th, 8th fed. cirs.), US Supreme Ct. Assoc., ptnr. Allegretti Newitt Witoff McAndrews, Chgo., 1969—88; founding ptnr. McAndrews Held Malloy, Chgo., 1988—. Mem. adv. coun. U. Notre Dame Law Sch., Ind., 2003—. Contbr. articles and book chpt. in field. Named one of Am.'s Leading Bus. Lawyers, Chambers U.S.A., 2002—, Worlds Leading Patent Law Experts, Euro Money Legal Media Group, 2003, 100 Ill. Super Lawyers, Chgo. Mag., 2005. Avocations: reading, golf, tennis, skiing. Office Phone: 312-775-8000.

**MALLOZZI, COS M.,** public relations executive; b. Utica, N.Y., Aug. 16, 1951; BA, Syracuse U., 1973. Pub. rels. coun. and legis. intern Congressman D. Mitchell, Washington, 1973—74; assr. pub. rels. dir., sports info. dir. Siena Coll., 1974—75; pub. rels. dir. SUNY, 1975-76; acct. supv. group mgr. Gibbs & Soell, Inc., N.Y.C., 1978—80, gen. mgr., 1980—81, exec. v.p., gen. mgr., 1981—88, pres., 1988—, CEO, 1993—. Office: Gibbs & Soell Inc 600 3rd Ave 6th Fl New York NY 10016-1903 E-mail: cmallozzi@gibbs-soell.com.*

**MALM, MIA,** actress; b. Ann Arbor, Mich., Oct. 18, 1962; d. William P. and Joyce A. (Rutherford) M. Student, San Francisco Sch. of the Arts, Herbert Berghof Studios, N.Y.C.; studied with Maria Vegh. Dance instr. Marin Ballet Sch., 1978-79. Appeared in (stage prodns.) Make Mine Disco, 1979, Dancin', 1981-83, 42nd Street, The Showgirl Musical, 1986, (films) Moscow on the

Hudson, Curtain Call, 1984, Joan-Lui, A Chorus Line, 1985, Ishtar, (TV) Dance Through Time, 1978. Mem. Actors' Equity Assn., Screen Actors Guild, AFTRA, NOW, Planned Parenthood. Avocations: drawing, watercoloring, reading.

**MALM, RICHARD ALLAN,** lawyer; b. Pensacola, Fla., Aug. 6, 1949; s. Frank Stuart and Darlene Mae (Nelson) M.; m. Robbie Jean Gatchel, Sept. 4, 1971; children: Jonathan, Kathryn, Margaret. BSEE, Iowa State U., 1971; JD with honors, Drake U., 1974. Bar: Iowa 1974, U.S. Dist. Ct. (no. and so. dists.) Iowa 1974, U.S. Ct. Appeals (8th and 7th cirs.) 1978, U.S. Supreme Ct. 1985. Assoc. Dickinson, Throckmorton, Parker, Mannheimer & Raife, Des Moines, 1974-78, ptnr., 1978—2005, Dickinson Mackama, Tyler & Hogan, Des Moines, 2005—. Mem. ABA, Iowa Bar Assn., Des Moines C. of C., Order of Coif, Tau Beta Pi, Eta Kappa Nu. Democrat. Home: 5812 N Waterbury Rd Des Moines IA 50312-1340 Office: Dickinson Mackamas Tyler & Hogan PC 699 Walnut St Ste 1600 Des Moines IA 50309-3944 Business E-Mail: rmalm@dickinsonlaw.ctr.

**MALM, ROGER CHARLES,** lawyer; b. Hot Springs, SD, July 8, 1949; s. Harry Milton and Angeline Mae (Johnson) M.; m. Sandra M. Metz, July 15, 1972; children: Andrew, Elliott, Nicholas. BA, St. Olaf Coll., 1971; JD, U. ND, 1974. Bar: N.D. 1974, Ariz. 1975, Minn. 1980, U.S. Dist. Ct. N.D. 1974, U.S. Dist. Ct. Ariz. 1976, U.S. Ct. Appeals (9th cir.) 1981, U.S. Supreme Ct. 1981, U.S. Ct. Appeals (8th cir.) 1982, U.S. Dist. Ct. Minn. 1985, U.S. Claims Ct. 1985, U.S. Tax Ct. 1988. Ptnr. Brink, Sobolik, Severson, Malm & Albrecht, P.A., Hallock, Minn., 1980—; county atty. Kittson County, Minn., 1995—. Pres. N.W. Minn. County Atty.'s Coun. Hospice dir. Kittson County Hospice, Inc., 1984—; bd. dirs. Cmty. Theatre, Hallock, 1987—, Greater Grand Forks Cmty. Theater, 1991-95, N.W. Minn. Found., 2004—. Mem. ABA, Ariz. Bar Assn., N.D. Bar Assn., Minn. Bar Assn. (mem. bd. govs. 1993-2000). Lutheran. Avocations: skiing, sailing. Office: Brink Sobolik Severson Malm & Albrecht PO Box 790 Hallock MN 56728-0790 Office Phone: 218-843-3686. Personal E-mail: brink@rural-access.com.

**MALMAN, LAURIE L.,** law educator; b. 1946; BA, Vassar Coll., 1968; JD, NYU, 1971. Bar: NY 1972. Assoc. Sullivan & Cromwell, NYC, 1971-79; instr. NYU Sch. Law, 1979-80, asst. prof. law, 1980-83, assoc. prof., 1983-86, prof., 1986—. Co-author: Federal Income Tax Problems, Cases, and Materials, 1994. Mem.: ABA, NY State Bar Assn. Office: NYU Sch Law Vanderbilt Hall Rm 430I 40 Washington Sq S New York NY 10012-1099 Office Phone: 212-998-6166. E-Mail: malman@juris.law.nyu.edu.

**MALMGREN, HARALD BERNARD,** economist; b. Boston, July 13, 1935; s. Berndt Birger and Magda Helena (Nilsson) M.; m. Patricia A. Malmgren, 1959 (div. 1975); children: Karen Philippa, Britt Patricia, Erika Nina; m. Linda V. Einberg, Oct. 3, 1987; children: Markus Harald, Liivia Linda, Viivianne Vaike. BA summa cum laude, Yale U., 1957; postgrad., Harvard U., 1959; PhD, Oxford U., 1961. Asst. prof. dept. engring. and econs. Cornell U., Ithaca, NY, 1961—62; head econ. group Inst. for Def. Analyses, Washington, 1962—64; asst. U.S. trade rep. Exec. Office Pres. The White House, Washington, 1964—69; sr. fellow Overseas Devel. Coun., 1969—71; amb., dep. U.S. trade rep., 1972—75; sr. fellow Woodrow Wilson Internat. Ctr. for Scholars, Washington, 1975—76; prof. George Washington U., Washington, 1976—77; pres. Malmgren, Inc., Washington, 1977—; mng. dir. Malmgren, Golt, Kingston, Ltd., London, 1979—99; chmn. Malmgren O'Donnell, London, 1998—2001, Cordell Hull Inst., Washington, 2001—. Adv. coun. Ctr. Strategic and Internat. Studies, Washington, 1987-97; adv. Senate Fin. Com., Washington, 1970-71, 75-76, Interaction Coun., 1985—. Author: International Economic Peace Keeping, 1972; co-author: Assisting Developing Countries, 1972; editor: Pacific Basin Development, 1972; bd. editors: The International Economy, 1987—, The Washington Quarterly, 1987-95, The World Economy, 1980-90; contbr. articles to profl. jours. Mem. Am. Econ. Assn., Met. Club, Reform Club. Home: Summerfield Farm 7620 Cannonball Gate Rd Warrenton VA 20186-7304 Office Phone: 202-466-8740. Business E-Mail: hm@malmgrenglobal.com.

**MALMONT, ANDREA G.,** education educator; b. Arlington, Pa., Mar. 27, 1969; d. Bruce and Valerie Malmont; children from previous marriage: Stephanie Summers, Paige Summers. AS, BS, U. Gt. Falls Mont., 1995, MEd, 1998; EdD, Duquesne U., Pitts., 2005. Cert. tchr. Mont., Alaska. Tchr. Cascade (Mont.) Sch. Dist., Gt. Falls Sch. Dist.; tng. & curriculum specialist USAF, Eielson AFB, Alaska; prof. Shippensburg (Pa.) U. Praxis testing cons. Shippensburg U., 2001—, mem. pro-sem com., 2002—, mem. elem. edn. com., 2004—; rsch. cons. Axiology Jours., 2003—05. CPR and first aid ARC, Fairbanks, Alaska; foster parent Cumberland Valley Animal Shelter, Chambersburg, Pa. Mem.: AAUW, Am. Edul. Rsch. Assn. Office: Shippensburg U 3595 Eagle Dr Chambersburg PA 17201 Office Phone: 717-477-1724. Business E-Mail: agmalm@ship.edu.

**MALMQUIST, CARL PHILLIP,** psychiatrist; b. St. Paul, Mar. 10, 1934; s. Phillip C. and Lillian Viola (Kahler) M.; m. Arlyn Virginia Bodal (dec. 1984); children: Derek, Jay. BA summa cum laude, U. Minn., 1954, MD, 1958, MS in Philosophy of Sci., 1961. Diplomate Am. Bd. Psychiatry and Neurology, Am. Bd. Child Psychiatry, Am. Bd. Adult Psychiatry; cert. forensic psychiatry, added qualification in forensic psychiatry. Intern Columbia Med. Ctr., NYC, 1963—64, U. Minn., Mpls., 1962—63; assoc. prof. dept. psychiatry U. Mich., 1965—67; assoc. prof. Inst. Child Devel. U. Minn., 1967—70, prof., dir. child and adolescent psychiatry, 1971—72, prof. criminal justice, 1972—80, prof. social psychiatry, dept. sociology, 1980—. Cons. Hennepin County Dist. Ct., Mpls., 1967—; mem. commn. of mentally disabled ABA, 1985. Author: Handbook of Adolescence, 1980, Homicide: Psychiatric Perspectives, 1996, 2d edit., 2006; mem. editl. bd. Psychiat. Anns., 1981; contbr. articles to profl. jours. Fellow Am. Psychiat. Assn. (disting. sr.; commn. on jud. action 1994—), Am. Coll. Psychiatrists, Am. Orthopsychiat. Assn., Am. Acad. Child Psychiatry, Am. Acad. Psychiatry and Law (Segmour Pollock Disting. Achievement award 2004), Am. Coll. Forensic Psychiatry; mem. Group for Advancement Psychiatry, Am. Psychopathol. Assn. Episcopalian. Home: 5010 Bruce Ave Minneapolis MN 55424-1318 Office: Univ Minn 6600 France Ave S Ste 545 Minneapolis MN 55435-1804 Office Phone: 952-926-8180. Business E-Mail: malmqu01@atlas.socsci.umn.edu.

**MALMSTAD, JOHN EARL,** literature and language professor; b. Bismarck, ND, June 25, 1941; s. Manley Ellsworth and Joyce Evelyn (David) M. BA summa cum laude with distinction and departmental honors in Russian Lang. and Lit., Northwestern U., 1963; MA in Slavic Langs. and Lits., Princeton U., 1965, PhD in Slavic Langs. and Lits., 1969; AM (hon.), Harvard U., 1985. Instr. Columbia U., N.Y.C., 1968-69, asst. prof. Russian Lit., 1969-73, assoc. prof., 1973-79, prof. Slavic langs. and lits., 1979-85; Samuel Hazzard Cross prof. Slavic langs. and lits. Harvard U., Cambridge, Mass., 1985—, assoc. dean, 1993-94. Vis. assoc. prof. Stanford U., 1971-72, U. Calif. Berkeley, 1977-78; vis. prof. Harvard U. fall 1982; cons., referee NEH translation awards; lectr. in field; attendee internat. symposia. Editor: (with others) The Poetry of Mikhail Kuzmin (3 vols.), 1977, The Poetry of Andrei Bely (3 vols.), 1982-85, Gibel Senatora, 1986, Vladislav Khodasevich Sobranie sochinenii, 1983, Andrei Bely, Spirit of Symbolism, 1987, Readings in Russian Modernism to Honor Vladimir Markov, 1993, Mikhail Kuzmin: Zhizn' Tvorchestvo, Epokha, 1996, Andrey Bely-Ivanov-Razumnik Perepiska, 1998, Mikhail Kuzmin: A Life in Art, 1999, K.N. Bugaeva Vospominaniia o Belom, 2001; Russian book rev. editor Slavic Rev., 1975-86; assoc. editor Russian Rev., 1986-88; mem. editl. bd. Feniks, Opyty, Novoe Literaturnoe obozrenie, Experiment, Philologica, Diaspora; manuscript rev. profl. jours., univ. presses; contbr. articles to profl. jours. Woodrow Wilson fellow, 1963, NDFL fellow Columbia U., 1963-66, Princeton U., 1967-68, Fulbright-Hays fellow, 1966-67, spring 1981, spring 1987, Woodrow Wilson Dissertation fellow, 1966, ACLS fellow, 1972, Rsch. fellow Russian Inst. Columbia U., summer 1977, 79, 83, 84, IREX fellow, 1975, John Simon Guggenheim fellow, 1980-81; ACLS grant-in-aid, summer, 1980, IREX/ACLS grantee exch. Acad. Scis. USSR, fall 1981, spring 1987, 91, IREX travel grantee Moscow, 1992, Am. Coun. Internat. Edn. grantee, Moscow, 2003. Mem. MLA, Am. Assn. Advancement of Slavic Studies, Assn.

Tchrs. of Slavic and East European Langs., Inst. d'Etudes Slaves (Paris), Phi Beta Kappa. Avocations: fine arts, ballet, reading. Home: 8A Cogswell Ave Cambridge MA 02140-2001 Office: Harvard U Dept Slavic Langs/Lit Barker Ctr, 12 Quincy St Cambridge MA 02138 E-mail: malmstad@fas.harvard.edu.

**MALMUTH, NORMAN DAVID,** research scientist; b. Bklyn., Jan. 22, 1931; s. Jacob and Selma Malmuth; m. Constance Nelson, 1970; children: Kenneth, Jill. AE, U. Cin., 1953; MA in Aero. Engring., Polytech. Inst. of N.Y., 1956; PhD in Aeronautics, Calif. Inst. Tech., 1962. Rsch. engr. Grumman Aircraft Engring. Corp., 1953-56; preliminary design engr. N.A. Aviation Div., L.A., 1956-68; teaching asst. Calif. Inst. Tech., L.A., 1961; mem. maths. sci. group Rockwell Internat. Sci. Ctr., 1968-75, project mgr. fluid dynamics rsch., 1975-80, mgr. fluid dynamics group, 1980-82, sr. scientist, project mgr., 1982—. Cons. Aerojet Gen., 1986—89; lectr. UCLA, 1971—72; mem. adv. group for aerospace R&D Fluid Dynamics Panel, 1995; vis. scientist Rensselaer Poly. Inst.; vis. assoc. Calif. Inst. Tech., 2003; chair NATO RTO/AVT meeting, Prague, Czech Republic, 2004. Referee AIAA Jour.; bd. editors Jour. Aircraft; contbr. articles to Jour. of Heat Transfer, Internat. Jour. Heat Mass Transfer, and others. Named Calif. Inst. Tech. fellow; recipient Outstanding Alumnus award Univ. Cin., 1990. Fellow AIAA (Aerodynamics award 1991. lectr. meeting 2005), Am. Phys. Soc.; mem. Am. Acad. Mechanics, Am. Inst. Physics (fluid dynamics divsn.), Soc. Indsl. and Applied Math. Achievements include patent in Methods and Apparatus for Controlling Laser Welding, hypersonic transition delay; pioneering development of high aerodynamic efficiency of hypersonic delta wing body combinations, hypersonic boundary layer stability, transonic wind tunnel interference, plasma aerodynamics, flow control web dynamics, combined asymptotic and numerical methods in fluid dynamics and aerodynamics. Home: 182 Maple Rd Newbury Park CA 91320-4718 Office: Rockwell Sci Co PO Box 1085 1049 Camino Dos Rios Thousand Oaks CA 91360-2362 Business E-Mail: nmalmuth@rwsc.com.

**MALO, MICHELE LEE,** marketing professional; b. Chgo., Dec. 21, 1972; d. William Reining and Candyce Lee Collins; m. James John Malo, Oct. 4, 2003. B of Advt., U. Nebr., 1996; MBA with honors, Lake Forest Grad. Sch. Mgmt., 2003; postgrad., Lake Forest Grad. Sch. Mgmt. Internat. Bus. Specialization, 2005. Mktg. asst. Allied Domecq, Chgo., 1996—98, field mktg. specialist, 1998—2000; asst. promotions mgr. Kraft Foods, Glenview, 2000—02, assoc. promotions mgr., 2002—03; assoc. bus. mgr Oscar Mayer, 2003—04; customer mktg. mgr. Kellogg's, Elmhurst, 2004—06, bus. unit mgr. biscuit, 2006—. Breast cancer fundraising com. Women in POP. Mem.: Women's Food Svc. Forum, Am. Mktg. Assn., Alpha Sigma Alpha. Avocation: softball. Office: Kellogg 545 Lamont Rd Elmhurst IL 60126 Office Phone: 630-956-9792. E-mail: esmalo@yahoo.com.

**MALONE, CAROLYN LUCIA MARINO,** education educator; b. Manhattan, Kans., July 14, 1944; d. John and Viola Rolander Marino; 1 child, Jesse David Marino Kramer. PhD in History of Art and Medieval Studies, U. Calif., Berkeley, 1973. Vis. lectr. U. Mich., Ann Arbor, 1973, Harvard U., Cambridge, Mass., 1973; asst. prof. U Mass., Amherst, Mass., 1974, Vassar Coll., Poughkipsie, NY, 1974—75, Princeton U., NJ, 1975—81; assoc. prof. U. So. Calif., LA, 1981—. Author: (excavations and archaeological interpretation) Les Fouilles de Saint Bénigne de Dijon (1976-1978) et le problème de l'église de l'an mil, Bulletin Monumental 138, 1980 (Courtland-Elliott prize, Medieval Acad. Am., 1982), (liturgical and political interpretation) Facade as Spectacle: Ritual and Ideology at Wells Cathedral, Brill Series: Studies in Medieval and Reformation Traditions, 2004. Fellow excavations, Saint-Bénigne in Dijon, Samuel H. Kress Found., 1976, Nat. Endowment for Humanities, 1977—78, Am. Coun. Learned Socs., 2002, Am. Assn. of U. Women, 2002; St.-Bénigne fellow, Graham Found., 1998. Mem.: So. Calif. Art Historians Assn. (assoc.; v.p. 1996—99), Medieval Assn. of the Pacific (assoc.; bd. dirs. 1986—89), Medieval Acad. of Am. (assoc.), Phi Beta Kappa (hon.). Home: 476 36th St Manhattan Beach CA 90266 Office: Univ Southern Calif Dept History of Art Los Angeles CA 90089 Office Phone: 213-740-4569. Personal E-mail: cmalone@usc.edu.

**MALONE, CLAUDINE BERKELEY,** financial and management consultant; b. Louisville, May 9, 1936; d. Claude McDowell and Mary Katharine (Smith) M.; BA, Wellesley Coll., 1963; MBA, Harvard U., 1972. CPA, Md. Systems engr. IBM Corp., Washington, 1964; sr. systems analyst Crane Co., Chgo., 1966; contr., mgr. data processing Raleigh Stores, Washington, 1967-70; asst. prof. Harvard U., 1972-76, assoc. prof., 1977-81; pres., CEO, Fin. and Mgmt. Consulting Inc., Bethesda, Md., 1981-; vis. prof. Georgetown U., 1982-84, U. Va., 1984-87; dir. Scott Paper Co., Houghton Mifflin Co., Campbell Soup Co., Boston Co., Dart Group Inc., Hasbro Inc., 1994-, Novell Inc., 2003-; trustee Penn Mut. Life Ins. Co. Chmn. Bus. for Reagan-Bush Com. Mass., 1980; trustee Wellesley Coll., 1982-. Recipient Candace award, 1982. Mem. Assn. Women CPA's, UN Assn., Wellesley Coll. Alumnae Assn., Washington Wellesley Club. Episcopalian. Office Phone: 703-821-8861.

**MALONE, DAVID L.,** broadcast technician; b. Troy, NY, Aug. 11, 1959; s. Fredrick G. Malone and Dorthy A. Duffy. AAS, Schenectady County C.C., NY, 1985. Asst. tv engr. NY Network, Albany, 1987—. Mem.: Math. Assn. Am. (assoc.). Independent. Roman Catholic. Avocations: photography, computers, chess, mathematics, entomology. Office Phone: 518-443-5333. Personal E-mail: dmalone1@yahoo.com. E-mail: malonedl@nyn.suny.edu.

**MALONE, DAVID MICHAEL,** diplomat, educator; b. Ottawa, Canada, Feb. 7, 1954; s. Paul Thomas Malone and Deirdre Lavalette Ingram. BA, Univ. Montreal, Montreal, Can., 1972; MPA, Kennedy Sch. of Govt., Harvard U., Cambridge, MA, 1980; DPhil, Oxford U., Eng., 1997. Various positions in can. fgn. min. and at can. diplomatic missions in cairo, amman and kuwait Govt. of Can., 1975—90; can. rep. to the un's ecosoc N. Y. and Geneva, NY, 1990—92; amb., dep. permanent rep. Can. Permanent Mission to the UN, N. Y., NY, 1992—94; dir. gen., policy, internat. orgn. and global issues bureaus Can. Ministry of Fgn. Affairs and Internat. Trade, Ottawa, Canada, 1994—98; pres. Internat. Peace Acad., N. Y., NY, 1998—2004; asst. dep. min. global issues Fgn. Affairs Can., 2004—06; high commr. for Can. to India and amb. of Can. to Bhutan and Nepal, 2006—. Adj. prof. law N.Y. U. Sch. of Law, 1999; adj. prof. internat. rels. Institut des Etudes Politiques (Sciences Po), Paris, 2001. Author: The UN Security Council from the Cold War to the Twenty First Century; contbr. articles to profl. jour. Address: 7/8 Shantypath Chanakyapuri New Delhi 110 021 India Office Phone: 613-944-2273. Business E-Mail: david.malone@international.gc.ca.

**MALONE, DAVID ROY,** educational association administrator, director; b. Beebe, Ark., Nov. 4, 1943; s. James Roy and Ila Mae (Griffin) M.; m. Judith Kaye Huff, June 20, 1965 (div. Feb. 1990); m. Deborah W. Thomas, Jan. 23, 2004; 1 child, Michael David. BSBA, U. Ark., 1965, JD, 1969, MBA, 1982. Bar: Ark. 1969, U.S. Dist. Ct. (we. dist.) Ark. 1969, U.S. Tax Ct. 1972, U.S. Ct. Appeals (8th cir.) 1972, U.S. Supreme Ct. 1972. Pvt. practice, Fayetteville, Ark., 1969-72; atty. City of Fayetteville, 1969-72; asst. prof. bus. U. Ark., Fayetteville, 1972-76, asst. dean law, 1976-91; mem. Ark. Ho. of Reps., 1980-84, Ark. Senate, 1984—2002; co-chair Ark. Found., 1991—2002, Ark. Tchr. Ret. Sys., 2003—. Chair Senate edn. com., 1997-2002, co-chair legis. coun., 1999-2000; bd. dirs. Bank of Elkins, 1976-98, S.W. Edn. Devel. Lab., Austin, Tex., 1988-94; legal adv. coun. So. Regional Edn. Bd., Atlanta, 1991-2002. Contbr. articles to profl. jours.; bd. dirs. Ark. Law Rev., 1978-92; contbg. author U. Ark. Press, 1989. Mayor City of Fayetteville, 1979-80; mem. Jud. Article Task Force, Little Rock, 1989-91; chair Motor Voter task force, 1994-95; bd. dirs. Music Festival Ark., 1989-91, Washington County Hist. Soc., 1993-96; bd. dirs. Walton Arts Ctr. Found., 1994-2000, chmn., 1994-98; trustee Washington County Law Libr., 1970-84; chmn. Ark. Tuition Trust Authority, 1997-99. Recipient Svc. award, Ark. Mcpl. League, 1980, Disting. Svc. award, Ark., 1988, Lucas Svc. award, Ark. Alumni Assn., 1998, award, Walton Coll. Bus., U. Ark., 2004. Mem. Ark. Bar Assn. (ho. of dels. 1977-81, award of merit 1980, exec. 1981-82, Outstanding Lawyer-Citizen award 1990), Washington County Bar Assn., Ark. Inst. Continuing Legal Edn. (bd. dirs. 1979-88), Fayetteville C. of C. (bd. dirs. 1984-99), Ark. Genealogy Soc. (bd. dirs. 1990-99). Democrat. Methodist.

Avocations: genealogy, stamp collecting/philately. Home: 804 N Arthur St Little Rock AR 72205-2902 Office: 1400 W Third St Little Rock AR 72201 Office Phone: 501-682-1827. Business E-Mail: david.malone@atrs.state.ar.us.

**MALONE, EMBRY,** property manager, advocate; b. Louisville, Mar. 9, 1954; BA in European History, Pepperdine U., 1977. Mgr. Pelican Properties, Stone Mountain, Ga., 1988—; owner ABA Franchise/The Gwinnett Gwizzlies. Cmty. activist Nat. Assn. Cmty. Devel., Atlanta, 1993—2003. AWP scholar, Pepperdine U., Malibu, 1976—77. Mem.: Pepperdine U. Alumni Assocs. (assoc.). Office: PO Box 870273 Stone Mountain GA 30087 Personal E-mail: palucanx@aol.com.

**MALONE, JAMES HIRAM,** graphics designer, journalist, writer; b. Winterville, Ga., Mar. 24, 1930; s. Ralph and Sarah Lena (Echols) M.; m. Mary Louise Liebaert, 1972 (div. 1982); children: Andrew Ralph, Matthew Martin. Student, Morehouse Coll., 1949-50, Coll. Art and Design, 1959-62. Art dir., prodn. mgr. Better Brochures, Inc., Detroit, 1963-65; graphics mgr. Fed. Dept. Stores, Detroit, 1965-69; sr. art cons. Northgate Ad Agy., Detroit, 1969-75; sr. graphics designer Montgomery Ward Regional Hdqs., Southfield, Mich., 1975-80; layout/prodn. designer K-Mart Internat. Hdqs., Troy, Mich., 1980-83; ad/promotions creative dir. Atlanta Jour./Constitution, 1983-90; fine art prodr., painter Bianco Art Collections of Atlanta, Marietta, Ga., 1990-92; cartoonist, newspaper columnist/reporter Atlanta News Leader, Union City, Ga., 1992—. Author, artist: Ralph cartoon strip, 1998, Here and There Poetry, Blues Poetry, 1954, Grandma Sarah's Closet, 1960, Brother, 1970, Malone's Atlanta, 1986, No-Job Dad, 1992, The Cart, 1994, April Mae Jones Coloring Book, 1999; contbr. The Total Cartoonist, 1983, Lure of the Local, 1997, Landscape Narratives, 1998, (novel) If I Live, 2003, (juvenile) Joey Grows and Knows, 2005; co-author songs Talk to Your Child, Willie Lives in the Streets, 1986, Homeless Hope, 1987, The TAP Song, 1995, artist: (literacy drawings) Say (Simply Apply Yourself), 1988, contr. Word-Up Anthology, 1990, (paintings) BIG (Black Inventors Gifts), 1991; one-man shows include AAA Art Gallery, Detroit, 1963-67, Richard Russell Hall Gallery, Atlanta, 1985, C.W. Hill Gallery, Atlanta, 1990, Walker St. Gallery, Atlanta, 1992, Alma Simmons Gallery, 1986-94, The Atlanta Project Collaboration Ctr., 1994, Atlanta's Auburn Ave. Rsch. Libr., African Am. Culture and History Gallery, 1999, Tchg. Mus. South, 1999-2001, Decatur Bapt. Ch., 2000; exhibited in group shows at Red Cross European Exchange Touring Art Exhbn., 1949, Atlanta U., 1949, 53-55, Contemporary Art Studio Gallery, Detroit, 1962, 64-67, 75, Detroit Mus. Art, 1968, Wayne State Coll. Cmty. Gallery, Detroit, 1969, Kumarsi Mart Art Gallery, Detroit, 1970, Scarab Club Mus., Detroit, 1974, United Auto Workers, Detroit, 1977, Salon Internat. De La Caricature, Montreal, Can., 1980-83, 85-86, 88, Artistic Directions Gallery, Atlanta, 1983, Nexus Gallery, Atlanta, 1984, 89, Ctr. Creative Studies Coll. Art and Design Alumni Exhibits, Detroit, 1986-92, Spelman Coll., Atlanta, 1987, Mattress Factory, 1987, 89, Nat. Black Arts Festival, Atlanta, 1988-92, Ga. State U., 1989, Ruth Hall Hodges Gallery, Atlanta, 1990-93, TULA Galleries, Atlanta, 1990, Seven Stages, 1990, 96, EarthFactory, Atlanta, 1991, Art Station, Atlanta, 1991, Atlanta Life, 1992, Trinity Art Gallery, 1992, Samari Art Gallery, 1993, Mobile (Ala.) Coll., 1993-94, Albany Mus. Art, 1994, Alma Simmons Gallery, Atlanta, 1994, Atlanta Project Hdqs., 1994, Avery Gallery, 1995; Buttermilk Bottom Art Proj., 1995-96, Atlanta's Civic Ctr., 1995-96, Alma Simmons Gallery, 1995-96, Atlanta's Auburn Ave Rsch. Libr., African Am. Culture and History Gallery, 1996, City Hall East Gallery, 1996-97, Atlanta Olympic Park, 1997, Eddies' Alley, 1997, Miles Gallery, 1997, House of Colors, 1998, Annie McPheeters Art Gallery, 1999, Tchg. Mus. South, 1999—, Atlanta Hartsfield Airport, 2000, New Orleans Art Galleries, 2000, Kennesaw State U. Gallery, 2000, Southwest Cafe Gallery, 2005, Homecoming: 20th Century African Am. Masters, 2005, Walt Disney's movie scenery, 2001-, Motion Through Art, 2002, Pilgrimage to Paradise, Gallery on Greene, 2002, Youth Gallery, 2003, Atlanta Biennial, 2003, Mills Srs. Ctr. Collection, 2003, Habersham Gardens, 2004, South Fulton Art Show, 2004; represented in permanent collections including Atlanta U., Hatch-Billups, N.Y., Ga. Artists Register, Atlanta, Bianco Collections, Ga. Rsch. libr. African-Am. culture and history, 1995, RepoHistory Assn., 1996, neighborhood schs. mentor Fed. Dept. Stores, Detroit, 1964-69; motivator, sch. lectr. Atlanta Jour./Constitution, 1983-90, minority job fairs guide, 1985; bd. dirs. Neighborhood Planning Unit J, Atlanta, 1984—, Bankhead Hwy. Revitalization Project, Atlanta, 1990—; arts cons. Fulton County Cmty. Arts Task Force, Atlanta, 1990—; com. chmn. Jimmie Carter's West Fulton and Douglass Atlanta Cluster Project, 1992—; active Feed The Homeless, Inc., Atlanta Olympics Com., Atlanta Mayor's Bicycle Paths Commn., 1995; com. chmn. Atlanta-Fulton County Action Authority Assn., 1994, North Ave Civic League Assn., 2002, The Atlanta Contemporary Studios, 2003. Recipient George H. Clapp Meml. Found. award Art Inst. Pitts., 1949, Nat. Art award, Scholastic Art Awards Contest, Atlanta U. Nat. Art award, 1949, Nat. Cartoonist Soc. scholar, 1958, Editorial Cartoon award Nat. Newspapers Pubs. Assn., 1973, Bronze Jubilee Cmty. award WPBA TV, Atlanta, 1986, Alumni Art award Ctr. Creative Studies, Coll. Art and Design, Detroit, 1986, Atlanta Symphony Art award, 1986, Youth Motivation award Merit Employment Assn., 1987-89, So. Drawl Art Exhbn. award, 1993, Atlanta's Centennial Olympic Park Art award, 1997, Annie L. McPheeters Cmty. Medallion award, 1998, Million Man March Srs. award, 1998, Cmty. award Together Atlanta, 1999; grantee Atlanta Jour./Constitution, 1986, Nexus Family History Artbook Project, 1994, Avant Gardening Tour 2000, Daimler/Chrysler Art award, 2002. Mem. Assn. Am. Cultures, 1980, High Mus. Art, 1st World Writers (v.p. 1993-94), Internat. Black Writers (cons., pres. 1996), Atlanta Writing Resource Ctr., Nat. Conf. Artists, Friends of Atlanta/Fulton County Libr., Buttermilk Bottom Cmty. Assn. (cons., v.p. 1996, pres. 1998), Individual Visual Artists' Coalition, Laughing Trees Assn. (CEO 2000), Keep Atlanta Beautiful (bd. mem. 2004). Democrat. Baptist. Avocations: poetry, photography, tennis, rummage sales, reading. Home: 1796 North Ave NW Atlanta GA 30318/4441 Office Phone: 404 794 0948. Personal E-mail: j.l.t.malone@att.net. E-mail: laughingtrees@worldnet.att.net.

**MALONE, JAMES RICHARD,** manufacturing company executive; b. Cleve., Dec. 2, 1942; s. William R. and Marian (Bentley) M.; BSc, Ind. U., 1965; m. Linda Malone; children: Deanna Lynn, Lisa Suzanne, Zachary, Gabriel. With Gen. Motors, Bendix, Cummins Engine, 1969-70; with Western Acadia, Chgo., 1970-74; v.p. mfg. Haskell of Pitts., 1971-74; pres., chief exec. officer Mgmt. Concepts Co., Pitts., 1974-79; pres., CEO Facet Enterprises Inc., Tulsa, 1979, Purolator Products Co., Tulsa, Anchor Glass Container Corp., Grimes Aerospace, Cenveo, 2005-; former founding, mng. ptnr., Qorval LLC, Naples, Fla.; bd. dirs. Sooner Fed. Savs. and Loan, Red Ball Freight Co., Maclenburg-Duncan Inc. Mem. exec. com. Tulsa Philharm., Indian Nations council Boy Scouts Am., Tulsa Global Trade Found., Govs. Task Force on Econ. Devel.; bd. dirs. Tulsa Ballet Theatre; bd. dirs. Achievement of Tulsa, pres., 1986. Mem. Young President's Orgn., UN Bus. Council, Tulsa Club, So. Hills. Country Club, Golf Club of Okla., Castle Pines Golf Club. Republican. Methodist. Office: Cenveo 8310 S Valley Hwy Englewood CO 80112

**MALONE, JEAN HAMBIDGE,** educational consultant; b. South Bend, Ind., Nov. 23, 1954; d. Craig Ellis and Dorothy Jane (Piechorowski) Hambidge; m. James Kevill Malone, July 8, 1978; children: Julia Mae, James Kevill III, John Thomas. BS in Edn., Butler U., 1976, MS in Edn., 1977. Tchr. Indpls. Pub. Schs., 1977-78; dir. student center and activities Butler U., Indpls., 1978-87. Trustee Pleasure Meml. scholarship, 1977-80; bd. dirs. Heritage Place of Indpls., 1983-88, Ind. Office Campus Ministries, 1985-87, 89—91, Campfire of Cen. Ind., 1980-84, 86-87, Intercollegiate YMCA, Indpls., 1985-87, 89-90, Indpls. Jr. League, 1989—, Indpls. Urban Parish Coop, 1987-90, v.p., pres., 1991, 92; bd. dirs. Gennesaret Free Clinic of Indy, 1992-94; mem. overseers coun. Camp Delafield Children with Dyslexia, 1993-95, bd. pres., 1997-2000; bd. dirs. Dyslexia Inst. Ind., 1996—, bd. pres., 1997-2000; mem. Commn. Youth Archdiocese, 2000-01; community advv. for the homeless of Indpls. Recipient Outstanding Faculty award, Butler U., 1980. Mem. Ind. Assn. Women Deans (v.p. bd. dirs. 1987-88), Adminstrs. and Counselors (bd. dirs. 1982-83), Internat. Dyslexia Assn. (mem. Ind. br.

1992—), Kappa Delta Pi, Phi Kappa Phi, Alpha Lambda Delta, Kappa Kappa Gamma. Roman Catholic. Office: 5256 N Illinois St Indianapolis IN 46208-2636 Personal E-mail: jhmalone2@aol.com.

**MALONE, JENA,** actress; b. Lake Tahoe, Nev., Nov. 21, 1984; d. Debbie. Actress (films) Contact, 1997, Stepmom, 1998, The Book of Stars, 1999, For Love of the Game, 1999, Donnie Darko, 2001, Life as a House, 2001, Corn, 2002, The Dangerous Lives of Altar Boys, 2002, The Badge, 2002, American Girl, 2002, The United States of Leland, 2003, Cold Mountain, 2003, Saved!, 2004, Howl's Moving Castle, 2004, Bickford Shmeckler's Cool Ideas, 2005, The Ballad of Jack and Rose, 2005, Pride & Prejudice, 2005, (TV films) Hidden in America, 1996, Hope, 1997, Ellen Foster, 1997, Cheaters, 2000, The Ballad of Lucy Whipple, 2001, Hitler: The Rise of Evil, 2003, guest appearances Punk'd, 2004, On-Air with Ryan Seacrest, 2004, Dennis Miller, 2004, Tonight Show with Jay Leno, 2004, actress (Broadway plays) Doubt, 2006. Mailing: c/o UTA 9560 Wilshire Blvd Beverly Hills CA 90212*

**MALONE, JIMMY,** radio personality; m. April Malone; 1 child, Angela. Radio host WMJI, Cleve., 1961—. Stand-up comedian. Co-host (radio shows) Knuckleheads in the News, 1961—, The Lanigan & Malone Show, 1991—. Active Cleve. Scholar Program, Providence House, Greater Cleve. Hunger Task Force. Co-recipient (with John Lanigan) Large Market Personality of Yr., NAB Marconi Radio Awards, 2003; named Radio and TV Coun. Students' Broadcaster of Yr.; named to, Shaker Heights Alumni Hall of Fame. Office: WMJI 105.7 4th Fl 6200 Oak Tree Blvd Independence OH 44131 also: WMJI 105.7 FM 6th Fl 310 W Lakeside Ave Cleveland OH 44113 E-mail: malone@wmji.com.

**MALONE, JOHN C.,** media company executive; b. Milford, Conn., Mar. 7, 1941; m. Leslie. BS in Elec. Engring. and Econ., Yale U., 1963; MS in Indsl. Mgmt., John Hopkins U., 1964, PhD in Ops. Rsch., 1967; LHD (hon.), Denver U., 1992. With econ. planning rsch. and devel. Bell Telephone Labs/AT&T, 1963—68; joined McKinsey & Co., 1968; group v.p. Gen. Instrument Corp., 1970—73; formerly pres. Jerrold Electronics Corp. (subs. Gen. Instrument Corp.); pres., CEO Tele-Comms., Inc., Denver, 1973—96; chmn., CEO Tele-Comms., Inc. (merged with AT&T Corp.), Denver, 1996-99; chmn. Liberty Satellite, 1996—2000, Liberty Media Corp., Denver, 1990—, CEO, 2005—06. Bd. dirs. IAC/InterActiveCorp., 2001—04, Bank of New York, 1986—, UnitedGlobalCom, Inc., Discovery Communications, CATO Inst., Cablevision Systems Corp.; bd. dirs. Liberty Media Corp.; bd. dirs. The Nature Conservancy; bd. dirs., chmn. emeritus Cable Television Laboratories, Inc. Bd. dirs. Nature Conservancy, CATO Inst. Named Man of Yr. award, TVC Mag., 1981; named one of Forbes' Richest Americans, 2006; recipient Wall Street Transcript's Gold award for cable industry's best CEO, 1982, 1985, 1986, 1987, Wall Street Transcript Silver award, 1984, 1989, NCTA Vanguard award, 1983, Women in Cable Betsy Magness Fellowship Honoree, U. Pa. Wharton Sch. Sol C. Snider Entrepreneurial Ctr. Award of Merit for Disting. Entrepreneurship, Am. Jewish Com. Sherrill C. Corwin Human Rels. award, Comm. Tech. Mag. Svc. and Tech. award, Bronze award, Fin. World CEO of Yr. Competition, 1993, Hopkins Disting. Alumnus award, 1994. Mem.: Nat. Cable. TV Assn. (dir. 1974—77, treas. 1977—78, dir. 1980—93, Vanguard award 1983). Office: Liberty Media Corp 12300 Liberty Blvd Englewood CO 80112*

**MALONE, JOHN I.,** pediatrics educator, biomedical researcher; b. Altoona, Pa., Oct. 10, 1941; s. W. Paul and Olive (Romine) M.; m. Gloria Joyce Cromer, Sept. 5, 1964; children: John Irvin Jr., Michael A., Jennifer A., W. Andrew. BS, Pa. State U., 1963; MD, U. Pa., 1967. Diplomate Am. Bd. Pediatrics, Am. Bd. Pediatric Endocrinology; cert. diabetes educator. Straight pediatric intern Children's Hosp. Phila., 1967-68, resident, 1968-69, research fellow div. biochem. devel. and molecular diseases, 1969-71; instr. pediatrics U. Pa. Sch. Medicine, Phila., 1971-72; chief resident Hosp. of U. Pa., 1971-72; asst. prof. U. South Fla. Coll. Medicine, Tampa, 1972-76, assoc. prof., 1976-80, chief divsn. pediatric diabetes & metabolic diseases, 1976—, prof., 1980—, co-dir. Diabetes Ctr., 1979—. Co-dir. Fla. Camp for Children and Youth with Diabetes, Tampa, 1973—, pres., 1990; mem. clin. and sci. adv. bd. Children's Diabetes Found. at Denver, 1976-86; dir. Suncoast Regional PKU Program, 1976—, Suncoast Regional Diabetes Program, 1976—, chief pediat. endocrinology, diabetes and metabolism, 1995—; mem. Fla. Gov.'s Diabetes Adv. Coun., 1979—; mem. Internat. Study Group Diabetes in Children and Adolescents, Paris, 1982—; vis. prof., cons. in pediatric endocrinology Uniformed Svcs. U. Health Scis., Bethesda, Md., 1990-98; mem. staff various hosps. Contbr. over 110 articles Sci., New Eng. Jour. Medicine, Jour. Pediatrics, Am. Jour. Human Genetics, Am. Jour. Diseases of Children, Diabetes, Jour. Fla. Med. Assn., Diabetes Care, Jour. Clin. Investigation, Jour. Clin. Psychiatry, European Jour. Pediatrics, Proc. NAS, Pediatrics Rsch., Pediatrician, Diabetes Care, Pediatrics, Am. Jour. Med. Scis., Am. Jour. Med. Genetics, Clin. Pediatrics, also chpts. to books. Bd. dir. Diabetes Trust Fund, Birmingham, Ala., 2002—. Mem. AAAS, Am. Acad. Pediatrics, Am. Diabetes Assn. (program chmn. youth coun. 1987-88), Lawson Wilkins Pediatric Endocrine Soc., So. Soc. for Pediatric Rsch. (pres. 1986-87), Am. Fedn. for Clin. Rsch., Soc. for Pediatric Rsch., N.Y. Acad. Sci., Am. Inst. Nutrition, Am. Pediatric Soc., Am. Soc. for Clin. Nutrition, Soc. for Inherited Metabolic Disorders. Achievements include research on the metabolic causes of diabetes associated complications and research on the development and prevention of diabetes in relatives of patients with insulin-dependent diabetes. Office: U South Fla Coll Medicine 12901 Bruce B Downs Blvd Tampa FL 33612-4742 Office Phone: 813-974-5777. E-mail: jmalone@hsc.usf.edu.

**MALONE, JOSEPH JAMES,** mathematics professor, researcher; b. St. Louis, Sept. 9, 1932; s. Joseph James and Aurelia Theresa (Schomaker) M.; m. Dorothy Sue Cleary, Nov. 24, 1960; children: Michael, Barbara, Philip, Patrick. BS, St. Louis U., 1954, MS, 1958, PhD, 1962. Instr. math. Rockhurst Coll., Kansas City, Mo., 1960-62; asst. prof. U. Houston, 1962-67; assoc. prof. Tex. A&M U., College Station, 1967-70, prof., 1970-71, Worcester (Mass.) Poly. Inst., 1971-2000, prof. emeritus, 2000—, chmn. dept. math., 1971-78. Contbr. articles to profl. jours. Mem. adv. schs. bd. Town of Westborough (Mass.), 1974-83, 84-87, fin. com., 1992-98, selectman, 1998-2001, fin. com., 2001—. With U.S. Army, 1954-56. Mem. Am. Math. Soc., Math. Assn. Am. Democrat. Roman Catholic. Achievements include research in near-ring theory and group theory. Home: 45 Adams St Westborough MA 01581-3610 Office: Worcester Poly Inst 100 Institute Rd Worcester MA 01609-2280 E-mail: jjmalone@wpi.edu.

**MALONE, KARL,** retired professional basketball player; b. Summerfield, La., July 24, 1963; m. Kay Malone; 4 children; 1 child, Cheryl Ford (Plays in WNBA). Student, La. Tech. U., 1981—85. Basketball player Utah Jazz, Salt Lake City, 1985—2003, LA Lakers, 2004—05. Mem. U.S. Olympic Basketball Team, 1992, 96. Founder Karl Malone Foundation for Kid's; works with Utah Special Olympics. Named NBA Most Valuable Player, 1997, 1999; named one of 50 Greatest Players in NBA History, 1996; named to NBA All-Rookie team, 1986, NBA All-Star team, 1988—89, 1991—2001, 2003, All-NBA 1st team, 1989—99, All-NBA 2d team, 1988, NBA All-Defensive 1st team, 1997—99; recipient All-Star Game Most Valuable Player award, NBA, 1989, All-Star game Most Valuable Player award co-recipient, 1993, Gold medal, U.S. Olympic Basketball Team, 1992, 1996. Achievements include being co-leader most seasons (11) with 2000 points, 1987-95.

**MALONE, MARK HUGH,** music educator; b. Miami, Fla., Jan. 29, 1952; s. Wallace Marvin and Jackie Lou (Thornton) Malone; m. Patricia Ann Sharpe, June 14, 1980; children: Meagan Elizabeth, Andrew Kent. BS in Social Studies Edn., Fla. State U., 1974; BA in Humanities, Rollins Coll., 1977; MusM, Fla. State U., 1979, MusD, 1981. Dir. choral music Osceola HS, Kissimee, Fla., 1974—78; music specialist W.I. Thames Elem., Hattiesburg, Miss., 1982—85; dir. choral music Pearl River CC, Poplarville, Miss., 1985—2006; dean Winters Sch. Music, William Carey U., Hattiesburg, Miss., 2006—. Contbr. articles to profl. jours. Named Outstanding Young Men in Am., 1983; recipient Headwae Tchg. award, Miss. State Legis., 2006, Outstanding Faculty Mem., Pearl River Cmty. Coll., 1988. Mem.: Am. Choral

Dir. Assn. (nat. two yr. coll. chmn. 2000—06, southern divsn. show choir chmn. 1992—98), Phi Tu Alpha Sinforia. Avocations: travel, reading, spectator sports, college pennant collecting. Office: William Carey U 498 Tuscan Ave Hattiesburg MS 39401

**MALONE, NANCY,** actress; b. Queens Village, NY; d. James and Bridget (Sheilds) M. Freelance actress, dir., producer, writer. Performer (TV series) The First Hundred Years, Naked City, The Long, Hot Summer (Best Performance by an Actress award); Broadway debut in Time Out For Ginger, other stage performances include Major Barbara, The Makropoulis Secret, A Touch of the Poet, The Trial of the Catonsville Nine; touring performances include The Chalk Garden, The Seven Yr. Itch, A Place For Dolly; actress (films) The Violators, I Cast No Shadow, An Affair of the Skin, Intimacy, The Trial of the Cantonsville Nine, The Man Who Loved Cat Dancing, Capricorn One; producer (TV series) including Bionic Woman, 1978, Husbands, Wives and Lovers, 1978, The Great Pretender, 1984, (special) Bob Hope: The First 90 Years, 1993 (Emmy award, Outstanding Variety, Musical or Comedy Special, 1993), Womanspeak, 1983; dir. (TV series) Dynasty, 1984-87, Hotel, 1984-87, Colbys, 1985, Cagney and Lacey, 1987, Star Trek Voyager, 1997, Burning Zone, 1997, Fame I.A. 1997-98, Rosie O'Niel (Emmy nomination), Sisters (Emmy nomination), Melrose Place, 1992-99, Beverly Hills, 1990-2000, Picket Fences, Judging Amy, 1999, Resurrection Blvd., 2000-02; producer, dir. (film) There Were Times Dear, 1986 (John Muir Trustees award, Cine Golden Eagle, Blue Ribbon); founder Nancy Malone Prodns., 1975, Lilac Prodns., 1979. Fellow Leaky Found.; mem. Am. Film Inst. (mem. founder), Women in Film (trustee, Chrystal award, Founders award 1996). Office: Guild Mgmt PHA 9911 W Pico Blvd Los Angeles CA 90035-2703 Home: 4604 Ledge Ave Toluca Lake CA 91602-1536

**MALONE, RICH L.,** financial services company executive; Positions in IT dept. Fed. Home Loan Bank, Des Moines; prin. info. tech. Edward D. Jones & Co., 1979—, mem. mgmt. com., 1985—, mem. exec. com., 1999—. Dir. F5 Networks Inc., Seattle, 2003—. Named one of Top 5 CIOs in securities and investment industry, Wall St. and Tech. mag. CIO Elite Survey, 2001, Premier 100 IT Leaders, Computerworld, 2005. Office: Edward Jones 12555 Manchester Rd Saint Louis MO 63131*

**MALONE, ROBERT K.,** lawyer; b. Bklyn., 1959; BA, Cath. Univ. Am., 1981; JD, Seton Hall Univ., 1984. Bar: NJ 1985. Staff to Hon. Bill Bradley US Senate, Wash., DC, 1979—81; law clerk, Hon. William H. Gindin US Bankruptcy Ct. (Dist. NJ), 1985—86; prtnr., co-head, bus. fin., restructuring practice group Drinker Biddle & Reath LLP, Florham Park, NJ. Office: Drinker Biddle & Reath 500 Campus Dr Florham Park NJ 07932-1047 Office Phone: 973-549-7080. Office Fax: 973-360-9831. Business E-Mail: robert.malone@dbr.com.

**MALONE, ROBERT ROY,** artist, art educator; b. McColl, SC, Aug. 8, 1933; s. Robert Roy and Anne (Matthews) M.; m. Cynthia Enid Taylor, Feb. 26, 1956; 1 child, Brendan Trevor. BA, U. N.C., 1955; MFA, U. Chgo., 1958; postgrad., U. Iowa, 1959. Instr. art Union U. Jackson, Tenn., 1959-60, Lambuth Coll., 1959-61; asst. prof. art Wesleyan Coll., Macon, Ga., 1961-67, assoc. prof., 1967-68, W.Va. U., 1968-70, So. Ill. U., Edwardsville, 1970-75, prof., 1975—2000, prof. emeritus, 2000—. One-man shows at Gallery Illien, Atlanta, 1969, De Cinque Gallery, Miami, 1968, 71, Ill. State Mus., Springfield, 1974, U. Del., Newark, 1978, Elliot Smith Gallery, St. Louis, 1985, Merida Galleries, Louisville, 1985, Yvonne Rapp Gallery, Louisville, 1990, 92-93, 96, 98, 2000, 04, St. John's Coll., Santa Fe, 1991, Uzelac Gallery, Pontiac, Mich., 1997, others; group shows include Bklyn. Mus., 1966, Assoc. Am. Artists Gallery, NYC, 1968, Mus. d'Art Modern, Paris, 1970, DeCordova Mus., 1973-74, St. Louis Art Mus., 1985, Wake Forest U., 1985, New Orleans Mus. Art, 1990, Dakota Internat., Vermillion, 1994, Springfield Art Mus., Mo., 2004; represented in permanent collections including Smithsonian Instn., Washington, USIA, Washington, Libr. of Congress, Calif. Palace of Legion of Honor, San Francisco, NY Pub. Libr., NYC, Victoria and Albert Mus., London, Speed Mus. Chgo. Art Inst., Indpls. Mus. Art, Humana Inc., Louisville, State of Ill. Ctr., Chgo., Speed Mus., Louisville, N. Ill. U., Capital Devel. Bd., Ill.; co-editor: Contemporary American Printmakers, 1999 (English and Chinese edits.). Recipient numerous regional, nat. awards in competitive exhbns.; Ford fellow, 1977, So. Ill. U. at Edwardsville sr. research scholar, 1976, 1984. Home: 600 Chapman St Edwardsville IL 62025-1260

**MALONE, ROBERT WALLACE,** surgeon; s. Edgar Wallace and Nancy Adams Malone; m. Jill Glasspool, Feb. 17, 1979; children: William Zachary, Spencer James. AA, Santa Barbara C.C., Calif., 1982; BS in Biochemistry, U. of Calif., Davis, 1984; MS in Biology, U. of Calif., La Jolla, 1989; MD, Northwestern U., Chgo., 1991. Rsch. scientist Vical, Inc, San Diego, 1989; pathology resident U. of Calif., Davis, 1991—92, rsch. fellow, 1992—93, asst. prof. pathology, 1993—97; asst. prof. pathology U. of Md., Sch. of Medicine, Balt., 1997—2000; chief of lab. sci., dir. of tissue banking USUHS Clin. Breast Care Program, Bethesda, Md., 2000—01; pres. and founder Gene Delivery Alliance, Inc, Rockville, Md., 2001; assoc. dir, clin. rsch. Dynport Vaccine Co., LLC, Frederick, Md., 2002—; assoc. prof. of surgery Uniformed Services U. of the Health Sci., Bethesda, Md., 2001. Cons. Inovio, Oslo, 2001—02; sr. cons. Mgmt. Systems Designers, Inc, Vienna, 2001—02; med. dir. Molecular Histology, Montgomery Village, Md., 2002. Contbr. chpts. to books. Recipient Trainee Investigator award, Am. Fedn. for Clin. Rsch., 1993, Svc. to the Coll. award, Santa Barbara C.C., 1981—82, Giannini Found. fellow, Bank of Am., Giannini Found., 1992—93, Henry Christian Award for Excellence in Rsch., Am. Fedn. for Clin. Rsch., 1992, 1st Pl., Northwestern AOA Rsch. Symposium competition for Med. Students, Northwestern U. AOA, 1989; fellow Edmonson Summer fellow, UC Davis Dept. of Med. Pathology, 1984, Pre-Doctoral fellow, USUHS, 1986—88, grantee Pres.'s Undergraduate Fellowship grantee, U. Calif.-Davis, 1983—84, Med. Scholars Program grantee, Univ of Calif. Davis Med. Ctr., 1992—93, Grant for RNA structure modeling, San Diego Supercomputer Ctr., 1988; scholar MD./Ph.D. scholar, Northwestern U., 1984—86. Mem.: AAAS, European Gene Therapy Soc., Bioelectrochem. Soc., NY Acad. of Sci., Gene Therapy/Molecular Biology Internat. Soc. Achievements include invention of electroporation gene delivery into lung; patents for direct DNA delivery; genetic (DNA) vaccination; mucosal polynucleotide vaccination; invention of nuclease inhibitors for non-viral gene therapy; patents pending for nuclease inhibitors for non-viral gene therapy; invention of skin electroporation for genetic vaccination. Avocations: carpentry, kayacking, animal husbandry, mountain climbing. Personal E-mail: gtinventor@hotmail.com. E-mail: maloner@dynport.com.

**MALONE, THOMAS FRANCIS,** academic administrator, meteorologist; b. Sioux City, Iowa, May 3, 1917; s. John and Mary (Hourigan) M.; m. Rosalie Doran, Dec. 30, 1942; children: John H., Thomas Francis, Mary E., James K., Richard K., Dennis P. BS, S.D. Sch. Mines, 1940, D.Eng., 1962; Sc.D, MIT, 1946; L.H.D., St. Joseph Coll., West Hartford, Conn., 1965; Sc.D. (hon.), Bates Coll., 1988. Instr. MIT, 1942-43, asst. prof., 1943-51, assoc. prof., 1951-56; dir. Travelers Rsch. Ctr., Travelers Ins. Co., Hartford, Conn., 1955-56, dir. rsch., 1956-69, sr. v.p., 1968-70, chmn. bd., 1961-70; dean Grad. Sch., U. Conn., Storrs, 1970-73; chmn. bd. Ctr. for Environment and Men, 1970-71; dir. emeritus Holcomb Rsch. Inst., Butler U., Indpls., 1983—; scholar in residence St. Joseph Coll., 1983-98; Nat. Scis. fellow Resources for Future, 1983-84; Univ. Disting. scholar N.C. State U., 1991—98. Chmn. bd. Univ. Corp. for Atmospheric Rsch., 1973—76; mem. Conn. Weather Control Bd., 1959—73; mem. panel on sci. and tech. com. on sci. and astronautics U.S. Ho. of Reps., 1960—70; nat. adv. com. on air pollution HEW, 1962—66; mem. sci. info. coun. NSF, 1962—66; rep. Am. Geophys. Union to U.S. Nat. Commn. for UNESCO, 1963—73, chmn. U.S. Nat. Commn., 1965—67; mem. nat. adv. com. on oceans and atmosphere, 1972—75; mem. Conn. Rsch. Commn., 1965—71; mem. com. application sci. and tech. New Eng. Coun.; chmn. Nat. Motor Vehicle Safety Adv. Coun., 1967—70; mem. sci. adv. com. climate impact assessment and response program UN Environ. Program, 1992—; mem. adv. com. on accreditation Conn. Dept. Higher Edn., 2000—02; mem. acad. adv. bd. S.D. Sch. Mines and Tech., 1991—2002; bd.

dirs. Conn. Acad. for Edn., 2001—02. Editor: Compendium of Meteorology, 1951; contbg. editor: Environment, 1992-99; bd. editors: Jour. of the Marine Tech. Soc., 1995-99. Bd. dirs. Engrs. Joint Coun., 1968-70; bd. govs. Ins. Inst. Hwy. Safety, 1968-70; mem. oversight rev. bd. Nat. Acid Precipitation Assessment Program, 1990-96; corporator Hartford Sem., 2003—. Recipient Spl. Citation for Patriotic Svc. US War Dept., 1946, Robert M. Losey award Inst. Aero. Sci., 1960, Charter Oak Leadership medal Greater Hartford C. of C., 1962, Charles Franklin Brooks award, 1964, Cleveland Abbe award Am. Meteorol. Soc., 1968, Conn. Conservationist of Yr. award, 1966, Guy E. March Silver medal S.D. Sch. Mines, 1976, Internat. Meteorol. Orgn. prize, 1984, Internat. St. Francis Assissi prize for environment, 1991, AAAS Internat. prize, 1994, Irving award Distance Edn. Consortium, 1997, Disting. Alumni award S.D. Sch. Mines, 1998, Living Legend award St. Joseph Coll. 2006; named to S.D. Hall of Fame, 2003; named KEN Practitioner of Yr., Entuovation Internat., 2003; N.C. State U. disting. scholar, 1990-99, emeritus, 1999- Fellow AAAS (internat. sci. coop., 1994), N.Y. Acad. Scis., Am. Meteorol. Soc. (pres. 1960-62), Am. Geophys. Union (past pres., sec. internat. participation 1994, Waldo E. Smith award 1986); mem. NAS (chmn. geophysics rsch. bd. 1969-76, chmn. bd. on internat. orgns. and programs, dep. fgn. sec. 1969-73, fgn. sec. 1978-82), NRC (space application bd. 1973-77), Am. Acad. Arts and Scis., Internat. Coun. Sci. Unions (v.p., sec.-gen. sci. com. problems environ. 1970-76, treas. 1978-82) Am. Geog. Soc. (coun. 1971-77), Royal Irish Acad. (hon.), Conn. Acad. Sci. and Engring. (exec. scientist 1987-91, 97-2000, Lifetime Disting. Svc. award, 2004), Acad. Polit. Scis., Sigma Xi (bd. dirs. 1983-96, pres. 1988-89, dir. Sigma Xi Ctr. 1992-95, chief scientist 1996-98). Home: 275 Steele Rd Apt 504B West Hartford CT 06117 Office Phone: 860-920-6357. Personal E-mail: tfmalone@aol.com.

**MALONE, THOMAS W.,** business educator, researcher; b. Roswell, N.Mex., June 2, 1952; s. Ernest P. Jr. and Virginia Malone; m. Joan L. Goldberg, Aug. 28, 1988; children: Robert, Laura. BA in Math. Scis. magna cum laude, Rice U., 1974; MA in Psychology, Stanford U., 1977, MS in Engring.-Econ. Sys., 1978, PhD in Psychology, 1980. Cons. for computer-based instrn. Region IV Edn. Svc. Ctr., Houston, 1974-75; rsch. intern Xerox Corp., Palo Alto Rsch. Ctr., Calif., 1979-80, mem. rsch. staff, 1980-83; from asst. prof. to assoc. prof. MIT, Sloan Sch. Mgmt., Cambridge, Mass., 1983-89, Patrick McGovern prof. info. sys., 1989—, dir. Ctr. for Coord. Sci., 1989—2006, head info. tech. group, 2000—, dir. Ctr. Collective Intelligence, 2006—. Vis. prof. Harvard Bus. Sch., Boston, 1992, IESE Bus. Sch., Barcelona, 2001-02; co-dir. Initiative on Inventing the Orgns. of 21st Century, MIT, Sloan Sch. Mgmt., 1994-99, Douglas Drane Career Devel. assoc. prof. info. tech. and mgmt., 1985; co-founder, cons. Palladian Software, Cambridge, 1984-88, Agility Sys., Waltham, Mass., 1989-91; mem. adv. bd. Perot Sys. Corp., Dallas, 1992-98; co-founder, chmn. Phios Corp., Cambridge, 1996—, CEO, 1998-99; mem. adv. bd. ELance, Inc., Sunnyvale, Calif., 2000—, Oco Corp., Wayland, Mass., 2000—; bd. dirs. Seriosity, Inc.; spkr. and presenter in field. Author: The Future of Work, 2004, others; contbr. articles to profl. jours.; patentee in field. U.S. Presdl. scholar U.S. Presdl. Scholars Commn., 1970; grad. fellow NSF, 1976. Mem. Assn. for Computing Machinery (program chair conf. on computer supported coop. work 1993-94), Phi Beta Kappa. Office: MIT Sloan Sch Mgmt E53-333 Cambridge MA 02142 Office Phone: 617-253-6843. Business E-mail: malone@mit.edu.

**MALONE, WALLACE D., JR.,** retired bank executive; b. Dothan, Ala., 1936; married. BS, U. Ala., 1957; MBA, U. Pa., 1960. With First Nat. Bank, 1959-71, SouthTrust Corp. (acquired by Wachovia), Birmingham, Ala., 1972; chmn., CEO & pres. SouthTrust Corp., Birmingham, Ala., 1981—2004; vice chmn. Wachovia Corp., Charlotte, NC, 2004—06. Named to Univ. Ala. Bus. Hall of Fame, 2001.

**MALONE, WILLIAM GRADY,** retired lawyer; b. Minden, La., Feb. 19, 1915; s. William Gordon and Minnie Lucie (Hortman) M.; m. Marion Rowe Whitfield, Sept. 26, 1943; children: William Grady, Gordon Whitfield, Marion Elizabeth, Helen Ann, Margaret Catherine. BS, La. State U., 1941; JD, George Washington U., 1952. Bar: Va. 1952, U.S. Supreme Ct. 1971. Statis. analyst Dept. Agr., Baton Rouge, 1941; investigator VA, Washington, 1946-59, legal officer, dep. gen. counsel, asst. gen. counsel, 1959-79; pvt. practice law Arlington, Va., 1979-97. Editor: Fed. Bar News, 1972-73. Pres. Aurora Hills Civic Assn., 1948-49; spl. asst. to treas. Com. of 100, 1979-81, chmn., 1982-83; pres. Children's Theater, 1968-69; trustee St. George's Episc. Ch., 1979—; chmn. Arlington County Fair Assn., 1979-83. Lt. col. AUS, 1941-46, ETO. Decorated Legion of Merit; recipient Disting. Svc. award, 1979, 3 Superior Performance awards, 1952-72, Outstanding Alumni award George Washington Law Sch., 1978 Mem. Fed. Bar Assn. (pres. D.C. chpt. 1970-71, nat. pres. 1978-79), Va. Bar Assn., Arlington County Bar Assn., Nat. Lawyers Club (dir.), Arlington Hotel Dist Lions, Ft. Myer Officers Club. Home: Apt 1523 900 N Taylor St Arlington VA 22203 E-mail: wgmalone@juno.com. *Success is not measured by dollars accumulated but by service to others.*

**MALONEY, CAROLYN BOSHER,** congresswoman; b. Greensboro, NC, Feb. 19, 1948; d. R.G. and Christine (Clegg) Bosher; m. Clifton H.W. Maloney, 1976; children: Christina, Virginia. BA, Greensboro Coll., 1968. Cmty. affairs coord. welfare relie. prog. Bd. Edn., NYC, 1972—75, spl. asst. ctr. career and occupl. edn., 1975—76; legis. aide housing com. NY State Assembly, 1977, sr. prog. analyst cities com., 1977—79; exec. dir. adv. coun. Office of NY State Senate Minority Leader Manfred Ohrenstein, 1979—82, dir. spl. projects, 1980—82; mem. City Coun. from Dist. 8, NYC, 1983-93, US Congress from 14th NY dist., 1993—, chair Ho Dem. Caucus Task Force on Homeland Security, 2003—, ranking Ho. Dem. joint econ. com., 2005—, ranking minority mem. domestic and internat. monetary policy, trade and tech. subcommittee, 2003—, mem. govt. reform com., ranking minority mem. census subcommittee, 1999—. Mem. US del. Fourth World Conf. on Women, Beijing, Internat. Conf. on Population and Devel., The Hague, Netherlands. Active Assn. for a Better NY, Manhattan Women's Polit. Caucus. Decorated Mil. Order of the Purple Heart; recipient Spl. Impact award, Healthy Mothers, Healthy Babies, 2000, Women's Leadership award, UN Family Planning, 2002, Disting. Pub. Svc. award, Nat. Family Planning and Reproductive Health Assn., Ellis Island Medal of Honor, Global Peace award, Peace Action, Queens Women of Distinction award, Queen's Women's Polit. Caucus. Mem.: Hadassah (Myrtle Wreath award), NOW, NAACP. Democrat. Presbyterian. Office: US Ho Reps 2331 Rayburn Ho Office Bldg Washington DC 20515-3214 Office Phone: 202-225-7944.*

**MALONEY, JAMES HENRY,** former congressman, real estate developer; b. Quincy, Mass., Sept. 17, 1948; s. James Henry Jr. and Katherine Smith (Murphy) M.; m. Mary Angela Draper, Aug. 16, 1980; children: Kate, Anna, Ellen. BA cum laude, Harvard U., 1972; JD, Boston U., 1980. Vol. VISTA, Gary, Ind., 1969—70; exec. dir. Cmty. Action Com. Danbury, Conn., 1974—78; atty. Pinney, Payne, VanLenten, Burrell, Wolfe & Dillman, P.C., Danbury, 1980—86; ptnr. Dice, Maloney & Lenz, P.C., Danbury, 1986—93, Maloney, Leaphart & Assocs., PC, Danbury, 1995—97; mem. Conn. Senate, Hartford, 1987—95, 105-107th Congresses from 5th Conn. dist., 1997—2003, mem. armed svcs. com., mem. fin. svcs. com.; pres., gen. counsel Conn. Inst. Cmtys., Inc., 2003—; COO Main St. Devel. Corp., 2003—. Democrat. Roman Catholic. Avocation: sailing. Office Phone: 203-743-9760. E-mail: JamesHMaloney@aol.com.

**MALONEY, JOHN JOSEPH,** writer; b. N.Y.C., Jan. 15, 1929; s. John J. and Breda T. (O'Leary) M.; m. Helen Martin; children: Peter, Elizabeth, Mary Ellen. BA, Fordham Coll., 1951. City editor Patent Trader, Mt. Kisco, N.Y., 1953-59; news bureau mgr. N.Y. Stock Exchange, N.Y.C., 1959-63; dir. pub. rels. Lehman Bros., N.Y.C., 1963-71, Warnaco, Inc., Bridgeport, Conn., 1971-77; v.p. charge of media rels. Citigroup (formerly Citicorp/Citibank), N.Y.C., 1977-91; writer Easton, Conn., 1991—. Cons. capital formation markets Kenyan govt., 1991, Bulgarian govt., 1999. With U.S. Army, 1951-53. Avocation: sailing. Home: 65 Sport Hill Pkwy Easton CT 06612-2239

**MALONEY, KRISTEN,** gymnast; b. Hacketstown, NJ, Mar. 10, 1981; d. Richard and Linda. Mem. U.S. Gymnastics Team, 1994—2001, UCLA Gymnastics Team, 2000—. Mem. U.S. World Championships Team, 1997, 99, U.S. Gymnastics Team Sydney Olympics, 2000. Recipient numerous awards, 1st pl. Am. Classic, 1997, 98, 1st pl. (3) Foxsport Challenge, Sydney, 1997, 1st team, 1st balance beam, 1st floor exercise 1st AA, Internat. Team Championships, 1998, 1st team, 1st AA, Pacific Alliance Champiaonships, Winnipeg, Can., 1998, 1st balance beam Goodwill Games, 1998, others. Mem. Parketts Club. Avocations: reading, music, movies, shopping. Office: UCLA Women's Gymnastics PO Box 24044 Los Angeles CA 90024

**MALONEY, MARY D.,** lawyer; BA, U. Akron, 1984; JD summa cum laude, Cleve. State U., 1987; LLM, Case Wester Res. U., 1995. Bar: Ohio 1987. With Jones Day, Cleve., 1987—, ptnr., 2001—. Mem.: Ohio State Bar Assn. Office: Jones Day North Point 901 Lakeside Ave Cleveland OH 44114-1190

**MALONEY, MARYNELL,** lawyer; b. Hutchinson, Kans., Jan. 14, 1955; d. Robert Edgar and Marian Ellen (Benson) Baker; m. Michael D. Maloney, Nov. 30, 1977; children: Michelle M., Erica O., Dennis Jr. BA, Oberlin Coll., 1975; MA, Trinity U., San Antonio, 1978; JD, St. Mary's U., San Antonio, 1980. Cert. by Tex. bd. of legal specialization. Assoc. Law Offices Pat Maloney, P.C., San Antonio, 1981-82; ptnr., owner Maloney & Maloney, San Antonio, 1982—. Bd. dirs. San Antonio Internat. Keyboard Competition, 1988-90; bd. govs. St. Peters/St. Joseph's Children's Home, San Antonio, 1989-92. Mem. ACLU of Tex. (bd. dirs. 1990—), v.p. 1995-96, SACLU 1990—), Am. Trial Lawyers Assn., State Bar Tex., Tex. Trial Lawyers Assn. (assoc. bd. dirs. 1989-90, bd. dirs. 1991-2002, dir. emeritus 2002—, cert. personal injury trial law), San Antonio Bar Assn., San Antonio Trial Lawyers Assn. (pres. 1991-92). Democrat. Avocations: reading, writing, films. Office: Maloney & Maloney PC 2000 Milam 115 E Travis San Antonio TX 78205 Office Phone: 210-227-7000. Business E-Mail: marynell@maloneyandmaloney.com.

**MALONEY, MAUREEN MURPHY,** social sciences educator; b. N.Y.C., Nov. 16, 1941; d. Cyril Bernard Murphy and Monique Louissiane Jacques; m. Paul K. Maloney, Dec. 5, 1964; children: Jennifer, Paula, Edward. Diploma, Holy Name Sch. Nursing, 1962; BS in Psychology, Sacred Heart U., 1982; M in Applied Psychology, Fairfield U., 1986; D Ednl. Leadership summa cum laude, U. Bridgeport, 2003. RN N.J. Head nurse neurosurgery Columbia Presbyn. Med. Ctr., N.Y.C., 1962—65; prof. Housatonic C.C., Bridgeport, Conn., 1993—, chmn. dept. behavioral and social scis., 2006—. Adj. prof. Norwalk C.C., 1987—93. Recipient award for Tchg. Excellence and Disting. Svc., Housatonic Coll., 2004. Mem.: APS, ASCD, APA, AAUP, Am. Psychological Soc. Roman Catholic. Avocations: reading, skiing, tennis, classical music, opera. Office: Housatonic CC 900 Lafayette Ave Bridgeport CT 06608

**MALONEY, MICHAEL PATRICK,** lawyer, mediator, arbitrator; b. Syracuse, N.Y., June 1, 1944; s. Randolph Bartholomew and Alice Mary (Loban) M.; m. Jane McBurney, May 21, 1977; children: Christopher, Kara. AB, Georgetown U., 1966; MBA, Cornell U., 1968, JD, 1971. Bar: N.Y. 1972. Assoc. Donovan Leisure Newton and Irvine, N.Y.C., 1971-78; asst. dir. div. market regulation SEC, Washington, 1978-79; sr. v.p., gen. counsel, sec. Orion Capital Corp., N.Y.C., 1979-98; pres. OSOWA Enterprises, LLC, 1998—. Sec., bd. dirs. Carden Sch. Maui. Mem.: Am. Corp. Counsel Assn., Am. Soc. Corp. Secs. Home: 891 Holopuni Rd Kula HI 96790 E-mail: osowa@aol.com

**MALONEY, MILFORD CHARLES,** retired internal medicine educator; b. Buffalo, Mar. 15, 1927; s. John Angelus Maloney and Winifred Hill; m. Dione Ethyl Sheppard. BS, Canisius Coll., 1947, postgrad., 1947-49; MD, U. Buffalo, 1953. Diplomate Am. Bd. Internal Medicine. Rsch. chemist Buffalo Electrochem. Co., 1947-49; internship Mercy Hosp./Georgetown U., 1953-54; med. residency Buffalo VA Hosp., 1954-56; cardiology fellow Buffalo Gen. Hosp., 1956-57; chmn. dept. medicine Mercy Hosp., 1966-94, program dir., internal medicine residency Buffalo, 1972-89; with steering com. Assn. Program Dirs. in Internal Medicine, 1976, coun. mem., 1977-80; clin. prof. medicine SUNY, Buffalo, 1981-94; trustee Am. Soc. Internal Medicine, 1984-90, edn. leader, European seminar, 1987, edn. leader, So. Am. seminar, 1988; faculty instr. Christopher Wren Assn. Coll. William and Mary, Williamsburg, Va., 1997—. Bd. dirs. Internal Medicine Ctr. for Advancement and Rsch. Edn., Ctr. Excellence in Aging and Geriatric Health, Williamsburg, Va., chmn. devel. com.; pres. Heart Assn. Western N.Y., Buffalo, 1969; sr. cancer rsch. physician Roswell Park Meml. Cancer Inst., 1959-62; mem. internal medicine liaison com. N.Y. State, 1980-90; faculty instr., mem. curriculum com. Christopher Wren Assn. Coll. William & Mary, Williamsburg, Va., 1997-99 Editor newsletter N.Y. State Soc. Internal Medicine, 1972-78. Bd. dirs. Health Sys. Agy. Western N.Y., Buffalo, 1981; mem. exec. com., bd. dirs. Blue Cross Western N.Y., Buffalo, 1987; mem. bd. regents Canisius Coll., Buffalo, 1987; mem. pres. assocs. SUNY, Buffalo; founding mem. Greater Williamsburg Va. Symphony Soc., 1998; bd. dirs. Va. Symphony, Norfolk, 2001; bd. dirs., dir. devell. Williamsburg Ctr. for Excellence in Aging and Geriatric Health, 2004. Capt. M.C., U.S. Army, 1957-59. Recipient award of merit N.Y. State Soc. Internal Medicine, 1980, Man of Yr. award Heart Assn. Western N.Y., 1982, ann. honoree award Trocaire Coll. 1986, Disting. Alumni award Canisius Coll., 1991, Berkson Excellence award in tchg. and art of medicine, SUNY at Buffalo, 1992, Outstanding Med. Tchg. Attending award Mercy Hosp./SUNY Med. Residents, 1994, Lifetime Career Achievement award Med. Alumni Assn. SUNY, Buffalo, 2005, Heritage award Mercy Hosp. Found., Buffalo, N.Y., 2005; named to Sports Hall of Fame, Canisius Coll., 1978. Master ACP (pres. emeritus, Upstate Physician Recognition award 1989); fellow Am. Coll. Cardiology; mem. AMA (SUNY rep. 1986-94, rep. to sect. med. schs. at ann. meetings 1984-94, chmn. sect. on internal medicine 1990-91), Am. Soc. Internal Medicine (bd. dirs. Internal Medicine Ctr. for Advancement of Rsch. Edn. 1988-91, trustee 1984-90, pres. 1990-91, chmn. long range planning com., rep. to Federated Coun. on Internal Medicine 1990-91, rep. nat. practice parameters and guidelines com. 1989-91, Scroll of Honor benefactor for Internal Medicine Ctr. for Advancement of Rsch. and Edn. 1991), Va. State Soc. Internal Medicine (ex officio mem. exec. com., bd. dirs.), N.Y. State Soc. Internal Medicine (pres. 1974-75), Alumni Assn. SUNY (pres. 1975), Med. Soc. County Erie (pres. 1991-82), Va. Soc. Internal Medicine (hon.), Greater Williamsburg Va. Symphony Soc. (founding mem. 1998, editor newsletter 1998-2003). Home: 116 Cove Point Ln Williamsburg VA 23185-8613 E-mail: mcmaloney@widomaker.com.

**MALONEY, ROBERT E., JR.,** lawyer; b. San Francisco, Sept. 17, 1942; s. Robert E. and Mara A. (Murphy) M.; children: Michael, Sarah, Paul. BA magna cum laude, U. Portland, 1964; JD summa cum laude, Willamette U., Salem, Oreg., 1967. Bar: Oreg. 1967, Wash., U.S. Dist. Ct. Oreg., U.S. Dist. Ct. (we. dist.) Wash., U.S. Dist. Ct. (ea. dist.) Wash., U.S. Ct. Appeals (9th cir.). Ptnr. Lane Powell PC, Portland, 1967—; chmn., profl. svcs. counsel Bounce Back Oreg., 2003. Bd. dirs., sec. Norm Thompson Outfitters, Inc., Portland; mem. bd. visitors Willamette U. Law Sch., 1985-98, chair, 1993-95, mem. exec. com., 1992-97; past chair, mem. exec. com. Portland Trial Dept.; lawyers del. 9th Cir. Jud. Conf., 1995-98; chmn., pres. adv. coun. U. Portland, 2001—; mem. adv. coun. Oreg. Ct. Appeals, 2004-. Bd. dirs. Oreg. chpt. Multiple Sclerosis Soc., 1995-02, Children's Cancer Assn., 2002—, Oreg. Ind. Coll. Found., 2004—; chmn., Oreg. Lawyers Against Hunger, 1997-99; judge pro tem Multnomah County Cir. Ct., 1994-98. Mem. ABA (co-chair products liability com., trial practice com. 1988-93), Am. Assn. R.R. Trial Counsel, Fedn. Ins. Corp. Counsel, Oreg. Assn. Def. Counsel (bd. dirs. 1988-95 sec. 1991-92, v.p. 1993-94, pres. 1994), Fed. Bar Assn. (exec. com. Oreg. divsn. 1988-96, pres. 1994-95), Multnomah Athletic Club. Republican. Roman Catholic. Office: Lane Powell PC 601 SW Second Ave Ste 2100 Portland OR 97204-3158 Office Phone: 503-778-2105. Office Fax: 503-778-2200. Business E-mail: maloneyr@lanepowell.com.

**MALONEY, ROBERT KELLER,** ophthalmologist, medical educator; b. May 1, 1958; AB in Mathematics summa cum laude, Harvard U., 1979; MA in Philosophy, Politics and Econs., Oxford (Eng.) U., 1981; MD, U. Calif.,

San Francisco, 1985. Diplomate Am. Bd. Ophthalmology. Rsch fellow dept. physiology Cambridge (Eng.) U., 1985; intern U. Calif., L.A., 1985-86; resident Wilmer Ophthal. Inst. Johns Hopkins Hosp., Balt., 1986-89; Heed fellow cornea and refractive surgery Emory U., Dept. Ophthalmology, Atlanta, 1989-91; clin. prof. ophthalmology Jules Stein Eye Inst. Sch. Medicine U. Calif., 2005—, assoc. prof. ophthalmology Jules Stein Eye Inst. Sch. Medicine L.A., 1991—2004; dir. Maloney Vision Inst., L.A., Calif., 1998—. Bd. dirs. Lasik Inst., Calhoun Vision; cons. in field. Contbr. numerous articles to profl. jours.; presenter and spkr. in field; assoc. editor (N.Am.) Jour. Refractive and Corneal Surgery, 1991-95; internat. editl. bd. European Jour. Implant and Refractive Surgery, 1995; reviewer Am. Jour. Ophthalmology, Ophthalmology, Archives of Ophthalmology, Jour. Cataract and Refractive Surgery, Ophthalmic Surgery and Lasers; editl. bd. Ophthalmology Times. Rhodes scholar, 1979, Heed Found. fellow, 1989-90, Heed/Knapp fellow, 1990-91, John Harvard scholar, 1978; recipient Detur and Edward Whitaker prizes, Harvard U., Rsch. to Prevent Blindness Career Devel. award, 1992, Mericos Whittier award, 1997, VISX Star Surgeon award, 1999, 2000. Mem. Am. Acad. Ophthalmology (long-range planning com. 1989-92, quality of care com. 1987-91, retina preferred practice pattern subcom., refractive errors preferred practice pattern subcom.; chmn. ann. meeting program com. for young ophthalmologists, 1990-92; adv. group to ad hoc com. on orgnl. design 1991, young ophthalmologists' com. 1992-94; Honor award 1993, 97, Sr. Achievement award 2002, Secretariat award 2003), Assn. Rsch. in Vision and Ophthalmology, Internat. Soc. Refractive Surgery (Disting. Lans Refractive Surgery award 2001), Calif. Assn. Ophthalmology, Max Fine Corneal Soc., Phi Beta Kappa. Office: Maloney Vision Inst Ste 900 10921 Wilshire Blvd Los Angeles CA 90024 Office Phone: 310-208-3937.

**MALONEY, SEAN M.,** computer company executive; Mgr. applications engring. Intel U.K. Intel Corp., country mgr. Intel U.K., dir. mktg. Intel Europe, gen. mgr. Asia Pacific ops., tech. asst. to chmn. and chief exec., 1992—95, mgr. sales and mktg. activities Asia Pacific, 1995—99, sr. v.p., 1999—2001, exec. v.p. and dir. sales and mktg. group, exec. v.p., gen. mgr. Intel Comm. Group, 2001—. Bd. dirs. Cadence Design Sys., U.S./China Bus. Coun. Office: 2200 Mission College Blvd Santa Clara CA 95052

**MALONEY, SEAN PATRICK,** lawyer, former federal official; b. Sherbrooke, Que., Can., July 30, 1966; s. James Francis and Joan Caroline (Daley) Maloney; life ptnr. Randy Florke; 3 adopted children. Student, Georgetown Sch. Fgn. Svc., Washington, 1984-86; BA, U.Va., 1988, JD, 1992. Bar: NY 1993, DC 1994. Assoc. Willkie Farr & Gallagher LLP, NYC, 1992-97, 2003—; asst. to Pres., staff sec. The White House, Washington, 1997—2000; v.p., gen. counsel Kiodex, Inc., NYC, 2000, CEO, 2000—03. Grantee Next Generation Leadership fellowship, Rockefeller Found., 2002—03. Avocations: soccer, running. Office: Willkie Farr & Gallagher LLP 787 Seventh Ave New York NY 10019-6099 Office Phone: 212-728-8598. Office Fax: 212-728-9598. E-mail: smaloney@willkie.com.*

**MALONEY, SEAN ROBERT,** physician, biomedical engineer; b. L.A., Feb. 21, 1949; s. Robert Edward and Virginia Elizabeth (Walsh) M.; m. Susan Marie Howard, Aug. 15, 1981; children: Michael Patrick, Matthew Robert, John Howard. BSChemE, BS in Phys. Scis., U. Calif., Davis, 1975; MD, Emory U., 1980; MSME, Stanford U., 1984. Diplomate Am. Bd. Electrodiagnostic Medicine, Nat. Bd. Med. Examiners, Am. Bd. Phys. Medicine and Rehab. Process control engr. Atlantic Richfield and Hanford (Wash.) Co., 1975-76; intern/resident phys. medicine and rehab. Stanford (Calif.) U., 1980-83; asst. med. dir., dir. spinal cord injury unit Thoms Rehab. Hosp., Asheville, N.C., 1984-85; pvt. practice Asheville, 1985—; sole proprietor, biomedical engr. Sean R. Maloney & Co., Asheville, 1989—; asst. clin. prof. surgery orthop./rehab. Bowman Gray Sch. Medicine, 1995—. Presenter in field. Article reviewer Archives Phys. Medicine & Rehab., 1988—; patentee intraoral controller. Col. Asheville Buncombe County Christian Mission Free Med. Clinic, 1992—. With U.S. Army, 1968-72. Grantee Nat. Inst. Neurol. Disorders and Stroke, 1990, 92-93, 96-98, Bapt. Hosp. Inc., 1995-98. Fellow AIChE, So. Soc. Phys. Medicine and Rehab., Am. Med. Soc., Buncombe County Med. Soc. Democrat. Roman Catholic. Avocations: dixieland jazz, tennis. Home: 2036 Rossmore Road Clemmons NC 27012

**MALONEY, SIMONE,** accountant; b. Manchester, NH, Sept. 11, 1936; d. Henri and Emilia Carignan; m. Anthony Maloney, Aug. 30, 1958; children: Paul, Charles, James. BS in Acctg., So. Univ. N.H., 1981. Cert. tax profl., practitioner of taxation. Receptionist, telephone operator, acctg. supr. Travelers Ins. Co., Manchester, 1966-76, auditor, 1976-79; pvt. practice as acct. and bookkeeper, also tax svcs. Manchester, 1981—. Vol. Boy Scouts Am., campaign to reelect Robert Shaw Mayor City of Manchester, 1985, presdl. campaign Congressman Phil Crane, 1980, Congressman Bill Zeliff, 1990; candidate for alderman City of Manchester, 1983; office mgr. campaign Congressman Bob Smith, 1983-84, treas., 1985-86; elected Selectman Ward 2, Manchester, 1992-95, appointed moderator, 1996, elected moderator, 1997—; sec. Greater Manchester Federated Rep. Women's Club, 1987; treas. Manchester Rep. Com., 1989-92, 96—, sec., chmn. Ward 2 Rep. Com., 1987-88. Recipient Bella Duperron award, Manchester Rep. Party, 2003, Clarence Ferry Appreciation award, Manchester Ward 2 Rep. Com., 2004. Mem.: Nat. Soc. Tex. Profls., Nat. Federated Rep. Women, Smithsonian Inst. Roman Catholic. Avocations: sewing, reading, travel, swimming. Home and Office: 171 Russell St Manchester NH 03104-3770

**MALONEY, TERRY,** horticulturist, educator; b. Corning, N.Y., June 15, 1955; s. Robert Francis Maloney Sr. and Shirley Lucille (Borden) Maloney; m. Sylvaine Marie Senechal, Oct. 26, 1991. Student, Cornell U., 1973—75. Rm. mgr. Corning Hilton Inn., 1975—80; horticulturist cons. Corning, 1979—84; ops. cons. various orgns., 1984—2002; owner, advisor Earth Centre, North Myrtle Beach, SC, 1998—. Educator, advisor, owner Spiritual Growth Horticulture, North Myrtle Beach, 2002—; horticulturist Surf Golf and Beach Country Club, North Myrtle Beach, 2003—04; cons. Mkt. St. Restoration Agy., Corning, 1979—84, City of Corning, 1980—84. Author: Rewriting Religion, 2004; contbr. articles to profl. jours. Recipient Citizen award for Volunteer Work, Mkt. St. Assn., Corning, 1983. Mem.: Am. Horticultural Soc., Am. Acad. Religion. Avocations: gardening, theology, string theory, writing. Home and Office: 2483 Burning Tree Ln Little River SC 29566-9325

**MALONEY, THERESE ADELE,** insurance company executive; b. Sept. 15, 1929; d. James Henry and F. Adele (Powers) M. BA in Econs., Coll. St. Elizabeth, Convent Station, N.J., 1951; AMP, Harvard U., 1981. CPCU. With Liberty Mut. Ins. Co., Boston, 1951-94, asst. v.p., asst. mgr. nat risks, 1974-77, v.p., asst. mgr. nat. risks, 1977-79, v.p., mgr. nat. risks, 1979-86, sr. v.p. underwriting mktg. and adminstrn., 1986-87, exec. v.p. underwriting, policy decision, 1987-94, asst bd. dirs.; pres. and bd. dirs. subs. Liberty Mus. (Bermuda) Ltd., 1981-94, LEXCO Ltd.; cons. Exec. Svc. Corp., 1994—2002. Bd. dirs., dep. chmn. Liberty Mut. (U.K.) Ltd., London; bd. dirs. Liberty Mut. Ins. Co., Liberty Mut. Fire Ins. Co., Liberty Mut. Life Assurance Co., Liberty Fin. Cos.; mem. faculty Inst. Northeastern U., Boston 1969—74; mem. adv. bd., risk mgmt. studies Ins. Inst. Am., 1977—83; mem. adv. coun. Suffolk U. Sch. Mgmt., 1984—96; mem. adv. com. to program in internat. bus. rels. Fletcher Sch. Law and Diplomacy, 1985—94; cons. Exec. Svc. Corp., Boston, 1994—2002. Trustee Coll. St. Elizabeth, N.J., 1993-02. Mem. Soc. CPCUs (past pres. Boston chpt.), Univ. Club, Boston Club, Neighborhood Club of Quincy. Personal E-mail: therese.maloney@verizon.net.

**MALONEY, WILLIAM JAMES,** dentist, educator; b. White Plains, NY, Feb. 16, 1967; BS, Siena Coll., Loudonville, N.Y., 1989; DDS, NYU, 1992. Faculty NYU Coll. Dentistry, NY, 2000—. Contbr. articles to profl. jours. Mem.: ADA. Office: 12 Ellis Pl Ossining NY 10562

**MALOOF, GILES WILSON,** academic administrator, educator, author; b. San Bernardino, Calif., Jan. 4, 1932; s. Joseph Peters and Georgia (Wilson) M.; m. Mary Anne Ziniker, Sept. 5, 1958 (dec. Oct. 1976); children: Mary

Jane, Margery Jo. BA, U. Calif., Berkeley, 1953; MA, U. Oreg., 1958; PhD, Oreg. State U., 1962. Petroleum reservoir engr. Creole Petroleum Corp., Venezuela, 1953—54; mathematician electronics divsn. rsch. dept. US. Naval Ordnance Rsch. Lab., Corona, Calif., 1958—59; asst. prof. math. Oreg. State U., Corvallis, 1962—68, rsch. assoc. dept. oceanography, 1963—68, vis. prof. math., 1977—78; prof. math. Boise State U., Idaho, 1968—, head dept., 1968—75, dean grad. sch., 1970—75. Author, reviewer of coll. textbooks; contbr. to profl. jours. Served with Ordnance Corps, AUS, 1950, 54-56. Recipient Carter award, 1963, Mosser prize, 1966, Oreg. State U., Alumni Found. scholar Tchg. award Boise State U., 2000. Mem. Math. Assn. Am., Am. Math. Soc. Indsl. and Applied Math., N.W. Coll. and Univ. Assn. for Sci. (dir., pres. 1990-92), N.W. Sci. Assn. (trustee 1977-80), Assn. We. Univs. (edn. and rsch. com. 1993-2001), Sigma Xi, Pi Mu Epsilon, Phi Kappa Phi. Home: 1400 Longmont Ave Boise ID 83706-3730 E-mail: giles@diamond.boisestate.edu.

**MALOOF, SAM,** woodworker; b. Chino, Calif., Jan. 24, 1916; m. Alfreda Ward, 1948 (dec. 1998); m. Beverly Wingate, 2001. With VORTOX, 1934—39, Harold Graham Industrial Designer, 1940—41; graphic artist Millard Sheets, 1946—48; design project in Iran and Lebanon US State Dept., 1959, design project in El Salvador, 1963. Former pres. So. Calif. Designer; former trustee Southeast Region Am. Craft Coun., former chmn. Acad. Fellows; former bd. dir. US sect. World Craft Congress. Exhibitions include Calif. Design I-XI, 1954—71, Smithsonian Inst., Washington, 1970, Renwick Gallery, Smithsonian Am. Art Mus., 1971, 1992, 2004, Mus. Contemporary Art, Chgo., 1976, Vatican Mus., Rome, 1978, Vice President's House, Washington, DC, 1980, J.M. Kohler Arts Ctr., Sheboygan, Wis., 1983, Barnsdell Art Ctr., LA, 1984, Anderson Ranch Arts Ctr., Aspen, Colo., 1984—85, Euphat Gallery, Cupertino, Calif., 1986, Joanne Lyon Gallery, Apsen, 1987, Laguna Beach Mus. Art, 1988, Dallas Mus. Art, 1989, University Art Gallery, Riverside, Calif., 1993, LA County Fair, 1993, Chgo. Internat. New Art Forms Exposition, Navy Pier Joanne Rapp Gallery, 1993, Wustum Mus. Fine Arts, 1993, Connell Gallery, Atlanta, Ga., 1996, Craft and Folk Art Mus., LA, 2003, Ruth Chandler Williamson Gallery at Scripps Coll., 2004, public collections, Minn. Art Mus., 1959, Oakland Art Mus., Calif. 1969, 1984, Fine Art Mus., Boston, 1976, The White House, 1981, St. Louis Art Mus., 1983, Carter Presdl. Library, 1985, Dallas Art Mus., 1986, Met. Mus. Art, NYC, 1988, Phila. Mus. Art, 1981, 1991, Renwick Gallery, 1992, Toledo Mus. Art, Ohio, 1992. Served with U.S. Army, 1941—45. Mailing: c/o Sam and Alfreda Maloof Found for Arts and Crafts 5131 Carnelian St Alta Loma CA 91701*

**MALOOLEY, DAVID JOSEPH,** electronics and computer technology educator; b. Terre Haute, Ind., Aug. 20, 1951; s. Edward Joseph and Vula (Starn) Malooley. BS, Ind. State U., 1975; MS, Ind. U., 1981. Supr. Zenith Radio Corp., Paris, Ill., 1978—79; assoc. prof., electronics and computer tech. Ind. State U., Terre Haute, 1979—; cons. in field. Served to 1st lt. U.S. Army, 1975-78. Mem.: Nat. Fire Protection Assn., Am. Assn. Indsl. Tech., Soc. Mfg. Engrs., Instrument Soc. Am. (sr.), Epsilon Pi Tau, Pi Lambda Theta, Phi Delta Kappa. Democrat. Home: 11420 Spring Creek Rd Terre Haute IN 47805-9679 Office: Ind State U Dept Electronics and Computer Tech Terre Haute IN 47809-0001 Office Phone: 812-237-3395. Business E-Mail: dmalooley@indstate.edu.

**MALOON, JERRY L.,** lawyer, director; b. Union City, Ind., June 23, 1938; s. Charles Elias and Bertha Lucille (Creviston) M.; children: Jeffrey Lee, Jerry Lee II. BS, Ohio State U., 1960, MD, 1964; JD, Capital U. Law Sch., 1974. Intern Santa Monica (Calif.) Hosp., 1964-65; tng. psychiatry Ctrl. Ohio Psychiat. Hosp., 1969, Menninger Clinic, Topeka, 1970; clin. dir. Orient (Ohio) Devel. Ctr., 1967-69, med. dir., 1971-83; assoc. med. dir. Western Electric, Inc., Columbus, 1969-71; cons. State Med. Bd. Ohio, 1974-80; pvt. practice law Columbus, 1978—; pres. Jerry L. Maloon Co., L.P.A., 1981—. Medicolegal cons., 1972—; pres. Maloon, Maloon & Barclay Co., L.P.A., 1990-95; guest lectr. law and medicine Orient Devel. Ctr. and Columbus Devel. Ctr., 1969-71; dep. coroner Franklin County (Ohio), 1978-84 Dean's coun. Capital U. Law Sch. Capt. M.C., AUS, 1965-67. Fellow: Columbus Bar Found., Am. Coll. Legal Medicine; mem.: ATLA, AMA, ABA, Am. Profl. Practice Assn., Columbus Trial Lawyers Assn., Ohio Trial Lawyers Assn., Columbus Bar Assn., Ohio Bar Assn., Ohio State U. Alumni Assn., U.S. Trotting Assn., The Country Club at Muirfield Village, Ohio State U. Pres.'s Buckeye Club. Office: 9155 Moors Pl North Dublin OH 43017 Home: 9155 Moors Pl N Dublin OH 43017-8220 Office Phone: 614-798-1616. Personal E-mail: maloonmdjd@columbus.rr.com.

**MALORATSKY, LEO G.,** electrical engineer; b. Zaporoghe, U.S.S.R., Apr. 28, 1939; arrived in U.S., 1989; s. German M. Maloratsky and Slava I. Grinberg; m. Helena A. Vinitsky, Oct. 3, 1968; children: Artem, Anna. MSEE, Moscow Aviation Inst., 1962; PhD, Moscow Inst. Telecomm., 1967. Rsch. scientist Electrotech. Inst., Moscow, 1962—79; asst. prof. Moscow Inst. Radio, Electronics and Automation, 1968—88; sr. rsch. scientist Automation Lab., Moscow, 1979—89; vis. scholar Northeastern U., Boston, 1989; sr. engr. M/A-COM, Boston, 1990; v.p. REC, Boston, 1991—92; staff engr. Allied Signal, Ft. Lauderdale, Fla., 1992—97; prin. engr. Rockwell Collins, Melbourne, Fla., 1997—. Author: Microminiaturization of Microwave Components and Devices, 1976, Passive RF and Microwave Integrated Circuits, 2003; co-author: Design and Calculation of Microwave Stripline Elements, 1972, Design of Microwave Devices, 1983, Microwave Devices and Screens, 1990. Mem.: IEEE. Home: 2160 N Hwy A1A Apt 205 Indialantic FL 32903 Office: Rockwell Collins PO Box 1080 Melbourne FL 32902 Personal E-mail: lhmal@earthlink.net.

**MALOTT, JOHN RAYMOND,** writer, consultant, not-for-profit executive; b Kankakee, Ill, Nov 5, 1946; s Raymond Roderick and Ruth Pearl (Jacobs) M.; m. Hiroko Iwami, Nov. 23, 1971; children: David Iwami, Rumi Justine. BA, Northwestern U., 1967; grad., Nat. War Coll., 1983. Civilian advisor US Dept. State, Vietnam, 1969-70, China desk officer Washington, 1970-71, Am. consul Kobe, Japan, 1971-73, 1st sec. Am. Embassy Tokyo, 1974-77, Sri Lanka desk officer Washington, 1977-78, India desk officer, 1978-80; Am. consul Bombay, 1980-82; with Nat. War Coll. Washington, 1982-83; dep. dir. Japan Affairs, 1983-85; spl. asst. to Under Sec. State Econ. Affairs, 1985-86; Am. consul gen. Osaka, Japan, 1986-89; dir. Japan Affairs Washington, 1989-91; sr. seminar, 1991-92; dep. asst. sec. state South Asian Affairs, 1992-93; sr. advisor to Undersec. State for Econ. Affairs, Washington, 1993-95; U.S. amb. to Malaysia Dept. State, 1995-98; exec. chmn. Malott & Assocs., 1999—; pres. World Affairs/Coun. of Orange County, 2000—02; mng. dir. Manatt Jones Global Strategies, 2003—06; sr. advisor Manatt, Phelps & Phillips, LLP, 2003—06; pres., CEO Japan-Am. Soc. Wash., DC, 2006—. Author: Partners, 1992. Recipient Vietnam Svc. award, 1970, Meritorious Honor award Dept. State, 1982, Superior honor award, 1991. Presbyterian. Home: 5911 Reservoir Heights Ave Alexandria VA 22311-1017 Office Phone: 202-833-2210. Business E-Mail: jmalott@us-japan.org.

**MALOUF, WALDY,** food service executive; m. Meg Malouf; children: Max, Merrill. Grad., Culinary Inst. Am., 1975. With The Four Seasons, La Côte Basque, St. Regis Hotel, La Cremaillere, Banksville, NY, Hudson River Club, The Rainbow Rm.; chef, owner Beacon Restaurant, N.Y.C. Tchr. The New Sch., Macy's DeGustibis; judge various culinary competitions; trading chef N.Y. State Dept. Econ. Devel., N.Y. Wine and Grape Found.; guest chef numerous host countries; active James Beard Found.; regional chef-cons. N.W./KLM Airlines; bd. dirs. Culinary Inst. Am. Alumni Assn. Author: (books) The Hudson River Valley Cookbook: A Leading American Chef Savors the Region's Bounty, 1995 (One of Yr.'s Ten Best, N.Y. Times), Magnificent Meats, 2000; featured House Beautiful, Met. Home, N.Y. mag., Ladies' Home Jour., Food and Wine, Paper, numerous Japanese mags. and guide books, appeared Time Out New Morning, CNN, The Food Network, CBS Latin Am., CBS Saturday Morning, Brazilian TV, N.Y. 1 News. Active Share Our Strength, God's Love We Deliver, Culinary Inst. Am., City Meals-on-Wheels, Green Chimneys; bd. dirs. Ballet Sch. Stamford, Conn. Named Great Chef N.Y., James Beard Found.; recipient 1st prize, 3rd Ann. Cointreau Recipe Contest, 1992, Golden Ann. Gala honors, Culinary

---

Inst. Am., 1996. Mem.: Am. Inst. Wine and Food (co-chair ann. marketplace tasting, bd. dirs. N.Y. chpt.). Office: Beacon Restaurant 25 West 56th St New York NY 10019 Office Phone: 212-332-0500. E-mail: waldyny@aol.com.

**MALOUFF, FRANK JOSEPH,** health care association executive; s. Phillip Francis and Lillian Aileen Malouff; m. Virginia Lynn Frye, Aug. 24, 1968; children: Lynnea, Joseph, J. Daniel, David. BS in Journalism, U. Colo., Boulder, 1969; MS in Health Adminstrn., U. Colo., Denver, 1974; LLD (hon.), Ohio Coll. Podiatric Medicine, 1988. Program adminstr. U. Colo. Health Scis. Ctr., Denver, 1974-83; exec. dir. Ohio Podiatric Med. Assn., Columbus, 1983-89, Am. Podiatric Med. Assn., Bethesda, Md., 1989-98, Am. Soc. Therapeutic Radiology and Oncology, Fairfax, Va., 1998—2002; prin. and CEO JVF Mgmt., Chantilly, Va., 2002—. Bd. dir. Neurologic Disease Found., Fairfax, Va.; lectr. in field Leader Boy Scouts Am., various locations; mem. Fairfax County Med. Res. Corps. 1st lt. U.S. Army, 1969—72, Korea. Mem. Am. Soc. Healthcare Execs. (officer 1977-81, Disting. Svc. award 1982, past dir.), Am. Soc. Assn. Execs., Area 26 Coun., Spl. Olympics Va. Roman Catholic. Avocation: lay church ministry. Office: JVF Mgmt PO Box 2234 Centreville VA 20122

**MALOUIN, JEAN-LOUIS,** adult education educator; b. Three-Rivers, Que., Can., Oct. 5, 1943; m. Hélène Pépin; children: Pascale, Philippe. B in Commerce, Université Laval, Que., 1965, MSc, 1966; PhD, UCLA, 1970. Prof. Bus. Sch., U. Laval, 1966-89, dir. OSD dept., 1971-75, 78-79, assoc. dean acad. affairs, 1979-84, dean, 1984-89; dean faculty of bus. U. Alta., Edmonton, Alta., Canada, 1989-92; dean faculty of adminstrn. U. Ottawa, Ottawa, Ont., Canada, 1992 2000. Coord. Can. Consortium for the Support of the Sea PhD program; bd. dirs. Corel Corp., 1997—2003, Acerra Corp. Editor: The Generation of Scientific Administrative Knowledge, 1986; co-author: L'Innovation Technologique dans les PME Manufacturières: études de cas enquête, 1992. Bd. dirs. Centre québécois de Productivité, du Vêtement, Montréal, 1983-86, Nat. Rsch. Ctr. London, 1986-87, Banff Sch. Advancement Mgmt., 1989-92. Mem. Can. Fedn. Deans (v.p. 1987), Edmonton C. of C. (bd. dirs. 1989-92). Home: 1410 Clay Ct Gloucester ON Canada K1C 4T2 Business E-Mail: malouin@uottawa.ca.

**MALOVANY, HOWARD,** lawyer; b. Dayton, Ohio, July 6, 1950; m. Cynthia Jane Shilt, Sept. 18, 1976. BA, Ohio State U., 1972; JD, U. Toledo, 1977; MBA, U. Dayton, 1985. Bar: Ohio 1977, Ill. 1997. Staff atty., asst. sec. Nat. Cash Register Corp., Dayton, 1977-85; counsel Outboard Marine Corp., Waukegan, Ill., 1985-89, asst. sec., counsel, 1989—93, sec., sr. counsel, 1993—96; asst. sec., sr. counsel William Wrigley Jr. Co., Waukegan, 1996-98, sec., gen. counsel Chgo., 1998-2001, v.p., sec., gen. counsel, 2001—. Mem.: ABA, Am. Soc. Corp. Secretaries (mem. corp. practice & technology com. 1995—97), Toledo Internat. Law Soc. (founder), Ohio State Bar Assn., Ill. State Bar Assn. Office: William Wrigley Jr Co 410 N Michigan Ave Chicago IL 60611-4213 Office Phone: 312-645-4223. Business E-Mail: hmalovany@wrigley.com.

**MALOW, BETH,** director; d. Monroe and Theresa Malow; m. Stephen E. Pert, Sept. 22, 1991; children: Austin Pert, Daniel Pert. MD, Northwestern U., Chgo., Ill., 1986. Diplomate Am. Bd. Neurology, Am. Bd. Sleep Medicine. Intern Beth Israel Med. Ctr., N.Y.C., 1987—88; resident Harvard-Longwood, Boston, 1988—91; fellow NIH, Bethesda, Md., 1991—94; dir. Sleep Disorders Ctr. Vanderbilt U., Nashville, 2003—. Office Phone: 615-322-0283.

**MALPHURS, ROGER EDWARD,** biomedical marketing executive; b. Lake Worth, Fla., Dec. 15, 1933; s. Cecil Edward and Muriel Thelma (Ward) M.; m. Carolyn Sue Calapp, Feb. 2, 1963(div. 1993); children: Steven, Brian, Darren, Regina, Victoria. BS, U. Utah, 1961; D of Chiropractic, Palmer Coll. Chiropractic West, 1990. Cert. med. technologist; lic. chiropractor, Calif., Ariz. Supr. spl. chemistry Cen. Pathology Lab., Santa Rosa, Calif., 1968-73; mgr. lab. Cmty. Hosp., Santa Rosa, 1973-76; supr. chem., staff asst. Meml. Hosp., Santa Rosa, 1976-85; pres., CEO R.E. Malphurs Co., Sunnyvale, Calif., 1972—95; tech. writer Maximus, Inc., Rancho Cordova, Calif., 2004—. Owner, developer REMCO Mktg. Assocs., Santa Rosa, 1970—71; pvt. commodity trader, 1974—; owner Better Bus. Forms and Typeset, Santa Rosa, Calif., 1977—81; commodity pool operator, 1979—81; dept. mgr. immunochemistry Spectra Labs, Fremont, Calif., 1990—95; clin. trials cons. hematology, tech. writer Abbott Diagnostics, Santa Clara, Calif., 1995—2000; tech. writer Healtheon/WebMD, Santa Clara, Calif., 2000—01; tech. writer, project mgr. Hewlett-Packard, Roseville, Calif., 2000—04. Author: A New, Simple Way to Win at Blackjack, 1972. Served as squadron commdr. CAP USAF Aux., 1982-84. Mem. APHA, Am. Chiropractic Assn., Calif. Chiropractic Assn., Optimists Internat. (youth awards chmn. 1969-74), Toastmasters (sec./treas. 1988-89), Rep. Senatorial Inner Circle. Republican. Avocations: flying, computers, pistol shooting, painting, writing.

**MALT, RONALD BRADFORD,** lawyer; b. Boston, Aug. 1, 1954; s. Ronald A. and Geraldine (Sutton) M.; m. Sharon Lynn Harford, Feb. 14, 1981; 2 children. AB, Harvard U., 1976, JD, 1979. Bar: Mass. 1979. Assoc. Ropes & Gray, Boston, 1979-86, ptnr., 1987—; policy com., 1993—, chmn., 2004—; dir. Fenway Ptnrs., Inc., N.Y.C., 1999—. Asst. treas. Butler Capital Corp., N.Y.C., 1983—; sec. to adv. bd. Mezzanine Lending Assocs., N.Y.C., 1983— Mem. corp. Mass. Gen. Hosp., Boston, 1989—; trustee Butler Found., 1989—, Butler Fund for the Environment, 2004-, Black River Environ. Improvement Assn., Inc., 1991—. Republican. Episcopalian. Office: Ropes & Gray One International Pl Boston MA 02110 Office Phone: 617-951-7318. Office Fax: 617-951-7050. Business E-Mail: bmalt@ropesgray.com.

**MALTBY, FLORENCE HELEN,** library science educator; b. Sumner, Iowa, Mar. 2, 1933; d. Harold George and Blanche Theresa (Gritzner) Garland; m. George Robert Maltby, June 3, 1964 (dec. Oct. 1985); 1 child, Patricia Garland Maltby Clark. BA, U. No. Iowa, Cedar Falls, 1954; MS in Libr. Sci., U. Ill., 1960, cert. advanced study librarianship, 1967. Cert. literary braille transcriber. Elem. sch. libr. Barrington (Ill.) Pub. Sch., 1954-57, USAF Dependent Sch. Europe. Sculthorpe, Eng., 1957-58, Ramstein, Fed. Republic of Germany, 1958-59, Wiesbaden, Fed. Republic of Germany, 1960-61; grad. asst. U. Ill., Champaign, 1959-60; reference asst., instr. Libr. Cen. Mich. U., Mt. Pleasant, 1961-63; asst. prof. libr. sci. Southwest Mo. State U., Springfield, 1963-66, 67-80, assoc. prof. libr. sci., 1980-97; instr. libr. sci. U. Ill. Champaign, 1966-67; archivist Diocese of Springfield-Cape Girardeau, 2001—04, 2006—. Evaluator North Cen. Assn., Springfield, 1989, Dept. Elem. and Secondary Edn., Mo. Sch. Improvement, 1989; com. mem. Children's Lit. Festival, Springfield, 1990, treas., 1991. Contbr. to Masterplots II: Juvenile and Young Adult Fiction, 1991, 97. Mem. AAUP, ALA, Assn. Libr. and Info. Sci. Edn., Mo. Assn. Sch. Librs. (mem. standards rev. com. for state sch. libr. media standards 1994), Mo. Conf. Diocesan Archivists, Beta Phi Mu, Alpha Beta Alpha, Kappa Delta Pi. Roman Catholic. Avocations: reading, piano, organ.

**MALTBY, RICHARD ELDRIDGE, JR.,** theater director, lyricist; b. Ripon, Wis., Oct. 6, 1937; s. Richard Eldridge and Virginia (Hosegood) D.; m. Janet Brenner, 1987; children: Nicholas Avery, David Stevenson, Jordan Brenner, Emily Celia, Charlotte Perry. BA, Yale U., 1959. Dir., lyricist: Starting Here, Starting Now, 1977 (Grammy nomination); dir.: Ain't Misbehavin', 1978 (NY Drama Critics Circle award, Drama Desk award, Obie award Best Musical, Tony award Best Dir.), Baby, 1983 (3 Tony award nominations), Closer Than Ever, 1989 (2 Outer Critics' Circle awards, Best Off-Broadway Musical, Best Score), Nick and Nora, 1993 (Tony award nomination for best score), Big, 1996 (Tony award nomination for best score) Ring of Fire: The Johnny Cash Musical Show, 2005; dir., co-lyricist: Song and Dance, 1985 (Tony award nomination); co-lyricist: Miss Saigon, 1989 (London Evening Standard Best Musical, London Drama Critics award, 3 Tony awards); dir. Fosse, 1999 (Best Musical: Tony award, Outer Critics Cir. award, Drama Desk award), The 60's Project, 2005. Mem.: Soc. Stage Dirs. and Choreographers, Dramatists Guild, ASCAP.*

---

**MALTER, JAMES SAMUEL,** pathologist, educator; b. Tooele, Utah, May 18, 1956; s. Robert Henry Malter and Evvajean (Harris) Mintz; m. Elaine Gadzicki, May 26, 1988. AB, Dartmouth Coll., 1979; MD, Washington U., 1983. Diplomate Am. Bd. Clin. Pathology. Resident in pathology U. Pa., Phila. 1983-88, chief resident, 1987-88; asst. prof. pathology Tulane U., New Orleans, 1988-91; dir. exptl. pathology Tulane Med. Ctr., New Orleans, 1988-91; dir. Blood Ctr., 1989-91; asst. prof. pathology Sch. Medicine U. Wis., Madison, 1991-97; med. dir. Blood Bank U. Wis. Hosp. & Clinic, Madison, 1991—; prof. pathology Sch. Medicine U. Wis., Madison, 1997—. Mem. editl. bd. Hepatology jour., 1991—. Recipient Nat. Rsch. Svc. award NIH, 1986-88, Clin. Investigator award NCI-NIH, 1988-91, Ind. Investigator award NIH, 1991—. Mem. Am. Assn. Blood Banks, Am. Assn. Pathologists, Am. Coll. Pathologists (diplomate). Office: U Wis Hosp & Clinic Dept of Pathology 600 Highland Ave # B4 263 Madison WI 53792-0001

**MALTHOUSE, EDWARD CARL,** finance educator; s. Edward R. and Elinor H. Malthouse; m. Elisabeth Geyer, Mar. 23, 2004; children: Thomas Bernhard, Niklas Edward, Ellen Ingeborg. BS in Marh., Augustana Coll., Rock Island, Ill., 1988; PhD in Stats., Northwestern U., Evanston, Ill., 1995; MS in Operational Rsch., Southampton U., England, 1990. Assoc. prof. Northwestern U., Evanston, Ill., 1997—. Achievements include research in Media Marketing. Office: Northwestern U 1870 Campus Dr Evanston IL 60208 Office Phone: 847-467-3376.

**MALTIN, LEONARD,** commentator, writer; b. NYC, Dec. 18, 1950; s. Aaron Isaac and Jacqueline (Gould) M.; m. Alice Tlusty, Mar. 15, 1975; 1 child, Jessica Bennett. BA, NYU, 1972. Mem. faculty New Sch. for Social Rsch., N.Y.C., 1973-81; curator Am. Acad. Humor, N.Y.C., 1975-76; guest curator dept. film Mus. Modern Art, N.Y.C., 1976; film critic and corr. Entertainment Tonight, Hollywood, Calif., 1982—; columnist Modern Maturity, 1996-99; film critic Playboy Mag., 1998—2004. Adj. prof. Sch. Cinema & TV, U. So. Calif., 1998—. Author: Movie Comedy Teams, 1970, rev. edit., 1985, Behind the Camera (reprinted as The Art of the Cinematographer), 1971, The Great Movie Shorts (reprinted as Selected Short Subjects), 1971, The Disney Films, 1973, rev. edit., 2000, The Great Movie Comedians, 1978, Of Mice and Magic: A History of American Animated Cartoons, 1980, rev. edit., 1987, The Great American Broadcast, 1997; co-author: Our Gang: The Life and Times of the Little Rascals, 1977, reprinted as The Little Rascals: The Life and Times of Our Gang, 1992; editor: Leonard Maltin's Movie & Video Guide, 1969, rev. annually, Leonard Maltin's Movie Encyclopedia, 1994, Leonard Maltin's Family Film Guide, 1999; producer, writer, host (video) Cartoons for Big Kids, 1989; writer (TV spl.) Fantasia: The Making of a Disney Classic, 1990; writer, host (video) The Making of The Quiet Man, 1992, The Making of High Noon, 1992, Cartoon Madness: The Fantastic Max Fleischer Cartoons, 1993, Cliffhanger!, 1993; co-host Hot Ticket, 2001-04; co-prodr., host (film series) Walt Disney Treasures, 2001—. Recipient Distinction award, Am. Soc. Cinematographers, 2005. Mem. Authors Guild, Soc. for Cinephiles (pres. 1990, Man of Yr. 1973), L.A. Film Critics Assn. (pres. 1995-96). Office: c/o Entertainment Tonight Paramount TV 5555 Melrose Ave Los Angeles CA 90038-3112

**MALTZ, ROBERT,** surgeon; b. Cin., July 21, 1935; s. William and Sarah (Goldberg) M.; m. Sylvia Moskowitz, Aug. 24, 1958; children: Mark Edward, Deborah Lynn, Steven Alan, David Stuart. BS in Zoology, U. Cin., 1958, MD, 1962. Diplomate Am. Bd. Otolaryngology. Intern Cin. Gen. Hosp., 1962-63; resident Barnes Hosp., St. Louis, 1965-69; asst. prof. surgery Stanford U. Med. Ctr., Palo Alto, Calif., 1969-71; asst. prof. otolaryngology U. Cin. Med. Ctr., 1971-75, assoc. prof. otolaryngology, 1975—; dir. dept. otolaryngology Jewish Hosp., Cin., 1992—. Chief divsn. head and neck surgery, dept. otolaryngology and maxillofacial surgery U. Cin. Med. Ctr., 1972-76; bd. dirs. Cancer Control Coun., U. Cin. Med. Cntr.; cons. Bur. Crippled Children's Svcs., State of Ohio; on staff Univ. Hosp., Cin., Jewish Hosp., Cin., Children's Hosp. Med. Ctr., Bethesda Hosp., Cin.; del. to numerous profl. confs.; mem. health affairs adv. cmty. Mut. Ins. Co.; mem. mng. bd. PIE Mut. Ins. Co.; bd. dirs. UCATS, 1995-98, trustee Health Found. Greater Cin., 1997-2006, vice-chmn., 2000-01, chmn. 2001-03, chmn. program com., 2000-01; instr. short term courses in field; pres.-elect alumni exec. coun. U. Cin. Coll. Medicine, 1998-2000, pres., 2000-02. Contbr. articles to profl. jours. Bd. dirs. Jewish Cmty. Rels. Coun.; bd. trustees Cin. Art Acad., 1998—; faculty adv. com. U. Cin.; trustee Health Found. Fund, 2002-, vice-chmn., 2002-03, chmn., 2003—05. Capt. USAF, 1963-65, PTO. USPHS fellow, 1968-69; Eli Lilly Co. grantee, 1971-76, Burroughs Wellcome Co., 1972. Fellow ACS, Am. Acad. Facial and Reconstructive Surgery (edn. com. 1972, future plans com. 1973-75, sci. program com., budget and fin. com. 1975, chmn. credentials com., secst. 1980-85), Royal Soc. Health, Internat. Cosmetic Surgeons, Am. Acad. Cosmetic Surgeons, Am. Assn. Cosmetic Surgeons (sec.-treas. 1976-81); mem. Am. Acad. Otolaryngology and Head and Neck Surgery, Am. Coun. Otolaryngology, Soc. Univ. Otolaryngologists, Pan-Am. Assn. Oto-Rhino-Laryngology and Broncho-Esophagology, Ohio State Med. Assn., Cin. Acad. Medicine (trustee 1992-95, treas. 1993-95, pres. 1996-97, chmn. pub. rels. com. 1980, chmn. comm. com. 1994-96, chmn sply. soc. com. 1995, legis. com. 1985, editl. bd. 1994-96, jud. com. 1995—2004, chmn. managed care med. com. 1997-2002), U. Cin. Alumni Assn. (bd. govs. sec. 1994, fin. v.p. 1995, 1st v.p. 1996, pres. 1997-98), Acad. Medicine Found. (bd. dirs., v.p., pres. 2002—2004), Cin. Ear, Nose and Throat Soc., Losantiville Country Club (bd. govs. 1996-2004, pres. 1999-2001), Omicron Delta Kappa, Sigma Sigma, Sigma Alpha Mu. Avocations: tennis, golf, travel. Home: 2601 Willowbrook Dr Cincinnati OH 45237-3725 Office: 10496 Montgomery Rd Cincinnati OH 45242-5223 Office Phone: 513-984-1190. Personal E-Mail: maltz@cinci.rr.com.

**MALTZAN, MICHAEL THOMAS,** architect; b. Ronlyn Heights, N.Y., Oct. 10, 1959; s. William George and Jacqueline (Cain) M.; m. Amy Louise Murphy, Sept. 25, 1988. Student, Wentworth Inst. Tech., 1977-79; BFA, RISD, 1984, BArch, 1985; MArch with letter of distinction, Harvard U., 1988. Lic. architect, Calif. Architect The Architects, Glastonbury, Conn., 1978-80, Williamd D. Warner Assocs., Exeter, R.I., 1980-83, Steven Lerner Assocs., Providence, 1983-84, Schwartz/Silver Assocs., Boston, 1984-86, Machado-Silvetti Assocs., Boston, 1986-88, Frank O. Gehry Assocs., L.A., 1988-95; pvt. practice architecture L.A., 1995—. Prof. RISD, Providence, 1987, Harvard U., Cambridge, Mass., 1988; co-instr. UCLA, 1989, U. Waterloo, 1993, RISD, 1995, Harvard U., 1999, USC, 2002; vis. prof. GSD, 2003; invited jury critic Harvard U., RISD, Ariz. State U., Tempe, Calif. Coll. Arts and Crafts, San Francisco, U. So. Calif., L.A., UCLA, Iowa State U., Ames, Miami (Ohio) U. Prin. works include Inner-City Arts, L.A., 1994 (PA award), Getty Digital Lab, 1997, Hilghman-Horn Ctr. Arts, 1997 (AIA award), Hergott-Shepard Residence, 1998 (AIA awards), Kidspace Mus., Pasadena, Calif., 1998 (PA award), UCLA Hammer Mus., 1999, MOMA ONS, 2002 (AIA awards), World Trade Ctr. Team, 2002, Fresno (Calif.) Met. Mus., 2002 (AIA awards), Giardini Di Porta Nuova, Milan, Italy, 2004, Vancouver (Can.) Art Gallery, 2004. Recipient Collegiate Gold medal AIA, Young Archs. award. Office: 2801 Hyperion Ave # 107 Los Angeles CA 90027-2571 Office Phone: 323-913-3098.

**MALTZMAN, IRVING MYRON,** psychology professor; b. Bklyn., May 9, 1924; s. Israel and Lillian (Mass) M.; m. Diane Seiden, Aug. 21, 1949; children— Sara, Kenneth, Elaine. BA, NYU, 1946; PhD, State U. Iowa, 1949. Mem. faculty UCLA, 1949—, assoc. prof., 1957—60, prof. psychology, 1961—94, chmn. dept., 1970—77, prof. emeritus, 1994—. Co-author: Handbook of Contemporary Soviet Psychology, 1969, Alcoholism: A Review of it Characteristics, Etiology, Treatments, and Controversies, 2000. Fellow: APA, AAAS; mem.: Psychonomic Soc., APS, Phi Beta Kappa, Sigma Xi. Home: 11260-22B Overland Ave Culver City CA 90230-5559 Office Phone: 310-825-2909.

**MALUCHNIK, ROSEMARY PELLICORE,** elementary school educator; b. Chgo., Ill., Oct. 25, 1947; d. Henry Joseph Pellicore and Genevieve Gorski; m. Jerome Anthony Maluchnik, June 22, 1980; 1 child, Joshua Anthony. BS in Edn., Northern Ill., 1969; MS in Edn. Tchr. Elgin Pub. Schools,

1969—84, 1995—. Mentor to new tchrs., 2001, 02, 03, 04, 05, 06; contbr. to kindergarten curriculum, 1995—96. Mem.: NEA, Elgin Tchr. Assn., Internat. Reading Assn., Ill. Edn. Assn. Home: 221 W Beech Dr Schaumburg IL 60193

**MALUGEN, J.T. (JOE THOMAS),** retail executive; BS, Univ. Mo., Columbia; JD, Samford Univ.; LLM in taxation, NYU. Atty., Ala., 1978—92, Mo., 1978—92; co-founder, chmn., CEO Movie Gallery Inc., Dothan, Ala., 1985—, pres., 2002—. Bd. dir. Helen Keller Found.; mem. dean's adv. bd. Cumberland Sch. Law Samford Univ.; mem. dean's strategy council NYU Sch. Law. Office: Movie Gallery Inc 900 W Main St Dothan AL 36301*

**MALVEAUX, FLOYD JOSEPH,** dean; BS, Creighton U., 1961; MS, Loyola U.; PhD in Microbiology and Pub. Health, Mich. State U., 1968; MD, Howard U., 1974; postgrad., Washington Hosp. Ctr., 1974—76, Johns Hopkins U., 1976—78. Asst. prof. microbiology Howard U. Med. Sch., Washington, 1968—70, chmn. microbiology, assoc. prof. microbiology and medicine, 1989—94, dean, v.p. health affairs, prof. microbiology and medicine, 1995—; mem. faculty Johns Hopkins U., Balt., 1984—89. Founder, pres. Urban Asthma and Allergy Ctr., Balt., 1986—89; mem. numerous med. panels; lectr. in field. Contbr. articles to profl. jours. Recipient Nat. Rsch. Svc. award, NIH, Clemens von Pirquet Rsch. award, Georgetown U. Sch. Medicine, 1991; grantee, Nat. Inst. Allergy and Infectious Diseases, Nat. Heart, Lung and Blood Inst. of NIH, Hasbro Children's Found., Robert Wood Johnson Found.; Vivian B. Allen Found. fellow. Mem.: NAACP (life), Inst. Medicine, Kappa Alpha Psi, Sigma Pi Phi, Sigma Xi, Alpha Omega Alpha. Office: Howard U Med Sch 520 W St NW Washington DC 20059-0001

**MALY, KURT JOHN,** computer science educator; b. Modling, Austria, Aug. 20, 1944; came to U.S., 1969; s. Anton and Editha (Gneist) M.; m. Christiana Peterlik, Mar. 18, 1972; 1 child, Angela Claudia. Diplom Ingenieur summa cum laude, U. Tech., Austria, 1968; MS, Courant Inst. NYU, 1970, PhD, 1973. Asst. prof. U. Minn., Mpls., 1972-78, assoc. prof., 1978-85, acting head, 1980-82, head, 1982-85; eminent prof., chmn. computer sci. Old Dominion U., Norfolk, Va., 1985—, Kaufman prof., 1991—. Hon. prof. Chengdu U. of Sci. and Tech., People's Republic of China, 1986—, Hefei U., People's Republic of China, 1991—; Guangxi Computer Inst., People's Republic of China, 1993—; bd. dirs. Inst. of Info. Tech., Ctr. for Innovative Tech., Blacksburg, Va., 1988-92; bd. dirs., exec. co-dir. Microelectronic and Info. Scis. Ctr., Mpls., 1980-85. Author: Fundamentals of the Computing Sciences, 1978; assoc. editor: Jour. for Microcomputer Application Tech., PRC; contbr. articles to profl. jours. Served with Austrian Air Force, 1963-64. Fellow Sorbonne U., Paris, 1966, Courant Inst., N.Y.C., 1968-72. Mem. Assn. Computing Machinery, IEEE, Sigma Xi. Roman Catholic. Office: Old Dominion U Norfolk VA 23529 Office Phone: 757-683-4817. E-mail: maly@cs.odu.edu.

**MALY, MICHAEL KIP,** lawyer; b. San Antonio, Tex., July 18, 1945; BA with honors, U. Tex., 1967; JD, U. Calif., 1975. Bar: Calif. 1975, U.S. Dist. Ct. Calif. (no., ea., ctrl. dist.). Mng. ptnr. Winston & Strawn LLP, San Francisco, 2003—. Spkr. in field; mem. arbitration panel San Francisco Superior Ct. Contbr. articles to profl. jours. Lt USN, 1967—72. Mem.: ABA. Office: Winston & Strawn LLP 101 California St San Francisco CA 94111-5802 Office Phone: 415-591-1424. Office Fax: 415-591-1400. Business E-Mail: mmaly@winston.com.

**MAMAT, FRANK TRUSTICK,** lawyer; b. Syracuse, N.Y., Sept. 4, 1949; s. Harvey Sanford and Annette (Trustick) M.; m. Kathy Lou Winters, June 23, 1975; children: Jonathan Adam, Steven Kenneth. BA, U. Rochester, 1971; JD, Syracuse U., 1974. Bar: D.C. 1976, U.S. Ct. Appeals (D.C. cir.) 1976, Fla. 1977, U.S. Supreme Ct. 1979, U.S. Dist. Ct. (ea. dist.) 1983, U.S. Ct. Appeals (6th cir.) 1983, Mich. 1984, U.S. Dist. Ct. (no. dist.) Ind. 1984. Atty. NLRB, Washington, 1975—79; assoc. Proskauer, Rose, Goetz & Mendelsohn, Washington, N.Y.C. and L.A., 1979—83, Fishman Group, Bloomfield Hills, Mich., 1983—85, ptnr., 1985—87; sr. ptnr. Honigman, Miller, Schwartz and Cohn, 1987—94; pres., CEO Morgan Daniels Co., Inc., West Bloomfield, Mich., 1994—; ptnr. Clark Klein & Beaumont, P.L.C., Detroit, 1995—96, Clark Hill, P.L.C., Detroit, 1996—2003, mem. exec. com., 1999—2001; ptnr. Dickinson Wright, PLLC, 2003—. Bd. dirs. Mich. Food and Beverage Assn., Air Conditioning Contractors of Am., Air Conditioning Contractors of Mich., Am. Subcontractors Assn., Mich. Mfrs. Assn. Labor Counsel, Jewish Vocat. Svcs., Constrn. Fin. Mgmt. Assn., Mich. Assn. Home Builders. Gen. counsel Rep. Com. of Oakland County, 1986—; chmn. Constrn. Code Commn. Mich., 1993—; bd. dirs. 300 Club, Mich., 1984-90; pres. 400 Club, 1990-93, chmn., 1993—, chmn. bd., Am. Soc. of Employers, 2003-2005; mem. Associated Gen. Contractors Labor Lawyers Coun.; mem. Rep. Nat. Com. Nat. Rep. Senatorial Com., Presdl. Task Force, Rep. Labor Coun., Washington; city dir. West Bloomfield, 1985-87; pres. West Bloomfield Rep. Club, 1985-87; chmn. bd. trustees Am. Soc. Edn. Found., 2005—; fin. com. Rep. Com. of Oakland County, 1984-93; pres. Oakland County Lincoln Rep. Club, 1989-90; bd. dirs. camping svcs. and human resources com. YMCA, 1989-93, Anti-Defamation League, 1989—; vice chmn. Lawyers for Reagan-Bush, 1984; v.p. Fruehauf Farms, West Bloomfield, Mich., 1985-88; mem. staff Exec. Office of Pres. of U.S. Inquiries/Comments, Washington, 1981-83. Fellow Coll. Labor and Employment Attys.; mem. ABA, FBA, Mich. Bar Assn., Fla. Bar Assn. (labor com. 1977—), Rep. Nat. Lawyers Assn., Mich. Bus. and Profl. Assn., Am. Acad. Constrn. and Labor Attys. (exec. dir. 1998—), Am. Subcontractors Assn. (Southeastern Mich., bd. dirs.), Founders Soc. Detroit Bar Assn., Assn. Corp. Growth (Detroit chpt.), Oakland County Bar Assn., B'nai B'rith (v.p. 1982-83, trustee 1987-88, bd. dirs. Detroit Barristers unit 1983-91, pres. 1985-87), Am. Soc. Employers (chmn. 2003—), Oakpointe Country Club, Detroit Soc. Clubs, Skyline Club, Fairlane Club, Detroit Athletic Club, Renaissance Club, Econ. Club Detroit. Office: Dickinson Wright PLLC 500 Woodward Ave Ste 4000 Detroit MI 48226 also: Morgan Daniels Co Inc 5484 Crispin Way Rd West Bloomfield MI 48323-3402 Office Phone: 313-223-3169. Business E-Mail: fmamat@dickinsonwright.com. E-mail: fmamat@aol.com.

**MAMATEY, VICTOR SAMUEL,** historian, educator; b. North Braddock, Pa., Feb. 19, 1917; s. Albert Paul and Ola (Darnek) Mamatey; m. Denise M. Perronne, Nov. 20, 1945; children: Albert R., Peter V. Student, Wittenberg Coll., 1938-39, U. Chgo., 1939-40; AM, Harvard U., 1941; PhD, U. Paris, 1949. Asst. prof. history Fla. State U., Tallahassee, 1949-55, assoc. prof., 1955-58, prof., 1958-67, chmn. dept. history, 1964-67; rsch. prof. hist. U. Ga., Athens, 1967-82, acting dean Coll. Arts and Scis., 1972-73. Vis. prof. Columbia U., 1961, Tulane U., 1963. Author: The United States and East Central Europe, 1914-18, 1957, Soviet RussianImperialism, 1964, (with Geoffrey Brunn) The World in the Twentieth Century, 1967, The Rise of the Hapsburg Empire, 1526-1815, 1971, (with Radomir Luza) History of the Czechoslovak Republic, 1918-1948, 1973. With U.S. Army, 1942-46. Guggenheim fellow, 1959. Mem. Am. Hist. Assn. (George Louis Beer prize for best book on internat. history 1958), Am. Assn. For Advancement Slavic Studies. Home: Alterra 134 1780 Hermitage Blvd Tallahassee FL 32308

**MAMELE, RICHARD LOUIS,** lawyer; b. Madison, S.D., Apr. 15, 1949; s. Clayton Carl and Marcella Grace (Hoff) M.; m. Paula Brillante, Oct. 12, 1980 (div. Feb. 1988); 1 child, Jenna Megan; m. Barbara Hessey, Mar. 17, 1991; 1 child, Clayton Colt. BS in Polit. Sci., Belmont (N.C.) Abbey Coll., 1971; JD, U. Fla., 1974. Bar: Fla. 1975, U.S. Supreme Ct. 1981, U.S. Dist. Ct. (mid. dist.) Fla. 1977; bd. cert. marital and family law; cert. family law medicine. Assoc. Hutchison & Morris, Sanford, Fla., 1975-78; ptnr. Hutchison Morris & Mamele, Sanford, 1978; sr. ptnr., pres. Hutchison Mamele & Coover, Sanford, 1991—. Dir., counsel Heathrow Art Festival, Lake Mary, Fla., 1994—. Mem. Seminole County Bar Assn. (pres. 1979-84), Inn of Ct., Timacuan Country Club. Bd. govs. 1996—), Kiwanis Internat. Avocations: golf, skiing, travel. Home: 487 Flora Creek Ct Lake Mary FL 32746-2201 Office: Hutchison Mamele & Coover 230 N Park Ave Sanford FL 32771-1242

**MAMER, JAMES MICHAEL,** secondary school educator; b. LA, Oct. 8, 1948; s. James Robert and Annette (Babue) M.; m. Jessica Puma, Aug. 31, 1963. BA in Polit. Sci., Calif. Poly. U., Pomona, 1970; MA in Internat. Studies, Immaculate Heart Coll., 1990. Tchr. Irvine (Calif.) Unified Sch. Dist., 1978—. Mentor tchr. Irvine Sch. Dist., 1988-95. Mem. editl. bd. Global Pages, L.A., 1991-96. Recipient Global Teaching award Western Internat. Studies Consortium, L.A., 1991, Am. Coun. Internat. Edn. award, 1998, Human Rights Edn. award Internat. Studies Edn. Project, 2004; Fulbright-Hays grantee, India, 1977; Coe fellow, 1984. Mem. Nat. Coun. Social Studies (Nat. Social Studies Tchr. of Yr. 1992), Irvine Tchrs. Assn. Democrat. Avocation: reading. Home: 29102 Kommers Ln Silverado CA 92676-9726 Personal E-Mail: jmamer@earthlink.net.

**MAMER, JOHN WILLIAM,** business educator; b. July 4, 1954; BA, BS, U. Calif., Davis, 1975; MS, U. Calif., Berkeley, 1978, PhD, 1982. Analyst Manalytics Inc., 1977-78; rsch. intern Xerox Corp., 1979-80; from asst. prof. to prof. U. Calif., L.A., 1981-96, prof., 1996—. Lectr. in field. Referee Mgmt. Sci., 1982—, Ops. Rsch., 1984—, Jour. Econ. Dynamics and Control, 1984, 88; contbr. over 15 articles to profl. jours. Mem. Inst. Mgmt. Sci. (organizing chmn. 1994, arrangements chmn. 1995), Ops. Rsch. Soc. Am. Office: The Anderson School UCLA PO Box 951481 Los Angeles CA 90095-1481

**MAMER, STUART MIES,** lawyer; b. East Hardin, Ill., Feb. 23, 1921; s. Louis H. and Anna (Mies) M.; m. Donna E. Jordan, Sept. 10, 1944; children: Richard A., John S., Bruce J. AB, U. Ill., 1942, JD, 1947. Bar: Ill. bar 1947. Assoc. Thomas & Mulliken, Champaign, 1947-55; partner firm Thomas, Mamer & Haughey, Champaign, 1955—. Lectr. U. Ill. Coll. Law, Urbana, 1965-85; Mem. Atty. Registration and Disciplinary Commn. Ill., 1976-82 Chmn. fund drive Champaign County Community Chest, 1955; 1st pres. Champaign County United Fund, 1957; Pres., dir. U. Ill. McKinley Found., Champaign, 1957-69; trustee Children's Home and Aid Soc. of Ill., v.p., 1977-96. Served as pilot USAAC, 1943-45. Mem. Am. Coll. Trust and Estate Counsel (bd. regents 1984-90), Pillar of Champaign County Bar Assn., Phi Beta Kappa, Phi Gamma Delta. Republican. Presbyterian. Home: 101 W Windsor Rd # 3105 Urbana IL 61802-6663 Office: Thomas Mamer & Haughey LLP 30 E Main St Fl 5 Champaign IL 61820-3629 Office Phone: 217-351-1500. Business E-Mail: smamer@tmh-law.com.

**MAMET, DAVID ALAN,** playwright, theater producer; b. Chgo., Nov. 30, 1947; s. Bernard Morris and Lenore June (Silver) Mamet; m. Lindsay Crouse, Dec. 1977 (div.); m. Rebecca Pidgeon, Sept. 22, 1991. BA, Goddard Coll., Plainfield, Vt., 1969; DLitt (hon.), Dartmouth Coll., 1996. Artist-in-residence Goddard Coll., 1971-73; artistic dir. St. Nicholas Theatre Co., Chgo., 1973-75; guest lectr. U. Chgo., 1975, 79, NYU, 1981; assoc. artistic dir. Goodman Theater, Chgo., 1978; assoc. prof. film Columbia U., 1988. Chmn. bd. Atlantic Theater Co. Author: (plays) The Duck Variations, 1971, Sexual Perversity in Chicago, 1973 (Village Voice Obie award, N.Y. Drama Critics Cir. award), Reunion, 1973, Squirrels, 1974, American Buffalo, 1976, A Life in the Theatre, 1976, The Water Engine, 1976, The Woods, 1977, Lone Canoe, 1978, Prairie du Chien, 1978, Lakeboat, 1980, Donny March, 1981, Edmond, 1982 (Village Voice Obie award, 1983), The Disappearance of the Jews, 1983, The Shawl, 1985, Glengarry Glen Ross, 1984 (Pulitzer prize for drama, N.Y. Drama Critics Cir. award), Speed-the-Plow, 1987, Bobby Gould in Hell, 1989, The Old Neighborhood, 1991, Oleanna, 1992, The Cryptogram, 1994, Ricky Jay and His 52 Assistants, 1994; author: (one act) Death Defying Acts, 1995; author: Boston Marriage, 1999, Romance, 2005, (screenplays) The Postman Always Rings Twice, 1979, The Verdict, 1980, The Untouchables, 1986, House of Games, 1986; author: (with Shel Silverstein) Things Change, 1987; author: We're No Angels, 1987, Homicide, 1991, Hoffa, 1991, Oleanna, 1994, The Edge, 1996, The Spanish Prisoner, 1996, Wag the Dog, 1997, Ronin, 1998, The Winslow Boy, 1999, State & Main, 2000, Lakeboat, 2001, Hannibal, 2001, (children's books) Warm and Cold with drawings by Donald Sultan, 1985, The Duck and the Goat, Jafsie & John Henry, 1999, Bar Mitzvah, 1999, (essays) Writing In Restaurants, 1986, SomeFreaks, 1989, on Directing Film, 1990, The Cabin, 1992; actor: (essays) Make-Believe-Town, 1996; author: (novels) The Village, 1994, The Old Religion, 1996, True and False, 1996, 3 Uses of the Knife, 1996, Wilson, 2001, Passover, The Duck and the Goat, 1996, Henrietta, 1999, the Hero Pony, 1990, (poetry) The China Man, 1999, Wilson, 2000; dir.: (films) House of Games, 1986, Oleanna, 1994, The Spanish Prisoner, 1996, The Winslow Boy, 1988, State and Main, 2000, Catastrophe, 2000, Homicide, 1991, Things Change, 1988; assoc. prodr. (films) Hoffa, 1992; dir.: (plays) Dangerous Corner, 1995; exec. prodr.: (TV films) Lansky, 1999, A Life in the Theater, 1993; prodr.: Lip Service, 1988; writer, dir. (films) Heist, 2001, creator, writer (TV series) The Unit, 2006. Recipient Outer Critics Circle award for contbn. to Am. theater, 1978, Acad. award nominee for best screenplay adaptation, 1983, 1998, Common Wealth Award Distinguished Svc., 2004, Screen Laurel Award, Writers Guild Am., 2005; Rockefeller grantee, 1977, CBS Creative Writing fellow, Yale U. Drama Sch, 1976—77. Office: David Mamet 2 Northfield Plz Northfield IL 60093-1294*

**MAMLOK, URSULA,** composer; b. Berlin, Feb. 1, 1928; d. John and Dorothy Lewis; m. Dwight G. Mamlok, Nov. 27, 1947. Student, Mannes Coll. Music, 1942-45; MusB, Manhattan Sch. Music, 1955, MusM, 1958. Faculty dept. music NYU, 1967-74, CUNY, 1971-74; prof. composition Manhattan Sch. Music, N.Y.C., 1968—2003. Composer numerous works including Variations and Interludes for 4 percussionists, 1973, Sextet, 1977, Festive Sounds, 1978, When Summer Sang, 1980, piano trio Panta rhei, 1981, 5 recital pieces for young pianists, 1983, From My Garden for solo viola or solo violin, 1983, Concertino for wind quintet, strings and percussion, 1984, Der Andreas Garten for voice, flute and harp, 1986, Alariana for recorder, clarinet, bassoon, violin and cello, 1986, 3 Bagatelles for harpsichord, 1987, 5 Bagatelles for clarinet, violin, cello, 1988, Rhapsody for clarinet, viola, piano Inward Journey for Piano, 1989, Sonata for violin and piano, 1989, Music for flute, violin, cello, 1990, Girasol, a sextet for flute, violin, viola, cello and piano, 1991, Constellations for orch., 1993, Polarities for flute, violin, cello, piano, 1995, Festive Sounds for Organ, String Quartet II, 1996-97, Two Thousand Notes for Piano, 2000-01, Confluencies for Clarinet, Violin, Cello, Piano, 2002, Rückblick for Saxophone and Piano, 2002, piano pieces for 25th anniversary archive Woman and Music, 2004, 2 Bagatelles for String Quartet, rev., 2004. Recipient Opus One Rec. award Am. Composers Alliance, 1987, Serge Koussevitzky Found. commn., 1988, Walter Hinrichsen award Acad. Inst. Arts and Letters, 1989, commn. San Francisco Symphony, 1990; Nat. Endowment Arts grantee, 1974, Am. Inst. Acad. Arts and Letters grantee, 1981, 89, Martha Baird Rockefeller grantee, 1982; John Simon Gugenheim fellow, 1995. Mem. Am. Soc. Univ. Composers, Am. Women Composers, N.Y. Women Composers, Internat. League Women Composers, Am. Music Ctr., Internat. Soc Contemporary Music (bd. dirs.), Fromm Found. Commn., Am. Guild Organists Continuum Centre. Address: 315 E 86th St New York NY 10028-4714 *In my music, I have never striven for novelty nor originality for its own sake. Rather, my primary concern as a composer has been the consolidation of older and newer techniques, as they best serve the work at hand.*

**MAMLOK, WALTER JOSEPH,** music educator, musician; b. Bronx, N.Y., Jan. 4, 1949; s. Julius Alvin and Ruth Mamlok; m. Carol Diane Rubin, Aug. 26, 1972; children: Charna Beth Westervelt, Elena Susanne. BA in Music Edn., U. Hartford, 1971; MS, Ctrl. Conn. State U., 2000. Cert. profl. educator Conn. State Bd. Edn., 1994. Music tchr. Wethersfield (Conn.) Bd. Edn., 1971—75, 1976—80, Wolcott (Conn.) Bd. Edn., 1975—76; mgmt. Kemp Enterprises, South Windsor, Conn., 1980—88; music tchr. Newtown (Conn.) Bd. Edn., 1988—99, Meridan (Conn.) Bd. Edn., 1999—2001; music tchr. gr. 6-12 Capitol Region Ednl. Coun., Hartford, Conn., 2001—04; mid. sch. music tchr. Bloomfield (Conn.) Bd. Edn., 2004—. Dir., condr. Strictly Swing Jazz Band, Bloomfield, 1977—; bass clarinetist Local 400 Pops Band, Rocky Hill, Conn., 1988—; musician Capital Winds Ensemble, Hartford, 1990—; clarinetist Klezical Tradition Klezmer Band, Fairfield, Conn., 1994—. Contbr. articles to profl. jours. Mem. Dem. Town Com., Bloomfield, 2004; v.p. bd. dirs. Temple Beth Sholom, Manchester, 1985—95, tchr., 1991—99; pres. Temple Beth Sholom Nursery Sch., Manchester, Conn., 1982—86. Mem.:

Music Educators Technologists Assn. (treas., sec., charter), Conn Music Educators Assn., Conn. Edn. Assn. (assoc.), Music Educators Nat. Conf. (assoc.). Democrat. Jewish. Avocations: music, sports. Home: 1 South Ridge Dr Bloomfield CT 06002-5009 Office: Bloomfield Board of Education 390 Park Ave Bloomfield CT 06002 Office Phone: 860-286-2622. Personal E-mail: wmamlok@comcast.net. Business E-Mail: wmamlok@blmfld.org.

**MAMOUN, JOHN SAMI,** dentist; b. Livingston, NJ, Dec. 1, 1976; m. Ghena Mamoun. BA in Polit. Sci., U. Pa., Phila., 1999; DMD, U. Medicine and Dentistry NJ, Newark, 2003. Dentist Sunbeam Dentistry, Manalapan, NJ, 2006—. Contbr. articles to profl. jours. Recipient Eagle Scout award, 1995. Fellow: Acad. Gen. Dentistry. Avocation: piano. Office: Sunbeam Dental LLC 100 Craig Rd Ste 106 Manalapan NJ 07726

**MAMPRE, VIRGINIA ELIZABETH,** communications executive; b. Chgo., Sept. 12, 1949; d. Albert Leon and Virginia S. (Joboul) M. BA with honors, U. Iowa, 1971; Masters degree, Ind. U., 1972; spl. cert., Harvard U., 1981, Purdue U., 1999. Cert. tchr. Harris Intern WTTW-TV Sta., Chgo., 1972, asst. dir., 1972-73; prod. and dir. WSIU/WUSI-TV Sta., Carbondale, Ill., 1973-74; instr. So. Ill. U., Carbondale, 1972-77; prog. and prod. mgr. WSIU/WUSI-TV, Carbondale, 1974-77; prog. dir. KUHT-TV Sta., Houston, 1977-83; pres. Victory Media, Inc., Houston, 1984-89, Mampre Media Internat., Houston, 1984—. Cons. Corp. Pub. Broadcasting, Washington, 1981—83; bd. dirs. TVPC; program bd. Ea. Ednl. Network; spkr., presenter in field Europe, Asia, Australia, S. Am. Contbg. author/editor to mags. including Focus, 1989, News & Views, 1987-88, In the Black, 1984-93, Festivals; creator: (report card campaign) Multi-media, U.S., 1985—; exec. prodr. TV spls., pub. affairs and info., 1977-83 (awards 1978-91). Pres. Child Abuse Prevention Coun., Houston, 1984—97; chmn. exhbns. Mayor's 1st Hearing, Children and Youth, Houston, 1985—88; rep. Houston 2nd World Conf. on Mayors, Japan, 1989; bd. govs. Houston Read Commn., pres., 1995—2001, chair adv. bd., 1993—2001; mem. nat. faculty Ctr. Children's Issues, 1995—97; pres. Episcopal Ch. Women, 2002—, 2006; pres. bd. dirs. Houston Fin. Coun., 1983—; bd. dirs. Child Abuse Prevention Network, 1990—97; chmn. bd. dirs., gala chair Crime Stoppers Houston, 1984—99; founder, bd. dirs. Friends of WSIU-TV, 1974—77; chmn. St. Kevork/ACYO Nat. Sports Fair, St. John the Divine, 1990; mem. exec. bd. Nat. Com. To Prevent Child Abuse, 1990—97; pres., bd. dirs. Fedn. Houston Profl. Women Found., 1996; bd. dirs. Humanities Tex., 1998—, Tex. Coun. Humanities, Operation Rainbow, 1997—, pres. bd. gala chair; bd. dirs. Kellogg Fellows Leadership Alliance; adv. bd. Southwest Area Media Project. Fellow W.K. Kellogg Found., Battle Creek, Mich., 1987-90; recipient award for Excellence Pres. Pvt. Sector, White House, Washington, 1987, Ohio State U., Columbus, 1983, Feddersen award for excellence in Pub. TV Ind. U., Bloomington, 1981, Heritage award Child Abuse Prevention Coun., 1990, Dona J. Stone Founders award Nat. Assn. for Prevention of Child Abuse, 1990; named among Outstanding Women Vols. for community, civic and profl. contbns., Fedn. Houston Profl. Women, 1989; honoree Woman on Move, 1997. Mem.: Houston Culinary Guild (pres. 2006—), Internat. Festivals Events. Assn. (officer 1994—2003, sec. 1994—, bd. dirs. 1995—2002, creator Mampre Media Internat. Leadership Devel.), Profls. in Culinary Arts (pres. 2002—), TV Program Conf. (sec. bd. 1990—), Ctr. Bus. Women's Devel., Nat. Assn. Programming TV Execs., Nat. Assn. Ednl. Broadcasters (presenter nat. conv. 1975—76), Houston Fed. Profl. Women (del. 1986—93, chmn. 1994—, pres.), Am. Women in Radio and TV (bd. dirs. 1985—, nat. v.p. 1986—90, award 1987, pres. Houston chpt. 1990), Kellogg Fellows Leadership Alliance (bd. trustees), Dau. of the King, Christ in the Arts (chair), Dephians, Tex. Lyceum (v.p., bd. dirs. 1990—96). Republican. Episcopalian. Avocations: photography, swimming, sailing, languages, travel. Office: Mampre Media Internat 5123 Del Monte Dr Houston TX 77056-4391 Office Phone: 713-960-9849. Personal E-Mail: mampremedi@aol.com.

**MAMRACK, WILLIAM H.,** tax specialist; b. Canonsburg, Pa., June 7, 1943; BBA, U. Mich., 1965. Tax mgr. Arthur Andersen and Co., 1971—77, tax ptnr., 1978—84, head Memphis tax divsn., 1984—89; v.p. taxes Ga. Pacific, Atlanta, 1992—. Active Salvation Army; mem. adv. coun. Boys and Girls Clubs; mem. Tex. Execs. Inst. Mem.: AICPA, Pa. Inst. CPA's, Ga. Soc. CPA's, Am. Forest & Paper Assn. (tax subcom.). Office: Ga Pacific 133 Peachtree St NE Atlanta GA 30303

**MAMTANI, MANJU RAMESHLAL,** geneticist, researcher; b. Nagpur, India, Oct. 12, 1974; arrived in U.S., 2004; d. Rameshlal Tekchand and Savitri Rameshlal Mamtani; m. Hemant Kulkarni, Feb. 23, 2004. MBBS, Indira Gandhi Govt. Med. Coll., Nagpur U., India, 1997; MD, Govt. Med. Coll. Nagpur U., India, 2003. Cert. Maharashtra Med. Coun., 1997. Rsch. fellow U. Tex. Health Sci. Ctr., San Antonio, 2004—. Patron mem. Lata Med. Rsch. Found., Nagpur, 2001—; joint sec. Thalassemia Soc. India, Nagpur, 2001—. Kathak dance. Achievements include research in Waist circumference as a predictor of type 2 diabetes; MCV and MCH as predictors of thalassemia. Avocations: travel, dancing, painting. Home: 7458 Louis Pasteur Dr Apt #1205 San Antonio TX 78229 Office: UTHSCSA 7703 Floyd Curl Dr San Antonio TX 78229 Office Phone: 210-567-0103. Business E-Mail: mamtani@uthscsa.edu.

**MAMULA, PETAR,** gastroenterologist, director; b. Zagreb, Croatia, July 14, 1965; s. Bozidar and Danica Mamula; m. Gordana-Dana Grozdanic, Dec. 3, 1994; 1 child, Emil Niko. MD, U. Zagreb, 1991. Lic. pediat. gastroenterologist Am. Bd. Pediat. Pediat. gastroenterologist Children's Hosp. Phila., 2001—. Dir. endoscopy ste. Children's Hosp. Phila., 2001—. Achievements include research in new drug therapies and gastrointestinal endoscopy. Office Phone: 215-590-9146. Office Fax: 215-590-3606.

**MAMUT, MARY CATHERINE,** retired entrepreneur; b. Calabria, Italy, Oct. 17, 1923; came to U.S., 1928; d. Carmelo Charles and Caterina (Tripodi) Cogliandro; m. Michael Matthew Mamut, May 15, 1954; children: Anthony Carl, Charles Terrance. Student, Stenotype Comml. Coll., 1946-50. Sec. to pres. Thomas Goodfellow, Inc., Detroit, 1942-50; asst. to v.p. R.G. Moeller Co., Detroit, 1951-52; sec. to pres. United Steel Supply Co., Detroit, 1952-54; sec. to libr. Farmington (Mich.) Schs., 1962-68; real estate agt., 1969; owner, mgr. Crystal Fair, Birmingham, Mich., 1969-88, ret. Mich. Tchr. Stenotype Comml. Coll., Detroit, 1952-54. Vol. Henry Ford Mus., Dearborn, Mich., 1989-90, Greenfield Village, 1989-90, West Bloomfield Libr., 1993-95. Recipient World Lifetime Achievement award Am. Biog. Inst. U.S.A., 1993. Mem. Am. Bus. Women's Assn., Birmingham-Bloomfield C. of C., Profl. Secs. Internat., NAFE. Roman Catholic. Avocations: reading, music, art, theater. Home: 7423 Coach Ln West Bloomfield MI 48322-4022

**MAN, DANIEL,** plastic surgeon; married; 3 children. MD, Tel Aviv U., 1973. Lic. Maine, 1976, Del., 1976, Ky., 1978, Fla., 1981, cert. in Plastic and Reconstructive Surgery Am. Bd. Plastic Surgery, 1981. Intern in gen. surgery Tel Hashomer Hosp., Ramat Gan, Israel, 1972—73; resident in gen. surgery Montefiore Hosp., Bronx, NY, 1974—76; resident in surgery Wilmington Gen. Hosp., Del., 1976—78; resident in plastic and reconstructive surgery U. Louisville, 1978—80; pvt. practice Boca Raton, Fla., 1981—. Presenter in field; profl. interviewee in field various mags., newspapers, and TV programs. Author: The Art of Man: Faces of Plastic Surgery, 1998, The New Art of Man: Faces of Plastic Surgery, 2002; contbr. books, anthologies, and profl. jours. in field. Named Dr. Man Day in his honor, Boca Raton, Fla., 2001; recipient Humanitarian of Yr. award, Palm Beach County Victim Svcs., 2001, Letter of Recognition for Humanitarian Contbns., Fla. State Senator M. Mandy Dawson, 2001, Fla. State Senator Tom Rossin, 2001, US Congressman Robert Wexler, 2001, US Senator Bill Nelson, 2001, US Senator Bob Graham, 2001, Gov. Jeb Bush, 2001; Hand fellowship, U. Louisville, 1978—80, Microvascular fellowship, 1980. Fellow: Am. Soc. Laser Surgery and Medicine; mem.: AMA, Y-ME Fla. (founding bd. mem. 1982—87, med. advisor 1982—87), Lipolysis Soc. N.Am., Broward County Soc. Plastic Surgeons, Palm Beach County Soc. Plastic Surgeons, Palm Beach County Med. Soc., Am. Soc. Aesthetic Plastic Surgery, Am. Soc. Plastic Surgeons. Office: 851 Meadows Rd Ste 222 Boca Raton FL 33486 Office Phone: 561-395-5508.

**MAN, LAWRENCE KONG,** architect, art dealer; b. Kowloon, Hong Kong, July 4, 1953; s. Hon-Kwong Man and Sau-Ching Luk. Student, U. Redlands, 1971-72; BArch, U. Oreg., 1977; MArch, Harvard U., 1978. Registered architect, Mass.; Calif. Designer, project architect Shepley Bulfinch Richardson & Abbott, Boston, 1978-86; project designer, project architect E. Verner Johnson & Assoc., Boston, 1987-91; owner Lawrence Man Architect, Cambridge, Mass., 1992-95, L.A., 1994—. Prin. works include Kromka House, L.A., Calif., LMAN Studio, L.A., Chu House, Downey, Calif., Fong House, San Marino, Calif., Tighe Summer House, Sagamore Beach, Mass, Frozen Fusion Juice Bar, L.A. schs., Fed. Credit Union, L.A., Pub. Mus. Grand Rapids, Mich. (AIA Grand Valley Disting. Bldg. award 1997), LCP Studio, Somerville, Mass., New Asia Restaurants, Danvers and Arlington, Mass., Tai Pan Restaurant, Cambridge, Mass. (Honor award AIA 1993, New Eng. award Excellence in Architecture 1993, Design Excellence award Nat. Orgn. Minority Architects 1993), Ti-Sales Office, Sudbury, Mass. (Design Excellence award Nat. Orgn. Minority Architects 1993), Dental Clinic, Reading, Mass. (AIA Interior Architecture award 1992, Interior Design Project award Am. Soc. Interior Designers 1991, Boston Exports citation AIA 1990, Boston Soc. of Architects/New Eng. Healthcare Assembly honor award, 1994), Mus. Ctr. Union Terminal, Cin. (Reconstrn. award 1991), Ramesses Pavilion Boston Mus. Sci. (Double Vision award/Double Silver Soc. Environ. Graphics 1990), Smithsonian South Quadrangle Mus., Washington (Boston Exports award/citation AIA 1990, Honor award AIA 1989), U. Vt. Student Ctr., Burlington, Campus Ctr. Study and Libr. addition Franklin & Marshall Coll., Andover (Mass.) Co. Corp. Hdqs., Emerson Hosp., Concord, Mass., pvt. residences, others. Avocations: dance, travel, music. Office: 949 Chung King Rd Los Angeles CA 90012 Office Phone: 213-628-3883. Business E-Mail: info@lawrencemanarchitects.com. *There are ups and downs in life. It is more rewarding to experience them all, no matter how hard it may get sometimes. It allows you to become a more complete person. That is, in my view, a true achievement.*

**MAN, PANG LING,** retired psychiatrist; b. Hong Kong, China; arrived in U.S., 1963; s. Kwong Cheung and Loy-Ho Man; m. Hope Man, Mar. 8, 1958; children: Ching, Dick, Linda. Degree, Queen Coll., Hong Kong, 1953; MD, Sun Yat-Sen U., 1958. Intern, resident U. Hosp., Gaungzhen, China, 1958—60; intern Grade Hosp., Winnipeg, Canada, 1963—64; resident Worcester State Hosp., Mass., 1964—67; instr. psychiatry U. Louisville, 1967—71; asst. prof. psychiatry Wayne State U., Detroit, 1971—78, assoc. prof. psychiatry, 1978—98, ret., 1998. Dir. rsch. Northville Regional Psychiatric Hosp., Mich., 1971—98, asst. dir. edn., 1971—90. Author: Handbook of Acupuncture Anesthesia, 1973; contbr. articles to profl. jours. Vol. physician Chinatown Free Clinic, Detroit, 1971—90. Fellow: Am. Psychiatric Assn., Am. Bd. Neurology and Psychiatry. Avocations: golf, travel, swimming, ping pong/table tennis, dance. Home: 6504 Horsemans Canyon Dr Walnut Creek CA 94595

**MANABE, SHARI A.,** education educator; m. Layne Manabe. BS, Ind. State U., 1991; MS, U. Hawaii, Manoa, 1993. Lic. Teacher State of Hawaii Dept. of Edn., 1996, cert. Adapted Physical Educator Nat. Consortium for Physical Edn. and Recreation for People with Disabilities, 2001. Secondary tchr. King Kekaulike H.S., Pukalani, Hawaii, 1995—96, Lahaina Intermediate Sch., Hawaii, 1996—97, Lokelani Intermediate Sch., Kihei, Hawaii, 1997—2001, Ctrl. Mid. Sch., Honolulu, 2001—03, Aiea Intermediate Sch., Hawaii, 2003—. Mem.: Am. Assn. for Health, Physical Edn., Recreation and Dance (assoc.), Am. Coll. of Sports Medicine (assoc.), Nat. Strength and Conditioning Assn. (assoc.), Hawaii Assn. for Health, Physical Edn., Recreation and Dance (life). Office: Aiea Intermediate Sch 99-600 Kulawea St Aiea HI 96701 Office Phone: 808-486-7230.

**MANABE, SYUKURO,** meteorologist; b. Shikoku-chuo-shi, Uma-Gun, Ehime-ken, Japan, Sept. 21, 1931; arrived in U.S., 1958; s. Seiichi and Sueko (Akashi) M.; m. Nobuko Nakamura, Jan. 21, 1962; children: Nagisa M., Yukari C. BS, Tokyo U., 1953, MS, 1955, DS, 1958; DSc (hon.), McGill U., 2004. Rsch. meteorologist U.S. Weather Bur., Washington, 1958-63; sr. rsch. meteorologist Geophys. Fluid Dynamics Lab. NOAA, Washington, 1963-68, sr. rsch. meterologist geophys. fluid dynamics lab. Princeton, NJ, 1968-95, mem. sr. exec. svc. of U.S., 1979-95, sr. scientist, 1995-97; dir. global warming rsch. program Frontier Rsch. Sys. for Global Change, Yokohama, Japan, 1997—2001; vis. rsch. collaborator, Program in Atmospheric and Oceanic Scis. Princeton U., 2002—03. Lectr. with rank of prof. Princeton U., 1968-98; joint sci. com. World Climate Rsch. Program, 1981-87; bd. atmospheric sci. and climate NRC, 1988-91; com. on Geoscis., Environ. and Resources, NRC, 1990-93, climate rsch. com., 2001-03; panel on climate and global change NOAA, 1988-97. Recipient Gold medal U.S. Dept. Commerce, 1970, Presdl. Rank Meritorious Exec. award Pres. of U.S., 1989, Blue Planet prize Asahi Glass Found., 1992, Asahi prize Asahi Daily Found., 1996, Volvo Environ. prize Volvo Found., 1997, Milankovitch medal European Geophys. Soc., 1998. Fellow AAAS, Am. Geophys. Union (Revelle medal 1993), Am. Meteorol. Soc. (hon.: Meisinger award 1967, 2d half century award 1977, Rossby medal 1992), Japan Meteorol. Soc. (hon.: Fujiwara award 1966); mem. NAS, Acad. Europaea (fgn.), Royal Soc. Can. (fgn.). Achievements include first numerical modeling study of global warming. Home: 6 Governors Ln Princeton NJ 08540-3666 Office: Princeton U Sayre Hall Forrestal Campus PO Box CN710 Princeton NJ 08544-0710 Business E-Mail: manabe@splash.princeton.edu.

**MANAHAN, JOAN ELSIE,** health and physical education educator; b. Haskell, N.J., Jan. 18, 1940; d. Edward A. and Elsie G. (Beckmann) M. BA, Trenton State Coll., 1962; MA, Columbia U., 1966, EdD, 1975. Tchr., coach Bloomfield (N.J.) Bd. Edn., 1962-97; ret. Cons. Nat. Dairy Coun., 1970s. Cons. (book): Basic Stuff: Motor Learning and Performance; contbr. articles to profl. jours. Grantee A+ For Kids Tchr. Network, Inc., 1992-93; recipient Proclamation, N.J. State Legislature, 1997. Mem. NEA, AAHPERD (pres. 1980u, 1990u), Am. Archvy Assn. N J AHPERD, N.J. Athletic Assn. (treas. 1966-67, co-editor newsletter 1982-88), archery tournament chairperson 1965-75), N.J. Edn. Assn., Essex County Coaches Assn., Kappa Delta Pi, Pi Lambda Theta. Roman Catholic. Avocations: collecting playing cards and swizzle sticks, life master bridge. E-mail: jem7152002@yahoo.com.

**MANAS, GERALD BENNETT,** information technology manager; b. Phila., Mar. 15, 1960; s. Sidney Ralph and Barbara M. Manas; m. Sharon Erica Olson, Sept. 10, 1989; 1 child, Elizabeth Rose. Student, Temple U., 1978-79. Cert. project mgmt. Am. Mgmt. Assn., project mgmt. profl. Project Mgmt. Inst., Microsoft Project Users Group. Programmer Alfred Angelo, Inc., Willow Grove, Pa., 1978-81, Pepper, Hamilton & Scheetz, Phila., 1981-82; programmer, analyst Hurst Performance, Warminster, Pa., 1982-85; sys. analyst C&D Power Sys., Plymouth Meeting, Pa., 1985-87; mgr. product devel. Centennial Sys., Wayne, Pa., 1987-89; mgr. edn. Responsive Software Solutions, Wayne, 1989-90; client mgr. Alliance Cons., Phila., 1990—2003, Rohm and Haas, Phila., 2003—. Pres. Manas Comm., Inc., Phila., 1995-96; chmn. round table Del. Valley Computer Users Group, Phila., 1987—88. Author: (articles) Project Mgmt. According to Napoleon, 2002, Lessons Learned from Napoleon, 2002, Lessons From the Rise and Fall of the Roman Empire; songwriter Sept. Forever, 1996. Vol. contr. Project Mgmt. Inst. Mem.: Nat. Acad. Songwriters, Alliance Francaise Phila., Delaware Valley Entrepreneur's Club (pres., founder 1994—96). Democrat. Jewish. Avocations: music, art, photography, writing, french studies. Office: Rohm and Haas 7th Fl E-Bus 100 Independence Mall W Philadelphia PA 19106 Office Phone: 215-341-6413.

**MANASSAH, JAMAL TEWFEK,** electrical engineer, educator, management consultant; b. Haifa, Palestine, Feb. 23, 1945; s. Tewfek George and Alia Nasrallah (Kardoush) M.; m. Azza Tarek H.I. Mikdadi, Mar. 16, 1979; children: Tala, Nigh. BSc, Am. U., Beirut, Lebanon, 1966; MA, Columbia U., 1968, PhD, 1970. Mem. Inst. Advanced Study, Princeton, N.J., 1970-72, 74-79; prof. Am. U. Beirut, 1972-75; chief sci. adviser Kuwait Inst. Sci. Rsch., 1976-81; COO Kuwait Found., 1979-81; prof. dept. elec. engring. CUNY, N.Y.C., 1981—. Cons. Columbia Radiation Labs., N.Y.C., 1970-73, Ford Found., N.Y.C., 1973-79, NSF, Washington, 1978-83; chmn. Internat.

Symposium Series, Kuwait, 1979-81; mng. dir. Khayatt and Co., Inc., N.Y.C., 1982; organizing com. Chem. Rsch. Applied to World Needs II, 1980-83; mem. Welfare Assn., Geneva, 1984-92; steering com. Internat. Workshop on Laser Physics, 1993-2000. Editor: Alternate Energy Sources (2 vols.) 1981; (with others) Advances in Food Producing Systems for Arid and Semiarid Lands (2 vols.), 1981, Innovations in Telecommunication (2 vols.), 1982, (with others) Transient Coherent Phenomena, 1995, Elementary Mathematical and Computational Tools for Electrical and Computer Engineering Using MATLAB®, 2001, (with others) Coherent and Nonlinear Optics and Spectroscopy, 2002; mem. editl. bd. Internat. Jour. Laser Physics, 1994—, Laser Physics Letters, 2004—; contbr. articles to profl. jours. Commr. Lebanese Boy Scouts Assn., Beirut, 1972-75; adviser internat. program NSF, 1979-83; bd. dirs. CUNY Rsch. Found., 2001-03. Columbia U. faculty fellow, 1966-68, Pfister fellow, 1968-70; grantee NSF, 1982-87; recipient ABI Key award, 1987, Commemorative medal of honor, 1988; named Man of Yr., 1990. Mem. Assn. Mems. of Inst. for Advanced Study, Princeton Club. Christian Orthodox. Achievements include discovery of resonant absorption coefficient frequency shift; collective Lamb shift, pion minus condensation in nuclear matter, blackbody frequency shift; dynamical Lorenz shift, reflectivity frequency shift, induced coherent pulse compression, induced spectral broadening; induced frequency shift, three-photons frequency shift, twin peaks in second harmonics generation; induced waveguiding and focusing, time-space superspike, non-linear compression of noise correlation time, soliton phases; coherently inhibited amplification, induced channeling, delayed reflectivity, two-color photon echos; superradiance without inversion, pressure induced optical cavities, periodicity enhanced precocious superradiant transition, acousto-induced reflectivity shift; research in statistical field theory, nonlinear and quantum optics, photonics, ultrafast phenomena and new technologies assessment. Home: 55 E 87th St Apt 15G New York NY 10128-1051 Office: CUNY Dept Elec Engring Convent Ave New York NY 10031 Office Phone: 212-650-8133. Business E-Mail: manassah@ccny.cuny.edu.

**MANASSE, HENRI RICHARD, JR.,** pharmaceutical executive; b. Amsterdam, The Netherlands, Nov. 27, 1945; came to U.S., 1954, naturalized, 1963; s. Henri David and Janny Lynn (Borst) M.; m. Arlynn Hem, Aug. 9, 1969; children: Bryan, Sheralynn. BS in Pharmacy, U. Ill., Chgo., 1968; MA, Loyola U., Chgo., 1972; PhD, U. Minn., 1974; DSc (hon.), Campbell U., 1997, Union U., 1997, Mercer U., 1998, LI U., NY, 2004. Lic. pharmacist, Ill. Rsch. pharmacist Xttrium Labs., Chgo., 1968-69; asst. to dean Coll. Pharmacy U. Ill., Chgo., 1969-72, asst. prof. pharmacy adminstrn., 1974-77, assoc. dean, 1977-80, acting dean, 1980-81, dean, prof., 1981-93, interim vice chancellor for health svcs., 1992-93; prof. coll. pharmacy and medicine U. Iowa, v.p. for health scis., 1993-96; exec. v.p.-designate Am. Soc. Health-Sys. Pharmacists, 1996—, CEO, exec. v.p., 1997—. Sr. policy fellow Ctr. on Drugs and Pub. Policy, U. Md., 1988—; mem. Ill. Bd. Pharmacy, Springfield, 1982-94; pub. mem. Am. Soc. Hosp. Pharmacists Commn. on Credentialling, Bethesda, Md., 1984-86; chair bd. dirs. Nat. Patient Safety Found., 1999-2001, chair bd. govs., 2006; mem. adv. bd. PEW Found. Health Professions Edn. Reform Commn.; bd. dirs. Am. Soc. Cons. Pharmacists Rsch. and Edn. Found.; pres. Coun. on Credentialing in Pharmacy, 1998—02; mem. quality quest prize selection com. Am. Hosp. Assn.; co-chair safe practices steering com. Nat. Quality Forum, 2001-04, adv. com. on exec. leadership; mem. sentinel events adv. com. JCAHO Sentinel, 2002—; cons. FDA Adv. Com. on Risk Mgmt. and Drug Safety; expert on patient safety Bd. Pharmacy Practice, profl. sec., 2005—, Internat. Pharm. Fedn.; JCAHO mem. Internat. Adv. Com. on Patient Safety. Mem. editl. bd. Am. Jour. Hosp. Pharmacy, 1990-92; contbr. chpts. to books and articles to profl. jours. Pres. Downers Grove Sch. Bd. Caucus, Ill., 1984-85; bd. dirs. mem. svc. Westside Holistic Ctr., Chgo., 1979-89. Recipient Lederle Faculty award Lederle Pharm. Co., 1975, Outstanding Achievement award U. Minn., 1998; named Alumnus of Yr., U. Ill. Alumni Assn., 1983. Jesse E Stewart Svc. award, U. of Illinois, 2004. Fellow Inst. Medicine Chgo.; mem. Am. Assn. Colls. Pharmacy (pres., adminstrv. bd. 1982-86, bd. dirs. 1984-86, pres. 1988-89), Am. Soc. Health Sys. Pharmacists, Nat. Acad. Scis., Inst. Medicine, Am. Pharm. Assn., Am. Soc. Assn. Execs. Baptist. Avocations: computers, international travel. Home: 10118 Vanderbilt Cir Rockville MD 20850-4674 Office: ASHP 7272 Wisconsin Ave Bethesda MD 20814 Office Phone: 301-657-3000. Business E-Mail: hrmjr@ashp.org.

**MANATT, CHARLES TAYLOR,** lawyer; b. Chgo., June 9, 1936; BS, Iowa State U., 1958; JD, George Washington U., 1962. Bar: Calif. 1962, U.S. Supreme Ct. 1967, D.C. 1985. Ptnr. Manatt, Phelps & Phillips, Washington, now chmn.; U.S. ambassador Dominican Republic, 1999—2001. Bd. editors George Washington Law Rev., 1960-62. Pres. Calif. Bankers Assn.; chmn. Nat. Democratic Inst., Calif. Dem. Com., Nat. Dem. Com., Internat. Found. for Election Sys.; chmn. bd. trustees George Washington U.; bd. dirs. Mayo Clinic; trustee Mus. Am. History. Mem. ABA, Calif. State Bar, L.A. County Bar Assn., San Fernando Valley Bar Assn. (pres. 1971-72), Century City Bar Assn., Phi Delta Phi, Delta Sigma Rho. also: Manatt Phelps & Phillips Trident Ctr E Tower 11355 W Olympic Blvd Los Angeles CA 90064-1614 Office: Manatt Phelps Phillips 700 12th St NW Ste 1100 Washington DC 20005-4075

**MANATT, RICHARD,** retired education educator; b. Odebolt, Iowa, Dec. 13, 1931; s. William Price and Lucille (Taylor) M.; m. Sally Jo Johnson, Aug. 20, 1952; children— Tamra Jo, Ann Lea, Joel Price; m. Jacquelyn M. Nesset, Feb. 25, 1970; 1 child, Megan Sue. BSc, Iowa State U., 1953, MS, 1956; PhD, U. Iowa, 1964. Prin. Oskloosa (Iowa) Schs., 1959-62; rsch. assoc. U. Iowa, Iowa City, 1962-64; mem. faculty Iowa State U., Ames, 1964—, prof., 1972—, chmn. dept. ednl. adminstrn., 1970-80, 93-98, dir. Sch. Improvement Model Projects, 1980—, prof., 1998—2002, prof. emeritus, 2002—. Cons. performance evaluation for public and independent schs.; disting. vis. prof. Calif. State U., L.A. Author: Educator's Guide to the New Design, When Right is Wrong, Fundamentalists and the Public Schools, Clinical Manual for Teacher Performance Evaluation Compendias of Professional Growth Plans (computer software program) Computer Assisted Teach Evaluation/Supervision. Served with AUS, 1953-55. Named Disting. Prof., Nat. Acad. Sch. Execs., 1979. Regents' Prof. Edn., 1994; recipient faculty citation Iowa State U. Alumni Assn., 1998, Margaret White Grad. Faculty award, 2001, Pres.'s award NAACP, 2002. Mem. NEA, NASSP, ASCD (Outstanding Cons. 1981), Am. Assn. Sch. Adminstrs., Phi Kappa Phi, Phi Delta Kappa, Delta Chi. Democrat. Methodist. Home: 2926 Monroe Dr Ames IA 50010-4362 Office Phone: 515-232-0202. Business E-Mail: rmanatt@iastate.edu.

**MANBECK, ALEXANDRA T.,** lawyer; b. Saigon, Vietnam, Aug. 6, 1955; arrived in US, 1973; d. Tinh Nguyen and Sarah Tran; m. Peter C. Manbeck, May 1, 1990; children: Lara, Courtney. BS in chemistry, Tex. Tech U., 1979; MS in petroleum engring., U. So. Calif., 1980, degree in petroleum engring., 1992; JD, Columbia U., 1990. Bar: NY 1991, US Patent Office 1992, Calif. 1995. Petroleum engr. Chevron Corp., LA, 1980—86; assoc. atty. Hughes Hubbard & Reed, NYC, 1990—91, Morgan & Finnegan, NYC, 1991—93; v.p. Bear Stearns, NYC, 1993—95; gen. counsel Nguyen Tin Legal Svc., San Diego, 1995—; pvt. practice Cross River, NY, 1995—. Contbr. articles to profl. jours. Founder Assn. Vietnamese Vets., San Diego, 1999—. Recipient Harlan Fiske Stone prize in constl. law, Columbia U., 1988; Harlan Fiske Stone scholar, 1989. Mem.: Westchester Bar Assn. Home: PO Box 449 Cross River NY 10518 Office: Nguyen Tin Legal Svcs 4531 University Ave San Diego CA 92105 Office Phone: 619-563-3588. Fax: 212-504-6626. E-mail: manbeckjd@optonline.net.

**MANBECK, HARVEY B.,** agricultural and biological engineer, educator; b. Reading, Pa., Jan. 11, 1942; m. Glenda Manbeck; children: Eric, Christina. BS, Pa. State U., 1963, MS in Agrl. Engring., 1965; PhD in Engring., Okla. State U., 1970. Rsch. assoc. agrl. engring. dept. Pa. State U., 1965, instr. agrl. engring. dept., 1966, prof. agrl. engring., 1980-96; asst. prof. agrl engring. dept. U. Ga., 1970-75, assoc. prof. agrl. engring. dept., 1977-80; assoc. prof., extension agrl. engr. Ohio State U., 1975-77; adminstrv. internrash. office Pa. Agrl. Experiment Sta., 1991-92; Disting. prof. agrl. engring. Pa. State U., 1996—2004, Disting. prof. emeritus Pa., 2004— interim head agrl. and biol. engring. dept. Pa., 1996—98. Vis. prof. agrl. engring. U. Manitoba, 1986-87,

Shenyang Agrl. U., 1988; interim dir. Housing Rsch. Ctr., Pa. State U., 1995. Contbr. chpts. to books and articles to profl. jours. Coach Little League Baseball, 1981-84, leader YMCA Indian Princess Longhouse, 1983-85, Webelo's Cub Scouts 1984, com. mem. Troop 31 Boy Scouts of Am. 1985—. Recipient Outstanding and Premier Tchg. award, Outstanding Rsch. award Coll. of Engring., Pa. State U., Atherton Excellence in Tchg. award Pa. State U., Black award for rsch. excellence Coll. Agrl. Scis., Pa. State U. Mem. ASCE, Am. Soc. Agrl. Engrs. (mem. structures group, vice chair 1978-79, chair, 1979-81, Pa. State sect. sec.-treas. 1983-84, chair 1985-86, trustee 1992-94, tech. dir. S.E. divsn. 1993-95, Henry Giese S & E award 1990), Nat. Frame Builders Assn. (mem. editl. rev. com. for the post-frame profl., chair 1988—), Ga. Soc. Profl. Engrs (state dir. at large 1974-75, named Outstanding Young Engr. of the Year, 1972, recipient Outstanding Chpt. Pres. award, 1974, various other coms.), Ohio Soc. Profl. Engrs., Forest Products Rsch. Soc., Gamma Sigma Delta (internat. sec. 1998—), Alpha Epsilon, Sigma Xi, numerous others. Achievements include development of standard designs and specs for hardwood glulam highway bridges, authorship of national engineering practice for post-frame structural diaphragm design, development of FEM for predicting thermal pressures in grain bins, development of FEM for predicting structural performance of wood-framed, metal-clad diaphagm evaluation of creep response of wood I-joist floor systems, lateral stability of composite wood I-joists and development of standards for ventilation of confined space storage systems in agriculture. Home: 912 Anna St Boalsburg PA 16827-1214 Office: Penn State U 210 Agr Engring Bldg University Park PA 16802 Business E-Mail: Hmanbeck@psu.edu.

**MANCALL, ELLIOTT LEE,** neurologist, educator; b. Hartford, Conn., July 31, 1927; s. Nicholas and Bess Tuch M.; m. Jacqueline Sue Cooper, Dec. 27, 1953; children: Andrew Cooper, Peter Cooper. BS, Trinity Coll., Hartford, 1948; MD, U. Pa., 1952. Diplomate Am. Bd. Psychiatry and Neurology. Intern Hartford Hosp., 1952-54; clk. in neurology Nat. Hosp. Nervous Disease, London, 1954-55; asst. resident neurology Neurol. Inst. NY, 1955-56; resident in neuropathology Mass. Gen. Hosp., 1956-57, clin. and rsch. fellow, 1957-58; tchg. fellow neuropathology Harvard Med. Sch., 1956-57; from asst. prof. neurology to assoc. prof. Jefferson Med. Coll., 1958-65; prof. medicine Hahnemann Med. Coll. and Hosp., 1965-76; prof. neurology Med. Coll. Pa.-Hahnemann U., 1993-95; prof. neurology, chmn. dept. Hahnemann Med. Coll. and Hosp., 1976-93; prof. neurology Jefferson Med. Coll., Phila., 1995—, interim chmn. dept. neurology, 1997—2003. Dir. Hahnemann U. ALS Clinic, 1985-95; chmn. bd. dirs. Phila. Profl. Stds. Rev. Orgn., 1981-84. Author: (with others) The Human Cerebellum: A Topographical Atlas, 1961; (with B.J. Alpers) Clinical Neurology, 1971, Essentials of the Neurological Examination, 1971, 81; contbr. articles to profl. jours. With USN, 1945—47. Recipient Christian R. and Mary F. Lindback award, 1969, Oliver Meml. prize ophthalmology U. Pa., 1952. Fellow Am. Acad. Neurology (alt. del. to AMA 1982-86, gen. editor CONTINUUM 1991-2003, A.B. Baker award for excellence in neurol. edn. 1997, Presdl. award 2003); mem. Am. Neurol. Assn., Am. Assn. Neuropathology, Assn. Rsch. in Nervous and Mental Diseases, Soc. Neurosci., AAUP, Pa. Med. Peer Rev. Orgn. (dir. 1979-84), Phila. Neurol. Soc., Alpers Soc. Clin. Neurology, Coll. Physicians Phila., Sydenham Coterie, Phila. County Med. Soc., Pa. State Med. Soc., AMA (sec.-treas. sect. coun. neurology 1983-86), Am. Med. Soc. on Alcoholism, Neurology Intersoc. Liaison Group, Intersoc. Com. Neurol. Resources, Assn. Univ. Prof. Neurology (pres. 1988-90), Soc. for Exptl. Neuropathology, Am. Bd. Med. Specialities (exec. bd., chmn. com. study of evaluation procedures, 1992-99, rep. accreditation com. continuing med. edn. 1998—, chair accredidation coun., 2003—), Am. Bd. Psychiatry and Neurology (v.p. 1990, del. to Am. Bd. Med. Spltys., dir. 1983-91, emeritus dir. 1991—, cons. 2004-), Pa. Blue Shield (profl. adv. coun. 1991-98). Democrat. Jewish. Home: PO Box 498 Lafayette Hill PA 19444-0498 Office: Ste 200 900 Walnut St Philadelphia PA 19107 Office Phone: 215-955-0707. Business E-Mail: elliott.mancall@jefferson.edu.

**MANCALL, JACQUELINE COOPER,** library and information scientist, educator; b. Phila., Mar. 31, 1932; d. Morris and Bertha Cooper; m. Elliott Lee Mancall, Dec. 27, 1953; children: Andrew Cooper, Peter Cooper. BA, U. Pa., 1954; MS, Drexel U. Sch. Libr. and Info. Sci., 1970, PhD, 1979. Adminstrt. Miquon Sch., Pa., 1966—67, libr., 1967—76; tchg. asst. Drexel U., Phila., 1976—78, rsch. assoc., 1978, asst. prof., assoc. prof., 1979—89, prof., 1989—. Chair Phila. Children's Reading Round Table, 1982—84, mem. steering com., 1979—89; mem. faculty coun. Drexel U., 1984—89, chair faculty coun., 1987—89, mem. senate, 2000—05, chair senate, 2001—02; mem. sch. libr. survey com. State Libr. Pa., 1993; cons. Author (with M.C. Drott): Measuring Student Information Use: A Guide for School Library Media Specialists, 1963; author: (with E.S. Aversa) Management of Online Search Services in Schools, 1989; author: (with Sandra Hughes-Hassell) Collection for Management Youth, 2005; rsch. editor: Sch. Libr. Media quar., 1982—88, mem. editl. bd.; Jour. Libr. and Info. Sci. Edn., 1981—86, mem. editl. adv. bd.: Multimedia Schs.; contbg. editor: Cath. Libr. World, 1981—85; contbr. chapters to books, articles to profl. jours. Bd. dirs. Friends of William Jeannes Meml. Libr., Plymouth Meeting, Pa., 1976—79; pres. bd. dirs. Miquon Sch., 1964—66. Recipient Ann. award, Phila. Sch. Libr., 1994. Mem.: ALA (adv. com. office info. tech. 1995—97, continuing edn. task force 1995—98, co-chair ICONect evaluation com. 1996—2000, libr. congress nat. digital libr. adv. com. 1997, pub. awareness com. 1997—99, dir. KidsConnect 2000—02), Am. Assn. Sch. Libr. (chmn. continuing edn. com. 1985—87, rsch. stats. com. 1988—92, v.p./pres.-elect 1993, pres. 1994. Disting. Svc. award 1999), Pa. Sch. Librs. Assn. (chmn. profl. std. com. 1980—82, bd. dirs. 1984—87, chmn. profl. std. com. 1991—). Outstanding Contbr. award 1997), Phi Delta Kappa, Beta Phi Mu, Pi Gamma Mu. Democrat. Jewish. Office: Drexel U Coll Info Sci & Tech Philadelphia PA 19104 Office Phone: 215-895-2473. Business E-Mail: jackie.mancall@drexel.edu.

**MANCERO, MARIA CELMIRA,** psychologist; b. Angola Aug. 19, 1971 d. Jose Carlos and Otilia Ferreira Mancebo. BA. Providence Coll., 1993; MA, Conn. Coll., 1997; PhD, Hofstra U., 2002. Lic. Psychologist RI, 2004. Project dir., rsch. psychologist Butler Hosp., Providence, 2001—; instr. Brown Med. Sch., Providence, 2004—. Clin. psychologist, Providence, 2005—; vis. asst. prof. Conn. Coll., New London, 2003—. Recipient Psychiatry Rsch. Mentor award, Brown Med. Sch., 2004—05. Mem.: APA (assoc.), Assn. for the Advancement of Behavior Therapy (assoc.). Office: Butler Hosp 345 Blackstone Blvd Providence RI 02906 Office Phone: 401-455-6216.

**MANCHESTER, KENNETH EDWARD,** electronics executive, consultant; b. Winona, Minn., Mar. 22, 1925; s. Laurence Edwin and Daisy Idel (Finley) M.; m. Bonnie Lee Hardgrave, June 24, 1946; children: Cynthia Lee, David Scott. AB, San Jose State Coll., 1949; MS, Stanford U., 1950, PhD, 1955. Sr. chemist Shell Devel. Co., Emeryville, Calif., 1955-62; head chemistry sect. Sprague Electric Co., North Adams, Mass., 1962-63, head chemistry dept., 1963-69, dir. semiconductor rsch., devel. and engring., 1969-79, dir. quality assurance and reliability Worcester, Mass., 1979-85, v.p. corp. R & D North Adams, 1985-89, Sprague fellow, 1985; cons. semiconductor industry, 1989—. Lectr. Rensselaer Poly. Inst., Troy, N.Y., 1967. Contbr. articles to profl. jours.; patentee in field. Chmn. com. Troop 70 Boy Scouts Am. Sgt. U.S. Army Ground Forces, 1943-46, ETO. Mem. Am. Chem. Soc., AIME, Optimist Club, Sigma Xi. Democrat. Avocations: woodworking, golf. E-mail: kmbucko@netzero.com.

**MANCHESTER, PAUL BRUNSON,** economist; b. Winsted, Conn., Oct. 7, 1942; s. Elbert Grant and Eleanor Elizabeth (Jones) M.; m. Ruth Elaine Garbisch, Oct. 25, 1969; children: Sarah H., Daniel P. BA, Yale U., 1964; PhD, U. Minn., 1973. Vol. Peace Corps, Colombia, 1964-66; teaching assoc. U. Minn., Mpls., 1966-69; prof. Mary Washington Coll., Fredericksburg, Va., 1971-74; cons. U.S. Dept. Treasury, Washington, 1974-75; asst. prof. Cath. U. Am., Washington, 1974-78; cons. Robert R. Nathan Assocs., Washington, 1975-78; economist joint econ. com. U.S. Congress, Washington, 1978-89; econ. adviser to U.S. senator U.S. Senate, Washington, 1988; sr. economist U.S. League Savs. Insts., Washington, 1989-90; economist Office Thrift Supervision, Washington, 1990-91; fin. economist U.S. Dept. HUD, Washington, 1991—. Contbr. articles to profl. jours. Pres. Woodmoor-

Pinecrest Citizens' Assn., Silver Spring, Md.; del. Allied Civic Group, Silver Spring. Mem. Am. Econ. Assn., Soc. Govt. Economists, Nat. Economists Club (v.p. 1985, 87, bd. dirs. 1989-92), Yale Club Washington (bd. dirs., v.p. 2004-2005). Lutheran. Avocations: tennis, skiing, bowling. Home: 105 Lexington Dr Silver Spring MD 20901-2546 Office: US Dept HUD 451 7th St SW Rm 8212 Washington DC 20410-0001

**MANCHESTER, STEVEN HERBERT,** writer, educator; b. Fall River, Mass., Nov. 4, 1967; s. William and Nancy Ann Manchester; children: Isabella Emma children: Evan Steven, Jacob Alexander. AA, Bristol C.C., Fall River, Mass., 1989. Prison investigator Mass. Dept. Corrections, Bridgewater, 1989—98. Writing instr. Southcoast Learning Network, New Bedford, Mass., 2002—03. Author: (novels) The Unexpected Storm - The Gulf War Legacy, At The Stroke of Midnight, Jacob Evans, A Father's Love, 6-5; A Different Shade of Blue, (movie) Gooseberry Island. Vol. lectr. Straight Ahead Ministry, Taunton, Mass., 2000—03. Sgt. U.S. Army, 1990—91, Operation Desert Storm. Decorated SW Asia Svc., Liberation of Kuwait, Nat. Def. citations U.S. Army. Mem.: VFW (assoc.). Avocations: reading, running, travel, weightlifting. Home and Office: 55 Summerfield Ave Somerset MA 02725 Personal E-mail: shmanchester@statestreet.com. E-mail: paula1271@attbi.com.

**MANCHESTER, SUSAN JEAN,** lawyer, artist; b. Oklahoma City, July 15, 1950; d. Frederick J. and Jean (Ball) Hoyt. BA in Art Edn., Okla. State U., 1972; JD, Okla. U., 1980. Bar: Okla. 1980, U.S. Dist. Ct. (we. dist.) Okla. 1981, U.S. Ct. Appeals (10th cir.) 1981, U.S. Dist. Ct. (ea. dist.) Okla. 1987. Profl. artist, Oklahoma City, 1973-80; atty./asst. atty. gen. Okla. Atty. Gen.'s Office, Oklahoma City, 1980-81, dep. chief criminal divsn., 1981-82, chief criminal divsn., 1982-83; assoc. McClelland, Collins, Bailey, Bailey & Manchester, Oklahoma City, 1983-86; ptnr. Miskovsky, Sullivan, Taylor & Manchester, 1987-91, Taylor & Manchester, 1991—2003; pvt. practice Oklahoma City, 2003—. Panel trustee we. dist. Okla. US Bankruptcy Ct., 1994—, bankruptcy trustee U.S. Bankruptcy Ct. (we. dist) Okla., 1994— Named to Outstanding Young Women of Am., 1983-84; invitational artist Okla. Bi-Centennial Showing, 1983. Mem. ABA, Oklahoma County Bar Assn., Okla. Bar Assn., Assn. Trial Lawyers Am., Phi Delta Phi. Office: 1412 N Dewey Oklahoma City OK 73103-2217

**MANCHIN, JOE, III, (JOSEPH MANCHIN III),** governor, former state official; b. Farmington, W. Va., Aug. 24, 1947; s. John and Mary Manchin; m. Gayle Conelly; children: Heather, Joseph IV, Brooke. BS in Bus. and Econs., W.Va. U., 1970. Operator Manchin's Carpet Center, Marion County, W.Va., 1970; mem. W.Va. Ho. of Dels., 1982—86, W.Va. State Senate, 1986—92; sec. of state State of W.Va., Charleston, 2001—05, gov., 2005—. Past chmn. banking and ins. com. W.Va. State Senate, past vice chair fin. com., past chair rule making rev. Democrat. Office: Office of Governor 1900 Kanawha Blvd East Charleston WV 25305 Office Phone: 304-558-8860.*

**MANCINI, ERNEST ANTHONY,** geologist, educator, researcher; b. Reading, Pa., Feb. 27, 1947; s. Ernest and Marian K. (Filbert) M.; m. Marilyn E. Lee, Dec. 27, 1969; children: Lisa L., Lauren N. BS, Albright Coll., 1969; MS, So. Ill. U., 1972; PhD, Tex. A&M U., 1974. Petroleum exploration geologist Cities Svc. Oil Co., Denver, 1974-76; asst. prof. geology U. Ala., Tuscaloosa, 1976-79, assoc. prof., 1979-84, prof., 1984—, Disting. Rsch. prof., 2005—. State geologist, oil and gas supr. State Ala., Tuscaloosa, 1982-96; regional dir. Ea. Gulf Region of the Petroleum Tech. Transfer Coun., 1995—; founding dir. Ctr. Sedimentary Basin Studies, U. Ala., 1998—. Contbr. articles to profl. jours. Geol. Soc. Am. fellow; recipient Nat. Coun. Citation Albright Coll., 1983, Pratt-Haas Disting. Lectr. Am. Assn. Petroleum Geologists, 1987-88. Mem. Geol. Soc. Am. (past chmn. S.E. sect.), Am. Assn. Petroleum Geologists (A.I. Levorsen petroleum geology Meml. award Gulf Coast Assn., geol. socs. sect. 1980, chair rsch. com. 2001-04, assoc. editor, 2003-04, editor, 2004—, Disting. Educator award 2000), Assn. State Geologists (hon., past pres.), Am. Geol. Inst. (pres., Ian Campbell medal 2004), Nat. Assn. State Univs. and Land-Grant Colls. (past chair, mineral and energy resources sect. mem. bd. natural resources), Soc. Econ. Paleontologists and Mineralogists Gulf Coast sect. (hon., past pres.), Paleontol. Soc. (past pres. southeast sect.), Ala. Geol. Soc. (past pres.), Gulf Coast Assn. Geol. Scis. (hon., Outstanding Educator award 1998), Sigma Xi (past chpt. pres.), Phi Kappa Phi (past chpt. pres.), Phi Sigma. Presbyterian. Home: 15271 Four Winds Loop Northport AL 35475-3325 Office: U Ala Dept Geol Scis PO Box 870338 Tuscaloosa AL 35487-0338 Business E-mail: emancini@geo.ua.edu.

**MANCINI, JOHN,** editor, publishing executive; b. NYC; m. Laura Litterello; 2 children. BA in Comm. Arts, LI Univ-C.W. Post. Reporter Greenwich Time, 1982—83; copy editor Stamford Advocate, Conn., 1983—85; presentation editor NY Times, 1995; dep. met. editor NY Post, 1995—96, met. editor, 1999—2001; founding editor-in-chief LI Voice, 1996—99; editorial asst. Newsday, 1980—82, copy editor, graphics editor, Sunday news editor, night city editor, day city editor, NY edition, 1985—95, met. editor, 2001—03, asst. mng. editor/NY, 2003—04, exec. v.p., editor, 2004—. Office: Newsday 235 Pinelawn Rd Melville NY 11747-4250 Office Phone: 631-843-4177. Office Fax: 631-843-4719. Business E-Mail: john.mancini@newsday.com.*

**MANCINI, RICHARD ALAN,** music educator; s. John Desmond and Ruth Ardelle Mancini; m. Denise Michelle Sager, June 26, 1999. BA in Edn., Ctrl. Wash. U., MusM. Educator Naselle (Wash.) Sch. Dist., 1985—2001, Camas (Wash.) Sch. Dist., 2001—. Min. music, worship leader Camas (Wash.) Assembly Dog, 2001—02; min. music, dir. choir Calvary Cmty. Ch., Longview, Wash., 1985—98. Named Citizen of Yr., Pacific County D.A.R.E. Officers, 1995. Avocations: travel, model building, disney, exercise. Office: Camas High School 26900 SE 15th St Camas WA 98607 Office Phone: 360-817-4441.

**MANCINO, DOUGLAS MICHAEL,** lawyer; b. May 8, 1949; s. Paul and Adele (Brazaitis) M.; m. Carol Keith, June 16, 1973. BA, Kent State U., 1971; JD, Ohio State U., 1974. Bar: Ohio 1974, U.S. Tax Ct. 1977, Calif. 1981, D.C. 1981. Assoc. Baker & Hostetler, Cleve., 1974-80; ptnr. Memel & Ellsworth, L.A., 1980-87, McDermott, Will & Emery, L.A., 1987—. Bd. dirs. Health Net of Calif. Inc. Author: Taxation of Hospitals and Health Care Organizations, 2000, (with others) Hospital Survival Guide, 1984, Navigating the Federal Physician Self-Referral Law, 1998; (with F. Hill) Taxation of Exempt Organizations, 2002; co-author quar. tax column Am. Hosp. Assn. publ. Health Law Vigil, (with L. Burns) Joint Ventures Between Hosps. and Physicians, 1987; contbr. articles to profl. jours. Chmn. bd. dirs. The Children's Burn Found.; bd. dirs. Kent State U. Found., Inc. Mem. ABA (tax, bus., real property, probate and trust sects., chair exempt orgns. com. 1995-97, coun. dir. 1999—), Calif. State Bar Assn. (tax, bus. law sects.), Ohio Bar Assn., Calif. State Bar, D.C. Bar Assn., Am. Health Lawyers Assn. (bd. dirs. 1986-95, pres. 1993-94), Calif. Soc. for Healthcare Attys., Bel Air Country Club, The Regency Club, Calif. Yacht Club. Office: McDermott Will & Emery 2049 Century Park E Fl 34 Los Angeles CA 90067-3101 E-mail: dmancino@mwe.com.

**MANCINO, JOHN GREGORY,** software company executive; b. N.Y.C., Nov. 14, 1946; s. John D. and Carmela A. Mancino. BA, Colgate U., 1968. Chief appraiser Rusciano Appraisers & Cons., N.Y.C., 1968-70; v.p. Pisces Prodns., Boulder, Colo., 1971-73; v.p. ops. Celestial Seasonings, Inc., Boulder, Colo., 1973-84, also dir.; dir. Strategic Info. Group, 1994—; founder, owner DeviceWorks Co., 2002—. Bd. dirs. Computer Connection, Inc., Mr. Software, Inc., Spruce St. Mktg., Inc., Fortune 44 Co., Inc.; pres., bd. dirs. Decision Makers Software, 1984—; chmn. Generation 5 Tech., 1985-89, Preferred Bus. Investments, Ltd., 1986-90; founder, dir. DeviceWorks Co., 2002—. Author: (software) Tattletale, 1991. Office: 214 Mountain Meadows Rd Boulder CO 80302-9256 E-mail: jmancino@decismkr.com.

**MANCOFF, NEAL ALAN,** lawyer; b. Chgo., May 7, 1939; s. Isadore and Sarah (Leviton) M.; m. Alys Belofsky, June 26, 1966; children: Wesley, Frederick, Daniel. BBA, U. Wis., 1961; JD, Northwestern U., 1965. Bar: Ill. 1965, U.S. Dist. Ct. (no. dist.) Ill. 1965. Assoc. Aaron Aaron Schimberg & Hess, Chgo., 1965-72, ptnr., 1972-80. Schiff Hardin & Waite, Chgo., 1980—. Author: Qualified Deferred Compensation Plans, 1983, Nonqualified Deferred Compensation Agreements, 1987. Lst lt. U.S. Army, 1961-62. Mem. Chgo. Bar Assn. (chmn. employee benefits com. 1984). Office: Schiff Hardin LLC 7500 Sears Tower Chicago IL 60606

**MANCUSI, ROBERTO FRANCESCO COSTANTINO,** vocalist, educator; b. Kenosha, Wis., Aug. 15, 1971; s. Robert Arnold Emory Tapley and Diane Jean Broughton; m. Staci Lyn Peiffer, July 27, 1996; children: Daniel Richard children: Matthew Robert. MusB in Performance, Simpson Coll., Indianola, Iowa, 1994; MusM in Performance, U. Mo., Kansas City, 1998, DMA in Performance, 2004. Dir. music Franksville United Meth. Ch., Franksville, Wis., 1998—99; adj. voice faculty Baker U., Baldwin City, Kans., 2001—04; asst. prof. Ea. N.Mex. U., 2004—. Treas., bd. dirs. Opera Kadopera, Raytown, Mo., 2002—04, set designer/builder, 2002. Singer: (opera) Amahl and the Night Visitors, Magic Flute, Cosi fan tutte, Manon, Ariadne auf Naxos. Friends of the Conservatory Music scholar, U. Mo. Conservatory of Music, 2001—02. Mem.: Nat. Assn. Tchrs. of Singing, Lambda Chi Alpha (risk mgr. 1992—93, v.p. 1993—94). Avocations: videophile, magic, walking. Home: 710 W 16th Ln Portales NM 88130-7220 Personal E-mail: rmancusi1@yahoo.com

**MANCUSI-UNGARO, CAROL,** conservator, educator; BA, Conn. Coll.; MA in history of art and conservation, NYU Inst. Fine Arts. Chief conservator The Menil Collection, Houston, 1983—2001; founding dir. Ctr. for Tech. Study of Modern Art Harvard U. Museums, Cambridge, Mass., 2001—; dir. conservation Whitney Mus. Am. Art, NYC, 2001—; sr. lectr. in history of art and conservation Harvard U., Cambridge, Mass. Recipient Coll. Art Assn./Heritage Preservation Award for Distinction in Scholarship and Conservation, 2004. Office: Harvard U Art Museums 32 Quincy Ave Cambridge MA 02138

**MANCUSO, JOHN HENRY,** retired lawyer, bank executive; b. Utica, N.Y., June 5, 1944; arrived in U.S., 1987; s. Sam A. and Frances H. (Nelson) M.; m. Etel Tumma, July 18, 1970; children: Christa E., John A. BA in English magna cum laude, Boston Coll., 1968; MA in English, Lehigh U., 1970; MS in Higher Edn. Adminstrn., Syracuse U., 1973, PhD in Higher Edn. Adminstrn., 1978, JD, 1975. Bar: (NY) 1999. Assoc. Hiscock & Barclay, Syracuse, 1976-80, ptnr., 1981-90; gen. counsel Key Bank of N.Y., Albany, 1992-94; sr. v.p., dep. gen. counsel KeyCorp, Cleve. and Albany, NY, 1990—2001, exec. v.p., gen. counsel, 2001—03; gen. counsel, sec. Key Bank Nat. Assn., Cleve., 1994—2003, vice chmn., 2001—03. Mem. U.S. Senate Banking Com. Task Force on Fin. Modernization Bill, 1998; adj. prof. law Syracuse U., 1976-87, tchr. higher edn. adminstrn. grad. sch.; English tchr. at various colls., secondary schs., 1968-73; spkr. in field; bd. dirs. Key Bank Nat. Assn., Key Corporate Capital Inc., KeyCorp Ins. Co. Ltd. Author: Home Equity Update: A Manual for Lenders and Lawyers, 1989; co-author: Compliance Examinations Update for Financial Institutions, 1985-2001, The Law of Truth in Lending: 1989, Supplement, Reporting to Bank Regulators: Requirements and Forms Manual, 1990, Bank Regulatory Update: Beyond Consumer Issues, 1995-97; contbr. numerous articles to profl. publs. Chmn. planning bd. Village of Manlius, N.Y., 1983-86; trustee Cleve. Hearing and Speech Ctr., 2000-03; bd. dirs. St. Mary's Sem., Cleve., 2003-05. Mem. Am. Bankers Assn. (bank counsel com. 1996-98), Am. Coll. Consumer Fin. Svcs. Lawyers (founding mem., 2001), N.Y. State Bar Assn. (chair bus. law sect. 1994-95, chmn. consumer fin. svcs. com. bus. law sect. 1988-91, chmn subcom. on equal credit opportunity/truth-in-lending 1985-86, chmn. subcom. on credit cards/fair credit billing 1982-83), N.Y. State Bankers Assn. (mem. lawyers retail legis. com. 1992-94, ops. and payments sys. com. 1988-90, legal advisor to residential mortgage com. of consumer banking divsn. 1986-87, mem. lawyers adv. com. 1994-2003), Consumer Bankers Assn. (mem. ad hoc com. on bank investment products 1993-97, mem. lawyers com. 1987-97), Justinian Soc., Order of Coif. Republican. Avocations: skiing, golf, tennis, reading, chess. Home (Summer): 3908 Forest Glen Blvd #202 Naples FL 34114 Home: 3908 Forest Glen Blvd Apt 202 Naples FL 34114-3584 E-mail: johnmanc@comcast.net.

**MANCUSO, JOSEPH EDWARD,** medical psychotherapist; b. Rockford, Ill., Dec. 1, 1955; s. Robert and Anne Mancuso. Student, Bradley U., Peoria, Ill., 1974-76; BA in Psychology, Marquette U., 1984, MEd in Ednl. Psychology, 1987. Diplomate Am. Bd. Med. Psychotherapists; LCSW, Wis.; lic. profl. counselor, alcohol and drug abuse counselor, Wis.; cert. trauma responder and trauma specialist. Child care worker Community Care Svcs. Inc., Milw., 1978—79; day care dir. Mich. Street Day Care, Milw., 1979—80; adminstrv. unit clk. Milw. Jewish Nursing Home, 1980—81; day care tchr. St. Mary's Children's Sch., Milw., 1983—84; psychotherapist Wis. Correctional Svcs., Milw., 1984—90; coord. alcohol and other drug abuse St. Mary's Psychiat. Hosp., Milw., 1990-92; pvt. practice Lighthouse Clinic, Milw., 1993—2004; emergency rm. social worker Sinai Samaritan Med. Ctr., Milw., 1994-99; intake psychotherapist psychiat. svcs. Behav. Health Intake Ctr.-Sinai Samaritan Med. Ctr., Milw., 1999-2000; childrens psychotherapist Sinai Samaritan Med. Ctr., Milw., 2000—02, adult psychotherapist, 2002—03, geriatric psychotherapist, 2003; program psychotherapist Aurora Psychiat. Hosp., Wauwatosa, Wis., 2003. Cons., presenter in field. Cartoonist, published and shown in galleries throughout Milw. Mem. APA, Wis. Psychol. Assn. (assoc.), Am. Ment. Rsch. Assn., Assn. Traumatic Stress Specialists. Avocations: hiking, drawing, painting, birdwatching. Home: 1612 E Hartford Ave Milwaukee WI 53211-3036 Office: Aurora Psychiat Hosp 1220 Dewey Ave Wauwatosa WI 53213 Office Phone: 414-454-6695.

**MANCUSO, JULIA,** skier, Olympic athlete; b. Reno, Nev., Mar. 9, 1984; d. Ciro and Andrea Mancuso. Mem. U.S. Winter Olympics Team, 2006; designer Super Jules Underwear. Mem.: U.S. Ski Team. Achievements include Am. record for medals and gold medals, Jr. World Championships Downhill Skiing; bronze medal in Super-G and Giant Slalom, World Championships, 2005; gold medal in Giant Slalom, Olympic Winter Games, Torino, 2006. Avocations: surfing, water-skiing, mountain biking, kiteboarding. Office: US Ski and Snowboard Assn 1500 Kearns Blvd Park City UT 84060*

**MANCUSO, MICHAEL JOHN,** retired corporate financial executive; Grad., Villanova U.; MBA, Ea. Coll. Exec. in fin. mgmt. space systems divsn. GE; CFO land systems divsn. Gen. Dynamics, Falls Church, Va., 1993-94, v.p., comtr., 1994-97, sr. v.p., CFO, 1997—2006. Bd. dir. SPX Corp., 2005—, Agere Systems Inc., 2006—, Shaw Group Inc., 2006—. Mailing: SPX Corp Bd Directors 13515 Ballantyne Corp Pl Charlotte NC 28277*

**MANCUSO, MONICA LAUGHLIN,** educational administrator; d. Earl Francis and Mary Catherine Asping Laughlin; m. Bart Louis Mancuso, Aug. 17, 1974; children: Frances Mancuso Chauvin, DDS, Mary Mancuso White, Andrew Vincent, Luke Everett. BS, La. State U., Baton Rouge, 1975; BA, U. La. at Lafayette, 1982; Med, Nicholls State U., Thibodaux, Louisiana, 1989; PhD, La. State U., Baton Rouge, 2004. Tchr. La. State Bd. Edn., 1983, Elem. Sch. Prin. La. State Bd. Edn., 1995, Parish or City Supr. of Instrn. La. State Bd. Edn., 1995, Prin. La. State Bd. Edn., 1996. Tchr. Diocese of Houma-Thibodaux, Morgan City, La., 1975—80, St. Mary Parish Sch. Bd., Centerville, 1983—86, 1987—91, sch. prin., 1991—2001, supr. of instrn., 2001—. Mem. adv. bd. La. Tech. Coll., Young Meml. Campus, Morgan City, La., 2003—. Recipient St. Mary Parish Tchr. of Yr. award, St. Mary Parish Sch. Bd., 1991, Outstanding Earth Sci. Tchr. award, Nat. Assn. Geology Tchrs., 1991, grant, La. Urban Forestry Coun., 1996—97, St. Mary Parish Prin. of Yr. award, St. Mary Parish Sch. Bd., 1997. Mem.: Am Sch. Prin. Assn. (bd. mem.; mem. Ther 1721 Dale St Morgan City LA 70380 Office: St Mary Parish Sch Bd PO Box 170 Centerville LA 70522 Office Phone: 337-836-9661. Personal E-mail: mmancuso@atvci.net. E-mail: mmancuso@stmary.k12.la.us.

**MANCUSO, PETER,** medical educator; b. Somerville, NJ, July 15, 1962; s. Joseph and Anita Mancuso; m. Alison Maud Hightower, Sept. 17, 1987; children: Jonathan Hightower, Christopher Hightower, Amanda Catherine. BS, Purdue U., West Lafayette, Ind., 1985; MS, U. Tenn., Knoxville, 1987, PhD, 1996. Food scientist Ragu Foods, Shelton, Conn., 1987—90, rsch. food scientist, 1990; grad. student rsch. and tchg. asst. U. Tenn., Knoxville, 1990—96; postdoctoral rsch. fellow U. Mich. Med. Ctr., Ann Arbor, 1997—99; asst. prof. U. Mich., Ann Arbor, 2000—. Rsch. asst., U. Tenn. Grad. Sch. Medicine, 1994—96, grantee, NIH, 1997—98, rsch. fellow, Am. Lung Assn. of Mich., 1999—2000, rsch. grantee, Am. Lung Assn., 2001—03, NIH-Heart, Lung, and Blood Inst., 2006—. Mem.: Am. Assn. of Immunologists (assoc.), Am. Thoracic Soc. (assoc.). Lutheran. Achievements include research in role of leptin in pulmonary innate host defense. Avocation: cycling. Office: U of Mich 1420 Washington Hts Ann Arbor MI 48109-2029 Office Phone: 734-615-5158.

**MAND, MARTIN GARY,** financial executive; b. Norfolk, Va., Sept. 26, 1936; s. Meyer J. and Lena (Sutton) M.; m. Shelly Cohen, Aug. 29, 1965; children: Gregory S., Michael E., Brian C. BS in Commerce, U. Va., 1958; MBA, U. Del., 1964. Various fin. staff and mgmt. positions E.I. du Pont de Nemours & Co., Wilmington, Del., 1961-81, v.p. taxes and fin. svcs., 1981-84, v.p., comptr., 1984-88, v.p., treas., 1989-90; sr. v.p., CFO, Nortel Networks, Mississauga, Ont., Canada, 1990—93, exec. v.p., CFO, 1993—94; chmn. pres., CEO Mand Assocs., Ltd., Wilmington, 1995—. Bd. dirs. Mizuho Corp Bank U.S.A., N.Y.C., Townsends, Inc., Wilmington, Del., Factory Card and Party Outlet, Naperville, Ill.; pres. Fin. Execs. Rsch. Found., 1988—90. Co-author: (book) Partnering for Performance: Unleashing the Power of Finance in the 21st Century Organization, 2000. Lt. USN, 1958-61. Mem. Fin. Execs. Inst., Am. Mgmt. Assn. (chmn. fin. coun.). Office: 618 Berwick Rd Ste 100 Wilmington DE 19803-2204 Office Phone: 302-478-5644. Personal E-mail: mandassociates@comcast.net.

**MANDAL, PRABIR KUMAR,** biologist, educator; s. Paresh Chandra and Arati Mandal; m. Anita Choudhury, Jan. 29, 1988; 1 child, Sunny. BSc in zoology with honors, U. N.Bengal, India, 1978—81, MSc in Cytogenetics, 1981—84; PhD, Bhopal U., India, 1990—93. Rsch. scientist U. Hawaii, Honolulu, 1998—2003; vis. asst. prof. U. N.Fla., Jacksonville, Fla., 2003—. Grantee Fla. Sea Grant Seminar grant award, U. Fla., 2005—06. Office: Univ N Fla 4567 St Johns Bluff Rd S Jacksonville FL 32224

**MANDARICH, DAVID D.,** real estate corporation executive; b. 1948; With Majestic Savs. and Loan, 1966-67, MDC Holdings Inc., Denver, 1977—, bd. dir., 1980—89, 1994—, chmn. Richmond Am. Homes, 1990—93, exec. v.p. real estate, 1993—94, co-COO, 1994—96, COO, pres., 1999—. Office: MDC Holdings 4350 S Monaco St Denver CO 80237*

**MANDEL, ADRIENNE ABRAMSON,** state legislator; b. Irvington, N.J., Sept. 30, 1936; d. Nathaniel and Florence (Lebovitz) Abramson; m. Emanuel Mandel, 1958; children: Lisa Mandel-Trupp, David. BA, Rutgers U., 1958; MA, George Washington U., 1984. Exec. program cert.: Harvard U., JF Kennedy Sch. Govt. 2003. Chairwoman, vice chairwoman Precinct 13-56, 1979-94; parole officer, social svc. case worker N.J. Dept. Inst. & Agencies, 1958-60; survey interviewer U.S. Census Bur., 1973-77; monitoring and evaluation specialist Divsn. Labor Svc., Montgomery County Govt., 1979-81; asst. dir. Sr. Ctr. Divsn. Elder Affairs, Dept. Family Resources, 1981-84; staff asst. Office Chief Adminstr., 1984-85; legis. rep. Office Intergovt. Rels., 1985-94; mem. Md. State Legislature, 1995—, mem. commerce govt. matters com., 1995—2002, mem. health and govt. ops., 2003—, dep. majority whip, 2003—. Pres. Women's Caucus, 2002-03; bi-county chair Montgomery County Del., 1998—; health issues chair Nat. Order Women Legislators, 1999—; mem. exec. bd. Nat. Found. Women Legislators, 2004—. Named one of Md. Top 100 Women, The Daily Record, 2002, 2004; recipient Woman of Valor award, B'nai B'rith Women, 1972, MD Profl. Driver Educators Legis. of Year, 1998, MD League Conservation Voters Environ. Leadership award, Nat. Capitol Homecare Assn. Pres. award, 2001, MD Nurses Assn. Legislator of Yr., 2002, Montgomery County NOW Legislator of Yr., 2003, Significant Contribution to Med. Cmty. award, Montgomery County Med. Soc., 2005. Mem. Women's Polit. Caucus, Mothers Against Drunk Driving, Md. Govt. Rels. Assn., Montgomery County Ethnic Heritage Festival, LWV, Alpha Psi Omega, Delta Phi Delta.

**MANDEL, BABALOO,** scriptwriter; b. NYC; 6 children. Screenwriter: (with Lowell Ganz) Night Shift, 1982, (with Bruce Jay Friedman) Splash, 1984 (Academy award nomination best original screenplay 1984), (with Dan Aykroyd) Spies Like Us, 1985, Vibes, 1988, Parenthood, 1989, City Slickers, 1991, A League of Their Own, 1992, (with Billy Crystal) Mr. Saturday Night, 1992, Greedy, 1994, City Slickers II: The Legend of Curley's Gold, 1994, (with Billy Crystal) Forget Paris, 1995, Multiplicity, 1996, Father's Day, 1997, Edtv, 1999, Where the Heart Is, 2000, Robots, 2005, Fever Pitch, 2005; writer: (TV series) Happy Days, 1974-84, Laverne and Shirley, 1976-83, Herndon, 1983; writer, assoc. prodr.: Gung Ho, 1986; creator (TV series) Knight and Daye, 1989; appearances include (film) Splash, 1984, (TV) Naked Hollywood, 1991. Office: Creative Artists Agy 9830 Wilshire Blvd Beverly Hills CA 90212-1804

**MANDEL, CAROL,** librarian; b. Bklyn., Dec. 18, 1946; d. Irwin Daniel and Charlotte Mandel; m. Vincent T. Covello. BA magna cum laude, U. Mass., 1968; MSLS with honors, Columbia U., 1970, MA in Art History, 1975. Reference libr. Northeastern U. Libr., Boston, 1970; architecture and fine arts cataloger Columbia U. Librs., NYC, 1971-75, asst. to head original monographs cataloging dept., 1975-77, head original monographs cataloging dept., 1977-79, dir. tech. svcs., 1986-91, dir. tech. and networked info. svcs., 1991-93, dep. univ. libr., 1993—99; assoc. exec. dir. Assn. Rsch. Librs., Washington, 1979-83; asst. assoc. univ. libr. assess svcs. U. Calif., San Diego Librs., 1983-86; dean libr. NYU, 1999—. Mem. coop. cataloging coun. Libr. Congress, 1993-95, mem. seminar on copy cataloging, 1992, cons., 1985; reviewer, panelist, site visitor NEH, 1978-94; panelist NEA Title II-C grant program Dept. Edn., 1982, 84, 86, 89; mem. pres.'s commn. on tech. processing Rsch. Librs. Group, 1991, mem. bibtech steering com., 1988-90; presenter in field. Contbr. articles to profl. publs. Grantee NEH, 1989-83, 83-86, 89-93, 93—, Dept. Edn., 1989-95. Mem. ALA (vice chair tech. svcs. dirs. of large rsch. librs. discussion group 1992, editorial bd. 1993—, chair various coms., Margaret Mann citation for outstanding profl. achievement in cataloging or classification 1994), Assn. Rsch. Librs. (cons. 1983-86, project dir. microform project, CONSER A&I coverage project), Coun. on Libr. Resources (chair bibliographic svcs. study com. 1987-93, cons.), Ctr. for Rsch. Librs. (mem. acad. adv. panel 1992—). Office: Columbua U Librs 535 W 114th St New York NY 10027-7035 also: Bost Libr Rm 1134 NYU 70 Washington Sq S New York NY 10012 Office Phone: 212-998-2444. Office Fax: 212-995-4070. E-mail: carol.mandel@nyu.edu.*

**MANDEL, HAROLD GEORGE,** pharmacologist, educator; b. Berlin, June 6, 1924; came to U.S., 1937, naturalized, 1944; s. Ernest A. and Else (Crail) M.; m. Marianne Klein, July 25, 1953; children: Marcia Mandel Halgren, Audrey Lynn Todd. BS, Yale U., 1944, PhD, 1949. Lab. instr. in chemistry Yale U., 1942-44, 47-49; rsch. assoc. prof. pharmacology George Washington U. Sch. Medicine and Health Scis., 1949-50, asst. rsch. prof., 1950-52, assoc. prof. pharmacology, 1952-58, prof., 1958—, chmn. dept. pharmacology, 1960-96. Advanced Commonwealth Fund fellow Molteno Inst. Cambridge (Eng.) U., 1956; Commonwealth Fund fellow U. Auckland (N.Z.) and U. Med. Scis., Bangkok, Thailand, 1964; Am. Cancer Soc. Eleanor Roosevelt Internat. fellow Chester Beatty Research Inst. London, 1970-71; Am. Cancer Soc. scholar U. Calif., San Francisco, 1978-79; fellow Med. Research Council toxicology unit, Carshalton, Eng., 1986; Burroughs Wellcome Rsch. travel grant, Carshalton, 1988; hon. rsch. fellow dept. biochemistry and molecular biology U. Coll., London, 1993, 96, 97; mem. com. problems drug safety NRC-NAS, 1965-76, mem. com. on toxicology, 1978-82, mem. various panels, 1981-86; mem. cancer chemotherapy com. Internat. Union Against Cancer, 1966-73, fellow, Lyon, France, 1989; mem. external rev. com. Howard U. Cancer Research Center, 1972-74; cons. Bur. Drugs, FDA,

1975-79, EPA, 1978-82; mem. toxicology adv. com. FDA, 1975-78; mem. med. research service merit rev. bd. in alcoholism and drug dependence VA, 1975-78; mem. cancer spl. program adv. com. Nat. Cancer Inst., 1974-78, chmn., 1976-78; mem. Nat. Large Bowel Cancer Project Working Cadre, 1980-84; mem. Kettering award selection com. GM Cancer Rsch. Found., 1979-81; bd. advisors Roswell Park Cancer Inst., Buffalo, 1972-74. Editorial bd.: Jour. Pharmacology and Exptl. Therapeutics, 1960-65, field editor, 1978-94; editorial bd.: Molecular Pharmacology, 1965-69, Rsch. Comm. in Chem. Pathology, Pharmacology, 1972-98, Cancer Drug Delivery, Selective Cancer Therapeutics, 1983-92, Cancer Research, 1974-76, assoc. editor, 1977-81. Served with AUS, 1944-46. Recipient John J. Abel award in pharmacology Eli Lilly and Co., 1958, Disting. Achievement award Washington Acad. Scis., 1958, Golden Apple Teaching award AMA, 1969, 85, 97, Sci. Emeritus award Soc. Biology & Medicine, 1999. Mem. AAAS, Am. Chem. Soc., Am. Soc. Biochemistry and Molecular Biology, Am. Soc. Pharmacology and Exptl. Therapeutics (pres. 1973-74), Am. Assn. Cancer rsch., Assn. Med. Sch. Pharmacology (pres. 1976-78), Nat. Caucus of Basic Biomed. Sci. Chairs (chmn. 1991—), Citizens Pub. Rsch. and Edn. Funding (sec. 1996-99), Cosmos Club (Washington), Sigma Xi, Alpha Omega Alpha. Democrat. Achievements include research, numerous publs. on cancer chemotherapy, mechanism of growth inhibition, antimetabolites, drug disposition, chemical carcinogenesis. Home: Apt 302 4956 Sentinel Dr Bethesda MD 20816-3594 Office: George Washington U Sch Medicine and Health Scis Dept Pharmacology and Physiology 2300 I St NW Washington DC 20037-2336 Office Phone: 202-994-3542. Business E-Mail: phmhgm@gwumc.edu. E-mail: hgmandel@verizon.net.

**MANDEL, HERBERT MAURICE,** civil engineer; b. Port Chester, N.Y., May 11, 1924; s. Arthur William and Rose (Schmeiser) M.; m. Charlotte Feldman, Aug. 22, 1954; children: Rosanne Mandel Levine, Elliott D., Arthur M. BSCE, Va. Poly. Inst., 1948; M Engring., Yale U., 1949. Registered profl. engr., N.Y., Conn., Fla., Md., Mich., Minn., Ohio, Pa., Va., W.Va. Structural engr. Madigan Hyland Co., L.I., N.Y., 1949-50; v.p. GAI Cons., Inc., Monroeville, Pa., 1986—2004, prin. staff cons., 1993—2004, sr. staff cons., 2004—. Resident engr., Chgo., 1961, Atlanta, 1962, project. mgr., N.Y.C., 1963-70, Honolulu, 1970-74, v.p., N.Y., 1974, sr. v.p., Pitts., 1977-86; mem. faculty Yale U., 1948-49; adj. faculty Bklyn. Poly. Inst., 1956-64, U. Pitts., 1986; gen. chmn. 6th Internat. Bridge Conf., Pitts., 1989. Prin. works include (prin.-in-charge) Williamstown-Marietta Bridge, W.Va.-Ohio, Dunbar Bridge, W.Va., I-64 Bridge over Big Sandy River, W.Va.-Ky., Davis Creek Bridge, Charleston, W.Va., Tygart R. Bridge, W.Va., Easley Bridge, Bluefield, W.Va., Fayette Sta. Bridge, Fayetteville, W.Va., Mon Valley Expwy., W.Va., King Coal Hwy, W.Va., Romney Bridge, W.Va., (project mgr.) Newport Bridge, Narragansett Bay, R.I., (designer/project engr.) Hackensack River Bridge, N.J., Housatonic River Bridge, Conn., Arthur Kill Vertical Lift R.R. Bridge, S.I., N.Y., 62d St. Bridge, Pitts., Savannah River Cantilever Bridge, Ga., I-84 Bridges, Danbury, Conn., (structural rehab. designer) Avondale Bridge, N.J, Lincoln Bridge, N.J., B&O R.R. Bridge, Vincennes, Ind., Hawk St. Viaduct, Albany, N.Y., Congress Ave. Bridge, Austin, Tex., Ohio St. Bridge, Buffalo, Panhandle Bridge, Pitts.; project dir. design and constrn. Pitts. Light Rail Transit Sys., 1977-84; designer Elizabeth R. Tunnel, Norfolk, Va., 1950. Served to 1st lt. U.S. Army, 1943-46, 50-52, ETO. Fellow ASCE, Soc. Am. Mil. Engrs.; mem. NSPE, Engrs. Soc. We. Pa. (exec. com. Internat. Bridge Conf. 1986—), gen. chmn. 1988-89), Am. Rlwy. Engring. and Maintenance of Way Assn. (steel structures specifications com. 1974—), Profl. Engrs. in Pvt. Practice (bd. govs. 1994-96, profl. devel. com. 1995-97), Pa. Profl. Engrs. in Pvt. Practice (state vice-chmn. 1992-94, chmn. 1994-96), Pa. Soc. Profl. Engrs. (dir. Pitts. chpt. 1995-98), Internat. Assn. Bridge and Structural Engring., Assn. for Bridge Constrn. and Design, Engrs. Club Pitts., Tau Beta Pi, Chi Epsilon, Omicron Delta Kappa, Phi Kappa Phi, Pi Delta Epsilon, Scabbard and Blade. Jewish. Home: 920 Parkview Dr Pittsburgh PA 15243-1116 Office: GAI Cons Inc 385 Waterfront Dr E Homestead PA 15120-5005 Business E-Mail: h.mandel@gaiconsultants.com.

**MANDEL, HOWIE,** actor, comedian; b. Toronto, Ont., Can., Nov. 29, 1955; m. Terry Mandel, Mar. 1980; children: Jacklyn Perry, Riley, Alex. Actor: (films) Gas, 1981, The Funny Farm, 1983, (voice) Gremlins, 1984, A Fine Mess, 1986, Walk Like a Man, 1987, Little Monsters, 1989, (voice) Gremlins 2: The New Batch, 1990, Magic Kid II, 1994, Spin Cycle, 2000, Tribulation, 2000, (voice) The Tangerine Bear, 2000, Hansel & Gretel, 2002, (voice) Pinocchio 3000, 2004, (TV series) Laugh Trax, 1982, (voice) Muppet Babies, 1984-91, St. Elsewhere, 1983, 85, 88, Good Grief, 1990-91, The Amazing Live Sea-Monkeys, 1992; exec. prodr.) Howie Mandel on Ice, 1997, The Legend of Willie Brown, 1998, The Howie Mandel Show, 1998, Hidden Howie, 2005—; host: Howie Mandel's Sunny Skies, 1995, Deal or No Deal, 2005—; comedian various nightclubs and venues; opening act for Diana Ross, Las Vegas. Office: c/o 3 Arts Entertainment 9460 Wilshire Blvd 7th Fl Beverly Hills CA 90212*

**MANDEL, IRWIN DANIEL,** dentist; b. Bklyn., Apr. 9, 1922; s. Samuel A. and Shirley (Blankstein) M.; m. Charlotte Lifschutz, Apr. 1, 1944; children: Carol, Nora, Richard. BS, CCNY, 1942; DDS, Columbia U., 1945; DSc (hon.), U. Medicine and Dentistry N.J., 1981, U. Göteborg, 1984, Columbia U., 1996. Rsch. asst. Dental Sch. Columbia U., 1946-48, mem. faculty Dental Sch., 1946—, prof. dentistry, dir. div. preventive dentistry Dental Sch., 1969-84, dir. Ctr. Clin. Rsch. in Dentistry Dental Sch., 1984-91, assoc. dean rsch., 1991-92; prof. emeritus Dental Sch., 1992—; pvt. practice dentistry, 1946-68; vis. prof. various dental schs.; chmn. oral biology and medicine study sect. Nat. Inst. Dental Rsch., 1974-76. Co-author: The Plaque Diseases, 1972; contbr. over 250 articles to profl. jours., chpts. to books. Active local chpt. Peace Action, Physicians for Social Responsibility. Lt. Dental Corps USNR, 1945-46, 52-54. Recipient Career Scientist award, N.Y.C. Health Rsch. Coun. 1969—72. Leadership award in periodontology Tufts U. Dental Sch., 1971, Internat. award, U. Conn. Sch. Dental Medicine, 1979, Seymour J. Kreshover NIDR Lectr. award, 1986, Townsend Harris medal, CCNY, 2000. Fellow AAAS, Am. Coll. Dentists; mem. ADA (chmn. coun. dental rsch. 1978-80, Gold medal for excellence in rsch. 1985), Dental Soc. (Henry Spenadel award 1973, Jarvie-Burkhart Internat. award 1990), Am. Assn. Dental Rsch. (pres. 1980), Am. Assn. Pub. Health Dentists (Disting. Svc. award 1991), Fed. Dentair Internat. (W. D. Miller prize 1992), Internat. Assn. Dental Rsch. (Salivary Rsch. award 1994, Disting. Svc. award 2001), N.Y. Acad. Scis., Sigma Xi, Omicron Kappa Upsilon. Home: 1305 Holly Ln Cedar Grove NJ 07009 Office: 630 W 168th St New York NY 10032-3702 Personal E-mail: irwinmandel@optonline.net.

**MANDEL, JACK N.,** manufacturing executive; b. Austria, July 16, 1911; s. Sam and Rose M.; m. Lilyan, Aug. 14, 1938 (dec.) Student, Fenn Coll., 1930-33. Founder, former pres., chmn. Premier Indsl. Corp., Cleve.; chmn., pres. Manbro Corp.; exec. dir. Parkwood Corp.; gen. ptnr. Courtland Assocs. Former mem. exec. com. NCCJ; former life trustee Wood Hosp.; trustee Fla. Soc. for Blind; life trustee South Broward Jewish Fedn., Cleve. Jewish Welfare Fedn.; former pres., life trustee Montefiore Home for Aged; pres. adv. bd. Barry U.; hon. trustee Hebrew U.; trustee Tel Aviv U. Mus. of the Diaspora; life trustee The Temple, Woodruff Found.; trustee Cleve. Play House. Mem. Beachmont Country Club, Commede Club, Union Club. Office: Parkwood Corp 2829 Euclid Ave Cleveland OH 44115-2413

**MANDEL, JOEL EMANUEL,** orthopedist; b. BKlyn., Mar. 1, 1930; s. Morris and Minnie Mandel. BA, NY U., 1951; MS, Ga. Inst. Tech., 1952; MD, Chgo. Med. Sch., 1956. Diplomate Am. Bd. Med. Examiners, Am. Bd. Orthop. Surgery, Am. Bd. Profl. Disabled Cons. Intern D.C. Gen. Hosp., 1956—57; resident in gen. surgery VA Hosp., 1957—58; resident in orthopedic surgery D.C. Gen. Hosp. 1958—60, N.Y. U., Bellevue, 1960—61; pres., founding ptnr. The New City (N.Y.) Orthopedic Group, P.C., 1961—85; med. dir. Post-Trauma Med. Svcs., New Windsor, NY, 1985—. Host weekly radio program Medicine Today, 1973—76. Mem. editl. bd. Jour. Disability, 1990—93, Disability, 1995—96. Bd. govs. Rockland County (N.Y.) Health Complex, 1977—88; mem. coord. coun. Rockland County Emergency Med. Svc., 1977—81. Recipient Rockland County Dist. Svc. award, 1973. Fellow:

ACS, NY State Soc. Surgeons, Am. Acad. Orthop. Surgeons, Internat. Coll. Surgeons, Am. Acad. Disability Evaluating Physicians (bd. dirs. 1988—93, sec. 1990—93); mem.: Rockland County Med. Soc. (dir. pub. rels. 1967—73, exec. com. 1967—76, peer rev. com. 1973—85, pres. 1974—75, chmn. bd. censors 1975—76), Orange County Med. Soc. (peer rev. com. 1987—, exec. com. 1991—), Ea. Orthop. Assn., NY State Soc. Orthop. Surgeons (bd. dirs. 1976—82). Avocations: sailing, windsurfing, computer science, astronomy. Office: Post-Trauma Med Svc PC 833 Blooming Grove Tpk New Windsor NY 12553 Office Phone: 845-561-2000. E-mail: bonedoc@frontiernet.net.

**MANDEL, JOSEPH DAVID,** academic administrator, lawyer; b. NYC, Mar. 26, 1940; s. Max and Charlotte Lee (Goodman) M.; m. Jean Carol Westerman, Aug. 18, 1963; children: Jonathan Scott, Eric David. AB, Dartmouth Coll., 1960, MBA with distinction, 1961; JD, Yale U., 1964. Bar: Calif. 1965. Law clk. U.S. Ct. Appeals, 9th cir., L.A., 1964-65; lectr. law U. So. Calif. Law Ctr., L.A., 1965-68; assoc. atty. Tuttle & Taylor, L.A., 1965-69, mem., 1970-82, 90-91, of counsel, 1984-90; vice chancellor UCLA, 1991—, lectr. in law, 1993, 2001—02; v.p., gen. counsel, sec. Natomas Co., San Francisco, 1983. Bd. dirs. LRN, The Legal Knowledge Co., 1993-2005. Mem. bd. editors Yale Law Jour., 1962-64. Pres. Legal Aid Found., L.A., 1978-79; trustee Southwestern U. Sch. Law, 1982, UCLA Pub. Interest Law Found., 1981-82, L.A. County Bar Found., 1974-79, 82, Coro Found., 1989-92, UCLA Armand Hammer Mus. Art and Cultural Ctr., 1995—, Geffen Playhouse, Inc., 1995-98, Coro So. Calif. Ctr., 1985-92; bd. dirs. pub. coun., 1989-94, cmty. v.p., 1992-94; mem. L.A. Bd. Zoning Appeals, 1984-90, vice-chmn., 1985-86, 89-90, chmn., 1986-87; mem. L.A. City Charter Reform Commn., 1996-99; bd. dirs. Western Justice Ctr. Found., 1989—, v.p., 1992-95, 1st v.p., 1995-97, sr. v.p., 1997-99, pres., 1999-03; bd. dirs. Harvard Water Polo Found., 1990-96; bd. govs. Inner City Law Ctr., 1991-05; chair Blue Ribbon Screening Com. to Select Insp. Gen., L.A. Police Commn., 1999; mem. bd. overseers Inst. for Civil Justice, RAND, 1999—; bd. dirs. Children's Law Ctr. L.A., 2003—. Recipient Maynard Toll award Legal Aid Found. of L.A., 1991, Shattuck-Price award L.A. County Bar Assn., 1993, West Coast Liberty award Lambda Legal Def. and Edn. Fund, 1994, Cmty. Achievement award Pub. Coun., 1996, Stanley Mosk Liberty Through Justice award ADL, 2003; named One of Calif.'s 100 Most Influential Attys. by Calif. Bus. Jour., 2000. Mem. State Bar Calif. (legal svcs. trust fund commn. 1985-87, chmn. 1985-86), Yale U. Law Sch. Assn. (exec. com. 1983-88, 90-96, v.p. 1986-88, chmn. planning com. 1990-92, pres. 1992-94, exec. com. 1994-96), mem. alumni Coun. Dartmouth Coll., 1992-95, Dartmouth Coll. Assn. Alumni (exec. com. 1997-2002, v.p. 2001-02), L.A. Co. Bar Assn. (trustee 1974, 1975-81, v.p. 1977-78, pres. 1978-79, pres.-elect 1979-80, pres. 1980-81, chair pro bono coun. 1988-87), Order of Coif. Democrat. Home: 15478 Longbow Dr Sherman Oaks CA 91403-4910 Office: UCLA Office of the Chancellor 2135 Murphy Hl Los Angeles CA 90095-1405 Office Phone: 310-206-1355. Business E-Mail: jmandel@conet.ucla.edu.

**MANDEL, JUDITH LYNN,** primary school educator; b. Mpls., June 20, 1936; d. Lloyd L. and Gussie Miller Elzas; m. Seymour L. Mandel (div.); children: Lloyd J., Paula J. Cert. of X-Ray Tech., U. Minn., Mpls., 1958; BEd, Nat. Lewis U., Evanston, Ill., 1979. Substitute tchr. pub. schs., Wilmette and Winnetka, Ill., 1979—83; tchr. 2d grade Solomon Schechter Sch., Skokie, Ill., 1984—85; tchr. Haugan Sch., Chgo., 1986—90, Patrick Henry Sch., Chgo., 1991—. Vol. in pediatrics dept. Evanston Hosp., Ill.; den mother cub scouts Boy Scouts Am., Wilmette; leader brownie troop Girl Scouts U.S., Wilmette. Mem.: Chgo. Tchrs. Union, North Shore Sr. Ctr., Chgo. Bot. Gardens, Kappa Delta Pi, Alpha Epsilon Phi. Jewish. Avocations: rug hooking, exercise, reading, antiques, gardening. Home: 245 Essex Pl Wilmette IL 60091 Personal E-mail: judylyn2@aol.com.

**MANDEL, KARYL LYNN,** accountant; b. Chgo., Dec. 14, 1935; d. Isador J. and Eve (Gellar) Karzen; m. Fredric H. Mandel, Sept. 29, 1956; children: David Scott, Douglas Jay, Jennifer Ann. Student, U. Mich., 1954-56, Roosevelt U., 1956-57; AA summa cum laude, Oakton Community Coll., 1979. CPA, Ill; registered investment advisor; lic. life ins. providor. Pres. Excel Transp. Service Co., Elk Grove, Ill., 1958-78; tax mgr. CTB, Ltd., CPAs, Northbrook, Ill., 1981-83; tax ptnr. Chunowitz, Teitelbaum & Baerson, CPA's, Northbrook, Ill., 1984—. Sec-treas. Lednam, Inc., Coffee Break, Inc.; mem. acctg. curriculum adv. bd. Oakton C.C., Des Plaines, Ill., 1987—; pres. Lednam Enterprises, LLC, 2001—. Contbg. author: Ill. CPA's News Jour., Acctg. Today. Recipient State of Israel Solidarity award, 1976. Mem. AICPA, Am. Soc. Women CPA, Women's Am. ORT (pres. Chgo. region 1972-74, v.p. midwest dist. 1975-76, nat. endowment com., nat investment adv. com.)), Ill. CPA Soc. (chmn. estate and gift tax com. 1987-89, legis. contact com. 1981-82, pres. North Shore chpt., award for Excellence in Acctg. Edn., Bd. dirs. 1989-91), Chgo. Soc. Women CPA, Chgo. Estate Planning Coun., Nat. Assn. Women Bus. Owners, Lake County Estate Planning, Coun., Greater North Shore Estate Planning Coun. Office: 401 Huehl Rd Northbrook IL 60062-2300 Business E-Mail: klm@ctbltld.com

**MANDEL, LESLIE ANN,** investment advisor, writer; b. Washington, July 29, 1945; d. Seymour and Marjorie (Syble) Mandel; m. Arthur Herzog III, Oct. 27, 1999. BA in Art History, U. Minn., 1967; cert., N.Y. Sch. Interior Design, 1969. Cert. Brailled Libr. Congress. Pres. Leslie Mandel Enterprises, Inc., N.Y.C., 1968—; sr. v.p. Maximum Entertainment Network, L.A. and N.Y.C., 1988-90; pres. Rich List Co., 1968—; pres., CEO Mandel Airplane Funding and Leasing Corp., N.Y.C., Hong Kong, China and Mongolia, 1990—; CEO Mandel-Khan Inc., Ulaanbaatar, Mongolia, 1994—, Travel Safe: keep hers, keep his, 2002—. Fin. advisor Comml. Inc., Mpls., 1986—; Devine Comm./Allen & Co., NY, Del., Utah, N.Mex., NY, N.Y. WUWV, Utah KBER, WKTC-AM-FM, 1984—89, Am. Kefir Corp., N.Y.C., 1983—89, Shore Group (Internat., Guyana), Flight Internat., 1991; founder The Rich List Co., 150 internat. catalogs, mags. and fundraising lists; joint venture Mongolian Ind. Broadcasting Channel, Ulaanbaatar, 1995; pres., owner Mandel Airplane Funding and Leasing Corp.; rep. Israeli Govt. IAI Satellite, China, Romania, Costa Rica, Mongolia, Amos Satellite Network, China, 1992—; advisor rep. Gt. Wall Corp., Long March Corp., China, 1992—, Chinese Silk, 1993—, Am. Oil Refinery, 1993—; bd. dirs. Coastal Equipment Co., Bristol Airlines; cons. Exclusive Miat Airlines, Mongolia; purchasing agt. People's Republic of China-Aircraft; advisor Aeropostalis, Mexico, 1994—95; photographer; lectr. UN Internat. Direct Mail; advisor Aruba Airlines, Mexicana Airlines; aircraft agt., bd. dirs. Lazorlines Landing Equipment, 1997—; lease Estafada Airlines 757-200-C, 2000—, Chile Airlines 757-200C, 2002; advisor Guyana 2000 Airlines; ptnr. Laserline/Vulcan Power Plant, Greece, 2005—, China, 2005—. Photographer: Vogue, 1978, New Earth Times, 1995, Fortune mag.; Braille transcriber: The Prophet (Kalil Gibran), 1967, Getting Ready for Battle (R. Prawe Jhabuala), 1967; exec. prodr. film: Hospital Audiences, 1975 (Cannes award 1976); author: Hungry at the Watering Hole, Garden Island, 1636-1990, 1998, Expedition: In the Steps of Ghengis Kahn, 1994; advisor Port Liberté Ptnrs., 1988-94; contbr. articles to profl. jours. N.Y.C. advisor Correctional Assn., Violeta B. de Chamarro for Pres. of Nicaragua Campaign. Recipient Inst. for the Creative and Performing Arts fellowship, N.Y.C., 1966, Appreciation cert. Presdl. Inaugural Com., Washington, 1981. Fellow N.Y. Women in Real Estate, Explorers Club (lectr. on Mongolia, fin. com., housing, student, hospitality and Lowell Thomas coms., reciprocity com.); mem. Com. on Am. and Internat. Fgn. Affairs, Lawyers Com. on Internat. Human Rels., Bus. Exec. Nat. Security, Venture Capital Breakfast Club, The Coffee Club House, Sigma Delta Tau, Sigma Epsilon Sigma. Democrat. Avocations: painting, writing, fishing, canoeing, horseback riding, breeding cockatiels. Home: 4 E 81st St New York NY 10028-0235 Office: Mandel-Khan Inc/Po Box 97 care Boldbaatar Mandel Kahn Ulaanbaatar 210648 Mongolia also: Leslie Mandel Enterprises PO Box 294 Wainscott NY 11975-0294 also: PO Box 294 Wainscott NY 11975-0029 Office Phone: 212-737-8917. Personal E-mail: mandelair@aol.com. E-mail: richlistco@aol.com.

**MANDEL, MAURICE, II,** lawyer, educator, mediator; b. Hollywood, Calif. s. Maurice and Wynne Mandel BSBA, U. So. Calif., 1971, MEd, 1972; JD, We. State U., 1979. Bar: Calif. 1980, U.S. Dist. Ct. (ctrl. dist.) Calif. 1982, U.S. Ct. Appeals (fed. and 9th cirs.) 1983, U.S. Dist. Ct. (we. dist.) Tenn. 1987, U.S. Dist. Ct. Ariz. 1990, U.S. Dist. Ct. (so. dist.) Calif. 1991, U.S. Supreme Ct. 1991, cert. level I ski instr. PSIA Nat. Acad. 1998, settlement officer, USDC-CDCa. Tchr. Orange County Sch. Dist., Calif., 1972—82; pvt. practice law Newport Beach, Calif., 1982—; fed. settlement officer CDCA, 1998—. Instr. Coastline C.C., 1987-95, prof., 1995—, Acad. Senate, Parlimentarian 1996-99; prof. law Irvine (Calif.) U. Coll. Law, 1994-98; instr. Bear Mountain Calif. Ski Sch., 1996—, Ziet Maros, 1998—; FBA/OCC Mandatory Continuing Legal Edn. provider, 1994—, COURSE Vail Colo. Alpine World Cup Finals, 1997, Alpine World Championships, 1999, World Cup, 1999, COURSE St. Anton am Arlberg, Alpine World Championships, 2001, COURSE Ladies' Norams, Snowbasin, Utah, 2001, COURSE XIX Olympic Games, Salt Lake City, 2002, Alpine Ski, COURSE St. Moritz, Switzerland, Alpine World Championships, 2003, COURSE Bormio Italy Alpine World Championships, 2005, others Counselor Troy Camp, 1969-72; chmn. Legal Edn. for Youth, 1984-86; active Ctr. Dance Alliance, Orange County, 1986-97; JOC racing dir. So. Calif., 1998-2000; mem. Friends Am. Ballet Theatre, Opera Pacific Guild, Opera Pacific Bohemians, Calypso Soc., World Wildlife Found., L.A. County Mus. Art, Newport Beach Art Mus., Met. Mus. Art, Laguna Beach Mus. Art, Smithsonian Instn., Friend of Ballet Pacifica, Friends of Joffrey Ballet; assoc. U.S. Ski Team, 1975—; com. assoc. U.S. Olympics, 1988—; 100th Olympics vols., 1996, XIX Olympics, 2002; F.I.S. vol., 1997—, COURSE Alpine World Cup Finals, Vail, Colo., 1997, Alpine World Championships, 1999, 2001, 03, 05, XIX Olympics, 2002; alumni and scholarship com. Beverly Hills H.S Recipient cert. of appreciation U.S. Dist. Ct., L.A., 1985, U.S. Dist. Ct. Mediation award D.C., 2000, Thwarted Thwart award Newport Harbor C. of C., 1989, 1996, Tovarich award Kirov Ballet, 1989, 92, Perostroika award Moscow Classical Ballet, 1988-89, 94, Ziet Maros award 1998, 99, 2000, Skrisivi Nogi award Bolshoi Ballet, 1990, Marinskii Dance award St. Petersburg, 1993; ABT Romeo & Juliet, 1996, 2d Pl. award JOC Slalom, 1998, 1st pl. award, 2000, 2d pl. award Big Bear Instrs. Giant Slalom, 2000, 1st pl. award JOC Concourse, 2000, 14th pl. nat. standing JCNA Slalom, 1999 Mem. ABA, ATLA, Assn. Bus. Trial Lawyers, Fed. Bar Assn., (founding pres. Orange County chpt. 1986, nat. del. 1988-90, founder criminal indigent def. panel 1986, com. Nat. Chpt. Activity award 1987, Nat. Membership award 1987, Chpt. Svc. award 1989, nat. regional membership chmn. 1990, spl. appointee nat. membership com. 1991), Calif. Bar Assn. (Pro Bono awards 1989-89), Pres.'s Coun. (founder 1996—), Orange County Bar Assn. (instr. Coll. Trial Advocacy, 1994—, legal edn. for youth com. 1982-90, chmn. 1985, fed. practice com., sports com., mandatory fee arbitration com. 1992—, lawyer's referral svc. com. 1984-98, Merit award 1986), Orange County Bar Found. (trustee 1984-87), Newport Harbor Bar Assn., Trial Lawyers Assn., Calif. Employee Lawyers Assn., Plaintiff Employee Lawyers Assn., Bar Leaders Coun. Dist. 8, U.S. Calif. Alumni Assn., Mensa, Cougar Club Am., So. Calif. Cougar Club, San Diego Cougar Club, So. Calif. Jaguar Owners Assn., Balboa Yacht Club Avocations: skiing, yachting. Home: PO Box 411 Newport Beach CA 92662 Office Phone: 949-759-7799. Personal E-mail: MMANDEL2@aol.com.

**MANDEL, MICHAEL S.,** lawyer; b. Charlotte, NC; BA, Univ. NC, Chapel Hill, 1971, JD, 1974, MA in Urban and Regional Planning, 1974. Bar: NC 1974, DC 1975. Dir. Urban Govt. Affairs Nat. Assn. Home Builders; spl. asst. to sec. US Dept. Housing and Urban Devel., Washington, 1979—81; assoc. Akin Gump Strauss Hauer & Feld LLP, Washington, 1981—85, now ptnr., head real estate sect. Washington. Mem.: ABA, NC Bar Assn., DC Bar Assn. Office: Akin Gump Strauss Hauer & Feld LLP Robert S Strauss Bldg 1333 New Hampshire Ave NW Washington DC 20036-1564

**MANDEL, MORTON,** molecular biologist; b. Bklyn., July 6, 1924; s. Barnet and Rose (Kliner) M.; m. Florence H. Goodman, Apr. 1, 1952; children: Robert, Leslie. BCE, CUNY, 1944; MS, Columbia U., 1949 PhD in Physics, 1957. Scientist Bell Telephone Labs., Murray Hill, NJ, 1956-57; asst. prof. physics dept. Stanford (Calif.) U., 1957-61; scientist Gen. Telephone & Telegraph, Mountain View, Calif., 1961-63; rsch. assoc. dept. genetics Stanford U., 1963-64; rsch. fellow Karolinska Inst., Stockholm, 1964-66; assoc. prof. sch. of medicine U. Hawaii, Honolulu, 1966-68, prof., 1968—; founder, dir. Hawaii Biotechnology Group, Inc., 1982-95. Cons. Fairchild Semiconductor, Hewlett Packard, Lockheed, Rheem, Palo Alto, Calif., 1957-61. Contbr. articles to profl. jours. Lt. (j.g.) USN, 1944-46. Recipient Am. Cancer Soc. Scholar award Am. Cancer Soc., 1979-80, Eleanor Roosevelt Internat. Cancer fellowship, 1979; named NIH Spl. fellow Karolinska Inst., 1964-66. Fellow Am. Phys. Soc.; mem. Sigma Xi. Achievements include citation classics; optimal conditions for mutagenesis by N-methyl-N-nitro-N-nitrosoguanidine in E. coli K12; calcium dependent bacteriophage DNA infection. Office: Dept Biochemistry 1960 E West Rd Honolulu HI 96822-2319 Home: 250 Hammond Pond Pkwy Apt 303N Chestnut Hill MA 02467-1519

**MANDEL, SHELDON LLOYD,** dermatologist, educator; b. Mpls., Dec. 6, 1922; s. Maurice and Stelle R. M.; m. Patricia E., Oct. 15, 1978; 1 child, Melissa A. BA, U. Minn., Mpls., 1943, BS, 1944, BM, MD, U. Minn., Mpls., 1946. Diplomate Am. Bd. Dermatology, 1953. Intern U. Okla., 1946-47; resident Valley Forge (Pa.) Gen. Hosp., 1947—49, VA Hosp., Mpls., 1949—51, VA Hosp. and U. Minn. Mpls., 1949—51; pvt. practice dermatology Mpls., 1951—; prof. clin. dermatology U. Minn., Mpls., 1970—. Contbr. articles to profl. jours. Capt. MC, U.S. Army, 1947-49. Fellow Royal Soc. Medicine (Britain), Am. Acad. Dermatology (life); mem. AMA, Minn. Med. Soc., Noah Worcester Dermatol. Soc. (bd. dirs. 1988-91), Internat. Dermatol. Svc. Address: Downtown Dermatology PA 825 Nicollet Mall Ste 1629 Minneapolis MN 55402-2705

**MANDEL, STEPHEN, JR.,** financier; m. Susan Mandel. Grad., Dartmouth, 1978. Retail analyst Goldman, Sachs & Co., 1985—87, v.p., retail analyst NY, 1987—90; retail analyst Tiger Mgmt. Corp., 1990—97; CEO Lone Pine Capital, 1998—. Office: Lone Pine Capital LLC 2 Greenwich Plz Greenwich CT 06830-6353

**MANDELBAUM, HAROLD NEIL,** accountant; b. Englewood, N.J., Sept. 13, 1967; s. Diane M. (Kaufman) Kubik; m. Shari Patt, Sept. 9, 1995. BA in Econs., Syracuse U., 1990; BS in Acctg., William Paterson Coll., 1993. CPA; CFP; cert. personal fin. specialist; lic. ins. N.Y.; lic. securities. Broker Lehman Brothers, N.Y.C., 1990—91; acct. NSCSA Am. Svc., S.I., NY, 1992; acct., fin. cons. Joseph A. Salamo, CPA, N.Y.C., 1992—96; Harold N. Mandelbaum CPA, PFS, CFP, N.Y.C., 1996—. Mem. AICPA, N.Y. State Soc. CPA. Office: 555 5th Ave Fl 9 New York NY 10017-2416 Office Phone: 212-949-0500 x 225. Business E-Mail: hnmandelbaum@nyc.rr.com.

**MANDELBAUM, JAY,** diversified financial services company executive; B, Princeton U., NJ; MBA, Harvard Bus. Sch. Cons. McKinsey & Co.; v.p. corp. devel. Primerica Corpn., 1992; sr. exec. v.p. Pvt. Client Sales and Mktg. Salomon Smith Barney, vice chmn., CEO Pvt. Client Grp., 2000—02; head strategy and bus. devel. Bank One Corpn., 2002; officer J.P. Morgan Chase & Co., exec. v.p. strategy. Office: JP Morgan Chase & Co 270 Park Ave New York NY 10017-2070*

**MANDELBROT, BENOIT B.,** mathematician, research scientist, educator; b. Warsaw, Nov. 20, 1924; arrived in U.S., 1958; s. Charles and Belle (Lurie) M.; m. Aliette Kagan, Nov. 5, 1955; children: Laurent, Didier. Diploma, Ecole Polytechnique, Paris, 1947; MS in Aeronautics, Calif. Inst. Tech., 1948; PhD in Math., U. Paris, 1952; DS (hon.), Syracuse U., 1985, Laurentian U., Ont. Can., 1986, Boston U., 1987, SUNY, 1988, U. Bremen, Germany, 1988, U. Guelph, Ont., Can., 1989, Pace U., 1989, U. Dallas, 1992, Union Coll., 1993, Buenos Aires, 1993, U. Tel Aviv, 1993, Open U., U.K., 1998, Athens U. Bus. and Fin., Greece, 1998, U. St. Andrews, Scotland, 1999, Emory U., 2002, Politecnico di Torino, Italy, 2005, U. Bari; AM (hon.), Yale U., 2000. Postdoctoral mem. and Rockefeller scholar Inst. for Advanced Study, Princeton, NJ, 1953—54; jr. prof. math. U. Geneva, 1955-57, U. Lille and Ecole

Polytechnique, Paris, 1957-58; rsch. staff mem. IBM Watson Rsch. Ctr., Yorktown Heights, NY, 1958-74, IBM fellow, 1974-93, IBM fellow emeritus, 1993—; vis. prof. engring. Yale U., New Haven, 1970, prof. math. scis., 1987—99, Sterling prof., 1999—2004, Sterling prof. emeritus, 2005—; Battelle fellow Pacific Northwest Nat. Lab. 2005—. Vis. prof. econs. Harvard U., 1962-63, applied math., 1963-64, 84-87, U. Paris, 1966, physiology Einstein Coll. Medicine, 1970, Coll. France, 1973, math., 1979-80, Inst. Hautes Etudes Sci. Bures, 1980, Mittag-Leffler Inst., Sweden, 1984, 2001, 02, 04, Max Planck Inst. Math, Bonn, Germany, 1988, Cambridge, 1990, 2005, Oxford U., 1990, Imperial Coll., London, 1991; Hitchcock prof. U. Calif., Berkeley, 1992; visitor MIT, 1953, Inst. lectr., 1964-; spkr. and organizer profl. confs. Author: Logique, langage et théorie de l'information, 1957, Les objets fractals: forme, hasard et dimension, 1975, 4th edit., 1995, Fractals: Form, Chance and Dimension, 1977, The Fractal Geometry of Nature, 1982, La Geometria della Natura, 1987, Fractals and Scaling in Finance: Discontinuity, Concentration, Risk, 1997, Fractales, hasard et finance, 1997, Multifractals and 1/f Noise: Wild Self-Affinity in Physics, 1999, Nel mondo dei frattali, 2001, Gaussian Self-Affinity and Fractals: Globality, The Earth, 1/f Noise and R/S, 2002, Fractals and Chaos: The Mandelbrot Set and Beyond, 2004; (with M.L. Frame) Fractals, Graphics and Mathematics Education, 2002, (with R.L. Hudson) The MisBehavior of Markets: A Fractal View of Risk, Ruin, and Reward, 2004; books translated into many langs.; contbr. articles to profl. jours. Recipient Franklin medal Franklin Inst., 1986, Alexander von Humboldt Preis, 1987, Caltech disting. svc. award, 1988, Moet-Hennessy Sci. and Art prize, 1988, Harvey prize, 1989, Nev. prize U. Nev. Sys., 1991, Wolf prize for physics, 1993, Honda prize, 1994, Medal of City of Paris, 1996, John Scott award City of Phila., 1999, L.F. Richardson medal European Geophys. Soc., 2000, Sven Berggren prize, Lund, Sweden, 2002, Japan prize for Sci. and Tech., 2003, Fin. Times (Germany) award, 2004, Waclaw Sierpinski prize, 2005 Wladislaw Orlicz medal, 2005, Casimir Funk award Piasa, 2005, officer Legion of Honor, France; Guggenheim fellow, 1968. Fellow AAAS, IEEE (Charles Proteus Steinmetz medal 1988), Am. Acad. Arts and Scis., European Acad. Arts, Scis. and Humanities, Am. Phys. Soc., French Physics Soc. (hon.), Inst. Math. Stats., Econometric Soc., Am. Geophys. Union, Am. Statistic Assn.; mem. NAS U.S.A. (Barnard medal 1985), Am. Philos. Soc., Internat. Statis. Inst. (elected.), Am. Math. Soc., Norwegian Acad. Sci. and Letters (fgn. mem.), Sigma Xi (nat. lectr. 1980-82, Procter prize 2002). Achievements include origination of theory of fractals geometry, a nascent interdisciplinary theory of roughness; this theory provides mathematical conjectures including very difficult ones, and also provides practical tools to handle financial data, mountains, clouds, fractures of metals, dynamic attractors, and all other shapes and phenomena in nature or man's works that are equally irregular or broken-up at all scales; the best known fractal is called Mandelbrot set. Home and Office: Battelle Cambridge Office 222 Third St Ste 3100 Cambridge MA 02142 Office Phone: 617-577-7254 ext. 2012. Business E-Mail: benoit.mandelbrot@yale.edu.

**MANDELL, FLOYD A.,** lawyer; b. Chgo., June 17, 1948; s. Marvin M. and Estelle (Witt) M.; m. Pamela Sue Cohen, Aug. 31, 1975; children: Chad, Craig. BA magna cum laude, No. Ill. U., 1970; JD, U. Ill., Champaign, 1973. Bar: Ill. 1973, Fla. 1973. Assoc. Dettishell, McAuliffe & Hifestiter, Chgo., 1973-76; sr. ptnr. Katten Muchin Zavis Rosenman, Chgo., 1976—. Dir. Chgo. Bar Assn., 1978-80; planning chmn. Ill. Continuing Legal Edn., Intellectual Property Litigation, Chgo., 1985—. Cpl. USAR, 1969-73. Office: Katten Muchin Zavis Rosenman 525 W Monroe St Ste 1600 Chicago IL 60661-3693 Office Fax: 312-577-8982. E-mail: floyd.mandell@kmzr.com.

**MANDELL, GERALD LEE,** internist, educator; b. N.Y.C., Aug. 20, 1936; s. Herman and Sylvia (Keller) M.; m. Judith Rensin Mandell, Dec. 22, 1960; children: James, Pamela, Scott. BA, Cornell U., 1958; MD, Cornell U., N.Y.C., 1962. Diplomate Am. Bd. Internal Medicine. Intern, resident NY Hosp. Cornell Med. Ctr., NYC, 1965-67; instr. Med. Coll., Cornell U., N.Y.C. 1968-69; asst. prof. U. Va., Charlottesville, 1969-71, assoc. prof., 1972-75, prof., 1976—, Owen R. Cheatham prof. sci., 1981—, chief infectious diseases, 1970–2002. Editor: Principles and Practice of Infectious Diseases, 1979, 6th edit., 2005. Lt. comdr. USPHS, 1963-65. Recipient MERIT award NIH, 1986; named Outstanding Alumnus, Cornell Med. Coll, 2002. Master ACP; fellow AAAS, Infectious Diseases Soc. Am. (pres. 1994, Bristol award 2000), Nat. Inst. Allergy and Infectious Diseases (adv. coun.), Inst. Medicine; mem. Assn. Am. Physicians, Am. Soc. Clin. Investigation, Phi Beta Kappa, Alpha Omega Alpha. Jewish. Avocations: photography, tropical fish, sculling. Office: U VA Health Scis Ctr MR4 Rsch Bldg Rm 2112 PO Box 801341 Charlottesville VA 22908-1341 Office Phone: 434-924-5942, 434-924-9663. Office Fax: 434-982-0002. Business E-Mail: gm@virginia.edu.

**MANDELL, GORDON KEITH,** aerospace engineer; b. NYC, Mar. 6, 1947; s. Bertram Herman and Maria Catherine (O'Hagan) M. BS, MIT, 1969, MS, 1970. Rsch. aerospace engr. MIT, Cambridge, 1972—; aero. cons. Eagle River, Alaska, 1972—76; designated engring. rep., 1976—82; aerospace engr. FAA, Anchorage, 1982—. Author/editor: Topics in Advanced Model Rocketry, 1973; mng. editor Model Rocketry mag., Cambridge, 1968-72; contbr. articles to profl. jours. Fellow, NSF, 1969; scholar, Grumman Aerospace Corp., 1965. Mem.: Search for Extraterrestrial Intelligence Inst., Nat. Space Soc., Nat. Assn. Rocketry, Planetary Soc., Tau Beta Pi, Sigma Gamma Tau, Sigma Xi. Avocations: rural living, model building, home computing. Home: PO Box 671388 Chugiak AK 99567-1388 Office: FAA Aircraft Cert Office ACE-115N 222 W 7th Ave Unit 14 Anchorage AK 99513-7587 Business E-Mail: gkm1441@mtaonline.net.

**MANDELL, JAMES,** health facility executive, urologist, educator; b. SI, NY, Feb. 20, 1945; s. Gustave and Rose (Zimmerman) M.; m. Valerie Steele, Jan. 20, 1967; children: Joshua Lindstrom, Jeremy Hill, Bethany Shalom. AA, U. Fla., l965; MD, U. Fla. Coll. Medicine, l970; MS, Union U., 1999. Am. Bd. Diplomate Urology 1979. Intern U. Fla. Sch. Medicine, Gainesville, 1970-71, resident in surgery, 1971-72; resident in urology U. NC Sch. Medicine, Chapel Hill, 1974-71, fellow in pediatric urology, 1977-78, asst. prof. surgery and pediatrics, 1979-84, assoc. prof., 1984-85; dir. pediatric urology NC Meml. Hosp., Chapel Hill, 1979-85; instr. surgery Harvard U. Med. Sch., Boston, 1978-79, asst. prof. surgery (urology), 1985-90, assoc. prof. surgery, urology, 1990-94, prof. surgery (urology); prof. surgery and pediat., chief divsn. urology, exec. med. dir. Albany Med. Coll., NY, 1994-97, dean NY, 1996-2000; fellow in surgery (urology) Children's Hosp., Boston, 1978-79, asst. in surgery (urology), 1985-90, sr. assoc. surgery, 1990-94, CEO, pres., 2000—. Contbr. numerous articles to med. jours., clpts. to books. Lt. comdr. M.C., USNR, 1972-74. Fellow ACS, Am. Acad. Pediatrics; mem. Am. Urol. Assn. (New England sec.), Soc. Pediatric Urology (exec. com. 1988-92), Soc. Univ. Urologists (pres. 2001-02). Avocations: fishing, skiing, tennis. Office: Children's Hosp Boston Dept Urology Hunnewell 3 300 Longwood Ave Boston MA 02115-5724 Office Phone: 518-355-2080, 617-355-6000. Office Fax: 617-730-0474. Business E-Mail: james.mandell@childrens.harvard.edu.

**MANDELL, JOHN F.,** chemical engineer, educator; BS in Civil Engring., U. Mass., Amherst, 1966; MS in Engring. Mechanics, Case Western Reserve U., Cleve., 1968; PhD in Materials, MIT, Cambridge, 1971. Rsch. assoc. MIT, 1971—81, prin. rsch. assoc., 1981—88; prof. Mont. State U., Bozeman, 1988—. Vis. rsch. Swiss Fed. Labs. for Testing Materials and Rsch., Dübendorf, Switzerland, 1974. Contbr. articles to profl. jours. Recipient Outstanding Rsch. and Devel. Partnership award, US Dept. Energy, 2003. Office: Chem and Biol Engring Dept Mont State U Bozeman 306 Cobleigh Hall Bozeman MT 59717 E-mail: JohnM@coe.montana.edu.*

**MANDELSTAM, CHARLES LAWRENCE,** lawyer; b. Brookline, Mass., July 6, 1927; s. Felix and Sarah (Odence) M.; m. Gloria Messinger, June 2, 1957; children: Emily F., Peter D. BA, Harvard Coll., 1949; LLB, Yale U. 1952. Bar: Conn. 1952, NY 1953, DC 1953. Mem. staff office gen. counsel Internat. Ladies' Garment Workers Union, N.Y.C., 1952—56; assoc. Kaye, Scholer, Fierman, Hays & Handler, N.Y.C., 1956—60; ptnr. Dornbush Mensch Mandelstam & Schaeffer, LLP, N.Y.C., 1968—2004, McLaughlin & Stern, LLP, N.Y.C., 2004—. Comment editor Yale Law Jour., 1951-52; contbr.

articles Yale Law Jour., 1951, 52 Bd. dirs. Samuel Rubin Found., 1975-2005 Mem. Assn. Bar City N.Y., Phi Beta Kappa. Home: 27 W 86th St New York NY 10024-3615 Office: 260 Madison Ave New York NY 10016 Office Phone: 212-448-1100.

**MANDELSTAM, STANLEY,** physicist; b. Johannesburg, Dec. 12, 1928; came to U.S., 1963; s. Boris and Beatrice (Liknaitzky) M. BSc, U. Witwatersrand, Johannesburg, 1952; BA, Cambridge U., Eng., 1954; PhD, Birmingham U., Eng., 1956. Boese postdoctoral fellow Columbia U., N.Y.C., 1957-58; prof. math. physics U. Birmingham, 1960-63; asst. rsch. physicist U. Calif., Berkeley, 1958-60, prof. physics, 1963-94, prof. emeritus, 1994—. Vis. prof. physics Harvard U., Cambridge, Mass., 1965-66, Univ. de Paris, Paris Sud, 1979-80, 84-85. Editorial bd. The Phys. Rev. jour., 1978-81, 85-88; contbr. articles to profl. jours. Recipient Dirac medal and prize Internat. Ctr. for Theoretical Physics, 1991. Fellow AAAS, Royal Soc. London, Am. Phys. Soc. (Dannie N. Heineman Math. Physics prize 1992). Jewish. Office: U Calif Dept Physics Berkeley CA 94720-7300

**MANDELSTAMM, JEROME ROBERT,** lawyer; b. St. Louis, Apr. 3, 1932; s. Henry and Estelle (London) M.; m. Carolyn A. White; stepchildren: John M. Gagliardi, Maria A. Amundson, Amy E. Gagliardi. AB, U. Pa., 1954; LL.B., Harvard U., 1957. Bar: Mo. 1957. Since practiced in, St. Louis; ptnr. Greenfield, Davidson, Mandelstamm & Voorhees, 1969—81, Schmitz, Mandelstamm, Hawker & Fischer, 1981—82; pvt. practice St. Louis, 1982—. Bd. dirs. Legal Aid Soc. City and County St. Louis, 1967-75, pres., 1969-70; bd. dirs. Lawyers Reference Service Met. St. Louis, 1976-83, chmn., 1978-83; bd. dirs. Mo. Legal Aid Soc., 1977-82; mem. 22d Jud. Cir. Bar Com., 1983-85, gen. chmn., 1984-85. Mem. St. Louis County Bd. Election Commrs., 1973-77. Served with AUS, 1957. Mem. ABA, Mo. Bar Assn., Am. Arbitration Assn. (panel of arbitrators 1984-2003), Bar Assn. Met. St. Louis (v.p. 1974-75, treas. 1975-76, William L. Weiss award for Svcs. to the Bar and the Cmty. 2004). Home: 7217 Princeton Saint Louis MO 63130-3000 Office: 1010 Market St Ste 1600 Saint Louis MO 63101-2082

**MANDERS, KARL LEE,** neurosurgeon; b. Rochester, N.Y., Jan. 21, 1927; s. David Bert and Frances Edna (Cohan) Mendelson; m. Ann Laprell, July 28, 1969; children: Karlanna Butler, Maidena Fulford;children from previous marriage: Karl, Kristine Myers, Kerry. Student, Cornell U. 1946; MD, U. Buffalo, 1950. Diplomate Am. Bd. Neurol. Surgery, Am. Bd. Clin. Biofeedback, Am. Bd. Hyperbaric Medicine, Am. Bd. Pain Medicine, Nat. Bd. Med. Examiners. Intern U. Va. Hosp., Charlottesville, 1950-51, resident in neurol. surgery, 1951-52, Henry Ford Hosp., Detroit, 1954-56; pvt. practice indpls., 1956—. Med. dir. Cmty. Hosp. Rehab. Ctr. Pain, 1973—92; chief hosp. med. and surg. neurology Cmty. Hosp., 1983, 93; coroner Marion County, Ind., 1977—85, 1992—96. *Over 45 years in practice of Neurological Surgery and the development of one of the first multidisciplinary pain centers in the country over a quarter of a century ago. Dr. Manders also established the first hyper-baric centers in Indiana. He has also served as Marion County coroner in Indianapolis for twelve years and his continued interest in forensic medicine have developed into further development of medical-legal consultation services.* With USN, 1952—54, Korea. Recipient cert. Achievement, Dept. Army, 1969. Disting. Physician award, Cmty. Hosp., 1997. Cert. of Distinction, Ind. State Med. Assn., Am.'s Top Surgeon award, Cosumers Rsch. Coun. Am., 2002. Fellow: ACS, Harvey Cushing Soc., Am. Acad. Neurology, Internat. Coll. Surgeons; mem. James McClure Surg. Soc., Am. Bd. Med. Psychotherapists (mem. profl. adv. coun.), James A. Gibson Anat. Soc., Internat. Soc. Aquatic Medicine, Interurban Neurosurg. Soc., Ctrl. Neurol. Soc., Am. Acad. Pain Medicine, Midwest Pain Soc. (pres. 1988), Am. Pain Soc., Nat. Assn. Med. Examiners, Royal Soc. Medicine, Ind. Coroners Assn. (pres. 1979), Soc. Computerized Tomography and Neuroimaging, Am. Soc. Stereotaxic and Functional Neurosurgery, N.Am. Spine Soc., Internat. Back Pain Soc., Pan Am. Med. Assn., Acad. Psychosomatic Medicine, Biofeedback Soc. Am., Pan Pacific Surg. Assn., Soc. Cryosurgery, Am. Assn. Biofeedback Clinicians, Am. Acad. Forensic Soc., Undersea Med. Soc., Am. Holistic Med. Assn. (co-founder), Am. Soc. Contemporary Medicine and Surgery, Am. Coll. Angiology, NY Acad. Scis., Am. Assn. Study Headache, Internat. Assn. Study Pain, Congress Neurol. Surgery, Highland Country Club, Brendonwood Country Club. Home and Office: 5845 High Fall Rd Indianapolis IN 46226-1018 Office Phone: 317-546-6691. Personal E-mail: annlmanders@comcast.net.

**MANDERS, SUSAN KAY,** artist; b. Burbank, Calif., Dec. 29, 1948; d. Gus H. and Erika (Stadelbauer) M.; m. Alan D. Yasnyi, Dec. 18, 1992; children: Brian Mallut. Attended. U. Guadalajara, 1969; BA, Calif. State U., 1971; postgrad., UCLA, Otis Parsons, LA. 1985, Royal Coll. of the Arts, London, 1987; grad., Silicon Digital Arts. Owner, dir., tchr. The Art Experience Sch. and Gallery, Studio City, Calif., 1978—. Cons. in field. U.S. artist Athens (Greece) Summer Olympic Games, 2004; exhibitions include UN World Conf. on Women, Beijing, 1996, LA, NY, Chgo., Beverly Hills, Irvine, San Francisco, New Orleans, 1990—, prin. works include Steel Sculpture, Harry Ross Industries, 2003, Represented in permanent collections Nat. Mus. Women in the Arts, Smithsonian, Washington. Docent UCLA; active Tuesday's Child, Pillars of Hope Project San Fernando Valley County Fair, 1995. Mem. AAUW, LA Art Assn., Beverley Hills Art Assn., Nat. Mus. Women in the Arts, Nat. Assn. Univ. Women, LA County Mus. of Art, Dada, LA, Mus. Contemporary Art Coun., Women in Animation, Nat. Assn. Univ. Women, Vidamation Assn. (bd. dirs.). Office: The Art Experience 11830 Ventura Blvd Studio City CA 91604-2617 Office Phone: 818-506-7806. Personal E-mail: susanmanders@aol.com.

**MANDERSCHEID, LESTER VINCENT,** agricultural economics educator; b. Andrew, Iowa, Oct. 9, 1930; s. Vincent John and Alma (Sprank) M.; m. Dorothy Helen Varnum, Aug. 29, 1953; children: David, Paul, Laura. Jane. BS, Iowa State U., 1951, MS, 1952; PhD, Stanford U., 1961. Grad. asst. Iowa State U., Ames, 1951-52, Stanford (Calif.) U., 1952-56; asst. prof. Mich. State U., East Lansing, 1956-65, assoc. prof., 1965-70, prof., 1970-73, prof., assoc. chmn., 1973-87, prof., chmn., 1987-92, prof., 1992-95, prof. emeritus, 1996—, coord. Grad. Sch., 1993—. Reviewer Tex. A&M Agrl. Econ. Program, College Station, 1989; cons. Consortium Internat. Earth Sci. Info. Network, Ann Arbor, 1990. Co-author: Improving Undergraduate Education, 1967; contbr. articles to jours. in field. Pres. parish coun. St. Thomas, East Lansing, 1984-87; coll. coord. United Way, East Lansing, 1983-84; pres. bd. dirs. Cristo Rey Cmty. Ctr., 1998-2001. Recipient Disting. Faculty award Mich. State U., 1977. Mem. Am. Agrl. Econ. Assn. (pres. 1988-89, bd. dirs. 1982-85, excellence in teaching award 1974), Am. Statis. Assn., Am. Evaluation Assn., Am. Econ. Assn., University Club, Sigma Xi (pres. 1986-87), Phi Kappa Phi (pres. 1979-80). Roman Catholic. Home: 2372 Burcham Dr East Lansing MI 48823-3885 Office: Mich State U Dept of Agrl Econs Circle Dr East Lansing MI 48824-1039 Office Phone: 517-355-0301. Business E-Mail: mandersc@msu.edu.

**MANDERSCHEID, RONALD WILLIAM,** program administrator; b. La-Crosse, Wis., Sept. 28, 1943; s. William Joseph and Norene Elsine (Batten) M.; m. Frances Elizabeth Fedkiw, Sept. 1, 1973; children: William Derrick, Kristen Elizabeth, Erika Marie. BA maxima cum laude, Loras Coll., 1965; MA, Marquette U., 1967; PhD, U. Md., 1975; Cert., Fed. Exec. Inst., 1986. Rsch. assist. U. Md., College Park, 1970—72; rsch. assoc. NIMH, Adelphi, Md., 1972—75, sr. rsch. sociologist, 1975—80, chief evaluation rsch. sect. Rockville, Md., 1980—81, chief stats. rsch. br., 1981—92; acting dir. divsn. state and cmty. sys. devel. Ctr. Mental Health Svcs., Rockville, 1992—93, chief survey & analysis, 1992—2006; dir. mental health and substance use program Constella Group, Rockville, 2006—. Cons. George Washington U., Washington, 1978-83, WHO, 1993—, Pan Am. Health Orgn., 1995—, Columbia U., 1998-2001; mem. Internat. Consortium Mental Health Policy & Rsch., 2000—; adj. prof. dept. mental health Johns Hopkins U., Balt., 2006—. Author, editor: Mental Health in the United States, 1987, 90, 92, 94, 96, 98, 2000, 02, 04; editor: System Science and the Future of Health, 1976; prodr.: Making the Numbers Work for You, 1987; spl. editor Jour. of Washington Acad. Scis., 2000, Internat. Jour. Mental Health, 2005;contbr. articles to profl. jours. Active West Montgomery Citizens Assn., Potomac, Md., 1983—.

With U.S. Army, 1967-69. Decorated Army Commendation medal; recipient Disting. Alumni award, Loras Coll., 1998, Sec. Disting. Svc. award, Dept. Health and Human Sevcs., 1999, 2004, 2005, 2006, Mental Health Stats. Improvement Program Leadership award, 2001, 2006, Irving Blumberg Humanitarian award, Am. Assn. for Psychosocial Rehab., 2002. Fellow Washington Acad. Scis. (life, pres. 1987-88), World Acad. Art and Sci.; mem. APHA (chair mental health 1997-98, Mental Health Sect. award 2000, Mental Health Chairperson's Disting. Svc. award 2001, Consumer Leadership award 2003), N.Y. Acad. Scis., Am. Sociol. Assn. (chmn. various coms. 1983-91, chmn. com. fed. stds. sociologists 1983-88), Soc. for Gen. Sys. Rsch. (chmn. Washington chpt. 1976—), Ea. Sociol. Soc. (exec. com. 1979-84, chmn. various coms., Peter Gellman award 1984), D.C. Sociol. Soc. (pres. 1992-93), Fed. Exec. Inst. Alumni Assn. (exec. bd. 1997-2005, chair policy issues com. 1995-2000, pres. 2003, pres. found. 2003—), Meritorious Svc. award 1999), Soc. Applied Sociology (Nat. Sociol. Practice award 1995), Nat. Assn. State Mental Health Program Dirs. (Disting. Svc. award 2006, Pub. Svc. tribute 2006), Am. Coll. Mental Health Admimstrs. (Saul Feldman Lifetime Achievement award 2003, Disting. Svc. award 2006), Nat. Coun. Cmty. Behavioral Healthcare (Pub. Svc. award 2006), Cosmos Club, Alpha Kappa Delta (pres. 1972-73), Delta Epsilon Sigma, Phi Kappa Phi. Avocations: coin collecting/numismatics, reading. Office: Constella Group 6003 Exec Blvd Ste 400 Rockville MD 20852 Office Phone: 301-571-0240 432, 240-574-2607. Business E-Mail: ronald.manderscheid@samhsa.hhs.gov. E-mail: rmanderscheid@constellagroup.com.

**MANDIBERG, DAVID MICHAEL,** sculptor; b. Detroit, June 30, 1942; s. Jack Norman and Helen (Jaffe) M. Student, Art Students League, N.Y.C., 1965-68, San Francisco Art Inst., 1970-71, Ctr for Creative Studies, Detroit, 1991-93; BA, Wayne State U., 1981. Tchr. sculpture Cunniff Studio Gallery, Lake Orion, 1995-96. One-man shows include Cunniff Studio Gallery, Lake Orion, Mich., 1989, 91, 93-95, 97, Swann Gallery, Detroit, 1997, 99; exhibited in group shows at Detroit Artists Market, 1970, Helen Cunniff Studio Gallery, Lake Orion, 1987, 88, 90, Detroit Focus Gallery, 1988, Ariel Gallery, N.Y.C., 1988, 89, Sculptors Guild Mich., Detroit, 1993, Gallery One Twenty Eight, N.Y.C., 1994, 96, Scarab Club, Detroit, 1998, Mus. Contemporary Art, Pontiac, Mich., 1999, State of the Art Gallery, Ithaca, N.Y., 2002, See Spot Gallery, Ithaca, 2003; represented in permanent collections Rosemary McNaughton, Toronto, Can., Helen Cunniff, Lake Orion, Mich., Swords into Plowshares Peace Ctr., Detroit, Dr. Jack Levine, N.Y.C., Sol Lewitt, N.Y.C., Takao Nagai, Chgo., Irving Berg, Detroit, Joan Brace, Lake Orion, Mich., Mus. New Art, Detroit; sculptures include life-size David, Life, Psalm, Reality, Peace at Swords into Ploughshares Peace Ctr., Detroit, busts of William Clinton, Andy Warhol, Dr. Elliot Laby, Dr. Jack and Helen Mandiberg; Progress-3 part woodcarving, Stardom; TV appearances include Metro Art and Book Talk, Channel 11, Media One, 1999. Recipient 12 award ribbons Metro Carvers Mich., 1994-97, 2d place award for sculpture Sister Kenny Inst., Mpls., 1991; scholar Art Students League, 1966-67. Mem. Sculptors Guild Mich. (treas. 1992-97), Metro Carvers Mich., Detroit Blues Soc. (bd. dirs. 1994-96), Met. Detroit Recorder Soc., Nat. Sculpture Soc. Avocations: playing piano, guitar and recorder, italian, tennis. Home: Apt 101 2688 Patrick Henry St Auburn Hills MI 48326-2241 Studio: Ste 318 40 W Howard St Pontiac MI 48342-1293 E-mail: dmandiberg@aol.com.

**MANDIL, I. HARRY,** nuclear engineer; b. Istanbul, Turkey, Dec. 11, 1919; s. Harry Robert and Bertha (Presente) M. (parents Am. citizens); m. Beverly Ericson, June 22, 1946; children: Jean Dale, Eric Robert. BS, U. London, 1939; MS, MIT, 1941; grad., Oak Ridge Sch. Reactor Tech., 1950; DSc (hon.), Thiel Coll., Greenville, Pa., 1960. Devel., design process controls for textile mills and chem. plants Norcross Corp., 1941-42, asst. to pres. charge field engring., 1946-49; asst. to tech. dir. naval reactors br. reactor devel. div. AEC, 1950-54, dir. reactor engring. div. Bur. Ships, Navy Dept. and chief reactor engring. br. Naval Reactors, 1954-64; prin. officer, dir. MPR Assos., Inc. (engrs.), Washington, 1964-85, cons., dir. Alexandria, Va., 1985—. Developer nuclear power for propulsion naval vessels, also for Shippingport Atomic Power Ctrl. Sta.; mem., sec. Energy Adv. Bd., Washington, 1990-93; mem. corp. vis. com. for nuclear engring. dept. MIT, 1984-93; mem. sr. tech. rev. group for plutonium, Amarillo, Tex., 1995-99. Author numerous papers in field. Served with USNR, 1942-46. Recipient Naval Letter of Commendation, 1946, Meritorious Civilian Svc. award Navy Dept., 1952, ASME Prime Movers award, 1956, Disting. Civilian Svc. award. 1959. Mem. Nat. Acad. Engring. Home: 150 Moorings Park Dr K302 Naples FL 34105 Office: 320 King St Alexandria VA 22314-3238 Office Phone: 703-519-0200. Office Fax: 703-519-0224.

**MANDL, ALEX J(OHANN),** telecommunications company executive; b. Vienna, Dec. 14, 1943; came to U.S., 1958, naturalized, 1968; s. Otto William and Charlotte J. (Peshek) M.; m. Nancy J. Scott, June 10, 1967; 1 dau., Melanie. BA, Willamette U., 1967; MBA, U. Calif., Berkeley, 1969. With Boise Cascade Corp., 1969-80, dir. internat. fin., asst. treas., then fin. chmn. Boise, Idaho, 1973-80; sr. v.p. fin. and corp. planning Seaboard System R.R. Co., Jacksonville, Fla., 1980-85; sr. v.p. corp. devel. and adminstrn. CSX Corp., Richmond, Va., 1985-86; chmn., CEO CSX Tech., 1986-88, Sea-Land Corp. subs. CSX Corp., Iselin, N.J., 1988-91; exec. v.p. comm. svc. group AT&T, N.Y.C., 1991-96; chmn., CEO Teligent, Vienna, Va., 1996—. Bd. dirs. CSX Comm., CSX Transp., Inc., Richmond Renaissance, Cybernetics and Systems Inc. Trustee Jacksonville Art Mus. Mem. Fin. Execs. Inst., Soc. Internat. Treasurers, Young Pres. Orgn., Bus. Week Corp. Planning 100, Mgmt. Policy Council, Council Planning Execs. (conf. bd.), Fin. Execs. Inst. (com. on corp. fin.). Clubs: River, University, The Bull and Bear. Office: Taligent 7925 Jones Branch Dr Mc Lean VA 22102-3321

**MANDL, HERBERT JAY,** rabbi; b. Balt., Jan. 9, 1945; s. Sigmund and Ruth (Lefkowitz) M.; m. Barbara Sue Toltzis, Aug. 18, 1968; children: Aron M., Seth S., Debra A., Miriam D. AB, Johns Hopkins U., Balt.. 1965: MHL Jewish Theol. Sem., 1967. DDiv, 1994; PhD, U. Montreal, 1981. Ordained rabbi, 1969. Lectr. U. Alta., Edmonton, 1969-71; sr. rabbi Beth Shalom Synagoge, Edmonton, Alta., Can.. 1969-71; asst. rabbi Congregation Shaar Hashomayim, Montreal, Que., Can., 1971-77; sr. rabbi Kehilath Israel Synagogue, Kansas City, Mo., 1977—; chaplain Overland Park Police Dept., Kans., 2000—. Adj. prof. U. Mo., Kansas City, 1978-80, Rockhurst Coll., adj. prof., 1989—; chaplain Kansas City Police Dept., 1988—. Bd. dirs. Shalom Geriatric Group, Kansas City, 1985-1990, Jewish Fedn., Kansas City, 1977—; chmn. State Mo. Health Facilities Rev. Commn., Jefferson City, 1980-86; chmn. Kansas State Holocaust Commn., Topeka, 1987—; mem. Kansas City Sister City Commn., 1980—, Kans. Pub. Disclosure Commn., 1991-97. Mem. Rabbinical Assembly (com. Jewish law and standards 1989-94), Internat. Order Police Chaplains, Rabbinical Assn. Kansas City (pres. 1980-81, 94-96), Union for Traditional Judaism (panelist on Jewish law 1985—), B'nai Brith, Rabbinic Cabinet United Jewish Cmtys., Fedn. of North Am. Office: Kebilath Israel Synagogue 10501 Conser St Shawnee Mission KS 66212-2600 Office Phone: 913-642-1880. Personal E-mail: hjm18@aol.com.

**MANDL, ROBERT,** application developer; b. Romania; s. Paul and Eva Mandl. MSc in Math., MIT, Cambridge, Mass., MSEE, PhD in Engring., PhD in Linguistics. Sr. software engr. Softech, Waltham, Mass., 1980—83; mgr. software engring. Analogic Corp., Peabody, Mass., 1983—89; sr. software engr. Info. Engring., Bedford, Mass., 1990; cons. AT&T Bell Labs., North Andover, Mass., 1991—95; prin. engr. Digital Equipment Corp., Littleton, Mass., 1996—2001; ind. rschr. Cambridge, 2001—. Author software; compiler, editor: MIT Folk Dance Club Song Book, 1975; contbr. articles to profl. jours.; presenter in field. Mem.: IEEE, NY Acad. Sci., IEEE Computer Soc., Linguistic Soc. Am., Math. Assn. Am., Sigma Xi. Avocations: languages, running, hambo, dance. Home: Box 397199 Cambridge MA 02139

**MANDL, WILLIAM JOHN,** electronics engineer, researcher; b. Los Angeles, Calif., Apr. 8, 1939; s. Bernard William Mandl and Teresa Rooal; m. Mary Louise Mullins, Nov. 25, 1950; children: Kathryn Ingrid McCarron, Stephen Mingus, Joseph William. AA, East LA Coll., 1957—59; BS, Calif. State U. at LA, 1959—62; MS, U. So. Calif., 1963—65. Rsch. engr. Rockwell Internat., Downey, Calif., 1960—64; sr. rsch. engr. RCA, Van Nuys,

Calif., 1964—67, Litton Systems, Woodland Hills, Calif., 1967—69; v.p. mktg. Macrodata, Los Angeles, 1969—76; new products mktg. mgr. EM&M, Woodland Hills, Calif., 1976—78; pres. Hometech Corp., Los Angeles, 1978—81; dir. of engring. Aerojet, Azusa, Calif., 1981—94; pres. Amain Electronics Co., Reno, 1994—. Asst. of engring. Calif. State U. at LA, 1964—67. Contbr. articles to profl. jours. Recipient 1998 SBIR Phase II Quality award, US Army, 1998. Achievements include patents for method and apparatus for multiplexed oversampled analog to digital modulation; system for digitally driving addressable pixel matrix; residential monitoring and control system; low power EPROM logic cell and log arrays there of; garbage collection system for a symbolic digital processor. Home: 5429 Greenview Ct Reno NV 89502 Office: Amain Electronics Co 3983 South McCarran Blvd Unit 466 Reno NV 89502 Office Phone: 775-825-6001. Home Fax: 775-825-6002; Office Fax: 775-825-6002. Personal E-mail: wmandl@aol.com.

**MANDLE, EARL ROGER,** academic administrator, former museum director; b. Hackensack, N.J., May 13, 1941; s. Earl and Phyllis (Key) M.; m. Gayle Wells Jenkins, July 11, 1964; children: Luke Harrison, Julia Barnes. BA cum laude, Williams Coll., 1963; MA, NYU, 1967, cert. in Museum Training, 1967, postgrad.; DFA (hon.), U. Toledo, 1983, Kenyon Coll., 1986; PhD, Case Western Reserve U., 2002; DFA (hon.), Brown U., 2003. Intern in drawings Met. Mus. Art, NYC; intern in sculpture and architecture Victoria and Albert Mus., London, 1966-67; assoc. dir. Mpls. Inst. Arts, 1967-74, Toledo Mus. Art, 1974-76, dir., 1977-88; dep. dir. Nat. Gallery Art, Washington, 1988-93; pres. RISD, Providence, 1993—. Chmn. exec. com. Am. Fedn. Arts, 1987-93; mem. adv. panel New Zealand-U.S. Arts Found., Nas. Mgmt. Inst.; trustee Internat. Exhbns. Found., Sterling & Francine Clark Art Inst., Spanish Found. for Restoration of Toledo (Spain); mem. NEA, Nat. Com. Standards in Arts, 1992-94, steering com. 1993-94; mem. adv. council Nat. Mus. Act, Smithsonian Instn.; mem. adv. com. on mus. mgmt. J. Paul Getty Trust; adv. bd. Charles Hosmer Morse Found., Inc., Wexner Ctr., 1986, search com. dirs., 1988; chmn. U.S. Com. on Restoration of Toledo; cons. Nat. Mus. Western Art, Tokyo, Kerr Found., Oklahoma City; chair cultural adv. council Netherlands-Am. Amity Trust, Inc., Annual Coun. Retreats, 1990, 91, co-chmn. agenda com., 1992, cultural diversity task force, 1993, chair Clinton adminstrn. liaison com., 1993; mem., exec. Ohio Arts Coun.; mem. exec. adv. com. Williams Coll. Mus. Art; mem. arts adv. com. Barnes Found.; com. for the preservation of the U.S. Treasury Bldg., hist. advisor, 1989-93; vis. prof. Robert Sterling Clark Prof. of Art Williams Coll., Williamstown, Mass., 1993; mem. bd. trustees, sec. Art Mus. Assn., 1983, v.p. 1985, pres. 1986; com. mem. Art Against Aids, 1987, The Barnes Found. Conservation, 1992; founding trustee Coun. Mus. and Edn. in the Visual Arts, 1971; exec. com. Intermuseum Conservation Assn., 1977; appted. to Nat. Coun. Arts, Pres. Reagan, 1988, Pres. Bush, 1990-94; mem. search adv. com. U.S. State Dept. Curator, 1992; resource cons. Arts Edn. Partnership Working Group Subcommittee, Nat. Ctr. Arts Edn., 1992-93;bd. mem. Indian-dependent Coll. Art & Design (AICAD), Fraunhofer Gesellschaft; hon. bd. mem. Sterling & Francine Clark Art Inst., Toledo Mus. Art; testimony to the adv. bd. Nat. Mus. African Art, Smithsonian Instn., 1990; adv. session for bd. trustees The Textile Mus., Wash., D.C., 1993. Contbr. to profl. mags. and jours. Chmn., bd. dirs. Health and Edn. Leadership for Providence, 1996-99; trustee Providence Found., 1996, Toledo Arts Commn. 1975-78, Toledo Hosp., 1979, pub. rels. Com., 1979-88; mem. City Film Commn., 1995, Coun. Ambs; bd. dirs. Cranston Print Works, 1994-99; mem. adv. bd. Corp. Design Found., 1995, Alliance of Artists' Cmtys., chmn. com. on trustees, 1997-99; mem. nat. policy bd. Ams. for Artists, 1998; mem. steering com. Nat. Endowment for Arts, 1999; bd. trustees nom. com. Am. Red Cross, Toledo chpt., 1976, chmn. youth com.; founder English Speaking Union, Mpls. chpt., 1974; trustee long range planning com. Maumee Valley Country Day Sch., 1983-84, v.p., chmn. com. on trustees, 1987-88; Mayor's com. planning, City of Perrysburg, Ohio, 1985; mem. Rotary, vice-chmn. internat. svc. com., 1987, chmn. 75th anniversary sculpture com. 1987; design review bd. Toledo 1% for Art, 1978-88; mem. Toledo Bicentennial commn. 1974-76; mem. Toledo's com. of One Hundred, Cultural Task Force, 1987; bd. mem. Toledo's Cmty. And Cultural Arts Ctr., 1983; mem. Toledo Econ. Planning Coun., Cmty. and Cultural Programs Subcommittee, chmn. design com., 1981; mem. Toledo Exec. Forum, 1974-81, Toledo Mayor's Citizen Forum, 1975, Toledo Mayor's Com. on Renaissance Bldg. Redevelopment, 1983, Toledo Modern Art Group, 1974-1981, Toledo Sesquicentennial Commn., 1986-87, Young Pres. Org., Wash. Metro chpt., 1988-91, Greater Providence C. of C., 1994-; mem. task force com. Toledo Pub. Sch. "Partners in Edn.", 1981; coord. and speaker United Way Campaign Toledo, Company Program, 1975-81; mem. Warren/Sherman City Venture Project Mobility/Land Use Design Use com., 1977; mem. corp. bd. Trustcorp, Inc., audit, loan and nom. com., 1981-88. Decorated by the His Majesty Juan Carlos Knight of the Order of Isabel the Cath., Spain, 1985; Andover teaching fellow, 1963-64; Ford Found. fellow, 1966; Nat. Endowment Arts fellow, 1974; recipient Am. Hellenic Educational Progressive award, 1983, Distinguished Citizen for Art award Ohio Art Edn. Assn., 1983, Resolution for Leadership award Ohio Senate, 1983, Governor's award State of Ohio, 1983, Marketer of the Year award Am. Marketing Assn., 1983. Mem. Am. Assn. Mus. (trustee, v.p.), Art Mus. Assn. (pres.), Assn. Art Mus. Dirs., Am. Arts Alliance (trustee, policy com.), Coll. Art Assn. (mem. pres.' adv. bd.), Ohio Found. for Arts, Ohio Art Coun., Am. Assn. 18th Century Studies (treas.), Young Pres. Orgn., R.I. Ind. Higher Edn. Assn., Am. Fedn. Arts (chmn. exec. com., chmn. exhbn. com. 1985-93), R.I. Commodores, Confrerie des Chevaliers du Tastevin, Phi Kappa Phi. (hon. mem.), Providence Art Club, Univ. Club, Title Club, Century Club (N.Y.C.), The Answer Club, Williams Club (N.Y.C.), Carranor Hunt and Polo Club, Catawba Island Yacht Club, The Toledo Club (mem, trustee 1977-88), Hope Club. Office: RISD Office of President 2 College St Providence RI 02903-2784

**MANDLER, GEORGE,** psychologist, educator; b. Vienna, June 11, 1924; came to U.S., 1940, naturalized, 1943; s. Richard and Hede (Goldschmied) M.; m. Jean Matter, Jan. 19, 1957; children: Peter Clark, Michael Allen. BA, NYU, 1949; MS, Yale U., 1950, PhD, 1953; post grad., U Basel, Switzerland, 1947-48. Asst. prof. Harvard U., 1953-57, lectr., 1957-60; prof. U Toronto, 1960—65; prof. psychology U. Calif., San Diego, 1965-94, chmn. dept. psychology 1965-70, prof. emeritus, 1994—; dir. Ctr. Human Info. Processing, U. Calif., San Diego, 1965-90. Hon. rsch. fellow Univ. Coll. London, 1977-78, 82-90, vis. prof., 1990—. Author: Mind and Emotion, 1975, (German edit.), 1980, Mind and Body, 1984, (Japanese edit.); 1987, Cognitive Psychology, 1985, Japanese edit., 1991, Human Nature Explored, 1997, Interesting Times, 2001, Consciousness Recovered, 2002; co-author: (with W. Kessen) The Language of Psychology, (Italian edit.), 1959, (with J.M. Mandler) Thinking: From Association to Gestalt, 1964; contbr. articles and revs. to profl. jours.; editor: Psychol. Rev., 1970-76. Served with U.S. Army, 1943-46. Fellow Ctr. for Advanced Study in Behavioral Scis., 1959-60; vis. fellow Oxford U., Eng., 1971-72, 78; Guggenheim fellow, 1971-72. Fellow AAAS, Am. Acad. Arts and Scis.; mem. AAUP, Am. Assn. Advancement Psychology (1974-82); Psychonomic Soc. (governing bd., chmn. 1983), Am. Psychol. Soc., Am. Psychol. Assn. (pres. div. exptl. psychology 1978-79, pres. div. gen psychology 1982-83, mem. coun. reps. 1978-82, William James prize 1986), Internat. Union Psychol. Scis. (U.S. com. 1985-90), Soc. Exptl. Psychologists, Fedn. Behavioral Psychol. and Cognitive Scis. (pres. 1983). Home: 1406 La Jolla Knoll La Jolla CA 92037-5236 Office: U Calif San Diego Dept Psychology La Jolla CA 92093-0109 also: 3 Perrins Lane London NW3 1QY England Business E-Mail: gmandler@ucsd.edu.

**MANDLER, JEAN MATTER,** psychologist, educator; b. Oak Park, Ill., Nov. 6, 1929; d. Joseph Allen and May Roberts (Finch) Matter; m. George Mandler, Jan. 19, 1957; children: Peter Clark, Michael Allen. Student, Carleton Coll., 1947-49; BA with highest honors, Swarthmore Coll., 1951; PhD, Harvard U., 1956. Rsch. assoc. lab. social rels. Harvard U., 1957-60; rsch. assoc. dept. psychology U. Toronto, Ont., Canada, 1961-65; assoc. rsch. psychologist, lectr. U. Calif. at San Diego, La Jolla, 1965-73, assoc. prof., 1973-77, prof. psychology, 1977-88, prof. of cognitive sci., 1988—96, disting. prof., 1996—2000, disting. rsch. prof., 2000—; mem. adv. com. memory and cognitive processes NSF, 1978-81. Hon. rsch. fellow U. Coll. London, 1978-89, vis. prof., 1990—; hon. mem. Med. Rsch. Coun. Cognitive Devel. Unit, 1982-98. Author: (G. Mandler) Thinking: From Association to Gestalt,

1964, Stories, Scripts and Scenes, 1984, The Foundations of Mind: Origins of Conceptual Thought, 2004 (APA Divsn. 7 Eleanor Maccoby Book award 2005); assoc. editor Psychol. rev., 1970-76; mem. editl. bd. Child Devel., 1976-89, Discourse Processes, 1977-94, Jour. Exptl. Psychology, 1977-85, Text, 1979-97, Jour. Verbal Learning and Verbal Behavior, 1980-88, Lang. and Cognitive Processes, 1985—, Cognitive Devel., 1990-99, Jour. Cognition and Devel., 1999—; contbr. articles to profl. jours Pres. San Diego Assn. Gifted Children, 1968-71; v.p. Calif. Parents for Gifted, 1970-71; mem. alumni council Swarthmore Coll., 1975-78. NIMH research grantee, 1968—81, NSF research grantee, 1981—99. Fellow: APA (mem. exec. com. divsn. 3 1983—85), Am. Acad. Arts and Scis.; mem.: Soc. Exptl. Psychologists, Cognitive Devel. Soc., Cognitive Sci. Soc., Psychonomic Soc. (mem. governing bd. 1982—87, chmn. 1985—86), Phi Beta Kappa. Office: U Calif San Diego Dept Cognitive Sci 9500 Gilman Dr La Jolla CA 92093-0515 Business E-Mail: jmandler@ucsd.edu.

**MANDLES, MARTINN HEROE,** facility services company executive; b. Tacoma, Nov. 1, 1940; m. Connie Mandles; children: Melanie, Valarie Barsky. BS in Engring., Stanford U., 1964. Pilot U.S. Navy, 1964—68; dir., western corp. opers. Microdot Inc., 1969—72; v.p., mem. bd. dirs., exec. com., 1992—96, chmn. bd., 1997—. Dir. Nat. Multi-Housing Coun., Washington, 1988—90, Bldg. Owners & Mgrs. Assn. of Greater L.A., 1995—. Founding dir. Century City C. of C., 1971—, chmn. bd., 1994; trustee Jewish Big Brothers & Sisters Assn., 1977—; charter mem. Fraternity of Friends of the L.A. Music Ctr., 1978—; trustee The Hebrew U. of Jerusalem, 1996—, vice chmn., dir. western region Am. Friends, 1996—. Lt. comdr. USN. Named Century City Citizen of Yr., Century City C. of C., 1986. Mem.: The Regency Club (L.A.), Hillcrest Country Club (L.A.). Home: 2465 Century Hill at 10100 Galaxy Way Los Angeles CA 90067

**MANDRA, YORK T.,** geology educator; b. NYC; s. Raymond and Irene (Farruggio) M.; m. Highoohi Kechijian, Jan. 26, 1946. BA, U. Calif., Berkeley, 1947, MA in Paleontology, 1949; PhD in Geology, Stanford U., 1958. From instr. to assoc. prof. geology San Francisco State U., 1950-63, prof., 1964—2004, head geology sect., chmn. dept., 1960-67, prof. emeritus, 2005—. Vis. prof. U. Aix-Marseille, France, 1959, Syracuse U., summer 1963, U. Maine, summer 1969, U. Calif., Santa Barbara, summers 1972—2002; rsch. assoc. U. Glasgow, 1959, Calif. Acad. Scis., 1966-88; vis. scientist New Zealand Geol. Survey, fall 1970; disting. fellow in geol. scis. U. Calif., Santa Barbara, 2001—. Contbr. numerous articles to profl. jours. Pres. David S. Sohigian Found., 1975—. Served with USAAF, 1942-46. Recipient Neil A. Miner Disting. Coll. Teaching award, 1984; Danforth Found. teaching fellow, 1958, NSF fellow, 1959; NSF rsch. grantee, 1967-77. Fellow Geol. Soc. Am. (Sr.), Calif. Acad. Scis., Calif. Acad. Scis.; mem. Assn. Geology Tchrs. (pres. Far Western sect. 1953-54, 73-74, Robert Wallace Webb award 1977). Avocations: walking, reading, music. Office: San Francisco State U Dept Geoscis 1600 Holloway Ave Dept Geoscis San Francisco CA 94132-1722 E-mail: ytjmandra@sfsu.edu.

**MANDRACCHIA, VINCENT JOSEPH,** podiatrist; b. Bklyn., Oct. 5, 1950; s. Vincent and Eva (DiGiamBattista) M.; m. Denise Mary Wardell, June 1, 1991; 1 child, Michael. BS, St. Francis Coll., 1972; D in Podiatric Medicine, Pa. Coll. Podiatric Medicine, 1976. Elaborate Am. Bd. Podiatric Surgery. Resident in foot surgery Met. Hosp., Phila., 1976-78; chmn. sect. on podiatric surgery Springfield (Pa.) Hosp., 1989—; podiatrist Family Foot Care Assocs., PA, Sewell, N.J. Author: (textbook) Foot Surgery, 1989; contbr. articles to profl. jours. Mem. active status U.S. Power Squadrons, 1980. Fellow Am. Coll. Foot Surgeons; mem. Am. Med. Writers Soc., Pi Delta. Republican. Roman Catholic. Avocation: boating. Office: Family Foot Care Assocs Washington Med Arts Bldg RR 1 Sewell NJ 08080-9501

**MANDRELL, BARBARA ANN,** singer, entertainer, actress, producer, writer; b. Houston, Dec. 25, 1948; d. Irby Matthew and Mary Ellen (McGill) M.; m. Kenneth Lee Dudney, May 28, 1967; children: Kenneth Matthew, Jaime Nicole, Nathaniel. Grad. high sch. Country music singer and entertainer, 1959—, performed throughout U.S. and in various fgn. countries; mem., Grand Ole Opry, Nashville, 1972—; star TV series Barbara Mandrell and the Mandrell Sisters, 1980-82, Barbara Mandrell: Get to the Heart, 1987; albums include Midnight Oil, Treat Him Right, He set My Life To Music (Grammy award, Dove award 1983), This Time I Almost Made It, This is Barbara Mandrell, Midnight Angel, Barbara Mandrell's Greatest Hits, Christmas at Our House, 1987, Morning Sun, 1990, Greatest Country Hits, 1990, Standing Room Only, 1993; star TV series Barbara Mandrell and the Mandrell Sisters, 1980-82, TV movie Burning Rage, 1984, TV specials Barbara Mandrell, Something Special, 1985, The Lady is A Champ, (TV) The Wrong Girl, 1999, Stolen from the Heart, 2000; guest star TV series The Commish, Touched By an Angel, Dr. Quinn, Medicine Woman, Baywatch, Diagnosis Murder, (TV series) Sunset Beach, 1997-98, Touched By an Angel, 1994, Love Boat: The Next Wave, 1998, others; author (with George Vecsey): Get To the Heart: My Story, 1990; co-exec. (TV) Get to the Heart: The Barbara Mandrell Story, 1997; discs include No Nonsense, 1990, Key's in the Mailbox, 1991, The Best of Barbara Mandrell, 1992, The Ultimate Barbara Mandrell, 1994, The Barbara Mandrell Collection, 1995, Fooled By a Feeling, 1995. Named Miss Oceanside, Calif., 1965; Named Most Promising Female Singer, Acad. Country and Western Music, 1971; Female Vocalist of Yr., 1978; Female Vocalist of Yr., Music City News Cover Awards, 1979; Female Vocalist of Yr., Country Music Assn., 1979, 81, Entertainer of Yr., 1980, 81, 95; People's Choice awards (9), 1983-87. Mem. Musicians Union, Screen Actors Guild, AFTRA, Country Music Assn. (v.p.) Mem. Order Eastern Star. Home: PO Box 620 Hendersonville TN 37077-0620 Office: Creative Artists Agy 3310 W End Ave Fl 5 Nashville TN 37203-1028

**MANDRY, CHRISTINE M.,** public information officer; b. Waukegan, Ill., June 16, 1961; d. Jamon and Linda (Lambert) LaPonsie; m. Dennis Ralet d Mandry; children: Sherri Ann, Casey Lynn, Nicole, Rebekah. BS, Auburn U., 2000, MPA, 2003. Cert.: (legal asst.); victim svcs. officer. Records tech. Adminstrv. Office of Cts., Montgomery, Ala.; restitution coord. Dist. Atty.'s Office, Montgomery, 2000—. Softball coach Millbrook Girls Softball League; vol. Victims of Crime and Leniency, Elmore County Humane Soc., Montgomery County Habitat for Humanity. Mem.: Ala. Victim Svc. Officer Assn., Nat. Orgn. Victim Assistance, Am. Soc. for Pub. Adminstrs., Nat. Fastpitch Coaches Assn., Lady Mustangs Booster Club (treas.). Home: 40 Green Ct Deatsville AL 36022 Office: Dist Atty's Office 100 South Lawrence St Montgomery AL 36102 Office Phone: 334-832-2545. Personal E-mail: cmandry@justice.com. Business E-Mail: christinemandry@mc-ala.org.

**MANDYAM, GIRIDHAR DHATI,** electronics engineer; b. Dallas, Tex., Oct. 15, 1967; s. Mandyam Dhati and Revathi Srinath; m. Chitra Mandyam, Feb. 1, 1973; 1 child, Atulya Dhati. BSEE, So. Meth. U., Dallas, 1985—89; MSEE, U. So. Calif., L.A., 1991—93; PhD, U. N.Mex, Albuquerque, 1994—96. Engr. Rockwell Internat., Richardson, Tex., 1989—91, Qualcomm Inc., San Diego, Calif., 1993—94; mem. of group tech. staff Tex. Instruments, Dallas, Tex., 1996—98; sr. rsch. engr. Nokia Rsch. Ctr., Irving, Tex., 1998—2000, prin. scientist, 2000—02 dir., 2002—04, San Diego, 2004—06; chief technologist, sr. mem. Nokia Mobile Phones, Irving, Tex., 2006—. Adj. prof. U. Tex. at Dallas, Richardson, 2001—. Mem.: IEEE. Achievements include patents for 13 issued US patents.

**MANEA, NORMAN,** writer, educator; b. Suceava, Bukovina, Romania, July 19, 1936; came to U.S., 1988; s. Marcu and Janeta (Braunstein) M.; m. Josette-Cella Boiangiu, June 28, 1969. MS in Engring., Inst. Constrn., Bucharest, Romania, 1954. Engr. Romania, 1959-74; writer, 1969-86; fellow Deutscher Akademischer Austauschdienst, West Berlin, Germany, 1987; fellow Internat. Acad. Scholarship and the Arts Bard Coll., Annandale On Hudson, NY, 1989-92, writer in residence, 1992-96, Francis Flournoy prof. in European studies and culture, 1997—. Author: October, eight o'clock, 1992, On Clowns: The Dictator & the Artist, 1992, Compulsory Happiness, 1993, The Black Envelope, 1995, The Hooligan's Return, 2003; contbr. articles, stories to profl. jours. Recipient MacArthur Found. award, 1992, Nat. Jewish

Book award Jewish Book Coun., 1993, Literary Lion award Nat. Pub. Libr., 1993, Nonino Internat. Lit. prize, Italy, 2002, Napoli prize for internat. fiction, 2004, Holtzbrinck prize Am. Acad. in Berlin, 2005; Guggenheim grantee, 1992; Fulbright fellow, 1988. Mem. Am. PEN, Berlin Acad. Art. Office: Bard Coll Dept Lang and Lit Annandale On Hudson NY 12504

**MANEKER, MORTON M.,** lawyer; b. NYC, Nov. 14, 1932; s. Arthur and Estelle (Hochberg) M.; m. Roberta S. Wexler, 1985; children: Meryl Colle, Amy Jill, Marion Kenneth. AB, Harvard U., 1954, LL.B., 1957. Bar: NY 1957. Assoc. Shearman & Sterling, 1957—62; trial atty. antitrust divsn. Dept. Justice, 1962—63; ptnr. Proskauer Rose LLP, N.Y.C., 1963—94; ret., 1994. Trustee Beth Israel Hosp., N.Y.C., 1977—2001. Mem. Am. Law Inst., N.Y. State Bar Assn., Harmonie Club. Jewish. Home: 30 E 65th St New York NY 10021-7013 Office Phone: 212-439-9737. Personal E-mail: maneker@aol.com.

**MANEKER, ROBERTA S(UE),** public relations executive; b. N.Y.C., July 9, 1937; d. Maxwell Roy and Esther (Gerson) Scheff; m. Hannan Wexler, June 4, 1961 (div. 1983); children: Daniel, Joanna Bayer; m. Morton M. Maneker, June 1, 1985. BA, Oberlin Coll., 1957. Mng. editor True Love mag., N.Y.C., 1960-62; publicity dir. Capt. Kangaroo, CBS, N.Y.C., 1962-66; syndicated columnist Oleg Cassini, N.Y.C., 1967-69; freelance writer, N.Y.C., 1967-70; dir. pub. rels. Direct Mktg. Assn., N.Y.C., 1983-85, v.p. pub. rels., 1985-87; v.p. pub. rels. Christie's, N.Y.C., 1987-91, sr. v.p. corp. comm./mktg., 1991-94; freelance cons. mktg. and pub. rels., 1995—; mktg. dir. Phillips Auctioneers, 2000-01; mktg. cons. Lechters, Inc., 2000, dir. 1991-2001. Contbr. articles to publs. Ford Found. scholar, 1953-57. Trustee Jewish Home and Hosp., 1996-04, chmn. Manhattan Divsn., 2000-03; trustee Oberlin Coll., 1997—, mem. exec. com., 2004-2006, hon. treas, 2006—; chmn. vis. com. Allen Meml. Art Mus., 2002—. Mem. Oberlin Coll. Alumni Assn. (pres. 1989-91), Phi Beta Kappa

**MANELLA, NORA MARGARET,** judge; BA with high hons. in Italian, Wellesley Coll., Mass., 1972; JD, U. So. Calif., 1975. Bar: Calif. 1976, U.S. Ct. Appeals (5th cir.) 1976, D.C. Ct. Appeals 1978, U.S. Dist. Ct. (ctrl., so., no. and ea. dists.) 1980-81, U.S. Ct. Appeals (9th cir.) 1982. Law clk. to Hon. John Minor Wisdom U.S. Ct. Appeals (5th cir.), New Orleans, 1975-76; legal counsel Subcom. on Constn., Senate Com. on Judiciary, Washington, 1976-78; assoc. O'Melveny & Myers, Washington and L.A., 1978-82; asst. U.S. atty. U.S. Dept. Justice, LA, 1982—90, trial asst. major crimes, 1982-85, dep. chief, criminal complaints, 1986-87, chief criminal appeals, 1988-90; judge LA Mcpl. Ct., 1990-92, 1998—2006, LA Superior Ct., 1992-93, U.S. Dist. Ct. (ctrl. dist.) Calif., LA, 1998—; justice pro tem Calif. Ct. of Appeal 2d appellate dist. LA, 1992, assoc. justice, 2006—; U.S. Atty. (ctrl. dist.) Calif. U.S. Dept. Justice, LA, 1994—98. Instr. U.S. Atty. Gen. Advocacy Inst., 1984-86, Calif. Jud. Coll., 1992-93; mem. Atty. Gen.'s Adv. Com., 1994-95. Mem. editl. bd. State Bar Criminal Law Newsletter, 1991-92. Mem. adv. bd. Monroe H.S. and Govt. Magnet, 1991-94; acad. specialist USAID Delegation, 1993; judge L.A. Times Cmty. Partnership Awards, 1993; bd. councilors Law Sch. U. So. Calif., 1996—. Mem. Am. Law Inst., Calif. Judges Assn., Nat. Assn. Women Judges, Calif. Women Lawyers, Women Lawyers L.A., Phi Beta Kappa, Order of the Coif. Office: Calif Ct of Appeal 2d Appellate Dist LA 300 South Spring St Los Angeles CA 90013 Office Phone: 213-830-7443. Business E-Mail: arlene.chavez@jud.ca.gov.

**MANELLI, DONALD DEAN,** scriptwriter, film producer; b. Burlington, Iowa, Oct. 20, 1936; s. Daniel Anthony and Mignon Marie (Dean) M.; m. Susan Linda Allen, June 16, 1964 (div. Aug. 1973); children: Daniel, Lisa. BA, U. Notre Dame, 1959. Communications specialist Jewel Cos., Melrose Park, Ill., 1959; script writer Coronet Films, Chgo., 1960-62; freelance writer Chgo., 1962-63; creative dir. Fred A. Niles Communications Ctrs., Chgo., 1963-67; sr. writer Wild Kingdom NBC-TV, Chgo., 1967-70; freelance film writer, producer Chgo., 1970-76; pres. Donald Manelli & Assocs., Inc., Chgo. and Paris, 1976—. Screenwriter, prodr. more than 225 documentary films, 1970—, numerous episodes Wild Kingdom, 1967-82 (Emmy award 1969, 70). Recipient numerous awards various orgns. including N.Y. Internat. Film Festival, Houston Internat. Film Festival, Berlin, Paris, Venice Internat. Film Festivals, CINE, 1976—. Mem. Writers Guild Am. Roman Catholic. Avocations: photography, travel, tennis. also: 1 Rue Goethe 75116 Paris France Office: Donald Manelli And Associates 175 N Harbor Dr Ste 4901 Chicago IL 60601-7892 E-mail: dmanelli@earthlink.net. *A simple truth is played out in most lives: what we believe ourselves to be, we are. We may be tested with our own failed efforts and plain bad luck, but our personal vision gives us strength. Success brings satisfaction and the responsibility to help others form and follow their own visions.*

**MANES, STEPHEN GABRIEL,** concert pianist, educator; b. Bennington, Vt., Apr. 11, 1940; s. Julius H. and Edna E. (Silberstein) M.; m. Frieda Green, July 7, 1963; children: Sonya Ruth, Daniel Ira. BS, Juilliard Sch. Music, 1961, MS, 1963; postgrad. (Fulbright fellow), Acad. Music, Vienna, 1963-64. Vis. instr. music Oberlin Coll. Conservatory, Ohio, 1966-67; asst. prof. Ball State U., Muncie, Ind., 1967-68; prof. music U. Buffalo-SUNY, 1968—, chair, 1989-93, 99—; co-music dir. Sebago-Long Lake Region Chamber Music Festival, North Bridgton, Maine, 1982-85. Concert piano soloist maj. orchs. U.S. and abroad; debuts in Washington, 1962, N.Y.C., 1963, Vienna, Austria, 1964, Berlin, 1975, Amsterdam, 1975, London, 1975, chamber music concerts, radio, TV appearances, four-hand piano recitals with Frieda Manes in U.S., Australia, Can. and P.R.; rec. artist Orion Master Records, 1974—, Spectrum Records, 1986—; mem. Baird Piano Trio, 1986-90, 2000—. Recipient Kosciuszko Chopin prize, 1960, Town Hall award Concert Artists Guild, 1962; finalist Leventritt Internat. Competition, 1962; Harriet Cohen Internat. Beethoven prize, 1964 Mem. Music Tchrs. Nat. Assn. Coll. Music Soc., Am. Fedn. Musicians. Home: 89 High Park Blvd Amherst NY 14226-4210 Office: U Buffalo-SUNY Dept of Music 222 Baird Hall Buffalo NY 14260-4700

**MANESS, ELEANOR PALMER,** researcher; b. Raleigh, N.C., June 24, 1935; d. Oren Alston and Lillian Way Palmer; m. Charles B. Maness, Feb. 1, 1955 (dec. July 1989); children: Reid, Brian, Teresa. BA, Meredith Coll., 1958. Tchr. St. Timoth Sch., Raleigh, 1958—64; rsch. analyst N.C. State U., Raleigh, 1966—99; cons., 1999—. Contbr. articles to sci. jours. Recipient L.M. Ware Rsch. award, Am. Soc. for Hort. Sci., 1974, Excellence in Environment Rsch. award, Fed. Hwy. Adminstrn., 1997. Presbyterian. Avocations: hiking, swimming, gardening, rock hunting, fishing. Home: 2104 Gray Walsh Dr Wilmington NC 28405

**MANETTA, AMEDA AVRILL,** social sciences educator; d. Malcolm James and Mabel Manetta; children: Lola P Sutherland, Morgan J. J. Sutherland. BA in Sociology, The U. of Western Ont., London, Ont., Can., 1988; BSW, The U. of Western Ont., 1989; MSW, U. of Western Ont., 1990; PhD, Va. Commonwealth U., 1997. Faculty Stephen F. Austin State U., Nacogdoches, Tex., 1997—98; assoc. prof. Winthrop U., Rock Hill, SC, 1998—. Bd. dirs. Safe Passage, Inc, Rock Hill, SC, 2003—. Contbr. articles to profl. jours., chapters to books. Mem. profl. adv. bd. Home Care Connections, Richmond, Grantee, Winthrop Faculty grantee, 1999, Stephen F. Austin Faculty grantee, 1998. Mem.: NASW (bd. dirs. 2001), Coun. on Social Work Edn., Am. Assn. of Suicidology. Office: Winthrop University 128 Bancroft Bldg Rock Hill SC 29733 Business E-Mail: manetta@winthrop.edu.

**MANETTA, RICHARD L.,** chemicals executive, lawyer; b. 1945; BA, U. Mich.; JD, Wayne State U. Legal advisor Detroit City Coun., 1973—74; chief supervising asst./corp. counsel City of Detroit Law Dept., 1974—78; asst. gen. counsel for automotive safety and product litigation Ford Motor Co., 1989—94, asst. gen. counsel for discovery, 1994—99, assoc. gen. counsel for litigation, 1999—2000, dep. gen. counsel, dir. regulatory compliance, 2000—01; chmn. v.p., gen. counsel The Dow Chem. Co., Midland, Mich., 2001—04, corp. v.p., spl. counsel to pres., 2004—05. Spkr. in field. Recipient

Pres. award, Nat. Bar Assn., 2001, award, Wolverine Bar Assn., 2001, Access to Justice award, State of Mich., 2003. Fellow: Mich. State Bar Found. (life); mem.: ABA, Mich. Gen. Counsel Assn., Mich. State Bar. Home: 59 Lake Shore Rd Grosse Pointe MI 48236

**MANEY, JACK LOGAN,** mathematician, educator; b. Crookston, Minn., Nov. 26, 1976; s. Daniel and Ardis Maney, George High (Stepfather); m. Geraldean Lynn Baxter, Aug. 7, 2005. BS in Math., ND State U., 1999; PhD in Math., N.D. State U., 2004. Grad. tchg. fellow ND State U., Fargo, 2003—04; asst. prof. math. U. SD, Vermillion, 2004—. Mem.: Math. Assn. Am., Am. Math. Soc. Democrat. Avocations: computers, mathematics. Office: U SD Dept Math Scis 414 E Clark St Vermillion SD 57069 Office Phone: 605-677-5997. Business E-Mail: jmaney@usd.edu.

**MANEY, MICHAEL MASON,** lawyer; b. Taihoku, Japan, Aug. 13, 1936; s. Edward Strait and Helen M. M.; m. Suzanne Cochran, Oct. 22, 1960; 1 child, Michele. BA, Yale U., 1956; MA, Fletcher Sch. Law and Diplomacy, Tufts U., 1957; LL.B., U. Pa., 1964. Bar: N.Y. 1966, D.C. 1977. Case officer CIA, 1957-61; law clk. Justice John Harlan, Supreme Ct. U.S., Washington, 1964-65; asso. Sullivan & Cromwell, N.Y.C., 1965-70, ptnr., 1971—77, 1981—2003, mng. ptnr. Washington, 1977-81, sr. counsel, 2004—. Law fellow Salzburg Seminar in Am. Studies, 1967; mem. bd. overseers Fletcher Sch. Law and Diplomacy. 1st lt. USAF, 1957-61. Mem. ABA, Am. Law Inst., Am. Coll. Trial Lawyers, N.Y. State Bar Assn., Union Club, Down Town Assn., Madison Beach Club, Madison Country Club, Met. Opera Club, New Haven Country Club. Address: 48 Neptune Ave Madison CT 06443-3210 Office: Sullivan & Cromwell LLP 125 Broad St New York NY 10004-2498 Office Phone: 212-558-3800. Business E-Mail: maneym@sullcrom.com.

**MANGA, MICHAEL,** earth science educator, geophysicist; b. Hamilton, Ont., Can., July 22, 1968; s. Pran and Louise Manga; m. Susan Storch. BSc, McGill U., Montreal, Que., Can., 1990; SM, Harvard U., 1992, PhD, 1994. Miller rsch. fellow Miller Inst. for Basic Rsch. Sci., Berkeley, Calif., 1994—96; asst. prof. U. Oreg., Eugene, 1996—2001; assoc. prof. earth & planetary sci. U. Calif., Berkeley, 2001—. Named a MacArthur fellow, John D. and Catherine T. MacArthur Found., 2005; recipient Career award, NSF, 1997—2001; fellow, Sloan Found., 2001. Fellow: Am. Geophys. Union (James B. Macelwane medal 2002). Office: Univ Calif Berkeley 307 McCone Hall Berkeley CA 94720-4767 Business E-Mail: manga@seismo.berkeley.edu.

**MANGAN, JOHN LEO,** retired electric power industry executive, international trade specialist; b. Lakewood, Ohio, May 24, 1920; s. Mark A. and Celia M. Mangan; m. Mildred J. Livingston, June 21, 1946; children: John, Scott. BSME, Carnegie Inst. Tech., 1942. Registered profl. engr., Mass., N.Y. Turbine design engr. Gen. Electric Co., Lynn, Mass., 1946-48, turbine application and sales engr. Fitchburg and Lynn, Mass., Schenectady, St. Louis, 1948-55, mgr. gas turbine indsl. sales Schenectady, 1955-60, mgr. gas turbine product planning, 1960-64, mgr. turbine bus. strategy devel., 1966-86; mgr. turbine indsl. customer requirements Boeing Co., Seattle, 1964-66. Contbr. articles profl. jours., chpts. in books; inventor in field. Mem. com. Boy Scouts Am., 1955-59, 64-66; bd. dirs. United Way Schenectady County, Inc., 1991-96, chmn. 1992-93. 1st lt. U.S. Army, 1942-46. Recipient Profl. and Social Activities award GE, 1977, cert. of merit N.Y. State Assembly, 1995. Fellow ASME (v.p. 1975-79, bd. govs. 1983-87, Gas Turbine citation, Centennial medal 1980, Dedicated Svc. award 1988); mem. Internat. Combustion Engine Coun. (permanent com. 1974-81, v.p. 1977-81), Mohawk Golf Club (Schenectady). Home: 1345 Ruffner Rd Niskayuna NY 12309-2505

**MANGAN, TERENCE JOSEPH,** retired federal agency administrator; b. Utica, N.Y., Feb. 17, 1938; BA, St. Mary's Coll., 1961; MA, St. Albert's Coll., 1965; postgrad. in pub. adminstrn., U. So. Calif., 1972-76; Grad., FBI Nat. Acad., N.W. Law Enforcement Exec., 1986. Cert. Wash. State Criminal Justice Tng. Commn., Calif.; cert. Gov.'s Rev. Team Child Abuse Svscs., 1986. With Seaside Police Dept., Calif., 1967—72, Lakewood Police Dept., Calif., 1972-76, chief, dir. cmty. safety Calif., 1976; chief Bellingham Police Dept., Wash., 1976—87, Spokane Police Dept., Wash., 1987—98; ret., 1998; mem. FBI Leadership Devel. Inst. FBI Nat. Acad., Quantico, Va., 1998—2006; program mgmt. FBI Nat. Exec. Inst. and Major City Chiefs Program. Past chair Wash. Stae Criminal Justice Tng. Commn., working group counterterrorism, futures; mem. Mgmt. Adv. Group Organized Crime and Narcotics Enforcement; apptd. to death investigations coun. Spl. Task Force on Child Abuse, Gov.'s Criminal Justice Adv. Bd.; master mentor Waspc's Exec. Leadership Inst., coord. N.W. Law Enforcement Command Coll. Program; mem. Wash. Law Enforcement Exec. Forum, past chair; mem. Wash. State Inst. Cmty. Oriented Policing. Mem. archdiocesan steering com. Ann. Catholic Appeal, 1982; chair fund-raising drives Am. Cancer Soc., Am. Heart Assn., Salvation Army, Easter Seal Soc., Assn. Retarded Citizens; bd. advs. Holy Names Ctr.; exec. bd. Inland Empire coun. Boy Scouts Am.; bd. dirs. Spokane Goodwill Industries, United Way, Whatcom County, Calif. Paul Harris fellow Rotary Internat., 1986; recipient citation U.S. Secret Svc., 1969, Congl. Com. Internal Security, 1971, Svc. award City of Seaside, 1972, Disting. Svc. award City of Lakewood, Wash. Assn. Sheriffs and Police Chiefs, 1978-81, Cmty. Svc. award Wash. Toastmasters Internat., 1980, Pres. award Pacific Luth. U., 1981; named Police Officer of Yr. Nat. Exch. Club, 1979, Lawman of Yr. VFW, 1980, Law Enforcement Officer of Yr. VFW, 1980, Secret Svc. Honor award, 1998, Defender of Freedom award, 1998. Mem. Internat. Assn. Chiefs of Police (life)(com. terrorism), Nat. Coun. Crime and Delinquency, Wash. Assn. Sheriffs and Police Chiefs (life mem.; past pres.), Internat. Peace Artch Law Enforcement Coun., VFW (life). Roman Catholic. Office: FBI Acad L Msu Rm 112 Quantico VA 22135-0001 Office Phone: 703-632-3164. Business E-Mail: tmangan@fbiacademy.edu.

**MANGANARO, FRANCIS FERDINAND,** naval officer; b. Providence, Feb. 27, 1925; s. Ralph and Ada Susanna (Hobden) M.; m. Carol Anne Slater, Sept. 8, 1948; children: Carol Sue, William Francis, John Thomas, Linda Anne, Mary Kathryn. Student, U. R.I., 1943-44; BS in Elec. Engring. U.S. Naval Acad., 1944-47; Post MD, Naval Engr., MIT, 1956; cert., Advanced Mgmt. Program, Harvard U. Sch. Bus., 1971; cert. pub. utilities exec. program, U. Mich., 1984. Registered profl. engr., Conn. Commd. ensign U.S. Navy, 1947, advanced through grades to rear adm., 1975; served in destroyers Atlantic Fleet, 1947-49; served in submarines Pacific Fleet, 1949-53; repair officer, submarines Pearl Harbor Naval Shipyard, 1956-59; design project officer, submarines Bur Ships, 1959-63; inspection and planning officer Office Supr. of Shipbldg. Groton, Conn., 1963-68; prodn. officer Portsmouth Naval Shipyard, 1968-72; comdg. officer Puget Sound Naval Shipyard, 1972-76; chmn. navy claims settlement bd. Naval Material Command, 1976-78; vice comdr. Naval Sea Systems Command Washington, 1978-80; ret. Naval Sea Systems Command), 1980. V.p., dir. GPU Nuclear Corp., 1980-90; cons. Burns & Roe Utility Mgmt. Cons., 1990-94; cons. Raytheon Engrs. & Constructors, Inc., 1994-96. Decorated DSM, Legion of Merit. Mem. Soc. Naval Architects and Marine Engrs., Am. Soc. Naval Engrs., Sigma Xi, Tau Beta Pi, Beta Psi Alpha. Personal E-Mail: ffm48@comcast.net.

**MANGANELLO, TIMOTHY M.,** auto parts company executive; B of Mech. Engring., U. Mich.; postgrad., Harvard U.; grad., Chrusler Inst. Program. Product engring. mgr. Chrysler Corp., 1973—81; sales mgr. PT Components, 1981—88; v.p. ops. BorgWarner TorqTransfer Systems, Inc., Muncie, Ind., 1995—99, pres., gen. mgr. Chgo., 1999—2001; v.p. Borg-Warner, Inc., 1999—2001, exec. v.p., 2001—02, pres., COO, 2002—03, pres., CEO, 2003, chmn., CEO, 2003—. Mem. bd. dirs. Bemis Co., Inc. Office: Borgwarner 3850 Hamlin Rd Auburn Hills MI 48326-2872*

**MANGANO, LOUIS,** lawyer; b. Passaic, N.J., Sept. 19, 1939; s. Salvatore and Mary Mangano; m. Arlene M. Triolo, Sept. 20, 1964; children: Kenneth L., Eileen M., Louis M., Michael S. BS in Bus. Administrn., Seton Hall U., 1970; MA in Criminal Justice, John Jay Coll., 1973; JD, Seton Hall U., 1979. Bar: N.J. 1981, U.S. Dist. Ct. N.J. 1981, U.S. Supreme Ct. 1985. With Elmwood Park (N.J.) Police Dept., 1966-83; pvt. practice atty. Elmwood

Park, 1981—. Adj. prof. Fairleigh Dickinson U., Rutherford, N.J., 1973-75, Jersey City (N.J.) State Coll., 1973-75; asst. prof. William Paterson Coll., Wayne, N.J., 1983-84. Trustee, pres. Elmwood Park (N.J.) Bd. Edn., 1980-83, 89-93; borough atty. for Elmwood Park, N.J., 2005—. With U.S. Army, 1959-61. Mem. Bergen County Bar Assn. Office: PO Box 305 395 River Dr Elmwood Park NJ 07407-1622 Office Phone: 201-796-2727.

**MANGASARIAN, OLVI LEON,** education educator, research scientist; b. Baghdad, Iraq, Jan. 12, 1934; s. Leon Ohannes and Josephine Mangasarian; m. Claire Natalie Garabedian, June 14, 1959; children: Leon Charles, Jeffrey Thomas, Aram Andrew. BSE, Princeton U., 1954, MSE, 1955; PhD, Harvard U., Cambridge, Mass., 1959. Mathematician Shell Devel. Co., Emeryville, Calif., 1959—67; prof. U. Wis., Madison, 1967—2003, John von Neumann prof. emeritus, 2003—; rsch. scientist U. Calif. at San Diego, La Jolla, 2002—. Author: (scientific book) Nonlinear Programming, 1969 (INFORMS Lanchester prize for Math. Programming in Machine Learning and Data Mining, 2000). Office Phone: 608-262-6593. Business E-Mail: olvi@cs.wisc.edu.

**MANGELSDORF, THOMAS KELLY,** psychiatrist, consultant; b. St. Louis; s. Albert Henry and Hazel (Kelly) M.; m. Helen Louise Kareth, Apr. 12, 1958 (div. Jan. 1986); children: Ellen S., Steven T., Thomas K. Jr., Laura E. BS, U. Notre Dame, 1952; MD, St. Louis U., 1956. Diplomate Am. Bd. Psychiatry and Neurology (examiner 1968, 95); forensic expert in psychiat. trauma. Cons. in mental health various municipalities and pvt. practice, 1972—. Author and editor computerized system to interpret Minn. Multiphasic Personality Inventory profiles. Served to capt. U.S. Army, 1960-62. Fellow: Am. Psychiat. Assn. Avocation: sailing. Office Phone: 314-997-5440. Personal E-Mail: tkm18@charter.net.

**MANGER, WILLIAM MUIR,** internist, educator, writer, research scientist; b. Greenwich, Conn., Aug. 13, 1920; s. Julius and Lilian (Weissinger) M.; m. Lynn Seymour Sheppard, May 30, 1964; children: William Muir, Jr., Lilian Wade (Mrs. Porter Fleming), Stewart Sheppard, Charles Seymour. BS, Yale U., 1944; MD, Columbia U., 1946; PhD, Mayo Found., U. Minn., 1958. Diplomate Nat. Bd. Med. Examiners, Am. Bd. Internal Medicine. Intern Presbyn. Hosp., NYC, 1946-47, resident, 1949-50, asst. physician, 1957—2001; fellow internal medicine Mayo Found., 1950-55; dir. Manger Rsch. Found., 1961-77; clin. asst. attending physician Columbia divsn. Bellevue Hosp., 1964-68; asst. attending physician NYU Bellevue Hosp., 1969-77, assoc. attending physician, 1977-83, attending physician, 1983—; instr. medicine Columbia U. Coll. Physicians and Surgeons, 1957-66, assoc. medicine, 1966-70, lectr. emeritus, 1891—. Asst. attending physician Presbyn. Hosp., 1966—68; asst. clin. prof. medicine NYU Med. Ctr., 1968—75, assoc. clin. prof. medicine, 1975—83, clin. prof. medicine, 1983—; mem. devel. com. Mayo Clinic, 1981; vice chmn. bd. Manger Hotels, Inc., 1957—73; mem. nat. high blood pressure edn. program NIH. Co-author: Chemical Quantitation of Epinephrine and Norepinephrine in Plasma, 1959, Pheochromocytoma, 1977, Clinical and Experimental Pheochromocytoma, 1996, 100 Questions and Answers About Hypertension, 2001, Our Greatest Threats, 2006; author: Catecholamines in Normal and Abnormal Cardiac Function, 1982; editor, co-author: Hormones and Hypertension, 1966; editor: Am. Lecture Series in Endocrinology, 1962-75; guest editor First Irvine H. Page Internat. Hypertension Rsch. Symposium, 1990; contbr. articles to profl. and lay jours. Mem. bd. govs. St. Albans Sch., Washington, 1958-64, 67-73, 83-89, chmn., 1967-69; trustee Found. Rsch. in Medicine and Biology, 1971-77, Buckley Sch., 1975-85, Lycee Francais, NY, 1996-98, Found. for Advancement Internat. Rsch. in Microbiology, 1977-82, Thyroid Found., 1980-85; mem. bd. visitors Boston U. Med. Sch., 1992—; trustee Found. for Depression and Manic Depression, 1978-89, pres., 1980-89; elder Presbyn. Ch., 1968-70, 92-93, trustee, 1962-67, 80-84, deacon, 1959-61; founder Values Initiative Tchg. About Lifestyle program to combat obesity, 2002. Lt. (j.g.) M.C., USNR, 1947-49. Recipient Mayo Found. Alumni award for Meritorious Rsch., 1955, Disting. Alumnus award, 1992. Fellow ACP, Acad. Psychosomatic Medicine, Am. Geriatric Soc., Coun. on Geriatric Cardiology, NY Acad. Medicine (admission com. 1976-78, edn. com. 1979-92) Am. Coll. Cardiology, Am. Coll. Clin. Pharmacology, Royal Soc. Health, Am. Inst. Chemists; Nat. Hypertension Assn. (founder, trustee, chmn. 1977—), AMA, Am. Soc. Internal Medicine, NY State Med. Soc., NY County Med. Soc., Am. Heart Assn. (fellow coun. on circulation and coun. for high blood pressure rsch.), Inter-Am. Soc. Hypertension, Internat. Soc. Hypertension, Am. Soc. Hypertension (designated hypertension specialist), Am. Thoracic Soc., NY Acad. Sci., AAAS, Am. Physiol. Soc., Am. Chem. Soc., Am. Soc. Pharmacology and Exptl. Therapeutics, Am. Soc. for Clin. Pharmacology and Therapeutics, Clin. Autonomic Rsch. Soc., Am. Autonomic Soc., Med. Strollers, NYC, Endocrine Soc., Pan Am. Med. Assn., Harvey Soc., Soc. Exptl. Biology and Medicine, Rsch. Discussion Group (founding mem., sec.-treas. 1958-80), Am. Fedn. Clin. Rsch. Am. Soc. Nephrology, Royal Soc. Medicine (affiliate), Fellows Assn. Mayo Found. (v.p., pres. 1953), Mayo Alumni Assn. (v.p. 1981-82, exec. com. 1981-89, pres. elect 1982-85, pres. 1985-87), Chatecholamine Club (founder, sec.-treas. 1967-80, pres. 1981-82), Pheochromocytom Rsch. Support Orgn. (pres. and treas. 2005—), Drs. Mayo Soc., Plummer Soc., Albert Gallatin Assocs., The 1941 Soc., New Eng. Soc., SAR (chmn. admissions com. 1959-67, bd. mgrs. 1959-67, 69-70), Soc. Colonial Wars, Soc. of the Cin., Sigma Xi, Nu Sigma Nu, Phi Delta Theta, Explorers, Meadow (L.I., NY), Univ. Club, NY Athletic Club (NYC), Southampton Bathing Corp. Achievements include research on the mechanism of salt-induced hypertension, the mechanism whereby potassium lowers blood pressure and prevents stroke, and on pheochromocytoma. Home: 8 E 81st St New York NY 10028-0201 Fax: 212-447-7032. Office Phone: 212-689-0873. Personal E-Mail: nathypertension@aol.com.

**MANGES, JAMES HORACE,** investment banker; b. NYC, Oct. 8, 1927; s. Horace S. and Natalie (Bloch) M.; m. Joan Brownell, Oct., 1969 (div.); m. Mary Seymour, 1974 (div. Oct. 2000); children: Alison, James H. Jr. Grad. Phillips Exeter Acad., 1945; BA, Yale U., 1950; MBA, Harvard U., 1953. With Kuhn, Loeb & Co., N.Y.C., 1954-77, ptnr., 1967-77; mng. dir. Lehman Bros., Kuhn Loeb Inc., N.Y.C., 1977-84, Shearson Lehman, Inc., N.Y.C., 1984-90; adv. dir. Lehman Bros., N.Y.C., 1990-96. Dir. Baker Industries, 1967—77, Proudfoot PLC (U.K.), 1996—98; dir., exec. com. Metromedia, Inc., 1970—86. Trustee The Episcopal Sch., 1978-92, St. Bernard's Sch., 1985-2000, Phillips Exeter Acad., 1985-89, mem. trustee coun., 1989-95; mem. Ctr. Strategic and Internat. Studies, Washington. Mem. Bond Club, Yale Club (N.Y.C.), Century Country Club (Purchase, N.Y.), Harvard Club (N.Y.C.). Home: 888 Park Ave New York NY 10021-0235 Office: #2016 45 Rockefeller Plz New York NY 10111-0100

**MANGIAPANE, JOSEPH ARTHUR,** information technology executive; b. NYC, Aug. 1, 1926; s. Michael and Rose D'Amico M.; m. Marcia Balut, Oct. 30, 1954 (div. Apr. 1974); children: Rosemarie, Michael, Diana, Joseph J., Susan. BS, Fordham U., 1950. Stress analyst Republic Aviation, Farmingdale, NY, 1951-55; pvt. practice cons., 1955-58; sect. mgr. Aerojet-Gen., Sacramento, 1958-61; project engr. Pratt & Whitney Aircraft, East Hartford, Conn., 1961-71; pvt. practice cons., 1971-79; pres. Joseph A. Mangiapane & Assocs., Inc., Tampa, Fla., 1979-92. Author numerous tech. reports. Served as cpl. USAAF, 1945-47, ETO. Named Knight in Equestrian Order of Holy Sepulchre of Jerusalem Southeastern Lieutenancy of U.S., 2004. Fellow: AIAA (assoc.); mem.: Pine Acres Club (Wethersfield, Conn. chpt.) (pres. 1968—69), Equestrian Order of the Holy Sepulchre of Jerusalem (Southeastern Lieutenancy) (knight 2004). Republican. Roman Catholic. Avocations: reading, photography, genealogy. Home: 5410 Aragon Ct Tampa FL 33624-4884 Personal E-Mail: jam50ram@earthlink.net.

**MANGINI, ERIC,** professional football coach; b. Hartford, Conn., Jan. 19, 1971; s. Carmine and Nancy Mangini; m. Julie Mangini; children: Jake, Luke. BA in Polit. Sci., Wesleyan Coll., 1994. Asst. coach Cleve. Browns, 1995—96, Balt. Ravens (formerly Cleve. Browns), 1996—97; defensive asst., quality control coach NY Jets, 1997—99; defensive backs coach New

England Patriots, 1999—2005, defensive coord., 2005—06; head coach NY Jets, 2006—. Achievements include asst. coach, Super Bowl Champion New England Patriots, 2001, 2003, 2004. Office: c/o NY Jets 1000 Fulton Ave Hempstead NY 11550*

**MANGIOLA, MARK,** information technology executive; Exec. v.p. KBLCOM/Time Warner; CEO @Home Solutions; pres., CEO Postive Comm.; ptnr. Canaan Ventures, Menlo Park, Calif. Mem. bd. dir. Midstream Tech., TVIA, Zolo. Office: Canaan Ventures 2765 Sand Hill Rd Menlo Park CA 94025 Office Phone: 650-854-8127. Office Fax: 650-854-8127.*

**MANGION, RICHARD MICHAEL,** health facility administrator; b. Haverhill, Mass., Apr. 26, 1941; s. Michael Anthony and Evelyn (Cote) M.; m. Gail Elizabeth Donne, Apr. 27, 1968; children: Catherine Jean, James Richard, Ian Kyle. BBA, Suffolk U., 1963; MBA, Syracuse U., 1965; MPH, U. Calif., Berkeley, 1972. Asst. adminstr. Nashua (N.H.) Meml. Hosp., 1972-75, assoc. adminstr., 1975-77; pres. and chief exec. officer Harrington Meml. Hosp., Southbridge, Mass., 1977—. Lectr. U.N.H., Durham, 1972-74. Pres. Tri-Community Devel. Corp., Southbridge, 1983-88. Capt. USAF, 1966-70. Fellow Am. Coll. Health Care Execs. (regent Mass. area B 1995-99); mem. Am. Hosp. Assn., Mass. Hosp. Assn., Ctrl. Mass. Hosp. Coun. (pres. 1982-84), Ctrl. Mass. Health Care Found., Tri-Cmty. C. of C. (pres. 1983-84). Clubs: Hosp. Supts. Lodges: Rotary. Democrat. Roman Catholic. Avocations: tennis, swimming, hiking. Home: 50 Old Village Rd Sturbridge MA 01566-1069 Office: Harrington Meml Hosp 100 South St Ste 1 Southbridge MA 01550-4047 Office Phone: 508-765-9771 x 3451. E-mail: rmangion@harringtonhospital.org.

**MANGLA, SUNDEEP,** radiologist, research scientist; s. Kishan Chand and Sushila Mangla; m. Minh-Nhut Yvonne Dang, Oct. 4, 2003; 1 child, Ronin Tai Satyam. MD, N.E. OH U., Rootstown, 1992. Resident in diagnostic radiology Coll. Medicine, N.E. OH U., Canton, 1992—97; fellow in diagnostic neuroradiology U. So. Calif., LA, 1997—98; fellow in interventional neuroradiology and neuroendovascular surgery Yale U., New Haven, 1998—99, U. Iowa, Iowa City, 1999—2000; asst. prof. interventional neuroradiology Columbia and Cornell Univs., NYC, 2000—03; dir. interventional neuroradiology, radiology rsch. SUNY Downstate Health Sci. Ctr., Bklyn., 2003—. Dir. radiology rsch. SUNY Downstate Health Sci. Ctr., 2006—. Contbr. articles to profl. jours. Local educator stroke awareness SUNY Health Sci. Ctr., Bklyn., 2003—06. Grantee, Columbia U. NY, 2002—03. Mem.: Neurocritical Care Assn., Am. Soc. Neuroradiology, Am. Soc. Interventional and Therapeutic Neuroradiology. Achievements include patents pending for endovascular and endoluminal robotics, nano-robotics. Avocations: tennis, basketball, travel, cooking, international and independent cinema. Office: SUNY Downstate Health Sci Ctr 450 Clarkson Ave Box 1189 New York NY 10203 Office Phone: 718-270-4141. Office Fax: 718-270-7241. Business E-Mail: smangla@downstate.edu.

**MANGLANO-OVALLE, INIGO,** sculptor; BA in Art with highest honors, Williams Coll., 1983, BA in L.Am. and Spanish Lit. cum laude, 1983; MFA in Sculpture, Sch. Art Inst. Chgo., 1989. One-man shows include Mus. Contemporary Art, Chgo., 1993, 1997, Andera Rosen Gallery, N.Y.C., 1996, Contemporary Arts Ctr., Cin., 1997, Inst. Cultural Cabanas Mus., Guadalajara, Mex., 1997, Max Protech Gallery, N.Y.C., 1998, Southeastern Ctr. Arts, Winston-Salem, N.C., 1998, Henry Art Gallery, U. Wash., Seattle, 1999, exhibited in group shows at U. Ill., Chgo., 1992, 1993, U. Wis., Eau Claire, 1992, Sch. Art Inst. Chgo., 1992, Walker Arts Ctr., Mpls., 1992, Randolph St. Gallery, Chgo., 1992, 1996, No. Ill. U. Art Gallery, 1992, Terrain Gallery, San Francisco, 1992, 1998, Mexican Fine Arts Ctr. and Mus., Chgo., 1992, Otis Gallery, L.A., 1993, Berlin Gallery Mus. Modern Art, 1994, Lowe Art Mus., U. Miami, 1996, Mus. Contemporary Art, Chgo., 1996, Ariz. State U. Art Mus., Phoenix, 1998, Christopher Grimes Gallery and Track 16 Gallery, Santa Monica, Calif., 1998, Represented in permanent collections Mus. Contemporary Art, Chgo., also corp. collections, work represented in numerous publs. Recipient spl. projects award, Ill. Arts Coun., 1993; Hutchinson fellow, Williams Coll., 1983—85, fellowship award, Ill. Arts Coun., 1992, Gt. Cities fellow, U. Ill. Coll. Urban Planning, Chgo., 1995, Orion fellow, U. Victoria, B.C., Can., 1995, visual artist fellow, NEA, 1995, internat. artist residency fellow, ArtPace Found., San Antonio, 1997, grantee, Chgo. Dept. Cultural Affairs, 1992, 1993, 1994. Address: care Max Protech Gallery 511 W 22d St New York NY 10011-1109

**MANGLONA, JOHN A.,** commonwealth supreme court justice; b. Rota, Northern Marianas, June 12, 1959; m. Mona V. Monglona; 2 children. BA in Polit. Econ., U. Calif., Berkeley, 1981; JD, Creighton U., 1984; LLM in Taxation, U. Pacific, 1988. Pvt. practice; assoc. judge Commonwealth Superior Ct., 1998—2000; justice Commonwealth Supreme Ct., 2000—. Designated justice Guam Supreme Ct., 1999—2003. Office: House Justice Guma Hustisia, Imwaal Aweewe PO Box 502179 Saipan MP 96950-2179 Business E-Mail: supreme.court@saipan.com.*

**MANGLONA, RAMONA V.,** judge, former attorney general; b. 1967; BA, U. Calif., 1990; JD, U. N.Mex., 1996. Bar: New Mex. Bar Assn. 1997, No. Mariana Islands Bar Assn. 1997. Asst. atty. gen., 1997—2002; atty. gen. No. Mariana Islands, Saipan, 2002—03; assoc. judge Commonwealth Superior Ct., 2003—. Office Phone: 670-236-9751.

**MANGO, WILFRED GILBERT, JR.,** construction executive, real estate company executive; b. Weehawkin, NJ, July 11, 1940; s. Wilfred Gilbert and Mildred B.M.; children from previous marriage; Christian P., Peter H.; m. Charlene Holt, Feb. 14, 1985; children: Alison L., David H. BS, Lehigh U., 1963; MBA, NYU, 1969. With Hurdman & Cranstown, N.Y.C., 1963-69; dir. fin. Thomas Crimmins Contracting Co., N.Y.C., 1969-77; v.p. fin., mgr. fin. controls ITT Teleplant, Inc., N.Y.C., 1977-78; v.p. fin. George A. Fuller Co. div. Northrop Corp., N.Y.C., 1978-81, now pres., CEO, dir., 1981—; chmn., CEO Fuller Internat. Devel. Ltd. Past chmn. bd. trustees Marymount Manhattan Coll., The Stanwich Sch., Greenwich, Conn.; adv. bd. N.Y. Real Estate Inst.; bus. adv. coun. emeritus Lehigh U.; bus. coun. Lighthouse for the Blind; mem. Urban Land Inst. Mem.: Bell Haven Club, Univ. Club, Lehigh U. N.Y. Club. Home: 40 Carrington Dr Greenwich CT 06831-3119 Business E-Mail: wmango@fullerdev.com.

**MANGOLD, ARCHIE WAYNE, II,** insurance agent; b. Pekin, Ill., Dec. 8, 1973; s. Archie Wayne, Sr. and Rebecca Ann Mangold. BA in English, U. No. Iowa, 1996. Bean walker Arthur Milikins Farm, Hedrick, Iowa, 1991; tel. sales rep. APAC Customer Svcs., Oskaloosa, Iowa, 1995, tel. sales rep., ins. agt., 1996—2002. Editor: Literary: Mag. Writing, 1990—2000. Home and Office: PO Box 116 117 1/2 1st Ave W #12 Oskaloosa IA 52577 Office Phone: 641-672-2976.

**MANGOLD, JOHN FREDERIC,** manufacturing executive, retired military officer; b. La Grange, Ill., Jan. 24, 1927; s. John Frederic and Helvig Victoria (Anderson) M.; m. Margaret Ellen Gore. Oct. 25, 1947; children: John, Andrew, Jennifer. BS, U.S. Naval Acad., 1947; MSEE, U.S. Naval Postgrad. Sch., Monterey, Calif., 1958. Registered profl. engr., Conn. Commd. ensign USN, 1947, advanced through grades to comdr., 1962, comdg. officer nuclear submarine U.S.S. Halibut, 1962—63, comdg. officer nuclear tng. unit, 1963—67, ret. 1967; v.p. mfg. Combustion Engring., Inc., Windsor, Conn., 1972—78, group pres., 1982—86, v.p. utility boilers, 1990—91; pres. Vetco, Inc., Ventura, Calif., 1978—82; cons., 1992; pres. Detrex Corp., Southfield, Mich., 1992—93, ret., 1993. Bd. dirs. Detrex Corp. Mem. IEEE, U.S. C. of C. (energy com. 1984-87). Republican.

**MANGOLD, ROBERT PETER,** artist; b. North Tonawanda, N.Y., Oct. 12, 1937; Student, Cleve. Inst. Art, 1956-59; B.F.A., Yale U., 1961, M.F.A., 1964. Instr. art Sch. Visual Arts, N.Y.C., 1963—, Hunter Coll., 1964-65, Cornell U., Skowhegan Summer Art Sch., 1968 Exhbns. include. Whitney Mus. Am. Art, N.Y.C., 1968, 73, 79, 83, Albright-Knox Art Gallery, Buffalo, 1970, 78, Solomon R. Guggenheim Mus., N.Y.C., 1971, Documenta, Kassel, W. Ger.,

1972, VI, 1977, VII, 1982, La Jolla Mus. Contemporary Art, 1974, Mus. Contemporary Art, Chgo., 1974, N.Y. Cultural Center, 1974, Mus. Modern Art, N.Y.C., 1975, 76, Sidney Janis Gallery, N.Y.C., 1977, Ink, Zurich, 1978, Kunsthalle Bielefeld, W.Ger., 1979, Paula Cooper Gallery, N.Y.C., 1982, 84, 91, Protetch-McIntosh, Washington, 1978, Berkeley & Newberger Mus., Purchase, N.Y., 1985-86, Bard Coll., 1985, Ritter Klagenfurt, Austria, 1992-93; one-person exhbn. Daniel Weinberg Gallery, Los Angeles, 1984, 92, Akron Art Mus., 1984, Lisson Gallery, London, 1990, Pace Gallery, 1992, Le Consortium Dijon, France, 1992, Acad. Inst. Arts & Letters, 1992; retrospective exhbn., Stedelijk Mus., Amsterdam, 1982; represented in permanent collections, Solomon R. Guggenheim Mus., Mus. Modern Art, Whitney Mus. Am. Art, N.Y.C., Mus. Fine Arts, Houston, La Jolla Mus. Contemporary Art, Tate Gallery, London, Stedelijk Mus., Contemp. Art Amsterdam, Stedelijk van Abbemuseum, Eindhoven, Kunsthaus, Zurich, Art Inst. Chgo., Rhona Hoffman Gallery, Chgo., Donald Young Gallery, Chgo., Tex. Gallery. Recipient award Nat. Council on Arts, 1966; Guggenheim grantee, 1969 Mailing: c/o Whitney Museum 945 Madision Ave New York NY 10021

**MANGOLD, SYLVIA PLIMACK,** artist; b. NYC, Sept. 18, 1938; d. Maurice and Ethel (Rein) Plimack; m. Robert Mangold. Student, Cooper Union, 1956-59; BFA, Yale U., 1961. Exhibited one-person shows Daniel Weinberg Gallery, San Francisco, 1974, 75, Fischbach Gallery, N.Y.C., 1974, 76, Fischbach, 1974, 76, Annemarie Verna Gallery, Zurich, 1978, 91, 97, Droll-Kolbert Gallery, N.Y.C., 1978, 80, Young Hoffman Gallery, Chgo., 1980, Ohio State U., Columbus, 1980, Pa. Acad., 1981, Contemporary Arts Mus., Houston, 1981, Madison Art Ctr., (Wis.), 1982, Brooke Alexander, Inc., 1982, 83, 84, 85, 86, 89, 92, 95, Duke Art Mus., N.C., 1982, Rhona Hoffman Gallery, Chgo., 1982, 85, Tex. Gallery, 1986, Fuller Goldeen Gallery, San Francisco, 1987, U. Mich, Ann Arbor, 1992, Minn. Inst. Arts, 1992, Grunwald Ctr. for Graphic Arts, UCLA, 1992, Neuberger Mus. Art, SUNY, Purchase, 1993, Davison Art Ctr., Wesleyan U., Middletown, Conn., 1993, Albright-Knox Art Gallery, Buffalo, 1994, Wadsworth Atheneum, Hartford, Conn., 1994, Blaffer Gallery U. Houston, 1994, Mus. Fine Arts, Boston, 1994, Herbert F. Johnson Museum, 1998, Cornell U., Ithaca, N.Y., 1998, Alexander and Bonin N.Y., 2000, 2003; group shows at Young Hoffman Gallery, Chgo., 1979, Walker Art Ctr., Mpls., 1979, Droll-Kolbert Gallery, 1979, Denver Art Mus., 1979, U. So. Calif., 1979, Honolulu Acad. Art, 1979, Oakland Mus., (Calif.), 1979, Univ. Art Mus. of U. Tex.-Austin, 1979, Cornell U., Ithaca, N.Y., 1979, The New Museum of Contemporary Art, N.Y.C., 1979, Nat. Museum, Belgrade, Yugoslavia, 1979, Internat. Biennial Ljibliana, Yugoslavia, Phoenix Art Mus., 1979, Art Latitute Gallery, N.Y.C., 1980, Thorpe Intermedia Gallery, Sparkhill, N.Y., 1980, U. Colo. Art Galleries, Boulder, 1980, Nina Freudenheim Gallery, Buffalo, 1980, U.S. Pavillion of Venice Biennial, 1980-81, Indianapolis Museum of Art, 1980, Civici Musei e Gallerie di Storia e Arte, Sala Ajace, Udine, Italy, 1980, Young Hoffman, Chicago, 1980-81, Delahurty, Dallas, 1980, Museum of Modern Art, 1981, Wesleyan U. Art Gallery, 1981, Davison Art Ctr., Middleton, Conn., 1981, Virginia Museum of Fine Arts, Richmond, 1981, Oakland Museum, Calif. 1981, Inst. Contemporary Art of U Pa., Phila, 1980-81, Yale U. Art Gallery, 1981, San Antonio Mus. Art, 1981, Indpls. Mus. Art, 1981, Tucson Mus. Art, 1981, Pa. Acad., 1981, Mus. Art of Carnegie Inst., Pitts., 1981, Brooke Alexander, Inc., N.Y.C., 1982, Ben Shahn Ctr. Visual Arts, 1982, Castle Gallery, Coll. of New Rochelle, N.Y., 1983, Thomas Segal Gallery, Boston, 1982-83, Siegel Contemporary Art, N.Y., 1983, Freedman Gallery, Albright Coll., Reading, Pa., 1983, Fuller Goldeen, San Francisco, 1983, Yale U. Art Gallery, New Haven, 1983-84, 86, Wilcox Gallery, Swarthmore, Pa., 1984, The Hudson River Mus., Yonkers, N.Y., 1984, Sardonia Art Gallery, Wilkes Coll., Wilkes-Barre, Pa., 1985, Kent State U. Gallery, Ohio, 1985, Brooke Alexander, N.Y., 1985, John C. Stoller Co., Minn., 1985, Knight Gallery, Spirit Sq. Arts Ctr., Charlotte, N.C., 1986, Mus. Art, R.I. Sch. Design, Providence, 1986, Yale U. Gallery, 1986, CUNY, 1986-87, Lorence Monk Gallery, N.Y.C., Vanguard Gallery, Phila., 1986-87, Aldrich Mus., Ridgefield, 1986-87. Flander's Contemporary Art, Mpls., 1987, Annemarie Verna Galerie, Zurich, 1988, U. N.C., 1988, R.I. Sch. Design, 1988, Grace Borgenicht Gallery, N.Y.C., 1988, Fay Gold Gallery, Atlanta, 1988, U. N.C., Greensboro, Three Rivers Arts Festival, Pitts., 1989, Cin. Art Mus., New Orleans Mus. Art, Denver Art Mus., Pa. Acad. Fine Arts, 1989, U. Mich., 1992, Mpls. Inst. Arts, 1992, Grunwald Ctr. Graphic Arts, UCLA, L.A., Neuberger Mus. Art, SUNY Purchase, 1993, Davison Art Ctr., 1993, Montgomery Glasoe Fine Art, Mpls., 1993, Yale U. Art Gallery, New Haven, 1993, Daniel Weinberg Gallery, Santa Monica, Calif., 1993, Museum of Fine Arts, Boston, 1993, Barbara Mathes Gallery, N.Y.C., 1993, Nina Freudenheim Gallery, Buffalo, 1993, Kansas City Gallery of Art, U. Mo., 1994, Midtown Payson, N.Y.C., 1994, Katonah Museum of Art, N.Y., 1994, Rhona Hoffman Gallery, Chgo., 1994, Feigen Inc., Chgo., 1994, Brooke Alexander, N.Y.C., 1994, Elga Wimmer Gallery, N.Y.C., 1995, Aargauer Kunsthaus Aarau, Austria, 1995, The Am. Acad. of Arts and Letters, N.Y.C., 1995, Andre Zarre Gallery, N.Y.C., 1996, Aspen Art Museum, Colo., 1996, The Am. Acad. of Arts and Letters, N.Y.C., 1996, Anne Marie Verna Gallery, Zurich, Switzerland, 1997, Queens Museum of Art, 1997, Aspen Art Museum, 1997, U. Gallery, Fine Arts Ctr., U. Mass., Amherst James Graham & Sons, N.Y.C., 1997, The Museum of Modern Art, 1997, Seattle Art Museum, 1997, State U., N.Y., 1998, N.Y.U. Dowd Fine Arts Gallery, 1998, The Am. Acad. of Fine Arts and Letters, 1998, Karen McCready Fine Art, 1999, Alexander and Bonin, N.Y.C., 1999, Henry Art Gallery, Seattle, 2000, Small Work, Nina Freudenheim Inc., Buffalo, Whitney Mus., 2006, and numerous others; exhibited in permanent collections, Albright-Knox Art Gallery, Buffalo, Allen Meml. Art Mus., Oberlin, Ohio, Bklyn. Mus., Dallas Mus. Fine Arts, Detroit Inst. Art, Mus. Fine Arts, Houston, Indpls. Mus. Art, Madison (Wis.) Art Ctr., Milw. Art Mus., Yale U. Art Gallery, Mus. Modern Art, N.Y.C., Mus. Fine Arts, U. Utah, Tampa (Fla.) Mus., Walker Art Mus., Mpls., Whitney Mus. Am. Art, N.Y., Weatherspoon Art Gallery, Greensboro, N.C., Wadsworth Atheneaum, Hartford, U. Mich., Utah Mus. Fine Art, Museum of Fine Arts, Boston, N.Y.C. Public Library, Smith Coll. Museum, Northampton, Mass., Achenbach Found. for Graphic Arts, San Francisco, St. Louis Art Museum The Tampa Museum, Art Inst. Chgo., Milwaukee Art Mus. Fort Worth Tex., Indpls. Mus. Art, Telfair Mus. Art, Savannah Ga. Achievements include work reviewed in newspapers and mags. Office    Phone:    212-367-7474.    Business    E-Mail: gallery@alexanderandbonin.com

**MANGONE, GERARD J.,** maritime law educator; b. NYC, Oct. 10, 1918; s. Gerard Francis and Viola (Schumm) M.; m. Emma Haddad, Apr. 13, 1958; children— Cleopatra, Regina, Flaminia. AB, CCNY, 1938; MA, Harvard, 1947, PhD (Charles Summer prize), 1949. Asst. prof. polit. sci. Wesleyan U., Middletown, Conn., 1948-51; assoc. prof. Swarthmore Coll., 1951-56; prof. polit. sci. and internat. relations Syracuse U., 1956-67; dir. grad. overseas tng. program, exec. officer Maxwell Grad School Overseas Operations, 1958-60; exec. asst. to dean Maxwell Grad. Sch., 1961-64, asso. dean dir. internat. relations program, 1961-67; dean Coll. Liberal Arts, v.p.; provost Temple U., Phila., 1967-69; sr. fellow Woodrow Wilson Internat. Ctr., 1970-72; prof. internat. law U. Del., Newark, 1972-74, dir. Ctr. for Study of Marine Policy, 1973-89, H. Rodney Sharp prof. internat. law and orgn., 1975-89, univ. rsch. prof. internat. and maritime law, 1989—, prof. legal studies, 2001—, coord. grad. studies, 1976-79; adj. prof. Maine Maritime Acad., 1992—94. Vis. prof. Trinity Coll., Mt. Holyoke Coll., Yale, Princeton, Johns Hopkins; Tagore law prof. U. Calcutta, 1979; disting. lectr. U. Ind., 1980; vis. scholar U. Western Australia, 1983, 87, Peking U., 1984, Capetown U., 1986, 89, U. Natal, 1989, Hanyano U., 1994, Hong Kong U., 1994; mem. Presdl. Commn. Trust Territory Pacific, 1963; cons. AID, 1965-67, Nat. Commn. Marine Resources and Engring. and State Dept., 1967-73, UN, 1965, U.S. Corps Engrs., 1975; vice chmn. exec. com. Commn. Study Ocean. Peace; exec. dir. Pres.' Commn. on UN, 1970-71; dir. diploma program, shipping and pt. mgmt. Pt. of Singapore, 1990-97. Author: The Idea and Practice of World Government, 1951, A Short History of International Organization, 1954, The Elements of International Law, 2d edit, 1967, Marine Policy for America, 1977, 2d edit., 1989; Law for the World Ocean, 1981, Mangone's Concise Marine Almanac, 2d edit., 1991, United States Admiralty Law, 1997; co-author, editor: The Art of Overseamanship, 1958, The Overseas Americans, 1960, European Political Systems, 1960, UN Administration of Economic and Social Programs, 1966, Energy Policies of the World, 3 vols, 1976-79, Internat. Straits of the World, 14 vols., 1978-2004; editor: Future of Gas and Oil from Sea, American

Strategic Minerals, 1984; editor in chief: Marine Policy Reports, 1981-91, Internat. Jour. Marine and Coastal Law, 1991—. Capt. AUS, 1942-46, maj. res., 1946-54. Mem. Am. Soc. Internat. Law, Internat. Law Assn., Maritime Law Assn., Port of Wilmington Maritime Soc. (bd. dirs. 1980-, chmn. 1989, Francis Alison award 1983), Alison Soc. (sec. 1990—), Del. Acad. Sci. (pres. 1993), Cosmos Club (Washington), Harvard Club (N.Y.C.). Home: 201 Unami Trl Newark DE 19711-7508 Office: Univ Del Grad Coll Marine Studi Newark   DE   19716   Office   Phone:   302-831-8087.   E-mail: gmangone@udel.edu.

**MANGOUNI, NORMAN,** publishing executive; b. Detroit, Oct. 19, 1932; s. Nazareth Lazarus and Isabelle (Garabedian) M.; m. Anahid Apelian, May 10, 1964; 1 child, Marie-Isabelle. AB, U. Mich., 1954; MS, Columbia U., 1955; postgrad., U. Mich., 1957-58. Reporter Ann Arbor (Mich.) News, 1957-59; editor Mich. Alumnus, U. Mich., Ann Arbor, 1959-62; sr. editor Coll. Entrance Exam. Bd., N.Y.C., 1962-64; dir. fin. aid U. Miami, Coral Gables, Fla., 1965-66; dir. State U. N.Y. Press, Albany, 1966-78; pres., gen. editor Scholars' Facsimiles & Reprints, Ann Arbor, Mich., 1972—; pres. Caravan Books, Ann Arbor, Mich., 1972—, Acad. Resources Corp., Las Vegas, Nev., 1988—; corr. DuPont-Columbia Survey and Awards, 1976-78; rep. to com. on standards in field of library work, documentation and related pub. practices Am. Nat. Standards Inst., 1974-78. Exec. asst. to majority caucus Mich. State Senate, 1964; dir. summer session Am. Coll. Switzerland, 1979, 81, 82. Co-translator: The Gaucho Martin Fierro, 1974; contbr. articles to profl. jours.; mem. editorial bd. Ararat mag. 1962-66, 77-78. Served to lt. USAF, 1955-57. Mem. Rotary, Mensa, Phi Sigma Kappa, Sigma Delta Chi, Phi Alpha Delta. Home: PO Box 5934 Carefree AZ 85377 Office Phone: 480-575-9945. E-mail: maxinmin@umich.edu.

**MANGRAVITE, RONALD,** education educator, writer; MFA, UCLA, LA; BA (highest hons.), U. Calif., Berkeley; prep. Lawrenceville Sch., NJ. Instr. Juilliard Sch., NYC, 1974—76; assoc. artistic dir. Attic Theatre, Detroit, 1985—90; instr. Am. Film Inst., LA, 1991—2000, U. of Miami, Coral Gables, 2001—02; theatre, film critic Miami New Times, New Times Broward/Palm Beach, Miami, 2001—05; asst. prof. U. Miami, Coral Gables. Author: (stage play) Back in the Saddle premiered NY, 1981, Behind the Chutes premiered NY, 1981, The Lewis & Clark Expedition, premiered Ashland, OR, 1983, The Rewrite premiered San Francisco, 1983, Jean Baptiste Pointe du Sable: Black Man in the Wilderness premiered Detroit, 1988, Madame Cadillac premiered Detroit, 1989, The Great Divide, 2005; screenwriter (feature film) Kennedy Boulevard, 2006, co-author (non fiction book) The Screenwriter's Manual, 2005, The Complete Screenwriter's Manual, 2006; dir.(writer): (short film) The Queen of the Sea, 2002, My Father's Hopes (Silver Palmetto Piccolo Spoleto Short Film Festival, 2004); prodr.: (film) For Liberty, 2006. Recipient First prize, Fla. Press Assn., 2003, Silver Palmetto, Piccolo Spoleto Festival, 2004 for My Father's Hopes, Best Film, Miami Film Festival Collaboration Film Contest, 2002 for The Queen of the Sea, Best Screenplay, 2002 for The Queen of the Sea, Best of the Fest citation, Silver Images Film Festival, 2002 for My Father's Hopes. Mem.: U. Film and Video Assn., Dramatists Guild (assoc.). Office: Univ of Miami 5100 Brunson Dr Coral Gables FL 33146 Office Phone: 305-284-5219. Business E-Mail: mangravite@miami.edu.

**MANGRUM, RICHARD LEE,** flight educator; s. Milagro Castillo and Jesse Bowen Mangrum; m. Shannon Dee Robbins, Nov. 19, 1993; children: Cameron Naghavi, Vanessa Evans. BSBA, Phillips U., Enid, Okla., 1996; MS in Natural and Applied Sci., Okla. State U., Stillwater, EdD in Applied Ednl. Studies in Aviation, 2003. Cert. airframe and powerplant mechanic FAA, 1988, flight instr. FAA, 1994, lic. airline transport pilot FAA, 2003. With USAF, 1982—92, advanced through grades to staff sgt., 1992; asst. chief flight instr. Okla. State U., Stillwater, 1999—2003; asst. and chief flight instr. Kent State U., Ohio, 2003—. Flight instr. Spartan Sch. of Aeronautics, Tulsa, Okla., 1994—99. Min. of discipleship Broadman Bapt. Ch., Cuyahoga Falls, Ohio, 2005. Decorated Fgn. Svc. medal USAF, Desert Storm Campaign medal; recipient Tech. Tchg. Excellence award, Epsilon Pi Tau, 1. Mem.: Jour. of Applied Studies in Aviation (corr.; contbg. editor 2004), Nat. Intercollegiate Flying Assn. (assoc.; Region III rep. 2006), Aircraft Owners and Pilots Assn. (assoc.), U. Aviation Assn. (assoc.), Epsilon Pi Tau (assoc.). Conservative. Southern Baptist. Avocation: travel. Office: Kent State Univ 4020 Kent Rd Stow OH 44224 Office Phone: 330-672-1933. Personal E-mail: no1av8or@sbcglobal.net. Business E-Mail: rmangrum@kent.edu.

**MANGUAL, JESUS A.,** army officer; b. San Juan, P.R., Nov. 20, 1949; BA in Econs., Norwich U., 1973; MS in Contracts and Acquisition Mgmt., Fla. Inst. Tech., 1986; grad., Army Command/Gen. Staff Coll., Indsl. Coll. Armed Forces. Commd. 2d lt. U.S. Army, 1973, advanced through grades to col.; comdr. 46th Corps Support Group, Ft. Bragg, N.C., 1995-97; chief supply policy divsn. Army DCSLOG, Pentagon, Washington, 1997-98; exec. officer, mil. asst. to Dep. Asst. Sec. Def., Pentagon, Washington, 1995; dep. for acquisition and readiness U.S. Army Soldier and Biol. Chem. Command, Soldier Sys. Ctr., Natick, Mass., 1998-2000, also installation comdr., 1998-2000; comdr. Def. Supply Ctr. Phila. U.S. Army Def. Logistics Agy., Phila., 2000—02; dir. force projection and distbn. Office Dep. Chief Staff G-4 U.S. Army, Washington, 2000—04. Decorated Legion of Merit with one oak leaf cluster, others; recipient Meritorious Svc. award Nat. IMAGE, Inc., 2002.

**MANGUM, GARTH LEROY,** retired economist; b. Delta, Utah, July 23, 1926; s. James L. and Golda (Elder) M.; m. Marion Poll, Nov. 20, 1953; children: Stephen, David, Mary, Elizabeth. BS, Brigham Young U., 1956; MPA, Harvard U., 1958, PhD, 1960; JD, U. Utah, 1989. Instr. econs. Harvard U., 1960; asso. prof. econs. Brigham Young U., 1960-63; sr. staff analyst Presdl. R.R. Commn., 1961; research dir., subcom. employment and manpower U.S. Senate, 1963-64; exec. dir. President's Com. Manpower, 1964-65; exec. sec. Nat. Com. Tech. Automation and Econ. Progress, 1965-66; research prof. econs. George Washington U., 1967-71; co-dir. George Washington U. (Center Manpower Policy Studies), 1967-69; Max McGraw prof. econs. and mgmt. U. Utah, Salt Lake City, 1969-97, prof. emeritus, 1997—, dir. Inst. Human Resource Mgmt., 1950-64; adj. prof. edn. leadership Brigham Young U., 2003—; lectr. U. Tel Aviv, Israel, 1969, 84, Am. Seminar at Salzburg, 1975, U. South Africa, 1977, Monash U., Australia, 1984; spl. mediator Fed. Mediation and Conciliation Svc., 1962-63; mem. Adv. Coun. Vocat. Edn., 1966-67; vice chmn. Nat. Manpower Policy Task Force, 1966-69, chmn., 1969-71; mem. Nat. Coun. on Employment Policy, 1976—, chmn., 1979-81, sec.- treas., 1990-2002; chmn. Nat. Inst. Career Edn., 1976-81; cons. fed., state and local govts., bus. firms, govts. of, Saudi Arabia, Kuwait, Jordan, Yemen, Bahrain, United Arab Emirates, Indonesia, Yugoslavia, Romania, Uganda, Nigeria, Israel, South Africa, Russia, Korea, China, others; cons. AID, ILO, World Bank; also arbitrator. Author: The Operating Engineers: Economic History of a Trade Union, 1964, MDTA, Foundation of Federal Manpower Policy, 1968, The Emergence of Manpower Policy, 1969, Federal Work and Training Program in the 1960's, 1969, Economic Opportunity in the Ghetto, 1970, Human Resources and Labor Markets, 1971, Career Education: What It Is and How To Do It, 1972, A Decade of Manpower Development and Training, 1973, Career Education and the Elementary School Teacher, 1973, Career Education in the Middle/Junior High School, 1973, Manpower Planning for Local Labor Markets, 1974, Career Education for the Academic Classroom, 1975, Employability, Employment and Income, 1976, Career Education in the High School, 1976, Your Child's Career, 1977, The Lingering Crisis of Youth Unemployment, 1978, Coming of Age in the Ghetto, 1978, Job Market Futurity, 1979, The Coal Industry and its Industrial Relations, 1985, Capital and Labor in American Copper, 1992, Labor Struggle In The Post Office, 1992, The Mormons War on Poverty, 1993, Union Resilience in Troubled Times, 1994, Portable Pension Plans for Casual Labor Markets, 1995, Transnational Industrial Marriages, 1996, The Rise, Fall and Replacement of Industry-Wide Bargaining in the Basic Steel Industry, 1996, Programs in Aid of the Poor, 8th edit., 2003, On Being Poor in Utah, 1997, The Public Employment Svc. In a One Stop World, 1998, Poverty Ain't What It Used To Be, 1999, Confronting The Youth Demographic Challenge, 2000, The Persistance of Poverty in the United States, 2003; also articles, monographs.; editor: The Manpower

Revolution: Its Policy Consequences, 1965, Automation and Economic Progress, 1966, Metropolitan Impact of Manpower Programs, 1973, The T in CETA, 1981, Of Heart and Mind: Social Policy Essays in Honor of Sar A. Levitan, 1996 (dec. Dec. 4, 2000); children: Logan Grant, Chase Lee. MusB, U. of Wis., Poor: Solutions for Today's Economyy, 2005 With USAAF, 1944-45. Mem. Ch. of Jesus Christ of Latter-day Saints (missionary 1950-53, bishop 1971-78, other positions). Home: 2130 Ridgewood Way Bountiful UT 84010-1632 Personal E-mail: garthmangum@aros.net.

**MANGUSO, JOHN A.,** museum director; b. Bklyn., May 30, 1945; s. Angelo Michael and Rose Rita Manguso; m. Barbara Louise Carlson, Apr. 22, 1967; children: Matthew J., Joseph A. BA, U. Fla., 1967, MA, 1977. Commd. 2d lt. US Army, 1967, advanced through grades to lt. col., 1987, ret., 1995; dir. Ft. Sam Houston (Tex.) Mus., 1978—. Advisor Soc. for Preservation of Historic Ft. Sam Houston, 1984—. Editor: (monograph) No Place for Kindness - the POW Diary of Ray Bodine, 1983; author: The Post at San Antonio, 1845-1879, 2002. Decorated Bronze Star, Air medal, Meritorious Svc. medal. Republican. Roman Catholic. Office: Ft Sam Houston Mus 1590 Stanley Rd Ste 36 Fort Sam Houston TX 78234 Office Phone: 210-221-1886.

**MANHART, GRANT LEE,** music educator; b. Columbus, Ohio, July 6, 1957; s. Harold Eugene and Sharon Lee Manhart; m. Nicole Marie Hiar, Oct. 4, 1996 (dec. Dec. 4, 2000); children: Logan Grant, Chase Lee. MusB, U. of Wis., Madison, WI, 1977—81; MusM - trumpet performance, U. of Cin. - Coll. Conservatory of Music, Cincinnati, OH, 1981—83; MusD - trumpet performance, Ind. U., Bloomington, IN, 1986—94. First Aid CPR ARC, 1987. Trumpet artist Salsa Picante Band, San Juan, PR, 1989—94; factory sales Keystone RV, Elkhart, Ind., 1996—97; head wrangler Cheley Colo. Camps, Estes Park, Colo., 1976—78; assoc. prof. of music No. State U., Aberdeen, SD; trumpet artist Buddy Rich Band, Various, NY, 1984—85, Carol Channing-Rita Moreno show, Various, Elkhart Symphony, Elkhart, Ind., Carmine Cavallero/Herb Jeffires/June Valli Show, Various, Calif., Dreamgirls Broadway Show, New York, NY; leader Jif and the Choosey Mothers Band, Bloomington, Ind.; trumpet artist Columbia Artists Gene Krupa Band, LA, 1991—92, Jimmy Coe Band, Indianapolis, Ind., 1987—94. Composer: (music for band) Various titles for band, jazz ensemble, pep band, (trumpet teaching method) Manhart's Trumpet Method; author: (internet music masterclass) Improving the Trumpet Section, High Notes for Trumpets. Artist in residence Gt. Live Music Productions, Aberdeen, SD, 1998—2003, Elkhart, Ind., 1995—98, Madison, Wis., 1977—81. Recipient 2002 Outstanding Faculty Award, No. State U. Found., 2002, Coclaser Award, U. of Cin. Bands, 1983, Gold Key, Gold Spurs, Cheley Colo. Camps, 1975, Performance Award-Teaching, No. State U., 2001. Mem.: Am. Federations of Musicians Union Local 131 (licentiate; active mem. 1977—2003), Pi Kappa Lambda (licentiate; active mem. 2000—03), Phi Beta Mu (licentiate; mem. 2001—03). Achievements include development of Dr. Manhart's Summer Jazz Workshops; design of Fishing Lure Badger Coppertail; Compositions: Multiple, for jazz ensemble, pep band, marching band; first to Distance Learning: Music Masterclasses in South Dakota; Continuing the teachings of William Adam, combining Gestalt and Zen psychology, principles of Tai Chi and athletic performance in the teaching of trumpet and music in general. Avocations: fishing, lure making, cedar strip canoe building, woodworking, gardening, ice skating, golf. Office: Northern State Univ 1200 S Jay St Aberdeen SD 57401 E-mail: manhartg@northern.edu.

**MANHART, MARCIA Y(OCKEY),** art museum director; b. Wichita, Kans., Jan. 14, 1943; d. Everett W. and Ruth C. (Correll) Yockey; children: Caroline Manhart Sanderson, Emily Alexandrea Morrison. BA in Art, U. Tulsa, 1965, MA in Ceramics. 1971. Dir. edn. Philbrook Art Ctr., Tulsa, 1972-77, exec. v.p., asst. dir., 1977-83, acting dir., 1983-84; exec. dir. Philbrook Mus. Art (formerly Philbrook Art Ctr.), Tulsa, 1984—2003; exec. dir., trustee The Judith and Jean Pape Charitable Foun., 2004—. Instr. Philbrook Art Ctr. Mus. Sch., Tulsa, 1963-72; gallery dir. Alexandre Hogue Gallery, Tulsa U., 1967-69; NEH Challenge Grant panelist, 1991; presenter to AAM Conv., 1991; MAAA Craft Fellowship panelist, 1988, 93, NEA Craft Fellowship panelist, 1990; NEA spl. exhbn. panelist, 1996; curator nat. touring exhibit Nature's Forms/Nature's Forces: The Art of Alexandre Hogue, 1984-85; co-curator internat. exhbn.: The Eloquent Object, 1987-90; curator Sanford and Diane Besser Collection exhbn., 1992. Author essays in field. Vis. com. Smithsonian Instn./Renwick Gallery, Washington, 1986; cultural negotiator Gov. George Nigh's World Trade Mission (Okla.), China., 1985; com. mem. State Art Coll. of Okla., 1985—; mem. Assocs. of Hillcrest Med. Ctr., 1983-88, exec. com., 1985-88; com. mem. Neighborhood Housing Services, 1985-87; mem. City of Tulsa Arts Commn., 1996-2003; steering com. Harwelden Isnt. for Aesthetic Edn., 1983; com. mem. River Parks Authority, 1976; mem. Jr. League of Tulsa Inc., 1974-78; adv. panel mem. Nat. Craft Planning Project, NEA, Washington, 1978-81; craft adv. panel mem. Okla. Arts and Humanities Council, 1974-76; juror numerous art festivals, competitions, programs; reviewer Inst. Mus. Services, Washington, 1985, 88, 92, 95, 98; auditor Symposium on Language & Scholarship of Modern Crafts, NEA and NEH, Washington, 1981; nominator MacArthur Fellows Program, 1988; panelist Lila Wallace Reader's Digest Internat. Artists Fellowship, 1992, panelist Pew Charitable Trust, 1996. Recipient Harwelden award for Individual Contbrn. in the Arts, 1989, Gov.'s award State of Okla., 1992. Mem. Gillespie County Hist. Soc. (bd. dirs. 2005—), Phi Beta Kappa. Home: 105 S Cherry St Fredericksburg TX 78624 Office Phone: 830-997-7347. E-mail: mmanhart@austin.rr.com.

**MANHEIM, CAMRYN,** television and film actress; b. Caldwell, NJ, Mar. 8, 1961; d. Jerry and Sylvia Manheim; 1 child, Milo Jacob. BFA, UC Santa Cruz, 1984; MFA, NYU, 1987. Actor: (TV series) The Practice, 1997—2004 (Emmy award for Outstanding Supporting Actress in a Drama Series, 1998, Golden Globe award for Best Performance by an Actress in a Supporting Role, 1999); (TV films) Jackie's Back!, 1999, The Loretta Claiborne Story, 2000, Jenifer, 2001; (TV miniseries) The 10th Kingdom, 2000, A Girl Thing, 2001, Elvis, 2005; actor, prodr. (TV films) Kiss My Act, 2000, (film) Bonfire of the Vanities, 1990, The Road to Wellville, 1994, Jeffrey, 1995, Eraser, 1996, Romy and Michele's High School Reunion, 1997, David Searching, 1998, Wide Awake, 1998, Mercury Rising, 1998, Happiness, 1998 (Nat. Bd. Rev. award, 1998), Fool's Gold, 1998, Joe the King, 1999, What Planet are You From?, 2000, East of A, 2000, The Laramie Project, 2002, Just Like Mona, 2003, Scary Movie 3, 2003, Twisted, 2004, Marilyn Hotchkiss' Ballroom Dancing and Charm School, 2005, Dark Water, 2005, An Unfinished Life, 2005; guest appearances Law and Order, Touched By an Angel, New York Undercover, Ally McBeal, Oh Baby, Chicago Hope, Will and Grace; writer: (off-Broadway play) Wake Up, I'm Fat, 1995; theater appearances include N.Y. Shakespeare Festival, Lincoln Ctr., Yale Repertory, N.Y. Theatre Workshop, Classic Stage Co., Home for Contemporary Theater. Office: Creative Artists Agy 9830 Wilshire Blvd Beverly Hills CA 90212

**MANHEIMER, HEIDI,** cosmetics company executive; Diploma in Bus. Mgmt., Ithaca Coll., 1985. Various buying and mgmt. positions Bloomingdales; v.p. cosmetics Barneys NY; with Bluemercury.com, 1999; gen. mgr. Beauty.com; exec. v.p. Shiseido Cosmetics (Am.) Ltd., pres., 2002—06, CEO, 2006—. Bd. dirs. Fragrance Found. Recipient Skin Sense award, Skin Cancer Found., 2005. Office: Shiseido Cosmetics Am Ltd 178 Bauer Dr Oakland NJ 07436-3131*

**MANHOLD, JOHN HENRY,** dental educator, consultant; b. Rochester, N.Y., Aug. 20, 1919; s. John Henry and Helen Martha (Shulz) Manhold; m. Beverly Schecter, 1953 (div. 1969); 1 child: m. Enriqueta Andino, Mar. 20, 1971. BA, U. Rochester, 1940; MD, Harvard U., 1944; MA, Washington U., 1956. Instr. Coll. Medicine Tufts U., Boston, 1948—50; asst. prof., chmn. gen. and oral pathology Coll. Dentistry U. Washington, St. Louis, 1954—56; from asst. prof. to prof., chmn. dept. gen. and oral pathology Seton Hall Coll. Medicine and Dentistry (now U. Medicine and Dentistry N.J.), Newark, 1956—87; emeritus prof. 1987—89; ret. 1989. Cons. Johnson & Johnson, New Brunswick, NJ, 1960—70, Richardson-Vicks, Shelton, Conn., 1981—87, Los Produits Associes, Geneva, 1965—87, Health Care Devel. Group N.J., 1990—2005, Health Care Devel. Group Pa., 1990—2005, Consumer Comm. Network N.Y., 1990—2005, Consumer Comm. Network

Conn., 1990—; lectr. in field. Author: Introductory Psychosomatic Dentistry, 1956, Outline of Pathology, 1960; editor: Clinical Oral Diagnosis, 1965; author: Tissue Respiration and Oxigenating Agents, 1977, Practical Dental Management: Patients and Practice, 1984; author: (in 4 langs.) Illustrated Dental Terminology: A Lexicon for the Dental Profession, 1985; author: (with others) Handbook of Pathology, 1987; editor: Clinical Preventive Dentistry Jour., 1979—92; contbr. articles to profl. jours. Named Disting. Alumni, Harvard U., 1989; named to Sr. Soc. Harvard Sch. Dental Medicine, 1984; recipient Pres. award, Alumni Assn. U. Medicine and Dentistry N.J., 1980, Letter Appreciation, Asara Mihara former min. Japan, 1980, Cert. Achievement, U. Md., 1965. Fellow: Acad. Psychosomatic Medicine (pres. 1977—78, sec. 1975—76, treas. 1976—78), Internat. Coll. Dentists, Am. Coll. Dentists; mem.: APA, Internat. Assn. Dental Rsch., Am. Soc. Clin. Pathologists, Moon Valley Country Club, St. Petersburg Yacht Club, Sigma Xi. Home and Office: 26027 N 44th Ave Glendale AZ 85310 Office Phone: 623-434-6647. E-mail: kupferce@cox.net, eltigreviejo@yahoo.com.

**MANI, NANDITA S.,** medical librarian; b. Edmonton, Alberta, Canada, Jan. 31, 1978; d. Rajam Subra and Anu Subra Mani; m. Scotia Meeshan Roopnarine; 1 child, Maya Mani Roopnarine. BA, U. Concordia, Edmonton, Alberta, Can., 1999; M in Libr. and Info. Sci., Wayne State U., Detroit, 2003, postdoc. in instrnl. tech., 2006—. Cert. computer sys. tech. Northern Alberta Inst. Tech., 2000. Sys. analyst Cross Cancer Inst., Edmonton, Alberta, Canada, 1999—2001; info. sys. libr. Shiffman Med. Libr. Wayne State U., Detroit, 2003—05; med. libr. Sladen Libr. Henry Ford Hosp., 2005—. Presenter at profl. confs. Contbr. articles to profl. jours. Mem.: Met. Med. Libr. Group (mem. newsletter com. 2004—06), Med. Libr. Assn. (mem. minority student scholarship jury 2006—), Beta Tau, Beta Phi Mu. Office: Henry Ford Hosp 2799 W Grand Blvd Detroit MI 48202 Office Phone: 313-916-5335. E-mail: nmani@wayne.edu.

**MANIBUSAN, JOAQUIN V.E., JR.,** magistrate judge; b. Sinajana, Guam, Dec. 10, 1949; s. Joaquin and Alejandrina M.; m. Eileen Bordallo; children: Joaquin III, Erwin, Michael, Maria. BA in Polit. Sci., U. Calif., Berkeley, 1971, JD, 1974. Asst. atty. gen. Govt. of Guam, 1975-77; pvt. practice Guam, 1977-95; judge Superior Ct. of Guam, Agana, Guam, 1995—2004; magistrate judge Dist. of Guam, 2004—. Vice-chmn., mem. Chalan Pago (Guam)-Ordot Mcpl. Planning Coun.; mem. Ret. Srs. Vol. Program; chmn., mem. Guam chpt. ARC; mem. Chalan Pago Parish Coun.; mem. Jr. Holy Name Soc. (pres.), Knights of Alter (v.p.). Office: Dist Ct of Guam 3d Floor US Courthouse Hagatna GU 96910

**MANIKA, JOHN FRANCIS,** computer systems educator, computer information systems analyst; b. Phila., Jan. 22, 1922; s. John F. and Mary T. (Johnston) M.; m. Marie Susan Valeo, Feb. 20, 1944; 1 child, Suzanne Manika Frauenhoffer. A in Bus. Adminstrn., U. Pa., 1967, BBA, 1979, postgrad., 1979-85; grad., U.S. Army Mgmt. Sch., 1968. Mgmt. analyst, internal mgmt. com. VA, 1946-49; mgr. mgmt. engring. dept. Aviation Supply Office, USN, 1949-51, mgr. mgmt. engring. dept. Shipbldg. Activity, 1951-53; dir. mgmt. planning dept. U.S. Army Ordnance Dist., Phila., 1953-59; computer sys. mgr., sys. analyst Def. Logistics Agy., 1959-79; faculty Peirce Coll., Phila., 1967-98, profl. computer info. sys., 1979-98, chmn. computer info. system dept., 1982-89. Adj. instr. Temple U., 1951-56; cons. in field, 2000—. Capt. U.S. Army, 1942-46; lt. col. USAR ret. Fellow Assn. Data Comm. Users (chmn. ednl. com. 1986-86); mem. AAUP, Am. Soc. Profl. Cons., Toastmasters (past pres., founder Mil. Clothiers chpt.), Wharton Club, U. Pa. Faculty Club.

**MANILOW, BARRY (BARRY ALAN PINCUS),** singer, composer; b. N.Y.C., June 17, 1946; s. Harold Pincus and Edna M. Student, N.Y. Coll. Music. Former positions include mailroom CBS; film editor WCBS-TV. Dir. music Callback series, Ed. Sullivan's Pilots; dir. music, condr., arranger, producer for Bette Midler, singer and composer; recorded hit songs: Can't Smile Without You, I Write the Songs, At the Copa (Grammy award, best male pop performance, 1979), Mandy, Looks Like We Made It, Let Me Be Your Wings; albums include Barry Manilow I, 1973, Barry Manilow II, 1974, Tryin' to Get the Feeling, 1975, This One's For You, 1976, Live, 1977, Even Now, 1977, One Voice, 1979, Barry, 1980, A Nice Boy Like Me, 1980, If I Should Love Again, 1981, Here Comes the Night, 1982, Oh, Julie!, 1982, 2 A.M. Paradise Cafe, 1984, Manilow, 1985, Swing Street, 1987, Live on Broadway, 1987, Barry Manilow, 1989, Because It's Christmas, 1990, Showstoppers, 1991, Live in Britain, 1993, Singin' with The Big Bands, 1994, Summer of '78, 1996, Manilow Sings Sinatra, 1998, Here at the Mayflower, 2001, A Christmas Gift of Love, 2002, 2 Nights Live, 2004, The Essential Barry Manilow, 2005, Love Songs of the 50's, 2006; (video) The Best of Me: The Greatest Hits Tour, 1993; star TV movie Copacabana, 1985, Because It's Christmas: Barry Manilow, 1991; appeared TV specials The Barry Manilow Special (Emmy award, 1977), The Second Barry Manilow Special, also Big Fun on Swing Street, 1988, Barry Manilow: SRO on Broadway, 1989; TV appearances include Murphy Brown, 1993, Ally McBeal, 2001, Will & Grace, 2003, American Idol, 2004, Dancing With the Stars, 2006; Broadway prodn.: Barry Manilow at the Gershwin, 1989; author Sweet Life: Adventures on the Way to Paradise; recipient Spl. Tony award, 1977, Ruby award After Dark mag. 1976, Photoplay Gold medal award 1976. Recipient Emmy award for Individual Performance in a variety or music program (Music and Passion), 2006. Office: William Morris Agy 1325 Ave of the Americas New York NY 10019*

**MANIN, YURI IVANOVICH,** mathematician; b. Simferopol, Crimea, Russia, Feb. 16, 1937; s. Ivan Gavrilovich and Rebecca Zinovievna (Miller) M.; m. Marianna Z. Rosenfeld (div.); 1 child, Dimitri Yurievic; m. Xenia Glebovna Semenova, May 30, 1975. MS, Moscow U., 1958; PhD in Math., Math. Inst., Acad. Scis., Moscow, 1960. Leading rsch. scientist Steklov U. 1960—; prof. & chair mathematics Moscow U., 1965—91; dir. Max Planck Inst. for Mathematics, Bonn, 1995—2005; prof. mathematics Northwestern U., 2002—. Vis. prof. Harvard U., MIT, Coll. de France, Montreal (Que., Can.) U., Utrecht (The Netherlands) U., others. Author: Cubic Forms, 1972, Mathematics and Physics, 1981, Gauge Fields and Complex Geometry, 1988. Recipient award Moscow Math. Soc., 1963, Lenin award for work in algebraic geometry USSR Govt., 1967, Brouwer medal Netherlands Math. Soc., 1987, Erwin Plein Nemmers prize in mathematics, Northwestern U., 1994, King Faisal Internat. prize in sci., 2002. Fellow Am. Acad. Arts and Scis.; mem. Acad. Scis. Russia (corr.), Royal Acad. Scis. of the Netherlands (fgn. mem.), Academia Europaea, Acad. de Scis. Inst. France (fgn.). Avocations: literary criticism, studies in psycholinguistics. Office: Northwestern U 2033 Sheridan Rd Evanston IL 60208 Business E-Mail: manin@mpim-bonn.mpg.de.

**MANION, BONNIE J.,** volunteer, poet, composer; b. South Bend, Ind., Apr. 13, 1942; d. Serge A. and Inez (Reed) Rivard; m. Paul T. Manion, Aug. 12, 1961; children: Christine, Sheila, Stephanie, Michael, Daniel, John Brian. BS in Elem. Edn., DePaul U., 1965; grad. lay ministry leadership program, Cath. Diocese, Peoria, Ill., 1988. Cert. elem. tchr. Ill. Author: Soul Search, 2002; contbr. poetry to mags. and books. Host family Rotary Internat., Hoopeston, Ill., 1985, 1995, 1996, 2002; vol. Hosp. Auxiliary, Little League, United Way, Lions Club, local libr.; Hoopeston Music Boosters; vol. Dem. Party, Danville, Ill., 1972—2004; tchr. CCD programs St. Anthony's, Hoopeston, 1969—89, lay pastoral care min., 1985—2006; presenter diocesan programs Cath. Diocese, Peoria, Ill., 1980—2005. Recipient Pere Marquette Medal, Cath. Diocese, Peoria, 2001. Mem.: St. Davids' Christian Writers' Assn., Mary Hartwell Catherwood Book Club. Avocations: painting, poetry, hiking.

**MANION, DANIEL ANTHONY,** federal judge; b. South Bend, Ind., Feb. 1, 1942; s. Clarence E. and Virginia (O'Brien) Manion; m. Ann Murphy Manion, June 29, 1984. AB, U. Notre Dame, 1964; JD, Ind. U., 1973. Bar: Ind., U.S. Dist. Ct. (no. dist.) Ind., U.S. Dist. Ct. (so. dist.) Ind. Dir., indsl. devel. Ind. Dept. Commerce, 1968—73; dep. atty. gen. State of Ind., 1973—74; from assoc. to ptnr. Doran, Manion, Boynton, Kamm & Esmont, South Bend, 1974—86; judge U.S. Ct. Appeals (7th cir.), South Bend, 1986—. Mem. Ind.

State Senate, Indpls., 1978—82; dir. St. Joseph Bank & Trust Co., 1979—86. With U.S. Army, 1965—66. Office: US Ct Appeals US Courthouse & Federal Bldg 204 S Main St Rm 301 South Bend IN 46601-2122*

**MANIS, MELVIN,** psychologist, educator; b. N.Y.C., Feb. 18, 1931; s. Alex and Hanna (Oyle) M.; m. Jean Denby, May 28, 1954; children: Peter Eugene, David Denby. AB in Psychology, Franklin and Marshall Coll., 1951; PhD, U. Ill., 1954. Instr. psychology U. Pitts., 1956-58; rsch. psychologist Ann Arbor VA Med. Ctr., Mich., 1958-89; prof. psychology U. Mich., Ann Arbor, 1966-98, assoc. chmn. dept., 1990-91; ret., 1998. Author: Cognitive Processes, 1966, An Introduction to Cognitive Psychology, 1971; editor Jour. Personality and Social Psychology, 1980-84. With USPHS, 1954—56. Mem.: APA, Soc. Exptl. Social Psychology, Racquet, Phi Beta Kappa. Democrat. Jewish. Home: 20 Harvard Pl Ann Arbor MI 48104-1726 Business E-Mail: Melmanis@umich.edu.

**MANISCALCO, IGNATIUS ANTHONY,** chemistry professor; b. NYC, June 25, 1944; m. Rosemarie Genevieve Taglianetto; children: Ronald Matthew, Frank Stephen. BS, Manhattan Coll., Riverdale, NY, 1965; PhD, Fordham U., Bronx, 1971. Instr. U. Va., Charlottesville, 1970—71; prof. Springfield Coll., Mass., 1971—. Mem.: Am. Chem. Soc., Agawam Lions Club. Achievements include development of Utilizing Computer Technology in Education. Office: Springfield Coll 263 Alden St Springfield MA 01109 Office Phone: 413-748-3381. E-mail: tonym@spfldcol.edu.

**MANISCALCO, JOSEPH,** artist, educator; b. Tampa, Fla., Feb. 24, 1921; s. Michaelangelo and Rosa (Belluccia) M.; m. Ann Lynn Laurence Cadman, Sept. 24, 1954 (div. June 1962); children: Michael, James, Elizabeth, Robert; m. Barbara Ann Fisher Insley, Jan. 3, 1976. Student, Art Students League of N.Y., 1939-41, 46-49. Portrait artist, 1941—. Lectr. in field; judge exhbns. Represented in permanent collections including Mich. Supreme Ct., U.S. House of Reps., Nat. Archives, Washington. With U.S. Army, 1942-46, ETO and PTO. Recipient Fitch award Mich. Acad. Letters, Arts and Sci., Artistic Excellence and Cmty. Commitment award Wayne County Coun. of the Arts, 1992. Mem. Scarab Club (bd. dirs. 1967—, pres. 1972-73, 80-81, 4 gold medals, 1st prize Silver Medal Show), Prismatic Club of Detroit (pres. 2000), Grosse Point Theatre (scenic artist), Fine Art Soc. of Detroit (chmn. art com. 1975), Adcraft Club of Detroit. Avocations: acting and singing in community theater productions, church choral singing. Home: 41110 Fox Run Rd #108 Novi MI 48377

**MANISCALCO-THEBERGE, MARY ELIZABETH,** surgeon, medical educator; b. Portsmouth, Va., Sept. 1, 1956; d. Joseph Jack and Elizabeth Mary Maniscalco; m. Daniel Martin Theberge, June 23, 1984; children: Matthew John Theberge, Danielle Elizabeth Theberge. BS, Old Dominion U., 1978; MD, Ea. Va. Med. Sch., 1981. Diplomate Am. Bd. Surgery, Am. Bd. Critical Care. Commd. 2d lt. US Army, 1981, advanced through grades to col.; chmn. dept. surgery Walter Reed Army Med. Ctr., Washington, 2001. Cons. to surgeon gen. US Army, 1994—2002. Mem. forward in hope com. St. Thomas a Becket Cath. Ch., Reston, Va., 2003. Recipient William Clements award for excellence in edn., Uniformed Svcs. U., Bethesda, Md., 1994. Disting. Alumni award, Old Dominion U., 2003. Fellow: ACS (pres. Med. Washington chpt. 2003—04, mem. com.); mem.: AMA, Soc. Critical Care Medicine (chmn. coun. local chpt.), Am. Coll. Breast Surgeons. Office: US Army Walter Reed Army Med Ctr Dept Surgery 6900 Georgia Ave NW Washington DC 20307

**MANJILI, MASOUD H.,** immunologist, educator; b. Manjil, Iran, Sept. 23, 1962; arrived in U.S., 1999; s. Mahmoud Hajizadeh Manjili and Farandokht Kamran; m. Fariba Azimi, Sept. 26, 1962; children: Saeed H. children: Razieh H., Fahimeh H. DVM, U. Tehran Vet. Sch., Iran, 1990; PhD, Vet. Sch., Sydney, Australia, 1996. Rsch. assist. U Sydney, 1996—96; asst. prof. Razi Vaccine & Serum Rsch. Inst., Hessarak, Tehran, Iran, 1997—99; rsch. affiliate Roswell Pk. Cancer Inst., Buffalo, 1999—2002, instr., 2003—04; asst. prof. Massey Cancer Ctr., Va. Commonwealth U., Richmond, 2004—, mem. scientist, 2006—; mng. editor Frontiers in Biosci., 2005—. Cons. Pasteur Inst., Tehran, 1997—99. Editor: Frontiers in Biosci., 2005—; contbr. articles to profl. jours. Recipient The AACR Inglenook Scholars-in-Training award, 2003; grantee, The N.Y. State Breast Cancer Rsch. and Edn. Fund, 2001, Roswell Pk. Alliance Found., 2003, NIH, 2005—, Susan G. Komen Breast Cancer Found., 2005—. Mem.: Internat. Soc. Biol. Therapy of Cancer, North Am. Hyperthermia Soc., Am. Assn. Immunologists, Am. Assn. for Cancer Rsch. Achievements include research in HSP110-HER-2/neu chaperone complex vaccine induces protective immunity against spontaneous mammary tumors in HER-2/neu transgenic mice. Office: Va Commonwealth U Sch Medicine/Massey Cancer Ctr Dept Microbiology and Immunology Box 980037 Richmond VA 23298 Office Phone: 804-828-8779. Business E-Mail: mmanjili@vcu.edu.

**MANKEL, FRANCIS XAVIER,** retired principal, priest; b. Knoxville, Tenn., Nov. 8, 1935; s. George Whitehead Sr. and Willia Frances (Duncan) M. BA, St. Ambrose U., 1957; STB, St. Mary's Sem. and U., Balt., 1959, STL, 1961; MEd, Loyola Coll., Balt., 1965. Ordained priest, Roman Cath. Ch. 1961. Assoc. pastor Our Lady of Fatima Ch., Alcoa, Tenn., 1961—62, Holy Ghost Ch., Knoxville, 1962-67; tchr. Knoxville Cath. H.S., 1961—67, prin., 1967-79; pastor Sacred Heart Ch., Lawrenceburg, Tenn., 1979-84, St. John Neumann Ch., Knoxville, 1984-87, Sacred Heart Cathedral, Knoxville, 1987-97, Holy Ghost Ch., Knoxville, 1997—. Chancellor Cath. Diocese Knoxville, 1988-96, vicar gen., 1988-98, 99—; supt. Cath. Schs., Diocese of Knoxville, 1989-92. Bd. dirs. Knoxville area chpt. ARC, 1986—2005; sch. bd. Knoxville Cath. HS, 1967—79, 1984—85, 1987—; com. mem. Sacred Heart Cathedral Sch., Knoxville, 1987—97, St. Joseph Sch., Knoxville, 1997—. Mem. Knoxville Ministerial Assn. Home and Office: 111 Hinton Ave Knoxville TN 37917-6418 Office Phone: 865-522-2205. Personal E-mail: hgchurch@bellsouth.net.

**MANKIEWICZ, FRANK F.,** journalist, writer; b. NYC, May 16, 1924; s. Herman J. and Sara (Aaronson) M.; m. Holly Jolley, 1952 (div.); children: Joshua, Benjamin; m. Patricia O'Brien, 1988. AB, UCLA, 1947; MS, Columbia U., 1948; LL.B., U. Calif.-Berkeley, 1955. Bar: Calif. 1955, D.C. 1985. Engaged in journalism, Washington and Los Angeles, 1948-52; practice law Beverly Hills, 1955-61; dir. Peace Corps, Lima, Peru, 1962-64, Latin Am. regional dir. Washington, 1964-66; press sec. Senator Robert F. Kennedy, 1966-68; syndicated columnist and TV news commentator, 1968-71; nat. polit. dir. Presdl. campaign of Senator George McGovern, 1971-72; columnist Washington Post, 1976-77; pres. Nat. Pub. Radio, 1977-83; vice-chmn. Hill and Knowlton (formerly Gray and Co.), 1983—. Author: Perfectly Clear: Nixon from Whittier to Watergate, 1973, U.S. v. Richard M. Nixon: The Final Crisis, 1974, With Fidel: A Portrait of Castro and Cuba, 1975, Remote Control: Television and the Manipulation of American Life, 1977; contbr. articles to newspapers and mags. Served with inf. AUS, 1943-46 Office: Hill and Knowlton 600 New Hampshire Ave NW Washington DC 20037-2403 Office Phone: 202-944-5104.

**MANKIEWICZ, THOMAS FRANK,** screenwriter, director, producer; b. L.A., June 1, 1942; s. Joseph Leo and Rosa M. Student, Yale U., 1959-63. Filmmaker-in-residence Dodge Coll. Film and Media Arts, Chapman U., Orange, Calif., 2006. Author: (book, Broadway musical) Georgy!, 1970; screenwriter: (teleplay, musical spl.) Movin' with Nancy, 1967, The Sweet Ride, 1968, (teleplay, musical spl.) The Beat of the Brass, 1968, Diamonds Are Forever, 1971, Live and Let Die, 1973, The Man With with the Golden Gun, 1974, The Eagle Has Landed, 1976, The Cassandra Crossing, 1977, Ladyhawke, 1985; screenwriter, co-prodr.: Mother, Juggs and Speed, 1976; creative cons.: Superman, 1978, Superman II, 1980; dir. (teleplay, tv pilot) Hart to Hart, 1979-80, (screenplay) Dragnet, 1987, Delirious, 1991, (cable tv series) Tales from the Crypt, 1992, (cable tv movie) Taking the Heat, 1993; exec. prodr. Hot Pursuit, 1985. Bd. dirs. William Holden Wildlife Found., L.A., 1995—. Mem. Greater L.A. Zoo Assn. (bd. trustees 1997—, chmn.

2002--), Motion Picture Acad. Arts and Scis. (bd. govs. 1979-81), Thoroughbred Owners Calif. (bd. dirs. 2005). Avocations: wildlife conservation, thoroughbred horse racing and breeding. E-mail: mankone@earthlink.net.

**MANKILLER, WILMA PEARL,** retired tribal leader; b. Stilwell, Okla., Nov. 18, 1945; d. Charley and Clara Irene (Sitton) M.; m. Hector N. Olaya, Nov. 13, 1963 (div. 1975); children: Felicia Marie Olaya, Gina Irene Olaya; m. Charlie Soap, Oct. 13, 1986. Student, Skyline Coll., San Bruno Coll., 1973, San Francisco State Coll., 1973-75; BA in Social Sci., Union Coll., 1977; postgrad., U. Ark., 1979; DHL (hon.), U. New Eng., 1986; PhD in Pub. Svc. (hon.), R.I. Coll., 1989; DHL (hon.), Yale U., 1990; PhD (hon.), Dartmouth Coll., 1991; LLD (hon.), Mills Coll., 1992. Cmty. devel. dir. Cherokee Nation, Tahlequah, Okla., 1977-83, dep. chief, 1983-85, prin. chief, 1985-95; Montgomery fellow Dartmouth Coll., 1996. Author: Mankiller: A Chief and Her People, 1993; co-editor: The Readers Companion to the History of Women in the U.S., 1998. Recipient Donna Nigh First Lady award Okla. Commn. for Status of Women, 1985, Am. Leadership award Harvard U., 1986, Elizabeth Blackwell award, 1996, Dorothy Height Lifetime Achievement award, 1997, Presdl. Medal of Freedom, 1998; inducted Okla. Women's Hall of Fame, 1986. Avocations: reading, writing. Home: PO Box 308 Park Hill OK 74451-0308

**MANKIN, DONALD AARON,** management consultant, writer; b. Phila., Apr. 22, 1942; s. Harry and Eva Mankin; m. Katherine Braun, Apr. 5, 1945. BSEE, Drexel U., 1964; PhD in Engring. Psychology, Johns Hopkins U., 1968. Asst. prof. Lehigh U., Bethlehem, Pa., 1968—75; vis. rsch. assoc. U. So. Calif., L.A., 1975—76; assoc. prof. U. Houston, 1976—78, U. Md., University College, 1978—80; vis. rsch. assoc. The Rand Corp., Santa Monica, Calif., 1980—81; prof. Antioch U., L.A., 1981—88; program dir. Calif. Sch. Profl. Psychology, L.A., 1988—90; sr. cons. GammaVision, Inc., Seattle, 1990—92; self-employed cons. L.A., Calif., 1992—94; dean Calif. Sch. Profl. Psychology, 1994—99; prof. Alliant Internat. U., 1999—2002; pres. Co:e-laboration Design Assoc., Venice, Calif., 2002—. Author: (book) Toward a Post Industrial Psychology; editor: Classics of Industrial and Organizational Psychology; author: Teams and Technology, Business without Boundaries. Mem.: Acad. of Mgmt., Tau Beta Pi. Jewish. Avocations: avant garde jazz, exercise, travel. Office: Co:e-laboration Design Assoc 230 Market St Venice CA 90291 Office Phone: 310-401-0092. Home Fax: 310-401-0165; Office Fax: 310-401-0165. Personal E-mail: dmankin@comcast.net.

**MANKIN, HENRY JAY,** orthopedist, educator, health facility administrator; b. Pitts., Oct. 9, 1928; s. Hyman Isaac and Mary (Simons) M.; m. Carole Jane Pinkney, Aug. 20, 1952; children: Allison Joan, David Philip, Keith Pinkney. BS magna cum laude, U. Pitts., 1952, MD, 1953; MA (hon.), Harvard U., 1973. Diplomate Am. Bd. Orthopaedic Surgery (mem. bd. 1976-82, pres. bd. 1980-81). Intern U. Chgo. Clinics, 1953-54; resident orthopaedics Hosp. for Joint Diseases, N.Y.C., 1957-60; instr. orthopaedics U. Pitts. Sch. Medicine, 1960-62, assoc. prof., 1962-64, assoc. prof., 1964-66; prof. orthopaedics Hosp. for Joint Diseases and Mt. Sinai Sch. Medicine, 1966-72; chief orthopaedics Mass. Gen. Hosp., Boston, 1972-96, chief orthopaedic oncology, 1972—. Edith M. Ashley prof. orthopaedics Harvard Med. Sch., 1972—; mem. surgery B study sect. NIH, 1969-73; mem. adv. com. on surg. treatment FDA, 1973-75; corporator Boston Five Cent Savs. Bank, 1982-83; mem. exec. com. Am. Bd. Med. Spltys., 1982-85; adv. council on grad. med. edn., 1986-96; mem. Nat. Arthritis Avd. Bd., 1986-89; mem. human resources and research rev. group A Nat. Inst. Arthritis, Metabolism and Digestive Diseases, 1981-85, chmn., 1983-85. Assoc. editor Arthritis and Rheumatism, 1967-77, Jour. Bone and Joint Surgery, 1967-82; mem. editorial bd. Jour. Orthopedic Research, 1982-85; trustee Jour. Bone and Joint Surgery, 1985-91, chmn. bd., 1988-91; contbr. more than 560 articles to profl. med. jours. Served to lt. comdr. USNR, 1955-57. Fellow ACS, Royal Coll. Surgeons (hon.); mem. Am. Acad. Orthopaedic Surgeons, Acad. Orthopaedic Soc. (pres. 1991-92), Am. Orthopaedic Assn. (pres. 1982-83), Orthopaedic Research Soc. (pres. 1969-70), Musculoskeletal Tumor Soc. (pres. 1991-92), Brit. Orthopaedic Research Soc., Argentine Orthopedic Assn. (hon.), N.Y. Acad. Medicine (chmn. orthopaedic sect. 1971-72), Am. Rheumatism Assn., Soc. Internat. Chirurgerie Orthopaedice et Traumatologia, Hip Soc., Interurban, Forum Orthopaedic clubs, Brit. Orthopaedic Assn. (hon.), Can. Orthopaedic Assn. (hon.), Australian Orthopaedic Assn. (hon.), N.Z. Orthopaedic Assn. (hon.), Japanese Orthopaedic Assn. (hon.), Israel Orthopaedic Assn. (hon.), Thai Orthopaedic Assn (hon.). Office: Mass Gen Hosp 55 Fruit St Boston MA 02114-2696 Business E-Mail: hmankin@partners.org.

**MANKIN, ROBERT STEPHEN,** diversified financial services company executive; b. NYC, Mar. 26, 1939; s. Samuel Harry Mankin and Dorothy (Rosenblum) Goldstein; m. Joyce Marie Cabel, June 13, 1971 (div.); children: Seth Howard, Laura Nicole, Gina Danielle; m. Ruth Irwin, July 20, 2002. BA cum laude, Bklyn. Coll., 1961; MBA, Bernard Baruch Coll., 1970; Dr. Profl. Studies with distinction, Pace U., 1982. Mgr. ABC, N.Y.C., 1969-71, Babcock and Wilcox, N.Y.C., 1971-74; v.p. Chase Manhattan Bank, N.Y.C., 1974-84; sr. v.p. 1st Interstate Bank, N.Y.C., 1984-87; mng. dir., co-head fixed income, mem. mgmt. com. Nomura Securities Internat., N.Y.C., 1987-94; mng. dir. Paine Webber, N.Y.C., 1994-95; pres., CEO Lakeside Fin. Svcs., Hoboken, NJ, 1995—; COO Thomson Fin. Electronic Settlements Group, Boston, 1997-98; acting pres. Ocwen Tech. Exch., West Palm Beach, Fla., 1999; CEO Sutton Strategic, LLC, 2001—02. Bd. dirs., sec. Nomura Mortgage Capital Corp., N.Y.C.; bd. dirs., pres., CEO Nomura Asset Capital Corp., N.Y.C., 1988-94; trustee Hudson Inst., 2004— Contbr. articles to profl. jours. Mem. Planning Forum, Assn. for Computing Machinery, Assn. Computer Programmers and Analysts (chmn. bd. 1971).

**MANKIW, GREGORY (NICHOLAS GREGORY MANKIW),** economics professor, former federal official; b. Trenton, N.J., Feb. 3, 1958; s. Nicholas and Dorothy (Sawchak) Mankiw; m. Deborah Jean Roloff, June 16, 1984. AB, Princeton U., 1980; PhD, MIT, 1984. Staff economist Coun. Econ. Advisers, Washington, 1982-83; instr. MIT, Cambridge, 1984-85; asst. prof. econs. Harvard U., Cambridge, 1985-87, prof. econs., 1987—; mem., chmn. Coun. Econ. Advisers Exec. Office of the Pres., Washington, 2003—05. Research assoc. Nat. Bureau of Economic Research; advisor Fed. Reserve Bank of Boston, Congressional Budget Off.; mem. test devel. comm. ETS. Author: Macroeconomics, 1992, Principles of Economics, 1998; contbr. articles Am. Economic Review, Jour. of Polit. Economy, Quarterly Jour. of Economics, The NY Times, The Financial Times, The Wall Street Journal, Fortune. Recipient Presidential Young Investigator award NSF, 1986. Office: Harvard U Dept Econs Littauer 223 Cambridge MA 02138*

**MANKOFF, DAVID ABRAHAM,** nuclear medicine physician; b. July 10, 1959; BS in Physics summa cum laude, Yale U., 1981; MD, PhD in Bioengring., U. Pa., 1988. Diplomate Am. Bd. Internal Medicine, Am. Bd. Nuclear Medicine. Rsch. scientist UGM Med. Sys., Phila., 1988-89, dir. engring., 1989-90; rsch. assoc. nuclear medicine sect. U. Pa., Phila., 1988-90; resident in internal medicine U. Wash., Seattle, 1990-92, resident in nuclear medicine, 1992-96, asst. prof. radiology, 1996—2001, assoc. prof. radiology, 2001, assoc. prof. medicine, 2002—; assoc. prof. bioengring., 2005—. Office: Divsn Nuc Medicine U Wash Med Ctr Box 356113 1959 NE Pacific St Seattle WA 98195-0001 Office Phone: 206-598-4727. Business E-Mail: dam@u.washington.edu.

**MANKOFF, RONALD MORTON,** retired lawyer; b. Gettysburg, S.D., Oct. 13, 1931; s. Harry B. and Sarah (Frank) M.; m. Joy Faith Shechtman, Nov. 3, 1959; children: Jeffrey Walker, Douglas Frank. BSL, U. Minn., JD, 1954; LLM in Taxation, NYU, 1959. Bar: Minn. 1954, Tex. 1959. With Leonard, Street & Deinard, Mpls., 1957-58; research analyst Inst. Jud. Adminstrn., N.Y.C., 1958-59; assoc. Lyne, Blanchette, Smith & Shelton, Dallas, 1959-60; ptnr. Durant and Mankoff, Dallas, 1960-85; pres. Brice & Mankoff P.C., Dallas, 1985-89, Mankoff, Hill, Held & Metzger, L.L.P., Dallas, 1989-95; chmn./gen. counsel RAC Fin. Group, Inc. (now 1st Plus Fin Group, Inc.), 1994-96. Lectr. law Sch. Law, So. Meth. U., 1974-77; speaker in field. Contbr. articles to profl. jours. Mem. Dallas Mcpl. Libr., 1973—75, Mayor's Task Force on Child Care, 1984; chmn. bd. Dallas chpt. Am. Cancer Soc.,

1976—77, bd. dirs. Tex. divsn., 1981—94; chmn. Dallas Crusade, 1974—75, bd. dirs., mem. exec. com., 1963—88; mem. exec. com. Nat. Pooled Income Fund, Coun. Jewish Welfare Fedns. and Funds, 1975—77; adv. dir. Dallas Cmty. Chest Trust Fund, 1976—78; chmn. Found. Dallas Jewish Fedn., 1976—77; pres. Temple Emanu-el Dallas, 1977—79; bd. dirs. Jewish Fedn. Greater Dallas, 1977—79, 1999—2002, Dallas Civic Opera, 1981—83, World Union Progressive Judaism, 1981—90; mem. S.W. regional liaison com. IRS, 1980—83; mem. exec. com. Union Am. Hebrew Congregations, 1979—89, trustee, 1979—97, chmn. nat. coll. com., 1983—87, vice chmn. bd. dirs., 1984—88, vice chmn. devel. commn., 1997—99; sec. Dallas Assembly, 1979—84; mem. exec. com. Dallas Jewish Cmty Rels. Coun., 1982—83, Com. for Qualified Judiciary, 1982—; sec. Child Care Partnership, 1984—86, bd. dirs., 1986—88, Dallas Women's Found., 1985—89, mem. adv. coun., 1989—, chair adv. coun., 1997—99; bd. dirs. Am. Jewish Com., 1982—88, pres. Dallas chpt., 1986—90; bd. dirs. Tex. coun. Girl Scouts U.S., 1982—85; bd. dirs. Goodwill Industries of Greater Dallas, 1979—83, Title One Home Improvement Lender's Assn., 1994—96; bd. govs. Dallas Symphony Assn., 1988—92, 1998—; chmn. Temple Emanu El Found., 1988—95; bd. dirs. Dallas Inst. Humanities and Culture, 1998—2005, mem. adv. coun., 2005—; bd. dirs. Ctr. for Interreligious Understanding, 2001—05, Cardio-Pulmonary Rsch. Inst., 2002—, Jane's Due Process, Inc., 2002—, Cmty. Home for Adults Found., 2001—. Lt. (j.g.) USN, 1954—57. Mem. ABA, State Bar Tex., Dallas Bar Assn., Columbian Country Club (bd. dirs. 1967-73), LaJolla Country Club, Crescent Club, Park Cities Club, Zeta Beta Tau, Delta Sigma Rho. Democrat. Jewish. Home: 22 Lakeside Pk Dallas TX 75225 Address: 8510 El Paseo Grande La Jolla CA 90237 Personal E-mail: ron@mankoff.com.

**MANLEY, AUDREY FORBES,** retired academic administrator, pediatrician, retired military officer; b. Jackson, Miss., Mar. 25, 1934; d. Jesse Lee and Ora Lee (Buckhalter) Forbes; m. Albert Edward Manley, Apr. 3, 1970. AB with honors (tuition scholar), Spelman Coll. Atlanta, 1955; MD (Jesse Smith Noyes Found. scholar), Meharry Med. Coll., 1959; MPH, Johns Hopkins U.-USPHS traineeship, 1987; LHD (hon.), Tougaloo Coll., Miss., 1990, Meharry Med. Coll., Nashville, 1991; LLD (hon.), Spelman Coll., 1991, Tskegee U., 1998; DSc (hon.), Coll. New Rochelle, 1998, Morehouse Coll., 2002, U. Del., 2002. Diplomate: Am. Bd. Pediatrics. Intern St. Mary Mercy Hosp., Gary, Ind., 1960; from jr. to chief resident in pediatrics Cook County Children's Hosp., Chgo., 1960—62; NIH fellow neonatology U. Ill. Rsch. and Ednl. Hosp., Chgo., 1963—65; staff pediatrician Chgo. Bd. Health, 1963—66; practice medicine specializing in pediatrics Chgo., 1963—66; assoc. Lawndale Neighborhood Health Ctr. North, 1966—67; asst. med. dir., 1967—69; asst. prof. Chgo. Med. Coll., 1966—67; instr. Pritzker Sch. Medicine, U. Chgo., 1967—69; asst. dir. ambulatory pediatrics, asst. dir. pediatrics Mt. Zion Hosp. and Med. Center, San Francisco, 1969—70; med. cons. Spelman Coll., 1970—71; med. dir. family planning program, chmn. health careers adv. com., 1972—76; med. dir. Grady Meml. Hosp. Family Planning Clinic, 1972—76; commd. officer, advanced though grades to rear adm. USPHS, 1976—97; chief genetic diseases services br. Office Maternal and Child Health, Bur. Community Health Services, Rockville, Md., 1976—81; acting assoc. adminstr. clin. affairs Office of Adminstr. Health Resources and Services Adminstrn., 1981—83, chief med. officer, dep. assoc. adminstr. planning. evaluation and legis., 1983—85; sabbatical leave USPHS Johns Hopkins Sch. Hygiene and Pub. Health, 1986—87; dir. Nat. Health Service Corps.; asst. surgeon gen. US Dept. Health & Human Services, 1988, dep. asst. sec. for health, 1989—93, acting asst. sec. health, 1993, dep. asst. sec. health & intergovtl. affairs, 1993—94, dep. surgeon gen., acting dep. asst. sec. for minority health, 1994—95, acting surgeon gen., 1995—97; pres. Spelman Coll., 1997—2002, pres. emerita, 2003—04; pres. History Makers, 2003. Mem. U.S. del. UNICEF, 1990-94, Am. Acad. Family Physicians (pub. adv. bd.), Am. Coun. Learned Socs., Am. Med. Assn. Minority Affairs Consortium (sr. advisor), Ctrs. for Disease Control Found. (bd. visitors), Morehouse Sch. Medicine (clin. Prof. Pediats., Pub. Health Lectr.), Rollins Sch. Pub. Health Emory U (Commrs., Adv. Coun., Ga. Leadership Commn. Organ, Tissue, Blood Marrow donation amont African Ams. Author numerous articles, reports in field; artist permanent collections Nat. Acads. Sci., Spelman Coll. Alumnae Hall of Fame, 2005. Trustee Spelman Coll., 1966-70; The Coll. Fund (UNCF com. Archives, Hist. Govtl. Affairs Com.), Coun. Fgn. Rels., bd. dirs. coun. Ind. Colls.; bd. dirs. March of Dimes, 1998, Nat. Merit Scholarship Corp.; Nat. Minority Mil. Mus. Found. Edl. Adv. Coun., Am. Cancer Soc. Found., CDC Found., Compas Compact, Downtown Atlanta Chpt. Rotary, Atlanta 2000 Adv. Com., Quality Edn. for Minorities; adv. bd. Atlanta Regional Health Summit, Commerce Club, Ga. Found. Ind., Food and Drug Adv. Com., publ. advisory bd. Am. Acad. Family Physicians, sr. advisor AMA Minority Affairs Consortium, bd. visitors CDC Found., hon. advisor coun., charter mem. The Children's Inn at NIH, mem. Coun. on Fgn. Rels., Adv. Com., vaccine and biologics com. Food and Drug Adminstrn., mem. Health Careers Exploring Advisory Com., Tribal Colls.; chair, advisory group Univ. S.Carolina Rural Health Initiative. Rear adm. USPHS. ret. USPHS. Recipient Meritorious Svc. award USPHS, 1981, Mary McLeod Bethune award Nat Coun. Negro Women, 1979, Dr. John P. McGovern Ann. Lectureship award Am. Sch. Health Assn., Disting. Alumni award Meharry Med. Coll., 1989, Spelman Coll. 108 Founder's Day Convocation, 1989, Disting. Svc. medal USPHS, 1992, Hildrus A. Poindexter award OSG/PHS, 1993, numerous other svc. and achievement awards; named to African Americans in Sci., Engring., and Medicine Portrait Collection, Nat. Acads., 2005. Fellow Am. Acad. Pediatrics; mem. Nat. Inst. Medicine of Nat. Acad. Sci., Nat. Med. Assn., APHA, AAUW, AAAS, Coun. Fgn. Rels., Spelman Coll. Alumnae Assn. (Hall of Fame 2005), Meharry Alumni Assn., African Am. Collection Portraits of NAS, Operation Crossroads Africa Alumni Assn. Atlanta C. of C., Rotary, Delta Sigma Theta (hon.), Phi Beta Kappa. Address: 2807 18th St NW Washington DC 20009 Office Phone: 202-462-5214. Personal E-mail: amanley009@aol.com, amanley007@netaccess.com.

**MANLEY, EDWARD HARRY, JR.,** professional association administrator, food prevention director, retired military officer; b. Staten Island, NY, Sept. 12, 1941; s. Edward H. and Dorothy I.; m. Judith Manley; children: Deborah Szymchack, Michael E. BS, Cornell U., 1975; MS, Rollins Coll., 1978. Cert. HACCP mgr., 2003. Joined USN, 1959, commd. ensign, 1970, advanced through grades to lt. comdr., 1979; food svc. dir. Naval Hosp., Annapolis, Md., 1972-73; asst. food svc. dir. Nat. Naval Med. Ctr., Bethesda, Md., 1971-72; food svc. dir. Naval Regional Med. Ctr., Orlando, Fla., 1975-80, ret. 1980; food svc. dir. North Broward Hosp., Pompano Beach, Fla., 1981-89; pres. Creative Food Concepts, Inc.; founder Workaholics Internat. Network, 1999—; pres. VIP Food Safety; HACCP and food safety tng. worldwide. Mem. adv. bd. Mid-Fla. Tech. Food Svc. Program, 1978-80, Atlantic Vo-Tech Dietetic Program, 1981-89; chmn. Skills Std. Bd., Hospitality and Tourism. Mem. evaluation team Hennessey award US Air Force, 1982; mem. adv. bd. Broward C.C., 1985—. Ed Manley Scholarship Fund established, 1984; named Disting. Health Care Food Svc. Adminstr., 1985, Master Cert. Food Exec., 2002; recipient Peter Gust Economou award, 1987. Mem. Internat. Food Svc. Exec. Assn. (pres. Orlando br. 1979-80, pres. South Fla. br. 1983-84, internat. sec.-treas. 1986-87, chmn. bd. 1988-1989, pres. 1989-2006, Mem. of Yr. Orlando br. 1978, South Fla. br. 1984, Disting. Svc. award 1984, Dignified Order of the Dinner Gong 2001), Cornell Hotel Soc. (treas. Las Vegas 2001—), Fla. Restaurant Assn. (bd. dir. 1980), Am. Soc. Hosp. Food Svc. Adminstrn. (sec. South Fla. chpt.), Cornell of Ctrl. Fla. Club, Naval Tng. Officers Club (pres. 1978-80), Pompano Sq. Mall Walkers Club (founder). Home and Office: 2609 Surfwood Dr Las Vegas NV 89128-1282 E-mail: hq@workaholic.com.

**MANLEY, FRANK,** language educator, writer; b. Scranton, Pa., Nov. 13, 1930; s. Aloysius F. and Kathryn L. (Needham) M.; m. Carolyn Mary Holliday, Mar. 14, 1952; children: Evelyn, Mary. BA, Emory U., 1952, MA, 1953; PhD, Johns Hopkins U., 1959. Instr., then asst. prof. Yale U., New Haven, 1959-64; assoc. prof., then prof. dept. English Emory U., Atlanta, 1964-2000, chmn. dept., 1968-70, Candler prof. English, 1982-2000, dir. creative writing program, 1990-2000, retired, 2000. Editor: The Anniversaries (John Donne), 1963, (with R. Sylvester) De Fructu qui ex Doctrina Percipitur,

1967, All Fools (George Chapman), 1968, A Dialogue of Comfort (St. Thomas More), vol. 12, 1977 and Epistola ad Pomeranum, vol. 7, 1990, Yale edit. More's complete works; author: Resultances, 1980 (Devins award for poetry 1980), Two Masters (co-winner Gt. Am. New Play Contest 9th Ann. Humana Festival New Am. Plays 1985), (with F. Watkins) Some Poems and Some Talk About Poetry, 1985, Within the Ribbons: 9 Stories, 1989, (play) The Trap, 1993, The Cockfighter: a Novel, 1998, Among Prisoners: Stories, 2000, (poems) The Emperors, 2001, True Hope: A Novel, 2002. With U.S. Army, 1953—55. Guggenheim Found. fellow, 1966-67, 78-79; recipient NEH transl. program fellowship, 1981-83, Nat. Endowment Arts Creative Writing Fellowship in Fiction, 1995-97, Disting. Teaching award, 1984, Univ. scholar/tchr. of yr. award, 1989, Disting. Alumnus award The Marist Sch., 1993. Roman Catholic. Home: 401 Adams St Decatur GA 30030-5207 also: Doublehead Gap Rd Ellijay GA 30540 Business E-Mail: fmanley@emory.edu.

**MANLEY, JAMES L.,** molecular biologist, educator; PhD. Julian Clarence Levy prof. life scis. Columbia U., NYC. Contbr. articles to sci. jours.; editor: Molecular and Cellular Biology; assoc. editor: Gene Expression. Fellow: Am. Acad. Arts & Scis. Office: Dept Biol Scis Columbia U 1117 Fairchild Ctr MC 2410 New York NY 10027 E-mail: jlm2@columbia.edu.*

**MANLEY, JANET ZEEGERS,** retired small business owner; b. Grosse Pointe, Mich., July 4, 1933; d. Frank and Maria Elisabeth (Voncken) Zeegers; m. Richard Edward Manley, Dec. 3, 1955; 1 child, David Richard. A in Bus., Mich. State U., 1953. Owner, ptnr., mgr. Zeegers Electric, Center Line, Mich., 1950-91; sec., stenographer Mopar divsn. Chrysler Corp., Center Line, 1953-55; libr. aide Houghton Lake Pub. libr., Mich., 1970-94; mgr. salesperson Carolyn's Book Nook, Houghton Lake, Mich., 1980-88. Sec. bd. edn., Houghton Lake, Mich., 1976-99, Mid-Mich. Libr. League Bd., Cadillac, 1970—, Mich. Libr. Assn., Lansing, 1985—. Recipient award of Distinction, Mich. Assn. Sch. Bds., 1994, Master Bd. Mem. award, 1996. Mem. Am. Bus. Women's Assn. (com. chair 1987—, Woman of Yr., 1995). Avocations: non-fiction reading, needlecrafts, travel, nature, youth activities. Home: 6119 W Nestel Rd Houghton Lake MI 48629-8202

**MANLEY, JOAN A(DELE) DANIELS,** retired publishing executive; b. San Luis Obispo, Calif., Sept. 23, 1932; d. Carl and Della (Weinmann) Daniels; m. Jeremy C. Lanning, Mar. 17, 1956 (div. Sept. 1963); m. Donald H. Manley, Sept. 12, 1964 (div. 1985); m. William G. Houlton, May 31, 1991. BA, U. Calif., Berkeley, 1954; DBA (hon.), U. New Haven, 1974; LLD (hon.), Babson Coll., 1981. Sec. Doubleday & Co., N.Y.C., 1954-60; sales exec. Time Inc., 1960-66, v.p., 1971-75, group v.p., 1975-84, also bd. dir.; circulation dir. Time-Life Books, 1966-68, dir. sales, 1968-70, pub., 1970-76; chmn. bd. Time-Life Books Inc., 1976-80. Vice chmn. bd. Book-of-the-Month Club, Inc., N.Y.C., until 1984; supervising dir. Time-Life Internat. (Nederland) B.V., Amsterdam, until 1984; mem. exec. bd. Coll. Letters and Sci. U. Calif., Berkeley, Calif., 2005— Past trustee Mayo Found., Rochester, Minn., Nat. Repertory Orch., William Benton Found.; former mem. adv. coun. Stanford U. Bus. Sch., Haas Sch. Bus. U. Calif. Named to Direct Mktg. Hall of Fame, 1993; U. Calif.-Berkeley fellow, 1989. Mem. Assn. Am. Pubs. (past chmn.).

**MANLEY, JOHN FREDERICK,** political scientist, educator; b. Utica, NY, Feb. 20, 1939; s. John A. and Gertrude Manley; children from previous marriage: John, Laura; m. Kathy Lynn Sharp, 1991; 1 child, Cole Sharp Manley. BS, Le Moyne Coll., 1961; PhD, Syracuse U., 1966. Asst. prof. polit. sci. U. Wis., 1966, assoc. prof., 1969-71; prof., chmn. dept. polit. sci. Stanford U., 1977-80. Fellow Center for Advanced Study in Behavioral Scis., 1976-77; vis. prof. Stanford in Oxford, 1996. Author: The Politics of Finance, 1970, American Government and Public Policy, 1976; author, co-editor: The Case Against the Constitution, 1987. Congressional fellow, 1963-64; Brookings Instn. fellow, 1965-66; Guggenheim fellow, 1974-75; Fulbright fellow U. Bologna, 1992. Office: 152 Greens Farms Rd Westport CT 06880-6215 E-mail: manley48@msn.com.

**MANLEY, JOHN HUGO,** computer company executive, educator; b. Highland Park, Mich., July 9, 1932; s. Hugo Edward and Linda Amelia (Kuure) M.; m. Josephine Theresa Catanzaro, Sept. 3, 1958; children: Lisa Linn, Michele Ann, John David, Marc Darrin. B. Metall. Engring., Cornell U., 1955; MS Indsl. Engring., U. Pitts., 1965, PhD, 1971. Metall. engr. GE, Schenectady, NY, 1955—56; commd. 2d lt. USAF, 1956, advanced through grades to lt. col., 1973, ret., 1976; asst. to dir. Johns Hopkins Applied Physics Lab., Laurel, Md., 1976—80; exec. ITT Corp., Stratford, Conn., 1980—83; v.p. Nastec Corp., Southfield, Mich., 1983—85; dir. emeritus Software Engring. Inst. Carnegie Mellon U., Pitts., 1985—87; pres., chmn. Computing Tech. Transition, Inc., Wilmington, Del., 1983—2004; prof. emeritus mfg. and info. tech. sys. engring.; dir. mfg. sys. engring. program U. Pitts., 1987—2002. Tech. advisor. bd. Tartan Inc., Pitts.; com. on nat. weather svc. modernization NRC, 1991-94. Editor-in-chief Jour. Systems and Software, 1978-82; contbr. articles to profl. jours. Pres. Point Field Community Assn., Millersville, Md., 1979-80; v.p. Greater Severna Park Coun., Severna Park, Md., 1980. Lt. col. USAF, 1955-76, Vietnam. Decorated Legion of Merit, Bronze Star. Mem. IEEE Computer Soc. (TC exec. bd.), Soc. Mfg. Engrs., Gulf Harbour Golf & Country Club. Republican. Episcopalian.

**MANLEY, JOHN PAUL,** former Canadian government official; b. Ottawa, Ontario, Canada, Jan. 5, 1950; s. John Joseph and Mildred Charlotte (Scharf) Manley; m. Judith Mary Rae, Apr. 21, 1973; children: Rebecca Jane, David John, Sarah Kathleen. Attended, Carleton U.; Doctorate (hon.), U. Ottawa. Law clerk for Rt. Hon. Bora Laskin Chief Justice Can., 1976-77; chair Ottawa-Carleton Bd. Trade, 1985-86; min. Industry Govt. of Can., 1993-2000, min. Western Econ. Diversification, min. Atlantic Can. Opportunities Agy., 1996, min. for Can. Econ. Devel. for Que. Regions, 1996-2000; min. fgn. affairs, 2000—02; chair cabinet com. on pub. security and anti-terrorism, 2001—; dep. prime minister of Can., 2002—03; min. of fin, 2002—03. Chmn. cabinet com. on pub. security and anti-terrorism Ho. of Commons, Ottawa, Canada, 2001—, min. infrastructure and crown corps., 2002, polit. min. for Ontario and chmn. cabinet com. on econ. union and social union, 2002—03; bd. dir. Nortel Networks, 2004—. Elected to H. of C. g.e., 1988. Named Time Can. Mag. Newsmaker of the Yr., 2001. Avocation: marathon running. Office: McCarthy Tetrault LLP The Chambers Ste 1400 40 Elgin St Ottawa ON K1P Canada E-mail: manlej@parl.gc.ca

**MANLEY, JUDITH L.,** director; b. Columbus, Ohio; B in Bus., Ohio State U., 1970; MEd, Xavier U., 1986. Copy writer advt. agy., Columbus, 1970—74; program asst. Ohio State U., Columbus, 1974—. Advisor, counselor, tchr. dept. Spanish and Portuguese Ohio State U., Columbus, 1991—. Author poems. Commr. Greater Hilltop Area Commn., Columbus, 1989—; bd. dirs. Greater Hilltop Cmty. Devel. Corp., Columbus, 1989—; alumnae Leadership Columbus, Columbus, 1993; mem. citizens' adv. coun. Columbus Devel. Ctr. Named Vol. of the Month, Children's Hosp., Columbus, 2002; recipient Pres.'s Vol. Svc. award, 2003, 2004, 2005, Va. Denman Vol. award, 2004. Mem.: ACA, Am. Assn. Tchrs. Spanish and Portuguese. Avocations: writing, photography, music, theater.

**MANLEY, NANCY JANE,** environmental engineer; b. Ft. Smith, Ark., Sept. 13, 1951; d. Eugene Hailey and Mary Adele (Chave) M. BSE, Purdue U., 1974; MSE, U. Wash., 1976; postgrad., U. Minn., 1976-77; grad., Air Command and Staff Coll., 1984, Exec. Leadership Devel. Program Dept. Def., 1988. Lic. profl. engr., Ga.; registered environ. mgr.; bd. cert. environ. engr. Am. Acad. Environ. Engrs. Sanitary engr. Minn. Dept. Health. Mpls., 1976-77; sanitary engr. water supply EPA, Chgo., 1977, leader primacy unit water supply Atlanta, 1977-79, leader tech. assistance team, 1979-82; chief environ. and contract planning, project mgr. Grand Bay Range design USAF, Moody AFB, Ga., 1982-84; dep. base civil engr. Carswell AFB, Tex., 1984-86, Scott AFB, Ill., 1986-89, mem. tech. adv. com. Scott AFB master plan study Belleville, Ill., 1986-89, dep. base civil engr. Robins AFB, Ga.,

1989-91, acting chief engr., 1990-91, chief pollution prevention divsn., dir. environ. mgmt., 1991-93; chief engr. divsn. 78 Civil Engr. Group, Robins AFB, Ga., 1993—. Mem. Fla. Tech. Adv. Com. for Injection Wells, Tallahassee, 1980-82, Nat. Implementation Team for Underground Injection Control Program, Washington, 1979-82, tech. panel Nat. Groundwater Protection Strategy Hearings, 1981; judge Internat. Sci. and Engring. Fair, 1986. Active various ch. activities, 1969-74, St. Louis Math. and Sci. Network Day, 1989, Adopt-a-Sch. Program, Lebanon, Ill., 1987-89; sec. Perry Area Hist. Soc., 1991-93; vol. Meals-on-Wheels, Girl Scouts U.S., Ga. Voluntary Tech. Assistance Group, others, various locations, 1982—; founder, crisis intervention counselor Midwest Alliance, West Lafayette, Ind., 1970-74; scientist by mail Boston Mus. Sci., 1989-99, Mathcounts, 1991—; mentor Purdue U., U. Washington, others, 1986—. Named Engr. of Yr., Robins AFB, 1997, 2000, 2003, Air Force Material Command, 1998, 2000, Ga. Engr. of Yr., Ga. Soc. Profl. Engrs., 2001, USAF Civilian Engr. of Yr., 2003, Fed. Engr. of Yr., 2004; named to Gallery Women Engrs., NAE, 2006; recipient Recipient Presdl. Point of Light award, USAF, 1991, Disting. Govt. Svc. award, Dallas/Ft. Worth Fed. Exec. Bd., 1986, Lady of the Black Knights award, 19th Air Refueling Wing, 1991, Celebration of Women in Engring. award, Nat. Acad. Engring., 2000. Fellow ASCE (vol. Ga. sect., Govt. Civil Engr. of Yr. 2005), NSPE (chpt. bd. dirs. 1994, 96, 97—, v.p. local chpt. 1994-95, pres.-elect local chpt. 1995-96, pres. 1996-97, 2001, nat. govt. and legis. affairs com. 1999—, state dir. 2000—, Govt. Civil Engr. of Yr. 2005), Soc. Am. Mil. Engrs. (local membership and contingency coms., local bd. dirs., profl. soc. liaison, 1998, sec. 1999-2001, exec. bd. 2003—); mem. Soc. Women Engrs. (sr., regional mem.-at-large rep. 1990-93, local officer 1979-82, 84-86), Am. Women in Sci. Achievements include assignment as 1st woman dep. base civil engr. USAF, Carswell AFB; first woman engineer hired by U.S. Environmental Protection Agency. Office: 778 CES/CEC 775 Macon St Robins Afb GA 31098 Office Phone: 478-926-3533 ext. 28100. Personal E-mail: nanjmanley@cs.com. Business E-mail: nancy.manley@robins.af.mil.

**MANLEY, RICHARD WALTER,** insurance company executive; b. Malone, N.Y., Dec. 26, 1934; s. Walter E. and Ruth (St. Mary) Manley; m. Linda Kimberlin, Dec. 18, 1965; children: Stephanie, Christopher. BS in Bus., U. So. Miss., 1960. Cert. real estate broker. Account exec. Colonial Life and Accident, Hattiesburg, Miss., 1960-63; dist. mgr. Oklahoma City, 1963-66, regional dir. Denver, 1966-76, zone dir., 1976-82; pres. Commonwealth Gen. Group, Denver, 1982-98, Manley Properties Inc., Denver, 1982-90, Richard W. Manley Commonwealth Gen. Grps., Inc., Denver, 1982—. Cons. Capitol Am. Life Ins. Co., Cleve., 1987—96; bd. dirs. Mercy Hosp., Denver, 1982—87. With USAF, 1956—59. Mem.: Cherry Hills C. of C., Rotary, Alpha Tau Omega. Roman Catholic. Avocations: golf, racquetball, running. Home: 6510 E Lake Pl Englewood CO 80111-4411 Office Phone: 303-220-1114. E-mail: dickmanley@speakeasy.net.

**MANLEY, ROBERT EDWARD,** lawyer, economist; b. Cin., Nov. 24, 1935; s. John M. and Helen Catherine (McCarthy) M.; m. Roberta L. Anzinger, Oct. 21, 1971 (div. 1990); 1 child, Robert Edward. ScB in Econs, Xavier U., 1956; AM in Econ. Theory, U. Cin., 1957; JD, Harvard U., 1960; postgrad., London Sch. Econs. and Polit. Sci., 1960, MIT, 1972. Bar: Ohio 1960, U.S. Supreme Ct. 1970. Pvt. practice law, Cin., 1960—; chmn. Manley Burke, 1977. Taft teaching fellow econs. U. Cin., 1956-57, vis. lectr. community planning law Coll. Design, Architecture and Art, 1967-73, adj. assoc. prof. urban planning Coll. Design, Architecture, Art and Planning, 1972-81, adj. prof., 1981—, adj. prof. law, 1980—. Author: Metropolitan School Desegregation, 1978, (with Robert N. Cook) Management of Land and Environment, 1981, others; chmn. editl. adv. bd. Urban Lawyer, 1986-95. Mem. Hamilton County Pub. Defender Commn., 1976-79; trustee HOPE, Cin., Albert J. Ryan Found.; counsel, co-founder Action Housing for Greater Cin.; mem. Spl. Commn. on Formation U. Cin. Health Maintenance Orgn., Mayor Cin. Spl. Com. on Housing; chmn. Cin. Environ. Adv. Coun., 1975-76; trustee The Americas Fund for Ind. Univs., 1987-2000; trustee Ohio Planning Conf., 1982-91, pres., 1987-89, trustee, 1987-90; sec. Cin. Mounted Patrol Com., 1993—; active Bd. Cin. Downtown Coun., 1991-98. Mem. ABA (coun. sect. local govt. law 1976-80, 81-85, 88-92), Ohio Bar Assn., Cin. Bar Assn., Am. Judicature Soc., Law and Soc. Assn., Nat. Coun. Crime and Delinquency, Harvard U. Law Sch. Assn. Cin. (pres. 1970-71), Am. Econ. Assn., Am. Acad. Polit. and Social Sci., Queen City Club, Explorers Club (N.Y.C.) (trustee, sec. Clark chpt. 1992—), Athenaeum Club (Phila.), S.Am. Explorers (Lima, Peru). Republican. Roman Catholic. Office: Manley Burke 225 W Court St Cincinnati OH 45202-1052 Office Phone: 513-721-5525. E-mail: rmanley@manleyburke.com.

**MANLY, MARC EDWARD,** lawyer; b. Knoxville, Tenn., Mar. 11, 1952; s. William Donald and Jane (Wilden) M.; m. Colby A. Chapman, July 20, 1974; children: Justin C., Allison C. BA summa cum laude, Amherst Coll., 1974; MA in Econs., JD magna cum laude, U. Mich., 1977. Bar: Ill. 1978, D.C. 1988, U.S. Dist. Ct. (no. dist.) Ill. 1978. Assoc. Sidley & Austin, Chgo., 1978-84, ptnr., 1986—94; with AT&T, 1995—2000; mng. dir., law & govtl. holdings, gen. counsel, sec. Newpower Holdings, Inc., 2000—02; exec. v.p., chief legal officer Cinergy Corp., 2002—. Mem. ABA, Order of Coif, Phi Beta Kappa. Office: Cinergy Corp 139 E 4th St Cincinnati OH 45202

**MANLY, SARAH LETITIA,** retired state legislator, ophthalmic photographer, angiographer; b. Greenville, S.C., Feb. 1, 1927; d. Victor Harris and Elsie Clippard (Burnett) Gillespie; m. Basil Manly IV, Sept. 11, 1947; children: Sarah Manly Cornish, Basil V, Jean Manly McDowell, Mary Manly Mounce. BS cum laude, Furman U., 1947; postgrad., MIT, 1972; MEd, Clemson U., 1974; postgrad., Cambridge (Eng.) U., 1981. Cert. physics tchr., Pa., S.C.; cert. retinal angiographer. Ward sec. Roper Hosp., Charleston, S.C., 1947; analytical chemist Parker Labs., Charleston, 1948; tchr. sci. Upper Darby (Pa.) Sch. Dist., 1961-63; tchr. physics Sch. Dist. Greenville (S.C.) County, 1963-64, 70-76; ophthalmic photographer Basil Manly IV, MD, Greenville, 1976; 961 lectr. physics Clemson (S.C.) U., 1979-81. Cons. MIT, Cambridge, 1972-75, Georgetown U., Washington, 1974-76, NASA, Houston, 1974-76. Editor, cons. physics study guides MIT, 1972-75; editor lab. materials NASA, 1974-76; contbr. articles to profl. jours. Trustee Sch. Dist. Greenville County, 1976-88. Named S.C. Legislator of Yr., S.C. Sch. Bds. Assn., 1991, Hon. Alumnus of Phi Beta Kappa, 1994. Mem. Greenville County Med. Aux. (sec. 1953-54), Delta Kappa Gamma. Democrat. Baptist. Avocations: travel, reading, volunteering. Home: 201 Robin Ln Greenville SC 29605

**MANN, AIMEE,** singer, songwriter; b. Richmond, Va., Aug. 9, 1960; m. Michael Penn. Vocals, bass 'Til Tuesday, 1983—89; solo artist, 1993—. Singer: (albums) (with 'Til Tuesday) Voices Carry, 1985, Welcome Home, 1986, Everything's Different Now, 1988, (solo) Whatever, 1993, I'm With Stupid, 1995, Bachelor No. 2, 2000, Lost in Space, 2002, (songs) Save Me, 1999 (nom. for Acad. Award for Original Song, 1999). Office: SuperEgo Records 511 Ave of the Americas #197 New York NY 10011

**MANN, ALFRED,** pharmaceutical executive; b. Portland, Oreg., 1925; MS in Physics, UCLA; DHL (hon.), U. So. Calif., 2001, Johns Hopkins U., 2001. Chmn., CEO MannKind Corp., Sylmar, Calif.; chmn., co-CEO Advanced Bionics Corp.; chmn. emeritus MiniMed Inc.; founder, chmn. Med. Rsch. Group, Inc.; chmn., CEO Siemens-Pacesetter, Inc. and predecessor Pacesetter Sys., Inc.; pres. Spectrolab, Heliotek. Chmn. bd. trustees Alfred Mann Found., 1985—, Alfred Mann Inst., U. So. Calif.; U. So. Calif. trustee mem. bd. overseers Keck U. So. Calif. Sch. Medicine; chmn. So. Calif. Biomed. Coun., Second Sight, LLC, Allecure Corp., Quallion, LLC, CTL Immunotherapy, Inc., Pharm. Discovery Co., Inc. Named Man of Yr. WISE Sr. Svcs., 1999, Humanitarian of Yr., House Ear Inst., 1999; named one of 10 Most Influential People on Tch Coast, La. Times, 1999, Forbes' Richest Americans, 2006; recipient Spirit of Edison award for cmty. svc., Thomas Edison State Coll., 1999, Vision of the Future award, RP Internat., 1999, Reynolds Soc. Achievement award, Harvard Med. Sch., 1999. Fellow: Am. Inst. Med. and Biol. Engring.; mem.: NAE. Office: MannKind Corp 28903 N Ave Paine Valencia CA 91355 also: Alfred Mann Found PO Box 905 Valencia CA 91380*

**MANN, BRUCE ALAN,** lawyer, bank executive, investment banker; b. Chgo., Nov. 28, 1934; s. David I. and Lillian (Segal) M.; m. Naomi Cooks, Aug. 31, 1980; children: Sally Mann Stull, Jonathan Hugh, Andrew Ross. BBA, U. Wis., 1955, SJD, 1957. Bar: Wis. 1957, N.Y. 1958, Calif. 1961. Assoc. Davis, Polk & Wardwell, N.Y.C., 1957-60, Pillsbury, Madison & Sutro, San Francisco, 1960-66, ptnr., 1967-83; adminstrv. mng. dir. L.F. Rothschild Unterberg Towbin, San Francisco, 1983-87; ptnr. Morrison & Foerster, San Francisco, 1987—; sr. mng. dir. W.R. Hambrecht & Co, San Francisco, 1999—2003. Cons. SEC, 1978; vis. prof. law Georgetown U., 1978; lectr. in field. Contbr: (with Mattson) California Corporate Practice and Forms, 1999; contbr. articles to profl. jours. Served with USAR, 1957. Mem.: NASD (gov.-at-large 1981—83), ABA (chmn. fed. regulation of securities com. 1981—83, mem. bus. law sect. coun. 1996—99, standing com. on ethics and profl. responsibility 1997—2003, chmn. com. on venture capital 2000—03), Bar Assn. San Francisco (bd. dirs. 1974—75), State Bar Calif., Am. Law Inst., The Family Club. Office: Morrison & Foerster 425 Market St Ste 3100 San Francisco CA 94105-2482 E-mail: bmann@mofo.com.

**MANN, BRUCE H.,** law educator, historian; b. 1950; AB, AM, Brown U., 1972, JD, 1975, M in Philosophy, 1975; PhD, Yale U., 1977. Bar: Conn. 1975, Tex. 1984. Asst. prof. U. Conn., 1977-79, assoc. prof., 1979-81; vis. assoc. prof. U. Tex., 1981-83; assoc. prof. Washington U., St. Louis, 1983-84, prof., 1984-87, U. Pa., Phila., 1987-88, prof. law and history, 1988—2003, Leon Meltzer prof. law & prof. history, 2004—. Editor Law & History Rev., 1987—; Constl. fellow NEH, 1987-88. Mem. Am. Soc. for Legal History (bd. dirs. 1987-89), Law and Soc. Assn., Phi Beta Kappa. Office: U Pa Law Sch 3400 Chestnut St Philadelphia PA 19104-6204 Office Phone: 215-898-6728. Office Fax: 215-573-2025. E-mail: bmann@law.upenn.edu.

**MANN, CEDRIC ROBERT,** retired health facility administrator, oceanographer; b. Auckland, N.Z., Feb. 14, 1926; came to Can., 1949; s. Duncan and Winifred Mary (Hood) M.; m. Muriel Frances May, Dec. 19, 1950; 1 child, Robin Carl B.Sc., U. N.Z., Auckland, 1948, M.Sc., 1950; PhD, U. B.C., Vancouver, Can., 1953; D.Eng., N.S. Tech. Coll., Halifax, Can., 1972. Physicist Naval Research Establishment, Halifax, N.S., Can., 1953-61; oceanographer Atlantic Oceanographic Lab., Halifax, N.S., Can., 1961-75, dir., 1975-78; dir. gen. Bedford Inst. Oceanography, Halifax, N.S., Can., 1978-79, Inst. Ocean Scis., Sidney, B.C., Can., 1979-87. Assoc. prof. Dalhousie U., Halifax, 1961-75; commn. sci. adv. bd. Intergovtl. Oceanographic Commn., Paris, 1978-81; mem. Can. Climate Planning Bd., Ottawa, 1983-86; chmn. Sea Use Council, Seattle, 1981-86. Contbr. articles to profl. jours. Fellow Royal Soc. Can.; mem. Can. Meteorol. and Oceanographic Soc. (life, recipient J.P. Tully medal in Oceanography, 1994). Anglican. Avocations: golf, gardening. Home: 301-2373 Henry Ave Sidney BC Canada V8L 2B4

**MANN, CLARENCE CHARLES,** retired real estate company officer; b. Oradell, N.J., Oct. 15, 1929; s. Clarence Theodore and Martha Barbara (Koster) M.; m. Joan Elizabeth Schnoor, Nov. 25, 1951 (div. Jan. 1985); 1 child, Gary John; life ptnr., Stephen Garrett. BA, NYU, 1951; MA, U. Pa., 1958, Am. U., Beirut, Lebanon, 1963. Commd. 2d. lt. U.S. Army, 1951, advanced through grades to col., ret., 1977; def. attache to Jordan, 1973-77; mktg. mgr. Litton Industries, Jordan, Saudi Arabia, 1977-81; mktg. mgr. Mid-East Hughes Aircraft Co., Fullerton, Calif., 1981-91; dir. relocation ERA Gem Realty, Tucson, 1992-97; realtor Realty Execs., Tucson, 1997—2005. Author: Abu Dhabi: Birth of an Oil Shaikhdom, 1964. Decorated Legion of Merit. Avocations: music, gardening, travel. Office: relowebaz@comcast.net. Business E-Mail: relowebaz@comcast.net.

**MANN, DAVID,** energy and services company executive; b. Drummondville, Que., 1939; m. Lois Dyer Mann; children: Geoffrey, Peter, Gillian. B.Commerce, Dalhousie U., Halifax, N.S., 1961, B.Laws, 1965; M.Laws, U. London, 1966. With Cox Hanson O'Reilly Matheson, Halifax, 1967-96, mng. ptnr., 1974-91; pres., CEO Emera Inc. and Nova Scotia Power Inc., 1996—; also bd. dirs. Bd. dirs., chmn. Emera Fuels, Maritimes & N.E. Pipeline L.P., L.L.C.; chmn. Bangor Hydro-Electric Co.; bd. dirs. Logistec Corp., Can. Coun. Chief Exec., Emera, Inc., Nova Scotia Power, Inc. Can. Electricity Assn., Conf. Bd. of Can., Atlantic Inst. Market Studies. Gov. Olympic Trust of Can.; mem. adv. bd. Dalhousie Sch. Bus.; with Atlantic Salmon Fedn.; bd. dirs., chmn. Found. for Ednl. Exch. between Can. and U.S. (The Can.-U.S. Fulbright Program). Queen's Counsel, 1982. Fellow: Coll. Law Practice Mgmt. Avocations: golf, sailing, skiing, fly fishing, cooking. Office: Emera Inc PO Box 910 Halifax NS Canada B3J 2W5 Fax: (902) 428-6112. E-mail: david.mann@emera.com.

**MANN, DAVID SCOTT,** lawyer; b. Cin., Ohio, Sept. 25, 1939; s. Henry M. and Helen Faye M.; m. Elizabeth Taliaferro, Oct. 5, 1963; children: Michael, Deborah, Marshall. AB cum laude, Harvard Coll., 1961, LLB magna cum laude, 1968. Bar: Ohio 1968. Assoc. Dinsmore & Shohl, Cin., 1968-74, ptnr., 1974-83, Taliaferro and Mann, Cin., 1983-92; councilman City of Cin., 1974-92, mayor, 1980-82, 91; mem. 103d Congress 1st Ohio dist., Washington, 1993-94; mem. armed svcs. com., mem. jud. com. Washington; of counsel Thompson, Hine and Flory, Cin., 1995-96; pvt. practice Mann & Mann, LLC, Cin., 1997—. Adj. prof. Coll. Law U. Cin., 1995—2002. Editor Harvard Law Rev., 1966-68, notes editor, 1967-68; contbr. articles to profl. jours. Mem., chmn. Cin. Bd. Health, 1972-74. With USN, 1961-65. Mem. Cin. Bar Assn. Democrat. Methodist. Home: 568 Evanswood Pl Cincinnati OH 45220-1527 Office Phone: 513-621-2888. Business E-Mail: david@mannandmannlaw.com.

**MANN, DAVID WILLIAM,** minister; b. Elkhart, Ind., Apr. 17, 1947; s. Herbert Richard and Kathryn (Bontrager) M.; m. Brenda Marie Frantz, June 7, 1969; children: Troy, Todd, Erika. BA, Bethel Coll., 1969; MDiv, Campus life dir. Youth for Christ, Elkhart, 1969-77; denominational youth dir. Missionary Ch., Ft. Wayne, Ind., 1977-81, Christian edn. dir., 1981-88, U.S. dir. missions, 1990—; assoc. dir. World Ptnrs., Ft. Wayne, 1988-90. Dir. Missionary Ch. Vol. Svc., Ft. Wayne, 1983—, World Ptnrs. USA, 1998—. Author: (with others) Youth Leaders Source Book, 1985; contbr. articles to profl. jour. Mgr. Little League, Ft. Wayne, 1981-89, bd. dirs. 1986. Recipient Alumnus of the Year award, Bethel Coll., 2003. Mem. Nat. Assn. Evangelicals, Evangelical Fellowship of Mission Agys. (nat. bd. dirs. 1999—), Denominational Execs. in Christian Edn. (chmn. 1988), Aldersgate Pub. Assn. (bd. dirs. 1985, 87), Nat. Christian Edn. Assn. (exec. com. 1987-89). Avocations: baseball, skiing, fishing, woodworking. Office: Missionary Ch PO Box 9127 Fort Wayne IN 46899-9127 Office Phone: 260-747-2027. E-mail: manndw@aol.com.

**MANN, DONEGAN,** lawyer; b. Birmingham, Ala., Mar. 6, 1922; s. Ephriam DeValse and Edna Atkins (Donegan) M.; m. Frances Virginia Hindman, Apr. 6, 1957 (dec. May 1993); m. Frances M. Jenkins, Jan. 7, 1995 (dec. Dec. 1997). Student, Birmingham-So., 1940-41; AB, George Washington U., 1947, JD, 1950. Bar: U.S. Dist. Ct. 1950, U.S. Ct. Appeals (D.C. cir.) 1950, U.S. Ct. Claims 1957, U.S. Supreme Ct. 1961, U.S. Ct. Appeals (fed. cir.) 1982. Acting bur. counsel Civil Aeronautics Bd., Washington, 1953-55; gen. rates atty. GAO, Washington, 1955-57; spl. rate counsel Gen. Svcs. Adminstrn., Washington, 1957-60; assoc. Wolf & Case, Washington, 1960-66; sr. atty., office gen. counsel. U.S. Dept. Treasury, Washington, 1966-79; of counsel Shands & Stupar, Washington, 1979-82; pvt. practice Washington, 1984—. Pres. Friends of Historic Great Falls Tavern, Inc., Potomac, Md., 1977-80, bd. dirs., 1980-83. With USN, 1943-46, PTO. Mem. ABA (treas. pub. contracts com. 1965-66, chmn. awards com. 1975-76, sec. award st. lawyers' divsn. 1991, counsel sr. lawyers divsn., 1995-97, chmn. guardianship and conservatorship com. 1989-95, sr. lawyers' divsn. task force to reform guardianship laws 1992-94, vice chmn., chmn. probate and trust com., 1995—, chmn. citizenship com. 1996-97, vice chmn. Law Day and citizenship com. 1997—), FBA, Fed. Energy Bar Assn., D.C. Bar Assn., Montgomery County Hist. Soc. (exec. v.p. 1980-83, bd. dirs. 1984-86). Democrat. Episcopalian. Avocations: fishing, hunting, golf, tennis, gardening.

**MANN, ERIC LOUIS,** retired military officer, mathematics professor, researcher; b. July 22, 1952; BA in Math., Albion Coll., 1974; MSc in Sys. Mgmt. and Logistics Sys., U. So. Calif., 1980; MAT in Elem. Tchg. and Ednl. Tech., Colo. Coll., 1997; post grad. diploma in Ednl. Psychology, U. Conn., 2002, student, 2003—. Cert. Elem. Tchr. (kindergarten through eighth grade) NH, Elem. Tchr. (kindergarten through sixth grade) Conn., Mid. Sch. Math. Tchr. Conn., Mid. Sch. Earth Sci. Tchr. Conn. Advanced through grades to lt. col. USAF, 1975—96, ret. lt. col., 1996; intern tchr. Rockrimmon Elem., 1996—97; tchr. Atkinson Acad., NH, 1997—98, editor, pub. In Their Own Words; sci., math, Am. history tchr. Bow Meml. Mid. Sch., NH, 1998—2002, gifted and talented coord., 2001—02, mathcounts, math. team coach, Jason project coord., conv. coord., math. olympiads, continental math. league, Mandelbrot competition, space explorers mission to moon coord.; bridge builders club supr., physics course coord., FIRST LEGO team organizer, gifted and talented resource website developer, editor lit. jour., chess club establisher; math. tchr. Hall Meml. Sch., Willington, Conn., 2002—03; vis. prof. Purdue U., 2003—, webmaster project M3 U. Conn., 2003—, webmaster project M3, 2003, editor project M3 newsletters, moderator on-line profl. discussion bd. project M3, rsch. assoc. project M3, 03, on-line course developer, mentor, 04; presenter in field, 2004—05. Contbr. articles to profl. jours. in field, manuals in field. Decorated Group Achievement award NASA, Commendation medals USAF, Achievement medals, Meritorious Svc. medals, Orgnl. Excellence awards, Outstanding Unit awards, Air Force Assn. award, Dept. Def. Joint Svc. Commendation medal, Master Space Ops. badge, Named one of Twelve Airmen of Air Force award, Named 1st Space Wing Jr. Officer of Quarter, Named Hdqs. North Am. Def. Command Jr. Officer of Quarter, Named Hdqs. Air Force Space Command Jr. Officer of Quarter, Named Strategic Air Command Communication Area Airman of Quarter; Quality of Life Improvement grant, USAF, New Boston Air Sta., 1990, Space Explorers On-line Simulation Project, Jefferson Pilot Fin. grant, Bow Meml. Mid. Sch., 1990, FIRST LEGO League grant, Bow PTO, 2001, Blue Chip Sch. Tech. grant, State of Conn., Hall Meml. Sch., 2003. Mem.: NSTA, Sch. Sci. and Math. Assn., Ind. Coun. Tchrs. Math., Nat. Coun. Tchrs. Math., Nat. Coun. Suprs. Math., Ind. Assn. for Gifted, Nat. Assn. Gifted Children, Assn. Supervision and Curriculum Devel., Kappa Delta Pi, Pi Lambda Theta.

**MANN, FRANK BERT,** artist, educator; b. Washington, Apr. 22, 1950; s. Frank Bert and Wilda Vendetta Kaufman. BS, High Point Univ., 1972; BA, George Washington Univ., 1978; MFA, Pratt Inst., 1981. Guest lectr. Corcoran Sch. of Art, Washington, 1979, Pa. State U., Reading, 1986-87, Pratt Inst., Bklyn., 1987-88, Parsons Sch. Art & Design, NYC, 1996-97, Iona Coll., New Rochelle, NY, 2005. Exec. dir. Colaborative Projects, Inc., NY, 1987-88, Basicarts Network, NY, 1989-90; vis. artist Coalition for the Homeless Camp, 1997, Children's Friends for Life, NY, 1997, Project for St. Cyrils Ch., NY, 1992. Author: Eye of the Painter, 1997; illustrator (film) Nerves, 1993; exhibitions include Biennale Internat., Florence, Italy, 2001 (Lorenzo Il Magnifico medal in painting, 2001), live interview series and DVD, A Special Program in Three Parts: The Art of Frank Mann, 2005, Represented in permanent collections Guggenheim Mus., NYC, Mus. Contemp. Art, Nice, France. U.S. rep. Biennale Internazionale, Florence, 1999, 2001. Recipient Mable Sanger Webb award, Ford Found., 1980, Lorenzo le Magnifico medal, Internat. Dell'Arte Contemporanea, 2001; grantee, N.Y. State Coun. Arts, 1988, N.Y. City Dept. Cultural Affairs, 1989. Mem.: Assn. D'Art Internat., Contemporary Artists' Guild, Am. Soc. Contemporary Artists (v.p. 2003—), Drawing Soc., Artists Equity (bd. dirs. 2000—03, v.p. 2003—), Am. for the Arts. Lutheran. Home and Office: 212 E 34th St Apt 3E New York NY 10016-4846 Office Phone: 212-689-9003. Personal E-mail: fmann100@hotmail.com.

**MANN, GEORGE STANLEY,** diversified financial services company executive, real estate company officer; b. Toronto, Ont., Can., Dec. 23, 1932; s. David Philip and Elizabeth (Green) M.; children: Michael, Tracy. Attended. North Toronto Collegiate Sch.; LLD (hon.), U. Windsor. Ptnr. Mann & Martel Co. Ltd., 1959-68, CEO, 1968-70, United Trust Co., 1970-76; pres. Unicorp Canada Corp., Toronto, 1972-76, chmn. bd., 1976-90; dir. Nat. Bank Canada, 1978-91; chmn. bd. Union Gas Ltd., 1986-93; owner Townsview Properties Ltd., Toronto, 1984—. Pres. chmn. bd. Lincorp Holdings, Inc., N.Y.C. Bd. govs. Mt. Sinai Hosp., Toronto. Mem. Oakdale Golf & Country Club (Toronto), High Ridge Country Club (Palm Beach, Fla.), Mar-a-Lago Club (Palm Beach, Fla.), Trump Internat. Golf Club (Palm Beach, Fla.). Avocation: golf. Home: #10 Bellair St Ste 302 Toronto ON Canada M5R 3T8 also: 505 South County Rd Palm Beach FL 33480 Office: 2 St Clair Ave W Ste 1004 Toronto ON Canada Office Phone: 416-922-1500.

**MANN, J. KEITH,** retired law educator, arbitrator; b. May 28, 1924; s. William Young and Lillian Myrle (Bailey) M.; m. Virginia McKinnon, July 7, 1950; children: William Christopher, Marilyn Keith, John Kevin, Susan Bailey, Andrew Curry. BS, Ind. U., 1948, LLB, 1949; LLD, Monmouth Coll., 1989. Bar: Ind. 1949, D.C. 1951. Law clk. Justice Wiley Rutledge and Justice Sherman Minton, 1949-50; pvt. practice Washington, 1950; with Wage Stblzn. Bd., 1951; asst. prof. U. Wis., 1952, Stanford (Calif.) U. Law Sch., 1952-54, assoc. prof., 1954-58, prof., 1958-88, prof. emeritus, 1988—, assoc. dean, 1961-85, acting dean, 1976, 81-82, cons. to provost, 1986-87. Vis. prof. U. Chgo., 1953; mem. Sec. of Labor's Adv. Com., 1955-57; mem. Pres.'s Commn. Airlines Controversy, 1961; mem. Presdl. Emergency Bds. or Bds. of Inquiry, 1962-63, 67, 71-72; spl. master U.S. vs. Alaska, U.S. Supreme Ct., 1980-97. Editor book rev. and articles Ind. U. Law Jour, 1948-49. Ensign USNR, 1944-46. Sunderland fellow U. Mich., 1959-60; scholar-in-residence Duke U., 1972. Mem. ABA, AAUP, Nat. Acad. Arbitrators, Indsl. Rels. Rsch. Assn., Acad. Law Alumni Fellows Ind. U., Order of Coif, Tau Kappa Epsilon, Phi Delta Phi. Democrat. Presbyterian. Home: 850 Webster St Apt 425 Palo Alto CA 94301-2884 Office: Stanford U Sch Law Stanford CA 94305-8610

**MANN, JACK MATTHEWSON,** bottling company executive; b. Marshall, Tex., Apr. 14, 1932; s. Jack Slater and Mary (Matthewson) M.; m. True Sandlin, Sept. 4, 1954 (div. 1989); children: Jack, Robert, Daniel, Nathaniel; m. Glenda Copeland Grimes, Sept. 17, 2005. Student, N.Mex. Mil. Inst., 1952; BBA, U. Tex., 1954; MBA, Harvard U., 1960. Credit analyst Republic Nat. Bank, Dallas, 1959; ptnr. coord. Humble Oil and Refining Co., Baytown, Tex., 1960-61; asst. sales mgr. The Made-Rite Co., Marshall, Tex., 1957-58; asst. gen. mgr. The Made Rite Co., Marshall, Tex., 1961-63, gen. mgr. Longview, Tex., 1963-92, pres., 1972—, owner, chmn., 1982—; v.p. Longview Econ. Devel. Corp., 1994-2000, treas., 1995-96, pres., 1996-97. Mem. pres.'s adv. coun. Le Tourneau U., 1994—97; mem. devel. coun. U. Tex.-Tyler Longview U. Ctr., 2000—, pres., 2004—. Exec. com. Rep. Party Tex., 1962-65; mem. Trinity Episcopal Ch., Longview, 1963-, sr. warden, jr. warden, treas.; mem. exec. bd. Episcopal Diocese Tex., Houston, 1974-76; mem. small bus. adv. com. Tex. Dept. Commerce, 1988-91. Mem.: Nat. Dr. Pepper Bottlers Assn. (pres. 1983—85), Tex. Soft Drink Assn. (pres. 1972), Longview C. of C. (dir. 1965—68, 1984—86), Pinecrest Country Club, Longview Summit Club (gov. 1982—94). Avocation: University of Texas athletics. Office: The Made Rite Co PO Box 3283 Longview TX 75606-3283 Home: 21 Tallwood Ln Longview TX 75605

**MANN, JAMES L.,** computer company executive; Degree in bus. adminstrn., Wichita State U. Pres., COO Bradford Nat. Corp., NYC, 1981—83; COO SunGard Data Sys. Inc., Wayne, Pa., 1983—86, pres., CEO, 1986—87, chmn., pres., CEO, 1987—2000, chmn., CEO, 2000—02, chmn., 2002—05, bd. dir., 2006—. Past chmn. Info. Tech. Assn. Am. With USAF. Office: Sungard Data Sys Inc 680 E Swedesford Rd Wayne PA 19087*

**MANN, JAMES ROBERT,** former congressman; b. Greenville, S.C., Apr. 27, 1920; s. Alfred Cleo and Nina (Griffin) M.; m. Virginia Thomason Brunson, Jan. 15, 1945; children— James Robert, David Brunson, William Walker, Virginia Brunson. BA, The Citadel, 1941, LLD (hon.), 1978; JD, U. S.C., 1947. Bar: S.C. 1947, U.S. Ct. Appeals (4th cir.) 1948, U.S. Supreme Ct. 1970. Practice in, Greenville, 1947—; del. S.C. Ho. of Reps. from, Greenville County, 1949-52; solicitor 13th Jud. Circuit, 1953-63; mem. 91st-95th Congresses 4th Dist. SC. Sec. Greenville County Planning Commn., 1963-67;

Trustee Greenville Hosp. System, 1965-68; bd. govs. Greenville Shriners Hosp., 1983-90. Served to lt. col. AUS, 1941-46; col. USAR ret. Mem. Am., S.C., Greenville County bar assns., Am. Judicature Soc., Greater Greenville C. of C. (pres. 1965), V.F.W. (dep. comdr. 1951-52), Am. Legion. Lodges: Mason; Shriners; Kiwanis; Elks; Woodmen of World. Democrat. Baptist. Office: 414 Univ Park Greenville SC 29601

**MANN, JOAN ELLONA,** artist, editor; b. Seattle, Aug. 21, 1931; d. Henry Hughes and Jeanetta Maurine (Baker) Jacobsen; m. Hugh Mann, Sept. 2, 1955 (div. Aug. 1981); children: Susan, Kristi, Steven, Nancy, Roy. BA in Journalism, U. Wash., 1953, BFA in Sculpture, 1970, MFA in Sculpture, 1985. Reporter East Side Jour., Kirkland, Wash., 1953-55; med. editor Virginia Mason Med. Ctr., Seattle, 1965-69; info. specialist Continuing Edn. News Svc. U. Wash., Seattle, 1969-73; editor Seattle Arts Commn., 1973-77; pub. info. officer King County Arts Commn., Seattle, 1973-90; owner, mgr. Joan Mann, Editor, Seattle. Sculptures include multi-media floor sculpture Trident, Ship of Fools, 1988 (award); shows include U. Wash. Henry Gallery, 1971; group shows include Roscoe Louie Gallery, Seattle, 1975, Univ. Unitarian Gallery, 1978, U. Wash. Henry Gallery, 1987, U. Wash. Meany Hall, 1987, SJW Studios, Seattle, 1988, Seattle Ctr. Opera House, 1988, PNAC, Bellevue, 1988, Ctr. for Contemporary Art, Seattle, 1989. Precinct del. Wash. Dem. Com., Seattle, 1992. Recipient 2d and 3d place ann. awards Wash. Press Women, 1971, 1st prize Ctr. for Contemporary Art, 1989; travel grantee Goethe Inst., Berlin, 1988. Mem. Women in Comm. (Nat. Clarion award 1974), Allied Arts Seattle (adv. bd. 1990—), Seattle Art Mus. Roman Catholic. Avocations: photography, skiing, hiking on beaches, travel.

**MANN, JOHN MARTIN,** minister; b. McKeesport, Pa., Nov. 18, 1946; s. Glenn Grant and Mary Dorothy (Flaherty) M. BA, Clarion State Coll., 1967; MDiv, Duke U., 1970, ThM, 1972; D Ministry, Wittenberg U., 1976. Ordained to ministry Luth. Ch. in Am., 1972. Pastor 1st Luth. Ch., Edinboro, Pa., 1971-82; sr. pastor St. John's Luth. Ch., Erie, Pa., 1982-91. Instr. Edinboro State Coll., 1971-82; adj. prof. religion Thiel Coll. Greenville, Pa., 1980-82, baccalaureate preacher, 1980-84, trustee, 1974-80, 82—; chmn. synod vocations examining com. N.W. Pa.-W.Va. Synod, 1984-88; chmn. intersynodical vocations candidacy com. N.W. Pa.-Allegheny Synods, 1988-90; chmn. ch. vocations examining com. N.W. Pa. Synod, 1990—; chmn. Luth. Coalition of Erie, 1990-91; dean Cond. I, Northwestern Pa. Synod, 1991—, faculty post grad Family Systems Seminars, 2004. Contbr. articles to profl. jours. Bd. dirs. Luth. Home, Erie, 1976-79, 82—, Inter-Ch. Ministries N.W. Pa., 1979-84, South Erie Hillside Cmty. Orgn., 1982—, Holy Trinity Cmty. Ctr., Erie, 1984-88, Nesting Inn, 1988—, Hospice Met. Erie, 1988—; chmn. Erie City Strategy for Luths., 1989—; pastor Trinity Luth. Ch., Canton, Ohio, 1992—; pres. UrbanArk Urban Ministry Coalition; active ELCA N.E. Ohio Synod, ecumenical com., chmn. synod outreach com., 1998—, dean conf., Canton, mission planner, Urban Strategy com.; founding chmn. Interfaith Roundtable of Canton and N.W. Neighborhood Assn.; covenant commr. Youngstown Roman Cath. Diocese, N.E. Ohio Synod. Recipient Outstanding Young Man of Am. award Jaycees, 1982. Mem. Luth. Assn. Larger Ches., Am. Assn. Pastoral Counselors, Luth. Campus Ministry Assn., Interdenominational Ministerial Assn. (sec.), Canton Downtown Pastors Assn., Synod Evangelism Com. Home: 6671 Firestone Ave NE Canton OH 44721-2514 Office: Trinity Luth Ch 415 Tuscarawas St W Canton OH 44702-2017 Office Phone: 330-456-0124. Personal E-mail: trinity415@sbcglobal.net. In a global environment where fundamentalist religions create division and terrorism, we need a constructive, reappropriation of faith in God.

**MANN, KATINKA,** artist; b. N.Y.C., June 28, 1925; Vis. artist Morris & Rose Markowitz Polaroid Corp. at Boston Mus. Fine Arts, 1983. One-woman shows include Ctrl. Hall Gallery, Port Washington, N.Y., 1974, 76, 77, 79, N.Y.C., 1982, 84, Hansen Gallery, N.Y.C., 1976, 77, 79, Heckscher Mus., Huntington, N.Y., 1977, Fairleigh Dickinson U., Hackensack, N.J., 1985, Real Art Ways, Hartford, Conn., 1985, Marymount Manhattan Coll., N.Y.C., 1986, Islip Art Mus., East Islip, N.Y., 1986, Phlia. Art Alliance, 1987, Silvermine Galleries, New Canaan, Conn., 1987, Dowling Coll. Gallery, Oakdale, N.Y., 1987, Art Gallery Port Washington Libr., Port Washington, N.Y., 1996, Space 504 Gallery, N.Y.C., 1998, Heckscher Mus. Art, Roslyn, N.Y., 2001; exhibited in numerous group shows including most recently A.I.R. Gallery, N.Y.C., 2000, Martin Art Gallery, Muhlenberg Coll., Allentown, Pa., 2002, Hofstra Art Mus., Hempstead, N.Y., 2002, Hillwood Art Mus., Brookville, N.Y., 2003, El Instituto Nacional de Bellas Artes, San Miguel de Allende, Mex., 2003, Nasau County Mus. Art, Roslyn, N.Y., 2004, Heckscher Mus. Art, Huntington, N.Y., 2003; represented in permanent collections Bklyn. Mus., Islip Art Mus., Polaroid Internat. Corp., Boston, Russ Togs Corp., N.Y., Nassau C.C., Guggenheim Mus., N.Y.C., Mus. Modern Art, N.Y.C., Princeton Univ., Nat. Mus. Am. Art, Smithsonian Instn., Washington, Brit. Mus., London, Phila. Mus. Art, N.Y Pub. Libr., N.Y.C., San Francisco Mus. Modern Art, Houston Mus. Fine Arts, numerous pvt. collections. Mem. Am. Abstract Artists (treas. 1989-96, 2002—). Home: 290 9th Ave Apt 13H New York NY 10001 Personal E-mail: katinkamann5@aol.com.

**MANN, KENNETH HENRY,** marine ecologist; b. Dovercourt, Essex, Eng., Aug. 15, 1923; arrived in Can., 1967, naturalized, 1975; s. Harry and Mabel (Ashby) M.; m. Isabella Gilmour Ness, Apr. 18, 1946; children: Ian Malcolm, Sheila Helen, Colin Gilmour. BSc, U. London, 1949, DSc, 1965; PhD, U. Reading, 1953. Lectr. zoology, then reader U. Reading, Eng., 1949-64; 64-67; sr. biologist marine ecology lab. Bedford Inst. Oceanography, Dartmouth, Can., 1967-72, dir. marine ecology lab., 1980-87, sr. rsch. scientist, 1987-93, emeritus rsch. scientist, 1993—. Prof., chmn. biology Dalhousie U., Halifax, N.S., Canada, 1972—80, adj. prof. biology, 1980—2002. Author: Leeches: Their Structure, Physiology, Ecology and Embryology, 1961, Ecology of Coastal Waters: A Systems Approach, 1982, Ecology of Coastal Waters: Implications for Management, 2000; co-author (with J. Lazier): Dynamics of Marine Ecosystems: Biological-Physical Interactions in the Sea, 1991, 3d edit., 2005; co-author: (with R.S. Barnes) Fundamentals of Aquatic Ecology, 1991, Korean edit., 2002; editor, contbr.: (with T. Platt and R. Ulanowicz) Mathematical Models in Biological Oceanography, 1981, (with F. Wulff and J.G. Field) Network Analysis in Marine Ecology, 1989, (with A. Payne, K. Brink and R. Hilborn) Benguela Trophic Functioning, 1992; editor Jour. Animal Ecology, 1966—70. Served with Royal Air Force, 1942-46. Fellow Royal Soc. Can.; mem. Am. Soc. Limnology and Oceanography. Home: 23 Woodward Cres Halifax NS Canada B3M 1J6 Office: Bedford Inst Oceanography Box 1006 Dartmouth NS Canada B2Y 4A2 Office Phone: 902-426-3696. Personal E-mail: ken.mann@ns.sympatico.ca.

**MANN, KENNETH WALKER,** retired minister, psychologist; b. Nyack, NY, Aug. 22, 1914; s. Arthur Hungerford and Ethel Livingston (Walker) M. AB, Princeton U., 1937; STB, Gen. Theol. Sem., N.Y.C., 1942; MS, U. Mich., 1950, PhD, 1956. Ordained priest Episcopal Ch., 1942; diplomate Am. Assn. Pastoral Counselors; lic. clin. psychologist, Calif., Conn.; lic. marriage, family and child counselor, Calif. Vicar in Valley Cottage, Pearl River, NY, 1941-43; priest in charge Yonkers, NY, 1943-45; ret. minister, 1945—. Dir. youth work and Christian edn. Diocese L.A., 1945-47; curate in Beverly Hills, Calif., 1947-49; counselor Bur. Psychol. Svcs. U. Mich., 1951-52; chaplain, clin. psychologist dept. psychiatry St. Luke's Hosp., N.Y.C., also priest-psychotherapist Cathedral St. John Divine, N.Y.C., psychol. examiner ministerial candidates Diocese N.Y., 1952-58; assoc. chaplain Hosp. Good Samaritan, L.A., 1958-65; exec. pastoral svcs., exec. coun. Episc. Ch. N.Y.C., 1965-70; program officer Acad. Religion and Mental Health, N.Y.C. 1970-72; sr. adviser profl. affairs Inst. Religion and Health, 1972-74; sr. psychol. staff Silver Hill Found., New Canaan, Conn., 1974-84; pres. Rockland County (N.Y.) Mins. Assn., 1942-43; exec. sec. social svcs. commn. Diocese N.Y., 1943-45; chmn. div. pastoral svcs. Diocese L.A., 1945-47; field dir. Western region Acad. Religion and Mental Health, 1958-61; assoc. nat. chaplain U.S Power Squadrons, 1956-57. Author: On Pills and Needles, 1969, Deadline for Survival—A Survey of Moral Issues in Science and Medicine, 1970; contbr. articles to profl. jours. Pres. Adoption Inst. L.A., 1964; mem. edn. com. Calif. Heart Assn., 1962-64; trustee, treas. Acad. Religion and Mental Health, 1954-59, mem. profl. bd., 1960-70; trustee Vis. Nurse Assn. L.A., 1963-65,

Children's Home Soc. Calif. in L.A., 1964-65, North Conway Inst., 1966-80. USPHS grantee, 1950-51. Fellow AAAS; mem. APA (chmn. com. rels. between psychology and religion 1956-58), Western Psychol. Assn., Calif. Psychol. Assn., L.A. County Psychol. Assn., N.Y. Acad. Scis., Planetary Soc., Assembly Episc. Hosps. and Chaplains, Upper Nyack Tennis Club, Princeton Club N.Y., Exch. Club Beverly Hills (pres.). Republican. Home: 32 Tallman Ave Nyack NY 10960-1606 *I have strongly held to the principle that the total "health" of mankind cannot be considered apart from the values and aspirations by which people live, and by which they may even be prepared to die. Amidst the confusions that exist today over loyalties, traditions, and ideals, many are asking: What is the right way to behave? How should I think? What kind of person am I supposed to be? To help such people in quandary to live responsibly, and still be true to their individuality, is a large task, but it is one that is central to a religious ministry. It has always been my chief concern.*

**MANN, LAURA ANN,** soprano; MusB, Eastman Sch. Music, 1965, MusM, 1972; Dr.Mus.Arts, U. Md., 1995; studied with Herbert Brauer Kammersanger, Berlin, Germany; studied with Edwin McArthur, N.Y.; studied with Edith Lang Kammersangerin, Lubeck, Germany; studied with David Garvey, studied with Stefan Scaggiari and Rayburn Wright, studied with Julius Huehn, studied with Anna Kaskas, studied with John Maloy, studied with Kammersanger Hans Hotter, studied with Louise Urban, studied with Leon Major, studied with Rhoda Levine, studied with Ted van Griethaesen, studied with Franchelle Dorn, studied with Kammersanger Heinz Rehfuss, studied, studied with Gerd Albrecht, studied with Christof Perick, studied with Richard Woitach. Prin., owner vocal studio Vocal Advancement, Fairfax, Va., 1979—. Prof. voice Tex. A&I U., Kingsville, Tex., 1984—85; asst. prof. voice Tex. Tech. U., Lubbock, Tex., 1984—86; vis. prof. voice We. Carolina U., Cullowhee, NC, 1986—88; prof. voice Anne Arundel C.C., Annapolis, Md., 1989—94; adj. prof. voice and opera George Mason U., Fairfax, Va., 1995—2001, dir. opera, 1995—, mem. women's studies faculty, 1998—, tchr. stage movement, French, German diction; presenter in field; lectr. in field; clinician and adjudicator. Singer: (CD) The Joy of Christmas, 1996, Operas, (albums) Christ Is Born, Laura Mann In Recital, Songs of Light and Joy, 2002, (CD) Laura Mann in Concert, 1996, (one-act, one-person opera/monodrama) The White Cliffs; soloist: Berlin Philharm., Swiss Chamber Orch., Prague Chamber Ensemble, Rochester Philharm., Buffalo Philharm., Richmond Symphony, Oklahoma City Symphony, Asheville Symphony, Dallas Baroque Ensemble, Kennedy Ctr. Concert Hall, German Embassy, French Embassy, Mexican Embassy. Named a Internat. Opera Singers Competition Semi-Finalist, Ctr. Contemporary Opera, N.Y.C.; recipient Performer's Cert. in Voice and Opera, Eastman Sch. Music, Senatorial award, U. Md. Coll. Pl., 1995; grantee, Prince George's Arts Coun., 1993—96, Va. Commn. Arts, 2000—, Fulbright grant, Martha Rockefeller grant. Mem.: Music Tchrs. Nat. Assn., Internat. Alliance for Women in Music, Opera Am., Nat. Acad. Recording Arts and Scis., South Tex. Assn. Tchrs. Singing, Nat. Assn. Tchrs. Singing, Pi Kappa Lambda. Office: Music Dept George Mason Univ 4400 University Dr Fairfax VA 22030-4422 Office Phone: 703-217-8615, 703-995-1586. E-mail: opera_tunity@peoplepc.com

**MANN, LOUIS EUGENE,** financial planner; b. Balt., Jan. 24, 1947; s. Manfred and Ruth Eleanor (Kates) M.; m. Marjorie Ruth Friedman, Mar. 23, 1971; children: Lisa Renee, Brian Michael. Student, Balt. Poly. Inst., 1964, Towson State Coll., 1964-67; postgrad., U. Pa., 1969-70; CFP, Coll. for Fin. Planning, 1993. CFP; securities licenses; lic. ins. broker, N.J., Pa., Calif. Clk. Food Fair Stores, Inc., Balt., 1964-68; v.p. Friendly Grocer, Inc., Cherry Hill, N.J., 1968-79; sales mgr. Frito-Lay Inc., Cinnaminson, N.J., 1979-82; salesman N.Y. Life Ins. Co., Cherry Hill, 1982-89; ptnr. Custom Fin. Svcs., Marlton, N.J., 1988-93; pres. Louis E. Mann Fin. Svcs., Inc., Mt. Laurel, N.J., 1993—; comptroller Shusterman & Davis, LLC, Phila., 1996-2000; exec. v.p. Orion Fin. Svcs. LLC, Phila., 2001. Developer: (math. formula) Law of Squares of Consecutive Numbers, 1963. Mgr., coach Greentree Athletic Assn., Mount Laurel, N.J., 1985-94; pres. Congregation Beth Tikvah Men's Club, Marlton, 1988-89, 90-91, 94-95, bd. dirs., exec. bd. mem., 1994-95. Recipient Coll. scholarships State of Md.-Senatorial and Ednl., 1964. Mem. Delaware Valley Inst. CFPs, Fin. Planning Assn., Million Dollar Round Table (membership unit. 1984), Rotary Club of Moorestown (com. chmn. bd. dirs 1984-94, 1st v.p. 1996-97, pres. 1997-98), Rotary Internat. (dist. planned giving chmn. Dist. 7500, 1994-95, asst. dist. ann. giving chair dist. 7500 2001-03), Fedn. Jewish Men's Clubs (trustee Mid-Atlantic region 1995-96) Democrat. Jewish. Avocations: sports, music, gardening, reading. Home: 121 Colony Pl Mount Laurel NJ 08054-2404 Office Phone: 856-988-5453. E-mail: manncfp@aol.com, louis@mannfinacial.net.

**MANN, MARION,** pathologist, educator; b. Atlanta, Mar. 29, 1920; s. Levi James and Cora (Casey) Mann; m. Ruth Maurine Reagin, Jan. 16, 1943; children: Marion Jr., Judith Walk. BS in Edn., Tuskegee Inst., Ala., 1940; MD, Howard U., 1954; PhD, Georgetown U., 1961; grad., 1965, U.S. Army War Coll., 1970; DSc (hon.), Georgetown U., 1979, U. Mass., 1984, Tuskegee U., 1998; grad., U.S. Army War Coll., 1970. Diplomate Nat. Bd. Med. Examiners, Am. Bd. Pathology. Intern USPHS Hosp., Staten Island, NY, 1954—55; resident Georgetown U. Hosp., 1956—60; practice medicine, specializing in pathology Washington, 1961—; instr. pathology Georgetown U., 1960—61; professorial lectr. Georgetown U. Sch. Medicine, 1970—73; asst. prof. pathology Howard U. Coll. Medicine, 1961—67, assoc. prof., 1967—70, prof., 1970, dean, 1970—79; v.p. rsch. Howard U., 1980—91. Capt. U.S. Army, 1942—50, brig. gen. Res. U.S. Army. Mem.: Nat. Acad. Scis., Inst. Medicine, Sigma Pi Phi, Alpha Omega Alpha. Home: 1453 Whittier Pl NW Washington DC 20012-2845 Office: 520 W St NW Washington DC 20059-0001

**MANN, MICHAEL E.,** physicist, educator, climatologist; b. Amherst, Mass., Dec. 28, 1965; s. Larry N. and Paula (Finesod) M. AB in Applied Math and Physics (honors), U. Calif., Berkeley, 1989; MS in Physics, MPhil in Physics, Yale U., 1991, MPhil in Geology and Geophysics, 1993, PhD in Geology and Geophysics, 1998. Rsch. asst., dept. chemistry Univ. Calif., Berkeley, 1985-88, rsch. assist., dept. materials sci., 1988-89; teaching asst., dept. physics Yale Univ., New Haven, Con., 1989-90, rsch. asst., 1990, teaching asst., 1990—96; Alexander Hollaender Disting. postdoctoral rsch. fellow Dept. Energy, 1996—98; adj. asst. prof. dept. geosciences U. Mass., 1997—98, rsch. asst. prof., dept. geosciences, 1998—99; asst. prof., dept. environ. sciences U. Va., 1999—2005; assoc. prof., dept meterology (joint appt. dept. geosciences and earth and environ. systems inst.) Pa. State U., 2005—, dir., Earth System Sci. Ctr., 2005—. Invited lectr. in field; scientific advisor to US Govt. (White House OSTP) on climate change, 1999—2000; invited advisor NOAA Global Change and Climate Panel, Boulder, Colo., 1999; mem. of Working Group, Internat. PAGES/CLIVAR, 2000—; panel mem. NOAA Climate Change Data and Detection Program, 2000—; IAMAS delegate for US/Internat. Comm. on Climate, 2002—; mem. steering com. NSF Marine Earth Systems History Panel, 2003—; chair organizing com. NAS, Frontiers of Sci. symposium, 2003; co-chair Workshop on Past Millennia Climate Variability, Wengen, Switzerland, 2006; provided testimony to US House of Representatives, Energy and Commerce Com. hearing, 06. Contbr. articles to profl. jours., chpts. to books;refereed Nature, Science, Climatic Change, Geophysical Research Letters, Jour. Climate, JGR-Oceans, JGR-Atmospheres, Paleoceanography, Climate Dynamics, Eos, Internat. Jour. Climatol., Water Resources Research, Holocene, Atmospheric & Solar-Terrestrial Physics, GSA Today, Earth and Planetary Science Letters, Global & Planetary Change, Water Resources Research, Climate Research, NRC/NAS, NSF, NOAA, DOE grant programs; public outreach to CBS, NBC, ABC, CNN, CNN headline news, The Weather Channel, BBC, NPR, PBS, WCBS, Time, Newsweek, Life, US News & World Report, Economist, Scientific American, New Scientist, National Geographic, Discover, Science News, Science, Rolling Stone, Mother Jones, Cosmos, Popular Science, USA Today, New York Times, New York Times "Science Times", Washington Post, Wall Street Journal, Boston Globe, London Times, Irish Times, Le Monde, AP, UPI, Reuters, Scripps Howard, and numerous other television/print media,; mem. editl. adv. bd, Scientific American, Scientific American 50, 2003-, The Holocene, 2005-; editor, Jour. of Climate, 2000-02; co-founder,

contbr. (website) RealClimate.org, 2004-(named one of the top 25 Sci. and Tech. website, Scientific American, 2005). Named one of 50 Leading Visionaries in Sci. and Tech., Scientific American, 2002, Website: RealClimate.org (co-founded, 2004) chosen as one of top 25 Science and Technology websites, 2005; recipient Josiah Willard Gibbs prize for outstanding rsch. and scholarship in Physics, Yale U., 1989, Phillip M. Orville prize for outstanding dissertation in the earth sciences, Yale U., 1997, Article (Mann, et. al Global-scale temperature patterns and climate forcing over the past six centuries, Nature, 1998) selected for fast moving fronts, Inst. Scientific Information, 2002, Outstanding Scientific Paper award for article: Observed and Simulated Multidecadal Variability in the Northern Hemisphere, Climate Dynamics, 2000), NOAA Office of Oceanic and Atmospheric Research (OAR), 2002, John Russell Mather Paper award article: Mann, et. al. A Distinctly Interdecadal Signal of Pacific Ocean-Atmosphere Interaction, Journal of Climate), Assn. Am. Geographers, 2005. Mem. Am. Meteorol. Soc.(com. on probability & statistics, 2003-05), Am. Geophysical Union (mem. adv. bd., Earth Interactions, 2001-02), European Geophysical Soc., Geol. Soc. Am., Am. Physical Soc., AAAS, Sigma Xi Research conducted with colleagues concluded that the Northern Hemisphere was the warmest it has been in 2,000 years. The research was known as the "hockey-stick" graph because it compared the sharp curve of the hockey blade to the recent sharp rise in temperatures and the stick's long shaft to centuries of previous climate stability. Office: Pa State Univ Dept Meterology University Park PA 16802 Office Phone: 814-863-4075. Office Fax: 814-865-3663. Business E-Mail: mann@psu.edu.*

**MANN, MICHAEL KENNETH,** film director, film producer; b. Chgo., Feb. 5, 1943; m. Summer Mann, 1974; 4 children. Student, U. Wis., London Film Sch. Dir.: (documentaries) 17 Days Down the Line, 1972; screenwriter, dir. (films) The Keep, 1983, Manhunter, 1986, screenwriter, exec. prodr., dir. Thief, 1981, screenwriter, prodr., dir. The Last of the Mohicans, 1992, Heat, 1995 (Dir., Screenwriter, Prodr. Acad. award nominee), The Insider, 1999, Ali, 2001, Miami Vice, 2006, dir., prodr. Collateral, 2004, prodr. The Aviator, 2004, screenwriter (TV films) River of Promises, 1977, screenwriter, dir. The Jericho Mile, 1979 (Best Dir. award Dir. Guild Am., Emmy award, 1979), screenwriter Swan Song, 1980, screenwriter, exec. prodr., dir. L.A. Takedown, 1989, screenwriter, exec. prodr. (TV miniseries) Drug Wars: The Camarena Story, 1990 (Emmy award, 1990), screenwriter (TV series) Police Story, 1973, Starsky and Hutch, 1975, Bronk, 1975, screenwriter, dir. Vega$, 1978, screenwriter, exec. prodr. Miami Vice, 1984; exec. prodr.: (TV series) Robbery Homicide Division, 2002—03. Mem.: Dirs. Guild, Writers Guild. Office: c/o Creative Artists Agy 9830 Wilshire Blvd Beverly Hills CA 90212-1804*

**MANN, MICHAEL MARTIN,** engineering executive; b. NYC, Nov. 28, 1939; s. Herbert and Rosalind (Kaplan) M.; m. Mariel Joy Steinberg, Apr. 25, 1965. BSEE, Calif. Inst. Tech., 1960, MSEE, 1961; PhD in Elec. Engring. and Physics, U. So. Calif., 1969; MBA, UCLA, 1984. Cert. bus. appraiser, profl. cons., mgmt. cons., lic. real estate broker, Calif. Mgr. high power laser programs office Northrop Corp., Hawthorne, Calif., 1969-76; mgr. high energy laser systems lab. Hughes Aircraft Co., El Segundo, Calif., 1976-78, mgr. E-0 control systems labs., 1978-83, asst. to v.p., space & strategic, 1983-84; exec. v.p. Helionetics Inc., Irvine, Calif., 1984-85, pres., chief exec. officer, 1985-86, also bd. dirs.; ptnr. Mann Kavanaugh Chernove, 1986-87; sr. cons. Arthur D. Little, Inc., 1987-88; chmn. bd., pres., CEO, Blue Marble Devel. Group, Inc., 1988—; exec. assoc. Ctr. Internat. Cooperation and Trade, 1989—91; sr. assoc. Corp. Fin. Assocs., 1990—91; exec. assoc. Reece and Assocs., 1991—92; mng. dir. Blue Marble Ptnrs. Ltd, 1991—; chmn. bd. dirs., CEO Blue Marble Ptnrs., 1992—; chmn., CEO, En Compass Techs., Inc., Torrance, Calif., 1994-98; chmn. En Compass Knowledge Systems, Inc., 2000—. Mem. Army Sci. Bd., Dept. Army, Washington, 1986-91; chmn. Ballistic Missile Def. Panel, Directed Energy Weapon Panel, Rsch. and New Initiatives Panel; cons. Office of Sec. of Army, Washington, 1986—, Inst. of Def. Analysis, Washington, 1978—, Dept. Energy, 1988—, Nat. Riverside Rsch. Inst., 1990—; bd. dirs. Datum, Inc., 1988—, Fail-Safe Tech., Corp., 1989-90, Safeguard Health Enterprises, Inc., 1988—, Am. Video Communications, Inc., Meck Industries, Inc., 1987-88, Decade Optical Systems, Inc., 1990—, Forum Mil. Application Directed Energy, 1992—, Am. Bus. Consultants, Inc., 1993—; chmn. bd. Mgmt. Tech., Inc. 1991—, Encompass Tech., Inc., 1994-98; bd. dirs., mem. adv. bd. Micro-Frame, Inc., 1988-91; chmn. bd. HLX Laser, Inc., 1984-86; bd. dirs. Cons's. Roundtable, 1992—, Am. Bus. Cons., Inc., 1993—, Country Home Bakers, Inc., 1999—, C.L.E.A.R., Inc., 1999—; chmn. TEC, 1999—; rsch. assoc., mem. extension teaching staff U. So. Calif.; L.A., 1964-70; chmn. Ballistic Missile Def. Subgroup, 1989-90, Tactical Directed Energy Weapons Subgroup, 1988-90; chmn., chief exec. officer Mgmt. Tech., Inc., 1991—; dir. Am. Bus. Cons., Inc., 1993—; faculty mem. Asia Pacific Inst., 1998—; faculty Nat. Technol. U., 1997—. Mem. editl. bd. Calif. High-Tech Funding Jour., 1989-90; contbr. articles to profl. jours.; patentee in field. Adv. com. to Engring. Sch., Calif. State U., Long Beach, 1985—; chmn. polit. affairs Am. Electronics Assn., Orange County Coun., 1986-87, exec. com., 1986-88; adv. com. Calif. congressmen, 1985—; dean's coun. UCLA Grad. Sch. Mgmt., 1984-85; bd. dirs. Archimedes Circle U. So. Calif., 1983-85, Ctr. for Innovation and Entrepreneurship, 1986-90, Caltech/MIT Venture Forum, 1987-91; chmn. adv. coun., adj. prof., indsl. and sys. engring. U. So. Calif., 1996—; bd. examiners Nat. Quality Award, 1998—2000. Hicks fellow in Indsl. Rels. Calif. Inst. Tech., 1961, Hewlett Packard fellow. Mem. IEEE (sr.), So. Calif. Tech. Execs. Network, Orange County CEO's Network, Orange County CEO's Roundtable, Pres. Roundtable, Nat. Assn. Corp. Dirs., Aerospace-Def. CEO's Roundtable, Am. Def. Preparedness Assn., Security Affairs Support Assn., Acad. Profl. Cons. and Advisors, Internat. Platform Assn., Inst. Mgmt. Cons. (bd. dirs. So. Calif. chpt.), Pres. Assn., Cons. Roundtable Forum for Corp. Dirs., King Harbor Yacht Club, Fourth of July Yacht Club. Republican. Avocations: sailing, photography, writing. Home: 4248 Via Alondra Palos Verdes Peninsula CA 90274-1545 Office: Encompass Knowledge Sys Inc 100 Corporate Pointe Ste 210 Culver City CA 90230 Office Phone: 310-981-9200. E-mail: mmmann@encompassknowledge.com.

**MANN, NANCY LOUISE (NANCY LOUISE ROBBINS),** entrepreneur; b. Chillicothe, Ohio, May 6, 1925; d. Everett Chaney and Pauline Elizabeth R.; m. Kenneth Douglas Mann, June 19, 1949 (div. June 1979); children: Bryan Wilkinson, Laura Elizabeth. BA in Math., UCLA, 1948, MA in Math., 1949, PhD in Biostatistics, 1965. Sr. scientist Rocketdyne Divsn. Rockwell Internat., Canoga Park, Calif., 1962-75; tech. staff Rockwell Sci. Ctr., Thousand Oaks, Calif., 1975-78; rsch. prof. UCLA Biomath., L.A., 1978-87; pres., CEO, owner Quality Enhancement Seminars, Inc., L.A., 1982—; pres., CEO Quality and Productivity, Inc., L.A., 1987—. Curriculum adv. UCLA Ext. Dept. of Bus. and Mgmt., L.A., 1991—; mem. com. on Nat. Statistics, Nat. Acad. Scis., Washington, 1978-82; mem adv. bd. to supt. U.S. Naval Posgrad. Sch., Monterey, Calif., 1979-82. Co-author: Methods for Analysis of Reliability and Life Data, 1974; author: Keys to Excellence, 1985, The Story of the Deming Philosophy, 2d edit., 1987, 3d edit., 1989; contbr. articles to profl. jours. Recipient award IEEE Reliability Soc., 1982, ASQC Reliability Divsn., 1986. Fellow Am. Statis. Assn. (v.p. 1982-84); mem. Internat. Statis. Inst. Office: Quality Productivity Inc 10724 Wilshire Blvd # 711 Los Angeles CA 90024-4463

**MANN, OSCAR,** retired physician, internist, educator; b. Paris, Oct. 13, 1934; arrived in U.S., 1953; s. Aron and Helen (Biegun) Mann; m. Amy S. Mann, July 19, 1964; children: Adriana, Karen. AA with distinction, George Washington U., 1958; MD cum laude, Georgetown U., 1962. Diplomate Am. Bd. Med. Examiners, Am. Bd. Internal Medicine, Am. Bd. Cardiovasc. Disease, cert. advanced achievement in internal medicine. Intern Georgetown U. Med. Ctr., Washington, 1962-63, jr. asst. med. resident, 1963-64, clin. fellow in cardiology with Proctor Harvey program, 1965-66; sr. asst. resident in medicine Georgetown svc. D.C. Gen. Hosp., Washington, 1964-65; clin. prof. medicine Georgetown U. Sch. Medicine, 1995—; nat. chmn. med. alumni fund Georgetown U. Med. Sch., Washington, 1993-95; pvt. practice internal medicine and cardiology, Washington, 1966-99. Mem. med. nursing com. Georgetown U. Med. Ctr., mem. adv. com. CME, mem. tchg. adv. com.,

opthalmology dept. rev. com., surgery dept. rev. com., faculty com., search com. for a new dean for acad. affairs; appointed coun. to the dean Georgetown U. Sch. Medicine, 1977—; mem. Instnl. Self Study Task Force. Author: A Journey of Hope, 2005; contbr. articles to profl. jours. Nat. chmn. med. alumni fund Georgetown U., 1997—99. With U.S. Army, 1953—55, with U.S. Army, 1953—55. Recipient Mead Johnson Postgrad. Scholar ACP, 1964—65, Physicians Recognition award, AMA, 1987—96, Advanced Achievement in Internal Medicine, 1987, John Carroll award, Georgetown U. 1999. Fellow: ACP, Am. Coll. Chest Physicians, Am. Coll. Cardiology; mem.: AMA, Med. Soc. D.C., Am. Heart Assn. (coun. clin. cardiology), Am. Soc. Internal Medicine, Georgetown U. Alumni Assn. (bd. govs. 1993—, chair med. alumni bd. 1995—, nat. chmn. med. alumni fund 1997—99), Cosmos Club, Phi Delta Epsilon, Alpha Omega Alpha. Home: 5137 Yuma St NW Washington DC 20016 E-mail: oscarmann@comcast.net.

**MANN, RICHARD ALAN,** physician, educator; b. Bklyn., Dec. 18, 1952; s. Daniel Isaac and Claire Ethel (Spiller) M.; m. Judith Fleischer, Aug. 6, 1977; 1 child, David Michael Mann. BS in Math., Union Coll., Schenectady, N.Y., 1973; MS in Biophysics, SUNY, Buffalo, 1975; MD, Albert Einstein Coll. Medicine, The Bronx, N.Y., 1979. Diplomate Am. Bd. Internal Medicine. Intern Grad. Hosp. U. Pa., Phila., 1979-80; resident Temple U. Hosp., Phila., 1980—82; clin. nephrology fellow Hosp. U. Pa., Phila., 1982—83, rsch. fellow, 1983—86; asst. prof. medicine Rutgers U. Med. Sch., New Brunswick, NJ, 1986—93; assoc. prof. medicine, microbiology and molecular genetics; physician Robert Wood Johnson Med. Sch., New Brunswick, 1993—, med. dir. Kidney/Pancreas Transplant Program, 1993—; mem. grad. program in microbiology and molecular genetics Rutgers U., Piscataway, NJ, 1989—. Antiviral drug adv. com. FDA, Rockville, Md., 1993—; spl. study sect. NIH, Bethesda, Md., 1994; NIH Reviewers Res.; State Dept. Task Force, Operation Desert Storm, 1991. Contbr. over 50 articles, chpts. and abstracts to profl. jours. Recipient Young Investigator award Nat. Kidney Found., 1987, Nat. Med. award Kidney and Urology Found. Am., 2004, named one of Best Drs. in Am., 1996-2006, others; grantee NIH, 1988-93, William Lightfoot Schultz Found., 1987-88, UMDNJ Found., 1987-88. Mem. Am. Soc. Nephrology (co-chair basic immunology free comm. session 1989, 90), Am. Fedn. for Clin. Rsch., Am. Heart Assn. (Coun. on the Kidney in Cardiovascular Disease), Nat. Kidney Found., Nephrology Soc. N.J., Am. Assn. for Lab. Animal Sci., Am. Soc. Transplantation, Alpha Omega Alpha (Acad. Excellence and Outstanding Tchg. award 1995). Office: UMDNJ Robert Wood Johnson Med Sch Acad Health Sci Ctr CN-19 New Brunswick NJ 08903 Business E-Mail: mannri@umdnj.edu.

**MANN, RICHARD O.,** public relations consulting company executive; b. NYC, July 1, 1933; s. Otto and Ruth (Buchwald) M.; m. Anne Marie Seidenschwang, Apr. 28, 1956; children: Melinda, Susan, Carolyn. BA in History and Polit. Sci., Hofstra U., 1955. Reporter Newsday, Garden City, NY, 1951-56; pub. rels. v.p., cons. Carl Byoir & Assoc., NYC, 1957—76; v.p. corp. affairs Mack Trucks, Inc., Allentown, Pa., 1976-79; v.p. pub. rels. Transway Internat., NYC, 1979—85; pres. Mann Assoc., Danbury, Conn., 1985—. Track and field ofcl., U.S. Internat. meets, including 1984 Olympics, 1970—. Bd. dirs. Vol. Ctr. Westchester County. 1st It. U.S. Army, 1956-57. Mem. Met. Golf Writers Assn., Mt. Kisco Country Club. Republican. Presbyterian. Avocations: golf, sports. Home and Office: 63 Woodcrest Ln Danbury CT 06810 E-mail: romsport@sbcglobal.net.

**MANN, ROANNE L.,** federal judge; b. 1951; BA, Yale U., 1972; JD, Stanford U., 1975. Bar: N.Y. 1975. Asst. dist. atty. Manhattan Dist. Atty.'s Office, N.Y.C., 1975-76; law clk. U.S. Ct. Appeals for D.C. Circuit, Washington, 1976-77; spl. asst. to asst. atty. gen. civil divsn. U.S. Dept. Justice, Washington, 1977-78; asst. U.S. atty., chief appeals, sr. litigation counsel U.S. Atty.'s Office for So. Dist. N.Y., N.Y.C., then dept. chief criminal divsn., 1978-86; ptnr. Stein, Zauderer, Ellenhorn, Frischer & Sharp, N.Y.C., 1986-94; magistrate judge for ea. dist. N.Y., U.S. Magistrate Ct., Bklyn., 1994—. Mem.: Fed. Bar Coun. Office: US Magistrate Ct 225 Cadman Plz E Brooklyn NY 11201-1818 Office Phone: 718-260-2350.

**MANN, ROBERT CHRISTOPHER,** communications educator, television producer, television personality; b. Bklyn., Mar. 18, 1953; s. Alvin Charles and Marion Theresa (Hensch) M.; 1 child, Christopher Robert. BA, Fordham U., 1975; MA, Montclair State U., 1993. Radio newscaster, sportscaster Sta. WOBM-AM-FM, Toms River, NJ, 1976-77; TV host, prodr. United Artists Cable (now Cablevision), Oakland, NJ, 1977-84; on air host Sta. WNET-TV, N.Y.C., 1983-85; feature reporter Sta. WOR-AM, N.Y.C., 1985; prof. comm., chair dept. Caldwell (N.J.) Coll., 1988—; TV host, prodr. Mann Media Inc., Bergenfield, NJ, 1989—. Mem. faculty coun. Caldwell Coll., 1990—. Host, prodr. (TV show) Healthview From Hackensack U. Med. Ctr., 1989— (Percy award 1990), Healthtalk, 1996—; host (radio program) Healthbeat, 1991— (Percy award 1996). Class father Roy Brown Mid. Sch., Bergenfield, 1994; vol. TV host Am. Cancer Soc., Bergen County, N.J., 1996. Recipient Cable Programming award Cable TV Network N.J., 1996. Mem. AFTRA, Nat. Acad. Cable Programming (CableACE award (3), 1984-85), Soc. Profl. Journalists, AAUP. Avocations: tennis, travel, movies, baseball. Home: 163 Phelps Ave Bergenfield NJ 07621-1422 Office: Caldwell Coll 9 Ryerson Ave Caldwell NJ 07006-6109 E-mail: profmann@aol.com.

**MANN, SALLY,** photographer; b. Lexington, Va., 1951; married; children: Emmett, Jessie, Virginia. Student, Putney Sch., 1966-69, Bennington Coll., 1969-71, Praestegaard Film Sch., Denmark, 1971-72, Aegean Sch. Fine Arts, Greece, 1971-72; BA summa cum laude, Hollins Coll., 1974, MA, 1975; DFA (hon.), Corcoran Coll., 2006. Guest lectr. Honolulu Acad. Arts, 1989, Women Photog. Conf., 1989, Md. Inst. Art, 1989, Bard Coll., 1989, San Francisco Cameraworks, 1990, Photog.-Retrospect/Prospect Conf., 1990, others; instr. Maine Photog. Workshops, 1985-89, Palm Beach Photog. Workshops, 1987-89, Ctr. Photog. Woodstock, 1988, 90, Internat. Ctr. Photog., N.Y., 1989, Image Found., Honolulu, 1989, Okla. Arts Found., 1989, Friends Photog. Workshops, 1990. One-woman shows include Cleve. Ctr. Contemporary Art, 1990, Edwynn Houk Gallery, Chgo., 1990, 92, Tartt Gallery, Washington, 1990, Md. Art Pl., Balt., 1991, Houk Friedman, N.Y., 1992-94, Mus. Contemporary Photog., Chgo., 1993-94, Mus. Modern Art, N.Y., 1991, Milw. Mus. Art, 1991, Whitney Mus. Am. Art, N.Y., 1991, Met. Mus. Art, N.Y., 1991, Frumpkin Adams Gallery, N.Y., 1994, Elizabeth Leach Gallery, Portland, Oreg., 1994, Bard Coll., Mass., 1994, Wellesley Coll., Mass., 1995, Edwynn Houk Gallery, N.Y., 1997, Gagosian Gallery, Calif., 1997; exhibited in group shows Corcoran Gallery Art, Washington, 1977, Va. Mus. Fine Arts, Richmond, 1988, New Orleans Mus. Art, 1990; represented in permanent collections Addison Gallery Am. Art, Andover, Mass., Balt. Mus. Art, Birmingham (Ala.) Mus. Art, Boston Mus. Fine Art, In Response to Place: Photographs from The Nature Conservancy's Last Great Places, Corcoran Gallery Art, 2001, Hirshhorn Mus. and Sculpture Garden, Nat. Mus. Am. Art, Smithsonian Inst., Washington, Met. Mus. Art, N.Y., Mus. Modern Art, N.Y., Whitney Mus. Am. Art, N.Y., San Francisco Mus. Art, Va. Mus. Fine Arts, Richmond, Gagosian Gallery, NYC, 2006, others; author/photographer: (with Ann Beattie) Second Sight: The Photographs of Sally Mann, 1984, (with Reynolds Price) At Twelve: Portraits of Young Women, 1988, Imediate Family, 1992, Still Time, 1994, What Remains, 2003. Fellow Nat. Endowment Arts, 1982, 88, 92, Guggenheim Found., 1987, Southeastern Ctr. Contemporary Arts, 1989, Artists Visual Arts, 1989; named Best Photographer in Am., Time Mag., 2001.*

**MANN, SAM HENRY, JR.,** retired lawyer; b. St. Petersburg, Fla., Aug. 2, 1925; s. Sam Henry and Vivian (Moore) M.; m. Mary Joan Bishop, Sept. 7, 1948; children: Vivian Louise, Sam Henry III, Wallace Bishop. BA, Yale U., New Haven, Conn., 1948; LLB, Fla. U., Gainesville, 1951, JD, 1967. Bar: Fla. 1951, U.S. Dist. Ct. (mid. and so. dists.) Fla. 1951, U.S. Ct. Appeals (5th cir.) 1955, U.S. Ct. Appeals (11th cir.) 1996, U.S. Supreme Ct. 1971. Ptnr. Greene, Mann, Rowe, Stanton, Mastry & Burton, St. Petersburg, 1951-84, Harris, Barrett, Mann & Dew, St. Petersburg, 1984—, ret., 2001. Trustee, v.p. Mus. Fine Arts, St. Petersburg, 1980-94, Eckerd Coll., St. Petersburg, 1976-79, Webb Sch., Bell Buckle, Tenn., 1966-75; bd. dirs. Regional Cmty. Blood Ctr., St. Petersburg, 1966-93, Fla. Blood Svcs., 1993-94, mem.

emeritus 1996—; mem. Disting. Alumni Soc. Webb Sch.; mem., chmn. H. Milton Rogers Heart Found.; bd. dirs., pres. Family and Children's Svc., Inc., 1956-61. Lt. (j.g.) USNR, 1943-48. Fellow Am. Coll. Trial Lawyers, Am. Bar Found., Fla. Bar Found.; mem. ABA, Fla. Bar Assn., Fla. Supreme Ct. Hist. Soc., Am. Counsel Assn., Def. Rsch. Inst., Internat. Assn. Def. Counsel, Pinellas County Trial Lawyers Assn., Nat. Assn. Railroad Trial Counsel, Fla. Def. Lawyers Assn., Assn. Hostp. Attys., Bay Area Vanderbilt, St. Petersburg Bar Assn., Yale and U. Fla. Alumni Assns., Phi Alpha Delta, Delta Kappa Epsilon. Republican. Presbyterian. Avocations: travel, boating, gardening. Home: 531 Brightwaters Blvd NE Saint Petersburg FL 33704 Office: Harris Barrett Mann Dew Pa 8083 38th Ave N Saint Petersburg FL 33710-1029 Business E-Mail: mjbmann@aol.com.

**MANN, SEYMOUR ZALMON**, retired political science professor, labor union administrator; b. Chgo., Mar. 29, 1921; s. Morris and Sarah (Julius) M.; m. Irene Eincig, Aug. 30, 1942; children: Martin R., Sheldon H., Jeanette P. Student, Wright Coll., 1938-40; BE, No. Ill. U. (formerly No., Ill. State Tchr.'s Coll.), 1942; MA, U. Chgo., 1948, PhD, 1951. Instr. polit. sci. Triple Cities Coll., Syracuse U., 1948-51; asst. prof. Harpur Coll., State U. N.Y., 1951-55, asso. prof. polit. sci., 1955-60, chmn. dept., 1953-58; dir. pub. adminstrn. and met. affairs program, prof. govt. So. Ill. U., Edwardsville, 1960-67; chmn., prof. urban affairs dept. urban affairs Hunter Coll./CUNY, 1967-77; dir. Urban Research Center, 1967-68, chmn. dept. urban affairs, 1968-73; dep. to execs. dist. council 37, Am. Fedn. State, County and Mcpl. Employees, AFL-CIO, 1977-79; prof. govt. and public adminstrn., assoc. dir. Nat. Center Public Productivity, John Jay Coll. Criminal Justice, CUNY, 1980-86. Vis. expert Office Pub. Affairs, High Commr.'s Office, Germany, 1954; cons. Southwestern Ill. Govtl. Study Commn., 1961-62; vis. prof. U. So. Calif. Sch. Pub. Adminstrn., 1967; co-author. Ill. U.-State Agy. Coun., 1965-67; chmn. nat. commn. on urban affairs Am. Jewish Congress, 1977-81, mem. nat. governing coun., 1991-97; cons., coord. spl. projects dist. coun. 37 Am. Fedn. State, County and Mcpl. Employees, N.Y.C., 1972-77, dep. to dir., DC 37, 1977-82. Author: (with others) From the Wagner Act to the Taft-Hartley Act, 1950, (with Charlotte B. Smart) Land Use and Planning in the Cleveland Metropolitan Area, 1959, (with R.R. Boyce) Urbanism in Illinois: Its Nature Importance and Problems, 1965, Chicago's War on poverty, 1966; contbr. to: Cases in State and Local Government, 1961, Cases in American National Government and Politics, 1978, The Politics of Productivity: State and Local Focus, 1980, Labor Management Cooperation and Worker Participation: A Public Sector Focus, 1989, play Summing Up in Public Voices, 1993, The Purple Automobile and the Newspapers Girl, 2003; contbr. poetry to anthologies, vols. of poetry; mem. editl. bd. Pub. Voices. Served with AUS, 1943-45, ETO. Fellow Social Sci. Research Council, 1949-50; Fulbright prof. W. Germany, 1953-54; Fulbright prof. Tel Aviv (Israel) U., 1974-75 Mem. Am. Soc. for Pub. Adminstrn. (pres. St. Louis met. chpt. 1964-65), Am. Arbitration Assn. (nat. labor panel), Soc. of Children's Book Writers and Illustrators, Poetry Soc. Va., Live Poets Soc. (Alexandria, Va.). Home and Office: 203 S Yoakum Pky Apt 1111 Alexandria VA 22304-3731 Office Phone: 703-823-3547. Personal E-Mail: szmann@comcast.net. *It will have to be left to others to judge what success I may have obtained. There have, however, been some guiding principles which seemed to have given direction to my life's course and undoubtedly impacted on whatever professional recognition has come my way. These include: a profound respect for democratic ideology— particularly the notion that each person should have the opportunity to achieve his/her fullest potential; a clear recognition that wisdom and knowledge are not the same; and that listening is harder than talking, though it is the most important element in human communication.*

**MANN, STEPHEN ASHBY**, financial consultant; b. Richmond, Va., Feb. 20, 1947; s. Milton Ashby and Rebecca (George) Mann; m. Patricia Ann Kofron, Aug. 25, 1982; 1 child, Michael Joseph Ashby stepchildren: Christine Ford, Tracy Kofron. BS in Gen. Bus., Va. Poly. Inst. and State U., 1970. Cert. sr. advisor, CLU. Supr. mfg. Brown & Williamson Tobacco Corp., Petersburg, Va., 1970—72; pres. Cumberland Woodyard, Va., 1972—79; mgr. Ragland Woodyards, Goochland, Va., 1980—81; advt. mgr., reporter Gazette Newspapers, Goochland, 1982—85; fin. counselor, ins. and fin. planner Peoples Security Ins. Co., Mechanicsville, Va., 1986—98, Monumental Life Ins. Co., Mechanicsville, Va., 1999—2003; v.p. Roberts-Funai Ins. Agy., Richmond, 2003—. Pres. Millquarter Property Owners Assn., Powhatan, Va., 1987. Named to All-Star Honor Roll, Ins. Sales Mag., 1989—90; Life Underwriters Tng. Coun. fellow. Fellow: Life Underwriters Tng. Coun.; mem.: SCV (lt. comdr. Powhatan 1980—82, inspector gen. state divsn 1981, nat. adc 1982—83, comdr.), All Harley Drag Racing Assn. (Racer of Yr. Award 1996, nat. ranked # 4 st. eliminator 1996—97, nat. ranked #2 super sport 1999, ranked #6 in East, 13th Nat. 2002, ranked #1 in East, 7th Nat. 2003), Richmond Assn. Ins. and Fin. Advisors (bd. dirs. 1989—92), Assn. Health Ins. Agts., Soc. Fin. Svc. Profls., Nat. Assn. Ins. and Fin. Advisors (Nat. Quality Award 1986, Nat. Sales Achievement Award 1986, Nat. Health Inst. Award 1986), Sons of South Motorcycle Club, Masons (master 1990, Samis Grotto treas. 1991—93, master 1994, 16th dist. blood coord. 1995—96, chaplain Powhatan Lodge # 295 1995—2006, Scottish Rite, life mem. Royal Arch), Golden Key Soc. (hon. mem. 1991—96). Republican. Baptist. Avocations: organ, history, motorcycling, piano. Home: 1433 E Overlook Dr Powhatan VA 23139 Office: Roberts & Funai Ins Agy Richmond VA 23236 Personal E-Mail: pamann@verizon.net.

**MANN, THEODORE R.**, lawyer; b. Czechoslovakia, Jan. 31, 1928; came to U.S., 1929, naturalized, 1930; s. Aaron and Bertha (Schreiber) M.; m. Rowena Joan Weiss, 1954; children: Julie Ellen, Rachel Beth, Marcus Eliyahu. Pvt. practice, Phila., 1953—2005; counsel Pa. Securities Commn., 2005—. Chmn., pres. Nat. Jewish Cmty. Rels. Adv. Coun., 1976-80; Conf. Pres. Major Am. Jewish Orgns., 1978-80; Nat. Conf. Soviet Jewry, 1981-83; Am. Jewish Congress, 1984-88; founding chmn. Mazon-A Jewish Response to Hunger, 1985-90, Project Nishma, 1988-97; exec. com. chair Israel Policy Forum, 1997-2001; trustee internat. coun. New Israel Fund, 2002-. Alumni fellow, Temple U. Office: 2401 Pennsylvania Ave 17A4 Philadelphia PA 19130 E-mail: tmann@wolfblock.com.

**MANN, THOMAS**, reference librarian; b. Chgo., Feb. 21, 1948; BA, St. Louis U., 1966; MLS, La. State U., 1979; PhD, Loyola U., Chgo., 1975. Pvt. investigator B & L Assocs., Baton Rouge, 1976—77; reference libr. La. State U. Libr., Baton Rouge, 1979—80, Mullen Libr., Cath. U. Am., Washington, 1980—81, Libr. Congress, Washington, 1981—. Author: A Guide to Library Research Methods, 1987, Library Research Models, 1993, The Oxford Guide to Library Research, 2005. Mem.: Cosmos Club. Office: Library of Congress 101 Independence Ave SE Washington DC 20540-4660 Office Phone: 202-707-5173.

**MANN, THOMAS EDWARD**, political scientist; b. Milw., Sept. 10, 1944; s. Edward Emil and Eleanor (Hoffman) M.; m. Sheilah Rosenhack, June 4, 1976; children: Edward Matthew, Stephanie Rachael. BA, U. Fla., 1966; MA, U. Mich., 1968, PhD, 1977. Staff assoc. Am. Polit. Sci. Assn., Washington, 1970-76, asst. dir., 1977-81, exec. dir., 1981-87; co-dir. congress project Am. Enterprise Inst., Washington, 1979-81; dir. govtl. studies Brookings Instn., 1987-99, W. Averell Harriman sr. fellow in Am. governance, 1991—. Mem. bd. overseers Nat. Election Study, 1987-94, chmn., 1990-94. Author: Unsafe At Any Margin, 1978; co-author: Vital Statistics on Congress, 1980, 82, 84-85, 87-2002; Renewing Congress, 1992, 93, The New Campaign Finance Sourcebook, 2005, The Broken Branch, 2006; co-editor: The New Congress, 1981, The American Elections of 1982, 1983, Media Polls in American Politics, 1992, Values and Public Policy, 1994, Elections at Home and Abroad, 1994, Congress, the Press, and the Public, 1994, Intensive Care: How Congress Shapes Health Policy, 1995,Campaign Finance Reform, A Source Book, 1997, The Permanent Campaign and Its Future, 2000, Governance for a New Century: Japanese Challenges, American Experience, 2002, Inside the Campaign Finance Battle, 2003, Party Lines: Competition, Partisanship, and Congressional Redistricting, 2005; editor: A Question of Balance: The President, The Congress and Foreign Policy, 1990. Mem. Democratic Nat. Com.'s Commn. on Presdl. Nomination and Party Structure, 1975-78; mem.

tech. com. Dem. Nat. Com. Commn. on Presdl. Nominations, 1981-82, The Fairness Commn., 1985. U. Mich. NDEA grad. fellow, 1966-69; Am. Polit. Sci. Assn. Congl. fellow, 1969-70 Fellow Am. Acad. Arts and Scis., Nat. Acad. Pub. Adminstrn.; mem. Coun. on Fgn. Rels., Phi Beta Kappa (Frank J. Goodnow award, Charles E. Merriam award). Home: 6508 Goldleaf Dr Bethesda MD 20817-5837 Office: Brookings Instn 1775 Massachusetts Ave NW Washington DC 20036-2103 Business E-Mail: tmann@brookings.edu.

**MANN, TRUE SANDLIN**, psychologist, consultant; b. Longview, Tex., Aug. 4, 1934; d. Bob Murphy and Stella True (Williams) Sandlin; m. Jack Matthewson Mann, Sept. 4, 1954 (div. Dec. 1989); children: Jack Matthewson Jr., Bob Sandlin, Daniel Williams, Nathaniel Currier. BS, Stephen F. Austin State U., Nacogdoches, Tex., 1973, MA, 1977; PhD, East Tex. State U., 1982. Lic. psychologist, Tex., Ark. Instr. Stephen F. Austin State U., 1975-76, vis. asst. prof. psychology, 1986-87; instr. East Tex. State U., Commerce, 1980-81; postdoctoral fellow Southwestern Med. Sch., Dallas, 1982-83; pvt. practice, Longview, Tex., 1983-92; psychologist dept. family practice U. Tex. Health Sci. Ctr., Tyler, 1990-92; dir. psychol. svcs. St. Michael's Hosp., Texarkana, Tex., 1992-93; cons. psychologist, Longview, 1993—. Weekly newspaper columnist HARBUS, Cambridge Mass., 1959-60; cons. Made-Rite Co., Longview, 1989—. Mem. candidate com. Assoc. Reps. Tex., Austin, 1990—; bd. dirs. Mental Health Assn. Tex., 1977-82, 84-92, Longview Symphony, 1995-99, Dallas Opera Guild, 1999—, Longview Mus. of Art, 1995; mem. Leadership Tex., 1988—. Mem. APA, Tex. Psychol. Assn., N.E. Tex. Field Ornithologists. Episcopalian. Avocations: photography, travel, history. Home: 1906 N 4th St Longview TX 75601-3202 Office: 1203 Montclair St Longview TX 75601-3565

**MANN, WILLIAM CRAIG**, lawyer; b. Norwalk, Ohio, Nov. 17, 1953; s. Abraham and Shirley (Smith) M. BA, Case Western Res. U., Ohio, 1976; JD, U. Dayton, Ohio, 1979. Bar: Ohio 1979, U.S. Dist. Ct. (no. dist.) Ohio 1979, U.S. Supreme Ct. 1986, U.S. Dist. Ct. (so. dist.) Ohio 1988. Law clk. Ohio Supreme Ct., Ohio, 1985-86; pvt. practice Cleve., 1986-87; assoc. Wolske and Blue, Columbus, Ohio, 1987-97; ptnr. Sunbury, Mann & Young, Columbus, Ohio, 1997-99; of counsel Mitchell, Allen, Catalano & Boda, Columbus, 1997—. Spkr. various orgns. in field, including Ohio Legal Ctr. Inst., Ohio Acad. of Trial Lawyers; mem. Ohio Supreme Ct. commn. on professionalism, 1997-2002 Contbr. articles to profl. jours. Bd. dirs. United Way, Huron County, Ohio, 1983; mem. exec. and cen. coms. Huron County Dem. Com., 1976-79. Mem. Ohio State Bar Assn. (ethics com. 1987—), Columbus Bar Assn., Ohio Acad. Trial Lawyers (pres. 2001—), Franklin County Trial Lawyers Assn. (pres. 2001-2002. Avocations: football, history, economics. Home: 2041 Ramblewood Ave Columbus OH 43235-7340 Office: Mitchell Allen Catalano & Boda 580 S High St Ste 200 Columbus OH 43215 Office Phone: 614-224-4114. Personal E-mail: mannlaw99@aol.com.

**MANNE, HENRY GIRARD**, lawyer, consultant, economist, educator, retired dean; b. New Orleans, May 10, 1928; s. Geoffrey and Eva (Shainberg) M.; m. Bobbette Lee Taxer, Aug. 19, 1968; children: Emily Kay, Geoffrey Adam. BA, Vanderbilt U., 1950; JD, U. Chgo., 1952; LL.M., Yale U., 1953, J.S.D., 1966; LLD, U. Seattle, 1987, U. Francisco Marroquin, Guatemala, 1987, George Mason U., 2000. Bar: Ill. 1952, N.Y. 1969. Practice in Chgo., 1953-54; assoc. prof. St. Louis U. Law Sch., 1956-57, 59-62; vis. prof. law U. Wis., Madison, 1957-59; prof. George Washington U. Law Sch., 1962-68; Kenan prof. law and polit. sci. U. Rochester, 1968-74; vis. prof. law Stanford (Calif.) Law Sch., 1971-72; disting. prof. law, dir. Law and Econs. Center, U. Miami Law Sch., 1974-80; prof. law Emory U. Law and Econs. Ctr., Atlanta, 1980-86; dean Law Sch., chmn. Law and Econs. Ctr. George Mason U., 1986-96, univ. prof., 1986-99, dean emeritus, 2000—. Vis. prof. law U. Wis., Madison, 1957-59, Stanford (Calif.) Law Sch., 1971-72, U. Chgo. Law Sch., 2000-02; dir. Econs. Insts. Fed. Judges, 1976-89. Author: Insider Trading and the Stock Market, 1966, (with H. Wallich) The Modern Corporation and Social Responsibility, 1973, (with E. Solomon) Wall Street in Transition, 1974, Med. Malpractice Guidebook: Law and Economics, 1985; editor: (with Roger LeRoy Miller) Gold, Money and the Law, 1975; editor: Economic Policy and the Regulation of Corporate Securities, 1968, The Economics of Legal Relationships, 1975; editor: (with James Dorn) Econ. Liberties and the Judiciary, 1987; contbr. to Wall St. Jour. Served to 1st lt. USAF, 1954—56. Recipient Salvatori award Excellence in Acad. Leadership, 1994, award for excellence in pvt. enterprise edn. Freedom Found., 1992; named Cultural Laureate of Va., 1992; Adj. scholar Cato Inst. Fellow Am. Law and Econs. Assn. (hon. life; named one of four Founders of Law ad Econs.), Mont Pelerin Soc., Order of Coif, Phi Beta Kappa. Achievements include pioneered work in economics of corporation law, including first economic analysis of a "market for corporate control" and the first economic analysis of insider trading; started first economics program for judges; introduced numerous innovations into legal education. Avocation: golf. Office Phone: 239-287-0183, 239-596-7972. E-mail: Henry@themannes.com.

**MANNELLA, CARMEN A.**, research scientist; b. Buffalo, June 15, 1947; s. Patrick and Nicolina Mannella; m. Linda J. Thomann, Apr. 8, 1950; children: Marc P., Susan N. BS in Physics, Canisius Coll., Buffalo, 1969; PhD in Biophysics, U. Pa., Phila., 1974. Rsch. scientist Wadsworth Ctr., Albany, NY, 1979—, dir. divsn. molecular medicine, 1994—. Prof. U. Albany, Albany, 1986—; adj. prof. Rensselaer Poly. Inst., Troy, NY; mem. staff health rsch. svc. Health Rsch., Inc., Rensselaer, NY, 2001—. Mem. editl. bd.: Jour. Bioenergetics and Biomembranes, 1992—. Recipient Disting. Alumnus award, Canisius Coll., 2000; fellow, Roswell Pk. Cancer Inst., Buffalo, 1974—76, NIH, 1974—76, St. Louis U. Med. Sch., 1976—78; grantee, NSF, 1981—99, 1991—99; Peter Coleman fellow, Ben Gurion U., Beer Sheeva, Israel, 2006. Mem.: Albany Conf. Found. (bd. dirs. 1989), Mitochondrial Rsch. Soc. (mem. sci. adv. bd. 2001), Biophysical Soc. (chair bioenergetics subgroup 2001—04), DiGamma, Alpha Sigma Nu, Sigma Xi. Achievements include research in development of electron tomography & application to mitochondria other biological structures characterization of mitochondrial channel, VDAC by electron crystallography & other biophysical techniques. Office: Wadsworth Center Empire State Plaza Albany NY 12201-0509 Office Phone: 518-474-0109. Office Fax: 518-402-5381. Personal E-mail: carmmann@aol.com. E-mail: carmen@wadsworth.org.

**MANNELLY, PATRICK J.**, former beverage company executive; With Johnston Coca-Cola Bottling Group, The Coca-Cola Co.: group v.p. Ea. N.Am. group; divsn. gen. mgr. So. Calif. divsn.; CFO Western N.Am. group; corp. v.p., fin. & adminstrn. Coca-Cola Enterprises, Inc., Atlanta, 1998, CFO, 1999—2004.

**MANNERS, PAMELA JEANNE**, secondary school educator; b. Holyoke, Mass., Mar. 20, 1951; d. Francis Edward and Helen Mary (Kurtyka) Herbert; div. 1985; children: Tracy, Kristen. BA, U. So. Miss., 1986, MEd, 1993. Cert. elem. edn. K-3, 4-8, secondary Eng., Social Studies; cert. elem. prin., secondary prin., elem. and secondary adminstrn. Registrar Michel Mid. Sch., Biloxi, Miss., 1987-88, tchr. Eng. and Social Studies, 1988-90, tchr. reading/law related edn., 1990-95; curriculum coord. Biloxi Pub. Schs., 1995-98; administrator Fernwood Jr. High Sch., Biloxi Pub. Schs., 1998-2000; dir. ABA Reading Curriculum Program, 1999-95; prin. Michel Jr. H.S., Biloxi Pub. Schs., 2000—04, Biloxi H.S., 2004—. Law-related edn. trainer Miss. Law-Related Edn. Ctr., Jackson, 1990-2002; law-related trainer Ctr. Civic Edn., Calabasas, Calif., 1993; law-related trainer Constitutional Right Found., 1994-2002. Participant program Lawyer in Every Class Miss. Bar Assn., Jackson, 1990-93 On-site regional grantee Miss. Bar/Dept. Justice, 1992; A+ Site recognition U.S. Dept. Edn. Mem. Leadership Gulf Coast C. of C. (edn. com. 1996—). Roman Catholic. Office: Biloxi Pub Schs 1845 Richard Dr Biloxi MS 39532 Business E-Mail: pamela.manners@biloxischools.net.

**MANNES, ELENA SABIN**, film and television producer, television director; b. NYC, Dec. 3, 1943; d. Leopold Damrosch and Evelyn (Sabin) M. BA, Smith Coll., 1965; MA, Johns Hopkins U., 1967. Rschr. Pub. Broadcast Lab. Nat. Ednl. TV, N.Y.C., 1968-70; writer Sta. WPIX-TV, N.Y.C., 1970-73; assignment editor Sta. ABC-TV, N.Y.C., 1973-76; prodr., writer Sta. WCBS-TV, N.Y.C., 1976-80; prodr. CBS News, N.Y.C., 1980-87, Pub. Affairs

TV/Bill Moyers PBS Documentaries, N.Y.C., 1987-90. Ind. documentary dir. and prodr., 1987—. Recipient Emmy award NATAS, 1984, 85, 87, 90, 94, 96, 2002, Peabody award, 1985, Cine Golden Eagle award, 1988, 90, 93, 94, 95, 99, Robert F. Kennedy Journalism award, 1989, DGA awards, 1987, 90. Mem. Writers Guild Am., Dirs. Guild Am., Am. Film Inst. (dir. Workshop for Women). Avocations: tennis, still photography.

**MANNICK, JOHN ANTHONY**, surgeon; b. Deadwood, S.D., Mar. 24, 1928; s. Alfred and Catherine Elizabeth (Schuster) M.; m. Alice Virginia Gossard, June 9, 1952; children— Catherine Virginia, Elizabeth Eleanor, Joan Barbara. BA, Harvard U., 1949, MD, 1953. Diplomate: Am. Bd. Surgery (dir. 1971-77). Intern Mass. Gen. Hosp., 1953-54, resident in surgery, 1956-60; instr. in surgery to asst. prof. Med. Coll. Va., 1960-64; asso. prof. to prof. surgery Boston U., 1964-76, chmn. div. surgery, 1973-76; Moseley prof. surgery Harvard U., 1976-94, Moseley Disting. prof. surgery, 1994—; dir. ednl. programs Harvard Med. Internat., 1994-96; chmn. dept. surgery Peter Bent Brigham Hosp. and Brigham and Women's Hosp., Boston, 1976-94. Mem. surgery, anesthesiology and trauma study sect. NIH, 1978-82, mem. medicine study sect., 1967-70; rsch. com. Med. Found., Inc., 1970-76. Author: (with others) Modern Surgery, 1970, Core Textbook of Surgery, 1972, Surgery of Ischemic Limbs, 1972, The Cause and Management of Aneurysms, 1990; mem. editorial bd. AMA Archives of Surgery, 1973-84, Clin. Immunology and Immunopathology, 1972-84, Surgery, 1982-97, Brit. Jour. Surgery, 1982-92, European Jour. Vascular Surgery, 1984-96, Shock, 1997—; mem. editl. bd. Advances in Surgery, 1979—, editor, 1984-86; mem. editl. bd. Jour. Vascular Surgery, 1984-97, assoc. editor, 1990-97; also articles. Served to capt. M.C. USAF, 1954-56. Markle scholar in acad. medicine, 1961-66 Fellow ACS (gov.), Royal Coll. Surgeons (hon., Eng.), Royal Coll. Surgeons (hon., Edinburgh), Vascular Soc. Gt. Britain and Ireland (hon.); mem. Am. Fedn. Clin. Rsch., Am. Assn. Immunologists, Am. Soc. Exptl. Pathology, Soc. Clin. Investigation, Soc. Clin. Surgery, Soc. Univ. Surgeons (Lifetime Achievement award 2005), Soc. Surg. Chmn. (sec. 1985-87, pres. 1987-88), Am. Surg. Assn. (pres. 1989-90), Internat. Cardiovascular Soc. (recorder N.Am. chpt., 1973-76, pres. N.Am. chpt. 1991-92, internat. v.p. 1993, Disting. Svc. award 2002), Soc. Vascular Surgery (pres. 1981), N.E. Surg. Soc., New Eng. Soc. Vascular Surgery (pres. 1994-95), Royal Coll. Surgeons (hon., Australasia) So. Surg. Assn., So. Soc. Vascular Surgery (hon.), Surg. Infection Soc., Halstead Soc., Lifeline Found. (pres. 1997-2002), Shock Soc. (Sci. Achievement award 2000), Phi Beta Kappa. Home: 81 Bogle St Weston MA 02493-1056 Office: 75 Francis St Boston MA 02115-6110 Office Fax: 617-582-6169.

**MANNING, CHARLES W.**, university chancellor; b. Mar. 18, 1943; s. Charles Manning; m. Sharon Fischer; children: Shannon, Charles, Kelly. BS in Chemistry, McDaniel Coll., 1965; PhD in Analytical Chemistry, U. Md., 1969; postgrad., Johannes Gutenberg U., Mainz, Germany, 1969—70. Sr. staff assoc. Nat. Ctr. Higher Edn. Mgmt. Systems, Boulder, Colo., 1971-74; asst. provost, asst. prof. chemistry U. Mo., Kansas City, 1974-79; exec. exec. dir. acad. relations Colo. Commn. Higher Edn., Denver, 1979-81, dep. exec. dir., 1982-88; v.p. acad. affairs U. No. Colo., Greeley, 1981-82; exec. vice chancellor Okla. State Regents for Higher Edn., Oklahoma City, 1988-90; chancellor U. System W.Va., Charleston, 1991-2000, Tenn. Bd. Regents, Nashville, 2000—. Cons. as v.p. for planning and fin. Fed. U., Ceara, Brazil, 1976-77; presenter in field. Contbr. articles to profl. jours. Capt. U.S. Army, 1970-71. Office: Tenn Bd Regents 1415 Murfreesboro Pike Ste 350 Nashville TN 37217-2829

**MANNING, CHRISTOPHER ASHLEY**, finance educator, consultant; b. L.A., June 26, 1945; s. Ashley and Vivian LaVerne (Wagner) M.; m. Cathy Ann Nichols, July 30, 1977 (div. Sept. 1993). BS, San Diego State U., 1967; MBA, Northwestern U., 1971; PhD, UCLA, 1983. Corp. loan officer Security Pacific Nat. Bank, L.A., 1971-75; v.p. fin. Solitude Ski Resort, Bravo Ski Corp., Salt Lake City, 1975-78; pres. Sequoia Spa Co., L.A., 1976-79, Manning and Co., L.A., 1971-86, Manning's Little Red Piano Shop, L.A., 1971-86; instr. corp. fin. Pepperdine U., L.A., 1979-83; instr. corp. fin. and real estate Long Beach (Calif.) State U., 1983-86; assoc. prof. fin. Loyola Marymount U., L.A., 1986-92, prof. fin., 1992—. Mng. prin. Denver office Houlihan Valuation Advisors, 1993-94; founder, mng. prin. Manning Advisors. Mem. editl. bd. Jour. of Real Estate Rsch., 1988-90, 91-93, 94-96, 97-99, 2003—; contbr. articles to profl. jours. 1st lt. U.S. Army, 1967—70. Decorated Bronze Star. Mem.: Am. Real Estate Soc. (bd. dirs. 1994—96, 1997—99, v.p./program chair 2000—01, bd. dirs. 2000—, pres.-elect 2001—02, pres. 2002—03), Phi Eta Sigma, Beta Gamma Sigma. Republican. Episcopalian. Home and Office: Manning Advisors 29438 Quailwood Dr Palos Verdes Peninsula CA 90275-4929 Office Phone: 310-541-0353. Business E-Mail: CManning@lmu.edu.

**MANNING, DAVID GEOFFREY**, ambassador; b. Dec. 5, 1949; m. Catherine Manning. With Mexico and Central Am. Dept. British Fgn. and Commonwealth Office, 1972—74, third sec. to second sec. Warsaw, 1974—77, second sec. to first sec. New Delhi, 1977—80, with Soviet Dept., 1980—82, dep. head, Policy Planning Dept., 1982—84, first sec. Paris, 1984—88, counselor-on-loan to Cabinet Office, 1988—90, counselor, head of chancery Moscow, 1990—93, head, Eastern Dept., 1993—94, head, Policy and Planning staff, 1994—95, dep. undersecretary, 1998—2000; fgn. policy adviser to Prime Min., London, 2001—03; amb. and mem. U.K. Del. to NATO, Brussels, 2001; British amb. to Israel, Tel Aviv, 1995—98, to the U.S., Washington, 2003—. U.K. mem. Internat. Conf. on Former Yugoslavia, 1994. Recipient Knight Commander, Order of St. Michael and St. George. Office: Embassy of Britain 3100 Mass Ave NW Washington DC 20008

**MANNING, DENNIS J.**, insurance company executive; m. Kathy Manning; 3 children. BBA, Notre Dame U. Ins. agent Guardian Life Ins. Co. Am., Houston, 1983—91, v.p. life mktg., agy. distbn., 1991—2000, COO, 2000—02, pres., 2002—, CEO, 2003—. Bd. trustees Forman Sch., Litchfield, Conn. With U.S. Army, in Vietnam. Office: 7 Hanover Sq New York NY 10004-2616*

**MANNING, ELI (ELISHA NELSON MANNING)**, professional football player; b. Jan. 3, 1981; s. Archie and Olivia Manning. BA in Mktg., U. Miss., 2003. Quarterback N.Y. Giants, East Rutherford, NJ, 2004—. Recipient Maxwell award, 2003, Johnny Unitas Golden Arm award, 2003. Achievements include selected #1 overall NFL Entry Draft, 2004; comes from a prestigious family with brother Peyton and father Archie both great NFL quarterbacks. Office: c/o New York Football Giants Giants Stadium East Rutherford NJ 07073*

**MANNING, ERIC**, computer scientist, educator, dean, researcher; b. Windsor, Ont., Can., Aug. 4, 1940; g. George Gorman and Eleanor Katherine (Koehler) M.; m. Betty Gelling, Sept. 16, 1961 (div. Jan. 18, 2005); children: David, Paula. BSc, U. Waterloo, Ont., 1961, MSc, 1962; PhD, U. Ill., 1965. Registered profl. engr., B.C. With MIT and Bell Tel. Labs., 1965-68; prof. computer sci. U. Waterloo, 1968-86, founding dir. computer comms. networks group, 1973-82; founding dir. Inst. for Computer Rsch., 1982-86; prof., dean engring. U. Victoria, B.C., Canada, 1986-92, prof. computer sci., elec. engring., 1993-2000, New Media Ctr./Nortel Networks Prof. Network Performance, 2000—03; prin. scientist, strategic advisor Sysor R&D Inc., 2003—. NewMIC Chief Scientist, Networks Cluster, 2000-03; dir. Natural Sci. and Engring. Rsch. Coun. Can., exec. com., chair strategic grants com., 1982-87; dir. Comm. Rsch. Ctr., Govt. of Can., 1995-97, Consortium for Software Engring. Rsch., Ottawa, 1997-99; trustee B.C. Advanced Sys. Found., 1986-93; dir. Sci. Coun. B.C., 1988-91, B.C. Microelectronic Corp.; adv. com. on artificial intelligence NRC, 1987-91; internat. rsch. adv. com. Alta. Informatics Ctr. Rsch. Excellence, 2002-; IBM chair computer sci. Keio U. Yokohama, 1992-93; hon. prof. South East U., Nanjing, China; guest prof. Tokyo U. Tech., 2005— Author: Fault Diagnosis of Digital Systems, 1970; contbr. articles to profl. jours V.p. Greater Victoria Concert Band, 1995-96; trumpet sect., Sooke Philharm. & 5th Field Arty. Band, Royal Can. Arty. Fellow IEEE, Engring. Inst. Can.; mem. Assn. Computing Machinery (mem. snowbird com. 1999—), Assn. Profl. Engrs. B.C., Soc. for Computer

Simulation, Can. Inst. for Advanced Rsch. (adv. com. on artificial intelligence and robotics 1986-90), Can. Assn. for Computer Sci. (pres. 1994-2000), Can. Soc. for Fifth Generation Rsch. (trustee 1987-88), B.C. Microelectronics Soc. (bd. dirs. 1986-87). Avocations: amateur radio, scuba diving, sailing, flying, musical performance. Home: 440 Simcoe St #1431 Victoria BC Canada V8V 1L3 Office: U Victoria Faculty Engring PO Box 3055 Victoria BC Canada V8W 3P6 Business E-Mail: eric.manning@engr.uvic.ca.

**MANNING, GEORGE TAYLOR,** lawyer; b. June 27, 1948; s. Howard M.; children: Nell, Taylor; m. Catherine Zick, Apr. 9, 1999. BA, U. NC, 1970; JD, Columbia U., 1973. Bar: NY 1974, DC 1982, GA 2001. Assoc. Chadbourne, Parke & Whiteside, NYC, 1973-78, ptnr. NYC and Washington, 1982-85; asst. US Atty. So. Dist., NYC, 1978-82; ptnr. Jones, Day, Reavis & Pogue, Washington, 1985—99; ptnr.-in-charge Atlanta office Jones Day, 2000—. Office: Jones Day Ste 800 1420 Peachtree St NE Atlanta GA 30309-3053 Office Phone: 404-581-8400. Business E-Mail: gtmanning@jonesday.com.

**MANNING, J. RICHARD,** lawyer; b. Seattle, Nov. 2, 1932; BA, Seattle U., 1954; LLB, Gonzaga U., 1960. Bar: Wash. 1960. Pvt. practice, Seattle. Chmn. Seattle adv. coun. Am. Arbitration Assn., 1985—96, Bd. Govs., 1997—2000; Mem. Law Adv. Bd. Gonzaga U., 1988—; pres. Wash. State Bar Assn., 2002—03. Chair US Supreme Ct. Hist. Soc., Wash., 2005—. Recipient Nat. Outstanding Svc. award, Am. Arbitration Assn., 1988, Wash. Law and Politics Super Lawyer award, Top 100 Lawyers award, 2002—04. Mem.: ABA, Wash. State Bar Assn. (pres. 2003), Assn. Trial Lawyers Am., King County Bar Found. (pres. 1991—93), Am. Judicature Soc., King County Bar Assn. (pres. 1995—96). Office: 925 Logan Bldg 500 Union St Seattle WA 98101 Office Phone: 206-623-6302. Business E-Mail: jmb@seanet.com.

**MANNING, JAMES E.,** social studies educator; b. Tucson, Ariz., May 4, 1957; s. Beth Manning; m. Cynthia Oney; children: Thomas E., Matthew W. BA, Humboldt State U., Arcata, Calif., 1979. Tchg. credential Calif. Social studies tchr. Salida Mid. Sch., Salida, 1986—. Del. to ann. conf. United Meth. Ch., Hughson, Calif., 1999—2006. Nominee Tchr. of the Yr., Calif. League of Mid. Schs., 2004. Mem.: Salida Tchr. Assn. (Sch. Bell award 1989). Office Phone: 209-545-1633. Business E-Mail: jmanning@salida.k12.ca.us.

**MANNING, JEROME ALAN,** retired lawyer; b. Bklyn., Dec. 31, 1929; s. Emanuel J. and Dorothy (Levine) M.; m. Naomi Jacobs, Oct. 31, 1954; children: Joy, Stephen, Susan. BA, NYU, 1950, LLB, 1952; LLM, Yale U., 1953. Bar: N.Y. 1953, Fla. 1977. Assoc. Joseph Trachtman, NYC, 1956-61; ptnr. Stroock & Stroock & Lavan, N.Y.C., 1961-96; prof. NYU Sch. Law, 1956-96. Editor: NYU Law Rev.; author: Estate Planning, 1980, rev. edit., 2005, Estate Planning for Laymen, 1992. Trustee N.Y.U. Sch. Law. Capt. USAF, 1953-56. Home: 1661 Pine St #911 San Francisco CA 94109-3457 Office Phone: 212-806-6030. Personal E-Mail: jmanning@stroock.com.

**MANNING, JOHN F.,** law educator; b. LA, Apr. 11, 1961; AB in History, summa cum laude, Harvard U., 1982, JD magna cum laude, 1985. Bar: Pa. 1986, Calif. 1990. Law clk. to Judge Robert H. Bork US Ct. Appeals DC Cir., 1985; atty.-advisor Office Legal Counsel US Dept. Justice, 1986—88; law clk. to Justice Antonin Scalia US Supreme Ct., 1988; assoc. Gibson, Dunn & Crutcher, Washington, 1989—91; asst to US Solicitor Gen., 1991—94; prof. Columbia Law Sch., NYC, 1994—2004, Harvard Law Sch., Cambridge, Mass., 2004—. Office: Harvard Law Sch 1563 Massachusetts Ave Cambridge MA 02138 Office Phone: 617-495-5547. Business E-Mail: jmanning@law.harvard.edu.

**MANNING, JOHN WARREN, III,** retired surgeon, medical educator; b. Phila., Nov. 24, 1919; s. John Warren Jr. and Edith Margaret (Reagan) M.; m. Muriel Elizabeth Johnson, Oct. 11, 1944; children: John, Melissa, Susan. BS in Chemistry with honors, Ursinus Coll., 1940; MD, U. Pa., 1943; postgrad., 1978. Diplomate Am. Bd. Surgery. Naval intern Pa. Naval Hosp., 1946; resident Saginaw (Mich.) Gen. Hosp., 1947-50; preceptor Dr. H.M. Bishop, 1950-52; pvt. practice Saginaw, 1950—. Sr. staff mem. Saginaw Gen. Hosp., St. Luke's Hosp., Saginaw; past chief of surgery, chmn. tissue com. St. Mary's Hosp., Saginaw; cons. VA Hosp., Saginaw; assoc. clin. prof. surgery Mich. State U., assoc. prof. surgery, 1976-92, prof. emeritus, 1992—; mem. search com. Saginaw Coop. Hosp. Center; author: articles to profl. publs. Lt. USN, 1942-46, PTO. Fellow ACS; mem. AMA, Mich. State Med. Soc., Saginaw Surg. Soc., Soc. Abdominal Surgeons, Am. Coll. Angiology, Soc. Am. Gastrointestinal Endoscopic Surgeons. Office: 4515 Gratiot Rd Saginaw MI 48603-6261 Office Phone: 989-793-0712.

**MANNING, JOHN WILLARD,** lawyer; b. Miles City, Mont., Mar. 8, 1950; s. Frank Willard Manning and Mary Kathryn (Williams) Murphy; m. Margaret Jean Connors, Dec. 11, 1987; children: Dan Marsh, Sean Marsh, Megan Marsh, Molly Manning. AB, Dartmouth Coll., 1972; JD, Stanford U., 1975. Bar: N.Y. 1977, Mont. 1983. Assoc. Davis Polk & Wardwell, N.Y.C., 1975-80, Dorsey & Whitney, Great Falls, Mont., 1980-83, ptnr., corp. practice group, 1984—, ptnr.-in-charge, Great Falls and Missoula offices. Bd. dirs. Neighborhood Housing Services, Great Falls, 1986-, Native Am. Ctr., Great Falls, 1987-90, Mont. Overthrust Energy Found., Great Falls, 1983-. Mem. Mont. Securities Task Force, Mont. Venture Capital Network. Avocations: skiing, golf, reading. Office: Dorsey & Whitney 507 Davidson Bldg 8 Third St N Great Falls MT 59403-1566 also: Dorsey & Whitney Ste 600 Millenium Bldg 125 Bank St Missoula MT 59802-4407 Office Phone: 406-727-3632, 406-721-6025. Office Fax: 406-727-3638, 406-543-0863. Business E-Mail: manning.jack@dorsey.com.

**MANNING, KENNETH ALAN,** lawyer; b. Buffalo, July 22, 1951; s. Jack Edwin and Dorothea Ann (Ruhland) Manning; children: Michael John, Kathryn Ann. BS in Engring. Sci., SUNY, Buffalo, 1974, JD, 1977. Bar: N.Y. 1978, U.S. Dist. Ct. (we. dist.) N.Y. 1978, U.S. Dist. Ct. (no. dist.) N.Y. 1980, U.S. Ct Appeals (2d cir.) 1993, U.S. Ct. Appeals (3d cir.) 1990. Confidential law asst. to assoc. justice Appellate Divsn. 4th Dept., Buffalo, 1977—79; assoc. Phillips, Lytle, Hitchcock, Blaine & Huber, Buffalo, 1979—84; ptnr. Phillips Lytle LLP, Buffalo, 1985—. Vol. Lawyers Project, Erie County, 1985-2002, Criminal Appeals Program, Erie County, 1988-89; mem. Western N.Y. region NCCJ. Woodburn fellow SUNY, Buffalo, 1973-76. Mem. ABA (TIP sect.), N.Y. State Bar Assn. (ins. negligence sect.), Erie County Bar Assn., Gyro Club (pres. 1988), Park Club. Avocations: sports, hunting. Home: 167 Leicester Rd Buffalo NY 14217-2113 Office: Phillips Lytle LLP 3400 HSBC Ctr Buffalo NY 14203-2887 Office Phone: 716-847-7041.

**MANNING, KENNETH PAUL,** specialty chemical company executive; b. NYC, Jan. 18, 1942; s. John Joseph and Edith Helen (Hoffmann) M.; m. Maureen Lambert, Sept. 12, 1964; children: Kenneth J., John J., Elise, Paul, Carolyn, Jacqueline. BME, Rensselaer Poly. Inst., 1963; postgrad., George Washington U., 1965-66; MBA in Ops. Rsch., Am. U., 1968. With W.R. Grace & Co., NYC, 1973-87, v.p. European consumer divsn., 1975-76, pres. ednl. products divsn., 1976-79, pres. real estate divsn., 1979-81, v.p. corp. tech. group, 1981-83, pres., CEO, Ambrosia Chocolate Co. divsn. Milw., 1983-87; prodp. v.p. Sensient Technologies Corp., Milw., 1987-89, exec. v.p., dir., 1989-92, pres., COO, dir., 1992-96, pres., CEO, dir., 1996—, chmn., CEO, 1997—. Bd. dirs. Badger Meter, Inc., Milw., Saddle Brook, N.J. Served as lt. USN, 1963-67; rear adm. USNR, ret. Decorated Legion of Merit, Nat. Def. medal, others. Mem. ASME, Am. Chem. Soc., Navy League, U.S. Naval Inst., Naval Res. Assn., Milw. Metro Assn. Commerce (bd. dirs.), Knights of Malta. Republican. Roman Catholic. Office: Sensient Techs Corp 777 E Wisconsin Ave Milwaukee WI 53202-5304

**MANNING, KEVIN JAMES,** academic administrator; b. N.Y.C., Nov. 8, 1944; s. James and Helen (Gurry) M.; m. Sara Garrity; children: Elizabeth Ann, Meagan Garrity, Kevin James. BA in Theater, Webster U., St. Louis, 1967; MS in Pers., Shippensburg (Pa.) U., 1976; PhD in Ednl. Adminstrn., Ohio State U., 1982; attended, Inst. Ednl. Mgmt., Harvard U., 1989 Adminstr., intr. Webster U., St. Louis, 1967-68; mgmt recruiter L.S. Brady, Inc., St. Louis, 1969; adminstr. Washington U., St. Louis, 1969-71; admis-

sions counselor Elizabethtown (Pa.) Coll., 1972-76, dir. admissions, 1976-80, spl. asst. to pres., 1982-83; rsch. asst. Ohio State U., Columbus, 1980-82; chief staff Gov.'s Commn. Higher Edn., Harrisburg, Pa., 1983-84; v.p. devel. Immaculata (Pa.) Coll., 1984-2000; pres. Villa Julie Coll., Md., 2000—. Workforce adv. panel Commonwealth of Pa. Mem. attractions com. Phila. Econ. Devel. Coalition, 1988—; bd. trustees Peirce Coll., 1998—2001; mem. oversight com. Vision 2030; bd. dirs. Chester County Export Ctr., Exton, Pa., 1990. Mem. Sr. Devel. Officers Phila. (chmn. 1995-96), Great Valley C. of C. (bd. dirs.). Avocations: reading, art, films, golf. Home: 1907 Billy Barton Cir Reisterstown MD 21136 Office: Villa Julie Coll 1525 Greenspring Valley Rd Stevenson MD 21153-0641 E-mail: prs-mann@mail.vjc.edu.

**MANNING, LAURA SHELTON,** assistant principal; b. Danville, Va., Dec. 22, 1952; d. Jennings Bryan and Mary Garland Shelton; m. Anthony D. Manning, June 29, 2001; children: Nicole Worsham, Victor Hall, Kristina Hall, Zachery Hall. BA cum laude, Averett Coll., Danville, 1973; MA, Adams State Coll., Alamosa, Colo., 1991; prin.'s lic., U. Denver, 1995. Tchr. sci. and social studies Halifax (Va.) County Acad., 1973—78; tchr. sci. Henrico County Sch. Dist., Richmond, Va., 1979—83; tchr. sci., asst. prin. Douglas County Sch. Dist., Castle Rock, Colo., 1983—2001; asst. prin. Catalina Foothills Sch. Dist., Tucson, 2001—. Com. mem. Grace Counseling Svcs., Englewood, Colo., 1994—96; cons. Team Work, Englewood, 1991—95; mem., singer Cross Point Promise Band; organizer, singer Catalina Foothills Faculty Ensemble. Co-chair drama team Grace Chapel, Englewood, 1990—2004; presenter, cons. Adoption Alliance, Denver, 1991—2001. Named Inspirational Tchr., Boettches Scholarship Com., 1991. Mem.: ASCD, Kid Ariz. (bd. dirs. 2004—), Phi Delta Kappa. Avocations: music, drama, gardening, reading, swimming. Home: 8509 E Hodgman Pl Tucson AZ 85747

**MANNING, LAUREN FORSHAY,** financial service company executive; b. Belleville, NJ, Feb. 15, 1961; d. Thomas Owen Pritchard; m. Kenneth DeMille Butler, Dec. 12, 1991 (div. Mar. 1998); m. Gregory Peter Manning, March, 2000; 1 child, Tyler. BA, Fordham U., N.Y.C., 1981-84; postgrad. in bus., N.Y.U., 1985—. Cert. Series 7, 63 NASD, SEC. Asst. v.p. Lehman Bros., Inc., N.Y.C., 1985-86; asst. v.p., v.p. Dean Witter Reynolds, Wayne, N.J., 1986-88; sales mgr. Reuters Am., N.Y.C., 1988-91; regional sales mgr. Fusion Sys. Corp., N.Y.C., 1991-93; v.p. bus. devel. Cantor Fitzgerald Securities, N.Y.C., 1993-96, ptnr., 1994—, v.p. sales Market Data Corp., 1996-97, sr. v.p., dir. global information svcs., 1997—. Pres., chmn. Perry St. Assn., N.Y.C., 1999—; jr. com. mem. N.Y.C. Ballet, 1997. Mem.: Fin. Womens Assn., Women's Bond Club. Avocations: golf, horseback riding, real-estate. Personal E-mail: laurenmanning@nyc.rr.com.

**MANNING, MARTHA MARY,** writer, psychologist; b. Chgo., Aug. 18, 1952; d. John Eugene and Mary Louise M.; m. Brian J. Depenbrock, Oct. 20, 1973; 1 child, Keara. BA with high honors, U. Md., College Park, 1974; MA, Cath. Univ. Am., 1978, PhD, 1981. Postdoctoral fellow McLean Hosp./Harvard Med. Sch., Boston, 1981-83; asst. prof. George Mason U., Fairfax, Va., 1983-88; pvt. practice Alexandria, Va., 1994-96. Psychology instr., 1989-93. Author: A Season of Mercy, 1985, Undercurrents: A Life Beneath the Surface, 1995, Chasing Grace, 1996; co-author: Restoring Intimacy: A Patients Guide to Maintaining Relationships During Depression, 1999, All Seasons Pass: Grieving & Miscarriage, 2000; columnist, Salt of the Earth, 1993-96; contbr. to popular mags. including Health, Mirabella, New Woman, Ladies' Home Jour., Glamour, U.S. Cath., N.Y. Times Book Rev., Family Therapy Networker, Washington Post. Recipient Merit award Associated Ch. Press, 1994, 96, Best Mag. Column Cath. Press Assn., 1995, Presdl. award for Patient Advocacy, Am. Psychiat. Assn., 1996, Stephen Logan award Nat. Alliance for Mentally Ill. Office: Arielle Eckstut James Levine Comm Inc care FWI 307 7th Ave 1904 New York NY 10001

**MANNING, MICHAEL J.,** lawyer; b. Wichita, Kans., July 18, 1944; BA, U. Kans., 1966; JD, Washburn U., 1969. Bar: Kans. 1969, D.C. 1970. Mem. Fulbright & Jaworski LLP, Washington. Mem.: ABA, Fed. Energy Assn., D.C. Bar, Phi Alpha Delta. Office: Fulbright & Jaworski Market Sq 801 Pennsylvania Ave NW Fl 3-5 Washington DC 20004-2623

**MANNING, MICHAEL NICHOLAS,** actor, singer, guitarist, broadcaster, journalist; b. Cin., Apr. 5, 1958; s. Nicholas George and Catherine. BA in psychology, U. Cin., 1999. Regional mktg. and develop. mgr. SCA Wolff Sys., Redmond, Wash., 1986—90; mktg. and pub. rels. cons. Manning & Assoc., Dallas, 1989—90, KERA-TV 13 (PBS), Dallas, 1990—2003; news anchor, reporter CBS Radio Network, NYC, 1999—2000; prodr. CBS Westwood One affilitates, 1990—95; comml. copywriter, scriptwriter, host Saturday Main Event Weekend Music mag., 1990—95, dir. mktg. and promotions, 1995—98; news anchor WBAP News Network / Talk 820 AM (ABC Network), NYC, 2001—03; helicopter reporter WLWT-TV5 (NBC), Cin., 2003—04. Strategic cons. alt. plan of reorgn. US Airways, Crystal City, Va., 2004. Author: (poems) No Artificial Flowers During the Mowing Season, 1990, (short stories) Bread Crumbs for Sale, 2006; contbg. editor: Airways mag., 1995—; actor(voice over): (pilot for cable TV series) When Dreams Come True, 2004, (radio and TV) in 6,000 and more commls.; contbr. numerous mag. articles; actor, narrator: Turning Back Time: A Tribute to the 35th Anniversary of "Bullitt" with Steve McQueen; actor: Out of Our Heads Improv Comedy Group, 2003—04; interviewed for: Billboard mag., 1996. Chmn. pub. rels. No. Tex. chpt. Lupus Found. Am., 1987—93, bd. dirs.; mem. adv. bd. Families for the Rainforest, Carrollton, Tex., 1998—2005. Recipient Vol. Svc. award, Lupus Found. Am., 1993. Mem.: AFTRA (actor 2003—), Pan Am World Airways Hist. Found. (mus. com. 2006—). E-mail: michaelmanninginfo@gmail.com.

**MANNING, NANCY CHRISTINE,** retired elementary school educator; d. Alexander Anthony and Millie (Burczak) Pawlikowski; m. Richard Wayne Manning. BS in Elem. Edn. cum laude, East Stroudsburg U., 1971. Cert. Family Math. instr. Rutgers U., 1994 Tchr. Green Twp. Bd. Edn., Greendell, NJ, 1971—2003; ret. Treas. Green Twp. Edn. Assn., Greendell, 1978—2002. Recipient Tchr. Recognition award, NJ Dept. Edn., 1993. Avocations: reading, gardening, cooking, baking, quilting.

**MANNING, PETER KIRBY,** criminal justice educator; b. Salem, Oreg., Sept. 27, 1940; s. Kenneth Gilbert and Esther Amelia (Gibbard) M.; m. Victoria Francis Shaughnessy, Sept. 1, 1961 (div. 1981); children: Kerry Patricia, Sean Peter, Merry Kathleen; m. Betsy Cullum-Swan, Aug. 4, 1991 (div. 1997). BA, Willamette U., 1961; MA, Duke U., 1963, PhD, 1966; MA (hon.), Oxford U., Eng., 1983. Instr. sociology Duke U., 1964-65; asst. prof. sociology U. Mo., 1965-66, Mich. State U., East Lansing, 1966-70, assoc. prof. sociology and psychiatry, 1970-74, prof., 1974—; prof. criminal justice, 1993—, Beto chair lectr. Sam Houston State U., 1990; Ameritech lectr. E. Ky. U., 1993; vis. lectr. U. Las Andes, Meridá Venezuela, 2002-03, 2005; vis. prof. U. Victoria, 1968, MIT, 1982, SUNY, Albany, 1982, U. Mich., 1990—91, York U., Toronto, 1999; vis. sr. scholar Northeastern U. Coll. Criminal Justice, 2001, E.V. and E.M. Brooks chair; cons. Nat. Inst. Law Enforcement and Criminal Justice, U.S. Dept. Justice, Rsch. Triangle Inst., NSF, Nat. Health and Med. Rsch. Coun., Australia, 1980—, Social Sci. Rsch. Coun. Eng., AID, Jamaica, 1991, Sheehy com. Police Pay and Performance, England, 1993. Author: Sociology of Mental Health and Illness, 1975, Police Work, 1977, 2d edit., 1997, The Narcs' Game, 1980, 2d edit., 2003, Semiotics and Fieldwork, 1987, Symbolic Communication, 1988, Organizational Communication, 1992, Private Policing, 1999, Policing Contingencies, 2003, others; also book chpts., articles in profl. jours.; cons. editor series: Principal Themes in Sociology; co-editor Sage Series in Qualitative Methods, Crime, Law and Social Change, 2004—; mem. editl. bd. numerous jours. in social scis. Recipient Bruce Smith Sr. award Acad. Criminal Justice Scis., 1993, O.W. Wilson award, 1997, Charles H. Cooley award Mich. Sociol. Assn., 1994; NDEA fellow, 1962-64, NSF fellow, 1965, fellow Balliol Coll. Oxford U., 1982-83, vis. fellow Wolfson Coll., Oxford U., 1981, 82-83, fellow, 1984-86; Am Bar Found. fellow, 1998; Rockefeller resident, Bellagio, Italy, 2000. Mem. Am. Soc. Criminology, Am. Sociol. Assn., Acad. Criminal Justice Scis., Brit. Soc. Criminology, Internat. Sociol. Assn., Midwest Sociol. Soc., Soc. Study Social Problems, Soc. Study Symbolic Interaction (spl.

recognition award 1990, v.p. 1992-93, program chair 1993), Internat. Soc. Semiotics and Law. Office: Northeastern U Coll Criminal Justice Boston MA 02115 Office Phone: 617-373-7748. Personal E-mail: manningpk@hotmail.com.

**MANNING, PEYTON WILLIAMS,** professional football player; b. New Orleans, Mar. 24, 1976; s. Archie and Olivia Manning; m. Ashley Thompson, Mar. 17, 2001. BA in Speech Communications, U. Tenn., 1998. Quarterback Indpls. Colts, 1998—. Appeared in The Pro Bowl (AFC), 1999, 2000, 01, 03, 04, 05. Named NFL Co-MVP, AP, 2003, NFL MVP, 2004, NFL Offensive Player of the Yr., 2004, Pro-Bowl MVP, 2004; named to NFL All-Pro Team, 2005; recipient Espy Award for Best College Football Player, 1998, Espy Award for Best NFL player, 2004. Achievements include led NFL in completions and passing yards 2000, 2003; holds the NFL single season record for most touchdown passes (49), 2004; holds the NFL single season record for best passing rating (121.1), 2004. Office: Indianapolis Colts PO Box 535000 Indianapolis IN 46253-5000 also: Indianapolis Colts 7001 West 56th Strreet Indianapolis IN 46254*

**MANNING, ROBERT HENDRICK,** retired audio-visual services executive; b. Soerabaja, Java, Indonesia, Aug. 23, 1941; s. William and Gertrude (Unk) Manning. BS, No. Mich. U., 1974. Lic. capt. USCG. Instr. sailing USCG Acad., New London, Conn., 1959-63; dir. audio visual/media svcs. No. Mich. U., Marquette, 1965-93, capt. univ. rsch. vessel, 1977-79, dir. audio visual svcs. emeritus; dir. devel. Bresnan Comm. Co., Marquette, 1993-97. Comm. cons., 1996—. Host (TV series) Ask the Doctors, Sta. WNMU-TV, 1977—98. Pub. rels. dir. Charter Comm., 2000—02. Mem.: Marquette-Alger County Med. Soc. (hon.; exec. dir. 1975—2000). Avocations: astronomy, sailing, amateur radio. Home and Office: PO Box 309 Marquette MI 49855-0309

**MANNING, ROBERT THOMAS,** internist, educator; b. Wichita, Kans., Oct. 16, 1927; s. Thomas Earl and Mary Francis (Schlegel) M.; m. Jane Bell, July 29, 1949; children: Mary Kay Fausch, Phillip Carson, Ann Shiba. AB, Wichita U., 1950; MD, Kans. U., 1954; DHL, Med. Coll. Hampton Rds., 1991. Diplomate Am. Bd. Internal Medicine. Intern Kansas City (Mo.) Gen. Hosp., 1954-55; resident Kans. U., Kansas City, 1955-58; from asst. prof. to prof. Kans. U. Med. Ctr. Sch. of Medicine, Kansas City, 1958-71, assoc. dean students, 1969-71; dean Eastern Va. Med. Sch., Norfolk, Va., 1971-74, chmn., prof. internal medicine, 1974-77; prof. internal medicine U. Kans. Sch. of Medicine, Wichita, 1977-93; prof. emeritus U. Kans. Sch. Medicine, Wichita, 1993—; assoc. dean, clin. affairs U. Kans. Sch. of Medicine, Wichita, 1985-89; chmn. internal medicine U. Kans. Sch. Medicine, Wichita, 1987—89; pres. Wesley Med. Rsch. Inst., 1986-88. Nat. cons. surgeon gen. USAF, 1973-78. Author: Major's Physical Diagnosis, 9th edit., 1982; contbr. articles to profl. jours. Pres. Kans. Health Ethics, Inc., 1994-96. Served with USAAC, 1945-47. With US Army Air Corps, 1945—47. Recipient Advanced Achievement award Am. Bd. Internal Medicine, 1987. Fellow ACP (laureate Kans. chpt., bd. govs. Kans. 1984-88); mem. Am. Fedn. Clin. Rsch., Cen. Soc. Clin. Rsch., Am. Assn. Study Liver Disease, Sigma Xi, Alpha Omega Alpha. Presbyterian. Avocations: woodworking, golf. Home: 126 Trail Of The Flowers Georgetown TX 78628-4814 Personal E-mail: rmannsun@cox.net.

**MANNING, SYLVIA,** language educator; b. Montreal, Que., Can., Dec. 2, 1943; came to U.S., 1967; d. Bruno and Lea Bank; m. Peter J. Manning, Aug. 20, 1967; children: Bruce David, Jason Maurice BA, McGill U., 1963; MA, Yale U., 1964, PhD in English, 1967. Asst. prof. English Calif. State U.-Hayward, 1967-71, assoc. prof., 1971-75, assoc. dean, 1972-75; assoc. prof. U. So. Calif., 1975-94, prof., assoc. dir. Ctr. for Humanities, 1975-77, assoc. dir. Ctr. for Humanities, 1975-77, chmn. freshman writing, 1977-80, chmn. dept. English, 1980-83, vice provost, exec. v.p., 1984-94; prof. English U. Ill., Champaign, 1994—, v.p. for acad. affairs, prof. English, 1994—, interim chancellor Chgo., 1999-2000, chancellor, 2000—. Author: Dickens as Satirist, 1971; Hard Times: An Annotated Bibliography, 1984. Contbr. essays to mags. Woodrow Wilson fellow, 1963-64, 66-67 Mem. MLA, Dickens Soc. Office: U of Ill Office of Chancellor 2833 University Hall 601 S Morgan St Chicago IL 60607-7100 Office Phone: 312-413-3350.

**MANNING, WILLIAM FREDERICK,** retired photographer; b. Gardner, Mass., Aug. 18, 1920; s. Seth Newton and Jennie May (Bennett) M.; m. Yvonne J.Z. Winslow, Feb. 29, 1964; children: Pamela Ann, Jeffrey Newton. AA, Boston U., 1950, BS in Comm., 1952. With AP, Boston, 1951-53; photographer UPI, Boston, 1953-88; ret., 1988. Contbr. photos to books, mags., newspapers throughout the world. Served with USN, 1940-46, PTO. Recipient Look 1st Prize All Sports award, 1958; Pictures of the Yr. award U. Mo., 1964, 74; Nat. Headliners Club award for outstanding syndicate photography, 1974. Mem. Boston Press Photographers Assn., Nat. Headliners Club, Delta Kappa Alpha. Congregationalist. Home: 23 Sunset Dr Beverly MA 01915-2319

**MANNINO, EDWARD FRANCIS,** lawyer, educator; b. Abington, Pa., Dec. 5, 1941; s. Sante Francis and Martha Anne (Hines) M.; m. Mary Ann Vigilante, July 17, 1965 (div. 1990); m. Antoinette K. O'Connell, June 25, 1993; children: Robert John, Jennifer Elaine. BA with distinction, U. Pa., 1963, LLB magna cum laude, 1966. Bar: Pa. 1967. Law clk. 3d cir. U.S. Ct. Appeals, 1966-67; assoc. Dilworth, Paxson, Kalish & Kauffman, Phila., 1967-71, ptnr., 1972-86, co-chmn. litigation dept., 1980-86, sr. ptnr., 1982-86; sr. prin. Elliott, Mannino & Flaherty, PC, Phila., 1986-90; chmn. Mannino Griffith PC, Phila., 1990-95; sr. ptnr. Wolf, Block, Schorr & Solis-Cohen, Phila., 1995-98; ptnr., chair litig. practice Akin, Gump, Strauss, Hauer & Feld LLP, Phila., 1998—. Hearing examiner disciplinary bd. Supreme Ct. Pa., 1986—89, mem. adv. com. on appellate ct. rules, 1989—95; lectr. Temple U. Law Sch., 1960—69, 1971—72, mem. Phila. Mayor's Sel. and Tech. Adv. Com., 1976—79; project mgr. Pa. Environ. Master Plan, 1973; chmn. Pa. Land Use Policy Study Adv. Com., 1973—75; chmn. adv. com., hon. faculty history dept. U. Pa., 1980—85, lectr. Am. history, 2001—. Author: Lender Liability and Banking Litigation, 1989, Business and Commercial Litigation: A Trial Lawyer's Handbook, 1995, The Civil RICO Primer, 1996; mem. editl. bd. Litigation mag., 1985-87, Comm. Lending Litigation News, 1988-2001, Bank Bailout Litigation News, 1989-93, Bus. Torts Reporter, 1988—, Practical Litigator, 1989—2003, Civil RICO Report, 1991-2001; contbr. articles to profl. jours. Pres. parish coun. Our Mother of Consolation Ch., 1977-79; bd. overseers U. Pa. Sch. Arts and Scis., 1985-89, chmn. recruitment and retention of faculty com.; commonwealth trustee Temple U., 1987-90, audit, bus. and fin. coms. Named one of Nation's Top Litigators Nat. Law Jour., 1990, Pa.'s Top Ten Trial Lawyers, 1999, Best Lawyers in Am., Am.'s Leading Bus. Lawyers. Fellow Am. Bar Found., ABA (chmn. various coms.), Am. Law Inst., Hist. Soc. U.S. Dist. Ct. Ea. Dist. Pa. (bd. dirs.), Pa. Bar Assn., Phila. Bar Assn. (gov. 1975), Bar Assn. Soc., Order of Coif, Phi Beta Kappa, Phi Beta Kappa Assocs. Democrat. Office: Akin Gump Strauss Hauer Et Al One Commerce Sq Ste 2200 2005 Market St Philadelphia PA 19103-7014 Office Phone: 215-965-1340. Office Fax: 215-965-1210. Business E-Mail: emannino@akingump.com.

**MANNIX, KEVIN LEESE,** lawyer, political organization executive; b. Queens, NY, Nov. 26, 1949; s. John Warren Sr. and Editta Gorrell M.; m. Susanna Bernadette Chiocca, June 1, 1974; children: Nicholas Chiocca, Gabriel Leese, Emily Kemper. BA, U. Va., 1971, JD, 1974. Bar: Oreg. 1974, U.S. Ct. Appeals (9th cir.) 1976, U.S. Supreme Ct. 1978, Guam 1979. Law clk. to judge Oreg. Ct. Appeals, Salem, 1974—75; asst. atty. gen. Oreg. Dept. Justice, Salem, 1975—77, Govt. of Guam, Agana, 1977—79; judge adminstr. law Oreg. Workers' Compensation Bd., Salem, 1980—83; assoc. Lindsay, Hart, Neil & Weigler, Portland, Oreg., 1983—86; prin. Kevin L. Mannix Profl. Corp., Salem, 1986—. Chmn. St. House Sch. Bd., Salem, 1981-86; pres. Salem Cath. Schs. Corp., 1985; v.p. Salem Cath. Schs. Found., 1985-88, pres., 1988-90, 91-94, 2000—; pres. bd. dirs. Blanchet Sch., 1995-; vice chair Oreg. Rep. Party, 1998-2000, chmn., 2003-05; state rep., 1989-2001; state sen., 1998-99. Mem. Marion Bar Assn., Rotary (bd. dirs. East

Salem 1985-89, pres. 1987-88), KC. Republican. Avocations: photography, scuba diving, travel. Home: 375 18th St NE Salem OR 97301-4307 Office: 2003 State St Salem OR 97301-4349 Office Phone: 503-364-1913.

**MANNS, ESSIE JEANETTE DELANEY,** advocate; b. Roanoke, Va., June 20, 1946; d. Walter Leon Delaney and Nanny Rebecca Minor Delaney Volley; divorced; children: Christa Manns Hall, Robert Marcellus Jr. AAS, Va. Western C.C., Roanoke, 1979; BA in Psychology/Sociology, Mary Baldwin Coll., Staunton, Va., 1987; MA in Psychology, PhD in Psychology, Am. State U., Honolulu, 1998. Self-employed seamstress, Columbus, Ohio, 1968—73, Roanoke, 1973—76; daycare provider Social Svcs., Roanoke, 1973—76; pub. rels. coord. Roanoke Valley Outreach Assn., 1976—77; parent coord. counselor Opportunity Industrialization Ctr., Roanoke, 1977—78; peer counselor Va. Western C.C., Roanoke, 1978—79; GS-4 nursing asst. Salem (Va.) Vets. Med. Ctr., 1980—85; outreach worker 23d Dist. Juvenile Ct., Roanoke, 1983—85; project fundraiser, alcohol and drug abuse counselor, battered women's counselor Total Action Against Poverty, Roanoke, 1987—89; project image counselor Social Svcs. 5th Planning Dist., Roanoke, 1989. 3d v.p. labor and industry So. Christian Leadership Conf., 1992—97; co-pres. Washington Pk. Alliance for Neighborhoods, Roanoke, 1998—; co-founder, pres. STRIVE Econ. Empowerment, Inc., Roanoke, 1998—; bd. dirs. Cmty. Orgn. for Rsch. and Devel., Roanoke, 1976—, S.W. Va. Cmty. Devel. Fund, Roanoke, 1979—. Recipient Outstanding Svcs. award, S.W. Va. Cmty. Devel. Fund, 1980—85, Vol. of Yr. award, Total Action Against Poverty, 1994, Svc. Learning Program award, Roanoke Coll., 2001, Dr. Martin Luther King Jr.'s Drum Major for Justice award, So. Christian Leadership Conf., 2002, Timeless Enthusiasm Dedication Hard Work award, Inner City for Selective Devel., Roanoke, 2003. Baptist. Achievements include Roanoke Gladiators Wrestling Team joining STRIVE, a chartered community service organization, 2004. Avocation: human and civil rights. Home: 1826 10th St NW Roanoke VA 24012 Office: Economic Empowerment Inc 1826 10th St NW Roanoke VA 24012 E-mail: ejdmanns@aim.com.

**MANNWEILER, MARY-ELIZABETH,** painter; b. Norwood, Ohio, June 23, 1916; d. Wilbur Lawrence Young Davis and Augusta Minnis (Newman) Davis; m. Robert Mays Lang, Sr., May 25, 1940 (dec. July 1981); children: Robert Mays Lang, Jr., Gary Davis Lang, Virginia Elizabeth Lang Crawford; m. Gordon Bannatyne Mannweiler, Apr. 17, 1982 (dec. Aug. 2001). Student, Miami U., Oxford, Ohio, 1935-37. Portrait painter; permanent collections; donated (with husband) stained glass window to Congl. Ch., Naugatuck, Conn. Past pres. Athena Club, Freeport, N.Y., Woodbury (Conn.) Women's Club, 1977-78, Watertown (Conn.) Art League; past dir. Waterbury (Conn.) Symphony Orch.; pres. Mary Elizabeth and Gordon Mannweiler Found., Naugatuck, Conn.; trustee YMCA, Naugatuck; mem. scholarship com. Naugatuck H.S., 2003. Recipient blue ribbons for artwork; Paul Harris fellow Rotary, 2001; music room named in honor of Mr. and Mrs. Mannweiler Conn. Jr. Republic, Litchfield, 1997m Meml. Vol. award Naugatuck YMCA, 2005. Mem. DAR (regent Ruth Floyd Woodhull chpt. 1966-67, pres.). Home: 435 Hillside Ave Naugatuck CT 06770-2727

**MANNY, CARTER HUGH, JR.,** architect, foundation administrator; b. Michigan City, Ind., Nov. 16, 1918; s. Carter Hugh and Ada Gage (Barnes) M.; m. Mary Alice Kellett, Dec. 6, 1942 (dec. Jan. 1994); children: Elizabeth, Carter Hugh III; m. Maya Moran, Dec. 27, 1995. AB magna cum laude, Harvard U., 1941, Indsl. Adminstr., 1942; Taliesin fellow, Scottsdale, Ariz., 1946; BS in Architecture, Ill. Inst. Tech., 1948. With Murphy/Jahn (name formerly Naess & Murphy and C.F. Murphy Assocs.), Chgo., 1948-83, partner, 1957-61; dir. 1st Citizens Bank, Michigan City, Ind., 1970-86; sr. v.p. Murphy/Jahn (name formerly Naess & Murphy and C.F. Murphy Assocs.), 1978-83. Mem. adv. com. on architecture Art Inst. of Chgo., 1982—; oversight com. Ill. Inst. Tech. Sch. of Architecture, Chgo., 1989-94; trustee Graham Found. Advanced Studies in Fine Arts 1956-74, exec. dir., 1972-93, hon. trustee, 1994—. Projects include O'Hare Internat. Airport, Chgo., FBI Hdqrs, Washington, First Nat. Bank Chgo, Chgo. Civic Center, Chgo. Bd. Trade. Fellow AIA (pres. Chgo. chpt. 1973, dir. Ill. council 1972-73); Soc. Archtl. Historians (dir. 1982-85), Chgo. Bldg. Congress (dir. 1978-83); mem. Phi Beta Kappa, Mich. City Yacht Club, Arts Club, Cliff Dwellers Club (Chgo., hon.). Home: 200 Lake Ave Michigan City IN 46360 also: 50 Parftridge Dr San Rafael CA 94901

**MANO, NICOLAS P.,** research scientist; b. Arcachon, France, Mar. 15, 1973; s. Michel and Francoise Mano. PhD, Bordeaux U., France, 1995—2001. Rsch. assoc. U. Tex., Austin, 2001. Recipient prize of ISE, Oronzio De Nora Found., 2004; grantee Oronzio De Nora Indsl. Electrochem. fellowship, Electrochem. Soc., 2005. Mem.: Bioelectrochemical Soc. (Luigi Galvani prize 2003), Internat. Soc. Electrochemistry, Electrochem. Soc., Am. Chem. Soc. Achievements include first to miniature membrane-less biofuel cell operating under physiological conditions; demonstrated the operation of a miniature membrane-less biofuel cell in a living plant, a Grape; demonstrated that the electrically wired enzyme, bilirubin oxidase, catalyzes the four electron electroreduction of oxygen to water at a lesser overpotential than the classical Platinum. Office: Univ Tex 1 University Sta - #C0400 Austin TX 78712 Office Phone: 512-471-8892. E-mail: mano@mail.utexas.edu.

**MANOFF, RICHARD KALMAN,** advertising executive, writer, public health service officer, consultant; b. Bklyn., June 24, 1916; s. Kalman and Sarah (Glatman) M.; m. Lucy B. Deutscher, Nov. 27, 1942; children: Robert K., Gregory P. BS, CCNY, 1937, postgrad., 1940. Asst. regional dir. War Manpower Commn., 1942-45; marketing dir. Welch Grape Juice Co., 1949-53; v.p. Kenyon & Eckhardt Advt., N.Y.C., 1953-56; pres., chmn. bd. Richard K. Manoff Inc. Advt., N.Y.C., from 1956; now pres. Manoff Internat. Inc.; spl. adv. mktg. and communications to exec. dir. UNICEF, 1980—. Dir. Thomas J. Lipton, Inc.; adj. prof. dept. health Scis. Sargent Coll. Allied Health Professions, Boston U., 1978—; lectr. pub. health Columbia U. Sch. Medicine, 1982-83; Mem. U.S. del. FAO World Conf. Rome, Italy, 1966; spl. advisor UNICEF and WHO, 1968-78; cons. spl. mission to Food and Agr. Ministry, Govt. India, AID, 1969; Ford Found. offices Pub. Edn. Pub. Broadcasting for children's TV; participant 1st World Conf. on Social Communication for Devel. Mass Communications, Mexico, 1970, 7th Asian Advt. Congress, Delhi, 1970, 3d Western Hemisphere Nutrition Congress, Fla., 1971, Internat. Conf. Nutrition. Nat. Devel. and Planning, Mass. Inst. Tech., 1971, Symposium Eating Patterns and Their Influence on Purchasing Behavior and Nutrition, Nev., 1971, Nutrition Workshop, AID, 1971, 9th Annual Summer Workshop Family Planning, 1971, 4th & 5th Seminar Workshop on Mgmt. and Planning of Population Family Planning Programs, 1971, New Products Symposium, 1971, Communication Seminar series Cornell U., 1971, Exploration The Frontiers of Nutritional Edn. Seminar, 1972, 9th Internat. Congress of Nutrition, Mexico, 1972, East-West Center Comml. Resources Conf. on Family Planning, Hawaii, 1972; Protein adv. group UN Systems Annual Mtg., 1973; mem. panel White House Conf. Food, Nutrition and Health, 1969; mem. Sec.'s Adv. Com. on Population Affairs, Dept. HEW, 1971-76; mem. adv. com. Population Reference Bur., Washington, 1977—, Population Inst., 1980—; mem. Nelson A. Rockefeller's Commn. on Critical Choices for Ams.; cons. HRSA Healthy Start Campaign to reduce infant mortality, 1991; bd. dirs. Population Comm. Internat.; Martin J. Forman Meml. lectr., Washington, 1993. Author: Social Marketing: New Imperative for Public Health, 1985. Bd. dirs. Planned Parenthood World Population, Pathfinder Fund, Boston, 1977-80, United Nutrition Edn. Found., Alexandria, Va., 1978—; mem. com. on internat. nutrition programs NAS-NRC, 1973; founder, mem. Com. for Shakespeare Festival, N.Y.C.; bd. visitors Grad. Sch. and Univ. Ctr., CUNY; mem. nat. bd., cons. to the pres. Henry J. Kaiser Family Found., 1987-91; dir. City Coll. Fund, 1990—. Recipient 5th Ann. Global award for media excellence Population Inst., China, 1985, Townsend Harris medal Alumni Assn. CCNY, 1986. Mem. Am. Advt. Assn. Agcy. (gov. 1967—; sec.-treas. 1975—), Population Comms. Internat. (dir. 1992—), Friars Club, Harmonie Club (N.Y.C.), Century Assn. Home: 322 E 57th St New York NY 10022-2949

**MANOOGIAN, RICHARD ALEXANDER,** manufacturing executive; b. Long Branch, N.J., July 30, 1936; s. Alex and Marie (Tatian) Manoogian; m. Jane Manoogian; children: James, Richard, Bridget. BA in Econs, Yale U., 1958. Asst. to pres. Masco Corp., Taylor, Mich., 1958-62, exec. v.p., 1962-68, pres., 1968-85, chmn. bd., CEO, 1985—. Chmn., dir. Mascotech, Inc., Trimas Corp.; dir. First Chgo. NBD Corp., Bank One Corp., Ford Motor Co. Metaldyne Corp., Detroit Renaissance, Am. Bus. Conf. Chmn. Alex & Marie Manoogian Found.; pres. & treas. Richard & Jane Manoogian Found.; co-founder Mackinac Island Cmty. Found., 2003; trustee U. Liggett Sch. State Dept. Fine Arts Comsn., Founder's Soc., Detroit Inst. Arts, Center for Creative Studies; trustee coun. Nat. Gallery Art. Mem. Yale Alumni Assn. Clubs: Grosse Pointe Yacht, Grosse Pointe Hunt, Country Club Detroit, Detroit Athletic. Office: Masco Corp 21001 Van Born Rd Taylor MI 48180-1300*

**MANOS, CHRISTOPHER LAWRENCE,** lawyer, mediator; b. Ft. Bragg, N.C., July 1, 1952; m. B.J. Osmon, June 14, 1974; children: Monica, Kelly. BS, U.S. Mil. Acad., 1974; JD, U. N.D., 1982. Bar: Mont. 1983, U.S. Dist. Ct. (Mont.) 1983, U.S. Ct. Appeals (9th cir.) 1983. Assoc. to ptnr. Moore, O'Connell, Refling & Manos, Bozeman, Mont., 1982-92; ptnr. Biglen & Manos, Big Timber, Mont., 1992—97, Manos law firm, 1997; part-time dep. county atty. Sweet Grass county, 1992—98; county atty, 1998—2001. Trainer for mediators Ctr. for Collaborative Solutions and Alternative Dispute Resolution Assocs., Bozeman and Palo Alto, Calif., 1990—. Contbr. articles to profl. jours. Bd. dirs. Mont. Pub. TV, Bozeman, 1985-92, Mont. Coun. for Internat. Visitors, Bozeman, 1992; mem. Mont. Stat Bar Dispute Resolution Com., Helena, Mont., 1989—. Capt. U.S. Army, 1974-79. Col. USAR (ret.), 1979-2004. Mem. Assn. Conflict Resolution, Am. Arbitration Assn., State Bar Mont. (pres. 2001-02), Soc. Profls. in Dispute Resolution. Office Phone: 406-442-7660.

**MANOSEVITZ, MARTIN,** psychologist; b. Mpls., June 22, 1938; s. Julius and Ethel (Cohen) M.; m. Carolyn Heather Margulius, Sept. 17, 1959; children— Bradley, Jason. BA, U. Minn., Mpls., 1960, PhD, 1964. Diplomate in clin. psychology, psychoanalysis Am. Bd. Profl. Psychology. Asst. prof. psychology Rutgers U., 1964-67; asst. prof. psychology U. Tex., Austin, 1967-69, assoc. prof., 1969-75, prof., 1975-87; pvt. practice clin. psychology Austin, 1975-99, Aspen, Colo., 1999—. Adj. prof. psychology U. Tex., 1987-93; dir. psychol. svcs. CPC Capital Hosp., Austin, 1987-93, Shoal Creek Hosp., Austin, 1994-99; allied profl. staff Aspen Valley Hosp., 2000—. Trustee Austin-Travis County Mental Health-Mental Retardation Center, 1978-80. Fellow APA (bd. dirs. divsn. psychoanalysis, 1999-2000, membership chmn. 1997-2000, bd. mem. at large 1999-2000, treas. 2003-05), Acad. Psychoanalytic Psychology; mem. Colo. Psychol. Assn. (bd. dirs. 2005-06, pres.-elect 2006), Austin Soc. for Psychoanalytic Psychology (pres. 1994-95), Denver Psychoanalytic Soc. Office: Ste 200 106 S Mill St Aspen CO 81611 Mailing: PO Box 7976 Aspen CO 81612 E-mail: mmanosev@earthlink.net.

**MANOWITZ, PAUL,** biochemist, researcher, educator; b. Monticello, NY, Dec. 13, 1940; s. Jacob M. and Rose (Levine) M.; m. Joyce L. Swartz, June 16, 1968; children: Neal J., Lauren H. BA in Chemistry with honors, Cornell U., 1962; PhD in Biochemistry, Brandeis U., 1967. Fellow NYU Sch. Medicine, 1967-70, instr., 1970-72; asst. prof. psychiatry U. Medicine and Dentistry N.J. Robert Wood Johnson Med. Sch., Piscataway, 1972-78, assoc. prof. psychiatry, 1978-96, prof. psychiatry, 1996—. Rsch. cons. VA Med. Ctr., Lyons, N.J., 1987—. Mem. editl. bd. Jour. of Studies on Alcohol, 1993—2003; contbr. articles to profl. jours. Mem. AAAS, Internat. Soc. for Biomed. Rsch. on Alcoholism, Am. Soc. Human Genetics, Am. Soc. Neurochemistry, Soc. Biol. Psychiatry, Rsch. Soc. on Alcoholism. Home: 7 Guernsey Ln East Brunswick NJ 08816-3506 Office: U Medicine and Dentistry NJ Robert Wood Johnson Med Sch 671 Hoes Ln Piscataway NJ 08854-5627 Office Phone: 732-235-4347.

**MANRIQUE, JUSTO RAFAEL,** economist, educator; s. Justo Liberio and Renee Pilar (Gutierrez) Manrique; m. Luz Liliana Torres, June 11, 1980; children: Justo Luis, Daniel Antonio, Carlos Javier. BS in Econs., Nat. Agrarian U., Lima, Peru, 1980; MSc in Agrl. Econs., Iowa State U., Ames, 1988, PhD. in Agrl. Econs., 1992. Chair St. Louis U. Madrid Campus, Madrid, 1995—2001; asst. prof. econs. U. Houston - Downtown, 2002—06, asst. chair, 2004—. Recipient McGraw Hill/Irwin Disting. Paper award, 2005, Allied Acads. Disting. Rsch. award, 2005; Organized Rsch. grantee, U. Houston - Downtown, 2003 -2004. Mem.: Acad. of Internat. Bus. US SW Chpt. Office: Univf Houston - Downtown One Main Street Suite 1007-N Houston TX 77002-1001 Office Phone: 713-221-8209. Office Fax: 713-226-5238. E-mail: manriquej@uhd.edu.

**MANSAGER, ERIK DONN,** adolescent counselor; b. Montevideo, Minn., Feb. 19, 1955; s. DeWane Earle and Wynona Mary (Tucker) M.; m. Helen Adams, Nov. 1, 1980; children: Ryan Adam, Alyssa Drew. BA, St. Thomas Theol. Sem., 1977; MA, U. Ariz., 1981. Human svc. specialist State Ariz. Dept. Econ. Security, Casa Grande, 1978-81, supr. Coolidge, 1983-86, trainer Phoenix, 1984-90, child sexual abuse prevention specialist, 1986-88; teaching parent Children's Behavioral Services, Las Vegas, Nev., 1981-83; jud. supervision program mgr. Casa de los Ninos Crisis Shelter, Tucson, 1988-89; asst. dir. Casade los Ninos Crisis Shelter, 1989-90; adolescent substance abuse counselor Sci. Applications Internat. Co., Germany, 1990-91, adolescent substance abuse clin. supr., 1991—. Cons. Gila River Indian Community, Sacaton, Ariz., 1985-89. Author: Team Staffings, 1987. Co-chmn. Youth Issues Council, Coolidge, 1985-86. Mem. Am.'s Inst. Adlerian Studies (cert. profl. studies), N. Am. Soc. Adlerian Psychology, Adlerian Soc. Ariz. (pres. 1987-88, editor newletter 1986-90). Democrat. Roman Catholic. Avocations: profl. guitarist, teaching, sch. writings, theol./psychol. studies. Home: Auf der Warte 19 6367 Karben Germany

**MANSBACH, CHARLES,** gastroenterologist, researcher; b. Norfolk, Va., Aug. 21, 1937; m. May Lynn Mansbach; 1 child, Johnathan. BA, Yale U., New Haven, Conn., 1963; MD, NYU, N.Y.C., 1963. Lic. internal medicine Am. Bd. of Internal Medicine, gastroenterology Am. Bd. of Internal Medicine. Assoc. prof. of medicine Duke U. Med. Ctr., Durham, NC, 1970—86; prof. of medicine and physiology U. of Tenn., Memphis, 1986—. Lt. cdr. USNR, 1968—70. Recipient Rsch. award, NIH, 1975—2001, Merit Rev. grant, VA, 1971—2006. Achievements include research in Identified the pre-chylomicron transport vesicle. Office: Univ Tenn Ste 240 920 Madison Ave Memphis TN 38163 Office Phone: 901-448-5813. Business E-Mail: cmansbach@utmem.edu.

**MANSBERGER, ARLIE ROLAND, JR.,** surgeon; b. Pitts., Oct. 13, 1922; s. Arlie Rol and Mayme (Smith) M.; m. Anna Ellen Piel, July 27, 1946; children— Ellen Lynn, John Arlie, Leigh Ann. BA, Western Md. Coll., 1943, D.Sc. (hon.), 1947; MD, U. Md., 1947, D.Sc. (hon.), 1978. Diplomate: Am. Bd. Surgery (dir., vice chmn.). Intern U. Md. Hosp., 1947-49, resident in surgery, 1949-54; chief wound shock br. biophysics div. Army Chem. Center, 1954-56; instr. surgery U. Md., 1956-59, asst. prof., 1959-61, assoc. prof., 1961-69, prof. surgery, 1969-73; clin. dir. shock-trauma unit, 1962-73; prof. surgery, chmn. dept. Med. Coll. Ga., Augusta, 1973-91; prof. surgery emeritus, chmn., 1991—. Cons. surgeon Dwight David Eisenhower Army Med. Center, VA Hosp. Editor: Essence of General Surgery, 1975; chmn. editorial bd.: Bull. U. Md, 1971-73; editor-in-chief: The Am. Surgeon, 1973-89; surg. editor: Resident and Staff Physician, 1979-91; contbr. articles to profl. jours., chpts. to books. Trustee Western Md. Coll., 1971—, med. Research Found. Ga., 1973-91; bd. dirs. Nicholas J. Pisican Found., 1993—. Served to col. U.S. Army, 1943-46, 54-56. Recipient Man of Yr. award U. Md., 1970, 72, Golden Apple teaching award U. Md., 1968, 72, Disting. Faculty award Med. Coll. Ga., 1979, Gold Medal Alumni award U. Md., 1989, Disting. Svc. award (medal) Southeastern Surg. Congress, 1990. Fellow A.C.S. (gov.); mem. Am. Surg. Assn., Soc. Univ. Surgeons, So. Surg. Assn., Soc. Internationale de Chirurgie, Am. Assn. Surgery of Trauma, Southeastern Surg. Congress, Soc. Surgery of Alimentary Tract, AMA, Soc. Consultants to Armed Forces, Med. Assn. Ga. (editorial bd. 1987-92), Am. Bd. Family

Practice (bd. dirs. 1987-92), 29th Div. Assn., Alpha Omega Alpha (Tchg. award 2001). Episcopalian. Home: One 7th St Unit 1502 Augusta GA 30901-1343 Office: Dept Surgery Med Coll Ga Augusta GA 30912 E-mail: ellenmansberger@aol.com.

**MANSBERY, SARAH HUNTSMAN,** music educator; b. Wilmington, N.C., Dec. 26, 1979; d. John Robert and Rebecca Gallagher Huntsman; m. Ryan Thomas Mansbery, June 16, 2001. MB, U. N.C., 2001; MusM, Ill. State U., 2003. Cert. music therapist. Music educator Carolina Beach Elem. Sch. Wilmington, NC, 2004—; music therapist Wilmington, NC, 2004—. Mem.: Am. Music Therapy Assn., Music Educators Nat. Conf., Alpha Xi Delta. Methodist. Office: Carolina Beach Elem Sch 400 S Fourth St Carolina Beach NC 28428 Home: 7021 Farrington Farms Dr Wilmington NC 28411 E-mail: smansber@nhcs.k12.nc.us.

**MANSBRIDGE, JANE JEBB,** political scientist, educator; b. N.Y.C., Nov. 19, 1939; d. Ronald and Georgia St. Claire (Mullen) Mansbridge; m. Christopher Jencks; 1 child, Nathaniel Mansbridge Jencks. BA, Wellesley Coll., 1961; MA, Harvard U., 1966, PhD, 1971. Asst. prof. polit. sci. U. Chgo., 1973-80; assoc. prof. Northwestern U., Evanston, Ill., 1980-86, prof. polit. sci., 1986-91, Jane W. Long prof. arts and scis., 1991-96; prof. J.F. Kennedy Sch. Govt. Harvard U., 1996-98, Adams prof. polit. leadership and democratic values, 1998—. Author: Beyond Adversary Democracy, 1980, Why We Lost the ERA, 1986; editor: Beyond Self-Interest, 1990; editor: (with Susan M. Okin) Feminism 2 vols., 1994; editor: (with Aidon Morris) Oppositional Consciousness, 2001; mem. editorial bd. Signs, Jour. Polit. Philosophy. Russell Sage Found. scholar, 1991-92; fellow Inst. for Advanced Study, 1985-86, Rockefeller Humanities, 1982-83, NSF, 1971-72, Ctr. Advanced Study in the Behavioral Scis., 1997-98, 2001-02, Radcliffe medal Radcliffe Grad. Soc., 2004; fellowship Radcliffe Inst. Advanced Study, 2004-05. Mem. Am. Acad. Arts and Scis., Am. Polit. Sci. Assn. (v.p 1992-93, program chair 1990, exec. com. 1987-89, coun. 1987-89, pres. Women's Caucus 1996, Schuck award 1988, Kammerer award 1987), Soc. Advancement of Socio-Econs. (pres. 1992-93), Internat. Polit. Psychology Assn. (governing coun. 1993-94). Office: JF Kennedy Sch Govt 79 JFK St Cambridge MA 02138-5801 Office Phone: 617-495-9343.

**MANSELL, DARREL LEE, JR.,** language educator; b. Canton, Ohio, Apr. 9, 1934; s. Darrel Lee and Virginia (Shepherd) M.; m. Elizabeth Meihack, Jan. 1957 (div. July 1970); 1 child, Benjamin Lloyd; m. Adriana Saviane, July 16, 1983. BA, Oberlin Coll., 1956; student, Oxford U., 1961—62; PhD, Yale U., 1963; MA (hon.), Dartmouth Coll., 1975. Instr. Dartmouth Coll., Hanover, NH, 1962-64, asst. prof., 1964-68, assoc. prof., 1968-74, prof., 1974-99, prof. emeritus, 1999—. Author: The Novels of Jane Austen, 1973; contbr. articles to scholarly jours. Mem.: Jane Austen Soc. N.Am. (founding patron), Phi Beta Kappa. Home: 2 Dana Rd Hanover NH 03755-2227 Office: Dartmouth Coll Dept English Hanover NH 03755

**MANSELL, HENRY J.,** archbishop; b. NYC, Oct. 10, 1937; Student, Cathedral Coll., St. Joseph's Sem. and Coll., N.Am. Coll., Gregorian U.; BA, St. Joseph Sem., Yonkers, 1959; Lic. Sacred Theology, Gregorian U., Rome, 1963; postgrad., Catholic U. Am., 1965. Ordained priest, NY, 1962; parish priest in various parishes NYC & Westchester County; auxiliary bishop Archdiocese of NY, 1992—95; titular bishop Marazanae, NYC, 1993-95; bishop Diocese of Buffalo, NY, 1995—2003; archbishop Archdiocese of Hartford, Conn., 2003—. Dir. Office of Parish Councils, 1972. Office: Archdiocese of Hartford 134 Farmington Ave Hartford CT 06105-3784

**MANSELL, JOYCE MARILYN,** retired special education educator; b. Minot, N.D., Dec. 17, 1934; d. Einar Axel and Gladys Ellen (Wall) Alm; m. Dudley J. Mansell, Oct. 31, 1954; children: Michael, Debra Mansell Richards. BS, U. Houston, 1968; MEd, Sam Houston State U., 1980. Cert. provisional elem. tchr. 1-8, provisional mentally retarded tchr., provisional lang. and/or learning disabilities tchr., provisional prof. elem. tchr. gen. 1-9, reading specialist. From 1st grade tchr. to 3rd grade tchr. Johnson Elem. Sch., 1968-77; spl. edn. tchr. mentally retarded/learning disabled Meml. Parkway Jr. HS, 1982-86, Waller Mid. Sch., 1986-90; spl. edn. tchr. mentally retarded Royal Mid. Sch., Tex., 1990-95, Royal HS, 1995-96; ret., 1996. Tchr. Am. sign lang. for retarded students in pub. schs. Lutheran. Avocations: painting, bridge, reading, fishing, travel. Home: 2155 Paso Rello Dr Houston TX 77077-5622 Personal E-mail: dmansell@hal-pc.org.

**MANSELL, JUSTIN DENNIS,** optical engineer, consultant; b. LA, Oct. 21, 1973; s. Dennis Mansell and Mary Lou Dowling; m. Tahmina Rahman Mansell, Mar. 21, 2004; 1 child, Rhianna Jada. PhD in Elec. Engring., Stanford U., Calif., 2002. Intern Sandia Nat. Labs., Albuquerque, 1993—96, NASA Glenn Rsch. Ctr., Ohio Aerospace Inst., Cleve., 1993—94; rsch. asst. Stanford U., Robert L. Byer's Rsch. Group, 1996—2002; engring. cons. Wavefront Sciences Corp., Albuquerque, 1996—99; founder, v.p., chief tech. officer AgilOptics, Inc. (formerly Intellite, Inc.), 2000—02; pres., founder Mansell & Assocs., LLC, 2002—06; chief engr. Qynergy Corp., 2002—03; v.p., chief tech. officer MZA Assocs. Corp., 2004—; pres., founder Active Optical Sys., LLC, 2005—. Contbr. articles to profl. jours. Pres. N.Mex Gymnastics Judges Assn., Albuquerque, 2003—05. Mem.: SPIE (assoc.), IEEE (assoc.), USA Gymnasics (assoc.), Optical Soc. Am. (assoc.). Achievements include patents for automated pupil remapping with binary optics; silicon micromachined deformable mirror; apparatus and method for evaluating a target larger than a measuring aperture of a sensor; sub-lens spatial resolution Shack-Hartmann wavefront sensing; patents pending for new concepts in advanced optics. Avocation: gymnastics coach. Office: Active Optical Systems LLC 2021 Girard Ste 150 Albuquerque NM 87106 Office Phone: 505-245-9970 184. Personal E-mail: jmansell@mansellassociates.com. Business E-Mail: jmansell@aos-llc.com.

**MANSELL, KEVIN B.,** retail executive; b. St. Louis; Student, U. Mo. Joined Venture Store divsn. May Dept. Stores, 1975, positions in merchandising and buying; divsn. merchandise mgr. Kohl's Corp., Menomonee Falls, Wis., 1982—87, named gen. merchandise mgr., 1987, sr. exec. v.p. merchandising and mktg., 1998—99, pres., 1999—, also bd. dirs, 1999—. Office: Kohl's Corp N56 W17000 Ridgewood Dr Menomonee Falls WI 53051*

**MANSFIELD, CHRISTOPHER CHARLES,** lawyer; b. 1950; m. Laura Mansfield; children: Carolyn, Brendan. BA in economics, Boston Coll., 1972, JD, 1975. Bar: Mass. 1975. With Liberty Mut. Ins. Co., Boston, 1975—, assoc. gen. counsel, 1981—83, v.p., gen. counsel, 1985—88, sr. v.p., gen. counsel, 1988—, bd. dirs. Employers Ins. Co., Wausau, New Eng. Legal Found.; bd. overseers RAND Corp. Inst. Civil Justice. Trustee Trust Fund Commn., Dedham, Mass.; bd. dirs. Pine St. Inn, Boston. Office: Liberty Mut Ins Co PO Box 140 175 Berkeley St Boston MA 02117-5066

**MANSFIELD, EDWARD PATRICK, JR.,** advertising executive; b. Warren, Pa., Oct. 29, 1947; s. Edward Patrick and Frieda (Dahler) M.; m. Norma L. Johnson, Apr. 17, 1971. AS in Acctg., Jamestown Bus. Coll., 1967; BS in Mktg. Advt., Myers U., 1970. Promotion mgr., ad dir. The News-Herald, Lake County, Ohio, 1973-77; dir. advt. The Eagle, Butler, Pa., 1977-78; dir. mktg. Baltimore Mag., 1978-79; asst. to The Washingtonian, Washington, 1979—. Founder, chmn. Warm-A-Heart Fund, 1988—; bd. dirs. Columbia Lighthouse for the Blind, 1988—, chmn., 1988-93; bd. dirs. The Lighthouse. Avocations: amateur radio, boating. Home: 347 Cottswold Pl Riva MD 21140-1528 Office: Washingtonian Mag 1828 L St NW Ste 200 Washington DC 20036-5169 Office Phone: 202-296-1246, 202-296-3600. Business E-Mail: emansfield@washingtonian.com.

**MANSFIELD, GORDON HALL,** federal agency administrator; BA, Villanova U., 1964; JD, U. Miami, 1976. Commd. U.S. Army, 1964, co. comdr. 101st Airborne Divsn. Vietnam; lawyer Ocala, Fla.; various positions including assoc. exec. dir. govt. rels. Paralyzed Vets. Am., 1981—89, exec. dir. Washington, 1993—2001; asst. sec. fair housing and equal opportunity U.S. Dept. Housing and Urban Devel., 1989—93; asst. sec. congl. and legis. affairs

U.S. Dept. Vets. Affairs, Washington, 2001—04, dep. sec., 2004—. Decorated Bronze Star, Purple Heart (2), Combat Infantryman's badge, Presdl. Unit Citation. Office: US Dept Vets Affairs 810 Vermont Ave NW Rm 1004 Washington DC 20420

**MANSFIELD, JAMES E.,** marketing professional, consultant; b. Phila., Feb. 15, 1973; s. James E. and Mary T. M.; m. Heather L. Creps, Sept. 9, 2000. BS in Biology, Villanova U., 1994; MBA, U. Chgo., 1999. Mktg. rep. Johnson & Johnson/Janssen Pharms., Titusville, N.J., 1995-96, sales rep. Chgo., 1996-97, hosp. specialist, 1997-98; mgr. Knoll Pharm., Chgo., 1998-99; dir., client mgmt. IMS Health, Chgo., 1999—. Bd. dirs. Am. Cancer Soc., 1996-99. E-mail: jmansfield@us.imshealth.com.

**MANSFIELD, JOHN H.,** law educator; b. Morristown, NJ, Oct. 12, 1928; AB in History, Harvard U., 1952, LLB, 1956. Bar: Calif. 1956, Mass. 1962. Law clk. to Justice Roger Traynor Calif. Supreme Ct., 1956—57; law. clk. to Justice Felix Frankfurter US Supreme Ct., 1957—58; asst. prof. law Harvard Law Sch., Cambridge, Mass., 1958—61, prof., 1961—, John H. Watson, Jr. prof. law, 1985—. Co-editor (with Weinstein, Abrams and Berger): Evidence: cases and materials, 1997; author: Personal Laws in India, 2001. Mem.: Assn. for Asian Studies. Office: Harvard Law Sch 1563 Massachusetts Ave Cambridge MA 02138 Office Phone: 617-495-3141. Office Fax: 617-496-4913. Business E-Mail: jmans@law.harvard.edu.

**MANSFIELD, KAREN LEE,** lawyer; b. Chgo., Mar. 17, 1942; d. Ralph and Hilda (Blum) Mansfield; children: Nicole Rafaela, Lori Michele. BA in Polit. Sci., Roosevelt U., 1963; JD, DePaul U., 1971; student U. Chgo., 1959-60. Bar: Ill. 1972, U.S. Dist. Ct. (no. dist.) Ill. 1972. Legis. intern Ill. State Senate, Springfield, 1966-67; tchr. Chgo. Pub. Schs., 1967-70; asst. CNA Ins., Chgo., 1971-73; law clk. Ill. Apellate Ct., Chgo., 1973-75; sr. trial atty. U.S. Dept. Labor, Chgo., 1975—, mentor Adopt-a-Sch. Program, 1992-95. Contbr. articles to profl. jours. Vol. Big Sister, 1975-81; bd. dirs. Altgeld Nursery Sch., 1963-66, Ill. div. UN Assn., 1966-72, Hull House Jane Addams Ctr., 1977-82, Broadway Children's Ctr., 1986-90, Acorn Family Entertainment, 1993-95; active Oak Park Farmers' Market Commn., 1996-2002; rsch. asst. Citizens for Gov. Otto Kerner, Chgo., 1964-70; del. Nat. Conf. on Status of Women, Chgo., 1964-70; del. Nat. Conf. on Status of Women, 1968; candidate for del. Ill. Constl. Conv., 1969. Mem. Chgo. Council Lawyers, Women's Bar Assn. Ill., Lawyer Pilots Bar Assn., Fed. Bar Assn. Unitarian. Clubs: Friends of Gamelan (performer), 99's Internat. Orgn. Women Pilots (legis. chmn. Chgo. area chpt. 1983-86, legis. chmn Nat. Cen. sect. 1986-88, legis. award 1983, 85). Home: 204 S Taylor Ave Oak Park IL 60302-3307 Office: US Dept Labor Office Solicitor 230 S Dearborn St Fl 8 Chicago IL 60604-1505

**MANSFIELD, WILLIAM L.,** manufacturing executive; BS, Drexel Univ.; MBA, Lehigh Univ. Mgmt. positions through v.p. Valspar Corp., Mpls., 1977—91, v.p. packaging & coatings, 1991—98, sr. v.p. packaging & indsl. coatings, 1998—2000, sr. v.p. arch., automotive, specialty & packaging coatings, 2000—02, exec. v.p., 2002—04, exec. v.p., COO, 2004—05, pres., CEO, 2005—. Office: Valspar Corp 1101 3d St S Minneapolis MN 55415*

**MANSI, JOSEPH ANNEILLO,** public relations company executive; b. Oct. 8, 1935; s. Joseph C. and Vinnie (Chirico) M.; m. Mary P. Fusco, Aug. 1, 1959; children: Karen M. D'Attore, Joanne V. Dimenna. BS, NYU, 1957. Newsman Internat. News Service, UPI, 1953-58; mem. pub. relations staff Lawrence Orgn., N.Y.C., 1960-63; acct. supr. Philip Lesly Co., N.Y.C., 1963-67; dir. corp. communications Ward Foods, Inc., N.Y.C., 1967-72; dir. pub. relations Metromedia Inc., N.Y.C., 1973-75; pres. Corp. Relations Network, Inc., N.Y.C., 1975-80; mng. ptnr. KCSA Pub. Rels. Worldwide, N.Y.C., 1980—. Served with AUS, 1958-60. Mem. Pub. Rels. Soc. Am. (accredited). Home: 10 Beatrice Ln Glen Cove NY 11542-1202 Office: KCSA Pub Rels Worldwide 800 2nd Ave New York NY 10017-4709 Office Phone: 212-896-1205. Personal E-mail: jmansi@kcsa.com.

**MANSKE, ROBERT C.,** physical therapist, educator; b. Topeka, Kans., Sept. 16, 1966; s. Robert Warren and Judith Lynn (Kimbell) Manske; m. Julia Oler, Jan. 25, 1992; children: Rachael Elizabeth, Halle Grace. B in Phys. Edn., Wichita State U., Kans., 1991, M in Phys. Therapy, 1994, EdM, 2000. Cert. athletic trainer, nat. strength and conditioning cert. Mem. staff Via Christi Regional Med. Ctr., Wichita, 1994—97, mem. staff phys. therapy dept., 1998—; mem. staff Gundersen Luth. Sports Medicine, LaCrosse, Wis., 1997—98; mem. staff dept. phys. therapy Wichita State U., 1998—. Contbr. articles to profl. jours. Mem.: Nat. Strength and Conditioning Assn., Nat. Athletic Trainers Assn., Kans. Phys. Therapy Assn. (chair rsch. com., Instr. of Yr. 2003), Am. Phys. Therapy Assn. (bd. spity. cert. 2002), Alpha Eta. Office: Wichita State U Dept Phys Therapy 1845 N Fairmount Wichita KS 67260 Home: 2623 Keywest Ct Wichita KS 67204 Office Phone: 316-978-3702. E-mail: robert.manske@wichita.edu.

**MANSNERUS, LAURA,** news correspondent; Staff writer NY Times, editor Week in Review, corr. Trenton Bur. Office: NY Times Trenton Bur PO Box 021 Trenton NJ 08625-0021 also: NJ State House 125 W State St Trenton NJ 08625-0021*

**MANSON, ANNE,** music director; Grad., Harvard U.; postgrad., King's Coll., London, Royal Coll. Music, Royal Northern Coll. Music; studied with Norman Del Mar, James Lockhart. Music dir. Kansas City (Mo.) Symphony, 1998—. Condr. Mecklenburgh Opera, 1991, Endymion Ensemble, 1992-93, London Mozart Players, 1993-94, BBC Scottish Symphony and Iceland Symphony Orch., 1994-95, Northern Sinfonia, Resedentie Orch. in The Hague, Ensemble Inter Contemporain, Paris, 1996-97, Bournemouth Symphony Orch., Royal Scottish Nat. Orch., 1997-98. Dir. operas The Emperor of Atlantis, Die Weisse Rose, Manekiny, Hansel and Gretel, Marriage of Figaro, Cosi fan Tutte, The Magic Flute, Il Combattimento, Echoes, Royal Opera House, Don Pasquale, Don Giovanni, English Touring Opera, House of the Dead, Salzburg Festival, Lohengrin, Blood Wedding, 1992-93, Petrified, The Place Theatre, London, 1992, Brundibar, Queen Elizabeth Hall, London, 1993, Craig's Progress, 1994, Boris Godunov, Vienna State Opera, 1994, Vanessa, 1994-95, Rise and Fall of the City of Mahagonny, Netherlands Touring Opera, 1996, Dangerous Liaisons, Washington Opera, 1997, Voices, Berlin Biennale, 1997-98. Marshall scholar Royal Coll. Music; Conducting fellow Royal Northern Coll. Music.

**MANSON, JOANN ELISABETH,** endocrinologist; b. Cleve., Apr. 14, 1953; d. S. Stanford and Therese (Palay) M.; m. Christopher N. Ames, June 12, 1979; children: Jennifer, Jeffrey, Joshua Simon. AB magna cum laude, Harvard U., 1975; MD, Case Western Res. U., 1979; MPH, Harvard Sch. Pub. Health, 1984, DPH, 1987. Bd. cert. internal medicine; bd. cert. in subspecialty of endocrinology and metabolism. Intern and resident internal medicine NEDH, Harvard Med. Sch., Boston, 1979-82; fellowship in endocrinology U. Hosp. Boston, Mass., 1982-84; rsch fellow in medicine Brigham and Women's Hosp., Boston, 1984-87, Andrew W. Mellon Found. fellow, 1987-89, dir. endocrinology, co-dir. women's health divsn. preventive medicine, 1993—, chief divsn. preventive medicine, 1999—; staff physician, consulting endocrinologist Harvard Vanguard Med. Assocs., Peabody, Mass., 1986—2003; prof. medicine Harvard Med. Sch., Boston, 1999—, Elizabeth Brigham prof. women's health, 2003—. Mem. editl. bd.: Jour. Women's Health, 1996—, Menopause, 2004—; contbr. chapters to books, more than 500 articles to profl. jours.; author, editor: several books and textbooks. Vol. physician Lynn (Mass.) Shelter for the Homeless, 1989-93; med. adv. bd. Harvard Health Letter, Boston, 1992—, Greater Boston (Mass.) Diabetes Soc., 1993—, Harvard Women's Health Watch, Boston, 1993—; vol. Am. Heart Assn., 1994—. Named Hero in Women's Health, Am. Health for Women Mag., 1997, one of Top 10 Champions of Women's Health, Ladies Home Jour., 2000, one of Top Docs for Women, Boston mag., 2001; recipient Connors award for outstanding leadership in women's health, 1999-, Woman in Sci. award, Am. Med. Women's Assoc., 2003, Henry I. Bowditch award for excellence in pub. health Mass. Med. Soc., 2002. Fellow ACP, ACE; mem. AMA, Am. Med. Women's Assn., Am. Heart Assn., Am. Diabetes Assn.,

Women's Health Initiative (mem. steering com.), Assn. Am. Physicians, Alpha Omega Alpha. Avocations: reading, hiking, music, travel. Home: 14 Washington St Beverly MA 01915-5820 Office: Brigham and Women's Hosp 900 Commonwealth Ave E Fl 3 Boston MA 02215-1204 Office Phone: 617-278-0871. Business E-Mail: jmanson@rics.bwh.harvard.edu.

**MANSON, JOSEPH LLOYD, III,** lawyer; b. Richmond, Va., May 5, 1949; s. Joseph Lloyd Jr. and Nan Smith (Copley) M.; divorced; children: Martha Stuart, Joseph Scott, Rachel Smith. BS, U. Va., 1970; JD, Emory U., 1974. Assoc. Verner, Liipfert, Bernhard & McPherson, Washington, 1974—80; ptnr. Verner, Liipfert, Bernhard, McPherson & Hand, 1981—2002, co-chmn. exec. com., 1998—2001; ptnr. Piper, Rudnick, 2002—05, Baker & Hostetler, 2005—. Pres., CEO, bd. dirs. Barrow Grocery Co., DBM Group; mem. internat. bd. advisors Thailand Creative and Design Ctr. Founder Alexandria Youth Sports Found., 1993, Emory U. Law Sch. Coun.; bd. dirs. Mesa Air Group; trustee St. Stephens and St. Agnes Sch. Found. 2d lt. U.S. Army, 1973. Mem. ABA (ry. and airline labor law com., co-chmn. mgmt. 1993-94), D.C. Bar Assn. Republican. Episcopalian. Avocations: music, tennis, theater, movies. Office: Baker & Hostetler 1050 Connecticut Ave NW Washington DC 20036 Office Phone: 202-861-1543. Business E-Mail: jmanson@bakerlaw.com.

**MANSON, LEWIS AUMAN,** energy executive; b. Cleve., July 12, 1918; s. Lewis Frederick and Ina Josephine (Auman) Manson; m. Shirley Anne Traeger, Jan. 27, 1982; children: Lewis, Jean, Phillip, Edward, Anita. Student, Gen. Motors Tech. U., 1943-44, Purdue U., 1942-43, Rice U., 1950-54. Cons. numerous oil, gas, and mining cos., 1951-57; cons. The Space Agy., Washington, 1958-59, Douglas Aircraft, El Segundo, Calif., 1964; dir. Copper Range Mines, Wyo., 1965; dir. explorations, cons. Nico Internat., S.A. de C V., Mex., 1968 71; builder Spring, Tex., 1971-74; dir. conductor explorations Minerals of the Sun, S.A. de C.V., Honduras, 1975; dir. Asheville Petroleum Corp., Ill., 1976; conductor explorations Neozoic Minerals & Petroleum, Ltd., Colo., N.Mex., Tex., 1976-77; conductor explorations, dir. Primal Energy Rsch. Found., Houston, 1982—. Pres. Transzoic Orebody Locators, Ltd., Vancouver, BC, Pleiades Petroleum Corp., Lexington, Tenn., Houston; pres., bd. dirs. Neozoic Geophys. Survey, Ltd., 1999; lectr. grade schs., HS, Kiwanis, and Rotary, 1962—. Author: The Discovery of the Primal Energy Transverter, 1966, Birth of the Moon, 1978, Origins of Solar Flares and Keys to Predicting Them, 1978, Automatic Recording of Deep Space (interplanetary) Gravity, 1978, Arriving Ionospheric High Energy (Solar Generated), 1978, Out of the Grey Mist, 1992, Life's Continuum, 1992, The Real Origin of Stellar Energy, 1993, The Great Mystery, 1994, Why the Earth Quakes, 2003; patentee in field. Scoutmaster Boy Scouts Am., Houston, 1956—63; cubmaster Cub Scouts, Pasadena, Calif., 1962. With Ind. N.G., 1942—43. Republican. Achievements include patents in field; developed and placed in service new equipment, The Affinity System, that indicates petroleum or gas from the surface to any depth and defines if commercial quality. Avocations: mountain climbing, boating, archaeology, woodworking. Office: Primal Energy Rsch Found 31 Rush Haven Dr The Woodlands TX 77381-3227 also: Neozoic Geophysical Survey Ltd 31 Rush Haven Dr The Woodlands TX 77381 Office Phone: 281-419-0446. Personal E-mail: manson.a7311@sbcglobal.net.

**MANSON, MARILYN (BRIAN HUGH WARNER),** musician; b. Canton, OH, Jan. 5, 1969; s. Hugh and Barbara Warner; m. Dita Von Teese, Dec. 3, 2005. Music journalist, 1987—89; co-founded band Marilyn Manson & the Spooky Kids, 1989; band signed to Nothing Records as Marilyn Manson, 1992. Founder art movement Celebritarian Corp., 1996. Performer: (albums) Portrait of an American Family, 1994, Smells Like Children, 1995, Antichrist Superstar, 1996, Remix & Repent, 1997, Mechanical Animals, 1998, The Last Tour on Earth, 1999, Holy Wood (In the Shadow of the Valley of Death), 2000, The Golden Age of Grotesque, 2003, Lest We Forget, 2004, (songs) Sweet Dreams, 1995, The Beautiful People, 1996 (one of 100 Greatest Videos Ever Made, MTV, 1999), Tourniquet, 1997, The Dope Show, 1998 (Rolling Stone Best Video of Yr., Billboard Maximum Vision award, 1998), Rock is Dead, 1999, I Don't Like the Drugs (but the Drugs Like Me), 1999, Disposable Teens, 2000, The Fight Song, 2001, The Nobodies, 2001, Tainted Love, 2002, mOBSCENE, 2003, This is the New Shit, 2003, Personal Jesus, 2004; composer: WWF Smackdown! theme song, 2001—; co-author: (autobiography) The Long Hard Road Out of Hell, 1998; contbr.: film soundtracks From Hell, 2001, The Matrix, 1999, Book of Shadows: Blair Witch 2, 2000, Resident Evil, 2002, Queen of the Damned, 2002, Bowling for Columbine, 2002; actor: (films) Lost Highway, 1997, Jawbreaker, 1998, Party Monster, 2003, The Heart is Deceitful Above All Things, 2004, Rise, 2005, Living Neon Dreams, 2005, (video games) Area 51 (voice only), 2005; actor, dir., exec. prodr. (films) Doppelherz, 2003. Rev. Church of Satan, 1994. Nominee 3 Grammy Awards, 5 MTV Video Music awards; named one of 100 Greatest Artists of Hard Rock, VH1, 2000; recipient 4 S. Fla. Slammies. Avocations: painting, writing. Office: Nothing Records 635 W Lakeside Ave Cleveland OH 44113 also: Interscope Geffen A&M Records 2220 Colorado Ave Santa Monica CA 90404*

**MANSON, PAUL NELLIS,** plastic surgeon; b. Kansas City, Mo., Dec. 28, 1943; s. Emanuel and Alice Winifred (Olson) M.; m. Kathryn Garland, 1968; children: Ted, Jenner. BA in Chemistry, Northwestern U., 1965, MD, 1968. Prof., chmn. plastic surgery Johns Hopkins Sch. Medicine, Balt., 1990—. Maj. U.S. Army, 1970-73. Republican. Presbyterian. Office: 8152 F McElderry Wing 601 N Caroline St Baltimore MD 21287-0981 Office Phone: 410-955-9469.

**MANSON, ZYNORA DAVIS,** music educator, minister; b. Richmond, Va., Sept. 9, 1954; d. Henry and Ada Ellis Davis; m. Isaiah Jacob Manson, Aug. 8, 1993; children: Elizabeth Nicole, Chenaniah Jacob, Lateisha Rene', Isaiah Jacob Jr. BS in Music Edn., Norfolk State U., 1979. Profl. collegiate cert. Va., 1979. Sec. Henrico County Govt., Richmond, Va., 1977—??, 1st music Fairfax County Pub. Schs., 1979—86, Henrico County Pub. Schs., Richmond, 1986—. Composer: (music book and music cd's) Catch Zynora's SOL Songs. Pastor Bethany Bapt. Ch., Sandston, Va., 1996—2005. Finalist Tchr. award of Excellence, REB, 2005; named Jacob L. Adams Tchr. of Yr., 1991, 1992, Henrico Music Educator of Yr., 2002; recipient Telly award, Henrico County Pub. Schs., Channel 36, 2001, Disting. Communicator award, Channel 36, Henrico County, 2001. Mem.: Va. Music Educators Assn. (assoc.). Democrat. Baptist. Avocations: walking, travel, skating. Home: 1070 Nash Rd Sandston VA 23150 Office: Prophetic Full Tone Praise Ministries In 1070 Nash Rd Sandston VA 23150 Office Phone: 804-737-7042. Office Fax: 804-737-7042. Personal E-mail: pftpm@aol.com.

**MANSOUR, GEORGE P.,** Spanish language and literature educator; b. Huntington, W.Va., Sept. 4, 1939; s. Elia and Marie (Jarrah) M.; m. Mary Ann Rogers, Dec. 27, 1961; children: Alicia, Philip. AB, Marshall U., 1961; MA, Mich. State U., 1963, PhD, 1965. Assoc. prof. Mich. State U., East Lansing, 1968-77, prof., 1977—, chmn. dept. Romance and Classical langs., 1982—. Cons. Mich. Dept. Edn., Lansing, 1984-85. Contbr. articles to profl. jours., including Hispania, Revista de estudias, hispanicos, also chpts. to books. Mem. Am. Assn. Tchrs. Spanish and Portuguese (v.p. 1969-71), Mich. Fgn. Lang. Assn. (pres. 1982-84). Democrat. Mem. Eastern Orthodox Ch. Avocations: pysanky, golf. Home: 1303 Lucerne Dr Dewitt MI 48820-9528 Office: Mich State U Dept Romance & Classical Langs East Lansing MI 48824 Office Phone: 517-285-1487. Personal E-mail: mansour1515@yahoo.com.

**MANSOUR, KAMAL A.,** cardiothoracic surgeon; b. Nov. 25, 1929; m. Sylvia Cleopatra Sideros, June 19, 1956; 1 child, Sylvia Frederica. M.B., B.Ch., Ein Shams U., Cairo, Egypt, 1954. Diplomate Am. Bd. Surgery, Am. Bd. Thoracic Surgery; lic. physician, Ga. Intern Tanta (Egypt) Gen. Hosp., 1954-55; surgeon Bapt. Hosp., Ajlun, Jordan, 1956-60, Gaza, Egypt, 1961-62; asst. resident in surgery Ch. Home & Hosp., Balt., 1962-63; asst. and chief resident in surgery Ga. Bapt. Hosp., Atlanta, 1963-66; asst. and chief resident cardio thoracic surgery Emory U. Hosp., Atlanta, 1966-68; pvt. practice specializing in cardiothoracic surgery Atlanta, 1968—. Active staff Emory U.

Hosp., Grady Meml. Hosp., Crawford W. Long Hosp., Henrietta Egleston Children's Hosp., VA Hosp., Piedmont Hosp.; instr. surgery Emory U. Sch. Medicine, 1968-71, asst. prof. surgery, 1971-76, assoc. prof. surgery, 1976-87, prof. cardiothoracic surgery, 1987—. Contbr. numerous articles to profl. jours. Fellow ACS, Am. Coll. Cardiology, Am. Coll. Chest Physicians, Am. Coll. Angiology, Southeastern Surg. Congress; mem. Council on Critical Care, Am. Assn. Thoracic Surgery, Am. Heart Assn., Soc. Thoracic Surgeons, So. Thoracic Surg. Assn. Internat. Coll. Surgeons (vice regent Ga.), Am. Thoracic Soc., Ga. Surg. Soc., AMA, Med. Assn. Ga., Med. Assn. Atlanta, N. Am. Soc. Pacing and Electrophysiology (founding mem.), Internat. Soc. for Diseases of the Esophagus, Gen. Thoracic Surg. Club. Home: 823 Lullwater Rd NE Atlanta GA 30307-1239 Office: The Emory Clinic 1365 Clifton Rd NE Atlanta GA 30322-1013 Office Phone: 404-778-3554. E-mail: kamal_mansour@emoryhealthcare.org.

**MANSOUR, TAG ELDIN,** pharmacologist, educator; b. Belkas, Egypt, Nov. 6, 1924; came to U.S., 1951, naturalized, 1956; s. Elsayed and Rokaya (Elzayat) M.; m. Joan Adela MacKinnon, Aug. 6, 1955; children— Suzanne, Jeanne, Dean. DVM, Cairo U., 1946; PhD, U. Birmingham, Eng., 1949, DSc, 1974. Lectr. U. Cairo, 1950-51; Fulbright instr. physiology Howard U., Washington, 1951-52; sr. instr. pharmacology Case Western Res. U., 1952-54; asst. prof., assoc. prof. pharmacology La. State U. Med. Sch., New Orleans, 1954-61; assoc. prof., prof. molecular pharmacology Stanford U. Sch. Medicine, 1961—, chmn. dept. pharmacology, 1977-91, Donald E. Baxter prof., 1977-98, prof. emeritus, 1999—. Cons. USPHS, WHO, Nat. Acad. Scis.; Mem. adv. bd. Med. Sch., Kuwait U.; Heath Clarke lectr. London Sch. Hygiene and Tropical Medicine, 1981 Author: Chemotherapeutic Targets in Parasites, 2002; contrbr. sci. articles to profl. jours. Commonwealth Fund fellow, 1965; Macy Found. scholar NIMR, London, 1982. Fellow AAAS; mem. Am. Soc. Pharmacology and Exptl. Therapeutics, Am. Soc. Biochemistry and Molecular Biology, Am. Heart Assn., Sierra Club, Stanford Faculty Club. Office: Stanford Sch Medicine Dept Molecular Pharm CCSR 269 Campus Dr Stanford CA 94305-5174

**MANSOURI, LOTFOLLAH (LOTFI MANSOURI),** retired performing company executive; b. Tehran, June 15, 1929; s. Hassan and Mehri (Jalili) M.; m. Marjorie Anne Thompson, Sept. 18, 1954; 1 child, Shireen Melinda. AB, UCLA, 1953. Asst. prof. UCLA, 1957-60; resident stage dir. Zurich Opera, 1960-65; chief stage dir. Geneva Opera, 1965-75; gen. dir. Can. Opera Co., Toronto, Ont., 1976-88, San Francisco (Calif.) Opera, 1988—2001, gen. dir. emeritus, 2001—; dramatic coach Music Acad. West, Santa Barbara, Calif., 1959; dir. dramatics Zurich Internat. Opera Studio, 1961-65, Centre Lyrique, Geneva, 1967-72; artistic adviser Tehran Opera, 1973-75; opera adviser Nat. Arts Centre, Ottawa, Ont., 1977; v.p. Opera America, 1979—. Operatic cons. dir. Yes, Giorgio, MGM, 1981; dir. opera sequence for film Moonstruck (Norman Jewison), 1987; stage dir. Fla. Grand Opera Mus. Acad. of West. Guest dir. opera cos. including Met. Opera, San Francisco Opera (70 prodns.), N.Y.C. Opera, Lyric Opera of Chgo., L.A. Opera, guest dir. opera cos. San Diego Opera, guest dir. opera cos. including Teatro Colon, Buenos Aires, Utah Opera, Canadian Opera Co. (30 new prodns.), Houston Grand Opera, La Scala, Covent Garden, Verona Opera, Kirov Opera, Australian Opera, Vienna Staatsoper, Vienna Volksoper, Salzburg Festival, Amsterdam Opera, Holland Festival, Nice (France) Opera, Festival D'Orange, France, Verona Arena Festival; co-author: An Operatic Life, 1982. Decorated chevalier Order Arts and Letters (France), 1992. Mem. Am. Guild Mus. Artists, Can. Actors Equity Assn. Achievements include initiating above-stage projection of subtitles as a simultaneous translation of opera, 1983. Office: Columbia Artists Management Llc 1790 Broadway # 6 New York NY 10019-1412 Office Phone: 415-387-9967. E-mail: lotfimansori@hotmail.com.

**MANSUETO, JOSEPH DANIEL,** publisher; b. East Chicago, Ind., Sept. 3, 1956; s. Mario Daniel and Sara Wilda (Smart) M. BBA, U. Chgo., 1978, MBA, 1980. Securities analyst Harris Assocs., Chgo., 1983-84; founder, chmn., prin. Morningstar, Chgo., 1984—, CEO, 1984—96, 2000—. Named one of Forbes' Richest Americans, 2006; recipient Rosenthal Award for Excellence in Investment Research, Univ. Chgo., 1992, KPMG Peat Marwick High Tech Entrepreneur of Yr. award, 1993, Disting. Entrepreneurial Alumnus award, Univ. Chgo., 2000. Office: 225 W Wacker Dr Chicago IL 60606 Office Phone: 312-696-6000.*

**MANTEGNA, JOE ANTHONY,** actor, playwright; b. Chgo., Nov. 13, 1947; s. Joseph Anthony and Mary Ann (Novelli) M.; m. Arlene Vrhel, Oct. 3, 1975; children: Mia Marie, Gina Cristine. Student, Goodman Sch. of Drama, Chgo., 1967-69. Author: (play) Bleacher Bums, 1979 (Emmy award 1979); appeared in plays including Glengarry Glen Ross, 1984-86 (Tony award, Jeff award), Speed-the-Plow, Trumbo, 2005; appeared in films Compromising Positions, 1984, Offbeat, 1985, Money Pit, 1986, 3 Amigos, 1986, Critical Condition, 1986, House of Games, 1987, Suspect, 1987, Weeds, 1987, Things Change, 1988 (Best Actor award Venice Film Festival 1988), Wait Until Spring Bandini, 1990, Alice, 1990, The Godfather Part III, 1990, Queens Logic, 1991, Homicide, 1991, Bugsy, 1991, Body of Evidence, 1992, Family Prayers, 1993, Searching for Bobby Fischer, 1993, Airheads, 1994, Baby's Day Out, 1994, Stranger Things, 1995, Above Suspicion, 1995, Forget Paris, 1995, For Better or Worse, 1996, Albino Alligator, 1996, Eye for an Eye, 1996, Up Close and Personal, 1996, Thinner, 1996, Persons Unknown, 1996, National Lampoon's Favorite Deadly Sins, 1995, Captain Nuke and the Bomber Boys, 1995, Underworld, 1997, The Wonderful Ice Cream Suit, 1998, Jerry and Tom, 1998 (also exec. prodr.), Conundrum, 1998, Celebrity, 1998, Error in Judgement, 1998, Boy Meets Girl, 1998, Airspeed, 1998, Hoods, 1998, The Runner, 1999, More Dogs Than Bones, 1999, Liberty Heights, 1999, Fall, 2000, The Last Producer, 2000, (voice) The Trumpet of the Swan, 2001, Laguna, 2001, Off Key, 2001, Mother Ghost, 2002, Unlo Nino, 2003, Stateside, 2004, Pontormo, 2004, Nine Lives, 2005, Edmond, 2005, The Kid and I, 2005; TV films include Elvis, 1979, Comrades of Summer, 1992, The Water Engine, 1992, State of Emergency, 1994, The Last Don, 1997, A Call to Remember, 1997, Fall Down, 1997, Merry Christmas George Bailey, 1997, The Rat Pack, 1998, The Last Don II, 1998, Spenser: Small Vices, 1999, My Little Assassin, 1999, Thin Air, 2000, Walking Shadow, 2001, and Thou Shalt Honor, 2002, Women vs. Men, 2002, A Very Married Christmas, 2004; TV series include Comedy Zone, 1984, First Monday, 2002, Joan of Arcadia, 2003-05; numerous TV guest appearances including Bosom Buddies, The Greatest American Hero, Frasier, The Simpsons, Rugrats, others. Recipient Drama Desk Award N.Y. Drama Desk, 1984. Mem. Actors Equity, Screen Actors Guild, Am. Fedn. TV and Radio Artists. Office: Tri Richard Stable 321 W 44th St Ste 805 New York NY 10036-5404

**MANTEL, SAMUEL JOSEPH, JR.,** management educator, consultant; b. Indpls., Nov. 17, 1921; s. Samuel Joseph and Beatrice Smith (Talmas) M.; m. Dorothy Jean Friedland, June 28, 1950 (dec. July 27, 2005); children— Michael Lee, Samuel Joseph, III, Margaret Irene, Elizabeth Baer. AB, Harvard U., 1948, MPA, 1950, PhD, 1952. Asst. prof. social sci. Ga. Inst. Tech., 1953-56; asst. then assoc. prof. econs., dir. Econs.-in-Action program, Case Western Res. U., 1956-69; prof. mgmt. and quantitative analysis U. Cin., 1969-89, prof. emeritus quantitative analysis and ops. mgmt., 1989—, Joseph S. Stern prof. mgmt., 1973—89, prof. emeritus, 1989, exec. dir. Grad. Ctr. for Mgmt. of Advanced Tech. and Innovation, 1987—89, emeritus, 1989. Mgmt. cons., condr. mgmt. seminars. Author: Cases in Managerial Decisions, 1964, Project Management: A Managerial Approach, 1985, 5th edit., 2003, Operations Management for Pharmacists: Strategy and Tactics, 1992, Project Management in Practice 2d edit., 2005; contbr. chapters to books, articles to profl. jours. Vice pres. Jewish Fedn. Cin., 1978-80; past pres., life mem. Cin. Hillel Found., Cleve. Hillel Found.; historian Rockdale Temple, 1969-77; mem. mgmt. and adminstrn. com. Anti-Defamation League, B'nai B'rith, 1976; trustee Jewish Hosp., Cin., 1975-84, Sarah Marvin Found. for Performing Arts, 1990—; mem. mgmt. adv. com. Cin. Police Dept., 1991-92. Maj. USMCR, 1942-46, 51-53. Decorated D.F.C. with 3 oak leaf clusters, Air medal with 11 oak leaf clusters; Econs.-in-Action fellow, 1955; fellow Inst. Policy Rsch., 1980; named Prof. of Year, Delta Sigma Pi, 1974. Mem. IEEE, Project Mgmt. Inst., Iota Epsilon, Beta Gamma Sigma. Home: 608 Flagstaff Dr Cincinnati OH 45215-2525 Personal E-mail: mantelsj@email.uc.edu.

**MANTELL, SUZANNE RUTH,** editor; b. West Orange, N.J., Nov. 26, 1944; d. Milton A. and Florence B. M.; m. Peter Gray Friedman, 1985; 1 child, Erica Mantell Friedman Student, U. Chgo., 1962; B.F.A., Pratt Inst., 1967. Formerly assoc. editor Harper's mag., N.Y.C., exec. editor, 1977-80; editor Harper's Bookletter, 1974-77, Learning Mag., 1980-81, Family Learning Mag., 1983-84; reader Book of the Month Club, 1985-87, 91-99; editor Travel Bookstore Catalogue, Banana Republic, 1985-87; assoc. editor The N.Y. Observer, N.Y.C., 1987-91; acting Book News editor Pubs. Weekly, 1992-93, contbg. editor, 1993—. Also lectr. mag. writing Stanford U., U. Calif. at Santa Cruz. Consulting editor Spelman Coll. Messenger, 1994-98; columnist L.A. Times Book Review, 1998-99; arts editor New Times L.A., 1999-2001; author Art of the State: Vermont, 1998. Mem. PEN, PEN West USA, Nat. Book Critics Circle. Home: 101 Warwick Pl South Pasadena CA 91030-4062

**MANTELLA, TINO J.,** former medical association administrator; m. Deb Mantella; children: Cara, Dana, Brock. MS, Temple U.; postgrad., Columbia U. Inst. Non-Profit Mgmt. Pres. and CEO Arthritis Found., 2001—03; consultant Georgia Center for Nonprofits, 2003—. Office: Georgia Ctr for Nonprofits 50 Hurt Plaza SE Ste 845 Atlanta GA 30303

**MANTELLO, JOSEPH,** theater director; b. Rockford, Ill. Dec. 27, 1962; Studied acting, N.C. Sch. Arts, 1984; studied directing, Cir. Repertory Co. Co-founder Edge Theater, N.Y.C., 1984. Dir.: (plays) Imagining Brad, 1989, Nebraska, 1991, Coq au Vin, 1991, Babylon Gardens, 1991, Three Hotels, 1993, Fat Men in Skirts, 1994, Blue Window, 1996, The Santaland Diaries, 1996, God's Heart, 1997, Schmucks, 1998, Lillian, 1998, Corpus Christi, 1998, Bash, 1999, The Mineola Twins, 1999—2000, The Vagina Monologues, 1999—2003, Another American: Asking & Telling, 1999, Assassins, 2001, A Man of No Importance, 2002 (Broadway plays) What's Wrong with the Picture?, 1994, Love! Valour! Compassion!, 1994—97 (Obie award), Proposals, 1997, Design for Living, 2001, Take Me Out, 2002 (Lucille Lortel award for oustanding dir., 2003, Drama Desk award nom. for outstanding dir. of a play, 2003, Tony award best dir. of a play, 2003), Frankie and Johnny in the Clair de Lune, 2002, Wicked, 2003—04 (Tony nom. best dir. of a musical, 2004, Drama Desk award best book of a musical, 2004), Assassins, 2004— (Tony award best dir. of a musical, 2004), Glengarry Glen Ross, 2005; actor: Angels in America, 1994 (Drama Desk award for best featured actor in a play, 1994). Recipient Outer Critics Cir. award, Helen Hayes award, Clarence Derwent award, Joe A. Callaway award. Office: Creative Artists Agy 9830 Wilshire Blvd Beverly Hills CA 90212

**MANTEUFFEL, ROBERT LEE,** lawyer; b. St. Francis, Kans., July 15, 1955; s. Walter Junior and Winnie Belle Manteuffel; m. Martha Ann Hatten, Mar. 8, 1980; children: Jessica Ann, Laura Alean. BA in Math., with distinction, Va. Mil. Inst., Lexington, 1977; MS in Ops. Rsch., USAF Inst. Tech., Wright-Patterson AFB, Ohio, 1985; JD, So. Meth. U., Dallas, 1991. Bar: Tex. 1991, US Dist. Ct. (no. dist.) 1992, US Dist. Ct. (so. dist.) 1994, US Dist. Ct. (ea. dist.) 1994, US Dist. Ct. (we. dist.) 1994. Platoon leader, staff officer 3d Armored Cavalry Regiment and US Army Operational Test and Evaluation Agy., Ft. Bliss, Tex., 1978—79; exec. officer 4th Tng. Brigade US Army, Ft. Knox, Ky., 1979, platoon leader, exec. officer, co. comdr., 3d Bn., 68th Armor, 8th Infantry Divsn. Mannheim, Germany, 1979—82; force structure analyst US Army TRADOC Analysis Ctr., Ft. Leavenworth, Kans., 1985—88; clk., atty. Bailey & Williams, Dallas, 1990—92; atty. Fowler, Wiles & Keith, LLP, Dallas, 1992—98, Kane, Russell, Coleman & Logan, PC, Dallas, 1998—. Mng. staff editor Southwestern Law Jour., 1990—91. Dir., adv. bd. West Dallas Youth and Family Ctr., 1995—2001; bd. dirs. Dallas Market Ctr. Rotary Club, 2002—05; chair Berkner Area Exchange Club, 2004—05; chair libr. com. Dallas Bar Assn. 2002. Capt. U.S. Army, 1977—88. Named one of Outstanding Young Men of Am., 1985; recipient Mil. Parachute Badge, 1975, Silver medal for Army scholarship, Am. Legion, 1976, medal, Am. Vets. of WWII, 1977, John H. French medal, Va. Mil. Inst., 1977, Jackson-Hope medal (first honor), 1977, Army Svc. ribbon, 1977, Overseas Svc. ribbon, 1982, Army Commendation medal, 1982, Meritorious Svc. medal, 1988; Hatton W. Sumners scholar, So. Meth. U. and Hatton W. Sumners Found., 1988—91. Mem.: Dallas Bar Assn., State Bar Tex., Coll. of State Bar Tex., Kappa Alpha Order, Omega Rho, VMI Alumni Assn., Phi Delta Phi. Republican. Methodist. Avocations: music, reading, jogging, swimming, bicycling. Home: 4817 Copper Mountain Ln Richardson TX 75082 Office: Kane Russell Coleman and Logan PC 1601 Elm St Ste 3700 Dallas TX 75201 Office Phone: 214-777-4267. Fax: 214-777-4299. E-mail: rmanteuffel@krcl.com.

**MANTEY, ELMER MARTIN,** food company executive; b. Malone, Tex., July 20, 1926; s. Edward G. and Margaret H. Mantey; m. Donna May Scritsmier, Dec. 27, 1948; children: Patricia Mantey Rooks, Carol Mantey Callis, Cynthia Mantey Stockdale. BS in Chemistry with honors, Bradley U., 1949. Chemist, plant mgr. Am. Petrochem. Co., Mpls., 1949—63, v.p. ops., 1963—66; v.p. Polychem. Group Whittaker Corp., L.A., 1966—69, pres. textile divsn., 1969—71; CEO, pres., chmn. bd. dirs. Flavorite Labs. Inc., Memphis, 1971—89; chmn. emeritus; bd. dirs. Craig Halum Corp., 1971—92. Bd. dirs. A.M. Todd Co., dir. emeritus; bd. dirs. The Dupps Co.; chmn. emeritus Chrichton Coll. Trustee John Brown U., 1991-2000. Served with USN, 1944-46. Mem. Rotary (Memphis) Home: 6925 Sugar Maple Cv Memphis TN 38119-5619

**MANTHE, CORA DE MUNCK,** real estate company executive; b. Alton, Iowa, Oct. 10, 1928; d. Cornelius John and Bessie Bell (Miller) De Munck; m. Carl Robert Manthe, Apr. 5, 1952 (dec. Dec. 1987); children: Barry Paul, David Glenn. BA in Econs., U. Iowa, 1950; postgrad., U. Wis., Madison and Oshkosh, 1972-75; grad., Realtors Inst., 1983. Cert. residential appraiser. Rsch. analyst Dept. Def., Washington, 1951-52; social work investigator Dane County, Madison, 1960-62; civic hostess Welcome Wagon, Beaver Dam, Wis., 1963-70; real estate broker "C" Manthe Realty, Ltd., Beaver Dam, 1979—, property mgr., investment mgr., pres., treas., 1982—. Deacon Grace Presbyn. Ch., 1974-77, elder, 1979-82, ruling elder, 1989-92; staff worker Kohl Senate Campaign, 1994. Mem. AAUW (life), Beaver Dam C. of C., U. Iowa Alumni Assn. (life), Optimist Internat. (life). Avocations: bridge, golf, travel, reading. Home and Office: 404 Declark St Beaver Dam WI 53916-1714 *Attendance at meetings, classes, family reunions throughout the world has consumed time. The Crystal Cathedral California Hour of Power Television Ministry has been a participating meeting place for me since the early 70s. The International Platform Association in wAshington, D.C., featuring classes in Speech, Journalism, Art, Acting, etc. has been attended. Charitable work includes Optimist International and the American Association of University Women with their emphasis on Women's issues has taken time and endeavors.*

**MANTHEY, RICHARD DALE,** retired lawyer, health products executive; b. Olivia, Minn., Dec. 23, 1935; s. Alvin R. and Sidonia (Klatt) M.; m. Karen J. Peterson, Sept. 6, 1959 (dec. Mar. 1985); children: Steven, Jana, Kari, John, Rebecca; m. Lynn E. Graham, Aug. 9, 1986. BS in Pharmacy (Rexall award 1960), S.D. State U., 1960; JD, U. Minn., 1967. Bar: Minn. 1967, Ill. 1970, D.C. 1987, U.S. Supreme Ct. 1987. Sales rep. Eli Lilly & Co., Indpls., 1962-64, atty., 1967-70; atty., then asst. corp. sec., dir. regulatory affairs Am. Hosp. Supply Corp., Evanston, Ill., 1970-79, corp. sec., dep. gen. counsel, 1979-85; assoc. gen. counsel Baxter Travenol Labs., Deerfield, Ill., 1986-87; ptnr. Burditt, Bowles & Radzius, Washington, 1987-90, McKenna & Cuneo, Washington, 1990-96; sr. v.p. regulatory scis. C.R. Bard, Inc., Murray Hill, NJ, 1996-2000. Author articles in field.; Editorial adv. staff: Med. Devices and Diagnostic Industry, 1979. Mem. bd. edn. Libertyville H.S., 1984-87; mem. governing bd. Spl. Edn. Dist. of Lake County, Ill., 1985-87; trustee N.J. Ctr. for Visual Arts. With AUS, 1954-56. Mem. Health Industry Mfrs. Assn. (chmn. law sect. 1976), Health Industry Assn. (chmn. legal com. 1973), Am.

---

Soc. Corp. Secs. (corp. practices com. 1983-88, group pres. 1985-86, Chgo. regional group 1986-87), D.C. Bar Assn., Univ. Club (Evanston, Ill., bd. dirs. 1984-86). Home: 11608 Stonewall Jackson Dr Spotsylvania VA 22553

**MANTHEY, FRANK ANTHONY,** physician, director; b. NYC, Dec. 2, 1933; s. Frank A.J. and Josephine (Roth) M.; m. Douglas Susan Falvey, Sept. 14 1958 (div. 1979, dec. 1989); children: Michael P., Susan M., Peter J.; m. Doris Jean Pulley, Oct. 11, 1979. BS, Fordham U., 1955; MD, SUNY, Syracuse, 1958. Diplomate Am. Bd. Anesthesiology, Am. Bd. Med. Examiners. Intern Upstate Med. Ctr., Syracuse, 1958-59; resident in anesthesiology Yale-New Haven Med. Ctr., 1962-64; physician Yale-New Haven Hosp., 1964-75; pvt. practice medicine Illmo, Mo., 1975-79; dir. Manthey Med. Clinic, Elkton, Ky., 1979—. Clin. instr. anesthesiology Yale U. Med. Sch., New Haven, 1964-69, asst. clin. prof. anesthesiology, 1969-75; cons. Conn. Dept. Aeros., Hartford, 1969-70; sr. med. examiner Fed. Aviation Adminstrn., Illmo, 1975-79. Contbr. articles to profl. jours. Chmn. gen. works Little Folks Fair, Guilford, Conn., 1967-71; mem. Rep. Town Com., Guilford, 1969-75; chmn. Guilford Sch. Bldg. Com., 1973-75; mem. Todd County (Ky.) Bd. of Health, 1999—. Capt. USAF (M.C.), 1956-62. Mem.: Flying Physicians Assn. (v.p. NE chpt. 1973—75, v.p. nat. 1974—75, 1979—80, bd. dirs. 1970—73, 1975—78, bd. dirs. nat. 1975—78), Aerospace Med. Assn. (assoc. fellow 1973—75), Ky. Med. Assn., Mercedes Benz ClubAm., Alpha Kappa Kappa. Avocations: stamp collecting/philately, coin collecting/numismatics, aviation, auto restoration, skiing. Home: 105 Sunset Dr Elkton KY 42220-9257 Office: Manthey Family Practice Clinic 203 Allensville St PO Box 368 Elkton KY 42220-0368 Office Phone: 270-265-2531. Personal E-mail: giantsinky@earthlink.net.

**MANTHEY, THOMAS RICHARD,** lawyer; b. St. Cloud, Minn., May 5, 1942; s. Richard Jesse and Dolores Theresa (Terhaar) M.; m. Janet S. Barth, Dec. 18, 1965; children: Molly, Andrew, Luke. BA cum laude, St. John's U., Collegeville, Minn., 1964; JD cum laude, Harvard U., 1967. Bar: Minn. 1967. Assoc. Dorsey & Whitney, Mpls., 1967-73, ptnr. real estate dept., 1974—, also mem. Indian and gaming law practice group, chmn. real estate workout practice group. Contbr. articles to profl. jours. Capt. U.S. Army, 1968-70. Mem. Minn. State Bar Assn. (real estate sect.), Hennepin County Bar Assn. (real estate sect.). Roman Catholic. Avocations: volleyball, golf, fishing. Home: 9958 Wellington Ln Woodbury MN 55125-8459 Office: Dorsey & Whitney 50 S 6th St Ste 1500 Minneapolis MN 55402-1553

**MANTLE, RAYMOND ALLAN,** lawyer; m. Judith Ann LaGrange, Nov. 26, 1967; children: Amanda Lee, Rachel Ann, Leah Amy. BSBA summa cum laude, BA summa cum laude, Kent State U., 1961; LLB cum laude, NYU, 1964. Bar: N.Y. 1964, N.J. 1976, Fla. 2005, U.S. Supreme Ct. Asst. counsel Gov. Nelson A. Rockefeller, N.Y., 1964-65; assoc. Paul Weiss Rifkind Wharton & Garrison, 1967-69; mem. Varet & Fink P.C. (formerly Milgrim Thomajan & Lee, P.C.), N.Y.C., 1969-95; ptnr. Piper & Marbury L.L.P., N.Y.C., 1995-98; mem. Reitler Brown & Rosenblatt LLC (formerly Brock Silverstein, LLC), 1998—2003, counsel, 2004—. Lectr. in computer law field. Contbr. author: Doing Business in China and Intellectual Property China, 1990—. Capt. U.S. Army, 1965—67. Mem.: Fla. Bar, N.Y. State Bar Assn. (co-chmn. ann. meeting seminar on intellectual property 2000—05, co-chair intellectual property sect. internat. com., exec. com. intellectual property sect.). Republican. Methodist. Office: Reitler Brown & Rosenblatt LLC 800 3rd Ave Fl 21 New York NY 10022-7604 also: 4745 Sutton Park Ct Ste 602 Jacksonville FL 32224 Office Phone: 904-821-4885. E-mail: rmantle@reitlerbrown.com.

**MANTON, WILLIAM INWOOD,** geologist, educator; b. Durban, Natal, South Africa, Feb. 8, 1937; arrived in U.S., 1964; s. Geoffrey Charles Manton and Constance Irene Melsens; m. Renee Southernwood Manton, Dec. 9, 1982; m. Janet Rae Humphrey, Sept. 1, 1968 (div. May 15, 1982); children: Gabrielle Marcelline, Iris Irene, Piers Kingsley, Geoffrey Leonard. BSc with honors, U. of the Witwatersrand, Johannesburg, South Africa, 1959, MSc, 1962, PhD, 1964. Prof. U. Tex. Dallas, Richardson, 1964—. Recipient Best paper award, Soc. Toxicology, 1997. Episcopalian. Achievements include research in applied techniques of geochemistry to toxicology and showed that most of lead in blood is derived from stores in bone. Demonstrated that blood lead rises in pregnancy due to bone resorption; made fundamental observations pertaining to lead poisoning from gunshot wounds, acquisition of lead by young children and role of lead in amyotrophic lateral sclerosis. Avocations: antique furniture, classical languages. Home: 300 Ridgewood Richardson TX 75080-1912 Office: Univ Tex Dallas PO Box 830688 Richardson TX 75083-0688 Personal E-mail: inwood@attbi.com. E-mail: manton@utdallas.edu.

**MANTONI, PHILIP JOSEPH,** retired principal, education educator; b. Springfield, Mass., Dec. 3, 1944; s. Adelino Philip and Mary (Barberis) M.; m. Susan Beth Hartley Mantoni, Aug. 4, 1973; 1 child, Christian Philip. BSE in Elem. Edn., North Adams State Coll., Mass., 1969; MEd in Edn., Springfield Coll., 1979; C.A.G.S. in Adminstrn., Westfield State Coll. Mass., 1988. Tchr. Washington Sch., Springfield, 1969-77, Ecology Ctr. of Springfield, 1977-89; asst. prin. New North Cmty. Sch., Springfield, 1989-90; prin. A.G. Zanetti Elem. Sch., Springfield, 1990-95, Alice B. Beal Sch., Springfield, 1995—2002; ret., 2002. Exec. bd. South End Cmty. Ctr., 1992—; mem. chmn., exec. bd., bldg. rep. Springfield Fedn. Tchrs.; adj. faculty Bay Path Coll., Long Meadow, Mass., 2005—. Mem. Springfield Citywide Sch. Centered Decision Making Team, 1993-99; chmn. Springfield Park Commn., 1982-91; mem. Forest Park Zool. Soc. Edn. and Curriculum Com., 1981-89; mem. Olmstead grants Com. for Forest Park, 1986-88; mem. Springfield Schs. Sci. Curriculum Com., 1978-83; mem. Springfield Mcpl. Planning Bd., 1983-91. Mem.: Springfield Elem. Prins. Assn. (treas. 1992—93, sec. 1993—94, v.p. 1994—95). Home: 41 Texel Dr Springfield MA 01108-2637 Office: Alice B Beal Sch 285 Tiffany St Springfield MA 01108-3333 Personal E-mail: pjmsiri@hotmail.com.

**MANTONYA, JOHN BUTCHER,** lawyer; b. Columbus, Ohio, May 26, 1922; s. Elroy Letts and Blanche (Butcher) M.; m. Mary E. Reynolds, June 14, 1947 (dec. 1987); children: Elizabeth Claire, Mary Kay, Lee Ann; m. Carole L. Lugar, Sept. 28, 1989. AB cum laude, Washington and Jefferson Coll., 1943; postgrad., U. Mich. Law Sch., 1946—47; JD, Ohio State U. 1949. Bar: Ohio 1949. Assoc. A.S. Mitchell, Atty., Newark, Ohio, 1949—50, C.D. Lindrooth, Newark, 1950—57; ptnr. firm Lindrooth & Mantonya, Newark, 1957—74; firm John B. Mantonya, 1974—81, John B. Mantonya, L.P.A., 1981—. Mem. North Fork Local Bd. Edn., 1962-69; adv. com. Salvation Army, Licking County, 1965—; Mayor of Utica, Ohio, 1953-59. Served with AUS, 1943-45. Mem. ABA, Ohio Bar Assn., Licking County Bar Assn. (pres. 1967), Phi Delta Phi, Beta Theta Pi. Home: 11055 Reynolds Rd Utica OH 43080-9549 Office: 3 N 3rd St Newark OH 43055-5506 Personal E-mail: jb.mantonya@alltel.com.

**MANTOVANI, JOHN F.,** pediatric neurologist; b. St. Louis, Jan. 17, 1949; s. John F. and Marinelle Mantovani; children: John R. and Ann Marie. BA cum laude, U. Evansville, 1971; MD, U. Mo., 1974. Diplomate Am. Bd. Pediat., Am. Bd. Psychiatry and Neurology in child neurology and in neurodevel. disabilities. Resident pediatrics, neurology, fellow child neurology Washington U.-St. Louis Childrens Hosp., 1974-79; practitioner adult and child neurology Dean Clinic, Madison, Wis., 1979-84; dir. child neurology, vice chmn. dept. pediatrics St. John's Mercy Med. Ctr., St. Louis, 1984—. Clin. assoc. prof. neurology U. Wis., Madison, 1980-84; instr. clin. pediatrics and neurology Washington U., 1985-95, asst. prof., 1995-99, assoc. prof., 1999—; vice chmn. neurodevel. disabilities com. Am. Bd. Psychiatry and Neurology. Mem. editl. bd., vice chmn. Dev. Med. and Child Neurology; Contbr. articles to profl. jours. Fellow Am. Acad. Pediatrics, Am. Acad. Cerebral Palsy and Devel. Medicine (bd. dirs. 1994-2003, v.p. 1997-98, pres.-elect 1999, pres. 2000); mem. AMA, Am. Acad. Neurology (vice chmn. Neurodevel. Disabilities Exam. com.), Child Neurology Soc., Alpha Omega Alpha. Office: 621 S New Ballas Rd Ste 5009 Saint Louis MO 63141-8232

---

**MANTSCH, HENRY HORST,** chemistry professor; b. Mediasch, Transylvania, Romania, July 30, 1935; emigrated to Can., 1968; s. Heinrich Johann and Olga Augusta (Gondosch) M.; m. Amy Emilia Kory, Nov. 2, 1959; children: Monica, Marietta. BSc, U. Cluj, Transylvania, 1958, PhD, 1964. Rsch. scientist Romanian Acad. Sci., Cluj, 1958-65, Tech. U. Munich, Germany, 1966-68; with NRC, Ottawa, Can., 1968-72; prof. biochemistry U. Cluj, 1973-74, Liebig U., Giessen, Germany, 1975-76; head molecular spectroscopy NRC, Ottawa, 1977—; mem. Can. Rsch. Coun., Ottawa, 1977-91, Winnipeg, 1992—2002; sci. counsellor Can. Embassy, Berlin, 2002—. Adj. prof. Carleton U., Ottawa, 1978-90, U. Ottawa, 1990-92, U. Manitoba, Winnipeg, 1992—. Contbr. articles to profl. jours.; patentee in field. Recipient medal Ministry of Edn., Bucharest, 1972, Humboldt Found. medal Bonn, 1980, Herzberg award, 1984, Marcus Marci medal, 1998; Chem. Inst. Can. fellow, 1979, Royal Soc. Can. fellow, 1982. Mem. Am. Biophys. Soc., Soc. Applied Spectroscopy, Chem. Inst. Can. (chmn. biol. chem. divsn. 1980-81), Can. Spectroscopy Soc. (nat. exec. com. 1981-90), Can. Biophys. Soc. (sec. 1999—). Office: Can Embassy Leipziger Platz 17 10117 Berlin Germany E-mail: henry.mantsch@international.gc.ca.

**MANUEL, CHARLIE (CHARLES FUQUA MANUEL JR.),** professional baseball manager; b. Northfork, W.Va., Jan. 4, 1944; children: Charles Jr., Julie. Outfielder Minn. Twins, 1963-74; with LA Dodgers, 1974-75, Yakult Swallows and Kintetsu Buffaloes, Japan, 1976-81; scout Minn. Twins, 1982; mgr. class A Wisconsin Rapids, 1983; various coaching and mgr. positions, 1983-99; mgr. Cleve. Indians, 1999—2002; special asst. to gen. mgr. Phila. Phillies, 2003—04, mgr., 2004—. Inducted Salem-Roanoke Baseball Hall of Fame, 1995. Office: c/o Philadelphia Phillies 1 Citizens Bank Way Philadelphia PA 19148*

**MANUEL, JERRY,** former professional sports team manager; b. Hahira, Ga., Dec. 23, 1953; m. Renette Caldwell; children: Angela, Jerry, Anthony, Natalie. Switch-hitting infielder Detroit Tigers, 1972, Class A Lakeland, Class AAA Toledo, 1973, Class AAA Evansville, 1974-75, Detroit Tigers, 1975-76, Montreal, Can., 1980-81, San Diego, 1982, Class AAA Iowa, 1983, Class AAA Denver, 1984; scout White Sox, 1985; player, coach Indpls. orgn., 1986, infield instr.; 1987; minor-league fielding coord. Expos orgn., 1988-89; mgr. Class AAA Indpls. Montreal Expos Sys., 1991; coach maj. league baseball Montreal Expos, 1991-96; mgr. Chgo. White Sox, 1997—2003. Bench coach Fla. Marlins, 1997. Named So. League Mgr. of Yr., 1992.

**MANUEL, PETER JAY,** poet, librettist, literature and language professor; b. Framingham, Mass. s. John Lewis and Jane Dorothy (Bohlin) Manuel. BA English, U. So. Maine, 1982, MFA in Creative Writing, 2005. Warehouse worker Loring, Short & Harmon, Portland, 1989—95; clk. Portland Pub. Libr., 1992—95; dishwasher Embassy Suites Hotel, Portland, 1998—2002, prep cook, 2002—03, Maverick's Restaurant, Portland, 2004; adj. prof. English So. Maine C.C. South Portland, 2003—. Organizer Geno's Live Poets' Soc., Portland, 2000—. Mem. Trinity touring performance poetry act, 2002—05. Mem.: Maine Writers and Pubs. Alliance, Acad. Am. Poets (assoc.), Planned Parenthood. Democrat. Jewish. Avocation: music. Home: 312 Congress St # 4 Portland ME 04101 Office: So Maine C C 2 Fort Rd South Portland ME 04106 Office Phone: 207-741-5500. E-mail: pjm@gwi.net.

**MANUEL, RALPH NIXON,** retired private school executive; b. Frederick, Md., Apr. 21, 1936; s. Ralph Walter and Frances Rebecca (Nixon) M.; m. Sarah Jane Warner, July 22, 1960; children: Mark, David, Stephen, Bradley. AB, Dartmouth Coll., 1958; M.Ed., Boston U., 1967; PhD, U. Ill., 1971. Assoc. dean Dartmouth Coll., Hanover, NH, 1971-72, dean of freshmen, 1972-75, dean, 1975-82; pres. Culver (Ind.) Acad. and Culver Edn. Found., 1982-99. Bd. dirs. Ind. Sch. Cen. States, 1986-99, chair, 1993-95. Mem. Assn. Mil. Colls. and Schs. of U.S. (pres., bd. dirs.), Nat. Assn. Ind. Schs. (bd. dirs. 1995-99).

**MANUEL, SANDRA LORRAINE,** minister; b. Lakewood, NJ, July 29, 1951; d. Samuel Blackstone and Curtis Burnett; m. Alexander Manuel, July 12, 1967 (dec. Feb. 27, 1995); children: Darnell, Tasha, Alexia;. Diploma in nursing, Charles Gregory Sch. Nursing, 1985; B in Religious Edn., United Bible Coll., 1991. RN NJ; cert. student group adviser Kean U., 00. HIV and AIDS instr. NJ Dept. Criminal Justice, Police Tng. Commn., NJ; med. supr. NJ Tng. Sch. for Boys, Jameburg; head nurse, group advisor Kean U., Union, NJ; pastor Mission of Faith Ministry, Neptune, NJ. Pres. Euphrates Project, Neptune, NJ; developer workshop on non-violence Tchg. Non-Violence: Begin in Infancy, 1996. Organizer: first gospel program for cable TV in Monmouth County. Active Neighborhood Leadership Initiative Cmty. Found. of NJ, Morristown, 2002. Recipient plaque, Harde Hank Cable, 1984, Letter of Accomodation, NJ Tng. Sch., 1990. Mem.: Nat. Coun. Netro Women. Avocation: bird watching. Home: PO Box 653 Neptune NJ 07753

**MANUELIAN, LUCY DER,** art historian, architecture educator; b. Arlington, Mass. AB in English lit., Radcliffe Coll.; MA in Art History, Boston U., 1975, PhD in Art History, 1980. Head tchg. fellow Boston U., 1975-76; vis. lectr. Framingham State Coll., 1979-80; archivist Armenian Archtl. Archives Project, 1979—84; holder lectureship in Armenian Art and Architecture Tufts U., 1984—89, Arthur H. Dadian and Ara Oztemel prof. Armenian Art and Architecture Medford, 1989—. Mus. cons. Dartmouth Coll.; author, narrator 4 TV documentaries on Armenian art; holder lectureship in Armenian art and architecture Tufts U., 1984; lectr. Harvard U., 1984—89, McGill U., 1984—89, Boston U., 1984—89, Boston Coll., 1984—89, U. Mass., 1984—89, Northeastern U., 1984—89. Author: Armenian Architecture, 4 vols., 1981—88, Dictionary of Middle Ages, 1982—89, Dictionary of Art, The Gregorian Collection-Armenian Rugs, 1983, Weavers, Merchants and Kings: The Inscribed Rugs of Armenia, 1984; author, prodr. Lost Treasure of Christianity: The Ancient Monuments of Armenia; contbr. chapters to books, articles to profl. jours. Fellow to USSR, 1977-78, fellow Bunting Inst., Radcliffe Coll., 1971-73; Samuel H. Kress grantee Boston U., 1975, 78, Rsch. grantee Nat. Assn. for Armenian Studies and Rsch. to USSR, 1972, 78; sr. scholar grantee Am. Coun. Learned Socs./Soviet Acad. Scis., 1983; recipient Jack H. Kolligian award Nat. Assn. Armenian Studies and Rsch., 1981, Boyan award Armenian Students Assn., Woman of Achievement award Armenian Internat. Women's Assn., 1994, Kohar award Armenian Rugs Soc.; named to Boston U. Acad. Disting. Alumni, 1986, Armenian of Yr., Masons, 1990. Mem. Armenian Acad. Sci. (cons. Art Inst. symposium 1990—), Nat. Assn. Armenian Studies and Rsch. (adv. bd. 1991—), Soc. Armenian Studies, Aga Khan Program Islamic Architecture (affiliate), Middle East Studies Assn., Coll. Art Assn., Medieval Acad. Accademia Tiberina Rome (assoc.), Assn. Internat. Etudes Armeniennes, Nat. Assn. Armenian Studies and Rsch. (hon. life), Phi Beta Kappa (hon. Radcliffe Coll.). Achievements include research in archaeology with ground penetrating radar technology; medieval American Armenian architecture sculpture and illuminated manuscripts, the crusades; restoration of 5 medieval Armenian churches. Avocations: music, piano, tennis. Office Phone: 617-484-0668. Business E-Mail: lucy.manuelian@tufts.edu.

**MANVILLE, STEWART ROEBLING,** archivist; b. White Plains, N.Y., Jan. 15, 1927; s. Leo and Margaret (Roebling) Manville; m. Ella V. Grainger, Jan. 19, 1972 (dec.). Student, U. Wyo. 1944-46; BS, Columbia U. 1962. Various office positions, NYC, 1947-51, 56-58; asst. stage dir. several European opera houses, 1951-55; editor Jas. T. White & Co., 1959-63; archivist, curator Percy Grainger Library, White Plains, 1963—. Author: The Manville/Manvel Families in America; contbr. articles to mags. and newspapers. Mem.: SAR, Archivists Round Table Met. NY, St. Nicholas Soc. NY, Westchester Trails Assn. (pres. 2001—05), Brit. Music Soc., Société des Antiquaires de Picardie, Victorian Soc. Am. (past. dir. N.Y. chpt.), Nat. Trust Hist. Preservation. Mem. Soc. Of Friends. Office: 7 Cromwell Pl White Plains NY 10601-5005 Office Phone: 914-948-7436.

**MANYAK, MICHAEL JOHN,** urologist, educator, researcher; b. Flint, Mich., Mar. 25, 1951; m. Rebecca Bruning; children: Rachel, Susannah, Timothy. BA, U. Notre Dame, 1973; MD, U. of East, Manila, 1979. Intern, then resident in gen. surgery Booth Meml. Med. Ctr., Flushing, N.Y., 1980-82; resident in urology George Washington Univ. Med. Ctr., Washington, 1982-84, chief resident, 1984-85, instr. urology, 1988-89, asst. prof., 1989-91, assoc. prof., 1991—, prof. urology engrng. microbiology and tropical medicine, 1996—; v.p. med. affairs Cxtogen Corp., 2005—. Mem. adv. bd. Nat. Kidney and Urological Disease, 1992—; dir. urological rsch. George Washington U. Med. Ctr., 1992—, acting chmn. 1995. Contbr. articles to profl. jours. Adv. bd. aerospace medicine NASA. Fellow Nat. Cancer Inst., 1985-88; scholar Am. Urol. Assn., 1986-88. Fellow Explorers Club (nat. bd. dirs. 1996-06, chmn. sci. adv. bd., Sweeney medal); mem. Internat. Soc. Cryptozoology (field med. advisor), Am. Urol. Assn. (chmn. tech. coun. 1995). Office: Cytogen Corp 650 Coll Rd U St Princeton NJ 08540 Office Phone: 609-750-8281. Business E-Mail: mmanyak@cytogen.com.

**MANYAM, BALA VENKATESHA,** medical researcher; neurology educator; b. Bangalore, India, Oct. 15, 1942; came to U.S., 1972; s. Kolar Venktesha and Swarnam (Venktesha) Iyer; m. Rani Manyam; 1 child, Shaila. MB, BS, Bangalore Med. Coll., 1967. Diplomate Am. Bd. of Psychiatry and Neurology. With Thomas Jefferson U., Phila., 1975-83, 83-84, asst. prof. pharmacology, 1981-83, assoc. prof. pharmacology, 1983-84; staff neurologist VA Med. Ctr., Wilmington, Del., 1975-80, asst. chief neurology, 1982-84; assoc. prof. neurology Sch. of Medicine So. Ill. U., Springfield, 1984-92, prof., 1992—99, dir. neurology residency program, 1993—99; prof., dir. Plummar Movement Disorder Ctr., Scott & White Clinic, Tex. A&M U. HSC Coll. Medicine, 1999—2005. Founding dir. Parkinson's Disease & Movement Disorders Clinic, Springfield, 1984—99; mem. NIH/NCCAM Coun., 2004—, Contbr. numerous articles to profl. jours.; mem. cditl. bd. Phytotherapy Rsch., patentee in field. Grantee NIH, VA, various founds. Fellow Am. Acad. Neurology; mem. World Fedn. Neurology (rsch. com.), Am. Neurologic Assn., Am. Soc. Pharmacology and Exptl. Therapeutics. Hindu. Achievements include research in drug development from herbs for neurological diseases. Avocations: creative writing, history of medicine, collecting old coins and stamps, photography, Indian art.

**MANZ, CARL WALTON,** surgeon, educator; b. Eau Claire, Wis., Feb. 15, 1938; s. Walton Robert and Beatrice (Hartvigh) M.; m. Diane Mary Johnson, June 28, 1958; children: James W., Barbara D., Robert C. BS, U. Wis., 1960, MD, 1963; MS, U. Minn., 1971. Diplomate Am. Bd. Gen. Surgery. Practice medicine specializing in gen. and vascular surgery Midelfort Clinic, Eau Claire, 1971—. Asst. clin. prof. dept. family practice U. Wis., Madison, 1979—. Served to capt. USAR, 1964-66. Fellow ACS; mem. Wis. Med. Assn., Tri-County Med. Assn. Avocations: biking, swimming. Home: 4442 Meadow Ln Eau Claire WI 54701-7407 Office: Midelfort Clinic 733 W Clairemont Ave Eau Claire WI 54701-6117 Office Phone: 715-838-6140. Business E-Mail: manz.carl@mayo.edu.

**MANZ, CHARLES CRAIG,** management educator; BA, MBA, Mich. State U.; PhD, Penn State U. Nirenberg prof. bus. leadership U. Mass., Amherst, 1997—. Author: The Art of Self-Leadership: Strategies for Personal Effectiveness in Your Life and Work, 1983, Mastering Self-Leadership: Empowering Yourself for Personal Excellence, 1992, 4th edit., 2006, The Power of Failure: 27 Ways to Turn Life's Setbacks Into Success, 2002, Emotional Discipline: The Power to Choose How You Feel, 2003; co-author: Superleadership, 1990, Business Without Bosses: How Self-Managing Teams are Building High-Performance Companies, 1993, Company of Heroes: Unleashing the Power of Self-Leadership, 1996, For Team Members Only, 1997, The Leadership Wisdom of Jesus: Practical Lessons for Today, 1998, 2005, Teamwork and Group Dynamics, 1999, The Wisdom of Solomon at Work: Ancient Virtues for Living and Leading Today, 2001, The New Super Leadership: Leading Others to Lead Themselves, 2001, Fit to Lead: The Proven 8-Week Solution for Shaping Up Your Body, Your Mind and Your Career, 2004, Temporary Sanity: Instant Self-Leadership Strategies for Turbulent Times, 2005, The Greatest Leader Who Wasn't: A Leadership Fable, 2005. Office: U Mass Sch of Mgmt Amherst MA 01003

**MANZARI, LAURA LYNN,** law educator; b. N.Y., Jan. 4, 1959; d. Charles John and Rose Marie (Lepik) Slepetis; m. Peter Michael Manzari, Aug., 19, 1988. BA, Queen's Coll., 1979, MLS, 1986; JD, St. John's U., 1982. Bar: N.Y. 1983. Claim atty. Allstate Ins. Co., Lake Success, N.Y., 1984-85; law libr. Parker Chapin Flattau & Klimpl, N.Y.C., 1985; libr. Pace U., N.Y.C., 1987-89; assoc. prof. L.I. U., Greenvale, 1989—, dept. head Libr. and Info. Sci. Libr., 2000—. Contbr. articles to profl. jours. Mem. ALA, AAUW, Greater N.Y. Assn. Coll. and Rsch. Librs., Nassau County Libr. Office: LI U B Davis Schwartz Meml Libr Greenvale NY 11548 E-mail: manzari@liu.edu.

**MANZELLO, DEREK PAUL,** marine biologist; b. Elk Grove Village, Ill., July 16, 1980; s. Samuel and Cathy Manzello. Grad. summa cum laude, U. Miami, 2002. Rsch. asst. NOAA, Miami, Fla., 2001—. Contbr. articles to profl. jours. Office: Rosenstiel School/Univ of Miami/MBF 4600 Rickenbacker Causeway Miami FL 33149 Office Phone: 305-421-4145. Business E-Mail: dmanzello@rsmas.miami.edu.

**MANZI, JIM P.,** computer software company executive; b. N.Y.C., Dec. 22, 1951; s. Walter Edward and Ann (Smirka) M.; m. Glenda Baugh, May 20, 1978 BA, Colgate U., 1973; MAL.D., Fletcher Sch., Tufts U., 1979. Editorial asst. Nat. Rev. Mag., N.Y.C., 1973-74; news reporter Gannet Newspapers, Port Chester, N.Y., 1974-77; cons. McKinsey & Co., Los Angeles, Boston and N.Y.C., 1979-82; v.p. mktg. and sales Lotus Devel. Corp., Cambridge, Mass., 1983-84, pres., 1984-86, 89-1996, CEO, 1986-1996; pres., CEO Industry Net, 1996. Recipient In-Depth Reporting award AP, N.Y., 1976, 77, Investigative Reporting award N.Y. State Pubs. Assn., 1976, 77.

**MANZO, EDWARD DAVID,** lawyer; b. N.Y.C., Nov. 23, 1950; BS in Physics, Poly. Inst. Bklyn., 1972; JD cum laude, SUNY, Buffalo, 1975. Bar: N.Y. 1976, Ill. 1979, U.S. Patent and Trademark Office 1976, U.S. Ct. Appeals (fed. cir) 1982, U.S. Supreme Ct. 1982. Assoc. Darby & Darby, P.C., N.Y.C., 1975-77; group patent counsel Schlumberger Ltd., N.Y.C., 1977-79; ptnr. Cook, Wetzel & Egan, Chgo., 1979-85, 88-90, Jenner & Block, 1985-88; sr. ptnr. Cook McFarron & Manzo, Ltd., Chgo., 1990-99; sr. ptnr., exec. v.p., treas., CFO Cook, Alex, McFarron, Manzo, Cummings & Mehler, Ltd., Chgo., 1999—. Instr. DePaul U., Chgo., 1989-91, 2002-03; mem. adv. bd. DePaul Law Sch., 2002—. Author (with others): Intellectual Property Law in Illinois, 1988; contbr. articles to profl. jours. Bd. dirs. Concertante di Chgo., 1997-2004; Lake Forest Symphony. 2004—; grantor Edward Manzo Patent Law scholarship DePaul Law Sch., 2001-03, Law Lectures, 2004-06. Jaeckle Fleishman grantee, 1973. Mem. Am. Intellectual Property Law Assn., Intellectual Property Law Assn. Chgo. (chmn. litigation com. 2002-05, bd. mgrs. 2005—), Stradivari Soc., Sicilian Am. Cultural Assn. (treas. 1996-98, v.p. 1998-99, pres. 2000-02) Office: Cook Alex McFarron Manzo Cummings & Mehler Ltd 200 W Adams St Ste 2850 Chicago IL 60606-5206 Office Phone: 312-236-8500. Business E-Mail: emanzo@cookalex.com.

**MANZULLO, DONALD A.,** congressman, lawyer; b. Rockford, Ill., Mar. 27, 1944; s. Frank A. Sr. and Catherine M.; m. Freda Teslik; children: Neil, Noel, Katie. BA in Polit. Sci./Internat. Rels., American U., 1967; JD, Marquette U. Law Sch., 1971. Atty., 1970—; mem. U.S. Congress from 16th Ill. Dist., 1993—. Mem. House Com. on Internat. Rels., subcom. internat. econ. policy and trade, subcom. on Asia and the Pacific, House Com. on small bus., chmn. on subcom. on tax, fin. and exports, Banking Com. and its capital markets, securities and govt.-sponsored enterprises subcom. Mem. No. Ill. Alliance for Arts, Friends of Severson Dells, Citizens Against Govt. Waste, Rep. Nat. Com. Recipient George Washington honor medal for excellence in pub. comm. Freedoms Found., Valley Forge, Pa., 1991. Mem. ABA, Ill. Bar Assn., Ogle County Bar Assn. (pres. 1971, 73), Nat. Legal Found., Acad. Polit. Sci., Ill. Press Assn., Ill. C. of C., Oregon City C. of C., Nat. Land Inst.,

Nat. Fedn. Ind. Bus., Ogle County Hist. Soc., Aircraft Owners and Pilots Assn., Ogle County Pilots Assn., Ill. Farm Bur., Ogle County Farm Bur. Republican. Office: US Ho of Reps 2228 Rayburn House Office Bldg Washington DC 20515-1316

**MAO, AIWU,** physician, radiologist; b. Shanghai, June 1956; s. Zhen Long Mao and Peifang Shi; m. Feng Ping Zhou; 1 child, Yiming. MD, Shanghai Secondary Mil. Med. U. Internship Shanghai Tian Shan Hosp., 1976—77; resident St. Luke's Hosp., 1982—87; asst. dir., attending physician Xian Xia Hosp.; dep. dir. St. Luke's Hosp., dep. dir. The Interventional Dept. Prof. Shanghai Secondary Med. Sch., Shanghai Worker's Med. Sch.; cons. YueYang Hosp., Rui Jing Hosp. Editor: Interventional Radiology-Non Vascular, Chinese Med. Jour. of the Lenient Treatment of Cancer, Jour. of Interventional Radiology, International Therapy of Cancer; contbr. articles to profl. jours. Named Top Ten Physicians of Shanghai, 2004; recipient Progress of Sci. and Tech. of Shanghai award, The Shanghai People's Gov., 1999, 2000, 2001, 2002, Outstanding Person of Health, Dept. China, 2003, Outstanding Specialist, Shanghai, 2003. Mem.: The Chinese Anti-Cancer Assn. Achievements include patents in field. Avocations: music, travel. Home: West Tian Shan Road Shanghai 200335 China Office: St Lukes Hospital Yu Yuan Road Shanghai 200050 China Personal E-mail: mawzfp@yahoo.com.on.

**MAO, CHANGXUAN,** statistician; s. Yunzhang Mao and Weiqing Yao; m. Wei Zhang, July 6, 1998; 1 child, Colin Yue. PhD, Pa. State U., State College, 2001. Asst. prof. dept. stats. U. of Calif., Riverside, 2002—. Contbr. articles to profl. jours. Fellow: Internat. Statis. Inst.; mem.: Inst. of Math. Stats., Am. Statis. Assn. Office: U Calif Dept Stats Riverside CA 92521 Office Phone: 951-827-2561.

**MAO, EN,** information scientist, educator, research scientist; b. Hefei, Anhui, China, Aug. 31, 1973; d. Peiji Mao and Xia Liu; life ptnr. Acky Li. BBA, So. Ark. U., Magnolia, 1994; MBA, Ark. State U., Jonesboro, 1996; PhD, U. Memphis, 2001. Asst. prof. U. Wis., Milw., 2000—. Mem. editl. bd. Jour. Global Info. Tech. Mgmt., Greensboro, NC. Recipient Orgnl. Leadership award, Global Info. Tech. Mgmt. Assn., 2002, 2003, 2004, Gold Star Teach award, U. Wis., Milw., 2005; Curriculum Devel. grant, U. Wis., Milw. Ctr. Internat. Edn., 2001, 2003, 2004. Mem.: Global Info. Tech. Mgmt. Assn., Assn. Info. Sys. Office: Univ Wis Milw 3202 N Maryland Ave Milwaukee WI 53201 Office Phone: 414-229-4556. Office Fax: 414-229-6957. E-mail: enmao1@gmail.com.

**MAO, LI,** molecular biologist, educator; b. Nanjing, China, July 16, 1957; s. Xiqiu Mao and Yihe Huang; m. Jialing Xu, Dec. 25, 1982; children: Melissa Shanshan, Roger Tiger. MD, Nanjing Med. U., China, 1977—82. Diplomate China, 1982. Attending surgeon Nanjing Med. U. Hosp., China, 1989—95; rsch. fellow Johns Hopkins Med. Sch., Balt., 1992—95; asst. prof., medicine U. Tex., M.D. Anderson Cancer Ctr., Houston, 1995—99, assoc. prof., medicine, 1999—2004, prof., medicine, 2004—; exec. v.p., chief tech. officer Cangen Internat., Irvine, Calif., 2001—02. Advisor Panacea Pharmaceuticals, Washington, 2003—. Mem.: AACR (corr.). Office: Univ Texas MD Anderson Cancer Ctr Unit 432 PO Box 301402 Houston TX 77230-1402 Office Phone: 713-792-6363. Office Fax: 713-796-8655. E-mail: lmao@mdanderson.org.

**MAO, RUIXUAN (RICK MAO),** dean; arrived in US, 1986; s. Junye Mao and Wenhua Wu; m. Mi Hu, Oct. 6, 1980; m. Kangquan Zhou, Nov. 15, 1967 (div. May 9, 1980); children: Shufan, Guxia, Guyang Alex. BS, S.W. China Teachers U., Chongqing, 1964; MS, U. Tenn., Knoxville, 1986, PhD, 1993. Asst. prof. to assoc. prof. English S.W. China Teachers U., Chongqing, Sichuan, China, 1964—86; grad. asst. U. Tenn., Knoxville, 1986—89, instr. Chinese, 1989—90, grad. tchg. asst., 1990—92; asst. prof. English and coord. English edn. Philander Smith Coll., Little Rock, 1992—95, chair of divsn. of edn., assoc. prof. of edn., 1995—98; assoc. dir. instl. rsch. and planning The Ross Sch., East Hampton, NY, 1998—2002; dean liberal arts and social sci. Elgin C.C., Ill., 2002—05, dean comms. and behavioral sci., 2005—. Dir. instrn. and rsch. srs. S.W. China Teachers U., Chongqing, 1982—86, dir. internship program, 1982—86; English editor natural sci. series S.W. China Teachers U. Jour., 1979—86; translator Chinese edit. Sci. Am. Jour., 1980—85; editor Internat. Edn. Jour., Knoxville, Tenn., 1986—. Editor: (textbooks) English (Volumes I-VIII), 1973—75, Tunnel English (Volumes 1-3), 1974, Teacher's Manual for English (Volumes 1-6), 1976. Recipient Multicultural Presentation award, Little Rock Dist. U.S. Army Corps of Engrs., 1993, Extraordinary Contbn. award, The Ross Sch., 2002; grantee, Ark. State Dept. Higher Edn., 1995—98, Ill. C.C. Bd., 2003—; Historically Black Colls.and Univs., 1997; Hilton A. Smith fellow, U. Tenn., Knoxville, 1988—89. Mem.: Rotary (Elgin Breakfast chpt.). Avocations: bridge, ping pong/table tennis. Office: Elgin CC 1700 Spartan Dr Elgin IL 60123 Office Phone: 847-214-7455. Office Fax: 847-622-3048. Business E-Mail: rmao@elgin.edu.

**MAO, WEIDONG,** communications engineer, technology executive; arrived in U.S., 1986; s. Yuhai Mao and Qinglin; m. Rachel Zhang; children: Angela, Julia. BS, Beijing U., 1986; PhD in Elec. Engring., Princeton U., NJ, 1991. Sr. mem. rsch. staff Philips Electronics, Briarcliff Manor, NY, 1990—94; dir. telecom. unit Gen. Instrument, Horsham, Pa., 1994—97; co-founder, chief tech. officer MoreCom, Horsham, 1997—2000; v.p. tech. Liberate Tech., San Carlos, Calif., 2000—03; fellow Comcast, Phila., 2003—. Key contbr. Moving Picture Expert Group, 1990—96; invited spkr. Nat. Cable TV Assn., 2004; panelist Cable TV Labs., 2004. Wallace Meml. fellowship, Princeton U., 1989—90. Mem.: Soc. Motion Picture and TV Engrs., Soc. Cable Telecomm. Engrs., IEEE. Achievements include invention of digital TV system with synchronized www content; channel changer in a switched video system; apparatus and method for web-casting over digital TV; pioneer of digital cable, video on demand, and interactive television. Office: Comcast Cable 1500 Market St Philadelphia PA 19102 Business E-Mail: weidong_mao@cable.comcast.com.

**MAPEL, DOUGLAS WAYNE,** epidemiologist, educator, pulmonologist, critical care specialist; b. Torrejon U.S. AFB, Madrid, Spain, Apr. 14, 1961; m. Cynthia Caruso-Mapel; children: Xena, Sierra. BS in Chemistry, U. Tex., Arlington, 1984; MD, U. Tex., Galveston, 1988; MPH, U. N.Mex., 1996. Diplomate Am. Bd. Internal Medicine, Am. Bd. Pulmonary Diseases, Am. Bd. Critical Care Medicine. Resident Tex. Tech. U., Lubbock, 1988—92; fellow U. N.Mex., Albuquerque, 1992—96, asst. prof., 1996—2000, clin. prof., 2001—; med. dir. Lovelace Respiratory Rsch. Inst., Albuquerque, 2001—03, Lovelace Clinic Found., Albuquerque, 2003—; sr. ptnr. Progressive Med. Intensivists, 2003—06; founding ptnr., pres., CEO, Critical Care Cons. of Ariz., 2006—. Co-author: (book) Rom's Occupational Medicine, 1998, Occupational Disorders of the Lung, 2001. Fellow: Am. Coll. Chest Physicians; mem.: ACP, Am. Thoracic Soc. Home: PO Box 67050 Albuquerque NM 87193 Office: Lovelace Clin Found 2309 Renard Pl SE Ste 103 Albuquerque NM 87106 Office Phone: 505-262-7857. Business E-Mail: doug@lcfresearch.org.

**MAPEL, WILLIAM MARLEN RAINES,** retired bank executive; b. Maryville, Mo., Sept. 17, 1931; s. William and Evelyn (Raines) M.; m. Gail Manchee, June 21, 1958; children: Daniel B., Susan L., Stephen W. BA, Yale U., 1953. Indsl. relations asst. Union Carbide Corp., N.Y.C., 1953-57; with Citibank (N.A.), N.Y.C., 1957-88, asst. cashier, 1959-62, asst. v.p., 1962-64, v.p., 1964-69, sr. v.p., 1969-88. Bd. dirs. Churchill Capital Ptnrs., Atlantic Salmon Fedn., Que.-Labrador Found. Bd. dirs. Miramichi Salmon Assn. Mem. U.S. Srs. Golf Assn., Woodway Country Club, Pine Valley Golf Club, Anglers Club, Wolf's Head, Delta Kappa Epsilon. Home: 40 Pasture Ln Darien CT 06820-5618

**MAPES, GLYNN DEMPSEY,** newspaper editor; b. NYC, July 15, 1939; s. John George and Dorothy (Glynn) M.; m. Elizabeth Adlum, Apr. 13, 1963; children—Timothy Glynn, Susannah Glynn. BA, Williams Coll., 1961. Reporter Wall St. Jour., San Francisco, 1965-67, bur. chief Phila., 1967-70, fgn. editor N.Y.C., 1970-71, bur. chief, 1971-75, Page One editor, 1975-88,

Reports editor, 1988-89, bur. chief London, 1989-93, money and investing editor N.Y.C., 1993-99, asst. mgn. editor, 1999—. Served to lt. (j.g.) USN, 1961-65. Mem.: Bronx Opera Chorus, London Concert Choir Club, Collegiate Chorale Club. Democrat. Home: 37 W 12th St Apt 2H New York NY 10011-8503 Office: Wall St Jour 200 Liberty St New York NY 10281-1003 E-mail: gmapes@pipeline.com.

**MAPES, KIMBERLY R.,** biology educator; d. Jeffrey S. and Frances M. Mapes. BA in Biology, Cedarville (Ohio) U., 2000; M in Edn., Roberts Wesleyan Coll., Rochester, N.Y., 2005. Cert. profl. tchr. N.Y. Acad. support instr. Brighton H.S., Rochester, 2001—03, biology tchr., 2004—. Mem.: Am. Biology Tchrs. Avocation: travel.

**MAPLE, M. BRIAN,** physics professor; b. Nov. 20, 1939; BS in Physics with distinction, San Diego State U., 1963, AB in Math with distinction, 1963; MS in Physics, U. Calif., San Diego, 1965, PhD in Physics, 1969. Asst. rsch. physicist U. Calif., San Diego, 1969—75, assoc. prof. physics, 1973—75, assoc. prof. physics, 1975—81, prof. physics, 1981—90, assoc. rsch. physicist Inst. for Theoretical Physics Santa Barbara, 1980, Bernd T. Matthias endowed chair in physics San Diego, 1990—, dir. Ctr. Interface and Materials Sci., 1990—; Bernd T. Matthias scholar Ctr. for Materials Sci. Los Alamos Nat. Lab., N.Mex., 1993; dir. Inst. for Pure and Applied Phys. Scis. U. Calif., 1995—, chair dept. physics, 2004—, disting. prof. physics, 2005—. Vis. scientist U. Chile, Santiago, 1971, 1973; vis. prof. Inst. de Fisica Jose Balseiro, San Carlos de Bariloche, Argentina, 1974; lectr. in field; mem. rev. com. materials sci. and tech. divsn. Argonne Nat. Lab., 1983-90, chmn., 1987; mem. rev. com. Office of Basic Energy Scis. Rev. of the Materials Sci. Program at Lawrence Livermore Nat. Lab., 1985; mem. exec. com. High Flux Isotope Reactor User's Group, Oak Ridge Nat. Lab., 1984-91; mem. user's com. Francis Bitter Nat. Magnet Lab., 1984-87; mem. rev. com. materials scis. program rev. Ames Lab., 1990-93; mem. scientific adv. bd. CONNECT, 1990—; mem. adv. coun. Glenn T. Seaborg Inst. for Transactinium Sci. Lawrence Livermore Nat. Lab., 1991—. Co-editor: Applied Physics A, 1983-93, Superconductivity in d- and f-Band Metals, 1980, Valence Fluctuations in Solids, 1982, Superconductivity in Ternary Compounds, Vols. 32, 34, 1982, Proceedings of the Internat. Conf. on Strongly Correlated Electron Sys., 1994; guest editor Spl. Issue of Materials Rsch. Soc. Bulletin on High Tc Superconductors, 1989, 2 Spl. Issue of Materials Rsch. Soc. Bulletin on High Tc Superconductors, 1990, Handbook on the Physics and Chemistry of Rare Earths, Vols. 30, 31, High Temperature Superconductors, 2001; mem. editl. bd. Superconductivity Review. Recipient Lockheed Leadership scholarship, 1958-60, Rotary Club scholarship, 1958-60, Calif. State scholarship, 1961-62, John Simon Guggenheim Meml. Found. fellowship, 1984, Disting. Alumnus of Yr. award U. Calif., San Diego, 1987, Disting. Alumnus of Yr. award San Diego State U. Coll. Scis., 1988; inducted into Chula Vista HS Hall of Fame, 1990; recognized as one of world's most highly cited rschrs. Inst. Sci. Info., 2000. Fellow AAAS, Am. Physical Soc. (various positions selection com. for internat. prize on new materials, 1982-91, mem. exec. com. divsn. condensed matter physics 1985-89, vice-chmn. to chmn. divsn. 1986-88, mem. com. on meetings 1992-96, David Adler lectureship award 1996, centennial speaker 1998-99, Humboldt Rsch. award 1998, Frank H. Spedding award 1999, James C. McGroddy prize in New Materials 2000, Bernd T. Matthias prize Internat. Conf. Materials and Mechanisms of Superconductivity and High Temperature Superconductors 2000); mem. NAS, Am. Vacuum Soc., Materials Rsch. Soc., Calif. Catalysis Soc., Sigma Xi. Achievements include research in experimental condensed matter physics including superconductivity, magnetism, valence fluctuation and heavy fermion phenomena, strongly correlated election phenomena low temperature and high pressure physics, surface science and catalysis. Office: U Calif San Diego Dept Physics IPAPS 0319 9500 Gilman Dr La Jolla CA 92093-0319 E-mail: mbmaple@ucsd.edu.

**MAPLE, MARILYN JEAN,** educational media coordinator; b. Turtle Creek, Pa., Jan. 16, 1931; d. Harry Chester and Agnes (Dobbie) Kelley; 1 child, Sandra Maple. BA, U. Fla., 1972, MA, 1975, PhD, 1985. Journalist various newspaper including Mountain Eagle, Jasper, Ala., Boise (Idaho) Statesman, Daytona Beach (Fla.) Jour., Lorain (Ohio) Jour.: account exec. Frederides & Co., N.Y.C.; prodr. hist. films Fla. State Mus., Gainesville, 1967-69; writer, dir., prodr. med. and sci. films and TV prodns. for 6 medically related colls. U. Fla., Gainesville, 1969—. Pres. Media Modes, Inc., Gainesville. Author: On the Wings of a Butterfly; columnist Health Care Edn. mag.; contbr. Fla. Hist. Quar. Recipient Blakslee award, 1969, spl. award, 1979; Monsour lectr., 1979. Mem. Health Edn. Media Assn. (bd. dirs., awards 1977, 79), Phi Delta Kappa, Kappa Tau Alpha. Home: 1927 NW 7th Ln Gainesville FL 32603-1103 Office: U Fla PO Box 16J Gainesville FL 32602-0016 Personal E-mail: mmaple@atlantic.net.

**MAPLES, JIMMIE KAY,** mechanical engineer; b. Berryville, Ark., Jan. 11, 1940; s. William Floyd and Edith (Bowman) M.; m. Beverly Florence Hadden, June 12, 1965 (div. Dec. 1968); children: Myrtle Venita, Beverly Sue; m. Sharon Gay Jennings Stewart (div. June 1974). BSME, U. Ark., 1962; MSRP, S.W. Mo. State U., 1991. Registered profl. engr., Mo., Ala., Ga., W.Va., Ark. Assoc. engr. Lockheed Aircraft Service Co., Ontario, Calif., 1962-63; design engr. McDonnell Aircraft Co., St. Louis, 1965-68; bookkeeper, salesman, co-owner Glen Isle Shoes, Springfield, Mo., 1969-72; mech. engr. Warren and Goodin, Inc., Springfield, 1972-77; engr. systems and equipment Piper Aircraft Corp., Lakeland, Fla., 1977-81; sr. facility engr. Zenith Electronics Corp., Springfield, 1981-88; with Boone Internat. Corrugated Svcs., Inc., Waco, Tex., 1988-89; cons., author Maples Enterprizes, Springfield, 1989—; v.p. Corrugated Mech. Svcs. Inc., Nixa, Mo., 1990-95, Heartland Electronics Corp., 1995-97; engr. Godwin & Assocs., 1997—; treas. Mohawk Quality Remodeling Inc., 2000—. Mem. Boone County Hist., Harrison, Ark., Carroll County Hist. and Geol., Berryville, The Air Force Hist. Found., White River Valley Hist. Soc. Served with U.S. Army, 1963-65. Mem. Air Force Assn., Am. Aviation Hist. Soc., Nat. Cong. Res., The Rich Family Assn., U. Ark. Alumni Assn., Frontiersmen Camping Fraternity (Royal Rangers Daniel Boone chpt.) Democrat. Mem. Assembly of God. Avocations: stamp collecting/philately, genealogy, computers. Home: 2545 W Swallow St Springfield MO 65810-3623 also: Godwin & Assocs 1200 E Woodhurst Bldg P Springfield MO 65804 E-mail: godwinae@aol.com, jkmtree@aol.com.

**MAPLES, MARY LOU,** elementary school educator; Tchr. kindergarten Lessie Moore Elem. Sch., Pineville, La., 1974-97; early childhood Title I supr. Media Ctr., Pineville, 1997—. Recipient La. Tchr. of Yr. award La. Dept. Edn., 1992. Office: Media Ctr PO Box 1230 Alexandria LA 71309-1230 E-mail: maplesml@cox.netmail.com.

**MAPLES, MICHAEL D.,** career military officer; b. Bonham, Tex. m. Lynn; children: Meredith, Katherine, Elizabeth. Graduate, US Mil. Acad., 1971; MA in Organizational Behavior, Pacific Lutheran U. Commd. 2d. lt. US Army, 1971, advanced through grades to lt. gen., 2005; stationed at Ft. Lewis, Wash., Republic of Korea; tng. mgmt. officer Ft. Sam Houston, Tex.; various assignments Desert Shield/Desert Storm; sr. military aide to sec. US Army; comdr. Babenhausen, Hungary; dep. chief staff ops. US Army Europe, Tazar, Hungary, asst. chief of staff G3, V Corps Heidelberg, Germany; asst. divsn. comdr. (support) 1st Armored Divsn. US Army, dir. mil. support, Office Dep. Chief of Staff for Ops. & Plans, dir. ops., readiness & mobilization; commdg. gen. US Army Field Artillery Ctr., Ft. Sill, Okla., 2001—03; vice dir., dir. mgmt. The Joint Staff, The Pentagon, 2003—05; dir. Def. Intelligence Agy., 2005—. Decorated Legion of Merit with oak leaf cluster, Bronze Star medal, Def. Superior Svc. award with oak leaf cluster, Meritorious Svc. medal with three oak leaf clusters, Army Commendation medal with oak leaf cluster, Army Achievement medal, French Croix du Guerre with silver star. Office: Def Intelligence Agy 7400 Def Pentagon Washington DC 20301*

**MAPLES, PHILIP G.,** museum director; s. Philip B Maples and Jessie Hazel Galligan; m. Karen E Ritz, Mar. 26, 1977; children: Philip C, Susan E MA, SUNY, Brockport, N.Y., 1976. Curator of decorative arts Mattatuck Mus., Waterbury, Conn., 1971—72; asst. curator for registration Old Mus. Village of Smith's Clove, Monroe, NY, 1972; hist. rschr. and preparator Cayuga County Historian's Office, Auburn, NY, 1972—73; curator/dir. Arcade Hist. Soc., Arcade, NY, 1989—92, Baker-Cederberg Mus. and Archives, Rochester, NY, 1989—. Author: (institutional history) To Serve the Community: a Sesquicentennial History of Rochester General Hospital, 1847 to 1997, (monograph) Outline for an Emergency Medical Services History Program, Organizing a Healthcare History Program; contbr. articles in field to profl. jours. Fellow: Co. of Mil. Historians. Office: Baker-Cederberg Museum and Archives 333 Humboldt St Rochester NY 14610 Office Phone: 585-922-1847. Office Fax: 585-922-0018. Personal E-mail: p_maples@msn.com. E-mail: phil.maples@viahealth.org.

**MAPLESDEN, CAROL HARPER,** marriage and family therapist, music educator; b. Phila., Aug. 27, 1947; d. Emmitt Dewain and Helen Esther (Davison) Harper; m. James Paul Maplesden, May 27, 1967; children: Andrew James, Elizabeth Elvira. BA, Holy Family Coll., Phila., 1979; MA, La Salle U., Phila., 1984. Cert. counselor Nat. Bd. Cert. Counselors, lic. profl. counselor of mental health Del., Pa. Child, youth and family therapist People Acting To Help (PATH), Phila. 1983-86, Benjamin Rush Cmty. Mental Health, Phila., 1987-88; clin. dir. N.E. Treatment, Phila., 1988-89; outpatient supr. Interact Com. Mental Health, Phila., 1989; program supr. Cath. Charities Christopher House, Trenton, N.J., 1989-90; dir. Carden Family Inst., Phila., 1984—, CEO, 1984—, instr. keyboard, organist, vocal performer, vocal choir and handbell choir dir. Carden music div., 1993—. Seminar lectr. in Phila. area. Author: (piano course and audio tape) Young Beginnings Piano Course, Part I, 1993. Mem.: APA, NRC (hon. bus. chmn. 2004), ACA, Internat. Assn. Marriage and Family Counselors, Daus. Am. Colonists (chpt. vice regent 2006—), Daughters Union Vets. Civil War (Pa. state pres. 2001—02). Republican. Methodist. Avocations: history studies, genealogy, crafts. Office Phone: 215-741-4234.

**MAPOTHER, THOMAS CRUISE** See **CRUISE, TOM**

**MAPP, ALF JOHNSON, JR.,** writer, historian, educator; b. Portsmouth, Va., Feb. 17; s. Alf Johnson and Lorraine (Carney) M.; m. Hartley Lockhart, Mar. 28, 1953; 1 son, Alf Johnson III; m. Ramona Hartley Hamby, Aug. 1, 1971. *A 13-th generation Virginian in paternal descent and 12th in maternal, Mapp is the son of Alf Johnson Mapp, Sr., internationally honored public educator. He is a direct descendant of Alfred the Great and Charlemagne. Ancestors include more than 60 persons with separate sketches in the Encyclopedia Britannica.* AA, Coll. William and Mary, 1945, AB summa cum laude, 1961; LLD (hon.), Old Dominion U., 2006. Editorial writer Portsmouth Star, 1945-46, assoc. editor, 1946-48, editorial chief, 1948-54; news editor, editorial writer Virginian-Pilot, Norfolk, 1954-58; free-lance writer, 1958—; lectr. Old Dominion U., 1961-62, instr., 1962-67, asst. prof. English and history, 1967-73, asso prof. English, journalism, creative writing, history, 1973-79, prof., 1979-82, eminent prof., 1982-89, eminent scholar, 1989-92, eminent scholar emeritus, 1992—, Louis I. Jaffe prof. English, 1990-92; Louis I. Jaffe prof. emeritus, 1992—. Radio commentator WSAP, Portsmouth, Va., 1947-48; profl. lectr., 1984—; frequent analyst or guest on radio and TV including individual stas. and Universal Studio and BBC radio networks, CBS-TV, 1985—, C-SPAN, 1998—, PBS, 2001, NPR, 2001, CNN, 2001—, World-Wide Ave Maria Network, 2005.; mem. Nat. Jefferson-Hemings Scholars commn., 2001-2002. *Mapp's writings have circulated around the world in nine languages. The Worldware Encyclopedia of the States lists him as one of the two most important historians, and one of the seven most important writers in any category, born in 20th century Virginia. One of America's leading biographers, he is one of the world's three principal living authorities on Thomas Jefferson. He is the author of internationally acclaimed works on American and British history, and is an outstanding scholar in cultural history and interdisciplinary studies. He is in demand nationally and internationally as an informative and lively speaker and interviewee. "Reared in an intellectual family with high ethical standards, enthusiasm for the arts, and a firm belief in hard work, I also had impressed on me that advantages conferred obligations. In an historic environment, I became aware of my generation's responsibility to those that had preceded it (to preserve the good that they had created) and to those who would follow (to create things that would enrich their lives). This concept, with personal ambition, imbues my professional life"* Host TV series Jamestown to Yorktown, 1975-77; author: The Virginia Experiment, 1975, 3d edit., 1987, Frock Coats and Epaulets, 1963, 5th edit., 1996, America Creates Its Own Literature, 1965, Just One Man, 1968, The Golden Dragon: Alfred the Great and His Times, 1974, 4th edit., 1990, Thomas Jefferson: A Strange Case of Mistaken Identity, 1987, 3d edit., 1989 (Book-of-Month Club feature selection 1987), Thomas Jefferson: Passionate Pilgrim, 1991, 3d edit., 1993 (Book-of-Month Club feature selection 1991), (novel) Bed of Honor, 1995, 2d edit., 2000, Three Golden Ages: Discovering the Creative Secrets of Renaissance Florence, Elizabethan England, and America's Founding, 1998, Faiths of our Fathers: What America's Founders Really Believed, 2003 (prize book Coun. Am.'s 1st Freedom 2005); co-author: Chesapeake Bay in the Revolution, 1981, Portsmouth: A Pictorial History, 1989, Constitutionalism: Founding and Future, 1989, Constitutionalism and Human Rights, 1991, Great American Presidents, 1995; mem. editl. bd. Jamestown Found., 1967—; author lyrics for symphonic composition, world debut with Va. Symphony, 1998; nationally distributed AP editl., 1998; contbr. to N.Y. Times, Wall St. Jour., other newspapers and mags. Mem. Portsmouth-Norfolk County Savs. Bond Com, 1948-51, Va. Com. on Libr. Devel., 1949-50; mem. publs. com. 350th Anniversary of Rep. Govt. in the Western World, 1966-69, War of Independence Commn., 1967-83; chmn. Portsmouth Revolutionary Bicentennial Com., 1968-81; chmn. awards jury Baruch award United Daus. Confederacy-Columbia U., 1976, mem., 1980; chmn. Portsmouth Mus. and Fine Arts Commn., 1983-85, Southeastern Va. Anglo-Am. Friendship Day, 1976, Bicentennial Commemoration of Cornwallis' Embarkation for Yorktown, 1981, World Premiere of Mary Rose Marine Archeol. Exhibit, 1985; mem. grant rev. com. Va. Commn. for the Arts, 1986-87; bd. dirs. Portsmouth Pub. Libr., 1948-58, v.p., 1954-56; bd. dirs. Va. Symphony, 1986-87, trustee, 1987—; mem. taxes and mandates com. City of Portsmouth, 1982-86; mem. adv. com. City Mgr. of Norfolk, 1988-94; bd. dirs. Portsmouth Area Cmty. Chest, 1948-52, Va. YMCA Youth and Govt. Found., 1950-52; mem. All-Am. cities com. for award-winning city Nat. League Municipalities, 1976; bd. advisors Ctr. Study Interactive Learning, Pasadena, Calif., 1993—; mem. steering com. Old Dominion U. Friends of the Libr., 1994-2002, dir., 1995-2002; trustee Coun. for Am.'s First Freedom, 1994-98; chair ad hoc com. Joint Portsmouth-Suffolk Libr., 1999-2004; dir. Va. R.R. Mus., 2000—. Named Portsmouth Young Man of Year, 1951; recipient honor medal Freedoms Found., 1951, Disting. Rsch. award Old Dominion U., 1987, Great Citizen award Hampton Roads 8 Cities, 1987, Notable Citizen award Portsmouth, Va., 1987; English award Old Dominion Coll., 1961; Troubadour, Great Tchrs. award, 1969; Outstanding Am. Educator award, 1972, 74; Nat. Bicentennial medal Am. Revolution Bicentennial Adminstrsn., 1976; medal Comité Francais du Bicentenaire de l'Independence des Etats-Unis, France, 1976; (with Ramona Mapp) Nat. Family Svc. award Family Found. Am., 1980; Laureate award Commonwealth of Va., 1981; Disting. Alumnus award Old Dominion U., 1982; Liberty Bell award Portsmouth Bar Assn., 1985; Old Dominion U. Triennial Phi Kappa Phi Scholar award, 1986, 91; History medal Great Bridge Chpt.Daus. Am. Revolution; Portsmouth Downtown Merchants award, 1984, 85, Nat. Founders and Patriots award, 1995; Old Dominion U. Outstanding Achievement award, 1995; Gladstone Hill Friend of the Arts award (with Ramona H. Mapp), 1995, Richard Hakluyt award for Am. history, 2002, First Freedom Tchg. Excellence awrd named in his honor Coun. for Am.'s 1st Freedom, 2005; named to Order of the Crown of Charlemagne, 1993. Mem. Am. Hist. Assn., Va. Hist. Soc., Portsmouth Hist. Soc. (historiographer 1975-82, v.p. 1982-84, pres. 1985), Norfolk Hist. Soc. (dir. 1965-72), No. Neck Hist. Soc., Hist. Socs. Eastern Va. (dir. 1971—), SAR, Am. Assn. U. Profs., Authors Guild, Va. Library Assn. (legislative com. 1950-51), Poetry Soc. Va. (pres. 1974-75, adv. com. 1976—), Va. Writers Club, Assn. Preservation of Va. Antiquities, Order of Cape Henry (dir. 1970—, nat. pres. 1975-76), Jamestowne Soc. (chief historian 1975-77, internat. sec. state 1978-79), English Speaking Union (dir. 1976-77), Modern Lang. Assn., Order of First Families Va. 1607-1624 (councillor 1996-99), Nat.

Historians Circle, Phi Theta Kappa, Delta Phi Omega (chpt. pres. 1961), Phi Kappa Phi. Baptist. Home: Willow Oaks 2901 Tanbark Ln Portsmouth VA 23703-4828 Office Phone: 757-484-6273.

**MAPP, EDWARD CHARLES,** speech educator; b. NYC, Aug. 17, 1929; s. Edward Cameron and Estelle Viola (Sampson) Mapp; children: Andrew, Elmer, Everett. BA, CCNY, 1953; MS, Columbia U., 1956; PhD, NYU, 1970. Tchr. Bd. Edn., N.Y.C., 1957-64; dir. librs. N.Y.C. Tech. Coll. CUNY, 1964-77, dean of faculty Borough of Manhattan CC N.Y.C., 1977-81, prof. speech and communication, 1983-92, prof. emeritus, 1994—; vice chancellor City Colls. Chgo., 1982-83. Commr. N.Y. Commn. Human Rights, 1987—94, vice chair, 1992—94; treas. univ. faculty senate CUNY, 1974—77; model, 1994—2002. Compiler Books for Occupational Education Programs, 1971, Directory of Blacks in Performing Arts, 1978, Directory of Blacks in Performing Arts, 2d edit., 1990; editor: (book) Puerto Rican Perspectives, 1974; author: African-Americans and the Oscar, 2003, Blacks in American Films: Today and Yesterday, 1972, Wednesday at Weeksville, 2005; co-author: (book) A Separate Cinema, 1992; columnist: Movie/TV Mktg., 1979—91. Mem. Bklyn. Borough Pres. Adv. Panel, 1981—84; mem. exec. com. Com. Pub. Higher Edn., N.Y.C., 1978—81; bd. dirs. UN Assn. N.Y., 1975—78; trustee N.Y. Met. Ref. and Rsch. Agy., 1980—82. Named Comms. Educator of Yr., City Coll. N.Y., 2005; named to Black Collectors Hall of Fame, 1992; recipient Founders Day award, NYU, 1970, award, Acad. Motion Picture Arts and Scis., 1996. Mem.: Theatre Libr. Assn., Black Filmmakers Found., Audelco, Friends Thirteen (bd. dirs. 2000—, 1st vice chmn. 2003—05, chmn. 2005—), Archons Colophon (convenor 1985—86). Democrat.

**MAQBOOL, MUHAMMAD,** physics professor; b. Mardan, Pakistan; s. Alam Zeb and Rawasia Begum; m. Huma Riaz; 1 child, Malaika. MS in Med. Physics, Birmingham U., Eng., 1990; PhD, Ohio U., Athens, 2005. Rsch. asst. Ohio U., Athens, 2003—05; asst. prof. physics Mt. Olive Coll., NC, 2005—. Tchg. asst. Ohio U., Athens, 2001—03. Contbr. articles to profl. jours.; mem. editl. bd.: RNA, Molecular and Cellular Biology, RNA Biology. Commonwealth scholar, Commonwealth Assn. UK, 1997. Mem.: Am. Phys. Soc. (assoc.). Home: 901B East Harding Dr Goldsboro NC 27534 Office: Mount Olive Coll 634 Henderson St Mount Olive NC 28365 Office Phone: 919-658-7498. Personal E-mail: mmaqbool@gmail.com. E-mail: mmaqbool@moc.edu.

**MAQUAT, LYNNE E.,** biomedical researcher; Grad., U. Conn.; PhD in Biochemistry, U. Wis., Madison. Postdoctoral rschr. McArdle Lab. Cancer Rsch. U. Wis., Madison; rsch. scientist Roswell Pk. Cancer Inst.; mem. faculty to prof. biochemistry and biophysics James P. Wilmot Cancer Ctr. U. Rochester Med. Ctr., NY, 2000—. Contbr. articles to profl. jours.; mem. editl. bd.: RNA, Molecular and Cellular Biology, RNA Biology. Recipient Davey Meml. award, Outstanding Cancer Rsch., 2002. Fellow: Am. Acad. Arts & Scis.; mem.: Am. Soc. Cell Biology (mem. pub. info. com. 1992—), RNA Soc. (dir. 2000—02, pres. 2006—). Office: Dept Biochemistry and Biophysics U Rochester Sch Medicine and Dentistry 601 Elmwood Ave Box 712 Rochester NY 14642 E-mail: Lynne_Maquat@urmc.rochester.edu.*

**MARA, PATRICK SCOTT,** mathematics educator; b. Pueblo, Colo., Oct. 13, 1948; s. John Henry and Erma Lee Mara; m. Sally Ann Sabo, June 12, 1969; children: Tammy Cappellucci, Jeffrey. BS, Colo. State U., Ft. Collins, 1970, MS, 1972. Tchr. Highland H.S., Thornton, Colo., 1972—73, East H.S., Pueblo, Colo., 1973—85; math. specialist Sch. Dist. #60, Pueblo, 1985—86; tchr. South H.S., Pueblo, 1986—, chair math. dept., 1990—. Named Best Tchr. in Pueblo, Readers of the Pueblo Chieftain, 2006; recipient Presdl. award, NSF, 1989, Tchr. award, Milken Family Found., 1990, Disney award, Disney Channel, 1996. Fellow: Internat. Acad. Sci.; mem.: Nat. Coun. Tchrs. Math. Home: 633 Goodnight Pueblo CO 81005 Office: South HS 1801 Hollywood Pueblo CO 81005

**MARABLE, MANNING,** social science educator, writer; b. Dayton, Ohio, May 13, 1950; s. James Palmer and June (Morehead) M.; m. Hazel Ann Harris, Nov. 13, 1976; children: Malaika, Joshua, Sojourner. AB in History, Earlham Coll., 1971; MA in History, U. Wis., 1972; PhD in History, U. Md., 1976; D (hon.), SUNY, New Paltz, 2000. Lectr. Black studies Smith Coll., Northampton, Mass., 1974-76; assoc. prof., chair polit. sci. dept. Tuskegee (Ala.) Inst., 1976-78; assoc. prof. Africana Studies Ctr. Cornell U., Ithaca, NY, 1979-82; prof. econs. and history Fisk U., Nashville, 1982-83; prof. sociology, chair dept. Africana and Hispanic studies Colgate U., Hamilton, NY, 1983-86; prof. sociology Purdue U., West Lafayette, Ind., 1986-87; prof., chair dept. Black studies Ohio State U., Columbus, 1987-89; prof. polit. sci., rsch. assoc. Ctr. for Studies of Ethnicity and Race U. Colo., Boulder, 1989—93; dir. Inst. Rsch. in African-Am. Studies, prof. history Columbia Univ., NYC, 1993—. Luce Disting. prof. Williams Coll., Williamstown, Mass., 1982, 84; bd. dirs. Oral History of the Left, N.Y.U., 1983—; cons. Congl. Black Caucus, Washington, 1982—, Black Elected Dems. of Ohio, Columbus, 1988—. Author: How Capitalism Underdeveloped Black America, 1983, Race, Reform and Rebellion, 1984, Black American Politics, 1985 (book of yr. Socialist Rev. jour. 1986), W.E.B. Du Bois: Black Radical Democrat, 1986 (book of yr. Gustavus Myers Ctr. U. Ark. 1987), African and Caribbean Politics, 1987, Beyond Black and White: Transforming African-American Politics, 1995, (Book of Yr.Gustavus Myers Ctr. Study Human Rights, Univ. Ark., 1996), Speaking Truth to Power: Essays on Race, Resistance & Radicalism, 1996, Let Nobody Turn Us Around, 1999, The Great Wells of Democracy; The Meaning of Race in American Life, 2002, Living Black History: How Re-Imagining the African-American Past Can Remake America's Racial Future, 2006; co-editor (with Myrlie Evers Williams) The Autobiography Of Medgar Evers: A Hero's Life and Legacy Revealed Through His Writings, Letters, and Speeches, 2005; mem. editl. bd. Rev. Black Economy, 1983-87, Jour. Sport and Social Issues, 1983-87, The Witness, 1984—94. Grantee Columbus Found., 1989, Arthur J. Felberbaum award of Brecht Forum, 1989. Office: 758 Schermerhorn Extension Columbia Univ 1200 Amsterdam Ave New York NY 10027 E-mail: marable1@manningmarable.net.*

**MARABLE, SIMEON-DAVID,** artist; b. Phila., May 10, 1948; s. Daniel Berry and Marsima (Maddela) M.; m. Pamela Joyce Sorenson, June 1, 1969; children: Simeon-David dePaul, Daniel-Dale Christopher (dec.), Jason-Andrew Bartley, Jo Anna Lee, Benjamin Arthur Kurtis. BA in Art and English, Lea Coll., Minn., 1970; postgrad., Tyler Sch. Art, Phila. Art tchr. 7-8th grade Pennsbury Sch. Sys., Pa., 1970—88; Art tchr. 9-10th grade Charles H. Boehm H.S., Pennsbury, 1988—, Medill Bair H.S., Pennsbury, 1990—; Art tchr. 9-12th grade Pennsbury H.S. W, 2002—. Tchr. Neshaminy Adult Edn., 1972-82; resident artist Middletown Hist. Assn., 1976, Three Arches Corp., 1975, tex.; founder, creator Rivulet Art 2000. Permanent collections include Albert Lea (Minn.) Libr., chapel Ft. Dix, N.J., pencil/charcoal Am. Eagle superimposed over outline Levittown, Pa., James A. Michener Mus., 2003; portraits of Mr. Mike Schmidt, Mr. Lee Elia; creator Phila. City of Champs logo, 50th anniversary logo Fairless Hills, Pa. 1951-2001 Celebration; creator children's ednl. programs Falls Twp. 300th Pa. statehood; artwork represented in Middletown Twp. calendar, 1992, Falls Twp. calendar, 1992; creator Olde Phila. Ednl. Program and Pa. Statehood Program, Nat. Rep. Conv., Phila., 2000; creator scale model homes exhibit Pa. Hist. Mus., 2002; author: Levittown Pennsylvania 1952-2002 A Garden Community, 2002; sketch presented to Gov. of Pa. 2002, papers written of John S. Levitt, 2005, Raymond Fletcher Proffitt, profl. pilot and close friend of William J. Levitt, 2005. Vol. Rep. Nat. Conv., Phila., 2000; mgr. Boys Soccer League, Boys Little League, Middletown Twp.; sr. Babe Ruth coach, mgr. Langhorne Athletic Assn., 1988-89; sr. coach Babe Ruth League, 1989; J.V. baseball coach, 1989; mem. Presdl. Task Force; elected to Nat. Trust for Hist. Preservation, 1995; involved with ednl. program Honoring the 200th Anniversary U.S. Constn. Commemorative Olde Phila. Constn. Atty.; curator Levittown Exhibit, Pa.; pres. Levittown Internationally Known Communities Inc., 2003—; program dir. Dream of America 1952 Photographs and Memorabilia of Levittown and Bucks County, Pa., Snowball Gate Dr. Levittown Exhibit Ctr, 2003. Served in USAR, 1970. Named Artist of Yr., Albert Lea Lions Club, 1970. Mem. Buck County Art Educators (pres.

1973-74), Levittown Artists Assn., Nat. Soc. Arts and Lit., Internat. Platform Assn. Roman Catholic. Achievements include development of Levitt Mobile that houses memorabilia and photog. of the 1950's in Buck's Co., Pa. Home: 18 Spindletree Rd Levittown PA 19056-2215 Office: Levittown Exhibit Ctr North 283 Snowball Dr Levittown PA 19056 Office Phone: 215-945-4558. Personal E-mail: amx_12345@hotmail.com.

**MARADIAGA KIEFFER-AANONSEN, NORA LUDMILA,** language educator; b. La Ceiba, Honduras, Dec. 18, 1957; arrived in U.S., 1980; d. Carlos Maradiaga and Ana Ludmila Kieffer-Maradiaga; m. Richard Alfred Aanonsen, June 8, 2002. AA, El Camino C.C., Torrance, Calif., 1989; BA in Global Politics, Spanish Lit., Calif. State U., Dominguez Hills, 1993, MA, 1995; postgrad., Calif. Coast U., Santa Ana, 1999. Bilingual tchr. asst. LA Unified Sch. Dist., 1981—90, bilingual spl. edn. trainee, 1990—94; bilingual spanish educator Compton (Calif.) Sch. Dist., 1994—2000; Spanish educator Compton Coll., 1997—, Spanish prof. upward bound math. and sci. program, 2002—. Spanish translator Compton Coll., 1999—2001, student campus climate surveys, 1997, 98, 2000. Mem.: Calif. Tchr. Assn., Calif. Bilingual Edn., El Camino Coll. Student Assn., Dominguez Hills U. Student Assn., Alpha Phi. Democrat-Npl. Roman Catholic. Avocations: reading, acting, jogging, travel, martial arts. Home: 15327 Mansel Ave Lawndale CA 90260 Office: Compton C C 1111 E Artesia Blvd Compton CA 90221 E-mail: noraludmila1@aol.com

**MARADUDIN, ALEXEI A.,** physics professor; b. San Francisco, Dec. 14, 1931; BS, Stanford U., 1953, MS, 1954; PhD in Physics, Bristol U., 1957; D (hon.), U. Pierre et Marie Curie, Paris, 1986. Rsch. assoc. physicist U. Md., College Park, 1956—57, rsch. asst. prof., 1957—58; asst. rsch. prof. Inst. Fluid Dynamics & Applied Math., 1958—60; physicist Westinghouse Rsch. Labs., Churchill Borough, Pa., 1960—65; cons. semiconductor br. U.S. Naval Rsch. Lab., Washington, 1958—60, Los Alamos Sci. Lab., N.Mex., 1965—67, 1983—89, Gen. Atomic Divsn. Gen. Dynamics Corp., 1965—71; prof. physics U. Calif., Irvine, 1965—, chmn. dept., 1968—71. Recipient Alexander von Humboldt U.S. Sr. Scientist award, 1980—81. Fellow: AAAS, Am. Phys. Soc., Optical Soc. Am., Inst. Physics (U.K.); mem.: Phi Beta Kappa, Sigma Xi, Tau Beta Pi. Office: U Calif Irvine Dept Physics & Astronomy Frederick Reines Hl # 2180 Irvine CA 92697-4575 Office Phone: 949-824-5943. Business E-Mail: aamaradu@uci.edu.

**MARAMAN, KATHERINE ANN,** judge; b. Los Alamos, N.Mex., Aug. 13, 1951; d. William Joseph and Katherine Ann (Thorpe) Maraman. BA, Colorado Coll., 1973; JD, U. N.Mex., 1976. Bar: N.Mex. 1976, Guam 1978, Trust Territory Pacific Islands, Commonwealth of No. Mariana Islands, U.S. Ct. Appeals (9th cir.), U.S. Supreme Ct. Draftsperson N.Mex. Legis. Coun. Svc., Santa Fe, 1976—77; atty. Brooks & Klitzkie, P.C., Agana, Guam, 1977—84; pvt. practice Agana, 1985—88; counsel Office of Gov., Agana, 1988—94; judge Superior Ct., Agana, 1994—. Mem. asst. legis. counsel Guam Legis., Agana, 1977—80, mem. minority counsel, 1981—87; bd. dirs. Pub. Defender Svc. Corp., Agana, 1988—94. Trustee Guam Ter. Law Libr., 1994—; counsel Rep. Party, Agana, 1981—94; deacon First Presbyn. Reformed Ch., Agana; bd. dirs. Guam Rehab. and Workshop, Inc., Tumon, Guam, 1983—95. Mem.: Guam Bar Assn. Office: Superior Ct Guam 120 W Obrien Dr Hagatna GU 96910-5174

**MARAMOROSCH, KARL,** virologist, educator; b. Vienna, Jan. 16, 1915; came to U.S., 1947, naturalized, 1952; s. Jacob and Stefanie Olga (Schlesinger) M.; m. Irene Ludwinowska, Nov. 15, 1938; 1 dau., Lydia Ann. MS magna cum laude in Entomology, Agrl. U., Warsaw, Poland, 1938; student, Poly. U. Bucharest, Rumania, 1944-46; fellow, Bklyn. Bot. Garden, 1947-48; PhD (predoctoral fellow Am. Cancer Soc. 1948-49), Columbia, 1949. Civilian internee in, Rumania, 1939-46; asst., then assoc. Rockefeller U., N.Y.C., 1949-61; sr. entomologist Boyce Thompson Inst., Yonkers, NY, 1961-74, program dir. virology and insect physiology, 1962-74; prof. microbiology Waksman Inst., Rutgers U., New Brunswick, NJ, 1974-85; prof. entomology Cook Coll., Rutgers U., New Brunswick, 1985—, Robert L. Starkey prof., 1983—; vis. prof. agr. U. Wageningen, Netherlands, 1953, Cornell U., 1957, Rutgers U., 1967-68, Fordham U., 1973, Hokkaido U., Sapporo, Japan, 1980, Justus Liebig U., Giessen, Ger., 1983. Mendel lectr. St. Peters Coll., Jersey City, 1963; virologist FAO to Philippines, 1960; Disting. Vis. prof. Fudan U., Shanghai, 1982; cons. FAO-UN, World-wide survey, 1963; chmn. U.S.-Japan Coop. Seminar, 1965, 74, 85; mem. panel food and fiber Nat. Acad. Scis., 1966; cons. rice virus diseases AID-IRRI, Hyderabad, India, 1971; cons. UNDP, Bangalore, India, 1978-79; virologist FAO/UNDP, Sri Lanka, 1981, 82, 83, Mauritius, 1985; AIBS lectr., 1970-72, Found. Microbiology Nat. lectr., 1972-73, Fulbright Disting. lectr., Yugoslavia, 1972, 78; mem. tropical medicine and parasitology study sect. NIH, 1972-76; chmn. 1st-3d Internat. Confs. Comparative Virology, 1969, 73, 76. Author: Comparative Symptomatology of Coconut Diseases of Unknown Etiology, 1964; editor: Biological Transmission of Disease Agents, 1962, Insect Viruses, 1968, Viruses, Vectors and Vegetation, 1969, Comparative Virology, 1971, Mycoplasma Diseases, 1973, Viruses, Evolution and Cancer, 1974, Invertebrate Immunity, 1975, Legume Diseases in the Tropics, 1975, Invertebrate Tissue Culture: Research Applications, 1976, Invertebrate Tissue Culture: Applications in Medicine, Biology and Agriculture, 1976, Aphids as Virus Vectors, 1977, Insect and Plant Viruses: An Atlas, 1977, Viruses and Environment, 1978, Practical Tissue Culture Applications, 1979, Leafhopper Vectors and Plant Disease Agents, 1979, Vectors of Plant Pathogens, 1980, Invertebrate Systems in Vitro, 1980, Vectors of Disease Agents, 1981, Mycoplasma Diseases of Trees and Shrubs, 1981, Mycoplasma and Allied Pathogens of Plants, Animals and Human Beings, 1981, Plant Diseases and Vectors: Ecology and Epidemiology, 1981, Invertebrate Cell Culture Applications, 1982, Pathogens, Vectors and Plant Diseases: Approaches to Control, 1982, Subviral Pathogens of Plants and Animals, 1985, Viral Insecticides for Biological Control, 1985, Biotechnology Advances in Insect Pathology and Cell Culture, 1987, Mycoplasma Diseases of Crops, 1988, Invertebrate and Fish Tissue Culture, 1988, Biotechnology for Biological Control of Pests and Vectors, 1991, Viroids and Satellites: Molecular Parasites at the Frontier of Life, 1991, Plant Diseases of Uncertain Etiology, 1992, Insect Cell Biotechnology, 1994, Arthropod Cell Culture Systems, 1994, Forest Trees and Palms: Diseases and Control, 1996, Invertebrate Cell Culture: Novel Directions and Biotechnology Applications, 1997, Invertebrate Cell Culture: Looking Toward the XXI Century, 1997, Biotechnology and Plant Protection in Forestry Sci., 1998, Maintenance of Human, Animal, and Plant Pathogen Vectors, 1999; Methods in Virology, 1964-84, Advances in Virus Research, 1972—; Archives of Virology, 1973-78, Intervirology, 1973-77, Advances in Cell Culture, 1979-89, Jour. Virological Methods, 1980-; editor in chief Jour. NY Entomol. Soc., 1972-84; assoc. editor: Virology, 1964-68, 75-79. Recipient Sr. Rsch., Lalor Found., 1957, Nat. Ciba-Geigy award in agr., 1976, Wolf prize in agr., Wolf Found., Israel, 1980, Jurzykowski prize in biology, 1980, Disting. Svc. award, Am. Inst. Biol. Scis., 1983, Khailshanker Durlabhji award, Jaipur, 1993, Lifetime Achievement award, Soc. In Vitro Biology, 2001. Fellow AAAS (hon., Campbell award 1958), Entomol. Soc. Am. (L.O. Howard Disting. Achievement award 2006), Am. Phytopath. Soc., N.Y. Acad. Scis. (A. Cressy Morrison prize natural sci. 1951, chmn. div. microbiology 1960-60, rec. sec. 1960-61, v.p. 1962-63), Nat. Acad. Scis. India (hon.); mem. Harvey Soc., Growth Soc., Phytopath. Soc., Indian, Japan, Can. phytopath. socs., Leopoldina Acad., Internat. Com. Virus Nomenclature, Electron Microscopy Soc., Am. Soc. Microbiology (Waksman award 1978), Soc. In Vitro Biology (Tissue Culture Assn., pres. N.E. br. 1978-81, pres. history br. 1988-90, Disting. Lifetime Achievement award 2001), Soc. Invertebrate Pathology (founder's lectr. Adelaide 1990, Founder's honoree Sapporo 1998), Internat. Assn. Medicinal Forest Plants (pres. 1989—), Sigma Xi (pres. Rugers chpt. 1978). Home: 17 Black Birch Ln Scarsdale NY 10583-7456 Office: Rutgers U Dept Entomology New Brunswick NJ 08901 Business E-Mail: maramors@rci.rutgers.edu.

**MARAN, DAVID,** lawyer; b. Newark, Nov. 4, 1958; m. Denise Del Sordo; married 1984; children: Rachel, Joseph, Daniel. BS in Math., Union Coll., 1980; JD, N.Y. Law Sch., 1984. Bar: N.J. 1985, U.S. Dist. Ct. N.J. 1985.

Assoc. Joe Maran, Newark, 1985-87; ptnr. Maran & Maran, Newark, 1987—2002, Maran & Maran PC, 2001—. Home: PO Box 200282 Newark NJ 07102-0305 Office Phone: 201-622-5303. Business E-Mail: dmaran@njmalpractice.com.

**MARAN, STEPHEN PAUL,** astronomer; b. Bklyn., Dec. 25, 1938; s. Alexander P. and Clara F. (Schoenfeld) M.; m. Sally Ann Scott, Feb. 14, 1971; children: Michael Scott, Enid Rebecca, Elissa Jean. BS, Bklyn. Coll., 1959; MA, U. Mich., 1961, PhD, 1964. Astronomer Kitt Peak Nat. Obs., Tucson, 1964-69; project scientist for orbiting solar observatories NASA-Goddard Space Flight Center, Greenbelt, Md., 1969-75; head advanced systems and ground observations br. NASA-Goddard Space Flight Ctr., 1970-77, mgr. Operation Kohoutek, 1973-74, sr. staff scientist Lab. for Astronomy and Solar Physics, 1977-95; asst. dir. Space Scis. for Info. and Outreach, 1995—2004. Cons. Westinghouse Rsch. Labs., 1966; vis. lectr. U. Md., College Park, 1969-70; sr. lectr. UCLA, 1976; press officer Am. Astron. Soc., 1985—; A. Dixon Johnson lectr. in sci. comm., Pa. State U., 1990; vis. scholar Univ. Ctr. Ga., 1997; lectr. on astronomy cruises and eclipse tours. Author: (with John C. Brandt) New Horizons in Astronomy, 1972, 2d edit., 1979, Arabic edit., 1979, (with Jacqueline Mitton) Gems of Hubble-Superb Images from the Hubble Telescope, 1996, Astronomy for Dummies, 1999, 2d edit. 2005, German edit. 2000, 2d German edit. 2004, French edit. 2001, Chinese edit. 2001, Russian edit. 2004, Dutch edit. 2005; editor: Physics of Nonthermal Radio Sources, 1964, The Gum Nebula and Related Problems, 1971, Possible Relations Between Solar Activity and Meteorological Phenomena, 1975, New Astronomy and Space Science Reader, 1977, A Meeting with the Universe, 1981, Astrophysics of Brown Dwarfs, 1986, The Astronomy and Astrophysics Encyclopedia, 1991; assoc. editor: Earth, Extraterrestrial Scis, 1969-79; editor: Astrophys. Letters, 1974-77, assoc. editor, 1977-85; contbg. editor Air & Space/Smithsonian, 1990—; mem. editl. adv. bd. Astronomy Mag., 1997—, Astronomy and Geophysics, 1997—; contbr. articles on astronomy, space to popular mags. Named Disting. Visitor Boston U., 1970; recipient Group Achievement awards NASA, 1969, 74, Exceptional Achievement medal, 1991, Klumpke-Roberts award Astron. Soc. of Pacific, 1999. Fellow AAAS; mem. Internat. Astron. Union (editor daily newspaper 1988, Minor Planet 9768 named Stephenmaran in honor 2000), Am. Astron. Soc. (Harlow Shapley vis. lectr. 1981—), press. officer 1985—), Royal Astron. Soc., Am. Phys. Soc., Am. Geophys. Union. Office: Am Astronomical Soc Ste 400 2000 Florida Ave NW Washington DC 20009 Office Phone: 202-328-2010 116. Business E-Mail: maran@aas.org.

**MARANCHIE, JODI KATHLEEN,** urologist, oncologist, researcher; d. Joseph Steven Maranchie and Marylin Diane Brown; m. Leonard Joseph Appleman, Sept. 25, 1999; children: Mark Campbell Appleman, Katherine Sandra Appleman. BS in Biochemistry, Brown U., Providence, 1989; MD, Northwestern U. Med. Sch., Chgo., 1993. Bd. cert. Am. Bd. Urology, 2004. Asst. prof. surgery and cell biology U. Mass. Med. Sch., Worcester, 2002—06; asst. prof. urology U. Pitts., 2006—. Dir. urologic oncology U. Mass., 2004—06. Fellow, Harvard Program Urology, 1999, Urologic Oncology Br. Nat. Cancer Inst., 2002; grantee, Nat. Inst. Diabetes and Digestive and Kidney, 2003—. Fellow: ACS; mem.: Assn. Women Urology, Am. Urologic Assn., Soc. Urologic Oncology. Achievements include research in Molecular Genetics of Renal Cell Carcinoma.

**MARANO, ANTHONY JOSEPH,** cardiologist; b. White Plains, NY, Apr. 14, 1934; s. Anthony Joseph and Mary Antoinette (Perrotta) M.; m. Mary Regina Marbach, Aug. 23, 1958; children—Thomas, Kathryn, Michele. BA, Williams Coll., 1956; MD, Cornell Med. Coll., 1960. Diplomate Am. Bd. Internal Medicine, Am. Bd. Cardiovasc. Disease. Intern Bellevue Hosp., NYC, 1960-61; resident St. Luke's Hosp., NYC, 1970-86; NIH fellow in cardiology Mt. Sinai Hosp., NYC, 1963-64, rsch. assoc., 1964-75; clin. assoc. in medicine Coll. Physicians and Surgeons, NYC, 1970-86; pres. med. staff White Plains Hosp., 1984-86, chief cardiology, 1985-91, chief cardiology emeritus, 1991—, bd. dirs., 1983-88; cons. in cardiology Burke Rehab. Ctr.; med. dir., founder Paramedic Ambulance, White Plains, 1976-82. Contbr. articles to profl. jours. Trustee Pace U., NYC, 1975—, Home Savs. Bank, White Plains, 1973-90; bd. dirs. YMCA, White Plains, 1978-82; team physician White Plains HS, 1967—; cons. physician Dept. Pub. Safety, White Plains, 1968—; cons. physician City of White Plains Sch. System, 1994—98; bd. dirs. Westchester County Sports Hall of Fame, 1993—; alumni trustee Tyng Found., Williams Coll., 1994—. Tyng scholar Williams Coll., 1952-59; recipient Outstanding Achievement award Emergency Med. Svcs. Coun., 1982, YMCA Ctrl. Westchester Cmty. Svc. award, 2006; named to White Plains HS Hall of Fame, 1998; Anthony J. Marano MD Cardiac Care Unit at White Plains Hosp. Ctr. named in his honor, 2005. Fellow ACP, Am. Coll. Cardiology; mem. AMA, Am. Coll. Sports Medicine, Am. Heart Assn., NY State Heart Assn. (bd. dirs. 1982-85), Westchester Heart Assn. (v.p. 1983-86, pres. 1987-90), Univ. Club (White Plains, pres. 1970-71) Westchester Country Club (Harrison, NY), Phi Beta Kappa. Avocations: gardening, swimming. Home: 46 Eagle Ct White Plains NY 10605-5116 Office: 15 North Broadway White Plains NY 10605 Office Phone: 914-948-8838.

**MARANO, RICHARD MICHAEL,** judge; b. Waterbury, Conn., June 22, 1960; s. Albert Nicholas and Angeline Domenica (Viotti) M.; m. Eileen N. Barry. BA, Fairfield U., 1982; JD, Seton Hall U., 1985. Bar: Conn. 1985, US Dist. Ct. Conn. 1985, US Tax Ct. 1986, US Supreme Ct. 1990, US Ct. Appeals (2d cir.) 1991; cert. criminal trial advocate. Assoc. Moynahan, Ruskin, Mascolo & Mariani, Waterbury, 1985-87; ptnr. Marano & Diamond, Waterbury, 1987—2001, Marano Law Offices, 2001—04; superior ct. judge, 2004—. Bd. of examiners Nat. Bd. Trial Advocacy, 1999-2004 Author: History of the Order Sons of Italy of Waterbury, Connecticut, 1995, Connecticut Criminal Legal Forms, 1999, Vote Your Conscience: The Last Campaign of George McGovern, 2003; co-author: Growing Up Italian and American in Waterbury, 1997; co-editor: Counsel for the Defense, 1991-93, editor, 1993-98; contbr. law articles to conn. Bar Jour. Bd. dirs. Italian-Am. Dem. Club, Waterbury, 1988-2004, Ctrl. Naugatuck Valley HELP, 1992-2005, Anderson Boys Club, 1989-2002, pres. 1996-98, Waterbury Housing Police Fund, 1992-94, Waterbury Crime Stoppers Inc., 1994-97; pres. Conn. Young Dems., 1981-82; state coord. McGovern for US Presdl. campaign, 1983-84; campaign mgr. Orman for Congress, 1984; active Oxford Dem. Town Com., 2002-2004; commr. Waterbury Pub. Assistance, 1986-88, Waterbury Fire Bd., 1996-98; justice of the peace, Waterbury, 1989-99; gen. counsel Waterbury Dem. Town Com., 1990-96; trustee Our Lady of Lourdes Ch., 1993—; alderman City of Waterbury, 1988-90; mem. adv. bd. Housatonic coun. Boy Scouts Am., 2004—, v.p., 2006—; mem. bldg. com. Oxford H.S., 2004. Mem. Nat. Assn. Criminal Def. Lawyers (life), Conn. Criminal Def. Lawyers Assn. (pres.-elect 1997-98, pres. 1998-99), Conn. Italian-Am. Bar Assn. (pres. 1993-95), Waterbury Bar Assn. (bd. dirs. 1993-02, pres. 1996-98), New Haven County Bar Assn., Nat. Italian-Am. Bar Assn. (Conn. delegate 1993-04), Sons of Italy (pres. lodge #66 1994-96), Unico Club (pres. Waterbury chpt. 1997-99), Cath. Lawyers Guild, Conn. Acad. Cert. Trial Lawyers, Nat. Eagle Scout Assn. (life), Elks, Alpha Mu Gamma, Pi Sigma Alpha. Roman Catholic. Home: 24 Lake Dr Oxford CT 06478-1172 E-mail: richardmarano@aol.com.

**MARASH, DAVID,** television news correspondent; b. Atlanta, May 3, 1942; s. Jack Paul and Ina (Havelin) M. BA cum laude, Williams Coll., 1964; postgrad., Rutgers U. Newsman stas. in Mass., N.J. and N.Y., 1959-72; news corr., anchorman Sta. WCBS-TV, N.Y.C., 1973-77, 81-82; newsman 20/20, ABC-TV News, N.Y.C., 1978-81, NBC-TV, N.Y.C., 1983-85; anchorman Sta. WRC-TV, Washington, 1985-89; corr. ABC Nightline, Washington, 1989—2006; co-anchor Al Jazeera English Lang. Network, Washington, 2006—. Mem. faculty Rutgers U., 1964-67, Williams Coll., 1970, 71, Ramapo (N.J.) State Coll., 1976. Bd. dirs. Com. to Protect Journalists, 1981—, chmn., 1983-85. Recipient Overseas Press Club award, 1972, N.Y. area Emmy award, 1976, 83, Nat. Emmy award, 1980, Washington area Emmy award 1986, 88, 89. Office: Al Jazeera English Lang Network 1600 K St NW Washington DC 20006*

**MARAVELIAS, CHRISTOS THEODOROS,** engineering educator; b. Athens, Greece, Aug. 26, 1973; arrived in US, 1999; s. Theodoros Maravelias and Flora Maravelia. Diploma, Nat. Tech. U., Athens, 1996; MSc, London Sch. Econ., 1997; PhD, Carnegie Mellon U., Pitts., 2004. Rsch. asst. Carnegie Mellon U., 1999—2004; asst. prof. U. Wis., Madison, 2004—. Manuscript reviewer jours. in field; organizer confs. in field. Contbr. articles to profl. jours. Recipient Career award, NSF, 2006; fellow, Alexander Onassis Found., 1999, U. Wis., 2004. Mem.: AIChemE, Inst. Indsl. Engrs., Inst. Ops. Rsch. and Mfmt. Sci. Office: U Wis 1415 Engineering Dr Madison WI 53706

**MARAVIGLIA, BRUNO,** physicist, researcher; b. Pescia/Pistoia, Tuscany, Italy, Apr. 29, 1938; s. Narciso and Nada (Guidi) M.; m. Maria Antonietta Macri, Jan. 31, 1992; 1 child, Beatrice. Master's degree, U. Florence, Italy, 1962; postgrad., La Sapienza U., Rome, 1964. Researcher Nat. Inst. Nuclear Physics, Rome, 1962-68; asst. prof. physics Duke U., Durham, NC, 1969-70; assoc. prof. Inst. Physics La Sapienza U., Rome, 1970-79, prof. physics, 1980—, dir. Postgrad. Sch. Med. Physics, 1986—, dir. dept. physics, 1992-95. Vis. prof. dept. physics U. B.C., Vancouver, Can., 1977-78; dir. magnetic resonance and brain function E. Fermi Sch. Physics., 1998 Editor: Physics of NMR Spectroscopy, 1988, Nuclear Magnetic Double Resonance, 1992, (book procs.) XXIII Congress Ampere, 1986; contbr. over 170 articles to profl. jours.; mem. editorial bd. Jour. Magnetic Resonance, 1992-99, Magnetic Resonance in Medicine, 1986—, Applied Magnetic Resonance, 1990—, Solid State Nuclear Magnetic Resonance, 1995—. Mem. coun. Mus. of Physics and Sci. Ctr. E. Fermi, Rome, 2000—. Mem. Internat. Soc. Magnetic Resonance (com. mem. 1985—), Soc. Magnetic Resonance in Medicine, Italian Phys. Soc., Groupement Ampere (v.p. 1986-94, pres. 1994-2000). Avocations: skiing, hiking, archaeology. Home: Via Jacopo Sannazzaro 82 00141 Rome Italy Office: La Sapienza U Dept Physics P le Aldo Moro 2 00185 Rome Italy Office Phone: +39 06 4454859. E-mail: bruno.maraviglia@romal.infn.it.

**MARAVOLO, NICHOLAS C.,** biology professor; b. Chgo., Dec. 4, 1940; s. Nicholas and Mary Ann Maravolo. SB, U. Chgo., 1962, MS, 1964, PhD, 1966. Prof. biology Lawrence U., Appleton, Wis., 1966—. Author: numerous articles in refereed jours. Mem.: Am. Assn. Plant Biologies. Office: Lawrence Univ PO Box 599 Appleton WI 54912 Business E-Mail: nicholas.c.maravolo@lawrence.edu.

**MARAYNES, ALLAN LAWRENCE,** filmmaker, television producer; b. N.Y.C., Apr. 26, 1950; s. Harry and Dorothy (Kaufman) Maraynes; m. Bitsy Healy, Oct. 14, 1978; children: Sean, Megan, Matthew. BA, Queens Coll., 1972; MA, Loyola U., L.A., 1974. Assoc. prodr. CBS News, N.Y.C., 1976-77, prodr. 60 Minutes, 1974-88, writer, dir. 60 Minutes, 1976-88; pres. No. Films, N.Y.C., 1988-90; exec. prodr. "SST" program ABC, N.Y.C., 1989; prodr. 20/20 ABC News, N.Y.C., 1990-93, sr. investigative prodr. 20/20, 1994-96; sr. investigative prodr. Dateline NBC, N.Y.C., 1996—. Lectr. New Sch., N.Y.C., 1979, Columbia U., N.Y.C. Author: (plays) A Straight Line to the Market Place, 1975, (screenplays) Smithereens, 1999, Track Rats, 2005. Recipient Emmy award, NATAS, 1981, 1985, 1988, 1989, 1991, 1993, 1995, 1997, 1998, 2002, 2004, George Foster Peabody award, 1989, 2000, Edward R. Murrow award, 1997, 1998, 2000, Investigative Reporters and Editors award, 1997, 2000—01, DuPont Columbia Journalism award, 2000, George Polk award, 2000, Overseas Press Club award, 2002. Mem.: NATAS, Writers Guild Am. Office: NBC 30 Rockefeller Plz Fl 2 New York NY 10112-0036 E-mail: ALLAN.MARAYNES@NBC.COM.

**MARAZITA, MARY LOUISE,** genetics researcher; b. Cheboygan, Mich., June 13, 1954; m. Richard T. McCoy, 1984; 5 children. BS, Mich. State U., East Lansing, 1976; PhD in Genetics, U. N.C., 1980. Fellow U. So. Calif., 1980-82; statistician, instr. UCLA, 1982-86; asst. prof. human genetics Med. Coll. Va., 1986-93; dir. Palate-craniofacial Ctr. U. Pitts., 1993-00, head divsn. oral biology, 1999—, asst. dean for rsch. Sch. Dental Medicine, 2000-2001, assoc. dean rsch., 2001—, dept. chair, 2006—. Instr. biomath. U. Calif., 1984-86; asst. prof. dentistry Med. Coll. Va., 1992-93; assoc. prof. human genetics and oral maxillofacial surgery U. Pitts., 1993-97, prof. human genetics and oral and maxillofacial surgery, 1997—, prof. psychiatry, 2003—. Fellow Am. Coll. Med. Genetics, Am. Cleft Palate Assn., Am. Soc. Human Genetics, Internat. Genetic Epidemiol. Soc., Internat. Assn. Dental Rsch. Achievements include research in genetics of cleft lip, cleft palate and other craniofacial anomalies, including statistical genetic analysis and gene mapping studies. Office: U Pitts Divsn Oral Biology/Genetics Ste 500 Cellomics Bldg/100 Technology Dr Pittsburgh PA 15219 Business E-Mail: marazita@sdmgenetics.pitt.edu.

**MARBAIS, PETER CHRISTIAN,** language educator; b. East Liverpool, Ohio, July 1, 1973; s. James and Margaret Marbais. PhD, Kent (Ohio) State U., 2005. Instr. English Hutchinson (Kans.) CC, 2000—06; asst. prof. Mt. Olive (NC) Coll., 2006—. Mem.: Internat. John Bunyan Soc., Am. Soc. Eighteenth-Century Studies. Home: 5134 Berry Rose Way Cary NC 27511 Office: Mount Olive Coll 634 Henderson St Mount Olive NC 28365 Office Phone: 919-658-7850. Business E-Mail: pmarbais@moc.edu.

**MARBLE, DUANE FRANCIS,** geography educator, researcher; b. Seattle, Dec. 10, 1931; s. Francis Augustus and Beulah Belle (Simmons) M.; m. Jacquelynne Hardester, Aug. 18, 1957; children: Kimberley Eileen Wood, Douglas Craig. BA, U. Wash., 1953, MA, 1956, PhD, 1959. Asst. prof. real estate U. Oreg., Eugene, 1959; asst. prof. regional sci. U. Pa., Phila., 1960-63; from assoc. prof. geography to prof. geography Northwestern U., Evanston, Ill., 1963-73, assoc. dir. Transp. Ctr., 1966-73; prof. geography and computer sci. SUNY at Buffalo, Amherst, NY, 1973-87; prof. geography and natural resources Ohio State U., Columbus, 1987-98, prof. emeritus, 1998—. Courtesy prof. U. Oreg., 2003—. Chmn. com. on geog. data sensing and processing Internat. Geog. Union, 1980-88; bd. dirs. Castlereagh Enterprises, Phoenix; founder Internat. Symposium Spatial Data Handling; mem. steering com. Pleiades Ancient Geography Project, 2005—; cons. on geog. info. systems to U.S. Bur. Census, UN, also pvt. orgns. Editor: Intro Readings in GIS, 1990, Taylor & Francis, 1990-95; author computer program (best software award Assn. Am. Geogs. 1990); mem. editl. bd. Annals of Assn. Am. Geography, 2000-05, Internat. Jour. of Geographic Info. Sys., 1987-97. Recipient Legend in Leadership award, Environ. Sys. Rsch. Inst., 1997, Making a Difference award, 2004. Mem.: Florence Urban Renewal Adv. Com., Assn. Am. Geographers (sr. assoc. 2005, honors 1993). Home: 2226 Primrose Ln Florence OR 97439-7627 Personal E-mail: dmarble@oregonfast.net.

**MARBURGER, JOHN HARMEN, III,** federal official; b. S.I., N.Y., Feb. 8, 1941; s. John H., Jr. and Virginia A. (Smith) M.; m. Carol Preston Godfrey, June 12, 1965; children: John Harmen, Alexander Godfrey. BA in Physics magna cum laude, Princeton U., 1962; PhD in Applied Physics (NASA trainee), Stanford U., 1967; LHD (hon.), Hofstra U., 2000; DS (hon.), Stony Brook U., 2002, Moscow State U., 2002. Physicist Goddard Space Flight Center, NASA, 1962—63; asst. prof. physics and elec. engring. U. So. Calif., Los Angeles, 1966—69, assoc. prof., 1969—75, prof., 1975—80, chmn. physics dept., 1972—75, interim dean Coll. Letters, Arts and Scis., 1976—77, dean Coll. Letters, Arts and Scis., 1977—80; pres. SUNY, Stony Brook, 1980—94, prof. physics and elec. engring., 1994—98; pres. Brookhaven Sci. Assoc., 1998—2001; dir. Brookhaven Nat. Labs., 1998—2001, Off. Sci. & Tech. Policy, Washington, 2001—. Cons. laser fusion program Lawrence Livermore Labs., 1972-76; chmn. N.Y. State fact finding panel on Shoreham Nuclear Power Facility, 1983; chmn. bd. trustees Universities Rsch. Assn., 1988-94; co-chair NASULGC Bd. on Oceans and Atmosphere, 1992-93; bd. dirs. N.Y. State Edn. and Rsch. Network Inc., 1986-98; bd. dirs. chair L.I. Rsch. Instn., 1989-95; bd. dirs. L.I. High Tech. Incubator Corp., 1992-98, chair 1994-98. Contbr. articles to tech. pubs. Bd. dirs. Mus. at Stony Brook, 1980-92, 94-98, L.I. Assn., Inc., 1983-93, 98—, Action Com. for L.I., 1980-83, L.I. Forum for Tech., Inc., 1980—, Rsch. Found. SUNY, 1990—; bd. trustees Princeton U., 1985-89; chmn. N.Y. State Energy Office Rev. Commn., 1980-81, Suffolk County (N.Y.) Task Force on Priorities in Fin., 1980-81; campaign chmn. United Way of L.I., 1991-92. Recipient Shuichi

Kusaka Meml. Prize Princeton U., 1962 Fellow AAAS, APS; mem. Assn. of Colls. and Univs. State of N.Y. (pres. 1988-90), Coleman Chamber Music Assn. (bd. dirs. 1969-80). Office: OSTP Eisenhower Exec Office Bldg 17th and Pennsylvania Ave NW Washington DC 20502*

**MARBURY, RITCHEY MCGUIRE, III,** engineering executive, surveyor; b. Albany, Ga., May 18, 1938; s. Ritchey McGuire and Shirley Kathryn (VanHouten) M.; m. Fonda Gayle Starnes, June 16, 1962; children: Mary Kathryn, Ritchey McGuire IV. BCE, Ga. Tech. Inst., 1960, M in City Planning, 1966. Registered profl. engr., Ga., Fla., Idaho, Ala.; land surveyor, Ga. V.p. Marbury Engring. Co., Albany, Ga., 1965-78, pres., chmn. bd., 1981—; pres. Marbury, Ritter, Scott & Turner, Inc. Albany, 1970-78, 81-92, Marbury Assocs., Inc., 1991—, Idaho Boise Mission of Latter-day Saints Ch., 1978-81; sr. prin. EMC Engring. Svcs., 2004—. Presenter seminars on total quality mgmt. to nat. convs. of Am. Cons. Engrs. Coun., Design Constrn. Quality Inst., Sml. Firm Coalition of Cons. Engrs., Assn. for Project Mgrs. Exec. bd. Boy Scouts Am., Southwest Ga., 1982—. Served to 1st lt. U.S. Army, 1963-65. Mem. NSPE (South Ga. chpt. pres. 1993-95), Am. Cons. Engrs. Coun., Surveying and Mapping Soc. of Ga. (bd. dirs. 1966-78), Ga. Planning Assn., Home Builders Assn. (bd. dirs. 1985-86), Rotary. Mem. Lds Ch. Avocations: fishing, writing, music, computer, golf. Home: 1824 Green Valley Dr Albany GA 31707-3116 Office: 2334 Lake Park Dr Albany GA 31707-3132 Office Phone: 229-435-6133. Business E-Mail: ritchey_marbury@emc-eng.com. *Always be a role model of Christlike behavior and do those things that make a significant differenc for good. Do what's right simply because it's the right thing to do. The greatest results come through kindness.*

**MARBURY, STEPHON,** professional basketball player; b. Feb. 20, 1977; children: Stephanie, Xaviera. Student, Ga. Inst. Tech., 1996. Guard Minn. Timberwolves, 1996—98; guard, forward N.J. Nets, 1998—2001; guard Phoenix Suns, 2002—04, N.Y. Knicks, 2004—. Mem. U.S. Olympic Basketball Team, Athens, 2004. Hosts The Stephon Marbury Basketball Classic. Named National High School Player of the Year (Abraham Lincoln H.S.) by Parade Magazine, 1995; named to 1996-97 NBA All-Rookie First Team, NBA All-Star game, 2001, 2003. Office: c/o NY Knickerbockers 2 Pennsylvania Plz New York NY 10121*

**MARBURY, VIRGINIA LOMAX,** insurance and investment executive; b. Ruston, La., June 25, 1918; d. Dallas Daniel and Della (Southern) Lomax; m. William A. Marbury Jr., Sept. 5, 1943; children: Rebekah, Caroline. BA, La. Tech. U., 1936, LLD (hon.), 1987; MusB, La. State U., 1938. Exec. v.p. Marbury Corp., Ruston, La., 1944—; sec.-treas. Bankers Life La., Ruston, 1959—. 1st v.p., membership chmn. Lincoln Parish Mus. and Hist. Soc., Ruston, La., 1992—. Recipient Tower Medallion award La. Tech. U., 1991. Mem. Shreveport Symphony Soc. Republican. Episcopalian. Office: Marbury Corp 601 N Trenton St Ruston LA 71270-3840

**MARBUT, ROBERT GORDON,** communications executive, electronic security and broadcast executive, investor; b. Athens, Ga., Apr. 11, 1935; s. Robert Smith and Laura Gordon (Powers) M.; m. Margo Susan Spitz, Sept. 24, 1989; children: Robert Gordon, Laura Dodd, Michael Powers, Marcy Lizbeth. B Indsl. Engring., Ga. Inst. Tech., 1957; MBA with distinction, Harvard U., 1963. Registered profl. engr., Calif. Engr. Esso Standard Oil Co., Baton Rouge, 1957; corp. dir. engring. and plans Copley Press, La Jolla, Calif., 1963-70; v.p. Harte-Hanks Newspapers, Inc., San Antonio, 1970-71; pres., CEO Harte-Hanks Comm., Inc., San Antonio, 1971-91, also chmn. bd., 1991; founder, chmn., CEO Argyle Comm., Inc San Antonio, 1992—; founder, CEO, dir. Argyle TV Holding, Inc., San Antonio, 1993-95; co-founder, chmn., CEO Argyle TV, Inc., San Antonio, 1994-97; chmn., co-CEO Hearst-Argyle TV, Inc., N.Y.C., 1997-2000, chmn., 2001—02; co-mng. ptnr. Argyle Global, LP, 2001—; founder, chmn., CEO SectecGLOBAL, Inc., 2002—. Dir. AP, 1979—88, vice chmn., 1987—88; chmn. Newspaper Advt. Bur., 1988—90, exec. com. dir., 1974—89, 1982—90; bd. dirs. Valero Energy Corp., Tupperware, Inc., Hearst-Argyle TV, Inc., Bus. Execs. Nat. Security; mem. adv. bd. U. Ga. Henry W. Grady Sch. Journalism, 1975—83, Ga. Tech., 1978—81, 1998—; founding mem. Am. Bus. Conf., 1981—89; mem. U. Tex. Centennial commn., 1981—83; pres. adv. coun. U. Tex. Coll. Comm., 1982—83; bd. dirs. Up With People, 1983—2001, exec. com., 1984—2001; instr. Armstrong Coll., 1951, Calif. State U., L.A., 1964, Woodbury Coll., 1964. Author: (with Healy, Henderson and others) Creative Collective Bargaining, 1965. Coordinating chmn. San Antonio Target 90 commn., 1983-84; campaign chmn. United Way, San Antonio, 1985, chmn. bd. trustees 1988-89; vice chmn. Tex. select com. on Tax Equity, 1987-89; mem select com. Tex. Revenues, 1991-92; mem. Tex. World Trade Coun., 1986-87. Capt. USAF, 1958-61. Salzburg Inst. Am. Studies sr. fellow, 1997—; recipient Isaiah Thomas award Rochester Inst. Tech., 1980, EXCEL award in comm., 1987, People of Vision award, 1991; selected to Acad. Disting. Engring. Alumni Ga. Tech., 1995. Mem. Am. Newspaper Pubrs. Assn. (chmn. task group on future, chmn. telecomm. com. 1974-81, bd. dirs. 1976-84, chmn. future task group), So. Newspaper Pubrs. Assn. (pres. 1979-80, dir. 1975-81, treas. 1977), Am. Newspaper Pubrs. Assn. Found. (trustee 1976-79), Tex. Daily Newspaper Assn. (pres. 1979, Tex. Newspaper Leader of Yr., 1981), N.Y. Met. Club, Doubles, San Antonio Country Club, Argyle Club, Greater San Antonio C. of C., Delta Tau Delta (Alumni Achievement award 2000), Omicron Delta Kappa, Phi Eta Sigma. Office: Hearst-Argyle Television Inc 200 Concord Plaza Dr Ste 700 San Antonio TX 78216-6941

**MARCDANTE, KAREN JEAN,** medical educator; b. Milw., Sept. 15, 1955; d. Willard Karl and Beth Elaine (Maule) Kohn; m. Mark Wendelberger, Aug. 5, 1978 (div. Sept. 1985); m. Anthony Marcdante, Oct. 17, 1998. Student, Marquette U., 1973-76; MD, Med. Coll. Wis., 1980. Diplomate Am. Bd. Pediat. & Pediat. Crit. Care, Resident in pediat Med Coll Wis, affiliated hosps., Milw., 1980-83; instr. pediat. Med. Coll. Wis., Milw., 1983-85, asst. prof. pediat., 1987-94, assoc. prof. pediat., 1994-2000—, assoc. dean curriculum, 1997—2003, vice-chair edn. dept. pediat., 1994—; fellow in pediatric critical care U. Calif., San Francisco, 1985-87; vice chief staff Children's Hosp. Wis., Milw., 1995-97. Dir. Respiratory Care Svcs., 1992-98, Transport Program, 1998—; chief dept. pediat. Children's Hosp. Wis., 1991-95, dept. critical care 1993-95, mem. numerous coms., including care mgmt. steering com., 1994—, critical care com., 1991—, pres.-elect, 2003-05; pres. med. dental staff, 2005—. Contbr. numerous articles to profl. jours. Recipient New Investigator award Assn. Am. Med. Colls., 1992, Cert. Leadership award YWCA and Marquette Electronics Found., 1992, Laureate award Ctrl. Group Ednl. Affairs, 1997; grantee Dept. HHS, 1996—. Mem. Am. Acad. Pediat. (pub. rels. chair Wis. chpt. 1988-91, sec.-treas. 1990-95, v.p. 1995-96, chair careers and opportunities 1996-2001), Soc. Critical Care Medicine (chair task force on quality improvement pediat. 1994-96, quality indicator devel. work group 1997-98, Presdl. citation 1996, 97), Coun. on Med. Student Edn. in Pediat. (co-chair task force on tchg. methods 1991-96, nominating com. 1993-95, exec. com. 1996-99, sec.-treas. 1997-99). Business E-Mail: kwendel@mcw.edu.

**MARCEAU, JUDITH MARIE,** retired elementary school educator, small business owner; b. Gardner, Mass., Aug. 10, 1946; d. George Joseph and Bernice Victoria (Johnson) Babineau; m. James Victor Krymowski, Aug. 20, 1976 (div. Mar. 1985); children: Kathryn Victoria, Kenneth James; m. Glen Francis Marceau, Aug. 30, 1989. Grad., Sch. Worcester Art Mus., 1967; BFA, Clark U., 1971. Tchr. elem. art Quabbin Regional Pub. Schs., Barre, Mass., 1967-70, Gardner (Mass.) Pub. Schs., 1970—2003, ret., 2003; propr. Babineau's Corner Antiques Shop, Hubbardston, 2003—. Author, editor: Fascinating Facts of Gardner, 1977, 2d edit., 1999, Hubbardston as Seen Through the Eyes of its Children, 1987; author numerous poems. Active Hubbardston Hist. Commn.; vol. Hubbardston Recycling Initiative; bd. dirs. Gardner Edn. Assn., 1975-86; bd. dirs. Youth Advocacy and Counseling Ctr., Gardner, 1979-82. Recipient Citation of Outstanding Edn. City of Gardner, 1994, 2000, Cert. of Commendation, Mayor of City of Gardner, Cert. of Achievement Gardner Pub. Sch. Com., 2004. Mem. Mass. Tchrs. Assn., Nat. Tchrs. Assn. Achievements include my third grade class 2000-01 petitioned for a bill to declare offical state colors to be cranberry, green and blue for Mass. This became a law signed by Gov. Mitt Romney in Dec. 2004 (students in 7th). Avocations: writing history, poetry, antiques, watercolor painting, sketching. Home: 221 Gardner Rd Hubbardston MA 01452-1655 Office: Babineau's Corner Antiques 221 Gardner Rd Hubbardston MA 01452 Office Phone: 978-632-2840.

**MARCEAU, YVONNE,** ballroom dancer, educator; b. Chgo., July 13, 1950; BFA, U. Utah, 1972; AA, Imperial Soc. Ballroom Dance. Ballet dancer Ballet West; ptnr. with Pierre Dulaine, 1976; founder, artistic dir. Am. Ballroom Theatre, N.Y.C., 1984-93; educator dance divsn. Julliard Sch., N.Y.C., 1993—. Guest tchr. Sch. Am. Ballet, N.Y.C.; tchr. ballroom dancing Juilliard Sch. Appearances include The Smithsonian Inst., JFK Ctr. for Performing Arts, N.Y. State Theater, N.Y.C., Sadlers Wells, London, (Broadway and London show) Grand Hotel, 1989-92, toured with Pierre Dulaine and Am. Ballroom Theatre worldwide. Recipient Recipient Brit. Theatrical Arts Championships 4 times, Spl. Astaire award, Dance Educator awards, Outstanding Achievement in Dance award Nat. Coun. Dance Am., 1992, Dance Mag. award, 1993.

**MARCEL-CALDERON, LINDA,** music educator; m. Gene Calderon. MusB, Brigham Young U.; MusM, SUNY, Potsdam; EdD, Columbia U. Assoc. prof. music Bergen C.C., Paramus, NJ, 1987—. Author: Discover the Power of Music Listening, 2001. Recipient award, NISOD, 2005; Princeton U. fellow, 2005—. Coll. Music Soc. Office: Bergen CC 400 Paramus Rd Paramus NJ 07652-1508 Office Phone: 201-447-7143. Business E-Mail: lmarcel@bergen.edu.

**MARCELLA, JOSEPH,** information scientist; BA in Biochemistry, Temple U., 1970. Computer operator/sys. programmer, asst. mgr. King Kullen Grocery Co./Gen. Fire & Casualty, L.I., 1971-72; asst. v.p., electronic banking Bank of Am., Las Vegas, 1972-83; sr. v.p., dir. info. svcs. Norwest/Wells of Nev., Las Vegas, 1983-96; chief info. officer, dir. info. technologies City of Las Vegas, 1997—. Bd. dirs., past pres. Bank Adminstrn. Inst.; past pres., v.p. Nev. Clearing House Assn.; bd. dirs. Western Payments Alliance; mem. Rules Com. Nat. Automated Clearning House, Task Force to Build Acad. Advanced Tech., Focus Sch. Partnership program. Mem. South Nev. Entities Tech. Alliance (bd. dirs.). Office: City Las Vegas Dept Info Techs City Hall 5th Fl 400 Stewart Ave Las Vegas NV 89101-2927

**MARCH, JAMES GARDNER,** social sciences educator; b. Cleve., Jan. 15, 1928; s. James Herbert and Mildred (MacCorkle) M.; m. Jayne Mary Dohr, Sept. 23, 1947; children: Kathryn Sue, Gary Clifton, James Christopher, Roderic Gunn. BA, U. Wis., 1949; MA, Yale U., 1950, PhD, 1953; PhD (hon.), Copenhagen Sch. Econs., 1978, Swedish Sch. Econs., 1979, U. Wis., Milw., 1980, U. Bergen, 1980, Uppsala U., 1987, Helsinki Sch. Econs., 1991, Göteborg U., 1998, U. Poitiers, 2001, Budapest U. Econs., 2003. From asst. prof. to prof. Carnegie Inst. Tech., 1953-64; prof. psychology, sociology, dean Sch. Social Scis. U. Calif., Irvine, 1964-70; prof. mgmt., higher edn., polit. sci. and sociology Stanford (Calif.) U., 1970-95, prof. emeritus, 1995—. Cons. in field; mem. Nat. Council Ednl. Research, 1975-78, Nat. Sci. Bd., 1968-74; mem. sociol.-social psychology panel NSF, 1964-66; social sci. tng. com. NIMH, 1967-68; mem. Assembly Behavioral and Social Sci., NRC, 1973-79, chmn. com. on aging, 1977-82, chmn. com. on math., sci., tech. edn., 1984-86 Author: (with H.A. Simon) Organizations, 1958, 2nd edit., 1993, (with R.M. Cyert) A Behavioral Theory of the Firm, 1963, 2nd edit., 1992, Handbook of Organizations, 1965; (with B.R. Gelbaum) Mathematics for the Social and Behavioral Sciences, 1969; (with M.D. Cohen) Leadership and Ambiguity, 1974, 2nd edit., 1986, Academic Notes, 1974; (with C.E. Lave) An Introduction to Models in the Social Sciences, 1975; (with J.P. Olsen) Ambiguity and Choice in Organizations, 1976, Aged Wisconsin, 1977, Autonomy as a Factor in Group Organization, 1980, Pleasures of the Process, 1980, Slow Learner, 1985; (with R. Weissinger-Baylon) Ambiguity and Command, 1986, Decisions and Organizations, 1988; (with J.P. Olsen) Rediscovering Institutions, 1989, Minor Memos, 1990, A Primer on Decision Making, 1994, Fornuft og Forandring, 1995; (with J.P. Olsen) Democratic Governance, 1995; The Pursuit of Organizational Intelligence, 1999, (with M. Schulz and X. Zhou) The Dynamics of Rules, 2000, Late Harvest, 2000; (with M. Augier) The Economics of Choice, Change and Organization, 2002, (with M. Augier), Models of a Man, 2004, Footprints, 2005, Valg, Vane ag Vision, 2005, (with T. Weil) On Leadership, 2005; contbr. articles to profl. jours. Fellow Ctr. Advanced Study in Behavioral Scis., 1955-56, 73-74; recipient Wilbur Lucius Cross medal Yale U., 1968, Viipuri prize, Finland, 2004, Herbert Simon award, Hungary, 2005; decorated knight 1st class Royal Norwegian Order of Merit, comdr. Order of Lion of Finland. Mem. NAS, APA, Nat. Acad. Edn., Accademia Italiana di Economia Aziendale, Royal Swedish Acad. Scis., Norwegian Acad. of Sci. and Letters. Am. Acad. Arts and Scis., Am. Econ. Assn., Am. Polit. Sci. Assn. (v.p. 1983-84, John Gaus award 1997, Wildavsky award 2004), Am. Sociol. Assn., Acad. Mgmt. (Disting. Scholar award 1999), Russell Sage Found. (trustee 1985-94, chmn. 1990-93), Finnish Soc. Scis. and Letters, Citigroup Behavioral Scis. Rsch. Coun. (chmn. 1994-2000), Am. Philos. Soc., Phi Beta Kappa, Sigma Xi. Home: 501 Portola Rd Box 8136 Portola Valley CA 94028 Office Phone: 650-424-4344. Business E-Mail: march@stanford.edu.

**MARCH, KEVIN P.,** electronics executive: BS Economics, U. Pittsburgh, 1983, MBA, 1984. Various positions including dir. fin., contr. semicondr. units Tex. Instruments, Dallas, 1984—97, v.p., fin. planning mgr. global ops., 1997—2002, contr., 2002—03, sr. v.p., CFO, 2003—. Mem. Fin. Exec. Internat., Conf. Bd.'s Coun. Fin. Exec. Office: Texas Instruments MS 3905 7839 Churchill Way Dallas TX 75266-0199*

**MARCH, MICHAEL F.,** propulsion systems analyst, consultant; b. Detroit, Mar. 3, 1962; s. Stanley and Dorothy M. AAS in Archtl. Design, Macomb C.C., Warren, Mich., 1983: BS in Mech. Engring., Lawrence Technol. U., 1986; ME, U. Fla., 1994. Sr. analytical engr. United Techs. Corp.-Pratt & Whitney, West Palm Beach, Fla., 1986-93; pvt. practice propulsion analysis cons. Tullahoma, Tenn., 1994—. Mem. ASME.

**MARCHAK, MAUREEN PATRICIA,** anthropology and sociology educator, academic administrator; b. Lethbridge, Alta., Can., June 22, 1936; d. Adrian Ebenezer and Wilhelmina Rankin (Hamilton) Russell; m. William Marchak, Dec. 31, 1956; children: Geordon Eric, Lauren Craig. BA, U. B.C., Vancouver. Can. 1958, 1970. Asst. prof. U. B.C., Vancouver. 1972-75, assoc. prof., 1975-80, prof., 1980—, head dept. anthropology and sociology 1987-90, dean faculty arts, 1990-96, disting. scholar in residence Peter Wall Inst., 2000—, prof., dean emerita of arts, 2001—; sr. rsch. fellow Ctr. Internat. Rels. Liu Inst. for Study of Global Issues, 2002—, interim dir., 2005—06. Author: Ideological Perspectives on Canada, 1975, 2d edit., 1981, 3d edit., 1988, In Whose Interests, 1979, Green Gold, 1983 (John Porter award 1985), The Integrated Circus, The New Right and The Restructuring of Global Markets, 1991, Logging the Globe, 1995, Falldown, Forest Policy in British Columbia, 1999, Racism, Sexism and the University, the Political Science Affair at UBC, 1996, God's Assassins. State Terrorism in Argentina in the 1970's, 1999 (Wallace J. Ferguson prize, Hon. Mention), Reigns of Terror, 2003, Global Pieces, 2006; author, co-editor: Uncommon Property, 1987; mem. editl. bd. Can. Rev. Sociology and Anthropology, Montreal, 1971-74, Studies in Polit. Economy, Ottawa, Ont., Can., 1980-87, Current Sociology, 1980-86, Can. Jour. Sociology, 1980-84. Bd.-C. Studies, 1988-90, 2000-04. Bd. dir., chair ethics com. Univ. Hosp., 1992-93; trustee Cedar Lodge Trust Soc., 1989-92; mem. adv. coun. Ecotrust. 1991-93, bd. dir., 1993-97. Eco-trust Can., 1995-99; chmn. bd. dir. B.C. Bldgs. Corp., 1992-95; mem. B.C. Forest Appeals Commn., 1992-2002; bd. govs. U. B.C., 1999-2001; bd. dir. Pub. Svc. Employees for Environ. Ethics, 2002-04; mem. sector study steering com. Can. Coun. Profl. Fish Harvesters, 2002—05. Named Woman of Distinction, YWCA, 1999. Fellow Royal Soc. Can. (v.p. Acad. II 1994-98, pres. Acad. II 1998-2000); mem. Can. Sociology and Anthropology Assn. (pres. 1979-80, other offices), Internat. Sociol. divsn., Can. Polit. Sci. Assn.,

Assn. for Can. Studies, Forest History Soc. (mem. exec. com. 1991-92). Avocations: hiking, swimming, travel, listening to music. Home: 4455 W Ist Ave Vancouver BC Canada V6R 4H9 Office Phone: 604-822-9958. E-mail: pmarchak@interchange.ubc.ca.

**MARCHALONIS, JOHN JACOB,** immunologist, educator; b. Scranton, Pa., July 22, 1940; s. John Louis and Anna Irene (Stadner) M.; m. Anne B. Caldwell, 1969 (div. 1976); 1 child, Lee; m. Sally Ann Sevy, May 5, 1978 (div. 2003); children: Elizabeth, Emily. AB summa cum laude, Lafayette Coll., 1962; PhD, Rockefeller U., 1967. Grad. fellow Rockefeller U., 1962-67; fellow Am. Cancer Soc. Walter and Eliza Hall Inst. Med. Research, 1967-68; asst. prof. biomed. scis. Brown U., 1969-70; head molecular immunology lab. Walter and Eliza Hall Inst. Med. Research, Melbourne, Australia, 1970-76; head cell biology and biochemistry sect. Frederick Cancer Research Ctr., 1977-80; adj. prof. dept. pathology U. Pa., 1977-83; prof., chmn. dept. biochemistry and molecular biology Med. U. S.C., Charleston, 1980-88; prof., chmn. dept. microbiology and immunology U. Ariz., Tucson, 1988—2004, prof. pathology, 1991—, prof. medicine, 1992—. Bd. dirs. Type Tissue Culture Collection; vis. prof. human immunology Pierre et Marie Curie U., Paris, 2001. Author: Immunity in Evolution, 1977; editor: Comparative Immunology, 1976, the Lymphocyte: Structure and Function, 1977; (with N. Cohen) Self/Non-Self Discrimination, 1980; (with G.W. Warr) Antibody as a Tool, 1982, The Immunobiology and Molecular Biology of Parasitic Infections, 1983, Antigen-Specific T Cell Receptors and Factors, 1987, The Lymphocyte: Structure and Function, 2d edit., 1987; (with Carol Reinisch) Defense Molecules, 1989; (with Gregory Beck, Edwin L. Cooper and Gail S. Habicht) Primordial Immunity, 1994; editl. bd. jours. in field. Active Nat. Commn. Damon Runyon-Walter Winchel Cancer Fund. Named among 1,000 most highly cited sci. authors Inst. for Sci. Info.; Frank R. Lillie fellow, 1974; grantee in field. Fellow Am. Inst. Chemists, Am. Acad. Microbiology; mem. AAAS, Am. Assn. Immunology, Am. Soc. Biol. Chemists and Molecular Biologists, Henry Kunkel Soc., Sigma Xi, Phi Beta Kappa. Episcopalian. Achievements include development of microchemical (radioimmunochemical) approaches for proteins and surface receptors of living cells; characterization of immunoglobulin-like antigen receptors of thymusderived lymphocytes; application of synthetic peptide technology to antibodies, T cell receptors and autoimmunity; pioneered investigation of the molecular evolution of immunity, peptides therapies for acquired immunodeficiency and autoimmunity. Home: 5661 N Camino Arturo Tucson AZ 85718-3933 Office: U Ariz Health Sci Ctr Tucson AZ 85724-0001 Personal E-mail: jmarchalonis@yahoo.com.

**MARCHAN, MARISSA L.,** social worker; b. Muntinlupa, Philippines, Sept. 6, 1960; arrived in U.S., 1976; d. Vedasto A. and Matilde V. Layola Sr.; m. Leon P. Marchan Jr.; children: Lesley-Anne, Matt-Derek. Grad., h.s. Bookkeeper Dave Morken Sailmakers, Honolulu, 0979—80; fund raising sec. Hawaii Heart Assn., Honolulu, 1980—81; data entry Hawaiian Fin., Honolulu, 1981—83; accts. payable Paul, Hastings, Janofsky, L.A., 1983—90; acctg. clk. Powerine Oil Co., Santa Fe Springs, Calif., 1990—92; family support specialist DA Family Support Divsn., Las Vegas, 1996—. Author: A Marriage Made in Heaven and Hell, 2003. Avocations: sewing, interior decorating, painting. Personal E-mail: marissamarchan@netzero.com.

**MARCHAND, MICHAEL J.,** judge, career military officer; b. Rice, Minn. BA, St. John's U., Collegeville, Minn., 1970; JD, U. Minn.; grad., Armed Forces Staff Coll., Indsl. Coll. Armed Forces. Commd. JAGC, U.S. Army, 1974, asst. staff judge advocate Ft. Sam Houston, Tex., 1974—77, US Army Forces Command, Ft. McPherson, Ga., 1977—79; instr., sr. instr. contract law JAG Sch., Charlottesville, Va., 1980—83; dep. staff judge advocate U.S. Army Transp. Ctr. and Ft. Eustis, Ft. Eustis, Va., 1983—85; plans officer Office of the JAG, Washington, 1986—88; staff judge advocate 6th Inf. Divsn. (Light) Alaska, 1988—91, U.S. Army Garrison, Ft. Polk, La., 1991—93; chief administrv. law divsn. Office of JAG, Washington, 1994—95, exec. to JAG, 1995—97, asst. JAG for civil law and litigation, 1997—98; comdr. U.S. Army Svcs. Agy., 1998—2001; chief judge U.S. Army Ct. Criminal Appeals, 1998—2001; asst. JAG, JAGC U.S. Army, 2001—. Decorated Legion of Merit, Meritorious Svc. medal with 3 oak leaf clusters, Army Commendation medal with one oak leaf cluster, Army Achievement medal with one oak leaf cluster, Nat. Def. Svc. medal with one svc. star, Army Staff Identification Badge. Office: Office of JAG US Army Pentagon Washington DC 20310-1500

**MARCHANT, BYRON,** lawyer; b. Chgo., July 1, 1957; 1 child, Rebecca. BS with merit, US Naval Acad., 1978; JD, U. Va., 1987. Bar: DC 1987, NY 1987, NJ 1988. McCook assoc. Sidney Austin Brown & Wood, Washington; with FCC, 1989—95; gen. counsel Telecommunications Systems, Inc., Annapolis, Md.; ptnr. Patton Boggs, Washington, 1996—97; sr. v.p., gen. counsel BET Holdings, Inc., Washington, 1997—98, exec. v.p., chief adminstrv. officer, gen. counsel, 1998—. Chair, E-Commerce com. DC C. of C. Recipient Trailblazer award, Minority Corp. Counsel Assn., 1999. Mem.: PEN, Washington Lawyers Com. for Civil Rights and Law, Fed. Comm. Bar Assn., US Supreme Ct. Bar, ABA. Avocations: swimming, skiing, golf, bicycling. Office: BET Holdings Inc 1235 W St NE Washington DC 20018-1211*

**MARCHANT, DAVID JUDSON,** lawyer; b. Oakland, Calif., Jan. 12, 1939; s. Luther Brusie and Marian Hand (Fisher) M.; m. Susan Robbins (div. 1980); children: Michael Hilton, Robbins Fisher, Lauren Payton. BA, U. Calif., Berkeley, 1961; JD, U. Calif., San Francisco, 1967. Bar: Calif. 1967. Atty. Calif. Pub. Utilities Commn., San Francisco, 1967—68; ptnr. Graham & James, San Francisco, 1974—95; sr. counsel MCI Telecom, Corp., San Francisco, 1996—98; of counsel Davis, Wright, Tremaine, San Francisco, 1999—2000; ptnr. Davis Wright Tremaine LLP, San Francisco, 2001—. Mem. ABA (pub. utility law sect.). Office: Davis Wright Tremaine One Embarcadero Ctr Ste 600 San Francisco CA 94111

**MARCHANT, GARY ELVIN,** lawyer; b. Squamish, BC, Can., July 5, 1958; came to U.S., 1986; s. Leonard Roy and Elsie Christine (Anderson) M. BSc, U. B.C., 1980. PhD, 1986; MPP, Harvard U., 1990. JD magna cum laude, 1990. Bar: Mass. 1991, D.C. 1993. Assoc. Kirkland & Ellis. Washington, 1990-95, ptnr., 1995—99; assoc. prof. Ariz. State Univ. Coll. Law, Tempe, Ariz., 1999—2003, prof., 2003—; dir. Ctr. Study Law, Sci. & Tech., Ariz. State Univ., 2001—. Editor-in-chief, Harvard Jour. Law & Tech.; editor, Harvard Environ. Law rev.; assoc. ed., Nonlinearity in Biology, Toxicology and Medicine; contr. articles to profl. jours. Mem. Risk Rsch. Inst.-Air and Waste Mgmt. Assn., Environ. Law inst., AAAS, Soc. Risk Analysis, N.Y. Acad. Sci., Soc. Social Studies of Sci. Office: Arizona State University School of Law PO Box 877906 Tempe AZ 85287-7906

**MARCHANT, KENNY,** congressman; b. Bonham, Tex, Feb. 23, 1951; m. Donna Marchant; children: Luke, Matthew, Kenny, Dallas. BA, So. Nazarene U., Bethany, Okla., 1974; attended, Nazarene Theol. Sem., Kansas City, Mo., 1975—76; DHL (hon.), So. Nazarene U., Bethany, Okla., 1999. Mem. City Coun., Carrollton, Tex., 1980—84; mayor Carrollton, Tex., 1984—87; mem. Tex. State Ho. Reps., Austin, 1987—2004, US Congress from 24th Tex. dist., 2005—, mem. transp. and infrastructure com., mem. edn. and the workforce com., mem. govt. reform com. Mem. adv. bd. Children's Med. Ctr. Named Top Ten Legislator, Tex. Monthly mag., Citizen of Yr., Metrocrest C. of C., Legislator of Yr., Tex. Mcpl. League. Republican. Nazarene. Office: US Ho Reps 501 Cannon Ho Office Bldg Washington DC 20515-4324 Office Phone: 202-225-6605.*

**MARCHESE, LISA MARIE,** lawyer, educator; b. Seattle, Sept. 13, 1962; d. John Sebastian and Joanne Spino Marchese. BA, Cath. U. Am., 1984; JD, Georgetown U. Law Ctr., Washington, D.C., 1987. Bar: Wash. 1988, Oreg. 2003, U.S. Supreme Ct. 1998, U.S. Dist. Ct. (ea. and we. dists.) Wash. 1998, U.S. Ct. Appeals (9th cir.) 2003. Legis. counsel Hon. Daniel J. Evans, Washington, 1983—88; sr. dep. pros. atty. King County Prosecutor's Office, Seattle, 1989—98; ptnr. Stafford Frey Cooper, 1998—2006, Dorsey & Whitney LLP, Seattle, 2006—. Adj. law prof. U. Wash. Law Sch., 1999—;

Seattle U. Sch. Law, 2000—; faculty mem. Nat. Inst. Trial Advocacy, 1999—; bd. mem. Coalition Women Lawyers, 2000—02; spkr. in field. Contbr. articles to various law jours. Mem.: Washington Women Lawyers, Phi Beta Kappa. Roman Cath. Avocations: sports, opera, reading, golf. Office: Dorsey & Whitney LLP 45 Bank Centre 1420 Fifth Ave #3400 Seattle WA 98101 Office Phone: 206-903-2379. Business E-Mail: marchese.lisa@dorsey.com.

**MARCHESE, MICHAEL JAMES, JR.,** radiation oncologist; b. N.Y.C., Mar. 9, 1955; s. Michael James Sr. and Mabel Gladys (Rosero) M.; m. Kathryn Allen, Aug. 7, 1982 (div. May 1993); 1 child, Michael James III; m. Kathleen Spahr, Oct. 18, 1997; 1 child, Melissa June. BA magna cum laude, NYU, 1976; MD, Baylor Coll. Medicine, 1979. Diplomate Am. Bd. Radiology. Intern Monmouth Med. Ctr., Hahnemann Med. Coll., Long Branch, NJ, 1979—80; resident and chief resident radiation therapy Presbyn. Hosp., Columbia U. Coll. Physicians and Surgeons, N.Y.C., 1980—83, asst. attending physician radiation oncology, 1983—87; resident brachytherapy svc. Meml. Sloan Kettering Cancer Ctr., Cornell U. Med. Coll., N.Y.C., 1982; asst. clin. prof. radiation oncology Columbia U. Coll. Physicians & Surgeons, N.Y.C., 1983—84, asst. prof. radiation oncology, 1984—87; attending staff radiology/radiation oncology Cmty. Med. Ctr., Toms River, NJ, 1987—96, Kimball Med. Ctr., Lakewood, NJ, 1994—, Med. Ctr. Ocean County, Brick, NJ, 1996—; dir. Ocean Radiation Therapy Ctr., Toms River, NJ, 1997—2005, Ctr. for Advanced Radiation Oncology, Toms River, NJ, 2005—. Investigator Nat. Cancer Inst., 1983-87, investigator radiation therapy oncology group, 1983-87, 95—, physician surveyor, 1983-85, investigator cancer and leukemia group B, 1986-87, investigator Ea. Coop. Oncology Group, 1995—; physician surveyor practice accreditation program Am. Coll. Radiology, 1986-87; Cancer liason Am. Coll. Surgeons, Kimball Med. Ctr., 2001-04. Author: (with others) Radiation Therapy of Gynecological Cancers, 1987, Frontiers of Radiation Therapy and Oncology, vol. 22, 1988; contbr. articles to profl. jours. Bd. dirs. Am. Cancer Soc., Ocean County, N.J., 1993—, v.p., 1993-94, pres., 1994-98, chief med. officer, 2000-01. Recipient Resident/Fellow award Am. Radium Soc., Travel award European Soc. Therapeutic Radiology and Oncology, Clin. Oncology Career Devel. award Am. Cancer Soc., Physician of the Year, Amer. Canc. Soc., 1998; fellow Am. Coll. Radiation Oncology. Fellow Am. Coll. Radiation Oncology; mem. Am. Soc. Therapeutic Radiology and Oncology, Am. Soc. Clin. Oncology, Acad. Medicine N.J., Radiation Rsch. Soc., N.Y. Acad. Scis., Ocean County Med. Soc. (trustee 1997—, pres. 2005—), Med. Soc. N.J. (del. 2000—). Roman Catholic. Home: 44 Lake Shore Dr Red Bank NJ 07701-5840 Office: Center for Advanced Radiation Oncology 512 Lakehurst Rd Toms River NJ 08755-5029 Office Phone: 732-240-0053. Personal E-mail: mjmmd44@yahoo.com.

**MARCHESE, RICHARD B.,** manufacturing executive; V.p. fin., CFO Ga. Gulf Corp., Atlanta, 1993—. Mem. bd. dir. Bluelinx Holdings, Nalco Holding Co., Quality Distbr.

**MARCHESE, RONALD THOMAS,** ancient history and archaeology educator; b. Fresno, Calif., Mar. 17, 1947; s. John Anthony and Julie Rita (Ferrarese) M.; m. Marcia Lynn Schneider, Apr. 6, 1974 (div. Apr. 1980); 1 child, Stephanie Jo; m. K. Werdin, 1988; children: Alexander Joseph, Kayla Marie. BA summa cum laude, Calif. State U., Fresno, 1970; MA, N.Y.U., 1972, PhD with distinction, 1976; postgrad., Columbia U., 1972-73. Asst. prof. Va. Poly. Inst., Blacksburg, 1976-77; asst. to assoc. prof. ancient history and archaeology U. Minn., Duluth, 1977-87, prof., 1987—. Rsch. assoc. dept. classics NYU, 1972—74; evaluator grant proposals NEH, NSF; excavator numerous sites in Israel, Turkey, and Greece; lectr. in field. Author, editor 7 books; author articles on nomadic material culture, religious textiles, and sacred relics from the American Orthodox Churches of Istanbul, Turkey. Recipient Fulbright-Hays Sr. Research fellowship, Turkey, 1984-85, 91-92, The Am. Council Learned Socs. fellowship, 1977-78, NDEA Title VI Fgn. Languages fellowship, 1972-75, Spl. Commendation for Excellence award Phi Alpha Theta, 1979; grantee NEH, 1978, 80, nat. Geographic Soc., 1974, Andrew Mellon Found., NSF, Ford Found., 1971-72, U. Minn., others; McKnight fellow, 2004—. Mem. NEH, Nat. Assn. Scholars, Coun. for Internat. Exchange, Am. Coun. Learned Socs., Fulbright Alumni Assn., Phi Alpha Theta, Sigma Xi, Alpha Phi Omega. Roman Catholic. Avocations: tennis, golf, horseback riding. Home: 5789 220th St N Forest Lake MN 55025-9677 Office Phone: 218-726-8507. Business E-Mail: rmarches@d.umn.edu.

**MARCHESI, VINCENT THOMAS,** biochemist, educator; b. NYC, Sept. 4, 1935; married, 1959; six children. BA, Yale U., 1957, MD, 1963; PhD in Pathology, Oxford U., Eng., 1961. Intern, resident in pathology Wash. U., St. Louis, 1963-65; rsch. assoc. cell biology Rockefeller U., NYC, 1965-66; staff assoc. Nat. Cancer Inst., Bethesda, Md., 1966-68; chief sect. chem. pathology Nat. Inst. Arthritis, Metabolism & Digestive Disorders, 1968—72; assoc. prof. pathology Sch. Medicine Yale U., New Haven, 1972-73, prof. pathology and cell biology Sch. Medicine, chmn. dept. biology, 1973—89; chief pathology Yale-New Haven Hosp., New Haven, 1973—79; dir. Boyer Ctr. Molecular Medicine, Yale U. Sch. Medicine, New Haven, 1989—. Cons. Miles Pharm., West Haven, Conn., 1982—. Editor-in-chief FASEB Jour., 1996—; editor: Laboratory Investigation, —, Molecular Mag., —, BCMD, —. Bd. dirs. Am. Cyanamid, N.J., 1992-94. Lt. comdr. USPHS, 1966-68. Recipient Borden Undergrad. Med. Rsch. award, Yale U., 1963, Parke Davis Meritorious award in exptl. pathology, 1973, Karl Landsteiner award, 1983, Rous-Whipple Rsch. award. Am. Assn. Pathology, 1989. Mem. Inst. Medicine-NAS, Am. Soc. Cell Biology, Am. Assn. Pathologists (former pres.), Am. Assn. Immunologists, Am. Soc. Investigative Pathology, Am. Soc. Biological Chem., Biophysical Soc. Avocations: tennis, history. also: Boyer Ctr Molecular Medicine 295 Congress Ave Rm 109 New Haven CT 06519-1418

**MARCHESSEAULT, ANITA,** music educator; b. Moosup, Conn., June 15, 1917; d. Henry Marchesseault and Rose Brault; ptnr. Anita. MusB. Laval U., 1950; MusM, Boston U., 1957, D Mus. Arts, 1970. Cert. music tchr. Music tchr. Schs. of Mt. Royal, Montreal, Que., Canada. 1935-52; prof. music, piano and organ tchr. band dir. Notre Dame Coll., Manchester, NH, 1952—. Ch. organist, pvt. piano tchr., Manchester, 1952—. Recipient Key to City. Mem. Music Tchrs. Nat. Assn. (cert. chair 1968—), N.H. Music Tchrs. Assn. (Music Tchr. of Yr. 1970). Home: 357 Island Pond Rd #1 Manchester NH 03109

**MARCHETTI, MICHAEL JOSEPH,** director; s. Phillip Frank and Sarah Jane Marchetti; m. Antonella Maltese. May 4, 2002; 1 child. Alexander Phillip. BA in English, Coll. N.J., 1997, MA in English. 2002. Coord. grad. student svcs. Coll. N.J., Ewing, 2001—03, asst. scheduling mgr., 2003—05, sr. bus. analyst Oracle/Peoplesoft implementation, 2004—06; dir. grad. enrollment and admissions U. N.J., Phila., 2006—. Adj. prof. Coll. N.J., Ewing, 2003—06; pres. TCNJ Staff Senate, Ewing, NJ, 2005—06; presenter in field. Vol. Susan G. Komen Breast Cancer Found. Race for the Cure, Lawrenceville, NJ, 2005, Am. Heart Assn. Heart Walk, Hamilton, NJ, 2005. Nominee TCNJ Shaw Staff Excellence award, 2004, Best Screenplay, N.J. Internat. Film Festival, 2006. Mem.: Mid. States Assn. Collegiate Registrars and Officers of Admission, MLA. Avocations: travel, screenwriting. Office: Univ Sci Phila Forty-Third St Philadelphia PA 19104 Personal E-mail: mike.marchetti@tcnjalumni.org.

**MARCHETTI-PONTE, KARIN,** lawyer, land conservation consultant; b. Devens, Mass., Nov. 3, 1951; d. Robert Joseph and Patricia (Morico) M.; children: Haley Warden, Henry Warden, Christopher W. Kaiser. BA summa cum laude, U. Maine, 1975, JD, 1978. Bar: Mass. 1979, Maine, 1979. Reporter Sta. WGBH-TV, Portland, Maine, 1978-79; news anchorperson Sta. WMTW-TV, Poland Spring, Maine, 1977-78; atty., founder Advocates, Inc., Portland, 1979-80; assoc. corp. counsel City of Portland, 1980-83; vol. Peace Corps, Tunisia, 1983-84; gen. counsel, clk. Maine Coast Heritage Trust, Topsham, Maine, 1985—; ptnr. Land Conservation Legal Svcs., Bernard, Maine, 1992—. Spkr. Land Trust Alliance, 1988—. Lincoln Inst., 1992, Nat. Land Conservation Leadership Program, Washington, 1997—, Georgetown U. Law Taxings Conf. Co-author: Conserving Land with Conservation

Easements, 1999, Conservation Easement Handbook, Easement Drafting Guide, 2005. Office: Land Conservation Legal Svcs PO Box 100 Hebron ME 04238-0100 also: Maine Coast Heritage Trust Topsham ME 04086 also: PO Box 100 Bernard ME 04612-0100

**MARCHI, SERGIO SISTO,** Canadian government official; b. Buenos Aires, May 12, 1956; s. Ottavio and Luisa (D'Agostinis) M.; m. Laureen Storozuk, Oct. 1, 1983. BA with honors, York U., Toronto, 1979. Alderman City of North York, 1982-84; M.P. for York West dist. Ho. of Commons, Ottawa, 1984-99, min. citizenship and immigration, 1993-96; min. of environment, 1996-97; min. internat. trade Govt. Canada, 1997-99; Canadian amb. of UN and WTO Permanent Missions of Can. to Office of UN, Geneva, 2000—05; chmn. WTO Coun. for Trade in Svcs., 2000—01; chair working party on accession of Ukraine WTO, 2000—; mem. policy adv. commn. WIPO, 2000—; chair gen. coun. WTO, 2002—03; pres. Legacy House of Investments, Geneva. Mem. cabinet coms. on treasury bd.; social policy and program review. Mem. Cabinet Com. on Treas. bd., Social Policy and Program Review; vice chmn. North York Planning Bd., Toronto, 1982-84, Standing Com. on Transport, Ottawa, 1990-93; chmn. Nat. Liberal Caucus, Ottawa, 1990-93. Liberal Party Can.

**MARCHINA, DARLENE B.,** religious coordinator; b. Hammond, Ind., May 8, 1947; d. Walter A. and Paula Skibinski; m. Robert M. Marchina, June 25, 1977; children: Patrick, Ryan, Kevin, Kyle. BA in elem. edn., St. Mary of the Woods Coll., 1969; MS in edn., Purdue U., 1973; BA in theology, Cal. Coll. of St. Joseph, 1984. Tchr. St. Casimir Sch., Hammond, Ind., 1969—79; coordr. religious edn. St. Elizabeth Seton, Valparaiso, Ind., 1983—99; coordr. sch. visits Diocese of Gary, Merrillville, Ind., 2000—, coord. safe environ. program, 2003—. Mem. Nat. Cath. Edn. Assn. Catholic. Avocations: reading, sewing, needlecrafts, tap dancing. Home: 4069 Bush Hill Ct Crown Point IN 46307 Office: Diocese of Gary 9292 Broadway Merrillville IN 46410 Office Phone: 219-769-9292. E-mail: dmarchin@dcgary.org.

**MARCHIONINI, GARY JOSEPH,** information science educator; b. Altoona, Pa., Sept. 12, 1949; s. Arthur and Claudia (Serventi) M.; m. Suzanne Bernhardt, July 10, 1970; children: Brian, Deanna. BA, Western Mich. U., 1971; MEd, Wayne State U., 1974, PhD, 1981. Tchr. math. East Detroit (Mich.) Pub. Schs., 1971-78; inservice specialist, rschr. Wayne State U., Detroit, 1978-82, asst. prof. inst. tech., 1982-83; asst. prof. info. sci. U. Md., College Park, 1983-90, assoc. prof. info. sci., 1990-95, prof. info. sci., 1995-98; Boshamer prof. info. sci. U. N.C., Chapel Hill, 1998—. Expert NSF, Washington, 1989-90; adj. prof. George Washington U., Washington, 1992. Author: Information Seeking in Electronic Environments, 1995; contbr. articles to profl. jours. Grantee: NSF, 1987-90, Harvard U., Annenberg Corp. Pub. Broadcasting, 1988-93, Coun. on Libr. Resources, 1990-91, Nat. Libr. Medicine, 1992, NASA, 1993-94. Mem. Assn. for Computing Machinery, Am. Soc. for Info. Sci. (Rsch. award 1997), Am. Soc. Rsch. Assn., Assn. for Advancement Computers in Edn. Office: U NC 203 Maning Hill Chapel Hill NC 27599-0001

**MARCHIORI, MASSIMO,** computer scientist; BS in math., MS in math., PhD in computer sci. Rsch. scientist MIT Lab. Computer Sci., World Wide Web Consortium; rsch. scientist dept. computer sci. U. Venice, Italy. Contbr. articles to profl. jour. Named one of Top 100 Young Innovators, MIT Tech. Review, 2004; recipient award for Innovative Rsch., Gini Found., Young Scientist award, IBM, Lifetime Mem. award, Oxford Soc.

**MARCIALIS, ANGELO VINCENT,** music educator, musician; b. Bronx, NY, Nov. 19, 1958; s. Vincent John and Mary Concetta Marcialis. BA in Music, Berklee Coll. Music, 1980; MA in Edn. and Music, Manhattanville Coll., 1991. Cert. state cert. adjudicator NY State Sch. Music Assn., tchr. mentor NY State Union Tchrs. Regional dir. Music on the Move, Staten Island, NY, 1982—84; dir. of bands Chester (N.Y.) Union Free Sch. Dist., 1985—87, Enlarged City Sch. Dist. Middletown, NY, 1987—2003; dir. ensembles Washingtonville (NY) Schs., 2003—. Historian, archivist, trumpeter, jazz clinician Orange County (N.Y.) Music Educators Assn., 1987—. Author: Supplementary Method for Beginning Trumpet Players, 1992. Recruiter Green Party, Orange County, 2000. Mem.: N.Y. State Band Dirs. Assn., Internat. Trumpet Guild, N.Y. State Music Assn. Avocations: gardening, baseball, hiking, bicycling. Home: 3712 Whispering Hills Chester NY 10918-1530 Office: Washingtonville Sch 38 W Main St Washingtonville NY 10992 Office Phone: 845-497-2200 ext 21197. Personal E-mail: trumpethead@hotmail.com.

**MARCIALIS, ROBERT LOUIS,** planetary astronomer; b. NYC, Sept. 14, 1956; s. Louis Angelo and Joan Regina (Dippolito) M. SB in Aero. and Astronautical Engring., MIT, 1978, SB in Earth and Planetary Scis., 1980; MS in Physics and Astronomy, Vanderbilt U., 1983; PhD in Planetary Scis., U. Ariz., 1990. Tchg. asst. dept. earth and planetary scis. MIT, Cambridge, 1976—80; lab. instr. dept. physics and astronomy Vanderbilt U., Nashville, 1981, 1982—83, rsch. assist. Arthur J. Dyer Obs., 1981—82; rsch. assist. Lunar and Planetary Lab. U. Ariz., Tucson, 1983—86, rsch. assoc., 1986—90; postdoctoral fellow Jet Propulsion Lab., Pasadena, Calif., 1990—92; adj. faculty Pima C.C., Tucson, 1992—; sr. rsch. specialist U. Ariz., 1996—. Founding mem. Pluto/Charon Mut. Eclipse Season Campaign. Contbr. articles to Nature, Bull. Am. Astron. Soc., Astron. Jour., Minor Planet Circular, Lunar and Planetary Sci., Sci., Jour. Brit. Astron. Assn., Astrophys. Jour., Icarus, also others. Instr. water safety ARC, 1981-82; ednl. counselor MIT, 1983—; fastpitch softball umpire, 1975—. Rsch. fellow NASA, 1986-89. Mem. AAAS, Am. Astron. Soc., Am. Geophys. Union, Astron. Soc. Pacific, Internat. Occultation Timing Assn., Sigma Pi Sigma. Roman Catholic. Achievements include discovery of water ice on surface of Pluto's moon Charon; construction of an albedo map for surface of Pluto; research on Pluto, Charon and Triton, icy satellites, outer solar system formation and evolution, solar system photometry, occultation astronomy, construction and calibration of Imager for Mars Pathfinder, cameras for the Mars Polar Lander and Mars Phoenix missions and Mars Odyssey gamma ray spectrometer. Office: U Ariz Lunar Planetary Lab Tucson AZ 85721-0001 E-mail: umpire@lpl.arizona.edu.

**MARCIANO, LISA OGGIONI,** musician, music educator; b. Englewood, N.J., May 3, 1958; d. Mario Luciano and Angela Ciotti Oggioni; m. William David Marciano, May 1, 1982; children: Richard Gregory, Jessica Christine. MusM, Manhattan Sch. of Music, 1981; postgrad., Westminster Choir Coll., Princeton, N.J., 1996. Cert. tchr. of music K-12 N.J. Dept. of Edn. Dir. of music, organist Ch. of the Good Shepherd, Bergenfield, NJ, 1980–96; music tchr. k-8 Paramus (N.J.) Pub. Schs., 1981–84; music tchr. 6-8 George Washington Mid. Sch., Ridgewood, NJ, 1984–86; choral dir. 9-12 Pascack Valley Regional H.S., Hillsdale, NJ, 1986–88; dir. of music, organist Ch. of the Ascension, New Milford, NJ, 1996–2002; dir. of music ministries St. John the Evangelist Roman Cath. Ch., Bergenfield, 2002—. Liturgical musician Archdiocese of Newark, 1995—, Fordham U., N.Y.C., 2005—; piano tchr., New Milford, 1977—. Coordinating musician (music dir.) for 9/11 svcs. Bergenfield Mayor and Coun., 2004. Mem.: Nat. Assn. of Pastoral Musicians (dir. of music ministries 2002). Roman Catholic. Home: 636 Stockton St New Milford NJ 07646 Office: Saint John the Evangelist Roman Cath Ch 29 N Washington Avenue Bergenfield NJ 07621 Office Phone: 201-384-0101. Personal E-mail: opus58@optonline.net.

**MARCIANO, MAURICE,** apparel executive; b. France; CEO Guess?, L.A., co-chmn. Office: Guess Inc 1444 S Alameda St Los Angeles CA 90021-2433

**MARCIL, WILLIAM CHRIST, SR.,** publisher, broadcast executive; b. Rolette, N.D., Mar. 9, 1936; s. Max I. and Ida (Fuerst) M.; m. Jane Black, Oct. 15, 1960; children: Debora Jane, William Christ Jr. BSBA, U.N.D. 1958. Br. mgr. Community Credit Co., Mpls., 1959-61; with Forum Comms. Co., Fargo, N.D., 1961—, pres., pub., CEO, 1969—. Pres. Forum Comm. Found.; past bd. dirs. North Ctrl. region Boy Scouts Am. With U.S. Army, 1958-59. Mem. Inland Newspaper Press Assn., N.D. Press Assn., Am.

Newspaper Pubs. Assn. (past dir., chmn.), Fargo Morehead C. of C., N.D. State C. of C. (past pres.), U.S. C. of C. (past chmn.), Sigma Delta Chi, Lambda Chi Alpha. Lodges: Masons, Shriners, Elks. Republican. Office: Forum Comm Co 101 5th St N Fargo ND 58102-4826 Home: 1618 S 8th St Fargo ND 58103

**MARCIN, ROBERT H.,** automotive executive; BBA, SUNY, 1971; MBA, Calif. State U., 1973. With Ford Aerospace, San Jose, Calif., 1973—89; exec. v.p., dir., external & employee affairs First Nationwide Fin. Corp., 1989—93; dir., compensation planning office Ford Motor Co., 1993—95, dir., internat. labor affairs, 1995—98, exec. dir., labor affairs, 1998—2000; sr. v.p., human resources Visteon Corp., Dearborn, Mich., 2000—03, sr. v.p., corp. relations, 2003—. Bd. dirs. Med-i-bank, Inc., Am. Soc. Employers, Mich. Office: Visteon Corp 1700 Rotunda Dr Dearborn MI 48120

**MARCINEK, MARGARET ANN,** nursing education administrator; b. Uniontown, Pa., Sept. 29, 1948; d. Joseph Hugh and Evelyn (Bailey) Boyle; m. Bernard Francis Marcinek, Aug. 11, 1973; 1 child, Cara Ann. RN, Uniontown Hosp., 1969; BSN, Pa. State U., 1970; MSN, U. Md., 1973; EdD, W.Va. U., 1983. Staff nurse Presbyn. U., Pitts., 1970-73; instr. nursing W.Va. U., Morgantown, 1973-77, asst. prof., 1977-80, assoc. prof., 1980-83, California U. Pa., 1983-87, prof., 1987—2004, dept. chmn., 1985—2004, assoc. provost, 2004—. Program evaluator Commn. on Collegiate Nursing Edn.; mem. adv. coun. In Home Health, Inc.; mem. adv. coun. Albert Gallatin VNA. Contbg. author: Critical Care Nursing; contbr. articles to profl. jours. Mem.: ANA, Commn. on Collegiate Nursing Edn. (site evaluator), Oncology Nursing Soc., Sigma Theta Tau. Business E-Mail: marcinek@cup.edu.

**MARCINKOSKI, ANNETTE MARIE,** retired elementary school educator; b. Akron, Ohio, Aug. 2, 1933; d. Frank J. and Barbara (Popielarczyk) M. BS, U. Akron, 1955; MA, U. Mich., 1959. Tchr. Flint (Mich.) Pub. Schs., 1955-63; tng. tchr. Coop. Tchr. Edn. Program, 1963-69, elem. tchr., 1969—92. Active Big Sister program; sponsor Jr. Red Cross, 1959-63; tchr. Confraternity of Christian Doctrine; precinct del. Dem. Com. Mem. United Tchrs. of Flint (del. rep. assembly, instn./profl. devel. com.), Mich. Edn. Assn. (bd. dirs. 1978-80, pres. Region X, 1976-77, exec. com. 1986-90), NEA (regional dir. 1973-78), Elem., Kindergarten and Nursery Educators, Assn. Childhood Edn. Internat. (sec. Flint 1959-62, treas. Mich. 1970-72, pres. Mich. 1973-75), AAUW (v.p. 1967-69, area rep. in edn. 1969-72), Cath. Bus. Women (sec. 1970-72, del. Coun. State Congrs. 1974-76), Flint Area Reading Coun., Mich. Reading Assn., Mich. Edn. Spl. Svcs. Assn. (trustee 1983-92, v.p. 1990), Flint Cmty. Schs. Edn. Fund (bd. govs. 1984-88), Flint Classroom Support Fund (bd. trustees 1988-92, exec. dir. 1992—), Theta Phi Alpha (advisor GM Inst. chpt. 1973-85, chmn. bd. dirs. 1973-79, sec. Founders Found., 1978-80, nat. treas. 1980-82, chmn. nat. bd. dirs. 1986-88), Delta Kappa Gamma (pres. 1990-92), Phi Delta Kappa (del. 1981-84, 86-88). Home: 1911 Laurel Oak Dr Flint MI 48507-6038 Office: 923 E Kearsley St Flint MI 48503-1900

**MARCO, CURA A.,** medical educator; s. Jorge and Martha Cura; m. Natalia Martinez, Aug. 17, 1970; children: Victoria Cura, Emilia Cura. MD, Cath. U. Cordoba, Argentina, 1995. Cert. Am. Bd. Radiology, 2003. Asst. U. Tex. Health Sci. Ctr., San Antonio, 2005—. Contbr. articles to profl. jours. Fellow Interventional Radiology, Columbia U., 2003. Mem.: Soc. Interventional Radiology (assoc.), Am. Coll. Radiology (assoc.), Radiol. Soc. N.Am. (assoc. Cert. Merit 2002, Cum Laude award 2002), Am. Roentgen Ray Soc. (assoc. Cert. Merit 2005), Am. Heart Assn. (assoc.). Office Phone: 210-567-5564.

**MARCO, MITCHELL,** artist; b. Atlantic City, May 25, 1977; s. Peter and Jennifer Marco. BFA, Sch. Visual Arts, 1999. Curator Sleight of Hand Salena Gallery L.I. U., Bklyn., 2003. One-man shows include Pelham Art Ctr., NY, 2003, exhibited in group shows at Mus. Contemporary Art, Balt., 2000, Rosenberg Art Gallery Hofstra U., Hempstead, N.Y., 2002, Parrish Art Mus., Southampton, N.Y., 2003, Boulder Mus. Contemporary Art, Colo., 2004, Exit Art, N.Y.C., 2004, 2005, 2006, George Adams Gallery, 2004; creator: The Sophisticated Animal, 2003, Out of the Aviary, 2004, The Unnatural Glow of Significance, 2004. Recipient Alexander Rutsch award, Pelham (N.Y.) Art Ctr., 2003. Office: PO Box 1808 New York NY 10025

**MARCOCCIA, LOUIS GARY,** accountant, academic administrator; b. Syracuse, NY, Nov. 6, 1946; s. George A. and Rose J. (Misita) M.; m. Susan Evelyn Miller, June 21, 1974; 1 child: Rachel Kathryn. BS, Syracuse U., 1968, MS, 1969; EdD, U. Pa., 2003. CPA NY. Acct. Price Waterhouse & Co., Syracuse, NY, 1969-75; dir. internal audit Syracuse U., 1975-76, comptroller, 1976-82, v.p., comptroller, 1982-95, sr. v.p. bus., and fin., 1985-95, sr. v.p. bus., fin. and adminstrv. svcs., 1995—. Bd. dirs. Syracuse Bd. Chase Manhattan Bank, Syracuse Divsn., 1985-2001, Lincoln Life and Annuity Co. N.Y., Univ. Hill Corp., Upstate Med. Univ. Found.; pres. Syracuse U. Hotel and Conf. Ctr., LLC; spkr. Harvard U. Inst. Ednl. Mgmt., 1984-88, 90-91. Pres. parish coun. St. Michael's Ch., Syracuse, 1985-88; pres. Syracuse U. Theatre Corp., 1987—; bd. dirs. Friends of Burnet Park Zoo, 1987-93, Syracuse U. Press., 1982—, Syracuse Sports Corp., 1990-91. Mem. AICPA, N.Y. Soc. CPA, Nat. Assn. Accts., Fin. Execs. Inst., Inst. Internal Auditors. Clubs: Drumlins (pres. 1976—); Century. Republican. Roman Catholic. Avocations: swimming, tennis. Home: Hedge Ln Cazenovia NY 13035 Office: Syracuse U Off ExecVP and CFO 900 S Crouse AveSte 620 Syracuse NY 13244-2130 Business E-Mail: lmarcocc@syr.edu.

**MARCOGLIESE, RICHARD J.,** energy executive; BSChemE, NYU. Various operational and tech. supervisory positions Benicia refinery, Baton Rouge refinery, refining and supply hdqs. and Bayway refinery Exxon; v.p., gen. mgr. Benicia refinery Valero Energy Corp., sr. v.p. strategic planning San Antonio, 2001—02, sr. v.p. refining ops., 2002, v.p. refining ops. Office: Valero Energy Corpn PO Box 696000 San Antonio TX 78269 6000

**MARCONE, ANGELA T.,** music educator; b. Clinton, SC, Feb. 27, 1959; d. Dewey C. Traylor and Dveda D. Stroud; m. Stephen F. Marcone, Oct. 9, 1998 (separated); 1 child, Abigail Rose. AS in computer sci., NY Tech. Coll., 1979; MusB, William Paterson U., 1997. Cert. music tchr. K-12. Asst. mgmt., svc. distribution IBM, Paramus, NJ, 1983—92; instr. computer software Productivity Point Inst., NJ, 1990—99, Cir. Profl. Edn., Paoli, Pa., 1990—99, Midland Park (NJ) HS Continuing Edn., 1990—99; vocal coach, instr. self employed, Wayne, NJ, 1997—; owner, tchr. Vocal Performance Studio, Pompton Lakes, NJ, 2003—; music tchr. Pub. Edn., NJ, 2001—. Author various computer software manuals; performer (singer): HarmonyTryx. Mem.: NY Tchrs. Singing Assn., Nat. Assn. Tchrs. Avocations: gardening, singing, mountain biking. Office Phone: 973-831-0450. Personal E-mail: angietryx@msn.com.

**MARCOPOULOS, GEORGE JOHN,** history professor; b. Salem, Mass., June 30, 1931; s. John George and Urania Christou (Moustakis) M. BA, Bowdoin Coll., 1953; MA, Harvard U., 1955, PhD, 1966. Instr. Tufts U., Medford, Mass., 1961-66, asst. prof., 1966-71, assoc. prof., 1971-92, prof., 1992—2006, prof. emeritus, 2006. Contbr. articles to profl. jours. and Am. Ann. yearbooks. Bd. dirs. Gerondelis Found., Inc., Lynn, Mass., 1987—; treas., 1994—. Recipient Seymour Simcher award for disting. tchg. and advising Tufts U., 1997, 2006, Outstanding Contbn. to Grad. Studies award Tufts U., 2006; Mellon Faculty Devel. grantee Tufts U., 1983. Mem. Phi Beta Kappa. Greek Orthodox. Avocations: music, films, reading, performing arts, excursions. Office Phone: 617-627-3758. Business E-Mail: gjm1953@comcast.net.

**MARCOSSON, THOMAS I.,** management consultant, advertising executive; b. NYC, Jan. 31, 1936; s. Mark and Mollie (Schreiber) M.; m. Carla F. Hunt, May 15, 1988; children: Mark, Susan, Samuel, Jill. Student, Union Coll., Schenectady, 1953-55; BS, NYU, 1959. CPA NY. Mgr. Touche Ross & Co., N.Y.C., 1959-63; v.p. fin., dir. Superior Surg. Mfg. Co., Inc., Huntington, NY, 1964-66; div. pres., gen. mgr. OEI div., Vernitron Corp., Great Neck, NY, 1967-71; controller Allied Maintenance Corp., N.Y.C., 1972-75, v.p. fin.,

1975-82; chief fin. officer Remco Maintenance Corp., N.Y.C., 1982-84, exec. v.p., chief operating officer, 1984-88; pres. MBW Advt. Network Inc., N.Y.C., 1988-89; founder, pres. Dunmarc Assocs., Inc., N.Y.C., 1989—; pres., dir. Square Arch Realty Corp., N.Y.C., 1986—2004. Exec. v.p. Greater Talent Network, Inc., 1991—; co-founder, dir. Village Alliance Bus. Improvement Dist., 1993-2004. Office: 437 5th Ave 7th Fl New York NY 10016 Office Phone: 212-645-4200. Personal E-mail: tmarcosson@nyc.rr.com.

**MARCOTT, CURTIS ALLEN,** chemist, researcher; b. Mpls., Apr. 8, 1952; s. Allen Henry and Marion Lorraine (Grahl) M.; m. Susan Frances Marshall, Apr. 28, 1984; children: Steven, Pamela. BA, Concordia Coll., 1974; PhD, U. Minn., 1979. Rsch. fellow Procter & Gamble, Cin., 1979—. Mem. editl. adv. bd. Vibrational Spectroscopy, 1990-99, Analytical Chemistry, 1995-97, 2004—, Applied Spectroscopy, 1998—. Named Cin. Chemist of Yr., 2001. Mem. Coblentz Soc. (bd. mgrs. 1990-94, Williams-Wright award 1993). Home: 10125 Cliffwood Ct Cincinnati OH 45241-1086 Office: Procter & Gamble Co Miami Valley Innovation Ctr Cincinnati OH 45253-8707 Office Phone: 513-627-2806. E-mail: marcott.ca@pg.com.

**MARCOTTE, MICHAEL STEVEN,** municipal official; b. New Orleans, Jan. 17, 1951; s. Steven Stephen and Gloria Catherine (DeValcourt) Marcotte; m. Mary Jane Kilgore, May 28, 1972; children: Matthew David, Margaret Katherine. BA, M of Environ. Engring., Rice U., 1973. Cert. profl. engr, DC, Tex, Colo. Engr., sr. engr., mgr. Turner, Collie & Braden, Inc., Houston, 1973—82; chief maintenance engr. water divsn. City of Houston, 1982—83, mng. engr. water divsn., 1984—85, asst. to dir. Pub. Works dept., 1985—87, exec. asst. to dir. Pub. Works dept., 1987—88, acting dir. dept. planning and devel., 1988—89; dir. Dallas Water Utilities, 1989—95; dir. econ. devel. City of Dallas, 1995—97; chief engr. D.C. Water & Sewer Authority, 1997—2004; dir. pub. works City Houston, 2004—. Fellow: ASCE; mem.: Houston Galveston Area Coun., Am. Acad. Water Resource Engrs., Am Acad Environ Engrs (trustee), Tex Water Conservation Asn (bd dirs), Met. Washington Coun Govts, Water Environ Fedn (life), Am Water Works Assn. (life; trustee Rsch. Found.). Presbyterian. Avocation: high school and college sports official. Home: 204 Travis St Apt 2D Houston TX 77002-1775 Office: City Houston 611 Walker 25th Fl Houston TX 77002 Office Phone: 713-837-0037. Personal E-mail: marcottem@prodigy.net.

**MARCOTTE, PAUL HENRY,** state representative; b. LaCrosse, Wis., Jan. 26, 1928; m. Kathleen Marcotte; 4 children. BA, St. John's Univ., 1951. V.p. Gateway Foods, Inc., 1958—69; dir. comms. IGA Internat. Hdqs., 1969—75; exec. v.p., dir. mktg. Convenient Food Mart, Inc., 1975—84; exec. v.p. Ohio Valley AFM Inc., 1984—95; State Rep. House of Rep., Dist. 60, 1994—2006. Chair Boone County Rep. Party, 1993—94; mem. Capital Projects & Bond Oversight Licensing and Occupations; Vice chair State Gov.; mem. transportation. T/4, CAC USAR. Caucuses: Am. Legis. Exch. Coun.(ALEC); mem. Nat. Homeland Sec. working Group, 2002-present; chair, Trade & Transp. Task Force, 2001-05 Republican. Roman Catholic. Office: Capitol Capitol Annex, Rm 413E Frankfort KY 40601 also: Dist 10674 Palestine Dr Union KY 41091

**MARCOTTE, PAUL JOHN,** neurosurgeon, educator; b. Ottawa, Ont., Can., Oct. 15, 1958; (parents Can. and Am. citizens); s. Paul John and Elinor Ann (Simeone) M. BSc, U. Ottawa, 1980, MD, 1984. Intern Ottawa Civic Hosp., 1984-85; resident U. Ottawa, 1985-90, asst. prof., 1990-92; fellow in spinal surgery Barrow Neurol. Inst., Phoenix, 1991-92; assoc. prof. U. Pa., Phila., 1993—. Contbr. articles to profl. jours., chpts. to books. Fellow: ACS, Royal Coll. Physicians and Surgeons (Can.); mem.: Can. Congress Neurol. Surgeons, Am. Assn. Neurol. Surgeons, Congress Neurol. Surgeons. Roman Catholic. Avocations: hockey, model railroading, automobiles. Office: Hosp U Pa 3400 Spruce St Philadelphia PA 19104-4206

**MARCOUX, CARL HENRY,** insurance company executive, writer, historian; b. San Francisco, Jan. 6, 1927; s. Henry Roderick and Margaret (Carlin) M.; m. Ana Virginia Penate-Melara, Nov. 11, 1967; children: Eric Henry, Grant Reynold. BA, Stanford U., 1950; MBA, Golden Gate U., San Francisco, 1958; MA in Latin Am. History, U. Calif., Irvine, 1988; PhD in Latin Am. History, U. Calif., Riverside, 1994. Gen. mgr. Nat. Union Ins. Co., Pitts., 1953-68; exec. v.p. Transam. Ins. Co., 1968-85. Author: (novels) Sailing West, 2001. Served with U.S. Mcht. Marine, 1944-46; USAF, 1951-53. Mem. Stanford Alumni Assn. Republican. Home: 1967 Port Cardigan Pl Newport Beach CA 92660-5347

**MARCOUX, JULIA A.,** midwife; b. St. Helens, Eng., Aug. 7, 1928; d. Robert Patrick and Margaret Mary Theresa (Whelly Ashall; m. Albert Marcoux, Apr. 23, 1955; children: Stephen, Ann Marie, Richard, Michael, Maureen, Patrick, Margaret, Julie. Diploma, Withington Hosp., Manchester, England, 1950; grad., Cowley Hill Hosp., St. Helens, England, 1952; BS in Pub. Adminstrn., St. Joseph's Coll. RN, Conn.; lic. midwife, Conn. Nurse, labor, delivery rm. and nursery Day Kimbal Hosp., Putnam, Conn.; sr. nurse Marianapolis Prep. Sch., Thompson, Conn.; occupational nurse U.S. Post Office, Hartford, Conn.; pvt. duty and gerontology nurse Conn. ctrs. in field. Contbr. articles to profl. jours. Named Internat. Cath. Family of Yr., 1982.

**MARCOUX, WILLIAM JOSEPH,** lawyer; b. Detroit, Jan. 20, 1927; s. Lona J. and Anna (Ransom) C.; m. Kae Marie Sanborn, Aug. 23, 1952; children: Ann K., William C. BA, U. Mich., 1949, JD, 1952. Bar: Mich. 1953. Pvt. practice, Pontiac, Mich., 1953; assoc. McKone, Badgley, Domke and Kline, Jackson, Mich., 1953-65, ptnr., 1965-75; dir. Marcoux, Allen, Schomer, Bower, Nichols, Kendall and Lindsey, PC, Jackson, Mich., 1975—. Mem. exec. bd. Great Sauk Trail council Boy Scouts Am., 1965-66; bd. dirs. Jackson County United Way, pres., 1983-84. Served with USNR, 1945-46. Recipient Silver Beaver award Boy Scouts Am., 1969, Disting. Citizen award Lund O'Lakes coun. Boy Scouts Am., 1991. Fellow Am. Coll. Trial Lawyers, Mich. State Bar Found.; mem. Mich. State Bar Assn., Jackson County Bar Assn. (pres. 1979-80), Jackson Rotary Club (pres. 1963-64), Country Club of Jackson, Clark Lake Yacht Club (commodore 1959). Methodist. Home: 1745 Malvern Dr Jackson MI 49203-5378 Office: Marcoux Allen et al PO Box 787 Jackson MI 49204-0787 Office Phone: 517-787-4100. Personal E-mail: wmarcoux@marcouxallen.com.

**MARCOVICI, MICHAEL,** investment company executive; b. 1969; V.p., private banking and investment group Merrill Lynch & Co., Chgo. Named one of 40 Under Forty, Crain's Bus. Chgo., 2005. Office: Merril Lynch & Co Ste 2500 33 W Monroe St Chicago IL 60603-5409*

**MARCOVITZ, LEONARD EDWARD,** retail executive; b. Bismarck, N.D., Sept. 6, 1934; s. Jacob and Frieda Marcovitz. Asst. mgr. Greengard's Clothing, Mandan, ND, 1955-58; mgr. K-G Men's Stores, Inc., Bismarck, 1958-61, Billings, Mont., 1961-69, v.p. store ops., 1969-73; pres. Leonard's Men's Stores, Yakima, Wash. and Billings, Mont., 1973-77; chief exec. officer K-G Retail div. Chromalloy Am. Corp., Englewood, Colo., 1977-81; pres. DeMarcos Men's Clothing, Casper, Wyo., 1982—, Idaho Falls, Idaho, 1984—, Billings, Mont., 1986-96, Twin Falls, Idaho, 1996—, Ft. Collins, Colo., 1999—, Boise, Idaho, 2000, DeMarcos Men's Clothing, Boise Town Square, 2002. With N.D. Nat. Guard, 1954—61, with Mont. Nat. Guard, 1961—63. Mem. Menswear Retailers Am. (past dir.). Order of Demolay (Degree of Chevalier 1952, Internat. Master Councilor 1953, Demolay Dad 1959), Elks. Home: PO Box 777035 Henderson NV 89077

**MARCUCCIO, PHYLLIS ROSE,** retired educational association administrator, editor; b. Hackensack, N.J., Aug. 25, 1933; d. Filippo and Rose (Henry) Marcuccio. AB, Bucknell U., 1955; MA, George Washington U., 1976. Trainee Time, Inc., 1956—57; art prodn. for mags. of Med. Econs., Inc., 1958—60; mem. staff Nat. Sci. Tchrs. Assn., Washington, 1961—99; assoc. editor Sci. and Children, 1963, editor, 1964—93, dir. divsn. elem. edn. 1974—78, dir. divsn. program devel. and continuing edn., 1978—83, pub., 1993—99; dir. publs. Nat. Sci. Tchrs. Assn., 1983—99, assoc. exec. dir., 1990—99; pub. Dragonfly, 1996—99. Lectr., cons. in field. Author (photographer, illustrator numerous articles); co-author: Investigation in Ecology, 1972; editor: Science Fun, 1977, Science Fun, 2d edit., 1994; Selected Readings for Students of English as a Second Language, 1966; compiler: Opportunities for Summer Studies in Elementary Science, 1968, Opportunities for Summer Studies in Elementary Science, 2d edit., 1969, pub.: Sci. and Children, 1993—99, Dragonfly Mag., 1997—99. Apptd. commr. Rockville (Md.) Housing Authority, 1981—91, chairperson, 1984—86; bd. dirs. Nat. Sci. Resource Ctr., NAS, 1986—96, Hands on Sci. Outreach, Inc., 1991—2001; pres. East Rockville Civic Assn., 2000—; elected mem. City Coun. of Rockville, 2005—. Recipient Citizenship medal, DAR, 1951, Golden Lamp award, Edpress, 1998. Mem.: AAAS, NSTA (life), Pocono Environ. Edn. Ctr. (bd. dirs. 1993—98), Sci. Tchg. Assn. N.Y. (Outstanding Svc. to Sci. Edn. award 1987), Ednl. Press Assn. Am. (regional dir. 1969—71, sec. 1979—, Disting. Achievement award 1969, 1971—74, 1976, 1977, Eleanor Fishburn award 1978, Disting. Achievement award 1980, 1988, 1993, 1995), The Washington Forum, Washington edn. Press Assn. (treas. 1966—67, pres. 1975—76), Ohio Coun. Elem. Sch. Sci. (life), Nat. Assn. Industry Edn. Coop. (bd. dirs. 1980—86), Nat. Press Club (Silver Owl), Am. Nature Study Soc., Coun. Elem. Sci. Internat. (Internat. award for outstanding contbns. sci. edn. 1971, 1972, 1986, 1994), Kiwanis Internat., Sigma Delta Chi, Phi Delta Kappa, Phi Delta gamma, Theta Alpha Phi. Home: 406 S Horners Ln Rockville MD 20850-1556 E-mail: marcu@erols.com.

**MARCUM, DEANNA BOWLING,** library administrator; b. Salem, Ind., Aug. 5, 1946; d. Anderson and Ruby (Mobley) Bowling; m. Thomas P. Marcum, June 13, 1974; 1 child, Ursula. BA, U. Ill., 1967; MA, So. Ill. U., 1969; MLS, U. Ky., 1971; PhD, U. Md. 1991. Tchr. Deland-Weldon (Ill.) High Sch., 1967-68; instr. English U. Ky., Lexington, 1969-70, cataloging librarian, 1970-73, asst. to dir., 1973-74; asst. dir. pub. svcs. Joint U. Librs., Nashville, 1974-77; mgmt. tng. specialist Assn. Rsch. Librs., Washington, 1977-80; sr. cons. Info. Systems Cons., Inc., Washington, 1980-81; v.p. Coun. on Libr. Resources, Washington, 1981-89; dean Sch. Libr. and Info. Sch. Cath. U., Washington, 1989-92; dir. pub. svcs. and collections mgmt. Libr. of Congress, Washington, 1993-95, assoc. libr., 2003—; pres. Coun. on Libr. Resources and Info., Washington, 1995—2003. Adv. bd. So. Edn. Found., Atlanta, 1986-91; chmn. grants com. Coun. on Libr. resources, Washington, 1990-94. Author: Good Books in a Country Home, 1993, Development of Digital Libraries, An American Perspective, 2001, Digital Library Development: View from Kanazawa, 2005; co-author: (with Richard Boss) The Library Catalog, 1980, On-Line Acquisitions Systems, 1981; contbr. articles to profl. jours. Pres., Commn. on Preservation and Access, 1995—. Mem. ALA, Am. Studies Assn., Orgn. Am. Historians, Am. Antiquarian Soc. (adv. bd. 1989—), Beta Phi Mu, Phi Kappa Phi. Home: 3315 Wake Dr Kensington MD 20895-3218 Office: Coun on Libr and Info Resources Ste 500 1755 Massachusetts Ave NW Washington DC 20036-2124 Office Phone: 202-707-6240. E-mail: dmarcum@loc.gov.

**MARCUS, ABIR A.,** psychiatrist; arrived in US, 1995; d. Assaad Aziz Abdel-Sayed and Nadra Nassry Sourial; divorced; 1 child, Gina Marie. MD with honors, Ain Shams U., Cairo, 1991. Diplomate Am. Bd. Psychiatry and Neurology, Am. Bd. Med. Specialties, lic. psychiatrist NJ, NY. Intern Ain Shams Med. Sch., Cairo, 1992—93, instr. forensic medicine and toxicology, 1994—95; resident in psychiatry NJ Med. Sch., Newark, 1996—2000; fellow, asst. prof. Robert Wood Johnson, Piscataway, NJ, 2000—01; pvt. practice Hazlet, NJ, 1999—. Adj. asst. prof. Robert Wood Johnson Med. Sch., Piscataway, 2001—; task force com. for curriculum devel. in psychotherapy tng. for residents U. Medicine and Dentistry NJ Med. Sch., Newark, 1999—2000; cons. CPC Behavioral Health Care, Red Bank, NJ, 2001—; cons. in field. Contbr. articles to profl. jours. Recipient Physician's Recognition award, AMA, 1999, 2005; scholar, Nat. Inst. Drug Abuse. Mem.: Am. Psychiatric Assn. (assoc. mem.), Neurosci. Edn. Inst., Am. Soc. Clin. Psychopharmacology, NJ Psychiat. Assn. (pres. resident chpt. 1999, pres. 2000, early career psychiatry com., pub. com., disaster preparedness com., resident and med. student com.), Am. Psychiat. Assn., Am. Acad. Addiction Psychiatry, Am. Soc. Addiction Medicine. Avocations: reading, travel, ballroom dancing, salsa dancing. Office: 32 Village Ct Hazlet NJ 07730 Office Phone: 917-204-5960. Personal E-mail: abirmarcus@aol.com.

**MARCUS, ALAN C.,** public relations consultant; b. NYC, Feb. 26, 1947; s. Percy and Rose (Fox) M.; m. Judith Lamel. June 21, 1979; 1 child, Allison. Student, Hun Sch. of Princeton, 1965. Dir. pub. rels. Bergen County Rep. Com., Hackensack, N.J., 1968; clk. N.J. Gen. Assembly, Trenton, 1969, sec. to majority party of assembly, 1970; pres. The Marcus Group, Inc., Secaucus, 1971—. Adj. prof. Rutger U. Grad. Sch., 1986-88. Trustee Nat. Leukemia Assn., 1978-82, Hun Sch. of Princeton, 1977-88, Passaic River Coalition, 1980-82. Recipient Youth Enterprise award Jim Waiter Corp., 1972. Mem. Pub. Rels. Soc. Am. (pres., bd. dirs. N.J. chpt. 1976-77, N.J. chpt. Pres. award 1975), N.J. C. of C., N.J. Bus. and Industry Assn., N.J. Press Assn., Alpine Country Club. Office: 300 Lighting Way Secaucus NJ 07094-3672 also: 50 W State St Trenton NJ 08608-1220

**MARCUS, AMY DOCKSER,** reporter; b. Boston; B magna cum laude, Harvard Univ. Reporter Am. Lawyer, 1987—88; news asst. Wall St. Jour., 1988—89, staff reporter, Boston, 1989—2000, Middle East corr, 1991—98, staff reporter, Boston, 2002—; reporter Money Mag., 2000—02. Author: The View From Nebo: How Archaeology Is Rewriting the Bible and Reshaping the Middle East, 2000. Recipient first place, NY State Bar Assn. Media Awards, 1990, honorable mention, single article category, Benjamin Fine Awards for Outstanding Edn. Reporting, 1999, Pulitzer Prize for beat reporting, 2005; grantee Harvard Med. Sch. media fellowship, 2004, CASE media fellowship, Univ. Pitt. Cancer Ctr., 2005.

**MARCUS, BERNARD,** lawyer, arbitrator, mediator; b. Wilkes-Barre, Pa., Mar. 10, 1924; m. Frances Frank; children: Kate, Aaron, Charles, Mary. Student, U. Pa., 1941-43, Carnegie-Mellon U., 1943-44; LL.B., Harvard U., 1948; postgrad., Loyola U. of South, New Orleans, 1958. Bar: D.C. 1949, La. 1958. Atty. legis. reference service Library of Congress, 1949-50; acting counsel small bus. com. Ho. of Reps., 1950; atty. NLRB, Washington, Un. Buffalo and New Orleans, 1950-57; assoc. Deutsch, Kerrigan & Stiles, New Orleans, 1957-58, ptnr., 1958-95, mng. ptnr., 1985-89, emeritus ptnr., 1995—2004; of counsel Lehmann, Norman & Marcus, New Orleans, 2004—. Cons. Dept. State, 1965-69; labor arbitrator Am. Arbitration Assn., Fed. Mediation and Conciliation Svc., Arbitration Forum, USDA, U.S. Dept. Def., U.S. Dept. Transp., U.S. Dept. Justice, U.S. Dept. Labor, U.S. Dept. Interior, U.S. Dept. Treasury, USDA, City of Oklahoma City, City of Fort Worth, Computer Sci., City of Houston, Houston Met. Transit Authority, Internat. Paper Co., Inland Paper, ADM Corp., PPG Industries, Ga. Pacific Corp., Westvaco, Hertz, Schering Plough, Chevron, Bryan Foods, SBC Corp., Verizon, GTE, GAF, Citgo, Conoco Phillips Petroleum Co., others. Author: Congress and the Monopoly Problem, 1950; contbr. to casebooks. Pres. New Orleans Jewish Community Center, 1973-75; mem. Nat. Jewish Welfare Bd., 1974-83; bd. dirs. New Orleans Jewish Welfare Fedn., Jewish Family and Children's Service, New Orleans, Communal Hebrew Sch.; v.p. New Orleans Home for Jewish Aged, 1977-80, Florence Heller Rsch. Found. Served U.S Army, 1943-46. Mem. ABA, Fed. Bar Assn., La. Bar Assn., New Orleans Bar Assn. (exec. com. 1971-74), D.C. Bar Assn., Nat. Acad. Arbitrators. Home: 630 Burdette St New Orleans LA 70118-3937 Office: Texaco Bldg Ste 2050 400 Poydras St New Orleans LA 70130 Office Phone: 504-680-6045. Business E-Mail: bmarcus@lnmlaw.com.

**MARCUS, BERNARD,** retired retail executive; b. Newark, 1929; married. BS, Rutgers U., 1954. V.p. Vornado Inc., 1952-68; pres. Odell Inc., 1968-70; v.p. Daylin Inc., 1970-73; with Handy Dan Home Improvement, 1972-78; co-founder (ex. chmn. and CEO) Home Depot Inc., Atlanta, 1978—2002, ret., 2002. Exec. advisor Chief Exec. Leadership Inst., Yale U. Sch. Mgmt. Chmn., founder Marcus Found. Inc., Marcus Inst., 1991—; founder Ga. Aquarium, Marcus Devel. Resource Ctr., DC; bd. mem. City of Hope, Duarte, Calif., Shepherd Spinal Center, Atlanta, Am. Jewish Com., Atlanta Jewish Found. Named one of Forbes Richest Americans, 2006. Office: The Marcus Found 2455 Paces Ferry Rd SE Atlanta GA 30339-4024*

**MARCUS, BESS H.,** psychologist, medical educator, health facility administrator; PhD, Auburn U., Ala. Lic. psychologist RI. Prof. psychiatry and human behavior Brown U., Providence, 2000—; dir. Ctrs. for Behavioral and Preventive Medicine The Miriam Hosp., Providence, 2005—. Mem. rsch. adv. com. Lifespan Academic Med. Ctr., Providence, 2005—; mem. expert panel on population and prevention sci. Am. Heart Assn., 2003—. Mem. editl. bd. Jour. Phys. Activity & Health; contbr. articles to profl. jours., chapters to books. Named Active Living by Design Person of the Yr., Robert Wood Johnson Found., 2004. Office: Ctrs for Behavioral and Preventive Medicine 1 Hoppin St Ste 500 Providence RI 02903 Office Phone: 401-793-8000.

**MARCUS, CLAUDE,** advertising executive; b. Paris, Aug. 28, 1924; s. Jacques and Louise (Bleustein) M.; m. Claudine Pohl, May 27, 1948; children: Michele, Pierre, Anne-Marie, Isabelle. Diploma in Econs., U. Paris, 1947; Lic., Paris Law Sch., 1947. Sec. gen. Publicis, Paris, 1948-55, dir. comml. to dir. gen. adjoint, 1961, dir. gen., 1962-68; mng. dir. Publicis Conseil, Paris, 1968-83; pres. Publicis Internat., Paris, 1984-88; vice-chmn. Publicis Comm., Paris, 1988—96. Decorated chevalier de la Legion d'Honneur. Mem. Bur. Verification de la Publicite (vice-chmn.), Racing Club (France). Home: 12 Rue Felicien David 75016 Paris France Office: Publicis 133 Champs Elysees 75008 Paris France Personal E-mail: claudius6@wanadoo.fr.

**MARCUS, EDWARD,** economist, educator; b. Bklyn., Apr. 29, 1918; s. Herman and Rose (Marayna) M.; m. Mildred Rendl, Aug. 10, 1956. BS, Harvard, 1939, MBA, 1941; student, King's Coll., Cambridge U., Eng., 1946-47; PhD, Princeton, 1950. Economist Fed. Res. Bd., 1950-52; prof. econs. Bklyn. Coll., 1952-81, chmn. dept., 1966-79. Cons. Nat. Acad. Scis., 1959, UN Conf. Trade and Devel., 1966; dir. Syracuse U. Maxwell Sch. Nigerian Project, 1961; participant Internat. Econometrics Assn., Amsterdam, Holland, 1968 Author: Canada and the International Business Cycle, 1927-1938, 1954, (with Mildred Rendl Marcus) Investment and Development Possibilities in Tropical Africa, 1960, International Trade and Finance, 1965, Monetary and Banking Theory, 1965, Economic Progress and the Developing World, 1971, Economics, 1978. Served with AUS, 1941-42, to comdr. USCGR, 1942-46. Grantee Merrill Found., 1953 Mem. AAUP, Am. Econ. Assn., Canadian Econ. Assn., N.Y. Met. Econ. Assn. (pres. 1966-67), Am. Fin Assn., Royal Econ. Soc., Econ. Soc. South Africa, New Canaan Hist. Soc. (treas. 1983—), Phi Beta Kappa.

**MARCUS, EDWARD LEONARD,** lawyer, political organization worker; b. Bklyn., June 14, 1927; s. Isaac Horatio and Dorothy (Kirchsten) M.; m. Phyllis Betzes, Sept. 19, 1948 (div. 1984); children: Shelley A., Susan E., Nicole Marie; m. Lisa E. Munson, 1984 (div. 1989); m. Lorraine Jill Surprenant, Aug. 9, 1989. BA, Yale Coll., 1948, LLB, LLD, 1950. Bar: Conn. 1950, U.S. Dist. Ct. Conn. 1952, U.S. Ct. Appeals (2d dist.) 1954, U.S. Supreme Ct. 1955. Sr. ptnr. Marcus Law Firm, New Haven, Conn., 1950—. Mem. Overseas Pvt. Invest Corp, Washington, 1978-81; bd. dirs. exec. com. Branford (Conn.) Savs. Bank, Boca Raton (Fla.) First Nat. Bank. Alderman City of New Haven, 1951-56; majority leader State Senate, Conn., 1958-70; chmn. Commn. Inter Govt. Rels., 1962-70, senate majority leader, 1958-70; chmn. Coun. State Govts., 1968-69; del. Dem. Nat. Conf., 1976, 92, 96; mem. Conn. Tourism Task Force, 1991—; mem. Dem. State Ctrl. Com., Conn., 1986—, chmn. fin. com., 1991-92; chmn. Conn. del. Dem. Nat. Conv., 1992, 96, 2000. Mem. ABA, Nat. Trial Lawyers Am. (bd. dirs., sec.), Conn. Bar Assn., New Haven Bar Assn. Democrat. Avocations: tennis, swimming. Home: 100 Stony Creek Rd Branford CT 06405-3236 Office: Marcus Law Firm 111 Whitney Ave Ste 2 New Haven CT 06510-1261 Business E-Mail: emarcus@marcuslawfirm.com.

**MARCUS, ERIC PETER,** lawyer; b. Newark, Aug. 31, 1950; s. John J. and Alice M. (Zeldin) M.; m. Terry R. Toll, Oct. 9, 1983. BA, Brown U., 1972; JD, Stanford U., 1976. Bar: N.Y. 1977, NJ 1977. Assoc. Kaye, Scholer, Fierman, Hays & Handler LLP, N.Y.C., 1976-84, ptnr., 1985—. Contbr. articles to profl. jours. Mem. Phi Beta Kappa. Office: Kaye Scholer LLP 425 Park Ave New York NY 10022-3506

**MARCUS, ERIC ROBERT,** psychiatrist; b. NYC, Feb. 16, 1944; s. Victor and Pearl (Maddow) M.; m. Eslee Samberg, Nov. 24, 1985; children: Max, Pia. AB, Columbia U., 1965; MD, U. Wis., 1969. Diplomate Am. Bd. Psychiatry and Neurology. Intern NYU Med. Ctr. Bellevue Hosp., 1969-70 resident Columbia Presbyn. Med. Ctr.-NY State Psychiat. Inst., 1972-75; dir. St. Marks Free Clinic, NYC, 1971-75; from co-dir. to dir. neuropsychiat//diagnostic treatment unit Columbia-Presbyn. Med. Ctr., NYC, 1975-84; dir. med. student edn. in psychiatry Columbia U. Coll. Physicians and Surgeons, NYC, 1981—; supervising-tng. analyst Columbia U. Ctr. for Psychoanalytic Tng.-Rsch., NYC, 1994—; clin. prof. psychiatry and social medicine Columbia U. Coll. Physicians and Surgeons, NYC, 1995—. Bd. govs. student health Columbia U., 1986-2003. Author: Psychosis and Near Psychosis, 1992, 2d edn., 2003; mem. editl. bd.: The Psychoanalytic Study of Society, 1989—94, Jour. Clin. Psychoanalysis, 1998—2002; co-editor: Psychiatry, 1998; contbr. articles to profl. jours. Recipient Weber Rsch. award Columbia U. Psychoanalytic Ctr., 1991, O'Connor Tchg. award, 1995, Columbia U. Presdl. award for Outstanding Tchg., 1999. Fellow: NY Acad. Medicine, Am. Coll. Psychoanalysts, Am. Psychiat. Assn. (pres. NY County Dist. 2002—03, Roeske award 1991); mem.: Assn. Psychoanalytic Medicine (pres. 1999—2001), Am. Psychoanalytic Assn. (chmn. com. on univ. and med. edn. 1999—2005, mem. editl. bd. Jour. 2000—03, Sabshin award 2003). Avocations: classical music, photography, swimming, reading. Office: Columbia U Dept Psychiatry 1051 Riverside Dr New York NY 10032-1013 Office Phone: 212-427-0543.

**MARCUS, FRANK ISADORE,** cardiologist, educator; b. Haverstraw, NY, Mar. 23, 1928; s. Samuel and Edith (Sattler) M.; m. Janet Geller, June 30, 1957; children: Ann, Steve, Lynn. BA, Columbia U., 1948; MS, Tufts U., 1951; MD cum laude, Boston U., 1953. Diplomate Am. Bd. Internal Medicine (subspecialty cardiovasc. diseases). Intern Peter Bent Brigham Hosp., Boston, 1953-54, asst. resident, 1956-57, research fellow in cardiology, 1957-58; clin. fellow in cardiology Georgetown U. Hosp., 1958-59, chief med. resident, 1959-60; chief of cardiology Georgetown U. Med. Service, D.C. Gen. Hosp., Washington, 1960-68; instr. medicine Georgetown U. Sch. Medicine, 1960-63, asst. prof., 1963-68, assoc. prof., 1968; prof. medicine, chief cardiology sect. U. Ariz. Coll. Medicine, Tucson, 1969-82, disting. prof. internal medicine (cardiology), 1982-99, emeritus prof., 1999—, dir. electrophysiology, 1982—2001; prin. investigator multidisciplinary study of right ventricular dysplasia Nat. Heart, Lung and Blood Inst., 2001—. Cons. cardiology VA Hosp., Tucson, 1969, USAF Regional Hosp., Davis-Monthan AFB, Tucson, 1969; mem. panel drug efficacy study, panel on cardiovascular drugs Nat. Acad. Scis.-NRC, 1967-68; chmn. undergrad. cardiovascular tng. grant com. HEW-NIH, 1970; dir. Arrhythmia Svcs., 1996-2001. Editor: Modern Concepts of Cardiovascular Disease, 1982—84; mem. editl. bd. Circulation, 1974—81, Current Problems in Cardiology, 1975—79, Cardiovascular Drugs and Therapy, 1986—2000, New Trends in Arrythmias, 1984—, Jour. Am. Coll. Cardiology, 1983—87, 1996—2000, Am. Jour. Cardiology, 1984—, Jour. Cardiovasc. Drugs and Therapy, 1991—2000, Pacing and Clin. Electrophysiology, 1995—, Annals of Noninvasive Electrocardiology, 1996—, Cardiology, 2000—, Jour. Electrocardiology, 2005—; contbr. articles to profl. jours. Chmn. Washington Heart Assn. High Sch. Heart Program, 1968-70. Served to capt. USAF, 1954-56. Recipient Career Devel. award NIH, 1965, Student AMA Golden Apple award Georgetown U. Sch. Medicine, 1968, Disting. Alumni award Boston U. Sch. Medicine, 2003, Master Clinician award Coun. Clin. Cardiology, 2005; Mass. Heart Assn. fellow, 1957-58; John and Mary Markle scholar, 1960-65; grantee Nat. Heart, Lung and Blood Inst., 2001—. Fellow Coun. on Clin. Cardiology Am. Heart Assn., ACP (Ariz. laureate award 1987), Am. Coll. Cardiology (bd. govs. Ariz. 1984-87, asst. sec. 1987-89, trustee); mem. Assn. Univ. Cardiologists, Inc. (v.p. 1989-90, pres. 1990-91), Ariz. Heart Assn. (dir. 1970, v.p. 1972-73, chmn. rsch. com. 1970-72), So. Ariz. Heart Assn. (dir. 1969), N.Am. Soc. Pacing and Electrophysiology, Alpha Omega Alpha. Home: 4949 E Glenn St Tucson AZ 85712-1212 Office: U Ariz Univ Med Ctr 1501 N Campbell Ave Tucson AZ 85724-0001 Office Phone: 502-626-1416. Business E-Mail: fmarcus@u.arizona.edu.

**MARCUS, GREIL GERSTLEY,** critic; b. San Francisco, June 19, 1945; s. Gerald Dodd and Eleanore (Hyman) M.; m. Jenelle Bernstein, June 26, 1966; children: Emily Rose, Cecily Helen. BA, U. Calif., Berkeley, 1967, MA, 1968. Record editor Rolling Stone mag., San Francisco and N.Y.C., 1969-70, book columnist, 1975-80, Calif. Mag., L.A., 1982-83, 88-90; pop music columnist Music Mag., Tokyo, 1978-94, New West mag., L.A., 1978-82, Artforum mag., N.Y.C., 1983—87, 1991—98, Village Voice newspaper, N.Y.C., 1986—91, Interview Mag., N.Y.C., 1992—; dir. Falter newspaper, Vienna, 1997-98; cultural columnist N.Y. Times, 1998, Esquire mag., 1998-99; music columnist Salon.com, 1999—2003, City Pages, 2003—04. Presenter in field. Author: Mystery Train: Images of America in Rock 'n Roll Music, 1975, U.S. rev., 1982, 90, 97 (Brit., German, Greek, Dutch, Japanese, Italian and French edits.), Real Life Rock (Japanese), 1984, Lipstick Traces: A Secret History of the 20th Century, 1989 (Brit., Italian, Spanish, German, French and Turkish edits.), Dead Elvis: A Chronicle of a Cultural Obsession, 1991 (Brit., French, Japanese and German edits., rev. 1999), Ranters and Crowd Pleasers: Punk in Pop Music, 1977-92, 93, In The Fascist Bathroom: Writings on Punk, 1999 (Brit., German and US edits.), The Dustbin of History (Brit. and German edits.), 1995, Invisible Republic: Bob Dylan's Basement Tapes, 1997 (Brit., Italian, German, Dutch and French edits.), Double Trouble: Bill Clinton and Elvis Presley in a Land of No Alternatives, 2000, rev. edit., 2001 (Brit. edit.), The Old, Weird America: The World of Bob Dylan's Basement Tapes, 2001, The Manchurian Candidate (Brit. edit.), 2002, Like a Rolling Stone: Bob Dylan at the Crossroads (Brit., German, French, Italian edits.), 2005, The Shape of Things to Come: Prophecy and the American Voice, Brit. edit., 2006; editor: Stranded, 1979, rev. 1996, Psychotic Reactions and Carburetor Dung (Lester Bangs), 1987, (with Sean Wilentz) The Rose and the Briar: Death, Love and Liberty in The American Ballad, 2004; contbr. criticism to publs. including Creem, Express-Times, New Mus. Express, Another Room, RAW, Rock and Roll Confidential, Threepenny Rev., Representations, Common Knowledge, La Nouvelle Revue Francaise; curator Whitney Mus. Arm. Art, N.Y., 1998.

**MARCUS, GWEN ELLEN,** sculptor; b. N.Y.C. d. David Oscar and Doris (Sherman) M. BS, NYU, 1977. One-woman shows include Galeries Lafayette Trump Tower, NYC, 1994, exhibited in group shows at Catharine Lorillard Wolfe Art Club Inc., 2002, Wobun Abbey, Bedfordshire, Eng., 2002, Sudeley Castle, Gloucestershire, Eng., 2002, Stoneleigh Abbey, Warwickshire, Eng., 2002, Castle Howard, Yorkshire, Eng., 2002, Chi Mej Mus., Taiwan, 2002—06, Ind. U., 2003, Gallery North, Setacket, NY, 2003, Salmagundi Art Club Annual Exhbn., NYC, 2006 (award), others. Recipient Elliot Liskin Meml. award, Salmagundi Photography & Sculpture Exhbn., N.Y., 1993, Excellence award, 1994, BBI award, 1995, Excellence award, Knickerbocker Artists, Washington, 1993, cert. Merit, Nat. Acad. Design Mus., N.Y., 1996, Elliot Liskin award, 2001, Coun. Am. Artists Soc. award, 1998, Michael Gressel Meml. award, 2001, Sculpture award, Art Students League NY, 2005. Fellow Nat. Sculpture Soc. (bd. dirs. 2001-06, Tallix Foundry Prize 69th annual exhibition, 2002); mem. Allied Artists Am. (Philip Eisenberg award 1990, Lindsey Morris Meml. award 1994, Gold Medal 1996, Josephine Beardsley Sander Meml. award 1999, 2001, Elliot Liskin Meml. award 2002, Mem. and Assocs. award, 2005), Catharine Lorillard Wofe Art Club (Medal of Honor 1993, Harriet W. Frishmuth Meml. award 1994, Anna Hyatt Huntington Bronze Medal 1995, CLWAC Centennial award 1996, Paul Manship Meml. award 2003-), Pen and Brush Club (sculpture soc., Solo Show award 1995, Leonard J. Meiselman Meml. award 1997, Charlotte Dunwiddie Meml. award 2001, Josephine B., Sandor mem. award, 2002), Am. Medallic Sculpture Assn., Nat. Assn. Women Artists Inc., Hudson Valley Art Assn., Inc. (Agop Agopoff award 1998, Gold Medal honor 2000), Am. Artist Profl. League Inc. (Medal of Honor 1994, 95, 96, 2005, Pres.'s award 1995, Granville Carter Meml. award 1998, Frank C. Wright Meml. award 1999, Am. Artists Fund award 2001, Kathryn Thayer Hobson Meml. award 2004), Nat. Sculpture Soc. (Gloria medal 1996), Medallic Sculpture Assn. (bd. dir.), Audubon Artists, Inc. (Gold medal 1998, Renee and Chaim Mem. award 2002), Art Students League NY (Sculpture award, 2005), Am. Profl. League (Gold medal of honor 2005). Avocations: travel, theater, music, dance, volunteer work. Home and Office: 401 E 80th St Apt 19E New York NY 10021-0651 Office Phone: 212-744-2114. Business E-Mail: marcustudio@aol.com.

**MARCUS, HARRIS LEON,** materials science educator; b. Ellenville, N.Y., July 5, 1931; s. David and Bertha (Messite) M.; m. Leona Gorker, Aug. 29, 1962; children: Leland, M'Risa. BS, Purdue U., 1963; PhD, Northwestern U., 1966. Registered profl. engr., Tex. Tech. staff Tex. Instruments, Attleboro, Mass., 1966—68, Rockwell Sci. Ctr., 1968—70, group leader, 1971—75; prof. mech. engring. U. Tex., Austin, 1975—79, Harry L. Kent Jr. prof. mech. engring., 1979—90, Cullen Found. prof., 1980—95, dir. ctr. for Materials Sci. and Engring., 1979—95; prof. materials sci. and engring., dir. Inst. for Material Sci., U. Conn., 1995—. Cons. numerous orgns. Contbr. more than 300 articles to profl. publs. Recipient U. Tex. faculty U. Tex. Engring. Found., 1983; Krengel lectr. Technion, Israel, 1983; Alumni Merit medal Northwestern U., 1988, Disting. Purdue Univ. Engring. Alumnus award, 1994. Fellow Soc. Am. Metals; mem. ACS, AIME (bd. dirs. Metall. Soc. 1976-78, 84-86), Materials Rsch. Soc., Conn. Acad. Sci. and Engring. Achievements include 24 patents. Home: 78 Ellise Rd Storrs Mansfield CT 06268-1424 Office: Inst Materials Scis 97 N Eagleville Rd Unit U-3136 Storrs Mansfield CT 06269-3136 Office Phone: 860-486-4623. Business E-Mail: hmarcus@ims.uconn.edu.

**MARCUS, JAMES ELBERT,** manufacturing executive; b. Helena, Ala., July 3, 1949; s. James Edward and Ora Dee (Shanks) M.; m. Willie Mae Murry, June 30, 1980; children: Charsie Latrice, Chareka Lenita, Carlisle Lamar. BS in Biology, Chemistry, Tuskegee U., 1971. Soft drink technician Custom Canners, Inc., Norcross, Ga., 1972-73; comml. inventory supr. Washington Inventory Svc., Inc., Atlanta, 1973-76; shipping and receiving specialist Norrell Temporary Svc., Atlanta, 1977-78; enology lab. technician Monarch Wine Co., Atlanta, 1978-80; R & D technician Pave-Mark Corp., Atlanta, 1980-82; mfg. tech. support specialist Dynatron Bondo Corp., Atlanta, 1982-85; equipment operator Circuit City, Inc., Atlanta, 1985-86; air filter technician Comml. Air Filter Co., Atlanta, 1987-88; owner, pres. Marcus Industries, Atlanta, 1989—, Group 38 Transp. Svcs., Inc., Atlanta, Group 38, Inc. Bus. Concerns, Atlanta. Sub-contractor, advt. distbr., investment profl., 1998. Prin. developer pavement marking material, 1981. Cub scout master Southeastern dist. Traveler's Rest Mt. Pleasant Bapt. Ch. Boy Scouts Am., 1988, 89, 90. Mem.: Nat. Hon. Soc. Pershing Rifles. Democrat. Baptist. Avocations: basketball, bowling, writing, electronics, billiards. Home: 2009 Rocking Ter Conley GA 30288-2109 Personal E-mail: mae7673@aol.com.

**MARCUS, JEFFREY M.,** science educator; b. Bronx, July 20, 1973; s. Martin J. and Laura E. Marcus; m. Joanne E. Seiff, June 28, 2000; children: Lucy Seiff, Harry Seiff, Sally Seiff. BA, Cornell U., 1995; MPhil, Cambridge U., Eng., 1996; PhD, Duke U., 2002. Cert. tchg. coll. biology Preparing Future Faculty Program, Duke U. Asst. prof. dept. biology Western Ky. U., Bowling Green, Ky., 2003—. Contbr. articles to profl. jours. Fellow, Howard Hughes Med. Inst., 1996—2002; grantee, Ky. Nat. Sci. Found., 2003—04, NIH, 2004—09; scholar, Cornell U., 1991—95; James B. Duke fellowship, Duke U., 1996—2001, Churchill scholarship, Cambridge U., 1995—96. Mem.: AAAS, Soc. of Systematic Biologists, Soc. of Ky. Lepidopterists (pres. 2005—06), Soc. for Integrative and Comparative Biology, Soc. for the Study of Evolution, Soc. for Devel. Biology, Genetics Soc. of Am., Sigma Xi, Phi Beta Kappa. Achievements include research in Butterfly genetics, development, and evolution; invention of FaSSTIR mapping to improve mapping of genes on Drosophila X chromosome; first to First to successfully introduce foreign genes into butterflies via transposon mediated germ line transformation. Avocations: photography, gardening, album collecting. Office: Western Ky U # 11080 1906 College Heights Blvd Bowling Green KY 42101-1080 Office Phone: 270-745-2043. Office Fax: 270-745-6856. E-mail: jeffrey.marcus@wku.edu.

**MARCUS, KENNETH L.,** federal official; m. Stephanie Marcus. Grad., Willams Coll.; JD, U. Calif., 1991. Litigation ptnr.; gen. dep. asst. sec. fair housing and equal oppty. U.S. Dept. HUD; dep. asst. sec. edn. for enforcement U.S. Dept. Edn., delegated the authority of asst. sec. edn. for civil rights, 2003—05; staff dir. U.S. Commn. on Civil Rights, 2004—. Office: US Commn Civil Rights 624 Ninth St NW Ste 700 Washington DC 20425 Office Phone: 202-376-7700. Office Fax: 202-376-7672. Business E-Mail: kmarcus@usccr.gov.

**MARCUS, LEE EVAN,** small business owner, consultant, accountant; b. Cleve., 1953; s. Morton and Bluma Marcus. BA in English, Amherst Coll., 1975. CPA, Fla. Audit staff acct. Arthur Andersen, Tampa, 1976-78; tax mgr. Price Waterhouse, Miami, Fla., 1978-83; controller Williams Island Assocs., Ltd., North Miami Beach, Fla., 1983-84; corp. contr. Suncoast Land Devel. Co., Inc., and Affiliates, Stuart, Fla., 1984-85; fin. officer, contr. Haydn Cutler Cos., Ft. Worth, 1985-89; pres. Global Solutions Co., Plantation, Fla., 1989-2000, Positive Changes Broward, Inc., Sunrise, Fla., 2000—. Office Phone: 954-942-1120. Personal E-mail: LeeMcpa@aol.com.

**MARCUS, LINDA SUSAN,** dermatologist; b. Bklyn. d. Nathaniel and Eugenia (Portnay) Marcus; m. Ronald Carlin, July 5, 1976; children: Robert Adam, Neal Marc. BS, Adelphi U., Garden City, N.J., 1970; MD, Downstate Med. Sch., Bklyn., 1975. Diplomate Am. Bd. Dermatology. Intern Long Island (N.Y.) Jewish Med. Ctr., 1975-76; resident in dermatology Columbia-St. Luke's, N.Y.C., 1976-77, Boston U.-1ufts U., 1977-79; pvt. practice Wyckoff, NJ, 1980—. Dir. dermatology Valley Hosp., Ridgewood. Contbr. articles to profl. jours. Mem. Am. Acad. Dermatology (editor pamphlet editl. bd.), Am. Soc. Dermatol. Surgeons, Internat. Soc. Dermatol. Surgeons, N.J. Dermatol. Soc. (program dir.), N.J. North Dermatol. Soc. (co-chair). Avocations: swimming, ice skating. Office: 271 Godwin Ave Wyckoff NJ 07481-2057 Office Phone: 201-891-4373. Personal E-mail: sexyderm@earthlink.com.

**MARCUS, MARIA LENHOFF,** lawyer, educator; b. Vienna, June 23, 1933; came to U.S., 1938, naturalized, 1944; d. Arthur and Clara (Gruber) Lenhoff; m. Norman Marcus, Dec. 23, 1956; children: Valerie, Nicole, Eric. BA, Oberlin Coll., 1954; JD, Yale Law Sch., 1957. Bar: N.Y. 1961, U.S. Dist. Ct. (so. and ea. dists.) N.Y. 1962, U.S. Ct. Appeals (2d cir.) 1962, U.S. Supreme Ct. 1964. Assoc. counsel NAACP, N.Y., 1961-67; asst. atty. gen. N.Y. State, N.Y.C., 1967-78; chief litigation bur. Atty. Gen. N.Y. State, 1976-78; adj. assoc. prof. NYU Law Sch., 1976-78; assoc. prof. Fordham U. Law Sch., N.Y.C., 1978-86, prof., 1986—, Joseph M. McLaughlin prof., 1997—. Arbitrator Nat. Assn. Securities Dealers; chair subcom. interrogatories U.S. Dist. Ct. (so. dist.) N.Y., 1983-85. Contbr. articles to profl. jours. Named Tchr. of Yr., Fordham Law School Students, 2001. Fellow N.Y. Bar Found.; mem. Assn. Bar City of N.Y. (v.p. 1995-96, long range planning com. 1996-2000, exec. com. 1976-80, com. audit 1988-95, labor com. 1981-84, judiciary com. 1975-76, cimm. civil rights com. 1972-75), N.Y. State Bar Assn. (exec. com. 1979-81, ho. dels. 1978-81, com. constitution and by-laws 1984-93), N.Y. Women's Bar Assn. (Pres.'s award 1999). Office: Fordham U Law Sch 140 W 62nd St New York NY 10023-7485

**MARCUS, MITCH,** musician, composer; b. N.Y., July 3, 1975; s. Philip and Ravena H. Marcus; m. Sarah Ellen Clagett, Mar. 29, 2003. BMus in Jazz Studies, Ind. U., Bloomington, 1997. Mus. dir., tenor saxophone Mitch Marcus Quintet, Berkeley, Calif., 1997—; tenor saxophone, piano The Japonize Elephants, Bloomington, Ind., 1996—; composer Counterpointe, Berkeley, 2000—; mus. dir., tenor saxophone, keyboards, vocals Donovan, San Francisco, 2004—; soprano, tenor saxophone Matt Small Chamber Ensemble, San Francisco, 2004—. Piano acocmpanist Oakland Ballet, Calif., 2000—, Berkeley Ballet Theatre, 1999—. Composer (band leader, arranger): (albums) Mitch Marcus Quintet Entropions, 2002; musician (saxophonist) Mitch Marcus Quintet + 13 "The 50", 2005, Mitch Marcus Quintet - Live at Yoshie, 2004, Japanese Elephants. Mem.: Chamber Music Am.

**MARCUS, PAUL,** law educator; b. NYC, Dec. 8, 1946; s. Edward and Lillian (Rubin) M.; m. Rebecca Nimmer, Dec. 22, 1968; children: Emily, Beth, Daniel. AB, UCLA, 1968, JD, 1971. Bar: Calif. 1971, U.S. Dist. Ct. (cen. dist.) Calif. 1972, U.S. Ct. Appeals (D.C. cir.) 1972, U.S. Ct. Appeals (7th cir.) 1976. Law clk. U.S. Ct. Appeals (D.C. cir.), 1971-72; assoc. Loeb & Loeb, L.A., 1972-74; prof. law U. Ill., Urbana, 1974-83; dean Coll. Law U. Ariz., Tucson, 1983-88, prof., 1988-92; Haynes prof. law Coll. William and Mary, Williamsburg, Va., 1992—, interim dean, 1993-94, 97-98. Reporter, cons. Fed. Jud. Ctr. Commn., Nat. Com.on the Right to Counsel. Author: The Entrapment Defense, 1989, 3d edit., 2003, The Prosecution and Defense of Criminal Conspiracy, 1978, 5th edit., 2002, Gilbert Law Summary, 1982, 8th edit., 2004, Criminal Law: Cases and Materials, 1982, 5th edit., 2003, Criminal Procedure in Practice, 2001, 2d edit., 2003. Office: Coll William & Mary Law Sch PO Box 8795 Williamsburg VA 23187-8795 Office Phone: 757-221-3900. Business E-Mail: pxmarc@wm.edu.

**MARCUS, PHILIP,** dean; b. N.Y.C., Nov. 26, 1946; s. Max and Rosaline Marcus; m. Rovena Shreck, Aug. 24, 1969; children: Mitchell Howard, Brian Seth, Alyssa Robyn. BS in Pharmacological Scis., Columbia U., N.Y.C., 1969; MD, SUNY, Bklyn., 1973; MPH, Johns Hopkins U., Balt., 2001. Diplomate internal medicine Am. Bd. Internal Medicine, 1976, pulmonary diseases Am. Bd. Internal Medicine, 1978, critical care medicine Am. Bd. Internal Medicine, 1999. Assoc. dean, curriculum devel. NY Coll. Osteo. Medicine, Old Westbury, NY, 2001—; chief, divsn. pulmonary medicine St. Francis Hosp., Roslyn, NY, 2003– 06. Contbr. articles various profl. jours. Fellow: ACP, Am. Coll. Chest Physicians (chair, practice mgmt. com. 2004—06). Avocation: travel. Office: NY Coll Osteo Medicine 233 E Shore Rd Great Neck NY 11023 Office Phone: 516-482-7810. Home Fax: 516-482-3760; Office Fax: 516-482-3760. Personal E-mail: pmarcus192@aol.com. E-mail: pmarcus@nyit.edu.

**MARCUS, PHILIP IRVING,** virology educator, researcher; b. Springfield, Mass., June 3, 1927; s. Julius and Marley Amelia (Speir) M.; m. Angela Joan Francis, Dec. 4, 1953; children: Craig F., Wendy L., Valerie L. BS, U. So. Calif., 1950; MS, U. Chgo., 1953; PhD, U. Colo., 1957. Asst. prof. biophysics U. Colo. Sch. Medicine, Denver, 1957-60; asso. prof. microbiology Albert Einstein Coll. Medicine, Bronx, NY, 1961-66, prof., 1967-69; prof. microbiology U. Conn., Storrs, 1969-75, head dept., 1969-75, prof. virology, 1969—; dir. Biotech. Ctr., 1990-95, 2002—, Bd. of Trustees Disting. prof., 2003—. Dir. Nat. Cancer Inst. Program Project, 1973-83; cons. NIH, NSF; mem. sci. adv. coun. Damon Runyon-Walter Winchell Cancer Fund, 1970-74, Am. Cancer Soc., 1986-88, Am. Found. for AIDS Rsch., 1990—. Editor Jour. Cellular Physiology, 1969-96; editor in chief Jour. Interferon Rsch., 1984-95, Jour. Interferon & Cytokine Rsch., 1995—2002; sr. cons. editor, 2003—; contbr. numerous articles to profl. jours.; patentee in field. Served with USAAC, 1945-47. Recipient USPHS rsch. career devel. award, 1960-70, excellence in rsch. award U. Conn. Alumni Assn., 1987; NIH grantee, 1960-94, NSF, USDA grantee. Mem. AAAS, Am. Soc. Microbiology, Am. Soc. Cell Biology, Am. Soc. Virology, Brit. Soc. Microbiology, Internat. Soc. Interferon and Cytokine Rsch. (hon.), Soc. In Vitro Biology, Harvey Soc., Conn. Acad. Sci. and Engring. Achievements include development of the Marcus Theory of electron transfer reactions in chemical systems and RRKM theory of unimolecular reactions. Home: 24 Thompson Rd Storrs Mansfield CT 06268-1806 Office: U Conn Dept Molec & Cell Biol U-3044 Storrs Mansfield CT 06269 Office Phone: 860-486-4254. E-mail: philip.marcus@uconn.edu.

**MARCUS, PHILLIP RONALD,** management consultant; b. Newark, Aug. 4, 1947; s. Samuel and Sophie (Hackmeyer) M. BS in Indsl. Engring., N.J. Inst. Tech., 1969; MBA, Seton Hall U., 1971; PhD, Nova Southeastern U., 1998. Cons. Metro Four Cons., Bloomfield, N.J., 1982-85; sr. cons., 1985-87, v.p., 1987—95, sr. v.p., 1995—. Vis. asst. prof. Del. State U., 1999—2000;

substitute asst. prof. CUNY, 2000—01; lectr. in field. Contbr. articles to profl. jours. Cons., Residents for Community Action, Newark, 1974—; chmn. Newarkers for Good Govt., 1974-86, 90-96; pres. Essex Residents for Effective Govt., Bloomfield, 1975-87. Named Man of Yr. Newarkers for Good Govt., 1982, 86, 93. Mem. ASME, AIAA, Acad. Mgmt., Assn. for Global Bus., Inst. Indsl. Engrs., Assn. MBA Execs. Democrat. Jewish. Avocation: politics. Office: Metro Four Consultants 13 Municipal Plaza PO Box 1428 Bloomfield NJ 07003-1428

**MARCUS, RICHARD GREENWALD,** manufacturing executive; b. NYC, Sept. 24, 1947; s. Robert Greenwald and Natalie (Snider) M.; m. Beth Applebaum; children: Teri Applebaum, Todd Snider. SB, MIT, 1969, SM, 1971. Sales and mktg. assoc. Am. Biltrite Inc., Wellesley Hills, Mass., 1971-83, v.p., 1981-83, pres., 1983—. Office: Am Biltrite Inc 57 River St Wellesley MA 02481-2013

**MARCUS, RICHARD SARGON,** research scientist; AB, U. Pa., 1954, BSEE, 1955; MSEE, MIT, 1957, EE, 1958. Rsch. fellow MIT Rsch. Lab. for Electronics, 1955-58; prin. rsch. scientist MIT Lab. for Info. and Decision Systems, 1958-62, 67—; sr. systems engr. Itek Corp., 1962-67. Editl. bd. Info. Processing and Mgmt., Jour. of Intelligent Info. Systems; reviewer other jours. Mem. Am. Soc. for Info. Sci. (Best article of Yr. to Jour.), Assn. for Computing Machinery, Assn. for Computational Linguistics. Achievements include research on modeling of indexing and retrieval processes for bibliographic and textual databases and the application of those models in the development of expert search assistance systems. E-mial. Office: MIT LIDS 77 Mass Ave Rm 32D-558 Cambridge MA 02139-4307 E-mail: rmarcus@mit.edu.

**MARCUS, RUDOLPH ARTHUR,** chemist, educator; b. Montreal, July 21, 1923; arrived in U.S., 1949, naturalized, 1958; s. Myer and Esther (Cohen) Marcus; m. Laura Hearne, Aug. 27, 1949 (dec. Jan. 2003); children: Alan Rudolph, Kenneth Hearne, Raymond Arthur. BS in Chemistry, McGill U., 1943, PhD in Chemistry, 1946, DSc (hon.), 1988, U. Chgo., 1983, Poly. U., 1986, U. Göteborg, Sweden, 1987, U.N.B., Can., 1993, Queens U., 1993, U. Oxford, Eng., 1995, Yokohama Nat. U., Japan, 1996, U. N.C., 1996, U. Ill., 1997, Technion-Israel Inst. Tech., 1998, Polytechnic U. Valencia, 1999, Northwestern U., 2000, U. Waterloo, Can., 2002. Rsch. staff RDX Project, Montreal, 1944—46; rsch. assoc. NRC of Can., Ottawa, Ont., 1946—49, U. N.C., 1949—51; asst. prof. Poly. Inst. Bklyn., 1951—54, assoc. prof., 1954—58, prof., 1958—64, acting head, div. phys. chem., 1961—62; prof. U. Ill., Urbana, 1964—78, head, div. phys. chem., 1967—68; prof. Arthur Amos Noyes prof. chem. Calif. Inst. Tech., Pasadena, 1978—; vis. prof. theoretical chem. U. Oxford, 1975—76; Baker lectr. Cornell U., Ithaca, NY, 1991; Linnett vis. prof. chemistry Cambridge (Eng.) U., 1996; hon. prof. Fudan U., Shanghai, 1994—; hon prof. Inst. Chem. Chinese Acad. Scis., Beijing, 1995—; hon. fellow Univ. Coll., Oxford, 1995—; hon. prof. Tianjin U., China, 2002, China Ocean U., 2002, Dalian Inst. Chem. Physics, Dalian, China, 2005, Wenzhou Med. Coll., Wenzhov, China, 2005. Professorial fellow Univ. Coll., Oxford, 1975—76; mem. Courant Inst. Math. Scis., NYU, 1960—61; trustee Gordon Rsch. confs., 1966—69; assoc. mem. Ctr. Advanced Studies, U. Ill., Urbana, 1968—69; chmn. bd. dirs. Gordon Rsch. confs., 1968—69, mem. coun., 1965—68; mem. rev. panel Argonne Nat. Lab., 1966—72, chmn., 1967—68; mem. rev. panel Brookhaven Nat. Lab., 1971—74; mem. rev. com.Radiation Lab., U. Notre Dame Radiation Lab., U. Notre Dame, 1975—80; mem. panel on atmospheric chemistry climatic impact com. NAS-NRC, 1975—78, mem. com. kinetics of chem. reactions, 1973—77, chmn., 1975—77, mem. com. chem. scis., 1977—79; lectr. in field, 1982; mem. com. to survey opportunities in chem. scis., 1982—86; mem. math. panel Internat. Benchmarking of U.S. Rsch. Fields, 1996—97; mem. panel on accountability of federally funded rsch. Com. on Sci., Engring. and Pub. Policy, 2000—01; adv. com. for chemistry NSF, 1977—80; external adv. bd. NAS Ctr. Photoinduced Charge Transfer, 1990—; mem. presdl. chairs com., Chile, 1994—96; advisor, Ctr. for Molecular Scis. Chinese Acad. Scis. and State Key Lab. for Structural Chemistry of Unstable and Stable Species, Beijing, 1995—; co-hon. pres. 29th Internat. Chemistry Olympiad, 1997; hon. visitor Nat. Sci. Coun., China, 1999. Former mem. editl. bd. Jour. Chem. Physics, Am. Rev. Phys. Chemistry, Jour. Phys. Chemistry, Accounts Chem. Rsch., Internat. Jour. Chem. Kinetics Molecular Physics, Theoretica Chimica Acta, Chem. Physics Letters, Faraday Trans., Jour. Chem. Soc., editl. bd. Laser Chemistry, 1982—, Advances in Chem. Physics, 1984—, World Sci. Pub., 1987—, Internat. Revs. in Phys. Chemistry, 1988—, Progress in Physics, Chemistry and Mechanics (China), 1989—, Perkins Transactions 2, Jour. Chem. Soc., 1992—, Chem. Physics Rsch. (India), 1992—, Trends in Chem. Physics Rsch. (India), 1992—, hon. editor Internat. Jour. Quantum Chemistry, 1996—. Named Hon. Citizen, City of Winnipeg, 1994, Treasure of L.A., Ctrl. City Assn., 1995; recipient Anne Molson prize in chem., McGill U., 1943, Sr. U.S. Scientist award, Alexander von Humboldt-Stiftung, 1976, Electrochem. Soc. Lecture award, 1979, 1996, Robinson medal, Faraday divsn. Royal Soc. Chemistry, 1982, Centenary medal, 1988, Chandler medal, Columbia U., 1983, Wolf prize in chemistry, Wolf Found., Israel, 1985, Nat. medal of Sci., 1989, Evans award, Ohio State U., 1990, Nobel prize in Chem., 1992, Hirshfelder prize in Theoretical Chemistry, U. Wis., 1993, Golden Plate award, Am. Acad. Achievement, 1993, Lavoisier medal, French Chem. Soc., 1994, Oesper award, U. Cin., 1997, Key to City of Taipei, Taiwan, 1999, William Jost lectr. and medal, Deutsche Bunsenges and Acad. Sci., Göttingen, 1999, Susquicentennial medal, Polytech U.; fellow Alfred P. Sloan, 1960—61, NSF sr. postdoctoral, 1960—61; scholar Sr. Fulbright-Hays, 1972. Fellow: AAAS, Royal Soc. Can. (hon.), Internat. Acad. Quantum Molecular Sci. (hon.), Chinese Acad. Scis. (hon.), Internat. Soc. for Theoretical Chem. Physics (hon.), Internat. Soc. Electrochemistry (hon.), Royal Soc. Chemistry (hon.), Royal Soc. (London) (hon.), Am. Acad. Arts and Scis. (hon.; exec. com. western sect., co-chmn. 1981—84, rsch. and planning com. 1989—91); mem.: NAS (hon.), Am. Chem. Soc. (past divsn. chmn., mem. exec. com., mem. adv. bd. petroleum rsch. fund, Irving Langmuir award in chem. physics 1978, Peter Debye award in physic. chemistry 1988, Willard Gibbs medal Chgo. sect. 1988, S.C. Lind Lecture, East Tenn. sect. 1988, Theodore William Richards medal Northwestern sect. 1990, Edgar Fahs Smith award Phila. sect. 1991, Ira Remsen Meml. award Md. sect. 1991, Pauling medal Portland, Oreg., and Puget Sound sect. 1991, Auburn-Kosolapoff award 1996, Theoretical Chemistry award 1997, Top 75 Chem. & Engring. News award 1998), Am. Phys. Soc., Lit. and Hist. Soc., Univ. Coll. Dublin (hon.), European Acad. Scis. (hon.), Korean Chem. Soc. (hon.), Am. Philos. Soc. (hon.; coun. mem. 1990), Alpha Chi Sigma. Achievements include development of the Marcus Theory of electron transfer reactions in chemical systems and RRKM theory of unimolecular reactions. Home: 331 S Hill Ave Pasadena CA 91106-3405 Office Phone: 626-395-6566. Business E-Mail: ram@caltech.edu.

**MARCUS, RUTH BARCAN,** philosopher, educator, writer, lecturer; b. N.Y.C. d. Samuel and Rose (Post) Barcan; divorced; children: James Spencer, Peter Webb, Katherine Hollister, Elizabeth Post. BA, NYU, 1941; MA, Yale U., 1942, PhD, 1946; DLH (hon.), U. Ill., 1995. Rsch. assoc. in anthropology Inst. for Human Relations, Yale U., New Haven, Conn., 1945-47; AAUW fellow U. Chgo., 1947-48; vis. prof. (intermittently) Northwestern U., 1950-57, Guggenheim fellow, 1953-54; asst. prof., assoc. prof. Roosevelt U., Chgo., 1957-63; NSF fellow 1963-64; prof. philosophy U. Ill. at Chgo., 1963-70, head philosophy dept., 1963-69; fellow U. Ill. Center for Advanced Study, 1968-69; prof. philosophy Northwestern U., 1970-73; Reuben Post Halleck prof. philosophy Yale U., 1973-93; sr. rsch. scholar, 1994—. Fellow Ctr. Advanced Study in Behavioral Sci., Stanford, Calif., 1979; vis. fellow Inst. Advanced Study, U. Edinburgh, 1983, Wolfson Coll., Oxford U., 1985, 86; vis. fellow Clare Hall, Cambridge U., 1988, lifetime mem. coll. rooms, 1989—; past or present mem. adv. coms. Princeton U., MIT, Calif. Inst. Tech., Cornell U. Humanities Ctr., Columbia U., UCLA, Ohio State U., U. Calif. Santa Barbara, Carnegie Mellon, Brown U., U. Va., U. Tex., others; disting. vis. prof. U. Calif., Irvine, 1995—. Author: Modalities, 1993; editor: The Logical Enterprise, 1975, Logic Methodology and Philosophy of Science VII, 1986; mem. editorial bd. Past or Present Metaphilosophy, Monist, Philos. Studies, Signs, Jour. Symbolic Logic, The Philosophers Annual; editor,

contbr. to profl. jours. and books. Recipient Machette prize for contbn. to profession; Medal, College de France, 1986, Wilbur Cross medal Yale U., 2000; Mellon sr. fellow Nat. Humanities Ctr., 1992-93; vis. disting. prof. U. Calif., Irvine, 1994, 96, 97, 98, 99, 2000; fellow Conn. Acad. Arts and Scis. Fellow Am. Acad. Arts and Scis.; mem. Coun. on Philos. Studies (pres. 1988-90), Assn. for Symbolic Logic (past exec. coun., exec. com. 1973-83, v.p. 1980-82, coun. 1980-85, pres. 1982-84), Am. Philos. Assn. (past sec., treas., nat. bd. dirs. 1977-83, pres. ctrl. divsn. 1975-78, chmn. nat. bd. officers 1977-85), Philosophy of Sci. Assn., Inst. Internat. Philosophie (past exec. com., v.p. 1983-86, pres. 1990-93, hon. pres. 1994—), Fedn. Internat. Philosophy (exec. com., steering com. 1985-99), Elizabethan Club (v.p. 1989, pres. 1989-90), Phi Beta Kappa. Office: Yale U Dept Philosophy PO Box 208306 New Haven CT 06520-8306 E-mail: ruth.marcus@yale.edu.

**MARCUS, SHELDON,** school policy and administration educator; b. N.Y.C., Aug. 4, 1937; s. Manny and Sarah (Lande) M.; m. Phyllis Knight; children: Beth, Jonathan, Evan. BA, CCNY, 1959, MS, 1960; EdD, Yeshiva U., 1970. Tchr. N.Y.C. Pub. Schs., 1959—68; lectr. social sci. CUNY, 1965—68; mem. faculty Fordham U., N.Y.C., 1968—70, chmn. divsn. urban edn., 1970—76, assoc. dean grad. edn. Tarrytown campus, 1976—93, prof., 1993—. Mem. exec. bd. tchr. corps program U.S. Office Edn., 1974-82; trustee Doctoral Assn. N.Y., 1973-82; co-dir. Fordham Inst. for Rsch. on Supervision and Tchg., 1992-94, Fordham U./N.Y.C. Supts. Network, 1995—. Author or co-author: Conflicts in Urban Education, 1970, Hot Button Issues, 2006; Urban Education: Crisis or Opportunity?, 1972; Father Coughlin: The Tumultuous Life of the Priest of the Little Flower, 1973, (nominated for Pulitzer Prize); The Urban In-Service Education Experience, 1977; Administrative Decision Making in Schools: A Case Study Approach to Strategic Planning, 1986, Strategic Planning: A Case Study Approach to Administrative Decision Making. Case Teaching Notes, 1987, Hot-Button Issues In Today's Schools; contbr. articles to profl. jours. Recipient Scanlon award for contbns. to edn., 1992, Adminstr. of Yr. award, Phi Delta Kappa, 1993. Mem. Am. Edl. Rsch. Assn. (proposal reviewer 1992-97). Home: 36 Pocantico River Rd Pleasantville NY 10570-3510 Office: Fordham U Sch Educ Tarrytown NY 10591 Office Phone: 718-817-5677. Business E-Mail: marcus@fordham.edu.

**MARCUS, STANLEY,** federal judge; b. NYC, 1946; BA, CUNY, 1967; JD, Harvard U., 1971. Law clerk Hon. John Bartels, US Dist. Ct. (ea. dist.), NY; assoc. Botein, Hays, Sklar & Herzberg, NYC, 1974-75; asst. atty. U.S. Dist. Ct. (ea. dist.)NY, 1975-78; spl. atty., dep. chief U.S. organized crime sect. Detroit Strike Force, 1978-79, chief U.S. organized crime sect., 1980-82; US atty. So. Dist. of Fla., Miami, 1982-85; judge US Dist. Ct. (so. dist.) Fla., Miami, 1985-97, US Ct. Appeals (11th cir.), 1997—. Mem. Fed. Bar Assn., Fla. Bar Assn, NY Bar Assn. Mem. U.S. Army, 1968—74. Office: US Ct of Appeals 11th Cir 99 NE 4th St Rm 1262 Miami FL 33132-2185*

**MARCUS, STEVEN IRL,** electrical engineering educator; b. St. Louis, Apr. 2, 1949; s. Herbert A. and Peggy L. (Polishuk) M.; m. Jeanne M. Wilde, June 4, 1978; children: Jeremy A., Tobin L. BA, Rice U., 1971; SM, MIT, 1972, PhD, 1975. Research engr. The Analytic Scis. Corp., Reading, Mass., 1973; asst. prof. U. Tex., Austin, 1975-80, assoc. prof., 1980-84, prof., 1984-91, assoc. chmn., dept. elec. and computer engring., 1984-89, L.B. Meaders prof. engring., 1987-91; prof. elec. and computer engring. U. Md., College Park, 1991—, acting chair dept., 2000-01, chair, 2001—05, dir. Inst. for Sys. Rsch., 1991-96, acting chair, 2000-01. Cons. Tracor Inc., Austin, 1977, 90, ALPHATECH Inc., Arlington, 1999-02. Assoc. editor Math. of Control Signals and Systems, 1987-02, Jour. on Discrete Event Dynamic Systems, 1990-00, Acta Applicandae Mathematicae, 1983—. NSF fellow, 1971-74; Werner W. Dornberger Centennial Teaching fellowship in engring., U. Tex., Austin, 1982-84. Fellow IEEE (prize paper awards com. 1985-88, field awards com. 1989-90, assoc. editor Transactions Info. Theory 1990-92), IEEE Control Systems Soc. (bd. govs. 1985-90, chmn. conf. on decision and control program com. 1983, chmn. working group on stochastic control and estimation 1984-87, assoc. editor Transactions Automatic Control 1980-81); mem. Am. Math. Soc., Soc. Indsl. and Applied Math. (corr. editor Jour. Control and Optimization 1990—, editor-in-chief 2000-05), Acta Applicandae Math., 1983—, Eta Kappa Nu, Tau Beta Pi. Home: 9516 Thornhill Rd Silver Spring MD 20901-4836 Office: U Md Inst Sys Rsch 2219 Ave Williams Bldg 115 College Park MD 20742-0001

**MARCUS, WILLIAM MICHAEL,** rubber and vinyl products manufacturing company executive; b. Boston, Jan. 31, 1938; s. Richard and Diana (Litch) M.; m. Cynthia Steinman, Dec. 9, 1962; children: Melanie, Daniel, Richard. BS in Bus. Adminstrn., Babson Inst., 1959. With Am. Biltrite Inc., Wellesley Hills, Mass., 1960—, exec. v.p., treas., 1983—, also dir. Bd. dirs. Congoleum Corp. Served with U.S. Army, 1960-61. Office: American Biltrite Inc 57 River St Wellesley Hills MA 02481-2013

**MARCUSA, FRED HAYE,** lawyer; b. Paterson, NJ, Jan. 31, 1946; s. Harry and Alice Marcusa; m. Andrea Disario, June 28, 1986; children: Michael, Daniel. AB, Dartmouth Coll., 1967; JD, U. Pa., 1970. Bar: N.Y. 1971. Assoc. Davis, Polk & Wardwell, NYC, 1970-79; v.p., gen. counsel The Coca-Cola Bottling Co. of NY, Inc., 1979-81; sr. ptnr. corp. & fin. dept. Kaye Scholer LLP, NYC, 1981—. Office: Kaye Scholer LLP 425 Park Ave New York NY 10022-3506 Office Phone: 212-836-8433. E-mail: fmarcusa@kayescholer.com.

**MARCUSE, ADRIAN GREGORY,** academic administrator; b. NYC, Mar. 25, 1922; s. Maxwell Frederick and Mildred Ann (Hitter) M.; m. Janet Constance Radlo, Oct. 28, 1945 (dec. Mar. 22, 1980); children: Nancy Ruth Marcuse Marshall, Sally Ann Marcuse Crawford, Elizabeth Susan Marcuse; m. Betty Jane Lieberman Rossman, Jan. 11, 1985; 1 stepchild, Ann Betty Rossman Schurtz. BS, MIT, 1942, MS, 1946, LLD (hon.), Lab Inst. Merchandising, 1992. Production mgmt. engr. N.Y., Fla. Rsch. assoc. MIT, Cambridge, Mass., 1945-46; rsch. scientist United Aircraft Co., E. Hartford, Conn., 1946-47; application engr. Westinghouse Electric Corp., Boston, N.Y.C., 1947-60; consulting engr. pvt. practice, N.Y.C., 1955-62; v.p. mktg. and sales Corrosion Control Corp., N.Y.C., 1960-62; sales and merchandising mgr. B. Altman & Co., N.Y.C., 1962; v.p., COO Lab. Inst. of Merchandising, N.Y.C., 1962-72, pres., CEO, 1972—2002, pres. emeritus, counsel to pres., 2002—. Pres. LIM Fashion Edn. Found., N.Y.C., 1978—; mem. Assn. Regionally Accredited Prvt. Colls. and Univs., Washington, 1990-93. Charter commr. City of Glen Cove, N.Y., 1964, chmn. bd. engrs., 1964-68, mem. planning bd., 1980-87; past treas. Community Concert Assn., Glen Cove; past trustee and budget chmn. North Country Reform Temple, Glen Cove; past mem. YMCA Fund-Raising Coun., Glen Cove 1st lt. USAAF, 1942-45, PTO. Mem.: Assn. Proprietary Colls., Sigma Beta Delta, Sigma Xi. Republican. Avocations: sailing, bicycling, travel, theater. Office: Lab Inst of Merchandising 12 E 53rd St Fl 2 New York NY 10022-5268 Home: 356 Golfview Rd #306 North Palm Beach FL 33408 Business E-Mail: amarcuse@limcollege.edu.

**MARCUSE, DIETRICH,** retired physicist; b. Koenigsberg, East Prussia, Germany, Feb. 27, 1929; arrived in US, 1957; s. Richard and Gertrud (Stolp) M.; m. Haide Schwarz, Jan. 13, 1959; children: Christina, Mikel. Diplom Physiker, Freie Universität, Berlin, 1954; Doktor Ingenieur, Karlsruhe Universität, 1962. Mem. tech. staff Siemens and Halske, Berlin, 1954-57, AT&T Bell Labs., Holmdel, NJ, 1957-94, dist. mem. tech. staff, 1982-94; ret., 1994. Vis. rsch. prof. U. Md., Balt. County, 1995-99. Author: Principles of Quantum-Electronics, 2d edit., 1980, Light Transmission Optics, 2d edit., 1982, Theory of Dielectric Optical Wave-guides, 1972, 2nd edit.,1991, Principles of Optical Fiber Measurements, 1981; also over 200 articles. Fellow IEEE (Quantum Electronics award 1981), Optical Soc. Am. (Max Born award 1989). Personal E-mail: dmarcuse@optonline.net.

**MARCUSS, ROSEMARY DALY,** economist; b. Stamford, Conn., Aug. 27, 1945; d. Eugene Lawrence and Margaret Mary (Murphy) Daly; B.A. in Econs. cum laude, Newton (Mass.) Coll., 1967; M.S., U. Md., 1973, Ph.D.,

1979; m. Stanley J. Marcuss, July 6, 1968; children— Elena Daly, Aidan Stanley. Jr. staff economist President's Council of Econ. Advisers, 1968-70; economist, asst. to pres. Am. Fedn. State, County and Mcpl. Employees, Washington, 1973; economist, mgmt. cons. Data Resources, Inc., Washington, 1974-78; dep. asst. dir. tax analysis Congressional Budget Office, Washington, 1980-83, asst. dir. tax analysis, 1983-98; dep. dir. Bur. Econ. Analysis, Washington, 1998—; pres. Nat. Assn Bus. Econ., 2005-. NSF fellow, 1970-73. Mem. Am. Econ. Assn., Nat. Tax Assn., Tax Inst. Am., So. Econ. Assn., Soc. Govt. Economists, Nat. Economists Club, Nat. Assn. Business Economists (v.p. 2003-), Washington Women Economists. Home: 4616 29th Pl NW Washington DC 20008-2105 Office: Congressional Budget Office 2nd & D Sts SW Washington DC 20515-0001

**MARCUSS, STANLEY JOSEPH,** lawyer; b. Hartford, Conn., Jan. 24, 1942; s. Stanley Joseph and Anne Sutton (Leone) M.; m. Rosemary Daly, July 6, 1968; children: Elena Daly, Aidan Stanley. BA, Trinity Coll., 1963, Cambridge U., 1965, MA, 1968; JD, Harvard U., 1968. Bar: D.C., N.Y., Conn., U.S. Supreme Ct. Staff atty. office of gen. counsel HUD, Washington, 1968; atty. firm Hogan and Hartson, Washington, 1968-73; counsel to internat. fin. subcom. U.S. Senate Com. on Banking, Housing and Urban Affairs, 1973-77; dep. asst. sec. for trade regulation Dept. Commerce, Washington, 1977-78, sr. dep. asst. sec. for industry and trade, 1978-79, acting asst. sec. for industry and trade, 1979-80, acting asst. sec. for trade regulation, 1980; mem. firm Milbank, Tweed, Hadley & McCloy, Washington, 1980-93, Bryan Cave, 1993—. Former adj. prof. Am. U. Law Sch. Author: Effective Washington Representation, 1983; mem. bd. overseers U. Calif. Berkeley Law Jour.; contbr. articles to profl. jours. Former trustee Trinity Coll., Hartford. Marshall scholar. Mem. ABA, D.C. Bar (former chmn., steering com. internat. law div.), Phi Beta Kappa. Home: 4616 29th Pl NW Washington DC 20008-2105

**MARCUVITZ, NATHAN,** physicist, educator; b. Bklyn., Dec. 29, 1913; s. Samuel and Rebecca (Kainer) M.; m. Muriel Spanier, June 30, 1946; children— Andrew, Karen. B.E.E., Poly. Inst. Bklyn., 1935, M.E.E., 1941, D.E.E., 1947; Laurea Honoris Causa, Politecnico Di Torino, 1993; D in Engring. (hon.), Polytechnic U., 2000. Engr. RCA Labs., 1936-40; research asso. Radiation Lab., Mass. Inst. Tech., 1941-46; asst. prof. elec. engring. Poly. Inst. Bklyn., 1946-49, asso. prof., 1949-51, prof., 1951-65; dir. Poly. Inst. Bklyn. (Microwave Research Inst.), 1957-61; v.p. research, acting dean Poly. Inst. Bklyn. (Grad. Center), 1961-63, prof. electrophysics, 1961-66, dean research, dean, 1964-65; asst. dir. def. research and engring. Dept. Def., Washington, 1963-64; prof. applied physics N.Y.U., 1966-73; prof. electrophysics Poly. Inst. N.Y., 1973—; prof. emeritus, 1978—. Vis. prof. Harvard U., spring 1971. Author: Waveguide Handbook, Vol. 10, 1951, (with L. Felsen) Radiation and Scattering of Waves, 1973; also numerous articles. Recipient Microwave Career award IEEE Microwave Theory and Techniques Soc., 1985. Fellow IEEE (Heinrich Hertz medal 1989); mem. Nat. Acad. Engring., Am. Phys. Soc., Sigma Xi, Tau Beta Pi, Eta Kappa Nu. Home: Apt 1403 7225 Pelican Bay Blvd Naples FL 34108-5524 Personal E-mail: marc@rama.poly.edu.

**MARCY, GEOFFREY W.,** astronomer, physicist, educator; BA in Physics & Astronomy (summa cum laude), UCLA, 1976; PhD in Astronomy & Astrophysics, U. Calif., Santa Cruz, 1982. Fellow Carnegie Inst., Wash., 1982—84; full prof. physics & astronomy San Francisco State U., 1984—96, disting. prof., 1997—99, adjunct prof. physics & astronomy, 1999—; prof. astronomy U. Calif., Berkeley, 1999—. Mem. Com. on the Status of Women in Astronomy, 1994—97, NASA Working Group: Origins of Solar Systems, 1998—2000, NASA Working Group: Terrestrial Planet Finder, 1998—2001; dir. Ctr. for Integrative Planetary Sci., 2000—; Bunyan lectr., physics dept. Stanford U., 1997; G. Darwin Lecture Royal Astronomical Soc., 2000; NSF Disting. Lectr., 00; prin. investigator NASA Space Interferometry Mission, 2001; Sackler Lectr. U. Leiden, 2001; Niels Bohr Lecture N.B. Inst., 2005. Author numerous scientific articles in peer-reviewed jours., newspapers, and mag.; appearances include ABC Nightline, CBS Nightly News, NBC Today Show, BBC Horizons, CNN News, PBS, Late Show with David Letterman. Named Person of Week, ABC News Hour, 1996, Alumnus Yr., U. Calif. Santa Cruz, 1997, Calif. Scientist of the Yr., 2000, Space Scientist Yr., Discover Mag., 2003; recipient Manne Siegbahn award, Swedish Acad., 1996, Internat. Assn. Universities Commn. 51 Bioastronomy Medal of Honor (First Ever Issued), 1997, Certificate of Recognition (First Ever Issued), Extrasolar Planetary Found., 1999, UCLA Alumni Profl. Achievement award, 1999, Carl Sagan award, Am. Astronautical & Planetary Soc., 2002, Exceptional Scientific Achievement medal, NASA, 2003, Shaw prize, 2005. Fellow: Calif. Acad. of Sci.; mem.: NAS (Henry Draper medal 2001), Astronomical Soc. of Pacific (bd. dirs. 1997—99, pub. bd. 1997—2002), Am. Astronomical Soc. (bd. of councilors 1998—2000, Beatrice M. Tinsley prize 2002). Made First Zeeman Measurements of Magnetic Fields for Solor-Type Stars; found Paucity of Brown Dwarfs Orbiting Stars; developed the method of Precise Doppler Measurements; discovered 70 of the first 100 Extrasolar Planets known; found evidence that the Solar System maybe peculiar; discovered the first system of planets around a sun-like star; discovered first transiting planet around another star; discovered the first candidate Saturn-Mass planets; discovered the first extrasolar planet orbiting beyond 5AU; co-discovered the first Neptune-Sized Planets: Gliese 436b and 55 Cancri e. Office: U Calif 417 Campbell Hall Berkeley CA 94720 Office Phone: 510-642-1952. Office Fax: 510-642-3411.*

**MARCY, KEVIN MICHAEL,** film producer, lawyer; BS, U. Nev., Reno, 1974—78; JD, U. So. Calif., L.A., 1978—81. Bar: Calif. 1981. Atty. Kinsella, Boesch, Fujikawa & Towle, L.A., 1981—83; assoc. prodr. Paramount Pictures, L.A., 1983—87, 1995; asst. to Dan Aykroyd Applied Action Rsch., L.A., 1987—95, prodr., 2003—; Snake River Productions, Malibu, Calif., 1996—2003; assoc. prodr. Miramax Films, L.A., 2003. V.p., guest rels. Ho. of Blues, L.A., 1994; cons. Hitplay Media, L.A., 2000. Prodr.: (films) The Testimony of Taliesin Jones, 2000, (short film) Mr. Bill Goes To Law School; assoc. prodr. (films) The Naked Gun, 1988, The Coneheads, 1993, Scary Movie 3, 2003. Mem.: Ho. of Blues Found. (life), Dan Aykroyd Biker Gang (life), Phi Kappa Phi (life), Beta Gamma Sigma (life), Delta Sigma Pi (life).

**MARDELL, CAROL DOLORES,** psychology professor; b. Chgo., Nov. 30, 1935; d. Albert and Lee (Mandel) Goldstein; m. Howard Mardell, Nov. 21, 1956 (div. Nov. 1977); children: Benjamin, Dina, Ruth; m. Moshe Marcel Czudnowski, Nov. 13, 1978 (div. Nov. 2002). BS, U. Ill., 1956; MA, U. Chgo., 1958; PhD, Northwestern U., 1972. Tchr. various schs., Skokie and Highland Park, Ill., 1956-70; dir. research project Ill. Office Edn., Chgo., 1971-73; asst. prof. edn. Northwestern U., Evanston, Ill., 1973-74; from asst. to assoc. prof. Northeastern Ill. U., Chgo., 1974-78; assoc. prof. edn. No. Ill. U., DeKalb, 1978-86, prof. edn., 1986-92. Vis. prof. Nat. Taiwan Normal U., Taipei, 1983-84, Université Laval, Quebec City, Can., 1984-85, Inst. Edn., Stockholm, 1990. Co-author: Special Education for the Early Childhood Years, 1981, 2d edition 1987, Developmental Indicators for the Assessment of Learning-Revised (DIAL-R), 1983, Assessing Young Children, 1996, Developmental Indicators for the Assessment of Learning (DIAL-3), 1998, Parents' Observations of Infants and Toddlers (Point), 2006. Dir. Project LINKS, 1987-90. Mem. Am. Psychol. Assn., Council for Exceptional Children, Internat. Acad. Rsch. in Learning Disabilities, Learning Disabilities Assn., Nat. Assn. for Edn. Young Children, Phi Kappa Phi, Alpha Lambda Delta, Pi Lambda Theta, Phi Delta Kappa, Kappa Delta Pi. Home and Office: 26300 Village Ln Apt 403 Bonita Springs FL 34134-7014 Office Phone: 216-588-1270. Business E-Mail: dialcarol@prodigy.net.mx, dialcarol@gmail.com.

**MARDEN, BRICE,** artist; b. Bronxville, NY, Oct. 15, 1938; s. Nicholas Brice and Kathryn (Fox) Marden; m. Pauline Thalia Baez, 1960 (div. 1964); 1 child, Nicholas Brice; m. Helen Regina Harrington, Nov. 7, 1968; children: Maya Mirabelle Zahara, Melia Io Bricia. Student, Fla. So. Coll., 1957—58; BFA, Boston U., 1958—61; attended, Yale U. Summer Sch. Music and Arts, 1961; MFA, Yale U., 1961—63. Security guard Jewish Mus., NYC, 1963—64; gen. asst. to Robert Rauschenberg, 1966; inst. Sch. Visual Arts, NY, 1969—74. Pres. Plane Image, Inc. Exhibited in one man shows including Wilcox Gallery, Swarthmore, Pa., 1964, Bykert Gallery, NYC, 1966, 68-70, 72-74, Galerie Yvon Lambert, Paris, 1969, 73, Galleria Francoise Lambert, Milan, Italy, 1970, 73, Konrad Fischer, Dusseldorf, Fed. Republic of Germany, 1971-73, 75, 80, Gian Enzo Sperone, Turin, Italy, 1971, 77, Locksley-Shea Gallery, Mpls., 1972, 74, Jack Glenn Gallery, Corona del Mar, Calif., 1973, Cirrus Gallery, Los Angeles, 1974, Sable-Castelli Gallery, Toronto, Can., 1974, Contemporary Arts Mus., Houston, 1974, Loretto Hilton Gallery, St. Louis, 1974, Ft. Worth Art Mus., Tex., 1974, Mpls. Inst. Arts, 1975, D'Allesandro/Ferranti, Rome, 1975, Solomon R. Guggenheim Mus., NYC, 1975, Sperone Westwater Fischer, NYC, 1976, Max Protech Gallery, Washington, 1977, Bell Gallery, Providence, 1977, Jean and Karen Bernier, Athens, 1977, Pace Gallery, NYC, 1978, 80, 82, 84, Kunstraum, Munich, 1979, Inst. für Moderne Kunst, Nurnberg, Fed. Republic of Germany, 1979, Ink, Zurich, 1980, Stedelijk Mus., Amsterdam, 1981, Daniel Weinberg Gallery, Los Angeles, 1984, Mary Boone Gallery, NYC, 1987, Mary Boone/Michael Werner Gallery, NYC, 1988, 89, Gallery Montenay, Paris, 1988, Anthony d'Offay Gallery, London, 1988, Van Straaten Gallery, Chgo., 1989, Galerie Michael Werner, Cologne, 1990, Kunsthalle im Kulturhaus Palazzo, Baselland, Switzerland, 1991, Gagosian Gallery, NY, 1993, Mus. Fine Arts, Boston, 1993, Matthew Marks Gallery, NY, 1993, 95, 96, 98, Dia Ctr. for the Arts, NY, 1993, Walker Art Ctr., Mpls., 1993, Menil Collection, Houston, 1993, Mus. Nat. Ctr. de Arte, Madrid, 1993, Kunstmus., Bonn, Germany, 1993, Tate Gallery, London, 1993, Mus. d'Art Moderne de la Ville de Paris, 1993, Balt. Mus. Art, 1993, Curwen Gallery, London, 1993, Kunstmus. Basel, 1995, Mus. fur Gegenwartskunst, 1995, Mus. Fridericianum, Kassel, 1995, Kunsthalle, Bern, 1995, Vienna Secession, 1995, Stedelijk, Amsterdam, 1995, St. Louis Art Mus., 1995, Pace Gallery, NY, 1996, Thomas Ammann Fine Art AG, Zurich, Switzerland, 1997, Staatliche Graphisch Sammlung, Munchen, 1998, Kunstmus., Winterthur, Switzerland, 1998, Wexner Art Ctr., Ohio, 1999, Fogg Art Mus., Cambridge, Mass., 1999, Dallas Mus. Art, 1999, Etchings, Margo Leavin Gallery, LA, 2001, Serpentine Gallery, London, 2001, Drawing the Line: A Retrospective of Drawings, 2002, Alumni Gallery, Boston U., 2003, Attendants, Bears, and Rocks, Matthew Marks Gallery, NY, 2003, An Empty Space, Akira Ikeda Gallery, NY, 2005; represented in group shows including Lyman Allen Mus., New London, Conn., 1960, Leo Castelli Gallery, NYC, 1966, Park Place Gallery, NYC, 1966, Ithaca Coll. Mus. Art, NY, 1967, Krannert Art Mus., Champaign, Ill., 1967, Bykert Gallery, 1967-68, 70-71, 74, Inst. Contemporary Art, Phila., 1967, U. Omaha, 1967, Mus. Fine Arts, Houston, 1967, Clemson U. Sch. Architecture, 1968, Vassar Coll. Art Gallery, Poughkeepsie, NY, 1969, Stadtische Kunsthalle, Dusseldorf, 1969, Ft. Worth Art Mus., 1969, 74, Carmen Lamanna Gallery, Toronto, 1969, Whitney Mus. Am. Art, NYC, 1969, 71, 73, 77, 83, Locksley-Shea Gallery, 1970, Albright-Knox Gallery, Buffalo, 1970, Found. Maeght, St. Paul-de-Vence, France, 1970, Utah Mus. Fine Arts, Salt Lake City, 1970, Minn. Mus. Art, St. Paul, 1971, Henry Gallery, Seattle, 1972-73, Ariz. State U., Tempe, 1972, Ga. Mus. Art, Athens, 1972, Mus. Contemporary Art, Chgo., 1972, 86, Indpls. Mus. Art, 1972, Walker Art Ctr., Mpls., 1972, Univ. Art Mus., Berkeley, Calif., 1972, Art Inst. Chgo., 1972, Mus. Friderichianum and Neue Gallerie, Kassel, Fed. Republic of Germany, 1972, Galerie Yvon Lambert, 1972, Yale U. Art Gallery, New Haven, 1973, Genthofte Kunstvenner and Genthofte Kommune, Denmark, 1973, Stadtisches Mus., Monchengladbach, Fed. Republic of Germany, 1973, I.C.C., Antwerp, Belgium, 1973, Centro Communitario di Brera, Milan, 1973, Royal Coll. Art, London, 1973, Parcheggio di Villa Borghese, Rome, 1974, Kathonah Gallery, NY, 1974, Nat. Gallery of Victoria, Australia, 1974, Art Gallery of New South Wales, Australia, 1974, Art Gallery of South Australia, Akelaide, 1974, West Australian Art Gallery, Perth, 1974, City of Auckland Art Gallery, Australia, 1974, Westfalischer Kunstverein, Munster, Fed. Republic of Germany, 1974, Scottish Arts Council, Edinburgh, 1974, Mus. Modern Art, NYC, 1974, 76, Rice Mus. and Sewall Gallery, 1975, Rijksmuseum Kroller-Muller, Otterlo, Holland, 1975, Basel (Switzerland) Kunstmuseum, 1975, Kunstahlle, Zurich, 1976, Staatliche Kunsthalle, Baden-Baden, Fed. Republic of Germany, 1976, Graphische Sammlung Albertina, Vienna, 1976, Sidney Janis Gallery, NYC, 1977, Wildenstein and Co., London, 1980, Bklyn. Mus., 1980, Mus. Contemporary Art, Los Angeles, 1983, Hayden Gallery, Cambridge, Mass., 1983, Pratt Inst. Gallery, NYC, 1983, Gallery Maeght Lelong, NYC, 1983, The Renaissance Soc., Chgo., 1984, Blum Helman Warehouse, NYC, 1984, Daniel Weinberg Gallery, Los Angeles, 1985, Guggenheim Mus., NYC, 1985, Condeso Lawler Gallery, NYC, 1985, Mary Boone Gallery, 1985, Carnegie Inst., Pitts., 1985, Ft. Lauderdale Mus. Art, Fla.,1986, P.S. 1, LI City, 1986, Charles Cowles Gallery, NYC, 1986, Musee d'Art Moderne, Paris, 1986, Los Angeles County Mus., 1986, Gemeentemuseum, The Hague, The Netherlands, 1986, Ludwig Mus., Kolm, Fed. Republic of Germany, 1986, Galerie Nachst St. Stephan, Vienna, 1986, CAPC Musee d'Art Contemporain de Bordeaux, France, 1986, Anthony d'Offay Gallery, London, 1987, The Sara Hilden Art Mus., Tampere, Finland, 1988, Carnegie Mus. Art, Pitts., 1988, Musee d'art contemporain, Lyon, 1988, Hirschl and Adler Modern, New York, 1989, Whitney Mus. Am. Art, NY, 1989, Albright Knox Art Gallery, Buffalo, Ctr. for the Fine Arts, Miami, Fla., Milwaukee Art Mus., Wis., Yale U. Art Gallery, New Haven, Conn., 1989, The Albertina, Vienna, 1990, Musee du Louvre, Paris, 1990, The Mus. of Modern Art, New York, 1992, Margo Leavin Gallery, LA, 1992, The Balt. Mus. Art, 1992, Kassel, Germany, 1992, The Aldrich Mus., Ridgefield, Conn., 1993, Luhring Augusting, NY, 1994, Nat. Gallery, Washington, 1994, The Art Inst. Chgo., 1995, Nat. Mus. Modern Art, Tokyo, 1995, Whitney Mus. Am. Art, NY, 1995, Musee national d'art modern, Centre Georges Pompidou, 1995, Mus. Contemporary Art, Chgo., 1996, La Biennale di Venizia, Venice, Italy, 1997, Mitchell-innes & Nash, NY, 1998, Hirshhorn Mus. and Sculpture Garden, Washington, Miami Art Mus., Fla., 1999-2000, Carnegie Mus. Art, Pitts., 2000, Serpentine Gallery, London, 2000, Kunst Mus., Luzern, Switzerland, 2000, Instituto Nazionale Per La Gradica, Rome, 2001, Archivio di Stato, Torino, Italy, 2002, Landesmuseum fur Kunst und Kulturgeschichte, Munster, Germany, 2002, Boston U. Gallery, 2002, Matthew Marks Gallery, NYC, 2002, Daros Collection, Zurich, Switzerland, 2003, Not Exactly Photographs, Fraenkel Gallery, San Francisco, 2004, A Minimal Future? Art as Object, Mus. Contemporary Art, LA, 2004, Singular Forms (Sometimes Repeated), Guggenheim Mus., NYC, 2004, Matisse to Freud: A Critic's Choice, Brit. Mus., London, 2005, Imageless Icons: Abstract Thoughts, Gagosian Gallery, London, 2005, Contemporary Voices, Mus. Modern Art, NYC, 2005. Fellow: Am. Acad. Arts and Sci. Office: 131 Varick St Rm 1003 New York NY 10013-1417 Home: Hydra Greece*

**MARDEN, KENNETH ALLEN,** advertising executive; b. Dec. 12, 1928; s. Allen H. and Doris (Littlefield) M.; m. Julia Lee Black, June 11, 1949; children: Priscilla Anne, Emily Gage. BA, U. Maine, 1950. Hosp. salesman Johnson & Johnson, New Brunswick, NJ, 1959-61, product dir. hosp divsn., 1962-68, advt. and pub. rels. mgr. hosp. divsn., 1969-71, group product dir. patient care divsn., 1972-74, advt. dir. patient care divsn., 1974-78; v.p. E.J. Axelrod, Inc., N.Y.C., 1978-80; v.p. account mgmt. Vicom/FCB, Phila., 1980-87; pres. Am. Kennel Club, N.Y., 1987-90. Cons. on dog legislation, 1990—, also bd. dirs.; pres. Crossing Creek Comm., 1991—; bd. dirs. The Dog Mus., 1995—. 1st lt. U.S. Army, 1951-53; capt. Med. N.G., 1956-59. Mem. Dog Writers Assn. Am., German Shorthaired Pointer Am. Club (del. 1976—, v.p. 1985-86), Eastern German Shorthaired Pointer Club (pres. 1972-74, 94-98), Jersey Rag Racers (pres. 1994-96), Katahdin German Shorthaired Pointer Club of Greater Portland, Nat. Animal Interest Alliance (bd. dirs. 1994—), Nat. Breed Clubs Alliance (v.p. 1996-2000). Republican. Episcopalian. Home: 183 E River Rd Whitefield ME 04353 Office: Crossing Creek Communications 183 E River Rd Whitefield ME 04353 Office Phone: 207-549-4783. Business E-Mail: kam@akc.org. E-Mail: kmarden@earthlink.net.

**MARDER, BARBARA HERMLING,** theater educator, department chairman; b. Peoria, Ill., Oct. 5, 1941; d. Harold Otha and Elizabeth Kendall Hermling; m. Stuart Charles Marder, Jan. 28, 1972; children: Joshua Gerold, Jody Elicia. MA, George Washington U., Washington, 1968. Cert. advanced profl. study in tech. Johns Hopkins U., 1980. Theatre arts faculty Anne Arundel C.C., Arnold, Md., 1978—2002, chair performing arts, 2002—. Dir.: (theatre) All My Sons (Cert. Merit, Am. Coll. Theatre Festival, 2000). Chair scholarship AAUW, Severna Park, Md., 2000—04. Mem.: Assn. for Theatre in Higher Edn. (2 yr. coll. conf. planner 2006—). Avocations: water sports, travel. Office: Anne Arundel Community College 101 College Pkwy Arnold MD 21012 Office Phone: 410-777-7030. Business E-Mail: bhmarder@aacc.edu.

**MARDER, EVE ESTHER,** neuroscientist, educator; b. NYC, May 30, 1948; d. Eric Marder and Dorothy Silverman. AB, Brandeis U., 1969; PhD, U. Calif., San Diego, 1974. Postdoctoral fellow U. Oreg., Eugene, 1975, Ecole Normale Superieure, Paris, 1976-78; from asst. prof. to assoc. prof. Brandeis U., Waltham, Mass., 1978-90, prof., 1990—; program dir. Sloan Ctr. for Theoretical Neuroscience; chief editor Jour. of Neurophysiology, 2002—, Forbes lectr., 2000. Founding editor: Jour. Computational Neurosci.; mem. editorial bd., Jour. Exptl. Biology, Jour. Neurobiology, curr. biol; jour. comp. physiol A; curr. opinion in Neurobiology; jour. of comp. neurology; contbr. papers and chpt. to sci. jour. Trustee Grass Found. Coun., 1999—2002. Recipient Javits award in neurosci. NINDS, 1987, Investigators award McKnight Found., 1994, NIMH Merit award, 1995; Alfred P. Sloan Found. fellow, 1978; McKnight scholar, 1978. Fellow AAAS, Am. Acad. of Arts and Sci., Women in Neuroscience, Biophysical Soc. (trustee). Office: Brandeis U Volen Ctr Waltham MA 02454

**MARDER, JOHN ADAM,** lawyer; b. Fall River, Mass., Jan. 17, 1960; s. Everett Joseph and Brenda Joan (Leviss) M.; m. Bonnie Jane Webber, Nov. 11, 1989; 1 child, Max Phillip. BA, Bates Coll., 1982; JD, Calif. Western Sch. Law, 1985. Bar: Calif. 1986, U.S. Dist. Ct. (ctrl. dist.) Calif. 1989. Dep. dist. atty. San Bernardino D.A., 1985-87; atty. Home Ins. Co., L.A., 1987; ptnr. Morris, Polich & Purdy LLP, 1987-94; mng. ptnr. Manning & Marder Kass Ellrod Ramirez LLP (formerly Manning, Marder & Wolfe LLP), L.A. 1994—. Gen. counsel Internat. Assn. Spl. Investigation Units, So. Calif. Chapter; bd. dirs. Athens Found. Named a Super Lawyer, Law & Politics, 2005; named Calif. Atty. of the Yr., Calif. Lawyer mag., 2005. Office: Manning & Marder Kass Ellrod Ramirez LLP 660 S Figueroa St 23rd Fl Los Angeles CA 90017*

**MARDER, MICHAEL ZACHARY,** dental educator, researcher; b. N.Y.C., Aug. 30, 1938; s. Joseph Theodore and Rhea (Greenspun) M.; (widowed); children: Sherri Ellen, Robert Whitney. Student, Tufts U., 1959; DDS, Columbia U., 1963. Diplomate: Am. Bd. Oral Medicine. Practice dentistry, NYC, 1963-66, 68—; asst. Sch. Dental and Oral Surgery, Columbia U., NYC, 1963-66, instr., 1968, asst. clin. prof., 1968-72, assoc. clin. prof., 1972-76, NYC clin. prof. dentistry, 1976—, rschr., 1963—; dir. oral medicine, 1972-84; dir. clin. cancer trg., 1993—; attending dental surgeon Presbyn. Hosp., 1972-76; assoc. attending dentist, 1976-82; attending dentist, 1982—; cons. Good Samaritan Hosp., Suffern, NY. Lectr. field. Author 2 textbooks in dental medicine; contbr. chpts. to med. and dental textbooks, articles to profl. jours. Served to capt. US Army, 1966-68. Recipient Cert. Achievement US Army, 1968. Fellow NY Acad. Dentistry; mem. ADA, Internat. Assn. Dental Rsch., Am. Acad. Oral Medicine, Frist Dist. Dental Soc. NY, Omicron Kappa Upsilon, Sigma Xi. Office: 119 W 57th St New York NY 10019-2303 Office Phone: 212-265-8291. Business E-Mail: mzm2@columbia.edu.

**MARDIKIAN, PAUL,** conservator; b. Rambouillet, France, Apr. 15, 1963; s. Jacques Mardikian and Martine Boivin; m. Pascale Nicole Nahmias, July 13, 1996; children: Victor, Rose. MA in Archaeology and Art History, Sch. of the Louvre, Paris, 1984—89; MS in Conservation Scis. and Techniques, Sorbonne U., Paris, 1987—91. Profl. Diver Class IB GRASM, Marseille, France, 1994, cert. in Comml. Surface Supplied Diving Von's Diving Svcs., Charleston, S.C., 2001, Radiation Safety Officer, Hunley Conservation Lab. Advanced Testing Tech., 2000. Conservator Rsch. Lab. Valectra, Electricité de France, Direction des Etudes et Recherches, St-Denis, France, 1988—90; conservation intern Can. Parks Svc. Underwater Archaeology Conservation Lab., Ottawa, Ont., Canada, 1990—91; hon. rsch. fellow We. Australian Maritime Mus. Lab., Fremantle, Australia, 1991—92; head conservator Underwater Conservation Lab. Archeolyse Internat., Cannes, France, 1992—99; sr. conservator, H.L. Hunley project Friends of the Hunley, Inc., Warren Lasch Conservation Ctr., North Charleston, SC, 1999—. Contbr. articles to profl. jours. Recipient Laureat, Fondation Marcel Bleustein-Blanchet pour la vocation, 1990, Salavin-Fournier, Fondation de France, 1990, Fondation Electricite de France, 1991. Mem.: ICOM-CC, Soc. for Hist. Archaeology (assoc.), Am. Inst. for Conservation (assoc.). Achievements include the preservation of shipwreck materials including metals, organics, composite artifacts, large and/or complex metal assemblies; development of the conservation of numerous artifacts from ancient shipwrecks in the Mediterranean to American Civil War vessels or WWII composite materials; first to conserve & analyze of artifacts from the RMS Titanic (1912), CSS Alabama (1863), H.L Hunley (1864) for Electricite de France Research Lab, France or Naval Historical Center in Washington, D.C; research in the use of sub critical fluids in the conservation of archaeological metals in collaboration with Clemson U. Office: Warren Lasch Conservation Ctr 1250 Supply St North Charleston SC 29405 Office Phone: 843-743-4865 x 15. Office Fax: 843-744-1480. E-mail: mardikian@hunley.org.

**MARDILOVICH, IVAN P.,** education educator, researcher; b. Stolbtsy, Belarus, Sept. 21, 1952; s. Peter L and Elena I (Zvytsevich) Mardilovich; m. Galina A Semyonov, Apr. 23, 1977; children: Anastasia I, Katerina I. MSc, Belarus State U., 1975; PhD in phys. chemistry, Russian U. of Peoples' Friendship, 1982. Sr. rsch. scientist Nat. Acad. Sci. Belarus, Minsk, 1985—99; rsch. assoc. prof. Worcester Poly. Inst., Mass., 1999—. Sci. sec. of the divsn. of chem. and earth sciences NAS of Belarus, Minsk, Belarus, 1998—99. Sec.- gen. Internat. Fedn. of Chem. Societies, Minsk, Belarus, 1993—2000. Recipient Bronze medal, USSR Exhbn. of the Nat. Economy Achievements, 1985. Achievements include developed and characterized unique Pd and Pd-alloy membranes on porous supports for high temperature hydrogen separation and for a variety of hydrogen-related processes. Office: Worcester Polytechnic Institute 100 Institute Rd Worcester MA 01609 Office Phone: 508-831-5474. Business E-Mail: ivanpm@wpi.edu.

**MARDINLY, GEORGE JOHN,** lawyer; s. Rose and John Mardinly; m. Jeanette Mardinly. JD, Temple U., Phila. 1996. Owner The Law Offices of George J. Mardinly, Rumson, NJ, 2001—. Contbr. Phila. Orch., Boston Symphony. Office: The Law Offices of George J Mardinly PO Box 338 Rumson NJ 07760 Office Phone: 1-732-212-0196. Home Fax: 1-732-212-9411; Office Fax: 1-732-212-9411. Personal E-mail: gmardinly@aol.com.

**MARDINLY, SUSAN J.,** musician, music educator; d. Ashe John Mardinly and Jane Elizabeth Fish; m. Fred Dale Shinkle, Feb. 21, 1998; children: Deborah Ruth Goodman, Sarah Nancy Goodman. MusB, New Eng. Conservatory of Music, 1969; MusM, U. Hartford, 1991; D in Musical Arts, U. Conn., 2004. Voice tchr., Seymour, 1979—84, Waterbury, Conn., 1985—91; voice tchr. dept. chair Hartford Conservatory, Hartford, Conn., 1992—99; voice tchr. arts adminstr. U. Conn., Storrs, 1992—96; voice tchr. The Hartt Sch. Cmty. Divsn., Hartford, Conn., 2005—. Lectr. recitals, 1978—; ch. soloist, choir dir., 1978—; dir. Chamber Musicians' Alliance, New Haven, 1979—83; operatic/oratorio soloist various ocs., 1979—99; co-chair Ann. Concert of Music by Women Composers, Hartford, 2001—. Author (editor, arranger): (book) Barbara Strozzi and The Pleasures of Euterpe, 21 other publ. vocal works by Barbara Strozzi; musician (soprano soloist, chorister): Conn. Opera, 1966—92; contbr. articles to profl. jours. Benefit concerts Conn. Hospice, Branford/Litchfield, 1982—93, St. Vincent de Paul Shelter, Waterbury, Conn., 1992—99; publicity chair Naugatuck (Conn.) Teen Theater, 2006—; dir. music St. Anthony Ch., Litchfield/Prospect, Conn., 1992—99; soprano soloist Ch. of Good Shepherd, Hartford, Conn., 1991—; mem. Musical Club Hartford, 1991—. Recipient Nine Dir. Music awards, Naugatuck Teen Theater, Conn., 1991; Doctoral fellow, U. Conn., 1993—96, Wagenlis scholar, 1994, Rsch. grantee, 1995. Mem.: Conn. Music Educators Assn. (cert. adjudicator 1995—), Conn. Nat. Assn. Tchrs. of Singing (judge 1981—; Conn. winner; New Eng. Regional Finalist Artist award 1982), AGMA (profl. liason 1986—92), Mu Phi Epsilon (life; two term sec.

1966—68), Pi Kappa Lambda (life). Avocations: travel, poetry, cooking. Office: Hartt Sch Bloomfield Ave Hartford CT 06117 Office Phone: 860-768-8562. Personal E-mail: susanmardinly@aol.com.

**MARDIROSIAN, TOM,** actor, playwright; b. Buffalo, Dec. 14, 1947; s. Matthew and Afro (Karahos) M. BA inTheatre, U. Buffalo, 1972. Tchr. U. Buffalo, 1972-75; drama coach Studio Arena Theater, Buffalo, 1972-75. Broadway performances include: The Magic Show, Cuba and His Teddy Bear, Happy Education, feature films include: Tootsie, 1982, Alphabet City, 1984, Trading Places, 1983, Power, 1986, The Rosary Murders, 1987, Shakedown, 1988, New York Stories, 1989, Betsy's Wedding, 1990, Presumed Innocent, 1990, The Dark Half, 1993, Don Juan DeMarco, 1995, On the Q.T., 1999, Razor's Edge, 1999, Lady in the Water, 2006, (TV films) Seizure: The Story of Kathy Morris, 1980, Muggable Mary, Street Cop, 1982, The Neighborhood, 1982, Rockabye, 1986, True Blue, 1989, Kojak: None So Blind, 1990, Quiet Killer, 1992, Miss Rose White, 1992, With Murder in Mind, 1992, If Looks Could Kill, 1996, Voice from the Grave, 1996; performer numerous off-Broadway plays; playwright: Saved from Obscurity, 1988 (Drama Desk nomination), Subfertile, 1990. With U.S. Army, 1967-69. Mem. SAG, AFTRA, Actors Equity Assn. Home: 210 W 16th St Apt 1C New York NY 10011-6132*

**MARDIS, ELIZABETH WILLIAMS,** occupational health nurse; b. Colbert County, Ala., July 31, 1953; d. Bobby Joe and Nell Elizabeth (Cochran) Williams; m. Danny Richard Mardis, Dec. 18, 1976; children: Paige, Patrick. Diploma nursing, Sanford U., 1973; BS in Nursing, U. North Ala., 2004. Cert. occupl. health nurse; cert. occupl. hearing conservationist. Occupl. health mgr. Huntsville Hosp., Ala., Goodyear Dunlop Tire Corp., Huntsville, Ala.; occupl. health nurse Delphi Automotive Systems, Athens, Ala.; dir. case mgmt Parkway Med. Ctr., Decatur, Ala., emergency rm. supr.; asst. dir. nursing svcs. Lawrence County Hosp., Moulton, Ala.; patient edn. and infection control nurse Humana Hosp., Russelville, Ala. Instr. prepared childbirth. Mem. Am. Assn. Occupl. Health Nurses, Case Mgmt. Soc. Am., Assn. Occupl. Health Profls. in Healthcare. Home: 2006 Cotaco Valley Trl SE Decatur AL 35603-5145 Office Phone: 256-265-8042. Business E-Mail: eliza093@hhsys.org.

**MARDIS, HAL KENNEDY,** urological surgeon, educator, researcher; b. Lincoln, Nebr., Apr. 4, 1934; s. Harold Corson and Marie (Swaim) M.; m. Janet Reimers Schenken, June 22, 1956; children: Michael Corson, Anne Lucille, Jeanne Marie. BS, U. Nebr., Lincoln, 1955; MD, U. Nebr., Omaha, 1958. Diplomate Am. Bd. Urology. Intern Nebr. Meth. Hosp., Omaha, 1958-59, med. dir. The Stone Ctr., 1966—; resident in urology Charity Hosp. La., New Orleans, 1959-62, chief resident in urology, 1962-63; pvt. practice Omaha, 1965—; instr., asst. prof. La. State U. Sch. Medicine, New Orleans, 1963-65; asst. prof., assoc. prof. surgery U. Nebr. Med. Ctr., 1965-85, prof., 1985—. Investigator North Cen. Cancer Treatment Group, Rochester, Minn., 1988—, Technomed Internat., Inc., Danvers, Mass., 1988—; cons. Boston Sci. Corp., Watertown, Mass., 1988—. Assoc. editor Jour. Stone Disease; contbr. articles to Jour. AMA, So. Med. Jour., Jour. Urology, Urology, Urol. Clinics N.Am., Seminars in Interventional Radiology. Sec., pres. Omaha Symphony Assn., 1973-76; advisor United Arts Omaha, 1983-88. Recipient Outstanding Contbn. award dept. surgery U. Nebr. Med. Ctr., 1990. Fellow ACS; mem. AMa (del. med. staff sect. 1983-86), Am. Urol. Assn. (pres. South Cen. chpt. 1990-91, 1st prize 1976, best clin. exhibit award 1977, Gold Cane achievement award 2001), Am. Lithotripsy Soc. (pres. 1989-90), Alpha Omega Alpha (pres. 1991-92). Republican. Achievements include development of guidewire techniques for angiography and endourology, thermoplastic internal ureteral stent; description of benefits of hydrophilic polymers for endourologic devices. Office: The Urology Ctr 111 S 90th St Omaha NE 68114-3907 Office Phone: 402-397-9800, 402-680-3553. Personal E-mail: hkmardis@cox.net.

**MARDUEL, ALIX,** venture capitalist; MD, U. Paris. Med. residency, Paris; postdoctoral fellowship U. Calif., San Francisco, Stanford U.; assoc. med. dir. ICI Pharma (now AstraZeneca), France, England; gen. ptnr. Sofinnova Ventures, 1990—97; mng. dir. Alta Partners, San Francisco, 1997—. Bd. dirs. Cytos Biotechnology, 2000—, Corcept Therapeutics, 2001—, Syntonix, 2002—, NeurogesX, Metabolex, Inc., Genteric, Memory Pharm.; actively involved with the creation of several life sci. co. in the US and Europe, including Millennium Pharm., CV Therapeutics, Medicine Co., Genset & Aviaron. Office: Alta Partners One Embarcadero Ctr Ste 4050 San Francisco CA 94111

**MARECEK, JEANNE,** psychologist, educator; b. Berwyn, Ill., May 28, 1946; d. Frank J. and Josephine (Serio) M. BS, Loyola U., Chgo., 1968; MS, Yale U., 1971, PhD, 1973. From asst. prof. to prof. psychology Swarthmore (Pa.) Coll., 1972—, chmn. dept., 1986—91, 1994—95, 1998—99, head women's studies program, 1996—99. Fulbright sr. lectr., Sri Lanka, 1988. Co-author: Making a Difference: Psychology and the Construction of Gender; contbr. numerous articles to profl. jours. and chpts. to books. Bd. dirs. Women in Transition, Phila., 1980-86; vice patron Nest, Hendala, Sri Lanka, 1995—; bd. dirs. Women's Therapy Ctr., Phila., 1996-2004, CHOICE, Phila., 2006—. Fellow Swedish Collegium for Advanced Study in Social Scis., 1997; various fed. research grants. Mem. APA, Assn. for Asian Studies, Am. Inst. Sri Lanka Studies (sec. 1995-2000, pres. 2001—), Am. Overseas Rsch. Ctrs. (mem. exec. coun.). Office: Swarthmore Coll Dept Psychology 500 College Ave Swarthmore PA 19081-1306 Business E-Mail: jmarece1@swarthmore.edu.

**MARÉE, KATHLEEN NANCY,** retired language educator; b. Belleville, NJ, Nov. 8, 1942; d. Jacobus and Marie Theresa (Lilore) Marée. BA, Rutgers U., Newark, N.J., 1965; MA in Tchg. magna cum laude, Fairleigh Dickinson U., Rutherford, N.J., 1970. Elem. French tchr. Freehold (N.J.) Elem. Schs., 1965—66, River Edge (N.J.) Elem. Schs., 1966—71, dept. head and fgn. langs. in elem. sch. rep.; elem. French tchr. Hanahouli Elem. Sch., Honolulu, 1971—73; pub. rels. coord. Oceanic Cablevision, Honolulu, 1974—75; pub. rels. rep., adminstrv. asst. Hawaii State Legis., Honolulu, 1975; ESL instr., head tchr., asst. coord. New Intensive Course in English program U. Hawaii at Manoa, Honolulu, 1976—79; founder, pres., dir. Lang. Inst. Hawaii, Honolulu, 1979—86; advisor, coord. study cultural tours Internat. Pacific Asian Consortium, Honolulu, 1979—86; ESL instr. Fairleigh Dickinson U., Seton Hall U., Rutgers U., NJ, 1987—89; ESL lectr. and adj. Bergen CC, Paramus, NJ, 1989—2000. Pub. rels. Fgn. Lang. Elem. Sch., 1966—71; chairperson N.J. Assn. Tchrs. Fgn. Langs. Elem. Sch., 1970—71. ESL tchr., coord. employment Vietnamese Immigrant Vol. Assistance, Honolulu, 1975; mem., ESL sponsor CIVITAN, Honolulu, 1980—86. Grantee, East-West Ctr.-Culture Learning Inst., 1975—76. Avocations: reading, oil painting.

**MAREINISS, DARREN PETER,** lawyer, physician; b. Hoboken, N.J., Nov. 15, 1972; s. Martin Charles Mareiniss and Jeanette Schwarz Young; m. Alexandra Morgan, Aug. 16, 1997. AB cum laude, Dartmouth Coll., Hanover, N.H., 1994; MD, NYU Sch. Medicine, N.Y.C., 1999; JD, U. Pa., Phila., 2005. Law medicine/surgery N.Y., 2000, N.J., 2003, instr. advanced trauma and life support ACS, 2005. Surg. intern NYU Med. Ctr./Bellevue Hosp., N.Y.C., 1999—2001; surg. resident U. Tex. Southwestern Med. Ctr., Dallas 2001—02; med. staff Gracie Sq. Hosp., N.Y.C., 2002—03; cons. Woodcock Washburn, LLP, Phila., 2003; assoc. atty. Bickel & Brewer, Dallas 2004—; sr. legal and med. advisor U. Md. Ctr. for Health and Homeland Security, 2006—. Lectr. Tex. Back Inst., Bioethics and Trauma. Contbr. articles to medical and legal jours. Recipient Letters Academic citation, Dartmouth Coll., 1991—93, N.Y. U. Sch. Medicine, 1996; Jaqua scholarship, Dartmouth Coll., 1993. Mem.: AMA, Am. Coll. Legal Medicine (mem. bioethics com 2004—, mem. grad. com. 2004—), Alpha Omega Alpha. Achievements include research in genetics and bioethics. Home: 3432 Mount Vernon Way Plano TX 75025 Office: Bickel & Brewer 4800 Bank One Ctr 1700 Main St Dallas TX 75201 Home Fax: 214-653-1015; Office Fax: 214-653-1015. Personal E-mail: dpmmd@sbcglobal.net. E-mail: dzm@bickelbrewer.com.

**MAREK, JOYCELYN,** publishing executive; m. Andrew Marek; children: Allison, Matthew. BBA, U. Houston, 1978; postgrad., Northwestern U., 1996, Hearst Mgmt. Inst., 1997-98. Rsch. analyst Houston Chronicle, 1978, chief analyst, 1978-84, asst. rsch. mgr., 1984-85, rsch. mgr., 1985-88, display advt. dir., 1988-90, mktg. dir., 1990-95, v.p. mktg. and electronic products, 1995—. Bd. dirs., exec. com. Sheltering Arms; mem. mktg. com. Houston Symphony; former bd. dirs. Houston Advt. Fedn. Mem. Am. Mktg. Assn. (edn./intern chair, past pres. Houston chpt.), Newspaper Assn. Am. (former chair market devel. and promotion coun.). Avocations: tennis, reading, golf. Office: Houston Chronicle PO Box 4260 Houston TX 77210-4260

**MARELLA, PHILIP DANIEL,** broadcasting company executive; b. Italy, Sept. 9, 1929; came to U.S., 1930; s. T. Joseph and Julia (Santolina) M.; m. Lucinda Minor, Dec. 30, 1955; children: Philip Daniel, Laura Ann, William Scott. BS, Calif. State U., 1955; MS, Syracuse U., 1956. Account exec. WGR-TV, Buffalo, 1956-57; account exec., sales mgr. WIIC-TV, Pitts., 1957-66; gen. mgr. WCHS-TV, Charleston, W.va., 1966-68; v.p. radio and television Rollins, Inc., Atlanta, 1968-70; pres. WAVY-TV, Inc., Tidewater, Va., 1970—; v.p. ops. Lin Broadcasting, Inc., N.Y.C.; also dir.; pres., owner WMGC-TV, Binghamton, NY, 1978-86; CEO, pres. Pinnacle Comm., Inc., 1987—. CEO Pinnacle Broadcasting Co., 1987; owner radio stas. WFXC-FM, WDUR, WFXK, Raleigh, N.C., WRNS-AM-FM, WANG-FM, WMSQ-AM, WERO-FM, WCPQ, WDLX-AM, Coastal, N.C., WKOO-FM, WKJA-FM, Jacksonville, N.C., WYAV-FM, WRNN-FM, WMYB-FM, WYAK-FM, Myrtle Beach, S.C., KLLL-AM-FM, KONE-FM, KMMX-FM, Lubbock, Tex., WYNG-FM, Evansville, Ind., WSOY-AM-FM, WDZQ-FM, WDZ-AM, WCZQ-FM, Decatur, Ill., WPXX-FM, Danville, Va.; bd. dirs. Radio Advt. Bur., N.C. Assn. Broadcasters. Bd. dirs. Salvation Army, 1966-68; bd. dirs., v.p. United Fund; bd. dirs. Portsmouth chpt. ARC, Tidewater Regional Health and Planning Commn.; bd. dirs., v.p. Binghamton Symphony. Served with USMC, 1948-49, 50-52. Mem. Nat. Assn. Broadcasters (v.p., radio advt. bd. dirs.), Va. Assn. Broadcasters, N.C. Assn. Broadcasters (bd. dirs.), Nat. Adv. Bur. (bd. dirs.), Variety Club Pitts., Radio and TV Club, Portsmouth C. of C. (pres.-elect), Norfolk C. of C., Newport News C. of C., Cavalier Golf and Yacht Club (Virginia Beach, Va.), N.Y. Athletic Club, Binghamton Country Club, Boca Raton Club and Resort. Home: 2073 Cheshire Rd Binghamton NY 13903-3199 Address: 2924 S Ocean Blvd # A4 Boca Raton FL 33432

**MARGALITH, HELEN MARGARET,** retired librarian; b. N.Y.C., Nov. 19, 1914; d. Louis and Caroline (Stern) Fleischer; m. Aaron Margalith, Jan. 26, 1947 (dec.); children: Carol Lenore, Joan Louise. BA, Hunter Coll., 1936, MA, 1944; MLS, Columbia U., 1958. Editl. corr. Book of the Month Club, 1936-47; rschr. libr. N.Y.C. Bd. Edn., 1955-80; prof. pibr. Touro Coll., N.Y.C., 1980-90; mentor in libr. Empire State Coll., SUNY, 1991—. Cons. in field. Fellow Royal Soc. Medicine (libr. com., gerontology com., history of medicine com.); mem. Ch. and Synagogue Libr. Assn. (book reviewer), Internat. Honor Soc. Women in Edn., Am. Geolinguistic Assn. (bd. dirs. 2003—), Am. Soc. Geolinguistics, Delta Kappa Gamma Democrat. Avocations: reading, travel, research. Home: 205 W End Ave Apt 25S New York NY 10023-4804

**MARGER, EDWIN,** lawyer; b. N.Y.C., Mar. 18, 1928; s. William and Fannie (Cohen) M.; m. Kaye Sanderson, Oct. 1, 1951; children: Shari Ann, Diane Elaine, Sandy Ben; m. L. Suzanne Smyth, July 5, 1968; 1 child, George Phinney; m. Mary Susan Hamel, May 6, 1987; 1 child, Charleston Faye. BA, U. Miami, 1951, JD, 1953. Bar: Fla. 1953, Ga. 1971, D.C. 1978. Pvt. practice, Miami Beach, Fla., 1953—67, Atlanta, 1971—90, Jasper, Ga., 1990—. Gen. counsel Physicians Nat. Risk Retention Group, 1988-91, Physicians Reliance Assn., 1988-91, Physicians Nat. Legal Def. Corp., 1988-91; spl. asst. atty. gen. Fla., 1960-61; atty., agt. Republic of Haiti, 1962-67, City of Port-au-Prince for Transp. and Housing, 1962, Dominican Republic for Trade and Industry, 1964-65; of counsel Richard Burns, Miami, 1967—. Contbr. articles to profl. jours. Tchr. Nat. Inst. Trial Advocacy; mem. Miami Beach Social Svc. Commn., 1957; chmn. Fulton County Aviation Adv. Com., 1980—; chmn. Pickens County Airport Adv. Com., 2004-06; trustee Forensic Scis. Found., 1984-88, v.p., 1986-88; lt. col., a.d.c. Gov. Ga., 1971-74, 80-84; col., a.d.c. Gov. La., 1977-87; Khan Bahador and mem. exiled King of Afghanistan Privy Coun., 1980—. With USAAF, 1946-47. Fellow Am. Acad. Forensic Scis. (chmn. jurisprudence sect. 1977-78, sec. 1976-77, bd. dirs. 1978-79, exec. com. 1983-86); mem. ATLA, ABA, Fla. Bar Assn. (exec. com. 1971-83, bd. govs. 1983-87, 90-94, exec. com. 1993-94), State Bar Ga. (chmn. sect. environ. law 1974-75, aviation law sect. 1978, bd. govs. 1999-2005, stds. of the profession com.), Ga. Trial Lawyers Assn., Nat. Assn. Criminal Def. Lawyers, Ga. Assn. Criminal Def. Lawyers, Am. Judicature Soc., Am. Arbitration Assn. (commn. panel 1978), Inter-Am. Bar Assn. (sr.), World Assn. Lawyers (founding), Lawyer-Pilots Bar Assn. (founding, v.p. 1959-62), VFW, Rotary, Lions, Navy League, U.S. Naval Inst. Advocates Club, Lawyers Club Atlanta. Office: 44 N Main St Jasper GA 30143-1501 Office Phone: 706-253-3060. Personal E-mail: admin@edmarger.com.

**MARGESON, THEODORE EARL,** judge; b. New Glasgow, NS, Can., Aug. 15, 1938; children: Theodore Jason, Mark Andrew Earl. BA, Mt. Allison U., Sackville, NB, Can., 1959, BEd, 1960; LLB, Dalhousie U., Halifax, NS, 1965. Barrister, solicitor, notary pub. Tchr. Shelburne HS, NS, 1960—61, New Glasgow HS, 1961-62; barrister, solicitor New Glasgow and Toronto, Ont., 1965-90; judge Tax Ct. of Can., Ottawa, 1990—. Bd. dirs. NS Legal Aid. Recipient Confedn. medal Govt. of Can., 1992; Jubilee medal, 2003. Mem. Can. Judges Conf., NS Barrister's Soc. (mem. of coun.), Continuing Legal Edn. Soc. (dir.). Avocations: golf, hockey, squash. Office: Tax Ct of Can 200 Kent St 3d Fl Ottawa ON Canada K1A OM1 Office Phone: 613-992-1994.

**MARGETON, STEPHEN GEORGE,** law librarian; b. Elizabeth, N.J., Mar. 22, 1945; s. Louis George and Josephine A. (Bednarik) M.; m. Margaret Mary Salter, May 14, 1977; children: Catherine Ann, Elizabeth Ann AB Mt St Mary's Coll., 1967; JD, George Washington U., 1970; MSLS, Cath. U., 1973. Reference librarian Am.-Brit. law div. Library of Congress, Washington, 1968-72; law libr. Steptoe & Johnson, Washington, 1972-85; librarian Supreme Ct. of U.S., Washington, 1985-88; dir. Judge Kathryn J. DuFour Law Libr. The Cath. Univ. Am., 1988—. Instr. George Mason Law Sch., Arlington, Va., 1977-80. Mem. Am. Assn. Law Libraries, Internat. Assn. Law Libraries., Am. Soc. Internat. Law. Office: Cath U Am Judge Kathryn J DuFour Law Libr 3600 John Mccormack Rd NE Washington DC 20064-0001

**MARGIOTTA, JOSEPH M.,** printing company executive; b. Staten Island, N.Y., Aug. 14, 1973; s. Sam and Vickie Margiotta. Student, Union County Coll., N.J., 2001—. Pres. Paragon Forms and Paper Co., N.Y.C., 1992— Author poetry. Home: 1541 Cooper Rd Scotch Plains NJ 07076-2521

**MARGIOTTA, MARY-LOU ANN,** application developer; b. Waterbury, Conn., June 14, 1956; d. Rocco Donato and Louise Antoinette (Carosella) M. AS Gen. Edn., Mattatuck C.C., Waterbury, 1982; BSBA, Teikyo Post U., 1983; MS Computer Sci., Rensselaer Polytech. Inst., 1989. Programmer analyst Travelers Ins. Co., Hartford, Conn., 1985-87; sr. programmer analyst Conn. Bank and Trust Co., East Hartford, Conn., 1987-88; programmer analyst Ingersoll-Rand Corp., Torrington, Conn., 1990-91; sr. programmer analyst Orion Capital Cos. Inc., Farmington, Conn., 1991-92; pres., prin. software engr. A.M. Consultants, New Britain, Conn., 1992—. Pres. C++ Spl. Interest Group, 1995-96; bd. dirs. Object Oriented Users Group, 1995-96; tech. team leader Computer Scis. Corp., East Hartford, Conn., 1998-, Asnuntuck C.C., Enfield, Conn., 2003; adj. prof. Ctrl. Conn. State U., New Britain, 2000, New Eng. Tech. Inst., New Britain, Conn., 2002. Mem. social action com. St. Helena's Parish, West Hartford, Conn., 1988-95; advisor Jr. Achievement, Waterbury, 1981-83; tutor Traveler's Ins. Co. Tutorial Program, West Hartford, 1986-87; trainer CPR, ARC, Hartford, 1986-87; mem. Lang. and Cultural Adoptation Programs, Conn. and Mass., 1998— Clayborn Pell grantee Post Coll., 1982-83, State of Conn. grantee, 1982-83; recipient Citation, Jr. Achievement, 1982; Bd. Trustees scholar Post Coll., 1982-83. Mem. IEEE (chairwoman membership devel., Conn. chpt.), Am. Aculturation Assocs. (bd. dirs.), Toastmasters Internat., Tau Alpha, Beta Gamma. Roman Catholic. Avocations: european travel, gourmet cooking, reading, tennis, golf. Home: 210 Brittany Farms Rd Ste E New Britain CT 06053-1282 Office Phone: 860-229-3496. E-mail: raebedet@aol.com.

**MARGITIĆ, MILORAD R.,** language educator, researcher; b. Kragujevac, Serbia, June 6, 1934; arrived in USA, 1963; s. Radomir B. and Olga J. Margitić; m. Susan E. Kent, Oct. 5, 1969; children: Alexandra Margitic, Tatiana Margitic. MA Candidatus Degree, Univ. of Leiden, Leiden, the Netherlands, 1963; PhD French, Wayne State Univ., Detroit, Mich., 1971. Tchg. asst., instr., asst. prof. (French) Wayne State Univ., Detroit, 1963—72; asst. prof. (French) Univ. of Chgo., Chgo., 1972—78; asst. prof., assoc. prof., prof. (French) Wake Forest Univ., Winston-Salem, NC, 1978. Author: (book) Essai sur la mythologie du Cid, 1976, La Suivante, comédie, de Pierre Corneille, édition critique, 1978, La Galerie du Palais, ou l'amie rivale, comédie, de Pierre Corneille, édition critique, 1981, Corneille comique: Nine Studies of Pierre Corneille's Comedy with an Intro. and a Bibliography, 1982, Actes de Wake Forest/ procs. of the NASSCFL 19th Ann. Conf., 1987, Le Cid, tragi-comédie, de Pierre Corneille, édition critique, 1989, Cornelian Power Games: Variations on a Theme in Pierre Corneille's Theater from "Mélite" to "Polyeucte", 2002. Recipient Scholarship (full stipend), Universitair Asyl Fonds/ Holland, 1960—63, Outside evaluator in tenure and promotion cases, UCLA, Vassar Coll., U. Ga., Loyola U.; grantee Publ. Subsidy Grant, Univ. of Chgo., 1975. Democrat. Serbian Orthodox. Achievements include played the accordion professionally from 1950-1959 and semi-professionally from 1959-1972. Avocation: play accordion as a hobby. Office: Wake Forest Univ Dept of Romance Lang PO Box 7566 Winston Salem NC 27109 Home: 5435 Stone Crossing Dr Winston Salem NC 27104-3744

**MARGO, KATHERINE LANE,** family physician, educator; d. Warren Wilson and Virginia (Penney) Lane; m. Geoffrey Myles Margo, Apr. 20, 1980; 1 child, Benjamin stepchildren: Jenny, Judy. BA, Swarthmore Coll., 1974; MD, SUNY Health Sci. Ctr. Syracuse, 1978. Cert. in family medicine. Resident physician St. Joseph's Hosp., Syracuse, 1979-82; attending physician Health Svcs. Assn., Syracuse, 1982-90, asst. med. dir. for quality assurance, 1985-90; asst. prof. family medicine SUNY-HSC at Syracuse, 1990-94; mem. residency faculty Harrisburg (Pa.) Hosp., 1994-2000; med. dir. Harrisburg Kline Family Practice Ctr., 1996-2000; assoc. residency dir. Harrisburg Family Practice Residency, 1997-2000; predoctoral dir. Dept. Family Practice Cmty. Medicine U. Pa., 2000—, asst. prof., assoc. dir. family practice residency, 2000—. Clin. assoc. prof. Allegheny Med. Sch., 1997—2000. Contbr. articles to profl. jours. Bd. trustees Pt. Choice, Syracuse, 1993—94; chair med. com. Planned Parenthood, Syracuse, 1984—94; bd. dirs. Planned Parenthood Susquehanna Valley, 1996—2000; active Friends of Chamber Music, Syracuse, 1985—94; keyboard player Old World folk Band. Recipient Exemplary Tchg. award, Pa. Acad. of Family Practice, 2003, Penn Pearls Tchg. award, U. Pa. Sch. Medicine, 2004. Mem.: Am. Acad. Family Practitioners (v.p. Syracuse chpt.), Soc. Tchrs. of Family Medicine (chair group on predoctoral edn. 2003—04). Democrat. Avocations: music, theater, gardening, birdwatching. Home: 426 Carpenter Ln Philadelphia PA 19119-3040 Office: Univ Pa Dept Family Practice Community Medicine 2 Gates 3400 Spruce St Philadelphia PA 19104 Office Phone: 215-662-8777. E-mail: margok@uphs.upenn.edu.

**MARGO, ROD DAVID,** lawyer; b. Johannesburg, Republic of South Africa, Feb. 14, 1950; came to U.S., 1978; s. Cecil Stanley and Marguerite Giselle (Polné) M. BCom, U. Witwatersrand, 1970, LLB cum laude, 1973; D.Civil Laws, McGill U., 1979. Bar: Ga. 1979, Calif. 1981, DC 1996, solicitor, NSW, Australia, 2004. From assoc. to ptnr. Condon & Forsyth, L.A., 1980—. Lectr. aviation law UCLA, 1981-98; adj. prof. law Inst. Air and Space Law, Montreal, Can. Author: Aviation Ins. 3d edit., 2000; co-author: Shawcross & Beaumont on Air Law, 4th rev. edit., 2006. Fellow: Royal Aero. Soc.; mem.: L.A. County Bar Assn. Office: Condon & Forsyth 1901 Avenue Of The Stars Ste 850 Los Angeles CA 90067-6010 Office Phone: 310-557-2030. Business E-Mail: rmargo@condonlaw.com.

**MARGOLIASH, EMANUEL,** biochemist, educator; b. Cairo, Feb. 10, 1920; s. Wolf and Bertha (Kotler) M.; m. Sima Beshkin, Aug. 22, 1944; children: Reuben, Daniel. BA, Am. U., Beirut, 1940, MA, 1942, MD, 1945. Rsch. fellow, lectr., acting head cancer rsch. labs. Hebrew U., Jerusalem, 1945-58; rsch. fellow Molteno Inst. Cambridge (Eng.) U., 1951-53; Dazian fellow Nobel Inst., 1958; rsch. assoc. U. Utah, Salt Lake City, 1958-60, McGill U., Montreal, Que., Canada, 1960-62; rsch. fellow Abbott Labs., North Chicago, Ill., 1962-69, sr. rsch. fellow, 1969-71, head protein sect., 1962-71; prof. biochemistry and molecular biology Northwestern U., Evanston, Ill., 1971-90, prof. chemistry, 1985-90, Owen L. Coon prof. molecular biology, 1988-90, Owen L. Coon prof. molecular biology emeritus, 1990—; prof. biol. scis. U. Ill., Chgo., 1989—, coord. lab. for molecular biology, 1990-93. Mem. com. on cytochrome nomenclature Internat. Union Biochemistry, 1962-75; mem. adv. com. Plant Research Lab., Mich. State U./AEC, 1967-72; co-chmn. Gordon Research Conf. on Proteins, 1967 Editl. bd. Jour. Biol. Chemistry, 1966-72, Biochem. Genetics, 1966-80, Jour. Molecular Evolution, 1971-82, Biochemistry and Molecular Biology Internat., 1981-99, Jour. Protein Chemistry, 1982-86, Chemtracts, Biochem. Molecular Biology, 1990-99; contbr. over 280 articles and revs. to sci. jours. Rudi Lemberg fellow Australian Acad. Sci., 1981; Guggenheim fellow, 1983 Fellow Am. Acad. Arts and Scis., Am. Acad. Microbiology, Am. Inst. Chemists; mem. Nat. Acad. Scis., Biochem. Soc. (Keilin Meml. lectr. 1970), Harvey Soc. (lectr. 1970-71), Am. Soc. Biochem. Molecular Biology (publs. com. 1973-76), Am. Chem. Soc., Am. Soc. Microbiology, Can. Biochem. Soc. N.Y. Acad. Sci., Ill. Acad. Sci., Am. Soc. Naturalists, Sigma Xi (sat. lectr. 1972-73, 74-77). Home: 353 Madison Ave Glencoe IL 60022-1009 Office: Biochem istry Molecular & Cell Biology Hogan Hall 2-100 Northwestern U Evanston IL 60208-3500 Office Phone: 847-491-5620.

**MARGOLICK, DAVID,** journalist, writer; B. Univ. Mich.; JD, Stanford Univ. Legal reporter NY Times, NYC, 1981—86, nat. legal affairs editor, law columnist, 1987—94, bur. corr. San Francisco, 1994—96; contbg. editor Vanity Fair mag., NYC, 1996—. Author: Undue Influence: The Epic Battle for the Johnson & Johnson Fortune, 1993, At the Bar: The Passions and Peccadilloes of American Lawyers, 1996, Strange Fruit: Billie Holiday, Cafe Society, and an Early Cry for Civil Rights, 2000, Beyond Glory: Joe Louis vs. Max Schmeling, and a World on the Brink, 2005. Nominee Pulitzer prize (4 times). Office: Vanity Fair 4 Times Sq New York NY 10036*

**MARGOLIN, BRUCE M.,** lawyer; LLB, U. So. Calif., 1963, JD, 1966. Bar: Calif. 1967, U.S. Dist. Ct. 1967, Ct. Dist. Calif. 1971. Pvt. practice, W. Hollywood, Calif. Dir. Nat. Orgn. Reform Marijuana Laws. Contbr. articles to profl. jours. Elected to State Calif. Dem. Com. Recipient Cert. Appreciation, ACLU. Mem.: Nat. Assn. Criminal Def. Lawyers (co-chmn. ethics com.), Criminal Cts. Bar Assn., Century City Bar Assn. (Criminal Def. Atty of Yr. 1999). Ran for governor of California in the 2003 recall election; contributed to the development of the California Prop 215 Medical Marijuana Initiative. Office: 8749 Holloway Dr West Hollywood CA 90069 Office Phone: 310-276-2231. Office Fax: 310-652-1501. E-mail: bmargolin@aol.com.

**MARGOLIN, ERIC MITCHELL,** lawyer; b. NYC, Mar. 31, 1953; s. Benjamin and Muriel (Leibowitz) Margolin BA, SUNY, Buffalo, 1974; JD, Georgetown U., 1977. Bar: NY 1978. Staff atty. Met. Life Ins. Co., NYC, 1977-79; atty. Chesebrough-Pond's Inc., Greenwich, Conn., 1979—81, sr. atty., 1982—85; v.p., gen. counsel, sec., dir. Health-Tex Inc., NYC, 1985—92; v.p., gen. counsel, sec. The He-Ro Group Ltd., NYC, 1992—93; v.p., gen. counsel, sec. Tire Kingdom Inc. (now TBC Corp.), West Palm Beach, Fla., 1993—2000; sr. v.p., gen. counsel, sec. Advance Auto Parts Inc., Roanoke, Va., 2001—. Mem.: ABA. Office: Advance Auto Parts Inc 5673 Airport Rd Roanoke VA 24012 Office Phone: 540-561-3225. Business E-Mail: emargolin@advanceautoparts.com.

**MARGOLIN, HAROLD,** metallurgical educator; b. Hartford, Conn., July 12, 1922; s. Aaron David and Sonia (Krupnikoff) M.; m. Elaine Marjorie Rose, July 4, 1946; children: Shelley, Deborah, Amy. B in Engring., Yale U., 1943; M in Engring., Yale Univ., 1947, DEng, 1950. Rsch. assoc./scientist divsn. rsch. NYU, N.Y.C., 1949-56, assoc. prof. metall. engring., 1956-62, prof., 1962-73; prof. phys. metallurgy Poly. U. N.Y., Bklyn., 1973-93, disting. rsch. prof., 1993—2003, 2004—05. Theodore W. Krengel vis. prof. Technion, Haifa, Israel, 1983; cons. in field. Contbg. author books; contbr. articles to profl. publs.; patentee in field. With USNR, 1944-46. Fellow Am. Soc. Metals (edn. award N.Y. chpt. 1967); mem. Metall. Soc. (honoree symposium in his name San Francisco 1994), ASM Internat., TMS. Democrat. Jewish. Home: 81 Stony Run New Rochelle NY 10804-3415 Personal E-mail: hmemxox@aol.com. *Achievement, work, and refusal to accept defeat are intimately intertwined.*

**MARGOLIN, JEAN SPIELBERG,** artist; b. NYC, Oct. 12, 1926; d. Jack and Ida (Grossman) Spielberg and Bess Liebowitz Spielberg (stepmother); m. Paul Margolin, May 19, 1946 (dec. Mar. 1989). Student, Ind. U., 1951-55, Skowhegan Sch. Painting/Sculp., 1954. Tchr. painting and drawing Ind. U., Bloomington, 1954-55; curator group show Pace U. Gallery, N.Y.C., 1984. Paintings exhibited John Herron Art Mus., Indpls., 1952-55, J.B. Speed Art Mus., Louisville, 1953, Cin. Mus. Art, 1955, L.A. County Mus. Art, 1956, A.C.A. Gallery, N.Y.C., 1959-60, Pa. Acad. Fine Arts, Phila., 1962, Heckscher Mus., Huntington, N.Y., 1964, Skowhegan Benefit Exbhn., Nat. Arts Club, N.Y.C., 1974, Arthouse, Storrs, Conn., 1979, Landmark Gallery, N.Y.C., 1980-82, Pace U. Gallery, N.Y.C., 1980, 84, The Artists Choice Mus., Alex Rosenberg Gallery, N.Y.C., 1983; paintings exhibited by appointment only, N.Y.C., 1985—. Recipient 1st prize purchase award for painting Skowhegan Sch. Painting and Sculpture, 1954, scholar, 1954. Home: 4 Washington Square Vlg Apt 12S New York NY 10012-1908

**MARGOLIN, LEON,** physician; BA with high honors, BSc with high honors, Bar-Ilan Univ., Israel, 1994; MD, Hebrew Univ Hadassah Med. Sch., 2002; PhD, Hebrew Univ. Hadassah Med. Sch., 2002. Internship Staten Island Univ. Hosp., 2002; physician AECOM, Bronx, NY, 2003—. Contbr. scientific papers. Recipient Kaye Prize, 1999, Pratt Found. award, 2001; scholar Scholarship of Dean of Students, Bar-Ilan Univ., 1991—94, Scholarship for MD/PhD program, Hadassah Med. Sch.-Hebrew Univ., 1994—99. Jewish. Achievements include patents for mask for headache relief. Avocations: reading, travel. Home: 3450 Wayne Ave Apt 10A Bronx NY 10467

**MARGOLIN, PHILLIP MICHAEL,** lawyer; b. NYC, Apr. 20, 1944; s. Joseph Harold and Eleonore (Leftcourt) M.; m. Doreen Stamm, Dec. 22, 1968; children: Daniel Scott, Ami Elaine. BA, Am. U., Washington, 1965; JD, NYU, 1970. Bar: Oreg. 1972, U.S. Dist. Ct. Oreg. 1973, U.S. Ct. Appeals (9th cir.) 1974, U.S. Supreme Ct. 1977. Tchr. N.Y.C. Pub. Schs., 1968-70; law clk. to chief judge Oreg. Ct. Appeals, Salem, 1970-71; dep. dist. atty., spl. agt. Multnomah County, Portland, Oreg., 1971-72; pvt. practice Portland, 1973, 80-86; ptnr. Nash & Margolin, Portland, 1977-80, Margolin & Margolin, Portland, 1986—. Lectr. in field. Author: Heartstone, 1978, The Last Innocent Man, 1981, Gone But Not Forgotten, 1994, Heartstone, 1995, After Dark, 1995, The Burning Man, 1996, Wild Justice, 2000, The Associate, 2001, Ties That Bind, 2003, Sleeping Beauty, 2004, Lost Lake, 2005, numerous short stories; contbr. articles to profl. jours. Vol. Peace Corps., Liberia, 1965-67; coach Hayhurst Elem. Chess Team, Portland, 1981—. Mem. Oreg. Criminal Def. Lawyers Assn., Oreg. State Bar Assn. Democrat. Jewish. Avocations: chess, writing, swimming. Office: Margolin & Margolin 621 SW Morrison St Ste 1025 Portland OR 97205-3813*

**MARGOLIN, ROBERT JEREMY,** lawyer; b. Kansas City, Mo., Mar. 21, 1935; s. Abraham Eugene and Florence Margolin; m. Dorothy Ann Macy, Sept. 20, 1959; 1 child, Kathryn R. Margolin Richter. BA, Dartmouth Coll., 1957; JD, LLB, U. Mich., 1960. Bar: Mo. U.S. Ct. Appeals (8th cir.). Ptnr. Margolin and Kirwan, Kansas City, Mo.—. Bd. dirs. Kansas City Kings, Feld Leasing. Asst. editor Mich. Law Rev. Bd. dirs. Menorah Med. Ctr., Kansas City, Kansas City Philharm. Assn.; mem. exec. com. Jewish Vocat. Svc., Kansas City. Mem. ABA, Nat. Basketball Assn. (bd. govs.), Mo. Bar Assn., Kansas City Bar Assn. Avocations: golf, skiing. Home: 1628 River Ridge Williamsburg VA 23185-7546 E-mail: bobj757@aol.com.

**MARGOLIN, SOLOMON BEGELFOR,** pharmacologist, consultant; b. Phila., May 16, 1920; s. Nathan and Fannie (Begelfor) M.; m. Gerda Levy, Jan. 17, 1947 (div. Feb. 1985); children: David, Bernard, Daniel; m. Nancy A. Cox, Apr. 30, 1987. BSc, Rutgers U., 1941, MSc, 1943, PhD, 1945. Asst. Rutgers U., New Brunswick, NJ, 1943-45; rsch. biologist Silmo Chem. Co., Vineland, NJ, 1947-48; rsch. pharmacologist Schering Corp., Bloomfield, NJ, 1948-52, dir. pharmacology dept., 1952-54; chief pharmacologist Maltbie Labs., Belleville, NJ, 1954-56, Wallace Labs, Carter-Wallace, Inc., Cranbury, NJ, 1956-60, dir. pharmacology dept., 1960-64, v.p. biol. rsch., 1964-68; pres. AMR Biol. Rsch., Inc., Princeton, NJ, 1968-78; from prof., chmn. pharmacology dept. to emeritus prof. St. George's (Grenada) U. Sch. Medicine, 1978—; pres. MARNAC, Inc., Dallas, 1990—. Author: Harper's Handbook Therapeutic Pharmacology, 1981; author: (with others) Physiological Pharmacology, 1963, World Review, Nutrition and Dietetics, 1980; contbr. more than 100 articles to profl. jours. Mem. AAAS, Endocrino Soc., Am. Chem. Soc., Soc. Exptl. Biology and Medicine, Am. Soc. Pharmacology and Exptl. Therapeutics, N.Y. Acad. Scis., Drug Information Assn. Achievements include over 40 U.S., European, and Japanese patents for prevention and treatment of fibrotic lesions, multiple sclerosis and other neurodegenerative disorders; research in anti-histamines anti-cholinergics, endorphins, sedative-hypnotics, tranquilizers, muscle relaxants, glucocorticoids, cardiovascular agents, anti-inflammatory drugs, anti-fibrotic agents, multiple sclerosis agents. Home: 6723 Desco Dr Dallas TX 75225-2704 E-mail: marnacinc@aol.com.

**MARGOLIS, BERNARD ALLEN,** library administrator; b. Greenwich, Conn., Oct. 2, 1948; s. Sidney S. and Rose (Birkenfeld) M.; m. Amanda Batey, Nov. 2, 1973. BA in Polit. Sci., U. Denver, 1970, MLS, 1973; Doctorate (hon.), Wentworth Inst. Tech., 1999. Cert. libr., Mich. Life. asst. Denver Pub. Libr., 1970-72; br. head Virginia Village Libr., Denver Pub. Libr., 1972-73; dep. dir. Monroe County Libr. Sys., Mich., 1973-75; dir. Raisin Valley Libr. Sys., Monroe, 1976-88, Pikes Peak Libr. Dist., Colorado Springs, Colo., 1988-97; pres. Colo. Ctr. for Books, 1989-92, Colo. Ctr. for the Book, 1993-97, Boston Pub. Libr., 1997—. Cons. in libr. pub. rels., 1976—; founding trustee United Colo. Investment Trust, 1993-95; chmn. Colo. Gov.'s Conf. on Libr. and Info. Svcs., 1990; lectr. Western Mich. U., Kalamazoo, 1978-81; appraiser rare books, Monroe, Colorado Springs, 1970—. Contbr. articles to profl. jours.; mem. editl. bd. Bottom Line Mag. Fin. Mgmt. for Librs., 1986—. Bd. dirs. Friends of the Book, Back Bay Assn., Monroe Sr. Citizens Ctr., 1976-80, Monroe Fine Arts Coun., 1978-81, Am. the Beautiful Centennial Celebration, Inc., 1993, Boston Libr. Consortium, 1993-97, Downtown Colorado Springs, Inc., 1994-97, Friends of Copley Sq., Care & Share, Inc., 1994-95, vice chmn., 1995, chmn., 1995-97; chmn. Blue Cross-Blue Shield Consumer Coun., Detroit, 1984-88; adv. bd. Access Colo. Libr. and Info. Network, 1991-97, Mercy Meml. Hosp., Monroe, 1984-86, 5th Congl. Art Competition Com., 1992-97; Dem. candidate for Mich. Senate, 1986; allocations com. Pikes Peak United Way, 1988-91, chmn., 1990-91, bd. dirs., 1990-91; chmn. Great Pikes Peak Cowboy Poetry Gathering, 1990-92, 94-96; del. White House Conf. on Libr. and Info. Scis.; mem. El Paso County, Colo. Retirement Bd., 1995-97, sec., 1996-97; fellow Boston Found., 1998—; overseer Hancock Shaker Village, Pittsfield, Mass., 1999—; leadership mgmt. com. Assn. Rsch. Librs., 2003—. Recipient Mayoral Cert. Commendation award Denver, 1972, 73; named Mich. Libr. of Yr., 1985, Colo. Libr. of Yr., 1990, commendation John F. Kennedy Ctr. for Performing Arts, 1993, Frank Waters award Pikes Peak Writer's Conf., 1996. Mem.: ALA (cons. ann. swap and shop 1979—84, governing coun. 1982—; endowment trustee 1989—93, chmn. resolutions com. 1991—92, sr. endowment trustee 1993—2001, John Cotton Dana award 1977, 1991, Libr. Awareness Idea Search award Washington 1982), Pub. Libr. Assn., Libr. Adminstrv. Mgmt. Assn., Colo. Libr. Assn. (legis.com., Intellec-

tual Freedom award 1993), Internat. Fedn. Libr. Assns. and Instns., New Eng. Libr. Assn., Mass. Libr. Assn. Democrat. Jewish. Office: Boston Pub Libr Copley Sq 700 Boylston St Boston MA 02116 Office Phone: 617-536-5400 x4475. Business E-Mail: bmargolis@bpl.org.

**MARGOLIS, BRUCE LEWIS,** human resources executive; b. Bklyn., Nov. 16, 1944; s. Laurance Nathan and Augusta Margolis; m. Simone Braipson, Aug. 11, 1974; children: Mathew, Jessie Lara. BS, Bklyn. Coll., 1965; MA, Western Res. U., 1967; PhD, Case Western Res. U., 1970. Human resource dir. Jewel Food Stores, Melrose Park, Ill., 1978-80; v.p. human resources Jewel Cos., Chgo., 1980-84; dir. human resources devel. Household Merchandising, Des Plaines, Ill., 1984-86; v.p. human resources TJ Maxx, Framingham, Mass., 1986-95; sr. v.p. human resources The Marmaxx Group, Framingham, 1995; exec. v.p., chief human resources officer TJX Cos., Inc., 2002—. Corp. psychologist Jewel Cos. Inc., Chgo., 1974-78; sect. chief NIOSH, Cin., 1971-74; psychophysiologist Bur. of Occpl. Safety and Health, USPHS, 1970-71; staff psychologist Psychol. Resource Svcs., Cleve., 1968-70. Co-author: Managers Guide to Developing Subordinate Managers, 1980; editor: The Human Side of Accident Prevention, 1975. Bd. dirs. Metro West YMCA, Framingham, 1997-98, Employers Against Domestic Violence, 1997-2000. Avocation: tennis. Office: TJX Cos Inc 770 Cochituate Rd Framingham MA 01701 Office Phone: 508-390-1000.

**MARGOLIS, DANIEL HERBERT,** lawyer; b. 1926; s. Morris Abraham and Miriam M.; m. Anabel Tendler, Dec. 23, 1951 (dec.); children: Peter, Beth, Laura, James; m. Sidney Millman Moore, Feb. 5, 1983. BA, Johns Hopkins U., 1948; LLB, Harvard U., 1951. Bar: DC 1951, U.S. Supreme Ct. 1959. Atty. adv. Office Price Stblzn., Washington, 1951-52; trial atty. Antitrust divsn. Dept. Justice, Washington, 1952-56; sr. ptnr. Bergson, Borkland, Margolis & Adler, Washington, 1962—86, McGuire, Woods, Battle & Boothe, Washington, 1986-89, Patton, Boggs LLP, Washington, 1989—2001; sr. counsel DC Office of Corp. Counsel, 2001—03; prin. Law Offices of Daniel H. Margolis, 2003—. With USN, 1945—46. Fellow: ABA; mem.: Coll. Counsel. Arbitrators. Avocations: sailing, skiing, cooking.

**MARGOLIS, DAVID I(SRAEL),** industrial manufacturing executive; b. NYC, Jan. 24, 1930; s. Benjamin and Celia (Kosofsky) M.; m. Barbara Schneider, Sept. 7, 1958; children: Brian, Robert, Peter, Nancy. BA, CCNY, 1950, MBA, 1952; postgrad., NYU, 1952-55. Asst. treas. Raytheon Co., 1956-59; treas. IT&T, N.Y.C., 1959-62; with Coltec Industries Inc., N.Y.C., 1962-95, pres., 1968-91, CEO, 1984-95, chmn. bd. dirs., 1985-95; chmn. exec. com., 1995-99. Mem. bd. trustees NY Presbyn. Hosp.; bd. overseers NYU Stern Sch. Bus. Mem.: Coun. Fgn. Rels.

**MARGOLIS, EMANUEL,** lawyer, educator; b. Bklyn., Mar. 18, 1926; s. Abraham and Esther (Levin) Margolis; m. Edith Cushing (div.); m. Estelle Thompson, Mar. 1, 1959; children: Elizabeth Margolis-Pineo, Catherine, Abby Margolis Newman, Joshua, Sarah Margolis Marsh. BA, U. N.C., 1947; MA, Harvard U., 1948, PhD, 1951; JD, Yale U., 1956. Bar: Conn. 1957, U.S. Dist. Ct. Conn. 1958, U.S. Supreme Ct. 1969. Instr. dept. govt. U. Conn., 1951-53; assoc. Silberberg & Silverstein, Ansonia, Conn., 1956-60, Wofsey Rosen Kweskin & Kuriansky, Stamford, Conn., 1960-96, ptnr., 1966-96, of counsel, 1996—. Arbitrator State of Conn., 1984—85; adj. prof. Quinnipiac U. Sch. Law, 1986—. Sr. editor: Conn. Bar Jour., 1971—80, 1983—, editor-in-chief, 1980—83; contbr. articles to profl. jours. Nat. bd. dirs. ACLU, 1975—79; mem. Westport (Conn.) Planning and Zoning Commn., 1971—75; chmn. Conn. CLU, 1988—95, legal advisor, 1995—; mem. exec. com. Yale Law Sch., 2000—04. With U.S. Army, 1944—46. Decorated Purple Heart; recipient 1st award for Disting. Svc. to Conn. Bar, Conn. Law Tribune, 1987, Champion of Liberty award, Conn. Def. Lawyers Assn, 2004. Fellow: Conn. Bar Found. (James W. Cooper fellow 1996); mem.: ABA, Am. Arbitration Assn. (arbitrator 1998—, trial referee 1985—), Nat. Assn. Criminal Def. Lawyers, Conn. Bar Assn. (human rigts sect. 1970—73). Home: 72 Myrtle Ave Westport CT 06880-3512 Office Phone: 203-327-2300. Personal E-mail: emesq@optonline.net.

**MARGOLIS, GERALD JOSEPH,** psychiatrist, psychoanalyst; b. Bronx, N.Y., May 7, 1935; s. Max and Sophie (Siegel) M.; m. June Edelman Greenspan, July 13, 1976; children: David J., Peter S., Steven J. AB, U. Rochester, 1957; MD, U. Chgo., 1960; postgrad., Inst. Phila. Am. Psychoa., 1972. Diplomate in psychiatry Am. Bd. Psychiatry and Neurology. Intern to resident in psychiatry Upstate Med. Ctr. SUNY, Syracuse, 1960-64; instr. psychiatry, 1966-67; from instr. to clin. prof. psychiatry Med. Sch. U. Pa., Phila., 1967—. Practice medicine specializing in psychiatry and psychoanalysis, Cherry Hill, NJ; tng. and supervising analyst Inst. of the Psychoanalytic Ctr. Phila. Contbr. articles to profl. jours. Served with M.C., USAF, 1964-66. Mem.: AMA, Med. Socl N.J., Camden County Med. Soc., Psychoanalytic Ctr. Phila. (tng. and supervising analyst), Am. Psychiat. Assn., Am. Psychoanalytic Assn. (cert.), B'nai B'rith, Phi Beta Kappa. Office: One Mall Dr Ste 930 Cherry Hill NJ 08002-2194 Office Phone: 856-667-1055.

**MARGOLIS, JAY M.,** clothing executive; b. N.Y.C., Feb. 11, 1949; s. Mac and Sarah Margolis; m. Donna Brenda Polsky, June 12, 1972; children: Jared Michael, Stacey Allyse. BA, Queens Coll., N.Y.C., 1971. Asst. mdse. mgr. Manhattan Shirt Co., N.Y.C., 1972-74; mdse. mgr. Arrow Shirt Co., N.Y.C., 1974-78; pres. Yves St. Laurent-Biderman Inc., N.Y.C., 1978-81, Ron Chereskin div. Cluett Peabody, N.Y.C., 1981-83, Claiborne Mens-Liz Claiborne Inc., N.Y.C., 1983-86; group pres., exec. v.p. corp. Liz Claiborne Inc., N.Y.C., 1986-88, vice chmn., 1988—92; pres., vice chmn. Tommy Hilfiger, 1992—95; chmn., CEO Esprit de Corp., 1995—99, E7th.com, 1999—2001; pres. splty. bus. group Reebok Internat. Ltd., 2001, pres., COO, 2001—04; group pres. apparel Limited Brands, Inc., 2005—. Mem. bd. Fathers Day/Mothers Day Coun. Mem. City Athletic Club. Avocations: skiing, swimming, tennis, environmental studies. Office: Limited Brands Inc 3 Limited Pkwy Columbus OH 43216

**MARGOLIS, JULIUS,** economics professor; b. NYC, Sept. 26, 1920; s. Sam and Fannie (Weiner) Margolis; m. Doris Lubetsky, Oct. 30, 1942; children: Jane S., Carl W. BSS, CCNY, 1941; PhM in Econs, U. Wis., 1943; MPA in Econs, Harvard, 1947, PhD, 1949. Instr. econs. Tufts Coll., 1947-48 asst. prof. econs. and planning U. Chgo., 1948-51; asst. prof. econs Stanford (Calif.) U., 1951-54; prof. econs. and engring. econ. systems, 1964-69; prof. bus administrn. U. Calif., Berkeley, 1954-64, prof. econs. Irvine, 1976—; prof., dir. Fels Ctr. Govt. U. Pa., 1969-76. Cons. govt. and industry, 1958—; dir. Ctr. Global Peace and Conflict Studies, 1985—. Author (with others): The Public Economy of Urban Communities, 1965, The Northern California's Water Industry, 1966, Public Economics, 1969, Public Expenditure and Policy Analysis, 1984; contbr. articles to profl. jours. With U.S. Army, 1943—46. Mem.: Royal Econ. Soc., Am. Econ. Assn. Home: 45 Whitman Ct Irvine CA 92617-4059 Office: U Calif Dept Econ Irvine CA 92697-0001 Office Phone: 949-854-3911. Business E-Mail: jmargoli@uci.edu.

**MARGOLIS, LAWRENCE STANLEY,** federal judge; b. Phila., Mar. 13, 1935; m. Doris May Rosenberg, Jan. 30, 1960; children: Mary Aleta, Paul Oliver. BSME, Drexel U., 1957; JD, George Washington U., 1961. Bar: D.C. 1963. Patent examiner US Patent Office, Washington, 1957-62; patent counsel Naval Ordnance Lab., White Oak, Md., 1962-63; asst. corp. counsel Washington, 1963-66; atty. criminal div., spl. asst. U.S. atty. US Dept. Justice, Washington, 1966-68, asst. US atty. DC, 1968-71; US magistrate judge US Dist. Ct., Washington, 1971-82; judge US Ct. Fed. Claims, Washington, 1982—97, sr. judge, 1997—; chmn. task force on discovery reform US Claims Ct., Washington, chmn. alt. dispute resolution com. Space and Bldg. com., chmn. Ct. Security Com., mem. mgmt. com., mem. budget com. Judl. Ctr. Editor-in-chief The Young Lawyer, 1965-66, D.C. Bar Jour., 1967-73; bd. editors The Dist. Lawyer, 1978-82. Trustee Drexel U., 1983-89; bd. govs. George Washington U. Alumni Assn., 1978-85, 93-96. Recipient Contbn. award D.C. Jaycees, 1966, Svc. award Boy Scouts Am., 1970, Alumni Svc. award George Washington U., 1976, Disting. Alumni Achievement award George Washington U., 1985, Disting. Alumni Achievement award Drexel U.,

1988, Drexel 100 award, 1992, Alternative Dispute Resolution award Ctr. for Pub. Resources, 1988, Alternative Dispute Resolution Svc. award Ct. of Fed. Claims, 1996, Alumni Recognition award George Washington U., 1996. Fellow Inst. Jud. Adminstrn., Am. Bar Found.; mem. ABA (chmn. jud. adminstrn. divsn., Disting. Svc. award 1981), ABA Nat. Conf. Spl. Ct. Judges (chmn., Disting. Svc. award 1978), D.C. Jud. Conf., Bar Assn. D.C. (bd. dirs. 1970-72, jour. editor-in-chief, Chmn. of Yr. award, Contbn. award young lawyers sect. 1983), Fed. Bar Assn., George Washington U. Nat. Law Assn. (pres. D.C. chpt. 1974-76, nat. pres. 1983-84), Univ. Club., Rotary (bd. dirs. Washington 1984-90, pres. 1988-89, dist. gov. 1991-92, Rotarian of Yr. 1984, Rotary Internat. Rep. to the World Bank and Orgn. of Am. States, 1998-99, pres. Rotary Found. 1999-00, Rotarian of the Decade 2005), Charles Fahy Am. Inn of Ct. (Nat. Program award, 1997), Phila. Cen. High Sch. Alumni (bd. mgrs. 2001-05). Office: US Ct Fed Claims 717 Madison Pl NW Ste 703 Washington DC 20005

**MARGOLIS, MARK NEAL,** actor; b. Phila., Nov. 26, 1939; s. Isidore and Fanya (Fried) M.; m. Jacqueline Petcove, June 3, 1962; 1 child, Morgan. Studied with, Stella Adler, Lee Strasberg, Bill Hickey, Barbara Loden. Actor: (films) Short Eyes, 1977, Going in Style, 1979, Dressed to Kill, 1980, You Better Watch Out, 1980, The Avengin, 1982, Diner, 1982, Eddie Macon's Run, 1983, Scarface, 1983, Far From Poland, 1984, The Cotton Club, 1984, The Bedroom Windo, 1987, The Secret of My Succe$s, 1987, The Rosary Murders, 1987, White Hot, 1989, Glory, 1989, Tales from the Darkside: The Movie, 1990, Delta Force: The Colombian Connection, 1990, 1492: Conquest of Paradise, 1992, Where the Rivers Flow North, 1994, Ace Ventura: Pet Detective, 1994, Squanto: A Warrior's Tale, 1994, I Shot Andy Warhol, 1996, The Pallbearer, 1996, Absolute Power, 1997, Trouble on the Corner, 1997, Above Freezing, 1998, Pants on Fire, 1998, 18 Shades of Dust, 1999, The Thomas Crown Affair, 1999, Mickey Blue Eyes, 1999, End of Days, 1999, Flawless, 1999, Angela, 2000, Requiem for a Dream, 2000, Dinner Rush, 2000, Hannibal, 2001, The Tailor of Panama, 2001, Hard Ball, 2001, Bridget, 2002, Infested, 2002, Particles of Truth, 2003, 2BPerfectlyHonest, 2004, Hose of D, 2004, Stay, 2005, The Fountain, 2006, others; (TV series) The Guiding Light, 1994, Santa Barbara, 1990, Oz, 1998-99, (TV films) Muggable Mary, Street Cop, 1982, Rage of Angels, 1983, Doubletake, 1985, Almost Partners, 1987, Lady Mobster, 1988, Columbo: Columbo Cries Wolf, 1990, Descending Angel, 1990, Boss of Bosses, 2001, (Broadway prodns.) The World of Sholom Aleichem, Infidel Caesar); (off-Broadway prodns.) Three Americanisms, My Uncle Sam, Balm in Gilead, Hospitality, Child of the Clay Country, The Big Knife, others; (regional theatre) The Substance of Fire, Ghosts, Love Me or Leave Me, Once in a Lifetime, The Boys Next Door, A Shayna Maidel, Hunting Cockroaches, The Seagull, Split Decision, The Front Page, Broken Glass, Quills; TV guest appearances include Kojak, 1977, The Equalizer, 1986, 87, 88, Crime Story, 1987, Quantum Leap, 1989, Mancuso, FBI, 1990, Star Trek: The Next Generation, 1990, Jake and the Fatman, 1990, The Antagonists, 1991, Law & Order, 1992, 97, 2001, New York Undercover, 1994, Prince Street, 1997, 2000, Now and Again, 1999, 100 Centre Street, 2001, The Practice, 2002, Hack, 2002, Ed, 2003, 04, Sex and the City, 2004, Law & Order: Criminal Intent, 2004, Crossing Jordan, 2005. Office: HWA Talent Reps 220 E 23d St Ste 400 New York NY 10010

**MARGOLIS, NADIA,** language educator, translator, medievalist; b. Neuilly-sur-Seine, France, Apr. 27, 1949; came to U.S., 1950; d. Morton Margolis and Diane Seyfort-Ruegg Kensler; m. Peter Kenneth Marshall, May 23, 1984. BA, U. N.H., 1971; PhD, Stanford U., 1977. Lectr. in French Stanford (Calif.) U., 1976-77; editorial asst. Medieval Acad. of Am., Cambridge, Mass., 1977-78; asst. prof. in French Amherst (Mass.) Coll., 1978-85; assoc. prof. French U. Utah, Salt Lake City, 1985-89; rsch. assoc. Inst. Advanced Study in Humanities/U. Mass., Amherst, 1993—. Asst. coach Jr. World Cycling Championships, Trexlertown, Pa., 1978; adj. instr. French, U. Mass., 1992-93, vis. lectr. in comparative lit., 1993; panelist NEH, Washington, 1984, 86-87; cons. Garland Medieval Series, N.Y.C., 1992—, for composer Richard Einhorn, 1994, for Capella Films, 1994; rsch. profl. Ctr. Nat. Sci. Rsch., Paris, 1973—; vis. assoc. prof. French U. Calif., Santa Barbara, 2002, UCLA, 2003, U. Mass., 2005, Mt. Holyoke Coll., 2006; vis. prof French Mt. Holyoke Coll., 2006. Author: Joan of Arc in History, Literature and Film; co-author, co-editor: Christine de Pizan, 2000, Women in the Middle Ages: An Encyclopedia, 2004, co-translator: Book of the Duke of True Lovers, 1991. Author, panel mem. Bicycle Safety/Bike Path com., Amherst, 1984. Miner Crary fellow Amherst Coll., 1979, NEH Ind. fellow, 1981; Rsch. grant Am. Philos. Soc., 1982. Mem. Modern Lang. Assn., Soc. Rencesvals, Medieval Acad. of Am., Christine de Pizan Soc. (sec. 1991—, editor newsletter 1991-96), Internat. Courtly Lit. Soc. Democrat. Jewish. Avocations: bicycling, gardening, drawing, painting. Home: 75 Amherst Rd Leverett MA 01054-5402 Office Phone: 413-548-9721. Personal E-Mail: margolis@rcn.com.

**MARGOLIS, PHILIP MARCUS,** psychiatrist, educator; b. Lima, Ohio, July 7, 1925; s. Harry Sterling and Clara (Brunner) M.; m. Nancy Nupuf, July 26, 1959; children: Cynthia, Marc, David, Laurence. BA magna cum laude, U. Minn., 1945, MD, 1948. Diplomate Am. Bd. Psychiatry and Neurology, 1966 (examiner 1973—1999, 2003-), recert. com., 1998-2004. Intern Milw. County Hosp., 1948-49; resident VA Hosp. and U. Minn., 1949-52, Mass. Gen. Hosp. and Harvard U., Boston, 1952-54; instr. U. Minn., Milw., 1953-55; asst. prof. dept. psychiatry Med. Sch., U. Chgo., 1955-60, assoc. prof., 1960-66; prof. psychiatry Med. Sch. U. Mich., 1966—, prof. cmty. mental health, 1968—; prof. psychiatry emeritus L.S.A., 1997—, instr., 1977-97; chief psychiat. inpatient service U. Chgo. Hosps. and Clinics, 1956-66; dir. Civil Forensic Tng. Program, 1997—. Cons. Forensic Psychiat. Ctr., State of Mich., 1972—; coord. med. student edn. program, 1975-78, dir., 1978-82; cons. Turner Geriatric Clin., 1978-86, cons. Breast Cancer Clinic, 1988, Powertrain subs. Gen. Motors, 1984—, Dept. Mental Health, U.S. Dept. Justice; assoc. chief clin. affairs U. Mich. Hosps., 1981-85, chair legis. govt. com., 1996—, chmn. ethics com., profl. rev. com. PSRO Area VII, 1982-86, PROM, 2003—; mem. Mich. State Bd. Medicine, 1984-89, chmn. 1992-94, senate adv. com. Univ. Affairs., 1986-89; spl. com. on profl. conduct and ethics Fedn. of State Med. Bds., 1998—, Mich. del., 1988-96, FLEX Com. Nat. Bd. Med. Examiners, 1988-98; civil liberties bd. U. Mich., 1995-2004, chmn., 1996-2002, gen counsel adv. com., 2002—; dir. Civil Forensic Tng. Program, 1997—. Author: Guide for Mental Health Workers, 1970, Patient Power: The Development of a Therapeutic Community in a General Hospital, 1974; also articles.; cons. editor: Community Mental Health jour., 1967—. Recipient Commonwealth Fund fellow award, 1964, Career Svc. award, 1992, Resident Appreciation award, 1991. Fellow: Am. Coll. Psychiatrists (chmn. bylaws com. 1997—), Am. Psychiat. Assn. (life; chmn. membership com. 1979—83, coms. ethics com. 1983—86, trustee 1985—88, sec. 1989—91, chmn. ethics appeals bd. 1989—, cons. steering com. on practical guidelines 1991—, budget com. 1991—, mem. assembly 1992, exec. com. edn. and career devel. 1993—, pres. Lifers 1994—, recertification com. 1998—, mem. pub. funding com. 2001—, assembly rep. 2003—, newsletter editor 2003—, cons. mem. com. 2004—, mem. audit com. 2004—, annual Lifers award 1999); mem.: Am. Acad. Psychiatry and Law (com. on psychoanalytic edn. 1995—, edn. com. 1998, texas midwest chpt. 1998—2000, forensic tng. com. 2005—, pres. 2001—02), Am. Acad. Psychoanalysis, Mich. State Med. Soc. (bioethics com. 1989—, com. on med. licensure and discipline 1995—, legis. and evaluations com. 1995—, mental health liaison com. 1995—, liaison com. Gen. Motors 1998—, chair 2000—, chair com. on med. licensure and discipline 2000—), Mich. Psychiat. Soc. (pres. 1980—81, chmn. ethics com. 1983—86, resolutions officer student rights responsibilities 1996—, chmn. legislation and govt. com. 1996—, v.p. 2000—, chmn. nom. com. 2004, Career Achievement award 2000), Washtenaw County Med. Soc. (exec. coun. 1983—, chmn. ethics com. 1983—87, pres. 1987—88, editl. bd. 1995—, chair legis. comm. 1999—). Home: 228 Riverview Dr Ann Arbor MI 48104-1846 Office: 2101 Commonwealth Blvd Ste B Ann Arbor MI 48105-0722 Office Phone: 734-647-8762. Business E-Mail: margolis@umich.edu.

**MARGOLIS, SHERRY,** newscaster; m. Jeff Zaslow, 1987; children: Jordan, Alexandra, Eden. BA in English, SUNY, Buffalo. Anchor and reporter WKBW-TV, Buffalo; reporter WJBK-TV, Detroit, 1984—, anchor "In the News", co-anchor 5am and noon news. Named Best Newscast in Mich., AP, 1990; recipient Best News Anchor Emmys, NATAS, 1993, 1999, Emmy Reporting, 2002. Office: WJBK-TV FOX 2 PO Box 2000 Southfield MI 48037-2000

**MARGOLIS, SIMEON,** physician, educator; b. Johnstown, Pa., Mar. 29, 1931; s. Edward Charles and Bella (Kantor) M.; m. Mary Alice Kahl, May 29, 1954; children: Karen Ann Margolis Griswold, Susan, Amy Elizabeth Harden. BA, Johns Hopkins U., 1953, MD, 1957, PhD, 1964. Intern Johns Hopkins Hosp., Balt., 1957—58, asst. resident, 1958—59; sr. asst. surgeon USPHS, Bethesda, Md., 1959—61; rsch. fellow Johns Hopkins Sch. Medicine, Balt., 1961—64; chief resident Johns Hopkins Hosp., 1964—65; asst. prof. medicine and biol. chemistry Johns Hopkins Sch. Medicine, Balt., 1965—68, assoc. prof., 1968—77, prof., 1977—, assoc. dean acad. affairs, 1984—90, assoc. dean faculty affairs, 1990—92. Mem. metabolism study sect. NIH, Bethesda, 1971-75, mem. gen. clin. rsch. ctrs. com., 1976-80, mem. nat. diabetes bd., 1984-88; mem. endocrine and metabolic drugs adv. com. FDA, Rockville, Md., 1979-82. Editor Johns Hopkins Med. Letter Health After 50, 1991—; contbr. articles to profl. jours., chpts. to books. Pres. 3d Dist. Citizens, Balt., 1970. Sr. asst. surgeon USPHS, 1959-61. Nat. Heart Inst. grantee, 1965-85. Mem. Am Diabetes Assn., Endocrine Soc., Am. Soc. Clin. Investigation, Am. Soc. Biol. Chemists, Am. Inst. Nutrition, Am. Soc. Clin. Nutrition, Coun. Atherosclerosis Rsch. Avocations: tennis, stamps. Office: Johns Hopkins Hosp 1830 Bldg Rm 336 Baltimore MD 21287-0001 E-mail: smargoli@jhmi.edu.

**MARGOLIS, THOMAS IRA,** vitreoretinal ophthalmologist; s. Herbert and Barbara M.; m. Robin Deborah Small, Mar. 12, 1989; children: Rebecca, Joshua, Jennifer. BA summa cum laude, U. Pa., 1984; MD magna cum laude, Harvard U., 1989. Cert. Am. Bd. Ophthalmology. Intern Cedars Sinai Med. Ctr., L.A., 1989-90; resident Wills Eye Hosp., Phila., 1990-93; fellowship (vitreoretinal) Tufts U.-New Eng. Eye Ctr., Boston, 1993-95. Instr. ophthalmology Tufts U. Med. Sch., Boston, 1993-96; hosp. staff AtlantiCare Regional Med. Ctr., Shore Meml. Hosp., Somers Point, N.J. Contbr. sci. articles to profl. jours. and chpt. to book. Recipient Benjamin Franklin scholar U. Pa., 1980-84, Laurence B. Ellis scholar Harvard Med. Sch., 1987; named one of "Top Docs", N.J. Monthly, 2003, 05, 06, Phila. (Pa.) Mag., 2004, 05, 06, NJ Life, 2005. Mem. AMA, Am. Acad. Ophthalmology, N.J. Acad. Ophthalmology, N.J. Med. Soc., Atlantic County Med. Soc. (pres.-elect 2006), Wills Eye Hosp. Soc., N.J. Retina Soc., Am. Soc. Retina Specialists, Phi Beta Kappa. Jewish. Avocations: running, skiing, golf, tennis, travel. Office: Retinal and Ophthalmic Cons PC 1500 Tilton Rd Northfield NJ 08225-1827 also: 2466 E Chestnut Ave Vineland NJ 08360 also: Ste 102 211 S Main St Cape May Court House NJ 08210 Office Phone: 609-646-5200. E-mail: vitrector@aol.com.

**MARGOLIUS, HARRY STEPHEN,** pharmacologist, physician; b. Albany, N.Y., Jan. 29, 1938; s. Irving Robert and Betty (Zweig) M.; m. Francine Rockwood, May 22, 1964; children: Elizabeth Anne, Craig Matthew. BS, Union U., 1959, PhD, 1963, MD, U. Cin., 1968. Diplomate Nat. Bd. Med. Examiners, 1969, chmn. pharmacology test com., 1990-94. Intern, resident Harvard Med. Svc. Boston City Hosp., 1968-70, pharmcology rsch. assoc., 1970-72; sr. clin. investigator NHLBI NIH, Bethesda, 1972-74; assoc. prof. pharmacology, asst. prof. medicine Med. U. S.C., Charleston, 1974-77, prof. pharmacology, assoc. prof. medicine, 1977-80, prof. pharmacology, prof. medicine, 1980—, chmn. pharmacology, 1989—. Cons. NIH, FDA, VA, NSF, Washington, Bethesda, 1975—; mem. editorial bd. Am. Heart Assn., Dallas, 1980—. Editor: Kinins IV, 1986, Renal Function, Hypertension and Kallikrein-Kinin System, 1988; contbr. numerous articles to profl. jours. Commdr. USPHS, 1967-74. Recipient S.C. Gov.'s award for sci. S.C. Acad. Scis., 1988, Frey-Werle Commemorative medal for biomed. rsch., 1997; Burroughs-Wellcome scholar, 1976; vis. scholar U. Cambridge, Eng., 1980-81; sr. fellow Fitzwilliam Coll., 1996; NIH grantee, 1975—; named Theodore Cooper Meml. Lectr., 1995. Fellow Coun. for High Blood Pressure Rsch., Am. Heart Assn.; mem. Am. Soc. for Pharmacology and Exptl. Therapeutics, Am. Soc. for Clin. Investigation and 10 additional med., sci. socs. Jewish. Achievements include studies of the role of kallikreins and kinins in human and animal forms of hypertension; discovery of abnormalities which signify roles in causing high blood pressure. Office: Medical Univ SC Coll Medicine 171 Ashley Ave Charleston SC 29425-0001

**MARGON, BRUCE HENRY,** astrophysicist, educator; b. NYC, Jan. 7, 1948; s. Leon and Maxine E. (Margon) Siegelbaum; 1 dau., Pamela. AB, Columbia U., 1968; MA, U. Calif.-Berkeley, 1971, PhD, 1973. Asst. rsch. astronomer U. Calif.-Berkeley, 1973—76; assoc. prof. astronomy UCLA, 1976—80; prof. astronomy U. Wash., Seattle, 1980—2001, chmn., 1981—87, 1990—95, sci. dir. Sloan Digital Sky Survey, 1998—99; assoc. dir. Space Telescope Sci. Inst., Balt., 2001—. Bd. govs. Astrophys. Rsch. Consortium, Inc., Seattle; chmn. bd. dirs. AURA, Inc., Washington; co-investigator Hubble space telescope NASA, Washington, 1977—. NATO postdoctoral fellow, 1973-74; Sloan Found. rsch. fellow, 1979-83 Fellow AAAS, Am. Phys. Soc.; mem. Internat. Astron. Union, Am. Astron. Soc. (Pierce Prize 1981) Royal Astron. Soc. Office: Space Telescope Sci Inst 3700 San Martin Dr Baltimore MD 21218 Business E-Mail: margon@stsci.edu.

**MARGOSHES, MIRIAM KAGAN,** information specialist; b. Cambridge, Mass., Feb. 10, 1932; d. Baruch and Raizel (Rozinko) Kagan; m. Marvin Margoshes, Aug. 7, 1955; children: Bethia Anne, Sara Amy, Jessa Abi, Dan Raphael. BS, Simmons Coll., 1953; MS, CUNY, 1976. Cert. libr. media specialist, N Y Libr. aide Harvard U. Libra. Cambridge, 1947 33; asst. libr. Wheelock Coll., Boston, 1954-57; libr., cons. Combined Book Exhibit, Briarcliff Manor, N.Y., 1971-73; instrnl. svcs. libr. Westchester C.C., Valhalla, N.Y., 1974-77; libr. dir., editor Pergamon Press, Inc., Elmsford, N.Y., 1978-83; libr. supr. Joseph E. Seagram & Sons, N.Y.C., 1984-87; sr. rsch. assoc. House of Seagram, N.Y.C., 1987-92; database specialist Towers Perrin, Valhalla, 1992—2004, ret., 2004; sr. database specialist IC/KM; part-time libr. Hastings Pub. Libr., 2005—. Cons. D.C. Welfare Dept., Washington, 1965-70; libr. cons. Pocantico Hills (N.Y.) Sch., 1973-74. Contbr. articles to profl. jours. Trustee Bethesda-Chevy Chase (Md.) Libr. Bd., 1968-71; dist. leader Tarrytown Dem. Com., 1972-74; trustee Temple Beth Abraham, Tarrytown, N.Y., 1980-89, 100th Anniversary publicity com., 1999-2000; chmn., sec. Warner Libr. Bd., Tarrytown, 1982, 84-94; trustee, sec. Westchester Libr. Sys. Bd., Elmsford, 1984-89, v.p. adv. com.; with Kerry/Edwards office, N.Y.C., 2004; libr. vol. Anti-Defamation League, 2004-05; vol. Mus. Modern Art, 2005-. Recipient Luminary award Westchester Libr. Sys., 1999. Mem. Spl. Librs. Assn., Hadassah. Avocations: travel, cultural anthropology, aerobics. Personal E-mail: mirkamar@cloud9.net.

**MARGRAF, FRANCIS JOSEPH, JR.,** marine biologist, educator; b. Atlantic City, N.J., Oct. 17, 1947; s. Francis J. and Henrietta K. Margraf; m. Wennona A. Brown, Apr. 17, 1982; children: Jason Dirk, Marissa Leigh. BS, Cornell U., 1970; MS, PhD, Tex. A&M U., 1978. Unit leader, prof. fisheries Ohio Coop. Fish and Wildlife Rsch. Unit Ohio State U., Columbus, Ohio, 1980—87; unit leader, prof. fisheries W.Va. Coop. Fish and Wildlife Rsch. Unit W.Va. U., Morgantown, W.Va., 1987—95; unit leader, prof. fisheries Md. Coop. Fish and Wildlife Rsch. Unit U. Md. Ea. Shore, Princess Anne, Md., 1995—99; unit leader, prof. fisheries Alaska Coop. Fish and Wildlife Rsch. Unit U. Alaska, Fairbanks, Alaska, 1999—. Presenter in field. Contbr. over 100 articles to profl. jours. Fellow: Am. Inst. Fisheries Rsch. Biologists (dist. dir. 2003—); mem. Am. Fisheries Soc. (life; v.p. we. divsn. 2003—04, pres. we divsn. 2005—06, Disting. Svc. award 2001), Mastiff Club of Am. (pres. 1997—99). Office: AK-CFWRU Univ Alaska Fairbanks 210A Irving I Fairbanks AK 99775-7020 Office Phone: 904-474-7661. Business E-Mail: joe.margraf@uaf.edu.

**MARGULES, CECELIA,** composer, poet; b. Stockholm, Apr. 11, 1947; d. Morris Berkowitz; m. Rubin Margules, June 5, 1971; children: Julie, Rachyl, Adam. BA, Bklyn. Coll., 1970; Interior Design Degree, N.Y. Sch. Interior Design. Design cons. ARM Mgmt. Co., Bklyn., 1985—. Composer N.Y.C. Parks Dept., Emma Lazarus tribute, 2004, Celebration '350'. Contbr. articles and poetry to profl. jours.; contbg. editor Harmony, 1987; composer: (songs) Guiliani, 1987, New Sinai Sound, 2005. Chmn. Yossi Berger Holocaust Study Ctr., 1990—; cultural chmn. Jewish Heritage, N.Y.C.; bd. dirs. Jewish Cmty. Rels. Coun., N.Y.C, 2000—. Recipient State of Israel Bonds award, 1996, Woman of Valor award, Coun. Jewish Orgns., 2003, 1st prize Zionist nat. song contest, Am. Zionist Movement, 1998. Mem.: Emunah of Am. (v.p., Woman of the Yr. 1991). Jewish. E-mail: ceceliaproductions@yahoo.com.

**MARGULIES, JAMES HOWARD,** editorial cartoonist; b. Bklyn., Oct. 8, 1951; s. Henry Norman and Miriam Margulies; m. Martha Anne Golub, May 21, 1978; children: Elana, David. BFA, Carnegie-Mellon U., 1973. Editorial cartoonist Jour. Newspapers, Springfield, Va., 1980-84, Houston Post, 1984-90, The Record, Hackensack, NJ, 1990—. Syndicated cartoonist various newspapers, 1985—. Author: My Husband Is Not a Wimp, 1988, Hitting Below the Beltway, 1998; contbr. columns to profl. jours.; cartoons featured on TV programs. Mem. leadership com. Jewish Community Ctr., Houston, 1987, 88. Recipient Best Cartoon award Population Inst., 1985, Global Media award, 1985, 2d Place Editl. award Pavillion of Humor, 1985, Judges award World Hunger Media awards, 1986, Katie award Press Club of Dallas, 1989, Best Black and White Illustration in Advt. and Graphic Arts Addy award Houston Advt. Fedn., 1990, John Peter Zenger award N.Y. State Bar Assn., 1992, Nat. Headliner award for editl. cartoons Press Club of Atlantic City, 1996, 1st prize Fischetti Editl. Cartoon Competition, Columbia Coll., Chgo., 1996, Deadline Club award for editl. cartoons N.Y. chpt. Soc. Profl. Journalists, 1998, 1st pl for editl. cartoons Garden State Assn. of Black Journalists, 1999-2003, 3d Pl. Nat. Headliner awards for Editl. Cartoons. Press Club of Atlantic City, 2003, 04; named One of Texans Who Made the Eighties Winter, Ultra mag., 1990, Cartoonist of the Yr. Nat. Press Found., 2005, Berryman Cartoonist of Yr. Nat. Press Found., DC, 2005. Mem. Assn. Am. Editl. Cartoonists. Avocation: running. Office: The Record 150 River St Hackensack NJ 07601-7155 Office Phone: 201-646-4468. E-mail: jimmarg@aol.com.

**MARGULIES, JULIANNA,** actress; b. Spring Valley, NY, June 8, 1966; BA, Sarah Lawrence Coll., 1989. Actor (films) Out for Justice, 1991, Traveller, 1997, Paradise Road, 1997, A Price Above Rubies, 1997, The Newton Boys, 1998, The Big Day, 1999, What's Cooking, 2000, (voice only) Dinosaur, 2000, Ten Unknowns, 2001 (Lucille Lortel Award for outstanding featured actress, 2001), The Man From Elysian Fields, 2001, (voice only) Love Gets You Twisted, 2002, Ghost Ship, 2002, Evelyn, 2002, Slingshot, 2005, The Darwin Awrds, 2006, Snakes on a Plane, 2006; (TV series) Philly Heat, 1994, ER, 1994-2000 (Emmy award for supporting actress Drama, 1995, Golden Globe award winner, 1998, SAG award winner 1997, 98, 99); (TV mini-series) The Grid, 2004; (TV movies) The Mists of Avalon, 2001, Jenifer, 2001, Hitler: The Rise of Evil, 2003; (TV appearances) Law & Order, 1993, Murder, She Wrote, 1993, Homicide: Life on the Street, 1994, Scrubs, 2004, The Sopranos, 2006; (theater appearances) The Substance of Fire, At Home, Fefu and Her Friends, The Substance of Fire, Living Expenses, Dan Drift, Book of Names, Balm in Gilead, In the Boom Boom Room, The Vagina Monologues, 2000, Festen, 2006. Office: c/o William Morris Agency 151 S El Camino Dr Beverly Hills CA 90212*

**MARGULIES, MARTIN B.,** lawyer, educator; b. N.Y.C., Oct. 6, 1940; s. Max N. and Mae (Cohen) M.; m. Beth Ellen Zeldes, July 26, 1981; children: Max Zeldes, Adam Zeldes. AB, Columbia Coll., 1961; LLB, Harvard U., 1964; LLM, NYU, 1966. Bar: N.D. 1968, N.Y. 1974, Mass. 1977, Conn. 1988, U.S. Dist. Ct. Mass. 1977, U.S. Ct. Appeals (2d cir.) 1984, U.S. Supreme Ct. 1995. Asst. prof. law U. N.D., Grand Forks, 1966-69; editor-in-chief Columbia Coll. Today, Columbia U., N.Y.C., 1969-71; assoc. editor Parade Mag., N.Y.C., 1971-72; assoc. prof. law Western New Eng. Law Sch., Springfield, Mass., 1973-76; Bernard Hersher prof. law U. Bridgeport, Conn., 1977-92; Neil H. Cogan Pub. Svc. prof. law Quinnipiac U., 1997-99, prof. law, 1992—2005, prof. emeritus, 2005—. Author: The Early Life of Sean O'Casey, 1970; contbr. articles to profl. jours. Cooperating atty. Conn. Civil Liberties Union, Hartford, 1979—, bd. dirs., 1982-94; bd. dirs. Conn. Attys. for Progressive Legislature, New Haven, 1982; bd. dirs. ACLU, 1987-94, mem. free speech-assn. and poverty constl. rights com., 1988-94; chmn. bd. dirs. Fairfield County Civil Liberties Union, 1982-87, Hampden County Civil Liberties Union, 1976-78; bd. dirs. Civil Liberties Union Mass., Boston, 1975-78, Greater Springfield Urban League, 1976-78, Conn. Civil Liberties Union, 1982-94, ACLU, 1987-94, Ctr. for First Amendment Rights, Inc., 1993—. Named one of Best Lawyers in Am.: 2006; recipient Media award, NY State Bar Assn., 1972, Gavel award, ABA, 1973, Outstanding Tchr. award, U. Bridgeport Law Sch., 1986, 1987. Mem. Mass. Bar Assn., N.Y. State Bar Assn. Jewish. Home: 79 High Rock Rd Sandy Hook CT 06482-1623 Office: Quinnipiac Univ Sch Law 275 Mt Carmel Ave Hamden CT 06518-1947 Office Phone: 203-582-3252. Personal E-mail: mmargulies023@earthlink.net.

**MARGULIES, ALEXANDER RAFAILO,** physician, educator; b. Belgrade, Yugoslavia, Mar. 21, 1921; arrived in U.S., 1946; s. Rafailo and Olga (Weiss-Belic) Margulis; m. Hedvig Hricak, Feb. 26, 1983; 1 child, Peter Hricak. Student: U. Belgrade, 1939—41, student, 1945—46; MD, Harvard U., 1950; Doctorate (hon.), Aix-Marseille U., 1980, Med. Coll. Wisc., 1986, Cath. U. Louvain, 1986, Karolinska Inst., Stockholm, 1986, U. Munich, 1987, U. Toulouse, 1987, U. Montpellier, 1993, U. Novi Sad, 2005. Diplomate Am. Bd. Radiology. Intern Henry Ford Hosp., Detroit, 1950—51; resident in radiology U. Mich. Hosps., 1951—53; jr. clin. instr. U. Mich., 1953—54, instr., then asst. prof. U. Minn., 1954—59; asst. prof. sch. medicine Washington U., St. Louis, 1959—60, assoc. prof. to prof., 1960 63; prof. radiology, chmn. dept. U. Calif., San Francisco, 1963—89, dir. magnetic resonance Sci. Ctr., assoc. chancellor spl. projects, 1989—93, spl. cons. to vice chancellor, 1993—2000; clin. prof. radiology Cornell U. Weill Med. Coll., N.Y.C., 2000—; radiologist N.Y.-Presbyn. Med. Ctr., 2000—. Radiologist in chief U. Calif. Hosps., 1963—89; cons. VA Hosp., Letterman Gen. Hosp., San Francisco, U.S. Naval Hosp., Oakland, Calif.; cons. in radiology Office Surgeon Gen., 1967—71. Author (with others): Roentgen Diagnosis of Abdominal Tumors in Childhood, 1957; editor: Modern Alimentary Tract Radiology; co-editor: Alimentary Tract Roentgenology; editl. bd. Calif. Medicine, 1964—74, Radiology, 1975—93, assoc. editor Investigative Radiology, 1980—89; editor: Opinion in Radiology, 1988—91; author: Be in Charge: A Leadership Manual, 2002. Capt. U.S. Army, 1957—59. Recipient Cannon medal, Soc. Radiol., 1977, Gold medal, Am. Roentgen Ray Soc., 1988, J.P. Allyn medal, P. Roberts Rsch. Inst., 1989, Gold medal, Am. Coll. Radiology, 1999, UCSF medal, 2000. Fellow: Royal Coll. Radiologists (hon.); mem.: AMA (cons. drugs 1961—), Internat. Soc. Strategic Studies in Radiology (founding pres. 1995—99), Royal Coll. Radiologists of Thailand, Polish Soc. Radiology, Thai Coll. Radiology, Chinese Radiol. Soc., Russian Radiol. Soc., Royal Coll. Surgeons Ireland, French Radiol. Soc., Swiss Radiol. Soc., Italian Radiol. Soc., Russian Acad. Scis. (fgn.), Serbian Acad. Scis. (fgn.), Soc. Magnetic Resonance in Medicine (pres. 1983), Calif. Acad. Medicine (pres. 1973—74), San Francisco Radiol. Soc. (pres. 1973—74), Radiol. Soc. N.Am. (Gold medal 1983), Am. Gastroenterological Assn. Univ. Radiologists (pres. 1966—67, chmn. adv. com. acad. radiology 1971, pres. 1971), Roentgen Ray Soc., NAS-Inst. Medicine, Japan Radiol. Soc. (hon.), German Radiol. Soc. (hon.), Rocky Mountain Radiol. Soc. Office: NY Presbyn Hosp Rm N-09 Box 141 525 E 68th St New York NY 10021-4870 Business E-Mail: arm2001@med.cornell.edu.

**MARGULIS, GREGORY A.,** mathematics professor, researcher, science educator; b. Moscow, Feb. 24, 1946; came to U.S., 1991; s. Alexander Y. Margulis and Tsilya M. Oshorenko; m. Raisa T. Kristal, Aug. 30, 1972; 1 child, Boris. Diploma, Moscow U., 1967, PhD, 1970; DSc, Belorussian Acad. Scis., Minsk, 1983. Rschr. Inst. Problems in Info. Transmission, Soviet Acad. Scis., Moscow, 1970-91; prof. math. Yale U., New Haven, 1991—. Mem. sci. adv. coun. Math. Scis. Rsch. Inst., Berkeley, Calif., 1993-97; mem. sci. adv. bd. Clay Math. Inst., Cambridge, Mass., 2003—. Author: Discrete Subgroups of Semisimple Lie Groups, 1991; mem. editl. bd. math. jours. Recipient prize for young mathematicians Moscow Math. Soc., 1968, Fields medal Internat. Math. Union, 1978, Humboldt Found. prize, 1995, Lobachevski prize Russian Acad. Scis., 1996, Wolf prize in math. Wolf Found., Israel, 2005. Mem. AAAS (fgn. hon.), NAS. Avocations: chess, jogging, swimming. Home: 20 Vista Ter New Haven CT 06515-2402 Office: Yale U Dept Math 10 Hillhouse Ave Dept Math New Haven CT 06511-6814

**MARGULIS, HEIDI,** health products executive; Licensure analyst Humana, Inc., 1985—95, v.p. govt. affairs, 1995—2000, sr. v.p. govt. affairs, 2000—. Mem. fed. adv. com. to streamline regulations to ensure quality health care svcs., 2002; mem. com. on Medicare edn. HFCA. Mem.: Women's Polit. Forum (bd. dirs.), Bus. and Profl. Women (pres. 1978—79), Bus. Roundtable, Health Care Leadership Coun., Am. Assn. Health Plans (policy, legis., advocacy and strategic planning coms.). Office: Humana Inc 500 W Main St Louisville KY 40202

**MARGULIS, HOWARD LEE,** lawyer; b. St. Louis, Oct. 7, 1961; s. Lawrence and Rosalyn Rae (Chait) M.; children: Jennifer Lynne, Michelle Lisa, David Jonathan. BA in History, Northwestern U., 1984; JD summa cum laude, Ill. Inst. Tech., 1987. Bar: Ill. 1987, N.J. 1990, N.Y., 1999, U.S. Dist. Ct. (no. dist.) Ill. 1987, U.S. Dist. Ct. N.J. 1990, U.S. Ct. Appeals (7th and D.C. cirs.) 1988, U.S. Ct. Appeals (9th and 3d cirs.) 1989, U.S. Dist. Ct. (ea. and so. dists.) N.Y. 1998, U.S. Dist. Ct. (ea. dist.) Mich. 1998, U.S. Ct. Appeals (2d cir.) 1998; registered lobbyist, N.J. Assoc. Seyfarth, Shaw, Fairweather & Geraldson, Chgo., 1987-89, Saiber Schlesinger Satz & Goldstein, Newark, 1989-90; spl. counsel Guardian Life Ins. Co., Iselin, NJ, 1990-91; gen. counsel Energy Consortium, Inc., Iselin, NJ, 1991—94, Skadden Arps Slate Meagher & Flom, Newark, 1994—99; ptnr. Baker & McKenzie, NYC, 1999—2002, Holland & Knight, NYC, 2002—05, Troutman Sanders LLP, NYC, 2005—. Active Middlesex County Human Rels. Commn., 1997—. IIT Acad. scholar, 1984-87. Mem. N.Y. State Bar Assn., NYC Bar Assn. (energy law steering com.), N.J. Assn. Energy Engrs. (pres. 1992-94, sr. dir. 1992-2004). Democrat. Office: Troutman Sanders LLP The Chrysler Bldg 405 Lexington Ave New York NY 10174 E-mail: howard.margulis@troutmansanders.com.

**MARGULIS, LYNN (LYNN ALEXANDER),** evolutionist, educator; b. Chgo., Mar. 5, 1938; d. Morris and Leone Alexander; m. Carl Sagan, June 16, 1957; children: Dorion Sagan, Jeremy Sagan; m. Thomas N. Margulis, Jan. 18, 1967; children: Zachary Margulis-Ohnuma, Jennifer Margulis di Properzio. AB, U. Chgo., 1957; AM, U. Wis., 1960; PhD, U. Calif., Berkeley, 1965; Doctorate (hon.), U. Montreal, Can., 1987, U. Valencia, Spain, 2001; DSc (hon.), Southeastern Mass. U., North Dartmouth, 1989, Westfield State Coll., Mass., 1989, Plymouth State Coll., NH, 1991, Tulane U., New Orleans, 1996, U. Montreal, 1997, Autonomous U. Madrid, 1998, Union Coll. Schenectady, NY, 2001, San Francisco U., Quito, Ecuador, 2001, Rutgers U., New Brunswick, 2004, Bates Coll., Lewiston, Maine, 2005, Tufts U., Medford, Mass., 2006, NC State U., Raleigh, 2006; Dr.rer.nat (hon.), U. Oldenburg, Germany, 1999. Mem. faculty Boston U., 1966—68, asst. prof. biology, 1967—71, assoc. prof., 1971—77, prof., 1977—88, Univ. prof., 1986—88; Disting. Univ. prof. U. Mass., Amherst, 1988—. Sherman Fairchild Disting. scholar Calif. Inst. Tech., 1976—77; vis. prof. dept. microbiology U. Autónoma de Barcelona, Spain, 1986, Spain, 88; Disting. univ. prof. U. Mass. Author: Origin of Eukaryotic Cells, 1970, Symbiosis in Cell Evolution, 1981, Early Life, 1982, 2d edit., 2002, Symbiosis in Cell Evolution, 2d edit., 1993, Microcosmos Videos, 1999; editor (with Mitchell Rambler and René Fester): Global Ecology, 1989; editor: (with others) Handbook of Protoctista, 1990; co-editor (with René Fester): Symbiosis as a Source of Evolutionary Innovation: Speciation and Morphogenesis, 1991; co-editor: Concepts of Symbiogenesis: A Historical and Critical Study of the Research of Russian Botanists, 1992, Environmental Evolution: Effects of the Origin and Evolution of Life on Planet Earth, 1992, Environmental Evolution: Effects of the Origin and Evolution of Life on Planet Earth, 2d edit., 2000, Glossary of Protoctista, 1993; co-editor: (with Dorion Sagan) What Is Sex?, 1998; co-editor: Slanted Truths: Essays on Gaia, Evolution and Symbiosis, 1997, What is Life?, 1995, Diversity of Life: The Illustrated Guide to the Five Kingdoms, 2d edit., 1999; co-author: Five Kingdoms, 1982, 3d edit., 1998, Microcosmos, 1986; co-author: (with Dorion Sagan) Origins of Sex, 1986; co-author: Garden of Microbial Delights, 1988, 2d edit., 1998, Biospheres From Earth To Space, 1988, Mystery Dance: On the Evolution of Human Sexuality, 1991, What Happens to Trash and Garbage: An Introduction to the Carbon Cycle, 1993, Living Sands: Mapping Time and Space with Forams, 2000, Early Life, 2d edit., 2002, Acquiring Genomes: A Theory of the Origins of Species, 2002, Peces Luminosos: Historias de Ciencia y Amor, 2002, Una Revolucion en la Evolucion, 2002; co-author: (with Andrew Wier) Vol. I Cells and Reproduction, Vol. II Evolution and Diversity; co-author: (with Lorraine Olendzenski) (videos) Looking at Microbes, An Introduction to the Microbiology Laboratory for Students, Symbiotic Planet. A New Look at Evolution, 1997; contbr. chapters to books, articles to profl. jours. Recipient Nat. Medal Sci., 1999, Humboldt Prize, 2002, Commonwealth of Mass. award; Guggenheim fellow, 1979. Fellow: AAAS; mem.: NAS, Soc. Sci. Rsch. Soc., Evolutionary Protistology (co-founder), Sigma Xi (pres. 2005—06). Office: U Mass Dept Geosci 611 No Pleasant St Amherst MA 01003-9297 Mailing: PO Box 671 Amherst MA 01004-0671 Office Phone: 413-545-3244. *We must, as E. M. Forster admonished, "only connect" and lower our population's growth rate. The sciences, the quest for knowledge about the universe and life are intrinsically related. Like all other species ever to have lived on Earth, ours too will be replaced. The quality of that demise depends directly on preservation of habitat of our planetmates directly on our own population growth rates by presentation of habitat of our planetmates.*

**MARI, GIANCARLO,** obstetrician, gynecologist, educator; b. Salerno, Italy, Apr. 17, 1957; s. Michele Mari and Cecilia Scola; m. Laura Detti, May 2006; children: Michael C, Camilla A. MD, U. Naples, Italy, 1982. Resident ob-gyn. U. Parma, Italy, 1982—84, U. Napoli, Italy, 1984—86; resident ob-gyn. Sch. Medicine Yale U., New Haven, 1990—94, fellow maternal-fetal medicine Sch. of Medicine, 1994—96, asst. prof. ob-gyn. Sch. of Medicine, 1995—2000, assoc. prof. ob-gyn. Sch. of Medicine, 1999—2000; assoc. prof. ob-gyn. U. Va., Charlottesville, Va., 2000—02; prof. ob-gyn. U. Cin., 2002—04, Wayne State U., Detroit, 2004—. Dir. diagnostic endoscopy and fetal therapy Wayne State U., mem.instl. rev. bd. Hutzel Hosp., 2006; dir. prenatal diagnosis and fetal therapy U. Cin., 2002—04, U. Va., 2000—02; rsch. fellow Baylor Coll. Medicine, Houston, 1997—2000. Author: Twin-Twin-Transfusion Syndrome International Registry (The best of SMFM 1998 award SGI, 1998); mem. editl bd.: European Jour. Ob-gyn. in Reproductive Biology, Prenatal Diagnosis and Fetal Therapy. Named Top reviewer, Am Jour. Ob-Gyn.; named one of Best Doctors in Am., 2004, 2006; recipient Best Paper award, Soc. Perinatal Obstetricians, 1993, John J Meehan-Clifford R. Miller award, Dept. Ob-gyn., Yale U., 1994. Fellow: Am. Coll. Ob-gyn.; mem.: Internat. Soc. Ultrasound in Ob-gyn. (mem. editl. bd.), Soc. Gynecologic Investigation, Soc. Maternal Fetal Medicine. Roman Catholic. Achievements include discovery of non-invsive diagnosis of fetal anemia-Many children have and will have a happy life because of this discovery. Office: Wayne State University John R Detroit MI 48202 Office Phone: 313-993-1379. Personal E-mail: giancarlomari@hotmail.com. Business E-Mail: gmari@med.wayne.edu.

**MARIA, BERNARD L.,** pediatric neurologist; b. Montreal, Que., Can., Jan. 23, 1958; s. Maurice A. and Margaret Maria; m. Barbara E. Maria, Nov. 28, 1983; 1 child, Alexander. DEC, Coll. Marguerite-Bourgeois, Montreal, 1976; MD, U. Sherbrooke, Can., 1981; MBA, U. Fla., 1995. Diplomate Am. Bd. Pediatrics, Am. Bd. Neurology and Psychiatry. Resident in pediatrics McGill U., Montreal, 1981-83; resident in neurology Johns Hopkins U., Balt., 1983-86; fellow in neuro-oncology M.D. Anderson, Houston, 1986-88; asst. prof. U. Toronto, Ont., Can., 1988-90; assoc. prof. U. Fla., Gainesville, 1990-98, prof., 1998—, divsn. chief, 1990—. Founding dir. neuro-oncology group Johns Hopkins Hosp., 1984-86; founding dir. neuro-oncology program U. Fla., 1990—; lectr. in field. Editor consensus in Child Neurology, 1997—; Current Mgmt. in Child Neurology, 1999, 2002, 05; guest-editor Seminar in Child Neurology, 1997; guest editor Jour. Child Neurology, 2002-; mem. editl. bd. Jour. Child Neurology, 1995—; Pediat. Neurology, 1997—; reviewer jours. in field; contbr. articles to med. jours., chpt. to book; author monographs in field. Grantee NSC Found., 1988-90, Brain Rsch. Found., 1988-90, U. Fla., 1990, ORDCR Found., 1990, 91-97, Sigma-Tau Pharms., 1992, Stop! Children's Cancer, Inc., 1991-92, 96-97, Abbot Pharms., 1992, Parke Davis Pharms., 1992, Nat. Cancer Inst., 1992, 93, Children's Miracle Network, 1995, Depotech, Inc., 1994, Glaxo, Inc., 1995, Genetic Therapy, Inc., 1995, 96, Sturge-Weber Found., 1995, LAVFW, 1997-98, Glaxo Wellcome, 1997, Parke Davis, 1997, State of Fla., 1997-99, NINDS, 1999—, Medeva, 1998-99. Mem. AMA, Child Neurology Soc. (bylaws com. 1990-95, fin. com. 1995—), Soc. for Pediat. Rsch., Soc. for Neurosci., Pediat. Oncology Group, Profs. of Child Neurology, Internat. Child Neurology Assn., Am. Acad. Pediat., Am. Acad. Neurology, Am. Soc. Clin. Oncology, Am. Pediat. Soc., Soc. Neuro-Oncology. Office: MUSC PO Box 250514 173 Ashly Ave Ste 409 Charleston SC 29425 Office Phone: 843-792-7715. Business E-Mail: mariabl@musc.edu.

**MARIAM, THOMAS FRED,** public relations executive, radio producer; b. NYC, Feb. 26, 1957; s. Rudolph Karl and Lisa Gertrud (Silbermann) Mariam; m. Alyce Beth Appleman, Aug. 20, 2000; children: Michael Reese, Madison Leah. BA in Polit. Sci., Columbia U., 1978; MS in Broadcast Journalism, Boston U., 1980. News dir. Sta. WNBP, Newburyport, Mass., 1979-80; sports dir. Sta. WKCR-FM, NYC, 1976-78; editor, writer The Wall St. Jour. Report, NYC, 1980-84; nat. copy editor Dow Jones News Svc., NYC, 1984; dir. news svcs. Am. Stock Exch., NYC, 1984-95; sr. v.p. Rubenstein Assoc. Pub. Rels., NYC, 1995-96; sr. mgr. pub. rels. Booz-Allen & Hamilton, NYC, 1996-99; dir. mktg. and comm. Cadwalader, Wickersham & Taft, NYC, 1999-2000; dir. global comm. Clifford Chance Rogers & Wells LLP, 2000—02; pres. Mariam Comms. LLC, 2002—; prodr., co-host The Metro Golf Show, 2003—. Radio sports reporter Sports Final Radio Network, 1987—; NY corr. The Sports File, 1989-93. Producer, host (radio program) Amex Business Talk, 1985-94; freelance radio sports reporter, 1986—. Voting mem. Self-Help, Inc., N.Y.C., 1985-92; trustee Congregation Habonim. Mem. ABA, Legal Mktg. Assn., N.Y. Fin. Writers Assn. (bd. dirs. 1992-99), Radio-TV News Dirs. Assn., Pub. Rels. Soc. Am. (v.p. Westchester-Fairfield chpt. 2002—), Deadline Club N.Y., Nat. Assn. Broadcasters, Nat. Assn. Sportscasters and Sportswriters, Columbia Club N.Y. (dir.-at-large 1984-96, activities chmn. 1986-94, 1st v.p. 1988-96). Democrat. Jewish. Home and Office: 89 Country Ridge Dr Rye Brook NY 10573-1046 Office Phone: 914-939-4294. E-mail: tom@mariam.biz.

**MARIANI, JOHN F.,** writer; b. N.Y.C., Aug. 27, 1945; s. Eligio Alfonse and Renee Theodora (Sofia) Mariani; m. Galina Stepanoff-Dargery, May 28, 1977; children: Michael, Christopher. BA, Iona Coll., 1967; MA, Columbia U., 1968, PhD, 1973. Author: Dictionary of Italian Food and Drink, 1998, Encyclopedia of American Food and Drink, 1999, The Italian-American Cookbook, 2001. Trustee Village of Tuckahoe, Tuckahoe, NY, 1990—. Mem.: Wine Media Guild. Home and Office: 8 Henry St Tuckahoe NY 10707

**MARIANI, MICHAEL MATTHEW,** lawyer; b. West Pittston, Pa., Sept. 25, 1950; s. Stephen Francis and Tulia Felicia (DelCorso) M.; m. Patricia Mary Leptak, June 26, 1976; children: Kathryn Elizabeth, Michael Joseph. BS with honors, Wilkes Coll., 1972; JD, St. John's U., Jamaica, N.Y., 1975; LLM, NYU, 1980. Bar: N.Y. 1976, U.S. Dist. Ct. (so. and ea. dists.) N.Y. 1976, U.S. Tax Ct. 1980. Law sec. to presiding judge Surrogate's Ct., New City, N.Y., 1976-80; assoc. Law offices of Edward S. Schlesinger P.C., N.Y.C., 1981-97; sr. v.p., trust counsel Fiduciary Trust Co. Internat., N.Y.C., 1997—. Adj. prof. law St. John's Univ. Sch. Law, Jamaica, NY, 2005—. Co-author: New York Probate, 1986, supplements 1987-2006; contbr. articles to profl. jours. Trustee Cath. Charities, Diocese of Bklyn., 1981—2005, treas., 1985—87, v.p., 1987—89, pres., 1989—91; bd. dirs. Mercy Home for Children, Bklyn., 1989—97, mem. advl. bd., 1997—; mem. profl. adv. bd. Calvary Hosp., 2002—; mem. Heritage bd. dirs. Am. Heart Assn., 2004—. Recipient Benemerenti medal Pope John Paul II, 1997. Mem. ABA (real property, probate and trust law sects.), N.Y. State Bar Assn. (trusts and estates sects.), Assn. Bar City N.Y. Democrat. Home: 53-32 215th St Bayside NY 11364-1835 Office: 600 Fifth Ave New York NY 10020-2302 Office Phone: 212-632-3255. Business E-Mail: mmariani@ftci.com.

**MARIANO, ANA VIRGINIA,** retired pathologist; b. Baguio City, The Philippines, Nov. 20, 1938; came to US, 1963; d. Celestino Chuongco and Ana (Teanco) Juan; m. Gregorio Torres Mariano, June 4, 1966; children: Joel, Eric, Greg, Anita. AA, St. Tomas, Manila, 1957, MD, 1962. Bd. cert. in anatomic pathology and clin. pathology Am. Bd. Pathology; lic. physician, NY, Pa. Med. intern Youngstown Hosp., Ohio, 1963; pathology resident I RI Hosp., Providence, 1964; pathology resident II-IV Wayne State U. Med. Sch., Detroit, 1965-68; assoc. pathologist Newark-Wayne Cmty. Hosp., Newark, NY, 1979-83; interim pathologist Clifton Springs Hosp., NY, 1983; lab. dir. and acting lab. dir. VA Med. Ctr., Altoona, Pa., 1997—, staff pathologist, 1997-99. Locum tenens Altoona Hosp., Pa., 1999-2001; mem. courtesy med. staff Newark-Wayne Cmty. Hosp., 1983-92, Clifton Springs Hosp., NY, 1983-89; mem. adv. bd. Cath. Physicians Guild, Rochester, NY, 1991-92; cons. in pathology VA Med. Ctr., Altoona, 1993-96. Tchr. religious edn. St. Michael's Ch., Newark, 1978-80, 82-84. Fellow Am. Soc. Clin. Pathologists, Coll. Am. Pathologists. Roman Catholic. Avocations: swimming, aerobics, gardening. Home and Office: 320 Bristol Ln Hollidaysburg PA 16648-2901

**MARIANO, ROBERT A.,** retail executive; BS, Univ. Ill., Chgo.; MBA, Univ. Chgo., 1987. V.p-r dairy ops., mfg., retail ops. Dominick's Finer Foods, sr. v.p. mktg., perishable mdse., pres., COO, 1995—96, pres., CEO, 1996—98; commr. Ill. Gaming Bd., 2001—02; chmn., CEO, pres. Roundy's Supermarkets Inc., Milw., 2002—. Office: Roundy's Supermarkets Ste 100 875 E Wisconsin Ave Milwaukee WI 53202 Mailing: Roundy's Supermarkets PO Box 473 Milwaukee WI 53201-0473*

**MARICONDA, NICHOLAS GERARD,** music educator, musician; b. Bridgeport, Conn., Mar. 2, 1954; s. Nicholas Thomas and Elena (DiMenna) Mariconda; m. Barbara Marie Johnson (div.); children: Glenn, Marissa. BS in Music Edn., U. Bridgeport, 1976, MS in Music Edn., 1977. Cert. tchr. Conn. Instrumental music tchr. Staples HS, Westport, Conn., 1977—92, band dir., 1992—. Cons. in field. Mem.: Conn. Music Educators Assn., Conn. Edn. Assn., Music Educators Nat. Conf. Democrat. Roman Catholic. Avocations: exercise, running.

**MARIENTHAL, GEORGE,** telecommunications industry executive; b. Kansas City, Mo., Nov. 15, 1938; s. George and Sadie (James) M.; children: Shawn Ann Capon, Patrick James, Shannon Lee Van Winter. BS, U.S. Naval Acad., 1962; MS, Stanford U., 1963; MBA, Am. U., 1974. Sr. rsch. assoc. Logistics Mgmt. Inst., Washington, 1967-71; dir. regional ops. EPA, 1971-75, dir. water policy, 1984-85; dep. asst. sec. def. Dept. Def., Washington, 1975-81; v.p. Survival Tech., Inc., Bethesda, Md., 1981-84; dep. asst. sec. agr. Dept. Agr., Washington, 1985-86; dep. adv. programs Titan Systems, Inc., 1986-87; mktg. Computer Scis. Corp., Falls Church, Va., 1987-89; v.p. Verizon Business, Vienna, 1989—. Bd. dirs. Home Security Title Ins. Co. Served with USAF, 1962-67. Mem.: Nat. Def. Indsl. Assn., Internat. Telephone Pioneers Assn., Armed Forces Comms. and Electronics Assn., Masons. Republican. Episcopalian. Home: 2157 Sandcastle Ct Annapolis MD 21403-5505 Personal E-mail: george.marienthal@verizonbusiness.com.

**MARIER, ROBERT L.,** dean, hospital administrator; b. Mar. 29, 1943; m. Joanne Cain Marier; 2 children. AB, Boston Coll., 1965; MD, Yale U., 1969; MHA, Tulane U., 1994. Diplomate Am. Bd. Internal Medicine and Infectious Diseases. Intern in internal medicine Mass. Gen. Hosp., Boston, 1969-70, asst. resident in medicine, 1970-71; epidemic intelligence svc. officer Nat. Ctr. Disease Control USPHS, Atlanta, 1971-73; clin. rsch. fellow in inflammatory

disease Yale U., New Haven, 1973-75, asst. prof. medicine, 1975-78; assoc. prof. medicine La. State U., New Orleans, 1978-83, acting head sect. infectious disease, 1982-83, dir. intro. to clin. medicine, 1982-85, dir. residency program, 1982-86, prof. medicine, 1983—, dir. office infection control, 1982—91; med. dir. Med. Ctr. La., 1982—92; chmn. Dept. Pub. Health La. State U. Sch. Medicine, New Orleans, 1993—95, dean, 1995—2002; acting dean La. State U. Sch. Pub. Health, New Orleans, 2003—04, dir. Health Policy and Systems Mgmt. Program; CEO La. Pub. Hosp. Sys., 1997—99. Vis. physician Yale-New Haven Hosp., 1975-78. Fellow ACP, Infectious Disease Soc. Am.; mem. AMA, La. State Med. Soc., Orleans Parish Med. Soc., Alpha Omega Alpha. Office Phone: 504-599-1396. Office Fax: 504-568-6905. E-mail: rmarier@lsuhsc.edu.*

**MARIETTA, ELIZABETH ANN,** real estate broker; b. Oshkosh, Wis., Feb. 28, 1954; d. Frederick Damler and Connie Steiger Dempsey; children: Hunter H. Student, U. Autonima, Guadalajara, Mex., 1974; BA in Architecture, U. N.Mex., 1979. Lic. Oreg. Real Estate Compass Realty. Project mgr. drafting Hutchinson, Brown & Ptnrs., Architects, Albuquerque, 1978-80; engr. facilities constrn. mgmt. divsn. Albuquerque Ops. Office, 1982-90, engr. quality engring. divsn., 1982-90, engr. budget and resources mgmt., 1982-90, site mgr. uranium mill tailings remedial action project, 1982-90, environ. engr. performance assessment divsn., 1995—98; sect. chief indsl. tech. Bonneville Power Adminstrn., Portland, Oreg., 1990—. Employee support sounding bd. Bonneville Power Adminstrn., Portland, 1990-91, women's resource group, 1990-93. Author: Ricochet Stepparenting. Mem. City Club Portland, 1990-91. Mem.: Coun. Women Realtors, Le-Tip Coalition of Women, Ind. Real Estate Brokers Assn., Network Orgn. Avocations: reading, sailing, travel, scuba diving. Home: 580 First St Lake Oswego OR 97034-3115 Office Phone: 503-675-2995, 503-753-5558.

**MARIK, PAUL ELLIS,** physician; b. Johannesburg, Mar. 26, 1958; arrived in U.S., 1992; s. Colin Sigmund and Jocelyn (Feldman) M.; m. Kathryn Phillips Marik, June 22, 1992; 1 child, Emma. MBBch, U. of the Witwatersrand, Johannesburg, 1981, M in medicine, 1988, BSc in pharmacology (hons.), 1989; FCP, Coll. Medicine, Johannesburg, 1987. Attending physician Baragwanath Hosp., Soweto, South Africa, 1988-92, Detroit Medical Ctr., Detroit, 1992-94, St. Vincent Hosp., Worcester, Mass., 1994—. Office: St Vincent Hosp Dept Critical Care 25 Winthrop St Dept Critical Worcester MA 01604-4543

**MARIL, DAVID C.,** editor; b. Balt., Apr. 2, 1950; s. Herman and Esta Cook Maril. BA in English, Clark U., 1972. Sports editor News Recorder, Worcester, Mass., 1972-75, Milford (Mass.) Daily News, 1975-2000; news copy editor, Sunday columnist Brockton (Mass.) Enterprise, 2000—, mem. contract negotiative bd., 2006—. V.p Herman Maril Paintings, Balt., 1995—; sports editor AP Assn. Editor, writer Baseball Odyssey supplements, 1977-98 (award UPI 1988); columnist Off the Field, 1999. Bd. dirs Highwood Condo Assn., Franklin, Mass., 1995—; mem. cable adv. com. Town of Franklin, 1988-91; mem. art adv. bd. Univ. Coll. of Univ. Md., 2001—. Recipient sports column awards UPI, 1986, 87, New Eng. Newspaper Assn., Boston, 1999, Cmty. Newspapers, Needham, Mass., 1999. Mem. Baseball Writers Assn. (Hall of Fame voter), Soc. Baseball Rsch., Boston Baseball Writers (bd. dirs.). Avocations: reading, cinema history, baseball history. Home: 37 Highwood Dr Franklin MA 02038 Office Fax: 774-571-2130. Personal E-mail: dmoriole13@yahoo.com.

**MARIMOW, WILLIAM K.,** editor; b. Phila., Aug. 4, 1947; s. Jay and Helen Alma (Gitnig) M.; m. Diane K. Macomb, Oct. 18, 1969; children: Ann Esther, Scott Macomb. BA, Trinity Coll., Conn., 1969. Asst. editor Comml. Car Jour., Chilton Co., Bala Cynwyd, Pa., 1969-70; asst. to econ. columnist Phila. Bull., 1970-72; staff writer Phila. Inquirer, 1972—, city hall bur. chief, 1979-81, editor Main Line Neighbors, 1986-87, N.J. editor, 1987-89, city editor, 1989-91; city editor, asst. to pub. Phila. Inquirer and Daily News, 1991-93; met. editor Balt. Sun, 1993, assoc. mng. editor, 1993-95, mng. editor, 1995-2000, editor, sr. v.p., 2000—04; mng. editor Nat. Pub. Radio, Washington, 2004—05, v.p. news, 2006—. Instr. urban studies U. Pa., 1979; instr. English Rutgers U., Camden, NJ, 1981; nominating jury Pulitzer Prize, 1991—92, 1996—97, 2002—03; bd. fellows Trinity Coll., 1998—2000; mem. adv. bd. Knight Ctr. for Specialized Journalism at U. Md., 1999—2000; bd. visitors U. Md. Sch. Journalism, 2000—; mem. nat. adv. bd. Poynter Inst., 2004—. Recipient 1st pl. award for team reporting Phila. Press Assn., 1977, 1st pl. award for deadline reporting AP Mng. Editors of Pa., 1977, Pub. Svc. awards, 1978, 85, Nat. Pub. Svc. award Sigma Delta Chi, 1978, 1st pl. award for best news story Sigma Delta Chi Phila., 1977, 2nd pl. award for deadline reporting, 1980, Pub. Svc. awards, 1978, 85, Pub. Svc. awards Sigma Delta Chi N.J., 1978, Pulitzer prize for disting. pub. svc., 1978, Pulitzer prize for investigative reporting, 1985, Silver Gavel award ABA, 1978, 82, Roy W. Howard Pub. Svc. award Scripps-Howard Found., 1978, Robert F. Kennedy Journalism award, 1978, 2nd pl. award for investigative reporting Keystone Press Assn., 1978, 85, 1st pl. award for best news story, 1982, Media Achievement award Phila. Bar Assn., 1982, William Schnader award Pa. Bar Assn., 1982, Nat. Headliners award, 1985, Trinity Coll. Alumni Achievement award, 1984; Nieman fellow Harvard U., 1982-83. Mem. Am. Soc. Newspaper Editors, Pen and Pencil Club, Investigative Reporters and Editors, Inc. (1st place for radio reporting, 2004). Office: Nat Pub Radio 635 Mass Ave NW Washington DC 20001

**MARIN, DEBORAH B.,** psychiatrist, educator; b. Cleve., Oct. 9, 1957; d. Emanuel and Klara Blumenthal; m. Michael Marin; children: Lea, Max. BA, Wellesley Coll., 1979; MD, Mt. Sinai Med. Sch., 1984. Resident Mt. Sinai Med. Ctr., NYC, 1984—88; fellowship Cornell U., 1988—92; vice chair, prof. psychiatry Mt. Sinai Med. Ctr., NYC, 1992—, exec. v.p. for strategic devel., chief med. officer, 2004—; dean clin. rsch. Mt. Sinai Med. Sch., NYC, 2003—. Office: Mt Sinai Med Ctr 1425 Madison Ave New York NY 10029 E-mail: deborah.marin@mssm.edu.

**MARIN, JACKIE WILLIS,** music educator, pianist; b. Morehead City, NC, July 19, 1948; d. Fred Swindell, Sr. and Frances Bell Willis. BA, East Carolina U., Greenville, N.C., 1972, MA, 1977; diploma, Inst. of Children's Lit., Conn., 1988. Adj. music Tarrant County Coll. System, Hurst, Tex., 1992—; Collin County Coll. Sys., Plano, Tex., 1992—2000; pvt. vocal coach North Mesquite HS, Tex., 2000—05; soloist, pianist 2d Ch. of Christ Scientist, Oak Cliff, Tex., 2003—. Vocal coach Victory Outreach Ch. Choir, Dallas, 2006; regional vocal judge Tex. Young Artist Competition, Ft. Worth, 2005, Ft. Worth, 06, U. Interscholastic League, Ft. Worth, 2005, Ft. Worth, 06. Mezzo-soprano soloist Canturbury and Salisbury Cathedrals, Lovers Lane United Methodist Choir, 1997—98. Recipient Regional Winner, Nat. Assn. Tchrs. of Singing, U. Fla., 1971, State Winner, N.C. Fedn. Music Clubs, 1972, Regional Winner, 1972. Avocations: reading, walking, sightseeing. Home: 808 S Galloway Ave Mesquite TX 75149 Personal E-mail: jini@ev1.net.

**MARIN, MICHAEL L.,** vascular surgeon; b. June 7, 1956; BS, SUNY, Stony Brook, 1978; MD, Mt. Sinai Sch. Medicine, 1984. Bd. cert. surgery 1992. Intern in surgery Columbia-Presbyn. Med. Ctr., NYC, 1984—85, resident in surgery, 1985—89, chief resident surgery, 1989—90; fellow in transplant surgery Coll. Physicians and Surgeons, Columbia U., NYC, 1987—88; fellow in vascular surgery Montefiore Med. Ctr., NYC, 1990—92, attending physician surgery, 1992—96, Albert Einstein Coll. Medicine, NYC, 1992—96, asst. prof. surgery, 1992—96, assoc. prof. surgery, 1996—; attending physician surgery Bronx Municipal Hosp. Ctr., NYC, 1992—96, N. Cent. Bronx Hosp., NYC, 1992—96, Mt. Sinai Med. Ctr., NYC, 1996—, assoc. prof. surgery, 1996—, prof. vascular surgery, 1999—, prof. surgery, 1999—. Office: Mt Sinai Med Ctr Dept Surgery 14th Fl 5 E 98th St New York NY 10029-6501 Office Phone: 212-241-5392.

**MARIN, MONA,** epidemiologist; d. Constantin and Ioana Marin. MD, U. Medicine, Iasi, Romania, 1990. Asst. prof. U. Medicine and Pharmacy, Bucharest, Romania, 1997—2002; med. epidemiologist Centers for Disease Control and Prevention, Atlanta, 2002—. Recipient Secs. award for Disting. Svcs., US HHS, 2004.

**MARIN, ROSARIO,** state agency administrator, former federal agency administrator; b. Mexico City, Mex., Aug. 4, 1958; m. Alex Marin; children: Eric, Carmen, Alvaro. BS bus. adminstrn., Calif. State U., L.A., 1983, LLD (hon.), 2002; grad., Harvard U., 1998. With City Nat. Bank, Beverly Hills, 1981—86; chief legis. affairs Calif. Dept. Devel. Svcs., 1992—93; chair Calif. State Coun. Developmental Disabilities, 1994—96; asst. dep. dir. Calif. State Dept. Social Svcs., 1996—97; dep. dir. Gov.'s Office Cmty. Rels., L.A., 1997—98; mayor City of Huntington Park, Calif., 1999—2000; 41st U.S. treas. U. S. Dept. Treasury, Washington, 2001—03. Mem. Calif. Integrated Waste Mgmt. Bd., Sacramento, 2004—, chmn., 2004—. Recipient Rose Fitzgerald Kennedy award, U.N., 1995, Excellence in Pub. Svc. award, Latino Perspective Conf., 2000, Alumna of the Year, Calif. State U., 2002. Office: Calif EPA Hdqs 1001 I St PO Box 4025 Sacramento CA 95812

**MARINACCIO, CHARLES LINDBERGH,** lawyer, consultant; b. Stratford, Conn., Dec. 10, 1933; BA, U. Conn., 1957; JD with honors, George Washington U., 1962. Bar: Conn. 1962, D.C. 1982. Trial lawyer U.S. Dept. Justice, Washington, 1963-69; advisor supervisory and regulation div. Fed. Res. Bd., Washington, 1969-73; dir., exec. sec. law enforcement assistance adminstrn. U.S. Dept. Justice, Washington, 1973-75; gen. counsel banking housing and urban affairs com. U.S. Senate, Washington, 1975-84; commr. SEC, Washington, 1984-85; ptnr. Kelley, Drye & Warren, Washington, 1985-94; ind. cons. Washington, 1995—. Apptd. by Pres. Clinton to bd. dirs. Securities Investor Protection Corp.; dir. Ameritrade Holding Corp., 1997—2002. Home and Office: 4911 Massachusetts Ave NW Washington DC 20016-4310

**MARINACCIO, LEE ANTHONY,** lawyer; b. Buffalo, Aug. 24, 1944; s. Anthony John and Leona Laura (Perrone) M.; m. Katherine Ann Kimball, Apr. 6, 1968; children: Lee Anne Lynn, Carla Maria, Laura A., Anna Maria, Anthony John. BA, Elmhurst (Ill.) Coll., 1967; JD, Loyola U., 1971. Bar: Ill. 1971, U.S. Dist. Ct. (no. dist.) Ill. 1972, U.S. Dist. (no. dist.) Ind. 1973, U.S. Ct. Appeals (7th cir.) 1972, U.S. Supreme Ct. 1977. Asst. states atty. DuPage County, Wheaton, Ill., 1971-72; with Office Drug Abuse Law Enforcement, U.S. Dept. Justice, Chgo., 1972-74, Hammond, Ind., 1973-74; asst. U.S. atty. no. Ill. dist. U.S. Atty. Office, Chgo., 1974—75; 1st asst. state atty. Kane County, Geneva, Ill., 1975; ptnr. Botti, Marinaccio Ltd., Oakbrook, Ill., 1975—. Mem. family law com. DuPage County, 1977—, mem. family ct. task force, 1996-99. Mem. ABA, Ill. Bar Assn., DuPage Co. Bar Assn., Kane Co. Bar Assn., Justinian Soc. Lawyers. Office: 720 Enterprise Dr Oak Brook IL 60523-1908 Office Phone: 630-573-8585. Office Fax: 630-573-8586. Business E-Mail: lam@botti-law.com.

**MARINCOLA, ELIZABETH MARK,** nonprofit executive; b. New Haven, Conn., Aug. 31, 1959; d. James B.D. and Jean M. (Rambar) Mark; m. Francesco M. Marincola, Jan. 1, 1982; children: James Paul, Paula Rambar, Rachel Angela. AB, Stanford U., 1981, MBA, 1986. Dir. devel. Stanford (Calif.) U. Hosp., 1987-90; dep. dir. policy rsch. analysis NIMH, Rockville, Md., 1990-91; exec. dir. The Am. Soc. Cell Biology, Bethesda, Md., 1991—2005; pres. Science Service, 2005—; pub. Science News, Wash., DC. Mem. cell biology com. of visitors NSF, 2001; com. for divsn. on earth and life studies Nat. Acad. Sci., 2001—; mem. PubMed Ctrl. Nat. adv. com. Nat. Libr. of Medicine Nat. Inst. Health, 2000-03; 20th Annual Fae Golden Kass lectr. Harvard Med. Sch., 1999; mem. adv. bd. Krasnow Inst. for Advanced Study, George Mason U., 2002—; elected first citizen mem. Am. Soc. Cell Biology, 2003; mem. Joint Steering Com. for Pub. Policy, 1991—, exec. dir., 1991-2005; pres. Sci. Svc. and Sci. News. Mem. strategic adv. bd. Thomson Sci., 2005—; bd. dirs., mem. fin. com. Pub. Libr. Sci., 2005—. Home: 10110 Chapel Rd Potomac MD 20854-4143 Office: Science Service 1719 N St NW Washington DC 20036 Office Phone: 202-785-2255. Business E-Mail: emarincola@sciserv.org.

**MARINE, CLYDE LOCKWOOD,** agricultural products supplier, consultant; b. Knoxville, Tenn., Dec. 25, 1936; s. Harry H. and Idelle (Larue) M.; m. Eleanor Harb, Aug. 6, 1958; children: Cathleen, Sharon. BS in Agr., U. Tenn., 1958; MS in Agrl. Econs., U. Ill., 1959; PhD in Agrl. Econs., Mich. State U., 1963. Sr. market analyst Pet Milk Co., St. Louis, 1963-64; mgr. market planning agr. chems. div. Mobile Chem. Co., Richmond, Va., 1964-67; mgr. ingredient purchasing Central Soya Co., Ft. Wayne, Ind., 1970-73, corp. economist, 1967-70, v.p. ingredient purchasing, 1973-75, sr. v.p., 1975-90; pres. Marine Assocs., Ft. Wayne, 1991—; bd. dirs. SCAN, 1992—. Mem. agrl. policy adv. com. U.S.D.A. Bd. dirs. Ft. Wayne Fine Arts Found., 1976-79, Ft. Wayne Pub. Transp. Corp., 1975-83, Libr. Found.; commr. Metro Human Rels. Commn.; v.p. Ft. Wayne Philharm., 1974-76. Served with U.S. Army, 1959-60. Mem. Nat. Soybean Processors Assn. (chmn.), U.S.C. of C., Am. Agrl. Econs. Assn., Am. Feed Mfrs. Assn. (chmn. purchasing coun.). Clubs: Ft. Wayne Country. Episcopalian. Office: Marine Assocs 4646 W Jefferson Blvd Fort Wayne IN 46804-6842 Office Phone: 260-436-4180. E-mail: lmarine@proparkwest.com.

**MARINE, MICHAEL W.,** ambassador; b. NYC, 1947; married; 2 children. BA in Chinese history, summa cum laude, U. Calif., Santa Barbara, 1974. With U.S. Dept. State, Washington, 1985—, various positions, 1985—91; dep. chief of mission U.S. Embassy, Suva, Fiji, 1991—93, charge d' affaires, 1993—94, minister counselor for consular affairs Bonn, 1994—95, Moscow, 1995—97, dep. chief of mission Nairobi, Kenya, 1997—2000, charge d' affaires, 1999, dep. chief of mission Beijing, 2000—04; US amb. to Vietnam US Dept. State, Hanoi, 2004—. Joined Fgn. Svc., 1975, consular officer, 1979—81, polit. officer, Hong Kong, 1982—85. Advanced through grades to capt. USMC, 1967—71. Office: 4550 Hanoi Pl Washington DC 20521*

**MARINE, SUSAN SONCHIK,** analytical chemist, educator; b. Maple Heights, Ohio, May 10, 1954; d. Stephen Robert and Gloria Ann (Hach) Sonchik; m. Michael David Marine; 1 child, Matthew Robert Marine. BS in Chemistry magna cum laude, John Carroll U., Cleve., 1975; MS in Analytical Chemistry, Case Western Res. U., Cleve., 1978; PhD in Phys. Chemistry, Case Western Res. U., 1980. Asst. chemist Horizons Research Inc., Beachwood, Ohio, 1974-75; chemist specialist Standard Oil of Ohio, Warrensville Heights, Ohio, 1975-79; organic chemistry br. mgr. Versar, Inc., Springfield, Va., 1980-83; mgr. gas chromatography program IBM Instruments Inc., Danbury, Conn., 1983-87, radiation safety officer, 1985-87; expert witness, cons. Martin, Craig, Chester & Sonnenschein, Chgo., 1981-83; advt. engr. in advanced lithography IBM Corp., Essex Junction, Vt., 1987-95; vis. assoc. prof. chemistry Centre Coll., Danville, Ky., 1995-98; asst. prof. chemistry and biochemistry, coord. tech. program Miami U., Middletown, Ohio, 1998—2004; spl. term appointment energy sys. divsn. Argonne Nat. Lab., Ill., 2003—05; assoc. prof. chemistry and biochemistry, coord. tech. program Miami U., Middletown, Ohio, 2004—. Vis. asst. prof. chemistry and math. Heritage Coll., 1991—92; spkr. in field. Author: African Walking Safari, 1985; editl. adv. bd. Jour. Chromatographic Sci., 1977-93, guest editor, 1987. Mem. Danbury Conservation Commn., 1986-87, tchr. and tutor chemistry, 1985-89, 91-92, 94; troop leader Lake Erie coun. Girl Scouts U.S.A., 1971-80, Southwestern Conn., 1983-87; leader explorer post Cleve. coun. Boy Scouts Am., 1977-78; managerial advisor Jr. Achievement, Warrensville Heights, Ohio, 1977-78; judge State or Regional Sci. Fair, 1977, 80, 89-91, 99, 2000, Odyssey of the Mind, 1994; asst. leader Internat. Folk Dancers, Newtown, Conn., 1985-87; tchr. religion, 1981-84, 87-90, 93-94; mem. sch. bd. John XXIII Elem. Sch., 2004—. Recipient Overall Best Paper award Eastern Analytical Symposium, 1984, First Gas Chromatograph award IBM Instruments Inc., 1985, contbn. award (tech. paper) 10th Internat. Congress of Essential Oils, Flavors, Fragrances, Washington, 1986. Mem. ASTM (exec. com. E-19 1985-2000, chmn. subcom. 1986-2000, vice chmn. arrangements 1994-98), Am. Chem. Soc. (chmn. membership com. Green Mountain sect. 1988-89, chmn. 1990-91, local coord. Nat. Chemistry Week 1991, 93-98,

2002-04, mem. nat. com. on technician affairs 2005, 2006, nat. com. on cmty. activities 2005, Phoenix award 1994, 97, Salute to Excellence award 2004), Iota Sigma Pi (pres. N.E. Ohio chpt. 1978-79, mem.-at-large fin. mgr. 1993-97, nat. v.p. 1996-99, nat. pres. 1999-2002, immediate past pres. 2002-05), No. Vt. Canoe Cruisers (treas. 1990-92), Green Mountain Steppers (sec. 1993-95), Centre Coll. Outdoors Club (faculty advisor 1996-98), Miami U. Middletown Chemistry Club (faculty advisor 2003-04), Miami U. Middletown Ski and Snowboard Club (faculty advisor 2004—), Phi Theta Kappa (faculty advisor Miami U. Middletown 2004—). Roman Catholic. Avocations: camping, dance, travel. Home: 4667 Sebald Dr Franklin OH 45005-5328 Office: Miami U Middletown 4200 E University Blvd Middletown OH 45042-3458 Business E-Mail: mariness@muohio.edu.

**MARINEAU, PHILIP ALBERT,** apparel executive; b. Chgo., Oct. 4, 1946; s. Philip Albert and Bernice (Collins) Marineau; m. Susan Anne Graf, June 28, 1969. AB in History, Georgetown U., 1968; MBA, Northwestern U., 1970. Coordinator sales research The Quaker Oats Co., Chgo., 1972-73, mktg. asst., 1973-74, asst. brand mgr., then brand mgr., 1974-78, product group mgr., 1978-80, dir., then v.p. product mgmt., 1980-85, pres. grocery specialties div., 1985-87, exec. v.p. grocery specialties and market devel., 1987-88, exec. v.p. internat. grocery products, 1988, exec. v.p., U.S. grocery products, 1989-93, pres., COO, 1993-96; pres. & COO Dean Foods Co., 1996; pres. & CEO Pepsi-Cola N. America, 1997-99, Levi Strauss & Co., San Francisco, 1999—2006. Bd. mem. Meredith Corp. Bd. dirs. Travelers and Immigrant Aid, Chgo., 1987; bd. mem. Georgetown Univ., Kaiser Permanente, Am. Inst. Pub. Svc.; adv. bd. Kellogg Sch. Mgmt. Northwestern U., Vietnam Veterans Meml. Fund; trustee Northlight Theatre, Evanston, Ill., 1985; bd. mem. Holy Family Day Home, Golden Gate Nat. Parks Conservancy. Mem.: Am. Mktg. Assn. (Steuart Hendersen Britt award 1987), Westmoreland Country Club (Wilmette, Ill.). Office: Levi Strauss & Co 1155 Battery St San Francisco CA 94111*

**MARINELLI, JANICE,** broadcast executive; b. N.Y., 1958; m. Thomas Mazza; 3 children. BS in Comm., St. John's U., NY. Rsch. analyst TeleRep; sr. rschr. Lorimar TV, Katz TV Group; acct. exec. Buena Vista TV, 1985, dir. sales western divsn., exec. v.p., 1996—99, pres. Burbank, Calif., 1999—. Office: Buena Vista TV 500 S Buena Vista St Burbank CA 91521*

**MARINELLI, ROD,** professional football coach; b. Rosemead, Calif., July 13, 1949; m. Barbara Marinelli; children: Chris, Gina. Attended, Univ. Utah, 1968, Calif. Lutheran, 1970—72. Asst. coach Rosemead Highschool, Calif., 1973—75; defensive line coach Utah St. U., 1976—81, offensive line/spl. teams coach, 1982; defensive line coach U. Calif., 1983—91; asst. coach, defensive line coach Ariz. State U., 1993—95; defensive line coach U.S.C., 1995—96, Tampa Bay Bucaneers, 1996—2006; head coach Detroit Lions, 2006—. Served in U.S. Army, 1969, Vietnam. Recipient All-Am. honors, NAIA, 1972. Office: Detroit Lions 222 Republic Drive Allen Park MI 48101*

**MARINER, JONATHAN D.,** major league baseball executive; m. Mildred Mariner; children: Brian, Phillip, Matthew. BS in Acctg., U. Va.; MBA, Harvard U. CPA. Sr. fin. analyst to sr. mgr. MCI Comm., Washington; various positions including sr. mgr. mergers and acquisitions, strategic planning and budgets, and controller insurance ops. Ryder Truck Rental, Fla.; v.p. fin. and adminstrn. Greater Miami Convention and Visitors Bur.; v.p., CFO Fla. Panthers Hockey Club, 1993—94; CFO Pro Player Stadium; pres. Marlins Ballpark Devel. Corp.; exec. v.p., CFO Fla. Marlins Baseball Club, 1992—2000; COO, CFO Charter Schs. USA, 2000—02; exec. v.p., CFO Major League Baseball, 2002—. Bd. dirs. Charter Schs. USA, BankAtlantic Bancorp, Ryan, Beck and Co., Steiner Leisure Ltd. Chmn. Broward Cmty. Coll. Found. Bd.; mem. advisory bd. U. Va. McIntire Sch. Commerce, Pine Crest Sch., Ft. Lauderdale, Fla. Named one of 101 Most Influential Minorities in Sports, Sports Illustrated mag. Avocation: martial arts. Office: Major League Baseball 245 Park Ave 31st Fl New York NY 10167

**MARINER, LINDA KETTERMAN,** minister; d. Charles Albert and Margaret Jane Hearn; m. Howard Paul Ketterman, Sept. 20, 1957 (dec. Oct. 14, 1990); children: Howard Paul Ketterman Jr., Jane Elizabeth Ruark; m. William Bentley Mariner, Feb. 24, 1994 (dec. July 2000). AA in Chem. Dependency Counseling, Wor-Wic C.C., 2000. Course of Study Wesley Theol. Sem., Wash., DC, 2001, License to Preach Drew Theol. Sem. Madison, NJ., 1992, Ordained Deacon United Meth. Ch., 2001. Cert. nursing asst. McCready Meml. Hosp., Crisfield, Md., 1978—85; adminstr. day care ctr. Little Lambs, Ocean Pines, Md., 1991—93. Pastor Sharptown-Asbury Charge, Md., 1993—99, Nanticoke-West Side Parish, Md., 1999—2002. Named Mother of Yr., Asbury United Meth. Ch., 1978, Rookie of Yr., Am. Cancer Soc., 1991, Vol. of Yr., Kent County C. of C., 2005; recipient Gov's award for Voluntarism, State of Md., 2004, Martin Luther King, Jr. Humanitarian award, Chester Valley Mins. Assn., 2005. Mem.: Lion's Club (dist. chaplain 1999—2000, dist. chaplain 2004—05), Phi Theta Kappa. Home: 6190 Rock Hall Rd Rock Hall MD 21661 Office: Rock Hall United Meth Charge PO Box 66 Rock Hall MD 21661 Office Phone: 410-639-2144.

**MARINESCU, DAN CRISTIAN,** computer sciences educator, consultant; b. Craiova, Dolj, Romania, Mar. 4, 1942; s. Nicolae and Aurelia Marinescu; m. Gabriela Magdalena Sezon; 1 child, Andrei. PhD in EECS, Polytechnic Inst., Bucharest, Romania, 1972—75. Prof. computer sci. Purdue U., West Lafayette, Ind., 1984—2001, U. Ctrl. Florida, Orlando, 2001—02; sr. rschr. GSI, Darmstadt, Fla., Germany, 1980—84, Inst. Atomic Physics, Bucharest, Hungary, Romania, 1965—79; assoc. prof. Polytechnic Inst., Bucharest, Hungary, Romania, 1970—79. Vis. prof. INRIA Rocquencourt, Paris, 2000—00, Paris, 1999—99, IBM Rsch., Yorktown Heights, NY, 1985—85, Intel Supercomputer Sys., Portland, 1992—92. Author: Internet-Based Workflow Management, 2002; contbr. articles to profl. jours., 1987. Recipient Grand Challenge, National Science Foundation, 1995, 2002, Virtual Lab for Computational Biology, Nat. Sci. Found., 2001—, Workflow Management, 2001—, 3D Reconstruction of Viruses, 2000—. Greek Orthodox. Avocations: skiing, photography, travel. Home: 14449 Dover Forest Dr Orlando FL 32828 Office: Computer Sci Dept UCF 4000 Central Florida Blvd Orlando FL 32816 E-mail: danc.marinescu@gmail.com.

**MARINETTI, GUIDO V.,** biochemistry professor; b. Rochester, N.Y., June 26, 1918; s. Michael and Nancy (Lippa) M.; m. Antoinette Francione, Sept. 19, 1942; children: Timothy D., Hope L. BS, U. Rochester, 1950, PhD, 1953. Research biochemist Western Regional Lab., Albany, Calif., 1953-54; instr. U. Rochester, NY, 1954-57, asst. prof., 1957-60, assoc. prof., 1960-66, prof. sch. medicine and dentistry, 1966—97; prof. emeritus dept biochemistry and biophysics, 1997—. Cons. Eastman Kodak, 1978, Rochester Gas & Electric, 1979 Author: Disorders of Lipid Metabolism, 1990; editor: Lipid Chromatographic Analysis, 3 vols., 1969, 2nd edit., 1976; contrb. 160 pub. articles in sci. jours. Served with USAAF, 1942-46. Recipient Nat. Infantile Paralysis award, 1952; recipient Glycerine Research award, 1957; NSF grantee, 1953; recipient Lederle Med. Faculty award, 1955, 56 Mem. Am. Soc. Biol. Chemists, Am. Chem. Soc., AAAS, Sigma Xi, Phi Beta Kappa Achievements include research in membrane structure and function, biochemistry of phospholipids, phosphatidylinositiol metabolism in isolated synaptomsomes.

**MARING, MARY MUEHLEN,** state supreme court justice; b. Devils Lake, ND, July 27, 1951; d. Joseph Edward and Charlotte Rose (Schorr) Muehlen; m. David Scott Maring, Aug. 30, 1975; children: Christopher David, Andrew Joseph. BA in Polit. Sci. summa cum laude, Moorhead State U., 1972; JD, U. N.D., 1975. Bar: Minn., N.D. Law clk. Hon. Bruce Stone, Mpls., 1975—76; assoc. Stefanson, Landberg & Alm, Ltd., Moorhead, Minn., 1976—82, Ohnstad, Twichell, Breitling, Rosenvold, Wanner, Nelson, Neugebauer & Maring, West Fargo, ND, 1982—88, Lee Hagan Law Office, Fargo, ND, 1988—91; pvt. practice Maring Law Office, Fargo, 1991—96; justice ND Supreme Ct., Bismarck, ND, 1996—. Women's bd. mem. 1st Nat. Bank, Fargo, 1977-82; career day speaker Moorhead Rotarians, 1980-83; mem. Court Svcs. Com., 1996-, Jud. Compensation, subcom. of Jud. Conf., 1998-,

Five-State Jud. Conf. Planning Com., 1997-98, 99-2000; chmn. Gender Fairness Implementation Com., 1997-, Jud. Conf. Exec. Bd., 1998-, chair-elect, 2004-05, chair, 2005, Juvenile Drug Ct. Study, planning and Implementation Com., 1998-2000, Juvenile Drug Ct. Adv. Com., 2000-, Personnel Policy bd., 1999-2004, Govs. Drug and Alcohol Policy Adv. Bd., 1999-2001, N.Dak. Commn. on Drug and Alcohol Abuse, 2002-, No. Plains Ethics Inst., 2000-, Juvenile Policy Bd., 2001-, Jud. Edn. Com., 2005-, Jud. Planning Com., 2001-, Harold Schafer Leadership Ctr. Com. Contbr. note to legal rev.; note editor N.D. Law Rev., 1975. Mem. ABA (del. ann. conv. young lawyers sect. 1981-82, bd. govs. 1982-83), Minn. Women Lawyers, N.D. State Bar Assn. (bd. govs. 1991-93), Clay County Bar Assn. (v.p. 1983-84), N.D. Trial Lawyers Assn. (pres. 1992-93), Internat. Soc. of Barristers, Nat. Assn. of Women Judges (dist. 10 dir. 2001-03). Roman Catholic. Office: ND Supreme Ct 600 E Boulevard Ave Dept 180 Bismarck ND 58505-0530*

**MARINI, ANN MARIE,** medical researcher, educator; b. Stamford, Conn., May 27, 1949; d. Alfred Francis and Theresa Maryann Marini; m. Robert Henry Lipsky, Sept. 6, 1990; 1 child, Sarah. BA, Erskine Coll., 1971; PhD, Georgetown U., 1978, MD, 1980. Diplomate Am. Bd. Internal Medicine, Am. Bd. Psychiatry and Neurology. Med. resident U. Mass., Worcester, 1980-83; neurology resident Albert Einstein Coll. Medicine, Bronx, N.Y., 1983-86; post-doctoral fellow NIH, Bethesda, Md., 1986-93; staff neurologist Dept. Vet. Affairs, Washington, 1993-94; asst. prof. Uniformed Svcs. U. Health Scis., Bethesda, 1994-2001, assoc. prof., 2001—. Mem. Am. Acad. Neurology (tech. and therapeutics subcom. 1994-99), Soc. for Neurosci., Sigma Xi. Office: Uniformed Svcs U Health Scis 4301 Jones Bridge Rd Bethesda MD 20814-4712 Office Phone: 301-295-9686. Business E-Mail: amarini@usuhs.mil.

**MARINI, FRANK NICHOLAS,** political science and public administration educator; b. Melrose Park, Ill., June 18, 1935; s. Joseph and Lillian Lee (Stuart) M.; m. Elsie McKaskle Marini; children: Lisa M., Katherine D. BA, Ariz. State U., 1960, MA, 1961; PhD, U. Calif., Berkeley, 1966. Instr. U. Mo., Columbia, 1963-64; asst. prof. polit. sci. U. Ky., 1966-67; asst. prof. Syracuse U., 1967-70; assoc. prof., asso. dean Syracuse U. (Maxwell Sch.), dir. public adminstrn. programs, 1970-73; dean Coll. Arts and Letters, San Diego State U., 1973-80; provost U. acad. affairs Calif. State U., Fullerton, 1980-84, sr. adviser chancellor's office, 1984-85; sr. v.p., provost U. Akron, Ohio, 1985-90, prof. pub. adminstrn., urban studies, polit. sci. Ohio, 1990-96, prof. emeritus Ohio, 1996—. Author pamphlets; contrb. numerous articles to profl. jours.; editor: Toward a New Public Administration, 1971; mng. editor: Public Administrn. Rev, 1967-77; editor-in-chief Jour. Pub. Administrn. Edn., 1994-96. Served with USAF, 1954-58. Mem. Am. Soc. Pub. Adminstrn.

**MARINI, ROBERT CHARLES,** environmental engineering executive; b. Quincy, Mass., Sept. 29, 1931; s. Larry and Millie (Cirillo) M.; m. Myrna Lydia Pellegrini, June 26, 1955 (dec. June 1994); children: Debra, Robert Charles, Larry; m. B. Anne Jones, May 27, 1995. BSCE (hon.), Northeastern U., 1954, doctorate (hon.), 1997; SMSE, Harvard U., 1955, postgrad. in advanced mgmt., 1985. Registered profl. engr., Mass., N.Y., Calif., Mich., Va. Jr. engr. Camp Dresser & McKee Inc., Boston, 1955-56, project engr., 1958-64, assoc., 1964-67, ptnr., sr. v.p., 1967-77, pres. environ. engring. div., 1977-82, exec. v.p., 1982-84, pres., 1984-90, CEO, 1989-98, chmn. bd. dirs., 1998—99, vice chmn. bd. dirs., 1999-2001, chmn. emeritus, 2001—. Mem. civil engring. adv. com. Worcester (Mass.) Poly. Inst., 1980-90, U. Mass., 1986-90, U. Tex., Austin, 1989-91, chmn., 1991-92, mem. engring. found. adv. coun., 1991-98; trustee South Shore Savs. Bank, 1990—, audit com., 2001-. Contbr. articles to profl. jours. Dir. nat. coun. Northeastern U., Boston, 1983-2004, mem. corp. bd., 1983-2004, bd. overseers, 1985-89, trustee, 1989-2004; chmn. Leadership Phase Century II Fund, 1989-91, chmn. devel. com., 1991-98, vice chmn. bd. trustees, 1997-2004, vice chmn. emeritus, 2004-; bd. dirs. Mass. Bus. Round Table, chmn. vice chmn., 1995-97, chmn., 1997-99. Recipient Disting. Eagle Scout award Boy Scouts Am., 1986, Mass. Patriots award Old Colony Coun., 1998, W. Erwin Story award, 1991, Outstanding Civil Engring. Alumni award Northeastern U., 1992, Outstanding Alumni award, 1993; named Man of Yr., Don Orione, 1999. Fellow ASCE (hon., Opal award 2003), NAE, Boston Soc. Civil Engrs. (hon.); mem. Am. Pub. Works Assn. (Man of Yr. award New Eng. chpt. 1981), Am. Water Works Assn., Mass. Soc. Profl. Engrs. (Young Engr. of Yr. award 1966), Am. Acad. Environ. Engrs. (diplomate, trustee at large 1989-92, v.p. 1992-93, pres.-elect 1993-94, pres. 1994-95, Stanley E. Kappe award 1992, Gordon Maskew Fair award, 2005), Water Environment Fedn. (hon., N.E. chpt., Founders award 1999), Internat. Assn. Water Pollution Rsch. and Control, Engring. Soc. New Eng. (New Eng. award 1994), Greater Boston C. of C. (bd. dirs. 1997-99), Water Environ. Rsch. Found. (bd. dirs. 1991-93), Tau Beta Pi, Phi Kappa Phi. Roman Catholic. Home: 1 Nevin Rd Weymouth MA 02190-1610 Office: Camp Dresser & McKee Inc 50 Hampshire St Cambridge MA 02139 Office Phone: 617-452-6000. Business E-Mail: marinirc@cdm.com.

**MARINIS, THOMAS PAUL, JR.,** lawyer; b. Jacksonville, Tex., May 31, 1943; s. Thomas Paul and Betty Sue (Garner) M.; m. Lucinda Cruse, June 25, 1969; children: Courtney, Kathryn, Megan. BA, Yale U., 1965; LLB, U. Tex., 1968. Bar: Tex. 1968. Assoc. Vinson & Elkins, Houston, 1969-76, ptnr., 1977—. Bd. mem. Phoenix House of Tex., Inc. Fellow Tex. Bar Found.; mem. ABA (sec. taxation sect. 1986-87), Houston Country Club, Houston Ctr. Club, Coronado Club. E-mail: tmarinis@velaw.com.

**MARINO, CAROLYN,** psychologist; b. Pensacola, Aug. 16, 1951; d. Dayton, Jr. Robinson and Henen Louise Swanson; m. Matthew J. Marion, Dec. 17, 1984 (div.); 1 child, Colen Alexander 1 stepchild, Klaudia Marguerite. MA in Asian studies, U. Mich., 1975; MA in English lang. and lit., U. Ala., 1981, PhD in Clin. Psychology, 1993. Editor, rschr. dir. publs. Ala. Internat. Trade Ctr., Tuscaloosa, 1981—83; grad. lectr. English dept. The Compassionate Friends, Tuscaloosa, 1983—84, U. Ala., Tuscaloosa, 1984—86, lectr. English dept., 1988, clin. Psychology intern Birmingham, 1991—92; grad. lectr. English dept. Ind. Crisis Fedn., Purdue U., 1987—88; clin. Psychology intern U.S. Vets. Adminstrn., Tuscaloosa, 1995—2006. Author (editor): AITC Newsletter, 1981— (Dir., Publ. and Rsc. award, 1983). Grantee Nat. Def. and Leadership Scholarship, U. Mich., 1976—78, Grad. Council Fellowship, U. Ala., 1985—86. Democrat. Methodist. Home: 3308 University Blvd E Tuscaloosa AL 35404

**MARINO, DAN,** sports broadcaster, retired professional football player; b. Pitts., Sept. 15, 1961; BA in Comm., U. Pitts., 1983. Quarterback Miami Dolphins, 1983—99; co-host Inside the NFL, HBO, 2000—, NFL Today, CBS, 2002—. Film appearance: Ace Ventura: Pet Detective, 1994; co-author (with David Hyde): Dan Marino: My Life in Football, 2005. Named All-Am. team quarterback, The Sporting News, 1981, Rookie of Yr., 1983, NFL All-Pro team, 1984—86, MVP, Nat. Football League, 1984—85; named to Pro Bowl Team, 1983—87, 1991—92. Achievements include having the NFL career record for most games (12) with 400 or more yards passing; NFL records for most seasons (6) with 4,000 or more yards passing, most seasons (9) with 3,000 or more yards passing, 1984-92; most consecutive games (4) with four or more touchdown passes, 1984; NFL record for lowest percentage (2.03) of passes intercepted by a rookie, 1983; NFL record for most games (17) with four or more touchdown passes, 1984; inducted to the Pro Football Hall of Fame, 2005. Office: 1100 Avenue of the Americas New York NY 10036

**MARINO, EUGENE LOUIS,** publishing executive, director; b. N.Y.C., Jan. 7, 1929; s. Salvatore A. and Florence M. (Casabona) M.; m. Patricia Ryan, Mar. 11, 1948; children: Jeanette, Anthony, John, Eugene III. Student, Columbia U., 1945-48. Credit mgr. Sears, Roebuck Inc., L.I., NY, 1951-60; gen. credit mgr. Davison-Paxon div. R.H. Macy, Inc., Atlanta, 1960-63, Grand-Way div. Grand Union Co. N.Y.C., 1963-66; v.p. gen. credit mgr. Consumer Products div. Singer Co., N.Y.C., 1966-75, Grolier, Inc., Danbury, Conn., 1975-90; ret. Officer, v.p., gen. credit mgr. dir. numerous subsidiaries.

Recipient Quarter Century cert. Internat. Consumer Credit Assn., 1981. Mem. Mchts. Rsch. Coun., Internat. Consumer Credit Assn., Nat. Assn. Credit Mgmt., Alpha Sigma Phi. Home: 4858 Tivoli Ct Sarasota FL 34235-3653 E-mail: elmarino@comcast.net.

**MARINO, GIOVANNI,** surgeon; b. Catania, Italy, Dec. 23, 1969; s. Salvatore and Rosetta (Rapisarda) Marino. MD with honors, U. Catania, 1993, PhD, 2001. Cert. in Medicine 1993, in General Surgery with honors Italian Bd. Surgery, 2001. Internship U. Catania, Dept. Plastic Surgery, 1992—93; chief med. officer Italian Air Force, Rieti Mil. Base, Italy, 1994—95; fellow Dept. of Surg. Oncology, San Luigi Hosp., Catania, 1999—2001; primary care physician Italian Health Sys., Vizzini, Italy, 2001. Vis. fellow U. Pisa (Italy) Dept Surg. Endoscopy, 1996—97; vis. fellow Great Ormond St. Hosp., London, 1999; instr. surgery Thomas E. Starzl Transplantation Inst., U. Pitts., 2003—05. Author: Experimental Models of Liver Transplantation, 1998, Abdominal Surgery Today, 1999, Laparoscopic Approach to the Essential Varicocele, 2000, Surgery in Old Age, 2000; contbr. articles to profl. jours. Chief med. officer Italian Air Force, 1994—95, Rieti, Italy. Recipient S.I.S.M Scholarship, Italian Soc. of Med. Students, 1992, Fulbright Scholarship, Thomas E. Starzl Transplantation Inst., Fulbright Commn., 2001-2002. Mem.: Surg. Soc. Catania, European Assn. for Endoscopic Surgery, Internat. Liver Transplantation Soc., Italian Soc. Young Surgeons, Italian Soc. Endoscopic Surgery, Sicilian Soc. Surgery, Med. Soc. Catania. Achievements include first to perform laparoscopic robot assisted andrenalectomy; use a robot AESOP to perform endoscopy operations. Personal E-mail: marinog@unict.it.

**MARINO, IGNAZIO ROBERTO,** transplant surgeon, educator, researcher; b. Genoa, Italy, Mar. 10, 1955; s. Pietro Rosario and Valeria (Mazzanti) M.; m. Rossana Parisen-Toldin, Sept. 15, 1990; 1 child, Stefania Valeria. Maturità-Classica, Coll. of Merode, Rome, 1973; MD, Cath. U., Rome, 1979. Diplomate Nat. Bd. Gen. Surgery, Nat. Bd. Vascular Surgery. Intern, then resident Gemelli U. Hosp., Rome, 1979-84; temp. asst. dept. surgery Cath. U., Rome, 1981, asst. prof. surgery, 1983-92; asst. prof. surgery Transplantation Inst. U. Pitts., 1991-95, assoc. prof. surgery Transplantation Inst./, 1995-99; prof. surgery postgrad. Sch. Microsurgery, Exptl. Surgery U. Milan, 1994—; prof. surgery Sch. Medicine U. Perugia, 1994—; attending surgeon U. Pitts. Med. Ctr., Pitts., 1991—2002; assoc. dir. transplant divsn. VA Med. Ctr., Pitts., 1992—2002; attending surgeon Children's Hosp. Pitts., 1993—; prof. surgery Transplantation Inst., U. Pitts., 1999—2002, Thomas Jefferson Med. Coll., Phila., 2002—; dir. divsn. transplantation Thomas Jefferson U. Hosp., Phila., 2004—; sen. Repub. of Italy, 2006—. Mem. surg. team 1st and 2d baboon to human liver transplants U. Pitts. Med. Ctr., 1992-93; dir. European med. divsn., 1990-92; nat. ad hoc donations com. United Network for Organ Sharing, 1995—; cons. Nat. Transplant Com. Italy, 1999—; regional com. Organ Procurement Orgn. for Sicily, 1999—; mem. Nat. Tech. Commn. for Informative Campaign on Organ Donation of Italy, 1999—, Nat. Ctr. Transplantation of Italy, 2000—; co-founder, pres. Imagine ONLUS, 2005—; senator Italian Republic, chmn. standing health com. Italian Senate. Author: New Technique to Avoid the Revascularization Syndrome in Liver Transplantation, 1985 (Ann. prize Italian Soc. Surgery, 86), New Technique in Liver Transplantation, 1996 (De Angelis award, 86); mem. editl. bd.: Clin. Transplantation, Leadership Medica, Transplantation, Jour. Investigative Surgery; contbr. more than 590 sci. articles to profl. jours. Co-founder, pres. Imagine, 2005-. Grantee Italian Nat. Coun. Rsch., 1979, 86-93, Gastroenterology Soc., 1988; recipient award Inst. Nazionale Previdenza Dirigenti Aziende Industriali, 1982. Mem. ACS, Am. Soc. Transplantation Surgeons, Am. Soc. Transplant Physicians, Italian Soc. Surgery, Transplantation Soc. (grant 1988), European Soc. for Organ Transplantation, Soc. Surgeons Under 40 (ann. prize 1986), Cell Transplant Soc. (founding mem.), Acad. Surg. Rsch., Soc. Critical Care Medicine, Internat. Liver Transplantation Soc., Italian Order Journalists, Assn. Italian Corrs. in N.Am. (assoc.), Xenotransplantation Club (founding mem.), Internat. Coll. Surgeons, Assn. for Acad. Surgery, Nat. Assn. VA Physicians, Univ. Physician Practice Assn., Xenotransplantation Assn., Am. Assn. for the Study of Liver Diseases. Avocations: reading (history books), sailing, scuba diving, yoga. Home: Corso Italia 29 Rome 00198 Italy Office: Thomas Jefferson U Ste 605 Coll Bldg 1025 Walnut St Philadelphia PA 19107-5083 Office Phone: 215-955-4845. Business E-Mail: ignazio.marino@jefferson.edu.

**MARINO, LOUIS J(OHN),** mathematics educator; b. Whitestone, N.Y., May 3, 1949; s. Lewis F. and Lillian (Sheilds) M.; m. Sheila Burris, Dec. 19, 1969; children: Sheila Noelle, Heather Michelle. BS, U. Tenn., 1971, MS, 1975; MA in Teaching, U. S.C., 1977; AS in Engring., Piedmont Tech. Coll., 1981. Cert. tchr., S.C., learning disabled, 2002-; elem. edn., 2001-, nat. bd. candidate, 2004. Salesman Harper Bros., Inc., Greenwood, S.C., 1971-72; tchr. Orangeburg County (S.C.) Sch. Dist. 5, 1975-76, Greenwood County (S.C.) Sch. Dist. 50, 1976-77; mgr. Burger King, Greenwood, 1977-79; tchr. Laurens County (S.C.) Sch. Dist. 55, 1980-94; math. tchr. Long Cane Acad., McCormick, SC, 1994-95, math tchr., 2000—01; entrepreneur, 1995-98; security agent Omnisec, Greenville, SC, 1998-99; math tchr. McCormick Mid. Sch., 2002—, Greenville County Sch. Dist., 2002—; math and sci. tchr. Woodmont Mid. Sch., 2002—05; spl. edn. tchr. Calhoun Falls H.S., 2005—. Adj. prof. Limestone Coll., Spartanburg, S.C., 1978-79, Piedmont Tech. Coll., Greenwood, 1979-81. S.C. Dept. Edn. grantee, 1986. Mem. Laurens County Edn. Assn. (pres. 1991-92, sec. 1980-83, 90-91), assn. rep. 1984-94, mem. svcs. 1984-86, chmn. membership com. 1988-89), Nat. Model Railroad Assn., 2001—, Phi Delta Kappa. Democrat. Presbyterian. Avocations: astronomy, model trains, coin collecting/numismatics. Home: 103 Essex Ct Greenwood SC 29649-9561

**MARINO, MICHAEL FRANK, III,** lawyer; b. Little Falls, N.Y., Feb. 19, 1948; s. Michael Frank and Betty (Roberts) M.; m. Catherine Viladesau Aug. 11, 1971 (div. Nov. 1996); m. Ann Duffield Feb. 15, 1997; children: Michael John, Lisa Kathryn, Matthew Christopher. BS, Cornell U., 1971; JD, Syracuse U., 1974; LLM, Georgetown U., 1982. Bar: D.C. 1975, U.S. Dist. Ct. D.C. 1975, U.S. Ct. Mil. Appeals 1975, N.Y. 1976, U.S. Dist. Ct. (ea. and we. dists.) Va. 1977, U.S. Dist. Ct. Md. 1980, U.S. Ct. Appeals (4th cir.) 1982, Va. 1982, U.S. Ct. Appeals (9th cir.) 1994. Civilian employee head rels. br. Office of the Judge Adv. of the Navy, Washington, 1975-76; spl. asst. to the gen. counsel Office of Sec. of Navy, Washington, 1977; asst. gen. counsel labor and employment Office of the Gen. Counsel of the Navy, Washington, 1978; assoc. Pierson, Ball & Dowd, Washington, 1978-81; prin. Boothe, Prichard & Dudley, Fairfax and Mc Lean, Va., 1981-87, McGuire, Woods, Battle & Boothe, Mc Lean, 1987-89, Reed, Smith, Shaw & McClay, N.Y., 1989-2000, Hunton & Williams, McLean, Va., 2000—. Labor group head, Washington, Va.; mng. ptnr. McLean Office. Author: Virginia Employer's Guide to Labor Law, 1987; co-author: New York Employer's Guide, 1989, 1992—2001, Florida Labor and Emloyment Law, 2001, Labor Employment Law in Pennsylvania, 1994. Mem. planning com. SMU Multi State labor Law Conf., Dallas; chmn. Arlington (Va.) Chamber Employee Rels. Com.; bd. dirs. Arlington Chamber; mem. Va. Chamber Mgmt. Rels. Com. Richmond, 1980—; bd. dirs. Dan Marino Found. Capt. USMC, 1971-78. Mem.: ABA (labor law com. 1974—, Pro Bono award 2000), N.Y. Bar Assn. (labor law com. 1974—), Va. Bar Assn. (labor law com. 1974—, sec.-treas. labor law sect. 1995, vice chair 1996—97), D.C. Bar Assn. (labor law com. 1974—). Roman Catholic. Avocations: exercise, boating. Office: Hunton & Williams 1751 Pinnacle Dr Ste 1700 Mc Lean VA 22102-3836 E-mail: mmarino@hunton.com.

**MARINO, MIGUEL ANGEL,** engineering educator; b. Cienfuegos, Cuba, Nov. 10, 1940; arrived in US, 1967; s. Ramon and Julia Marino; m. Irma Padovani, July 27, 1968; 1 child, Raquel Christina. AA, Andrew Coll., 1959 BS, N.Mex. Inst. Mining and Tech., 1962, MS, 1965; PhD, UCLA, 1972. Asst. geohydrologist N.Mex. State Engrs. Office, Santa Fe, 1964; asst. hydrologist Ill. State Water Survey, Champaign, 1965-69; from asst. prof. to assoc. prof. U. Calif., Davis, 1972—80, prof., 1980-99, prof. above-scale, 1999—2003, disting. prof., 2003—. Author: Groundwater and Seepage, 1982, Regional Management of Water

Resources, 2001, Integrated Water Resources Management, 2001, (monograph) Subsurface Flow and Contamination, 1987; contbr. articles to profl. jours. Pres./elect Am. Inst. of Hydrology, 2003—05; v.p. Internat. Commn. Water Resources Sys.; bd. dirs. Univs. Coun. Water Resources. Recipient Warren A. Hall medal, Univs. Coun. Water Resources. Fellow: Am. Geophys. Union, Am. Water Resources Assn. (hon.); mem.: ASCE (hon. Outstanding Jour. Paper awards 1986, 1990, Julian Hinds award 1996, Richard R. Torrens award 1986), Internat. Assn. Hydrol. Scis. (Best Paper award), Am. Inst. Hydrology (pres.-elect, cert.), Am. Water Resources Assn., N.Y. Acad. Scis., Sigma Xi, Tau Beta Pi. Home: 813 Harrier Pl Davis CA 95616-0173 Office: Univ Calif 139 Veihmeyer Hall Davis CA 95616 Office Phone: 530-752-0684. Business E-Mail: MAMarino@ucdavis.edu.

**MARINO, NANCY A.,** marketing professional; b. N.Y.C., Aug. 11; d. Thomas and Ruth Firriolo; m. J. Richard Marino. BA in Mktg., Hunter Coll., 1971. Exec. v.p. AMC, NYC, 1990—97; pres., CEO Frederick Atkins, NYC, 1997—99; pres. Linmark, NYC, 1999—2002, SVP Brond Devel. Worldwide Sourcing, 2002—04; exec. dir. NMG Consulting Corp., NYC, 2004—05; sr. v.p. global sourcing Sara Lee Branded Apparel, 2005—. Bd. dirs. USA-ITA, N.Y.C., Cotton Inc., N.Y.C.; mem. steering com. Fashion Group Internat., N.Y.C., 1999—. Mem. found. bd. Fashion Inst. Tech., N.Y.C., 1999—. Mem.: Retail Mktg. Soc. (bd. dirs. 1998—). Office: 1000 E Hanes Mill Rd Winston Salem NC 27105 Office Phone: 516-448-9994. Personal E-mail: nancymarino@earthlink.net.

**MARINO, NATALIE MARIE,** artist; b. Elizabeth, NJ, July 4, 1957; d. John T. and Stefana (Sarullo) Marino; m. Anthony Paul D'Alessio, Aug. 28, 1968 (div. 1998); 1 child, Stephanie Elsbeth; m. Brian James Blackmore, Mar. 27, 1998; children: Jonathan Brian, Ronnie Marin, Stefana. BA, NYU, 1969; postgrad., New Sch., N.Y.C., 1969-72; cert., N.J. Ctr. Visual Arts, 1977. Tchr. mural projects to at-risk populations, Paterson, 2004—05. One-woman shows include Exxon Corp., Linden, NJ, 1985, Florence Gallery, Dallas, 1985, Rosalyn Sailors, Phila., 1993, ART Insights, NY, Marino Galleries, Millburn, NJ, 1994, 96, YMCA Patterson, NJ, 2004; exhibited in group shows at NJ State Mus., 1979, Bergen Cmty. Mus., Paramus, NJ, 1980, Nat. Art Club, NYC, 1981, Lincoln Ctr., NYC, 1983, Cork Art Gallery, NYC, 1983, Phila. Port of History Mus., 1984, others; represented in permanent collections including Rosalyn Sailor Gallery and Mus. Fine Art, Margate, NJ, Phila., Tom Weiner's Art Insights, NYC, Marino Galleries, Inc., Millburn, Ward St. YMCA, Crown Roll Leaf; editor, designer: Once Upon a Star, 2003; illustrator (book) A Place in the Sky, Andrew's Dragon; author: (screenplay) The Successor, 1989; illustrator: Art Lovers Cookbook, 1975, A Place in the Sky, 2003, Tappi and Her Shiny Black Tap Shoes, 2003, Andrews Dragon, 2004, Once Upon a Star, 2004, The Light in My Room, 2006, Tee Ball, Butterflys Wings and Magical Things, They Say I Have ADHD; I Say Life Sucks, 2006; host cablecast series Art Forum; prodr., dir. video and TV programs. Vol. cons. N.J. Ctr. for Visual Arts, Summit, 1989; trustee TV 36, Communities on Cable, Summit, 1989; judge for sr. citizen art shows, Newark, 1989. Recipient Bee Co. award Pastel Soc. Am., 1981, European Banner of Arts, Accademia d'Europa, 1984; grantee Union County Divsn. Art and Cultural Affairs, N.J. State Coun. Arts, Union County Cultural Commn., 1985-86, Ludwig Vogelstein Found., 1989, Patterson Divsn. Art and Cultural Affairs, 2004, 05, Crown Gold Leaf Corp., 2004, Passaic County Cultural Commn., 2004, 05 Fellow Artists Equity, Women's Caucus for Art, Riker Hill Art Park (exec. com.); mem. N.J. Ctr. Visual Art (award 1979). Home: PO Box 225 Springfield NJ 07081-0225

**MARINO, RALPH J.,** rehabilitation services professional; BS in Biopsychology, Eckerd Coll., 1978; MD, Jefferson Med. Coll., 1982; MS in Clin. Epidemiology, U. Pa., 1998. Bd. cert. Am. Bd. Phys. Medicine and Rehab., Minn., 1988, cert. subsplty. spinal cord injury medicine Am. Bd. Phys. Medicine and Rehab., Minn., 2000. Assoc. prof., dept. rehab. medicine Mt. Sinai Sch. Medicine, NYC, 1998—2002, Jefferson Med. Coll. Thomas Jefferson U., 2002—. Clin. dir., spinal cord injury svc. Thomas Jefferson U. Hosp., 2002—; assoc. dir. rsch., dept. rehab. medicine Jefferson Med. Coll., Phila., 2002—. Recipient Physician Scientist award, NIH, 1993—98. Mem.: Am. Congress Rehab. Medicine (treas. 2002), Am. Spinal Injury Assn. (chair neurol. standards com. 1999, mem. bd. govs. 2003). Office: Thomas Jefferson U 132 South 10th St Ste 375 Main Philadelphia PA 19107 Office Phone: 215-955-5756. Office Fax: 215-955-5152.

**MARINO, SHEILA BURRIS,** education educator; b. Knoxville, Nov. 24, 1947; d. David Paul and Lucille Cora (Maupin) Burris; m. Louis John Marino, Dec. 19, 1969; children: Sheila Noelle, Heather Michelle. BS, U. Tenn., 1969, MS, 1971, EdD, 1976; postgrad., W.Va. U., Europe, Clemson U. Elem./early childhood tchr. Knoxville City Schs., 1969-71; cooperating tchr. U. Tenn., Knoxville, 1969-71; dir. early childhood edn./tchr. Glenville (W.Va.) State Coll., 1971-72, Colo. Women's Coll., Denver, 1972-73; asst. prof. edn. Lander U., Greenwood, SC, 1973-75; instr., spl. asst. to coord. elem./early childhood edn. U. Tenn., 1975-76; dir. clin. experiences, asst. dean Lander U. Sch. Edn., 1976—93, dean, 1993-94, dir. sci. discovery program, 1995—; prof. edn., dir. tchg. fellows program, 1995—. Cons. in field; dir. Creative Activities Prog. for Children, Lander U., 1979—; mem. W.Va. Gov.'s Early Childhood Adv. Bd., 1971-72, Gov.'s Team of Higher Edn. Profls. on Comprehensive Plan for S.C. Early Childhood Edn., 1982. Contbr. articles to profl. jours. and books; author: International Children's Literature, 1989. Bd. dirs. Greenwood Lit. Coun., v.p., 1990, pres., 1991; bd. dirs. St. Nicholas Speech and Hearing Ctr., Greenwood, pres., 1992; bd. dirs. Old Ninety-Six coun. Girl Scouts U.S.A., 1987-92; vol. March of Dimes Program, Greenwood, 1987; vice chair Greenwood County First Steps, 2004—. Mem. AAUW (pres. 1990-92), AAUP, SNEA (state advisor 1981-88, 98-99), S.C. Student Edn. Assn., Piedmont Assn. Children and Adults with Learning Disabilities (pres. 1986-93, exec. bd.), Learning Disabilities Assn. S.C. (pres. 1990-94), S.C. Edn. Assn., S.C. Assn. for Children Under Six, So. Assn. for Children under Six, S.C. Assn. Tchr. Educators, Piedmont Reading Coun. (v.p. 1985-86, 90-91, pres. 1986-88, 91-92, 96-97), S.C. Coun. Internat. Reading Assn. (exec. bd. 1986-88, 91-96), Delta Kappa Gamma (pres. Epsilon chpt. 1984-88, 92-94, mem. exec. bd.), Pi Lambda Theta, Kappa Delta Pi (pres. U. Tenn. chpt. 1974-75), Phi Delta Kappa (v.p. 1988-90, pres. Lander U. chpt. 1990-91, 94-96, 2005—). Democrat. Presbyterian. Avocations: reading, gardening, swimming, music, arts and crafts. Home: 103 Essex Ct Greenwood SC 29649-9561 Office: Lander U Stanley Avenue Greenwood SC 29649

**MARINO, THOMAS A.,** prosecutor, lawyer; b. 1952; AA, Williamsport Area C.C., 1983; BA, Lycoming Coll.; JD, Dickinson U. Assoc. McNerney, Page, Vanderlin & Hall, Williamsport, Pa., 1988—96; dist. atty. Lycoming County, Pa., 1996—2002; US atty. (mid. dist.) Pa. US Dept. Justice, 2002—. Office: US Atty's Office PO Box 309 Scranton PA 18501*

**MARINO, WILLIAM FRANCIS,** telecommunications industry executive, consultant; b. Phila., Dec. 28, 1948; s. William F. and Edith Ellen (Dougherty) M.; m. Mary Ellen Klems, Sept. 29, 1979; children: Kiersten Leigh, Meghan Lyn. Student, Ohio State U., 1967; BS in Fin. and Acctg., Widener U., 1970. Sr. acctg., fin. positions U.S. Steel Corp., Pitts., 1970-83; v.p. U.S. Steel Credit Corp., Pitts. 1983-85; dir. fin. programs CIS Corp., Syracuse, N.Y., 1985, v.p. instl. sales, 1986; pres. CIS Credit Corp., Syracuse, N.Y., 1987, v.p. fin., 1988; v.p., chmn. reorganization com. Continental Info. Systems Corp., Syracuse, N.Y., 1989; v.p. fin., CFO ITEC Corp., Lake Bluff, Ill., 1990-91, pres., CEO, 1991—; Global Telecom Svcs. Corp., 2000—. Advisor, cons. Chong & Assocs., N.Y.C. 1989. Advisor Hiawatha coun. Boy Scouts Am., Syracuse, 1987; dir. Cystic Fibrosis Found., Syracuse, 1987-88. Recipient Century award Boy Scouts Am., Syracuse, 1988. Mem. Am. Assn. Equipment Lessors, Am. Mgmt. Assn., Fin. Execs. Inst., Aircraft Owners & Pilots Assn. Republican. Avocations: flying, cross country skiing. Home: 8763 Muirfield Dr Naples FL 34109-4352 Office: Global Telecom Svcs Corp 8763 Muirfield Dr Naples FL 34109-4352 Personal E-mail: billmarino@comcast.net.

**MARINO, WILLIAM J.,** insurance executive; Various positions Prudential Ins. Co. Am., 1968-91, Horizon Blue Cross & Blue Shield of N.J., Inc., Newark, 1991-94; pres., CEO Horizon Blue Cross & Blue Shield of NJ Inc, Newark, 1994—. Mem. exec. com. Blue Cross/Blue Shield Assn. (BCBSA), chair Inter-Plan Operating Com. and Emerging Issues of BCBSA, bd. dirs. of Health Insurance Assn. of America, Nat. Inst. for Health Care Mgmt. Trustee, chmn. United Way of Essex and West Hudson, N.J., campaign chmn. 1993-94; chmn., bd. dirs., mem. exec. com. Regional Bus. Partnership; trustee N.J. Network Found., St. Peter's Coll., Newark Mus.; bd. pres. advisors Fairleigh Dickinson U.; mem. chief justice com. on efficiency N.J. Jud. Sys.; past trustee Kessler Inst. for Rehab., Inc. Mem. N.J. State C. of C., past chmn. bd. dirs., exec. com. Blue Cross/Blue Shield Assn. (BCBSA), Inter-Plan Operating Com., mem. Emerging Issues Com. of BCBSA, bd. dirs. Health Insurance Assn. of Amer., Nat. Inst. for Health Care Mgmt. Office: Horizon Blue Cross/Blue Shield NJ Inc 3 Penn Plz E Newark NJ 07105-2245*

**MARINO, ANNE WINDFOHR,** rancher, museum administrator; b. Fort Worth, Tex., Nov. 10, 1938; d. James Goodwin Hall and Anne (Burnett) Hall Tandy; m. John Louis Marion, 1988; 1 child, Anne Phillips Grimes. Attended, Univ. Tex., Austin, Univ. Geneva, Switzerland. Chmn. Burnett Oil Co.; pres. Burnett Ranches Ltd., 6666 Ranch, Guthrie, Tex., Burnett Found., Forth Worth, Tex. Chmn. Georgia O'Keeffe Mus., Santa Fe; trustee Kimbell Art Mus., Forth Worth, Tex.; trustee, former chmn. & pres., chmn. acquisition com. Modern Art Mus., Forth Worth, Tex.; past trustee Mus. Modern Art, NYC; mem. bd. regents Texas Tech Univ.; dir. emeritus Nat. Cowboy Hall of Fame; mem. exec. com. Forth Worth Stock Show; honorary bd. mem. Nat. Cowgirl Hall of Fame, West. Heritage Ctr. Named Great Woman of Texas, Fort Worth Bus. Press, 1993; named one of Top 200 Collectors, ARTnews Mag., 2003—; Forbes Richest Americans, 2006; recipient Charles Goodnight award, 1993, Golden Deed honoree, Fort Worth Exchange Club, 1993, Fern Sawyer award, Nat. Cowgirl Hall of Fame, 1994, Gov. award for excellence in the arts, New Mex., 1996, Boss of the Plains award, Ranching Heritage Ctr., 2000. Mem.: Tex. & S.W. Cattle Raisers Assn. (honorary v.p.), Am. Quarter Horse Assn. (honorary v.p., Merle Wood Humanitarian award 1999). Mailing: Burnett Ranches Ltd PO Box 130 Guthrie TX 79236

**MARION, JOHN LOUIS,** former fine arts auctioneer and appraiser; b. NYC, Nov. 27, 1933; s. Louis John and Florence Adelaide (Winters) Marion; m. Anne Burnett Windfohr, May 26, 1988; children from previous marriage: John L., Deborah Mary, Therese Marie, Michelle Marie. BS, Fordham U., 1956; postgrad., Columbia U., 1960—61. With Sotheby Parke Bernet Inc., N.Y.C., 1960—, dir., 1965—, v.p., 1966—70, exec. v.p., 1970—72, pres., 1972—87; chmn. bd. Sotheby's Inc., N.Y.C., 1975—, now hon. chmn. Bd. dirs. Sotheby Holdings Inc., London, Mus. N.Mex. Sys. Chmn. fine arts NYC divsn. Am. Cancer Soc., 1983—; vice chmn. bldg. steering com. Dobbs Ferry (NY) Hosp., 1975; bd. dirs. Internat. Found. Art Rsch.; Ctr. for Hope. Lt. (j.g.) USN, 1956—60. Named one of Top 200 Collectors, ARTnews Mag., 2004—. Mem.: Appraisers Assn. Am., Vintage Club, Shady Oaks Club, Eldorado Club, Lotos Club. Avocation: Collector of 17th and 18th century European art; modern and contemporary art.

**MARION, JOHN MARTIN,** instructional technology educator; b. Fitchburg, Mass., Jan. 11, 1947; s. Don Louis and Violet Pearl Marion; m. Joann Elizabeth Trzcinski, Aug. 8, 1970; children: Benjamin Andrew, Jessica Noelle. BS in Edn., Fitchburg State Coll., 1969, MEd, 1971; postgrad., Pepperdine U. Tchr. Groton (Mass.) Dunstable Regional Schs., 1969-84; computer tchr. Littleton (Mass.) Pub. Schs., 1985-86; computer coord. K-12 8th grades Newburyport (Mass.) Pub. Schs., 1986-90; assoc. dean Acad. Computing Endicott Coll., Beverly, Mass., 1990—98; dir. tech. Reading (Mass.) Pub. Schs., 1998-2000; media tech. specialist Dracut Pub. Schs., Mass., 2000—03; tech. edn. specialist Jefferson County (Colo.) Pub. Schs., 2003—. Instr. Merrimack Edn. Ctr., Chelmsford, Mass., 1990-92; trainer, cons. Logo Computer Sys., Inc., N.Y.C., 1984-90; tchr. trainer Lego-Decta, Lego Sys., Inc., Enfield, Conn., 1987-90; mem. adv. bd. Claris Software Co.; bd. dirs. Mass. Computing Using Educator, 1989-90; master tchr. trainer Intel-Teach to the Future program Jefferson Pub. Schs., 2004—, info. literacy adv. com., 2004—. Bd. dirs. Reading Cmty. TV, Inc., 1998-99. Fulbright scholar tchr. exch., Southampton, Eng., 1973-74. Mem.: ASCD, Internat. Tech. Edn. Assn., Internat. Soc. Tech.in Edn., Phi Delta Kappa. Office: Jeffco Schs 9201 W Columbine Dr Littleton CO 80128-4140 Home: 29191 Shadow Mountain Dr Conifer CO 80433-8612 Office Phone: 303-982-4130. Personal E-mail: jmarion@aol.com.

**MARION, LINDA SHEETZ,** psychology professor; b. Reading, Pa., Mar. 27, 1947; d. Lester William and Betty Jane Sheetz; m. David J. Marion, Nov. 24, 1985; children: Elana Beth, Daniel William Benjamin. MEd, Temple U., 1971; MS, Drexel U., 1998, PhD, 2004. Lic. psychologist Pa., 1978. Psychologist pvt. practice, Berwyn, Pa., 1978—89; educator Drexel U. Phila., 2000—; rschr. U. NSW, Sydney, Australia, 2004—04; program mgr. saturday scholars Drexel U., 2004—. Contbr. articles to profl. jours. Recipient Rsch. award, Assn. Coll. & Rsch. Librs., 2001, Belver C. Griffith Rsch. award, Coll. Info. Sci. & Tech., 2004. Mem.: ALA, Am. Soc. Info. Sci. and Tech., Beta Phi Mu. Office: Drexel U 3001 Market St Philadelphia PA 19104 Office Phone: 215-895-6107. Office Fax: 215-895-2153.

**MARION, MARJORIE ANNE,** English language educator, educational consultant; b. Winterset, Iowa, May 6, 1935; d. Virgil Arthur and Marilyn Ruth (Sandy) Hammon; m. Robert H. Marion, Dec. 20, 1964; 1 child, Kathryn Ruth BA, Colo. Coll., 1958; MA, Purdue U., 1969; postgrad., Inst. Mgmt. Lifelong Edn. Harvard U., 1981. Chairperson English dept. Lincoln-Way H.S., New Lenox, Ill., 1964—68; dir. pub. rels. U. St. Francis, Joliet, Ill., 1968—70, chairperson English dept., 1971—75, chairperson humanities and fine arts divsn., 1975—79, coord. instrnl. devel., 1979—80, dir. continuing edn., 1980—84, acting v.p. acad. affairs, 1984—85, dean faculty, 1985—89, assoc. prof. English, 1989—97, dir. Freshman Core Program, 1993—95, dir. Writing Ctr., 1996, prof. emeritus, 1997—. Cons. to presdtl. search U. St. Francis, 2001—02; mem. vis. team North Ctrl. Assn., Joliet and Lockport, Ill., 1975—79; lectr. at ednl. workshops and instns.; condr. writing workshops for adults returning to coll., 1995—; TV and radio appearances regarding lifelong edn., Chgo., St. Louis, Albuquerque, Phoenix, 1982—85; lectr. writing workshops. Author: A Guide to Writing for the Faint at Heart, 1996; author monograph; drama critic Joliet Herald News, 1970-82 Phoenix. Cath. Franciscan Charisma Coun., 2005—06. Recipient Pres.'s award Coll. St. Francis, 1975 Mem. Am. Assn. Higher Edn., Nat. Coun. Tchrs. English, Nat. Acad. Advising Assn. Roman Catholic. E-mail: mamarion1@msn.com.

**MARION, SHAWN,** professional basketball player; b. Waukegan, IL, May 7, 1978; Student, Vincennes U., Ind., UNLV. Player Phoenix Suns, 1999—. Mem. Team USA, Goodwill Games, Brisbane, Australia, 2001, Team USA, World Championships, Indpls., 2002, US Olympic Basketball Team, Athens, Greece, 2004. Named to All-Rookie second team, 2000, NBA All-Star Game, 2003, 2005, All-NBA Second team, 2005. Achievements include Won Gold medal with team USA, Goodwill Games, 2001. Office: c/o Phoenix Suns 201 E Jefferson St Phoenix AZ 85004*

**MARION, WINIFRED ZENORINI,** retired elementary school educator; b. Fairview, N.J., Oct. 12, 1929; d. Leopold and Anna (Saldarini) Zenorini; m. Louis William Marion, Nov. 29, 1952; children: William Harvey. BA with honors, Ladycliff Coll. N.Y., 1951; MEd with honors, Paterson State Coll., 1968; MEd, Fairleigh Dickinson U., 1975-78; student, Caldwell Coll., 1977, Monmouth Coll., 1980, Columbia Tchrs Coll., 1989-91. Cert. tchr., N.J. Elem. sch. tchr., Tenafly Pub. Schs., 1951-54, 62-92, ret., 1992; edn. dir. UNICEF, 1986-90; elem. sch. tchr. Ramsey, 1959-60, Franklin Lakes, N.J., 1961; piano tchr.; condr. ednl. and UNICEF workshops. Tchr. Confrat. of Christian Doctrine, Mt. Carmel Ch., Tenafly, 1962-72; active UN Assn. 1980-90, chair edn. dept., 1985-86, film edn. chair pub. schs. Englewood/Tenafly chpt., 1987-91; travel agent Benson Travel, 1990-2002; mem. planning bd. Mt. Carmel Ch., Tenafly, 1975, parish lay minister, 1975-77; mem. parish renewal group St. Mary's Ch., Dumont, N.J., 1981-92, eucharistic min., 1989-2002; active UNICEF card program League of Women/Jr. Women's Club, Tenafly, 1980-87, vol. Holy Name Hosp., 1994-2004, Hackensack Med. Ctr., 1997-2001; mem. Blue Army World Apostolate of Fatima, Washington, N.J., 1983—, Greenpeace Nat. Wildlife, Mus. Nat. History, Environ. Spl. Olympics, Def. Better World Soc., Covenant House; vol. Holy Name Hosp., 1992-2001, 2003—; AARP Friends of the Tenafly & Dumont Libr., 1990—, vol. reader Tenafly Children's Libr. Dept., 1993-96. Recipient award Northern Valley-Englewood/Tenafly chpt. UN Assn., 1980, Gov.'s Tchr. cert. Recognition, 1991; Ladycliff Coll. scholar, 1950. Mem. NJ Ret. Edn. Assn., Nat. Ednl. Assn. Ret., Bergen County Ret. Edn. Assn. (life), AAUW, Tenafly Edn. Assn. (negotiations rep. 1973-78, exec. elem. rep. 1990—), Home Sch. Edn. Assn. (rep. Tenafly Sch. System 1988-90) N.J. Edn. Assn., Bergen County Edn. Assn. (life), Smithsonian Inst., World Vision, Nat. Geographic Soc., Met. Opera Fund and Guild, Holy Trinity Ch., Our Lady Fatima Chapel, Paquanock, NJ, 2003-, Sierra Club. Republican. Roman Catholic. Avocations: opera, ballet, travel, oil painting, plate collector. Home: 11 Florence Ave Cresskill NJ 07626

**MARIOTTO, MARCO JEROME,** dean, psychology educator, researcher; b. Ill., Oct. 21, 1946; s. Marco Anibele and Sally (Hughes) M.; m. Danita Irene Czyzewski, May 4, 1985; children: Ana-Sofia Antonia, Marco Luca. BS, U. Ill., 1968, PhD, 1974. Diplomate Am. Bd. Sexology, Am. Bd. Forensic Examiners; lic. psychologist; cert. sex therapist, cert. health svcs. provider. Asst. rsch. dir. Adolf Meyer Ctr. Rsch. Units, Decatur, Ill., 1972-74; psychologist U.S. Army Acad. Health Scis., San Antonio, 1974; asst. prof. Purdue U., West Lafayette, Ind., 1975-79; assoc. prof. U. Houston, 1979-90, supervisory psychologist, 1979—, prof., 1990—, dept. chmn., 1994—99, founding dean grad. and profl. studies, 1999—. Cons. NIMH, Bethesda, Md., 1977—, NSF, Washington, 1980-84, Nat. Inst. Drug Abuse, Bethesda, 1986-89; adj. prof. U. Tex. Health Scis., Houston, 1980—. Contbr. chpts. to books and articles to profl. jours.; also rsch. monographs and tech. reports. Forensic cons. Harris County Dist. Atty.'s Office, Houston, 1988—, ABA, 1989—; founding mem. Gulf Coast Consortium on Mental Health, Houston and Galveston, Tex., 1989. Capt. U.S. Army, 1968-74. Named one of top 35 Young Scientist Profls. Jour. Cons. and Clin. Psychology, 1988; David Ross fellow Purdue U., 1977. Mem. APA, Am. Psychol. Soc.; mem. AAAS, Midwestern Psychol. Assn. (local rep. 1979—), Sigma Xi. Achievements include co-devel. of TSBC/SRIC planned access infosystem for rsch. and svc. for patients in residential treatment settings; rsch. in observational measurement in mental health, schizophrenia, chronic mental patients. Office: U Houston Office of the Dean Grad and Profl Studies Houston TX 77204-2012 Office Phone: 713-743-9088. Business E-Mail: mmariotto@uh.edu.

**MARIS, ANTHONY, JR.,** environmental services administrator; s. Anthony J. and Elpis Alice Maris; m. Jennifer A. Maris, July 25, 1978; children: Kevin R., Traci T. BA, U. Calif., Santa Barbara, 1974. Registered environ. health specialist Calif., cert. underground storage tank inspector Internat. Code Coun., landfill inspector Solid Waste Assn. N.Am. Owner Sam's Kosher Style Deli, Fair Oaks, Calif., 1976—84; quality control supr. Capital Beverage Packers, Sacramento, 1984—92; environ. health specialist Calaveras County Environ. Health Dept., San Andreas, Calif., 1992—. Grantee, Calif. State Water Resources Bd., 2005. Mem.: Calif. Environ. Health Assn. (audio/visual chair 1999), Calif. Conf. Dirs. of Environ. Health (pool tech. adv. com. 1995—, food tech. adv. com. 2000—), The Cephalonian Soc., Am. Hellenic Edn. Progressive Assn. Democrat. Greek Orthodox. Avocations: hiking, boating, skiing, home maintenance. Office: Calaveras County Environ Health 891 Mountain Ranch Rd San Andreas CA 95249 Office Phone: 209-754-6690. E-mail: tmaris@co.calaveras.ca.us.

**MARIS, STEPHEN S.,** lawyer, educator; b. Dallas, Dec. 19, 1949; children: Shane, Kara. BS, Stephen F. Austin State, 1971; JD, So. Meth. U., 1975. Bar: U.S. Dist. Ct. (no. dist.) Tex. 1975, U.S. Dist. Ct. (ea. dist.) Tex. 1986, U.S. Dist. Ct. (so. dist.) Tex. 1992, U.S. Ct. Appeals (5th cir.) 1980, U.S. Ct. Appeals (11th cir.) 1981, U.S. Supreme Ct. Tex. 1975. Assoc. Passman & Jones, Dallas, 1975-80, ptnr., 1980-87, Fulbright & Jaworski, Dallas, 1987-97, Jenkens & Gilchrist, Dallas, 1997—. Prof. So. Ill. U., 1979-80, So. Meth. U., Dallas, 1980—; mem. faculty Nat. Inst. Trial Advocacy, 1980—. Editor: Southwest Law Journal, 1973-75. Mem. ABA, State Bar Tex., Dallas Bar Assn., Barristers, Order Coif, Phi Delta Kappa. Office: Jenkens & Gilchrist 1445 Ross Ave Ste 3200 Dallas TX 75202-2785 Office Phone: 214-855-4155. E-mail: smaris@jenkens.com.

**MARISTUEN, KEITH A.,** lawyer; b. Malta, Mont., 1953; BA with high honors, Univ. Mont., 1975, JD with honors, 1978. Mem. Bosch, Kuhr, Dugdale, Martin & Kaze PLLP, Havre, Mont. Mem.: ABA, Mont. State Bar Assn. (pres. 2004). Office: Bosch Kuhr Dugdale Martin & Kaze PLLP 335 Fourth Ave PO Box 7152 Havre MT 59501 Office Phone: 406-265-6706. Business E-Mail: kmaristuen@bkdlaw.org.

**MARITZ, W. STEPHEN,** marketing professional, service executive; b. St. Louis; BS, Princeton U., 1980. With Maritz Inc., Fenton, Mo., 1983—; dir. sales, 1993—95, vice chmn. bd., 1994—, sr. v.p., 1995—97, pres., COO 1997—98, CEO, pres., 1998—2001, chmn., CEO, 2001—. Bd. dir. Laclede Group Inc. Bd. dir. St. Louis Regional Chamber and Growth Assn. Office: Maritz 1375 N Highway Dr Fenton MO 63099*

**MARIUCCI, STEVE,** professional football coach, former college football coach; b. Iron Mountain, Mich., Nov. 4, 1955; m. Gayle Mariucci; 4 children. Football coach No. Mich. U., 1978-79, Calif. State U., Fullerton, 1980-82; asst. head coach U. Louisville, 1983-84; receivers coach Orlando Renegades U.S. Football League, 1985; quality control coach L.A. Rams, 1985; receivers/spl. teams coach U. So. Calif. Trojans, L.A., 1986, wide receivers/spl. teams coach, 1987-89, quarterbacks coach, offensive coord. 1990-91; quarterbacks coach Green Bay (Wis.) Packers, 1992-95; head coach U. Calif. Golden Bears, 1996-98, San Francisco 49ers, 1996—2003, Detroit Lions, 2003—05.

**MARIYA, DEBORAH LUETHJE,** minister; b. Long Beach, Calif., Feb. 26, 1953; d. Betty and Keith Luethje; m. Sam John Tangredi, May 21, 1994. BA. Augustana Coll., 1977; MDiv, Garrett-Evangelical Theol. Sem., 1984; D in Ministry, Wesley Theol. Sem., 2003. Ordained United Meth. Ch., 1983. Assoc. pastor Wesley United Meth. Ch., Muscatine, Iowa, 1982—83; pastor Danbury United Meth. Ch. and Oto United Ch. of Christ, Iowa, 1984—86, Dawson-Cooper-Greenbrier United Meth. Chs., Iowa, 1986—90; commd. lt. j.g. USN, 1988, advanced through grades to lt. comdr.; comd. chaplain USS Cape Cod, San Diego, 1990—93; hosp. chaplain, Protestant chapel pastor Nat. Naval Med. Ctr., Bethesda, Md., 1993—95; Protestant chaplain USNS Comfort, Balt., 1993—95; squadron chaplain Amphibious Squadron Five, San Diego, 1995—96; supr. chaplain Command Chaplains Assistance Team. Comdr. Naval Surface Force, U.S. Pacific Fleet, San Diego, 1996—98; comd. chaplain, chapel pastor Naval Security Sta., Washington, 1998—2000; ret. USN, 2000; pastor Chicamuxen (Md.) United Meth. Ch., 2001—; with Joint Mil. Attaché Sch., 2004—. Chaplain CAP, U.S. Air Force, Forest Glen, Md., 1994—. Author: Holy Places: Sacred Sites in Washington, DC and the Surrounding Region. County election ofcl. Bd. Elections, Arlington, Va., 2001—03; elder Iowa ann. conf. United Meth. Ch., 1986; deacon Iowa annual conf., 1983. Decorated Navy and Marine Corps Commendation Medal (five awards) Sec. of the Navy, Armed Forces Expeditionary Medal Sec. of Def., South West Asia Svc. Medal-three awards, Kuwait Liberation Medal Govt. of Saudi Arabia, Kuwaiti Freedom Medal Govt. of Kuwait, Navy and Marine Corps Achievement Medal Sec. of the Navy, Nat. Def. Medal Sec. of Def. Mem.: Balt.-Washington Ann. Conf. of United Meth. Ch., Navy Mut. Aid Assn. (resident dir. 1994—99), Mil. Chaplains Assn., Navy League, Women in Mil. Svc. for Am. Meml. Methodist. Mailing: USDAO Athens 801 15th St Ste 1401 Arlington VA 22202 Office: Chicamuxen United Meth Ch PO Box 2338 La Plata MD 20646 Home: USDAO Athens PSC 108 Box 21 Apo AE 09842 Personal E-mail: debmariya@aol.com.

**MARJANCZYK, JOSEPH ANICETUS,** priest; b. Elizabeth, N.J., Apr. 17, 1921; s. Joseph John and Catherine Frances (Cwik) M. BA, Seton Hall U., 1941; MDiv, Darlington Sem., 1975. Ordained priest Roman Cath. Ch., 1945; named monsignor, 1979. Asst. pastor St. Valentine's Ch., Bloomfield, NJ, 1945-72; pastor St. Adalbert's Ch., Elizabeth, 1972-83, Our Lady of Mt. Carmel Ch., Bayonne, NJ, 1983-96; named protonotary apostolic, 1988; vicar episcopal South Hudson Vicariate, 1991—96; prof. Polish Master Sch. Fgn. Langs., Seton Hall U., 1948-60; pastor emeritus Our Lady of Mt. Carmel Ch., Bayonne, 1996—. Chmn. pers. bd. Archdiocese of Newark, 1972-74, mem. pastoral coun., 1972-83, archdiocesan trustee 1975-86; chmn. adminstrv. com., mem. exec. bd. Archdiocesan Pastoral Coun., 1972-84; dean Union County East Deanery, 1975-83; Polish Apostolate rep. Nat. Conf. Cath. Bishops Com. on Migration, 1989-96, chmn. Polish adv. bd. to conf. office for pastoral care of migrants and refugees, 1989-96. Chmn. bd. dirs. Polish Cultural Found., 1974-90, 92-97, 98-2000; trustee Seton Hall U., 1978-96, Immaculate Conception Sem., South Orange, N.J., 1979-86; commr. bd. edn. City of Elizabeth, 1979-83; nat. chaplain Polish Army Vets. Assn. Am., 1980-98; founder, pres. emeritus N.J. chpt. John Paul II Found., 1986-2000; chmn. exec. bd. Polish chapel renovation and rededication Nat. Shrine of Immaculate Conception, Washington, 1988. Decorated Gold Order of Merit (Republic of Poland), 1988; recipient Polish Apostolate Pride of Polonia award, 1996, Nat. Polish Priests' Assn. award, 2006; named Canon of Cathedral chpt. Archdiocese Warsaw, Poland, 1995. Mem. Archdiocesan Polish Clergy Soc. (hon. pres. 1979—), Polish Am. Priests Assn. (exec. com. 1991-99, Nat. award 2006), Polish Am. Congress, Polish Am. Hist. Assn., N.J. Hist. Soc., Polish Am. Numis. Assn., Polonians Club, KC. Home: PO Box 456 Point Pleasant NJ 08742-0456

**MARJORAM, PAUL,** medical educator, researcher; b. Bishop's Stortford, Eng., Sept. 17, 1962; s. Lloyd Victor Marjoram and Daphne Jean Younger. BSc, Warwick U., Eng., 1984; diploma, Cambridge U., Eng., 1986; PhD, Queen Mary Coll., London, 1989. Postdoctoral rsch. fellow Queen Mary Coll., 1989—92, Monash U., Melbourne, Australia, 1992—95; rsch. asst. prof. U. So. Calif., LA, 1995—98, asst. prof., 1999—. Office: U So Calif Dept Preventive Medicine 1540 Alcazar St CHP-220 Los Angeles CA 90089-9011 Office Phone: 323-442-0111.

**MARK, DANIEL BENJAMIN,** cardiologist; b. Boston, Aug. 1, 1953; s. Vernon H. and Alexandra M.; m. M. Lee Cheney. BA, Hampshire Coll., 1974; MD, Tufts U., 1978; MPH, Harvard Sch. of Pub. Health, 1979. Intern U. Va. Hosp., Charlottesville, 1979-80, resident, 1980-82; fellow Duke U. Med. Ctr., Durham, N.C., 1982-85, assoc. in medicine, 1985-86, asst. prof. of medicine, 1987-92, assoc. prof. of medicine, 1993-98, prof. of medicine, 1998—, dir. Outcomes Rsch. and Assessment Group, 1994—. Editor: Am. Heart Jour., 1996—; author: (book) Acute Coronary Care; contbr. articles to numerous profl. jours. and publs. Recipient Rsch. Excellence award Assn. of Pharmacoecons. and Outcomes Rsch., 1997. Fellow: ACP, AHA (rsch. com. 2002—), Am. Soc. Clin. Investigation, Am. Coll. Cardiology (guideline com. AHCPR-NIH Unstable Angina Guideline 1994, database R&D com. 1998—2001, Coronary Stent Consensus Guidelines 2001—02, Exercise Testing Guidelines 2002); mem.: European Soc. Cardiology, Assn. Am. Physicians, Assn. Health Svcs. Rsch., Soc. for Med. Decision Making. Office: Duke Clin Rsch Inst 2400 Pratt Ave Rm 311 Durham NC 27705-3976 E-mail: daniel.mark@duke.edu.

**MARK, HANS MICHAEL,** physicist, former federal agency administrator; b. Mannheim, Germany, June 17, 1929; arrived in U.S., 1940, naturalized, 1945; s. Herman Francis and Maria (Schramek) M.; m. Marion G. Thorpe, Jan. 28, 1951; children: Jane H., Rufus J. AB in Physics, U. Calif., Berkeley, 1951; PhD, MIT, 1954; ScD (hon.), Fla. Inst. Tech., 1978; DEng (hon.), Poly. U. NY, 1982, Milw. Sch. Engring., 1991; LHD (hon.), St. Edward's U., 1993; ScD (hon.), Royal Mil. Coll. Sci., U.K., 2004; DEng (hon.), Tri-State U., 2005. Rsch. assoc. MIT, Cambridge, 1954-55, asst. prof., 1958-60; rsch. physicist Lawrence Radiation Lab. U. Calif., Livermore, 1955-58, 60-69, exptl. physics divsn. leader, 1960-64, assoc. prof. nuc. engring. Berkeley, 1960-66, prof., 1966-69, chmn. dept. nuc. engring., 1964-69, lectr. dept. applied sci. Davis, 1969-73; cons. prof. engring. Stanford (Calif.) U., 1973-84; dir. NASA-Ames Rsch. Ctr., 1969-77; undersec. Air Force, dir. Nat. Reconnaissance Office USAF, Washington, 1977-79, sec. Air Force 1979-81; dep. adminstr. NASA, Washington, 1981-84; chancellor U. Tex. Sys., Austin, 1984-92; prof. aerospace engring. and engring. mechanics U. Tex., Austin, 1988—; dir. defense rsch. and engring. Dept. Def., Washington, 1998-2001. Mem. Pres.'s Adv. Group Sci. and Tech., 1975-76; bd. dirs. Astronautics Corp. Am.; trustee Poly. U., 1984—. Author: (with N.T. Olson) Experiments in Modern Physics, 1966; (with E. Teller and J.S. Foster, Jr.) Power and Security, 1976; (with A. Levine) The Management of Research Institutions, 1983, The Space Station-A Personal Journey, 1987, (with Victor G. Szebehely) Adventures in Celestial Mechanics, 1998; also numerous articles; editor: (with S. Fernbach) Properties of Matter Under Unusual Conditions, 1969; (with Lowell Wood) Energy in Physics, War and Peace, 1988. Recipient Disting. Svc. medal NASA, 1972, 77, medal for exceptional engring. achievement, 1984, Exceptional Civilian Svc. award USAF, 1979, Disting. Pub. Svc. medal, Dept. Def., 1981, 2001, Sec.'s Gold medal Dept. Energy, 2001. Fellow AIAA (hon., Von Karman lectr. astronautics 1992), Am. Phys. Soc.; mem. NAE, Am. Nuc. Soc., Am. Geophys. Union, Coun. Fgn. Rels., Cosmos Club. Achievements include research on nuclear energy levels, nuclear reactions, applications, nuclear energy for practical purposes, atomic flourescence yields, measurement X-rays above atmosphere, spacecraft and experimental aircraft design. Office: U Tex Dept Aerospace Engring/Engr Austin TX 78712 Office Phone: 512-471-5077. Business E-Mail: hmark@mail.utexas.edu.

**MARK, HON FONG LOUIE,** cytogeneticist; m. Roger Mark; children: Yvonne, Roger Jr., Seamus. PhD, Brown U. Diplomate Am. Bd. Med. Genetics. Postdoctoral fellow in med. genetics R.I. Hosp., Providence, asst., assoc. dir. cytogenetics, fellow molecular biology, dir. cytogenetics, clin. cytogeneticist Cancer & Leukemia Group B, 1990—99; pres., CEO KRAM Corp., 1994—; dir. human genetics RIDOH, 1999—2001; exec. dir. RIACA, 2001—02; dir. cytogenetics dept. Presbyn. Lab. Svcs., Charlotte, NC, 2002—04; dir. cytogenetics Boston U. Sch. Medicine, 2004—, clin. prof., 2004—. Instr. pathology Brown U., Providence, asst. prof. pathology; clin. prof. Brown Med. Sch., 1998—; assoc. mem. Maine Toxicology Inst., 1993—; chair grants rev. com. mem., prenatal diagnosis com., chair cancer genetics com., steering com.; grant reviewer NIH, U.S. Army Breast Cancer Rsch. Program, U.S. Army Prostate Cancer Rsch. Program; reviewer numerous other panels. Author: Medical Cytogenetics, 2000; mem. editl. rev. bd. Applied Cytogenetics, Pathobiology, Exptl. and Molecular Pathology, Cancer Genetics and Cytogenetics; contbr. 200 articles to profl. jours. Recipient award Time Mag. Essay Writing Contest, Balfour award, Award R.I. Found.; NSF rsch. grantee Brown U., co-grantee Dept. Energy; Florence Seibert postdoctoral fellowship AAUW Ednl. Found.; North Providence Citizens scholar, Fruithill Jr. Women's Club scholar; others. Fellow Am. Coll. Med. Genetics; mem. AAAS, Am. Soc. Human Genetics, Assn. Genetic Technologists, Sigma Xi.

**MARK, JAMES B. D.,** surgeon, educator; b. Nashville, June 26, 1929; s. Julius and Margaret (Baer) M.; m. Jean Rambar, Feb. 5, 1957; children: Jonathan, Michael, Margaret, Katherine. BA, Vanderbilt U., 1950, MD, 1953. Intern, resident in gen. and thoracic surgery Yale-New Haven Hosp., 1953-60; instr. to asst. prof. surgery Yale U., 1960-65; assoc. prof. surgery Stanford U., 1965-69, prof., 1969-97, prof. emeritus, 1997—; Johnson and Johnson prof. surgery, 1978—97, head div. thoracic surgery, 1972-97, assoc. dean clin. affairs, 1982-92; chief staff Stanford U. Hosp., 1988-92. Governing bd. Health Systems Agy., Santa Clara County, 1978-80; sr. Fulbright-Hays fellow, vis. prof. surgery U. Dar es Salaam, Tanzania, 1972-73 Mem. editl. bd.: Jour. Thoracic and Cardiovasc. Surgery, 1986-94, World Jour. Surgery, 1995-2003, The Pharos, 2002—; contbr. numerous articles to sci. jours. Bd. dirs. Stanford U. Hosp., 1992-94. With USPHS, 1955-57. Fellow ACS (pres. No. Calif. chpt. 1980-81), Am. Coll. Chest Physicians (pres. 1994-95); mem. Am. Assn. Thoracic Surgery, Am. Surg. Assn., Western

Surg. Assn., Pacific Coast Surg. Assn., Halsted Soc. (pres. 1984), Western Thoracic Surg. Assn. (pres. 1992-93), Calif. Acad. Medicine (pres. 1978), Santa Clara County Med. Soc. (pres. 1976-77). Home: 921 Casanueva Pl Stanford CA 94305-1001 Office: Stanford U Med Ctr CVRB Stanford CA 94305 Office Phone: 650-723-6649. E-mail: jbdm@stanford.edu.

**MARK, JONATHAN L,** lawyer; b. N.Y.C., Oct. 18, 1947; s. Sandor and Ruth (Weiss) M.; m. B. Kathleen Munguia, May 25, 1986; children: Ramona G., Sandor A. AB, Dartmouth Coll., 1969; JD, Columbia U., 1974. Bar: N.Y., Calif., U.S. Dist. Ct. (so. and ea. dists.), N.Y., U.S. Ct. Appeals (2d cir.). Law clk. to presiding justice U.S. Dist. Ct. (so. dist.) N.Y., N.Y.C., 1974-75; assoc. Cahill Gordon & Reindel, N.Y.C., 1975-82, ptnr., 1982—. Office: Cahill Gordon & Reindel LLP 80 Pine St Fl 17 New York NY 10005-1790 Office Phone: 212-701-3100. Personal E-mail: jmark58@aol.com.

**MARK, JUDI,** actress, choreographer; b. Chgo., Mar. 20; d. Leonard and Dorothy March. BS in Edn., So. Ill. U.; postgrad., San Diego State U., U.S. Internat. U. Performing Arts. Dancer U.S. Internat. Dance Theatre, Balboa Park Theatre, San Diego. Founder, choreographer Judi Mark & Co.; dance instr. P.S. 190, N.Y.C., 1986—; elem. tchr. Dade County Schs., 1970-74. Appeared in (stage prodns.) West Side Story, The Rose Tattoo, The Rainmaker, Time and Involvement, (films) Deathtrap, 1982, Turk 182!, 1985, Private Resorts, 1986, (TV) Miami Vice. Mem. AFTRA. Jewish. Avocation: travel.

**MARK, KENNETH DEAN,** museum director, educator; b. Harrisburg, Pa., Nov. 13, 1950; s. Clifford Kenneth and Catherine Elsie Mark; m. Beth L. Hostetler, July 15, 1972; children: Ryan, Sally Mark Young. BA, Messiah Coll., Grantham, Pa., 1972; MEd, Shippensburg U., Pa., 1975. Tchr. cert. Pa., 1972. 6th grade tchr. Mechanicsburg Area Sch. Dist., Pa., 1972—84, 5th grade tchr., 1984—2002, master tchr., 1990—2002; asst. dir. Oakes Mus., Messiah Coll., Grantham, Pa., 2001—05, dir., 2005—. Adj. lectr. in edn. Messiah Coll., Grantham, Pa., 1988—2001. Named Elem. Tchr. of Yr., Mechanicsburg Area Sch. Dist., 1991; recipient Disting. Svc. to Pupils, 1974, 1976, 1982, 1989, Salute to Tchg. award, Pa. Acad. Profession of Tchg., 1990. Mem.: NEA, Pa. State Edn. Assn., Pa. Sci. Tchrs. Assn., Mid-Atlantic Assn. Mus., Am. Assn. Museums. Independent. Protestant. Avocations: golf, reading, swimming, RVing. Office: Oakes Mus Natural History One College Ave Box 3029 Grantham PA 17027 Office Phone: 717-796-1800 x 7190. Office Fax: 717-691-6046. Business E-Mail: kmark@messiah.edu.

**MARK, MARY ELLEN,** photographer; b. Phila., Mar. 20, 1940; d. A. DeRoy and Beatrice (Silverman) M.; m. Frank Anthony Macaoge, 1963 (div. 1964); m. Martin Bell. BA, U.Pa., 1962; MA, Annenberg Sch. Communication, 1964. Lectr., presenter workshops in field. One-woman shows include Photographers Gallery, London, 1976, Castelli Graphics, NYC, 1978, Olympus Gallery, London, 1981, Seson Art Gallery, U. Calif-Santa Cruz, Calif. Mus. Photography, Riverside, Drew U., NJ, 1982, Gallery of Fine Arts, Daytona Beach Community Coll., Fla., Friends of Photography, Carmel, Calif., 1983, Allen Street Gallery, Dallas, 1985, Birmingham (Ala.) Mus. of Art, 1989; numerous others; exhibited in group shows at Photokina, Cologne, 1973, Sidney Janis Gallery, NYC, 1976, Internat. Ctr. of Photography, NYC, 1979, Bibliotheque Nationale, Paris, 1979, Corcoran Gallery of Art and George Eastman House, NY, U. Colo., 1982, Eaton Shoen Gallery, San Francisco, 1983, Barbican Art Gallery, London, 1985, Munich Stadt Mus., 1985, Walker Art Ctr., Mpls., 1986, Portland (Maine) Mus. Art, 1986, Castle Gallery, New Rochelle, NY, Hillwood Art Gallery, Greenvale, NY, UN 40th Anniversary Photography Exhibit, 1985, Paris Opera, 1988, Zeitgenossischen Photography, Frankfurt, 1989, numerous others; author: Passport, 1974, Ward 81, 1979, Falkland Road: Prostitutes of Bombay, 1981, Streetwise, 1988, Mary Ellen Mark: Indian Circus, 1993, A Cry for Help: Stories of Homelessness and Hope, 1996, Mary Ellen Mark: American Odyssey, 1999, Twins, 2003, Exposure, 2005, others; contbr. articles, photographs to profl. publs., mags. Fulbright scholar, 1965-66; grantee USIA, 1975, NEA, 1977, 80, NY State Coun. for Arts, 1977, NEA, 1979-80; recipient Page One award The Newspaper Guild of NY, 1979, First Pl. Feature Picture Stroy U. Mo., 1980, Canon Photo Essayist award Life Mag., 1983, 1st prize Robert F. Kennedy Journalism, 1985, Philippe Halsman award ASMP, Photojournalism award George W. Polk, 1988. Mem. Am. Assn. Soc. Mag. Photographers.

**MARK, MELVIN,** mechanical engineering educator, consultant; b. St. Paul, Nov. 15, 1922; s. Isadore William and Fannye (Abrahamson) M.; m. Elizabeth J. Wyner, Sept. 9, 1951; children: Jonathan S., David W., Peter B. B.M.E., U. Minn., 1943, MS, 1946; Sc.D (Teaching, Research fellow), Harvard, 1950. Registered profl. engr., Mass., Minn. Instr. N.D. State U., 1943-44, U. Minn., 1945-47; project mgr. Gen. Electric Co., Lynn., Mass., 1950-52; mgr. Raytheon Co., Wayland, Mass., 1952-56; cons. engr., 1956—; prof. Lowell Technol. Inst., 1957-59, dean faculty, 1959-62; prof. mech. engring. Northeastern U., Boston, 1963-84, dean engring., 1968-79, provost, sr. v.p. for acad. affairs, 1979-84. Vis. lectr. Mass. Inst. Tech., 1955, Brandeis U., 1958; vis. prof. U. Mass., 1984-86; mem. Mass. Bd. Registration of Profl. Engrs. and Land Surveyors, 1990-2001. Author: Thermodynamics: An Auto-Instructional Text, 1967, Concepts of Thermodynamics, 1975, Thermodynamics: Principles and Applications, 1979, Engineering Thermodynamics, 1985; contbr. articles to profl. jours. Served with USAAF, 1944-45. Recipient prize Lincoln Arc Welding Found., 1947. Hon. fellow ASME (fellow 1948-50); mem. Am. Soc. Engring. Edn., Sigma Xi, Tau Beta Pi, Pi Tau Sigma, Phi Kappa Phi. Achievements include patents in field. Home: 17 Larch Rd Waban MA 02468-1413 E-mail: mel@cartesianinc.com.

**MARK, MICHAEL LAURENCE,** retired music educator; b. Schenectady, N.Y., Dec. 1, 1936; s. David and Ruth (Garbowitz) M.; m. Lois Nitekman, Jan. 28, 1942; children: Michelle, Diana. BM, The Cath. U. of Am., 1958, DMA, 1969; MA, George Washington U., 1960; M in Music Edn., U. Mich., 1962 Tchr. Prince George's County, Md. Pub. Schs., 1958-60, 61 dir. assoc. prof. music Morgan State U., Balt., 1966-70; supr. music Auburn (N.Y.) Enlarged Sch. Dist., 1970-72; dir. music Elmira (N.Y.) Enlarged Sch. Dist., 1972-73; assoc. prof., sch. music Cath. U. Am., Washington, 1973-81; dean grad. sch., prof. music Towson (Md.) U., 1981-95, prof. music, 1995-98, prof. emeritus, 1998; pres. Spectrum Assocs., Inc. Mem editl. com. five jours. in field. Author: Contemporary Music Education, 1978, 3rd rev. edit., 1996, Source Readings in Music Education History, 1982, 2nd edit., 2002; co-author: A History of American Music Education, 1992. Mem. Music Educators Nat. Conf. (numerous coms., Music Educators Hall of Fame), Coll. Music Soc., Md. Music Educators Assn. (pres. 1999-2003). Avocations: travel, woodworking. E-mail: mimark@comcast.net.

**MARK, PETER,** performing company executive, conductor; b. N.Y.C., Oct. 31, 1940; s. Irving and Edna M.; m. Thea Musgrave, Oct. 2, 1971. BA (Woodrow Wilson fellow), Columbia U., 1961; MS, Juilliard Sch. Music, 1963. Prof. music and dramatic art U. Calif., Santa Barbara, 1965-94. Fellow Creative Arts Inst., U. Calif., 1968-69, 71-72; guest condr. Wolf Trap Orch., 1979, N.Y.C. Opera, 1981, L.A. Opera Theater, 1981, Royal Opera House, London, 1982, Hong Kong Philharm. Orch., 1984, Jerusalem Symphony Orch., 1988, Tulsa Opera, 1988, Compania Nacional de Opera, Mexico City, 1989, 92, N.Y. Pops, Carnegie Hall, 1991. Concert violist U.S., S.Am., Europe, 1961-67; artistic dir., condr. Va. Opera, Norfolk, 1975—, art dir., 1978—; condr.: Am. premier of Mary, Queen of Scots (Musgrave), 1978; World premier of A Christmas Carol (Musgrave), 1979, of Harriet, the Woman Called Moses (Musgrave), 1985, of Simon Bolivar (Musgrave), 1984, Porgy and Bess, Buenos Aires, Mexico City and São Paulo, 1992, Orlando Opera Co., 1993, Richmond Symphony, 1993, Salome, 1994, Krakow Opera, 1995, Pacific Opera Victoria (Can.), 1996, Cleve. Opera, 1996, Festival Internacional-Torre del Lago, Italy, 1996, The Flying Dutchman, 1996, Orfeo et Euridice, 1999, Rodelinda, 2000, Elektra, 2002, Die Walkure, 2002, Andrea Chenier, 2003, Fidelio, 2004, Tristan und Isolde, 2005. Recipient Elias Lifchey viola award Juilliard Sch. Music, 1963; named hon. citizen of Norfolk (Va.) Mem. Musicians Union, Phi Beta Kappa. Office: Va Opera PO Box 2580 Norfolk VA 23501-2580 Office Phone: 757-627-9545 x 3337. Business E-Mail: pmark@vaopera.com.

**MARK, REUBEN,** consumer products company executive; b. Jersey City, Jan. 21, 1939; s. Edward and Libbie (Berman) M.; m. Arlene Slobzian, Jan. 10, 1964; children: Lisa, Peter, Stephen. AB, Middlebury Coll., 1960; MBA, Harvard U., 1963. With Colgate-Palmolive Co., N.Y.C., 1963—, pres., gen. mgr. Venezuela, 1972-73, Can., 1973-74, v.p., gen. mgr. Far East div., 1974-75, v.p., gen. mgr. household products div., 1975-79, group v.p. domestic ops., 1979-81, exec. v.p. 1981-83, chief operating officer, 1983-84, pres., 1983-86, CEO, 1984—, chmn. bd., 1986—. Lectr. Sch. Bus. Adminstrn. U. Conn., 1977; bd. dirs. Time Warner, 1993—, Cabela's Inc., Colgate-Palmolive Co., Pearson PLC. Served with U.S. Army, 1961. Mem. Soap and Detergent Assn. Jewish. Avocation: jogging. Office: Colgate-Palmolive Co 300 Park Ave Fl 8 New York NY 10022-7499*

**MARK, RICHARD KUSHAKOW,** internist; b. N.Y.C., Feb. 11, 1951; s. Eugene and Gertrude (Kushakow) M.; m. Harriet Bass, Sept. 17, 1989; children: Sabrina, Ari, Etan. BS, Hofstra U., 1972; MD, U. Autonomous Guadalajara, 1976, SUNY, Bklyn., 1977. Diplomate Am. Bd. Internal Medicine. Resident in medicine Maimonides Med. Ctr., Bklyn., 1977-82; clin. instr. medicine Downstate Med. Ctr., Bklyn., 1982-90, asst. prof. medicine, 1990-93; prof. clin. medicine CUNY, 1993—; pvt. practice internal medicine Bklyn., 1982—. Dept. attending emergency Cabrini Med. Ctr., N.Y.C., 1982-84; med. cons. The Lighthouse. Author: Consumer's Guide to Preventive Medicine, 1996. Mem. N.Y.C. Coalition for the Homeless, 1986—, The Children's Fund., N.Y.C., 1990—. Recipient Cmty. Svc. award Borough of Bklyn., 1986, Physicians Recognition award AMA, 1993-97, Preceptorship award ACP, 1996, Tchr. of Yr. Maimonides Clin. Tchg. award CUNY, 1995, 96, 97, 98, 99, 2001, 02, 04, recipient Tchr. of Yr. award, 1982, 83, Citizen of Yr. award C.O.C.I.G, 2002 Fellow ACP; mem. Acad. Medicine, Inter-Am. Coll. Medicine, King's County Med. Soc. Democrat. Jewish. Avocations: sailing, photography, skiing. Office: 8023 19th Ave Brooklyn NY 11214-1753

**MARK, SHELLEY MUIN,** economist, educator; b. China, Sept. 9, 1922; came to U.S., 1923, naturalized, 1944; s. Hing D. and S. (Wong) M.; m. Janet Chong, Sept. 14, 1946 (dec. Mar. 1977); children— Philip, Diane, Paul, Peter, Steven; m. Tung Chow, July 8, 1978. BA, U. Wash., 1943, PhD, 1956; MS, Columbia, 1944; postgrad. (Ford Found. fellow), Harvard, 1959-60. Fgn. news reporter CBS, NY, 1945-46; instr. U. Wash., 1946-48; asst. prof. Ariz. State Coll., 1948-51; territorial economist OPS, Honolulu, 1951-53; prof. econs. U. Hawaii, 1953-62, dir. econ. rsch., 1959-62; dir. planning and econ. devel. State of Hawaii, 1962-74, state land use commr., 1962-74, state energy coord., 1973-74; dir. Office Land Use Coordination EPA, Washington, 1975-77; prof. econs. U. Hawaii, 1978—. Rsch. fellow East-West Ctr., Inst. Econ. Devel. and Policy, 1984-94; Asian advisor Internat. Ctr. Econ. Growth, 1992—; sr. advisor Dept. Bus., Econ. Devel. and Tourism, Hawaii, 1995-2002; vis. scholar Harvard U., 1986; vis. faculty Grad. Sch. People's Bank of China, 1988; also econ. cons. Philippines Inst. Devel. Studies, Devel. Rsch. Ctr. State Coun., China, Peoples Bank of China, Beijing, also other orgns.; mem. Gov.'s Adv. Com. Sci. and Tech., 1963-74, Oahu Transp. Policy Com., 1964-74, Regional Export Expansion Coun., 1964-74. Author: Economics in Action, 4th edit., 1969, Macroeconomic Performance of Asia-Pacific Region, 1985, Development Economics and Developing Economies, 1990, US Trade Policy, Asian Economic Interdependence, and the South China Growth Triangle, 1996; editor: Economic Interdependence and Cooperation in Asia-Pacific, 1993, Asian Transitional Economies, 1996; contbr. articles to profl. jours. Bd. dirs. U. Hawaii Rsch. Corp.; bd. dirs. Coun. State Planning Agys., pres., 1973-74, hon. mem., 1975—; governing bd. Coun. State Govts., 1972-74. Recipient Sackett Meml. award Columbia, 1944 Mem. Hawaii Govt. Employees Assn. (pres. univ. chpt., dir. 1958-59), Am. Econ. Assn., Royal Econ. Soc., Western Regional Sci. Assn. (pres. 1974-75, dir.), Phi Beta Kappa, Sigma Delta Chi. Mem. United Ch. of Christ. Home: 2036 Keaumoku St Honolulu HI 96822-2526 Personal E-Mail: smark5@hotmail.com.

**MARKARD, MARLENE MARIA,** lawyer; b. N.Y.C., Sept. 29, 1971; d. Hildegarde Maria (Von Stehr) Markard; m. Adam Edward Hirshfield, May 6, 2000. Music cert., Mannes Coll. Music, 1989; internat. baccalaureate, UN Internat. Sch., 1989; BA cum laude, Columbia U., 1992; JD, Cardozo Sch. Law, 1998. Bar: N.Y. 1999. Corp. lawyer Camhy Karlinsky & Stein LLP, N.Y.C., 1998—2000, McDermott Will & Emery, N.Y.C., 2000, Greenberg Traurig LLP, N.Y.C., 2000—; lic. real estate broker. Dir. Choices Theatre Project, N.Y.C., 1997—; mentor Barnard Coll., N.Y.C., 2002—. Mem.: ABA, N.Y. State Bar Assn., Bar Assn. of City of N.Y. Office: Greenberg Traurig LLP 200 Park Ave New York NY 10166 Home: 422 E 72nd St Apt 15b New York NY 10021-4619

**MARKEE, KATHERINE MADIGAN,** librarian, educator; b. Cleve., Feb. 24, 1931; d. Arthur Alexis and Margaret Elizabeth (Madigan) M. AB, Trinity Coll., Washington, 1953; MA, Columbia U., 1962; MLS, Case Western Res. U., 1968. Employment mgr. br. store tng. supr. The May Co., Cleve., 1965-67; assoc. prof. libr. sci., data bases libr. Purdue U. Libr., West Lafayette, Ind., 1968—96, libr. spl. collections, 1996—2006, oral history libr., 2006—. Contbr. articles to profl. jours. Mem. ALA, AAUP, Spl. Librs. Assn., Ind. Online Users Group, Sigma Xi (Rsch. Support award 1986). Avocations: photography, sailing, gardening. Office: Purdue U Libr 504 W State St West Lafayette IN 47907-2058 Office Phone: 765-496-1323. Business E-Mail: kmarkee@purdue.edu.

**MARKEE, RICHARD L.,** retail executive; BS in Econ., U. Wis. Buyer Famous-Barr May Co.; v.p., divisional mdse. mgr. Target Stores Dayton Hudson Corp.; from v.p., gen. mdse. mgr. Kids "R" Us Divsn. to vice chmn. Toys "R" Us, Inc., Wayne, NJ, 1990—2003, vice chmn., 2003—, pres. U.S. Toy Stores, 2003—06, interim CEO, 2005—06; pres. Babies "R" Us, 2004—. Chmn. bd. Kids in Distressed Situations, Inc., bd. dir. Office: Toys R Us Inc 1 Geoffrey Way Wayne NJ 07470-2030*

**MARKEL, GREGORY ARTHUR,** lawyer; b. NYC, Aug. 6, 1945; s. Edward and Ann (Larkin) M.; m. Dorothy Flanagan (div. 1979); 1 child, Kimberly; m. Belinda Elizabeth Heym, May 3, 1981; children: Alexis, Amy, William. BA in Econs., Columbia U., 1967; MBA in Fin. and Acctg., U. Mich., 1968; JD, Yale U., 1972. Bar: N.Y. 1972, U.S. Dist. Ct. (so. and ea. dists.) N.Y. 1974, U.S. Ct. Appeals (2nd cir.) 1975, U.S. Ct. Appeals (3rd cir.) 1978, U.S Dist. Ct. (no. dist.) Calif. 1984, U.S. Ct. Appeals (9th cir.) 1984, U.S. Ct. Appeals (11th cir.) 1987. Assoc. Cravath, Swaine & Moore, N.Y.C., 1972-80; ptnr. Davis, Markel & Edwards, 1980-93, Orrick, Herrington & Sutcliffe, N.Y.C., Brobeck Phleger & Harrison LLP, N.Y.C.; ptnr., chmn. litig. dept., mem. mgmt. com. Cadwalader Wickersham & Taft LLP, N.Y.C., 2002—. Tv, radio commentator on legal issues; mem. securities litig. panel Ann. Inst. Securities Regulation, 1999, 2000, 01, 02, 03, 04, 05; bank commentator, instr., 2004—05. Contbr. articles to profl. jours. and chpts. to publs. in field. Named one of Leading Securities Litig. Def. Attys., Chambers U.S.A., 2005's Top Litigators for Comml. Litig., Best Lawyers in Am.; Top 500 Attys. in Country; LawDragon.com; named to, Best Lawyers in N.Y. Fellow N.Y. Bar Found.; mem. ABA (mem. litig. and antitrust sects., litig. co-chair subcom. on fed. rules rev. of the pretrial practices and discovery com.), N.Y. State Bar Assn. (mem. comml. litig. sect.), Fed. Bar Coun., Univ. Club (N.Y.C.). Office: Cadwalader Wickersham & Taft LLP 1 World Fin Ctr New York NY 10281 Office Phone: 212-504-6112. Office Fax: 212-504-6666. Business E-Mail: greg.markel@cwt.com.

**MARKEL, HOWARD,** physician, educator; b. Detroit, Apr. 23, 1960; s. Samuel and Bernice Markel; m. Marcia Deborah Gordin, Sept. 20, 1987 (dec. Oct. 1988); m. Kate Gelya Levin, Aug. 17, 1997; children: Bess Rachel, Samantha Louise. AB in English Lit. summa cum laude, U. Mich., 1982, MD cum laude, 1986; PhD in History of Sci., Medicine & Tech., Johns Hopkins U., 1994. Diplomate Am. Bd. Pediat., 1989. Intern, resident Johns Hopkins Hosp. & Sch. Medicine, Balt., 1986-89, fellow, gen. pediat. and adolescent medicine, 1989—91, fellow, history medicine 1989—93; asst. prof. pediatrics, communicable diseases U. Mich., Ann Arbor, 1993-98, assoc. prof. pediatrics, communicable diseases, 1998—2002, George E. Wantz prof.

history medicine, 2000—, prof. pediat. and communicable diseases, prof. history, 2002—, prof. pub. health psychiatry, 2004—. Dir. Ctr. for History of Medicine, U. Mich., 1996—. Author: The H.L. Mencken Baby Book, 1990, The Portable Pediatrician, 1992, The Portable Pediatrician, 2nd edit., 2000, The Practical Pediatrician, 1996 (Child Mag. Book of Yr., 1997), Quarantine! East European Jewish Immigrants and the New York City, 1997 (Arthur Viseltear prize, APHA, 2003), When Germs Travel, 2004. Recipient Nat. Rsch. Svc. award, NIH, 1991, James A. Shannon Dirs. award, 1996, Burroughs Wellcome Fund 40th Ann. History Medicine award, 1996, History of Medicine award, Nat. Libr. Medicine, NIH, 2005—; scholar Robert Wood Johnson Found., 1996—2000. Fellow: Am. Acad. Pediat.; mem.: Am. Pediat. Soc., Soc. Pediat. Rsch., Am. Assn. History Medicine (exec. coun. 1994—97). Democrat. Jewish. Office: U Mich Ctr for History of Medicine 100 Simpson Meml Inst 102 Observatory Ann Arbor MI 48109-0725 Office Phone: 734-647-6914. Business E-Mail: howard@umich.edu.

**MARKEN, WILLIAM RILEY**, editor-in-chief; b. San Jose, Calif., Sept. 2, 1942; s. Harry L. and Emma Catherine (Kraus) M.; m. Marilyn Tonascia, Aug. 30, 1964; children— Catherine, Elizabeth, Michael, Paul Student, Occidental Coll., 1960-62; BA, U. Calif., Berkeley, 1964. Editor-in-chief Sunset Mag., Menlo Park, Calif., 1981-96, eHow.com, 1999-2001, Garden Design Mag., 2001—. Bd. dirs. Calif. Tomorrow, 1979-83; pres. League to Save Lake Tahoe, 1994-97. Avocations: tennis, skiing, basketball.

**MARKER, CARL W.**, diversified financial services company executive; BS in Computer Sci., U. Oreg. Fin. sys. analyst, Mercedes-Benz, Gen. Motors; pres. IMS Capital Mgmt., Portland, Oreg., CIO. Bd. dir. Clackamas County Libr. Found. Mem.: Portland (Oreg.) Soc. Fin. Analysts. Office: IMS Capital Management 8995 SE Otty Rd Portland OR 97266

**MARKER, MARC LINTHACUM**, lawyer, investor, entrepreneur; b. LA, July 19, 1941; s. Clifford Harry and Voris (Linthacum) M.; m. Sandra Vocom. Aug. 29, 1965; children: Victor, Gwendolyn. BA in Econs. and Geography, U. Calif.-Riverside, 1964; JD, U. So. Calif., 1967. Asst. v.p., asst. sec. Security Pacific Nat. Bank, L.A., 1970-73; sr. v.p., chief counsel, sec. Security Pacific Leasing Corp., San Francisco, 1973-92; pres. Security Pacific Leasing Corp., San Francisco, 1977-85, dir., 1977-92. Bd. dirs., sec. Voris, Inc., 1973-86; bd. dirs. Refiners Petroleum Corp., 1977-81, Security Pacific Leasing Singapore Ltd., 1983-85, Security Pacific Leasing Can. Ltd., 1989-92; lectr. in field. Served to comdr., USCGR. Mem. ABA, D.C. Bar Assn; Club: Army and Navy. Republican. Lutheran.

**MARKER, SHAUN JAMES**, lawyer; b. Lockport, N.Y., July 27, 1980; s. James Leroy and Nancy Lou Marker. BA magna cum laude, SUNY, Buffalo, 2002; JD cum laude, New Eng. Sch. Law, 2005. Bar: Fla. 2005. Law clk. Law Offices Timothy McCarthy, Medford, Mass., 2002—05, NMS Comm. Corp., Framingham, Mass., 2004; assoc. Powers, McNalis, Torres & Teebagy, West Palm Beach, Fla., 2005—. Articles editor: New Eng. Jour. Criminal and Civil Confinement, 2004—05. Mem.: ABA, Fla. State Theta, Golden Key, Phi Beta Kappa. Home: 8149 B Bridgewater Ct West Palm Beach FL 33406 Office: Powers McNalis Torres & Teebagy 1601 Belvedere Rd Ste 500S West Palm Beach FL 33406

**MARKERT, CYNTHIA ALLIN**, artist; b. Oak Ridge, Tenn., Apr. 7, 1954; d. George Wilbur and Barbara Anderson Allin. BFA, U. Tenn., 1977. Exhibitions include So. Living Mag. Dream Ho., Atlanta, Bennett Gallery, Alexis Georges, New Orleans, Circa Gallery, Setting the Stage Artspace, Alexandria, Va., DC Space, Washington, Veni Vidi Vici, Zenith Gallery, Fla. Design Mag., Susan Key Gallery, Knoxville, Tenn., Vetrum Gallery, Asheville, NC, Michael B. Tusing Gallery, Staunton, Va., Impeccable Art, Winston Salem, NC, Kress Emporium, Asheville, Hanson Gallery, Knoxville, Studio E Gallery, Jupiter, Fla., Raiford Gallery, Roswell, Ga., C.J. Varnum Gallery, Palm Beach, Fla., Louis Aronow Gallery, San Francisco, Through the Lens Gallery, Knoxville, Tenn., World Grotto Marketplace, Vagabondia, archives, Nat. Mus. Women in the Arts, Washington, commns. include, Stanford U. Dept. Lively Arts, No. Ky. U. Dept. Dance, U. Tenn. Dept. Theatre, Pandora's Books, Knoxville, Tenn. Festival Ballet, Tressa'a Jazz Club, Asheville, New Millennium Writings, Image Conscious of San Francisco, Spiral Licensing of Cherre, France. Office: Markert Du Jour PO box 724 Knoxville TN 37901 Office Phone: 865-523-8696. Business E-Mail: cynthia@cynthiamarkert.com.

**MARKERT, MARY LOUISE**, pediatrics educator; MD, Duke U., 1982. Dir. Duke General Clinical Research Center Duke U., Durham, NC, 1982, resident, 1982-84, assoc. prof. pediatrics, 1984—; asst. prof immunology; chmn. American Board of Allergy & Immunology, 1998—. Office: Duke U DUMC Box 3010 368 Jones Bldg Durham NC 27710

**MARKEY, EDWARD JOHN**, congressman; b. Malden, Mass., July 11, 1946; s. John E. and Christine M. Markey; m. Susan Blumenthal. BA, Boston Coll., 1968, JD, 1972. Bar: Mass. Mem. Mass. Ho. of reps., 1973-76, U.S. Congress from 7th Mass. dist., 1976—, New Eng. Congl. Caucus, N.E.-Midwest Econ. Advancement Coalition, Dem. Study Group; mem. energy and commerce com. Mem. editorial staff: Boston Coll. Law Rev. Served with USAR, 1968-73. Mem. Mass. Bar Assn. (Mass. Legislator of Year 1975) Clubs: K.C. Democrat. Roman Catholic. Home: 7 Townsend St Malden MA 02148-6322 Office: US Ho of Reps 2108 Rayburn House Office Bldg Washington DC 20515-2107 Office Phone: 202-225-2836. Office Fax: 202-226-0092.

**MARKEY, JAMES IAN**, music educator, tenor; b. N.Y.C. s. Joseph and Linda Markey. BA, Coastal Carolina U., Myrtle Beach, 2001, MAT, 2003. Cert. tchr. N.C., S.C. Chorus tchr. Canton Mid. Sch., NC, 2003—. Tenor Junaluska Singers, NC, 1999, Glenn Draper Singers, Chattanooga, 2000—. Mem.: Am. Choir Dirs. Assn., Music Educators N.C., N.C. Educators Assn. Methodist. Home: 100 Kilgore PO Box 1137 Lake Junaluska NC 28745 Office Phone: 828-646-3467. Office Fax: 828-646-3478.

**MARKEY, JAMES KEVIN**, lawyer; b. Springfield, Ill., July 15, 1956; s. James Owen and Marjorie Jean (Diesness) M.; m. Allison Markey; children: Lauren, Katherine. BBA with highest honors, U. Notre Dame, 1977, JD cum laude, U. Mich., 1980; MBA, U. Chgo., 1987; LLM in Taxation, DePaul U., 1993. CPA Ill.; bar: Ill. 1980. Assoc. Chapman & Cutler, Chgo., 1980-81; atty. Quaker Oats Co., Chgo., 1981-84; corp. counsel Baxter Healthcare Corp., Deerfield, Ill., 1984-90; v.p. law and other positions Motorola, Inc., Schaumburg, Ill., 1990-2000; v.p., chief counsel-securities and internat. Kellogg Co., Battle Creek, Mich., 2000—. Mem. ABA, Beta Alpha Psi, Beta Gamma Sigma. Avocations: racquetball, running, bridge. Home: 3541 Sandhill Ln Portage MI 49024 Office: 1 Kellogg Sq Battle Creek MI 49017-3534 E-mail: jim.markey@kellogg.com.

**MARKEY, JOHN K.**, lawyer; b. Melrose, Mass., Aug. 1, 1947; BS cum laude, Boston Coll., 1969, JD, 1973. Bar: Mass. 1974. Asst. dist. atty. Middlesex County, 1974-77; asst. US atty. Dist. Mass., 1978; mem. Mintz, Levin, Cohn, Ferris, Glovsky and Popeo PC, ptnr., Litig., chmn., pro bono com. Mem.: Boston Bar Assn. (task force on drugs & the cts., com. on state cts.study, chmn. criminal law sect. 1990—92), Mass. Bar Assn., ABA. Address: Mintz Levin Cohn Ferris Glovsky & Popeo PC 1 Financial Ctr Fl 39 Boston MA 02111-2621 Office Phone: 617-348-1686. Office Fax: 617-542-2241. Business E-Mail: jmarkey@mintz.com.

**MARKEY, MAURICE**, food products executive; b. 1966; With Goodyear Tire & Rubber Co., Kraft Foods, Inc., 1994, mktg. dir., spoonables divsn. Chgo. Mktg. appoint New Schools for Chgo., Ill., 2005. Office: Kraft Foods Inc 3 Lakes Dr Winnetka IL 60093 Office Fax: 847-646-6005.*

**MARKEY, RANDOLPH DAVID**, marketing professional; s. Robert Guy and Carol Sogg Markey; m. Molly Clare Sinelar; children: Max, Isabel. MBA, Weatherhead Sch. At Case Western Res. U. Nat. sales mgr. Matrix

Essentials, Inc., Cleve., 1990—94; dir., mktg. Bristol-Myers Squibb, 1994—2000; mng. dir. Parkland Group, 2000—03; mng. ptnr. Capital Acceleration Ptnrs., 2003—. Bd. dirs. Sogg Found., Corp. Bd., OEM Labeling, Inc., LaVar Holdings, Inc., Phylogy, Inc.; chmn. bd. dirs. Geotrac, Inc. Contbr. chapters to books. Mem.: Social Venture Ptnrs., Assn. for Corp. Growth, Turnaround Mgmt. Assn.

**MARKEY, WILLIAM ALAN**, health facility administrator, consultant; b. Cleve., Dec. 29, 1927; s. Oscar Bennett and Claire (Feldman) M.; m. Irene Nelson, Oct. 31, 1954; children: Janet Ellen Markey-Hisakawa, Suzanne Katherine Markey-Johnson. Student, Case Inst. Tech., 1945—48; BA, U. Mich., 1950; MS, Yale U., 1954. Resident in hosp. adminstrn. Beth Israel Hosp., Boston, 1953-54; asst. dir. Montefiore Hosp., Pitts., 1954-56; asst. adminstr. City of Hope Med. Ctr., Duarte, Calif., 1956-57; adminstrv. dir., 1957-66; assoc. dir. cancer hosp. project, instr. pub. health U. So. Calif. Sch. Medicine, 1966-67; asst. clin. prof. pub. health and cmty. medicine, 1968-70, asst. prof., 1970-75, dep. dir. regional med. programs, 1967-71; adminstr. Health Care Agy., County of San Diego, 1971-74, health svcs. cons., 1974-75; dir. Maricopa County Dept. Health Svcs., Phoenix, 1975-79, cons., 1979-80; adminstr. Sonoma Valley Hosp., Calif., 1980—83. Lectr. pub. health Sch. Pub. Health, UCLA, 1969-74; lectr. cmty. medicine Sch. Medicine, U. Calif., San Diego, 1973-75; cons. LA County Dept. Hosps., 1966-71, cons. Hosp./Health Svcs., 1983—; CEO Chinese Hosp., San Francisco, 1985-86, 90-91; adj. instr. Golden Gate U., 1992-96. Mem. bd. edn. Duarte Unified Sch. Dist., 1967-72, pres., 1970-72; bd. dir. Hosp. Coun., Calif., 1963-67, sec., 1966-67, Duarte Pub. Libr. Assn., 1965-72, Duarte-Bradbury chpt. Am. Field Svc., 1965-72, Duarte-Bradbury Cmty. Chest, 1961-68, Cmty. Christ. Calif. Ariz. Health Svcs. Agy., 1975-80, Vis. Nurse Assn. The Redwoods, Santa Rosa, Calif., 1985-86, Sonoma Greens Homeowners Assn., 1990-95, 2002-05, Sonoma City Opera, 1987, 93, United Way, Sonoma, 1996—; com. chmn. Sonoma County Bd. Realtors, 1990-92; active Sonoma County Multiple Listing Svc., 1987-97; mem. Sonoma County Human Svcs. Commn., 2003-. With AUS, 1950-52. Fellow Am. Coll. Health Care Execs. (life); mem. Am. Hosp. Assn. (life), APHA, Royal Soc. Health, Calif. Hosp. Assn. (trustee 1966-69, dir. 1966-69), Internat. Fedn. Hosps., Hosp. Coun. No. Calif. (dir. 1981-83), Kiwanis, Rotary (past pres. Duarte). Home: 866 Princeton Dr Sonoma CA 95476-4186 Office Phone: 707-996-2212.

**MARKEY, WINSTON ROSCOE**, aeronautical engineering educator; b. Buffalo, Sept. 20, 1929; s. Roscoe Irvin and Catherine L. (Higgins) M.; m. Phoebe Anne Sproule, Sept. 10, 1955; children: Karl Richard, Katherine Ilse, Kristina Anne. BS, MIT, 1951, ScD, 1956. Engr. MIT, 1951-57, asst. prof., 1957-62, assoc. prof., 1962-66, prof., 1966—; undergrad. officer, 1988-2000, dir. Measurement Systems Labs., 1961-89. Chief scientist USAF, 1964-65, mem. sci. adv. bd., 1966-69 Author: (with J. Hovorka) The Mechanics of Inertial Position and Heading Indication, 1961; Assoc. editor: AIAA Jour, 1963-66. Recipient Exceptional Civilian Service award, USAF, 1965. Mem. Sigma Xi, Tau Beta Pi, Gamma Alpha Rho. Home: 11 Edgewood Rd Lexington MA 02420-3501 Office: MIT Bldg 33-208 Cambridge MA 02139 Office Phone: 617-253-2923. Personal E-mail: wrmarkey@earthlink.net. Business E-Mail: wrmarkey@mit.edu.

**MARKEZICH, RON**, information technology executive; BA in Mgmt. Info. Sys., U. Notre Dame. With electronics and high tech. group Accenture (formerly Andersen Consulting); joined Microsoft, 1998; gen. mgr. fin. and adminstrn. info. tech. Microsoft Info. Tech., gen. mgr. info. tech. client svcs., gen. mgr. global tech. svcs.; CIO, v.p. managed solutions Microsoft Corp., Redmond, Wash., 2004—. Office: Microsoft Corp 1 Microsoft Way Redmond WA 98052-6399*

**MARKGRAF, CHERYL LEE**, church musician, conductor; d. Paul George and Jennie Marie Markgraf; life ptnr. Charlotte Ruth McLendon; 1 child, Melissa Renne Prado Hernandez. BA, Concordia U., 1981; MusM, Oberlin U., 1984; MA, U. Wis., 1989. Cert. min. parish music Concordia U., 1981. Music instr. Gethsemane Luth. Ch., St. Paul, 1977—82; condr. Concordia Coll., 1977—83, St. Paul All City Elem. Orch., 1980—82, Minnetonka Civic Orch., Minnetonka, Minn., 1987—88; dir. music Nativity Luth. Ch., Mpls., 1982—86, Holy Nativity Luth. Ch., New Hope, 1990—91; min. parish music Zion Luth. Ch., Hopkins, 1986—90; min. music, parish ministry asst. St. Alban's Episcopal Ch., Edina, 1995—; music dir., condr. Mpls. Southside Singers, Mpls., 1997—. Sec. Bd. Congl. Life, Evang. Luth. Ch. Am., Mpls., 1992—95; mem. Mpls. Area Synod Worship Com., 1993—95; membership chair Twin Cities Choirmasters Assn., Mpls., 1995—97. Mem.: Am. Guild Organists, Am. Choral Dirs. Assn., Am. Guild English Handbell Ringers, Air Force Assn. (sec. Gen. E.W. Rawlings chpt. 2005—). Avocation: travel. Office: St Alban's Episcopal Ch 6716 Gleason Rd Edina MN 55439 Office Phone: 952-941-3065. Business E-Mail: tukster1@msn.com.

**MARKGRAF, J(OHN) HODGE**, chemist, educator; b. Cin., Mar. 16, 1930; s. Carl A. and Elizabeth (Hodge) M.; m. Nancy Hart, Apr. 4, 1957; children: Carrie G., Sarah T. AB, Williams Coll., 1952; M.Sc., Yale U., 1954, PhD, 1957; postgrad., U. Munich, W. Ger., 1956-57. Research chemist Procter & Gamble Co., Cin., 1958-59; asst. prof. chemistry Williams Coll., Williamstown, Mass., 1959-65, assoc. prof., 1965-69 prof., 1969-98, Ebenezer Fitch prof. chemistry, 1977-85, 94-98, prof. emeritus, 1998—, provost, 1980-83, v.p. for alumni relations and devel., 1985-94, coll. marshal, 1995-98. Vis. prof. U. Calif., Berkeley, 1964—65, 1968—69, 1976—77, Duke U., 1983—84, 2001, U. Houston, 1999, Williams Coll., 2002—04, 2006, Mass. Coll. Liberal Arts, 2005—06. Contbr. articles to profl. jours.; patentee in field. NSF sci. faculty fellow, 1964-65; NSF grantee, 1961-63, Am. Chem. Soc.-Petroleum Rsch. Fund grantee, 1965-72, 93-95, Merck & Co. grantee, 1967, Rsch. Corp. grantee, 1963, 75, 90-92, Pfizer Inc. grantee, 1996, 97, 98, Camille and Henry Dreyfus Found. grantee, 2000-01, 04-05 Mem.: Am. Chem. Soc., Phi Beta Kappa, Sigma Xi. Home: 104 Forest Rd Williamstown MA 01267-2029 Office: Williams College Dept Chemistry Williamstown MA 01267-2692 E-mail: j.hodge.markgraf@williams.edu.

**MARKHAM, CHARLES HENRY**, neurologist; b. Pasadena, Calif., Dec. 24, 1923; s. Fred Smith and Maziebelle Valeta (Glover) M.; m. Kathleen Tiernan, Sept. 29, 1945 (div. 1971); children: Charles H., Arthur Tiernan, Daphne, James Daniel; m. Lisa Wells Overly, July 10, 1971; children: John Wells, Sara Brennan. Student, Colo. Sch. Mines, 1941-43; AB, Stanford U., 1947, MD, 1951. Intern, med. asst. resident Lane Hosp., San Francisco, 1950-52; fellow in neurology Children's Med. Ctr., Boston, 1952-53; asst. resident Boston City Hosp., 1953-54, chief resident, 1954-55; asst. prof. neurology UCLA Sch. Medicine, 1958-65, assoc. prof., 1965-70, assoc. prof. neurology, 1970-71, prof. neurology, 1971-94, prof. emeritus, 1994—; rsch. prof. dept. psychology U. Calif., Santa Barbara, 1995—. Sci. dir. Dystonia Med. Rsch. Found., Chgo., 1985-94, mem. bd. trustees, 1994—; sci. dir. Hereditary Disease Found., L.A., 1979-81; mem. adv. bd. Am. Parkinson Disease Assn., N.Y.C., 1976-83; attending physician UCLA Sch. Medicine, 1957—, cons. in neurology St. John's Hosp., Santa Monica, Calif., 1960-94. Contbr. articles to profl. jours.; author numerous books and abstracts. Trustee Westlake Sch. for Girls, L.A., 1965-74, St. Matthews Parish Sch. L.A., 1985-87; bd. dirs. Jubilee Christian Acad., 1996-99, Wildling Mus., 1997-2005, Las Positas Park Found., 1998-2000. With U.S. Army, 1943-45, ETO. Grantee NIH, NASA. Mem. Am. Acad. Neurology, AAAS, Am. Bd. Psychology and Neurology, Am. Epilepsy Soc., Am. Neurol. Assn., Am. Pain Soc., Am. Soc. for Gravitational and Space Biology, Bárány Soc. (Hallpike-Nylen prize 1990), Internat. Brain Rsch. Org., Internat. League Against Epilepsy, L.A. Soc. Neurology and Psychiatry, N.Y. Acad. Scis., Soc. for Neurosci., Western Inst. on Epilepsy, Rsch. Soc. for Parkinson Disease and Movement Disorders (pres. 1984-2000). Republican. Achievements include research in L-dopa and medical and surgical therapy for Parkinson's disease, dystonia, brain stem mechanisms for vestibular and quick and slow eye movements, long-term exposure to microgravity, space motion sickness, vestibular response to gravity, alcohol. Personal E-mail: cmarkham1@cox.net.

**MARKHAM, CLAIRE AGNES (M. CLARE MARKHAM)**, retired chemistry educator, consultant; b. New Haven, Aug. 12, 1919; d. James J. and Agnes V. (Manning) M. BA, St. Joseph Coll., West Hartford, Conn., 1940, DHL (hon.), 1989; PhD, Cath. U. Am., 1952. Joined Sisters of Mercy, Roman Cath. Ch., 1940. Tchr. chemistry and math. Sacred Heart H.S., Waterbury, Conn., 1945-49; mem. faculty chemistry St. Joseph Coll., 1952-97, cons. instl. advancement, 1996—, prof. emeritus in chemistry, 1997—. Dept. chair St. Joseph Coll., 1959-70, dean Grad. Sch., 1979-87, asst. to pres. acad. affairs, 1987-95; dir. numerous tchr. insts., 1959-89; mem. vis. faculty Calvin's Lab., NSF, U. Calif., Berkeley, 1967-68. dir. CT Talent Prog., 2002-03. Contbr. articles to profl. jours.; editor sci. series McGraw Hill, 1966-60. Undersec. for Energy, Office of Policy and Mgmt., State of Conn., Hartford, 1977—79; mem. adv. com. Permanent Commn. Status of Women, Hartford, 1995—; mem. adv. coun. Dept. Higher Edn., State of Conn., Hartford, 1970—80; energy advisor Nat. Gov.'s Assn., 1977—79; bd. dirs. Conn. Energy Co-op, 2000—03. Recipient Equity award AAUW, 1992, Sci. Advocacy award, CSTA, 2002, award for outstanding sci. adv. Conn. Sci. Tchrs. Assn., 2002; Faculty fellow NSF, Trondheim, Norway, 1967, Travel grantee, cons., Madras, India, 1974-77. Fellow Conn. Acad. for Edn.; mem. AAAS, Am. Chem. Soc. (councilor 1968-88, chair Conn. Valley sect. 1955-67, 20 Yr. award 1988), Conn. Acad. Sci. and Engring. (founding mem., chair tech. bd. 1994-98), Sigma Xi (sect. chair 1993-95). Democrat. Avocations: photography, music, literature. Home: 1678 Asylum Ave West Hartford CT 06117-2791 Office: St Joseph Coll West Hartford CT 06117 Office Phone: 860-231-5501. Business E-Mail: cmarkham@sjc.edu.

**MARKHAM, IAN STEPHEN**, theology studies educator, dean; b. Crediton, England, Sept. 19, 1962; arrived in U.S., 2001; s. Stephen Keith Markham and Beryl Evelyn Walker; m. Lesley Patricia Bunn, July 4, 1987; 1 child, Luke Stephen Austin. BTh, Kings Coll., London, Eng., 1985; MLitt, Cambridge univ., Cambridge, Eng., 1990; PhD ethics, Exeter Devon, Exeter, Eng., 1994. Lectr. in theology Univ. Exeter, Devon, England, 1989—96; prof. of theology and pub. life Liverpool Hope Univ., Liverpool, England, 1996—2001; dean of the seminary, prof. of theology and ethics Hartford Seminary, Conn., 2001—. Coun. mem. and dir. Advt. Stds. Authority, London, 1993—99; Teape lectr., India, 2004; vis. prof. Leeds Metro. U., 2005. Author: Plurality and Christian Ethics, 1994, Truth and the Reality of God, 1999, Why Bother With Ethics, 2006; editor: September 11: Religious Perspectives on the causes and Consequences, 2002, Theology of Engagement, 2003, Globalization, Ethics and Islam: The Case of Bediuzzaman Said Nursi, 2005. Mem.: Am. Acad. of Religion. Office: Hartford Seminary 77 Sherman St Hartford CT 06105 Office Phone: 860-509-9536. Business E-Mail: markham@hartsem.edu.

**MARKHAM, JESSE WILLIAM**, economist, educator; b. Richmond, Va., Apr. 21, 1916; s. John James and Edith (Luttrell) M.; m. Penelope Jane Anton, Oct. 15, 1944; children: Elizabeth Anton Markham McLean, John James, Jesse William. AB, U. Richmond, 1941; postgrad., Johns Hopkins U., 1941-42, U.S Fgn. Svc. Sch., 1945; MA, Harvard U., 1947, PhD, 1949. Acct. E.I. duPont de Nemours Co., Richmond, 1935-38; tchg. fellow Harvard U., 1946-48; asst. prof. Vanderbilt U., 1948-52, assoc. prof., 1952-53; chief economist FTC, Washington, 1953-55; assoc. prof. Princeton U., 1955-57, prof. econs., 1957-68; prof. Harvard Grad. Sch. Bus. Adminstrn., 1968-72, Charles Edward Wilson prof., 1972-82, prof. emeritus, 1982—; prof. Harvard U. Ext. Svcs., 1984—. Vis. prof. Columbia U., 1958; Ford Found. vis. prof. Harvard Grad. Sch. Bus. ADminstrn., 1965-66; rsch. prof. Law and Econs. Ctr., Emory U., 1982-84; rsch. staff, mem. bd. editors Patent Trademark Copyright Rsch. Inst., George Washington U., 1955-70; econs. editor Houghton Mifflin Co., 1961-71; U.S. del. commn. experts on bus. practices European Productivity Agy., OEEC, 1956, 57, 58, 59, 61; vis. prof. Harvard U., 1961-62; dir. Ford Found. Seminar Region II, 1961; adv. com. mktg. to sec. commerce, 1967-71; mem. Am. Bar Assn. Commn. to study FTC, 1969. Author: Competition in the Rayon Industry, 1952, The Fertilizer Industry: Study of an Imperfect Market, 1958, The American Economy, 1963, (with Charles Fiero and Howard Piquet) The European Common Market: Friend or Competitor, 1964, (with Gustav Papnek) Industrial Organization and Economic Development, 1970, Conglomerate Enterprise and Public Policy, 1973, (with Paul Teplitz) Baseball Economics and Public Policy, 1982; sect. on oligopoly Internat. Encyc. Social Scis.; contbr. articles to econ. jours. Del. People to People Diplomacy Mission to USSR, 1989; active Boy Scouts Am.; chmn. Harvard Parents Com., 1969-72. Served as 1t. USNR, World War II. Ford Found. rsch. prof., 1958-59. Mem. Am. Econ. Assn., U.S.C. of C. (econ. policy com.), Harvard Club (N.Y.C., Sarasota, Fla.), The Cedars Club, Phi Beta Kappa. Episcopalian. Home: 4425 Gulf Of Mexico Dr Longboat Key FL 34228-2403 Office: Harvard U Grad Sch Bus Adminstrn 300 Cumnock Boston MA 02163

**MARKHAM, REED B.**, education educator, consultant; b. Alhambra, Calif., Feb. 14, 1957; s. John F. and Reeda (Bjarason) M. BA, MA, Brigham Young U., 1982; BS, Regents Coll., 1981, MA, 1982; MPA, U. So. Calif., 1983; MA, UCLA, 1989; PhD, Columbia Pacific U., 1991. Mem. faculty Brigham Young U., Provo, Utah, 1984, Calif. State U., Fullerton and Long Beach, 1984, Northridge, 1985, El Camino Coll., Torrance, Calif., 1986, Orange Coast Coll., Costa Mesa, Calif., 1986, Pasadena (Calif.) Coll., 1986, Fullerton (Calif.) Community Coll., 1986; instr., mem. pub. rels. com. Chaffey (Calif.) Coll., 1986-87; prof., CARES dir. Calif. State Poly. U., Pomona, 1987-98; adj. prof. Calif. State U., L.A., 1992-93, dir. Ctr. for Student Retention, 1995—; prof. East L.A. Coll., 1996-98, Salt Lake C.C., 1998—; adj. prof. Fla. C.C.-Jacksonville, 2005—; mem. governing bd. U. Coll. of Caribbean, 2005. Rsch. asst. to pres. Ctr. for the Study of Cmty. Coll., 1985; mem. faculty Riverside (Calif.) Coll., 1989-90, Rio Hondo (Calif.) Coll., 1989-90, English Lang. Inst., 1994, Calif. Poly Summer Bridge, 1989-95, East L.A. Coll.; adj. prof. Citrus Coll., 1998—; speechwriter U.S. Supreme Ct., Washington, 1980; cons. gifted children program Johns Hopkins U./Scripps Coll., Claremont, Calif., 1987-88; mem. faculty PACE Program East L.A., 1995-96; faculty East L.A. Coll., 1996-97; adj. prof. U. So. Calif., 1998—; prof. Salt Lake C. C., 1998-99; mem. Pres.'s Coalition for Am. Reads Challenge, 1999; mem. Olympic News Svc. 2002, 2001-. Author: Power Speechwriting, 1983, Power Speaking, 1990, Public Opinion, 1990, Advances in Public Speaking, 1991, Leadership 2000: Success Skills for University Students, 1995, Excellence in Public Speaking, 1997; co-author: Student Retention: Success Models in Higher Education, 1996, Upward Bound Program Grant Proposal, 1996, Making Marriage Magnificent, 1998; editor Trojan in Govt., U. So. Calif., 1983; editl. bd. mem. Edn. Digest, Speaker and Gavel, Innovative Higher End., Pub. Rels. Rev., Nat. Forensic Jour., The Forensic Educator, Clearinghouse for the Contemporary Educator, Hispanic Am. Family Mag.; writer N.Y. times, Christian Sci. Monitor; ednl. columnist San Bernardino (Calif.) Sun., 1992-98. VOICE, 2000-01; contbg. editor Great Lives, 2002, American Lives, 2004. Pres. bd. trustees Regents Coll., 1986; appointed to Pres.'s Coalition for Am. Reads Challenge; mem. Olympic News Svc., 2001—; mem. Coun. Study of Cmty. Colls., 2002—; torchbearer Olympic Winter Games, 2002; unit commr. Boy Scouts of Am., 2002; bd. govs. Univ. Coll. of Caribbean, 2005. Mem. Am. Comm. Assn., Doctorate Assn. N.Y. Scholars, Nat. Assn. Pvt. Nontraditional Colls. (accrediting com. 1989—), Pub. Rels. Soc. Am. (dir.-at-large inland empire 1992-93, faculty advisor), Ctr. Study Cmty. Colls. Mem. Lds Ch. Office: Salt Lake CC Comm Dept PO Box 30808 Salt Lake City UT 84130-0808 Office Phone: 801-957-4183. Personal E-mail: rljmarkham@comcast.net. Business E-Mail: markhare@slcc.edu.

**MARKIDES, KYRIAKOS SOCRATES**, gerontology educator; b. Nicosia, Cyprus, Mar. 21, 1948; arrived in U.S., 1968; s. Socrates and Persoulla Markides; m. Evelyn A. Stanton, Dec. 18, 1971; 1 child, Michael. BA, Bowling Green State U., 1972; MA, La. State U., 1973, PhD, 1976. Asst. prof. U. Tex. Health Sci. Ctr., San Antonio, 1976—82, assoc. prof., 1982—87; prof. U. Tex. Med. Br., Galveston, 1987—; Annie and John Gnitzinger Endowed prof., 1999—. Author (with others): Older Mexican Americans, 1983, Aging and Ethnicity, 1987, Retirement in Industrialized Societies, 1987, Aging and Health, 1989, Aging, Stress and Health, 1989, Minorities, Aging and Health, 1997; mem. editl. bd. The Gerontologist Jour., 1980—, founding editor Jour. of Aging and Health, 1989—. Grantee Rsch. grantee,

Nat. Inst. Aging, 1980—, Hogg Found., 1984—. Rockefeller Found. Fellow: Am. Coll. Epidemiology, Gerontol. Soc. Am.; mem.: APHA, Population Assn. Am., Am. Sociol. Assn. Office: Univ Tex Med Branch Galveston TX 77550 Office Phone: 409-772-2551. E-mail: kmarkide@utmb.edu.

**MARKIEWICZ, LESZEK,** research biochemist; b. Sowliny, Krakow, Poland, Sept. 10, 1928; came to U.S., 1965; s. Jan and Maria (Drozdowicz) M. MS, Coll. Agr., Krakow, 1956; PhD, Coll. Agr., 1963. Rsch. assoc. Polish Acad. Sci., Krakow, 1955-63; adj. Coll. Agr., 1964-65; rsch. assoc. Cornell U. Coll. Agr., Ithaca, N.Y., 1965-67, Inst. for Muscle Disease, Inc., N.Y.C., 1968-74; rsch. biochemist dept. neurology U. Calif. Sch. Medicine, San Francisco, 1974-79; rsch. asst. prof. dept ob-gyn and reproductive sci. Mt. Sinai Sch. Medicine, N.Y.C., 1982—. Contbr. more than 50 articles to Jour. Steroid Biochemistry, Endocrinology, Jour. Clin. Endocrinology and Metabolism, also chpts. to books. Mem. Endocrine Soc., N.Y. Acad. Scis. Office: Mt Sinai Med Ctr One Gustave L Levy Pl New York NY 10029

**MARKIN, KAREN MARY,** research scientist, journalist; b. Hartford, Conn., Jan. 20, 1957; d. Walter Anthony Markin, Katherine Irene Markin; m. Benjamin Adams Cray, June 6, 1987; 1 child, Colleen Cray. BA, Clark U., 1979; MA, Ohio State U., 1986; PhD, U. NC, 1993. Reporter The Day, New London, Conn., 1975—85; dir. rsch. devel. U. R.I., Kingston, RI, 1999—. Head law divsn. asst. for Edn. in Journalism and Mass Comm., Columbia, SC, 2004—05; dir. Ctr. for Humanities U.R.I. Kingston, 2001; proposal reviewer NSF, Arlington, 1999—2004, U.S. Dept. Edn., Washington, 1998—2001. Author (govt. publ.): Ballot Access, volumes 2-4, 1995. V.p. program AAUW, Middletown, RI, 1997—99, pres. Westerly, RI; program panelist AAUW Ednl. Found., 2002—. Mem.: Nat. Coun. Univ. Rsch. Adminstrs., Internat. Comm. Assn., Phi Beta Kappa (treas. RI chpt.). Office: Univ Rhode Island Rsch Office 70 Lower College Rd Kingston RI 02881

**MARKIN, SHEILA RUBEN,** community relations executive; b. Rochester, NY, July 11, 1932; d. William Saul and Sara Gitin Ruben; m. Lawrence T. Markin, June 13, 1954; children: Linda, Amy. BA in Am. Studies, Smith Coll., 1954; postgrad., U. Rochester, 1970—72, Rochester Inst. Tech., 1978. Asst. soc. editor Lawton (Okla.) Constitution Morning Press, 1954—55; fashion model Sibley's B. Forman Co., Rochester, NY, 1956—70; designer product safety program BRX Inc., Rochester, 1974; consumer rep. Park Edge Supermarkets, Rochester, 1979—80; crews supr. U.S. Census Bur., Brighton, NY, 1980; tutor Rochester Sch. Dist., 1981—84; dir. edn. and cmty. rels. Rochester Human Parts Bank, 1983—87; children and family advocate Rochester, 1981—. Author: (newsletter) Tissues Vol. 1-3, 1984—87, curriculum materials. Children's advocate CASA, Sarasota, Fla., 2000—; organizer landscape com. Villa Palmeras Homeowners Assn., Sarasota; bd. dirs. Canandaigua (NY) Lake Pure Waters, 1981—85, Jewish Home of Rochester, 1986—90. Mem.: Smith Coll. Club Sarasota (treas. 2002—). Avocations: weaving, photography, golf, reading, gardening. Home: 4348 Camino Madera Sarasota FL 34238

**MARKISON, BRIAN A.,** pharmaceutical executive; BS, Iona Coll. 1982. Various mktg. and sales positions Bristol-Myers Squibb, 1982—98, sr. v.p., neuroscience/infectious disease, pres. neuroscience/infectious disease/dermatology, v.p., operational excellence and productivity, 1998—2001; pres. Bristol-Myers Squibb's Oncology, Virology and Oncology Therapeutics, 2001—04; COO King Pharm., Inc., Bristol, Tenn., 2004, pres. & CEO, 2004—. Bd. dir. King Pharm., Inc., Bristol, Tenn., 2004—. Office: King Pharmaceuticals Inc 501 Fifth St Bristol TN 37620

**MARKLAND, FRANCIS SWABY, JR.,** biochemist, educator; b. Phila., Jan. 15, 1936; s. Francis Swaby Sr. and Willie Lawrence (Averritt) M.; m. Barbara Blake, Jun. 27, 1959 - April 5, 1996; children: Cathleen Blake, Francis Swaby IV. BS, Pa. State U., 1957; PhD, Johns Hopkins U., 1964. Postdoctoral fellow UCLA, 1964-66, asst. prof. biochemistry, 1966-73; vis. asst. prof. U. So. Calif., Los Angeles, 1973-74, assoc. prof., 1974-83, prof., 1983—, acting chmn. dept. biochemistry, 1986-88, vice-chmn., 1988-92, assoc. dean for sci. affairs, 2004—. Cons. Clin. Lab. Med. Group, LA, 1977-88, Cortech, Inc., Denver, 1983-88, Maret Corp., Wayne, Pa., 1996-2000; founder Pivotal BioSis., Inc., 2003-; mem. biochem., endocrinology study sect. NIH, 1986-90, mem FLAIR prog., rev. NIH NCI, 2002-2003, Contbg. editor: Toxicon, Jour. Natural Toxins; contbr. articles to profl. jours.: Mem. Angeles Choral, L.A. Capt. USNR, 1957-59, ret. Recipient NIH rsch. career devel. award USPHS, NIH, 1968-73; rsch. grantee Nat. Cancer Inst., 1979-86, 91-93, Nat. Heart Lung and Blood Inst., 1984-88, 95-2002, State of Calif. Breast Cancer Rsch. Program, 1995-2002, State Calif. Cancer Rsch. Program, 2000-03, U.S. Army Prostate Cancer Rsch. Program, 2004—, Komen Found., 2004—; fellow study sec. reviewer Western region Am. Heart Assn., 2003-06 . Mem. AAAS, Am. Soc. Biochem. and Molecular Biology, Am. Chem. Soc., Internat. Soc. on Toxinology, Internat. Soc. on Thrombosis and Haemostasis (subcom. exogenous hemostatic factors, chair 1994-96, co-chair 1999—), Am. Assn. Cancer Rsch., Am. Soc. Hematology, Sigma Xi, Alpha Zeta. Avocations: singing, aerobics, golf. Office: U So Calif Keck Sch Medicine Cancer Rsch Lab Rm 106 1303 N Mission Rd Los Angeles CA 90033-1020 Business E-Mail: markland@usc.edu.

**MARKLE, CHERI VIRGINIA CUMMINS,** nurse; b. N.Y.C., Nov. 22, 1936; d. Brainard Lyle and Mildred (Schwab) Cummins; m. John Markle, Aug. 26, 1961 (dec. 1962); 1 child, Kellianne. RN, Ind. State U. and Union Hosp., 1959; BS in Rehab. Edn., Wright State U., 1975; BSN, Capital U., 1987; postgrad. in nursing adminstrn., Wright State U., 1987-89; MS, Calif. Coll. Health Sci. Administration, 1994; postgrad., Columbia Pacific U., 1996-2000. Cert. clin. hypnotherapist Nat. Guild Hypnotherapists. Coordinator Dayton (Ohio) Children's Psychiat. Hosp., 1962-75; dir nursing Stillwater Health Ctr., Dayton, 1975-76; head nurse psychiat. clinic VA, Dayton, 1976-91, N.Y.C.; sr. supr. VA, Dayton, 1977-85, nurse coord. alcohol rehab., 1985 86; DON Odd Fellows, Springfield, Ohio, 1987-88, Miami Christel Manor, Miamisburg, Ohio, 1988-99; DON, rehab. cons. NMS Tng. Sys., Dayton, 1989-91. Psychiat. nurse VA Med. Ctr., N.Y. Rehab., 1991, mem. com. women vets., 1991-93; advisor Calif. Coll. Health Sci. Newspaper columnist Golden Times, Clark County. Bd. dirs. Temple Universal Judaism, 1992, 97; mem. Town and Village Synagogue, 1999—. 1st lt. USAF, 1959-61. Mem. ANA (cert. adminstr. 1983, cert. gerontology 1984), AAUW, Nurse Mgrs. Assembly, Gerontol. Nurse Assembly, Rehab. Soc., Nat. Guild Hypnotherapists, Internat. Assn. Counselors and Therapists, Nat. Coun. Jewish Women, Jewish War Vets. (sr. vice comdr. Post 1), Wright State U. Alumni Assn., Am. Legion (life), Hadassah, Women's City Club N.Y., Gilbert and Sullivan Soc., Internat. Consortium Parse Scholars, Alpha Sigma Alpha, Sigma Theta Tau. Democrat. Jewish. Avocations: cats, reading, music, needlecrafts, swimming, grandchildren. E-mail: cherimarklern@yahoo.com.

**MARKLEY, KENNETH ALAN,** psychologist; b. Harrisburg, Pa., Sept. 30, 1933; s. Charles Donald and Gladys Elizabeth (Wallis) M.; m. Susan Watson, Sept. 14, 1957; children: Jennifer Elaine, Christopher David. BA, Dickinson Coll., 1955; postgrad., Syracuse U., 1955-57; MA, NYU, 1959; postgrad., Ref. Episcopal Seminary, 1966-68, PhD, 1968. Cert. psychologist, Pa.; ordained to gospel ministry Evangelical Ch. Alliance, 1978. Sch. psychologist Ctrl. Dauphin Schs., Harrisburg, 1959; exec. dir. United Cerebral Palsy Treatment Ctr., Camp Hill, Pa., 1960-64; ea. dir. Narramore Christian Found. and Rosemead (Calif.) Grad. Sch., 1964—2000. Mem. faculty Dickinson Coll., Carlisle, Pa., 1963-64; propr. Oldtimers Antique Clocks. Author: Our Speaker This Evening, 1974. Bd. dirs. cmty. civic and religious orgns. Served 1st lt. Adj. Gen. Corps AUS, 1955-57. Mem. Am. Psychol. Assn., Pa. Psychol. Assn., Phi Kappa Psi. Mem. Brethren in Christ. Address: 104 N 26th St Camp Hill PA 17011-3616

**MARKLEY, WILLIAM C.,** lawyer; b. Salina, Kans., Dec. 21, 1945; m. Marcia A. Markley. BS, US Naval Acad., 1967; JD, Hastings Coll. Law, 1974. Sr. v.p., gen. counsel, sec. Jacobs Engring. Group Inc., Pasadena, Calif. Mem.: L.A. County Bar Assn., ABA, State Bar Calif., Am. Corp. Counsel Assn.

Office: Jacobs Engring Group Inc 1111 S Arroyo Pky Pasadena CA 91105 Home: 2105 Sunnybank Dr La Canada Flintridge CA 91011-1358 Office Phone: 626-578-6855. Office Fax: 626-578-6990. Business E-Mail: Bill.Markley@Jacobs.com.

**MARKMAN, ARTHUR BRIAN,** psychology professor; b. Plainfield, NJ, Feb. 28, 1966; s. Edward Steven and Sondra Rae (Gold) M.; children: Lucas Gabriel, Niv, Eylam. BS, Brown U., 1988; MA, U. Ill., 1990, PhD, 1992. Vis. asst. prof. Northwestern U., Evanston, Ill., 1991-93; asst. prof. psychology Columbia U., N.Y.C., 1993-98; assoc. prof. U. Tex., Austin 1998—2003, prof., 2003—06, Annabel Irian Worsham Centennial prof. psychology, 2006—. Fellow Inst. for Innovation, Creativity and Capital, 2005—. Author: Knowledge Representation, 1999; author: (with D.L. Medin and B.H. Ross) Cognitive Psychology, 2000, 2005; editor: Magellan Books, 2004—, Categorization Inside and Outside the Laboratory, 2005—, Cognitive Science, 2005—; co-editor: Cognitive Dynamics, 2000—, Human Factors in Remote Sensing Imagery, —; assoc. editor Psychonomic Bull. and Rev., 2004—05, mem. editl. bd. Jour. Exptl. Psychology, Learning, Memory and Cognition, 1995—2000, Memory and Cognition, 1998—2005, Cognitive Science, 2000—05, Psychonomic Bull. and Rev., 2003—04, Cognitive Psychology, 2005; contbr. articles to profl. jours. Fellow Inst. Innovation Creativity and Capital; mem. APA, Am. Psychol. Soc., Cognitive Sci. Soc. (exec. officer), Am. Assn. for Artificial Intelligence, Psychonomic Soc., Sigma Xi, Phi Kappa Phi. Achievements include seminal research on parallels between analogy and similarity; research on the role of comparison in decision-making, motivational influences in decision making and categorization and research on motivation. Office: U Texas Dept Psychology 1 University Station A8000 Austin TX 78712 E-mail: markman@psy.utexas.edu.

**MARKMAN, JON,** business journalist; Grad., Duke U., Columbia U. Grad. Sch. Journalism. Editor, investments columnist, investigative reporter LA Times, 1984—97; mng. editor, columnist MSN Money, 1997—2002; co-portfolio mgr. Helios Equity Fund, LLC; sr. investment strategist Pinnacle Investment Advisors, LLC; editor, founder StockTactics Advisor, 2002—. Author: Swing Trading, Online Investing. Recipient award, Soc. Profl. Journalists, 2001, Gerald Loeb award for disting. fin. journalism, 2002.

**MARKMAN, RONALD,** artist, educator; b. Bronx, N.Y., May 29, 1931; s. Julius and Mildred (Berkowitz) M.; m. Barbara Miller, Sept. 12, 1959; 1 dau., Ericka Elizabeth. B.F.A. Yale U., 1957, M.F.A., 1959. Instr. Art Inst. Chgo., 1960-64; prof. fine arts Ind. U., 1964—. Color cons. Hallmark Card Co., 1959-60 One-man shows Kanegis Gallery, 1959, Reed Coll., 1966, Terry Dintenfass Gallery, 1965, 66, 68, 70, 76, 79, 82, 85, The Gallery, Bloomington, Ind., 1972, 79, Indpls. Mus., 1974, Tyler Sch. Art, Phila., 1976, Franklin Coll., 1980, Dart Gallery, Chgo., 1981, Patrick King Gallery, Indpls., 1983, 86, John Heron Gallery, Indpls., 1985, New Harmony Gallery, 1985, Mitchell Gallery, St. John's Coll., Annapolis, Md., 2005; two-man show Dintenfass Gallery, 1984; group shows include Kanegis Gallery, Boston, 1958, 60, 61, Boston Arts Festival, 1959, 60, Mus. Modern Art, 1959, 66, Whitney Mus., N.Y.C., 1960, Art Inst. Chgo., 1964, Gallery 99, Miami, Fla., 1966, Ball State Coll., 1966, Butler Inst., 1967, Indpls. Mus., 1968, 69, 72, 74, Phoenix Gallery, N.Y.C., 1970, Harvard U., 1974, Skidmore Coll., 1975, Am. Acad. Arts and Letters, 1977, 89, Tuthill-Gimprich Gallery, N.Y.C., 1980, Patrick King Gallery, 1988, numerous others; represented in permanent collections Met. Mus. Art, Mus. Modern Art, Art Inst. Chgo., Library of Congress, Cin. Art Mus., Bklyn. Mus., Ark. Art Center, others; commns. include 5 murals Riley Children's Hosp., Indpls., 1986; installation Evanston (Ill.) Art Ctr., 1989, 2-part installation Ortho Child Care Ctr., Raritan, N.J., 1991; illustrator Acid and Basics-A Guide to Acid-Base Physiology, 1992. Served with U.S. Army, 1952-54. Recipient Ind. Arts Commn. award, 1990, 93; Fulbright grantee, Italy, 1962, grantee Ctr. for New TV, Chgo., 1992; Lilly Endowment fellow, 1989, honorable mention, Ohio Film Festival, 1995. Home and Office: 1623 Saint Margarets Rd Annapolis MD 21401-5540

**MARKMAN, RONALD ABRAHAM,** psychiatrist, lawyer; b. Tel-Aviv, Israel, Aug. 29, 1936; s. Irving and Hadassa Markman; m. Nitza Artsiel, June 3, 1962; children: Sharon Debra Himmelstern, David Philip, Michael Elliot. MD, UCLA, 1956—60; JD, U. West LA, 1975—79, Bar: Calif. State Bar 1979; MD Calif. State Med. Bd., 1961. Assoc. clin. prof. USC Sch. Medicine, L.A., 1967—84; attending Cedars-Sinai Med. Ctr., L.A., 1973—; asst. clin. prof. psychiatry U.C.L.A. Sch. Medicine, L.A., 1984—. Med. dir. Airport Marina Counseling Svc., L.A. Author: (non-fiction book) Alone with the Devil (NY Times Best Seller (paperback), 1988), Obsessed; contbr. profl. articles-Am. Jour. of Psychiatry. Bd. mem. Sinai Temple, L.A., 1971—73. Capt. USMC, 1961—63. Fellow: Am. Psychiat. Assn. (disting. life); mem.: Calif. Psychiat. Assn., L.A. County Bar Assn., Am. Acad. Psychiatry & Law, So. Calif. Psychiat. Soc. Avocations: tennis, jogging, bicycling, travel, skiing. Office: PO Box 1272 Beverly Hills CA 90213 Office Phone: 310-276-1482. E-mail: rammdjd@pol.net.

**MARKMAN, SHERMAN,** investment banker, venture capitalist, financial consultant; b. Denver, Aug. 21, 1920; s. Abe and Julia (Rosen) M.; m. Paula Elaine Henderson; children: S. Michael, Joan, Levi. Student, So. Meth. U., 1962-64. V.p. Lester's Inc., Oklahoma City, 1940-59; exec. v.p. Besco Enterprises, San Francisco, 1960-61; sr. v.p. Zale Corp., Dallas, 1962-69; pres. CAC Fin. Group, Dallas, 1965; pres., CEO Zale Leased Jewelry divsn., 1965-69; CEO Designcraft Industries, N.Y.C., 1969-75, Tex. Internat. Export Co., Dallas, 1975—. Fin. cons. Vocat. Video, Huntington, N.Y., Consol. Transplant Network, Metairie, La., Slane Devel. Co., Columbus, Thera-Test Diagnostic Labs., Chgo., Clarity Devel., Orlando, Fla., Kemper Mil. Acad., Boonville, Mo., Soft-Trac Info. Systems, Jasper, Ala.; fin. project analyst, AFL-CIO; client referal arrangement The Dai-Ichi Kangyo Bank, Ltd., GMACCM, Chgo.; charter mem. N.Y. Ins. Exch.; guest lectr. fin. risk confs., 1982—, spkr. Am. Real Estate Investment Conf., London, 1986; pres., CEO The Markman Fin. Orgn., Dallas, 1973 . Contbr. articles to profl. jours. Vol. social worker Presbyn. Hosp., Dallas; mem. Dallas Co. World Affairs, 1962—; active NCCJ. With USMCR, 1942-45, PTO. Mem. Press Club, City Club (Dallas), India Temple Club (Oklahoma City), L.A. Athletic Club, Columbian Golf and Country Club (Addison, Tex.), Young Men's Philanthropic League (N.Y.C.). Address: 3013 W Country Hill Dr Tucson AZ 85742 Personal E-mail: shermanmarkman@aol.com.

**MARKMAN, STEPHEN J.,** state supreme court justice; b. Detroit, June 4, 1949; s. Julius and Pauline Markman; m. Mary Kathleen Sites, Aug. 25, 1974; children: James, Charles. BA, Duke U., 1971; JD, U. Cin., 1974. Legis. asst. to Rep. Edward Hutchinson, Mich., 1975, Rep. Tom Hagedorn, Minn., 1976—78; chief counsel, staff dir. subcom. on const. U.S. Senate Com. on Judiciary, 1978—85, dep. chief counsel, 1983; asst. atty. gen. Office Legal Policy, Dept. Justice, Washington, 1985-89; U.S. atty. U.S. Dept. Justice, Detroit, 1989-93; mem. Miller, Canfield, Paddock & Stone, Detroit, 1993—95; judge Mich. Ct. Appeals, 1995—99; justice Mich. Supreme Ct., Lansing, Mich., 1999—. Prof. constitutional law Hillsdale Coll. Author numerous articles appearing in Stanford Law Review, U. Chicago Law Review, U. Mich. Jour. of Law Reform, Am. Criminal Justice Law Review, Barrister's Law Jour., Harvard Jour. of Law & Public Policy, Detroit Coll. of Law Review. Fellow: Mich. Bar Found.; mem.: ABA, One Hundred Club, Am. Inns of Ct. Office: Mich Supreme Ct Hall of Justice 925 W Ottawa St Fl 6 Lansing MI 48915 Office Phone: 517-373-9449.*

**MARKO, MARLENE,** psychiatrist; b. N.Y.C., July 3, 1945; m. Loren R. Skeist; children: Marc, David, Sarah. BA, Sarah Lawrence Coll., 1967; MD, Mt. Sinai Sch. Medicine, 1972. Diplomate Am. Bd. Psychiatry. Intern Lenox Hill Hosp., 1973; resident Mt. Sinai Hosp., 1976; clin. instr. Mt. Sinai Sch. Medicine.

**MARKOE, FRANK, JR.,** lawyer, health facility administrator; b. Balt., Sept. 5, 1923; s. Frank and Margaret (Smith) M.; m. Margaret McCormack (div.); children: Andrée Markoe Caldwell, Ritchie Harrison Markoe Scribner. AB, Washington and Lee U., 1947; LLB, U. Md., 1950. Bar: Md. 1950. Pntr.

Karl F. Steinmann, Balt., 1948-50, 50-53, Cable & McDaniel, Balt., 1954-55; gen. counsel, dir. Emerson Drug Co., Balt., 1955-56, adminstrv. v.p., 1957-58; v.p., sec., dir., gen. counsel Warner-Lambert Pharm. Co., 1958-67, exec. com., sr. v.p., dir., gen. counsel, sec., 1967-69, exec. asst. chmn. bd., 1970-71, sr. v.p., 1971-73; exec. v.p. Warner-Lambert Co., Morris Plains, NJ, 1973-77, vice chmn. bd., 1977-81; vice chmn. adv. bd. NY Hosp.-Cornell Med. Ctr. 1987—, also chmn. major gifts com. Capital Campaign; hon. holder Alfred E. Driscoll chair Fairleigh Dickinson U. Bd. dirs. NJ Coll. Medicine and Dentistry, Bd. Internat. Broadcasting, Radio Free Europe/Radio Liberty, Kips Bay Boys; bd. dirs., exec. com., pres. NJ Ballet. With USAAF, 1942-45, PTO. Mem. US C. of C., Proprietary Assn. (former), US C. of C. (dir.), Pharm. Mfrs. Assn. (bd. dir., exec. com.), NJ State C. of C. (bd. dir.), Phi Beta Kappa. Home and Office: 201 Grenville Rd Hobe Sound FL 33455-2414

**MARKOFF, JOHN,** reporter; b. Oakland, Calif., Oct. 24, 1949; m. Leslie Terzian. Bachelors, Whitman Coll., Walla Walla, Washington, 1971; Masters, U. Oreg., 1976. Covered tech. and def. industry Pacific News Svc., San Francisco, 1977—81; reporter, editor Infoworld, 1981—83; wrote column on personal computers San Jose Mercury, 1983—85; west coast editor Byte Mag., 1984—85; reporter San Francisco Examiner, 1985—88; reporter, bus. sect., computer and tech. NY Times, 1988—. Adj. faculty Stanford U., 2002—; lectr. U. Calif. Berkeley Sch. Journalism. Co-author (with Lennie Siegel): The High Cost of High Tech, 1985; co-author: (with Katie Hafner) Cyberpunk: Outlaws and Hackers on the Computer Frontier, 1991; co-author: (with Tsutomu Shimomura) Takedown: The Pursuit and Capture of America's Most Wanted Computer Outlaw, 1996. Recipient award for best new reporting, Software Pub. Assn., 1988, Gerald Loeb award, UCLA Anderson Sch. Mgmt. Office: NY Times 201 Spear St San Francisco CA 94105 Office Phone: 415-836-6700. Business E-Mail: markoff@nytimes.com.*

**MARKOFF, STEVEN C.,** finance company executive; CEO, pres., founder A. Mark Fin., Santa Monica, Calif., 1965—. Co-chmn. A. Mark Entertainment Film Prodn. Co., 2004; dir. Goldline Internat.; chmn. Careside Inc. Dir. ACLU Found. Southern Calif., 1979—; dir. Mgmt. Edn. Associates UCLA, 1986—92, dir. bd. visitors Grad. Sch. Mgmt., 1986; dir. Hollywood Cmty. Hosp., 1982—91. Office: A Mark Financial Corporation 233 Wilshire Blvd Ste 200 Santa Monica CA 90401-1227*

**MARKOS, CHRIS,** retired real estate company executive; b. Cleve., Nov. 25, 1926; s. George and Bessie (Papathatou) Markos; m. Alice Zaharopoulos, Dec. 11, 1949 (dec.); children: Marilyn Martin, Irene Matthews, Betsy Feierabend; m. Marilyn Gardanier, Nov. 8, 2002; children: Kathleen Mitchell, Patricia Hickle. BA, Case Western Reserve, Cleve., 1960; LLB, LaSalle U., Chgo., 1964. Cert. gen. real estate appraiser Ohio. Pres. Brooklyn Realty Co., Cleve., 1953—63; vice-pres. Herbert Laronge Inc., Cleve., 1963-76; v.p. Calabrese, Racek and Markos Inc., Cleve., 1976-83, Herbert Laronge Inc., Cleve., 1983-87, pres., 1987-88; v.p. Cragin Lang, Inc., Cleve., 1989-91; sr. cons. Grubb & Ellis, Cleve., 1991-93; sr. v.p. Realty One Appraisal Divsn., Independence, Ohio, 1993-98. Pres. Alcrimar Inc., 1988—1998. Co-author: Ohio Supplement to Modern Real Estate Practice, 5th-7th edits.; cons. editor, co-author: Modern Real Estate Practice in Ohio, 1st-3rd edits. Bd. dirs. Meyers U., Cleve., 1984-97. With U.S. Army, 1945-46. Mem. Am. Soc. Appraisers (sr., pres. 1973, state dir. 1975), Cleve. Bd. Realtors (hon. life mem., pres. 1974, Realtor of Yr. award 1976). Republican. Greek Orthodox. Home: Corinthian Condominium 936 Intracoastal Dr Apt 6-H Fort Lauderdale FL 33304 Personal E-mail: alcrimar@webtv.net. *Everyone's life has a beginning and an ending. It is what happens between these two points that makes up the essence of a person.*

**MARKOSKI, JOSEPH PETER,** lawyer; b. Floral Park, NY, Nov. 7, 1948; s. Stephen Nicolas and Josephine Veronica (Lapkofsky) Markoski; m. Julie Ann Angus, June 30, 1979; children: Katherine, Caroline, Peter. BSFS, Georgetown U., 1970, JD, 1973. Bar: DC 1973. Law clk. Hon. Thomas A. Flannery US Dist. Ct., Washington, 1973-74; assoc. Wilkinson, Cragun & Barker, Washington, 1975-80, ptnr., 1980-82, Squire, Sanders & Dempsey, Washington, 1982-96, mng. ptnr., 1991-96, mng. ptnr. Europe London, 1996—, mng. ptnr. DC & Tysons Corner, Va. Offices, chmn., Comm. Practice Group. Co-chmn. task force on open network initiatives Strategic Planning Group of U.S. CCITT Nat. Com., 1988-92; bd. dirs. Cmty. Lodgings, Inc. Co-author: Internat. Telecommunications Handbook, 1986; contbr. articles to profl. jours. Capt. USAR, 1970—78. Mem. ABA (vice-chmn. common carrier com. sci. and tech. sect. 1986-88, internat. common carrier project 1980-86), Fed. Commn. Bar Assn. (com. common carrier practice and procedure 1980—), Computer Law Assn., bd. dirs., chmn. telecomm. bar liaison com. 1994-96), Internat. Bar Assn. (mem. comm. and internat. computer and tech. law coms.), Am. C. of C. (Eng.). Democrat. Roman Catholic. Office: Squire Sanders & Dempsey LLP 1201 Pennsylvania Ave NW PO Box 407 Washington DC 20044-0407 also: Squire Sanders & Dempsey LLP 8000 Towers Crescent Dr 14th Floor Vienna VA 22182-2700 Office Fax: 703-720-7801, 202-626-6780. Business E-Mail: jmarkoski@ssd.com.

**MARKOVICH, PATRICIA H.,** economist; b. Oakland, Calif. MS in Econs., U. Calif., Berkeley; postgrad., Stanford U. Cert. emergency mgmt. planner. Pvt. practice polit. and econs. cons.; former aide to majority whip Oreg. Ho. of Reps.; lectr., instr. various Calif. instns., Chemeketa (Oreg.) Coll., Portland (Oreg.) State U.; commr. City of Oakland, Calif. Chairperson, bd. dirs. Cable Sta. KCOM; econ. and emergency mgmt. cons. Mem. Piedmont (Calif.) Gen. Plan Commn. NSF grant Oreg. Grad. Rsch. Ctr., Lilly Found. grant. Mem.: Nat. Coordinating Coun. Emergency Mgmt., Mensa.

**MARKOVICH, VOYA R.,** information technology executive; arrived in US, 1969; s. Rista A. and Draga S. Markovic; m. Anita M. Sica, Jan. 9, 1951; children: Michael children: Steven. BS in Chemistry, U. Belgrade, Serbia, 1966; MS in Chemistry, Poly. Inst. NY, 1981. Analytical chemist Community Labs., Inc., N.Y.C., 1969—81, devel. project mgr. IBM, Endicott, NY, 1981—2002; sr. v.p., chief tech. officer, gen. mgr. R&D and IP, Endicott Interconnect Techs., Inc., Endicott. Sr. tech. staff mem. IBM, Endicott, 1996—2002, mem. Acad. of Tech., 1997—2002. Contbr. chapters to books. Mem.: IEEE (assoc.), Electronic Components Tech. Conf. (assoc.), Internat. Printed Circuits (assoc.), Integrated Electronics Engring. Ctr. (assoc.), Internat. Microelectronics Packaging Soc. (assoc.). Achievements include 168 US patents in field; some of the patents include Direct Chip Attach on Laminate Packaging; Full Additive Process - Copper Bondable Surface (CBS); Z Interconnection for Organic Packaging; High Performance Core Board Technology; invention of High Speed Board design. Avocations: travel, technology, politics. Home: 3611 Joel Dr Endicott NY 13760 Office: Endicott Interconnect Technologies Inc 1701 North Street Endicott NY 13760 Office Phone: 607-755-1978. Personal E-mail: markovichv@yahoo.com, voyarm@aol.com. Business E-Mail: v.markovich@eitny.com. E-mail: voya.markovich@eitny.com.

**MARKOVITS, ANDREI STEVEN,** political science professor; b. Timisoara, Romania, Oct. 6, 1948; came to U.S., 1960, naturalized, 1971; s. Ludwig and Ida (Ritter) M. BA, Columbia U., 1969, MBA, 1971, MA, 1971, MPhil, 1974, PhD, 1976. Mem. faculty NYU, 1974, John Jay Coll. Criminal Justice, CUNY, 1974, Columbia U., 1975; rsch. assoc. Inst. Advanced Studies, Vienna, Austria, 1973-74, Wirtschafts und Sozialwissenschaftliches Inst., German Trade U. Fedn., Düsseldorf, Germany, 1979, Internat. Inst. Comparative Social Rsch., Sci. Ctr. Berlin, 1980; asst. prof. govt. Wesleyan U., Middletown, Conn., 1977-83; assoc. prof. polit. sci. Boston U., 1983-92; prof., chair dept. politics U. Calif., Santa Cruz, 1992-99; prof. dept. polit. sci., 1999—; prof. dept. Germanic langs. and lit. and dept. polit. sci. U. Mich., Ann Arbor, 1999—2003, Karl W. Deutsch Collegiate prof. comparative politics and German studies, 2003—; Fulbright prof. U. Innsbruck, Austria, 1996. Vis. prof. Tel Aviv U., 1986, Osnabrück U., 1987, Bochum U., 1991, Harvard U., 2002—03, St. Gallen (Switzerland) U., 2004, Hebrew U., 2005, Dortmund U., 2006; sr. rsch. assoc. Ctrl. European Studies Harvard U., 1975—99. Author, editor books and papers in field; TV and radio commentator. Univ. Pres.'s fellow Columbia U., 1969, B'nai B'rith Found. fellow, 1976-77, Kalmus Found. fellow, 1976-77, Ford Found. fellow, 1979,

Hans Boeckler Found. fellow, 1982 Inst. for Advanced Study Berlin fellow, 1998-99; N.Y. State scholar Columbia U., 1969. Mem. N.Y. Acad. Scis., Am. Polit. Sci. Assn., Internat. Polit. Sci. Assn., AAUP. Home: 718 Onondaga St Ann Arbor MI 48104-2611 Office: Univ Mich 3110 Modern Lang Bldg 812 E Washington St Ann Arbor MI 48109-1275 Office Phone: 734-764-8018. Personal E-mail: andreimarkovits@cs.com. Business E-Mail: andymark@umich.edu.

**MARKOWITZ, DEBORAH LYNN,** state official; b. Tarrytown, N.Y., Sept. 14, 1961; d. Gerald Harvey and Sandra Lee (Schulner) M.; m. Paul William Markowitz, June 19, 1988; children: Aviva Lee, Sandra Rose, Ari David. BA with honors, Vt., 1982; JD magna cum laude, Georgetown U., 1987. Bar: Vt. 1988, U.S. Dist. Ct. Vt. 1989. Assoc. Covington & Burling, Washington, 1987-88; assoc. Langrack, Sperry & Wool, Burlington, Vt., 1988-90; Dir. Law Ctr. Vt. League of Cities and Towns, Montpelier, Vt., 1990—97; devel. cons. Vt. Law Sch., South Royalton, 1997—; sec. of state State of Vt., 1998—. Adj. faculty Vt. Law Sch., South Royalton, 1992; examiner Vt. Bd. Bar Examiners, Montpelier, 1994-98. Contbr. articles to profl. jours. Bd. dirs. Ctrl. Vt. Cmty. Action Agy., Vt. Hist. Soc.; trustee Woodbury Coll. Mem. ABA (state and local govt. sect.), Vt. Bar Assn. (mcpl. com.), Internat. Mcpl. Lawyers Assn. (chair pers. sect. 1993—), Nat. Assn. Secs. of State (pres.), Nat. Mus. of Women in the Arts (bd. dirs. Vt. chpt.), Order of Coif. Democrat. Avocations: cross country skiing, singing, sketching, gardening. Office: Office Sec of State Redstone Bldg 26 Terrace Street, PO Box 9 Montpelier VT 05609-0001 Office Phone: 802-828-2148. Office Fax: 802-828-2496. E-mail: dmarkowitz@sec.state.vt.us.*

**MARKOWITZ, GERALD E.,** historian, educator; b. N.Y.C., July 12, 1944; s. Irving and Esther Wittes Markowitz; m. Andrea Ades, Nov. 25, 1994; children: William, Elena Kennedy, Eva Vasquez, Anton Vasquez. BA, Earlham Coll., Richmond, Ind., 1965; PhD, U. of Wis., 1971. Disting. prof. history John Jay Coll., CUNY, N.Y.C., 1970—, Grad. Ctr., CUNY, N.Y.C., 1990—; adj. prof. sociomed. sci. Mailman Sch. of Pub. Health, Columbia U., N.Y.C., 2002—. Mem., bd. of dirs. Am. Social History Project, N.Y.C., 2002—. Author (with David Rosner): (book) Deceit and Denial: The Deadly Politics of Industrial Pollution, Deadly Dust: Silicosis and the Politics of Industrial Disease in Twentieth Century America (Outstanding Academic Book of 1991 by Choice, 1991); author: (with Marlene Park) Democratic Vistas: Post Offices and Public Art in the New Deal; author: Are We Ready: Public Health Since 9/11; editor (with David Rosner): Slaves of the Depression: Workers Letters About Life on the Job, Dying for Work: Workers' Safety and Health in Twentieth Century America; contbr. articles to profl. jours. Recipient Arthur Viseltear Award for Outstanding Contribns. to the History of Pub. Health, Med. Care Sect., APHA, 2000, Award for Disting. Work in Occupl. and Environ. Health, N.Y. Com. for Occupl. Health; grantee Power and Pollution: The Politics of Indsl. Disease, NSF, 2001—02, Interpretative Rsch. grantee, NEH, 1992—94, 1987—89, History of Occupl. Safety and Health grantee, Milbank Meml. Fund, 1985—86, The Un-Natural History of Pub. Health grantee, Robert Wood Johnson Investigator Awards in Health Policy Rsch., 2002—. Mem.: Am. Soc. for Environ. History, Orgn. of Am. History, Am. Hist. Assn. Office: John Jay College 899 Tenth Ave New York NY 10019 Office Phone: 212-237-8458. E-mail: gmarkowitz@jjay.cuny.edu.

**MARKOWITZ, HARRY MAX,** finance and economics educator; b. Chgo., Aug. 24, 1927; s. Morris and Mildred (Gruber) M.; m. Barbara Gay. PhB, U. Chgo., 1947, MA, 1950, PhD, 1954. With research staff Rand Corp., Santa Monica, Calif., 1952-60, 61-63; chmn. bd., tech. dir. Consol. Analysis Ctrs., Inc., Santa Monica, 1963-68; prof. UCLA, Westwood, 1968-69; pres. Arbitrage Mgmt. Co., N.Y.C., 1969-72; pvt. practice cons. N.Y.C., 1972-74; prof. Wharton Sch., U. Pa., 1972—74; with research staff T.J. Watson Research Ctr. IBM, Yorktown Hills, NY, 1974-83; prof. Rutgers U., 1980—82; Marvin Speiser Disting. Prof. of Fin. and Econs. Baruch Coll. CUNY, N.Y.C., 1982-93; dir. rsch. Daiwa Securities Trust Co, Jersey City, 1990-2000; prin., owner Harry Markowitz Co., 1993—; rsch. prof. dept. econs. U. Calif. San Diego. V.p. Inst. Mgmt. Sci., 1960-62. adv. bd. Jour. Investment Mgmt. Author: Portfolio Selection: Efficient Diversification of Investments, 1959, Mean-Variance Analysis in Portfolio Choice, 1987; co-author: SIMSCRIPT Simulation Programming Language, 1963; co-editor: Process Analysis of Economic Capabilities, 1963. Recipient John von Neumann Theory prize Opns. Rsch. Soc. Am. and Inst. Mgmt. Sci., 1989, Nobel Prize in Econs., 1990. Fellow Econometric Soc., Am. Acad. Arts and Scis., Am. Fin. Assn. Office: Ste 245 1010 Turquoise St San Diego CA 92109*

**MARKOWITZ, MARTIN H.,** biomedical researcher; b. NYC, Nov. 22, 1953; BA in Biology, SUNY, Buffalo, NY, 1974; MD, Stanford U., 1978. Cert. internal medicine 1981, med. oncology 1983, hematology 1984. Intern, medicine Mt. Zion Hosp. and Med. Ctr., U. Calif., San Francisco, 1978-79, resident, medicine, 1979—81; clin. fellow, hematology/oncology Cornell Med. Coll., NY, 1981—82, rsch. fellow, hematology/oncology NY, 1982—83, chief clin. fellow, instr., dept. medicine, divsn. hematology/oncology, 1983—84; asst. attending physician Hosp. for Spl. Surgery, 1985; attending adult hematologist Regional Comprehensive Hemophilia Diagnostic and Treatment Ctr., Cornell Med. Coll., 1986; attending hematologist/oncologist Spellman Ctr. for the Treatment of HIV Related Disease, St. Clare's Hosp., NY, 1985—89; acting dir. Spellman Ctr., St. Clare's Hosp., NY, 1989; attending staff, dept. of medicine, divsn. hematology/oncology Lenox Hill Hosp., NY, 1985—90; vis. assoc. physician Rockefeller Univ. Hosp., NY, 1995—96; clin. fellow, divsn. infectious diseases NYU/Bellevue, NY, 1991—92; rsch. fellow Aaron Diamond AIDS Rsch. Ctr., NY, 1992—94, staff investigator NY, 1994—, clin. dir., 1998—; adj. assoc. physician, divsn. infectious diseases Cornell Med. Coll., 1996—; assoc. physician Rockefeller Univ. Hosp., NY, 1996—; assoc. prof. Rockefeller U., NY, 2000. Instr., dept. medicine/div. hematology/oncology Cornell Med. Coll., 1984—85; instr., dept. medicine NYU, 1994—95; asst. prof., dept. medicine, divsn. infectious diseases NY Med. Sch., NY, 1995—96; assoc. prof. clin. investigation Rockefeller Univ., NY, 2000—. Editor: Journal of AIDS; review assignments Journal of American Med. Assn., Journal of Virology, Lancet, Journal of Infectious Diseases, AIDS and Human Retroviruses, PNAS, AIDS after PNAS. Named 10th Annual Mothers' Voices, 2001; recipient AMFAR award of Courage, NY, 2001. Mem.: Infectious Disease Soc. of Am., Am. Soc. Microbiology, Phi Beta Kappa. Achievements include research in HIV therapeutics and pathogenesis. Office: Aaron Diamond AIDS Rsch Ctr 455 First Ave 7th Fl New York NY 10016 E-mail: mmarkowitz@adarc.org.

**MARKOWITZ, MARTY (MARTIN MARKOWITZ),** city manager; b. Bklyn., Feb. 14, 1945; m. Jamie Markowitz, 1999. BA, Bklyn. Coll., 1970. Organizer Flatbush Tenants Coun., 1971; elected to NY State Senate, Albany, 1979—2002, past mem. aging com., civil svc. and pensions com., health com., housing and cmty. devel. com., labor com.; borough pres. Brooklyn, 2002—. Chair Initiative for a Competitive Brooklyn; creator Seaside Summer Concert Series, Coney Island, Martin Luther King, Jr. Concert Series, Flatbush. Mem. NAACP (life), Midwood Jewish Ctr., City Urban League. Office: 209 Joralemon St Brooklyn NY 11201 Office Phone: 718-802-3700.*

**MARKOWITZ, SAMUEL SOLOMON,** chemistry professor; b. Bklyn., Oct. 31, 1931; s. Max and Florence Ethel (Goldman) M.; children: Michael, Daniel, Jonah; m. 2d Lydia de Antonis, Oct. 31, 1993. BS in Chemistry, Rensselaer Poly. Inst., 1953; MA, Princeton U., 1955, PhD, 1957; postgrad., Brookhaven Nat. Lab., 1955-57. Asst. prof. chemistry U. Calif., Berkeley, 1958-64, assoc. prof., 1964-72, prof., 1972—. Faculty sr. scientist Lawrence Berkeley Lab., 1985—. Fellow of nuclear physics Weizmann Inst. Sci., Rehovot, Israel, 1973-74. Mem. Bd. Edn. of Berkeley Unified Sch. Dist., 1969-73, pres. bd., 1972-73. Recipient Elizabeth McFeely D'Urso Meml. Pub. Ofcl. award Alameda County Edn. Assn., 1973; LeRoy McKay fellow Princeton U., 1955, Charlotte Elizabeth Proctor fellow Princeton U., 1956, NSF postdoctoral fellow U. Birmingham, Eng., 1957-58, NSF sr. postdoctoral

fellow Faculte des Scis. U. Paris a Orsay, Laboratoire Joliot-Curie de Physique Nucleaire, 1964-65. Fellow AAAS; mem. Am. Chem. Soc. (bd. dirs. Calif. sect., chmn. 1991, 93-94, Nat. Councilor, 1990-, Walter Petersen award 2003), Am. Phys. Soc., Am. Inst. chemists, N.Y. Acad. Scis., Calif. Inst. Chemists, Sigma Xi. Home: 555 Pierce St # 245 Albany CA 94706 Office: U Calif Dept Chemistry Berkeley CA 94720-1460 Office Phone: 510-642-2922. Business E-Mail: markowit@cchem.berkeley.edu.

**MARKS, BOBBY KEES,** academic administrator; b. Alexandria, La., May 17, 1934; s. Frank Arnold and Alma Lucille (Kees) M.; m. Colleen Ann McDonald, July 28, 1956; children: Denice Leanne, Donna Deanne. BBA, Lamar U., 1956; MBA, North Tex. State U., 1960; PhD, U. Ark., 1966. Salesman Gulf Supply Co. Inc.,Beaumont, Tex., 1956-59; instr. Sam Houston State U., Huntsville, Tex., 1960-63, asst. prof., 1964-66, assoc. prof., 1966-67, prof., 1967—, dir. dept. econs., 1968-69, dean coll. bus. adminstrn., 1969-84, v.p., 1984-95; interim pres., 1995-96; pres., 1996—2001; instr. U. Ark., Fayetteville, 1963-64. Bd. dirs. 1st Nat. Bank-South, Huntsville, Walker County Indsl. Devel. Corp., Huntsville, pres. Mem. planning commn. City of Huntsville, 1983-85; chmn. bd. dirs. Huntsville Leadership Inst., 1981-82, Elkins Lake Bapt. Ch., Huntsville, 1974—. Served with U.S. Army, 1957-58. Mem. Ozark Econs. Assn. (pres. 1971-72), Tex. Coun. Collegiate Educators for Bus. (pres. 1980-81), Assn. Chief Acad. Officers of So. States (v.p. 1994, pres. 1995), Soc. for Coll. and Univ. Planning, Planning Forum (bd. dirs. Houston chpt. 1986-87), Assn. Tex. Colls. and Univs. (bd. dirs. 1997—, exec. com. 1997—), Coun. Pub. Univ. Press. and Chancellors (exec. com. 1997—), Tex. Internat. Edn. Consorium (exec. com. 1998—, chmn. 2000-01), Huntsville/Walker County C. of C. (bd. dirs. 1979-81, 88-91, Pres.'s Key Mem. award 1981, pres. 1990, Lifetime Achievement award 2000), Rotary (pres.-elect Huntsville 1971-72), Beta Gamma Sigma. Office: Sam Houston State U PO Box 2026 Huntsville TX 77341-2026

**MARKS, BRUCE,** performing company executive, choreographer; b. NYC, Jan. 23, 1937; s. Albert and Helen (Kosersky) M.; m. Toni Pihl Petersen, Jan. 27, 1966 (dec. May 1985); children: Erik Antony, Adam Christopher, Kenneth Rikard. Student, Brandeis U., 1954—55, Juilliard Sch., 1955—56; DFA, D, Northeastern U., 1997. Prof. U. Utah, 1981, 1984—86; artistic dir. Boston Ballet Co., 1985—97, artistic dir. emeritus, 1998—. Mem. dance adv. panel Nat. Endowment for Arts, 1979, chmn. internat. selection com., 1979, chmn. dance adv. panel, 1981, mem. nat. adv. bd. on arts and edn., 1989; bd. dirs., mem. exec. com., Dance/USA 1989, 92—, chmn., 1990-92, chmn. govt. affairs, 1992—; mem. U.S.-USSR Commn. on Dance and Theatre Studies, Am. Coun. Learned Socs./IREX; mem. jury Internat. Moscow Internat. Ballet Competition, 1989; mem. arts in edn. adv. coun. Harvard U., 1997; chmn. 3d Japan Internat. Ballet and Modern Dance competition, 1999; jury mem. Prague Internat. Ballet Competition, 2001; artistic advisor Ft. Worth/Dallas Ballet, 2000-01; tchr. 1st Seoul (Korea) Internat. Dance Competition, 2004. Prin. dancer Met. Opera, 1956-61, Am. Ballet Theatre, 1961-72, Royal Swedish Ballet, 1963, Festival Ballet, London, 1965, Royal Danish Ballet, 1971-76; artistic dir. Ballet West, Salt Lake City, 1976-85; choreographer Eliot Feld Ballet Co., 1970, Royal Danish Ballet, 1971-76, Netherlands Dance Theatre, 1974, Ballet West, 1976-85; artistic fellow Aspen Inst. for Humanistic Studies, 1979—. Bd. dirs. Am. Arts Alliance, 1983-85, Am. Coun. for Arts, 1985—; Dance U.S.A., 1988-94, chmn., 1990-92; chmn. U.S.A. Internat. Ballet Competition, Jackson, Micc., 1990—, vice chair jury Helsinki, Finland, 1991, judge Helsinki Ballet Competition 1995; mem. nat. adv. bd. on arts and edn. NEA, 1989-91; mem. internat. jury 1st and 2d Japan Internat. Ballet Competition, Nagoya, Japan, 1993, 96, 2005, Am. jury for Prix de Lausanne, 1994, 98; mem. Brandeis Creative Arts Awards Commn., 1993, chmn. Brandeis Creative Arts Awards Dance, 1994; chair Grants to Dance Cos. panel NEA, 1993, overview panel, 1994; chmn. 3d Japan Internat. Ballet Competition, Nagoya, 1999; artistic advisor Ft. Worth/Dallas Ballet, 2000-2001; mem. Princess Grace Awards panel, 2005. Recipient Disting. Svc. award for artistic prodn. Nat. Govs. Assn., 1994, Capezio award Balletmakers, Inc., 1995, Dance Mag. award, 1997, Honors award Dance/USA, 1998, Proscenium award, Boston, 2001, Juilliard medal Svc. to Arts, 2005

**MARKS, CHARLES,** surgeon, educator; b. Kiev, Ukraine, Jan. 28, 1922; came to U.S., 1963; s. Abe and Sonia (Beck) M.; m. Joyce Wernick, Dec. 11, 1949; children: Malcolm, Peter, Ian, Anthony. MD, U. Cape Town, south Africa, 1945; MS, Marquette U., 1966; PhD, Tulane U., 1973. Intern and surg. resident Groote Schuur Hosp., Cape Town, 1946-49; surg. resident Royal Coll. Surgeons Affiliated Hosps., London, 1950-53; cons. surgeon Salisbury (Rhodesia) Gen. Hosp., 1953-63; assoc. prof. surgery Marquette U. Med. Sch., Milw., 1963-67; dir. dept. surgery Mt. Sinai Hosp., Cleve., 1967-71; assoc. clin. prof. surgery Case Western Res. U. Sch. Medicine, Cleve., 1967-71; prof. surgery La. State U. Sch. Medicine, New Orleans, 1971-88; sr. attending surgeon Charity, VA, Touro and Hotel Dieu Hosps., New Orleans, 1971—88; med. exec. dir. Fla. Dept. Corrections, Charlotte, Fla., 1994-97. Cons. cardiothoracic surgeon Ministry of Health, Govt. Zimbabwe, Harare, 1989-94; Hunterian prof. Royal Coll. Surgeons, 1956. Mem. bd. govs. Drs. Hosp. Sarasota, 1997-2004, chmn. bd. govs., 2001—; mem. inner senatorial com. Rep. Party, Washington, 1997—. Recipient Schlieder Rsch. award, 1975. Fellow ACS, Royal Coll. Physicians Edinburgh, Am. Coll. Cardiology; mem. Internat. Cardiovasc. Soc., Am. Transplantation Soc., New Orleans Surg. Soc. (pres.). Republican. Avocations: tennis, golf, travel. Home: # 1517 988 Blvd of the Arts Sarasota FL 34236

**MARKS, CHARLES CALDWELL,** retired investment banker, retired manufacturing executive; b. Birmingham, Ala., June 1, 1921; s. Charles Pollard and Isabel (Caldwell) M.; m. Jeanne Vigeant, Jan. 12, 1945 (dec.); children: Randolph C., Margaret Marks Porter, Charles P.; m. Alice V. Scott, Sept. 18, 1999. Student, Birmingham U., 1930-38; BS in Physics, U. of South, 1942; grad. mgmt. seminar, Harvard U., 1957; DCL (hon.), U. of the South, 1989; LLD (hon.), U. Ala., Birmingham, 1990. With Owen-Richards Co. (name changed to Motion Industries, Inc. 1970), Birmingham, 1946—, chmn. bd., 1952-73, pres., 1973-83; vice chmn. bd. Porter White & Yardley Cos., Inc., 1984-92, ret., 1992. Bd. dirs. emeritus Genuine Parts Co., BE & K Inc., emeritus; bd. dirs., chmn. Birmingham br. Fed. Res. Bank of Atlanta. Bd. dirs. So. Rsch. Inst., exec. com., 1987-95, dir. emeritus, 1995—2001; bd. govs. Indian Springs Sch., dir. emeritus, 1995—; pres., bd. dirs. Workshop for Blind, Birmingham, 1958-61, Children's Aid Soc. Birmingham, 1962; chmn. Com. of 100, Birmingham, 1963; co-chmn. United Appeals of Jefferson County, 1963; trustee, regent U. of South; chmn. St. Vincent's Found., 1980-81, pres., 1987; bd. dirs. U. Ala.-Birmingham Rsch. Found., Exec. Svcs. Corps. of Birmingham, 1984-96. Lt. USNR, WWII, ATO, MTO. Named to Ala. Bus. Hall of Fame, 2005. Mem. The Club, Redstone Club, John's Island Club, Mountain Brook Club, Ala. Newcomen Soc., Blue Key, Phi Beta Kappa, Sigma Alpha Epsilon. Episcopalian. Home: 500 Olde English Ln Apt 516 Birmingham AL 35223-1078 Office: Ste 104 402 Office Park Dr Birmingham AL 35223

**MARKS, CHARLES DENNERY,** insurance consultant; b. New Orleans, Nov. 22, 1935; s. Sidney Leroy Marks and Melanie Dennery; m. Gillian E. Otter, Sept. 1, 1963; children: Elizabeth Dennery, Richard Dennery. BA, Yale U., 1957. CLU; ChFC; accredited estate planner; cert. long term care, cert. sr. advisor; chartered advisor for sr. living. With Charles Dennery, Inc., 1959-63; sales rep. Prudential Ins. Co., New Orleans, 1964-97. Past bd. dirs. Boys Club Greater New Orleans, Big Bros. Greater New Orleans, United Way; past pres. Goodwill Rehab. Ctr.; vice-chmn. Jr. Achievement; active Temple Sinai Synagogue; bd. dirs. Am. Coll., 2000-2003, 2005, exec. com., 2001-2003; bd. dirs. Am. Coll. Found., 2001-05. 1st lt. U.S. Army, 1957-59. Recipient award Volunteer Activist, 1983. Mem.: Nat. Assn. Ins. and Fin. Advisors (vice chmn. fin. com. 1993—99, mem. audit com. 2003—, pres. Greater New Orleans chpt. 1983, Man of Yr. 1981), Million Dollar Round Table (exec. com. 1990—94, pres. 1993, Top of the Table 1986—89), New Orleans Estate Planning Coun. (pres. 1986—87), La. Assn. Ins. and Fin. Advisors (pres. 1986—87, Advisor of Yr. 1985, Advisor or Yr 1987, Advisor of Yr. 2002),

Soc. Fin. Svc. Profls. (pres. New Orleans chpt. 1984—85), Life and Health Found. for Edn. (life; chmn. 1996—98). Republican. Home and Office: 1525 Eleonore St New Orleans LA 70115-4242 Personal E-mail: cdmdrt@msn.com.

**MARKS, DAVID HUNTER,** civil engineering educator; b. White Plains, N.Y., Feb. 22, 1939; s. Sidney M. and Jean (Berger) M.; div.; 1 child, Joanna; m. Lilian Kemp, Dec. 17, 1998. BCE, Cornell U., 1962, MS in Environ. Engring., 1964; PhD, Johns Hopkins U., 1969. Registered profl. engr.: N.Y., Mass.; registered hydrologist, Am. Inst. Hydrology. Sr. sanitary engr. USPHS, Phila., 1964-66; asst. prof. civil engring. MIT, Cambridge, Mass., 1969-72, assoc. prof., 1972-75, prof., 1975—, head dept., 1985-92, dir. program in environ. edn. and rsch., 1991-2000, James Mason Crafts prof., 1992-2000, Goulder Family prof., 2001—; coord. Alliance for Global Sustainability, 1996—; dir. Ctr. Environ. Initiatives, 1997-2001, Lab. for Energy and the Environment, 2001—. Office: Mit 1 Amherst St Rm E40-455 Cambridge MA 02139-4307 Office Phone: 617-253-1992. E-mail: dhmarks@mit.edu.

**MARKS, DEBRA JANE,** special education educator; b. Rockville Centre, NY, Aug. 22, 1948; d. Warren Godfrey and Beth Hyman; m. Michael Joel Marks, Aug. 23, 1969; children: Melissa, Stephanie, Karen. BS in Elem. Edn., U. Cin., 1970; M in Elem. Edn., LI U., 1973; cert. in spl. edn., Hofstra U., 1998. Tchr. 6th grade Hillside Grade Sch., New Hyde Park, NY, 1970—74; HS tchr. Jericho (NY) Jewish Ctr., 1978—80; owner Happily Ever After, Plainview, NY, 1985—89; from spl. edn. tchr. asst. to spl. edn. tchr. Nassau BOCES, Wantagh, NY, 1994—2000; spl. edn. tchr. W.T. Clarke Mid. Sch., East Meadow, NY, 2000—. Presenter in field; participant Nat. Svcs. Learning Conf., Phila., 2006; facilitator parallel report card devel. for spl. edn. W.T. Clarke Mid. Sch., 2005; coord., pres. Penny Harvest Exec. Svc. Learning Club, 2000—06. Contbr. chpts. to sch. dist. curriculum books. Named Founder's Day Honoree, East Meadow Sch. Dist., 2004—06; recipient, Nat. Wall of Tolerance Recognition, 2006; grantee, Common Cents NY, 2001—06, Future Corps, Newsday, 2004—06. Mem.: Spl. Edn. PTA (tchr. rep. 2004—06), Penny Harvest Exec. Svc. Learning Club, Martin Luther King Racial/Cultural Awareness Club (awareness com. 2004—05), Kappa Delta Pi. Avocations: travel, reading, golf. Office: WT Clarke Mid Sch 740 Edgewood Dr Westbury NY 11590

**MARKS, ED,** editor; Asst. culture editor NY Times. Office: NY Times 229 W 43rd St New York NY 10036 Office Phone: 212-556-5131. Office Fax: 212-556-1516.*

**MARKS, GERALD,** surgeon, educator; b. Bklyn., Apr. 14, 1925; s. Maurice and Lee (Leib) M.; m. Barbara Ann Hendershot, Nov. 25, 1950; children: Richard M., James M., John H. Grad., Villanova U., 1945; MD, Jefferson Med. Coll., 1949. Diplomate: Am. Bd. Surgery, Am. Bd. Colon and Rectal Surgery (examiner). Intern Jefferson Med. Coll. Hosp., Phila., 1949-51, resident in surgery, 1952-57, resident in proctology, 1953-54, asst. dir. Tumor Clinic, 1959-68; practice medicine specializing in gen. and colorectal surgery Phila., 1957—; asst. chief surgery Phila. Gen. Hosp., 1957-70, chief Proctology Clinic, 1968-70, coordinator student surg. edn. Jefferson Surg. Service, 1960-70; attending physician in surgery Thomas Jefferson U. Hosp., 1957-95, sec. med. staff, 1974-77, dir. Comprehensive Rectal Cancer Ctr., Colorectal Surgery Residency Program, exec. dir. Colorectal Surgical Found., 1984-95, co-dir. Colorectal Cancer Genetics Ctr.; dir. div. internat. surg. edn. and practice Ctr. for Research in Med. Edn. and Health Care; instr. surgery Jefferson Med. Coll., 1958-67, assoc. in clin. surgery, 1967-68, clin. assoc. prof. surgery, 1974-78, prof., 1978-95; chief sect. colorectal surgery, cons. in colon-rectal surgery Pa. Hosp.; cons. in colon-rectal surgery VA Hosp., Coatesville, Pa., 1959—, San Juan, P.R., 1968—, Wilmington, Del., 1977—; cons in colon-rectal surgery USN Regional Med. Ctr., Phila., 1977—; Edgar Deissler prof. surgery Allegheny U. Health Scis., 1995—2001, dir. comprehensive rectal cancer ctr., 1995—98, dir. GI surg. endoscopy, 1995. Adj. prof. surgery U. Pa. Sch. Medicine; sr. investigator, Lankenan Inst. for Med. Rsch.; dir. Internat. Network Comprehensive Rectal Cancer Ctrs., 1997-; chmn. Marks Colorectal Surg. Found.; clin. prof. surgery Drexel U. Sch. Medicine, 2001; Deissler prof. surgery and founding dir. divsn. colorectal surgery Hahnemann Med. Coll. of Allegheny U., 1995-2000 Sr. editor Surg. Endoscopy, Ultrasound and Interventional Techniques Jour.; assoc. editor Diseases of the Colon and Rectum Jour., 1977—; cons. editor Pa. Medicine; editl. cons. bd. mem. Gen. Surgery News, 1991, Jour. Surg. Techn.; contbr. articles to profl. jours.; developed colonscopic colon teaching model; solo artist exhbn. in watercolor painting in Italy and U.S Chmn. Marks Colorectal Surg. Rsch. Found. Served with USN, 1943-46; served to capt. M.C. USAF, 1951-52. Recipient 7th Ann. Jonathan M. Wainwright award, Moses Taylor Hosp., Scranton, Pa., 1989; Ann. Alumni Achievement award, Jefferson Med. Coll.; named Man of the Yr., Jewish Nat. Fund, Lifetime Achievement award Northeast Soc. of Colon and Rectal Surgeons, 2004 Mem. ACS (rep. to bd. govs. 1983, council Met. Phila. chpt.), AMA, Pa. Soc. Colon and Rectal Surgery (pres. 1981-82), Am. Soc. Colon and Rectal Surgeons (v.p. 1989), Am. Soc. Clin. Oncology, Internat. Soc. Univ. Colon and Rectal Surgeons, Coll. Physicians Phila., Internat. Fedn. Socs. Endoscopic Surgeons (founding pres. 1991-2000), Royal Micro. Society (affiliate), Ea. Surg. Soc., Phila. Acad. Surgery (mem. council), Pa. Med. Soc., Phila. County Med. Soc. (bd. dirs., v.p., chmn. publs. com.; pub. affairs com., v.p. 1986—), Soc. Surgery Alimentary Tract, Am. Soc. Gastrointestinal Endoscopy, Italian Soc. Gastrointestinal Endoscopy (hon.), Am. Soc. Gastrointestinal Endoscopic Surgeons (founder, pres. 1980, bd. govs., honoree Annual Gerald Marks Lectureship, former chmn. internat. rels. com., Dist. Svc. award, 1997, Lifetime Achievement award, 2004), Italian Soc. Surgery (hon.), Northeastern Soc. Colon and Rectal Surgeons (past pres.), Jefferson Vol. Faculty Assn. (pres. 1973-74, Brady Cancer Rsch. Inst. award, 1997), Am. Soc. Colon and Rectal Surgeons (v.p. 1989—), Abruzzi Surg. Soc. (hon.), European Assn. Endoscopic Surgeons, Endolaparoscopic Surgeons of Asia, Puerto Rico Chpt. Am. Coll. Surgeons, Alpha Omega Alpha Home: 45 Fairview Rd Narberth PA 19072-1328 Office: 100 Lancaster Ave # 3-west Wynnewood PA 19096-3411 Office Phone: 610-645-9093. E-mail: marksg@mlhs.org.

**MARKS, HERBERT EDWARD,** lawyer; b. Dayton, Ohio, Nov. 3, 1935; s. I.M. and Sarah S. M.; m. Marcia Frager; children: Jennifer L., Susan E. AB with high distinction, U. Mich., 1957; JD, Yale U., 1960; postgrad., George Washington U. Law Sch., 1965-67. Bar: Ohio 1960, D.C. 1964, U.S. Supreme Ct. 1965. Law clk. to chief judge U.S. Ct. Claims, 1964-65; assoc. Wilkinson, Cragun & Barker, Washington, 1965-69, ptnr., 1969-82, Squire, Sanders & Dempsey, Washington, 1982—2003, sr. counsel, 2003—, sr. counsel Presdl. Inaugural Coms., 1969, 73, 81; chmn. U.S. State Dept. Adv. Panel on Internat. Telecom. Law, 1987—91; mem. adv. com. on internat. comm. and info. policy U.S. State Dept., 1988—91, 2002—; mem. U.S. del. ITU European Telecom. Devel. Conf., 1991, ITU Plenipotentiary Conf., 1998, ITU Coun., 2000, 04; mem. ITU Sec. Gen.'s Expert Group, 1999—2002; vice chmn. ITU Treaty Working Group, 2004—; bd. dirs. Vet. Legal Svc. Program, 2004—. Contbr. articles to legal jours. Served to capt. JAG USAF, 1960-64. Mem. ABA (chair sci. and tech. sect. 1990-91), Computer Law Assn. (pres. 1975-77, bd. dirs. 1972-85, adv. bd. 1985—), Fed. Comms. Bar Assn., Cosmos Club, Kenwood Golf and Country Club, Phi Beta Kappa. Office: Squire Sanders & Dempsey 1201 Pennsylvania Ave NW PO Box 407 Washington DC 20044-0407 also: 5317 Cardinal Ct Bethesda MD 20816-2908 Office Phone: 626-626-6624.

**MARKS, JAMES FREDERIC,** pediatric endocrinologist, educator; b. Pitts., Dec. 18, 1928; s. Alfred Mozelle and Cecil (Cuff) M.; m. Susan Grace Benson, Nov. 18, 2001; 1 child, Roland Phillip. BA, Princeton U., 1950; MD, Harvard U., 1954; MPH. U. Pitts. 1984. Intern Montefiore Hosp., Pitts., 1954-55; resident in pediatrics Children's Hosp. Pitts., 1955-57; rsch. fellow in pediatric endocrinology U. Pitts., 1959-61; asst. prof. dept. pediatrics U. Tex. Southwestern Med., Dallas, 1961-68, assoc. prof. pediatrics, 1968-98, clin. prof. internal medicine, 2001—, clin. prof. pediatrics, 2004—. Bd. dirs. State Newborn Screening Program, Tex., 1980-98. Contbr. articles to profl. bulls., chpts. to med. textbooks. Capt. U.S. Army, 1957-59. Sr. rsch. fellow USPHS, 1983-84. Mem. Am. Diabetes Assn. (bd. dirs. Tex.

affiliate 1992-97), Am. Acad. Pediatrics, Endocrine Soc., Soc. for Pediatric Rsch. Achievements include research in thyroid function in infancy, delineation of early clinical course in Lesch-Nyhan disease, observations on the possible genetic factors in diabetic microvascular disease. Office: U Tex Southwestern Med 5323 Harry Hines Blvd Dallas TX 75390-7208 Office Phone: 214-648-3767.

**MARKS, JAMES GARFIELD, JR.,** dermatologist; b. Trenton, N.J., May 19, 1945; s. James Garfield and Lavinia May (Ellis) M.; m. Joyce Lynne Turner, Aug. 9, 1969; 1 child, Shannon. BA, Wilkes Coll., 1967; MD, Temple U., 1971. Intern Geisinger Med. Ctr., Danville, Pa., 1971-72; resident Wilford Hall USAF Med. Ctr., San Antonio, 1975-78; clin. instr. dermatology U. Tex. Health Sci. Ctr., San Antonio, 1978-80; staff dermatologist Pa. State U. Coll. Medicine, Hershey, 1980—, asst. prof., 1980-85, assoc. prof., 1985-91, prof. dermatology, 1991—; chair dept. dermatology Hershey Med. Ctr. Team leader Cosmic Ingredient Rev. Expert Panel. Author: Atlas of Differential Diagnosis in Dermatology, 1998, Principles of Dermatology, 2006, Handbook of Contact Dermatitis, 2000, Contact and Occupational Dermatology, 2002, Principles and Practice of Dermatology, 1990, 2d edit., 1996, Occupational Skin Diseases, 1999, Conn's Current Therapy, 1988, 2d edit., 1989; author: (with others) Principles of Clinical Diagnosis, 1992, Dermatology, 2003; contbr. articles to profl. jours. Bd. dirs. Braun Sta. East Cmty., 1976. Maj. USAF, 1972-80. Decorated Meritorious Svc. Commendation meadl; Am. Acad. Dermatology Exch. fellow, 1984; recipient Roerig Pharms. Challenges in Dermatology Ednl. award, 1982. Mem. Am. Acad. Dermatology, Am. Contact Dermatitis Soc. (v.p. 1993, pres. 2001), N.Am. Contact Dermatitis Group, Pa. Acad. Dermatology, Phila. Dermatology Soc., European Soc. Contact Dermatitis, Soc. Investigative Dermatology, Assn. Mil. Dermatologists, Dermatology Found., Lions (v.p. 1982, pres. 1983). Office: Hershey Med Ctr 500 University Dr # 850 Hershey PA 17033 2360 Office Phone: 717-531-8307. E-mail: jmarks@psu.edu.

**MARKS, JAMES S.,** public health service administrator; b. May 13, 1948; AB cum laude, Williams Coll., 1969; MD, SUNY, Buffalo, 1973; MPH, Yale U., 1980. Diplomate Am. Bd. Pediatrics. Intern in pediat. U. Calif., San Francisco, 1973-74; resident in pediat., 1974-75, chief resident pediatric outpatient dept., 1975-76; fellow Robert Wood Johnson Clin. Scholars Program Yale U., New Haven, 1978-80; resident in preventive medicine Ctrs. for Disease Control, Atlanta, 1977-78, 1981-82, chief epidemiology and rsch. br., nutrition divsn., 1982-84, asst. dir. preventive medicine residency program, 1985-87, dir. divsn. reproductive health, 1987, coord. for chronic disease control activities, 1987-88, acting dir. divsn. diabetes transl., 1988-89, acting dir. divsn. chronic disease control, 1990-91, dir. divsn. reproductive health, 1992-95, dir. Nat. Ctr. Chronic Disease Prevention/Health Promotion, 1995—2004, acting dir., 2004; adj. assoc. prof. Emory U. Sch. Pub. Health, Atlanta, 1990—; sr. v.p., dir. health group Robert Wood Johnson Found., 2004—. Asst. surgeon general, 1996—; editor Chronic Disease Notes and Reports, 1989-92; clinic physician Planned Parenthood of San Francisco Teen Clinic, San Francisco, 1975-76; cons. physician Ohio Dept. Health Bur. Preventive Medicine, 1978-79; cons. PAHO Consultative Group on Perinatal Care, Washington, 1982, WHO Malaysia Ministry of Health, 1982, 83, WHO Maternal and Child Health Unit Geneva, 1983, World Bank China Program Third Health Project, 1988, 1991, World Bank Poland, Health Promotion/Chronic Disease Prevention, 1992, World Bank China, Seventh Health Project, 1993. Contbr. articles to profl. jours, chpts. to books. Exec. sec. Diabetes Tech. Adv. com., 1989-92; liaison mem. Nat. Diabetes Adv. Bd., 1988-89; mem. Diabetes Mellitus Interagy. Coording. com., 1988-89; mem. subcom. adult edn., Am. Cancer Soc., 1987-92; staff White House Task Force on Infant Mortality, 1989; presenter in field. Epidemic Intelligence Svc. Officer USPHS Field Svcs. Divsn., 1976-78. Recipient Alexander D. Langmuir award, 1978, CDC Group award, 1984, Commendation Medal USPHS, 1984, and many other awards and citations. Fellow Am. Coll. Epidemiology; mem. APHA (active in com. work), Inst. Medicine, Am. Epidemiol. Soc., Soc. Epidemiol. Rsch., Am. Acad. Pediat. (com. pediatric rsch. 1994-95), Internat. Epidemiol. Assn., Physicians for Social Responsibility, Soc. on Med. Decision Making, Epidemic Intelligence Svc. Alumni Assn., Sigma Xi. Home: 15 Houghton Rd Princeton NJ 08540-3300 Office: Robert Wood Johnson Found PO Box 2316 College Rd East and Rte 1 Princeton NJ 08543*

**MARKS, JOHN,** engineer, consultant; adopted s. Cyril Bernard Marks and Laura Mary Kings; m. Gina Roberta Anne Hawkins, Jan. 18, 2003. B, U. Sussex, 1974. High Voltage Switching, C.e.g.b. Uk, 1990. Owners engr. Croatin Power Authority, Zagreb, Croatia, 2001—03; cons. engr. Tampa Electric Co, Tampa. Tech. dir. Cts (Uk) Ltd, Southampton, England, 1990—95. Sr. engr. (power) T.P.C., Taipei, Taiwan, 1979—84. Flt.lt. Brit. Mil., 1963—68. Mem.: IEEE. Conservative. Church Of England. Avocations: travel, swimming, rugby, music, reading. Office Phone: 813-657-2404. Home Fax: +(34)96676165. Personal E-mail: johnmarks4@aol.com.

**MARKS, JONATHAN BOWLES,** mediator, arbitrator; b. Dec. 17, 1943; s. Herbert Simon Marks and Rebecca (Bowles) Marks Hawkins; m. Nandita Wagle, Dec. 18, 1971; children: Joshua Benegal, Natasha. BA cum laude, Harvard U., 1966, JD cum laude, 1972. Asst. U.S. Atty., Washington, 1973-76; assoc. Munger, Tolles & Rickershauser, L.A., 1976-78, ptnr., 1979; counsel, assoc. dir. planning and evaluation Peace Corps, Washington, 1979-80; gen. counsel Internat. Devel. Coop. Agy., Washington, 1980-81; dispute resolution cons. Washington, 1981-82; pres. EnDispute, Inc., Washington, 1982-94; vice chmn. Jams-EnDispute, Washington, 1994-99; prin. MarksADR, LLC, Washington, 1999—. Home: 4410 Chalfont Pl Bethesda MD 20816-1804 Office: 4833 Rugby Ave Ste 301 Bethesda MD 20814 Office Phone: 301-907-4712. Business E-Mail: jmarks@marksadr.com.

**MARKS, LAWRENCE EDWARD,** psychologist, educator; b. NYC, Dec. 28, 1941; s. Milton and Anne (Barmes) M.; m. Joya Ellen Cazes, Dec. 24, 1963; children: Liza, Laura. AB Hunter Coll. N.Y.C., 1962; PhD, Harvard U., Cambridge, Mass., 1965; PhD honoris causa, Stockholm U., 1994. Rsch.-assoc. prof. Yale U., New Haven, 1966-84; asst.-assoc. fellow John B. Pierce Lab., New Haven, 1966-84; prof. epidemiology and psychology Yale U., New Haven, 1984—; fellow John B. Pierce Lab., New Haven, 1984—, dir., 1999—. Author: Sensory Processes: The New Psychophysics, 1974, The Unity of the Senses, 1978. Named to Hall of Fame, Hunter Coll., N.Y.C., 1985; recipient Jacob Javits award NIH, Washington, 1987. Fellow AAAS, Am. Psychol. Assn., Am. Psychol. Soc., N.Y. Acad. Sci. Democrat. Jewish. Achievements include elucidation of common principles underlying sensory processes in various sense modalities; development of validational scheme for quantifying magnitudes of sensory experience; indication of role of cross-modal (synesthetic) perception in relation to language and literature. Home: 48 Maplevale Dr Woodbridge CT 06525-1118 Office: John B Pierce Lab 290 Congress Ave New Haven CT 06519-1403 Office Phone: 203-562-9901. Business E-Mail: marks@jbpierce.org.

**MARKS, LESTER,** automotive dealership owner; b. June 1953; Bd. mem. Cultural Arts Coun. of Houston/Harris County; patron Seattle Art Mus.; bd. dirs. Art League Houston, 2004—. Named one of Top 200 Collectors, ARTnews Mag., 2004. Avocation: Collector of Contemporary art. Home: 2808 Rice Blvd Houston TX 77005-3046

**MARKS, LILLIAN SHAPIRO,** secretarial studies educator, retired, writer, editor; b. Bklyn., Mar. 16, 1907; d. Hayman and Celia (Amsterdam) Shapiro; m. Joseph Marks, Feb. 21, 1932; children: Daniel, Sheila Blake, Jonathan. BS, NYU, 1928. High sch. tchr., N.Y.C., 1929-30; tchr. Evalina de Rothschild Sch., Jerusalem, 1930-31; social worker United Jewish Aid Bklyn., 1931-32; tchr. Richmond Hill High Sch., 1932-40, Andrew Jackson High Sch., Cambria Heights, NY, 1940-71; staff Vassar Summer Inst. 1946; mem. faculty New Sch. Social Rsch., N.Y.C., 1977-87; ret., 2006. Vol. tchr. English Israel schs., 1987—2000. Am. editor: Teeline, A System of Fast Writing, 1970; author: College Teeline, 1977, College Teeline Self Taught, 1988, Touch Typing Made Simple, 1985; contbr. articles to profl. lit. jours. Mem. Am. Fedn. Tchrs. Democrat. Home and Office: 300 E46 St 17J New York NY 10017

**MARKS, MARILYN,** trailer company executive; b. 1952; BS, U. Tenn., 1975. Acct. Ernst & Ernst, Chattanooga, 1975-76; with Deloitte, Haskins & Sells, Chattanooga, 1976-79; v.p. corp. planning The Dorsey Corp., Chattanooga, 1979-87; pres., chmn. of bd., CEO Dorsey Trailers, Atlanta, 1987-97, chmn. bd., 1997—.

**MARKS, MARTHA ALFORD,** writer; b. Oxford, Miss., July 27, 1946; d. Truman and Margaret Alford; m. Bernard L. Marks, Jan. 27, 1968. BA, Centenary Coll., 1968; MA, Northwestern U., 1972, PhD, 1978. Tchr. Notre Dame High Sch. for Boys, Niles, Ill., 1969-74; teaching asst. Northwestern U., Evanston, Ill., 1974-78, lectr., lang. coord., 1978-83; asst. prof. Kalamazoo (Mich.) Coll., 1983-85; writer Riverwoods, Ill., 1985—2002. Cons. WGBH Edn. Found., Boston, 1988-91, Am. Coun. on the Tchg. of Fgn. Langs., 1981-92, Ednl. Testing Svcs., 1988-90, Peace Corps., 1993. Co-author: Destinos: An Introduction to Spanish, 1991, 96, Al corriente, 1989, 93, 97, Que tal?, 1986, 90; author: (workbook) Al corriente, 1989, 93; contbr. articles to profl. jours. Mem. Lake County (Ill.) Bd., Forest Preserve Commn., 1992-2002; co-founder Lake County Conservation Alliance; co-founder Reps. for Environ. Protection, 1995, pres. Reps. for Environ. Protection. Office Phone: 505-889-4544.

**MARKS, MERTON ELEAZER,** lawyer, international arbitrator, mediator, consultant; b. Chgo., Oct. 16, 1932; s. Alfred Tobias and Helene Fannie (Rosner) M.; m. Radee Maiden Feiler, May 20, 1966; children: Sheldon, Elise Marks Vazelakis, Alan, Elaine Marks Ianchiou (dec.). BS, Northwestern U., 1954, JD, 1956. Bar: Ill. 1956, U.S. Ct. Mil. Appeals 1957, Ariz. 1958, U.S. Dist. Ct. Ariz. 1960, U.S. Ct. Appeals (9th cir.) 1962, U.S. Supreme Ct. 1970; cert. arbitrator U.S. Dist. Ct. Ariz. Assoc. Moser, Compere & Emerson, Chgo., 1956-57; ptnr. Morgan, Marks & Rogers, Tucson, 1960-62; asst. atty. gen State of Ariz., Phoenix, 1962-64; counsel indsl. commn., 1964-65; from assoc. to ptnr. Shimmel, Hill, Bishop & Greunder, Phoenix, 1965-74; ptnr. Lewis & Roca, Phoenix, 1974—2001; prin. Merton E. Marks, PC, 2001—. Judge Pro Tempore Ariz. Ct. Appeals, 1994; CPR Inst. Dispute Resolution Inter-Insurer Arb. Panel; spl. master Ariz. Superior Ct., 2001—; U.S. and internat. alternative dispute resolution cons.; lectr. in field. Contbr. articles to profl. jours., columns. Past trustee Ariz. Opera Co., past chmn. endowment commn.; past mem. U.S. Olympic Com. for Ariz. Capt. JAGC, USAR, 1957-64. Fellow Chartered Inst. Arbitrators (London); mem. ABA (trial, tort and ins. practice sect., chmn. spl. com. on fed. asbestos legis. 1987-89, chmn. workers compensation and employers liability law com. 1983-84, dispute resolution sect., 2005-06), Am. Bd. Trial Advs., Am. Coll. Legal Medicine, Am. Arbitration Assn. (panelist, mediator), Internat. Bar Assn. (sect. on bus. law, product liability, internat. litig. com., ins. com., arbitration com.), State Bar Ariz. (chmn. workers compensation sect. 1969-73), Fedn. Def. and Corp. Counsel (chmn. pharm. litig. sect. 1989-91, chmn. workers compensation sect. 1977-79, v.p. 1978-79, 81, bd. dirs. 1981-89, mem. products liability sect., mem. reinsurance sect., chmn. alternative dispute resolution sect. 2005-06), Internat. Assn. Def. Counsel, Ariz. Assn. Def. Counsel (pres. 1976-77), Maricopa County Bar Assn., Pima County Bar Assn., Def. Rsch. Inst. (drug and device com., chmn. workers compensation com. 1977-78), Assn. Internat. de Droit des Assurances (cert. arbitrator), Reinsurance and Ins. Arbitration Soc., Nat. Assn. Securities Dealers Dispute Resolution (bd. arbitrators), Internat. C. of C. Office: Scottsdale Exec Office Pk 8655 E Via De Ventura Ste G200 Scottsdale AZ 85258-3321 also: 850 N Kolb Rd Tucson AZ 85710-1333 Office Phone: 602-840-0808. Personal E-mail: memarkspc@earthlink.net.

**MARKS, MICHAEL E.,** electronics executive; BA, MA, Oberlin Coll.; MBA, Harvard U. Pres., CEO Metcal Inc., Menlo Park, Calif.; CEO Flextronics Internat. Ltd., Singapore, 1994—2005, chmn., 2006—; mem. Kohlberg Kravis Roberts & Co., Menlo Park, Calif., 2005—. Bd. dir. SanDisk Corp. Office: KKR Ste 200 2800 Sand Hill Rd Menlo Park CA 94025*

**MARKS, MICHAEL J.,** lawyer; b. 1938; AB, Cornell U., 1960; JD, U. Chgo., 1963. Assoc. Stroock & Lavan, 1964—70, Chun, Kerr & Dodd, 1970—72; counsel Kelso, Spencer, Snyder & Stirling, 1972—75; asst. gen. counsel Alexander & Baldwin Inc., Honolulu, 1975—80, v.p., gen. counsel, 1980—84, v.p., gen. counsel, sec., 1984—85, sr. v.p., gen. counsel, sec., 1985—. Office: Alexander & Baldwin Inc 822 Bishop St Honolulu HI 96813-3925

**MARKS, PAUL ALAN,** oncologist, cell biologist, educator; b. NYC, Aug. 16, 1926; s. Robert R. and Sarah (Bohorad) Marks; m. Joan Harriet Rosen, Nov. 28, 1953; children: Andrew Robert, Elizabeth Susan Marks Ostrer, Matthew Stuart. AB with gen. honors, Columbia U., 1945, MD, 1949, DSc (hon.), 2000; D in Biol. Sci. (hon.), U. Umbino, Italy, 1982; PhD (hon.), Hebrew U., Jerusalem, Israel, 1987, U. Tel Aviv, 1992; DSc (hon.), Ben Gurion U., Beer Sheva, Israel, 2003. From fellow to prof. Coll. Physicians and Surgeons Columbia U., N.Y., 1952—67, prof. medicine Coll. Physicians and Surgeons, 1967—82, dean faculty of medicine, v.p. med. affairs Coll. Physicians and Surgeons 1970—73, dir. Comprehensive Cancer Ctr. Coll. Physicians and Surgeons, 1972—80, v.p. health scis. Coll. Physicians and Surgeons, 1973—80; prof. cell biology and genetics Coll. Medicine Cornell U., N.Y.C., 1980—; prof. medicine Grad. Sch. Med. Scis., 1983—; pres., CEO Meml. Sloan-Kettering Cancer Ctr., N.Y.C., 1980—99, pres. emeritus, 2000—. Instr. Sloan Medicine George Washington U., 1954—55; cons. VA Hosp., N.Y.C., 1962—66; attending physician Presbyn. Hosp., N.Y.C., 1967—82, Meml. Hosp. for Cancer and Allied Diseases, 1980—; prin. investigator, Devel. Cell Biology Sloan-Kettering Inst. for Cancer Rsch., 1980—; adj. prof. Rockefeller U., 1980—; vis. physician Rockefeller U. Hosp., 1980—; bd. sci. counselors divsn. cancer treatment Nat. Cancer Inst., 1980—83; hon. staff N.Y. Hosp., 1981—; steering com. Frederick Cancer Rsch. Facility Nat. Cancer Inst., 1982—86; chmn. program adv. com. Robert Wood Johnson Found., 1983—89; adv. com. on NIH to Sec. HHS, 1989—90, 1993—98; external adv com. Intramural Rsch. Program Rev. NIH gen. com. NYPRHA, 1996; tech. adv. group UN Assn. U.S.; com. adv. scis. Pritzker Sch. Medicine U. Chgo., 1977—88; William Dameshek vis. prof. hematology Mt. Sinai Med. Ctr., 1985; nat. vis. com. CUNY Med. Sch., 1986—89; trustee Feinberg Grad. Sch. Weizmann Inst. Sci., Rehovot, Israel, 1986—; vis. prof. Coll. de France, 1988; Alpha Omega Alpha vis. prof. N.Y. Med. Coll., 1990; Mario A. Baldini vis. prof. Med. Sch. Harvard U., 1991; sci. adv. bd. City Hope Nat. Med. Ctr., Duarte, Calif., 1987—92, Raymond and Beverly Sackler Found., Inc., 1989, Jefferson Cancer Inst., Phila., 1989, PTC Biotech., Inc., 2002—, Ikonysis, 2004—, Merck, Inc., 2004—05; mem. Found. Biomed. Rsch., 1989—; sci. adv. com. Imperial Cancer Rsch. Fund, 1994—2003; sr. adv. Lazard Freres, 2000—; co-founder, sec. and vice chmn. Aton Pharma, Tarrytown, NY, 2001—04; internat. adv. coun. Singapore Econ. Devel. Bd., 2000—03; dir. Dreyfus Mutual Funds, NC, 1998—2005; lectr. Nobel Forum, Karolinska Inst., Sweden, 2004. Author: 11 books; mem. editl. bd.: Blood, 1964—76, editor-in-chief; 1978—82, mem. editl. bd.: Jour. Clin Investigation, 1970—71, editor-in-chief:, mem. editl. bd.: Cancer Treatment Revs., 1981—, Japanese Jour. Cancer Rsch., 1985—, Molecular Reprodn. and Devel., 1988—, Cancer Investigation, 1989, Sci., 1990, Current Opinion Oncologic Endocrine and Metabolic Drugs, 1998, expert analyst: Chemistry and Molecular Biology edit. of Chemtracts, 1990—92, mem. adv. bd.: Internat. Jour. Hematology, 1992, Stem Cells, bd. contrbg. editors: Blood Cells, Molecules and Diseases, 1994, Comité des Sages, 1994; contbr. over 400 articles to profl. jours. Trustee St. Luke's Hosp., 1970—80, Roosevelt Hosp., 1970—80, Presbyn. Hosp., 1972—80, Metpath Inst. Med. Edn., 1977—79, Hadassah Med. Ctr. Jerusalem, 1996; mem. jury Albert Lasker Awards, 1974—82; bd. dirs. Revson Found., 1976—91, Am. Found. for Basic Rsch. Israel, Israel Acad. Scis., 1991; mem. tech. bd. Milbank Meml. Fund, 1978—85; bd. govs. Friends of Sheba Med. Ctr., Tel Hashomer; mem. commn. sci. and tech. Mayor, N.Y.C., 1984—87; mem. commn. Shoreham Nuc. Plant Gov., N.Y.C., 1983; mem. task force biomed. rsch. and tech. Mayor, N.Y.C., 1999. Recipient Stevens Triennial prize, 1960, Swiss-Am. Found. award, 1965, Centenary medal, Inst. Pasteur, 1987, Found. for Promotion of Cancer Rsch. medal, Japan, 1984, Disting. Svc. medal, Robert Wood Johnson Found., 1989, Outstanding Achievement award, U. Innsbruck, 1991, Pres.'s Nat. Medal Sci., 1991, Japan Found. for Cancer Rsch. award,

1995, Lifetime Achievement award, Greater N.Y. Hosp. Assn., 1997, Am. Italian Cancer Found., 1999, Humanitarian award, Breast Cancer Rsch. Found., 2000, Disting. Lifetime Achievement award, Healthcare Chaplaincy, NY, 2001, John Stearns award, NY Acad. Medicine, 2002, Annie Blount Storrs Humanitarian award, Calvary Hosp., NY, 2002; fellow Commonwealth Fund fellow, Pasteur Inst., 1961—62; Ayrey fellow, 1985. Master: ACP, Coll. Physicians and Surgeons (Gold medal 1994); fellow: AAAS, Pasteur Inst. Paris (Commonwealth Fund fellow 1961—62), Am. Acad. Arts and Scis., Royal Soc. Medicine; mem.: NAS (chmn. Acad. Forum Adv. Com. 1980—81, chmn. sect. med. genetics, hematology and oncology 1980—83, coun. 1984—87, del. biol. warfare com. Internat. Security and Arms Control 1986—89, bd. dirs. 2002), N.Y. Acad. Sci. (bd. dirs. 2002—), European Acad. Scis., UN Assn. U.S.A. (tech. adv. group), Weizmann Inst. Sci. (bd. govs. 1976—, gov. emeritus, Israel), Third World Acad. Scis. (advisor), Soc. Study Devel. and Growth, Japan Soc. Hematology (Disting. lectr. 1989, Disting. lectr. 1989), Soc. Devel. Biology, Internat. Soc. Devel. Biologists, Harvey Soc. (pres. 1973—74), Assn. Am. Physicians, Am. Soc. Hematology (pres.-elect 1983, pres. 1984, chmn. adv. bd. 1985), Soc. Cell Biology, Assn. Am. Cancer Insts. (bd. dirs. 1983—88), Am. Assn. Cancer Rsch., Am. Soc. Human Genetics (past mem. program com.), Am. Soc. Biol. Chemists, Italian Assn. Cell Biology and Differentiation (hon.), Chinese Anti-Cancer Assn. (hon.), Japanese Cancer Assn. (hon.), Am. Soc. Clin. Investigation (pres. 1972—73), Am. Fedn. Clin. Rsch. (past councillor Ea. dist.), Red Cell Club (past chmn.), Inst. Medicine (coun. 1973—76, chmn. com. study resources clin. investigation with NAS 1988), Univ. Club, Soc. Interurban Clin. Club, Century Assn., Alpha Omega Alpha. Office: Meml Sloan-Kettering Cancer Ctr 1275 York Ave New York NY 10021-6094 Office Phone: 212-639-6568. Business E-Mail: paula_marks@mskcc.org.

**MARKS, RAMON PAUL,** lawyer; b. Washington, Dec. 9, 1948; s. Matthew J. and Simone V. (Van de Meulebroeke) M.; m. Susan Eleanor MacCarthy; children: Robert Justin, Timothy Matthew, Fletcher MacCarthy. AB magna cum laude, Dartmouth Coll., 1971; MA, Johns Hopkins U., 1973; JD, U. Va., 1976. Bar: N.Y. 1977, Tex. 1983, U.S. Dist. Ct. (so. dist.) Tex. 1984, U.S. Ct. Appeals (5th cir.) 1984, U.S. Ct. Internat. Trade 1988, U.S. Dist. Ct. (so. dist.) N.Y. 1989, U.S. Ct Appeals (fed cir.) 1989. Assoc., Alexander & Green, N.Y.C., 1976-77; corporate atty. Schlumberger Ltd., N.Y.C., 1978; asst. legal counsel services, techniques Schlumberger Paris, 1978-80; gen. counsel Schlumberger Well Services, Houston, 1980-84; sec., gen. counsel Dowell Schlumberger, Inc., Houston, 1984-85; asst. gen. counsel Schlumberger Ltd., Houston, 1986-87; ptnr. Marks & Murase, N.Y.C., 1987.; ptnr., Dorsey & Whitney, NYC, 1997; ptnr., internat. litig., Arnold & Porter, NYC, 2005—. Mem. dean's coun. John F. Kennedy Sch. Govt., Harvard U. Mem. Assn. Bar City NY, Bus. Execs. Nat. Security (bd. dirs., co-chmn. policy com.), Phi Beta Kappa. Office: Arnold & Porter 399 Park Ave New York NY 10022-4690 Office Phone: 212-715-1145. Office Fax: 212-715-1399. Business E-Mail: ramon.marks@aporter.com.

**MARKS, RICHARD DANIEL,** lawyer; b. NYC, June 21, 1944; s. Morris Andrew and Dorothy (Schill) M.; m. Cheryl L. Hoffman, Nov. 13, 1971. BA, U. Va., 1966; JD, Yale U., 1969. Bar: D.C., U.S. Ct. Appeals (3rd, 4th, 8th, 11th and D.C. cir.), U.S. Supreme Ct. Assoc. Dow, Lohnes & Albertson, Washington, 1972-78, ptnr., 1978-97, Vinson & Elkins, Washington, 1997-2000, Davis Wright Tremaine, Washington, 2000—. Co-author: Legal Problems in Broadcasting, 1974. Trustee U. Va. Coll. Found. 2001-03. Capt. U.S. Army, 1970-72. Mem. ABA (chmn. contracting for computer com., sect. for sci. and tech., computer law div., chmn. computer law divsn. 1994-2002, chmn. HIPAA task force 2002—), chmn. program cmte. (2003-2004), Fed. Comms. Bar Assn., Am. Law Inst., Computer Law Assn. (dir. 1999-2002), Capital Area Assn. Flight Instrs. (pres. 1989-90), UVA Club of Washington (pres. 1991-92). Avocations: aviation, skiing. Office: Davis Wright Tremaine LLP 1500 K St NW Ste 450 Washington DC 20005-1272 Business E-Mail: richardmarks@dwt.com.

**MARKS, ROBERT GALE,** music educator; b. Mt. Kisco, N.Y., Nov. 7, 1954; s. Cecil Gale and June Marie Marks; m. Karen Lavaughn Ullman, Nov. 25, 1978; 1 child, Kimberly Dawn. MusB in Edn., Heidelberg Coll., Tiffin, Ohio, 1977; MA in Edn., Muskingum Coll., New Concord, Ohio, 2003. Tchr. vocal music Caldwell (Ohio) Exempted Village Schs., 1977—81; specialist elem. music Rolling Hills Local Schs., Byesville, Ohio, 1983—84; dir. vocal music Cambridge (Ohio) Mid. Sch. and H.S., 1984—. Dir. music First United Meth. Ch., Cambridge, 1990—; interim dir. choral soc. Muskingum Coll., New Concord, Ohio, 1991—92; assoc. condr. Muskingum Coll. Choral Soc., New Concord, 1992—98; guest condr. Camerata Choir, Wheeling, W.Va., 1995—96; lectr. in field. Dir.(music): (plays) Cambridge (Ohio) Performing Arts Ctr., 1995—2006. Mem.: Nat. Cambridge Edn. Assn., Ohio Edn. Assn., Ohio Music Edn. Assn. (pres. dist. 9 1986—88), Music Educators Nat. Conf. Democrat. Methodist. Avocations: computers, travel. Home: 1610 Quail Hollow Drive Cambridge OH 43725 Office: Cambridge High School 65328 Creek Road Cambridge OH 43725 Office Phone: 740-435-1100 1267. Personal E-mail: rgmarks@adelphia.net.

**MARKS, ROBERTA BARBARA,** artist, educator; b. Savannah, Ga.; d. Philip W. and Eleanore (Margolis) Dilner; children: Jeffery Allen, Steven Craig. BFA, U. Miami, Coral Gables, Fla., 1980; MFA, U. South Fla., 1981. Instr., lectr. multi-media, lectr., vis. artist to numerous art schs., including U. South Fla., Tampa, 1998-05. Custom House Mus., Armory Art Ctr., Palm Beach, Fla., 2002, Key West, Fla., 2003, Galerie Jonas, Neuchatel, Switzerland, 2003, Chgo. Anderson Ranch Art Sch., Colo., 2004, U. South (Tampa) Fla., U. Miami Lowe Art Mus., Fla., Armory Art Ctr., Palm Beach, Fla., Valparaiso U., Ind., Rochester Inst. Tech. Am. Sch. of Crafts, N.Y., Galerie de Koull, Murten, Switzerland, Santa Fe Community Coll., Gainesville, Brookfield Craft Ctr., Conn., Fla. Keys Community Coll., U. Wis.-Milw., Parson Sch. Design, Key West (Fla.) C.C., 1991, Am. Embassy, Bern, Switzerland, 1993; juror Riverside Avondale Preservation Art Festival, Jacksonville, Fla., 1981, Ybor Square Art Festival, Tampa, 1980, Miami Lakes Art Festival, Fla., 1975. One woman shows include Brevard Community Coll., Melbourne, Fla., 1982, Cocoa, Fla., 1982, Coventry Galleries, Ltd., Tampa, 1983, Barbara Gillman Gallery, Miami, 1984, 87, Tennessee Williams Fine Arts Ctr., Key West, 1985, Garth Clark Gallery, NYC, 1985, Fred Gros Gallery, Key West, 1985, Key West Art and Historical Soc. East Martello Mus. and Gallery, 1985, U. Miami New Gallery, Fla., 1987, Katie Gingrass Gallery, Milw., 1987, Zimmerman Saturn Gallery, Nashville, 1987, Bern, Zurich Switzerland, 1988, Galerie Alte Krone, Altstadt, Biel, Switzerland, 1990, Helander Gallery, NYC, 1990, Gump's Gallery, San Francisco, 1990, Helander Gallery, NYC, 1991, LeMieux Gallery, New Orleans, 1991, Helander Gallery, Palm Beach, 1992, Galerie Etc., Bern, 1992, Galerie Bel Arte, Lengnau, Switzerland, 1992, Lucky Street Gallery, Key West, 1994-05, Barbara Gillman Gallery, Miami, 1994-05, Galerie Vinelz, Switzerland, 1994, Galerie Quattro, Zurich, 1994, many others; exhibited in group shows at Netsky Gallery, Miami, 1982, The Craftsman's Gallery, Scarsdale, N.Y., 1982, Garth Clark Gallery, Los Angeles, 1983, Nelson-Atkins Mus. Art, Kansas City, Mo., 1983, Am. Craft Mus., NYC, 1984, N. Miami Mus. and Art Ctr., 1985, Joanne Lyon Gallery, Aspen, Colo., 1984, Key West Art and Hist. Soc. East Martello Mus. and Gallery, 1985, Garth Clark Gallery, NYC and Los Angeles, 1985, 24X24, Ruth Siegel Ltd., NYC, 1987, Artforms Gallery, Louisville, 1986, The Pvt. Collection Women Artists, Ohio, 1987, East Martello Mus., Key West, Fla., 1990, East Martello Mus., Key West, Fla., 1990, Philharmonic Ctr. for Arts, Naples, Fla., 1993, Ctr. for Arts, Vero Beach, Fla., 1993, Helander Gallery, Palm Beach, 1993, Gingrass Gallery, Milw., 1993, many others; represented in permanent collections Mint Mus., Charlotte, NC, N.Mex Mus. Fine Arts, Sante Fe, Smithsonian Instn., Renwick Gallery, Rochester Inst. Tech. Fine Arts Dept., U. Utah Mus., U. South Fla. Fine Arts Dept., Galerie du Manoir, La Chaux-de-Fonds, Switzerland, Valencia Community Coll., Okum Gallery, Victoria and Albert Mus., London, IBM, Jacksonville, Fla., AT&T, NYC, Custom Ho. Mus., Key West, Fla., 2002, U. South Fla., Galerie Jonas, Neuchatel, Switzerland, 2003, Lucky St. Gallery, 2005, Mint Mus., Charlotte, NMex. Mus. Fine Arts, Sante Fe, others. Recipient Regional Visual Artist fellow, Miami, Fla., 1990, also numerous awards. Mem. World Craft Council, Artists Equity Assn., Internat. Sculpture Ctr.

**MARKS, STEPHEN J.,** neurologist, educator; b. Bklyn., Aug. 30, 1953; s. Ansel R. Marks and Frances L. Carpenter; m. Cindy G. Marks, Mar. 27, 1994; children: Jordan, Avery. BA, Colgate U., 1979. Diplomate Am. Bd. Neurology & Psychiatry. Intern Lenox Hill Hosp., NYC; resident Mt. Sinai Hosp., NYC; assoc. prof. N.Y. Med. Coll., Valhalla, 1987—. Team neurologist N.Y. Jets, Hempstead, 1986. Co-author: (chapter) Principle & Practice of Emergency Medicine, 1992, (book), 1997. Fellow: Am. Heart Assn. (mem. stroke coun.); mem.: Soc. Neuroscience, Nat. Stroke Assn., Am. Acad. Neurology. Avocations: skiing, windsurfing. Office: Dept Neurology Munger Pavilion, NYMC Valhalla NY 10595

**MARKS-MORGAN, LINDA LEE,** music educator; b. Oshkosh, Wis., July 4, 1952; d. Lawrence Ernst Marks and Carol Camilla Olson-Marks; m. David C. Morgan, Apr. 3, 1999. MusB in Voice Performance, U. Wis., Oshkosh, 1974, MusB in Edn., 1975, MFA in Choral Conducting, 1979; specialist in edn., U. Louisville, 2001. Choral tchr. Appleton (Wis.) Pub. Sch., 1975—81, Palm Bay (Fla.) H.S., 1981—82, Walpole (Mass.) Pub. Sch., 1982—84, Cambridge (Mass.) Pub. Sch., 1984—98, Jefferson County Pub. Sch., Louisville, 1998—. Mem.: Am. Choral Dirs. Assn., Ky. Music Educators Assn., Kappa Delta Pi. Home: 6405 Gunpowder Ln Prospect KY 40059 Office: Farnsley Mid Sch 3400 Lees Ln Louisville KY 40216

**MARKULIS, HENRYK JOHN,** career military officer; b. Columbia, SC, July 10, 1945; s. Henryk F. Markulis and Judith E. (Taylor) Kassman; children: Mark C., Melinda L. BA, U. Buffalo, 1968; MA, Ctrl. Mich. U., 1977. Commd. USAF, 1969; advanced through ranks to col.; aircraft cmdr. 53d Weather Recon Squadron Ramey AFB, PR, 1970-74; gunship aircraft cmdr. 16th Spl. Ops. Squadron Korat RTAB, Thailand, 1974-75; cmdr. 437th Field Maintenance Squadron Sect. Charleston AFB, SC, 1975-78; exercise and contingency support 1701st Mobility Support Shaw AFB, SC, 1978-82; air staff action officer Joint Chiefs of Staff Pentagon, 1982-84; chief internat. programs Singapore, Malaysia & Brunei, 1984-93; dep. cmdr., chief staff Iceland Def. Force NATO, 1993-95, ret., 1995; pres., CEO Internat. Security and Mktg. Cons., 1996—. Cons. Nissan Motor Acceptance Corp., 1996—, Infiniti Fin. Svcs., 1996—, Project Boreas, 2006-. Mem. Am. Legion, VFW, Mil. Officers Assn. Am., Aircraft Owners and Pilots Assn., Army Navy Country Club, Order of Daedalians, Kiwanis, KC (4th degree). Avocation: golf. Office: 52 Union St Hamburg NY 14075 Home: 56 Union St Hamburg NY 14075-4910 Office Phone: 716-646-1589. E-mail: colonelm@adelphia.net.

**MARKUS, KENT RICHARD,** lawyer; b. Cleve., Feb. 1, 1959; s. Richard and Carol (Slater) M.; m. Susan Mary Gilles, Apr. 15, 1987; 1 child Robinson Reno. BS, Northwestern U., 1981; JD with honors, Harvard U., 1984. Bar: Ohio 1984, U.S. Dist. Ct. (no. dist.) Ohio 1984, U.S. Dist. Ct. (so. dist.) Ohio 1996, U.S. Ct. Appeals (6th cir.) 1988. Jud. clk. to Hon. Alvin I. Krenzler U.S. Dist. Ct. (no. dist.) Ohio, Cleve., 1984-86; litigation assoc. Gold, Rotatori, Schwartz & Gibbons, Cleve., 1986-89; transition dir. Ohio Atty. Gen. Office, Columbus, 1990-91, first asst. atty., chief of staff, 1991-93; counsel to dep. atty. gen. U.S. Dept. Justice, Washington, 1994, dep. assoc. atty. gen., 1994-95, acting asst. atty. gen. legis affairs, 1995, counselor to atty. gen, 1996-98, dep. chief of staff, 1997-98; prof., dir. Nat. Ctr. for Adoption Law & Policy, Capital U. Law Sch., 1998—. Adj. prof. law Cleveland-Marshall Coll. Law, 1987-88. Co-editor: Trial Handbook for Ohio Lawyers, 2nd edit., 1988; contbn. editor for law Webster's New World Dictionary, 4th edit., 1999. Past bd. dirs., past legis. chair Handgun Control Fedn. of Ohio, 1984-93; adv. coun. Northwestern U. Sch. Speech, 1985—; spl. projects dir. Celeste for Gov. Com., Cleve., 1986; campaign mgr. Lee Fisher for Atty. Gen., Cleve. and Columbus, 1989-90; bd. dirs., former trustee, life mem. Cleve. NAACP, 1986-87; chief of staff Dem. Nat. Com., Washington, 1993-94; at-large mem. bd. dirs. SEARCH, Inc., 2000-; bd. dirs Ohio Legal Assistance Found. 2002-; chair Ctr. Ohio Neighborhood Safety Working Group, 2003-. Named Rising Star of Dem. Party, Campaigns and Elections mag., 1991. Mem. ABA, Ohio State Bar Assn. (former chair young lawyers divsn.), Columbus Bar Assn. Home: 5636 Indian Hill Rd Dublin OH 43017-8209 Office: Capital Univ Law Sch 303 E Broad St Columbus OH 43215-3201 E-mail: kmarkus@law.capital.edu.

**MARKUS, LAWRENCE,** retired mathematics professor; b. Hibbing, Minn., Oct. 13, 1922; s. Benjamin and Ruby (Friedman) M.; m. Lois Shoemaker, Dec. 9, 1950; children: Sylvia, Andrew. BS, U. Chgo., 1942, MS, 1946; PhD, Harvard U., 1951. Instr. meteorology U. Chgo., 1942-44; rsch. meteorologist Atomic Project, Hanford, 1944; instr. math. Harvard U., 1951-52; instr. Yale U., 1952-55; lectr. Princeton U., 1955-57; asst. prof. U. Minn., Mpls., 1957-58, assoc. prof., 1958-60, prof. math., 1960-93, assoc. chmn. dept. math., 1961-63, dir. control scis., 1964-73, Regents' prof. math., 1980-93, Regents' prof. emeritus, 1993—, dir. Control Sci. and Dynamical Sys. Ctr., 1980-89. Leverhulme prof. control theory, dir. control theory ctr. U. Warwick, Eng., 1970-73, Nuffield prof. math., 1970-85, hon. prof., 1985—; regional conf. lectr. NSF, 1969; vis. prof. Yale U., Columbia U., U. Calif., U. Warsaw, 1980, Tech. Inst. Zurich, 1983, Peking U. (China), 1983; dir. conf. Internat. Ctr. Math., Trieste, 1974; lectr. Internat. Math. Congress, 1974, Iranian Math. Soc., 1975, Brit. Math. Soc., 1976, Japan Soc. for Promotion Sci., 1976, Royal Instn., London, 1982, U. Beer Sheva, Israel, 1983; vis. prof. U. Tokyo, 1976, Tech. U. Denmark, 1979; mem. panel Internat. Congress Mathematicians, Helsinki, 1978; sr. vis. fellow Sci. Rsch. Coun., Imperial Coll., London, 1978; mem. UNESCO sci. adv. com. Control Symposium, U. Strasbourg, France, 1980; IEEE Plenary lectr., Orlando, Fla., 1982; Sci. and Engring. Rsch. Coun. vis. prof. U. Warwick, Eng., 1982-90; Neustadt Meml. lectr. U. So. Calif., 1985, prin. lectr. symposium U. Minn., 1988, dir. NSF workshop, 1989, prin. lectr. symposium in honor of his 75th birthday, 1997; Tate lectr. U. Cin., 1998; chmn. Conf. Markus-80, 2002; adv. bd. Office Naval Rsch., Air Force Office Sci. Rsch. Author: Flat Lorentz Manifolds, 1959, Flows on Homogeneous Spaces, 1963, Foundations of Optimal Control Theory, 1967, rev. edit., 1985, Lectures on Differentiable Dynamics, 1971, rev. edit., 1980, Generic Hamiltonian Dynamical Systems, 1974, Distributed Parameter Control Systems, 1991, Boundary Value Problems and Symplectic Algebra, 1998, Multi-Interval Linear Ordinary Boundary Value Problems and Complex Symplectic Algebra, 2001, Elliptic Partial Differential Operators and Symplectic Algebra, 2003, Infinite Dimensional Complex Symplectic Spaces, 2004; editor Internat. Jour. Nonlinear Mechanics, 1965-73, Jour. Control, 1963-67; mem. editl. bd. Proc. Georgian Acad. Sci. Math., 1993—; contbr. articles to profl. jours Lt. (j.g.) USNR, 1944-46. Recipient Rsch. prize Internat. Conf. Nonlinear Oscillations, Ukrainian Acad. Sci., Kiev, 1969, Festschrift volume, 1993; Fulbright fellow Paris, 1950; Guggenheim fellow Lausanne, Switzerland, 1963. Fellow Royal Soc. Edinburgh (hon.); mem. Am. Math. Soc. (past mem. nat. coun.), Am. Geophys. Soc., Soc. Indsl. and Applied Math. (past nat. lectr.), Phi Beta Kappa, Sigma Xi. Office: 109 Vincent Hall 206 Church St S Minneapolis MN 55455 Business E-Mail: markus@math.umn.edu.

**MARKUS, MAURA,** bank executive; BA summa cum laude, Boston Coll., Mass.; MBA, Harvard U. Joined Citibank, N.Y.C., 1987, pres. North Am. Retail Distbr. Group, 2000—. Office: CBNA One Court Sq 49th Fl Long Island City NY 11120

**MARKUS, RAMSEY,** dermatologist; m. Jodi Markus. Diplomate Am. Bd. Dermatology. Dermatologist Baylor Dermatology, Houston, 2000—.

**MARKUS, RICHARD M.,** judge, arbitrator; b. Evanston, Ill., Apr. 16, 1930; s. Benjamin and Ruby M.; m. Carol Joanne Slater, July 26, 1952; children: Linda, Scott, Kent. BS magna cum laude, Northwestern U., 1951; JD cum laude, Harvard U., 1954. Bar: D.C. 1954, Ohio 1956, Fla. 1994. Appellate atty., civil div. Dept. Justice, Washington, 1954-56; ptnr. civil litigation law firms Cleve., 1956-76, 89-98; judge Cuyahoga County (Ohio) Common Pleas Ct., 1976-80, Ohio Ct. Appeals, 1981-88. Instr. M.I.T., 1952-54; adj. prof. Case Western Res. U. Law Sch., 1972-78, 84-87, Cleve. State U. Law Sch., 1960-80, prof. 1999-2000; prof. Harvard Law Sch., 1980-81; mem. Nat. Commn. on Med. Malpractice, 1971-73; chmn. Nat. Inst. Trial Advocacy, 1978-81, trustee 1971—. Author: Trial Handbook for Ohio Lawyers, all

edits., 1971—, Ohio Evidence Rules with Commentary, 1999; contbr. articles to profl. jours.; editor Harvard U. Law Rev, 1952-54. Republican nominee Justice of Ohio Supreme Ct., 1978; bd. dirs. Luth. Metro Ministry, 1988—, Fairview Luth. Hosp., 1985—. Mem. Ohio State Bar Assn. (pres. 1991-92), Cuyahoga County Bar Assn., Greater Cleve. Bar Assn. (trustee 1967-70, 85-90), Assn. Trial Lawyers Am. (nat. pres. 1970-71), Ohio Acad. Trial Lawyers (pres. 1965-66), Phi Beta Kappa, Pi Mu Epsilon, Delta Sigma Rho, Phi Alpha Delta. Home and office: Pvt Judicial Svcs Inc 3903 N Valley Dr Cleveland OH 44126-1716 Office Phone: 440-356-2728. E-mail: judgemarkus1@cs.com.

**MARKUS, ROBERT MICHAEL,** retired journalist; b. Chgo., Jan. 30, 1934; s. David White and Anna (Tonkonogy) M.; m. Leslie Winnifred Ator, Aug. 25, 1962; children— Catherine Mary, Patricia Anne, Michael Hughes. B.J., U. Mo., 1955. Gen. assignment reporter Moline (Ill.) Dispatch, 1955-59; successively copy editor, sports columnist, feature writer, baseball writer, coll. sports writer, hockey writer Chgo. Tribune, 1959-96, ret., 1996. Mem. Northbrook (Ill.) Caucus, 1967. Served with U.S. Army, 1956-58. Recipient Nat. Headliner award as best columnist, 1973; named Ill. Sports Writer of Year, 1970, 71, 72 Mem. Football Writers Assn. Am., Baseball Writers Assn. Am., Am. Auto Racing Writers and Broadcasters Assn. Home: 3000 Holiday Dr 1501 Fort Lauderdale FL 33316

**MARKUSON, RICHARD K.,** former pharmaceutical association executive; Mem. adv. com. on pharmacy practice Nat. Assn. Bds. Pharmacy, pres.; exec. dir. Idaho State Bd. Pharmacy; adj. prof. pharmacy law Idaho State U.; chmn. Nat. Assn. Bds. Pharmacy, 2002—04. Mem.: Idaho State Pharm. Assn., Idaho Soc. Health Sys. Profls. (life). Office: 280 N 8th St Ste 204 Boise ID 83702

**MARKWELL, DICK R(OBERT),** retired chemist; b. Muskogee, Okla., Feb. 20, 1925; s. Alex J. and May (Albright) M.; m. Virginia Ann Gass, Aug. 28, 1949 (dec. Nov. 2002); children: Steven R., Scot L., Eric R., Cheryl F.; m. Marjorie H. Melville, Feb. 20, 2003. BS, Wichita State U., 1948, MS, 1950; PhD, U. Wis., 1956. Commd. 2d lt. U.S. Army, 1951, ret. lt. col., 1967; with Office Chief Rsch. and Devel.; assoc. prof. chemistry San Antonio Coll., 1967-74; chemist Corpus Christi Dept. Health, 1975-77; supr. chemistry sect. lab. div. San Antonio Met. Health Dist., 1977-87. With USMC, 1942-45. Mem. Am. Chem. Soc. Home: 7887 Broadway Unit 501 San Antonio TX 78209-2537

**MARLAND, ALKIS JOSEPH,** leasing company executive, computer scientist, educator, financial planner; b. Athens, Greece, Mar. 8, 1943; arrived in U.S., 1961, naturalized, 1974; s. Basil and Maria (Pervanides) Mouradoglou; m. Anita Louise Malone, Dec. 19, 1970 (dec. Mar. 27, 2003); children: Andrea Weber, Alyssa. BS, Southwestern U., 1963; MA, U. Tex., Austin, 1967; MS in Engring. Adminstrn., So. Meth. U., 1971. CLU; cert. data processing, enrolled agt., fund specialist, ChFC, CFP, accredited tax advisor, accredited tax preparer. With Sun Co., Richardson, Tex., 1968-71, Phila., 1971-76; mgr. planning and acquisitions Sun Info. Svcs. subs. Sun Co., Dallas, 1976-78; v.p. Helios Capital Corp. subs. Sun Co., Radnor, Pa., 1978-83; pres. ALKAN Leasing Corp., Wayne, Pa., 1983—, also bd. dirs. Prof. dept. computer scis. and bus. adminstrn. Ea. Coll., St. Davids, Pa., 1985—87; prof. math. Villanova (Pa.) U., 1987—89. Contr. Christian Counseling and Ednl. Found., 2003—05; bd. dirs. Radnor Twp. Sch. Dist., 1987—91, Delaware County Intermediate Unit, 1988—91. Mem.: IEEE, Assn. Investment Mgmt. and Rsch., Phila. Union League, World Affairs Coun. Phila., Fgn. Policy Rsch. Inst., Phila. Fin. Assn. (mem. award 1988, sec. 1989—92, bd. dirs. 1989—92), Fin. Planning Assn. (treas. 2000—01, bd. dirs. Phila. Tri-State Area 2000—04, pres.-elect 2002, pres. 2003, chmn. 2004), Fin. Analysts Phila., Nat. Assn. Pub. Accts., Nat. Assn. Tax Practitioners, Nat. Assn. Enrolled Agts., Inst. Cert. Fin. Planners (bd. dirs. Phila. Tri-State Area 1993—99, v.p. membership 1994—95, treas. 1995—99), Am. Assn. Equipment Lessors, Fin. Svc. Profls., Data Processing Mgmt. Assn., Assn. Computing Machinery, Main Line C. of C., Masons, Rotary (pres. 1989—90, asst. gov. 1990—92, 1993—94, treas. dist. 7450 2002—, Wayne). Republican. Home: 4 Starling Ct Phoenixville PA 19460 Office: PO Box 1063 Oaks PA 19456-1063 Office Phone: 610-293-1059. Personal E-mail: almarland@aol.com.

**MARLAS, JAMES CONSTANTINE,** diversified financial services company executive; b. Chgo., Aug. 22, 1937; s. Constantine J. and Helen (Cotsirilos) M.; m. Kendra S. Graham, 1968 (div. 1971); m. Glenn Close, 1984 (div. 1987); m. Marie Nugent-Head, 1993. AB cum laude, Harvard U., 1959; MA in Jurisprudence, Oxford U., Eng., 1961; JD, U. Chgo., 1963. Bar: Ill. 1963, N.Y. 1966. Assoc. firm Baker & McKenzie, London and N.Y.C., 1963-66; exec. v.p. South East Commodity Corp., N.Y.C., 1967-68; chmn. bd. Union Capital Corp., N.Y.C., 1968—; vice chmn. bd. Mickelberry's Food Products Co., N.Y.C., 1970-71; pres., dir. Mickelberry Comm. Corp., 1972—, chief exec. officer, 1973—; chmn. bd. Mickleberry Commn. Corp.; chmn. bd., CEO Newcourt Industries, Inc., 1976—. Chmn. bd. dirs. Bowmar Instrument Corp., chmn. exec. com., 1983-92. Co-editor: Univ. Chgo. Law Rev, 1962-63; Contbr. articles to profl. jours. Bd. dirs. N.Y.C. Opera, Commanderie de Bordeaux, Brasenose Coll. Charitable Found. Mem. Am. Fgn. Law Assn., Young Pres.'s Orgn. Clubs: Boodle's (London); Knickerbocker (N.Y.C.), Racquet and Tennis (N.Y.C.). Office: Mickelberry Comm Corp 405 Park Ave New York NY 10022-4405

**MARLATT, MICHAEL JAMES,** lawyer; b. LA, Jan. 15, 1957; s. James Raymond and Norma Jean (Greenfield) M.; m. Donna Marie Healey, Apr. 13, 1985. BA, U. So. Calif., Calif. Poly., Pomona, 1981; JD, Pepperdine U., 1984. Bar: Calif. 1984, U.S. Dist. Ct. (ctrl. dist.) Calif. 1985, U.S. Supreme Ct. 1990. Project liaison U. So. Calif., Sch. Medicine, L.A., 1975-78; documentation rschr. NASA-Jet Propulsion Lab., Pasadena, Calif., 1978-81; ptnr. Thompson & Colegate, Riverside, Calif., 1984—. Bd. dirs. Assn. So. Calif. Def. Counsel, L.A., U. Calif., Riverside; lectr. Calif. Trial Lawyers Assn., 1991-94, Princeton U., 1993, U. Amsterdam Law Sch., 1994, Loma Linda (Calif.) U. Sch. Medicine, 1991-94, 99, 2001-03, Boston Coll. Law Sch., 1997, U. London, 1998; chair Am. Legal Sys. Internat. Law Program Civil Litigation U. of Calif., 1997; lectr., spkr. to vis. cos. on health care, 1988—; radio commentator Stas. KCKC, KCAL, KMEN and KPRO. Pres. U. Calif., Riverside, 1996—2000, mem. steering com.NCAA/ Big West Athletic Assn., 2003; v.p. Mission Inn Found., 1996—98, pres., 1999—2001; mem. bioethics com. Riverside Cmty. Hosp., 1999—2002; bd. dirs. Humane Soc.; bd. visitors Calif. Bapt. U., 2003—; Mem. attr. com. Calif. Rep. Party, Sacramento, 1990—93; bd. dirs. U. Calif., Riverside, Mission Inn Found., Riverside County Regional Med. Ctr., ARC, 2002—; bd. regents La Salle Cath. Pasadena, 2002—; bd. visitors Calif. Bapt. U., 2003—; chair Riverside County Regional Med. Ctr., 2005—. Mem. Am. Bd. Trial Advocates, So. Calif. Assn. Hosp. Risk Mgrs. (bylaws com. 1996-99), Victoria Country Club, Lincoln Club Riverside County, Phi Alpha Delta. Roman Catholic. Avocations: rare book collecting, collegiate athletics, travel. Office: Thompson & Colegate PO Box 1299 3610 14th St Riverside CA 92501-3843 Office Phone: 951-682-5550. Business E-Mail: mmarlatt@tclaw.net.

**MARLAY, ROBERT CHARLES,** physicist, engineer; b. Seaside, Oreg., Dec. 19, 1946; s. Myron George Jr. and Margaret Alice (Bump) M.; m. Nancy Evelyn Tate, Oct. 18, 1980; children: Jennifer Lynn, Sarah Elizabeth. BS in Engring., Duke U., 1969; MS, MIT, 1971, M City Planning, 1971, PhD in Nuc. Engring., 1983. Profl. engr., D.C. Engr. Office of Policy U.S. Dept. Energy, Washington, 1977-83, engr. office of energy conservation, 1983-85, scientist office of energy rsch., 1985-89, dir. office of energy strategy devel., 1989-90, dir. office of program rev. & analysis, office of policy, 1990-92, dir. office tech. policy, 1992-93, dir. office sci. policy, 1993—; dep. dir. U.S. Climate Change Tech. Program, 2001—. Contbr., editor (govt. publ.) Nat. Energy Strategy, 1991. Bd. trustees Seabee Meml. Scholarship Assn., 1999-; bd. visitors Pratt Sch. Engring. Duke U., 2003-. Lt. Civil Engring. Corps, USNR, 1971-74, rear admiral, 1997-2001, ret. 2001. Mem. AAAS, Internat. Assn. for Energy Econs., Sigma Xi. Achievements include development of quantitative methods for characterizing structural change in industrial economies; development of a national energy strategy; use of technology assess-

ments to guide federal funding priorities for energy research and development, national strategy for climate change technology development. Office: US Dept Energy 1000 Independence Ave SW Washington DC 20585-0001 Business E-Mail: robert.marlay@hq.doe.gov.

**MARLEN, JAMES S.,** chemical, plastics and building materials manufacturing company executive; b. Santiago, Chile, Mar. 14, 1941; came to U.S., 1961; m. Carolyn S. Shields, Jan. 23, 1965; children: James, Andrew, John. B.S. chem engring., U. Ala., 1965; MBA, U. Akron, 1971. With GenCorp., Akron, Ohio, 1965-93, engring., mktg. and gen. mgmt. positions domestic and internat. ops., 1977—80; group pres. fabricated plastics GTR Coated Fabrics Co., 1980-87; pres. consumer and indsl. sects. GenCorp Polymer Products, Akron, Ohio, 1988—; v.p. and officer GenCorp, Akron, 1988-93; pres., CEO Ameron Internat. Corp., Pasadena, Calif., 1993—. Bd. dirs. Ameron, Inc., chmn. bd. dirs., pres. and CEO, 1995—; dir. A. Schulman, Inc., Tamco Steel, Parsons Corp.; gen. and hon. chmn. Nat. Inventors Hall of Fame Induction, 1993. Bd. dirs. YMCA Met. L.A., The Employers Group of Calif., Town Hall of L.A., gov.; mem. the Beavers; dir. L.A. Sports Coun.; mem. bd. visitors Anderson Sch. Bus., UCLA, 1999-2001. Mem. Chem. Mfrs. Assn. (past pres.), Assocs. Caltech, Calif. C. of C., L.A. C. of C. (dir.), Portage Country Club (Akron, Ohio), Calif. Club (L.A.), Annandale Golf Club (Pasadena), L.A. Country Club, Valley Hunt Club (Pasadena), Soc. Fellows of Huntington Libr. (L.A.), Birnam Wood Golf Club (Santa Barbara, Calif.). Office: Ameron Internat Corp 245 S Los Robles Ave Pasadena CA 91101-2820

**MARLER, JOAN,** writer, educator; b. Chico, Calif., June 6, 1947; d. William Thomas Marler and Grace Elizabeth Paddock; m. Dan Dimitrov Smith, Jan. 1, 1975; 1 child, Sorrel Smith. BA in Dance, Mills Coll., Oakland, CA, 1969; MA in Archaeomythology, Sonoma State U., Rohnert Park, Calif., 1998. Instr. folk and ethnic dance Santa Rosa (Calif.) Jr. Coll., 1975—; prof. archaeomythology Calif. Inst. Integral Studies, San Francisco, 1996—. Radio prodr. KPFA, Berkeley, 1982—96; vis. prof. art history Sonoma State U., Rohnert Park, 1998; adj. faculty New Coll. Calif., San Francisco, 1998—2001; founder, dir. Inst. Archaeomythology. Editor: From the Realm of the Ancestors: An Anthology in Honor of Marija Gimbutas, 1997; author: (article in anthology) Treasures: Studies in Honor of Ivan Marazov, 1998, In Le radici prime dell'Æuropa: Gli intrecci genetici, linguistici, storici, 2002, In Women in Transition: Voices, 2001, Il Mito e il Cueto della grande Dea, 2003, Die Diskriminierung der Matriarchatsforschung, 2003, Notable American Women, 2003; editor: (jour.) ReVision Jour., (by Marija Gimbutas) Civilization of the Goddess, 1991, Jour. of Archaeomythology. Founding mem. Monastery Project. Grantee, Calif. Inst. Integral Studies, 2000. Mem.: Anthrop. Assn. Am. (assoc.). Office: Institute of Archaeomythology PO Box 1902 Sebastopol CA 95473 Office Phone: 707-823-7727. Business E-Mail: jmarler@archaeomythology.org.

**MARLETT, JUDITH ANN,** nutritional sciences educator, researcher; b. Toledo; BS, Miami U., Oxford, Ohio, 1965; PhD, U. Minn., 1972; postgrad., Harvard U., 1973-74. Registered dietitian. Therapeutic and metabolic unit dietitian VA Hosp., Mpls., 1966-67; spl. instr. in nutrition Simmons Coll., Boston, 1973-74; asst. prof. U. Wis., Madison, 1975-80, assoc. prof. dept. nutritional scis., 1981-84, prof. dept. nutritional scis., 1984—. Cons. U.S. AID, Leyte, Philippines, 1983, Makerere U., Kampala, Uganda, 2005; acting dir. dietetic program dept. Nutritional Scis. U. Wis., 1977-78, dir., 1985-89; cons. grain, drug and food cos., 1985—; adv. bd. U. Ariz. Clin. Cancer Ctr., 1987-95; sci. bd. advisors Am. Health Found., 1988—; reviewer NIH, 1982-2004; vis. prof. Makerere U., Kampala, Uganada, 2005; spkr. in field. Mem. editl. bd. Jour. Sci. of Food and Agrl., 1989—, Jour. Food Composition and Analysis, 1994-2000, Jour. of Nutrition, 2002—; contbr. articles to profl. jours. Mem. NIH (Diabetes amd Digestive and Kidney Disease spl. grant rev. com. 1992-96), Am. Soc. Nutrition, Am. Dietetic Assn. Achievements include research on human nutrition and disease, dietary fiber and gastrointestinal function. Office: U Wis Dept Nutritional Sci 1415 Linden Dr Madison WI 53706-1527 Office Phone: 623-972-5221. Business E-Mail: jmarlett@nutrisci.wisc.edu.

**MARLETTE, DOUGLAS NIGEL,** editorial cartoonist, comic strip creator; b. Greensboro, N.C., Dec. 6, 1949; m. Melinda Hartley; 1 child, Jackson Douglas. Student, Fla. State U. Editorial cartoonist The Charlotte (N.C.) Observer, 1972-87, The Atlanta Constn., 1987-89, N.Y. Newsday, N.Y.C., 1989—; syndicated to over 200 newspapers through L.A. Times Syndicate, Inc., 1988—. Creator syndicated comic strip Kudzu; works reproduced in Time, Newsweek, Christian Century, Rolling Stone, Der Spiegel, Esquire mags., also textbooks and encys.; author: The Emperor Has No Clothes, If You Can't Say Something Nice, Drawing Blood, Kudzu, 1982, Preacher, The Wit and Wisdom of Will B. Dunn, 1984, Just A Simple Country Preacher, 1985, It's a Dirty Job But Somebody Has To Do It, There's No Business Like Soul Business, 1987, Chocolate is My Life, Shred This Book, I Am Not a Televangelist, Doublewide with a View, 1989, In Your Face, A Cartoonist At Work, 1991, (novels) Magic Time, 2006;, (children's book) The Before and After Book, Even White Boys Get the Blues, 1992, Gone With the Kudzu, 1995; co-wrote screenplay "EX", TV appearances include ABC's Nightline, Good Morning Am., Today Show, CBS Morning News, Nat. Pub. Radio's Morning Edition; syndicated animated editorial cartoons NBC Today Show. Nieman fellow, 1st for editorial cartoonist, Harvard U.; recipient Nat. Headliners award 1983, 88, Robert F. Kennedy Meml. award 1984, Sigma Delta Chi Disting. Service award 1986, First Amendment award 1986, 1st Pl. award John Fischetti Editorial Cartoon Competition, 1986, The Golden Plate Acad. of Achievement award, 1991; named to Register of Men and Women Who Are Changing Am., Esquire Mag., 1984; recipient Pulitzer Prize for editorial cartooning Newsday, 1988; 1st Prize, John Fischetti Editorial Cartoon Competition, 1990. Office: Sarah Crichton Books Author Mail Farrar Straus & Giroux 19 Union Sq West New York NY 10003*

**MARLEY, DAMIAN ROBERT NESTA (JR. GONG),** reggae artist; b. Kingston, Jamaica, July 21, 1978; s. Bob Marley and Cindy Breakspeare. Performer: (albums) Mr. Marley, 1996, Halfway Tree, 2001 (Grammy award, Best Reggae Album, 2002), Welcome to Jamrock, 2005 (Vibe mag. Boomshot award, 2005, Grammy award, Best Reggae Album, 2006, Grammy award, Best Urban/Alternative Performance, 2006, Best Album, Internat. Reggae & World Music Awards, 2006); performer: (with Stephen & Julian Marley) Educated Fool, 2001; performer: (songs) There for You, 2005, Welcome to Jamrock, 2005 (Music of Black Origin award, Best Song, Internat. Reggae & World Music Awards, 2006, Best Music Video, Internat. Reggae & World Music Awards, 2006). Co-recipient Songwriter of Yr. (with Stephen Marley), Internat. Reggae & World Music Awards, 2006; recipient Bob Marley award for Entertainer of Yr., 2006, Recording Artist of Yr., 2006. Rastafarian. Office: Ghetto Youths Internat Ste A21 16115 SW 117th Ave Miami FL 33177 Office Phone: 305-969-7111.*

**MARLING, KARAL ANN,** art history educator, social sciences educator, curator; b. Rochester, NY, Nov. 5, 1943; d. Raymond J. and Marjorie (Karal) M. PhD, Bryn Mawr Coll., 1971. Prof. art history and Am. studies U. Minn., Mpls., 1977—. Author: Federal Art in Cleveland, 1933-1943: An Exhibition, 1974, Wall-to-Wall America: America: A Cultural History of Post-Office Murals in the Great Depression, 1982, 2d edit., 2001, The Colossus of the Roads: Myth and Symbol Along the American Highway, 1984, 2d edit., 2000, Tom Benton and His Drawings: A Biographical Essay and a Collection of His Sketches, Studies and Mural Cartoons, 1985, Frederick C. Knight (1898-1797), 1987, George Washington Slept Here: Colonial Revivals and American Culture, 1876-1986, 1988, Looking Back: A Perspective on the 1913 Inaugural Exhibition, 1988, Blue Ribbon: A Social and Pictorial History of the Minnesota State Fair, 1990; author: (with John Wetenhall) Iwo Jima: Monuments, Memories, and the American Hero, 1992; author: Edward Hopper, 1992, As Seen on T.V.: The Visual Culture of Everyday Life in the 1950's era, 1994, Graceland: Going Home with Elvis, 1995; editor (with Jessica H. Foy): The Arts and the American Home, 1890-1930, 1994; editor: Norman Rockwell, 1997, Designing the Disney Theme Parks: The Architecture of Reassurance, 1997, Merry Christmas! Celebrating America's Greatest Holiday, 2000, Looking North, 2003, Debutante, 2004, Old Glory Unfurled, 2004, Norman Rockwell: America's Favorite Painter, 2005, Behind The Magic: 50 Years of Disneyland, 2005, Designs on The Heart: The Homemade Art of Grandma Moses, 2006; contbr. essays to catalogs. Recipient award Minn. Humanities Commn., 1986, Book History award Minn., 1994, Robert C. Smith award Decorative Arts Soc., 1994, award Internat. Assn. Art Critics, 1998; Woodrow Wilson fellow, fellow Luce Found. Office: 1920 S 1st St Ste 1301 Minneapolis MN 55454-1190 Office Phone: 612-339-6172. Business E-Mail: marli001@umn.edu. E-mail: kmarling@mn.rr.com.

**MARLON, ANTHONY M.,** healthcare company executive, cardiologist; m. Renee Marlon. Graduate, Coll. of Holy Cross, Mass., 1963; internship, residency in cardiology, Stanford Univ., 1967—72. Intern, resident, cardiology fellow Stanford (Calif.) U., 1967-72; chief cardiology U. Med. Ctr. So. Nev., 1972-85; pvt. practice cardiology, from 1972; founder, chmn. bd., CEO Sierra Health Svcs., Inc., Las Vegas, Nev., 1984—. Office: Sierra Health Svcs Inc 2724 N Tenaya Way Las Vegas NV 89128

**MARLOW, EDWARD A.,** former army officer; b. Cleve., Nov. 22, 1946; m. Gari Ann Dill, Sept. 20, 1975. AA, Long Beach City Coll., 1971; cert., Officer Candidate Sch., Ft. Benning, 1974, Basic Infantry Officer Course, 1976; student, Am. Law Inst., N.Y., 1979-80; cert., Advance Armor Officer Course, Ft. Knox, 1982, U.S. Army Command and Gen. Staff Coll., 1986; BS in Bus. Mgmt. and Polit. Sci., SUNY, 1987; MPA, U. So. Calif., 1990; cert., Advance Intelligence Officer Course, Ft. Huachuca, 1991. Registered investment adv. with SEC, 1997-99. Commd. 2d lt. inf. U.S. Army, 1974, advanced through grades to maj., 1988; chief real property br. Mil. Dept., Sacramento, 1968—2004; pres. and dir. TEAM Mgmt. Corp., 1998—2003; pres. Western Res. Corp., Goldfield, Nev., 2000—, bd. dir.; CEO TEAM Internat., LLC, Sacramento, 2004—; pres. and CEO TEAM Profl. Svcs., LLC, 2004—; team leader Real Property Acquisition Program US Army Corps Engrs., L.A., 2005—; CEO Edward A. Marlow, LLC, 2005—. Del. Korean Svc. Vets. Revisit Program, Seoul, Republic of Korea, 1975. Mng. sr. ptnr. Caribbean Basin Latin Am. Devel. Orgn., Sacramento, 1988-98; trustee Hosp. Relief Fund Caribbean, Inc., Washington, 1989-92; mem. Caribbean Pvt. Sector Disaster Coord. subcom. White House Internat. Disaster Adv. Com., 1991-92; sr. ptnr. Caribbean Basin Latin Am. Devel. Orgn. Endowment Group, Sacramento, 1992—; chair bd. trustees CABALADO Relief Fund, Inc., 1993-99; provided disaster assistance and med. equipment to Glendon Hosp., Plymouth, Montserrat, West Indies, 1994-95; mem. Park and Recreation Com. Found., Santa Barbara, Calif. (steering com. 2004-); pre. Petersen Automotive Mus., 2005—; supporter santa Barbara County Sheriff's Coun., 2005—. Mem.: Euclid City Schs. Alumni Assn., U. So. Calif. Gen. Alumni Assn., Am. Assn. Retired Persons, DAV (life), 200 Checkered Flag Club. Avocations: sailing, fishing. Office Phone: 916-961-9382. E-mail: emarlowe_teamwrc@yahoo.com.

**MARLOW, IAN MICHAEL,** real estate company executive; b. Bklyn., Jan. 18, 1975; s. David Zachary and Ann Marlow. BSChemE, Rensselaer Poly. Inst., 1996. Environ. engr. Dept. Def., NY, 1993-96; nuc. engr. Dept. Energy, NY, 1996-97; v.p., dir. info. scis. Homestead Ins. Co., Florham Park, NJ, 1997-99; v.p., chief engring. and mktg. officer Signet Star Re, Florham Park, 1999—; exec. v.p., COO, CIO The Gale Co. LLC, Florham Park, 2002. Mem. Datawarehousing Inst., Phi Lambda Phi (Nat. Engring. award). Avocations: sailing, automobiles, travel. Home: 18 Garrity Terrace Pine Brook NJ 07058

**MARLOW, PATRICIA BAIR BOND,** realtor; b Altoona, Pa., Dec. 3, 1932; d. John Lesley and Gladys Marie Bair; m. Neal Nelson Jensen Bond, Aug. 7, 1953 (dec. July 1963); children: John Scott Bond, Lisa Suzanne Moody, Lesley Ann Stephen; m. Laurin Purcell Marlow, Apr. 4, 1967. Student, Mary Washington Coll., 1950-52. Realtor Everitt/Luby, Dallas, 1971-80; with Merrill Lynch, Dallas, 1980-89; realtor Adleta Fine Properties, 1989—. Contbr. poetry to anthologies. Recipient Diamond Summit. Mem. Dallas Mus. Art, Dallas Arboretum, Les Femmes du Monde, Dallas Mus. Art League, Tex. Kidney Found., Salvation Army (women's aux.). Avocation: watercolor painting. Home: 5336 Nashwood Ln Granbury TX 76049 Office: Adleta Fine Properties 5950 Berkshire Ln Dallas TX 75225 Personal E-mail: patti@pattimarlow.com.

**MARLOWE, KATHLEEN SCOTT,** employment analyst; b. Vanadium, N.Mex., Apr. 14, 1947; d. Noah Anthony Scott and Evelyn Marie Dunagan; m. William D Marlowe, Aug. 5, 1988; 1 child, James Martin Graham. BA, N.Mex State U., 1974. Sr. equal employment opportunity fed. agy. decision analyst Dept. of Homeland Security, Washington, 2003—05; equal employment opportunity analyst New London, Conn., 2005—. Fed. equal employment opportunity complaint analyst Dept. of Navy, Washington, 1992—2003. Chair, bd. of deacons First Presbyn. Ch., Arlington, Va., 1999—2000. Presbyterian. Avocation: foreign travel. Personal E-mail: kmarlowe@comcast.net.

**MARLOWE, WILLIE,** artist, fine arts educator; b. Whiteville, NC, Jan. 17, 1943; d. John David and Tessie Ernestine (McLawhorn) M.; m. Thomas Blakeslee Speight, July 11, 1980. Student, Pa. Acad. Fine Arts, Phila., 1964; BS, East Carolina U., 1965; MFA, U. Idaho, 1969; postgrad., Peace Coll. 1993. Instr. dept. art Skidmore Coll., Saratoga Springs, NY, 1970-74, mentor univ. without walls, 1972-74; instr. dept. art Columbia-Greene C.C., Hudson, NY, 1973-74; instr. Empire State Coll. SUNY, Albany, 1974; prof. Dept. Visual Arts Sage Coll., Albany, 1977—; chmn. The Sage Colls., Albany, 1979-81. Co-founder, instr. Saratoga Arts Workshop, Saratoga Springs, N.Y., 1970-74; watercolor tchr. abroad Sage Colls., Scotland, Ireland, 2001; tchr. Somerville Coll., Oxford U., Eng., 1992; vis. artist U. Ga. studies abroad program, Cortona, Italy, 1989; vis. artist, Wexford Arts Ctr., Ireland, 1998, artist-in-residence for Ptnrs. of the Americas, Barbados, W.I., 1986, The Millay Colony for the Arts, Austerlitz, N.Y., 1999; artist selection com. Albany Ctr. Gallery, 1998; internat. artists' residency Cill Rialaig Project, Dallindelllgo, Ireland, 2005. Emily Harvey Found., Venice, 2006; lectr. in field. One-woman shows include The Mint Mus. Art, Charlotte, NC, 1971, Schenectady Mus., NY, 1975, Marist Coll., Poughkeepsie, NY, 1976, Stockton State Coll., Pomono, NJ, 1977, Greenville Mus. Art, NC, 1982, 97, Ann Grey Gallery The Casino, Saratoga Springs, NY, 1985, The Barrett Art Gallery Utica Coll. Syracuse U., NY, 1986, The Atrium Gen. Electric Corp. R&D Ctr., Schenectady, 1988, Forum Gallery, Gütersloh, Germany, 1992, Albany Ctr. Gallery, 1992, 97, McHenry County Coll., Crystal Lake, Ill., Main St. Gallery, Dobbs Ferry, 1995, The Wexford Arts Ctr., Ireland, 1998, The Saratoga Arts Ctr., Saratoga Springs, NY, 2000, Fondo del Sol Gallery and Visual Arts Ctr., Washington, 2002, Barrett Arts Ctr., Poughkeepsie, NY, 2002, Gallery C, Raleigh, 2003, Color and Space traveling solo show, NC, 2006; exhibited in group shows at Fulton St. Gallery, Troy, NY, 2003, Adirondack CC, Queensbury, NY, 2006, Gallery Neptune, Bethesda, Md., 2005, Wexford (Ireland) Arts Ctr., 2004, Art Ctr. for the Capital Region, Troy, NY, 2002, Reprize Internat. Invitational Show, Wexford Arts Ctr., Ireland, 2002, Martinez Gallery, Troy, NY, 2002, Artemisia Gallery, Chgo., 2000, 03, Nexus Gallery, NYC, 1997-99, Gang Gallery, NYC, Eng. & Co., London, 1993, Steinbaum-Krauss Gallery, NYC, 1990, Stux Gallery, Boston, 1987, Nat. Mus. Women Arts, Washington, 1987, Westbeth Gallery, NYC, 1994, Clocktower, NYC, 1986, Rice Gallery The Albany Inst. History & Art, 1986, Deborah Davis Fine Arts, Hudson, 2003-04, 06, Firlefanz Gallery, Albany, 2004, Gallery 100, Saratoga Springs, 2004, U. West Eng., Bristol, 2004, Nat. Coll. Art and Design, Dublin, Ireland, 2004; represented in pvt. collections; represented in permanent collections Legis. Offices Empire State Plz., Albany, First Albany Corp., Md. Dept. Econ. & Cmty. Devel., Balt., Quad Graphics, Boston, SUNY Albany, NC Nat. Bank, Charlotte, Greenville Mus. Art, East Carolina U., Greenville, NC Boston Pub. Libr., Budapest Gallery, Russell Sage Coll., Troy, Mint Mus. Art, Charlotte, NC, Four Winds Ctr., Saratoga Springs, U. Mus. SUNY Albany, Bullard and McLeod & Assocs., Inc., Albany, NY, Rocky Mount Art Ctr., NC, Adirondack CC, NY; co-curator and curator for mail art shows. Recipient Purchase award in painting Hudson Mohawk Regional Ann., SUNY Albany, 1977, 95, 97, honorable mention in watercolor The Oswego Art Guild, N.Y., 1986, medal Internat. Art Competition Metro Arts, Inc., Scarsdale, N.Y., 1986, honorable mention in painting

Third Ann. Nat. C.C. Miniature Painting Show, Lexington, 1987, Sywer award, 1995, and numerous others; N.Y. State Coun. on the Arts grantee Barrett Art Gallery Syracuse U., 1986, grantee Artists' Space, 1988, Spl. Opportunity grant N.Y. Found. Arts. Mem.: Nat. Assn. Women Artists, Albany Inst. History and Art, Fulton St. Gallery, Albany Ctr. Gallery, Woman's Caucus For Art. Avocations: painting, visual poetry, mail art. Personal E-mail: info@williemarlowe.com.

**MARMARELIS, VASILIS ZISSIS,** engineering educator, writer, consultant; b. Mytilini, Greece, Nov. 16, 1949; arrived in US, 1972; s. Zissis P. and Elpis V. (Galinos) M.; m. Melissa Emily Orme, Mar. 12, 1989; children: Zissis Eugene and Myrl Galinos. Diploma in elec. and mech. engring., Nat. Tech. U. Athens, 1972; MS in Info. Sci., Calif. Inst. Tech., 1973, PhD in Engring. Sci., 1976. Rsch. fellow Calif. Inst. Tech., Pasadena, 1976—78; asst. prof. U. So. Calif., L.A., 1978—83, assoc. prof., 1983—88, prof., 1988—, also dir. biomed. simulations resource, 1985—, chmn. dept. biomed. engring., 1990—96; pres. Multispec Corp., L.A., 1986—2000. Author: Analysis of Physiological Systems, 1978, translated in Russian 1981, translated in Chinese 1990; Advanced Methods of Physiological Systems Modeling, vol. I, 1987, vol. II, 1989, vol. III, 1994, Nonlinear Dynamic Modeling of Physiological Systems, 2004; contbr. numerous articles to profl. jours. Fellow: IEEE, Am. Inst. for Med. and Biol. Engring.; mem.: N.Y. Acad. Scis., Biomed. Engring. Soc., Neural Networks Soc. Achievements include invention of Artemis mammography system. Office: Univ So Calif DRB160 Los Angeles CA 90089-1111

**MARMER, ELLEN LUCILLE,** pediatrician, cardiologist; b. Bronx, N.Y., June 29, 1939; d. Benjamin and Diane (Goldstein) M.; m. Harold O. Shapiro, June 5, 1960; children: Chori, Brenda. DS in Chemistry, U. Ala., 1960; MD, U. Ala., Birmingham, 1964. Cert. Nat. Bd. Med. Examiners; diplomate Am. Bd. Sports Medicine, Bd. Pediat., Bd. Qualified and Eligible Pediatric Cardiology, Bd. cert. sports medicine. Intern Upstate Med. Ctr., Syracuse, NY, 1964-65, resident, 1965-66; fellow in pediatric cardiology Columbia Presbyn. Med. Ctr.-Babies Hosp., N.Y.C., 1967-69; pvt. practice Hartford, Vernon, Conn., 1969—. Examining pediatrician child devel. program Columbia Presbyn. Med. Ctr.-Babies Hosp., N.Y.C., 1967, instr. pediat., 1967-69; dir. pediatric cardiology clinic St. Francis Hosp., Hartford, 1970-80; asst. state med. examiner, Tolland County, Conn., 1974-79; sports physician Rockville (Conn.) High Sch., 1976—; advisor Cardiac Rehab. com., Rockville, 1984-90; mem. bd. examiners Am. Bd. Sports Medicine, 1991—, chmn. credentials com., 1991-93. Mem. Vernon Town Coun., 1985-89; bd. dirs. Child Guidance Clinic, Manchester, Conn., 1970—; life mem. Tolland County chpt. Hadassah, v.p., 1969-70, pres., 1970-72, bd. dirs., 1973-74; mem. B'nai Israel Congregation and Sisterhood, Vernon, 1969—, chmn. youth commn., 1970-72; mayor Town of Vernon, 2003--. Recipient Outstanding Svc. award Indian Valley YMCA, 1985. Fellow Am. Acad. Pediat., Am. Coll. Cardiology, Am. Coll. Sports Medicine; mem. Conn. Med. Soc., Am. Heart Assn. (mem. coun. cardiovasc. disease in young 1969—, chmn. elect New Eng. regional heart com. 1990-91, mem. Heritage affiliate 1998—), Conn. Heart Assn. (bd. dirs 1974-75, 83-84, pres. 1986-88), Heart Assn. Greater Hartford (bd. dirs. 1970-89, mem. exec. com. 1972-73, 79-84, pres. 1982-84), Tolland County Med. Assn. (sec. 1971-72), Vis. Nurse and Cmty. Care Tolland County, LWV (state program chairperson Vernon chpt. 1971-73). Democrat. Jewish. Avocation: sports. Office: 520 Hartford Tpke Vernon Rockville CT 06066 Office Phone: 860-870-9366.

**MARMER, NANCY,** editor; b. N.Y.C., Nov. 19, 1932; d. Carl and Frances Marmer; m. Gerald Jay Goldberg, Jan. 23, 1954; 1 child, Robert. BA magna cum laude, Queens Coll., 1954; postgrad., U. Minn., 1954-57, UCLA, 1968-71. L.A. corr. Art Internat., 1965-67; West Coast editor Artforum, 1976-77; sr. editor Art in America, N.Y.C., 1979-81, exec. editor, 1981-83, book rev. editor, 1983-97, mng. editor, 1983-97, editor-at-large, 1997-98, contbg. editor, 1998—. Lectr. Mellon seminar R.I. Sch. Design, 1983; lectr. art criticism Visual Arts dept. U. Calif., San Diego, 1978; faculty expository writing Dept. English, U. Minn., 1954-57. Author: The Modern Critical Spectrum, 1962; contbr. numerous articles to profl. jours.; art critic/reviewer for Art in America, Art Internat., Artforum, L.A. Times. Recipient Samuel Kress Found. Award in Art History; Nat. endowment for the Arts fellow in art criticism. Mem. Phi Beta Kappa. E-mail: 102424.711@compuserve.com.

**MARMION, DANIEL KEITH,** school librarian; b. Colo. m. Diana Mary Manttan; 1 child, Jennifer Lynn. Assoc. dir. librs. U. Notre Dame, 2000—; asst. dean librs. Western Mich. U. Office: Univ Notre Dame 221 Hesburgh Library Notre Dame IN 46556 Office Phone: 574-631-3811.

**MARMOL, GUILLERMO G. (GIL MARMOL),** information technology executive; BA in engring. and applied physics magna cum laude, Harvard Coll., 1975; MBA with distinction, Harvard Bus. Sch., 1978. Former dir., sr. ptnr. McKinsey & Co. Inc.; sr. mgmt. to v.p. and chmn. operating com. Perot Systems, 1995—98; CEO, dir. Luminant Worldwide Corp., 1998—2000; pres. Marmol & Assoc., 2000—03; divsn. v.p. bus. process outsourcing portfolio EDS, Plano, Tex., 2003—. Mem. bd. Ctr. Free Cuba, Washington. Office: EDS Corp HQ 5400 Legacy Dr Plano TX 75024 Office Phone: 972-604-6000. Office Fax: 972-605-6033.

**MARMOR, MICHAEL,** epidemiologist, educator; married; 2 children. BA, Queens Coll., CUNY, 1966; MA, SUNY, Stony Brook, 1968, PhD, 1972. Program assoc. Rockefeller Found., NYC, 1971—74; asst. rsch. scientist Brookhaven Nat. Lab., Upton, NY, 1974—75. Asst. prof. NYU Sch. Medicine, NYC, 1975—78, rsch. assoc. prof., 1980—84, assoc. prof., 1984—92, prof., 1992—; prof. environ. medicine and medicine, 1994—; asst. dean NY State Coll Vet Medicine, Cornell U., Ithaca, NY, 1970—80. Contbr. more than 100 articles to sci. jours. Grantee, NIH, 1980—. Fellow: Am. Coll. Epidemiology. Office: NYU Sch Medicine 650 First Ave Rm 560 New York NY 10016-3240 Office Phone: 212-263-6667.

**MARMOR, MICHAEL FRANKLIN,** ophthalmologist, educator; b. NYC, Aug. 10, 1941; s. Judd and Katherine (Stern) M.; m. C. Jane Breeden, Dec. 20, 1968; children: Andrea K., David J. AB, Harvard U., 1962, MD, 1966. Diplomate Am. Bd. Ophthalmology. Med. intern UCLA Med. Ctr., 1967; fellow neurophysiology NIMH, 1967-70; resident in ophthalmology Mass. Eye and Ear Infirmary, Boston, 1970-73; asst. prof. ophthalmology U. Calif. Sch. Medicine, San Francisco, 1973-74; asst. prof. surgery (ophthalmology) Stanford (Calif.) U. Sch. Medicine, 1974-80, assoc. prof., 1980-86, prof., 1986—, head. div. ophthalmology, 1984-88, chmn. dept., 1988-92, dir. Basic Sci. Course Ophthalmology, 1993—. Faculty mem. program in human biology Stanford U., 1994; chief ophthalmology sect. VA Med. Ctr., Palo Alto, 1974-84; mem. sci. adv. bd. No. Calif. Soc. to Prevent Blindness, 1984-92, Calif. Med. Assn., 1984-92, Nat. Retinitis Pigmentosa Found., 1985-95. Author: The Eye of the Artist, 1997, Degas Through his own Eyes, 2002; editor: The Retinal Pigment Epithelium, 1975, The Effects of Aging and Environment on Vision, 1991, The Retinal Pigment Epithelium: Function and Disease, 1998; editor-in-chief Doc. Ophthalmologica, 1995-99; history editor: Survey of Ophthalmology; editl. bd. Healthline; contbr. more than 250 articles to BioMed Ctrl. jour. 50 chpts. to books. Mem. affirmative action com. Stanford U. Sch. Medicine, 1984-92. Sr. asst. surgeon USPHS, 1967-70. Recipient Svc. award Nat. Retinitis Pigmentosa Found., Balt., 1981, Rsch. award Alcon Rsch. Found., Houston, 1989; rsch. grantee Nat. Eye Inst., Bethesda, Md., 1974-94. Fellow Am. Acad. Ophthalmology (bd. councillors 1982-85, pub. health com. 1990-93, rep. to NAS com. on vision 1991-93, mus. com. 2004—). Honor award 1984, Sr. Honor award 1996), Cogan Ophthalmology Hist. Soc. (pres. 2003—); mem. Internat. Soc. Clin. Electrophysiology of Vision (v.p. 1990-98, dir. stds.), Assn. Rsch. in Vision and Ophthalmology, Internat. Soc. for Eye Rsch., Macula Soc., Retina Soc. Democrat. Avocations: tennis, bicycling, chamber music (clarinet), art history. Office: Stanford U Sch Medicine Dept Ophthalmology Stanford CA 94305-5308

**MARMOR, THEODORE RICHARD,** political science professor; b. Bklyn., Feb. 24, 1939; s. James and Mira Bernice (Karpf) M.; m. Jan Schmidt, Oct. 20, 1961; children— Laura Carleton, Sarah Rogers BA, Harvard U., 1960, PhD, 1966; postgrad., Wadham Coll., Oxford U., Eng., 1961-62. Asst. and assoc. prof. polit. sci. U. Wis.-Madison, 1967-69; assoc. prof. pub. affairs U. Minn.-Mpls., 1970-73; prof. U. Chgo., 1973-79; prof. polit. sci. Yale U., New Haven, 1979—, chmn. Ctr. Health Studies, 1979-85, prof. pub. mgmt. Sch. Orgn. and Mgmt., 1983—. Vis. fellow Russell Sage Found., 1987-88; cons., lectr. in field. Author: The Politics of Medicare, 1973, 2d edit., 2000, Political Analysis and American Medical Care, 1983, Understanding Health Care Reform, 1994; co-author: Health Care Policy, 1982, America's Misunderstood Welfare State, 1992; editor: Poverty Policy, 1971, National Health Insurance, 1980, Social Security: Beyond the Rhetoric of Crisis, 1988, Why Some People Are Healthy and Others Not, 1994, Jour. Health Politics Policy and Law, 1980-84, JHPPL; contbr. articles to profl. jours. Mem. Council on Fgn. Relations, N.Y.C., 1979-80, Pres.' Commn. on 1980s, 1980; social policy adviser Walter Mondale Presdl. Campaign, 1984. Can. Inst. Advanced Rsch. fellow, 1987—; fellow Adlai Stevenson Inst., J.F.K. Inst. Politics. Fellow Inst. Medicine, Nat. Acad. Social Scis.; mem. U.S. Squash Racquets Assn. (bd. dirs. 1983—), Century Assn., United Oxford and Cambridge Club, Lawn Club. Democrat. Jewish. Home: 139 Armory St Hamden CT 06517-4005 Office: Yale Univ Sch of Mgmt 135 Prospect St New Haven CT 06520-8200

**MARMORSTEIN, VICTORIA E.,** lawyer; BA with distinction, Univ. Okla., 1973; JD, Am. Univ., 1977; LLM, Univ. Va., 1978. Bar: DC 1977, NY 1980, Calif. 1989. Ptnr., global chair, fin. and real estate dept. Latham & Watkins, LA. Adj. prof., UCLA Sch. of Law. Editor: Va. Jour. of Internat. Law; author: numerous articles in profl. publications. Named in Chambers & Partners Guide to America's Leading Lawyers for Bus., 2004, in Euromoney's Legal Group Guide to the World's Leading Securitization Lawyers; named one of Top Women Lawyers in LA, LA mag., 2004. Mem.: Phi Beta Kappa. Fluent in Spanish. Office: Latham & Watkins Ste 4000 633 W Fifth St Los Angeles CA 90071-2007

**MARNAY, CHRIS,** research scientist; b. Stourport-on-Severn, Worcestershire, Eng., May 3, 1950; m. Nyla Marquis, Aug. 1, 1975. PhD, U. Calif., Berkeley, 1993. Staff scientist Ernest Orlando Lawrence Berkeley Nat. Lab., Calif., 1984—. Achievements include co-developer of microgrid concept. Office: Berkeley Lab 1 Cyclotron Rd MS 90R4000 Berkeley CA 94720-8136 Office Phone: +1.510.486.7028. Office Fax: +1.510.486.7976. Business E-mail: c_marnay@lbl.gov.

**MARNELL, ANTHONY AUSTIN, II,** architect; b. Riverside, Calif., Mar. 30, 1949; s. Anthony Austin and Ida Marie (Comforti) M.; m. Sandra Jean Graf, June 24, 1972 (div.); children: Anthony, Alisa. BArch, U. So. Calif., 1972. Architect, draftsman firms in Calif. and Nev., 1969-72; project coordinator Zuni Constrn. Co., Las Vegas, Nev., 1973-74; office mgr. architect Corrao Constrn. Co., Inc., Las Vegas, Nev., 1973-74, 1974-82; founder, CEO, chmn. bd. Marnell Corrao Assocs., Las Vegas, Nev., 1982—; pres. Marinelli Internat., Inc., Las Vegas, Nev., 1978—, A.A. Marnell II, Architect, Las Vegas, Nev., 1978—, Air Continental Jet Charter, Inc., Las Vegas, Nev., 1980-99; chmn., CEO Rio Hotel & Casino (acquired by Harrah's), 1986—99. Mem. ethics com. Nev. Bd. Architects, 1974; chmn. bd. Rio Hotel & Casino, Inc., 1986—, Focus 2000, Inc., 1989—, Prin. works include Mirage, Rio, Maxim Hotel, Treasure Island, Boulder Station, Sundance Hotel, Sam's Town, Excalibur; additions to Caesar's Palace, Desert Inn, Sands, Stardust, California, Frontier and Dunes Hotels (all Las Vegas), Caesar's, Atlantic City, others. Mem. Founders Bd. U. Nev., Las Vegas. Mem. Nat. Council Archtl. Registration Bds., Post Tensioning Inst. YPO (Nev. chmn. 1990). Roman Catholic. Office: Marnell Corrao Assoc Inc 222 Via Marnell Way Las Vegas NV 89119 Office Phone: 702-739-2000. Office Fax: 702-739-2005.*

**MARNEROS, ALEXANDER GEORG,** physician, researcher; MD summa cum laude, U. Cologne, Germany, 2003; PhD, Harvard U. and U. Oslo, Boston and Norway, 2004. Rsch. assoc. Med. Sch. and Dental Sch. Harvard U., Boston, 2003—05, sr. rsch. assoc. Dental Sch., 2006—. Editl. reviewer Harvard U., 2001—. Contbr. articles to profl. jours. Recipient Macula Degeneration prize, ProRetina eingetragener Verein, Germany, 2004; scholar, Boehringer Ingelheim Fonds, 2001. Mem.: Am. Soc. Matrix Biology (grantee 2002), German Dermatol. Soc., Assn. Rsch. in Vision and Ophthalmology (grantee 2006). Achievements include research in generation of a mouse model for age-related macular degeneration; characterization of the role of vascular endothelial growth factor and collagen XVIII/endostatin for ocular development; characterizing the genetics of keloids.

**MARNEY, SAMUEL ROWE, JR.,** allergist, immunologist, educator; b. Bristol, Va., Feb. 15, 1934; m. Elizabeth Ann Bingham, Oct. 1, 1966; children: Samuel Rowe III, Annis Morison. BA in Chemistry, U. Va., 1955, MD, 1960. Diplomate Am. Bd. Internal Medicine, Am. Bd. Allergy and Immunology; cert. in Diagnostic Lab. Immunology, 1988. Staff physician VA Hosp., Nashville, 1968—69, clin. assoc., 1969—71, clin. investigator, 1971—74, staff physician, infectious disease and allergy cons., 1974—; asst. prof. medicine Med. Ctr. Vanderbilt U., Nashville, 1971—76, assoc. prof., 1976—, dir. allergy and immunology, 1974—. Vis. investigator Scripps Clinic and Rsch. Found., La Jolla, Calif., 1973-74. Capt. USAF, 1962—64, Korea. Fellow ACP, Am. Acad. Allergy and Immunology, Am. Coll. Allergy and Immunology; mem. Southeastern Allergy Assn. (pres. 1986-87, Hal M. Davison Meml. award, 1981, 99), Tenn. Soc. Allergy and Immunology. Home: 4340 Sneed Rd Nashville TN 37215-3242 Office: Vanderbilt U Med Ctr Allergy & Immunology 2611 W End Ave Nashville TN 37203-6013 Office Phone: 615-936-2727. Business E-Mail: samuel.marney@vanderbilt.edu.

**MAROHN, WILLIAM D.,** consumer products company executive; BSME, Univ. Toledo, 1964. With Whirlpool Corp., 1964—98, division v.p., 1979—84, v.p., 1984—87, pres. Kenmore appliance group, 1987—89, exec. v.p. No. Am. ops., 1989—91, pres. Whirlpool Europe, 1992, pres., COO, 1992—97, vice chmn., 1997—98; dir. Newell Rubbermaid, Atlanta, 1999—, chmn., 2004—. Bd. dir. Cooper Tire & Rubber, Hanson Cold Storage. Dir. Mich. Jobs Commn.; chmn. Whirlpool Found., Lake Mich. Coll. Found.; mem. vis. com. Univ. Mich. Sch. Bus. Served USAF, Ohio & Mich. Air Nat. Guard. Recipient Gold T award, Univ. Toledo, 1997. Office: Newell Rubbermaid Ste 600 10 B Glendale Pkwy Atlanta GA 30328*

**MARON, MARC,** radio personality, comedian, actor, writer; b. 1963; m. Mishna Wolf. Stand-up comic, 1986—; host Short Attention Span Theater, Comedy Central; co-host (with Mark Riley) Morning Sedition, Air Am. Radio, 2004—. Performer: (one-man show) Jerusalem Syndrome, 2000; author: (book) Jerusalem Syndrome: My Life as a Reluctant Messiah, 2001; actor: (films) Los Enchiladas!, 1999, Almost Famous, 2000; guest appearances (comedian) Late Show with David Letterman, Late Night with Conan O'Brian, (documentaries) Left of the Dial, 2005. Jewish. Office: Air America Radio 641 Avenue Of The Americas Fl 4 New York NY 10011-2038

**MARONDE, ROBERT FRANCIS,** internist, pharmacologist; b. Monterey Park, Calif., Jan. 13, 1920; s. John August and Emma Florence (Palmer) M.; m. Yolanda Cerda, Apr. 15, 1970; children: Robert George, Donna F. Maronde Varnau, James Augustus, Craig DeWald. BA, U. So. Calif., 1941, MD, 1944. Diplomate: Am. Bd. Internal Medicine. Intern L.A. County-U. So. Calif. Med. Ctr., 1943-44, resident, 1944-45, 47-48; asst. prof. physiology U. So. Calif., L.A., 1948-49, clin. instr. medicine, 1949-60, assoc. clin. prof. medicine, 1960-65, assoc. prof. medicine and pharmacology, 1965-67, prof. medicine and pharmacology, 1968-90, emeritus, 1990—, prof. emeritus, 1990—; spl. asst. v.p. for health affairs, 1990—. Cons. FDA, 1973, Medco Containment Co. Inc. 1991-97, State of Calif. Dept. Health Svcs., 1993; mem. adv. panel State of Calif., 1997—. Served to lt. (j.g.) USNR, 1945-47. Fellow ACP; mem. Am. Soc. Clin. Pharmacology and Therapeutics, Alpha

Omega Alpha. Home: 785 Ridgecrest St Monterey Park CA 91754-3759 Office: 2025 Zonal Ave Los Angeles, CA 90089-0110 Business E-Mail: marone@usc.edu. *Scientific integrity, objectivity, concern for the quality of life and adherence to the ethics of Nuremberg are ingredients for the evaluation of therapy for human illness. This is the ultimate objective of the practice of medicine.*

**MARONE, JAMES MATTHEW,** music educator; b. Batavia, N.Y., Apr. 23, 1967; s. John T. and Jane P. Marone. MusB in Music Edn., SUNY, Fredonia, 1989; MusM in Music Edn., Fla. State U., Tallahassee, 1992. Music tchr. Sweet Home Cen. Schs., Amherst, NY, 1997—, Olean (N.Y.) City Sch. Dist., 1997. Mem.: Internat. Soc. of Bassists. Home: 74 Bondcroft Dr Amherst NY 14226 Office: Sweet Home Central Schools 1901 Sweet Home Road Amherst NY 14228 Personal E-mail: jmarone@adelphia.net.

**MARONE-CINZANO, ENRICO,** apparel designer; BS in Bus. Studies, Babson Coll. Co-founder (with Natalie Chanin) Project Alabama, Florence, Ala., 2000—. Recipient Cooper Hewitt National Design award nomination, 2005, Artisan Advocate award. Office: Project Alabama 6534 County Rd 200 Florence AL 35633*

**MARONEY, JANE PERKINS,** former state legislator, consultant; b. Boston, July 29, 1923; d. John Henry and Mary (Boland) Perkins; m. John Walker Maroney, July 7, 1956; children: Jane Maroney El Dahr, John Walker Jr. Student, Radcliffe Coll., 1940—41, Katharine Gibbs Sch., 1941—42; LHD (hon.), Golden Beacom Coll., 1995. Elected ofcl. Del. Gen. Assembly, Dover, 1978-98; former project mgr. Milbank Meml. Fund, N.Y.C. Del. Family Law Commn., 1990—99, Health and Human Devel. Com., 1984—99; moderator, panelist Pub. Policy Conf., annually; past mem. Jr. League Wilmington (Del.); vice chair Creative Grandparenting, Inc., 1999—; pres. Lincoln Club of Del., 2002—03; trustee Christiana Care Health Sys., 2000—; mem. bd. Health and Nursing Scis. U. Del., 1998—; bd. dirs. YWCA, New Castle County, Family and Workplace Connection, Coord. Coun. Children with Disabilities, chmn., 1990—91; pres. adv. coun. Girl Scouts Del.; mem. adv. bd. Del. Internat. Yr. of Family, March of Dimes, Inst. Human Behavior; bd. dirs. Afghanistan-Del. Cmtys. Together, 2001—, St. Michaels Sch. and Nursery, 2000—. Named 1 of 10 Best Rep. Legislators of Yr., Pres. Reagan, 1985; named to, Women's Hall of Fame, Del., 1996, Outstanding Legislator of Yr., Easter Seals of Del., 1998; recipient Outstanding Svc. to Children award, Acad. Pediat., Disting. Svc. award, Del. Bar Assn., Alfred R. Shands Disting. Svc. award, 1992, Order of Merit award, U. Del., 1993, J. Donaldson Brown Disting. Svcs. award, Children and Family Svcs. Del. to Dr. & Rep. Maroney, 1992, Nathan Davis award, AMA, 1996, Order of the First State award, Gov. of Del., 1998, Advocacy and Leadership in Children's Issues award, Epilepsy Found. Del., 2000, Outstanding Lifetime Contbn. award, Health Edn. Network Del., 2001, Cmty. Builder award, Nat. Conf. for Cmty. and Justice, 2001, Woman Pioneer award, Boy Scouts Am., 2001, Liberty Bell award, Del. State Bar Assn. Law Day, 2003, Carrie Chapman Catt award, Wilmington LWV, 2004. Roman Catholic. Avocations: public policy, continuing education. Fax: 302-478-2677. Personal E-mail: jpmaroney@aol.com.

**MARONEY, THOMAS JOSEPH,** lawyer; b. Nassau County, N.Y., Sept. 27, 1955; s. George Edward and Elaine (Murphy) M.; m. Michelle Carol Entin, Nov. 15, 1997; children: Susan Isabella, Caroline Sara, Laura Ellen. BA, Siena Coll., 1977; JD, St. John's U., 1980. Bar: N.Y. 1982, U.S. Ct. Appeals (fed. dist.) 1981. Shareholder, founding ptnr. Hawkins, Feretic, Daly, Maroney & Hayes, P.C., N.Y.C., 1990—2005, Maroney O'Connor LLP, N.Y.C., 2005—. Mem. com. on character and fitness Appellate Divsn., N.Y. State, 1998. Mem. N.Y. State Bar Assn. (exec. com., torts, ins., compensation law sect.), N.Y. County Lawyers Assn., N.Y. Trial Lawyers, Def. Assn. N.Y. Office: Maroney O'Connor LLP 11 Broadway New York NY 10004 Office Phone: 212-530-3909. E-mail: tmaroney@maroneyoconnorllp.com

**MARONEY, THOMAS P.,** lawyer, political party executive; AB, Marshall U.; JD, Am. U. Pvt. practice, Charleston, WV. Chmn. W.Va. State Dem. Party, 1996—.

**MARONI, DONNA FAROLINO,** biologist, researcher; b. Buffalo, Feb. 27, 1938; d. Enrico Victor and Eleanor (Redlinska) Farolino; m. Gustavo Primo Maroni, Dec. 16, 1974. BS, U. Wis., 1960, PhD, 1969. Project assoc. U. Wis., Madison, 1960-63, 68-74; Alexander von Humboldt fellow Inst. Genetics U. Cologne, Fed. Republic Germany, 1974-75; Hargitt fellow Duke U., Durham, NC, 1975-76, rsch. assoc., 1976-83, rsch. assoc. prof., 1983-87; sr. program specialist N.C. Biotech. Ctr., Research Triangle Park, 1987-88, dir. sci. programs div., 1988-92, v.p. for sci. programs, 1992-94, ret., 1995. Mem. adv. com. MICROMED at Bowman Gray Sch. Medicine, Winston-Salem, NC, 1988—94; mem. sci. adv. bd. NC Biosci. Fund, LLC, 1998—99, Minority Sci. Improvement Alliance for Instrn. and Rsch. in Biotech, Ala. A&M U., Normal, 1990—91. Contbr. over 20 articles and revs. to profl. jours. Grantee NSF, 1977-79, NIH, 1979-82, 79-83, 82-87. Mem. Genetics Soc. Am., N.C. Acad. Sci., Inc. (bd. dirs. 1983-86), Sigma Xi (mem. exec. com. Duke U. chpt. 1989-90). Achievements include research in electron microscopy, evolution of chromosomes, chromosome structure, evolution of mitosis, and mitosis and fungal phylogeny. Personal E-mail: dmaroni@email.unc.du.

**MAROONE, MICHAEL E.,** car and truck sales executive; b. 1962; CEO Maroone Car & Truck Sales, Pembroke Pines, Fla.; COO, pres. AutoNation Inc., Ft. Lauderdale, Fla., 1999—. Bd. dir. Intercontinental Bank; chmn. South Fla. Internat. Auto Show, 1995. Bd. dir. Dan Marino Found., Boys and Girls Club of Broward County, Children Cancer Caring Ctr., Police Athletic League. Named Humanitarian of Yr., Transflorida Bank; recipient Chmn.'s award, Ford Motor Co., Quality Dealer award, Time mag. Mem.: Fla. Automotive Dealers Assn. (bd. dir.), South Fla. Chevrolet Dealers Mktg. Assn. (pres. 1994), South Fla. Auto Truck Dealers Assn. (pres. 1994). Office: AutoNation Inc 110 S E 6th St Fort Lauderdale FL 33301*

**MAROONEY, RICHARD T.,** lawyer; b. Garden City, N.Y. BS, BA cum laude, Boston Coll., 1991; JD with distinction, Hofstra Univ., 1994. Bar: N.Y. 1995, US Dist. Ct. So. & Ea. Dist. N.Y. 1996, US Dist. Ct. We. & No. Dist. N.Y. 1998. Ptnr., Litigation Practice Group King & Spalding LLP, New York. Editor (assoc.): Hofstra Law Rev. Office: King & Spalding LLP 1185 Ave of the Americas New York NY 10036 Office Phone: 212-556-2242. Office Fax: 212-556-2222. Business E-Mail: rmarooney@kslaw.com.

**MAROOTIAN, DOROTHY,** artist; b. New Haven; BFA, Cooper Union, NYC, 1978. Asst. art dir. Neiman-Marcus, Dallas; art dir. Bullock's, LA; freelance designer, art dir.; artist KCET, Channel 28; tchr. Chouinard Art Sch.; art dir. Max Factor. Artist: A Taste of Texas; designer Christmas wrap, Nieman Marcus; artist (permanent collections) USAF, Wash. DC, artist (altar pieces) St. Gregory Armenian Ch., Pasadena, St. Mary Armenian Ch., Costa Mesa Recipient painting awards Pasadena Art Soc., Irvine Creative Art Guild, Costa Mesa Art League; award for paper design Portfolio Mag. Mem.: Orange County Fine Arts. Home: 69 Claret Irvine CA 92614-7942 Office Phone: 949-786-9645.

**MAROSAN, GEORGE,** plastic surgeon; b. Oradea, Romania. Apr. 20, 1955; s. Bela and Irene Marosan; m. Boglarka Hagya, June 1, 1986; children: Zoltan George, Nandor Christopher. BA, SUNY at Buffalo, 1978; MA, Roswell Pk. Cancer Inst., Buffalo, 1981; MD, Rush Med. Coll., Chgo., 1983. Diplomate Am. Bd. of Plastic Surgery, 1994. Gen. surgery resident Rush Univ. Hosp., 1983—84, Jersey City Med. Ctr., 1984—85, David Grant USAF Med. Ctr., Calif., 1986—89; plastic surgery resident Walter Reed Army Med. Ctr., Washington, 1990—92; plastic surgeon Bellevue Plastic Surgeons, Bellevue, Wash., 1996—. Lt. col. USAF, 1985—95. Decorated Air Force Commendation medal. Fellow: ACS; mem.: Am. Soc. for Laser Medicine and Surgery, Hungarian Med. Assn. of Am., Wash. Soc. of Plastic Surgeons, N.W. Soc. of Plastic Surgeons, Am. Soc. for Aesthetic Plastic Surgery, Am. Soc. of Plastic

Surgeons. R-Consevative. Avocations: Tae Kwon Do, hiking, soccer. Office: Bellevue Plastic Surgeons 11820 Northup Way E-190 Bellevue WA 98005 Office Phone: 425-450-1994. Office Fax: 425-284-1803. E-mail: gmarosan@hotmail.com.

**MAROTTA, JOSEPH THOMAS,** medical educator; b. Niagara Falls, N.Y., May 28, 1926; emigrated to Can., 1930; s. Alfred and Mary (Montemuro) M.; m. Margaret Hughes, Aug. 31, 1953; children: Maureen, Patricia, Margaret, Fred, Thomas, Jo Anne, Michael, Martha, John, Virginia. MD, U. Toronto, 1949. Trainee in internal medicine U. Toronto, 1949-52; trainee in neurology Presbyn. Hosp., N.Y.C., 1952-55, U. London, Eng., 1955-56; mem. faculty U. Toronto, 1956—; prof. medicine, 1969—; former assoc. dean clin. affairs U. Toronto (Faculty of Medicine), 1981-89; hon. prof. of neurology U. Western Ontario, 1990—. Fellow Royal Coll. Physicians (Can.); mem. Alpha Omega Alpha, Phi Chi. Home and Office: 46 Carnforth Rd London ON Canada N6G 4P6 Office Phone: 519-642-4698. Business E-Mail: jtmarotta@rogers.com.

**MAROVITZ, SANFORD EARL,** English language and literature educator; b. Chgo., May 10, 1933; s. Harold and Gertrude (Luster) M.; m. Eleonora Dimitsa, Sept. 1, 1964. BA with honors, Lake Forest Coll., 1960; MA, Duke U., 1961, PhD, 1968. Instr. English Temple U., 1963-65; Fulbright instr. U. Athens, Greece, 1965-67; from asst. prof. English to prof. Kent State U., Ohio, 1967-96, prof. emeritus, 1996—. Vis. prof. English, Shimane U., Matsue, Japan, 1976-77, chair, 1987-92; co-dir. Melville Among the Nations, Greece, 1997. Co-editor: Artful Thunder: Versions of Romanticism in American Literature in Honor of Howard P. Vincent, 1975, Melville Among the Nations: Proceedings, 2001; co-author: Bibliographical Guide to the Study of the Literature of the U.S.A., 5th edit., 1984; author: Abraham Cahan, 1996; contbr. articles to profl. jours. Nat. trustee Lake Forest Coll., 1990-98. With USAF, 1953-57. Woodrow Wilson fellow, 1960-61; recipient Disting. Svc. Citation Lake Forest Coll., 1985, Disting. Tchg. award Kent State U., 1985, Presdl. Citation Shimane U., 1998. Mem.: MLA, Jack London Soc., Coll. English Assn. (Robert Miller award for best article in CEA Critic 2000), R.W. Emerson Soc., Saul Bellow Soc., W.D. Howells Soc. (v.p. 2000—01, pres. 2002—03, editor The Howellsian 2004—), Aldous Huxley Soc. (curator 1998—), Nathaniel Hawthorne Soc., Melville Soc. (sec. 1994—96, pres. 1998), Phi Beta Kappa, Phi Beta Delta, Omicron Delta Kappa. Democrat. Jewish. Home: 1155 Norwood St Kent OH 44240-3342 Office: Kent State U Dept English Kent OH 44242-0001 E-mail: smarovit@kent.edu.

**MAROZSAN, JOHN ROBERT,** retired publishing company executive; b. Trenton, N.J., Oct. 25, 1941; s. John Nichols and Anna Mary (Lacko) M.; m. Anne Marie Gousha, Mar. 18, 1983; children— Andre J., Marc J., Carl B. A.S., Trenton Jr. Coll., 1965; BA, Trenton State Coll., 1967; MA, Harvard U., 1969. Tchr. Princeton Pub. Sch., N.J., 1967-68; coordinator secondary pub. Ginn and Co., Boston, 1969-72; program mgr. Lexington, Mass., 1972-75; v.p., editor-in-chief Aspen Publishers, Inc., Rockville, Md., 1975-80; sr. v.p pub., 1980-85; pres. Aspen Pubs., Inc., Gaithersburg, 1986-96; COO Commerce Clearing House, Riverwoods, Ill., 1996-97; pres., CEO Commerce Clearinghouse, Riverwoods, Ill.; ret., 1999. Bd. dirs. Innodata. Bd. dirs. Hospice Caring, Wolters Klumen, U.S. Bd.; bd. examiners Henry B. Betts Found.; bd. govs. WUSA One and Only Award. With USAF, 1959-63. Recipient Sci. award NSF, 1968. Mem. Newsletter Assn. Am., Rotary, North Star Owners Assn. (pres. 1998-2001). Home: 220 E Prospect Ave Lake Bluff IL 60044 E-mail: jmarozsan@sbcglobal.net.

**MARPLE, DOROTHY JANE,** retired church executive; b. Abington, Pa., Nov. 24, 1926; d. John Stanley and Jennie (Stetler) M. AB, Ursinus Coll., 1948; MA, Syracuse U., 1950; Ed.D., Columbia U. Tchrs. Coll., 1969; L.H.D., Thiel Coll., 1965, Gettysburg Coll., 1979, Ursinus Coll., 1981; D. Humanitarian Services, Newberry Coll., 1977; DD, Trinity Luth. Sem., 1987. Counselor, asst., office dean undergrad. women Women's Coll., Duke, 1950-53; dean women, fgn. student adv. Thiel Coll., 1953-61; asst. social dir. Whittier Hall, Columbia Tchrs. Coll., 1961-62; exec. dir. Luth. Ch. Women, Luth. Ch. Am., Phila., 1962-75; asst. to bishop Luth. Ch. Am., 1975-85; coord. Transition Office Evang. Luth. Ch. Am., 1986-87; asst. gen. sec. ops. Nat. Coun. Chs. of Christ in U.S., N.Y.C., 1987-89. Coord. Luth. Ch. in Am. commn. on function and structure, 1970-72; chairperson Luth. World Fedn. Commn. Ch. Cooperation, 1983-90; mem. bd. dirs. Luth. Theol. Sem., Gettysburg, 1989-98; bd. trustees United Bd. Christian Higher Edn. in Asia, 1989-98. Home: 8018 Anderson St Philadelphia PA 19118-2936

**MARPLE, THOMAS FRANKLIN,** columnist, reporter; b. Winchester, Va., June 24, 1956; s. Thomas Franklin Marple Jr. and Mary Ellen Marple. BS in Mgmt., Shenandoah U., 1980. Reporter The Journal, Martinsburg, W.Va., 1997—2001; writer Mid-Atlantic Thoroughbred, Timonium, Md., 2001—, Horsemen's Jour., Austin, Tex., 2000—, Md. Jockey Club and Preakness Media Rels., 2002—. With U.S. Army, 1980—82. Named Best Sports Columnist, W.Va. Press Assn., 2001. Mem.: W.Va. Sports Writers Assn., W.Va. Breeders Assn. (publicity dir. 2001—). Avocations: fishing, bicycling, weightlifting, basketball, gardening. Home: 1801 Sam Mason Rd Bunker Hill WV 25413 Office Phone: 304-229-5370. E-mail: hallowedhaha@aol.com.

**MARQUARDT, CHRISTEL ELISABETH,** judge; b. Chgo., Aug. 26, 1935; d. Herman Albert and Christine Marie (Geringer) Trolenberg; children: Eric, Philip, Andrew, Joel. BS in Edn., Mo. Western Coll., 1970; JD with honors, Washburn U., 1974. Bar: Kans. 1974, Mo. 1992, U.S. Dist. Ct. Kans. 1974, U.S. Dist. Ct. (we. dist.) Mo. 1992. Tchr. St. John's Ch., Tigerton, Wis., 1955-56; pers. asst. Columbia Records, L.A., 1958-59; ptnr. Cosgrove, Webb & Oman, Topeka, 1974-86, Palmer & Marquardt, Topeka, 1986-91, Levy and Craig P.C., Overland Park, Kans., 1991-94; sr. ptnr. Marquardt and Assocs., L.L.C., Fairway, Kans., 1994-95; judge Kans. Ct. Appeals, 1995—. Mem. atty. bd. discipline Kans. Supreme Ct., 1984—86; mem. Kans. Sentencing Commn., 2004—, Kans. Criminal Justice Recodification, Rehab. and Restoration Com., 2004—. Mem. editorial adv. bd. Kans. Lawyers Weekly, 1992-96; contbr. articles to legal jours. Bd. dirs. Topeka Symphony, 1983-92, 95-2002, Arts and Humanities Assn. Johnson County, 1992-95, Brown Found., 1988-90; hearing examiner Human Rels. Com., Topeka, 1974-76; local advisor Boy Scouts Am., 1973-74; bd. dirs., mem. nominating com. YWCA, Topeka, 1979-81; bd. govs. Washburn U. Law Sch., 1987-2002, v.p., 1996-98, pres., 1998-2000, disting. alumni, 2004; mem. dist. bd. adjudication Mo. Synod Luth. Ch., Kans., 1982-88. Named Woman of Yr., Mayor, City of Topeka, 1982; Obee scholar Washburn U., 1972-74; recipient Jennie Mitchell Kellogg Atty. of Achievement award, 1999, Phil Lewis medal of Distinction, 2000, Atty. of Achievement award Kans. Women Attys. Assn., Disting. Svc. award Washburn U. Law Sch., 2002, 04; named Disting. Alumni, Washburn U. Fellow: Kans. Bar Found. (trustee 1987—89), Am. Bar Found.; mem.: ABA (mem. ho. dels. 1988—, chmn. specialization com. 1991—93, lawyer referral com. 1993—95, state del. 1995—99, bar svcs. and activities 1995—99, bd. govs., program and planning com. 1999—2002, bd. govs. 1999—2002, ctrl. and ea. European law initiative 2001—02, African law coun. 2002—04, del-at-large ho. of dels. 2002—, standing com. on jud. independence 2004—, 2004—), Law and Organizational Econ. Ctr. (bd. dirs. 2000—02), Am. Bus. Women's Assn. (lectr., corr. sec. 1983—84, pres. career chpt. 1986—87, named one of Top 10 Bus. Women of Yr. 1985), Topeka Bar Assn., Kans. Trial Lawyers Assn. (bd. govs. 1982—86, lectr.), Kans. Bar Assn. (sec., treas. 1981—85, bd. dirs. 1983—, v.p. 1985—86, pres. 1987—88, mem., lawyer referral com. 1999—). Home: 3408 SW Alameda Dr Topeka KS 66614-5108 Office: 301 SW 10th Ave Topeka KS 66612-1502 E-mail: marquardt@kscourts.org.

**MARQUARDT, DAVID F.,** venture capitalist; BSME, Columbia U., 1973; MBA, Stanford U., 1979. Design engr., devel. mgr. Diablo Systems; assoc. Instl. Venture Associates, 1979—80; founding ptnr. Tech. Venture Investors, 1980—95; founding gen. ptnr. August Capital, Menlo Park, Calif., 1995—. Founding mem. bd. dirs. Microsoft Corp., 1981—; bd. dirs. Alibre Inc., AutoTradeCenter Inc., NetCell Corp., Seagate Tech. Inc., Westbridge Tech.

Inc., Netopia Inc., 1990—, Tumbleweed Comm. Corp. Inc., 1997—, Six Apart Ltd., 2004—. Mem.: Nat. Venture Capital Assn. (past pres.), We. Assn. Venture Capitalists (past pres.). Office: August Capital 2480 Sand Hill Rd Ste 101 Menlo Park CA 94025

**MARQUARDT, STEVE ROBERT,** advocate; b. St. Paul, Sept. 7, 1943; s. Robert Thomas and Dorothy Jean (Kane) M.; m. Judy G. Brown, Aug. 4, 1968; 1 child, Sarah. BA in History, Macalester Coll., 1966; MA in History, U. Minn., 1970, MLS, 1973, PhD in History, 1978. History instr. Macalester Coll., St. Paul, 1968-69; cataloger N.Mex. State U. Libr., Las Cruces, 1973-75; acting univ. archivist, acting dir. Rio Grande Hist. Collections N. Mex. State U. Libr., Las Cruces, 1973-74; acquisitions librarian Western Ill. U. Libr., Macomb, 1976-77, head cataloger, Online Computer Libr. Ctr. coord., 1977-79; asst. dir. resources & tech. svcs. Ohio U. Libr., Athens, 1979-81; dir. librs. U. Wis., Eau Claire, 1981-89; dir. univ. librs. No. Ill. U., DeKalb, 1989-90; dir. librs. U. Wis., Eau Claire, 1999-96; dean of librs. S.D. State U., Brookings, 1996—. Editor Jour. Rio Grande History, 1974; contbg. editor: Library Issues, 1994-2003; contbr. articles to profl. jours. Coord. Amnesty Internat. Adoption Group 275, Eau Claire, 1985-88; pres. Chippewa Valley Free-net, 1994-96. Mem. ALA, Assn. Coll. and Rsch. Librs. (chmn. performance measures in acad. librs. com. 1985-89). Lutheran. Avocation: bicycling. Office: Rancho Mosquito 9383 123rd Ave SE Lake Lillian MN 56253-9777 Office Phone: 605-688-5106, 320-664-4231. E-mail: marquardt.steve@gmail.com.

**MARQUESS, LAWRENCE WADE,** lawyer; b. Bloomington, Ind., Mar. 2, 1950; s. Earl Lawrence and Mary Louise (Coberly) M.; m. Barbara Ann Bailey, June 17, 1978; children: Alexander Lawrence, Michael Wade. BSEE, Purdue U., 1973; JD, W.Va. U., 1977. Bar: W.Va. 1977, Tex. 1977, U.S. Dist. Ct. (so. dist.) W.Va. 1977, U.S. Dist. Ct. (no. dist.) Tex. 1977, Colo. 1980, U.S. Dist. Ct. Colo. 1980, U.S. Ct. Appeals (10th cir.) 1980, U.S. Supreme Ct. 1984, U.S. Dist. Ct. (no. dist.) Ohio 1988, U.S. Ct. Appeals (DC cir.) 1997, U.S. Dist. Ct. Nebr. 1999. Assoc. Johnson, Bromberg, Leeds & Riggs, Dallas, 1977-79, Bradley, Campbell & Carney, Golden, Colo., 1979-82, ptnr., 1983-84, Stettner, Miller & Cohn P.C., 1984-87, Nelson & Harding, Denver, 1987-88, Heron, Burchette, Ruckert & Rothwell, 1989-90, Harding & Ogborn, 1990-94, Otten, Johnson, Robinson, Neff & Ragonetti, Denver, 1994-2001, Littler Mendelson, P.C., Denver, 2001—, mng. shareholder, 2001—. Mem. faculty Am. Law Inst. - ABA Advanced Labor and Employment Law Course, 1986, 87. Mem.: ACLU, ABA (labor, antitrust and litig. sects.), Colo. Bar Found., Coll. Labor and Employment Lawyers, 1st Jud. Dist. Bar Assn., Denver Bar Assn., Colo. Bar Assn. (co-chmn. labor law com. 1989—92), Nat. Rlwy. Hist. Soc., Sierra Club. Democrat. Methodist. Home: 11883 W 27th Dr Lakewood CO 80215-7000 Office: Littler Mendelson PC 1200 17th St Ste 1000 Denver CO 80202 Office Phone: 303-362-2840. Business E-Mail: lmarquess@littler.com.

**MARQUEZ, ALFREDO C.,** federal judge; b. 1922; m. Linda Nowobilsky. BS, U. Ariz., 1948, JD, 1950. Bar: Ariz. Practice law Mesch Marquez & Rothschild, 1957-80; asst. atty. gen. State of Ariz., 1951-52; asst. county atty. Pima County, Ariz., 1953-54; adminstrv. asst. to Congressman Stewart Udall, 1955; judge U.S. Dist. Ct. Ariz., Tucson, 1980-91, sr. judge, 1991—. Served with USN, 1942-45 Office: US Dist Ct US Courthouse Rm 327 405 W Congress Ste 6180 Tucson AZ 85701-5060

**MÁRQUEZ, DAVID W.,** state attorney general; b. Wendling, Eng., 1945; married; 3 children. BS, Northwestern U.; JD, U. Wis. Law Sch. Bar: Alaska 1973. With private law firm, Anchorage; gen. counsel Alyeska Pipeline Service Co.; assoc. gen. counsel ARCO, v.p., chief counsel ARCO Alaska, Anchorage, v.p. external affairs and environment, health, & safety; atty. gen. State of Alaska, Juneau, 2005—. Chief asst. atty. gen., legis. and regulations sect. Alaska Dept. Law; acting dep. atty. gen. Civil Divsn. for Dept. Law; bd. dir. Alaska Permanent Fund Corp. Bd., 2005—. Bd. chair Jr. Achievement Alaska, Alaska State CofC. U.S. Army, Vietnam. Republican. Office: PO Box 110300 Juneau AK 99811-0300 Office Phone: 907-465-2133. Office Fax: 907-465-2075. Business E-Mail: Attorney_General@law.state.ak.us.

**MARQUEZ, VICTOR E.,** medical researcher; naturalized, US, 1987; BS in pharmacy, Ctrl. U. of Venezuela, Caracas, 1966; MS in medicinal chemistry, U. Mich., Ann Arbor, 1968, PhD, 1970. Postdoctoral training Nat. Cancer Inst., 1970—71; positions in pvt. industry Venezuela, 1971—76; vis. scientist Nat. Cancer Inst., 1977—87, granted tenure, 1987, now chief Lab. Medicinal Chemistry, head Organic Chemistry Sect., Lab. Medicinal Chemistry. Achievements include holding over 20 US patents. Office: Lab Medicinal Chemistry Nat Cancer Inst at Frederick 376 Boyles St PO Box B Frederick MD 21702-1201 Office Phone: 301-846-5954. Office Fax: 301-846-6033. E-mail: marquezv@dc37a.nci.nih.gov.

**MÁRQUEZ-MAGAÑA, LETICIA MARIA,** biology professor; b. Sacramento, Aug. 15, 1963; d. Jesús José and Guadalupe María Márquez; married; children: Joaquín, Elías. BS,MS in Biol. Scis., Stanford U., 1986; PhD in Biochemistry, U. Calif., Berkeley, 1991. Postdoctoral fellow Stanford (Calif.) U., 1991—94; asst. prof. biology San Francisco State U., 1994—99, assoc. prof. biology, 1999—2004, prof. biology, 2004—, microbial geneticist, 1994—. Contbr. articles to profl. jours., including Jour. Bacteriology and Jour. Biol. Chemistry. Motivational spkr. to minority students, No. Calif., 1994—; mentor to UC San Fransico Tchg. postdoctoral fellows, 2002—. Named Hispanic Powerhitter, Hispanic Engr. mag., 2003; named one of 100 Most Influential Hispanics, Hispanic Bus. mag., 1998. Mem.: AAAS (Mentor award 2001), Soc. Advancement of Chicanos and Native Americans in Sci. (e-mentor for K-12 educators 2001—, bd. dirs. 1989—91), Am. Soc. Microbiology. Office: San Francisco State U Dept Biology 1600 Holloway Ave San Francisco CA 94132 E-mail: marquez@sfsu.edu.

**MARQUIS, KATHLEEN,** librarian, archivist; b. Chgo., Sept. 20, 1954; d. Stewart Dent and Ruth Marquis; m. Mark A. Greene. BA in History, U. Mich., Ann Arbor, Mich., 1977; MLS, Simmons Coll., Boston, Mass., 1981. Archival asst. History Women in Am. Arthur and Elizabeth Schlesinger Libr., Cambridge, Mass., 1978—81; reference archivist MIT, Cambridge, 1981—90; reference assoc. Minn. Hist. Soc., St. Paul, 1990—98; head reference and access Bentley Hist. Libr. U. Mich., Ann Arbor, Mich., 1999—2002; adult svcs. libr. Albany County Pub. Libr., Laramie, Wyo., 2002—. Contbr. articles to profl. jours. Mem.: Wyo. Territorial Prison Hist. Assn. (sec. 2006—), Midwest Archives Conf. (mem. coun. 2002—05), Soc. Am. Archivists (co-chmn. program com. 1984—2005, chmn. nominating com.). Office Phone: 307-721-2580.

**MARR, CARMEL CARRINGTON,** retired state official; b. Bklyn., June 23, 1921; d. William Preston and Gertrude Clementine (Lewis) Carrington; m. Warren Marr II, Apr. 11, 1948; children: Charles Carrington, Warren Quincy III. BA, Hunter Coll., 1945; JD, Columbia U., 1948. Bar: N.Y. 1948, U.S. Dist. Ct. (ea. dist.) N.Y. 1951, U.S. Dist. Ct. (so. dist.) N.Y. 1951. Clk. Dyer & Stevens, N.Y.C., 1948-49; pvt. practice N.Y.C., 1949-53; adviser legal affairs U.S. mission to UN, N.Y.C., 1953-67; sr. legal officer Office Legal Affairs UN Secretariat, 1967-68; mem. N.Y. State Human Rights Appeal Bd., 1971-91, N.Y. State Pub. Svc. Commn., 1971-86; cons. Gas. Rsch. Inst., 1987-91. Lectr. N.Y. Police Acad., 1963-67. Contbr. articles to profl. jours. Mem. Nat. Soc. Wom's. Com. Edn. and Employment of Women, 1963-64; mem. Nat. Gen. Svcs. Pub. Adv. Council, 1969-71; mem., former chmn. adv. coun. Gas. Rsch. Inst.; mem. chmn. tech. pipeline safety standards Dept. Transp., 1979-85; former mem. task force Fed. Energy Regulatory Commn. and EPA to examine PCBs in gas supply system; past chmn. gas com. Nat. Assn. Regulatory Utility Commrs.; past pres. Great Lakes Conf. Pub. Utilities Commrs., mem. exec. com.; mem. UN Devel. Corp., 1969-72; bd. dirs. Amistad Rsch. Ctr., New Orleans, 1970—, chmn. bd. dirs., 1981-94; bd. dirs. Bklyn. Soc. Prevention Cruelty to Children, Nat. Arts Stblzn. Fund, 1984-93, hon. bd. mem., 1998, Prospect Park Alliance, 1987-98; bd. visitors N.Y. State Sch. Girls, Hudson, 1964-71; mem. exec. bd. Plays for Living,

N.Y.C., 1968-75; pres. bd. dirs. Billie Holiday Theatre, 1972-80; mem. nat. adv. coun. Hampshire Coll.; pres.'s coun. Tulane U., 1988-95. Mem. Phi Beta Kappa, Alpha Chi Alpha, Alpha Kappa Alpha. Republican. Episcopalian.

**MARR, DANIEL G.,** food products executive; Divsn. v.p., N. Tex. Coca-Cola Enterprises, 1988—92, divsn. v.p., gen. mgr., E. Tex., 1992—96, v.p., mktg., 1996—2000, sr. v.p., chief customer officer, 2000—03, pres., N.Am. sales, 2003—. Office: Coca-Cola Enterprises 2500 Windy Ridge Pkwy Atlanta GA 30339

**MARR, PETER,** actor, host, comedian; b. Nebr., Apr. 1, 1974; Actor: (films) Armadillo!, 1999, The Lack Of Luxury, Proverbial Justice, Letters To Lauren; (TV series) The Bold and the Beautiful, 2000, 2001; host (TV series) Kitchen Accomplished, Food Network, 2004, 10 Things You Must Know, DIY, All-Star Kitchen Makeover, 2005, My Celebrity Home, 2006, (TV special) Mobile Home Disaster, Warner Bros., 2005; performer: The Comedy Store, Improv Olympic West.*

**MARR, PHEBE ANN,** retired historian, educator; b. Mt. Vernon, NY, Sept. 21, 1931; d. John Joseph and Lillian Victoria (Henningsen) Marr. BA, Barnard Coll., N.Y.C., 1953; PhD, Harvard U., Cambridge, Mass., 1967. Rsch. assoc. ARAMCO, Dhahran, Saudi Arabia, 1960-62; dir. mid. east program Fgn. Svc. Inst., 1963-66; asst. prof. Stanislaus State Coll., Turlock, Calif., 1970-71, assoc. prof., 1971-74; assoc. prof. history U. Tenn., Knoxville, 1974-85, chmn. Asian studies program, 1977-79. Cons. ARAMCO, 1979-83. Author: The Modern History of Iraq, 1985, 2d edit., 2003; co-editor: Riding the Tiger: Middle East Challenge After the Cold War, 1993; contbr. articles to profl. jours. Bd. dirs. Mid. East Policy Coun., 2004. Rsch. fellow Mid. East Ctr., Harvard U., Cambridge, Mass., 1968-70, sr. fellow Nat. Def. U., Washington, 1985-97, Woodrow Wilson Ctr. fellow, 1998-99, Coun. on Fgn. Rels., U.S. Inst. Peace fellow, 2004-06. Mem. Mid. East Inst., Mid. East Studies Assn. Home and Office: 2902 18th St NW Washington DC 20009-2954 Office Phone: 202-462-3580. Personal E-mail: marrphebe@aol.com.

**MARR, ROBERT BRUCE,** physicist, researcher; b. Quincy, Mass., Mar. 25, 1932; s. Ralph George and Ethel (Beals) M.; m. Nancy Rosa Parkes, June 12, 1954; children: Richard, Jonathan, Rebecca. BS, MIT, 1953; MA, Harvard U., 1955, PhD, 1959. Research asso. Brookhaven Nat. Lab., Upton, NY, 1959-61, asso. physicist, 1961-64, physicist, 1964-68, sr. physicist, 1968-95, assoc. chmn. applied math. dept., 1974-75, 83-88, chmn., 1975-78; ret., 1995. Adj. assoc. prof. Columbia U., 1969; lectr. SUNY at Stony Brook, 1969-70, vis. prof. dept. computer sci., 1979; guest mathematician U. Colo., 1970; vis. mathematician Lawrence Berkeley Lab., 1978; cons. NSF, NIH, 1969—. Contbr. articles to profl. jours. Served with U.S. Army, 1958-59. NSF grantee, 1974 Mem. Soc. for Magnetic Resonance in Medicine (trustee 1982-87, sec.-treas. 1984-86, treas. 1986-87). Home: 368 Private Rd Patchogue NY 11772-5827

**MARRA, THOMAS M.,** investment company executive; Grad., St. Bonaventure U. Assoc. actuary Hartford Fin. Svcs. Group, 1980, v.p., dir. of individual annuities, 1990—94, head, individual life and annuities divsn., 1994—98, exec. v.p., 1996—2000, sr. v.p., 1994—96, dir. investment products divsn., 1998—2000, exec. v.p., 2000—, COO, Hartford Life, 2000—, pres., Hartford Life, 2002—. Mem., office of the chmn. Hartford Fin. Svcs. Group, 2000—; past chmn. Nat. Assn. of variable annuities. Mem. Bushnell Ctr. for the Performing Arts. Fellow: Soc. of Actuaries; mem.: Am. Acad. of Actuaries. Office: Hartford Financial Services Group Hartford Plaza 690 Asylum Ave Hartford CT 06115

**MARRACK, PHILIPPA CHARLOTTE,** immunologist, researcher; b. Ewell, Eng., June 28, 1945; m. John Kappler, 1974; children: Kate, Jim. BA, U. Cambridge, 1967, PhD in Biology, 1970. Post-doctoral fellow, lab. rschr. U. Calif., San Diego, 1971-73; post-doctoral rschr. fellow U. Rochester, NY, 1973-79, assoc. prof. NY, 1974-75, asst. prof. immunology NY, 1975-79, assoc. prof. NY, 1980-85; prof. dept. microbiology and immunology U. Colo. Health Scis. Ctr., Denver, 1988—94, prof. integrated dept. of Immunology, 1994—, prof., dept. biochemistry and molecular biology, prof. medicine; head, div. of basic immunology Nat. Jewish Ctr. for Immunology and Respiratory Medicine, Denver, 1988—90; prof. dept. biophysics, biochemistry and genetics U. Colo. Health Scis. Ctr., Denver, 1985-88; head, div. of Basic Immunology Nat. Jewish Medical and Rsch. Ctr., Denver, 1998—99, sr. faculty mem., Integrated Dept. of Immunology; investigator Kappler and Marrack Rsch. Lab. Howard Hughes Med. Inst., Chevy Chase, Md., 1986—. Mem. dept. medicine Nat. Jewish Hosp. and Rsch. Ctr., Denver, 1979—. Contbr. articles to profl. jours.; mem. editl. bds. Cell, Science, and Journal of Immunology. Served on panels for Am. Cancer Soc., US NIH, Burroughs Wellcome Fund. Recipient Cancer Rsch. award Cancer Rsch. Inst., 1991, Wellcome Found. lecturer Royal Soc., 1990, Paul Ehrlich and Ludwig Darmstädter prize, 1993, Louisa Gross Horwitz prize, 1994, Women's Excellence Scis. award Fedn. Am. Socs. Exptl. Biology, 1995, Women in Sci. award, L'Oreal-UNESCO, 2004. Mem. NAS, Royal Soc., Am. Assn. Immunologists (pres. 2000-2001, Lifetime Achievement award, 2003), Brit. Soc. Immunology, Internat. Union of Immunological Societies (past pres.). Office: Howard Hughes Med Inst Natl Jewish Med and Rsch Ctr 1400 Jackson St 5th fl Goodman Bldg Denver CO 80206*

**MARRAM, ELLEN R.,** investment company executive; BS, Wellesley Coll., 1968; MBA, Harvard U., 1970. Pres. grocery divsn. Nabisco, 1987—88; pres., CEO Nabisco Biscuit Co., 1988—93, Tropicana & Tropicana Beverage Corp., 1993—98; exec. v.p. Seagram Ltd., 1998—99; pres., CEO EfdCon, Stamford, Conn., 1999; mng. dir. N. Castle Partners, 2000—. Bd. dirs. Ford Motor Co., N.Y. Times Co., Eli Lilly and Co. Bd. dirs. WJ Presbyn. Hosp., Lincoln Ctr. Theater Families and Work Inst. City Meals on Wheels. Office: N Castle Partners 138 E Putnam Ave Greenwich CT 06830

**MARRELLA-DAVIS, CHRISTY ELIZABETH,** history educator; b. Camden, NJ, July 27, 1972; d. Richard and Rosanna Marrella; m. Steven Gary Davis, Jr., Apr. 3, 2004. BA, La Salle U., 1994; MA, Villanova U., 2005. Cert. social studies tchr. NJ, 1994. Tchr. history Samuel S. Yellin Sch., Stratford, NJ, 1994—96, Beck Mid. Sch., Cherry Hill, NJ, 1996—99, Rosa Internat. Mid. Sch., Cherry Hill, NJ, 1999—. Mem. history curriculum com. Cherry Hill Bd. of Edn., NJ, 1997—2003. Leadership scholarship, W.W. Smith Found., 1991-1994, China Study Travel grant, Tchg. East Asia, 2001, James Madison fellow for NJ, James Madison Fellowship, 2003-2005. Mem.: Nat. Coun. For Social Studies. Roman Catholic. Avocations: golf, traveling, singing, running. Home: 311 Tearose Ln Cherry Hill NJ 08003 Office: Cherry Hill Bd of Edn 45 Ranaldo Terr Cherry Hill NJ 08035 Office Phone: 856-429-5600.

**MARRERO, VICTOR,** federal judge, lawyer; b. Santurce, PR, Sept. 1, 1941; s. Ezequiel Marrero and Josefina (Sanabria) Santos M.; m. Veronica M. White, Dec. 1987. BA, NYU, 1964; LLB, Yale U., 1968; postgrad. (Fulbright scholar), U. Sheffield, Eng., 1966-67. Bar: N.Y. 1982. Exec. dir. NYC Dept. City Planning, 1973-74; spl. counsel to comptroller City of N.Y., 1974-75; 1st asst. counsel to gov. State of N.Y., Albany, 1975-76; chmn. NYC City Planning Commn., 1976-77; commr. N.Y. State Divsn. Housing and Cmty. Renewal, N.Y., 1977-79; under-sec. HUD, Washington, 1979-81; ptnr. Tufo & Zuccotti, N.Y.C., 1982-85, Brown & Wood, N.Y.C., 1986-93; amb., U.S. rep. UN Econ. and Social Coun., N.Y.C., 1993-97; amb., permanent U.S. rep. OAS, Dept. State, Washington, 1998-99; judge U.S. Dist. Ct. (So. Dist.), NYC, 1999—. Vis. lectr. Yale U. Law Sch., New Haven, 1986, Columbia U. Law Sch., 1991-93. Trustee N.Y. Pub. Libr., 1989—, SUNY, Albany, 1985-93, Cooper Union, 1989-93, Consolidated Edison Co., 1988-93; bd. dirs. P.R. Legal Def. and Edn. Fund., N.Y.C., 1972-86, N.Y. Telephone Co., 1987-93; chmn. N.Y. State Chief Judge's Com. to Improve Availability of Legal Svcs., 1988-90. Mem. ABA (Pro Bono Publico award 1993), N.Y. State Bar Assn. (Root/Stimson Pub. Svc. award 1992), Assn. Bar City N.Y. (mem.

com. modern cts. 1980-93, exec. com. 1986-89, judiciary com. 1991-92, v.p. 1992-93). Office: US Courthouse 500 Pearl St Rm 660 New York NY 10007-1502 Office Phone: 212-805-6374.

**MARRETT, CAROLINE DENISE,** special education educator; b. Queens, NY, Jan. 15, 1962; d. Cyril Pratt, Sr. and Jennie Pratt; m. Phillip Marston Marrett, Oct. 10, 1987; children: Phillip Charles, Dwayne Anthony, Sylvia Nicole. BS in Elem. Edn., SUNY, Buffalo, 1984; MA in Learning Disabilities, Columbia U., NYC, 1986, MA in Spl. Edn., 1986; diploma in sch. administrn. & supervision, St. John's U., Queens, 2003; student in Spl. Edn., U. Ctrl. Fla., Orlando, 2004—. Tchr. borough transition coord. office of supt. of Manhattan high schs. HS of Graphic Communication Arts, NYC, 1982—93; tchr. trainer specialist Spl. Edn. Tchr. Resource Ctr., Queens, 1993—98; administrator Law, Govt. & Cmty. Svc. HS, Queens, NY, 1998—99; spl. edn. tchr. Volusia County Sch. Bd., Deltona, Fla., 2000—02, Volusia County Pub. Sch. Bd., Deltona, Fla., 2003—04. Student mem. Coun. for Exceptional Children, Arlington, Va. Scholar Project Lead, U. Ctrl. Fla., 2004—, The Holmes Partnership, 2004—. Mem.: Phi Delta Kappa Internat., Am. Ednl. Rsch. Assn., Coun. Exceptional Children. Home: 1631 N Normandy Blvd Deltona FL 32725 Personal E-mail: cmarrett@mail.ucf.edu.

**MARRETT, CORA B.,** science educator; b. Richmond, Va., June 15, 1942; d. Horace Sterling and Clora Ann (Boswell) Bagley; m. Louis Everard Marrett, Dec. 24, 1968. BA, Va. Union U., 1963; MS, U. Wis., 1965, PhD, 1968. Asst. prof. U. N.C., Chapel Hill, 1968-69; from asst. to assoc. prof. Western Mich. U., Kalamazoo, 1969-73; from assoc. to full prof. U. Wis., Madison, 1973-97; asst. dir. NSF, Arlington, Va., 1992-96; provost, vice chancellor for acad. affairs U. Mass., Amherst, 1997—2001; sr. v.p. for acad. affairs U. Wis. System, 2001—. Mem. sci. adv. panel U.S. Army, Washington, 1976-77; mem. Naval Rsch. Adv. Com., Washington, 1978-81, Pres. Commn. on the Accident at Three Mile Island, 1979; bd. govs. Argonne (Ill.) Nat. Lab., 1983-90, 96-99. Editor: Research in Race and Ethnic Relations, 1988, Gender and Classroom Interaction, 1990. Resident fellow NAS, 1973-74; fellow Ctr. for Advanced Study in Behavioral Scis., 1976-77. Mem. AAAS, ASA, Phi Kappa Phi. Avocations: reading, travel, film appreciation. Home: 7517 Farmington Way Madison WI 53717 Office: Office Acad Affairs U of Wisconsin System 1620 Van Hise Hall Madison WI 53706 Office Phone: 608-262-3826. E-mail: cmarrett@uwsa.edu.

**MARRETT, MICHAEL MCFARLENE,** chaplain; b. Greenwich Town, Surrey, Jamaica, Oct. 7, 1935; s. Kenneth Louis and Ivy Lynmae (McFarlane) M.; m. Margery Eva Mugford, Jan. 29, 1984. Cert. gen. ordination, Oxford (Eng.) U., 1961; cert. edn. in English lang., London U., 1967; MDiv. Gen. Theol. Sem., 1969, STM, 1970, N.Y. Theol. Sem., 1972; postgrad., Princeton Theol. Sem., 1972-73, Columbia U., 1973-75; BA, Fordham U., 1974; postgrad., The Coll. of Preachers, 1979, Yale U., 1979-81; PhD, NYU, 1980; MS, So. Conn. State U., 1982. Lic. pastoral counselor, Md.; cert. profl. mental health clergy, chaplain and fellow of Coll. Chaplains; nat. cert. bereavement facilitator Am. Acad. Bereavement; diplomate Am. Psychotherapy Assn. Staff chaplain St. Elizabeths Hosp., Washington, 1986-99; ret., 1999. Author: The Lambeth Conferences and Women Priests, 1981. Appointed commissary Diocese of Akoko, West Africa, 1984, appointed hon. canon St. Stephens Cathedral, 1987. Mem. Assn. Clin. Pastoral Edn. (clin.), Am. Assn. Christian Counselors, Am. Assn. Family Counselors. Home: PO Box 48232 1902 C St NE Washington DC 20002-6714

**MARRIN, CHARLES AINSWORTH STAVELEY,** cardiovascular and thoracic surgeon, educator; b. Santa Monica, Calif., Dec. 19, 1947; s. Charles Ainsworth and Cecilia Margaret (Staveley) M.; m. Marian Anthon Bruen, Apr. 19, 1976; 1 child, Minet A. B. MB, BS, U. London, Royal Free Hosp. Sch. Medicine, London, 1971. Ho. physician Willesden Gen. Hosp., London, 1971, Royal Free Hosp., London, 1972; resident in gen. surgery St. Luke's Hosp. Ctr., N.Y.C., 1973-76, chief resident, 1976-77, fellow in cardiovasc. surgery, asst. physician, 1977; fellow in cardiovasc. surg. rsch. Coll. Physicians and Surgeons, Columbia U., N.Y.C., 1978; resident in cardiovasc. and thoracic surgery Columbia-Presbyn. Med. Ctr., N.Y.C., 1979-80, chief resident, 1980; staff surgeon Hitchcock Clinic and Dartmouth-Hitchcock Med. Ctr., Lebanon, N.H., 1981—; prof. surgery Dartmouth (N.H.) U. Med. Sch., 2000—. Author chpts. to books; contbr. articles to profl. jours. Co-prin. investigator Am. Heart Assn., 1993—; co-investigator U.S. Agy. for Health Care Policy and Rsch., 1993—. Fellow ACS, Am. Coll. Cardiology, Am. Coll. Chest Physicians; mem. AMA, Am. Assn. Thoracic Surgery, Soc. Thoracic Surgeons.

**MARRINAN, SUSAN FAYE,** lawyer; b. Vermillion, SD, May 29, 1948; BA, U. Minn., 1969, JD, 1973. Bar: Minn. 1973, Wis. 1973. Atty. Carlson Cos., Plymouth, Minn., 1973-74, Prudential Ins. Co., Mpls., 1974-75; v.p., gen. counsel, corp. sec. H.B. Fuller Co., St. Paul, 1977—90; gen. counsel, sec. Snap-On, Inc., Kenosha, Wis., 1990—92, v.p., gen. counsel, sec., 1992—2004, v.p., sec., chief legal officer, 2004—. Fundraiser Am. Cancer Soc.; bd. dirs. Family Svcs. St. Paul, Childrens Theatre Co. Mem. Am. Assn. Corp. Counsel (bd. dirs. Minn. chpt. 1986—), Am. Corp. Counsel Assn. (bd. dirs. 1997-02). Republican. Avocation: running. Office: Snap-On Inc 2801 80th St Kenosha WI 53141

**MARRIOTT, DAVID W.,** lawyer; b. Salt Lake City, June 10, 1967; BA magna cum laude, Brigham Young Univ., 1991; JD, NYU, 1994. Bar: NY 1995. Law clk., Hon. Albert J. Engel US Ct. of Appeals, 6th Cir.; law clk., Hon. Eugene F. Lynch US Dist. Ct., No. Dist. Calif.; assoc. Cravath Swaine & Moore LLP, NYC, 1996—2003, ptnr., litig., 2003—. Staff editor NYU Jour. Internat. Law and Politics. Office: Cravath Swaine & Moore LLP Worldwide Plz 825 Eighth Ave New York NY 10019-7475 Office Phone: 212-474-1430. Office Fax: 212-474-3700. Business E-Mail: dmarriott@cravath.com.

**MARRIOTT, JOHN W., III,** hotel executive; BS, Univ. Utah. 1985. With Marriott Internat. Inc., Washington, 1976—, sr. v.p. mid-Atlantic region, exec. v.p. global sales & mktg., bd. dir., 2002—, exec. v.p. lodging, 2003—05, vice chmn., 2005—. CEO J.W.M. Family Enterprises, 2006. Named one of Forbes Richest Americans, 2006. Office: Marriott internat Inc Marriott Dr Washington DC 20058*

**MARRIOTT, JOHN WILLARD, JR.,** lodging and senior living executive; b. Washington, Mar. 25, 1932; s. John Willard and Alice (Sheets) M.; m. Donna Garff, June 29, 1955; children: Deborah, Stephen Garff, John Willard, David Sheets. BS in Banking and Fin., U. Utah, 1954. V.p. Marriott Hot Shoppes Inc., 1959-64, exec. v.p. bd. dirs., 1964; pres. Marriott Corp., 1964—, CEO, 1972—; chmn. bd. Marriott Internat., Inc. (formerly Marriott Corp.), 1985—. Bd. dirs. GM, U.S.-Russia Bus. Coun., Host Marriott Svcs. Corp., Naval Acad. Endowment Trust. Trustee Nat. Geog. Soc.; mem. nat. adv. bd. Boy Scouts Am.; mem. Bus. Coun., Bus. Roundtable.; exec. com. World Travel and Tourism Coun. Lt. USNR, 1954-56. Recipient Bus. Leader of Yr. award, Georgetown U. Sch. Bus. Administrn., 1984, Svc. Above Self award, Rotary Club at JFK Internat. Airport, 1985, Am. Mgr. of Yr. award, Nat. Mgmt. Assn., 1985, Golden Chain award, Nations's Restaurant News, 1985, Hall of Fame award, Consumer Digest Mag., 1985, Citizen of Yr. award, Boy Scouts of Am., 1986, Restaurant Bus. Leadership award, Restaurant Bus. Mag., 1986, Gold Plate award, Am. Acad. Achievement, 1986, Hall of Fame, Am. Hotel and Motel Assn., 1986, Hall of Fame award, Culinary Inst. of Am., 1987, Hospitality Exec. of Yr. award, Pa. State U., 1987, Bronze winner in Fin. World's Chief Exec. Officers award, 1988, Silver Plate award Lodging Hospitality Mag., 1988, Chief Exec. Officer of Yr. Chief Exec. Officer Mag., 1988, Signature award CA chpt. Nat. Multiple Sclerosis, 1988, Excellence Cmty. award Suburban Md., 1993, Silver Plate award Internat. Foodsvc. Mfrs. Assn., 1993, Good Scout award Boy Scouts Am. Greater N.Y. Coun., 1990, Trendsetter award Foodsvc. Cons. Soc., 1989

Mem. Conf. Bd., U.S. C. of C., Bald Peak C.C. (N.J.), Avenel Golf Club, Sigma Chi. Mem. LDS Ch. Clubs: Burning Tree (Washington), Met. (Washington). Office: Marriott Intl Inc 1 Marriott Dr Washington DC 20058-0001*

**MARRIOTT, MARCIA ANN,** business and economics educator, health facility administrator; b. Rochester, N.Y., Mar. 21, 1947; d. Coyne and Alice (Schleper) M.; children: Brian, Jonathan. AA, Monroe C.C., Rochester, 1967; BS, SUNY, Brockport, 1970, MA, 1975; PhD, S.W. U. La., 1985. Program adminstr. N.Y. Dept. of Labor, N.Y.C., 1970-75; employment mgr. Rochester Gen. Hosp., 1975-77, salary adminstr., 1982-98, compensation mgr., 1996—; corp. dir. wage and salary dept. Gannett Newspapers, Rochester, 1977-80; compensation and benefits adminstr. Sybron Corp., Rochester, 1980-82; compensation mgr. Rochester Gen. Hosp., 1996—; dir. compensation Via Health, Rochester, 1995-98; pres. Compensation Link, 1997—; prof. Grad. Sch. Bus. Rochester Inst. Tech., 1998—2003, SUNY, Brockport, 1998—2003. Instr. N.Y. State Sch. Indsl. Rels., Cornell U., N.Y.C., 1976-79; assoc. prof. Rochester Inst. Tech., 1978—, Monroe C.C., 1981—, dir. career adv. coun., 1989—; assoc. prof. SUNY, Brockport; assoc. prof. Nazareth Coll., 1998; dir. Rochester Presbyn. Home, Health-91, 96—, v.p. bd. dirs., 1997-98, pres. bd. dirs., 1998—; dir. area hosp. coun. Kidney Svc. Ctrs., Rochester, 1988-91; cons. in field. Author: (pamphlets) Guideline for Writing Job Descriptions, 1983, (manual) Career Planning Manual, 1985, (booklet) Guideline for Writing Criteria-Based Job Descriptions, 1988, Skill-based Job Descriptions: A Quality Approach, 1994, Redesigning the Performance Appraisal Process, 1996. Campaign mgr. Carter Campaign Commn., Rochester, 1975; mem. coun. Messiah Luth. Ch., Rochester, 1991-94. Davenport-Hatch Found. grantee, 1973, Wegman Found. grantee, 1975. Mem. Am. Compensation Assn., Single Adopted Parents Group (pres. 1988-93). Avocations: tennis, hiking, reading, swimming, skiing. Office: Rochester Gen Hosp 1425 Portland Ave Rochester NY 14621-3095

**MARRIOTT, MICHEL,** reporter; married; 3 children. BA in Philosophy and Journalism, Morehead State U., 1976; MA in Journalism, Northwestern U., 1977. Reporter Marion Chronicle-Tribune, Ind., 1977, Courier-Jour., Louisville, Washington Post, Phila. Daily News; gen. editor Newsweek mag., NY, 1994—95; reporter NY Times, 1987—94, reporter, Style Dept., 1995—98, tech. reporter Circuits Sect., 1998—. Adj. prof. Grad. Sch. Journalism Columbia U.; prof., Dept. Communication, Film & Video City Coll. NY; frequent contbr. Ann. Men's Issue Essence mag.; contbr. Esquire mag.; prof. Antioch Writer's Workshop. Author: Hedz; co-author: (screenplays) (based on his NY Times series) New Jersey Drive, 1995 (Pulitzer prize nominee). Recipient Outstanding Achievement award, Nat. Assn. Black Journalists, 1981; Nieman fellow, Harvard U., 2002. Office: Circuits Sect NY Times 229 West 43rd St New York NY 10036 Office Phone: 212-556-7803. Office Fax: 212-556-1448. E-mail: marr@nytimes.com.*

**MARRIOTT, RICHARD EDWIN,** hotel and contract services executive; b. Washington, Jan. 9, 1939; s. John Willard and Alice Taylor (Sheets) M.; m. Nancy Peery, Mar. 20, 1962; children: Julie Ann, Sandra, Karen, Mary Alice. BS, U. Utah, 1963; MBA, Harvard U., 1965. With Marriott Corp., Washington, 1965—, group v.p. restaurant ops., 1976-78, corp. group v.p. restaurant and theme park ops., 1979-84, exec. v.p., 1984, vice chmn., 1986—92; chmn. Host Marriott Corp., 1992—. Chmn. bd. dirs. Media Corp., 1973—; bd. dirs. Riggs Nat. Bank of Washington. Mem. Nat. Commn. Against Drunk Driving; trustee Boys Clubs Am., Dole Found. for Employemnt of Persons with Disabilities; chmn. Marriott Found. People with Disabilities. Named one of Forbes Richest Americans, 2006. Mem. Nat. Restaurant Assn., Sigma Chi. Mem. Lds Ch. Office: Host Marriott Corp Suite 1500 6903 Rockledge Dr Bethesda MD 20817*

**MARRIS, ROY O.,** agriculturist, consultant; b. Bogata, Tex., Oct. 6, 1922; s. Dick and Clara E. Marris; m. Myrle A. Marris, May 7, 1927; children: Dicky O., Donna, Dwight. MS, Sam Houston State U., 1951. Cert. real estate appraiser, Tex. Tech., 1953, Tex. A & M, 1966. Technician soil conservation USDA, Palestine, Tex., 1953—64, supr. Farmers Home Adminstrn. Nacogdoches, Tex., 1964—65, Ft. Worth, 1965—72; advisor to young farmers and ranchers Bogata, 1972—. Mem. Civil Def. Orgn., Ft. Worth, 1965—72; former membership chmn. Farm Bur. Tex.; former county chmn. Dem. Primary, Red River, Tex., former election judge; deacon First Bapt. Ch., 1954—. With U.S. Army, 1942—45. Mem.: Agr. Workers. Democrat. Baptist. Achievements include research in program on animal breeding to determine the sex of animal at breeding time. Avocations: raising and training spotted horses, cow dogs. Home: 13614 Farm Rd 410 S Bogata TX 75417-3652

**MARRO, ANTHONY JAMES,** retired newspaper editor; b. Middlebury, Vt., Feb. 10, 1942; s. Francis James and Esther Martha (Butterfield) M.; m. Jacqueline Helen Cleary, June 5, 1965; 1 child, Alexandria. BA in History, U. Vt., 1965; MS in Journalism, Columbia U., 1968. Reporter Rutland (Vt.) Herald, 1964-67, Newsday, L.I., NY, 1968-74, chief Washington bur., 1979-81, mng. editor, 1981-86, exec. editor, 1986-87, editor, 1987—2003; reporter Newsweek, Washington, 1974-76, N.Y. Times, Washington, 1976-79. Co-recipient Pulitzer prizes for Pub. Service Reporting, 1970, 74.

**MARRON, DONALD BAIRD,** venture capitalist; b. Goshen, NY, July 21, 1934; m. Catherine D. Calligar. Student, Baruch Sch. Bus., 1949-51, 55-57. Investment analyst NY Trust Co., NYC, 1951-56, Lionel D. Edie Co., 1956-58; mgr. research dept. George O'Neill & Co., 1958-59; pres. D.B. Marron & Co. Inc., NYC, 1959-65. Mitchell Hutchins & Co. Inc. (merger with D.B. Marron & Co. Inc. 1965), NYC, 1965-69, pres., chief exec. officer, 1969-77; pres. PaineWebber Inc. (merger with Mitchell Hutchins & Co. Inc. 1977), NYC, 1977—80, CEO, 1980—2000, chmn. bd., 1981—2000; co-founder, former chmn. Data Resources, Inc., 1969—79; chmn. UBS Am., 2000—03; chmn., CEO, founder Lightyear Capital, LLC, NYC 2000— Dir NYSE 1974-81; bd. mem. Fannie Mae 2001-06, Shinsei Bank 1999-2005; chmn. Collegiate Funding Svcs. 2004-06; gov., vice chmn. Securities Industry Assn. 1974-77; gov. NASD 1997-2001. Chmn. Ctr. for Study of the Presidency; vice chmn. & former pres. bd. trustees Mus. of Modern Art, N.Y.C; mem. adv. bd. UBS Art Collection; mem. bd. overseers and mgrs. Meml. Sloan-Kettering Cancer Ctr.; trustee Charles A. Dana Found., Ctr. for Strategic & Internat. Studies (private sector co-chmn. Nat. Commn. on Retirement Policy); bd. dirs. NYC Partnership; mem. Govs.'s Sch. and Bus. Alliance Task Force, NY; former mem. Pres. Commn. on The Arts and The Humanities; former vice chmn. Calif. Inst. for the Arts. Named one of Top 200 Collectors, ARTnews Mag., 2004—. Mem.: Council on Fgn. Rels. Avocation: collector of 19th century European, modern & contemporary art. Office: Lightyear Capital LLC 11th Fl 375 Park Ave New York NY 10152 Business E-Mail: dbmarron@lycap.com.

**MARRON, PAMELA ANNE,** artist; b. Hackensack, N.J., Nov. 16, 1945; d. Chester Charles and Edith Anne Marron. AA, Parsons Sch. Design, N.Y.C., 1968; postgrad., Stanford U., Calif., 1970. Mem. art com. Stratton Art Festival, Stratton Mountain, Vt.; founder, art com. Elm St. Arts, Manchester, Vt. Archtl. Digest, 1998, Women Artists Calendar, 1999, one-woman shows include Stratton Arts Festival, 1974—94, Park McCullough House, Bennington, Vt., 1976, The Hoosac Sch., NY, 1978, Garden Gallery, Londonderry, Vt., 1980, AVA Gallery, Hanover, N.H., 1984, Castleton State Coll., Vt., 1986, Pindar Gallery, N.Y.C., 1987, Northstar Gallery Show, Stratton Mountain, 1989—2002, Avanti Gallery, Lambertville, N.J., 1990, Nicholas Roerich Mus., N.Y.C., 1990, Lotus Gallery, Cambridge, Mass., 1990, Vt. State House, Montpelier, 1992, Chaffee Art Ctr., Rutland, Vt., 1994, Elm St. Arts, Manchester Center, Vt., 1994, 95, 1994, 1995, Gallery Two, Woodstock, Vt., 1995, Olde Moon Gallery, Breckenridge, Colo., 1998, Grayson Gallery, Woodstock, 1999, Gardner Colby Gallery, Naples, Fla., 2001, Schenectady Mus., 2004, Haddad Lascano Gallery, Great Barrington, Mass., 2005, Redux Gallery, Dorset, Vt., 2005, Nancy Price Gallery, Jamaica, Vt., 2005, Doreset Theater Festival, 2005, Art at Vt. Ctr. of Art, 2006, So. Vt. Coll. Manchester Center, 1975, '79, 2006, Beside Myself Gallery, Arlington, Vt., 1982, 86, 90, Cove Gallery, Wellfleet, Mass., 1991, 97, Represented in permanent collections Lotus Corp., Omni Corp., N.Y.C., Yoder Brothers

Internat., Barherton, Ohio, numerous group exhbns. Recipient Max Beckman scholarship, 1967, 1968, Jurors award, Berkshire Mus., 1978, Stratton Art Festival, 1983, 1988, Jay Conaway award, 1987, 1990. Mem.: Vt. Coun. on Arts, So. Vt. Art Ctr. (art com., numerous art exhbns., Jurors award 1998). Avocations: singing, swimming, walking. Home: Box 563 Dorset VT 05251 Office Phone: 802-867-2246.

**MARRONE, PHILIP A.,** chemical engineer; b. Everett, Mass., Jan. 9, 1968; s. Robert F. and Carol A. Marrone. BS, Columbia U., NYC, 1990; MS, MIT, Cambridge, Mass., 1992, PhD, 1998. Mgr. Arthur D. Little, Inc., Cambridge, 1998—2002, FOCIS Assocs. (a Geo-Centers Co.), Newton, Mass., 2002—05; chem. engr. Sci. Applications Internat. Corp. (SAIC), Newton, 2005—. Contbr. chapters to books; editor: (workshop procs.) Supercritical Water Oxidation — Achievements and Challenges in Commercial Applications; contbr. articles to profl. jours. Named Class Valedictorian, Sch. Engring. and Applied Sci., Columbia U., 1990; recipient Charles F. Bonilla medal for Outstanding Academic Merit, 1990, Illig medal for high GPA and commendable proficiency in studies, 1990. Mem.: AIChE (mem. career and profl. svcs. com. Boston sect. 2005—), Sigma Xi. Avocations: road biking, hiking, kayaking, travel, skiing. Home: 20 Ship Ave #21 Medford MA 02155 Office: SAIC 7 Wells Ave Newton MA 02459 Office Phone: 617-618-4686. Office Fax: 617-618-4697. Business E-Mail: philip.a.marrone@saic.com.

**MARROW, TRACY See ICE-T**

**MARRS, JAMES F., JR., (JIM MARRS),** writer, journalist, educator; b. Ft. Worth, Dec. 5, 1943; s. James Marrs; m. Carol Ann Worcester, May 25, 1968; children: Cathryn Nova Ayn, Jayme Alistar. BA in Journalism, U. North Tex., 1966; postgrad., Tex. Tech. Coll., 1967-68. Editor/owner Magpie Mag., 1963-64; sports/news writer, cartoonist Denton (Tex.) Record Chronicle, 1965-66; reporter, copy editor, cartoonist and photographer Lubbock (Tex.) Avalanche-Jour., 1967-68; news and feature writer, cartoonist, photographer Lubbock Sentinel, 1968; reporter, feature writer, photographer, cartoonist Ft. Worth Star-Telegram, 1968-80; prodr. "Texas Roundup" Sammons Cable TV, Ft. Worth, 1982-83; scriptwriter Spindletop Prodns., Dallas, 1982-83; pub. rels. cons. The Mktg. Group, Dallas, 1982-83; pubr., co-owner The Springtown (Tex.) Current, 1983-84; comm. dir. Continental State Bank, Springtown, 1985-95. Editl. page editor Campus Chat, North Tex. State U., 1965-66; part-time copywriter, pub. rels. dir., cartoonist Jerre R. Todd & Assocs., 1972-74, dir. spl. projects, account exec., pub. rels. dir., 1980-81; editor/pub. and co-owner Cowtown Trails, Ft. Worth, 1983-84; faculty Ctr. Continuing Edn. U. Tex., Arlington, 1976—; comm. dir. N.E. HealthCare Ctr., Hurst, Tex., 1985-86. Author: Crossfire: The Plot That Killed Kennedy, 1989, Alien Agenda, 1997, Rule by Secrecy, 2000, Psi Spies, 2001, The War on Freedom, 2003, Inside Job, 2004; scriptwriter, dir. video: Fake, 1991, The Many Faces of Lee Harvey Oswald, 1992, Aurora, The Secret of Redgate, 2004, The Terror Conspiracy, 2006; contbr. articles to profl. jours. Prodr. Tex. Gridiron Show, Ft. Worth, 1978-79, dir., 1980; chmn. pub. info. subcom. Ft. Worth Mayor's Com. on Employment of Handicapped, 1979-82; co-chmn. Springtown Centennial Com., 1984; workshop tchr. Operation CLASP, Neighborhood Adv. Coun., Community Devel. Block Grant, City of Ft. Worth, 1984; community rels. cons. All Church Home for Children, Ft. Worth, 1984-95. With USAR, 1969-70. Recipient White Helmet award Ft. Worth Fire dept., 1969, 71, Assoc. Press writing awards, 1969-76, Nat. Writing award Aviation/Aerospace Writers Assn., 1972, Human Rights Leadership award Freedom Mag., 1993; named Arts and Entertainment Newsmaker of the Yr., Tex. Gridiron Club, 2003, Soc. Profl. Journalists, 1991. Mem. Tex. Mil. Hist. Soc., Springtown Optimist Club, Beta Sigma Phi, Sigma Delta Chi. Libertarian. Methodist. Avocation: civil war reenactor. Home and Office: Wise Comms PO Box 189 Springtown TX 76082-0189 Office Phone: 940-433-2916. Business E-Mail: jmarrs@ntws.net.

**MARS, FORREST E., JR.,** candy company executive; s. Forrest Mars Sr.; m. Virginia Cretella, Oct. 20, 1955 (div. Jan. 1990); children: Victoria B., Valerie A., Pamela D., Marijke E. Grad., Yale U., 1953. Chmn. bd. dirs., former CEO Mars Inc., Mc Lean, Va. Named one of World's Richest People, Forbes mag., 2006, Forbes Richest Americans, 2006. Office: Mars Inc 6885 Elm St Mc Lean VA 22101-3810*

**MARS, JACQUELINE BADGER,** food products executive; m. David Badger, 1961 (div.); 3 children; m. Harold Vogel, 1986 (div.). Degree in anthropology, Bryn Mawr Coll., 1961. Co-owner Mars, Inc., McLean, Va., 1973—, corp. v.p., 1990—. Trustee Bryn Mawr Coll.; bd. trustee mem.-at-large Washington Nat. Opera. Named one of World's Richest People, Forbes, 2000—, Forbes Richest Americans, 2006. Office: Mars Inc 6885 Elm St Mc Lean VA 22101

**MARS, JOHN FRANKLYN,** candy company executive; b. 1935; m. Adrienne Mars. Student, Yale U., 1957. Chmn. Kal Kan Foods Inc.; co-pres. Mars Inc., 1973—, CEO, 2000—. Named one of Forbes Richest Americans, 2006. Office: Mars Inc 6885 Elm St Mc Lean VA 22101

**MARSALIS, BRANFORD,** musician; b. Breaux Bridge, LA, Aug. 26, 1960; s. Ellis Marsalis. Student, So. U., 1978, Berklee Coll. Music, 1979-81. Mem. Art Blakey big band, 1980, Art Blakey's Jazz Messengers, 1981, Wynton Marsalis Quintet, 1982—85; incl. saxophonist, 1983—; bandleader The Tonight Show, L.A., 1992-95. Rec. Artist: (with Wynton Marsalis) Wynton Marsalis, 1981, Think of One, 1983, Hot House Flowers, 1984, Black Codes (From the Underground), 1985, Popular Songs...The Best of Wynton, 2001, (with Dizzy Gillespie) New Faces, 1984, Closer to the Source, 1984, (with Miles Davis) Decoy, 1984, (with Andy Jaffe) Manhattan Projects, 1984, (with Kevin Eubanks) Opening Nights, 1985, (with Carole King) City Streets, 1989, (with Art Blakey) Concord Jazz Heritage Series, 1979, Live at Montreux and Northsea, 1980, Keystone 3, 1982, Art Blakey (Timeless), 2001, (with Harry Connick Jr.) We Are in Love, 1990, Songs I Heard, 2001, (with James Taylor) New Moon Shine, 1991, Hourglass, 1997, New Moon Shine/Never Die Young..., 2000, (with Bela Fleck) Tales From the Acoustic Planet, 1994, Ten From Little Worlds, 2003, Little Worlds, 2003, (with Sting) Dream of the Blue Turtles, 1985, Bring on the Night, 1986, Nothing Like the Sun, 1987, The Soul Cages, 1991, Mercury Falling, 1996, Strange Fruit, 1997, Brand New Day, 1999, and appeared on many other recordings; (solo albums) Romances for Saxophone, 1986, Royal Garden Blues, 1986, Renaissance, 1986, Random Abstract, 1987, Trio Jeepy, 1988, Crazy People Music, 1990, The Beautiful Ones Are Not Yet Born, 1991, Bloomington, 1991, I Heard You Twice the First Time, 1992, Dark Keys, 1996, Requiem, 1999, Contemporary Jazz, 2000, Creation, 2001, Footsteps of Our Fathers, 2002, Romare Beardon Revealed (Live), 2003, Steep Anthology, 2004; appears on:(Guru) Jazzmatazz, 1995; composer various pieces including No Backstage Pass, Solstice, Waiting for Rain, (video) David and Goliath, 1993, (film) Bring on the Night, 1985, Throw Momma From The Train, 1987, School Daze, 1988, Mo' Better Blues, 1990, The Music Tells You, 1992, Mr. and Mrs. Loving, 1996, Eve's Bayou, 1997, Men in Black soundtrack, 1997, and others (TV movie) To My Daughter with Love, 1994. Winner Down Beat magazine's readers' poll, best soprano sax player, 1991-92; Grammy award, Best Pop Instrumental 1994 for "Barcelona Mona" with Bruce Hornsby.

**MARSALIS, WYNTON,** musician; b. New Orleans, Oct. 18, 1961; s. Ellis and Dolores Marsalis. Studied with John Longo; student, New Orleans Ctr. for Performing Arts, Berkshire Music Ctr., Juilliard Sch. Music, 1979-81. Music dir. Lincoln Ctr. Jazz Orch. Trumpet soloist with New Orleans Philharm. Orch., 1975, recitalist with New Orleans Ctr. for Creative Arts, 1979, played with various New Orleans and NYC orchs., with Art Blakey's Jazz Messengers, 1980—81, Herbie Hancock's V.S.O.P. quartet, formed own group, 1981, albums Fathers and Sons, 1982, Hummel/Haydn/L. Mozart Trumpet Concertos, 1983 (Grammy award, 1983), Wynton Marsalis (Grammy award), Handel, Purcell, Torelli, Fasch, Moler, Trumpet Concertos, 1983, Hot House Flowers, 1984, Black Codes from the Underground, 1985 (2 Grammy awards), J Mood, 1986, Carnaval, Marsalis Standard Time, Vol. 1, 1987

(Grammy award), Majesty of the Blues, 1989, Standard Time, Vol. 3, 1990, Intimacy Calling Standard Time, Soul Gestures in Southern Blue, Vols. 1, 2, 3, 1991, Blue Interlude, 1992, Citi Movement, 1993, In This House, On This Morning, 1994, Wynton Marsalis, 1995, Popular Songs: The Best Of Wynton Marsalis, 2001, All Rise, 2002, Unforgivable Blackness, 2004, The Magic Hour, 2004, Baroque Music For Trumpets, 2005, Trumpet Concertos, 2005, Live At The House Of Tribes, 2005, (with others) The All-American Hero, Live at Bubba's, In Gabriel's Garden, Sound of Jazz, All American Hero, 1996, Blood on the Fields, Jump Start and Jazz, Crescent City Xmas Card, 1997, Standard Time, Vol. 5: The Midnight Blues, One by One, Gold Collection, 1998. Named Jazz Musician of Yr., Downbeat readers' poll, 1982, 1984—86, 1989, Best Trumpet Player, Downbeat critics' poll, 1984, Acoustic Jazz Group of Yr., 1984, Best Trumpet Player, Downbeat readers' poll, 1985; named one of America's 25 Most Influential People, Time mag., 1996, 100 Most Influential People, Time Mag., 2006; recipient Grammy award for best solo jazz instrumental, 1983—85, Grammy award for best solo classical performance with orch., 1984—85, Grammy award for best jazz instrumental performance with group, 1985, 1987, musician of the Year, Down Beat Readers, 1992, Pulitzer prize for music, 1997, Algur H. Meadows award, Southern Meth. Univ. 1997, Nat. Medal of Arts, Nat. Endowment for the Arts, 2005, Most Influential Black Americans, Ebony mag., 2006.*

**MARSCHILOK, EDWARD,** music educator, musician; b. Troy, N.Y., Jan. 11, 1952; s. Edward Joseph and Dorothy Mathilda Marschilok; m. Linda June Crowell, June 23, 1979; children: Edward Andrew, Christine Ann. BMusEd, SUNY Coll., Potsdam; MSc, Syracuse U., N.Y., 1979; PhD, SUNY, Albany, 1993. Cert. sch. adminstr. and supr. N.Y., tchr. music K-12 N.Y. Tchr. and dir. music Cooperstown Ctrl. Schs., N.Y., 1974—77, 1978—84; dir. bands Hudson Falls Ctrl. Schs., 1984—86; assoc. in music edn. N.Y. State Edn. Dept., Albany, 1986—. Performing musician, 1974—; advisor N.Y. State Sch. Music Assn., 1986—; content reviewer and project coord. Theatre: A Resource Guide for Standards-Based Instrn., Music: A Resource Guide for Standards-Based Instrn. Tchr. religious edn. program Sacred Heart Ch., 2000—; v.p. and bd. mem. Empire State Youth Orch., Schenectady, NY, 1996—; bd. mem. Concerted Effort, N. Chatham, NY, 2002—. Named honoree for Advancing Edn. Theatre, N.Y. State Theatre Edn. Assn., 2003. Mem.: Am. Fedn. Musicians, N.Y. State Sch. Music Assn. (Disting. Svc. award 1996). Roman Catholic. Avocations: woodworking, motorcycling, auto repair. Office: NY State Edn Dept Rm 320EB 89 Washington Ave Albany NY 12234

**MARSCHKE, SEAN M.,** police captain, emergency management director; s. Gregory G. and Catherine A. Marschke; m. Laurel L. Lischka, Oct. 22, 1994; 1 child, Caylyn C. AS in Police sci., Waukesha County Tech. Coll., Pewaukee, Wis., 1991; BS in Criminal Justice Adminstrn., Mt. Senario Coll., Ladysmith, Wis., 2000; grad., Northwesten U. Sch. Police Staff and Command, 2001, FBI Law Enforcement Exec. Devel. Seminar, Wis., 2003, Nat. Fire Acad., Md., 2005. Cert. Unified Tactical Instr. Wis. Dept. Justice. Law enforcement ranger Wis. Dept. Natural Resources, Eagle, 1991—92; police officer Village of Merton, Wis., 1991—97; police capt. Village of Sturtevant (Wis.) Police Dept., 1992—; emergency mgmt. dir. Village of Sturtevant, 1998—. Tng. and mgmt. cons. Fall River (Wis.) Police Dept., 1996—; tng. cons. Randolph (Wis.) Police Dept., 1996—2006, Fox Lake (Wis.) Police Dept., 1996—2006, Rio (Wis.) Police Dept., 1996—2006. Appointee Racine County Local Emergency Planning Com., 2002—. Named Law Enforcement Officer of Yr., VFW Post # 9929, 1994; recipient Traffic Safety Enforcement award, Wis. Dept. Transp., 1996, Commendation, Office of Dir. of Pub. Safety, Village of Sturtevant, 1999, John Edgar Hoover Meml. award, Am. Police Hall of Fame, 2001, Commendation, Office of Dir. of Pub. Safety, Village of Sturtevant, 2001, 2002, Office of Dir. Pub. Safety, Village of Sturtevant, 2003. Mem.: NRA (life; police firearms instr. 1992—), Internat. Assn. Chiefs of Police, FBI Law Enforcement Exec. Devel. Assn. (assoc.), Internat. Law Enforcement Educators Trainers Assn. (assoc.), Nat. Fire Acad. Alumni Assn., Loyal Order of Moose (assoc.). Roman Catholic. Avocations: camping, hunting, boating, hiking. Office: Village of Sturtevant 2801 89th St Sturtevant WI 53177 Office Phone: 262-886-7229. Personal E-mail: sgtsmm@yahoo.com

**MARSCIARELLI, GARRY KENT See MARSHALL, GARRY**

**MARSDEN, BRIAN GEOFFREY,** astronomer; b. Cambridge, Eng., Aug. 5, 1937; arrived in US, 1959; s. Thomas and Eileen (West) M.; m. Nancy Lou Zissell, Dec. 26, 1964; children: Cynthia Louise, Jonathan Brian. BA, Oxford U., U.K., 1959, MA, 1963; PhD, Yale U., 1965. Rsch. asst. Yale U., New Haven, 1959-65; lectr. astronomy Harvard U., Cambridge, Mass., 1966-83; astronomer Smithsonian Astrophys. Obs., Cambridge, 1965—; assoc. dir. planetary scis. Harvard-Smithsonian Ctr. for Astrophysics, Cambridge, 1987—2002. Dir. Ctrl. Bur. Astron. Telegrams, 1968-2000, Minor Planet Ctr. Internat. Astron. Union, 1978—. Editor: The Earth-Moon System, 1966, The Motion, Evolution of Orbits and Origin of Comets, 1972, Catalogue of Orbits of Unnumbered Minor Planets, 1996, Catalogue of Cometary Orbits, 2003. Recipient Merlin medal Brit. Astron. Assn., 1965, Goodacre medal, 1979, Alcock lectureship, 2003; Van Biesbroeck award U. Ariz., 1989, Camus-Waitz prize Société astronomique de France, 1993, Dirk Brouwer award Am. Astron. Soc., 1995, Lacchini prize Unione Astrofili Italiani, 2001. Fellow Royal Astron. Soc. (Svc. award astronomy and geophysics 2006); mem. Am. Astron. Soc. (chmn. div. on dynamical astronomy 1976-78), Internat. Astron. Union (pres. commn. 1976-79, 00-03), Astron. Soc. Pacific, Sigma Xi. Office: Harvard-Smithsonian Ctr Astrophysics 60 Garden St Cambridge MA 02138-1516 Business E-Mail: bmarsden@cfa.harvard.edu.

**MARSDEN, GEORGE M.,** history professor, writer; b. Feb. 25, 1939; BA in History, Haverford Coll., 1959; BD, Westminster Theol. Sem., 1963; MA, Yale U., 1961, PhD in Am. Studies, 1965. Asst. in instrn. Yale U., 1964—65, instr., asst. and assoc. prof., 1965—74; prof. dept. history Calvin Coll., 1974—86, dir. MA in Christian Studies Program, 1980—83; prof. history of Christianity in Am. Duke U., The Divinity Sch., 1986—92; Francis A. McAnaney prof. history U. Notre Dame, Ind., 1992—. Vis. prof. ch. history Trinity Evang. Div. Sch., Deerfield, Ill., 1976—77; vis. prof. history U. Calif. Berkeley, California, 1986, Berkeley, 90. Author: The Evangelical Mind and the New School Presbyterian Experience, 1970, Fundamentalism and American Culture: The Shaping of Twentieth-Century Evangelicalism, 1980, Reforming Fundamentalism: Fuller Seminary and the New Evangelicalism, 1987, Religion and American Culture, 1990, Understanding Fundamentalism and Evangelicalism, 1991, The Soul of the American University, 1994, The Outrageous Idea of Christian Scholarship, 1997, Jonathan Edwards: A Life, 2003 (The Grawemeyer award in Religion, U. Louisville, 2005); assoc. editor: social scis. Christian Scholar's Rev., 1970—77; editor: (mem. sr. editl. bd.) The Reformed Jour., 1980—90. Fellow, Calvin Ctr. for Christian Scholarship, 1979—80, John Simon Guggenheim Meml. Found.; grantee, J. Howard Pew Freedom Trust, 1988—92; Younger Humanists fellow, NEH, 1971—72, Calvin Rsch. fellow, 1982—83. Mem.: Am. Soc. Ch. History (coun. mem. 1983—86, pres. 1992), Inst. for the Study of Am. Evangelicals (mem. adv. coun. 1989—). Office: Univ Notre Dame 321 Decio Faculty Hall Notre Dame IN 46556 E-mail: marsden.1@nd.edu.*

**MARSDEN, HERCI IVANA,** classical ballet artistic director; b. Omis-Split, Croatia, Dec. 2, 1937; d. Ante and Magda (Smith) Munitic; m. Myles Marsden, Aug. 10, 1957 (div. 1976); children: Ana, Richard, Mark.; m. Dujko Radovnikovic, Aug. 27, 1977; 1 child, Dujko. Student, Internat. Ballet Sch., 1955. Mem. corps de ballet Nat. Theatre, Split, 1954-58; founder Braecrest Sch. Ballet, Lincoln, RI, 1958—, State Ballet of R.I., Lincoln, Wood—, artistic dir., 1976—. Artistic dir. U. R.I. Classical Ballet, Kingston, 1966—, lectr., 1966—. Office: Brae Crest School of Ballet 52 Sherman Ave Lincoln RI 02865-3809 Office Phone: 401-334-2560. Business E-Mail: hmarsden@stateballet.com.

**MARSDEN, JAMES (JAMES PAUL MARSDEN),** actor; b. Stillwater, Okla., Sept. 18, 1973; m. Lisa Linde Marsden, July 22, 2000; children: Jack, Mary James. Student, Okla. State U. Actor: (films) No Dessert Dad, Til You

Mow the Lawn, 1994, Public Enemies, 1996, Campfire Tales, 1997, Disturbing Behavior, 1998, Gossip, 2000, X-Men, 2000, Sugar & Spice, 2001, Zoolander, 2001, Interstate 60, 2002, X2, 2003, The 24th Day, 2004, The Notebook, 2004, Heights, 2004, The Alibi, 2006, 10th & Wolf, 2006, X-Men: The Last Stand, 2006, Superman Returns, 2006; (TV films) In the Line of Duty: Ambush in Waco, 1993, Search and Resume, 1994, 919 Fifth Avenue, 1995, Gone in a Heartbeat, 1996, One the Edge of Innocence, 1997, Bella Mafia, 1997; (TV series) Boogies Diner, 1994, Second Noah, 1996—97, Ally McBeal, 2001—02. Office: BWR Pub Rels 9100 Wilshire Blvd Sixth Fl W Tower Beverly Hills CA 90212*

**MARSE, MELISSA J.,** music educator, concert pianist; d. John Pat and Linda Marse. MusB, U. of Tex., Austin, 1996; MusM, Yale U., New Haven, Conn., 1998; PhD in Music in Collaborative Piano, New Eng. Conservatory, Boston, 2002; postgrad, Juilliard Sch., N.Y.C., 1999. Prof. Houston Bapt. U., 2006—; artist in residence Kinkaid Sch., Houston; tchg. fellow Harvard U., Boston; adj. prof. Tex. State U., San Marcos. Pres. U. Tex. Fine Arts Coun. Austin. Musician (soloist): (Breckenridge Music Festival) Beethoven Emperor Concerto; piano soloist Aspen Music Festival, vocal coach faculty Mannes Art Song Inst., orchestral pianist (film music prodns.), soloist/chamber musician (worldwide). V.p. America's Dream Chamber Artists, N.Y., NY, 2003—06. Mem.: Tex. Music Educators Assn., Nat. Guild of Piano Tchrs. (assoc.), Music Tchres. Nat. Assn. (assoc.). Personal E-mail: mjmarse@yahoo.com.

**MARSEE, SUSANNE IRENE,** vocalist; b. San Diego, Nov. 26, 1941; d. Warren Jefferson and Irene Rose (Wills) Dowell; m. Mark J. Weinstein, May, 1987; 1 child, Zachary. Student, Santa Monica City Coll., 1961; BA in History, UCLA, 1964; postgrad., Juilliard, 1969, La. State U., 1991—92. Mem. voice faculty Am. Mus. and Dramatic Acad., N.Y.C., 1994-97, Pitts. Civic Light Opera Acad., 1997—2000, Duquesne U., 1998-2000; artist's lectr. Carnegie Mellon U., 2000—. Appeared with numerous U.S. opera cos., 1970—, including N.Y.C. Opera, San Francisco Opera, Boston Opera, Houston Grand Opera; appeared with fgn. cos., festivals, Mexico City Bellas Artes, 1973, 78, Canary Islands Co., 1976, Opera Metropolitana, Caracas, Venezuela, 1977, Spoleto (Italy) Festival, 1977, Aix en Provence Festival, France, 1977, Calgary, Alta., Can., 1986; recorded Tales of Hoffmann, ABC/Dunhill Records; TV appearances include Live from Lincoln Center, Turk in Italy, Cenerentola, 1989, Live from Wolftrap Roberto Devereux, 1975, Rigoletto, 1988, A Little Night Music, 1990, Marriage of Figaro, 1991, (PBS TV) Rachel, La Cubana; recs. and CDs Anna Bolena with Ramey, Scotto, Roberto Devereux with Beverly Sills, Roberto Devereux with Monserat Caballé Carreras, Tales of Hoffmann with Beverly Sills, Rigoletto with Quilico and Carreras; videotape Roberto Devereux with Beverly Sills. Recipient 2d place award Met. Opera Regional Auditions, 1968, San Francisco Opera Regional Auditions 1968; named winner Liederkranz Club Contest, 1970; Gladys Turk Found. grantee, 1968-69; Corbett Found. grantee, 1969-73; Martha Baird Rockefeller grantee, 1969-70, 71-72 Mem. AFTRA, Am. Guild Mus. Artists (past bd. dirs.), Nat. Assn. Tchrs. of Singing (past bd. dirs. for N.Y.). Democrat.

**MARSELLA, ANTHONY JOSEPH,** psychologist, educator; b. Cleve., Sept. 12, 1940; m. Joy Anne Marsella, June 22, 1963; children: Laura Joy, Gianna Malia. BA in Psychology with honors, Baldwin-Wallace Coll., 1962; PhD in Clin. Psychology, Pa. State U., 1968; PhD (hon.), U. Copenhagen, D (hon.), 1999. Lic. psychologist, Hawaii. Intern Worcester (Mass.) State Hosp., 1966-67; Fulbright rsch. scholar Alteneo de Manila U., Quezon City, The Philippines, 1967-68; postdoctoral rsch. scholar NIMH Culture-Mental Health Program, East-West Ctr., Honolulu, 1968-69; prof. psychology, dir. clin. studies program U. Hawaii, Honolulu, 1969—, dir. disaster and humanitarian assistance program, 2001—. Dir. WHO Psychiat. Rsch. Ctr., Honolulu; cons. Inst. Stress Rsch. of Karolinska Inst., Stockholm, Divsn. Mental Health, WHO, Geneva; v.p. acad. affairs U. Hawaii, 1985-89; vis. prof. Melbourne U., Monash U., Korea U., King George Med. Coll., India, Shanghai Psychiat. Inst., Ateneo de Manila U., Johns Hopkins U., Balt.; lectr. in field Author 10 books and over 150 articles to profl. jours. and chpts. to books; assoc. editor: Encyclopedia of Psychology; jour. reviewer. Recipient Medal of Highest Honor, Soka U., Tokyo, 1995. Fellow APA (Internat. Advancement of Psychology award 1997); mem. Hawaii Psychol. Assn., Amnesty Internat., Psi Chi, Omicron Delta Kappa, Sigma Xi. Home: 8925 Nesbit Lakes Dr Alpharetta GA 30022-4039

**MARSH, BENJAMIN FRANKLIN,** lawyer; b. Toledo, Apr. 30, 1927; s. Lester Randall and Alice (Smith) M.; m. Martha Kirkpatrick, July 12, 1952; children: Samuel, Elizabeth. BA, Ohio Wesleyan U., 1950; JD, George Washington U., 1954. Bar: Ohio 1955. Pvt. practice law, Toledo, 1955—88; assoc., ptnr. Doyle, Lewis & Warner, Toledo, 1955—71; ptnr. Ritter, Boesel, Robinson & Marsh, Toledo, 1971—88; mem. Marsh & McAdams, Maumee, 1988—98; pers. officer AEC, 1950—54; asst. atty. gen. State of Ohio, 1969—71; asst. solicitor City of Maumee, 1959—63, solicitor, 1963—92; mem. Marsh McAdams, Ltd., Maumee, 1999—. Mem. U.S. Fgn. Claims Settlement Commn., Washington, 1990-94; counsel N.W. Ohio Mayors and Mgrs. Assn., 1990-2000; regional bd. rev. Indsl. Commn. Ohio, Toledo, 1993-94; mem. Ohio Dental Bd., 1995-2000; trustee Corp. for Effective Govt., 1998-2003; mem. Ohio Elections Commn., 2001—, chmn. 2003-04 U.S. rep. with rank spl. amb. to 10th Anniversary Independence of Botswana, 1976; past pres. Toledo and Lucas County Tb Soc.; co-chmn. citizens for metro pks.; past mem. Judges Com. Notaries Pub.; former mem. Lucas County Bd. Elections; former chmn. bldg. commn. Riverside Hosp., Toledo; past trustee Com. on Rels. with Toledo, Spain; past chmn. bd. trustee Med. Coll., Ohio; past treas. Coglin Meml. Inst.; chmn. Lucas County Rep. Exec. Com., 1973-74; precinct commiteeman, Maumee, 1959-73; legal counsel, bd. dirs. Nat. Coun. Rep. Workshops, 1960-65; pres. Rep. Workshops, Ohio, 1960-64; alt. del. Rep. Nat. Conv., 1964; candidate 9th dist. U.S. Ho. of Reps., 1968; adminstrv. asst. to Rep. state chmn. Ray C. Bliss, 1954; chmn. Lucas County Bush for Pres.; 1980; co-chmn. Reagan-Bush Com. for Northwestern Ohio, 1980, vice chmn. fin. com. Bush-Quayle, 1992; co-chmn. Ohio steering com. Bush for Pres., mass. nat. steering com., 1988; del. Rep. Nat. Conv., 1988; past bd. dirs. Ohio Tb and Respiratory Disease Assn.; apptd. Ohio chmn. UN Day, 1980, 81, 82; adminstrv. asst. Legis. Svc. Commn., Columbus, 1954-55; mem. Lucas County Charter Commn., Toledo, 1959-60; vice-chmn. U.S. Nat. Commn. for UNESCO, mem. legal com., del. 17th gen. conf., Paris, 1972, U.S. observer meeting of nat. commns., Africa, 1974, Addis Ababa, Ethiopia; past mem. industry functional adv. com. on stds. trade policy matters; mem. nat. def. exec. res. Dept. Commerce; active Am. Bicentennial Presdl. Inauguration, Diplomatic Adv. Com. With USNR, 1945-46. Named Outstanding Young Man of Toledo, 1962. Mem. ABA, Maumee C. of C. (past pres.), UN Assn., Ohio State Bar Assn., Toledo Bar Assn., Ohio Mpcl. League (past pres.), Am. Legion (1st vice comdr. Toledo Post), Lucas County Maumee Valley Hist. Soc. (past pres.), Internat. Inst. Toledo, Ohio Mcpl. Attys. Assn. (past pres.), Orgn. Security and Cooperation in Europe (registration supr., adjudicator, elections supr. in Bosnia), West Lake Erie Hist. Soc. (Ohio Hist. Soc., Canal Soc. Ohio, Toledo Mus. Art, Ohio Wesleyan U. Alumni Assn. (past pres.), Ohio State Bar Found., Toledo Bar Found., Rotary, Toledo Country Club, Capitol Club Columbus, Torch Club Toledo (bd. dirs.), Navy League, Omicron Delta Kappa, Delta Sigma Rho, Theta Alpha Phi, Phi Delta Phi. Presbyterian. Home: 1624 Swan Creek Ln Toledo OH 43614 Office: 204 W Wayne St Maumee OH 43537-2125 Office Phone: 419-893-4880. Personal E-mail: bmarsh124@aol.com.

**MARSH, BRUCE DAVID,** geologist, educator; b. Munising, Mich., Jan. 4, 1947; s. William Roland and Audrey Jane (Steinhoff) M.; m. Judith Anne Congdon, Jan. 24, 1970; children: Hannah Eyre, William Noah. BS, Mich. State U., 1969; MS, U. Ariz., 1971; PhD, U. Calif.-Berkeley, 1974. Geologist, geophysicist Anaconda Co., Tucson, 1969-71; asst. prof. dept. earth/planet sci. Johns Hopkins U., Balt., 1974-78, assoc. prof., 1978-81, prof., 1981—. Chmn., 1989-93; vis. professor Calif. Inst. Tech., Pasadena, U. Maine, 1992-93; co-chmn. Gordon Rsch. Conf. on Inorganic Geochemistry, Holderness, N.H., 1983-84; advisor NASA, Washington, 1975-84, NSF, Washington, 1978-90, NRC, 1985-91; Hallimond lectr. Mineral. Soc. Great Britain and

Ireland, 1995. Assoc. editor Geology, 1981-83, Jour. Volcanology and Geothermal Rsch., 1978—, Jour. Petrology, 1986—; editor Jour. Volcanology and Geothermal Rsch., 1985—. Fellow Geol. Soc. Am. (assoc. editor Bulletin 1986-92), Royal Astron. Soc., Mineral. Soc. Am., Am. Geophys. Union (sec. sect. on volcanology, geochemistry and petrology 1984-86, pres. elect 1988-90, pres. 1990-92, Bowen award 1993, Daly lecture 2000); mem. Model A Ford Club Am. Achievements include being named in honor of research in Antarctica, Marsh Cirque, a glacial valley in the Olympus Mountains. Office: Johns Hopkins U Dept Earth-Planetary Scis 322 Olin Hall Baltimore MD 21218 Office Phone: 410-516-4652. Business E-Mail: bmarsh@jhu.edu.

**MARSH, CARYL AMSTERDAM,** retired curator, retired psychologist; b. N.Y.C., Mar. 9, 1923; d. Louis and Kitty (Weitz) Amsterdam; m. Michael Marsh, Sept. 3, 1942 (dec. 1993); children: Susan E., Anna L. BA, Bklyn. Coll., 1942; MA, Columbia U., N.Y.C., 1946; PhD, George Washington U., 1978. Lic. psychologist, D.C. Asst. cultural attache Am. Embassy, Paris, 1946-48; psychologist D.C. Recreation Dept., 1957-69; spl. asst. Smithsonian Instn., Washington, 1966-73; curator exhbns. Nat. Archives, Washington, 1978-85, sr. exhbns. specialist, 1985-86; dir. traveling psychology exhbn. Am. Psychol. Assn., 1986-93, sr. advisor, 1993-95; chair humanities seminars in sci. mus. Assn. Sci. Tech. Ctrs., 1994—2001; ret. 2003. Rsch. fellow exptl. gallery Smithsonian Instn., 1992; rsch. cons. Nat. Zoo, 1981-92, Smithsonian Folk Life Festival, Nat. Mus. Am. History, 1977-78; organizer Discovery Room Nat. Mus. Natural History, 1969-73; cons. Meyer Found., 1964-66; advisor Lemelson Ctr. for Study of Invention and Innovation, Nat. Mus. Am. History, 1999-2000. Editor: Exhibition: The American Image, 1979. Organizer Anacostia Neighborhood Mus., Washington, 1967, bd. dirs., 1974—, v.p. 1993—; sec. D.C. Commn. on Arts and Humanities, 1987—; pres. Pre-Sch. Parents Coun., Washington, 1956-57; adv. bd. Youth Alive, 1997-99. Fellow Nat. Mus. Am. Art, 1975-77; vis. scholar Nat. Mus. Am. Art, 1978—; grad. fellow CUNY, 1945-46; scholar George Washington U., noted for Disting. Contbn. to Pub. Understanding of Psychology, APA, 1993. Mem. AAAS, APA (Outstanding Svc. award 1992, Disting. Contbn. to Pub. Understanding of Psychology award 1993), D.C. Psychol. Assn., Am. Assn. Mus., Mus. Edn. Roundtable (bd. dirs. 1983-87). Home and Office: 10450 Lottsford Rd # 3011 Mitchellville MD 20721-2734

**MARSH, CLAY BRADEN,** pulmonologist, researcher; b. Charleston, W.Va., Nov. 15, 1958; s. Don and Geraldine Marsh; m. Gail Marsh; children: Cameron, Matthew, Rachel. BS, W.Va. U., 1981, MD, 1985. Diplomate Am. Bd. Internal Medicine, 1988, Am. Bd. Pulmonary Medicine, 1993, Am. Bd. Critical Care Medicine, 1994. Clin. instr. rsch. divsn. pulmonary and critical care medicine Ohio State U., Columbus, 1993—95, asst. prof. medicine, 1995, assoc. prof. medicine, 1998—2004, prof. medicine, 2004—, vice chmn. rsch. dept. internal medicine, 2000—, interim dir. divsn. pulmonary, allergy and critical care medicine, 2002—03, dir. divsn. pulmonary, allergy, critical care and sleep medicine, 2003—; investigator Davis Heart and Lung Rsch. Inst., Columbus, 1998—; dir. Ctr. Critical Care and Respiratory Medicine, 2005—; assoc. dir. Davis Heart and Lung Rsch. Inst., Columbus, 2000—; resident in internal medicine Ohio State U., Columbus, 1985—88, chief resident in internal medicine, 1989—90, fellow in pulmonary and critical care medicine, 1990—92. Mem. sect. study lung, biology and pathology NIH, Washington, 2003—04. Recipient Presdl. award, Am. Lung Assn. Ohio, 2003. Mem.: Am. Soc. Biochemistry and Molecular Biology, Stanley Sarnoff Found. (sci. bd.), Fedn. Am. Soc. Exptl. Biology, Ohio Thoracic Soc., Am. Thoracic Soc. Home: 2266 Club Rd Columbus OH 43221 Office: Pulmonary Critical Care OSU 473 W 12th Ave Columbus OH 43210 Office Phone: 614-293-9309. Business E-Mail: clay.marsh@osumc.edu.

**MARSH, DON ERMAL,** supermarket executive; b. Muncie, Ind., Feb. 2, 1938; s. Ermal W. and Garnet (Gibson) M.; m. Marilyn Faust, Mar. 28, 1959; children: Don Ermal, Jr., Arthur Andrew, David Alan, Anne Elizabeth, Alexander Elliott. BA, Mich. State U., 1961. With Marsh Supermarkets, Inc., Indpls., 1961—, pres., 1968—, chmn. CEO, also dir. Chmn. FoodPAC, Washington, 1991; bd. dirs. Nat. City Bank, Indpls., Ind. Energy, Inc., Indpls.; gov. World Econ. Forum—Food & Agro, Geneva. Bd. dirs. Corp. Community Coun., Culver Fathers Assn., Food Industry Crusade Against Hunger, Charlene S. Lugar Birth Defects Grant Fund, Am. Arbitration Assn. Ctrl. Ind. Corp., Econ. Club Indpls., Hanover Coll., other; bd. mem. Ind. Assn. Cities and Towns; mem. adv. com. on food distbn. Western Mich. U.; mem. Conner Prairie Pioneer Settlement Adv. Coun.; mem. Indpls. Mus. Art.; mgmt. coun. Am. Mgmt. Assn. Mem. Am. Mgmt. Assn., Mgmt. Execs. Soc., Gen. Mgmt. Coun., Internat. Food Congress, Assn. of Publicly Traded Cos. (bd. dirs., past chmn.), Food Mktg. Inst. (bd. dirs.), Indpls. C. of C., Ind. State C. of C. (bd. dirs.), Ind. Retail Coun. (bd. dirs.), Nat. Soc. Chgo., Chief Execs. Orgn., World Bus. Coun., Newcomen Soc. N.Am., Internat. Ctr. for Cos. of Food Trade and Industry (past chmn., bd. dirs.), Food Merchandisers Edn. Coun., Nat. Assn. Convenience Stores, Nat. Assn. Food Rsch., World Pres. Orgn., Young Pres. Orgn. Alumni, Nat. Soc. Fund Raising Execs., Well House Soc., Am. Bus. Club, Ind. Fiscal Policy Inst., Nat. Soc. Chgo., Ind. U. Varsity Club, Crooked Stick Golf Club, Columbia Club, Delaware Country Club, The Hundred Club Indpls., Indpls. Athletic Club, Marco Polo Club, Meridian Hills Country Club, Skyline Club, Masons, Elks, Pi Sigma Epsilon, Lambda Chi Alpha Found., Sigma Phi Omega. Republican. Presbyterian. Office: Marsh Supermarkets Inc 9800 Crosspoint Blvd Indianapolis IN 46256-3350

**MARSH, DONALD PETE,** chaplain; b. Redfield, S.D., Dec. 9, 1951; s. Vernon Glen Marsh and Esther Virgina (Bramble) Parrish; m. Vickie Lynn Schwersinske, Dec. 17, 1978; children: Rebecca, Amy, Stephanie. BA magna cum laude, Columbia Union Coll., 1974; MDiv, Andrews U., 1979; DMin, Fuller Theol. Sem., 1999. Pastor Mich. Conf. Seventh-Day Adventists, Lansing, 1978-89, Chesapeake Conf. Seventh-Day Adventists, Gambrills, Md., 1985-89; chaplain resident Holy Cross Hosp., Silver Spring, Md., 1989-90; dir. pastoral care Avista Adventist Hosp., Louisville, Colo., 1990— Chmn. ethics com. Avista Hosp., Louisville, 1992—. Mem. Am. Coll. Pastoral Supervision and Psychotherapy (convener North Denver chpt.), Assn. Death Edn. and Counseling, Seventh-Day Adventists Healthcare Chaplains Assn. (pres.-elect 2004-05, pres. 2005—), Boulder County Safehouse Spiritual Support Team. Avocations: music, bicycling, photography. Office: Avista Adventist Hosp 100 Health Park Dr Louisville CO 80027-9583 E-mail: donmarsh@centura.org.

**MARSH, DORIS ELAINE,** retired ballet school owner; b. Saginaw, Mich., Sept. 14, 1931; d. William Henry and Elizabeth Ann (Bates) M. BA, U. Mich., 1953, MA, 1956; postgrad. U. Toronto, Ont., Can., 1954-55, Mich. State U., 1968. Owner, tchr. Doris Marsh Sch. Ballet, Saginaw, 1956—2004; tchr. Saginaw Pub. Schs., 1956-70; dir. summer dance program Delta Coll., University Ctr., Mich., 1964-83, assoc. prof. art history, 1970-71; instr. Saginaw Valley State U., University Ctr., 1971-81, adj. prof. art history, 2002—; dir., pres. Saginaw Valley Dancers, 1975-90, artistic dir. 1975—2004; ret. 2004. Choreographer Fischer Opera Haus, Frankenmuth, Mich., 1973-74; dance critic Saginaw News, 1986—; part time tchr., 2004—. Choreographer, costume designer: (ballets) The Nutcracker, 1980, All In Fun, 1980, Clair de Lune, 1980, Summer, 1983, Festival, 1990, Saturday Night at Flossie's, 1990, Sea Interludes, 1991, The Firebird, 1991; contbr. articles to profl. jours. Pres. Saginaw Valley Dance Council, 1972-73; mem. program com. Temple Theater Arts Assn., Saginaw, 1982-87; bd. dirs. Saginaw Community Concerts, 1960-80. Recipient All Area Arts award Saginaw Enrichment Commn., 1996. Mem. Mich. Dance Assn., Imperial Soc. Tchrs. of Dancing (assoc.). Avocations: photography, folk dance, hiking, travel, reading. Home: 2701 Willard St Saginaw MI 48602-3431

**MARSH, ELLA JEAN,** pediatrician; b. Chgo., Dec. 16, 1941; d. Charles and Eleanor (Canfield) M. BA, St. Mary of Woods Coll., Ind., 1963; DO, Chgo. Coll. Osteo. Medicine, 1971. Diplomate Am. Coll. Osteo. Pediatricians (chmn. evaluating com. 1981-89), Nat. Osteo. Bds., Am. Bd. Pediats., Am. Bd. Osteopathic Pediatricians. Intern Doctor's Hosp., Columbus, Ohio, 1971-72; resident in pediatrics Chgo. Coll. Osteo. Medicine, 1972-74, asst.

prof., 1974-78, assoc. prof. pediatrics, 1978-82; assoc. prof. W.Va. Coll. Osteo. Medicine, 1975-86; clin. assoc. prof. pediatrics South Eastern Osteo. Sch. Medicine, 1984-96, chmn. pediatric and newborn nursery, 1982-94; assoc. dir. med. edn. Orlando (Fla.) Gen. Hosp., 1985-88. Mem. staff Arnold Palmer Children's Hosp., Fla. Hosp., Health Ctr.; pediatric cons. Nat. Bd. Osteo. Examiners; lectr., cons. in field. Alumni bd. dirs. St. Mary of Woods Coll., 1992-95, Ctrl. Fla. Primary Care, 1994-97. Donald Bucknar Moore scholar, 1963. Fellow Am. Coll. Osteo. Pediatricians (v.p. 1986, pres. 1988), Am. Coll. Pediatricians, Am. Acad. Pediats.; mem. AMA, Am. Osteo. Assn., Fla. Osteo. Assn., Fla. Med. Soc., Orange County Med. Soc., Cen. Fla. Pediatric Soc., Chgo. Coll. Osteo. Medicine Alumni Assn., Am. Coll. Osteo. Pediatricians, Am. Acad. Pediatricians, Irish Am. Pediatric Soc., Am. Acad. Osteopathy Roman Catholic. Home: 8210 Imber St Orlando FL 32825-8233

**MARSH, GARY MARTIN,** environmental biostatistician epidemiologist educator; b. Wheeling, W.Va., Jan. 27, 1952; s. Floyd Martin and Alma Elizabeth (Custer) M.; m. Valerie A. Marsh, Aug. 28, 1991; children: Brian, Eric, Gregory, Anastasia. BS cum laude, U. Pitts., 1973, MS, 1974, PhD in Biostatistics, 1977. From asst. prof. to prof. Grad. Sch. Pub. Health U. Pitts., 1978—. Asst. dir. Ctr. Environ. Epidemiology, Pitts., 1983-92. Contbr. over 150 reviewed publs. in field. Den leader Boy Scouts Am., 2000—04. Recipient Adolf Kammer Merit in Authorship award, Am. Coll. Occup. and Environ. Medicine, 1979. Fellow Am. Coll. Epidemiology; mem. Am. Statis. Assn., Internat. Soc. Environ. Epidemiology, Soc. Occupl. Environ. Health, Soc. Epidemiol. Rsch., Brit. Occupl. Health Soc., Delta Omega. Avocations: Karate, performance driving, classical music, Tae Kwon Do. Office: U Pitts 130 Desoto St Pittsburgh PA 15213-2535 Office Phone: 412-624-3032. Business E-Mail: gmarsh@pitt.edu.

**MARSH, JOAN KNIGHT,** educational film, video and computer software company executive, publishing executive; b. Apr. 8, 1934; d. E. Lyle and Ruth (Hopkins) Knight; m. Alan Reid Marsh, Sept. 27, 1958; children: Alan Reid, Clayton Knight. BA, Tex. Tech U., 1956. Owner, pres. MarshMedia, Kansas City, Mo., 1966—. Tchr. evaluation guides. Mem. ctrl. governing bd. Children's Mercy Hosp., 1996-05; mem. coun. Family Study Ctr., U. Mo., Kansas City, 1983-89. Children's Relief Assn. Mercy Hosp., Kansas City, 1984—, pres., 1989-91; chmn., hon. co-chmn. Rose Brooks Ctr. Cabaret, 1995, 2000; pres. Friends of Children's Mercy Hosp., 1996-98; chmn. The Jewel Ball, 1997, Great Ball of China II, 1999, Genevieve Byrne Spkr. Series ARC Kansas City chpt., 2004. Mem. Jr. League (sustaining chmn. 1982-84, Cmty. Svc. award 1999), Gamma Phi Beta. Republican. Presbyterian. Avocations: egyptology, filmology. Office Phone: 816-523-1059.

**MARSH, JOSEPH FRANKLIN, JR.,** retired academic administrator; b. Charleston, W.Va., Feb. 24, 1925; s. Joseph Franklin and Florence (Keller) M. Student, Concord Coll., 1941-42, W.Va. U., 1942-43; AB, Dartmouth Coll., 1947; student, Nat. Inst. Pub. Affairs, Washington, 1947-48; M.P.A., Harvard U., 1949; LL.D., Davis and Elkins Coll., 1968; L.H.D., Alderson-Broaddus Coll., 1982. Cons. Hoover Commn., Washington, 1948; instr. in gt. issues Dartmouth, 1952—54, instr. econs., 1953—55, asst. prof., 1955—59; pres. Concord Coll., Athens, W.Va., 1959—73, pres. emeritus, 1985—; ednl. cons., 1973—74; pres. Waynesburg (Pa.) Coll., 1974—83, pres. emeritus, 1983—; v.p. The Armand Hammer United World Coll. of the Am. West, Montezuma, N.Mex., 1984—85; pres. Marsh Edn Cons., Athens, W.Va., 1985—. Dir. One Valley Bank of Mercer County, 1987-98, hon. dir., 1998-2000. Contbr. articles to profl. jours. Mem. State Dept. Ednl. Mission to U.A.R., 1964, Mercer County (W.Va.) Planning Commn., 1964-74, 83-94, hon., 1994—; vice chmn. W.Va. Com. for Constl. Amendments, 1966; mem. regional coun. Internat. Edn. Study Mission to Europe, 1970; bd. dirs. Am. Assn. State Colls. and Univs., 1972-73, Regional Coun. for Internat. Edn., 1973, Hospice Care Mercer County, W.Va., 1987-91, Faculty Merit Found. W.Va., 1990—, Greater Mercer County Charitable Found., W.Va., 1998-02, exec. com. 2001-02, chmn., pres., 1998-2001; bd. dirs. Charitable Found. of the Virginians, Inc., 2002-05, Pa. Assn. Ind. Colls. and Univs., 1974-83, exec. com. 1980-82; bd. dirs. Pa. Commn. for Ind. Colls. and Univs., 1974-83, sec.-treas., 1976-77, vice chmn., 1977-80, chmn., 1980-82; trustee Found. Ind. Colls. Pa., 1974-83, mem. exec. com., 1979-82; bd. visitors Midway Coll., Ky., 1979-93; adv. com. Pa. State Coun. Higher Edn., 1980-82; trustee Concord Coll. Found., 1986, bd. dirs. 1987—; active Town of Athens Planning Commn., 1986-94, pres. commn. 1987-94; bd. trustees, Princeton (W.Va.) Cmty. Hosp. Found., 1989-98, vice chmn., 1989-97; Gov's. appointee to bd. dirs. State Coll. System W.Va., 1989-96, chmn. adminstrv. com., 1990-91, vice chmn. of bd., 1991-95, chmn., 1995-96; gov's appointee to the W.Va. Parkways, Econ. Devel. and Tourism Authority, 1998—2006, asst. sec., 2001-02, sec., 2002-03, vice chmn., 2003-04; gov's appointee Edn. Commn. of the States, 1998-2002. Served as gunnery officer USNR, 1943-46. Named Outstanding Young Man, W.Va. Jr. C. of C., 1960; recipient Alumnus of Yr. award Concord Coll., 1973, Golden Alumnus award, 1992, Outstanding Alumnus award for Career Achievement, 1996; Outstanding Citizen award Athens Woman's Club, 1992, Total Community Involvement Award, Town of Athens, WV, 2001; Rotary fellow Oxford (Eng.) U., 1950-52. Mem. AAUP, Am. Assn. Univ. Adminstrs., Am. Econ. Assn., Royal Inst. Pub. Adminstrn., Oxford Union Debating Soc. (life), Oxford Soc. (life), Pa. Soc., Duquesne Club (Pitts.), Univ. Club (Bluefield), Masons, Rotary (dist. gov. 1992-93), The Guild of Carillonneurs N.Am. (hon.), Phi Beta Kappa, Phi Tau, Phi Delta Pi, Phi Sigma Kappa, Alpha Kappa Psi (hon.). Methodist. Home: 106 First Ave Athens WV 24712 Office: PO Box 734 Athens WV 24712-0734 Office Phone: 304-384-9816.

**MARSH, JOSEPH VIRGIL,** real estate broker, retired investment advisor; b. Winston-Salem, N.C., Apr. 28, 1952; s. Gilliam Hughes and Dovie Elizabeth (Watson) Marsh. Student, Surry CC, 1970-72, US Govt. Schs., Md., SC, Washington, 1972-74; BSEE, U. Md., 1976; diploma, NY Inst. Fin., 1978, NYU, 1978, MBA, 1980. Cert. comml. real estate broker N.C. With Joint Armed Svcs. Tech. Liaison, Washington, 1974-75; cons. Ararat, NC, 1975-76; corr., cons. individuals, bus. on tech. matters Ararat, NC, 1977—. Registered advisor SEC, 1981—2000. Active U.S. Presdl. Task Force, 1981—2000; founder Marsh Found., 1989; tech. liaison NASA, 1992. Recipient Presdl. medal of merit, Pres. of U.S., 1988, 1990. Mem.: VFW (hon.), Coun. Civilian Tech. Advisers, Internat. Assn. Sci. Devel., Inds. Cons. Assns., Internat. Entrepreneurs Assn., Armed Forces Assn. Republican. Office: Hwy 2019/2026 Ararat NC 27007-0178 Office Phone: 336-374-4405. Office Fax: 336-374-4405.

**MARSH, KEVIN B.,** energy executive; b. Atlanta; married; 2 children. CPA. Group mgr. tech. acctg. S.C. Electric & Gas Co., 1984—89, v.p., contr., CFO, 1996—, former v.p. corp. planning; former v.p. fin., treas., contr. SCANA Corp., Columbia, SC, CFO, 1996—, sr. v.p., 1998—. Past bd. dirs. Palmetto Place Children's Emergency Shelter; bd. dirs. Bus. Devel. Corp. of S.C. Mem.: AICPA. Methodist. Office: SCANA Corp 1426 Main St Columbia SC 29218

**MARSH, MARIAN E.,** voice educator; b. San Mateo, Calif., Apr. 5, 1936; d. Richard Harding and Helen McGregor (Grant) Marsh; m. David Wade, Sept. 18, 1955. Voice tchr. Sonoma State U., Rohnert Park, Calif., 1965—70, U. Calif., Santa Cruz, 1974—88, Dominican U., San Rafael, Calif., 1975—; pvt. practice Calif., 1962—. Cruise ship entertainer, 1970—82, 1993, 95. Singer: San Francisco Symphony, LA Philharmonic, Oakland Symphony, Sinfonia Nat.; singer: (soloist) Schola Cantorum, De Anza Coll., San Francisco Civic Chorale, Winifred Baker Chorale, Coll. Marin, Diablo Valley Coll., San Mateo Masterworks Chorale, Contra Costa Chorale, Peninsula Singers, Coll. Marin Cmty. Chorus. Organist various chs., Calif., 1950—60, soloist San Francisco, 1964—97, Temple Emanuel, San Francisco 1960—96; organist dir. Ch. of Nativity, San Rafael, Calif., 2002—. Recipient Met. Opera award, 1963, 1965, East Bay Opera League award, 1964. Mem.: Music Tchrs. Assn. (scholarship chair), Nat. Assn. Tchrs. Singing, Womens Musicians Club (pres., v.p., recital chair). Episcopalian. Home: 91 Grande Paseo San Rafael CA 94903 Office: Dominican Univ 50 Acacia San Rafael CA 94901 Personal E-mail: davidmarionsong@aol.com

**MARSH, MARTHA H.,** hospital administrator; BS, U. Rochester; MPH, MBA, Columbia U. Pres. and CEO Matthew Thornton Health Plan, Dartmouth-Hitchcock Med. Ctr., 1986—94; sr. v.p., profl. svcs. and managed care and v.p, managed care U. Pa. Health Sys., 1994—98; COO U. Calif.-Davis Health Care Sys., 1999—2002; dir. Hosp. and Clinics U. Calif.-Davis Medical Ctr., 1999—2002; pres. and CEO Stanford (Conn.) Hosp. and Clinics, 2002—. Apptd. by Pres. Bush Nat. Infrastructure Adv. Coun., 2003; bd. dirs. Calif. Healthcare Assoc., Integrated Healthcare Assoc., Blue Cross of Calif. Hosp. Relations Com. Office: Stanford Hosp 300 Pasteur Dr Ste H3200 Stanford CA 94305 Office Phone: 650-723-4000.*

**MARSH, MERRILYN DELANO,** sculptor, artist, painter; b. Larchmont, N.Y., Dec. 26, 1923; d. Merrill Potter and Hazel (Holmes) Delano; m. George Estabrook Marsh, Sept. 18, 1954; children: Merrill Delano, George Estabrook Jr., Robert Houston. Diploma, Sch. of Mus. of Fine Arts, Boston, 1946, cert., 1947; postgrad., Acad. Grande Chaumière, Paris, 1947-48. Art tchr. Choate Sch., Brookline, Mass., 1948, 49, Brookline Cmty. Ctr., 1948, 49; pvt. art tchr. Newton, Mass., 1948-49; comml. sculptor for display and mfg. cos., 1948-55; sculpture tchr. De Cordova Mus., Lincoln, Mass., 1950-54. Juror for numerous art exhbns., New Eng. area, 1954-55, 72-74. One-woman show at Copley Soc. of Boston, 1996; commd. 7 reliefs for Sch. for Environ., Levine Sci. Ctr., Duke U., Durham, N.C., 1994, bronze statue for cloister garden St. Andrew's Episcopal Ch., Wellesley, Mass., 1995, bronze portrait reliefs for Houston and Sargent Athletic awards Tufts U., Medford, Mass., 1997, 2 bronze reliefs, Ellis Oval Athletic Field Tufts U., 2001, bronze portrait relief of Clarence P. "Pop" Houston, Houston Hall, Tufts U., 1965, bronze portrait relief for Rocco J. Carzo Cage, Cousens Gymnasium, Tufts U., 2002, others; profiled in Wellesley Weston Mag., 2006. Mrs. David Hunt Sculpture scholar Mus. Fine Arts, 1947; recipient Katherine Thayer Hobson award Pen and Brush Soc., 1991, Best in Show award Juliani Gallery, 1991, Pres.'s Cup award for golf Wellesley (Mass.) Country Club, 1998, 2d Pl. award Wellesley Soc. Artists, 2003, Hon. mention Wellesley Soc. Artists Spring Show, 2004, Margaret E. Fearnside Meml. award Wellesley Soc. Artists Fall Show, 2004. Mem. Copley Soc. Boston (Copley master, Maria Maravigna award 1988, 1st prize in sculpture and large works 1994, other awards, 1983, 89), New Eng. Sculptors Assn. (bd. dirs. 1986, award 1988), Wellesley Soc. Artists (awards 1985, 87, 89, 91-92, 95, 2001-02, 2d pl. award 2003, bd. dirs. 1970, 88—, Hon. Mention award 2004, Margaret E. Fearnside Meml. award 2004), Cambridge Art Assn. (Jack Schultz award, 2000, other awards 1993-94). Republican. Episcopalian.

**MARSH, MICHELE,** former newscaster; married; 1 child. Anchor/reporter WABI-TV, Bangor, Maine, KSAT-TV, San Antonio, WCBS, 1979-96; co-anchor WNBC/News Channel 4 at 6 p.m., N.Y.C., 1996—2003. Recipient Emmy awards for Best Broadcast (3). Office: WNBC-TV 30 Rockefeller Plz New York NY 10112-0002

**MARSH, MILES L.,** paper company executive; b. 1947; With various divsns. Dart & Kraft Inc., Gen. Foods USA; chmn., CEO Pet Inc., St. Louis, until 1995; pres., CEO Ft. James Corp., Richmond, 1995—, chmn. bd., 1996—, chmn., CEO Deerfield, Ill. Office: Fort James Corp 1919 S Broadway Green Bay WI 54304-4905

**MARSH, MILTON R.W.,** composer; b. Hamilton, Bermuda, Sept. 29, 1945; arrived in U.S., 1964; s. Milton Murray and Gwendolyn Isadora Marsh; children: Tanya, Jonathan Milton, Milton Andre. Cert. in Edn., London U., 1964; MB, Berklee Coll. Music, Boston, 1969; MusM, New Eng. Conservatory, Boston, 1971. Cert. tchr., adminstr. Calif. Music cons. Nat. Ctr. for Afro-Am. Artists, Boston, 1970—71; vis. prof. SUNY, Oneonta, 1972—73, prof., dir. Afro-Am. music studies Buffalo, 1973—77. Cons. Nat. Ctr. for Afro-Am. Artists, Boston, 1970—71. Author: (music) Monism, 1975, Continuum, 1985, We Are Not Alone, 2003. Recipient grant, Artist Found. Office: Alankara Records PO Box 230635 Boston MA 02123-0635 Office Phone: 781-979-2417. Office Fax: 781-324-4922. E-mail: mmarsh8113@aol.com, alankara@msn.com.

**MARSH, PATRICIA GUYTON,** humanities educator; b. Columbus, Miss., Mar. 17, 1947; d. Rickman Keith and Dora Hankins Guyton; m. Robert Tate Marsh, May 13, 1973; 1 child, Erin Tate. BA in Speech, Miss. State U., Starkville, 1968; MA in Theatre, U. Miss., Oxford, 1972, postgrad., 1972, postgrad., 2005, U. South Ala., Mobile, Miss. U. for Women, Columbus. Cert. English, speech and theatre tchr. Miss., Ala., Ga., Fla. Instr. Sidney Lanier Jr. HS for Boys, Macon, Ga., 1969, Warner Robins Sr. HS, 1969—71, U. Miss., Oxford, 1971—72, East Miss. Jr. Coll., Scooba, 1973, Pasco Comprehensive HS, Dade City, Fla., 1973—74, Pasco C.C., Dade City, Fla., 1974—75, Ala. Christian Coll., Mobile, 1975—76, St. Paul's Episcopal Sch., Mobile, 1976—2003, Columbus HS, 2003—04, East Miss. CC, Mayhew, 2004—. Adjudicator song writing divsn. Hank Williams Internat. Music Festival; adjudicator State 4H Oratorical Contest; guest lectr. Ala. Pub. Rels. Coun.; moderator Evenings with Ala. Writers series Spring Hill Coll.; actress Manhattan Theatre Co., NYC; actress, dir. Entertainer Dinner Theatre, Mobile, Ala.; dir. Granada Little Theatre, Miss., Warren Robins Little Theatre, Ga.; choreographer music and theatre depts. U. Miss.; dir. winning prodns. Southeastern Theatre Conf., Secondary Sch. Divsn., Crystal City, Va., Louisville. Dir. featured performer An Evening with Tennessee's Ladies Tennessee Williams Tribute, Columbus, 2005; mem. com. Roast and Boast, Columbus, 2005; dir. An Army of Stars benefit Salvation Army; site dir. Kaleidoscope benefit festival United Cerebral Palsy. Named Ala. Speech/Theatre Tchr. of Yr.; recipient Disting. Tchr. award, White House Commn. on Presdl. Scholars, Best Actress award, Southeastern Theatre Conf., Cmty. Theatre Divsn., Miss. State U., Joe Jefferson Playhouse, Mobile, Mobile Theatre Guild, Azalea City News and Review, Mobile; Pres. scholar, Miss. State U. Mem.: Ala. Speech Assn. (sec.), Ala. Theatre Assn. (sec.), Ala. Coun. Theatre/Speech, Southeastern Theatre Conf. Republican. Methodist. Avocations: travel, gardening, antiques, theatre, football. Home: 509 7th St South Columbus MS 39701 Office: East Miss CC PO Box 100 Mayhew MS 39753-0100

**MARSH, RICHARD CHARLES,** psychologist, educator, writer; b. LA, Jan. 20, 1942; s. Lazar William and Miriam Rose Marsh; m. Sandra Marian Combs, Sept. 27, 1975; children: Shaun Eric, Alexander Dendry, Andrew Tatanka. AB, U. Calif., Berkeley, 1964; MS, UCLA, 1969, Purdue U., 1970; PhD, Utah State U., 1971. Registered psychologist Nat. Register of Health Providers in Psychology, 1978. Expert witness Superior Ct., County of Alameda, Oakland, Calif., 1984—, Superior Ct., County of Contra Costa, Martinez, Calif., 1984—; pvt. practice Albany, Calif., 1983—. Intern Ky. State Mental Hosp., Lexington, 1972—73; psychol. asst. William Zehv, Ph.D., Beverly Hills, Calif., 1974—76; dir. project team Medper Corp., Chatsworth, Calif., 1979—80, CEO, 1981—85; cons. psychologist San Fernando Valley Problem Back Pain Clinic, Panorama City, Calif., 1977—79; dir. R.C. Marsh, Ph.D. & Assocs., Beverly Hills, 1981; chmn. dept. psychology Ctr. Neuro Skills, Bakersfield, Calif., 1983; instr. U. Calif. Extention, Berkeley, 1985—87; owner Through the Courthouse Door Seminars, Albany, Calif., 1992—. Fellow, NIMH, 1966-1967, 1968, 1971, Brain Rsch. Inst., Dept. Anatomy, UCLA, 1972, US Pub. Health, 1966-1967, 1971. Fellow: Am. Coll. Forensic Psychology; mem.: APA, Am. Psychology - Law Soc. Achievements include discovery of Dendritic Bundles (neuroanatomical substrate for ephapsis); development of Medical Patient Personality Inventory (Medper); research in Cytoarchitecture of Spinal Cord Grey Matter. Office: Clin & Forensic Psychology 1035 San Pablo Ave Ste 7 Albany CA 94706 Office Phone: 510-559-8412.

**MARSH, RICHARD H.,** utilities company executive; BA, Kent State U.; MA in Clinical Psychology, U. Akron; MBA. CFA. Joined Ohio Edison, 1980, various financial positions, 1980—91; treasurer Ohio Edison (merged with Centerior Energy to form FirstEnergy), 1991—97; v.p. finance FirstEnergy Corp., Akron, Ohio, 1997, v.p., CFO, 1998—2001, sr. v.p., CFO, 2001—. Chmn. Utility Pension Fund Study Group; mem. fin. adv. com. Edison Elec. Inst. Mem. advancement coun. Coll. Bus. Admin. U. Akron, v.p. alumni coun.; chair We. Reserve Girl Scout Coun.; trustee FirstEnergy Found., H.M.

Life Opportunity Services; mem. advisory com. for Master of Sci. in Fin. Engring. prog. Kent State U. Mem.: Cleve. Soc. Security Analysts. Office: First Energy Corp 76 S Main St Akron OH 44308-1890*

**MARSH, ROBERT HARRY,** chemicals executive; b. Camden, N.J., Sept. 6, 1946; s. Harry Louis and Margaret Charlotte (Starke) M. BA, BSME, Rutgers U., 1969; MBA in Mgmt. and Fin., Temple U., 1980. Registered profl. engr., N.J., Pa., Del. From mech. engr. to mech. specialist and project engr. Rohm & Haas Engring., Bristol, Pa., 1967—76; from staff engr. to sr. engring. specialist Hercules, Inc., Wilmington, Del., 1976—80, sr. fin. analyst for corp. strategic planning, 1980—81, sr. bus. analyst bus. group, 1982—83; mgr. bus. analysis Himont, Inc., 1983—86, dir. strategy and planning, 1986—88, dir. bus. mgmt., 1988—91, mng. dir. China, 1991—95, dir. strategy, 1991—95; founder R.H. Marsh & Assoc. Internat. Mgmt., Bethlehem, Pa., 1995—; pres., prin., CEO, chmn. bd. dirs. Internat. Bus. and Mktg. Mgmt., 1996—. Founder, bd. dirs. various cos., 1995—. Contbr. articles to profl. jours. Active Haddonfield (N.J.) Civic Affairs, Bethlehem (Pa.) Civic Affairs, Wesley Meth. Ch., Bethlehem, Pa., 2001—. Mem.: NSPE, ASME (vice chmn. awards com. 1980, membership chmn. 1982, nat. power com. 1977—84), Engrs. Club Phila., Pyramid Club Phila., Beta Gamma Sigma. Home: 225 Flagstone Dr Bethlehem PA 18017 Personal E-mail: rbtmarsh@verizon.net.

**MARSH, ROBERT MORTIMER,** sociologist, educator; b. Everett, Mass., Jan. 22, 1931; s. Henry Warren and Ruth (Dunbar) M.; children: Eleanor L., Christopher S.H., Diana E. Student, Boston U., 1948-50; AB, U. Chgo., 1952; MA, Columbia, 1953, PhD, 1959. Fellow Ford Found., Japan, Taiwan, Hong Kong, 1956-58; instr. sociology U. Mich., 1958-61; asst. prof. sociology Cornell U., 1961-65; asso. prof. Duke, 1965-67; mem. faculty Brown U., 1967—, prof. sociology, 1968—, chmn. dept., 1971-75. Manpower personnel and tng. rsch. prof. U.S. Naval Acad., Annapolis, 1987-88; vis. prof. Nat. Tsing Hua U., Taiwan, 1991. Author: The Mandarins: The Circulation of Elites in China, 1961, Comparative Sociology: A Codification of Cross-Societal Analysis, 1967; (with H. Mannari) Modernization and the Japanese Factory, 1976, Organizational Change in Japanese Factories, 1988, The Great Transformation: Social Change in Taipei, Taiwan Since the 1960s, 1996; also articles; assoc. editor Adminstrv. Sci. Quar., 1963-67, Jour. Comparative Family Studies, 1970-74; co-editor: (with J. Michael Armer) Comparative Sociological Research in the 1960s and 1970s. East Asian Inst. summer fellow Chinese Columbia, 1955; Ford Found. and Guggenheim Found. fellow Japan, 1969-70; Japan Soc. Promotion Sci. fellow, 1976, 83; Chiang Ching Kuo Found. and Nat. Sci. Coun. fellow (Taiwan, Republic of China), 1991-93. Mem. Am. Sociol. Assn., Ea. Sociol. Assn., Assn. Asian Studies, Internat. Studies Assn. (exec. com. comparative interdisciplinary studies sect. 1971-76), Japan Human Rels. Assn. (councilor 1970—). Office: Dept Sociology Brown Univ Providence RI 02912-0001 Business E-Mail: robert_marsh@brown.edu.

**MARSH, WENDY K.,** pharmacist, lawyer; b. Chgo., Dec. 13, 1967; d. Roger W. and Sheila P. Hartung; m. Matthew D. Marsh, Oct. 16, 1998; children: Darby J., Tate D. BS, Drake U., Des Moines, Iowa, 1990—90, JD, 1994. Registered pharmacist Iowa. Pharmacist Sun Drug Village Sq., Johnston, Iowa, 1990—96; assoc. McKee, Voorhees & Sease, PLC, Des Moines, 1999—2000, mem., 2001—. Contbr. articles to profl. jours. Vol. Big Bros. Big Sisters Iowa, Des Moines, 2000—05; chair intellectual property divsn., inventor's com. ABA, Washington, 1998—99; legal counsel vol. Des Moines Jaycees, 1994—97; chair intellectual property com. Iowa Bar Assn., 2001—02; bd. dirs. Des Moines YMCA Camp, 2000—03, Project SEMI Bd., Des Moines, 2004—05. Recipient Outstanding Svc. award, Des Moines Jaycees, 1997. Mem.: Iowa Intellectual Property Law Assn. (sec. 2004—05, pres.-elect 2005—), Am. Intellectual Property Law Assn., Am. Pharm. Assn. Office: McKee Voorhees & Sease PLC 801 Grand Ave Ste 3200 Des Moines IA 50309 Office Fax: 515-288-1338. Business E-Mail: marsh@ipmvs.com.

**MARSHAK, ALAN HOWARD,** electrical engineer, educator; b. Miami Beach, Fla., Mar. 21, 1938; s. Jerome and Yetta (Feiner) M.; children: Jerry Brian; m. Joan Grode Milner, May 25, 1997. BScEE, U. Miami, 1960; MS, La. State U., 1962; PhD, U. Ariz., 1969. Asst. prof. elec. engring. La. State U., Baton Rouge, 1969-73, assoc. prof., 1973-78, prof., 1978—2002, chmn. dept. elec. and computer engring., 1983—2002, prof. emeritus, 2002—. Vis. prof. Electron Device Rsch. Ctr., U. Fla., Gainesville, 1979-80; tech. reviewer NSF, 1976—, panelist, 1993-96; panelist NRC, 1993, 2001, 04; mem. Southeastern Ctr. Elec. Engring. Edn., 1984-2002, life mem., 2002—, chmn., CEO, 1992-2001, trustee, 1994—; spkr. profl. confs. Tech. referee various jours. including Solid-State Electronics, Jour. Applied Physics; editor: Device and Process Modeling, IEEE Trans. Electron Devices, 1991-2001; author: (with D. J. Hamilton and F. A. Lindholm) Principles and Applications of Semiconductor Device Modeling, 1971, Basic Experiments in Electronics: A Laboratory Manual, 1978, also 56 tech. papers. NSF grad. trainee, 1967-69; grantee, 1970, 73, 75, 78; named F.H. Coughlin/CLECO prof. of elec. engring., 1993. Fellow IEEE (life); mem. Electron Devices Soc., Sigma Xi, Eta Kappa Nu. Home: 113 Clipper Cove Lafayette LA 70508-7023

**MARSHAK, HARRY,** plastic surgeon; b. LA, Oct. 1, 1961; s. Herbert and Pearl (Engelson) M. BS, U. Calif., Riverside, 1981; MD, UCLA, 1984. Diplomate Am. Bd. Surgery, Am. Bd. Plastic Surgery. Pvt. practice, Beverly Hills, Calif., 1991—. Fellow ACS (hon.), Internat. Coll. Surgeons; mem. Am. Soc. Plastic and Reconstructive Surgeons, Calif. Soc. Plastic Surgery, Am. Soc. for Aesthetic Plastic Surgery. Republican. Avocation: sports. Office: 120 S Spalding Dr Ste 300 Beverly Hills CA 90212-1841 Office Phone: 310-657-7600. Personal E-Mail: drharrymarshak@aol.com.

**MARSHAK, MARVIN LLOYD,** physicist, researcher; b. Mar. 11, 1946; s. Kalman and Goldie (Hait) M.; m. Anita Sue Kolman, Sept. 24, 1972; children: Rachel Kolman, Adam Kolman. BA in Physics, Cornell U., 1967; MS in Physics, U. Mich., PhD in Physics, 1970. Rsch. assoc. U. Minn., Mpls., 1970-74, from asst. prof. to assoc. prof., 1974-83, prof. physics, 1983-96, dir. grad. studies in physics, 1983-86, prin. investigator high energy physics, 1982-86, head Sch. Physics and Astronomy, 1986-96, sr. v.p. for acad. affairs, 1996-97, Morse-Alumni disting. tchg. prof. physics, 1996—, Inst. of Tech. prof., 2004—, dir. residential coll., 1997—2005, faculty legis. liason, 1997—2001, chair univ. senate consultative exec. com., 2004—05. Contbr. articles to profl. jours. Trustee Children's Theatre Co., 1989-94. Fellow: Am. Phys. Soc. Home: 2855 Ottawa Ave S Minneapolis MN 55416-1946 Office Phone: 612-624-1312. Business E-Mail: marshak@umn.edu.

**MARSHAK, ROBERT REUBEN,** retired dean, medical educator, veterinarian; b. NYC, Feb. 23, 1923; s. David and Edith (Youselovsky) Marshak; m. Ruth Emilie Lyons, Dec. 4, 1948 (div. 1983); children: William Lyons, John Ball, Richard Best; m. Margo Post Marshall, June 25, 1983. Student, U. Wis., 1940—41; DVM, Cornell U., 1945; DVM (hon.), U. Bern, 1968; MA (hon.), U. Pa., 1971. Diplomate Am. Coll. Vet. Internal Medicine (charter). Practice vet. medicine, Springfield, Vt., 1945—56; prof., chmn. dept. medicine Sch. Vet. Medicine, U. Pa., Phila., 1956-58; prof. medicine Grad. Sch. Medicine, 1957—64; chmn. dept. clin. studies Sch. Vet. Medicine, 1958—73; dir. Bovine Leukemia Research Center, 1965—73; dean Sch. Vet. Medicine, 1973—87; co-dir. Center on Interactions Animals and Soc. 1975—79, also mem. grad. group com. in comparative med. scis.; prof. medicine, chief sect. epidemiology and pub. health Sch. Vet. Medicine U. Pa., 1990—93, prof. medicine emeritus, 1993—, dean emeritus, 1987—. Adv. bd. Pa. Dept. Agr., 1973—87; chmn. Gov.'s STudy Group on Horse Racing Industry in Pa., 1979; del. to evaluate vet. med. and rsch. Chinese Ministry Agr.; adv. com. Stround Water Rsch. Ctr., 1992; adv. coun. Coll. Vet. Medicine, Cornell U., 1993—; animal use and care com. Calif. Inst. Tech., 2003—. Contbr. articles to profl. jours. Sci. adv. bd. Sch. Vet. Medicine The Hebrew U., Jerusalem, 1984—, rev. com., 1997—; trustee Upland Country Day Sch., 1988—91; animal adv. com. City of Phila., 1989—93; pres. rev. com. Koret Sch. Vet. Medicine Hebrew U. Jerusalem, 1997—98; bd. dirs. Humane Soc. U.S., 1978—82, Bide-a-wee Home Assn., 1980—85. With U.S. Army, 1943—44. Recipient Disting. Vet. award, Pa. Vet. Med. Assn., 1984, Barnraiser award, Pa. Farmers Assn., 1987. Fellow: Phila. Coll. Physicians; mem.: NAS Inst.

Medicine (sr.), Pa. Vet. Med. Assn., Am. Vet. Med. Assn., John Morgan Soc. (pres. 1967—68), Phila. Zool. Soc. (bd. dirs. 1986—87), James A. Baker Inst. for Animal Health (mem. adv. coun. 1977—), Westminster Kennel Club, Phi Zeta, Sigma Xi. E-mail: rmarshak@caltech.edu.

**MARSHALL, ALAN GEORGE,** chemistry and biochemistry educator; b. Bluffton, Ohio, May 26, 1944; s. Herbert Boyer Marshall Jr. and Cecile (Mogil) Rosser; m. Marilyn Gard, June 13, 1965; children: Gwendolyn Scott, Brian George. BA in Chemistry with honors, Northwestern U., 1965; PhD in Phys. Chemistry, Stanford U., 1970. Instr. II U. B.C., Vancouver, Can., 1969-71, asst. prof., 1971-76, assoc. prof., 1976-80; prof. chemistry and biochemistry, dir. Chem. Instrument Ctr. Ohio State U., Columbus, 1980—93; prof. chemistry and biochemistry Fla. State U., Tallahassee, 1993—, disting. rsch. prof., 1999, Kasha prof., 2000—06, Robert O. Lawton prof., 2006—. Dir. Ion Cyclotron Resonance Program Nat. High Magnetic Field Lab., 1993—. Author: Biophysical Chemistry, 1978, Fourier Transforms in NMR, Optical and Mass Spectroscopy, 1990; editor: Nat. High Magnetic Field Lab. ICR/ION Trap newsletter, 1986—92, Rapid Comm. in Mass Spectrometry, 1998—2005; mem. editl. bd. Rapid Comm. in Mass Spectrometry, 2005—; mem. editl. adv. bd.: Analytical Chemistry, 1990—92, mem. editl. bd.: Internat. Jour. Mass Ion Procs., 1987—, Jour. Am. Soc. Mass Spectrometry 1989—97; mem. editl. bd. (jour.) Jour. Am. Soc. Mass Spectrometry 1999—2002; mem. editl. bd.: Mass Spectrometry Rev., 1994—, Jour. Magnetic Resonance, 1996—2000, Chemometrics and Intelligent Lab. Systems, 1986—89, Ency. of Mass Spectrometry, 2000—, mem. internat. editl adv. bd.: ACS Ency. of Chem. Instrumentation, 1992—95; contbr. articles to profl. jours. Recipient Disting. Scholar award, Ohio State U., 1988, award in analytical chemistry, Ea. Analytical Symposium, 1991, Maurice F. Hasler award, Spectroscopy Soc. Pitts., 1997, Two-Yr. Creativity award, NSF, 1997, gold medal, N.Y. Soc. Applied Spectroscopy, 1998, Pitts. Spectroscopy award, Spectroscopy Soc. Pitts., 2002; grad. fellow, NSF, 1965—69, Alfred P. Sloan rsch. fellow, 1976. Fellow: AAAS, Soc. Applied Spectroscopy, Am. Phys. Soc.; mem.: Am. Soc. Mass Spectroscopy (bd. dirs. 1991—93, 2003—, pres. 2004—06, Disting. Contbn. award 1999), Soc. Applied Spectroscopy (hon.; chmn. local sect. 1990—93), Am. Chem. Soc. (Akron Sect. award 1988, award in chem. instrumentation 1990, Frank H. Field and Joe L. Franklin award in mass spectrometry 1995, award in analytical chemistry 2002, Herty medal (Ga. sect.) 2003, Fla. sect. award 2003, So. Chemist award (Memphis sect.) 2004), Internat. Mass Spectrum Soc. (Thomson medal 2000). Office: Fla State U Nat High Magnetic Field Lab 1800 E Paul Dirac Dr Tallahassee FL 32310-4005 Office Phone: 850-644-0529. Business E-Mail: marshall@magnet.fsu.edu.

**MARSHALL, ALTON GARWOOD,** real estate agent, consultant; b. Flint, Mich., Sept. 19, 1921; s. William Robert and Lela Christine (Brabon) M.; m. Mary Lee Golden, June 22, 1945 (div. July 1971); children: William A., Stephen B., Bruce S., Mary Ann Marshall Trebian, John L.; m. Sarah Elizabeth DeLand, Sept. 4, 1971; 1 child, Sarah Graham. BA, Hillsdale Coll., 1942; MS, Syracuse U., 1948, LLD (hon.), 1974; D Pub. Service & Bus. Adminstrn. (hon.), Hillsdale Coll., 1980. Sec. utility regulations pub. svc. commn. N.Y. State, Albany, 1953-61, dep. dir. div. budget, 1961-65, exec. officer, then sec. to gov., Office of Gov., 1965-70; pres., bd. dirs. Rockefeller Ctr., N.Y.C., 1971-81; pres. A.G. Marshall Assocs., N.Y.C., 1981—; chmn., pres., chief exec. officer Lincoln Savs. Bank, N.Y.C., 1984-88, chmn., chief exec. officer, 1988-91, also bd. dirs. Mem. exec. com. Nat. Realty Com., Washington, 1970-99; bd. dirs. N.Y. State Electric & Gas Corp., 1971-98; ind. gen. ptnr. Equitable Capital Ptnrs. and Equitable Capital Ptnrs. Retirement Fund, 1989-99; trustee Hudson River Trust, 1991-97. Mem. exec. com., steering com. Assn. for a Better N.Y., 1971—; mem. exec., landmarks and polit. action coms. Real Estate Bd. N.Y.; chmn. Nat. Adv. com. on Drug Abuse Problems, 1990-92. Sr. fellow The Nelson A. Rockefeller Inst. Govt., 1991-94. Mem. Am. Soc. Real Estate Counselors. Office: Alton G Marshall Assocs Inc 136 E 79th St New York NY 10021-0328 Office Phone: 212-407-2514.

**MARSHALL, BARRY JAMES,** gastroenterologist; b. Kalgoorlie, Western Australia, Australia, Sept. 30, 1951; came to U.S., 1986; s. Robert William and Marjory Jean (Donald) M.; m. Adrienne Joyce Feldman, Dec. 27, 1972; children: Luke, Bronwyn, Caroline, Jessica. MBBS, U. Western Australia, Perth, 1974, postgrad., 1986. Intern Sir Charles Gairdner Hosp., Western Australia, 1975-76, resident Western Australia, 1976-77, registrar medicine, 1977-78, Royal Perth Hosp., 1979-82, Fremantle Hosp., 1983-84, microbiology register Western Australia, 1984; Nat. Health and Med. Rsch. Coun. (NHMRC) rsch. fellow, Gastroenterology Royal Perth Hosp., 1985-86; research fellow, prof. medicine U. Va. Sch. Med., Charlottesville, 1986—94; chief med. officer TRI-MED Distributors Pty Ltd, Australia, 1990—; prof. rsch. in internal medicine Univ. Va., 1996; clin. prof. medicine Univ. Western Australia, 1997, clin. prof. microbiology, 1999, Nat. Health and Med. Rsch. Coun. sr. rsch. fellow, 2003. Cons. Procter and Gamble Co., Cin., 1984—, Delta West Perth, 1985—; founder, Helicobacter Found., 1994-; bd. dirs. JARM Pty. Ltd., Perth, 1987—. Edited Helicobacter Pioneers Firsthand accounts from the scientists who discovered helicobacters, 1892-1982, 2002 Named one of Outstanding West Australians, Perth Jaycees, 1985; research grantee Australian Nat. Health and Med. Rsch. Coun., 1985-86; recipient Albert Lasker Clin. Med.Rsch. award, Albert and Mary Lasker Found., 1995, Gairdner Found. Internat. award, 1996, DR AH Heineken prize for Medicine, Amsterdam, 1998, Florey medal, Canberra, 1998, Buchnan medal, Brit. Soc. Medicine, 1998, Benjamin Franklin medal for Life Sciences, Phila., 1999, Keio Med. Soc. prize, 2002, Australian Centenary medal, 2003; co-recipient (with J. Robin Warren) Warren Alpert prize, 1994, Australian Med. Assn. award, 1995, Paul Ehrlich prize, 1997, Nobel prize for Physiology or Medicine, 2005. Fellow Royal Australian Coll. Physicians, Am. Coll. Gastroenterolgy; mem. Australian Med. Assn., Australian Gastroent. Soc. Achievements include Inventor Clotest (rapid urease test), 1985, Carbon-14 Urea Breath Test, 1985; co-discoverer Helicobacter Pylori bacilli in stomach of patients with gastritis and peptic ulcers, 1982; first person to culture Helicobacter Pylori bacilli. Avocations: computer hardware and software, photography, skin diving, american cuisine. Office: Nat Health and Med Rsch Coun Helicobacter pylori Rsch Lab Rm 1 11 L Block QEII Med Centre Nedlands 6009 Australia also: TRI-MED Distributors Pty Ltd 105 Hay St Subiaco 6008 Australia Mailing: TRI-MED Distributors Pty Ltd Locked Bag 15 Subiaco 6904 Australia*

**MARSHALL, BRIAN LAURENCE,** federal official; b. Kingston-on-Thames, Eng., Apr. 6, 1941; arrived in US, 1949; s. John and Marguerite Elizabeth (Sandele) Marshall. BA in European History, U. N.C., 1963; MS in Internat. Mgmt., Am. Grad. Sch. Internat. Mgmt., Glendale, Ariz., 1973. Commd. 2d lt. USAF, 1964, advanced through grades to capt., 1972; instr. Armed Forces Air Intelligence Tng. Ctr., Denver, 1965-68; intelligence analyst Task Force Alpha, Nakhon Phanom, Thailand, 1968-69; intelligence systems analyst Hdqs. Tactical Air Command, Langley AFB, Va., 1969-72, resigned, 1972; sr. analyst Computer Scis. Corp., Falls Church, Va., 1974-87; dir. U.S. membership and pubs. U.S.-Mexico C. of C, Washington, 1987-91; v.p. pub. affairs bd. dirs. N.Am. Free Trade Assn., Washington, 1991-96; v.p., bd. dirs. N.Am. Trade and Investment Group, Washington, 1997-99; with U.S. Dept. State, 2005—; dept. state adviser Govt. of Iraq, US Embassy, Baghdad, 2005—. Contract team leader strategic planning studies and analyses U.S. Dept. Def., Joint Chiefs Staff, Washington, 1976—82; regional oper. supr. elections in Bosnia Orgn. Security and Coop. in Europe (OSCE), 1997, election supr., Bosnia and Kosovo, 1997—98, Bosnia and Kosovo, 2000; internat. trade cons., 1998—2005; long and short term observer, Belarus, 2001, Belarus, 04, Azerbaijan, 03, Ukraine, 04. Contbr. articles to booklets and newsletters. Bd. dirs. Columbia Plz. Tenants Assn., Washington, 1981—84; vol. Pres. Ford Com., Washington, 1976. Mem.: VFW, Washington Mgmt. and Bus. Assn. (vice chmn. 1981—83, treas. 1987—91), Thunderbird Alumni Assn. (pres. Washington chpt. 1980—87), Fgn. Policy Assn. (group leader discussion program), World Affairs Coun., Assn. Former Intelligence Officers, Has House Harriers. Republican. Avocations: jogging,

tennis, travel, discussion groups, reading. Home: 5304 Albemarle St Bethesda MD 20816-1827 Office: US Embassy Baghdad Irmo/Moi APO AE 09316 Personal E-mail: brnmarsh@hotmail.com.

**MARSHALL, CHARLES,** communications company executive; b. Vandalia, Ill., Apr. 21, 1929; s. William Forman and Ruth (Corson) M.; m. Millicent Bruner, Jan. 2, 1953; children: Ruth Ann, Marcia Marshall Rinek, William Forman, Charles Tedrick. BS in Agr. U. Ill., 1951. With Ill. Bell Telephone Co., 1953-59, 61-64, 65-70, 71-72, 77-81, pres., chief exec. officer Chgo., 1977-81; with AT&T, 1959-61, 64-65, 70-71, 76-77, 81-89; chmn., chief exec. officer Am. Bell, Morristown, N.J., 1983-84, AT&T Info. Systems, 1984-85; vice chmn. AT&T, N.Y.C., 1985-89. Bd. dirs. Moorings Park, Naples; trustee U. Ill. Found.; vice-chmn. Naples Philharm. Soc. for the Arts. Served to 1st lt. USAF, 1951-53. Mem.: Chgo. Club, Club of Pelican Bay, Comml. Club Chgo., Econ. Club Chgo. Avocations: fishing, golf, reading. Home: 6001 Pelican Bay Blvd Ph B Naples FL 34108-8168

**MARSHALL, CHARLES NOBLE,** rail transportation executive; b. Phila., Feb. 18, 1942; s. Donnell and Cornelia Lansdale (Brooke) M.; m. Ann Shaw Donovan, Jan. 12, 1971; children: Elizabeth, Caroline, Cornelia, Edward BS in Engring., Princeton U., 1963; JD, U. Mich., 1967. Bar: Md. 1967, D.C. 1975, Pa. 1978. Atty. Balt. & Ohio R.R., Balt. and Cleve., 1967-73; gen. atty. So. Ry., Washington, 1973-78; gen. counsel commerce Conrail, Phila., 1978-83, v.p mktg., 1983-85, v.p. mktg. and sales, 1985-89, sr. v.p. devel., 1989-95; pres., COO Genesee & Wyoming Inc., 1997—2005, vice chmn., 2005—06; sr. v.p. industry affairs Farmrall Sys., Inc., 2006—. Bd. dirs. Phila. Reg. Port Authority, Rails to Trails Conservancy, Pa. Hort. Soc.

**MARSHALL, CODY,** bishop; Bishop Ch. of God in Christ, No. Ill. Mem. Ch. Of God In Christ. Office: Freedom Temple Church of God in Christ 6028 S Champlain Ave Chicago IL 60637-2512

**MARSHALL, CONSUELO BLAND,** federal judge; b. Knoxville, Tenn., Sept. 28, 1936; d. Clyde Theodore and Annie (Brown) Arnold; m. George Edward Marshall, Aug. 30, 1959; children: Michael Edward, Laurie Ann. AA, L.A. City Coll., 1956; BA, Howard U., 1958, LLB, 1961. Bar: Calif. 1962. Dep. atty., City of LA, 1962-67; assoc. Cochran & Atkins, LA, 1968-70; commr. LA Superior Ct., 1971-76; judge Inglewood Mcpl. Ct., 1976-77, LA Superior Ct., 1977-80, US Dist. Ct. (ctrl dist.) Calif., LA, 1980—, chief judge, 2001—. Lectr. U.S. Information Agy. in Yugoslavia, Greece and Italy, 1984, in Nigera and Ghana, 1991, in Ghana, 1992. Contbr. articles to profl. jours.; notes editor Law Jour. Howard U. Mem. adv. bd. Richstone Child Abuse Center. Recipient Judicial Excellence award Criminal Cts. Bar Assn., 1992, Ernestine Stalhut award; named Criminal Ct. Judge of Yr., U.S. Dist. Ct., 1997; inducted into Langston Hall of Fame, 2000, Outstanding Jurist Award, LA County Bar Assn., 2005; rsch. fellow Howard U. Law Sch., 1959-60. Mem. State Bar Calif., Century City Bar Assn., Calif. Women Lawyers Assn., Calif. Assn. Black Lawyers, Calif. Judges Assn., Black Women Lawyers Assn., Los Angeles County Bar Assn., Nat. Assn. Women Judges, NAACP, Urban League, Beta Phi Sigma. Office: US Dist Ct 312 N Spring St Los Angeles CA 90012-4701

**MARSHALL, DALE ROGERS,** academic administrator, political scientist, educator; b. Mar. 22, 1937; m. Donald J. Marshall; children: Jessica, Cynthia, Clayton. BA in Govt., Cornell U., 1959; MA in Polit. Sci., U. Calif., Berkeley, 1960; PhD in Polit. Sci. with distinction, UCLA, 1969. Lectr. in polit. sci. UCLA, 1969-70, U. Calif., Berkeley, 1970-72, from asst. prof. to prof. Davis, 1972-86, faculty asst. to vice chancellor acad. affairs, 1980-82, assoc. dean Coll. Letters and Scis., 1983-86; acting pres. Wellesley (Mass.) Coll., 1987-88, dean of coll., prof. polit. sci., 1986-92; pres. Wheaton (Mass.) Coll., 1992—. Mem. exec. bd. Calif. Assembly Fellowship Program, 1980-86; bd. trustees, bd. overseers Newton-Wellesley Hosp., 1989-93; bd. trustees Cornell U., Ithaca, N.Y., 1983-93, chair Cornell Fund, co-chair Coll. Arts and Scis. Capital Campaign, 1990-93; bd. trustees New Eng. Zenith Fund, New Eng. Mut. Life Ins. Co., 1995—; bd. dirs. Am. Student Assistance Guarantor, Am. Student Assistance Corp, 1994-2001. Author: (with John C. Bollens) Guide to Participation: Field Work, Role Playing Cases and Other Forms, 1973, (with Roger Montgomery) Housing Policy for the 80's, 1980, (with Rufus P. Browning and David H. Tabb) Protest is Not Enough: The Struggle of Blacks and Hispanics for Equality in Urban Politics, 1984 (APSA Ralph J. Bunche award for best book on ethnic rels. 1985, Gladys Kammerer award for best book in Am. policy 1985); editor: Urban Policy Making, 1979, (with David K. Leonard) Institutions of Rural Development for the Poor: Decentralization and Organizatonal Linkages, 1982, (with Rufus P. Browning and David H. Tabb, co-editor) Racial Politics in American Cities, 1990, 3d edit., 2003; mem. editl. bd. Am. Polit. Sci. Rev., 1972-76, Pub. Adminstrn. Rev., 1985-86; contbr. articles to profl. jours. Woodrow Wilson fellow, 1959-60, Calif. Regents fellow, 1966-67, 67-68; NSF grantee, 1976-78, 79-80; recipient Disting. Teaching award Significant Contbn. to Status of Women citation Chancellor's Com. on Status of Women at U. Calif. at Davis, 1978. Mem. Am. Polit. Sci. Assn. (mem. exec. coun. 1974-76, v.p. 1985-86, mem. nominating com. 1988-90), Western Polit. Sci. Assn. (mem. exec. coun. 1973-75, pres. 1984-85), Nat. Acad. Pub. Adminstrn., Nat. Assn. Ind. Colls. and Univs. (bd. dirs.), Assn. Ind. Colls. and Univs. Mass. (exec. com.), Mortar Bd., Phi Beta Kappa, Phi Kappa Phi. Office: Wheaton Coll Office of Pres Norton MA 02766 E-mail: dmarshal@wheatonma.edu

**MARSHALL, DANTE,** lawyer; JD, Ohio State U., Columbus, 2003. Law clk. to Law Firm Byron L. Potts & Co., LPA, Columbus, Ohio, 2001—03; atty. Law Firm of DMEG, Atlanta, 2003—. Mem.: ABA, Cobb County Bar Assn., Black Entertainment and Sports Law Assn., Atlanta Bar Assn., Ga. State Bar Assn. Office: Law Firm DMEG 1970 Cliff Valley Way Ste 250 Atlanta GA 30329 Office Phone: 404-320-5212. Office Fax: 404-320-5214. E-mail: info@dmeglaw.com

**MARSHALL, DEBRA LYNN,** secondary school educator; b. Charleston, W.Va., July 7, 1956; d. James L. Marshall and Lena B. Bailey. BA in English cum laude, Ohio State U., Columbus, 1998; MEd in English, Ohio State U., 1999. Tchr. H.S. English Piqua (Ohio) City Sch., 1999—2003, Moreno Valley (Calif.) Unified Schs., 2003—. Adj. faculty Edison C.C., Piqua, 2001—03; coord. Ohio Writing Project, Piqua, 2000—02. Author: (short stories) Super Boy, 2003 (Hon. Mention award Sinclair C.C., 2003). Mem. pub. rels. team Spring Arts Show The Piqua (Ohio) Arts Coun., 2003. Mem.: NEA, Nat. Coun. Tchrs. English, Calif. Assn. Tchrs. English, Calif. Tchrs. Assn. Avocations: dog training, painting, cello. Office: CanyonSprings High School 23100 Cougar Canyon Dr Moreno Valley CA 92557 Office Phone: 951-571-4760. E-mail: marshalld4@adelphia.net.

**MARSHALL, DONALD E.,** mathematics professor; s. Donald and Jeanne Cawley Marshall; m. Marianne Jensen, Sept. 2, 1972; children: Kirsten Jensen, Bjorn J., Hans-Peter. PhD, UCLA, L.A., 1976. Prof. math. U. Wash., Seattle, 1976—, chair, dept math., 1998—2001; vis. prof. Mittag-Leffler Inst., Royal Swedish Acad. of Scis., Djursholm, Sweden, 1982—83, U. Bergen, Norway, 2003—04. Cons. Jet Propulsion Lab, Pasadena, Calif., 1975. Contbr. scientific papers. Recipient Disting. Svc. Award, UCLA, 1976; grantee Royalty Rsch. Fund, U. Wash. 1995—96, 2002—03; scholar Nat. Merit Scholarship, 1966; Thord-Gray Fellowship, American-Scandinavian Found., 1982-1983, NSF-NATO Postdoctoral Fellowship, NSF. Mem.: Am. Math. Soc. Office: Univ Wash Box 354350 Dept Math Seattle WA 98195-4350 Office Phone: 206-543-9352. Office Fax: 206-543-0397. E-mail: marshall@math.washington.edu.

**MARSHALL, DONALD GLENN,** English language and literature educator; b. Long Beach, Calif., Sept. 9, 1943; s. Albert Louis and Margaret Corinne (Morrison) M.; m. Kathleen Bonann, June 21, 1975; children: Stephanie Deborah, Zachary Louis AB summa cum laude, Harvard U., 1965; MPhil, Yale U., 1969, PhD, 1971. Asst. prof. English UCLA, 1969-75; from assoc. prof. to prof. English U. Iowa, Iowa City, 1975-90; honors dir. U. Iowa Coll Liberal Arts, 1981-85; prof. English dept. U. Ill., Chgo., 1990—2003, head dept., 1990—2000; prof. Great Books Pepperdine U., Malibu, Calif., 2003—. Editor: Philosophy as Literature/Literature as Philosophy, 1986, The Force of Tradition: Response and Resistance in Literature, Religion, and Cultural Studies, 2005; compiler: Contemporary Critical Theory: A Selective Bibliography, 1993; translator: (with Joel Weinsheimer) Truth and Method by Hans-Georg Gadamer, 1989; contbr. articles and revs. to profl. jours. Recipient Bell prize Harvard U., 1965, Webster prize Yale U., 1967; NEH Younger Humanist fellow, 1973-74; grantee UCLA, U. Iowa Mem.: MLA, Ill. Humanities Coun. (bd. dirs. 1994—2000, active Chgo. Humanities Festival 1997—2003), The Poetry Found. (pres. 1998—2000, bd. dir. 1996—), Conf. Christianity and Lit. (bd. dirs. 2000—03). Democrat. Roman Catholic. Office: Pepperdine U Divsn Humanities and Tchr Edn 24255 Pacific Coast Hwy Malibu CA 90263 Office Phone: 310-506-7654. Business E-Mail: Donald.Marshall@pepperdine.edu.

**MARSHALL, DOUGLAS WILLIAM,** health research administrator, educator; b. Indpls., July 1, 1943; s. William Pryor and Virginia (Guthrie) M.; m. Heidi Christina Amenda, May 30, 1985; 1 child, W. Parker. BA, Denison U., Granville, Ohio, 1965; AM, U. Mich., 1967, PhD, 1976. Western field mgr. U. Mich. Alumni Assn., San Francisco, 1967-69; assoc. curator W.L. Clements Libr. Am. History U. Mich., Ann Arbor, 1970-82; project dir. Campbell-Ewald Co., Warren, Mich., 1982-83; sr. account exec. N.W. Ayer, Inc., Detroit, 1984; mgr. strategic planning GM, Detroit, 1985-91; program mgr. GM Internat., Detroit, 1991-96; CEO Onkoservices, Detroit, 1996-97; v.p. new bus. devel. Innovative Solutions in Healthcare, Detroit, 1997-99; prin. Blitz and Assoc. LLC, 2000—05; v.p. bus. devel. Idetix Inc., 2005—. Adj. assoc. prof. radiation oncology Sch. Medicine, Wayne State U., Detroit, 1996-2000; coord. program in history of discovery U. Mich., Ann Arbor, 1973-81. Co-author: (with H.H. Peckham) Campaigns of the American Revolution: An Atlas Manuscript Maps, 1976; exec. editor Terrae Incognitae: Annals of the Soc. for the History of Discoveries, 1975-82, editor: Research Catalog of Maps of America to 1860, 4 vols., 1972; writer, narrator: (with U. Mich. TV series) Maps: Horizons to Knowledge, 1981. Dir. Gt. Lakes region Am. Cancer Soc. Found., 1996-2005; mem. dean's adv. bd. Rackham Grad. Sch., U. Mich., 1999—; mem. S.E. Mich. strategic planning bd. United Found., Detroit, 1982-83; trustee City of Grosse Pointe Found., 2004—. Rsch. fellow Nat. Geog. Soc., 1977; recipient Bicentennial award Bicentennial Commn., State of Mich., 1974; Fulbright lectr. U.S. Fulbright Commn., Helsinki U., 1980-81; William Andrews Clark postdoctoral fellow UCLA, 1979. Mem. Mich. Map Soc. (pres. 1984-85), Soc. for the History of Discoveries (coun. 1979-81), Bohemian Club Calif. Episcopalian. Home: 545 University Pl Grosse Pointe MI 48230-1639 also: 7090 Windemere PO Box 152 Harbor Springs MI 49740 Office: 21 Kercheval Ave Ste 270 Grosse Pointe MI 48236 Business E-Mail: marshall@karmanos.org.

**MARSHALL, ELAINE FOLK,** state official; b. Lineboro, Md., Nov. 18, 1945; d. Donald and Pauline Folk; m. Bill Holdford; 5 stepchildren. BS in Textiles and Clothing, U. Md., 1968; JD, Campbell U., 1981; D (hon.), Meredith Coll., 2004, Lees McRae Coll., 2005. Bar: N.C., U.S. Dist. Ct. (ea. and mid. dists.), U.S. Ct. Appeals (4th cir.), U.S. Supreme Ct. Tchr., 1968—75; owner retail bus., 1968-79; assoc. Bain Law Firm, Lillington, NC, 1981-84; ptnr. Bain & Marshall, Lillington, 1985-92, Marshall & Marshall, Lillington, 1993-96; sec.of state State of N.C., 1997—. Legal advisor Bus. and Profl. Women, N.C., 1982-90; mem. 15th dist. N.C. Senate, 1993-94, N.C. Capital Planning Commn., 1993-94, 1997-, N.C. Cts. Commn., 1993-94, bd. mem. Nat. Electronic Commerce Coord. Coun., 2001-03, 2005—, v.p., 2005-06, bd. mem. Nat. Assn. Secretaries of State, 2001-04. Bd. dirs. Harnett County United Way, 1987-97, N.C. 4-H Devel. Fund, Inc., 1990—, N.C. Rural Econ. Fund, 1993-95, N.C. Bd. Econ. Devel., 1993-94, 97—, N.C. Ctr. Pub. Policy Rsch., 1994-99, N.C. Justice Acad. Found., 1994-98; mem. Divine St. United Meth. Ch.; founding chmn., hon. chmn. Harnett HelpNet Children, 1992—; trustee Meredith Coll., 1997-2002. Recipient N.C. Friends Ext. award, 1992, Spl. Achievement award, N.C. Acad. Trial Lawyers, 2000, Alumni of Yr. award, N.C. 4-H Found., Lifetime Achievement award, 2003, Best of Breed, In the Arena awards, Ctr. Digital Govt., 2002, Top 25 award, Govt. Tech. Mag., 2003, Atty. of Yr. award, N.C. Assn. Women Attorneys, 2004, Women in Bus. award RBC Centura Bank and Triangle Bus. Jour., 2005, Hon. Gold Record award Recording Industry Am., 2005, U.L. Lab. award, 2005, Get Real award Internat. Anti Counterfeit Coalition, 2005. Fellow N.C. Inst. Polit. Leadership (bd. dirs. 1996—); mem. Women's Forum N.C., Gamma Sigma Delta, Delta Kappa Gamma. Democrat. Office: 2 S Salisbury St Raleigh NC 27601 Office Phone: 919-807-2005. Business E-Mail: emarshall@sosnc.com.

**MARSHALL, ELLEN RUTH,** lawyer; b. NYC, Apr. 23, 1949; d. Louis and Faith (Gladstone) M. AB, Yale U., 1971; JD, Harvard U., 1974. Bar: Calif. 1975, D.C. 1981, N.Y. 1989. Assoc. McKenna & Fitting, LA, 1975-80; ptnr. McKenna, Conner & Cuneo, LA and Orange County, Calif., 1980-88, Morrison & Foerster, LLP, Orange County, 1988—2003, Manatt, Phelps & Phillips LLP, Orange County, 2003—. Mem. ABA (bus. law sect., mem. savs. inst. com., mem. asset securitization com., tax sect., mem. employee benefits com.), Orange County Bar Assn., Center Club (Costa Mesa, Calif.), Yale Club (N.Y.C.). Office: Manatt Phelps & Phillips LLP 695 Town Ctr Dr Costa Mesa CA 92626

**MARSHALL, FRANCIS JOSEPH,** aerospace engineer; b. NYC, Sept. 5, 1923; s. Francis Joseph and Mary Gertrude (Leary) M.; m. Joan Eager, June 14, 1952; children— Peter, Colin, Stephen, Dana. BS in Mech. Engring., CCNY, 1948; MS, Rensselaer Poly. Inst., 1950; Dr. Eng. Sci., N.Y. U., 1955. Engr. Western Union Co., N.Y.C., 1948, Gen. Electric Co., Schenectady, 1948-50; engr. Wright-Aero Corp., Woodridge, NJ, 1950-52; group leader Lab. for Applied Scis., U. Chgo., 1955-60; instr. Ill. Inst. Tech., 1957-59; prof. Sch. Aeros. and Astronautics, Purdue U., West Lafayette, Ind., 1960—. Engr. U.S. Naval Underseas Warfare Center, Pasadena, Calif., 1966-68; faculty fellow NASA-Langley, 1969-70; vis. prof. Inst. Tech. Mara-Midwest Univs. Consortium for Internat. Activities, Malaysia, 1989 Contbr. articles to profl. jours. Served with U.S. Army, 1943-46. Decorated Combat Inf. badge.; Rsch. grantee NASA, 1970-76; Fulbright scholar, Turkey, 1988-89. Assoc. fellow AIAA; mem. Am. Soc. Engring. Edn., AAUP. Home: 120 Leslie Ave West Lafayette IN 47906-2410 Office: Sch Aeros and Astronautics Purdue U West Lafayette IN 47907

**MARSHALL, FRANK W.,** film producer, director; b. L.A., Sept. 13, 1946; m. Kathleen Kennedy. Student, UCLA. Location mgr.: The Last Picture Show, 1971, What's Up Doc?, 1972; assoc. prodr.: Paper Moon, 1973, Daisy Miller, 1974, At Long Last Love, 1975. Nickelodeon, 1976, The Driver, 1978; line prodr.: Orson Welles' The Other Side of the Wind (unreleased), Marin Scorsese's The Last Waltz, 1977; prodr.: (films) Raiders of the Lost Ark, 1981 (Academy award nomination for best picture 1981), Noises Off, 1992; (with Steven Spielberg) Poltergeist, 1982; (with Spielberg, Quincy Jones, and Kathleen Kennedy) The Color Purple, 1985 (Academy award nomination for best picture 1985), (with Kathleen Kennedy and Kane Startz) Indian in a Cupboard, 1995; (with Spielberg and Kennedy) Empire of the Sun, 1987, Always, 1989; (with Robert Watts) Who Framed Roger Rabbit, 1988; (with Kennedy and Gerald R. Molen) Hook, 1991; (with Kennedy) Milk Money, 1994, The Sixth Sense, 1999, Snow Falling on Cedars, 1999, A Map of the World, 1999, Signs, 2002, The Young Black Stallion, 2003, The Bourne Supremacy, 2004, Roving Mars, 2006; exec. prodr.: (films) The Warriors, 1979, Twilight Zone-The Movie, 1983; (with George Lucas) Indiana Jones and the Temple of Doom, 1984; (with Kennedy and Spielberg) Gremlins, 1984, The Goonies, 1985, Back to the Future, 1985, Young Sherlock Holmes, 1985, *batteries not included, 1987, Dad, 1989, Back to the Future Part II, 1989, Gremlins 2: The New Batch, 1990, Back to the Future Part III, 1990, Joe Versus the Volcano, 1990, Cape Fear, 1991, We're Back! A Dinosaur's Story, 1993; (with Kennedy) Fandango, 1985; (with Kennedy, Spielberg, and David Kirschner) An American Tail, 1986; (with Kennedy and Art Levinson) The Money Pit, 1986; (with Kennedy, Spielberg, Peter Guber, and Jon Peters) Innerspace, 1987; (with Kennedy, Lucas, and Spielberg) The Land Before Time, 1988; (with Kennedy and Lucas) Indiana Jones and the Last Crusade, 1989; (with Kennedy and Kirschner) An American Tail: Fievel Goes West,

1991; (with Chris Meledandri) Swing Kids, 1993; (with Kennedy and Molen) A Far Off Place, 1993, Swing Kids, 1993, Congo, 1995, The Sports Pages, 2001, The Bourne Identity, 2002, Mr. 3000, 2004; exec. prodr. (with Spielberg, Robert W. Cort, and Ted Field), dir.: Arachnophobia, 1990; dir.: Alive, 1993, Congo, 1995, Eight Below, 2006; exec. producer: TV Roger Rabbit and the Secret of Toontown; prodr., dir. TV Johnny Bago. Address: Kennedy-Marshall Co 1351 4th St Fl 4 Santa Monica CA 90401-1358*

**MARSHALL, GAILEN DAUGHERTY, JR.,** allergist, educator; b. Houston, Sept. 9, 1950; s. Gailen D. and Evelyn C. (Gresham) M.; m. Elizabeth M. Marek, Nov. 5, 1978; children: Sarah Elizabeth, Jonathan David, Rebecca Marie. BS, U. Houston, 1972; MS, Tex. A&M U., 1975; PhD, U. Tex., 1979, MD, 1984. Rsch. sci. U. Tex., Galveston, 1981-84; rsch. fellow U. Iowa, Iowa City, 1985-86; lab. dir. Biotherapeutics Inc., Memphis, 1986-88; chief med. resident Bapt. Meml. Hosp., Memphis, 1988-89; assoc. dir. Rsch. for Health Inc., Houston, 1989-90; dir. divsn. allergy and immunology U. Tex., Houston, 1990—2004, clin. asst. prof. medicine, 1990-91, asst. prof. medicine, 1991—98, assoc. prof. medicine and pathology, 1998—2003, prof., 2003—04; vice chair medicine, dir. divsn. clin. immunology and allergy U. Miss. Med. Ctr., Jackson, Miss., 2004—, prof. medicine and pediatrics. Mem. sci. adv. com. Carrington Labs., Dallas, 1992-94; mem. Merck Rhinitis Adv. Bd., 2002-05, Genentech/Novartis Adv. Bd., 2003—. Mem. editl. bd. Molecular Biotherapy, 1992-93, Cancer Biotherapy, 1994-96, Allergy Procs., 1994-2003, Annals Allergy, Asthma and Immunology, 1995-99, Jour. Interferon Cytokin Rsch., 1999-2005, Clin. Immunology, 2001-05, Jour. Clin. Immunology, 2002-05, Cellular Molecular Allergy, 2003-05; editor-in-chief Annals of Allergy, Asthma and Immunology, 2006—; contbr. articles to profl. jours. Judge Greater Houston Sci. Fair, 1992—; adv. bd. Merck Rhinitis, 2002-04, Grenentech Worch's, 2003-05. Fellow ACP, Am. Coll. Allergy and Immunology, Am. Acad. Allergy-Immunology (chair com.); mem. Tex. Allergy-Immunology Soc. (chair com., bd. dirs. 1999-2002), Greater Houston Allergy Soc. Republican. Baptists. Avocations: classical music, fishing. Office: U Miss Med Ctr 2500 N State St Jackson MS 39216 Office Phone: 601-815-5527. Business E-Mail: gmarshall@umsmed.edu.

**MARSHALL, GARRY K. (GARRY KENT MARSCIARELLI),** film producer, director, writer; b. N.Y.C., Nov. 13, 1934; m. Barbara Marshall, Mar. 1963; children: Lori, Kathleen, Scott. BS, Northwestern U. Writer Jack Paar Show, Joey Bishop Show, Danny Thomas Show; writer (TV series) Make Room For Daddy, 1953, The Dick Van Dyke Show, 1961, The Lucy Show, 1962, Gomer Pyle, USMC, 1964, I Spy, 1965, Barefoot in the Park, 1970, Love, American Style, 1969; writer (TV films) Sheriff Who, 1967 (also prodr.), The Murdocks and the McClays, 1970; writer, creator, prodr. (TV series) Hey Landlord, 1966; writer, creator (TV film) Wednesday Night Out, 1972; dir., exec. prodr. (TV series) The Odd Couple, 1970; creator, dir., prodr. Evil Roy Slade, 1972; creator, writer, exec. prodr., dir. Happy Days, 1974, Laverne and Shirley, 1976 (co-creator), Mork and Mindy, 1978; writer, prodr.(films) How Sweet It Is, 1968, The Grasshopper, 1970; screenwriter, dir. (films) Flamingo Kid, 1984, The Other Sister, 1999; dir. (films) Young Doctors in Love, 1982 (also exec. prodr.), Nothing in Common, 1987 (also prodr.), The Lottery, 1987, Overboard, 1987, Beaches, 1988, Pretty Woman, 1990, Frankie & Johnny, 1991 (also prodr.), Exit to Eden, 1994 (also prodr.), Dear God, 1996, Runaway Bride, 1999, The Princess Diaries, 2001, Raising Helen, 2004, The Princess Diaries 2:Royal Engagement, 2004; dir. (TV series) Me and the Chimp, 1972 (also creator, exec. prodr.), Blansky's Beauties, 1977 (also prodr.), Herndon, 1983 (also exec. prodr.), Murphy Brown, 1988; creator, dir., exec. prodr. (TV films) Dominic's Dream, 1974; actor (film) The Phony American, 1961, Maryjane, 1968, Psych-Out, 1968, Grand Theft Auto, 1977, Lost In America, 1985, Jumpin' Jack Flash, 1986, Secret Agent OO Soul, 1990, Soapdish, 1991, A League of Their Own, 1992, Statistically Speaking, 1995, With Friends Like These, 1998, Never Been Kissed, 1999, This Space Between Us, 2000, It's a Shame About Ray, 2000, Can't Be Heaven, 2000, Tomcats, 2001, The Hollywood Sign, 2001, (voice) The Majestic, 2001, Orange County, 2002, Mother Ghost, 2002, Devil's Knight, 2003, The Long Ride Home, 2003, They Call Him Sasquatch, 2003, Lucky 13, 2005, (voice) Chicken Little, 2005; actor (TV films) But Seriously, Folks, 1986, The Last Shot, 1993, The Twilight of the Golds, 1997 (also exec. prodr.), Frank Capra's American Dream, 1997, CHiPs '99, 1998; exec. prodr. (TV series) Who's Watching the Kids, 1978, Angie, 1979, Joanie Loves Chachi, 1982; (TV films) Beanes of Boston, 1979; guest appearances include Dick Van Dyke Show, 1965, 1966, Hey Landlord, 1967, The Odd Couple, 1974, Happy Days, 1975, Laverne & Shirley, 1976, Vega$, 1980, Murphy Brown, 1994-1997 (several episodes), The Naked Truth, 1997, The Simpsons (voice) 1999, Mad TV, 2000, Three Sisters, 2001, 2002, Monk, 2002, Sabrina, The Teenage Witch, 2002, Father of the Pride (voice), 2004, Unscripted, 2005, and several others. Office: Pkwy Prodns 10202 Washington Blvd Culver City CA 90232-3119*

**MARSHALL, GARY S.,** lawyer; b. Charlottesville, Va., 1952; AB magna cum laude, Princeton U., 1974; JD, Coll. William and Mary, Williamsburg, Va., 1979. Bar: Va. 1979, U.S. Dist. Ct. Ea. Dist. Va. 1979, US Dist. Ct. We. Dist. Va. 1980, US Ct. Appeals 4th Cir. 1979, US Ct. Appeals 8th Cir. 1988, US Ct. Appeals 7th Cir. 1997. Ptnr. McGuireWoods LLP, Richmond, Va., 1987—, chair firm labor & employment dept. Adj. prof. labor law U. Richmond, 1984—87. Mem.: ABA (mem. sect. labor & employment 1994—). Office: McGuireWoods LLP One James Ctr 901 E Cary St Richmond VA 23219-4030 Office Phone: 804-775-1013. Office Fax: 804-698-2104. Business E-Mail: gmarshall@mcguirewoods.com.

**MARSHALL, GERALD FRANCIS,** optical engineer, consultant, physicist; b. Seven Kings, Eng., Feb. 26, 1929; BSc in Physics, London U., 1952. Physicist Morganite Internat., London, 1954—59; sr. rsch. devel. engr. Ferranti Ltd., Edinburgh, Scotland, 1959—67; project mgr. Diffraction Limited Inc., Bedford, Mass., 1967—69; dir. engring. Medical Lasers, Inc., Burlington, Mass., 1969—71, staff cons. Speeding Systems, Troy, Mich., 1971—76; dir. optical engring. Energy Conversion Devices, Inc., Troy, Mich., 1976—87; sr. tech. staff specialist Kaiser Electronics, San Jose, Calif., 1987—89; cons. in optics design and engring., 1989—. Editor, contbg. author: Laser Beam Scanning, 1985, Optical Scanning, 1991, Handbook of Optical and Laser Scanning, 2004. Fellow: Internat. Soc. Optical Engring. (bd. dirs. 1991—93), Optical Soc. Am. Achievements include patents in field. Home and Office: 410 Dusenbury St Niles MI 49120-1468

**MARSHALL, GERALD LEE,** mathematician, educator; b. Franklin County, N.C., June 27, 1947; s. George Eugene Marshall and Roberta Odell Perry; m. Judy Faye Beck, Nov. 24, 1971; 1 child, Kera Beck; m. Karen Louise Gebhart, June 19, 1971 (div.); children: Katharine Elizabeth, Katrina Marie. BSChE, N.C. State U., 1969; ThM in Christian Theology, Luther Rice Sem., 1997; MLS, Fla. State U., 1977; MDiv in New Testament Greek, Luther Rice Sem., 1976, DMin Theol. Libr., 1979; AA, C.C. Chgo., Wiesbaden, Germany, 1985; MA in Math., U. Ala., 1997; PhD in Math Edn., Ill. State U., 2000. Ordained Christian min. So. Bapt. Conv., 1985. Pastor Aschaffenburg Bapt. Ch., Germany, 1985—87; adj. lectr. C.C. Chgo., Wiesbaden, Germany, 1984—87; min. edn. Hillsboro Heights Bapt. Ch., Huntsville, Ala., 1987—89; supr. environ. svcs. Huntsville Hosp. Sys., 1989—98; adj. instr. Calhoun C.C., Decatur, Ala., 1989—98, Heartland C.C., Bloomington, Ill., 1998—2000; head. math. dept. Tri-County Tech. Coll., Pendleton, SC, 2001—. V.p. Tri-County Tech. Edn. Assn., Pendleton, SC, 2002—04; master presenter Nat. Inst. for Staff and Orgnl. Devel., Austin, Tex., 2002; presenter S.C. Tech. Edn. Assn., Myrtle Beach, SC, 2002—02. Contbr. articles to profl. jours. Capt. USAF, 1969—72, U.S. and Thailand. Grantee NSF, 2000—02, Sustainable Univs. Initiatives, 2002. Mem.: S.C. Math. Assn. Two-Yr. Colls. (pres. 2004—), S.C. Coun. Tchrs. Math., Nat. Assn. Math. Tchr. Educators, Am. Math. Assn. Two-Year Colls., Nat. Coun. Tchrs. Math., Math. Assn. Am. Southern Baptist. Avocations: travel, mathematics history. Home: 2701 Bellview Rd Anderson SC 29621 Office: Tri-County Tech Coll P O Box 587 Pendleton SC 29670 Office Phone: 864-646-1368. Business E-Mail: gmarshal@tctc.edu.

**MARSHALL, GRAYSON WILLIAM, JR.,** materials scientist, biomedical engineer, health sciences educator, dentist; b. Balt., Feb. 12, 1943; s. Grayson William and Muriel Marie Marshall; m. Sally Jean Rimkus, July 4, 1970; children: Grayson W. III, Jonathan Charles. BS in Metall. Engring., Va. Poly. Inst., 1965; PhD in Materials Sci., Northwestern U., 1972, DDS, 1986; MPH, U. Calif., Berkeley, 1992. Cert. dentist. Rsch. assoc., design and devel. ctr. Northwestern U., Evanston, Ill., 1972-73, NIH fellow, 1973, instr. Dental and Med. Schs. Chgo., 1973-74, asst. prof. Dental Sch., 1974-78, assoc. prof. Dental Sch. and Grad. Sch., 1978-87; prof. preventive and restorative dental scis. U. Calif., San Francisco, 1987—, chief biomaterials sect., 1985-92, chmn. biomaterials and bioengring. divsn., 1992—, vice chmn. rsch., 2005—. Chmn. oral and craniaofacial scis. program U of Calif., San Francisco, 2002—, UCSF Grad. Coun., 2003-05; guest scientist Lawrence Livermore Nat. Lab., 1989-2000, Lawrence Berkeley Nat. Lab., 1989—; cons. oral biology and medicine study sect. NIH, 1988-92; dir. Clin. Rsch. Unit, 1992-96, Dentist-Sci. Award Program, 1996-2004, Integrated DDS-PhD Program, 1996—, Comprehensive Oral Health Rsch. Tng. Program, 2001—. Contbr. articles to profl. jours. and books Mem. City of Larkspur Heritage Preservation Bd., 1998—, chmn., 2006—. Recipient Spl. Dental Rsch. award Nat. Inst. Dental Rsch., 1975, Rsch. Lectr. award U. Calif., San Francisco, 1994; vis. fellow U. Melbourne, Australia, 1981. Fellow: AAAS, Acad. Dental Materials (exec. sec. 1983—85, chmn. credentials 1984—91, bd. dirs. 1985—93, mem. editl. bd. Scanning Microscopy 1987—93, sec. 1988—91, pres. 1991—93, Cells and Materials 1992—2000, sect. editor 1993—2000, Jour. Oral Rehab. 1994—, Dent Mater 1998—, Am. Jour. Dentistry 2004—), Am. Coll. Dentists, Internat. Coll. Dentists; mem.: AIME, APHA, ADA (assoc. editor Jour. ADA 2002—05), U.S. Power Squadrons, U.S. Naval Inst., Calif. Pub. Health Assn.-North, Calif. Acad. Scis., N.Y. Acad. Scis., Am. Assn Dental Rsch. (bd. dirs. 1996—98, San Francisco coun. 1997—), Microscopy Soc. Am., Am. Soc. Metals, Am. Coll. Sports Medicine, Internat. Assn. Dental Rsch. (Chgo. sect. officer 1978—80, dental materials coun. 1990—96, pres. 1998—99), Soc. Biomaterials, Am. Dental Edn. Assn. (sect. officer 1981—83), Omicron Kappa Upsilon, Sigma Gamma Epsilon, Sigma Xi, Alpha Sigma Mu. Avocations: swimming, sailing, hiking, travel. Office: U Calif Dept Preven & Restor Dental Scis San Francisco CA 94143-0758 Office Phone: 415-476-9119. Business E-Mail: gw.marshall@ucsf.edu, gwmarshall@lbl.gov.

**MARSHALL, GREGORY K.,** food service executive; m. LaNese Marshall; 4 children. Bachelor's Degree, Colo. Coll.; MBA, U. Denver. V.p. mktg. Nobel/Sysco Food Svcs. Co., Denver; sr. v.p. Sysco Corp., Houston, 1993—, CEO Sygma Network Inc., 1993—. Office: Sysco Corp 1390 Enclave Pkwy Houston TX 77077-2099

**MARSHALL, HELEN M.,** city manager; m. Donald E. Marshall; children: Donald Jr., Agnes Marie. BA, Queens Coll.; student, L.I. U. Dir. Langston Hughes Libr., 1969; Elmcor Testing Assessment and Placement Program; mem. NY State Assembly, Dist. 35, 1983—91; city councilwoman Dist. 21, NYC, 1992—2001; borough pres. Queens, 2001—. Chmn. stds. and ethics com., mem. edn., housing and bldg. and environ. protection coms. Dem. nat. committeewoman, N.Y., 1975; del. Dem. Nat. Conv., 1980; mem. Nat. Dem. Exec. Com., N.Y. State assemblywoman, Dist. 35, 1983-91, past mem. cities, election law, higher edn., labor and transp. coms., chairwoman airport devel. subcom., 1985; vice chairwoman Women's Legis. Caucus, 1985, past chairwoman standing com. on state-fed. rels. Office: 120-55 Queens Blvd Kew Gardens NY 11424 Office Phone: 718-286-3000. E-mail: Marshall4Queens@aol.com.*

**MARSHALL, HEMAN ALEXANDER, III,** lawyer; b. Roanoke, Va., Feb. 15, 1950; s. Heman Alexander Jr. and Jeanne (Martin) M.; children: Alexander Tevis, Claiborne Henebry, Courtney Littlepaige; m. Judith Skaff, July 6, 1996. BA, U. Va., 1972, JD, 1975. Bar: Va. Assoc. Woods, Rogers, Muse, Walker & Thornton, Roanoke, Va., 1975-80, ptnr., 1981-85, Woods, Rogers & Hazlegrove, P.L.C., Roanoke, Va., 1985-93, prin., 1994—, pres., 1995—2001, chmn., 1997—2002. Contbr. articles to profl. jours. Bd. dirs. Binaba Found., 2003—, Nat. Conf. Cmty. and Justice, Roanoke, 2000—04, Art Mus. Western Va., 2000—04. Fellow Va. Law Found., Am. Bar Found.; mem. ABA, Va. State Bar (chmn. health law sect. 1988-89, antitrust law sect. 1989-90), Va. Bar Assn. (chmn. health law sect. 1991-92, bd. govs. 2000-04, chmn. law practice mgmt. divsn. 2002-04), Health Law Sect. Governing Coun., Roanoke Bar Assn., Am. Health Lawyers Assn. Home: 6629 Cotton Hill Rd Roanoke VA 24018-6915 Office: Woods Rogers PLC 10 S Jefferson St Ste 1400 Roanoke VA 24011-1331 Office Phone: 540-983-7654. Business E-Mail: marshall@woodsrogers.com.

**MARSHALL, HOWARD LOWEN,** musicologist, retired music educator; b. Nokesville, Va., July 21, 1931; s. Howard Hampton and Florence Annie (Nash) Marshall; m. Doris Mae Rosencranz, July 14, 1962. B in Music Edn., Shenandoah U., 1952; MusM, U. Cin., 1958; PhD, U. Rochester, 1968. Asst. prof. music Lake Forest (Ill.) Coll., 1966-73; Charles B. Thompson prof. music Mercer U., Macon, Ga., 1974—98, Charles B. Thompson emeritus prof. music, 1998—, chmn. dept. music, 1974-97. Author: The Four-Voice Motets of Thomas Crecquillon, Symbolism in Schubert's Winterreise in Studies in Romanticism, The Motets of Georg Prenner. Lt. comdr. USNR. Mem.: Am. Musicological Soc., Phi Kappa Lambda, Phi Mu Alpha. Avocation: photography. Home: 7 W Harbor Pond Rd West Boothbay Harbor ME 04575

**MARSHALL, JAMES CREEL,** congressman; b. Ithaca, NY, Mar. 31, 1948; s. Robert Creel and Mary Elizabeth (Pie) M.; m. Camille Hope, Mar. 17, 1976; children: Elizabeth, Robert Creel III. AB, Princeton Univ., 1972; JD, Boston Univ., 1977. Bar Ga. 1977. Mayor City of Macon, 1995—97; mem. US Congress from 3rd Ga. dist., 2003—. Contbr. articles to profl. jours. Pres. Macon Heritage Assn., 1989-90, Leadership Macon, 1988-90; commn. Macon Housing Authority, 1988-95; mem. bd. govs. State Bar Ga., 1995—, mem. adv. bd. US Conf. of Mayors, 1997—; co-chair econ. devel. Nat. Conf. of Dem. Mayors, 1996—, chair criminal justice com. Ga. Mcpl. Assn., 1997—. With US Army, 1968-70, Vietnam. Mem. Macon Bar Assn. (pres. 1992-93), Palaver Club of Macon, League of Women Voters. Democrat. Roman Catholic. Avocations: reading, sports, hunting, piddling. Office: US Ho Reps 502 Cannon Ho Office Bldg Washington DC 20515-1003

**MARSHALL, JEFFERY M.,** retail executive; b. Greenwich, Conn. Studied, Julliard; B in comparative lit., Columbia U. Programmer Honeywell Info. Systems; with United Telecommunications; v.p. info. and tech. The Men's Wearhouse Inc., 1996—98, v.p., chief info. officer, 1998—2003, sr. v.p., chief info. officer, 2003—05 Kohl's Corp., 2005—. Named one of Premier 100 IT Leaders, Computerworld, 2005. Office: Kohl's Corp N56 W17000 Ridgewood Dr Menomonee Falls WI 53051*

**MARSHALL, JEFFREY SCOTT,** mechanical engineer, educator; b. Cin., Feb. 10, 1961; s. James C. and Norma E. (Everett) M.; m. Marilyn Jane Patterson, July 16, 1983; children: Judith K., Eric G., Emily J., Paul E. BS summa cum laude, UCLA, 1983, MS, 1984; PhD, U. Calif., Berkeley, 1987. Asst. rsch. engr. U. Calif., Berkeley, 1988; engr. Creare, Inc., Hanover, NH, 1988-89; from asst. to assoc. prof. dept. ocean engring. Fla. Atlantic U., 1989-93; from assoc. prof. to prof. dept. mech. engring. U. Iowa, Iowa City, 1993—2001, prof., 2001—06, chair dept. mech. and indsl. engring., 2001—06; prof. U. Vt., Burlington, Vt., 2006—, dir. Sch. Engring., 2006—. Assoc. editor Jour. Fluids Engring.; contbr. articles to profl. jours.; textbook author. Recipient Young Investigator award, 1992-95. Fellow ASME (assoc. editor jour. Fluids Engring. 2001-04, Henry Hess award 1992); mem. Am. Phys. Soc., Tau Beta Pi. Achievements include research in fluid mechanics, three-dimensional vortex dynamics and vortex-structure interaction, particulate flows, and thin film flows. Office: U Iowa Dept Mech & Indsl Engring Iowa City IA 52242 Office Phone: 319-335-5817. Business E-Mail: jeffrey-marshall@uiowa.edu.

**MARSHALL, JO TAYLOR,** social worker; b. N.Y.C. BA, Sarah Lawrence Coll., 1957; MSW, Columbia U., 1959. Cert. clin. social worker, NY, NJ; bd. cert. diplomate. Caseworker Youth Cons. Svcs., 1960-62; program cons. Social Work Recruiting Ctr., 1962-63; casework supr. Louise Wise Svcs., 1963-68; faculty field instr. sch. social work Columbia U., N.Y.C., 1968-70; coord. social work vol. and student tng. programs St. Lukes/Roosevelt Hosp. Ctr., 1970-75; asst. dir. fieldwork, faculty lectr. in health care Columbia U., N.Y.C., 1975-78; dir. social work and psychiat. emergency svcs. Morristown Meml. Hosp., 1978—95; social worker pvt. practice, 1995—2002; ret., 2002. Adj. prof. Columbia U.; adv. bd., faculty Nat. Discharge Planning Inst. SUNY, Buffalo; prin. speaker, cons. Hosp. Assn. Pa., 1983, Mid-Atlantic Health Congress, 1985, VA, East Orange, N.J., 1986, Hosp. Assn. Tenn., 1987; adv. com. Rutgers GGrad. Sch. Social Work; mem. multidisciplinary state rev. com. for discharge planning standards in N.J. Contbr. articles to profl. jours.; produced and cons. on numerous film and TV prodns. Named Dir. of Yr., N.J. Hosp. Social Work, 1989-90. Mem.: NASW, Acad. Cert. Social Workers, Soc. Hosp. Social Work Dirs. (exec. bd., pres. N.J. chpt. 1988—89, chmn. nat. media task force). Achievements include The New Welcome Terrace at Columbia Grad. Sch. of Social Work named in her honor. Home (Winter): 1230 Hillsboro Mile Hillsboro Beach FL 33062-1344 Home (Summer): PO Box 40 Far Hills NJ 07931-0040 Office Phone: 908-553-5444. Personal E-mail: jomase@msn.com.

**MARSHALL, JOAN** See HELPERN, JOAN

**MARSHALL, JOHN CROOK,** internal medicine educator, researcher; b. Blackburn, Lancashire, Eng., Feb. 28, 1941; came to US, 1976; s. Albert Acey and Marion Miller (Crook) M.; m. Marilyn Dallas Parry, Sept. 20, 1969; children: Samantha Jane, Susannah Crook. BS, Victoria U., Manchester, Eng., 1962, MB, ChB, 1965, MD, 1973. Diplomate Am. Bd. Internal Medicine. Intern Manchester Royal Infirmary, 1965-66; resident Brompton Hosp., Nat. Heart Hosp., Nat Hosp. Queen Sq., London, 1966-69, Hammersmith Hosp., London, 1966-69, rsch. fellow, 1969-72; lectr. U. Birmingham, Eng., 1972-76; assoc. prof. internal medicine U. Mich., Ann Arbor, 1976-79, prof., 1979-91, chief endocrinology and metabolism, 1987-91; prof. U. Va., Charlottesville, 1991—, dir. Ctr. for Rsch. in Reprod., 1996—. Sci. counselor NIH, Bethesda, Md., 1983-84. Editor: Endocrinology Jour., 1979-84, Endocrinology Text, 1990—; contbr. articles to profl. jour. Grantee NIH, 1977-. Fellow ACP, Royal Coll. Physicians, Royal Soc. Medicine; mem. Ctrl. Soc. for Clin. Rsch. (coun. 1983—), Assn. Am. Physicians, Am. Soc. for Clin. Investigation, Am. Clin. and Climatological Soc. Anglican. Avocations: vintage racing cars, golf. Office: U Va Sch Medicine Dept Internal Medicine Charlottesville VA 22908-0001 Business E-Mail: jcm9h@virginia.edu.

**MARSHALL, JOHN DAVID,** lawyer; b. Chgo., May 19, 1940; s. John Howard and Sophie (Brezenk) M.; m. Marcia A. Podlasinski, Aug. 26, 1961; children: Jacquelyn, David, Jason, Patricia, Brian, Denise, Michael, Catherine. BS in Acctg., U. Ill., 1961; JD, Ill. Inst. Tech., 1965. CPA Ill.; bar: Ill. 1965, U.S. Tax Ct. 1968, U.S. Dist. Ct. (no. dist.) Ill. 1971. Ptnr. Mayer, Brown & Platt, Chgo., 1961—. Bd. dirs. Levinson Ctr. for Handicapped Children, Chgo., 1970—75. Named an Ill. Super Lawyer, Law & Politics, 2004. Fellow Am. Coll. Probate Counsel; mem. Ill. Bar Assn., Chgo. Bar Assn. (agribus. com. 1978—, trust law com. 1969-95, probate practice com. 1969—, com. on coms. 1983-00, vice chmn. 1988-89, chmn. 1989-90, legis. com. of probate practice com. 1983—, chmn. and vice chmn. legis. com. of probate practice com. 1983-84, rules and forms com., 1996—, chmn. exec. com. probate practice com. 1982-83, vice chmn. exec. com. 1981-82, sec. exec. com. 1980-81, div. chmn. 78-79, div. vice chmn. 1977-78, div. sec. 1976-77, Appreciation award 1982-83), Chgo. Estate Planning Council. Clubs: Union League (Chgo.). Roman Catholic. Home: 429 N Willow Wood Dr Palatine IL 60074-3831 Office: Attorney at Law 1300 E Woodfield Rd Schaumburg IL 60173 Business E-Mail: jmarshall@ncc-cpa.com.

**MARSHALL, JOHN ELBERT, III,** foundation executive; b. Providence, July 2, 1942; s. John Elbert Jr. and Millicent Edna (Paige) M.; m. Diana M. Healy, Aug. 16, 1968; children: Nelson John, Priscilla Anne. BA, Brown U., 1964. Advt. mgr. U.N. Alloy Steel Corp., Boston, 1968-70; devel. officer Brown U., Providence, 1970—72, assoc. dir. devel., 1972—75; exec. dir. R.I. Found., Providence, 1975—79; v.p. Kresge Found., Troy, Mich., 1979-82, exec. v.p., 1982-87, pres., 1987—, trustee, 1991—, CEO, 1993—2006. Former chmn. Mich. Cmty. Found. Youth Project. Bd. dirs. United Way Cmty. Svcs., Detroit Downtown Partnership, New Detroit, City Year Detroit, Detroit 300 Conservancy Endowment, Detroit Riverfront Conservatory, Health Found. for the Ams., Assn. Hole in the Wall Camps Found.; former bd. dirs. Mich. Campus Compact, Mich. Nonprofit Forum, Coun. Mich. Founds., Detroit Cmty. Devel. Funders Collaborative; former bd. dirs., vice chmn. Family Svc. Detroit and Wayne County; past pres. Bloomfield Village Assn.; former trustee Coun. on Founds., Washington; mem. com. CFSEM Greenways Initiative; mem. capital improvement program Detroit Pub. Schs.; mem. pres.'s leadership coun. Brown U. Office: The Kresge Foundation 2701 Troy Ctr Dr Ste 150 Troy MI 48084-4755*

**MARSHALL, JOHN HARRIS, JR.,** geologist, oil industry executive; b. Dallas, Mar. 12, 1924; s. John Harris and Jessie Elizabeth (Mosley) M.; m. Betty Eugenia Zarecor, Aug. 9, 1947 (dec. 2003); children: John Harris III, George Z., Jacqueline Anne. BA in Geology, U. Mo., 1949, MA in Geology, 1950; LHD, Garrett Evangelical Theolgical, 1996. Registered geologist Calif., Wyo., Ky., Tex. Geologist Magnolia Oil Co., Jackson, Miss., 1950-59; assoc. geologist Magnolia/Mobil Oil, Okla. City, Okla., 1959-63; from dist. and divsn. geologist to chief geologist worldwide Mobil Oil Corp., various, 1963-81, gen. mgr. exploration for Western Hemisphere N.Y.C., 1981-82; chief geologist Ambrex, 1982—84; prin., owner Marshall Energetics, Inc., Dallas, 1982—. Dir. exploration Anschutz, 1985-91; pres. Summit Oil and Gas Worldwide, 1993-99, Madera Prodn. Co., 1992—; adv. bd. Salvation Army, Manhattan, 1980-82; trustee The Sci. Place, Dallas, 1995-2002, pres. adv. coun. U. Mo., mem. plan giving com., 2004— Mem. geology devel. bd. U. Mo., past pres., 1982-, pres. Coll. Arts and Sci. devel. program, 1996—, mem. devel. coun., 1996-2000, arts and scis. strategic devel. bd., 2000—; councilman, City of Warr Acres (Okla.), 1962-63; active United Meth. Ch., 1951—, Boy Scouts Am., 1960-68; trustee Found. of Evangelism, United Meth. Ch., 1984-, chair, 1988-96. With U.S. Army, 1943—46. Decorated 3 Battle Stars U.S. Army; recipient Curator's medal, U. Mo., 1949, Disting. Alumni Svc. award, 1996, Arts and Sci. award, The Mosaic Soc., U. Mo., 2000, Faculty-Alumni award, U. Mo., 2001, Hon. Life Mem., Geology Devel. Bd., U. Mo., 2004. Mem. Am. Assn. Petroleum Geologists (Pub. Svc. award 2000), Am. Geol. Inst., Am. Geol. Soc. (Dallas, Alaska, Oklahoma City; L.A. Basin pres. 1969-70), Rocky Mountain Assn. Geologists, N.Y. Acad. Sci., Pacific Petroleum Geologists, Am. Sci. Affiliation, Assn. Christian Geologists, United Meth. Gen. Bd. of Discipleship (nat. hispanic evangelization com., 2003-), Meth. Men Club, Denver Petroleum Club, Sigma Xi. Democrat. Office: 9526 Moss Haven Dr Dallas TX 75231-2608 Office Phone: 214-220-4300 4307.

**MARSHALL, JOHN HENRY,** lawyer; b. Paterson, NJ, July 31, 1949; s. Henry Leland and Elizabeth Marion (Bates) M.; m. Jan (Eastman), May 4, 1979. BA, Dartmouth Coll., 1971, Cambridge U., Eng., 1973; JD, Yale U., 1977. Bar: Vt. 1977, U.S. Dist. Ct. Vt., 1978. Assoc. Downs Rachlin Martin, St. Johnsbury, Vt., 1977—82, ptnr., 1982—, mng. ptnr., 2003—. Mem. Vt. Health Care Authority Adv. Com. Universal Access Plan, 1992. Chmn. Dist. Environ. Commn., St. Johnsbury, 1981-90; mem. Governor's Blue Ribbon Commn. on Health Care, 1991; chmn. Vt. Cmty. Found., 2002-00; chmn. Vt. Pub. TV. 2002-04. Capt. U.S. Army, 1973-74. Mem. Vt. Bar Assn. (chmn. environ. law com. 1987-92, chmn. health law com. 1994-96). Office: Downs Rachlin Martin PLLC 90 Prospect St Saint Johnsbury VT 05819-0099 Home: PO Box 19 Peacham VT 05862-0019 Business E-Mail: jmarshall@drm.com.

**MARSHALL, JOHN PATRICK,** lawyer; b. Bklyn., July 3, 1950; s. Harry W. and Mary Margaret (Kelly) M.; m. Cheryl J. Garvey, Aug. 10, 1975; children: Kelly Blake, Logan Brooke. BA, Rutgers U., 1972; JD cum laude,

N.Y. Law Sch., 1976. Bar: N.Y. 1977, N.J. 1977, U.S. Dist. Ct. N.J. 1977, U.S. Dist. Ct. (so. and ea. dists.) N.Y. 1978, U.S. Ct. Appeals (3rd cir.) 1982, U.S. Dist. Ct. (no. dist.) N.Y. 1991. Assoc. Kelley Drye & Warren, N.Y.C., 1976-84, ptnr., 1985-98; pres., CEO Metro Ventures, Inc., Short Hills, NJ, 1997—. Pres., CEO Metro Ventures, Inc. Mem. editl. bd. N.Y. Law Sch. Law Rev., 1975-76, staff mem., 1974-75; contbr. articles to profl. jours. Jud. screening com. N.Y. Dem. Com., N.Y. New Dem. Coalition, 1988; exec. v.p. Humanitarian Found. for Nicaragua; sec. Respect for Law Found., 1996; active So. Dist. N.Y. Mediation Panel, 1994—, Coun. on Jud. Adminstrn., 1996-98. Fellow Am. Bar Found.; mem. ABA, N.Y. County Lawyers' Assn. (sec. 1984-87, mem. com. on Supreme Ct. 1984-94, mem. legal edn., admission to bar and lawyer placement com. 1983-93), Am. Arbitration Assn. (mem. nat. panel arbitrators N.Y. and N.J. regions 1991—, mem. corp. counsel com. 1993-98), Assn. of Bar of City of N.Y. (sec. judiciary com. 1989-92, mem. com. on arbitration 1994-96, sec. coun. on judical adminstrn. 1996-98). Home and Office: 50 Highland Ave Short Hills NJ 07078-2812 E-mail: marshall.highland@prodigy.net.

**MARSHALL, JOHN PAUL,** broadcast engineer; came to U.S., 1967. Degree, U. Grenoble, 1963; student, U. Munich, 1964—65, San Francisco State U., 1969—71, John O'Connell Tech. Inst., 1973—74. Cert. Novell adminstr., cert. broadcast technologist, A+ computer svc. technician Microsoft Cert. Profl.; cert. Networkplus Tech., Microsoft Cert. Profl., Microsoft Cert. Sys. Engr. Mem. faculty law and econ. scis. U. Grenoble, France, 1963—64; mem. Expo '67 staff City of Montreal, Que., Canada, 1967; filmmaker Cinemalab, San Francisco, 1970; engr. film and TV Able Studios, San Francisco, 1971—73; engr. radio and TV Sta. KALW-FM (Nat. Pub. Radio), San Francisco, 1973—74; broadcast engr. Sta. KRON-TV (NBC), San Francisco, 1974—91; intern Centre d'Informatique et de Maintenance Automatisme, 1993; founder Marshall U.S.A., San Francisco, 1994; freelance broadcast engr. KPIX-TV (CBS), KGO-Radio (ABC), KSFO-Radio (ABC), KPST-TV, San Francisco, 1995—2001; adminstr. Thomson Prometric, San Francisco, 2003—. Freelance audio visual tech. advisor, San Francisco area, 1975—, lectr. radio, TV, motion pictures, 1975—, cons. customized electronic effects; tech. advisor, assoc. Broadkast Skills Bank. Translator tech. pubs. and manuals, 1975—. Mus. dir.; participant in theater prodns., 1950-59; active Boy Scouts Am. Govt. of France scholar, 1960-63. Mem. Rolls Royce Owners Club Found. (life), Internet Soc., Soc. Broadcast Engrs. (cert. broadcast networking technologist), Elec. Tech. Assn. Avocations: classical pianist, polyglot, world traveler. Personal E-mail: jpm1221@sbcglobal.net. *Personal philosophy: (French proverb) Aide toi, le ciel t'aidera--Use your own resources and you will always receive a helping hand from heaven.*

**MARSHALL, JOHN TREUTLEN,** lawyer, educator; b. Macon, Ga., Nov. 1, 1934; s. Hubert and Gladys (Lucas) M.; m. Katrine White, May 1, 1959; children: Allison, Rebecca, Paul, Mary Anne. BA, Vanderbilt U., 1956; LLB, Yale U., 1962. Bar: Ga. 1962, U.S. Dist. Ct. (no., mid. and so. dists.) Ga. 1962, U.S. Ct. Appeals (5th cir.) 1962, U.S. Supreme Ct. 1978, U.S. Ct. Appeals (11th cir.) 1982. Ptnr. Powell Goldstein LLP, Atlanta, 1962—. Comm. bd. visitors Ga. State U. Law Sch., 2005—; chmn. No. Dist. Ga. Bar Coun., 1989; chmn. Ga. State Bar Commn. on Continuing Lawyer Competency, 1991-93, Ga. State Commn. on Stds. of Profession, 1996—; bd. dirs. Ga. Eye Bank, Inc., Atlanta Bar Found. Bd. editor: Yale Law Jour. Trustee Ga. Inst. Continuing Legal Edn., 1983—90; chmn. adv. bd. Atlanta Vol. Lawyers Found.; bd. dirs. Atlanta Legal Aid, 1972—73. Capt. USMC, 1959—62. Recipient S. Phillip Heiner award Atlanta Vol. Lawyers Assn., 1992, A. Gus Cleveland award Ga. Commn. on Continuing Legal Edn., Tradition of Excellence award State Bar Ga., 1995, Disting. Svc. award, Ga. State Bar, 2006, Professionalism award Am. Inns of Ct. (11th Jud. Cir.), 2005. Fellow: Ga. Bar Found., Am. Bar Found. (bd. dirs.), Am. Acad. Appellate Lawyers, Am. Coll. Trial Lawyers (state chmn. 1985—86); mem.: ABA (ho. of dels. 1976—86, Harrison Tweed award 1986), Ga. Inst. Trial Advocacy (chmn. 1982—83), Atlanta Bar Assn. (pres. 1974—75, Charles E. Watkins Jr. award 1988, Leadership award 1996), Atlanta Bar Found. (bd. dirs.), State Bar Ga. (chmn. stds. profession com., Disting. Svc. award 2005), Am. Arbitration Assn., Lawyers Club. Office: Powell Goldstein LLP One Atlantic Ctr Fl 14 1201 W Peachtree St NW Atlanta GA 30309-3488 Office Phone: 404-572-6615. Business E-Mail: jmarshall@pogolaw.com.

**MARSHALL, JONATHAN,** foundation administrator, journalist; b. NYC, Jan. 20, 1924; s. James and Lenore (Guinzburg) M.; m. Maxine Besser, Apr. 6, 1955; children: Lucinda, Laura, Robert Louis, Jonathan Herbert. BA in Econs., U. Colo., 1946; postgrad., U. N.C., 1947—49; MS in Journalism, U. Oreg., 1962; LHD (hon.), Ariz. State U., 1994. Program assoc. Planning Dept., West Chester County, NY, 1949—52; editor, pub. Ariz. mag., NYC, 1953-58, Scottsdale Daily Progress, Ariz., 1963-87; program assoc. Ford Found., NYC, 1958-59; pres. New Hope Found., NYC, 1985-98, Marshall Fund, Scottsdale, Ariz., 1987—92. Pulitzer prize juror, 1983, 84; Ruhl fellow lectr. U. Oreg., 1986, Allen lectr., 91. Author: Reunion in Norway, 2005; former mem. editl. bd. Amicus Jour.; contbr. articles to various publs., including Masthead, ASNE Bull., Quill, Amicus Jour. Chmn. Oreg. Vols. for Stevenson, 1960, Ariz. Grandparents Day, 1972, 73; bd. dirs. Ariz. Theatre Co., Phoenix Art Mus., Nat. Com. for Effective Congress; former mem. bd. dirs. Am. Jewish Com., Camelback Hosp., Phoenix Urban League, Phoenix Symphony Assn. Recipient Nat. Phys. Fitness Leadership award U.S. Jaycees, 1973, Ariz. Newspapers' Master Editor-Pub. award, 1978, Disting. Svc. award Ariz. Press Club, 1988, Ariz. Philanthropist award Nat. Soc. Fundraising Execs., 1997, Ariz. State U. Coll. Liberal Arts, 1988, Pub. Interest award Ariz. Ctr. for Law in Pub. Interest, 1998, John W. Creasman award for excellence Ariz. State U., 1999, Martin Luther King, Jr. Diversity Champion award, 2001; named Ariz. Civil Libertarian of Yr., 1996; inducted into Ariz. Newspapers Hall of Fame, 1996; named to U. Oreg. Journalism Sch. Hall of Achievement, 2001. Mem. Nat. Conf. Editl. Writers, Am. Soc. Newspapers Editors (past mem. editl. bd. Bull.), Soc. Profl. Journalists (1st Amendment award 1979). Democrat. Jewish.

**MARSHALL, JOSEPH ROMAN, JR.,** electrical engineer; b. Chgo., Feb. 13, 1956; s. Joseph Roman Marshall and Eleanor Louise Woodward; m. Suzanne Lasseigne, May 19, 1979. BSEE, Purdue U., 1978, MSEE, 1979. Cert. fed. systems arch. Assoc. engr. Banking Products-IBM, Charlotte, N.C., 1979-81, sr. assoc. engr., 1981-83, staff engr., 1983-84; staff engr. common attachments Printer Products-IBM, Charlotte, 1984-86, adv. engr., 1986-87; adv. engr. VLSI architecture Fed. Systems-IBM, Manassas, Va., 1987-89, chief engr., 1989-92; prin. investigator Fed. Sys.-IBM/Loral, Manassas, Va., 1992-95; lead sys. engr. space processors Fed. Sys.-Loral, Manassas, Va., 1994-95, chief engr. futurebus & space profile devel., 1995-97; sr. sys. engr. Lockheed Martin Fed. Sys., 1997—2000; sr. prin. sys. engr. BAE Sys., 2000—, sys. arch. reconfigurable processing sys., 2001—. Working group participant Bus Architecture Stds. Com., IEEE, Piscataway, N.J., 1991-97; charter organizer Dependability Working Group, 1992-94. Newsletter editor Ascension Coun. #9285 K.O.C., Prince William County, Va., 1988—, lectr. 1995-98, adv., 2001—; bd. dirs. Woodbine Woods Civic Assn., 1997—. Fellow AIAA (assoc., computer publs. chair, computer sys. tech. com. 1993—, tech. program conf. com. 2005, chmn. conf. session 2005, 06); mem. IEEE (sr., editor P896.10 Std. 1994-97, session chair space processors and interconnects Aerospace Conf. 2004—). Achievements include successful demonstration of ASCM fault tolerance-completely autonomous error recovery in spaceborne computer system; publication of 10 disclosures; co-program chair of workshop on integrating error models in error injections; patents in field; patents pending. Office: BAE Systems MVA 01-012 9300 Wellington Rd Manassas VA 20110-4122

**MARSHALL, JOSHUA MICAH,** publisher, blog writer, columnist, editor, political journalist; b. St. Louis, Mo., Feb. 15, 1969; m. Millet Israeli, 2005. Grad., Princeton U., 1991; PhD in American History, Brown U. Assoc. editor to Washington editor The American Prospect, 1998—2001; founder, editor, publisher talkingpointsmemo.com; editor, publisher TPMCafe.com, 2005—; contbg. editor The Washington Monthly, Washington; contbg. writer, columnist The Hill, Washington; columnist Time.com. Blog writer TPMmuckraker.com. Contbg. writer Salon.com; contbr. articles to the Atlantic Monthly,

Boston Globe, Financial Times, Foreign Affairs, LA Times, NY Republic, New Yorker, NY Post, NY Times and Slate; guest appearances CNN, CNBC, C-Span, Fox and MSNBC. Office: The Hill 1625 K St NW Ste 900 Washington DC 20006 Address: The Washington Monthly 1319 F St NW Ste 710 Washington DC 20004*

**MARSHALL, JOSIE,** secondary school educator; b. American, Idaho, Dec. 26, 1942; BS, U. Idaho, MS in Edn. Nat. bd. cert. tchr. 1999. Tchr. Sacajawea Jr. H.S., Lewiston, Idaho. Recipient Idaho Middle Sch. Tchr. of the Yr. award, 1997—98; Tom Wright fellow. Mem.: Idaho Edn. Assn. (bd. mem.), Nat. Bd. for Profl. Tchg. Stds. (bd. mem.). Office: Sacajawea Jr HS 3610 12th St Lewiston ID 83501*

**MARSHALL, JULIE ARNITZ,** biology educator; d. Jospeh and Mary Arnitz; m. David Marshall, July 25, 1998; children: Devin, Jordyn. BS in Biology, Cornell U., Ithaca, N.Y., 1992, MA in secondary sci. edn., 1993. Sci. edn. Fairport HS, NY, 1993—. Office: Faiport HS 1358 Ayrault Rd Fairport NY 14450

**MARSHALL, KATHLEEN,** choreographer, theater director; Mem. exec. bd. Soc. Stage Dirs. and Choreographers. Asst. choreographer (Broadway plays) Kiss of the Spider Woman, 1993—95, She Loves Me, 1993—94, Damn Yankees, 1994—95, choreographer Swinging on a Star, 1996 (Drama Desk nomination), 1776, 1997—98, Ring Round the Moon, 1999, Kiss Me, Kate, 1999—2001 (Tony nom. best choreography, 2001, Laurence Olivier nom. best choreography, 2002, Drama Desk nomination, Outer Critics Circle nomination, Astaire Award nomination), Seussical, 2000—01, Follies, 2001 (Outer Critics Circle award nomination), Little Shop of Horrors, 2003; dir. (Broadway plays) Wonderful Town, 2003 (Tony nom. best dir. musical, 2004, Drama Desk award best choreography, 2004); choreographer (Broadway plays) Wonderful Town, 2003 (Tony award best choreography, 2004), The Pajama Game, 2005 (Outer Critics' Cir. award, outstanding choreography, 2006, Drama Desk award outstanding choreography, 2006, Tony award, best choreography, 2006), (TV films) The Music Man, 2003. Recipient Mr. Abbott Award, Stage Directors & Choreographers Found., 2005. Office: Ste 702 311 W 43rd St New York NY 10036*

**MARSHALL, KATHLEEN ANN,** elementary school educator; b. Winchester, Conn., Dec. 18, 1951; d. Richard Bartholomew and Jeannine Rose Marshall. AA with honors, Bay Path Jr. Coll., 1978; BS with honors, U. Hartford, 1980, MEd with honors, 1988; Sixth Yr. Degree with honors, So. Conn. State U., 1998. Tchr. Riverside Sch., Torrington, Conn., 1980—81, Oliver Wolcott Sch., Torrington, 1981—84, 1986—87, Litchfield HS, Conn., 1984—86; tchr. elem. sch. Archdiocese Hartford, Bloomfield, Conn., 1987—2000; freelance subs. tchr. Conn., 2004—. Tchr. catacism St. Francis Assisi Ch., Torrington, 1981—89, 1999—2002; pvt. tutor, Torrington, 2006. Vol. Big Bros. Big Sisters, Conn., 1997—. Mem.: ASCD. Avocations: reading, walking, doll collecting. Home: 420A Migeon Ave Torrington CT 06790

**MARSHALL, KATHRYN SUE,** lawyer; b. Decatur, Ill., Sept. 12, 1942; d. Edward Elda and Frances M. (Minor) Lahniers; m. Robert S. Marshall, Sept. 5, 1964 (div. Apr. 1984); children: Stephen Edward, Christine Elizabeth; m. Robert J. Arndt, June 25, 1988 (dec. 1999). BA, Lake Forest Coll., 1964; JD, John Marshall Law Sch., Chgo., 1976. Intern U.S. Atty.'s Office, Chgo., 1974—76; mng. ptnr. Marshall and Marshall Ltd., Waukegan, Ill., 1976—84; pvt. practice Waukegan, 1984—93, Preemptive Solutions, Wash. Contbr. articles to profl. jours. Bd. dirs., v.p. Lake Forest (Ill.) Fine Arts Ensemble; bd. dirs. Island Hosp. Health Found.; mem. steering com. Equal Justice Coalition; cert. jud. Dem. candidate Lake County, Ill.; bd. dirs. Camerata Soc., Lake Forest. Fellow: ABA (gov. 1993—96), Coll. Law Practice Mgmt., Ill. Bar Assn.; mem.: Navy League (life). Avocations: boating, reading, travel.

**MARSHALL, KENNETH ROBERT,** retired music educator; b. Aurora, Ill., May 18, 1939; s. John Redman and Gladys Marie Marshall. MusB, U. Ill., 1961, BS in Music Edn., 1962, MusM, 1963; BS in Hospitality Mgmt., Fla. Internat. U., 1980. Cert. evaluator Fla. Dept. Revenue. Choral dir. various high schs., Ill., Fla., 1963—68; dir. choral activities Brevard C.C., Cocoa, Fla., 1968—75; dir. choral activities, tchr. English Internat. Sch. Bangkok/Thai U., 1975—79; U.S. customs product clearance/tangible personal property Sunbelt Internat. Shoppers/Osceola Co. Property Dep. Appraiser, Orlando and Kissimmee, Fla., 1979—90; full time ch. musician, organist. dir. 1st United Meth. Ch., Sanford, Fla., 1990—92; med. records transcriptionist Leesburg (Fla.) Regional Med. Ctr., 1992—95; assoc. prof. humanities Valencia C.C., Orlando, Fla., 1995—2003; organist, dir. music Faith Viera (Fla.) Luth. Ch., 2004—. Tchr., counselor various high schs. and coll.s, Fla., 1963—2003; part-time ch. musician, 1975—95. Named Prof. of the Semester, Phi Theta Kappa, 1999—2000. Mem.: Am. Guild Organists (assoc.; regional officer 1968—75), Am. Choral Dirs. Assn. (life; state and conv. planning positions 1965—75), Phi Mu Alpha. Republican. Methodist/Lutheran. Avocations: animals, stamp collecting/philately. Office Phone: 321-636-5504. Personal E-mail: jsbach@cfl.rr.com.

**MARSHALL, KERRY JAMES,** artist; b. Birmingham, Ala., Oct. 17, 1955; BFA, Otis Art Inst., L.A., 1978. Prodn. designer Praise House & Sankofa, 1991; assoc. prof. U. Ill., Chgo. Art instr. L.A. City Coll., 1980-83; art faculty L.A. S.W. Coll., 1981-85; adj. asst. prof. Sch. Art and Design, U. Ill., Chgo., 1993-94. One man exhibits include James Turcotte Gallery, L.A., 1983, Pepperdine U., Malibu, 1984, Koplin Gallery, 1985, 91, Studio Mus. Harlem, 1986, Terra Incognito, Chgo. Cultural Ctr., 1992, Jack Shainman Gallery, N.Y.C., 1993, 95, Koplin Gallery, Santa Monica, Calif., 1993, Cleveland Ctr. Contemporary ARts, 1994, Drawings III, Koplin Gallery, Santa Monica, 1993, Markts of Resistance, White Columns Gallery, N.Y.C. 1993, 43rd Biennial of Contemporary Am. Painting, Corcoran Gallery Art, Washington, 1993, Document X, Kassel, Germany, 1997, Whitney Biennial Whitney Mus. Am. Art, N.Y.C., 1997, Saddlebrook Coll. Art Gallery, Mission Viejo, Calif., 1994, Addison Gallery Am. Art, 1997; contbr. articles to profl. jours. Recipient Herb Alpert award Cal Arts, 1997; fellow Nat. Endowment Arts Visual Art, 1991, John D. and Catherine T. MacArthur Found., 1997; visual arts grantee Ill. Arts Coun., 1992; grantee Tiffany Found., 1993, Disting. Artist Fellowship and Stillwater Found. grant, Coll. Fine Arts, U. Tex., Austin, 2004. Mem. Ill. Arts Coun. Office: 4122 S Calumet Ave Chicago IL 60653-2649*

**MARSHALL, KEVIN A.,** director; b. Bronx, NY, June 9, 1950; s. Aldon Eddie and Winifred Ann Marshall; m. Marlene Ann Cassella, Dec. 30, 1972; children: Jeffrey Aldon, Bryan Matthew. BA, William Paterson U., Wayne, NJ, 1972; MFA, Ohio U., Athens, 1974. Head grad. program in theatre mgmt. and arts adminstrn. U. Ala./Ala. Shakespeare Festival, Tuscaloosa, 1982—88; dir. Sch. Theatre and Dance U. Fla., Gainesville, 1998—. Bus. mgr. Festival Players, Chattanooga, 1979—82; house mgr. Manhattan Theatre Club, NYC, 1979; exec. dir. Johnson City Area Arts Coun., Tenn., 1982; ho. mgr. Ala. Shakespeare Festival, Anniston, Ala., 1983—84. Co-author: Theatre Management: A Successful Guide to Producing Plays on Commercial and Non-Profit Stages; editor: Theatre Mgmt. Jour. V.p. Chattanooga Wine Tasters, 1981—82; active Assn. Arts Adminstrn. Educators, Pitts., 1991—92, Tenn. Theatre Assn., Nashville, 1981—82, Appalachian Coun. for the Arts, Bristol, Tenn., 1982. Recipient Druid Arts award, Arts Coun. Tuscaloosa County, 1992. Mem.: Southeastern Theatre Conf., Assn. for Theatre in Higher Edn. (treas. 1990—95). Roman Catholic. Avocation: travel. Home: 4064 SW 98th Terrace Gainesville FL 32608 Office: University of Florida PO Box 115900 Gainesville FL 32611 Office Fax: 352-392-5114. Business E-Mail: kmarshall@arts.ufl.edu.

**MARSHALL, KIMBERLY,** music educator, musician; b. May 9, 1959; Grad. Gold medal organist, Lyon Conservatory of Music, 1978; student 1st prize organ, Montpellier U., Toulouse, France, 1981; BA in French, U. N.C., Chapel Hill, 1982; PhD in Music, Univ. Coll., Oxford, Eng., 1986. Performer in concerts Australia, Eng., Mexico and U.S. live and on the radio, Del.,

1980—; vis. tchr. master classes St. Giles Organ Sch., Royal Coll. Music, Royal Coll. Organists, London, 2000; performer recitals on renovated organs in Europe and U.S., 2004—05; project leader Goteborg (Sweden) GoArt, 1996—2000. Author: (books) Iconographical Evidence for the Late Medieval Organ in French, English and Flemish manuscripts, 1989; editor: Late Medieval Organ Music: Before 1460, 2000, Renaissance Organ Music: 1500-1550, 2004; author: (essay collection) Rediscovering the Muses: Women's Musical Traditions, 1993; contbr. articles and reviews to profl. jours. Recipient 1st prize, St. Alban's Internat. Organ Interpretation Competition, 1985; grantee thesis grant, U. Oxford, Eng., 1984, Rsch. grant, Pew Meml. Trust, 1987; scholar Morehead scholarship, U. N.C., Chapel Hill, 1977—82, Marshall scholarship, U. Oxford, 1982—85, Fulbright Rsch./Tchg. scholarship, 1990. Office: Ariz State U Sch of Music Box 870405 Tempe AZ 85287 E-mail: kimberly.marshall@asu.edu.

**MARSHALL, LAWRENCE C.,** law educator; b. Jan. 10, 1959; m. Michelle Oberman, Mar. 17, 1996; children: Rachel, Steven, Jonathan, Hanna, Noa. BA, Beth Hatalmud Coll., Jerusalem, 1979; JD summa cum laude, Northwestern U., 1985; LHD (hon.), Nat.-Louis U., 2003. Bar: Ill. 1987. Law clk. to Chief Judge Patricia M. Wald US Ct. Appeals DC Cir., 1985-86; law clk. to Assoc. Justice John Paul Stevens US Supreme Ct., Washington, 1986-87; of counsel Mayer, Brown & Platt, 1989—93; assoc. prof. Northwestern U. Sch. Law, Chgo., 1987—99, prof. law, 1989—99, co-founder, legal dir. Ctr. on Wrongful Convictions, 1999—2005; prof. law Stanford Law Sch., 2005—; David and Stephanie Mills dir. clin. edn., 2005—. Exec. dir. ROFEH, Inc., Boston, 1979-81; field rep. Devel. Corp. for Israel, Boston, 1981-82. Co-recipient Pro Bono Award, ABA, 1996, Cmty. Svc. Award, Mexican Legal Def. Fund, 1996; named Illinoisan of Yr., Ill. Newsbroadcasters' Assn., 2003; recipient Robert H. Childres Award for Tchg. Excellence, Northwestern U. Sch. Law, 1989, 2003, Mario Cuomo Act of Courage Award, Death Penalty Focus of Cailf. 1999. Mem. Chgo. Inns of Ct. (barrister). Office: Stanford Law Sch Crown Quadrangle 559 Nathan Abbott Way Stanford CA 94305-8610 Office Phone: 650-723-7572. E-mail: lmarshall@stanford.edu.

**MARSHALL, MARGARET HILARY,** state supreme court justice; b. Newcastle, Natal, South Africa, Sept. 1, 1944; came to U.S., 1968; d. Bernard Charles and Hilary A.D. (Anderton) M; m. Samuel Shapiro, Dec. 14, 1968 (div. Apr. 1982); m. Anthony Lewis, Sept. 23, 1984. BA, Witwatersrand U., Johannesburg, 1966; MEd, Harvard U., 1969; JD, Yale U., 1976; LHD (hon.), Regis Coll., 1993. Bar: Mass. 1977, U.S. Dist. Ct. Mass., U.S. Dist. Ct. N.H., U.S. Dist. Ct. D.C., U.S. Dist. Ct. (ea. dist.) Mich., U.S. Tax Ct., U.S. Ct. Appeals (1st, 11th and D.C. cirs.), U.S. Supreme Ct. Assoc. Csaplar & Bok, Boston, 1976-83, ptnr., 1983-89, Choate, Hall & Stewart, Boston, 1989-92; v.p., gen. counsel Harvard U., Cambridge, Mass., 1992-96; justice Mass. Supreme Jud. Ct., 1996-99, chief justice, 1999—. Mem. jud. nominating coun., 1987-90, 92; chairperson ct. rules subcom. Alternative Dispute Resolution Working Group, 1985-87; mem. fed. appts. commn., 1993; mem. adv. com. Supreme Judicial Ct., 1989-92, mem. gender equality com., 1989-94; mem. civil justice adv. group U.S. Dist. Ct. Mass., 1991-93; spl. counsel Jud. Conduct Commn., 1988-92; trustee Mass. Continuing Legal Edn., Inc., 1990-92. Trustee Regis Coll., 1993-96; bd. dirs. internat. Design Conf., Aspen, 1986-92, Boston Mcpl. Res. Bur., 1990-94, Supreme Judicial Ct. Hist. Soc., 1990-94, sec., 1990-94. Fellow Am. Bar Found. (Mass. state chair); mem. Boston Bar Assn. (treas. 1988-89, v.p. 1989-90, pres.-elect 1990-91, pres. 1991-92), Internat. Women's Forum, Mass. Women's Forum, Boston Club, Phi Beta Kappa (hon.). Office: Supreme Judicial Court 1 Pemberton Sq Ste 2-500 Boston MA 02108-1717*

**MARSHALL, MARK F.,** lawyer; b. 1954; BS, U.S.D., 1977, JD, 1981. Bar: S.D. 1981, U.S. Dist. Ct. S.D. 1981, U.S. Ct. Appeals (8th cir.) 1981, U.S. Supreme Ct. 1984. Law clk. hon. Fred J. Nichol, 1981-83; ptnr. Bangs, McCullen, Butler, Foye & Simmons, Rapid City, SD, 1983-96; of counsel Johnson, Heideprim, Miner, Marlow & Janklow, Sioux Falls, SD, 1996—2000; magistrate judge U.S. Dist. Ct. S.D., Sioux Falls, 1996-2000; ptnr. Davenport Law Firm, Sioux Falls, 2000—. Office: 206 W 14th St Sioux Falls SD 57105 Office Phone: 605-336-2880. Business E-Mail: mmarshall@dehs.com.

**MARSHALL, MARTIN VIVAN,** business administration educator, consultant; b. Kansas City, July 22, 1922; s. Vivan Dean and Marie (Church) M.; m. Rosanne Borden, Sept. 5, 1951 (dec. Feb. 8, 1986); children: Martin Dean, Michael Borden, Neil McNair; m. Hildegard Meyer, June 24, 1988. BA, U. Mo., 1943; MBA, Harvard U., 1947, D.C.S., 1953. Instr. mktg. and advt. U. Kans., 1947-48; mem. faculty Harvard U., 1948—, Henry R. Byers prof. bus. adminstrn., 1960—, chmn. mktg. area faculty, 1962-66, chmn. Smaller Co. Mgmt. Program, 1981-84, chmn. Owner/Pres. Mgmt. Program, 1985-94, mem. faculty Inst. Ednl. Mgmt., 1981-90, endowed chair, Martin Marshall prof. bus. adminstrn., 1999. Cons. U.S. and internat. bus., 1950—; dir. ann. seminar mktg. and advt. Am. Advt. Fedn., 1958-78; vis. profl. mktg. IMEDE Mgmt. Inst., Lausanne, 1965-66; sr. prof., ednl. dir. Internat. Mktg. Inst., 1967-71; vis. prof. Indian Inst. Mgmt., Agra, 1968, IPADE, Mexico City, 1969, U. Melbourne, Australia, 1977, 79; bd. dirs. Western Stone & Metal.; lectr. Templeton Coll., Oxford, summer 1998. Author: Automatic Merchandising, 1954, (with N.H. Borden) Advertising Management, 1960, Notes on Marketing, 1983, 88, 90, 92, 93, 2002, 2004. Bd. dirs. Youth Svcs. Internat., Inc., 1994-97, Moclean Co., 1998-99. Served to lt. (s.g.) USNR, 1943-46. Home: 130 Mount Auburn St Apt 309 Cambridge MA 02138-5779 Office: Harvard U Cumnock Hall Boston MA 02163 Office Phone: 617-497-0840.

**MARSHALL, MICHAEL BORDEN,** marketing executive; b. Boston, Mar. 16, 1957; s. Martin Vivan and Rosanne (Borden) M.; m. Susan Diane (Parks), June 15, 1991; children: Samantha Rosanne, Brenton Alexander. BA, Oberlin Coll., Ohio, 1979; MBA, Harvard U., Cambridge, Mass., 1983. Analyst Benton and Bowles, Inc., N.Y.C., 1977—80; mktg. mgr. Thor Metal Works, Ltd., Syracuse, NY, 1980—81; asst. mgr. Am. Express Co., N.Y.C., 1982; sr. analyst Bank of Boston Corp., 1982—85; cons. John Hancock Mut. Life Ins. Co., Boston, 1985—89; corp. v.p. N.Y. Life Ins. Co., N.Y.C., 1989—. Cons. assoc., Bank Mktg. Assn., Boston, 1983-89, N.Y., 1991—; advisor bus. analysis, Arthur D. Little, Inc., Cambridge, Mass., 1985-93. Contbr. articles to profl. journals. Mem. adv. bd. Youth Enrichment Svc. Boston, 1984-90; treas. St. James Episcopal Ch., North Salem, N.Y., 1996-99; jr. warden, 2005-06. Recipient Jerome Davis Award Oberlin Coll., 1979, Copeland Sect. Award Harvard Bus. Sch., 1982, Corp. Spl. Award John Hancock Exec. Com., 1986. Mem. Am. Mktg. Assn. (sr. v.p. 1984-93), Mktg. Sci. Inst. (bd. dir. 1985-89), Life Ins. Mktg. and Rsch. Assn. (devel. bd. 1991-98, markét rsch. com. 1995—, chmn. 2002-03, market rsch. conf. com. 2004-), Coun. on Fin. Competition (adv. bd. 1991—, markét rsch. com. 2004—), Soc. Ins. Strategists (founding mem.), Fin. Industry Rsch. Study Team (founding mem.), Am. Coun. on Life Ins. (rsch. advisor 1994-2003), N.Y. Mktg. Coun., Harvard Club. Office: NY Life Ins Co 1 Rockwood Rd Sleepy Hollow NY 10591 Business E-Mail: mmarshall@newyorklife.com.

**MARSHALL, NATALIE JUNEMANN,** economics professor; b. Milw., June 13, 1929; d. Harold E. and Myrtle (Findlay) Junemann; m. Howard D. Marshall, Aug. 7, 1954 (dec. 1972); children: Frederick S., Alison B.; m. Phillip Shatz, May 27, 1988. AB, Vassar Coll., 1951; MA, Columbia U., 1952, PhD, 1963. JD, 1994. Instr. Vassar Coll., Poughkeepsie, NY, 1952-54, 59, 59-60, 63, assoc. prof. econs., 1973-75, v.p. for student affairs, 1975-80, v.p. for adminstrn. and student services and prof. econs., 1980-91, prof. econs., 1991-94; teaching fellow Wesleyan U., Middletown, Conn., 1955-56; from asst. prof. to prof. econs. SUNY, New Paltz, 1964-73; prof. econs. Vassar Coll., Poughkeepsie, NY, 1973-94; of counsel Donoghue, Thomas, Auslander & Drohan, Hopewell Junction, NY, 1997—. Editor (with Howard Marshall): The History of Economic Thought, 1968; editor: Keynes, Updated or Outdated, 1970; author (with Howard Marshall): Collective Bargaining, 1971. Trustee St. Francis Hosp., 1979-88, Area Fund Dutchess County, 1981-87, Coll. New Rochelle, 1994-2000, Hudson Valley Philharm., 1985-92, pres., 1989-91. Mem. AAUP, Am. Assn. Higher Edn., Am. Econ. Assn., AAUW (v.p. N.Y. State div. 1964-66), Poughkeepsie Vassar Club (pres. 1965-67). Home: 157 Skidmore Rd Pleasant Valley NY 12569-5001

**MARSHALL, PATRICK C.,** lawyer; b. San Francisco, Aug. 8, 1954; BA, Whitman Coll., 1976; JD with honors, Univ. Wash., 1979. Bar: Wash. 1979, Calif. 1984. Ptnr. Pillsbury Winthrop Shaw Pittman, San Francisco, 1984—; office mng. ptnr., 2004, co-leader Litigation sect., leader San Francisco Litigation sect. Mem.: San Francisco Bar Assn. Office: Pillsbury Winthrop Shaw Pittman 50 Fremont St San Francisco CA 94105 Office Phone: 415-983-7233. Office Fax: 415-983-1200. Business E-Mail: patrick.marshall@pillsburylaw.com.

**MARSHALL, PENNY (C. MARSHALL, CAROLE PENNY MARSHALL),** director, actress; b. NYC, Oct. 15, 1943; d. Anthony W. and Marjorie Irene (Ward) M.; m. Michael Henry (div.); 1 child, Tracy Lee; m. Robert Reiner, Apr. 10, 1971 (div. 1979). Student, U. N.Mex., 1961-64. Appeared on numerous television shows, including The Odd Couple, 1972-74, Friends and Lovers (co-star), 1974, Let's Switch, 1974, Wives (pilot), 1975, Chico and the Man, 1975, Mary Tyler Moore, 1975, Heaven Help Us, 1975, Saturday Night Live, 1975-77, Happy Days, 1975, Battle of Network Stars (ABC special), 1976, Barry Manilow special, 1976, The Tonight Show, 1976-77, Dinah, 1976-77, Mike Douglas Show, 1975-77, Merv Griffin Show, 1976-77, Blansky's Beauties, 1977, Network Battle of the Sexes, 1977, Laverne and Shirley (co-star), 1976-83, Entertainment Tonight's Presents: Laverne and Shirley Together Again, 2002; TV films More Than Friends, 1978, Love Thy Neighbor, 1984, Challenge of a Lifetime, 1985, The Odd Couple: Together Again, 1993; guest appearances include Mary Tyler Moore, 1975, Happy Days, 1975, Chico and the Man, 1975, Mork & Mindy, 1978, Bosom Buddies, 1982, Taxi, 1983, The Simpsons (voice), 1990, Frasier, 2004, I'm With Her, 2004; appeared in motion pictures How Sweet It Is, 1967, The Savage Seven, 1968, The Grasshopper, 1970, 1941, 1979, Movers and Shakers, 1985, She's Having a Baby, 1988, The Hard Way, 1991, Hocus Pocus, 1993, Get Shorty, 1995, Stateside, 2004; dir. films: Jumpin' Jack Flash, 1986, Big, 1988, Awakenings, 1990 (exec. prodr.), A League of Their Own, 1992 (exec. prodr.), Renaissance Man, 1994 (exec. prodr.), The Preacher's Wife, 1996, The Time Tunnel: The Movie, 1999, Special Delivery, 1999, Riding in Cars with Boys, 2001 appeared in TV movie Jackie's Back, 1999; prodr. TV series A League of Their Own, 1993 (also dir. pilot), Dynasties, 2003, Crossover, 2004; dir. (TV Series) Working Stiffs, 1979; prodr. films Getting Away With Murder, 1996, With Friends Like These, 1998, Risk, 2003; exec. prodr. Calender Girl, 1993. Avocations: needlepoint, jigsaw puzzles, antique shopping. Office: c/o William Morris Agy 151 El Camino Dr Beverly Hills CA 90212

**MARSHALL, RAYMOND CHARLES,** lawyer; b. Aquadilia, PR, July 23, 1953; 1 child, Kyle. BA summa cum laude, Coll. Idaho, 1975; JD, Harvard U., 1978. Bar: Calif. 1978, D.C. 1989. Ptnr. Bingham McCutchen LLP, San Francisco, co-chmn. white-collar crime & bus. regulation practice group. Chmn. Calif. Supreme Ct. Adv. Multi-Jurisdictional Practice, 2004. Co-author: Environmental Crimes, 1992; contbr. chpt. to manual; contbr. articles to profl. jours. Bd. dirs. Nat. Multiple Sclerosis Soc. Northern Calif. chpt., 1992—; adv. bd. United Negro Coll. Fund Northern Bay Area Chpt., 1992—; bd. trustees Alta Bates Found., 1994—; adv. coun. mem. San Francisco Sports Coun. Recipient San Francisco Neighborhood Legal Assistance Found. award, 1989, Earl Warren Legal Svcs. award NAACP Legal Def. & Ednl. Found., 1990, Unity award Minority Bar Coalition, 1992, Cmty. Svc. award Wiley Manuel Law Found., 1994, Disting. Jesuit award Anti-Defamation League, 2001. Mem. ABA (met. bar caucus exec. com. 1992-94, vice-chmn. natural resources & energy litigation com. 1989-93, environmental crimes com. 1990-92, nominating com. conf. of minority ptnrs. in maj. corp. law firms 1991, commn. on women in the profession 1994-95, co-chmn. environmental crimes subcom. of white collar crime com. 1994-95), Nat. Bar Assn., Calif. State Bar (bd. govs. 1995—, pres. 1998-99), Charles Houston Bar Assn. Avocations: travel, sports. Office: Bingham McCutchen LLP Three Embarcadero Ctr San Francisco CA 94111 Office Phone: 415-393-2348. Business E-Mail: raymond.marshall@bingham.com.

**MARSHALL, RICHARD PAUL, JR.,** lawyer; b. Lincoln, Nebr., June 7, 1949; s. Richard P. and Betty Jean (Schleuning) M.; m. Mary Elizabeth Van Bloom, Jan. 28, 1970; 1 child, Sydna Suzanne. BA, U. Nebr., 1974; JD cum laude, Creighton U., 1979. Bar: Tex. 1979, U.S. Dist. Ct. (so. dist.) Tex. 1979, U.S. Ct Appeals (5th cir.) 1979, U.S. Dist. Ct. (we. dist.) Tex. 1988. Briefing atty., law clk. to presiding justice U.S. Ct. Appeals (5th cir.), Houston, 1979-80; assoc. Scott, Douglass & Keeton, Austin, Tex., 1980-83; ptnr. Scott, Douglass & Luton, Austin, 1984—. Editor-in-chief Creighton Law Rev., 1978-79. Bd. dirs. Swim-A-Long fundraiser Juvenile Diabetes Found., Austin, 1987-89; commr. Travis County Rural Fire Prevention Dist. 1, 1990-96. Mem. Tex. Bar Assn. (oil, gas and mineral law sect., litigation sect.), Travis County Bar Assn., Phi Alpha Delta (Scholastic Achievement award 1979). Democrat. Presbyterian. Avocations: golf, swimming, music, motorcycles, sport shooting. Office: Scott Douglass & Luton One American Ctr 600 Congress Ave Ste 1500 Austin TX 78701-2589 Home: 103 Coyote Trl Round Mountain TX 78663-6006

**MARSHALL, RICHARD TREEGER,** lawyer; b. NYC, May 17, 1925; s. Edward and Sydney (Treeger) M.; m. Dorothy M. Goodman, June 4, 1950; children: Abigail Ruth Marshall, Stanley Marshall; m. 2d Sylvia J. Kelley, June 10, 1979. BS, Cornell U., 1948; JD, Yale U., 1951. Bar: Tex. 1952, U.S. Ct. Appeals (5th cir.) 1966, U.S. Ct. Appeals (10th cir.) 1980, U.S. Supreme Ct. 1959; lic. Tex. Dept. Ins. Pvt. practice, El Paso, Tex., 1952-59, 61-79; assoc. Fryer & Milstead, El Paso, 1952; sr. ptnr. Marshall & Wendorf, El Paso, 1959-61, Marshall & Volk, El Paso, 1979-81; sr. atty. Richard T. Marshall & Assocs., PC, El Paso, 1981-85; sr. ptnr. Marshall, Thomas & Winters, El Paso, 1985-87; sr. atty. Marshall & Winters, 1987-88, Marshall, Sherrod & Winters, 1988-90; pvt. practice El Paso, 1990—. Instr. polit. sci. U. Tex., El Paso, 1961-62; instr. ins. law C.L.U. tng. course Am. Coll.; officer, dir. Advance Funding, Inc., El Paso; mem. El Paso Estate Planning Coun., Editor El Paso Trial Lawyers Rev., 1973-80; contbr. articles to profl. jours. Mem. ABA, ATLA (sec. personal injury law sect. 1967-68, nat. sec. 1969-70, sec.-treas. environ. law sect. 1970-71, vice chmn. family law litigation sec. 1971-72), El Paso Bar Assn., El Paso Trial Lawyers Assn. (pres. 1965-66), Roscoe Pound-Am. Trial Lawyers Found. (commn. on profl. responsibility 1979-82), Soc. Cert. Sr. Advisors, Nat. Assn. Charitable Estate Counselors. Office: 5959 Gateway Blvd W El Paso TX 79925-3331 Office Phone: 915-779-6627. Business E-Mail: marshall@texseniorlaw.com.

**MARSHALL, ROBERT,** film director, television director, theater director, choreographer; b. Madison, Wis., Oct. 17, 1960; Grad., Carnegie-Mellon U., 1982. Broadway dancer, N.Y.C. Dir.: (plays) Chicago, 1992; co-choreographer (Broadway plays) Kiss of the Spider Woman, 1993; choreographer (Broadway plays) Damn Yankees (revival), 1994, Victor/Victoria, 1995, A Funny Thing Happened On the Way to the Forum (revival), 1996; overseer dance sequences (TV films) Mrs. Santa Claus (CBS), 1996; choreographer (TV films) Rogers and Hammerstein's Cinderella (ABC), 1997, (films) The Cradle Will Rock, 1998; dir.(with Sam Mendes): (Broadway plays) Cabaret (revival), 1998 (Dora Mavor Moore award),: (TV films) Annie, 1999 (Emmy award, Am. Choreography award), (uncredited): (Broadway plays) Suessical, 2000,: (films) Chicago, 2002 (Nat. Bd. Rev. award, Dirs. Guild of Am. award, nominated for Oscar award), Memoirs of a Geisha, 2005. Recipient Mr. Abbott Award, Stage Directors & Choreographers Found., 2005. Office: c/o Paul Martino ICM 40 W 57th St New York NY 10019*

**MARSHALL, ROBERT CHARLES,** computer company executive; b. Berwyn, Ill., June 19, 1931; s. Joseph H. and Rose M.; m. Sarane Virruso, Aug. 1, 1954; children—Joseph, Lisa, Jim. BSE.E., Heald Engring. Coll., 1956; MBA, Pepperdine U., 1976. Engr. Lawrence Radiation Lab. Livermore, Calif., 1956-64; systems engr. Electronics Assos., Palo Alto, Calif., 1964-69; v.p. mfg. Diablo Systems, Hayward, Calif., 1969-75; with Tandem Computers, Inc., Cupertino, Calif., 1975—, sr. v.p., chief operating officer, dir., 1979-96; pres., CEO InfoGear, 1996-97; gen. ptnr. Selby Venture Ptnrs., 1998—. Served with U.S. Army, 1952-54. E-mail: Bob@selbyventures.com.

**MARSHALL, ROBERT LEWIS,** musicologist, educator; b. NYC, Oct. 12, 1939; s. Saul and Pearl (Shapiro) M.; m. Traute Maass, Sept. 9, 1966; children— Eric, Brenda. AB, Columbia U., 1960; M.F.A., Princeton U., 1962, PhD, 1968; postgrad., U. Hamburg, W. Ger., 1965. Instr. dept. music U. Chgo., 1966-68, asst. prof., 1968-71, assoc. prof., chmn. dept., 1972-78, prof., 1978-83, Brandeis U., 1983-2000, chmn. dept., 1985-93, incumbent endowed chair Louis, Frances and Jeffrey Sachar prof. music, 1986-2000; emeritus, 2000—. Vis. assoc. prof. Princeton U., 1971-72; endowed prof. Univ. Ala., 1994; mem. rev. bd. rsch. materials program NEH, 1982, rev. bd. edits., 1991. Author: The Compositional Process of J.S. Bach, 2 vols., 1972, The Music of Johann Sebastian Bach: The Sources; The Style; The Significance, 1989, Mozart Speaks: Views on Music, Musicians and the World, 1991, Dennis Brain on Record: A Comprehensive Discography of His Solo, Chamber, and Orchestral Recordings, 1996; editor New Bach Edit., Eighteenth Century Keyboard Music, 1994, 2d edit., 2003; contbr. articles to musical jours. in U.S., Gt. Brit., Germany. Mem. music adv. bd. Ill. Arts Council, 1977-79. Recipient Deems Taylor award ASCAP, 1990; NEH fellow, 1978-79; Hon. Harold Spivacke consultantship Library of Congress. Mem. Am. Musicol. Soc. (bd. dirs. 1974-75, v.p. 1985-86, editl. bd. jour. 1975-80, rev. editor 1986-89, chmn. publs. com. 1994-99, Otto Kinkeldey prize 1974, hon. 2003), New Bach Soc. (chmn. Am. chpt. 1977-80), Phi Beta Kappa. Home: 100 Chestnut St Newton MA 02465-2538 E-mail: rmarshal@brandeis.edu.

**MARSHALL, RON,** retail executive; BS with honors, Wright State U. V.p., CFO Barnes & Noble Bookstores; sr. v.p., CFO Dart Group Corp., Md., 1991-94; exec. v.p., CFO Pathmark Stores, NJ, 1994-98; pres. Nash Finch Co., Mpls., 1998—2002, CEO, 1998—. Mem. Food Mktg. Inst. (bd. dirs.). Office: Nash Finch Co 7600 France Ave S Ste 200 Minneapolis MN 55435-5920*

**MARSHALL, RUSSELL FRANK,** consulting company executive; b. Fort Madison, Iowa, Sept. 10, 1941; s. William Frank and Dorothy Eleanor (Mikels) M.; m. Mary Jean Bailey, June 19, 1966; children: William Russell, Robert Scott (dec.); Gregory Howard. AB, Monmouth Coll., 1963; MS, U. Ill., 1965, PhD, 1971. Rsch. engr. Materials Rsch. Lab, Urbana, Ill., 1970-75; mgr. acad. computing Drake U., Des Moines, 1975-80; v.p. GMI Ltd., Des Moines, 1980-83; sr. v.p., treas. Communication Devel. Co., West Des Moines, 1983-96; pres. Marshall Assocs., West Des Moines, Iowa, 1996—; dir. info. svcs. Grand View Coll., Des Moines, 1996—. Contbr. articles to profl. jours. Active Boy Scouts Am., 1982—; mem. Des Moines Cmty. Theatre. Grantee AEC, 1964-71. Mem. Assn. Computing Machinery, Am. Phys. Soc., Assn. Info. Tech. Mgrs., Des Moines Symphony Assn. Presbyterian. Avocations: music, reading. Home: 1625 19th St West Des Moines IA 50265-1622 Business E-Mail: rmarshall@gvc.edu.

**MARSHALL, SHEILA HERMES,** lawyer; b. NYC, Jan. 17, 1934; d. Paul Milton and Julia Angela (Meagher) Hermes; m. James Josiah Marshall, Sept. 30, 1967; 1 child, James J.H. BA, St. John's U., N.Y.C., 1959; JD, NYU, 1963. Bar: N.Y. 1964, U.S. Ct. Appeals (2d, 3d, 5th and D.C. cirs.), U.S. Supreme Ct. 1970. Assoc. LeBoeuf, Lamb, Greene & MacRae, N.Y.C., 1963-72, ptnr., 1973—95, of counsel, 1996—. Specialist in field. Mem. ABA, N.Y. State Bar Assn., Assn. of Bar of City of N.Y. Republican. Home: 325 E 72nd St New York NY 10021 Office: LeBoeuf Lamb Greene & MacRae 125 W 55th St New York NY 10019-5369 Office Phone: 212-424-8624. Business E-Mail: shmarsha@llgm.com.

**MARSHALL, SIRI SWENSON,** lawyer; BA, Harvard U., 1970; JD, Yale U., 1974. Bar: NY 1975. Assoc. Debevoise & Plimpton, 1974-79; atty., sr. atty., asst. gen. counsel Avon Products Inc., NYC, 1979-85, v.p. legal affairs, 1985-89, sr. v.p., gen. counsel, 1990-94, Gen. Mills, Inc., Mpls., 1994—; bd. dirs. CPR Internat. Inst. Dispute Resolution, Internat. Inst. for Conflict Prevention and Resolution, Ameriprise Fin. Trustee Mpls. Inst. Arts. Office: Gen Mills Inc Number One Gen Mills Blvd Minneapolis MN 55426

**MARSHALL, THOMAS CARLISLE,** applied physics professor; b. Cleve., Jan. 29, 1935; s. Stephen Irby and Bertha Marie (Bieger) M.; children—Julian, John B.sc., Case Inst. Tech., 1957; M.Sc., U. Ill., 1958, PhD, 1960. Asst. prof. elec. engring. U. Ill., 1961-62; mem. faculty Columbia U., 1962—2006, asst. prof. elec. engring., 1962-65, assoc. prof., 1965-70, prof. engring. sci., 1970-78, prof. applied physics, 1978—2006. Author: Free Electron Lasers, 1985, Book of the Toade, 1992; contbr. more than 160 articles to profl. jours. Research grantee Dept. Energy, Office Naval Research, NSF. Fellow: Am. Phys. Soc. (study group on directed energy weapons 1985—87); mem.: Free Electron Lasers and Advanced Concepts in Accelerator Physics. Office: Columbia U 213 Mudd Bldg New York NY 10027 Office Phone: 212-854-3116. E-mail: tcm2@columbia.edu.

**MARSHALL, TOM,** publishing executive; b. Shreveport, La., 1954; With Lousiana Life; pub. Alaska mag., 1987—89; gen. mgr. Cooking Light, 1991—98; v.p. mktg. So. Living, 1998—2003; v.p., pub. Sunset, N.Y.C., 2003—. Recipient Gen. Excellence Nat. Mag. award, 1983. Office: Sunset Time and Life Bldg 20th Fl 1271 Avenue of the Americas New York NY 10020 Office Phone: 212-522-9058. E-mail: marshallt@sunset.com.

**MARSHALL, VINCENT DE PAUL,** industrial microbiologist, researcher; b. Washington, Apr. 5, 1943; s. Vincent de Paul Sr. and Mary Frances (Bach) M.; m. Sylvia Ann Kieffer, Nov. 15, 1969; children from previous marriage: Vincent de Paul III, Amy. BS, Northeastern State Coll., Tahlequah, Okla., 1965; MS, U. Okla. Health Sci. Ctr., Oklahoma City, 1967, PhD, 1970. Rsch. assoc. U. Ill., Urbana, 1970, postdoctoral fellow, 1971-73; rsch. scientist The Upjohn Co., Kalamazoo, Mich., 1973-74, rsch. head, 1975, sr. rsch. scientist, 1976-91, sr. scientist, 1991-2000; cons., 2000—. Mem. editl. bd. Jour. of Antibiotics, 1990-2001, Jour. Indsl. Microbiology, 1989-2001, Devels. in Indsl. Microbiology, 1990, contbr. numerous articles to profl. jours., chpts. to books; patentee in field. Served with U.S. Army Nat. Guard, 1960-65. NIH predoctoral fellow, 1967-70; NIH postdoctoral fellow, 1971-73. Fellow Am. Acad. Microbiology; mem. Soc. for Indsl. Microbiology (membership com. 1988-90, co-chair edn. com. 1989-93, local sects. com. 1991-96, chair nominating com. 1993-94, mem. nominating com. 1999-2000, co-chair program com. 1993-94, dir. 1994-96, pres. So. Great Lakes Sect. 1992-95), Am. Soc. Microbiology, Am. Soc. Biochemistry and Molecular Biology, Internat. Soc. for Antimicrobial Activity of Non-Antibiotics (sci. adv. bd.). Sigma Xi. Republican. Lutheran. Home and Office: 203 Paisley Ct Kalamazoo MI 49006-4359 Office Phone: 269-349-3795. E-mail: vince3795@aol.com.

**MARSHALL, WILLIAM, III,** think-tank executive; b. Norfolk, Va., 1952; m. Katryn S. Nicolai; children: Olivia, William. BA in English and History, U. Va., 1975. Reporter Richmond Times-Dispatch; various positions on Capitol Hill and electoral politics; policy dir. Dem. Leadership Coun., 1985-89; pres. Progressive Found., 1989—; pres., founder Progressive Policy Inst., Washington, 1989—. Sr. editor 1984 House Dem. Caucus policy, Renewing America's Promise; participant in drafting nat. legis., including a demonstration project for vol. nat. svc. Nat. Cmty. Svc. Act of 1990; press sec., spokesman, speechwriter for 1984 U.S. Senate campaign of current N.C. Gov. Jim Hunt; speechwriter, policy analyst for late U.S. Rep. Gillis Long of La., chmn. of House Dem. Caucus; spokesman, speechwriter 1982 U.S. Senate campaign of former Va. Lt. Gov. Dick Davis. Co-editor: Mandate for Change, 1992; contbr. articles to profl. jours. Office: Progressive Policy Inst 600 Pennsylvania Ave SE Ste 400 Washington DC 20003-4350

**MARSHALL, WILLIS HENRY,** psychiatrist; s. Willis Henry Sr. and Pauline Elizabeth (Murphy) M.; m. Carolyn Mae Kowalski; children: Louann Lorinda Marshall Johnson, John Willis. AB cum laude, U. Evansville, Ind., 1958; MD, Ind. U., Bloomington, 1961. Cert. psychiatry Am. Assn. Psychiat. Medicine, 2005; Intern Detroit Meml. Hosp., 1961-62; resident psychiatry Mental Health Inst., Cherokee, Iowa, 1965-67, 69-70, staff psychiatrist, 1967-69, Mental Health Ctr., Muskegon, Mich., 1970-71; pvt. practice psychiatry Madison, Tenn., 1974-85, Bowling Green, Ky., 1987-98; staff psychiatrist chief admission svc., staff psychiatrist treatment unit Mid. Tenn. Mental Health Inst., Nashville, 1981—85, staff psychiatrist evaluation unit forensic svcs. div., 1985—87, chief of staff, 1986-87; forensic psychiatrist State of Tenn., 1981—87; staff psychiatrist Moccasin Bend Mental Health Inst., Chattanooga, 1998—2003; staff psychiatrist, med. dir. Crisis Stabilization Unit Vol. Behavioral Health Svcs. Ctr., Chattanooga, 2003—05, outpatient psychiatrist, 2005—. Part-time staff psychiatrist Ottawa County Mental Health Ctr., Grand Haven, Mich., 1971-73, Tenn. Dept. Mental Health and Mental Retardation Mid. Tenn. Mental Health Inst., Nashville, 1981-87, Lifeskills, Inc., Glasgow, Ky., Franklin, Ky., 1987-89; psychiat. cons. Allegan County Mental Health Ctr., Allegan, Mich., 1973; med. svcs. cons. dept. of forensic svcs. Mid. Tenn. Mental Health Inst., Nashville, 1983-84; clin. asst. prof. psychiatry dept. allied health Trevecca Nazaraene Coll., Nashville, 1985-87; part-time pvt. practice psychiatry, Muskegon, Mich., 1970-74, Madison, Tenn., 1974-87; assoc. clin. dir. mental health unit Med. Ctr., Bowling Green, Ky., 1987-91; preceptor, asst. clin. prof. physician asst. program U. Ky., 1988-91; acting med. dir. Rivendell Children's Psychiat. Hosp., Bowling Green, 1989; med. dir. adult mental health unit Rivendell of Ky., 1992-94. Commd. officer, surgeon USPHS, 1962-65. Recipient AMA Physicians Recognition award, 1969, 79, 83, 86, 89, 92, Exemplary Psychiatrist award Nat. Alliance for Mentally Ill, 1993. Mem. Am. Psychiat. Assn. (life, art assn. 1976—), Ky. Med. Assn., Warren County Med. Soc., Am. Profl. Practice Assn., Am. Acad. Clin. Psychiatrists, Am. Assn. of Psychiat. Medicine, Am. Physicians Art Assn., NRA, Nat. Geog. Soc., AAA Automobile Club, Gallatin Gun Club, Alpha Omega Alpha. Avocations: sculpture, photography, painting, hunting, fixing old guns. Home: 5115 Silver Ln Apison TN 37302-9594 Office: 420 Bell Ave Chattanooga TN 37405 Personal E-mail: willishmarshall@aol.com.

**MARSHALL-BEASLEY, ELIZABETH,** landscape architect; b. Wilton, Conn., Mar. 14, 1959; d. Hamilton West Marshall, Jr. and Mary Barno Marshall; m. James W. Beasley, Jr., Nov. 28, 1986. BA, Princeton U., 1981; M in Landscape Arch., Fla. Internat. U., 1998. Policy analyst N.J. Legislature, 1981; field devel. dir. The Rouse Co., 1984; devel. mgr. Disney Devel. Co., Orlando, Fla., 1988; devel. dir. Norton Mus. Art, West Palm Beach, Fla., 1995; state orgn. dir. Jeb Bush for Gov., Tallahassee, 1996; project mgr., apprentice Morgan Wheelock Inc., West Palm Beach, 1999—2001; cons. Elizabeth Marshall-Beasley, West Palm Beach, 2001—02; pres. Elizabeth Marshall-Beasley, MLA, West Palm Beach, 2003—. Pres. coun. Nat. Pub. Radio, Washington, 2001—; gov. apptd. Bd. Landscape Arch., Tallahassee, 2002—; bd. dirs. Habitat for Humanity, West Palm Beach, New Horizon Svc. Dogs, Orlando. Sponsor Nantucket Conservation Found.; mem. curriculum com. Fla. A&M U. Grad. Sch. Arch.; active US VA Task Force Health and Rehab. Gardens; apptd. mem. City West Palm Beach Art in Pub. Places Commn.; mayor Art in Pub. Places Commn., 2006—. Recipient, ADDY, 1987, Comml. Project of 1989, Architecture Record, 1989; Fairchild Tropical Gardens: Off Site Collection Grad. scholar, 1997. Mem.: Am. Soc. Landscape Arch. (cert.), Sigma Alpha Lambda, Phi Kappa Phi. Episcopalian. Avocations: travel, theater. Office: Ste 1500 505 S Flagler Dr West Palm Beach FL 33401 E-mail: em-b@landplandesign.com.

**MARSHALL-CHAPMAN, PAULA,** food products executive; d. Paul Marshall. BS in Bus., Okla. City U., 1983, PhD in commercial sci., 1993. CEO Bama Companies, Tulsa, Okla., 1984—. Adv. bd. Fed. Reserve Bank, Kans. City; bd. dirs. Am. Fidelity Corp., Bank of Oklahoma, Helmerich and Payne. Pres. Okla. Quality Found. Bd.; trustee Tulsa Community Found.; mem. Ronald McDonald Advisory Bd.; chmn. Salvation Army Advisory Bd.; bd. mem. U. Tulsa. Named Advocate of the Year, Domestic Violence Intervention Services, 2000; named to Bus. Hall of Fame, Okla. Dept. of Commerce, 1998, Hall of Fame, Sales and Mktg. Executives Internat. Academy of Achievements, 1999; recipient Entrepreneur of Yr. award, Ernst & Young LLP, 1997, Pinnacle award, Sales and Mktg. Executives Internat. Academy of Achievements, 1999, Outstanding Philanthropist award, 2001, Amigo of the Year, Tulsa Hispanic C. of C., 2001. Mem.: Women's Foodservice Forum (bd. mem), Tulsa C. of C. (past chair). Office: Bama Companies 2745 E 11th St Tulsa OK 74104

**MARSHALL-DANIELS, MERYL,** mediator, executive coach; b. LA, Oct. 16, 1949; d. Jack and Nita Corinblit; m. Raymond Daniels, Aug. 19, 2000. BA, UCLA, 1971; JD, Loyola Marymount U., L.A., 1974. Bar: Calif. 1974. Dep. pub. defender County of L.A., 1977—; sole practice L.A., 1977—78; ptnr. Markman and Marshall, L.A., 1978—79; sr. atty. NBC, Burbank, Calif., 1979—80, dir. programs, talent contracts bus. affairs, 1980, asst. gen. atty. N.Y.C., 1980—82, v.p., compliance and practices Burbank, 1982; v.p. program affairs Group W Prodns., 1987—89, sr. v.p. future images, 1989—91, TV prodr., Meryl Marshall Prodns., 1991—93; pres. Mediation Ptnrs. and Two Oceans Entertainment Group, 1991—. Chmn., Nat. Women's Polit. Caucus, Westside, Calif., 1978-80; mem. Calif. Dem. Ctrl. Com., 1978-79; mem. Hollywood Women's Polit. Com., 1988; bd. mem. George Foster Peabody Awards. Mem.: Women in Film, Acad. TV Arts and Scis. (treas. 1985, bd. govs. 1989—2001, treas. 1993—97, chmn. bd., CEO 1997—2001). Democrat. Jewish. Office: Two Oceans Consulting Group 2017 Lemoyne St Los Angeles CA 90026 E-mail: merylmarsh@aol.com.

**MARSHANSKY, VLADIMIR NIKOLAEVICH,** medical educator, biochemist, cell biologist; arrived in US, 1998; s. Nikolay Ivanovich and Avrora Sergeivna (Sorokina) Marshansky; 1 child, Serguei Vladimirovich. MSc in Med. Biophysics, Bio-Med. Faculty of Russian State Med. U., Russia, 1980; PhD in Biochemistry, Biol. Faculty Moscow State U., Russia, 1984. Cert. physician-biophysicist Russian State Med. U., 1980. Prof. and dir. dept. biochemistry of faculty of sci. Javeriana U., Bogota, Colombia, 1989—92; rsch. asst. prof. dept. medicine U. Montreal, Canada, 1993—98; asst. prof. medicine dept. medicine Harvard Med. Sch., Boston, 2003—. Contbr. chapters to books, articles to profl. jours. Mem.: Am. Diabetes Assn., Am. Soc. for Biochemistry and Molecular Biology, Proteomic Soc., Can. Soc. of Biochemistry and Molecular Biology, The Am. Physiol. Soc., Am. Soc. for Cell Biology, The Salt and Water Club. Office: Program in Membrane Biology and Nephrology Divsn Mass Gen Hosp Harvard Med Sch 185 Cambridge St Ste 8212 Boston MA 02114 Business E-mail: vladimir_marshansky@hms.harvard.edu.

**MARSTON, EDGAR JEAN, III,** lawyer; b. Houston, July 5, 1939; s. Edgar Jr. and Jean (White) M.; m. Graeme Meyers, June 21, 1961; children: Christopher Graham, Jonathan Andrew. BA, Brown U., 1961; JD, U. Tex., 1964. Bar: Tex. l964. Law clk. to presiding justice Supreme Ct. Tex., Austin, 1964-65; assoc. Baker & Botts, Houston, 1965-71; ptnr. Bracewell & Patterson, L.L.P., Houston, 1971-89, 96—; of counsel, 1990-96; exec. v.p., gen. counsel Southdown, Inc., Houston, 1987-95, also bd. dirs. Mem. ABA, Tex. Bar Assn., Tex. Bar Found., Houston Bar Assn., Houston Country Club, Coronado Club. Episcopalian. Avocations: hunting, fishing, stamp collecting/philately, reading. Office: Bracewell & Giuliani LLP 711 Louisiana St Ste 2300 Houston TX 77002-2770 Office Phone: 713-221-1315. E-mail: edgar.marston@bracewellgiuliani.com.

**MARSTON, MICHAEL,** economist, consultant; b. Oakland, Calif., Dec. 4, 1936; s. Lester Woodbury and Josephine (Janovic) Marston; m. Alexandra Lynn Geyer, Apr. 30, 1966; children: John, Elizabeth. BA, U. Calif., Berkeley, 1959; postgrad., London Sch. Econs., 1961-63. Cert. rev. appraiser Nat. Assn. Rev. Appraisers and Mortgage Consultants, 1984. V.p. Larry Smith & Co., San Francisco, 1969—72, exec. v.p. urban econ. divsn., 1969—72; chmn. bd. Keyser Marston Assocs., Inc., San Francisco, 1973—87; gen. ptnr. The Sequoia Partnership, 1979—91; pres. Marston Vineyard and Winery, 1982—, Marston Assocs., Inc., 1982—. Pres. The Ctr. Individual and Instnl. Renewal, 1996—. Contbr. articles to profl. jours. Mem. spkr. bus. Am. Embassy, London, 1961—63; mem. Gov.'s Issue Anlysis Com. and Spkr. Bur., 1966; v.p., bd. dirs. Dem. Forum, 1968—72; chmn. San Francisco Waterfront Com., 1969—86; v.p. People for Open Space, 1972—87, mem. exec. com., 1972—87; chmn. fin. com. San Francisco Planning and Urban Rsch. Assn., 1976—87, bd. dirs., 1976—87, mem. exec. com., 1976—87, treas., 1976—87; bd. trustees Cathedral Sch. Boys, 1981—82, Marin Country

Day Sch., 1984—90; pres. Presidio Heights Assn. Neighbors, 1983—84; mem. Napa Valley Vintners, 1986—, mem. gov. affairs com.; v.p. St. Luke's Sch., 1986—91; chmn. Presidio Com., 1991—; v.p., trustee Youth for Svc. Served to lt. USNR. Mem.: Napa Valley Vintners, Calif. Vintage Wine Soc., World Congress Land Policy, Urban Land Inst., Pacific Union Club, Bohemian Club, Order of Golden Bear, Chevalier du Tastevin, Lambda Alpha. Home: 3375 Jackson St San Francisco CA 94118-2018 Personal E-mail: marstonmichael@yahoo.com. *Personal philosophy: Success is what you do with what you have not what others think or what is in vogue.*

**MARTE-BAUTISTA, HELEN I.,** retired performing arts educator; d. Diosdado and Modesta Inocencio Marte; 1 child, Andreliz Marte Bautista. MA, San Francisco State U., 1970. Cert. Calif. State credential. Educator, staff devel. San Francisco Unified Sch. Dist., 1968—98. Commr. San Francisco Pub. Libr., 2000—; trustee Am. Libr. Trustee Assn., Chgo., 2002—. Choreographer (prodn.) dance drama, Santa Cruzan (Dance-in-Residence award, 1968). Pres. City Celebration, Inc. Ethnic Dance Festival, San Francisco, 1984—88; sec., bd. mem. Kearny St. Housing Corp., Inc., San Francisco, 1986; pres. Friends of the San Francisco Commn. and Status of Women, 1986—88; treas. YWCA - San Francisco, Marin and San Mateo County, 1990—96; treas. Mayor's Protocol Office San Francisco/Manila Sister City Com., 1996; citizen adv. mem. Presidio Redevel. U.S. Dept. of Interior, San Francisco, 1997—99; sec., mem. bd. Internat. Hotel Sr. Housing Corp., Inc., San Francisco, 1998. Recipient Summer/Residence Citizenship award, Ethical Union Soc., Philippine Scouts Assn., U. Calif., Berkeley, 1961, Merit award outstanding pub. svc., San Francisco Mayor's Office Diane Feinstein, 1984, Human Rights award, San Francisco, Human Rights Commn., 1985; grantee Spl. Edn. program bilingual tchrs., U. San Francisco, 1979; Melvin Jones fellow, Lion's Found., 2005. Mem.: Delta Kappa Gamma (assoc.; pres. 1982—84, Beta Chi chpt.), Am. Fedn. of Teachers (assoc.; mem. of the bd. 1971—76), Fil-Am. Lions Club San Francisco (pres.), Am. Lions Club San Francisco (assoc.; mem. of the bd. 1988, Presdl. award 1996). Avocations: travel, art, music, literature, dance. Office Phone: 415-557-4233.

**MARTEL, EVA LEONA,** accountant; b. Bristol, Conn., Feb. 14, 1945; d. Samuel L. and Irene A. (Beaulieu) Martel. BS in Acctg., N.H. Coll., 1986; MBA, Plymouth State U., 1990. Cert. mgmt. acct.; cert. continuing edn. educator. Accts. payable Elliot Hosp., Manchester, N.H., 1971-79, bookkeeper, 1979-84, dir. acctg., 1984-94; portfolio mgr. Optima Health Inc., Manchester, N.H., 1994-97; mgr. managed care contracting, 1997-98, dir. managed care, 1998-2000; exec. dir. managed care Elliot Hosp., 2000—. Adj. faculty N.H. Coll., 1991—; speaker Daniel Webster coun. Boy Scouts Am., Manchester, 1988, Med. Assts. Workshop, 1997; mem. supervisory com. of bd. Telephone Credit Union, 2004—; panel mem. edn. seminar, 1993. Treas. N.H. Indian Coun., 1980-84; vol. United Way, Manchester, 1988—, accountexec., 1990, 91; mem. adv. coun. health care adminstrn. N.H. Coll., 1990, faculty advisor weekend program, 1990-91; vol. N.H. Heart Assn., 1990-92; bd. dirs. N.H. chpt. Am. Cancer Soc., 1991—; road race com. Elliot Hosp., 2000. Mem. NAFE, Hosp. Fin. Mgmt. Assn., Speaker's Bur. (smoke free com., recycling com. 1991), IMA, Healthcare Fin. Mgmt. Assn, Telephone Credit Union (supr. com., 2004—). Roman Catholic. Avocations: physical fitness, reading, music, writing, teaching. Home: 129 Riverledge Dr Goffstown NH 03045-6203 Office Phone: 603-663-6181. Business E-Mail: emartel@elliot-hs.org.

**MARTEL, JOHN SHELDON,** lawyer, writer; b. Stockton, Calif., Jan. 1, 1931; s. Henry T. and Alice L. M.; m. Bonnie Martel; children: John Sheldon, Melissa Ann. BS, U. Calif.-Berkeley, 1956, JD, 1959. Bar: Calif. 1959. Dep. dist. atty., Alameda County, 1960-61; assoc. trial atty. firm Bronson, Bronson & McKinnon, San Francisco, 1961-64; ptnr. firm Farella, Braun & Martel, San Francisco, 1964—. Lectr., mem. adv. bd. Hastings Ctr. for Trial and Appellate Adv., 1983—. Author: (novels) Partners, 1988, Conflicts of Interest, 1994, The Alternate, 1999, Billy Strobe, 2001; author, editor legal publs.; composer-writer popular songs; profl. musician. Pilot USAF, 1951-54. Winner Am. Song Festival awards, 1978-80, 82, 85, 87. Fellow Am. Coll. Trial Lawyers (state chmn. 1985-87, bd. regents 1993-98); mem. ABA (litigation, antitrust, tort and ins. sects.), Calif. Bar Assn., San Francisco Bar Assn. (former chair litigation sect.), Am. Bd. Trial Advocates (bd. dirs. 1991-93), Am. Fedn. Musicians, Phi Delta Phi, Kappa Sigma. Office: Farella Braun & Martel 235 Montgomery St Ste 3100 San Francisco CA 94104-2902 Office Phone: 415-954-4422. E-mail: jmartel@fbm.com.

**MARTELET, FRANCOIS R.,** pharmaceutical executive; b. Dijon, France, Feb. 17, 1960; m. Marie Santiard, July 9, 1991; children: Marie-Alix, Alexandre, Astrid-Marie. Degree in Bus., Dijon U., MD. Internat. mktg. trainee F. Hoffmann-La Roche, 1991—92, product mgr. Stockholm, 1992—94, group product mgr., 1994—95, internat. product mgr. Basel, Switzerland, 1996—96; head regional oncology, Europe, Middle East, Africa Eli Lilly Corp., London, 1996—99; bus. unit head Benelux Schering-Plough, Brussels, 1999—2000; v.p. pharma oncology intercontinental region, Latam, Asia-Pacific, CEE, Middle East, Africa) Novartis Pharma, East Hanover, NJ, 2001—03; regional head, Cen. and Ea. Europe, Mid. East, Africa Novartis, Munich, 2003—; Basel, Switzerland, 2003—05; v.p. oncology worldwide, human health divsn. Merck & Co., Inc., Whitehouse Station, NJ, 2005—. Lt.-col. French Army Res., 1992—2005. Decorated Medaille des Services Militaires Volontaires. Roman Catholic. Avocations: skiing, horseback riding. Home: 25 Deer Chase Rd Morristown NJ 07960 Office: Merck & Co Inc WS30-10 One Merck Dr PO Box 11 Whitehouse Station NJ 08889-0140 Office Phone: 908-423-6160. Personal E-mail: francoismartelet@yahoo.com. Business E-mail: francois_martelet@merck.com.

**MARTEN, GORDON CORNELIUS,** agronomist, educator, federal agency administrator; b. Wittenberg, Wis., Sept. 14, 1935; s. Clarence George and Cora Levina (Verpoorten) M.; m. Lynette Joy Hanson, Sept. 9, 1961; 1 dau., Kimberly Joy. BS, U. Wis., 1957; MS, U. Minn., 1959, PhD, 1961; postgrad., Purdue U., 1962; DSc (hon.), U. Minn., 2006. Rsch. agronomist U.S. Dept. Agr., U. Minn., St. Paul, 1961-72, supervisory rsch. agronomist, rsch. leader, 1972-89; adj. prof. agronomy U. Minn., St. Paul, 1971-96; assoc. dir. USDA-Agr. Rsch. Svc., Beltsville, Md., 1989-96; prof. emeritus U. Minn., St. Paul, 1996—. Mem. governing body and U.S. rep. to OECD Biol. Resource Mgmt. Program, Paris, 1990-96; adminstrv. coun. USDA Sustainable Agrl. Rsch. and Edn. Program, 1993-95. Assoc. editor: Crop Sci., 1972-74; sr. editor USDA Handbook Near Infrared Reflectance Spectroscopy: Analysis of Forage Quality, 1985, rev. edit., 1989; mem. edit. bd. Sci. of Food and Agriculture, 1985-90; contbr. numerous articles to profl. jours. NSF grad. fellow, 1959-61; recipient Merit award Am. Forage and Grassland Coun., 1976, Outstanding Svc. award, 1981, Civil Servant of Yr. award Twin Cities, Minn., 1976, Cert. of Merits, USDA Agrl. Rsch. Svc., Northrup King Faculty Outstanding Performance award U. Minn., 1986, Superior Svc. award USDA, 1987; named to Hall of Fame, Wausau Wis. Sch. Dist., 1998. Fellow: Crop Sci. Soc. Am. (bd. dirs. 1975—77), Am. Soc. Agronomy; mem.: Agronomic Sci. Found. (trustee 1984—89), Coun. Agr. Sci. and Tech. (bd. dirs. 1985—90), Am. Forage and Grassland Coun. (bd. dirs. 1977—80), North Suburban St. Paul Golden K Kiwanis (bd. dirs. 1998—2001), Biol. Club, Sigma Xi, Phi Kappa Phi, Delta Theta Sigma, Alpha Zeta, Gamma Sigma Delta (Adminstrn. award of merit Nat. Capital Area 1994). Lutheran. Home: 1312 Willow Cir Roseville MN 55113-3235

**MARTENS, ERWIN W.,** risk management consultant; BSc in Computer Sci., U. N.D., 1983, MA in Econs./Stats., 1985. Profl. hockey player, Germany; with Coopers & Lybrand, 1985; founder Analytic Info. Mgmt., Inc., Toronto; global market risk mgmt., dep. head global risk mgmt. and credit suisse Group; sr. v.p. Lehman Bros.; exec. v.p., chief risk officer TIAA-CREF, N.Y.C., 2003—. Mem. U. N.D. Alumni Bd. Named Buy Side Risk Mgr. of Yr., Risk Mgmt. Mag., 2000. Office: TIAA-CREF 730 3d Ave New York NY 10017

**MARTENS, HARVEY ARTHUR,** retired government worker, academic administrator; b. Bancroft, S.D., Mar. 19, 1928; s. Henry Martens and Anna Naeve; m. Barbara Colwell, Oct. 7, 1956 (div. Jan. 0, 1979); children: Craig Colwell, Eric Harvey, Douglas Henry. BS in Polit. sci., S.D. State U., 1951; MPA, Maxwell Sch., Syracuse U., N.Y., 1952, PhD, 1973. Asst. to dir. Navy Adminstrv. Office, Washington, 1952—58; head, mgmt. devel. staff Navy Mgmt. Office, Washington, 1958—62; mgmt. analyst U.S. Dept. of Agr., Washington, 1962—64; dir. spl. projects ASPA, Washington, 1964—65; dir. pub. adminstrn. programs, lectr. in pub. adminstrn. Maxwell Sch., Syracuse U., NY, 1965—73; project dir. Nat. Acad. of Pub. Adminstrn., Washington, 1970—71; dir. rsch. & planning, prof. pub. adminstrn. U. of Nebr., Omaha, 1973—77; dir. grants, prof. pub. adminstrn. Drake U., Des Moines, 1978—86; dir. grants Des Moines U., 1986—93. Editor: Navy Mgmt. Rev., 1960—62, ASPA News, 1962—64; author: (study report) The Orgn. and Adminstrn. of Federally Funded Cmty. Mental Health Ctrs. Press. Ea. Nebr. Nutrition for Elderly, Omaha, 1974—77, Neighborhood Housing Svcs. of Des Moines, 1985—89; chpt. pres. AARP, West Des Moines, Iowa; adv. com. of Polk County sr. svcs. Area Agy. on Aging, Des Moines, 1996—2003; mem. Older Iowans Legislature, Des Moines, 1998—2003; north am. adv. com. Internat. Coun. of Unitarian and Universalists, Prague, Czech Republic, 1999—2003; moderator, summer patio ch. First Unitarian Ch., Des Moines, 1985—2000. Lt. col. USAR, 1951—88, cpl. U.S. Army, 1953—55. Decorated Nat. Def. Svc. medal U.S. Army, Meritorious Svc. medal 103d Corps Command; Scholarship, Syracuse U., 1951—52, Hixson Fellow, Kiwanis Internat., 1997. Mem.: Coun. Fgn. Rels. (Omaha), Am. Humanist Assn. (life), Torch Club Internat. (club pres. 1999—2000), Kiwanis Internat., Mason, Scottish Rite, Shriner. Liberal. Unitarian Universalist. Avocations: travel, genealogy. Home: 2935 Rutland Ave Des Moines IA 50311-3916 Personal E-mail: hmartens4@mchsi.com.

**MARTENS, JUERGEN A.,** pharmaceutical executive; b. Pirmasens, Germany, July 7, 1955; s. Wolfgang and Isolde Martens; m. Denise M. Cook, Apr. 7, 1996; 1 child, Michael L. Hand. Diploma in chemistry, U. Marburg, Germany, 1984, PhD, 1987; M in Tech. Mgmt., U. Pa., Phila., 1998. V.p. pharm. tech. devel. Nektar Therapeutics, San Carlos, Calif., 2000—05; corp. v.p. ops. Mankind Corp., Danbury, Conn., 2005—. Office: Mankind Corporation One Casper St Danbury CT 06810 Office Phone: 203-790-3122. Business E-Mail: jmartens@mannkindcorp.com.

**MARTENSEN, BARBARA,** electronics executive; BS in Math., U. Ariz. With Motorola Semiconductor Products, 1978—99; global info. officer Avnet, Inc., Phoenix, 1999—2001, corp. v.p., sr. v.p. integrated bus. solutions, 2001—. Office: Avnet Inc 2211 S 47th St Phoenix AZ 85034

**MARTHELL, YVETTE JESSICA,** photographer, educator, filmmaker; b. Orange, Calif., Sept. 22, 1976; d. Eliott and Armonica Marthell. BA in Film and Video Prodn., Long Beach U., Calif., 2003. Owner Photography by Yvette, Long Beach, Calif., 2000—; instr. photography, 2001—. Office: Artesia HS 12108 Del Amo Blvd Lakewood CA 90715-1516

**MARTI, KURT,** chemistry professor; b. Berne, Switzerland, Aug. 18, 1936; came to U.S., 1965; s. Werner Marti and Emma H. (Habegger) M.; children: Andres Niklaus, Stefan Kurt, Lorenz Roman. MS, U. Berne, 1963, PhD, 1965. Postgrad. research chemist U. Calif.-San Diego, La Jolla, 1965-68, asst. prof., 1969-74, assoc. prof., 1974-80, prof., 1980—; vis. prof. phys. rsch. lab. Ahmedabad, India, 1977, U. Berne, Switzerland, 1977, 95. Vis. prof. U. Bordeaux, France, 1983, 94; mem. rev. panel Lunar Sci. Inst., Houston, 1971-74, 91-93; lunar sample analysis planning team mem. Johnson Space Ctr., Houston, 1975-78; lectr. in field. Assoc. editor Geochim. Cosmochim. Acta, 1985-95. Grantee NASA, 1971—; Guggenheim fellow, 1976. Fellow Meteoritical Soc.; mem. AAAS, Am. Geophys. Union, Am. Chem Soc. Home: 13424 Calais Dr Del Mar CA 92014-3524 Office: U Calif San Diego Dept Chemistry La Jolla CA 92093-0317 E-mail: kmarti@ucsd.edu.

**MARTI, PAUL EDGAR, JR.,** architect, educator; b. Wichita, Sept. 7, 1929; s. Paul Edgar and Edna Clareen (Conley) M.; m. Audrey Lee Marti, Mar. 15, 1933; children: Dane Eric, Kara Lynn. BArch, Kans. State U., 1953; MA, U. Calif., Berkeley, 1958. Architect Murphy-Mackey, St. Louis, 1955—57, Hellmuth-Obata-K, St. Louis, 1958—62; v.p. Smith-Entzeroth, Clayton, Mo., 1962—88, Paul Marti Assocs. Architects, St. Louis, 1988—. Juror Am Plywood Assn. awards, Seattle, 1973; instr. archtl. tech. Washington U., St. Louis, 1979—85. Contbr. articles in field to profl. jours. Alderman, 1986—; chmn. bd. St. Louis U. Cupples Hist. Mansion, 1995-2000; mayor, City of Oakland, Mo., 2001-; pres. Mayors Small Cities of St. Louis, 2004. Served with USAF, 1953-55. Citation of merit Am. Plywood Assn., 1978; Honor award, landmarks Assocs., 1996. Mem. AIA (award of merit St. Louis 1970, bd. dirs.), Alpha Tau Omega, Clayton Mo. Optimists (pres. 1968). Home: 105 Minturn Ave Saint Louis MO 63122-4842 Office: Paul Marti Architects 34 N Brentwood Blvd Ste 1 Saint Louis MO 63105-3746 Office Phone: 314-725-9006. Business E-Mail: martiarchitect@mailstation.com.

**MARTI, VIRGIL,** artist; b. St. Louis, 1962; BFA, Washington U., 1984; MFA, Temple U., 1990; student, Skowhegan Sch., 1990. Paley Gallery, Moore Coll. Art and Design, Phila., 1992, one-man shows include Samuel S. Fleisher Art Meml., 1994, White Columns, N.Y., 1996, Thread Waxing Space, 1998, exhibited in group shows at Cmty. Edn. Ctr., Phila., 1992, Larry Becker Cmty. Edn. Ctr., 1992, Inst. Contemporary Art, Boston, 1993, Vox Populi, Phila., 1994, Caren Golden Fine Art, N.Y., 1994, Ea. State Penitentiary, Phila., 1995, 88 Room, Boston, 1995, Nexus, Phila., 1996, Beavery Coll. Art Gallery, Glenside, Pa., 1996, The Fabric Workshop and Mus., Phila., 1997, exhibited in group shows, Columbus, 1997, exhibited in group shows, Mus. Am. Art of Pa. Acad. Fine Arts, Phila., 1998, Whitney Biennial, Whitney Mus. Am. Art, 2004, Represented in permanent collections Art Resources Transfer, Inc., N.Y., The Fabric Workshop and Mus., Phila., Phila. Mus. Art, Victoria and Albert Mus., London. Recipient Louis Comfort Tiffany Found. award, 1997; Art Matters fellow, 1995, Pew Fellow in the Arts, 1995, Pa. Coun. Arts fellow, 1997.

**MARTIA, DOMINIC FRANCIS,** academic administrator; b. Canton, Ohio, May 9, 1935; s. Joseph James and Anita (Cimadevilla) Martia; m. Roberta Christine Abel, Feb. 13, 1954; children: Laura Ann, Paul Abel. BA, Roosevelt U., 1962; MA, U. Chgo., 1963; PhD, Loyola U., Chgo., 1972. Assoc. prof. English Roosevelt U., Chgo., 1972—93, asst. to pres., 1972—76, dean grad. divsn., 1976—79, v.p. student svcs., 1979—93, prof. English and humanities, 1993—2000, prof. emeritus, 2000—. Author: Getting Verse, 1989, Present, Tense, Direct Light, 2002, Light Meters, 2005, numerous poems; contbr. articles to profl. jours. Scholarship com. Stone Found., Chgo., 1981—2000. With U.S. Army, 1954—56. Fellow, Woodrow Wilson Found., 1962. Mem.: Nat. Assn. Scholars. Avocation: writing. Home: 5318 Huntingwood Ct Sarasota FL 34235 Personal E-mail: dfmar@webtv.net.

**MARTIGNETTI, FRANK ANTHONY, III,** music educator, church music director; b. New Rochelle, NY, July 22, 1976; s. Frank Anthony and Edith Ann Martignetti. BA, U. Rochester, 1999; MusB, Eastman Sch. Music, 1999; MusM, U. Cin. Coll., 2002. Cert. privisional educator music Conn., 2004. Dir. music H.S. in Cmty., New Haven, 2003—, St. Paul's Luth. Ch., Bridgeport, Conn., 2003—. Adj. prof. music U. Bridgeport, 2005—. Mem.: Nat. Assn. Music Edn., Am. Guild Organists (Greater Bridgeport chpt.), Am. Choral Dirs. Assn., Conn. Music Educators Assn. (regional festival chorus chair, mem. com. urban schs. 2003). Office: High Sch in Cmty 175 Water St New Haven CT 06511 Personal E-mail: frank.martignetti@new-haven.k12.ct.us.

**MARTIKAINEN, A(UNE) HELEN,** retired health specialist educator; b. Harrison, Maine, May 11, 1916; d. Sylvester and Emma (Heikkinen) M. AB, Bates Coll., 1939, DSc (hon.), 1957; MPH, Yale U., 1941; DSc, Harvard U., 1964; DSc (hon.), Smith Coll., 1969. Health edn. sec. Hartford (Conn.) Tb and Pub. Health Assn., 1941; cons. USPHS, 1942—49; chief health edn. WHO, Geneva, 1949—74; chair internat. affairs AAUW-NC, 1986—94, rep. to NC Coalition on Aging, 2001—; bd. dirs., 2001—; mem. NC Health Adv.

Bd. for Aging, 2001—. Hon. trustee Bridgton Acad., North Bridgton, Maine; mem. NC Women's Forum, 1984—; bd. dirs. NC Ctr. of Laws Affecting Women, Inc.; bd. dirs. West Triangle chpt. UNA-USA; chair residents health and social svcs. com., residents com., residents com. for cmty. rels. Carol Woods. Recipient Delta Omega award Yale U., Nat. Adminstrv. award Am. Acad. Phys. Edn., Key award Bates Coll., Internat. Svc. award, France, 1953, Prentiss medal, 1956, Spl. medal, cert. for internat. health edn. svc. Nat. Acad. Medicine for France, 1959, Profl. award Soc. Pub. Health Educators, 1963, Benjamin Elijah Mays award Bates Coll. Alumni Assn., 1989, Legacy of Leadership honoree Pines of Carolina coun. Girl Scouts U.S., 2002; named to Bridgeton Acad. Hall of Fame, Maine, 2003. Fellow APHA (chmn. health edn. sect., Excellence award 1969); mem. AAUW, LWV, Women's Internat. League for Peace and Freedom, U.S. Soc. Pub. Health Educators, Internat. Union Health Edn. (Parisot medal, tech. adviser), Acad. Phys. Edn. (assoc.), NC Coun. Women's Orgns. (mem. coun. assembly 1988-92, Women of Distinction award 1989), Phi Beta Kappa. Home: 3113 Carol Woods 750 Weaver Dairy Rd Chapel Hill NC 27514-1443 Personal E-mail: ahm3113@hotmail.com.

**MARTIN, ALBERT CHARLES,** manufacturing executive, lawyer; b. San Lucido, Italy, Sept. 20, 1928; s. Joseph and Carmela M.; m. Jean Perrin, Aug. 22, 1953 (dec.); children: Lynne, Ken; m. Frances Doughty, June, 1996. BS, Mich. State U., 1952; MS, U. Mich., 1953; JD, Detroit Coll. Law, 1962. Bar: Mich. 1962. Corp. counsel, sec. Udylite Corp., Detroit, 1963-68; corp. counsel Hooker Chem. Corp., N.Y.C., 1968-70, Grow Chem. Co., N.Y.C., 1970-71; group v.p. Leeds & Northrup Internat., North Wales, Pa., 1971-79, pres., 1979—. Served with U.S. Army, 1946-48. Mem. Mich. Bar Assn. E-mail: franal8@aol.com.

**MARTIN, ALICE HOWZE,** prosecutor; b. Memphis, Apr. 25, 1956; married; 3 children. BSN, Vanderbilt U., 1978; JD, U. Miss., 1981. Bar: Tenn. 1981, Miss. 1981, Ala. 1989. Asst. U.S. atty. U.S. Attys. Office, Memphis, 1983-89; ptnr. Harris Harris & Martin, Florence, Ala., 1989-94; dist. mcpl. judge City of Florence, Ala., 1993—97; judge Cir. Ct. State of Ala., 1997—99; U.S. Atty. (no. dist.) Ala. US Dept. Justice, 2001—. Avocations: travel, skeet shooting. Office Phone: 205-244-2001. E-mail: Alice.Martin@usdoj.gov.*

**MARTIN, ALLEN,** retired lawyer; b. Manchester, Conn., Aug. 12, 1937; s. Richard and Ruth Palmer (Smith) M.; m. Bonnie Reid, Sept. 8, 1979; children: Elizabeth Palmer, Samuel Bates. BA, Williams Coll., 1960, Oxford U., 1962; LLB, Harvard U., 1965. Ptnr. Downs, Rachlin and Martin, Burlington, Vt., 1971—2002. Chmn. bd. dirs. Wicor Ams., 1991—; bd. dirs., chmn. compensation com. IDX Systems Corp., 1999-2006; bd. dirs., chmn. fin. com. Union Mut. Ins. Co., New Eng. Guaranty Ins. Co.; mem. Vt. Jud. Responsibility Bd., vice-chmn., 1978-80; trustee Vt. Law Sch., 2000-04. Chmn. Vt. Bd. Edn., 1978-83; chmn. Vt. Rep. Party, 1991-95; mem. Rep. Nat. Com., 1991-95, 97-99. Mem.: ABA, Am. Law Inst. (life). Republican. Home: PO Box B Six Chimneys Orford NH 03777 Office Phone: 603-640-6100. E-mail: amartin@valley.net.

**MARTIN, ANDREA LOUISE,** actress, comedienne, writer; b. Portland, Maine, Jan. 15, 1947; m. Bob Dolman, 1980 (div.); children: Joe, Jack. Grad., Emerson Coll. Appearances include (plays) Hard Shell, 1980 (off-Broadway debut), Sorrows of Stephen, 1980, What's a Nice Country Like You Doing in a State Like This?, 1974, She Loves Me, My Favorite Year, 1993 (Tony award, Featured Actress in a Musical), (films) Cannibal Girls, 1973, Black Christmas, 1974, Wholly Moses!, 1980, Soup for One, 1982, Club Paradise, 1986, Innerspace, 1987, Martha Ruth and Eddie, 1988, Worth Winning, 1989, Boris and Natasha, 1989, Rude Awakening, 1989, Too Much Sun, 1991, Stepping Out, 1991, All I Want for Christmas, 1991, (voice) The Itsy Bitsy Spider, 1992, Striking Distance, 1993, Bogus, 1996, (voice) Anastasia, 1997, Wag the Dog, 1997, The Rugrats Movie (voice), 1998, Bartok the Magnificent, 1999, Believe, 2000, Loser, 2000, Recess: Schools Out (voice), 2001, All Over the Guy, 2000, Jimmy Neutron: Boy Genius, 2001, My Big Fat Greek Wedding, 2002, New York Minute, 2004, The Producers, 2005, The TV Set, 2006, How to Eat Fried Worms, 2006, (TV) Second City TV, 1977-81, That Thing on ABC, 1978, Torn Between Two Lovers, 1979, The Robert Klein Show, 1981, Kate and Allie, 1982, The Comedy Zone, 1984, Late Night Film Festival, 1985, Second City Twenty-Fifth Anniversary, 1985, Martin Short Concert for the North Americas, 1985, The Smothers Brothers Comedy Hour, 1988, Poison, 1988, The Martin Short Show, 1994, Earthworm Jim, 1995, Life...and Stuff, 1997, Damon, 1998, Committed, 2001, My Big Fat Greek Life, 2003, others; (TV movie) Charles Dickens' David Copperfield, 1993, Gypsy, 1993, In Search of Dr. Seuss, 1994, Harrison Bergeron, 1995, My Funny Valentine, 2000, The Kid, 2001, Sick in the Head, 2003, Kim Possible: A Sitch in Time, 2003, (voice) Jimmy Neutron: Attack of the Twonkies, 2005; TV host Women of the Night II, 1988, Second City Fifteen Anniversary Special, 1988, Andrea Martin: Together Again, 1989; actress/writer: TV series SCTV Network 90, 1981-83 (2 Emmy awards 1982, 83), SCTV Channel, 1983-84, TV pilot From Cleveland, 1980; also The Completely Mental Misadventures of Ed Grimley, 1988-90 (voice of Mrs. Freebus).*

**MARTIN, ANDREW AYERS,** lawyer, physician, educator; b. Toccoa, Ga., Aug. 18, 1958; s. Wallace Ford and Dorothy LaTranquil (Ayers) M.; children: William Ayers, Malorie Ayers. BA, Emory U., Atlanta, 1980, MD, 1984; JD, Duke U., 1988. Bar: Calif. 1989, La. 1990, D.C. 1991; diplomate Am. Bd. Pathology, Nat. Bd. Med. Examiners; lic. physician, La., Miss., Ark. Intern in pediatrics Emory U./Grady Meml. Hosp., Atlanta, 1984; intern Tulane U./Charity Hosp., New Orleans, 1989-90, resident in anatomic and clin. pathology, 1990-94; surg. pathology fellow Baylor Coll. Medicine, Houston, 1994-95; law clk. Ogletree, Deakins, Smoak, Stewart, Greenville, SC, summer 1986, Thelen Marrin Johnson Bridges, L.A., summer 1987, Duke Hosp. Risk Mgmt., 1987-88; assoc. Haight Brown Bonesteel, Santa Monica, Calif., 1988; pvt. practice L.A. 1999 physician/atty. Tulane Med. Ctr./Charity Hosp., New Orleans, 1989-94, Baylor Coll. Medicine/Tex. Med. Ctr., Houston, 1994-95; lab. dir. King's Daus. Hosp., Greenville, Miss., 1995—; asst. clin. prof. pathology Tulane U.; lab. dir., owner Vicksburg Pathology Lab., Bolivar Med. Ctr., Cleveland, Miss.; staff pathologist Delta Regional Ctr., Greenville, Miss., N.W. Miss. Regional Medical Ctr., Clarksdale, Miss., No. Sunflower County Hosp., Ruteville, Miss., Tallahatchie County Hosp., Charleston, Miss. Sr. ptnr. Mid-South Pathology Assocs.; med. dir. of labs. Vicksburg Pathology Lab., N.W. Miss. Regional Med. Ctr., Bolivar Med. Ctr., Delta Regional Med. Ctr., North Sunflower County Hosp. 1997—, Tallahatchie (Miss.) County Hosp., N.W. Miss. Regional Med. Ctr., Clarksdale, Lab Corp., Southaven, Miss., Tallahatchie County Hosp.; adj. faculty Moorhead U.; bd. dirs. Martin Bldrs., Inc., Toccoa; mem. AIDS Legis. Task Force for La.; case cons. Office of Tech. Assessment, Washington; tech. cons. and autopsy extra Oliver Stone's "JFK"; adj. clin. faculty Moorhead Coll. Contbr. articles to profl. jours.; author: Reflections on Rusted Chrome (book of poetry). Fellow Coll. Am. Pathologists, Coll. Legal Medicine, La. State Med. Soc. (del. meeting 1992-93). Home: 935 Lakehall Rd Lake Village AR 71653-6096 also: 4104 Alabama Ave Kenner LA 70065-5603 also: 3850 Old Highway 27 Vicksburg MS 39180-8829 Office: Mid-South Pathology Assocs PO Box 5880 Greenville MS 38704-5880

**MARTIN, ANN BODENHAMER,** minister, writer; d. Richard Clinton and Vera von Hein Bodenhamer, Jewel Little Bodenhamer (Stepmother); children: Richard Clinton Elliott, Mark Andrew Elliott. BA, PhD, Univ of Ar, Southwestern Univ, Ark., Fla. and USVI. Lic. FCC First Class, FCC, 1965. Sr. min. Unity of Palm Springs, Calif., 1987—. Home: Post Office Box 1508 Palm Springs CA 92263-1508 Office: Unity of Palm Springs 815 South Camino Real Palm Springs CA 92264

**MARTIN, ANNA MARIE,** music educator; b. Sturgis, Mich., June 3, 1944; d. Robert Stanislas Sutula and Evelyn Mae Good; m. James Summer Martin, May 19, 1979. B of Music Edn., Wichita State U., 1966; MA, Ball State U., 1973. Orch. dir. Elkhart (Ind.) Comty. Schs., 1966—76; choral dir. Rutherford (N.C.) County Schs., 1982—87; orch. dir. Charlottesville (Va.) Pub. Schs.,

1987—88, Prince William County Schs., Manassas, Va., 1988—. Indsl. tng. and pub. rels. CTS Corp., Elkhart, 1976—79; adj. prof. music Gardner Webb Coll., Shelby, NC, 1980—82, Converse Coll., Spartanburg, SC, 1980—82; ch. music dir. St. Francis Episcopal Ch., Rutherfordton, NC, 1986—87; condr. Reston (Va.) Chamber Orch., 1991—94, Nova/Manassas Comty. Orch., Manassas, 1993—95; coord. Presdl. Exch. Program to Ekaterinburg, Russia, 1995—97. Mem.: Am. String Tchrs. Assn., Music Edn. Nat. Conf., Am. Fedn. Tchrs. Home: 8341 Gaither St Manassas VA 20110 Office: Stonewall Jackson H S 8820 Rixlew Ln Manassas VA 20108

**MARTIN, ARTHUR MEAD,** lawyer; b. Cleveland Heights, Ohio, Mar. 29, 1942; s. Bernard P. and Winifred (Mead) M. AB, Princeton U., 1963; LLB, Harvard U., 1966. Bar: Ill. 1966, U.S. Dist. Ct. (no. dist. Ill.) 1969, U.S. Ct. Appeals (7th cir.) 1970, U.S. Supreme Ct. 1980, U.S. Ct. Appeals (fed. cir.) 2000. Instr. law U. Wis., Madison, 1966-68; assoc. Jenner & Block, Chgo., 1968-74, ptnr., 1975—2003. Co-trustee Dille Family Trust, 1982—. Author: Historical and Practice Notes to the Illinois Civil Practice Act and Illinois Supreme Court Rules, 1968-88. Trustee 4th Presbyn. Ch., Chgo., 1996-99, sec. 1997-99, exec. com. 1997-99; mem. nominating com., 2006—; bd. dirs. Stop Colon/Rectal Cancer Found., 1998—; founding bd. mem. Alliance for the Great Lakes, 2005, chair nominating com., 2005—. Mem. ABA, Am. Law Inst., Ill. Bar Assn., Chgo. Bar Assn. (bd. editors 1972-86), Ill. State Hist. Soc. (adv. bd. 1998-99, bd. dirs. 1999—, exec. com. 1999—, fin. com. 1999—, treas. 2002—), Ill. Centennial Bus. Com., Lake Mich. Fedn. (bd. dirs. 1993-2002, 03—, exec. com. 1994-2002, treas. 1994-99, 2001-02, sec. 1999-2001), Law Club Chgo., Legal Club Chgo. Office: Jenner & Block 1 IBM Plz Fl 4400 Chicago IL 60611-7603 Business E-mail: amartin@jenner.com.

**MARTIN, BENJAMIN GAUFMAN,** ophthalmologist; b. Louisville, Aug. 18, 1937; s. Benjamin and Catherine L. Martin; m. Caroline Sue Martin, May 25, 1975; children: Benjamin, Lori, Tamara, Farrell, Steven, David. BME, U. Louisville, 1954, M. Engring., 1973; MD, U. So. Calif., 1964. Design engr. Philco/Ford, Palo Alto, Calif., 1957-60; rsch. engr. N.Am./Rockwell, Inglewood, Calif., 1961-63; intern Wright-Patterson Med. Ctr., Dayton, Ohio, 1964-65; ophthalmology resident Wilford Hall Med. Ctr., San Antonio, 1968-71; commd. USAF, 1963, advanced through grades to col., ret., 1980; CEO Cape Coral (Fla.) Eye Ctr., 1980—. With USN, 1954-57. Decorated Legion of Merit, DFC, Bronze Star, Air medal. Mem.: DFC Soc., Daedalions, Elks, Shriners, Masons. Republican. Lutheran. Office: Cape Coral Eye Ctr 4120 Del Prado Blvd S Cape Coral FL 33904-7165 Office Phone: 239-542-2020.

**MARTIN, BOE WILLIS,** lawyer; b. Texarkana, Ark, Oct. 6, 1940; s. E.H. and Dorothy Annette (Willis) M.; m. Carol J. Edwards, June 12, 1965; children: Stephanie Diane, Scott Andrew. BA, Tex. A&M U., 1962; LLB, U. Tex., 1964; LLM, George Washington U., 1970. Bar: (Tex.) 1964. Law clk. Tex. Supreme Ct., 1966-67; assoc. Snakard, Brown & Gambill, Ft. Worth, 1967-69, assoc., ptnr., 1971-72; asst. counsel US Senate Labor and Pub. Welfare Com., 1969; legal asst. U.S. Senator Ralph W. Yarborough, 1969-71; assoc., ptnr. Stalcup & Johnson, Dallas, 1972-77; assoc. ptnr. Coke & Coke, Dallas, 1977-80; ptnr., shareholder Johnson & Gibbs, Dallas, 1981—95, Bell, Nunnally & Martin, Dallas, 1996—. Vis. prof. law So. Meth. U. Sch. Law, 1972-73, 75, 88-89, 95, 1999-2000, 2002-06, U. Tex. Sch. Law, 1977, 79, U. Houston Law Ctr., 2005. Contbr. articles to profl. jours. Staff Carter-Mondale Campaign, 1976, 80; cons. to v.p. of US, 1977-80; cons. Mondale for Pres. Campaign, 1983-84, Dukakis for Pres. Campaign, 1988; dep. coord. of visit of Pres. Mikhail Gorbachev to State of Minn., 1990. Capt. US Army, 1966-69. Mem. ABA, Tex. Bar Assn., Dallas Bar Assn. Democrat. Methodist. Home: 4055 Sweetwater Dr College Station TX 77845-964 Office: Bell & Nunnally & Martin 3232 Mckinney Ave Ste 1400 Dallas TX 75204-2426 Business E-Mail: boem@bellnunnally.com.

**MARTIN, BOSTON FAUST,** neurosurgeon; b. Tampa, fla., June 1, 1927; s. Boston Francis and Cantherina Heidi Martin; m. Roselle Bayot, May 26, 1988; children: Sandrine, Nathalie, Samantha, Arielle. BS, Howard U., 1949; BMS, U. Fribourg, Switzerland, 1954; MD, U. Geneva, 1958. Diplomate Am. Bd. Neurological and Orthopedic Surgeons, Am. Bd. Minimally Invasive Spinal Surgery. Intern in gen. surgery Danbury (Conn.) Hosp., 1959-60; resident in gen. surgery Stamford (Conn.) Hosp.-Yale U. Affiliate, 1960-61; resident in neurology Met. Hosp., N.Y.C., 1961-62; resident in neurosurgery NYU Bellevue Med. Ctr., N.Y.C., 1962-65; chief resident in neurosurgery NYU Med. Ctr., N.Y.C., 1965-66, fellow in neurosurgery, 1966-67; interim chief neurol. surgery sect. Sch. Medicine and Univ. Hosp., U. P.R., San Juan, 1969-70, asst. prof. neurosurgery, 1969-75; clin. instr. in neurol. surgery NYU, 1966-67; clin. instr. in rehab. medicine U. Medicine and Dentistry N.J./N.J. Med. Sch., Newark, 1978-86, clin. instr. surgery, 1996—; attending neurosurgeon Hosp. Ctr. at Orange, NJ, 1976—, Meadowlands Hosp. Med. Ctr., Secaucus, NJ, 1981—, chief neurol. surgery, 1998—; attending neurosurgeon Christ Hosp., Jersey City, 1987—. Pvt. practice, West Orange, 1976—; attending neurosurgeon Doctors Hosp., Santuce, 1970-75, Matilde Brenes Hosp., Bayamon, P.R., 1970-75, San Jorge Hosp., Santice, P.R., 1970-75, Tchrs. Hosp., Haty Rey, P.R., 1971-75, Auxilio Muto Hosp., Hato Rey, 1971-75, Presbyn. Hosp., Santuce, 1972-75; asst. attending neurosurgeon Knud-Hansen Meml. Hosp., St. Thomas, V.I., 1967-69, U. P.R. Univ. Hosp., 1969-75; attending neurosurgeon East Orange Gen. Hosp., 1976-86, chief neurol. surgery, 1990-2000; chief spinal cord injury svc. VA Med. Ctr., East Orange, 1975-84; active attending neurosurgeon Newark Beth Israel Med. Ctr., 1998—; presenter in field. Co-author: the Conus Medullaris: Physiological Anatomy and Clinical Considerations. 1987; contbr. articles to profl. jours. Lt. col., flight surgeon USAF, 1984-90. Recipient Cert. of Merit Lions Club Internat., 1969, Disting. citation DAV, 1977, spl. trophy for disting. svc. DAV, 1979. Mem. ACS, AAUP, Internat. Coll. Surgeons, Acad. Medicine N.J., Congress Neurol. Surgeons (mem. internat. com 1974, socio-econ. com. 1974-76, med. legal sub-com. 1978-84), Societe de Neuro-Cirurgie De Langue Francaise, N.J. Neurosurg. Soc., Assn. Mil. Surgeons U.S., Am. Acad. Neurol. and Orthopedic Surgeons, Air Force Assn., Orange Mountain Med. Soc., Alpha Phi Alpha. Office: 81 Northfield Ave West Orange NJ 07052-5338

**MARTIN, BOYCE FICKLEN, JR.,** federal judge; b. Boston, Oct. 23, 1935; s. Boyce Ficklen and Helen Artt Martin; m. Mavin Hamilton Brown, July 8, 1961; children: Mary V.H., Julia H.C., Boyce Ficklen III, Robert C.G. II. AB, Davidson Coll., 1957; JD, U. Va., 1963. Bar: Ky. 1963. Law clk. to Hon. Shackelford Miller, Jr. U.S. Ct. Appeals (6th cir.), Cin., 1963—64; asst. to US atty (we. dist.) Ky US Dept. Justice, Louisville, 1964, U.S. atty. (we. dist.) Ky., 1965; instructor Louisville Law school, 1965—67; pvt. practice Louisville, 1966—74; 1st asst. Office of the County Attorney, Jefferson County, 1970—74; judge Jefferson Circuit Ct., Louisville, 1974—76; chief judge Ky. Ct. Appeals, 1976—79; judge US Ct. Appeals (6th Cir.), Cin. and Louisville, 1979—, chief judge, 1996—2003. Jud. coun. U.S. Ct. Appeals (6th cir.), 1979—96, chmn., 1996—; mem. Jud. Conf. of U.S. 1996—, exec. com., 1998—. Trustee Isaac W. Bernheim Found., Louisville, 1981—97, chmn. 1982—95; trustee Blackacre Found., Inc., Louiville, 1983—94, chmn., 1986—94; trustee Hanover (Ind.) Coll., 1982—, vice-chmn., 1992—97, chmn., 1998—; exec. bd. Old Ky. Home coun. Boy Scouts of Am., 1968—72; pres. Louisville Zool. Commn., 1971—74; vestry mem. St. Francis in the Fields Episcopal Ch., Harrods Creek, Ky., 1979—83; bd. vis. Davidson (N.C.) Coll., 1980—86, trustee, 1994—98. Capt. JAGC U.S. Army, 1958—66. Fellow: Am. Bar Found.; mem.: ABA (com. effective appellate advocacy Conf. Appellate Judges), Louisville Bar Assn., Ky. Bar Assn., Fed. Bar Assn., Am. Judicature Soc., Inst. Jud. Adminstrn. Office: US Ct Appeals 209 US Courthouse 601 W Broadway Louisville KY 40202-2227*

**MARTIN, BRIAN,** Olympic athlete; b. Palo Alto, Calif., Jan. 19, 1974; Student, Denver U. Luge racer with 2 man team, back driver, 1988—; mem. U.S. 1st Olympic Team; named to devel. team, 1989. Named winner, World Cup Races (4), 1997—98, All-Japan Championships, Nagano; recipient Bronze medal Luge Men's Doubles, Nagano Olympics, Japan, 1998, World

Cup, 1998, Silver medal, Bell Atlantic Nat. champion, 1998, Silver medal, Luge Challenge Cup, 2000, Bronze medal, World Championship, 2000, 2005. Address: US Luge Association 35 Church St Lake Placid NY 12946-1805

**MARTIN, C. D.,** lawyer; b. Seminole, Okla., Mar. 24, 1943; BS, U. North Tex., 1964; LLB, U. Tex., 1967. Bar: Tex. 1967, N.Mex. 1967, U.S. Dist. Ct. N.Mex., U.S. Dist. Ct. (we. and no. dists.) Tex. Mem., mng. ptnr. Hinkle, Hensley, Shanor & Martin, L.L.P., Midland, Tex., 1986—. Mem. adv. bd. dirs. Wells Fargo Bank Tex., Midland Bank. Mem. Midland Planning and Zoning Commn., 1979-82, chmn., 1982; mem. adv. coun. Sch. Arts and Scis., U. Tex. at Permian Basin; trustee Permian Basin Petroleum Mus., gen. counsel; past dir. U. Tex. Law Sch. Found. Fellow Tex. Bar Found. (life), N.Mex. Bar Found.; mem. ABA, State Bar Tex., State Bar N.Mex., Midland County Bar Assn. (pres. 1984-85), Phi Delta Phi. Office: Hinkle Hansley, Shanor & Martin LLP PO Box 3580 Midland TX 79702-3580 Business E-Mail: bud@hinklelawfirm.com.

**MARTIN, CAMERON,** artist; b. Bklyn., 1970; BA, Brown U., 1994; attended, Whitney Mus. Ind. Study Program, NY, 1996. One-man shows include The Future Lasts Forever, Howard House, Seattle, 1999, Future Views, Tate, NY, 1999, Angstrom Gallery, Dallas, 2000, Three Pictures, Howard House, Seattle, 2001, New Paintings, Kevin Bruk Gallery, Miami, 2001, Standstill, Artemis Greenberg Van Doren Gallery, NY, 2002, Never Rider, Gallery Min Min, Tokyo, 2003, Clear Skies, Artemis Greenberg Van Doren Gallery, NY, 2004, A Turn Pale, Gallery Min Min, Tokyo, 2004, exhibited in group shows at Home, Bellevue Art Mus., Wash., 1994, Northwest Ann., Ctr. Contemporary Art, Seattle, 1995, Images Lost & Found, Chassie Post Gallery, NY, 1996, Apartments, Artra, Milan, Italy, 1997, Landscapes, Meyerson Nowinski Gallery, Seattle, 1998, Open, Tate, NY, 1998, Other Paintings, Huntington Beach Art Ctr., Calif., 1999, Twice Born: Beauty, Mills Gallery, Boston, 2000, Flat File, Bellwether Gallery, Bklyn., 2000, Three Painter, Lawrence Rubin Greenberg Van Doren Fine Art, NY, 2001, Guide to Trust No. 2, Yerba Buena Ctr. Arts, San Francisco, 2002, Linger, Artemis Greenberg Van Doren Gallery, NY, 2002, Everybody Knows This is Nowhere, Kevin Bruk Gallery, Miami, 2002, City Mouse/Country Mouse, Space 101, Bklyn., 2003, How Come, Stux Gallery, NY, 2003, Nature Boy, Elizabeth Dee Gallery, NY, 2003, Giverny, Salon 94, NY, 2003, Whitney Biennial, Whitney Mus. Am. Art, 2004, Colored Pencil, KS Art, NY, 2004, About the House, Howard House, Seattle, 2004, Stay Inside, Shoshana Wayne Gallery, Santa Monica, Calif., 2004. Recipient Pollock-Krasner Foundation Award, 2000; Samuel T. Arnold Fellowship, 1994, Artists Giverny Fellowship & Residency, France, 2001. Mailing: c/o Artemis Greenberg Van Doren Gallery 730 Fifth Ave 7th Floor New York NY 10019

**MARTIN, CAROL JACQUELYN,** artist, educator; b. Ft. Worth, Tex., Oct. 6, 1943; d. John Warren and Dorothy Lorene (Coffman) Edwards; m. Boe Willis Martin, Oct. 6, 1940; children: Stephanie Diane, Scott Andrew. BA summa cum laude, U. North Tex., 1965; MA, U. Tex., El Paso, 1967. Tchr. Edgemere Elem. Sch., El Paso, 1965—66, Fulmore Jr. H.S., Austin, Tex., 1966—67, Monnig Jr. H.S., Ft. Worth, 1967—68, Paschal H.S., Ft. Worth, 1968—69; instr. Tarrant County Jr. Coll., Ft. Worth, 1968—69, 1971—72; instr. English Eastfield C.C., Dallas, 1981; instr. Richland C.C. Dist., 1982; instr. art Meml. Student Ctr. UPlus Tex. A&M U., 2002—03; instr. art Brenham Fine Arts League, 2006. Artist Vt. Studio Ctr., 1998; press sec. Senator Gaylord Nelson, Washington, 1969—71. Editor The Avesta Mag., 1964-65; various art exhbns Mem. Nat. Mus. Women in Arts; mem. Brenham Fine Arts League, Friends of Meml. Student Ctr.-Opera and Performing Arts Soc., The Woman's Club. Mem. Lone Star Art Guild, Brazos Valley Art League, Brazos Valley Symphony Soc., Mortar Board, Alpha Chi, Sigma Tau Delta, Kappa Delta Pi, Delta Gamma Democrat. Methodist. Avocations: travel, photography, skiing, painting. Address: 4055 Sweetwater Dr College Station TX 77845-9650

**MARTIN, CHARITY KAY,** academic librarian, educator; b. Tulsa, Sept. 29, 1968; d. Carlton D and Sondra K Stokes; m. Tim L. Martin, Dec. 4, 1999; 1 child, Connell D. BA in Psychology, Northeastern State U., Tahlequah, Okla., 1990; MA in History, U. Kans., Lawrence, 1993; MS in Libr. Sci., U. North Tex., Denton, 1997. Asst. prof. univ. librs. U. Nebr., Lincoln, 1997—2003, assoc. prof. univ. librs., 2003—. Advisor - history Praeger/Greenwood Pub. Group Libr. Adv. Bd., Westport, Conn., 2005—; advisor Lincoln Sch. of Commerce Libr. Adv. Bd., 1998—2004. Author: (journal article) Various Professional Journals; contbr. articles to profl. jours. Recipient First Step award, Wiley Profl. Devel. Grant, 1999; grantee Diversity Rsch. grantee, ALA - Office of Diversity, 2006, Coll. and U. Sect. Rsch. grantee, Nebr. Libr. Assn. - C&U Sect., 1999, 2003. Mem.: N.Am. Serials Interest Group (program planning com., co-chair 2001—03), Nebr. Libr. Assn. (tech. svcs. roundtable treas., webmaster 1997—2001, new mems. round table chair, vice-chair, sec., treas. 1998—2003), ALA. Democrat-Npl. Christian. Avocations: yoga, reading, gardening. Office: Univ of Neb - Lincoln Univ Libraries 322 Love Library Lincoln NE 68588-4100 Office Phone: 402-472-2517. Office Fax: 402-472-2534. E-mail: cmartin3@unl.edu.

**MARTIN, CHARLES E.,** music educator; b. Berwyn, Ill., Aug. 1, 1955; s. Tom and Ruth Martin; m. Pegy R. Martin, Sept. 3, 1957; children: Nicholas, Nathan. MusB, Iowa State U., 1978; MusM, Ariz. State U., 1982. Cert. tchr. k-12 Ill., Iowa. Dir. band Maquoketa Midi. Sch., Ill., 1978—80, Lewis Ctrl. H.S., Council Bluffs, Iowa, 1982—95, H.L. Richards H.S., Oak Lawn, Ill., 1995—. Musician-on-call Des Moines Symphony, Phoenix Symphony, Omaha Symphony. Summer Music fellow, Northwestern U., 1994. Mem.: NEA, Nat. Music Educators Conf., Ill. Music Educators. Home: 5521 W 99th St Oak Lawn IL 60453-3817 Office: HL Richards HS 10601 S Ctrl Ave Oak Lawn IL 60453 Office Phone: 708-499-2550 ext 5096. E-mail: chuck.martin@chsd218.org, charlesemartin@comcast.net.

**MARTIN, CHARLES FONTAINE,** management consultant; b. New Orleans, La., Sept. 28, 1945; s. Fontaine and Lillian Lyons (Galt) M.; m. Martha Ann Spaulding, Mar. 25, 1972; children: Ethan, Amy, Susan. AB, Harvard Coll., 1966; PhD, U. Calif., Berkeley, 1973. Applied mathematician GE Space Divsn., Sunnyvale, Calif., 1972-76, system engr. Valley Forge, Pa., 1976-78; mgr. data systems engring. TASC, Reading, Mass., 1978-84; mgr. systems analysis Booz, Allen & Hamilton, Lexington, Mass., 1984-87; pres. Chas. F. Martin Assocs., Inc., Concord, Mass., 1987-94; v.p. Mfg. Cons. Ptnrs., Concord, 1995-96; sr. cons. Spectrum Tech. Group, Woburn, Mass., 1997-98; product mkt. mgr. i2 Techs., Cambridge, Mass., 1998—2001; dir. product mgmt. Valogix, Saratoga, NY, 2001—03; sr. dir. ops. rsch. Viewlocity, Dallas, 2003—04. Chmn. Greater Boston SIGSOFT, Burlington, Mass., 1990-92. Author: (guidebook) Sierra Whitewater, 1974, (textbook) User-Centered Requirements Analysis, 1988. Pres. bd. Solutions at Work, 1997-98. Mem. IEEE Computer Soc., Assn. Computing Machinery, Sierra Club (race chmn. River Touring sect. 1969-71). Office Phone: 603-526-7387. Business E-Mail: charlesmartin@acm.org.

**MARTIN, CHARLES NEIL, JR.,** health care management company executive; b. Florence, Ala., Dec. 11, 1942; s. Charles Neil Sr. and Hazel Lucy (Hawkins) M. BS, So. Coll., Chattanooga, 1964. Adminstr. El Reposo Nursing Home, Florence, 1964-66, Parkwood Convalescent Ctr., Chattanooga, 1966-67; project dir. Tenn. Hosp. Assn., Nashville, 1967-68, asst. dir., 1968-69; v.p. Gen. Care Corp., Nashville, 1969-76, exec. v.p., 1976-79, pres., COO, 1979-80; sr. v.p. HCA, Nashville, 1980-85, exec. v.p., 1985-87, also bd. dirs.; pres., chief operating officer HealthTrust, Inc., Nashville, 1987—92; chmn., pres., CEO OrNda HealthCorp., 1992—97; chmn., CEO Vanguard Health Sys., Nashville, 1997—. Bd. dirs. Equicor, Nashville, 1986—; bd. dirs. Cystic Fibrosis Found., Nashville, 1987. Office: Vanguard Healthcare 20 Burton Hills Blvd Nashville TN 37215*

**MARTIN, CHESTER Y.,** sculptor, painter; b. Chattanooga, Nov. 2, 1934; s. Woodfin Ballenger and Mabel Willett (Young) M.; m. Patricia Ann Parnell, Aug. 15, 1963; 1 child, Sharon Elizabeth (Mrs. Christopher Pruitt). Student, U. Chattanooga, 1952-55, 60-61, Internat. Medallic Workshop-Pa. State U.,

1984. Freelance artist, Chattanooga, 1967-86; sculptor, engraver U.S. Mint, Phila., 1986-92. One-man shows include Hunter Mus. Art, Chattanooga, 1979; group shows: Kottler Galleries, N.Y.C., 1966; Internat. Exposition Contemporary Medals, Italy, 1983, Sweden, 1985, Finland, 1990; U.S. Dept. State, 1984, Nat. Sculpture Soc., N.Y.C., 1984, 85, 99, Cast Iron Gallery, N.Y.C., 1992, Internat. Exhbn. of Contemporary Medals, Brit. Mus., London, 1992, Hungarian Nat. Gallery, Budapest, 1994, Neuchatel, 1996, Nat. Sculpture Soc., N.Y.C., 1999, Weimar, 2000, Paris Mint, 2002, Lisbon, 2004; numerous others; permanent collections: British Mus., London; Smithsonian Instn.; Food and Agrl. Orgn., Rome; Am. Numismatic Soc., N.Y.C.; Julius Wile Sons and Co., N.Y.C.; Brookgreen Gardens, S.C., U.S. Mint, Phila., Belmont U., Nashville; major comms.: World Food Day Medal, UN, 1984, others; other major works: History of Chattanooga Mural, 1974; theme painting of Br. Colonial Ft. Loudon, 1975; Centennial Mural for Chattem Inc., Chattanooga, 1980; sculptured Congl. Bicentennial Silver Dollar, 1989, Eisenhower Centennial Dollar reverse, Mt. Rushmore Dollar obverse, 1991; designer Andrew Wyeth Congl. medal, 1989, George H.W. Bush Presdl. medal reverse; designer Yosemite Nat. Park Centennial Congressional Medal, 1991, Gen. Colin L. Powell Congressional Medal, 1992, White House Bicentennial Dollar reverse, 1992; designer mural Chattanooga Met. Airport, 1999. Served with USAF, 1956-60. Recipient numerous art awards, most recent being Purchase award Benedictine Art Competition, 1975, Medallic Sculpture award Am. Numismatic Assn., 1993. Mem. Fedn. Internationale de la Medaille (Am. del.), Am. Medallic Sculpture Assn. (v.p. 1987). Methodist. Avocation: modern languages. Mailing: 4110 Sunbury Ave Chattanooga TN 37411-5232 Office Phone: 423-698-3561. E-mail: cymppm@comcast.net.

**MARTIN, CHRIS,** vocalist; b. Devon, England, Mar. 2, 1977; m. Gwenyth Paltrow, 2003; children: Apple Blythe Alison, Moses. Student in Ancient World Studies, U. Coll. London. Sign painter; vocalist, pianist, rhythm guitarist Coldplay, 1998—. Singer: (albums) Parachutes, 2000 (Grammy award: Best Alternative Music Album, 2001), A Rush of Blood to the Head, 2002 (Grammy awards: Best Alternative Music Album, 2002, Best Rock Performance By A Duo Or Group With Vocal for song "In My Place", 2002, Record Of The Yr. for song "Clocks", 2003), Live 2003, 2003, X&Y, 2005, Love, Actually, 2006. Recipient Favorite Alternative Artist (Coldplay), Am. Music Awards, 2005. Office: Capital Records 1750 North Vine St 10th Fl Hollywood CA 90028*

**MARTIN, CLARENCE EUGENE, III,** lawyer; b. Martinsburg, W.Va., Mar. 24, 1946; s. Clarence Eugene Jr. and Catherine Dubois (Silver) M.; m. Judith Anne Gray; 2 children: McKenna Gray Martin, Morgan Elizabeth Martin. AB in English, U. Ariz., 1968; JD, Cath. U., Washington, 1974; hon. doctorate (hon.), Shepherd U. Bar: W. Va. 1974, D.C. 1974, Md. 1987, Pa., 1992, U.S. Dist. Ct. D.C. 1975, U.S. Ct. Appeals (D.C. cir.) 1975, U.S. Dist. Ct. (no. dist.) W.Va. 1976, U.S. Dist. Ct. (so. dist.) W.Va., U.S. Dist. Ct. Md. 1986, U.S. Ct. Appeals (4th cir.) 1976, U.S. Supreme Ct. 1979, U.S. Dist. Ct. (no. and ea. dists.) Pa. 1984, U.S. Ct. Appeals (3d cir.) 1984. Asst. couonsel U.S. Ho. Reps., Washington, 1974-75; trial atty. U.S. Dept. Justice, 1975-76; assoc. Martin & Seibert, L.C., Martinsburg, 1976-79, ptnr., 1979—. Bd. dirs. Mchts. & Farmers Bank, Martinsburg, W.Va. Legal Svcs. Plan. Author: (seminar) Impeachment of Witnesses, 1984; co-author ABA publ. Emerging Problems Under the Federal Rules of Evidence, 2d edit., Bad Faith Litigation, The Ethics of Surveillance. Mem. W.Va. Ho. Dels., Charleston, 1976-82; trustee Nat. Parks and Conservation Assn., Washington, 1980-85; bd. govs. Def. Trial Counsel W.Va., 1984-92; commr. Interstate Commn. Potomac River Basin, 1980-86, U.S. Commn. on Agrl. Workers, 1988-94; bd. advs. Shepherd Coll. (Am. del.), mem. Jurisprudence Scholastic Achievement award, 1993-2004; mem. Greater Ea. Panhandle Ch. Com., 1988—, chmn. 1988—; chmn. St. Joseph's Parish Coun., 1997-99; pres. Washington-Balt. chpt. Patrons of the Arts in the Vatican Mus.; bd. dirs. Region IX Planning and Devel. Coun., Holy Family Hosp. Found.; mem. Berkeley County Devel. Authority; commr. U.S. Commn. on Agr. Workers, 1998-1999; trustee Nat. Pks. and Conservation Assn., 1980-85. Recipient Am. Jurisprudence Scholastic Achievement award, 1972, Assn. Govt. Employees award, 1980. Fellow W.Va. Bar Found.; mem. ABA, W.Va. Bar Assn. (pres. 1990-91), W.Va. State Bar, D.C. Bar Assn., Berkeley County Bar Assn. (pres. 1984), Nat. Assn. R.R. Trial Counsel, Am. Legis. Exch. Coun., Am. Judicature Soc., Def. Rsch. Inst., D.C. Bar Assn., Md. Bar Assn., Ya. Bar Assn., Am. Bd. Trial Advocates (bd. dirs. 1986-94), Internat. Assn. Def. Counsel, Def. Trial Counsel of W.Va. (founding mem., bd. dirs. 1984-92), Md. Def. Trial Counsel, W.Va. Law Inst., Berkeley County Roundhouse Authority (chmn. 1999—), W.Va. C. of C. (sec., mem. exec. com., bd. dirs. 2003—, sec. 2006), John Carroll Soc., KC, Univ. Club, Order of Malta (bd. dirs. 2003-), Order of the Holy Sepulchre, Constantinian Order St. George (bd. dirs.), W.Va. Edn. Alliance (bd.dirs.), Conf. U.S. Ct. Appeals for 4th Cir. (life). Home: Pendleton House 6393 Jordan Nollville Rd Martinsburg WV 25401-8866 Office: Martin & Seibert LC PO Box 1286 Martinsburg WV 25402-1286 Office Phone: 304-262-3213. E-mail: cemartin@martinandseibert.com.

**MARTIN, CLAUDE RAYMOND, JR.,** marketing consultant, educator; b. Harrisburg, May 11, 1932; s. Claude R. and Marie Teresa (Stapf) M.; m. Marie Frances Culkin, Nov. 16, 1957; children: Elizabeth Ann, David Jude, Nancy Marie, William Jude, Patrick Jude, Cecelia Marie. BS, U. Scranton, Pa., 1954, MBA, 1963; PhD, Columbia U., NYC, 1969. Newsman Sta. WILK-TV, Wilkes-Barre, Pa., 1953-55; news dir. Sta. WNEP-TV, Scranton, Pa., 1955-60; dir. systems Blue Cross & Blue Shield Ins., Wilkes-Barre, 1960-63; lectr. mktg. St. Francis Coll., Bklyn., 1964, U. Mich., Ann Arbor, 1965-68, asst. prof., 1968-73, assoc. prof., 1973-77, prof., 1977-80, Isadore and Leon Winkelman prof. retail mktg., 1980—92, chmn. mktg. dept., 1986-90, prof. retail mktg. Isadore and Loen Winkerman, 1992—. Bd. dirs. Perry Drug Stores, cons. mktg., 1983-89; spl. cons. on rsch. changes in U.S. currency Fed. Res. Sys., 1978—; pub. mem. Nat. Advt. Rev. Bd., 1989-94. Contbr. articles to profl. jours. Trustee U. Scranton, 1996—. Served with USNR, 1955-57. Mem. Acad. Mktg. Sci., Am. Mktg. Assn., SW Mktg. Assn., Bank Mktg. Assn., Assn. Consumer Rsch., Am. Collegiate Retailing Assn., Am. Acad. Advt. (Disting. Fellow). Roman Catholic. Home: 1116 Aberdeen Dr Ann Arbor MI 48104-2812 Office Phone: 734-971-1897. Personal E-mail: claudemartinjr@hotmail.com.

**MARTIN, CLYDE VERNE,** psychiatrist; b. Coffeyville, Kans., Apr. 7, 1933; s. Howard Verne and Elfrieda Louise (Moehn) Martin; m. Barbara Jean McNeilly, June 24, 1956; children: Kent Clyde, Kristin Claire, Kerry Constance, Kyle Curtis. Student, Coffeyville Coll., 1951—52; AB, U. Kans., 1955, MD, 1958; MA, Webster Coll., St. Louis, 1977; JD, Thomas Jefferson Coll. Law, L.A., 1985. Diplomate Am. Bd. Psychiatry and Neurology. Intern Lewis Gale Hosp., Roanoke, Va., 1958—59; resident in psychiatry U. Kans. Med. Ctr., Kansas City, 1959—62, Fresno br. U. Calif.-San Francisco, 1978; staff psychiatrist Neurol. Hosp., Kansas City, 1962; practice medicine specializing in psychiatry Kansas City, Mo., 1964—84; founder, med. dir., pres. bd. dirs. Mid-Continent Psychiat. Hosp., Olathe, Kans., 1972—84; adj. prof. psychology Baker U., Baldwin City, Kans., 1969—84; staff psychiatrist Atascadero State Hosp., Calif., 1984—85; clin. prof. psychiatry U. Calif., San Francisco, 1985—; chief psychiatrist Calif. Med. Facility, Vacaville, 1985—87. Pres., editor Corrective and Social Psychiatry, Olathe, 1970—84, Atascadero, 1984—85, Fairfield, Calif., 1985—97; cons. psychiatrist Brit. Health Svc. Plymouth (Eng.) Trust, 1999—2001. Contbr. articles to profl. jours. Bd. dirs. Meth. Youthville, Newton, Kans., 1965—75, Spofford Home, Kansas City, 1974—78; del. Kans. East Conf. Meth. Ch., 1972—80, bd. global ministries, 1974—80. Served to capt. USAF, 1962—64, ret. col. USAF. Scholar Oxford Law and Soc., 1993. Fellow: Am. Orthopsychiat. Assn., World Assn. Social Psychiatry, Royal Soc. Health (London), Am. Assn. Mental Health Profls. in Corrections, Am. Psychiat. Assn.; mem.: AMA, Assn. Mental Health Adminstrs. (cert.), Am. Assn. Sex Educators, Counselors and Therapists (cert.), Assn. for Advancement Psychotherapy, St. James Club (London), Capitol Hill Club (Washington), Marines Meml. Club (San Francisco), Pi Kappa Alpha, Phi Beta Pi. Office Phone: 707-688-3790. Personal E-mail: cvkcmartin@msn.com.

**MARTIN, CRAIG ALLEN,** infectious diseases pharmacist; b. Covington, Ky., Sept. 27, 1974; s. Donald Wayne Martin and Margie Ann Pittman; m. Valerie Beth Perkins, June 20, 1998; children: Tyler Coleman, Caleb Andrew. PharmD, U. Ky., 1999. Registered pharmacist Ky. Infectious diseases clin. pharmacy specialist U. Ky., Lexington, 2002—. Mem. Southland Christian Ch., Lexington. Recipient Best Practice Award, Am. Soc. Health Sys. Pharmacists, 2004, Clinician of Yr. award, Soc. Infectious Diseases Pharmacists, 2005. Mem.: Rho Chi. Office: U Ky Med Ctr Pharmacy Svcs C117 800 Rose St Lexington KY 40536 Office Phone: 859-257-1558. E-mail: cmart2@email.uky.edu.

**MARTIN, CRAIG LEE,** engineering company executive; b. Dodge City, Kans., Nov. 23, 1949; s. Ray N. and Nadia C. Martin; m. Diane E. Hensley, Mar. 19, 1977. BSCE, U. Kans., 1971; MBA, U. Denver, 1982. Project mgr. Martin K. Eby Constrn. Co., Wichita, Kans., 1972-83; exec. v.p., COO CRSS Constructors, Inc., Denver, 1983-89; exec. v.p. CRSS Comml. Group, Houston, 1989-90; sr. v.p. CRSS Capital, Houston, 1990-92, CRSS Inc., Houston, 1992-94; pres. CRSS Architects, Inc., Houston, 1992-94; sr. v.p. ops. Jacobs Engring. Group Inc., 1994-95; pres. Jacobs Constructors, Inc., 1994-95; sr. v.p. gen. sales and mktg. to pres. Jacobs Engring. Group, Inc., Pasadena, Calif., 1995—2000, exec. v.p. global sales, 2000—02, pres., 2002—, CEO, pres., 2006—. Adv. bd. Constrn. Bus. Rev., 1993—. Bd. govs. Woodbury U. Sch. Bus. Mem. ASCE. Avocations: golf, clay shooting. Home: 930 S El Molino Ave Pasadena CA 91106-4414 Office: Jacobs Engring Group Inc 1111 S Arroyo Pkwy Pasadena CA 91105-3254 Office Phone: 626-578-6813. Business E-mail: craig.martin@jacobs.com.

**MARTIN, CURTIS,** professional football player; b. Pitts., Pa, May 1, 1973; 1 child. Student, U. Pitts. Running back New Eng. Patriots, Foxboro, Mass., 1995—98, N.Y. Jets, 1998—. Named to Pro Bowl, 1995, 1996, 1998, 2001, 2004. Achievements include led NFL in rushing, 2004; rushed for over 1,000 yards in each of his first 10 NFL seasons; became NY Jets all-time rushing leader, 2004. Office: care NY Jets 1000 Fulton Ave Hempstead NY 11550-1030*

**MARTIN, DANIEL C.,** surgeon, gynecologist, educator; b. St. Louis, Apr. 7, 1946; s. Dan Allen and Ruth Keel (Fields) M.; m. Glenn Ann Blakemore, July 1, 1970; children: Josh, Adam. BS in Physics, Emory U., Atlanta, 1968, MD, 1972. Diplomate Am. Bd. Ob-Gyn. Rsch. asst. physics and radiology Emory U., Atlanta, 1968-69; intern, resident, fellow, instr. The Johns Hopkins Med. Instns., Balt., 1972-77; from asst. prof. to clin. asst. prof. U. Tenn., Memphis, 1977-90, clin. assoc. prof., 1990—2005, clin. prof., 2005—; surgeon Reproductive Surgery, P.C., Memphis, 1977—. Gynecologist, reproductive surgeon Bapt. Meml. Hosp., 1977—; Axel Munthe presenter, Naples, Italy, 1992; guest spkr.Annual Japanese Endometriosis Symposium, Osaka, 1994, 2004; dir. gynecologic laser and endoscopy workshops, 1982-93. Editor: (textbooks) Lasers in Endoscopy, 1990, Laparoscopic Appearance of Endometriosis, 1990, Manual of Endoscopy, 1990, Atlas of Endometriosis, 1993, Endoscopic Management of Gynecologic Disease, 1996. Picker Found. fellow Emory U., 1969; Tex. Assn. Ob-Gyn. hon. fellow, 1989; recipient Bridges trophy for athletics Emory U., 1968, Codman surg. award, 1982, 83, Video award Am. Fertility Soc., 1992, Physician Recognition awrd Endometriosis Assn., 1995; named one of Best Drs. Am. Woodward and White Inc., 1992, 94, 96, 98, 00,02, 04, Hon. mem. Australian Gynecol. Endoscopy Soc., 1993, named to Sports Hall of Fame, Emory Coll., 2002. Mem. ACOG (sect. chair jr. fellows Md.), Tenn. Med. Assn., Memphis and Shelby County Med. Soc. (comm. on laser safety in med. facility), Am. Assn. Gynecol. Laparoscopists (pres. 1990-91, Videoendoscopy award 1993), Gynecologic Surgery Soc. (pres. 1994-96, chmn. bd. 1996-98), Australian Gynecol. Endoscopy Soc. (hon.), Argentinian Ob-Gyn. Soc. (hon.). Office Phone: 901-751-0300, 901-751-0300. Personal E-mail: drdanmartin@aol.com.

**MARTIN, DANIEL RICHARD,** pharmaceutical executive; b. Lima, Peru, June 9, 1937; s. James Marion and Clemmy Caroline (Valencia) M.; m. Barbara Artemis Cyrus, June 23, 1962; children: Daniel Richard Jr., John Alexander, Christopher Andrew. BA, Cornell U., 1958; MS, Columbia U., N.Y.C., 1959. Area sales supr. Schering Corp., Bloomfield, NJ, 1960-64; assoc. McKinsey & Co. N.Y.C., 1964-69; treas. Harper & Row, Pubs., N.Y.C., 1969-72; mng. dir. Merck & Co., Rahway, NJ, 1972-77; group v.p. Bell & Howell Co., Chgo., 1977-80; pres. Howland Martin Corp., N.Y.C., 1980-85; pres. Sterling Europe, Middle East, Africa Sterling Drug, Inc., N.Y.C., 1986-89; pres., CEO, also bd. dirs. E-Z-EM, Inc., Westbury, NY, 1990-97; pres., also bd. dirs. Milestone Scientific, Inc., Livingston, NJ, 1998-99. Adj. prof. mgmt. Pace Univ., NYC, 1996—; bd. mgrs. Country Life PLC, 2005. Co-chmn. Accion Internat., Cambridge, Mass., 1988-98; trustee Bangor (Maine) Theol. Sem., 1991-2000, Key and Candle Found., 2006; dir. Americas Found.; bd. dirs., fin. com. White Plains (N.Y.) Hosp. Decorated Order of Merit (Ecuador). Mem. Coun. on Fgn. Rels., Americas Soc., Cornell Club (N.Y.C.). Independent. Congregationalist. Home: 31 Rochambeau Dr Hartsdale NY 10530-3017 E-mail: drm1937@aol.com.

**MARTIN, DAVID ALAN,** law educator; b. Indpls., July 23, 1948; s. C. Wendell and Elizabeth Bowman (Meeker) M.; m. Cynthia Jo Lorman, June 13, 1970; children: Amy Lynn, Jeffrey David. BA, DePauw U., 1970; JD, Yale U., 1975. Bar: D.C. Law clk. to Hon. J. Skelly Wright U.S. Ct. Appeals (D.C. cir.), 1975—76; law clk. to Hon. Lewis F. Powell U.S. Supreme Ct. Washington, 1976—77; assoc. Rogovin, Stern & Huge, Washington, 1977—78; spl. asst. bur. human rights and humanitarian affairs U.S. State Dept., Washington, 1978—80; from asst. prof. to assoc. prof. U. Va. Sch. Law, Charlottesville, 1980—86, prof., 1986—91, Henry L. & Grace Doherty prof. law, 1991—2003, F. Palmer Weber Rsch. prof. civil liberties and human rights, 1992—95, 2000—03, Warner-Booker disting. prof. internat. law, 2003—, Class of 1963 rsch. prof., 2004—. Cons. Adminstrv. Conf. U.S., Washington, 1988-89, 91-92, U.S. Dept. Justice, 1993-95, U.S. Dept. of State, 2003-04; gen. counsel U.S. Immigration and Naturalization Svc., 1995-98. Author: Immigration: Process and Policy, 1985, 5th edit., 2003, Asylum Case Law Sourcebook, 1994, 5th edit., 2005, The Endless Quest: Helping America's Farm Workers, 1994; editor: The New Asylum Seekers, 1988, Immigration Admissions, 1998, Immigration Controls, 1998, Rights and Duties of Dual Nationals: Evolution and Prospects, 2002, Immigration Stories, 2005; bd. editors Am. Jour. Internat. Law, 2004—; contbr. articles to profl. jours. Nat. governing bd. Common Cause, Washington, 1972-75; elder Westminster Presbyn. Ch., Charlottesville, 1982-84, 89-92; bd. dirs. Internat. Rescue Com., 2000-03. German Marshall Fund Rsch. fellow, Geneva, 1984-85. Mem. Am. Soc. Internat. Law (v.p. 2003-05, Book award 1986), Internat. Law Assn. Democrat. Office: U Va Sch Law 580 Massie Rd Charlottesville VA 22903-1738 Office Phone: 434-924-3144.

**MARTIN, DAVID ALLEN,** application developer, computer scientist; b. Louisville, Ky., Oct. 27, 1953; s. Philip Allen and Finas Ellen Martin; m. Rhonda Faye Martin, Apr. 12, 1998; children: Benjamin Lloyd, Sarah Beth Richert, Patricia Ellen, Bradley Alan Richert. MS in Computer Sci., U. Louisville, Louisville, Ky., 1977. Chief tech. officer A. L. Sewell Co., Inc., Louisville, 1980—92, Computer Contractors Internat. Dana Point, Calif., 1992—97, e-PULSETrak.com, Louisville, 1997—. Cons. software bus. solutions Computer Contractors Internat., Dana Point, Calif., 1992—97. Author: (software) Traker; co-author: e-PULSETrak.com. Deacon Midlane Pk. Bapt. Ch., Louisville, 2004—06. Bapt. Avocations: travel, computers, reading, investments. Home: 17006 Polo Fields Lane Louisville KY 40245 Office: e-PULSETrakcom 4220 Bardstown Road Louisville KY 40218 Office Phone: 502-371-3106. Home Fax: 502-459-2955; Office Fax: 502-459-2955. Business E-Mail: davidm@e-pulsetrak.com.

**MARTIN, DAVID BRITON HADDEN, JR.,** lawyer; b. Beverly, Mass., Dec. 9, 1946; s. David Briton Hadden and Mary Louise (Ward) M.; m. Martha Bacon, June 21, 1969; children: Charlotte, Jessica, Benjamin Ward. BA, Yale U., 1969; JD, U. Va., 1976. Bar: Va. 1976, D.C. 1977. Assoc. Dunnells, Duvall, Bennett & Porter, Washington, 1976—79, Dickstein, Shapiro &

Morin, Washington, 1979—80; spl. counsel SEC, Washington, 1980—84, spl. counsel to chmn., 1984—85, dir. divsn. corp. fin., 2000—02; assoc. Hogan & Hartson, Washington, 1985—87, ptnr., 1987—99, Covington & Burling, Washington, 2002—, chmn., Securities Practice Group, co-head corp. practice area. Mng. editor U. Va. Law Review, 1975-76. Bd. dirs. Jubilee Jobs, 1998—; trustee Westover Sch., 1998—, SEC Hist. Soc., 2004—. Mem. Metro. Club. Office: Covington & Burling LLP 1201 Pennsylvania Ave Washington DC 20004-2401 Office Phone: 202-662-5128. Office Fax: 202-778-5128. Business E-Mail: dmartin@cov.com.

**MARTIN, DAVID EDWARD,** health sciences educator; b. Green Bay, Wis., Oct. 1, 1939; s. Edward Henry and Lillie (Luckman) M. BS, U. Wis., 1961, MS, 1963, PhD, 1970. Ford Found. research trainee Wis. Regional Primate Ctr., Madison, 1967-70; asst. prof. health scis. Ga. State U., Atlanta, 1970-74, assoc. prof., 1974-80, prof., 1980-91, regents prof., 1992-00, regents prof. emeritus, 2000—. Affiliate scientist Yerkes Primate Rsch. Ctr., Emory U., Atlanta, 1970—98; US rep to Internat. Olympic Acad., 1978; sport medicine rsch. assoc. US Olympic Com., 1981—84; chmn. sports scis. USA Track and Field; mem. coaching staff US teams to world championships in distance running, Rome, 1982, Gateshead, England, 83, Budapest, Hungary, 94, Vilamoura, Portugal, 2000, Fukuoka, Japan, 06, head coach, Paris, 1980, Madrid, 84, Hiroshima, Japan, 85, Warsaw, 87, Antwerp, Belgium, 91; mem. Olympic med. support group Atlanta Olympic Games. Author: Laboratory Experiments in Human Physiology, 4th edit., 1980, The Marathon Footrace, 1979, La Corsa Di Maratona, 1982, The High Jump Book, 1982, The High Jump Book, 2d edit., 1987, Respiratory Anatomy and Physiology, 1987, Training Distance Runners, 1991, Training Distance Runners, 2d edit., 1997, Training Distance Runners, German edit., 1992, Training Distance Runners, Spanish edit., 1995, Training Distance Runners, Japanese edit., 2001, The Olympic Marathon, 2000. Trustee Ga. Found. for Athletic Excellence. Named Disting. prof. Ga. State U., 1975, 81, 85 Fellow Am. Coll. Sports Medicine; mem. Internat. Soc. Olympic Historians, Am. Physiol. Soc., Atlanta Track Club. Home: 510 Coventry Rd Apt 13A Decatur GA 30030-5038 Office: Ga State U Dept Cardiopul Care Atlanta GA 30303 Office Phone: 404-651-1499. E-mail: drdave@gsu.edu.

**MARTIN, DAVID HUBERT,** internist, epidemiologist, educator; b. Detroit, Mar. 24, 1943; s. Hubert Cillis and Mable Anita (Stewart) M.; m. Jane Ellen Schlichtemeier, Nov. 22, 1970; children: Jennifer, Jason. BA with distinction, U. Kans., 1965; MD cum laude, Harvard Coll., 1969. Diplomate Nat. Bd. Med. Examiners, Am. Bd. Internal Medicine, Infectious Disease Subspecialty Bd. Am. Bd. Internal Medicine. Intern Bronx (N.Y.) Mcpl. Hosp. Ctr., 1969-70; staff assoc. Nat. Inst. Allergy and Infectious Diseases, Mid. Am. Rsch. Unit, NIH, Panama Canal Zone, 1970-73; med. resident U. Wash. Affiliated Hosps., 1973-75; sr. fellow in infectious diseases U. Wash., 1976-78; chief resident in medicine USPHS Hosp., Seattle, 1975-76, staff internal medicine clinic, 1975, attending physician internal medicine, 1976-78, staff dept. internal medicine New Orleans, 1979-81; staff Hotel Dieu Hosp., New Orleans, 1982-94; clin. asst. prof. medicine La. State U. Med. Sch., New Orleans, 1979-81, asst. prof. medicine divsn. infectious diseases, 1981-82, assoc. prof. medicine divsn. infectious diseases, 1982-88, assoc. prof. microbiology, 1986-88, prof. internal medicine and microbiology, 1988, asst. chief sect. infectious diseases, 1988-89, chief sect. infectious diseases, 1990—, Harry E. Dascomb M.D. prof. of medicine, 1990—. Instr. dept. medicine U. Wash. Med. Sch. Medicine, Seattle, 1975-78, acting asst. prof. medicine, 1978-79; chmn. infection control com., chmn. instnl. rev. bd. human rsch. com., chmn. antibiotic utilization com., sec. rsch. and editl. com., sec. animal welfare com. USPHS Hosp., New Orleans, 1979-81, dep. chief clin. rsch. dept., 1979-81, chmn. credentials com., 1980-81; mem. infection control com. Hotel Dieu Hosp., New Orleans, 1983-84, chmn. pharmacy and therapeutics com., 1988-94, mem. infection control com., 1990-94; vis. physician Charity Hosp. (now Med. Ctr. of La. at New Orleans), New Orleans, 1982—; chmn. antibiotics com., 1982—; dir. infection control program, 1993—, chmn. infection control com., 1993—, vice chmn. pharmacy and therapeutics com., 1995—; chmn. comprehensive medicine head search com. La. State U. Med. Sch., 1989-90, dept. medicine faculty promotion com., 1988—; AIDS policy com., 1992; adv. bd. La. State Labs., 1993—, State La. Pub. Health Lab. Adv. Com., 1994—, U.S. Pub. Health Region 6 Infertility Prevention Adv. Com., 1995—; mem. nat. STD treatment guidelines com. Ctrs. Disease Control, 1993, 98, nat. Chlamydia and gonorrheadiagnosis guidelines com., 1997—; dir. La. STD/HIV rsch. ctr., 2001-04, Gulf South STI/TM Collaborative Rsch. Ctr., 2004—. Peer reviewer various jours. including Sexually Transmitted Diseases, The Jour. of Infectious Diseases, The Am. Jour. of the Med. Scis., Archives of Internal Medicine, Clin. Infectious Diseases, New Eng. Jour. Medicine, Annals Internal Medicine, Jour. AMA; contbr. chpts. to books and articles to profl. jours. Dir. La. STD/HIV Rsch. Ctr., 2002—. With USPHS, 1970-82. Achievements include established the first chlamydia laboratory in the Gulf South. Fellow ACP (La. chpt. program chmn. 1994-95), Infectious Diseases Soc. Am.; mem. Internat. Soc. for Sexually Transmitted Disease Rsch. (bd. dirs. 1991-99, chmn. 1995 meeting organizing com., pres. 1993-95, sec.-treas. 1999—), Am. Fedn. for Clin. Rsch., Am. Sexually Transmitted Diseases Assn. (v.p. 1992-94, pres. 1994-96), Am. Soc. for Microbiology, European Soc. for Clin. Microbiology and Infectious Diseases, Soc. for Clin. Investigation La./Miss. Infectious Diseases Soc. (bd. dirs., sci. program chmn. 1993, pres. 1997-99), Phi Beta Kappa. Achievements include research in the effect of sexually transmitted microorganisms on pregnancy outcome, antibiotic treatment of sexually transmitted diseases and in particular C. trachomatis, epidemiology of C. trachomatis in normal populations, chancroid and other genital ulcer diseases. Office: La State U Med Sch 1542 Tulane Ave New Orleans LA 70112-2825 Office Phone: 504-568-5031.

**MARTIN, DAVID JERNER,** education educator; b. N.Y.C., Aug. 12, 1934; s. Henning J. and Ruth J. Martin; m. Mary Lou Pierson, Sept. 13, 1958; children: David, Steven, Elizabeth. BA in Chemistry, Hope Coll., Holland, Mich., 1956; MS in Gen. Sci., Syracuse U., N.Y., 1974; PhD in Sci. Edn., Ga. State U., Atlanta, 1991. Cert. mid. sch. and HS sci., math. tchr. Ga., N.Y. Tchr. sci. and math. Van Hornesville Ctrl. Sch., NY, 1958—60, Arabian Am. Oil Co., Dhahran, Saudi Arabia, 1960—71, coord. sci. curriculum, 1971—75, coord. profl. devel., 1975—82; pres. Human Resources Devel. Internat., Marietta, Ga., 1982—86; tchr. sci. Marietta H.S., 1986—89; prof. sci. edn. Kennesaw State U., Marietta, 1990—, dir. Grad. Studies Edn. and Tchr. Edn. Svcs., 1996—2000. Author: Elementary Science Methods: A Constructivist Approach, 1997, 2006, Constructing Early Childhood Education, 2000, Building Teachers: A Constructivist Approach to Introducing Education, 2007; editor, cons. The Weather Classroom, 1992. Exec. dir. Ga. Jr. Acad. Sci., 1994—2000; counselor Kappa Delta Pi, 1994—2002. Mem.: NSTA, Ga. Sci. Tchrs., Ga. Acad. Sci., Southeastern Assn. Edn. Tchrs. Sci., Assn. Edn. Tchrs. Sci., Nat. Assn. Rsch. Sci. Tchg. Avocations: classical violin, chamber music. Business E-Mail: dmartin1@kennesaw.edu.

**MARTIN, DAVID S.,** retired secondary school educator, administrator; b. N.Y.C., May 14, 1941; s. Perry Johnson and Polly Edith (Shedlov) M.; m. Florence E. Martin, Jan. 14, 1989; children: Drew Michael, Amy Davida. BA, Adelphi Coll., 1962, MA, 1966; profl. cert., Hofstra U., 1969. Cert. secondary tchr., sch. dist. adminstr., N.Y. Adj. assoc. prof. Pace U., White Plains, N.Y., 1978-92; tchr., computer coord. Jericho (N.Y.) Pub. Schs., 1962-99. Author: Teachers Manual for Introduction to Pascal; co-author: How To Prepare for SAT II: Physics, 6th edit.; also author other books; contbr. articles to profl. jours. Fulbright-Hays grantee, 1967-68; recipient Grand award L.I. Sci. Congress, 1958, Disting Achievement award Electronic Learning, 1983, Outstanding Accomplishment award RITEC, 1984. Mem.: IEEE (sr.), N.Y. State United Tchrs., Assn. Computing Machinery, Am. Assn. Physics Tchrs., Jericho Retirees Assn., Flambeau, Sigma Pi Sigma, Phi Delta Kappa, Omicron Delta Kappa. Home: 25 Cedar Ln N Glen Head NY 11545-1703

**MARTIN, DAVID STANDISH,** education educator; b. New Bedford, Mass. Aug. 24, 1937; s. Theodore Tripp and Elinor Louise (Raymond) M.; m. Susan Katherine Orowan, June 30, 1962. BA, Yale U., 1959; MEd, Harvard U., 1961, CAS, 1968; PhD, Boston Coll., 1971. Cert. tchr., prin. Tchr. Newton

(Mass.) Pub. Schs., 1961-68, asst. prin., 1969-70; teaching asst. Boston Coll., Chestnut Hill, Mass., 1968-69; curriculum dir. Beverly (Mass.) Pub. Schs., 1970-73; prin. Mill Valley (Calif.) Pub. Schs., 1973-75, curriculum dir., 1975-80; chmn. dept. edn. Dominican Coll., San Rafael, Calif., 1978-80; coordinator undergrad. tchr. edn. Gallaudet U., Washington, 1980-85, dean sch. edn. and human svcs., 1985-95, prof. edn., 1995—2001, prof., dean emeritus, 2002—. Cons. Curriculum Devel. Assocs., Washington, 1975-2001; mem. bd. examiners Nat. Coun. Accreditation Tchr. Education; bd. dirs. USA-SINO Tchr. Education Consortium, Western Pa. Sch. for the Deaf; Fulbright fellow U. Witwatersrand, South Africa, 2003, 04, Open U., 2005, vis. rsch. prof. Author: Case Studies in Curriculum, 1989; editor: Cognition, Education and Deafness, 1985, Advances in Cognition Education and Deafness, 1991; co-editor, author: Assessing Deaf Adults, Curriculum for Deaf Learners; contbr. articles to profl. jours. Grantee Dept. Edn., 1970, 85, Knight Found., 1995-2001, Ford Found., 1998-2001. Mem. D.C. Assn. Colls. Tchr. Edn. (pres. 1989-92), Assn. for Supervision and Curricum Devel., Nat. Coun. for Social Studies, Am. Ednl. Rsch. Assn., Am. Assn. Colls. for Tchr. Edn. (bd. dirs.), Coun. for Exceptional Children, Phi Delta Kappa, Kappa Delta Pi (chair publ.), Ednl. Consulting Schs. and Univs. (prof., dean emeritus 2002-). Democrat. Unitarian Universalist. Avocations: genealogy, sailing, classical organ, astronomy. Home and Office: 10 Colonial Farm Cir Marstons Mills MA 02648 Personal E-mail: davidchina_2000@yahoo.com.

MARTIN, DENISE ANN, safety and environmental health manger; d. Richard Frank and Jeannine Carol Salisbury; m. Gerald Lee Martin, June 10, 1972; children: Katrina Ann Martin Davenport, Brent Lee. BS, Colo. State U., Ft. Collins, 1974. Rsch. assoc. Colo. State U., Ft. Collins, Colo., 1988—91; microbiologist Ctrs. for Disease Control, Ft. Collins, Colo., 1991—2005, alternate responsible official select agts. program, 2005—. Contbr. articles to profl. jours. including Jour. Virology (Charles C. Shepard Sci. award, 2002, James Nakano Citation, 2002). Recognition 8pl. Recognition award, USPHS, 1994, Honor award, Nat. Ctr. for Infectious Diseases, 1994, Group award, 1996, 2003, Spl. Asct of Svc. award, 1996, 2001, Sec.'s Disting. Svc. award, DHHS, 1997, 2000—01. Achievements include research in West Nile diagnostic serology techniques. Avocations: singing, sewing, travel, reading, music. Office: Ctrs for Disease Control & Prevention Foothills Campus 1300 Rampart Rd Fort Collins CO 80522 Office Phone: 970-221-6484. Business E-Mail: dzm9@cdc.gov.

MARTIN, DIANNE LESLIE, artist, educator; b. Boston, Apr. 8, 1940; d. James Donald and Ina (Mac Lerie) M.; m. William Paul Kennedy, June 15, 1961 (div. June 1978). BFA in Painting, RISD, 1965; MA in Painting, U. Iowa, 1968. Head art dept. Spence Sch., N.Y.C., 1971—95; dir. Spence Gallery, 1996—2004; represented by Markel/Sears Works on Paper, N.Y.C., 1991—98. Reader advanced placement art portfolios Ednl. Testing Svc., Princeton, N.J., 1993-98; mem. nat. devel. com. Advanced Placement Studio Art, 2002—05. One-woman shows include Noho Gallery, NYC, 1981-82, 85, 2003. Leonarda Di Mauro Gallery, NYC, 1984, 87, Interchurch Ctr, NYC, 2002, Brodsky Gallery, Princeton, NJ, 2002; exhibited in group shows at Bklyn. Mus., 1975, Women in the Arts Found., NYC, 1978, Salgamundi Club, NYC, 1979, Bjorn Lindgren Gallery, NYC, 1982, Ethel Putterman Gallery, Orleans, Mass., 1982, 83, Queens (NY) Mus., 1985, Newmark Gallery, NYC, 1989, Mus. of the Nat. Arts Found., NYC, 1989, Ceres Gallery, NYC, 1990, Citicorp Ctr., Long Island City, NY, 1992, Broome St. Gallery, NYC, 1997, Whitney Art Works, Greenport, NY, 2001-02, Inst. for Am. U., U. Rome, Md. Inst., U. Washington, 2001-03, Citicorp Ctr., 2005-06; represented in permanent collections David Rockefeller Jr., Pfizer, Inc., Pepsico, J.C. Penney, Inc., Southeast Bank, Manhattan Musicians Union, Warburg Pincus, Inc. Resident fellow Va. Ctr. Creative Arts Sweetbrier Coll., 1995. Personal E-mail: paintergreen@aol.com.

MARTIN, DONALD A., mathematics professor; BS, MIT, 1962; MS, U. Chicago, 1965. Prof. mathematics UCLA. Junior fellow Harvard U., 1965—67. Recipient Shared Carol Karp prize, Assn. for Symbolic Logic, 1988; grantee Sloan Found. Fellowship, 1971—73, Guggenheim Fellowship, 1989—90. Fellow: Am. Acad. of Arts & Sciences. Office: UCLA Dept Mathematics 7935 Mathematical Sciences Bldg Los Angeles CA 90095

MARTIN, DONALD EUGENE KEMP, mathematics professor, statistician; b. Balt., July 8, 1958; s. Donald Winfrey Kemp and Sylvia Cooke Martin; m. Antoinette Johanna Ware, Apr. 12, 1992; children: Donald Benjamin Kemp, Johnathan Antonio. BS, U. Md., College Park, 1982, MA, 1987, PhD, 1990. Math. statistician US Dept. Energy, Washington, 1991—94; assoc. prof. Howard U., 1994—; math. statistician US Census Bur., 2000—. Contbr. articles to profl. jours. Fellow, NASA/ASEE, 1997—99; grantee, Howard U., 1995. Mem.: Am. Statis. Assn. Office: Howard University Mathematics Department Washington DC 20059 Office Phone: 202-806-6837. E-mail: donald.e.martin@census.gov.

MARTIN, DONNA LEE, retired publishing company executive; b. Detroit, Aug. 7, 1935; d. David M. Paul and Lillian (Paul); m. Rex Martin, June 5, 1956; children: Justin, Andrew. BA, Rice U., 1957. Mng. editor trade dept. Appleton-Century-Crofts Co., N.Y.C., 1961-62; dir. publs. Lycoming Coll., Williamsport, Pa., 1966-68; editor Univ. Press of Kans., Lawrence, 1971-74; mng. editor Andrews McMeel Publ., Kansas City, Mo., 1974-80, v.p., editorial dir., 1980-95, v.p., editor-at-large, 1995-98; v.p. Universal Press Syndicate, Kansas City, 1980-98. Lectr. U. Mo., Kansas City, Johnson County Cmty. Coll., Kans.; free-lance writer, editor; cons. editor Kans. City Star Books. Author: (adaptation) Charles Dickens' A Christmas Carol: Adapted for Theatre; co-author (with Melissa Hayden) The Nutcracker Ballet; contbr. articles to profl. jours. Named Disting. Alumna Rice U., 1990. Mem. Ctrl. Exchange (Kansas City), The Groucho Club (London), Phi Beta Kappa. Home: 6810 W 66th Ter Shawnee Mission KS 66202-4147 Business E-Mail: donnamartin@kc.rr.com.

MARTIN, EDWARD CURTIS, JR., landscape architect, educator; b. Albany, Ga., Aug. 21, 1928; s. Edward Curtis and Mildred Lee (Tyler) M.; m. Roberta Inman Parker, Mar. 18, 1967; children: Edward Curtis III, Andrew Parker. BFA, U, Ga., 1950, M of Landscape Architecture, 1969. Landscape arch. Norman C. Butts Landscape Contractor, Atlanta, 1950, M.T. Brooks Office of Landscape Architecture, Birmingham, Ala., 1950-56; Univ. landscape arch., horticulturist Miss. State U., 1956-70, prof. landscape architecture, 1970-92, Disting. prof., 1988, prof. emeritus, 1993—, part-time prof., 1992—93; originator, chmn., lectr. Miss. Landscape Design Symposium, 1957—2005. Guest lectr. U. San Luis Potosi, Mex., 1990. U. Mex. Sch. Architecture, Mexico City, 1991. La. State U. 1990, 91, 92, 94, 96, Biendenharn Found., Monroe, La., 1991, Longue Vue Found., New Orleans, 1991; guest instr. in field: originator, lectr. Garden Design Workshops, Miss. State U., 1988-2001; host numerous flower and garden shows and tours abroad; So. hist. gardens lectr. Miss. U. for Women, 1997, 98, 99, 2000; photog. landscape archtl. rsch. study: Europe, 1958, 66, 74, 85, S.Am., 1960, Israel, 1993, 95, Greece, Turkey, 1998; vis. prof. La. State U., 1990-93, 94, 97; instr. landscape design Bot. Gardens, Huntsville, Ala., 1996; host, lectr. hist. so. gardens in Miss. River, New Orleans to Vicksburg, Delta Queen Steamboat, 1994, others; instr. ecology tour Copper Canyon, Mex., 1994; spkr. and lectr. in field. Author: Landscape Plants in Design, A Photographic Guide, 1983; co-author: Home Landscapes, Planting Design and Management, 1994; invited to participate in Attingham Summer Program in Hist. Preservation (English country houses and gardens) Eng., 1985; author/photographer of 80-captioned slide series, one on Home Landscapes, another on Urban Landscape Design for use by Nat. Coun. State Garden Clubs, Inc., 1994. Mem. Miss. State Bd. Landscape Archs. for Profl. Registration, 1973-74; mem. Starkville (Miss.) Park and Recreation Bd., 1973-79; mem. civic beautification com. Black Mountain, N.C., 2002—; bd. visitors Warren Wilson Coll., Asheville, NC, 2002—; elder Trinity Presbyn. Ch., Starkville, Miss., Warren Wilson Presbyn. Ch. and Coll. Chapel, Asheville, N.C.; tour guide Biltmore Estate, Asheville, N.C., 2003— Recipient Silver Seal award Nat. Coun. State Garden Clubs 1969, honoree 1995, Landscape Heritage award Fraser Found. Calif. 1986, Helent S. Hull Lit. award, 1996; Paul Harris fellow Rotary Internat., 1998; reception area (lobby)

of Miss. State U. Dept. Landscape Architecture donated in his honor by Garden Clubs Miss. Inc., 2003. Fellow Am. Soc. Landscape Archs. (chmn. edn. com. 1960-61, pres. Miss. sect. S.W. chpt. 1975, chmn. S.W. chpt. ann. awards com. 1976, trustee Miss. chpt. 1977-81, nominated Jot Carpenter Tchg. medal Miss. chpt. 2006); mem. So. Garden History Soc., Nat. Coun. State Garden Clubs (chmn. landscape design 1993-97, Appreciation cert. 2005), Garden Clubs Miss. (bd. dirs. 1958—, Silver Trophy 1961, Spl. Silver award 1980, Gold trophy 1993, Appreciation citation 2005). Presbyterian. Home: 464 Chapel Rd Black Mountain NC 28711-2640 Office: Dept Landscape Architecture Box 9725 Mississippi State MS 39762-9725

MARTIN, EDWIN WILSON, corporate director, columnist, educational consultant; b. Oceanside, NY, Sept. 3, 1931; s. Edwin Wilson and Jean (Carbone) Martin; m. Peggy Smith, Sept. 5, 1953 (div. Oct. 2005); children: Scott Andrew, Bruce Leslie. AB, Muhlenberg Coll., Pa., 1953; MA, U. Ala., 1955; PhD, U. Pitts., 1961; D of Humane Letters (hon.), Emerson Hall, Boston, 1984; D of Sci. Edn. (hon.), Muhlenberg Coll., Pa., 1981; D. of Humane Letters (hon.), LI U., 1995. Asst. prof. speech, assoc. prof. pathology U Ala., 1960—66; dir. sub-com. on handicapped US Ho. Reps., 1966—67; dep. assoc. commr. edn. US Office of Edn., 1967—69; assoc. commr., dir. Bur. Edn. Handicapped, 1969—79; dep. commr. edn. US Dept. HEW, 1979—80; asst. sec. edn. US Dept. Edn., 1980—81; lectr. in edn. Harvard U., 1979—81; adj. prof. edn. Columbia U., 1982—91; pres., CEO Nat. Disability Svcs., NY, 1981—94, pres. emeritus NY, 1994—; ret., 1994. Bd. dirs. Pall Corp., NY; mem. adv. bd. Roslyn Bank Divsn., NY Cmty. Bank, 2004—. Columnist: Venice Gondolier Sun, 2003—; contbr. articles to profl. jours., chapters to books. Mem. Mayor's Adv. Com. on Spl. Edn., NYC, 1987—90, govs. adv. com. on rehab., NY, 1990—94; bd. mem. Golden Beach Assn., Inc., Venice, 1995—98; mem Rd. Zoning Appeals, 2004—05. Recipient Alexander Graham Bell award, Alexander Graham Bell Assn. for the Deaf, 1978, Disting. Leadership award, US Dept. Edn., 1986. Fellow: Am. Speech, Lang. and Hearing Assn.; mem.: Coun. for Exceptional Children (v.p., pres.-elect, pres., past pres. divsn. learning disabilities 1996—2000, Wallin award 1979), Jacaranda West Country Club (mem. nominating com. 2005, mem. green com. 2006). E-mail: tiltingatwindmilk@comcast.net.

MARTIN, ELLIOT EDWARDS, theatrical producer; b. Denver, Feb. 25, 1924; m. Marjorie Cuesta, Oct. 7, 1949; children: Richard, Linda Lisa. Student, U. Denver, 1943-46. Actor, singer, stage mgr., assoc. producer Theatre Guild, N.Y.C. and London, 1947-53; prodn. stage mgr. 20 Broadway plays and musicals, 1953-61; theatrical producer Never Too Late, Nobody Loves an Albatross, N.Y.C., 1962-66; theatre producer London, 1963; mng. dir. Center Theatre Group, Music Ctr., Los Angeles, 1966-71; producer Elliot Martin Prodns., N.Y.C., 1972—. Mem. exec. nd. Nat. Theatre of the Deaf, Chester, Conn., 1981-, Westport-Weston Arts Council, 1976- Prodns. on Broadway include: Dinner at Eight, 1966, More Stately Mansions, 1967, Abelard and Heloise, 1971, Emperor Henry IV, 1973, A Moon for the Misbegotten, 1973 (spl. Tony award), When You Comin' Back, Red Rider, 1974 (Outer Critics award), Of Mice and Men, 1975, Touch of the Poet, 1976, Dirty Linen and New Found Land, 1977, Caesar and Cleopatra, 1977, Kingfisher, 1979, Clothes for a Summer Hotel, 1980, Kingdoms, 1981, American Buffalo, 1981, Angels Fall, 1983, Glengarry Glen Ross, 1984 (Pulitzer prize), Woza Albert, 1984, American Buffalo, 1984, Harrigan 'n' Hart, 1985, Arsenic and Old Lace (Broadway and nat. tour), 1986-87, Joe Turner's Come and Gone (7 Tony nominations, NY Drama Critic's award best play), 1988, Steel Magnolias (nat. tour), 1989, The Circle, 1989-90, Shadowlands, 1990-91, Breaking Legs, 1991-92, She Loves Me (9 Tony noms.), 1993-94, Death of a Salesman, 1999, A Moon For the Misbegotten, 2000, Down the Gaden Paths, 2001, I'm Not Rappaprot, 2002, The Oldest Living Confederate Widow Tells All, 2003. Mem. bd. assocs. U. Bridgeport, 1978-83. Recipient Tony award for most innovative revival, 1977-78, Larry Tajiri award for outstanding contbn. to arts Denver Post, 1970, Congl. commendation, 1970, Profl. Achievement award U. Denver, 1987. Mem. Platform Speakers Am., League NY Theatres and Prodrs. (gov.), Am. Friends of Theatre (pres.), Players Club, NY Athletic Club (NYC). Republican. Office Phone: 212-245-4176.

MARTIN, FLORA Y., music educator; b. Bellefontaine, Ohio, Dec. 8, 1946; d. Chalmer W. Yoder and Clarabell Dachenbach; m. Victor Ray Martin, June 14, 1969; 1 child, Danielle Reneé. BA, Ea. Mennonite Coll., 1969; MusM, Manhattan Sch. Music, 1973. Pvt. voice tchr., Balt., 1973; voice tchr. Roland Park County Sch., Balt., 1973—2002, Salisbury (Md.) U., 1994; assoc. prof. Prince George's C.C., Largo, Md., 1985—; mem. voice faculty Peabody Conservatory, Balt., 2003—. Singer Balt. Opera, 1978—92, Bel Canto Singers of Balt. Music Club, 1984—92. Presbyterian. Avocations: antiques, sewing, scrapbooks, travel. Home: 5821 Glenkirk Ct Baltimore MD 21239 Office: Prince George's CC 301 Largo Rd Largo MD 20774

MARTIN, FRANCES LEE, nursing educator; b. Filbert, Pa., Sept. 17; d. Mack and Nellie (Allen0 Marshall; 1 child, Tanya. Diploma in nursing, Fordham Hosp., 1951; BSN, Hunter Coll., 1957, MSN, 1964; MS in Edn., Bklyn. Coll., 1974. Instr. nursing Cumberland Hosp., Bklyn., 1959-61; substitute tchr. Sara Hale Vocat. HS, Bklyn., 1963-64; instr. Meth. Sch. Nursing, Bklyn., 1964-70; asst. prof., then assoc. prof. Coll. S.I., NY, 1970—; instr. Coney Island Hosp., Bklyn., 1989. Mem. adv. bd. CRTS South Beach Psychiat. Ctr., S.I., NY, 1981—; mem. adv. bd. NY Urban League, S.I. 1988—, vice chairperson, 1990—; clin. cons. Regents Coll., Mineola, NY, 1988—; presenter in field. Author: Nurse Test Medical-Surgical Nursing, 1992; contbg. author: Nursing Decision, 1982; contbr. articles to profl. pubis. Vol. tutor First Univ. Bapt. Ch., S.I., NY, 2005. Mem. ANA (cert.), AAUP, NAACP, Assoc. Degree Orgn. Nursing Edn., Nat. League Nursing, NY Urban League, Sigma Theta Tau. Democrat. Avocations: theater, tennis, reading, sewing. Home: 27 Kathy Pl Apt 3A Staten Island NY 10314 5920 Office: Coll of 715 Ocean Ter Staten Island NY 10301-4542

MARTIN, FRED, artist, academic administrator; b. San Francisco, June 13, 1927; s. Ernest Thomas and Leona (Richey) M.; m. Genevieve Catherine Fisette, Jan. 29, 1950 (dec.); children: T. Demian, Fredericka C., Anthony J.; m. Stephanie Zuperko Dudek, 1992. BA, U. Calif., Berkeley, 1949, MA, 1954; postgrad., Calif. Sch. Fine Arts, 1949—50. Registrar Oakland (Calif.) Art Mus., 1955-58; dir. exhbn. San Francisco Art Inst., 1958-65, 1965-75, dir. coll., 1983-92, dean acad. affairs; represented by Green Gates Gallery and Press, Oakland. Exhibited one man shows, Zoe Dusanne Gallery, Seattle, 1952, M.H. deYoung Meml. Mus., San Francisco, 1954, 64, Oakland Mus. Calif., 1958, 2003, San Francisco Mus. Modern Art, 1958, 73, Dilexi Gallery, San Francisco, 1961, Minami Gallery, Tokyo, 1963, Royal Marks Gallery, NYC, 1965-70, Hansen Fuller Gallery, San Francisco, 1974, 75, 76, Quay Gallery, San Francisco, 1979, 81, 84, Natsoulas Gallery, Davis, Calif., 1991, Belcher Studios Gallery, San Francisco, 1994, Frederick Spratt Gallery, San Jose, 1996, Ebert Gallery, San Francisco, 1997, 98, 99, 2001, 2003, Art and Consciousness Gallery/John F. Kennedy U., Berkeley, 1997, Shasta Coll., 1998, Han Art Contemporaine, Montreal, 1999, Sanchez Art Ctr., 2003, Collector's Gallery of Oakland Mus., 2004, Paul Sunderholm Gallery, 2004; represented in permanent collections, Mus. Modern Art, NYC, San Francisco Mus. Modern Art, Oakland Art Mus., Whitney Mus., Fogg Mus.; author: Beulah Land, 1966, Log of the Sun Ship, 1969, Liber Studiorum, 1973, A Travel Book, 1976, From an Antique Land, 1979; Bay area corr.: Art Internat., 1967-69, 75-76; contbg. editor Art Week, 1976-93. Recipient prizes Oakland Art Mus., 1951, 58, prizes San Francisco Mus. Art, 1957, 58, prizes Richmond (Calif.) Art Ctr., 1962, prizes Nat. Found. for Arts, 1970. Home: 232 Monte Vista Ave Oakland CA 94611-4922 Office: San Francisco Art Inst 800 Chestnut St San Francisco CA 94133-2206

MARTIN, FREDERICK NICHOLS, school system administrator; s. Frederick Wight and Elizabeth Foltz Martin. BA., Princeton U., N.J., 1994; MEd, Harvard U, Cambridge, 2000. Tchr. Arthur Morgan Sch., Burnsville, NC, 1995—99, clk. sch., 2001—03; admissions dir. The Meeting Sch., Rindge, NH, 2003—. Bd. dir. Pendle Hill, Wallingford, Pa., 2002—, Kestrel Ednl.

Adventures, Gloucester, Mass., 2005—. Mem. Soc. Friends. Home: 120 Thomas Rd Rindge NH 03461 Office: The Meeting Sch 120 Thomas Rd Rindge NH 03461 Office Phone: 603-899-3366. Personal E-mail: frederick@meetingschool.org.

MARTIN, FREDERICK NOEL, audiology educator; b. N.Y.C., July 24, 1931; s. Philip and Mildred Ruth (Austin) M.; m. Mary Catherine Robinson, Apr. 4, 1954; children: David C., Leslie Anne. BA, Bklyn. Coll., 1957, MA, 1958; PhD, CUNY, 1968. Audiologist, Lenox Hill Hosp., N.Y.C., 1957-58; Audiologist Ark. Sch. for the Deaf, Little Rock, 1958-60; dir. audiology Bailey Ear Clinic, Little Rock, 1960-66; mem. faculty Bklyn. Coll., 1966-68, U. Tex., Austin, 1968—, endowed prof. audiology, 1982—. Author: Introduction to Audiology, 1975, 8th edit., 2003, interactive CD ROM, 2003, Pediatric Audiology, 1978, Medical Audiology, 1981, Basic Audiometry, 1986, Essentials of Audiology, 2006; editor: Remediation of Communication Disorders, Vol. 10, 1978, Hearing Disorders in Children, 1986, Effective Counseling in Audiology, 1994, Hearing Care for Children, 1996, Exercises in Audiometry, 1998; contbr. numerous articles to profl. jours. Served with USAF, 1951-55. Fellow Am. Speech-Language Hearing Assn., Am. Acad. Audiology; mem. Tex. Speech-Lang.-Hearing Assn., Am. Auditory Soc., Tex. Acad. Audiology. Home: 8613 Silver Ridge Dr Austin TX 78759-8144 Office: U Tex Austin TX 78712 Business E-Mail: fnmartin@mail.utexas.edu.

MARTIN, GARY JOSEPH, medical educator; b. Chgo., Mar. 12, 1952; m. Helen Gartner; children: Daniel T., David G. BA in Psychology, U. Ill., 1974, MD, 1978. Diplomate Am. Bd. Internal Medicine, Am. Bd. Cardiovascular Disease, Nat. Bd. Med. Examiners; lic. physician, Ill. Intern, resident internal medicine Northwestern U. Med. Sch., Chgo., 1978-81, instr. medicine, 1981-82, asst. prof. medicine, 1984-90, assoc prof., 1990-96, prof., 1996—, divsn. chief, divsn. gen. internal medicine, 1988-2001, assoc. chmn. dept. medicine, 1998-2000, vice chmn. dept. medicine, 2001—; cardiology fellow Loyola U. Med. Ctr., 1982-84; attending physician Northwestern Meml. Hosp./Northwestern Med. Faculty Found., Chgo., 1984—; chief med. resident, attending physician Northwestern Meml. Hosp., Chgo., 1981-82; dir. primary care clerkship Nat. Ctr. for Advanced Med. Edn., 1984—. Chmn. outpatient utilization rev. and quality assurance com., 1985-93; chmn. Northwestern Meml. Hosp./Lakeside VA Rsch. Com., 1988-91; dir. tng. gen. internal medicine residency program, 1985-95; bd. dirs. com. Northwestern Med. Faculty Found., 1993—; cons. health care divsn. Ernst & Young, 1991—; peer reviewer Faculty Devel. Rev. Com. Panel 1. 1994. Contbr. articles to profl. jours. Fellow Buehler Ctr. on Aging, Fellow Am. Coll. Cardiology; mem. ACP, Soc. Gen. Internal Medicine, Am. Heart Assn. Office: Northwestern U Med Sch Divsn Gen Internal Medicine 675 N Saint Clair St Ste 18-200 Chicago IL 60611-5929

MARTIN, GARY WAYNE, lawyer; b. Cin., Feb. 14, 1946; s. Elmer DeForrest and Nellie May (Hughes) M.; m. Debra Lynn Goldsmith, June 25, 1982; children: Christopher, Jeremy, Joie, Casey. BA, Wilmington Coll., 1967; JD, U. Cin., 1974. Bar: Fla. 1974. Bd. dirs. Fowler White Boggs Banker, Tampa, Fla., 1974—. Lt. USNR, 1967-71. Mem. Harbour Island Athletic Club. Republican. Avocation: tennis. Office: Fowler White Gillen Boggs Villareal & Banker 501 E Kennedy Blvd Ste 1600 Tampa FL 33602-5240 Office Phone: 813-228-7411. Business E-Mail: gmartin@fowlerwhite.com.

MARTIN, GEORGE (GEORGE WHITNEY MARTIN), writer; b. N.Y.C., Jan. 25, 1926; s. George Whitney and Agnes Wharton (Hutchinson) M. BA, Harvard U., 1948; student, Trinity Coll., Cambridge U., Eng., 1950; LL.B., U. Va., 1953. Bar: N.Y. 1955. With firm Emmet, Marvin & Martin, N.Y.C., 1955-59; engaged in writing, 1959—. Author: The Opera Companion, A Guide for the Casual Operagoer, 1961, 5th edit., 1999, The Battle of the Frogs and Mice, An Homeric Fable, 1962, 2d edit., 1987, Verdi, His Music, Life and Times, 1963, 4th edit., 2001, The Red Shirt and The Cross of Savoy, The Story of Italy's Risorgimento, 1748-1871, 1969, Causes and Conflicts, The Centennial History of the Association of the Bar of the City of New York, 1870-1970, 1970, 2d edit., 1997, Madam Secretary: Frances Perkins, 1976, The Damrosch Dynasty, America's First Family of Music, 1983, Aspects of Verdi, 1988, 2nd edit., 1993, Verdi at the Golden Gate, San Francisco in the Golden Years, 1993, Twentieth Century Opera, A Guide, 1999, CCB: The Life and Century of Charles C. Burlingham, New York's First Citizen, 1858-1959, 2005; contbr. articles to profl. jours., mags. Recipient Erwin N. Griswold award, 2006. Home: 53 Crosslands Dr Kennett Square PA 19348-2010 Office Phone: 610-388-0529.

MARTIN, GEORGE J., JR., lawyer; b. Port Chester, N.Y., June 7, 1942; s. George J. and Eileen Ann (Buckley) Martin; m. Joanne L. Frost, Aug. 21, 1965 (div. May 1986); children: Amy Anne, Ryan Frost; m. Anna Marie Cipriati, June 21, 1986; stepchildren: Marissa McCreay, Jill McCreay. BA, Georgetown U., 1964, JD, 1967. Bar: N.Y. 1969, conseil juridique: France 1977. From assoc. to ptnr. Mudge Rose Guthrie Alexander & Ferdon, N.Y.C., 1967-95; ptnr. Coudert Bros., N.Y.C., 1995—2004; of counsel Greenberg Traurig, LLP, N.Y.C., 2005—. Mem.: French Heritage Soc. (gen. counsel dir.). Roman Catholic. Office: Greenberg Traurig LLP Met Life Bldg 200 Park Ave New York NY 10166 Home: 374 Union St Brooklyn NY 11231-4912 Office Phone: 212-801-2101. Personal E-mail: george0607@nyc.rr.com. Business E-Mail: marting@gtlaw.com.

MARTIN, GEORGE MONROE, pathologist, gerontologist, educator; m. Julaine Ruth Miller, Dec. 2, 1952 (dec.); children: Peter C., Kelsey C., Thomas M., Andrew C. BS, U. Wash., 1949, MD, 1953. Diplomate Am. Bd. Pathology, Am. Bd. Med. Genetics. Intern Montreal Gen. Hosp., Que., Canada, 1953-54; resident, instr. U. Chgo., 1954-57; instr., prof. U. Wash., Seattle, 1957—2003, prof. emeritus, 2003—. Vis. scientist Dept. Genetics Albert Einstein Coll., NYC, 1964, Rockefeller U. 1998-99, UCLA, 2000, chmn. dept. Gordon Confs. Molecular Pathology, Biology of Aging, 1974-79; chmn., nat. res. Plan on Aging Nat. Inst. on Aging, Bethesda, Md., 1985-89; dir. Alzheimer's Disease Rsch. Ctr. U. Wash., 1985—; assoc. dir. 1999—; dir. emeritus, 2003-. Editor Werner's Syndrome and Human Aging, 1985, Molecular Aspects of Aging, 1995; editor-in-chief: Science of Aging Knowledge Environment, 2000-06; contbr. articles in field to profl jours. Active Fedn. Am. Scientists, Human Rights Comm., Inst. Medicine. With USN, 1945—46. Recipient Allied Signal award in Aging, 1991. Rsch. medal Am. Aging Assn., 1992, Kleemeier award, 1994, Paul Glenn award for aging rsch., 1998, Longevity Prize, IPSEN Found., 2002; named Disting. Alumnus, U. Wash. Sch. Medicine, 1987; USPHS rsch. fellow dept. genetics, Glasgow U., 1961-62; Eleanor Roosevelt Inst. Cancer Rsch. fellow Inst. de Biologie, Physiologie, Chimie, Paris, 1968-69; Josiah Macy faculty scholar Sir William Din Sch. Pathology, Oxford (Eng.) U., 1978-79; Humboldt Disting. scientist dept. genetics U. Wurzburg, Germany, 1991. Fellow: AAAS, Tissue Culture Assn. (pres. 1986—88), Gerontol. Soc. Am. (chmn. Biol. Sci. 1979, pres. 2003. Brookdale award 1981, Lifetime Achievement award for rsch. in alzheimer's disease World Alzheimer's Congress 2000); mem.: Am. Fedn. Aging Rsch. (pres. 1999—2001, sci. dir. 2003—), Am. Soc. Investigative Pathology, Am. Soc. Human Genetics, Am. Assn. Univ. Pathologists (emeritus), Inst. Medicine. Democrat. Avocations: travel, jazz, reading. Home: 2223 E Howe St Seattle WA 98112-2931 Office: U Wash Sch Medicine Dept Pathology Rm K543 Seattle WA 98195 Office Phone: 206-543-5088. Business E-Mail: gmmartin@u.washington.edu.

MARTIN, GEORGE RAYMOND RICHARD, writer; b. Bayonne, N.J., Sept. 20, 1948; s. Raymond and Margaret (Brady) M.; m. Gale Burnick, Nov. 15, 1975 (div. Dec. 1979). BS summa cum laude, Northwestern U., 1970; MS cum laude, 1971. Journalism intern Medill News Service, Washington, 1971; sportswriter, pub. relations officer N.J. Dept. Parks, Bayonne, 1971; coordinator communications and edn. Cook County (Ill.) Legal Assistance Found., Chgo., 1972-74; instr. journalism Clarke Coll., Dubuque, Iowa, 1976-78, writer-in-residence, 1978-79. Founder, chmn. Windy City Sci. Fiction Writers' Workshop, Chgo., 1972-76 Author sci. fiction: A Song for Lya, 1976, Songs of Stars and Shadows, 1977, Sandkings, 1981, Dying of the Light, 1977, Windhaven, 1981, Fevre Dream, 1982, The Armageddon Rag, 1983,

Songs the Deadmen Sing, 1983, Nightflyers, 1985, Tuf Voyaging, 1986, Portraits of His Children, 1987, A Game of Thrones, 1996, A Feast for Crows, 2005 (No. 1 on Publishers Weekly hardcover bestseller list); editor: New Voices I, 1977, New Voices II, 1979, New Voices III, 1980, New Voices IV, 1981, John W. Campbell Awards vol. 5, 1984, Night Visions 3, 1987, Wild Cards, 1987, Aces High, 1987, Jokers Wild, 1987, Aces Abroad, 1988, Down & Dirty, 1988, Ace in the Hole, 1990, Dead Man's Hand, 1990, One-Eyed Jacks, 1991, Jokertown Shuffle, 1991, Double Solitaire, 1992, Dealer's Choice, 1992, Turn of the Cards, 1993, Card Sharks, 1993, Marked Cards, 1994, Black Trump, 1995, Deuces Down, 2002, Draws Five, 2006; story editor The Twilight Zone, CBS-TV, 1987; prodr. Beauty and the Beast, CBS-TV, 1987-88; exec. prodr. Doorways, (ABC-TV), 1992-93; contbr. short stories to mags. Mem. Sci. Fiction Writers Am. (dir. Central region 1977-79, v.p. 1996-97), Writers Guild Am. West. E-mail: georr@aol.com.

**MARTIN, GREGORY KEITH,** lawyer, mayor; b. Conway, SC, Nov. 7, 1956; s. George Henry Martin and Julia Ann (Johnson) M. Land. BS in Fin. Mgmt., Clemson U., 1979; JD, U. S.C., 1983. Bar: S.C. 1983. Intern U.S. Senate, 1980; law clk. to presiding judge 15th Jud. Cir. Ct., Conway, 1983; assoc. Johnson & Martin, Conway, 1983-88, ptnr., 1988-93, Martin & Smith, Conway, 1993-98; mayor City of Conway, 1995—; sole practice Gregory K. Martin, PC, Conway, 1998—. Mem. Conway Planning Commn., 1986-89, chmn., 1989; bd. dirs. Conway-Main St. U.S.A., 1986-90, chmn., 1988; mem. Conway Rd. Appeals, 1987-89, Horry County Bd. Archtl. Rev., 1987-90; mem. Conway City Coun., 1991-94; pres., Horry County Hist. Soc., 1988, 90, mayor pro tem, 1994; mem. adv. bd. Pee Dee Heritage Ctr., 1988-2003. Mem. ABA, S.C. Bar Assn., Horry County Bar Assn., Sigma Nu, Phi Delta Phi. Methodist. Avocations: tennis, coin collecting/numismatics. Home: 706 Elm St Conway SC 29526-4373 Office: PO Box 736 Conway SC 29528-0736 Office Phone: 843-248-2089. E-mail: gkm11aw@sccoast.net.

**MARTIN, GREGORY S.,** air force officer; b. Ft. Meyer, Va., Apr. 24, 1948; m. Wendy Bliss; children: Tracie, Todd, Tyler. BS, USAF Acad., 1970; M in Bus. Mgmt., Ctrl. Mich. U., 1977; attended, Nat. War Coll., 1985-86. Commd. 2d lt. USAF, 1970, advanced through grades to brig. gen., 1993, student, pilot tng. Laredo AFB, Tex., 1970-71, student F-4 replacement tng. George AFB, Calif., 1971-72, f-4 fighter pilot 388th tactical fighter wing Korat Royal Thair Air Base, Thailand, 1972, F-4 flight leader 421st tactical fighter squadron Udorn Royal Thai Air Base, Thailand, 1972-73, F-4 instr. pilot 49th tactical fighter wing Holloman AFB, N.Mex., 1973-76, air staff tng. assignment officer, Pentagon Washington, 1976-77, aide to chief of staff of air force, Pentagon, 1977-78, F-15 instr. pilot and flight comdr. 461st tactical fighter tng. squadron Luke AFB, Ariz., 1978-81, chief of wing tng. 12th tactical fighter squadron ops. officer, then comdr. 67th tactical fighter squadron 18th tactical fighter wing Kadena Air Base, Japan, 1981-85, divsn. chief CONUS bases, units, then divsn. chief tactical programs for Air Staff's directorate programs and resources, Pentagon Washington, 1986-88, vice comdr. 49th tactical fighter wing Holloman AFB, 1988-89, exec. officer to comdr., then asst. dep. chief of staff of plans tactical air command Langley AFB, Va., 1989-90, comdr. 479th tactical tng. wing Holloman AFB, 1990-91, comdr. 33d fighter wing Eglin AFB, Fla., 1991-93, comdr. 1st fighter wing Langley AFB, 1993—. Decorated Legion of Merit with 1 oak leaf cluster, DFC, Meritorious Svc. medal with 3 oak leaf clusters, Air medal with 11 oak leaf clusters, Air Force Commendation medal.

**MARTIN, GUY,** lawyer; b. Los Angeles, Jan. 22, 1911; s. I.G. and Mary Pearl (Howe) M.; m. Edith Kingdon Gould, Oct. 12, 1946; children— Guy III, Jason Gould, Christopher Kingdon, Edith Maria Theodosia Burr. AB, Occidental Coll., 1931; BA (1st class hons.), Oxford U., 1934, MA, 1944; LL.B., Yale, 1937. Bar: N.Y. 1938, D.C. 1947. Practiced with Donovan, Leisure, Newton & Lumbard, N.Y.C., 1938-41; gen. counsel All Am. Aviation, Inc., 1942, Am. Mexican Claims Commn., U.S. Dept. State, 1945-47; ptnr. Martin, Whitfield, Smith & Bebchick (and predecessors), Washington, 1952-80; counsel Martin and Smith (and predecessors), 1981-86; pres., vice chmn. bd., dep. chief exec. officer Internat. Bank, 1981-86; with Law Office of Saltzstein & Martin, 1988-99. Served with USN; sea duty 1942-45. Mem. ABA, Assn. of Bar of City of N.Y., Bar Assn. D.C., Phi Beta Kappa, Sigma Alpha Epsilon. Clubs: Yale, Brook, Knickerbocker (N.Y.C.); Metropolitan, City Tavern (Washington). Episcopalian. Home: 3300 O St NW Washington DC 20007-2813

**MARTIN, HAROLD G.,** engineering consultant; b. Scotland, Pa. s. Abram Earl and Eula Mae Martin; m. Christina Shipley Martin, June 5, 1948; children: Susan (dec.), Judith Krieger, Bruce. BSCE, Pa. State U., 1944. Stress analyst, chief structures Fairchild Republic Co., Hagerstown, Md., 1967-70, mgr. tech. engring., 1970-71, chief problem analysis and corrective action Alo Program, 1977-81, chief quality engring., 1981, project engr. F14, FAA airworthiness coord., 1981-84; engring. cons., FAA designated engring. rep. Waynesboro, Pa., 1984—. Mem. sch. bd. Waynesboro Area Sch. Bd., 1978-84. Staff sgt. U.S. Army, 1944-46. Mem.: Mid Atlantic Air Mus., Am. Aviation Hist. Soc., Soc. of Automotive Engineers. Avocations: auto restoration, travel, writing, boating, fishing. Home and Office: 833 Anthony Ave Waynesboro PA 17268

**MARTIN, HARRY C.,** lawyer; Graduate, Univ. Va.; JD with honors, George Washington Univ. Ptnr. Fletcher, Heald, Hildreth PLC, Arlington, Va. Columnist Broadcast Engring. mag., 1981—, Radio mag., 1997—; frequent spkr. NAB, state broadcast industry conventions, regular panelist Kagan Radio Summit seminars. Bd. dir. Univ. Va. Club of Washington. Mem.: Fed. Comm. Bar Assn. (asst. secy-secy. 1997—99, asst. treas.-treas. 2000—02, pres.-elect 2003—04, pres. 2004—05, exec. com. 1994—2002). Office: Fletcher Heald & Hildreth 11th Fl 1300 N 17th St Arlington VA 22209 Office Phone: 703-812-0415. Office Fax: 703-812-0486. Business E-Mail: martin@fhhlaw.com.

**MARTIN, HARRY CORPENING,** lawyer, retired state supreme court justice; b. Lenoir, NC, Jan. 13, 1920; s. Hal C. and Johnsie Harshaw (Nelson) M.; m. Nancy Robiou Dallam, Apr. 16, 1955; children: John, Matthew, Mary. AB, U. N.C., 1942; LLB, Harvard U., 1948; LLM, U. Va., 1982. Bar: N.C. 1948. Pvt. practice, Asheville, NC, 1948-62; judge NC Superior Ct., Asheville, 1962-78, NC Ct. Appeals, Raleigh, 1978-82; justice NC Supreme Ct., 1982-92; ptnr. Martin & Martin, Attys., Hillsborough, 1992—. Adj. prof. U. N.C. Law Sch., 1983-92, Duke U., 1990-91, Dan K. Moore disting. vis. prof., U. N.C Law Sch., 1992-94; sr. conf. atty. U.S. Ct. Appeals for 4th Cir., 1994-99; chief justice Supreme Ct. ea. bd. of Cherokee Indians, 2000—, ret. With U.S. Army, 1942-45, South Pacific. Mem. U.S. Supreme Ct. Hist. Soc., N.C. Supreme Ct. Hist. Soc. (pres.). Democrat. Episcopalian. Home: 1 Hilltop Rd Asheville NC 28803-3017 Office: Cherokee Supreme Ct PO Box 1629 Cherokee NC 28719 Office Phone: 828-497-1077. E-mail: judgemartin@bellsouth.net.

**MARTIN, HARRY STRATTON, III,** law educator, law librarian; b. Hartford, Conn., Jan. 22, 1943; AB in History, Harvard U., 1965; JD, U. Minn., 1968; MLS, U. Pitts., 1971. Bar: Minn. 1968. Instr. U. Liberia, Monrovia, 1969—71; asst. libr. U. Tex., 1972—74, assoc. libr., 1975—76; libr. and asst. prof. Georgetown U., Washington, 1976—81; libr., prof. Harvard Law Sch., Cambridge, Mass., 1981—2002, Henry N. Ess III libr., prof., 2002—. Editl. bd. Computer Law Jour., 1979—, Westlaw, 1989—91. Contbr. articles to profl. jours. Mem.: Am. Libr. Assn., Am. Law Libr., New England Law Libr. Consortium (pres. 1995—97), Beta Phi Mu. Office: Harvard Law Sch Areeda 511 1563 Massachusetts Ave Cambridge MA 02138 Business E-Mail: martin@law.harvard.edu.

**MARTIN, HELEN LOENE,** minister; b. Muleshoe, Tex., Dec. 27, 1941; d. Benjamin Franklin and Vella Dean Hays; m. K. Ray Martin, Feb. 2, 1960; children: David (Deceased) Ray, Daniel Dean. Pastoral Counsel, Inst. of Pastoral Counseling, Akron, Ohio, 1994; Assoc. of Bibl. Sch., Harvest Conf. (IPHC), Wichita, Kans., 1994. Ordained minister Pentecostal Ch., 1993. Care pastor Abundant Life Ch., Hutchinson, Kans., 1988—93; evangelist Internat.

Pentecostal Holiness Ch., Okla., 1994—98; asst. conf. supt. Harvest Conf., Wichita, Kans., 1996—2000, evangelism dir., 2006—, bd. dirs., 2005; care pastor Eagles Nest Ch., Wichita, Kans., 1997—99; ch. planter, pastor New Beginnings Christian Fellowship Ch., Minneapolis, Kans., 2001—. Ch. planter (Russia) IPHC, Okla., 1994; missionary to Mex. Abundant Life Ch. Hutchinson, Kans., 1987—91; missionary to Nicaragua Internat. Pentecostal Holiness Ch., Okla., 1998. Editor: (ch.newspaper) A Conversation with God. Bd. dirs. Love Inc., Minneapolis, Kans., 2004—06. Recipient Svc. and Outstanding Acad. award, Harvest Conf., 2000, Servant's award, 2006, Appreciation award, 2006. International Pentecostal Holiness Church. Avocation: piano. Office Phone: 785-392-2858.

**MARTIN, HELEN SCHATKOWSKI,** music educator, television producer; b. Phila., Apr. 15, 1940; d. Edwin Oscar Schatkowski and Helen Emma Schumann; children: Scott Thomas, Michelle Linda. BA, U. Calif., San Diego, 1987; scholarship student, Eastman Sch. Music, 1958—68; student, Ind. Univ. Sch. Music; student, of Josef Gingold. Instr. Ctr. for Young Musicians, London, 1979—83, Moravian Coll., Bethlehem, Pa., 1987—91; artist in residence Mt. Pocono H.S., Mt. Pocono, Pa., 2000—02; instr. Fretless Studio, Easton, Pa., 2000—; founder, dir. Mt. Jefferson Inst. for Music and the Arts, Easton, Pa., 2003—. Author: (instl. video) Violin For Musicians; prodr.: (instl. video) Violin For Musicians (Finalist, NY Festivals, 2000); author: (plays) Secret Life of Antonio Vivaldi; performer; author: (violin method for adults) Forever Fretless; prodr.: (TV series) Music a la Mode; musician: (TV series) Music a la Mode. Recipient Chamber Music Award of Merit, Nat. Fedn. of Music Clubs, 2002. Mem.: Music Tchrs. Nat. Assn. Achievements include development of forever fretless string method; research in language aspects of music, blending essential musical literacy and the skills of playing by ear. Office Phone: 610-704-8461.

**MARTIN, HENRY ALAN,** public defender; b. Nashville, Sept. 5, 1949; s. James Alvin and Mary Elizabeth (Long) M.; m. Gloria B. Ballard, May 9, 1975; children: Nathan Daniel, Anna Elizabeth. BA, Vanderbilt U., 1971, JD, 1974. Bar: Tenn. 1975, U.S. Dist. Ct. (mid. dist.) Tenn. 1975, U.S. Ct. Appeals (6th cir.) 1976, U.S. Supreme Ct. 1979. Pvt. practice, Nashville, 1975-76; ptnr. Haile & Martin, P.A., Nashville, 1976-82; assoc. firm Barrett & Ray, P.C., Nashville, 1982-85; fed. pub. defender U.S. Dist. Ct. (mid. dist.) Tenn., Nashville, 1985—. Mem. adv. com. on rules criminal procedure U.S. Judicial Conf., 1994-99. CO-author, co-editor trial manual, Tools for the Ultimate Trial, 1985, 2d edit., 1988; contbr. articles to profl. jours. Del., Witness for Peace, Managua, Nicaragua, 1987. Mem. ABA (coun. criminal justice sect. 1993-96), NACDL, Assn. Fed. Defenders (pres. 1995-98), Nashville Bar Assn., Napier Looby Bar Assn., Tenn. Assn. Criminal Def. Lawyers (bd. dirs. 1978-94, pres. 1984-85, Pres.'s award 1988). Democrat. Avocations: jogging, swimming. Home: 3802 Whitland Ave Nashville TN 37205-2432 Office: Fed Pub Defender 810 Broadway Ste 200 Nashville TN 37203-3861 Office Phone: 615-736-5047. Business E-Mail: henry_martin@fd.org.

**MARTIN, IONIS B.,** artist, educator; b. Chgo., 1936; d. Francis Wright and Hattie Robinson Bracy; m. Allyn Aubrey Martin; 1 child, Allyn Bracy-Fletcher. BS, Fisk U., 1957; MEd, U. Hartford, 1968; MFA, Pratt Inst., Bklyn., 1987. Y-teen assoc. dir. YWCA of Greater Hartford, 1957—59; homefinder Conn. Child Welfare Assn, New Haven, 1959—61; art tchr. Arsenal elem sch. Hartford Bd. Edn., Conn., 1961, art tchr. Weaver H.S., 1961—67; lectr., adj. prof. Ctrl. Conn. State U., New Britain, 1985; h.s. art tchr. Bloomfield Bd. Edn., Conn., 1971—2001. Co-founder, sec. treas., v.p. bd. dirs. Artist Collective, Hartford, 1972—2006; trustee Wadsworth Athenaeum Mus. Art, Hartford, 1978—97; corporator Hartford Art Sch., U. Hartford, West Hartford, 2001—06; sec. Skidmore Coll. Author: A Curriculum Sampler. Co-trustee Ella Burr McManus Trust, Hartford, 1985—2006; bd. dirs. Ancient Burial Ground, Hartford, 1998—2005, Huntington House Mus., Windsor, Conn., 2001—05., DuBois Inst. fellow Harvard U., 1994, Through Young Black Eyes grantee, Conn. Commn. on the Arts, Artist fellow, Skidmore Coll. Mem.: The Links, Art Works Gallery, Delta Sigma Theta. Home: 1234 Prospect Avenue Hartford CT 06105 Office Phone: 860-202-4017. Personal E-mail: dr.a.martin@snet.net.

**MARTIN, IRENE ELIZABETH,** librarian, writer; b. Southsea, England, July 8, 1946; arrived in U.S., 1973; d. Harold and Evelyn (Thistleton) Bennell; m. Kent Oliver Martin, Apr. 25, 1973; children: Varsha Serena, Menoka Sybilla. BA with honors, York U., Can., 1969; BLS, U. Toronto, 1970; MLS, U. B.C., 1975. Ordained priest Diocese Olympia, 1992. Libr. Cambrian Coll., Sudbury, Canada, 1970—71; reference libr. Meml. U. Library, St. John's, Nfld., 1971—73; libr. Skamokawa Cmty. Libr., Skamokawa, Wash., 1974—. Advisor Wahkiakum County Bicentennial Com., Cathalmet, Wash., 1975—76, Columbia River Estuary Data Devel. Program, Astoria, Oreg., 1977—82; adv. Pacific States Marine Fisheries Commn., 2005—; rsch. asst. and cons. Oreg. Atty. Gen., Portland, 1979—80; guest curator furniture Wash. state exhibit Seattle Mus. History and Industry, 1986. Editor: Strictly Fish, A Seafood Cookbook, 3d edit., 1988, Index to the Gray's River Builder and the Skamokawa Eagle, 1983, Skamokawa: Sad Years, Glad Years, 1985, Legacy and Testament, the Story of Columbia River Gillnetters, 1994, The Beach of Heaven, A History of Wahkiakum County, 1997, Lewis and Clark in the land of the Wahkiakum, 2003, Sea Fire, Tales of Jesus and Fishing, 2003, A Social Snapshot of the Columbia River Gillnet Fishery, 2005, (video) Work is Our Joy: The Story of the Columbia River Gillnetter, 1990; contbr. articles to profl. jours. Pres. N.W. Fishermen's Wives Assn., Astoria, Oreg., 1984; bd. dirs. and historian Friends of Skamokawa Found., 1986; bd. dirs. St. James Family Ctr., 1985—, Lower Columbia Regional Fisheries Enhancement Group, 2003—05. Grantee, Wash. State Library Commn., 1983, 1984, Wash. Commn. on Humanities, 1984, Nat. Coastal Resources Research and Devel. Inst., 1986. Episcopalian. Home: PO Box 83 Skamokawa WA 98647-0083

**MARTIN, J. CLARK,** lawyer; b. Washington, DC, May 10, 1940; BSEE, La. State U., 1963, JD, 1966. Bar: La. 1966, Tex. 1970. Ptnr., co-head Intellectual Property / Technical Litig. Sect. Vinson & Elkins LLP, Houston. Fellow: Tex. Bar Found. Office: Vinson & Elkins LLP First City Tower 1001 Fannin St, Ste 2300 Houston TX 77002 Office Phone: 713-758-2400. E-mail: cmartin@velaw.com.

**MARTIN, JACK,** physician; b. Northport, Ala., Aug. 11, 1927; s. Marvin Oscar and Glenavis (Rice) M.; m. Ann Inman, Apr. 7, 1957; children: Sarah, Richard, Charles Randall, Robert. BS, U. Ala., 1949; MD, Vanderbilt U. 1953. Intern Charity Hosp., New Orleans, 1953-54; resident in adult and child psychiatry Cin. Gen. Hosp., 1954-58; dir. child psychiatry U. Tex. Health Scis. Ctr., Dallas, 1958-67, clin. prof. child psychiatry, 1967—; med. dir. Shady Brook Rsch. Ctr., Richardson, Tex., 1963-81; physician pvt. practice, Dallas, 1981—. With USNR, 1945-47. Independent. Episcopalian. Avocations: bridge, golf. Office: 3636 Dickason Ave Dallas TX 75219-4911 Office Phone: 214-528-3095. Personal E-mail: jam4757@aol.com.

**MARTIN, JACK,** federal agency administrator; m. Bettye Martin; children: Randy, Ingrid. BS, MBA, Wayne State U.; postgrad., U. Minn. CPA. With Gen. Motors Corp., Detroit; various mgmt. positions Control Data; cons. acct. Touche Ross & Co. (now Deloitte and Touche); mng. dir., CEO founder Jack Martin and Co. P.C., CPAs, 1975—; chmn., acting CEO Home Fed. Savings Bank, Detroit, 1995—; chmn. provider reimbursement rev. bd. U.S. Dept. Health and Human Srvcs., 1991—94; CFO US Dept. Edn., Washington, 2001—. Chmn. of bd. Health Alliance Plan; mem. investment com. Mercy Health Sys. (now Trinity Health); chair Mich. adv. com. U.S. Civil Rights Commn.; v.p. Merrill Palmer Inst. Wayne State U. Treas. Alzheimer's Assn. Mem.: AICPA (mem. practice stds. subcom.), Det. Athletic Club (bd. dirs.). Office: Dept Edn Office CFO 400 Maryland Ave SW Rm 4E313 Washington DC 20202-4110 Office Phone: 202-401-0085, 202-401-0477. Office Fax: 202-401-0006. E-mail: jack.martin@ed.gov.

**MARTIN, JACQUELINE BRIGGS,** writer; b. Maine; m. Rich Martin; children: Sarah, Justin. Author: Bizzy Bones and Moosemouse, 1986, Bizzy Bones and the Lost Quilt, 1988, Bizzy Bones and Uncle Ezra, 1984, Button, Bucket, Sky, 1998, The Finest Horse in Town, 1992, Grandmother Bryant's Pocket, 1996 (Lupine award 1996), The Green Truck Garden Giveaway: A Neighborhood Story and Almanac, 1997, Good Times on Grandfather Mountain, 1992, Higgins Bend Song and Dance, 1997, Snowflake Bentley, 1998 (Caldecott Award 1999, Lupine Award 1998), Washing the Willow Tree Loon, 1995, The Lamp, The Ice and The Boat Called Fish, 2001, The Water Gift and the Pig of the Pig (Lupine award 2003), 2003, On Sand Island, 2003. Office: Houghton Mifflin Co Juvenile Dept Boston MA 02116

**MARTIN, JACQUES,** professional hockey coach, professional sports team executive; b. St. Pascal, Ont., Can., Oct. 1, 1952; Coach St. Louis Blues, 1986-88; asst. coach Chgo. Blackhawks, 1988-96; head coach Ottawa Senators, 1996—2004, Fla. Panthers, 2004—. Recipient Jack Adams award, 1999. Office: c/o Florida Panthers 1 Panther Pkwy Miami FL 33323*

**MARTIN, JAMES,** retired education educator; b. Crawfordsville, Ind., July 5, 1931; children: Neil Shorey, Tammi York. BS, Purdue U., Lafayette, Ind., 1954. Bus. software cons. Self-Employed, 1977—93; computer instr. KVCC, Fairfield, Maine, 1993—. Home: P O Box 324 Newport ME 04953 Office: Kennebec Valley CC Fairfield ME Office Phone: 2074535000. Personal E-mail: jmartin74@verizon.net. E-mail: jmartin@mit.edu.

**MARTIN, JAMES CHARLES,** physician; b. Coleman, Tex., 1948; MD, U. Tex. San Antonio, 1973. Resident Bexar County Hosp., San Antonio, 1973-76; clin. prof. U. Tex. Health Sci. Ctr.; physician pvt. practice, 1976-96; dir. residency program Santa Rosa Family Practice, 1996—. V.p. med. affairs Christus Sauta Rosa, 2004—; review com. for party medicine ACGME, 2005—. Mem. Am. Acad. Family Physicians (pres. 2002-03), Am. Bd. Family Practice (pres. 1997-98), Tex. Med. Assn. Office: Ste 4703 333 N Santa Rosa San Antonio TX 78207-3108 Office Phone: 210-704-2551. E-mail: james.martin@christushealth.org.

**MARTIN, JAMES DOUGLAS,** neurologist; b. Cullman, Ala., Dec. 10, 1926; s. Charles L. and Sylvia J. (Johnson) M.; m. Elizabeth Mason, June 22, 1956; children: James, Julia, Ann. BA, Vanderbilt U., 1949, MD, 1959. Diplomate Am. Bd. Psychiatry and Neurology. Med. intern U. Va., Charlottesville, Va., 1959-60, neurology resident, 1960-63; fellow in neuropathology Harvard Med. Sch., Boston, 1963-65; asst. prof. neurology W. Va. U., Morgantown, 1965-70, assoc. prof., 1970-72, prof., 1972—. Fellow Am. Acad. Neurology. Office: W Va Univ Dept Neurology PO Box 9180 Morgantown WV 26506-9180

**MARTIN, JAMES FREDERICK,** media consultant; b. Sebring, Fla., June 29, 1944; s. George William and Elizabeth (Knudson) Martin; m. Hope Hamilton McCulloch, May 31, 1969; children: Faith Hamilton, Aimee Leavenworth. BFA in Visual Comm., Syracuse U., 1967; MA in Non-Verbal Communication, Mich. State U., 1968. Film producer Foote, Cone & Belding, Chgo., 1968-73, sr. producer, v.p., 1973-77, exec. producer, 1977-80, dir. broadcast prodn., 1980—83, dir. advt. services, 1983-84, sr. v.p. global broadcast prodn., 1984—2002; broadcast prodn. cons. Jim Martin, Glenview, Ill., 2003—. Home and Office: 1115 Normandy Ln Glenview IL 60025-3211 Office Phone: 847-998-4549. E-mail: jamesfm@earthlink.net.

**MARTIN, JAMES HANLEY,** state attorney general; b. NYC, Dec. 22, 1960; s. James Patrick and Josephine Anne (Hanley) M. AB, Georgetown U., 1983; JD, Fordham U., 1986. Bar: N.J. 1986, U.S. Dist. Ct. N.J. 1986, N.Y. 1987, D.C. 1988, U.S. Dist. Ct. (so. and ea. dists.) N.Y. 1991, U.S. Ct. Appeals (D.C. and 3d cirs.) 1991, U.S. Supreme Ct. 1991. Dep. atty. gen. State of N.J., Newark, 1987—2003, dep. atty. gen. Litig., sect., 2003—04, asst. atty. gen. Litig. Trenton, 2004—. Mem. ABA, Am. Judicature Soc., Mercer County Bar Assn., N.J. State Bar Assn., D.C. Bar Assn. Roman Catholic. Office: State of NJ Divsn Law PO Box 112 25 Market St Trenton NJ 08625-0112

**MARTIN, JAMES JOHN, JR.,** systems analyst, retired research and development company executive; b. Paterson, NJ, Feb. 3, 1936; s. James John and Lillian (Lea) M.; m. Lydia Elizabeth Bent, June 11, 1954; children: David, Peter, Laura, Daniel, Lucas. BA, U. Wis.-Madison, 1955; postgrad., Div. Sch., Harvard U., 1955-57; MS, Navy Postgrad. Sch., 1963; PhD, MIT, 1965. Commd. ensign USN, 1957, advanced through grades to comdr., 1971, ret., 1977; sector v.p. Sci. Applications Internat. Corp., La Jolla, Calif., 1977-95. Author: Bayesian Decision Problems and Markov Chains, 1967; editor: On Not Confusing Ourselves, 1991; contbr. articles to profl. jours. Bd. dirs. Mil. Conflict Inst., 1986-92. Decorated Legion of Merit. Mem. Internat. Inst. Strategic Studies, Ops. Research Soc. Am., Mil. Ops. Research Soc. (bd. dirs. 1974-77). Democrat. Avocation: cooking. Home: 6603 Aranda Ave La Jolla CA 92037-6216

**MARTIN, JAMES KAY,** management consultant; b. Montreal, Que., Sept. 20, 1948; s. Douglas and Margaret Martin; m. Emma Lim Abrenica, Sept. 12, 1986. B of Math., U. Waterloo, Ont., 1970; PhD, U. Toronto, 1974. Sr. analyst Health & Welfare, Ottawa, 1974-79; asst. dir. transfer payments Social Devel. Ministry, Ottawa, 1980-84; exec. dir. planning Dept. Agr., Ottawa, 1984-90; exec dir. regulatory affairs Treasury bd. Can., Ottawa, 1990-96; dir. gen. Internal Audit and Risk Mgmt. Human Resources Can., Ottawa, 1997—2004; dir. gen. audit and evaluation Human Resources and Skills Devel., Ottawa, 2004—05; pres. JK & E Martin Cons., Inc., Ottawa, 2005—. Chmn. regulatory mgmt. group OECD, Paris, 1993-96. Contbr. articles to profl. jours. Chmn. grad. students union U. Toronto, 1973, mem. bd. govs., 1974. Fellow Nat. Rsch. Coun., 1970, Ont. Inst. for Edn., 1971, Can. Coun., 1972, 73. Mem. Ottawa Humane Soc. Roman Catholic. Avocations: running, canoeing, skiing, swimming. Office Phone: 613-614-3012. E-mail: martin.jk@rogers.com.

**MARTIN, J(AMES) KENNETH,** music educator; b. Washington, Jan. 20, 1947; s. Samuel M. Jr. and Georgia Irene (O'Dell) Martin; m. Nancy Gravley; children: Sara L., Susan I. Yancey. BA, Wake Forest U., 1969; postgrad., Vanderbilt Div. Sch., 1971; M Ch. Music, So. Bapt. Theol. Sem., 1981, D Mus. Arts, 1983. Pres., gen. mgr. Martin Asphalt Paving, Inc., Clinton, Md., 1972—77; min. music and edn. Hillandale Bapt. Ch., Adelphi, Md., 1977—79; prof. of music Campbellsville (Ky.) U., 1985—, chmn. faculty 1989—90, 2004—05. Tchr. Russian Bapt. Pastors Sch., St. Petersburg, 1994, Siberian Bapt. Pastors Sch., Irkutsk, Russia, 1997, Irkutsk, 98; prof. of music Campbellsville U. Brazil Program, Recife, Brazil, 2002—; part-time or interim min. of music various chs., 1974—2004. Composer: (choral arrangement) My Old Kentucky Home, 1989; singer, actor: solo voice recitals in U.S. and Brazil; actor: (outdoor hist. music drama) Hoofprints on the Stairs, 1999—; contbr. revs., articles to profl. publs. Dir. choir, founder Capital Bapt. Chorale, 1976—79; mem. Lebanon Cmty. Choir, Ky., Mid-Ky. Chorus St. Catharine; deacon Pa. Ave. Bapt. Ch., Washington, 1972—75, Campbellsville Bapt. Ch., 1991—94; mem. Louisville Bach Soc.; organizer and dir. Martin Family Reunion, Mayodan, NC, 1972—. Named Hon. Chaplain, USN Chief of Chaplains, 1983; recipient Honors award cert. in Ministry, So. Bapt. Theol. Sem. Sch. of Ch. Music, 1981; Garrett fellow, So. Bapt. Theol. Sem., 1981—83. Mem. Music Conf., Nat. Assn. Tchrs. of Singing, Am. Choral Directors Assn., Phi Mu Alpha Sinfonia. Baptist. Avocation: genealogy. Home: 624 North Central Ave Campbellsville KY 42718 Office: Campbellsville U 1 University Dr Campbellsville KY 42718 Office Phone: 270-789-5340. Office Fax: 270-789-5524. E-mail: jkmartin@campbellsville.edu.

**MARTIN, JAMES KIRBY,** historian, educator; b. Akron, Ohio, May 26, 1943; s. Paul Elmo and Dorothy Marie (Garrett) M.; m. Karen Wierwille, Aug. 7, 1965; children: Darcy Elizabeth, Sarah Marie, Joelle Kathryn Garrett. BA summa cum laude, Hiram Coll., 1965; MA, U. Wis., 1967, PhD, 1969.

Asst. prof. history Rutgers U., New Brunswick, NJ, 1969-73, assoc. prof., 1973-79, prof., 1979-80, asst. provost, 1972-74, v.p. acad. affairs, 1977-79; vis. prof. Rutgers Ctr. of Alcohol Studies, 1978-88; prof. history U. Houston, 1980-97, disting. univ. prof., 1997—, chmn. dept., 1980-83; vis. prof. history Rice U., Houston, 1992. Chmn. bd. sponsors Papers of Thomas Edison Project, 1977-80; founding ptnr. PastQuest Rsch. Svcs., 1999. Author: Men in Rebellion, 1973, In the Course of Human Events, 1979, (with M.E. Lender) A Respectable Army: The Military Origins of the Republic, 1982, 2d edit., 2006, (contemporary mil. reading list), Drinking in America: A History, 1982, rev. edit. 1987, (with others) America and Its Peoples, 1989, 5th edit. 2004, concise edit. 1995, Benedict Arnold: Revolutionary Hero, 1997 (Homer D. Babbidge, Jr. award), audio edit., 2001,(with J.T. Glatthaar) Forgotten Allies: Oneida Indians and the American Revolution, 2006; editor: Interpreting Colonial America, 1973, 2d edit. 1978, The Human Dimensions of Nation Making, 1976, (with K. Stubaus) The American Revolution, Whose Revolution?, 1977, 81, (with M.E. Lender) Citizen-Soldier: The Revolutionary War Journal of Joseph Bloomfield, 1982 (R.P. McCormick prize), Ordinary Courage: The Revolutionary War Adventures of Joseph Plumb Martin, 1993, 2d edit., 1999; mem. editl. bd. Papers of William Livingston Project, 1973-80, Houston Rev., 1981-2003, N.J. History, 1986—, Conversations with the Past Series, 1993-95; gen. editor Am. Social Experience Series, 1983-2002. Recipient N.J. Soc. of the Cin. prize for Disting. Achievement in Am. History, 1995, Hiram Coll. Alumni Achievement award, 1996. Mem. Tex. Assn. for Advancement History (bd. dirs. 1981-93, v.p. 1986-90), Inst. for Internat. Bus. Analysis (adv. coun. 1982-86), Am. Hist. Assn. (Beveridge-Dunning prize com. 1990-93), Orgn. Am. Historians, So. Hist. Assn., Soc. Historians Early Am. Republic (adv. coun. 1985-88), Soc. for Mil. History, Phi Beta Kappa, Phi Kappa Phi, Pi Gamma Mu, Omicron Delta Kappa, Phi Alpha Theta. Office: U Houston Dept History 524 Arnold Hall Houston TX 77204-3003

**MARTIN, JAMES LARENCE,** dentist, educator; b. Dubuque, Iowa, Sept. 3, 1940; s. James Larence and Ada Virginia (Boone) M.; m. Willie Mae Walker, Jan. 23, 1941; children: Linda Gail, James Larence III, John Lance. BS, Loras Coll., Dubuque, 1959, LittD, 1982; MS, Tenn. State U., 1960; DDS, Meharry Med. Coll., 1966; MPH, U. Mich., 1975. Dental dir. children and youth Meharry Med. Coll., Nashville, 1967-72, acting dir. children and youth program, 1972-73, dir. primary dental svcs., 1973-75, coord. dental component Ctr. for Health Care Rsch., 1975-77, prof., 1981—; owner Martin Dental, Nashville, 1980—. Dental cons. Medically Dedicated, Washington, 1992—; pres. faculty senate Meharry Med. Coll., 1989-93, mem. pres.'s exec. mgmt. team, 1989-93, dir. divsn. dental public health 1999—, chmn. dept. dental pub. health, 1999—. Contbr. articles to profl. jours., chpts. to books. Bd. regents Loras Coll., 1997—. Recipient Meritorious Svc. award Acad. Oral Medicine, 1977. Mem. ADA, Am. Pub. Health Assn. (med. com.), Am. Assn. Pub. Health Dentistry, Nat. Assn. Cmty. Health Ctrs., Am. Acad. Goil Foil Operators, Soc. of the Upper 10th, Nashville Area C. of C., Beta Kappa Chi, Phi Sigma. Avocations: reading, swimming, photography. Home: 3515 Geneva Cir Nashville TN 37209-2524 Office: 908 34th Ave N Nashville TN 37209-2502 Office Phone: 615-327-4499. Personal E-mail: jmarti3817@aol.com.

**MARTIN, JAMES ROBERT,** identification company executive; b. Indpls., Mar. 31, 1943; s. Walter and Helen (Snider) M.; m. Jan. 24, 1970 (div. Dec. 1990); children: Julia, Justin; m. Tamara Hicks, Dec. 21, 1991; stepchildren: Hunter Hoskins, Laura Hoskins. BA, DePauw U., 1965; MBA, Ind. U., 1967. Bus. analyst TRW, Inc., Redondo Beach, Calif., 1967-70; fin. analyst Internat. Industries, Beverly Hills, Calif., 1970; v.p. fin., treas. A & E Plastik Pak Co., Inc., Industry, Calif., 1970-75; pres. Plasti-Line, Inc., Knoxville, Tenn. 1975-92, chmn., CEO, 1992—. Bd. dirs. 1st Am. Corp., Nashville, Signal Thread Co., Chattanooga, Tenn. Bd. dirs. Knoxville Symphony Soc., 1976, Knoxville United Way, 1986, Knoxville Mus. Art; bd. dirs., chmn. fin. com. Thompson Cancer Survival Ctr., Knoxville, 1985. Mem. Chief Execs. Orgn., Club LeConte (bd. dirs.), East Tenn. Automobile Club (bd. dirs.), St. Francis Yacht Club, Cherokee Country Club. Aspen Mountain Club. Republican. Episcopalian. Home: 1029 Scenic Dr Knoxville TN 37919 Office: ImagePoint PO Box 59043 Knoxville TN 37950-9043

**MARTIN, JAMES RUSSELL,** lawyer; b. Columbus, Ohio, June 24, 1947; s. Robert Wells and Gwendolyn (Collins) M.; m. Susan Virginia Jarman, Aug. 4, 1973; children: James Russell Jr., Elizabeth Collins. BA in History, Denison U., 1969; JD, U. Denver, 1972. Bar: Colo. 1972, U.S. Dist. Ct. Colo. 1972. Assoc. Brundage & Yates, Denver, 1973; asst. atty. gen. State of Colo., Denver, 1974-76; v.p. Butterwick Enterprises Ltd., Denver, 1978-81, pres., 1981-83; ptnr. Baker & Hostetler LLP, Denver, 1985—2004; sr. v.p., gen. counsel, clerk Bluegreen Corp., Boca Raton, Fla., 2004—. Mem. ABA, Colo. Bar Assn., Denver Bar Assn. Avocations: skiing, tennis, bicycling. Office: Bluegreen Corp 4960 Conference Way N Boca Raton FL 33431*

**MARTIN, JAMES VICTOR, JR.,** foreign service officer, writer; b. Tokyo, Nov. 15, 1916; (parents Am. citizens); s. James Victor Sr. and Esther Belle (Ludwig) M.; m. Elizabeth Shaler Smith, June 28, 1941; children: Sarah Martin Brown, Susan P. Martin, David Ludwig Martin. BA, DePauw U., 1938; MA, Tufts U., 1939, PhD, 1948; postgrad. in Japanese lang., Harvard U., 1941—42, Yale U., 1948—49; student, Nat. War Coll., 1961—62. Vice consul U.S. Consulate Gen., Bombay, 1946-48; polit. officer, head transl. sect. Office of Polit. Adviser, Tokyo, 1949-50; econ. officer U.S. Consulate Gen., Kobe-Osaka, Japan, 1951-53; prin. officer U.S. Consulate, Fukuoka, Japan, 1953-56; officer-in-charge Japanese Affairs U.S. Dept. State, Washington, 1956-58, personnel planning staff, 1958-61; chief polit. sect. U.S. Embassy, Rangoon, Burma, 1962-64; polit. adviser Office of U.S. High Commn. to the Ryukyu Islands, Okinawa, 1964-67; polit. counselor U.S. Embassy, Canberra, Australia, 1968-70; country dir. for Australia, N.Z. and Pacific Islands, U.S. Dept. State, Washington, 1970-73. Lectr. Far East internat. rels. Am. U., Washington, summer 1961; occasional lectr. U.S. Asian policy U. Md. Extension, Okinawa 1965-67; cons. Pacific Inlands, U.S. Dept. of Interior, Washington, 1973-74. Contbr. articles to profl. jours. Trustee Japan-Am. Soc. Washington, Inc., 1982-89; bd. dirs. Com. Cmty. Democracies-USA, Washington, 1983-92, v.p., 1986-87; sec., treas. Com. Cmty. Democracies, Washington, 1985-88. Lt. USN, 1941-46, PTO. Mem. Assn. for Asian Studies, Mid-Atlantic Region Coll. Assn. for Asian Studies (treas. 1972-76), Diplomatic and Consular Officers Ret. Methodist. Avocation: painting.

**MARTIN, JAY GRIFFITH,** lawyer; b. Washington, Oct. 13, 1951; s. Drexel Reese and Joyce (Towne) M.; m. Jackie Werdt; 1 child, Trevor. BBA, So. Meth. U., 1973, MPA, JD, So. Meth. U., 1976. Bar: Tex., D.C., U.S. Ct. Appeals (5th cir.), U.S. Dist. Ct. (so. dist.) Tex., U.S. Dist. Ct. D.C., U.S. Supreme Ct. Counsel Pennzoil Co., Houston, 1976-78, sr. counsel, 1978-81; divsn. counsel The Superior Oil Co., Houston, 1981-85; sr. counsel Mobil Natural Gas, Houston, 1985-87, gen. counsel, 1987-91; asst. gen. counsel Mobil Oil Corp., Fairfax, Va., 1991-96; ptnr. Andrews & Kurth LLP. Washington, 1996-2000, Phelps Dunbar LLP, Houston, 2000—01, Winstead Sechrest & Minick, Houston, 2001—04; v.p., chief compliance officer, sr. deputy Gen. Coun. Baker Hughes, Inc., Houston, 2004—. Mem. sr. adv. bd. Bus. Laws Inc., Chesterland, Ohio, 1997—; mem. adv. bd. Inst. Transnat. Arbitration, Southwestern Legal Found., 1996—. Oil and Gas sect. of Inst. Am. and Internat. Law. Author: Environmental Management Systems, 1998. Dispute Resolution and the Use of Alternatives (ADR), 2000, Environmental Dispute Resolution, 2002; mem. editl. bd.: Natural Gas Contracts, 1991—; contbr. over 60 articles on energy and environ. topics to profl. jours. Chmn. fundraising com. So. Meth. U., Washington, 1996—97, mem. dean's adv. coun. Sch. Law, 1995—; trustee Rocky Mountain Mineral Law Found., 2003—. Named Tex. Super Atty., Tex. Monthly Mag., 2004; named one of World's Outstanding Energy Lawyers, Euromoney, 1997, 2000, 2001, 2003. Fellow: State Bar Coll. of Tex., Tex. Bar Found., State Bar Tex. (life; adv. bd. 1985—, chmn. corp. counsel sect. 1990—91, mem. corp counsel sect. adv. bd. 2003—04, mem. coun. for oil, gas and resources sect. 2003—, coun. oil and gas sect. 2003—, dir. Tex. C-Bar); mem.: Instit. Am. and Internat. Law (adv. bd. 2004), Fed. Bar Assn. (chmn. 1986—87, bd. dirs. 1990—92, antitrust sect. 1991—98, chmn. internat. energy com. 1997—), Delta Theta

Phi, Rocky Mountain Law Inst. (trustee 1991—), Am. Soc. Internat. Law, Assn. Internat. Petroleum Negotiators, Houston Bar Assn. (mem. internat. com. 2006—), ABA (litig. sect. rep. on ABA coord. com. on energy law 1991—97, sect. pub. utility law 1991—, chmn. natural resources, energy and environ law internat. energy com. 1996—98, exec. coun., budget chmn. sect. on environment, energy and law 1996—, liaison to Fed. Energy Bar Assn. 1997—, ad hoc mem. of com. 1997—, sr. liaison oversight responsibility for all energy and resource coms. 1998—, vice chmn. sect. on environment, energy and resources' natural gas and), Energy Bar Assn. (mem. antitrust sect. 1986—87, chmn. internat. energy com. 1998—99, chmn. internat. com.), Internat. Bar Assn. (sect. energy and natural resources 1994—), D.C. Bar Assn. (internat.sect.), Tex. Bar Assn. (dir. Tex.). Avocations: history, current events and politics, tennis, golf, jogging, rugby. Home: 10623 Gawain Houston TX 77024-1828 Office: c/o Baker Hughes Inc 3900 Essex Ln Ste 1200 Houston TX 77027-5177 Office Phone: 713-439-8439. Business E-Mail: jay.martin@bakerhughes.com.

**MARTIN, JAY HERBERT,** psychoanalyst, language professor, political science professor; b. Newark, Oct. 30, 1935; s. Sylvester K. and Ada M. (Smith) M.; m. Helen Bernadette Saldini, June 9, 1956; children: Helen E., Laura A., Jay Herbert. AB with honors, Columbia U., 1956; MA, Ohio State U., 1957, PhD, 1960; PhD in Psychoanalysis, So. Calif. Psychoanalytic Inst., 1983. Instr. English Pa. State U., 1957-58; instr., then asst. to assoc. prof. English and Am. Studies Yale U., New Haven, 1960-68; prof. English and comparative culture U. Calif., Irvine, 1968-79; asst. prof. psychiatry and human behavior, clin. supr. residency program Calif. Coll. Medicine Calif. Coll. Medicine U. Calif.-Irvine, 1978—96; Leo S. Bing prof. English and Am. lit. U. So. Calif., L.A., 1979-96, dir. undergrad. program in Am. studies, 1968-69, dir. program in comparative culture, 1969-71, dir. edn. abroad program, 1971 75; prof. govt., Edward S. Gould prof. humanities Claremont McKenna Coll., 1996—; dir. civilization program Claremont (Calif.) McKenna Coll., 1996—2000, acting dir. Gould Ctr. for Humanistic Studies, 1998-2000, prof., English, grad. sch., 2004—. Instr. psychoanalysis So. Calif. Psychoanalytic Inst., 1984-96; Bicentennial prof. Am. lit. and culture Moscow State U., USSR, 1976, Dai Ho Chun (Wisdom) chair Prof. U. Hawaii, 2000-01; dir. NEH summer sems., 1976, 77; mem. evaluation com. dept. pvt. post-secondary edn. State of Calif., 1986; lectr. in field; cons. in field Author: (criticism and biography) Conrad Aiken: A Life of His Art, 1962, Harvests of Change: American Literature 1865-1914, 1967, Nathanael West: The Art of His Life, 1970 (U. Calif. Friends Libr. award), Robert Lowell, 1970, Always Merry and Bright. The Life of Henry Miller, 1978, (U. Calif. Friends of Libr. award), Phi Kappa Phi Best Faculty Publ. prize U. So. Calif., transl. in French, Japanese and German), (fiction) Winter Dreams: An American in Moscow, 1979, Who Am I This Time, Uncovering the Fictive Personality, 1988 (trans. Portuguese), Burlington No. Found. award 1989); Swallowing Tigers Whole, 1996, A Corresponding Leap of Love: Henry Miller, 1996, Henry Miller's Dream Song, 1996, Journey to Heavenly Mountain, 2002 (ForeWord mag. Book of Yr. prize), The Education of John Dewey, 2003, Cased as Catalysts, 2005, Only God: A Biography of Yogi Ramsuratkumar, 2005, International Reserach on Global Affairs, 2005; author one hour radio drama, William Faulkner. Sound Portraits of Twentieth-Century Humanists, starring Tennessee Williams, Glenn Close, Colleen Dewhurst, Nat. Pub. Radio, 1980; author one-act docudrama Trial Days in Coyocoan, Antioch Rev., 2001; author sects. 24 books including most recently American Writing Today, vol. I, 1982, The Haunted Dusk: American Supernatural Fiction, 1820-1902, 1983, Frontiers of Infant Psychiatry, vol.II, 1986, Centenary Essays on Huckleberry Finn, 1985, Robert Lowell: Essays on the Poetry, 1987, William Faulkner: The Best from American Literature, 1989, The Homosexualities: Reality, Fantasy and the Arts, 1991, Life Guidance Through Literature, 1992, Biography and Source Studies, 1995, William Faulkner and Psychology, 1995, Psychotherapy East and West, 1996, Readings on Huckleberry Finn, 1999, John Fante: A Critical Gathering, 2000, Uncollected Works By...Paul Laurence Dunbar, 2000, American Literature of the Civil War, 2004, Blackwell Companion to Modernist Literature and Culture, 2004,Cases as Catalysts, 2005, Only God: A Biography of Ramsuratkumar, 2005, International Research on Global Affairs, 2005; editor: Winfield Townley Scott (Yale series recorded poets), 1962, Twentieth Century Interpretations of the Waste Land: A Collection of Critical Essays, 1968, Twentieth Century Views of Nathanael West, 1972, A Singer in the Dawn: Reinterpretations of Paul Laurence Dunbar (with intro.), 1975, Economic Depression and American Humor (with intro.), 1986; mem. editl. bd. Am. Lit., 1978-81, Humanities in Society, 1979-1983; editor-in-chief Psychoanalytic Edn., 1984-89; editor Humanitas/Communitas, 1998-2000; appearances on TV and radio including Connie Martinson Talks Books, Barbara Brunner Nightline, Sonya Live in L.A., Oprah Winfrey Show, C-SPAN, 1988-89; contbr. numerous articles and revs. to profl. jours., bulls. Pres. Friends of Irvine Pub. Libr., 1974-75; mem. com. for Freud Mus. Recipient Fritz Schmidl Meml. prize for rsch. applied psychoanalysis Seattle Assn. Psychoanalysis, 1982, Marie H. Briehl prize for child psychoanalysis, 1982, Franz Alexander prize in psychoanalysis, 1984, Disting. Writers award Antioch Rev., 2004; Morse rsch. fellow, 1963-64, Am. Philos. Soc. fellow, 1966, J.S. Guggenheim fellow, 1966-67, Rockefeller Found.humanities sr. fellow, 1975-76, Rsch. Clin. fellow So. Calif. Psychoanalytic Soc. 1977-81, Rockefeller fellow, Bellagio, Italy, 1983, NEH sr. fellow, 1983-84; Durfee Found. fellow to China, 2004; fellow Bogliasco Found. Liguria Ctr. for Arts and Humanities, 2004. Mem. So. Calif. Am. Studies Assn. (pres. 1969-71), Am. Studies Assn. (exec. bd. 1969-71, del. to MLA Assembly 1974, chmn. Ralph Gabriel prize com. 1975-77), MLA (chmn. prize com. Jay B. Hubbell Silver medal in Am. lit. 1978-84), Nat. Assn. Arts and Letters (prize com. 1987-88), Nat. Humanities Faculty (advisor to Valhalla High Sch., El Cajon, Calif. 1979-81), Nat. Am. Studies Faculty, Internat. Psychoanalytic Assn., Internat. Assn. Empirical Aesthetics, Internat. Assn. U. Profs. English, Internat. Karen Horney Soc., Newport Psychoanalytical Inst., Phi Beta Kappa. Home: 748 Via Santo Tomas Claremont CA 91711-1569 Office Phone: 909-398-0193. Personal E-mail: helenjay@comcast.net. Business E-Mail: jmartin@mckenna.edu.

**MARTIN, JEAN H.,** retired interior designer; d. Irving William and Doris Gaffield Howland; m. Raymond Ray Martin, Feb. 28, 1976; children from previous marriage: Darron G. Spalty, Maren Jane Spalty Halliday. At, Rider Coll., Trenton, N.J., Rochester Inst. Tech., N.Y. Lic. interior designer State of Fla. Interior designer Lauer Furniture, Rochester, NY, 1962—67; sr. interior designer Sibley's, 1967—79, Burderes, Boca Raton, Fla., 1979—92; owner Jean H. Martin Interiors, Boca Raton and Weeki Wachee, 1992—; ret., 1995. Design advisor Schlegel Mfg., Rochester, NY, Gioia Mfg., Case Hoyt Printing, George Ballard, Inc., Norman Matthews, Loxahatchie Club, CEO Federated Dept. Stores. Prin. works include NY Lab. Supply, NYC, Ian Calder Nat. Enquirer, Hypaloso, Fla., Mr. and Mrs. John Graeme residence, 1985, Johnson-Higgens de Venezuela. Sec. and v.p. Rochester C. of C., 1962—79; pres. and charter mem. Satin Wood Twig Rochester North Side Hosp., 1962—79; charter mem. Opus Soc. Boca Raton Symphony, Boca Raton and Ft. Lauderdale, 1979—, Boca Mus. Art, 1979—. Named Most Outstanding Designer, Burdines, 1985; named to Rochester Jr. League Showcase, 1980. Mem.: Am. Soc. Interior Designers, Philanthropic Ednl. Orgn., Glen Lakes Country Club, Stafford Country Club. Avocations: golf, skiing, bowling, big game fishing.

**MARTIN, JERRY LEE,** organization executive, educator; b. Turkey, Tex., Oct. 16, 1941; m. Abigail L. Rosenthal, 1998. Student, San Diego State Coll. 1961; BA in Polit. Sci., U. Calif., Riverside, 1963; MA in Philosophy and Polit. Sci., U. Chgo., 1966; PhD in Philosophy, Northwestern U., 1970; DHL (hon.), Thomas More Coll. Liberal Arts, 2003. Assoc. prof. U. Colo., Boulder, 1967-74, chmn. dept. philosophy, 1979-81, assoc. prof., 1974-84, adjunct prof., 1984—; rsch. analyst House Rep. Rsch. Com., 1982-87; legis. asst. Congressman Han Brown, 1982-87; dir. divisn. edn. programs NEH, Washington, 1987-88, asst. chmn. studies and evaluation, 1988-89, asst. chmn. programs and policy, 1989-95, acting chmn., 1993. Adj. prof. Georgetown U., 1993-95; adj. scholar Am. Enterprise Inst., 1999—; dir. Ctr. Study Values and Social Policy, U. Colo., Boulder, 1981-82; founding mem. organized rsch. program State of Colo., 1981-82; mem. exec. com. faculty adv. coun. Colo. Commn. Higher Edn., 1980-82; pres. Am. Coun. Trustees

and Alumni, 1995-2004, chmn., 2004—; spkr. in field, frequent guest on radio and TV. Contbr. articles to profl. jours. Mem. Gov.'s Blue Ribbon Commn. on Higher Edn., 1998—2000. Andrew W. Mellon Found. Congl. fellow, 1992-93. Mem. AAUP (state pres. 1977-79), Am. Philos. Assn., Soc. Historians Early Am. Republic, Am. Polit. Sci. Assn., Soc. Social, Polit. and Legal Philosophy. Avocations: tennis, baseball, history. Home: 145 C Selner Ln Doylestown PA 18901 Office: Am Coun Trustees and Alumni 1726 M Street NW # 800 Washington DC 20036

**MARTIN, JESSE LAMONT,** actor; b. Rocky Mountain, Va., Jan. 18, 1969; s. Jesse Reed Watkins and Virginia Price. B, NYU. Actor: (TV series) 413 Hope St., 1997—98, Law & Order, 1990, Law & Order: Spl. Victims Unit, 1999, Law & Order: Criminal Intent, 2001, Law & Order: Trial By Jury, 2005; (TV films) Deep in My Heart, 1999, A Christmas Carol, 2004; (films) Restaurant, 1998, Burning House of Love, 2002, Season of Youth, 2003, Rent, 2005. Bd. dirs. Jonathan Larson Performing Arts Found.*

**MARTIN, JOANNE,** social sciences educator; b. Salem, Mass., Sept. 25, 1946; d. Richard Drake and Nathalie (Ashton) M.; m. Beaumont A. Sheil, July 9, 1977; 1 child, Beaumont Martin Sheil. BA, Smith Coll., 1968; PhD in Social Psychology, Harvard U., 1977; PhD in Econs. and Bus. Adminstrn. (hon.), Copenhagen Bus. Sch., 2001; PhD (hon.), Vrije U., Amsterdam, 2005. Assoc. cons. McBer & Co. (formerly Behavior Sci. Ctr. of Sterling Inst.), 1968-70, dir. govt. mktg., 1970-72; asst. prof. orgnl. behavior Grad. Sch. Bus., Stanford (Calif.) U., 1977-80; assoc. prof. grad. sch. bus. Stanford U., 1980-91, prof. grad. sch. bus., 1991—, dir. doctoral programs, grad. sch. bus., 1991-95, Fred H. Merrill prof. orgn. behavior and, by courtesy, sociology, 1996—. Sec. faculty adv. bd. Stanford U., 1995—96, vice chair adv. bd., 1996—97; vis. scholar Australian Grad. Sch. Mgmt. U. N.S.W., 1989—90, Copenhagen Bus. Sch., 1998, 2004, vis. scholar dept. psychology Sydney (Australia) U., 1989—90; Ruffin fellow bus. ethics Darden Grad. Sch. Bus. Adminstrn. U. Va., 1990; mem. bd. advisors iMahal, 1990—; bd. dirs. C.P.P., Inc., 1993—2003; mem. internat. adv. bd. Internat. Ctr. for Rsch. in Orgnl. Discourse, Strategy and Change; Bus. Sch. rep. Stanford U., 1995—; vis. scholar U. Tech. Sydney, 2004—05. Mem. editl. bd. Adminstrv. Sci. Qtrly., 1984—88, Jour. Social Issues, 1981—83, Acad. Mgmt. Jour., 1984—85, Social Justice Rsch., 1985—90, Jour. Mgmt. Inquiry, 1991—, Orgn., 1994—, Jour. Mgmt. Studies, 1996—2004, Gender, Work and Organization, 1998—, Orgn. Studies, 2003—, Scandinavian Jour. Mgmt., 2003—, consulting editor Internat. Jour. Mgmt. Reviews, 1998—; co-author: five books; contbr. over 60 articles to profl. jours. and edited books. Recipient Centennial medal for contbns. to soc. Harvard U. Grad. Sch. Arts and Scis., 2002; Lena Lake Forrest Rsch. fellowship Bus. and Profl. Women's Found., 1978, James and Doris McNamara Faculty fellowship Grad. Sch. of Bus., Stanford U., 1990-91, Grad. Sch. Bus. Trust Faculty fellow, 2005-06. Fellow: APA, Am. Psychol. Soc., Acad. Mgmt. (rep.-at-large 1983—85, divsn. program chair 1985—87, divsn. chair 1987—89, nat. bd. govs. 1992—95, we. divsn. Promising Young Scholar award 1982, Nat. Disting. Educator award 2000, We. Divsn. Disting. Scholar award 2003, Orgn. and Mgmt. Divsn. Disting. Scholar career achievement award 2005); mem.: Nat. Assn. Corp. Dirs. (adv. bd. 2000—04). Office: Stanford U Grad Sch Bus Littlefield Ctr 353 Stanford CA 94305 Office Phone: 650-723-4791.

**MARTIN, JOHN C.,** pharmaceutical company executive; b. 1952; MBA in Mktg., Golden Gate U.; PhD in Organic Chemistry, U. Chgo. With Syntex Corp., 1978-84; dir. antiviral chemistry Bristol-Myers Squibb, 1984-90; v.p. R&D Gilead Sciences Inc., Foster City, Calif., 1990-95, COO, 1995-96, pres., CEO, 1996—. Mem. Ctrs. for Disease Control/Health Resources and Svcs. Adminstrn. Advisory Com. on HIV and STD Prevention and Treatment, Nat. Inst. Allergy & Infectious Diseases Coun., 2000—03; chmn. Bay Area Bioscience Ctr., 1999—2001, Calif. Healthcare Inst. Bd. trustee U. Chgo., Golden Gate U. Recipient Isbell award, Am. Chemical Soc., Gertrude B. Elion award for Scientific Excellence, Internat. Soc. for Antiviral Rsch. Mem.: Internat. Soc. for Antiviral Rsch. (pres. 1999—2000). Achievements include invention of of the drug ganciclovir. Office: Gilead Scis Inc 333 Lakeside Dr Foster City CA 94404*

**MARTIN, JOHN CHARLES,** lawyer; b. Sheridan, Wyo., Apr. 17, 1953; s. Charles S. and M. Louise (Ago) M.; m. Michele Pacifico, Dec. 9, 1989; children: Laura, Travis John, Hallie Jane. BS with high honors, U. Wyo., 1974; JD, Georgetown U., 1979. Bar: D.C., Wyo. Lawyer Hettinger & Leedy, Riverton, Wyo., 1979-80, Dept. of Interior, Washington, 1981-82, Dept. of Justice, Washington, 1982-85; ptnr., Environ. Health & Safety, Natural Resources, Litigation & Dispute Resolution practices Patton Boggs LLP, Washington, 1985—, mem. exec. com. Co-author: The Corporate Counsel's Guide to Environmental Law, 1989, Handbook on Environmental Law, 1989, Clean Water Handbook, 1990, Handbook of Environmental Law, 1994; contbr. articles to profl. jours. Mem. Wyo. Bar Assn., D.C. Bar Assn. Roman Catholic. Office: Patton Boggs LLP 2550 M St NW Washington DC 20037-1350 Office Phone: 202-457-6032. Office Fax: 202-457-6315. Business E-Mail: jmartin@pattonboggs.com.

**MARTIN, JOHN DRISCOLL,** school administrator; b. Chgo., July 28, 1954; s. Walter Roy and Constance Kathleen (Driscoll) M.; children: Patrick, Kelsey; m. Caroline J. Martin, Mar. 28, 1996. BA, Augustana Coll., 1976; MA, Northwestern U., 1982. Cert. tchr., Ill. Tchr. J.D. Darnall High Sch., Geneseo, Ill., 1976-77, St. Viator High Sch., Arlington Heights, Ill., 1977-79, Hoffman Estates (Ill.) High Sch., 1979-88, athletic dir., 1988-90, Adlai E. Stevenson High Sch., Lincolnshire, Ill., 1990—. Adv. com. Ill. High Sch. Assn., Bloomington, 1989-92; master tchr. Gov.'s Master Tchr. Program, 1984—. Mem. AAHPERD, Ill. Assn. Health, Phys. Edn., Recreation and Dance, Nat. Athletic Adminstrs. Assn., Ill. Athletic Dirs. Assn. (conf. chair 1995, cert. athletic adminstr.). Avocations: golf, reading. Office: 1 Stevenson Dr Lincolnshire IL 60069-2824 E-mail: jmartin@district125.k12.il.us.

**MARTIN, JOHN E,** psychologist, educator; b. Wyandotte, Mich., Apr. 24, 1949; s. John E and Eileen E Martin; m. Mary Lois Horton, Sept. 8, 1972; children: Valerie, Matthew, Andrew, Alison. BA, Sacred Heart Coll., 1971; specialist in sch. psychology, Eastern Mich. U., 1975; PhD in clin. psychology, U. Detroit, 1995. Cert. National School Psychologist Nat. Assn. of Sch. Psychologists, 1976, lic. Psychologist Mich. Dept. Commerce, 1995. Sch. psychologist Wayne Westland Schools, Westland, Mich., 1975—88, adminstr., 1988—93; adj. prof. Eastern Mich. U., 1984—86; clin. psychologist Lifespan Cmty. Ctr., Garden City, Mich., 1995—97; test cons. Wide Range Inc., Wilmington, Del., 1994—; adj. prof. U. Detroit, 1993—; assoc. prof., 2005—; sch. psychologist Wayne Westland Schools, 1993—. Cons. psychologist Psychological Corp., Chgo.; psychology intern Hawthorne Ctr., 1991—92; cons. psychologist Tchg. Resources, Chgo., 1990—95. Editor: (crisis manual) Addressing Crises, 2004. Mem.: Mich. Assn. Sch. Psychologists, Nat. Assn. Sch. Psychologists, Knights of Columbus. Avocations: golf, hiking, baseball. Home: 25309 Bridlepath Farmington MI 48335 Office: Univ Detroit Mercy Psychology Dept 4001 W McNichols Detroit MI 48221 Personal E-mail: schoolpsych424@yahoo.com.

**MARTIN, J(OHN) EDWARD,** architectural engineer; b. LA, Oct. 23, 1916; s. Albert C. and Carolyn Elizabeth (Borchard) M.; m. Elizabeth Jane Hines, May 27, 1944; children: Nicolas Edward, Peter Hines, Sara Jane McKinley Reynolds, Christopher Carey, Elizabeth Margaret Ferguson. Student, U. So. Calif., 1934-36; BS in Archtl. Engring., U. Ill., 1939. Registered profl. engr., Calif., Ill. Structural engr. Albert C. Martin & Assocs., L.A., 1939-42, ptnr. 1945-75, mng. ptnr., 1975-86. Founding mem. bd. trustees Thomas Aquinas Coll., Santa Paula, Calif., 1971-98, emeritus, 1998. Lt. CEC, USNR, 1942-45. Fellow ASCE; mem. Structural Engrs. Assn. Calif., Cons. Engrs. Assn. Calif., Jonathan Club (bd. dirs. 1978-81), Calif. Club, Ranchero Visitadores, Valley Hunt Club, Flintridge Riding Club, West Hills Hunt Club (Master of Fox Hounds 1975-88), Saddle & Sirloin Club, Heritage Found., Traditional Mass Soc. (founder), Pacific Legal Found. (charter). Republican. Roman Catholic. Avocation: horseback riding. Office: AC Martin Pntrs 444 S Flower St Los Angeles CA 90017-3475 Home: 1763 Royal Oaks Dr Apt C3 Bradbury CA 91010-1981 Fax: 626-440-0889.

**MARTIN, JOHN F.,** management consultant; B.Mgmt.Sci., MIT, 1989; M.Mgmt., Northwestern U., Evanston, Ill., 1995. Bus. systems analyst CUC Internat., Inc., Stamford, Conn., 1989—91, product mktg. mgr., 1991—93; prin. cons. PriceWaterhouseCoopers L.L.P., N.Y.C. and Chgo., 1995—98; mgr. Deloitte Cons., N.Y.C., 1999; COO Soliloquy, Inc., N.Y.C., 1999—2001, Medrium, Inc., San Francisco, N.Y.C., 2001—04; pres. JFM OPS Cons. LLC, N.Y.C., 2005—. Prodr. album The First Line rock band. Mem.: Delta Kappa E0psilon (past pres., past exec. mem. intrafraternity coun.). Avocations: scuba diving, skiing, reading, basketball. Office: JFM OPS Cons LLC New York NY

**MARTIN, JOHN JOSEPH,** journalist; b. NYC, Dec. 3, 1938; s. John and Marie Agnes (Jacobsen) M.; children from previous marriage: Sophie Suzanne, Claire Catherine; m. Katherine Fitzhugh, Feb. 14, 1987. BA in Journalism, San Diego State U., 1995. Copy editor, reporter San Diego Union, 1958-62; copy editor Augusta (Ga.) Chronicle, 1963, N.Y. Times Internat. Edit., Paris, 1964-65; editorial asst. Temple Fielding Publs., Mallorca, Spain, 1965-66; reporter, producer Sta. KCRA-TV News, Sacramento, 1966-75; corr. ABC-TV News, 1975—2002. Adj. prof. Columbia U. Grad. Sch. of Journalism, 2002—. Editor, pub. Aztec Tennis Reporter, 1999—; contbg. writer Tennisone.com, 2000-02. Juror DuPont-Columbia Awards, 2005—. Served with U.S. Army, 1962-64. Recipient Nat. Headliner awards, 1980, 89, Emmy award, 1993, George Polk award, 1994, DuPont-Columbia U. Gold baton, 1994, Nat. Assn. Black Journalists award, 2002, Peabody award, 2002. Mem. AFTRA, U.S. Tennis Assn., Coffee House Club N.Y.C., Nat. Press Club, Overseas Press Club, U.S. Tennis Writers Assn.

**MARTIN, JOHN L.,** airport executive; Dir. San Francisco Internat. Airport, 1999—. Office: San Francisco Airport Commn PO Box 8097 San Francisco CA 94128-8097

**MARTIN, JOHN LEWIS,** state legislator; b. Eagle Lake, Maine, June 5, 1941; s. Frank and Edwidge (Raymond) M. BA in History and Govt., U. Maine, 1963, postgrad., 1963-64. Tchr. Am. govt. and history Ft. Kent (Maine) Community High Sch., 1966-72; instr. U. Maine, Ft. Kent, 1972-89, asst. prof., 1989—; mem. from Eagle Lake and St. Francis dist. Maine Ho. of Reps., 1964-94, minority fl. leader, 1970-74, speaker of ho., 1975-94, chmn. com. on energy & natural resources, 1994-95, mem. from dist. 151, 1998-2000. Mem. Maine Senate, Dist. 1, 2000—, chmn. com. natural resources, 1999-2004, human svcs., chmn. rules com.; adj. lectr.; mem. intergovtl. rels. com. Nat. Legis. Conf., 1970-74; chmn. Maine Land Use Regulation Commn., 1972-73, Maine Bur. Human Rels., 1972, State Legis. Leaders Found., 1979-83; mem. exec. bd. Nat. Conf. State Legislatures, chmn. state-fed. assembly, 1985-86, chair task force on reapportionment, 1987-88, vice chmn. budget, fiscal and rules com., 1986-87, v.p., 1988-89, pres.•elect, 1989-90, pres., 1990-91, immediate past pres., 1991-92; mem. exec. com. New Eng. Caucus of State Legislatures, 1978-95, chmn., 1982; mem. regional exec. com. Nat. Dem. State Legis. Leaders Assn., 1991-95, chmn., 1987-89; bd. dirs. Found. for State Legislatures, 1988-94; mem. exec. com. Dem. Nat. Com., 1991-94; pres. Ambulance Svc. Inc., 1975—. Trustee Eagle Lake Water and Sewer Dist., 1966—, No. Maine Gen. Hosp., Eagle Lake, Ea. Maine Health Care, 1991-92, No. Maine Med. Ctr., 1966—; mem. rural health steering com. Nat. Acad. for State Health Policy; advisor White House Task Force on Health Care Reform; dir. intergovtl. affairs Nat. Health Care Campaign, 1994; trustee Maine Med. Ctr., Ft. Kent. Mem. New Eng. Polit. Sci. Assn. Democrat. Home: PO Box 250 Eagle Lake ME 04739-0250 Office: Maine Senate State House Augusta ME 04333-0003 Office Phone: 207-444-5556.

**MARTIN, JOHN RANDOLPH,** judge; b. Lexington, Ky., May 26, 1948; s. Harry and Geraldine (Gray) M.; m. Jacqueline Lauren Snyder, Apr. 24, 1976; 1 child, Lauren Elizabeth. BA, U. Okla., 1973, MA, 1976, JD, 1980. Bar: Okla. 1981, U.S. Ct. Mil. Appeals 1981, U.S. Dist. Ct. (we. dist.) Okla. 1982, S.C. 1983, U.S. Ct. Appeals (10th cir.) 1983, U.S. Dist. Ct. S.C. 1984, U.S. Ct. Appeals (4th cir.) 1984, U.S. Supreme Ct. 1995. Assoc. Finkel, Georgaklis et al, Columbia, SC, 1984-86; ptnr. Mumford, Wishart & Martin, North Myrtle Beach, SC, 1986-87, Gertz, Kastanes, Moore & Martin, North Myrtle Beach, SC, 1987-91; with Office of Hearings and Appeals Social Security Adminstrn., Columbia, SC, 1991—. Lt. col. ret. U.S. Army, 1967-70, Vietnam, 1975-78, with Res. 1970-74, 78-81, 84-97, Desert Storm, JAGC, 1981-84. Mem. NRA, Masons, Shriners, Elks, Phi Delta Phi, Pi Kappa Alpha. Republican. Episcopalian. Avocations: singing, shooting. Office: Office of Hearing and Appeals 1927 Thurmond Mall Blvd Ste 200 Columbia SC 29201-2375

**MARTIN, JOHN THOMAS,** physician, author, educator; b. Cleve., June 8, 1924; s. Clarence Henry and Clara May (Feeney) M.; m. Marion Elizabeth George, Feb. 18, 1946; children: Thomas R., David B., Richard G., Janet E., Patricia L., Robert W. MD, U. Cin., 1948. Commd. 1st lt. USAF, 1949, advanced through grades to maj., 1953; instr. in anesthesiology Lackland AFB Hosp., San Antonio, 1953-55; asst. chief USAF Sch. Anesthesiology, Lackland AFB, 1955-57; attending anesthesiologist Baylor U. Hosp., Dallas, 1957-58; cons. dept. anesthesiology Mayo Clinic, Rochester, Minn., 1958-72, head Meth sect. anesthesiology, 1966-72; assoc. clin. prof. anesthesiology, 1968-72; chmn. dept. anesthesiology Ochsner Med. Ctr., New Orleans, 1972-74; clin. assoc. prof. anesthesiology Tulane U. Sch. Medicine, New Orleans, 1972-74; prof. anesthesiology Med. Coll. Ohio, Toledo, 1974-90, chmn. dept. anesthesiology, 1980-89, emeritus prof. anesthesiology, 1990—. Editor, author: Positioning Patients Anesthesia/Surgery, 1978, 2d edit., 1987, 3d edit., 1997; editor ASA Handbook of Hosp. Facilities for Anesthesia, 1972, 2d edit., 1974; contbr. articles to profl. jours. Chmn. conductor selection com. Rochester Symphony Orch., 1963-66; pres. Rochester Civic Music, 1965. Mem. Internat. Anesthesia Rsch. Soc. (chmn. 1979-81, trustee 1965-90), Minn. Soc. Anesthesiologists (pres. 1966-67), Ohio Soc. Anesthesiologists (pres. 1988-89), Am. Med. Writers Assn. (pres. Minn. chpt. 1970-71), Assoc. Physicians Med. Coll. Ohio (bd. dirs. 1974-89), Am. Soc. Anesthesiology, Sigma Xi, Alpha Omega Alpha, Sigma Chi, Phi Chi. Republican. Avocations: medical writing, computers, music, fishing. Office: Med Coll of Ohio PO Box 10008 Toledo OH 43699-0008 Home: 4306 Todd Dr Sylvania OH 43560-3297

**MARTIN, JOHN WILLIAM, JR.,** retired lawyer, automotive executive; b. Evergreen Park, Ill., Sept. 1, 1936; s. John William and Frances (Hayes) M.; m. Joanne Cross, July 2, 1966; children: Amanda Hayes, Bartholomew McGuire. AB in History, DePaul U., 1958, JD, 1961. Bar: Ill. 1961, D.C. 1962, N.Y. 1964, Mich. 1970. Antitrust trial atty. Dept. Justice, Washington, 1961-62; assoc. Donovan, Leisure, Newton & Irvine, N.Y.C., 1962-70; sr. atty. Ford Motor Co., Dearborn, Mich., 1970-72, assoc. counsel, 1972-74, counsel, 1974-76, asst. gen. counsel, 1976-77, assoc. gen. counsel, 1977-89, v.p., gen. counsel, 1989-99; ret., 1999. Contbr. articles to profl. jours. Trustee DePaul U., 1998—; bd. dirs. Ctr. Social Gerontology, Inc., Nat. Women's Law Ctr., Friends of Legal Svcs. Corp. Mem.: Am. Law Inst., Assn. Gen. Counsel, Little Traverse Yacht Club (commodore). Republican. Roman Catholic. Personal E-mail: jwmartinjrsail@netscape.net.

**MARTIN, JOHNNY BENJAMIN,** accountant; b. Gainesville, Ga., June 9, 1947; s. John Daniel and Helen Amanda (Meeks) M.; m. Mary Sue West, June 8, 1969; 1 child, Tammye Michelle. BBA, U. Ga., Athens, 1969, MA, 1971. CPA, Ga. Tchr. high sch. Hall County Sch. Systems, Gainesville, 1969-70; instr. acctg. Austin Peay State U., Clarksville, Tenn., 1972-76; instr. bus. Gainesville Jr. Coll., 1976-77; cont. Home Fed. Savs. and Loan, Gainesville, 1977-83; ptnr. Kendrick & Jessup, CPA's, Gainesville, 1983-92; pvt. practice Gainesville, 1992—. Mem. AICPA, Ga. Soc. CPAs, Civitan (bd. dirs., treas. 1981-82, treas. 1986-87), Phi Kappa Phi, Beta Gamma Sigma. Democrat. Baptist. Home: 3751 Robinson Dr Oakwood GA 30566-3408 Personal E-mail: johnnybmartin@netzero.com.

**MARTIN, JOSEPH BOYD,** dean, neurologist, educator; b. Bassano, Alta., Can., Oct. 20, 1938; s. Joseph Bruce and Ruth Elizabeth (Ramer) Martin; m. Rachel Ann Wenger, June 18, 1960; children: Bradley, Melanie, Douglas, Neil. BSc, Eastern Mennonite Coll., Harrisonburg, Va., 1959; MD, U. Alta., 1962; PhD in Anatomy, U. Rochester, NY, 1971; MA (hon.), Harvard U., 1978; ScD (hon.), McGill U., 1994, U. Rochester, 1996, U. Wis., 1997, U. Alta., 1998. Resident in internal medicine Univ. Hosp., Edmonton, Alta. 1962—64; resident in neurology, fellow in neuropathology Case-Western Res. U., Cleveland, Ohio, 1964—67; rsch. fellow U. Rochester, NY, 1967—70; mem. faculty McGill U. Faculty Medicine, Montreal, Canada, 1970—78, chair, dept. neurology and neurosurgery, 1977—78; prof. medicine and neurology, neurologist-in-chief Montreal Neurol. Inst., 1976—78; Bullard prof. neurology, chief dept. neurology svc. Mass. Gen. Hosp., Boston, 1978—89; Julieanne Dorn prof. neurology Harvard U. Med. Sch., 1984; dean Sch. Medicine U. Calif., San Francisco, 1989—93; chancellor U. Calif., San Francisco, 1993—97; dean faculty medicine Harvard U., Boston, 1997—. Mem. med. adv. bd. Gairdner Found., Toronto, 1978—83, 1997—2005; adv. coun. neurol. disorders program Nat. Inst. Neurol., Communicative Disorders and Stroke, 1979—82; mem. scientific adv. bd. Encyclopedia of Neuroscience, 1993—, Alzheimer Rsch. Forum, 1998—; internat. adv. bd. Neuroscience, Neurology & Psychaitry, 1993—; bd. dir. Baxter, 2002—, Cytyc Corp., Scientific Learning Corp; chmn. bd. dirs. New England Healthcare Inst., 2006—. Co-author: Clinical Neuroendocrinology, 1977, The Hypothalamus, 1978, Clinical Neuroendocrinology: A Pathophysiological Approach, 1979, Neurosecretion and Brain Peptides: Implications for Brain Functions and Neurological Disease, 1981, Brain Peptides, 1983; editor: Harrison's Principles of Internal Medicine, 1980—99; mem. editl. bd. Human Brain Mapping, 1993—, Neuroreport, 1993—99, The Neuroscientist, 1994—, New England Journal of Medicine, Annual of Neurology and Science, mem. search com. for editor Archives of Neurology, 1995—; contbr. articles to profl. jours. Recipient Moshier Meml. gold medal, U. Alta. Faculty Medicine, 1962, John W. Scott gold med. award, 1962, Abraham Flexner award, AAMC, 1999; scholar, Med. Rsch. Coun. Can., 1970—75. Fellow: Am. Acad. Arts and Scis.; mem.: NAS, Inst. of Medicine, Assn. Am. Physicians, Soc. Neurosci., Royal Coll. Phys. and Surg. Can., Am. Physiol. Soc. (Bowditch lectr. 1978), Am. Neurol. Assn. (pres. 1990). Office: Dean Faculty Medicine Harvard U 25 Shattuck St Boston MA 02115-6027 Office Phone: 617-432-1501. E-mail: joseph_martin@hms.harvard.edu.

**MARTIN, J(OSEPH) PATRICK,** lawyer, judge; b. Detroit, Apr. 19, 1938; s. Joseph A. and Kathleen G. (Rich) Martin; m. Denise Taylor, June 27, 1964; children: Timothy J., Julie D. AB magna cum laude, U. Notre Dame, 1960; JD with distinction, U. Mich., 1963; postgrad., London Sch. Econs., 1964. Bar: Mich. 1963, U.S. Dist. Ct. (ea. dist.) Mich. 1963, U.S. Ct. Appeals (6th cir.) 1967, U.S. Supreme Ct. 1979, U.S. Dist. Ct. (we. dist.) Mich. 1981, U.S. Ct. Fed. Claims 1990. Spl. asst. to gen. counsel Ford Motor Co., Dearborn, Mich., 1962; assoc. Dykema, Wheat, Spencer et al, Detroit, 1963-66; from assoc. to ptnr. Poole Littell Sutherland, Detroit, 1966-76; sr. atty., ptnr., shareholder Butzel Long, Detroit and Birmingham, Mich., 1976-94; sr. atty., shareholder Vlcko, Lane, Payne & Broder PC, Bingham Farms, Mich., 1994-96; sr. atty. Gourwitz and Barr PC, Southfield, Mich., 1996-99; pvt. practice, 2000—; adminstrv. law judge State of Mich., 2002—. Arbitrator Am. Arbitration Assn., Southfield, Mich., 1968—, Nat. Assn. Security Dealers, 1988—, NY Stock Exch., 1991—, Constrn. Arbitration Svcs., Mt. Clemens, 2005—; adj. prof. remedies and alternative dispute resolution U. Detroit Law Sch., 1989—, Wayne State U. Law Sch., 1996—, Cooley Law Sch., 2001—; state ct. administry. office approved mediator all Mich. cts. under new ADR rules; case evaluator, mediator, discovery master Oak County Cir. Ct., Pontiac, Mich., 1985—; mediator Lex Mundi, Coll. Mediators, 1992—; case evaluator, mediator Mediation Tribunal Assn. Wayne County Cir. Ct., 1992—, Oakland County Dist. Cts., 1998—, Wayne County Dist. Cts., 1998—, Wayne County Probate Ct., 2002—; moderator Mich. State Ct. Appeals, 1995—. Author, editor: Laches-Oak County Bar Assn. Legal Jour., 1984, 1992, 1996, Real Property Rev., 1989—90, Mich. Law Weekly, 1990, ADR Newsletter, 2000. Scholar, Cook Found., Ford Found., London, 1963—64. Mem.: ABA, Oakland County Bar Found., Mich. State Bar Found., Oakland County Bar Assn. (chair fed. ct. com., chair Mich. dist. ct. com., mem. ADR com., bd. dirs.), State Bar Mich. (chair alternative dispute sect.). Roman Catholic. Avocations: gardening, golf, walking. Home and Office: 1663 Hoit Tower Dr Bloomfield Hills MI 48302-2630 Fax: 248-932-0368. Personal E-mail: jpatrickmartin@comcast.net.

**MARTIN, JOSEPH ROBERT,** retired corporate financial executive; b. Phila., Dec. 9, 1947; s. Robert and Elva Ruth (Griffen) M.; m. Catherine Marie Kelly, Sept. 5, 1970; children: Joseph Robert Jr., Jennifer H., Patrick F., Kathleen K., Mariah E. BS, Embry Riddle U., 1974; MBA, U. Maine, 1976. Sr. corp. fin. analyst Keyes Fibre Co., Waterville, Maine, 1976—80; mgr. fin. analysis and planning Schlumberger, Fairchild, South Portland, Maine, 1980—83; divsn. contr. Schlumberger, Factron, Clifton Park, NY, 1983—84; corp. contr. VTC, Inc., Bloomington, Minn., 1984—87, v.p. fin., CFO, 1987—88, sr. v.p., CFO, 1989—90; dir. fin. Nat. Semiconductor, South Portland, Maine, 1990—91; v.p. fin. std. products group Nat. Semicondr., Santa Clara, Calif., 1991—95; v.p. fin. worldwide ops. Nat. Semiconductor, Santa Clara, Calif., 1995—96; exec. v.p., CFO, vice chmn. bd. dirs. Fairchild Semiconductor, South Portland, Maine, 1996—2006; ret., 2006. Bd. visitors U. So. Maine, 1998—2001; pres.'s bd. advisors Embry-Riddle Aero. U., 2000—04, trustee, 2004—; bd. dirs. Brooks Automation LLC, Chelmsford, Mass.; bd. dirs. Synqor, Inc., Hudston, Mass., Soitec, Inc., Bernin, France. Served to capt. U.S. Army, 1967-72, Vietnam. Decorated D.F.C., Purple Heart, Bronze Star medal, Air medal, Vietnamese Cross of Gallantry, Army Commendation medal. Home: 17 Stornoway Rd Cumberland Foreside ME 04110 Office: JR Martin Co 14 Lantern Ln Cumberland Foreside ME 04110 Office Phone: 207-781-2825. E-mail: joe@jrmandco.com.

**MARTIN, JOSEPH VINSON,** neuroscientist, educator; b. Boston, Sept. 17, 1952; s. James Cullen and Mary Louise (Echols) M.; m. Jean Ann Rusteberg, Apr. 27, 1989; 1 child, Lara Jean. BA, Northwestern U., Evanston, Ill., 1973; PhD, U. So. Calif., 1987. Cert. Am. Nurses creditialing Ctr. Rsch. asst. L.A. Harbor Commn., 1978—79; chemist NIMH, Bethesda, Md., 1982—87; postdoctoral rsch. assoc. SUNY, Stony Brook, 1987—88, rsch. instr.; asst. prof. Biology Dept., Rutgers U., Camden, NJ, 1989—95, assoc. prof., 1995—2004, prof., 2004—. Proposal reviewer NSF; manuscript reviewer European Jour. Pharmacology, Pharmacology Biochemistry and Behavior, Sleep; lectr. in field. Contbr. articles to profl. jours. Recipient Nat. Merit Letter of Commendation, 1969, Editor's Choice award, Internat. Soc. Poetry; NSF Undergrad. Summer Rsch. fellowship, 1972, NIMH Predoctoral Rsch. fellowship, 1977-78, Rutgers U. Acad. Svc. Increment award, 1991, 93, 98, 2000-06, NSF grantee, 1994-97, 98-2001, 2002-04, 2004—; Dean's Citation, UMDNJ. Mem. AAAS, Assn. Profl. Sleep Socs., Internat. Brain Rsch. Orgn., N.J. Acad. Sci., N.Y. Acad. Scis., Sleep Rsch. Soc., Soc. for Neuroscience. E-mail: jomartin@camden.rutgers.edu.

**MARTIN, JUDITH MORAN,** lawyer; b. Ann Arbor, Mich., Feb. 10, 1943; d. D. Lawrence and Donna E. (Webb) Moran; children: Laura M. Buford, Paul M. Martin, A. Lindsay McGill. BA, U. Mich., Ann Arbor, 1963; postgrad., U. Jean Moulin, Du Droit, Lyon, France, 1981; JD, U. Minn., Mpls., 1982. Bar: Minn. 1982, Fla. 1991, Colo. 1994, U.S. Tax Ct. 1989, U.S. Dist. Ct. Minn. 1984, U.S. Ct. Appeals (8th cir.) 1989. Tax supr., dir. fin. planning, asst. nat. dir. Coopers & Lybrand, Mpls., 1981-84; dir. fin. planning Investors Diversified Services subs. Am. Express, Mpls. and N.Y.C., 1984-85; sr. tax mgr., dir. fin. planning KPMG Peat Marwick Main & Co., Mpls., 1985-89; prin. Gray Plant Mooty Mooty & Bennett, P.A., Mpls., 2000—02; owner, mng. ptnr. Martin & Assoc., P.A, Mpls., 1989—2000, 2002—. Faculty Minn. CLE, 1994; adv. bd. Nicollet/Ebenezer, 1996; instr. continuing profl. edn., Minn. Soc. CPAs, 1982-86, continuing legal edn., 1983-84, individual, trust and estate provisions Tax Reform Act 1986, continuing legal edn. estate planning 1994. Mem. M. C. of C. Campaign, Downtown Coun. Campaign, Mpls., 1982-84, Metro Tax Planning Group, 1984-86, Mpls. Estate Planning Coun., 1985-99, Planned Giving Coun.; class chmn. fundraising campaign U. Minn. Law Sch., Mpls., 1985, 98; bd. dirs. Ensemble Capriccio, chmn.

fundraising com., 1998-2002; usher Christ Presbyn. Ch., Edina, Minn., 1983—; mem. adv. coun. on planned giving ARC. Mem. ABA (task force on legal fin. planning), Minn. Bar Assn., Hennepin County Bar Assn., Fla. Bar Assn., Colo. Bar Assn., Minn. Planned Giving Coun., Am. Assn. Ind. Investors (speaker), Am. Soc. CLUs, Minn. Soc. CLUs, Minn. Women Lawyers, Fla. Women Lawyers, Lex Alumnae, U. Mich. Alumni Assn. (coun. govs. 1989-2003, scholarship chmn.), U. Minn. Alumni Club (bd. dirs. 1996, coun. govs. 1988-96, pres., treas. mem. com.), Interlachen Club, Lafayette Club, Montana Club, U. Minn. Alumni Assn. (mem. univ. issues com., nat. bd. dirs. 1996-99), The Woman's Club Mpls. Home: 5232 West 70th St Edina MN 55439 Office: Martin & Assoc PA 3800 American Blvd W #270 Minneapolis MN 55431 Office Phone: 952-857-2424. Business E-mail: judith@martinandassociates.com.

**MARTIN, JUDITH SYLVIA,** journalist; b. Washington, Sept. 13, 1938; d. Jacob and Helen (Aronson) Perlman; m. Robert Martin, Jan. 30, 1960; children: Nicholas Ivor, Jacobina Helen. BA, Wellesley Coll., 1959; DHL (hon.), York Coll., 1985, Adelphi U., 1991. Reporter-critic, columnist Washington Post, 1960—83; syndicated columnist United Feature Syndicate, N.Y.C., 1978—; columnist Microsoft, 1996—. Critic-at-large Vanity Fair, 1983—84. Author: The Name on the White House Floor, 1972, Miss Manners' Guide to Excruciatingly Correct Behavior, 1982, Gilbert, 1982, Miss Manners' Guide to Rearing Perfect Children, 1984, Common Courtesy, 1985, Style and Substance, 1986, Miss Manners' Guide for the Turn-of-the-Millennium, 1989, Miss Manners on (Painfully Proper) Weddings, 1996, Miss Manners Rescues Civilization, 1996, Miss Manners' Basic Training: Communications, 1997, Miss Manners' Basic Training: Eating, 1997, Miss Manners' Basic Training: The Right Thing to Say, 1998, Miss Manners' Guide to Domestic Tranquility, 1999, Star-Spangled Manners, 2002, Miss Manners Guide to Excruciatingly Correct Behavior (Freshly Updated), 2005, No Vulgar Hotel, The Desire and Pursuit of Venice, 2007. Bd. dirs. Friends of Scuola San Rocco. Recipient Nat. Humanities medal, 2005. Mem. Cosmos Club, Literary Soc. Office: United Feature Syndicate 200 Madison Ave Fl 4 New York NY 10016-3911 Business E-mail: MissManners@unitedmedia.com.

**MARTIN, JULIE A.,** retired insurance company executive; BS, Tex. Tech. U.; MS in Fgn. Svc., George Washington U., MBA in Fin. Dir. investment missions program Overseas Pvt. Investment Corp., investment ins. officer, regional mgr. ins. dept., mng. dir. L.Am. and Caribbean ins. dept., mng. dir. policy and underwriting, chief underwriter polit. risk ins. dept., dep. v.p. ins., v.p. ins., 1997—. Office: Overseas Pvt Investment Corp 1100 New York Ave NW Washington DC 20527-0001

**MARTIN, JUNE JOHNSON CALDWELL,** journalist; b. Toledo, Oct. 06; d. John Franklin and Eunice Imogene (Fish) Johnson; m. Erskine Caldwell, Dec. 21, 1942 (div. Dec. 1955); 1 child, Jay Erskine; m. Keith Martin, May 5, 1964. AA, Phoenix Jr. Coll., 1941; BA, U. Ariz., 1943, 59; postgrad., Ariz. State U., 1939, 40. Freelance writer, 1944—; columnist Ariz. Daily Star, Tucson, 1956-59, 70-94, book reviewer, 1970-94, co-founder Ann. Book and Author Event; editor Ariz. Alumnus mag., Tucson, 1959-70; ind. book reviewer, audio tape columnist Tucson, 1994—; coord. S.W. Books of Yr. sponsored by Tucson Pima Pub. Libr., Ariz., 2000—. Panelist, co-producer TV news show Tucson Press Club, 1954-55, pres., 1958. Contbg. author: Rocky Mountain Cities, 1949; contbr. articles to World Book Ency., and various mags. Mem. Tucson CD Com., 1961; vol. campaigns of Samuel Goddard, U.S. Rep. Morris Udall, U.S. amb. and Ariz. gov. Raul Castro. Recipient award Nat. Headliners Club, 1959, Ariz. Press Club award, 1957-59, 96, Am. Alumni Coun., 1966, 70. Mem. Nat. Book Critics Circle, Ariz. Press Women, Jr. League of Tucson, Tucson Urban League, PEN U.S.A. West, Planned Parenthood So. Ariz., Tucson Press, Pi Beta Phi. Democrat. Methodist. Home: Desert Foothills Sta PO Box 65388 Tucson AZ 85728-5388

**MARTIN, KAREN SIEBENTHAL,** community health nurse; b. Bloomington, Ill., Sept. 15, 1942; d. Arthur A. and Evelyn R. (Ehresman) Siebenthal; m. Stanley A. Martin. Mar. 31, 1963; children: Steven, Kathleen, Kelly. Diploma, Meth. Hosp. Sch. Nursing, 1963; BSN, U. Iowa Coll. Nursing, 1969; MS in Nursing, U. Nebr. Coll. Nursing, 1977. Staff nurse, dir. nursing Champaign (Ill.)-Urbana Pub. Health, 1966-67, 69-73; dir. rsch. Vis. Nurse Assn. Omaha, 1978—93. Prin. investigator Nat. Ctr. for Nursing Rsch., 1989—93; health care cons., 1993—; adj. prof. Midland Luth. Coll. Driven Nursing, Fremont, Nebr., 1994—; vis. prof. Japan and Taiwan, 1998, U.K., 2000—01, Ireland, 2001; workshops and cons. Europe, 1992—93, Canada, 1997, New Zealand, 2000, Austria, 02, Slovenia, 02, Wales, 03, Canada, 03, England, 04, Taiwan, 06, Republic of Korea, 06; co-chair Omaha Sys. Internat. Conf., St. Paul, 2001, Milw., 03, Minn., 05; spkr. in field; bank of nurse experts Internat. Coun. Nurses, 2002. Author: 5 books, 1 translated into Japanese; editor: Home Health Focus, 1994—2000; mem. editl. adv. bd.: Pub. Health Nursing, 1996—, mem. editl. bd.: Outcomes Mgmt. for Nursing, 1997—2003, Home Care Provider, 1996—2001, bd. of review: Nursing Outlook, 1990—; contbr. articles to Australian, Japanese and Dutch profl. jours. Recipient Alumnus of Yr. award Meth. Med. Ctr. of Cen. Ill. Sch. Nursing, Peoria, Ill., 1995; named Disting. Alumus, U. Iowa Coll. Nursing, Iowa City, 2006. Mem.: Am. Acad. Nursing (expert panel on electronic networks 1995—97, expert panel on informatics 2002—), APHA, ANA (Congress of Nursing Practice 1994—98, dist. bd. dirs. 1999—2001), Nat. Assn. County and City Health Officials, Am. Med. Informatics Assn., Internat. Coun. Nurses (internat. classification of nursing practice adv. com. 1994—), Midwest Nursing Rsch. Soc., N.Am. Nursing Diagnosis Assn., Sigma Theta Tau.

**MARTIN, KATE ABBOTT,** lawyer; b. Pasadena, Calif., Mar. 11, 1952; BA, Pomona Coll., 1973; JD, U. Va., 1977. Bar: D.C. 1978, U.S. Ct. Appeals (D.C. cir.) 1979, U.S. Supreme Ct. 1989. Assoc. Nussbaum, Owen & Webster, Washington, 1977-83, prin., 1983-88; dir. Nat. Security Litigation Project ACLU, Washington, 1988-92, dir. Ctr. for Nat. Security Studies, 1992—. Office: Gelman Libr 2130 H St NW Ste 701 Washington DC 20037-2521

**MARTIN, KATHLEEN SUZANNE,** librarian; b. San Diego, Nov. 9, 1950; d. Theodore Finley and Betty (Balton) M.; m. William Scherr Renninger; children: Elizabeth Martin, Theodore Renninger, Margaret Renninger. AB, San Diego State U., 1973; MLS, UCLA, 1978. Libr. Ginsburg, Feldman & Bress, Washington, 1980-84, Cohen & Uretz, Washington, 1984-85, Davis, Polk & Wardwell, Washington, 1985-94; head libr. Morgan, Lewis & Bockius LLP, Washington, 1994—2000; dir. librs. McKenna Long & Aldridge LLP, Washington, 2005—. Editor: (newsletter) Law Library Lights, 1985-86; contbr. articles to jours. Mem. Spl. Librs. Assn., Am. Assn. Law Librs. (bd. dirs.), Law Librs. Soc. Washington (rec. sec. 1987-89, pres. 1990-91). Office: McKenna Long & Aldridge LLP 1900 K St NW Washington DC 20006 E-mail: kmartin@mckennalong.com.

**MARTIN, KEITH,** lawyer; b. Mpls., May 5, 1953; s. L. John and Lois Ann (Henze) M. BA, Wesleyan U., 1974; JD, George Washington U., 1977; MSc, London Sch. Economics, 1978. Bar: DC 1978, NY 1985. Legis. asst. to Sen. Henry M. Jackson, Washington, 1974-77; legis. counsel to Sen. Daniel Patrick Moynihan, 1979-82; ptnr. Chadbourne & Parke LLP, Washington, 1983—, mng. ptnr., 1989-93. Democrat. Office: Chadbourne & Parke LLP 1200 New Hampshire Ave NW Washington DC 20036 Office Phone: 202-974-5674. E-mail: kmartin@chadbourne.com.

**MARTIN, KENNETH J.,** pharmaceutical executive; BA magna cum laude, Hofstra U. CPA. Audit mgr. Arthur Andersen LLP; various positions including asst. dir. corp. compliance, asst. v.p., dir. compliance and asst. comptroller Wyeth (then Am. Home Products), 1984—95; pres. Am. Home Foods, 1995-97, Whitehall-Robins Healthcare, 1997—98; sr. v.p., CFO Wyeth-Ayerst Pharmaceuticals, 1998—2000, Wyeth, 2000—, exec. v.p., CFO, 2002—06, vice chmn., CFO, 2006—. Office: Wyeth Corp 5 Giralda Farms Madison NJ 07940*

**MARTIN, KENYON,** professional basketball player; b. Saginaw, Mich., Dec. 30, 1977; BA in Criminal Justice, U. Cin. Player N.J. Nets, 2000—04, Denver Nuggets, 2004—. Player U.S. Nat. Sr. Team, 2003. Named Nat. Player of Yr., AP, 2000; named to NBA All-Rookie First Team, 2001, NBA All-Star Game, 2004. Office: c/o Denver Nuggets 1000 Chopper Cir Denver CO 80204

**MARTIN, KEVIN J.,** federal agency administrator; b. Charlotte, NC, 1966; m. Catherine Jurgensmeyer Martin. BA, U. N.C., Chapel Hill; M Pub. Policy, Duke U.; JD, Harvard U. Bar: Fla., D.C. Law clk. to Hon. William M. Hoeveler U.S. Dist. Ct., Miami; assoc. Wileu, Rein & Fielding, Washington; with Office Coun. Counsel; legal advisor to commr. Harold Furchtgott-Roth FCC, 1997—99; deputy gen. counsel Bush Campaign, 1999—2000; with transition team Bush-Cheney; spl. asst. to the Pres. for econ. policy The White House, Washington, 2000—01; commr. FCC, 2001—, chmn., 2005—. Named one of Top 40 Lawyers Under 40, Nat. Law Jour., 2005. Mem.: D.C. Bar Assn., Fla. Bar Assn., Fed. Comm. Bar Assn. Republican. Office: FCC 445 12th St SW Rm 8B201 Washington DC 20554 Fax: 202-418-0982.

**MARTIN, KEVIN JOHN,** nephrologist, educator; b. Dublin, Jan. 18, 1948; came to U.S., 1973; s. John Martin and Maura Martin; m. Grania E. O'Connor, Nov. 16, 1972; children: Alan, John, Ciara, Audrey. MB BCh, Univ. Coll. Dublin, 1971. Diplomate Am. Bd. Internal Medicine, Am. Bd. Nephrology. Intern St. Vincent's Hosp., Dublin, 1971-72, resident, 1972-73, Barnes Hosp., St. Louis, 1973-74, fellow, 1974-77; asst. prof. Washington U., St. Louis, 1977-84, assoc. prof., 1984-89; prof. dir. div nephrology St. Louis U., 1989—. Contbr. numerous articles to med. jours. Office: Saint Louis Univ Med Ctr 3635 Vista Ave Saint Louis MO 63110-2539

**MARTIN, LAURA KEIDAN,** lawyer; b. Detroit, Oct. 8, 1964; BA, U. Mich., 1986; JD, Harvard U., 1989. Bar: Ill. 1989. Ptnr. Katten Muchin Rosenman LLP, Chgo. Mem.: ABA, Nat. Health Lawyers Assn., Ill. Assn. Healthcare Attys. (bd. dirs., pres.), Chgo. Bar Assn. (chair antitrust law com. 2004—05). Office: Katten Muchin Rosenman LLP 525 W Monroe St Chicago IL 60661 Office Fax: 312-902-5487, 312-577-8951. E-mail: laura.martin@kattenlaw.com.

**MARTIN, LAURABELLE,** property manager; b. Jackson County, Minn., Nov. 3, 1915; d. Eugene Wellington and Mary Christina (Hansen) M. BS, Mankato State U., 1968. Tchr. rural schs., Renville County, Minn., 1936-41, 45-50, Wabasso (Minn.) Pub. Sch., 1963-81; pres. Renville Farms and Feed Lots, 1982-86. Author: Hist. Biography of Joseph Renville, 1996; poet: Nat. Libr. Poetry (Silver Cup award, 2003). Pres. Wabasso (Minn.) Edn. Assn., 1974-75, publicity chmn., 1968-74; sec. and publicity agt. Hist. Renville Preservation Com., 1978-86; publicity chmn., sec. Town and Country Boosters, Renville, 1982-83. Recipient Outstanding Achievement in Poetry Award, Internat. Soc. Poets. Mem. Genealogy Soc. Renville County, Am. Legion Aux. Democrat. Lutheran. Avocations: antique furniture, travel, sewing, poetry. Home and Office: 334 NW 1201st Rd Holden MO 64040-9378

**MARTIN, LELAND MORRIS (PAPPY MARTIN),** historian, educator; b. Patrick Springs, Va., Aug. 8, 1930; s. Rufus Wesley and Mary Hilda (Biggs) M.; m. Mildred Greer, May 12, 1956; children: Lee Ann Geneve, Mitzi Jo. AB, Berea Coll., 1953; MS, U. Tenn., 1954; grad., Air War Coll., Maxwelll AFB, Ala., 1978; MA in History, U Tex. Pan-Am., 1993; cert. machinist, Tex. State Tech. Coll., 1997, AAS in Machining Technology-Tool and Die Making, 1999. Enlisted USAF, 1954, advanced through grades to col., 1977; comdr. RAF, Greenham Common, Welford, 1974-76; comdt., comdr. Mil. Airlift Command Noncommissioned Officers Acad., McGuire AFB, NJ, 1976-79; vice comdr., comdr. RAF Mildenhall and RAF Chicksands, England, 1979-83; chief of staff 21st Air Force, McGuire AFB, 1983-84; pres. Air Force Phys. Evaluation Bd., Randolph AFB, NJ, 1984-86; ret., 1986; dep. exec. dir. Confederate Air Force, Harlingen, Tex., 1986-88; exec. dir. Am. Airpower Heritage Found., Harlingen, 1986-88; tchg. asst., lectr. in history U. Tex. Pan Am., Edinburg, 1989-93; adj. prof. history Tex. State Tech. Coll., Harlingen, 1994—2001. Co-chair (with Sir Douglas Bader) 1976 Internat. Air Tatoo at RAF Greenham Common; chair Air Fete 80 and 81, RAF Mildenhall, Eng. Co-editor: History of Military Assistance Command, Vietnam, 1970. Decorated Legion of Merit with two oak leaf clusters, Bronze Star; Cross of Gallantry (Vietnam); recipient Amb.'s award Ct. St. James, London, 1974, 83. Mem. Air Force Assn., Am. Watchmakers and Clockmakers Inst., Nat. Assn. Watch and Clock Collectors, Brit. Officers Club Phila. (hon.), Rotary (gov. internat. dist. 5930 1995-96), Phi Alpha Theta, Phi Kappa Phi. Presbyterian. Avocations: clock repairs, photography, golf, fishing. Home: 3001 Emerald Lake Dr Harlingen TX 78550-8621

**MARTIN, LINDA GAYE,** demographer, economist; b. Paris, Ark., Dec. 17, 1947; d. Leslie Paul and Margie La Verne (Thomas) Martin. BA in Math., Harvard U., 1970; MPA, Princeton U., 1972, PhD in Econs., 1978; DHL (hon.), Marlboro Coll., 2002; D in Pub. Policy (hon.), Pardee U., 2006. Dir. mgmt. info. sc. ctrs. bur. purchased social svcs. for adults City of N.Y., 1972—74; rsch. assoc., rsch. dir. U.S. Ho. of Reps. Select Com. on Population, Washington, 1977—79; rsch. assoc. East-West Population Inst., Honolulu, 1979—89, assoc. dir., 1982—84; asst. prof. econs. U. Hawaii, Honolulu, 1979—81, assoc. prof., 1981—89, prof., 1989; dir. com. on population Nat. Acad. Scis., Washington, 1989—93; dir. domestic rsch. divsn., v.p. RAND, Santa Monica, Calif., 1993—95, v.p. for rsch. devel., 1995—99; pres. Population Coun., N.Y.C., 1999—2004; scholar in residence Inst. Medicine, 2004—. Mem. neurosci. behavior and sociology of aging rev. com. Nat. Inst. on Aging, Bethesda, 1991—95; chair panel on aging in developing countries NAS, Washington, 1987, mem. com. on population, 1993—99, mem. panel on internat. aging data, 1999—2001; mem. peer rev. oversight group NIH, 1998—2004. Editor: The ASEAN Success Story, 1987; co editor: Demographic Change in Sub-Saharan Africa, 1993, The Demography of Aging, 1994, Racial and Ethnic Differences in the Health of Older Americans, 1997; author: (monograph) The Graying of Japan, 1989; co-author: Disability in America, 2004; contbr. articles to profl. jours. Mem. adv. coun. Woodrow Wilson Sch. Pub. and Internat. Affairs, Princeton U., NJ, 2000—. Recipient Fulbright Faculty Rsch. award, Coun. for Internat. Exch. of Scholars, 1988. Mem.: AAAS (adv. coun. 2003—06, chair elect social, econ. and polit. scis. sect. 2004—), Population Assn. Am. (bd. dir. 1991—93), Internat. Union for Sci. Study Population, Gerontol. Soc. Am. Democrat. Office: Inst of Medicine 500 5th St NW Rm 863 Washington DC 20001 Home: 3419 Mansfield Rd Falls Church VA 22041

**MARTIN, LISA DEMET,** lawyer; b. Pa., 1959; BA with honors, Wellesley Coll., 1980; JD, U. Pa., 1984. Bar: Mo. 1984. Ptnr., mem. exec. com. Bryan Cave LLP, St. Louis. Durant scholar Wellesley Coll. Mem. Phi Beta Kappa. Office: Bryan Cave LLP One Metropolitan Sq, Ste 3600 211 N Broadway Saint Louis MO 63102 Office Phone: 314-259-2125. E-mail: lmartin@bryancave.com.

**MARTIN, LISA MARIE,** sociologist; d. Concetta and Donald Reid (Step-father). Student, Case Western Res. U., 1997. Rsch. asst. Case Western Res. U., Cleve., 1997—2001; mgr., biostatis. and epidemiology Inova Heart & Vascular Inst., Cardiac Surgery Rsch., Falls Church, Va., 2001—. Mem.: APHA, Am. Sociol. Assn. Avocation: animal welfare. Office: Inova Heart & Vascular Inst Cardiac Surgery Res 3300 Gallows Rd Falls Church VA 22042 Office Phone: 703-776-7071. Business E-mail: lisa.martin@inova.com.

**MARTIN, LOREN WINSTON,** allergist; b. Albertsville, Ala., Apr. 20, 1938; s. Loren G. and Byrda G. (Crotwell) M.; m. Vivian Elizabeth Sanger Martin, Dec. 29, 1960; children: Lori Ann, Karen Lynn, James Winston. BA in Chemistry, Duke U., 1959; MD, U. Tenn., 1962. Lic. physician, Ariz. Rotating internship Fitzsimons Army Hosp., Denver, 1963; med. residency Honolulu, 1964-67; med. officer U.S. Army, 1962-70; fellowship allergy U. Colo., Denver, 1970-71; pvt. practice Tucson, 1971—. Decorated Bronze Star. Fellow Am. Acad. Allergy & Immunology, Am. Coll. Allergy & Immunology; mem. Pima County Med. Soc. Republican. Office: 1661 N Swan Rd Ste 300 Tucson AZ 85712-4053 Office Phone: 520-795-1185.

**MARTIN, LYNN MORLEY,** former secretary of labor; b. Evanston, Ill., Dec. 26, 1939; d. Lawrence William and Helen Catherine (Hall) Morley; children from a previous marriage: Julia Catherine, Caroline; m. Harry D. Leinenweber, Jan. 1987; stepchildren: Jane, John, Stephen, Justin, Thomas Leinenweber. BA, U. Ill., 1960. Former tchr. pub. schs.; mem. Ill. Ho. of Reps., 1977-79, Ill. Senate, 1979-81, 97th-101st Congresses from 16th Ill. Dist., 1981-91; sec. Dept. of Labor, Washington, 1991-93; faculty Northwestern U., 1993—2000. Bd. dirs. Dreyfus Funds, Procter & Gamble Co., Constellation Energy Group; mem. Coun. Fgn. Relations, Chgo. Network. Co-chmn. Bush-Quayle Presdl. campaign, 1988. Named one of Outstanding Young Women in Am., U.S. Jaycees; named Rep. Woman of the Yr., 1989; named a Mother of the Yr., Nat. Mother's Day Com., 1992; 1st woman elected to leadership post in House of Reps., 1982. Mem. AAUW, Jr. League, Phi Beta Kappa (hon. doctorate). Republican.

**MARTIN, MALCOLM ELLIOT,** lawyer; b. Buffalo, Dec. 11, 1935; s. Carl Edward and Pearl Maude (Elliot) M.; m. Judith Hill Harley, June 27, 1964; children: Jennifer, Elizabeth, Christina, Katherine. BA, U. Mich., Ann Arbor, 1958, JD, 1962. Bar: N.Y. 1963, U.S. Ct. Appeals (2nd cir.) 1966, U.S. Supreme Ct. 1967. Assoc. Chadbourne & Parke LLP (formerly Chadbourne Parke Whiteside & Wolff), NYC, 1962-73, ptnr., Trusts, Estates & Pvt. Clients Practice Groups, 1974—. Dir., sec. Carl and Dorothy Bennett Found., Inc.; sec., counsel Copper Devel. Assn., Inc. With U.S. Army, 1958—60. Mem. ABA, NY State Bar Assn., Assn. Bar City NY, St. Andrew's Soc. NY, Met. Opera Guild, Oratamin Club (Blauvelt, NY), Nyack Boat Club, Rockefeller Ctr. Club, Copper Club (NYC). Office: Chadbourne & Parke LLP 30 Rockefeller Plz Fl 31 New York NY 10112-0129 Office Phone: 212-408-1040. Office Fax: 212-541-5369. Business E-mail: mmartin@chadbourne.com.

**MARTIN, MARCELLA EDRIC,** retired community health nurse; b. Rosedale, Miss., Jan. 25, 1930; d. Amos and Alma Allen; m. Reuben Clifton Martin, Jan. 25, 1969; children: Brunetta, Jacqueline, Cornell, Constance. Student, Marygrove Coll., Detroit, 1971; ADN, Highland Park Sch. Nursing, Mich., 1979; ThB, Cmty. Bible Coll., Detroit, 1968. Lic. LPN. Nurse VA Hosp., Ann Arbor, Mich., Crittendon Hosp., Detroit, Vis. Nurses Assn., Detroit. Instr. Charles H. Mason Bible Sch., Detroit, 1991—95; mem. C.O.G.I.C. Bus. owners Assn., 1982—. Author: Women Who Struggle, 2001; prodr.: (plays) And Didn't Those Knees Bow, 2004. Founder Prime of Life Adult Foster Care Home, 1979, Somebody's Got To Care Min., 2003; mem. Nat. Campaign Tolerance-The Wall of Tolerance, 2003; missionary over women Chs. of God in Christ, 1986—2002; vol. Redford Geriatric Home, Mich., 1999—. Named to Wall of Tolerance, New Civil Rights Meml. Ctr., Montgomery, Ala., 2003; recipient Spirit of Detroit award, City of Detroit, 1978, 2000, 2002, Disting. Citizen of Detroit award, 1980, Testimonial Resolution award, 1985. Mem.: Detroit Writers Guild. Democrat. Pentecostal Ch. Avocations: reading, writing. Home: 25332 Shiawassee Cir Apt 106 Southfield MI 48034 Personal E-mail: reumarone@comcast.net.

**MARTIN, MARCI,** writer, former advertising specialist; b. Corsicana, Tex., Oct. 20, 1927; d. Roy Rhoston McNutt and Maggie Mae Price; m. Harold Durward Martin, May 31, 1947 (dec. Dec. 15, 1998); children: Jennifer Ann Martin Svihus, Gary(dec.). Student, North Tex. State U., 1945—46, So. Meth. U., Dallas, 1946, Miracosta Coll., Oceanside, Calif., 1990—91. Bus. rep. Southwestern Bell, Dallas, 1946—55; advt. rep. Christian Sci. Monitor, San Diego, 1982—89. Author: Go To Hell and Make a U-Turn, 1996, rev. edit., 2000, Secrets and Lies, 2000, License To Steal, 2001, (short stories, essays, articles) The Muse on My Shoulder, 2001, Tangled Webs, 2004, Out of Bounds - dead Dots, 2005, Dirty Genes, 2006; co-editor: A Way With Murder, An Anthology by Arizona Mystery Writers, 2004; editor, ghost writer: Much Ado About Something, 2003. Vol. prison chaplain, San Diego, 1989—95. Recipient 1st pl. for poetry, Nat. U., 1991, 3d pl. for essay, Writer's Jour., 2d pl. and hon. mention, Ann. Showcase Writers Club, 1994, Tangled Webs 2d pl., Jim Woods prize, 2002. Mem.: Sisters in Crime, Ariz. Mystery Writers (coord./pres. 1998—), Soc. Southwestern Authors (mentor 1998—), Mystery Writers Am. Avocation: golf. Home: 3011 W Sawmill Spring Trail Tucson AZ 85742

**MARTIN, MARCIA GRAY,** retired architecture educator, artist, designer; b. Chgo., May 18, 1932; d. Harry Gray and Emma Bernstein; children: Elizabeth Anne, Charles Brandon. BArch, Ill. Inst. Tech., 1956; attended, De Paul Law Sch., 1957—58, U. Chgo., 1948—50; MA in Liberal Studies, North Ctrl. Coll., 1997. Freelance architect designer, Chgo., 1956—79; instr. architecture Coll. Dupage, Glen Ellyn, Ill., 1980—88, prof. architecture, 1989—2004, coord. architectural programs, 2000—04, prof. emeritis, 2004—; asst. art gallery Inspire Fine Art, Chgo., 2004—. Head traveling exhibition Coll. Dupage, 2001—; illustrator, artist Wheaton History Ctr., Ill., 1985—. Author: (books) Wheaton, USA, 1991, Architectural Drafting, 1997. Sec. Wheaton Historic Preservation Coun.; mem. City Wheaton Historic Com., Ill., 1992—93, Landmark Preservation Coun., Wheaton, 1990—2004; pres. Waterford Condominium Assn., Wheaton, 2005—; mem., bd. dirs. Dupage Art League, Wheaton, 1980—85; pres. bd. dirs. Wheaton Historic Preservation Coun.; bd. dirs. Waterford Condominium Assn., Wheaton. Recipient Wisdom & Coun. award, Wheaton Youth Outreach, 1990. Achievements include created one of the few undergraduate historic preservation education programs. Home: 455 W Front St #302 Wheaton IL 60187 E-mail: marciagraymartin@yahoo.com.

**MARTIN, MARGARET ANNE See STEELE, ANITA**

**MARTIN, MARIE ANN,** art association administrator; b. Winthrop, Mass., July 13, 1963; d. Charles and Ann Marie-Kelly Murray; m. Harold Glen Martin; children: Garrison Cash, Carson Carter, Grace Elane. AA, Nat. Pk. C.C., Hot Springs, Ark., 2005; postgrad., Henderson State U., Arkadelphia, Ark., 2005—. Banking Principles, New Eng. Banking Inst./Boston, MA, 1983; Mass Marketing New Eng. Banking Inst./Boston, MA, 1984. Founder Elberta Arts Coun. and Humanities, Nashville, Ark., 2000—; exec. dir. Fine Arts Ctr. Hot Springs, 2002—04. Music dir. Maranatha Bapt. Ch., Nashville, 1996—99. Juror/judge/curator (exhibition) Elberta Arts Juried Art Exhibit, curator (fine art exhibits) Fine Arts Center Exhibitions, Elberta Arts Center Exhibits. Mem. Literacy Coun. Howard County, Nashville, Ark., 2001—02. Recipient Svc. to Arts, Fine Arts Ctr. Hot Springs, 2004; Mid Am. Singers scholar, Nat. Pk. C.C., 2004—05, Tuition scholar, Henderson State U., 2005—. Mem.: Alpha Chi Omega. Avocations: president's list-national park comm. coll -2005, dean's list-henderson state university -2006. Home: 6207 A Gould Pl Texarkana TX 75503 Office: Elberta Arts Council & Humanities 109 S Main St Nashville AR 71901 Office Phone: 870-451-9966. E-mail: mmartinmarie@aol.com.

**MARTIN, MARILYN MANN,** retired media specialist; b. Greencastle, Ind., July 14, 1939; d. Emil Albert and Edith Costa Mann; m. Max Lee Martin; children: Michael Lee, Melanie Sue Martin Boesen. BS, Ind. State U., 1960, MS, 1970, MS, 1988. Tchr. Latin, sch. libr. Greencastle H.S., Ind., 1960; libr., media specialist Greencastle H.S., 1971—2002, ret., 2002. Mem. tech. connections com. Greencastle H.S., 1997-98; exec. bd. Stone Hills Libr. Svcs., Bloomington, Ind., 1990-96. Mem.: NEA, ASCD, Greencastle Classroom Tchrs. (scholarship chmn. 1985—2002), Assn. Ind. Media Educators (dist. advocacy chmn. 1998), Ind. Coop. Libr. Svcs., Ind. Libr. Found., Ind. Ret. Tchrs. Assn., Ret. Sr. Vol. Program, Nat. Home Gardening Club, Down-to-Earth Garden Club, Phi Kappa Phi. Avocations: gardening, reading, volunteering.

**MARTIN, MARK,** race car driver; b. Batesville, Ark., Jan. 9, 1959; m. Arlene Martin; children: Heather, Rachel, Stacy, Matthew Clyde. Profl. race car driver, 1978—; driver Winston Cup, 1981—. Named winner, ASA Championship, 1978, 1979, 1980, 1986, AC Delco 500, 1989, Pontiac 500, 1989, Pontiac Excitement 400, 1990, Tyson/Holly Farms 400, 1990, Hardee's 500, 1991, Hanes 500, 1992, Mello Yello 500, 1992, Bud 500, 1993, Montain Dew So. 500, 1993, Slick 50 500, 1993, The But at the Glen, 1993, 1994, 1995, Hooters 500, 1994, Winston 500, 1995—97, Tyson 400, 1995, VAW-GM 500, 1995, Savemart 300, 1997, MENA 400, 1997, Las Vegas 400, 1998, Tex. 500, 1998, Calif. 500, 1998, Miller Lite 400, 1997, Goody's Headache Powder 500, 1998, VAW-GM Quality 500, 1998, MBNA Gold 400, 1998, 1999, Dura-Lube/Big KMart 400, 1999, IROC Championship, 1999, Goody's Body Pain 500, 2000, Coca-Cola 600, 2002, MBNA America 400 Dover International Speedway, 2004, Calif. 200, 2006, Daytona 250, 2006. Office: Roush Racing 122 Knob Hill Rd Mooresville NC 28117-6847 also: care NASCAR 1801 W Internat Speedway Bd Daytona Beach FL 32114*

**MARTIN, MARK D.,** State Supreme Court Justice; b. Apr. 29, 1963; s. M. Dean and Ann Martin. Student, U. Dayton, 1981; BS summa cum laude, Western Carolina U., 1985; JD (hon.), U. NC, 1988; grad., Nat. Jud. Coll., 1993; LLM, U. Va., 1998. Bar: N.C., U.S. Dist. Ct. (ea. and mid. dists.) N.C., U.S. Ct. Appeals (4th cir.), U.S. Supreme Ct. Law clk. to Hon. Clyde H. Hamilton U.S Dist. Ct., Columbia, SC, 1988-90; pvt. practice McNair Law Firm, Raleigh, NC, 1990-91; legal counsel to gov. Office of Gov., Raleigh, NC, 1991-92; superior ct. judge Jud. Dist. 3A, Greenville, NC, 1992-94; judge NC Ct. Appeals, 1994-99; assoc. justice NC Supreme Ct., 1999—. Mem. legis. and law reform com. Conf. Superior Ct. Judges, 1993—94; sec. N.C. Jud. Conf., 1997—99; adj. prof. law U. N.C., Chapel Hill; adj. faculty N.C. Ctrl. U. Sch. Law; sr. lecturing fellow Duke U. Law Sch., 2005—; chair Chief Justice's Commn. Future NC Bus. Ct., 2003—05. Editor-in-chief: Jour Internat. Law and Comml. Regulation. Office coord. United Way Ann. Combined Campaign, 1991, 1992; mem. master plan adv. com. N.C. Dept. Correction, 1992; mem. N.C. Coun. Women, 1992. Recipient Order Long Leaf Pine, 1992, Disting. Alumnus award, Western Carolina U., 1995, Svc. award, City of Raleigh Cmty. Svc. Dept.; Lloyd C. Balfour fellow, N.C. Inst. Polit. Leadership fellow, 1992, Coun. State Govt. Toll fellow, 2001. Mem.: ABA (mem. editl. bd. Judges' Jour., mem. coalition justice com., mem. commn. state ct. funding, mem. John Marshall award rev. com., mem. nominating com., exec. com. appellate judges conf.), Appellate Judges Ednl. Inst. (mem. planning com. 2005), Mortar Bd., Wake County Bar Assn. (bd. dirs., C.L.E. presenter 2003—), Assn. N.C. Women Attys., N.C. Assn. Black Lawyers, N.C. Bar Assn. (mem minorities profession com. 1995—2001, mem. multidisciplinary practice task force 1999—2001, v.p. 2000—01, mem. litig. sect. coun. 2000—03, mem. strategic planning emerging trends com. 2001—, mem. program com. 2004 Brown v. Bd. Edn. 50th anniversary), Carolina Law Alumni Assn. (bd. dirs.), U. N.C. Law Davis Soc., Internat. Hon. Soc., Beta Gamma Sigma, Delta Sigma Phi (scholar 1986), Phi Kappa Phi, Alpha Lambda Delta, Omicron Delta Epsilon, Pi Gamma Mu, Phi Kappa Phi, Alpha Lambda Delta. Office: NC Supreme Ct PO Box 1841 Raleigh NC 27602-2170 Office Phone: 919-733-3714. Business E-mail: maj@sc.state.nc.us, mmartin@sc.state.nc.us.

**MARTIN, MARY-ANNE,** art gallery owner; b. Hoboken, NJ, Apr. 26, 1943; d. Thomas Philipp and Ruth (Kelley) Martin; m. Henry S. Berman, June 9, 1963 (div. 1976); 1 child, Julia Coyote. Student, Smith Coll., 1961—63; BA, Barnard Coll., 1965. Head dept. painting Sotheby Parke Bernet, N.Y.C., 1971-78; founder Latin Am. dept. Sotheby's, N.Y.C., 1977, sr. v.p., 1978-82; pres. Mary Anne Martin, Fine Art, N.Y.C., 1982—. Mem.: Art Dealers Assn. Am. (sr. v.p.). Avocations: art collecting, scuba diving. Office: 23 E 73rd St New York NY 10021-3522 Business E-mail: mail@mamfa.com.

**MARTIN, MELISSA CAROL,** radiological physicist; b. Muskogee, Okla., Feb. 7, 1951; d. Carl Leroy and Helen Shirley (Hicks) Paden; m. Donald Ray Martin, Feb. 14, 1970; 1 child, Christina Gail. BS, Okla. State U., 1971; MS, UCLA, 1975. Cert. radiol. physicist Am. Bd. Radiology, radiation oncology Am. Bd. Med. Physics. Asst. radiation physicist Hosp. of the Good Samaritan, L.A., 1975-80; radiol. physicist Meml. Med. Ctr., Long Beach, Calif., 1980-83, St. Joseph Hosp., Orange, Calif., 1983-92, Therapy Physics, Inc., Bellflower, Calif., 1993—. Cons. in field. Editor: (book) Current Regulatory Issues in Medical Physics, 1992. Fund raising campaign divsn. mgr. YMCA, Torrance, Calif., 1988-92; dir. AWANA Youth Club-Guards Group, Manhattan Beach, Calif., 1984—. Named Dir. of Symposium, Am. Coll. Med. Physics, 1992. Fellow Am. Coll. Med. Physics (chancellor western region 1992-95, treas. 2004-05), Am. Assn. Physicists in Medicine (profl. coun. 1990-95, treas. 1998-2003, bd. dirs. 1994-2003), Am. Coll. Radiology (econs. com. 1992-95, govt. rels. com. 1998—, councilor at large 2001-, common. on med. physics 2002-); mem. Calif. Med. Physics Soc. (treas. 1991-98), Am. Soc. for Therapeutic Radiology and Oncology, Health Physics Soc. (pres. So. Calif. chpt. 1992-93), Am. Brachytherapy Soc. Baptist. Avocation: christian youth group dir. Home: 507 Susana Ave Redondo Beach CA 90277-3953 Office Phone: 310-612-8127. Personal E-mail: melissamartin@compuserve.com. Business E-mail: melissa@therapyphysics.com.

**MARTIN, MICHAEL TOWNSEND,** sports association executive, marketing professional, consultant; b. NYC, Nov. 21, 1941; s. Townsend Bradley and Irene (Redmond) M.; m. Jennifer Johnston, Nov. 7, 1964 (div. Jan. 1977); children: Ryan Bradley, Christopher Townsend; m. Jean Kathleen Meyer, Mar. 1, 1980 Grad., The Choate Sch., 1960; student, Rutgers U., 1961-62. Asst. gen. mgr. N.Y. Jets Football Club, N.Y.C., 1968-74; v.p. NAMANCO Prodns., N.Y.C., 1975-76; v.p., gen. mgr. Cosmos Soccer Club, N.Y.C., 1976-77; exec. asst. Warner Communications, N.Y.C., 1978-84; owner, operator Martin Racing Stable, N.Y.C., 1983—; pres. Sports Mark, Inc., N.Y.C., 1990—2003. Bd. dirs. Mote Marine Labs., Sarasota, Fla., Animal Rescue Coalition, Coun. of Visitors, Woods Hole Marine Biol. Lab., Nat. Lighthouse Ctr. and Mus., Lemur Conservation Found., Ringling Sch. Art and Design; program com. WNET Channel 13; bd. advisors The Pennington Sch., Dir's Cir. Scripps Instn. Oceanography Mem. Athletics Congress (life, cert. official 1984—), U.S. Tennis Assn. (life), Internat. Oceanographic Found. (Miami life mem.), Fla. Thoroughbred Breeders Assn., Quogue Field Club, The Union Club. Republican. Episcopalian. Avocation: collecting inuit (eskimo) art. Home: 131 E 69th St Apt 11A New York NY 10021-5158 Office: 575 Madison Ave Ste 1006 New York NY 10022-2511 Office Phone: 212-980-9525. Personal E-mail: mmarti1237@aol.com.

**MARTIN, MURRAY D.,** manufacturing executive; Pres. Dictaphone Canada, 1987—90, Pitney Bowes copier systems, 1990—98, Pitney Bowes Internat., 1998—2001; group pres. global mailstream solutions Pitney Bowes Inc., Stamford, Conn., 2001—04, exec. v.p., 2003—04, pres., COO, 2004—. Bd. dir. Brink's Inc. Office: Pitney Bowes Inc 1 Elmcroft Rd Stamford CT 06926-0700*

**MARTIN, NOEL,** graphics designer, educator; b. Syracuse, Ohio, Apr. 19, 1922; s. Harry Ross and Lula (Van Meter) M.; m. Coletta Ruchty, Aug. 29, 1942; children: Dana, Reid Cert. in Fine Arts, Art Acad. Cin., Doctorate (hon.), 1994. Designer Cin. Art Mus., 1947-93, asst. to dir., 1947-55; freelance designer for various ednl., cultural and indsl. orgns., 1947—; instr. Art Acad. Cin., 1951-57, artist-in-residence, 1993—. Design cons. Champion Internat., 1959-82, Xomox Corp., 1961—, Federated Dept. Stores, 1962-83, Hebrew Union Coll., 1969—; designer-in-residence U. Cin., 1968-71, adj. prof., 1968-73; mem. adv. bd. Carnegie-Mellon U., R.I. Sch. Design, Cin. Symphony Orch., Am. Inst. Graphic Arts; lectr. Smithsonian Instn., Libr. of Congress, Am. Inst. Graphic Arts, Aspen Design Conf., various additional schs. and orgns. nationally. One man shows include Contemporary Arts Ctr., Cin., 1954, 71, Addison Gallery Am. Art, 1955, R.I. Sch. Design, 1955, Soc. Typographic Arts, Chgo., 1956, White Mus. of Cornell U., 1956, Cooper & Beatty, Toronto, Ont., Can., 1958, Am. Inst. Graphic Arts, 1958, Ind. U., 1958, Ohio State U., 1971; exhibited in group shows at Mus. Modern Art, N.Y.C., Library of Congress, Musee d'Art Moderne, Paris, Grafiska Inst., Stockholm, Carpenter Ctr., Cambridge, Gutenberg Mus., Mainz, U.S. info. exhbns. In Europe, South America and USSR; represented in permanent collections Mus. Modern Art, Stedelijk Mus., Amsterdam, Cin. Art Mus., Boston Mus. Fine Arts, Cin. Hist. Soc., Library of Congress; contbr. to various publs. Served to sgt. U.S. Air Force, 1942-45 Recipient Art Directors medal, Phila., 1957, Sachs award, Cin., 1973, Lifetime Achievement award Cin. Art Dirs., 1989. Office Phone: 513-731-1287.

**MARTIN, OLIVIA JEAN,** social studies educator; b. L.A., Nov. 08; d. Henry and Stella Martin. BA in Clin./Physiol. Psychology, U. So. Calif., 1990; MA in Edn. Adminstrn., Azusa Pacific U., 2005. Mgr. Eastman West, Montebello/Buena Park, Calif.; asst. mgr. Hortman Jewelers; peer coll. tutor East LA Coll., Monterey Park, Calif., 1985—86; facilitator U. So. Calif.-Biomed. Rsch. Program, L.A., 1987—91; behavioral counselor, nutritional specialist Nutri Sys., West Covina, Calif.; tchr. asst. Franklin Adult H.S., L.A.; elem. tchr. L.A. Unified Sch. Dist., 1994—2001; asst. dir. curriculum L.A. Archdiocese/San Gabriel Mission H.S., 2001—02, sci. tchr., 2000—01; mid. sch. social studies and sci. tchr. Azusa (Calif.) Unified Sch. Dist., 2002—06, dist. mgmt. trainee, 2004—06. Participant Olive Crest Cruise for Kids, L.A., 2004; hon. mem. exec. bd. Azusa PTA Coun., 2004—06; fundraiser Corvettes United Spl. Wish Found., L.A., 1999—2005. Recipient Merit award, Gov. of Calif., 1998—2000, Congl. award, Rep. Edward Roybal, L.A., 1986, Best Facilitator AP Biology award, U. So. Calif., 1989. Mem.: ASCD, NEA, Calif. Assn. Bilingual Edn. (v.p. Azusa Canyon chpt.), Nat. Coun. Social Studies, Assn. Calif. Supts. and Adminstrs., Corvettes Ltd. Club, Phi Lambda Theta. Republican. Roman Catholic. Avocations: racquetball, auto shows, auto racing. Home: PO Box 80892 San Marino CA 91118-9982

**MARTIN, PATRICK J.,** technology company executive; b. 1941; BS in math., Iona Coll.; MS in Elec. Engring., Doctorate in Elec. Engring., George Washington U.; grad. exec. edn. program, Harvard U. With US Dept. Agriculture; exec. Xerox Corp., pres. N.Am. solutions group; chmn., pres., CEO StorageTek, Louisville, Colo., 2000—. Past mem. bd. dirs. US C. of C., US/China Bus. Coun.; bd. trustees George Washington U.; adv. bd. com. George Washington U. Sch. Engring.; adv. com. Ohio State U. Fisher Sch. Bus. Recipient Jonas Bronck award, Bronx Hist. Soc., 2001, Ellis Island Medal Honor, 2003. Office: Storage Tech 1 Storage Tek Dr Louisville CO 80028

**MARTIN, PAUL,** former Prime Minister of Canada; b. Windsor, Ont., Can., Aug. 28, 1938; s. Paul Joseph and Eleanor (Adams) M.; m. Sheila Ann Cowan, Sept. 11, 1965; children: Paul William, Robert James, David Patrick. BA in Philosophy and History, U. Toronto, Can., 1962, LLB, 1965. Bar: Ont. 1966. Exec. asst. to pres. Power Corp. Can. Ltd., 1966-69, v.p., 1969-71; v.p. spl. projects Consol.-Bathurst Ltd., 1971-73; v.p. planning and devel. Power Corp., Can., 1973-74; pres. Can. S.S. Lines Ltd., Montreal, 1974-80, CEO 1976-80; pres., CEO CSL Group Inc., 1980-88; M.P. Ho. of Commons, 1988—; min. for fed. office of regional devel. Govt. of Can., Ottawa, 1993-95, min. fin., 1993—2002, prime min., 2003—06; leader Liberal Party Can., 2003—06. Co-chair Nat. Platform Com. of Liberal Party of Can. Author: Making History: The Politics of Achievement; co-author (with Chaviva Hosek): Creating Opportunity: The Liberal Plan for Canada. Former mem. C.D. Howe Inst. Policy Analysis Com., Birt, N.Am. Com., Ctr. Rsch. Action on Race Rels.; former bd. dirs. Can. Coun. Christians and Jews; founding dir. emeritus North-South Inst., Can., Coun. Native Bus.; bd. govs. Concordia U., coun., v.p., past mem. bd. advisors; inaugural chair G-20, 1999. Liberal. Avocations: sports, reading.

**MARTIN, PAUL CECIL,** physicist, researcher; b. Bklyn., Jan. 31, 1931; s. Harry and Helen (Salzberger) M.; m. Ann Wallace Bradley, Aug. 7, 1957; children: Peter, Stephanie Glennon, Daniel. AB, Harvard U., 1952, PhD, 1954. Mem. faculty Harvard U., Cambridge, Mass., 1957—, prof. physics, 1964-82, J. H. VanVleck prof. pure and applied physics, 1982—, emeritus prof. physics, 1972-75, dean divsn. engring. and applied scis., 1977-98, assoc. dean Faculty Arts and Scis., 1981-98, dean rsch. and info. tech., 1998—. Vis. prof. Ecole Normale Superieure, Paris, 1963, 66. U. Paris, Orsay, 1971; mem. materials rsch. adv. coun. NSF, 1986-89; bd. dirs. Mass. Tech. Pk. Corp., 1990—, exec. com., 1992—. Bd. editors: Jour. Math Physics, 1965-68, Annals of Physics, 1968-82, Jour. Statis. Physics, 1975-80, Proc. Nat. Acad. Scis., 2000—. Bd. dirs. Assoc. Univs. for Rsch. in Astronomy 1979-85; bd. dirs. Assoc. Univs., Inc., 1981—, exec. com., 1986-90, 92-94, chmn. bd. dirs., 1996-2000. NSF postdoctoral fellow, 1955; Sloan Found. fellow, 1959-62; Guggenheim fellow, 1966, 71 Fellow: AAAS (chair physics sect. 1986), Am. Phys. Soc. (councillor-at-large 1982—84, panel on pub. affairs 1983—86, chmn. nominating com. 1994), Am. Acad. Arts and Scis., NAS. Office: Harvard U Dept Physics Cambridge MA 02138 E-mail: martin@harvard.edu.

**MARTIN, PAUL EDWARD,** lawyer; b. Atchison, Kans., Feb. 5, 1928; s. Harres C. and Thelma F. (Wilson) M.; m. Betty Lou Crawford, Aug. 28, 1954; children: Cherry G., Paul A., Marylou. BBA, Baylor U., 1955, LLB, 1956; LLM, Harvard U., 1957. Bar: Tex. 1956, Pa. 1958. Assoc. Ballard, Spahr, Andrews & Ingersoll, Phila., 1957-58; ptnr. Fulbright & Jaworski, Houston, 1959-77; shareholder Chamberlain, Hrdlicka, White, Williams & Martin, 1977—; instr. in estate planning U. Houston. Exec. com. Met. Houston March of Dimes, 1980-82; chmn. deacons West Meml. Bapt. Ch., 1979-80; trustee Baylor U., 1970-89, Meml. Hosp. Sys., 1975—, Fgn. Mission Bd., So. Bapt. Conv.; pres. Baylor U. Devel. Coun., 1973-74. Lt. comdr. USN, 1947-53. Fellow Am. Coll. Trust and Estate Coun.; mem. ABA (sect. real property, probate and trust law and sect. taxation), State Bar Tex., Houston Bar Assn., Houston Estate and Fin. Forum (pres. 1965-66), Houston Bus. and Estate Planning Coun., Houston Club, Phi Delta Phi. Republican. Co-author: How to Live and Die with Texas Probate. Home: 126 Lakeside Dr Montgomery TX 77356 Office: Chamberlin Hrdlicka Et Al 1200 Smith St Ste 1400 Houston TX 77002-4401 Office Phone: 713-654-9637. Office Fax: 713-658-2553. Business E-Mail: paul.martin@chamberlainlaw.com.

**MARTIN, PAUL ROSS,** editor; b. Lancaster, Pa., May 14, 1932; s. Paul Rupp and Amanda (Minnich) M.; m. Julia Ibbotson, June 5, 1954 (div. Apr. 1979); children: Monica Martin Goble, Julia, Paul Jr., Barbara, Drew, Eric. BA, Dartmouth Coll., 1954. Reporter, wire editor Lancaster New Era, Lancaster Newspapers Inc., 1954-60; copyreader, makeup editor Wall St. Jour. divsn. Dow Jones & Co., N.Y.C. 1960-63, copy editor nat. news, 1963-69, editor bus. and fin. column, 1969-72, nat. copydesk chief, 1972-75, page one sr. spl. writer, 1975-90, asst. to mng. editor, 1990-93, asst. mng. editor, 1993—2002. Editor: The Possible Dream, 1978, Retirement Without Fear, 1981, Wall Street Journal Style Book, 1981, 4th edit., 1995, The Wall Street Journal Guide to Business Style and Usage, 2002; co-author, editor: American Dynasties Today, 1983. Bd. dirs. Cmty. Bd. 1, S.I., N.Y., 1976-80. Mem. N.Y. Fin. Writers Assn. (past officer). Avocations: basketball, tennis, travel. Office: Wall St Jour 200 Liberty St New York NY 10281-1003 E-mail: paul.martin-sr@wsj.com.

**MARTIN, PETER GERARD,** computer technician, consultant, secondary school educator; b. Weymouth, Mass., May 2, 1952; s. John Augustine and Jean Anita (Murphy) M.; m. Elizabeth Anne Collins, Aug. 24, 1974; children: Derek Grant, Erin Jean. BA, Nasson Coll., 1974; MS, U. R.I., 1979; postgrad., Boston Coll., U. So. Maine, 1977, 79; MA, Columbia Pacific U., 1991; PhD, U. Heriseau, 2000. Computer programmer Baybank Data Services, Waltham, Mass., 1975-76; mathematician Factory Mut. Engring., Norwood, Mass., 1976-78; tchr. Kennebunk (Maine) High Sch., 1978-79; v.p. strategic planning The Foxboro (Mass.) Co., 1979-84, systems cons., 1984-85, mgr. system product planning, 1986-88, v.p. market strategies and comm., 1996-99, v.p. corp. mktg., 1999—; v.p. mktg. Intec Controls Corp., 1993-94; v.p. Automation Rsch. Corp., 1996. Instr. Dean Jr. Coll., Franklin, Mass. 1980-96; tech. cons. Balance Inc., Wiscassett, Maine, 1985-89. Author: Dynamic Performance Management: A Path to World Class Manufacturing, 1992, Bottom-Line Automation, 2001; contrbr. articles to profl. jours. Pres. East Woonsocket Coun. Parent Council, R.I., 1983-85; mem. Parents Involvement Com., Woonsocket, 1985; Cub Scout den leader, Woonsocket, 1985-86; instr. religious edn. Our Lady of Lourdes Ch. Mem. Soc. Mfg. Engrs., Mfrs. Automation Protocol Users Group, Inst. Soc. of Am. Roman Catholic. Avocations: camping, tennis, boating. Office: The Foxboro Co Bristol Park 351-2C Bristol Park Foxboro MA 02035 E-mail: pmartin@foxboro.com.

---

**MARTIN, PETER ROBERT,** psychiatrist, pharmacologist; b. Budapest, Hungary, Sept. 6, 1949; came to U.S., 1980; s. Nicholas M. and Eva (Horvat) M.; m. Barbara Bradford, Dec. 23, 1985; 1 child, Alexander Bradford. BSc with honors, McGill U., Montreal, Que., Can., 1971, MD, CM, 1975; MSc, U. Toronto, Ont., Can., 1978. Diplomate Am. Bd. Psychiatry and Neurology, Psychiatry, Addiction Psychiatry. Resident in internal medicine U. Toronto, Can., 1975-76, resident in psychiatry, 1978-80; fellow clin. pharmacology Addiction Rsch. Found., Toronto, 1976-78; chief sect. clin. sci. Nat. Inst. on Alcohol Abuse & Alcoholism, Bethesda, 1983-86; assoc. prof. Vanderbilt U. Sch. Medicine, Nashville, 1986-92, prof., 1992—, dir. divsn. addiction medicine, 1986—, dir. addiction ctr., 1994—; dir. Vanderbilt Inst. for Coffee Studies, 1999—. Vis. scientist Lab. of Clin. Sci., NIMH, Bethesda, Md., 1980-83; investigator John F. Kennedy Ctr. for Rsch. on Human Devel., Nashville, 1993—. Fellow Royal Coll. Physicians (Can.), Am. Psychiat. Assn. (disting.); mem. AAAS, Am. Soc. Clin. Pharmacology and Therapeutics, Am. Acad. Addiction Psychiatry, Rsch. Soc. on Alcoholism, Internat. Soc. Biomed. Rsch. in Alcoholism. Office: Psychiatric Hosp at Vanderbilt Ste 3068 1601 23rd Ave South Nashville TN 37232-8650 Office Phone: 615-322-3527. E-mail: peter.martin@vanderbilt.edu.

**MARTIN, PETER WILLIAM,** lawyer, educator; b. Cin., Apr. 11, 1939; s. Wilfred Samuel and Elizabeth (Myers) M.; m. Ann Wadsworth, Nov. 28, 1964; children: Leah, Elliot, Isaac. BA, Cornell U., 1961; JD, Harvard U., 1964. Bar: Ohio 1964. Atty. AF Gen. Counsel's Office, 1964-67; asso. prof. law U. Minn., 1967-71; vis. asso. prof. law Cornell U., 1971-72; prof. law, 1972—, dean, 1980-88, Edward Cornell prof. law, 1989-92, Jane Foster prof. law, 1992—; co-dir. Legal Info. Inst., 1992—2003; pres. Ctr. for Computer Assisted Legal Instrn., 1986-88. Cons. Adminstrv. Conf. U.S., 1977-79; reporter Am. Bar Assn. Task Force on Lawyer Competency and the Role of the Law Schs. Author: The Ill-Housed, 1971, (with others) Social Welfare and the Individual, 1971, Cases and Materials on Property, 1974, 3d edit., 1992, Social Security Law, 2006, Basic Legal Citation, 2006, Social Security Plus, 1994, Introduction to Copyright, 2004; editor Jour. Legal Edn., 1985. Chmn. Ithaca Bd. Zoning Appeals, 1974-79. Served to capt. USAF, 1964-67. Mem. ABA (out of the box commn., vice chmn., task force on law schs. and legal profession 1990-92), Am. Bar Found. (vis. com.), Am. Assn. Law Schs. (chmn. law and computers sect. 1987-88, 93-94). Office: Cornell U Law Sch Myron Taylor Hall Ithaca NY 14853 E-mail: martin@lii.law.cornell.edu.

**MARTIN, PHILLIP DWIGHT,** bank consulting company executive, mayor; b. Nevada, Mo., Jan. 4, 1943; s. E. Dwight and Berniece E. (Leedy) M. BS, U. Mo., 1964, MBA, 1965, cert. math. and bus. edn., 1966. Tchr. Warsaw (Mo.) Pub. Schs., 1966—68; investment analyst Bus. Men's Assurance Co. Am., Kansas City, Mo., 1968—70; exec. v.p. Farmer's Bank Walker, Mo., 1970—71; banking cons. Howard J. Blender Co., Dallas, 1971—84; chmn. Profit Motivators Internat., Inc., Boulder, Colo., 1984—2002; mayor City of Walker, Mo., 1986—2000, 2002—; math. tchr. El Dorado Springs, Mo., 2002—. Bd. dirs. Nev. Regional Med. Ctr., 2004—. Mem. Walker R-4 Alumni Assn. (exec. com. fellow. scholarship com., pres. 1994-96). Home: 214 E Marvin Ave Walker MO 64790-9106 E-mail: pdm19@neighborlink.us.

**MARTIN, PHILLIP HAMMOND,** lawyer; b. Tucson, Jan. 4, 1940; s. William P. and Harriet (Hammond) M.; m. Sandra E. Chandler, June 17, 1961 (div. Mar. 1989); children: Lisa, Craig, Wade, Ryan; m. Erika Zetty, May 9, 1990. BA, U. Minn., 1961, JD, 1964. Bar: Minn. 1964, U.S. Tax Ct. 1967, U.S. Dist. Ct. Minn. 1968, U.S. Ct. Appeals (8th cir.) 1973, U.S. Supreme Ct. 1981, U.S. Claims Ct. 1983, U.S. Ct. Appeals (fed. cir.) 1983, U.S. Ct. Appeals (7th cir.) 1989. Assoc. Dorsey & Whitney, Mpls., 1964-69, ptnr., 1970—. Home: 487 Portland Ave Saint Paul MN 55102-2216 Office: Dorsey & Whitney LLP Ste 1500 50 S 6th St Minneapolis MN 55402-1498 Office Phone: 612-340-2845. Business E-Mail: martin.phil@dorsey.com.

**MARTIN, PRESTON,** finance company executive, consultant; b. L.A., Dec. 5, 1923; s. Oscar and Gaynell (Horn) M.; 1 child, Pier Preston. BS in Fin., U. So. Calif., 1947, MBA, 1948; PhD in Monetary Econs., U. Ind., 1952. Prof. fin. Grad. Sch. Bus. Adminstrn. U. So. Calif., 1950-60; prin. in houseбldg. firm, 1952-56; cons. mortgage fin. and consumer fin. instns., 1954-57; commr. savs. and loan State of Calif., 1967-69; chmn. Fed. Home Loan Bank Bd., Washington, 1969-72; founder, CEO PMI Mortgage Ins. Co., 1972-80; chmn., CEO Seraco Group subs. Sears, Roebuck & Co., 1980-81, also bd. dirs. parent co.; chmn. CEO WestFed Holdings Inc., L.A., 1986-92, SoCal Holdings, Inc., L.A., 1987-93, H.F. Holdings, Inc., San Francisco, 1986, Honolulu Fed. Bank, Honolulu. Vice-chmn. Fed. Res. Bd., Washington, 1982-86; founder Fed. Home Loan Mortgage Corp., 1970—; prof. bus. econ. and fin. Inst. Per Lo Studio Orgn. Aziendale, Turin, Italy; bd. dirs., chmn. audit com. ITLA Capital Corp Author: Principles and Practices of Real Estate, 1959; co-author: The Complete Idiot's Guide to the Federal Reserve, 2003. Mem. President's Commn. on Housing, 1980-81; prin. Coun. Excellence in Govt., Washington. Recipient House and Home award, 1969; award Engring. News Record, 1971; Turntable award Nat. Assn. Home Builders, 1973; Housing Hall of Fame award, Nat. Assn. Home Builders, 2001. Mem. Lambda Chi Alpha. Presbyterian. Office Phone: 415-283-3224.

**MARTIN, QUINCY, III,** career planning administrator; b. Tacoma, Wash., Apr. 18, 1973; s. Quincy Martin Jr. and Jean Betty Martin. MEd in Counseling and Devel., Lamar U., 2005. Dir. career svcs. Lamar U., Beaumont, Tex., 2003—. Mem. Leadership Ky., Fort Mitchell, 2002—03; facilitator Leadership Beaumont, Tex., 2003—04. Named Ky. Col., Ky. Gov. Paul E. Patton, 2003. Mem.: Houston Area Consortium of Career Ctrs. (pres. 2004—05). Office: Lamar Univ PO Box 10012 Beaumont TX 77710 Home: 1865 Euclid Beaumont TX 77705 Personal E-mail: quincymartin@hotmail.com. Business E-Mail: quincy.martin@lamar.edu.

**MARTIN, QUINN WILLIAM,** lawyer; b. Fond du Lac, Wis., 1948; s. Quinn W. and Marcia E. Martin; m. Jane E.; children: Quinn W., William J. BSME, Purdue U., 1969; postgrad., U. Santa Clara, 1969-70; JD, U. Mich., 1973. Bar: Wis. 1973, U.S. Dist. Ct. (ea. dist.) Wis. 1973, U.S. Ct. Appeals (7th cir.) 1973. Sales support mgr. Hewlett-Packard, Palo Alto, Calif., 1969-70; assoc. Quarles & Brady, Milw., 1973-80, ptnr., 1980—. Bd. dirs. Associated Bank Milw., U-Line Corp., Gen. Timber and Land, Inc., Fond du Lac. Chmn. Gov. McCallum Trans Com., Wis., U. Mich. Law Sch. Fund; bd. dirs. Milw. Zool. Soc., Found. for Wildlife Conservation. Mem. ABA, Wis. Bar Assn., Milw. Club, Ozaukee Country Club, Chaine des Rottiseurs, Delta Upsilon (sec.), Milw. Club, Rotary. Office: Quarles & Brady 411 E Wisconsin Ave Ste 2550 Milwaukee WI 53202-4497

**MARTIN, R. BRAD,** retail executive; b. Nov. 5, 1951; BA, Univ. of Memphis, 1976; MBA, Vanderbilt Univ., 1980. Mem. Tenn. Ho. Reps., 94th dist., 1973—82; chmn. Saks Inc., Birmingham, 1997—, CEO, 1989—. Bd. dir. Saks Inc., Birmingham, Ala., 1984—, First Tenn. Corp., Harrah's Entertainment, Pilot Corp. Achievements include being youngest person elected to Tenn. Gen. Assembly. Office: Saks Inc 750 Lakeshore Pkwy Birmingham AL 35211-4400*

**MARTIN, R. KEITH,** business and information systems educator, consultant; b. Seattle, Sept. 5, 1933; s. Jerome Milton and Winifred (Gifford) M.; m. Carolyn Joanne Carosella, June 15, 1957; children: Jefferson, Sean, Jennifer, Katherine. AB, Whitman Coll., 1955; MBA with high honors, CCNY, 1965; PhD, U. Wash., 1973. Registered, lic. profl. engr.; cert. data processing, cert. systems profl., cert. computer profl. Div. mgr. Campus Merchandising Bur., Inc., NYC, 1955-56; sales rep. IBM, Seattle, 1956, Svc. Bur. Corp. subs. IBM, NYC, 1957-58; specialist mgmt. adv. svcs. Price Waterhouse & Co., NYC, 1959-65, Seattle, 1965-66, mgr., 1966-67; dir. mgmt. systems dept. U. Wash., 1967-71, lectr. dept. acctg. Sch. Bus. Adminstrn., 1971-73; asst. prof. dept. accountancy Baruch Coll., CUNY, 1973-76, assoc. prof., 1977-79, prof. acctg. Fairfield U., 1979-84, prof. acctg. and info. systems, 1984-94, assoc. dean Sch. Bus., 1980-82, dean, 1982-93, acting dean grad. Sch. of Communications, 1988-90, prof. info. systems and

---

ops. mgmt., 2001—05, prof. emeritus, 2005—, dept. chmn., 1999—2002, holder Stephen and Camille Schramm chair in bus., 2000—04. V.p. Eastalco Systems, 1971-72; faculty fin. div. Am. Mgmt. Assn., 1963-64; part-time lectr. Bellevue C.C., 1967-69, Shoreline Community Coll., 1968-72, Seattle U., 1971-72; program dir., summer program at Heslier (Rotterdam) 2000, 2001, Nat. Univ. Galway, 2003. Co-author: Management Control of Electronic Data Processing, 1965; author: Management Information Systems in Higher Education: Case Studies at Three Universities, 1973, Effective Business Communications, 1976, 79, 91, Systems Development and Computer Concepts, 1977; assoc. editor: Industry Guides for Accountants and Auditors, 2 vols., 1980; mem. editorial rev. bd. Dickenson Pub. Co., 1974-75, Prentice-Hall, Inc., 1977-78, 87-88, 90-91, Reston Pub. Co., 1977-78, Jour. Acctg. Edn., 1981-83; featured roles (Amateur Comedy Club prodns.) Guys and Dolls, Our Town, The Fantastics, The Night of the Iguana, The Rainmaker, My Fair Lady; stage mgr. Some Assembly Required, Arcadia, Murder by the Book, Night Watch; house mgr.(plays) The Real Thing, The Tempest, play com., 2004—, chmn., 2005-06; author numerous monographs; contbr. numerous articles to profl. jours. Mem. Mendelssohn Choir of Conn., Amateur Comedy Club, Westchester Chordsmen, Litchfield Norwestones; trustee Westchester County Hist. Soc. Recipient cert. of appreciation Am. Mgmt. Assn., 1966, cert. of merit for disting. service to Mgmt. Scis., 1969, for disting. service to info. systems profession, 1973; Merit award Assn. Systems Mgmt., 1971, Achievement award, 1972, Internat. award World Assn. for Case Method Rsch. and Application, 1996, 2002; cert. for service City of Seattle, 1973; named Outstanding Young Man Am., 1970, One of 300 Outstanding Alumni, Whitman Coll., 1979; Kellogg fellow, 1971-72, Price Waterhouse faculty fellow, 1976. Mem.: NSPE, AAUP, Am. Acctg. Assn., Soc. Mgmt. Info. Systems, NY Soc. Profl. Engrs., Soc. Cert. Data Processors, Assn. Computing Machinery, Data Processing Mgmt. Assn., Assn. Systems Mgmt. (sec. 1968—69, v.p. 1969-70, pres. Pacific NW chpt. 1970—71), Inst. Mgmt. Accts. (assoc. dir. NY chpt. 1963—64, 1975—85, Seattle chpt. 1967—70), Acad. Creative Tchg. (exec. bd. 1998—), World Assn. Case Method Rsch. and Application (adv. bd. 1996—99, exec. bd. dirs. 1999—, vice-chair internat. case stds. setting com. 2001—), Am. Inst. Indsl. Engrs. (dir. Seattle chpt. 1967—70, chmn. regional conf. 1969), Westchester County Hist. Soc. (trustee 2005—), Amateur Comedy Club, Brookville Field Club, Beta Alpha Psi, Phi Delta Kappa, Mu Gamma Tau, Beta Gamma Sigma, Phi Delta Theta (province pres. 1986—87). Home: 39 Sheldon Ln Litchfield CT 06759 Personal E-mail: rkmartin6221@msn.com.

**MARTIN, RAYMOND BRUCE,** plumbing equipment manufacturing company executive; b. N.Y.C., Oct. 23, 1934; s. Raymond M. and Margaret (Lennon) M.; m. Suzanne Ruth Longpre, Sept. 3, 1960; 1 son, Christopher Haines. AB, Villanova U., 1956. With Corning (NY) Glass Works, 1956-68, nat. plumbing sales mgr., 1966-68; v.p. mktg. Briggs Mfg. Co., Warren, Mich., 1968-69, v.p., gen. mgr. plumbing fixture div., 1969-72, pres., CEO, chmn. bd. Water Control Internat. Inc., Troy, Mich., 1972-91; pres., CEO W/C Technology Corp., 1991—2002; chmn. Intertech Corp., 2003—; mem. plumbing harmonization Fed. N.Am. Free Trade Delegation, 1992; ret., 2002. Served with AUS, 1957-58. Mem. Am. Soc. Plumbing Engrs., Plumbing Mfrs. Inst. (chmn. HUD Task Group 1981-82, chmn. com. 1983-86, chmn. fed. water conservation com. 1988-90, chmn. flushing devices com. 1999—, chmn. info. tech. com. 2002—), Am. Soc. Sanitary Engrs. (chmn. std. com. pressurized flushing devices 2004), ASME (panel 19, chmn. definitions task group 1993-94, chmn. water closet hydraulic performance task group 1993-94, chmn. flushing devices com. 2000-02). Republican. Roman Catholic.

**MARTIN, RENEE COHEN,** forensic document examiner, author, expert witness; b. Bklyn., Feb. 26, 1928; d. Aref Max and Eleanora (Cofino) Cohen; m. Howard Martin Kessler, Dec. 24, 1950 (div. 1978); children: Kenneth S., Laurel R. Van Blarcum, Elena A. Covert (dec.), Julia M. Diplomate Nat. Assn. Document Examiners, 2000, cert. Nat. Assn. Document Examiners, 1979. Pres. Handwriting Cons., Inc., Princeton, N.J., 1950-90, chief exec. officer, 1965-85; pres., chief exec. officer Questioned Documents, Inc., 1985—, exec. dir. forgery forensics (c) a Div-f, 1995—. Coord. Metamorphosis II, Princeton, 1984-86; frequent lectr., presenter workshops; adj. prof. Mercer County CC, NJ, 1985-87. Author: Your Script is Showing, 1969, Secrets of Handwriting, 1970, Scriptease, 1976, Experts in Court, 1986, Handwriting Analysis, 1971, Mensa Cooks Book, 1989, (videotape, handbook, workbook) Personalysis Dynamics, 1990, Forgery Protection Tips, 1989; contbr. articles to profl. jours. Com. mem. East Windsor Democratic Club, 1983-84, sgt.-at-arms, 1984, sec., 1986-87; mem. Mercer County Commn. on Women, 1989-91; mem. Ea. Windsor (N.J.) Local Assistance Bd., 1995-98. Recipient Woman of Yr. award Hightstown Bus. and Profl. Women Club, 1974, Honor from Chapel of the Four Chapels. Mem. Nat. Assn. Document Examiners (co-founder, life, chmn. diplomate com., Examiner of Yr. 1984, past pres. 1979-83, diplomate 1993), Evidence Photographers Internat. Coun., Nat. Forensic Soc. (co-founder), Friends of N.J. Librs. (pres. 1980-85), Mensa (Ctrl. N.J. program chmn. 1984, local sec. 1984-86, bd. dirs. 1986-88, author Compiled Mensa Cooks' Book 1987, mem. local scholarship com. 1994—), Princeton Area (N.J.) C. of C. (chair small bus. coun. 1996), Nat. Assn. Document Examiners. Office Phone: 609-452-7030. Personal E-mail: forgerynet@aol.com.

**MARTIN, RENWICK D.,** lawyer; b. 1947; AB, Stanford U., 1969; JD, Harvard U., 1972. Bar: NY 1975. With Sidley Austin LLP, NYC, 1972—, specialist asset-backed securities area, 1977—, mem. mgmt. and exec. coms. Mem.: ABA. Office: Sidley Austin LLP 787 Seventh Ave New York NY 10019 Office Phone: 212-839-5319. Office Fax: 212-839-5599. Business E-Mail: rmartin@sidley.com.

**MARTIN, REX,** manufacturing executive; Chmn., pres., CEO Nibco, Elkhart, Ind. Office: NIBCO Inc 1516 Middlebury St PO Box 1167 Elkhart IN 46515-1167

**MARTIN, RICHARD D.,** social studies educator; b. LA, Nov. 13, 1952; s. Earl D. and Hazel Mae Martin; m. Susan L. Telles, Apr. 12, 1975; 1 child, Vanessa. AA, East LA CC, 1972; BA, Calif. State U., LA, 1974, MA, 1978. Tchr. Wilson Mid. Sch., Pasadena, Calif., 1975—78, Marshall Sch., Pasadena, 1978—88, Blair HS, Pasadena, 1988—89, South Pasadena Mid. Sch., Calif., 1989—91, South Pasadena HS, 1991—. Vol. Fred Jordan Mission, LA, 1998—. Mem.: Tchrs. Assn. South Pasadena (contract negotiator 2003—, rep. coun. 2002—04), South Pasadena Chinese/Am. Club. Baptist. Avocation: Shotokan karate. Home: 524 Valmont Dr Monrovia CA 91016 Office: South Pasadena Schs 1401 Fremont South Pasadena CA 91030

**MARTIN, RICHARD H.,** principal; b. Washington, Pa., Feb. 25, 1956; s. Henderson E. and Margaret Roxena Martin; m. Lori Confer Martin, Nov. 6, 1982. BS in Edn., Calif. State Coll., 1978, MA in Comms., 1980; EdD in Edn. Adminstrn., W.Va. U., 1991. Cert. tchr., supr., prin., supt. schs. Asst. to dean Calif. State Coll. 1978-80; tchr. Turkeyfoot Sch. Dist., Confluence, Pa., 1980-81, Somerset (Pa.) Sch. Dist., 1981-82, Frazier Sch. Dist., Perryopolis, Pa., 1982-85, dept. chair, 1985-90, prin., 1990-96, Mt. Lebanon Sch. Dist., Pitts., 1996-99, Bethlehem Ctr. High Sch., 1999—. Cons. W.Va. Dept. of Edn., Charleston, 2000—. Intermediate Unit #1, Calif., 1982-90; mem. safety coun. Mt. Lebanon Sch. Dist., Pitts., 1997—; trainer in IDEA Allegheny Intermediate Unit, Pitts., 1998—; adj. asst. prof. W.Va. U., 1991—. Contbr. articles to profl. jours. Recipient Cmty. Svc. award Perrypolis Heritage Soc., 1991. Mem. NASSP/PASSP, AASA, ASCD, CEFPI, Mt. Lebanon Found., Masons (floor officer 1985—), Monessen Commandery Knights Templar (floor officer 1985—), Shriners, Uniontown Masons, Phi Delta Kappa. Avocations: fly fishing, hunting, good cigars. Home: 225 Nobles Rd Brownsville PA 15417-9283 Personal E-mail: martinlm@peoplepc.com.

**MARTIN, RICHARD J.,** food wholesale executive; Exec. v.p., CFO Rykoff-Sexton, Wilkes-Barre, Pa.; sr. v.p. fin. & adminstrn., CFO Cert. Grocers Calif., 1998-2000; CFO, exec. v.p. fin. & adminstrn. Unified Western Grocers, Inc., Commerce, Calif., 2000—. Office: Unified Western Grocers Inc 5200 Sheila St City Of Commerce CA 90040

**MARTIN, RICHARD JAY,** medical educator; b. Detroit, May 16, 1946; s. Peter Aaron and Tillie Jean (Munch) M.; m. Helene Iris Horowitz, Dec. 23, 1967; children: Elizabeth Hope, David Evan. BS, U. Mich., 1967, MD, 1971. Diplomate Am. Bd. Internal Medicine and Pulmonary Disease. Intern, Ariz., 1971-72; resident Tulane U., New Orleans, 1974-76; pulmonary fellow, 1976-78; asst. prof. medicine U. Okla., Okla. City, 1978-80, U. Colo., Denver, 1980-85, assoc. prof., 1985-92, prof., 1992—. Dir. Cardiorespiratory Sleep Rsch., Nat. Jewish Med. and Rsch. Ctr., Denver, 1980-89, staff physician, 1980-, head divsn. pulmonary medicine, 1993-2005, vice-chair dept. medicine, 1997-2004, acting chair dept. medicine, 2004-2005, chair dept. medicine, 2006—. Author: Cardiorespiratory Disorders During Sleep, 1984, 2d edit., 1990, (with others) Current Therapy in Internal Medicine, 1984, Clinical Pharmacology and Therapeutics in Nursing, 1985, Interdisciplinary Rehabilitation of Multiple Sclerosis and Neuromuscular Disorders, 1984, Drugs for the Respiratory System, 1985, Current Therapy in Pulmonary Medicine, 1985, Abnormalities of Respiration During Sleep, 1986, Mitchell's Synopsis of Pulmonary Medicine, 1987, Pulmonary Grand Rounds, 1990, Asthma and Rhinitis, 1994, The High Risk Patient: Management of the Critically Ill, 1995, Manual of Asthma Management, 1995, 2000, Severe Asthma: Pathogenesis and Clinical Management, 1995, Curret Pulmonology, 1995, Pulmonary and Respiratory Therapy Secrets, 1996, (book chpts.) Lung Biology in Health and Disease, 1995, 3d edit., 2000, Allergy, 1997, Asthma, 1997, Emergency Asthma, 1999, Difficult Asthma, 1999, Asthma and Rhinitis, 1999, Imaging of Diffuse Lung Disease, 2000, Manual of Asthma Management, 2000, Severe Asthma, 2001, Asthma Critical Debates, 2002, Inhaled Steroids in Asthma, 2002, The Merck Manual, 2002, Current Review of Asthma, 2003; editor: Nocturnal Asthma: Mechanisms and Interventions, 1993, Cardiothoracic Interrelationships in Clinical Practice, 1997; author, editor: Nocturnal Asthma: Mechanisms and Treatment, 1993, Combination Therapy for Asthma and Chronic Obstructive Pulmonary Disease, 2000; mem. editl. bd. Chronobiology Internat., 1997—, Am. Jour. Respiratory and Critical Care Medicine, 1994-98, Bronchial Asthma: Index and Review, 1996-97; assoc. editor: Clinical Care for Asthma, 1995-97; contbr. articles to profl. jours. Pres. Congregation Rodef Shalom, Denver, 1984-85; regional v.p. United Synagogues of Am., Denver, 1988-89. Named Disting. Lectr., Royal Coll. Physicians and Surgeons Can., 1998, Cardio-Pulmonary Congress, Argentina, 1998, Assn. Argentina Allergy and Immunology, 2001; recipient Best Paper in Internal Medicine award, Okla. Soc. Interna. Medicine, 1977—78, U. Okla. Gastroenterology sect, 1977, Amb. award, Nat. Jewish Med. and Rsch. Ctr., 2002; grantee Am. Lung Assn., Va., U. Okla. Lung Assn., NIH, Parker B. Francis Found.; Pulmonary fellow, Am. Lung Assn., 1977—79, James F. Hammarsten Outstanding fellow, U. Okla. Health Scis. Ctr., 1978. Mem. ACP, Am. Thoracic Soc., Am. Fedn. for Clin. Rsch., Am. Coll. Chest Physicians (Disting. scholar in respiratory health 2003—), Colo. Trudeau Soc., Western Soc. Clin. Investigation. Avocations: biking, golf, Karate. Office: Nat Jewish Med Rsch Ctr 1400 Jackson St Denver CO 80206-2761 Office Phone: 303-398-1847. Business E-Mail: martinr@njc.org.

**MARTIN, RICHARD KELLEY,** lawyer; b. Tulsa, June 30, 1952; s. Richard Loye and Maxine (Kelley) M.; m. Reba Lawson, June 12, 1993; children from previous marriage: R. Kyle, Andrew J. BA, Westminster Coll., 1974; JD, So. Meth. U., 1977. Bar: Tex. 1977, U.S. Tax Ct. 1979. Ptnr. Akin, Gump, Strauss, Hauer & Feld, LLP, Dallas, 1977-95, Haynes and Boone LLP, Dallas, 1995—. Bd. dirs. Goodwill Industries, Dallas, 1986-91; bd. dirs. mem. bd. dirs. Greater Dallas Youth Orchs., 1987-90; bd. dirs., v.p., pres. Big Bros. and Sisters Met. Dallas, 1988-91; bd. dirs. Tejas coun. Girl Scouts U.S., 1997-2001, Salvation Army, Dallas, 2003-. Mem. Tex. Bar Assn., Salesmanship Club Dallas. Republican. Methodist. Office: Haynes and Boone LLP 2505 N Plano Rd Ste 4000 Richardson TX 75082-4101 Office Phone: 972-739-8634. Business E-Mail: rick.martin@haynesboone.com.

**MARTIN, RICHARD PETER,** classics educator, consultant; b. Boston, May 19, 1954; s. Nicholas Richard and Marie Eileen (Daly) M.; children: Catherine, Thomas. AB, Harvard U., 1976, AM, 1978, PhD, 1981. Teaching fellow Harvard U., Cambridge, Mass., 1978-81; from asst. to assoc. prof. Princeton (N.J.) U., 1981-94, prof., 1994—99; Antony and Isabelle Raubitschek Prof. of Classics Stanford U., 2000—. Author: Healing, Sacrifice and Battle, 1983, The Language of Heroes, 1989, Myths of the Ancient Greeks, 2003; editor: Bulfinch, Mythology, 1991. Class of 1936 preceptor Princeton U., 1984-87. Devel. grantee Apple Computer Co., 1989. Fellow Onassis Found.; mem. Am. Philol. Assn., Celtic Studies Assn. of N.Am., Irish Texts Soc. Democrat. Roman Catholic. Office: Stanford Univ Bldg 20 Main Quad Stanford CA 94305-2080 Business E-Mail: rpmartin@stanford.edu.

**MARTIN, RICKY (ENRIQUE MARTIN MORALES IV),** vocalist, actor; b. San Juan, PR, Dec. 24, 1971; Member. Menudo, 1984—89. Singer: (albums) Ricky Martin (Spanish), 1991, Me Amaras, 1993, A Medio Vivir, 1995, Vuelve, 1998 (Grammy award for Best Latin Pop Album, two Billboard Latin Music awards), Ricky Martin, 1999 (two MTV Video Music awards, Teen Choice award for Favorite Male Artist, two Billboard Music awards, Am. Latino Media Arts award for Male Entertainer of Yr., Billboard Latin Music award for Latin Pop Track of Yr., two World Music awards), Sound Loaded, 2000 (nominated for two MTV Video Music awards), La Historia, 2001, Platinum Rhythm, 2001, The Best of Ricky Martin, 2001, Coleccion De Oro: A Medio Vivir, 2002, Medio Viir, 2002, Almas del Silencio, 2003, I Don't Care, 2005, Life, 2005; contbr. (albums) Boleros Voz y Sentimiento, 1993, Gigantes de la Cancion, 1994, Hey Jude: Tributo a Los Beatles, 1995, Voces Unidas, 1996, Music of the World Cup, 1998, Billboard Latin Music Awards Superstar Hits, 1999, 2000 Grammy Nominees, 2000; actor: (TV series) General Hospital, 1994—95, Barefoot in Paradise, 1996; (films) Les Diables, 2002; (Broadway plays) Les Miserables, 1996. Founded Ricky Martin Found., San Juan, PR, 2000, launched People for Children initiative, 2004; Goodwill Ambassador UNICEF, 2004—. Recipient Hispanic Heritage award, Hispanic Heritage Found., 2002, Lifetime Achievement award, Univision Premios Lo Nuestro, 2004, Internat. Humanitarian award, Internat. Ctr. Missing & Exploited Children, 2005. The Others prize for social svc., Salvation Army, 2006, Person of Yr., Latin Recording Acad., 2006. Office: Sony Music Latin 550 Madison Ave New York NY 10022-3211 also: Ricky Martin Found Santurce Sta PO Box 13534 San Juan PR 00908-3534

**MARTIN, ROBERT BRUCE,** chemistry professor; b. Chgo., Apr. 29, 1929; s. Robert Frank and Helen (Woelffer) M.; m. Frances May Young, June 7, 1953. BS, Northwestern U., 1950; PhD, U. Rochester, 1953. Asst. prof. chemistry Am. U., Beirut, Lebanon, 1953-56; research fellow Calif. Inst. Tech., 1956-57, Harvard U., 1957-58; asst. prof. chemistry U. Va., Charlottesville, 1959-61, assoc. prof., 1961-65, prof., 1965—, chmn. dept., 1968-71. Spl. fellow Oxford U., 1961-62; Program dir. Molecular Biology Sect., NSF, 1965-66 Author: Introduction to Biophysical Chemistry, 1964. Fellow AAAS; mem. Am. Chem. Soc. Home: 620 Sand Hill Rd #314D Palo Alto CA 94304

**MARTIN, ROBERT D.,** former hospital executive; m. Theresa Martin. PhD in econ. & fin., Southern Methodist U.; MA in econ. & fin., Southern Methodist U.; graduate, U. North Tex. Sr. v.p., fin. and admin. Scottsdale Meml. Health Sys., 1989—95; chief adminstrv. officer, treas. Mayo Clinic, Scottsdale, Ariz.; exec. dir., Clinical Care Assocs. U. Pa. Health Sys., 1997—99, COO, CFO, 1999—2001, interim CEO, 2000—01, CEO, 2001—03.

**MARTIN, ROBERT DAVID,** judge, educator; b. Iowa City, Oct. 7, 1944; s. Murray and G'Ann (Holmgren) Martin; m. Ruth A. Haberman, Aug. 21, 1966; children: Jacob, Matthew, David. AB, Cornell Coll., Mt. Vernon, Iowa, 1966; JD, U. Chgo., 1969. Bar: Wis. 1969, US Dist. Ct. (we. dist.) Wis. 1969, US Supreme Ct. 1973, US Dist. Ct. (ea. dist.) Wis. 1974. Assoc. Ross & Stevens, S.C., Madison, Wis., 1969-72, ptnr., 1973-78; chief judge U.S. Bankruptcy Ct. We. Dist. Wis., 1978—. Instr. gen. practice course U. Wis. Law Sch., 1974, 76, 77, 80, lectr. debtor/creditor course, 1981-82, 83, 85, 87, 2001, farm credit seminar, 1985, advanced bankruptcy problems, 1989, 91, 96; co-chmn. faculty Am. Law Inst.-ABA Fin. and Bus. Planning for Agr., Stanford U., 1979; faculty mem. Fed. Jud. Ctr. Schs. for New Bankruptcy Judges, 1985-96; chmn. Ann. Continuing Legal Edn. Wis. Debtor Creditor Conf., 1981—. Author: (book) Bankruptcy: Annotated Forms, 1989; co-author: Secured Transactions Handbook for Wisconsin Lawyers and Lenders, Bankruptcy-Text Statutes Rules and Forms, 1992, Ginsberg and Martin on Bankruptcy, 4th edit, 1996. Chmn., bd. dirs., mem. exec. com. Turnaround Mgmt. Svc. Wis. and Upper Mich.; bd. dirs., mem. exec. com. Luth. Social Svc. Assn., 1997—2002. Mem.: Wis. State Bar, Nat. Bankruptcy Conf., Nat. Conf. Bankruptcy Judges (bd. govs. 1989—91, sec. 1993—94, v.p. 1994—95, pres. 1995—96), Am. Coll. Bankruptcy. Office: 120 N Henry Rm 340 PO Box 548 Madison WI 53701-0548 Office Phone: 608-264-5188.

**MARTIN, ROBERT EDWARD,** architect; b. Dodge City, Kans., Mar. 17, 1928; s. Emry and Alice Jane (Boyce) M.; m. Billie Jo Lange, Aug. 16, 1952 (div. Feb. 1970); m. Kathryn M. Arvanitis, June 26, 1971; children: Lynn, Amy, Blaine. Student, McPherson Coll., 1946-48; BArch, U. Cin., 1954. Registered architect, Ohio. Architect Samborn, Steketee, Otis & Evans, Inc., Toledo, 1956-58; prin. Schauder & Martin, Toledo, 1958-72; The Collaborative, Inc., Toledo, 1972-93. Mem. Bd. Examiners Archs., Ohio, 1985-95, pres., 1989-94; bd. examiners Nat. Coun. Archtl. Registration Bds., 1986-95, edn. com., 1992; chmn. site design divsn. Archtl. Registration Exam., 1989, 90, 91; mem. Nat. Coun. Archtl. Registration Bds. Grading, 1987-94; chmn. study of Toledo Fire & Rescue Dept., Corp. for Effective Govt., 1994. Artist numerous paintings. Mem. Toledo Planning Commn., 1971-74, Toledo Zoning Appeals Bd., 1973, Toledo Bd. Bldg. Stds., 1967-84, Citizens Fire Adv. Commn., 1974-80, Citizens Urban Area Adv. Commn., 1962, Toledo Area Coun. Govts., 1977-80, Com. of 100, Toledo, 1987-89, Spectrum Friends Fine Arts, Inc., Toledo; chmn. bd. Toledo Area Govtl. Rsch. Assn., 1981-90; chmn. Corp. for Effective Govt., Study of Toledo Fire and Rescue Dept., 1994; chmn. Cystic Fibrosis, Toledo, 1985. Served to capt. USAF 1954-56. Recipient numerous watercolor awards. Fellow AIA (pres. Toledo chpt. 1966, Arch. of Yr. 1993), Archs. Soc. Ohio (pres. 1975), Ohio Watercolor Soc. (trustee 1999—), N.W. Ohio Watercolor Soc., Toledo Fedn. Art Socs. (pres. 1989, 90), Spectrum, Tile Club (v.p.), Toledo Artists Club, Sylvania Country Club, Toledo Club, Rotary, Masons, Shriners, Jesters. Mem. Ch. of Brethren. Avocation: painting. Home: 5119 Regency Dr Toledo OH 43615-2946 Office: 1700 N Reynolds Rd Toledo OH 43615-3628 Office Phone: 419-531-5753.

**MARTIN, ROBERT SIDNEY,** former museum director; b. Houston, Aug. 13, 1949; s. Sidney A. and Elizabeth Ann Martin. BA, Rice U., 1971; MLS, U. N. Tex., 1979; PhD, U. N.C., 1988. Libr. assoc. U. Tex., Austin, 1972-76; debt claims adjustor US Gen. Acctg. Office, Washington, 1977; libr. U. Tex., Arlington, 1977-80; instr. Sch. Libr. and Info. Sci. U. Wis., Madison, 1984; assoc. dean Librs. La. State U., Baton Rouge, 1985-95; dir. libr. Tex. State Libr. and Archives Commn., Austin, 1995—99; prof., interim dir. Sch. Library and Info. Studies, Texas Women's U., 2001; dir. The Inst. Mus. & Library Services, Washington, 2001—05. Co-author: Contours of Discovery, 1982, Maps of Texas and the Southwest, 1513-1900, 1984 (Kate Broock Bates award 1985); editor: Scholarly Communication in an Electronic Environment: Issues for Research, 1993, Carnegie Denied: Communities Rejecting Carnegie Library Construction Grants, 1993; mem. editl. bd. Am. Archivist, 1994-01, Libr. Quar., 1995-01. Mem. ALA (councilor 1998-01), Nat. Assn. Govt. Archivists and Records Adminstrs. (mem. exec. bd. 1996—), Tex. Map Soc. (v.p. 1996-00), Book Club Tex. (v.p. 1996-00). Avocations: hiking, photography, music.

**MARTIN, ROBERT WILLIAM,** retired utilities executive; b. Toronto, Ont., Can., June 7, 1936; s. William George and Evelyn Irene (Phillips) M.; m. Patricia Lorraine Norris, June 27, 1959; children: Stephen Gregory, Robert Scott, Adrienne Christine Teron. BASc., U. Toronto, 1958. Pres., CEO Consumers Gas, Toronto, 1980—92. Bd. dirs. Aldridge Inc., HSBC Bank Can., Allied Properties Income Trust. Hon. gov. York U.; bd. dir. York U. Found.; past chmn. Toronto Symphony Orch. Recipient Meritorious Svc. award, U. Toronto, 1983, Arbor award, U. Ontario, Queen's Jubilee medal, 125 Yrs. Confederators medal, Govt. of Can., 1992. Mem.: Assn. Profl. Engrs. Ont., Toronto Club, Mad River Golf Club. Home: 118 Farnham Ave Toronto ON Canada M4V 1H4 Office Phone: 416-972-0970.

**MARTIN, ROBERT WILLIAM,** econometrician; b. Elizabeth, N.J., Nov. 14, 1961; s. Edward Robert Martin and Vivienne Angela Schaul; m. Nancy Leigh Lannan, Sept. 16, 2006. BA in English, U. N.C., 1984, BA in Econs., 1985; MA in Econs., Clemson U., 1989. Rsch. asst. dept. econs. Clemson (S.C.) U., 1988-89, lectr., policy analyst Ctr. Policy Studies, 1989-90; econometrician, exec. mgr. Bd. Econ. Advisors, Columbia, S.C., 1990—. Cons. Clemson U., 1990; adj. instr. Midlands Tech. Coll.; Columbia; adj. faculty mem. of the yr. Sch. of Social & Behavioral Sciences, 1997; mem. S.C. budget and control bd. Grad. Leadership Acad., 2003. Contbr. articles to profl. jours. Mem. Am. Econ. Assn., Nat. Assn. Bus. Economists (Carolinas chpt. regional v.p. and sec.), Western Econ. Assn. Internat., Omicron Delta Epsilon, Sigma Tau Delta. Avocations: golf, running, woodworking. Home: 6503 Christie Rd Columbia SC 29209-2049 Office: Bd Econ Advisors Rembert Dennis Bldg 1000 Assembly St Ste 446 Columbia SC 29201 Office Phone: 803-734-4637. Business E-Mail: rmartin@drss.state.sc.us.

**MARTIN, ROBLEE BOETTCHER,** retired cement manufacturing executive; b. St. Louis, Apr. 7, 1921; s. Henry W. and Esther (Boettcher) M.; m. Lillian Seegraves, July 15, 1940; children: Mary Katherine, Bruce Daniel, Amy Lee. BS in Chem. Engring., Columbia U., 1943, MS in Chem. Engring., 1947; D.Sc. in Bus. Adminstrn. (hon.), Cleary Coll., 1962. Prodn. supr. Monsanto Chem. Co., St. Louis, 1944-49; dir. research and devel. Miss. Lime Co., Ste. Genevieve, Mo., 1949-59; pres. Dundee Cement Co., Mich., 1959-69; v.p. Fruehauf Corp., gen. mgr. Fruehauf Bldgs. div.), Detroit, 1969-72; pres. Presidents Assn. div. Am. Mgmt. Assn., N.Y.C., 1972-74; pres. insulation div. Keene Corp., Princeton, NJ, 1974-76; chmn. chief exec. officer Kaystone Cement Co., Bath, Pa., 1976-89, Giant Cement Co., Harleyville, SC, 1985-89; sr. v.p., dir. Giant Group Ltd., Beverly Hills, Calif., 1985-89. Served to lt. (j.g.) USNR, 1944-46, PTO. Mem.: Phi Lambda Upsilon, Tau Beta Pi, Sigma Xi. Baptist. Home: 2590 Elms Plantation Beach Charleston SC 29406

**MARTIN, ROGER BOND,** landscape architect; b. Virginia, Minn., Nov. 23, 1936; s. Thomas George and Audrey (Bond) M.; m. Janis Ann Kloss, Aug. 11, 1962; children: Thomas, Stephen, Jonathan. BS with high distinction, U. Minn., 1958; M. Landscape Arch., Harvard U., 1961. Asst. prof. U. Calif.-Berkeley, 1964-66; from assoc. prof. to prof. emeritus U. Minn., Mpls. 1966—99, prof. emeritus, 1999—; owner Roger Martin & Assoc., site planners and landscape architects, Mpls., 1966-68, 99—; prin. InterDesign, Inc., Mpls., 1968-84, Martin & Pitz Assocs., Inc., 1984-98; vis. prof. U. Melbourne, 1979-80. Vis. prof. coll. architecture U. Minn., 2000—05. Prin. works include Minn. Zool. Gardens, 1978 (merit award Am. Soc. Landscape Archs., 1978), Mpls. Pkwy. Restorations, 1972—87 (merit award, 1978, Minn. Classic award Am. Soc. Landscape Archs., 1994), South St. Paul Ctrl. Sq., 1978 (merit award, 1978), Festival Park, Chisholm, Minn., 1986 (merit award, 1986), Miss. Wildlife Refuge Visual Image assessment (merit award, 1989), Nicollet Island Park, Hennepin Avenue Master Plan, 1995 (merit award, 1995), North Shore Scenic Byway Plan (Honor award, 2005). Recipient Fredrick Mann award for svc. to edn. U. Minn., 1990, Disting. Educator award Sigma Lambda Alpha, 1990, Bradford Williams medals for outstanding articles in landscape Architecture mag., 1968, 69, Minn. chpt. Lob Pine award for outstanding svc. to Landscape architecture, 1988, Mpls. Com. on Urban Environ. award for design of Whittier Park, 1997; fellow Am. Acad. in Rome, 1962-64. Mem. Am. Soc. Landscape Archs. (pres. Minn. chpt. 1976-79, trustee 1980-84, nat. pres. 1987, chmn.-elect coun. fellows 1991, chmn. 1992-94, past chmn. 1994-96, Pub. Svc. award 1985, Minn. chpt. Classic award 1994, 1st Valued Places award 2005), Nat. Coun. Instrs. Landscape Architecture (pres. 1973-74), Can. Soc. Landscape Archs. (hon-.);jury, 911 Pentagon Mem.,2003; Minn. WWII Mem. 2003 Home and Office: 2912 45th Ave S Minneapolis MN 55406-1829 Business E-Mail: marti009@tc.umn.edu.

**MARTIN, ROGER HARRY,** retired college president; b. N.Y.C., June 26, 1943; s. Edwin Diller and Emma (Neuenburg) M.; m. Susan Bradford, Aug. 29, 1970; children: Katherine R., Emily G. BA, Drew U., 1965; BD, Yale U., 1968, STM, 1969; DPhil, Oxford U., Eng., 1974. Program officer Edn. Incentive Program, N.Y.C., 1969-70; devel. officer NYU, 1970-71, 75-76; asst. dir. devel. Rensselaer Polytech Inst., Troy, NY, 1974-75; asst. prof. history, exec. asst. to pres. Middlebury (Vt.) Coll., 1976-80; assoc. dean Harvard Div. Sch., Cambridge, Mass., 1980-86; prof. history, pres. Moravian Coll., Bethlehem, Pa., 1986-97; pres. Randolph-Macon Coll., 1997—2006, ret., 2006. Author: Evangelicals United: Ecumenical Stirrings in Pre-Victorian Britain, 1795-1830, 1983. Bd. dirs. Brit. Schs. and Univs. Found., NYC. Mem. Harvard Club (N.Y.C.). Mem. Soc. Of Friends. Avocations: skiing, running. Home: 1321 Crown Ct Mamaroneck NY 10543

**MARTIN, ROGER JOHN,** computer scientist; b. Ft. Atkinson, Iowa, Sept. 11, 1947; s. Raymond Charles and Jane K. (Kuennen) M.; m. Jane Degnan, Nov. 21, 1970; children: John, Kathryn, Susan, Jacquelyn. BS in Computer Sci., Iowa State U., 1969, MS in Computer Sci., 1971. Computer specialist Naval Ship R & D Ctr., Bethesda, Md., 1971-76; supervisory sys. analyst Exec. Office of Pres., Washington, 1976-82; computer scientist, mgr. software engring. group Inst. Computer Scis. and Tech., Nat. Inst. Stds. and Tech., Washington, 1982-92, chief sys. and software tech. divsn., 1993-95, mgr. software methods, 1995-96; mgr. stds. strategy. Sun Microsys., Palo Alto, Calif., 1996—2002; dir. software AOL-TW, Dulles, Va., 2002—. Program co-chmn. Conf. on Software Maintenance, 1985, gen. mgr., 1987; gen. chmn. Computer Stds. Comf., 1988. Soccer coach Montgomery Country Recreation Dept., Rockville, Md., 1979-83; treas., del. Mill Creek Towne Elem. Sch. PTA, Rockville, 1981-84, pres., 1986-87; Magruder clustr PTA coord., 1984-856; leader Cub Scouts Am., Rockville, 1983-84, asst. troop scoutmaster, 1984-92. Recipient award for tech. excellence Interagy. Com. on Info. Resources Mgmt., 1989, Fed. Computer Week 100 award, 1992, cert. of recognition Nat. Bur. Stds., 1983, bronze medal Dept. Commerce, 1984, silver medal, 1989, Hans Karlsson award IEEE, 1995, Standards Medallion, 1992. Mem. Assn. for Computing Machinery, IEEE Computer Soc. (chmn. working group on test methods for POSIX 1986-93, tech. com. on conformance testing 1989-94, mem. tech. com. on operating sys. project mgmt. com. 1991-93, cert. of recognition 1987, Meritorious Svc. award 1991, Stds. medal 1992). Home: 1102 Round Pebble Ln Reston VA 20194-1002 Office: AOL 44900 Prentice Dr Sterling VA 20166 Office Phone: 703-265-6203. E-mail: rjmartin99@aol.com.

**MARTIN, SANDRA ANN,** special education educator, writer; b. Sewickley, Pa., Feb. 9, 1954; d. Antoni S. and Marian M. Jankiewicz; m. Stephen Patrick Martin, June 26, 1976; children: Caitlin Lauren, Alyssa Ann. BS in Edn., Bloomsburg U., Pa., 1976; M in Edn., Shippensburg U., Pa., 1979. Learning disabilities and emotional support resource rm. tchr. southwestern sch. dist. Lincoln Intermediate Unit # 12 Emory Markle Intermediate Sch., Hanover, Pa., 1976—77; learning disabilities and emotional support tchr. grades 6-12 math, reading, and lang. arts resource rm. settings Lincoln Intermediate Unit # 12 New Oxford (Pa.) Jr. HS, 1977—79, learning disabilities tchr. grades 7-9 math, reading, and lang. arts resource rm. settings, 1979—83; learning disabilities tchr. grades 6-8 math, reading, and lang. arts resource rm. settings New Oxford Mid. Sch., 1983—88, learning support tchr. grades 7-8 math, reading, and lang. arts resource rm. and inclusion settings Lincoln Intermediate Unit, 1988—96, learning support tchr. grades 7-8 math, reading, and lang. arts resource rm. and inclusion settings Conewago Valley Sch. Dist., 1996—. Spkr. in field, 2000—; supr. spl. edn. tchrs. Western Md. Coll., Shippensburg U., 1997—98. Author: Breaking the Sound Barrier to Fluent Reading, Level 1, 2002, Mathopedia, Level 1, Level 2, 2003. Chaperone, dance instr. New Oxford Mid. Sch., 1990—2003, drama coach, 1977—85; chaperone, dance instr. Girl Scouts, New Oxford, 1993—99; fundraiser Immaculate Conception Ch., New Oxford. Finalist Pa. Tchr. of Yr., 2004; named one of Outstanding Educators of Adams County. Mem.: NEA, Pa. State Edn. Assn., Coun. Exceptional Children (divsn. learning disabilities), New Oxford Area C. of C. Avocations: travel, concerts, Broadway plays and musicals, antiques, spectator sports. Home: 316 Lincoln Way W New Oxford PA 17350 Office: Conewago Valley Sch Dist 130 Berlin Rd New Oxford PA 17350 Office Phone: 717-624-4513. Personal E-mail: martinsandy@hotmail.com. Business E-Mail: specialtypublishers@hotmail.com.

**MARTIN, SHANE PATRICK,** education educator, consultant; b. L.A., Aug. 7, 1958; s. Robert Curtis and Lucille Catherine (Koch) M. BA in History, Loyola Marymount U., 1980; MDiv, Jesuit Sch. Theology, Berkeley, Calif., 1991, ThM, 1992; PhD, U. So. Calif., 1995. Cert. secondary tchr., Calif. Mem. faculty Bellarmine Coll. Prep. Sch., San Jose, Calif., 1984, 85-88, dir. campus ministry, 1987-88; grad. tchg. asst. Jesuit Sch. Theology, 1990-92; lectr. Loyola Marymount U., L.A., 1994-95, assoc. prof. edn., 1995—2004, coord. secondary edn., 2000—02, acting coord. bilingual and multicultural edn. programs, 1999-2000, assoc. dean edn., 2002—04, acting dean edn., 2004—05, dean, 2005—, prof., 2005—. Adj. prof. U. San Francisco, 1996—; cons., sr. assoc. Karadenes & Assocs., L.A., 1998—; sr. rsch. cons. Imoyase Group, Inc., 2001-. Author: Cultural Diversity in Catholic Schools, 1996, Equity, Advocacy and Diversity: New Directions for Catholic Schools, 2004. Pres. Assn. Jesuit Colls. and Univs. Edn. Coun., 2003—; trustee Loyola H.S., L.A., 1997—98; bd. dirs. Greendot Pub. Charter Schs., 2000—; bd. dirs. chmn. com. Coun. on Anthropology and Edn., 1998—2004; bd. dirs. Teach for Am., L.A., Calif. Charter Schs. Assn. Grantee, Loyola Marymount U., 1996, 1998—99, 2001—04. Mem. Am. Anthrop. Assn., Am. Edn. Rsch. Assn., Am. Assn. for Colls. Tchr. Edn., Assn. Tchr. Educators, Nat. Assn. for Multicultural Edn., Nat. Cath. Edn. Assn. (McGivney Meml. Fund grantee 1993), Nat. Coun. for Accreditation Tchr. Edn. (bd. examiners 2004—). Avocations: travel, cultural events, music, technology, mentoring. Office: Loyola Marymount U Sch Edn 1 LMU Dr UH Ste 2100 Los Angeles CA 90045-2659 Office Phone: 310 338-7301 Business E-Mail: smartin@lmu.edu.

**MARTIN, STANLEY ALLEN,** lawyer; b. Logansport, Ind., Apr. 9, 1955; s. Richard James and Helen Elizabeth M.; m. Kellie Lea McCabe, Aug. 14, 1988. BS, MIT, 1977; JD, Boston Coll., 1984. Bar: Mass. 1985, U.S. Dist. Ct. Mass. 1985, U.S. Ct. Appeals (1st cir.) 1985, N.H. 1986, U.S. Dist. Ct. N.H. 1987. Prin. Stan Martin, Designer/Builder, Andover, Mass., 1977-84; assoc. Gadsby & Hannah LLP, Boston, 1984-91, ptnr., 1992—2001, Holland & Knight LLP, Boston, 2001—. Lectr. Northeastern U., Boston, 1989—95, MIT, 2000—01. Author: Mechanic's Liens, Performance and Payment Bonds under Massachusetts Law, 1989, 7th rev. edit., 1996; co-author: Architect-Engineer Liability Under Massachusetts Law, 1985, 5th rev. edit., 1990; contbg. author ann. Aspen Construction Law Update, 1995—; contbr. articles to profl. jours. Bd. dirs. Andover Com./A Better Chance-ABC, 1981—84, Associated Gen. Contractors of Mass., 1999—2001, Boston Archtl. Ctr., 2000—04, Edgewood Retirement Cmty., 2001—. Mem. ABA (pub. contract sect., chair region I 1990-96), Am. Arbitration Assn. Constrn. Industry Panel, Mass. Bar Assn. (chair pub. law sect. 1993-94), Internat. Bar Assn., N.H. Bar Assn. Home: 7 Pendant Ct Andover MA 01810-6305 Office: Holland & Knight LLP 10 St James Ave Boston MA 02116 E-mail: stan.martin@hklaw.com.

**MARTIN, STANLEY DONALD,** publishing executive, editor; b. Hamilton, Bermuda, Jan. 1, 1942; s. John Hewitt Mitchell and Dorothy Emily Martin; life ptnr. Lillian Guardino; children: Danamarie, Torilyn Martin Dunn, Mary K. children: Grant Shelton Kilbourne, Thayne Mitchell. BA In Journalism, Idaho State U., 1964; MBA, MS in Journalism, U. Utah, 1970. Commercial Pilot NW Aviation, 1978. Editor & pub. Straus Newspapers, Inc., Monroe, NY, 1986—; v.p. mktg. News Voice Newspapers, Inc., Highland Park, Ill., 1985—86. Pres. & pub. Hammell Newspapers of Fla., Clewiston, Fla., 1982—85. Contbg. editor: (newspapers) Various Publications (Over 150 awards in pub. industry). Mem. Rotary Internat., Warwick, NY, 1982—2003. Capt. U.S. Army Signal Corps, 1965—68, Germany. Mem.: N.Y. Press Assn. (assoc.). Avocations: travel, aviation. Office: Straus Newspapers Inc 45 Gilbert St Ext Monroe NY 10950

**MARTIN, STEPHEN F.,** chemist, educator, researcher; BS, U. N.Mex., 1968; PhD, Princeton U., 1972. Alexander von Humboldt stipendiat Inst. fur Organische Chemie U. Munich, 1972-73; NIH postdoctoral fellow MIT, 1973-74; M. June and J. Virgil Waggoner Regents Chair in chemistry U. Tex., Austin. Contbr. articles to profl. jours. Recipient Rsch. Career Devel. award NIH, 1980-85, Arthur C. Cope Scholar award Am. Chem. Soc., 1996, Alexander von Humboldt Sr. Scientist award, 1995-97, Japan Soc. for Promotion of Sci. award, 2001, Wyeth Rsch. award, 2003. Fellow: AAAS. Office: Chem & Biochem Dept Univ Texas 1 University Sta A5300 Austin TX 78712-1095 Office Phone: 512-471-3915. E-mail: sfmartin@mail.utexas.edu.

**MARTIN, STEVE,** actor, comedian; b. Waco, Tex., Aug. 14, 1945; s. Glenn and Mary Lee Martin; m. Victoria Tennant, Nov. 20, 1986 (div. 1994). Student, Long Beach State Coll., UCLA. Exec. prodr. TV show Domestic Life, 1984. TV writer for Smothers Bros. (co-winner Emmy award 1969), Sonny and Cher, Pat Paulsen, Ray Stevens, Dick Van Dyke, John Denver, Glen Campbell; nightclub comedian; guest and host appearances NBC's Saturday Night Live, Tonight Show; appeared on Carol Burnett Show; starred in TV spls. Steve Martin: A Wild and Crazy Guy, 1978, Comedy is Not Pretty, 1980, Steve Martin's Best Show Ever, 1981; rec. comedy albums Let's Get Small, 1977 (Grammy award 1977), A Wild and Crazy Guy, 1978 (Grammy award 1978), Comedy is Not Pretty, 1979, The Steve Martin Brothers, 1982; actor, screenwriter (films) The Absent Minded Waiter, 1977 (Academy award nomination best short film 1977), The Jerk, 1979, Pennies From Heaven, 1981, Dead Men Don't Wear Plaid, 1982, The Man With Two Brains, 1983, All of Me, 1984 (Nat. Soc. Film Critics award best actor 1984, New York Film Critics' Circle award best actor 1984), Three Amigos, 1986 (also exec. prodr.), Roxanne, 1987 (also exec. prodr.), (Nat. Soc. Film Critics award best actor 1988, Los Angeles Film Critics' award best actor 1988), L.A. Story, 1991; actor (films) Sergeant Pepper's Lonely Hearts Club Band, 1978, The Muppet Movie, 1979, The Kids Are Alright, 1979, The Lonely Guy, 1984, Little Shop of Horrors, 1986, Planes, Trains and Automobiles, 1987, Dirty Rotten Scoundrels, 1988, Parenthood, 1989, My Blue Heaven, 1990, Father of the Bride, 1991, Grand Canyon, 1991, Housesitter, 1992, Leap of Faith, 1993, Mixed Nuts, 1994, Twist of Fate, 1994, Sgt. Bilko, 1995, The Spanish Prisoner, 1998, Bowfinger, 1999, Joe Gould's Secret, 2000, Novocaine, 2001, Bringing Down the House, 2003, Looney Tunes: Back in Action, 2003, Cheaper by the Dozen, 2003, Jiminy Glick in La La Wood, 2004, Shopgirl, 2005 (also writer, prodr.), Cheaper by the Dozen 2, 2005, The Pink Panther, 2006 (also writer); (theatre) Waiting For Godot, 1988; (television) And the Band Played On, 1993, Rutles 2: Can't Buy Me Lunch, 2002; screenwriter (films) Easy Money, 1983, Bowfinger, 1999; author: Cruel Shoes, 1977, Pure Drivel, 1998, Shopgirl, 2001; playwright Picasso at the Lapin Agile, 1993. Trustee L.A. Mus. Art. Named one of 50 Most Powerful People in Hollywood, Premiere mag., 2006; recipient Georgie award, Am. Guild Variety Artists, 1977, 1978, Grammy award, 1978, Mark Twain prize for Am. Humor, 2005. Office: PO Box 929 Beverly Hills CA 90213*

**MARTIN, SUSAN KATHERINE,** librarian; b. Cambridge, Eng., Nov. 14, 1942; came to U.S., 1950, naturalized, 1961; d. Egon and Jolan (Schonfeld) Orowan; m. David S. Martin, June 30, 1962. BA with honors, Tufts U., 1963; MS, Simmons Coll., 1965; PhD, U. Calif., Berkeley, 1983. Intern libr. Harvard U., Cambridge, Mass., 1963-65, systems libr., 1965-73; head systems office gen. libr. U. Calif., Berkeley, 1973-79; dir. Milton S. Eisenhower Libr. Johns Hopkins U., Balt., 1979-88, exec. dir. Nat. Commn. on Libraries and Info. Sci., 1988-90; univ. libr. Georgetown U., Washington, 1990-2001, tchr., cons., 2001—; pres. SKM Associates, 2001—; cons. dir. Marstons Mills Pub. Libr., 2003—05, dir., 2005—. Mem. libr. com. Princeton (N.J.) U., 1987—95; mem. vis. com. Harvard U. Libr., 1987—93, 1994—2000; bd. overseers for univ. libr. Tufts U., 1986—2001, Tufts U. Sch. Arts and Scis., 2001—06; cons. various librs. and info. cos., 1975—; mem. libr. adv. com. Hong Kong U. Sci. Tech., 1988—95; mem. acad. libr. adv. com. U. Md. Sch. Libr. and Info. Scis., 1994—96; mem. adv. bd. ERIC, 1990—92; mem. Chadwyck-Healey N.Am. Adv. Com. on Lit. Online, 1997—99; vice chair, chair Chesapeake Info. and Rsch. Libr. Alliance, 1996—98; cons. libr. devel. & fundraising, 1998—; spkr. in field; mem. adv. bd. Georgetown U. Libr., 2001—. Author: Library Networks: Libraries in Partnership, 1986—87; editor: Jour. Libr. Automation, 1972—77; co-editor: Portal: Libraries and the Academy, 2000—04; mem. editl. bd. Portal: Libraries and the Academy, 2005—; mem. editl. bd.: Advanced Tech./Librs., 1973—93, Jour. Libr. Adminstrn., 1986—2000, Libr. Hi-Tech., 1989—93, Jour. Acad. Librarianship, 1994—99; contbr. articles to profl. jours. Trustee Phila. Area Libr. Network, 1980—81; bd. dirs. Universal Serials and Book Exch., 1981—82, v.p., 1983, pres., 1984; trustee Capital Consortium, 1992—95; mem. bd. Potomac Internet, 1995—96; pres., trustee Marstons Mills Pub. Libr., 2002—03. Named Samuel Lazerow disting. lectr., Drexel U., 1984, L.I. U., 2002; recipient Simmons Coll. Disting. Alumni award, 1977; Coun. on Libr. Resources fellow, 1973. Mem.: ALA (coun. 1988—92, structure revision TF 1995—97, chair task force on external accrediting body 1999—2002), Assn. Coll. and Rsch. Librs. (pres. 1994—95, vis. program officer for scholarly com. 2002—03), Coalition for Networked Info. (leader working group 1990—92), Assn. Assoc. Colls. and Univ. Librs. (chair 1997—98), Libr. of Congress (optical disk pilot project adv. com. 1985—89), Assn. Rsch. Librs. (info. policy com. 1995—97, stats. com. 1988—2000), Librl. and Info. Tech. Assn. (pres. 1978—79), Rsch. Librs. Group (bd. govs. 1981—88, exec. com. 1985—87), Internat. Fedn. Libr. Assns. Commn. on Access to Info. and Freedom of Expression, Cranberry Shores Chorus (publicity coord. 2002—05, pres. 2005—, webmaster 2004—), Sweet Adelines Internat. (region 1 mgmt. team 2005—), Cosmos Club (libr. com. 1988—2005), Phi Beta Kappa (chair Georgetown U. chpt. 2000—01). Home: 10 Colonial Farm Cir Marstons Mills MA 02648 Office: Marston Mills Pub Library PO Box 9 2160 Main St Marstons Mills MA 02648 Office Phone: 508-428-5175. Business E-Mail: martin@skmassociates.net.

**MARTIN, THEODORE KRINN,** former university administrator; b. Blue Mountain, Miss., Jan. 2, 1915; s. Thomas Theodore and Ivy (Manning) M.; m. Lorene Garrison, Sept. 6, 1947; children: Glenn Krinn, Mary Ann, Janet Kay. AB, Georgetown Coll., Ky., 1935; MA, La. State U., 1941; PhD, George Peabody Coll., 1949. Tchr. Consol. Sch., Dumas, Miss., 1935-36; prin. Mississippi Heights Acad., 1936-39; tchr. Murphy High Sch., Mobile, Ala., 1940-41; registrar Miss. State U., 1949-53, registrar, adminstrv. asst. to pres., 1953-56, dean Sch. Edn., 1956-61, exec. asst. to pres., 1961-66, v.p., 1966-85, dir. Summer Sch., 1956-70, ret., 1985. Served as capt. AUS, 1941-46. T.K. Martin Ctr. for Tech. and Disability on Miss. State U. Campus named in his honor. Mem. Masons, Kappa Alpha, Phi Kappa Phi, Omicron Delta Kappa, Kappa Delta Pi, Phi Delta Kappa. Home: 1151 East Dr Starkville MS 39759-9491

**MARTIN, THOMAS A.,** psychologist; s. Thomas and Sandra J. Martin; children: Lauren A., Dalton T. D in Psychology, Adler Sch. Profl. Psychology, Chgo., 2000. Lic. psychologist Mo., 2001. Psychologist Mo. Rehab. Ctr., Mt. Vernon, 2002—; clin. asst. prof. U. Mo., Columbia, 2002—. Editor: (text book) Geriatric Neuropsychology: Practice Essentials. Office: Missouri Rehabilitation Center 600 N Main St Mount Vernon MO 65712 Office Phone: 417-461-5238.

**MARTIN, THOMAS JOHN,** pediatrician, sports medicine physician; b. Greensburg, Pa., July 4, 1934; s. John William and Mary DeTar Martin; m. Lois Darlene Miller, June 20, 1992; children: Jack T., Susan L. O'Malley, James S., David S. BS, Franklin and Marshall Coll., Lancaster, Pa., 1956; MD, U. Pitts., 1960. Diplomate Am. Bd. Pediats. Gen. practice medicine, Slippery Rock, Pa., 1961—62, 1964—65; pediat. resident Children's Hosp. of Pitts., 1965—67; assoc. in pediats. Geisinger Med. Ctr., Danville, Pa., 1967—75, chmn. pediats., 1975—95; dir. inpatient pediats. Aultman Hosp., Canton, Ohio, 1995—97; team physician, prof. Pa. State U., University Park, 1997—2004, clin. prof. pediats., Milton S. Hershey Med. Ctr., 2005—; assoc. program dir. family practice residency The Williamsport (Pa.) Hosp., 2004—; prof. emeritus dept. orthop. and rehab. Hershey Med. Ctr., 2005—. Adj. clin. assoc. prof. Jefferson Med. Coll., Phila.; team physician football, wrestling Pa. State U., University Park, 1997—2004; courtesy staff Lewistown (Pa.)

Hosp., 1999—2004; active staff Centre Cmty. Hosp., State College, Pa., 1997—2004, Children's Hosp. Med. Ctr. of Akron, Ohio, 1995—97; lectr. in field. Contbr. articles to profl. jours. Pres. Riverside Home and Sch., Pa., 1968—69; coach, organizer Danville H.S. Swim Team, 1974; pres. Riverside Home and Sch. Assn., 1968—69; mem. global mission com. Upper Susquehanna Synod Coun., 1999—; fin. com. Pine St. Luth. Ch., Danville, 1994—96, coun. mem., 1993—95, chmn. religious com., 1993—95; bd. dirs. Sunbury Area YMCA, Pa., 1976—84. Capt. U.S. Army, 1962—64. Named Citizen of the Yr., Elks, 1995; named to Geisinger's Pediat. Wall of Fame, 2005; recipient Honors for Exceptional Svc. to Children and Youth, Nat. Child Labor Com., N.Y.C., 1995. Mem.: AMA, Nat. Wrestling Coaches Assn., Pa. Med. Soc. (continuing med. edn. accreditation surveyor 1988—93), Am. Coll. Sports Medicine, Am. Acad. Pediats. (com. on sports medicine and fitness 1998—2004, exec. com. sect. on sports medicine 1997—2003, chpt. chmn. 1980—82), Lycoming County Med. Soc., Am. Bd. Pediats. Lutheran. Avocations: running, skiing, swimming, concerts. Home: 23 E Hayes Crossing Belleville PA 17004 Office: Susquehanna Health System 777 Rural Ave Williamsport PA 17701

**MARTIN, THOMAS LYLE, JR.,** academic administrator; b. Memphis, Sept. 26, 1921; s. Thomas Lyle and Malvina (Rucks) M.; m. Helene Hartley, June 12, 1943 (dec. Sept. 1983); children: Michele Marie, Thomas Lyle; m. Mildred L. Moore, June 5, 1984. B.E.E., Rensselaer Poly. Inst., 1942, M.E.E., 1948, D.Eng., 1967; PhD, Stanford U., 1951; DSc (hon.), So. Meth. U., 2004. Prof. elec. engring. U. N.Mex., 1948-53; prof. engring. U. Ariz., 1953-63, dean engring., 1958-63, U. Fla., Gainesville, 1963-66, So. Meth. U., Dallas, 1966-74; pres. Ill. Inst. Tech., Chgo., 1974-87, pres. emeritus. Capt. Signal Corps AUS, 1943-46. Mem. ASEE Hall of Fame. Fellow IEEE; mem. Nat. Acad. Engring. Achievements include being one of the founders of Dallas-Ft. Worth Internat. Airport. Home and Office: PO Box 167845 Irving TX 75016-7845

**MARTIN, THOMAS STEPHEN,** lawyer; b. NYC, Aug. 31, 1946; s. Stephen Paul and Kathleen Mary (Redmond) M.; m. Lynne Kathryn Mallory, Oct. 2, 1968; children: Laura Kathryn, Mallory Anne. BA maxima cum laude, King's Coll., 1968; JD, U. Chgo., 1972. Bar: DC 1973. Assoc. Steptoe & Johnson, Washington, 1972-75; spl. asst. to asst. atty. gen., civil div. Dept. Justice, Washington, 1975-76, asst. to solicitor gen., 1976-78, dep. asst. atty. gen. civil div., 1978-80, acting asst. atty. gen. civil div., 1981-82; ptnr. Venable, Baetjer, Howard & Civiletti, Washington, 1982-83, Jenner & Block, Washington, 1983-90; ptnr. litigation group Shearman & Sterling LLP, Washington, 1990—, mng. ptnr., dir. Appellate and Supreme Ct. Practice Group; mem. adv. com. fed. rules of civil procedure, 1980-84. Chmn. com. admissions and grievances US Ct. Appeals (DC cir.), 1991—. Comment editor: U. Chgo. Law Rev., 1971-72. Mem. ABA, DC Bar Assn., Am. Law Inst. Office: Shearman & Sterling LLP 801 Pennsylvania Ave NW Ste 900 Washington DC 20004-2604 Office Phone: 202-508-8040. Office Fax: 202-508-8100. Business E-Mail: tmartin@shearman.com.

**MARTIN, TONY,** humanities educator; b. Port of Spain, Trinidad, Feb. 21, 1942; arrived in U.S., 1969; s. Claude G. and Vida Beryl M. BSc in econ. with honors, U. Hull, 1968; MA, Mich. State U., 1970, PhD, 1973. Barrister-at-law Hon. Soc. Gray's Inn, London, 1965; asst. prof. history, African-Afro Am. studies U. Mich., Flint, 1971—73; assoc. prof. history and Africana studies Wellesley Coll., 1973—75, assoc. prof. Africana studies, 1975—79, prof. Africana studies, 1979—. Vis. prof. history U. Minn., 1975, The Colo. Coll., Colo. Springs, 1985-86; vis. prof. African-Am. Studies, Brown U., Providence, R.I., 1991, Brandeis U., Waltham, Mass., 1974, 81; hon. rsch. fellow U. of West Indies, Trinidad, 1986-87; lectr. DuBois-Padmore-Nkrumah, Ghana, 1990; cons. founds.; expert witness Congl. Hearings, 1987; guest lectr. numerous univs.; U.S., Can., Caribbean, Australia, Africa, Eng.; featured spkr. Conf. of Intellectuals of Africa and its Diaspora, Dakar, Senegal, 2004. Author: Race First, 1976, Literary Garveyism, 1983, The Pan-African Connection, 1983; reviewer articles for profl. jours.; contbr. articles to profl. jours., encys., and other ref. books, intro. to E. Franklin Frazier and Eric Williams, eds, The Economic Future of the Caribbean, 2004; contbg. editor profl. jours. Pres. Union of West Indian Students in Gt. Britain and No. Ireland, 1966—68. Recipient Rsch. award Am. Philos. Soc., Phila., 1990, Cmty. award Emancipation Support Com. Mem. Assn. of Caribbean Historians, African Heritage Studies Assn., Assn. for the Study of Classical African Civilizations (John Henrik Clarke Living Legacy award), Organ. Am. Historians. Office: Wellesley Coll Africana Studies Dept Wellesley MA 02481 Office Phone: 781-283-2564. E-mail: amartin@wellesley.edu.

**MARTIN, TRISA,** education and human development educator; d. Heber and Edna Jensen; m. Keith Martin, Sept. 4, 1970; children: David, Jonathan, Michelle, Steven, Deborah, Joseph. BS in Elem. Edn., Brigham Young U., 1970; MEd, U. Utah, 1973. Elem. tchr. Davis Sch. Dist., Farmington, Utah, 1970—73, substitute tchr. k-12, 1989—98; adj. prof. edn. and human devel. Salt Lake C.C., Salt Lake City, 1998—. Contbr. articles to mags. Edn. leader Women's Orgn., Bountiful (Utah) 30th Ward, 2000—03. Mem.: League of Utah Writers (pres. Bountiful chpt. 1995—96).

**MARTIN, VICKI JOAN,** biology professor; BS, U. N.C., Charlotte, 1970—74; MS, Wake Forest U., N.C., 1974—76, PhD, 1977—80. Postdoctoral fellow U. Alta., Edmonton, Canada, 1980—81; asst. prof. U. Louisville, Ky., 1981—83; asst. to assoc. prof. U. Notre Dame, Ind., 1983—99; prof. biology Appalachian State U., Boone, NC, 1999—, chair, dept. biology, 1999—2004. Dir. optical lab. U. Notre Dame, Notre Dame, 1983—99, dir. grad. studies, dept. biology, 1990—92; cons. Earth and Sky NPR, 1999—. Contbr. chapters to books, articles to profl. jours. and pubs. Recipient Career Advancement award, NSF, 1987—90, Frank O'Malley Undergraduate Tchg. award, U. Notre Dame, 1995—96, 100 Scholar's Rsch. award, Appalachian State U., 2004. Mem.: Nat. Coun. on Undergraduate Rsch. (elected councilor 2005—). Achievements include research in demonstration of visual pigments in primitive eyes of invertebrates. Office: Appalachian State Univ 572 Rivers St Boone NC 28608 Office Phone: 828-262-6923.

**MARTIN, VINCENT LIONEL,** retired manufacturing executive; b. Los Angles, June 29, 1939; s. Arthur Seymon and Alice Maria (Miller) M.; m. Janet Ann Dowler, Mar. 25, 1961; children: Jennifer Lynn, Karen Arlene, Timothy Paul. BS, Stanford U., 1960; MBA, Harvard U., 1963. Various staff positions FMC Corp, Chgo, 1966-74, gen. mgr. Crane and Excavator div. Cedar Rapids, Iowa, 1974-79; pres. Equipment Systems div. AMCA Internat. Corp., Houston, 1979-81, group v.p. Proliance, 1981-85; CEO, pres. Jason Inc., Milw., 1986-96, chmn. CEO, 1996-99, chmn., 1999—2004; ret. Bd. dirs. Jason Inc., Modine Mfg. Co., Proliance Internat. Inc. Mem. Phi Beta Kappa, Tau Beta Pi Republican. Presbyterian. Home: 2601 W Cedar Ln Milwaukee WI 53217-1138 Office: Jason Inc 411 E Wisconsin Ave Milwaukee WI 53202-4461 E-mail: Vmartin@jasoninc.com.

**MARTIN, VIVIAN BONITA,** journalist, educator; b. Mar. 29, 1956; d. Rutrell and Ruth Vivian (Robinson) Martin. MA in Am. Studies, Vt. Coll., 1997; PhD in Media and Culture, Union Inst., 2004. Reporter Hartford Courant, Conn., 1978—86, Op-ed columnist, 1997—2003; freelance writer, 1987—; assoc. prof. Dept. English Ctrl. Conn. State U., New Britain, 1999—. Reporter Conn. Law Tribune, 1989—90; mem. part-time faculty Ctrl. Conn. State U., 1996—99. Author: Astrocycles, 1990; contbr. articles to profl. jours. Recipient Best Op-ed Column award, Conn. Soc. Profl. Journalists. Mem.: Am. Sociol. Assn., Assn. for Edn. in Journalism and Mass Comm. Office: Central Conn State Univ 1615 Stanley Rd New Britain CT 06050 Office Phone: 860-832-2776. Business E-Mail: martinv@ccsu.edu.

**MARTIN, WILLIAM C.,** social studies educator, writer; b. San Antonio, Dec. 31, 1937; s. Lowell Curtis and Joe Bailey (Brite) M.; m. Patricia Gale Summerlin, Dec. 31, 1957; children: Rex Martin, Jeff Martin, Elisabeth Dale Martin Thomas. BA, Abilene Christian U., 1958, MA, 1960; BD, Harvard Divinity Sch., 1963; PhD, Harvard U., 1969. Instr. history Dana Hall Sch., Wellesley, Mass., 1965-68; instr. sociology Rice U., Houston, 1968-69, asst.

prof. sociology, 1969-73, assoc. prof. sociology, 1973-79, prof. sociology, 1979—, Chavanne prof. religion and pub. policy, 2005—, emeritus, 2005—, master Sid W. Richardson Coll., 1976-81, chair dept. sociology, 1983—86, 1989—94, 2003—04. Cons. films and TV documentaries; speaker in field. Author: These Were God's People, 1966, Christians in Conflict, 1972, A Prophet With Honor: Billy Graham Story, 1991 (Christianity Today's Critic's Choice award 1992), My Prostate and Me: Dealing With Prostate Cancer, 1994, With God on our Side: The Rise of the Religious Right in America, 1996; contbg. editor Tex. Monthly (Nat. Headliner award 1982); contbr. numerous articles to profl. jours. and pop mags.; numerous radio and TV appearances. Dir. House of the Carpenter, Inc., inner-city youth program, Boston, 1963-66, pres. and bd. dirs. non-profit housing corp.; bd. dirs. Fellowship Racial and Econ. Equality, 1970-71; mem. exec. com. Houston Coun. Human Rels. Recipient Nicholas Salgo Outstanding Tchr. award Rice U., 1971, 93, Brown Coll. award for Teaching in the Humanities Rice U., 1974, 76, George R. Brown Award for Superior Teaching, alumni Rice U., 1974, 76, 77, 84, for Excellence in Teaching, 1975, 82, Life Honor award, 1985, Sr. scholar James A. Baker III Inst. Pub. Policy; Chavenne sr. fellow for religion and pub. policy; grantee Am. Coun. Learned Socs. and Am. Philos. Soc., 1974. Mem. Am. Sociol. Assn., Soc. Scientific Study Religion, Religious Rsch. Assn., Tex. Inst. Letters (J. Frank Dobie/Paisano fellowship 1980). Democrat. Protestant. Avocation: bicycling. Home: 2929 Buffalo Speedway 312 Houston TX 77098 Office: Rice U Baker Inst MS40 6100 Main St Houston TX 77005-1892 Office Phone: 713-348-3481. Business E-Mail: wcm@rice.edu.

**MARTIN, WILLIAM EDWIN,** lawyer; b. Bowling Green, Ky., Oct. 16, 1943; s. John Edwin and Bess Carolyn (Matherly) M.; children: Anne Whitson, William Whitson; m. Jean Clinton Nelson, Aug. 1, 1981. BA, Vanderbilt U., 1965, JD, 1968. Bar: Tenn. 1968. Ptnr. Waller Lansden Dortch & Davis, Nashville, 1968-75; sr. ptnr. Harwell Martin & Stegall, Nashville, 1975-93; dep. asst. sec. for internat. affairs U.S. Dept. Commerce-NOAA, Washington, 1993-98; chmn. Will Martin Co., 1998—; sr. v.p. Pvt. Bus. Inc., Brentwood, Tenn., 1999; vice chmn. Tecniflex, Inc., Nashville, 2000—01; chmn. Imagic Corp., Nashville, 2000—01. Sr. fellow WWF, 1999—; chmn. Marine Stewardship Coun., London, 2005—; bd. dirs. Board Mem. Inc., Brentwood. Contbr. articles to profl. jours. and law revs. Dir. polar programs Wilderness Soc., Washington, 1990—92. Democrat. Episcopalian. Avocations: mountain climbing, photography, running, tennis, biking.

**MARTIN, WILLIAM FRANCIS, JR.,** lawyer; b. Lowell, Mass., Sept. 13, 1961; s. William F. and Patricia A. Martin; m. Martha Doherty, Oct. 23, 1988; children: William F. III, Daniel J., Jacqueline E. BA in English, Coll. of Holy Cross, Worcester, Mass., 1983; JD, Boston Coll., 1986. Bar: Mass. 1986, N.H. 1991. Law clk. to Hon. Joseph R. Nolan Mass. Supreme Jud. Ct., Boston, 1986-87; assoc. Hale and Dorr, Boston and Manchester, 1987-93; ptnr. Eno, Boulay, Martin Donahue, LLP (and predecessor firm), Lowell, 1994—. Bd. dirs. Lowell Parks and Conservation Trust, Lowell, 1991—; mem. Lowell Conservation Commn., 1993-94, chmn., 1994-99. Articles editor Boston Coll. Law Review, 1985-86. Mem. Lowell City Coun., 2000-2005; mayor City of Lowell, 2006—; bd. dirs. D'Youville Sr. Care, 1997—. Mem. Omicron Delta Epsilon, Order of the Coif. Home: 173 Clark Rd Lowell MA 01852 Office: Eno Boulay Martin & Donahue LLP 21 George St Lowell MA 01852 Office Phone: 978-452-8902. Business E-Mail: b.martin@ebmdattorneys.com.

**MARTIN, WILLIAM JOSEPH, II,** dean, educator; m. Joyce Martin; 2 children. MD, U. Minn. Resident in internal medicine Mayo Grad. Sch. Medicine, Rochester, Minn., fellow in pulmonary medicine; faculty and med. staff Mayo Clinic, Rochester, Minn., 1981—88; Floyd and Reba Smith prof. respiratory disease Ind. U. Sch. Medicine, 1988—2002, exec. assoc. dean clin. affairs, dir. divsn. pulmonary, allergy, critical care and occupl. medicine, 1988—2000; acting sr. v.p. U. Cin., 2002—03, Christian R. Holmes prof., dean Coll. Medicine, 2002—04, rsch. prof., 2004—. Pres. and CEO Ind. U. Med. Group; health policy fellow U.S. Sen. for Sen. Labor and Human Resources Com., 1995—96; funded prin. investigator Nat. Heart, Lung and Blood Inst. Mem.: Am. Thoracic Soc. (pres. 2000—01), Assn. Pulmonary and Critical Care Medicine Program Dirs. (past pres.), Am. Lung Assn. Ind. (past pres.). Office: Coll Medicine 231 Albert Sabin Way Cincinnati OH 45267

**MARTIN, WILLIAM RAYMOND,** retired financial manager; b. Phila., Oct. 16, 1939; s. Clyde Davis and Mary Anna (Coates) M.; m. Michaela Roberta Smink, Sept. 8, 1962 (div. 1969, dec. 2002); 1 child, James; m. Margaret Scouten, Oct. 16, 1970 (div. 1983); children: Mary Frances, Susanna; m. Joan Friedman Kennedy, Jan. 29, 1988 (div. 1999). BSME, Lehigh U., 1960; MBA, U. Pa., 1973. Mem. engring. staff Pa. R.R., 1960-65; asst. gen. mgr. Excelsior Truck Leasing, Phila., 1965-71; sr. policy analyst Assn. Am. R.R.s, Washington, 1973-76, mgr. engring. econ., 1976-78; mgr. fin. analysis So. Ry., Washington, 1978-83; dir. fin. planning Norfolk (Va.) So. Corp., 1984-92, asst. v.p. fin., 1992-95. Contbr. articles to profl. jours. Bd. dirs. Williams Sch., Norfolk, 1988—96, pres., 1992—96; bd. dirs. Va. Stage Co., Norfolk, 1995—2001, Feldman Chamber Music Soc., 2001—05, Norfolk Chamber Consort, 1998—2004, treas., 2001—04. Mem. ASME, Soc. Automotive Engrs., Mid Atlantic Roadracing Club. Home: 118 Woody's Ln Weems VA 22576

**MARTIN, WILLIAM ROYALL, JR.,** retired professional society administrator; b. Raleigh, NC, Sept. 3, 1926; s. William Royall and Edith Ruth (Crocker) M.; m. Betty Anne Rader, June 14, 1952; children: Sallie Rader Martin Busby, Amy Kemp Martin Lewis. AB, U.N.C., 1948, MBA, 1964; BS, N.C. State U., 1952. Chemist Stamford (Conn.) rsch. labs. Am. Cyanamid Co., 1952—54; chemist Dan River Mills, Danville, Va., 1954—56, Union Carbide Corp., South Charleston, W.Va., 1956—59; rsch. assoc. Sch. Textiles N.C. State U., 1959—63; tech. dir. Am. Assn. Textile Chemists and Colorists, Research Triangle Park, NC, 1963—73, exec. dir., 1974—96. Adj. assoc. prof. Coll. Textiles, N.C. State U., 1966-88, adj. assoc. prof., 1989-97; del. Internat. Orgn. Standardization, Pan Am. Standards Commn. With USNR, 1944—46. Fellow Am. Inst. Chemists, Soc. Dyers and Colourists, Textile Inst.; mem. Am. Chem. Soc., Coun. Engring. and Sci. Soc. Execs. (past pres. 1992-93), Fiber Soc., Am. Assn. Textile Chemists and Colorists, Masons, Rotary, Phi Kappa Phi, Phi Gamma Delta. Methodist. Home and Office: 224 Briarcliff Ln Cary NC 27511-3901 Office Phone: 919-467-9946. Personal E-mail: wrbrm@bellsouth.net.

**MARTIN, WILLIAM RUSSELL,** nuclear engineering educator; b. Flint, Mich., June 2, 1945; s. Carl Marcus and Audrey Winifred (Rosene) M.; m. Patricia Ann Williams, Aug. 13, 1967; children: Amy Leigh, Jonathan William. BSE in Engring. Physics, U. Mich., 1967; MS in Physics, U. Wis., 1968; MSE in Nuclear Engring., U. Mich., 1975, PhD in Nuclear Engring., 1976. Prin. physicist Combustion Engring., Inc., Windsor, Conn., 1976-77; asst. prof. nuclear engring. U. Mich., Ann Arbor, 1977-81, assoc. prof. nuclear engring., 1981-88, prof. nuclear engring., 1988—, dir. lab. for sci. computation, 1986—2001, chmn. nuclear engring., 1990-94, assoc. dean for acad. affairs Coll. Engring., 1994-99, dir. Ctr. for Advanced Computing, 2002—04; acting dir. Mich. Grid Ctr., 2002—04, chmn. nuclear engring., 2004—. Cons. Lawrence Livermore Nat. Lab., Livermore, Calif., 1982—, Los Alamos (N.Mex.) Nat. Lab., 1980-89, 2001—, IBM, Inc., Kingston, N.Y., 1984, Rockwell Internat., Pitts., 1985. Author: Transport Theory, 1979; author tech. and conf. papers. Recipient Glenn Murphy award Am. Soc. for Engring. Edn., 1993; Disting. scholar U. Mich. Coll. Engring., 1967; vis. fellow Royal Soc., London, 1989. Fellow Am. Nuclear Soc.; mem. Am. Phys. Soc., Soc. for Indsl. and Applied Math., IEEE. Avocations: running, reading, skiing, sailing. Home: 420 Huntington Dr Ann Arbor MI 48104 Office: U Mich Dept Nuclear Engring Ann Arbor MI 48109 Office Phone: 734-764-5534. Business E-Mail: wrm@umich.edu.

**MARTINA, CARLO JACK,** lawyer; b. Wyandotte, Mich., Jan. 1, 1954; s. Carlo and Matilda M.; m. Marie A. Pulte; children: Raphael, Ariel. BS with high distinction, U. Mich., 1976; JD, Wayne State U., 1979. Bar: Mich. 1979, U.S. Dist. Ct. (ea. dist.) Mich. 1980. Assoc. Provisor, Eisenberg et al, Southfield, Mich., 1979-81, Auslander, Babcock & Weiss, Southfield, Mich.,

1981-83; atty. pvt. practice, Southfield, Mich., 1983—. Mem. adv. bd. Legal Alternatives for Women, Southfield, 1985-87; co-founder Mich. br. Justice for Children, 1995-97; co-founder, co-publisher, co-owner MetroParent Mag., Southfield, 1987-95;; mem. task force Oakland County Family Ct., 2001—; lectr. in field. Legal expert (video) Latchkey Kids: Home Alone & Safe, 1994; author: Effective Discovery in Domestic Violence Litigation, 2002; contbr. chpts. to books, articles pub. to profl. jour. Mem. adv. bd. Gov.'s Internat. Yr. of Family Coun., Lansing, Mich., 1994-95, Roundtable of Christians, Muslims & Jews, Detroit, 1989-91, Anti-Defamation League, Southfield, 1988-90, Coalition Against Domestic Violence; scoutmaster Cub Scout Pack 1016, Birmingham, Mich., 1993-97. James P. Angel scholar U. Mich., 1977-79. Mem. Mich. Trial Lawyers Assn., Mich. Bar Assn. (bd. dirs., family law coun. 2001—, chmn. child support, alimony and friend of ct. com. 2002—, exec. bd. mem. family law coun. 2003—, lectr.), Oakland County Bar Assn. (co-chair family court com., friend of ct. subcom.), Wayne County Bar Assn. (family law divsn., liaison to Mich. Bar Assn., family law coun. 2001—, pres. 2004-05). Avocations: reading, fishing, furniture refinishing and home remodeling, model building. Office: 1158 S Main St Plymouth MI 48170-2214 Business E-Mail: MartinaLawOffice@aol.com.

**MARTINBOROUGH, SAMUEL NEIL,** music educator, conductor, musician; s. Gordon Ornsley and Waveney Vivina Martinborough. AA, Caribbean Union Coll., Trinidad, West Indies, 1986; MusB in Edn., Atlantic Union Coll., 1991; MA in Theatre Edn., Emerson Coll., 2000. Elem. educator Antigua SDA Sch., St Johns, Antigua and Barbuda, 1987—88; music educator South Lancaster Acad. and Browning Elem. Schs., 1991—96, Brookwood Sch., Manchester - by- the- Sea, Mass., 1996—2000; theatre educator Boston Arts Acad., 2001—02, music educator, 2002—. Choir dir. Indian Hill Arts, Inc, Littleton, Mass., 1997—2002, Sharing a New Song, Inc., Newton, Mass., 2001—03; gospel choir dir. Framingham State Coll, 1999—2002, Gordon Coll., Wenham, 1998—2002; dir. handbell choir Pilgrim Ch., Southborough, Mass., 1994—2000; vocalist New Eng. Spiritual Ensemble, Boston, 2000—04. Actor: Baby!, Annie, Guys & Dolls, King and I, How Bush Got Kerryed Away; author: Where in The World is Belle Voce de Cantar von Destrucken, Oh Black and Unknown Bards, Where in the World is Belle Noce de Cantor Von Destruchen, 2001—02, Oh Black and Unknown Bards, 2002—04. Recipient Silver medal, Mass. Instrumental and Choral Condr.'s Assn. Choral Competition, 1995, 1996, Gold medal, 1996, Silver and Bronze medals, 2004. Mem.: Handel and Haydn Soc. (vocalist Outreach Quartette 2000—), Boston Musician's Assn., Ctr. Black Music Rsch., Internat. Fedn. Choral Music, Am. Choral Dirs. Assn. (life). Avocations: roller-blading, reading, music. Home: PO Box 230913 Boston MA 02123-0913 Business E-Mail: exordiumma@aol.com

**MARTIN-BOWEN, LINDSEY,** freelance writer; b. Kansas City, Kans., Aug. 4, 1959; d. Lawrence Richard and V. Marie Pickett; m. Frederick E. Nicholson (div.); 1 child, Aaron Frederick; m. Edwin L. Martin (div.); 1 child, Ki Elise; m. Michael L. Bowen (div.). BA in English Lit., U. Mo. Kansas City, l972, MA in English and Creative Writing, 1988, postgrad., 1991-94; JD, U. Mo. Kansas City Sch. Law, Kansas City, 2000. Bar: Mo. 2001. Tech. editor Office Hearings and Appeals, U.S. Dept. Interior, Washington, 1976-77; reporter, photographer Louisville Times, 1982-83; reporter, features editor Sun Newspapers, Overland Park, Kans., 1983-84; assoc. editor Modern Jeweler, Overland Park and N.Y.C., 1984-85; writer Coll. Blvd. News, Overland Park, 1985-89, KC View, Kansas City, Mo., 1988-89; editor Number One, Kansas City, Mo., 1986-88, cons., 1988-89; copywriter Sta KXEO/KWWR Radio, Mexico, Mo., 1989; editorial asst. New Letters, 1985—; features writer, columnist The Squire, Prairie Village, Kans., 1990-95. Instr. lit., fiction writing, intro. to journalism, reporting, English, cultural studies, tech. writing, acad. writing and lit. U. Mo., Kansas City, 1986-88, 97-, Johnson County CC, 1988-95; fiction writer, 2002—; instr. world lit., writing Rockhurst U., 2002-03; tchr. English and fiction Longview CC, 1988-95, 97-98, 2004—; instr. writing and mass comm. Webster U., 1990; instr. world lit., Am. lit., women in lit., creative writing Penn Valley CC, 1993-97, faculty sponsor The Penn; owner, writer Paladin Freelance Writing Svc., Kansas City, 1988—; prodn. editor Nat. Paralegal Reporter, 1992-95, editor 1994-97, columnist; staff writer, columnist NPR, 1992-2005; writing contest judge New Letters, 1987-; judge poetry contest BkMk Press, U. Mo. Kansas City, 1998—; coord. written English proficiency test, U. Mo. Kans. City, 2005- Author: (novel) The Dark Horse Waits in Boulder, 1985, Deep City, 2005, Harvest, 2002, Denvie USA, 2003, Deep City, 2005, (poetry book) Second Touch, 1990, Standing on the Edge of the World, 2006, (fiction) Cicada Grove and Other Stories, 1992; author numerous poems; contbr. articles to profl. jours.; lead actress prodns. Coach House Players, 1969-70; extra Hdb film Truman, 1995; staff mem., contbr. UMKC Law Rev., 1997-99. Campaigner McGovern for Pres. Campaign, Kansas City, l97l-72. Regents scholar, l967; GAF fellow, 1986. Mem.: U. Mo.-Kansas City Alumni Assn. (media com. 1983-84), Phi Kappa Phi. Roman Catholic. Avocations: acrylic and oil painting, downhill skiing, music, Greek cooking, paralegal work. Office: U Mo Kansas City English Dept Cockefair Hall Rm 111 5100 Rockhill Rd Kansas City MO 64110-2481 Home: 1129 SE 7th St Lees Summit MO 64063-6442

**MARTINDALE, CARLA JOY,** retired librarian; b. Ladysmith, Wis., Sept. 9, 1947; d. Howard Walter and Audrey Elizabeth (Stanton) Martindale. BA, Mt. Senario Coll., 1970; MLIS, U. South Fla., 1990. Libr. Blackhawk Schs., South Wayne, Ind., 1975-79, Osceola County Libr., Kissimee, Fla., 1989-90, Fla. Tech. Coll., Orlando, 1991-92, Orlando Coll. South, 1993-98; ret., 1998; libr. U of Ctrl. Fla., 2003—. Vis. prof. distance learning libr. St. Leo (Fla.) U., 1999—2002; chair libr. 21st curriculum Phillips Coll., Orlando, 1995, acad. com., 1993—98, accreditation steering com., 1996. Named libr. in her honor, Orlando Coll. South, 1995. Avocations: reading, pets, stock investing. Home: 450 Narrows Dr Greers Ferry AR 72067 Personal E-mail: carlajoy52@yahoo.com

**MARTINE, CATHY,** telecommunications industry executive; BA in Econ., Coll. Mt. St. Vincent; MS, MIT; MBA, NYU Stern Sch. Branch mgr. AT&T Bus. Svcs., NYC; hired into mgmt. tng. prog. and had assignments in Network Ops., Fin., and Mktg. AT&T, gen. mgr., internat. consumer long distance bus., 1994—97, mktg. v.p., consumer svcs., 1997—99, v.p. internat. traffic mgmt., pres., internat. carrier svcs., 1999, led consumer long distance svcs., sr. v.p., Voice over Internet Protocol (VoIP), 2003, sr. v.p., Internet Telephony, Consumer Marketing and Sales Morristown, NJ, 2004—. Bd. dir. MIT Sloan Sch. Bd. of Gov., 1998—2001, US Telecommunications Tng. Inst., Washington, 1998—2001, Jersey Battered Women's Shelter, Brooklyn Acad. of Music, NYC, mem. fin. com.; bd. advisors Rutgers Sch. Bus.; co-lead Women of AT&T org. Sloan Fellow, 1993. Office: AT&T 412 Mount Kemble Ave Morristown NJ 07960-6654

**MARTINE, DAVID BUNN,** curator, artist; b. Southampton, NY, June 11, 1960; s. Thomas Siklos and Marjorie Carola Martinez. BFA in Advt. Design, U. Okla., 1982; MEd in Art Edn., Ctrl. State U., Edmond, Okla., 1983; cert., Inst. Am. Indian Arts, 1984. Ordained Spiritual Awareness Fellowship. Dir. Shinnecock Nation Cultural Ctr. and Mus, Southampton, 1992—93, curatorial asst., 2000—01, dir., curator, 2003—; mus. technician Nat. Mus. Am. Indian, Smithsonian Inst., 1994—96; retail sales agt. Deerfield Clothing and Supply, Southampton, 1994—96; mem. exhbn. crew Sotheby's, NYC, 1996; asst. to dir. Cultural and Civic Ctr. of Southampton, 1996—97. Sec. bd. dirs. Amerinda-Am. Indian Artists, Inc., NYC; mem. We'll Take Manhattan Native Arts Symposium, 2005. Book, We are Still Heer! The Algonzuin Peoples of Long Island, 1996, The Algonzuin Peoples of Long Island from Earliest Times to 1700, 1996, The Montaukett Indians of Eastern Long Island, 2001, mural, Am. Indian Cmty. House, NYC, 2005. Candidate Southampton Town Trust, 1991; mem. Shinnecock Nation Tribal Coun., 2000—02; mem. com. on racial justice Presbytery of L.I., 1987; cons. edn. com. Parrish Art Mus., 1988—89; mem. Am. Friends Svc. Com., NYC, 2001, Ft. Sill Chiricahua Apache Tribe, Okla. Grantee, Met. Mus. Art, NYC, 2005. Avocations: piano, poetry. Office: Shinnecock Nation Cultural Ctr and Mus PO Box 5059 Southampton NY 11969

**MARTINEAU, ROBERT JOHN,** retired law educator; b. Oconto, Wis., May 18, 1934; s. Francis Joseph and Gertrude (Schauer) Martineau; m. Constance Ann Zimmerman, Dec. 21, 1957; children: Robert John, Renee, Anne, Jeanne. BS, Coll. Holy Cross, 1956; JD, U. Chgo., 1959. Bar: Md. 1960, U.S. Supreme Ct. 1964, Iowa 1969, Wis. 1974. Law clk. to chief judge Md. Ct. Appeals, 1959-60; pvt. practice Md., 1960-68; asst. atty. gen. Md., 1964-65; assoc. prof. U. Iowa, 1968-71; prof., 1971-72; cir. exec. U.S. Ct. Appeals (8th cir.), Mo., 1972-74; exec. officer Wis. Supreme Ct., 1974-78; prof. U. Dayton, Ohio, 1978-80; prof. law U. Cin., 1980-88, disting. rsch. prof., 1988-93, emeritus, 1994—, assoc. dean, 1988-92, acting dean, 1985—86. Cons. Internat. Jud. Adminstrn., 1970—72, Fed. Jud. Ctr., 1978, Nat. Ctr. State Cts., 1978—79, 1987, Inst. Jud. Adminstrn., 1987—88, UN Devel. Program, Bhutan, 1999; spl. prof. U. Birmingham, England, 1987. Author: Wisconsin Appellate Practice, 1978, Judicial Reform in Wisconsin, in Court Reform in Seven States, 1980, Modern Appellate Practice-Federal and State Civil Appeals, 1983, Fundamentals of Modern Appellate Advocacy, 1985, Cases and Materials on Appellate Practice and Procedure, 1987; author: (with others) 2d edit., 2005; author: Appellate Justice in England and the United States: A Comparative Analysis, 1990, Drafting Legislation and Rules in Plain English, 1991; author: (with M. Salerno) Legal, Legislative, and Rule Drafting in Plain English, 2005. Reporter Wis. Supreme Ct. Com. Discipline Attys., 1975—77, Wis. Jud. Coun. Com. Appellate Practice and Procedure, 1976—78, Com. Contempt and Extraordinary Remedies, 1979—80; sec. Md. Constl. Conv. Commn., 1965—67, Md. Constl. Conv., 1967—68, Wis. Supreme Ct. Com. Study State Bar, 1975—77; mem. Iowa Mcpl. Laws Study Com., 1970—71, Wis. Legis. Coun. Com. Ct. Reorganization, 1977, Ohio Supreme Ct. Adv. Com. Rules, 1988—91; mem., reporter ABA Appellate Judges Conf. Com. Appellate Skills Tng., 1984—85, Com. Appellate Skills Tng., 1984—85; co-chair Com. Appellate Practice, 1986—88. Mem.: Am. Jud. Soc. (bd. dirs 1966—68), Md. Bar Assn. (reporter com. jud. selection 1962—64, v.p. 1967), Assn. Am. Law Schs. (ho. reps. 1982—87). Democrat. Roman Catholic. Office Phone: 941-488-0455. Personal E-mail: r.j.martineau@gmail.net.

**MARTINEK, CYNTHIA L.,** principal; b. Guthrie Ctr., Iowa, Nov. 4, 1953; d. Maurice Orville and Lillian Ann Leonard; m. Jerald Robert Martinek, Aug. 18, 1979; children: Christopher, Katherine. BS, Iowa State U., 1971, MS, 1976; EdD, Drake U., 1996. Cert. supt. Tchr. Terril (Iowa) Cmty. Sch. 1974—75, Mason City Cmty. Sch., 1976—87; elem. prin. CAL Cmty. Sch., Latimer, Iowa, 1987—93, Belmond-Klemine Sch., Iowa, 1993—. Adj. prof. Waldorf Coll., Forest City, Iowa, 2003—. Bd. dirs. YMCA, Belmond, 2003—05. Mem.: Nat. Assn. Elem. Sch. Prin., Belmond C. of C. (bd. dirs 2003—05), Phi Delta Kappa. Avocations: travel, art, exercise. Office: Belmond-Klemine Cmty Sch 611 4th St NE Belmond IA 50421

**MARTINEN, JOHN A.,** travel company executive; b. Sault Ste Marie, Mich., June 26, 1938; s. John Albert and Ina Helia (Jarvi) M. BS with highest honors, Mich. State U., 1960; JD, NYU, 1963. With Grace Line, N.Y.C., 1963—69; cons. Empresa Turistica Internat., Galapagos Cruises, Quito, Ecuador, 1969—70; regional mgr. Globus & Cosmos (Group Voyagers Inc.), N.Y.C., 1970—73, v.p., 1974—76, exec. v.p., 1977—78, pres., CEO 1979—92, Littleton, Colo., 1993—98, chmn., 1998; pres., CEO Vista Travel Ventures, Inc., Denver, 1999—2001; pres. Trafalgar Tours, Long Island City, NY, 2002; prin. Safe Passage Internat., Lakewood, Colo., 2003—. Root-Tilden Scholar, N.Y.U. Law Sch., 1960—63. Mem. Am. Soc. Travel Agts. (chmn. tour operating program 1996-99), U.S. Tour Operators Assn. (bd. dirs. 1993-99, treas. 1996-97, sec. 1998-99), Lotos N.Y., Wings Club (N.Y.), Columbine Country Club, Denver Athletic Club. Democrat. Home: 915 W End Ave Apt 7 A New York NY 10025 Office: Safe Passage Internat 3609 S Wadsworth Blvd Ste 565 Lakewood CO 80235 Office Phone: 800-777-7665. E-mail: JohnMartinen@TravelStrategies.net.

**MARTINETTI, RONALD ANTHONY,** lawyer; b. NYC, Aug. 13, 1945; s. Alfred Nathan and Frances Ann (Battipaglia) M.; m. Ky Le Du, June, 2002. Student, Hotchkiss Sch., 1959, Columbia U., 1966—68, U. Chgo., 1981-82; JD, U. So. Calif., 1982. Bar: Calif. 1982; U.S. Dist. Ct. (cen. and no. dists.) Calif. 1982, U.S. Dist. Ct. Ariz., 1992; U.S. Ct. Appeals (9th cir.) 1982. Ptnr. Kazanjian & Martinetti, Glendale, Calif., 1986—. Co-founder Am. Legends Website, 1995, Am. Legends Pub., 1996 Author: Nine Easy Ways to Strengthen Your Bad Faith Care in Discovery, 1991; co-author: Rights of Owners of Lost, Stolen or Destroyed Instruments Under UCC Section 3-804: Can They Be Holders in Due Course?, 1993, James Dean Story, 1995; contbr. articles to profl. jours., popular mags Mem. Calif. Bar Assn. Office: Kazanjian & Martinetti 520 E Wilson Ave Glendale CA 91206-4374 Office Phone: 818-241-1011. Office Fax: 818-241-2193. Personal E-mail: amlegends@aol.com.

**MARTINEZ, ADRIANA,** political organization worker, photographer; Student, U. Nev., Las Vegas; BA, Brooks Inst. Photography. Photography instr. C.C. So. Nev.; wedding photographer So. Nev. News Bur.; chair Nev. State Dem. Party, Las Vegas, 2003—. Mem.: PTA. Office: 1325 Vegas Valley Dr Ste C Las Vegas NV 89109-6219

**MARTINEZ, ALEX J.,** state supreme court justice; b. Denver, Apr. 1, 1951; m. Marla Carter; children: Julia, Maggie. Diploma, Phillips Exeter Acad., N.H., 1969; student, Reed Coll., 1969-72; BA, U. Colo., 1973, JD, 1976. Bar: Colo. 1976. Dep. state pub. defender, Pueblo and Denver, 1976-83; county ct. judge Pueblo, 1983-88; dist. ct. judge, 1988-97; justice Colo. Supreme Ct., Denver, 1997—. Supreme Ct. liaison Colo. Criminal Rules Com., Colo. Criminal Jury Instns.; chmn. Pub. Access Com., Jud. Edn. Com.; bd. dirs. Servicios de la Raza. Chmn. Pueblo adv. bd. Packard Found., 1993-96; chmn. site-based governing coun. Pueblo Sch. Arts and Scis., 1994-95; mem. site-based governing coun. Roncalli Mid. Sch., 1993-94; bd. dirs. Colo. U. Law Alumni. Mem. Colo. Bar Assn. (regional v.p. 1996-96), Colo. Hispanic Bar Assn., Pueblo Bar Assn. (mem. exec. coun. 1994-96), Pueblo Hispanic Bar Assn. Office: Colo Supreme Ct 2 E 14th Ave Denver CO 80203-2115*

**MARTINEZ, ALMA R.,** actress, theater director, educator; b. Monclova, Coahuila, Mex. Student, U. Guadalajara-Artes Plasticas, Mex., 1972-73, Ibero-Am. U., 1976, UNAM, Mexico City, 1976-77; BA in Theatre, Whittier Coll., 1984; MFA in Acting, U. So. Calif., 1995; postgrad., Stanford U., 1994—; student, Jerzy Grotowski Para Theatre, Berkeley, Calif., 1977, Lee Strasberg Theatre Inst., Hollywood, Calif., 1982, Royal Acad. Dramatic Arts, London, Eng., 1987, Mnouchkine/Theatre du Soleil, Paris, 1993. Asst. prof. theatre arts U. Calif., Santa Cruz, 2001—. Appeared in plays including In the Summer House, Lincoln Ctr., N.Y.C., Greencard, Joyce Theatre, N.Y.C., Zoot Suit, Mark Taper Forum, L.A., Bocon, Mark Taper Forum, L.A., Macbeth, Oreg. Shakespeare Festival, The Skin of Our Teeth, Oreg. Shakespeare Festival, Hello Dolly, Long Beach Civic Light Opera, A Christmas Carol, South Coast Repertory, House of Blue Leaves, Pasadena Playhouse, Sundance Inst., Sundance, Utah, Fuente Ovejuna, Berkeley Repertory Theatre, Burning Patience, San Diego Repertory Theatre, Marriage of Figaro, Ariz. Theatre Co., Sons of Don Juan, Asolo Theatre, Fla., Wait Until Dark, Pa. Stage Co., La Carpa de los Rasquachis, Teatro Campesino; TV appearances include Gen. Hosp., Twilight Zone, Sequin, Corridos (Peabody award), Tough Love, Dress Gray, The Boys, In a Child's Name, The Gambler Returns, Quiet Killer, The New Adam 12 (series regular), 500 Nations, Nash Bridges (guest star); film appearances include Ballad of a Soldier, Jacaranda, The Novice, Trial by Terror, Dollie Dearest, Maria's Story, For A Loves One, Soldado Razo, Shattered Image, Zoot Suit, Barbarosa, Born in East L.A., Under Fire, among others; dir. (plays) Bed of Stone, 1996, La Gran Carpa de los Rasquachis, 1997, Heroes & Saints, 2001. Active Assistance with Alcohol and Sobriety Uniting Latinas, United L.Am. Youth, Med. Aid for El Salvador, Save the Children, the Christian Children's Fund; vol. and charity work in refugee camps in Ethiopia, India, Thailand, Sri Lanka, and The Philippines; bd. dirs. Mexican Mus., El Teatro Compresing. Recipient Cert. of Appreciation El Teatro Campesino, 1978, Recognition award Barrio Sta., 1980, Alumni Hall of Fame, El Rancho H.S., 1982, Outstanding Hispanic Alumni award Whittier Coll., 1984; co-recipient with Anthony Quinn and Edward James Olmos Hispanic Entertainer of Yr., The Equitable Co., 1987; Escobedo

fellow Stanford U., 1996, Dorothy Danforth Compton Rsch. fellow, 1996. Mem. NATAS, AFTRA, SAG (John Dales scholar 1995-96, 98), TCG, Modern Lang. Assn., Assn. for Theatre in Higher Edn., Nat. Theatre Conf., Nat. Assn. Chicas and Chicano Studies, Actors Equity Assn. Address: JE Talent 323 Geary St #302 San Francisco CA 94102 Office: Univ Calif J-14 Theatre Arts Ctr Santa Cruz CA 95064 Business E-Mail: almamar@ucsc.edu.

**MARTINEZ, ANTONIO,** choir director, art director; b. Odessa, Tex., Dec. 15, 1972; s. Esmeralda Romero. Student, U. of Houston, 1996—2001. Chorister Houston Grand Opera, 1997—; dir. music Epworth-Parker United Meth. Ch., Houston, 1999—2000; dir. arts and worship St. Martin's Luth. Ch., Sugar Land, Tex., 2001—. Composer choral music. Sun. sch. tchr. St. Martin's Luth. Ch., Sugar Land, Tex., 2004—06. Mem.: Tex. Choral Dirs. Assn., Am. Choral Dirs. Assn. (Semi-Finalist, Student Conducting Awards 2001). D-Conservative. Lutheran. Avocation: computer building. Office: St Martin's Lutheran Church 1123 Burney Rd Sugar Land TX 77478 Office Phone: 281-980-0895. Office Fax: 281-980-0895. Personal E-mail: choirmaster@sbcglobal.net. E-mail: choirmaster@stmartinslc.org.

**MARTINEZ, ARTHUR C.,** consumer products company executive, former retail company executive; b. N.Y.C., Sept. 25, 1939; s. Arthur F. and Agnes (Caulfield) M.; m. Elizabeth Rusch, July 30, 1966; children: Lauren, Gregory. BSME, Polytech. U., 1960; MBA, Harvard U., 1965; LLD (hon.), Univ. Notre Dame, 1997. Dir. planning Internat. Paper Co., N.Y.C., 1967-69; asst. to pres. Talley Industries, Mesa, Ariz., 1969-70; dir. fin. RCA Corp., N.Y.C., 1970-73, v.p., 1973-80; sr. v.p., CFO Saks Fifth Ave. Inc., N.Y.C., 1980-84, exec. v.p., 1984-87, vice chmn., 1990-92; sr. v.p. & group chief exec. Batus Inc., Louisville, 1987-90; chmn., CEO Sears Merchandise Group, Chgo., 1992-95, Sears, Roebuck and Co., 1995—2000, chmn., CEO emeritus, 2000—; interim chmn., CEO Internat. Flavors & Fragrances Inc., NYC, 2006. Bd. dirs. PepsiCo, Inc., 1999-. Internat. Flavors & Fragrances, 2000-, IAC/InterActiveCorp., 2005-, Martha Stewart Living Omimedia, Inc.; dep. chmn. Fed. Res. Bank, Chgo.; former chmn. Nat. Minority Supplier Devel. Coun., Inc. Bd. dirs. Defenders of Wildlife, 1992—, Nat. Urban League; chmn. bd. trustees Polytech. U., 1990—; trustee Art Inst., Orch. Assn. Chgo. Symphony Orch.; bd. dirs. Northestern Meml. Hosp., Chgo. 1st lt. U.S. Army, 1961-63. Named CEO of Yr., Fin. World Mag., 1996; recipient T.C. and Elizabeth Clarke medallion Sch. of Bus., Coll. William and Mary, 1997, Olin Sch. of Bus. Excellence in Bus. award, Washington U., St. Louis, 1997. Mem. Nat. Retail Fedn. (chmn. bd. dirs.). Avocations: tennis, golf, gardening. Office: Internat Flavors & Fragrances 521 W 57th St New York NY 10019*

**MARTINEZ, BARBARA,** health insurance company executive; MBA, U. So. Calif.; MPH, Loma Linda U. With Delta Ins.Co., 1988—; dir. acct. svcs. Delta Dental; v.p. profl. svcs. PMI Dental Health Plan Delta Ins.Co., v.p. underwriting and fin., 1999—2001, sr. v.p., COO, 2001—; COO Delta Ins.Co., 2003—. Named one of Top 10 Latinos in Healthcare, LatinoLeaders mag., 2004. Office: Delta Dental Calif 100 1st St San Francisco CA 94105*

**MARTINEZ, BENJAMIN RAY,** security officer, retired military non-commissioned officer; b. Bakersfield, Calif., Apr. 13, 1955; s. Raymond Dominguez and Reba Lori Martinez; m. Carmencita Bugtong Adriatico, Dec. 6, 1986. Tech. cert., CC of Air Force, Gunther AFB, Ala., 1986, US Army Ordnance, Camp Roberts, Calif., 1999; tech. instr. cert., U. Calif., Long Beach, 2004. Security policeman USAF, San Antonio, 1973—86; wheel and track vehicle repairer Calif. Army N.G., Gardena, Calif., 1994—2002. Mentor North HS Army JROTC, Torrance, Calif.; mem. Easter Seals, USO; life mem. Rep. Nat. Party, San Bernardino, Calif., 1986—2004; mem. Rep. Presdl. Task Force. Staff sgt. USAF, 1973—86. Decorated Jts. Svcs. Commendation medal Supreme Hdqs. NATO, US Army 94th Engrs. Divsn. Coin; recipient letter of commendation and coin, US Dep. Sec. of Def. Hon. Rudy De Leon, 2000. Mem.: AARP, VFW, The Heritage Found., The Cousteau Soc., Nat. Geog. Soc., Disabled Am. Vets., US Army 9th/10th Cavalry (assoc.; sustaining mem. 1998—2004), Air Force Sgts. Assn. (life), Air Force Assn. (life), Inventors Workshop Internat. (assoc.), Nat. Inventors Hall of Fame, Planetary Soc., Nat. Space Soc., Paralyzed Vets. of Am., Am. Legion. Republican. Achievements include invention and patent for object retrieving device; contributor to the US Forces Coalition during Operation Iraqi Freedom. Avocations: world travel, ancient military histories, archaeology, paleontology-geology, arts and humanities. Home: 1250 Kendall Dr #D-305 San Bernardino CA 92407-5832 Personal E-mail: rangerthree@hotmail.com.

**MARTINEZ, BUCK,** baseball analyst; b. Nov. 7, 1948; married; 1 child. Student, Sacramento City Coll., Sacramento State U., Southwestern Mo. State U. Baseball player Kansas City, 1969-77, Milw., 1978-81, Toronto Blue Jays, 1981-86; color commentator World Series, Am. League Championship Telemedia Radio Network, 1982-88, color commentator All-Star Game, 1982-88, post-game analyst Major League Baseball coverage, 1982-88; analyst The Sports Network Toronto Blue Jays, 1986; reporter The Manager's Show and Sports Desk TSN, 1986, host The Boys of Winter and Knockout, 1986; analyst Wednesday night nat. telecasts Major League Baseball ESPN, 1992—2001; mgr. US Baseball, WBC, 2006. Author: (seasons with Toronto Blue Jays) From Worst to First, 1985, The Last Out, 1986.*

**MARTINEZ, CARLOS,** insurance agent; b. Havana, Cuba, Apr. 15, 1940; came to U.S., 1960; s. Serafin and Micaela (Contreras-Cutie) M.; m. Laurel Louise Hancock, Sept. 24, 1970; children: Carl Edward, Emily Louise. BS, Edison Inst., Havana, 1958; postgrad. studies in civil engring., U. Havana, 1959-60; AA, Miami-Dade C.C., Miami, Fla., 1968; BA, Fla. Atlantic U., 1971. Lic. ins. adjuster, Fla. Student rsch. asst. Fla. Atlantic U., Boca Raton, 1968-70; collection supr. Burdine's Dept. Stores, Miami, Fla., 1970-72; ins. adjuster Crawford and Co., Miami, 1972-75, All Risks Mgmt. Svcs., Miami, 1977, Allstate Ins. Co., Miami, 1975-77, Globe Adjustment Co., North Miami, 1977-86, Ins. Servicing & Adjusting Co., Miami, 1986 89; hr. mgr Crittenden Adjustment Co., Hollywood, Fla., 1989—. Mem. Young Ams. for Freedom, Boca Raton, Fla. 1968-71, Young Reps., Boca Raton, 1968-71. PO USN, 1960-61. Mem. S. Fla. Claims Assn. (assoc. mem.), Edison Inst. Alumni Assn., Fla. Atlantic U. Alumni Assn. Roman Catholic. Avocations: swimming, bicycle riding, history, sociology, insurance, law, gymnastics. Home: 3030 SW 123rd Ct Miami FL 33175-2250 Office: Crittenden Adjustment Co 1414 NW 107th Ave Ste 202 Miami FL 33172

**MARTINEZ, CARMEN MARIA,** ambassador; b. Pensacola, Fla., July 1950; married; 1 child. MA in Medieval History, MS in Nat. Security and Strategic Resources. Various positions U.S. Fgn. Svc., Sao Paulo, Brazil, 1981; chief of the consular sect. Quito, Ecuador, 1989—93; prin. officer U.S. consulate, Barranquilla, Colombia, 1993—94; dep. chief of mission US Dept. State, Maputo, Mozambique, 1997—99; prin. officer U.S. consulate, San Paolo, Brazil, 1999—2000; charge d'affaires to Burma US Dept. State, Rangoon, 2002—05; US amb. to Zambia Lusaka, 2005—. Office: US Dept State 2310 Lusaka Pl Washington DC 20521*

**MARTINEZ, DAVID GREY,** classicist, educator; b. Fort Smith, Ark., Mar. 10, 1952; s. Angel and Robbie Martinez; m. Meredith Anne Longley, Aug. 10, 1985; children: Julia Faith, Samuel David. PhD, U. Mich., Ann Arbor, 1985. Assoc. prof. classics U. Tex., Austin, 1990—2001, U. Chgo., 2001—. Author: Baptized for Our Sakes; A Leather Trisagion from Egypt, P. Michigan XVI: A Greek Love Charm from Egypt. Fellow, Ctr. for Hellenic Studies, 1997—99; Jr. fellow, NEH, 1995—96. Mem.: Soc. Biblical Lit., Am. Philological Assn., Am. Soc. Papyrologists (sec. 2000—06). Baptist. Office: Univ Chicago Dept Classics 1115 E 58th St Chicago IL 60637 Office Phone: 773-702-8232. Office Fax: 773-702-9861. Business E-Mail: davidm@uchicago.edu.

**MARTINEZ, DONNA F.,** federal judge; BA, U. Conn., 1973, MSW, 1975, JD, 1978. Bar: Conn. 1979. Corp. counsel City of Hartford, Conn., 1979-80; asst. U.S. atty. Office U.S. Atty., Hartford and New Haven, 1980-94; chief organized crime drug enforcement task force Dist. of Conn., New Haven, 1989-94; magistrate judge U.S. Magistrate Ct., Hartford, 1994—. Instr. trial practice Yale U. Law Sch., New Haven, 1996-2001. Mem. Conn. Bar Assn., Fed. Bar Assn., Hispanic Bar Assn., Fed. Magistrate Judges Assn., Am. Inns of Ct. (past. v.p., past pres.), Am. Leadership Forum (past bd. dirs.). Office: US Magistrate Ct 450 Main St Rm 262 Hartford CT 06103-3002 Office Phone: 860-240-3605.

**MARTINEZ, EURI ANTHONY,** music educator, small business owner; b. Tuy, Batangas, Philippines, Nov. 6, 1966; s. Galicano Paradero and Minda Tolentino Martinez; m. Maria Carolina Nuguid, Apr. 18, 1998; children: Erica Lourdes, Christian Anthony. MusB, North Pk. U., 1990. Prin., owner Martinez Music Studio, Carpentersville, Ill., 2002—. Adjudicator Sam & Rose Licata Meml., Chgo., 1995—. Granquist Music Competition, Geneva, 1997—, Festival of Music, Northwestern U., Evanston, Ill., 2005—. Choir dir. Filipino-Am. of the N.W. Suburbs, St. Mary Ch., Huntley, Ill.; organist, pianist St Gregory The Gt. Parish, Chgo., 1996—2000. Named to Filipino-American Hall Of Fame In Music, Via Times and The Chgo. Philippine Report TV, 1997; recipient Excellence In Music Instrn. award, Am. Music World, 1993. Mem.: Ill. Music Assn. (adjudicator 1996—, mem. scholarship bd. 1997—, sec. 1998—), Steinway Soc. Chgo., Northshore Music Tchrs. Assn., Ill. State Music Tchrs. Assn., Music Tchrs. Nat. Assn. Roman Cath. Avocations: travel, gardening, physical fitness. Office: American Music World 7727 N Milwaukee Avenue Niles IL 60743 Office Phone: 312-760-8795. Personal E-mail: euricarol@msn.com. E-mail: martinezmusic@yahoo.com.

**MARTINEZ, FERNANDO V.,** civil engineer; b. Blewett, Tex., July 2, 1927; s. Catarino G. and Refugia V. M.; m. Dora Garza, Sept. 27, 1953; children: Fernando G., Karen Martinez Solano, Edward A. BS in Civil Engring, Tex A&M U., 1951. Registered profl. engr., Tex. Field engr. Farnsworth & Chambers Co, Houston, Tex., 1953-54; design engr. Link Belt Co., Houston, 1954, Anderson Clayton & Co., Houston, 1954-59; project engr. Olin Mathieson Chem. Corp., Pasadena, Tex., 1959-80; project mgr. Mobil Oil Corp., Pasadena, 1980—. 1st lt. U.S. Army, 1951-53, Korea. Republican. Roman Catholic. Home: 710 Skylark Rd Pasadena TX 77502-4560 Office: Mobil Oil Corp 2001 Jackson Rd Pasadena TX 77501

**MARTINEZ, GUSTAVE See SOLOMONS, GUS JR.**

**MARTINEZ, HERIBERTO,** human resources manager; s. Ciprian Martinez and Dolores Gonzalez; m. Migdalia Centeno. BA in Mgmt., Inter Am. U., PR, 1983. Cert. human resources and labor law specialist. Labor law cons. Dept. of Labor, Arecibo, 1979—83; human resources mgr. Casera Foods Inc, Barceloneta, PR, 1983—93, Cardinal Health, Manati, PR, 1996—. Dir. Coop. Ahorro y Credito de Manati, 1996—2003; sec. PR Mustang Club, Aguadilla, 2002—04. Named Dir. of Yr., Coop. Ahorro y Credito de Manati, 1998; recipient recognition for work performance, Adminstrn. Accion Juvenil, 1976, Manuel A Perez / Nomination award, Dept. of Labor, 1983, Chmn. award, Cardinal Health, 2000. Mem.: Soc. Human Resource Mgmt. (assoc.), PR Mustang Club. Democrat. Roman Catholic. Avocations: guitar, electrical bass, baseball. Home: 222 Montecarlo St Monaco 3 Manati PR 00674 Office Phone: 787-621-3000.

**MARTINEZ, HERMINIA S.,** economist, banker; b. Havana, Cuba; came to U.S., 1960, naturalized, 1972; d. Carlos and Amelia (Santana) Martinez Sanchez; m. Mario Aguilar, 1982; children: Mario Aguilar, Carlos Aguilar. BA in Econs. cum laude, Am. U., 1965; MS in Fgn. Svc. (Univ. fellow); MS in Econs., Georgetown U., 1967, PhD in Econs., 1969; postgrad., Nat. U. Mex. Instr. econs. George Mason Coll., U. Va., Fairfax, 1967-68; researcher World Bank, 1967-69; instll. economist, devel. econs. dept., 1969-71; economist World Bank Latin Am. (Ctrl. Am., Mex., Venezuela, Ecuador, Panama and Dominican Republic, Washington, 1971-79; sr. loan officer for Middle East and North Africa World Bank, 1977—84, sr. loan officer, sr. economist Africa Region, 1988-91, prin. ops. officer pvt. sector fin. group Africa region, 1992-96, lead specialist, regional mgr., 1996-2000; pvt. practice fin., econ. devel., 2000—. Contbg. author: The Economic Growth of Colombia: Problems and Prospects, 1973, Central American Financial Integration, 1975. Mid-Career fellow Princeton U., 1988-89. Mem. Am. Econ. Assn., Soc. Internat. Devel., Brookings Inst. Latin Am. Study Group. Roman Catholic. Home: 5145 Yuma St NW Washington DC 20016-4336 Office: World Bank 1818 H St NW Washington DC 20433-0001

**MARTINEZ, IRIS,** state senator; b. Chgo. 1 child. Grad., Northeastern U., U. Ill., Chgo. Mem. Ill State Senate, Springfield, 2003—, mem. approprations II com., health and human svcs. com. and sbucom. on health care, vice chhair com. on ins. and pensions, mem. subcom. on mandates. Liaison to Hispanic Ministry. Committeewoman Ill. Dem. State Com.; mem. Dem. Nat. Com. Democrat. Catholic. Office: Capitol M-106 Capitol Bldg Springfield IL 62706 also: District 3024 N Pulaski Rd Chicago IL 60641 Home: 3154 W Grace St # 1 Chicago IL 60618-4529

**MARTINEZ, J. LEONARD,** aerospace executive; b. Colo. married; 3 children. Student, Adams State Coll., Alamosa, Colo.; grad., DeVry Inst., Phoenix, 1975; BS in Bus., MS in Mgmt., 1998; grad., Digital Internat. Mgmt. Edn. program, Fontainbleu, France. Various positions including mfg. dir. and gen. mgr. Digital Equipment Corp., 1975—90; dir. prodn. integration Sandia Nat. Labs., Albuquerque, 1995, dir. prodn. ops., v.p. defense product and svcs. divsn. (now mfg. sys., sci., tech.). Foster parent Heal the Children. Named one of 50 Most Important Hispanics in Govt., Edn., Hispanic Engineer and Info. Tech. mag., 2005; recipient Nat. Achievement award for exec. excellence, Hispanic Engineer mag.; grantee Sloan Fellow, Stanford Univ. Office: Sandia Nat Labs Dept 14000 MS 0149 PO Box 5800 Albuquerque NM 87185*

**MARTINEZ, JAMES PHILLIP,** music educator; b. Watsonville, Calif., Sept. 4, 1947; s. Joe Martinez and Rebecca Jartinez; m. Kem Frances Buffo, Oct. 5, 1968. MusB, Calif. State U., San Francisco, 1973. Cert. tchr. Calif. Musician Music From Bear Valley, 1972—88; music tchr. Richmond Unified Sch. Dist., El Sobrante, Calif., 1973—88, Jefferson Sch. Dist., Daly City, Calif., 1988—. Music instr. City Coll. San Francisco, 1981—2001; musician Orch. Baringuen, San Francisco, 1974—2006. With U.S. Army, 1967—70. Recipient Amoroso award, Calif. State U., San Francisco, 1972. Mem.: Calif. Music Edn. Assn. (bd. dirs. 1988—, treas. Bay sect. 1994—2005, mem. 2005, Pres.'s award Bay sect. 2005, Pres.'s award 2006) Phi Mu Alpha (pres. Eta Sigma chpt. 1971—73). Dfl. Roman Catholic. Avocations: snorkeling, photography, swimming.

**MARTINEZ, JENNY S.,** lawyer; BA cum laude, Yale U., 1993; JD magna cum laude, Harvard Law Sch., 1997. Bar: Va., DC. Law clk. to Honorable Guido Calabresi, US Ct. Appeals Second Circuit, 1997—98, Chambers of Justice Stephen Breyer, US Supreme Ct., 1998—99; assoc. legal officer to Judge Patricia Walk, UN Internat. Criminal Tribunal for Former Yugoslavia, 1999—2000; assoc. Jenner & Block LLC, 2000—03; sr. rsch. fellow, vis. lectr. Yale U., 2003—; asst. prof. law Stanford Law Sch., 2003—. Mng. editor Harvard Law Review; cons. Internat. Ctr. Transitional Justice, 2003—. Contbr. articles to profl. jours. Vol. tutor Thurgood Marshall Acad. Charter HS, Washington, 2001; vol. atty. DC Bar Law Firm Pro Bono Project, 2001; vol. cons. atty. Human Rights First, 2003—. Named one of Top 40 Lawyers Under 40, Nat. Law Jour., 2005; recipient Sears prize, Harvard Law, Temple Bar Scholar, Am. Inns Ct., 1999. Mem.: Hispanic Bar Assn. DC (v.p. internal affairs 2003—). Office: Stanford Law Sch 559 Nathan Abbott Way Stanford CA 94305-8610 Office Phone: 650-725-2749. Business E-Mail: jmartinez@law.stanford.edu.

**MARTINEZ, KATHRYN MARIE,** music educator; b. St. Paul, Dec. 20, 1957; d. Lloyd Gerald and Patricia Anne Schleusner; m. Michael David Martinez, Feb. 27, 1982 (div. Aug. 22, 1994); children: Kristin Marie, Kelly Anne. BA in Elem. Edn., Coll. St. Catherine, St. Paul, 1979. Tchr. grade 2 South Pk. Consol. Sch., Mpls., 1979—80, St. Peters Sch., North St. Paul, Minn., 1980—81; tchr. pre-sch. St Marks Ch., Independence, Mo., 1985—86; ind. piano tchr. Independence, Mo., 1985, Geneva, Ill., 1986, St.

Paul, 1987—. Accompanist St. Mary of the Lake, White Bear Lake, 1999—. Mem. pageant comm. Vadnais Heights Heritage Days, Minn., 1994, pageant co-dir., 1995—96. Recipient 1st Runner-up Miss Minn., 1978. Mem.: St. Paul Piano Tchr. Assoc. (3d v.p. 2002—), Minn. Music Tchr. Assoc. (mem. 1991—), Ea. Suburban Fed. Music Club (co-chair 2002—04, pres. 2005—). Catholic. Avocations: gardening, playing piano, travel, rubber stamping. Home and Office: 4309 Greenhaven Court Vadnais Heights MN 55127

**MARTINEZ, MARIA,** computer software company executive; BA in elec. engring., U. PR; MA in computer engring, Ohio State U. Various mgmt. and engring. positions AT&T Bell Labs.; v.p., gen. mgr. Internet Connectivity Solutions Divsn. Motorola Inc.; CEO Embrace Network, Inc.; corp. v.p. comm. and mobile solutions unit Microsoft Corp. Named an Elite Woman, Hispanic mag., 2004; recipient several process and quality awards. Achievements include led Motorola's launching of first CDMA comml. sys. in world; played a leadership role in Bell Lab's devel. of UNIX sys. for symmetries multiprocessing and high availability; patents for devel. and disk storage sys; launched first software platform and developed customer base for Embrace Networks, Inc; first female Hispanic named v.p. at Microsoft. Office: Microsoft Corp One Microsoft Way Redmond WA 98052-6399 Office Phone: 425-882-8080. Office Fax: 425-706-7329.

**MARTINEZ, MARITZA ARACELI,** elementary school educator; b. Mexico City, Mar. 23, 1969; d. Valente and Ethel Martínez. AA, LA City Coll., 1991; BA in Psychology, Calif. State U., LA, 1996, MA in Edn., 2005. Cert. tchr. Calif., reading credential Calif. Tchr. asst. Amnesty Program, LA, 1987—88, data entry asst.; data entry worker Ins. Co., LA, 1990—93; dean's asst. Health and Human Svcs., LA, 1993—98; tchr. LA Unified Sch. Dist., 1998—. Tchr. reading clinic Calif. State U., LA, 2004. Avocations: drawing, reading, jogging, movies. Home: 3054 Harrington Ave Los Angeles CA 90006 Office: LA Unified Sch Dist 107th St Elem Sch 147 E 107th St Los Angeles CA 90003

**MARTINEZ, MATTHEW GILBERT,** former congressman; b. Walsenburg, Colo., Feb. 14, 1929; children: Matthew, Diane, Susan, Michael, Carol Ann. Cert of competence, Los Angeles Trade Tech. Sch., 1959. Small businessman and bldg. contractor; mem. 97th-106th Congresses from 31st Calif. dist., 1982-2001; mem. edn. and labor com., fgn. affairs com. Mem. Monterey Park Planning Commn., 1971-74; mayor City of Monterey Park, 1974-75; mem. Monterey Park City Council, 1974-80, Calif. State Assembly, 1980-82; bd. dirs. San Gabriel Valley YMCA. Served with USMC, 1947-50. Mem. Congl. Hispanic Caucus, Hispanic Am. Democrats, Nat. Assn. Latino Elected and Apptd. Ofcls., Communications Workers Am., VFW, Am. Legion, Latin Bus. Assn., Monterey Park C. of C., Navy League (dir.) Lodges: Rotary. Democrat.

**MARTINEZ, MELQUIADES RAFAEL (MEL MARTINEZ),** senator, former secretary of housing and urban development; b. Sagua La Grande, Cuba, Oct. 23, 1946; arrived in US, 1962, naturalized, 1971; s. Melquiades C. and Gladys V. (Ruiz) M.; m. Kathryn Tindal, June 13, 1970; children: Lauren Elizabeth, John Melquiades, Andrew Tindal. AA, Orlando Jr. Coll., 1967; BA in Internat. Affairs, Fla. State U., 1969, JD, 1973. Bar: Fla. 1973, US Dist. Ct. (mid. dist.) Fla. 1973, US Supreme Ct. 1979, US Dist. Ct. (so. dist.) Fla. 1986; cert. Nat. Bd. Trial Advocacy. Civil trial atty., ptnr. Martinez, Dalton, Dellecker and Wilson, Orlando, Fla., 1973-85; ptnr. Martinez, Dalton, Dellecker, Wilson and King, 1985-98; chmn. Orange County, Fla., 1998-2001; sec. US Dept. Housing & Urban Devel., Washington, 2001—03; US senator from Fla., 2005—. Mem. Fla. Utilities Commn., 1994—97, pres., 1995—97; chmn. Fla. Growth Mgmt. Study Commn.; mem. com. banking, housing and urban affairs US Senate, com. energy and natural resources, com. fgn. relations, congressional-exec. commn. China, spl. com. aging. Bd. dirs. Cath. Social Svcs. Orlando, 1978-86; founder, chmn. Mayor's Hispanic Adv. Com., Orlando, 1981-82; chmn. bd. commrs. Orlando Housing Authority, 1983-86. Named one of 25 Most Influential Hispanics, Time Mag., 2005 Mem. Fla. Bar (bd. govs. young lawyers sect. 1980-81), Acad. Fla. Trial Lawyers (dir. 1981-85, treas. 1986-87, pres. 1988-89), 9th Jud. Cir. (jud. nomination commn. 1986), Congressional Hispanic Leadership Inst. Republican. Roman Catholic. Office: US Senate 317 Hart Senate Office Bldg Washington DC 20510 also: Landmark Ctr One Ste 475 315 East Robinson St Orlando FL 32801-4343 Office Phone: 202-224-3041, 407-254-2573. Office Fax: 202-228-5171.*

**MARTINEZ, MIGUEL ACEVEDO,** urologist, consultant, lecturer; b. Chihuahua, Mex., Aug. 18, 1953; came to U.S., 1956; s. Miguel Nuñez and Velia (Acevedo) M. AB, Stanford U., 1976; MD, Yale U., 1983. Diplomate Am. Bd. Urology. Intern U. S.C. Med. Ctr., 1983-84; resident in urology White Meml. Med. Ctr., L.A., 1984-89, urologist, 1989—. Cons., lectr. physician asst. program U. So. Calif., L.A., 1990—, clin. instr.; patient edn. cons. ICI Pharm., Del., 1991—, Zeneca's Speaker Forum; patient edn. and med. cons., lectr. Abbott Labs., 1991—; mem. edn.cons. several radio/TV stas., 1991—; mem. subcom. for diseases on kidney and transplantation NIH, Washington, 1991; mem. nat. Hispanic adv. bd. Pfizer Pharms., Inc., 1998—; mem. adv. bd. Glaxo Smith Kline, 2002—; cons. spkrs. bur. Pfizer, Bayer/ESK. Author: Intercellular Pathways, 1981. Polit. cons. Xavier Becerra, U.S. Congress, 1992, Martin Gallegos, Gil Cedillo, Calif. State Assembly, 1993, others; bd. dirs. Latino Ctr. for Prevention and Action in Health, Orange County, calif.; bd. govs., sec., rep. Zeneca Urology Econ. Summit, Washington, 1993; mem. Pfizer Nat. Hispanic Adv. Bd. Named One of Outstanding Young Men of Am., 1981, Philanthropic Leadership award Philanthropic Svc. Instns., 2006; Nat. Hispanic Med. Assn. Pub. Policy fellow, 2000-01. Mem. AMA, Nat. Hispanic Med. Assn. (public policy fellow), Am. Urological Assn., Calif. Med. Assn. (polit. action com. bd. dirs. 1997—, del.), L.A. Med. Assn. (polit. action com. 1992—), L.A. County Med. Assn., Yale Alumni Assn., Stanford Alumni Assn., L.A. Athletic Club. Office: White Meml Med Ctr Rm 500 1701 Cesar Chavez Ave Los Angeles CA 90033-2438 Office Phone: 323-224-6202. Personal E-mail: uromd@earthlink.net.

**MARTINEZ, NATALIE,** newscaster; b. Buffalo; Degree, SUNY, Buffalo. Anchor, reporter, prodr. at upstate N.Y. radio and TV stations; reporter and weekend anchor WXAA-TV, Albany, N.Y, primary anchor; co-anchor weekend morning news and reporter WMAQ-TV, Chgo., 2001—. Mem.: Nat. League Female Execs., Nat. Assn. of Hispanic Journalists, One Voice. Office: WMAQ-TV NBC Tower 454 N Columbus Dr Chicago IL 60611-5555 Office Phone: 312-836-5830.

**MARTINEZ, PEDRO JAIME,** professional baseball player; b. Manoquayabo, Dominican Republic, July 25, 1971; with LA Dodgers, 1992—93; pitcher Montreal Expos, 1994—97, Boston Red Sox, 1998—2004, NY Mets, 2005—. Named Minor League Player of Yr., Sporting News, 1991, Nat. League Earned Runs Average (ERA) Leader, 1997, Am. League Earned Runs Average (ERA) Leader, 1999—2003, Am. League Wins Leader, 1999, Am. League Strikeouts Leader, 1999, 2000, 2002, Am. League MVP, 1999; named to Am. League All-Star Team, 1998—2000, 2002, Nat. League All-Star Team, 1996—97, 2005; recipient Nat. League Cy Young award, 1997, Am. League Cy Young award, 1999, 2000. Achievements include being a member of World Series Champion Boston Red Sox, 2004; having over 200 career wins, 2006. Office: NY Mets 123 01 Roosevelt Ave Flushing NY 11368*

**MARTINEZ, PLACIDO,** energy executive; b. Cuba; BSc in Elec. Engring., Univ. New Orleans, 1981, MBA, 1988. Joined Entergy Corp., 1981, dir., distbn. ops., Ark., now v.p., ops. La. Named one of 50 Most Important Hispanics in Tech. & Bus., Hispanic Engr. & Info. Tech. mag., 2005.*

**MARTINEZ, RICARDO,** emergency medicine company executive; m. Robin Rosser. MD, La. State U. Sch. Medicine, 1980. Intern Lafayette (La.) Charity Hosp., 1980-81; resident Charity Hosp., New Orleans, 1983-85; vis. fellow accident rsch. unit Ctr. Automotive Engring./U. Birmingham, U.K., 1989; adminstr. Nat. Hwy. Traffic Safety Adminstrn, Washington, 1994—99; sr. v.p. health affairs Healtheon Web MD Corp., Atlanta, 1999—2000; pres.,

CEO Safety Intelligence Sys., Atlanta, 2000—04; exec. v.p. for med. affairs Schumacher Group, 2005—. Clin. prof. emergency medicine Emory U. Sch. Medicine, Atlanta. Mem.: Inst. Medicine. Home: 1254 Spring Creek Way Decatur GA 30033-2643 Office: 1275 Shiloh Rd NW Ste 2710 Kennesaw GA 30144

**MARTINEZ, RICHARD ISAAC,** research scientist, science administrator, music promoter and producer, education and health policy consultant; b. Havana, Cuba, Aug. 16, 1944; came to U.S., 1950; s. Joseph Louis and Susana (Nardea) M.; children: David B.J., Robyn S.M. BSc, McGill U., 1964; PhD in Chemistry, UCLA, 1976. Lab. asst. DuPont of Can. Ltd., Maitland, Ont., Canada, 1962; tchg. asst. McGill U., Montreal, 1964-65; tchg. and rsch. asst. San Diego State U., 1965-67; chemist Shell Chem. Co., Torrance, Calif., 1967-70; rsch. chemist UCLA, 1971-76, Dept. Commerce Nat. Inst. Standards and Tech., Gaithersburg, Md., 1976-92; CEO, pres. aDoReMe Prodns., 1990—; health scientist administr. Office Sci. Review, Nat. Inst. Gen. Med. Scis., NIH, Bethesda, Md., 1992—2006. Apptd. mem. City of Gaithersburg's Tech. and Innovation Com., 1998—. Contbr. over 40 articles to profl. publs., chpts. to books. Pres., chmn. bd. dirs Bethesda-Chevy Chase Jewish Cmty. Group, 1991-93. Fellow Coun. for Excellence in Govt., 1995-96, Sr. Fellow, 1996-; recipient I-R 100 award, 1983, Bronze medal U.S. Dept. Commerce, 1981; postdoctoral rsch. assoc. Nat. Acad. Scis., 1976-78; doctoral fellow UCLA, 1970-73. Mem. Am. Chem. Soc., Soc. Advancement of Chicanos and Native Ams. in Sci., Sigma Xi Sci. Rsch. Soc. Achievements include patents in methods for producing carbocyclic compounds, flue-gas desulfurization (I-R 100 award 1983); discovered dioxiranes (Ency. Brit. Yearbook of Sci. and the Future, 1979), metastable excited sulfur dioxide, vicinal hydroxy-substituted alkyl and oxoalkyl nitrates, peroxynitrates; research in development, standardization and application of MS/MS Tandem Mass Spectrometry for the study of the kinetics and mechanisms of complex ion-molecule reactions; rsch. on the kinetics and mechanisms of complex organic reaction systems relevant to oxidation and atmospheric chemistry (including the oxidation chemistry of olefins and sulfur compounds; free-radical reactions; ozone-olefin and ozone-sulfide reactions); developed cutting-edge rsch. methodologies. Office: aDoReMe Prodns PO Box 3616 Gaithersburg MD 20885-3616 Office Phone: 301-580-1850. E-mail: RM63F@verizon.net

**MARTINEZ, ROSE MARIE,** health science association administrator; PhD, Johns Hopkins Sch. Hygiene and Pub. Health. Former asst. dir. health fin. and policy U.S. Gen. Acctg. Office; sr. health rschr. Mathematica Policy Rsch.; dir. IOM Bd. Health Promotion and Disease Prevention, 1999—. Office: Inst of Med 500 Fifth St NW Washington DC 20001

**MARTINEZ, RUEBEN,** entrepreneur; b. Miami, Ariz., 1940; Profl. barber; owner, founder Libreria Martinez Books and Art Gallery, 1993—. Co-founder Latino Book Festival; founding mem. Santa Ana's Reading com.; spkr. in field. Named MacArthur Fellow, John D. and Catherine T. MacArthur Found., 2004. Office: Libreria Martinez 1110 N Main St Santa Ana CA 92701 Office Phone: 714-973-7900.

**MARTINEZ, TINO,** professional baseball player; b. Tampa, Fla., Dec. 7, 1967; Baseball player Seattle Mariners, 1988-95, N.Y. Yankees, 1996—2001, 2005—, St. Louis Cardinals, 2002—03, Tampa Bay Devil Rays, 2004. Mem. U.S. Olympic baseball team, 1988. Named to Am. League All-Star game, 1995, 1997. Achievements include mem. World Series Champions N.Y. Yankees, 1996, 1998-2000. Office: NY Yankees Yankee Stadium E 161 St and River Ave Bronx NY 10451

**MARTINEZ, TODD J.,** chemistry professor; BS, Calvin Coll., 1989; PhD, U. Calif., 1994. Fulbright fellow Fritz Haber Inst. Molecular Dynamics, Jerusalem; presdl. postdoctoral fellow U. Calif., LA, 1994—96; prof. U. Ill., Urbana-Champaign, 1996—. Faculty affiliate theoretical and computational biophysics group Beckman Inst. Advanced Sci. and Tech. Named a MacArthur fellow, John D. and Catherine T. MacArthur Found., 2005; recipient Beckman Young Investigator award, Beckman Found., 1999, Camille Dreyfuss Teacher-Scholar award, Camille & Henry Dreyfus Found., 2000, Rsch. Innovation award. Office: U Ill Dept Chemistry MC 712 600 S Mathews Urbana IL 61801 E-mail: tmartine@uiuc.edu.

**MARTÍNEZ, TOMÁS ELOY,** writer, journalist; b. Tucumán, Argentina, 1934; BA Spanish & Latin Am. Studies, U. Tucumán; MA, U. Paris; doctorates (hon.). Exec. editor Primera Plana, Buenos Aires, Panorama, Buenos Aires; editor La Opinión, Buenos Aires, Página 12, Buenos Aires, El Nacional, Caracas, Argentina; founder, exec. editor El Diario de Caracas; prof. Latin Am. Lit. U. Maryland, 1984—87; prof. Rutgers U., 1995—, dir. Latin Am. Studies Program, 1995—; syndicated columnist, 1995—. Dir. Ctr. Hemispheric Studies Rutgers U., 2000—, writer in residence, 2000—. Author: (essays) Structures of the Argentine Cinema, 1961, The Poetry of Ramos Sucre, 1981, The Argentine Dream, 1999, Requiem for a Lost Country, 2003, (short stories) The Commonplace Death, 1998, (novels) Sagrado, 1967, The Peron Novel, 1988, The Hand of the Master, 1991, Santa Evita, 1995, The Flight of the Queen, 2002 (Alfaguara Internat. Novel award), The Tango Singer, 2004. Woodrow Wilson Ctr. for Scholars fellowship, 1983, Guggenheim fellowship, 1987. Mem.: Com. to Protect Journalists. Office: RULAS Douglass Campus 105 George St New Brunswick NJ 08901-1414 also: NY Times Syndication Sales Corp 14th Fl 122 E 42nd St New York NY 10168 Office Phone: 732-932-0534, 732-932-9323 27, 212-499-3337. Office Fax: 212-499-3382. E-mail: eloy@rci.rutgers.edu.*

**MARTÍNEZ, YOLANDA R.,** social services administrator; b. Feb. 11, 1936; d. Eduardo R. and Consuelo (Rincon) Martínez; m. William Edward Hawkins, Mar. 27, 1963 (dec. May 11, 1996); children: Ricardo, Eduardo, William T. AA, San Bernardino Valley Coll., 1959; BA, U. Wash., 1974. Tchr. pub. schs., Calif., 1958—59; parole adviser, project dir., counselor Active Mexicanos, Seattle, 1972—76; instr. Everett (Wash.) C.C., 1975—76; rschr., translator Wash. State Coun. Crime and Delinquency, Seattle, 1977; program asst., minority affairs Seattle Ctrl. C.C.; cons. to cmty. offenders programs, 1977—81; sr. cmty. svc. rep. Seattle Dept. Human Resources, 1981—, ret., 2003; bus. owner Neighborhood Solutions, 2003—. Cons. in field. Author: Usted y La Ley, 1977. Translator ARC Lang. Bank, 1975—; chmn. Region 10 Chicago Task Force on Drug Abuse, 1977—79; mem. Seattle Cable Citizens Adv. Bd., 1988—90; v.p. Concilio for Spanish Speaking; state dir., mem. nat. exec. bd. League United L.Am. Citizens, 1980—82; chmn. Hispanic adv. bd. Seattle Cmty. Coll. Dist. 6, 1981—83; chmn. Seattle/Mazatlan Sister City Assn., 1981—83; v.p. Neighborhoods U.S.A., 1992—95, bd. dirs., 1986, United Way of King County; dist. adv. com. group health Northgate Clinic; del. White House Conf. on Families, L.A., 1980; bd. dirs. N.W. Kidney Ctr. Regional Coun., 2002; bd. mem. Northgate Chamber, 2002; Dem. precinct committeeman, 1968, 1970, 1988—2002; vol. worker various local and state polit. campaigns. Named One of 100 Women Role Models for Pub. Schs., State Office Pub. Instrn., Lake City Citizen of Yr., 2000; recipient Gov.'s citation, 1974, award for committment to higher edn., Seattle C.C. Dist., 1983, One of 10 Unsung Heroes in Seattle, Radical Women, 1983, Cmty. Svc. award, Am. G.I. Forum, 1984, Golden Maple Leaf award, Maple Leaf Cmty. Coun., 1991, Commn. award, Seattle Commn. on Children and Youth, 1991, 1993, assoc. mem., Eastern Washington U. Found., Seattle Works award, Cmty. Ambassador, 2001, Seattle Works Award, 2002. Mem.: Northgate C. of C. (founding mem.), Rotary. Home: 12018 17th Ave NE Seattle WA 98125-5116 E-mail: ymart@earthlink.net.

**MARTINEZ-CARBONELL, KARELIA,** not-for-profit fundraiser; b. Havana, Cuba, Jan. 6, 1962; arrived in U.S., 1968, naturalized; d. Francisco and Amada Martinez; m. Marino E. Carbonell, May 29, 1983; 1 child, Brenden Marino Carbonell. BA, Fla. Internat. U., Miami, 1994, MBA, 1997; DPA, Nova Southeastern U., Fort Lauderdale, Fla., 2002. Dir. devel. Carrollton Sch. of the Sacred Heart, Coconut Grove, Fla., 1998—. Bd. dirs. St. Philip's Episcopal Sch., Coral Gables, Fla., 1995—. Contbr. articles to profl. jours. Mem. Jr. League of Miami, Coral Gables, Fla., 1995—2002; adv. com. Blue Ribbon Ethics Commn., Miami, Fla., 2000—02. Mem.: Ocean Reef Club,

Riviera Country Club (arts com. 1992—2002), Pi Alpha Alpha. Republican. Roman Catholic. Avocations: reading, travel, research, writing. Office: Carrollton School of the Sacred Heart 3747 Main Highway Coconut Grove FL 33133 E-mail: kcarbonell@carrollton.org.

**MARTINEZ-FRAGA, PEDRO J.,** lawyer; b. Havana, Cuba, Sept. 9, 1960; BA with high honors, St. John's Coll., 1984; JD, Columbia U., 1987. Bar: Fla. 1988, DC 1988, US Dist. Ct. (so., mid. districts) Fla. 1988, US Ct. Appeals (11th cir.) 1989, US Dist. Ct. (Colo. dist.) 1991, US Supreme Ct. 1999. Adj. prof. law U. Miami, 2002—04; mem. com. Fla. Bar Rules of Civil Procedure, 1990—97, Fla. Bar Rules of Judicial administrn. 1996—97; chair com. Fla. Bar Code & Rules of Evidence, 1996; mem. ad hoc com. on rules and procedures US Dist. Ct., So. Dist. Fla. Author, editor Florida Civil Procedure, 2000, 2001, (chapters to books); contbr. articles to profl. journals. Dir. Cuban-Am. Endowment for Arts; bd. dirs. Miami Lighthouse for Blind, New World Sch. Arts; bd. mem. bd. visitors and governors St. John's Coll. Named 2001 Lawyer of the Americas, U. Miami Inter-Am. Law Review; named one of Top Lawyers in So. Fla., So. Fla. Legal Guide, 2001—05, Fla. Legal Elite, Fla. Trend Mag., 2004—05, Top Lawyers in Fla., Fla. Monthly Mag., 2004, Best Lawyers in Am., 2005—07; named to, Am. Law Inst., 1999, Best of the Bar, So. Fla. Bus. Jour., 2003—05; recipient Harlan Fiske Stone scholarship, 1987. Fellow: Am. Bar Found.; mem.: Hispanic Bar Assn., Am. Trial Lawyers Assn., Cuban-Am. Bar Assn., Dade County Bar Assn. (chair internat. law com. 2001—02, chair fed. ct. com. 1996), Internat. Bar Assn. Office: Greenberg Traurig LLP 1221 Brickell Ave Miami FL 33131 Office Phone: 305-579-0595. Office Fax: 305-579-0717. Business E-Mail: martinezp@gtlaw.com.

**MARTÍNEZ-LÓPEZ, CARMEN LEONOR,** management consultant, educator; b. Aracataca, Magdalena, Colombia, Oct. 13, 1956; d. Domingo Ramón Martínez and Alicia Esther Acosta de Martínez; m. Iván R. López, May 26, 2000. Licenciate in Ednl. Adminstrn., U. San Buenaventura, Medellín, Colombia, 1980; M in Ednl. Adminstrn., U. Antioquia, Medellín, 1989; specialist in Pub. Adminstrn., U. Escuela de Adminstrn. Publica, Medellín, 1995; specialist in Indsl. Rels., U. Escuela de Adminstrn. and Fin., Medellín, 1983, MBA, 2003; PhD in Internat. Bus., U. Tex.-Pan Am., Edinburg, 2003. Bd. dirs. Inst. Polictectico Jaime Isaza Cadavid, Medellín, 1980—82; dep. and bd. dirs. budget commn. Dept. de Antioquia, Medellín, 1982—84; regional mgr. Nat. Agy. Social Security, Medellín, 1983—86; pres. External Orgnl. Cons., Medellín, 1987—93; prof. rsch. and cons. U. Escuela de Adminstrn. and Fin., Medellín, 1989—92; adminstrv. mgr. Am. Med. Holding, Medellín, 1992—93; dept. chair Inst. Colombiano de Edn. Superior de Incolda, Cali, Colombia, 1993—96; rschr. and tchr. asst. U. Tex.-Pan Am., Edinburg, 1998—2003; asst. prof. CUNY, 2004—. Strategic planning cons. Am. Med. Holding, Medellín, 1989—92; strategic mgmt. cons. U. ICESI, Cali, 1995—96; strategic planning cons. Ednl. Cooperative Uraba, Apartadó, Antioquia, Colombia, 1999—2001; vis. prof. U. Monterrey, Mexico, 1999—2000. Dep. Dept. of Antioquia, Medellín, 1982—84; v.p. Colombian Conservative Party, Medellín, 1981—83; active Poly. Inst. Jaime Isaza, Medellín, 1980—82. Fellow: Ptnrs. of the Ams. (assoc.); mem.: Acad. Internat. Bus., Bus. Assn. L.Am. Studies, Acad. Mgmt. Conservative. Roman Catholic. Avocations: golf, soccer, travel. Office: CUNY S656 199 Chambers St New York NY 10007-1097 Home: Apt 3A 450 Halsted Rd New Rochelle NY 10805 Office Phone: 212-220-8389. Personal E-mail: carleo13@aol.com.

**MARTINEZ-MALDONADO, MANUEL,** academic administrator, dean, medical educator, physiology educator; b. Yauco, PR, Aug. 25, 1937; s. Manuel and Josefa Maldonado (Josefa Maldonado) Martinez; m. Nivia Elena Rivera, Dec. 18, 1959; children: Manuel, David, Ricardo, Pablo. BS, U. PR, 1957; MD, Temple U., 1961. Diplomate Am. Bd. Internal Medicine, Am. Bd. Nephrology. Intern St. Charles Hosp., Toledo, 1961—62; resident VA Hosp., San Juan, PR, 1962—65, chief resident, 1964—65; instr. U. Tex. Southwestern Med. Sch., Dallas, 1967—68; from asst. prof. to prof. medicine, co-dir. renal sect. Baylor Coll. Medicine, Houston, 1968—73; prof. medicine U. PR Sch. Medicine, 1973—90, prof. physiology, 1974—90; prof. medicine U. Caribbean, Bayamon, PR, 1980—90; chief med. svcs. VA Hosp., San Juan, 1973—90, co-dir. renal metabolic lab., 1973—90; prof., vice chmn. dept. medicine Emory U. Sch. Medicine, 1990—98; chief med. svcs. and clin. affairs Atlanta VA Med. Ctr., 1990—98; v.p. for rsch., prof. medicine Oreg. Health Scis. U., Portland, 1998—99, v.p. rsch., 1999—2000; pres., dean, prof. medicine and physiology Ponce Sch. Medicine, 2000—06. assoc. mem. nephrology com. Am. Bd. Internal Medicine, 1982—86; nat. adv. bd. gen. medicine B study sect. Nat. Inst. Arthritis, Metabolism and Digestive Diseases NIH; bd. sci. counselors, sci. advisors com. Nat. Heart, Lung and Blood Inst., NIH. Author: La Voz Sostenida, 1984, Palm Beach Blues, 1986, Por Amor al Arte, 1989, Hotel Maria, 1989, Isla Verde, 1999, Novela de Mediodia, 2003; film critic: El Reportero, 1983—86, El Mundo, 1987—90, editor/co-editor: in field, mem. editl. bd.: U. P.R. Press; editor: Am. Jour. of Med. Scis., 1994—98, Am. Jour. Kidney Disease, 1997—2002; contbr. over 200 articles to profl. jours. Com. mem. 500th Anniversary of Discovery Am., PR, 1987—92; bd. trustees Inst. Puerto Rican Culture and Performing Arts Ctr., 2001—05; trustee Corp. for Musical Arts, 2001—05; 1st Puerto Rican Lit., 2001—05; chair culture and recreation panel P.R. 2025; health com. Popular Dem. Com., PR, 1982—84; bd. dirs. All for P.R., Inc. Named one of Outstanding Young Men, P.R. C. of C., 1976; recipient Lederle Internat. award, 1966—67, Macy Faculty Scholar award, 1979—80, Grand Mobil prize medicine, Mobil Oil Corp., 1981, Disting. Alumnus award, Temple Med. Sch., 1988, Presdl. award, Nat. Kidney Found., 1988, Donald W. Seldin award, 1994, Disting. Physician award, P.R. Hosps. Assn., 1988, Orden del Cafetal award, Municipality of Yauco, 1989, Abelardo Díaz Alfaro award, Medicine & Humanites, 2002, Svc. Exec. award, P.R. Mfrs. Assn., 2005. Master: ACP; fellow: AAAS, Am. Heart Assn. (hypertension rsch. coun.), Coun. for High Blood Pressure Rsch.; mem.: Am. Acad. Arts and Scis. (hon. fgn.), Nat. Kidney Found. (chmn. pub. policy com. 1992—94), Consortium Southeastern Hypertension Ctrs. (bd. dirs.), Assn. Am. Physicians, Inter-Am. Soc. Hypertension Assn (bd. govs., chmn. 8th Sci. Congres 1989, U.S Pharmacopeial Conv. Cardio Renal Drugs com. 1990—96), L.Am. Soc. Nephrology (v.p. 1987—91, pres.-elect 1991—94, pres. 1994—96, Miatello award 1999), Am. Soc. for Clin. Investigation, So. Soc. Clin. Investigation (sec.-treas. 1983—85, pres. 1985—86, Founders medal 1990, Pub. Svc. medal, Donald W. Seldin award), Am. Soc. Nephrology (legis. liaison com., chmn. audit com. 1988), Inst. Medicine of NAS (com. on human rights 1987—92), Alpha Omega Alpha. Achievements include research in kidney physiology and pathophysiology, treatment of clinical disturbances of blood composition, clinical use of diuretics, mechanisms of the devel. of hypertension. Office Phone: 787-844-3710. Personal E-mail: martinem_pms@hotmail.com. Business E-Mail: mmartinez@psm.edu.

**MARTINEZ SANCHEZ, MARY ANN,** academic administrator; b. Redwood Falls, Minn., Apr. 9, 1963; d. Manuel and Doreen Roselyn Martinez; m. James Joseph Sanchez, May 13, 1989; 1 child, Joseph Manuel Sanchez. Grad., Duke U., Durham, NC, 1985; MA in Counseling Psychology, U. Notre Dame, Ind., 1992, PhD in Counseling Psychology, 1996. Instr. Ind. U., South Bend, 1993—94; psychologist Madison Ctr., South Bend, 1995—96; mem. faculty psychology Pima CC, Tucson, 1996—, chmn. dept. behavioral scis., 2000—. Mem.: APA, Psychology Tchrs. at CCs, Western Psychol. Assn. Democrat. Roman Catholic. Avocations: cooking, gardening, interior decorating. Office: Pima CC 2202 W Anklam Rd Tucson AZ 85709

**MARTÍNEZ-SOLÍS, LUIS FERNANDO,** journalist, writer, historian; b. Medellin, Antioquia, Colombia, Apr. 29, 1946; arrived in U.S., 1999; s. Edelberto A. Martínez-Márquez and Myriam C. Solís-Escobar; m. Alicia Ester Posada; children: Isabel Kristina, Ludoviko Ernesto, Enver Kamilo. BA in Journalism, Antioquia U., Medellin, 1987; Tchg. Cert., Nat. Learn Svc. SENA, Apartado, Colombia, 1996; Historian and Academic (hon.), Antioquia History Acad., Medellin, 1998. Speech writer CORVIDE, Medellin, 1992—99; human develoment SENA, Apartado, 1996—99; Spanish composition Cooperativ U., Turbo, Uraba, Colombia, 1997—98; comm. theory Apya Yala U., Apartado, 1997—98; columnist, editor El Periodiko, St. Louis, 1999—. Journalist Comunal Action, Medellin, 1970—85, Patriot Union,

Medellin, 1985—99. Author: (27 books) Geopolitics and Comunications, 1998; editor: (newspaper) EL PERIODIKO, 2001. Recipient Gold Medal, SEDUCA, 1987, Heroic Journalism award, SIP, 1989, Ariza Flower flower, COMFENALCO, 1998. Mem.: Universala Esperanto Asocio (rotterdam 1970—). Avocations: walking, athletics. Office: El Periodiko 2nd Fl 3337 Texas Ave Saint Louis MO 63118 Business E-Mail: elperiodiko@cs.com.

**MARTINEZ TUCKER, SARA,** educational association administrator; b. Laredo, Tex. BA, Univ. Tex., Austin, MBA with high honors. Reporter San Antonio Express-News; various positions through regional v.p. AT&T, 1981—97; pres., CEO Hispanic Scholarship Fund, San Francisco, 1997—. Bd. dir. Student Loan Mktg. Assn. (Sallie Mae), 2001—; mem. No. Am. diversity adv. bd. Toyota Motor Corp.; founding mem. Nat. Ctr. for Edn. Accountability; mem. steering com. Council for Aid to Edn., RAND Corp.; mem. Sec. of Edn.'s Commn. on Future of Edn., 2005. Mem. Chancellor's Council Univ. Tex., Austin, mem. adv. council, Coll. of Nat. Sci.; mem. adv. bd. Oxygen Media / Markle Found. Named Hispanic of the Year, Hispanic mag., 2000; named one of 80 Elite Hispanic Women, Hispanic Bus. mag., 2003, 25 Most Influential Hispanics, Time Mag., 2005. Office: Hispanic Scholarship Fund Ste 1500 55 Second St San Francisco CA 94105

**MARTING, MICHAEL G.,** lawyer; b. Cleve., Nov. 5, 1948; BA summa cum laude, Yale U., 1971, JD, 1974. Bar: Ohio 1974. Assoc. Jones Day, Cleve., 1974-83, ptnr., 1984—. Mem.: Chagrin Valley Hunt Club, Tavern Club (trustee local chpt. 1985—88, 2004—, treas., sec.), Cleve. Racquet Club, Union Club. Avocations: fly fishing, hurling, squash. Office: Jones Day N Point 901 Lakeside Ave E Cleveland OH 44114-1190 Office Phone: 216-586-7194. Business E-Mail: mgmarting@jonesday.com.

**MARTINI, PERRY JAMES,** educational consultant; b. Warren, Ohio, Apr. 20, 1948; s. Perry Enio and Angeline Martini; m. Jean Marie Gaby, Mar. 24, 1952; children: Yolanda Joan, Ellen Raffaela, Stephen Ray Collins, Bernadette Mitchell. BS, US Naval Acad., 1971; MA in Strategic Studies, Navy War Coll., 1989; MEd, Marymount U., 1994; MS, Salve Regina Coll., 1989; EdD, George Wash. U., 2000. Commd. ensign USN, 1971, advanced through grades to capt., ret., 1998; asst. sec. Higher Edn. Commn., Annapolis, Md., 1998—2000; assoc. dir. class giving US Naval Acad. Found., 2000—03; dir. exec. leadeship programs Acad. Leadership, King of Prussia, Pa., 2003—. Leadership cons. Acad. Leadership, King of Prussia, 2003—; adj. prof. Regent U., Alexandria, Va., 2001. Author: Inspiring Leadership: Character and Ethics Matter. Named to Ohio Football Hall Fame, Trumbull Hall Fame, 1990. Mem.: U.S. Naval Acad. Alumni Assn. (life; pres., trustee 1980—). Conservative. Avocations: travel, golf, reading, speaking. Home: 853 Holly Drive South Annapolis MD 21401 Office: Academy Leadership 10120 Valley Forge Circle King Of Prussia PA 19406 Office Phone: 610-783-0630. Personal E-mail: pjmartini@comcast.net. E-mail: pmartini@academyleadership.com.

**MARTINI, RICHARD K.,** theatrical producer; b. Bergenfield, NJ, Mar. 11, 1952; s. John F. and June L. (Fenton) M.; m. Susan C. Weaving, Aug. 1, 1981. BA, St. Francis Coll., Loretto, Pa., 1974; MEd, U. S.C., 1975. V.p. Am. Theatre Prodns., N.Y.C., 1975-81; pres. Edgewood Grp., N.Y.C., 1981-86; pres., owner KL Mgmt., N.Y.C., 1986—; owner, operator Martini Entertainment, Inc., N.Y.C., 1991—. Home: 201 E 37th St New York NY 10016-3159 Office: Martini Entertainment Co 1501 Broadway Ste 1401 New York NY 10036-5601

**MARTINI, WILLIAM J.,** former congressman, state commissioner, judge; b. Passaic, N.J. m. Gloria Martini; children: William Jr., Marissa. Degree, Villanova U., 1968; JD, Rutgers U., 1972. Elected mem. City Coun. of Clifton, N.J., Passaic County Bd. Chosen Freeholders, U.S. House of Reps., 1994-96; ptnr. Sills Cummis Radin Tischman Epstein & Gross PA, Newark; commr. Port Authority of N.Y. and N.J.; judge U.S. Dist Ct. N.J. Pres. Nicholas Martini Found.; trustee United Way of Passaic County, Ctr. Italian Am. Culture, Passaic Valley Coun. Boys Scouts of Am., Hackensack U. Med. Ctr., Freedom House. Republican.

**MARTINICO, JENNIFER MARIE,** music educator; b. Detroit; d. Joseph Michael and Kathleen Marie Martinico. B of Instrumental Music Edn., Wayne State U., 2003. Cert. tchr. Mich. Music specialist Herter Music Ctr., Saginaw, Mich., 2004; dir. of bands Alcona Cmty. Schs., Lincoln, Mich., 2004—. Musician St. John The Bapt. Ch., Alpena, Mich., 2004. Mem.: Delta Omicron (v.p., dir. musicals, sec., rush chair 1998—2003, Star of Delta Omicron 2002). Office: Alcona Cmty Schs 51 N Barlow Rd Lincoln MI 48742 Home: PO Box 171 115 Alger St Apt 2 Lincoln MI 48742 Personal E-mail: j_martinico@hotmail.com.

**MARTIN-LOWRY, BEVERLY ANNE,** writer, columnist; b. Washington, Oct. 25, 1948; d. James Aubrey and Gertha Mae Martin; m. Courtland Alan Milner, Apr. 20, 1968 (div. Oct. 17, 1989); children: Jennifer Anne Litton, Martin Alan Milner; m. Peter Hans Lowry, Dec. 29, 1999. CEO Pen 2 Paper, Ink, Live Oak, Tex., 2003—. Author: In October, I Turn Fifty! A Satirical Look Back on Life, 2000, Memoirs and Confessions: From Europe to the USA, 2001, (novels) Strong Appetites, 2004, Can't Cook Anonymous, 2004, The Most Unlikely Angel: A Trilogy of Love, Life, and Laughter, 2005; columnist: Sounding Off; contbr. articles to local newspapers. Mem.: Am. Legion (life). Republican. Presbyterian. Avocations: swimming, reading, travel. Office Phone: 210-646-9877. Personal E-mail: n2books@satx.rr.com.

**MARTINO, BABETTE,** artist; b. Jan. 4, 1956; d. Giovanni and Eva E. (Marinelli) M. Student, Pa. Acad. Fine Arts, Phila.; diploma, L'Accademia di Belle Arti, Firenze, Italy, 1970; BA, Temple U., Phila., 1972; MFA, U. Guanajuato, Mex., 1976. Painter, 1976—; fellow Yadoo, Saratoga Springs, N.Y., 1986, 88, 91, 1993, 95, Headlands Ctr for Arts, Sausalito, Calif., 1992. Fellow Yaddo, Saratoga Springs, N.Y., 1991, 88, 86, 84, 95; grad. teaching asst. Inst. Allende U. Guanajuato, Mex., 1975; instr. drawing Mohawk Valley Community Coll., Utica, N.Y., 1978-81; instr. painting Munson-Williams-Proctor Inst., Utica, 1978-80. Represented in collections at Art in Embassies State Dept., Washington, D.C., Price Waterhouse, Subaru Am., N.J., Blue Cross & Blue Shield Phila., Camden Country Cultural and Heritage Commn., N.J., Alexander & Alexander, Phila., Mohawk Valley Community Coll., Utica, Owensboro Nat. Bank, Ky., Gilberts Assocs., Pa., Mcpl. Ctr., Lawton, Okla., New Music West, Calif., Butler Inst. of Am. Art, Woodmere Art Mus., Owensboro Art Mus., Ky.; exhibitions include Suzanne Gross Gallery, Phila., Ptnrs. Gallery, Bethesda, Md., Tanzania Embassy, Dar Es Salaam, East Africa, Shippensburg U., Gov's. Mansion, Pa., Phila. U. City Art League, Butler Inst. Am. Art, Ohio, 2000, Hahn Gallery-Chestnut Hill, Phila., 2003, Dartmouth Coll., Hanover, NH, Gleria Prin., Ctr. Cultural El Nigromante San Miguel Allende, Mex., others; solo shows include Douglass Coll. Rutgers U., New Brunswick, N.J., 1990, Cudahy's Gallery, N.Y.C., 1990, NYU, N.Y.C., 1995, Markeim Art Ctr., Haddenfield, N.J., 2000, Salo Des Amis Gallery, Malvern, Pa., 2003, Pa. Coll., Williamsport, 2005, Butler Inst. Am. Art, Youngstown, Woodmere Art Mus., Phila. Grantee Mohawk Valley CC, 1980, Pa. Coun. Arts, 1984, NEA, 1985, GAP grant/ Pew fellow 2000, fellow Pollock-Krasner Found., NYC, 1992, Acad. Fine Arts, Pa., 2001,; named to Audubon Artists, 1984, Allied Artists Am., 1986; recipient 2d prize Atlantic City Art Show, 1976, 2d prize Camdon County (N.J.) Cultural & Heritage Commn., 1976, Grumbacher award and cert. merit Tex. Fine Arts Assn., 1977, Purchase award Lawton Jr. Svc. League, 1978, Ralph Fabri medal Allied Artists Am., 1988, 91, 60th Anniversary award Phillips Mill Assn., 1989, Painting award Assn. for Visual Artists, 1989, M Grumbacher Gold medal Allied Artists Am., NYC, 1989, G. Hitchcock Landscape in Sunlight award Nat. Acad. Design, NYC, 1990, Purchase award Milford Fine Arts Coun., 1991, F.T. McClintock award, Phillips Mill Art Assn., 1991, Lowe award Allied Artists Am., NYC, 1992, 1st prize Art of the State, State Mus. Pa., 1993, McNeely award Allied Artists Am., 1994, Tompson award Bianco Found., Pa., 1995, Pressman Ciocca and Smith award Bianco Found., 1996, Redenbaugh Painting award Phillips Mill, Pa., 1996, Willcox award No. Arts Coun., Nicolet Coll., Wis., 1998, Harvey award Phillips Mill, Pa., 1999, Everett

award Allied Artist Am., NYC, 1999, Thompson award Allied Artist Am., Meyerowitz award Audubon Artists, NYC, 1999, 1st award Nat. League of Am. Pen Women, 2000, Len G. Everett Meml. award Audubon Artists, 2000, Purchase award Pa. Acad. Fine Arts, 2000, PEW Fellow ship in Arts, Phila. 2000, Otto award Phillips Mill, Pa., 2001, Thompson award Allied Artists Am., 2001, GAP grant Pew Fellowship in Arts, 2001, Salmagundi award Audubon Artists, NYC, Excellence award Pa. Acad. Fine Arts, Maxwell award, Woodmere, Pa., 2002, Winsor-Newton award Audubon Artists, 2003, John Young-Hunter award Allied Artists Am., 2003, Ellen Penn Son Sutter award 2005, award in memory of Ellen Pearson Sutter-Phillips, Pa. Coun. Arts, 2005; grantee Pa. Coun. Arts Fellow: Pa. Acad. Fine Arts (M. Van Kirk award II 2004). Home: 1435 Manor Ln Blue Bell PA 19422-2021 Office Phone: 215-646-0822. Personal E-mail: babettemartino@hotmail.com.

**MARTINO, JOSEPH PAUL,** research scientist, researcher; b. Warren, Ohio, July 16, 1931; s. Joseph and Anna Elizabeth (Kubina) M.; m. Mary Lou Bouquot, May 18, 1957 (dec. Jan. 1988); children: Theresa, Anthony, Michael; m. Nancy McCoy, Dec. 28, 2000. AB in Physics, Miami U., Ohio, 1953; MSEE, Purdue U., 1955; PhD in Stats., Ohio State U., 1961; grad., Air War Coll., 1972. Commd. 2d lt. USAF, 1953, advanced through grades to col., 1973, project engr. armament lab. Wright-Patterson AFB, Ohio, 1955-58, mathematician Office Sci. Rsch. Washington, 1961-62, staff scientist Avionics Lab. Wright-Patterson AFB, 1972-73, dir. engring. standardization Def. Electronics Supply Ctr. Dayton, Ohio, 1973-75, ret., 1975; sr. scientist, rsch. inst. U. Dayton, 1975-93. Author: Technological Forecasting for Decision-making, 1972, rev. edit., 1983, 3d edit., 1992, A Fighting Chance-The Moral Use of Nuclear Weapons, 1988, Science Funding: Politics and Porkbarrel, 1992, Research and Development Project Selection, 1995, (novel) The Justice Cooperative, 2004; assoc. editor: Tech. Forecasting and Social Change Jour., 1968—. With USAF, 1953—75, col., 1973—75. Fellow IEEE (Centennial medal 1984), AAAS, AIAA (assoc.); mem. Inst. for Ops. Rsch. and Mgmt. Sci., Am. Soc. Engring. Mgmt., Engrs. Club of Dayton. Roman Catholic. Office Phone: 937-492-4729. Business E-Mail: j.p.martino@ieee.org.

**MARTINO, MICHAEL CHARLES,** entertainer, musician, actor; b. Phila., Sept. 10, 1950; s. Salvatore Joseph and Marie Angela (Langone) M. Grad. high sch., Upper Darby, Pa. Spokesperson/rep. Petosa Accordion Co., Seattle, 1979—; featured TV entertainer Mike Martino Show, Delaware County, Pa., 1987-89; accordion tchr. Drexel Hill, Pa., 1989—; featured artist Am. Accordion Soc. Conv., King of Prussia, Pa., 2003; actor TV series Hack, Channel 3, 2003. Entertainer, host, prodr. St. Jude's Children's Hosp. Marathon, King of Prussia, Pa., 1973; opening act comedian Morty Gunty, 1973, Pat Cooper, Phila., 1981; guest artist, entertainer Internat. Platform Assn. Conv., Washington, 1979, Am. Accordion Musicological Soc. Festival and symposium, King of Prussia, 2003; nite club performer Glen Mills, Pa., 1989; actor TV commls., Elkton, Md., 1979, Halloween Spl. KYW-TV, Phila., 1986, TV show Hack, 2003; performed radio contest jingle Sta. KISS 100 radio, Media, Pa., 1992; featured soloist Am. Accordian Festival, King of Prussia, Pa., 2003; opening act for broadway star Donna Theodore for Joe Theodore Fundraiser, Glassboro, NJ, 2005. Author: (movie) Forever Fiftys, 1990; composer, dir., prodr., actor: (video) Forever Fiftys; composer: (movie) That First September; creator, performer Suspended Triple Bellows Shake Technique for the Accordion, 1994; composer (ballad) Through the Music, Through the Words I Sing, 1995, (sung by Donna Theodore) Through the Music Through the Words I Sing, 1998; actor: (movie) Jesus' Son, 1999, (TV show) Hack, 2003; guest performer Accordion Conv., King of Prussia, 2003; featured in various articles. Recipient citation U.S. Ho. Reps., 1989, Proclamation Mike Martino Day Mayor Ward, Del. County, 1988, Danny Thomas Hon. award St. Jude's Hosp., Del. County, 1973, Mayor's Svc. award Upper Darby, Pa., 1994. Roman Catholic. Avocations: antique cars, dogs. Home: 2530 Stoneybrook Ln Drexel Hill PA 19026-1610 Office Phone: 610-789-5753.

**MARTINO, PETER DOMINIC,** financial software company executive, real estate developer, real estate broker, federal agency administrator, consultant, management consultant; b. NYC, Sept. 21, 1963; s. Rocco Leonard and Barbara Italia (D'Iorio) Martino; m. Manelle Victoria Nuñez, July 31, 2004; children: Elizabeth Marie, Arden Victoria. BS, U.S. Naval Acad., 1985; postgrad., Georgetown U., 2004—. Cert. cash mgr.; cert. Treasury profl. Commd. ensign USN, 1985, advanced through grades to lt., resigned, 1990; with USNR, 1990-99; from v.p. mktg. to exec. v.p., COO XRT, Inc., Wayne, Pa., 1990-93, pres., 1993-98, CEO, 1996-98; pres., CEO XRT-CERG Am., Inc., 1998-2000; exec. v.p. XRT-CERG S.A., Paris, 1998-2000; pres., CEO, chmn., founder CharitEx, Inc. N.Y.C., 2000—01; real estate broker Corcoran Group, N.Y.C., 2001—03; real estate developer, 2001—03; COO dept. homeland security Infrastructure Protection, U.S. Govt. Sr. Exec. Svc., Washington, 2003—04; pres., CEO, founder The Develop. Coun., LLC, Washington, 2004—05; legal rsch. asst. Law Ctr. Georgetown U., 2005; summer law assoc. Morgan Lewis & Bockius, LLP, 2006. Founder, dir. XRT Europe, Ltd., 1994-98; founder, dir., pres Four Star Software, Inc., Wayne, 1994-98; bd. dirs. Nat. Kidney Found. Delaware Valley; founder internet e-commerce bus. for charitable giving; mem. alternative dispute resolution divsn. Georgetown Law Barristers Coun., 2005-; mem. Georgetown Jour. Law and Pub. Policy. News editor: Georgetown Law Weekly, 2005. Mem. Kennedy Ctr. for Performing Arts, Phoenixville Borough Coun., 1993—94; Rep. committeeman, 1995—97; mem. coun. Nat. Italian Am. Found., 2003—; bd. dir. Nat. Kidney Found. Delaware Valley, 1997—2001, Martino Found., 1998—2003, World Affairs Coun. Phila., 1999—2001; adv. bd. Pres.'s Cir. Naval Acad. Found. 2002—03. Mem. ABA, Federalist Soc. Law and Pub. Policy Studies, Am. Constitution Soc., Cato Inst., Treasury Mgmt. Assn. Naval Acad. Alumni Assn., Naval Acad. Athletic Assn., Naval Acad. Sailing Squadron, Nat. Italian Am. Found. (coun. mem.), N.Y. Athletic Club, Pyramid Club (Phila.), Avalon Yacht Club, Army-Navy Club. Roman Catholic. Avocations: sailing, boating, real estate, fine wine, architecture. Home: 168 W Lake Dr Annapolis MD 21403 Office Phone: 410-991-5280. Personal E-mail: pmartino@igi.net, peter332@gmail.com. Business E-Mail: pdm32@law.georgetown.edu.

**MARTINO, RICHARD,** application developer, mathematician, educator; BS in Physics & Math. magna cum laude, Pa. State U., University Park, 1972—76. Cert. Toastmasters Internat., 1983. Adj. math. tchr. St. Petersburg Coll., Fla., 2003; software engring. project lead Medcere LLC, Clearwater, Fla., 2005—. Author: Return on Investment Theory of Human Motivation. Pres. adv. com. St. Jude Cathedral Sch., St. Petersburg, 2005—06. Recipient iDatix Impact award for outstanding software engring., iDatix Corp., 2005. Achievements include first to relational databases of entities. Avocation: gardening. Office: Richardmartinocom PO Box 1776 Clearwater FL 33757-1776 Business E-Mail: richard@richardmartino.com.

**MARTINO, ROBERT SALVATORE,** orthopedic surgeon; b. Clarksburg, W.Va., May 31, 1931; s. Leonard L. and Sarafina (Foglia) M.; m. Lenora Cappellanti, May 22, 1954; children: Robert Jr., Leslie L. Reckziegel. AB, W.Va. U., 1953, postgrad., 1955-56, BS in Medicine, 1958; MD, Northwestern U., 1960. Diplomate Am. Bd. Orthop. Surgery; lic. Ill., Calif., Ind. Intern Chgo. Wesley, 1960-61; resident dept. orthopaedic surgery Northwestern U., 1961-65, Chgo. Wesley Meml., 1961-62, Am. Legion Hosp. for Crippled Children, 1962-63, Cook County Hosp., Chgo., 1964, 64-65; orthopaedic surgeon Gary, Ind., 1965-67; orthopaedic surgeon Merrillville, Ind., 1967—. Fellow Nat. Found. Infantile Paralysis, 1956, Office of Vocat. Rehab., Hand Surgery, 1965; chief of staff St. Mary Med. Ctr., 1976, chief of surgery, 1974-85; chief of staff Gary Treatment Ctr./Ind. Crippled Children's Svcs., 1974-84; adj. asst. prof. anatomy Ind. U., 1978, clin. asst. prof. orthop. surgery, 1980, emeritus asst. prof. anatomy and cell biology Ind. U., 2003, emeritus clin. asst. prof. orthop. surgery, 2003; mem. Zoning Bd., 1989-90. Chmn. Planning Bd. Town of Dune Acres, 1992-96; bd. dirs. United Steel Workers Union Health Plan, 1994—; St. Mary's Med. Ctr., Chgo. mem. on Health Care Reform. Capt. U.S. Army, 1953-56. Fellow ACS (emeritus), Am. Acad. Orthop. Surgery (emeritus); mem. AMA, NRA, Ind. Med. Soc., Ill. Med. Soc., Chgo. Med. Soc., Ill. Orthop. Soc., Ind. Orthop. Soc., Mid-Am.

Orthop. Assn., Tri-State Orthop. Soc., Clin. Orthop. Soc. Home: 22 Oak Dr Dune Acres IN 46304-1016 Office Phone: 219-887-9506. Personal E-mail: indorth@aol.com, brutabobm@aol.com.

**MARTINS, NELSON,** physics professor; b. Santos, Brazil, Oct. 18, 1930; s. Aniceto and Angelica Martins; m. Maria Lucia, Jan. 8, 1959 (div. Sept. 1983); children: Flavia, Paulo. BS in Physics, Mackenzie U., São Paulo, Brazil, 1958; D in Physics, Pontifica U., Campinas, Brazil, 1977. Cert. physicist. Dir. engring. Mackenzie U., 1971-73, dir. Exact Sci., 1983-90; gen. dir. Ednl. Found., Barretos, Brazil, 1973-76; chief physics dep. Engring. Sch., Araraquara, Brazil, 1991; chief physics dept. U. Santo Amaro, São Paulo, 1990-92; dir. CCET Ctr. Exact Scis. and Tech., São Paulo, 1992-95. Author: (with others) Electriciy and Magnetism, 1973, Dimensional Analysis, 1980, Dynamics, 1982. Mem. Am. Assn. Physics Tcrhs., Brazil Soc. Physics. Office: Sorocaba Engring Sch Rod Sen Jose Ermirio Moraes Sorocaba 18001970 Brazil E-mail: nelson_martins30@yahoo.com.br.

**MARTINS, PETER,** ballet master, choreographer, dancer; b. Copenhagen, Oct. 27, 1946; arrived in U.S., 1967, naturalized, 1970; m. Lisa LaCour (div.); 1 child, Nilas; m. Darci Kistler. Pupil of Vera Volkova and Stanley Williams with Royal Danish Ballet. With N.Y.C. Ballet, 1967—, tchr., 1975, ballet master, 1981-83, co-ballet master-in-chief, 1983-89, ballet master-in-chief, 1990—. Tchr. Sch. Am. Ballet, 1975; artistic advisor Pa. Ballet, 1982—; participant, Voices of the Arts Kennedy Ctr. for Performing Arts, Washington, 2006. Mem. Royal Danish Ballet, 1965—67, prin. dancer including Bourn-onville repertory, 1967, guest artist NYC Ballet, 1967—70, prin. dancer, 1970—83, guest artist regional ballet cos. U.S., guest artist Nat. Ballet Can., Royal Ballet London, Grand Theatre Geneva, Paris Opera, Vienna State Opera, Munich State Opera, London Festival Ballet, Ballet Internat., Royal Danish Ballet, TV appearances in series of Balanchine works, 1974, appeared on PBS Dance in Am. series A Choreographer's Notebook: Stravinsky Piano Ballets by Peter Martins, 1984; choreographer Broadway musicals Dream of the Twins, 1982, On Your Toes, 1982, Song and Dance, 1985, Calcium Light Night, 1977, Tricolore-Pas de Basque sect., 1978, Rossini Pas de Deaux, 1978, ice ballet Tango-Tango, 1978, Dido and Aeneas, 1979, Sonate di Scarlatti, 1979, Eight Easy Pieces, 1980, Lille Suite, 1980, Suite from Histoire du Soldat, 1981, Capricio Italien, 1981, The Magic Flute, 1981, Symphony No. 1, 1981, Delibes Divertissement, 1982, Piano-Rag-Music, 1982, Concerto for Two Solo Pianos, 1982, Waltzes, 1983, Rossini Quartets, 1983, Tango, 1983, A Schubertiad, 1984, Mozart Violin Concerto, 1984, Poulenc Sonata, 1985, La Sylphide, 1985, Valse Triste, 1985, Eight More, 1985, We Are the World, 1985, Eight Miniatures, 1985, Ecstatic Orange, Tanzspiel, 1988, Jazz, 1993, Symphonic Dances, 1994, Barber Violin Concerto, 1994, Mozart Piano Concerto No. 17, 1994, X-Ray, 1995; author (autobiography): Far From Denmark, 1982. Named Knight of Order of Danneborg, Denmark, 1983; recipient Dance Mag. award, 1977, Golden Apple award, Cue, 1977, Merit award, Phila. Art Alliance, 1985, Liberty award, N.Y.C., 1986, H.C. Andersen Ballet prize, Royal Danish Theatre, 1988. Office: NY State Theater NYC Ballet 20 Lincoln Center Plz New York NY 10023-6913*

**MARTINSON, BRADLEY JAMES,** lawyer; b. Ortonville, Minn., Oct. 16, 1945; s. Edwin James and Helen Eleanor (Christenson) M.; m. Beth Louise Nelson, June 24, 1967; children: Sara, Timothy. BA, Concordia Coll., Moorhead, Minn., 1967; JD, U. Minn., 1973. Assoc. Robert Hillstrom & Assocs., Mpls., 1973-80; shareholder Hillstrom, Bale & Martinson, Mpls., 1980-85, Martinson, Schwartz & Corey, Mpls., 1985-87, Salmen, Brinkman & Martinson, St. Paul, 1987-90; shareholder, mng. ptnr. Tews, Squires, Martin & Martinson, Mpls., 1990-97; shareholder Law Offices of Bradley J. Martinson, Mpls., 1998—. Lt. U.S. Army, 1968-71. Mem. Midland Hills Country Club (pres. 1997-98). Home: 1928 29th Ave NW New Brighton MN 55112-1737 Office: 333 S 7th St Ste 1170 Minneapolis MN 55402 Office Phone: 612-335-9300. Business E-Mail: bmartinson@martinsonlaw.com.

**MARTINSON, CONSTANCE FRYE,** television personality, television producer; b. Boston, Apr. 11, 1932; d. Edward and Rosalind Helen (Sperber) Frye; m. Leslie Herbert Martinson, Sept. 24, 1955; 1 child, Julianna Martinson Carner. BA in English Lit., Wellesley Coll., 1953. Dir. pub. rels. Coro Found., LA, 1974-79; prodr., host KHJ Dimensions, LA, 1979-81, Connie Martinson Talks Books, LA, 1981—. Instr. dept. humanities UCLA, 1981—, bd. dirs. Friends of English; moderator, instr. U. Judaism; celebrity advisor Book Fair-Music Ctr., LA, 1986; advisor, moderator LA Times Festival Books, 1996; TV rep. LA Pub. Libr. LA Cityview, Sta. WNYE-TV. Author: Dramatization of Wellesley After Images, 1974; book editor, columnist: Calif. Press Bur. Syndicate, 1986—; columnist: Beverly Hills Courier, 1997—. Pres. Mayor's Adv. Coun. Volunteerism, LA, 1981—82; chmn. cmty. affairs dept. Town Hall of Calif., LA, 1981—85; bd. dirs. legal def. fund NAACP, LA, 1981—84. Mem.: Nat. Book Critics Assn., PEN, Am. Film Inst., Women in Cable, Jewish TV Network (bd. dirs. 1985—87), Mulholland Tennis Club, Wellesley Coll. Club (pres. 1979—81). Democrat. Jewish. Avocations: tennis, theater, reading. Home and Office: 2288 Coldwater Canyon Dr Beverly Hills CA 90210-1756 Personal E-mail: conniemartinson@qmail.com. Business E-Mail: talksbooks@lycos.com.

**MARTINSON, ELMER JAMES,** retired surgeon; b. Hinsdale, Ill., Nov. 16, 1917; s. Carl Jerome and Alma Ingebord (Berglin) Martinson; m. Peggy Jo Guy, Nov. 24, 1946; children: Thomas James, Carl John, Bruce Jeffrey, William Jay. BA, Union Coll., Lincoln, Nebr., 1937; MD, Loma Linda U., Calif., 1942. Diplomate Am. Bd. Surgery, 1956. Intern Mpls. Gen. Hosp., 1941—42, resident, 1946—49; surgeon Martinson Clinic, Wayzata, Minn., 1950—92; staff examiner Cancer Detection Ctr. U. Minn., Mpls., 1992—97; med. expert Social Security, Mpls., 1998—2005; ret., 2005. Maj. USAF, 1942—46. Fellow: ACS. Avocations: golf, painting, stamp collecting/philately, gardening. Home: 2799 Pheasant Rd Excelsior MN 55331

**MARTINSON, IDA MARIE,** medical/surgical nurse, educator, physiologist; b. Mentor, Minn., Nov. 8, 1936; d. Oscar and Marvel (Nelson) Sather; m. Paul Varo Martinson, Mar. 31, 1962; children: Anna Marie, Peter. Diploma, St. Luke's Hosp. Sch. Nursing, 1957; BS, U. Minn., 1960, M.N.A., 1962; PhD, U. Ill., Chgo., 1972. Instr. Coll. St. Scholastica St. Luke's Sch. Nursing, 1957—58, Thornton Jr. Coll., 1967—69; lab. asst. U. Ill. at Med. Ctr., 1970—72; lectr. dept. physiology U. Minn., St. Paul, 1972—82, asst. prof. Sch. Nursing, 1972—74, assoc. prof. rsch., 1974—77, prof. rsch., 1977—82; prof. dept. family health care U. Calif., San Francisco, 1982—2003, chmn. dept., 1982—90. Vis. rsch. prof. Nat. Taiwan U., Def. Med. Ctr., 1981; vis. rsch nursing Sun Yat-Sen U. Med. Scis., Guang Zhou, China, Ewha Women's U., Seoul, Republic of Korea, Frances Payne Bolton Sch. Nursing, Case Western Res. U., Cleve., 1994—96; chair, prof. dept. health scis. Hong Kong Poly. U., 1996—2000. Author: Mathematics for the Health Science Student, 1977; editor: Home Care for the Dying Child, 1976, Women in Stress, 1979, Women in Health and Illness, 1986, The Child and Family Facing Life Threatening Illness, 1987, Family Nursing, 1989, Home Health Care Nursing, 1989, Home Health Care Nursing, 2d edit., 2002; contbr. chapters to books, articles to profl. jours. Active Am. Cancer Soc. Recipient Book of Yr. award, Am. Jour. Nursing, 1977, 1980, 1987, 1990, Humanitarian award for pediat. nursing, 1993; fellow, Fulbright Found., 1991. Mem.: ANA, Inst. Medicine, Am. Acad. Nursing, Council Nurse Rschrs., Sigma Theta Tau, Sigma Xi. Lutheran. Address: 12149 E Movil Lake Rd NE Bemidji MN 56601 *The challenge of quality health care to all of society and the critical role nursing has to play in order to achieve this goal has motivated me throughout my professional life. The richness of talent in this country spurs me on.*

**MARTINSON, JACOB CHRISTIAN, JR.,** academic administrator; b. Menomonie, Wis., Apr. 15, 1933; s. Jacob Christian and Matilda Kate (Wisner) M.; m. Elizabeth Smathers, Apr. 29, 1962; children— Elizabeth Anne, Kirsten Kate. BA, Huntingdon Coll., Ala., 1954, LLD (hon.), 1993; MDiv, Duke U., 1957; DDiv, Vanderbilt U., 1972; grad., Inst. Ednl. Mgmt., Harvard U., 1981. Ordained elder United Methodist Ch. Minister Trinity

United Meth. Ch., Lighthouse Point, Fla., 1960-67; sr. minister First United Meth. Ch., Winter Park, Fla., 1967-71; supervising instr. Vanderbilt U. Div. Sch., Nashville, 1971-72; pres. Andrew Coll., Cuthbert, Ga., 1972-76, Brevard Coll., NC, 1976-85, High Point (N.C.) U., 1985—2005, hon. chancellor, 2005—; interim pres. Garrett-Evang. Theol. Sem., Evanston, Ill., 2006. Chmn. bd. dirs. First Union Nat. Bank (now Wachovia), High Point, 1989; lectr. St. Mary's Theol. Sch. St. Andrews, Scotland. Chmn. N.C. Friends of Higher Edn., 1986; mem. W.I.H. and Lula E. Pitts Found., Atlanta, 1972-76. Recipient Hickman Preaching award Duke U. Div. Sch.; Glen Slough scholar Vanderbilt U., 1971; hon. fellow Westminster Coll., Oxford, Eng., 1994; Rotary Paul Harris fellow. Mem. Brevard C. of C. (pres. 1979), High Point C. of C. (chmn. 1992), Piedmont Ind. Coll. Assn. (chmn. 1991-93), Carolinas Intercollegiate Athletic Conf. (pres. 1991-93), Phi Theta Kappa. Methodist. Avocation: mountain hiking. Home: 556 Crum Dr Lake Junaluska NC 28745 Office Phone: 828-456-5457. Personal E-mail: jmartinson@bellsouth.net.

**MARTINSON, JODY MARIE,** voice educator; b. St. Cloud, Minn., Apr. 1, 1975; d. James D. and Barbara R. Schindele; m. Todd E. Martinson, Sept. 1, 2001. BA in Musical Edn. and Vocal Performance, Coll. St. Benedict, 1997; MusM in Choral Conducting, St. Cloud State U., 2004. Dir. choral Sauk Rapids (Minn.) H.S., 1998—2000; pvt. voice tchr. Sauk Rapids, 1998; tchr. voice Ctrl. Lakes Coll., Brainerd, Minn., 2001—05; dir. music and liturgy Holy Spirit Cath. Ch., St. Cloud, Minn., 2000—. Bd. dirs. Minn. Ctr. Chorale, St. Joseph, Minn. Co-founder Those In Need Soldiers Holy Spirit Cath. Ch., 2003—. Mem.: Nat. Pastoral Musicians, Nat. Assn. Tchrs. Singing, Am. Choral Dirs. Assn. Roman Catholic. Avocations: piano, gardening, outdoors, painting. Home: 506 6th Ave N Sauk Rapids MN 56379 Office: Church of the Holy Spirit 2405 Walden Way Saint Cloud MN 56301

**MARTINSON, MICHAEL DAVID,** music educator, musician; b. Belling-ham, Wash., June 16, 1959; s. Elmer Emery Martinson and Rosalie Jo Kerr; m. Gerilynn Estella Hugg; children: David Michael, Benjamin Michael, Sarah Elisabeth. MusB, Western Wash. U., Bellingham, 1982; MusM, Western Wash. U., 1987. Cert. Type A tchr. Alaska, Type B adminstr. Alaska. Tchr. Bellingham Sch. Dist., 1982—83, Annette Island Sch. Dist., Metlakatla, Alaska, 1983—85, Kenai Peninsula Sch. Dist., Seward, Alaska, 1985—88, Anchorage Sch. Dist., Eagle River, Alaska, 1988—94, music supr., 1994—2005, Eagle River HS band tchr., 2005—. Musician: Vaughan Will-iams and Carol Tuba Concertos. Mem.: Music Educators Nat. Conf. (assoc.). Avocations: fishing, boating.

**MARTINUZZI, LEO SERGIO, JR.,** banker; b. Newton, Mass., Aug. 1, 1928; s. Leo Sergio and Jessica (Stewart) Martinuzzi; m. Helen Renfrew Gibson, Oct. 26, 1957 (dec. Oct. 1995); children: John James, Georgiana Gibson, Samuel Stewart; m. Sandra Stoison Schister, Nov. 18, 2004. BA, Harvard U., 1950; B.Litt., Oxford U., 1952. With Chase Manhattan Bank, NYC, 1956-81, asst. treas., 1960, asst. v.p. Japanese brs., 1961-64, v.p. Japanese brs., 1964-68, marketing exec. internat. staff, 1968-72, sr. v.p., 1971-81; corporate devel. officer Chase Manhattan Corp., 1972-75, group exec. info. services, 1975-81; chmn. Chase Econometric Assocs. Inc., 1975-80; sr. v.p. strategic planning Squibb Corp., NY, 1981-87, cons., 1988-91. Chmn. Strategic Dimensions, Inc., 1990—; adj. prof. econs. Edison CC, 1993-97. Lt. (j.g.) USNR, 1952-56. Home: 336 Galleon Dr Naples FL 34102-7638

**MARTO, PAUL JAMES,** retired mechanical engineering educator, consultant, researcher, dean; b. Flushing, N.Y., Aug. 15, 1938; s. Peter Joseph and Natalie Janet (Verrinoldi) M.; m. Mary Virginia Indence, June 10, 1961; children: Terese V. Marto Sanders, Paul J. Jr., Wayne T., Laura C., Marto Mahoney. BS, U. Notre Dame, 1960; SM, MIT, 1962, ScD, 1965. Asst. prof. Naval Postgrad. Sch., Monterey, Calif., 1965-69, assoc. prof., 1969-77, prof., 1977-85, disting. prof., 1985-96, chmn. dept. mech. engring., 1978-86, dean rsch., 1990-96, disting. prof. emeritus, 1996—. Cons. Modine Mfg. Co., Racine, Wis., 1986—. Editor: Power Condenser Heat, 1981; regional editor N.Am. Jour. of Enhanced Heat Transfer, 1993-98; editor-in-chief Internat. Jour. Transport Phenomena, 1997-2002, founding editor; contbr. articles to profl. jours. Bd. trustees Naval Postgrad. Sch. Found., Inc., 1997—. Lt. USN, 1965—67. Recipient Rear Adm. John J. Schieffelin award Naval Postgrad. Sch., 1976, Alexander von Humboldt U.S. Sr. Scientist award Humboldt Stiftung, Fed. Republic Germany, 1989-90, Disting. Civilian Svc. award Sec. of Navy, 1996. Fellow ASME (assoc. tech. editor Jour. of Heat Transfer 1984-90); mem. Am. Soc. Naval Engrs., Am. Soc. for Engring. Edn., Sigma Xi. Avocations: walking, tennis, music. Office: Naval Postgrad Sch Dept Mechanical Engring Code ME MX Monterey CA 93943 Office Phone: 831-659-0935. E-mail: pjmarto@aol.com.

**MARTOCCI, LEWIS NICHOLAS, III,** writer; b. Forrigga, Italy, July 10, 1960; s. Lewis Nicholas Martocci, Jr. and Maria Laub. AA in World History, Malone Coll. Naval Base Br., Sassabo, Japan, 1988; AA in Specialized Bus. Criminal Justice, Lehigh Valley Coll., Ctr. Valley, Pa., 2005. With USMC, 1978—99; dep. chief field agt. A&M Fugitive Recovery Agy., 2000—05. Author: (poetry books) From Within, 2001, Doodles of the Mind, 2002. Recipient Pres.'s Award for Lit. Excellence, Nat. Authors Registry, 2000. Mem.: Grange. Republican. Presbyterian. Avocations: reading, fishing, music, book collecting, antiques. Home and Office: 722 W Pennsylvania Ave Pen Argyl PA 18072 Office Phone: 610-657-0110. E-mail: max1887@nni.com.

**MARTON, KATHRYN WIDMAN,** secondary school educator; b. Newark, June 27, 1947; d. Rudolph William and Dorothy Mae (Bennett) Widman; m. Barry William Marton, Mar. 5, 1966; children: Barry Scott, Christopher James. BA in Edn., U. New Orleans, 1981, MEd, 1986, postgrad., 1986, 89. Cert. English tchr., reading specialist, La. Classrm. English tchr. Slidell H.S., La., 1981—, dept. chair, 1994—, master tchr., 1995—. Instr. English, Delgado Coll., Slidell, 1988. Greater New Orleans Writing Project fellow U. New Orleans, 1984; NEH fellowship grantee U. Buffalo, 1992. Mem. Nat. Coun. Tchr. English, Internat. Reading Assn., La. Reading Coun., Northshore Reading (past pres.). Avocations: reading, houseplants, antiques. Home: 1603 Rue Miramon Slidell LA 70458-2225 Office: Slidell HS 1 Tiger Dr Slidell LA 70458-2046 Office Phone: 985-643-2992.

**MARTONE, ERIC ANTHONY DOMENIC,** history educator; b. Nurem-berg, Bavaria, Germany, Sept. 29, 1978; s. Maria and Robert Cordery (Stepfather), Anthony Martone. BA in History cum laude, Pace U., Pleas-antville, NY, 2000; MA in Global History, Iona Coll., New Rochelle, NY, 2003; tchr. cert., Western Conn. State U., Danbury, 2003; French cert., U. Toronto, Canada, 2006. Cert. provisional educator history/social studies grades 7-12 Conn., 2006. Rsch. analyst Pitney Bowes, Stamford, Conn., 1999—2002; student tchr. North End Mid. Sch., Waterbury, Conn., 2003; tchr. Enlightenment Sch., Waterbury, 2004; history tchr. John F. Kennedy HS, Waterbury, 2004—. Creative cons. Teacher's Discovery, Auburn Hills, Mich., 2005—; vis. scholar Dickinson Coll., Carlisle, Pa., 2005. Author: (book) With a Little Help From My German Friend: Leopold II of Belgium and the Berlin Conference, 1884-85, 2003; translator: (drama) The Vampire/Catilina: Two Plays by Alexandre Dumas, 2003; contbr. encys. in field. Named Outstanding History Maj., History Dept., Pace U., 2000; grantee, Freeman Found., Wesleyan U., 2005; Presdl. scholar, Pace U., 1996—2000, All-American scholar, US Achievement Acad., 1999, All-Academic Team scholar, Tau Kappa Epsilon, 1999. Mem.: Conn. Educators' Assn., Waterbury Tchrs.' Assn., Nat. Educators' Assn., French Hist. Soc., Societe des Amis d'Alexandre Dumas, Alpha Chi, Pi Gamma Mu, Phi Alpha Theta, Tau Kappa Epsilon. Office: John F Kennedy HS 422 Highland Ave Waterbury CT 06708 Business E-Mail: emartone@waterbury.k12.ct.us.

**MARTONE, FREDERICK J.,** judge; b. Fall River, Mass., Nov. 8, 1943; BS, Coll. Holy Cross, 1965; JD, U. Notre Dame, 1972; LLM, Harvard U., 1975. Bar: Mass. 1972, Ariz. 1974, U.S. Dist. Ct. Mass. 1973, U.S. Dist. Ct. Ariz. 1974, U.S. Ct. Appeals (1st cir.) 1973, U.S. Ct. Appeals (9th cir.) 1974, U.S. Supreme Ct. 1977. Law clk. to Hon. Edward F. Hennessey Mass.

Supreme Judicial Ct., 1972-73; pvt. practice Phoenix, 1973-85; assoc. presiding judge Superior Ct. Ariz., Maricopa County, judge Phoenix, 1985-92; justice Supreme Ct. Ariz., Phoenix, 1992—2002; U.S. dist. judge Dist. of Ariz., 2002—. Editor notes and comments Notre Dame Law Rev., 1970-72; contbr. articles to profl. jours. Capt. USAF, 1965-69. Mem. ABA, Fed. Judges Assn., Maricopa County Bar Assn., Am. Judicature Soc., State Bar Ariz., Horace Rumpole Inn of Ct. Office: US Dist Ct Sandra Day O'Conner US Courthouse 401 W Washington St Spc 62 Ste 526 Phoenix AZ 85003-2158 E-mail: Frederick_Martone@azd.uscourts.gov

**MARTONE, PATRICIA ANN,** lawyer; b. Bklyn., Apr. 28, 1947; d. David Andrew and Rita Mary (Dullmeyer) Martone. BA in Chemistry, NYU, 1968, JD, 1973; MA in Phys. Chemistry, Johns Hopkins U., 1969. Bar: N.Y. 1974, U.S. Dist. Ct. (so. and ea. dists.) N.Y. 1975, U.S. Ct. Appeals (2d cir.) 1975, U.S. Ct. Appeals (1st cir.) 1981, U.S. Patent and Trademark Office 1983, U.S. Ct. Appeals (fed. cir.) 1984, U.S. Supreme Ct. 1984, U.S. Dist. Ct. (ea. dist.) Mich. 1985, U.S. Dist. Ct. (no. dist.) Calif. 1995. Tech. rep. computer timesharing On-Line Sys., Inc., NYC, 1969-70; assoc. Kelley Drye & Warren, NYC, 1973-77, Fish & Neave, NYC, 1977-82, ptnr., 1983—2004, Fish & Neave Intellectual Property Group at Ropes & Gray LLP, NYC, 2005—. Adj. prof. NYU Sch. Law, 1990—; mem. adv. coun. Engelberg Ctr. Innovation Law & Policy, 1996—; participating atty. Cmty. Law Offices, N.Y.C., 1974—78; atty. Pro Bono Panel U.S. Dist. Ct. (so. dist.) N.Y., 1982—84; lectr. Practising Law Inst., N.Y.C., 1995—, Aspen Law & Bus., 1990—95, Franklin Pierce Law Sch., 1992—97, Lic. Exec. Soc.; chair, bd. dirs. N.Y. Lawyers for the Pub. Interest, 1996—98, vice chair, 1998—2000, 2002—05, emeritus bd., 2006—; vice chair Legal Svcs., N.Y.C., 1982—84. Mng. editor NYU Law Sch. Rev. Law and Social Change, 1972-73; contbr. articles to profl. jours. Recipient Founder's Day award NYU Sch. Law, 1973; NSF grad. trainee Johns Hopkins U., 1968-69; NYU scholar, 1964-68. Mem. ABA, Assn. Bar City N.Y. (mem. environ. law com. 1978-83, trademarks, unfair competition com. 1983-86), Fed. Bar Coun., Fed. Cir. Bar Assn., Copyright Soc., Am. Chem. Soc., Licensing Execs. Soc., N.Y. Intellectual Property Law Assn., Univ. Club. Office: Fish & Neave Intellectual Property Group at Ropes & Gray LLP 1251 Ave of the Americas Fl 49 New York NY 10020-1105 Office Phone: 212-596-9021. Business E-Mail: patricia.martone@ropesgray.com.

**MARTONOSI, ANTHONY NICHOLAS,** biochemistry professor, re-searcher; b. Szeged, Hungary, Nov. 7, 1928; came to U.S., 1957; s. Antal and Anna (Zsoter) M.; m. Mary Alice Gouvea, May 2, 1959; children: Mary Anne, Anthony, Margaret, Susan. MD, U. Med. Sch., Szeged, 1953. Asst. prof. dept. physiology Med. Sch., Szeged, 1955-57; rsch. fellow Mass. Gen. Hosp., Boston. 1957-59; rsch. assoc. Retina Found., Boston, 1959-62, asst. dir. dept. muscle rsch., 1962-65; assoc. prof. biochemistry St. Louis U. Sch. Medicine, 1965-69, prof., 1969-79; prof. biochemistry SUNY Health Sci. Ctr., Syracuse, 1979-84. Albert Szent-Gyorgyi prof. U. Med. Sch., Szeged, Hungary, 1994; adj. prof. Kwangju Inst. f Sci. and Tech., Korea, 1994—; vis. scientist dept. biochemistry U. Birmingham, Eng., 1963-64. Author: The Development of Sarcoplasmic Reticulum, 2000; editor: The Enzymes of Biological Membranes, Vols. 1-4, 1976, 2d edit., 1985; Membranes and Transport, Vols. 1-2, 1982; contbr. over 180 articles to profl. jours.; mem. editl. bd. Biochimica et Biophysica Acta, 1988-96. Recipient Established Investigator award Am. Heart Assn., 1961-66; Rsch. grantee USPHS, NIH, 1959-89, NSF, 1963-96, Muscular Dystrophy Assn., 1975-89. Mem. Am. Soc. Biochemists and Molecular Biologists. Roman Catholic. Home: 110 Stan-wood Ln Manlius NY 13104-1412 Personal E-mail: gouveama@aol.com.

**MÁRTONYI, CSABA LÁSZLO,** retired ophthalmic photographer; b. Budapest, Hungary, Mar. 23, 1941; came to U.S., 1951; s. Louis Péter and Magda (Gyürky) M.; m. Elnajean Beyst, Sept. 4, 1976; 1 child, Erika Lyn. Cert. retinal angiographer. Chief photographer U. Mich. Photog. Svcs., Ann Arbor, 1967—71; dir. ophthalmic photography, dept. ophthalmology U. Mich., Ann Arbor, 1971—75, instr. dept. ophthalmic photography, 1975—80, asst. prof., 1980—83, assoc. prof., 1983—2000, assoc. prof. emeritus, 2000—. First author: Clinical Slit-Lamp Biomicroscopy and Photo Slit-Lamp Biomicrography, 1985; author, artist exhibit of eye images Landscapes of the Eye, 1993; author sci. exhibits. With U.S. Naval Air Res., 1965-67. Recipient Disting. Tchg. award Joint Commn. on Allied Health Pers. in Ophthalmology, 1997. Fellow Ophthalmic Photographers Soc. (parliamentarian 1988—, chair hon. life membership com. 1991—, fellowship com., pres. 1978-80, chair bd. certification 1978-84, chmn. editl. com. 1987-89, awards including top award for outstanding contbns. to ophthalmic photography), Am. Acad. Ophthal-mology (assoc., Honor award 1984, Sr. Honor award 2001). Avocations: guitar (classical-traditional), woodsculpting, fine art photography, tennis. Personal E-mail: martonyi1@msn.com.

**MARTORANA, BARBARA JOAN,** secondary school educator; b. N.Y.C., Oct. 18, 1942; d. Samuel and Joan Renee (Costello) M. BA, St. John's U., Jamaica, N.Y., 1970; MS in English Edn., St. John's U., 1972; advanced cert. computers in edn., L.I. U., 1988, profl. diploma in edn. adminstrn., 1990. Cert. sch. dist. adminstr., sch. adminstr. and supr., tchr. English grades 7-12, NY, Ed.D. Lit. Studies, Hofstra U., Hempstead, NY, 2003. Exec. sec. Am. Petroleum Inst., N.Y.C., 1960-65; exec. asst. to v.p. Goldring, Inc., 1965-67; exec. asst. Rsch. Inst. for Cath. Edn., 1967-69; English tchr. St. Martin of Tours Sch., Amityville, 1970-77, Oceanside Jr. HS, 1977-78, Freeport HS, 1979—. Rec. sec. Freeport (N.Y.) Tchr. Ctr. Policy Bd., 1986-89; co-chair Middle States Steering Com., Freeport, 1988-90; chair Freeport H.S. Shared Decision Team, 1992-93; adv. bd. L.I. Writing Project, Garden City, N.Y., 1993—, co-leader Summer Insts.; adj. prof. literacy studies dept. Hofstra U., N.Y., 1999—. Co-author: (textbooks) Writing Competency Practice, 1980, Writing Competency Practice-Revised and Expanded, 1989. With Seaford (NY) Rep. Club, 1975—. Mem. Nat. Coun. Tchrs. English (conf. on English edn.), N.Y. State English Coun., L.I. Writing Project. Avocations: reading, writing, travel. Office: Freeport HS 50 S Brookside Ave Freeport NY 11520-3114 Office Phone: 516-867-5300. Personal E-mail: engteech@aol.com.

**MARTORE, GRACIA,** publishing company executive; b. 1951; m. Joseph Martore; 2 children. BA, Wellesley Coll. Asst. treas. Gannett Co., Inc., Mc Lean, Va., 1985—93, v.p. Treasury Svcs., 1993, head Investor Rels., 1996—98, treas., v.p. Investor Rels., 1998—2001, sr. v.p., 2000—06, CFO, 2003—06, exec. v.p., CFO, 2006—. Office: Gannett Co Inc 7950 Jones Branch Dr Mc Lean VA 22107-0910*

**MARTORELL, CLAUDIA,** infectious diseases physician; b. San Juan, Puerto Rico, May 25, 1971; d. Edgar and Maria (Berrios) Martorell. BS in Gen. Sci., U. P.R., 1994, MD magna cum laude, 1998; MPH, Harvard U., 2004. Diplomate in internal medicine and infectious diseases Am. Bd. Internal Medicine. Trainee in internal medicine Baystate Med. Ctr. Tufts U., Springfield, Mass., 1998—2001, fellow in infectious diseases, 2001—02; rsch. fellow in social medicine, Commonwealth Fund/Harvard U. Fellowship in Minority Pub. Health Harvard Med. Sch., 2003—04; cons./clinical investigator Cmty. Rsch. Initiative of New England, Springfield, Mass., 2004—05, assoc. dir. rsch.-west, 2005—. Mass. Legis. Oversight Hearings on Health Disparities, 2004. Vol. HIV Awareness and Support Group Mochilas Salvavidas, 1997—98, Primary Health Care Clinics for Medically Underserved People., Lares, PR, 1996, Primary Health Care Clinics for the Underserved and Geriatric Population, Loiza, PR, 1993, Jarabacoba, Dominican Republic, 1993. Recipient Bristol Myers Squibb scholarship, 1997, NHMA resident leadership program, 2000, AMA Found. Leadership award, 2004. Mem.: ACP, AMA (governing coun. rep. Minority Affairs Consortium 2004—), Mass. Med. Soc., Mass. Infectious Diseases Soc., Nat. Hispanic Med. Assn. (Resident Leadership Program award 2001), Infectious Diseases Soc. Am., Alpha Omega Alpha. Avocations: Tae Kwon Do, piano, sports. Office: Cmty Rsch Initiative of New England Ste 30 780 Chestnut St Springfield MA 01107-1610 Office Phone: 617-534-2646.*

**MARTORI, JOSEPH PETER,** lawyer; b. NYC, Aug. 19, 1941; s. Joseph and Teresa Susan (Fezza) M. BS summa cum laude, NYU, 1964, MBA, 1968; JD cum laude, U. Notre Dame, 1967. Bar: DC 1968, U.S. Dist. Ct. DC 1968, U.S. Dist. Ct. Ariz. 1968, U.S. Ct. Appeals (9th cir.) 1969, U.S. Supreme Ct. 1977. Assoc. Sullivan & Cromwell, NYC, 1967-68, Snell & Wilmer, Phoenix, 1968-69; pres. Goldmar Inc., Phoenix, 1969-71; ptnr. Martori, Meyer, Hendricks & Victor, P.A., Phoenix, 1971-85, Brown & Bain, P.A., Phoenix, 1985-94, chmn. corp. banking & real estate dept., 1994—; chmn. bd. ILX Resorts, Inc., Phoenix. ILX Inc., Varsity Clubs Am. Inc. Author: Street Fights, 1987; also articles. Trustee Boys' Clubs Met. Phoenix, 1974-99; consul for Govt. of Italy, State of Ariz., 1987-97. Mem. ABA, State Bar Ariz., Maricopa County Bar Assn., Lawyers Com.for Civil Rights Under Law (trustee 1976—), Phoenix Country Club, Plaza Club (founding bd. govs. 1979-90). Republican. Roman Catholic. Office: ILX Resorts Inc 2111 E Highland Ave Ste 200 Phoenix AZ 85016-4786 Office Phone: 602-553-9444. Business E-Mail: jmartorisr@IXLresorts.com.

**MARTUCCI, VINCENT JAMES,** composer, pianist; b. Medford, Mass., Oct. 21, 1954; s. Vincent James Sr. and Grace Alice (Giorgio) M.; m. Elizabeth Nicoll Lawrence, Sept. 20, 1981; children: Katharine Amalia, James Lawrence. Student, Berklee Coll. Music, 1974—75; BA in Music, Colby Coll., 1977; studied with Hal Galper, N.Y.C., 1978—80; studied with Dave Holland, Woodstock, N.Y., 1982—84; MusM, SUNY Purchase, 2001. Lectr. music Alfred U., NY, 1978—80; registrar, instr. Creative Music Studio, Woodstock, 1980—82; owner, composer, performer Vinnie Martucci Prodns., West Hurley, NY, 1987—; prof. jazz studies SUNY, New Paltz, 1991—. Performer, composer, 1977—; free-lance composer, prodr. recs. and TV, 1986—; cons. synthesis and audio technique, 1985—; mem. U.S. Embassy tour concert series, Bogota, Colombia, 1991; participant conf. Internat. Assn. Jazz Educators, Boston, 1991; instr. music theory and piano Ashokan Fiddle & Dance, 1996—. Composer, performer, corporate spl. events The Dolphins, N.Am., S.Am., Europe, Can., including Newport Jazz at Saratoga, North Sea Jazz Festival, JVC Jazz Festival at Nice, France, The Hague, Holland, Jazz Mecca Festival, Holland, Pori Jazz Festival, Finland, Levercusen Jazz Festival Germany, Brubeck Family Project Tours, and many others, 1987—; performed with Hubert Laws, Nick Brignola, Livingston Taylor, Rory Block, Don Mclean; arranger radio concert series Karl Berger Composer, 1985; co-author, arranger Adventures of Comander Crumbcake - TV series, 1987; composer: (rec.) Malayan Breeze, 1991, network theme redesign package lifetime med. TV, 1988; travel channel, 1990, CNN-Daily Menus, 1991; composer, performer, arranger underscore CBS's As the World Turns, 1993—, NBC's Another World, 1993—, Guiding Light; co-composer: (rec.) Old World/New World, 1991, Ain't I a Woman, 1992; author instrnl. tape series Arranging and Recording Electronic Instruments, 1987—; co-prodr., performer, engr. music for theatrical prodns. McCarter Theatre (1 Tony award), Princeton, Asolo Theatre, Sarasota, Fla.; co-prodr., music for theatre prodn. Having Our Say, 1995—; performer, music dir. numerous live TV and radio performances; music dir. for Eileen Fulton star of As the World Turns, 1990-, music dir. Laurel Massé, 1997-; author: (book series) Introduction to Jazz Keyboards, Introduction to Blues Keyboards, Introduction to Rock Keyboards, 1997. Recipient 2d pl. jazz composition Billboard Mag., 1988. Mem. ASCAP, AFTRA, Am. Fedn. Musicians. Avocations: photography, bicycling, swimming. Home and Office: Vinnie Martucci Prodn 29 Pleasant Ridge Dr West Hurley NY 12491-5441 E-mail: tuchitune@aol.com.

**MARTUCCI, WILLIAM CHRISTOPHER,** lawyer; b. Asbury Park, N.J., Mar. 10, 1952; s. Frank and Evelyn (Gerrity) M.; children: Daniel Robert, William Sessions, John Andrew, James Christopher, Andrew Michael, Matthew Peter. AB magna cum laude, Rutgers U., 1974; JD with honors, U. Ark., 1977; LLM with honors, Georgetown U., 1981. Bar: Mo. 1977. Law clk. to presiding justice Mo. Ct. Appeals, Kansas City, 1977-78; assoc. Spencer, Fane, Britt & Browne, Kansas City, 1981-86, ptnr., 1987-99, Shook, Hardy & Bacon LLP, Kansas City, 2000—, leader Nat. Employment Litig. & Policy Group. Mem. practice and procedure com. Nat. Labor Relations Act; charter mem. Am. Employment Coun., 1993—; adj. prof. employment law U. Mo. Law Sch., Kansas City, 1998-95, chair minority affairs com. 1992-2002. Editor-in-chief Ark. Law Rev., 1976-77; contbr. articles to profl. jours. Chmn. adv. coun. Urban League Greater Kansas City Tng. Ctr., chmn. mentor program, 1988-2005; mem. Kansas City Civic Coun.; mem. Kansas City Tomorrow Leadership Program, 1992-93; adv. bd. Boys and Girls Club Kansas City, Reviving Baseball in the Inner City. Served to lt. JAGC, USN, 1978-81. Decorated Navy Commendation medal. Mem. ABA (employment and labor rels. com., EEO litigation com.), Mo. Bar Assn. (exec. com. continuing legal edn. 1987—, chair 1993-2000), Kansas City Bar Assn. (chmn. continuing legal edn. 1984-86, mem. exec. com. 1985-98, leadership award 1985, chmn. labor and employment law com. 1988-90, Pres. award 1992, 97), Lawyers Assn. Kansas City (mem. exec. com. young lawyers sect. 1981-82), Kansas City Club, Homestead Country Club, Rotary. Clubs: Kansas City. Republican. Roman Catholic. Office: Shook Hardy and Bacon 2555 Grand Blvd Kansas City MO 64105-2613 Home: 6429 Overbrook Rd Mission Hills KS 66208-1939 Office Phone: 816-474-6550. Business E-Mail: wmartucci@shb.com.

**MARTY, MARTIN EMIL,** theology studies educator; b. West Point, Nebr., Feb. 5, 1928; s. Emil A. and Anne Louise (Wuerdemann) Marty; m. Elsa Schumacher Marty, 1952 (dec. 1981); children: Frances, Joel, John, Peter, James, Micah, Ursula; m. Harriet Lindemann Marty, 1982. MDiv, Concordia Sem., 1952; STM, Luth. Sch. Theology, Chgo., 1954; PhD in Am. Religious and Intellectual History, U. Chgo., 1956; LittD (hon.), Thiel Coll., 1964; LHD (hon.), W.Va. Wesleyan Coll., 1967, Marian Coll., 1967, Providence Coll., 1967; DD (hon.), Muhlenberg Coll., 1967; LittD (hon.), Thomas More Coll., 1968; DD (hon.), Bethany Sem., 1969; LLD (hon.), Keuka Coll., 1972; LHD (hon.), Willamette U., 1974; DD (hon.), Wabash Coll., 1977; LLD (hon.), U. So. Calif., Valparaiso U., 1978; LHD (hon.), St. Olaf Coll., 1978, De Paul U., 1979; DD (hon.), Christ Sem.-Seminex, 1979 Capital U., 1980; LHD (hon.), Colo. Coll., 1980; DD (hon.), Maryville Coll., 1980, North Park Coll. Sem., 1982; LittD (hon.), Wittenberg U., 1983; LHD, Rosary Coll., 1984; LHD (hon.), Rockford Coll., 1984; DD (hon.), Va. Theol. Sem., 1984; LHD (hon.), Hamilton Coll., 1985, Loyola U., 1986; LLD (hon.), U. Notre Dame, 1987; LHD (hon.), Roanoke Coll., 1987, Mercer U., 1987, Ill. Wesleyan Coll., 1987, Roosevelt U., 1988, Aquinas Coll., 1988; LittD (hon.), Franklin Coll., 1988, U. Nebr., 1993; LHD (hon.), No. Mich. U., 1989, Muskingum Coll., Coe Coll., Lehigh U., 1989, Hebrew Union Coll. and Governors State U., 1990, Whittier Coll., 1991, Calif. Luth. U., 1993; DD (hon.), St. Xavier Coll. and Colgate U., 1990, Mt. Union Coll., 1991, Tex. Luth. Coll., 1991, Aurora U., 1991, Baker U., 1992; LHD (hon.), Luth. U., 1993; LHD, Calif. Luth. U., 1993, Midland Luth. Coll., 1995; DD, Hope Coll., 1993, Northwestern Coll., 1993; LHD (hon.), George Fox Coll., 1994, Drake U., 1994, Centre Coll., 1994, Fontbonne Coll., 1996; DD, Yale U., 1995; LHD (hon.), Otterbein Coll., 1996; ThD (hon.), Lycoming Coll., 1997; LHD, Dana Coll., 1998; LittD (hon.), Alma Coll., 1998, Concordia U. Portland, 1998, Niagara U., 1998; LHD (hon.), Kalamazoo Coll., 1999, William Jewell Coll., 1999; LittD, LittD, Lynchburg Coll., 2003; DD (hon.), Trinity Coll., 2001, Wake Forest U., 2003; DHum (hon.), Westminster Choir Coll., 2001; LHD (hon.), U. Scranton, 2001; DD (hon.), Wake Forest U., 2003; LHD (hon.), Ea. Mennonite U., 2003, Iona Coll.; LLD, Fordham U., 2005. Ordained to ministry Luth. Ch., 1952. Pastor, Washington, 1950—51; asst. pastor River Forest, Ill., 1952—56; pastor Elk Grove Village, Ill., 1956—63; prof. history of modern Christianity Div. Sch. U. Chgo., 1963—, Fairfax M. Cone Disting. Svc. prof., 1978—98, prof. emeritus, 1998—; assoc. editor Christian Century mag., Chgo., 1956—85, sr. editor, 1985—98; co-editor Ch. History mag., 1963—97. Pres. Park Ridge (Ill.) Ctr., 1989—, sr. scholar-in-residence, 1989—; pres. Am. Inst. for Study of Health, Faith and Ethics, 1985—89; dir. The Pub. Religion Project, 1996—99; interim pres. St. Olaf Coll., 2000—01. Author: A Short History of Christianity, 1959, The New Shape of American Religion, 1959, The Improper Opinion, 1961, The Infidel, 1961, Baptism, 1962, The Hidden Discipline, 1963, Second Chance for American Protestants, 1963, Church Unity and Church Mission, 1964, Varieties of Unbelief, 1964, The Search for a Usable Future, 1969, The Modern Schism, 1969, Righteous Empire, 1970, Protestantism, 1972, You

Are Promise, 1973, The Fire We Can Light, 1973, The Pro and Con Book of Religious America, 1975, A Nation of Behavers, 1976, Religion, Awakening and Revolution, 1978, Friendship, 1980, By Way of Response, 1981, The Public Church, 1981, A Cry of Absence, 1983, Health and Medicine in the Lutheran Tradition, 1983, Pilgrims in Their Own Land, 1984, Protestantism in the United States, 1985, Modern American Religion, The Irony of it All, Vol. 1, 1986, An Invitation to American Catholic History, 1986, Religion and Republic, 1987, Modern American Religion: The Noise of Conflict, Vol. 2, 1991; author: (with R. Scott Appleby) The Glory and the Power, 1992; editor (with Jerald C. Brauer): The Unrelieved Paradox: Studies in the Theology of Franz Bibfeldt, 1994; editor: (with Micah Marty) Places Along the Way, 1994; editor: Our Hope for Years to Come, 1995, Modern American Religion, Under God, Indivisible, Vol. 3, 1996, The One and the Many, 1997, The Promise of Winter, 1997, When True Simplicity is Gained, 1998, Politics, Religion, and the Common Good, 2000, Education, Religion, and the Common Good, 2001, Speaking of Trust, 2003, Vision of Utopia, 2003; When Faiths Collide, 2004, Protestant Voice in American Pluralism, 2004, Martin Luther, 2004; editor: (jours.) Context, 1969—; editor: Second Opinion; sr. editor: The Christian Century, 1956—98; contbr. articles to religious publs. Chmn. bd. regents St. Olaf Coll., 1996—2001, sr. regents, 2002—; dir. The Pub. Religion Project, 1996—2000. Recipient Nat. Medal Humanities, 1997, Alumni medal, U. Chgo., 1998. Fellow: Soc. Am. Historians, Am. Acad. Arts and Scis. (dir. fundamentalism project 1988—94); mem.: Am. Antiquarian Soc., Am. Acad. Religion (pres. 1987—88), Am. Cath. Hist. Assn. (pres. 1981), Am. Soc. Ch. History (pres. 1971), Am. Philos. Soc. Lutheran. Office: 239 Scottswood Rd Riverside IL 60546-2223 E-mail: memarty@aol.com.

**MARTYL, (MRS. ALEXANDER LANGSDORF JR.),** artist; b. St. Louis, Mar. 16, 1917; d. Martin and Aimee (Goldstone) Schweig; m. Alexander Langsdorf, Jr., Dec. 31, 1941; children: Suzanne, Alexandra. AB, Washington U., St. Louis, 1938. Instr. art dept. U. Chgo.; artist in residence Tamarind Inst., U. N.Mex., Albuquerque, 1974 Solo shows include, Calif. Palace of Legion of Honor, 1956, Chgo. Art Inst., 1949, 76, Feingarten Galleries, N.Y.C., Beverly Hills and Chgo., 1961, 62, 63, St. Louis, 1962, Feingarten Gallery, N.Y.C., 1963, L.A., 1964, Kovler Gallery, Chgo., 1967, Washington U., St. Louis, 1967, U. Chgo. Oriental Inst. Mus., 1970, Deson&Zaks Gallery, 1973, Fairweather-Hardin Gallery, 1977, 81, 83, Ill. State Mus., 1978, Fermilab, 1985, 91, Bklyn. Mus., 1986, Oriental Inst. Mus., 1987, Gibbes Art Mus., Charleston, S.C., 1988, Fairweather-Hardin Gallery, 1988, Tokyo Internat. Art Expo, 1990, State of Ill. Art Gallery, Chgo., 1990, Expo Navy Pier, Chgo., 1993, Printworks Gallery Ltd., Chgo., 1995, 97, 99, 2002, 04, Navy Pier, Chgo., 2003, 04, Oriental Inst. Mus., Chgo., Martyl: Nature/Artifice Ft. Wayne Mus. Art, 2000; represented in permanent collections, Met. Mus. Art, Chgo. Art Inst., Pa. Acad. Fine Arts, Ill. State Mus., Bklyn. Mus., DuSable Mus., Chgo., Los Angeles County Mus., Whitney Mus. Am. Art, Davenport (Iowa) Municipal Mus., St. Louis Art Mus., Washington U., U. Ariz., Arnot Gallery, Elmira, N.Y., Greenville (S.C.) Mus., Nat. Coll. Fine Arts, Hirshhorn Mus. and Sculpture Gallery, Rockford (Ill.) Mus. Recipient 1st prize City Art Mus., St. Louis, 1943, 44, Armstrong prize Chgo. Art Inst., 1947, William H. Bartels award, 1953, Frank Logan medal and prize, 1950, Walt Disney Purchase award L.A. (Calif.) Mus., Portrait of America Competition Purchase prize Colo. Springs Fine Arts Ctr., 1961, Hon. award AIA, 1962, Outstanding Achievement award YWCA. 1986, Artistic Contbn. to Cmty. award Schaumburg, Ill., 2005, Artistic Vision award Atomic Scientist, 2005, Artful Life award, 2005; grantee The Art Inst. Chgo., 2005; named Artist of Year Am. Fedn. Arts, 1958. Mem. Chgo. Network, Arts Club (Chgo.). Unitarian Universalist. *To be an artist means devoting a lifetime to an intensely difficult activity— one that requires concentration and skill. I've spent my time learning the power of color, line, shape and meaning. I like to think that I have opened out experiences people cannot reveal by themselves.*

**MARTYN, EVI,** music educator, musician; b. Athens, Greece, Nov. 12, 1941; arrived in U.S., 1965; d. Anastasios and Sophia (Alivizatos) Giannatos; BA, Royal Conservatory Athens, 1959; MA, Royal Conservatory Athens, Greece, 1959; PhD Music, Hochschule für Musik, Munich, Germany, 1963. Owner, founder Martyn Sch. Music, Los Alamitos, Calif., 1973—; chair keyboard dept., 1973—. Lectr., adjudicator, demonstrator numerous competitions, seminars, workshops etc. Author: Art of Piano Playing, 1988, The Root of Evil, 2005; contbg. author: Hellenic Voice; contbr. articles to profl. mags.; internat. performances include Wigmore Hall, London, Playel Hall, Paris, Merkin Hall, NYC, soloist SW Symphony of Utah, St. George, 2006. Performer at numerous benefit concerts including: D.C. Performing Arts Ctr., 1983, KLON Pub. Radio, Long Beach, Calif., Rotary Club Benefit for Needy, Huntington Beach, Calif., 1985, Hellenic U. Club, Loyola Marymount U., Calif., 1996. Recipient Excellent Artistic Evaluation, Internat. Comm. Agy., Washington, 1980, Award of Merit, Rotary Club of So. Calif., 1986, Knights of Pythias, 1993, The Andreas Sygros Gold medal, Greece Minister of Culture, First prize with gold medal, Royal Conservatory, Athens, 1959. Mem.: Internat. Assn. Music Competitions, Nat. Assn. Music Tchrs., Nat. Guild Piano Tchrs. (Named to Hall of Fame 1989). Avocation: swimming. Home Fax: 714-995-5699. E-mail: evimartyn@aol.com.

**MARTZ, CLYDE OLLEN,** lawyer, educator; b. Lincoln, Nebr., Aug. 14, 1920; s. Clyde O. and Elizabeth Mary (Anderson) M.; m. Ann Spieker, May 29, 1947; children: Robert Graham, Nancy. AB, U. Nebr., 1941; LLB, Harvard U., 1947. Bar: Colo. 1948, U.S. Ct. Appeals (D.C. cir.) 1968, U.S. Supreme Ct. 1969. Prof. U. Colo., Boulder, 1947-58, 60-62; jud. administr. State of Colo., Denver, 1959-60; ptnr. Davis, Graham & Stubbs, Denver, 1962-67, 69-80, 81-87, of counsel, 1988—; asst. atty. gen. U.S. Dept. Justice, Washington, 1967-69; solicitor U.S Dept. Interior, Washington, 1980-81; exec. dir. dept. natural resources State of Colo., 1987. Adj. prof. U. Denver, 1961-79, U. Colo., Boulder, 1988-96; cons. Pres. Materials Policy Commn., 1951; mem. Colo. Adv. Bd. Land Mgmt., 1967-69; bd. dirs., adv. bd. Natural Resources Law Ctr., 1982-2003. Author: Cases and Materials on Natural Resources Law, 1951, Water for Mushrooming Populations, 1954; co-author: American Law of Property, 1953, Water and Water Rights, 1963; editor, co-author: American Law of Mining. 1960. Co-chmn. Jud. Reorganization Commn., 1961-63; elder Presbyn. Ch., Boulder; pres. Rocky Mountain Mineral Law Found., 1961-62, others. Comdr. USN, 1942-58, PTO, with Res. Decorated Silver Star, Bronze Star, Letter of Commendation, Disting. Svc. award; honored by creation of Clyde O. Martz Natural Resources Scholarship Fund, 2002. Mem. ABA (chmn. natural resources sect. 1985-86), Fed. Bar Assn., Am. Health Lawyers Assn., Colo. Bar Assn. (chmn. water sect. 1957, chmn. mineral sect. 1961, award of merit 1962), Nat. Mining Assn. (Disting. Svc. award 1997), Order of Coif, Phi Beta Kappa. Democrat. Avocations: horticulture, woodworking, mountain climbing, skiing. Office: Davis Graham & Stubbs PO Box 185 Denver CO 80201-0185 Home: 970 Aurora Ave Apt A101 Boulder CO 80302-7239

**MARTZ, JUDY HELEN,** former governor; b. Big Timber, Mont., July 28, 1943; m. Harry Martz, June 23, 1965; children: Justin, Stacey. Owner, operator Martz Disposal Svc., Butte, Mont., 1971—; skater U.S. World Speed Skating Team, Japan, 1963, U.S. Olympic Team, Innsbruck, Austria, 1964; exec. dir. U.S. High Altitude Speed Skating Ctr., Butte, Mont., 1985-89; field rep. Senator Conrad Burns, 1989—95; lt. gov. State of Mont., Helena, 1997-2001, gov., 2001—05. Coach Mont. Amateur Speed Skating Assn.; bd. dirs. Youth Hockey Assn.; pres. adv. bd. U.S. Internat. Speed Skating Assn.; chair, Montanans for Judge Roberts (chief justice nominee), 2006. Bd dirs. St. James Cmty. Hosp., Legion Oasis HUD Housing Project. Named Miss Rodeo Mont., 1963; inducted Butte Sports Hall of Fame, 1987. Republican.*

**MARTZ, MIKE,** former professional football coach; b. Sioux Falls, S.D., May 13, 1951; BS summa cum laude, Fresno State. Asst. coach Los Angeles Rams, 1992—99, Washington Redskins, 1997-98; offensive coord. St. Louis Rams, 1999—2000, head coach, 2000—05; offensive coord. Detroit Lions, 2006—. Office: Detroit Lions Ford Field Ste 200 2000 Brush St Detroit MI 48226

**MARTZ, WILLARD HARRY,** physician; b. Camden, N.J., Dec. 2, 1934; s. Willard Weldon and Lena (Waldner) M. BA, Rutgers U., 1956; MD, Temple U., 1960. Intern Mt. Sinai Greater Miami, Miami Beach, Fla., 1960-61; resident VA, Long Beach, Calif., 1963-66; dermatologist So. Calif. Permanente Med. Group, L.A., 1966-69; pvt. practice Miami Beach, 1969-71; assoc. prof. clin. dermatology U. Miami, 1980-94, prof. clin. dermatology, 1994—. Cons. VA Hosp. of Miami. Fellow Am. Acad. Dermatology, Pacific Dermatology Assn.; mem. Nature Conservancy, Union of Concerned Scientists, Ctr. for Marine Conservation, Sierra, Alpha Omega Alpha. also: 333 W 41st St Ste 710 Miami Beach FL 33140-3608

**MARUNICK, MARK TIMOTHY,** medical educator, dental educator; b. Wyandotte, Mich., Feb. 11, 1951; s. Otto William and Jean Marunick; m. Robin Ann Edwards, Aug. 20, 1977; children: Mark Clinton, Piper Elizabeth. DDS, U. Mich. Dental Sch., 1975, MS in Removable Prosthodontics, 1980. Diplomate Am. Bd. Prosthodontics, 1991. Dir. maxillofacial prosthetics Wayne State U., Detroit, 1983—, assoc. prof., 2005—. Cons. maxillofacial prosthetics VA Hosp., Detroit, 2003—; dir. dental svcs. Detroit Med. Ctr., 2003—; adj. prof. U. Mich. Sch. Dentistry, Ann Arbor, 2001—. Editor (co-author): (text book) Maxillofacial Rehabilitation: Prosthodontic and Surgical Considerations. Bd. mem. Am. Cancer Soc., Southfield, Mich., 1989—94; examiner, splty. exam. prosthodontics State of Mich., 2002—05. Lt. comdr. USPHS, 1975—78. Recipient Clin. Oncology Career Devel. award, Am. Cancer Soc., 1987—89; grantee, NIH, Nat. Cancer Inst., 1986—91. Fellow: Am. Acad. Maxillofacial Prosthetics (pres. 2003—04), Am. Coll. Prosthodontists (pres. Mich. sect. 1992—94); mem.: ADA, Am. Acad. Maxillofacial Prosthetics (various positions 1991—2004), Kingery Prosthodontic Club, Mich. Soc. Prosthodontists (bd. dirs. 2002—05), Mich. Soc. Prosthodontists (pres. 1992—94), Am. Acad. Otolaryngology, Head and Neck Surgery (assoc.), Detroit Denture Clinic Club, Detroit Dist. Dental Soc., Mich. Dental Assn., Acad. Osseointegration. Avocation: gardening. Office: 5G - UHC 4201 Saint Antoine St Detroit MI 48201 Office Phone: 313-745-3096. Personal E-mail: mmarunic@med.wayne.edu.

**MARUOKA, JO ANN ELIZABETH,** retired information systems manager; b. Monrovia, Calif., Jan. 1, 1945; d. John Constantine and Pearl (Macovei) Gotsinas; m. Lester Hideo Maruoka, Nov. 8, 1973 (div. Aug. 1992); 1 child, John Nicholas Reyes-Burke; stepchildren: Les Scott Kaleohano, Lee Stuart Keola. BA with honors, UCLA, 1966; MBA, U. Hawaii, 1971. Office mgr. and asst. R. Wenkam, Photographer, Honolulu, 1966-69; computer mgmt. intern and sys. analyst Army Computer Sys. Command, Honolulu, 1969-78; reservations mgr. Hale Koa Hotel, Honolulu, 1978-79; equal employment opportunity specialist U.S. Army Pacific Hdqs., Honolulu, 1979-80, computer specialist, 1980-87, supervisory info. sys. mgr., chief info. tech. plans and programs, 1987-2001; ret., 2001. Bd. dirs. High Performance Computing and Comm. Coun., Tiverton, R.I.; Pacific v.p. Fedn. Govt. Info. Processing Couns., Washington, 1992-95. Active Nat. and Hawaii Women's Polit. Caucus, Honolulu, 1987—; pres. Fed. Women's Coun. Hawaii, Honolulu, 1976-77, advisor, 1977—. Recipient Svc. award Fed. Women's Coun. Hawaii, 1986, EEO Excellence award Sec. of Army, 1989, Pacific Fed. Mgr. award Honolulu-Pacific Fed. Exec. Bd., 1990, Info. Resources Mgmt. award Interagy. Com. on Info. Resources Mgmt., 1991, Lead Dog Leadership award Fedn. Govt. Info. Processing Couns., 1993; named One of Fed. 100 (Execs.) of Yr., Fed. Computer Week, 1996. Mem. AAUW, LWV (sec. Hawaii State Bd. 2003-05, dir. 2005—), Hawaii State League Women Voters (bd. dirs.), NAFE, Nat. Women's Polit. Caucus, Armed Forces Comm.-Electronics Assn. (Hawaii chpt., Internat. award for Info. Resources Mgmt. Excellence 1992), Assn. U.S. Army (Pacific Fed. Mgr. award 1990), Federally Employed Women (advisor Aloha and Rainbow chpts. 1977—), Army Signal Corps Regtl. Assn. (Bronze Order of Mercury 1997, Silver Order of Mercury, 2001), Hawaii Intergovt. Info. Processing Coun. (pres. 1988-89, svc. award 1989), Beta Gamma Sigma. Avocations: travel, reading, tai chi, theater. Personal E-mail: maruokaj@hawaii.rr.com.

**MARUPUDI, SAMBASIVA RAO,** surgeon, educator; b. Chintalapudi, India, July 1, 1952; arrived in US, 1976; s. Venkateswarlu and Nagendramma (Gaddipati) M.; m. Usha Nandipati, Mar. 25, 1976; children: Neena, Neelima. MB, BS, Guntur (India) Med. Coll., 1974. Diplomate Am. Bd. Surgery, Am. Bd. Colon and Rectal Surgery. Rotating internship St. Clare's Hosp., Schenectady, NY, 1976-77; resident in gen. surgery St. Agnes Hosp., Balt., 1977-78, Franklin Sq. Hosp., Balt., 1978-82; fellow in colon and rectal surgery U. Tex. Health Scis. Ctr., Houston, 1982-83; pvt. practice Amarillo, Tex., 1983—. Clin. asst. prof. dept. surgery Tex. Tech. U. Health Scis. Ctr., Amarillo, 1984—. Fellow ACS, Am. Soc. Colon and Rectal Surgeons, Internat. Coll. Surgeons; mem. AMA, Tex. Med. Assn., Potter-Randall County Med. Soc. (past pres.), Tex. Soc. Colon and Rectal Surgeons (past pres.). Republican. Hindu. Office: 800 Quail Creek Dr # 103 Amarillo TX 79124-1634 Office Phone: 806-358-7911. Personal E-mail: smarupdi@aol.com, drmarupudi@hotmail.com.

**MARUTOIU, CONSTANTIN CONSTANTIN,** chemistry professor, researcher; b. Stanesti, Romania, Feb. 4, 1949; s. Constantin Ioan and Floarea Ioana Marutoiu; m. Persida Livia Marutoiu, Aug. 22, 1974; children: Olivia Florena, Victor Constantin. MS, Babes-Bolyai U., Cluj-Napoca, Romania, 1973, PhD in Chemistry, 1986. Chemist Babes-Bolyai U., Cluj-Napoca, Romania, 1973—78, Raluca-Ripan Inst. Chemistry, Cluj-Napoca, Romania, 1978—80, rsch. chemist, 1980—82, sr. rsch. 3, 1982—90, sr. rschr. 2, 1990—93, sr. rschr. 1, 1993—2002; assoc. prof. Lucian Blaga U., Sibin, Romania, 2000—02, prof., 2002—. Author: Mycotoxin Anlysis, 2001, Drugs, 2002; contbr. articles to profl. jours. Recipient Gheorghe Spaou prize, Romanian Acad., 1998; grant, Leonardo da Vinci, 1999—2001, Relansin, 2002—03. Mem.: Romanian Analytical Chemistry Soc., Romanian Chemistry Soc. Avocations: history, music, fine arts. Home: Ion Nesven 12 400650 Cluj Napoca Romania Office: Lucian Blaga Univ Sibiu 7-9 Dr Ion Ratin St 2400 Sibiu Romania Office Phone: 0040 269 216069. Office Fax: 0040 269 212558. E-mail: cmarutoiu@email.re.

**MARUYAMA, GEOFFREY,** academic administrator, educator; children: Kristina, Daniel. PhD, U. So. Calif., 1977. From asst. prof. to prof. U. Minn., Mpls., 1976—, from asst. v.p. to vice provost, 1996—. Pres., sec. treas. Soc. Psychol. Study of Social Issues, Washington, 1996—2003. Author: (book) Basics of Structural Equation Modeling; author: (with Stan Deno) Research in Educational Settings; editor: (journal) Analyses of Social Issues and Public Policy. Office: U Minn 100 Church St SE Minneapolis MN 55455 Office Phone: 612-625-5861. Office Fax: 612-626-8388. Business E-Mail: geoff@umn.edu.

**MARUYAMA, MAGOROH,** business educator, researcher, consultant; b. Tokyo, Apr. 2, 1929; came to U.S., 1950; s. Shinsaku and Toyoko (Takashima) M.; m. Pierrette Duriez, Apr. 1966 (div. 1974); 1 child, Yukon; m. Kuniko Sakakibara, July 23, 1976; 1 child, Yuki. BA in Math., U. Calif., Berkeley, 1951; postgrad., U. Munich, U. Heidelberg, Fed. Republic of Germany, 1954-55, U. Copenhagen, 1955-57; PhD, U. Lund, Sweden, 1959. Asst. prof. human devel. U. Calif., Berkeley, 1960-62; rsch. assoc. psychology Stanford U., Calif., 1962-64; assoc. prof. psychology San Francisco State U., 1965-70; prof. computer sci. Antioch Coll., 1971-72; prof. systems sci. Portland (Oreg.) State U., 1973-76; vis. prof. anthropology and architecture U. Ill., Urbana, 1976-77; vis. prof. anthropology U. Uppsala, Sweden, 1982; vis. prof. mgmt. UCLA, 1983, Nat. U., Singapore, 1983-84; vis. prof. bus. administrn. U. Hawaii, Honolulu, 1984-86; prof. internat. bus. Aoyama Gakuin U., Tokyo, 1987-96, Aomori (Japan) Koritsu Daigaku, 1996—. Vis. prof. U. Oreg., U. Montpellier, France, 1986; cons. U.S. Dept. Commerce 1971 Can. Fed. Ministry Urban Affairs, 1974, NASA, 1975, Monsanto Chems., 1980, Volvo, Sweden, 1982. Fed. Motors of Indonesia, 1984, Technopolises Japan, 1984, MITI of Japan, 1985, Fujitsu, Japan, 1985, Hakuhodo, Japan, 1985, Gadelius, Sweden, 1988, Michelin, France, 1989, NEC, Japan, 1989-90, C. Itoh, Japan, 1990, OECD, France, 1990, Ministry of Rsch. and Tech., France, 1992. Author: The Second Cybernetics, 1963, Mindscapes and Science Theories, 1980, Mindscapes in Management, 1994, Heterogram Analysis, 1999, Interactive Heterogeneity, 2003. Sgt. USMC,

1952-54. Grantee NSF, NIMH, 1965-76. Fellow AAAS, APA; mem. Acad. Mgmt., Internat. Sociol. Assn., Sigma Xi, Pi Mu Epsilon Avocations: architecture, art design, music composition theory. Office Phone: 858-452-3826. Office Fax: 858-452-3826. Personal E-mail: kuniko_maruyama@sbcglobal.net.

**MARUYAMA, MICHELLE,** violinist; b. Washington; d. Xavier and Janet Maruyama. MusB, MusM, San Francisco Conservatory of Music. Asst. prin. second violin Santa Rosa Symphony, Santa Rosa, Calif., 2002—; violinist Marin Symphony, San Rafael, Calif., 2004—, Symphony Silicon Valley, San Jose; prin. second violin Napa Valley Symphony, Napa, Stockton Symphony, Stockton. Fellow New World Symphony, Miami Beach, Fla., 2003—04. Mem.: Am. Fedn. of Musicians.

**MARVEL, L. PAIGE,** federal judge; b. Easton, Md., Dec. 6, 1949; d. E. Warner Marvel and Louise H. Harrison; m. Robert H. Dyer, Jr., Aug. 9, 1975; children: Alex W. Dyer, Kelly E. Dyer. BA magna cum laude, Notre Dame Coll., 1971; JD with honors, U. Md., 1974. Bar: Md. 1974, U.S. Dist. Ct. Md. 1974, U.S. Tax Ct. 1975, U.S. Ct. Appeals (4th cir.) 1977, U.S. Supreme Ct. 1980, U.S. Ct. Claims 1981, D.C. 1985. Assoc. Garbis & Schwait, P.A., Balt., 1974-76, shareholder, 1976-85, Garbis, Marvel & Junghans, P.A., Balt., 1985-86; mem. Melnicove, Kaufman, Weiner, Smouse & Garbis, P.A., Balt., 1986-88; ptnr. Venable, Baetjer and Howard LLP, Balt., 1988-98; judge U.S. Tax Ct., Washington, 1998—. Mem. U. Md. Law Sch. Bd. Vis., 1995—2001; mem. adv. com. U.S. Dist. Ct. Md., 1991—93; mem. Commr.'s Rev. Panel on IRS Integrity, 1989—91. Co-editor procedure dept. Jour. Taxation, 1989-98; contbr. chpts. to books, articles to profl. jours. Active Women's Law Ctr., 1974-85, Md. Dept. Econ. and Cmty. Devel. Adv. Com., 1978-80; trustee Loyola-Notre Dame Libr., Inc., 1996-2003. Recipient Recognition award Balt. Is Best Program, 1981; named One of Md.'s Top 100 Women, The Daily Record, 1998; recipient MSBA Taxation section's Tax Excellence award, 2002. Fellow Am. Bar Found., Md. Bar Found.; Am. Coll. Tax Counsel (regent 1995-98); mem. ABA (sect. taxation coun. dir. 1989-92, vice-chair com. ops. 1993-95, Disting. Svc. award, Jules Ritholz award 2004), Am. Law Inst. (advisor restatement of law third, law governing lawyers), Md. Bar Assn. (chmn. taxation sect. 1982-83, bd. dirs. 1988-90, 96-98, Disting. Svc. award), Balt. Bar Assn. (at-large exec. coun.), Am. Tax Policy Inst. (trustee 1997-98), Serjeant's Inn. Avocations: golf, music, travel. Office: US Tax Ct 400 Second St NW Washington DC 20217-0001 Office Phone: 202-521-0740.

**MARVEL, THOMAS STAHL,** architect; b. Newburgh, N.Y., Mar. 15, 1935; s. Gordon Simis and Madelyn Emigh (Jova) M.; m. Lucilla Wellington Fuller, Apr. 19, 1958; children: Deacon Simis, Jonathan Jova, Thomas Stahl AB, Dartmouth Coll., 1956; MArch, Harvard U., 1962. Registered architect, N.C., P.R., Mass., N.Y. Designer Synergetics, Inc., Raleigh, NC, 1958; designer IBEC Housing, N.Y.C., 1959; ptnr., architect Torres-Beauchamp-Marvel, San Juan, PR, 1960-85, Marvel-Flores-Cobian, San Juan, PR, 1985-97; ptnr. Thomas S. Marvel Architects, San Juan, PR, 1997—. Prof. Sch. Architecture, U. P.R., Rio Piedras, 1967-89. Author: Antonin Nechodoma, Architect, 1994; co-author: Parish Churches of Puerto Rico, 1984. Works include Am. Embassy, Guatemala, 1973, U.S. Courthouse and Fed. Office Bldg., V.I., 1976, City Hall, Bayamon, P.R., 1978, Mcpl. Baseball Stadium, Bayamon, 1975, Am. Embassy, Costa Rica, 1986. Bd. dirs. St. John's Sch., San Juan, 1976-93. Recipient 1st award for regional coll. design U. P.R., Utuado, 1983; Harvard Grad. Sch. Design Julia Amory Appleton travelling fellow, 1962, Henry Klumb prize, 1991. Fellow AIA (bd. dirs. 1993-96, Design award for Fla. Caribbean region 1981, 84-85, 90-91); mem. P.R. Coll. Architects, Acad. Arts and Scis. Clubs: Harvard (N.Y.C.). Roman Catholic. Home: 450 Calle Del Valle San Juan PR 00915-3315 Office: Thomas S Marvel Architects 161 Calle San Jorge Santurce San Juan PR 00911-2018 Office Phone: 787-289-9494. Business E-Mail: tsmarvel@marvelarch.com.

**MARVIN, CHARLES ARTHUR,** law educator; b. July 14, 1942; s. Burton Wright and Margaret Fiske (Medlar) Marvin; m. Elizabeth Maureen Woodrow, July 4, 1970 (div. July 1987); children: Colin, Kristin; m. Elizabeth Dale Wilson, Mar. 20, 1999. BA, U. Kans., 1964; postgrad., U. Toulouse, France, 1964-65; JD, U. Chgo., 1968, M of Comparative Law, 1970. Bar: Ill. 1969. Legal intern EEC, Brussels, 1970; lectr. law U. Kent, Canterbury, England, 1970-71; asst. prof. law Laval U., Quebec City, Que., Canada, 1971-73; legal adv. Constnl., internat. and adminstrv. law sect. Can. Dept. Justice, Ottawa, Ont., 1973-76, dir. Adminstrv. Law Reform Project, 1983-85; assoc. prof. law U. Man., Winnipeg, Canada, 1976-77; dir. adminstrv. law project Law Reform Commn., Ottawa, 1977-80; prof. law Villanova (Pa.) U., 1980-83, Ga. State U., 1985—, assoc. dean, 1987-89. Legal advisor on adminstrv. code revision Govt. of Kazakhstan, 1993; law faculty devel. adviser, Bulgaria, 93; dir. internat. human rights law summer program Regent U. Sch. Law, 1998; USIS lectr., Ivory Coast, 98; Fulbright prof. Riga Grad. Sch. Law, Latvia, 2000—03; vis. prof. law Vytautas Magnus U., Lithuania, 2004—. Fulbright scholar, U. Toulouse, 1964—65; Summerfield scholar, U. Kans., 1961—64, Ford Found. Comparative Law fellow, 1968—70. Mem.: ABA, Can. Coun. Internat. Law, Internat. Law Assn., Internat. Bar Assn., Am. Fgn. Law Assn., Am. Soc. Internat. Law, Chgo. Bar Assn., Ill. Bar Assn., Phi Beta Kappa, Phi Delta Phi, Phi Beta Delta, Omicron Delta Kappa. Office: Ga State U Coll Law PO Box 4037 Atlanta GA 30302-4037 Office Phone: 404-651-2436. Business E-Mail: cmarvin@gsu.edu.

**MARVIN, CHARLES RODNEY, JR.,** lawyer; b. Elizabeth, N.J., Feb. 26, 1953; s. Charles Rodney and Doris Marie (Richards) Marvin; m. Carol Ann Welteroth, Aug. 30, 1975 (dec.); children: Kathryn, Kristin, Cynthia, Gregory; m. Nancy Agnes Ruggiero, Mar. 24, 2001; 1 stepchild, Susanna Myirski. BA in Econs., Mich. State U., 1975; JD, Boston U., 1978; LLM in Mil. Law, Judge Advocate Gen. Sch., 1987; LLM in Govt. Contracts, George Washington U., 1995. Bar: N.J. 1982, U.S. Dist. Ct. N.J. 1982, U.S. Ct. Mil. Appeals 1982, U.S. Ct. Appeals (fed. cir.) 1994, D.C. 1996, U.S. Ct. Fed. Claims 1996. Commd. 2nd lt. U.S. Army, 1975, advanced through grades to major, 1994, nuclear missile officer Schwaebisch Gmund, Germany, 1979-82; mil. prosecutor Fort Sill, Okla., 1983-86; sr. def. counsel U.S. Army Trial Def. Svc., Ft. Polk, La., 1987-89; trial counsel, chief protest br. U.S. Army Contract Appeals Divsn., Arlington, Va., 1990-94; ptnr., gov. contracts litig. Venable LLP (formerly Venable, Baetjer, Howard & Civiletti), Washington, 1994—. Mem. ABA (vice-chair, bid protest com., pub. contract sect. 1992-93), FBA, Bd. Contract Appeals Bar Assn. (bd. govs. 1993-96), Fed. Cir. Bar Assn., John Carroll Soc., Nat. Contract Mgmt. Assn., Bishop McNamara High School (bd. dirs.), Forestville, MD. Roman Catholic. Avocations: composing music, golf. Office: Venable LLP 575 7th St Washington DC 20004-1601 Office Phone: 202-344-4963. Office Fax: 202-344-8300.

**MARVIN, DAVID EDWARD SHREVE,** lawyer; b. Jan. 6, 1950; s. George Charles Marvin and Shirley Mae (Martin) Schaible; m. Mary Anne Kennedy, Sept. 16, 1972; 1 child, John. BS cum laude, Mich. State U., 1972; JD cum laude, Wayne State U., 1976. Bar: Mich. 1976, U.S. Dist. Ct. (ea. dist.) Mich. 1976, U.S. Dist. Ct. (we. dist.) Mich. 1978, U.S. Ct. Appeals (7th cir.) 1977, U.S. Ct. Appeals (6th cir.) 1979, U.S. Supreme Ct. 1979, U.S. Ct. Appeals (D.C. cir.) 1982, D.C. 1982. Asst. mgr. Allia Supply Co., Lansing, 1972-73; rsch. asst. Wayne State U., Detroit, fall 1975; jud. intern U.S. Dist. Ct., Detroit, summer 1975; shareholder Fraser Trebilcock Davis & Dunlap, P.C., Lansing, 1976—, chair Govt. Law dept., 1992—, v.p., 1997—, also bd. dirs. Pres. Red Rock Prodns., Inc., 1990-94; lectr. Inst. CLE, 1989; mem. qualifications rev. com. U.S. Dist. Ct. (we. dist.) Mich., 2001—. Exec. editor Wayne Law Rev., 1975-76; contbr. articles to law jours. Commr. Mich. Solar Resource Adv. Panel, Lansing, 1978-81, Mich. Commn. Profl. and Occupl. Licensure, 1981-83; chmn. Ingham County Energy Commn., Mason, Mich., 1978-80 (state bar for assembly 1985-88); dir., corp. sec. Friends Mich. Hist. Ctr., Inc., 1988-92; treas. Lansing Lawyer Referral Svc., 1981; state del. Nat. Solar Congress, Washington, 1978; hearing officer City of East Lansing, 1985; Tri-County Coun. of Bar Leaders (chmn. 1986); bd. dirs. East Lansing Edn. Found., 1990-92, Impression Five Sci. Mus., 1991-97; regional fin. chmn. Abraham for U.S. Senate, 1993-94, Abraham Senate 2000, 1995-2000; mem. transition team, Gov. Engler, 2000—03, Atty. Gen. Cox, 2002-03; exec. bd. chief Okemos coun. Boy Scouts Am., 1996—, pres. 2001-03. Recipient

Disting. Vol. award Tri-County Voluntary Action Ctr., 1990, Gov.'s Minuteman award, 1990, John W. Cummiskey award State Bar Mich., 1990, George Washington Honor medal Freedoms Found., 1990; named Outstandin Young Man Am., 1984, The Outstanding Young Lawyer in Mich., 1985-86, Small Bus. Adv. Yr., C. of C., 1991, Silver Beaver award Boy Scouts Am., 2003, Disting. Citizen, Boy Scouts Am., 2005; Wm. D. Traitel scholar, 1975. Fellow ABA, Am. Bar Found., Mich. State Bar Found. (life); mem. ABA, State Bar Mich. (com. chmn., sect. coun. 1982—, state chmn. 1988-89), Mich. Soc. Assoc. Execs., Ingham County Bar Assn. (pres. 1985-86), Pro Bono Lawyers Svc. (pres. 1982-83), Lansing Regional C. of C. (v.p. 1987), Mich. Audubon Soc. (bd. dirs. 1991-93), Mich. State Univ. Alumni Assn. (nat. bd. dirs. 1992—), State Capital Law Firm Group (nat. bd. dirs. 1989—, chmn. com. Can. 1990-93, chair pub. utility, energy and comm. sect. 1994—, nat. sec. 1996-97, vice-chmn. 1997-98, chmn. 1998-99), Downtown Coaches Club (bd. dirs., pres. 1987), Nat. Resource Ctr. on State Laws and Regulations (nat. bd. dirs. 1993-99, chmn. 1998-99), Mich. State U. Pres.'s Club, Rotary (bd. dirs. 1995-97, pres. 2004-05, Paul Harris fellow), Phi Alpha Delta, Phi Eta Sigma, Theta Delta Chi (pres. 1972). Republican. Home: 1959 Groton Way East Lansing MI 48823-1347 Office: Fraser Trebilcock Davis & Dunlap PC Boji Tower Fl 10 124 West Allegan Street Lansing MI 48933 Office Phone: 517-377-0830. Business E-Mail: dmarvin@fraserlawfirm.com.

**MARWEDEL, WARREN JOHN,** lawyer; b. Chgo., July 3, 1944; s. August Frank and Eleanor (Wolgamot) M.; m. Marilyn Baran, Apr. 12, 1975. BS in Marine Engring., U.S. Merchant Marine Acad., 1966; JD, Loyola U., Chgo., 1972. Bar: Ill. 1972, U.S. Dist. Ct. (no. dist.) Ill. 1972, U.S. Supreme Ct. 1974. Pres. Marwedel Minichello & Reeb, P.C., Chgo. With U.S. Merchant Marines, 1966-70. Mem. ABA (Ho. of Dels. 1989-96), Ill. Bar Assn., Chgo. Bar Assn., Maritime Law Assn.(1st v.p.), Propeller Club (Chgo. pres. 1982). Avocations: boating, reading, history. Office: Marwedel Minichello & Reeb PC President 10 S Riverside Plz Ste 720 Chicago IL 60606-3708 Office Phone: 312-902-1600. Personal E-mail: wjmmmandr@aol.com. Business E-Mail: wmarwedel@mmr-law.com.

**MARX, ANTHONY W.,** academic administrator; b. NYC, Feb. 28, 1959; s. Peter and Marion E. (Mankin) M.; m. Karen Barkey, Sept. 7, 1993; children: Joshua, Anna-Claire. Student, Wesleyan U., Middletown, Conn., 1977-79; BA, Yale U., 1981; MPA, Princeton U., 1986, MA, 1987, PhD, 1990. Adminstrv. aide to the pres. U. Pa., Phila., 1981-84; cons. SACHED Trust, Johannesburg, 1984, 86; vis. scholar Community Agy. for Social Enquiry, Johannesburg, 1988, 90; prof. polit. sci. Columbia U., NYC, 1990—2003; pres. Amherst Coll., 2003—. Rsch. asst. Ctr. for Ednl. Rsch. and Devel., Santiago, Chile, 1985; cons. UNDP, N.Y.C., 1991; vis. scholar Ctr. for Afro-Asian Studies, Rio de Janeiro, Brazil, 1993. Author: Lessons of Struggle, 1992, Making Race and Nation: A Comparison of the United States, South Africa and Brazil, 1998 (Ralph J. Bunche award Am. Polit. Sci. Assn. 1999, Barrington Moore prize Am. Social. Assn., 2000), Faith in Nation: Exclusionary Origins of Nationalism, 2003; contbr. articles to profl. jours. Trustee, treas. Fund for Edn. in South Africa, N.Y.C., 1991—94. Grantee J. D. and C.T. MacArthur Found., Chgo., 1989-90, Social Sci. Rsch. Coun., N.Y.C., 1992-93, U.S. Inst. Peace, Washington, 1992-93; named fellow H.F. Guggenheim Found., N.Y.C., 1994.; John Simon Guggenheim fellow, 1997. Office: Office of Pres 103 Converse Hall PO Box 5000 Amherst MA 01002-5000 Office Phone: 413-542-2234. E-mail: marx@amherst.edu.*

**MARX, DARRELYN MADONNA,** music educator, drama educator; b. Sauk Center, Minn., Apr. 19, 1951; d. Darrell and Jeanne Brawders; m. Kenneth Robert Marx, Apr. 2, 1991. BS in Edn., Speech/Theatre and Vocal Music, Minn. State U., Moorhead, 1974; MFA in Theatre, U. Ill., Champaign/Urbana, 1985. English, vocal music and drama instr. R.D. Parker Collegiate, Thompson, Man., Canada, 1974—82; grad. asst. U. Ill., Champaign/Urbana, 1982—85; vocal music and drama instr. New Trier H.S., Winnetka, Ill., 1985—2006. Bd. dirs. Stephen M. Hoenig Meml. Fund, Glencoe, Ill., 2005—. Recipient Jeff award for best supporting actress in a musical, Joseph Jefferson Com., Chgo., 2005; Sch. of Speech Summer fellow, Northwestern U., Evanston, Ill., 1988. Mem.: NEA, Ill. Theatre Assn., Ill. Edn. Assn. Achievements include development of Northern Illinois Theatre Educators. Avocations: acting, singing, theatre directing, choreography, dialect coaching.

**MARX, DAVID EARL,** chemistry professor, consultant; b. Nazareth, Pa., July 25, 1960; s. William John and Shirley Ackerman Marx; m. Patricia Ellen Wood, Feb. 17, 1996. BS, East Stroudsburg U., 1982; PhD, SUNY, Vestal, 1987. Assoc. prof. chemsitry U. Scranton, Pa., 1987—, chair dept. chemistry, 1998. Sci. cons. Sauquoit Industries, Inc., Scranton, Pa., 1992—98, Argentum Med. Corp., Chgo., 2000—, Cocciardi and Assocs, Inc., Mechanicsburg, Pa.; faculty sponsor U. Scranton, Pa., 1994. Deacon candidate Roman Cath. Ch., Scranton, Pa., 2001—04. ILI grant, NSF, 1992-1994, Ben Franklin Challenge grant, Commonwealth of Pa., 1999-2000, 2000-2001, CHE grant, NSF, 2001-2003. Mem.: Am. Chem. Soc., Sigma Xi, Phi Lamda Upsilon. Republican. Roman Catholic. Achievements include patents pending for Electroless Plating of fibers and fabrics with the aid of ultrasound. Home: 605 Timber Ln Clarks Summit PA 18411 Office: Univ Scranton Linden and Monroe Sts Scranton PA 18510 Business E-Mail: marxd1@scranton.edu.

**MARX, GARY DEAN,** educational consultant, futurist, think-tank executive; b. Manchester, SD, Nov. 28, 1938; s. Harvey Frederick and Lucille (Stemple) Marx; m. Judy Rae Marx, June 18, 1961; children: John Fredrick, Daniel Winston. BA, U. S.D., 1960. CAE, ASPR, APR. Newscaster, announcer, dir. KSOO radio and TV sta., Sioux Falls, SD, 1958-61; newscaster, announcer WOW radio and TV sta., Omaha, 1961-71; dir. comms. Westside Cmty. Schs., Omaha, 1971-77; exec. dir. comms. Jefferson County Pub. Schs., Denver, 1977-79; sr. assoc. exec. Am. Assn. Sch. Adminstrs., Arlington, Va., 1979-96, exec. dir. Leadership for Learning Found., 1996-98; pres. Ctr. for Pub. Outreach, Inc., Vienna, Va., 1998—. Sr. rsch. fellow Health, Energy and Productivity in Sch. project, Bethesda, Md., 2000-02; pub. rels. cons. Nat. Sch. Pub. Rels. Assn., Rockville, Md., 1972—; v.p., owner Sta. KOAK Radio, Red Oak, Iowa, 1977-82; v.p. Comms. Devel. Inc., Denver, 1974-76; chief evaluator CIVITAS Internat. Exch. Program, Calabasas, Calif., 2000—; cons., spkr. in field. Author: Radio...Your Publics are Listening, 1976; Radio...Get the Message, 1977; Excellence in Our Schools...Making it Happen, 1984; Public Relations for Administrators, 1984, 88; Working with the News Media, 1993; Preparing Students for the 21st Century, 1996, 99; The Future of Cmty., 1999; Preparing Schools and School Systems for the 21st Century, 1999; Ten Trends...Educating Children for a Profoundly Different Future, 2000, Future Focused Leadership...Preparing Schools, Students and Communities for Tomorrow's Realities, 2006, 16 Trends...Their Profound Impact on Our Future, 2006; contbr. articles to profl. jours. Founder, chmn. Keystone Cmty. Task Force, Omaha, 1970-77; mem. Omaha Parks and Recreation Bd., City of Omaha, 1975-77; mem. urban growth policy bd., 1976; mem. nat. adv. com. for restoration Statue of Liberty-Ellis Island Found,. NYC, 1984-86; mem. Horace Mann League, 1985-, bd. dirs. 2005—; mem. exec. com. edn. Commn. of Bicentennial of the US Constitution, Washington, 1986-92; bd. dir. Campaign for New Priorities, Washington, 1992-93; bd. dir., founder Coalition for America's Children, Washington, 1992-98; mem. steering com. Libr. of Congress, Ctr. for the Book, Washington, 1992-99, Goals 2000 Arts Edn. Partnership NEA, Washington, 1993-98, Civitas Internat., Brussels, Belgium, 1996—, Fulbright Scholars, selection com., 1998-; mem. design arts program steering com. NEA, Washington, 1993-94; mem. grants selection com. Alliance for Arts Edn., John F. Kennedy Ctr. for the Performing Arts, Washington, 1993-96, Nat. Tchr. of Yr. Program, Washington, 1979-99; mem. steering com., mem. selection com., judge Disney Salute to the Am. Tchr., Burbank, Calif., 1993-97; Emmy awards judge NATAS, NYC, 1995-97; mem. adv. bd. NBC The More You Know campaign, NYC, 1992-98; mem. nat. adv. bd. PBS, 1990-98; judge USA Today All USA Acad. Team, Arlington, Va., 1995-2000, Nat. History Day, 2002-; internat. cons., spkr., Ctr. for Civic Edn., Calabasas, Calif., 1996—, USIA, US Dept. State, Washington, 1996—; mem. steering com., facilitator Nat. Ctr. for Energy Mgmt. and Bldg. Techs., 2004—. Recipient Radio Advertising Bureau Commercial award, 1967. Mem. Nat. Sch. Pub. Rels.

Assn. (numerous offices and coms. 1971—, accredited, Pres.'s award 1999), Pub. Rels. Soc. Am. (accredited), Am. Soc. Assn. Exec. (cert.), Edn. Writers Assn. (bd. dir. 1979—), Am. Assn. Sch. Adminstrs. (Disting. Svc. award 2000), World Future Soc. (profl. mem.)Horace Mann League (bd. dirs., 2005—). Avocations: folk art, travel, reading, writing, photography. Office: Ctr for Pub Outreach 1831 Toyon Way Vienna VA 22182-3355 Office Phone: 703-938-8725. Personal E-mail: gmarxcpo@aol.com.

**MARX, JEFF,** composer, lyricist, lawyer, writer; BFA, U. Mich., 1993; degree, J.D. Cardozo Sch. Law, 1996; attended, BMI Lehman Engel Musical Theater Workshop, 1999. Bar: NY. Composer children's musicals Theatreworks/USA; composer various songs The Disney Channel. Author, pub. How to Win a High School Election, 1999, creator, co-writer (with Robert Lopez) (Broadway plays) Avenue Q, 2003 (Lucille Lortel award for best musical, 2003, Best Original Score Tony award, 2004, Lucille Lortel award best musical, 2003, Tony award best original score, 2004, Tony award best musical, 2004), composer, lyricist (with Robert Lopez) (plays) Kermit, Prince of Denmark (Kleban award). Mem.: BMI Lehman Engel Musical Theater Workshop. Office: care of John Buzzetti Gersh Agy 41 Madison 33d Fl New York NY 10010 Office Phone: 212-447-4747. Personal E-mail: jeffmarx@aol.com.

**MARX, MICHAEL WILLIAM,** language educator, writer; b. Phila., Nov. 1, 1951; s. Elmer Edward and Katharine Scott Marx. Student, Loyola U.; BA in Polit. Sci., Hobart Coll., 1973; MFA in Film Making, NYU, 1976; MA in English, Ind. State U., 2001. Freelance writer, Calif., 1976-90; owner, head chef Freelandville Novelist Cafe, Ind., 1990—95; pub. Marx & Marx Writers & Pubs., 1998—; instr. English lang. and lit. Ind. State U., Terre Haute, 1999—; instr. Lakeland Coll., Danville, Ill., 2000—01, Ivy Tech State Coll., Terra Haute & Greenfield, Ind., 2000—01, Mira Costa Coll., Oceanside, Calif., 2001—03, Southwestern Coll., Chula Vista, Calif., 2001—02, San Diego City Coll., 2001—, Palomar Coll., San Marcos, Calif., 2001—03, Miramar Coll., San Diego, 2001—03, Cuyumaca Coll., El Cajon, Calif., 2001—03, Inter-Am. Coll., National City, Calif., 2001—03, San Diego State U., 2002—, Nat. U., 2003—; instr. humanities, English, western civilization Art Inst. Calif., San Diego, 2004—; instr. Webster U., 2004—, Chapman U., 2004—. Tchr. Vincennes U., Ind., 1991—93, Ind. Bus. Coll., 1995. Author: (book) A War Ends, 1977, A War Ends, 2d edit., 1985 (Artisan award Acad. Fine Arts and Friends), Eric Greenfield: Middle American, 1987, Justus: A Utopia, 1999; columnist: North Knox Leader, 1997—98, Knox County Daily News, Wabash Weekly News, 1991—92; movie reviewer. Personal E-mail: michael@michaelwmarx.com.

**MARX, NICKI DIANE,** sculptor, painter; b. LA, Oct. 3, 1943; d. Donald F. and Ruth H. (Ungar) M. Student, U. Calif., Riverside, 1965, U. Calif., Santa Cruz, 1973. Represented by Nicki Marx Studio, Taos, N.Mex., Fred Kline Gallery, Santa Fe, N.Mex. One-woman shows include Palm Springs Desert Mus., 1977, Julie Artisans Gallery, NYC, 1975, Phoenix Art Mus., 1975, Weston Gallery, Carmel, Calif, 1981, Kirk de Gooyer Gallery, LA, 1982, Rocklands Gallery, Monterey, Calif., 1983, Fetish Gallery, Taos, 1988, Fenix Gallery, Taos, 1991, Earthworks, 1993, Lamberts, 1994, Stables Gallery, Taos, 1995, Fred Kline, 1995, Sun Cities Mus. Art, Ariz., 1996, Harwood Mus. Art, Taos, 1999, others; group exhbns. include E.P. Smith Gallery, Santa Cruz, 1994, Lumina Gallery, Taos, 1994, Cafe Gallery, Albuquerque, 1991, Bareiss Gallery, Taos, 1990, Ctr. for Contemporary Art, Santa Fe, 1989, Jordan Gallery, Taos, 1988-89, Stables Art Gallery, Taos, 1988, 94, Albuquerque State Fair Grounds, 1986, San Francisco Mus. Modern Art, 1977-78, Elements Gallery, Greenwich, Conn., 1977, Pacific Design Ctr., LA, 1976, Lester Gallery, Inverness, Calif., 1976, others; represented in pub. collections IBM, Milford, Conn., N.Y.C., San Jose, Calif., Bank of Am., San Francisco, The Continental Group, Inc., Stamford, Conn., Cedars-Sinai Hosp., LA, Farm Bur. Fedn., Sacramento, Calif., Sherman Fairchild Sci. Ctr., Stanford, Calif., Palm Springs (Calif.) Desert Mus., U. Ariz. State U. at Tempe, Mills Coll. Art Gallery, Berkeley, Calif.; exhibited in pvt. collections of Estate of Eugene Klein, Estate of Louise Nevelson, Estate of Georgia O'Keeffe, Fritz Scholder, Ray Graham, Bunny Horowitz, Sue and Otto Meyer, Burt Sugarman, Craig Moody, Paul Pletka, others; subject of numerous articles in jours. and mags. MacDowell Colony fellow, 1975; recipient Adolph and Esther Gottleib Found. grant, 1985. Studio: PO Box 128 Penasco NM 87553

**MARX, OWEN COX,** lawyer; b. Grosse Pointe, Mich., Oct. 17, 1947; s. Leo A. and Anne (Cox) M.; m. Patricia Windschill, Aug. 14, 1971; children: Patrick Cox, Molly Simser, Anne Windschill. BA, Coll. of St. Thomas, St. Paul, 1969; JD, Cath. U., Washington, 1972. Bar: Minn. 1972, N.Y. 1973. Law clk. to presiding justice Minn. Supreme Ct., St. Paul, 1972-73; assoc. Mudge, Rose, Guthrie & Alexander, N.Y.C., 1973-75, Dorsey & Whitney, Mpls., 1975-78, ptnr., 1979-86, ptnr., head London office, 1986-90, ptnr., corp. fin. internat. practice groups N.Y.C., 1990—, and co-chmn., project devel. and fin. Bd. dirs. Bush Mfg. Co., Detroit, Off Site Tech. Inc., Detroit, OFLA Receivables Corp., San Diego, Hercules (Cayman) Ltd., Cayman Islands. Mem. Internat. Bar Assn., Minn. Bar Assn., N.Y. Athletic Club. Republican. Roman Catholic. Office: Dorsey & Whitney 250 Park Ave New York NY 10177-1500 Office Phone: 212-415-9285. Office Fax: 212-953-7201. Business E-Mail: marx.owen@dorsey.com.

**MARX, PATRICIA ANNE,** education educator; d. August Frederick and Anna (Drol) Bianchi; m. Ronald Allen Marx; 1 child from previous marriage, Christopher D. Graham. BA, William Patterson U., 1969, M, 1976. Advanced profl. cert. Md. State Bd. Edn., Annapolis, Md., 2005. Tchr. grades 4 and 5 Greenwood Elem. Sch., Montgomery County, Md., 2000—. Presenter in field. Co-author: A Place to Hang Our Hats, Educational Leadership, 1998. Tchr.; mentor, 1990—; peer coaching demonstrator PG Co. Bd. Edn., Langley Park, Md., 1995—98. Nominee Disney Tchr. of Yr. award, 1999, 2000, 2004, Christa McAuliffe Outstanding Tchr. award, 2000. Home: 9530 Brigadoon Ln Frederick MD 21704 Office Phone: 301-924-3145. Personal E-mail: pmarteach@aol.com.

**MARX, RICHARD,** vocalist, musician; b. Chgo., Sept. 16, 1963; Songwriter, prodr., musician, singer; founder Signal 21 Records, 1999—. Musician: (albums) Richard Marx, 1987 (nominee Grammy award Best Male Rock Vocal Performance, 1988), Repeat Offender, 1989 (triple platinum album, nominee Grammy award Best Male Pop Vocal Performance, 1989), Rush Street, 1991, Paid Vacation, 1994 (platinum album), Flesh & Bone, 1997, Greatest Hits, 1997, Days in Avalon, 2000, The Best of Richard Marx, 2000, Ballads, 2003, My Own Best Enemy, 2004; appeared on: Dance with My Father, by Luther Vandross, 2003 (Grammy award Song of Yr., 2003).

**MARX, THOMAS GEORGE,** economist; b. Trenton, NJ, Oct. 25, 1943; s. George Thomas and Ann (Szymanski) Marx; m. Arlene May Varga, Aug. 23, 1969; children: Melissa Ann, Thomas Jeffrey, Jeffrey Alan. BS summa cum laude, Rider Coll., 1969; PhD, U. Pa., 1973. Fin. analyst Am. Cyanamid Co., Trenton, 1968; economist FTC, Washington, 1973; econ. cons. Foster Assocs. Inc., Washington, 1974-77; sr. economist GM, Detroit, 1977-79, mgr. indsl. econs., 1980-81, dir. econs. policy studies, 1981-83, dir. corp. strategic planning group, 1984-86, gen. dir. market analysis and forecasting, 1986-88, gen. dir. econ. analysis, 1988-90, gen. dir. issues mgmt. on industry govt. rels. staff, 1990-96, dir. econ. issues and analysis corp. affairs staff, 1996-97, dir. global climate issue, 1997—2005; dir., doctor of bus. adminstrn. prog. and sr. adminstrn. Coll. of Mgmt., Lawrence Tech. U., 2006—. Mem. faculty Temple U., Phila., 1972—73, U. Pa., Phila., 1972—73; adj. prof. Wayne State U. 1981—89, U. Detroit, 1988—, Lawrence Technol. U., 2005—. Assoc. editor: Bus. Econs. 1980—98, mem. editl. bd.: Akron Bus. and Econs., 1981—90; contbr. articles to profl. jours. With USAF, 1961—65. Mem.: Assn. Pub. Policy Analysts, Planning Forum, Western Econ. Assn., So. Econ. Assn., Econ. Soc. Mich., Detroit Area Bus. Economists (v.p.), Nat. Assn. Bus. Economists, Am. Econ. Assn., Nat. Econs. Club, Beta Gamma Sigma, Pi Gamma Mu. Roman Catholic. Home: 3312 Bloomfield Park Dr West Bloomfield MI 48323-3514 Office Phone: 248-204-3081. Personal E-mail: tmarx@ltw.edu.

**MARYA, MANUEL PAUL CLAUDE,** metallurgical and materials engineer; b. Nantes, France, July 1, 1972; s. Surendar Kumar and Annie Jeanne Suzanne (Crouau) Marya; m. Noriko Yao, Nov. 3, 2003. DUT in Mech. & Mfg. Engring., Inst. U. Nantes, France, 1990—92; BEng in Mech. Engring., U. Quebec, Can., 1992—95; MS in Metall. & Materials Engring., Colo. Sch. Mines, Golden, 1996—99, PhD in Metall. & Materials Engring., 1999—2001. Rsch. asst. Colo. Sch. Mines, Golden, Colo., 1996—2001, postdoctoral fellow, 2002, rsch. asst. prof., 2002—04; vis. scientist Gen. Motors Rsch. & Devel., Warren, Mich., 2002—04; sr. tech. staff Nanocoolers Inc., Austin, Tex., 2004—. Engring. trainee ECN Centre LASER, Nantes, France, 1990—94; rsch. asst. U. Nottingham, England, 1995; material & welding rsch. cons. Ecole Centrale Nantes, France, 1996—. Contbr. over 40 articles to profl. jours. and internat. conf. proceedings, chapters to books. Recipient Henry Granjon award, Internat. Inst. Welding, 2002; grantee, Ford, Visteon, Gen. Motors 2004—2004. Fellow: Am. Welding Soc.; mem.: Am. Soc. for Materials. Achievements include research in Magnesium Joining, Laser Processing Research, Alloy and Liquid Metal Development, Materials Processing, Coatings and Corrosion, etc; patents pending for Liquid Alloys, Product Development. Avocations: travel, art, reading. Home: 10801 Old Manchaca Rd Austin TX 78748 Office: Nano-Coolers Inc 5307 Industrial Oaks Blvd Ste 100 Austin TX 78735 Office Fax: 512-583-2075. Personal E-mail: mpmarya@hotmail.com. E-mail: mmarya@nanocoolers.com.

**MARYANSKI, FRED J.,** academic administrator; BA in Math., Providence Coll.; MA in Computer Sci., Stevens Inst. Tech.; PhD in Computer Sci., U. Conn. Faculty U. Conn., Storrs, 1983—; provost, 1999—2004; pres. Nev. State Coll., Henderson, 2005—. With Digital Equipment Corp., 1986—89. Office: Nev State Coll 1125 Nevada State Dr Henderson NV 89015

**MARYKS, ROBERT A.,** history professor; b. Torun, Poland, Nov. 9, 1967; s. Zbigniew Antoni and Leokadia Maryks. MA, U. Warsaw, 1992; BA in Theology, Pontificia Facoltà Teologica, Naples, 2001; PhD, Fordham U., 2005. State dipl. Spanish Ministry Of Edn. Spain, 1993, state dipl. Italian Inst. Italian Lang. and Culture, 2002. Prof. Latin, Italian and religion H.S., Warsaw, 1989—91; prof. religion Naples, 1994—96; prof. Italian Italian Embassy, Sarajevo, Bosnia-Herzegovina, 1996—97; tchg. asst. Fordham U., New York, 2003—04, tchg. fellow, 2004—05; adj. prof. Yeshiva U., New York, 2005—06, asst. prof., 2006—. Dir.: (festival) Internat. Ignatian Youth Festival and Miriam Makeba's Concert, Children Mine Victims Aid Program; co-organizer Princess Diana's visit to Sarajevo; translator: (book translation) John W. O'Malley's Trent And All That. Fellow rsch. assistantship and Presdl. scholarship; tchg. assistantship, Fordham U., 2002—05; grantee, 2005. Mem.: Am. Hist. Assn., Sixteenth Century Soc. and Conf., Renaissance Soc. Am. E-mail: rmaryks@yahoo.com.

**MARYLES, DAISY,** editor; B, City Coll. NY. Joined Publishers Weekly, NYC, 1965—, dept. editor, News, Bookselling, Mktg., exec. editor, 1986—. Author: (columns) Behind the Booksellers, Publishers Weekly. Recipient Harry Scherman Lifetime Svc. award, UJA-Fedn. NY pub. divsn., 2005. Office: Publishers Weekly 13th Fl 360 Park Ave S New York NY 10010-1710 Office Phone: 646-746-6767. Office Fax: 646-746-6631. Business E-Mail: dmaryles@reedbusiness.com.

**MARZIO, PETER CORT,** museum director; b. Governor's Island, N.Y., May 8, 1943; s. Francis and Katherine (Mastroberte) M.; m. Frances Ann Parker, July 2, 1979; children: Sara Lon, Steven Arnold. BA, Juniata Coll., 1965; MA, U. Chgo., 1966, PhD, 1969. Rsch. asst. to dir., then historian Nat. Mus. History and Tech., Smithsonian Instn., 1969-73, assoc. curator prints, 1977-78, chmn. dept. cultural history, 1978; dir., CEO Corcoran Gallery Art, Washington, 1978-82; dir. Mus. Fine Arts, Houston, 1982—. Instr. Roosevelt U., Chgo., 1966-68; assoc. prof. U. Md., 1967-70; chmn. Fed. Coun. on Arts and Humanities, 1997-2000. Author: Rube Goldberg: His Life and Works, 1973, The Art Crusade, 1976, The Democratic Art: An Introduction to the History of Chromolithography in America, 1979; editor: A Nation of Nations, 1976. Bd. dirs. Wallace Found. Sr. Fulbright fellow, Italy, 1973-74. Mem. Cosmos Club (Washington), Coronado Club (Houston), Assn. of Art Museum Directors (pres. 1988-89). Office: Mus Fine Arts 1001 Bissonet St PO Box 6826 Houston TX 77265-6826 Office Phone: 713-639-7300. E-mail: pmarzio@mfah.org.*

**MARZORATI, GERALD,** editor; b. Patterson, NJ, Feb. 8, 1953; BA, Villanova U., 1975. Editor SoHo (NY) News, Harper's Mag., NY, New Yorker Mag., 1994—98; editl. dir. NY Times Mag., NYC, 1998—2003, editor, 2003—06, asst. mng. editor, 2006—. Author: A Painter of Darkness: Leon Golub and Our Times, 1990 (PEN/Martha Albrand award). Office: The New York Times 229 W 43rd St New York NY 10036-3959*

**MARZULLI, JOHN ANTHONY, JR.,** lawyer; b. Orange, NJ, Jan. 3, 1953; s. John Anthony Sr. and Ruth Eileen (Dyer) M.; m. Penelope Bennett, Dec. 13, 1986; children: Emily Mooers, John A. III, Peter Bennett. BA magna cum laude, Middlebury Coll., 1975; JD, NYU Sch. Law, 1978. Bar: NJ 1978, NY 1979. Law clk. to Hon. George H. Barlow, Hon. Clarkson S. Fisher, and Hon. Anne E. Thompson US Dist. Ct., NJ, 1978-80; assoc. atty. Shearman & Sterling LLP, NYC, 1980-87, pntr., 1988—, chair, marketing com., head, UK mergers and acquisitions group London, 1990—96. Contbg. author: Corporate Restructuring, 1990, European Corporate Finance Law, 1990. Mem. ABA, NY State Bar Assn., Bar Assoc. City of NY, NJ Bar Assn., Order of Coif, Phi Beta Kappa. Office: Shearman & Sterling LLP 599 Lexington Ave New York NY 10022-6069 Office Phone: 212-848-8590. Office Fax: 646-848-8590. E-mail: jmarzulli@shearman.com

**MÁS, BEVERLEY BERLIN,** career planning advisor, counseling advisor; d. Hubert Irl Willits and Irene Ethel LaRue; m. Oscar Más, Apr. 30, 1977. BA in Psychology summa cum laude, Fla. Atlantic U., 2002. Secretarial supr. Ir. II & Manella Law Firm, Century City, Calif., 1981—91; freelance manuscript editor Palm Beach Gardens, Fla., 1991—99; academic advisor and counselor Palm Beach C.C., Palm Beach Gardens, 2002—, tutor English, biology, anatomy/physiology, 2002—; freelance life coach Palm Beach Gardens, 2002—. Trainer-recruiter Literacy Coalition Palm Beach County, Jupiter, Fla., 2000—02; presenter in field. Author short stories and poems. Group facilitator Murder and Suicide Survivors, L.A., 1994—95, Suicide Survivors, L.A., 1994—95; organizer Psychology Club Palm Beach C.C., Palm Beach Gardens, 1998—99, contbg mem. of president's strategic planning team, 1998—99, coll. amb. and student liaison; organizer of svc. of food and fin. svc. to needy families in cmty., v.p. of svc. Phi Theta Kappa Internat. Honors Soc., Palm Beach Gardens, 1998—99; ann. neighborhood vol. Am. Heart Assn., Palm Beach Gardens, 1999—2003, Am. Cancer Soc., Palm Beach Gardens, 1999—2003; leader Spl. Olympics, North Palm Beach, Fla., 1999—2000; organizer Halloween and Christmas parties for abused and underprivileged children Palm Beach County, Palm Beach Gardens, 1999—99; leader, vol. program for after-school tutorage Am. Reads Program, Jupiter, Fla., 2000—02; honoree, spkr., program presenter Nat. Collegiate Honors Coun. Nat. Convention, Chgo.; presenter Cognitive Aging Conf., Atlanta, 2000; v.p. Glenwood Homeowners' Assn., Palm Beach Gardens, 1998—99. Named Disting. Alumna, Harriet L. Wilkes Honors Coll., Fla. Atlantic U., 2004, 2005, Fla. Atlantic U., 2005; named to All USA Academic First Team, USA Today, 1999, All Fla. Academic First Team, Fla. State Legislature, 1999; recipient Spl. commendation as outstanding scholar in Ho. Resolution No. 9053, State Fla. Ho. Reps., 1999, State Poetry award, Fla. Collegiate Honors Coun., 2002, winning short story, Twentieth Century Lit. Conf., U. Louisville, Ky., 2002, Editors Choice award, Internat. Poetry Assn., 2005; scholar, Harriet L. Wilkes Honors Coll., Fla. Atlantic U., 2001; Guistewhite Scholar of the Yr., Phi Theta Kappa Internat. Honor Soc., 1999, Frederick DeHon scholar. Mem.: APA (life), SAG (life), Women in Film. (assoc.), Fed. Assn. Cmty. Colls. (assoc.), Greater Found. Women's Coun. (life), People for the Ethical Treatment of Animals (life), Physicians' Com. for Responsible Medicine (life), Soc. for the Study of Peace, Conflict, and Violence (life), Nat. Alliance for the Mentally Ill (life), Am. Fed. Variety Artists (life), Amnesty Internat. (life; women's action coun.), Psi Beta (v.p.

and chair edn. activities), Golden Key, Phi Kappa Phi, Phi Theta Kappa (Guistewhite scholar of the Yr. 1999), Nat. Soc. Collegiate Scholars (life). Achievements include research in age difference in effects of gaze avers; effects of age and encoding context on recognition of nouns and verbs; Aging and memory for self-performed tasks: effects of task difficulty and time pressure; Organizer of first Dream It Do It Club in nation (support group for non traditonal students). Home: 1502 15th Terr Palm Beach Gardens FL 33418-3613 Office: Palm Beach Community College 3160 PGA Blvd Palm Beach Gardens FL 33410-2893 Office Phone: 561-207-5338. E-mail: masb@pbcc.edu.

**MASA, GEORGE JOHN,** retired bank executive; b. Chgo., Apr. 29, 1947; s. George John Sr. and Barbara Ann (Kos) M.; m. Judy Ann Martin, Apr. 24, 1971; children: Kimberly Janine, Kristin Marie. BS in Commerce, De Paul U., 1969; cert. banking, Rutgers U., 1979; cert. mgmt., Pa. State U., 1987. Field bank examiner FDIC, Chgo., 1969-77, rev. examiner, 1977-82, asst. regional dir. Dallas, 1982-85, asst. dir. policy Washington, 1985-86, asst. dir. ops., 1986-89, regional dir. Chgo., 1989-91, San Francisco, 1991—2002; ret., 2002; dir. Gateway Bank, 2003. With USAR, 1970-76. Personal E-mail: gjmasa@aol.com.

**MASAGUTOV, VAKHID ERKINJONOVICH,** application developer; s. Erkinjon G Nazarov and Rumiya V Masagutova. BS in math. and computer sci., N.Mex State U., 1998—2002; Math Advanced Study, Pa. State U., 2000. Tester/ programmer IBM, Durham, NC, 2001; intern Charles River Analytics, Cambridge, 2003—04. Programmer Phys. Sci. Lab., Las Cruces, N.Mex., 1999—2002. VIGRE Grad fellowship, Purdue U., 2003. Achievements include development of algorithms for network reliability analysis. Personal E mail: vmasagut@math.purdue.edu.

**MASAKI, TAKAHISA,** translation company executive, educator; b. Kobe, Hyogo, Japan, Jan. 19, 1962; s. Hiroyuki and Keiko Masaki; m. Chieri Ogitani, Mar. 10, 1955. PhD, Hokkaido U., Sapporo, Japan, 1992. Co-chief rsch. divsn. Ishizu Seiyaku, Osaka, Japan, 1991—93; instr. medicine U. Utah, Salt Lake City, 1999—2001, rsch. asst. prof., 2001—; pres. Transl. SLEJ, 2001—. Pres. Utah Daigaku Japanese Assn., Salt Lake City, 2006—. Recipient Young Investigator award, Nat. Kidney Found., 2000—02, Forefronts Nephrology Symposium travel award, Internat. Soc. Nephrology, 2000; grantee, Nat. Kidney Found. Idaho & Utah, 2000—05. Mem.: Internat. Soc. Stem Cell Rsch. (assoc.), Am. Soc. Nephrology (assoc.). Achievements include patents for diagnosis kits. Avocations: skiing, golf, tennis, travel, gardening. Office Phone: 801-582-1565 5380. Personal E-mail: ctmasaki@hotmail.com.

**MASAND, PRAKASH S.,** psychiatrist, researcher; b. Bombay; US, 1984; s. Sham Masand; m. Sonia Masand; 1 child, Natasha. MD, Topiwala Nat. Med. Coll., Bombay, 1982. Cert. Am. Bd. Psychiatry and Neurology, 1990. Resident in psychiatry SUNY Upstate Med. U., Syracuse, 1985—88, prof. psychiatry, 1989—2001; fellowship in consultation liaison psychiatry Mass. Gen. Hosp., Harvard Med. Sch., 1988—99; consulting prof. psychiatry Duke U. Med. Ctr., Durham, NC, 2001—. Sect. editor Current Psychiatry Reports, Phila., 2002—. Contbr. chapters to books, articles to profl. jours. Local candidate fund raiser, Chapel Hill, NC. Named Tchr. of Yr., Dept. Psychiatry SUNY Upstate Med. U., 1990, 1996; named one of Americas Top Psychiatrists, 2004—05, Best Doctors in Am., 2005—06. Fellow: Am. Psychiat. Assn. Office: Psychcme Ste 1 110 Swift Ave Durham NC 27705 Office Phone: 919-286-3066.

**MASAOKA, JAN,** not-for-profit executive; BA, San Francisco State U. Regional dir. US–China Friendship Assn., 1978—80; bus. mgr. Cognos Assocs., 1982—83; fin. dir. Advocates for Women, 1983—85; dir. cons. svcs. Support Ctr. for Nonprofit Mgmt., 1988—90; exec. dir. CompassPoint Nonprofit Svcs., San Francisco, 1993—. Lectr. Grad. Sch. of Pub. Adminstrn. Golden Gate U., 1987—96. Writer, editor Board Café, 1999—, mem. nat. editl. adv. com. BoardSource, 1999—; contbr. articles to profl. jours. Chair bd. dirs. Asian & Pacific Islander Wellness Ctr.; founding pres., mem. bd. dirs. San Francisco Found. Cmty. Initiative Funds. Named Nonprofit Exec. of Yr, NonProfit Times, 2002; recipient Robert E. Kantor Medal, Pacific Grad. Sch. Psychology, 2000, Woman Warrior, Pacific Asian Am. Women's Bay Area Coalition, 2002; grantee Gerbode Fellowship, Sch. of Social Work, U. Calif., Berkeley, 2001. Office: CompassPoint Nonprofit Svcs Ste 200 731 Market St San Francisco CA 94103 Office Phone: 415-541-9000. Office Fax: 415-541-7780.*

**MASCETTA, JOSEPH ANTHONY,** principal; b. Canonsburg, Pa., Sept. 2, 1931; s. Joseph Alphonso and Amalia (Ciavarra) M.; m. Jean Verrone, June 18, 1960; children: Lisa Marie, Linda Jo, Lori Jean. BS, U. Pitts., 1954; MS, U. Pa., 1963; cert. advanced study, Harvard U., 1970. Cert. tchr. math., phys. scis.; adminstr. secondary sch., Pa. Tchr. chemistry Canonsburg High Sch., 1956-59, Mt. Lebanon High Sch., Pitts., 1959-75, chair sci. dept., 1967-75; coord. secondary curriculum Mt. Lebanon Sch. Dist., Pitts., 1975-81; prin. Mt. Lebanon Sr. High Sch., Pitts., 1981-91; ret., 1991; ednl. cons., 1991—. Vis. team Mid. States Assn. Colls. and Schs., Phila., 1967-78, chair vis. teams, 1981-96, Pa. state adv. com., 1988-91; sch. bd. and edn. commn. St. Patrick Sch., Canonsburg, 1972-85, 95-2002; tchr. undergrad. and grad. courses Duquesne U., Pitts., 1975-81; regional dir. Pa. Jr. Acad. Sci., Pitts., 1976-82; ednl. cons. Pitts. area schs., 1992—; quality edn. com. Pitts. Diocese, 1995-97. Author: Modern Chemistry Review, 1968, Chemistry the Easy Way, 1989, rev. edit., 2003, Barron's SAT II, Chemistry, 1994, 8th rev. edit., 2006; contbg. author: (ency.) Barron's Student Concise Ency., 1988, rev. 1994, Barron's New Student's Concise Ency., 1993, Perry Como Commemorative Booklet, 1998. Recipient Outstanding Tchr. award Spectroscopy Soc., 1973; grantee NSF, 1961, 62-63, 63, 67, 69 70, 73; nat. fellow GE, 1959 Mem. ASCD, Nat. Assn. Secondary Sch. Prins. (cert. recognition 1991), Pa. Assn. Curriculum & Supervision (exec. bd. dirs. 1985-87, regional pres. 1987), Western Pa. Assn. Curriculum & Supervision (v.p. 1983-85, pres. 1985-87, exec. bd. dirs. 1989-2001), Greater Canonsburg Heritage Soc., Italian-Am. Heritage and Cultural Soc. Washington County (chair scholarship com. 1992—), Phi Delta Kappa. Roman Catholic. Avocations: painting, writing. Home: 451 McClelland Rd Canonsburg PA 15317-2258 E-mail: jmascett@bellatlantic.net.

**MASCHERONI, ELEANOR EARLE,** marketing communications executive; b. Boston, June 6, 1955; d. Ralph II and Eleanor Forbes (Owens) Earle; m. Mark Mascheroni, May 30, 1981; children: Olivia Forbes, Isabella Starbuck, Rex Owens. AB, Brown U., 1977. Dept. adminstr. Sotheby Parke Bernet, N.Y.C., 1978-79; asst. dir. devel. Inst. Architecture and Urban Studies, N.Y.C., 1979-81; assoc. in pub. rels. Prudential Securities Inc., N.Y.C., 1981-84, asst. v.p., 1984-86, assoc. v.p., 1986-87, v.p., mgr., 1987-89, 1st v.p., dir. corp. commns., 1989—91; v.p. corp. comms. Zurich Scudder Investments, Inc., N.Y.C., 1991-95, prin., sr. v.p., dir. corp. comms., 1996-99, mng. dir., 1999—2001; CMO Ogilvy & Mather, 2001—. N.Y. Alumnae bd. govs. St. Timothy's Sch., Stevenson, Md., 1994—; trustee Hartley House, 2000—. Avocations: running, photography. Office Phone: 212-237-7239. Business E-Mail: eleanor.mascheroni@ogilvy.com

**MASCI, JOSEPH RICHARD,** medical educator; b. New Brunswick, N.J., Nov. 27, 1950; s. Joseph Nicholas and Delfina (Musa) M.; m. Elizabeth Bass, May 21, 1993; 1 child, Jonathan Samuel. BA, Cornell U., 1972; MD, NYU, 1976. Diplomate Am. Bd. Internal Medicine, Am. Bd. Infectious Diseases. Instr. medicine Boston U. Sch. Medicine, 1979—80, Mt. Sinai Sch. Medicine, NYC, 1982—84, asst. prof. clin. medicine, 1984—88, asst. prof. medicine, 1988—90, assoc. prof. medicine, 1990—2003; chief infectious diseases, 1999—2002; assoc. dir. medicine Elmhurst (NY) Hosp. Ctr., 1987—2002, dir. medicine, 2002—. Peer reviewer NIH, 1994—. Author: Primary and Ambulatory Care of the HIV-Infected Adult, 1992, Outpatient Management of HIV-Infection, 2d edit., 1996, 3d edit., 2001, Bioterrorism: A Guide for Hospital Preparedness, 2005. Recipient Dr Linda Laubenstien

award for Excellence in AIDS Care, 2002. Fellow Am. Coll. Chest Physicians; mem. ACP, Am. Soc. Microbiology, Assn. Program Dirs. Internal Medicine, Assn. Profs. of Medicine. Office: Elmhurst Hosp Ctr 79-01 Broadway Elmhurst NY 11373-1329

**MASDEU, JOSE CRUZ,** neurologist, health facility administrator; b. Madrid, Sept. 15, 1946; arrived in U.S., 1972; s. Jose and Maria Luisa Masdeu. MD, U. Madrid, 1969. Diplomate Am. Bd. Psychiatry and Neurology. Resident neurology Chgo. Med. Sch., 1972—75; fellow neuropathology Peter Bent Brigham Hosp., 1976—77; sect. chief neurology Hines VA Hosp., Ill., 1978—82; asst. prof. neurology Loyola U., 1978—82; head neurology sect. North Ctrl. Bronx (N.Y.) Hosp., 1982—87; assoc. attending staff Montefiore Med. Ctr., Bronx, 1982—87; assoc. prof. neurology Einstein, 1982—87; dir. neurology St. Vincent's Hosp./Med. Ctr., N.Y.C., 1987—; attending staff, clin. prof. neurology Bellevue Hosp./NYU Med. Ctr., N.Y.C., 1987—; prof., chmn. neurology dept. N.Y. Med. Coll./West County Med. Ctr., Valhalla, 1991—. Author (with C. Gonzalez, C.B. Grossman): Head and Spine Imaging, 1985; author: (with P. Brazis, J. Biller) Localization in Neurology, 4 edits., 1985—2001; author: (with L. Sudarsky, L. Wolfson) Gait Disturbances of Aging, 1997; editor-in-chief The HyperText Neurological Knowledgebase, 1999; co-editor: Encyclopedia of the Neurological Sciences, 2003; contbr. Named Outstanding New Citizen of Yr., Chgo. Citizenship Coun., 1977, Among Best Neurologists in N.Y., N.Y. Mag., 1991, 1996, Among 22 Best Neurologists in U.S., Am. Health Mag., 1996. Mem.: World Fedn. Neurology (chmn. neuroimaging rsch. group 1997—), Am. Soc. Neuroimaging (pres. 1994—96), Am. Acad. Neurology (chmn. neuroimaging sect. 1996—, chmn. subcom. practice com. 1990—, bd. dirs.). Roman Catholic. Avocation: Avocations: tennis, golf. Address: Neurology CUN Avda Pio XII 31008 Pamplona Spain

**MASEAR, CLAUDE,** music educator, musician; b. Bklyn., Mar. 16, 1964; s. Clyde Benjamin and Elizabeth Demetriades Masear. MusB cum laude, Bklyn. Coll., 1988, MusM, 1991—91; cert. in Sch. Adminstrn. and Supr., Bklyn. Coll., 1993; EdD, Columbia U., 1999; diploma in Ednl. Adminstrn., Coll. New Rochelle, 2001. Cert. music tchr. N.Y., 1992, sch. adminstr./Supervisor N.Y., 1998. Music educator Intermediate Sch. N.Y. City Schs., Hollis, NY, 1988—90, music educator Intermediate Sch Bklyn., 1990—91; music educator Lawrence (N.Y.) Pub. Schs., 1992, Hicksville (N.Y.) Pub. Schs., 1992—93, 1994—95, Huntington (N.Y.) Pub. Schs., 1993—94, 1995—. Asst. dir. Salute To Music Program N.Y. State Schs., Bklyn., 1990—93; concert master Spirit Improvisation Ensemble Columbia U., N.Y., 1995—; lectr. music edn. Bklyn. (N.Y.) Coll., Bklyn., 1996; presenter, balanced Mind Conf. L.I. U. C.W. Post Coll., 2001. Author: The Development And Field Test Of A Model For Evaluating Elementary String Programs, 1999; composer: (songs) Funky Town (Gold award N.Y. State Maj. Orgn. Festival, 1997), Rock Around The Clock (Silver award N.Y. State Maj. Orgn. Festival, 2000); musician Bouree For Solo Violin; conducted: Queens Borowide Concert, 1999. Coach 68 Precint Police Athletic League Youth Coun., Bklyn., 1981—93. Scholar, Teachers Coll., Columbia U., 1994. Mem.: N.Y. State Sch. Music Assn. (assoc.), Kappa Delta Pi (assoc.). Greek Orthodox. Achievements include development of standards for string instruction grades3-12; design of program evaluation models for public school music programs. Avocations: exercise, music, travel, cooking, languages. Office: Huntington Public Schools Woodhul Road Huntington NY 11743 Home: 12 College Dr Stony Brook NY 11790-2724 Office Phone: 631-673-2030. Personal E-mail: clmaedd@aol.com.

**MASEFIELD, OLIVER LESLIE PETER,** aerospace transportation executive, aerospace engineer; b. London, June 10, 1948; BSc in Aero. Engring., Loughborough U. of Tech., Loughborough, Leics, Eng., 1972; PhD in Aerodynamics, Loughborough U. of Tech., 1991. Chartered engr., Royal Aero. Soc., UK, 1978. Future projects engr. Hawker Siddeley Aviation, Kingston, Surrey, England, 1972—73; v.p. R & D Pilatus Aircraft Ltd, 6370 Stans, Switzerland, 1973—99; v.p. eclipse engring. Williams Internat., Walled Lake, Mich., 2000—01; v.p. engring. Eclipse Aviation Corp., Albuquerque, 2000—04; sr. v.p. Eclipse Aviation Corp, 2004—, sr, fellow, 2004—. Study group mem. Joint Aviation Authority, 1991—99; bd. mem., dir. Dynamic Test Centre, Biel, Bern, Switzerland, 1997—99; adv. bd. Mech. Engring., U. N.Mex., Albuquerque, 2002—; designated engring. rep., mech. sys., flight analyst FAA, 2006. Internat. editor (periodical) Jour. of Aircraft. Fellow: Royal Aero. Soc.; mem.: AIAA, Internat. Coun. of Aero. Scis. (program com. mem. 1990—), Internat. Coun. of Aero. Scis. (coun. mem. 1986—99), Swiss Soc. of Aero. Scis. (coun. mem. 1986—99). Achievements include led team which developed Pilatus PC-7, PC-9, PC-12 and PC-7 Mk II aircraft; led Pilatus team in partnership with Beech Aircraft, which obtained contract for JPATS trainer aircraft for USAF & USN; led team which first introduced Friction Stir Welding production in aviation; led team whic developed revolutionary Eclipse 500 personal jet aircraft. Avocations: reading, snow-boarding, squash, windsurfing, walking. Home: 819 El Alhambra Cir NW Albuquerque NM 87107 Office: Eclipse Aviation Corp 2503 Clark Carr Loop SE Albuquerque NM 87106 Office Phone: 505-724-1239. E-mail: oliver.masefield@eclipseaviation.com.

**MASEKELA, BARBARA JOYCE MOSIMA,** ambassador; 2 children. B, U. of Ohio. Chief of staff to Nelson Mandela, 1990—94; exec. dir. for public and corp. affairs De Beers Consol. Mines (ret. 2003); South African amb. to France and UNESCO, 1995—99, to the U.S., Washington, 2003—. Asst. prof. of English lit. Staten Island CC, NY, Rutgers U., NJ; trustee Nelson Mandela Children's Fund, Nelson Mandela Found.; various exec. and non-exec. directorships including Standard Bank of South Africa, South African Broadcasting Corp., and Internat. Mktg. Coun., 1999—2003. Achievements include founding African Nat. Congress Office of Arts and Culture. Office: Embassy of South Africa 3051 Mass Ave NW Washington DC 20008

**MASELLI, JOHN ANTHONY,** food products executive; b. N.Y.C., Feb. 18, 1928; s. Anthony and Livia M.; m. Brigitta Degenkolb, Dec. 26, 1948; children: Elisa, John A. Jr. BS in Chemistry, CCNY, 1947; MS in Chemistry, Fordham U., 1949, PhD in Chemistry, 1952. Dir. research and devel. Standard Brands, Stamford, Conn., 1952-64; mgr. product devel. M&M/Mars, Hack-ettstown, NJ, 1964-67; pres. OZ Food Corp., Chgo., 1967-79; v.p. tech. Nabisco Brands, East Hanover, NJ, 1979-85; v.p. corp. research and devel. RJR Nabisco, Winston-Salem, NC, 1985-87; sr. v.p. tech. Planters LifeSavers Co., Winston-Salem, 1987-91, cons., 1991—. Bd. dirs. Cultor Food Scis. (Finland), N.C. Biotech. Ctr., Sci-Works, Winston Salem, Winston Salem Symphony. Patentee in field. Bd. dirs. Chgo. Boy's Club, 1975-79, YMCA, Wilton, Conn, 1980-84. Mem. AAAS, ACS, Inst. Food Tech., Am. Soc. Bakery Engrs., Indsl. Biotechnology Assn., Indsl. Research Inst. Republican. Avocations: sailing, photography, music. Home: 529 Knob View Pl Winston Salem NC 27104-5107

**MASERITZ, GUY B.,** lawyer; b. Balt., June 5, 1937; m. Sally Jane Sugar, Mar. 30, 1961; children: Marjorie Ellen, Michael Louis. BA, Johns Hopkins U., 1959, MA in Econs., 1961; LLB, U. Md., 1966. Bar: Md. 1966, D.C. 1968, U.S. Supreme Ct. 1975, U.S. Dist. Ct. Md. 1979. Atty. SEC, Washington, 1966-70; asst. gen. counsel securities Am. Life Ins. Assn., Washington, 1971-74; atty. eval. sect., chief legis. unit antitrust divsn. U.S. Dept. Justice, Washington, 1974-78, spl. asst. U.S. atty. Alexandria, Va., 1978; pvt. practice Columbia, Md., 1978—. Author: U.S. Department of Justice Antitrust Report on Property-Liability Insurance Industry, 1977; contbr. articles to profl. jours. Mem. Howard County (Md.) Charter Revision Commn., 1979; bd. dirs. Howard County YMCA, 1997-99, disting. bd. mem. 1999; mem. Am. Inn of Ct., 2005—. With USAR, 1960-66. Mem. Md. Bar Assn., D.C. Bar Assn., Howard County Bar Assn., Greater Howard County C. of C. (dir., gen. counsel 1981-84). Office: Hobbits Glen 5040 Rushlight Path Columbia MD 21044-1295 Office Phone: 410-997-9400. Business E-Mail: consult@maseritzlaw.com.

**MASERU, NOBLE A.W.,** city health department administrator; b. Detroit; BS, Wayne State U.; MPH, Emory U. Sch. Medicine; PhD in Health Policy, Atlanta U. Founding dir., master of pub. health program Morehouse Sch.

Medicine, Atlanta; health policy scientist Morehouse Coll., Pub. Health Scis. Inst.; v.p., cmty. health Greater Detroit Area Health Coun. Inc., 1998—2000; dir. and health officer Detroit Dept. Health and Wellness Promotion, 2003—. Office: Detroit Dept Health & Wellness Promotion Herman Kiefer Health Complex 1151 Taylor Detroit MI 48202 Office Phone: 313-876-4300.

**MASEY, JACK,** exhibition designer; b. N.Y.C., June 10, 1924; s. Max and Anna Masey; m. Beverly Payeff-Masey, March 20, 2003. Student, Cooper Union, 1941-43; BFA, Yale U., 1950. Pres. MetaForm LLC, N.Y.C., 1979—; co. project mgr. for design of La. Pavilion, World Expo., New Orleans, 1984, Statue of Liberty Exhibit, N.Y.C., 1986; project mgr. for design Johnstown (Pa.) Flood Mus., 1988, Ellis Island Immigration Mus., N.Y.C., 1990; co. project mgr. for design of Nat. D-Day Mus., New Orleans, 1994, designer D-Day Invasion, Pacific Exhbn., 2000; co. project mgr. for design of Harry S. Truman Mus., Independence, Mo., 2001. Lectr. Sch. Art and Arch., Yale U., 1968—69; design cons. State Hermitage Mus., St. Petersburg, Russia, 1998; project mgr. design Fly-Girls of WWII exhibn. The Mighty Eighth Air Force Mus., Savannah, Ga., 2005. Cartoonist Esquire mag, 1946; exhibits officer, USIS, New Delhi, 1951-55; designer U.S. Pavilion, Kabul Internat. Fair, 1956; dir. design Am. Nat. Exhbn., Moscow, 1959, chief, East-West exhibits br. USIA, Washington, 1960-67; chief design U.S. Pavilion, Montreal (Que., Can.) World Expo, 1967, dep. commr. gen. for planning and design Osaka (Japan) World Expn., 1970; dir. design Am. Revolution Bicentennial Commn., Washington, 1971-73; dir. design and exhbns. Am. Revolution Bicentennial Adminstrn., 1974-77, design dir. Internat. Communication Agy., Washington, 1977—; designer: Medicine-U.S.A. exhbn. for, USSR exchange program, 1962, Tech.-Books exhbns., 1963; co-designer Visitor Center, UN, 2001. Served with AUS, 1943-45, ETO. Recipient Meritorious Service award USIA, 1959, Superior Service award, 1964, Superior Honor award, 1967, 75; award of excellence Fed. Design Council, 1975; Outstanding Achievement award, 1979; award of excellence Soc. Fed. Artists and Designers, 1971; Gold medal Art Dirs. Club, 1965; cert. of excellence Am. Inst. Graphic Arts, 1964; two Fed. Design Achievement awards for Contributions to Excellence in Design, U.S. Govt., 1984, Presdl. awards for Statue of Liberty Mus., 1986, for Ellis Island Immigration Mus., 1990. Home: 131 E 66th St Apt 3A New York NY 10021-6129 also: 137 E 25th St New York NY 10010-2314 Office Phone: 212-532-8580. E-mail: jackmasey@cs.com.

**MASH, DONALD J.,** college president; b. Oct. 12, 1942; children: Maria, Christina, Donnie (dec.). BS in Edn., Ind. U. Pa., 1960; MA in Geography, U. Pitts., 1966; PhD, Ohio State U., 1974. Teaching fellow U. Pitts. 1964-65; instr. geography U. Pitts.-Bradford, 1965-68; dean for student svcs. Ohio Dominican Coll., 1968-75; v.p. for student affairs George Mason U., Fairfax, Va., 1975-85, exec. v.p. adminstrn., 1985-88; pres. Wayne (Nebr.) State Coll., 1988-98; chancellor U. Wis.-Eau Claire, 1998—2005; exec. sr. v.p. U. Wis. Sys. Office: U Wis 1730 Van Hise Hall 1220 Linden Dr Madison WI 53706-4004 Office Phone: 608-262-4049. Business E-mail: dmash@uwsa.edu.

**MASHBURN, DONALD EUGENE,** education educator; b. Johnson City, Tenn., June 10, 1944; s. Harvey and Martha (McNeese) M.; m. Mary Juanita McKee, May 30, 1970; 1 child, Donna Sue. BS, East Tenn. State U., 1965, MS, 1971. Tchr. Cocke County High Sch., Newport, Tenn., 1965-66, John S. Battle High Sch., Bristol, Va., 1966-94, Wallace Mid. Sch., Bristol, 1994-97; tech. support tchr. Meadowview (Va.) Elem. Sch., 1997-98, Rhea Valley Elem. Sch., Damascus, Va., 1997-98, Valley Inst. Elem. Sch., Bristol, Va., 1997-98, Watanga Elem. Sch., Abingdon, Va., 1997-98; with Info. Sys. and Media Prodn., Abingdon, 1998-99; tchr. Washington Coll. Acad., Limestone, Tenn., 2001; substitute tchr. Washington County (Tenn.) Schs., 2002—04. Adj. faculty N.E. State Tech. C.C., Blountville, Tenn., 1994—99. Mem. Ruritan (sec. Conklin club 1986-91, 98, 2001-06, pres. 1985, 92, 99, 2000, Davy Crockett dist. treas. 1993, zone gov. 2003-04, lt. gov. 2004, dist. gov. 2005). Republican. Methodist. Avocations: computers, farming. Home and Office: 195 Mashburn Rd Telford TN 37690-3132 E-mail: donaldmashburn@comcast.net.

**MASHBURN, JAMAL,** professional basketball player; b. N.Y.C., Nov. 29, 1972; Grad., Ky. Coll. Forward Dallas Mavericks, 1993-97, Miami Heat, 1997-99, Charlotte Hornets, 1999—2004, Phila. 76ers, 2004—. Named to NBA All-Rookie First Team, 1994. Office: New Jersey Nets Continental Airlines Arena 50 Rte 120 East Rutherford NJ 07073*

**MASHBURN, JOSEPH L.,** architecture educator; BArch, U. Houston; MArch, Tex. A&M U. Registered arch. Vis. fellow U. Western Australia Sch. Arch. and Fine Arts; arch. dept. head Curtin U. Tech., Perth, Australia; prof. arch. Va. Poly. Inst.; with Tex. A&M U.; prof. arch. U. Houston, Gerald D. Hines Coll. Arch., dean, 1998—. Named to Arch. Hall of Fame, U. Houston, 1996; recipient Outstanding Alumni award, Tex. A&M U. Coll. Arch., 2002. Mem.: AIA. Office: Univ Houston Gerald D Hines Coll Arch 4800 Calhoun Rd Houston TX 77204

**MASHECK, JOSEPH DANIEL,** art critic, educator; b. NYC, Jan. 19, 1942; s. Joseph Anthony and Dorothy Anna (Cahill) M. AB, Columbia U., 1963, MA, 1965, PhD, 1973; MLitt, U. Dublin. 2001. Editorial researcher Bollingen Found.-Princeton U. Press, 1967-69; lectr. liberal studies Maidstone Coll. Art, Kent, England, 1968-69; preceptor in art history Columbia U., 1970-71; instr. art history Barnard Coll., 1971-73, asst. prof., 1973-82; lectr. visual and environ. studies Harvard U., Cambridge, Mass., 1983-86; assoc. prof. art history Hofstra U., Hempstead, NY, 1987-94, prof., 1994—. Coord. grad. program in humanities Hofstra Mus., Hempstead, 1991—99, curatorial cons., 1991—; visiting prof. history of art Edinburgh Coll. Art, Scotland, 2006—. Centennial fellow, Scotland, 2006—. Author: Historical Present: Essays of the 1970s, 1984, Smart Art (Point 1), 1984, Modernites: Art-Matters in the Present, 1993, Building-Art: Modern Architecture Under Cultural Construction, 1993, C's Aesthetics: Philosophy in the Painting, 2004; editor: Marcel Duchamp in Perspective 1975, reprint, 2002, Van Gogh 100, 1996, A.W. Dow's Composition, 1997; editor-in-chief Artforum mag., 1977-80. Bd. dirs. Crosby St. Project, N.Y., 1995-96; mem. adv. bd. Annals of Scholarship, 1998—. Samuel H. Kress Found. fellow, 1968-69, Nat. Endowment Arts fellow, 1972-73, 75-76, Guggenheim fellow, 1977-78; grantee Malevich Soc., 2003; Hon. Armiger, Coll. Arms, London Fellow Royal Soc. Arts, Soc. Antiquaries of Scotland; mem. AAUP, Coll. Art Assn., Internat. Assn. Art Critics, Artists Club (Dublin). Roman Catholic. Democrat. Office: Hofstra U Dept Fine Arts and Art History Calkins Hall Hempstead NY 11549

**MASHHOON, BAHRAM,** physicist, researcher; b. Tehran, Iran, Sept. 9, 1947; s. Hassan Mashhoon and Nosrat Dargahi; 1 child, Yasmin. BA, U. Calif., 1969; PhD, Princeton U., 1972. Assoc. prof. U. Mo., physics dept., Columbia, 1985—95; prof. U. Mo., 1995—. Author: (nonlocal theory of accelerated observers) Physical Review A, 1993. Home: 404 Victoria Dr Columbia MO 65201 Office: Department of Physics and Astronomy University of Missouri-Columbia Columbia MO 65211 Office Phone: 573-882-6526. E-mail: mashhoonb@missouri.edu.

**MASHNIK, STEPAN G.,** physicist; b. Brinzeni, Moldova, June 1, 1952; arrived in U.S., 1996, naturalized, 2004; s. George I. and Natalia G. Mashnik; m. Nadejda I. Sukhlova; children: Polina, Daria. BS, Kishinev State U., 1973; MS, Moscow State U., 1974; PhD, Joint Inst. Nuc. Rsch., Dubna, Russia, 1981; sr. rsch. diploma, Presidium Acad. Sci. USSR, Moscow, 1989. Jr. rsch. scientist Joint Inst. Nuc. Rsch., Dubna, 1975—82, sr. rsch. scientist, 1991—97; sr./jr. rsch. Acad. Sci. Moldova, Kishinev, 1982—91, leading rsch. scientist, 1991—2004; long term vis. staff mem. Los Alamos Nat. Lab., N.Mex., 1997—2001, staff mem. 2001—. Country coord. XXVIII Internat. Conf. High Energy Physics, Hamburg, 1996—97; mem. internat. sci. coun. Joint Inst. Nuc. Rsch., Dubna, 1992—95; mem. intermediate energy data group NEA/OECD, Paris, 1994—, liaison officer between Acad. Sci. JINR, Dubna, 1996—97; vis. rschr. Oak Ridge Nat. Lab., Tenn., 1995—96, Centre d'Etudes de Bruyeres-le-Chatel, France, 1996. Contbr. articles to profl. jours. Recipient Several Excellent Work and Dubna County awards, Joint Inst. Nuc.

Rsch., 1975—82, Investigations in Theoretical Physics award, Inst. Applied Physics, Acad. Sci. Moldova, 1983, Moldova Award for Young Scientists, Am. Medal of Honor, 2003; NASA Grant, Propagation Model for Cosmic Ray Species in the Galaxy, 2002—, CRDF Grant, Devel. of a Universal Intranuclear Cascade Type Model for Heavy Ion and Nucleon Induced Reactions at Intermediate Energies, 2001—. Mem.: Phys. Soc. Republic of Moldova, Internat. Nuc. Soc., Am. Nuc. Soc., Am. Phys. Soc. Avocations: swimming, travel, skiing, jogging. Office Phone: 505-667-9946. Office Fax: 505-667-1931. Personal E-mail: mashniks@qwest.net. Business E-mail: mashnik@lanl.gov.

**MASHOUF, MANNY,** apparel executive; b. Iran; m. Neda Mashouf; 1 child, Karim. BA in Polit. Sci., San Francisco State U., 1966. Founder & chmn. Bebe Stores Inc., San Francisco, 1976—. Mem. bus. adv. bd. San Francisco State U. Coll. Creative Arts. Named one of 400 Richest Americans, Forbes, 2006; named to San Francisco State U. Hall of Fame, 2003; recipient Alumnus of Yr. award, San Francisco State U., 2005. Office: Bebe Stores Inc 400 Valley Dr Brisbane CA 94005 Office Phone: 415-715-3900. Office Fax: 415-715-3939.*

**MASHOUR, STEVE,** pulmonologist; b. Hayward, Calif., Oct. 22, 1971; s. Farideh and Reza Mashhour; 1 child, Adam Jacob. BS, U. Calif., 1994; MD. U. Nev., 1998. Diplomate Am. Bd. Internal Medicine, pulmonary disease Am. Bd. Internal Medicine, critical care medicine Am. Bd. Internal Medicine. Pulmonologist, intensivist Pulmonary Medicine Assoc., Reno, 2004—06. Mem.: Am. Coll. Chest Physicians. Avocations: hockey, skiing, travel. Office: Pulmonary Medicine Assoc 236 W 6th St #100 Reno NV 89503 Office Phone: 775-329-9010. Personal E-mail: smashour@charter.net.

**MASI, DALE A.,** social sciences educator, research and development company executive; b. NYC; d. Alphonse E. and Vera Avella; children: Eric, Renee, Robin. BS, Coll. Mt. St. Vincent; MSW, U. Ill.; PhD Social Work, Cath. U. Lectr. Sch. Social Svcs., Ipswich, Eng., 1970-72; project dir. occupational substance abuse program, asso. prof. Boston Coll. Grad. Sch. Social Work, 1972-79; dir. Office Employee Counseling Svc., Dept. Health/Human Svcs., Washington, 1979-84; pres. Masi Research Cons., Inc., 1984—2005; prof. emeritus U. Md. Grad. Sch. Social Work, 1980—2004; adj. prof. U. Md. Coll. Bus. and Mgmt., 1980—2004, prof. emeritus, 2004—; lectr. Bacconi U., Milan, 2004—. Mem. IBM Mental Health Adv. Bd., 1990-95; cons. IBM, Toyota, Mobil Chm., The Washington Post, U.S. Ho. Reps., U.S. Postal Svc., White House, WHO, Bechtel Corp., other orgns. in pub. and pvt. sector; bd. advisors Nat. Security Inst., Wayside Youth and Family Support Network; USIA Ampart lectr. on alcohol, drugs and AIDS in the workplace; chair CMHS Joint Industry Alliance, 2002—; acad. advisor Northwestern U. Author: Human Services in Industry, Organizing for Women, Designing Employee Assistance Programs, Drug Free Workplace, AIDS Issues in the Workplace: A Response Model for Human Resource Management, The AMA Handbook for Developing Employee Assistance and Counseling Programs, Evaluating Your Employee Assistance and Managed Behavioral Care Program, Internat. Employee Assistance Anthology, I, II and III edits., Productivity Lost: Alcohol and Drugs in the Workplace; co-author: Shrink to Fit: Answers to Your Questions About Therapy; also over 40 articles. Named Disting. Scholar, Nat. Acad. Practice, 2001—; named to Employee Assistance Program Hall of Fame; recipient award, Employee Assistance Program Digest; fellow Fulbright fellow, 1969—70, 1994, AAUW postdoctoral fellow, 1962—64; Fulbright Sr. Specialist Canidate, 2002. Mem. AAUW, NASW (Internat. Rhoda G. Sarnat award 1993), Acad. Cert. Social Workers, Employee Assistance Profls. Assn. (nat. individual achievement award 1983), Fulbright Assn. (nat. bd.). Democrat. Roman Catholic. Office: 4 Copley Pl Suite 145 Boston MA 02116 Office Phone: 202-223-2399, 617-536-1930.

**MASI, JANE VIRGINIA,** marketing and sales consultant; b. June 6, 1947; d. Vincent Joseph and Virginia Marie (Beddow) Masi; m. Charles Walter Friedman, Feb. 14, 1976 (div. Sept. 1998). BA in Comms. and Psychology, Mercy Coll., N.Y., 1969; MA, New Sch. Social Rsch., 1979, postgrad., 1994. Asst. sales mgr. Chevron Chem., N.Y.C., 1969-71; writer, 1973-75; prnr. Masi-D'Angelo Constrn. and Devel. Assocs., N.Y.C., 1979-83; pres., founder Beddow Mills Inc., N.Y.C., 1982-85, Beddow Mfg. Inc., N.Y.C., 1983-85; co-pres. TRS Mktg. Inc., N.Y.C., 1985—. Founder Energy Works, 1985, Did You Know, 1989, Range Burgers, 1989, Terramor, 1989, In the Pink!, 1991, The Profl. Salon, 1991, Terramor Foods, 1991, Terramor Catering, 2003; founder, dir. TRS Inc. Profl. Suite, 1986—; pub. The Planetary Gazette, 2002-Happy Healing Hours cmty. svc. events concert, 2001-. Author 38 novellas. N.Y. Regents scholar, 1965-69. Mem. Soc. Ethical Treatment of Animals. Avocations: woodworking, carpentry, advocating animal rights, design psychology. Office: TRS Mktg Inc 44 E 32nd St Fl 11 New York NY 10016-5508 Office Phone: 212-685-2848. E-mail: terramor@earthlink.net.

**MASI, ROBIN,** artist, writer, educator; b. Palo Alto, Calif., July 29, 1960; d. Joseph Louis and Dale (Avella) M.; 1 child, Benjamin Westmont. BFA, Tufts U., 1983; MFA, Acad. of Art Coll., San Francisco, 1994. Adj. faculty fine arts Regis Coll., Weston, Mass., 1994-95, Endicott Coll., Beverly, Mass., 1995-96. Vis. faculty Sch. Mus. Fine Arts, 1996—. Author: Shrink-to-Fit: Answers to Your Questions About Therapy, 1998; exhibited in Boston, N.Y., Washington, San Francisco, 1980—; author (screenplay) Searching for Judith, 1997. Dir. The Women's Artist Database Project, 1992; creator The Varo Registry of Women Artists, 1995—; moderator Feminist Art History and Women Artist Listserves, 1996—. Democrat. Roman Catholic. E-mail: rmasi@ziplink.net.

**MASIE, ELLIOTT,** training executive; b. NYC, May 13, 1950; s. Harry H. and Dorothy (Gordon) M. BA, SUNY, 1972. Cons. Irish Ministry Health, Dublin, 1972-73; project evaluator NY State Dept. Edn., NY, 1973-76; dir. Nat. Student Leadership Ctr., Raquette Lake, NY, 1977—; pres. Masie Ctr., 1991—. Cons. Disney, CIA, 1990-91, Dow Chem., NASA, Panama C.Z., Bank of Am., Nat. Assn. Secondary Sch. Prins., Washington, 1985; rsch. fellow Picturetel Corp., 1996; mem. Oracle Adv. Edn. Bd., 1996; pres. Ziff Daus Inst., 1992-94; founder On-Line Learning Coun.; mem. White House Commn. on Tng. Opportunities, Nat. Govs. Assn.'s Commn. on Learning; bd. trustees Corporate Telelink Network. Author: Computers and Student Activities, 1984, The Computer Training Handbook, 1995, Learning in the Digital Age, others; host Microsoft TV. Trustee Skidmore Coll.; bd. dirs. Operation Respect Found.; trustee Nam Inst. Mem. Assn. Computer Tng. and Support (pres., dir. 1989—, founder 1989—), Nat. Tng. & Computer Projects (bd. dir., pres. Tools for Tng. 1992). Jewish. Avocation: technology. Office: Masie Ctr PO Box 397 Saratoga Springs NY 12866-0397

**MASIELLO, ANTHONY M. (TONY MASIELLO),** former mayor; b. Buffalo, 1947; s. Dan and Bridget M.; married; 1 child, Kimberly; m. Kathleen McCue; children: Kimberly, Ariel, Madeline Rose. BS, Canisius Coll.; LHD (hon.), Medaille Coll., Buffalo. Mem. North Dist. Buffalo Common Coun., 1971, councilman-at-large, 1976, coun. majority leader; mem. NY State Senate, 1980; mayor City of Buffalo, 1994-2005. Chair Democratic Conf.*

**MASIELLO, ROCCO JOSEPH,** air transportation executive, consultant; b. N.Y.C., Jan. 9, 1922; s. Joseph and Armanda (Mansueti) M.; m. Rita Elizabeth Amoruso, Feb. 11, 1945; children: Richard, Robin, Janet. Student, CCNY, 1946-48, Hofstra U., 1951-54. Registered profl. engr., Maine. With Pan. Am. World Airways, N.Y.C., 1950-59; v.p. maintenance and engring. U.S. Air Group, Pitts., 1959—73, Am. Airlines, Tulsa, 1973-82, s.v.p. ops. Dallas, 1982-86; founder, exec. v.p. USAfrica Airways, 1990-94, also bd. dirs; founder The Reston Group; aerospace cons., prin. R.J. Masiello and Assoc. Mem. Soc. Aerospace Engr., Royal Aero. Soc. Roman Catholic. Office Phone: 207-594-5223. E-mail: rjmasiello@aol.com.

**MASILELA, CALVIN ONIAS,** land use planner, educator; b. Bulawayo, Zimbabwe, Oct. 27, 1955; s. Stephen Masilela and Martha Ndiweni; m. Sibonisiwe Ntini; children: Zwelihle, Ayanda. BA in Urban Planning,

Westminster U., London, 1980; postgrad. diploma, U. Westminster, London, 1981; M in Urban and Regl. Planning, Va. Tech. U., 1983, PhD, 1989. Vis. prof. Indiana U. Pa., 1989—90, asst. prof., 1990—93, W.Va. U., 1993—99, assoc. prof., 1999—2001, dir. Ronald E. McNair scholars program, 1999—2001. Assoc. prof. Ind. U. of Pa., Indiana, 2001—. Bd. dirs. Mon Valley Green Space Coalition, Morgantown, 2000-01, dir. IUP McNair Scholars Program, 2003—. Recipient Outstanding Educator in Conservation Monongahela Soil Conservation Dist., 1999, Cheikh Anta Diop award Ctr. for Black Culture and Rsch. 1995, Urban Indicators award Univ. Consortium for Geographic Info. Sci. U.S. HUD, 2001; named Eberly Coll. Arts and Scis. Outstanding Tchr., 2000. Mem. Am. Planning Assn., Assn. Am. Geographers, Coun. Ednl. Opportunity, Mid-Eastern Assn. Ednl. Opportunity Pers., W.Va. Assn. Ednl. Opportunity Pers, Pa. Assn. Ednl. Opportunity Pers. Office: Dept Geography and Regional Planning Indiana U of Pa Indiana PA 15705 Home: 215 College Lodge Rd Indiana PA 15701 E-mail: cmasilel@iup.edu.

**MASIN, MICHAEL TERRY,** lawyer; came to U.S., 1954; BA, Dartmouth U., 1966; JD, UCLA, 1969, D.C. 1970. Assoc. O'Melveny & Myers, L.A., 1969-76, ptnr. Washington, 1976-91, mng. ptnr. N.Y.C., 1991-93; vice chair, pres. GTE, Irving, Tex., 1993—2000; vice chmn., pres. Verizon Comms., N.Y.C., 2000—02; vice chmn., COO Citigroup, N.Y.C., 2002—03; ptnr. O'Melveny & Myers, LLP, N.Y.C., 2004—. Trustee Carnegie Hall, W.M. Keck Found.; mem. dean's coun. UCLA Sch. Law Mem. Coun. on Fgn. Rels., The Brook. Republican. Methodist. Office: O'Melveny & Myers 7 Times Sq 30th Fl New York NY 10036 E-mail: mmasin@omm.com.

**MASINO, FRANK A.,** radiation oncologist; b. Newark, 1951; MD, Albert Einstein Coll. Medicine. 1978. Bd. cert. therapeutic radiology. Intern Med. Coll. Va., Richmond, 1978; resident in radiation therapy Yale-New Haven Hosp., 1979—82; radiation oncologist Stamford (Conn.) Hosp., 1982—. Office: Stamford Hosp 34 Shelburne Rd Stamford CT 06902-3628

**MASIO, RICHARD FRANK,** sales executive, director; b. Suffern, NY, Aug. 5, 1969; s. Janet and Richard Francis Masio; m. Eileen Mary Owen, Nov. 13, 1999; children: Amelia Channing, William Barrett. BA, CUNY. Sales dir. Sheridan Sq. Entertainment, NYC, 2004—05; dir. acquisitions IODA, San Francisco, 2005—. With U.S. Army, 1987—89. Decorated Meritorius Svc. medal US Army. Mem.: Lou Proctor Rotissary League (assoc.). Progressive. Office: IODA 537 Bryant San Francisco CA 94103 Office Phone: 415-777-4632. Personal E-mail: rich@iodalliance.com.

**MASKET, EDWARD SEYMOUR,** television executive; b. N.Y.C., Mar. 3, 1923; s. Isadore and Jennie (Bernstein) M.; m. Frances Ellen Rees, June 11, 1958 (div.); children: Joel Daniel, Johanna Rees Bettaeib, Kate Isobel Smiley. BS, CCNY, 1942; LLB, JD, Harvard U., 1949. Bar: N.Y. 1949. Atty., dir. bus. affairs, v.p. bus. affairs ABC, 1951-68; v.p. to exec. v.p. Columbia Pictures TV, Burbank, Calif., 1968-81; sr. v.p. adminstrn. Universal TV, 1982-86, exec. v.p. adminstrn., 1986-90, MCA TV Group, 1990-93; TV cons., 1994—98. Served as 2d lt. AUS, 1942-46, PTO. Mem. Motion Picture Pioneers, Phi Beta Kappa. E-mail: telemogul@aol.com.

**MASKET, SAMUEL,** medical association administrator; b. NYC, 1943; MD, N.Y. Med. Coll., 1968. Diplomate Am. Bd. Ophthalmology. Intern Bronx Mcpl. Hosp.-Einstein, N.Y.C., 1968—69; resident Metro Hosp. Ctr.-N.Y. Med., 1969—73; fellow Columbia-Presbyn. Med. Ctr., N.Y.C.; asst. clin. prof. ophthalmology UCLA; mem. staff West Hills Hosp., Canoga Park, Calif.; chmn. Am. Bd. Ophthalmology, Bala Cynwyd, Pa.; clinical prof. Jules Stein Eye Inst., Los Angeles, Calif. Fellow: Am. Acad. Ophthalmology; mem.: PAAO, ASCRS, AMA. Office: Am Bd Ophthalmology 111 Presidential Blvd Ste 241 Bala Cynwyd PA 19004-1012 also: 7230 Med Ctr Dr Ste 204 Canoga Park CA 91307 Office: Jules Stein Eye Inst 100 Stein Plaza UCLA Los Angeles CA 90095

**MASKIN, ERIC STARK,** economics professor; b. N.Y.C., Dec. 12, 1950; m. Gayle Sawtelle; children: Joseph, Charlotte. AB in Maths., Harvard U., 1972, AM in Applied maths., 1974, PhD in Applied Maths., 1976. Rsch. fellow Jesus Coll. Cambridge (Eng.) U., 1976-77; asst. prof. econs. MIT, Cambridge, Mass., 1977-80, assoc. prof. econs., 1980-81, prof. econs., 1981-84, Harvard U., Cambridge, 1985—2000; prof. social sci. Inst. for Advanced Study, Princeton, NJ, 2000—. Am. editor: Rev. of Econ. Studies, 1977-82; assoc. editor: Social Choice and Welfare, 1983—, Games and Econ. Behavior, 1988—; editor Quar. Jour. of Econs., 1984-90. Jour. Risk and Uncertainty, 1987-94; editor: Econs. Letters, 1992—. Churchill Coll. fellow, 1980-81; Guggenheim fellow, 1980-81, Sloan fellow, 1983-85, St. John's Coll. fellow, 1987-88. Fellow Econometric Soc. (hon., pres. 2003), Am. Acad. Arts and Sci., Brit. Acad. (corr.); mem. Am. Econ. Assn. Office: Inst for Advanced Study Einstein Drive Princeton NJ 08540 Office Phone: 609-734-8309.

**MASLACH, CHRISTINA,** psychology professor; b. San Francisco, Jan. 21, 1946; d. George James and Doris Ann (Cuneo) M.; m. Philip George Zimbardo, Aug. 10, 1972; children: Zara, Tanya. BA, Harvard-Radcliffe Coll., 1967; PhD, Stanford U., 1971. Prof. psychology U. Calif.-Berkeley, 1971—, vice provost for undergrad. edn., 2001—. Author: Burnout: The Cost of Caring, 1982; co-author: Influencing Attitudes and Changing Behavior, 1977, Maslach Burnout Inventory (rsch. scale), 1981, 2d edit., 1986, 3d edit., 1996, Experiencing Social Psychology, 1979, 4th edit., 2001, Professional Burnout, 1993, The Truth About Burnout, 1997, Preventing Burnout and Building Engagement, 2000, Banishing Burnout, 2005. Recipient Disting. Teaching award, 1987, Best Paper award Jour. Orgnl. Behavior, 1994, Prof. of Yr. award Carnegie/CASE, 1997. Fellow AAAS, APA, Am. Psychol. Soc., Soc. Clin. and Exptl. Hypnosis (Henry Guze rsch. award 1980), We. Psychol. Assn. (pres. 1989); mem. Soc. Exptl. Social Psychology. Democrat. Office: U Calif Office of Chancellor 200 California Hall # 1500 Berkeley CA 94720-1500 Office Phone: 510-642-9594. Business E-mail: maslach@berkeley.edu.

**MASLANKA, DANIEL CHESTER,** percussionist and music educator; b. Highland Park, Mich., Apr. 20, 1955; s. Chester J. and Irene F. (Baranski) M. MusB in Instrumental Edn. and Percussion Performance, Wayne State U., 1980. Cert. music education U. Mich. Ind. percussion instr., 1971—; asst. dir. band L' Anse Creuse High amd Mid. Schs., Mt. Clemens, Mich., 1979; head percussion dept. Ctr. Creative Studies div. Inst. Music and Dance, Detroit, 1985—; staff percussionist Birmingham (Mich.) Theater, 1984-95; co-owner Pro Percussion Ctr., Plymouth, Mich., 1996—2001. Mem. applied faculty Oakland U., Rochester, Mich., Macomb Cmty. Coll., Mt. Clemens; staff percussionist Church of Today weekly show, Sta. WKBD-TV, Detroit. Percussionist with nat. touring cos. of Cats, Big River, Phantom of the Opera, King and I, Am. Ballet Theater, (bus. and truck prodns.) Dancin', Fiddler on the Roof, A Chorus Line, Joseph and the Amazing Technicolor Dream Coat, various entertainers including Danny Thomas, Johnny Mathis, Dionne Warwick, Luciano Pavarotti, Marvin Hamlisch, with many groups including Brookside Jazz Ensemble, Detroit Symphony Orch., Golden Rain Percussion Ensemble, Mich. Opera Theatre; numerous TV and radio commls. and live jazz broadcasts. Mem. Percussive Arts Soc. (v.p. Mich. chpt.), Mich. Music Assn., Am. Guild Music.

**MASLANKA, SANDRA KAREN,** social worker, educator, educational consultant; d. Eugene Francis and Adella Cook; m. William Vincent Maslanka, Nov. 4, 1972; children: William Vincent, Jason Anthony, Craig Allan, Angela Sandra, Chaze Robert. AS in Pedology, C.C. Allegheny County, Pitts., 1991; BA in Psychology, Point State Pk., 1993; MSW, U. Pitts., 1995. Lic. social worker Pa., 1995. Educator various agys., Pitts., 1995—, social worker, 1995—2003. Cons. Skm Consultants, Pitts., 2002—. Author: (manual) A Comprehensive Grief Workshop, 2002. Mem.: NASW (assoc.). Office Phone: 724-625-6225. Personal E-mail: skm@nauticom.net.

**MASLIN, JANET,** critic; b. NYC, Aug. 12, 1949; d. Paul and Lucille (Becker) M.; m. Benjamin Cheever; children: John, Andrew. BA in Math., U. Rochester, 1970. Film and music critic The Boston Phoenix, 1972-76; film critic Newsweek, NYC, 1976-77; dep. film critic NY Times, NYC, 1977-93, chief film critic, 1993-99, now book critic. Office: NY Times 229 W 43rd St New York NY 10036-3959 Office Phone: 212-556-5801. Office Fax: 212-556-1516.*

**MASLOW, AARON D.,** lawyer; b. Bklyn., Dec. 19, 1956; s. Morris J. and Rosalind H. Maslow; m. Lori S. Fajnsod, Dec. 13, 1987; children: Rachel Francine, Sam Irvin, Bernard Jay. BA, Touro Coll., Bklyn., 1977; JD, Yeshiva U., N.Y.C., 1980. Bar: N.Y. 1981, U.S. Ct. Appeals (2nd cir.) 1984, U.S. Supreme Ct. 1985. Pvt. law practice, Bklyn., 1981—. Adminstrv. law judge N.Y.C. Taxi & Limousine Commn., 1983—87, 1992—98, atty. 1987—88; legal counsel N.Y.C. Bd. Elections, 1988—92; adminstrv. law judge N.Y.C. Parking Violations Bur., 1989—99; small claims arbitrator N.Y.C. Civil Ct. Bklyn., 1992—98; no-fault ins. arbitrator Am. Arbitration Assn., N.Y.C., 2002—. Contbr. articles to profl. jours. Candidate State Assembly, Bklyn., 1996, Justice of State Supreme Ct., Bklyn., 1997, 2002; active Kings County Dem. County Com., Bklyn., 1976—94, Kings County Rep. County Com., Bklyn., 1995—, 2d vice-chmn., 2001—04; v.p. Cong. Bnai Israel of Sheepshead Bay, Bklyn., 1990—91. Recipient Leadership award, Kings County Rep. Party, 2002. Mem.: Nat. Pk. Found., Ea. Nat. Pks. Assn., Bklyn. Bar Assn., Touro Synagogue Found., Found. Nat. Archives, Citizens Union, Smithsonian Inst., Nat. History Soc. Can., United Zembrover Soc. (life; sec.-treas. 2001—). Jewish. Avocations: travel, videography, history, philately. Home: 1761 Stuart St Brooklyn NY 11229

**MASLOW, WILL,** lawyer, legal association administrator; b. Kiev, Russia, Sept. 27, 1907; came to U.S., 1911, naturalized, 1924; s. Saul and Raeesa (Moonves) M.; m. Beatrice Greenfield, Dec. 21, 1933; children: Laura, Catha. AB, Cornell U., 1929; JD, Columbia U., 1931. Bar: N.Y. 1932, U.S. Supreme Ct. 1932. Reporter N.Y. Times, 1929-31; assoc. Arthur Garfield Hays, 1931-34; assoc. counsel Dept. Investigation, N.Y.C., 1934-36; trial atty., trial examiner NLRB, 1937-43; dir. field operations Pres.'s Com. Fair Employment Practice, 1943-45; gen. counsel Am. Jewish Congress, 1945—60, exec. dir., 1960-72. Faculty N.Y. Sch. Social Research, 1948-60; adj. prof. Coll. City N.Y., 1965-84. Editor: Boycott Report, 1977—94, Radical Islamic Fundamentalism Update, 1995—99. Trustee Meml. Found. for Jewish Culture; bd. dirs. Interracial Council for Bus. Opportunity, A. Philip Randolph Inst. Recipient Nat. award Jewish Coun. Pub. Affairs, 1998, award for def. of equal rights NY Bar Assn., 1963. Mem. World Jewish Congress (exec. com.), ACLU (dir. 1963-72), Am. Jewish Congress (Stephen Wise laureate 1972), Phi Beta Kappa. Home: 401 E 86th St New York NY 10028-6403

**MASNARI, NINO ANTONIO,** electrical engineer, educator; b. Three Rivers, Mich., Sept. 20, 1935; s. Antonio and Giovanna (Lupato) M.; m. Judy E. Guild, June 29, 1957; children: Michael A., Jeffrey P., Maria L. BSEE, U. Mich., 1958, MSEE, 1959, PhD, 1964. Electronics engr. R & D ctr. GE Schenectady, NY, 1967-69; lectr. rsch. assoc. U. Mich., Ann Arbor, 1964-67, assoc. prof. elec. engring., 1969-76, prof., 1976-79, dir. elec. physics lab., 1975-79; disting. prof. elec. and computer engring. NC State U., Raleigh, 1979—, head dept. elec. and computer engring., 1979-88, dir. Advanced Electronic Materials Processing Ctr., 1988-96, dean Coll. Engring., 1996—. Cons. in field. Raytheon predoctoral fellow 1962. Fellow IEEE; mem. Am. Soc. Engring. Edn., Materials Rsch. Soc., Sigma Xi, Phi Kappa Phi, Tau Beta Pi, Eta Kappa Nu. Achievements include patent for Process for Manufacturing Inertial Confinement Fusion Targets and Resulting Product. Office: NC State U Coll Engring Campus Box 7901 Raleigh NC 27695-7901

**MASNYJ, YURI,** painter, sculptor; b. Washington, 1976; BFA, Cooper Union, 1998. One-man shows include On Our Black Rainbow, Sutton Lane, London, 2004, A World of Interiors, Metro Pictures, NY, 2004, exhibitions include 126a, Bklyn. Front Gallery, 2001, Ballpoint Inklings, Geoffrey Young Gallery, Mass., 2002, New Topography, 2003, Radical Vaudeville, 2005, Shallow Interiors, Rivington Arms Gallery, NY, 2002, From Here On, Guild & Greyskhul, NY, 2003, The Night Has a Thousand Eyes, 2005, Drawings, Metro Pictures, NY, 2003, International Paper, Hammer Mus., Univ. Calif., LA, 2003, Happy Days Are Here Again, David Zwirner, 2004, Greater New York, PS 1 Mus. Modern Art, Long Island City, NY, 2005, Landings, Susan Inglett Gallery, NY, 2005, Square Dance, Galerie Jacky Strenz, Frankfurt, 2005, Whitney Biennial: Day for Night, Whitney Mus. Am. Art, NY, 2006, New York Drawings, Travesia Cautro, Madrid, 2006. Mailing: c/o Metro Pictures 519 West 24th St New York NY 10011*

**MASON, AIMEE HUNNICUTT ROMBERGER,** retired philosophy and humanities educator; b. Atlanta, Nov. 3, 1918; d. Edwin William and Aimee Greenleaf (Hunnicutt) Romberger; m. Samuel Venable Mason, Aug. 16, 1941 (dec. 1988); children: Olivia Elizabeth (Mrs. Mason Butcher), Christopher Leeds. BA, Conn. Coll., 1940; postgrad., Emory U., 1946-48; MA, U. Fla., 1979, PhD, 1980; MA. Stetson U., 1968. Model, coll. shop Saks Fifth Ave., N.Y.C.; jr. exec. merchandising G. Fox & Co., Hartford, Conn., 1940-41; air traffic contr. CAA, Atlanta, 1942; ptnr. Coronado Concrete Products, New Smyrna Beach, Fla., 1953-81; adj. faculty Valencia Jr. Coll., Orlando, Fla., 1969; instr. philosophy and Humanities Seminole C.C., Sanford, Fla., 1969. Area cons. ARC, 1947-50; del. Nat. Red Cross, Washington, 1949; founding mem. St. Joseph Hosp. Aux., Atlanta, 1950-53; v.p., treas. Nw Smyrna Beach PTA, 1955-60; bd. dirs. Atlanta Symphony Orch., Fla. Symphony Orch., 1954-59; mem Code Enforcement Bd., Edgewater, Fla., 1992-94. Lt. US-CGR, 1943-46. Recipient award in graphics Nat. Assn. Women Artists, 1939, 41. Mem. AAUP, AAUW (founding mem. New Smyrna Beach, exec. bd. 1984-85, chmn. scholarship com. 1984-87, coll./univ. liaison 1987-91, citizens code enforcement bd. Edgewater 1992-94), DAV, Am. Philos. Assn., Fla. Philos. Assn. (exec. coun. 1978-79), Collegium Phenomenologicum, Soc. Existencial and Phenomenological Philosophy, Soc. Phenomenology in Human Sci., Merleau Ponty Circle, Ital. Assn. Univ. Colls., Univ. Club Winter Park. Home: B216/218 1620 Mayflower Court Winter Park FL 32792

**MASON, BARBARA FOUNTAIN,** minister; d. Johnnie Lee and Eddie Fountain; m. William Lawrence Mason, June 12, 1956; children: Johnnie Ann Crawford, Lawrencina Mason Oramalu. AA, Calvary Bible Coll., Kansas City, Mo., 1977; BS in Local Ch. Edn., Calvary Bapt. Bible Coll., Grandview, Mo., 1980; MA Edn! Adminstrn., U.Mo., Kansas City, 1984; M in Religious Studies, Ctrl. Bapt. Theol. Sem., 1990; degree in spi. edn., Augsburg Coll., 2003. Pastor Little Flock Cmty. of Faith, Mpls., 1994—; tchr. Mpls. Pub. Schs., 1999—2003. Dir. Christian edn. Met. Missionary Bapt. Ch., Kans. City, Mo., 1977—90; asst. pastor Zion Bapt. Ch., Mpls., 1990—92; dir., ecumenical ptnrs. Greater Mpls. Coun. of Churches, 1993—94, dir., social policy, 1993—94. Bd. dirs. Salvation Army, Mpls., 1993—94, Battered Women's Orgn., Mpls., 1995—97; mem. Mayor's Coun. on Interfaith & Racial Partnerships, Mpls., 1996—98; bd. dirs. Exodus Cmty. Devel., Mpls., 2000—01; mem. Ministerial Alliance, Mpls., 1991—94; bd. dirs. Greater Mpls. Coun. of Churches, Mpls., 1992—93. Named Role Model for Youth, Bd. of Christian Edn., Met. Bapt. Ch., 1990; recipient Regional Workshop Facilitator award, Nat. Bapt. Pub. Bd., 1988; scholar Multicultural Educators' Program, Mpls. Pub. Schs., 2001—03. Mem.: LWV (bd. dirs. 1999—2001), Spl. Needs' Assn. Dfl. Bapt. Achievements include designed summer camp; development of a Christian pre-school; designed a teacher training class; designed a Bible Institute for lay leaders; development of a prayer ministry; outreach ministry; designed curriculum for character development; designed self-esteem program for juveniles; Founding Pastor of Little Flock Community of Faith. Home: 8712 Bass Creek Ave Minneapolis MN 55428 Office: Little Flock Comty Faith Ch 128 W 33rd Street Minneapolis MN 55408

**MASON, BOBBIE ANN,** writer; b. Mayfield, Ky., May 1, 1940; d. Wilburn A. and Christianna (Lee) M.; m. Roger B. Rawlings, Apr. 12, 1969. BA, U. Ky., 1962; MA, SUNY, Binghamton, 1966; PhD, U. Conn., 1972. Asst. prof. English Mansfield (Pa.) State Coll., 1972-79. Writer-in-residence, U. Ky., Lexington, 2001—. Author: Nabokov's Garden, 1974, The Girl Sleuth: A Feminist Guide to the Bobbsey Twins, Nancy Drew and Their Sisters, 1975,

2d edit., 1995, Shiloh and Other Stories, 1982 (PEN Hemingway award, Nat. Book Critics Circle award nominee, Am. Book award nominee, PEN Faulkner award nominee), 2d edit., 2001, In Country, 1985, 2d edit., 2005, Spence + Lila, 1988, 2d edit., 1998, Love Life, 1989, Feather Crowns, 1993 (Nat. Book Critic's Circle award nominee, So. Book award), Midnight Magic, 1998, Clear Springs, 1999 (Pulitzer prize finalist), Zigzagging Down a Wild Trail, 2001 (So. Book award), Elvis Presley, 2003 (Ky. Literary award), An Atomic Romance, 2005; editor: Missing Mountains, 2005, Nancy Culpepper, 2006; contbr. regularly to the New Yorker, 1980—; contbr. fiction to The Atlantic, Redbook, Paris Rev., Mother Jones, Harpers, N.Am. Rev., Va. Quar. Rev., Story, Ploughshares, So. Rev., Crazyhorse, DoubleTake; contbr. works Best American Short Stories, 1981, 83, The Pushcart Prize, Best of the Small Presses, 1983, 86, 97. Recipient O. Henry Anthology awards, 1986, 88, Hillsdale prize, 1999; grantee Pa. Arts Coun., 1983, 89, Nat. Endowment Arts, 1983, Am. Acad. and Inst. Arts and Letters, 1984; Guggenheim fellow, 1984. Mem.: PEN, Author's Guild, Fellowship of So. Writers. Office: Internat Creative Mgmt care Amanda Urban Apt 40 W 57th St New York NY 10019-4001 Business E-Mail: aurban@icmtalent.com

**MASON, CHARLES ELLIS, III,** magazine editor; b. Boston, Oct. 31, 1938; s. Charles Ellis, Jr. and Ada Brooks (Trafford) M. BA, Yale U., 1960. Loan officer State St. Bank, Boston, 1963-68; asso. editor Sail mag., Boston, 1968-74, exec. editor, 1974—. Author: (with Buddy Melges) Sailing Smart, 1983; editor: Best of Sail Trim, 1976, Best of SAIL Navigation, 1981. Mem. exec. com. Sierra Club Greater Boston Group, 1992-2004. Served with USNR, 1960-62. Office: Sail Publs 98 N Washington St Boston MA 02110 E-mail: charles.mason@primedia.com

**MASON, CHRISTOPHER MAY,** lawyer; b. Orange County, N.C., Nov. 4, 1957; s. Julian Dewey and Elsie (May) M. BA summa cum laude, U. N.C., 1979; JD magna cum laude, Duke U., 1983. Bar: N.Y. 1985, D.C. 1985, U.S. Dist. Ct. (so. and ea. dists.) N.Y. 1985, U.S. Dist. Ct. (no. and we. dists.) N.Y., 1989, U.S. Dist. Ct. D.C., 1995, U.S. Ct. Internat. Trade 1985, U.S. Temporary Emergency Ct. of Appeals 1985, U.S. Ct. Appeals (4th, 6th, 8th cirs.) 1985, U.S. Ct. Appeals (2d, 3d, 5th, 7th and 9th cirs.) 1988, U.S. Ct. Appeals (D.C. cir.) 1991, U. S. Supreme Ct. 1988. Law clk. to judge J. Clifford Wallace U.S. Ct. Appeals (9th cir.), San Diego, 1983-84; assoc. Cravath, Swaine & Moore, N.Y.C., 1984-89, Hunton & Williams, N.Y.C., 1989-91, ptnr., 1992-2000, Nixon Peabody LLP, N.Y.C., 2000—. Contbr. articles to profl. jours. Mem. ABA, Assn. of Bar of City of N.Y., N.Y. State Bar Assn., Fed. Bar Coun., Phi Beta Kappa, Order of Coif. Presbyterian. Office: Nixon Peabody LLP 437 Madison Ave New York NY 10022-7001 E-mail: cmason@nixonpeabody.com

**MASON, CONNIE JEANNE,** writer; b. Niles, Mich., Apr. 22, 1930; d. Frank G. and Frances (Coda) Roti; m. Lewis Gerald Mason, July 1, 1950; children: Jeri A. Vlasicak, Michelle A. Osborn, Mark. Grad. high sch., Buchanan, Mich. Author: Promise Me Forever, 1990, Brave Land, Brave Love, 1990, Surrender to The Fury, 1990, Ice @ Rapture, 1991, A Promise of Thunder, 1991, Lord Of The Night, 1991, Treasures Of The Heart, 1992, Tears Like Rain, 1993, Wind Rider, 1993, Sierra, 1994, The Lion's Bride, 1994, Taken By You, 1995, pure Temptation, 1995, Flame, 1996, A Love To Cherish, 1996, Shadow Walker, 1997, To Love A Stranger, 1997, Sheik, 1997, Viking!, 1998, The Black Knight, 1999 (N.Y. Times Extended Bestseller List), Pirate, 1998, Gunslinger, 1999, To Tempt a Rogue, 1999, The Black Knight, 1999 (N.Y. Times Extended List 1999), The Outlaws: Rafe, 2000, A Taste of Sin, 2000, The Outlaws: Jess, 2000, A Breath of Scandal, 2001, The Outlaws: Sam, 2001, The Dragon Lord, 2001, The Rogue and the Bastion, 2002, Lionheart, 2002, Seduced by a Rogue, 2003, The Laird of Stonehaven, 2003, The Last Rogue, 2004, The Pirate Prince, 2004, Gypsy Lover, 2005, A Knight's Honor, 2005, A Taste of Paradise, 2006, also novellas. Named Story Teller of Yr., Romantic Times, 1990; recipient Career Achievement award, 1994. Mem. Romance Writers Am., Novelists, Inc. Avocations: reading, travel.

**MASON, DEAN TOWLE,** cardiologist; b. Berkeley, Calif., Sept. 20, 1932; s. Ira Jenckes and Florence Mabel (Towle) M.; m. Maureen O'Brien, June 22, 1957; children: Kathleen, Alison. BA in Chemistry, Duke U., Durham, N.C., 1954; MD, Duke U., 1958. Diplomate Am. Bd. Internal Medicine, Am. Bd. Cardiovasc. Diseases, Nat. Bd. Med. Examiners. Intern, then resident in medicine Johns Hopkins Hosp., 1958-61; clin. assoc. cardiology dir., sr. asst. surgeon USPHS. Nat. Heart Inst., NIH, 1961-63, asst. sect. dir. cardiovascular diagnosis, attending physician, sr. investigator cardiology br., 1963-68; prof. medicine, prof. physiology, chief cardiovascular medicine U. Calif. Med. Sch., Davis-Sacramento Med. Center, 1968-82; dir. cardiac ctr. Cedars Med. Ctr., Miami, Fla., 1982-83; physician-in chief Western Heart Inst., San Francisco, 1983—2000; chmn. dept. cardiovascular medicine St. Mary's Med. Ctr., San Francisco, 1986-99, hon. med. staff, 2000—. Co-chmn. cardiovascular-renal drugs U.S. Pharmacopeia Com. Revision, 1970—75; mem. life scis. com. NASA; med. rsch. rev. bd. VA, NIH; prof. medicine (hon.) Peking Med. U., China, 1987; vis. prof. numerous univs.; cons. in field. Editor-in-chief Am. Heart Jour., 1980—96; contbr. chapters to books, articles. Recipient rsch. award. Am. Therapeutic Soc., 1965, Theodore and Susan B. Cummings Humanitarian award, Dept. State-Am. Coll. Cardiology, 1972, 1973, 1975, 1978, Skylab Achievement award, NASA, 1974, U. Calif. Faculty Rsch. award, 1978, Symbol of Excellence, Tex. Heart Inst., 1979, Disting. Alumnus award, Duke U. Sch. Medicine, 1979, award of Honor, Wisdom Soc., 1997, Medal of Honor, Winston Churchill Soc., 1998, Armand Hammer Creative Genius award, 1998, Dwight D. Eisenhower Admirable Am. of Achievement award, 1998, Eternal Jesus Christ award, 1998, Blessed Lord's Prayer award, 1998, Dean Towle Mason Eminent Physician of Wisdom award, 1998, Dean Towle Mason, M.D. Medal of Wisdom award. 2001. Cardiologist of the Century Wisdom award, 2001, Albert Schweitzer world Humanitarian of Wisdom award, 2002, Jonas Salk award for med. rsch., 2003, Albert Einstein Sci. Rsch. award, 2003, John Wayne Pioneer of Am. award, 2003, Ernest Hemingway award for maj. contbns. to med. lit., 2003, Will Durant Philosopher-Physician award, 2004, Paul Dudley White award for disting. svc. in cardiovasc. medicine, 2004, Newton Kugelmass Children's Cardiology Crusader award, 2004, Norman Vincent Peale Healing Power of Prayer award, 2005. Master Am. Coll. Cardiology (pres. 1977-78); fellow ACP, Am. Heart Assn., Am. Coll. Chest Physicians, Royal Soc. Medicine; mem. Am. Soc. Clin. Investigation, Am. Physiol. Soc., Am. Soc. Pharmacology and Exptl. Therapeutics (Exptl. Therapeutics award 1973), Am. Fedn. Clin. Research, N.Y. Acad. Scis., Am. Assn. U. Cardiologists, Am. Soc. Clin. Pharmacology and Therapeutics, We. Assn. Physicians, AAUP, We. Soc. Clin. Rsch. (past pres.), El Macero Country Club, Royal Soc. Medicine, Alpha Omega Alpha, Republican, Methodist. Home: 44725 Country Club Dr El Macero CA 95618-1047 Office: Western Heart Inst St Marys Med Ctr 450 Stanyan St San Francisco CA 94117-1079 Office Phone: 415-750-5598.

**MASON, DEIRDRE DIANNE,** secondary school educator; b. Cleve., Feb. 12, 1958; d. Richard Whiting and Ruth Elizabeth (Moody) M. BS, Ashland Coll., 1981; MS, Ohio State U., 1986. Cert. home economist. Grad. asst. Ohio State U., Columbus; adult regional cons./home econs. coord. Mansfield (Ohio) City Schs., home econs. tchr. Mem. Am. Home Econs. Assn., Ohio Home Econs. Assn., NEA, Ohio Edn. Assn., Mansfield Edn. Assn. (bldg. rep.), AAUW, ASCD, Nat. Mid. Sch. Assn., Ohio Mid. Sch. Assn., Am. Coun. on Consumer Interest, Kappa Omicron Phi.

**MASON, DERRICK,** professional football player; b. Detroit, Mich., Jan. 17, 1974; m. Marci Mason; children: Bailee My-Lin, Derrick Jr. Postgrad in comm., Mich. State Univ. Wide receiver Tenn. Titans, 1997—. Named to NFL Pro-Bowl, 2000, 2003. Achievements include the ninth player in NFL history to record consecutive seasons with more than 2,000 all-purpose yards; set NFL record for all-purpose yards (2,690), 2000.*

**MASON, DWAYNE L.,** lawyer; s. Leroy and Tillie Mason. BSChemE, Purdue U., 1984; JD, U. Houston, 1993. Bar: Tex. Supreme Ct. 1993, U.S. Patent & Trademark Office 1995. Ptnr. Matthew Joseph Shaddox & Mason, Houston, 1995—99, Winstead Secrest & Minick, Houston, 1999—2001, Akin

Gump Strauss Hauer & Feld, Houston, 2001—. Dir. Harris Coutny MUD 222, Houston, 1995—. Editl. bd.: Nanotechnology Law and Bus. Mem. emerging bus. coun. Greater Houston Ptnrship., 2001—. Named Top Minority IP Ptnr., AIPLA/MCCA, 2003, Top Lawyer, Tex. mag., 2004. Mem.: Kiwanis (chair legal com. 2001—). Office: Akin Gump Strauss Hauer & Feld LLP 1111 Louisiana St 44th Fl Houston TX 77002 Office Phone: 713-220-8186. Office Fax: 713-236-0822. Business E-Mail: dmason@akingump.com.

**MASON, EDWARD EATON,** surgeon; b. Boise, Idaho, Oct. 16, 1920; s. Edward Files and Dora Bell (Eaton) M.; m. Dordana Fairman, June 18, 1944; children— Daniel Edward, Rose Mary, Richard Eaton, Charles Henry. BA, U. Iowa, 1943, MD, 1945; PhD in Surgery, U. Minn., 1953. Intern, resident in surgery Univ. Hosps., Mpls., 1945-52; asst. prof. surgery U. Iowa, 1953-55, asso. prof., 1956-60, prof., 1961-91, prof. emeritus, 1991—, chmn. gen. surgery, 1978-91. Cons. VA Hosp.; trainee Nat. Cancer Inst., 1949-52 Author: Computer Applications in Medicine, 1964, Fluid, Electrolyte and Nutrient Therapy in Surgery, 1974, Surgical Treatment of Obesity, 1981; developer gastric bypass and gastroplasty for treatment of obesity; contbr. articles profl. jours. Served to lt. (j.g.) USNR, 1945-47. Fellow ACS; mem. AMA, Am. Surg. Assn., Western Surg. Assn., Soc. Univ. Surgeons, Internat. Soc. Surgery, Ctrl. Surg. Assn., Soc. Surgery Alimentary Tract, Am. Thyroid Assn., Am. Soc. Bariatric Surgery, Sigma Xi, Alpha Omega Alpha. Republican. Presbyterian. Home: 5 Melrose Cir Iowa City IA 52246-2013 Office: Univ Hosp Dept Surgery Iowa City IA 52242 Business E-Mail: edward-mason@uiowa.edu. *Continuity of interest and planning weaves the daily decisions into a whole cloth that does more than cover one's imperfections.*

**MASON, EILEEN B.,** federal arts administrator; b. Bklyn., 1943; m. Arthur Mason; children: Elizabeth, Laura. BA, Cornell U.; MPA, Am U. Tchr. math. and reading Hephzibah High Sch., Ga.; editor Little Brown, Boston; music adv. panelist Md. State Arts Coun.; v.p. grants Arts and Humanities Coun., Montgomery County, Md.; mgr. and adminstr. U.S. NRC, FERC; sr. dep. chmn. NEA, Washington, 2001—, acting chmn., 2002—03. Performer: (violinist) Cornell U. Symphony, MIT Symphony, Augusta Symphony, Am. U. Symphony Orchestra. Mem.: Phi Alpha Alpha. Office: NEA 1100 Pennsylvania Ave NW Washington DC 20506

**MASON, ELLSWORTH GOODWIN,** retired librarian; b. Waterbury, Conn., Aug. 25, 1917; s. Frederick William and Kathryn Loretta (Watkins) Mason; m. Rose Ellen Maloy, May 13, 1951 (div. Oct. 1961); children: Kay Iris Morice, Joyce Iris Lande; m. Joan Lou Shinew, Aug. 16, 1964; 1 child, Sean David. BA, Yale U., 1938, MA, 1942, PhD, 1948; LHD, Hofstra U., 1973; diploma, Inst. Children's Lit., 1996. Cert. Christian Writer's Guild. Reference asst. Yale Library, 1938-42; export license officer Bd. Econ. Warfare, 1942-43; instr. English Williams Coll., 1948-50; instr. humanities Marlboro (Vt.) Coll., 1951-52; serials libr. U. Wyo. Libr., 1952-54; reference libr. Colo. Coll. Libr., Colorado Springs, 1954-58; lectr., libr. Colo. Coll., 1958-63; prof., dir. libr. svcs. Hofstra U., Hempstead, NY, 1963-72; prof., dir. U. Colo. Librs., Boulder, 1972-76; freelance writer children's lit., 1995—. Libr. cons., 1958—; vis. lectr. Northwestern U., 1961, Colo. Coll., 1965, Syracuse U., 1965—68, Elmira Coll., 1966, Columbia U., 1966—68, Lincoln U., 1969, U. BC, Canada, 1969, U. Toronto, 1970, U. Tulsa, 1971, 76, U. Rutgers, 1971, U. Ill., 1972, Colgate U., 1972, Simmons Coll., 1972, U. Oreg., 1973, Hofstra U., 1974, U. N.C., 1976, U. Ala., 1976, Ball State U., 1977, U. Lethbridge, Canada, 1977, U. Ariz., 1981, Ariz. State U., 1981, Victoria U., New Zealand, 1983, U. Canterbury, New Zealand, 1983, U. Nev., Las Vegas, 1992, Remember Pearl Harbor Assn., 1993, 94; rsch. assoc. U. Calif., Berkeley, 1965; adj. prof. U. Ill., Urbana, 1968; pres. Mason Assocs., Ltd., 1977—; libr. value engr., 1992—. Author (with Walter and Jean Shine): A MacDonald Potpourri, 1988, The University of Colorado Library and Its Makers, 1876-1972, 1994; editor (with Stanislaus Joyce): The Early Joyce, 1955; editor Xerox U.M. edit., 1964, Norwood: Norwood Editions, 1977, Philadelphia (R. West), 1978, editor with Richard Ellmann The Critical Writings of James Joyce, 1959, 2d edit., 1989, editor Colorado College Studies, 1959—62, Critical Commentary on a Portrait of the Artist as a Young Man, 1966, The Bookover's Bounty, 1977—82; translator: Recollections of James Joyce (S. Joyce), 1950, Essais de J. Joyce, 1966, Escritos Criticos de James Joyce, Portuguese edit., 1967, Spanish edit., 1973, 1975, James Joyce's Ulysses and Vico's Cycle, 1973, Krittische Schriften v. James Joyce, 1975, Mason on Library Buildings, 1980; editor, compiler: Focus on Robert Graves, 1972—88, adv. editor: Focus on Robert Graves and His Contemporaries, 1988—; mem. editl. bd. Serial Slants, 1957—59, Choice, 1962—65, Coll. and Rsch. Librs., 1969—72, Serials Libr., 1977—98; contbr. articles to profl. jours. Mem. chancellor's coun. U. Tex., Austin, 1982—; exec. bd. U. Ky. Libr. Assocs., 1991—94, Concerned Christians in Ky., 1993—98, Littlefield Soc. U. Tex., Austin, 2004—. With USNR, 1943—46. Named Ky. Col., 1993; recipient Harry Bailly Spkr.'s award, Assn. Colls. Midwest, 1975; fellow, Coun. Libr. Resources, 1969—70; grantee, Am. Coun. Learned Socs., Econ. Facilities Labs., Hofstra U., U. Colo. Mem.: ALA (councilor-at-large 1961—65), Am. Christian Writers, Nat. Assn. Scholars, James Joyce Found. (chmn. sect. translation from Joyce 2d Internat. James Joyce Symposium 1969), Inst. Vico Studies, New Zealand Royal Forest and Bird Protection Soc., Conf. Editors Learned Jours., Alcuin Soc. Vancouver, Pvt. Librs. Assn., New Zealand Libr. Assn., Libr. Assn. (London), Bibliog. Soc. Am., Colo. Libr. Assn. (pres. so. dist. 1960—61), Black Am.'s PAC, Colo. Book Collectors (founder, pres. 1975—86), Ghost Town Club, Caxton Club, Archons of Colophon, Sigma Kappa Alpha (pres. 1969—70), Alpha Sigma Lambda. Home: 736 Providence Rd Lexington KY 40502-2267 also: 39 Discovery Dr Whitby New Zealand

**MASON, EMILY,** painter; b. NYC, 1932; d. Alice Trumbull Mason; m. Wolf Kahn. Attended, Bennington Coll., 1950—52; BFA, Cooper Union, NYC; DFA (hon.), Wheaton Coll., Mass., 2000. Tchr. Hunter Coll., NYC. Exhibitions include Grace Borgenicht Gallery NYC, Landmark Gallery NYC, Walker Kornbluth Gallery Fairlawn NJ, Thomas Babcor Gallery San Diego, MB Modern NYC, Virginia Lynch Gallery Tiverton R.I., Brattleboro Mus. Art. Mugar Art Gallery Colby-Sawyer Coll., David Findlay Jr. Fine Arts, NYC; represented in collections Springfield (Mass.) Mus., Rockefeller Group NYC, Ciba-Geigy Chemical Group Ohio Hon. trustee Brattleboro Mus. & Art Ctr., Vt. Grantee Fulbright Fellowship, Accademia delle Belle Arti, Venice, 1956. Mem.: NAD (academician).

**MASON, FRANK HENRY, III,** automotive executive, rental company executive; b. Paris, Tenn., Nov. 16, 1936; s. Frank H. and Dorothy (Carter) M.; children: Robert C., William C. B of Elec. Engring., Vanderbilt U., 1958; MS in Indsl. Mgmt., MIT, 1965. With Ford Motor Co., 1965-71; asst. controller Ford Brazil, Sao Paulo, 1971-74; mgr. overseas fin. dept. Ford Motor Co., Dearborn, Mich., 1974-76, asst. controller engine divsn., 1976-78, mgr. facilities and mgmt. svcs., 1978-81, controller Ford Motor Credit Co., Dearborn, Mich., 1981-87; dir. fin. Ford Fin. Svcs. Group, Dearborn, Mich., 1987-89; exec. v.p., chief fin. officer US Leasing, Internat., San Francisco, 1989-92; retired, 1992. Lt. USN, 1958-63.

**MASON, FRANK HERBERT,** artist, educator; b. Cleve., Feb. 20, 1921; s. Walter Harrison and Mildred Mary (Corbin) M.; m. Anne Cary Crosby, Mar. 12, 1966; 1 son, Arden Harriman. Student, Nat. Acad. Design, 1937-38, Art Students League, N.Y.C., 1938-51. Instr. fine arts Art Students League, 1951—. Represented in permanent collections at, Ch. of San Giovanni di Malta, Venice, Italy (Cross of Merit for eight canvas murals on life of St. Anthony of Padua Sovereign Mil. Order of Malta), Am. embassy, London, AEC, Washington, Duke U., Butler Inst. Am. Art, Indpls., Eureka Coll., 3 murals on naval history of Saudi Arabia at, King Faisal Naval Base, Jeddah; (mural) And the Gods Smiled on These, Houston. Served with AUS, 1945-46. Recipient North Am. Continent award Expn. Intercontinentale, Monaco, 1968 Mem. NAD (academician, past treas.), Nat. Mural Soc. Home: 385 Broome St New York NY 10013-3705

**MASON, GEORGE HENRY,** retired business educator; b. Chgo., Sept. 11, 1929; s. Robert De Main and Dorothy Wills (Belden) M.; m. Constance Eleanor Wolcott, May 14, 1960. AB, Kenyon Coll., 1955; MBA, Cornell U.,

1957; MF, Duke U., 1983. CFA. Investment officer Travelers Ins. Co., Hartford, Conn., 1957-88; exec.-in-residence U. Hartford, West Hartford, 1989—98. Vis. prof. Jagiellonian U., Cracow, Poland, 1996, Yang-En U., Quanzhou, Fujian, China, 1997. Co-author: Timberland Investments, 1992. Investment adv. coun. State of Conn., 1999—2003; tutor Literacy Vol. Greater Hartford, 2004—. Mem.: CFA Inst., Hartford Soc. Fin. Analysts, Farmington Hist. Soc. (bd. dirs. 2004—), Dataw Island Club, Mill Reef Club, Country Club of Farmington. Republican. Avocations: skiing, golf, writing.

**MASON, GREGG CLAUDE,** orthopedic surgeon, researcher; b. Schenectady, N.Y., July 28, 1958; s. George and Maureen (Murphy) M.; m. Dina Marie Sokolowski, June 16, 1990. BS in Chemistry magna cum laude, Allegheny Coll., 1980; MD, U. Pitts., 1984. Diplomate Am. Bd. Orthop. Surgery, Nat. Bd. Med. Examiners. Gen. surgery intern U. Colo./U. Colo. Med. Ctrs., Denver, 1984-85; orthopaedic rsch. fellow U. Pitts., 1985-86, resident in orthopaedic surgery, 1986-89; orthopedic surgeon U.S. Naval Hosp., Okinawa, Japan, 1989-92; pvt. practice, Erie, 1992—. Active staff St. Vincent Med. Ctr., St. Vincent Surgery Ctr., Hamot Med. Ctr., Union City Meml. Hosp.; lectr. in field. Contbr. articles to profl. jours. Comdr. M.C. USNR, 1980—. Recipient Outstanding Student Rsch. award U. Pitt. Sch. Medicine, 1984, Harold Henderson Sankey Orthop. award, 1984; rsch. grantee Competitive Med. Rsch. Fund., Presbyn.-Univ. Hosp. of Pitts., 1986-87, U. Pitts. Rsch. Devel. Fund, 1986-87. Disting. Alden scholar 1977, 78, 79, 80, Sandra Doane Turk scholar, 1979, Armed Svcs. Health Professions scholar, 1981-84. Fellow ACS, Internat. Coll. Surgeons, Mil. Soc. Orthop. Surgeons, Am. Acad. Orthop. Surgeons (tchg. seal 1993); mem. AMA, Pa. Orthop. Soc. (Best Rsch. Paper 1987, 88), Erie Orthop. Soc., U. Pitts. Med. Ctr. Orthop. Alumni., Am. Orthop. Soc. of Sports Medicine (Cabaud award 1988), Ea. Orthop. Assn. (Founders award 1988), Phi Beta Kappa. Office: Orthopaedic Surgeons Inc 204 W 26th St Erie PA 16508-1898 Office Phone: 814-454-2401.

**MASON, GREGORY WESLEY, JR.,** secondary school educator; b. Chgo., Jan. 21, 1963; s. Gregory Wesley and Diana (Burton) M.; m. LaTanya Yvonne Brown, June 8, 1991; children: Gregory Arthur, Timothy Michael. BS, Ill. State U., 1986; MEd, U. Ill., Chgo., 1996. Cert. secondary tchr., gen. adminstr., Ill. Instr. City Coll. Chgo., 1986-89; instr. project alert Roosevelt U., Chgo., 1989-91, counselor project upward bound, 1991-93; tchr. math. Bowen High Sch., Chgo., 1993-95, chmn. profl. planning adv. com., 1994-95; tchr. math. Whitney M. Young Magnet H.S., Chgo., 1995-2000, chmn. dept. math., 1997-2000; adminstr. Chgo. Pub. Schs., 2000—05; asst. prin. Sir Miles Davis Acad., 2005—. Instr. Ill. Math. and Sci. Acad., Aurora, summers 1993-96; lectr. Coll. Edn., Loyola U., Chgo., 1999-2001; tchr. coord. Golden Apple Found., 2000-01; mem. nat. adv. bd. Schs. and Scholars Program, Woodrow Wilson Nat. Fellowship Found. Mem. pres.'s coun. edn. com. Mus. Sci. and Industry; mem. Ill. Robotic Competition Adv. Bd. Named to Outstanding Young Men of Am., 1985. Mem. ASCD, Nat. Coun. Tchrs. Math., Ill. Coun. Tchrs. Math., Ill. Coun. for Coll. Attendance (bd. dirs. 1993-97), Nat. Assn. Secondary Sch. Prins., Benjamin Banneker Assn., Masons, Phi Delta Kappa. Avocations: swimming, chess, reading, stock trading, computers. Office: Miles Davis Acad 6723 S Wood St Chicago IL 60636 Home: 10500 S Oakley Chicago IL 60643 Business E-Mail: gmason@csc.cps.k12.il.us.

**MASON, HERBERT WARREN, JR.,** religion and history educator, author; b. Wilmington, Del., Apr. 20, 1932; s. Herbert Warren and Mildred Jane (Noyes) M.; m. Jeanine Young, June 25, 1982; children from previous marriage: Cathleen, Paul, Sarah. AB, Harvard U., 1955, AM, 1965, PhD, 1969. English tchr. Am. Sch. Paris, 1959-60; asst. prof. St. Joseph's Coll., Gorham, Maine, 1960-62; vis. lectr. Simmons Coll., Boston, 1962-63; vis. lectr. in Islamic Hist. Tufts U., Medford, Mass., 1965-66; teaching fellow in English Harvard U., Cambridge, Mass., 1962-66, teaching fellow in Islamic Hist., 1966-67; translator Bollingen Found., N.Y.C., 1968-72; prof. History and Religion Boston U., 1972-2000, William Goodwin Aurelio prof. history and religious thought, 2000—. U.K. cons. editor Banipal. Author: Reflections on the Middle East Crisis, 1970, Two Statesmen of Medieval Islam, 1971, Gilgamesh, 1971, 2d edit., 2003, The Death of al-Hallaj, 1979, Moments in Passage, 1979, (novel) Summer Light, 1980; translator: La Passion d'al-Hallaj, 4 vols., Bollingen Series (Louis Massignon), 1983, abridged 1 vol., 1994, A Legend of Alexander, 1986, Memoir of a Friend: Louis Massignon, 1988, Testimonies and Reflections, 1989, al-Hallaj, 1995, Haythu Taltaqi al-Anhar (novel in Arabic "Where the Rivers Meet"), 1999, English edit. 2003, (poems) Disappearances, 1999; co-editor: Humaniora Islamica; cons. editor Banipal, London; contbr. articles, essays, revs. fiction and poetry to popular fiction mags. Sec. Inter-racial Riverside Assn., Cambridge, Mass., 1965-67; trustee Bd. Charity of Edward Hopkins, Boston Athenaeum. Fellow Soc. for Values in Higher Edn.; mem. PEN (bd. dirs. Delos chpt.), Medieval Acad. Am., Am. Oriental Soc., Am. Acad. Religion, Mark Twain Soc., Inst. Internat. des Recherches Louis Massignon in Paris (dir. edn., v.p.), Am. Acad. Poetry, Japan Poetry Mus. (Iwate-Ken). Home: 9 Seaview Lane Newbury MA 01951 Office: Boston U 745 Commonwealth Ave Boston MA 02215-1401 Office Phone: 617-358-1777. E-mail: masonh@bu.edu, herbertwmason@comcast.net.

**MASON, JACKIE,** comedian, actor; b. Sheboygan, Wis., June 9, 1934; Stand-up comedian; performances include (theater) A Teaspoon Every Four Hours, 1969, The World According to Me! (one man show, Tony, Emmy and Ace awards 1987), Brand New, Politically Incorrect, 1994, Freshly Squeezed, 2005; (films) Operation Delilah, 1966, The Stoolie, 1972, The Jerk, 1979, History of the World Part I, 1981, Stroke of Genius, 1984, The Perils of P.K., 1986, Caddyshack II, 1988; TV appearances in Steve Allen, Ed Sullivan, Jack Paar, Garry Moore, Perry Como and Merv Griffin Shows, Johnny Carson, Arsenio Hall, Late Night with David Letterman; (TV series) Chicken Soup, The Jackie Mason Show; (TV movies) The Best of Times; (TV specials) Jackie Mason on Broadway (Emmy award for writing in a variety or music program 1988); records include The World According to Me!, Brand New. Recipient special Tony award, 1987, Emmy award for The Simpsons, 1991.

**MASON, JOAN ELLEN,** nurse; b. Reading, Pa., June 29, 1947; d. Richard Lenhart and Mary Jane (Miller) Fritz; m. W. Davis Mason, Feb. 12, 1977 (dec. Jan. 2002). RN, Temple U. Hosp. Sch. Nursing, 1968; BS in Nursing Edn., Temple U., 1971, EdM in Health Edn., 1981; postgrad., U. Pa. Staff nurse Temple U. Hosp., Phila., 1968-71; nursing instr. Phila. Gen. Hosp. Sch. Nursing, 1971-76; coord. staff devel. Meml. Hosp., Roxborough, Pa., 1976-84; clin. editor Springhouse Corp., Pa., 1984-94; nurse cons. Kelly Sci. Resources, 1995-98; adminstr., profl. nurse Bed and Breakfast Inn, Cape May, NJ, 1982—2003; nurse cons. Reading, 1999—2003, Orwigsburg, 2003—. Mem. exhibit com. Mus. Nursing History, Inc., 1988-2001. Editor Congl. Free Ch. of Christ newsletter; contbr. articles to profl. jours. Vol. Reading Mus., Berks Arts Coun., Am. Diabetes Assn. Mem. Mid-Atlantic Ctr. for Arts, Orwigsburg Women's Libr. Soc. Republican. Home: 225 Eisenhower Dr Orwigsburg PA 17961-1605

**MASON, JOHN LATIMER,** engineering executive; b. LA, Nov. 8, 1923; s. Zene Upham and Edna Ella (Watkins) Mason; m. Frances Howe Draeger, Sept. 1, 1950 (dec. June 1951); m. Mary Josephine Schulte, Nov. 26, 1954; children: Andrew, Peter, Mary Anne, John Edward. BS in Meteorology, U. Chgo., 1944; BS in Applied Chemistry, Calif. Inst. Tech., 1947, MS in Chem. Engring., 1948, PhD, 1950. Registered profl. engr., Calif. Engr. AiResearch Mfg. Co., Los Angeles, 1950-60; dir. engring. AiResearch Mfg. Co. div. Garrett Corp., Los Angeles, 1960-72; v.p. engring. Garrett Corp., Los Angeles, 1972-87; v.p. engring. and tech. Allied-Signal Aerospace Co., Los Angeles, 1987-88, cons., 1989-96; chmn. tech. adv. com. Indsl. Turbines Internat., Los Angeles, 1972-81, bd. dirs., 1980-88; adj. prof. engring. Calif. State U., Long Beach, 1992-96. Tech. adv. bd. Tex. Ctr. for Superconductivity. U. Houston, 1989-02, Ceryx Inc., 1998-2001; chair Calif. Coun. Sci. and Tech. Panel on Transp. R&D Ctr., 1993-94; bd. dirs. Planetary Sci. Inst., sec., 1998—; cons. Capstone Turbine Corp., 1994-98; workshop chmn. Transp. Rsch. Bd., 1998.; cons. Cleaire, Inc., 2001-03, Applied Rsch. and Tech., 2001-; ptnr. Applied Rsch. and Tech., 2001-06. Patentee in field. Chmn.

energy and environment com. FISITA Coun., 1990-94. 1st lt. USAAF, 1943-46, PTO. With USAF, 1946—57. Fellow AIAA, assoc. Soc. Automotive Engrs., bd. dirs. 1984-87, 90-93, pres.-elect 1989-90, pres. 1990-91, Performance Rev. Inst. chmn. 1990-91, bd. dirs. 1992-93; mem. AAAS, NRC of NAS, com. on alternative energy R&D strategies 1989-90, Office Sci. and Tech. Policy, Nat. Critical Techs. panel 1992-93, Inst. Medicine of NAS, com. on health effects of indoor allergens 1992-93, Nat. Acad. Engring., US Advanced Ceramics Assn. chmn. tech. com., bd. dirs. 1985-88, Am. Chem. Soc., Am. Ceramic Soc., Caltech Assocs., Sigma Xi assoc., Am. Soc. Mech. Engrs., Engrg. Adv. Bd., Univ. of So. Calif. Office Phone: 310-375-5161. Personal E-Mail: JL-Mason@cox.net.

**MASON, JOHN OLIVER,** freelance journalist, community activist, poet; b. Kingston, Pa., Aug. 1, 1957; s. Oliver B. and Dorothy Mae (Hunter) Mason. BA, Temple U., 1984. Editl. writer Temple News, Phila., 1983—85; writer Phila. Tribune, 1990—95, Irish Edition, Phila., 1990—95, Northeast Breeze, Rockledge, Pa., 1993—95, Germantown Courier, Phila., 1996—, Phila. Sunday Sun, 1996—, Chestnut Hill Local, 2000—, Milestones, 2000—, The Progressive, 2005—. Sec. Concerned Citizens of Delaware Valley, 1990; rec. sec. A. Philip Randolph Inst., Phila., 2001; mem. Jewish Labor Com., Phila., 1985. Avocations: stamp collecting/philately, reading, cultural activities. Office Phone: 215-843-0193. Personal E-Mail: jomason57@verizon.net.

**MASON, JOSEPH** See BUSHINSKY, JAY

**MASON, KAROL V.,** lawyer; b. Amityville, NY, Aug. 20, 1957; AB, Univ. NC, Chapel Hill, 1979; JD, Univ. Mich., 1982. Bar: Ga. 1983. Ptnr., chair, pub. fin. group Alston & Bird LLP, Atlanta. Notes editor Univ. Mich. Jour. Law Reform. Named Distinguished Young Alumna, Univ. NC, Chapel Hill, 1991. Mem.: Ga. Assn. Black Women Attys., Nat. Assn. Bond Lawyers. Office: Alston & Bird LLP One Atlantic Ctr 1201 W Peachtree St NW Atlanta GA 30309-3424 Office Phone: 404-881-7494. Office Fax: 404-881-7777. Business E-Mail: kmason@alston.com.

**MASON, KEVIN GEORGE,** military officer, military analyst; b. Queens, NY, Oct. 24, 1955; s. David Park Mason and Gisela Margarete Elsa Herbst; m. Sana Marie Francis, Aug. 7, 1991; 1 child, Katherine Elizabeth. BA, Mich. State U., 1974; MA, Boston U., 1992, U. Tenn., 1997, MS, 1998. Cert. tchr. Tenn., 2003. Commd. 2d lt. US Army, 1977, advanced through grades to maj.; mil. analyst Northrop-Grumman Info. Techs., Kaiserslautern, Rheinland-Pfalz, Germany, 1999—2003; dept. of Army, Grafenwoehr, Bavaria, 2003—. Decorated Meritorious Svc. medal US Army, Army Commendation medal, Army Achievement award. Mem.: VFW, Assn. US Army, Mil. Officers Assn. Am., Infantrymen Assn., Am. Hist. Assn. (life), Masons. Presbyterian. Avocations: history, hunting, fishing, travel. Office: Joint Multinational Training Center CMR 415 Box 3077 APO AE 09114 Office Phone: 496641836730. Personal E-mail: manchu19@aol.com. E-mail: kevin.mason1@us.army.mil.

**MASON, LINDA,** physical education educator, coach; b. Indpls., Jan. 29, 1946; d. Harrison Linn and Hazel Marie (Bledsoe) Crouch; divorced; children: Cassandra, Andrew. BS, Ind. U., 1968, MS, 1977. Cert. phys. edn. tchr., K-12, Ind. Tchr. phys. edn. Woodview Jr. H.S., Indpls., 1968—71; tchr. phys. edn., coach Ind. U.-Purdue U. Indpls., 1972—76; basketball coach Butler U., Indpls., 1976—84; head softball coach, asst. basketball coach Westfield Washington High Sch., Westfield, Ind., 1985; tchr. phys. edn., basketball coach Orchard Park Elem. Sch., Carmel, Ind., 1985—; tchr. elem. physical edn. Carmel-Clay Schs., Carmel 1985—; asst. varsity coach softball Carmel H.S., 1993—95, head varsity softball coach, 1996—99. Head coach Ind. Girls' H.S. All-Stars Basketball Team, Indpls., 1980. Named Coach of Yr. Dist. 4, Nat. Collegiate Athletic Assn., 1983, Coach of Yr. for softball ICGSA, 1997, coach ICGSA Girls All Stars, 1998. Mem. Delta Psi Kappa. Personal E-mail: peteacherl@msn.com. Business E-Mail: lmason@ccs.k12.in.us.

**MASON, LINDA,** broadcast executive; b. Middletown, NY; m. Cary Aminoff; 2 children. BA in Internat. Rels., Brown U., 1964; MS in Filmmaking, Syracuse U., 1965. Fellow Syracuse U.; reporter Providence Jour., RI; radio desk asst. CBS News, NY, 1966; news writer WCBS-TV, NY; writer, assoc. prodr. CBS Morning News, 1968—70, field prodr., 1971, sr. prodr., 1980—86; exec. prodr. CBS News (Weekend Broadcasts), 1986—92, CBS News Sunday Morning, 1987—92; exec.-in-charge Eye to Eye, CBS Mag., 1993—95, 60 Minutes...25 Years, 1993, 60 Minutes at 30, 1998; v.p. pub. affairs CBS News, 1992—, sr. v.p. standards and spl. projects NY, 2004—. Oversaw partnership between CBS News and the Smithsonian Institution, "Smithsonian Minutes", 1996; CBS News rep. working with other member networks to reform Voter News Svc. Helped develop "Before Your Eyes", CBS News, headed panel, author 87 page report examining the mistakes of Election Nght 2000, CBS News; exec. prodr.: "The Class of 2000", CBS Reports, CBS News/Time 100 Project. Recipient William Rogers award, 1991, Peabody award (Three), Edward R. Murrow award, RTNDA, Alfred I. duPont-Columbia U. award, Grand Prize of Robert F. Kennedy Journalism awards, Emmy awards (Thirteen), Honorable Mention, Overseas Press Club. Office: CBS News 524 N 57th St New York NY 10019-2924

**MASON, LOIS E. (J. DAY MASON),** painter, poet, actress, educator; b. Boston, May 4, 1919; d. Harold Monroe and Orpah Cecil (Smith) Scheibe; m. Lucien Bunce Day, June 21, 1941 (div. 1954); children: Felicity, Christopher, Sarah; m. Frederick Dike Mason, Apr. 27, 1964 (dec.); children: Frederick Dike III, Victoria, Johanna. Student, U. Leiden, Netherlands, 1939; BA, Oberlin (Ohio) U., 1940; postgrad., Cranbrook Acad. Art, Bloomfield Hills, Mich., 1941. Set-up and tchr. art dept. Pingree Sch., Hamilton Mass.; TV lectr. creative arts and writing, Mass. and Conn., 1949-58. Actress appearing in Alien Corn, Twelfth Night, Crucible, George Washington Slept Here, Philadelphia Story, Auntie Mame, Skin of our Teeth, Spoon River, Anything Goes, Call Me Madame, Seven Keys to Baldpate, Other People's Money, Quilters, Golden Pond, Cat on a Hot Tin Roof, Little Foxes, Lettice and Lovage, Close Ties, Grace and Glorie, others; set designer, decorator Auntie Mame, See How They Run, Tea House of the August Moon, Spoon River, Archie and Mehitable; author: Speaking to Strangers, 1987-88; one-woman shows include New Britain (Conn.) Mus., Am. Ballet, N.Y., Green Mountain Gallery, N.Y.C., Essex (Mass.) Inst., Marblehead Arts, Quadrom, Mast Cove, 6 Deering, Miles Hosp., Atty. Gen.'s Office, Kennebec Valley Art Assn., Chocolate Ch. Art Ctr., Maine Gallery, Kristina's, Oliver's, Islesboro Historic Soc., West Island Gallery, Bath, Maine. Ch. ladies com. Hamilton Hall, Salem, Mass., 1975—78; set designer Cmty. Theater, Swampscott, Mass., 1973—78. Recipient C. Law/Watkins fellowship Phillips Gallery, Mus., Washington, 1944-46. Mem. Nat. Assn. Women Painters, Conn. Acad., Silvermine, Maine Gallery, Kennebec Valley Arts, Chocolate Ch. Art Ctr., Marblehead Arts, Conn. Acad., Maine Writers and Publs. Avocations: cooking, sailing, gardening.

**MASON, MARILYN GELL,** library administrator, writer, consultant; b. Chickasha, Okla., Aug. 23, 1944; d. Emmett D. and Dorothy (O'Bar) Killebrew; m. Carl L. Gell, Dec. 29 1965 (div. Oct. 1978); 1 son, Charles E.; m. Robert M. Mason, July 17, 1981. BA, U. Dallas, 1966; M.L.S., N. Tex. State U., Denton, 1968; M.P.A., Harvard U., 1978. Libr. N.J. State Libr., Trenton, 1968-69; head dept. Arlington County Pub. Libr., Va., 1969-73; chief libr. program Metro Washington Coun. Govts., 1973-77; dir. White House Conf. on Librs. and Info. Svcs., Washington, 1979-80; exec. v.p. Metrics Rsch. Corp., Atlanta, 1981-82; dir. Atlanta-Fulton Pub. Libr., Atlanta, 1982-86, Cleve. Pub. Libr., 1986-99; writer, cons., 1999—. Trustee Online Computer Library Ctr., 1984-97; Evalene Parsons Jackson lectr. divsn. librarianship Emory U., 1981; commr. Nat. Commn. Libr. Info. Svcs., 2001-02; book project dir. Information for the 1980's, 1980 Author: The Federal Role in Library and Information Services, 1983, Strategic Management for Today's Libraries, 1999; editor: Survey of Library Automation in the Washington Area, 1977 Bd. visitors Sch. Info. Studies, Syracuse U., 1981-85, Sch. of Libr. and Info. Sci., U. Tenn.-Knoxville, 1983-85; trustee Coun. on

Libr. Resources, Washington, 1992-2000. Recipient Disting. Alumna award, N. Tex. State U., 1979, Herbert and Virginia White award, ALA, 1999; inducted into Ohio Libr. Coun. Hall of Fame, 1999. Mem. ALA (mem. council 1986—90), Am. Assn. Info. Sci., Ohio Library Assn., D.C. Library Assn. (pres. 1976-77) Home and Office: 2929 First Ave 1122 Seattle WA 98121 Office Phone: 850-445-2896. Personal E-mail: marilyngmason@earthlink.net. Business E-Mail: mgmason@oclc.org.

**MASON, MARSHA,** actress, theater director, writer; b. St. Louis, Apr. 3, 1942; d. James and Jacqueline M.; m. Gary Campbell, 1965 (div.); m. Neil Simon, Oct. 25, 1973 (div.). Grad., Webster Coll., Mo. Performances include cast broadway and nat. tour Cactus Flower, 1968; other stage appearances include The Deer Park, 1967, The Indian Wants the Bronx, 1968, Happy Birthday, Wanda June, 1970, Private Lives, 1971, You Can't Take It With You, 1972, Cyrano de Bergerac, 1972, A Doll's House, 1972, The Crucible, 1972, The Good Doctor, 1973, King Richard III, 1974, The Heiress, 1975, Mary Stuart, 1982, Amazing Grace, 1995, Night of the Iguana, 1996; one-woman show off-Broadway, The Big Love, Perry St. Theatre, 1988, Lake No Bottom, Second Stage, 1990, Escape From Happiness, With Naked Angels, 1994, Amazing Grace, 1998, House, 1998, (London) Prisoner of Second Avenue, 1999, Steel Magnolias, 2005; film appearances include Hot Rod Hullabaloo, 1966, Beyond the Law, 1968, Blume in Love, 1973, Cinderella Liberty, 1973 (recipient Golden Globe award 1974, Acad. award nominee), Audrey Rose, 1977, The Goodbye Girl, 1977 (recipient Golden Globe award 1978, Acad. award nominee), The Cheap Detective, 1978, Promises in the Dark, 1979, Chapter Two, 1979 (Acad. award nominee), Only When I Laugh, 1981 (Acad. award nominee), Max Dugan Returns, 1982, Heartbreak Ridge, 1986, Stella, 1988, Drop Dead Fred, 1990, I Love Trouble, 1994, Nick of Time, 1995, Two Days in the Valley, 1996, Bride & Prejudice, 2004, Bereft, 2004; (TV films) PBS series Cyrano de Bergerac, 1972, The Good Doctor, 1978, Lois Gibbs and the Love Canal, 1981, Surviving, 1985, Trapped in Silence, 1986, The Clinic, 1987, Dinner at Eight, 1989, The Image, 1990, Broken Trust, 1994, Dead Aviators, 1999, Life with Judy Garland:Me and My Shadows, 2001, The Long Shot: Believe in Courage, 2004; (TV series) Where the Heart Is, 1971, Love of Life, 1971-72, Young Dr. Kildare, 1972, Sibs, 1991; dir. (plays) Juno's Swans, 1987, Heaven Can Wait; dir. ABC Afternoon Spl. Little Miss Perfect, 1988; guest appearances include One Life to Live, 1993, Frasier, 1997, 1998 (Emmy Nom.), The Education of Max Bickford, 2002; author: Journey: A Personal Odyssey (Simon & Schuster), 2000. Personal E-mail: douhlem@newmexico.com

**MASON, MARSHALL W.,** theater director, educator, author; b. Amarillo, Tex., Feb. 24, 1940; s. Marvin Marshall and Lorine (Chrisman) M. BS in Speech, Northwestern U., 1961. Prof. Ariz. State U., 1994-2005, prof. emeritus, 2005; chief drama critic New Times, Phoenix, 1994-96. Founder, artistic dir. Circle Repertory Co., 1969-87, guest artistic dir., Ctr. Theater Group, 1988; dir. Broadway prodns. Redwood Curtain, 1993, The Seagull, 1992, Solitary Confinement, 1992, Burn This, 1987, As Is, 1985 (Drama Desk award, Tony nomination), Passion, 1983, Angels Fall, 1983 (Tony nomination), Fifth of July, 1981 (Tony nomination), Talley's Folly, 1980, (Pulitzer Prize, N.Y. Drama Critics Circle award, Tony nomination), Murder at the Howard Johnsons, 1979, Gemini, 1977, Knock Knock, 1976 (Tony nomination); Off-Broadway prodns. Book of Days, 2002, Sympathetic Magic, 1997, Robbers, 1997, Cakewalk, 1996, A Poster of the Cosmos/The Moonshot Tape, 1994, The Destiny of Me, 1992, Sunshine, 1989, Talley and Son, 1985, Childe Byron, 1980, Hamlet, 1979, Serenading Louie, 1976 (Obie award), Knock Knock, 1976 (Obie award), The Mound Builders, 1975 (Obie award), Battle of Angeles, 1974 (Obie award), The Sea Horse, 1974, The Hot L Baltimore, 1973 (Obie award); dir. numerous prodns. including Who's Afraid of Virginia Woolf?, Tokyo, 1985, Talley's Folly, 1982, London, Home Free! and The Madness of Lady Bright, 1968, Nat. Tour Sleuth, 1988, Regional Summer and Smoke, 1988, Whisper in the Mind, 1990, King Lear, 1998, The Elephant Man, London, 1998, Long Day's Journey into Night, 1998, Riga, 1999, Ginger, 2000; transl. Pirandello's Enrico IV, 2001; dir. Ghosts, 2001, Private Lives, 2002, The Drawer Boy, 2003, The Cherry Orchard, 2004, The Cripple of Inishman, 2004, The Member of the Wedding, 2005, Cat on a Hot Tin Roof, 2005, The Goat, 2006; dir. TV prodns. including Picnic, 1986, Kennedy's Children, 1982, The Fifth of July, 1983, The Mound Builders, 1975; author: Creating Lite on Stage, 2006. Recipient Vernon Rice award, 1975, Drama Desk award, 1977, Margo Jones award, 1977, Outer Critics Circle award, 1978, Theatre World award, 1979, Shubert's Vaughan award, 1980, Obie award for Sustained Achievement, 1983, Inge Festival award for lifetime achievement, 1990, Last Frontier award, 1994, award Ariz. Press Club, 1995, Erwin Piscator award, 1996, Millennium Mr. Abbott award, 1999, Creative Achievement award Ariz. State U., 2001. Mem. Soc. Stage Dirs. and Choreographers (pres. 1983-85), Dirs. Guild Am., Actors Equity Assn., Coll. Fellow of Am. Theater. Address: 165 Christopher St 5I New York NY 10014 Office Phone: 213-446-4144. E-mail: mwm@asu.edu.

**MASON, NANCY TOLMAN,** retired state agency administrator; b. Buxton, Maine, Mar. 14, 1933; d. Ansel Robert and Kate Douglas (Libby) M. Grad., Bryant Coll., Providence, R.I., 1952; BA, U. Mass., Boston, 1977; postgrad., Inst. Governmental Services, Boston, 1985, The Auditor's Inst., 1988. Asst. to chief justice Mass. Superior Ct., Boston, 1964-68; cmty. liaison Action for Boston Cmty. Devel., Boston, 1968-73; mgmt. cons. East Boston Cmty. Devel. Assn., Boston, 1973-78; asst. dir. Mass. Office of Deafness, Boston, 1978-86; dir. of contracts Mass. Rehab. Commn., Boston, 1986-98; ret., 1998. Cons. Jos. A Ryan Assocs., Boston and Orleans, Mass., 1981-86, Radio Sta. WFCC, Chatham, Mass., 1987-91, Networks, Inc., 2003-05. Author: Bromley-Heath Security Patrols, 1974, Reorganization of East Boston Community Development Corporation, 1976, How to Start Your Own Small Business, 1981. Bd. dirs. Deaf-Blind Contact Ctr., Boston, 1988-91; vol. Am. Cancer Soc., Winchester, Mass., 1986-93, Tax Equity Alliance Mass., 1994; treas. Sunset Bay Condo Assn., 1998-99, bd. dirs. 1998-2001, Highland Cemetery Assn., 2002-; mem. vestry Trinity Episc. Ch., Saco, Maine, 2005—. Recipient Good Citizen award DAR, 1950, Community Svc. award Northeastern U., 1986, Gov.'s citation for outstanding performance, 1993; named to Outstanding Young Women of Am., 1965. Mem. NOW, NAFE, Mass. State Assn. Deaf, Mass. Rehab. Commn. Statewide Cen. Office Dirs. (chair 1995-98, MRC procurement mgmt. team 1997-98, co-chair Take Your Daughters to Work Day 1998-99), Red Hat Soc. Democrat. Episcopalian. Avocations: reading, music, swimming, sign language. Address: 5 Elmwood Dr Saco ME 04072-2103

**MASON, PAUL,** broadcast executive; m. Evelyn Mason. Grad., Columbia Univ. High sch. teacher; freelance reporter ABC News, London, prod., exec. prod., 2000—04; sr. v.p., 2004—. Faculty, journalism Univ. Calif., Berkeley. Office: ABC News Fl 2 47 W 66th St New York NY 10023-6201

**MASON, RAYMOND ADAMS,** finance company executive; b. Lynchburg, Va., Sept. 28, 1936; s. Raymond Watsi and Marion (Adams) M.; married; children: Paige Adams, Pamela Ann, Carter Meade, Morgan Rand. BA in Econs., Coll. William and Mary, 1959. Rep. Mason & Lee Inc., Richmond, Va., 1960-62; founder, pres. Mason & Co. Inc., Newport News, Va., 1962-70; pres. Legg, Mason & Co., Inc., Washington, 1970-73, Legg, Mason Wood Walker, Inc., Balt., 1978—, chmn. bd. dirs.; chmn., chief exec. officer Legg Mason, Inc., 1981—. Chmn. regional firms com. N.Y. Stock Exchange, 1978-81. Trustee emeritus Endowment Assn., Coll. William and Mary; bd. dirs. emeritus William and Mary Sch. Bus. Adminstrn. Sponsors, Inc.; former trustee Balt. Mus. Art; former bd. dirs. Nat. Aquarium, Balt.; bd. dirs., exec. com., chair fin. com. Johns Hopkins Hosp.; chmn. bd., exec. com. Johns Hopkins U.; former chmn. bd. sponsors Sch. Bus. & Mgmt. Loyola Coll., Balt., 1980-88; bd. dirs. Greater Balt. Com., 1982-84, chmn., 1987-89; chmn. United Way Ctrl. Md.; former Nat. Assn. Securities Dealers (bd. govs. 1971-75, chmn. bd. govs. 1974-75), Securities Industry Assn. (bd. dirs. 1982—, chmn. 1985-86, bd. govs. 1984-88, chmn. bd. govs. 1987). Clubs: Ctr., Md., Balt. Country, L'Hirondelle, Elkridge Club, Balt. Country Club, New Orleans Country Club. Home: 1832 Circle Rd Baltimore MD 21204-6415 Office: Legg Mason Inc Bldg 100 Light St Baltimore MD 21202-6189

**MASON, RAYMOND E., JR.,** distributing company executive; b. Columbus, Ohio, Mar. 20, 1920; s. Raymond E. and Lula Estella (Potter) Mason; m. Margaret E. Edwards, Feb. 6, 1942; children: Raymond E. III, Michael D., Bruce R. BS, Ohio State U., 1941; grad., U.S. Command and Gen. Staff, 1962, U.S. Army War Coll., 1965; D of Bus. Sci. (hon.), Ohio State U., 2001; D (hon.), Franklin U., 2004; D of laws (hon.), Cumberland Coll., 2003. Ops. mgr. Suburban Motor Freight, Columbus, 1946-47; pres., gen. mgr. CFL Lines, Columbus, 1947-48; pres., chmn. Columbus Truck & Equipment Co., 1949—. Pres., chmn. REM Realty, Columbus, 1962—, Bode-Finn Co., Ltd., 1966—99; chmn. Ford Bros. Inc., Ironton, Ohio, 1975—79; mem. distbr. adv. coun. Mack Trucks; mng. dir. J. D. Ranch, Myakka City, Fla. Active Boy Scouts Am.; former trustee Freedoms Found. Valley Forge, Ohio Hist. Found.; vice-chmn. New Coll. Found.; dir. Mote Marine Lab. Ohio State U. Found.; chmn. bd. trustees emeritus Franklin U. With U.S. Army, 1941—45, maj. gen. USAR. Decorated Bronze Star medal with V for Valor, Legion of Merit, Silver Star; named State of Ohio Vet. Hall of Fame, 1997, Buckeye Boys State Hall of Fame, 1999, Ohio State U. ROTC Hall of Fame, Jr. Achievement Ctrl. Ohio Bus. Hall of Fame, 2000; recipient Pres. Unit citation, Truck Dealer of the Yr. award, Time mag., 1972, Good Scout award, Ctrl. Ohio Coun. Boy Scouts Am., Silver Beaver award, Boy Scouts Am., Silver Antelope award, Disting. Citizen of Yr. award, Centennial medal, Ohio State U., Pacesetters award, Coll. Bus. ISU, 1996, Virginia Steckler Internat. Svc. award, ARC, 1998, Lifetime Achievement award, Ohio State U., 1999, Harrison Sayre award, 2001, Philanthropist of the Yr., Columbus Found., 2001; Baden-Powell fellow, World Scout Found. Mem.: Ohio Truck Assn., Am. Truck Dealers, Ohio State U. Alumni Assn., Army War Coll. Alumni Assn., Armor Assn., U.S. Army Arty. Assn., Columbus Club, Rotary (past dist. gov., Man of Yr., Paul Harris fellow), Masons. Office: Columbus Truck Equipment Co PO Box 83250 Columbus OH 43203-0250 Home: 85 Sugar Mill Dr Osprey FL 34229-9067 Office Phone: 614-252-3111.

**MASON, RICHARD J.,** lawyer; b. Syracuse, N.Y., June 16, 1951; BA with high honors, U. Ill., 1973; MBA, U. Chgo., 1980; JD, U. Notre Dame, 1977. Bar: Ill. 1977. Ptnr., mem. exec. com. Ross & Hardies, Chgo., 1990—2003; ptnr. McGuireWoods, Chgo., 2003—. Adj. prof. law Kent Coll. Law, Ill. Inst. Tech., Chgo., 1984—. Bd. dirs. Ill. Farm Legal Educational Found., 1985-88. Fellow Am. Coll. Bankruptcy; mem. ABA (chmn. bus. bankruptcy subcom. on use and disposition of property under the bankruptcy code 1989—), Am. Bankruptcy Inst., Ill. State Bar Assn. (mem. banking and bankruptcy law sect. coun. 1986-88), Chgo. Bar Assn. (mem. bankruptcy and reorgn. com. 1978—). Office: McGuireWoods LLP 77 W Wacker Dr Ste 4100 Chicago IL 60601

**MASON, ROBERT MCSPADDEN,** information scientist, educator, dean; b. Sweetwater, Tenn., Jan. 16, 1941; s. Paul Rankin and Ruby May (McSpadden) M.; m. Betty Ann Durrence (div. 1980); children: Michael Dean, Donald Robert; m. Marilyn Killebrew Gell, July 17, 1981. SB, MIT, 1963, SM, 1965; PhD, Ga. Inst. Tech., 1973. Tech. staff mem. Sandia Labs., Livermore, Calif., 1965-68; rsch. scientist Ga. Inst. Tech., Atlanta, 1971-75, sr. rsch. scientist, 1975; prin. Metrics, Inc., Atlanta, 1975-80; pres. Metrics Rsch. Corp., Atlanta, 1980-86, Cleve., 1986-98, Tallahassee, 1998—; adj. prof. Weatherhead Sch. Mgmt. Case Western U., 1987-88, vis. prof., 1988-91, prof. for practice of tech. mgmt., 1991-98; dir. Ctr. Mgmt. Sch. Tech., 1988-96; Sprint prof. mgmt. and mgmt. info. sys. Coll. Bus. Fla. State U., Tallahassee, 1998—2005, chair mgmt. info. sys., 1998—2002; prof. info. sch. U. Wash., Seattle, 2006—, assoc. dean rsch., 2006—. Co-author: The Impact of Office Automation on Clerical Employment, 1985-00, 1985, Library Micro Consumer, 1986; co-editor: Information Services: Economics, Management, and Technology, 1981, Management of Technology V: Technology Management in a Changing World, 1996, Management of Technology, Sustainable Development, and Eco-Efficiency, 1998, Management of Technology: The Key to Prosperity in the Third Millenium, 2001; Am. editor Technovation, 1994-2005, sr. editl. bd., 2005—; mem. sr. editl. bd., 2006—; contbr. articles to profl. jours. Mem. Internat. Assn. for Tech. Mgmt. (newsletter editor 1992-93, program chair internat. conf., 1996, pres. 1996-98, mem. exec. com. 1998—). Republican. Presbyterian. Avocations: fly-fishing, skiing, sailing, scuba diving, photography. Home: 2929 1st Ave Unit 1122 Seattle WA 98121 Office: Info Sch U Wash Seattle WA 98195-2840 E-mail: rmmason@alum.mit.edu.

**MASON, RODNEY,** performing arts educator; b. Phila. Dancer Urban Colors, Portland, Oreg. Instr. hip-hop dance U. Arts Phila. Recipient Bessie Ward award, 2002.

**MASON, SALLY KAY FROST,** biology professor, academic administrator; b. N.Y.C., May 29, 1950; d. Michael and Alberta Viparina; m. John S. Frost, Aug. 1975 (div. Feb. 1982); m. Kenneth Andrew Mason, Mar. 17, 1990. BA in Zoology, U. Ky., 1972; MS in Cell/Devel. Biology, Purdue U., 1974; PhD in Cell/Devel. Biology, U. Ariz., 1978. Rsch. assoc Ind. U., Bloomington, 1978-80; asst. prof. biology U. Kans., Lawrence, 1981-88, assoc. prof. biology, 1986-91, prof. biology, 1991-2001, chair dept. physiology and cell biology, 1986-89, assoc. dean arts and scis., 1990-95, dean arts and scis., 1995-2001; provost, prof. biology Purdue U., West Lafayette, Ind., 2001—. Chmn. bd. Inproteo, 2003—; chmn. EHR adv. bd. NSF. 2005—; mem. exec. com. Nat. Assn. State U. and Land Grant Colls., 2002—; mem. Pres.'s Nat. Medal of Sci. Selection Com., 2006—. Mem. editl. bd. Pigment Cell Rsch., 1988-99; contbr. chpts. to books and articles to profl. jours. Dissertation fellow AAUW, 1977-78, Kemper Tchg. fellow U. Kans., Lawrence, 1997; grantee NSF, NIH, Washington, 1981—; Wesley Found. grantee Welsey Health Found., Wichita, Kans., 1991-93. Mem. Internat. Fedn. Pigment Cell Scis. (coun. mem. 1997-2000), Pan Am. Soc. for Pigment Cell Rsch. (coun. mem. 1988-98, pres. 1996-98), Coun. Colls. Arts and Scis. (bd. mem. 1997-99, pres. elect 1999-2000, pres. 2000-2001). Avocations: travel, reading, writing. Office: Purdue U Office of Provost Hovde Hall West Lafayette IN 47905 Office Phone: 765 494-9709 E-mail: sfmason@purdue.edu

**MASON, SCOTT MACGREGOR,** entrepreneur, inventor, consultant; b. NYC, Feb. 11, 1923; s. Gregory Mason and Mary Louise Turner; m. Mildred Davidson, Mar. 13, 1949 (div. 1970); children: Alan Gregory, Phoebe Louise, Caleb; m. Virginia Frances Perkins, May 5, 1970 (dec. 1990). AB, Princeton U., 1943; MS, NYU, 1947. Control chemist Firestone Tire & Rubber Co., Akron, Ohio, 1943-44; R & D chemist Am. Cyanamid Co. Rsch. Labs., Stamford, Conn., 1948-52; mgr. stearate dept. Warwick Chem. div. Sun Chem. Corp., Wood River Junction, R.I., 1952-58; cons., Stonington, Conn., 1958-59; instr. Williams Meml. Inst., New London, Conn., 1959-63; NSF fellow Brown U., Providence, 1963-64; Istr. Moses Brown Sch., Providence, 1964-70; owner, mgr. Innoventures, Wakefield, R.I., 1970—. Cons. Greene Plastics Corp., Canonchet, R.I., 1972-80, Dorette Inc., Pawtucket, R.I., 1982-83. Trustee Pine Point Sch., Stonington, 1956-62, pres. bd., 1959-61. With AUS, 1944-46, ETO. Named Tchr. of Week, Sta. WICE, Providence, 1967; summer rsch. fellow NSF, U. R.I., 1960. Mem. AAAS, N.Y. Acad. Scis. Achievements include patents in field. Avocations: tennis, fishing, snorkeling, photography, music. Office: Innoventures PO Box 369 Wakefield RI 02880-0369

**MASON, STEPHEN OLIN,** not-for-profit developer; b. Fresno, Calif., July 11, 1952; s. Olin James and Mary Edna (Moyer) Mason. BA, Bridgewater (Va.) Coll., 1974; MEd, James Madison U., 1979; PhD, Loyola U., Chgo. 1991. Asst. to the dir. student ctr. Bridgewater Coll., 1974-76; guidance counselor Woodlawn Elem. Sch., Sebring, Fla., 1976-77; asst. dean for student devel. Bridgewater Coll., 1977-81; dir. student life Roger Williams Coll., Bristol, R.I., 1981-83; assoc. dean for residential svcs. Dickinson Coll., Carlisle, Pa., 1983-84; v.p., dean student affairs Westmar Coll., LeMars, Iowa, 1984; rsch. assoc. to pres. Elmhurst (Ill.) Coll., 1986-87; v.p. student affairs Felician Coll., Chgo., 1987-88; dean students Huntingdon Coll., Montgomery, Ala., 1988-90; dir. devel. McPherson (Kans.) Coll., 1990-94, v.p. fin. svcs., 1994-97; exec. dir. Assn. of Brethren Caregivers, Elgin, Ill., 1997—2003; v.p. coll. adv. Manchester Coll., No. Manchester, Ind., 2004—05; exec. dir. Cmty. Found. Wabash County, No. Manchester, Ind., 2005—. Participant ARC Blood Drive, 1978—79; mem. allocations com.

United Way, Carlisle, 1984; adv. bd. mem. LeMars chpt. Siouxland Coun. for Alcoholism and Drug Abuse, 1984; site coord. for coat drive Mental Health Greater Chgo., 1985; dir.-at-large Alumni Bd. Bridgewater Coll., 1987—93; v.p. McPherson Habitat for Humanity, 1993, 1994, bd. dirs., 1993—96, pres., 1994; bd. dirs. McPherson Mus. and Arts Found., 1992—94, Assn. Brethren Caregivers, 1993—97, Assn. Anabaptist Risk Mgmt., 2000—03; governing coun., mem. adv. Bethany Hosp., 2001—02. Mem.: Brethren Benefit Trust (bd. dirs. 2002—). Avocations: calligraphy, theater, barbershop quartets, spelunking. Home: 106 S Merkle St North Manchester IN 46962 Office Phone: 260-982-5212. Business E-Mail: steve@cfwabash.org

**MASON, SUSAN E.,** social sciences educator, consultant; MAT in History, U. of Chgo., 1970; PhD, Columbia U., N.Y.C., 1981; MSSW, Columbia U., 1987; MS in Health Adminstrn., NYU, 1993. LCSW N.Y., 2004. Social work supr. LI Jewish Med. Ctr., Glen Oaks, NY, 1988—96; prof. of social work Yeshiva U., N.Y.C., NY, 1996—. Sr. ednl. cons. N.Y. State Social Work Edn. Consortium, N.Y.C. and Albany, NY, 2002—. Author: (book) Diagnosis Schizophrenia. Mem.: Coun. on Social Wk. Edn. (assoc.), NASW (assoc.), N.Y. Acad. Sci. (assoc.) Achievements include research in Mental health, child welfare, education, Gerontology. Office: WSSW/Yeshiva University 2495 Amsterdam Ave New York NY 10033 Office Phone: 212-960-0806. E-mail: masonse@yu.edu.

**MASON, TERRY,** city health department administrator, urologist; BS, Loyola U., 1974; MD, U. of Ill. Abraham Lincoln Sch. Medicine, 1978. Pres., ptnr. Prairie Med. Associates; chief Urology Mercy Hosp., Chgo.; assistant prof. surgery Abraham Lincoln Sch. Medicine U. of Ill.; commr. dept. public health City of Chgo., 2006—. Host radio prog. Doctor in the House WVON, Chgo. Author: Making Love Again, Renewing Intimacy & Helping Your Man Overcome Impotence, 1988. Recipient Physician of the Year, Nat. Med. Assn., 1999, Black Enterprise Best in Medicine award, 2001. Fellow: Am. Coll. Surgeons; mem.: World Impotence Assn. (regional dir.), Am. Urological Assn., Nat. Med. Assn. (nat. chmn.), AMA, Saltpond Redevelopment Inst., Ghana West Africa, NAACP. Office: City of Chgo Dept Health 333 S State St Ste 200 Chicago IL 60604 also: Prairie Med Assocs Ltd 2600 S Michigan Ste 303 Chicago IL 60616*

**MASON, THOMAS ALBERT,** retired lawyer; b. Cleve., May 4, 1936; s. Victor Lewis and Frances (Speidel) M.; m. Elisabeth Gun Sward, Sept. 25, 1965; children: Thomas Lewis, Robert Albert. AB, Kenyon Coll., 1958; LLB, Case-Western Res. U., 1961. Bar: Ohio 1962. Assoc. Thompson, Hine and Flory, Cleve., 1965-73, ptnr., 1973—2001; ret., 2002. Trustee Cleve. YMCA, 1975-94. Capt. USMCR, 1962-65. Mem. Am. Coll. Real Estate Lawyers, Ohio Bar Assn., Cleve. Bar Assn., The Country Club. Republican. Episcopalian. Avocations: tennis, golf. Home: 23375 Duffield Rd Cleveland OH 44122-3101 Office: Thompson Hine LLP 3900 Key Ctr 127 Public Sq Cleveland OH 44114-1291 Office Phone: 216-566-5519. E-mail: tom.mason@thompsonhine.com.

**MASON, THOMAS ALEXANDER,** historian, educator, author; b. Port Huron, Mich., Oct. 29, 1944; s. Frank Hallgren and Charlotte (Hamilton) M.; m. Christine Huguette Guyonneau, Aug. 11, 1984; 1 child, Charlotte Guyonneau. BA in History with highest honors, Kenyon Coll., 1966; MA, U. Va., 1970, PhD, 1975. Asst. prof. history Pembroke (N.C.) State U., 1976-79; assoc. editor Papers of James Madison, U. Va., 1979-86, acting editor, 1986-87; dir. publs. Ind. Hist. Soc., 1987—2001, v.p. publs., 2001—02; v.p. Ind. Hist. Soc. Press, 2002—. Author: Serving God and Mammon: William Juxon, 1582-1663, 1985; exec. editor: Traces of Indiana and Midwestern History, 1989—; editor: Documentary Editing, 1989-93, Mag. of Albermarle County History, 1984-86; co-editor: Papers of James Madison, congl. series, vols. 14-16, 1983-89, presdl. series, vol. 1, 1984; project dir.: Papers of Lew Wallace, 1992—; mem. editl. bd. Jour. of the Early Republic, 1991-95, Ency. of Indpls., 1990-94, Documentary Editing, 2002—; contbr. articles to encys. and scholarly jours. Served with USMC, 1966-68. Mem. Am. Assn. for State and Local History, Am. Hist. Assn., N.Am. Conf. on Brit. Studies, So. Hist. Assn., Assn. Documentary Editing (councillor-at-large 1999-2002, dir. publs. 1995-98, Disting. Svc. award 1993), Hist. Soc. of the Episcopal Ch. (sec. 1995—, bd. dirs. 1993—), English-Speaking Union U.S. (chmn. region VI 1996-2002, bd. dirs. 1995-2002, pres. Indpls. br. 1989-96, Lily Dabney scholar 1972, Merit award 2002), Raven Soc., Rotary (Indpls., bd. dirs. 1998-2000), Colonnade Club (Charlottesville), Royal Commonwealth Soc. (London), Omicron Delta Kappa (faculty sec. U. Va. 1984-86), Alpha Delta Phi. Episcopalian. Home: PO Box 20331 Indianapolis IN 46220-0331 Office: Ind Hist Soc 450 W Ohio St Indianapolis IN 46202-3269 E-mail: tmason@indianahistory.org.

**MASON, THOMAS R.,** utilities executive; BEE, Purdue U.; MBA, U. Chgo. Pres., COO CalEnergy Operating Svcs., Inc., 1995—99; sr. v.p. Calpine Power Co., San Jose, Calif., 1999, exec. v.p., pres., 1999—. Office: Calpine Power Co 50 W San Fernando St 5th Fl San Jose CA 95113 Office Phone: 408-995-5115. Office Fax: 408-995-0505.

**MASON, THOMASINE GRAYSON,** judge; b. Summerton, S.C., Nov. 7, 1918; d. James Fulton Grayson and Martha Anne Gentry; m. Edgar Fleming Mason, June 30, 1939 (dec.). BA, U. S.C., Columbia, 1938, LLB, 1942, JD, 1970. Certificate in cotton classing U. S.C., 1956. Tchr., West Columbia, SC, 1938—39; civil svc. rep. during World War II Atlanta, Athens and Charleston Navy Yard; gen. practice of law Manning, SC; trial atty. Dept. Justice, Washington, 1969—71; hearing office chief adminstrv. law judge, 1985—2002. Bd. trustees Clarendon Meml. Hosp., Manning, SC; state senator SC; del. Nat. Dem. Conv., 1980. Mem.: Richland County Bar Assn., S.C. Bar Assn., ABA, DAR, Am. Legion Aux., Alpha Delta Pi. Republican. Baptist. Avocation: jet-skiing. Office: Office of Hearings and Appeals 1927 Thurmond Mall Blvd Ste 200 Columbia SC 29201 Business E-Mail: thomasine.g.mason@ssa.gov

**MASON, WILLIAM,** opera company director; b. Chgo. m. Diana Davis; 2 children. MusB, Roosevelt U. Asst. to co-artistic dir. Pino Donati, 1962—66; asst. stage mgr. Lyric Opera Chgo., 1968—70; asst. to Felix Popper N.Y.C Opera, 1971; prod. stage mgr. Cin. Opera, 1972; stage mgr., asst. in musical preparation Light Opera of Manhattan, 1972; prod. mgr., asst. dir. Ohio-based Corbett Found., 1973; prod. dir. Lyric Opera Chgo., 1974—78, gen. dir., 1997—; artistic adminstr. San Francisco Opera, 1979—80. Mem. Lyric Children's Chorus, 1954—56. Office: Lyric Opera Chgo 20 N Wacker Dr Chicago IL 60606-2806*

**MASON, WILLIAM A(LVIN),** psychologist, educator, researcher; b. Mountain View, Calif., Mar. 28, 1926; s. Alvin Frank and Ruth Sabina (Erwin) M.; m. Virginia Joan Carmichael, June 27, 1948; children: Todd, Paula, Nicole, Hunter. BA, Stanford U., 1950, MS, 1952, PhD, 1954. Asst. prof. U. Wis.-Madison, 1954-59; research assoc. Yerkes Labs. Primate Biology, Orange Park, Fla., 1959-63; head dept. behavioral sci. Delta Primate Research Ctr., Tulane U., Covington, La., 1963-71; prof. psychology, research psychologist U. Calif., Davis, 1971-91, leader behavioral biology unit Calif. Primate Rsch. Ctr., 1972-96, prof. emeritus, 1991. Bd. dirs. Jane Goodall Inst., 1978-92, Karisoke Rsch. Ctr., 1980-86. Mem. Editorial bd. Animal Learning and Behavior, 1973-76, Internat. Jour. Devel. Psychobiology, 1980-92, Internat. Jour. Primatology, 1980-90; contbr. numerous articles to profl. jours., chpts. to books. With USMC, 1944-46. USPHS spl. fellow, 1963-64. Fellow AAAS, APA (pres. divsn. 6 1982, disting. sci. contbn. award 1995), Am. Psychol. Soc., Animal Behavior Soc.; mem. Internat. Primatological Soc. (pres. 1976-80, 81-84), Am. Soc. Primatologists (pres. 1988-90, disting. primatologist award), Internat. Soc. Devel. Psychobiology (pres. 1971-72, Best Paper of Yr. award 1976), Sigma Xi. Home: 2809 Anza Ave Davis CA 95616-0257 Office: U Calif Regl Primate Rsch Ctr 1 Shields Ave Davis CA 95616 Business E-Mail: wamason@ucdavis.edu.

**MASON, WILLIAM VANHORN,** dermatologist; b. Pitts., Jan. 8, 1930; AB, Harvard U., 1951; MD, Baylor Coll. Medicine, Houston, 1961. Diplomate Am. Bd. Dermatology. Pvt. practice, Albuquerque, 1979—; clin. prof. dermatology Sch. Medicine U. N.Mex., Albuquerque, 2003—. Lt. (j.g.) USN, 1951-54. Mem. Phi Beta Kappa, Alpha Omega Alpha. Office: 200 Oak St NE Ste 5 Albuquerque NM 87106-4740

**MASON-CHANEY, LISA,** curator; b. Paducah, Ky., Apr. 18, 1962; d. Billy C. and Doris Ann Mason; m. Kevin Chaney, Nov. 20, 1994; children: Courtney Ann Jones, Robert Wesley Jones. BFA, MA, We. Ky. U., 1989. Curatorial asst. Nat. Portrait Gallery, Washington, 1990—93; collections mgr. Soc. Cin. at Anderson House Mus., Washington, 1992—99; mus. dir. Ellicott City B&O RR Sta. Mus., Ellicott City, Md., 2000—04; curator, asst. dir. Hammond-Harwood House, Annapolis, Md., 2004—. Mem.: Am. Assn. Mus. (mid-atlantic rep. small museums com. 2003—), Mid-Atlantic Assn. Mus. (profl. com. coun. chair 2005—), Md. Assn. History Mus. (v.p. 2005—), Small Mus. Assn. (pres. 2005). Democrat. Avocations: travel, reading. Home: 313 Crandell Rd Severna Park MD 21146 Office: Hammond-Harwood House 19 Maryland Ave Annapolis MD 21401 Office Phone: 410-263-4683 x 12. E-mail: lmchaney@hammondharwoodhouse.org.

**MASON-HIPKINS, PATRICIA,** minister; b. Pitts., Pa. d. Oliver Ellwood and Clarice Jane Hipkins; widowed; children: Rodney Williams Jr., Rhonda Haynes, Gregory Williams. MDiv, Interdenominational Theol. Sem., 1984, D in Ministry, 1990. Assoc. minister Ch. of God in Christ, Atlanta, 1981—90; dir. enlistment Interdenominational Theol. Sem., Atlanta, 1990—93; ch. devel. pastor Presbyn. of Atlanta, 1994—2000; pastor Hazelwood Presbyn., Pitts., 2001—. Grief counselor Arlington Cemetery, Atlanta, 1998—2000; therapist Auberle Ctr. Dep. and Delinquent Youth, 2000; grief counselor Anegheny Cemetery, Pitts., 2000—01. Commr. Gen. Assembly PC USA, Louisville, 2004—; mem. Com. Racial and Social Justice, Pitts., 2001—05, Com. on Ministry; commr. New Ch. Devel. Mem.: Nat. Black Presbyn. Caucus, Theta Phi. Presbyterian. Avocation: interior decorating. Home: 1870 Graham Rd Pittsburgh PA 15235 Office: Hazelwood Presbyn Ch 5000 2nd Ave Pittsburgh PA 15207 Office Phone: 412-421-0947. Personal E-mail: drpatmason@aol.com.

**MASOTTI, LOUIS HENRY,** real estate educator, consultant; b. NYC, May 16, 1934; s. Henry and Angela Catherine (Turi) Masotti; m. Iris Patricia Leonard, Aug. 28, 1958 (div. 1981); children: Laura Lynn, Andrea Anne; m. Ann Randel Humm, Mar. 5, 1988. AB, Princeton U., 1956; MA, Northwestern U., 1961, PhD, 1964. Fellow Nat. Ctr. Edn. in Politics, 1962; asst. prof. polit. sci. Case Western Res. U., Cleve., 1963-67, assoc. prof., 1967-69, dir. Civil Violence Rsch. Ctr., 1968-69; sr. Fulbright lectr. Johns Hopkins U. Ctr. Advanced Internat. Studies, Bologna, Italy, 1969-70; assoc. prof. Northwestern U., Evanston, Ill., 1970-72, prof. polit. sci. and urban affairs, 1972-83, dir. Ctr. Urban Affairs, 1971-80, dir. Program in Pub. and Not-for-Profit Mgmt., Kellogg Sch. Mgmt., 1979-80, prof. mgmt. and urban devel. Kellogg Sch. Mgmt., 1983-94, dir. Real Estate Research Ctr. Kellogg Sch. Mgmt., 1986-88. Cons. in field; vis. assoc. prof. U. Wash., 1969; exec. dir. Mayor Jane Byrne Transition Com., Chgo., 1979; vis. prof. Stanford Sch. Bus., 1989—92, UCLA Sch. Mgmt., 1989—92; prof. dir. real estate mgmt. program U. Calif. Grad. Sch. Mgmt., Irvine, 1992—99; bd. dirs. Mfd. Home Cmtys., Inc., Facilities Mgmt. Internat., S. Calif. Physicans Ins. Co. Author: (book) Educaiton and Politics in Suburbia, 1967, Shootout in Cleveland, 1969, A Time to Burn?, 1969, Suburbia in Transition, 1973, The New Urban Politics, 1976, The City in Comparative Perspective, 1976; co-editor: Metropolis in Crisis, 1968, Metropolis in Crisis, 2d edit., 1971, Riots and Rebellion, 1968, The Urbanization of the Suburbs, 1973, After Daley: Chicago Politics in Transition, 1981, Downtown Development, 1985, Downtown Development, 2d edit., 1987; editor: Edn. and Urban Soc., 1968—71, Urban Affairs Quar., 1973—80; sr. editor: Devel. Quar., 1986—92, vice chmn. bd.; Ency. Issues Jour., 1986—92, BOMA Office Mag., 1990—95. Mem. Cleveland Heights Bd. Edn., 1967—69; devel. coord. high tech. State of Ill. - City of Chgo., 1982—83; Rsch. dir. Carl Stokes for Mayor Cleve., 1967; advisor to various congl., gubernatorial and mayoral campaigns Ohio, Ill., NJ, Calif. Lt. USNR, 1956—59. Recipient Disting. Svc. award, Cleve. Jaycees, 1967; fellow, Homer Hoyt Inst. Advanced Real Estate Studies; numerous rsch. grants, 1963—2000. Mem.: Internat. Econ. Devel. Coun., Nat. Assn. Indsl. Office Properties, Internat. Devel. Rsch. Coun., Internat. Assn. Corp. Real Estate Execs., Nat. Trust Hist. Preservation, Habitat, Urban Land Inst., Lambda Alpha Internat. Address: 2010 W Twinoaks Dr Prescott AZ 86305 Office Phone: 619-750-1703. Personal E-mail: louismasotti@cableone.net.

**MASRI, MERLE SID,** biochemist, consultant; b. Jerusalem, Palestine, Sept. 12, 1927; came to U.S., 1947; s. Said Rajab and Fatima M.; m. Maryjean Loretta Anderson, June 28, 1952 (div. 1974); children: Kristin Corinne, Allan Eric, Wendy Joan, Heather Anderson. BA in Physiology, U. Calif., Berkeley, 1950; PhD in Mammalian Physiology and Biochemistry, U. Calif. Berkeley, 1953. Rsch. asst. Dept. Physiology, Univ. Calif., Berkeley, 1950-53; predoctoral fellow Baxter Labs., Berkeley, 1952-53; rsch. assoc. hematology Med. Rsch. Inst., Michael Reese Hosp., Chgo., 1954-56; sr. rsch. biochemist Agrl. Rsch. Svc., USDA, Berkeley, 1956-87; supervisory rsch. scientist Agrl. Rsch. Svc., USDA, N.D. State U. Sta., Fargo, ND, 1987-89; pvt. practice as cons. Emeryville, Calif., 1989—. Lectr. in field. Contbr. articles to profl. jours.; chpts. to books. Recipient Spl. Svc. and Merit awards USDA, 1966, 76, 77, Superior Svc. award USDA, 1977. Mem. AAAS, Am. Chem. Soc., Am. Oil Chemists Soc., Am. Assn. Cereal Chemists, N.Y. Acad. Scis., Inst. Food Technologists, Commonwealth Club Calif., Internat. Platform Assn., World Affairs Coun. of No. Calif., Sigma Xi. Achievements include patents for detoxification of aflatoxins in agricultural crops and aflatoxin contaminated milk, improved dyeability of cotton fabrics and reduced dye and electrolyte discharge in plant effluent, new closed-circuit raw wool scouring technology to conserve water and energy and control pollution, synthesis and use of polymers and modification of biopolymers for wastewater treatment, and for encapsulation, enzyme immobilization, toxic heavy metals removal and textile finishing treatment, non-polluting new technology for scouring raw wool in a closed circuit with water recycling and re-use and waste effluent control; studied chlorination of water in food processing operations and water re-use and recycle and the generation of mutagens and means of improving disinfection efficiency and reducing mutagen formation, pharmacology, metabolism, and toxicology of natural and synthetic compounds, cereal and baking technology and wheat and durum quality, carbohydrate chemistry, fermentation and enology, confectionery, ceramic chemistry and digital graphic art image production; discovery of new methods and reagents for protein and amino acid residue modification and analysis, new mammalian metabolic pathways; development of other non-polluting textile finishing treatments (shrink, wrinkle, insect and fire resistance). Home: 9 Commodore Dr Emeryville CA 94608-1652

**MASRI, SAFWAN MALEK,** industrial engineer, educator; BS in Industrial Engring., Purdue U., 1982, MS in Industrial Engring., 1984; PhD in Industrial Engring. & Mgmt., Stanford U., 1988. Former prof. Stanford U., Santa Clara U.; prof. Columbia U., 1988—, vice dean, dir., MBA program, grad. sch. of bus., 1993—. Bd. dirs. ARAMEX Internat., Nuqul Group, Aregon, Sage Ventures; consultant Merrill Lynch, PaineWebber, Salomon Brothers, Deutsche Bank, Bankers Trust, Citibank, Ford Motor Co., Pfizer, IBM, Bahrain Inst. of Banking and Fin., UN; advisor to Queen Rania Al-Abdullah of Jordan; mem. adv. bd. UN Develop. Programme Project for Assessment of Arab Universities. Bd. dirs. Colbert Found., Friends for Life. Office: Columbia Bus Sch Uris Hall 3022 Broadway New York NY 10027

**MASS, M. F.,** allergist, immunologist; b. Phila., Feb. 24, 1945; m. Marilyn Halpern, June 12, 1966; children: Ellis, David. Student, U. Fla., 1963; BA, Brandeis U., 1966; MD, U. Fla., 1970; postgrad., U. Colo., Albany, NY, 1972, U. Colo., Denver, 1975. Intern Albany Med. Ctr., NY, 1970-71, residency, 1971-72; sr. residency U. Colo. Med. Ctr., Denver, 1972-73, postgrad. fellow/allergy-immunology, 1973-75; assoc. clin. prof. medicine U. Fla., Jacksonville, 1977—. Past chmn. dept. medicine Meml. Med. Ctr., Jacksonville; prin. investigator Jacksonville Ctr. for Clin. Rsch. Inventor skin chamber. Chmn. Duval County Environ. Protection Bd.; trustee Fla. CC at Jacksonville, 1999—, also bd. trustees. Maj. USAF, 1975-77. Health Professions scholar U. Fla. Fellow ACP, Am. Acad. Allergy and Immunology, Am. Coll. Allergy; mem. Duval County Med. Soc. (v.p., pres.-elect, pres.). Office: 3636 University Blvd S Ste B2 Jacksonville FL 32216-4223 Office Phone: 904-733-8200. E-mail: massjax@comcast.net.

**MASS, MICHAEL DON,** state legislator; b. McAlester, Okla., Oct. 29, 1951; s. Fred Jr. and Lois M.; m. Suzanne Kline; children: Elena, Angie, Micah, Lucas. Student, Grayson C.C., Sherman, Tex., Ea. Okla. State Coll. Mem. Ho. of Reps., 1991—. Dist. mgr. Pittsburg County Conservation Dist.; chair Okla. Dem. Party. Mem. McAlester C. of C. (exec. dir.), Latimer and Pittsburg County Cattlemen's Assn., Hartshorne C. of C. (v.p.). Democrat. Office: State Capitol Bldg Rm 501 2300 N Lincoln Blvd Oklahoma City OK 73105

**MASSA, CONRAD HARRY,** retired religious studies educator; b. Bklyn., N.Y., Oct. 27, 1927; s. Harry Frederick and Josephine W. (Lepold) M.; m. Anna W. Rossi, Aug. 19, 1951; children: Stephen Mark, Barbara Ann. AB with honors, Columbia U., 1951; M.Div., Princeton Theol. Sem., 1954, PhD, 1960; HHD, Lafayette Coll., 1987. Ordained to ministry Presbyn. Ch., 1954. Pastor Elmwood Presbyn. Ch., East Orange, NJ, 1954-57; asst. prof. homiletics Princeton Theol. Sem., 1957-61; sr. pastor Old First Ch., Newark, 1961-66, Third Presbyn. Ch., Rochester, NY, 1966-78; dean acad. affairs Princeton Theol. Sem., 1978-94, dean emeritus, 1994—, Charlotte W. Newcombe prof., 1978-95, Charlotte W. Newcombe prof. emeritus, 1995—. 1st moderator Synod of the Northeast, United Presbyn. Ch.; vis. prof. St. Bernard's Roman Cath. Sem., Rochester, 1968-70; keynote speaker 11th ann. conf. Inst. Theology, Yonsei U., Seoul, Republic of Korea, 1991. Author articles and book revs. Trustee Lafayette Coll., Easton, Pa., 1982-93. Served with U.S. Army, 1946-47. Mem. Acad. Homiletics, Am. Acad. Religion, Internat. John Bunyan Soc. Home: 9583 SW 90th St Ocala FL 34481-7495 E-mail: chm1@sprynet.com. *I have learned to try to understand all events and persons in terms of their relationships to other things, persons and events. While it is sometimes fruitful to isolate a particular and study it in its solitude, nothing and no one really exists in such isolation. This has become a guiding principle in my continued research and growth in those areas of greatest interest - religion, education and society.*

**MASSA, RICHARD WAYNE,** retired communications educator; b. Carona, Kans., May 2, 1932; s. Columbo and Ella (Whitehead) M.; m. Mary Lou Marshall, May 29, 1960 (div. 1969); m. Teresa Rose Ramirez, Mar. 19, 1971; children: Tod, Daphne, Sara. B in Journalism, U. Mo., 1954, MA, 1955; postgrad., U. Ark., 1964-65. Instr. U. Mo., Columbia, 1955, Miss. State Coll. for Women, Columbus, 1957-58; from instr. to assoc.prof. comm. Okla. Coll. for Women/Okla. Coll. Liberal Arts, Chickasha, 1958-69; assoc. prof. Mo. So. State Coll., Joplin, 1972-87, prof., 1987-99, head dept. comm., 1980-99, dir. Inst. Internat. Studies, 1996-99, acting head dept. lang. and lit., 1979-80; ret., 1999. V.p. Interpersonal Comm. Consultants, Oklahoma City, 1969-72. Co-author: Principal Ideas of Medieval and Renaissance Man, 1967, Contemporary Man in World Society, 1969; co-editor: Classical Readings for Contemporary Man, 1967, Inquisitive Man; His Quest for Truth, 1970. With U.S. Army, 1955-57. Recipient Gov.'s award for Excellence in Tchg., Mo. Dept. Higher Edn., Jefferson City, 1996. Home: 25399 Demott Dr Joplin MO 64801-6309 Personal E-mail: massa727@aol.com.

**MASSAD, JORDAN ELIAS,** mathematician; b. Tulsa, Okla., May 20, 1976; s. Joseph James and Darlene Ann Elizabeth Massad. BS, Worcester Poly. Inst., 1998; MS, N.C. State U., 2001, PhD, 2003. Html developer Worcester Poly. Inst., Mass., 1997—98; rsch. scientist Boeing Co., Bellevue, Wash., 1999—2000, Sandia Nat. Labs., Albuquerque, 2001—; rsch. fellow/asst. N.C. State U., Raleigh, NC, 1998—2003. Contbr. articles to profl. jours. Eucharitic min. and lector Cath. Campus Ministry, Worcester, Mass., 1994—98, Raleigh, NC, 1998—2003. Mem.: Soc. Physics Students, Soc. Photo-Optical Instrumentation Engineers (assoc.), Triangle Lebanese Assn., Nat. Apostolate of Maronites, So. Fedn. Syrian Lebanese Am. Clubs, Tau Beta Pi (life), Pi Mu Epsilon (life). Maronite Catholic. E-mail: krolj@alum.wpi.edu.

**MASSAD, STEPHEN ALBERT,** lawyer; b. Wewoka, Okla., Dec. 20, 1950; s. Alexander Hamilton and Delores Jean (Razook) Massad; children: Caroline, Sarah, Margaret. AB, Princeton U., 1972; JD, Harvard U., 1975. Bar: Tex. 1975. Assoc. Baker Botts LLP, Houston, 1975-82, ptnr., 1983—, corporate dept. chair, 1994—2002, mem. exec. com., 1995—2001, Office: Baker Botts LLP 3000 One Shell Plz 910 Louisiana St Houston TX 77002 Office Phone: 713-229-1475. Business E-Mail: stephen.massad@bakerbotts.com.

**MASSAD, SUSAN MOORE,** internist; b. NYC, 1938; MD, U. Calif., San Francisco, 1962. Bd. cert. internal medicine 1973. Intern Bellevue Hosp. Ctr., NYC, 1962—63, resident in medicine, 1963—64; resident San Francisco VA Hosp., 1967—68; fellow in ambulatory medicine U. Calif., San Francisco Med. Ctr., 1969—70; internist, clinical prof., dir. ambulatory internal medicine LI Coll. Hosp.

**MASSAD, TIMOTHY G.,** lawyer; b. New Orleans, July 30, 1956; AB magna cum laude, Harvard U., 1978, JD magna cum laude, 1984. Bar: NY 1985. Assoc. Cravath Swaine & Moore LLP, NYC, 1984—92, ptnr., corp., 1992—, resident ptnr. Hong Kong, 1998—2002. Corp. counsel Covenant House; vice chmn. Norwalk Redevel. Agy.; v.p. Norwalk C.C. Found. Mem.: ABA, NY State Bar Assn., Phi Beta Kappa. Office: Cravath Swaine & Moore LLP Worldwide Plz 825 Eighth Ave New York NY 10019-7475 Office Phone: 212-474-1164. Office Fax: 212-474-3700. Business E-Mail: tmassad@cravath.com.

**MASSAH, CHERILYN,** auditor; b. Dallas, Jan. 31, 1951; d. Herman Hiram and Mary Charleene (Thomas) Hill; m. Fathollah Massah, June 30, 1979. AA with highest honors, Tarrant County Jr. Coll., Hurst, Tex., 1982; BBA, U. Tex.-Arlington, 1987. CPA, Tex. Sr. auditor Def. Contract Audit Agy., Dallas, 1987—2006. Spl. Interest grantee Tarrant County Jr. Coll., 1982; nominated to Nat. Dean's List U. Tex.-Arlington, 1986-87. Mem. Assn. Govt. Accts., Beta Alpha Psi. Avocation: stamp collecting/philately. Home: 4708 Michelle Dr Arlington TX 76016-5339 Office: Def Contract Audit Agy 6321 Campus Circle Dr E Irving TX 75063 Personal E-mail: chmassah@comcast.net.

**MASSALSKI, THADDEUS BRONISLAW,** materials scientist, educator; b. Warsaw, June 29, 1926; came to U.S., 1959; s. Piotr and Stanislawa (Andrukaniec) M.; m. Sheila Joan Harris, Sept. 19, 1953; children: Irena, Peter, Christopher. B.Sc., Birmingham U., Eng., 1952, PhD, 1954, D.Sc., 1964; fellow, Inst. Study Metals, U. Chgo., 1954-56; D.Sc. (h.c.), Warsaw U., 1973. Lectr. Birmingham U., 1956-59; head. metal physics dir. Mellon Inst., Pitts., 1959-75, 1961—69; prof. metal physics and materials sci. Carnegie-Mellon U., 1966—. Vis. prof. U. Buenos Aires, 1962, Calif. Inst. Tech., 1962, Stanford, 1963, U. Calif., 1964, 66, Inst. Physics, Bariloche Argentina, 1966, 70, Harvard, 1969; exchange prof. Krakow (Poland) U., 1968; vis. scientist Nat. Bur. Standards, 1980-81; NAVSEA prof. Naval Postgrad. Sch., Monterey, Calif; chmn. bd. govs. Acta Metallurgica, Inc., 1992—96. Co-author: Structure of Metals, 3d edit, 1966, Advanced Physical Metallurgy, 1965; co-editor Progress in Materials Science, 1969—. Metall. Transactions, 1991—; editor-in-chief ASM/NIST Phase Diagram Program, 1980-2000; author papers and articles on alloy theory, crystallography, metal physics, meteorites. Guggenheim fellow Oxford U., 1965-66; recipient Alexander von Humboldt prize, 1991, Sendzimir prize Polish Inst. Arts and Scis. in Am., 1998. Fellow Am. Soc. Metals (gold medal 1993), Am. Phys. Soc., The Metals Soc. (gold medal 1995), Brit. Inst. Materials (hon.), Brit. Inst. Physics, AIME (Hume-Rotherly prize 1989); mem. Polish Acad. Sci. (fgn.), German Acad. Sci. (fgn.), Phys. Soc., Associazione Italiana di Metallurgia (Losana gold medal). Home: 900 Field Club Rd Pittsburgh PA 15238-2127 Office: Carnegie Mellon U 3303 Wean Hall Pittsburgh PA 15213

**MAS SANTOS, JORGE,** foundation administrator, telecommunications industry executive; s. Jorge Mas Canosa. BBA, U. Miami, 1984, MBA, 1985. Pres., CEO MasTec, Inc., 1994—99, dir., 1994—, chmn., 1998—; founder, chmn. Neff Corp.; chmn. Cuban Am. Nat. Found., 1999—. Exec. dir. Mas Family Scholarships, 1996—; bd. dirs. Nova Southeastern U. Office: Cuban Am Nat Found 1312 SW 27th Ave Miami FL 33145*

**MASSARO, TONI MARIE,** dean, law educator; BS, Northwestern U., 1977; JD, Coll. William and Mary, 1980. With Vedder, Price, Kaufman and Kammholz; tchr. law Washington and Lee U., U. Fla.; prof. law U. Ariz., Tucson, 1989—; Milton O. Riepe chair constl. law James E. Rogers Coll. Law, U. Ariz., Tucson, 1997—, dean, 1999—. Vis. prof. law Stanford U., U. N.C., Johann Goethe U., Frankfurt, West Germany. Author: Constitutional Literacy: A Core Curriculum for a Multi-Cultural Nation; contbr. numerous articles to law revs. Recipient Women on the Move award, YWCA, 2002. Fellow: Am. Bar Found.; mem.: Ariz. State Bar (Access to Justice com. 2003—04, Professionalism com. 2002—), Am. Law Inst., Am. Assoc. of Law Schs. (Academic Freedom and Tenure com. 2000—04). Office: U Ariz Coll Law Bldg 204a PO Box 210176 Tucson AZ 85721-0176 Fax: 520-621-9140. Office Phone: 520-621-1498. E-mail: massaro@law.arizona.edu.

**MASSENBURG, JOHNNYE SMITH,** speech pathology/audiology services professional, minister; b. Durham, N.C., July 4, 1954; d. John Franklin and Florence Rowland Smith; m. C. Warren Massenburg, Aug. 4, 1990 (dec. June 2005). BS in Speech Pathology and Audiology, Hampton U., Va., 1975; MS in Speech Pathology and Audiology, Towson State U., Md., 1978; PhD in Theology, Piedmont Theol. Sem., 2000. Lic. ordained minister Va. Speech pathologist and audiologist Balt. City Schs., 1975—78, Durham City Schs., NC, 1978—89; speech pathologist Richmond City Schs., Va., 1989—; pres. and CEO Massenburg & Massenburg Inc., Midlothian, 1990—; minister First Bapt. Ch., 1998—2006, Fifth Bapt. Ch., Richmond, 2006—. Named Woman of Yr., First Bapt. Ch., 1992, 2005; recipient Svc. award, Vets. Assn., 1993, 1994, 1998, Achievement award, Bus. Women Assn., 1994. Mem.: Am. Speech and Hearing Assn., Ministers Wives and Widows (treas. 1991—93). Democrat. Bapt. Avocations: singing, reading. Home: 13302 Farm Crest Ct Midlothian VA 23112 Office: Fifth Bapt Ch 1415 West Cary St Richmond VA 23220 Office Phone: 804-780-5078. E-mail: j_mass_midlo@att.net.

**MASSENBURG, TONY,** professional basketball player; b. July 31, 1967; BA, Univ. Md., 1990. G San Antonio Spurs, Tex., 2003—. Achievements include member, NBA Championship Team, 2005. Office: San Antonio Spurs One SBC Ctr San Antonio TX 78219

**MASSENGALE, MARTIN ANDREW,** agronomist, educator, university president; b. Monticello, Ky., Oct. 25, 1933; s. Elbert G. and Orpha (Conn) M.; m. Ruth Audrey Klingelhofer, July 11, 1959; children: Alan Ross, Jennifer Lynn. BS, Western Ky. U., 1952; MS, U. Wis., 1954, PhD, 1956, LHD (hon.), Nebr. Wesleyan U., 1987; DS (hon.), Senshu U., Tokyo, 1995. Cert. profl. agronomist, profl. crop scientist. Research asst. agronomy U. Wis., 1952-56; asst. prof., asst. agronomist U. Ariz., 1958-62, assoc. prof., assoc. agronomist, 1962-65, prof., agronomist, 1965-76, head dept., 1966-74, assoc. dean Coll. agr. assoc. dir. Ariz. Agr. Expt. Sta., 1974-76; vice chancellor for agr. and natural resources U. Nebr., 1976-81; chancellor U. Nebr.-Lincoln, 1981-91, interim pres., 1989-91; pres. U. Nebr., 1991-94, pres. emeritus, 1994, found. disting. prof. and dir., 1994—. Chmn. pure seed adv. com. Ariz. Agrl. Expt. Sta.; past chmn. bd., pres. Mid-Am. Internat. Agrl. Consortium; coord. com. environ. quality EPA-Dept. Agrl. Land Grand U.; past chmn. bd. dir. Am. Registry Cert. Profls. in Agronomy, Crops and Soils; bd. dir. Ctr. for Human Nutrition, Lincoln Ins. Group., Woodmen Accident & Life Co., LIG, Inc., Am. First, LLC, All Am. Enterprises, LLC; chair bd. dir. Agronomic Sci. Found., chmn. selection com; dir. devel. Secretariat, Filippo Maseri Florio World Prize Disting. Rsch. in Agr.; exec. com. U. Nebr. Tech. Park, LLC; mem. adv. bd. Nat. Agrl. Rsch., Ext., Edn. and Econs., 1998—, chair secs. nat. adv. bd., exec. com.; nat. adv. bd. Trees Am., 1998—. Chmn. NCAA Pres.'s Commn., 1988-91; distbn. revenue com., standing com. on appointments North Ctrl. Assn. Commn. on Insts. Higher Edn., 1991; trustee Nebr. Hist. Soc. Found.; bd. dir. Nebr. Hist. Soc.; bd. govs. Nebr. Sci. and Math. Initiative; mem. Knight Found. Commn. on Intercollegiate Athletics; bd. dir. Great Plains Funds, IBP, AGR Ednl. Found., 2004—; hon. life trustee Nebr. Coun. on Econ. Edn.; hon. lifetime trustee Nebr. Coun. on Econ. Edn.; bd. dir., trustee U. Nebr. Found. With U.S. Army, 1956-58. Named Midlands Man of Yr., 1982, to We. Ky. U. Hall of Disting. Alumni, 1992, DeKalb Crop Sci. Disting. Career award, 1996, Outstanding Educator Am., 1970, Wayne County H.S., Monticello, Ky., Charter Hall of Fame, 2002; recipient faculty recognition award Tucson Trade Mart., 1971, Ak-Sar-Ben Agrl. Achievement award, 1986, Agrl. Builders Nebr. award, 1986, Walter K. Beggs award, 1986, Vol. of Yr. award for disting. svc. Nebr. Coun. on Econ. Edn., IANR Team Initiation award, Agri award Triumph of Agr. Expn., 1999, Exemplary Svc. to Agr. award Nebr. AgRels. Coun., 2000, Friend of LEAD award Nat. LEAD Alumni Assn., 2001, Outstanding Pres. award All-Am. Football Found., 2001, Wagonmaster award Nebraskaland Found., 2006; named to Charter Hall of Fame, USDA, 2004; hon. state farmer degrees Ky., Ariz., Nebr. Future Farmers Am. Assn. Fellow AAAS (sect. chmn.), Crop Sci. Soc. Am. (past dir., pres. 1972-73, past assoc. editor, pres. western soc., Disting. Career award 1996), Am. Soc. Agronomy (past dir., vis. scientist program, past assoc. editor Agronomy Jour., Disting. Svc. award 1984); mem. Am. Grassland Coun., Ariz. Crop Improvement Assn. (bd. dir.), Am. Soc. Plant Physiology, Nat. Assn. Colls. and Tchrs. Agr., Soil and Water Conservation Soc. Am., Ariz. Acad. Sci., Nebr. Acad. Sci., Agrl. Coun. Am. (bd. dirs., issues com.), Coun. Agrl. Sci. and Tech. (bd. dir. budget and fin. 1979-82, 94-2005, treas., exec. com. 1997-2005), Nat. Assn. State Colls. and Land Grant Univs. (chmn. com. on info. tech. 1987-94, exec. com. 1990-92, bd. dir. 1992-94), Edn. Engring. Professions (mem. commn.), Coll. Football Assn. (chmn., bd. dir. 1986-88), Am. Assn. State Coll. and Univs. (task force instl. resource allocation), AAFL Enterprises LLC (bd. dir., 2004—), Assn. Am. Univs. Rsch. Librs. (steering com. 1992-94), Nebr. Crop Improvement Assn. (Disting. Svc. award), Grazing Lands Forum (pres.), Nat. C. of C. and Industry, Nebr. Diplomats Inc. (hon. diplomate), Nebr. Vet. Med. Assn. (hon.), Sigma Xi, Phi Kappa Phi, Gamma Sigma Delta (Merit award), Alpha Zeta, Phi Sigma, Gamma Alpha, Alpha Gamma Rho (bd. dir. ednl. found. 2004—, Bros. of the Century award), Phi Beta Delta, Golden Key, Innocents Soc., AGR Ednl. Found. (bd. dir., 2004—). Office: U Nebr 220 Keim Hall Lincoln NE 68583-0953 Office Phone: 402-472-4101. E-mail: mmassengale1@unl.edu.

**MASSENGILL, ELLEN WEBB,** librarian; b. Littlefield, Tex., Mar. 6, 1932; d. Lester L. and Bessie (Webb) M. BS, Tex. Tech U., 1953, MS, 1959; MLS, North Tex. State U., 1969. Homemaking tchr., Floyd, N.Mex., 1953-55, Crane, Tex., 1955-56, Seminole, Tex., 1956-68, Littlefield, Tex., 1971-73; libr. Odessa (Tex.) High Sch., 1969-71, Littlefield Jr. High Sch., 1973-82, Littlefield Ind. Sch. Dist., 1982-83, Littlefield High Sch. and Jr. High Sch., 1983-84, Littlefield High Sch., 1984-90, Littlefield High Sch. and Littlefield Primary Sch., 1990-2004; dist. area, state adv. bd. mem. Future Homemakers Am., N.Mex., Tex., 1954-68, adv. mem. nat. exec. coun., 1954-55; adv. Young Homemakers Tex., 1958-73. Mem. PTA; co-leader Girl Scouts U.S., 1948-49; del. Nat. Citizenship Coun., 1954. Recipient Home Econs. Scholarship award Borden Co., 1953, Panhellenic award Lubbock (Tex.) Panhellenic Soc., 1953; Forum award Tex. Tech. U., 1953. Mem. AAUW (reporter, historian, sec., parliamentarian 1956-68), ALA, Sch. Libr. & Info. Sci. Assn., Am. Home Econs. Assn., area Vocat. Assn., Tex. State Tchrs. Assn. (life), ALA, Tex. Libr. Assn. (life; sec. dist. 9), Tex. Classroom Tchrs. Assn., Vocat. Homemaking Tchrs. Assn. Tex., Tex. Home Econs. Assn., Lamb County Tchrs. Assn. (treas. 1984-89), Littlefield Classroom Tchrs. Assn. (treas. 1983-2005), Phi Kappa Phi, Phi Upsilon Omicron, Alpha Lambda Delta, Alpha Chi, Alpha Lambda Sigma, Beta Phi Mu, Delta Kappa Gamma (sec. Epsilon Delta chpt. 1984, charter mem. Iota Eta chpt., 2d v.p. 1987-89, 1st v.p. 1989-90, pres. 1990-92, 2d v.p. 1992-95, treas. 2000-. Alpha state constn. com. 1993-95). Republican. Baptist. Home: 510 E 6th St Littlefield TX 79339-3324 Office: 1100 W Waylon Jennings Blvd Littlefield TX 79339-3714

**MASSENGILL, MATTHEW H.,** data storage company executive; BE, Purdue U., 1983. Rsch. engr., infra detectors and imaging sys. Ford Aerospace and Commn. Corp., 1982—85; product engr. Western Digital Corp., Irvine, Calif., 1985—86, v.p. mktg. personal storage divsn., 1993—97, sr. v.p., gen. mgr. enterprise storage group Rochester, Minn., 1997—98, chief operating officer Irvine, Calif., 1998—2000, CEO, 2000—05, chmn. bd. dirs., 2001—05, exec. chmn. bd. dir., 2005—. Launched a startup software co., 1986; mgr. of ranch, Oreg., 1990—91; bd. dir. ViewSonic Corp. Bd. dir. Orange County Technology Action Network, Calif., THINK Together, (Orange County), Calif.; vice-chmn. CEO Roundtable program, Univ. Calif., Irvine; chmn. TechNet So.Calif. Recipient Outstanding Elec. Engring. Alumni award, Purdue Univ., 1998, Disting. Engring Alumni award, 2002. Office: Western Digital Corp 20511 Lake Forest Dr Lake Forest CA 92630-7741

**MASSEY, EDWIN R.,** college president; m. Jo Massey; 3 children. BS, Millsaps Coll.; MS in Marine Biology, U. Southern Miss., PhD in Zoology. Biology prof. Indian River Cmty. Coll., pres., 1988—. Bd. dirs. First Union Nat. Bank. Campaign co-chair United Way, Indian River county, 1995-96, campaign chair, 1991-93, pres. United Way of St. Lucie county, 1992-93; chmn. bd. dirs. Lawnwood Regional Med.; hon. co-chair Capital Campaign for Hospice; mem. St. Lucie County Econ. Devel. Coun.; chmn. high skill/high wage com. Region 20 JEP Bd.; co-chmn. program length and articulation com. SB 1688 Task Force; mem. legislative and high edn. articulation com. Coun. of Pres.; bd. dirs. Quad-County Tech. Prep/Sch.-to-Work Leadership; mem. Treasure Coast Educators' Coalition, Am. Coun. on Edn.'s Com. on Sci. and Math, State Articulation Coordinating com., State Correctional Acad. Adv. Bd.; chmn. Fla.'s statewide com. on accountability and effectiveness; chmn. stds./outcomes task force Divsn. of Cmty. Colls., chmn. performance based budgeting task force; chmn. trustee tng. com. SBCC; mem. adv. coun. Nat. World Class Acad.; mem. Commrs. Workforce Devel. Task Force; pres. Treasure Coast Lit. Soc.; adv. bd. mem. Ctr. for the Arts; active Martin County Bus. Devel. Bd., United Way Indian River County's Leadership Team, Pres. Coun. Steering Com., Jobs and Edn. Partnership Region 20 Bd.; mem. legis. com. Coun. Pres. Recipient Pres. award for Excellence Fla. Assn. of C.C., 1995; inducted Milsaps Coll. Sports Hall of Fame, 1994, St. Lucie County Sports Hall of Fame, 1996. Mem. Nat. Alliance Two-Yr. Coll. Athletic Adminstrs. (bd. dirs.), Fla. Assn. Colls. and Univs., Fla. Assn. C.C., Fla. C.C. Activities Assn. (past pres.), Fla. C.C. Athletic Assn. (past pres. exec. com.), Commn. on Colls. of the So. Assn. of Colls. and Schs., Am. Assn. of C.C., Southern Assn. of Cmty., Jr. and Tech. Colls. (pres. bd. dirs.), Fla. Coun. of C.C. Pres. (past chmn.), Indian River County Coun. 100, Ft. Pierce Breakfast club, Econ. Coun. Martin County, St. Lucie County C. of C. (bd. dirs., mem. higher edn. task force com.), Ft. Pierce Rotary Club. Office: Indian River CC 3209 Virginia Ave Fort Pierce FL 34981-5541

**MASSEY, ELEANOR NELSON,** school librarian, media specialist; b. Apr. 1, 1930; d. Walter K. and Jeanette (Perlman) Nelson; m. Marvin Donald Massey, June 29, 1952; children: Henry, David, Michael, Jonathan. BA, Douglass Coll., New Brunswick, N.J., 1952; postgrad., Rutgers U. Cert. ednl. media specialist. Children's librarian Westfield (N.J.) Pub. Library, 1952-55; librarian Franklin Jr. High Sch., Metuchen, N.J., 1959-61; media specialist Campbell Sch., Metuchen, 1962—2006; coordinator libraries Metuchen Pub. Schs., 1982—2006; ret., 2006. Dir. Woodbridge-East Brunswick Area Coordination Council, 1982-85; mem. interim planning com. N.J. Library Network, 1984-85; cooperating tchr. Kean Coll. and Rutgers U., 1975—; speaker; bibliographer. V.p. Sisterhood Neve Shalom, Metuchen, 1960; dir. Neve Shalom, 1959-60; bd. dirs. Union-Middlesex Regional Library Cooperative, Region IV, Inc., 1985-89; active Metuchen Cable TV Adv. Commn., 1994—. Title II Demonstration Library grantee State of N.J., 1974-76, Sch.-Pub. Libr. Coop. grantee 1986, Metuchen Edn. Found grantee for AuthorsLive program, 1999. Recipient N.J. Gov.'s Tchr. Recognition award, 1991. Mem. Ednl. Media Assn. N.J. (exec. bd. 1976-78), ALA, N.J. Library Assn., Ednl. Media Assn. Middlesex County (treas. 1982-83). Office: Campbell Sch Talmadge Ave Metuchen NJ 08840 Office Phone: 732-321-8776. E-mail: emassey@optonline.net.

**MASSEY, GARNETTA D.,** bank executive; Sr. v.p., head of bus. develop. and mktg. Harbor Bank of Md., Balt. Trustee Caroline Ctr.; mem. Greater Balt. Com. Named one of 25 Women to Watch, US Banker mag., 2005. Mem.: Balt. Mktg. Assoc. (mem. fin. com.). Office: Harbor Bank of Md 25 W Fayette St Baltimore MD 21201*

**MASSEY, HOWARD CLAYLAND,** writer; b. Coolidge, Ga., Oct. 21, 1925; s. Paul Lester and Ruby Dell Massey; m. Hilda Dodson Schroer, June 17, 1966; 1 child, Sondra Gayle Siegel; m. Edna Ann Weller (div.); 1 child, Richard Clayton. M in Plumbing and Heating, Lindsey Hopkins Tech. Edn. Ctr., Miami, 1958. Owner Ctr. Plumbing & Heating Corp., Miami-Dade, 1958—73; plans examiner Met. Bldg. & Zoning Dept., Miami-Dade, 1974—88; author Craftsman Book Co., Hollywood, Fla., 1978—85, Vero Beach, Fla., 1986—. Designer plumbing isometrics State of Fla. Lic. Bd., 1982—84; creator exam. questions Constrn. Industry Lic. Bd., Fla., 1983—85. Author: (tech. book) Plumber's Handbook, 1978, Basic Plumbing With Illustrations, 1980, Estimating Plumbing Costs, 1982, Plumber's Exam Preparation Guide, 1985, Planning Drain, Waste & Vent Systems, 1990, International Plumbing & Fuel Gas Codes, 2003, America's Ragged Edge, 2005, Deep Woods, 2006. Seaman 3d class USN, 1943—45. Mem.: Gideons Internat. Authors Guild. Republican. Home and Office: 1240 Fifth St Vero Beach FL 32962 E-mail: hcmhcm@bellsouth.net.

**MASSEY, JAMES EARL,** retired clergyman, retired educator; b. Ferndale, Mich., Jan. 4, 1930; s. George Wilson and Elizabeth (Shelton) M.; m. Gwendolyn Inez Kilpatrick, Aug. 4, 1951. Student, U. Detroit, 1949-50, 55-57; BTh, BRE, Detroit Bible Coll., 1961; AM, Oberlin Grad Sch. Theology, 1964; postgrad., U. Mich., 1967-69; DD, Asbury Theol. Sem., 1972, Ashland Theol. Sem., 1991, Huntington Coll., 1994; HumD, Tuskegee U., 1995; DD, Warner Pacific Coll., 1995; LittD, Anderson U., 1995; DD, Wash. and Jefferson Coll., 1997, North Park Theol. Sem., 1999. Ordained to ministry Ch. of God, 1951. Assoc. min. Ch. of God, Detroit, 1951-53; sr. pastor Met. Ch. of God, Detroit, 1954-76, pastor-at-large, 1976; spkr. Christian Brotherhood Hour, 1977-82; prin. Jamaica Sch. Theology, Kingston, 1963-66; campus min. Anderson Coll., Ind., 1969-77, asst. prof. religious studies Ind., 1977-79, assoc. prof. Ind., 1975-80, prof. N.T. and homiletics Ind., 1981-84; dean of chapel and univ., prof. religion and society Tuskegee U., Ala., 1984-89; dean, prof. preaching and bibl. studies Anderson Sch. Theology, 1995-99, dean emeritus, prof. at large, 1995—; dean emeritus Tuskegee U. Chapel, 1998—, 1998. Chmn. Commn. on Higher Edn. in the Ch. of God, 1968-71; vice chmn. bd. publs. Ch. of God, 1968-78; dir. Warner Press, Inc.; rsch. scholar Christianity Today Inst. Author: When Thou Prayest, 1960, The Worshipping Church, 1961, Raymond S. Jackson, A Portrait, 1967, The Soul Under Seige, 1970, The Church of God and the Negro, 1971, The Hidden Disciplines, 1972, The Responsible Pulpit, 1973, Temples of the Spirit, 1974, The Sermon in Perspective, 1976, Concerning Christian Unity, 1979; gen. editor: Christian Brotherhood Hour Study Bible, 1979, Designing the Sermon, 1980; co-editor: Interpreting God's Word for Today, 1982; editor: Educating for Service, 1984, The Spiritual Disciplines, 1985, The Bridge Between, 1988, Preaching From Hebrews, 1992, The Burdensome Joy of Preaching, 1996, Sundays at the Tuskegee Chapel, 1999, Aspects of My Pilgrimage: An Autobiography, 2002, Remembering William L. Dawson, 2004, African Americans and the Church of God, 2005, Stewards of the Story, 2005; mem. editl. bd. The Christian Scholar's Rev. Leadership mag.; mem. editl. bd., contbg. editor Vol I New Interpreter's Bible, 1990—; contbg. editor Preaching mag.; sr. editor Christianity Today mag. Mem. Corp. Inter-Vrsity Christian Fellowship; bd. dirs. World Vision. Served with AUS, 1951-53. Mem. Nat. Assn. Coll. and Univ. Chaplains, Nat. Com. Black Churchmen, Nat. Negro Evang. Assn. (bd. dirs. 1969-86). Office: 367 Beverly Rd Greensboro AL 36744-6034

**MASSEY, JAMES LEE,** electrical engineering educator; b. Wauseon, Ohio, Feb. 11, 1934; s. Charles Arnold Massey and Ethel (Pry) Sperry; m. Kathryn Jean Kramper, June 28, 1958 (div. 1977); children: Thomas A., Robert B., Peter C., John D.; m. Lis Kofod Mogensen, June 24, 1977; children: Flemming, Jesper. BSEE, U. Notre Dame, 1956; MSEE, MIT, 1960, PhD, 1962; D Tech. (hon.), U. Lund, Sweden, 1990. Prof. elect. engring. U. Notre Dame, Notre Dame, Ind., 1962-77; prof. system sci. UCLA, 1977-80; prof. elec. engring. Swiss Fed. Inst. Tech. Zurich, 1980—98, prof. emeritus, 1998—; adjunct prof. U. Lund, Sweden, 1999—. Author: Threshold Decoding, 1963. 1st lt. USMC, 1956-59. Recipient Marconi Fellowship, 1999. Fellow IEEE, Am. Acad. Arts & Sci.; mem. IEEE Info. Theory Soc. (Paper award 1964, Shannon lectr. 1988), Internat. Assn. for Cryptologic Rsch. 1986-88, Swiss Acad. Engring. Scis., U.S. Nat. Acad. Engring. Roman Catholic. Designed the International Data Encryption Algorithm. Office: Lund U PO Box 118 S-221 00 Lund Sweden

**MASSEY, JEANNE KELLY,** performing company executive; b. Charleston, SC, Oct. 30, 1938; d. Lawrence Lees and Margaret Augusta (Montgomery) Kelly; m. William Massey III, June 25, 1960 (div. 1994); children: Kelly Massey-Carlier, John Gant Massey. BA, Duke U., 1960; advanced libr. cert., William and Mary Coll., 1976. Founding libr. Jamestown Acad., Williamsburg, Va., 1974-77; pres. Va. State Ballet, Newport News, Va., 1978-82; founder, pres. Arts Resale of Williamsburg, Va., 1978-88; pres., gen. mgr. Mid-Atlantic Chamber Orch., Washington, 1985-98; exec. prodr. Benedictinus 2000 Internat. Order of Benedictines, 1997—2000; prodr. Annual World Bank Mozart Festival, 1991—. Commr. Va. Commn. for the Arts, Richmond, 1979-84; nat. exec. com. Children of the Am. Revolution, Washington, 1973-76; dir., pres. The Wyo. Condominium, Washington, 1988-91; mem. Arts Adv. Bd., Williamsburg, 1979-81. Recipient Platinum Violin award, Festival Williamsburg, 1984. Mem. DAR (pres. 1970-76), Jamestowne Soc., Jane Austen Soc. of N.Am., Phi Beta Kappa, Kappa Delta Pi, Sigma Delta Pi. Republican. Presbyterian. Avocations: walking, reading, concerts, museums, theater. Office: JKM Inc PO Box 21439 Washington DC 20009-0939 Fax: 202-337-1004. E-mail: jkminc@infionline.net.

**MASSEY, RAYMOND DAVID,** lawyer; b. Goldsboro, N.C., Oct. 13, 1946; s. Raymond L. and Dorris L. (Grant) Massey; m. Barbara A. Warner, Aug. 16, 1967; children: Suzanne, Christine. BA, Wofford Coll., Spartanburg, S.C., 1968; JD, U. S.C., Columbia, 1971; LLM in Taxation, Emory U., Atlanta, 1985. Bar: S.C. 1971, U.S. Dist. Ct. S.C. 1971, cert.: S.C. Supreme Ct. (specialist estate planning and probate law). Assoc. Perrin, Perrin & Mann, Spartanburg, Spartanburg, 1971—74; trust officer Bankers Trust of S.C., Columbia, SC, 1974—78; shareholder Brown, Massey, Evans, McLeod & Haynsworth, PA, Greenville, SC, 1978—. Pres. Greenville Estate Planning Coun., 1982; chair Cmty. Found. of Greater Greenville, 2001—02; dir. Greenville Hosp. Sys. Found., 2002—. Named to trusts and estates section, Best Lawyers in Am. Fellow: Am. Coll. Trust and Estate Counsel; mem.: S.C. Bar Assn. (chmn. probate, estate planning and trust sect. 1983), Greenville Bar Assn. (pres. tax sect. 1980—81), Poinsett Club, Greenville Country Club. Presbyterian. Office: PO Box 2464 Greenville SC 29602-2464 Office Phone: 864-271-7424.

**MASSEY, RAYMOND LEE,** lawyer; b. Macon, Ga., Sept. 25, 1948; s. Ford B. and Juanita (Sapp) M.; m. Lynn Ann Thielmeier, Aug. 23, 1967; children: Daniel, Caroline. BA, U. Mo., St. Louis, 1971; JD, U. Louisville, 1974. Bar: Mo. 1974, Ill. 1976, U.S. Dist. Ct. (ea. and we. dists.) Mo. 1974, U.S. Dist. Ct. (so. dist.) Ill. 1976, Tex. 1997. Assoc. Thompson & Mitchell, St. Louis, 1974-79; ptnr. Thompson & Mitchell (now Thompson & Coburn), St. Louis, 1979—. Mem. Maritime Law Assn. of U.S. (bd. dirs., chmn. ocean and river towing). Home: 3 Wild Rose Dr Saint Louis MO 63124-1465 Office: Thompson Coburn US Bank Ste 3400 Saint Louis MO 63101-1643 Office Phone: 314-552-6075. E-mail: rmassey@thompsoncoburn.com

**MASSEY, ROBERT UNRUH,** internist, educator, dean; b. Detroit, Feb. 23, 1922; s. Emil Laverne and Esther Elisabeth (Unruh) M.; m. June Charlene Collins, May 28, 1943; children: Robert Scott, Janet Charlene. Student, Oberlin Coll., 1939-42, U. Mich. Med. Sch., 1942-43; MD, Wayne State U., 1946. Intern, resident in internal medicine Henry Ford Hosp., Detroit, 1946-50; assoc. Lovelace Clinic, Albuquerque, 1950-68, chmn. dept. medicine, 1958-68, bd. govs., 1957-68; dir. med. edn. Lovelace Found. for Med. Edn. and Research, 1960-68; clin. assoc. U. N.Mex. Sch. Medicine, 1961-68; prof. medicine U. Conn. Sch. Medicine, Farmington, 1968-92, prof. emeritus, 1992—, assoc. dean for med. edn., 1968-71, dean Sch. Medicine, 1971-84, currently prof. emeritus dept. community medicine and health care, acting univ. v.p. for health affairs, 1975-76. Chief staff Newington VA Hosp., Conn., 1968-71; trustee Am. Assn. Med. Clinics, 1966-68; exec. com., regional adv. group Conn. Regional Med. Program, 1971-76; trustee, v.p. Capitol Area Health Consortium, 1974-78, pres., 1980-81. Editor-in-chief Conn. Medicine, 1986-99; editor Jour. of the History of Medicine and Allied Scis., 1987-91. Bd. dirs. Health Planning Coun., Inc., 1974-76; bd. dirs. Hartford Inst. for Criminal and Social Justice, 1976-80, Conn. Easter Seal Soc., 1977-85, Hospice Inst. Edn., Tng. and Rsch., 1979-81. With AUS, 1955-57; maj. Res. Fellow ACP; mem. Am. Group Practice Assn. (accreditation commn. 1968-78), Assn. Am. Med. Colls., Am. Assn. History of Medicine, Hartford County Med. Assn., AMA, Conn., Hartford med. socs., Am. Osler Soc., Beaumont Med. Club, Soc. Med. Adminstrs., Twilight Club (Hartford), Acorn Club, Sigma Xi, Alpha Omega Alpha. Roman Catholic.

**MASSEY, STEPHEN CHARLES,** rare book dealer, consultant; b. London, May 9, 1946; s. Charles Dudley and Sheila Florence (Browne) M.; divorced; 1 child, Sarah Louise. Grad. high sch., U.K. Cataloguer books and manuscripts Christie's, London, 1964-75; sr. dir. rare books and manuscripts dept. N.Y.C., 1975-96, sr. internat. cons., 1997-99. Fellow Pierpont Morgan Libr.; mem. The Grolier Club, The Old Book Table. Avocations: cinema, reading, running, music, fine arts. Office: Phone: 212-628-6930. Personal E-mail: scmassey@aol.com.

**MASSEY, THOMAS BENJAMIN,** retired university president; b. Charlotte, N.C., Sept. 5, 1926; s. William Everard and Sarah (Corley) M.; m. Bylee Hunnicutt Massey, July 10, 1968; children: Pamela Ann, Caroline Forest. AB, Duke U., 1948; MS, N.C. State U., 1953; PhD, Cambridge U., 1968. Assoc. dean students Ga. Inst. Tech., Atlanta, 1950-58; lectr. U. Md. Univ. Coll., 1960-66, dir. London, 1966—69, dir. Toyko, 1969-71, dir. Heidelberg (Fed. Republic of Germany), 1971-76, vice chancellor, 1976-78, chancellor, 1978-88, pres., 1988-98, pres. emeritus, 1998—. Served with USNS, 1943-46. Mem. APA, Univ. Continuing Edn. Assn., Am. Assn. Higher Edn., Internat. Confs. on Improving Learning and Tchg. at the Univ. (chair 1975—). Personal E-mail: benmassey@mac.com.

**MASSEY, WALTER EUGENE,** physicist, academic administrator; b. Hattiesburg, Miss., Apr. 5, 1938; s. Almon and Essie (Nelson) M.; m. Shirley Streeter, Oct. 25, 1969; children: Keith Anthony, Eric Eugene. BS, Morehouse Coll., 1958; MA, PhD, Washington U., St. Louis, 1966. Physicist Argonne (Ill.) Nat. Lab., 1966-68; asst. prof. physics U. Ill., Urbana, 1968-70; assoc. prof. Brown U., Providence, 1970-75, prof., dean of Coll., 1975-79; prof. physics U. Chgo., 1979-93; dir. Argonne Nat. Lab., 1979-84; v.p. for rsch. and for Argonne Nat. Lab. U. Chgo., 1984-91; dir. NSF, Washington 1991-93; sr. v.p. acad. affairs U. Calif. System, 1993-95; pres. Morehouse Coll., Atlanta, 1995—. Cons. NAS, 1973-76; mem. NSB, 1978-84; chair Sec. Energy Adv. Bd., 1997-99; bd. dirs. Mellon Found, Bank Am. Corp., McDonald's Corp., BP p.l.c.; mem. Gates Millennium Scholars Adv. Coun.; mem. coun. visitors Marine Biol. Lab.; mem. Pres.'s Coun. Advisors on Sci. and Tech., 1990-92, 01-. Contbr. articles on sci. edn. in secondary schs. and in theory of quantum fluids to profl. jours. Bd. fellows Brown U., 1980-90, Mus. Sci. and Industry, Chgo., 1980-89, Ill. Math. and Sci. Acad., 1985-88; bd. dirs. Urban League R.I., 1973-75; mem. Salzburg seminar, 1997—, Atlanta Symphony Orch., 1996—, Woodruf Art Ctr., 1995—, Atlanta Com. Polis, 1996-2004, Bhd. Project GRAD, Gt. Schs. Atlanta Bd., 2004-; trustee U. Chgo. Recipient over 25 hon. degrees; NAS fellow, 1961, NDEA fellow, 1959-60, AAAS fellow, 1962. Mem. AAAS (bd. dirs. 1981-85, pres.-elect 1987-88, pres. 1988-89,

chmn. 1989-90), Am. Phys. Soc. (councillor-at-large 1980-83, v.p. 1990), Smithsonian Inst. (bd. regents), Sigma Xi. Office: Morehouse Coll 830 Westview Dr SW Atlanta GA 30314-3773

**MASSEY, WILLIAM S.,** mathematician, educator; b. Granville, Ill., Aug. 23, 1920; s. Robert R. and Alma (Schumacher) M.; m. Ethel Heap, Mar. 14, 1953; children— Eleanor, Alexander, Joan. Student, Bradley U., 1937-39, MA (hon.), 2005. BS, U. Chgo., 1941, MS, 1942; PhD, Princeton, 1948. Mem. research dept. Princeton, 1948-50; from asst. prof. to prof. Brown U., 1950-60; prof. math. Yale, 1960—, Erastus L. Deforest prof. math, 1964-82, Eugene Higgins prof. math., 1983-91, Eugene Higgins prof. math. emeritus, 1991—, chmn. dept. math., 1968-71. Author: Algebraic Topology: An Introduction, 1967, Homology and Cohomology Theory, 1978, Singular Homology Theory, 1980, A Basic Course in Algebraic Topology, 1991; mem. editorial staff math. jours. Served as officer USNR, 1942-46. Fellow Am. Acad. Arts and Scis.; mem. Am. Math. Soc. Achievements include research in algebraic topology, differential topology, homotopy theory, fibre bundles. Home: 200 Leeder Hill Drive Hamden CT 06517-2729 Office: Yale U Math Dept PO Box 208283 New Haven CT 06520-8283

**MASSEY, WILLIAM WALTER, JR.,** sales executive; b. Lawrenceburg, Tenn., Sept. 21, 1928; s. William Walter and Bess Ann (Brian) M.; m. Virginia Claire Smith, Aug. 16, 1952; children: William Walter III, Laura Ann, Lynn Smith, Lisa Claire. BBA, U. Miami, Fla., 1949; BFA, U. Fla., 1969. Co-owner Massey Motors, Inc., Jacksonville, Fla., 1950—; v.p., dir. Atlantic Discount Co. Inc., Jacksonville, 1954-64; pres. Owners Surety Corp., Jacksonville, 1959—, General Svcs. Corp., Jacksonville, 1960-69, Owners Guaranty Life, Phoenix, 1960-64, Securities Guaranty Life, Phoenix, 1961-64, Fla. Properties, Inc., Jacksonville, 1961-66, Chi-Cha, Inc., Jacksonville, 1965-70, Univ. Square Properties, Jacksonville, 1969-80; v.p., sec./treas. Spring Forest Properties, Cashiers, NC, 1978—2001. V.p., dir. Southside Country Day School, Jacksonville, 1963-68; bd. dirs. Southside Atlantic Bank, Jacksonville, 1965-93. Exhibited in group shows at Internat., N.Y., 1970, Ball State U., 1972. Lt. USAF, 1950-1952. Mem. Ponte Vedra Club, River Club, Epping Forest Club, Deerwood Club, Sigma Chi. Methodist. Avocations: music, painting, writing. Office Phone: 904-398-6877. Office Fax: 904-642-8815.

**MASSEY-BURZIO, VIRGINIA,** librarian, writer; b. Greenfield, Mass., Apr. 5, 1943; d. Louis G. and Marie (Lamarche) Massey; m. Luigi Burzio, Dec. 1, 1978. BA, Trinity Coll., 1965; MLS, Drexel U., 1966. Cataloger Boston Pub. Libr., 1966—68; asst. docs. libr. Dartmouth Coll., Hanover, NH, 1968—71; docs. libr. Brandeis U., Waltham, Mass., 1971—73, head, docs. sect., 1973—83, head, reference dept., 1983—88, head, reader svcs., 1988—91; head, core libr. svcs. U. Md., College Park, 1991—; head, rsch. svcs. and collections dept. Johns Hopkins U., Balt., 1992—. Contbr. articles to jours. Recipient Isadore Gilbert Mudge award, Reference and User Services Assn., a divsn. of the ALA, 1999. Mem.: Assn. of Coll. and Rsch. Libraries, ALA. Achievements include development of Brandeis model of reference service. Avocations: creative writing, calligraphy, yoga. Office: Johns Hopkins Univ Milton S Eisenhower Libr 3400 N Charles St Baltimore MD 21218 Office Phone: 410-516-8366. E-mail: vmb@jhu.edu.

**MASSIE, CLIFFORD MICHAEL,** music company executive; b. Bklyn., May 11, 1957; s. Michael and Jennifer Massie. BA cum laude with honors, Brandeis U., 1979. Pres. The Hit House, Levittown, NY, 1987—, Shoot No Blanks Music Publishing, Bethpage, NY, 1987—. Producer/remixer Teena Marie, Gloria Gaynor, David Hasselhoff, Evelyn Champagne King, Promoter Jay-Z, Ja Rule, DMX, Ludacris, Ashanti, Janet Jackson, Mariah Carey, Aaliyah, Snoop Dogg, Brian McKnight. Recipient Songwriter 1st Place Billboard Mag. contest, 1988. Mem.: NMPA, NARAS, ASCAP. Achievements include numerous Gold and Platinum singles/albums. Home: 3700 Mallard Rd Levittown NY 11756 Office: The Hit House 3700 Mallard Rd Levittown NY 11756 also: Shoot No Blanks Music Pub PO Box 102 Bethpage NY 11714 Office Phone: 516-735-3452. Office Fax: 516-735-3329. Personal E-mail: cliffmassie@optonline.net.

**MASSIE, MICHAEL EARL,** lawyer; b. Stambaugh, Mich., Aug. 12, 1947; s. Glen E. and Bernice L. (Lambert) M.; m. Vicki L. Colmark, June 11, 1977; children: Christopher, Adam. BA, U. Ill., 1969, JD, 1972. Bar: Ill. 1972, U.S. Dist. Ct. (cen. dist.) 1989, U.S. Ct. Appeals (7th cir.) 1989. Pvt. practice, Galva, Ill., 1972—. Chair Ill. Com. Agrl. Edn. Fellow Am. Bar Found., Ill. Bar Found.; mem. ABA (chair, coun. mem. gen. practice sect. 1989—), Ill. State Bar Assn. (chmn. gen. practice sect. 1980, chmn. agrl. law com. 1980), Ill. Farm Legal Assistance Found. (chmn. bd. 1985-98), Henry County Bar Assn. (pres. 1977). Republican. Avocations: tennis, handball. Office: 115 NW 3rd Ave Galva IL 61434-1325

**MASSIE, TAMMY JEANNE PARLIMENT,** statistician; b. Suffern, N.Y., Jan. 4, 1972; d. Thomas Holden and Marjorie Eleanor (Wood) Parliment; m. Tristan Shaw Massie, Dec. 28, 1969. BS in Math., Stockton State Coll., 1994; MS in Stats., U. Ctrl. Fla., 1998; PhD in Biostatistics, Med. Coll. Va., Va. Commonwealth U., 2002. Grad. tchg. asst. U. Ctrl. Fla., Orlando, 1995—98; lfeguard, cast mem. Walt Disney World, Lake Buena Vista, Fla., 1996—98; statistician Whitehall Robins, Richmond, Va., 1999—2000; grad. rsch. asst. Med. Coll. Va., Va. Commonwealth U., 1998—2002; math. statistician Ctr. Vet. Medicine, FDA, Rockville, Md., 2002—04, Ctr. Drug Evaluation and Rsch., FDA, Rockville, 2004—. Statis. cons. U. Ctrl. Fla., 1995—98; statis. cons., biostatistical consulting lab student leader Med. Coll. Va., Va. Commonwealth U., 1998—2002. Contbr. to roundtable discussions, posters to sci. forums. Recipient Karl E. Peace award of Excellence, Med. Coll. Va., 2000—01; scholar Youth for Understanding Exch. Student award, Kraft Foods, 1990, Philip Morris Academic award, Philip Morris, 1992—94. Mem.: FDA Stats. Assn., Drug Info. Assn. (poster ann. meeting 2005), Soc. Clin. Trials (presenter ann. meeting 2003), Am. Statis. Assn., Assn. Women in Sci. Home: 171 Sharpstead Lane Gaithersburg MD 20878 Office: Food and Drug Administration-CDER 2901 Corporate Blvd Rockville MD 20850 Office Phone: 301-827-2549. Office Fax: 301-827-2577. Business E-Mail: tammy.massie@fda.gov.

**MASSIER, PAUL FERDINAND,** mechanical engineer; b. Pocatello, Idaho, July 22, 1923; s. John and Kathryn (Arki) M.; m. Miriam Parks, May 1, 1948 (dec. Aug. 1975); children: Marilyn Massier Schwegler, Paulette Massier Holden; m. Dorothy Hedlund Wright, Sept. 12, 1978. *Grandfather Ferdinand Massier pioneered the Baptist missionary movement in Bukovina and Galicia (Austria) during the late 1800's and early 1900's. Father John Massier, a cabinet maker, immigrated to the U.S. from Bukovina in 1903 and in 1951 was elected "Deacon for Life" by the First Baptist Church in Pocatello, Idaho. Mother Katie Arki immigrated from Croatia-Slavonia in 1906 and was an excellent cook and gardener. Daughter Marilyn, a flutist, was awarded "Musician of the Year" at Arcadia, California High School, where daughter Paulette, a violinist, was Concert Mistress of the orchestra. Both toured Europe with the American Youth Symphony Orchestra.* BSME, U. Colo., 1948; MSME, MIT, 1949. Cert. U. Idaho, So. Branch, 1943. Engr. Pan-Am. Refining Corp., Texas City, Tex., 1948; design engr. Maytag Co., Newton, Iowa, 1949-50; research engr. Boeing Co., Seattle, 1951-55; sr. research engr., supr. and dep. sect. mgr. Jet Propulsion Lab. Calif. Inst. Tech., Pasadena, 1955-84, task mgr., 1984-88, mem. tech. staff, 1989-94. *More than 40 years of engineering research and supervision led to: concepts and analysis of "far out" rocket propulsion systems such as antimatter, laser, nuclear, and metastable states; evaluation of rocket-engine fuel and oxidizer cooling capabilities including the upper limit of nucleate boiling for numerous liquid propellants such as hydrazine, nitrogen tetroxide, oxygen, alcohol, and many others; experimental determination of fluid mechanics and heat transfer phenomena for high-temperature compressible swirling flows in axisymmetric ducts and convergent-divergent nozzles; identification and evaluation of explanted heart valve prostheses; development of gas turbines for use as engines in trucks and boats and as air compressors.* Contbr. articles to profl. jours. Moderator Arcadia Congl. Ch., 1996-98; mem. Arcadia High Sch. Music Club, 1966-71. With U.S. Army, 1943-46. Recipient Apollo Achieve-

ment award NASA, 1969, Basic Noise Rsch. award NASA, 1980, Life Mem. Svc. award Calif. PTA, 1970, Layman of Yr. award Arcadia Congl. Ch., 1971, Mil. Unit Citation award, 1946. Fellow AIAA (assoc., Sustained Svc. award 1980-81); mem. AAAS, N.Y. Acad. Scis., Planetary Soc., Order of the Engr., Bukovina Soc. of the Ams., Sigma Xi, Tau Beta Pi, Pi Tau Sigma, Sigma Tau. Congregationalist. Achievements include 50% reduction of cooling requirements for rocket engines, experimental evaluation of heat transfer from thermally ionized gases at temperatures up to 13,000 degrees; experimental determination of starting characteristics, shock-wave structures, heat transfer and pressure distributions in supersonic diffusers led to the development of criteria for their design and their use as a means of simulating altitude conditions at ground level for static testing of rocket engines; experimental/analytical determination of the relationships of large-scale turbulent structures, density and temperature fluctuations, inverted velocity profiles, internally generated pure tones, twin jet shielding, and aircraft flight on noise emitted from aircraft supersonic jets; understanding of the formation of cenospheres during the combustion of heavy oils by analysis of electron microscope photo images of droplets and stages of formed globules and cenospheres gathered on slides during combustion experiments. Home: 764 Lava Falls Dr Las Vegas NV 89110

**MASSING, MICHAEL,** writer, media critic; BA, Harvard Coll.; MS, London Sch. Econs. and Polit. Sci. Former exec. editor Columbia Journalism Rev.; adj. prof. Columbia Sch. Journalism, Columbia Sch. for Internat. Affairs; co-founder Com. to Protect Journalists. Author: (nonfiction) The Fix: Solving the Nation's Drug Problem, 1998 (Washington Monthly's Political Book award), Now They Tell Us: The American Press and Iraq, 2004; contbr. articles NY Times mag., NY Rev. Books, New Yorker, Atlantic Monthly, Washington Post, LA Times, Nation, Am. Prospect, New Republic, Rolling Stone, Washington Monthly. Nat. adv. com. Innovators Combating Substance Abuse. Recipient Mongerson prize for investigative reporting, Northwestern Univ. Medill Sch. Journalism, 2005, Lettre Ulysses award for the art of reportage, 2005; grantee Alicia Patterson Fellowship for Journalism, 1989, MacArthur Fellowship, 1992. Mem.: PEN Am., NY Inst. for Humanities.*

**MASSMAN, RICHARD ALLAN,** lawyer; b. Beaumont, Tex., Aug. 19, 1943; s. Irwin Massman and Sylvia (Schmidt) Schwartz; m. Barbara Elaine Kessler; children: Jason Todd, Karen Faye. BS cum laude, U. Pa., 1965; JD cum laude, Harvard U., 1968. Bar: Tex. 1968; cert. in taxation, Tex. Bd. Legal Specialization. Assoc. Coke & Coke, Dallas, 1968-70, Johnson & Wortley, P.C. (formerly Johnson & Gibbs, P.C.), Dallas, 1970-71, ptnr., 1971-88, shareholder, 1988-94; of counsel Johnson & Wortley P.C., Dallas, 1994-95; sr. v.p., gen. counsel Hunt Consolidated, Inc., Dallas, 1994—. Lectr. So. Meth. U., Dallas, 1973; trustee Am. Beacon Funds, 2004—; bd. dirs. Retina Found. Southwest, 2004—. Chmn. Dallas Civil Svc. Bd., 1983; trustee Greenhill Sch., Dallas, 1985-92, vice chmn., 1990-92; bd. trustees Dallas Opera, 1999—. Recipient Jurisprudence award Anti-Defamation League, 2000. Mem. Am. Coll. Tax Coun., Tex. State Bar (chmn., sec. taxation 1983-84), Dallas Bar Assn. (chmn., sec. taxation 1978), Dallas Petroleum Club, Columbian Club, Trophy Club. Office: Hunt Consolidated Inc Fountain Pl 20th Fl 1445 Ross at Field Dallas TX 75202-2785

**MASSOF, ROBERT WILLIAM,** neuroscientist, educator; b. Minn., Jan. 2, 1948; m. Patricia Massof; children: Eric, Allison. BA, Hamline U., 1970; PhD, Ind. U., 1975. Postdoctoral fellow in ophthalmology Johns Hopkins U. Sch. Medicine, Balt., 1975-76, instr. ophthalmology, 1976-78, from asst. prof. to assoc. prof., 1978-91, prof. ophthalmology, 1991—; prof. neurosci., 1994—, prof. computer sci., 1994—, mem. staff applied physics lab., 2000—. Lectr. in field. Mem. editl. bd. Clin. Vision Scis., N.Y.C., 1986-94, Eye Care Technology/Computers in Eye Care, Folsom, Calif., 1992-96; patentee in field (5); contbr. articles to profl. jours. Recipient Manpower award, 1989, Tech. Transfer award NASA, 1993, Popular Mechanics Design and Engring. award, 1994, EyeCare Tech. Lifetime Achievement award, 1995, Richard E. Hoover Svc. award, 1995, Humanitarian award Lions, 2000, Disting. Svc. in Vision award Am. Pub. Health Assn., William Feinbloom award Am. Acad. of Optometry, 2000, Alfred W. Bressler prize Jewish Guild for the Blind, 2004. Fellow Optical Soc. Am. (chmn. edn. coun. 1993-95, bd. dirs. 1993-95), Am. Acad. Optometry; mem. Assn. for Edn. and Rehab. of the Visually Impaired, Soc. for Info. Display, Am. Congress Rehab. Medicine, Assn. Rsch. in Vision and Ophthalmology. Office: Johns Hopkins Univ Lions Vision Ctr 550 N Broadway Fl 6 Baltimore MD 21205-2020 Office Phone: 410-502-6246. E-mail: rmassof@lions.med.jhu.edu.

**MASSON, ROBERT HENRY,** paper company executive; b. Boston, June 27, 1935; s. Robert Louis and Henrietta Hill (Worrell) M.; m. Virginia Lee Morton, Dec. 28, 1957; children: Linda Anne, Kenneth Morton, Robert Louis, II. BA in Econs. cum laude, Amherst Coll., 1957; MBA, Harvard U., 1964. Fin. staff Ford Motor Co., Dearborn, Mich., 1964-68, mktg. services div. controller, 1968-70; pres. Knutson Constrn. Co., Mpls., 1970-72; v.p. fin., treas. Ellerbe, Inc., Bloomington, Minn., 1972-77; fin. dir. CirTech, Inc., Mpls., 1973-77; v.p. fin. transp. div. PepsiCo., Inc., Tulsa, 1977, corp. v.p., treas. Purchase, N.Y., 1978-80; v.p., treas. Combustion Engring., Inc., Stamford, Conn., 1981-86, v.p. fin. and internat. devel., 1986-87, v.p. venture fin. and internat. ops., 1988-90; v.p., CFO Parsons & Whittemore, Inc., Rye Brook, N.Y., 1990—. Mem. adv. bd. Fleet Bank, 1988—. Author: (with others) The Management of Racial Integration in Business, 1964. Pres. North Georgtown Homeowner's Assn., Birmingham, Mich., 1968-70, U.S. Presdl. Advance Man, 1972-76; trustee, finan. com. Naval Aviation Mus. Found. 1987—; trustee Hebron Acad., 1993-97; elder Presbyn. Ch. of Old Greenwich, 1992—. Served to lt. USN, 1957-62; lt. comdr. Res. Mem. Am. Forest and Paper Assn. (fin. com. 1991—), Fin. Execs. Inst. (com. on corp. fin. 1981—), Fairchester Treas. Group (pres. 1986), Lucas Point Homeowner's Assn. (pres. 1986-87), Theta Delta Chi. Clubs: Wayzata Yacht (dir.-treas. 1973-77), Riverside Yacht (assoc. treas. 1985-87). Office: Parsons & Whittemore Inc 4 International Dr Ste 5 Rye Brook NY 10573-1064

**MASSOUDI, BAHRAM BARRY,** management consultant; b. Tehran, Iran, 1960; arrived in U.S., 1977; BS, Syracuse U., N.Y., 1981; MEng, McGill U., Montreal, 1983; MBA, U. Wash., Seattle, 1992. Internat. compensation mgr. Schlumberger Ltd., Paris, 1984—90; principal Gemini Consulting, Morristown, NJ, 1992—99; founder, mng. ptnr. Cubicon LLC, Seattle, 1999—. Contbr. articles to profl. jours. Chmn. Arts Commn., Mercer Island, Wash., 2004. Avocations: jogging, photography, restoring old houses, gardening.

**MASSY, WILLIAM FRANCIS,** education educator, consultant; b. Milw., Mar. 26, 1934; s. Willard Francis and Ardys Dorothy (Digman) M.; m. Sally Vaughn Miller, July 21, 1984; children by previous marriage: Willard Francis, Elizabeth BS, Yale U., 1956; SM, MIT, 1958, PhD in Indsl. Econs., 1960. Asst. prof. indsl. mgmt. MIT, Cambridge, 1960-62; from asst. prof. to prof. edn. and bus. adminstrn. Stanford U., Calif., 1962-96, assoc. dean Grad. Sch. Bus. Calif., 1971, vice provost for rsch. Calif., 1971-77, v.p. for bus. and fin. Calif., 1977-88, v.p. fin. Calif., 1988-91, prof. emeritus, 1996—; prof. edn., dir. Stanford Inst. Higher Edn. Rsch., Calif., 1988-96; sr. v.p. P.R. Taylor Assocs., 1995-99; sr. rsch. Nat. Ctr. for Postsecondary Improvement, 1996—2002; pres. The Jackson Hole Higher Edn. Group, Inc., 1996—. Dir. Diebold, Inc., chmn. audit com., 2003-; mem. univ. grants com. Hong Kong, 1990-2003; mem. coun. Yale U., 1980-95; mgmt. cons. Stanford Mgmt. Co., 1991-93. Author: Stochastic Models of Buying Behavior, 1970, Marketing Management, 1972, Market Segmentation, 1972, Planning Models for Colleges and Universities, 1981, Endowment, 1991, Resource Allocation in Higher Education, 1996, Honoring The Trust, 2003, Remaking the American University, 2005; mem. editl. bd. Jour. Mktg. Rsch., 1964-70, Harcourt, Brace Jovanovich, 1965-71; contbr. articles to profl. jours. Bd. dirs. Palo Alto-Stanford chpt. United Way, 1978-80, Stanford U. Hosp., 1980-91, MAC, Inc., 1969-84, EDUCOM, 1983-86. Ford Found. faculty rsch. fellow, 1966-67 Mem. Am. Mktg. Assn. (dir. 1971-73, v.p. edn. 1976-77), Inst. Mgmt. Scis. Office: The Jackson Hole Higher Edn Group PO Box 9849 Jackson WY 83002-9849 Business E-Mail: bill@jhheg.com.

**MAST, BERNADETTE MIHALIC,** lawyer; BS, Ohio State U., 1982; JD magna cum laude, Case Western Res. U., 1988. CPA; bar: Ohio 1988; cert. prodn. and inventory mgr., systems profl. 1985. With Jones Day, Cleve., 1988—, ptnr., 2000—. Mem.: Cleve. Bar Assn. (real estate sect.), Ohio State Bar Assn. Office: Jones Day North Point 901 Lakeside Ave Cleveland OH 44114-1190

**MAST, KANDE WHITE,** artist; b. St. Louis, Mar. 10, 1950; d. Elliott Maxwell and Mary (Barritt) W. Student, U. Mo., 1968-70, Longview C.C., Kansas City, Mo., 1970-71. Portrait painter, free-lance artist, Albany, N.Y., 1973-74, Kansas City, 1974—; dir., tchr. Studio Kande, Sch. Fine Arts, Kansas City, 1983-86; founder, exec. dir. Art Ctr. Kansas City, 1986-90; behavioral foster parent, 1989—; master foster parent, 1992—. Mem. psychiat. diversion team, mental health rev. team Jackson County Divsns. Family Svcs., 1992-95. Portrait painter and free-lance artist. Pres., bd. dirs. Advocates for Children, Inc., 1996—; vol. Ozanam Home for Boys, Kansas City, 1987—, mem. adv. bd., 1991—; mem. Cmty. Response Team, Jackson County, Divsns. Family Svcs.; founding mem. Nat. Campaign for Tolerance. Named Therapeutic Foster Parent of Yr., 1992. Mem.: Code Pink: Women for Peace, Nat. Mus. of Women in Arts (charter). Home and Studio: 12406 Baltimore Ct Kansas City MO 64145

**MAST, KENT E.,** lawyer; b. Bryn Mawr, Pa., July 12, 1943; s. John Earl and Jeanette (Skokowski) M.; m. Deborah Frieson Helmer, June 29, 1998; children: Roger, Grier, Jensen, Jeffrey. AB in Politics, Princeton U., 1965; JD, Duke U., 1968. Bar: Ga. 1968, U.S. Ct. Appeals (5th cir.) 1968, U.S. Ct. Appeals (9th cir.) 1968, U.S. Ct. Appeals (11th cir.) 1981, U.S. Ct. Appeals (4th cir.) 1989. Assoc. Hansell & Post, Atlanta, 1968-73, ptnr., 1973-88, Hunton & Williams, Atlanta, 1988-90; sr. ptnr. Kilpatrick Stockton, Atlanta, 1990—2000; gen. counsel, corp. v.p. Equifax Inc., Atlanta, 2000—. Mem. ABA, Ga. Bar Assn., Atlanta Bar Assn., Consumer Data Industry Assn. (chmn.), Highlands Falls Country Club, Oceanside Country Club. Office: Equifax Inc 1550 Peachtree St NW Atlanta GA 30309-2639 Office Phone: 404-885-8009.

**MASTAGLIO, PETER JAMES,** lawyer; b. Flushing, NY, Sept. 21, 1941; s. George Washington and Katherine (Clancy) M.; m. Deidre Mary Twomey, Apr. 3, 1971; children: James Peter, Elizabeth Clare. BA, Manhattan Coll., 1963; JD, NYU, 1968. Bar: NY, Mass., US Dist. Ct. (ea. and so. dists.) N. 1971, US Ct. Appeals (2d cir.) 1975, US Supreme Ct. 1977. Assoc. Cullen & Dykman Bleakley Platt LLP (formerly Cullen & Dykman), Garden City, NY, 1969-77, ptnr., 1977—. Chmn. bd. dirs., trustee YMCA of LI, Huntington, NY, 1981—; mem. com. on character and fitness 2d, 10th and 11th Jud. Dists., Bklyn., 1986—. Capt. USMC, 1966-69. Mem. NY State Bar Assn., Nassau County Bar Assn. Avocations: history, basketball. Home: 25 Kensington Rd Garden City NY 11530-4240 Office: Cullen & Dykman Bleakley Platt LLP 100 Quentin Roosevelt Blvd Garden City NY 11530-4850 Office Phone: 516-357-3751. Office Fax: 516-357-3792.

**MASTEN, BARBARA JEAN,** education educator, department chairman; b. Toledo, Jan. 14, 1948; d. Joseph Anthony Czyzewski and Angela Rose Piorkowski; m. William Leonard Masten, Sept. 18, 1971; 1 child, Todd Michael. B in Edn., U. Toledo, 1970, M in Edn. Adminstrn., 1979. Sr. accountant and edn. and tchg. specialist Gen. Motors, Toledo, 1970—82; English instr. St. Ursula Acad., Toledo, 1983—89; instr. U. Toledo Cmty. Coll., 1989; assoc. prof./dept. chair Lourdes Coll., 1989—. Mem. adv. bd. Sch. Edn. Lourdes Coll., Sylvania, Ohio, 2003—, pres. faculty senate, 2005—06. Recipient Faculty Excellence award, Lourdes Coll., 1995, 2004. Mem.: Nat. Coun.Tchrs. English, Ohio Assn. Develop. Edn. Avocations: flower arranging, golf, reading. Office: Lourdes Coll 6832 Convent Blvd Sylvania OH 43560 Office Phone: 419-824-3758. Business E-Mail: bmasten@lourdes.edu.

**MASTEN, JACQUELINE GWENDOLYN,** small business owner; b. Brunswick, Maine, Oct. 24, 1941; d. Ralph Henry Bennet and Phyllis Estelle Crooker; children from previous marriage: Geraldine Frances Bullwinkel, Jennifer Lynn. Diploma in Bus., Pluss Sch. of Business, Portland, Maine, 1966. Shop owner Hudson Chair Caning Svcs., Hudson, NH, 1982; data entry operator Digital Corp., Nashua, NH, 1980; real estate landlady Hudson, NH, 1996—. Author: A Shaker Poetry Poetic History Book: A Tribute to My Aunt Eldress Gertrude Soule Shaker, 2003; contbr. poems to books. Named 1999 Poet of the Year, Famous Poets Soc., Nev., 1999, World Champion Amature, Internat. Soc. of Poets, 2001; recipient Shakespear medallion of Excellence, 2002. Mem.: New Eng. Saddlebred and Pony Assn., Quartzsite Roadrunner Gem and Mineral Club. Avocation: Shaker poetry writing, shaker tape chair seating, silversmith, gem faceting, lapidary. Personal E-mail: JGMas1025@aol.com.

**MASTERNAK, MICHAL MATEUSZ,** biotechnologist, educator, molecular biologist, researcher; arrived in US, 2002; s. Krzysztof and Danuta Masternak; m. Anna Idzinska, Aug. 14, 1999; children: Emilia, Adam. MS in Engring. and Biotechnology, August Cieszkowski Agrl. U. Poznan, Poland, 2000; PhD in Biol. Scis., Karol Marcinkowski U. Med. Scis., Poznan, 2002. Rschr. Inst. Human Genetics Polish Acad. of Scis., Poznan, 2000—02; vis. rsch. instr. So. Ill. U. Sch. Medicine, Springfield, 2002—04, rsch. asst. prof., 2004—. Recipient Samuel Goldstein Disting. Publ. award, Geron Corp., 2005. Office: So Ill Univ 801 N Rutledge Rm 4389 Springfield IL 62794-9628 Office Fax: 217-545-8006. Business E-Mail: mmasternak@siumed.edu.

**MASTERS, BETTIE SUE SILER,** biochemist, educator; b. Lexington, Va., June 13, 1937; d. Wendell Hamilton and Mildred Virginia (Cromer) Siler; m. Robert Sherman Masters, Aug. 6, 1960; children: Diane Elizabeth, Deborah Ann. BS in Chemistry, Roanoke Coll., 1959, D.Sc. (hon.), 1983; PhD in Biochemistry, Duke U., 1963. Postdoctoral fellow Duke U., 1963-66, advanced research fellow, 1966-68, assoc. on faculty, 1967-68; mem. faculty U. Tex. Health Sci. Ctr. (Southwestern Med. Sch.), Dallas, 1968-82, assoc. prof. biochemistry, 1972-76, prof., 1976-82, research prof. surgery, dir. biochem. burn research, 1978-82; prof. biochemistry, chmn. dept. Med. Coll. Wis., Milw., 1982-90; Robert A. Welch disting. prof. chemistry, dept. biochemistry U. Tex. Health Sci. Ctr., San Antonio, 1190—. Mem. pharmacology-toxicology rsch. rev. com. Nat. Inst. Gen. Med. Scis., NIH, 1975-79; mem. bd. sci. counselors Nat. Inst. Environ. Health Scis., 1982-86, chmn., 1984-86; mem. adv. com. on biochemistry and endocrinology Am. Cancer Soc., 1989-92, chmn., 1991-92, mem. coun. for extramural grants, 1998—; mem. phys. biochemistry study sect. NIH, 1989-90; mem. adv. com. to the dir. of NIH, 2001-04; chair nat. rsch. coun. study com. on identifying and assessing unintended effects of genetically engineered foods on human health NAS/Inst. of Medicine, 2002-04; vis. scientist Japan Soc. for Promotion Sci., 1978. Mem. editl. bd. Jour. Biol. Chemistry, 1976-81, 96-2001, Archives Biochemistry and Biophysics, 1991-94, Drug Metabolism and Disposition, 1993-, Nitric Oxide, Biology and Chemistry, 1996-, Internat. Union Biochemistry and Molecular Biology Life, 1999-; contbr. chpts. to books and articles, revs. and abstracts to profl. publs. Mem. coun. extramural grants Am. Cancer Soc., 1998-2000. Recipient Merit award Nat. Heart, Lung and Blood Inst., 1988-97, grantee, 1970—; recipient Excellence in Sci. award Fedn. Am. Socs. for Exptl. Biology, 1992; postdoctoral fellow Am. Cancer Soc., 1963-65, advanced rsch. fellow Am. Heart Assn., 1966-68, established investigator, 1968-73; rsch. grantee NIH, 1970—, Nat. Heart Lung Blood Inst., 1970—, Nat. Inst. Gen. Med. Scis., 1980—, Robert A. Welch Found., 1971-82, 90—; elected to Inst. Medicine of NAS, 1996. Fellow AAAS; mem. Am. Soc. Biochemistry and Molecular Biology (nominating com. 1983, coun. 1985-86, awards com. 1992-96, fin. com. 1993-98, publs. com. 1994-97, pres.-elect 2001, pres. 2002-04), Am. Soc. Pharmacology and Exptl. Therapeutics (exec. com. drug metabolism divsn. 1979-81, chmn. exec. com. 1993-94, bd. publs. trustees 1982-87, Bernard B. Brodie award 2000), Am. Chem. Soc., Assn. Am. Med. Colls. (adv. bd. biomed. rsch. 1995-98), Fedn. Am. Socs. for Exptl. Biology (bd. dirs. 1998—2002, v.p. 2001-02), Internat. Union Biochemistry and Molecular Biology (nominating com. 1994-97, chair

U.S. nat.com. 1997—), Phi Beta Kappa, Sigma Xi, Alpha Omega Alpha. Office: U Tex Health Sci Ctr Dept Biochemistry 7703 Floyd Curl Dr MSC 7760 San Antonio TX 78229-3900 Office Phone: 210-567-6627. E-mail: masters@uthscsa.edu.

**MASTERS, EDWARD EUGENE,** association executive, former foreign service officer; b. Columbus, Ohio, June 21, 1924; s. George Henry and Ethel Verena (Shaw) M.; m. Allene Mary Roche, Apr. 2, 1956; children: Julie Allene, Edward Ralston. Student, Denison U., 1942—43; BA with distinction, George Washington U., 1948; MA, Fletcher Sch. Law and Diplomacy, 1949; grad., Nat. War Coll., 1964. Joined U.S. Fgn. Svc., 1950; intelligence rsch. analyst Near East Dept. State, 1949-50; resident officer Heidelberg, Germany, 1950-52; polit. officer embassy Karachi, Pakistan, 1952-54; Hindustani lang. and area tng. U. Pa., 1954-55; consul, polit. officer Madras, India, 1955-58; intelligence rsch. specialist South Asia Dept. State, 1958-60, chief Indonesia-Malaya br. Office Rsch. Asia, 1960-61, officer-in-charge Thailand affairs Bur. Far Eastern Affairs, 1961-63; counselor for polit. affairs Am. embassy, Djakarta, 1964-68; country dir. for Indonesia Dept. State, 1968-70; dir. Office East Asian Regional Affairs, 1970-71; minister Am. embassy, Bangkok, 1971-75; amb. to Bangladesh, 1976—77; amb. to Indonesia, 1977—81; adj. prof. diplomacy Fletcher Sch. Law and Diplomacy, 1981-82; sr. v.p. Natomas Co., 1982-84; pres. Nat. Planning Assn., 1985-92, Edward Masters & Assocs., Washington, 1992—, U.S.-Indonesia Soc., 1994-2000, chmn., 2000—. Adj. prof. Sch. Advanced Internat. Studies, 2000—02. Mem. Am. Fgn. Svc. Assn., Cosmos Club, Phi Beta Kappa, Omicron Delta Kappa, Pi Gamma Mu, Delta Phi Epsilon. Home: 4101 Cathedral Ave NW Apt 1001 Washington DC 20016-7500 Personal E-mail: mastersdc@att.net.

**MASTERS, ELAINE,** religious studies educator, writer; b. Kansas City, Mo., Oct. 6, 1932; d. David Shepherd and Stella Frances (Ragan) M.; m. Donald Ramon Masters, Apr. 27, 1951; children: David, Vicki, Jennifer, Kevin. BS in Edn. with honors, U. Mo., Kansas City, 0968. Cert. tchr., Mo., Va. Tchr. grade 4 Am. Sch., Manila, 1956-57; tchr. grade 5 Escuela Gloria Felix, Caracas, Venezuela, 1960-62; tchr. grade 6 Okinawa Christian Sch., Urasoe, 1968-70; tchr. grade 5 Flint Hill Elem. Sch., Vienna, Va., 1970-73; tchr. Bible Inst. Hawaii, Honolulu, 1991-92; dir. Christian edn. St. Thomas United Meth. Ch., Manassas, Va., 1983-84; tchr. children's ministries Salvation Army, Kaneohe, Hawaii, 1991-94; owner Edon Industries, Quixtar, 1999—; reading and English tchr. Canaan Cmty. Gospel Ctr., Chinatown, Honolulu, 2004—. Evangelist, Hong Kong, Malaysia, Nigeria, Thailand, Honolulu; advisor Pentecostal Assemblies of Tribes, Chiang Mai, Thailand, 1991—; lectr. Christian Writers Workshop, 1993—2004; workshop leader Soc. Children's Book Writers and Illustrators, Honolulu, 2003, 04, 06; writer ednl. measurement Harcourt Brace, 1998—2005; workshop leader Conf. on Lit. and Hawaii's Children, 1998—2002; panelist Read to Me Internat. Conf., Honolulu, 2005. Author: Ali and the Ghost Tiger, 1967, Teach Us To Pray, 1970, Day Camp and Day Care Handbook, 1989, The Thief in Chinatown, 1998, Footloose the Mongoose and the Jumping Flea, 1999, Malia's Happy Birthday, 2000, Malia and Baby Brother, 2000, Where's Malia's Mama?, 2000, Where's Kimo's Daddy?, 2000, Yumi and Her Best-Forever Friend, 2000, Footloose the Mongoose and His Wonderful Ohana, 2001, Kalani and the Night Marchers, 2001, Momi, A Hawaiian Mermaid in the Land of Delight, 2001, Lullaby Moon, 2002 (Ka Palapala Po'okela Pub.'s award for best children's book fiction and non-fiction pub. in Hawaii, 2002), The Royal Waker-Upper, 2003, Momi's Birthday Surprise, 2006; contbr. articles to mags. and newspapers; inventor cricket transposer tool for musicians. Mem. spkr. bur. Alzheimer's Assn., Honolulu, 1991-97; mem. steering com. Children's Lit., Hawaii, 2001-04. Mem. Women's Aglow Fellowship Internat., Soc. Children's Book Writers and Illustrators (regional advisor State of Hawaii 1996-98). Avocations: travel, Hawaiian culture, languages. Home: 2355 Ala Wai Blvd Apt 502 Honolulu HI 96815-3404 Personal E-mail: eomasters@hotmail.com.

**MASTERS, GEORGE WINDSOR, JR.,** electrical engineer, educator; b. Annapolis, Md., Mar. 11, 1930; s. George and Ruby Lena (Jess) Masters; m. Barbara Lyons Wilson; children: Barbara Anne, George W. III. BS, MIT, 1952, MS, 1954; PhD, U. Fla., 1966. Mem. tech. staff Instrument Lab., MIT, Cambridge, 1952-55; sect. head Electromech. Rsch. Inc., Princeton, NJ, 1958-62; mem. sr. staff, sect. head flight control sect. The Aerospace Corp., El Segundo, Calif., 1962-75; chief engr. airborne sys. dept. USN Test Pilot Sch., Patuxent River, Md., 1975—2004; assoc. prof. elec. engring. Fla. Inst. Tech., Melbourne, 1984—2004; adj. assoc. prof. aviation sys. U. Tenn. Space Inst., Tullahoma, Tenn., 2004—. Recipient Meritorious Civilian Svc. award, Dept. of Navy, 2004. Mem. AIAA, IEEE, US Naval Inst., Elks, Kappa Sigma. Republican. Episcopalian. Home: 147 Brandi Way Winchester TN 37398 Office Phone: 931-393-7418. Personal E-mail: georgemasters@bellsouth.net. Business E-Mail: gmasters@utsi.edu.

**MASTERS, JOHN CHRISTOPHER,** psychologist, educator, writer; b. Terre Haute, Ind., Oct. 25, 1941; s. Robert William and Lillian Virginia (Decker) M.; m. Mary Jayne Capps, June 6, 1970; children— Blair Christopher, Kyle Alexander. AB, Harvard Coll., 1963; PhD, Stanford U., 1967. Asst. prof. Ariz. State U., Tempe, 1968-69; from asst. prof. U. Minn., Mpls., 1969-79; assoc. dir. Inst. Child Devel., 1974-79; Luce prof. pub. policy and the family, prof. psychology Vanderbilt U., Nashville, 1979-87, interim chair dept. psychology, 1986-88; pres. Profl. Mgmt. Group, Inc., 1991—; dir. Master Ventures, 1989—, Master Travel, 1989—. Assoc. editor: Child Development, 1973-76, Behavior Therapy: Techniques and Empirical Findings, 1974, 79, 88; editor: Psychol. Bull., 1987-89. Home: 4923 Old Oakleaf Dr Sarasota FL 34233-3947 Office Phone: 800-767-6162.

**MASTERS, JON JOSEPH,** corporate governance specialist, management consultant; b. N.Y.C., June 20, 1937; s. Arthur Edward and Esther (Shady) M.; m. Rosemary Dunaway Cox, June 16, 1962; children: Brooke Alison, Blake Edward. BA, Princeton U., 1958; JD, Harvard U., 1964. Bar: N.Y. 1965, U.S. Dist. Ct. (so. dist.) N.Y. 1965, U.S. Ct. Appeals (2d cir.) 1965. Cons. asst. to under sec. Dept. Army, 1961; mem. policy planning staff asst. sec. for internat. security affairs Dept. Def. Washington, 1962; mem. Pres. Johnson's Spl. Polit. Research Staff, Washington, 1964; assoc. Shearman & Sterling, N.Y.C., 1965-68, 69; mem. staff Bedford-Stuyvesant D & S Corp., Bklyn., 1968-69; v.p., sec., gen. counsel, dir. Baker, Weeks & Co., Inc., N.Y.C., 1969-76; co-founder, ptnr. Christy & Viener, N.Y.C., 1976-96; Vice-chmn. Robb, Peck, McCooey Specialist Corp., N.Y.C., 1996—98; prin. Lear, Yavitz & Assocs., N.Y.C., 1996-2001, mng. prin., 1998—2001; prin. Mercer Delta Cons., N.Y.C., 2001—02; chmn. Masters Governance Cons., LLC, N.Y.C., 2002—05; co-founder, prin. Masters-Rudnick & Assocs., LLC, NYC, 2005—. SEC adv. com. broker-dealer compliance, 1972-74; legal advisor NACD Blue Ribbon Commn. on CEO and Dir. Performance Evaluation, 1994; chmn. bd. Clear and Present Prodns., 1992-93; dir. Harris & Harris Group, Inc., 1992-98. Mem. implementation com. Econ. Devel. Task Force of N.Y. Urban Coalition, 1968; mem. bd. Internat. Social Service, Am. Br., Inc., 1978-83, pres., 1979-83; bd. dirs. The Arts Connection, 1979-85; mem. steering com. N.Y. Lawyers Alliance for Nuclear Arms Control, 1983-96. Served with USN, 1958-61. Mem. ABA, Assn. Bar City N.Y. (com. mcpl. affairs 1977-80). Office: 350 E 82 St New York NY 10028 Business E-Mail: jjmasters@mastersrudnick.com.

**MASTERS, JONATHAN EDWARD,** clinical psychologist; b. Northport, NY, Sept. 27, 1962; s. Edward Joseph and Janet (Pendleton) Masters. BA, Marist Coll., Poughkeepsie, NY, 1985; MA, Pepperdine U., LA, 1991, PsyD, 1998; PhD candidate, Inst. Contemporary Psychoanalysis, LA, 2003–. Cert. psychologist Ariz. Bd. Psychologist Examiners, 1999. Part-time lectr. in astronomy Vanderbilt Planetarium, Centerport, NY, 1979—84; psychology trainee NY State Office Mental Health, Poughkeepsie, 1985; behavioral specialist Psychol. Support Svcs., Mission Hills, 1990—94, Prairie Group Home, Hawthorne, 1991—94, Only a Place to Start, Inglewood, 1991—94; John B. Kelley Residential Treatment Ctr. for Men, LA, 1992—94, John B. Kelley Residential Treatment Ctr. for Women, LA, 1992—94; psychology trainee Cath. Psychol. Svcs., LA, 1993, U. So. Calif. Med. Ctr., LA, 1994;

predoctoral intern Pederson-Kraig Ctr., Huntington, NY, 1994—95; staff psychotherapist Advanced Ctr. Psychotherapy, Jamaica Estates, 1996—98; staff psychotherapist/psychologist New Hope Guild Ctr. for Children, Howard Beach, NY, 1996—99; clin. psychologist Paradise Valley Psychiat. Assocs., Phoenix, 2000—. Vol. Hurricane Katrina ARC, Phoenix, 2005. Mem.: APA (assoc.), SW Psychoanalytic Soc. (assoc.; practice com. mem. 2000, jour. group mem. 2000—01, chair program com. 2001—03, treas. 2004—05, bd. dirs. 2004—05). Office: Paradise Valley Psychiatric Assocs 4232 E Cactus Rd Ste 207 Phoenix AZ 85032 Office Phone: 602-494-8105. Personal E-mail: jmast99@cox.net.

**MASTERS, KEVIN S.,** psychology professor; b. Mass. s. Stanley W. and Joan E. Masters; m. Jill Masters; children: Sierra M., Hilary K., Christian S. PhD, Brigham Young U., Provo, Utah, 1989. Lic. Psychologist Utah, 1992. Prof. Utah State U., Logan, 1995—2004; assoc. prof., dir. of clin. tng. Syracuse U., NY, 2004—. Cons. psychologist Hillside Living Ctr., Logan, Utah, 2000—04. Contbr. articles to profl. jours. Cmty. U. Rsch. Initiative grant, State of Utah, 2003—04, 2002—03, Rsch. grant, Labor Commn. of Utah, 2001—02, Nat. Inst. on Aging, NIH, 2000—01. Mem.: APA (bd. dirs., divsn. 38 2002—), Coun. of Directors of Clin. Psychology Programs, Soc. of Behavioral Medicine (ann. conv. reviewer 2001—05). Office: Syracuse Univ 430 Huntington Hall Syracuse NY 13244 Office Phone: 315-443-3666. Office Fax: 315-443-4085. Business E-Mail: kemaster@syr.edu.

**MASTERS, LEE,** broadcast executive; married; 2 children. Student, Temple U. Various positions including programmer, sta. mgr., owner radio stas.; exec. v.p., gen. mgr. MTV, 1986—89; pres., CEO E! Entertainment TV, 1990—98; founder, pres., CEO Liberty Digital, 1999—2002; mem. bd. of dir. LodgeNet Entertainment Corp., 2002—. Conf. co-chair CTAM '96. Mem.: Nat. Cable TV Assn. (pub. affairs com., co-chair state and local govt. com., Vanguard award for programmers 1995). Office: LodgeNet Entertainment Corp 3900 W Innovation St Sioux Falls SD 57107

**MASTERS, ROBERT EDWARD LEE,** psychotherapist, sexologist; b. Jan. 4, 1927; s. Robert and Katherine (Leeper) Masters; m. Jean Houston, May 8, 1965. BA Philosophy, U. Mo., 1951; PhD Clin. Psychology, Humanistic Psychology Inst., 1974. Dir. Libr. Sex Rsch., N.Y.C., 1962—66, Sensory Imagery Program, 1965—69; dir. rsch. Found. for Mind Rsch., N.Y.C. and Ashland, Oreg., 1965—. Dir. Zarathustra Project, Pomona, 1980—99; co-dir. Human Capacities Tng. Program, Ramapo, NJ, 1982—99; pvt. practice psychotherapy, neural re-edn., aging and geropsychology programs; prin. tchr. Hypnotherapist Tng., Pomona, 1982—99; pres. Human Capacities Corp., Ashland, 1982—. Author: Eros and Evil, 1962, Forbidden Sexual Behavior and Morality, 1964, Mind Games, 1972, Listening to the Body, 1978, Psychophysical Method Exercises, vols. I-VI, 1983, The Goddess Sekhmet, 1987, The Masters Technique, 1987, Neurospeak, 1994, The Way to Awaken, 1997, Swimming Where Madmen Drown, 2002, numerous poems, short fiction, Literary and Art Criticism, 1952—60; co-author (with J. Houston): Varieties of Psychedelic Experience, 1966, Psychedelic Art, 1968; contbr. articles to profl. jours. With USN, 1945—46, PTO. Grantee, Erickson Found., 1966, Kleiner Found., 1968, Babcock Found., 1970, Doris Duke Found., 1972. Fellow: Am. Acad. Clin. Sexologists (founder): mem.: AAAS, APA, N.Y. Acad. Scis., Am. Psychotherapy Assn. (diplomate), Assn. Humanistic Psychology, Am. Assn. Sex Educators, Counselors and Therapists, Am. Bd. Sexology (clin. supr.). Office: Found Mind Rsch PMB 501 2305 Ashland St Ste C Ashland OR 97520-3777 Personal E-mail: hvhhbob@aol.com.

**MASTERS, ROGER DAVIS,** political scientist, educator, toxicologist; b. Boston, June 8, 1933; s. Maurice and S. Grace (Davis) M.; m. Judith Ann Rubin, June 6, 1956 (div. 1984); children— Seth J., William A., Katherine R.; m. Susanne R. Putnam, Aug. 25, 1984 BA, Harvard U., 1955; MA, U. Chgo., 1958, PhD, 1961; MA (hon.), Dartmouth Coll., 1974. Instr. dept. polit. sci. Yale U., 1961-62, asst. prof., 1962-67; assoc. prof. dept. govt. Dartmouth Coll., Hanover, NH, 1967-73, prof., 1973-98, John Sloan Dickey Third Century prof., 1980-85, chmn. dept., 1986-89, Nelson A. Rockefeller prof., 1991-98, prof. emeritus, 1998—, rsch. prof., 1999—. Cultural attache Am. Embassy, Paris, 1969—71; chmn. France-Am. Commn. Ednl. and Cultural Exch., 1969—71; vis. lectr. Yale U. Law Sch., 1988—89, Vt. Law Sch., 1993—94; sect. editor Social Sci., Info., 1971—; chmn. exec. com. Gruter Inst. Law and Behavioral Rsch., 1995—98; pres. Found. for Neurosci. and Soc., 1998—; mem. Get the Lead Out of Vt. Task Force, 2006. Author: The Nation Is Burdened, 1967, The Political Philosophy of Rousseau, 1968, The Nature of Politics, 1989, Beyond Relativism, 1993, Machiavelli, Leonardo, and the Science of Power, 1996, Fortune is a River, 1998; editor: Rousseau's Discourses, 1964, Rousseau's Social Contract, 1978; co-editor: Ostracism: A Social and Biological Phenomenon, 1986, Collected Writings of J.J. Rousseau, 1990—, Primate Politics, 1991, The Sense of Justice, 1992, The Neurotransmitter Revolution, 1994; editor Gruter Inst. Reader in Biology, Law, and Human Social Behavior, 1992. Served with AUS, 1955-57. Fulbright fellow Inst. d'Etudes Politiques, Paris, 1958-59, joint Yale U.-Social Sci. Rsch. Coun. fellow, 1964-65, Guggenheim fellow, 1967-68, Hastings Ctr. for Ethics and Life Scis. fellow, 1973-78. Mem. AAAS, Am. Polit. Sci. Assn., Assn. Polit. and Life Sci. (coun.), Am. Soc. for Legal and Polit. Philosophy, Internat. Soc. Human Ethology, Human Behavior Evolution Soc. Office: Dartmouth Coll Dept Govt Silsby Hall HB6108 Hanover NH 03755 Home: Valley Terrace Apt 214 2820 Christian St White River Junction VT 05001 Business E-Mail: roger.d.masters@dartmouth.edu.

**MASTERS, SHARON KAY,** sociologist, educator; d. John Joseph and Catherine Masters; m. William Charles Foege, Jr. BA, U. Buffalo, N.Y., 1975, MA, 1977, PhD, 1986. Instr. SUNY, Buffalo, 1978—82; rsch. assoc. Dept. Sociology and Anthropology N.Mex State U., Las Cruces, N.Mex., 1982—85; rsch. assoc. Fla. Mental Health Inst. U. South Fla., Tampa, Fla., 1987—87; sociology prof., Fla. So. Coll., Lakeland, Fla., 1987—. Dir. Women's Studies Program Fla. So. Coll., 2000—. Mem. com.target population and outcomes State Fla., 2000, mem. coun. child protection coun. health and human svcs. bd., 1999—2000; chmn. com. tchr. edn. program rev. Fla. Dept. Edn., Tallahassee, 1997—95; editor, action alert pub. affairs com. Planned Parenthood Ctrl. Fla., Lakeland Winter Haven, Fla., 1993—93; organizer women's history coll. and cmty. event Polk C.C. and Fla. So. Coll., Winter Haven, Fla., 2006; contbr. gun violence assessment Polk County League of Women Voters, 2000—04; bd. dir. Women's Resource Ctr., Winter Haven, Fla., 2001—, PACE Ctr. Girls, Inc. Polk County, Lakeland, 2000—. Named Faculty/Staff Vol. of Yr., Fla. So. Coll., 2006; fellow, NIMH, 1980—82, Nat. Humanities Ctr., 1996. Mem.: Nat. Women's Studies Assn., Fla. Consortium Women's Studies (chmn. conf. program 2005—, mem. organizing com. 2005—), Lakeland Dems. Club (bd. dirs. 2005—), Bookies Book Club. Democrat. Achievements include research in impact of modernization on the people of Easter Island; disaster aid programs and family recovery; life-stage responses to love canal crisis. Avocations: travel, gardening, environment. Office: Florida Southern College 111 Lake Hollingsworth Drive Lakeland FL 33801-5698 Office Phone: 863-680-4268.

**MASTERSON, CARLIN** See GLYNN, CARLIN

**MASTERSON, ELLEN HORNBERGER,** accountant; b. Ft. Smith, Ark., Feb. 19, 1951; d. Evans Zacharias and Nancy Cravens (Eads) H.; m. Conrad J. Masterson, Jr., Sept. 26, 1987. BA, Emory U., 1973; MBA, So. Meth. U., 1978. CPA, Mass. Staff acct. Coopers & Lybrand, Boston, 1973, gen. practice ptnr. Dallas, 1985—97; CFO Am. Gen. Corp., Houston, 1997—99; prin. PricewaterhouseCoopers, N.Y.C., 1999—. Instr. Sch. Mgmt. and Adminstry. Scis., U. Tex., Dallas, 1980-81. Bd. dirs. Shakespeare Festival Dallas, 1983-86, Leadership Dallas, 1985-86, USA Film Festival, 1986-88, Dental Health Program, Inc., 1986-88; mem. Jr. League, The 500, Inc.; workshop leader, vol. Cmty. Bd. Inc.; cons. Ctr. for Non Profit Mgmt. Mem. AICPA, Mass. Soc. CPAs, Tex. CPAs, So. Meth. U. MBA Alumni Assn., Kappa Kappa Gamma, Alpha Iota Delta, Beta Gamma Sigma. Presbyterian. Office: PricewaterhouseCoopers 300 Madison Ave 24th fl New York NY 10017

**MASTERSON, JAMES FRANCIS,** psychiatrist; b. Phila., Mar. 25, 1926; s. James Francis and Evangeline (O'Boyle) M.; m. Patricia Cooke, Jan. 28, 1950; children: James F., Richard K., Nancy. BS, U. Notre Dame, 1947; MD, Jefferson Med. Sch., Phila., 1951. Diplomate Am. Bd. Psychiatry, Am. Bd. Neurology. Intern Phila. Gen. Hosp., 1951-52; resident in psychiatry Payne Whitney Clinic, N.Y. Hosp., N.Y.C., 1952-55, chief resident, 1955-56, dir. adolescent OPD, 1956-66, head adolescent program, 1968-75, asst. attending psychiatrist, 1956-60, assoc. attending psychiatrist, 1960-70, attending psychiatrist, 1970—, dir. The Symptomatic Adolescent Research Project, 1957-67; dir. Masterson Group, P.C. for Study and Treatment Personality Disorders, N.Y.C., 1977—; Author: Psychotherapy of the Borderline Adolescent, Psychotherapy of the Borderline Adult, Countertransference, Narcissistic Personality Disorder, The Real Self, The Psychiatric Dilemma of Adolescence, The Test of Time: From Borderline Adolescent to Functioning Adult, The Personality Disorders: As Seen Through the Lens of Attachment Theory and Neurobiology Development of the Self, 2005; contbr. articles to profl. jours. Fellow Am. Psychiat. Assn., Am. Coll. Psychoanalysts; mem. AMA, Am. Coll. Psychoanalysis, N.Y. Soc. Adolescent Psychiatry (founder, past pres.), N.Y. County Med. Soc. Office: 60 Sutton Pl S New York NY 10022-4168 Office Phone: 212-751-4992. Business E-Mail: mastesnin@aol.com.

**MASTERSON, JOHN PATRICK,** retired language educator; b. Chgo., Mar. 15, 1925; s. Michael Joseph and Delia Frances (Dolan) M.; m. Jean Frances Wegrzyn, Aug. 18, 1956; children: Mary Beth, Michael, Maureen, Laura. BA, St. Mary of the Lake, 1947; MA, De Paul U., 1952; PhD, U. Ill., 1961. Chmn. English dept. De Paul U., Chgo., 1964-67, head humanities div., 1967-70, prof. English, 1970, dean Coll. Liberal Arts and Scis., 1970-76, prof. mgmt., 1976-80, 82-87, prof. emeritus, 1988—, dean Grad. Sch., 1980-82. Cons. in field. Recipient award Shell Oil Co., 1968, Via Sapientiae award De Paul U., 1987; fellow adminstrn. program Am. Coun. Edn. Roman Catholic. Home: 1922 Belleview Ave Westchester IL 60154-4345 Personal E-mail: mastersonjj@aol.com.

**MASTERSON, KENNETH RHODES,** lawyer; b. Kennett, Mo., Feb. 22, 1944; s. H. Byron and Mary (Rhodes) M.; children— Michael K., Elizabeth Megel, Grace Megel BA, Westminster Coll., 1966; JD, Vanderbilt U., 1970. Bar: Mo. 1970, Tenn. 1976. Ptnr. Thomason, Crawford & Hendrix, Memphis, 1976-79; v.p. legal Federal Express, Memphis, 1980-81, sr. v.p., gen. counsel 1981-93, sr. v.p., gen. counsel and sec., 1993-96, exec. v.p., gen. counsel and sec., 1996-98, FedEx Corp., Memphis, 1998—2005, cons., 2005—. Mem. ABA, Mo. Bar Assn., Am. Corp. Counsel Assn. Home: 8679 Classic Dr Memphis TN 38125-8824 Office: FedEx Corp 942 S Shady Grove Rd Memphis TN 38120-4117 Fax: 901-818-7590.

**MASTERSON, KLEBER SANLIN, JR.,** physicist; b. San Diego, Sept. 26, 1932; s. Kleber Sandlin and Charlotte Elizabeth (Parker) M.; m. Sara Ann Cooper, Dec. 21, 1957; children: Thomas Marshall, John Cooper. BS in Engring., U.S. Naval Acad., 1954; MS in Physics, USN, 1961; PhD in Physics, U. Calif., San Diego, 1963; student in Advanced Mgmt. Program, Harvard U., 1981—82. Commd. ensign USN, 1954, advanced through grades to rear adm., 1979, comdg. officer USS Preble Pearl Harbor, Hawaii, 1969-71, mgr. antiship missile def. project Washington, 1974-77, exec. asst. to sec. of Navy, 1977-79, asst. dep. comdr. Naval Sea Systems Command, 1979-81, chief Studies, Analyses and Gaming Agy., 1981-82, ret., 1982; prin. Booz, Allen and Hamilton, Inc., Arlington, Va., 1982-87, v.p. and ptnr., 1987-92; sr. v.p. Sci. Applications Internat. Corp., 1992-94; pres. The Riverside Group, Ltd., 1994—2005; ret. Bd. control U.S. Naval Inst., Annapolis, Md., 1971-82; bd. dirs. Mil. Ops. Rsch. Soc., 1984-90, pres., 1988-89; mem. divsn. rev. com. TSA divsn. Los Alamos Nat. Lab., 1996-2001, chmn. 1998-2001. Editor: Book of Navy Songs, 1954; contbr. articles on plasma and theoretical nuclear physics, computer science, radars, ops. rsch. to profl. publs. Active Historic Alexandria Resources Commn., 1998—, vice-chmn. 2001-02, chmn., 2002-04. Mem. Am. Phys. Soc., Am. Soc. Naval Engrs., U.S. Naval Acad. Alumni Assn. (pres. Washington chpt. 1989-90), U.S. Naval Acad. Found. (trustee 1991—), Soc. of the Cin. (chmn. edn. com. 1997-2001, asst. sec. gen. 2001-04, editor Cin. Fourteen 2001-04, treas. gen. 2004-), Mass. Soc. of the Cin. (mem. standing com., v.p. 1999-2001, pres. 2001-04), Sigma Xi. Achievements include development of NELIAC computer program and strategic simulation methodology. Home and Office: 101 Pommander Walk Alexandria VA 22314-3844 Office Phone: 703-548-6183. Personal E-mail: skidmasterson@cs.com.

**MASTERSON, MARY STUART,** actress; b. N.Y.C., June 28, 1966; d. Peter and Carlin Glynn Masterson. Theatre appearances include Alice in Wonderland, 1982, Been Taken, 1985, The Lucky Spot, 1987, Lily Dale, 1987, Three Sisters, 1991; TV movies include Love Lives On, 1985, City in Fear, 1980, Lily Dale, 1996, On the 2nd Day of Christmas, 1997; films: The Stepford Wives, 1975, Heaven Help Us, 1984, At Close Range, 1985, My Little Girl, 1986, Gardens of Stone, 1987, Some Kind of Wonderful, 1987, Mr. North, 1988, Chances Are, 1989, Immediate Family, 1989, Funny About Love, 1990, Married To It, 1990, Fried Green Tomatoes, 1991, Benny and Joon, 1993, Bad Girls, 1994, Radioland Murders, 1994, Heaven's Prisoners, 1996, Bed of Roses, 1996, Digging to China, 1997, Dogtown, 1997, The Postman, 1997, The Florentine, 1998, The Book of Stars, 1999, Black and Blue, 1999, The Book of Stars, 2000, Leo, 2002, West of Here, 2002; dir., writer for Showtime 2000; TV guest appearances include Amazing Stories, 1985, Inside the Actors Studio, 1994. Office: Creative Artists Agency 9830 Wilshire Blvd Beverly Hills CA 90212-1825

**MASTERSON, PETER,** actor, film producer; b. Houston, June 1, 1934; s. Carlos Bee and Josephine Yeager (Smith) M.; m. Carlin Glynn, Dec. 29, 1960; children: Carlin Alexandra, Mary Stuart, Peter Carlos. BA in History, Rice U., 1957. Appeared in Broadway plays Marathon '33, 1963, Blues for Mr. Charlies, 1964; title role in Trial of Lee Harvey Oswald, 1967; appeared in The Great White Hope, 1968, That Championship Season, 1974, The Poison Tree, 1973, (films) The Exorcist, 1972, Man on a Swing, 1973, The Stepford Wives, 1974; playwright The Best Little Whorehouse in Texas, 1978; dir. Broadway prodns. The Best Little Whorehouse in Texas, 1978 (Drama Desk award for Best Dir. of Musical 1978); co-dir., co-writer The Best Little Whorehouse Goes Public, 1994; dir. off-Broadway prodns. The Cover of Life, 1994, The Young Man from Atlanta (Pulitzer prize 1995); screenwriter The Best Little Whorehouse in Texas, 1980; prodr. (TV film) City in Fear, 1980; dir. films The Trip to Bountiful, 1985, Blood Red, 1986, Full Moon in Blue Water, 1987, Night Game, 1988, Convicts, 1989, Arctic Blue, 1993, Lily Dale, 1996, The Only Thrill, 1997, Mermaid, 1999, Lost Junction, 2001, Whiskey Sch., 2005. Mem. AFTRA, SAG, Actors Equity Assn., Soc. Stage Dirs. and Choreographers, Writers Guild Am., Actors Studio, Dirs. Guild Am., Seawanhaka Club, Corinthian Yacht Club, Tex. Corinthian Yacht Club.

**MASTERSON, WILLIAM A.,** retired judge; b. NYC, June 25, 1931; s. John Patrick and Helen Audrey (O'Hara) M.; m. Julie Dohrmann Cosgrove; children: Mark, Mary, Timothy, Barbara. BA, UCLA, 1953, JD, 1958. Bar: Calif. 1959, U.S. Supreme Ct. 1965. Assoc. Sheppard, Mullin, Richter & Hampton, L.A., 1952-62, pntr., 1962-79; pntr. Rogers & Wells, 1979-83, Skadden, Arps, Slate, Meagher & Flom, 1983-87; judge L.A. Superior Ct. 1987-92; justice Ct. Appeal, 1993-2000; ret., 2000. Author, editor: Civil Trial Practice: Strategies and Techniques, 1986. With inf. U.S. Army, 1953-55. Fellow Am. Coll. Trial Lawyers; mem. Order of Coif. Office: PO Box 190 Mendocino CA 95460

**MASTIN, LYNN P.,** biology professor; d. Forest Lynn and Martha Hamilton Purdom; m. Nathan Edgar Mastin, Dec. 21, 1974; 1 child, E. Thomas. BA in Biology, U. West Ga., Carrollton, 1971, MS in Biology, 1973. Microbiologist Ctrs. for Disease Control, Atlanta, 1974—76; instr. Oklahoma City Schs., 1979—82, South Okla. City Jr. Coll., Oklahoma City, 1982—84, Mid-Del Christian Sch., Oklahoma City, 1984—89, Life Christian Sch., Oklahoma City, 1989—90, Lee County Schs., Tupelo, Miss., 1992—99, Itawamba C.C.,

Fulton, Miss., 1999—. Tchr., musician Union Christian Assembly, Tupelo, 1990—. Mem.: Miss. State Tchrs. Assn. Office: Itawamba Cmty Coll 601 N Hill St Fulton MS 38843 Office Phone: 662-862-8369. E-mail: lpmastin@iccms.edu.

**MASTRAMICO, THOMAS J.,** music educator; s. Patsy and Theresa Mastramico; m. Jolene M. Bengiveno; children: Nicholas, Christa. B in Music Edn., Youngstown State U., 1977. Band dir., music instr., profl. trumpet player, Youngstown, 1977—. Mem.: KC, Ohio Music Educators Assn., Holy Name Soc.

**MASTRANDREA, PATRICIA,** elementary school educator, consultant; d. Nicholas Joseph Mastrandrea and Lucia Raia. BS in Elem. Edn., English, L.I. U., 1971, grad. in Media, 1975; Profl. diploma, CUNY, 1991. Cert. tchr. N.Y., 1991. Elem. tchr. Babylon UFSD, NY, 1971—; cons. N.Y. State United Tchrs. Edn. and Learning Trust, Latham, NY, 1985—. Chairperson Western Suffolk Tchr. Ctr., Deer Park, NY, 1985—89; lead facilitator Babylon Meml. Grade Sch., 1992—2001. Founder Western Suffolk Tchr. Ctr., 1985. Bd. dirs. Hidden Ponds HOA, Smithton, NY, 1998—2002. Recipient scholarship, Smithsonian Instn., 1978. Avocations: gardening, gourmet cooking, golf, tennis. Home: 158 Hidden Pond Cir Smithtown NY 11787 Office: Babylon Meml Grade Sch 169 Park Ave Babylon NY 11702 Office Phone: 638-893-7980. Office Fax: 631-893-7990. E-mail: patmaste@optonline.net.

**MASTRANTONIO, MARY ELIZABETH,** actress; b. Lombard, Ill., Nov. 17, 1958; d. Frank A. and Mary D. (Pagone) M. m. Pat O' Conn0r; 2 children Jack, Declan Student, U. Ill., 1976-78. Actress: (stage prodns.) Copperfield, 1981, Oh, Brother, 1981, Amadeus, 1982, Sunday in the Park with George, 1983, The Human Comedy, 1984, Henry V, 1984, Measure for Measure, 1985, The Knife, 1987, Twelfth Night, (feature films) Scarface, 1983, The Color of Money, 1986 (Acad. award nomination 1986), Slam Dance, 1987, The January Man, 1989, The Abyss, 1989, Fools of Fortune, 1990, Class Action, 1991, Robin Hood: Prince of Thieves, 1991, Consenting Adults, 1992, White Sands, 1992, Three Wishes, 1995, Two Bits, 1995, My Life So Far, 1999, Limbo, 1999, The Perfect Storm, 2000, Tabloid, 2001; TV miniseries Mussolini: THe Untold Story, 1985; TV films Uncle Vanya, 1991, Witness Protection, 1999, The Brooke Ellison Story, 2004; TV guest appearance Frasier, 1993, Without a Trace, 2005-2006. Office: Internat Creative Mgmt 8942 Wilshire Blvd Beverly Hills CA 90211-1934*

**MASTRIAN, STACEY LYNN,** singer, educator; MusB in Vocal Performance, The Cath. U. Am., Washington, D.C., 2000; MusM in Opera Performance, U. Md., Coll. Pk., 2002, student in Vocal Performanse, 2003—. Instr. U. Md., Coll. Pk., 2005—. Pvt. studio tchr., Balt., 2001—; adj. faculty Peabody Conservatory, Balt., 2006—. Singer: Vatican City, Georgian Radio, Susquehanna Orch., Blacksburg Orch., U. Md. Orch., Nova Annapolis Orch. Finalist, Palm Beach Opera Vocal Competition, 2005, Irma M. Cooper Opera Columbus Internat. Vocal Competition, 2005; named Disting. Tchg. Asst., U. Md., 2006; recipient Silver Medallion award, Rosa Ponselle Found., 1998, Benjamin T. Rome award, Cath. U., 2000, Discovery Series winner, Vocal Arts Soc., 2003, Hon. Mention award, Am. Bach Soc. Bethlehem Bach Choir Young Am. Singer Competition, 2004, Ulrich Grad. Competition winner, U. Md., 2004; fellow, Frank Huntington Beebe Fund for Musicians, 2002—03, U. Md., 2003—; grantee, Fulbright Found., 2002—03; scholar, U. Md., 2000—02, Nat. Italian Am. Found., 2001, Mu Phi Epsilon, 2004; Archdiscesan scholar, Cath. U., 1996—2000, Richard F. Gold Career grant, Shoshana Found., 2005. Mem.: Nat. Assn. Tchrs. Singing (First Pl. winner Mid Atlantic Regionals 1998), Phi Eta Sigma, Pi Kappa Lambda (Music). Personal E-mail: stacey@staceymastrian.com.

**MASTRO, VICTOR JOHN,** mathematician, educator; b. N.Y.C., Sept. 15, 1948; BS in Secondary Edn., Fordham U., 1970, MS in Secondary Edn., Math., 1973. Edn. cons., curriculum cons. Ind. Sch. 138-184, Bronx, N.Y., 1974-79; art sales cons. Intercraft Industries, Inc., Chgo., 1976-78; prof. coord. Hudson County C.C., Jersey City, N.J., 1979—; assoc. prof. math. Fordham U., Bronx, 1984—. Tutor vol. Hudson County C.C., 1979-92, faculty adviser, 1989-91; mentor, counselor Forum Italian Am. Educators, Bronx, 1982-87; speaker local radio programs; presenter workshops. Author multicultural and ethnomath. program, math. texts, videos and audio tapes, math. poem, math murals and collages, multicultural math; NFL contbr., author and historian; Bronx historian, rschr., contbr., author and mural and collage artist; contbr. articles to profl. publs. Mem. AAAS (text and video evaluator 1984-88), Am. Math. Assn., Nat. Coun. Tchrs. Math. (text evaluator). Roman Catholic. Achievements include development of multicultural mathematics programs for Afro-Americans, Native Americans, Hispanics, women, Italian, near- and far-East cultures. Home: 1907 Narragansett Ave Bronx NY 10461-1820 Office: Hudson County C C 168 Sip Ave Jersey City NJ 07306-3009

**MASTROENI, PABLO,** professional soccer player; b. Mendoza, Argentina, Aug. 26, 1976; Attended, N.C. State Univ. Midfielder Miami Fusion, 1998—2002, Colorado Rapids, 2002—, capt., 2004—. 48 caps US Nat. Soccer Team, 2001—; mem. U.S. World Cup Team, 2002, 06. Mailing: US Soccer Fedn 1801 S Prairie Ave Chicago IL 60616*

**MASTROIANNI, LUIGI, JR.,** physician, educator; b. New Haven, Nov. 8, 1925; s. Marion (Dallas) Mastroianni; m. Elaine Catherine Pierson, Nov. 4, 1957; children: John James, Anna Catherine, Robert Luigi. AB, Yale U., 1946; MD, Boston U., 1950, DSc (hon.), 1973; MA (hon.), U. Pa., 1970. Diplomate Am. Bd. Ob-Gyn. and Reproductive Endocrinology and Infertility. Intern, then resident ob-gyn. Met. Hosp. N.Y., 1950—54; fellow rsch. Harvard Med. Sch. and Free Hosp. for Women, Boston, 1954—55; instr. dept. ob-gyn, Yale U. Sch. Medicine. New Haven 1955—56; asst prof ob-gyn dept. Yale U., New Haven, 1956—61; prof. U. Calif., L.A., 1961—65; chief ob-gyn Harbor Gen. Hosp., L.A., 1961—65; William Goodell prof. ob.-gyn., chmn. dept. U. Pa. Sch. of Medicine, Phila., 1965—87, William Goodell prof. ob.-gyn. dept., dir. human reproduction div., 1987—96. Contbr. articles to profl. jours. Recipient Squibb prize, Pacific Coast Fertility Soc., 1965, Christian R. and Mary Lindback award, 1969, Gold medal, Barren Found., 1977, King Faisal prize in medicine, 1989. Pub. Recognition award, Assn. Profs. of Gynecology and Obstetrics, 1990, Disting. Svc. award, Soc. Study Reprodn., 1992, Rector's medal, U. Chile, 1993, Axel Munthe award, 1996, Resolve Svc. award, 1997, medal, Coll. Physicians of Phila., 1998. Mem.: Soc. for Study of Reprodn. (Disting. Svc. award 1992), Endocrine Soc., Soc. for Exptl. Biology and Medicine, Soc. Gynecology Investigation (Disting. Scientist award 2004), Inst. of Medicine of NAS, Am. Physiol. Soc., Am. Soc. for Reproductive Medicine, Am. Gynecol. Club, Am. Gynecol. and Obstet. Soc., ACOG, ACS, Chilean Soc. Ob-Gyn. (hon.), Uruguan Soc. Sterility and Fertility (hon.), Israel Soc. Ob-Gyn. (hon.), Soc. Espanola de Fertilidad (hon.), Peruvian Fertility Soc. (hon.), Argentina Fertility Soc. (hon.), Italian Soc. Ob-Gyns. (hon.), Brazilian Fertility Soc. (hon.), Assn. Profs. Ob-Gyn. (hon.), N.C. Gynecol. Soc. (hon.), Tex. Assn. Ob-Gyns. (hon.), Ctrl. Assn. Ob-Gyns. (hon.), Pacific Coast Fertility Soc. (hon.), Alpha Omega Alpha, Sigma Xi. Home: 561 Ferndale Ln Haverford PA 19041-1614 Office: Pa Fertility Care 3701 Market St Fl 8 Philadelphia PA 19104-5509 Office Phone: 215-662-2970.

**MASUCCI, MICHAEL JAMES,** artist; b. N.Y.C., Nov. 24, 1952; s. Allen A. and Frances Masucci; life ptnr. Kate Johnson, Sept. 30, 1969. Student, Arts Students League of N.Y., Parsons Sch. of Design, CUNY, 1972—74, Columbia U., 1974—76. Studio mgr. Alan Kaplan Studios, N.Y.C., 1978—79; master printer Modernage Photographics, N.Y.C., 1979—2002; CEO/dir. EZTV, Santa Monica, Calif., 1983—; video artist Bethune Theater-danse, L.A., 1986—2002, Loretta Livingston and Dancers, L.A., 2001—05. Co-creator, v.p. Rock Against Racism-USA, N.Y.C., 1978—80; faculty Otis Coll. of Art and Design, L.A., 2000—05; adv. bd. DV Expo, L.A., 2004—05; curator Hacking the Timeline, Santa Monica, Calif., 2006—. Prodr.: (feature film) Exile in Paradise, 1989 (AFI Retrospective, 1999); dir.: Quantum Entanglement, 2003; contbr. book.; cinematographer (documentary film) The

Sharpest Girl in Town, 1989 (commd. Mus. of Modern Art, NY, 1999); dir.: (documentary film) Zina Bethune in China, 1989 (AFI retrospective, 1999), Outside Looking In, 1996 (ICA-London Screening, 1996); contbr. articles to mags. and profl. jours. Judge for grants Roy Dean Film Awards, L.A., 2002—06; adv. bd. LA Theater Ctr., 1990—92, West Hollywood Mktg. Corp., Calif., 1990—92; bd. mem. Avaz Internat. Dance Theater, L.A., 2005—06; adv. bd. LA Free Clinic. Named one of Top 100 Prodrs., Prodr. Mag., 2000; recipient Artistic and Cmty. Svc. award, Dance Outreach/Bethune Theaterdanse, 1987, award, Changchun Film Studios, China, 1987, Artistic and Cmty. Svc. award, City of West Hollywood, 2001, Directing Award for Quantum Entanglement, Telly Awards, 2004, Curating award, James Irvine Found., 2005-6; Prodn. grant, Milken Found., 1989, Inst. of Contemporary Art, London, 1997, Exhbn. grant, West Hollywood Mktg. Com., 2000, Calif. Arts Coun., 2000, Online Exhbn. grant, Adobe Software, 2004-5, Artist grant, French Ministry of Culture, 2005-6, Prodn. grant, Santa Monica Cultural Affairs Dept., 2006, LA County Arts Commn., 2006. Mem.: L.A. Assn. of Ind. Video and Filmmakers (pres. 2006), Assn. of Ind. Video and Filmmakers, Assn. of Ind. Feature Film Prodrs., Assn. Computing Machinery Spl. Interest Group in Computer Graphics (chmn. digital video commitee 2002—03), Digital Video Expo (adv. bd. 2003—05). Achievements include invention of LiteCrane projection technology. Office: Eztv 1629 18th St #6 Santa Monica CA 90404 Office Phone: 310-829-3389. E-mail: mmasucci@eztvmedia.com.

**MASUI, YOSHIO,** zoology educator; b. Kyoto, Oct. 6, 1931; arrived in Can., 1969; s. Fusa and Toyo Masui; m. Yuriko Masui, May 9, 1959; children: Sayuri, Hitoshi. BSc, Kyoto U., 1953, MSc, 1955, PhD, 1961; DSc (hon.), U. Toronto, 1999. Asst. prof. Konan U., Kobe, Japan, 1965; rsch. staff biologist Yale U., New Haven, 1966-69, lectr., 1969; assoc. prof. U. Toronto, Ont., 1969-78, prof. Ont., 1978-97, prof. emeritus, 1997—, Konan U., 1999—. Recipient Manning award Manning Found., Calgary, Alta., 1991, Gairdner Internat. award Gairdner Found., Toronto, 1992, Albert Lasker Basic Med. Rsch. award, Lasker Found., 1998; named Officer, Order of Canada, 2003. Fellow Royal Soc. London., Royal Soc. Can. Achievements include discovery of Maturation Promoting Factor (MPF) and Cytostatic Factor (CSF) and their roles in cell divison control. Office: U Toronto Dept Zoology 25 Harbord St Toronto ON Canada M5S 3G5 Business E-Mail: masui@zoo.utoronto.ca.

**MASULIS, RONALD,** finance educator; children: Alexander Dunne, Laura Elizabeth. BA in Econs., Northeastern U., Boston, 1971; MBA, U. Chgo., 1974, PhD, 1976. James M. Collins prof. fin. Cox Sch. Bus., So. Meth. U., Dallas, 1986—90; Frank Houston prof. fin. Owen Grad. Sch.Mgmt., Vanderbilt U., Nashville, 1990—. Assoc. editor Jour. Fin. and Quantitative Analysis, 1985-, Rev. Fin. Studies, 1987-90, Jour. Fin. Econs., 1987-90, Jour. Fin., 1993-2000, Jour. Fin. Intermediation, 1989-95. Mem.: Western Fin. Assn. (exec. com. 1988—90), Fin. Mgmt. Assn. (academic dir. 2006—), Am. Fin. Assn. (dir. 1988—90). Office: Owen Grad Sch of Mgmt Vanderbilt Univ 401 21st Ave S Nashville TN 37203 Office Phone: 615-322-3687.

**MASULLO, ALFREDO SALVATORE,** dermatologist; b. Weehawken, N.J., June 27, 1949; s. Gustavo and Natalina (Caridi) Masullo; m. Linda Bonura, 1983. BA, Rutgers U., 1971; MD, U. Medicine and Dentistry N.J., Newark, 1975. Diplomate Am. Bd. Dermatology. Intern in internal medicine U. Medicine and Dentistry N.J., 1975-76, resident, 1976-77; resident in dermatology St. Lukes, Roosevelt and Columbia-Presbyn. Med. Ctr., N.Y.C., 1977-80; pvt. practice, Hackensack, NJ, 1980—. Attending physician Hackensack Univ. Med. Ctr., 1980 , Holy Name Hosp., Teaneck, N.J., 1980—. Fellow Am. Acad. Dermatology; mem. AMA. Office: 120 Prospect Ave Hackensack NJ 07601-2256 Office Phone: 201-488-0707.

**MASUMOTO, DAVID MAS,** writer, farmer; BA in Soc., U. Calif., Berkeley; MA in Cmty. Devel., U. Calif., Davis; attended, Internat. U., Tokyo, Japan. Farmer, Del Ray, Calif.; columnist USA Today, Los Angeles Times, The Fresno Bee. Writer in residence Iolani Sch., Honolulu, 2004. Author: Silent Strength, 1984, Country Voices, The Oral History of a Japanese American Family Farm Community, 1987, Home Bound, 1989, Epitaph For A Peach: Four Seasons on My Family Farm, 1995 (Julia Child Cookbook award, 1995, San Francisco Review Books Critics' Choice award, 1995), Harvest Son, Planting Roots in American Soil, 1998 (Calif. Book award, 1999), Four Seasons in Five Senses, Things Worth Savoring, 2003, Letters to the Valley, A Harvest of Memories, 2004. Bd. mem. Calif. Council for Humanities, 1994—, bd. co-chair, 1998—2001; bd. mem. James Irvine Found., 2002—. Recipient James Clavell Japanese Am. Nat. Literacy award, 1986, Breadloaf Writers Conf. fellowship, 1996. Mem.: Calif. Assn. of Family Farmers. Office: c/o Heyday Books PO Box 9145 Berkeley CA 94709*

**MASUR, JOSHUA MICHAEL,** lawyer; b. Bronx, N.Y, July 19, 1968; s. Milton Leon and Sandra Kazahn Masur, Victor Schuster (Stepfather) and Prudence Emery (Stepmother); m. Shelly Kristine Millar, Nov. 28, 1993; children: Julia Astrid, Jacob Nelson, Noah Marshall. AB, Columbia Coll., 1990; JD, Columbia Law Sch., 1996. Bar: Calif. 1999. Mgr. computer graphics studio Sudler & Hennessey Advt., N.Y., 1990—92; dir. consulting svcs. MESA Computer Sys., N.Y., 1992—94; freelance computer cons. and graphic designer N.Y., 1995—96; atty. Heller Ehrman White & McAuliffe, Menlo Park, Calif., 1999—2004, Mayer Brown Rowe & Maw LLP, Palo Alto, Calif., 2004—. Founder World Wide Web Artists' Consortium, N.Y., 1994—96. Recipient Comment Competition 1st prize, Berkeley Tech. Law Jour., 1999; grantee, Columbia U. Law Sch. Pub. Interest Law Found., 1986—90; scholar, Nat. Merit Scholarship Corp., 1986—87; Chancellor James Kent scholar, Columbia U. Law Sch., 1997—98, Chief Justice Harlan Fiske Stone scholar, 1996—99. Mem.: San Francisco Bay Area Intellectual Property Inn Ct. (assoc.; sec. 2004—, treas. 2004—). Democrat. Avocations: skiing, oenophile. Home: 440 Birch St Redwood City CA 94062 Office: Mayer Brown Rowe & Maw LLP 3000 El Camino Real Suite 2-300 Palo Alto CA 94306 Office Phone: 650-331-2053. Office Fax: 650-331-4553. Personal E-mail: josh@masur.us. Business E-Mail: jmasur@mayerbrownrowe.com.

**MASUR, KURT,** conductor, music director; b. Brieg, Silesia, Germany, July 18, 1927; Grad.. Nat. Music Schule, Breslau, Germany, 1944, Leipzig Conservatory, 1946-48; degree (hon.), U. Mich., Cleve. Inst. Music, Leipzig U., Westminster Choir Coll., Hamilton Coll. Repetiteur and conductor Halle Nat. Theatre, 1948-51; conductor Erfurt City Theatre, 1951-53, Leipzig City Theatre, 1953-55, Dresden Philharm., 1955-58; gen. music dir. Mecklenburg Staatstheater, 1958-60; mus. dir. Komische Oper Berlin, 1960-64; chief conductor Dresden Philharm., 1967-72; conductor Leipzig Gewandhaus Orch., 1970-96; mus. dir. New York Philharmonic, N.Y.C., 1991—2002; conductor London Philharm. Orch., 1989-92, 2000—; mus. dir. Orchestre National de France, Paris, 2002—; music dir. emeritus Philharmonic Soc. of NY, 2002—. Prof. Leipzig Acad. Music, 1975—; hon. board condr. Israel Philharm. Orch., 1992. Musician (tours include): Europe, S.Am., Japan, U.S., Can., Mid. East; musician: (rec. artist) Symphonies by Mendelssonn, Symphonies by Brahms, Symphonies by Bruckner, Symphonies by Beethoven, Symphonies by Schumann, Symphonies by Tchaikovsky, Prokofiev's Piano Concertos, Beethoven's Missa Solemnis. Mailing: The London Philharmonic Orchestra 89 Albert Embankment London SE1 7TP England*

**MASYS, DANIEL RICHARD,** medical educator, department chairman; b. Columbus, Ohio, Mar. 6, 1949; s. Paul John and Jane Marie (Mollenauer) M.; m. Linda Suzanne Bross, June 2, 1974; 1 child, Christopher. AB in Biochemistry, Princeton U., 1971; MD, Ohio State U., 1974. Diplomate Am. Bd. Internal Medicine. Staff hematologist, oncologist U.S. Naval Hosp., San Diego, 1980-84; chief ICRDB br. NIH, Bethesda, Md., 1984-86; dir. Lister Hill Nat. Ctr. Nat. Libr. Medicine, Bethesda, Md., 1986-94; dir. biomed. informatics, prof. Sch. Medicine U. Calif., San Diego, 1994—2004; prof. chair dept. biomedical informatics Vanderbilt U., 2005—. Assoc. editor Acad. Medicine jour., 1988-91, Jour. Am. Med. Informatics, Assn., 1994-2004. Mem. high performance computing White House Office of Sci., Washington, 1991-94; rep. Fed. Networking Coun., Washington, 1991-94. Capt. USPHS, 1984-94; NASA Adv. Aerospace Medicine, 2004-. Fellow: ACP, Am. Coll. Med. Informatics (exec. com. 1989—92, pres. 2006—); mem.: Nat. Acad.

Scis., Inst. Medicine, Am. Med. Informatics Assn. (bd. dirs. 1992—95, assoc. editor jour. 1993—, Pres.'s award 1992), Alpha Omega Alpha. Office: Vanderbilt Univ 416 EBL 2209 Garland Ave Nashville TN 37232-8340

**MATA, DAVID JOSEPH,** physician; b. Houston, Feb. 3, 1956; s. José and Josephine M.; m. Patricia M. Mata; children: Daniel José, Timothy John. BA in Biology, Point Loma Coll., 1978; postgrad., Calif. State U., L.A., 1978-80; MD, U. Minn., 1987. Diplomate Am. Bd. Family Practice, Nat. Bd. Med. Examiners. Resident in family medicine San Bernardino County Med. Ctr., Calif., 1987-90; med. dir. Salud Med. Ctr., Woodburn, Oreg., 1990-96; pvt. practice Hemet, Calif., 1996—. Adj. asst. prof. Oreg. Health Scis. U. Sch. Medicine, Portland, 1991—96; active staff mem. Salem Hosp., Oreg., 1992—96, Silverton Hosp., Oreg., 1992—96, Hemet Valley Med. Ctr., 1997—; vice-chair Family Medicine, 2000—02; coms, steering com. mem. Am. Lung Assn., Salem, 1992—94; med. dir. Ramona Manor Convalescent Hosp., 2002—, Heartland Hospice, Hemet, 2005—, Birth Choice, Hemet, 2001—. Expert witness to U.S. Congress, Oreg. Supreme Ct., 1992; counselor East L.A. Task Force, 1979-80; chaplain Boy Scouts Am., Hemet, 1998—; adv. com. San Jacinto Head Start, 1998—; vol. physician 20th World Jamboree Boy Scouts Am., Thailand, 2002-03. Geriatric Medicine fellow U. Minn., 1985, Med. Student Rsch. tng. grantee NIH, 1985, scholar Nat. Hispanic Scholarship Found, 1987; named one of 10 Outstanding Young Ams., U.S. Jr. C. of C., 1993, Outstanding Young Person of World, 1993; recipient Golden Aztec award Oreg. Human Devel. Corp., 1993, Citation of Merit award Oreg./Pacific Dist. Ch. of Nazarene, 1993, Mentorship award Dept. Family Medicine Oreg. Health Scis. U., 1993, Disting. svc. award Ch. of the Nazarene, Woodburn, Oreg., 1996; named Family Doctor of the Yr., Oreg., 1995; recipient Congl. Tribute, U.S. Ho. of Reps., 1994. Fellow Am. Acad. Family Physicians; mem. Nazarene Health Care Fellowship, Am. Acad. Family Physicians, Northwest Regional Primary Care Assn. (clinicians com. 1990-93), Riverside County Med. Assn., Calif. Med. Assn. Democrat. Mem. Ch. Of The Nazarene. Avocations: drawing, camping, church activities, public speaking. Office: Bldg B, Ste A 255 N Gilbert St Hemet CA 92543-4066 Office Phone: 951-765-1727.

**MATA, ELIZABETH ADAMS,** language educator, land investor; b. Raleigh, NC, Jan. 11, 1946; d. John Quincy Adams and Beulah Honeycutt; m. Juan Mata, June 21, 1968; children: Laura, Juan, Daniel. Student, Sweet Briar Coll., Paris, 1966-67; BA in French, Randolph-Macon Women's Coll., 1968; tchr. cert. in French and Spanish, N.C. State U., 1981; postgrad., U. Salamanca, Spain, 1983-86; MA in Spanish, NYU, 1986; cert. mentor tchr., N.C. State U., 1989; postgrad., Fordham U., 1994, U. N.C., 1995. Lic. real estate agt., N.C., 1991; cert. ESL tchr., 1999; Nat. Bd. cert. in Spanish, 2003. Tchr. ESL, Am. Inst., Madrid, 1968-69; tchr. English, Ay J Garriques, Madrid, 1968-74, pvt. classes, Madrid, 1975-78; tchr. French, Wake County Sch., Cary, NC, 1982—83, tchr. Spanish, Apex, NC, 1982—; instr. ESL Wake Tech. Coll., Raleigh, NC, 1999—; Fulbright tchr. U. del Mar del Plata, Argentina, 2001—. Cons. ETS, 1999—. Named Tchr. of Yr., Apex HS, 1992-93. Mem. Am. Assn. Tchr. Spanish and Portuguese, Univ. Coun. on Edn., Alpha Kappa Delta (Beta Omicron chpt. hist. 1996-98, v.p. 1998-2000). Democrat. Avocations: sculpting, reading, gourmet cooking, restoring antiques, writing. Home: 643 Kings Fork Rd Cary NC 27511-5711 E-mail: elimata@aol.com.

**MATALGAH, MUSTAFA MUHAMMAD,** engineering educator, researcher; b. Houfa, Irbid, Jordan, Jan. 11, 1964; BS, Yarmouk U., 1987; MS, Jordan U. Sci. and Tech., 1990; PhD, U. Mo., 1996. Prin. sr. engr., sr. planner Sprint, Overland Park, Kans., 1996—2002; asst. prof. elec. engring. U. Miss., Oxford, 2002—06. assoc. prof. elec. engring., 2006—. Adj. vis. faculty U. Mo., Kansas City, 2000. Reviewer book chpt.: John Wiley & Sons, Inc., reviewer funding proposals: U.S. Civilian R&D Found., editl. reviewer: Computer and Elec. Engring. Jour., Jour. Wireless Comm. and Networking, editl. reviewer proc.: 17th Internat. Conf. Parallel and Distributed Computing Sys., 2004; contbr. articles to profl. jours., chapters to books. Recipient Rsch. award, U. Miss., 2003—04, NASA, 2004—05. Mem.: IEEE. Achievements include being an expert in wireless and mobile communications; patents in field. Office: Univ Miss 302 Anderson Hall University MS 38677 Office Phone: 662-915-5381. Business E-Mail: mustafa@olemiss.edu

**MATALIN, MARY,** political consultant; b. Chgo., Aug. 19, 1953; d. Steven and Eileen Matalin; m. Artie Arnold (div.); m. James Carville, Nov. 25, 1993; 2 children. BA in Political Sci., Western Ill. Univ.; student, Hofstra Law Sch. With RNC, since the early 80's; voter contact dir. Reagan-Bush re-election campaign, 1984; chief staff to co-chmn. RNC, 1985; Midwest regional political dir. primary elections Bush-Quayle election campaign, 1988, dir. nat. victory '88 gen. election, 1988; polit. dir. George Bush's 1992 re-election campaign; co-host CNBC talk show, Equal Time, 1993—96; host radio show, CBS Talk Radio Network The Mary Matalin Show, 1996—98; co-host Crossfire, 1999—2001; asst. to the Pres. and Counselor to the V.P., 2001—02. Author (with James Carville): All's Fair: Love, War and Running for President, 1992; author: Letters to My Daughters, 2004; appearance: (TV political series) K-Street. Office: The Office of Mary Matalin 424 S Wash St Lower Level Alexandria VA 22314 Office Phone: 703-739-6006. E-mail: mary@matalin.info.

**MATANKY, JAMES E.,** real estate developer; b. Chgo., Sept. 23, 1960; s. Eugene and Gertrude M. BS, U. Ill., 1982, JD, 1985; LLM, Cambridge U., 1991. Bar: Ill. Lawyer Epton, Mullin & Druth, Chgo., 1985-86, Much, Shelist, Freed et al, Chgo., 1986-90, Curschman, Schubel & Weiss, Hamburg, Germany, 1990; pres. Matanky Realty Group, Inc., Chgo., 1991—. Bd. dirs. Chgo. Assn. Neighborhood Devel. Corp., West Humboldt Park Devel. Coun.; bd. dirs. Mus. Contemporary Art-Chgo. Renaissance Soc. U. Chgo., chair individual giving circle; pres. Am. Friends of Hebrew U. of Jerusalem; v.p. JCCs Chgo.; mentor retail devel. City of Chgo. Recipient Chgo. Neighborhood Devel. award, 2000, 06; Wexner fellow, 2006 Avocations: rowing, piano, architecture. Office: 200 N LaSalle St Ste 2350 Chicago IL 60601-1014 Office Phone: 312-337-1001. Office Fax: 312-337-5996.

**MATARASSO, ALAN,** plastic and reconstructive surgeon; b. NYC, Oct. 19, 1953; s. Daniel and Ethel M. BA magna cum laude, Boston U., 1975; MD, U. Miami, Miami, Fla., 1979. Diplomate Nat. Bd. Med. Examiners, 1980, Am. Bd. Plastic Surgery, 1986. Intern in dept. gen. surgery Albert Einstein Coll. Med., Montefiore Med. Ctr., Bronx, NY, 1979-80, resident in dept. gen. surgery, 1980—83, chief resident dept. gen. surgery, 1982—83, resident and chief resident dept. of plastic surgery, 1983—85; fellow aesthetic surgery Manhattan Eye, Ear and Throat Hosp., Lenox Hill Hosp., 1985, asst. attending surgeon, 1985—. Surgeon St. Luke's/Roosevelt Hosp. Ctr., 1986—; attending surgeon NY Eye and Ear Infirmary, 1986—; asst. attending surgeon, Lenox Hill Hosp., 2000—; now assoc. clin. prof. plastic surgery Albert Einstein Coll. Medicine, 1996—; expert cons., State NY, Dept. Health, Office of Profl. Med. Conduct. Contbr. chpt. Encyclopedia of Flpas, Mastery in Plastic Surgery; instrnl. course vol. Plastic Surgery Ednl. Found.; editor Clinics in Plastic Surgery.; sr. sci. editor Aesthetic Surgery Jour.; numerous profl. presentations; contbr. 100 articles to profl. jours. Bd. dirs. Sephardic Home For The Aged, Bklyn.; NE reg. coord., Ultrasonic Assisted Lipoplasty Reg. Workshops, 1996-98. Recipient Physicians Recognition award AMA, 1994, 2004; named one of Best Drs. in Am. Am. Health Mag., 1996, Best Doctors in N.Y., N.Y. Mag., 1996, 98-2005, Castle-Connolly Guide to the Best Drs., NY Metro Area. Fellow ACS, NY Acad. Medicine, Internat. Coll. Surgeons (USA) in Plastic Surgery; mem. Am. Assn. Plastic Surgeons (chair videotape com., 1996-99, symposium com., 1997-99, mem. teaching course subcom., 1996-, vice chair, 1998-99, program com., 1996-, Strategic Planning com., 1999-, travelling prof., 1999-2001, edu. commn.- 1999-2000, time and place com., 2000-, chair. corp. sponsorship com., 2000-, rep. to products/svcs. workshop, 2000, parliamentarian, 2001-2002); mem. Am. Soc. Aesthetic Plastic Surgery (bd. dirs.), Fla. Soc. Plastic and Reconstructive Surgeons, Internat. Soc. Aesthetic Plastic Surgeons (pub. edu. com., 2000), Lipoplasty Endowment for Plastic Surgery, Assn. for Academic Surgeons, Northeastern Soc. Plastic Surgeons (chmn., aesthetic symposium, 1998-99, bd. dirs.), NY Reg. Soc. of Plastic and Reconstructive Surgery (pres.), Soc. for Acad. Surgeons, Royal Soc. Medicine, England Oversee Fellow, Am. Cleft Palate Assn., Pan Am.

Med. Soc. (mem., sect. on Plastic and Reconstructive Surgery), Pan Pacific Surgical Assn., NY County Med. Soc. (Young Physician's Com., 1992-94, peer review com. I & II, 1993-, grievance com., 1993-, media com., 1993-), Med. Soc. State NY (social discipline com., 1994-, state legis. com., 1994-96), NY Reg. Soc. Plastic Surgeons, (exec. com. 1988-, sci. com. med. program chair, 1988-), NY State Soc. Surgeons, Rhinoplasty Soc. (bd. dirs.), Soc. of Laparoendoscopic Surgeons, So. Med. Assn., AMA, Am. Soc. Plastic Surgeons (Young Plastic Surgeons, 1987-89, Plastic Surgery Product Assessment Commn., 1991-92, CPT/ICD 9 Coding Workshop, 1991-96, Ad Hoc Com. 1992, mktg. com. 2000), Plastic Surgery Edu. com. (Computerized Exam, 1989, EF Teleplast, 1992-95, vis. scholar, 1993-94, Edu. Assessment, 1992, Internat. Symposia, 1993, chair, Resource Book Subcom. of Resident Information Com., 1995-98, rep. on Domsestic Clin. Symposia, 1997-, In-service Examination Com., Aesthetic and Breast Subcom., 2000, Device and Technique Assessment Com., 2000, Domestic Clin. Symposia Com., 2000), Aesthetic Surgery Edu. and Rsch. Found. (charter mem.), Skin Cancer Found. (med. adv. com., 1986-), Cancers and Careers.org (adv. bd. 2000). Office: 1009 Park Ave New York NY 10028-0936 Office Phone: 212-249-7500. Office Fax: 212-628-5000. Personal E-mail: matarasso@aol.com.

**MATARASSO, SETH L.,** dermatologic surgeon; b. Oct. 12, 1957; MD, U. Buffalo, 1984. Intern Beth Israel Med. Ctr., N.Y.C., 1984-85; resident Baylor Coll. Medicine, Houston, 1985-88; fellowship U. Calif. Sch. Medicine, San Francisco, 1989-90; clin. prof. dermatology Sch. Medicine U. Calif., San Francisco, 1990—. Lectr. in field. Contbr. articles to profl. jours. Fax: 415-362-7745.

**MATARAZZO, HARRIS STARR,** lawyer; b. Portland, Oreg. July 24, 1957; s. Joseph Dominic and Ruth Wood (Gadbois) M.; m. Judith Grace Hudson, Jan. 2, 1988. AB in Polit. Sci., Brown U., 1979; JD, Northwestern Sch. Law, Portland, 1983. Bar: Oreg. 1986, U.S. Dist. Ct. Oreg. 1986, U.S. Ct. Appeals (9th cir.) 1986, U.S. Supreme Ct. 1992. With Aitchison, Imperati, Paull, Barnett and Sherwood, Portland, 1986; assoc. Parks & Bauer, Salem, 1987-88; pvt. practice Portland, 1988—. Sprk. Mental Health and the Law conf. Med. Ednl. Svcs., Inc., 1995, 96. Contbr. to Criminal Law Handbook, 1994, 98, 2005. Mem. Hist. Preservation League Oreg., Portland, 1984—, Oreg. State Pub. Interest Rsch. Group, Portland, 1985—, The Old Ch. Soc., Portland, 1985—. bd. dirs. Bosco Milligan Found., Rape Survivors Inc., 1994, Lincoln H.S. Alumni Assn., 1995—, Morrison Ctr., 1996-2001, Network/Cascadia Housing, Inc., Oreg. Advocacy Ctr., 1998, 2000—, Italian Businessmen's Club, InAct, Inc., Rosemont Treatment Ctr. and Sch., 1998-99, Friends of Simon Benson House, 1998-2002, Parents Anonymous, 2001-02; mem. vestry Trinity Episcopal Ch., 1992-95, 2001-04; mem. Oreg. Advocacy Ctr. Mental Health Adv. Coun., 1996-2000; mem. planned giving com. Multnomah County Libr., 1997—2004. Mem. ABA, Fed. Bar Assn., Oreg. State Bar Assn., Oreg. Criminal Def. Lawyers Assn. (spkr. State of Mind. conf. 1990, Property Crimes conf. 1994), Multnomah County Bar Assn., Washington Bar Assn. Office: Bank Am Fin Ctr 121 SW Morrison St Ste 1020 Portland OR 97204-3140

**MATARAZZO, JOSEPH DOMINIC,** psychologist, educator; b. Caiazzo, Italy, Nov. 12, 1925; (parents Am. citizens); s. Nicholas and Adeline (Mastroianni) M.; m. Ruth Wood Gadbois, Mar. 26, 1949; children: Harris, Elizabeth, Sara. Student, Columbia U., 1944; BA, Brown U., 1946; MS, Northwestern U., 1950, PhD, 1952. Fellow in med. psychology Washington U. Sch. Medicine, 1950-51; instr. Washington U., 1951-53, asst. prof., 1953-55; rsch. assoc. Harvard Med. Sch., assoc. psychologist Mass. Gen. Hosp., 1955-57; prof., head med. psychol. dept. Oreg. Health Scis. U., Portland, 1957-96, prof. behavioral neurosci., 1996—. Mem. behavioral medicine study sect. NIH; nat. mental health adv. coun. NIMH; bd. regents Uniformed Svcs. U. Health Scis., 1974-80. Author: Wechsler's Measurement and Appraisal of Adult Intelligence, 5th edit., 1972, (with A.N. Wiens) The Interview: Research on its Anatomy and Structure, 1972, (with Harper and Wiens) Nonverbal Communication, 1978; editor: Behavioral Health: A Handbook of Health Enhancement and Disease Prevention, 1984; mem. editl. bd.: Jour. Clin. Psychology, 1962-96; cons. editor: Contemporary Psychology, 1962-70, 80-93, Intelligence: An Interdisciplinary Jour, 1976-90, Jour. Behavioral Medicine, 1977—; Profl. Psychology, 1978-94, Jour. Cons. and Clin. Psychology, 1978-85; editor: Psychology series Aldine Pub. Co, 1964-74; editor Williams & Wilkins Co, 1974-77; contbr. articles to profl. jours. With USNR, 1943-47; capt. Res. Recipient Hofheimer prize Am. Psychiat. Assn., 1962 Fellow AAAS, APA (pres. 1989-90), Am. Psychol. Assn. (divsn. health psychology 1978-89, mem. coun. reps. 1982-91, bd. dirs. 1986-90, Ann. Disting. Profl. Contbn. award 1991, Annual Gold Medal for Life Achievement in the Application of Psychology 2001); mem. Western Psychol. Assn. (pres. 1986-97), Am. Assn. State Psychology Bds. (pres. 1963-64), Nat. Assn. Mental Health (bd. dirs.), Oreg. Mental Health Assn. (bd. dirs., pres. 1962-63), Internat. Coun. Psychologists (bd. dirs. 1972-74, pres. 1976-77), Am. Psychol. Found. (pres. 1994-2000). Home: 1934 SW Vista Ave Portland OR 97201-2455 Office: Oreg Health Scis U Sch Medicine 3181 SW Sam Jackson Park Rd Portland OR 97239 Office Phone: 503-494-8644. Office Fax: 503-494-5972. Business E-Mail: matarazz@ohsu.edu.

**MATARAZZO, RUTH GADBOIS,** psychologist, educator; b. New London, Conn., Nov. 9, 1926; d. John Stuart and Elizabeth (Wood) Gadbois; m. Joseph D. Matarazzo, Mar. 26, 1949; children: Harris, Elizabeth, Sara. AB Brown U., 1948; MA, Washington U., St. Louis, 1950, PhD, 1955. Diplomate in psychology and clin. neuropsychology Am. Bd. Examiners Profl. Psychology. Rsch. fellow pediat. Washington U. Med. Sch., 1954-55; rsch. fellow psychology Harvard U. Med. Sch., 1955-57; asst. prof. med. psychology Oreg. Health Scis. U., Portland, 1957-63, assoc. prof., 1963-68, prof., 1968—, prof. emeritus, 1997—. Woman liaison officer Assn. Am. Med. Coll.s, 1979—90; cons. Tillamook Job Corps, Oreg. Bd. Med. Examiners, Social Security Adminstrn., Portland Ctr. Hearing and Speech. Author (E. Greif): (book) Behavioral Approaches to Rehabilitation: Coping with Change, 1982; contbr. chapters to books, articles to profl. jours., book reviews to jours. Bd. dirs. Portland Opera Assn., Morrison Child Guidance Clinic, Portland Chamber Orch., Neskowin Valley Sch., Hoover-Minthorn Mus. Fellow: APA (policy and planning bd., edn. and tng. bd., vice-chair accreditation bd., chair accreditation task force, accreditation bd., site visitor APA accreditation of grad. programs, coun. of reps.), Oreg. Psychol. Assn. (past pres.); mem.: AAAS, Portland Psychol. Assn. (past pres.), We. Psychol. Assn. (bd. dirs.), Sigma Xi. Home: 1934 SW Vista Ave Portland OR 97201-2455 Office Phone: 503-494-0279. Business E-Mail: matarazr@ohsu.edu.

**MATARIC, MAJA J.,** engineering educator; BS with honors in Computer Sci., U. Kans., 1987; SM in Computer Sci., MIT, Cambridge, 1990, PhD in Computer Sci. and Artificial Intelligence, 1994. Mem. tech. staff NASA Jet Propulsion Lab., Pasadena, Calif., 1988; cons. Advanced Rsch. and Devel. Grp. LEGO Futura, Cambridge, Mass., 1989—90; rsch. scientist Free U. Brussels, 1990, GTE Labs., Waltham, Mass., 1991; postdoctoral fellow MIT Artificial Intelligence Lab., 1994; asst. prof. computer sci. dept. and Volen Nat. Ctr. Complex Systems Brandeis U., Waltham, Mass., 1995—97; asst. prof. computer sci. dept. and neuroscience prog. U. So. Calif., LA, 1997—2001, assoc. prof., 2001—06, prof., 2006—. Vis. prof. Fed. Poly. Sch. Lausanne, Switzerland, 1994, Swedish Inst. Computer Sci., Stockholm, 1994; founding dir. Interaction Lab., 1995—; vis. rschr. ATR Human Info. Processing Rsch. Lab., Kyoto, 1996; dir. Robotics Rsch. Lab. U. So. Calif., LA, 1998—, assoc. dir. Inst. Robotics and Intelligent Systems, 1998—, founding dir. Ctr. Robotics and Embedded Systems, 2002—, sr. assoc. dean rsch. Viterbi Sch. Engring., 2006—; mem. sci. adv. bd. Evolution Robotics, Pasadena, Calif., 2002—; mem. academic adv. bd. Ctr. Neuromorphic Sys. Engring. Calif. Inst. Tech., 2002—05. Contbr. articles to profl. jours., chapters to books; assoc. editor: Adaptive Behavior Jour., 1995—, IEEE Transactions on Robotics and Automation, 2001—03, Internat. Jour. Humanoid Robotics, 2003—, mem. editl. bd.: Jour. Artificial Intelligence Rsch., 1999—2001, Internat. Jour. Autonomous Agents and Multi-Agent Systems, 2000—, mem. editl. adv. bd.: Internat. Jour. Advanced Robotic Systems, 2004—. Recipient Career award, NSF, 1996-2001, Paper award, Assn. Computing Machinery, 1999, TR100 Innovation award, MIT Tech. Rev., 1999, Early Career award,

IEEE Robotics and Automation Soc., 2000, Best Paper award, Hawaii Internat. Conf. Sys. Scis., 2003, Okawa Found. award, 2004. Mem.: IEEE Robotics and Automation Soc., Sigma Xi, Internat. Soc. Adaptive Behavior, Am. Assn. Artificial Intelligence (exec. com.), IEEE (sr.), Phi Kappa Phi. Office: Computer Sci Dept U So Calif 941 W 37th Pl MC 0781 Los Angeles CA 90089-0781 E-mail: mataric@usc.edu.*

**MATASAR, ANN B.,** retired dean, finance educator; b. NYC, June 27, 1940; d. Harry and Tillie (Simon) Bergman; m. Robert Matasar, June 9, 1962; children— Seth Gideon, Toby Rachel AB, Vassar Coll., 1962; MA, Columbia U., 1964, PhD, 1968; M of Mgmt. in Fin., Northwestern U., 1977. Assoc. prof. Mundelein Coll., Chgo., 1965-78; prof., dir. Ctr. for Bus. and Econ. Elmhurst Coll., Elmhurst, Ill., 1978-84; dean Roosevelt U., Chgo., 1984-92; prof. Internat. Bus. and Fin. Walter E. Heller Coll. Bus. Adminstrn. Roosevelt U., 1992—2005, prof. bus. emerita, 2005—. Dir. Corp. Responsibility Group, Chgo., 1978-84; chmn. long range planning Ill. Bar Assn., 1982-83; mem. edn. com. Ill. Commn. on the Status of Women, 1978-81 Author: Corporate PACS and Federal Campaign Financing Laws: Use or Abuse of Power?, 1986; (with others) Research Guide to Women's Studies, 1974, (with others) The Impact of Geographic Deregulation on the American Banking Industry, 2002, Women of Wine: The Rise of Women in the Global Wine Industry, 2006; contbr. articles to profl. jours. Dem. candidate 1st legis. dist. Ill. State Senate, no. suburbs Chgo., 1972; mem. Dem. exec. com. New Trier Twp., Ill., 1972-76; rsch. dir., acad. advisor Congressman Abner Mikva, Ill., 1974-76; bd. dirs. Ctr. Ethics and Policy, 1985-90. Named Roosevelt U. Chgo. Woman of Achievement, Mayor of Chgo., 1978. Fellow AAUW (trustee ednl. found. 1992-97, v.p. fin. 1993-97); mem. Am. Polit. Sci. Assn., Midwest Bus. Adminstrn. Assn., Acad. Mgmt., Women's Caucus for Polit. Sci. (pres. 1980-81), John Howard Assn. (bd. dirs. 1986-90), Am. Assembly of Coll. Schs. of Bus. (bd. dirs. 1989-92, chair com. on diversity in mgmt. edn. 1991-92), North Ctrl. Assn. (commr. 1994-97), Beta Gamma Sigma. Democrat. Jewish. Avocations: walking, biking, opera, crosswords. E-mail: amatasar@roosevelt.edu.

**MATASEJE, VERONICA JULIA,** sales executive; b. St. Ann's, Ontario, Can., Apr. 5, 1949; came to U.S., 1985; d. John and Anna Veronica M. Grad. H.S., Smithville, Can. Clk. typist, typesetter Crown Life Ins. Co., Toronto, 1966-70; typesetter Toronto Life/Calendar Mag., 1970-71; typesetter, exec. sec. Cerebrus Prodns. Ltd., Toronto, 1971-74; pres. Veron Prodns. Ltd., Toronto, 1975-81, Acclaim Records Inc., Toronto, 1981-88; pvt. health care provider Las Vegas, 1989-94; retail sales mgr. Top Cats, Las Vegas, 1994-00; pres. Abracadabra Music Corp., 2000—. Campaign vol. Dist. Atty., Las Vegas, 1994; vol. pilot Angel Planes, Las Vegas, 1989. Avocations: gardening, interior decorating, travel, music. Home: 4326 Caliente St Las Vegas NV 89119-5801 Office: Top Cats PO Box 61173 Las Vegas NV 89160-1173 E-mail: vm@abracadabramusic.com.

**MATAYOSHI, CORALIE CHUN,** lawyer, bar association executive; b. Honolulu, June 2, 1956; d. Peter J. and Daisy (Look) Chun; m. Ronald F. Matayoshi, Aug. 8, 1981; children: Scot, Kelly, Alana. BA, U. Calif., Berkeley, 1978; JD, U. Calif., San Francisco, 1981. Bar: Hawaii 1981, U.S. Dist. Ct. Hawaii 1981. Trial atty. U.S. Dept. Justice Antitrust, Washington, 1981-84; assoc. Chun, Kerr, & Dodd, Honolulu, 1984-86; exec. dir. Hawaii Inst. of CLE, Honolulu, 1987-90, Hawaii State Bar Assn., Honolulu, 1990—. Arbitrator Ct. Annexed Arbitration Program, Honolulu, 1992—; adv. bd. Channel 2 TV Action Line, Honolulu, 1993-96. Contbr. chapters to books. Bd. dirs. Neighborhood Justice Ctr., 1994-97, mediator, 1997—.

**MATCHAR, DAVID B.,** physician, researcher; b. Balt., Sept. 29, 1955; s. Joseph Charles and Evelyn M.; m. Barbara Fran Goldfinger, May 4, 1980; children: Emily Ruth, Benjamin Jacob, Daniel William. MD, U. Md., 1980. Diplomate Am. Bd. Internal Medicine. Prof. medicine Duke U. Med. Ctr., Durham, NC, 1985—; dir. Duke Ctr. Clin. Health Policy Rsch., 1985—. Fellow ACP, Soc. Gen. Internal Medicine (pres. so. sect. 1988), Am. Heart Assn., Soc. for Med. Decision Making (editl. bd., chair 1993 ann. meeting, trustee), Am. Acad. Neurology. Office: Duke Ctr Clin Health Policy Rsch 2200 W Main St Ste 220 Tower Durham NC 27705 Office Phone: 919-286-3399. Business E-Mail: match001@mc.duke.edu.

**MATCHETT, WILLIAM H(ENRY),** English literature educator; b. Chgo., Mar. 5, 1923; s. James Chapman and Lucy H. (Jipson) M.; m. Judith Wright, June 11, 1949; children: David H., Katherine C., Stephen C. BA with highest honors, Swarthmore Coll., 1949; MA, Harvard U., 1950, PhD, 1957. Teaching fellow Harvard U., Cambridge, Mass., 1953-54; instr. English lit. U. Wash., Seattle, 1954-56, asst. prof., 1956-61, assoc. prof., 1961-66, prof., 1966-82, prof. emeritus, 1982—. Author: Water Ouzel, 1955, The Phoenix and the Turtle, 1965, Fireweed, 1980, Shakespeare and Forgiveness, 2002, Elementary, 2004; numerous poems and articles; co-author: Poetry: From Statement to Meaning, 1965; editor: Modern Lang. Quar., Seattle, 1964-82. Mem. Soc. Friends. Home: 1017 Minor Ave Apt 702 Seattle WA 98104-1303

**MATECKI, PAUL L.,** lawyer; b. 1955; BA, Grinnell Coll., 1978; JD, St. Louis U., 1981. Bar: Mo. 1981, Fla. 1987. Corp. counsel Raymond James Fin., Inc., St. Petersburg, Fla., 1989—97, sr. v.p., 1989—, gen. counsel, dir. compliance, 2004—. Mem.: ABA, Assn. Corp. Counsel West Fla. Chpt. Office: Raymond James Fin Inc 880 Carillon Pky Saint Petersburg FL 33716 Office Phone: 727-567-1000. Office Fax: 727-567-8053.

**MATECZUN, JOHN MATTHEW,** career military officer; b. Albuquerque, Aug. 29, 1946; s. Alfred Jospeh and Margaret Ellen Mateczun; m. Elizabeth Kathleen Holmes; children: Erin Johnson, Adam Johnson, Laura. MD, U. N.Mex., 1978; MPH, U. Calif., Berkeley, 1982; JD, Georgetown U., 1988. Diplomate Am. Bd. Psychiatry and Neurology, Am. Bd. Forensic Psychiatry, cert. physician exec. 1999. Asst. divsn. surgeon, divsn. psychiatrist 3rd Marine Divsn., Okinawa, Japan, 1982—83; med. staff Nat. Naval Med. Ctr., Bethesda, Md., 1983—85, intern advisor, dir. transitional internship, 1985—87, chmn. dept. psychiatry, 1989—90, dir. med. svcs., 1990—91; force surgeon U.S. Marine Corps Forces Pacific, Camp Smith, Hawaii, 1991—94; chmn. dept. psychiatry Naval Regional Med. Ctr., Portsmouth, Va., 1987—89; dir. TRICARE Region 1, Washington, 1994—95; prin. dir. clin. svcs. Office of the Asst. Sec. of Def. (Health Affairs), Washington, 1995—97; chief med. officer Tricare Mgmt. Activity, Washington, 1997—99; comdf. officer Naval Hosp., Charleston, SC, 1998—2000; asst. chief ops. US Navy Bur. of Medicine and Surgery, Washington, 2000—01, chief staff, 2003, dep. surgeon gen., vice chair, 2005—; med. advisor to Chmn. Joint Chiefs of Staff, Washington, 2001—03; comdr. Naval Med. Ctr., San Diego, 2003—05; dep. surgeon gen. USN, 2005—; vice chief Bur. Medicine and Surgery, 2005—. Assoc. prof. clin. psychiatry Uniformed Svcs. U. Health Sciences. Contbr. chapters to books. Rear adm. M.C. USN, 1978—2004. Decorated Navy Disting. Svc. medal, Def. Superior Svc. Medal with Oak Leaf Cluster, Legion Merit with two gold stars, Bronze Star, Def. Meritorious Svc. medal, Meritorious Svc. medal with gold star, Navy/Marine Corps Commendation medal, Army Commendation medal, Navy/Marine Corps Achievement medal. Fellow: APA (disting.); mem.: Am. Coll. Physician Execs., Am. Acad. Psychiatry and the Law, Assn. Mil. Surgeons of the U.S. (life). Office: Bureau Medicine and Surgery 2300 E St NW Washington DC 20372

**MATEJKA, ROBERT,** chemicals executive; BBA in Acctg., Cleve. State U. V.p. fin. Rockwell Automation Co.; v.p. RPM Internat., Medina, Calif. 2000—, controller, 2000—, CFO, 2000—. Office: RPM International 2628 Pearl Rd Medina OH 44258

**MATELES, RICHARD ISAAC,** biotechnologist; b. NYC, Sept. 11, 1935; s. Simon and Jean (Phillips) M.; m. Roslyn C. Fish, Sept. 2, 1956; children: Naomi, Susan, Sarah. BS, MIT, 1956, MS, 1957, DSc, 1959. USPHS fellow Laboratorium voor Microbiologie, Technische Hogeschool, Delft, The Netherlands, 1959-60; mem. faculty MIT, 1960-70, assoc. prof. biochem. engring., 1965-68; dir. fermentation unit Jerusalem, 1968-77; prof. applied microbiology Hebrew U., Hadassah Med. Sch., Jerusalem, 1968-80; vis. prof. dept.

chem. engring. U. Pa., Phila., 1978-79; asst. dir. rsch. Stauffer Chem. Co., Westport, Conn., 1980, dir. rsch., 1980-81, v.p. rsch., 1981-88; sr. v.p. applied scis. IIT Rsch. Inst., Chgo., 1988-90; proprietor Candida Corp., Chgo., 1990—. Editor: Jour. Chem. Tech. and Biotech., 1972—; editor: (N.Am. edit.) Biotech., 2001—; editor: Penicillin: A Paradigm for Biotechnology, 1998, Directory of Toll Fermentation and Cell Culture Facilities, 2005; contbr. articles to profl. jours. Mem. Conn. Acad. Sci. Engring., 1981—; mem. vis. com., dept. applied biol. sci. MIT, 1980-88; mem. exec. com. Coun. on Chem. Rsch., 1981-85. Fellow Am. Inst. Med. and Biol. Engring.; mem. AICE, AAAS, SAR, Am. Chem. Soc., Am. Soc. Microbiology, Soc. for Gen. Microbiology U.K., Inst. Food Technologists, Soc. Chem. Ind. (U.K.) Union League, Sigma Xi. Home: 222 E Chestnut St Apt 10B Chicago IL 60611 Office: Candida Corp Ste 1310 220 S State St Chicago IL 60604 Office Phone: 312-431-1601. Business E-Mail: rmateles@candida.com.

**MATELIC, CANDACE TANGORRA,** museum director, educator; b. Detroit, Aug. 21, 1952; d. Paul Eugene and Madeline Marie (Tangora) M.; m. Steven Joseph Mrozek, Sept. 17, 1983 (div. Sept. 1987); 1 child, Madeline Rose. BA, U. Mich., 1974; MA, SUNY, Oneonta, 1977; postgrad. doctoral studies, SUNY, Albany. Interpretive specialist Living History Farms, Des Moines, 1978-80; mgr. adult edn. Henry Ford Mus./Greenfield Village, Dearborn, Mich., 1981-82, mgr. interpretive tng., 1982-84; dir., prof. mus. studies Cooperstown grad. program SUNY, Oneonta, 1985-94; exec. dir. Mission Houses Mus., Honolulu, 1994-96, Historic St. Mary's City, Md., 1997-98; pres./CEO CTM Profl. Svcs., Inc., 1999—, working leader, 2004—; founder, prin. The Cherry Valley Group, 2002—04. Cons. history mus., 1979—; lectr. tchr. nat. and regional confs., workshops, seminars, 1979—; frequent keynote spkr.; grant reviewer NEH and Inst. for Mus. Svc., Washington, 1982—, PEW Charitable Trusts, 2003; mem. guest faculty U. Victoria, B.C., 1993, 2000, 02, 03, B.C., 04, Naper Settlement, 2006, author distance learning course, 2002—; faculty Distance Cruise, 2004, 05. Author: (with others) Exhibition Reader, 1992, Strategic Interpretation and Program Plan for the Mill and Anselma, 2005; co-author: A Pictorial History of Food in Iowa, 1980, Survey of 1200-Plus Museum Studies Graduates, 1988; contbr. articles and videos on mus. interpretation, tng., orgnl. change and mentoring in mus., 1979—; author contr. procs. Trustee Motown Hist. Mus. 1985—2004; bd. dirs. Hawaii Youth Opera Chorus, 1996; project mgr. program plan for the Richard and Sarah Allen Ctr. for Faith, Freedom and Cmty. Mother Bethel Found., 2004-05. Mem. Am. Assn. State and Local History (sec., bd. dirs. 1988-93, program chmn. ann meeting 1988, mem. edn. com. 1996-99, co-chair task force on edn. and tng. 1994-96, faculty nat. workshop series 2001-04, Historic House Initiative), designed profl. tng. workshop series, 1999-00, Am. Living Hist. Farms and Agrl. Mus. (bd. dirs. 1980-88, pres. 1985, John T. Schlebecker award Lifetime Disting. Svc. 1996), Midwest Open Air Mus. Coordinating Coun. (founder, bd. dirs., pres. 1978-80, Candace Tangorra Matelic essay award competition established by MOMCC 2002), Am. Assn. Museums (mus. studies com. 1986-94), Internat. Coun. Museums, Nat. Trust for Hist. Preservation, Hawaii Museums Assn. (bd. dirs. 1994-96), So. Md. Mus. Assn. (bd. dirs. 1997-98). Democrat. Roman Catholic. Home and Office: 338 Navigators Dr Pawleys Island SC 29585-7068 Office Phone: 843-237-5078. Personal E-Mail: ctmatelic@sc.rr.com.

**MATEMA, ZSUN-NEE KIMBALL (ANNETTE K. MILLER),** social sciences educator; b. Washington, Jan. 11, 1944; d. Emmett Robinson Miller and Annette Kimball Brooks; m. John Fitzgerald Payne, Aug. 31, 1963 (div.); children: Kellie Jon, Jaanai Kimball, Myya Machel, Robin Annette. BA, U. D.C., 1982; MMsc, U. Metaphysics. Cert. in clin. hypnosis Am. Hypnosis Tng. Acad.; lic. practitioner of religious sci. Ch. of Religious Sci.; ordained metaphysical min.; cert. in cmty. mediation Fed. Mediation Svcs.; cert. tchr. social studies. Artistic dir. Annette's Theatre of Dance, Inc., Washington, 1968-78; prodr., writer Nat. Broadcast Corp., Washington, 1971-74; ednl. counseling cons. Something Better/A.K. Millers & Assocs., Silver Spring, Md., 1979-86; dir. cmty. edn. Am. Digestive Disease Soc., Bethesda, Md., 1986-88; cmty. outreach/arena stage multicult. audience devel. assoc. Washington, 1989-92; founding dir. Intercultural Edn. Exch., Washington, 1991—; prof. behavioral scis. Washington Saturday Coll., 1997—; founder, pres. Brannum Robinson Hist. Soc., Inc., 2001—; tchr. social studies Prince Georges Pub. Schs. Native Am. storyteller The Painted Gourd: Red & Black Voices, Washington, 1991—; hist. interpreter Mt. Vernon; colonial and Civil War reenactor DC Ladies Contraband Relief Soc., Washington, 1991—; cmty. policing trainer Met. Police Dept., Washington, 1993-97; nat. dir. All Nations Drum, Washington, 1996; pub. rels. coord. The Walk to Can., Silver Spring, Md., 1996; underground railroad historian Nat. Pk. Svc., Washington, 1996—; cmty. mediator Montgomery County Md., 1996—; nat. adv. bd. Trail of Dreams Walk from North to South, Washington, 1999; founder, prodr., writer (cable) Prejudice Picks on Children, 1988, Scripts, 1989, (radio drama) Underground Railroad Traveling Radio Show, 1998; playwright Tales from Tin Cup Alley, 1991; host, prodr. (radio) The Talking Feather, 2000—, Vital Signs, 2003—; author Elizabeth Keckley's Book of Good Measure; playwright Madame Elizabeth, 2001, Serpent Round My Tree, 2003; actor A Civil War Christmas, Discovery Channel, 2006; writer, rschr. Maryland National Road Project, 2001-06. Pub. programs chair Afro-Asian Rels. Coun., Washington, 1989-96; past vice chair Com. for Ethnic Affairs, Silver Spring, 1990-96; AFRIASIA founding dir. Cultural Alliance Greater Washington, 1991-94; cmty. mediator Human Rights Commn., Rockville, Md., 1994—; adv. bd. mem. NAACP, Silver Spring, 1996-98, com. mem. multicultural group, 1996-98; Native Am. adv. rep. Montgomery County Sch. Bd., 1996-97; tng. devel. com. mem. Nat. Area Crisis Response Team, Washington, 1997-99; founder Red Women for Good Medicine, 2006. Grantee Nat. Endowment for the Arts, Washington, 1974-76, Hawaii Arts in the Sch., Inc., Owau, Hawaii, 1994. Mem. Zeta Phi Beta. Avocations: colonial reenactment, creative wall art, travel. Office Phone: 301-257-0003. Personal E-Mail: zsunrise3@yahoo.com.

**MATERA, FRANCES LORINE,** elementary school educator; b. Eustis, Nebr., June 28, 1926; d. Frank Daniel and Marie Mathilda (Hess) Daiss; m. Daniel Matera, Dec. 27, 1973. Luth. tchrs. diploma, Concordia U., Seward, Nebr., 1947, BS in Edn., 1956; MEd, U. Oreg., Eugene, 1963. Elem. tchr. Our Savior's Luth. Ch., Colorado Springs, Colo., 1954—57; tchr. 5th grade Monterey (Calif.) Pub. Schs., 1957—59; tchr. 1st grade Roseburg (Oreg.) Schs., 1959—60; tchr. several schs. Palm Springs (Calif.) Unified Sch. Dist., 1960—93; tchr. 3rd grade Vista del Monte Sch., Palm Springs, Calif., 1973—93; ret., 1993. Named Tchr. of the Yr., Palm Springs Unified Schs. Mem. Kappa Kappa Iota (chpt. and state pres.). Personal E-mail: Franmatera7@aol.com.

**MATERIA, KATHLEEN PATRICIA AYLING,** nurse; b. Jersey City, Nov. 7, 1954; d. Donald Anthony and Muriel Cecilia (Joyce) Ayling; m. Francis Peter Materia, June 5, 1983; children: Christopher Michael, Donna Nicole. BSN, Fairleigh Dickinson U., 1976. RN, N.J. Critical care nurse Palisades Gen. Hosp., North Bergen, N.J., 1976-87; grad. nurse, 1976-77; nurse critical care unit North Hudson Hosp., Weehawken, NJ, 1977-78. Mem. Alpha Sigma Tau. Democrat. Avocations: bowling, dance.

**MATERNA, JOSEPH ANTHONY,** lawyer; b. Passaic, N.J., June 13, 1947; s. Anthony E. and Peggy Ann Materna; m. Dolores Corio, Dec. 14, 1975; children: Jodi, Jennifer, Janine. BA, Columbia U., 1969, JD, 1973. Bar: N.Y. 1975, Fla. 1977, U.S. Dist. Ct. (ea. and so. dists.) N.Y. 1977, U.S. Supreme Ct. 1977, U.S. Tax Ct. 1978, U.S. Ct. of Claims 1978. Trusts and estates atty. Chadbourne Parke Whiteside & Wolff, N.Y.C., 1973-76, Dreyer & Traub, N.Y.C., 1976-80, Finley Kumble Wagner Heine Underberg & Casey, N.Y.C., 1980-85; ptnr., head trusts and estates dept. Newman Tannenbaum Helpern Syracuse & Hirschtritt, N.Y.C., 1985-90; Shapiro Beilly Rosenberg Aronowitz Levy & Fox LLP, N.Y.C., 1990—2004, Solomon, Pearl, Blum, Heymann & Stich, LLP, N.Y.C., 2004—. Lectr. in field; expert witness in trusts and estate field ct. litigations, N.Y.C., 1999—. Contbr. articles to profl. jours. Chmn. planned giving com.; mem. bd. govs. Arthritis Found. N.Y. Chpt., N.Y.C.,

1980—; mem. bd. trustees, corp. treas. Cath. Interracial Coun., N.Y.C., 1992—; mem. bequests and planned gifts com. Cath. Archdiocese of N.Y., N.Y.C., 1988—; corp. sec. Arthritis Found. N.Y. chpt., N.Y.C., 1997—, mem. budget and fin. com., 2001—; mem. Meml. Sloan-Kettering Nat. Trusts and Estates Assocs. Recipient Planned Giving award Arthritis Found.-N.Y. Chpt., N.Y.C., 1994, Discovery Alliance award Arthritis Found.-N.Y. Chpt., N.Y.C., 1995; named Accredited Estate Planner, Nat. Assn. Estate Planners, Marietta, Ga., 1995. Mem. ABA, Fla. Bar (trusts and estate com.), N.Y. State Bar Assn. (com. on estates and trusts, com. on surrogate's ct.), Bar Assn. of the City of N.Y. (com. on surrogate's ct.), N.Y.C. Estate Planning Coun. (lectr., author), N.Y. County Lawyers Assn. (mem. com. on trusts and estates 1979—, com. on profl. ethics, com. on taxation 2000—, com. on surrogate's ct.), Queens County Bar Assn. (mem. com. trusts and estates 1990—, mem. com. on taxation, mem. com. on profl. ethics, com. on surrogate's ct.), Am. Judges Assn. (civil ct. arbitrator N.Y.C.), Am. Arbitration Assn. (panel of arbitrators), N.Y. State Trial Lawyers Assn., Richmond County Bar Assn. (com. on surrogates ct., com. on estate taxation), Columbia Coll. Alumni Assn. of Columbia U. (class pres. 1969—), Columbia Law Sch. Assn., S.I. Richmond-town Hist. Soc., Archdiocese N.Y., Regina Coeli Legacy Soc. Republican. Roman Catholic. Avocations: music, history, theater, lecturing, European travel. Home: 155 Johanna Ln Staten Island NY 10309-3604 Office: Solomon Pearl Blum Heymann & Stich LLP 40 Wall Street 35th Fl New York NY 10005 Office Phone: 212-267-7600. Business E-Mail: jmaterna@solpearl.com.

**MATERSON, EDWARD ARTHUR,** sculptor, artist; b. Bklyn., Jan. 25, 1935; m. Emily Jane Gilson, July 22, 1961; 1 child, Amy Elizabeth. Student, Cooper Union Art and Architecture, 1962. Graphic artist Guy Gannett Pub., Portland, Maine, 1966—99. Prin. works include Portrait of Nadia, Mus. Sports, Bucharest, Romania, Portrait of Joan Benoit, Portland, Running Cat, Limington, Maine, Joan Benoit, Portrait of Hannes Schneider, North Conway, NH, Portrait of Ge Erskine, South Portland, Maine. Arts commr. Cape Elizabeth (Maine) Arts Commn., 2001—03. With U.S. Army, 1958—60, Germany. Scholar, Cooper Union Advancement of Art and Arch., 1961. Avocation: sailing. Home: 2 Charles Rd Cape Elizabeth ME 04107 Personal E-mail: ematerso@maine.rr.com.

**MATERSON, RICHARD STEPHEN,** physician, educator; b. Phila., Feb. 11, 1941; s. Alfred Lawrence and June Eileen (Slakoff) Materson; m. Rosa Maria Navarro, Aug. 22, 1964; children: Lisa Gail, Lawrence Mark. MD, U. Miami, Coral Gables, Fla., 1965. Diplomate Am. Bd. Phys. Medicine and Rehab. Intern Walter Reed Gen. Hosp., Washington, 1965; resident Letterman Gen. Hosp., San Francisco, 1966—68; chief phys. medicine and rehab. Tripler Gen. Hosp., Honolulu, 1968—72; asst. prof. phys. medicine and rehab. Ohio State U., Columbus, 1972—76; assoc. clin. prof. phys. medicine and rehab. Baylor Coll. Medicine, Houston, 1976—93, prof., 1997—; pres. Materson MD, PA, Houston, 1976—2005; sr. v.p. for med. affairs, med. dir. Nat. Rehab. Hosp., Washington, 1990—97; prof. neurology George Washington U. Med. Ctr., Washington, 1994—97; med. v.p. Meml. Healthcare Sys., Houston, 1997—2005; prof. phys. medicine and rehab. U. Tex. Health Sci. Ctr., Houston, 1997—; fellow Kaiser Inst., 1999, 2001; chief med. officer Meml. Hermann Continuing Care Corp., 2000—02; v.p. med. devel. Hermann Healthcare Sys., 2002—05; ret., 2005. Med. dir. phys. medicine and rehab. Meml. Hosp. SE, Houston, 1978-90, Ctr. for Sports Medicine and Rehab., 1987-90, Electromyography Lab., 1978-90; faculty Kaiser Inst., 2000—. Co-author: Physical Medicine and Rehabilitation, 1977, 2d rev. edit., 1980, The Practice of Rehabilitation Medicine, 1982; co-editor: Management of Persons with Stroke, 1993; co-editor, author: The Non Surgical Management of Acute Low Back Pain, 1997, Pain Management, 1998; contbg. author: Practice of Medicine, 1978. Trustee Meml. Hosp. Sys., Houston, 1986—90, Nat. Rehab. Hosp., Washington, 1990—96; host family Experiment in Internat. Living, 1985—87; bd. dirs. Inst. for Religion and Health, Tex. Med. Ctr., 2002—, chmn. bd., 2006—. Served to maj. U.S. Army, 1965—72. Fellow Am. Acad. Phys. Medicine and Rehab. (pres. 1986-87, Distng. Pub. Svc. award, 1992, Walter J. Zeiter lectr., 1994), Am. Assn. Electrodiagnostic Medicine; mem. AMA (del. 1978-93), Phys. Medicine and Rehab. Edn. and Rsch. Found. (founder, pres. 1982-90, bd. dirs. 1983-2001), Houston Acad. Phys. Medicine and Rehab. (pres. 1979-80), Am. Acad. Pain Mgmt. (chmn. bd. advisors 1989-90, bd. adv. 1990-2005), Internat. Wine and Food Soc., Knights of Vine (master comdr. 1982—), Confrerie des Chevaliers du Tastevin, Chaine des Rotisseurs Jewish. Personal E-mail: rmaterson@earthlink.net.

**MATES, LAWRENCE A., II,** medical company executive, consultant; b. Toledo, Oct. 10, 1954; s. Lawrence A. and Phyllis A. (Thomas) M.; m. Ulrike D. Heermann, Dec. 23, 1977; children: Lawrence A. III, Jessica M. BS in Mktg. cum laude, Princeton U., 1976, MBA, 1977. Sales mgr. Technicare Corp., Cleve., 1977-80; dist. sales mgr. Siemens Med. Systems, Iselin, N.J., 1981-85; regional sales mgr. Digital Equipment Corp., Detroit, 1985-88; nat. sales mgr. Cemax, Inc., Fremont, Calif., 1988-92; exec. v.p. Philips Electronics, Cin., 1992-2000; sr. v.p. Siemens Med. Svcs., 2000—. Bd. dirs. Provident Nat. Bank. Bd. dirs. Cin. City Planners, 1994—, United Way, 1985-86, 92-96, Am. Cancer Soc., 1997-99. Mem. Med. Researchers Assn., Am. Hosp. Assn., Toledo Bus. Assn. (v.p. 1984-85), Ohio Young Men's Bus. Assn. (pres. 1985, chmn. 1992-93), Cin. Profl. Bus. Assn. (v.p. 1993—), Cin. Health Profls. (dir. 1994-95), Cin. Investors Ltd. (dir. 1994-98), Toledo Investors Ltd. (pres. 1986, 92), Cin. Bankers Club, Cin. Club, Univ. Club (v.p. 1993-96, pres. 1998-02), Sycamore Athletic Boosters (pres. 1996-98, bd. dirs. 1996—). Republican. Roman Catholic. Avocations: swimming, travel, wine collecting, automobiles, golf. Office Phone: 610-448-1517. E-mail: LMATES@aol.com.

**MATES, ROBERT EDWARD,** mechanical engineering educator; b. Buffalo, May 19, 1935; s. Cyril S. and Ruth Elizabeth Mates; m. Gail Paxson, June 4, 1960; children: Robert E., Elisabeth, Steven. BS, U. Rochester, 1957; MS, Cornell U., 1959, PhD, 1963. Lic. profl. engr. NY 1967. Instr. Cornell U., Ithaca, NY, 1958-61; asst. prof. SUNY, Buffalo, 1962-65, assoc. prof., 1965-69, chmn. mech. and aero. engring., 1967-70, 79-82, prof. mech. engring., 1969-97, dir. Ctr. Biomed. Engring., 1989-96, prof. emeritus, 1997—. Editor various symposium proceedings; contbr. articles to profl. jours. Mem. supt. adv. com. vocat. edn. Buffalo Pub. Schs., 1990—98. NIH spl. rsch. fellow, 1970-71, 78-79, H.R. Lissner award Am. Soc of Mechanical Engineers, 1995. Fellow ASME (chmn. winter ann. meeting com. 1989-93, mem.-at-large bd. comm. 1988-93, v.p. bd. comm. 1994-98), Am. Inst. for Med. and Biol. Engring. (founding, chmn. acad. coun. 1996-97); mem. AAUP, Biomed. Engring. Soc. (bd. dirs. 1991-94, chmn. awards com. 1991-92, mem. pub. bd. 1992-94), Am. Soc. Engring. Edn. Democrat. Episcopalian. Avocations: woodworking, tennis, sailing, bridge. E-mail: matesr@asme.org.

**MATES, SUSAN ONTHANK,** physician, educator, musician, writer; b. Oakland, Calif., Aug. 8, 1950; d. Benson and Lois (Onthank) M.; m. Joseph Harold Friedman, Dec. 10, 1978; children: Rebecca, Deborah, William. Student, Juilliard Sch. Music, 1967-69; BA magna cum laude with distinction, Yale Coll., 1972; MD, Albert Einstein Coll. Medicine, 1976. Cert. Am. Bd. Internal Medicine, Nat. Bd. Med. Examiners. Intern Boston City Hosp., 1976-77; fellow in gen. medicine Coll. of Physicians and Surgeons-Columbia U., N.Y.C., 1977-78; resident/fellow in infectious diseases Montefiore Hosp., Bronx, 1978-82; asst. prof. medicine Brown U., Providence, 1982-85, asst. prof. biochemistry, 1985-86, clin. assoc. prof. medicine, 1993-98; staff mem., former dir. R.I. State Tb Clinic, R.I. Dept. Health, Providence, 1986-96, cons. Tb program, 1987-96. Judge short story contest Providence Jour., 1994, 98; mem. jury R.I. Coun. Arts Fellowship; contbg. editor Pushcart Prize, Pushcart Press, 1995, 96, 97, 98, 99. Author: (fiction) The Good Doctor, 1994 (John Simmons Short Fiction Award, U. Iowa Press, 1994); contbr. sci. articles to profl. jours., stories to revs. and jours. and anthologies. Recipient Recognition award for young researchers AAUW, 1985, Clin. Investigator award NIH, 1984, R.I. Found. award, 1983; McDowell Colony fellow, 1995, Yaddo fellow, 1996; Symposium scholar in lit. and medicine for 21st Century, Brown U., 1997. Mem. Am. Med. Women's Assn., Poets and Writers, Alpha Omega Alpha.

**MATESKY, NANCY LEE,** music educator; b. West Point, Mo., Nov. 30, 1941; d. Enoch Ivy and Layla Nixon Miller; m. Michael Paul Matesky, Aug. 10, 1973; children: Angela Lynn, Michael Paul II. BS in Edn., U Ark., 1963, MS in Edn., 1971. Piano tchr. self employed, Tex., Ark., Wash., 1960—90; music tchr. Rogers Ark. Sch., 1963—64, Fayetteville Sch., Ark., 1964—65, Springdale Sch., Ark., 1965—70; instr. U Ark., Fayetteville, 1971—72; asst. prof. West Tex. State U, Canyon, 1972—75; prof. Shoreline CC, Seattle, 1976—. Founder, first pres. Ark. Elem. Music Educators Assn., 1965—67. Performer: Shoreline CC, 1981—98, Seattle Art Mus., 2000, 2002, Matesky-Swisher Two Piano Duo. Named one of Outstanding Young Women in Am., 1968; recipient Outstanding Young Educator award, Jaycees, 1967. Mem.: Music Educators Nat. Conf., Music Tchr. Nat. Assn. (assoc.), Seattle Ladies Musical Club, Sigma Alpha Iota (Nat. Coll. Leadership award 1963, Nat. Alumnae Leadership award 2001). United Meth. Home: 23004 35th Ave S E Bothell WA 98021-8913 Office: Shoreline CC 16101 Greenwood Ave N Shoreline WA 98133 Office Phone: 206-546-4618. Personal E-mail: opus.four@gte.net.

**MATHENY, ADAM PENCE, JR.,** child psychologist, educator, consultant, researcher; b. Stanford, Ky., Sept. 6, 1932; s. Adam Pence and Dorotha (Steele) Matheny; m. Ute I. Debus, July 10, 1962 (div.); m. Mary P. Tolbert, June 24, 1967 (div.); children: Laura Steele, Jason Gaverick. BS, Columbia U., 1958; PhD, Vanderbilt U., 1962. Sr. human factors engr. Martin Aerospace divsn., Balt., 1962—63; instr. Johns Hopkins U. Med. Sch., Balt., 1963—65; staff fellow Nat. Inst. Child Health and Human Devel., 1965—67; from asst. prof. to prof. pediat. U. Louisville Med. Sch., 1967—75; assoc. dir. to dir. Louisville Twin Study, 1986—. Mem. rev. panel NIH, 1991—95. Co-author: Genetics and Counseling in Medical Practice, 1969; contbr. articles to profl. jours. With USN, 1951—55. Recipient Outstanding Rsch. medal, U. Louisville. Fellow: APA, Am. Psychol. Soc., Am. Assn. Applied and Preventive Psychology, Internat. Soc. Twin Studies; mem.: AAAS, Internat. Soc. Infant Study, Internat. Soc. Behavior Devel., Behavior Genetics Assn., Soc. Rsch. Child Devel., Sigma Xi, Phi Beta Kappa. Office Phone: 502-634-0050. Business E-Mail: apmathol@louisville.edu. E-mail: adammatheny@aol.com.

**MATHENY, CHARLES WOODBURN, JR.,** former army officer, civil engineer, city official; b. Sarasota, Fla., Aug. 7, 1914; s. Charles Woodburn Sr. and Virginia (Yates) M.; m. Jeanne Felkel, July 12, 1942; children: Virginia Ann, Nancy Caroline, Charles Woodburn III. BSCE, U. Fla., 1936; grad. Army Command Gen. Staff Coll., 1944. Registered profl. engr., Ga., 1939; cert. surveyor Ga., 1939, lic. comml. pilot 1952. San. engr. Ga. State Dept. Health, 1939—39; civil engr. Fla. East Coast Rlwy., 1939—41; commd. 2d lt. F.A., USAR through ROTC U. Fla., 1936; 1st lt. F.A., USAR, 1939; vol. active army svc. F.A., US Army, 1941; commissioned 2d lt. F.A., US Army (Regular Army), 1942; advanced through grades to col. F.A., USAR, 1955; comdr. 351st Field Arty. Bn., 1944—45; commr. 33rd Field Arty. Bn., 1st Infantry Divsn., 1946; arty. staff officer 33rd Field Arty. Bn., 1st Inf. Divsn., 1947; gen. staff G-3 Plans Dept. Army, 1948—51; qualified Air Force liaison pilot, 1951; qualified Army aviator airplanes and helicopters, 1952; aviation officer 25th Infantry Divsn., Republic of Korea, 1952—53; sr. Army aviation advisor Korean Army, 1953; first dir. combat devel. dept. first dep. comdt. Army Aviation Sch., Ft. Sill, Okla., 1954—55; dep. dir. rsch., dep. dir. dept. tactics U.S. Army Field Arty. and Missile Sch., Ft. Sill, 1955—57; aviation officer 7th U.S. Army, Germany, 1957—58; Munich sub area comdr. So. Area Command, 1958—59; qualified sr. army aviator, 1959; dep. chief of staff for info. So. Area Command, 1960; Mich. sector comdr. VI Army Corps., 1961—62, ret., 1962; asst. dir. Tampa (Fla.) Dept. Pub. Works, 1963—81, ret., 1981. During World War II, Germany Commd., 351st field arty. Bn. in combat and occupation, 1945, also 33d field arty. bn., 1st Inf. Divsn., in occupation, 1946. Initiator and originator of tactical use of helicopters in Army, 1949, Army warrant officer helicopter aviator program and organization of first five Army Transp. Helicopter Co. move combat units battlefield authorized T.O. & E, 55-57, Oct. 24, 1950 by U.S. Army Chief of Staff Gen. J. Lawton Collins and establishment of a new U.S. Army pers. policy making U.S. Army helicopter pilots warrant officers instead of officers, 1950; 1st to envision army combat units and airphibious army divisions equipped with high performance helicopter mobility capable of land, sea or air warfare operations at 200 mph, 1950; initiated and prepared feasibility study signed by Army chief of staff, Gen. J. Lawton Collins ordering first feasibility tests of Army super-mobile inf. and arty. units equipped with helicopter mobility, 1951; pilot 1st combat observation mission in army helicopter, Korea, 1952; organizer, comdr., helicopter pilot 1st Army combat ops. using helicopter mobility to support inf. and engr. front line combat units 25th Inf. Divsn., Korea, 1952 proving feasibility of Army helicopter mobility on the battlefield; 1st to advocate, rsch., prepare orgn. plans and design of super-mobile Army combat units equipped with armed and unarmed helicopter mobility, with model designs of helicopters armed with missiles, rockets, etc. to equip proposed combat units, 1955-56; proposed development reconnaissance helicopter 1957 similar to Army O/R Comanche, RAH-66 reconnaissance helicopter later developed by Army; U.S. Army first to exploit and develop helicopter mobility due to Matheny's devotion to its early begining; pilot 100 combat observation missions, Korea, 1952-53; author 1st state legis. to establish profl. sch. civil engring. filed in Fla. Legis. by Sen. Julian Lane, 1974; mem. U.S. Army's Strategic Planning Com., 1950-51. Contbr. articles to profl. jours., popular mags. Troop com. Boy Scouts Am., 1965-73; active various cmty. and ch. activities; patron Tampa Art Mus., 1965-83, Tampa Cmty. Concert Series, 1979-82; bd. dirs. Tampa YMCA, 1967-71, Fla. Easter Seal Soc., 1978, Easter Seal Soc. Hillsborough County, 1971-84, hon. bd. dirs., 1984-95, treas., 1973-76, pres., 1977. Decorated Bronze Star with oak leaf cluster, Air medal with three oak leaf clusters; recipient of the Eagle Scout award, 1928; Letterman football U.F., 1933, 35; named to U. Fla. Student Hall of Fame, 1936. Mem. ASCE (pres. West Coast br., dir. Fla. sect. 1977, Engr. of Yr. award West Coast br. Fla. sect. 1979, life mem. 1980), Am. Soc. Profl. Engrs., Fla. Engring. Soc., Am. Pub. Works Assn. (pres. West Coast br. Fla. chpt. 1972, exec. com. Fla. chpt. 1972-77, v.p. 1977, pres. 1978), Ret. Officers Assn., Army Aviation Assn., SAR, Fla. Blue Key, Alpha Tau Omega, Sigma Tau. Episcopalian. Achievements include research in tactical use of helicopter aerial vehicles. Home: 3501 Bayshore Blvd Apt 1402 Tampa FL 33629-8901 Office Phone: 813-835-3426.

**MATHENY, EDWARD TAYLOR, JR.,** lawyer; b. Chgo., July 15, 1923; s. Edward Taylor and Lina (Pinnell) Matheny; m. Marion Elizabeth Shields, Sept. 10, 1947; children: Nancy Elizabeth, Edward Taylor III; m. Ann Spears, Jan. 14, 1984. BA, U. Mo., 1944; JD, Harvard, 1949. Bar: Mo. 1949. Pvt. practice, Kansas City, 1949-91; ptnr. firm Blackwell, Sanders, Matheny, Weary & Lombardi, 1954-91. Pres. St. Luke's Hosp., Kansas City, 1980-95; bd. dirs. Dunn Industries, Inc. Author: The Presence of Care (History of St. Luke's Hospital, Kansas City), 1997, A Long and Constant Courtship (The History of a Law Firm), 1998, The Rise and Fall of Excellence, 2000, The Pursuit of a Ruptured Duck (When Kansas Citians Went to War), 2001. Cmty. Svc. Broadcasting of Mid-Am., Inc., 1971—72; chmn. Citizens Assn. Kansas City, 1958; chmn. bd. St. Luke's Found., 1995; trustee U. Kansas City, 1980—96, Kansas City Cmty. Found., 1983—94, Eye Found., 1990—2000, H&R Block Found., 1996—, Jacob L. and Ella C. Loose Found., 1996—2005. Mem. Kansas City Bar Assn., Mo. Bar, River Club, Mo. Acad. Squires, Mission Hills Country Club, Phi Beta Kappa, Sigma Chi (Balfour Nat. award 1944) Episcopalian (chancellor emeritus Diocese West Mo.). Home: 4900 Central St Kansas City MO 64112 Office: 4801 Main St Kansas City MO 64121-6777

**MATHENY, KENNETH L.,** oil industry executive; b. Akron, Ohio; B in Acctg., U. Akron; MBA, Bowling Green State U. Dir. corp. fin. Marathon Oil Corp., Houston, 1988—89, dir. human resources, 1989—94, v.p. human resources and environment, 1994—97; v.p. contr. USX Corp., Pitts., 1997—2000, v.p. investor rels., 2000—02; v.p. investor rels. and pub. affairs Marathon Oil Corp., 2002—. Mem.: Petroleum Investor Rels. Assn., Nat. Investor Rels. Inst., Am. Inst. CPAs. Office: Marathon Oil Corp Corp Headquarters 5555 San Felipe Rd Houston TX 77056-2723

**MATHENY, PAMELA BEMKO,** secondary school educator; b. Orange, N.J., Nov. 6, 1953; d. Julian Boris and Olga Donelik Bemko; m. Michael Matheny; children: Joseph, Kathryn. BA in Spanish and Secondary Edn., Fla. So. Coll., 1975. Nat. bd. cert. tchr. 2005. Sci. tchr. Kathleen Jr. H.S. Lakeland, Fla., 1975-76; Spanish and English tchr. Lake Gibson Jr. H.S. Lakeland, 1976-83; Spanish tchr. Lakeland Sr. H.S., 1983—. Recipient 1st Pl. Nat. award for econ. edn. Nat. Coun. Econ. Edn., 1995, 97, Govs. award for excellence in econ. edn. State Econ. Coun., Tampa, Fla., 1995, 96, 97, 99, 2000, 01, 03, Leavey award for econ. edn. Freedoms Found., Valley Forge, Pa., 1997, Lakeland High Tchr. of the Yr. 1998, Walmart Tchr. of the Yr., 2000, World Lang. Tchr. of Yr., 2002; semi-finalist NASDAQ Edn. Found. and NCEE regional, 1999, 2000, 01. Mem. Am. Assn. Tchrs. Spanish and Portuguese, Fla. Fgn. Lang. Assn. (named to Tchr. Hall of Fame 2004), Polk County Fgn. Lang. Coun. (past pres.), Kappa Delta Pi. Republican. Presbyterian. Avocations: travel, reading, gourmet cooking. Home: 5327 Lisa Ave Lakeland FL 33813-3038 Office: Lakeland Sr HS 726 Hollingsworth Rd Lakeland FL 33801-5818 Office Phone: 813-499-2900. Personal E-mail: pamela.osthoff@polk-fl.net.

**MATHENY, RUTH ANN,** editor; b. Fargo, N.D., Jan. 17, 1918; d. Jasper Gordon and Mary Elizabeth (Carey) Wheelock; m. Charles Edward Matheny, Oct. 24, 1960. BE, Mankato State Coll., 1938; MA, U. Minn., 1955; postgrad., Universidad Autonoma de Guadalajara, Mex., 1956, Georgetown U., 1960. Tchr., U.S. and S.Am., 1938-61; assoc. editor Charles E. Merrill Pub. Co., Columbus, Ohio, 1963-66; tchr. Confraternity Christian Doctrine, Washington Court House, Ohio, 1969-70; assoc. editor Jr. Cath. Messenger, Dayton, Ohio, 1966-68; editor Witness Intermediate, Dayton, 1968-70; editor in chief, assoc. pub. Today's Cath. Tchr., Dayton, 1970—2002, editor-in-chief emeritus, 2002—; editor in chief Catechist, Dayton, 1976-89, Ednl. Dealer, Dayton, 1976-80; v.p. Peter Li, Inc., Dayton, 1980—. Editl. collaborator: Dimensions of Personality series, 1969—; co-author: At Ease in the Classroom; author: Why a Catholic School?, Scripture Stories for Today: Why Religious Education?; freelance writer, 1943—. Bd. dirs. Friends Ormond Beach Libr. Mem.: 3d Order St. Francis (eucharistic min. 1990—2006), Nat. Coun. Cath. Women. Home: 26 Reynolds Ave Ormond Beach FL 32174-7043 Office: Peter Li Ednl Group 2621 Dryden Rd Ste 300 Dayton OH 45439 Personal E-mail: chilermat@aol.com. *In a world that is constantly changing, a strong religious faith is a dependable compass through which we are able to stay on a positive, forward course.*

**MATHER, ELIZABETH VIVIAN,** healthcare executive; b. Richmond, Ind., Sept. 19, 1941; d. Willie Samuel and Lillie Mae (Harper) Fuqua; m. Roland Donald Mather, Dec. 26, 1966. BS, Maryville (Tenn.) Coll., 1963; postgrad., Columbia U., 1963-66. Tchr. Richmond Cmty. Schs., 1963-67, Indpls. Pub. Schs., 1967-68; systems analyst Ind. Blue Cross Blue Shield, Indpls., 1968-71, Ind. Nat. Bank, Indpls., 1971; med. cons. Ind. State Dept. Pub. Welfare, Indpls., 1971-78, cons. supr., 1978-86; systems analyst Ky. Blue Cross Blue Shield, Louisville, 1988-89; contracts specialist Humana Corp., Louisville, 1989—. Active Rep. Cen. Com. Montgomery County, Crawfordsville, 1976-86, Centenary Meth. Ch., adminstrv. bd., 1990. Mem. DAR (treas. 1963-66, sec. 1978-86). Avocation: designing and sewing clothes. Home: 6106 Partridge Pl Floyds Knobs IN 47119-9427 Office: 500 W Main St Fl 6 Louisville KY 40202-2946 Office Phone: 502-580-2519. Business E-Mail: emather@humana.com.

**MATHER, JOHN CROMWELL,** astrophysicist; b. Roanoke, Va., Aug. 7, 1946; s. Robert Eugene and Martha Belle (Cromwell) Mather; m. Jane Anne Hauser, Nov. 22, 1980. BA, Swarthmore (Pa.) Coll., 1968; PhD, U. Calif., Berkeley, 1974; PhD (hon.), Swarthmore Coll., 1994. NAS/NRC rsch. assoc. NASA/Goddard Inst. for Space Studies, N.Y.C., 1974-76; lectr. in astronomy Columbia U., N.Y.C., 1975-76; astrophysicist NASA/Goddard Space Flight Ctr., Greenbelt, Md., 1976—, head infrared astrophysics br., 1988-89, 90-93, sr. scientist, 1990, 93—, study scientist Cosmic Background Explorer Satellite, 1976-82, project scientist COBE, 1982—, prin. investigator FIRAS on COBE, 1976—. Chmn. external adv. bd. Ctr. for Astrophys. Rsch. in the Antarctic, U. Chgo., 1992—95; mem. lunar astrophysics mgmt. ops. working group NASA Hdqrs., Washington, 1992; study scientist Next Generation Space Telescope, 1995—2002; mem. NRC Bd. Physics and Astronomy, 1998—2001; sr. project scientist James Webb Space Telescope, 2002—. Author: The Very First Light with John Boslough, 1996; contbr. articles to profl. jours. Named to Hall of Fame, Newton HS Hall of Fame, NJ, 2003; recipient Nat. Space Achievement award, Rotary, 1991, Laurels award, Aviation Week and Space Tech., 1992, John Scott award, City of Phila., 1995, Mark. Aaronson Meml. prize, 1998, Franklin medal in Physics, 1999, Presdl. Rank award, NASA, 2003, Cosmology prize, Gruber Found., 2006. Fellow: AAAS (Rumford prize 1996), Am. Phys. Soc.; mem.: AIAA (Space Sci. award 1993), Soc. Photo-Optical Instrumentation Engrs. (George W. Goddard award 2005), Nat. Acad. Scis., Internat. Astron. Union, Am. Astron. Soc. (councilor 1998—2001, Dannie Heineman prize astrophysics 1993), Sigma Xi. Democrat. Unitarian Universalist. Achievements include proposed Cosmic Background Explorer Satellite, led team to successful launch in 1989; measured spectrum of cosmic microwave background radiation to unprecedented accuracy. Office: NASA/Goddard Space Flight Code 665 Greenbelt MD 20771-0001

**MATHER, LYNN,** law educator, political science professor; BA, Univ. Calif., Los Angeles; postgraduate, Univ. Wis., Univ. Calif., Berkeley; PhD, Univ. Calif., Irvine. Nelson A. Rockefeller prof. govt. Dartmouth Coll.; acting dir. Rockefeller Ctr. Social Sci., Dartmouth Coll.; prof. Law & Polit. Sci. SUNY Buffalo, 2002—; dir. Baldy Ctr. for Law & Social Policy, Buffalo, 2002—. Author: Plea Bargaining or Trial? The Process of Criminal Case Disposition; co-author: Divorce Lawyers at Work: Varieties of Professionalism in Practice (C. Herman Pritchett award, Am. Polit. Sci. Assn.); contbr. articles to profl. jour. Mem.: Am. Polit. Sci. Assn. (chair, Law & Cts. sect. 1993—94), Law & Soc. Assn. (pres. 2001—02). Office: University at Buffalo Law School 418 O'Brien Hall Buffalo NY 14260

**MATHER, MILDRED EUNICE,** retired archivist; b. Washington, Iowa, July 25, 1922; d. Hollis John and Delpha Irene (Cummings) Whiting; m. Stewart Elbert Mather, Aug. 7, 1955; children: Julie Marie, Thomas Stewart(dec.). Cert., Burlington and Des Moines, 1941, 1947, Stenotype Inst., 1948. Typist Burlington Willow-Weave, 1941-42, Burlington Basket Co., 1942; clk. typist U.S. Dept. War, Washington, 1942-43; supr. internat. conf. U.S. Dept. State, Washington, 1949-52; bookkeeper Iowa Wesleyan Coll., Mt. Pleasant, 1952-55; clk. typist Herbert Hoover Presdl. Libr., West Branch, Iowa, 1964-69, archives technician, 1964-72, archivist, libr., 1972-92, ret., 1992. With WAC U.S. Army, 1943—46. Mem.: Am. Legion, Order Ea. Star. Republican. Home: 1794 Garfield Ave West Branch IA 52358-9403

**MATHER, RICHARD BURROUGHS,** retired Chinese language and literature educator; b. Baoding, Hebei, China, Nov. 11, 1913; s. William Arnot and Grace (Burroughs) M.; m. Virginia Marjorie Temple, June 3, 1939; 1 dau., Elizabeth Temple. BA, Princeton U., 1935; B.Th., Princeton Theol. Sem., 1939; PhD in Oriental Langs, U. Calif., Berkeley, 1949. Ordained to ministry United Presbyterian Ch. U.S., 1939; pastor Belle Haven (Va.) Presbyterian Ch., 1939-41; asst. prof. Chinese U. Minn., Mpls., 1949-57, assoc. prof., 1957-64, prof., 1964-84. Mem. Am. Council Learned Socs. on Study of Chinese Civilization, 1979-81 Author: Shih-shuo hsin-yu, A New Account of Tales of the World, 1976, rev. edit., 2002, The Poet Shen Yueh (441-513), the Reticent Marquis, 1988, The Age of Eternal Brilliance: Three Poets of the Yung-ming Era, 2003; contbr. articles on medieval Chinese lit. and religion. Guggenheim fellow, 1956-57; Fulbright Hays grantee, 1956-57, 63-64; Am. Council Learned Socs. grantee, 1963-64 Mem. Am. Oriental Soc. (pres. 1980-81), Assn. Asian Studies. Democrat. Home: 1666 Coffman St Apt 108 Saint Paul MN 55108

**MATHER, ROGER FREDERICK,** retired music educator, writer; b. London, May 27, 1917; came to U.S., 1938; s. Richard and Marie Louise (Schultze) M.; m. Dorothea Meiner, Sept. 11, 1943 (div. Sept. 1971); children: Arielle Diane, Christopher Richard; m. Betty Louise Bang, Aug. 3,

---

1973. BA with honors, Cambridge U., 1938; MSc, MIT, 1940; MA in Metallurgy, U. Cambridge, 1941. Registered profl. engr., Ohio, Mich., Pa. Rsch. metallurgist Inland Steel Co., East Chicago, Ind., 1940-42; chief metallurgist Willys-Overland Motors, Toledo, 1942-46, Kaiser-Frazer Corp., Willow Run, Mich., 1946-50; project mgr. U.S. Steel Corp., Pitts., 1950-61; dir. rsch. engring. Mine Safety Appliances Co., Pitts., 1961-62; rsch. staff Du Pont Co., Wilmington, Del., 1962-63; chief nuclear power tech. br. NASA, Cleve., 1963-73; adj. prof. music U. Iowa, Iowa City, 1973-96; ret., 1996. Instr. pub. speaking and stage fright U. Iowa, 1983-85, Kirkwood C.C., Iowa City, 1983-85; cons. Miyazawa Flutes, U.S.A., Coralville, Iowa, 1985-90; lectr. U. Toledo; Mich. state examiner Registration of Profl. Engrs.; condr. numerous workshops, clinics, classes, and flute recitals regionally, nationally, Europe and Asia. Author: The Art of Playing the Flute, 1980, Vol. 2, 1981, Vol. 3, 1988; contbr. chpts. to several woodwind anthologies; pub., exec. editor The Romney Press, 1980—; contbr. poems to numerous poetry anthologies in US, Eng., numerous articles to sci. and music jours. Mem. Internat. Soc. Poets (Hall of Fame 1998, Poet of Merit 2002, Featured Artist 2005), Nat. Flute Assn. (life, cons.), The Pa. Assn., Mensa Episcopalian. Avocations: semi-professional photography, high fidelity sound reproduction contributions, alternative medicine. Home: 715 George St Iowa City IA 52246 Personal E-mail: bangmather@mchsi.com.

**MATHER, STEPHANIE JUNE,** lawyer; b. Kansas City, Mo., Dec. 5, 1952; d. Edward Wayne and H. June (Kunkel) M.; m. Miles Christopher Zimmerman, Sept. 23, 1988. BA magna cum laude, Okla. City U., 1975, JD with honors, 1980. Lawyer Pierce, Couch, Hendrickson, Johnston & Baysinger, Okla. City, Okla., 1980—88, Manchester, Hiltgen & Healy, P.C., Okla. City, 1989—90; sr. staff counsel Nat. Am. Ins. Co., Chandler, Okla., 1990—98; atty. for Edn. Law, Oklahoma City, 1998—, v.p., shareholder, 2003—. Asst. v.p. Lagere & Walkingstick Ins. Agcy., Inc., Chandler, Okla., 1993-98. Co-chair Lincoln County Dem. Party, 1991-92, 95-97; v.p. Lincoln County Dem. Women, 1992-95, pres., 1995-97; bd. dirs. Lincoln County Partnership for Children, 1994—; Gateway to Prevention and Recovery, 1996-97. Mem. Okla. Bar Assn. (editor, bd. editors, 1992-99), Lincoln County Bar Assn. (mem. libr. bd. 1990—), Nat. Sch. Bds. Assn. (coun. of sch. attys. 1998—), Okla. State Sch. Bds. Assn. (coun. of sch. attys. 1998—, bd. dirs. 2002-05, pres. 2005-), Lincoln County Profl. Women, Alpha Phi (treas. Cert. Okla. Alumnae 1997-99, Outstanding Okla. City Alumnae, 2005, Panhellenic Woman of Yr. Okla. City, 2005). Democrat. Avocations: reading, genealogy, ranching, cooking. Office: Center For Education Law 900 N Broadway Ave #300 Oklahoma City OK 73102-5828 Home: 808 Manvel Ave Chandler OK 74834-3858 also: 808 Marvel Ave Chandler OK 74834 Office Phone: 405-528-2800. E-mail: smather@cfel.com.

**MATHERS, MARSHALL See EMINEM**

**MATHERS, WILLIAM HARRIS,** lawyer; b. Newport, RI, Aug. 27, 1914; s. Howard and Margaret I. (Harris) M.; m. Myra T. Martin, Jan. 17, 1942; children: William Martin, Michael Harris, John Grinnell, Myra Tutt, Ursula Fraser. AB, Dartmouth Coll., 1935; LLB, Yale U., 1938. Bar: NY 1940. With Milbank, Tweed & Hope, 1938-48; mem. Milbank, Tweed, Hope & Hadley, 1948-57; v.p., sec., dir. Yale & Towne Mfg. Co., Stamford, Conn., 1957-60; ptnr. Chadbourne & Parke, 1960-75, counsel, 1983—; exec. v.p., gen. counsel, sec., dir. United Brands Co., 1975-82. Mayor, trustee Village of Cove Neck, N.Y., 1950-82; trustee Barnard Coll., 1958-69. Served to maj. U.S. Army, 1942-46. Mem. ABA, N.Y. State Bar Assn., Nassau County Bar Assn., Assn. of Bar of City of N.Y., New Eng. Soc. in City of N.Y., Casque and Gauntlet, Corbey Court, Piping Rock Club, Seminole Golf Club, N.Y. Yacht Club, Cold Spring Harbor Beach Club, Phi Beta Kappa, Psi Upsilon. Home: 1460 King George Farm Rd Sutton VT 05867 Office: 30 Rockefeller Plz New York NY 10112-0127 Office Phone: 212-408-5100.

**MATHES, EDWARD CONRAD,** architect; b. New Orleans, Mar. 10, 1943; s. Earl L. and Margaret (Gash) M.; m. Anne M. Ergenbright, Mar. 1, 1964 (div. June 2000); children: Margaret Elizabeth Hughes, Anne Catherine Aboud. BArch, U. Southwestern La., 1968. Registered arch., La., Miss., Fla., Tex., Ala., Ga., Tenn., Ky., N.C., S.C., W.Va., Conn. Tchr. U. Southwestern La., Lafayette, 1968-69; asst. to mng. arch. Rogers, Taliaferro, Kostritsky & Lamb, Balt., 1969; pres. Mathes, Bergman & Assocs., Inc., New Orleans, 1969-82, The Mathes Group, New Orleans, 1982—2000; chmn. MathesBrierre Architects, 1982—. Bd. dirs. New Orleans Mus. Art, 2006— Dean's adv. coun. U. La. Coll. of the Arts, Lafayette; bd. dirs. New Orleans Mus. Art. Chmn. Orleans Svc. Ctr., ARC, 1993-94; bd. dirs. City Park Improvement Assn., 1996—, pres. Recipient Am. Sch. and Univ. award, 1983, 1985, Partnership award, ARC, 1998, CEO's award, S.E. La. chpt. ARC, People's Choice award for music, comms., theatre complex, Loyola New Orleans, 1989, People's Choice award for Univ. Libr., 2000, Cert. Recognition Design Excellence, Nat. Orgn. Minority Architects, 2002. Mem.: AIA (pres. New Orleans chpt. 1989, Inst. scholar 1968—69, Honor award New Orleans Chpt. 1982, 1989, 2000, Honor award La. 1982, 1986, 2001), Constrn. Industry Assn. (pres. 1984—85, Honor award 1993), City Energy Club, Metairie Country Club, Pickwick Club, Rotary (pres. New Orleans 1985—86). Republican. Presbyterian. Avocations: tennis, travel. Home: # 4 Park Island Dr New Orleans LA 70122 Office: MathesBrierre Architects 201 Saint Charles Ave Fl 41 New Orleans LA 70170-4100 Office Phone: 504-586-9303. Business E-Mail: emathes@mathesbrierre.com.

**MATHES, JAMES R.,** bishop; b. Aug. 18, 1959; m. Teresa Yvette Sutton, Aug. 15, 1981; children: Rutherford Lee, Sarah Elizabeth Nam. BA magna cum laude, U. of the South, Sewanee, Tenn., 1982, MDiv, Va. Theol. Sem., Alexandria, 1991. Mascn. campaign dir. The Webb Sch., Bell Buckle, Tenn., 1983—85; math tchr. & coach St. Andrews-Sewanee Sch., St. Andrews, Tenn., 1985—86, dir. devel., 1986—89; asst. min. All Saints Episcopal Ch. Belmont, Mass., 1991—94; rector Church of St. James the Less, Northfield, Ill., 1994—2001; canon to the ordinary Episcopal Diocese of Chgo., 2001—05; bishop Episcopal Diocese of San Diego, 2005—. Episcopalian. Avocations: woodworking, backpacking, reading. Office: Episcopal Diocese of San Diego 2728 Sixth Ave San Diego CA 92103 Business E-Mail: jmathes@edsd.org.

**MATHES, RACHEL CLARKE,** voice educator, singer; b. Atlanta, Mar. 14, 1941; d. Frank Alfred and Jacqueline Woolfolk Mathes. MM, U. S.C., 1988, DMA, 1991. Leading soprano Stadttheater, Basel, Switzerland, 1966—66, Deutsche Opera Rhein, Duesseldorf, Germany, 1967—73, Met. Opera, N.Y.C., 1974—77; prof. voice U. Ala., Birmingham, 1983—. Elder, tchr. bible South Highland Presbyn. Ch., Birmingham, 1999—. Recipient Birmingham News Obelisk award, 1979, 1981, Ala. Music Hall Fame Contemporary award, 1987; scholar, Fulbright Found. 1962—63. Mem.: Nat. Fedn. Music Clubs, Nat. Assn. Singing, Pi Kappa Alpha. Office Phone: 205-934-8781.

**MATHES, STEPHEN JOHN,** plastic and reconstructive surgeon, educator; b. New Orleans, Aug. 17, 1943; s. John Ernest and Norma (Deutsch) M.; children: David, Brian, Edward. BS, La. State U., 1964; MD, La. State U., New Orleans, 1968. Diplomate Am. Bd. Surgery, Am. Bd. Plastic Surgery (dir. 1993—). Asst. prof. surgery Wash. U. St. Louis, 1977-78; assoc. prof. U. Calif., San Francisco, 1978-84, prof. surgery, 1984, prof. surgery, anatomy and cell biology, 1984-85, also bd. dirs. craniofacial anomalies; head plastic surgery sect. U. Mich., Ann Arbor, 1984-85, prof. surgery, 1984-85; prof. surgery, head plastic and reconstructive surgery div. U. Calif., San Francisco, 1985—, prof. growth and devel. Sch. Dentistry, 1985—. Pres. residency rev. com. Accreditation Coun. Grad. Med. Edn., 2004—05. Author: (textbook) Clinical Applications for Muscle and Musculocutaneous Flaps, 1983 (Best Med. Book award Physician's category, Am. Med. Writer's Assn., 1983), Clinical Atlas of Muscle and Musculocutaneous Flaps, 1979, Plastic Surgery Principles and Practice, 1990, Reconstructive Surgery, 1996; editor: Plastic Surgery, 2d edit., 2006; mem. editl. bd. Jour. Plascit and Resonstructive Surgery, 1991-98; contbr. articles to profl. jours. Recipient 1st prize plastic surgery scholarship contest Plastic Surgery Edn. Found., 1981, 83, 84, 86, 93, 99, Spl. Achievement award Am. Soc. Plastic Surgery, 1980, Best Sci. Paper,

---

Am. Soc. Aesthetic Plastic Surgery, 1981; grantee NIH, 1982-85, 86-90. Fellow ACS (chmn. adv. coun. on plastic and maxillofacial surgery 1999-02, gov. at large, mem. health policy steering com. 2000-06); mem. Am. Assn. Plastic Surgery (sec. 2005-06, Clinician of Yr. award 2001), Plastic Surgery Rsch. Coun. (pres. 1988), Am. Soc. Surgery of Hand, Am. Soc. Univ. Surgeons, Am. Soc. Plastic Surgery (Spl. Achievement award 2005), Am. Acad. Chairmen in Plastic Surgery (pres. 2001), Plastic Surgery Ednl. Found. (bd. dirs. 1994-04, pres. 2002-03, Disting. Svc. award 2005). Republican. Episcopalian. Avocations: gardening, tennis. Home: 2730 Broderick St San Francisco CA 94123 Office: Ste 503 350 Parnassus St San Francisco CA 94117-0001 Personal E-mail: sjmathes@pacbell.net. Business E-Mail: mathess@surgery.ucsf.edu.

**MATHESON, ALAN ADAMS,** law educator; b. Cedar City, Utah, Feb. 2, 1932; s. Scott Milne and Adele (Adams) M.; m. Milicent Holbrook, Aug. 15, 1960; children: Alan, David Scott, John Robert. BA, U. Utah, 1953, MS, 1957, JD, 1959; postgrad., Columbia U. Bar: Utah 1960, Ariz. 1975. Asst. to pres. Utah State U., 1961-67; mem. faculty Ariz. State U., Tempe, 1967—, prof. law, 1970—, dean, 1972, 1978-84, 89, 97-98. Bd. dirs. Ariz. Found. for Legal Svcs. and Edn. Pres. Tri-City Mental Health Citizens Bd., 1973-74. With AUS, 1953-55. Mem. ABA, Utah Bar Assn., Ariz. Bar Assn., Maricopa County Bar Assn., Phi Beta Kappa, Order of Coif. Democrat. Mem. Lds Ch. Home: 720 E Geneva Dr Tempe AZ 85282-3737 Office: Ariz State U Coll Law Tempe AZ 85287 Office Phone: 480-965-6503.

**MATHESON, ANN,** librarian, writer; b. Lochalsh, Wester Ross, Scotland, July 5, 1940; d. Alexander and Catherine (MacRae) M.; m. T. Russell Walker, Nov. 24, 1973. MA, U. St. Andrews, 1962; Diploma in Scottish Studies, U. Edinburgh, 1968, MLitt, 1970, PhD, 1979; Order of the Brit. Empire, 1998; DLitt, St. And, 1999. Asst. keeper Nat. Libr. Scotland, Edinburgh, 1975—83, keeper, 1983-2000; sec. gen. coun. U. Edinburgh, 2001—. Gen. sec. Ligue des Bibliothèques Européennes de Recherche, 1994-2000; chair lit. com. Scottish Arts Coun., 1997-2003; chair Consortium of European Rsch. Librs., 2000—, NEWSPLAN 2000, 1999—; specialist adviser Scottish Arts Coun., 2003—; spl. adviser Ligne de Bibliotheques Europeenes de Recherche, 2000—. Author: (with Mary Ferguson) The Scottish Gaelic Union Catalogue, vol. I, 1984, Theories of Rhetoric in the 18th-century Scottish Sermon, 1995; editor: (with Patrick Cadell) For the Encouragement of Learning, 1989; editor Transactions of the Edinburgh Bibliographical Society, 1973-83; contbr. articles and revs. to profl. jours. Decorated Order Brit. Empire. Mem.: Scottish Libr. Assn. (hon.), Ligue des Bibliothèques Européennes de Recherche (hon.). Home: Yewbank 52 Liberton Brae Edinburgh EH16 6AF Scotland E-mail: a.matheson@tinyworld.co.uk, ann.matheson@ed.ac.uk.

**MATHESON, JAMES DAVID (JIM MATHESON),** congressman; b. Salt Lake City, 1960; m. Amy Matheson; 2 children. BA in Govt., Harvard U., Cambridge, Mass., 1982; MBA, UCLA, 1987. Worked in energy industry, 12 yrs.; founder Matheson Grp., 1998; mem. US Congress from 2nd Utah dist., 2001—, mem. fin. svcs. com., mem. transp. and infrastructure com., mem. sci. com. Mem. Salt Lake Pub. Utilities bd., Scott M. Matheson Leadership Forum. Democrat. Mem. Lds Ch. Office: US Ho Reps 1222 Longworth Ho Office Bldg Washington DC 20515 Office Phone: 202-225-3011.*

**MATHESON, LINDA,** retired social worker; b. Martna, Estonia, Mar. 29, 1918; came to U.S., 1962, naturalized, 1969; d. Endrek and Leena Endrekson; m. Charles McLaren Matheson, Feb. 5, 1955. Diploma, Inst. Social Scis., Tallinn, Estonia, 1944; MS, Columbia U., 1966, D in Social Work, 1974. Diplomate clin. social work. Social work officer UN Rehab. and Resettlement Assn., Germany, 1946-48; social worker Victorian Mental Hygiene, Australia, 1955-62; rsch. assoc., social work project dir. Arthritis Midway House, N.Y.C., 1966-68; rsch. Columbia Presbyn. Med. Ctr., N.Y.C., 1971-75; field instr. Columbia U. Sch. Social Work, 1977-79, Columbia Presbyn. Med. Ctr., NYU Sch. Social Work, 1989-90; ret., 1992. Family Found. fellow, 1966, 89-90; grantee NIMH, 1969-72. Mem. Nat. Assn. Social Workers, Nat. Wildlife Fedn., Ctr. for Study of Presidency, Internat. Platform Assn., English Spkg. Union, Alliance Francaise, Columbia U. Alumni Assn., Met. Mus. N.Y. Lutheran. Home: 30-95 29th St Astoria NY 11102-2735

**MATHESON, NINA W.,** medical researcher; MLS, DSc. Libr. Ind. Univ. Libr., Bloomington, 1961—62; libr., asst. prof. Univ. Mo. Sch. Med., St. Louis, 1962—71; spl. asst. Nat. Libr. Med., Bethesda, Md., 1971—72, chief, office of prog. planning & evaluation, 1973—74, spl. expert cons., 1982—84; dir., asst. rsch. prof. Himmelfarb Health Sci. Libr., George Washington U., 1975—80; asst. dir. Assn. Am. Med. Coll., Washington, 1980—82; dir., assoc. prof. Welch Med. Libr., Johns Hopkins U., Balt., 1984—90, dir., prof. med. info., 1991—93, dir. emerita, prof. med info., 1994—. Named Disting. prof. nursing, Vanderbilt Sch. Nursing, 1976—82. Fellow: Am. Coll. Med. Informatics, Med. Libr. Assn. (bd. dir. 1977—80, 1982—84, pres. 1983, Ida & George Eliot prize 1995); mem.: Assn. Academic Health Sci. Libr. Dir. (pres. 1987—88), Phi Beta Kappa, Beta Phi Mu. Office: William H Welch Medical Library Johns Hopkins Univ 1900 E Monument St Baltimore MD 21205-2113

**MATHEU, FEDERICO MANUEL,** university chancellor; b. Humacao, P.R., Mar. 17, 1941; s. Federico Matheu-Baez and Matilde Delgado-Vazquez; m. Myrna Delgado-Miranda, May 30, 1963; children: Federico Antonio, Rosa Myrna, Alfredo Javier, David Reinaldo. BS in Chem. Engring. U. P.R., 1962; PhD in Phys. Chemistry, U. Pitts., 1971. Chem. engr. Commonwealth Oil Refining Co., 1962-63; mem. adminstrv. staff and faculty U. P.R., 1963-78, dir. Humacao Coll., 1976-78; chancellor San German campus Inter Am. U. P.R., 1978-91; exec. dir., gen. coun. on edn. Commonwealth of P.R., Hato Rey, 1991-96; chancellor U. Metropolitana-Ana G. Méndez U. System, 1996—. Cons. in field. Author papers, reports in field. Named Disting. Educator P.R. Jaycees, 1974 Mem. Colegio de Quimicos P.R., Am. Chem. Soc., Sci. Tchrs. Assn. P.R. (pres. 1975-76), P.R. Acad. Arts and Scis., Phi Delta Kappa, Phi Tau Sigma. Home: Parque de Villa Caperra No 17 Zuania St Guaynabo PR 00966 Office: UMET PO Box 21150 San Juan PR 00928-1150 Office Phone: 787-766-1743. Business E-Mail: um_fmatheu@suagm.edu.

**MATHEW, KIP,** music educator; b. Denton, Tex., Aug. 14, 1972; s. David C. and Nancy W. Mathew; m. Keri A. Peterson, June 22, 1974; children: Dakota W., Riley A. BS in Edn., N.W. Mo. State U., Maryville, 1995, MS in Edn., 2000. Cert. vocal music grades K-12 Mo. Vocal music dir. Harrisonville (Mo.) H.S., 2000—; dir. of music Harrisonville United Meth. Ch., 2002—06. Mem.: Barbershop Harmony Soc., Am. Choral Dirs. Assn., Music Educators Nat. Conf. Methodist. Avocations: choral writing and arranging, golf, card games. Office: Harrisonville H S 1503 E Elm Harrisonville MO 64701 Office Phone: 816-380-3273 ext. 6829. Office Fax: 816-380-5853. Personal E-mail: cdmathew@hotmail.com.

**MATHEWS, BARBARA EDITH,** gynecologist; b. Oct. 5, 1946; d. Joseph Chesley and Pearl (Cieri) Mathews. AB, U. Calif., 1969; MD, Tufts U., 1972. Diplomate Am. Bd. Ob-Gyn. Intern Cottage Hosp., Santa Barbara, Calif., 1972-73, Santa Barbara Gen. Hosp., 1972-73; resident in ob-gyn Beth Israel Hosp., Boston, 1973-77; clin. fellow in ob-gyn Harvard U., Boston, 1973-76, instr., 1976-77; gynecologist Sansum Med. Clin., Santa Barbara, 1977-98; sr. scientist Sansum Med. Rsch. Inst., 1998—; med. dir., gynecologist Women's Health Svcs., Santa Barbara, 1998—. Faculty mem. postgrad. course Harvard Med. Clinic, 1989-96, vice chmn. bd. dirs., 1994-96; dir. ann. postgrad course UCLA Med. Sch. Bd. dirs. Meml. Rehab. Found., Santa Barbara, Channel City Club, Santa Barbara, Music Acad. of the West, Santa Barbara, St. Francis Med. Ctr., Santa Barbara; mem. citizen's contg. edn. adv. coun. Santa Barbara C.C.; moderator Santa Barbara Cottage Hosp. Cmty. Health Forum. Author: (with L. Burke) Colposcopy in Clinical Practice, 1977; contbg. author Manual of Ambulatory Surgery, 1982. Bd trustees Furman U., Greenville, SC, 2005—, bd. dirs., 2005—. Fellow ACOG, ACS; mem. AMA, Am. Soc. Colposcopy and Cervical Pathology (dir.

1982-84), Harvard U. Alumni Assn., Tri-counties Obstet. and Gynecol. Soc. (pres. 1981-82), Birnam Wood Golf Club (Santa Barbara), Phi Beta Kappa. Home: 2105 Anacapa St Santa Barbara CA 93105-3503 Office: 2235 De La Vina St Santa Barbara CA 93105-3815 Office Phone: 805-687-7778. Office Fax: 805-687-0012.

**MATHEWS, CHRISTOPHER KING**, biochemist, educator; b. NYC, 1937; s. Frank Pelletreau and Alison Barstow (Murphy) M.; m. Catherine Anne Zitcer, June 19, 1960; children: Lawrence Stuart, Anne Catherine. BA in Chemistry, Reed Coll., 1958; PhD in Biochemistry (USPHS fellow), U. Wash., 1962. USPHS postdoctoral fellow in biochemistry U. Pa., 1962-63; asst. prof. biology Yale U., 1964-67; asso. prof. biochemistry U. Ariz. Coll. Medicine, 1967-73, prof. biochemistry, 1973-77; prof., chmn. dept. biochemistry and biophysics Oreg. State U., 1978—2002, Disting. prof., 1991, emeritus, 2002—. Mem. virology study sect. NIH, 1977-79, mem. microbial chemistry study sect., 1979-81; Tage Erlander guest prof. Swedish Nat. Sci. Rsch. Coun., 1994-95. Author: Bacteriophage Biochemistry, 1971, Bacteriophage T4, 1983; co-author: (with K.E. Van Holde) Biochemistry, 1990, 96, 2000; contbr. numerous articles on nucleotide and nucleic acid metabolism, biochemistry of virus replication, and regulation of cellular metabolism to profl. jours.; editl. bd. Jour. Virology, 1970-80, Archives Biochemistry and Biophysics, 1973-80, Jour. Biol. Chemistry, 1994-2005, Biochem. Molecular Biology Edn., 2000-, Faseb Jour., 2006-. Am. Cancer soc. scholar grantee, 1973-74; USPHS research grantee, 1964-2002; Am. Heart Assn. grantee, 1968-78; NSF research grantee, 1980-82, 83-86, 90-2006; Eleanor Roosevelt Internat. Cancer fellow, 1984-85; recipient Discovery award Med. Research Found. Oreg., 1986, Disting. prof. award Oreg. State U. Alumni Assn., 1988. Mem.: AAUP, AAAS, Am. Soc. Cell Biology, Am. Chem. Soc., Am. Soc. Microbiology, Am. Soc. Biochemistry and Molecular Biology. Home: 3336 SW Willamette Ave Corvallis OR 97333-1507/ Office: Dept Biochemistry and Biophysics Oreg State U Corvallis OR 97331-7305 Office Phone: 541-737-1865. Personal E-mail: mathewsc2@comcast.net.

**MATHEWS, DONNA MAE**, special education educator; b. Riverside, Calif., Dec. 3, 1968; m. Ronny Lynn Mathews, July 22, 1989; children: George Franklin Bemis, Jamie Lee, Russell Jay. BS, Ball State U., 2003. Cert. spl. edn. tchr. Idaho, 2004. Spl. edn. tchr. Twin Falls Sch. Districk, Twin Falls, Idaho, 2003—. Mem.: Coun. for Exceptional Children. Office: Twin Falls Sch Dist 411 Lincoln Elem 238 Buhl St N Twin Falls ID 83301 Office Phone: 208-733-6900. Personal E-mail: mathewsd2@tfsd.k12.id.us.

**MATHEWS, E. ANNE JONES**, retired library educator, academic administrator; b. Phila. d. Edmond Fulton and Anne Ruth (Reichner) Jones; m. Frank Samuel Mathews, June 16, 1951; children: Lisa Anne Mathews-Bingham, David Morgan, Lynne Elizabeth Bietenhader-Mathews, Alison Fulton Sawyer. AB, Wheaton Coll., 1949; MA, U. Denver, 1965, PhD, 1977. Field staff Intervarsity Christian Fellowship, Chgo., 1949-51; interviewer supr. Colo. Market Rsch. Svcs., Denver, 1952-64; reference libr. Oreg. State U., Corvallis, 1965-67; program dir. Ctrl. Colo. Libr. Sys., Denver, 1969-70; inst. dir. U.S. Office of Edn., Inst. Grant, 1979; dir. pub. rels., prof. Grad. Sch. Librarianship and Info. Mgmt. U. Denver, 1970-76, prof., dir. continuing edn., 1977-80; dir. office libr. programs, office ednl. rsch., improvement US Dept. Edn., Washington, 1986-91; dir. Nat. Libr. Edn., Washington, 1992-94; cons. Acad. Ednl. Devel., Washington, 1994—; cons. mil. installation vol. edn. rev. Am. Coun. on Edn., 1990—; from asst. prof. to prof., 1977—85; ret., 2004. Mem. adv. com. Golden H.S., 1973—77; faculty assoc. Danforth Found., 1974—84; mem. secondary sch. curriculum com. Jefferson County Pub. Schs., Colo., 1976—78; vis. lectr. Simmons Coll. Sch. L.S., Boston, 1977; mem. book and libr. adv. com. USIA, 1981—91; spkr. in field; cons. USIA, 1984—85; del. Internat. Fedn. Libr. Assns., 1984—93; mem. adv. coun. White House Com. on Librs. and Info. Svcs., 1991; cons. Walden U., Mpls., 2001. Author, editor 6 books; contbr. articles to profl. jours., numerous chpts. to books. Mem. rural librs. and humanities program Colo. planning and resource bd. NEH, 1982—83; bd. mgrs. Friends Found. of Denver Pub. Libr., 1976—82; pres. Faculty Women's Club, Colo. Sch. Mines, 1963—64; bd. dirs. Jefferson County Libr. Found., 1996—, v.p., 1997—2000. Mem.: ALA (visionary leaders com. 1987—89, mem. coun. 1979—83, com. on accreditation 1984—85, orientation com. 1974—77, 1983—84, pub. rels. com.), English Speaking Union, Assn. Libr. and Info. Sci. Edn. (comm. com. 1978—80, program com. 1977—78), Colo. Libr. Assn. (pres. 1974, bd. dirs. 1973—75, continuing edn. com. 1976—80), Mountain Plains Libr. Assn. (profl. devel. com. 1979—80, pub. rels. and publs. com. 1973—75, continuing edn. com. 1973—76), Am. Soc. Info. Sci. (chmn. pub. rels. 1971), Naples Philharm. League, Pelican Bay Women's League Fla., Mountain Rep. Women's Club (v.p. 1997—2000), Mt. Vernon (Colo.) Country Club, Cosmos Club (Washington). Avocations: travel, reading, museum and gallery activities, volunteer work. E-mail: afmathews2@earthlink.net.

**MATHEWS, HARRY BURCHELL**, poet, writer, educator; b. NYC, Feb. 14, 1930; s. Edward James and Mary (Burchell) M.; m. Niki de Saint Phalle, June 6, 1949 (div. 1964); 2 children; m. Marie Chaix, July 29, 1992. BA cum laude, Harvard Coll., 1952. Faculty Bennington Coll., Vt., 1978-80; vis. lectr. Hamilton Coll., Clinton, NY, 1979, Columbia Coll., NYC, 1982-83; Musée du Louvre, Paris, 1992; French Inst., London, 1996; vis. writer Brown U., Providence, 1988, Temple U., Phila., 1990, Magdalene Coll., Cambridge, England, 1992, Berliner Literarisches Colloquium, Berlin, 1994, Duke U., 1996, New Coll. of Calif., Brown U., San Francisco Art Inst., 1997, Key West Literary Seminar, 1999, Key West Writers Workshops, 2000, New Sch. U., 2002—05; Regents lectr. U. Calif., San Diego, 2001. Founding dir. Shakespeare & Co., Lenox, Mass.; bd. dirs. Dalkey Archive Press; lectr. in field at nat., internat. colls, art ctrs. and instns. Author: The Conversions, 1962, Tlooth, 1964, The Sinking of the Odradek Stadium, 1975, Country Cooking and Other Stories, 1980, Cigarettes, 1987, 20 Lines A Day, 1988, The Orchard, 1988, The Way Home, 1988, The American Experience, 1991, Singular Pleasures, 1993, The Journalist, 1994, The Human Country, 2002, My Life in CIA, 2005, (with A. Brotchie) Oulipo Compendium, 1998, (in French) Sainte Catherine, 2000; (poetry) The Ring, Poems 1956-69, 1970, The Planisphere, 1974, Trial Impressions, 1977, Selected Declarations of Dependence, 1977, Armenian Papers: Poems 1954-84, 1987, Out of Bounds, 1989, A Mid-Season Sky: Poems 1954-89, 1991, (in French) Le savoir des rois: poèmes à perverbes, 1976, Ecrits français, 1990; (essays) Immeasurable Distances: The Collected Essays, 1981, The Case of the Persevering Maltese: Collected Essays, 2003; trans.: A Man in a Dream (Georges Perec) 1975, The Laurels of Lake Constance (Marie Chaix) 1977, The Life: Memoirs of a French Hooker (Jeanne Cordelier), 1978, Blue of Noon (Georges Bataille), 1978, Ellis Island (Georges Perec) 1996, The Dust of Suns (Raymond Roussel) 1991, various jour. articles; pub., co-editor Locus Solus, 1960-62; Paris editor The Paris Review, 1989—94; contbr. poems, stories to anthologies, articles, criticisms, reviews to profl. jours. Decorated officer Ordre Arts et Lettres (France); recipient award Fiction Writing Am. Acad. Inst. Arts and Letters, NY, 1991, Am. award for lit., 1994; grantee Deutsche Akademische Austausch Dienst, Berlin, 1991; fiction writing grantee NEA, 1982. Mem. Ouvroir de Littérature Potentielle (Paris), Bielefelder Colloquium Neuer Poesie. Avocations: travel, music, making, back-country skiing, hiking, cooking. Home (Winter): Key West FL Home (Summer): Paris France E-mail: hmathews2@cs.com.

**MATHEWS, JACK SHERMAN**, foundation administrator, retired insurance company executive; b. Jacksonville, Ill., Aug. 28, 1924; s. Franklin Roosevelt and Helen Adeline Mathews; m. Elizabeth Caldwell Mathews, Jan. 17, 1943; children: Constance Lee Paige, John Harlan. BA, Ill. Coll., 1948; grad. Sch. Ins., Purdue U., 1988. Ins. agt. Equitable Life of NY, Jacksonville 1948—55; agy. v.p. Ctrl. Nat. Life, Jacksonville, 1955—68; gen. agt. Franklin Life, Springfield, Ill., 1969—84; dir. tng. John Deere Ins. Co., 1984—90, ins. broker, 1990—95; exec. dir. Jacksonville Pub. Schs. Found., 1995—. Pres. Jacksonville C. of C., 1951—52; consistery Valley of Springfield; alderman City of Jacksonville, 1953—61, bd. police and fire com., 1981—88. With Air Corps U.S. Army, 1943—44. Mem.: Elks, Shriners, Masons. Republican. Presbyterian. Avocations: reading, golf, travel. Home: 404 Westwinds Dr Jacksonville IL 62650 Office: Jacksonville Pub Schs Found 516 Jordan Jacksonville IL 62650 Office Phone: 217-243-9411 ext. 333. Business E-Mail: jmathews@jax117.morgan.k12.il.us.

**MATHEWS, JACK WAYNE**, journalist, film critic; b. LA, Dec. 2, 1939; s. Walter Edwin and Dorothy Helen (Friley) M.; m. Lucinda Lucille Herbert, Nov. 5, 1971; children: Darren Brady, Shelby Kay. BA, San Jose (Calif.) State Coll., 1965; MS, UCLA, 1966. Reporter Riverside (Calif.) Press, 1967-69; mktg. exec. Riverside Raceway, 1969-75; columnist, editor Rochester (N.Y.) Democrat & Chronicle, 1975-78; columnist, film critic Detroit Free Press, 1978-82, USA Today, L.A., 1982-85; columnist L.A. Times, 1985-89, film editor, 1989-91; film critic Newsday, L.I., 1991-99; film critic, movie editor N.Y. Daily News, 1999—. Co-host Cinema, PBS, 1995-98; juror Montreal World Film Festival, 1993. Author: The Battle of Brazil, 1987. Democrat. Office: 450 W 33rd St New York NY 10001-2681 Office Phone: 212-210-6344. Business E-Mail: jmathews@edit.nydailynews.com.

**MATHEWS, JENNIFER KATHLEEN**, librarian, editor; b. Birmingham, Ala., June 4, 1972; d. Charles Wayne Mathews and Helen Kathleen Mobley. BA, Wellesley (Mass.) Coll., 1993; M in Libr. and Info. Studies, U. of Ala. 2004. Copy asst. Oxmoor Ho., Birmingham, 1994—96; publications coord. Wellesley (Mass.) Coll., Wellesley, 1996—97; copy editor Solutions Integrator, Framingham, 1997—99, WebMD, Atlanta, 1999—2001; sr. editor A.D.A.M. Inc., Atlanta, 2002—03; grad. asst. U. of Ala., Tuscaloosa, 2003—. Contbr. web site design. EBSCO Libr. Scholarship, U. of Ala., 2004, 2005. Mem.: Soc. of Am. Archivists. Home: 1601 Mimosa Park Rd Tuscaloosa AL 35405

**MATHEWS, JESSICA TUCHMAN**, research executive, federal official, newswriter; b. NYC, July 4, 1946; d. Lester Reginald and Barbara (Wertheim) Tuchman; m. Colin D. Mathews, Feb. 25, 1978 (div.); children: Oliver Max Tuchman, Jordan Henry Morgenthau; m. Charles G. Boyd, Dec 31, 2005. AB magna cum laude, Radcliffe Coll., 1967; PhD, Calif. Inst. Tech., 1973. Congrl. sci. fellow AAAS, 1973-74; profl. staff mem. Energy and Environment subcom. House Com. on Interior and Insular Affairs, Washington, 1974-75; dir. issues and rsch. Udall Presdl. campaign, 1975-76; dir. Office of Global Issues NSC staff, Washington, 1977-79; mem. editorial bd. The Washington Post, 1980-82; v.p., dir. rsch. The World Resources Inst., Washington, 1982-92; dep. to undersec. for global affairs U.S. Dept. State, Washington, 1993; sr. fellow Coun. on Fgn. Rels., Washington, 1993-97; columnist Washington Post, 1991-97; pres. Carnegie Endowment Internat. Peace, Washington, 1997—. Mem. numerous adv. panels Office Tech. Assessment, NAS, AAAS, EPA; adv. com. Air Products Corp., 1995—99; bd. dirs. Somalogic Inc. Trustee Rockefeller Found., Century Found., Nuc. Threat Initiative; mem. Coun. Fgn. Rels.; bd. dirs. Joyce Found., Chgo., 1984—91, Inter-Am. Dialogue, 1991—2000, Surface Transp. Policy Project, 1991—2003, Radcliffe Coll., 1992—96, Carnegie Endowment for Internat. Peace, Washington, 1992—, Rockefeller Bros. Fund, N.Y.C., NY, 1992—96, Brookings Instn., Washington, 1995—2001. Mem.: Inst. Internat. Econs. (adv. com.), Fedn. Am. Scientists (bd. dirs. 1985—87, 1988—92), Trilateral Commn. Democrat. Jewish. Office: Carnegie Endowment Internat Peace 1779 Massachusetts Ave NW Washington DC 20036-2109 Office Phone: 202-939-2210.

**MATHEWS, JOAN HELENE**, pediatrician; b. Manchester, N.H., Feb. 3, 1940; d. John Barnaby and Helen A. Wlodkoski; m. Ernest Stephen Mathews, June 1, 1965; 3 children. BS, U. N.H., 1961; MD, Columbia U., 1965. Diplomate Am. Bd. Pediatrics. Med. intern Roosevelt Hosp., N.Y.C., 1965-66; pediatric resident Babies Hosp. Columbia Presbyn. Med. Ctr., N.Y.C. 1966-68, pediatric endocrine fellow Babies Hosp., 1968-70; instr. clin. pediat. Columbia U. Coll. Physicians and Surgeons, N.Y.C., 1973-77; asst. prof. pediat. Cornell U. Med. Coll., N.Y.C., 1977-81; clin. instr. pediat. Harvard Med. Sch., Boston, 1985—2003, clin. asst. prof. pediat., 2003—; clin. assoc. children's svc. Mass. Gen. Hosp., Boston, 1985—. Fellow: Am. Acad. Pediat.; mem.: Phi Beta Kappa. Office: 777 Concord Ave Cambridge MA 02138-1053 Office Phone: 617-876-6800. Office Fax: 617-876-5713.

**MATHEWS, LINDA MCVEIGH**, newspaper editor; b. Redlands, Calif. Mar. 14, 1946; d. Glenard Ralph and Edith Lorene (Humphrey) McVeigh; m. Thomas Jay Mathews, June 15, 1967; children: Joseph, Peter, Katherine. BA, Radcliffe Coll., 1967; JD, Harvard U., 1972. Gen. assignment reporter L.A. Times, 1967-69, Supreme Ct. corr., 1972-76, corr. Hong Kong, 1977-79, China corr. Beijing, 1979-80, editor op-ed page, 1980-81, dep. nat. editor, 1981-84, dep. fgn. editor, 1985-88, editl. writer, 1988-89, editor L.A. Times Mag., 1989-92; corr. Wall Street Jour., Hong Kong, 1976-77; sr. prodr. ABC News, N.Y.C., 1992-93; nat. editor N.Y. Times, N.Y.C., 1993-96; editor USA Today, McLean, Va., 1997—. Lectr.; freelance writer. Author (with others): Journey into China, 1982, One Billion: A China Chronicle, 1983. Mem. Women's Legal Def. Fund, 1972-76; co-founder, pres. Hong Kong Montessori Sch., 1977-79; bd. dirs. Ctr. for Childhood. Mem.: Fgn. Corrs. Club Hong Kong. Office: USA Today 7950 Jones Branch Dr Mc Lean VA 22108 Office Phone: 703-854-5581. Personal E-mail: LiMathews@aol.com. Business E-Mail: lmathews@usatoday.com.

**MATHEWS, LINNEA KOONS**, science educator, librarian; b. Waterville, Maine, Jan. 27, 1957; d. Edwin Donaldson and Elizabeth (Ortquist) Koons; m. Thomas Joseph Mathews, Oct. 11, 1986. BA, Colby Coll., 1979. Cert. phys. sci. and life sci. Dept. of Edn., Maine, 1988. Science tchr. SAD 39, Buckfield, Maine, 1987—2002, Mt Blue HS, Farmington, Maine, 2002—. Digital libr. Math. and Sci. Tchg. Excellence Collaborative, Portland, Maine, 2001—. Educator (devel. assessment tasks) Maine Assessment Portfolio, Local Assessment Development (Maine Math. and Sci. Alliance Tchr. Leader, 2004). Grantee MMSTEC Digital Libr., Nat. Science Found. Mem.: NSTA, Nat. Coun. Tchrs. Math., US Eventing Assn., Am. Connemara Pony Soc. Democrat. Achievements include development of MMSTEC Digital Library. Avocations: horseback riding, cooking, gardening. Home: 230 Lovejoy Pond Rd Fayette ME 04349 Office: Mt Blue HS 129 Seamon Rd Farmington ME 04938 Office Phone: 207-778-3561. Home Fax: 207-685-4465. Personal E-mail: tayfarm@aol.com. Business E-Mail: lmathews@mbhs.msad9.k12.me.us.

**MATHEWS, MICH**, computer company executive; Grad., U. Brighton, England. With Gen. Motors; pub. relations cons., U.K div. Microsoft Corp., head corp. pub. rels. group Redmond, Wash., 1993, v.p. corp. comms., 1993—, mem., bus. leadership team, 1999—. Office: Microsoft Corp Comms one Microsoft Way Redmond WA 98052-6399

**MATHEWS, NIKKI**, mathematics educator, science educator; b. Milwaukee, Wis., Mar. 31, 1974; d. Kathleen and John Geitz; m. Daniel Mathews, Aug. 6, 2001. BA in Elem. Edn., Lakeland Coll., 1997. Teaching Certificate for Elementary Education Dept. of Pub. Instrn. WI, 1997. Tchr. Holy Family Sch., Sheboygan, Wis., 1997—98; sci. tchr. Kiel Mid. Sch., Wis., 1998—2002; math and sci. tchr. John Long Mid. Sch., Grafton, Wis., 2002—. Daycare tchr. and asst. Learning Tree Acad., Howards Grove, Wis., 1992—97. Function com. mem. Am. Cancer Soc., Sheboygan, 1997—2001. Avocations: travel, creative arts. Office: John Long Mid Sch 700 Hickory St Grafton WI 53024

**MATHEWS, SHARON WALKER**, performing company executive, secondary school educator; b. Shreveport, La., Feb. 1, 1947; d. Arthur Delmar and Nona (Frye) Walker; m. John William (Bill) Mathews, Aug. 14, 1971; children: Rebecca, Elizabeth, Anna. BS, La. State U., 1969, MS, 1971. Dance grad. asst. La. State U., Baton Rouge, 1969-71, choreographer, 1975-76; 6th grade tchr. East Baton Rouge Parish, 1971-72, health phys. edn. tchr., 1972-74; dance instr. Magnet High Sch., Baton Rouge, 1975—; artistic dir. Baton Rouge Ballet Theatre, 1975—; dance dir. Dancers' Workshop, Baton Rouge, 1971—; choreographer Baton Rouge Opera, 1989-94, Univ. H.S. Musical Theatre, 1998—; choreographer Baton Rouge Gilbert and Sullivan Soc. summer musical La. State U., 2000, 2001; choreographer Baton Rouge Little Theater, 2000, 2002. Author: East Baton Rouge Parish Dance Curriculum. Mem. La. Supts. Task Force Arts in Edn., 1999—2001, La. Content Stds. Com. Dance, 2001, East Baton Rouge Parish Curriculum Com. Dance, 1997, La. Arts Consortium, 2000—, La. Arts Content Stds. Com., 2002—, La. Arts Content Revision Com., 2002—03. Named Dance Educator of the Yr., La. Alliance Health, Phys. Edn., Recreation and Dance; named to Univ. HS Hall of Distinction, 2003, Baton Rouge Magnet HS Hall of Fame, 2003; recipient Stream award for Artistic Excellence, S.W. Regional Ballet Assn., 1991, Mayor's Pres.'s award for Excellence in the Arts, 1999, Creative Ticket award for excellence in the arts, Kennedy Ctr., 2005. Mem.: La. Assn. Health, Phys. Edn., Recreation and Dance (dance chairperson 1995), Southwestern Regional Ballet Assn. (bd. dirs. 1981—, treas., exec. bd. dirs. 1989—92). Republican. Baptist. Office: Baton Rouge Ballet Theater 11017 Perkins Rd Baton Rouge LA 70884 Office Phone: 225-767-5814.

**MATHEWS, SYLVIA MARY**, foundation administrator; b. Hinton, W.Va., June 23, 1965; d. William Peter and Cleo P. M. AB, Harvard Coll., 1987; BA, Oxford U., 1990. Assoc. McKinsey & Co., N.Y.C., 1990-92; dep. dir. econ. policy Clinton/Gore '92, Little Rock, 1992; staff dir. Nat. Econ. Coun., Washington, 1993-94; chief of staff to Sec. Robert Rubin U.S. Dept. Treasury, Washington, 1995-96; dep. chief of staff to Pres. The White House, Washington, 1997-98; dep. dir. Office of Mgmt. & Budget, Washington, 1998—2001; COO, exec. dir., The Bill and Melinda Gates Found., Seattle, 2001—. Rhodes scholar, 1987. Mem. Coun. Fgn. Rels.; bd. dirs. MetLife, Inc., 2004- Democrat. Office: The Bill & Melinda Gates Found PO Box 23350 Seattle WA 98102

**MATHEWS, TIMOTHY NEWLYN**, lawyer; b. Morristown, NJ, June 9, 1975; s. James Llewellyn and Kathleen Brown Mathews; m. Catherine Rebecca Krzyzanowski, Jan. 3, 2004; 1 child, Moses Luke. BA summa cum laude, Rutgers U., Camden, NJ, 2000; JD magna cum laude, Rutgers U., 2003. Bar: Pa. 2003, NJ 2003. Rsch. asst. Rutgers U. Sch. Law, Camden, 2001—02; assoc. Chimicles & Tikellis, LLP, Haverford, Pa., 2003—. Legal rsch. and writing tchg. asst. Rutgers U. Sch. of Law, Camden, NJ, 2001—02. Editor: Rutgers Jour. Law and Religion. Dean's Merit scholar, Rutgers Sch. Law - Camden, 2000—03. Mem.: ABA, Del. County Field and Stream. Independent. Presbyterian. Avocations: sailing, trap and skeet shooting. Home: 1518 Delmont Ave Havertown PA 19083 Office: Chimicles & Tikellis LLP 361 West Lancaster Ave Haverford PA 19041 Office Phone: 610-642-8500. Office Fax: 610-649-3633. Business E-Mail: timothymathews@chimicles.com.

**MATHEWS, VALINDA GAIL**, theater educator, gifted and talented educator; b. Honolulu, Aug. 8, 1951; d. Harold Barr and Margarite Lillian Mathews. BS in Elem. Edn., Concordia U., Seward, Nebr., 1973; MS in Gifted Edn., Emporia State U., Kans., 1985. Cert. elem. tchr. Kans., K-12 gifted tchr. Kans., K-12 English lang. learning tchr. Kans., 6-12 speech/theater tchr. Kans. Head tchr. grades 4-8 Trinity Luth. Sch., Paola, Kans., 1974—77; tchr. grade 5, gifted tchr. grades 1-6 Louisburg Elem. Sch., Kans., 1977—82; gifted tchr. grades 7-9 Shawnee Mission Schs., Kans., 1982—94; gifted tchr. grades 6-9 Turner Schs., Kans., 1996—97; tchr. speech/theater Indian Trail Jr. H.S., Oletha, Kans., 1997—. Publicist Film Soc. Greater Kansas City, Mo., 1992—94; mem. internat. studies design team Olathe Schs., Kans., 2001—03. Vol. Bradley Campaign, L.A., 1969, McGovern Campaign, Seward, 1972, Moore Campaign, Shawnee Mission, 2000, 2002, 2004. Named Tchr. of Yr., Indian Trail Jr. H.S., 2001, Master Tchr. of Yr., 2001; named to Project Success, Emporia State U., 2003, Leadership Acad., Olathe Sch. Dist., 2003. Mem.: NEA, Ednl. Theatre Assn., Mensa, Phi Delta Kappa. Democrat. Mem. Christian Ch. Avocations: travel, music, photography, theater. Office: Olathe Pub Schs PO Box 2000 Olathe KS 66063 Office Phone: 913-780-7230.

**MATHEWSON, CHRISTOPHER COLVILLE**, engineer, geologist, educator; b. Plainfield, NJ, Aug. 12, 1941; s. George Anderson and Elsa Rae (Shrimpton) M.; m. Janet Marie Olmsted, Nov. 2, 1968; children: Heather Alexis, Glenn George Anderson. BSCE, Case Inst. Tech.; 1963; MS in Geol. Engring., U. Ariz., 1965, PhD in Geol. Engring., 1971. Registered profl. engr., Tex., Ariz.; profl. geologist Tex., Oreg., Alaska. Officer, lt. Nat. Ocean Survey, 1965-71; prof. Tex. A&M U., College Station, 1981—, Regents prof., 2005—. Mem. coun. of examiners Assn. State Bds. Geology, 1994—; cons., speaker in field. Author: Engineering Geology, 1981 (C.P. Holdredge award); contbr. articles to profl. publs. Chmn. College Station Planning and Zoning Commn., 1973—81; trustee Geol. Soc. Am. Found., 2001—03. Fellow Geol. Soc. Am. (chmn. engring. geology divsn. 1986-87, Meritorious Svc. award 1991); mem. Assn. Engring. Geologists (editor bull. 1981-88, pres. 1988-89, C.P. Holdredge award 1981, F.T. Johnston Svc. award 1995, exec. dir. 1998-2002), Am. Geol. Inst. (pres. 1991-92), Nat. Coal Coun., Internat. Assn. Engring. Geologists (chmn. U.S. nat. com. 1995-98). Office: Tex A&M U Dept Geology And Geophysics College Station TX 77843-3115 Office Phone: 979-845-2488. E-mail: mathewson@geo.tamu.edu. *Commitment and dedication to the mission will lead to its successful completion regardless of the odds.*

**MATHEWSON, GEORGE ATTERBURY**, retired lawyer; b. Paterson, N.J., Mar. 31, 1935; s. Joseph B. and Christina A. (Atterbury) M.; m. Ann Elizabeth, July 31, 1975' 1 child, James Lemuel. AB cum laude, Amherst Coll., 1957; LLB, Cornell U., 1960; LLM, U. Mich., 1961. Bar: N.Y. 1963. Atty officer spl. legal assts., trial atty. FTC, Washington, 1963-65; regional atty. N.Y. State Dept. Environ. Conservation, Liverpool, 1972-73; pvt. practice Syracuse, 1967—72, 1973—2002; of counsel Banac and Mathewson, Manlius, NY, 2002—04; ret., 2004. Adj. instr. bus. law Onondaga C.C., Syracuse, 1979-84. Author: 1984 Arrives in America, 2005. Bd. dirs. South Side Businessmen, 1971-72, 88-91, v.p., 1992, pres. 1993; elder Onondaga Hill Presbyn. Ch., 1979, 82-85; dir. Manilus C. of C., 1995, v.p., 1997; trustee Steuben County Hist. Soc., 2002—05, v.p. 2005; bd. dirs. Yates County Arts Coun., Inc. 2000—, sec., 2001. Mem. ABA, Fed. Bar Assn., N.Y. State Bar Assn. (former mem. state and county bar assn. coms.), Kiwanis (bd. dirs. Onondaga club 1988-89, v.p. 1989, pres. 1989-91). Patentee safety device for disabled airplanes.

**MATHEWSON, HUGH SPALDING**, anesthesiologist, educator; b. Washington, Sept. 20, 1921; s. Walter Eldridge and Jennie Lind (Jones) M.; m. Dorothy Ann Gordon, 1943 (div. 1952); 1 child, Jane Mathewson Holcombe; m. Hazel M. Jones, 1953 (div. 1976); children: Geoffrey K., Brian E., Catherine E. Brock, Jennifer A. Jehle; m. Judith Ann Mahoney, 1979 (div. 1990). Student, Washburn U., 1938-39; AB, U. Kans., 1942, MD, 1944. Intern Wesley Hosp., Wichita, Kans., 1944-45; resident anesthesiology U. Kans. Med. Ctr., Kansas City, 1946-48; pvt. practice specializing in anesthesiology Kansas City, Mo., 1948-69; chief anesthesiologist St. Luke's Hosp., Kansas City, 1953-69; med. dir., sect. respiratory therapy U. Kans. Med. Ctr., 1969-92, assoc. prof., 1969-75, prof., 1975-92, prof. anesthesiology emeritus, respiratory care edn., 1992—; examiner schs. respiratory therapy, 1975-95; oral examiner Nat. Bd. Respiratory Therapy; mem. Coun. Nurse Anesthesia Practice, 1974-78; prof. phys. therapy edn., 1993-98. Author: Structural Forms of Anesthetic Compounds, 1961, Respiratory Therapy in Critical Care, 1976, Pharmacology for Respiratory Therapists, 1977; contbr. articles to profl. publs.; mem. editl. bd. Anesthesia Staff News, 1975-84, Respiratory Care, 1980-90, cons. editor, 1980—, editor-in-chief Respiratory Mgmt., 1989-92. Pres. Overland Park Civic Band, 1997, Overland Park Orch., 1998-2001; trustee Kansas City Mus., Kansas City Conservatory of Music, 1993—. Served to lt. comdr. USNR, 1956. Recipient Bird Lit. prize Am. Assn. Respiratory Therapists, 1976, Spl. Recognition award Am. Assn. Nurse Anesthetists, 1997. Mem. Am. Soc. Anesthesiologists (pres. 1963), Kans. Soc. Anesthesiologists (pres. 1974-77), Kans. Med. Soc. (council), Phi Beta Kappa, Sigma Xi, Lambda Beta (hon.) Office Phone: 913-588-7287. Business E-Mail: hmathews@kumc.edu.

**MATHEWSON, MARK STUART**, lawyer, editor; b. Pana, Ill., Mar. 6, 1955; s. Raymond Glenn and Frances (King) M.; m. Barbara Jean Siegert, Oct. 30, 1980; children: Margie, Molly. BA, U. Wis., Madison, 1978; JD, U. Ill., 1984; MA, U. Iowa, 1985. Bar: Ill. 1985. Reporter Ill. Times, Springfield,

1985; asst. prof. Culver Stockton Coll., Canton, Mo., 1986—87; pvt. practice Pana, Ill., 1987—2000; mng. editor Ill. Bar Jour., Ill. State Bar Assn., Springfield, Ill. legal pub. 2000—. Home: RR 1 Box 2 Athens IL 62613-9787 Office: Ill State Bar Assn Ill Bar Journal Ill Bar Ctr Springfield IL 62701

**MATHIAS, ALICE IRENE,** business management consultant; b. N.Y.C., Mar. 2, 1949; d. Murray and Charlotte (Kottle) Mathias. BS in Math., Western New Eng. Coll., 1972. Programmer Carnation Co., L.A., 1973-78; programmer/analyst Cedars-Sinai Med. Ctr., L.A., 1978-79, Union Bank, L.A., 1979-81; group leader Kaiser Found. Health Plan, Pasadena, Calif., 1981-98; sr. cons. KPMG LLP, L.A., 1998—99; prin. Info. Tech. Mgmt., L.A., 1999—. Mem. NAFE, Am. Mgmt. Assn., L.A. County Mus. Art (sponsor), Smithsonian Inst., KCET Pub. TV, Choice In Dying, U.S. Holocaust Meml. Mus. (charter mem.). Caithness Collectors Club, Statue of Liberty Ellis Island Found. Home: 2031 Dracena Drive Apt 320 Los Angeles CA 90027 Office: Info Tech Mgmt 2031 Dracena Dr Ste 320 Los Angeles CA 90027

**MATHIAS, EDWARD JOSEPH,** merchant banker; b. Camden, NJ, Nov. 11, 1941; s. Edward Joseph and Zelma (Pollack) M.; 1 child, Ellen Susannah; m. Dale Lenzner, June 5, 2004. BA, U. Pa., 1964; MBA, Harvard U., 1971. Mng. dir. T. Rowe Price Assn., Inc., Balt., 1971-93, Carlyle Group Merchant Bank, Washington, 1994—. Spl. ltd. ptnr. Trident Capital, dir. Aether Sys. Trustee U. Pa. Lt. USN, 1964—69. Mem. Coun. Fgn. Rels., Harvard Club, Univ. Club (N.Y.C.), Columbia Country Club (Chevy Chase, Md.), Robert Trent Jones Golf Club (Manassas, Va.), Coral Beach Club (Bermuda), Carnegie Abbey (Portsmouth, R.I.), The Brook (N.Y.C.), Ctr. Club (Balt.), Met. Club (Wash. DC), Georgetown Club (Wash. DC), Talbot Country Club (Easton, Md.). Republican. Home: 2804 Q St NW Washington DC 20004 Office: The Carlyle Group 1001 Pennsylvania Ave NW Washington DC 20004-2505

**MATHIAS, JAMES D.,** lawyer; b. Washington, Mar. 6, 1961; BA magna cum laude, Amherst Coll., 1983; JD magna cum laude, Georgetown Univ., 1988. Bar: Md. 1988, DC 1996, US Dist. Ct. (Md., DC districts), US Ct. Appeals (4th cir.), US Tax Ct. Law clk. Hon. J. Frederick Motz US Dist. Ct. (Md. dist.); hiring ptnr. Balt. office DLA Piper Rudnick Gray Cary, 1997—2003, now ptnr., co-chair securities litig. group, co-chair hiring group Balt. Assoc. editor Georgetown Law Jour. Bd. dir. Babe Ruth Birthplace and Mus., 2003—; dir., fin. com. mem. Fund for Ednl. Excellence, 2002—. Mem.: ABA, Balt. City Bar Assn., Fed. Bar Assn. (bd. gov., Md. chapter 2002—), Serjeants Inn Law Club, Order of Coif. Office: DLA Piper Rudnick Gray Cary 6225 Smith Ave Baltimore MD 21209-3600 Office Phone: 410-580-4208. Office Fax: 410-580-3208. Business E-Mail: james.mathias@piperrudnick.com.

**MATHIAS, LESLIE MICHAEL,** electronic manufacturing company executive; b. Bombay, Dec. 17, 1935; arrived in US, 1957; s. Paschal Lawrence and Dulcine M.; m. Vivian Mae Doolittle, Dec. 16, 1962. BSc, U. Bombay, 1957; BS, San Jose (Calif.) State U., 1961. Elec. engr. Indian Standard Metal, Bombay, 1957; sales engr. Bleisch Engring. and Tool, Mt. View, Calif., 1958-60; gen. mgr. Meadows Terminal Bds., Cupertino, Calif., 1961-63; prodn. mgr. Sharidon Corp., Menlo Park, Calif., 1963-67, Videx Corp., Sunnyvale, Calif., 1967-68, Data Tech. Corp., Mt. View, 1968-69; pres. L.G.M. Mfg., Inc., Mt. View, 1969-83; pvt. practice plating cons. Los Altos, Calif., 1983-87; materials mgr. Excel Cirs., Santa Clara, Calif., 1987-91, 93-98, acct. mgr. 1991-93, materials mgr. 1993-98, internat. materials mgr., 2000—03; buyer Planned Parenthood, San Jose, Calif., 1998-2000; acct. mgr. Streamline Circuits, Santa Clara, Calif., 2003—04. Social chmn. Internat. Students, San Jose, 1958—59. Mem. Nat. Fedn. Ind. Bus., Calif. Cirs. Assn., Better Bus. Bur., Purchasing Assn., U.S. C. of C. Roman Catholic. Avocations: electronics, reading. Home: 20664 Mapletree Pl Cupertino CA 95014-0449 Office Phone: 408-727-1418. Personal E-mail: hopalongles@yahoo.com.

**MATHIAS, MARGARET GROSSMAN,** manufacturing company executive, leasing company executive; b. Detroit; d. D. Ray and Lila May (Skinner) Grossman; children: Deborah, Robert, Lesley, Jennifer, Mary. BA, Mt. Holyoke Coll.; cert., Am. Acad. Art. Artist and co-mgr. Mary Chase Marionettes, NYC; exec. v.p. Star Five Corp., Elkhart, Ind., 1975-88, pres., treas., chmn. bd., 1985-90; sec., chmn. bd. L & J Press Corp., Elkhart, 1985-91, also chmn. bd. dirs.; chmn., pres., CEO Magland Co., Elkhart, 1986—, Magco Inc., Elkhart, 1986—, pres., chmn., CEO Tech Products, Inc., Elkhart, 1992—. Mem. fin. com. United Fund, Elkhart; mem. parents adv. bd. Furman U., Greenville, SC, 1978-83, mem. art adv. bd. Mt. Holyoke Coll., South Hadley, Mass., 1982—; pres. Tri Kappa Svc. Orgn., Elkhart, 1965-66; trustee Stanley Clark Sch., South Bend, Ind., 1977-87; bd. dirs. Bridgework Theatre, Goshen, Ind., also Balt., 1996—; mem. adv. bd. Ruthmere 1910 House Mus. designated one of Am.'s castles, 1999—; instr., spkr. etiquette Montessori Schs., Elkhart, 1998—; vol. Dept. Edn., 2003, Art Inst. Chgo., 2003; weekly vol. dept. edn. Art Inst. Chgo. Recipient Lawson Top Sculpture Purchase award Midwest Mus. Am. Art. 1990. Mem. Elkhart C. of C., Elcona Country Club (Elkhart), Woman's Athletic Club (Chgo.), Thursday Club (Elkhart, pres. 1976). Republican. Avocations: sculpting, travel, skiing. Home: 1077 Greenleaf Blvd Apt 101 Elkhart IN 46514-3562 Office: 429 S Main St Elkhart IN 46516-3210

**MATHIAS, REUBEN VICTOR (VIC MATHIAS),** organization executive, real estate investor; b. Copperas Cove, Tex., Mar. 5, 1926; s. Alvin E. and Ella L. (Teinert) M.; m. Helen I. Thoresen, Jan. 28, 1950; children: Mona, Mark, Matt. BBA, U. Tex., 1950. Cert. Chamber Exec. Dist. mgr. W.A. Shaeffer Pen Co., Youngstown, Ohio, 1950-51; mgr. Cen-Tex Fair, Temple, Tex., 1951-52; dir. info. Tex. Assn. Soil Conservation Suprs., Temple, 1952-53; mgr. membership dept. Austin (Tex.) C. of C., 1953-56, chief exec. officer, 1956-82; dir. corp. devel. Franklin Corp., Austin, 1983-86; real estate and investments, 1987-92; pres. Tex. Travel Industry Assn., Austin, 1992-96. V.p. Austin Tours, Inc.; sec. Longhorn Caverns, Inc.; chmn. bd., instr. Inst. for Orgn. Mgmt., U. Houston; mgmt. cons. not-for-profit orgns., 1997-2003. Contbr. monthly editorial Thoughts While Thinking to Austin Mag., 1961-82. Pres. Austin USO Council, 1958-59; v.p. Beautify Tex. Council, 1975-77; founding pres. Discover Tex. Assn., 1969-71; chmn. Central Tex. Blood Donor Fund, 1979. Served with U.S. Army, 1944-46. Mem. Am. C. of C. Execs., Tex. C. of C. Execs. (pres. 1965), Rotary (pres. Austin 1985-86). Lutheran. Home: 3100 Mistywood Cir Austin TX 78746-7861 *You can find happiness only by giving it to others. Much of my life has been devoted to community building through voluntary action. The fact that my career has allowed me to stay in one community has made it possible for me to make and carry out long-term plans, both for the community and personally.*

**MATHIAS, ROBERT JOSEPH,** lawyer; b. Washington, Dec. 29, 1955; s. Wilbur J. and Elizabeth J. (Christenson) M.; m. Susan Joy Sawyer, Nov. 29, 1980; children: Christine Joy, Joan Castleton. BA, Yale U., 1977; JD, Harvard U., 1980. Bar: Md. 1980, D.C. 1993, U.S. Dist. Ct. Md. 1981, U.S. Ct. Appeals (4th cir.) 1981. Law clk. Hon. Joseph H. Young U.S. Dist. Ct., Balt., 1980-81; lawyer Piper & Marbury, L.L.P., Balt., 1981-83; U.S. atty. U.S. Atty's. Office, Balt., 1983-88; ptnr. Piper & Marbury, then Piper Marbury Rudnick & Wolfe, Balt., 1988—2004; ptnr., joint global litig. leader, chmn. U.S. Litigation practice DLA Piper Rudnick Gray Cary. Balt., 2005—, mem. US exec. com., Global Bd. Faculty Md. Inst. for Continuing Legal Edn. Firm rep. Ctr. for Pub. Resources Inst. for Dispute Resolution; bd. dirs. Pub. Justice Ctr., Cmty. Mediation Prog. 1999—; trustee, mem. exec. com. Balt. Mus. Art 2001-; trustee 2000-, pres. 2001-03 Calvert Sch., chair United Way Leadership Campaign. Recipient Leadership in Law award, Daily Record, 2004. Fellow, Am. Bar Found., Am. Coll. Trial Lawyers; mem. Serjeant's Inn, Fed. Bar Assn. (bd. govs.), Md. State Bar Assn. (jud. adminstrn. sect. coun.), Harvard Law Sch. Assn. of Md. (treas.), Yale Alumni Assn. of Md. (pres. 1991-94). Office: DLA Piper Rudnick Gray Cary 6225 Smith Ave Baltimore MD 21209-3600 Office Phone: 410-580-4209. Office Fax: 410-580-3209. Business E-Mail: robert.mathias@dlapiper.com.

**MATHIESON, GARRETT ALFRED,** insurance brokerage executive; b. Bronxville, N.Y., June 12, 1952; s. William Frederick and Susan (Prager) M.; m. Doris King, June 21, 1980; children: Christine, William. BA, Hobart Coll., 1974; MBA, N.Y. U., 1980. Account rep. Marsh & McLennan, N.Y.C., 1974-77; sr. broker Frank B. Hall & Co., N.Y.C., 1977-78; risk mgmt. cons. Marsh & McLennan, N.Y.C., 1978-80, cons. mgr.-asst. v.p., 1980-82, v.p., mgr. world consulting svcs., 1982-85; mng. cons. Towers Perrin Forster & Crosby, N.Y.C., 1985-86; sr. v.p. Jardine Ins. Brokers, N.Y.C., 1986-90; exec. v.p. Rollins Burdick Hunter, N.Y.C., 1990-92; chmn., CEO, Rollins Hudig Hall Pa., Phila., 1992-94; vice chmn. Aon Risk Svcs., 1994—99; pres., CEO Willis Risk Solutions, N.Y.C., 1999—. Seminar mgr. World Trade Inst., 1982-84. Contbr. articles to profl. jour. Mem.: Univ. Glee Club, Kiawah Island Club, Shenorock Shore Club, Siwanoy Country Club. Presbyterian. Avocations: vocal music, theater, golf, tennis.

**MATHIEU, GAIL DENNISE,** ambassador; b. N.J. m. Erick Mathieu; 1 child, Yuri. BA in Spanish and Latin Am. studies, Antioch Coll., 1973; JD, Rutgers U., 1976. Bar: N.J. 1976, D.C. 1977. Dep. chief of mission in Accra; U.S. observer UNESCO, 1991—95; dep. office dir. Pacific Island affairs US Dept. State, 1995—97; dep. office dir. of West African affairs, 1997—99, dep. chief of mission Accra, 1999—2002, U.S. amb. to Niger, 2002—. Asst. prosecutor City of Newark, NJ. Home: 2420 Niamey Pl Dulles VA 20189-2420

**MATHIEU, GEORGES VICTOR ADOLPHE,** artist; b. Boulogne, France, Jan. 27, 1921; s. Adolphe Mathieu d'Escandoeuvres and Madeleine Dupre d'Ausque. Student, Facultés de droit et des lettres, Lille, France. Tchr. English; mgr. pub. rels. U.S. Lines. Exhbns. include Paris, 1950, N.Y.C., 1952, Japan, 1957, Scandinavia, 1958, Eng., Spain, Italy, Switzerland, Fed. Republic Germany, Austria and S.Am., 1959, Middle East, 1961-62, Can., 1963, Musée Municipal d'Art Moderne, Paris, 1963, Galerie Charpentier, Paris, 1965, Musée Nat. d'Art Moderne, Paris, 1967, Musée de la Manufacture Nat. des Gobelins, 1969, Antibes, 1976, Ostend, 1977, Grand Palais, Paris, 1978, Wildenstien Gallery, N.Y.C., Dominion Gallery, Montreal, Que., Can., 1979, Musée de la Poste, Paris, 1980, Palais des Papes, Avignon, 1985, Galerie Sapone, Nice, 1987, Galerie Protée, Paris, 1988, Abbaye de Chateautoux, France, 1990, Musée de Boulogne Sur Mer, St. Germain en Laye, 1994, Refectoize des Jacobins, Toulouse, 1995, Jeu De Paume, 2002, Liege (Belguim), 2003, Milano (Italia), 2003; prin. works include Hommage à la Mort, 1950, Hommage au Marechal de Turenne, 1952, Les Capetiens Partout, 1954, La Victoire de Denain, 1963, Hommage à Jean Cocteau, 1963, Paris, Capitale des Arts, 1965, Hommages aux Freres Boisseree, 1967, Hommages à Condillac, 1968, La prise de Berg op Zoom, 1969, Election de Charles Quint, 1971, Matra-Salums, 1978, La Liberation de Paris, 1980, La liberation d'Orleans par Jeanne d'Arc, 1982, Le Massacre des 269, 1985, Paradis des Orages, 1988, Les enfants de Bogota, 1989, Rumeurs de Paradis, 1991; designed gardens and bldgs. for B.C. transformer factory, Fontenay-le-comte, 1966; 16 posters for Air France; tapestries; 18 medals for Paris Mint, 1971, new 10 F coin, 1974; creator Tachism; author: Audela du Tachisme; Le privilege d'Etre; De la Revolté à Rénaissance; La Réponse de l'Abstraction lyrique; L'Abstraction Prophetique, Les Massacre de la Sensibilité, Desormais, Seul en Face de Dieu, Mathieu: 50 Years of Creation; represented in 90 museums and pub. collections. Mem. Acad. Fine Arts.

**MATHIEU, HENRI DONAT** See **SAINT LAURENT, YVES**

**MATHIEU, MICHELE SUZANNE,** grant writer, computer scientist, consultant; b. Chgo., Mar. 24, 1950; d. Joseph Edward Mathieu and Mary Ellen Fisher; m. Robert Steven Harris, May 1, 1988 (dec. Sept. 2000); life ptnr. Kathryn Ruth Huff, Aug. 16, 2002. BS in Mktg., Regents Coll., Albany, N.Y., 1998; cert. web site design, Columbia Coll., Chgo., 2000; cert. in Perl and CGI Scripting, San Diego C.C., 2003. Microsoft cert. profl. Broadcast coord. Grey-North Advt., Chgo., 1967-71; head drama dept. Patricia Stevens Coll., Chgo., 1972; instr. beginning acting Ted Liss Sch. Performing Arts, Chgo., 1973-75; project coord. grants and contracts Am. Dietetic Assn., Chgo., 1974-81, adminstr. govt. affairs, 1981-86, mgr. licensure comm., 1986-90, adminstr. nutrition svcs. payment systems, 1990-94, team leader, health care fin. team, 1994-97, dir. health care fin. team, 1998—2000, dir. mem. web, 2000—01, dir. applications devel., 2001—02; Interactive Networks Plus Tech. Group, San Diego, 2003—04; pc imaging technician Knowledge Info. Solutions, San Diego, 2004; dir. grants and contracts Virtual Reality Med. Ctr., San Diego, 2004—. Grant proposal cons. various performance arts, Chgo., 1978-2000; med. reporter, writer various internat. clients, 1994-; PC cons., Chgo., 1994-2002, San Diego, 2002—. Editor Legis. Newsletter, 1981-86; contbg. editor Nutrition Forum, 1986, Courier, 1987—2002; contbr. articles to profl. jours., mags., newspapers. Website project mgr. DigitalEve, Chgo., 2001. Ill. Arts Coun. grantee, 1981. Mem. Am. Med. Writers Assn., Am. Soc. Assn. Execs. (Excellence in Govt. award 1989), WebSanDiego. Avocations: reading, fitness walking, sailing.

**MATHIEU, SUSAN LEIFER,** recreational therapist, educator; b. Long Beach, Calif., Nov. 13, 1952; d. Sally and Oscar Solomon Leifer; m. Jeff Mathieu, Mar. 20, 1976; children: Joseph Gabriel Mathieu 18, Daniel Jacob Mathieu 16. BA, Calif. State U., Long Beach, 1975, MS, 1992; EdD, U. La Verne, 1999. Cert. therapeutic recreation specialist Nat. Coun. Therapeutic Recreation, 1984. Lectr. Calif. State U., Dominguez Hills, 1990—2002, asst. prof. Long Beach, 2002—. Therapeutic recreation tng., cons. ChildNet, Long Beach. 1989—. Contbr. articles to profl. jours. Recreation commr. City of Long Beach, Parks, Recreation and Harbor Recreation Commn. 1981—85; bd. dirs. Jr. League, Long Beach, 1983—2005, PTA, Rancho Palos Verdes, Calif., 1994—99; sisterhood bd. dirs. Congregation Ner Tamid, Rancho Palos Verdes, Calif., 2000—04. Recipient Spl. Recognition award, Cath. Charities Family Shelter for Homeless, 1996, Golden Rule award, JC Penny, 1998. Mem.: Nat. Recreation and Pk. Assn. (assoc.; spkr. 1996—2005, Profl. award Pacific S.W. region 1984, 1994), Long Beach Area Child and Domestic Violence Coun. (assoc.; spkr.), Calif. Pk. and Recreation Soc. (assoc.; com. chair 1998—99, Outstanding Therapeutic Recreation Educator award 1996), Calif. State U. Long Beach Alumni Assn. (bd. dirs. 2004—05), Guild for Infant Survival (assoc.; parent support 1990—95), Chi Kappa Rho Gamma (assoc.; scholarship com. 2002—04, mem. women in leisure svcs.). Jewish. Achievements include first to introduced reading to former gang members in a residential treatment facility. Avocations: kayaking, drums, international folk dancing, developing comedy routines as a teaching tool, guitar. Office: Calif State Univ Long Beach 1250 Bellflower Blvd Long Beach CA 90840 Office Phone: 562-985-8075. Office Fax: 562-985-8154. Business E-Mail: smathieu@csulb.edu.

**MATHIEU BYERS, DEBORAH ANNE,** performing company executive; d. Edward F. and Marjorie V. Mathieu; m. Stephen Paul Byers, June 29, 1996. Studied with, Nafe Katter, Jerry Rojo, 1976—77; BFA, U. Conn., 1978; studied at, A.C.T., San Francisco, 1978; studied with, Ray Burke, 1978, Charles Hampton and Stuart Chenoweth, 1979; MA, San Francisco State U., 1979; studied with, Michael Graves, N.Y.C., 1984; master classes, Kate Collins, N.Y.C., 1987; studied at, Video Assoc., 1990, Three of Us Studios, N.Y.C., 1994, HB Studios, 1994. Exec. asst. to pres. and owner prodn. coord. Silver Blue Prodn., Inc., N.Y.C., 1982—86; freelance promoter and pub. rels. coord. Deborah Mathieu Consulting, Inc., 1984—90, designer makeup, hair and costume, 1987—90; assoc. casting dir. Stark Naked Prodn. Elsie Stark Casting, 1994—97; exec. asst. to owner R & V Internat. Inc., 1986—2002; chairperson acting technique dept. Sch. for Film and TV, 1995—2000; founder, president and producing artistic dir. Streetlight Prodn., Inc., 2000—; Pvt. acting coach, N.Y.C., 1995—. Dir.: (plays) Chamber Music, 1979, Ghost Sonata, 1978, Your Carolyn Skiddoo Period, 1995, Communion, 2002, Cityscapes, 2002, Yearning for the Fourth Grade, 2002, Leavin' the Life & Hangin' at Joe's, 2003, Faith, Hope and Charity, 2004, The American Dream and Other Fractured Fairy Tales, 2005; actor: Bus Stop, 1978, A Midsummer's Night Dream, 1978, West Side Story, 1978, Once a Thousand Days, 1979, Macbeth, 1979, Chamber Music, 1980, A Faded Rose, 1980, Comedy Tonite!, 1982, All Ye Faithful, 1982, Reasonable Circulation, 1983, Lullaby Eve, 1986, Law School Suicide, 1990, Mary Tudor, 1993, Mary Stuart, 1994,

The Knickerbockers, 1995, Nicola Sacco & Bartolomeo Vanezetti, 1999, Hamlet, 2001; dir.; actor: (plays) Leaving My Apartment & Other Urban Adventures, 2003; (films) The Deadliest Season, 1976, U.H.F., 1988, Guess Who?, 1989, Dreamstreets, 1989, Funny About Love, 1989, State of Grace, 1989, Quiet on the Set!, 1990, Heidi Loves Missy, 1993, Annie, 1995; (TV series) The Days and Nights of Molly Dodd, 1988—90, Saturday Night Live, 1994, (commercials and industrial films); choreographer Jumpers, San Francisco, 1977, The Darkening of the Light, 1978; costumer: The Tempest, 1978. Mem.: AFTRA, SAG, Theatre Comm. Guild, Actors Equity Assn., The Drama League. Democrat. Office: Streetlight Prodns 110-64 Queens Blvd PMB 175 Forest Hills NY 11375

**MATHILE, CLAYTON LEE,** pet food company executive; b. Portage, Ohio, Jan. 11, 1941; s. Wilbert and Helen (Good) Mathile; m. Mary Ann Maas, July 7, 1962; children: Cathy, Tim, Mike, Tina, Jennie. BA, Ohio No. U., 1962; postgraduate studies, Bowling Green State U., 1964; DBA (hon.), Ohio No. U., 1991. Acct. GM, Napoleon, Ohio, 1962-63, Campbell Soup Co., Napoleon, 1963-65, buyer, 1965-67, purchasing agt., 1967-70; gen. mgr. The Iams Co., Dayton, Ohio, 1970-75, v.p., 1975-80, chief exec. officer, 1980-90, chmn., 1990-99, also dir.; ret., 1999. Mem. Pet Food Inst.; bd. dirs. Midwest Grp., Cin., Bush Bros. Co., Knoxville, Tenn., The Iams Co., 1999—. Author: A Bus. Owner's Perspective on Outside Bds. Trustee Chaminade-Julienne HS, Dayton, 1987—, U. Dayton; mem. adv. bd. coll. bus. Ohio No. U., Ada, 1987—, also trustee. Named Best of Best Ctr. for Values Rsch., Houston, 1987; named one of 400 Richest Ams. Forbes mag., 2006. Mem. Am. Mgmt. Assn., Am. Agt. Assn. Roman Catholic. Avocations: travel, swimming, golf. Office: The Iams Co PO Box 13615 Dayton OH 45413-0615

**MATHIS, CATHERINE J.,** publishing executive; BS in Bus. Adminstrn., Univ. Minn., 1975, MBA in Mktg., Mgmt. Info. Sys., 1979. Mkt. rsch. analyst Internat. Paper Co., Purchase, NY, 1980—81, mgr. bus. sys., 1981—84, mgr. sales analysis, 1984—87, mgr. shareholder comm., 1987—92; former v.p. corp. rels. Overseas Shipholding Group Inc.; dir. investor rels NY Times Co., NYC, 1997—2000, v.p. corp. comm., 2000—; and spokesperson NY Times and The Times Co., 2000—. Dir. Nat. Investor Rels. Inst., 2005—. Office: Corp Comm NY Times Co 229 W 43rd St New York NY 10036 Office Phone: 212-556-1981. Business E-Mail: mathis@nytimes.com.*

**MATHIS, DONALD RAYMOND,** music educator; b. Omaha, Nebr., May 10, 1926; d. Howard Donald and Neva Morpheu Mathis; m. Joan DiVito; children: William, Christine, Barbara, Deborah, Mary Jane. MusB, Ill. Wesleyan U., 1949; MusM, Bradley U., 1952; MA, Westminster Choir Coll., 1956. Min. of edn. and music First Federated Ch., Peoria, Ill., 1949—51, Faith United Ch. of Christ, Chgo., 1951—53; prof. Westminster Choir Coll., Princeton, NJ, 1953—56; min. of music First Presbyn. Ch., St. Petersburg, Fla., 1956—73, Second Presbyn. Ch., Ft. Lauderdale, Fla., 1973—80; prof. Broward C.C., Ft. Lauderdale, Fla., 2000—. Pres. St. Petersburg (Fla.) Symphony, 1960—65; v.p. Fla. Philharmonic Chores, Ft. Lauderdale, Fla., 1990—2000; pres. Coun. of Churches, Ft. Lauderdale, Fla., 1958—70. Founder, musical dir. St. Petersburg Boy Choir, St. Petersburg, Fla., 1958—73, Fla. Singing Sons, Ft. Lauderdale, Fla., 1974—87. With USN, 1944—46. Mem.: Voice Found. Democrat. Presbyn. Avocation: sailing. Home: 1200 N Ft Lauderdale Bch Blvd Fort Lauderdale FL 33304 Office Phone: 954-673-2008. E-mail: donaldrmathis@bellsouth.net.

**MATHIS, JAMES FORREST,** retired petroleum company executive; b. Dallas, Sept. 28, 1925; s. Forrest and Martha (Godbold) M.; m. Frances Ellisor, Sept. 4, 1948; children: Alan Forrest (dec.), Lisa Lynn Lambeth. BSChE, Tex. A&M U., 1946; MS, U. Wis., 1951, PhD, 1953. Rsch. engr. Humble Oil & Refining Co., Baytown, Tex., 1946-49, 53-61, mgr. R & D, 1961-63, mgr. Splty. products planning, 1963-65; v.p. Exxon Rsch. & Engring. Co., Linden, NJ, 1966-68; sr. v.p., dir. Imperial Oil Ltd., Toronto, Ont., Canada, 1968-71; v.p. tech. Exxon Chem. Co., Florham Pk., NJ, 1971-80; v.p. sci. and tech. Exxon Corp., N.Y.C., 1980-84; ret., 1984. Cons. Arthur D. Little, 1985-92, ChemShare Corp., 1989-92; chmn. N.J. Commn. Sci and Tech., 1988-96; dir. Laser Recording Systems, Inc., 1989-93, N L Industries, 1985-86, Hanlin Corp., 1989-99, Beaver Lake Realty Co., 1995-98. Bd. dirs. Chem. Industry Inst. Toxicology, 1975-83, treas., 1977-80, chmn., 1980-83; bd. dirs. Tex. Inst. for Advancement of Chem. Tech., 2001-; trustee Wis. Alumni Rsch. Found., 1984-2004, pres., 1993-97; bd. mem. sci. and tech. of Nat. Rsch. Coun., 1987-89, chem. weapon stockpile demilitarization comn., 1998-2001. Served with AC, USNR, 1944-45 Recipient Disting. Alumni award Coll. Engring. Tex. A&M U., 1982, Disting. Svc. citation Coll. Engring. U. Wis., 1969. Fellow Am. Inst. Chem. Engrs. (interim exec. dir., sec. 1987-88, Robert L. Jacks award in Mgmt. 1985, Van Antwerpen award for Svc. to Inst. 1989); mem. AAAS, NAE, Am. Chem. Soc. (Earle B. Barnes award for Chem. Rsch. Mgmt. 1984), Sigma Xi, Phi Lambda Upsilon, Tau Beta Pi. Presbyterian. Achievements include 2 patents in field. Home: 2714 S Southern Oaks Dr Houston TX 77068-2600 Office Phone: 281-587-0117. Personal E-Mail: jfmathis@aol.com.

**MATHIS, JOHN PRENTISS,** lawyer; b. New Orleans, Feb. 10, 1944; s. Robert Prentess and Lena (Horton) M.; m. Karen Elizabeth McHugh, May 31, 1966; children: Lisa Lynne Mathis Kirkpatrick, Andrew P. BA magna cum laude, So. Meth. U., 1966; JD cum laude, Harvard U., 1969. Bar: Calif. 1970, D.C. 1975, U.S. Ct. Appeals (D.C. cir.) 1972, U.S. Ct. Appeals (5th cir.) 1975, U.S. Ct. Appeals (3d cir.) 1980, U.S. Supreme Ct. 1982. Assoc. Latham & Watkins, L.A., 1969-71; spl. asst. to gen. counsel FPC, Washington, 1971-72; gen. counsel Calif. Pub. Utilities Commn., San Francisco, 1972-74; assoc. Baker & Botts, Washington, 1974-76, ptnr., 1976-92, Hogan & Hartson, Washington, 1992—2000; v.p., assoc. gen. counsel regulatory affairs Edison Mission Energy, Washington, 2000—06. Mem. ABA (litig. sect., chmn. energy litig. com. 1985-89, divsn. dir. 1989-90, chmn. legis. com. 1990-94, rep. to coord. group energy law 1992-97), Fed. Energy Bar Assn., Harvard U. Law Sch. Assn. D.C. (past pres.), Congl. Country Club, Met. Club (Washington), Talbot Country Club (Easton, Md.). Republican. Episcopalian. Office: Edison Mission Energy 555 12th St NW Ste 640 Washington DC 20004 Personal E-Mail: john.p.mathis@gmail.com.

**MATHIS, KAREN J.,** lawyer, legal association administrator; b. Providence, Nov. 7, 1950; d. Charles H. Young and Elizabeth L. (Kriegal) Ballard; m. Stan A. Mathis, Sept. 7, 1970 (div. 1978). BA, U. Denver, 1972; JD, U. Colo., 1975; postgrad., U. Colo., Denver, 1975-76; LLD, Sienna Coll., 2003, Sturm Law Sch., U. Denver, 2005. Bar: Colo. Supreme Ct. 1975, U.S. Dist. Ct. 1975, U.S. Ct. Appeals (10th cir.) 1978, U.S. Tax Ct. 1980. Tax acct. Peat Marwick Mitchell, Denver, 1975-76; ptnr. Rothenberg & Mathis, Denver, 1976-79; sole practitioner Denver, 1979-80; assoc. Sterling & Simon PC, Denver, 1980-83; ptnr. Hughes & Dorsey, Denver, 1983-84; shareholder, dir. Sterling & Miller, Denver, 1984-86; pres. The Mathis Law Firm, Denver, 1986—2004; pres., CEO Mathis Asset Mgmt., Inc., Denver, 1989—2004; ptnr. McElroy, Deutsch, Mulvaney & Carpenter LLP, Denver, 2004—. Contbr. articles to profl. jours. Bd. dirs. CORRA, Denver, Planned Parenthood Rocky Mountains, Denver; bd. dirs., v.p. Rocky Mountain Meml. Soc., Denver; mem. adv. com. Colo. Dept. Social Svcs., Denver. Named Disting. Alumni U. Colo., 1992; recipient Order of the Coif (hon.) U. Colo., 2002 Mem. ABA (ho. of dels. 1982-, interim Colo. state del. 1992-2000, chair standing com. on mem., 1994-97, chair commn. on women in the profession, 1997-2000, chair ho. dels., 2000-02, chair gen. practice, solo & small firm section, 2002-03, pres-elect, 2005-06, pres., 2006-), Colo. Bar Assn. (1st v.p. 1992-93, bd. govs. 1983-, outstanding young lawyer in Colo.). Denver Bar Assn. Office: McElroy Deutsch Mulvaney & Carpenter LLP Mile High Ctr 1700 Broadway Ste 1900 Denver CO 80290

**MATHIS, LUSTER DOYLE,** academic administrator, political scientist, educator; b. Gainesville Ga., May 5, 1936; s. Luster and Fay Selena (Wingo) M.; m. Rheba Burch, June 5, 1958; children: Douglas James, Deborah Jane. AB, Berry Coll., 1958; MA, U. Ga., 1958, PhD (Univ. Alumni Found. fellow), 1966. Asst. prof. polit. sci. Brenau Coll., Gainesville, 1960-61; asso. prof. Calif. Baptist Coll., 1961-62, Belmont Coll., Nashville, 1962-64; asso. prof., head dept. polit. sci. W.Ga. Coll., Carrollton, 1965-68, prof., 1969-75, head dept., 1969-71, chmn. div. grad. studies, 1970-73; assoc. dean, 1972-75; research asso., asst. editor Papers of Thomas Jefferson Princeton U., 1968-69; v.p., dean of coll. Berry Coll., Mt. Berry, Ga., 1975-93, v.p. acad. affairs, 1993-99, provost, 1999-2000, coll. historian, prof. govt., 2000—03. Cons. Citizens Com. on Ga. Gen. Assembly. Co-author: Courts as Political Instruments, 1970. Mem. Ga. Democratic Charter Commn., 1974-75; mem. consumer adv. com. Floyd Med. Center, 1978-80. Fellow, Nat. Hist. Publs. Commn., 1968—68. Mem. Am. Assn. Higher Edn., Am. Conf. Acad. Deans, Ga. Polit. Sci. Assn. (pres. 1968-69). Democrat. Baptist. Office: 200 Salt Air Dr Unit 136 Saint Simons Island GA 31522 Business E-Mail: dmathis@berry.edu.

**MATHIS, MARSHA DEBRA,** customer service administrator; b. Detroit, Dec. 22, 1953; d. Marshall, Jr. and Anita Willene (Biggers) Mathis. BS, Fla. State U., 1978; MBA, Miss. Coll., 1982. With telecom. dept. Fla. State Dept. Safety, Tallahassee, 1973-76; asst. to chmn. Tallahassee Savs. and Loan Assn., 1976-78; sales engr. Prehler, Inc., Jackson, Miss., 1978-82; mktg. mgr. Norand Corp., Arlington, Tex., 1982-87; v.p. mktg. and sales Profl. Datasolutions, Inc., Irving, Tex., 1987-88; v.p. mktg. and sales, ptnr. Target Systems, Inc., Irving, 1988-89, also bd. dirs.; v.p. mktg. Profl. Datasolutions, Inc., Irving, 1990—2002, Onvance, Atlanta, 2002; v.p. bus. devel. Performance Retail, Austin, Tex., 2004—. Contbr. articles to profl. jours. Advisor Am. Diabetes Assn., Jackson, 1983—, Diabetes Found. Miss., Jackson, 1983—. Mem.: Network Exec. Women, Nat. Assn. Convenience Stores (mem. industry task force 1987—88), Nat. Adv. Group, Internat. Platform Assn. Republican. Roman Catholic. Avocations: scuba diving, sailing, reading, coin collecting/numismatics. Home: 1615 Purple Sage Dr Cedar Park TX 78613 Office: Dresser Wayne Bldg 2 Ste 101 6500 River Place Blvd Austin TX 78730 Office Phone: 512-527-6623. Personal E-mail: marshamathis@austin.rr.com. Business E-Mail: marsha_mathis@performanceretail.com.

**MATHIS, PRUDENCE MARCHMAN,** realtor; b. Throckmorton, Tex., Aug. 21, 1956; adopted d. Jack Robert and Grace Alma Hurst Brockman; m. Leonard Renfro Marchman, June 8, 1974 (div. May 4, 1990); children: Jeremy Robert Marchman, Caitlin Breanne Marchman; m. Jimmy Dale Mathis, June 9, 1990 (div. May 24, 1999). Student, Mountain View Coll., Dallas, 1985—90. Comml. ins. & workers compensation clk. Lovett-Meredith Clinic, Olney, Tex., 1977—79; credit corr., accounts receivable clk., fin. inventory control analyst, accounts payable clk., bid clk. Am. Hosp. Supply Co., Grand Prairie, Tex., 1979—85; credit analyst/adjuster Gifford-Hill & Co., Inc., Dallas, 1985—88; acctg. clk. - part-time Roy Rabenaldt, CPA, Farmers Branch, Tex., 1988—89; office mgr. Evelyn Cannon Showroom of Women's Apparel, Dallas, 1989—90; asst. office mgr./payroll coord. Site Concrete, Inc., Grand Prairie, 1990—94; customer svc. rep./accounts receivable collector Occupl. Health Centers, Dallas, 1994—95; human resources mgr., benefits specialist Site Concrete, Inc., Grand Prairie, 1995—98; exec. adminstrv. asst. Kelly Services for Johnson & Johnson Med., Arlington, Tex., 1998—2000; travel coord. Galactic Mktg., Arlington, Tex., 2000—01; human resources mgr. Site Concrete, Inc., Grand Prairie, 2001—02; ptnr. and co-owner Quest Residential & Comml. Properties, Ltd, Grand Prairie, Tex., 2002—, REALTOR, 2005—. Trainer Site Concrete, Inc., Grand Prairie, 2002—02. Vol. Habitat for Humanity, Grand Prairie, Tex., 2001—05; vol. adult leader and facilitator Boy Scouts Am., Grand Prairie, 1999—; mem. Grand Prairie C. of C.; mem. chancel choir First United Meth. Ch., Grand Prairie, 2001—02. Mem.: NAFE (assoc.), Women's Coun. of Realtors, Grand Prairie Bd. Realtors (mem. hospitality com., edn. com.), Metro Tex. Assn. Realtors, Tex. Assn. Realtors, Nat. Assn. Realtors, Am. Bus. Women's Assn. (assoc.; sec. 1999—2000), Phi Theta Kappa. Methodist. Avocations: reading, singing, photography, crocheting, travel. Office: 4116 S Carrier Pkwy Ste 280-827 Grand Prairie TX 75052 Personal E-mail: prudencemathis@comcast.net.

**MATHIS, SAMANTHA,** actress; b. N.Y.C., May 12, 1970; d. Bibi Besch. Actress: (films) Forbidden Sun, 1989, Pump Up the Volume, 1990, This is My Life, 1992, FernGully: The Last Rainforest (voice), 1992, Super Mario Bros., 1993, The Music of Chance, 1993, The Thing Called Love, 1993, Little Women, 1994, Jack and Sarah, 1995, How to Make an American Quilt, 1995, The American President, 1995, Broken Arrow, 1996, Museum of Love, 1996, Sweet Jane, 1998, Waiting for Woody, 1998, Freak City, 1999, The Simian Line, 2000, American Psycho, 2000, Attraction, 2000, The Punisher, 2004, (TV movies) Aaron's Way: The Harvest, 1988, Cold Sassy Tree, 1989, American Nuclear, 1989, Extreme Close-Up, 1990, 83 Hours 'Til Dawn, 1990, To My Daughter, 1990, Harsh Realm, 1999, Mermaid, 2000, Collected Stories, 2002; (TV series) Knightwatch, 1988-89, Aaron's Way, 1988, Harsh Realm, 1999, First Years, 2001; (TV miniseries) The Mists of Avalon, 2001. Office: Creative Artists Agy care Rick Kurtzman 9830 Wilshire Blvd Beverly Hills CA 90212-1804

**MATHIS, SHARON BELL,** retired writer, librarian, curator; b. Atlantic City, Feb. 26, 1937; d. John Willie and Alice Mary (Frazier) Bell; m. Leroy F. Mathis, July 11, 1957 (div. Jan. 1979); children: Sherie, Stacy, Stephanie. BA, Morgan State Coll., 1958; M.L.S., Catholic U. Am., 1975. Interviewer Children's Hosp. D.C., Washington, 1958-59; tchr. Holy Redeemer Elem. Sch., Washington, 1959-65, Charles Hart Jr. H.S., Washington, 1965-72; spl. edn. tchr. Stuart Jr. H.S., Washington, 1972-74; libr. Benning Elem.Sch., Washington, 1975-76, Friendship Ednl. Ctr. (now Patricia R. Harris Ednl. Ctr.), 1976-95, ret., 1995. Writer-in-charge children's lit. div. D.C. Black Writers Workshop; writer-in-residence Howard U., 1972-73 Author: Brooklyn Story, 1970, Sidewalk Story, 1971 (Council on Interracial Books for Children award 1970) (Teacup Full of Roses, 1972 (Outstanding Book of YY. award New York Times 1972), Ray Charles, 1973 (Coretta Scott King award 1974), Listen for the Fig Tree, 1974, The Hundred Penny Box, 1975 (Boston Globe-Horn Book Honor book 1975, Newbery Honor Book 1976), Cartwheels, 1977, Red Dog Blue Fly: Football Poems, 1991 (Children's Book of Yr. award Bank St. Coll. 1992), Red Dog Blue Fly. An American Bookseller (Pick of the List 1995), Running Girl: The Diary of Ebonee Rose, 1997, Ray Charles, 2001. Mem. bd. advisers lawyers com. D.C. Commn. on Arts, 1972. Nominated Books for Brotherhood list NCCJ, 1970; recipient D.C. Assn. Sch. Librs. award 1976, Arts and Humanities award Archdiocese of Washington Black Secretariat, 1987; Weekly Reader Book Club fellow Bread Loaf Writers Conf., 1970, MacDowell Colony fellow, 1978. Roman Catholic. *My success is due to the glorious African blood which flows throughout my body— and to the dignity, intelligence, strength, pride, efforts, and faith of my very creative parents and all people who have helped me.*

**MATHISEN, DOUGLAS J.,** thoracic surgeon; b. Spring Valley, Ill., 1948; MD, U. Ill. Diplomate Am. Bd. Thoracic Surgery, Am. Bd. Surgery. Thoracic surgeon Mass. Gen. Hosp., Boston, 1995—; assist. prof. thoracic surgery Harvard U. Med. Sch., 1989—99, Hermes C. Grillo prof. thoracic surgery, 1999—; chief general thoracic surgery Mass. Gen. Hosp. Fellow Am. Coll. Surgeons; mem. AMA, ACCPA, Am. Assn. Thoracic Surgery, Soc. Thoracic Surgery (bd. mem.), Cardiothoracic Surgery Network, Thoracic Surgery Directors Assn., Thoracic Surgery Found. for Rsch. & Edn., Soc. Thoracic Surgeons (treas.). Office: Mass Gen Hosp Thoracic Surgery Blake 1570 55 Fruit St Boston MA 02114 Business E-Mail: dmathisen@partners.org.

**MATHISEN, HOWARD,** psychologist, educator, minister; b. Bklyn., June 3, 1938; s. Olaf and Hjordis K. (Skjaerum) Mathisen; m. Sue Jane Andrews, June 13, 1960 (div. 1975); m. Kathleen Ann Poce, Sept. 20, 1980 (dec. 1987); m. Carolyn Anne Burroughs, Aug. 22, 1992. BA in Psychology, Taylor U., Upland, IN, 1956—60; MDiv, Phila. Theol. Sem., 1960—63; postgrad. in Theology, Luth. Theol. Sem., 1964—65; MA in Religion, Concordia Sem., St. Louis, 1966—67; postgrad. Alcoholism studies, Rutgers U., 1975; postgrad. in Psycholoy, Assumption Coll., Worcester, MA, 1971—76; DMin in Psychology, Andover Newton Theol. Sch., 1972—76. Lic. psychologist, Mass.; marriage and family therapist, Mass.; cert. diplomate of sex therapy Am. Assn. Sexuality Educators, Counselors and Therapists; diplomate in marital and sex therapy Am. Bd. Family Psychology; diplomate Am. Bd. Sexology. Pastor Christ Meml. Ch., Phila., 1962-66, Zion Luth. Ch., Webster,

Mass., 1967-73; dir. Human Svcs. Ctr. Hubbard Regional Hosp., Webster, 1973-81; pvt. practice psychology Boylston, Mass., 1976-81; co-dir. Counseling Affiliates, Worcester, Mass., 1981-97; dir. pastoral counseling Boston Road Clinic, Worcester, 1997—2001; dir. credentialing svcs. Capstan, Worcester, 1998-99; asst. pastor Concordia Luth. Ch., Worcester, 1975-98; dir. min. asst. program New Eng. Synod, Evangelical Luth. Ch., 1991—; psychologist Prescott Health Care, 2002—. Adj. instr. psychology Nichols Coll., Dudley, Mass., 1981, Assumption Coll., Worcester, 1983-86. Dean ctrl. Mass. conf. New Eng. Synod, Luth. Ch., 1988-90; bd. dirs. Luth. Svcs. Assn. New Eng., 1973-87, vice chmn., 1983-85, chmn., 1985-87; bd. dirs. Luth. Home of Worcester, 1987-92, chmn., 1987-89; chmn. bldg. com. Luth. Nursing Home, Worcester, 1977-79; chmn. Family Svcs. Com., 1981-83; mem. Mass. Adv. Com. Continuing Edn. for Nursing, 1979-81; bd. dirs. Family Planning Svcs. Ctrl. Mass., 1975-81; mem. tech. adv. subcom. substance abuse Ctrl. Mass. Health Sys. Agy., 1979-80. Fellow Acad. Family Psychology, Am. Acad. Clin. Sexologists; mem. APA, Am. Assn. Marriage and Family Therapy, Mass. Psychol. Assn., Mass. Assn. Marriage and Family Therapy, Acad. Managed Care Providers. Lutheran. Avocations: travel, photography. Home: 6 Camelot Cir Dudley MA 01571-6110 Office: Prescott Health Care 130 Linden St Worcester MA 01609-1969 Office Phone: 508-754-1803. E-mail: mathisen@charter.net.

**MATHIS-THORTON, DIANNA DAWN,** protective services official, writer, publishing executive, not-for-profit developer; b. Dallas, Tex., Nov. 16, 1967; d. Jimmie Lee and Billie Jo Mathis; m. Ryan Lee Thornton, Dec. 22, 2002. BS Home security, Fla. Met. Univ., 1989—. Cert. crime prevention inspector Tex., domestic violence counselor. Exec. sec. Sears logistic Svcs., Dallas, 1986—90; police officer Dallas police Depart., Dallas, 1991—; owner, pres. Mathis Pub. Co., Dallas, 1991—; founder, pres. Domestic Awareness, Dallas, 2003 —. Instr. safety first Dallas after sch. program, 2004—; future writers of Am., 2005—. Author: Dianna'a poetry of Life, 2001, Safety First Children's Guide, 2004, Future Writers of Am., 2005. Mem. counselor Victim relief Ministries, Dallas, 2004—; mentor, counselor Speak Life Ministries, Dallas, 1999—. Recipient Officer of the Yr, Woman of Dallas Inc., 1998, Nat. Assn. ins. Woman of Dallas Inc., 1998, Life Saving award, Dallas police dept., 1997. Mem.: Intenat. Code Coun. Christian. Avocations: reading, writing, poetry, movie scripts. Office: Dallas Police Dept 725 N Jim Miller Dallas TX 75217

**MATHOG, ROBERT HENRY,** otolaryngologist, educator; b. New Haven, Apr. 13, 1939; s. William and Tiby (Gans) M.; m. Deena Jane Rabinowitz, June 14, 1964; children: Tiby, Heather, Lauren, Jason. AB, Dartmouth Coll., 1960; MD, NYU, 1964. Diplomate Am. Bd. Facial Plastic and Reconstructive Surgery. Intern Duke Hosp., Durham, NC, 1964-65, resident surgery, 1965-66, resident otolaryngology, 1966-69; practice medicine, specializing in otolaryngology Mpls., 1971-77, Detroit, 1977—; chief of otolaryngology Hennepin County Med. Center, Mpls., 1972-77; asst. prof. U. Minn., 1971-74, asso. prof., 1974-77; prof., chmn. dept. otolaryngology Wayne State U. Sch. Medicine, 1977—. Chief otolaryngology Hennepin County Hosp., Mpls., 1972-77, Harper-Grace Hosps., Detroit, 1977—, Detroit Receiving Hosp., 1977-92; cons. staff VA Hosp., Allen Park, Minn., 1977—, Children's Hosp., Detroit, 1977—, Hutzel Hosp., Detroit, 1966, St. Joseph Mercy Hosp., Oakland, Mich., 2001; mem. adv. coun. Nat. Inst. Deaf and Other Communicable Disorders NIH, 1992-96; chief otolaryngology, head and neck surgery June Hosp., 1994-95; pres., chair Lin Haig Carlos, 1999-. Author: Otolaryngology Clinics of North America, 1976, Textbook of Maxillofacial Trauma, 1983; editor in chief Videomed. Edn. Systems, 1972-75; editor: Atlas of Craniofacial Trauma, 1992; contbr. articles to med. jours. Bd. dirs. Bexer County Hearing Soc., 1969-71; adv. coun. WIDCB, 1993. Maj. USAF, 1969-71; chmn. Lens Hearing Ctr. of S.E. Mich. Recipient Valentine Mott medal for proficiency in anatomy, 1961, Recognition award Wayne State Bd. Govs. Faculty, 1993; Deafness Rsch. Found. grantee, 1979-81, NIH grantee, 1986, 92, 96, Lawrence M. Weiner Alumni award Wayne State U. Sch. Med., 1999. Fellow ACS, Am. Acad. Otolaryngology, Head and Neck Surgery (Cert. award 1976, Cert. of Appreciation 1978), Am. Soc. Head and Neck Surgery, Triological Soc. (v.p. 1995-96, mtg. guest of honor 2002, Vice Presdl. Citation award 2004), Am. Otol. Soc., Am. Acad. Facial Plastic and Reconstructive Surgery (v.p. 1980), Am. Neurotology Soc.; mem. AMA, Am. Laryngol. Soc. (coun. 1994—), Am. Laryngol. Assn., Mich. Med. Soc., Am. Head and Neck Soc., Soc. Univ. Otolaryngologists (pres. 1995), Assn. Acad. Depts. Otolaryngology, Assn. Rsch. Otolaryngology (pres. 1981). Home: 27115 Wellington Rd Franklin MI 48025-1329 Office: 43494 Woodward Ste 210 Bloomfield Hills MI 48312 Also: Wayne State U Sch Med 540 E Canfield St Detroit MI 48201-1928

**MATHUR, ABHINAV,** research engineer; b. New Delhi, Feb. 26, 1979; s. Vijay Kumar and Manju Mathur. B in Engring., Netaji Subhas Inst. Tech., New Delhi, 2000; MS, Miss. State U. Starkville, 2002; PhD, Miss. State U., 2006. Elec. engr. Hughes Escorts Comm. Ltd., New Delhi, 1998, Compromintertech Pvt. Ltd., New Delhi, 1999—2000; grad. tchg. asst. dept. elec. and computer engring. Miss. State U., 2000—01, grad. rsch. asst. Engring. Rsch. Ctr., 2001—06; rsch. engr. Optech Internat., Inc., Kiln, Miss., 2006—. Pres. Indian Student Assn. Miss. State U., 2001—02. Finalist student paper contest, IEEE Internat. Geoscience and Remote Sensing Symposium, 2003; named Outstanding Internat. Grad. Student, Miss. State U., 2002; recipient Silver medal for best undergrad. project work, Netaji Subhas Inst. Tech., Delhi U., 2000, Bagley Coll. of Engring. Grad. Student Rsch. award, Office of Grad. Studies, Miss. State U., 2004, Rsch. Asst. of Yr. award elec. and computer engring. dept., Miss. State U., 2004; Barrier fellow dept. elec. and computer engring. 2002, 2004. Mem.: IEEE, Eta Kappa Nu. Office: Optech Internat Inc 7225 Stennis Airport Dr Ste # 400 Kiln MS 39556 Fax: 228-252-1007. Office Phone: 228-252-1004. E-mail: m_abhinav@hotmail.com.

**MATHUR, IKE,** finance educator; b. Jamshedpur, India, Nov. 22, 1943; arrived in U.S., 1961; s. Robert William and Ivy (Phillips) Mathur; children: Rebecca Lynn, Jason Gabriel. BS, Eastern Mich. U., 1965, MBA, 1968; PhD, U. Cin., 1974. Editor Am. Math. Soc., Providence, 1965-69; rsch. asst. U. Cin., 1969-72; instr. U. Dayton, Ohio, 1972-73; asst. prof. U. Pitts., 1973-77; assoc. prof. fin. So. Ill. U., Carbondale, 1977-81, prof., 1981—, chmn. fin., 1979-92, 94-95, dean Coll. Bus., 1992-94. Mgmt. trainer AID, Washington, 1978—81; Fulbright prof., Turku, Finland, 1983—84, Lisbon, Portugal, 1993. Author: Introduction to Financial Management, 1979, Cases in Managerial Finance, 1984, Personal Finance, 1989, Wealth Creation in Eastern Europe, 1992, Financial Management in Post Europe, 1992. Mem.: Fin. Mgmt. Assn., Midwest Fin. Assn., Western Fin. Assn., French Fin. Assn., Am. Fin. Assn. Avocations: running, martial arts, travel. Home: 4 Oxford Ln Glen Carbon IL 62034-1531 Office: So Ill U Coll Bus Carbondale IL 62901 Office Phone: 618-453-1421. Personal E-mail: imathur@msn.com. Business E-Mail: imathur@cba.siu.edu.

**MATHY, ROBIN MICHELLE,** writer, researcher; b. Portsmouth, Va., July 21, 1957; BS with honors in sociology with honors summa cum laude, Ariz. State U., 1985; MA, Ind. U., Bloomington, 1989; MSW, U. Minn., 2003; M in Internat. Rels., U. Cambridge, 2004; MS in Evidence Based Health Care, U. Oxford, 2005. Author: Male Homosexuality in Four Societies: Brazil, Guatemala, the Philippines, and the United States (Best Book in Print, NY Times Rev. of Books, 2002); contbr. articles to profl. jours., chapters to books; editor: Lesbian and Bisexual Women's Mental Health, 2004. Pres. GLBT&Q Suicide Prevention Coalition, Washington, 2003.

**MATHYS, GORDON D.,** accountant, educator; b. Hawkeye, Iowa, Jan. 15, 1947; s. Clarion and Darlene M Mathys; m. Janice R. Beltz, Aug. 30, 1969; children: Dalen M. Mathys-Cook, David M. BA, Upper Iowa U., Fayette, 1969; MEd, Iowa State U., Ames, 1992. Instr. Gates Bus. Coll., Waterloo, Iowa, 1969—71; Cedar Rapids Bus. Coll., Cedar Rapids, 1971—74; prof. Hawkeye C.C., Waterloo, 1974—. Author: (book) Computerized Accounting using Peachtree, Computerized Accounting using QuickBooks. Mem.: Iowa State Alumni Assn., Phi Kappa Phi. Avocation: gardening. Office: Hawkeye Community College 1501 East Orange Road Waterloo IA 50701 Office Phone: 319-296-2320.

**MATIA, PAUL RAMON,** retired judge; b. Cleve., Oct. 2, 1937; s. Leo Clemens and Irene Elizabeth (Linkert) M.; m. Nancy Arch Van Meter, Jan. 2, 1993. BA, Case Western Res. U., 1959; JD, Harvard U., 1962. Bar: Ohio 1962, U.S. Dist. Ct. (no. dist.) Ohio 1969. Law clk. Common Pleas Ct. of Cuyahoga County, Cleve., 1963-66, judge, 1985-91; asst. atty. gen. State of Ohio, Cleve., 1966-69, adminstrv. ast. to atty. gen. Columbus, 1969-70; senator Ohio State Senate, Columbus, 1971-75, 79-83; ptnr. Hadley, Matia, Mills & MacLean Co., L.P.A., Cleve., 1975-84, Porter Wright Morris & Arthur LLP, Cleve., 2005—; judge U.S. Dist. Ct. (no. dist.) Ohio, 1991-99, chief dist. judge 1999—2004, sr. judge, 2005. mem. 6th Cir. Jud. Coun., 1999—2004. Candidate Lt. Gov. Rep. Primary, 1982, Ohio Supreme Ct., 1988. Named Outstanding Legislator, Ohio Assn. for Retarded Citizens, 1974, Watchdog of Ohio Treasury, United Conservatives of Ohio, 1979; recipient Heritage award Polonia Found., 1988. Mem. Fed. Bar Assn., Ohio State Bar Assn., Cleve. Bar Assn., Club at Key Ctr. Avocations: skiing, gardening, travel. Office: Porter Wright Morris & Arthur LLP 925 Euclid Ave Ste 1700 Cleveland OH 44115-1483 Office Phone: 216-443-2548. Business E-Mail: pmatia@porterwright.com.

**MATIJEVIC, EGON,** chemistry professor; b. Otocac, Croatia, Apr. 27, 1922; came to U.S., 1957; s. Grgur and Stefica (Spiegel) M.; m. Bozica Biscan, Feb. 27, 1947. Diploma in Chem. Engring., U. Zagreb, 1944, PhD in Chemistry, 1948, D Habilitation in Phys. Chemistry, 1952; DSc (hon.), Lehigh U., 1977, M. Curie-Sklodowska U., Lublin, Poland, 1990, Clarkson U., 1992, Zagreb U., Croatia, 1998, Nat. U. San Martin, Buenos Aires, 2003, U. Ljubljana, Slovenia, 2003. Instr. chemistry U. Zagreb, 1944-47, sr. instr. phys. chemistry, 1949-52, privat dozent in colloid chemistry, 1952-54, dozent in phys. and colloid chemistry, 1955-56, on leave, 1956-59; rsch. assoc. Inst. Cinematography, Zagreb, 1948; rsch. fellow dept. colloid sci. U. Cambridge, England, 1956-57; vis. prof. Clarkson Coll. Tech., Potsdam, NY, 1957-59, assoc. prof. chemistry Potsdam, NY, 1960-62; prof. Clarkson U., Potsdam, NY, 1962-86, disting. univ. prof., 1986-99, LaMer prof. colloid and surface sci., 2000—; assoc. dir. Inst. Colloid and Surface Sci. Clarkson Coll. Tech., 1966-68, dir. inst., 1968-81, chmn. dept. chemistry, 1981-87. Vis. prof. Japan Soc. for Promotion Sci., 1973, U. Melbourne, Australia, 1976, Sci. U. Tokyo, 1979, 84, fgn. guest Inst. Colloid and Interface Sci., 82; vis. scientist U. Leningrad, Russia, 1977; advisor IAEA, Buenos Aires, 1978, Buenos Aires, 80; lectr. in field. Author: (with M. Kesler) General and Inorganic Chemistry for Senior High Schools, 11 edits., including Croatian, Macedonian, Hungarian, Italian, 1943-63; translator: Einfuhrung in die Stochiometrie (Nylen and Wigern), 1948; editor: (with Alter J. Weber) Adsorption from Aqueous Solution, 1968, Surface and Colloid Science, vols. 1-17, 1969-2002; contbr. numerous articles to profl. publs. Recipient Gold medal, Am. Electroplaters Soc., 1976, guest of honor 56th and 63d Colloid and Surface Sci. Symposia, Blacksburg, Va., 1982, Seattle, 1989, Boston, 2002, Egon Matijevic chair endowed in his name, Clarkson U., 1992. Mem. Am. Chem. Soc. (councilor divsn. colloid and surface chemistry 1982-87, chmn. 1969-70, Kendall award 1972, Langmuir Disting. Lectureship award 1985, Ralph K. Iler award 1993), Kolloid Gesellschaft (hon. life, Thomas Graham award 1985), Internat. Assn. Colloid Interface Sci. (pres. 1985-87), Chem. Soc. Japan, Inst. Colloid and Interface Sci. of U. of Tokyo (hon.), Phalanx Soc., Croatian Acad. Scis. and Arts (fgn.), Am. Ceramic Soc. (hon.), Materials Rsch. Soc. Japan (hon.), Acad. Ceramics (Italy), Croatian Chem. Soc. (hon., Bozo Tezak medal 1991), Sigma Xi (Clarkson Coll. Tech. chpt. award 1972, nat. lectr. 1987-89). Roman Catholic. Office: Ctr Advanced Materials Proc Clarkson U Dept Chem Potsdam NY 13699-5814 Business E-Mail: matiegon@clarkson.edu.

**MATIN, ARTHUR,** information technology executive; BS in biology, U. Rochester; MBA, U. Chgo. Managerial positions US and internat. sales ops. IBM, 1981—2000; sr. v.p. worldwide sales and mktg. CrossWorlds Software Inc., 2000—01; pres. Network Assoc., Inc., McAfee Security, 2001—04; exec. v.p. worldwide sales VERITAS Software Corp., Mountain View, Calif., 2004—. Office: VERITAS Software Corp 350 Ellis St Mountain View CA 94043

**MATIN, MOHAMMAD ABDUL,** electrical engineer, educator; s. Mohammed Abdul and Late Jahanara Majid; m. Nasima Akhtar, July 10, 1987; children: Mubeen Hamidul, Muqit Hamidul, Nafisa, Nadira, Samiha. PhD, Nottingham U., England, 1993. Lectr. Inst. Sci. Instrumentation, Dhaka, Bangladesh, 1987—93; rsch. assist. U. Nottingham, England, 1993—94; pdf, rsch. engr. McMaster U., Hamilton, Ont., Canada, 1994—98; sr. rsch. assoc. Toronto U., 1998—2000; asst. prof. Denver U., 2000—. Contbr. articles to profl. jours. Commonwealth scholar, Assn. Commonwealth Countries, Eng., 1990—93. Mem.: SPIE, IEEE (sr.; vice chair student activities 2004—), Optical Soc. Am., Rotary (dir. internat. svc. Englewood chpt. 2004), Sigma Xi. Achievements include patents for low threshold vertical cavity surface emitting lasers. Office: Univ Denver 2390 S York St Denver CO 80208 Office Phone: 303-871-2833. Office Fax: 303-871-4450. Business E-Mail: mmatin@du.edu.

**MATIS, NINA B.,** lawyer; b. NYC, June 23, 1947; AB cum laude, Smith Coll., 1969; JD, NYU, 1972. Bar: Ill. 1973. Ptnr. Katten Muchin Zavis Rosenman, Chgo. Adj. prof. law Northwestern U., 1984-87. Mem. Am. Coll. Lawyers, Urban Land Inst. Office: Katten Muchin Zavis Rosenman 525 W Monroe St Ste 1600 Chicago IL 60661-3693 Office Fax: 312-577-8686. E-mail: nina.matis@kmzr.com.

**MATJASKO, M. JANE,** anesthesiologist, educator; b. Harrison Twp., Pa., 1942; MD, Med. Coll. Pa., 1968. Diplomate Am. Bd. Anesthesiology. Resident in anesthesiology Md. Hosp., Balt., 1968-72; prof., chmn. anesthesiology U. Md., Balt., 1990—. Bd. dirs. Am. Bd. Anesthesiology. Mem. Am. Soc. Anesthesiologists, Assn. Univ. Anesthesiologists. Office: U Md Hosp Dept Anesthesiology 22 S Greene St Baltimore MD 21201-1544

**MATKOWSKY, BERNARD JUDAH,** mathematician, educator; b. N.Y.C., Aug. 19, 1939; s. Morris M. and Ethel H. M.; m. Florence Knobel, Apr. 11, 1965; children: David, Daniel, Devorah. BS, CCNY, 1960; M.E.E., NYU, 1961, MS, 1963, PhD, 1966. Fellow Courant Inst. Math. Scis., NYU, 1961-66; mem. faculty dept. math. Rensselaer Poly. Inst., 1966-77; John Evans prof. applied math., mech. engring. & math. Northwestern U., Evanston, Ill., 1977—, chmn. engring. sci. and applied math. dept., 1993-99. Vis. prof. Tel Aviv U., 1972-73; vis. scientist Weizmann Inst. Sci., Israel, summer 1976, summer 1980, Tel Aviv U., summer 1980; cons. Argonne Nat. Lab., Sandia Labs., Lawrence Livermore Nat. Lab., Exxon Research and Engring. Co. Editor Wave Motion—An Internat. Jour., 1979-99, Applied Math. Letters, 1987—, SIAM Jour. Applied Math., 1976-95, European Jour. Applied Math., 1990-96, Random and Computational Dynamics, 1991-97, Internat. Jour. SHS, 1992—, Jour. Materials Synthesis and Processing, 1992-2002, SIAM Monographs Math. Modeling and Computation, 2005—; mem. editl. adv. bd. Springer Verlag Applied Math. Scis. Series; contbr. chpts. to books, articles to profl. jours. Fulbright grantee, 1972-73; Guggenheim fellow, 1982-83 Fellow: AAAS, Am. Acad. Mechs.; mem.: Soc. Natural Philosophy, Com. Concerned Scientists, Conf. Bd. Math. Scis. (com. human rights math. scientists), Am. Assn. Combustion Synthesis, Am. Phys. Soc., Combustion Inst., Am. Math. Soc., Soc. Indsl. and Applied Math., Eta Kappa Nu, Sigma Xi. Home: 3704 Davis St Skokie IL 60076-1745 Office: Northwestern U Technological Institute Evanston IL 60208-0001 Office Phone: 847-491-5396. Business E-Mail: b-matkowsky@northwestern.edu.

**MATLIN, MARLEE,** actress; b. Morton Grove, Ill., Aug. 24, 1965; m. Kevin Grandalski, Aug. 29, 1993; 3 children Attended William Rainey Harper Coll. Appeared in films Children of a Lesser God, 1986 (Acad. award for best actress, Golden Globe award), Walker, 1987, Linguini Incident, 1990, The Player, 1992, Hear No Evil, 1993, It's My Party, 1996, When Justice Fails, 1998, Freak City, 1999; TV films: Bridge to Silence, 1989, Against Her Will: The Carrie Buck Story, 1994, When Justice Fails, 1997, Dead Silence, 1997, Where the Truth Lies, 1999; TV series: Reasonable Doubts, 1991-93; guest star: Picket Fences, 1993, 94-96 (Emmy nomination, Guest Actress-Drama

Series, 1994), Seinfeld, 1993 (Emmy nomination Guest Actress-Comedy Series, 1994), The Larry Sanders Show, 1992, Spin City, 1996, ER, 1999, Judging Amy, 1999, The West Wing, 2000—; author: Deaf Child Crossing, 2002

**MATLINS, STUART M.,** management consultant, publisher; b. NYC, July 25, 1940; s. Louis Karl and Lillian M. m. Andrea Cines, June 20, 1960 (div.); children: Seth, Andrew; m. Antoinette Leonard, Oct. 9, 1977. Student, London Sch. Econs., 1958-59; BS, U. Wis., 1960; AM, Princeton U., 1962, postgrad., 1962-63. Internat. economist Bur. Internat. Commerce, U.S. Dept. Commerce, Washington, 1963-66; cons. Booz Allen & Hamilton, Inc., N.Y.C., 1966-67, asst. to pres. internat./adminstrv. dir., 1967-70, v.p. internat. ops., 1970-71, v.p./mng. officer, instl. and pub. mgmt. div., 1971-74; pres. mgmt. cons. Stuart Matlins Assocs., Inc., Woodstock, Vt., 1974—. Chmn. bd. dirs. LongHill Ptnrs., Inc.; publisher Gemstone Press, Jewish Lights Pub., SkyLight Paths Pub. Bd. dirs. Health Edn. Found., Woodstock (Vt.) Area Jewish Cmty.; former chmn. overseers N.Y. Sch., Hebrew Union Coll.-Jewish Inst. Religion; bd. govs. Hebrew Union Coll.; trustee South Woodstock Fire Protection Assn., Inc., Mertens House, Woodstock, Vt.; mem. capital budget com. Town of Woodstock; mem. adv. bd. Abraham Geiger Coll., Germany; dir. Jewish Book Coun. Woodrow Wilson fellow, 1960-61, Herbert O. Peet fellow, 1961-62, Phillip A. Rollins fellow, 1962-63; recipient Am. Jewish Disting. Svc. award Hebrew Union Coll., 2006. Mem. Princeton Club. Office: LongHill Ptnrs Inc PO Box 237 Woodstock VT 05091-0237 also: Sunset Farm Offices Rt 4 Woodstock VT 05091

**MATLOCK, GINA RAE,** music educator; b. Oklahoma City, Sept. 1, 1968; d. Harold and Marge Dorris; 1 child, Keller Dwayne. B in Music Edn., So. Nazarene U., 1991. Tchr. music edn. Guthrie (Okla.) Pub. Schs., 1992—93, Hobbs (N.Mex.) Pub. Schs., 1993—95, Brownfield (Tex.) Pub. Schs., 1995—96, Lamesa (Tex.) Pub. Schs., 1996—2001, Kenneth Cooper Mid. Sch., Oklahoma City, 2001—. Home: 8109 NW 31st St Bethany OK 73008 Office: Kenneth Cooper Mid Sch 8001 River Bend Blvd Oklahoma City OK 73132 Office Phone: 405-720-9887.

**MATLOCK, GLEN,** musician; b. London, Aug. 27, 1956; Bassist Sex Pistols, 1975—77, The Rich Kids, various bands. Musician: (albums) Who's He Think He is When He's at Home?, 1996, Open Mind, 2000, On Something, 2004, (with the Sex Pistols) Never Mind the Bollocks...Here's the Sex Pistols, 1977, Anarchy in the UK: Live at the 76 Club, 1985, Live at Chelmsford Top Security Prison, 1990, Pretty Vacant, 1995, Back & There Again, 1997, (with the Rich Kids) Ghosts of Princes in Towers, 1978, (with Iggy Pop) Soldier, 1980, We Are Not Talking About Commercial S--t!, 1995, Heroin Hates You, 1997, Nuggets, 1999, (with Johnny Thunders) Que Sera, Sera, 1985, Born Too Loose, 1999, others; appears in (films) The Great Rock 'n' Roll Swindle, 1980, (documentaries) Sex Pistols Number 1, 1977, D.O.A., 1980, Punk & Its Aftershocks, 1980, The Filth & the Fury, 2000, 25 Years of Punk, 2001, End of the Century, 2003, Punk: Attitude, 2005; author: (autobiography) I Was a Teenage Sex Pistol, 1990. Named to Rock and Roll Hall of Fame, 2006.*

**MATLOCK, JACK FOUST, JR.,** diplomat; b. Greensboro, N.C., Oct. 1, 1929; s. Jack Foust and Nellie (McSwain) M.; m. Rebecca Burrum, Sept. 2, 1949; children: James, Hugh, Nell, David, Joseph. AB summa cum laude, Duke U., 1950; MA, Columbia U., 1952; cert., Russian Inst., 1952; LLD (hon.), Greensboro Coll., 1989, Albright Coll., 1992, Conn. Coll., 1993; LLD (hon.), Latvian Acad. Scis., 2002. Instr. Dartmouth, 1953-56; fgn. service officer Dept. State, 1956-91; assigned Washington, 1956-58, Am. Embassy, Vienna, 1958-60; Am. consul. gen. Munich, 1960-61; assigned Am. Embassy, Moscow, 1961-63, Accra, Ghana, 1963-66, Am. Consulate, Zanzibar, 1967-69, Am. Embassy, Dar es Salaam, Tanzania, 1969-70, Sr. Seminar in Fgn. Policy, Dept. State, 1970-71; country dir. for USSR State Dept., 1971-74; minister-counselor, dep. chief mission Am. Embassy, Moscow, 1974-78; diplomat-in-residence Vanderbilt U., Nashville, 1978-79; dep. dir. Fgn. Service Inst., Washington, 1979-80; chargé d'affaires ad interim Am. Embassy, Moscow, 1981; ambassador to Czechoslovakia, 1981-83; spl. asst. to pres., sr. dir. European and Soviet Affairs Nat. Security Council, 1983-87; U.S. ambassador to the Soviet Union, Moscow, 1987-91; sr. rsch. fellow Columbia U., N.Y.C., 1991-93, Kathryn and Shelby Collum Davis prof. Practice Internat. Diplomacy, 1993-96; George F. Kennan prof. Inst. for Advanced Study, Princeton, NJ, 1996-2001; John L. Weinberg/Goldman Sachs and Co. vis. prof. pub. and internat. affairs Princeton U., 2001—02; Sol Linowitz prof. internat. rels. Hamilton Coll., 2006. Author: Autopsy on an Empire: The American Ambassador's Account of the Collapse of the Soviet Union, 1995, Reagan and Gorbachev: How the Cold War Ended, 2004; compiler, editor: Index to J.V. Stalin's Works, 2d edit., 1971. Mem. Am. Acad. Diplomacy, Coun. on Fgn. Rels., Century Assn. N.Y., Am. Philos. Soc. Home: 940 Princeton Kingston Rd Princeton NJ 08540-4128 also: 32 Wagoner Hill Rd Fayetteville TN 37334 Office Phone: 609-252-1953. Personal E-mail: jfmatlock@patmedia.net. E-mail: matlock@ias.edu.

**MATLOCK, JOHN HUDSON,** science administrator, materials engineer; b. San Angelo, Tex., Nov. 23, 1944; s. Lee Hudson Jr. and Harriett (Kidder) M.; m. Kathe Lynne Reep, Sept. 3, 1966; children: Michelle, Joseph. B in Engring. Sci., U. Tex., 1967, MSME, 1969, PhD in Material Sci. and Engring., 1970; MBA, So. Ill. U., Edwardsville, 1976. Registered profl. engr., Mo., Wash., Oreg. Sr. rsch. engr. Monsanto Co., St. Peters, Mo., 1970-72, rsch. specialist, 1972-74, supt. tech. svcs., 1974-79; sr. staff engr. Mostek Corp., Carrollton, Tex., 1979-80, mgr. material tech. group, 1980-83; v.p. tech. SEH Am., Inc., Vancouver, Wash., 1983-90, exec. v.p., 1990-96, Komatsu Silicon Am., Hillsboro, Oreg., 1996, pres., CEO, 1997—2005; global officer Komatsu, Ltd., 1999—2003, sr. adv., 2006—; dir. Komatsu Electronic Metals, Ltd., 1999—. Mem. vis. com. Engring. Coll., U. Wash., Seattle, 1985-94, mem. indsl. adv. bd. Material Sci. and Engring., 1988-2000; mem. engring. adv. bd. Wash. State U., Pullman, 1984-96, adj. lectr., 1985; adj. prof. mech. engring., mem. grad. faculty Oreg. State U., Corvallis, 1985-90; adj. asst. prof. physics So. Ill. U., Edwardsville, 1973-76. Contbr. approximately 40 articles on silicon crystal growing and the effect of silicon properties on electronic device performance to profl. and trade jours. Bd. trustees 1st Ch. of God, Vancouver, 1988-91, tchr. adult ch. schs., 1986-91, 2001-02, spl. assignment missionary to Tanzania, 2006-; sch. bd. Kingsway Christian Sch., Vancouver, 1990-91; elder Sonrise Ch., Hillsboro, 2004-. Mem. Electrochem. Soc., Metall. Soc., AIME, Am. Soc. for Materials, Soc., Tau Beta Pi, Pi Tau Sigma, Phi Kappa Phi, Beta Gamma Sigma. Office Phone: 503-640-7000. Business E-Mail: jmatlock@komsil.com.

**MATLOCK, KENT,** advertising executive, public relations executive; BS, Morehouse Coll. Chmn., CEO Matlock & Assocs. Inc., 1984—. Office: Matlock Adv & Pub Rels Peachtree Pointe 1545 Peachtree St NE Ste 300 Atlanta GA 30309-2492

**MATLOCK-HETZEL, SUSAN,** psychologist, educator; d. John and Mary Matlock; m. Roderick Hetzel, Oct. 11, 1968. BS in Edn., U. Cen. Ark., 1985; MEd, Tex. A&M U., 1993, PhD, 2004. Lic. sch. psychologist N.Y., cert. tchr. N.Y., Tex. Home econs. tchr. Cameron (Tex.) Ind. Sch. Dist., 1985—88, Mexia (Tex.) Ind. Sch. Dist., 1988—92; grad. asst. sch. counseling program Tex. A&M U., College Station, Tex., 1992—93, grad. asst. sch. counseling helpline, 1993—97, grad. asst. sch. families, 1993—97; psychology intern Houston Ind. Sch. Dist., 1997—98; sch. psychologist Spencerport (N.Y.) Sch. Dist., 1999—2001, Rochester (N.Y.) Sch. Dist., 1999; dir. freshman yr. experience LeTourneau U., Longview, Tex., 2001—04, assoc. dean student svcs., 2004—05; staff psychologist Baylor U., Waco, Tex., 2005—. Coord. outreach Baylor U., Waco, 2005—06, instr. ednl. psychology, 2005—06; instr. freshman seminar LeTourneau U., Longview, 2001—05; adj. faculty student svcs. adminstrn. masters program Baylor U., Waco, 2006, lectr. in ednl. psychology, 2005—06, instr. dept. of curriculum and instrn., 2005—06; curriculum coord. freshman yr. experience LeTourneau U., Longview, 2001—04; grant writer in field. Author: (book chpt.) Review of the Sixteen PF Personal Career Development Profile. Chair luminaria com. Am. Cancer Soc. Relay for Life, Waco, 2005—06, team capt. Longview, 2001—04, team

mem. Spencerport, 1999—2001. Recipient Shining Star award, LeTourneau U., 2002, Tex. A&M Women Regency scholarship, Tex. A&M U., 1995. Mem.: APA (assoc.), Assn. for Christians in Student Devel. (assoc.), Christian Assn. for Psychol. Studies (assoc.), Tex. Psychol. Assn. (assoc.). Office: Baylor Univ #97060 209 Speight 1 Bear Pl Waco TX 76798-7060 Office Phone: 254-710-2467. Business E-Mail: susan_matlock-hetzel@baylor.edu.

**MATNEY, JUDY MCCALEB,** secondary school educator; b. Dumas, Tex., Jan. 31, 1944; d. Alex Truman McCaleb and Minnie May Curley; m. Roy Matney II, Dec. 21, 1963 (div. Jan. 1999); 1 child, Roy Matney III. BS in Chemistry, U. Tex., 1965; MEd in Math., Southwestern U., San Marcos, Tex., 1967. Cert. tchr. math., tchr. biology, tchr. chemistry, tchr. physics. Tchr. Taylor Ind. Sch. Dist., Tex., 1965—66, Austin Ind. Sch. Dist., Tex., 1967—69, Fort Bend Ind. Sch. Dist., Sugar Land, Tex., 1975—, head dept. sci. Active state textbook rev. panel Tex. Edn. Agy., Austin, 2001; active gov.'s block grants State Tex., Austin, 1983. Named Tex. State Tchr., Tex. Edn. Agy., 1981; recipient Termann Engring. award, Stanford U., 1997, Southwestern Region U.S. AP Physics Tchr. award, Coll. Bd., 1997, Excellence in Sci. award, Exxon. Mem.: Nat. Sci. Tchrs. (Excellence in Sci. Tchg. award). Avocation: computer technology. Home: 2911 Blue Lakes Missouri City TX 77459 Office: FBISD PO Box 1004 Sugar Land TX 77487-1004 Office Phone: 281-634-5600. Business E-Mail: 001JM318@fortbend.k12.tx.us.

**MATOAX, LOUISE,** mathematics professor, consultant; b. Gainesville, Aug. 13, 1961; d. Mary Leigh and George St.Clair Beers; 1 child, Canpaza. BS in Computer Sci., Mid. Tenn. State U., 1984, MS in Math., 1990. Cert. Software Quality Engr. # 324, Am. Soc. for Quality, 1997. Grad. tchg. asst. devel. studies dept. Mid. Tenn. State U., Murfreesboro, 1988—90; adj. prof. math. Santa Fe CC, Gainesville, 1990—91; math. instr. Miami Dade Coll. Kendall Campus, Fla., 1993—; adj. prof. math. and phys. edn. Pellissippi State Tech. CC, Knoxville, Tenn., 1992—93; hardware dept. Lowe's, Durham, NC, 1993; butcher, produce, grocery, front end, bakery delivery Whole Foods Market, Durham, NC, 1993; sr. product quality assurance test engr. WallData, Inc., Bellingham, Wash., 1994; math. instr. Bellingham (Wash.) Tech. Coll., 1994—95; sr. software quality engr. Component Internat., Inc., Mason, Ohio, 1996—98; prof. math. and physics in English ITESM, Colima, Mexico, 2000; sr. quality assurance engr. Raytheon Missile Sys., Tucson, 2001—02; math. instr. Hazard CC, Jackson, Ky., 2002—03. Rev. panel mem. The Ky. Jour. of Excellence in Coll. Tchg. and Learning, Jackson, Ky., 2002—03; math. curriculum cons. Educo, Inc., Miami, 2005; math. textbook reviewer Thompson, Brooks-Cole, Miami, 2005, McGraw-Hill Higher Edn., Miami, 2005—; math. curriculum cons. Edusun, Inc., Miami, 2006—. Author: (computerized algorithmic test bank) Test Bank. Mem. ACLU, Miami, 2004—06. Avocations: sewing, rug hooking, woodworking, writing, music. Personal E-mail: louise.matoax@gmail.com.

**MATOLAK, DAVID WILLIAM,** engineering educator; b. Johnstown, Pa., Aug. 29, 1961; s. William and Julia Matolak; m. Nancy Bigler Bigler, Dec. 15, 1961; children: Miranda Leigh, Madeleine Ruth. BS, Pa. State U., State College, 1983; MS, U. Mass., Amherst, 1987; PhD, U. Va., Charlottesville, 1994. Mem. tech. staff AT&T Bell Labs., North Andover, Mass., 1986—89; prin. engr. Loral Comm. Sys., Salt Lake City, 1994—96; lead comm. engr. The MITRE Corp., McLean, Va., 1996—98; sr. comm. engr. Lockheed Martin Global Telecom, Reston, Va., 1998—99; assoc. prof. Ohio U., Athens, 1999—. Aero. Comm. Rsch. grantee, NASA, 2000, Spread Spectrum Comm. Rsch. grantee, NSF, 2000—04, DARPA, 2001—04, Wireless Channel Characterization Rsch. grantee, NASA, 2004—06. Mem.: IEEE. Achievements include patents in field. Avocations: hiking, bicycling, old science fiction films. Office: Ohio University School EECS 322E Stocker Ctr Athens OH 45701 Office Phone: 740-593-1241.

**MATOS, CRUZ ALFONSO,** environmental consultant; b. N.Y.C., Mar. 6, 1929; s. José and Gertrudes (Manzanares) M.; m. Aurelia Santos, Dec. 13, 1963; children: Miguel, Veronica, Monica, Angélica. B Engring. Sci., Oxford U., 1957, M Engring. Sci., 1958; DSc (hon.), U. Met., P.R., 1995. Pres., CEO Fischer & Porter de P.R., 1964—69; asst. sec. dept. pub. works Govt. of P.R., 1969—70, exec. dir. Environ. Quality Bd., 1970—73, sec. dept. natural resources, 1973—75, cabinet mem., 1970—75; UN chief tech., dir. Inst. Marine Affairs, Trinidad and Tobago, 1975—79; UN Devel. Program regional rep. Barbados, Surinam, Dutch W.I., Trinidad and Tobago, 1979—80; UN chief tech. adviser South Pacific, dir. Com. for Coordination of Offshore Prospecting in the South Pacific, Suva, Fiji, 1980—89; ret., 1989. Advisor to pres. P.R. Senate for natural resources, the environ. and energy, 1993-97; advisor to exec. dir. UN Environ. Program for L.Am. and Caribbean, 1994-98; mem. various adv. panels and overseas mission U.S. NAS; mem. U.S. Nat. Commn. on Environment, Consejo Consultivo Recursos Naturales y Ambientales (apptd. Gov. P.R.), Com. Sobre Política Publica Energetíca P.R., Consejo Asesor Sobre Energia. Contbr. articles to sci. jours. and mags. Bd. dirs. Caribbean Environment and Devel. Inst. With U.S. Army, 1952-54. Named Dept. Natural and Environ. Resources bldg. the Dr. Cruz A. Matos Bldg., Govt. P.R., 2005, ann. scholarship for post grad. environ. studies Dr. Cruz A. Matos Scholarship, 2005; recipient Boriquen Conservation award, 1971; scholarship and bldg. named in his honor, Govt. P.R. 2005. Office: PO Box 7627-HC77 Playa Cerro Gordo Vega Alta PR 00692

**MATRANGA, FRANK PETER,** art educator, artist; b. L.A., Sept. 2, 1932; m. Casey Katherine Shields, Nov. 22, 1982. Degree, Pasadena C.C., 1953, U. So. Calif., 1960; MFA, L.A. State Coll., 1960. Cert. tchr. Calif., 1957. Tchr. h.s. art Whittier Sch. Dist., Calif., 1957—60, L.A. Sch. Dist., 1960—61; prof. art Los Angeles Harbor Coll., L.A., 1961—80; artist in residence Sue No Sato Ceramic Studio, Yokohama, Japan, 1977—79. Studio artist Matranga Stoneware, Manhattan Beach, Calif., 1960—. Ceramic murals, Historical Wall Sculptures (Outstanding Art Grad. L.A. State Coll., 1971), potter, pottery (Best In Show, 1995), ceramics, (many awards in exhibitions), potter, (hon. mention, 2002). With U.S. Army, 1954—55. Mem.: Am. Ceramic Soc. (pres. 1976—78). Avocations: skiing, travel, jazz, sport cars, photography. Home: 118 No Ardmore Ave Manhattan Beach CA 90266 Office: Matranga Stoneware 118 No Ardmore Ave Manhattan Beach CA 90266 Office Phone: 310-374-6044. Personal E-mail: frank@matrangastudios.com.

**MATROS, RICHARD K.,** insurance company executive; b. Queens, NY; m. Adrienne Matros; children: Carly, Chelsea, Alex. BA in Psychology, Alfred U.; MA in Gerontology, U. S.C. Facility adminstr. Extended Care Inc., Catered Living Inc.; regional adminstr., v.p. We. Ops. Beverly Enterprises Inc.; exec. v.p. ops. Care Enterprises, 1988—91, pres., COO, 1988—91, 1991—94, pres., CEO, 1994; pres., COO Regency Health Svcs. Inc., 1994—95, pres., CEO, 1995—97, Bright Now! Dental, 1998—2000; chmn., CEO Sun Healthcare Group, 2001—. Office: Sun Healthcare Group Ste 400 18831 Von Karman Ave Irvine CA 92612*

**MATSAKIS, ELIAS N.,** lawyer; b. Chgo., 1951; BA with honors, U. Chgo., 1971; JD cum laude, Harvard Law Sch., 1974. Bar: Ill. 1974. Ptnr. Holland & Knight LLP, Chgo., mem. dir. com. Staff mem. Harvard Civil Rights and Civil Liberties Law Review, 1972, lead author Navigating the Changing Tides of Managed Care and Health Reform, AMA. Mem. sch. bd. Dist. 225, Northfield Twp. Mem.: Comml. Law League Am., ABA, Hellenic Bar Assn. (Ill.). State Bar Assn., Chgo. Bar Assn. (chmn. pro se ct. com., young lawyers sect. 1977, David C. Hilliard award). Office: Holland & Knight LLP 131 S Dearborn St 30th Fl Chicago IL 60603 Office Phone: 312-715-5731. Business E-Mail: elias.matsakis@hklaw.com.

**MATSCHULLAT, DALE LEWIS,** lawyer; b. Ft. Sill, Okla., May 1, 1945; s. Wayne Emil and Harriet Jane (Bowman) M.; m. Eileen Joanne Davidson, Aug. 26, 1967; children— Robert Charles, Stephen Francis. AB, Stanford U., 1967, JD, 1970. Bar: N.Y., Wis. Law clk. U.S. Dist. Ct. (ea. dist.) N.Y.,

Bklyn., 1970-71; assoc. firm Davis, Polk & Wardwell, Manhattan, N.Y., 1972-77; former sector counsel Allis Chalmers Corp., Milw., from 1977, former gen. counsel; v.p., gen. counsel. Newell Rubbermaid Inc., Rockford, Ill., 1989—. Roman Catholic.

**MATSCHULLAT, ROBERT W.,** former consumer products company executive; b. Nov. 21, 1947; married. BA, Stanford U., 1969, MBA, 1972. CFO The Seagram Co. Ltd., 1995—99, vice chmn., 1995—2000; head worldwide investment banking Morgan Stanley & Co. Inc., 2000—04; non-exec. chmn. The Clorox Co., Oakland, Calif., 2004—05, interim chmn., CEO, 2006. Bd. dirs. The Clorox Co., 1999—, The Walt Disney Co., 2002—, McKesson Inc. Bd. dir. The Riverview Sch., East Sandwich, Mass. Mem.: Duke U. Parent's Assn. (nat. co-chmn.).

**MATSEN, FREDERICK ALBERT, III,** orthopedic educator; b. Austin, Tex., Feb. 5, 1944; s. Frederick Albert II and Cecilia (Kirkegaard) M.; m. Anne Lovell, Dec. 24, 1966; children: Susanna Lovell, Frederick A. IV, Laura Jane Megan. BA, U. Tex., Austin, 1964; MD, Baylor U., 1968. Intern Johns Hopkins U., Balt., 1971; resident in orthopaedics U. Wash., Seattle, 1971-74, acting instr. orthopaedics, 1974, asst. prof. orthopaedics, 1975-79, assoc. prof. orthopaedics, 1979-82, prof., 1982-85, 86—, adjunct prof. Ctr. Bioengring., 1985—, dir. residency program orthopaedics, 1978-81, vice chmn. dept. orthopaedics, 1982-85, acting chmn. dept. orthopaedics, 1983-84, prof., chmn. dept. orthopaedics, 1981—. Mem. Orthopaedic Residency Rev. Com., Chgo., 1981-86. Author: Compartmental Syndromes, 1980; editor: The Shoulder, 1990; contbr. articles to profl. jours., chpts. to textbooks; assoc. editor Clin. Orthopaedics, Jour. Orthopaedic Rsch., 1981—. Lt. comdr. USPHS, 1969-71. Recipient Traveling fellowship Am. Orthopaedic Assn., 1983, Nicholas Andry award Assn. Bone and Joint Surgery, 1979, Henry Meyerding Essay award Am. Fracture Assn., 1974. Mem. Am. Shoulder and Elbow Surgeons (founding, pres. 1991—), Am. Acad. Orthopaedic Surgeons (bd. dirs. 1984-85), Orthopaedic Rsch. Soc., Western Orthopaedic Assn., Phi Beta Kappa. Office: U Wash Dept Orthopaedics RK 10 1959 NE Pacific St Seattle WA 98195-0001

**MATSEN, JOHN MARTIN,** academic administrator, pathologist; b. Salt Lake City, Feb. 7, 1933; s. John M. and Bessie (Jackson) M.; m. Joneen Johnson, June 6, 1959; children: Marilee, Sharon, Coleen, Sally, John H., Martin K., Maureen, Catherine, Carl, Jeri. BA, Brigham Young U., 1958; MD, UCLA, 1963; DSc (hon.), U. Utah, 2006. Diplomate Am. Bd. Pediatrics, Am. Bd. Pathology, Spl. Competence in Med. Microbiology. Intern UCLA, 1963-65; resident Los Angeles County Harbor/UCLA Med. Ctr., Torrance, Calif., 1965-66; USPHS fellow U. Minn., Mpls., 1966-68, asst. prof., 1968-70, assoc. prof., 1971-74, prof., 1974, U. Utah, Salt Lake City, 1974—, assoc. dean, 1979-81, chmn. dept. pathology, 1981-93, univ. sr. v.p. health scis., dean Sch. Medicine, 1993-98. Pres. Associated Regional and Univ. Pathologists, Inc., Salt Lake City, 1983-93, chmn. bd. dirs., 1993-99. Author over 200 publs. in field. Recipient Sonnenwirth Meml. award Am. Soc. Microbiology, 1993, Disting. Svc. award Collegium Aesculapium Found., 2006, Am. Soc. for Clin. Pathology, 2006. Mem. Acad. Clin. Lab. Physicians and Scientists (pres. 1978-79), Assn. Pathology Chmn. (pres. 1990-92). Mem. Lds Ch.

**MATSKO, ANDREY B.,** research scientist; b. Kiev, Ukraine, June 28, 1971; arrived in US, 1997; m. Nelli A. Matsko, Nov. 16, 2002; 1 child, Matvey A. MSc in Physics with honors, Moscow State U., 1994, PhD, 1996. Postdoctoral rsch. assoc. Tex. A&M U., College Station, 1997–2001; sr. mem. tech. staff Jet Propulsion Lab Caltech, Pasadena, Calif., 2001—. Vis. scientist Max Plank Inst. Quantenoptick, 1998, 2000. Recipient Lew Allen award for excellence, Jet Propulsion Lab., 2005.

**MATSON, PAMELA ANNE,** environmental scientist, science educator; b. Eau Claire, Wis., Aug. 3, 1953; BS, U. Wis., 1975; MS, Ind. U., 1980; PhD, Oreg. State U., 1983. Prof. U. Calif., Berkeley, 1993—97; Goldman prof. environ. studies Stanford U., Calif., 1997—, Naramore dean sch. earth sci., 2002—. Contbr. articles to profl. jours.; editor: Annual Rev. of Environment & Resources. Fellow MacArthur fellow, 1995. Fellow: Am. Acad. Arts & Scis.; mem.: Nat. Acad. Sci. Achievements include research in interactions between the biosphere and the atmosphere; land-use changes on atmospheric change, analyzing the effects of greenhouse gas emissions resulting from tropical deforestization; intensive agriculture on the atmosphere, especially the effects of tropical agriculture and cattle ranching; development of agricultural productivity can be expanded without causing off-site environmental consequences. Office: Stanford U Sch Earth Scis Stanford CA 94305-2210

**MATSUDA, FUJIO,** retired academic administrator; b. Honolulu, Oct. 18, 1924; s. Yoshio and Shimo (Iwasaki) M.; m. Amy M. Saiki, June 11, 1949; children: Bailey Koki, Thomas Junji, Sherry Noriko, Joan Yuuko, Ann Mitsuyo, Richard Hideo. BSCE, Rose Poly. Inst., 1949; DSc, MIT, 1952; DEng (hon.), Rose Hulman Inst. Tech., 1975. Rsch. engr. MIT, 1952—54; rsch. asst. prof. engring. U. Ill., Urbana, 1954—55; asst. prof. to prof. engring. U. Hawaii, Honolulu, 1955—62, chmn. dept. civil engring., 1962—63, v.p. bus. affairs, 1973-74, pres., 1974-84, exec. dir. Rsch. Corp., 1984-94; pres. Japan-Am. Inst. Mgmt. Sci., Honolulu, 1994-96. Dir. Hawaii Dept. Transp., Honolulu, 1963-73; bd. dirs. C. Brewer & Co., Ltd., Buyco, Ltd., First Hawaiian Bank, BancWest Corp., Inc., Rehab. Hosp. of Pacific; chmn. bd. dirs. Pacific Internat. Ctr. High Tech. Rsch. Trustee Pacific Buddhist Acad., 2000—, chmn., 2004. With U.S. Army 1943—45. Recipient Honor Alumnus award Rose Poly. Inst., 1971, Disting. Svc. award Airport Ops. Coun. Internat., 1973; named Disting. Alumnus U. Hawaii, 1974, 91, Hawaii Engr. of Yr., 1972. Mem. NAE, NSPE, ASCE (Parcel-Sverdrup Engring. Mgmt. award 1986), Social Sci. Assn., Japan-Am. Soc. Hawaii (trustee 1976-84, adv. coun. 1984—), Japan-Hawaii Econ. Coun., Sigma Xi, Tau Beta Pi. E-mail: fmatsuda@hawaii.rr.com.

**MATSUDA, MASATAKE,** rail transportation executive; b. Hokkaido, Japan, 1936; Student, Hokkaido U. Chmn. E. Japan Rlwy. Co., Tokyo; joined Japan Nat. Rlwy., 1961, formerly Planning Mgr. of Office of Planning Mgmt., Planning Mgr. Hokkaido Hdqs., Dir.-Gen. Reconstruction Promotion Hdqs.; Mgmt. Dir. Corpn. Planning Hdqs. E Japan Rlwy Co. (Japan Rlwy. East-co. created after privatization of JNR 1987), Gen.-Mgr., V.P, Pres., 1993; current Chmn. Japan Rlwy. East. Dir. Mizuho Holdings Inc.; Pres. World Exec. Coun., Internat. Union of Railways (UIC); V.P. UIC, 2003—04; mem. Prime Min. Adv. Panel to oversee Privatization of Semi Governmental Expressway Corporations, 2003, resigned in protest of privatization scheme. Office: East Japan Railway 2-2-2 Yoyogi Shibuya-ku Tokyo 151-8578 Japan Office Phone: (3) 5334-1310. Office Fax: (3) 5334-1297.*

**MATSUDA, TAKAYOSHI,** surgeon, educator, biomedical researcher; b. Tonan, Japan, 1937; came to U.S., 1965; MD, Keio Gijuku U., Tokyo, 1963. Diplomate Am. Bd. Surgery. Rotating intern Cook County Hosp., Chgo., 1965-66, resident in surgery, 1966-71, dir. burn ctr., 1975-93; asst. prof. surgery Kyorin U., Tokyo, 1971-75; asst. prof. U. Ill., Chgo., 1977—; pres. TM & Assocs., Oak Park, Ill., 1994—; CEO, Matsuda Clean Energy Co., Oak Park, 2001—. Cons. alternative medicine, cons. leadership devel., fire freedom; investigator renewable energy; spkr. in field. Editl. bd. Jour. Burn Care Rehab., 1987-93; contbr. articles to profl. publ., chpt. to books. Recipient Jerry and Thelma Stergios award for Excellence in Basic Rsch., U. Ill. at Chgo., 1979, The Superior Pub. Serv. award, County of Cook, State of Ill., 1993. Fellow ACS; mem. Internat. Soc. Surgery, Internat. Soc. Burn Injuries, Am. Burn Assn., Am. Assn. Surgery Trauma, Soc. Critical Care Medicine, Chgo. Surg. Soc. Achievements include research in and devel. of a novel approach for the production of electricity without pollution; established the first human skin bank in the State of Illinois at the Burn Unit of Cook County Hospital, 1977. Office: TM & Assocs Alternative Medicine Cons 103 Bishop Quarter Ln Oak Park IL 60302-2672 Office Phone: 708-386-2522. Personal E-mail: takimatsuda@hotmail.com.

**MATSUDA, WAKOTO,** neurosurgeon, researcher; b. Onomichi, Hiroshima, Japan, Apr. 6, 1968; s. Tadao and Fujiko (Makihata) Matsuda; m. Kiyoe Nakazawa, Mar. 22, 1991; children: Shin, Nako, Tei. MD, U. Tsukuba, Japan, 1996. Diplomate in neurosurgery Japan Neurosrg. Soc. Resident dept. neurosurgery U. Tsukuba Hosp., 1996—2002; clin. fellow dept. neurosurgery Tsukuba Med. Ctr. Hosp., 2002—03; postgrad. dept. morphological brain sci. Grad. Sch. Medicine, Kyoto U., 2003—06; asst.prof. divsn. anatomy and cell biology, dept. anatomy Shiga U. Med. Sci., 2006—. Recipient Best Resident award, Inst. Clin. Medicine, U. Tsukuba, 2002; scholar, Iwadare Scholarship Found., 2003. Mem.: Japanese Assn. Anatomists, Japan Neuroscience Soc., Japanese Congress Neurological Surgeons, Japan Neurosurg. Soc. Office: Shiga U Med Sci Divsn Anatomy and Cell Biology Tsukinowa-cho Seya Ohsu Shiga 520292 Japan Office Phone: 81-757-548-2136. Office Fax: 81-77-548-2139. Personal E-mail: wako@mua.biglobe.ne.jp. Business E-Mail: matsuda@belle.shiga-med.ac.jp.

**MATSUI, CONNIE L.,** pharmaceutical executive; b. Piedmont, Calif. m. William Beckman; 2 children. BA, Stanford U., MBA, 1977. Various positions Wells Fargo Bank, 1977—91; sr. dir., planning and resource devel. IDEC Pharm., 1992—94, v.p., planning and resource devel., 1994—2000, sr. v.p., planning and resource devel., 2000—03; exec. v.p. corp. strategy and communication Biogen Idec Inc., 2003—. Bd. dirs. Halozyme Therapeutics, Inc., 2006—. Nat. pres. Girl Scouts Am., 1999—2002. Office: Biogen Inc 14 Cambridge Ctr Cambridge MA 02142

**MATSUI, DORIS OKADA,** congresswoman; b. Poston, Ariz., Sept. 25, 1944; m. Robert Takeo Matsui (dec. Jan. 1, 2005), Sept. 17, 1966; 1 child. BA in Psychology, U. Calif., Berkeley, 1966. Dep. dir. pub. liaison The White House, Washington, 1993—94, 1996—99, dep. asst. to the Pres. for pub. liaison, 1994—96; dir. govt. rels. Collier, Shannon & Scott PLLC, Washington, 1999—2005, mem. US Congress from 5th Calif. dist., 2005—. Mem. Clinton-Gore Transition Team, 1992—93; bd. trustees Woodrow Wilson Internat. Ctr. Scholars, Meridian Internat. Ctr., Calif. Inst. Bd., Arena Stage. Recipient Action for Breast Cancer Awareness award, Advocates award, Nat. Assn. Mental Health, Mentor award, U. So. Calif. -Sacramento Sch. Pub. Adminstrn., Newmyer award, Sidwell Friends Sch., Rosalie Stern award, U. Calif. Alumni Assn. Democrat. Methodist. Office: US Ho Reps 2310 Ho Office Bldg Washington DC 20515-0505 also: Robert T Matsui Fed Courthouse Ste 12-600 501 I St Sacramento CA 95814*

**MATSUI, HIDEKI,** professional baseball player; b. Kanazawa, Japan, June 12, 1974; Player Yomiuri Giants (Central League), Japan, 1992—2002, NY Yankees, 2003—. Major donor Japanese Red Cross Society for Tsunami Relief, 2004. Named MVP, Central League (Japan), 1998, 2000, 2002; recipient Golden Spirit Award, 1999, 2000. Achievements include being a member of Japan Series Championship team, 1994, 2000, 2002; recognized nine times as Japanese League All-Star; being a member of American League All-Star Team 2003; being the runner-up American League Rookie of the Year 2003. Office: c/o New York Yankees 161st St and River Ave Bronx NY 10452 Office Phone: 718-293-4300. Office Fax: 718-293-8431.

**MATSUKA, YURY V.,** biochemist, research scientist; b. Mariupol, Ukraine, Dec. 2, 1960; s. Alla and Vladimir Matsuka; 1 child, George. MS in Biophysics, Kyiv State U., Ukraine, 1983; PhD in Biochemistry, Palladin Inst. Biochemistry, Ukraine, 1989. Cert. Biology and Biophysics State Examinational Com., Ukraine, 1983, Biochemistry Supreme Certifying Com. at Coun. of Ministers of USSR, 1990. Biochemistry scientist Palladin Inst. of Biochemistry, NAS of Ukraine, Kyiv, 1983—91; vis. scientist ARC, Jerome H. Holland Lab. for the Biomedical Sciences, Rockville, Md., 1991—96; sr. rsch. scientist Wyeth Rsch., Dept. of Protein Chemistry, Rochester, NY, 1996—2003, prin. rsch. scientist Pearl River, NY, 2003—; sr. rsch. scientist Wyeth Rsch., Rochester, NY, 1996—2003, prin. rsch. scientist Pearl River, NY, 2003—. Jour. rev., wyeth rsch. rev. panel Wyeth Rsch., Pearl River, NY, 2003—. Author: (scientific manuscripts) several papers publ. in various jours. Recipient Above and Beyond award, Wyeth, 2003. Mem.: Am. Soc. for Biochemistry and Molecular Biology (corr.). Achievements include research in Fibrinolytic & Coagulation Systems, Bacterial, Molecular Pathogenesis. Office: Wyeth 401 N Middletown Rd Pearl River NY 10965 Office Phone: 845-602-8366.

**MATSUMORI, DOUGLAS,** lawyer; b. Salt Lake City, Oct. 22, 1947; BS, U. Utah, 1973; JD, Harvard U., 1976. Ptnr. Ray, Quinney & Nebeker PC, Salt Lake City. Mem. Utah State Bar, Phi Beta Kappa. Office: Ray Quinney & Nebeker PO Box 45385 Salt Lake City UT 84145-0385

**MATSUMOTO, CAROLEE SETSUKO,** researcher, education developer and administrator; b. Denver, Feb. 13, 1943; d. Harry Katsumi and Pearl Shizuho (Nakamura) M.; m. David Luther Gilbertson, Oct. 20, 1990. BA, Ea. Mich. U., 1965; MEd, Wayne State U., 1968; EdD, Harvard Univ., 1991. Cert. biology, sci. tchr., adminstr., Mass. Sci. tchr. Greenburgh Sch. Dist. #8, Hartsdale, NY, 1965-67; sci. dept., head tchr. Nagoya Internat. Sch., Japan, 1968-70; tchr. sci. grades 7-8 Brookline HS, Mass., 1970—73, tchr. biology, 1976—79, sci. supr., 1979-81; sci. dept. head Graded Am. Sch., Sao Paulo, Brazil, 1973-76; asst. supt. curriculum, instrn. Concord and Concord/Carlisle Pub. Schs., Mass., 1981-87; teaching fellow Harvard U., Cambridge, Mass., 1984-85; curriculum dir., prin. investigator Edn. Devel. Ctr., Newton, Mass., 1987-93, sr. project dir., sr. scientist, 1993—. Bd. dirs. New Eng. & Islands Reg. Lab., Andover, Mass., 1985-96, Lloyd Environ. Ctr., S. Dartmouth, Mass., 1990-97; mem. adv. coun. Collaboration for Equity, Am. Assn. for Advancement Sci., Washington, 1994-96; mem. Mass Dept. Edn. Cultural Proficiency Steering Com., 2006-; vis. scholar Stanford U., Palo Alto, 1993; rep. Carpe Vitam Found., Sweden; tchrs. 21, Wellesley, Mass.; bd. trustees New Bedford Oceanarium. Mem. ASCD, NSDC, Nat. Sci. Tchrs. Assn. Avocations: travel, photography. Home: 17 Arnold Pl New Bedford MA 02740-1604

**MATSUMOTO, ROGER LEE KEN,** research scientist, artist; b. Honolulu, May 28, 1952; s. Kazuichi Andrew and Reiko; m. Mary Clare Urlacher, Aug. 6, 1977; children: Michael(dec.), Steven, Brett. BS Physics, Seattle U., 1973; MS Ceramics, U. Wash., 1975. Engr. EDO We., Salt Lake City, 1976—79; mgr. product develop. Ceramatec, Inc., Salt Lake City, 1980—88; rsch. scientist Hercules, Wilmington, Del., 1988—92; sr. materials scientist GE, Newark, Del., 1992—. Photographer (permanent collections) 2 Palladium Prints, Phila. Mus. Art. Individual Artist Fellowship, Del. Divsn. Art, 2001. Mem.: Am. Recorder Soc. (pres. Brandywine chpt.). Achievements include patents in field. Avocations: bicycling, recorder. Home: 205 La Salle Way Newark DE 19711 Personal E-mail: palladium48@aol.com.

**MATSUMOTO, TERUO,** surgeon, educator; b. Fukuoka City, Japan, Jan. 2, 1929; came to U.S., 1956, naturalized, 1964; s. Yoshinari and Fumie (Hayashi) M.; m. Mary L. Cousino, July 29, 1961; children: Louisa Michi, Maria Chieko, Monica Mieko, Nelson Tateru. MD, Kyushu U., 1953, PhD, 1956. Diplomate Am. Bd. Surgery, Am. Bd. Gen. Vascular Surgery. Intern Cook County Hosp., Chgo., 1956-57; surg. resident Med. Coll. Ohio, Toledo, 1957-61; commd. capt. U.S. Army, 1961, advanced through grades to lt. col., 1965; gen. surgeon U.S. Army Camp Zama Hosp., Japan, 1961-65, chief surg. service, 1962-65, chief gen. surgery sect., 1962-65; chief dept. exptl. surgery Walter Reed Army Inst. Research, 1965-68, dir. U.S. Army Surg. Research, Pacific, 1968; assoc. prof. surgery Hahnemann Med. Coll. and Hosp., Phila., 1969-72; prof. surgery Hahnemann U., Phila., 1973—, chmn. dept. surgery, 1975-90, dir. divsn. vascular surgery, 1990—; pres. med. staff Hahnemann Med. Coll. and Hosp., 1979-81. Mem. sci. rev. com. NIH, cons. field surgeon for Office of Orphan Products Devel., FDA, 1986 Editor Emergency Surgery, Jour. Internat. Surgery, Jour. Critical Care Medicine, Jour. Internat. Cardiovascular Surgery; contbr. to profl. jours. and books. Recipient Sir Henry Wellcome medal and prize, 1965, gold medal Southeastern Surg. Congress, 1968, Outstanding Achievement award U.S. Army Sci. Conf., 1969, Golden Apple award Student AMA, 1972. Fellow Southeastern Surg. Congress, ACS,

Am. Coll. Angiology, Am. Assn. for Surgery of Trauma, Pan Am. Med. Assn., Assn. Surgery for Alimentary Tract, AMA, Japanese Coll. Surgeons, Internat. Cardiovascular Surgery, Soc. Vascular Surgery, AOA, Phila. Acad. Surgery, Pan Pacific Surg. Congress, Soc. Surg. Chairmen; mem. Council Cardiovascular Surgery, Soc. Surg. Oncology Home: 1026 Broadmoor Rd Bryn Mawr PA 19010-1934 Office: Hahnemann U Med Sch Philadelphia PA 19102

**MATSUSHIMA, AKIRA PAUL,** manufacturing executive; b. Tokyo, July 7, 1937; arrived in U.S., 1970; s. Hiromasa and Tomiko (Watanabe) Matsushima; m. Kathleen Sue Rowland, Aug. 18, 1968; children: John Hikaru, Karen Emi, Amy Kathryn. BS, Waseda U., Tokyo, 1961, MS in Mech. Engring., 1964; M in Mgmt., Northwestern U., 1981. Registered profl. engr., Calif. Asst. R & D mgr. NOK Corp. (Nippon Oil Seal Industry), Tokyo, 1961—85, mgr. rsch. planning, 1968-70; dir. engring. NOK-USA, Inc., LA, 1970-72, v.p., 1973-74, exec. v.p. Chgo., 1975-83, sec., 1979-82, dir., 1971-85; dep. gen. mgr. engring. divsn. NOK Corp., Tokyo, 1983-85; with Chgo. Rawhide Mfg. Co. (SKF), Elgin, Ill., 1985—98, sr. v.p., 1995-98; pres. Matsushima Mgmt., Palatine, Ill., 1999—. Japanese govt. del. Internat. Standardization Orgn., 1973—78; chmn. K. C. Engring. Ltd., Yokohama, Japan, 1989—95, pres., 1991—95; del. Motor Equipment Mfr. Assn./Japan Auto Mfr. Assn. Conf., 1990, 92, 94; exec. dir. U.S. ops. Yaguchi Seisakusho Co. Ltd., 1999—; bd. dirs. PLACO Co., Ltd., Saitama, Japan; bd. dirs., pres., sec., treas. ARAI Ams. Inc., Va. Beach, Va., 2001—; v.p., bd. dirs. Nihon Clin. Co., Inc., Va. Beach, 2002—04; comisario PT Arai Rubber Seal Indonesia, Jakarta, 2002—04; bd. dirs. Hi-Tech Arai, Inc., Madurai, India, 2000—; mem. Exec. Ptnrs., Coll. William and Mary, Grad. Sch. Bus., Williamsburg, Va., 2005—. Contbr. articles to profl. jours. Fund dr. chair western divsn. Jr. Achievement, Chgo., 1988—89, mem. governing bd., 1990—98, United Way Elgin, 1988—96, v.p. planning, 1991—92; pres. Oak Crest Residence, Elgin, 1993 95; commr. to gen. assembly Presbyn. Ch. U.S.A., 2001. Mem.: NSPE, Soc. Automotive Engrs. (adv. bd. seals com., cert. of Appreciation 1986), Internat. House Japan. Achievements include patents in field. Office: Matsushima Mgmt 1332 Shire Cir Palatine IL 60067-4727 Office Phone: 847-705-9130. Personal E-mail: apmatsu@aol.com.

**MATSUURA, KENNETH RAY,** counseling administrator; b. Urbana, Ill., July 17, 1954; s. George Shigeo and Sally Sueko (Kawasaki) M.; m. Peggy Ai Iwata, May 27, 1995; 1 child, Claire Miya Sara. BA, U. Calif., Santa Barbara, 1976; MA, UCLA, 1978, PhD, 1996. Career counselor Calif. State U. Dominguez Hills, Carson, 1984-85; grad. recruitment coord. U. Calif., Irvine, 1985-90; counselor/articulation officer Cerritos Coll., Norwalk, Calif., 1990—. Mem. accreditation teams Western Assn. Schs. and Colls., L.A., 1994, Alameda, 1999, mem. accreditation task force Project Renewal; chair South Coast Higher Edn. Coun.; co-chair region 8 articulation officers and transfer ctre. dirs.; program reviewer Am. Coll. Pers. Assn. Ann. conf., Washington, 1988; presenter to confs. UCLA grad. advancement program fellow, 1977—78. Avocations: singing, music. Home: 101 Santa Ynez Dr Arcadia CA 91007 Office Phone: 562-860-2451 2141. Business E-Mail: matsuura@cerritos.edu.

**MATTA, CHÉRIF FARID,** chemistry professor; b. Alexandria, Egypt, Sept. 8, 1963; arrived in Can., 1995, naturalized; s. Farid Alphonse Matta and Nabila Nassif Abdel Nour. B in Pharm. Sci., Alexandria U., 1987; grad. diploma in health, hosp. adminstrn., Sadat Acad., Nat. Inst. Higher Mgmt., Alexandria, 1994; PhD in Theoretical, Computational Chemistry, McMaster U., Hamilton, Ont., Can., 2001. Registered pharmacist Ministry Health, Egypt, 1987. 1st lt. pharmacist strategic med. supplies Naval Forces Hdqs., Alexandria, 1987—90; logistical support specialist WHO Regional Office Ea. Mediterranean, 1991—96; tchg. asst., grad. rschr. chemistry McMaster U., 1996—2001; postdoctoral fellow chemistry U. Toronto, 2002—04; Izaak Walter Killam postdoctoral scholar chemistry Dalhousie U., Halifax, Nova Scotia, Canada, 2004—; adj. prof. chemistry McMaster U., 2004—. Mem. bd. govs. McMaster U., 2000—01; mem. environ. workgroup Ont. Pub. Health Assn., 2002—; external referee Levrhumle Trust, 2003. Contbr. scientific papers and a book. Recipient John C. Polanyi prize in Chemistry, 2004, Chemistry Tchg. award CTFP, 2003-04; Killam fellow, 2004-06, Next Sci. fellow Biovision, 2003-05. Mem.: European Soc. Computational Methods in Sci. and Engring., Am. Chem. Soc., Can. Chem. Soc., Ont. Pub. Health Assn. Chem. Inst. Can. Achievements include pioneering research in theoretical chemistry with strong impact ranging from medicinal chemistry to surface science. Office: Dept Chemistry Dalhousie Univ Halifax B3H 4J3 Canada Office Phone: +1 (902) 494-7021. Personal E-mail: quantumjazz@hotmail.com.

**MATTA, MARK W.,** human resources specialist, manufacturing executive; BS, MA, St. Francis Coll. Employee rels. coord. Morgan Engring. Alliance, Ohio; labor rels. supr. Wiley Mfg., Port Deposit, Md.; employee rels. mgr. Frito-Lay, Kirkwood, NY; v.p. human resources Sherwin-Williams Co.; sr. v.p. human resources OfficeMax, Inc., Shaker Heights, Ohio, Winn-Dixie Stores, Inc., Jacksonville, Fla., 2003—. Bd. dirs. Students in Free Enterprise. Office: Winn-Dixie Stores Inc 5050 Edgewood Ct Jacksonville FL 32254

**MATTAR, PHILIP,** writer; b. Haifa, Palestine, Jan. 21, 1944; came to U.S. 1961; m. Evelyn Ann Keith, June 20, 1971; 1 child, Christina. MPhil, Columbia U., 1977, PhD, 1981. Exec. dir. Inst. for Palestine Studies, Washington, 1984-2001; assoc. editor Jour. Palestine Studies, Washington, 1985-2001; fellow Woodrow Wilson Ctr., 2001—02; sr. fellow U.S. Inst. Peace, 2002—03; guest scholar U.S. Inst. of Peace, 2003—04. Adj. lectr. history Yale U., 1981; adj. prof. history Georgetown U., 1990, 91, 94. Author: Mufti of Jerusalem, 1988, 2d edit., 1991; editor: Encyclopedia of the Modern Middle East and North Africa, 2004, Encyclopedia of the Palestinians, 2005; contbr. articles to profl. jours. including Fgn. Policy, Middle East Jour., Middle Ea. Studies. Mem. adv. com. Human Rights Watch/Middle East. Vis. scholar Columbia U., 1984; Fulbright-Hays Rsch. fellow, 1978. Mem. Middle East Studies Assn., Middle East Inst. Avocations: jogging, chess, reading, travel. E-mail: pjmattar@aol.com.

**MATTAUCH, ROBERT JOSEPH,** retired electrical engineering educator, retired dean; b. Rochester, Pa., May 30, 1940; s. Henry Paul and Anna Marie (Mlinarcik) M.; m. Frances Sabo, Dec. 29, 1962; children: Lori Ann, Thomas J. BS, Carnegie Inst. Tech., Pitts., 1962; MEE, N.C. State U., Raleigh, 1963, PhD, 1967. Asst. prof. elec. engring. U. Va., Charlottesville, 1966-70, assoc. prof. elec. engring., 1970-76, prof. elec. engring., 1976-83, Wilson prof. elec. engring., 1983-86, Standard Oil Co. prof. sci. and tech., 1986-89, chmn. dept. elect. engring., 1987-95, BP Am. prof. sci. and tech., 1989-95; Commonwealth prof., founding chair dept. elec. engring. Va. Commonwealth U., Richmond, 1995-99, dean engring., Commonwealth prof., 1999—2006, dean emeritus, Commonwealth prof., 2006—. Cons. The Rochester Corp., Culpepper, Va., 1983—88, Milltech Corp., Deerfield, Mass., 1985. Patentee: infrared detector; solid state switching capacitor; thin wire pointing method, whiskerless Schottky diode, controlled in-situ etch back growth technique. Bd. dirs. U. Va. Patent Found., 1989-95, Greater Richmond Technology Coun., 2001—, Va. Bioscis. Devel. Ctr., 2000—, Richmond Symphony Orch., 2003—. Recipient Excellence in Instruction of Engring. Students award Western Electric, 1980. Fellow IEEE (Centennial medal 1984); mem. Eta Kappa Nu (recipient Oustanding Prof. in Elec. Engring 1975), Sigma Xi, Tau Beta Pi, Sigma Pi Sigma. Office: Va Commonwealth U Office of the Dean PO Box 843068 Richmond VA 23284-3068 Office Phone: 804-440-6757. Business E-Mail: rjmattau@vcu.edu.

**MATTEI, IVAN E.,** lawyer; b. Dec. 13, 1955; BS summa cum laude, Georgetown U., 1979; JD magna cum laude, Harvard U., 1985. Bar: NY 1987. Mem. Debevoise & Plimpton LLP, NYC, 1987—. Adj. prof. Columbia Law Sch., 1994—97. Mem.: ABA, Assn. Bar of City NY. Office: Debevoise & Plimpton LLP 919 Third Ave New York NY 10022 Office Phone: 212-909-6060. Fax: 212-909-6836. E-mail: iemattei@debevoise.com.

**MATTEO, CHRISTINE E.,** librarian; b. Jersey City, May 26, 1952; d. Peter J. G. and Doris Ella (Stoffel) Dirschauer; m. Joseph A. Matteo, Sept. 9, 1978. BA in Psychology, Washington Coll., Chestertown, Md., 1974; MLS, Rutgers U., 1977. Cert. libr. N.J. Sr. libr., br. mgr. Ocean County Libr., Beachwood, NJ, 1976-78, prin. libr., br. mgr. Jackson, NJ, 1978-86, automation implementation mgr. Toms River, NJ, 1986-89, supervising libr. ctrl. svcs., 1989-91, chief libr. pub. svcs., 1991-95, chief libr. tech., 1995—2003, chief libr. adminstrn., 2003—. Mem. exec. bd., treas. Customers Dynix, Inc., Provo, Utah, 1989—91, Ctrl. Jersey Regional Libr., Freehold, 1994—96; editor, mem. steering com. Ocean County Libr. Master Plan, Toms River, 1984—85, 1991—92, 1997—98; mem. exec. bd. One Ease-E-Link, Toms River, 1998—2002; presenter in field, 2005—06. Mem.: ASPCA, ALA, N.J. Libr. Assn. (info. techs. sect., mem. LGBT Roundtable), World Future Soc., Animal Birth Control Inc., Monmouth County SPCa, Toms River Seaport Soc., Greenpeace, Humane Soc. U.S., Earthwatch, Tuckerton Seaport Soc. (charter), Environ. Def. Fund, World Wildlife Fund, Associated Humane Socs., Humane Soc. U.S., Toms River Yacht Club. Avocations: sailing, gardening, dog obedience, kayaking, science fiction. Office: Ocean County Libr 101 Washington St Toms River NJ 08753-7688 Office Phone: 732-349-6200. Business E-Mail: matteo_c@oceancounty.lib.nj.us.

**MATTERN, DOUGLAS JAMES,** think-tank executive; b. Creede, Colo., May 19, 1933; s. John A. and Ethel (Franklin) Mattern; m. Noemi E. Del Cioppo, May 4, 1963. Student, San Jose State U., 1956-58. Reliability engr. Intersil, Sunnyvale, Calif., 1973-80; sr. engr. Data Gen. Corp., Sunnyvale, 1981-87; staff engr. Apple Computer, Cupertino, Calif., 1987-97; sr. engr. Trimble Navigation, Sunnyvale, 1998-2000. Sec. Gen. World Citizens Assembly, San Francisco, 1975—86; dir. World Citizens Diplomats, Palo Alto, Calif., 1988—90; pres. Assn. World Citizens, San Francisco, 1989—; CEO World Citizens Found., San Francisco, 1977—; chmn. World Citizens Assembly, San Francisco, 1995, Taipei, Taiwan, 2001, Internat. Peace Conf., San Francisco, 2005. Author: Resolution to End the Arms Race, 1982, Looking for Square Two-Moving from War and Violence to Global Community, 2006; contbg. author: Building a More Democratic United Nations, 1991; editor: World Citizen Newsmag., 1973—; contbr. Bd. dirs. San Francisco chpt. UN Assn.; bd. dirs. War/Peace Found. With USN, 1951—55. Recipient Albert Einstein Peace award, Internat. World Educators for World Peace, 2001, Lifetime Achievement award for Love and Peace, Fowpal, 2005. Home: 2671 South Ct Palo Alto CA 94306-2462 Office: 55 New Montgomery St Ste 224 San Francisco CA 94105-3421 Office Phone: 415-541-9610. E-mail: worldcit@best.com.

**MATTERN, JOANNE,** writer, educator; b. Nyack, NY, Mar. 5, 1963; d. Robert Frederick and Genevieve Porri Gise; m. James Jude Mattern, June 16, 1990; children: Christina Xinwei, Leanne Pengjing, Grace Fuwan. BA in English, Hartwick Coll., 1985. Asst. editor Morrow Jr. Books, NYC, 1985—88; sr. editor, writer Troll Comms., Mahwah, NJ, 1988—95; freelance writer, 1995—. Author: (series) Wildlife of North America, 1998, Compete Like a Champion: Gymnastics, 1999, Barbie First-Grade Workbooks, 1999, Fisher-Price Little People Toddler Sticker Workbooks, 2000, Explorers, 2000—01, Working Together, 2001, Animal Geography, 2001, Safety First, 2000, Learning About Cats, 2000—01, Native Peoples, 2001, (children's books) Brer Rabbit in the Briar Patch, 1997, I Can't Believe My Eyes! Extraordinary Photos or Ordinary Things, 1997, Smart Thinking! Clever Ways Animals Make Their Lives Easier, 1997, Telling Time with Goofy, 1997, The Story of Molly Pitcher, 1999, The Trojan Horse, 1999, Big and Small, Homes for All: The Story of Bird Nests, 1999, From Flowers to Honey: The Story of Beekeeping, 1999, Mountain Climb, 1999, A Visit to the Past, 1999, Tower of Stone: The Story of a Castle, 1999, Claws and Wings and Other Neat Things, 2000, Power Rangers Power-Up Skills Learning Pads, 2000, Wishbone Adventures: Curse of Gold, 2000, Teletubbies Fun with Favorite Things Giant Coloring Activity Book, 2000, Animals Animals, 2001, People in the News: Tom Cruise, 2001, Nature's Greatest Hits, 2001, Reading Progress Indicators, 1998, Texas Assessment of Academic Skills, 2000, Reading Workbook, 2001, many others. Mem.: Soc. Children's Book Writers and Illustrators. Roman Catholic. Avocations: choral music, needlecrafts, church activities, reading, travel.

**MATTERSON, JOAN MCDEVITT,** physical therapist; b. Bryn Mawr, Pa., Feb. 24, 1949; d. William J. and Wanda Jean (Edwards) McD.; children: Brian, Jennie, Kira. BS in Biology, St. Joseph's U., Phila., 1973; cert. in Phys. Therapy, U. Pa., 1974. Assoc. pharmacologist, rschr. immunology and arthritis Prog. Phys. Therapy, P.A., Wilmington, Del., 1976-93, pediatric phys. therapist, 1974-81, pres., 1976-95; rehab. dir. Achievement Rehab.; phys. therapist Liberty Home Health, 1995—; rehab. dir. Office of Joan Matterson, 1995—, Integrated Health Svcs.- Kent, Smyrna, Del., 1996—; dir. rehab. Keystone Care Therapies, Media, Pa., 1997—, with Pain Mgmt. Ctr. Chester, Pa., 1999; with Hands on Health, Wilmington, 1999—2000; phys. therapist Hickory House Nursing and Rehab. Ctr., Honeybrook, Pa., 2000—; pvt. practice Wilmington, 2000—. Lectr. in field of low level laser therapy. Dep. gov. Am. Biog. Rsch. Inst.; mem. adv. bd. Internat. Biog. Rsch. Inst., Cambridge, Eng. Mem. NAFE, Am. Soc. Laser Medicine and Surgery, Internat. Platform Assn., Am. Acad. Pain (assoc.), Inst. Noetic Sci., Am. Bd. Forensic Examiners, N.Am. Assn. Laser Therapy, Internat. Exec. Service Corp. Avocations: dance, skiing, cooking. Office Phone: 610-457-9158. Personal E-mail: jnmttrsn711@aol.com.

**MATTES, MARTIN ANTHONY,** lawyer; b. San Francisco, June 18, 1946; s. Hans Adam and Marion Jane (Burge) M.; m. Catherine Elvira Garzio, May 26, 1984; children: Nicholas Anthony, Daniel Joseph, Thomas George. BA, Stanford U., 1968; postgrad., U. Chgo., 1968-69, U. Bonn, Germany, 1971; JD, U. Calif., Berkeley, 1974. Bar: Calif. 1974, U.S. Ct. Appeals (D.C., 5th and 9th cirs.) 1978, U.S. Dist. Ct. (no. dist.) Calif. 1979, U.S. Dist. Ct. (ea. dist.) Calif. 1991. Asst. legal officer Internat. Union Conservation of Nature and Natural Resources, Bonn, 1974-76; staff counsel Calif. Pub. Utilities Commn., San Francisco, 1976-79, legal advisor to pres., 1979-82, adminstrv. law judge, 1983, asst. chief adminstrv. law judge, 1983-86; ptnr. Graham & James, San Francisco, 1986-98, Nossaman Guthner Knox and Elliott, LLP, San Francisco, 1998—. Adv. group. Calif. Senate Subcom. on Pub. Utilities Commn. Procedural Reform, 1994. Mng. editor Ecology Law Quar., 1973-74; contbr. articles to profl. jours. Mem. Conf. Calif. Pub. Utility Counsel (treas. 1988-90, v.p. 1990-91, pres. 1991-92), Internat. Coun. Environ. Law, San Francisco Bar Assn., Fed. Comms. Bar Assn., Power Assn. No. Calif. Office: Nossaman Guthner Knox Elliott LLP 50 California St Fl 34 San Francisco CA 94111-4624 Office Phone: 415-398-3600. Business E-Mail: mmattes@nossaman.com.

**MATTESON, CAROL J.,** academic administrator; BS in Health Edn., Slippery Rock U. of Pa.; MS in Psychomotor Learning, U. Oreg.; PhD in Bus. Adminstrn., U. Pitts. Faculty Sturt Coll. of Edn., South Australia, Slippery Rock U., U. Maine, Augusta, Rowan U., NJ; asst. to pres. Slippery Rock U. of Pa.; dean coll. of bus. Bloomsburg U., Pa., provost and v.p. academic affairs Pa., 1992—95; exec. v.p. and provost Rowan U., NJ, 1995—2000; pres. Mt. Ida Coll., Newton, Mass., 2000—. Office: Mt Ida Coll 777 Dedham St Newton MA 02459

**MATTESON, CLARICE CHRIS,** artist, educator; b. Winnipeg, Man., Can., Sept. 2, 1918; came to U.S., 1922; d. Sergis and Nina (Balter) Alberts; m. D.C. Matteson, 1956 (dec. 1976); children: Kemmer, Gretchen. BA, Met. State U., 1976; MA in Liberal Studies, Hamline U., 1986; PhD in Humanities, LaSalle U., 1995. Mem. Orson Welles' staff, Hollywood, Calif., 1945-46; owner Hilde-Gardes Co., L.A., 1952—56; instr. art North Hennepin C.C., Brooklyn Park, Minn., 1975-81; instr. continuing edn. for women U. Minn., 1980. Prodr., host TV program Accent on Art, St. Paul, 1979—; instr. art Lakewood C.C., 1979, U. Minn., Bloomington (Minn.) Sch. Dist., 1980-2004, Mpls. Sch. Dist., St. Paul Sch. Dist., 1994-95, 03-04; guest artist Montserrat Gallery, Soho, N.Y.C, 1999; appeared as guest artist WCCO-TV, 1998; spkr. on TV, Am. Pen Women Spirituality and Creativity in Art, 2003. (one-woman shows) Decathlon Club, 1998, State Capital Rotunda, 1986, Lindbergh Home, 1988, Hamline U., 2002, exhibited (group shows) Mpls.

Inst. Art, 1994—98, Art in Bloom, 1999—2002, St. Paul, 2000, Landmark Ctr., Hamline U., St. Paul, 2002, U. Minn. Womens Club Art Show, 2003, Fairmount Hotel, 2002; Exhibited in group shows at Art in Bloom, 1999—2003; (represented by) Gov. Ventura's Ofcl. Residence and now by Gov. Jim Pawlenty, 2003—04, Montserrat Art Gallery, N.Y.C., Gallery 416, Mpls., Jean Stephen Art Gallery, 1999—2002, Premier Gallery, 2001—02, (corr.) Schaumburg (Ill) Newspapers, 1962—68; prodr.: (TV series, host) Kids Art, 1995—, (series program) Internat. Cafe Internet Arts, 1996—; patentee plastic products; prodr.: Men Aware TV, 2001—02, Punt, Pass, or Pie TV, 2001—02; composer: I Want You Near; Exhibited in group shows at Women's Club, 2002—03, exhibited in group shows, Gov. Ventura's and Gov. Tim Pawlenty's, 2001—05; composer: You Make a Difference, God is in my Heart. Active Minn. Orch. (WAMSO), Mpls., 1972—, vol. Recipient award for creative leadership Minn. Assn. for Continuing Adult Edn., 1977, Gold Cup award Bloomington Cable, 1989, Gov.'s Letter of Commendation, 1994; named Outstanding Grad. for past 25 yrs. Met. State U., 1997, Disting. Alumna John Marshall H.S., L.A., 2002, Outstanding Nominee of Grad. Students Met. State U., 2002; Park Cable TV grantee, 1982, Minn. Humanities Commn. grantee, 1985. Qem. ASCAP (award 1997-2003, award for popular music, 2003-04), AAUW (dir. arts com. 1989-90, bd. dirs. 1990-92), Am. Pen Women (Minn. chpt. 1994—, v.p. 1998), Internat. Biog. Assn. (dep. dir. Cambridge, Eng. 2001, participate art and comm. congress, 2001), Am. Composers Forum, Minn. Artists Assn., Minn. Territorial Pioneers (bd. dirs. 1995—, v.p. 1997-99, 1st v.p. 1999-2003, elected Minnesotan of Yr., 1999-2002, elected 1st v.p. 2003-04), Internat. Alliance for Women in Music, St. Paul Neighborhood Network (elected bd. dirs. TV station SPNN, 2002), N.Y. Neighborhood Network, Internat. Platform Speakers (award 1998), Mpls. Telecom. Network, Metro Cable Network, Adelphi Cable, Manhattan Cable, Duluth-Superior Cable, NDT, Eagan. Avocations: tennis, dance, writing children's books, composing liturgical music. Home and Office: 2119 Sargent Ave Saint Paul MN 55105-1126

**MATTESON, KARLA J.,** health science association administrator; BS in Chemistry, Beloit Coll., Wis., 1969; MS in Chemistry, Marquette U., 1976; PhD, Med. Coll. Wis., 1981. Postdoctoral fellow Baylor Coll. Medicine, Houston, 1981—83; former asst. dir. U. Tenn Devel. and Genetic Ctr., Knoxville; assoc. prof. med. genetics and pathology U. Tenn., Knoxville, 1986—, dir. biochem. and molecular genetics lab., 1986—; bd. dirs. Am. Bd. Med. Genetics, 1998—2001, exec. dir., 2001—. Fellow: Am. Coll. Med. Genetics; mem.: AAAS, Soc. for Inborn Metabolic Disorders. Office: U Tenn Grad Sch Medicine Ste 435 1924 Alcoa Hwy Knoxville TN 37920-6999 also: Am Bd Med Genetics 9650 Rockville Pike Bethesda MD 20814-3998*

**MATTESON, WILLIAM BLEECKER,** lawyer; b. NYC, Oct. 20, 1928; s. Leonard Jerome and Mary Jo (Harwell) M.; m. Marilee Brill, Aug. 26, 1950; children: Lynn, Sandra, Holly. Ba, Yale U., 1950; JD, Harvard U., 1953. Bar: N.Y. 1954. Clk. to judge Augustus N. Hand U.S. Ct. Appeals, 1953-54; clk. to U.S. Supreme Ct. Justice Harold H. Burton, 1954-55; assoc. firm Debevoise & Plimpton (and predecessors), N.Y.C., 1955-61, ptnr., 1961—98, Debevoise & Plimpton (European office), Paris, 1973-78; presiding ptnr. Debevoise & Plimpton, 1988-93. Lectr. Columbia U. Law Sch., 1972-73, 78-80. Trustee Peddie Sch., Hightstown, N.J., 1968-73, Kalamazoo Coll., 1972-77, Miss Porter's Sch., Farmington, Conn., 1977-83, N.Y. Inst. Spl. Edn., 1981-2004, Salk Inst., La Jolla, Calif., 1993-96, vice-chair, 1994-96, Statue of Liberty Ellis Island Found., 1996—, Hartford Found., 1990-95; active USA Bus. and Industry Adv. Com. to the Orgn. for Econ. Coop. and Devel., Paris, 1986-2000; chmn. Worldwide Bus. and Industry Adv. Com. 1994-96; vice chmn. U.S. Coun. for Internat. Bus., 1990-2000, hon. trustee. Mem. ABA, FBA, Internat. Bar Assn., N.Y. State Bar Assn., Assn. of Bar of City of N.Y. (chmn. securities regulation com. 1968-71), Harvard U. Law Sch. Assn. N.Y.C. (trustee 1968-73), Coun. Fgn. Rels., Union Club, Sky Club, Sankaty Head Club, John's Island Redstick, and Windsor Clubs, N.Y. Yacht Club. Office: Debevoise & Plimpton 919 3d Ave 47th Fl New York NY 10022 E-mail: wbmatteson@debevoise.com

**MATTESSICH, RICHARD VICTOR (ALVARUS),** business administration researcher; b. Trieste, Venezia-Julia, Italy, Aug. 9, 1922; s. Victor and Gertrude M.; m. Hermine Auguste Mattessich, Apr. 12, 1952. Mech. engr., Engring. Coll., Vienna, Austria, 1940; Diplomkaufmann, Hochschule für Welthandel, Vienna, 1944; Dr.rer.pol., Hochschule für Welthandel, 1945; Accademico Ordinario, Accademia Italiana di Economia Aziendale, Bologna, 1980—; D honoris causa, U. Complutense, Madrid, 1998. U. Montesquieux, Bordeaux, 2006, U. Malaga, 2006. Rsch. fellow Austrian Inst. Econ. Rsch., Vienna, 1945-47; instr. Rosenberg Coll., St. Gallen, 1947-52; dep. head Mt. Allison U., Sackville, Canada, 1953-59; assoc. prof. U. Calif., Berkeley, 1958-67; prof. econs. Ruhr U., Bochum, Germany, 1966-67; prof. indsl. adminstrn. U. Tech., Vienna, 1976-78; prof. bus. adminstrn. U. B.C., Vancouver, Canada, 1967-87; prof. emeritus, 1988—; Arthur Andersen & Co. Disting. chair, 1980-87. Vis. prof. Free U., Berlin, 1965, U. Social Scis., St. Gallen, Switzerland, 1965-66, U. Canterbury, 1970, Austrian Acad. Mgmt., 1971, 73, City Univ. Hong Kong, 1992, Chuo U., Tokyo, 1992; hon. prof. Centro Univ. Francesco de Vitoria, Madrid; mem. bd. nominations Acctg. Hall of Fame, Columbus, Ohio, 1978-87, 2004—; bd. govs. Sch. Chartered Accountancy, Vancouver, 1981-82; bd. dirs. Can. Cert. Gen. Accts. Rsch. Found., 1984-90, internat. adv. bd., 1993—. Author: Accounting and Analytical Methods, 1964, in German, 1970, in Japanese, 1972, in Spanish, 2002, Simulation of the Firm Through a Budget Computer Program, 1964, Instrumental Reasoning and Systems Methodology, 1978, Critique of Accounting: Foundational Research in Accounting, 1995, Professional Memoirs and Beyond, 1995, The Beginnings of Accounting and Accounting Thought, 2000; editor: Modern Accounting Research History, Survey and Guide, 1984, 89, 92, Accounting Research in the 1980s and Its Future Influence, 1991, French transl., 1993, others; mem. editl. bd. Theory and Decision Libr., Jour. Bus. Adminstrn., Economia Azlendale, Praxiology, Acctg., Bus. and Fin. History. Sec.-treas. Internat. House, U. B.C., 1969-70. Served to lt. Orgn. Todt., 1944-45. Recipient Lit. award AICPA, 1972, Haim Falk award Can. Acad. Acctg. Assn., 1991, highest rsch. award Acad. Accounting Historians, 2003, Hourglass award; Ford Found. fellow, 1961-62; Disting. Erskine fellow U. Canterbury, 1970; Killam sr. fellow U. B.C., 1971-72; nominated Nobel Meml. prize in Econs., 2002. Fellow Accademia Italiana di Economia Aziendale (accademico ordinario 1980—); mem. Am. Acctg. Assn. (lit. award 1972), Schmalenbach Gesellschaft, Verb. d. Hochschullehrer für Betriebswirtschaft (cert. adv. coun. 1976-78), Inst. Chartered Accts. of B.C. (bd. of govs. 1981-82), Austrian Acad. Scis. (corr.), Acad. Acctg. Historians (life). Achievements include pioneering analytical methods in accounting and the computerized spreadsheet. Office: U BC Sauder Sch Bus Vancouver BC Canada V6T 1Z2 Business E-Mail: Richard.Mattessich@sauder.ubc.ca. *Cautious optimism is the best long-run strategy.*

**MATTHAU, CHARLES MARCUS,** film director; b. N.Y.C., Dec. 10, 1965; s. Walter and Carol M. BA, U. So. Calif., 1986. Pres. The Matthau Co., L.A., 1987—. Bd. govs. Cedar Sinai Med. Ctr., L.A. Dir. motion picture Doin' Time on Planet Earth, 1990 (Saturn award Coun. Film Orgns., Silver Scroll award Acad. Sci. Fiction); dir., prodr. TV show Mrs. Lambert Remembers Love, 1993 (Golden Angel award Best TV Spl. 1993, Golden Medal award Best Drama Prodn. 1993, Grand award The Houston Internat. Film Festival); dir., prodr. motion picture The Grass Harp, 1996 (recipient Best Dir. Family Film awards 1996); dir. The Marriage Fool, 1998; dir. over 50 feature shorts. Nat. spokesperson Am. Lung Assn., L.A., 1989—; active Action on Smoking and Health, Washington, 1986—. Recipient Cine award, Coun. Non-Theatrical Events, Washington, 1985, Golden Seal award, London Amateur Film Festival, 1986, Platinum Circle award Am. Film Inst. Mem. Dirs. Guild Am.

**MATTHEI, EDWARD HODGE,** architect; b. Chgo., Dec. 21, 1927; s. Henry Reinhard and Myra Beth (Hodge) M.; m. Mary Nina Hoffmann, June 30, 1951; children: Edward Hodge, Suzanne Marie, Christie Ann, Laura Jean, John William. BS in Archtl. Engring. U. Ill., 1951. Registered arch. 17 states, including Ariz., Fla., Ill., Mich., N.Y., Wis., Calif.; cert. NCARB. Dir. health facilities planning and constrn. Child & Smith (architects and engrs.), Chgo.,

1951-60; sr. v.p. health facilities planning Perkins & Will, Chgo., 1960-74; ptnr. firm Matthei & Colin Assoc., Chgo., 1974-96; planning and archtl. design cons. Chgo., 1996—. Coun. chmn. Am. Nat. Standards Inst., 1983-89; lectr. 1st Internat. Conf. on Rehab. of Handicapped, Beijing, 1986, Design USA, Novosibirsk and Moscow, USSR, 1990. Editor: Inland Architect, 1956-58; prin. works health facilities projects, med. ctr. master plans including Akron (Ohio) Gen. Hosp., Heritage Hosp., Taylor, Mich., Rose Meml., Denver, Silver Cross Hosp., Joliet, Ill., Shands Tchg. Hosp. & Med. Sch., U. Fla., Gainesville, Mercy Hosp., Davenport, Iowa, Westlake Cmty. Hosp., Chgo., Highland Park (Ill.) Hosp., Ctrl. DuPage Hosp., Winfield, Ill., Nebr. Meth. Hosp., Omaha, Rockford (Ill.) Meml. Hosp., U. Ala. Med. Ctr., Birmingham, U. Calif. Sch. Medicine, Irvine, Kent Hall, U. Chgo., Holy Cross Hosp., Md., West Mich. Cancer Ctr. Second v.p. Nat. Easter Seal Soc., 1978; mem. bd. dirs. St. Scholastica H.S., Chgo., 1973-83, 86-96; mem. Welfare Coun. Greater Met. Chgo., 1965-72; chair profl. adv. coun. Nat. Easter Seal Soc., 1988-89. With AUS, 1946-47. Recipient Leon Chatelain award for barrier-free environ. Nat. Easter Seals Soc., 1979, Disting. Svc. award, 1990, 99, Meritorious Svc. award Am. Nat. Standards Inst., 1987, Speedy award Paralyzed Vets. Am., 1993. Fellow AIA (Disting. Svc. award Chgo. chpt. 1988); mem. Am. Hosp. Assn., Am. Assn. Hosp. Planning, Internat. Hosp. Fedn., Nat. Center Barrier Free Environ. (dir.), Builders Assn. Chgo., Chgo. Assn. Commerce and Industry. Home: 1437 W Glenlake Ave Chicago IL 60660-1801 Office: Matthei & Colin Assocs 332 S Michigan Ave Chicago IL 60604-4434

**MATTHEIS, THERESA JUDITH,** webmaster, educator; b. Bismarck, N.D., Apr. 11, 1977; d. Donald Harold and Judy Katherine Mattheis. BS in Elem. Edn., Dickinson State U., 2002. Vocal music educator Scranton Pub. Sch., Dickinson, ND, 2002—04; substitute tchr. Dickinson Pub. Schs., 2003—04; front desk clk. Hospitality Inn, Dickinson, 2004; with Am. Express, Dickinson, 2004—. Home: 112 2d Ave E Dickinson ND 58601 Office: Am Express 9330 64th Ave NE Dickinson ND 58601

**MATTHEW, LYN,** sales executive, consultant, marketing professional; b. Long Beach, Calif., Dec. 15, 1936; d. Harold G. and Beatrice (Hunt) Matthew; m. Wayne Thomas Castleberry, Aug. 12, 1961 (div. Jan. 1976); children: Melanie Castleberry, Cheryl Castleberry, Nicole Castleberry, Matthew Castleberry. BS, U. So. Calif., Davis, 1958; MA, Ariz. State U., 1979. Cert. hotel sales exec., meeting profl., hospitality mktg. exec., hospitality mgmt. exec. Pres. Davlyn Cons. Found., Scottsdale, Ariz., 1979-82; cons., vis. prof. Art Bus., Scottsdale, 1982—; pres., dir. sales and mktg. Embassy Stes., Scottsdale, 1987-98; pres. Matthew Enterprises, Inc., Scottsdale, 1998—. Vis. prof. Maricopa CC, Phoenix, 1979—, Ariz. State U., Tempe, 1980—83; cons. Women's Caucus Art, Phoenix, 1983—88; coun. adminstr. Lynn Andrews Prodns., 2001—. Author: The Business Aspects of Art, Book I, 1979, Book II, 1989, Marketing Strategies for the Creative Artist, 1985, Moxibustion Manual, 1999. Bd. dirs. Rossom Ho. and Heritage Sq. Found., Phoenix, 1987—88; trustee Hotel Sales and Mktg. Assn. Internat. Found., 1988—90, chmn., 1991—93, mem. exec. com., 1993—95. Recipient Cmty. Bldg. award, 2000. Mem.: Am. Orgn. Bodywork Therapies Asia (pres., state dir. 1999—2003), Ariz. Acad. Performing Arts (v.p. bd. dir. 1987—88, pres. 1988—89), Soc. Govt. Meeting Planners (charter bd. dir. 1987, nat. conf. co-chair 1993—94, Sam Gilmer award 1992), Meeting Planners Internat. (v.p. Ariz. Sunbelt chpt. 1989—91, pres. 1991—92, CMP cert. trainer 1995—, Supplier of the Yr. award 1984), Cert. Hospitality Mktg. Execs. (profl. designation tng. chair 1995), Hotels Sales and Mktg. Assn. Internat. (bd. dir. 1985—90, pres. Great Phoenix chpt. 1988—89, regional dir. 1989—90, mktg. exec. 1998—), Ariz. Vocat. Edn. Assn. (sec. 1978—80), Ariz. Women's Caucus Art (pres. 1980—82, hon. advisor 1986—87), Nat. Women's Caucus Art (v.p. 1981—83), Women in Higher Edn., Ariz. Visionary Artists (treas. 1987—88), Women Image Now (Achievement and Contbn. in Visual Arts award 1983), Coun. Whistling Elk (worldwide coun. adminstr. 2001—06).

**MATTHEW, NEIL EDWARD,** artist, educator; b. Anderson, Ind., Jan. 19, 1925; s. Mark Neil and Mary Bertha (Clifford) Matthew; m. Jeannette Morrow, Dec. 22, 1963 (dec. Aug. 30, 2000). BA in Edn., Ariz. State U., 1949; MFA, Ind. U., 1955; postgrad., U. Iowa, 1957-58, State Acad. of Fine Arts, Stuttgart, Germany, 1959-60. Tchr., art Covington (Ind.) Jr. HS, 1949-50, Clay HS, South Bend, Ind., 1955-57; instr. art Ind. U., Kokomo, 1960-64, from instr. to asst. prof. art. Indpls., 1964-71; from asst. to assoc. prof. Herron Sch. Art/Ind. U. Purdue U., Indpls., 1971-87, assoc. prof. emeritus, 1987—. Art exhibit judge Anderson Art Assn., 1970; rschr. salary studies AAUP, Ind. U. Purdue U., others. One-man shows include Lieber's Gallery, Indpls., 1962, 1968, Purdue U. Gallery, 1962, Ind. U. Med. Ctr., Indpls., 1966, Ind. U. Kokomo, 1967, Ind. U. Purdue U., Indpls., 1996, 1998, Lyman-Snodgrass Gallery, 1984, others, exhibited in group shows at Libr. Congress, 1956, 1958—59, Purdue U., 1966, 1969, Ind. Arts Competition, 1988, U. Ariz. Mus. Art, Tucson, 2005, exhibitions include, 2000, Represented in permanent collections Ctr. Creative Photography, Tucson, U. Ariz. Mus. Art, Ind. U. Purdue U., Indpls., Indpls. Mus. Art, Ind. U. Art Mus., Bloomington, Ind., Ind. State Mus., Indpls., Ind., Ctr. Creative Photography, 2003. With U.S. Army, 1950—52. Scholar, U. Iowa, 1957—58; Fulbright grantee, Stuttgart, 1959—60. Mem.: Coll. Art Assn., Fulbright Assn., Ctr. Creative Photography, Soc. Ind. Pioneers. Republican. Presbyterian. Avocations: travel, reading, history, fiction. Home: 5233 North Via Sempreverde Tucson AZ 85750-5967

**MATTHEWS, ALEXANDER,** health facility administrator; b. N.Y.C., Sept. 8, 1924; s. Matthew and Helen (Tertis) Fotopoulos; m. Ann Koutsatsa Matthews (dec.). m. Linda Kay Warren, Dec. 30, 1999; children: Andrew Philip, Lydia Ann. BA, Boston U., 1948; MD, SUNY, 1952. Diplomate Am. Bd. Surgery, Bd. Thoracic Surgery. Pvt. practice, 1960—90; med. dir. Des Moines Med. Exchange Program, Stavropal, Russia, 1990—95; chief med. officer Mil. Entrance Processing Sta., Des Moines, 1995—. Chief surgery, med. staff, bd. dirs. Iowa Luth. Hosp., Des Moines, 1962—90. Comdr. USPHS, 1952—59. Fellow: ACS, Am. Coll. Chest Physicians; mem.: Soc. Thoracic Surgeons. Home: 505 Glenview Dr Des Moines IA 50312 Office: Mil Entrance Processing Sta Dept Defense 2500 U Ave West Des Moines IA 50266-1480

**MATTHEWS, ALLAN FREEMAN,** geologist; b. Wakefield, Mass., May 27, 1916; s. Ralph Freeman Matthews and Mary (Morrill) Hill; m. Shirley Jean Spencer, Dec. 23, 1937 (div. Oct. 1955, dec. 1989); children: David Allan, Kim; m. Mary Cerantonio Thomas, Feb. 24, 1956 (div. Jan. 5, 1962); m. Doris Olive Haignere, June 26, 1962 (Dec. 2003). BA, Carleton Coll., Northfield, Minn., 1937; MS, Antioch Coll., Yellow Springs, Ohio, 1939; postgrad., Johns Hopkins U., Balt., 1939-40. Tech. editor Ceramic Industry Jour., Chgo., 1940-41; editor, chief U.S. Bur. of Mines, Washington, 1941-51; asst. dir., staff Pres.'s Materials Policy Commn., Washington, 1951-52; materials cons. Nat. Security Resources Bd., Washington, 1952-53; ops. analyst Johns Hopkins Ops. Rsch. Office, Chevy Chase, Md., 1953-54; program officer U.S. Agy. for Internat. Devel., Washington, 1954-75; editor, pub. Developing Country Courier, McLean, Va., 1978-85. Del. UN Global Modeling Conf., Paris, 1982; initiated citizens transnat. constl. conv., The Hague, Netherlands, 1998; chmn. constn. action group Alliance for Democracy, Waltham, Mass., 1997-99; minerals cons. Global 2000 Project, 1978-80; cons. and presenter in field. Author: Sovereigns Peacefully Take Charge, 1997, 2nd edit., 2005; editor: Minerals Yearbook, 1947-50; contbr. articles to profl. jours. and chpts. to books Dir. Streit Council for a Union of Democracies, Washington, 1957—; core planner 20/20 Vision, Washington, 1991-97; a founder The Reston Forum, 1990-92; pres. Waterford Sq. Condominium Assn., Reston, 1992; apptd. adv. bd. Phila. Two Orgn. Direct Democracy, 2001, Signatory of Natl. Initiative for Democracy. Lt. (j.g.) USN, 1944-46. Recipient Meritorious award U.S. Agy. for Internat. Devel., 1955, Commendation for Devel. Analysis, 1957; named Fellow in Geology, 1937-39. Mem. AAAS, ACLU, Democratic Socialists Am., Natural Resources Def. Coun., U N Assn., World Federalist Movement, Unitarian Universalist Assn., Fed. Am. Scientists, Phila. Two Direct Democracy, Soc. for Internat. Devel. (proposer continental fed. unions at N.Am. regional conf.

2000), Ctr. Def. Info, Initiative and Referendum Inst. Green Party. Achievements include evaluation of mineral resources adequacy and advancement of transnational constitutions. Home: Apt 624 900 N Taylor St Arlington VA 22203-1863 Personal E-mail: allan_matthews@comcast.net.

**MATTHEWS, ANDREA MORGAN,** soprano, educator; b. Needham, Mass., Nov. 6, 1956; d. Peter Dolan and Diane Perry Matthews; m. Kevin Hubbard, June 19, 1999. BA, Princeton U., 1978. Cert. counseling psychology Lesley U.; tchr. Alexander Tchg. Ctr., Cambridge. Voice instr. Wellesley (Mass.) Coll., 2001—. Singer (soprano): (Operas) Princeton Opera Assn., 1979, Mannes Mozart Project, 1980, Harrison Friends of Opera, 1981, Manhattan Opera, 1982, soprano: (Operas) San Diego Opera Ctr., 1982, Opera Shop, 1982, Va. Opera, 1984, Beethoven Soc., 1985, soprano: (Operas) Va. Opera, 1985, N.Y. Choral Soc., 1985, Kalamazoo Symphony, 1986, Mostly Mozart, 1986, 1987, Netherlands Dance Theatre, 1987, Piedmont Opera, 1987, Ctr. for Contemporary Opera, 1988, Greensboro Opera, 1988, Oratorio Soc. of N.Y., 1988, Stadttheater Aachen, 1990, 1991, 1992, Musica 2001 tour, 1992—93, Boston Symphony Orch., 1993, Springfield Symphony, 1994, Berkshire Opera, 1997, Boston Acad. Music, 1998, soprano: (Operas) Boston Acad. Music, 1999, 2000, 2002, The Bostonians, 2006. Recipient 2d prize, St. David's Soc. N.Y., 1979, 1980, Opera Co. of Boston, 1979, Grand prize, Providence Opera Theatre, 1980, 2d prize, N.Y. Singing Tchrs. Assn., 1981, 1st prize, Nat. Assn. Tchrs. of Singing, 1981, 2d prize, San Diego Opera Ctr., 1982, 1st prize, Oratorio Soc. N.Y., 1983, Disting. Career award, Needham HS, 1999; Grant, Nat. Inst. Music Theatre, 1986. Mem.: Nat. Assn. Tchrs. of Singing, Alexander Technique Internat. (tchg. mem. 1999—). Avocation: reading. Home: 204 Highgate St Needham MA 02492 Office: Wellesley Coll 106 Central St Wellesley MA 02481 Office Phone: 781-283-2077. Personal E-mail: alexanderteacher@earthlink.net.

**MATTHEWS, BRENDA J.,** human resources specialist; b. Hot Springs, Ark., Apr. 5, 1950; d. Earl Black and Mizella Roberts; m. Leonard Matthews, Nov. 22, 1979 (div. Jan. 1988); 1 child, Ebony. BA, U. Md., 1983; MA, Webster U., 1986. Sec. Dept. Vets. Affairs, Columbia, SC, 1984—87, pers. specialist Biloxi, Miss., 1987—88, Battle Creek, Mich., 1988—91, asst. pers. officer Salem, Va., 1991—96, assoc. chief human resources, 1996—2002, supr. human resources New Orleans, 2002—. Cons. ARC, Roanoke, Va., 2001—. Bd. dirs. ARC, Roanoke, 1995—2001, mem. exec. com., 1995—2001, chmn. vol. com., 2000—; mem. Kellogg Cmty. Leadership Acad., 1989. With U.S. Army, 1976—80. Recipient Chpt. Chmn.'s award, ARC, Roanoke, 2001. Mem.: Va. Soc. Human Resources Adminstrs. Avocations: reading, music, volunteer work, golf. Office: Dept Vets Affairs Med Ctr 1601 Perdido St New Orleans LA 70130

**MATTHEWS, BRIAN W.,** molecular biology educator; b. Mount Barker, Australia, May 25, 1938; came to U.S., 1967; s. Lionel A. and Ethlinda L. (Harris) M.; m. Helen F. Denley, Sept. 7, 1963; children: Susan, Kristine. BS, U. Adelaide, Australia, 1959, BS with honors, 1960, PhD, 1964, DSc, 1986. Mem. staff Med. Rsch. Coun., Cambridge, Eng., 1963-66; vis. assoc. NIH, Bethesda, Md., 1967-69; prof. molecular biology U. Oreg., Eugene, 1969—, chmn. dept. physics, 1985-86, dir. Inst. Molecular Biology, 1980-83, 90-92; Drummond lectr. U. Calgary (Can.), 1995. Advisor NSF, Washington, 1975-77; investigator Howard Hughes Med. Inst., 1989—; mem. U.S. Nat. Commn. for Crystallography, Washington, 1980-86, 88-90. Rsch. fellow Alfred P. Sloan Found., 1971, Guggenheim fellow, 1977; recipient Career Devel. award NIH, 1973, Faculty Excellence award Oreg. Bd. Edn., 1984, Discovery award Med. Rsch. Found. Oreg., 1987, Reed Coll. Vollum award, 1994, Stein and Moore award Protein Soc., 2000. Mem. NAS, AAAS, Crystallographic Assn., Am. Chem. Soc., Protein Soc. (pres. 1995-97), Biophysical Soc. (nat. lectr. 2001). Office: U Oreg HHMI Inst Molecular Biology Eugene OR 97403 Office Phone: 541-346-2572. E-mail: brian@uoxray.uoregon.edu.

**MATTHEWS, CHARLES R.,** academic administrator; m. Julia Matthews; 4 children. BA, U. Tex., Dallas; MA, Southwest Tex. State U. Bd. dirs. So. Bank & Trust; dir. Tex. Mcpl. Power Agency, 1979, bd. pres., 1982—83; mayor Garland, Tex., 1984; vice chmn. Tex. Turnpike Authority, 1987; commr. Railroad Commn. Tex., 1994—2005; chancellor Tex. State U. Sys., Austin, 2005—. Recipient Alfred M. Zuck Public Courage Award, Nat. Assn. Schs. of Pub. Affairs and Administrn, 2000, Tex. Mining and Reclamation Assn. Leadership Award, 2001. Office: Tex State U Sys Thomas J Rusk Bldg 200 E 10th St, Ste 600 Austin TX 78701-2407 Office Phone: 512-463-1808.

**MATTHEWS, CHARLES SEDWICK,** petroleum engineer, consultant; b. Houston, Mar. 27, 1920; s. Charles James and Zadoc Coleman (Sedwick) M.; m. Miriam Loraine Ormerod, June 2, 1945; children— Joan Gail, Wendy Loraine BSChemE, Rice U., 1941, MSChemE, 1943, PhD in Chemistry, 1944. Registered profl. engr., Tex. Engr. Shell Devel. Co. San Francisco, 1944-48, rsch. engr. Houston, 1948-56, dir. rsch., 1967-72; chief reservoir engr. Shell Oil Co., Houston, 1965, mgr. engring., 1972-73, sr. petroleum engring. cons., 1973-89. Engring. adv. com. Rice U., Houston, 1973-77; cons. Dept. Energy, Washington, 1974-78, adv. com., 1975-79; spl. asst. Nat. Petroleum Council, Washington, 1981-83; reserves com. Am. Petroleum Inst. Author: Pressure Buildup and Flow Tests in Wells, 1967; contbr. articles to profl. jours.; patentee in field. Chmn. Tex. Engrs. for Conservation, Houston, 1973 Recipient Disting. Alumnus award Rice U., 1994. Mem. NAE, Soc. Petroleum Engrs. (hon. mem., Lester Uren award 1975, disting. author, disting. lectr. 1968, Disting. lectr. emeritus 1986), Phi Beta Kappa, Sigma Xi, Tau Beta Pi, Phi Lambda Upsilon. Clubs: Houston, Meyerland (treas. 1982-85). Republican. Methodist. Avocations: swimming, fishing. Home: 5307 S Braeswood Blvd Houston TX 77096-4149

**MATTHEWS, CHARLES W., JR.,** oil industry executive; b. Houston, Tex., Feb. 27, 1945; BA, U. Tex., 1967; JD, U. Houston, 1970. Bar: Tex. 1970. Tenn. 1980, admitted to: U.S. Dist. Ct., So. Dist. Tex. 1975, U.S. Supreme Ct., U.S. Ct. Appeals, Dist. Columbia Circuit, U.S. Ct. Appeals, Fifth and Eleventh Circuits 1981. Trial atty. law dept. Exxon Corp., 1971-78, region atty. southeastern and southern region mktg. offices, 1978-81, assoc. gen. atty. litigation sect., gen. counsel & dir. Petroleum Casualty Co. and Exxon Risk Mgmt. Svcs., 1981-92; from assoc. gen. counsel law dept. to gen. counsel law dept. Exxon U.S.A., 1992; v.p., gen. counsel Exxon Mobil Corp., 1995—. Instr. State Bar Tex. Profl. Develop. Program, Litigating the Oil and Gas Case, 1988, U. Houston Law Found., mem. bd. trustees. Author: Recent Developments in Liability for Oil and Gas Operations, 1987. Nat. trustee Southwest Region Boys and Girls Club Am.; chair U. Tex. Chancellor's Coun., 2002; mem. bd. overseers Rand Inst. Civil Justice; mem. develop. bd. U. Tex. Recipient Alumnus of the Yr., Univ. of Houston, 2000. Fellow: Tex. Bar Found.; mem.: ABA (fellow, mem. com. corp. gen. counsel), Tex. Access Justice Commn. (commr. 2004—), Chief Legal Officers Roundtable, Am. Inns Ct. Found. (trustee, mem. leadership coun.), Nat. Ctr. State Courts (co-chair gen. counsel com. 2002—), Defense Rsch. Inst., State Bar Tex. (vice chmn. adminstrn. justice com. 1988, corp. counsel liaison to litigation section 1988—89), Ctr. Am. and Internat. Law (chmn. exec. com. 2002—, trustee), Internat. Assn. Def. Counsel Found. (chmn. corp. counsel com. 1991, v.p. 1993—95, bd. dirs. 2002—), Assn. Gen. Counsel, Dallas Bar Assn., Dallas Bar Found. (fellow, v.p.; gen. counsel), Houston Bar Assn. (bd. dirs. 1994—95, fellow), Order Barons. Office: Exxon Mobil Corp Law Dept 5959 Las Colinas Blvd Irving TX 75039-2298

**MATTHEWS, CHRISTIAN WILLIAM, JR.,** minister; b. Jersey City, Oct. 12, 1934; s. Christian William and Lydia Louise (Weller) M.; m. Elaine Louise Ochs, June 18, 1955; children: Christian William III, Patricia Louise, Judith Ann, Barbara Jean. BA, King's Coll., 1956; MRE, Ea. Theol. Sem., 1960, MDiv, 1962; MEd, U. Del., 1961; ThM, Princeton Theol. Sem., 1965; DD, Grove City Coll., 1988. Ordained to ministry Presby. Ch. (U.S.A.), 1962. Dir. Christian edn. United Presby. Ch. of Manoa, Havertown, Pa., 1959-62; asst. min. 1st Presby. Ch., Norristown, Pa., 1962-65; assoc. min. Marble Collegiate Ch., N.Y.C., 1965-68; sr. min. Fox Chapel Presby. Ch., Pitts., 1968-79, Christ Presby. Ch., Toledo, 1979-2000, 2d Presby. Ch., Balt., 2000—04, 1st Presby. Ch., Grand Haven, Mich., 2004—. Mem. The

Fellowship, Washington, Synod Gen. Coun. Presbyn. Ch. U.S.A.; chmn. Synod Evangelism; leader marriage and family seminars; mem. alumni fund bd. Princeton Theol. Sem.; mem. Kirk coun., Alma Coll.; cons. Presbyn. Ch. in U.S.A., Nat. Com. for Prison Reform, County Human Svc. Commn. Author: Lingering with Luke—A Study of the Life of Christ, 1976, Marriage and Family Study Course, 1983; developer (nat. program for Presbyn. chs.) Risk Evangelism; signer Lausanne Covenant of Internat. Congress on World Evangelization. Chmn. Com. for Ecol. Instrn.; founding pres. Samaritan Counseling Ctr.; sec. The Ability Ctr.; bd. dirs. area coun. Boy Scouts Am., Toledo Rotary Club, James C. Caldwell Cmty. Ctr., Met. Toledo Chs. United, AASK-Mid Am., Toledo Leadership Found.; mem. Coun. for Religion and Psychiatry. Mem.: Rotary Club of Toledo. Home and Office: 337 Sawgrass Ct Holland OH 43528-9210 Office Phone: 443-418-5593. Personal E-mail: DrCWMatthews@aol.com. *As I reflect upon life, I believe that God is at work in our world bringing together people of faith to meet the complex challenges confronting us at this time of history. Working together, we are able to encourage, strengthen, and support one another in meeting the needs of our world.*

**MATTHEWS, CHRISTOPHER JOHN,** political commentator, writer; b. Phila., Dec. 17, 1945; s. Herbert Charles and Mary Teresa (Shields) Matthews; m. Kathleen Ann Cunningham, 1980; children: Michael, Thomas, Caroline. BA in Economics, Coll. Holy Cross, 1967, LLD (hon.), 2003; grad. studies, U. NC; doctorate (hon.), St. Leo U., Loyola Coll., Md., Niagara U., Fontbonne Coll., Beaver Coll., New England Sch. Law, Anna Maria Coll., Chesnut Hill Coll. Legis. asst. to US Senator Frank Moss of Utah, 1971—73; staff mem. US Senator Edward Muskie of Maine; staff asst. US Senate Budget Com., 1974—77; speechwriter for Pres. Jimmy Carter, 1977—79; aide to Speaker of House Tip O'Neill US Ho. of Reps., 1981—87; polit. analyst CBS This Morning, 1987; bur. chief, columnist San Francisco Examiner, Washington, 1987—2000; past nat. syndicated columnist San Francisco Chronicle; past pres., CEO govt. rsch. corp., Washington; host Hardball with Chris Matthews CNBC, 1997—2002, MSNBC, 1999—; host syndicated program, The Chris Matthews Show, 2002—. Author: Hardball: How Politics is Really Played- Told By One Who Knows the Game, 1988, Kennedy & Nixon: The Rivalry That Shaped PostWar America, 1996, Now, Let Me Tell You What I Really Think, 2001, American: Beyond Our Grandest Notions, 2002, articles for The New Republic, US News and World Report, The NY Times, Christian Sci. Monitor, Am. Politics. Trade devel. advisor US Peace Corps, Swaziland, 1968—70. Recipient Lincoln Award, Union League of Phila. Democrat. Office: Hardball With Chris Matthews 30 Rockefeller Plz New York NY 10112

**MATTHEWS, CRAIG GERARD,** retired energy executive; b. Bklyn., Mar. 8, 1943; m. Carol O. Olsen, Sept. 10, 1971; children: Kenneth C., Bradford P., Melinda M. BCE, Rutgers U., 1965; MS in Indsl. Mgmt., Polytech. Inst. Bklyn., 1971. Vice chmn., COO, KeySpan Corp. (formerly Bklyn. Union Gas Co.), 1965—2002, ret., 2002; pres., CEO NUI Corp., 2004; ret., 2004—. Bd. dirs. Hess Corp., Nat. Fuel Gas; mem. adv. bd. Independence Cmty. Bank, Republic Fin. Chmn. Salvation Army, NY; bd. dirs. Bklyn. Philharm., Poly. Univ. Republican. Presbyterian. Home: 132 Canterbury Way Basking Ridge NJ 07920 Office Phone: 908-719-4290.

**MATTHEWS, DARRYL R., SR.,** not-for-profit fundraiser; m. Allison Paige Stinson; children: Julian, Blake, Darryl Jr. BSc in Polit. Sci. and Sociology, Ctrl. Mo. State Univ., 1977. Claims adjuster USF&G, Kansas City, Mo., 1977—78; asst. exec. sec. Alpha Phi Alpha Fraternity, Inc., Chgo., 1978—81; dir. mktg., membership Balt., 1983—93, dep. exec. dir., 1993—94, interim exec. dir., 1994—95, exec. dir., COO, 1995—96, sr. gen. pres. Baltimore, Md., 2005—; account exec. AT&T, Southwestern Bell, Am. Bell, Kansas City, 1981—83; exec. dir. mktg. Bingwa Software Co., Norcross, Ga., 1996—97; ind. cons. White House Presdl. Advance Office, 1997—98; exec. dir., COO Nat. Assn. of Black Accts., Inc., Greenbelt, Md., 1998—. Vice-chmn. bd. dirs. Martin Luther King Jr. Nat. Meml., Washington. Named one of Most Influential Black Americans, Ebony mag., 2006. Office: Nat Assn Black Accountants Inc 7249 A Hanover Pkwy Greenbelt MD 20770 Office Phone: 410-554-0040, 301-474-6222. Office Fax: 410-554-0054, 301-474-3114.*

**MATTHEWS, DAVE,** singer, musician; b. Johannesburg, Jan. 9, 1967; s. John and Val Matthews; m. Jennifer Ashley Harper, Aug. 10, 2000; children: Grace Anne, Stella Busina. Vocalist, guitarist The Dave Matthews Band, 1991—; founder ATO Records, 2000—. Bd. dirs. Farm Aid, 2001—. Musician: (albums) Remember Two Things, 1993, Under the Table and Dreaming, 1994, Crash, 1996 (Grammy award Best Rock Performance by a Duo Or Group, 1996), Live at Red Rocks, 1995, 1997, Before These Crowded Streets, 1998, Live at Luther College, 1999, Listener Supported, 1999, Live in Chicago 12-19-98, 2001, Everyday, 2001, Live at Folsom Field, Boulder Colorado, 2002, Busted Stuff, 2002, The Central Park Concert, 2003, The Gorge, 2004, (solo albums) Some Devil, 2003 (Grammy award Best Male Rock Vocal Performance, 2003); actor: (films) Where the Red Fern Grows, 2003, Because of Winn-Dixie, 2005. Office: ATO Records 157 Chambers St New York NY 10007

**MATTHEWS, DAVID,** clergyman; b. Indianola, Miss., Jan. 29, 1920; s. Albert and Bertha (Henderson) M.; m. Lillian Pearl Banks, Aug. 28, 1951; 1 dau., Denise. AB, Morehouse Coll., Atlanta, 1950; student, Atlanta U., 1950, Memphis Theol. Sem., 1965, Delta State U., Cleveland, Miss., 1969, 71, 72, D.D. (hon.), Natchez Jr. Coll., Miss., 1973, Morris Booker Meml. Coll., 1988. Ordained minister Nat. Baptist Conv. U.S.A., 1946; pastor chs. in Miss., 1951—, Bell Grove Baptist Ch., Indianola, 1951—; Strangers Home, Greenwood, 1958—. Tchr., chmn. dept. social sci. Gentry H.S., Indianola, 1958-83; moderator Sunflower Bapt. Assn., 1957—; v.p. Gen. Bapt. Conv. Miss., 1958—, former lectr., conv. congress religious edn.; v.p. Nat. Bapt. Conv. U.S.A., 1971-94; del. to Nat. Coun. Chs., 1960, supr. oratorical contest 1976; prin. Gen. Missionary Bapt. State Conv. Miss., 1974-98. Mem. Sunflower County Anti-Poverty Bd., 1965-71, Indianola Bi-Racial Com., 1965—; mem. Gov.'s Advisory Com.; col. on staff Gov. Finch, 1976-80; mem. budget com. Indianola United Fund, 1971—; chmn. bd. Indianola FHA, 1971—; trustee Natchez Jr. Coll.; mem. Miss. Gov.'s Research and Devel. Council, 1984—; apptd. mem. So. Govs. Ecumenical Coun. Infant Mortality, 1987. Served with U.S. Army, 1942-45, PTO. Recipient citation Morehouse Coll., 1950, citation Miss. Valley State Coll., 1956, J.H. Jackson Preaching award Midwestern Baptist Laymen Fellowship, 1974, Gov.'s Merit award, 1975, Human Svc. award Miss. Valley State U., 2004. Mem. NEA, Miss., Indianola Tchrs. Assns., Am. Bible Soc. (adv. coun. 1991-2000, student reform theol. sem. centennial edn. 1990—). Democrat. Baptist. Home: PO Box 627 Indianola MS 38751-0627 Fax: 662-887-9078. Personal E-mail: matthews3463@bills.net. *I have learned not to seek honors and success but to become so involved in worthwhile works that I lose myself and by such actions success and honors have come.*

**MATTHEWS, DAVID FORT,** career officer; b. Lancaster, NH, Sept. 25, 1944; s. Clinton Fort and Mabel Sawin (Oaks) M.; m. Eva Mae Horton, Nov. 10, 1990. BA, Vanderbilt U., 1966; MA, Mid. Tenn. U., 1973. Cert. acquisition mgmt. Rsch. and devel. officer U.S. Army Rsch. Inst., Washington, 1974-77; exec. officer 194th Maintenance Battalion-Camp Humphreys, Korea, 1978-79; career program mgr. U.S. Army Mil. Pers. Ctr., Washington, 1979-82; logistics staff officer Dep. Chief of Staff Logistics, Washington, 1982-83; team chief Chief of Staff Army Study Group, Washington, 1983-85; logistics div. chief Multiple Launch Rocket System Project Office, Huntsville, Ala., 1985-88; comdr. Ordnance Program Div., Riyadh, Saudi Arabia, 1988-90; project mgr. Army Tactical Missile System, Huntsville, 1990-94; sr. lectr. weapon systems acquisition Naval Postgrad. Sch., Monterey, Calif., 1994—. Decorated Legion of Merit, Bronze Star; recipient award as project mgr. of yr. Sec. of Army, 1991. Mem. Nat. Def. Indsl. Assn., Assn. U.S. Army. Avocations: sports, water-skiing, reading, scuba diving. Home: 83 High Meadow Ln Carmel CA 93923 Office: Naval Postgrad Sch Monterey CA 93943 Office Phone: 831-656-2360. Business E-mail: DMatthews@nps.navy.mil.

**MATTHEWS, DEWAYNE,** foundation administrator; b. Albuquerque, June 7, 1951; s. Robert and Irene Matthews; m. Gladys Gonzalez, Sept. 11, 1999. BS in Edn., U. N.Mex, 1974; MA, N.Mex Highlands U., 1980; PhD, Ariz. State U., 1992; LHD (hon.), Marycrest Internat. U., 1997. Exec. dir. N.Mex Commn. Higher Edn., Santa Fe, 1985—89; dir. programs Western Interstate Commn. Higher Edn., Boulder, Colo., 1992—2001; spl. asst. to pres. Edn. Commn. of the States, Denver, 2001—04; sr. rsch. dir. Lumina Found. for Edn., Indpls., 2005—. Pres. San Felipe Humanitarian Alliance, San Diego, 1980—2006. Home: 110 E Washington St Ste 1401 Indianapolis IN 46204 Office: Lumina Found for Edn 30 S Meridian St Ste 700 Indianapolis IN 46204 Office Phone: 317-951-5763. Office Fax: 317-951-5459. Business E-Mail: dmatthews@luminafoundation.org.

**MATTHEWS, EDWARD E.,** retired insurance company executive; b. 1931; AB, Princeton U., 1953; MBA, Harvard U., 1957. With Morgan Stanley & Co., 1957-73, named ptnr., 1967, mng. dir., 1970; v.p. Am. Internat. Group, Inc. (AIG), NYC, 1973—82, named exec. v.p., 1982, vice chmn. investments and fin. services, sr. vice chmn. investments and fin. services, 2001—02, also bd. dirs., 1973—2003; sr. adv., hon. dir., 2003—. Trustee emeritus Princeton U.; past chmn. bd. Princeton Investment Co.; bd. trustees Robert Wood Johnson Found., Princeton, NJ, 1994—; vice chmn. Princeton Med. Ctr.; trustee Princeton Day Sch. With U.S. Army, 1953—55. Office: Am Internat Group Inc 70 Pine St New York NY 10270*

**MATTHEWS, EDWIN SPENCER, JR.,** lawyer; b. Spokane, Wash., May 31, 1934; s. Edwin Spencer and Dorothy Chace (Ehrhardt) M.; m. Marie-Claude Paris, Dec. 19, 1959 (div. 1982); children: Nadia, Sylvie, Clarissa; m. Patricia L. Sills Barnes, Dec. 22, 1983; children: Paxton, Gillian. AB magna cum laude, Harvard U., 1956; Diplome d'Etudes Francaises, Inst. de Touraine, Tours, France, 1958; LLB, Yale U., 1962. Bar: N.Y. 1963, Calif. 1979, U.S. Supreme Ct. 1992; Conseil Juridique (France) 1965-79. Assoc. Coudert Bros., N.Y.C., 1962-65, Coudert Freres, Paris, 1965-69, ptnr., 1969-79, Coudert Bros., San Francisco, 1979-80, N.Y.C., 1980—2003, of counsel, 2003—05, Baker & McKenzie LLP, 2005—. Trustee Earthjustice Legal Def. Fund, San Francisco, 1984—, Steep Rock Assn., Washington, Conn., 1998-2004; bd. dirs. Friends of Earth Found., N.Y.C., 1979-85; bd. dirs. Friends of Earth Inc., Washington, Conn., 1970-85, pres., 1979-80; bd. dirs. Shepang River Assn., pres., 1995—. With U.S. Army, 1957-58. Mem. Assn. of Bar of City of N.Y. (com. on housing and urban devel. 1964-65, com. on capital representation, 1995-2003), Harvard Club, N.Y. Athletic Club. Democrat. Avocations: ocean sailing, carpentry, sculling, wilderness canoeing, photography. Home: 11 Harrison St New York NY 10013-2837 also: PO Box 493 Washington Depot CT 06794-0493 Office: Baker & McKenzie LLP 1114 Avenue Of The Americas New York NY 10036-7703

**MATTHEWS, ERIC JODDY,** film director; s. Matthew Gaddson and Leverna Ann Matthews. BFA, U. of Mich., 1993. Creative dir. Axentis Inc, Warrensville, Ohio, 2000—; dir./prodr. Madwerkz Studios, Euclid, Ohio, 1998—. Dir.: (feature film) 3 Penny Pawn; prodr.: (documentary) Freeze Defrost. Diary of Midwest Hip Hop (Best Documentary - Doubletake Film Festival, 2002); environmental design, Cleveland Browns PSL Monument; dir.: (3d animation 3 minute open) Sherwin Williams New Product 2000 Open, (feature film) Rundown; novel, Chicken Soup for the College Soul. Mentor Tremont Mentoring, Cleve/, 1990—99. Mem.: Midwest Filmmakers Alliance (pres. 2000—01), Siggraph, AIGA, Cleve. Advt. Assn., Midwest Maya User Group, Detroit Filmmakers Coalition, Music Video Producers Assn., Am. Ind. Comml. Producers. Avocations: painting, weightlifting, writing. Home: 1119 S Belvoir Blvd Cleveland OH 44121-2946 E-mail: ematthews@madwerkz.com.

**MATTHEWS, EUGENE EDWARD,** artist; b. Davenport, Iowa, Mar. 22, 1931; s. Nickolas Arthur and Velma (Schroeder) M.; m. Wanda Lee Miller, Sept. 14, 1952; children: Anthony Lee, Daniel Nickolas. Student, Bradley U., 1948-51; BFA, U. Iowa, 1953, MFA, 1957. Prof. fine arts emeritus, 1996—, dir. vis. artists program, 1985-96. Vis. artist Am. Acad. Rome, 1989. One-man shows include U. Wis., Milw., 1960, Brena Gallery, Denver, 1963, 65, 67, 70, 74, 76, 78, 80, 83, 88, Colorado Springs Fine Arts Ctr., 1967, Sheldon Art Gallery, U. Nebr., 1968, Denver Art Mus., 1972, James Yu Gallery, N.Y.C., 1973, 77, Dubins Gallery, L.A., 1981, Galeria Rysunku, Poznan, 1983, CU. Art Galleries, U. Colo., Boulder, 1996, Rule Art Gallery, Denver, 1998; exhibited in numerous group shows U.S., Europe, Africa, Asia; internat. watercolor exhbn. New Orleans, 1983, Louvre, Paris, Met. Mus. of Art, N.Y.C., Internat. Art - Cbr. Kyoto, Japan, Mus. of Modern Art, Rijeka, Yugoslavia, Taipei Fine Arts Mus., Taiwan, Republic of China, Internat. Watercolor Biennial-East/West, Champaign, Ill., 1997; represented in permanent collections Nat. Mus. Am. Art, Washington, Denver Art Mus., Butler Inst. Am. Art, Chrysler Art Mus., others. Recipient Penello d'Argento award Acitrezza Internazionale, 1958, S.P.Q.R. Cup of Rome, Roma Olimpionica Internazionale, 1959, Gold medal of honor Nat. Arts Club, N.Y.C., 1969, Bicentennial award Rocky Mountain Nat. Watercolor Exhbn., 1976, Am. Drawings IV Purchase award, 1982, others; fellow in painting Am. Acad. Rome, 1957-60, U. Colo. Creative Rsch. fellow, 1966-67. Mem. Watercolor U.S.A. Honor Soc. (charter). Home: 2865 Jay Rd Boulder CO 80301-1605

**MATTHEWS, GILBERT ELLIOTT,** investment banker; b. Brookline, Mass., Apr. 24, 1930; s. Martin W. and Charlotte (Cohen) M.; m. Anne Lisbeth Barnett, Apr. 20, 1958 (div. 1975); children: Lisa Joan, Diana Kory (dec. 1995); m. Elaine Rita Siegal Pulitzer, Jan. 2, 1978 (div. 1999); 1 child, Jennifer Rachel. AB, Harvard U., 1951; MBA, Columbia U., 1953. Chartered fin. analyst. Dept. mgr. Bloomingdale's, N.Y.C., 1955, 56-60; security analyst Merrill Lynch, N.Y.C., 1960; investment banker Bear, Stearns & Co., N.Y.C., 1960-95, gen. ptnr., 1979-85; mng. dir. Bear, Stearns & Co. Inc., 1985-86, sr. mng. dir., 1986-95, Sutter Securities Inc., San Francisco, 1995—, chmn. bd. dirs 1997—. Served on It. (j.g.) USN, 1953-56. Mem. N.Y. Soc. Security Analysts. Democrat. Jewish. Office: Sutter Securities Inc 555 California St Ste 3330 San Francisco CA 94104 Business E-Mail: gil@suttersf.com

**MATTHEWS, JACK (JOHN HAROLD MATTHEWS),** language educator, writer; b. Columbus, Ohio, July 22, 1925; s. John Harold and Lulu Emma (Grover) M.; m. Barbara Jane Reese, Sept. 16, 1947; children: Cynthia Ann Matthews Warnock, Barbara Ellen Matthews Saunders, John Harold. BA, Ohio State U., 1949, MA, 1954. Clk. U.S. Post Office, Columbus, 1950-59; prof. English Urbana Coll., Ohio, 1959-64, Ohio U., Athens, 1964-77, disting. prof., 1977—2003, disting. prof. emeritus, 2003—. Author: Bitter Knowledge, 1964 (Ohioana fiction award 1964), Hanger Stout, Awake!, 1967, The Charisma Campaigns, 1972, Sassafras, 1983, Crazy Women, 1985, Booking in the Heartland, 1986 (Ohioana Non-fiction award 1986), Ghostly Populations, 1986, Memoirs of a Bookman, 1989, Dirty Tricks, 1990, On The Shore of That Beautiful Shore (play), 1991, An Interview with the Sphinx (play), 1992, Storyhood As We Know It and Other Tales (stories), 1993, Booking Pleasures, 1996, (essays) Reading Matter, 2000, Schopenhauerova Vule, 2002, others. Served with USCG, 1943-45. Recipient numerous ind. artist awards Ohio Art Council, Major Artist award, 1989-90, Ohioana Career award, 2005, Guggenheim fellow, 1974-75 Mem. Phi Beta Kappa Home: 4314 Fisher Rd Athens OH 45701-9333 Office: Ohio U Dept English Athens OH 45701 Business E-Mail: matthej1@ohio.edu.

**MATTHEWS, JAMES SHADLEY,** lawyer; b. Omaha, Nov. 24, 1951; s. Donald E. and Lois Jean (Shadley) M.; m. Mary Kvaal, May 3, 1991; 1 child, Katherine. BA cum laude, St. Olaf Coll., 1973; JD, U. Ill., 1976; MBA, U. Denver, 1977. Bar: Minn. 1976, U.S. Dist. Ct. Minn. 1978. With Northwestern Nat. Life Ins. Co., Mpls., 1978-89, v.p., asst. gen. counsel, 1985-89; ptnr. Lindquist & Venum, Mpls., 1990—. Sr. v.p. gen. counsel Washington Square Capital, Inc., 1989; sec. NWNL Health Network, Inc., St. Paul, 1987-89; pub. dir. Minn. Health Reins. Assn., 1992-94; bd. dirs. Northstar Life Ins. Co., 2001-03; spkr. in field. Mem. ABA, Am. Health Lawyers Assn., Minn. Bar Assn. (chmn. health law sect. 1986-87). Office: Lindquist & Vennum IDS Ctr 80 S 8th St Ste 4200 Minneapolis MN 55402-2274 Office Phone: 612-371-3211. Business E-Mail: jmatthews@lindquist.com.

**MATTHEWS, JOHN,** human resources specialist, wholesale distribution executive; M in Finance. Various positions in human resources Costo Wholesale Corp., Issaquah, Wash., 1990—, sr. v.p., human resources and risk mgmt. Former comdr., logistics expert USN. Office: Costco Wholesale Corp 999 Lake Dr Issaquah WA 98027 Office Phone: 425-313-8100. Office Fax: 425-313-8103.

**MATTHEWS, JOSEPH MICHAEL,** lawyer; b. Grand Rapids, Mich., Apr. 28, 1952; s. Jordan Emmanuel and Anna Mae (Moose) M.; m. JoAnne Hatch, June 29, 1974; children: Megan, Kyle. BA, The Defiance Coll., 1974; JD, U. Miami, 1977. Bar: Fla. 1977, U.S. Dist. Ct. (so. dist.) Fla. 1978, D.C. 1979. Assoc. Paul, Landy & Beiley, Miami, 1977-79; spl. counsel State of Fla. Land Sales, Tallahassee, 1979-80; adj. faculty U. Miami, Coral Gables, Fla., 1981-85; ptnr. Murai, Wald, Biondo, Matthews & Moreno, P.A., Miami, 1980-89, Colson Hicks Eidson, Miami, 1989—. Spl. counsel U.S. Senator Bob Graham, 1989. Contbr. articles to profl. jours. Commr. 3rd Dist. Jud. Nominating Com., Miami, 1983-87; mem. Fla. Bd. Bar Examiners, Tallahassee, 1987-90. Fellow Internat. Acad. Trial Lawyers (dir., 2003-); mem. Am. Arbitration Assn. (dir. 2003—), ATLA (chair comml. litig. sect. 1994), ABA, Fla. Bar Assn., Acad. Fla. Trial Lawyers (chmn. comml. litigation sect. 1992), Dade County Bar Assn., Dade County Trial Lawyers Assn. (pres. 1996). Home: 2200 Segovia Cir Miami FL 33134-4834 Office: Law Firm of Colson Hicks Eidson 255 Aragon Ave 2d Fl Coral Gables FL 33134 E-mail: joseph@colson.com.

**MATTHEWS, JOSEPH VIRGIL,** musician, music educator; b. Taneyville, Mo., June 13, 1941; s. Roy Elza and Violet Myrtle (Redfern) Matthews. MusB in piano, Univ. Mo., Columbia, Mo., 1963, MA, 1965; Mus D, Ind. Univ., Bloomington, Ind., 1977. Piano tchr. Christian Coll. Prep Dept. Columbia, Mo., 1962—63; tchg. asst.-piano Univ. Mo., Columbia, Mo., 1963—64, Ind. Univ., Bloomington, Ind., 1964—65, 1969—72; asst. prof. Coll. of the Sch. of the Ozarks, Point Lookout, Mo., 1965—69; prof. music Chapman Univ., Orange, Calif., 1972—. Musician: (recitals) as soloist, accompanist, duo-pianist and soloist with orch., 1963—. Recipient Graves award in Humanities, Am. Coun. of Learned Soc., 1981, Valerie Scudder Disting. Tchng. award, Chapman Univ., 1989. Mem.: Music Tchr. Nat. Assn., Calif. Assn. of Profl. Music Tchr., Music Tchr. Assn. of Calif. (state co-chair, solo-concerto). Achievements include my students have won local, nat. and internat. prizes in piano competitions. Home: 5721-2 E Stillwater Ave Orange CA 92869 Office: Chapman Univ One Univ Dr Orange CA 92866 E-mail: matthews@chapman.edu.

**MATTHEWS, KATHLEEN SHIVE,** biochemistry educator; b. Austin, Tex., Aug. 30, 1945; d. William and Gwyn Shive; m. Randall Matthews. BS in Chemistry, U. Tex., 1966; PhD in Biochemistry, U. Calif., Berkeley, 1970. Post doctoral fellow Stanford (Calif.) U., 1970-72; mem. faculty Rice U., Houston, 1972—, chair dept., 1987-95, Wiess prof., 1989-96, Stewart Meml. chair, 1996—, dean natural scis., 1998—. Mem. BBCB study sect. NIH, Bethesda, Md., 1980-84, 86-88, BRSG adv. com., 1992-94; mem. adv. com. on rsch. programs Tex. Higher Edn. Coord. Bd., Austin, 1987-92; mem. undergrad. edn. initiative rev. panel Howard Hughes Rsch. Inst., Bethesda, 1991, mem. rsch. resources rev. panel, 1995, mem. predoctoral fellowships rev. panel, 2001, trustee S.W. Rsch. Inst., 2003—, Steering Com. Vinson & Elkins Women's Initiative Adv. Bd., 2001-06. Mem. editl. bd. Jour. Biol. Chemistry, 1988-93, assoc. editor, 1994-99; contbr. 140 reviewed papers. Fellow AAAS; mem. Am. Soc. Biochemistry and Molecular Biology (nominating com. 1993-94, 96-97, fin. com. 2001-2002), Protein Soc., Biophys. Soc. (pub. affairs com. 2002-05), Am. Chem. Soc., Phi Beta Kappa. Office: Rice Univ PO Box 1892 6100 Main St MS102 Houston TX 77005-1892 E-mail: ksm@rice.edu.

**MATTHEWS, LEONARD SARVER,** advertising and marketing executive; b. Glendean, Ky., Jan. 6, 1922; s. Clell and Zetta Price (Sarver) M.; m. Dorothy Lucille Fessler; children: Nancy, James, Douglas. BS summa cum laude, Northwestern U., 1948. With Leo Burnett Co., Inc., Chgo., 1948-75, v.p., dir., 1958-59, exec. v.p. charge mktg. services, 1959-61, exec. v.p. client svc., 1961-69, pres., 1970-75; asst. sec. commerce for domestic and internat. bus., 1976; pres., exec. com., dir. Young and Rubicam, 1977-78; pres. Am. Assn. Advt. Agys., 1979-89; co-founder Matthews & Johnston, Stamford, Conn., 1989-92; chmn. Next Century Media, 1992—99. Mem. adv. bd. Scripps Capital, San Diego. Ensign USCGR, 1942-46. Named to Advt. Hall of Fame, 1999. Mem. Advt. Coun. (life bd. dirs.), Sky Club (N.Y.C.), Pine Valley Golf Club (N.J.), Rancho Santa Fe Golf (Calif.), Georgetown Club (Washington), Delta Sigma Pi, Beta Gamma Sigma. Republican. Lutheran. Office: PO Box 2629 Rancho Santa Fe CA 92067-2629

**MATTHEWS, MANYALIBO JOSEPH,** physicist, researcher; b. Berkeley, Calif., Mar. 14, 1970; s. Kwame Mugodo and Elizabeth Rodriguez. BS, U. Calif., Davis, 1993; PhD in Physics, MIT, 1998. Part-time rsch. asst. Lawrence Berkeley Labs., 1988-91; cons. Lawrence Livermore (Calif.) Nat. Lab., 1994-95; mem. tech. staff Bell Labs., Lucent Technologies, Murray Hill, N.J., 1998—. Tech. cons., Bronx, N.Y., 1998-99; inventor in field. Chmn. Nat. Conf. of Black Physics Students, Cambridge, 1997; physics instr. Interphase Program, Cambridge, 1995; student mentor, advisor U. Calif., Davis, 1990-92. Grad. fellow NSF, 1993; Ronald E. McNair scholar U. Maine, 1992. Mem. Am. Phys. Soc., Materials Rsch. Soc., Alpha Phi Alpha (pres. U. Calif. 1991-93, advisor MIT 1996-98, Exceptional Svc. 1998). Avocations: saxophone, cooking, running, travel.

**MATTHEWS, MARGARET ELLEN,** physician; b. Quincy, Mass., Sept. 30, 1951; d. C. Dixon and Marion Louise (Strader) M.; children: Cora Lee, Tessa Ellice, Alicia Gale. BSN, Boston U., 1975, MSN, 1979; MD, Med. Coll. Pa., Phila., 1984. Diplomate Am. Bd. Family Practice. Staff nurse various hosps., Boston, 1975-80, Phila., 1980-84; staff nurse Med. Coll. Pa. Hosp., Phila., 1982-83; resident physician Cen. Maine Med. Ctr., Lewiston, 1984-87; physician The Health Ctr., Auburn, Maine, 1987-96; pvt. prac., 1996—. Office: 117 Goff St Auburn ME 04210-5024 Office Phone: 207-795-6970.

**MATTHEWS, MILDRED SHAPLEY,** freelance/self-employed editor; b. Pasadena, Calif., Feb. 15, 1915; d. Harlow and Martha (Betz) Shapley; m. Ralph Vernon Matthews, Sept. 25, 1937; children: June Lorrain, Bruce Shapley, Melvin Lloyd, Martha Alys. AB, U. Mich., 1936. Rsch. asst. Calif. Inst. Tech., Pasadena, 1950-61; bilingual editor, rsch. asst. Astron. Obs. Merate-Milan and Trieste, Italy, 1960-70; rsch. asst. Lunar-Planetary Lab., editor space sci. series U. Ariz., Tucson, 1970-96; retired, 1996. Contbr. articles to Sky and Telescope, Astronomia. Recipient Masursky Meritorious Svc. award div. planetary sci. Am. Astron. Soc., 1993. Avocations: classical music concerts, especially opera, travel. Home: 3154 Del Vina St Pasadena CA 91107

**MATTHEWS, NORMAN STUART,** retail executive; b. Boston, Jan. 13, 1933; s. Martin W. and Charlotte (Cohen) M.; m. Joanne Banks, June 11, 1956; children: Gary S., Jeffrey B., Patricia A. BA, Princeton U.; MBA, Harvard U. Ptnr. Beacon Mktg. and Advt. Assocs., N.Y.C., 1956-71; v.p. Broyhill Furniture Co., Lenoir, NC, 1971-73, E.J. Korvettes, N.Y.C., 1973-78; chief, chief exec. officer Gold Circle Stores, Columbus, Ohio, 1978-82; vice chmn. Federated Dept. Stores, Cin., from 1982, pres., chief oper. officer, 1987-88, retail cons., 1988—. Dir. Progressive Corp., Finlay Fine Jewelry, NYC, Henry Schein, Inc., Melville, NY. Office Phone: 212-308-5605. Personal E-mail: normanmatthews@yahoo.com.

**MATTHEWS, PAUL AARON,** lawyer; b. Memphis, May 7, 1952; s. Joseph Curtis and Sarah Rebecca M.; m. Roberta Bartow, July 29, 1978; children: Sarah Pierrepont, Elizabeth Barret. AB, Duke U., 1974; JD, Vanderbilt U., 1977. Bar: Tenn. 1977, U.S. Dist. Ct. (we. dist.) Tenn. 1977, U.S. Dist. Ct. (ea. dist.) Mich. 1987, U.S. Dist. Ct. (ea. dist.) Tenn. 1991, U.S. Ct. Appeals (6th cir.) 1991, U.S. Dist. Ct. (ea. and we. dists.) Ark. 1995, U.S. Dist. Ct. (mid. dist.) Tenn. 1998, U.S. Dist. Ct. (no. and so. dists.) Miss. 2000, U.S. Supreme

Ct. 1998; cert. in bus. bankruptcy law and consumer bankruptcy law, Am. Bd. Certification and Tenn. Comm. on Cont. Legal Edn. and Specialization, 1999. Assoc. Armstrong Allen, PLLC, Memphis, 1977-82, mem., 1982—2006, Bourland Heflin Alvarez Minor & Matthews PLC, 2006—. Chief justice Vanderbilt Law Sch. Moot Ct. Bd., Nashville, 1976—77. Co-author: Passport to Tennessee History, 1996; contbg. editor: Martindale-Hubbell Tenn. Law Digest, 1994—99; contbr. articles to profl. publs. Com. chmn. Memphis-in-May Internat. Festival, 1977-79, Tenn. Hist. Commn., 1987-97, 2005—; bd. dirs. Davies Manor Assn., Brunswick, Tenn., 1994-99, pres. 1996-97; mem. Leadership Memphis Class of 1987, alumni adv. coun., 2000—; trustee Tenn. Hist. Commn. Found., 1998—2005, Shelby County Hist. Commn., 1997-2004, vice-chmn. 1999, chmn., 2000-01; commr. Tenn. Wars Commn., 1994-97; vestry Episcopal Ch. of the Holy Communion, 1995-98; trustee St. Mary's Episcopal Sch., 2001—. Recipient Newman award Memphis Heritage, Inc., 1992. Fellow Tenn. Bar Found.; mem. ABA, SAR (Isaac Shelby chpt.), Am. Bankruptcy Inst., Tenn. Bar Assn., Memphis Bar Assn. (publs. coun. 1990-98, bd. dirs. 1999-2001, jud. practice and procedures com. 2000-02, vice chmn. professionalism com. 2003, chmn. 2004, task force on local rules of ct. 2004-), Memphis and Shelby County Mental Health Assn. (pres. 1984-85), Duke U. Alumni Assn. (pres. Memphis chpt. 1986-88), Descs. of Early Settlers of Shelby County (v.p. 1999-2003, pres. 2004-05), Sigma Alpha Epsilon. Episcopalian. Home: 4271 Heatherwood Ln Memphis TN 38117-2302

**MATTHEWS, RONDRA J.,** publishing executive; b. Inglewood, Calif., July 13, 1955; d. Nedra Plummer; m. Keith Matthews. BS in Behavioral Sci., High Point U.; MBA, Rollins Coll. Former pres. Better Bus. Bur, Ctrl. Fla.; various mgmt. positions Orlando (Fla.) Sentinel Comms., 1980—99, v.p., gen. mgr., 1999—2000; pres., pub., CEO Daily Press, Newport News, Va., 2000—06; publisher, CEO Baltimore Sun Co., 2006—. Bd. dirs. Peninsula Alliance for Econ. Devel., Hampton Roads Partnership, Greater Peninsula NOW; bd. advisors Christopher Newport U. Sch. Bus.; chair-elect bd. dirs. United Way of the Va. Peninsula. Office: Baltimore Sun Co 501 N Calvert St PO Box 137 Baltimore MD 21278-0001*

**MATTHEWS, ROY S.,** management consultant; b. 1945; BS, Lewis U., 1967; MBA, No. Ill. U., 1971. With Regis Paper Co., Chgo., 1967-68, Continental Ill. Nat. Bank, Chgo., 1968-69; instr. acctg. Marquette U., Milw., 1971-72; asst. dean Lewis U. Coll. Bus., Romeoville, Ill., 1972-78; mgr. Peat, Marwick, Mitchell & Co., Chgo., 1978-84; with George S. May Internat. Co., Park Ridge, Ill., 1984—, now v.p. fin., sec.-treas. With USAR, 1968-74. Office: George S May Internat Co 303 S Northwest Hwy Park Ridge IL 60068-4232

**MATTHEWS, STEVE ALLEN,** lawyer; b. Columbia, S.C., Oct. 11, 1955; s. Philip Garland and Vernecia Neely (Wilson) M.; m. Caroline Elizabeth FitzSimons, Sept. 26, 1987; children: Philip Garland II, Nathalie FitzSimons, Caroline Salley. BA in History, U. S.C., 1977; JD, Yale U., 1980. Bar: S.C. 1980, D.C. 1982. Assoc. Boyd, Knowlton, Tate & Finlay, Columbia, 1980—81, Dewey, Ballantine, Bushby, Palmer & Wood, Washington, 1981—85; spl. counsel to asst. atty. gen. Civil Rights Divsn. U.S. Dept. Justice, Washington, 1985—86, dep. asst. atty. gen. for jud. selection, Office of Legal Policy, 1986—88; exec. asst. to U.S. Atty. Gen., 1988; mem. Haynsworth Sinkler Boyd, PA, Columbia, 1988—, mng. ptnr., 2001—. Sec. Landmark Legal Found.; chair Gov.'s Edn. Reform Coun., SC, 2005. Mem. Federalist Soc., Nat. Assn. Bond Lawyers (bd. dirs. 1995-96), Am. Coll. Bond Counsel (bd. dirs. 1995-99), Collegiate Network, Inc. (chmn. bd. dirs.), Am. Intellectual Property Lawyers Assn., Cultural Coun. Richland and Lexington Counties, Phila. Soc., St. Andrews Soc. Columbia, Gov's Edn. Reform Coun. (chmn.). Office: Haynsworth Sinkler Boyd PA 1201 Main St Fl 22 Columbia SC 29201-3226 Office Phone: 803-779-3080. Business E-Mail: smatthews@hsblawfirm.com.

**MATTHEWS, STEVEN DEE,** retired music educator, pilot, educator; b. Evansville, Ind., Nov. 29, 1946; s. Gerald Dee and Rosemary (Sharp) M.; m. Barbara Jean Coffing, June 16, 1968; children: Steven Dee II, Eric Dean, Sarah Maryssa. BS, Oakland City Coll., 1968; MA, Ball State U., 1970. Cert. tchr., Ind.; cirrus instrn. U. N.D. and Cirrus Design Corp. Dir. bands Ferdinand (Ind.) Schs., 1968-69; asst. dir. bands Ball State U., Muncie, Ind., 1969-70; dir. bands Winamac (Ind.) High Schs., 1970-73, Marion (Ind.) High Sch., 1973-76; dir. instrumental music Harrison High Sch., Evansville, 1976-90, McGary Mid. Sch., Evansville, 1990—2002; ret., 2003; charter pilot, flight instr. Tri-State Aero, Evansville, 2003—. Scoutmaster Boy Scouts Am., Evansville, 1982-90, 2004—05. Mem. Ind. State Tchrs. Assn. (bd. dirs. 1995-2003, Lifetime Achievement award 2004), Evansville Tchrs. Assn. (bd. dirs. 1985-2003, v.p. 1999-2002, pres. 2003Pacesetter award 1999). Avocations: flying, boating, camping, travel. Home: 5707 Monroe Ave Evansville IN 47715-5047 Office: Tri-State Aero 6101 Flightline Dr Evansville IN 47725 Office Phone: 812-426-1221, 812-479-9088. E-mail: sdmatt@insightbb.com.

**MATTHEWS, THOMAS J.,** game company executive; BS in Fin., U. So. Calif., 1986. From pres. to pres., CEO, COO Global Gaming Distributors Inc. (acquired by Anchor Gaming), Reno; pres., CEO, chmn. Anchor Gaming (acquired by Internat. Game. Tech.), 1994—2001; COO Internat. Game Tech., 2001—, pres., 2003—, CEO, 2003—, bd. dirs. 2001—, chmn., 2005—. Office: International Game Technology 9295 Prototype Dr Reno NV 89521-8986*

**MATTHEWS, THOMAS MICHAEL,** former energy company executive; b. Luling, Tex., May 20, 1943; s. Chester Raymond and Mary Lucille (Stutts) Matthews; m. Sherry Dianne Klein, May 25, 1968; children: Stephanie Dianne, Leslie Michelle. BSCE, Tex. A & M U., 1965; postgrad., U. Okla., 1967, UCLA, 1975, Stanford U., 1988, Columbia U., 1993. Staff engr. Exxon Co. USA, Houston, New Orleans, 1965—69, project engr. L.A., 1974—76, div. engr. Houston, 1969—74, engring. mgr. Anchorage, 1976—78; v.p. Exxon Gas, Houston, 1978—81, Tenn. Gas/Tenneco, Houston, 1981—86, pres., 1986—89; v.p. engr. mgr. Texaco USA, Houston, 1989—; pres. Texaco Gas, 1990—93; pres., CEO Texaco Refining & Mktg., Inc.; v.p. Texaco, Inc.; pres. NGC Corp., 1996—98; chmn., CEO & pres. Avista Corp., Wash. Power Co., Spokane, 1998—2001; mem. bd. dir. Global Water Tech. Inc., Denver, 2002—. Dir. Offshore Tech. Ctr.; adv. coun. Tex. A and M U., 1987—89; bd. dirs. Inroads, Inc. Contbr. articles to profl. jours.; inventor in field. Pres., chmn. Ponderosa Forest Cmty. Coun., Houston, 1980—85; mem. PTO, Scenic Pk. Sch., Anchorage, 1976—78. Mem.: Gas Rsch. Inst., Natural Gas Supply Assn., Am. Petroleum Inst., Soc. Ga. Assn., NSPE (bd. dirs.), Northgate Forest Country Club, Petroleum Club, Soc. Petroleum Club. Republican. Lutheran. Avocations: skiing, golf, reading, running, singing. Office: 433 Park Pointe DR STE 250 Golden CO 80401-7602

**MATTHEWS, WARREN WAYNE,** state supreme court justice; b. Santa Cruz, Calif., Apr. 5, 1939; s. Warren Wayne and Ruth Ann (Maginnis) M.; m. Donna Stearns, Aug. 17, 1963; children: Holly Maginnis, Meredith Sample. BA, Stanford U., 1961; JD, Harvard U., 1964. Bar: Alaska 1965. Assoc. firm Burr, Boney & Pease, Anchorage, 1964-69, Matthews & Dunn, Matthews, Dunn and Baily, Anchorage, 1969-77; justice Alaska Supreme Ct., Anchorage, 1977—, chief justice, 1987—90, 1997—2000. Mem. Alaska Bar Ethics & Unauthorized Practices Com., Supreme Ct. Criminal Rules Revision Com., Alaska Sentencing Commn., 1990-93; former bd. mem., second v.p. Conference Chief Justices; chmn. Alaska Judicial Council, 1987-90, 1997-2000. Bd. dirs. Alaska Legal Services Corp., 1969-70. Mem. Alaska Bar Assn. (bd. govs. 1974-77), ABA, Anchorage Bar Assn. Office: Alaska Supreme Ct 303 K St Anchorage AK 99501-2013*

**MATTHEWS, WILLIAM,** health products executive; PhD in Cell Biology, Southwestern Med. Sch., Dallas. Scientist in stem cell biology Genentech Inc., 1992—97; co-founder, pres. Deltagen, Inc., Menlo Park, Calif., 1997—, CEO, 1998—. Fellow postdoctoral fellow, Harvard Med. Sch., Princeton U.

**MATTHEWS, WILLIAM DOTY,** lawyer, director, consumer products company executive; b. Oneida, N.Y., Aug. 25, 1934; s. William L. and Marjorie L. (Doty) M.; m. Ann M. Morse, Aug. 4, 1956; children: Judith Anne, Thomas John. AB, Union Coll., 1956; LLB, Cornell U., 1960. Bar: N.Y. 1960, D.C. 1962. Atty. divsn. corp. fin. SEC, Washington, 1960-62; assoc. Whitlock, Markey & Tait, Washington, 1962-69; gen. counsel Oneida (N.Y.) Ltd., 1973—86, from v.p. to exec. v.p., 1977-86, also dir., chmn., CEO, 1986-2000. Chmn., bd. dirs. Oneida Fin. Corp., Conmed Corp.; trustee, chmn. Oneida Savs. Bank. Alderman City of Oneida, 1972-79; mem. Madison County Bd. Suprs., 1984-86. Presbyterian. Home: 621 Patio Circle Dr Oneida NY 13421-1820

**MATTHEWS, WILLIAM R., JR., (BILL MATTHEWS),** headmaster; Former dir. of development St. Paul's Sch., Concord, NH, former vice rector, interim rector, 2005—. Office: St Paul's Sch 325 Pleasant St Concord NH 03301

**MATTHEWS, WYHOMME S.,** retired music educator, academic administrator; b. Battle Creek, Mich., July 22, 1948; d. Woodrow R. and LouLease (Graham) Sellers; m. Edward L. Matthews, Apr. 29, 1972; children: Channing DuVall, Triston Curran, Landon Edward, Brandon Graham. AA, Kellogg C.C., 1968; MusB, Mich. State U., 1970, MA, MusM, Mich. State U., 1972. Cert. elem. and secondary tchr., Mich. Tchr., vocal music dir. Benton Harbor (Mich.) Pub. Schs., 1971-72, dir. vocal music, 1972; dir. edn. head start program Burlington (N.J.) County, 1972-73; pvt. music tchr., 1973-89; tchr. Southeastern Jr. H.S., 1986-87, W.K. Kellogg Jr. H.S., 1987-89; chair visual and performing arts dept. Kellogg C.C., Battle Creek, Mich., 1989-99, dir. Eastern acad. Ctr., 1999—2003, ret., 2003. Part-time instr. Kellogg C.C., 1973—, dir. Eclectic Chorale, 1973-2005, dir., organizer Kellogg C.C. Eclectic Chorale Sacred Cultural Festival, 1979—, judge various contests; artistic dir. Battle Creek Sojourner Truth Monument Presentation Day, 1999; presenter in field. Pres. Dudley Elem. Sch., 1981-85; active Battle Creek Pub. Schs. PTA, Pennfield Pub. Schs. PTA, Mt. Zion African Meth. Episc. Ch.; v.p. Life Care Amb. Bd., 1990-2003; bd. dirs. Leila Aboretum Soc.; mem. Battle Creek Cmty. Found., Glen Cross Arts and Infrasture Fund; founder Echoes of Grace, 2005. Recipient Outstanding Cmty. Svc. award, 1975, Sojourner Truth award, 2000, George award, City of Battle Creek, 2000; fellow, Mich. State U., 1971. Mem. Mich. Music Tchr. Assn., Nat. Music Tchrs. Assn., Battle Creek Music Tchrs. Assn., Battle Creek Morning Music Club (bd. dirs.), Nat. Leadership Acad., Battle Creek Cmty. Concert Assn. Home: 466 Alton Ave Battle Creek MI 49017-3212 Personal E-mail: wmath5278@aol.com.

**MATTHIAS, GEORGE FRANK,** retired secondary school educator; b. Aug. 22, 1934; s. George and Marguerite (Blanchard) M.; m. Mary Jo Avery, Aug. 18, 1956; children: Todd Avery, Tara Lynn. BS, SUNY, Cortland, 1957; MS, Syracuse U., 1962; MA, Conn. Wesleyan U., 1970. Tchr. secondary earth sci. Belleville (N.Y.) Acad., 1957-58, Croton-Harmon H.S., Croton-on-Hudson, NY, 1961-89; tchr., prin. Raquette Lake (N.Y.) Elem. Sch., 1958-61; ret., 1989. Mem. N.Y. State Earth Sci. Syllabus Revision Writing Commn., 1967-70, 89-91; coord. Bur. of Sci. Edn., N.Y. State Dept. Edn., 1971-72; instr. Finger Lakes Inst., Alfred U., 1970; guest staff Coll. of St. Rose, summers 1984-85, 88-90; freelance cons. earth science edn.; item writer Nat. Testing Service, Nat. Assessment for Ednl. Progress, 1984; cons. in field. Author: (with Berey, Higham, Knabel, Maust) Observation and Interpretation in Earth Science, 1972; (with Daley and Higham) Earth Science: A Study of a Changing Planet, 1986; (with Deacon) Plate Tectonics, 1980; developer: (with Snyder) Individualized Earth Science Program, 1975-89; (with Snyderetal) Prentice-Hall General Science Series, 1986, NYS Student Performance Examination (Ed. Assessment), 1994; contbr. articles to profl. jours. NSF grant, 66-70; Merit fellow Shell, 1971. Mem. Nat. Assn. Geology Tchrs., Nat. Assn. Rsch. in Sci. Tchg., Sci. Tchrs. Assn. N.Y. State, N.Y. State United Tchrs., Am. Fedn. Tchrs. Home and Office: 143 Dutch St Montrose NY 10548-1505 Fax: 914-734-1725. E-mail: gfrmjmatt@mymailstation.com.

**MATTHIAS, JOHN EDWARD,** English literature educator; b. Columbus, Ohio, Sept. 5, 1941; s. John Marshall and Lois (Kirkpatrick) M.; m. Diana Clare Jocelyn, Dec. 27, 1967; children— Cynouai, Laura. BA, Ohio State U., 1963; MA, Stanford U., 1966; postgrad., U. London, 1967. Assoc. prof. dept. English U. Notre Dame, Ind., 1968-73, assoc. prof. fnd., 1973-80, prof. fnd., 1980—. Vis. fellow Clare Hall, Cambridge U., 1966-77, assoc., 1977—; vis. prof. dept. English, Skidmore Coll., Saratoga Springs, N.Y., 1975, U. Chgo., 1980. Author: Bucyrus, 1971, Turns, 1975, Crossing, 1979, Five American Poets, 1980, Introducing David Jones, 1980, Contemporary Swedish Poetry, 1980, Bathory and Lermontov, 1980, Northern Summer, New and Selected Poems, 1984, The Battle of Kosovo, 1987, David Jones: Man and Poet: A Gathering of Waves, 1991, Reading Old Friends, 1991, Swimming at Midnight, 1995, Beltane at Aphelion, 1995, Pages: New Poems and Cuttings, 2000, Working Progress, 2002, Three-Toed Gull: Selected Poems of Jesper Svenbro, 2003, New Selected Poems, 2004. Recipient Columbia U. Transl. award, 1978, Swedish Inst. award, 1981, Poetry award Soc. Midland Authors, 1984, Ingram Merrill Found. award, 1984, 90; Woodrow Wilson fellow, 1963, Lily Endowment fellow, 1993; Fulbright grantee, 1966. Mem. AAUP, PEN, Poets and Writers, Poetry Soc. Am. (George Bogin Meml. award 1990). Office: U Notre Dame Dept English Notre Dame IN 46556

**MATTHIES, FREDERICK JOHN,** civil and environmental engineer; b. Omaha, Oct. 4, 1925; s. Fred J. and Charlotte Leota (Metz) M.; m. Carol Mae Dean, Sept. 14, 1947; children: John Frederick, Jane Carolyn Matthies Goding BSCE, Cornell U., 1947; postgrad., U. Nebr., 1952-53. Bd. cert. Am. Acad. Environ. Engrs.; registered profl. engr. Nebr. Civil engr. Henningson, Durham & Richardson, Omaha, 1947-50, 52-54; sr. v.p. devel. Leo A. Daly Co., Omaha, 1954-90; cons. engr., 1990—. Lectr. in field; mem. dist. export coun. U.S. Dept. Commerce, 1981-83. Contbr. articles to profl. jours. Mem. Douglas County Rep. Cen. Com., Nebr., 1968-72; bd. regents Augustana Coll., Sioux Falls., S.D., 1976-89; bd. dirs. Orange County Luth. Hosp. Assn., Anaheim, Calif., 1961-62; Nebr. Humanities Coun., 1988-94, Omaha-Shizuoka City (Japan) Sister City Orgn.; trustee Luth. Med. Ctr., Omaha, 1978-82; mem. adv. bd. Marine Mil. Acad., Harlingen, Tex. 1st lt. USMCR, 1943-46, 50-52, Korea. Fellow ASCE, Instn. Civil Engrs. (London), Euro Engr. European Econ. Commn.; mem. NSPE, Am. Water Works Assn. (life), Air Force Assn., Am. Legion, VFW. Home: 950 Southridge Greens Blvd # 15 Fort Collins CO 80525-6726

**MATTHYS, DAVE,** music educator; Masters, Lewis and Clark Coll., 1987. Tchr. Portland Sch. District, 2000-03, Lake Oswego Sch. District, Oreg., 2003—. Mem.: Oreg. Band Dirs. Assn. (pres. 2002—03), Oreg. Music Educators Assn. Office Phone: 503-534-2425.

**MATTIA, DAVIDE,** materials engineer, researcher; b. Napoli, Italy, June 28, 1978; BS, MS, Università', Napoli. Rschr. Université' di Limoges, Limoges, France, 2003—04; EKU U., Tuebingen, Germany, 2004. Office: Drexel Univer Materials Engring 3141 Chestnut St Philadelphia PA 19104

**MATTICE, DEBORA J.,** special education educator, consultant; b. Concord, Calif., June 21, 1959; d. Fred Alexander and Sarah Elizabeth Elder; m. Galen Donald Mattice, July 24, 1993; 1 child, Paul Daniel Reininger. AS, Monroe C.C., 1990; BS, SUNY, Brockport, 1990; MS, Nazareth Coll., 1995; postgrad., Cumberland U. 2002. Cert. profl. tchg. State Dept. Edn., Tenn., permanent tchg. State of N.Y. Tchr. Rochester City Sch., 1993—94, spl. edn. tchr., 1995—96, Dede Wallace Sch., Nashville, 1996, Stones River Acad., Murfreesboro, Tenn., 1996—97, Metro Nashville Sch., 1997—. Notary pub., Tenn. Foster parent Dept. Children's Svcs., Davidson County. Mem.: Assn. Supr. and Curriculum Design, Christian Educators Assn., Nat. Geographic, Smithsonian Instn., Davison County Foster and Adoptive Care Assn. (sec. 2000—06), Am. Civil Liberties Union, Kappa Delta Epsilon Phi, Kappa Delta Pi. Democrat. Presbyterian. Avocations: reading, crafts, writing. Home: 5020 Sunshine Dr Antioch TN 37013 Office: John F Kennedy Mid Sch 2087 Hobson Pike Antioch TN 37013 Office Phone: 615-501-7900 1040.

**MATTICE, HARRY SANDLIN, JR.,** federal judge, former prosecutor; b. Chattanooga, Mar. 10, 1954; s. Harry Sandlin Sr. and Kathryn (McCoy) M.; m. Janet Lynn LeVan, Jan 4, 1975; children: Harry Sandlin III, Bryan Christopher, Kevin LeVan. BS, U. Tenn., Chattanooga, 1976; JD, U. Tenn., 1981. Bar: Tenn. 1981, US Dist. Ct. (ea. dist.) Tenn. 1981, US Ct. Appeals (6th cir.) 1984, US Tax Ct. 1984, US Claims Ct. 1984, US Dist. Ct. (we. dist.) Tenn. 1989. Staff acct. Deloitte, Haskins & Sells, Chattanooga, 1976-78; from assoc. to ptnr. Miller & Martin, Chattanooga, 1981—2000; shareholder Baker, Donelson, Bearman & Caldwell, Chattanooga, 2000—01; U.S. atty. (ea. dist.) Tenn. US Dept. Justice, 2001—05; judge US Dist. Ct. (ea. dist.) Tenn., Chattanooga, 2005—. Pres. Chattanooga Tax Practitioners; sr. counsel U.S. Senate Com. on Govtl. Affairs, Spl. Investigation, 1997. Asst. to pres. Chattanooga Goodwill Industries, 1988-92; chmn. Hamilton County Rep. Party, 1993-95. Mem. Order of Coif, Signal Mountain Golf and Country Club, Phi Kappa Phi. Episcopalian. Home: 609 Marr Dr Signal Mountain TN 37377-2280 Office: US Dist Ct Rm 104 900 Georgia Ave Chattanooga TN 37402

**MATTICE, HOWARD LEROY,** education educator; b. Roxbury, N.Y., Sept. 23, 1935; s. Charles Pierce and Loretta Jane (Ellis) M.; m. Elaine Grace Potts, Feb. 4, 1956 (dec. Jan. 2002); children: Kevin, Stephen. BA, King's Coll., 1960; MA, L.I. U., 1965, NYU, 1969; cert., CUNY, 1972; EdD, NYU, 1978. Cert. tchr. N.Y., clin. educators trainer, Fla. Dept. Edn. Social studies tchr. N.Y.C. Bd. Edn., 1961-90, mid. and jr. H.S. asst. prin., 1970-72, 73-75; assoc. prof. edn. and history Clearwater (Fla.) Christian Coll., 1990-92, chmn. divsn. edn., prof. edn. and history, 1992-99, prof. edn. and history, 2002—; social studies curriculum writer Accelerated Christian Edn., 2003; adj. prof. history DeVry U., 2004—. Adj. lectr. history S.I. C.C., CUNY, 1969-75; curriculum writer N.Y.C. Bd. Edn., 1985, Accelerated Christian Edn., Largo, Fla., 2003—; program reviewer Fla. Dept. Edn., Tallahassee, 1994—; item writer GED Testing Svc., Washington, 1988-92; mem. So. Assn. Colls. and Schs. Accreditation Team H.S., 1995—. Chmn. bd. New Dorp Christian Acad., S.I., 1973-90; chmn. bd. deacons New Dorp Bapt. Ch., S.I., 1981-90. Mem. ASCD, Assn. Tchr. Educators, Nat. Coun. Social Studies, So. Assn. Colls. and Schs. (h.s. accreditation review team 1995—). Avocations: reading, travel, gardening. Office Phone: 727-726-1153 ext. 259. Business E-Mail: howardmattice@clearwater.edu.

**MATTILA, MARY JO KALSEM,** elementary and art educator; b. Canton, Ill., Oct. 26, 1944; d. Joseph Nelson and Bernice Nora (Milbauer) Kalsem; m. John Peter Mattila, Jan. 27, 1968. BS in Art, U. Wis., Madison, 1966; student, Ohio State U., Columbus, 1972, Drake U., Des Moines, Iowa, 1981; MS in Ednl. Adminstrn., Iowa State U., Ames, 1988. Cert. tchr., prin., supr., adminstr., art tchr., secondary tchr., Iowa. Tchr. 2d grade McHenry Pub. Schs., Ill., 1966-67, Wisconsin Hts. Schs., Black Earth, Wis., 1967-69; substitute tchr. Columbus City Schs., Ohio, 1969-70; elem. art tchr. Southwestern City Schs., Columbus, 1972-73; adminstrv. intern Ames, Iowa, 1984-86; lead tchr. at Roosevelt Sch. Ames Cmty. Schs., 1986-87, art vertical curriculum chair, 1983-89, art educator, elem. and spl. edn., 1973—2003. Contbr. articles to profl. jours. Mem. human rels. commn. City of Ames, prevention policy bd. youth and shelter svcs., Breaking Down Barriers, Ames, Iowa, 2004—. Recipient Very Spl. Svc. award for Disting. Svc. in Very Spl. Arts, Gov. of Iowa, 1984. Mem.: LWV, Ctrl. Iowa Orchid Soc., Questers, Am. Orchid Soc. Avocations: collecting old stoneware jugs, growing orchids, reading. Home: 2822 Duff Ave Ames IA 50010-4710 Office: Ames Cmty Schs 415 Stanton Ave Ames IA 50014-7331

**MATTINA, MARYJANE INCORVIA,** chemist; b. N.Y.C., July 31, 1944; d. Ernest and Annette Incorvia; m. Charles F. Mattina, June 21, 1969; children: Emily, Matthew, Jenny. PhD, Colga U., New Haven, 1970. Head dept. analytical chemistry Conn. Agrl. Expt. Sta., New Haven, 1992—. Contbr. chapters to books, scientific papers to peer-rev. jours. Bd. sec. Shakesperience Productions Inc., Waterbury, Conn., 1999—. Recipient Best Paper award, Sigma Xi; grantee, Sci. To Achieve Results U.S. EPA, 1999—2002. Office: Conn Agrl Experiment Sta 123 Huntington St New Haven CT 06511 Office Phone: 203-974-8449. Business E-Mail: maryjane.mattina@po.state.ct.us.

**MATTINGLY, MACK FRANCIS,** former ambassador, former senator, entrepreneur; b. Anderson, Ind., Jan. 7, 1931; m. Carolyn Longcamp, 1957 (dec.); children: Jane, Anne; m. Leslie Ann Davisson, 1998. BS, Ind. U., 1957. Acct. supr. IND, Arvin, Ind., 1957-59; mktg. rep. IBM, Ga., 1959-79; owner, pres. M's Inc., Ga., 1959-79; U.S. senator from Ga., 1981-87; asst. sec. gen. def. support NATO, Brussels, 1987-90; amb. to Seychelles Dept. State, 1992-93. Spkr./author econ. def., fgn. policy, entrepreneur, 1993—; mem. U.S. Senate Com. Appropriations, chmn. legis. and mil. constrn. subcoms.; mem. energy and water devel., agt. rural devel., treasury, postal svc. and gen. govt., mil. constrn. legis. subcoms., U.S. Senate com. Banking, Housing and Urban Affairs, chmn. rural housing, econ. policy subcoms.; mem. select com. ethics, 1981-83, joint econ. com., 1983-87; chmn. Rep. Com. on Coms., mem. Rep. Senate Leadership, 1985-87, Holocaust Commn.; U.S. del. GATT, Geneva, 1982; bd. dirs. CompuCredit Corp.; hon. co-chmn. GMACC, Hemisphere, Inc. Author 40 U.S. Sen. Bills, Amendments and Resolutions. Sgt.-at-arms, Maj. Nat. Convs., del. Georgian Rep. Party Convs., 1964-90; chmn. 8th Dist. Goldwater for Pres., 1964, Ga. 8th Congl. Dist., Cand. U.S. Congress, 8th Dist., 1966; mem. Ga. Rep. Ctrl. Com.; mem. Ga. Exec. Com., vice chmn., 1968-75; chmn. Ga. Rep. Party, 1975-77; elected 1st Rep. U.S. Senator from Ga. since 1871, 1980; bd. dirs. NOVECON, Cumberland Preservation Soc., Inst. for Global Econ. Growth, Ga. Portts Authority; hon. bd. dirs. M.L. King Jr. Fed. Holiday Commn., Brunswick Golden Isles C. of C. Staff sgt. USAF, 1951-55. Recipient S.E. Father of Yr. award 1984, Ga. Wildlife Fed. Conservationist of Yr. award 1985, Selective Svc. System Dist. Svc. Gold medal 1985, Watchdog of Treasury award 1981-86, Nat. Taxpayers Union Taxpayers Best Friend award 1981-86, NFIB's Guardian of Small Bus. award 1981-86, Am. Security Coun. award 1981-86, Svc. Def. medal for Outstanding Pub. Svc. 1988. Episcopalian.

**MATTIODA, ANDREW LIGE,** research chemist, scientist; b. Hartshorne, Okla., Jan. 20, 1967; s. Tony and Gloria (Ranallo) Mattioda. AS, Ea. Okla. State Coll., Wilburton, 1987; BSc, East Ctrl. U., Ada, Okla., 1989; MSc in Chemistry, U. Okla., Norman, 1993, DSc in Chemistry, 1995. Cert. open water diver Profl. Assn. Diving Instrs., 1994, lic. pvt. pilot FAA, 2004. Environ. chemist Corps. Engrs. U.S. Army, Tulsa, Okla., 1995—99; vis. prof. U. Tulsa, 1999—2000, Rogers State U., Tulsa, 1999—2000; fellow Ames Rsrch.Ctr. NASA, Moffett Field, Calif., 2000—03, rsch. scientist Ames Astrochemistry Lab. SETI Inst. Mountain View, Calif., 2003—. Spkr. in field; lectr. in field. Contbr. articles to profl. jours. Coord. Mountain View Cath. Singles, Calif., 2000—02. Recipient Superior Performance Award, U.S. Army Corps. Engrs., 1996, Spl. Svc. Achievement award, 1997, Performance Evaluation award, 1997, 1998, Ark. Traveler award, Gov. Mike Huckabee, Ark., 2004; fellow Karcher Fellowship, U. of Okla, 1989, Nat. Rsch. Coun., 2000—03. Mem.: AAAS, Am. Chem. Soc. (chmn. organizing annual chemistry day Tulsa chpt. 1997—98, co-chmn. environ. chemistry symposia), Nat. Italian Am. Found., Planetary Soc., Nat. Space Soc., Aircraft Owners and Pilots Assn., PA Diving Instrs. Roman Catholic. Achievements include identifying the possibility that polycyclic aromatic nitrogen heterocycles are present in interstellar space; research in molecular spectroscopy of interstellar polycyclic aromatic hydrocarbons. Avocations: hiking, travel, scuba diving, flying, cooking. Office: SETI Institute NASA Ames Astrochemistry Ms245-6 Moffett Field CA 94035 Office Phone: 650-604-1075. Personal E-mail: andrew@mattioda.com. Business E-Mail: amattioda@mail.arc.nasa.gov.

**MATTIS, DANIEL CHARLES,** physicist, researcher; b. Brussels, Sept. 8, 1932; came to U.S., 1941; s. Joseph and Lucie (Applebaum) M. BS, MIT, 1953; MS, U. Ill., 1954, PhD, 1957. Mem. rsch. staff IBM, N.Y., 1959—65; prof. Belfer Grad. Sch. Yeshiva U., N.Y.C., 1965—78; Thomas Potts prof. Polytech., N.Y.C., 1978—80; prof. U. Utah, Salt Lake City, 1980—. Wei-Lun vis. prof. Chinese U. Hong Kong, 1997. Author: Theory of Magnetism, Vol. 1, 1981, Vol. 2, 1985, Many Body Theory, 1994, Statistical Mechanics Made Simple, 2003, Theory of Magnetism Made Simple, 2006; mem. editl. bd. Internat. Jour. Modern Physics; contbr. articles to profl. jours.

Fellow: Am. Phys. Soc. Achievements include 4 patents. Office: U Utah Dept Physics Salt Lake City UT 84112 Office Phone: 801-581-3690. Personal E-mail: mattis@physics.utah.edu, dancmat@comcast.net.

**MATTIS, TIM,** music educator; b. Richmond, Ind., Apr. 14, 1962; s. James Edward and Marjorie Jean (Earhart) Mattis; m. Tammie Lee Burr, June 7, 1986; children: Kristi Zachary and Elizabeth Ann. BA, Bluffton Coll., 1984; MusM, Bowling Green State U., 1997. Dir. music Ridgemont Local Sch. Dist., Ridgeway, Ohio, 1985—86, Perry Local Sch. Dist., Lima, Ohio, 1986—94; dir. bands Findlay (Ohio) City Sch. Dist., 1994—. Adj. instr. percussion Ohio No. U., Ada, 1990—91, Bluffton (Ohio) Coll., 1993—2001; performer Lima Marimba Ensemble, 1990—; dir., performer Pantasia Steelband, Findlay, 1997—. Spkr. Victims Impact Svcs., 2002—03; communion asst. Trinity Evangelical Luth. Ch., Findlay, 2000—, coun. mem., 2001—04. Named Disney Tchr. award, Walt Disney Corp., 2006; recipient Tchr. Who Made a Difference award, Findlay H.S., 2002, 2003, 2004, Golden Apple award for excellence in tchg., Findlay Rotary Club, 2005. Mem.: Ohio Edn. Assn., Ohio Music Edn. Assn., Music Educators Nat. Conf. Avocations: music performance, theatrical performance, collector Sinclair Service Station memorabilia. Home: 933 Laurel N Findlay OH 45840 Office: Findlay HS 1200 Broad AVe Findlay OH 45840

**MATTISON, DONALD ROGER,** gynecologist, toxicologist, educator, medical association administrator, public health service officer; b. Mpls., Apr. 28, 1944; s. Milford Zachary and Elizabeth Ruth (Davey) M.; m. Margaret Rose Libby, Jan. 28, 1967; children: Jon, Amy. BA cum laude in Chemistry and Math., Augsburg Coll., Mpls., 1966; MS in Chemistry, MIT, 1968; MD, Columbia U., 1973. Resident in ob-gyn Presbyn. Hosp., N.Y.C., 1973-75, 77-78; commd. officer, rsch. assoc. USPHS, 1975, advanced through grades to comdr., 1984; rsch. assoc. Nat. Inst. Child Health and Human Devel., NIH, Bethesda, Md., 1975-77, med. officer, 1978-84; assoc. prof. ob-gyn. U. Ark., Little Rock, 1984-87; prof. U. Pitts., 1987-90, assoc. prof. toxicology, 1984-88, prof., 1988-90, dean Grad. Sch. Pub. Health, prof., 1990-99; med. dir. March of Dimes, 1998—2002; sr. advisor to dirs. NICHD and CRMC, 2002—. Contbr. articles, abstracts, letters and editls. to profl. publs. Recipient Am. Chem. Soc. medal Minn. sect. Am. Chem. Soc., 1966, Assn. Am. Publs. award, 1983. Fellow AAAS; mem. APHA, Inst. of Medicine NAS, Soc. Risk Analysis (editl. bd. jour. 1988—), Pitts. chpt. Soc. Risk Analysis, Am. Assn. Cancer Rsch., N.Y. Acad. Sci., Am. Coll. Toxicology, Am. Fertility Soc., Soc. Gynecologic Investigation, Soc. Toxicology. Avocations: photography, computer sciences, fly fishing, cross country skiing. Office: NICHD/NIH 6100 Executive Blvd MSC 7510 Bethesda MD 20892 E-mail: mattisod@mail.nih.gov.

**MATTOLI, AGOSTINO MARRON,** management consultant; b. Rome, Feb. 23, 1938; s. Giorgio Mattoli and Doris Virginia Marron; m. Patrizia Chiavarelli Costa, June 11, 1966; children: Maurizio, Michele, Giorgio, Alessio, Agostino. BA in Arts and Sci., Rutgers U., 1962. Internat. advisor to pres. Fisvina, Rome, 1991-95; cons. Armemise Harva Found. Sci. Rsch. in Medicine, 1995—96; advisor, asst. to chmn. Armemise-Harvard Found. for Rsch. in Medicine, 1996—99; bd. dirs. Orders of the Royal House of Savoy, 2000—. Dir. bus. rels. Africa Ctr./Oil and Mineral Explorations, Rome and London, 1970—78. Editor, founder (journal) Cambridge Transcontinental, 1957 (Spl. Fgn. Student award, 1958). Cons. internat. ops. Red Cross, Rome, 1996-2001. Named a knight, officer, Savoy Order SS Maurizio & Lazzaro, senator, Sacro Romano Impero; recipient award for hunting achievements, Safari Club Internat., 1968—2000. Mem.: Gruppo Savoia, Royal Circolo Canottieri Tevere Remo (life socio sr. 1954), Sons of Am. Revolution, Inst. of The Holy Roman Empire. Roman Catholic. Avocations: travel, sailing, yachting, big game hunting. E-mail: trailmas@unete.cl.

**MATTOON, PETER MILLS,** lawyer; b. Bryn Mawr, Pa., Oct. 22, 1931; s. Harold Gleason and Marguerite Jeanette (Mills) M.; m. Mary Joan Henley, June 27, 1953; children: Pamela M. Zisselman, R. Stephen, Peter H., Philip P. AB, Dartmouth Coll., 1953; LLB, Harvard U., 1959; LLD (hon.), Widener U., 2001. Bar: Pa. 1960. Assoc. Ballard Spahr Andrews & Ingersoll, Phila., 1959-67; ptnr. Ballard Spahr Andrews & Ingersoll LLP, Phila., 1967—2001, sr. counsel, 2002—. Emeritus trustee Episcopal Acad., Merion, Pa., 1970—; past chmn.; trustee, v.p. Widener Meml. Found., Lafayette Hill, Pa., 1972—; trustee, vice-chmn. Thomas Jefferson U., Phila., 1989—; overseer Widener U. Law Sch., Wilmington, 1979—. Lt. USN, 1953-56. Office: Ballard Spahr Andrews & Ingersoll LLP 1735 Market St Fl 51 Philadelphia PA 19103-7599

**MATTOON, ROBERT H., JR., (SKIP MATTOON),** headmaster; m. Carolyn Orr; children: Danielle, Ashley. BA, Dartmouth Coll.; MA, PhD, Yale U. Former assoc. headmaster and dean of faculty Deerfield Acad.; head of sch. Hotchkiss Sch., Lakeville, Conn., 1996—. Former prof. Latin Am. history U. Ariz., U. Michigan. Trustee Bement Sch., Deerfield, Mass.; bd. chmn. Green Fields Country Day Sch., Tucson; bd. mem. Conn. Assn. of Independent Schools; mem. bd. dirs. Am. Secondary Schools for Internat. Students and Teachers. Grantee Fulbright-Hays Fellowship. Mem.: Assn. of Boarding Schools. Office: Hotchkiss Sch 11 Interlaken Rd PO Box 800 Lakeville CT 06039-0800

**MATTOON, SCOTT ALEXANDER,** private school educator; b. NYC, May 12, 1969; s. David Scott and Diana Mattoon; m. Dawn Rachel Gray, July 6, 1996; children: Ryland David, Avery Rachel. BA, Trinity Coll., 1991; MA, UCLA, 1994. Tchr. St. Mark's Sch. Tex., Dallas, 1991—92, UCLA, 1992—94, Collegiate Sch., NYC, 1997—2000; tchr., head lang. dept. Webb Sch. Calif., Claremont, 1994—97, Choate Rosemary Hall, Wallingford, Conn., 2000—. Vis. evaluator Chase Collegiate Acad., Waterbury, Conn., 2004. Recipient Excellence in Tchg. award, Webb Sch., 1996, Collegiate Sch., 1998—99; NEH ind. study grantee, Coun. Basic Edn., 1996. Mem.: Alliance Francaise, Am. Assn. Tchrs. French (chmn. nat. French contest 1997—2000). Office Phone: 203-697-2337. Business E-Mail: smattoon@choate.edu.

**MATTOS, WILLIAM HAROLD,** trade association administrator, publishing executive; b. Calif., July 4, 1952; s. Irma A. Mattos; children: Antoinette, Natalie. BS in Journalism, Calif. Polytech. State U., 1974; MS, U. Wis., 1975. Writer Agr. News Bur. U. Wis., Madison, Wis., 1975; editor, mgr. Agribusiness Pubs., Fresno, Calif., 1975—76; pres., pub. Mattos Newspapers, Inc., Newman, Calif., 1976—2006; pres. Calif. Poultry Fedn., Modesto, Calif., 1991—. Pres. Stanislaus County Fair Bd., Turlock, Calif., 1993, Agrl. Network, Sacramento, Calif., 1994—; pres., bd. regents Stanislaus State U. Bd. regents Stanislaus State U., Turlock, 1999; bd. govs., chmn. bd. Doctor's Hosp., Modesto, Calif., 2001; area 9 coord. Gov. George W. Bush for Pres., Modesto, 2000; campaign cabinet United Way of Stanislaus County, Modesto, 1999; bd. supr. Stanislaus County Bd. Suprs., 1990-91. Recipient John Silveira Meml. Svc. award Newman C. of C., 1990; named Outstanding Young Man of Am. Calif. Jaycees, 1986, Grand Marshall Newman Fall Festival, 1990, Disting. Citizen of Yr. Summer League Bseball, 1980; Paul Harris fellow Newman Rotary Club. Mem. Newman Rotary Club (Paul Harris fellow 1985), Phi Kappa Phi. Avocations: walking, swimming, travel, speaking. Office: Calif Poultry Fedn 4640 Spyres Way Ste 4 Modesto CA 95356 Personal E-mail: califpoultry@cs.com

**MATTOS GRELL, ELIZABETH,** artist; b. N.Y.C., Oct. 22, 1929; d. Percy Peter Allwork and Dorothy Edna Albers; m. Martin Grell, Feb. 14, 1981; children: Shelley(dec.), Debra, Lill. One-woman shows include Kipness Gallery, Westport, Conn., 1955, Bruce Mus., Greenwich, 1968—69, Rye N.Y. Libr., 1988, exhibited in group shows at Nat. Acad. Design, Manhattan, 1951, Greenwich Village Out Door Art Fair, 1951, Contempories, N.Y.C., 1960, White Barn, Greenwich, Conn., 1961, Somers Gallery, N.Y., 1983.

**MATTOX, JOHNNY LYNN,** biologist, educator; b. Corinth, Miss., Apr. 13, 1951; s. Oliver Lee Mattox Jr. and Margaret Joyce Mills; m. Glenda Jean Eaton, Aug. 11, 1973; children: Jason Lynn, Jenny Amanda, Julia Elizabeth. AA, NE Miss. C.C., Booneville, 1971; BA Edn., U. Miss., University, 1973; MSc, U. Miss., 1977; PhD, U. Miss., 1979. Tchr. sci. Kessuth H.S., Miss.,

1973—74; instr. sci. Itawamba C.C., Fulton, Miss., 1975—80; instr. Biology NE Miss. C.C., Booneville, 1981—2005; assoc. prof. Biology Blue Mountain Coll., Miss., 2005—. Adj. asst. prof. Miss. U. Women, Columbus, 1984—2000, U. Miss., University, 1991—93, 1996—, U. Tenn. Martin, Selmer, 2000—. Chmn. Sci. Edn. divsn. Miss. Acad. Sci., 1980—81; deacon Union Bapt. Ch., Kessuth, 1963—, treas., 1963—, organist, 1963—. Named to, Who's Who South/Southwest, 1981, Who's Who Miss., 1990, Who's Who Among America's Tchrs., 1994, 1996, 1998, 1999, 2000, 2004, 2005. Mem.: NSTA, SAR (Booneville chpt.), Nat. Assn. Biology Tchrs., Alcorn County Hist. Soc. (pres. 1982—83), Kessuth Hist. Soc. (pres. 1996—98), Kappa Delta Pi, Phi Theta kappa (advisor 1979—2005), Phi Kappa Phi. Baptist.

**MATTOX, ROBERT F.,** architectural firm executive; BArch, Rice U.; MBA, U. Mich. COO Payette Assocs. Inc., Boston, 1997—. Author: Financial Management for Architects; co-author: Success Strategies for Design Professionals. Fellow: AIA. Office: Payette Assocs Inc 285 Summer St Boston MA 02210-1522

**MATTOX, SHARON M.,** lawyer; b. Wichita Falls, Tex., Oct. 4, 1952; BA, Emporia State U., 1974; JD, U. Tex., 1974, PhD, 1978. Ptnr., co-head Adminstrv. / Environ. Law Sect. Vinson & Elkins LLP, Houston. Fellow: Tex. Bar Found. Office: Vinson & Elkins LLP First City Tower 1001 Fannin St, Ste 2300 Houston TX 77002 Office Phone: 713-758-4598. E-mail: smattox@velaw.com.

**MATTRAN, DONALD ALBERT,** management consultant, educator; b. Chgo., July 8, 1934; s. George Charles and Lucille Alice (Boule) M.; m. Betty Elena Flores, July 18, 1953 (div. Mar. 1988); children: Donald, Julie, Kimberly, Guy, Christy; m. Rose Lynn Castellano, May, 1988. B.Mus., U. Mich., 1957, M.Mus., 1960. Tchr. Van Buren Schs., Belleville, Mich., 1957-61; asst. prof. U. N.H., Durham, 1961-65, Boston U., 1965-66; assoc. prof. Hartt Sch. Music, West Hartford, Conn., 1966-82, dean, 1971-80; dir. Syracuse U. Sch. Music, NY, 1982-83; dean Sch. Fine and Performing Arts Montclair State Coll, Upper Montclair, NJ, 1983-87; pres. Sales Consultants of Sarasota (Fla.) Inc., 1987—. Cons. Music div. Kaman Corp., Bloomfield, Conn.; cons., evaluator Nat. Assn. Schs. of Music and Joint Commn. Theater and Dance Accreditation; guest condr. Hartford Symphony Orch., Hartt Opera Theatre, All-State Festivals, 1976-83, Soc. New Music, Syracuse, N.J. Sch. Arts Orch., 1985-87. Co-author: (with Mary Rasmussen) A Teacher's Guide to the Literature of Woodwind Instruments, 1966; condr.: rec. Concerto for Cello and Jazz Band, 1972. Chmn. adv. com. Prodigy Inc., Syracuse, 1982-86; trustee Conn. Opera Assn., 1977-80; bd. advs. Watkinson Sch. Creative Arts Program, Hartford, 1977-80; mem. humanities adv. com. N.J. Dept. Higher Edn., 1984—; mem. multi-disciplinary panel N.J. State Council on Arts, 1985-87; mem. adv. com. on auditions Met. Opera Nat. Council, 1984-87; mem. adv. com. Frank and Lydia Bergen Found., 1986-87. Mem. Nat. Assn. Schs. Music (exec. bd., sec. 1978-81). Home: Apt 204 888 Boulevard Of The Arts Sarasota FL 34236-4827 Office: 1343 Main St Ste 600 Sarasota FL 34236-5630 Office Phone: 941-365-5151. Business E-Mail: dmattran@scsarasota.com.

**MATTRICK, DONALD A.,** interactive entertainment software company executive; Founder, chmn. Distinctive Software Inc. (acquired by Electronic Arts in 1991), 1982—91; sr. v.p. N.Am. Studios, exec. v.p., gen. mgr. EA Canada, v.p. Electronic Arts, 1991—96, exec. v.p. N.Am. Studios, 1996—97, pres. Worldwide Studios, 1997—2005.

**MATTSON, CAROL LINNETTE,** social services administrator; b. Frederic, Wis., Oct. 3, 1946; d. Clarence Waldemar and Lucille Anna Mathilda (Bengtson) Hedlund; m. Wesley Harlan Mattson, June 24, 1967; 1 child, Aaron Ray. BS, U. Wis., Menomonie, 1968. Home econs. tchr. Luck (Wis.) High Sch., 1968-72; clk. Daniels Twp., Siren, Wis., 1973-75; family living instr. Wis. Indianhead Tech. Inst., New Richmond, 1974-77; aging program dir. Polk County, Balsam Lake, Wis., 1977—. Treas., bd. dirs. Polk County Transp. for the Disabled and Elderly, Inc., Balsam Lake, 1978—; mem. com. Long Term Support Com., Balsam Lake, 1985—. Mem. Wis. Assn. Nutrition Dirs., Wis. Assn. Aging Unit Dirs. Lutheran. Avocations: reading, needlecraft. Office: Polk County Aging Programs 300 Polk County Plz Ste 20 Balsam Lake WI 54810-9096

**MATTSON, CLARENCE RUSSELL,** safety engineer; b. Norwood, Mass., Nov. 3, 1924; s. Clarence R. and Jane P. (Dawson) M.; m. Constance W. Towne, June 7, 1953; children: Jennifer Lynn, Sue Ann. AA in Transp., Northeastern U., 1953, BBA, 1956. Cert. safety profl.; registered profl. engr., Calif. Ins. industry safety engr., 1953-62; mgr. accident prevention Dravo Corp., Pitts., 1962-72; corp. mgr. safety and environ. affairs Perini Corp., Framingham, Mass., 1972-84; dir. safety and eng. The Marr Co., South Boston, Mass., 1984; mng. dir. Long Beach-L.A. rail project Transit Ins. Adminstrs.-L.A. County Transp. Commn., 1984-86; v.p. tech. svcs. Fred S. James & Co., Short Hills, N.J., 1987-89; pres. Athena Assocs. Ltd., Safety Mgmt. Cons., Sunset Beach, N.C., 1990—. Deacon Scituate (Mass.) Congl. Ch. Recipient Disting. Svc. award Nat. Safety Council, 1988. Mem. Am. Soc. Safety Engrs., Nat. Safety Coun. (hon. life, past gen. chmn. constrn. exec. com., disting. svc. award 1988), Assn. Gen. Contractors Am. (past chmn. safety and health com., safety engrs. adv. com.), Nat. Constructors Assn., Vets. of Safety, Mass. Safety Coun. (bd. dirs.), Mass. Constrm. Safety Congress (bd. dirs.), Elks. Republican. Home and Office: 655 Kings Ct Sunset Beach NC 28468-5326

**MATTSON, FRANCIS OSCAR,** retired librarian, rare book dealer, curator; b. Boston, Aug. 17, 1931; s. Frans Oscar and Catherine (Carr) M. BA, Boston U., 1957, MA, 1959; MS, Sch. Library Sci., Simmons Coll., 1967. Cert. librarian. Teaching fellow Boston U., 1958-60; instr. Tufts U., Medford, Mass., 1960-64, State Coll. at Salem, Mass., 1964-65; librarian Boston Pub. Library, 1965-68, N.Y. Pub. Library, N.Y.C., 1969-95, curator rare books, 1981-88, chief spl. collections cataloging unit, 1988-93, curator Berg Collection of English and Am. Lit., 1991-95. Mem. adv. com. Small Press Ctr., 1984-88; mem. adv. bd. Biblion, 1990-95. Book rev. editor Printing History, 1983-86, contbg. editor Am. Book Collector, 1984-88. Staff sgt. USAF, 1952-56. Fellow Morgan Libr.; mem. Bibliog. Soc. of U. Va. (life), Am. Printing History Assn. (program chmn. ann. confs. 1983, 84, bd. dirs. 1985-90), Manuscript Soc. (trustee 1977-80, 83-86), Grolier Club., Am. Internationale de Bibliophilie, Browning Inst. (bd. dirs. 1975-90), Soc. for Preservation New Eng. Antiquities (life), Grolier Club. Home: 426 Hudson St New York NY 10014-3934

**MATTSON, JAMES STEWART,** lawyer, environmental scientist, educator; b. Providence, July 22, 1945; s. Irving Carl and Virginia (Lutey) M.; m. Carol Sandry, Aug. 15, 1964 (div. 1979); children: James, Birgitta; m. Rana A. Fine, Jan. 5, 1983. BS in Chemistry, U. Mich., 1966, MS in Environ. Health Scis., 1969, PhD in Water Resources Scis., 1970; JD with honors, George Washington U., 1979. Bar: D.C. 1979, Fla. 1983, U.S. Dist. Ct. D.C. 1979, U.S. Dist. Ct. (so. dist.) Fla. 1984, U.S. Ct. Appeals (D.C. cir.) 1979, U.S. Ct. Claims 1985, U.S. Supreme Ct. 1985, U.S. Ct. Appeals (11th cir.) 1985, U.S. Ct. Appeals (5th cir.) 1987, U.S. Ct. Appeals (fed. cir.) 1990. Staff scientist Gulf Gen. Atomic Co., San Diego, 1970-71; dir R & D Ouachita Industries, Inc., Monroe, La., 1971-72; asst. prof. chem. oceanography Rosenstiel Sch. Marine & Atmospheric Sci., U. Miami, 1972-76; phys. scientist NOAA, Washington, 1976-78; mem. profl. staff & congl. liaison Nat. Adv. Commn. on Oceans and Atmosphere, 1978-80; ptnr. Mattson & Pave, Washington, Miami, Key Largo, 1980-86, Mattson & Tobin, Key Largo, 1987-2000; founder/CEO Great House of Wine, Inc, Ft. Lauderdale, Fla. and Napa, Calif., 1997—2003; sole practitioner Key Largo, Fla., 2000—. Adj. prof. law U. Miami, 1983-93; cons. Alaska Dept. Environ. Conservation, 1981-91, cons. oil and hazardous material spills, natural res. damage assessment. Author: (with H.B. Mark) Activated Carbon: Surface Chemistry and Adsorption from Solution, 1971; editor (with others): Computers in Chemistry and Instrumentation, 8 vols., 1972-76; (with P.L. Grose) The Argo Merchant Oil Spill: A Preliminary Scientific Report, 1977, (with H.B. Mark) Water Quality Mea-

surement: Modern Analytical Techniques, 1981; contbr. articles to profl. jours. Candidate dist. 120 Fla. Ho. of Reps., 1994. Fellow Fed. Water Pollution Control Adminstrn., 1967-68; recipient Spl. Achievement award U.S. Dept. Commerce, 1976-77; Regents Alumni scholar U. Mich., 1963. Mem. ABA, Am. Chem. Soc. (chmn. Symposium on Oil Spill Indentification 1971), Order of Coif. Avocations: photography, hiking, sailing, scuba diving, fishing. Address: PO Box 586 Key Largo FL 33037-0586 Office Phone: 305-451-3951. Personal E-mail: mattsonj@bellsouth.net. Business E-Mail: jmattson@mattsonlaw.com.

**MATTSON, JOY LOUISE,** oncological nurse; b. Moline, Ill., Feb. 1, 1956; d. Norman O. and Jeanette (Squier) M.; m. Duncan F. Crannell, Sept. 9, 1988. BA magna cum laude, Bates Coll., 1977; MTS, Harvard U., 1982; BSN magna cum laude, Rutgers U., Newark, 1988; MLS, Rutgers U., 1993. R.N. N.J. Staff nurse oncology Muhlenberg Reg. Med. Ctr., Plainfield, NJ, 1987-88; staff nurse St. Lawrence Rehab. Ctr., Lawrenceville, NJ, 1989; clin. rsch. asst. G.H. Besselaar Assocs., Princeton, NJ, 1990-91; med. writer Convatec, Skillman, NJ, 1991-92, G.H. Besselaar Assocs., Princeton, NJ, 1992-94; sr. clin. safety assoc. Pfizer Inc., N.Y.C., 1994-99, sr. project mgr., antibiotics, 1999-2000, mgr. regulatory submissions, 2000—. Mem. Phi Beta Kappa. Home: 12610 Varny Pl Fairfax VA 22033-4383

**MATTSON, MARLIN ROY ALBIN,** health facility administrator, psychiatry educator; b. Bellingham, Wash., Apr. 25, 1939; s. Conrad Roy and Ruth Viola (Thompson) M. BA, U. Wash., 1961, MD, 1965. Diplomate Am. Bd. Psychiatry and Neurology. Intern and resident in medicine Cornell U. program at Bellevue and Meml. Hosps., N.Y.C., 1965-67; resident in psychiatry Payne Whitney Clin. The N.Y. Hosp., N.Y.C., 1969 72, chief resident in psychiatry, 1972-73, asst. med. dir., 1973-89, assoc. med. dir., 1989-99; asst. med. dir. quality assurance Westchester Divsn. N.Y. Hosp., White Plains, 1979-89, assoc. med. dir. quality assurance, 1989-93, head quality assurance program dept. psychiatry N.Y.C., 1979-94; assoc. med. dir. for quality mgmt. Dept. Psychiatry N.Y. Presbyn. Hosp., Payne Whitney Clinic and Westchester divsn., 1999—2001, assoc. vice chmn. quality mgmt., 2002—03, assoc. vice chmn. compliance, 2003—. Asst. prof. psychiatry Cornell U. Med. Coll., N.Y.C., 1973-79, assoc. prof. clin. psychiatry, 1979-2005, prof. clin. psychiatry, 2005—; sec. gen. faculty coun., 1999-2001, vice chmn. gen. faculty coun., 2001-03, chmn. gen. faculty coun., 2003—05, sr. coun. gen. faculty coun., 2005—; bd. visitors Manhattan Psychiat. Ctr., 1991—; bd. dirs. N.Y. County Health Svcs. Rev. Corp., N.Y.C., 1983-95; mem. stds. com. URAC/Am. Accreditation Health Care Commn., 1996-2000, bd. dirs., 2000—, mem. exec. com., 2005—, sec., 2006—. Editor Manual of Psychiat. Quality Assurance, 1992; contbr. numerous articles to profl. jours. Capt. U.S. Army Med. Corp., 1967-69, Korea. Fellow Am. Psychiat. Assn. (disting.,life mem. nat. com. on quality assurance 1988-95, chmn. 1992-95, mem. com. champus peer rev. program 1984-86, sec. N.Y. County dist. br. 1987-91, pres.-elect 1991-92, pres. 1992-93, co-pres. 1995-96, assembly rep. 1996-2003, cons. or mem. nat. com. on stds. and survey procedures 1996—), N.Y. Acad. Medicine (com. pub. health 1984-92, sec. sect. on psychiatry 1993-94, chmn 1994-95); mem. N.Y. State Psychiat. Assn. (chmn. peer rev. com. 1982-95, mem. com. econ. affairs 1995—), N.Y. County Med. Soc. (bd. dirs. 2002—), Republican. Episcopalian. Avocations: piano, european travel, theater, swedish-american organizations. Office: NY Presbyterian Hosp Payne Whitney 525 E 68th St Box 140 New York NY 10021-4885 Office Phone: 212-746-3775. E-mail: mmattson@med.cornell.edu.

**MATTSON, ROBERT MARVIN, JR.,** lawyer; b. Phila., May 13, 1948; s. Robert Marvin and Rillie Lee (Wright) M.; m. Carlene Kay Anderson; children: Michael Tyler, Jeffrey David. AB, Stanford U., 1971; M in Mgmt., Northwestern U., 1975, JD, 1975. Bar: Calif. 1975. Assoc. Morrison & Foerster, San Francisco, 1975-81, ptnr., 1981—, co-chair corp. practice. Mem. State Bar Calif. (exec. com. Bus. Law Sect. 1994-98, vice-chmn. 1997-98). Avocations: reading, travel, sports. Office: Morrison & Foerster LLP 19900 Macarthur Blvd Irvine CA 92612-2445 Office Phone: 949-251-7138. Office Fax: 949-251-0900. Business E-Mail: rmattson@mofo.com.

**MATTSON, STEPHEN JOSEPH,** retired lawyer; b. Abilene, Tex., Oct. 11, 1943; s. Joseph Martin and Dorothy Irene (Doyle) M.; m. Carole Kay Louise Mitchell, Mar. 13, 1965; children: Eric, Laura. BA (hon.), U. Ill., 1965, JD (hon.), 1970. Bar: Ill., 1970, U.S. Dist. Ct. (no. dist.) Ill. 1970. Assoc. Mayer, Brown, Rowe & Maw, Chgo., 1970—77, ptnr., 1978—2003, ret., 2003. Mem. ABA, Order of Coif.

**MATTSSON, AKE,** psychiatrist, physician; b. Stockholm, May 30, 1929; came to U.S., 1956, naturalized, 1964; s. Erik H. and Thyra (Bergtsson) M.; m. Margareta Fürst, Jan. 5, 1953; children: Erik, Peter, Nicholas; m. Judith Whitley Powell, Nov. 25, 2000. MB, Karolinska Inst., Stockholm, 1950, MD, 1955. Intern Vanderbilt U. Med. Sch., Nashville, 1955-56; resident in pediat. and child psychiatry Karolinska Hosp., Stockholm, 1958-60; fellow in child devel. Case Western Res. U. Med. Sch., 1957-58, resident in psychiatry and child psychiatry, 1960-64, asst. prof. psychiatry, 1964-70; prof. psychiatry and pediat. U. Va. Med. Sch., 1970-77, U. Pitts Med. Sch., 1977-78; prof. psychiatry and pediat., dir. divsn. child and adolescent psychiatry NYU Med. Sch., 1978-85, rsch. prof. psychiatry, 1985—; prof. psychiatry U. Va. Med. Sch., 1985-91; prof. psychiatry and pediat., dir. divsn. child and adolescent psychiatry Med. Sch., East Carolina U., Greenville, NC, 1991-97; med. dir. divsn. mental health V.I. Dept. Health, St. Thomas, 1997—2000; med. dir. Universal Health Care Mgmt. Svcs., Washington, 2004—, New Dimension, Inc., Washington, 2005—. Clin. prof. psychiatry Med. Sch. George Washington U., 2004—. Contbr. numerous articles to med. jours. Served with Swedish Navy, 1948-59. Fulbright-Hays grantee, 1975. Mem. Am. Psychiat. Assn., Am. Psychoanalytical Assn., N.Y. Psychiat. Soc., Am. Acad. Child Adolescent Psychiatry, N.Y. Acad. Scis., Soc. Biol. Psychiatry, Am. Acad. Psychiatry and the Law. Office: 700 New Hampshire Ave NW Apt 1409 Washington DC 20037 Office Phone: 202-333-1284.

**MATUANO, TONY,** chef Spiaggia, 1984. Author: (books) The Spiaggia Cookbook: Eleganza Italiana Cucina. Named one of Best New Chefs, Food & Wine, 1984; recipient Best Chef: Midwest award, The James Beard Found., 2005. Office: c/o Levy Restaurants 980 N Michigan Ave Chicago IL 60611 Office Phone: 312-664-8200.*

**MATUS, WAYNE CHARLES,** lawyer; b. NYC, Mar. 10, 1950; s. Eli and Alma (Platt) M.; children: Marshall Scott, Scott Adam. BA, Johns Hopkins U., 1972; JD, NYU, 1975. Law clk. Superior Ct. D.C., 1975-76; assoc. Marshall, Bratter, Greene, Allison and Tucker, N.Y.C., 1976-79, Christy & Viener, N.Y.C., 1979-83, ptnr., 1984—98, Salans Hertzfeld Heilbronn Christy & Viener, NYC, 1999—2001, Leboeuf Lamb Greene & MacRae, NYC, 2001—04, Mayer, Brown, Rowe & Maw LLP, NYC, 2004—. Faculty ABA-Am. Law Inst., 1988; neutral mediator comml. divsn. 1st jud. dist. Supreme Ct. State of NY Unified Ct. Sys., 1997—. Assoc. editor Nanotechnology Law and Bus. Jour., mem. editl. bd. ABA Model Jury Instructions for Trademarks, Trade Dress and Copyright; contbg. editor Commercial Corporate Strategies for Drafting and Negotiating. Mem. Assn. Bar City of NY (com. on computer law 1985-88, chmn. com. on state cts., subcom. on motion practice 1982-84, com. product liability 1994-97, com. on privacy 2003—), NY State Bar Assn. (com. on comms. and actions and complex civil litigation comml. fed. litigation sect. 1990-99, com. on Internet and litigation 2000—2002, lectr.), N.Y. Litigators Club (steering com. 1985—), Johns Hopkins U. Alumni Assn. (bd. dirs. met. NY chpt., v.p. 1988—2002, nat. alumni council 1996-2002, pres. 2002—, mem. The Sedona Conf. 2003-). Office: Mayer Brown Rowe & Maw 1675 Broadway New York NY 10019 Office Phone: 212-506-2122.

**MATUSCHAK, MARK G.,** lawyer; b. 1959; AB cum laude, Dartmouth Coll., 1981; JD, Columbia Univ., 1985. Bar: Mass., US Dist. Ct. (Mass. dist.), US Ct. Appeals (1st, 2d, 3d & Fed. cir.). Law clk. Judge Neil L. Lynch, Supreme Judicial Ct. Mass., 1984—85; assoc. to sr. ptnr. Wilmer Cutler Pickering Hale & Dorr, Boston, 1985—, vice chmn. Litigation dept. & mem.

Intellectual Property Litigation group. Mem.: Dartmouth Lawyers Assn., Boston Coll. Law Sch. Intellectual Property Am. Inn of Ct., Boston Bar Assn., Am. Intellectual Property Law Assn. Office: Wilmer Cutler Pickering Hale & Dorr 60 State St Boston MA 02109 Office Fax: 617-526-6559, 617-526-5000. Business E-Mail: mark.matuschak@wilmerhale.com.

**MATUS-MENDOZA, MARIADELALUZ,** language educator, sociologist; b. Mexico City, Apr. 10, 1961; arrived in U.S., 1991; d. MariadelaPaz Matus-Mendoza; m. Geoffrey Fitch, Sept. 3, 1993. BA in English Lit. and Applied Lang., Mex. Autonoman U., Mexico City, 1984; MA, Temple U., 1993, PhD, 1999. TA: Mex. Autonomon U., 1984—91; tchg. asst. Temple U., Phila., 1991—94, adj. instr., 1994—95, LuSulle U., Phila., 1995—98, U. Pa., Phila., 1996—99; asst. prof. Spanish U. Ctrl. Fla., Orlando, 1999—2001, Drexel U., Phila., 2001—. Cons. ETS, Princeton, NJ, 2001—. Mem.: MLA, Am. Assn. Tchrs. of Spanish and Portugese, Nat. Assn. Hispanic and Latino Studies. Roman Catholic. Office: Drexel Univ 229 N 33rd St Philadelphia PA 19104

**MATUSOW, STEVEN S.,** mathematics professor; b. L.A., Oct. 16, 1947; s. Alan Bernard and Judith Matusow; m. Lois Anne Levy, July 11, 1971; children: Rachel Beth, David Phillip. BA, U. Calif., Berkeley, 1970; MS, Santa Clara U., 1985. Cert. secondary edn. tchr. CTC/Calif., 1971. Tchr. math., physics, ind. study Campbell Union H.S. Dist., San Jose, Calif., 1971—93; prof. math. Evergreen Valley Coll., San Jose, Calif., 1995—. Pres. Campbell Edn. Assn./CTA/NEA, San Jose, Calif., 1988—91; senator EVC Acad. Senate, San Jose, Calif., 1999—2003. Bd. dirs. Temple Emanu-El, San Jose, Calif., 1996—98, Jewish Fedn., Los Gatos, Calif., 2002—03. Named Tchr. of Yr., Evergreen Valley Coll., 1998; recipient Regents' scholarship, U. Calif., Berkeley, 1965-1970; Innvation grant, Industry Initiatives for Sci. and Math Edn., 1998, Fund for Student Success grant, Chancellor's Office, Calif. C.C., 2000, grant, EVC Tchg. and Learning Ctr., 2005. Mem.: Nat. Coun. of Tchrs. of Math., Calif. Math. Coun. Democrat. Jewish. Achievements include development of alternative contractual education program. Avocations: white-water rafting, swimming/snorkeling, travel, cooking, yoga. Office: Evergreen Valley Coll 3095 Yerba Buena Rd San Jose CA 95135 Office Phone: 408-274-7900 6556. Business E-Mail: steve.matusow@evc.edu.

**MATUSZEK, JOHN MICHAEL, JR.,** environmental scientist, educator, consultant; b. Worcester, Mass., Apr. 16, 1935; s. John Michael and Felicia Martha (Shandruk) M.; m. Roberta Eva Cosman, Nov. 30, 1957; children: Debra-Jane Y., John Michael III, Kevin P., Jennifer R. BS in Chemistry with distinction, Worcester Poly. Inst., 1957; PhD in Nuclear Chemistry, Clark U., 1962. Dept. mgr. Teledyne Isotopes, Westwood, NJ, 1964-71; rsch. scientist in nuclear chemistry, radioactive waste mgmt., radiological health, environ. radioactivity and radiation N.Y. State Health Dept., Albany, 1971-2000; cons., owner JMM Cons. Svcs., Delmar, NY, 1992—. Adj. prof. Rensselaer Poly. Inst., Troy, N.Y., 1977-2003; prof. SUNY, Albany, 1996-99. Lt. comdr. USPHS, 1962-64. Mem.: Internat. Commn. Radionuclide Metrology. Avocations: skiing, music. Home and Office: JMM Cons Svcs 10 Fieldstone Dr Delmar NY 12054 E-mail: jmatuszek@verizon.net.

**MATUSZKO, ANTHONY JOSEPH,** research chemist, administrator; b. Hadley, Mass., Jan. 31, 1926; s. Joseph Anthony and Katherine (Narog) M.; m. Anita Colley, Oct. 26, 1956; children— Martha, Mary, Stephen, Richard. BA, Amherst Coll., 1946; MS in Chemistry, U. Mass., 1951; PhD in Chemistry, McGill U., 1953. Demonstrator in chemistry McGill U., Montreal, Que., Can., 1950-52; from instr. to assoc. prof. chemistry Lafayette Coll., Easton, Pa., 1952-58; head fundamental process div. Naval Propellant Lab., Indian Head, Md., 1958-62; program mgr. in chemistry Air Force Office Sci. Research, Washington, 1962-89; rsch. steering com. Dept. Def. Biotech., 1986-89; cons., Annandale, Va., 1989—. Contbr. articles to tech. jours. Patentee in field. Pres. Forest Heights PTA, Md., 1967. Served with U.S. Army, 1946-48. Named Hon. Fellow in Chemistry, U. Wis.-Madison, 1967-68, recipient Superior Performance award USAF, Outstanding Career Svc. award U.S. Govt. Fellow AAAS, Am. Inst. Chemists (life); mem. Am. Chem. Soc., Cosmos Club, Sigma Xi. Home: 4210 Elizabeth Ln Annandale VA 22003-3654

**MATYJASZEWSKI, KRZYSZTOF,** chemist, educator; b. Konstantynow, Poland, Apr. 8, 1950; arrived in U.S., 1985; s. Henryk and Antonina (Styss) M.; m. Malgorzata Kowalska, July 15, 1972; children: Antoni, Maria. BS, MS, Tech. U., Moscow, 1972; PhD, Polish Acad. Scis., Lodz, 1976; DSc, Lodz Poly., 1985; degree (hon.), U. Ghent, Belgium, 2002. Postdoctoral fellow U. Fla., 1977-78; rsch. assoc. Polish Acad. Scis., 1978-84, CNRS, France, 1984-85; asst. prof. chemistry Carnegie Mellon U., Pitts., 1985-89, assoc. prof., 1989-93, prof., 1993—, head dept. chemistry, 1994-98, J.C. Warner prof., 1998—, univ. prof., 2004—. Invited prof. U. Paris, 1985; vis. prof. U. Freiburg, 1988, U. Paris, 1990, 97, 98, 06, U. Bayreuth, 1991, U. Strasbourg, 1992, U. Bordeaux, 1996, U. Ulm, 1999, U. Pisa, 2000; adj. prof., U. Pitts., 2000-. Polish Acad. Sci., 2000-; cons. Dow Corning, Midland, Mich., 1988-89, Arco, Phila., 1990-92, GE, Schenectady, 1992-2000, Amoco, Naperville, Ill., 1994-97, Reilly Ind., Indpls., 1994—, Air Products, Allentown, Pa., 1994-97. Author 8 books; mem. editorial bd. Macromolecules, Macromolecular Synthesis, Jour. Polymer Sci., Jour. Macromolecular Sci.-Pure and Applied Chemistry, Jour. Inorganic and Organometallic Polymers, Polymer, others; editor Progress Polymer Sci., Ctrl. European Jour. Chemistry; contbr. chpts. to books, more than 600 articles to profl. jours.; 27 U.S. and 75 internat. patents in field. Recipient award Polish Chem. Soc., 1980, Polish Acad. Sci., 1981, Presdl. Young Investigator award NSF, 1989, Humboldt award for Sr. US scientists, 1999, Pitts. award, 2001, Polish Sci. Found. prize, 2004, UK Macro Group medal, 2005. Fellow: Internat. Union Pure and Applied Chemistry (corr. mem. polymer nomenclature), Polymer Materials Sci. Engring., Am. Chem. Soc. (Carl S. Marvel award 1995, Polymer Chemistry award 2002, Coop. Rsch. award 2004); mem.: NAE, Russian Acad. Scis.. Polish Acad. Scis. (fgn. mem. 2005), French Acad. Sci. (Elf chair 1998). Achievements include research in synthesis of well defined macromolecules via living and controlled polymerizations; organometallic polymers. Home: 9 Queens Ct Pittsburgh PA 15238-1519 Office: Carnegie Mellon U 4400 5th Ave Pittsburgh PA 15213-2617 Business E-Mail: matyjaszewski@yahoo.com.

**MATZ, DEBORAH,** former federal agency administration; m. Marshall Matz; children: Hayley, Peter. BS, Cornell U.; MA in Legis. Affairs, George Washington U. Cmty. devel. rep. U.S. Dept. Housing and Urban Devel., 1971—73; legis. asst. Congressman Peter Peyser; dir. Office Tech. Assessment, U.S. Congress; economist Joint Econ. Com.; chief of staff adminstrs. Farm Svc. Agy and Farmers Home USDA, dep. asst. sec. adminstrn., 1997—2001; exec. officer Liaison Office N.Am. Food and Agrl. Orgn., UN, 2001—02; mem. Nat. Credit Union Adminstrn., Alexandria, 2002—05.

**MATZ, JAMES RICHARD,** municipal official; BA with honors, U. Tex., 1961; postgrad., Mexico city U., 1961-62. Mktg. exec. Fluor Corp.; mem. diplomatic corps Dept. of State; commr. City of Harlingen, Tex., Cameron County. Mem. Pres.'s Exec. Interchange Program, Bank of Am.; mayor Palm Valley, Tex. Contbr. articles to profl. jours. Founder Harlingen Proud; founder, chmn. Valley Proud Environ. Coun., 1990; mem. citizen's exec. adv. coun. Rio Grande State Mental Health and Retardation Ctr.; bd. dirs. Harlingen, South Padre Island, San Benito Emergency Med. Svcs.; chmn. Tex. Reg. Cmty. Devel. Grant Rev. Com.; mem. Met. Planning Orgn., Cameron County; mem. exploration com. World Birding Ctr.; bd. dirs. Tex. Urban Forestry Coun.; mem. Tex. Energy Coord. Coun., Govt. Adv. Com. to U.S. Rep. to N.Am. Commn. for Environ. Coop.; past vice chmn. legis. policy com. on utility regulation and environment Tex. Mcpl. League; past chmn. City of Harlingen Utility Rate Rev. Bd., pub. works com. Harlingen Capital Improvement Adv. Bd.; past. bd. dirs. Rio Grande basin Sustainable Devel. Initiative, Border Trade Alliance, Area Health Edn. Ctr. Svcs., Keep Tex. Beautiful; former commr. Cameron County; past exec. com. Rio Grande Valley Emergency Mgmt. Coord. Coun., numerous others. Recipient Kind Found. Dist. Svc. award, 1990, Svc. Above Self award Harlingen Rotary, 1991, Tex. Urban Forestry Individual Accomplishment award, 1992, Harlin-

gen Proud, Chairman's award, 1992, Outstanding Dist. Gov., Keep Tex. Beautiful, 1995, Leadership award, 1995, Pres.'s Nat. Svc. award, 1995, Outstanding tex. Urban Forester award, 1996, State of Tex. Senate Resolution #989, 1995, Joint Resolution of Appreciation, San Benito City Commn. and San Benito Area C. of C., 1997, Tex. Environ. Excellence award Tex. Commn. Environ. Quality, 2004, Gulf Guardian award, 2004, Tex. Gov.'s Lonestar Cmty. Svc. award, 2005, Lone Star Land Steward award Tex. Parks and Wildlife Dept., 2006, Frederick Law Olmsted award Nat. Arbor Day Found., 2006. Mem. Harlingen Area C. of C. (past dir.), Assn. for Local Control of Utility Rates (past officer, dir.). Office: 900 Palm Valley Dr W Harlingen TX 78552

**MATZ, JENNI,** archivist, filmmaker; b. Queens, N.Y., Oct. 21, 1973; d. Manny and Bea Elizabeth Matz. MA Libr. Info. Sci., Simmons Coll., Boston, 2006. Asst. dir., editor Oreg. Pub. Broadcasting, Portland, 2001—03; mgr. and archivist Am. Comedy Archives, Boston, 2005—. Author and editor: Reminiscences and Remembrances of Herman and Aveve Cohen and the Chiswick Bookshop (1935-2001); prodr. and editor: (documentaries) Abe Lerner: A Life in Books; Reminiscences and Remembrances: The Boston Harbor Cleanup. Recipient Estelle Jussim award, Simmons Coll., 2006. Mem.: Assn. Moving Image Archivists. Office: Am Comedy Archives 120 Boylston St Boston MA 02116 Business E-Mail: jennifer_matz@emerson.edu.

**MATZ, SEAN CORMICK,** electrical engineer; b. Fullerton, Calif., July 31, 1959; s. Joseph Albert and Audrey Margaret Matz. BS in Math., U. Calif., Irvine, 1981, MS in Math., 1983, PhD in Elec. Engring., 2000; MSEE, Calif. Poly. U., Pomona, 1985. Mem. of the tech. staff Hughes Aircraft Co., Fullerton, Calif., 1986—88; staff engr. Walter Dorwin Teague Assoc., Pomona, Calif., 1989—92; engr./scientist The Boeing Co., Seal Beach, Calif., 2000—. Fellow Calif. Microelectronics and Computer Sci. fellow, U. of Calif., Irvine, 1993—94, Regents' fellow, 1996. Mem.: Math. Assn. of Am., IEEE. Independent-Republican. Roman Catholic. Avocations: reading, music, mathematics, computers. Home: 313 South Poinsettia Ave Brea CA 92821 Office: The Boeing Company 2800 Westminster Blvd Seal Beach CA 90740 Office Phone: 562-797-2839. Personal E-mail: smatz@cyberhotline.com. Business E-Mail: sean.c.matz@boeing.com.

**MATZDORFF, JAMES ARTHUR,** investment banker, internet marketing professional; b. Kansas City, Missouri, Jan. 3, 1956; BS, U. So. Calif., 1978, MBA, Loyola U., L.A., 1980. Comml. loan officer Bank Am. L.A., 1976—78; mng. dir. James A. Matzdorff and Co., Beverly Hills, Calif., 1978—. Mem. Rep. Nat. Com., 1980-. Mem. Am. Fin. Assn., Phi Delta Theta. Avocations: tennis, sailing, Karate, skiing. Home and Office: Ste 173 30872 So Coast Hwy Laguna Beach CA 92651 Office Phone: 800-348-4212. Business E-Mail: James@Projectsfinance.com.

**MATZIORINIS, KENNETH N.,** economist; b. N.Y.C., May 4, 1954; s. Neocles N. and Popi (Gregoratos) Matziorinis; m. Catherine Marina Astrakianakis, July 27, 1985; children: Anna Maria, Angela Ellen Fylitsa. BA, McGill U., 1976, MA, 1979, PhD, 1988. Cert. mgmt. cons. Asst. economist Nat. Bank Greece (Can.), Montreal, 1978-81; lectr. econs. McGill U., Montreal, 1977—; prof. econs. John Abbott Coll., Montreal, 1981—. Pres. Canbek Econ. Cons., Inc., Montreal, 1983—; econs. adviser to bd. dirs. Internat. Orgn. Psychophysiology, 1982-89; bd. dirs. Nat. Bank of Greece, Can.; dir. Hellas Capital, Inc. (Canada), 2001—. Author: Introduction to Macro Economics: An Applied Approach, 1988, 4th edit., 2005, Business Economics: Theory and Practice, 3d edit., 2005; editor: Vital Graphs of Canadian Economy, 1984; contbr. articles to profl. jours. V.p. Westmount Liberal Riding Assn., Montreal, 1975-77; bd. govs. McGill U., 1978-81, John Abbott Coll., 1988-91; chmn. bd. dirs. Cmty. Svc. Ctr. St. Louis, Montreal, 1978-80; bd. trustees Trafalgar Sch. for Girls, 2002—. Recipient Distinguished Tchg. award McGill U., 1993, 2006. Mem. Am. Econ. Assn., Am. Hellenic Ednl. and Progressive Assn., Can. Assn. Bus. Economists, Can. Econ. Assn., Que. Inst. Cert. Mgmt. Cons., Nat. Assn. Bus. Economists Greek Orthodox. Home: Laval 615 67th Ave Montreal PQ Canada H7V 3N9 Business E-Mail: canbekeconomics@videotron.ca.

**MATZKE, JAY,** internist; b. Sidney, Nebr., Oct. 2, 1956; m. Ann Matzke, Feb. 13, 1982; children: Alex, Jered, Sloan. B Medicine, U. Nebr. Med. Ctr., 1979, MD, 1983. Diplomate Am. Acad. Family Physicians. Resident in family practice U. Nebr. Med. Ctr., Nebr., 1984—86; ptnr. Martin Med. Clinic/Sidney Meml. Hosp., 1987—90; med. dir. Sidney Meml. Hosp. Addiction Ctr., 1987—89; staff physician Omaha Family Practice, 1990—96; ptnr. Immanuel Clinic/Immanuel Med. Ctr., 1990—96; med. dir. Immanuel/Alegent Health Sports Medicine, 1995—96; staff physician Meml. Health Care Sys., Seward, Nebr., 1997—, chief med. staff, 1999; med. dir. S.W. Rural Fire Dept., Nebr., 1998—; med. advisor Lancaster County Red Cross, Nebr., 1999—. Chmn. emergency cardiac care com. for Nebr. Am. Heart Assn., 1995—, instr. ACLS, 1984—; instr. ATLS ACS, 1986—. Dist. chmn. Boy Scouts Am., 2000—, pack com. chmn., 1997—98; trustee Nebr. Children's Home Soc., Nebr., 1999—; bd. dirs. Emergency Med. Svcs., 1998—; mem. pres.' adv. com. U. Nebr., 1997—2000; den leader Boy Scouts Am., 1985—87; chmn. ACLS Task Force, Nebr., 1992—95; pres., v.p., treas. Millard Sch. Bd., 1993—97; mem. Sidney City Coun., 1988—90; pres., charter mem. Cheyenne County Cmty. Ctr. Found., Inc., 1988—90; mem. bd. mission outreach, trustee Faith Luth. Ch., 1997—. Named Outstanding Young Nebraskan, Nebr. Jaycees, 1989, Outstanding Chamber Mem., Cheyenne County C. of C., 1988; recipient award of achievement, Nebr. Assn. Sch. Bds., 1995, 1996. Mem.: Am. Med. Soc. Sports Medicine.

**MAU, BOB,** statistician; b. Sheboygan, Wis., Sept. 1, 1950; s. Robert W. Mau and Lydia Welsch; m. Lynn Ellen Deschler, Sept. 29, 1979. BA, Lawrence U., Appleton, Wis., 1973; PhD, U. Wis., 1996. Mgr. rsch. program Wis. Survey Rsch. Lab., Madison, 1980—90; sr. scientist U. Wis., Madison, 1996—. Contbr. articles to profl. jours. Postdoctoral fellow Computational Molecular Biology, Sloan Found. / DOE, 1999—2001. Fellow: Royal Statis. Soc.; mem.: Soc. Molecular Biogol. Evolution, Inst. Math. Stats., Am. Statis. Soc. Achievements include research in the identification of genomic rearrangements using Markov chain Monte Carlo; Bayesian phylogenetic inference using Markov chain Monte Carlo; genome-wide detection of allelic substitution. Home: 207 E Racine Jefferson WI 53549 Office: Univ Wis - Madison 425 Henry Mall Madison WI 53706 Office Phone: 608-890-0172. Business E-Mail: bobmau@biochem.wisc.edu.

**MAU, C. S. See SALERNO, CHERIE**

**MAUCH, DIANE FARRELL,** music educator; b. Flushing, NY, Jan. 15, 1934; d. Edward Joseph Farrell and Adelaide Mary Hopkins; m. Robert Kurt Mauch, Aug. 24, 1963; children: Anneliese Farrell, Bronwen Adele. MusB, Manhattanville Coll., 1955; MusM, U. Mich., 1957; postgrad., Juilliard Sch. Music, Manhattan Sch. Music, Aspen Music Sch. Cert. tchr. Fla. Bd. Edn., ministry formation cert. Nat. Assn. Pastoral Musicians. Asst. prof. music Trevecca Coll., Nashville, 1973—77; music tchr. St. Bernard Acad., Nashville, 1976—82; music specialist Carrollton Sch., Coconut Grove, Fla., 1983—99; assoc. faculty vocal performance U. Miami, Coral Gables, Fla., 1994—. Music rep. Sch. Arts Planning, Ann Arbor, Mich., 1969—72; dir. Liturgy Com., Nashville, 1975—83; adj. prof. music Scarritt Coll., Nashville, 1976—80, Miami-Dade C.C., 1983—90; dir. edn. Fla. Grand Opera, Miami, 1990—93; del. Children Cultural Coalition, Miami, 1990—93; music rep. Visual and Performing Arts Steering Com., Miami, 1991—94; opera cons. Opera Am., Washington, 1992—94; choir dir. St. Mary's, Manchester, Mich., 1966—69, St. Lawrence Ch., North Miami Beach, Fla., 1984—86; soloist St. Henry, Nashville, 1975—82, Ch. by the Sea, Bal Harbour, Mich. 1991—2001. Contbr. chapters to books; performer (radio, concert, opera, oratorios). Chairperson Cmty. Concerts, Nashville, 1976—78; active Dade County Cultural Coalition, Miami, 1998—. Recipient Leadership award, Nat. Assn. Pastoral Musicians, Washington, 1980; grantee, NEA, 1977, NEH, 1991; scholar, Cambridge U., 2004. Mem.: Miami Music Tchrs. Assn., Music

Tchrs. Nat. Assn. (permanent nat. profl. cert., honors chair, v.p., scholarship chair), Nat. Assn. Tchrs. Singing (past officer, v.p., pres., auditions chair). Roman Catholic. Avocations: travel, linguistics and languages, choral singing. Home: 10645-C SW 113 Pl Miami FL 33176 Office: U Miami Foster Bldg San Amaro Dr Miami FL 33124

**MAUCH, ROBERT CARL,** energy and financial services executive; b. Cleve., Dec. 7, 1939; AMP, Harvard U., 1983; MS, U. Calif., Berkeley, 1965; BSChemE, Cleve. State U., 1962. V.p., gen. mgr., LP gas divsn. Amerigas Inc., Valley Forge, Pa., 1978-83; v.p. UGI Corp., Valley Forge, 1978-87, sr. v.p., 1987-90; dir. Ansutech, Inc., Valley Forge, 1981-82, Matheson Gas Products, Inc., Valley Forge, 1981-82; pres., dir. AP Propane Inc., Valley Forge, 1983-90, Amerigas Propane, Valley Forge, 1983-96; pres., CEO, dir. AmeriGas Inc., Valley Forge, 1991-96, Petrolane, Inc., Valley Forge, 1993-96, Amerigas, Inc. subs. UGI Corp., Valley Forge, 1990-96, AmeriGas Propane Inc. (gen. ptnr. AmeriGas Ptnrs. L.P.); chmn., CEO Anthem Holdings Corp., Valley Forge, 1997-98, AllianceOne Inc., Exton, 2000—2006. Bd. govs. Pa. Economy League, Phila., 1985-91; mem. World Affairs Coun., Phila., 1980-95. Mem.: Am. Collectors Assn., Propane Vehicle Coun. (chmn. 1994—), Waynesborough C. of C., Nat. Propane Gas Assn. (pres. 1978—, bd. dirs., exec. com.), Healthcare Fin. Mgmt. Assn. Lutheran. Avocations: tennis, reading, yoga, opera, weight training.

**MAUDERLY, JOE LLOYD,** pulmonary toxicologist; b. Strong City, Kans., Aug. 31, 1943; s. Joseph Park and Violet May (Cox) M.; m. Cheryl Gaines, Jan. 31, 1965; children: Laurie Jean, Jameson Lynn. BS, Kans. State U., 1965, DVM, 1967. Respiratory physiologist Inhalation Toxicology Rsch. Inst., Albuquerque, 1967-89, supr. pathophysiology group, 1976-89, dir., 1989-96; rsch. prof. medicine U. N.Mex., Albuquerque, 1988—; clin. prof. pharmacy, 1990—; sr. scientist, dir. external affairs Lovelace Respiratory Rsch. Inst., Albuquerque, 1997-99; v.p., dir. Nat. Environ. Respiratory Ctr., 1999—. Cons. in field; mem. EPA Clean Air Scientific Adv. Com., 1992-96, chair, 1997-2000. Assoc. editor Fundamental Applied Toxicology, 1989-94, editl. bd. exptl. lung rsch., 1983-2003; mem. editl. bd. Inhalation Toxicology, 2004—; contbr. articles to profl. jours., chpts. to books. Served to capt. USAF, 1967-69. Mem. Am. Thoracic Soc. (chmn. assembly of environ. and occupational health 1991-93, long-range planning com. 1991-94, sci. adv. com. 1993-96), Am. Physiol. Soc., Am. Vet. Med. Assn., N.Mex. Vet. Med. Assn., Soc. Toxicology (pres. inhalation specialty sect. 1994-95, career achievement award 1999). Republican. Home: 4517 Banff Dr NE Albuquerque NM 87111-2829 Office Phone: 505-348-9432. Business E-Mail: jmauderl@lrri.org.

**MAUDLIN, ROBERT V.,** economics and government affairs consultant; b. Wash., June 8, 1927; s. Cecil V. and Eva Jane (Wright) M.; m. Carole M. Jackson, Sept. 3, 1949; children: Lynda C., David V., Tim W.E. Student, MIT, 1945; BS, Am. U., 1951. Ptnr. C.V. & R.V. Maudlin, Washington, 1952-72, owner, 1972—. Mng. dir. Bur. Applied Econs., Washington, 1960—; sec. Nat. Assn. Scissors and Shears Mfrs., 1970-97; exec. dir. Joint Govt. Liaison Com., 1973-81; mem. Industry Sector Adv. Com. U.S. Dept. Commerce and U.S. Trade Rep., Washington, 1975-97; commr. Adv. Neighborhood Comm. of D.C., 1999—. Author econ. and statis. reports. Pres. Forest Hills Citizens Assn., Washington, 1964; chmn. Boy Scouts Am., Washington, 1972. 1st lt. C.E., AUS, 1945-47, USAR, 1947-55. Republican. E-mail: maudlin@alum.mit.edu.

**MAUDSLEY, RONALD R.,** finance company executive; With Transamerica Title, Sacramento, 1975—88, Fidelity Nat. Title Ins. Co., 1988—2002; exec. v.p. Fidelity Nat. Fin., Santa Barbara, Calif., 2002—, co-COO, 2002—. Office: Fidelity National Financial 4050 Calle Real Santa Barbara CA 93110

**MAUER, ALVIN MARX,** pediatrician, educator; b. LeMars, Iowa, Jan. 10, 1928; s. Alvin Milton and Bertha Elizabeth (Marx) M.; m. Theresa Ann McGivern, Dec. 2, 1950; children: Stephen James, Timothy John, Daria Maureen, Elizabeth Claire. BA, State U. Iowa, 1950, MD, 1953. Intern Cin. Gen. Hosp., 1953-54; resident in pediatrics Children's Hosp. Cin., 1954-56; fellow in hematology dept. medicine U. Utah, Salt Lake City, 1956-59; dir. div. hematology Children's Hosp.Cin., prof. dept. hematology, 1959-73; prof. dept. pediatrics U. Cin. Coll. Medicine, 1959-73; prof. pediatrics U. Tenn. Coll. Medicine, Memphis, 1973-97, prof. medicine, 1983-97, prof. emeritus, 1997—; dir. cancer program U. Tenn. Coll. Health Scis.; dir. St. Jude Children's Research Hosp., Memphis, 1973-83. Mem. hematology study sect. NIH; mem. clin. cancer investigation rev. com. Nat. Cancer Inst.; mem. com. on maternal and infant nutrition NRC. Author: Pediatric Hematology, 1969; editor: The Biology of Human Leukemia, 1990. Served with U.S. Army, 1946. Mem. Am. Soc. Hematology (pres. 1980-81), Assn. Am. Cancer Insts. (pres. 1980), am. Acad. Pediatrics (com. on nutrition), Am. Assn. Cancer Edn., Am. Soc. Clin. Investigation, Am. Fedn. Clin. Rsch., Assn. Am. Physicians, Am. Pediatric Soc., Cen. Soc. Clin. Investigation, Cen. Soc. Clin. Rsch., Internat. Soc. Hematology (pres. 1988-90, chmn. 1992-96, bd. councilors 1992-96), Am. Cancer Soc. (pres. Tenn. divsn. 1992-93), Midwest Soc. Pediat. Rsch., N.Y. Acad. Scis., Soc. Pediat. Rsch., Am. Assn. Cancer Rsch., Phi Beta Kappa, Sigma Xi, Alpha Omega Alpha. Democrat. Roman Catholic. Office: U Tenn Ctr for Health Scis Rm 808 910 Madison Ave Memphis TN 38103 Business E-Mail: amauer@utmem.edu.

**MAUER, J,** professional baseball player; b. St. Paul, Minn., Apr. 19, 1983; Catcher Minn. Twins, 2004—. Named to Am. League All-Star Team, MLB All-Star Game, 2006. Office: Minn Twins 34 Kirby Puckett Pl Minneapolis MN 55415*

**MAUER, LISA,** education educator; PhD, U. Minn., 1995—99. Asst. prof. Purdue U., West Lafayette, Ind., 2001—06, assoc. prof., 2006—. Cons. in field. Mem.: Inst. Food Technologists, Phi Beta Kappa. Office: Purdue Univ 745 Agriculture Mall Dr West Lafayette IN 47907 Office Phone: 765-494-9111. Business E-Mail: mauer@purdue.edu.

**MAUGANS, JOHN CONRAD,** lawyer; b. Miami County, Ind., May 10, 1938; s. Willis William and Evelyn Jeannette (Mills) M.; m. Judith M. Gallagher, Jan. 24, 1960 (dec. June 1984); children: Lisa Denise, Stacy Erin, Kristen Cherie; m. Jo Ella Middlekauff, June 7, 1985. AB, Manchester Coll. 1960; LLB with distinction, Ind. U., 1962, JD, 1969. Bar: Ind. 1962. Assoc. Barnes, Hickam, Pantzer & Boyd, Indpls., 1962-63; atty. pvt. practice, Kokomo, Ind., 1966—; ptnr. Bayliff, Harrigan, Cord & Maugans, Kokomo, Ind., 1969—. Guest lectr. Coll. Bus. Manchester Coll., 1966-80 Contbr. articles to profl. jours. Chmn. Howard fund dr. Manchester Coll., 1971; bd. dirs. Tribal Trials coun. Girl Scouts U.S.A., 1977-85, Vols. in Cmty. Svc., 1978-84, Home Health Care of Ctrl. Ind., Inc., 1983-89, Woodhaven Homeowners Assn., d002—; trustee Western Sch. Corp., 1986—, pres., 1991-93, 2003-2005; bd. dirs. Kokomo Park Band, Inc., 1989—; chmn. Christian Edn. com., Main St. Christian Ch., 1993—; mem. asset devel. and mktg. com. Cmty. Found. Howard County, Inc., 2000-05, mem. profl. adv. com., 2006—. Capt. AUS, 1963-66. Fellow Am. Trial Lawyers Assn. (Roscoe Pound chpt.), Ind. Bar Found.; mem. Ind. Bar Assn., Howard County Bar Assn. (pres. 1989), Ind. Trial Lawyers Assn., Manchester Coll. Alumni Assn. (chmn. area chpt. 1970, 88, 89, 90, 91), Manchester Coll. M. Alumni Assn. (pres. 1972), Am. Legion, Order of Coif, Phi Delta Phi. Home: 3274 Woodhaven Trl Kokomo IN 46902-5062 Office: PO Box 2249 123 N Buckeye St Kokomo IN 46904-2249 Office Phone: 765-459-3941. Business E-Mail: connie.maugans@bhcmlaw.com.

**MAUGER, CYNTHIA CARROLL,** secondary school educator; b. Pottstown, Pa., May 12, 1956; d. Walter W. and Eleanor LaRue (Schaeffer) Carroll; m. Lawrence J. Mauger, Mar. 26, 1983; children: Joshua Timothy, Jordan Michael, Caitlin Carroll. BS, Shippensburg (Pa.) U., 1978; postgrad., Pa. State U.; MA, Villanova (Pa.) U., 1995; postgrad., East Stroudsburg (Pa.) U., Ind. Wesleyan U. Cert. tchr. English, Pa. Tchr. secondary lang. arts

Boyertown (Pa.) Area Sch. Dist., 1978—. Mem. NEA, Pa. State Edn. Assn., Boyertown Area Edn. Assn. Home: 200 Edge Hill Rd Boyertown PA 19512-9807 Office Phone: 610-369-7435. Business E-Mail: cmauger@boyertownasd.org.

**MAUGERE, DENNIS PAUL,** historian, educator; b. Newark, Sept. 3, 1946; s. William John and Virginia Webb Maugere; m. Joanne Maria Cella, Sept. 21, 1974; children: Lisa Marie, Anthony Paul, Lauren Michelle. AS cum laude in History and Polit. Sci., Broward Jr. Coll., 1966; BA in hist., polit. sci., U. Fla., 1969, MA in tchg., am. hist., polit. sci., social founds. of edn., 1976. Cert. profl. social studies educator State Dept. Edn., Fla and NY. Human rels. specialist Broward County Commn. Govt., Ft. Lauderdale, Fla., 1977—80, Broward Employ. Tng. Admin., 1981—82; adj. prof., hist. govt. Broward CC, Pembroke Pines, Fla., 1984—99; hist. prof. Cooper City (Fla.) HS, 1984—. Chmn. Broward County Adv. Bd. for Disabled, Ft. Lauderdale, 1979—81; keynote spkr. South Fla Second Conf. on Handicapped, Hollywood, Fla., 1979. Author: (social studies course) The Warren Commission Report and The Assassination of President John F. Kennedy, 1998; performer: (talk show host) Concerns of the Disabled, Sta. WAVC-TV, 1977, Hotline for the Disabled, Sta. WKID-TV, 1978. Guest spkr. various comm. functions for handicapped issues. Named Leadership Coun. Wall of Tolerance Honoree, So. Poverty Law Ctr., 2005; recipient Citation of Merit award, Muscular Dystrophy Assn., Inc., 1978, Physically Handicapped, Inc., 1978, Award of Excellence, Nat. Assn. County Organ., 1978, Three Presdl. Invitations for Ann. Meeting Pres.'s Com. Employment of Handicapped, Pres. Carter Adminstrn., 1978—80, US Citizen Ambassador, Hist. Edn. Del. to Russia and Latvia selectee, Ariz. State U., 1993, honoree, Cmty. Leader's Banquet, Tamarac, Fla., 1993, Tchrs. Making a Difference award in the Lives of Fla. Children, Fla. Devel. Disabilities Coun., 2005. Mem.: Southern Poverty Law Ctr., Am. Hist. Assn., Phi Alpha Theta, Internat. Roman Catholic. Achievements include co-founder South Florida's 1st annual conference on the handicapped; development of numerous county ordinances for the rights of the handicapped. Office: Cooper City HS 9401 Stirling Rd Cooper City FL 33328 Office Phone: 754-323-0200. Office Fax: 754-323-0330. Personal E-mail: maugered@aol.com.

**MAUGHAN, DENITA RACHELLE,** psychologist; b. Sioux Falls, S.D., Nov. 24, 1971; d. Dennis Ray and Darlene Rosemarie Poppenga; m. Michael George Maughan, July 24, 1998; children: Mikaela Rayne, Maddox Michael. BS, Mankato (Minn.) State U., 1994, MA, 1996; PhD, U. Utah, 2004. Cert. pupil personnel svcs. Calif., 2003. Psychologist Panama-Buena Vista Union Sch. Dist., Bakersfield, Calif., 2002—. Contbr. articles to profl. jours. Mem.: NASP. Office Phone: 661-321-1906.

**MAUGHAN, SIR DERYCK,** former bank executive; Degree earned, King's Coll., Univ. of London, 1969, Stanford U., 1978. With Treasury Dept., United Kingdom, 1969—79, Goldman Sachs, 1979—83, Salomon Bros. Inc., 1983—97; mng. dir. Salomon Bros. Inc, 1986—91, COO N.Y.C. 1991-92, chmn., CEO, 1992—97; vice-chmn., CEO Citigroup, N.Y.C., 1998—2004; vice-chmn. NYSE, 1996—2000. Knighted for svcs. to Brit. bus. her majesty, The Queen, 2002.

**MAUKE, OTTO RUSSELL,** retired college president; b. Webster, Mass., Jan. 26, 1924; s. Otto G. and Florence (Giroux) M.; m. Leah Louison, June 18, 1950. AB, Clark U., 1947, A.M., 1948; PhD (Kellogg fellow), U. Tex., 1965. Tchr. history, acad. dean Endicott Jr. Coll., Beverly, Mass., 1948-65; acad. dean Cumberland County Coll., Vineland, NJ, 1966-67; pres. Camden County Coll., Blackwood, NJ, 1967-87, pres. emeritus. Served with U.S. Army, 1943-46. PTO. Home: 2119 E Lakeview Dr Sebastian FL 32958-8519

**MAUL, KEVIN JAY,** financial consultant, economist; BA, Shippensburg U., 1990; MA, U. Va., 1992. Economist USDA Econ. Rsch. Svc., Washington, 1991-92; fin. cons. Pricewaterhouse Coopers LLP, Washington, 1992-99, Resources Connection, McLean, Va., 1999-2000, Deloitte & Touche LLP, Washington, 2000—03, Callaway Ptnrs., LLC, Reston, Va., 2005—. Author: The Handbook of Mortgage Banking, 1993. Mem. Am. Econ. Assn., Mortgage Bankers Assn. Am. Lutheran. Avocations: music, travel, gardening, stamp collecting/philately.

**MAULDIN, JOHN INGLIS,** public defender; b. Atlanta, Nov. 6, 1947; s. Earle and Isabel (Inglis) M.; m. Cynthia Ann Balchin, Apr. 15, 1967 (div. Dec. 1985); children: Tracy Rutherford, Abigail Inglis; m. Linda W. Farmer, Nov. 7, 1998. BA, Wofford Coll., 1970; JD, Emory U., 1973. Bar: S.C. 1974, U.S. Ct. Appeals (4th cir.) 1974, U.S. Dist. Ct. S.C. 1975, U.S. Supreme Ct. 1978. Asst. pub. def. Defender Corp. Greenville County, S.C., 1974-76; ptnr. Mauldin & Allison, Greenville, 1977-92; pub. defender Greenville County, S.C., 1992—. Chair S.C. Commn. on Indigent Def., 1993-96; adj. prof. Greenville Tech. Coll., 1975-80; sec., treas. Def. Corp. Greenville County, 1979-92, bd. dirs. Speech Hearing and Learning Ctr., Greenville, 1977-90, pres., 1982; bd. dirs. Save Our Sons, 1995—, Palmetto Innocence Project, 2002—. Named S.C. Atty. Yr. ACLU, S.C., 1986. Mem.: SC Pub. Defender Assn. (bd. dirs. 1992—), SC Assn. Criminal Def. Lawyers (bd. dirs. 1997—99), SC Trial Lawyers Assn., Nat. Legal Aid and Defender Assn. (defender policy group 1999—, bd. dirs. 2002—), Nat. Assn. Criminal Def. Attys., Rotary, Sigma Delta Phi. Democrat. Methodist. Office: PO Box 10264fs Greenville SC 29603 Office Phone: 864-467-8522.

**MAULE, JAMES EDWARD,** law educator; b. Phila., Nov. 26, 1951; s. Edward Randolph George and Jennie Elisabeth (Zappone) M.; m. Susan Margaret Noonan, June 26, 1982 (div. May 1988); children: Catherine Edward, Sarah Margaret; m. Susan K. Garrison, Apr. 7, 1990 (div. 1991). BS cum laude, U. Pa. Wharton Sch., 1973; JD cum laude, Villanova U., 1976; LLM with highest honors, George Washington U., 1979. Bar: Pa. 1976, US Tax Ct. 1986. Atty.-adv. Office Chief Counsel to IRS Legis. and Regulations Divsn., Washington, 1976-78; atty.-adv. judge US Tax Ct., Washington 1978-80; asst. prof. law Dickinson Sch. Law, 1981-83; lectr. and tax program chmn. continuing legal edn., 1981-83; assoc. prof. Villanova Sch. Law, 1983-86, prof., 1986—. Lectr. continuing legal edn. Pa. Bar Inst., Harrisburg, Continuing Legal Edn. Satellite Network, Inc., 1988; lectr. state and local taxes Georgetown U. Law Ctr. Inst., 1992; sr. tax and tech. ptnr. Ctr. Info. Law and Policy, 1993—99; owner JEMBook Pub. Co., TaxJEM Inc.; co-owner Starjem LLC, 2001—04; lectr. continuing legal edn. Phila. Tax Conf., 1996, 2001. Author: Cases and Materials in Federal Income Taxation, 1981, 26th edit., 2006, Materials in Partnership Law and Taxation, 1985, 6th edit., 1991, Materials in Partnership Taxation, 1987, 28th edit., 2006, Materials in Introduction to Taxation, 1987, Cases and Materials in Introduction to the Taxation of Business Entities, 1992, 14th edit., 2006, Materials in Taxation of Fundamental Wealth Transfers, 1986;: 2d edit., 1988, Materials in Tax Consequences of Disposition of Property, 1983, Materials and Problems in Taxation of Property Dispositions I, 1987, Materials in Tax Planning for Real Estate, 1986, Materials in Estate and Gift Tax, 1983;: 3d edit., 1985, Materials in Taxation of Real Estate Transactions, 1986, 3d edit., 1992, Taxation of Residence Transactions, 1985, S Corporations: State Law and Taxation, 1989, (supplemental edits.), 1989, 1990, 1991, 1992, 1993, Materials and Problems in Computer Applications in the Law, 1990, 6th edit., 1995, Materials in Tax Policy, 1990, Materials in Digital Legal Practice Skills, 1996, Materials and Problems in Computer Applications in Tax Law, 1991, 8th edit., 1998, Better That 100 Witches Should Live, 1995, Materials in Decedents Estates and Trusts, 1997, 9th edit., 2006; co-author (with A. Clay): Preparing the 1065 Return, 1992, 1993; author: Continuing Legal Edn. Publs., 1981—; contbg. author: Federal Tax Service, 1989, Tax Practice Series, 1989—, Center for Computer-Assisted Legal Instruction, 2005—; contbr. articles to profl. jours., chapters to books, monographs; author, developer: Computer Assisted Legal Edn. Programs in Taxation, owner, author, editor: computer assisted tax law instruction TaxJEM Inc., cons., prin. author: ABA Section of Taxation Model S Corporation Income Tax Act and Commentary, 1989, author, editor: Report of the Subcommittee on Comparison of S Corporations and Partnerships, 1990, 1991, case and comment editor: Villanova Law Rev., 1975—76, columnist, mem. editl. bd.: S Corps. Jour., 1987—91, Jour. of Ltd. Liability Cos., 1994—98, BNA Tax Mgmt., 1994—. Recipient Disting. Author award,

BNA Tax Mgmt., 1993; Nat. Merit scholar, 1969—73. Mem. ABA (chair and reporter phaseout Elimination Project, Tax Simplification and Restructuring Com., sect. of taxation, cons., ex-officio mem. subcom. on state law, S Corp. com., chmn. subcom. on comparison of partnerships, mem. task force on pass-through entities, tax sect., former chmn. subcom. manuscripts and unpublished tchg. material, com. tchg. tax), Phila. Bar Assn. (lectr. tax sect. state and local tax CLE program 1991, fed. income taxes 1992—), Ctr. Info. Law and Policy, Order of Coif, Friars Sr. Soc. (Phila), Beta Alpha Psi. Home: 219 Comrie Dr Villanova PA 19085-1402 Office: Villanova U Sch Law Rm 12 299 N Spring Mill Rd Villanova PA 19085 Business E-Mail: maule@law.villanova.edu.

**MAULL, GEORGE MARRINER,** conductor, educator; b. Phila., Oct. 14, 1947; s. Frederick Dunlap and Helen Norbury (Jordan) M.; m. Marcia Eileen Korn, Aug. 13, 1984. MusB, U. Louisville, 1970, MusM, 1972; postgrad., Juilliard Sch. Music, 1976-78. Condr. Louisville Ballet Co., 1971-75; asst. condr. Opera Orch. N.Y., N.Y.C., 1976-78, N.J. Symphony Orch., Newark, 1979-80; music dir., condr. Bloomingdale Chamber Orch., N.Y.C., 1980-83, N.J. Youth Symphony, Summit, 1979—97, Philharm. Orch. N.J., Warren, 1987—2006; Condr. Laureate N.J. Youth Symphony, 1997; founder, artistic dir. The Discovery Orch., 2006—. Conductor: Carnegie Hall, N.Y.C., 1989, Lincoln Ctr., N.Y.C., writer, host, condr.: Philharmonic Orch. of N.J., Discovery Concert Bach to the Future, Am. Pub. TV, 2003 (Emmy nomination, 2004), Polish Nat. Radio Symphony Orch., 2001—02, Sono Lumina, 2001, featured in WNET mini-documentary Art Effects: Young and Noteworthy, 1988. Named Disting. Alumnus, U. Louisville, 1994. Mem. Am. Fedn. Musicians, Am. Symphony Orch. League (conducting fellow 1978, Nat. Cert. Merit 1980), Condr's. Guild. Episcopalian. Office: The Discovery Orch PO Box 4064 Warren NJ 07059-0064

**MAUN, MARY ELLEN,** computer consultant; b. NYC, Dec. 18, 1951; d. Emmet Joseph and Mary Alice (McMahon) M. BA, CUNY, 1977, MBA, 1988. Sales rep. N.Y. Telephone Co., N.Y.C., 1970-76, comml. rep., 1977-83, programmer, 1984-86; systems analyst Telesector Resources Group, N.Y.C., 1987-89, sr. systems analyst, 1990-95; pres. Sleepy Hollow (N.Y.) Techs., Inc., N.Y., 1995—. Corp. chmn. United Way of Tri-State Area, N.Y.C., 1985; recreation activities vol. Pioneers Am., N.Y.C., 1982—; active Sleepy Hollow Hist. Soc.; founder Mary Ellen Maun Philanthropic Found., 1998; dist. leader for Dem. Party Tarrytown Recipient Outstanding Community Service award, Calvary Hosp., Bronx, N.Y., 1984. Mem. N.Y. Health and Racquet Club, Road Runners. Avocations: antique restoration, classical music, skiing, running. Office: Sleepy Hollow Techs Inc 539 Martling Ave Tarrytown NY 10591-4719 Personal E-mail: havenhollow@msn.com.

**MAUNDER, ADDISON BRUCE,** agronomic research company executive; b. Holdrege, Nebr., May 13, 1934; s. Addison Haynes and Marie Sophia (Luebs) M.; m. Katherine Marlene Blum, Sept. 8, 1978; children: Lynda Diane, Christopher Allen. B.Sc., U. Nebr., 1956; M.Sc., Purdue U., 1958, PhD, 1960; DSc (hon.), U. Nebr., 1991; DAgr (hon.), Purdue U., 2003. With DeKalb AgResearch, Inc., Lubbock, Tex., 1960-96, sorghum breeder, 1960-61, dir. sorghum research, 1961-76, v.p. research, 1976-78, v.p. rsch., 1978-82; v.p. DeKalb-Pfizer Genetics, DeKalb, Ill., 1982-89; v.p. agronomic research DeKalb Plant Genetics, DeKalb, Ill., 1989-91; sr. v.p. DeKalb Genetics Corp., DeKalb, Ill., 1991-96; rsch. advisor Nat. Grain Sorghum Prodrs. Assn., 1997—. Bd. dirs. Diversity Mag., Washington, 1984-95; adj. prof. Tex. Tech. U., 1992—; pres. Nat. Grain Sorghum Prodrs. Found., 2004— Contbr. 13 chpts. to books and more than 70 articles to profl. jours. Mem. deans adv. com. Tex. Tech. U., Lubbock, 1983-86; chmn. external rev. INTSORMIL of U.S. AID, Lincoln, Nebr., 1980-2001; bd. dirs. Tex. Tech. U. Rsch. Found., 1986-92; mem. Nat. Plant Genetic Resources Bd., 1991-92, Nat. Plant Variety Protection Bd., 1991-94; mem. World Food Prize Com., 1997-2003. Recipient Gerald Thomas award Tex. Tech. U., 1974, Prodn. award Grain Sorghum Producers Assn., 1985, Genetics and Plant Breeding award for Industry, 1987, Indsl. Agronomy award, 1988, Purdue Disting. Alumni award, 1997, Monsanto Crop Sci. Disting. Career award, 2000, Pres.'s Disting Svc. award Am. Seed Trade Assn., 2001. Fellow AAAS, Am. Soc. Agronomy (bd. dirs. 1991-92), Crop Sci. Soc. Am. (bd. dirs. 1991-92, pres. 1995-96); mem. Am. Seed Trade Assn., Sigma Xi, Alpha Zeta. Republican. Achievements include development of plant products (150 hybrids) emphasizing yield, improved drought and insect resistance as well as nutritional quality. E-mail: texasgreenburg@aol.com.

**MAUNE, JAMES J.,** lawyer; b. N.Y.C., Dec. 10, 1942; s. John Lawrence Maune and Catherine Becker; m. Audrey L. De Nio, Sept. 6, 1965. BS in Physics, Manhattan Coll., 1964; MS in Electrophysics, Poly. Inst. Bklyn., 1968; JD cum laude, St. John's U., Jamaica, N.Y., 1976. Devel. engr. Wheeler Labs., Great Neck, NY, 1964—67; engr. Sadco Systems, Farmingdale, NY, 1968—70; sr. devel. engr. Hazeltine Corp., Green Lawn, NY, 1970—73, law clk., 1973—75; from law clk. to ptnr. Brumbaugh, Graves, Donohue & Raymond, N.Y.C., 1975—97; ptnr. Baker Botts, LLP, N.Y.C., 1997—97, ret., 2003. Lectr. Practicing Law Inst., N.Y.C., 1990—2002, Am. Intellectual Property Law Assn., Washington, 1995—2003; spl. prof. patent law Hofstra Law Sch., Hempstead, NY, 1989—94. Patentee in field. Adv. Tribunal-Diocese of Rockville Centre, NY, 1997—. Mem.: K.C. (St. Pius X chpt., Grand Knight 1992—93, 2004—05, Knight of Yr. 2002). Republican. Roman Catholic. Avocations: fishing, skiing. Home: 121 Harvard Dr Plainview NY 11803 Office Phone: 516-367-7066. E-mail: jmaune@pb.net.

**MAUNEY, BRANDI SAVAGE,** special education diagnostician; b. Miami, Mar. 5, 1976; d. Victor Martin and Yvonne Marie Savage; m. John David Mauney, Mar. 30, 1975. B in Psychology, Ga. Coll. and State U., 1999, M in Spl. Edn., 2004; student in Child, Youth and Human Svcs., Nova Southeastern U., 2005—. Cert. tchr. Profl. Stds. Commn. in Ga. Spl. edn. tchr. Henry County Bd. of Edn., McDonough, Ga. 2002—04, spl. edn. liaison/diagnostician, 2004—. Spl. edn. homebound tchr. for medically fragile Henry Count Bd. of Edn., McDounough, 2004—: Mem.: Collaboration Team: Direct On-going Tng. of Adminstrn. and Staff, State Monitoring Com. (assoc.), Continuous Improvement Monitoring Com. (assoc.), Interagency Child Coun. (assoc.; com. chair 2004—05), Sigma Alpha Iota (life; v.p. 1995—97). Republican. Baptist. Achievements include research in effects of Child-Find and Early Intervention. Avocations: music, swimming, yoga, travel, bicycling. Home: 70 Mountain Crt Covington GA 30016 Office: Henry County Bd Edn 33 N Zack Hinton Pkwy Mcdonough GA 30253 Office Phone: 770-316-5830. Personal E-mail: brandisavage@yahoo.com. E-mail: bmauney@henry.k12.ga.us.

**MAUNEY, THOMAS LEE,** set designer; b. Lexington, N.C., May 29, 1967; s. Thomas Pete and Iris Elnita (Washburn) M. BFA, U. N.C., Greensboro, 1990; MFA, U. Mont., 1995. Asst. tech. dir., designer Raleigh (N.C.) Little Theatre, 1989-90; tech. dir. U. Mont., Missoula, 1992-95; designer Big Fork (Mont.) Summer Playhouse, 1994-98; prodn. mgr., tech. dir. Raleigh Meml. Auditorium, 1998—2002, BTI Ctr. Performing Arts, 1998—2002. Freelance designer theatre and spl. events.

**MAUPIN, A. WILLIAM,** state supreme court justice; children: Allison, Michael. BA, U. Nev., 1968; JD, U. Ariz., 1971. Atty., ptnr. Thorndal, Backus, Maupin and Armstrong, Las Vegas, 1976—93; judge 8th Jud. Dist. Clark County, 1993—97; assoc. justice Nev. Supreme Ct., 1997—, chief justice, 2001—02. Bd. govs. Nev. State Bar, 1991—95. Mem.: Nev. Supreme Ct. (study com. to review jud. elections, chmn. 1995, alternate dispute resolution implementation com. chmn. 1992—96). Office: Nev Supreme Ct 201 S Carson St Carson City NV 89701-4702

**MAUPIN, ARMISTEAD JONES, JR.,** writer; b. Washington, May 13, 1944; s. Armistead Jones and Diana Jane (Barton) M. BA, U. N.C., 1966. Reporter News and Courier, Charleston, S.C., 1970-71, AP, San Francisco, 1971-72; account exec. Lowry Russom and Leeper, Pub. Rels., San Francisco, 1973; columnist Pacific Sun mag., San Francisco, 1974; publicist San Francisco Opera, 1975; serialist San Francisco Chronicle, 1976-77, 81, 83;

commentator Sta. KRON-TV, San Francisco, 1979; serialist San Francisco Examiner, 1986. Author: (novels) Tales of the City, 1978, More Tales of the City, 1980, Further Tales of the City, 1982, Babycakes, 1984, Significant Others, 1987, Sure of You, 1989, (omnibus) 28 Barbary Lane, 1990, (omnibus) Back to Barbary Lane, 1991, Maybe the Moon, 1992, The Night Listener, 2000; co-author: The Essential Clive Barker, 1999; librettist musical Heart's Desire, 1990; exec. prodr. (TV program) Armistead Maupin's Tales of the City, 1993; contbr. articles to N.Y. Times, L.A. Times, others. Lt. (j.g.) USN, 1967-70. Vietnam. Recipient Freedom Leadership award Freedoms Found., Valley Forge, Pa., 1972, Comms. award Met. Elections Com. L.A., 1989, Exceptional Achievement award ALA, 1990, Best Dramatic Serial award Royal TV Soc., 1994, Peabody award 1994, Outstanding Miniseries award, Gay and Lesbian Alliance Against Defamation, 1994, Best Miniseries award Nat. Bd. of Rev., 1994. Office: ICM Care Amanda Urban 40 W 57th St Fl 16 New York NY 10019-4098 Address: c/o Literary Bent PO Box 410990 Ste 528 San Francisco CA 94141 E-mail: inquiries@literarybent.com.*

**MAUPIN, ELIZABETH THATCHER,** theater critic; b. Cleve., Oct. 21, 1951; d. Addison and Margaret (Thatcher) M.; m. Jay Yellen, Dec. 29, 1995. BA in English, Wellesley (Mass.) Coll., 1973; M in Journalism, U. Calif., Berkeley, 1976. Editorial asst. Houghton Mifflin Co., Boston, 1973-74; reporter, movie critic Times-Standard, Eureka, Calif., 1976-78; theater and movie critic Chronicle-Telegram, Elyria, Ohio, 1978-79; movie critic Ledger-Star, Norfolk, Va., 1979-82; feature writer Va.-Pilot and Ledger-Star, Norfolk, 1982-83; sr. theater critic Orlando (Fla.) Sentinel, 1983—. Fellow Nat. Arts Journalism program Columbia U., 1995-96. Fellow Nat. Critics Inst.; mem. Am. Theatre Critics Assn. (exec. com. 1993-99, 05-06, chair 1996-99). Office: Orlando Sentinel 633 N Orange Ave Orlando FL 32801-1349

**MAUPIN, JOHN E., JR.,** college president; b. L.A., Oct. 28, 1946; m. Eilene; three children. Diploma, San Jose State Coll.; DDS, Meharry Med. Coll., 1972; MBA, Loyola Coll., Balt., 1979; LLD (hon.), Va. Union Univ., 1996; DSc (hon.), Morehouse Sch. Medicine, 1995. Dentistry resident Provident Hosp., Balt., 1973; dentist, capt. then advanced through grades to lt. col. U.S. Army Dental Corps/Walter Reed Med. Ctr., Washington, 1974-97; various health/dental positions including dep. commr. Balt. City Health Dept., 1981-87; CEO Southside Healthcare, Inc., Atlanta; exec. v.p. Morehouse Sch. of Medicine, Atlanta; pres. Meharry Med. Coll., Nashville, 1994—. Mem. adv. groups Nat. Com. on Fgn. Med. Edn. and Accreditation, Bd. of Scientific Counselors, Nat. Ctr. for Infectious Diseases, Managed Care Task Force, others; bd. dirs. Monarch Dental Corp., Am. Gen. Series Portfolio Co., U.S. Life Mut. Funds, others. Exec. coun. Boy Scouts of Mid. Tenn.; bd. dirs. Nashville Cmty. Found., BellSouth Sr. Classic at Opryland; former chair bd. dirs. United Way of Mid. Tenn.; former mem. bd. govs. Nashville Area C. of C., others. Recipient A.B. Cooper award North Ga. Dental Soc., 1994, Dentist of Yr. award, 1991, Mayor's Citation for outstanding pub. svc., Balt., 1987, others. Mem. Nat. Dental Assn. (del. dirs.), Nat. Med. Assn., Ga. State Med. Assn., Nat. Assn. Cmty. Health Ctrs., Nat. Assn. Health Care Execs., others. Office: Meharry Med Coll 1005 DB Todd Blvd Nashville TN 37208

**MAUPIN, KARIN LOUISE,** secondary school educator; d. Alfred Bertil and Kathryn Louise (Snapp) Swanson; m. Bernard Kent Fredrick Maupin, Aug. 11, 1973; children: Kristin Louise, Kevin Alfred. BA in Anthropology, Northwestern U., 1970, tchg. cert., 1972; postgrad., U. Ill., 1972—73, Aquinas Coll., 1994—95; M in Spl. Edn. and Learning Disabilities, Calvin Coll., 1998. Commodities trading asst. E.F. Hutton & Co., Chgo., 1972—73; comml. paper trader Montgomery Ward Credit Corp., Chgo., 1973—77; tchr. Creative Learning Ctr., Grand Rapids, Mich., 1982—83; program dir. Alternative Methods for Internat. Stability/Trees Corps., 1989—; tutor SLD Ctr., Grand Rapids, 1995—98; substitute tchr. Forest Hills Pub. Schs., Grand Rapids, 1996—97, tchr., 1997—. Odyssey of the Mind coach Forest Hills No. Middle Sch., Grand Rapids, 1995; adult sponsor F.O.M.E. Environ. Club Forest Hills No. H.S., 1995—98. Contbg. editor: mag. Our Children, 1991—93. Tutor Head Start Program, Grand Rapids, Mich., 1966, James Taylor Sch., Chgo., 1971, Cabrini Green Housing Project, 1976—77; vol. curator Field Mus. Natural History, Chgo., 1978—80; vol. curator, docent Grand Rapids Pub. Mus., 1981—83; bd. mem. Summerfest Ballet Sch., 1983—85; pres. Kent County Med. Soc. Aux., 1984—85; coord. Citizens Liability Action Com., 1984—87; legis. chmn. Mich. State Med. Soc. Aux., 1985—87; pres. Coffinberry Archaeol. Soc., 1988; bd. mem. Children's Inter-active Sci. Ctr., 1995—99, SLD Learning Ctr. Western Mich., 1995—99; rep. Northwestern U. Alumni, 1996—; mem. edn. com. Frederik Meijer Gardens, 1997—2001. Recipient Cert. Appreciation, Mich. State Med. Soc., 1987, AMA, 1987, Letter Appreciation for environ. stewardship, Former Pres. Gerald R. Ford, 1989, Achievement award, Global Releaf, 1990, Letter Appreciation for environ. stewardship, Pres. George Bush, 1992, Cert. Appreciation, Gov. Engler, Mich. Office of Governor, 1992, Cmty. Svc. award, Mich. Forestry & Park Assn., 1992, State Winner, Pres. Bush's Take Pride in Am., 1992, Nongovtl. Agy. award for environ. stewardship, Mich. Audubon Soc., 1993, Letter Appreciation, Kent County Commrs., 1994, Cert. Appreciation, Grand Rapids Pub. Schs., 1994, Pres. Clinton's Coun. on Sustainable Development, 1997. Avocations: travel, gardening, tennis, bicycling, golf. Office: Forest Hills Pub Schs 6590 Cascade Rd SE Grand Rapids MI 49506 E-mail: amistrees@aol.com.

**MAURER, ALAN HARVEY,** nuclear medicine physician; b. Atlantic City, N.J., Jan. 17, 1947; s. Franklin E. and Ruth L. (Cohen) M.; m. Marilyn Erber, May 21, 1981; children: Joshua, Benjamin, Molly. AB, ScB, Brown U., 1969; MS, U. Pa., 1971; MD, Temple U., 1975. Diplomate Am. Bd. Nuclear Medicine, Am. Bd. Internal Medicine. Dir. nuclear medicine Temple U. Hosp. and Sch. Medicine, Phila., 1981—. Contbr. sci. papers to profl. publs. Mem. Soc. Nuclear Medicine (pres. 2001-02), Radiologic Soc. N.Am., Tau Beta Pi, Sigma Xi, Alpha Omega Alpha. Achievements include invention of medical imaging devices. Office: Temple Univ Hosp Broad & Ontario Sts Philadelphia PA 19140

**MAURER, DAVID LEO,** lawyer; b. Evansville, Ind., Oct. 31, 1945; s. John G. Jr. and Mildred M. (Lintzenich) M.; m. Diane M. Kaput, Aug. 11, 1973; children: Eric W., Kathryn A. BA magna cum laude, U. Detroit, 1967, Cert. in Teaching, 1971; JD, Wayne State U., 1975. Bar: Mich., U.S. Dist. Ct. (ea. and we. dist.) Mich., U.S. Ct. Appeals (6th cir.) Cin. Law clk. Mich. Ct. Appeals, Detroit, 1976, Supreme Ct. Mich., Lansing, 1977-78; asst. U.S. atty. civil div. U.S. Dept. Justice, Detroit, 1978-81; assoc. to ptnr. Butzel, Long, Gust, Klein & Van Zile, Detroit, 1981-85; ptnr. Pepper, Hamilton & Scheetz (now Pepper Hamilton LLP), Detroit, 1985—. Guest lectr. Practicing Law Inst., 1988—, Nat. Bus. Inst., 1989—, U. Mich. Law Sch., U. Detroit Law Sch., 1990, Hazardous Waste Super Conf., 1986-87. Co-author: Michigan Environmental Law Deskbook, 1992; contbr. articles to profl. jours. and chpts. in books. Mem. Energy & Environ. Policy Com., 1988—, chairperson, 1989-90; mem. Great Lakes Water Resources Commn., 1986. Mem. State Bar Mich. (environ. couns. 1986-91, sec., treas., chairperson-elect, chairperson 1991-93). Office: Pepper Hamilton LLP 100 Renaissance Ctr Ste 3600 Detroit MI 48243-1157 Office Phone: 313-393-7448. Business E-Mail: maurerd@pepperlaw.com.

**MAURER, EVAN MACLYN,** museum director; b. Newark, Aug. 19, 1944; s. Myron P. and Belle (Cloth) M.; m. Naomi E. Maurer; children: Noah, Aaron. BA, Amherst Coll., 1966; MA, U. Minn., 1968; PhD, U. Chgo., 1974. Asst. dir. Mpls. Inst. Arts, 1971-73, dir., CEO, 1988—2005; curator Art Inst. Chgo., 1973-81; dir. Mus. Art, prof. U. Mich., Ann Arbor, 1981—88. Author: The Native American Heritage, 1977; co-author: Rising of the New Moon: A Century of Tabwa Art, 1986, Max Ernst: Beyond Surrealism, 1986, The Intelligence of Forms: An Artist Collect African Art, 1992, Visions of the People: A Pictorial History of Plains Indian Life, 1992. Recipient medal of Chevalier Order of Arts and Letters, French Govt., 2004.

**MAURER, FRANK W, JR.,** land trust administrator; b. Boston, Aug. 25, 1941; s. Frank W Sr. and Elizabeth M. Maurer; m. Lenora Ann Timm, Apr. 19, 1985; children from previous marriage: Pierre Crispin, Basil Gavin. *Father and namesake, Frank W Maurer, Sr., having a background in both engineer-*

*ing and physiology, was asked to work in secret at the beginning of WWII to design and produce high-altitude breathing equipment for Allied pilots to over-fly the Axis pilots with their then superior equipment. At the conclusion of the war, he returned all patents to the federal government, saying he could not profit from such a horrible event. For the rest of his life he was an inventor and designer. The family likes to think that his creative and social sensibilities live on in his children and grandchildren. Mother, Elizabeth M. Maurer, was always a free thinker, having voted for socialist, Norman Thomas, in her first presidential election. During my childhood, she was open minded in her approach to raising me and my siblings. Her role modeling allowed me to be the free thinker I became.* BA in Biology, Antioch Coll., 1964; PhD in Vertebrate Zoology and Ecology, Cornell U., 1968. Lic. vessel operator Calif. Asst. prof. biology U. Bosphorus, Istanbul, Turkey, 1968—71; lectr. zoology Nat. U. Lesotho, 1971—76; rsch. assoc. Swedish U. Agrl. Scis., Uppsala, 1977; interviewer 13 countries in Asia, 1978; owner, operator, dir. Rsch. Farm, Davis, Calif., 1978—; organic farmers' market prodr., 1978—; exec. dir., pres. Quail Ridge Wilderness Conservancy, Davis, 1989—; Environ. Edn. Farm Found., Davis, 1992—. Lectr. in field; cons. on openspace and conservation models for small landowners, Wyo., 2004—06. *Always among his goals are human rights, education, promoting environmental and open space programs, interwoven with artistic expression. In addition to starting an educational teaching farm in Davis, CA in 1978, he and his wife worked over 22 years to create a 2000 acre native habitat and wildlife reserve in Napa County by purchasing, via innovative fundraising strategies, land destined for development. He led the initiative to incorporate this reserve into the University of California's Natural Reserve System. Today's activities focus on public speaking, voting reform, habitat restoration, creating openspace and conservation models for small landowners, and using the art of hand-carved petroglyphs for teaching and commemorations.* Author: (legislation) Calif. State Grass Bill, 2004; petroglyphs, Calif. State Archives, 2000, 2004, Wash. State Archives, 2002, 2003, Assembly of Wales, 2003, Coun. of Cornwall, 2003, Parliament of Scotland, 2004, Oreg. State Archives, 2004, Nev. State Libr. and Archives, 2005, Utah State Archives, 2005, Wyo. State Archives, 2005; prodr.: (CD) Scottish Poetry, 2003, (ednl. videos) Quail Ridge Reserve, 1998, Reflections, 2000, (photobook) Portraits of a Vanishing Landscape A Pictorial Interpretation of the Western Sagebrush Steppe, 2006; contbr. articles to profl. publs. Registered pacifist US Draft Bd., 1966; activist Ctr. for Voting and Democracy, Takoma Park, Md., 2004—; Californians for Electoral Reform, Sacramento, 2004—. Recipient John Muir award, Davis Farmers Market, 1989, Conservation Achievement recognition, Napa County Land Trust, 1990. Mem.: Soc. Conservation Biology (life), Soc. Study of Evolution (life), Am. Soc. Mammalogy (life), Dixon Scottish Cultural Assn., Sacramento Caledonian Club. Green Party. Avocations: travel, hiking, birdwatching. Home: 25344 County Rd 95 Davis CA 95616 Office: Quail Ridge Wilderness Conservancy/ Environ Edn Farm Found 25344 County Rd 95 Davis CA 95616 Office Phone: 530-758-1387. Fax: 530-758-1316.

**MAURER, FREDERIC GEORGE, III,** bank executive; b. Grand Rapids, Mich., May 15, 1952; s. Frederic George and Rhea Marie (Annesser) Maurer. BA, St. Louis U., 1974, MBA, 1977. Dir. residence Marguerite Hall St. Louis U., 1977-79; internat. banking analyst Merc. Trust Co., St. Louis, 1979-80, banking rep. Latin Am., 1980-81, internat. officer, 1981-83, asst. v.p., 1983, Union Bank, L.A., 1983-86; asst. v.p. internat. sect. Centerre Bank, N.A., St. Louis, 1986-87, asst. v.p. portfolio mgmt. sect., 1987-88; with pvt. banking dept. Boatmen's Nat. Bank, St. Louis, 1988-90, v.p., 1990-97, Nations Bank, St. Louis, 1997-99, Bank Am., St. Louis, 1999-2001, Commerce Trust Co., St. Louis, 2001—06. Bank Midwest, N.A., St. Louis, 2006—. Bd. dirs. Assocs. St. Louis U. Librs., 1975—79, NCCJ, 1992—, Food Outreach, Inc., 2001—, Downtown/Marquette YMCA, 2003—; mem. dir.'s assn. Mo. Bot. Garden, 1986—; bd. dirs. Franciscan Missionary Union, 1996—2001. Internat. Bus. fellow, 1975—77. Mem.: DuBourg Soc., LA English-Speaking Union, Performing Arts Coun.-In the wings, Opera Guild, Robert Morris Assocs., Ctr. Internat. Banking Studies, U. Va., Alumni Coun. St. Louis U., Mo. Athletic Club (St. Louis), Noonday Club. Home: 849 Aldan Dr Saint Louis MO 63132-3501 Office: 1 N Brentwood Blvd Ste 100 Saint Louis MO 63105 Office Phone: 314-862-4953. Business E-Mail: maurerfg@dfckc.com.

**MAURER, GILBERT CHARLES,** media specialist; b. N.Y.C, May 24, 1928; s. Charles and Mildred (Petite) M.; m. Ann D'Espinosa. AB, St. Lawrence U., 1950; MBA, Harvard U., 1952. With Cowles Communications, Inc., NYC, 1952-71, Look Mag., 1952-62; pub. Venture mag., 1963-67; pres. Family Circle mag., 1967-69, v.p., dir. corporate planning, exec. com., 1969-71; sr. v.p., dir. F.A.S. Internat., Inc., 1971-73; v.p. mag. div. Hearst Corp., 1973-74, exec. v.p., 1974-76, pres. mag. div., 1976-90, also dir.; exec. v.p. The Hearst Corp., 1985-98, chief operating officer, 1990-98, cons. Mem. NY adv. bd. Salvation Army, 1979—; trustee Whitney Mus. Am. Art, 1983—, pres., 1994-98, trustee Norton Mus. of Art, 1998—; mem. vis. com. Medill Sch. Journalism Northwestern U., 1985-94, chmn., 1989-94; bd. dirs. Boys and Girls Club Am., 1986—, William Randolph Hearst Found., The Hearst Found.; mem. bd. mgrs. NY Bot. Garden, 1989. Mem. Mag. Pubs. Assn. (bd. dirs., chmn. 1979-81) Clubs: Harvard (NYC), Metropolitan (NYC). Office: Hearst 250 W 55th St New York NY 10019-5201

**MAURER, HAROLD MAURICE,** pediatrician; b. NYC, Sept. 10, 1936; s. Isador and Sarah (Rothkowitz) M.; m. Beverly Bennett, June 12, 1960; children: Ann Maurer Rosenbach, Wendy Maurer Linsky. AB, NYU, 1957; MD, SUNY, Bklyn., 1961. Diplomate Am. Bd. Pediatrics, Am. Bd. Pediatric Hematology-Oncology. Intern pediatrics Kings County Hosp., N.Y.C., 1961-62; resident in pediatrics Babies Hosp., Columbia-Presbyn. Med. Center, N.Y.C., 1962-64; fellow in pediatric hematology/oncology Columbia-Presbyn. Med. Center, 1966-68; asst. prof. pediatrics Med. Coll. Va., Richmond, 1968-71, asso. prof., 1971-75, prof., 1975—, chmn. dept. pediatrics, 1976-93; dean U. Nebr. Coll. Medicine, Omaha, 1993-98; chancellor U. Nebr. Med. Ctr., Omaha, 1998—. Chmn. Intergroup Rhabdomyosarcoma Study, 1972-98; exec. com. Pediatric Oncology Group. Editor: pediatrics, 1983, Rhabdomyosarcoma and Related Tumors in Children and Adolescence, 1991; mem. editorial bd. Am. Jour. Hematology, Journal Pediatric Hematology and Oncology, Medical and Pediatric Oncology, 1984-99; contbr. articles to profl. jours. Mem. Youth Health Task Force, City of Richmond., Gov.'s Adv. Com. on Handicapped., Gov.'s Homeland Security Policy Group, Nebr., 2002-; mem. coun. biodefense Assn. Academic Health Ctr., 2003—, coun. global health, 2003—, gov.'s homeland security policy group 2002—; mem. nat. com. on childhood cancer Am. Cancer Soc., bd. dirs. Va. divsn.; bd. dirs. Nebr. Med. Ctr., 1997—, Friends of Nat. Inst. Nursing Rsch., 2004-05; adv. com. Lisstratcom, 2004—. Served to lt. comdr. USPHS, 1964-66. Named Ak-Sar-Ben King C IX, 2005; recipient Midlander of Yr., Omaha World Herald Newspaper, 2004; grantee, NIH, 1974—98. Mem. Am. Acad. Pediatrics (com. oncology-hematology), Am. Soc. Hematology, Soc. Pediatric Rsch., Am. Pediatric Soc., Va. Pediatric Sic. (exec. com.), Assn. Med. Sch. Pediatric Dept. Chmn., Internat. Soc. Pediatric Oncology, Am. Soc. Clin. Oncology, Va. Hematology Soc., Am. Assn. Cancer Rsch., Am. Cancer Soc., Am. Soc. Pediatric Hematology-Oncology (v.p. 1990-91, pres. 1991-93, Lifetime Achievement award children's oncology group 2003), Sigma Xi, Coun. Deans AAMC, Gov.'s Blue Ribbon Commn., Alpha Omega Alpha. Republican. Jewish. Home: 9822 Ascot Dr Omaha NE 68114-3848 Office: U Nebr Med Ctr 986605 Nebraska Med Ctr Omaha NE 68198-6605 Business E-Mail: hmmaurer@unmc.edu.

**MAURER, JEFFREY STUART,** trust company executive; b. NYC, July 9, 1947; s. Herbert and Phoebe Maurer; m. Wendy S. Nemerov. BA, Alfred U., 1969; MBA, NYU, 1975; JD, St. John's U., 1976. With US Trust Co. NY, NYC, 1970—, pres., 1990; COO US Trust Co. NYC, 1994-2001, CEO, 2001—02, chmn., CEO, 2002—03; CEO Lehman Bros. Trust Co., N.A., 2003—. Trustee Alfred (N.Y.) U., 1984, North Shore L.I. Jewish Health Sys.; bd. dirs., treas. Children's Health Fund, N.Y.C., 1988; chmn. Hebrew Home Aged, Riverdale, NY; bd. dirs. Roundabout Theatre Co. Mem. ABA, N.Y. State Bar Assn., Glen Head Country Club, Harmonie Club. Jewish. Office: Lehman Bros Trust Co NA 605 Third Ave New York NY 10158 Office Phone: 212-476-5366. Business E-Mail: jeffrey.maurer@lehman.com.

**MAURER, KATHLEEN MARIE,** music educator, vocalist; b. Pitts. MusB in Vocal Performance, Butler U., Indpls., 1977; MusM in Vocal Performance, Bowling Green State U., Bowling Green, Ohio, 1979. Profl. opera singer Städtische Bühne Hagen, Hagen, Rheinland-Pfalz, Germany, 1983—85, Nationaltheater Mannheim, Mannheim, Baden-Württemberg, Germany, 1985—98; faculty assoc. in voice Wright State U., Dayton, Ohio, 1998—2003; asst. prof. of voice performance Ball State U. Sch. of Music, Muncie, Ind., 2003—. Singer: (orchestra concert) Handel's Messiah, (chamber music world première) Wildpeace (Deborah Netanel), (recital) Gesichte der Liebe (Faces of Love), (orchestral concert) Beethoven's Symphony No. 9, (oratorio) Mozart Requiem Mass, Saint-Saëns Christmas Oratorio, (opera) The Ballad of Baby Doe, Suor Angelica, (lecture recital) Poems of Love and the Rain (Ned Rorem), (recital) All About Love: A Romantic Recital, (chamber music world première) Within My Garden. Mem.: Vocal Arts Resource Network, Coll. Music Soc. (campus rep. 2005—06), Nat. Assn. of Tchrs. of Singing, Ball State U. Women's Club, Phi Kappa Phi, Pi Kappa Lambda. Avocations: attending concerts, handcrafts, reading. Office: Ball State University School of Music Muncie IN 47306 Business E-Mail: kmmaurer@bsu.edu.

**MAURER, MARGARET BEECHER,** librarian, educator; b. Akron, Ohio, Feb. 2, 1954; d. Marjorie Brandon and Carl J Beecher; m. Jeffrey Francis Maurer, Mar. 13, 1992. BA in english, Kent State U., 1972—76, MLS, 1984—86. Reference libr. Westlake Porter Pub. Libr., Westlake, Ohio, 1985—90; catalog dept. head, automation coord. Taylor Meml. Pub. Libr., Cuyahoga Falls, Ohio, 1990—98; asst. prof. KSU Libraries & Media Services, Kent, Ohio, 1998—; instr. (term) KSU Sch. of Libr. and Info. Sci., Kent, Ohio, 2003—. Editor, TechkNow Ohio Libr. Coun., 1994—. Contbr. articles to jours. Mem.: ALA, No. Ohio Tech. Services Librarians (chmn., sec., exec. com. mem.), Ohio Libr. Coun. (editor, TechkNOW), Academic Libr. Assn. of Ohio, PHI Beta MU Libr. Office: Kent State Univ Libr 370 Library PO Box 5190 Kent OH 44242-0001 Office Phone: 330-672-1702. E-mail: mbmaurer@kent.edu.

**MAURER, MARK CAREY,** music educator; b. Carlisle, Pa., Oct. 15, 1974; s. Carey Robert and Sharon Ann Maurer; m. Julie Florence McElwain, July 18, 1998; 1 child, Joshua Kenaniah. BS in Music Edn., Geneva Coll., Beaver Falls, Pa., 1998; BA in French Horn Performance, Geneva Coll., Beaver Falls. Pa., 1998. Tchr. mid. sch. chorus Elizabeth (Pa.) Forward Mid. Sch., 2000—. Bus. mentor Maurer Enterprises, Pitts., 2004—. Music dir. Providence Ref. Presbyn. Ch., Pitts., 1998—2006. Conservative. Avocations: music performance, music recording, philanthropy, theology. Home: 205 Broadway Street Extension North Versailles PA 15137 Office: Elizabeth Forward Mid Sch 401 Rock Run Rd Elizabeth PA 15037-2416 Office Phone: 412-896-2335.

**MAURER, RICHARD HORNSBY,** physicist; b. Reading, Pa., Apr. 27, 1942; s. Samuel Forest and Marian E. (Hornsby) M.; m. Marian Ross Harvey, May 3, 1975; children: Jonathan, Andrew. BS, L.I. U., 1964; PhD, U. Pitts., 1970. Postdoctoral fellow Bartol Rsch. Found., Swarthmore, Pa., 1970-73; environ. engr. AMP Inc., Harrisburg, Pa., 1973-81; physicist Applied Physics Lab. Johns Hopkins U., Laurel, Md., 1981—, reliability group supr. test and evaluation sect., 1986-94, instr. Whiting Sch. Engring., 1988—. Contbr. chpt. to: Space Systems Reliability and Survivability, 1994; contbr. articles to Jour. IEEE Transactions Nuclear Sci., Jour. Spacecraft and Rockets, Internat. Reliability Physics Symposium. Baseball mgr. Howard County Youth Program, Ellicott City, Md., 1985-97; lector St. John's Episcopal Ch., 1994-98. Mem. IEEE, Am. Soc. Quality Control, Am. Phys. Soc., Sigma Xi. Achievements include patent for fabrication of thermal batteries by multi-layer ceramic of organic printed circuit board methods; research on effects of radiation on electronic devices, on reliability of electronic packaging designs and gallium arsenide devices; development of portable neutron spectrometer. Office: Johns Hopkins U Applied Physics Lab 11100 Johns Hopkins Rd Laurel MD 20723-6005 Office Phone: 443-778-6482. Personal E-mail: ecmd@aol.com.

**MAURER, RICHARD MICHAEL,** investment company executive; b. Bethlehem, Pa., June 4, 1948; s. Richard Thomas and Anna Theresa (Bold) M.; m. Karen Coe, June 13, 1970; children: Christopher Coe, Mark Emerson. Student, Pa. State U., 1966-68; BS, Point Park Coll., 1971; MBA, U. Pitts., 1982. CPA Pa. Staff acct. Price Waterhouse, Pitts., 1972-74, tax acct., 1974, sr. tax acct., 1974-77, tax mgr., 1977-78; dir. taxes The Hillman Co., Pitts., 1978-85; pres. Maurer Ross & Co., Inc., Pitts., 1985—; co-mng. ptnr. Wesmar Ptnrs., Pitts., 1985—; chmn., CEO Admatic Industries, Inc., Pitts., 1998—. Bd. dirs. Women's Golf Unlimited, Inc., Admatic Industries, Inc., Maurer Ross & Co., Inc., Maurer & Ross, Inc. Bd. trustees Pa. State McKeesport U. Point Park U. Alumni. Mem. AICPA, Assn. Corp. Growth, Pa. Inst. CPAs, Rotary (past dir., past pres.), Oakmont Country Club, Duquesne Club, Lake Nona Golf Club. Office: PO Box 106 Murrysville PA 15668-0106 E-Mail: rmaurer@alltel.net.

**MAURER, ROBERT DISTLER,** retired industrial physicist; b. St. Louis, July 20, 1924; s. John and Elizabeth J. (Distler) M.; m. Barbara A. Mansfield, June 9, 1951; children: Robert M., James B.; Janet L. BS, U. Ark., 1948, LLD, 1980; PhD, MIT, 1951. Mem. staff MIT, 1951-52; with Corning Glass Works, NY, 1952-89, mgr. physics research, 1963-78, research fellow, 1978-89. Contbr. articles to profl. jours., chpts. to books; patentee in field. Served with U.S. Army, 1943-46. Recipient Indsl. Physics prize Am. Inst. Physics, 1978, L.M. Ericsson Internat. prize in telecommunications, 1979, Indsl. Rsch. Inst. Achievement award, 1988, Optical Soc. Am./IEEE Leos Tyndall award, 1987, Disting. Alumni award U. Ark., 1994, Am. Innovator award U.S. Dept. Commerce, 1995, Nat. Medal of Technology, 2000; decorated Purple Heart. Fellow IEEE (Morris N. Liebmann award 1978), Am. Ceramic Soc. (George W. Morey award 1976), Am. Phys. Soc. (New Materials prize 1989); mem. NAE (Charles Draper prize 1999), Nat. Inventors Hall of Fame. Home: 2572 W 28th Ave Eugene OR 97405

**MAURER, VIRGINIA GALLAHER,** law educator; b. Shawnee, Okla., Nov. 7, 1946; d. Paul Clark Gallaher and Virginia Ruth (Watson) Abernathy; m. Ralph Gerald Maurer, July 31, 1971; children: Ralph Emmett, William Edward. BA, Northwestern U., 1968; MA, Stanford U., 1969, JD, 1975. Bar: Iowa 1976. Tchr. social studies San Mateo H.S. Dist., Calif., 1969—71; spl. asst. to pres. U. Iowa, Iowa City, 1976—80, adj. asst. prof. law, 1979—80; affiliate asst. prof. law U. Fla., Gainesville, 1981, asst. prof. bus. law, 1980—85, assoc. prof., 1985—93, prof., 1993—, Huber Hurst prof., 1997—. Dir. Poe Bus. Ethics Ctr., 1998—, MBA program U. Fla., 1987, chair dept. mgmt., 1994-2003; vis. scholar Wolfson Coll., Cambridge, 1994; vis. prof. SDA Bocconi U., Milan, 1994-96, Helsinki Sch. Econs. and Bus., 1998, U. Catania, Sicily, 1999, 2002-03; cons. Gov.'s Com. on Iowa 2000, Iowa City, 1976-77, Fla. Banker's Assn., Gainesville, 1982, various law firms, 1995—; bd. dirs. Water & Air Rsch., Inc Contbr. articles to profl. jours.; jr. editor Am. Bus. Law Jour., 1989-90, mng. editor, 1990-91, editor-in-chief, 1992-94 Bd. dirs. Gainesville Chamber Orch., 1990-93; fundraising com. Pro Arte Musica, Gainesville, 1980-84; sr. warden, vestry Holy Trinity Episc. Ch., 1991-93, 99—, jr. warden, 2000-02; bd. dirs. Holy Trinity Found., Gainesville, 1991-93; com. charter and canon law Episc. Diocese Fla., 1994-96; bd. dirs. Samaritan Ctrs. of North Ctrl. Fla., Inc., 1995-97 Named Fla. Bluekey Disting. Faculty mem., 2004, Woman of Distinction, Alachua County, 2005. Fellow Soc. Advanced Legal Studies (UK); mem. ABA, AAUW, Acad. Legal Studies in Bus. (ho. of dels. 1989-90, exec. com. 1992, 98—, sec.-treas. 1998-99, v.p. 1999-2000, pres-elect 2000-01, pres. 2001-02, exec. com. 2002-), Southeastern Bus. Law Assn. (proc. editor 1984-87, treas. 1985-86, v.p. 1986-87, pres.-elect 1987-88, pres. 1988-89, Iowa Bar Assn., LWV, U. Fla. Athletic Assn. (bd. dirs., v.p. chmn. fin. com.), Gainesville Womens' Forum (bd. dirs. 1988-91), Fla. Women' Network (bd. dirs. 1995-99), Univ. Woman's Club (Gainesville, Fla.), Rotary (bd. dirs. 1989-91, dist. scholarship com. 1997-99, regional scholarship com. 2000, chair 2001), Beta Gamma Sigma, Kappa Alpha Theta, Delta Sigma Pi Home: 2210 NW 6th Pl Gainesville FL 32603-1409 Office: U Fla Grad Sch Bus Gainesville FL 32611 Office Phone: 352-392-1048. Business E-Mail: virginia.maurer@cba.ufl.edu.

**MAURICE, PATRICIA ANN,** geochemist, educator; b. Manchester, Conn., Sept. 3, 1960; d. Robert Aime and Helen (Kennedy) M.; m. Gregory Richard Madey; 1 child, Alexander Gregory. BA, Johns Hopkins U., Balt., 1982; MS, Dartmouth Coll., 1985; PhD, Stanford U., 1994. Project chief hydrogeochemistry U.S. Geol. Survey, 1985-89; asst. prof. geochemistry Kent (Ohio) State U., 1994-99, assoc. prof., 1999-2000, U. Notre Dame, Ind., 2000—. Assoc. editor Geochimica et cosmochimica Acta, 2000—; mem. editl. bd. Chem. Geology, 1999—; contbr. numerous articles to profl. jours. Mem. Am. Geophys. Union, Am. Chem. Soc., Clay Minerals Soc. Office: Univ of Notre Dame Dept Civil Eng/Geol Sci Notre Dame IN 46556

**MAURICE, PAUL,** professional hockey coach; b. Sault Ste. Marie, Ont., Canada, Jan. 30, 1967; m. Michelle; 1 child, Sydney. Asst. coach Detroit Jr. Red Wings, 1988-93, head coach, 1993-94, Hartford Whalers, 1995—97, Carolina Hurricanes, 1997—2003, Toronto Marlies, 2005—06, Toronto Maple Leafs, 2006—. Asst. coach NHL All-Star Game, 1997. Named runner up Coach of Yr. nominamtion OHL, 1995. Mem. Compuware Hockey Orgn. Office: Toronto Maple Leafs Air Canada Ctr 40 Bay St Ste 300 Toronto ON Canada*

**MAURIN, JAMES E.,** real estate executive; Grad. in aerospace engring., La. State U., 1970; MBA, Tulane U., 1972. Acct. Ernst and Ernst, New Orleans; mng. ptnr. Maurin-Ogden Properties, Covington, La., 1975—; chmn. Stirling Properties, Covington, La., 1975—. Mem. bus. sch. coun. Tulane U., La. State U.; bd. dirs. Ochsner Found. Hosp. Mem.: Internat. Coun. Shopping Ctrs. (chmn. 2004—05), World Pres.'s Orgn. (chmn. La. chpt. 2005), Urban Land Inst. (chmn. La. dist. coun. 2002—04). Office: Stirling Properties 109 Northpark Blvd Covington LA 70433-5005 Office Phone: 985-898-2022. Business E-Mail: jmau@stirlingprop.com.

**MAURO, ANTHONY PETER,** small business owner; b. Red Bank, NJ, Feb. 20, 1955; s. Peter Anthony and Dolores Joyce Mauro; m. Carol Jean Albanese, Sept. 22, 1985. BA, Montclair State U., 1977; MBA, Monmouth U., 1985. Dist., gen. mgr. Gen. Med. Corp., Edison, NJ, 1988—93; v.p. Eldercare Co., Edison, NJ, 1993—95; owner, pres. Camtec Industries, Inc., Colts Neck, NJ, 1995—. Author: Take Me On Safari!, 2003. Avocations: writing, hunting. Office: Camtec Industries Inc 28 Saddle Ridge Colts Neck NJ 07722

**MAURO, RICHARD FRANK,** retired lawyer, investment company executive; b. Hawthorne, Nev., July 21, 1945; s. Frank Joseph and Dolores D. (Kreimeyer) M.; m. LaVonne M. Madden, Aug. 28, 1965; 1 child, Lindsay Anne. AB, Brown U., 1967; JD summa cum laude, U. Denver, 1970. Bar: Colo. 1970. Assoc. Dawson, Nagel, Sherman & Howard, Denver, 1970-72, Van Cise, Freeman, Tooley & McClearn, Denver, 1972-73, ptnr., 1973-74, Hall & Evans, Denver, 1974-81, Morrison & Forester, Denver, 1981-84; of counsel Parcel & Mauro, P.C., Denver, 1984—; pres. Parcel, Mauro & Hultin, P.C., Denver, 1988-90; of counsel Parcel, Mauro P.C., Denver, 1992-99; pres. Sundance Oil Exploration Co., 1985-88; exec. v.p. Castle Group, Inc., 1992-97, pres., 1998—; Richard F. Mauro, P.C., 1999—; ptnr. Moye, Giles, O'Keefe, Vermeire & Gorrell, 1999—2003, ret., 2003. Adj. prof. U. Denver Coll. Law, 1981-84. Symposium editor: Denver Law Jour., 1969-70; editor: Colorado Corporation Manual; contbr. articles to legal jours. Pres. Colo. Open Space Coun., 1974; mem. law alumni coun. U. Denver Coll. Law, 1988-91. Francis Wayland scholar, 1967; recipient various Am. jurisprudence awards Mem. ABA, Colo. Bar Assn., Denver Bar Assn., Colo. Assn. Corp. Counsel. (pres. 1974-75), Am. Arbitration Assn. (comml. arbitrator), Order St. Ives, Denver Athletic Club (bd. dirs. 1986-89). Home: 2552 E Alameda Ave Unit 128 Denver CO 80209-3330 Office: 1225 17th St Fl 29 Denver CO 80202-5534 Personal E-mail: dick.mauro@comcast.net.

**MAURY, RICHARD,** painter; b. Washington, D.C., Nov. 6, 1935; Attended, U. Md., College Park, 1954—55, Corcoran Art Sch., 1956, The Art Students League, 1957—59, L'Academia delle belle Arti, Florence, Italy, 1960—62. Exhibitions include Capricorn Gallery Bethesda Md, 1968, Nat. Press Club Washington, 1971, Medici Gallery London, 1972, Gerold Wunderlich & Co. NYC, 1986-95, Forum Gallery NYC, 2001-03, Forum Gallery LA, 2003; represented in collections of Am. Express Co., Arnot Art Mus. Elmira NY, Art Students League NYC, Flint Inst. Arts, Mich., Met. Mus. Art NYC, New Britain Mus. Art, Conn., Fogg Mus. Cambridge Mass., Uffizi Gallery Florence Italy. Mem.: NAD (academician). Mailing: c/o Forum Gallery 5th Fl 745 Fifth Ave New York NY 10151

**MAU-SHIMIZU, PATRICIA ANN,** lawyer; b. Jan. 17, 1953; d. Herbert G. K. and Leilani (Yuen) Mau; 1 child, Melissa Rose. BS, U. San Francisco, 1975; JD, Golden Gate U., 1979. Bar: Hawaii 1979. Law clk. State Supreme Ct., Honolulu, 1979-80; atty. Bendet, Fidell & Sakai, Honolulu, 1980-81; legis. atty. Honolulu City Coun., 1981-83, House Majority Staff Office, Honolulu, 1983-84, dir., 1984-93; chief clk. Hawaii Ho. of Reps., 1993—. Mem. Hawaii Bar Assn., Hawaii Women Lawyers, Jr. League Hawaii. Democrat. Roman Catholic. Home: 7187 Hawaii Kai Dr Honolulu HI 96825-3115 Office: State House Reps 415 S Beretania St Rm 027 Honolulu HI 96813-2407 Office Phone: 808-586-6127. Business E-Mail: pat@capital.hawaii.gov.

**MAUSKOPF, ROSLYNN R.,** prosecutor; b. Washington, 1957; d. Barry and Regina Mauskopf. BA, Brandeis U., 1979; JD, Georgetown U., 1982. Asst. dist. atty. N.Y. County Dist. Atty.'s Office, 1982—95, dep. chief spl. prosecution bur., 1992, chief frauds bur., 1993; insp. gen. State of N.Y., 1995—2002; U.S. atty. U.S. Dept. Justice, (ea. dist.) N.Y., Bklyn., 2002—. Chair Moreland Commn. N.Y.C. Schs., 1999. Office: US Attys Office 147 Pierrepont St Brooklyn NY 11201*

**MAUSKOPF, SEYMOUR HAROLD,** history professor; b. Cleve., Nov. 11, 1938; s. Philip and Dora (Trompeter) M.; m. Josephine Mary Album, Aug. 9, 1964; children: Deborah, Philip, Alice. AB, Cornell U., 1960; PhD, Princeton U., 1966. Instr. history Duke U., Durham, NC, 1964-66, asst. prof., 1966-72, assoc. prof., 1972-80, prof., 1980—; dir. program in sci. tech. and human values, 1979-84, dir. Focus Interdisciplinary programs, 1995—2003. Author: Crystals and Compounds, Molecular Structure and Composition in Nineteenth Century French Science, 1976, (with M.R. McVaugh) The Elusive Science; Origins of Experimental Physical Research, 1915-1940, 1980; editor: The Reception of Unconventional Science by the Scientific Community, 1979, Chemical Sciences in the Modern World, 1993. Recipient Dexter award for outstanding achievement in history of chemistry, 1998, award Sci. and Religion Course Program, Ctr. for Theology and the Natural Scis., 2002; NSF postdoctoral fellow, 1971-72, Charles Price fellow Chem. Heritage Found., 2000; NSF grantee, 1974, 92-93; Am. Philos. Soc. travel grantee, 1979; Nat. Endowment for Humanities summer stipend, 1982; Edelstein internat. fellow in history chem. scis. and tech. Beckman Ctr. U. Pa. and Hebrew Univ., Jerusalem, 1988-89. Mem. History Sci. Soc. travel grantee, 1979-83, coun. 1993-95). Jewish. Office Phone: 919-684-2581. E-mail: shmaus@duke.edu.

**MAUST, EZMA MINNIE,** music educator; b. Palco, Kans., Jan. 29, 1914; d. Omer Cobb and Myrtle A. (Arnold) Bingham; m. Paul C. Maust Sr. (dec. 1986); children: Paul C. Jr., Patricia A., Lana E., Delores J. (dec.). Diploma, Sherwood Music Sch., Chgo., 1968; AA, Butte Coll., 1976; BA, Calif. State U., Chico, 1979. Cert. tchr., Kans., U.S., Nat. Music Tchrs. Assn., Kans. Music Tchrs., Nat. Cert. Tchr. (NCTM). Music tchr., Paradise, Calif., 1953—73, Paradise, Calif., 1974—92, Kans., 1993—. Tchr. ext. course Sherwood Music Sch., Chgo., 1960-83; organist various chs., Paradise, 1974-92; adjudicator Nat. Guild Piano Tchrs., 1987-97. Pres. Torrance (Calif.) chpt. PTA, 1962-63. Mem. Nat. Guild Piano Tchrs. (chmn. Paradise chpt. 1982-92), Honor Roll Guild Tchrs. (cert.), Kans. Music Tchrs. Assn Republican. Baptist. Avocations: sewing, crocheting, camping, painting. Home: 752 Beverly St Wichita KS 67218-2508 E-mail: cobbmaust@juno.com.

**MAUST, JOSEPH J.,** agricultural products supplier; Pres. Active Feed Co., Pigeon, Mich., 1984—. Office: Active Feed Co 7564 Pigeon Rd Pigeon MI 48755-9701

**MAUZ, HENRY HERRWARD, JR.,** retired naval officer; b. Lynchburg, Va., May 4, 1936; s. Henry Herrward and Rene C. (Ball) M.; m. Margaret Catherine O'Neill, June 6, 1959; children: Sheila, David, Lynn, Daniel. BS, U.S. Naval Acad., 1959; BSEE, US Naval Postgrad. Sch., 1965; MBA, Auburn U., 1970. Commd. ensign USN, 1959, advanced through grades to adm., 1992, various ships and shore duty assignments, 1977-80; strategy and concepts officer Office of Chief Naval Ops. Washington, 1980-82; comdg. officer USS England, San Diego, 1980-82, chief of staff Carrier Group One, 1982-83; ops./readiness officer SHAPE Belgium, 1983-85; comdr. Cruiser/Destroyer Group 12 Mayport, Fla., 1985-86; ops./plans officer to comdr. in chief Pacific Fleet, Pearl Harbor, Hawaii, 1986-88; comdr. Seventh Fleet Yokosuka, Japan, 1988-90; dep. chief Office Naval Op.s, Washington, 1991-92; comdr. in chief U.S. Atlantic Fleet, 1992-94; ret. USN, 1994. Pres. Naval Postgrad. Sch. Found. Decorated D.S.M. with four gold stars, Def. Superior Svc. medal, Legion of Merit, Bronze Star with combat V device. Mem. U.S. Naval Inst., U.S. Naval War Coll. Found., Naval Hist. Found., Monterey Peninsula Country Club, Army-Navy Country Club. Avocations: golf, skiing. Home: 1608 Viscaino Rd Pebble Beach CA 93953-3303

**MAVES, MICHAEL DONALD,** medical association executive; b. East St. Louis, Ill., Oct. 14, 1948; BS, U. Toledo, 1970; MD, Ohio State U., 1973; MBA, U. Iowa, 1988. Lic. physician, Iowa, Mo., Ill., D.C.; diplomate Am. Bd. Otolaryngology. Rsch. fellow Ohio State U. Coll. Medicine, Columbus, 1977; fellow head and neck surgery Columbia-Presbyn. Med. Ctr., N.Y.C., 1978, U. Iowa Hosps. and Clinics, Iowa City, 1980-81; asst. prof. otolaryngology, head and neck surgery Ind. U. Sch. Medicine, Indpls., 1981-84, U. Iowa Hosps. and Clinics, Iowa City, 1984-87, assoc. prof., 1987-88; chmn. dept. otolaryngology St. Louis U. Sch. Medicine, St. Louis, 1988-94; exec. v.p. Am. Acad. Otolaryngology, Head and Neck Surgery, Alexandria, Va., 1994—2001; pres. Consumer Healthcare Products Assn., Wash., DC, 1999—2001; exec. v.p., CEO AMA, Chicago, 2002—. Lectr. in field. Contbr. articles to profl. jours. Capt. U.S. Army, 1974-76. Recipient numerous awards including Honor award and Pres.'s award Am. Acad. Otolaryngology-Head and Neck Surgery; named one of Best 1000 Physicians in U.S., 1992, 94, One of Best 400 Cancer Doctors in Am., Good Housekeeping, 1992. Fellow ACS; mem. AMA (RBRVS update com.), Am. Cancer Soc., Am. Acad. Facial & Plastic Reconstructive Surgery.*

**MAVIMA, PAUL,** finance educator; b. Kwekwe, Zimbabwe, Sept. 25, 1963; arrived in U.S., 1994; s. Gabriel Tranos and Theresa Mavima; m. Sienna Ruregerero Juta, Dec. 2, 1989; children: Shingirirai, Michelle, Rumbidzai, Takunda. BS, U. Zimbabwe, Harare, 1986; MPA, U. Zimbabwe, 1991; PhD in Pub. Administrn., Fla. State U., 2000. Adminstrn. officer Govt. Zimbabwe, Harare, 1987—88; lectr. U. Zimbabwe, Harare, 1988—94; legis. policy analyst Fla. Legislature, Tallahassee, 2000; asst. prof. Grand Valley State U., Grand Rapids, Mich., 2000—. Cons. State of Fla., Tallahassee, 1996—98, Mich. Assn. United Ways, Lansing, 2002—. Contbr. articles to profl. jours. Initiator, founding bd. mem. Grand Rapids Food Sys. Coun., 2001. Fulbright fellow, U.S. Govt., 1994. Mem.: ASPA, S.E. Evaluation Assn., Acad. Mgmt. (Best Conf. Paper award 1997). Office: Grand Valley State Univ 401 W Fulton St Grand Rapids MI 49504 Home: 3826 Wedgewood Dr Sw Wyoming MI 49519-3194

**MAVROIDIS, PETROS,** law educator; LLB, U. Thessaloniki, 1982; LLM in EC Law, Institut d'Etudes Européennes, 1984; LLB, Brussels U., 1984; LLM, U. Calif., Berkeley, 1986; Dr iuris, U. Heidelberg, 1991. Prof. law, chair European Cmty. and Internat. Econ. Law U. of Neuchâtel, 1996—; Edwin B. Parker prof. of foreign and comparative law Columbia Law Sch., NYC, 2003—. Vis. prof. European U. Inst. (EUI), Florence, 1999—2000, Columbia U., 1999—2000, Institut d'Etudes Politiques, Paris, 1998—2002, Woodrow Wilson Sch., Princeton U., 2003; legal advisor World Trade Orgn. Vis. scholar Max-Planck-Institut, Heidelberg, Germany, 1988—90. Fellow: Am. Soc. Internat. Law. Office: Columbia Law Sch 435 W 116th St New York NY 10027 Office Phone: 212-854-0067. Office Fax: 212-854-7946. E-mail: pmavro@law.columbia.edu, pm2030@columbia.edu.

**MAVROUDI, MARIA,** philologist, educator; BA, U. Thessaloniki, 1990; MA, Harvard U., 1992, PhD, 1998. Postdoctoral fellow Byzantine studies Dumbarton Oaks, 2000—01; postdoctoral tchg. fellow Hellenic studies Princeton U., 2001—02; asst. prof. U. Calif., Berkeley, 2002—05, assoc. prof., 2005. Author: A Byzantine Book on Dream Interpretation: The Oneirocriticon of Achmet and its Arabic Sources, 2002. MacArthur fellow, 2004. Office: U Calif Berkeley 2223 Dwinelle Hall Berkeley CA 94720 Office Phone: 510-643-4413. E-mail: mavroudi@berkeley.edu.

**MAVROUDIS, JOHN M.,** lawyer; b. N.Y.C., July 24, 1947; s. Michael and Anna (Hariton) Mavroudis; m. Anne Drogaris; children: Michael, Lauren. JD cum laude, Syracuse Coll. Law, 1972. Bar: Fla. 1972, N.Y. 1973, N.J. 1975. Assoc. Patterson, Belknap & Webb, N.Y.C., 1972—74; sole practice N.Y.C., 1974—77; sr. ptnr. Nicolette & Mavroudis, P.A., Hackensack, NJ, 1978—83, Klinger, Nicolette, Mavroudis & Honig, P.A., 1984—89, Mavroudis & Rizzo, 1990—. Editor: Syracuse Law Rev., 1972. Trustee The Greek Orthodox Cathedral of St. John the Theologian, NJ, Hellenic Coll. and Holy Cross Greek Orthodox Sch. Theology, Brookline, Mass., 1987—91; gen. counsel Greek Orthodox Archdiocese Am., 1997—2000; bd. advisors Syracuse Coll. Law, 2005—. Served to capt. USAR. Recipient Ellis Island Medal of Honor, 1999; Archon of the Ecumenical Patriarchate Constantinople. Mem.: Bar Assn. City N.Y., Justinian Soc. Office: 690 Kinderkamack Rd # 300 Oradell NJ 07649-1524 Office Phone: 201-262-3000.

**MAVROVIC, PAUL J.,** information technology executive; s. Ivo and Erna Mavrovic. BS in Bus. Mgmt., U. Hartford, Conn., 1987—91. Cert. Info. Sys. Security Profl. ISC2, 2005. Dir., info. tech. svcs. Urea Technologies Inc., Hackensack, NJ, 1991—99; pres. Pm Tech Inc, Hackensack, 1999—. 2nd v.p. Edgewater Apts Inc., New York, NY, 2000—04. Mem.: ISC2. Office: Pm Tech Inc 1 University Plz Ste 304 Hackensack NJ 07601 Office Phone: 201-488-0700. Office Fax: 201-488-1062. Business E-Mail: paul@pmtechinc.net.

**MAW, NICHOLAS,** composer, music educator; arrived in US, 1984; s. Clarence Frederick Maw and Hilda Helen Chambers; children: Natasha Helen, Adrian Lindsay. Attended, Royal Acad. Music, 1955—58. Composition tutor Royal Acad. Music, London, 1964—66, Milton Avery Grad. Sch. Arts, Bard Coll., 1990—99; fellow commoner in creative arts Trinity Coll., Cambridge U., England, 1966—70; vis. prof. composition Yale Sch. Music, New Haven, 1984, 1985, 1989, Boston U. Sch. Fine Arts, 1986; prof. composition Peabody Conservatory Music, Balt., 1999—. Music panel mem. Arts Coun. Gt. Britain; coun. mem. Performing Right Soc. Composer: Odyssey, Violin Concerto, Dance Scenes, Shahnama, Little Concert, Sonata Nortturna, Hymnus, Life Studies, Scenes & Arias, Sinfonia, Sonata For Strings and Two Horns, American Games, La Vita Nuova, The Voice of Love, String Quartet No. 1, 2, 3 & 4, Chamber Music for Wind and Piano, Piano Trio, Flute Quartet, Ghost Dances, Roman Canticle, Night Thoughts for a solo flute, Sonata for Solo Violin, One Foot in Eden Still I Stand, Sophies Choice, Concert Suite, Voices of Memory, Spring Music, Summer Dances, The World in the Eveing, (Operas) One Man Show, The Rising of the Moon, Sophie's Choice. Recipient Lili Boulanger prize, 1959, Midsummer City of London prize, 1980, Sudler Internat. Wind Band prize, 1991, Elise L. Stoeger prize, Chamber Music Soc. Lincoln Ctr., 1993. Fellow: Assn. Profl. Composers (founding mem., first chmn.), Royal Acad. Music. Office: Peabody Inst Music Dept 1 E Mount Vernon Pl Baltimore MD 21202-2391

**MAWN, LOUISE ANN,** ophthalmologist, educator; b. Woburn, Mass., June 4, 1963; d. James Joseph and Rita Marie Mawn; m. Gregg Thomas Tarquinio, July 27, 1991; children: Jonathan Tarquinio, Amelia Tarquinio children: Abigail Tarquinio, Christopher Tarquinio. MD, Wake Forest U., 1990. Diplomate Am. Bd. Ophthalmology. Asst. prof. ophthalmology U. Nebr. Med. Ctr., Omaha, 1997—98, Vanderbilt U. Med. Ctr., Nashville, 1998—, asst. prof. neurol. surgery, 2003—. Prin. investigator rsch. grant Nat. Eye Inst., Bethesda, 2001—. Author: (book) Preseptal and Orbital Cellulitis, 2002; contbr. articles to profl. jours. Fellow: Am. Acad. Ophthalmology; mem.: Can. Soc. Oculplastic Surgeons, Europeon Soc. Ophthalmic Plastic and Reconstructive Surgeons. Office: Vanderbilt U Med Ctr 8014 Medical Center East Nashville TN 37232 Office Phone: 615-936-1960. Business E-Mail: louise.mawn@vanderbilt.edu.

**MAWS, TONY,** chef; b. Boston, 1970; m. Karolyn Maws. BA in Psych., U. Mich. Chef Restaurant Clio, Blue Room, La Rivore, Lyon, France, La Folie, Postrio, San Francisco, Coyote Café, Santa Fe; owner, exec. chef Cragie Street Bistrot, Boston, 2002—. Featured in Travel & Leisure mag., Gourmet mag., Boston Globe. Named Boston's Best Up-and-Coming Chef, Boston mag., 2005; named one of Am. Top 10 New Chefs, Food & Wine mag., 2005, Boston's Rising Stars, StarChefs.com, 2006. Avocations: Red Sox, skiing, travel, reading cookbooks. Office: Craigie Street Bistrot 5 Craigie Cir Cambridge MA 02138 Office Phone: 617-497-5511.*

**MAX, BUDDY (BORIS MAX PASTUCH),** musician; b. Jan. 25; m. Freda Max; 1 child, John. Musician, performer as America's Singing Flea Market Cowboy: albums include: Many Styles and Sounds of Buddy Max, 1980, The Great Nashville Star, 1984, The Story of Freda and Bud, 1985, Cowboy Junction Stars, 1985, Tribute to Challenger's Crew of 7, 1986, With Our Friends at Cowboy Junction, 1989, Little Circle B, 1990, Together-Our Masterpiece, 1991, The Life to Fame and Fortune, 1992, Orange Blossom Special, 1996, Hall of Fame, Gold Record Award Winning Buddy Max, 1996, Hall of Fame, Tribute to Bing Crosby, 2004, Tribute to Jimmy Rodgers, Meridian, Mo., 2005, A Tribute to Al Dexter, 2005, Hospice Citrus County, 2005; composer songs include When the Magnolia Tree Blooms in Lecanto, The Story of Barney Clark, Hang My Guitar on the Wall, John F. Kennedy, The Challenger, Where the Maple Syrups Flow, Little Circle B, Way Up on the Mountain, Desert Storm, When Do I Love You, The Pretty Girl on TV. Recipient World Hall of Fame award and gold medalion, 1997, numerous trophies, awards for benefit and non-profit shows Am. Heart Assn., Am. Lung Assn., Girl Scouts Am., Citizens of Citrus County Fla., Deaf Svcs. of Citrus County, Statue of Liberty trophy and coin award Cowboy Junction Opry Country Music Show, 2000 for song I Love Miss America, cert. Young Marines of Citrus County, 2002; named Ky. Col., Gov. Paul E. Patton, 2001. Address: care Cowboy Junction 3949 W Hwy 44 & Jct 490 Lecanto FL 34461-9232 Office Phone: 352-746-4754.

**MAX, ELIZABETH,** retired language educator; b. Ft. Worth, Oct. 9, 1924; d. Frederick Ward and Alice Louise (Matthews) Maxwell; m. Herbert Jones McCorkle, Sept. 22, 1945 (div. Oct., 1969); children: Anne McCorkle Moore, Louise Kate McCorkle, Bruce Ward McCorkle, Sallie Matthews McCorkle. BS, Tex. Woman's U., 1944; MSLS, U. North Tex., 1966; EdD, Okla. State U., 1974. Cert. secondary, elementary tchr., Tex., Okla.; cert. sch. librarian, elem. and secondary various schs., Tex., 1950—69; instr. libr. sci. We. Ill. U., Macomb, 1969—70; asst. prof., fine arts libr. Okla. State U., Stillwater, 1970—72, asst. prof., coord. Libr. Sci. Dept., 1972—76, assoc. prof., 1976—82, prof. emerita, 1990—; supt. English Edn., 1982—90. Cons. Skelly Oil Co., Tulsa, Okla., 1976, The Ctr. for Local Govt. Tech., 1983-84, Stillwater Library Sys. Bd., 1985, media reviewer Previews; book revs. Sch. Libr. Jour., 1976-77. Author (with others): Teaching the Short Story, 1996; mem. reader panel New York Times, 1996—2001, mem. New York Times Online Panel, 2002—; contbr. articles to profl. jours. Pres. Meml. Soc. Central Pa., 1994, 96-99; vol. Nat. Disaster Relief, ARC, 1991-96; mem. Dem. Nat. Com.; women's rights activist. Mem. NEA, ALA, Nat. Women's Studies Assn. (founder), Okla State U. Women's Coun. (founder, 2d chair), Okla. Adult and Continuing Edn., Nat. Collegiate Players, Stillwater Okla. Writer's Club (pres., 1985-89), Greek Sabbatical, Nat. Coun. Tchrs. of English (comparative and world lit. com. 1990-97), Gen. Soc. Mayflower Descs., Parents and Friends of Lesbians and Gays, Emily's List, NARAL, ACLU, Phi Delta Kappa, Phi Kappa Phi, Beta Phi Mu. Home and office: 2414 North Glenwood Dr Stillwater OK 74075 Personal E-mail: elizabethmax@earthlink.net.

**MAX, ERNEST,** surgeon; b. Vienna, Mar. 3, 1936; m. Silvia Neger, Mar. 18, 1964; children: Yvette Rosa, Oliver Fredrick. MD, U. Chile, 1961. Diplomate Am. Bd. Surgery, Am. Bd. Colon and Rectal Surgeons, Am. Bd. Laser Surgery. Intern Hosp. San Borja, Santiago, Chile, 1960-61, resident, 1962-63; fellow in gen. surgery, colon and rectal surgery Lahey Clinic Found., Boston, 1969-70; resident Sinai Hosp., Balt., 1971-72, The Western Pa. Hosp., Pitts., 1972-74; resident in colon and rectal surgery Hermann Hosp., Houston, 1974-75, staff, 1975—, Park Plz. Hosp., 1975—, Meml. Hosp. Southwest, 1975—, Meml. NW Hosp., 1975—, Diagnostic Ctr. Hosp., 1975—, The Methodist Hosp., 1976—, Meml. City Hosp., 1976—, Houston NW Med. Ctr., 1976—, St. Luke's Episcopal Hosp. 1981—, Cypress Fairbanks, 1983—; chief of staff Meml. Hosp., 1983; staff HCA Med. Ctr., 1986—; CEO Colon and Rectal Clinic PA, 1989—. Clin. assoc. prof. surgery Baylor Coll. Medicine; clin. instr. surgery U. Tex. Med. Sch., Houston. Author: (with others) Current Diagnosis, 1971. Recipient Walter A. Fansler Travel Edn. award Am. Soc. Colon and Rectal Surgeons, 1974, Harriet Cunningham award Tex. Med. Assn., 1988, Best of the Best award Tex. Med. Assc., 1989; The Purdue Fredrick fellow Am. Soc. Colon and Rectal Surgeons, 1974, Mem. Am. Coll. Surgeons, Tex. Med. Assn., Harris County Med. Soc., Tex. Soc. Colon and Rectal Surgeons (pres. 1982-83), Am. Soc. Laser Medicine and Surgery, Internat. Soc. Univ. Colon and Rectal Surgeons, Lahey Clinic Alumni Assn., Am. Soc. Colon and Rectal Surgeons, Tex. Gulf Coast Colon and Rectal Surgical Soc. (sec. treas. 1992—), Colombian Soc. Colo-Proctology (hon. mem.). Office: Colon & Rectal Clinic PA 6550 Fannin St Ste 2307 Houston TX 77030-2723 Office Phone: 713-790-9250. Business E-Mail: emax@crchouston.com.

**MAXCY, BRENDAN DAVID,** education educator; s. David Hunter and Janet Griffin Maxcy. BS in Edn., U. Maine, 1990; MEd, U. Tex., 1996, PhD in Ednl. Adminstrn., 2004. Cert. tchr. Tex., Va. Tchr. The McCallie Sch., Chattanooga, 1991—94, David Crockett H.S., Austin, Tex., 1996—2000; asst. prof. U. of Mo.-Columbia, 2004—. Contbr. articles to profl. jours. Fellow, U. of Tex. Grad. Sch., 1999—2000, 1994—96. Mem.: Am. Ednl. Rsch. Assn. Office: University of Missouri-Columbia 202 Hill Hall Columbia MO 65211 Office Phone: 573-882-1249. Office Fax: 573-884-5714.

**MAXEY, BETTY JIM,** elementary school educator; b. Halfway, Oreg., June 17, 1933; d. George Allen and Bessie Zoe (Wood) Bradford; m. Gale Edward Maxey, Sept. 3, 1955; 1 child, Melanie. BA, Northwest Nazarene Coll., 1955. Cert. tchr., Idaho. Tchr. Nampa Sch. Dist., Idaho, 1955-69, Ind. Sch. Dist. of Boise, Idaho, 1971—99. Mem. Idaho State Textbood Adoption Com., Boise, 1983-90. Mem. Delta Kappa Gamma. Mem. Ch. of Nazarene. E-mail: gmaxey@mindspring.com.

**MAXEY, DEBRA S.,** secondary school educator; b. Gueydan, La., July 17, 1952; d. Ira William Searle and Caldonia Vinson Campbell; m. William Dale Maxey, Nov. 25, 1972; 3 children: BS, McNeese State U., Lake Charles, La., 1973. Tchr., coach Odom Mid. Sch., Beaumont, Tex., 1974—76; tchr., head dept. Cathedral Christian HS, Beaumont, 1996—. Mem. Symphony League SE Tex., Beaumont, 1991, Art Mus. SE Tex., Beaumont 2003. Mem.: Nat. Coun. Social Studies. Mem. Assemblies Of God. Avocations: reading, travel, baseball. Office: Cathedral Christian HS 8200 Hwy 105 Beaumont TX 77713

**MAXEY, RANDALL W.,** medical researcher, health science association administrator; BPharm, U. Cin., 1966; MD, Howard U., 1972, PhD in Cardiovascular Pharmacology, 1972. Chmn. bd. trustees Nat. Med. Assn., Washington, 2001—02; med. dir. Pacific Rim Dialysis Ctr., L.A., Calif. Supr. med. dir. hosp. in Guam. Office: Nat Med Assn 1012 Tenth St NW Washington DC 20001

**MAXFIELD, GUY BUDD,** lawyer, educator; b. Galesburg, Ill., May 4, 1933; s. Guy W. and Isabelle B. Maxfield; m. Carol Tunick, Dec. 27, 1970; children: Susan, Stephen, Karen. AB summa cum laude, Augustana Coll., 1955; JD, U. Mich., 1958. Bar: NY 1959. Assoc. White & Case, NYC, 1958—63; prof. law NYU Sch. Law, NYC, 1963—; sr. counsel Fox Rothschild LLP. Author: Tennessee Will and Trust Manual, 1982, Federal Estate and Gift Taxation, 8th edit., 2002, Florida Will and Trust Manual, 1984, Tax Planning for Professionals, 1986; contbr. articles to law jours. Trustee Acomb Found., Newark, 1974—. With U.S. Treasury. Fellow Am. Coll. Tax Counsel; mem. ABA, Am. Law Inst., NY State Bar Assn., Order of Coif, Phi Beta Kappa. Office: NYU Sch Law 40 Washington Sq S New York NY 10012-1099 Office Phone: 561-835-9600. Office Fax: 561-835-9602. Business E-Mail: gmaxfield@foxrothschild.com.

**MAXFIELD, JOHN EDWARD,** retired university dean; b. Los Angeles, Mar. 17, 1927; s. Chauncey George and Rena Lucile (Cain) M.; m. Margaret Alice Waugh, Nov. 24, 1948; children— Frederick George (dec.), David Glen, Elaine Rebecca, Nancy Catherine, Daniel John. BS, Mass. Inst. Tech., 1947; MS, U. Wis., 1949; PhD, U. Oreg., 1951. Instr. U. Oreg., 1950-51; mathmatician U.S. Naval Ordnance Test Sta., China Lake, Calif., 1949-56, head computing br., 1956-57, head math. div., 1957-60, lectr. UCLA, 1951-60; head prof. dept. math. U. Fla., 1960-67; prof., chmn. dept. math. Kans. State U., 1967-81; dean Grad. Sch. and univ. research La. Tech. U., 1981-92, dean emeritus, 1992—; ret. La. Tech. U., 1992. Mem. Am. Math. Soc., Math. Assn. Am., Soc. Indsl. and Applied Math., Sigma Xi. Home: 209 E Louisiana Ave Ruston LA 71270-4417

**MAXFIELD, LOUISA FONDA GRIBBLE,** executive secretary; b. Waco, TX, Sept. 27, 1924; d. Theodore Miles and Louise Irwin Gribble; m. Jack G.S. Maxfield, July 21, 1951 (dec.); children: Martha Woodson Maxfield Cottingham, Elizabeth Fonda. BA, Randolph-Macon Woman's Coll., Lynchburg, Va., 1945; M Liberal Arts, So. Meth. U., Dallas, 1982. Editor, indsl. house organ Gen. Tire & Rubber Co., Waco, Tex., 1945—51; bus. mgr. Maxfield Clin./Hosp., Dallas, 1976—84, Covenant Presbyn. ch., Carrollton, Tex., 1984—99. Named Woman of Yr., Carrollton, Tex., 2004; Paul Harris fellow, Rotary Internat.

**MAXFIELD, PETER CHARLES,** state legislator, lawyer, educator; b. 1941; AB, Regis Coll., 1963; JD, U. Denver, 1966; LLM, Harvard U., 1968. Bar: Colo. 1966, Wyo. 1969. Trial atty. Dept. Justice, 1966-67; assoc. Hindry, Erickson & Meyer, Denver, 1968-69; asst. prof. U. Wyo. Coll. Law, 1969-72, assoc. prof., 1972-76 prof., 1976-96, dean, 1979-87, prof. emeritus, 1996—. Vis. assoc. prof. U. N.Mex., 1972-73; Raymond F. Rice Disting. prof. U. Kans., 1984; Chapman Vis. Disting. prof., U. Tulsa, 1987; vis. prof. U. Utah, 1992. Author: (with Garr Houghton) Cases and Materials on the Taxation of Oil and Gas and Natural Resources Transactions, 1990, (with Allen and Houghton) Taxation of Mining Operation, 1981, 97, 2002; (with Trelease and Dietrich) Natural Resources Law on American Indian Lands, 1977. Coord. Wyo. State Planning 1988-89; spl. asst. Gov. Wyo. 1989-90; Dem. nominee U.S. Ho. Reps., 1990; mem. Wyo. Environ. Quality Coun., 1991-93; mem. Wyo. Senate, Laramie, 1993-97; counsel Gov. Wyo., 2006. Mem. Omicron Delta Kappa, Pi Delta Phi, Order of the Coif (faculty). Home: 1159 Escalera St Laramie WY 82072-5020 Office: U Wyo Coll Law PO Box 3035 Laramie WY 82071-3035 Business E-Mail: petemaxfield@earthlink.net.

**MAXMAN, SUSAN ABEL,** architect; b. Columbus, Ohio, Dec. 30, 1938; d. Richard Jack Abel and Gussie (Brenner) Seiden; m. Rolf Sauer; children: Andrew Frankel, Thomas Frankel, Elizabeth Frankel, Melissa, Abby, William Jr., Madeleine Sauer. Student, Smith Coll., 1960; MArch., U. Pa., 1977; HHD, Ball State U., 1993, U. Detroit Mercy, 1997. Registered profl. arch. Pa., Mich., NH, Nat. Coun. Archtl. Registration Bds. Project designer Kopple Sheward & Day, Phila., 1978-80; ptnr. Maxman & Sutphin, Phila., 1983-87; prin. Susan Maxman & Ptnrs., Phila., 1984—. Mem. bd. overseers Grad. Sch. Fine Arts U. Pa.; past chmn.; mem. corp. vis. com. MIT; mem. Planning and Design Commn., Ga. Inst. Tech. Works include design of Women's Humane Soc. Animal Shelter, Bensalem, Pa. (Northeastern Sustainable Energy Assn. Comml. Bldg. award, 1994, Metal Constrn. Assn. award 1995, Gov.'s Award for Environ. Excellence 1997, AIA Pa. Hon. award 1997), Camp Tweedale-Freedom Valley Girl Scouts USA (AIA Honor award, 1991), Cusano Environ. Edn. Ctr. at John Heinz Nat. Wildlife Refuge at Tinicum, Phila. (US Dept. Energy Fed. Energy Saver Showcase award, US Dept. Interior Environ. Achievement award, Top Ten Green Bldg. award AIAA 2003, AIA Cote Top Ten Green Buildings award, 2003), Robert Lewis House (McArthur award 1985), Phila., Restoration Pennock Farmstead (Grand Prize Nat. Trust Hist. Preservation 1995), Canaan Valley Inst. Hdqs., Renovation of Second Bank of US, Phila., Navy Yard Bldg. 10 (Honor award, AIA, Phila. chpt., 2004, citation of merit, PA Historic Presercation award), Natural Lands Trust Hdqs. Expansion, Media, Pa. (N.E. Sustainable Energy Assn. Bldg. award 2004, Exemplary Sustainable Bldgs. Industry Coun. award 2005), Kutztown U., Pa. Sisters Servants of the Immaculate Heart of Mary Renovation of the Motherhouse (Mich. Hist. Preservation Network Bldg. award 2003, Top Ten Green Bldg. award AIAA 2006), Renovation of U. Pa. Nursing Edn. Bldg., Phila., Barbara C. Harris Camp and Conf. Ctr., Greenfield, NH, Chestnut Hill Nat. Bank, Phila., Somerset (Pa.) Hist. Ctr., Seneca Rocks Visitor Ctr., Seneca Rocks, W.Va., Fort Necessity/Nat. Rd. Interpretive Edn. Ctr., Farmington, Pa., The Woods Residence Hall at Penn State Berks, Reading, Roberts Hall Renovation and Addition U. Pa. Law Sch., Phila. Navy Yard Bldg. 10 Restoration (Merit citation Phila. chpt. AIAA 2004), others. Mem. Eco-Efficiency Task Force Pres. Coun. Sustainable Devel.; past chair Environ. Coun., Urban Land Inst.; mem. trustee's coun. for Pa. Women, U. Pa. Recipient Disting. Dau. Pa. award Gov. Tom Ridge, 1995, Excellence citation Engring. News Record, Shattering the Glass Ceiling award Women's Nat. Dem. Club, Mayor's commendation City Phila., citation Pa. Ho. Reps., Gov.'s award Environ. Excellence, 1997, Pa. Hist. and Mus. Commn. Preservation Achievement award Preservation Alliance Greater Phila.; named to Pa. Honor Roll of Women, Pa. Commn. for Women, 1996, named 1 of Pa.'s Best 50 Women in Bus. 1996. Mem. AIA (nat. pres. 1993), Pa. Women's Forum, Forum Exec. Women, Carpenter's Co. Phila. Avocation: sailing. Office: 1600 Walnut St Fl 2D Philadelphia PA 19103-5405 Office Phone: 215-985-4410. Business E-Mail: smaxman@maxmanpartners.com.

**MAX NIKIAS, See NIKIAS, CHRYSOSTOMOS**

**MAXON, DON CARLTON,** mining executive, construction executive, consultant; b. Downers Grove, Ill., Dec. 23, 1914; s. Norman T. and Agnes M. (Matteson) Maxon; m. Mary T. Quirk, June 14, 1941; children: Maureen, Don, Paul, Anne, Lee; m. Ella Luanne Roy, Dec. 10, 1971; 1 stepchild, Tom Roy. Founder and pres. Maxon Constrn. Co., Barrington, Ill., 1936, Gen. Mining & Devel. Co., Santa Fe, 1967—, U.S. Communities S.A., Panama, 1974, Taipei, Taiwan, 1986, Carson City, Nev., 1989—, Bonanza Mines Internat., 1987. Rancher; builder U.S. Gypsum Co. Rsch. Village, Barrington, 1963; founder City of Streamwood, 1954, City of Green Valley, Ariz., 1963; internat. fin. cons. Prem. pres.'s club Pres. Johnson and Kennedy; mem. Pockets of Poverty Commn. With Seabees USN, 1942—45. Named a Tenn. Squire; recipient design awards for family communities of Streamwood, Barrington Woods, Trout Valley, Ill., Parents Mag., 1953, 1959, 1960. Mem.: Nat. Assn. Home Builders (Pres.'s Land Planning first place award 1954), Gov.'s Club Ariz. Democrat. Roman Catholic. Achievements include research in methods for testing and extracting gold from complex ores; finest possible environment for quality of life and sci. applications of all disciplines needed for a self contained city of 150,000 population. Home: 2586 E Ave De Maria Tucson AZ 85718-3056

**MAXSON, LINDA ELLEN,** biologist, educator; b. N.Y.C., Apr. 24, 1943; d. Albert and Ruth (Rosenfeld) Resnick; m. Richard Dey Maxson, June 13, 1964; 1 child, Kevin. BS in Zoology, San Diego State U., 1964, MA in Biology, 1966; PhD in Genetics, San Diego State U./U. Calif., Berkeley, 1973. Instr. biology San Diego State U., 1966-68; tchr. gen. sci. San Diego Unified Sch. Dist., 1968-69; instr. biochemistry U. Calif., Berkeley, 1974; asst. prof. zoology, dept. genetics and devel. U. Ill., Urbana-Champaign, 1974-76, asst. prof. dept. genetics, devel. and ecology, ethology & evolution, 1976-79, assoc. prof., 1979-84, prof., 1984-87, prof. ecology, ethology and evolution, 1987-88; prof., head dept. biology Pa. State U., State College, 1988-94; assoc. vice-chancellor acad. affairs/dean undergrad. acad. affairs, prof. ecology and evolutionary biology U. Tenn., Knoxville, 1995-97; dean Coll. Liberal Arts & Scis., prof. biol. scis. U. Iowa, Iowa City, 1997—. Exec. officer biology programs Sch. Life Scis., U. Ill., 1981-86, assoc. dir. acad. affairs, 1984-86, dir. campus honors program, 1985-88; vis. prof. ecology and evolutionary biology U. Calif., Irvine, 1988; mem. adv. panel rsch. tng. groups behavioral biol. scis. NSF, 1990-94; rsch. assoc. Smithsonian Instn. Author: Genetics: A Human Perspective, 3d edit., 1992; mem. editl. bd. Molecular Biology Evolution; exec. editor Biochem. Sys. & Ecology, 1993-2001; contbr. numerous articles to scientific jours. Recipient Disting. Alumni award, San Diego State U., 1989, Disting. Herpetologist award, Herpetologists' League, 1993. Fellow: AAAS; mem.: Soc. Molecular Biology and Evolution (treas. 1992—94, sec. 1992—95), Soc. Study Evolution, Soc. for Study of Amphibians and Reptiles (pres. 1991), Am. Men and Women in Sci., Phi Beta Kappa. Office: U Iowa 240 Schaeffer Hall Iowa City IA 52242-1409 Business E-Mail: linda-maxson@uiowa.edu.

**MAXWELL, ANDERS JOHN,** investment banker; b. San Francisco, Oct. 3, 1946; s. John L. and Deborah A. M.; m. Carlene S. Maxwell, 2000; children by previous marriage: Lauren A., Colin A., Ian W., Erin C., Ryan N. BArch, U. Calif., Berkeley, 1969; MBA, U. Pa., 1971. Analyst GE, 1971-73; v.p. GE Credit Corp., Stamford, Conn., 1973-83; mng. dir. Dean Witter Reynolds Inc., N.Y.C., 1983-87; v.p. Kidder Peabody & Co., Inc., N.Y.C., 1987-88; prin. L.F. Rothschild & Co., N.Y.C., 1988; v.p. Smith Barney, Harris Upham & Co., Inc., 1989-91, Lazard Frères & Co., N.Y.C., 1991-92; ptnr. Benedetto, Gartland & Greene, N.Y.C., 1992-94; v.p., gen. mgr. GE Capital Corp., Stamford, Conn., 1994-96; dir. Salomon Smith Barney Inc., N.Y.C., 1997-98; mng. dir. Barington Capital Group, N.Y.C., 1998; mng. dir., ptnr. Peter J. Solomon Co., N.Y.C., 1999—. Capt. U.S. Army, 1971. Office: Peter J Solomon Co 520 Madison Ave New York NY 10022 Office Phone: 212-508-1683. Business E-Mail: amaxwell@pjsolomon.com.

**MAXWELL, BRIAN T.,** theatre and communications professor; b. Marlette, Mich., Sept. 20, 1961; s. Kenneth George and Roberta Kathleen Maxwell; m. Andrea Maxwell, Aug. 9, 1986; children: Brandon, Travis, Alyssa, Evan, Seth. BA in Comm., Cornerstone U., Grand Rapids, Mich., 1985; BS in Edn., Calvin Coll., Grand Rapids, Mich., 1985; MA in Theatre, Bowling Green State U., Ohio, 1986; PhD in Ednl. Theatre, NYU, N.Y.C., 2000. Prof. Bapt. Bible Coll., Clarkes Summit, Pa., 1986—. Dir. over 50 theatre prodns. Mem.: Christians in Theatre Arts. Avocations: reading, theater, films, worship. Home: 309 Lansdowne Ave Clarks Summit PA 18411 Office: Bapt Bible Coll 538 Venard Rd Clarks Summit PA 18411 Office Phone: 570-585-9437. Personal E-Mail: brianmaxwell@bbc.edu.

**MAXWELL, CARLA LENA,** dancer, choreographer, educator; b. Glendale, Calif., Oct. 25, 1945; d. Robert and Victoria (Carbone) Maxwell. Student, Bennington Coll., 1963-64; BS, Juilliard Sch. Music, 1967. Mem. Jose Limón Dance Co., N.Y.C., 1965, prin. dancer, 1969—, acting artistic dir., 1977-78, artistic dir., 1978—. Lectr., tchr. in field. Dancer soloist Louis Falco Dance Co., 1967—71, Harkness Festival at Delacorte Theater, N.Y.C., 1964—, artist-in-residence Gettysburg Coll., 1970—, Luther Coll., Decorah, Iowa, 1971—, U. Idaho, 1973—; guest tchr., performer Centre Internat. de la Danse, Vichy, France, 1976—; choreographer Function, 1970—, Improvisations on a Dream, 1970—, A Suite of Psalms, 1973—, Homage to José Linón, Place Spirit, 1975, Aadvark Brothers: Schwartz and Columbo Present Please Don't Stone the Clowns, 1975, Blue Warrior, 1975, Sonata, 1980, Keeping Still Mountain, 1987; featured Carlota, Dances for Isadora, La Malinche, Comedy, The Moor's Pavane, The Winged, There is a Time, The Shakers, Brandenburg Concerto No. 4, Translucence, Caviar, Missa Brevis, Day on Earth, Two Ecstatic Themes, A Choreographic Offering, The Exiles, Sacred Conversations; dancer toured East and West Africa, 1969. Recipient Dance Mag. award, 1995; N.Y. State Cultural Coun. grantee, 1971. Home: 7 Great Jones St New York NY 10012-1135 Office: Jose Limon Dance Fedn 611 Broadway Fl 9 New York NY 10012-2608

**MAXWELL, CLAIR D.,** musician, director, educator; s. Clair D. and Jill Maxwell; m. Kristene A. Osten, July 29, 1995; children: Owen K., Anna C. MusB, Baldwin-Wallace Coll., Berea, Ohio, 1989—93; MusM, Cleve. Inst. Music, 1995. Assoc. dir. music, organist Ch. We. Res., Pepper Pike, Ohio, 1994—95; artistic dir. Internat. Concert Series, Red Bank, NJ, 1995—2003; dir. music ministries United Meth. Ch., Red Bank, 1995—2003; assoc. dir. Shrewsbury Chorale, NJ, 1997—2002; adj. prof. music Brookdale CC, Lincroft, NJ, 2002; artistic dir. Celebrate the Arts, Doylestown, Pa., 2003—; dir. music & arts Doylestown Presbyn. Ch., Pa., 2003—. Composer: (song) The Only One, 1987; musician: (performance) Dreams Come True: Songs from the Heart, 1999, A Century of American Music, 2004, It's a Broadway Life, 2005; composer: (composition) In Response to the Call: 13 Responses for Worship, 2003, (hymn) Spirit Divine, We Lift Our Song, 2003. Finalist award, Ft. Wayne Nat. Organ Competition, 1995. Mem.: Presbyn. Assn. Musicians, Am. Guild English Handbell Ringers, Am. Choral Dirs. Assn., Royal Sch. Ch. Music, Am. Guild Organists, Omicron Delta Kappa. Avocations: reading, travel, bicycling. Home: 1 Walden Way Chalfont PA 18914 Office: Doylestown Presbyn Ch 127 E Court St Doylestown PA 18901 Office Phone: 215-348-3531. Business E-Mail: clairm@dtownpc.org.

**MAXWELL, DAVID E.,** academic executive, educator; b. NYC, Dec. 2, 1944; s. James Kendrick and Gertrude Sarah (Bernstein) M.; children: Justin Kendrick, Stephen Edward. BA, Grinnell Coll., 1966; MA, Brown U., 1968, PhD, 1974. Instr. Tufts U., Medford, Mass., 1971-74, asst. prof., 1974-78, assoc. prof. Russian lang. and lit., 1978-89; dean undergrad. studies, 1981-89; pres. Whitman Coll., Walla Walla, Wash., 1989-93; dir. Nat. Fgn. Lang. Ctr., Washington, 1993-99; pres. Drake U., Des Moines, 1999—. Chmn. steering com. Coop. Russian Lang. Program, Leningrad, USSR, 1981-86, chmn. 1986-90; cons. Coun. Internat. Ednl. Exch., 1974-94, bd. dirs., 1983-92, 93-94, vice chair, 1991-92, cons. Internat. Rsch. Exchs., 1976-83; mem. adv. bd. Israeli Lang. Project Inst. Contbr. articles to scholarly jours. Cmty. bd. dirs. Wells Fargo; bd. dirs. Iowa Wellness Coun.; bd. dirs. Greater Des Moines Partnership; pres. Des Moines Higher Edn. Collaborative, 2000—; bd. dirs. Downtown Cmty Alliance, Des Moines. Fulbright fellow, 1970-71, Brown U., 1966-67, NDEA Title IV, 1967-70; recipient Lillian Leibner award Tufts U., 1970; citation Grad. Sch. Arts and Scis., Brown U., 1991. Mem. MLA, Am. Coun. Edn. (commn. on internat. edn., pres.'s coun. on internat. edn.), Assn. Am. Colls., Assn. Am. Higher Edn., Brown U. Alumni Assn. (exec. com.), Bus. Higher Edn. Forum (bd. trustees, coun. econ. devel.), Phi Beta Kappa. Democrat. Avocations: tennis, running, music. Office: Drake Univ Office of the Pres 2507 University Ave Des Moines IA 50311-4505 Office Phone: 515-271-2191. Business E-Mail: david.maxwell@drake.edu.

**MAXWELL, DAVID OGDEN,** federal agency administrator, mortgage company executive; b. Phila., May 16, 1930; s. David Farrow and Emily Ogden (Nelson) M.; m. Joan Clark Paddock, Dec. 14, 1968. BA, Yale U., 1952; LLB, Harvard U., 1955. Bar: Pa. 1955, D.C. 1955. From assoc. to prin. Obermayer, Rebmann, Maxwell & Hippel, Phila., 1959-67; from ins. commr. to adminstrn. and budget sec. State of Pa., 1967-70; gen. counsel HUD, Washington, 1970-73; pres., CEO Ticor Mortgage Ins. Co., 1973-81; CEO Fannie Mae, Washington, 1981-91; dir. bus. and non-profit grps. Bd. dirs. Centre Ptnrs., L.P. Bd. dirs. Sta. WETA-TV; trustee emeritus Nat. Gallery Art. With USNR, 1955-59. Office: 5335 Wisconsin Ave NW Ste 440 Washington DC 20015-2052

**MAXWELL, DIANA KATHLEEN,** education educator, primary school educator; b. Seminole, Okla., Dec. 16, 1949; d. William Hunter and ImoJean (Mahurin) Rivers; m. Clarence Estel Maxwell, Jly 3, 1969; children: Amanda Hunter, Alexandra Jane. BS, U. Md., 1972; M of Secondary Edn., Boston U., 1974; PhD, U. Md., 1980. Cert. tchr., counselor, Tex. Tchr. Child Garden Presch., Adelphi, Md., 1969-71; tchr., dir. PREP Edn. Ctr., Heidelberg, Germany, 1972-74; tchr. N.E. Ind. Schs. Larkspur, San Antonio, 1974-77, 89-90, Headstart, Boyds, Md., 1978; tchg. asst. Coll. Edn. U. Md., College Park, 1978—80; dir., founder First Bapt. Child Devel. Ctr., Bryan, Tex., 1982-84; instr. English lang. Yonsei Med. Ctr., Seoul, Republic of Korea, 1985-87; instr. Incarnate Word Coll., San Antonio, 1987-89; tchr. kindergarten Fairfax County Pub. Schs., Kings Park, Va., 1990-94; tchr. Encino Park, San Antonio, 1994-95; lectr. U. Tex., San Antonio, 1995-96; multi-age tchr., theater arts tchr. Ft. Sam Houston Elem. Sch., San Antonio, 1996—. Cons. Sugar N'Spice Child Devel. Ctr., Kilgore, Tex., 1980—90; trainer region XX Tex. Edn. Assn. TOPPT, 2000—03. Contbr. articles to newspapers. Block chairperson March of Dimes, 1991-93, 2000-, Am. Heart Assn., Fairfax, Va., 1991, 92, San Antonio, 2000-06, Am. Diabetes Assn., Fairfax, 1992; judge speaking com. Burke Optimists, 1992, 93, judge writing competition N.E. Ind. Sch. Dist., 1996; judge speech/debate competition Tex. Forensics League, MacArthur H.S., N.E. Ind. Sch. Dist., 2003—; sec. Cole H.S. Cougar Club, Ft. Sam Houston, San Antonio, 1996-97, v.p., 1997-2002, chair project graduation, 2002—; Bible tchr. 1st Bapt. Ch., Alexandria, Va., 1993-95; tchr. kindergarten Trinity Bapt. Ch., San Antonio, 1995-99, 2005 tchr. 1st grade, 2001-05. Named one of Outstanding Young Women of Am., 1983; Md. fellow State of Md., 1978, 79; Tech. grantee Tex. Edn. Agy., San Antonio, 1990, State of Va. and Fairfax County, Springfield, 1991; recipient Yellow Rose of Tex. vol. award Gov. of Tex., 1996, Dean's Outstanding Tchg. award U. Tex., San Antonio, 1995-96, Ft. Sam Houston Hero award, 2001, 02. Mem. ASCD, Assn. Profl. Tchr. Educators. Avocations: oriental brush painting, singing, collecting butterflies, children/teacher advocate. Home: 2602 Country Square St San Antonio TX 78209-2235 Office: Ft Sam Houston Elem Sch 3370 Nursery Rd San Antonio TX 78234-1479 E-mail: kmaxwell@fshisd.net.

**MAXWELL, DONALD MALCOLM,** clergyman, theology studies educator; b. Watford, Eng., Apr. 6, 1934; s. Arthur S. and Rachel Elizabeth (Joyce) M.; m. Eileen J. Bolander, Aug. 25, 1955; children: Wendy E. Maxwell Henderson, D. Kevin. BA in Theology and Biblical Langs., Pacific Union Coll., 1956; MA in Systematic Theology, Andrews U., 1958; PhD in Biblical Studies New Testament, Drew U., 1968. Ordained to ministry Seventh-Day Adventist Ch., 1960. Pastor No. Calif. Conf. Seventh-Day Adventists, Oakland, Calif., 1956-64; instr. religion Union Coll., Lincoln, Nebr., 1964-65; prof. religion Walla Walla Coll., College Place, Wash., 1965-78, v.p. acad. affairs, 1978-83; pres. Pacific Union Coll., Angwin, Calif., 1983—2001, pres. emeritus, 2001, chmn. dept. religion, 2004—05; pastor Pacific Union Coll. Ch., 2002—03. Trustee Redbud Cmty. Hosp., Clearlake, Calif., 2002—. Recipient Charles Elliot Weniger award of excellence, 1996, Edn. award of excellence, 2001; Rockefeller fellow, 1967-68; Drew U. scholar, 1967-68; named Tchr. of Yr., Wash. State Auto Assn., 1971. Mem. Soc. Biblical Lit. Seventh-Day Adventist. Avocations: golf, boating, gardening. Office: Pacific Union Coll 1 Angwin Ave Angwin CA 94508-9713 Office Phone: 707-965-6206. Business E-Mail: mmaxwell@puc.edu.

**MAXWELL, J. B.,** financial consultant, marketing professional, consultant; b. Charleston, W.Va., Sept. 30, 1944; s. J. B. and Martha (Hornor) Maxwell; m. Valerie Ronson, Oct. 13, 1983; 1 child, Jennifer. BS, Salem (W.Va.) Coll., 1967; M in Mktg., Harvard U., 1970. Lic. real estate sales, ins., securities, registered commodity rep., accredited mgmt. cons. and fin. planner, registered fin. planner, investment advisor, accredited asset mgmt. specialist. Exec. Textron Inc., Providence, 1968-71; pres. Martech Inc. and 6 other cos., Portland, Maine, 1968—; v.p. E. F. Hutton Co., Portland, 1976-83; 1st v.p. fin. planning Dean Witter, Boston, 1983-90; pres. Planning Svcs. Corp., Boston, 1990-92; 1st v.p. Gruntal & Co., Inc., Boston, 1992—2003; with Ryan Beck & Co., Wellesley, Mass., 2003—. Author: handbooks, booklets; contbr. articles to profl. jours., Portland Coll. Art, 1980—93. Bd. dirs. Wellness Inst., Boston, 1990—91. Recipient Bronze award, Nat. Acad. Scis., 1962. Mem.: Nat. Assn. Security Dealers (former br. office mgr.), World Affairs Coun., Inst. Mgmt. Cons., Am. Mktg. Assn., Am. Mgmt. Assn., Internat. Assn. Fin. Planning, Boston C. of C., Rotary. Avocations: golf, woodworking, travel, literature. Home: 15 Bailey Road Arlington MA 02476 Office: Oppenheimer & Co 155 Federal St 14th Fl Boston MA 02110 Office Phone: 866-548-4763 4918. E-mail: j.b.maxwell@opco.com.

**MAXWELL, JACK ERWIN,** manufacturing executive; b. Cleve., July 17, 1926; s. Fred A. and Gertrude F. (Haug) M.; m. Martha Jane Miller, Dec. 28, 1966; children by previous marriage: Laura Jane, Fredric, Elizabeth Grant, Carla Moore, Linda Hanson. BS, Case Inst. Tech., 1949; MBA, Harvard U., 1952. Indsl. engr. Lincoln Electric Co., Cleve., 1952—53; mgr. purchase analysis Ford Motor Co., Dearborn, Mich., 1953—57; mgr. Booz, Allen & Hamilton, Inc., Detroit, 1957—69; v.p. corp. devel. Am. Motors Corp., Detroit, 1969—71; v.p. adminstrn., 1967—76, v.p. non-automotive subsidiaries, 1976—79, v.p. diversified ops., 1979—80; chmn., pres. Wheel Horse Products, Inc., South Bend, Ind., 1974—80; chmn., CEO Ingersoll Products Corp., Chgo., 1980—86; pres. Wellmax, Inc., 1974—. Served with USNR, 1944-46. Mem. Case Inst. Tech. Alumni Assn., Harvard Bus. Sch. Alumni Assn., Detroit Athletic Club, Detroit Econ. Club, Chgo. Club, Old Club, Tau Beta Pi, Theta Tau. Address: Ste 105-37 1000 S Old Woodward Ave Birmingham MI 48009 Office Phone: 248-646-3554. Personal E-mail: wellmaxx@earthlink.net.

**MAXWELL, JEROME EUGENE,** corporate executive; b. Princeton, Ill., June 2, 1944; s. Emmett Eugene and June (Erickson) M.; m. Cynthia Jane O'Connell, July 30, 1977; children: Eric Vaughn, Christina Dawn, Jeremy Emmett, Jason Daniel, Nicholas Mark. BSEE, So. Meth. U., 1967, MSEE, 1971. Maintainability engr. product support divsn. Collins Radio Co., Richardson, Tex., 1965-67, jr. engr. computer sic. divsn., 1967-70; sr. engr. TRW Electronics Products, Inc., Colorado Springs, Colo., 1970-73, mgr. engring., 1973-79, mgr. program mgmt. office, 1979-81, gen. mgr. space electronics mfg. divsn., 1981-86; pres., CEO G&S Sys., Inc., Bedford, Mass., 1986-87, Atec, Inc., Houston, 1987-91; v.p., divsn. dir. Nat. Sys. & Rsch. Co., Colorado Springs, 1992-94; pres., chmn. bd. dirs. Tech. Assocs. of Colo., Inc., Colorado Springs, 1994-96; pres., CEO Advanced Profl. Tng., Inc., Colorado Springs, 1996—. Patentee in field. Mem. adv. coun. U. Colo., Colorado Springs, 1973-86, U. So. Colo., Pueblo, 1974-78; Webelo leader, asst. pack leader Boy Scouts Am., 1976-77; fin. chmn. Ascension Luth. Ch., 1981-86; cons. to cmty. edn. coord. for computer sys. and equipment, 1980-86; mem. Soli Deo Gloria Choir, 1999—. Fellow: Nat. Assn. of Ch. Bus. Administr.; mem.: AIAA (sr.), Mesa Sertoma (charter, bd. dirs.), Assn. Old Crows (pres. space chpt.). Republican. Personal E-mail: president@yourtraining.net.

**MAXWELL, JOE (JOSEPH EDWIN MAXWELL),** former lieutenant governor; b. Kirksville, Mo., Mar. 17, 1957; s. Robert E. and Molly B. Maxwell; m. Sarah Baker; children: Megan, Shannen. BS in Secondary Edn., Social Studies, U. Mo., 1986, JD, 1990. Farmer, Rush Hill, Mo., 1976-78; ptnr., operator Maxwell Svc., Laddonia, Mo., 1978-84; rural mail carrier U.S. Postal Svc., Rush Hill, 1980-84; outstate field coord. Travis Morrison's Campaign for State Auditor, Mo., 1986; Mo. state field coord. Richard Gephardt for Pres., 1986-87; atty. pvt. practice Mexico, Mo., 1992—2001; mem. Mo. Ho. Reps., 1990-94, Mo. State Senate, 1995—2001; lt. gov. State of Mo., Jefferson City, 2001—05. Mem. Senate Appropriations, Judiciary, Labor and Indsl. Rels., Pub. Health and Welfare coms.; vice chair Elections, Corrections, and Vet's Affairs coms.; chair Commerce and Environment Com. Assoc. editor-in-chief Mo. Jour. of Dispute Resolution, 1989. Mem. Am. Legion, 1982—, adj. Post 510, 1982-84; mem. Young Dem. Clubs Mo., 1982—, jud. coun. Young Dems. Am., 1985, pres., 1984-87, 9th Congl. Dist. chmn., 1982; mem. Laddonia Bapt. Ch., 1975—, Sunday Sch. tchr. 1990-91, pulpit com.; bd. dirs. Handi-Shop Inc., Mexico, 1981-84, chmn. mfg. and mktg. com., 1982-84; bd. dirs. Boy Scouts Am. Troop 94, 1980-82. Recipient St. Louis Globe Dem. award for outstanding achievement, 1979, Cert. of

Appreciation, Troop 94, Boy Scouts Am., 1982, Mo.'s Outstanding Male Young Dem. award, 1987, George B. Freeman award for outstanding svc., 1987, Appreciation award Mo. Bar, 1992, Mo. Ho. of Reps. Resolution # 624 for exceptional svc. Mo., 1987, Mo. State Senate Resolution # 382 for exceptional svc. Mo., 1987; named one of Outstanding Young Men of Am., 1983, 85. Mem. Moose, Jaycees (Laddonia chpt. pres. 1978-79, coord. Laddonia Area Blood Drive, coord. Laddonia City Clean-up Day, chmn. Mexico Soybean Festival 1989, chmn. Lenten Breakfast 1990, Presdl. award of honor 1979), Kappa Delta Pi, Golden Key Nat. Honor Soc. Democrat.*

**MAXWELL, JUDITH,** think-tank executive, economist; b. Kingston, Ont., Can., July 21, 1943; d. James Ruffee and Marguerite Jane (Spanner) McMahon; m. Anthony Stirling Maxwell, May 8, 1970; 2 children. B in Commerce, Dalhousie U., 1963, LLD, 1991; postgrad., London Sch. Econs., 1965-66; LLD, Queen's U., 1992. Researcher Combines Investigation Br. Consumer and Corp. Affairs, Ottawa, Can., 1963-65; econs. writer, mem. editorial bd. Fin. Times, Montreal, Que., Can., 1966-72; dir. policy studies C.D. Howe Inst., Montreal, 1972-80; cons. Esso Europe Inc., London, Eng., 1980-82, Coopers & Lybrand, Montreal, Que., 1982-85; chmn. Econ. Council Can., Ottawa, Ont., 1985-92; exec. dir. Queen's-U. Ottawa Econ. Projects, 1992—. Dir. Can. Found. for Econ. Edn., 1985-88, Inst. for Rsch. on Pub. Policy, 1987-88. Author: Energy From the Arctic, 1973; (with C. Pestieau) Economic Realities of Contemporary Confederation, 1980; (with S. Currie) Partnership for Growth: Corporate University Education in Canada, 1984. Active Ont. Premier's Coun., 1988-90, Nfld. and Labrador Sci. and Tech. Adv. Coun., 1988-90. Mem. Can. Assn. Bus. Econs. (pres. 1976-77), Montreal Econs. Assn. (pres. 1975-76). Office: Canadian Policy Rsch Networks 600-250 Albert St Ottawa ON Canada K1P 6M1 Office Phone: 613-567-7500. E-mail: jmaxwell@cprn.org.

**MAXWELL, QUENTIN D.,** art educator; b. Smithville, Mo., Dec. 21, 1963; s. Loyd D. and Elma Jean Maxwell; m. Darla G. McKeefer, May 16, 1992; children: Amanda D. Simmonds, Evan J. Austin. BS, Coll. of Ozarks, 1995; MS in Counseling, SW Mo. State U., 2005. Cert. K-12 art tchr., secondary sch. counselor Mo. Tchr. Conway H.S., Mo., 1995—. Mem. Highland Pk. Ch. of God, Lebanon, Mo.; ch. spkr., mem. Gideons Internat., Lebanon, Mo., 1995—. Bonner Scholars Cmty. Svc. scholarship, Bonner Found., 1995-2005, Transitions Counselor Program grant, Mo. Dept. of Elem. and Secondary Edn., 2001-2003. Mem.: Kappa Delta Pi (life). Mem. Ch. Of God. Avocations: fishing, hunting, art, drawing, pottery. Office: Conway HS 726 W Jefferson Ave Conway MO 65632 Office Phone: 417-589-2941 1023. Business E-Mail: qmaxwell@conwayschooldistrict.com.

**MAXWELL, RAYMOND ROGERS,** retired accountant; b. Parmer County, Tex., Jan. 7, 1918; s. Frederick W. and Hazel Belle (Rogers) M.; m. Jeanne Hollarn, June 16, 1945 (dec. Dec. 1987); children: Donald R., Bruce Edward, Sabrina G. Ed B-J., Western Ill. State Tchrs Coll., 1941; MBA in Acctg., U. Fla., 1949; postgrad., UCLA, 1965-68. CPA, Fla., Calif. Asst. to bus. mgr. Western Ill. State Tchrs. Coll., Macomb, 1939-41; apprentice acct. Charles H. Lindfors, CPA, Ft. Lauderdale, Fla., 1946-48; acct/auditor Frederic Dunn-Rankin & Co, CPA, Miami, Fla., 1948-49; CPA staff Charles Costar, CPA, Miami, 1951; resident auditor/CPA prin. Raymond R. Maxwell CPA, Ft. Lauderdale, 1951-56; supt. pub. instrn. Broward County, Ft. Lauderdale, 1956-61; staff asst. in fin. North Am. Aviation, Inc., El Segundo, Calif., 1961-65; acctg. prin. Raymond R. Maxwell, CPA, Whittier, Calif., 1968-2000. Part-time tchr. asst. UCLA, 1965, teaching asst., 1966, 67; instr. Calif. Poly., 1967. Active precinct election bds., Whittier, L.A. County, 1989, 98-2000; 1st reader First Ch. of Christ, Scientist, Whittier, 1990-92, 96-98, exec. bd., 1989, exec. bd. chmn., 1993, participant Bible Explorations, 1991-92. 1st lt. USAAF, 1942-46. Recipient Am. Medal of Honor, Am. Bibliog. Inst., 2002. Republican. Avocations: dance, swimming, computers. One, with God, is a majority.

**MAXWELL, RICHARD ANTHONY,** retail executive; b. N.Y.C., Apr. 1, 1933; s. Arthur William and Mary Ellen (Winestock) M.; m. Jacqueline Ann Creamer, Oct. 27, 1962. Student, NYU, 1957-58, Acad. Advanced Traffic, 1959. Import ops. mgr. Associated Merchandising Corp., N.Y.C., 1950-52, 56-65; v.p. Associated Dry Goods Corp., N.Y.C., 1965-86, sr. v.p. mktg., 1980-82, exec. v.p. mktg., 1982-86; pres. A.D.G. Export Mktg., Florence, Italy, 1982-86, Associated Dry Goods Ltd., Hong Kong, 1983-86, Inter Textile Corp., 1987-89; with Matol Botanical Internat. Ltd.; exec. v.p. Matol World Corp., Montreal, Que., Canada, 1992-94; dir. Matol Botanical New Zealand, 1994-96; v.p. internat. ops. L'Aprina Internat. Inc., 1994-96; chief internat. officer Camelot Concept Co., Montreal, 1995-96; CFO Showcase Prodns., Phoenix, 1996; exec. v.p. Harmony House Internat., Phoenix, 1996-97, IGW Trust, Phoenix, 1997-99, Pre-Paid Legal Svcs., Inc., 1999—; pres. Team 39, Inc., Dunedin, Fla., 2000-2001; dir. Presley Promotions Inc., Memphis, 2001—02; pres., COO Home Farms Techs. Inc., Brandon, Man., Canada, 2002—. Mem. industry sector adv. com. Dept. Commerce, 1984-93; mem. shippers adv. com. Nat. Maritime Coun. Served with USAF, 1952-56. Recipient Silver medal for contbns. to trade expansion, Republic of China, 1980; appt. to rank of comdr. in Order of Merit in recognition of improvement of trade between Italy and U.S., Republic of Italy, 1985. Mem. Am. Assn. Exporters and Importers (past pres., dir.), Shippers Conf. Greater N.Y. (past pres., dir.), Nat. Retail Mchts. Assn. (vice chmn. fgn. trade com.), Nat. Com. Internat. Trade Documentation (past vice chmn. gen. bus. com.), Transp. Assn. Am., Italy-Am. C. of C. (past pres., dir.), Royal Soc. of Italian Legion of Merit (dir.). Home: 2408 Stag Run Blvd Clearwater FL 33765-1832

**MAXWELL, RICHARD CALLENDER,** retired lawyer, educator; b. Mpls., Oct. 7, 1919; s. Bertram Wayburn and Blossom (Callender) M.; m. Frances Lida McKay, Jan 27, 1942; children: Richard Callender, John McKay. BSL, U. Minn., 1941, LLB, 1947; LLD (hon.), Calif. Western U., 1983; LLD, Southwestern U., 1993. Assoc. prof. U. ND, 1947-49, U. Tex., 1949-51, prof., 1951-53; counsel Amerada Petroleum Corp., 1952-53; prof. UCLA, 1953-81; dean UCLA Sch. Law, 1959-69, Connell prof., 1979-81, Connell prof. emeritus, 1981—; Chadwick prof. Duke U. Sch. Law, 1981-89, Chadwick prof. emeritus, 1989—. Vis. prof. Columbia U., 1955; vis. Alumni prof. U. Minn., 1970-71; Fulbright lectr. Queen's U., No. Ireland, 1970; vis. Ford Found. prof. U. Singapore, 1971; Thompson prof. U. Colo., 1982; vis. prof. Hastings Coll. Law, 1976, Duke U., 1979-80, U. Tex., 1985; pres. Minn. Law Rev., 1946; chmn. Coun. Legal Edn. Opportunity, 1971-72; pres. Assn. Am. Law Schs., 1972; chmn. adv. com. law Fulbright Program, 1971-74, chmn. adv. com. U.K., 1974-77; mem. com. on gas prodn. opportunities NRC, 1977-78; mem. law sch. editl. ad. bd. West Pub. Co., 1971-94. Author: (with S. A. Riesenfeld) Cases and Materials on Modern Social Legislation, 1950, (with H.R. Williams and C.J. Meyers) Cases on Oil and Gas Law, 1956, 7th edit., (with Patrick H. Martin, Bruce M. Kramer), 2002, (with S.A. Riesenfeld) California Cases on Security Transactions, 1957, 4th edit. (with S.A. Riesenfeld, J.R. Hetland, W.D. Warren), 1991; West Coast editor Oil and Gas Reporter, 1953-. Mem. LA Employee Rels. Bd., 1971-74; bd. dirs. Constl. Rights Found., 1963-81; trustee Calif. Western U., 1979-81; bd. visitors Duke U. Sch. Law, 1973-79, chmn. bd. Pvt. Adjudication Ctr., 1984-89; bd. visitors Southwestern U. Sch. Law, 1981-90. Served to lt. comdr. USNR, 1941-46. Recipient Clyde O. Martz Tchg. award Rocky Mountain Mineral Law Found., 1994, Disting. Tchg. award, UCLA, 1977, Duke Law Sch., 1986, UCLA medal, 1982. Mem. ABA (com. on youth edn. for citizenship 1975-79, spl. com. on pub. understanding about the law 1979-84), Order of Coif (nat. exec. com. 1980-86). Office: Duke U Sch Law Durham NC 27708-0362 Office Phone: 919-613-7045. Personal E-mail: rcmaxwell@mindspring.com.

**MAXWELL, ROBERT EARL,** federal judge; b. Elkins, W.Va., Mar. 15, 1924; s. Earl L. and Nellie E. (Rexstrew) M.; m. Ann Marie Grabowski, Mar. 29, 1948; children— Mary Ann, Carol Lynn, Ellen Lindsay, Earl Wilson. LLD (hon.), Davis and Elkins Coll., 1984; LLB, W.Va. U., 1949. Bar: W.Va. 1949. Practiced in Randolph County, 1949; pros. atty., 1952-61; U.S. atty. for No. Dist. W.Va., 1961-64; judge U.S. Dist. Ct. (no. dist.) W.Va., Elkins, 1965—94, sr. judge, 1994—; judge Temp. Emergency Ct. of Appeals, 1980-89. Past chmn. budget com. Jud. Conf. U.S.; former mem. exec. com.

Nat. Conf. Fed. Trial Judges; former mem. adv. bd. W.Va. U. Mem. bd. advisors W.Va. U., past chmn.; bd. advisors Mary Babb Randolph Cancer Ctr. Recipient Alumni Disting. Svc. award Davis and Elkins Coll., 1969, Religious Heritage Am. award, 1979, Outstanding Trial Judge award W.Va. Trail Lawyers Assn., 1988, Order of Vandalia award W.Va. U., Outstanding Alumnus award, 1992, Tenured Faculty Mem. Recognition award Bd. Govs., Def. Trail Coun., W.Va., 1992, Cert. of Merit, W.Va. State Bar, 1994, Justitia Officium award Coll. of Law, W.Va. U., 1994, award of merit W.Va. Bar Assn., 2004, Lawyer Citizen of Yr. award, 2005, Humanitarian award Odd Fellows, 2005; fellow W.Va. Bar Found., 1999; Melvin Jones fellow Lions Internat. Found., 2001. Mem. Nat. Conf. Federal Trial Judges, Dist. Judges Assn. 4th Cir. (past pres.), Moose (life), Lions (life), Beta Alpha Beta (merit award), Elkins-Randolph County C. of C. (citizen of yr. 1994). Office: US Dist Ct No Dist PO Box 1275 Elkins WV 26241-1275 E-mail: judge_maxwell@wvnd.uscourts.gov.

**MAXWELL, ROBERT WALLACE, II,** lawyer; b. Sept. 6, 1943; s. Robert Wallace and Margaret Maxwell; m. Mamie Lee Payne, June 18, 1966; children: Virginia, Robert, William. BS magna cum laude, Hampden-Sydney Coll., 1965; JD with honors, Duke U., 1968. Bar: Ohio 1968. Assoc. Taft, Stettinius & Hollister, Cin., 1968—75, ptnr., 1975—88, Keating, Muething & Klekamp, Cin., 1988—. Instr. U. Cin. Sch. Law, 1975—76. Elder Wyoming Presbyn. Ch.; bd. dir. Contemporary Arts Ctr. of Cin., Cin. Ballet Co. Mem.: ABA, Am. Assn. Mus. Trustees. Republican. Home: 535 Larchmont Dr Cincinnati OH 45215-4215 Office: Keating Muething & Klekamp 1 E 4th St Ste 1400 Cincinnati OH 45202-3752 Office Phone: 513-579-6594. E-mail: rmaxwell@kmklaw.com.

**MAXWELL, ROBERT WILLIAM,** investment banker, financial analyst; b. Brentwood, Essex, Eng., June 19, 1948; s. William and Dilys Maxwell; m Vanessa Vorman; children: Duncan, Spencer, Kennon. BA in Econs., Manchester, Eng., 1970; MBA, Harvard U., 1977. Registered NASD Series 7 & 24. Lending officer Bank of Montreal Internat., Que., Canada, 1970—75; mgr. new ventures Freeport-McMoRan, New Orleans, 1977—87; pres., CEO Financing for Sci. Internat., Farmington, 1987—97; sr. v.p., CFO ProHealth Physicians, Farmington, 1997—99; mng. dir., founder Ironwood Capital Ltd., Avon, Conn., 1999—2001; prin. Brentwood Capital, LLC, Farmington, Conn., 2001—. Trustee Mooreland Hill Sch., Kensington, 1996—99; pres. Farmington Field Club, 2002—. Mem.: Harvard Club of N.Y. Business E-Mail: rmaxwell@brentwoodsecurties.com.

**MAXWELL, SARA (SALLY) ELIZABETH,** psychologist, educator, speech pathology/audiology services professional, director; b. DuQuoin, Ill., Jan. 23; d. Jean A. (Patterson) Green; m. David Lowell Maxwell, Dec. 27, 1960 (div. Mar. 1990); children: Lisa Marina, David Scott; m. James F. Manning, July 19, 1997 (div. Aug. 1998). BS, So. Ill. U., 1963, MS, 1964, MS in Edn., 1965; MEd, Boston Coll., 1982, PhD, 1992; postgrad., Harvard U., 1983. Cert. and lic. speech-lang. pathologist, early childhood specialist, guidance counselor, sch. adjustment counselor, behavior specialist, EMT. Clin. supr. Clin. Ctr. So. Ill. U., Carbondale, 1964-65, grad. clin. instr., 1965-66; speech/lang. pathologist, sch. adjustment counselor Westwood (Mass.) Pub. Schs., 1967-93; grad. faculty Emerson Coll., Boston, 1979-81; cons. Mass. Dept. Mental Health, Boston, 1979-82; grad. clin. supr. Robbins Speech/Hearing Ctr., Emerson Coll., Boston, 1979-82; predoctoral intern in clin. psychology South Shore Mental Health Ctr., Quincy, Mass., 1985-86, devel. and clin. staff psychologist Hingham and Quincy, 1989-93, emergency svcs. team and respite house manager Quincy, 1990-93; cons. Westwood Nursery Preschs., 1986-93; pvt. practice Twin Oaks Clin. Assocs., Westwood, 1986-88, South Coast Counseling Assocs., Quincy, 1989-93, South Shore Clin. Assocs., Ft. Lauderdale, Fla., 1993—2005; CEO Morpheus Music, 2005—. Cons. local collaboratives and preschs., Westwood, 1980-93; profl. workshops presenter Head Start, 1980; program specialist speech, lang., learning Broward County (Fla.) Schs., 1993-96, exceptional student edn. specialist, 1996-98; behavior specialist, 1999-2005; adj. prof. grad. sch. of psychology Nova Southeastern U., 1995-2005; chmn Broward County Action Rsch. Grant Project 2002-03; presenter Head Start, ASHA, CEC, APSC, IALP and other profl., nat. and state confs., 1980-99; invited lectr. to Sino-Am. Conf. on Exceptionality, Beijing Normal U., China, 1995. Contbr. articles to profl. jours., chpts. to textbooks. Mem. adv. coun. Westwood Bd. Health, 1977-80; emergency med. technician Westwood Pub. Schs. Athletic Dept., 1981. Vocat. Rehab. fellow So. Ill. U., 1964; Merit scholar Perry County, Ill., 1959-64, Credi meml. scholar So. Ill. U., 1964. Mem. Am. Speech & Hearing Assn. (nat. schs. com., nat. chairperson Pub. Sch. Caucus 1985-87), Am. Psychol. Assn., Assn. Psychiat. Svcs. for Children, Coun. Exceptional Children, Internat. Assn. of Logopedics, Rio Vista Civic Assn., Boston Coll. Alumni Assn., Harvard Club. Episcopalian. Avocations: squash, sailing, skiing. Office Phone: 760-668-1900. Personal E-mail: sally@morpheusmusic.com.

**MAXWELL, W(ILBUR) RICHARD,** retired management consultant; b. Troy, Ohio, June 20, 1920; s. Wilbur D. and Gertrude (McDowell) M.; m. Roberta Mae Kennedy, June 29, 1942 (dec.); children: Douglas R., Jean Ann. Student, Ohio Wesleyan U., 1938-41; BS, Richmond Profl. Inst. of Coll. William and Mary, 1955. Sec. Troy C. of C., 1948-50, Va. C. of C., 1950-55; asst. to pres./chmn. bd. Reynolds Metals Co., 1955-64; v.p., dir. Reynolds Fgn. Sales Inc., 1964-68; pres. Nat. Better Bus. Bur., 1968-70; pres., chief exec. officer Jr. Achievement, Inc., Stamford, Conn., 1970-82. Instr. Richmond Profl. Inst., part-time 1955-57; sponsor-trustee U. Va. Grad. Bus. Sch., 1963-72. Pres. Lancaster County Libr., 1984-85, Rappahannock Gen. Hosp. Found., 1988-90, Northern Neck Vocat.-Tech. Edn. Ctr., 1991-93; bd. dirs. Rappahannock Gen. Hosp., 1988-90, Richmond (Va.) Cmty. H.S., 1989-91; chmn. Northumberland County (Va.) Econ. Devel. Commn., 1994-97. Civilian specialist USAAC, USN, 1942-46. Recipient Albert Schweitzer award Hugh O'Brien Youth Fedn., 1982; inducted Jr. Achievement Profl. Hall of Fame, 1986. Mem. Indian Creek Yacht and Country Club (v.p., 1991-93, bd. dirs. 1991-93). Home: 13715 Richmond Pk Dr N #1203 Jacksonville FL 32224

**MAXWELL, WILLIAM LAUGHLIN,** retired industrial engineering educator; b. Phila., July 11, 1934; s. William Henry and Elizabeth (Laughlin) M.; m. Judith Behrens, July 5, 1969; children: Deborah, William, Judith, Keely BMechE, Cornell U., 1957, PhD, 1961. Andrew Schultz Jr. prof. dept. indsl. engring. Cornell U., Ithaca, NY, 1961-98. Author: Theory of Scheduling, 1967. Recipient Disting. Teaching award Cornell Soc. Engrs., 1968, Ralph S. Watts Tchg. award, 1997. Fellow Informs, Inst. Indsl. Engrs.; mem. Nat. Acad. Engring. Home: 106 Lake Ave Ithaca NY 14850-3537

**MAXWELL, WILLIAM STIRLING,** retired lawyer; b. Chgo., May 2, 1922; s. W. Stirling and Ethel (Bowes) Maxwell Reineke. AB with distinction, U. Mich., 1947, postgrad., 1946-49, JD, 1949. Bar: Ill. 1949, U.S. Ct. Mil. Appeals 1951, U.S. Supreme Ct. 1952. Assoc. Sidley & Austin, Chgo., 1949-60, 61, ptnr., 1962-84; now ret.; sr. legis. counsel U.S. Treasury, Washington, 1960-61. Trustee Mid-North Animal Shelter Found., Chgo., 1971—. Mem. Order of Coif, Phi Beta Kappa Clubs: Lawyers Club. Republican. Episcopalian. Home: PO Box 1839 Brookings OR 97415-0048

**MAXWELL DIAL, ELEANORE,** foreign language educator; b. Norwich, Connecticut, Feb. 21, 1929; d. Joseph Walter and Irene (Beetham) Maxwell; m. John E. Dial, Aug. 27, 1959. BA, U. Bridgeport, Conn., 1951; MA in Spanish, Mexico City Coll., 1955; PhD, U. Mo., 1968. Mem. faculty U. Wis., Milw., 1968—75, Ind. State U., Terre Haute, 1975—78, Bowling Green State U., Ohio, 1978—79; asst. prof. dept. fgn. lang. and lit. Iowa State U., Ames, 1979—85, assoc. prof., 1985—96, emerita assoc. prof., 1996—. Cons. pub. companies; participant workshops; del. First World Congress Women Journalists and Writers, Mex., 1975, mem. edn. commn. Contbr. articles, anthologies, and reviews to scholarly journals. Active governor's commn. on fgn. lang. and internat. studies, 1988-95. NDEA grantee, 1967, Ctr. Latin Am. grantee, 1972, NEH summer seminar UCLA, 1981, U. Calif. Santa Barbara, 1984. Mem. MLA, Am. Assn. Teachers Spanish and Portuguese, Midwest MLA, N. Ctrl. Coun. Latin Americanists, Midwest Assn. Latin Am. Studies.

Clermont County Geneal. Soc., Ohio Geneal. Soc., Story County Iowa Geneal. Soc., Caribbean Studies Assn., P.G. Wodehouse Soc., Phi Beta Delta, Phi Sigma Iota, Sigma Delta Pi. Home: 190 North St Batavia OH 45103-2911 Office: Iowa State U Ames IA 50011-0001

**MAXWORTHY, TONY,** mechanical and aerospace engineering educator; b. London, May 21, 1933; came to U.S., 1954, naturalized, 1961; s. Ernest Charles and Gladys May (Butson) M.; m. Emily Jean Parkinson, June 20, 1956 (div. 1974); children: Kirsten, Kara; m. Anna Barbara Parks, May 21, 1979 BS in Engring. with honors, U. London, 1954; MSE, Princeton U., 1955; PhD, Harvard U., 1959. Rsch. asst. Harvard U., Cambridge, Mass., 1955-59; sr. scientist, group supr. Jet Propulsion Lab., Pasadena, Calif., 1960-67; assoc. prof. U. So. Calif., L.A., 1967-70, prof., 1970—, Smith Internat. prof. mech. and aero. engring., 1988—, chmn. dept. mech. engring., 1979-89; cons. BBC Rsch. Ctr., Baden, Switzerland, 1972-82, J.P.L., Pasadena, Calif., 1968-80; lectr. Woods Hole Oceanographic Inst., Mass., summers 1965, 70, 72, 83. Forman vis. prof. aeronautics Technion Haifa, 1986; vis. prof. U. Poly., Madrid, 1988, Inst. Superiore Tech., Lisbon, 1988, Swiss Fed. Inst. Tech., Lausanne, 1989-95; assoc. prof. IMG, U. Joseph Fourier, Grenoble, 1980—, Ecole Superieure Physics and Indsl. Chemistry, Paris, 1995—; Shimizu vis. prof. Stanford U., 1996—, U. Canterbury, New Zealand, 2005—. Mem. editorial bd. Geophys. Fluid Dynamics, 1973-79, 88-96, Dynamic Atmospheric Oceans, 1976-83, Phys. Fluids, 1978-81, Zeitschrift fuer Angewandte Mathematik und Physik, 1987-96; contbr. articles to profl. jours. Recipient Humboldt Sr. Scientist award, 1981-93, G.I. Taylor medal Soc. Engring. Sci., 2003; life fellow Clare Hall, Cambridge U., 1974, 93—, Australian Nat. U., 1978, Nat. Ctr. Atmospheric Rsch., 1976, Glennon fellow U. Western Australia, 1990, F.W. Mosey fellow, 1993, Sr. Queen's fellow in marine scis. Commonwealth of Australia, 1984; sr. visitor DAMTP, Cambridge U., 1975—. Fellow: Am. Phys. Soc. (chmn. exec. com. fluid dynamics divsn. 1974—79, Otto Laporte award 1990), Am. Acad. Arts and Scis.; mem.: NAE, Oceanography Soc., European Geophys. Soc., Am. Geophys. Union. Office: U So Calif Dept Aerospace & Mech Engr Exposition Park Los Angeles CA 90089-1191 Business E-Mail: maxworth@usc.edu.

**MAY, ALAN ALFRED,** lawyer; b. Detroit, Apr. 7, 1942; s. Alfred Albert and Sylvia (Sheer) M.; m. Elizabeth Miller; children: Stacy Ann, Julie Beth. BA, U. Mich., 1963, JD cum laude, 1966. Bar: Mich. 1967, D.C. 1976; former reg. nursing home adminstr., Mich. Ptnr. May and May PC, Detroit, 1979—2001; ptnr., shareholder, v.p. Kemp Klein, Umphrey and May, P.C., Troy, Mich., 2001—05; CEO NCCJ, 2005. Spl. assst. atty. gen. State of Mich., 1970—; pres., instr. Med-Leg Seminars, Inc., 1978; lectr. Wayne State U., 1974; instr. Oakland U., 1969. Chmn. Rep. 18th Congrl. Dist. Com., 1983-87, now chmn. emeritus; chmn. 19th Congrl. Dist. Com., 1981-83; mem. Mich. Rep. Com., 1976-84; del. Rep. Nat. Conv., 1984, rules com., 1984; del. Rep. Nat. Conv., 1988, platform com., 1988; former chmn. Mich. Civil Rights Commn.; mem., vice chair Mich. Civil Svc. Commn., 1984-88; former trustee, mem. exec. bd. vice chmn. nat conf. for cmty. and justice NCCJ; trustee Temple Beth El Birmingham, Mich., past pres. exec. bd.; mem. Electoral Coll.; former bd. dirs. ADL, Mich.; bd. dirs. exec. bd., past pres. Detroit Region/Nat. Conf. Cmty. and Justice, Charfoos Charitable Found. Mem. Nat. Conf. Cmty. and Justice (former exec. bd., vice chmn., pres., CEO 2005—, interim pres. 2005), Detroit Bar Assn., Oakland County Bar Assn., Victors Club, Franklin Hills Country Club (past pres., bd. dirs.), President's Club. Home: 4140 Echo Rd Bloomfield Hills MI 48302-1941 Office: Kemp Klein Umphrey Endelman & May PC 201 W Big Beaver Rd Ste 600 Troy MI 48084 Office Phone: 248-528-1111. Business E-Mail: alan.may@kkue.com.

**MAY, ARTHUR W.,** retired academic administrator, educator; b. St. John's, Nfld., Can., June 29, 1937; s. William J. and Florence (Dawe) M.; m. Sonia Susan Streeter, Aug. 18, 1958; children: Stephen J., Heather E., Maria S., Douglas W. BSc with honors, Meml. U., St. John's, 1958; MSc, Meml. U., 1964; PhD, McGill U., Montreal, Que., Can., 1966; D of Univ. (hon.), U. Ottawa, 1988; DSc (hon.), Meml. U. Nfld., 1989; LLD (hon.), Brock U., 1992. Sci. adviser internat. fisheries Dept. Fisheries, Ottawa, Canada, 1971-73, dir. Nfld. biol. sta. St. John's, 1973-75, dir. gen. resource services Ottawa, 1975-78; asst. dep. minister Atlantic Dept. Fisheries and Oceans, Ottawa, 1978-82, dep. minister, 1982-86; pres. Natural Sci. and Engring. Rsch. Coun. Canada, 1986-90; pres., vice chancellor Meml. U. Nfld., St. Johns, 1990-99, ret., 1999—. V.p. Internat. Coun. For Exploration of Seas, Copenhagen, 1977-79; mem. Task Force on Atlantic Fisheries, Ottawa, 1982, Nat. Adv. Bd. Sci. and Tech., 1988-90, 94-95; Canadian rep. to NATO Sci. Com., 1990-97; bd. dirs. Canadian Millenium Scholarship Found., World Wildlife Can.; chmn. bd. One Ocean, 2001—. Contbr. articles to profl. jours. Served to sub. lt. Can. Navy, 1955-58 Decorated officer Order of Can.; recipient Gov.-Gen.'s medal Nfld. Dept. Edn., 1954, Meml. U. Nfld., 1958; named Alumnus of Yr., Meml. U. Nfld., 1983. Mem. N.W. Atlantic Fisheries Orgn. (pres. 1977-80) Anglican. Avocations: gardening, stamp collecting/philately. Office: Meml Univ Nfld 4003 Spencer Hall Saint John's NL Canada A1C 5S7 Home: St 303 25 Bonaventure Ave Saint John's NL Canada A1C 6N8

**MAY, AVIVA RABINOWITZ,** music educator, musician, linguist; b. Tel Aviv; naturalized, 1958; d. Samuel and Paula Pessia (Gordon) Rabinowitz; children: Chelley Mosoff, Alan May, Risa McPherson, Ellanna May/Gassman. AA, Oakton C.C., 1977; BA in Piano Pedagogy, Northeastern Ill. U., 1978. Folksinger, educator, musican Aviva May Studio/Piano and Guitar, 1948—; Sunday sch. dir. Canton (Ohio) Synagogue, 1952-54; nursery sch. tchr. Allentown (Pa.) Jewish Cmty. Ctr., 1954-56; Hebrew music tchr. Brith Shalom Cmty. Ctr., Bethlehem, Pa., 1954-62; Hebrew tchr. Beth Hillel Congregation, Wilmette, Ill., 1964-83; tchr. B'nai Mitzva, 1978; music dir. McCormick Health Ctrs., Chgo., 1978-79, Cove Sch. Perceptually Handicapped Children, Evanston, 1978-79; prof. Hebrew and Yiddish, Spertus Coll. Judaica, Chgo., 1980-89; Hebrew tchr. Anshe Emet Day Sch., 1989—, West Suburban Temple Har Zion, Oak Park, Ill., 1993—; music studio tchr. Cosmopolitan Sch., Chgo., 1992—. Tchr. continuing edn. Northeastern Ill. U., 1978-84, Niles Twp. Jewish Congregation, 1993—97, also Jewish Cmty. Ctrs., 1977-78; with Hebrew Spl. Investigations, Dept. Justice, Washington; music dir. Temple Emanuel Rosenwald Sch. Composer classical music for piano, choral work, folk songs; developer 8-hour system for learning piano or guitar; contbr. articles to profl. jours. Recipient Magen David Adom Pub. Svc. award 1973; grantee Ill. State, 1975-79, Ill. Congressman Woody Bowman, 1978-79. Mem. Music Tchrs. Nat. Assn., Ill. Music Tchrs. Assn., Organ and Piano Tchrs. Assn., Am. Coll. Musicians, Ill. Assn. Learning Disabilities, North Shore Music Tchrs. Assn. (charter mem., co-founder), Sherwood Sch. Music, Friends of Holocaust Survivors, Nat. Yiddish Book Exch., Nat. Ctr. for Jewish Films, Chgo. Jewish Hist. Soc., Oakton C.C. Alumni Assn., Northeastern Ill. U. Alumni Assn. Office: Aviva May Studio 410 S Michigan Ave Ste 920 Chicago IL 60605-1471 Office Phone: 773-348-8700.

**MAY, BRUCE BARNETT,** lawyer; b. Portland, Oreg., Apr. 16, 1948; s. Ralph Barnett May and Barbara (Newton) Evans; m. Deborah Sue Wright, Jan. 22, 1972; children: Alexander, Christopher, Elizabeth, Andrew. BA, Princeton U., 1971; JD, U. Oreg., 1978. Bar: Ariz. 1978. Ptnr. Jennings Strouss & Salmon, Phoenix, 1984—. Lectr. various bar and trade assns. Contbr. articles to profl. jours. Dir. Phoenix Mountain Preservation Coun., 1985-89; mem. Paradise Valley Urban Village Planning Com., Phoenix, 1985-87, Men's Art Coun., 1987-91, Phoenix Valley Partnership; mem. adv. bd. Corp. Supportive Housing; bd. Phoenix Revitalogation Coun.; mem. exec. bd. Phoenix Cmty. Alliance. Lt. (j.g.) USN, 1972-75. Mem. ABA (chmn. land sales regulation com., vice chair divsn. CLE, task force future of CLE, co-chmn. brokers and brokerage com.), Am. Coll. Real Estate Lawyers, Order of Coif. Republican. Episcopalian. Avocations: book collecting, running, boxing. Office: Jennings Strouss & Salmon 201 E Washington St Ste1100 Phoenix AZ 85004-2385 Office Phone: 602-262-5923. Business E-Mail: bmay@jsslaw.com.

**MAY, CECIL RICHARD, JR.,** academic administrator; b. Memphis, June 13, 1932; BA in biblical langs. magna cum laude, Harding U., MA in New Testament, MTh; LLD (hon.), Freed-Hardeman U., 1984. Min., Holly

Springs, Miss., 1954-57, Ripley, Miss., 1957-59, Pine Bluff Ch., Ctrl. Acad. Ch., Miss., 1959-60; dist. scout exec. Yocona Area Coun. Boy Scouts Am., Oxford, Miss., 1959-60; min. Ashland, Miss., 1961, Fulton, Miss., 1962-67, Eastside Campus Ch., Portland, Oreg., 1967-69; Bible tchr. Columbia Christian Coll., Portland, 1967-69; min. Vicksburg, Miss., 1969-76; dean Internat. Bible Coll., Florence, Ala., 1977-80; pres. Magnolia Bible Coll., Kosciusko, Miss., 1980-97; dean bibl. studies Faulkner U., Montgomery, Ala., 1998—, dir. annual Bible lectureship. Lectr. in field. Editor: Preacher Talk; assoc. editor: Magnolia Messenger; contbr. articles to profl. jours. Elder Vicksburg (Miss.) Ch., 1971-76, South Huntington St. Ch., Kosciusko, 1981-97, University Ch., Montgomery; active Boy Scouts Am., 1954-76; com. chair Kosciusko-Attala County C. of C., 1992; bd. dirs. Am. Cancer Soc., 1971-74, fin. campaign chmn., 1971; bd. dirs. Miss. Econ. Coun., 1985-86, 89-92, area vice-chmn., 1991-92; chmn. Attala County Med. Study Task Force, 1991-92. Recipient Disting. Christian Svc. award, Harding U., 2003. Mem. Nat. Assn. Ind. Coll. and Univs., Miss. Assn. Ind. Colls. (bd. dirs.), Evang. Theol. Soc., Miss. Assn. Colls. (bd. dirs.), Rotary Club (bd. dirs. 1983-85, pres. 1985-86). Achievements include Classroom Building at Magnolia Bible College named Cecil May Jr. Classroom Building, 1997. Office: Faulkner Univ 5345 Atlanta Hwy Montgomery AL 36109-3390 Office Phone: 334-386-7154. Business E-Mail: cmay@faulkner.edu.

**MAY, DEBRA HARDYMON,** librarian; b. Savannah; d. Charles Fletcher and Ruby Eloise Hardymon; m. Tony Kent May, July 23, 1993; 1 child, Brandon Reid Justice. AA, Maysville CC, 1973; BSc in Secondary English Edn., U. Ky., 1975, M in Libr. and Info. Sci., 2001; MA in English, Morehead State U., 1989. Cert. in Sch. Media Dept. Edn., Ky., 2001, Libr. Cert. Ky. Dept. Libr. and Archives, 2004. Tchr. English Tollesboro H.S., Vanceburg, Ky., 1980—82; homecare program coord. Buffalo Trace Area Devel. Dist., Maysville, Ky., 1982—83, Licking Valley Cmty. Action Program, Flemingsburg, Ky., 1983—88, homecare program supr., 1988—93, child care resource and referral coord., 1993—2000; social editor, proofreader Ledger Ind., Maysville, 2000—01; children's libr. Campbell County Pub. Libr., Cold Spring, Ky., 2003—. Bd. mem. Fleming Countians for Literacy, Flemingsburg, 1991—93. Mem. Women's Dems., Flemingsburg, 1990—93; mem. fin. com. Trinity United Meth. Ch., 2006; adv. bd. mem. Foster Grandparents, Maysville, 2003. Homecare Program grant, Buffalo Trace Area Devel. Dist., 1984—87, 1990—93. Mem.: Ky. Dept. Libr. and Archives. Democrat. Methodist. Avocations: reading, basketball, football, singing. Home: 1212 Dutch Ridge Augusta KY 41002 Office: Campbell County Public Libr 3920 Alexandria Pike Cold Spring KY 41076

**MAY, DONALD ROBERT LEE,** ophthalmologist, educator, academic administrator, farmer; b. Spring Valley, Ill., Nov. 26, 1945; BS in Liberal Arts and Scis. with high honors and distinction, U. Ill., 1968, MD, 1972. Diplomate Am. Bd. Ophthalmology, Nat. Bd. Med. Examiners. Rsch. fellow dept. ophthalmology U. Ill. Eye and Ear Infirmary, Chgo., 1971—72; intern Northwestern U. Sch. Medicine Meml. Hosps., Chgo., 1972—73; resident in ophthalmology U. Ill. Eye and Ear Infirmary, Chgo., 1973—76, instr. dept. ophthalmology, 1974—77, attending surgeon dept. ophthalmology, 1976—77, fellow in diabetic retinopathy study, diabetic retinopathy vitrectomy study, and retina and vitreous surgery, 1976—77; founder, dir. retina svc., dept. ophthalmology Wilford Hall USAF Med. Ctr., San Antonio, 1977—79; asst. prof. ophthalmology, founder, dir. Retina/Vitreous/Ocular Trauma Svc. U. Calif. Davis Sch. Medicine, Calif., 1979—81; assoc. prof., dir. retina, vitreous and ocular trauma svc. U. Calif. Sch. Medicine, Davis, 1984—89; dir. med. student edn. dept. ophthalmology, 1985—89; dir. ophthalmology Charity Hosp., 1985—89; prof. Tex. Tech U. Health Scis. Ctr., Lubbock, Tex., 1989—2001, chmn. dept. ophthalmology and visual scis. 1989—94, prof. dept. health orgn. mgmt., 1993—2001, assoc. dean Sch. Medicine, 1994—96. Co-investigator in the intraocular gentamicin prophylaxis study Govt. Erskine Hosp., Madurai, India, 1975, Dept. Ophthalmology, Audie Murphy VA Hosp., San Antonio, 1977—79, Martinez VA Hosp., Calif., 1979—84, VA Hosp., New Orleans, 1984—89, VA Med. Ctr., Big Spring, Tex., 1989—93, 1996—2001, VA Ctr., Lubbock, Tex., 1989—92, Lubbock, 1996—2001; vis. prof., Germany, 1984, Switzerland, 87; 1st v.p. U.S. Eye Injury Registry 1990—92, pres.-elect, 1992—94, pres., 1994—96; founder, med. dir. Tex. Eye Injury Registry, 1991—2001; cons. in field. Contbg. editor: Outcome/Fragmatome Newsletter, 1978—81; assoc. editor: Vitreorential Surgery and Tech., 1989—98, mem. editl. bd.: Jour. Eye Trauma, 1996—2001; contbr. articles to profl. jours.; appeared in numerous TV and radio programs. Com. mem. Sch. Medicine U. Calif., Davis, Tulane U. Sch. Medicine, New Orleans, Sch. Medicine Tex. Tech. U. Health Scis. Ctr.; bd. dirs. Lubbock Internat. Cultural Ctr., Inc., 1997—, chmn. ways and means com., 1998—2000, v.p. bd. dirs., 2004, pres. bd. dirs., 2005—; planning com., chmn. medicine and history com., liaison Vatican Mus. Exhbn. Found., 2001—02. Maj. USAF, 1973—80. Decorated Air Force Commendation medal. Mem.: AMA, ACS, Mil. Officers Assn. Am., Ill. Farm Bur., Ill. Agrl. Assn., Am. Farm Bur. Fedn., Soc. Med. Cons. Armed Forces, Vitreous Soc. (charter), Retina Soc., Schepens Internat. Soc., Tex. Tech. Rsch. Found. (bd. dirs. 1993—96), Tex. Ophthal. Assn. (chair edn. com. 1990—93, cons. 1990—93, nominating com. 1991—93), So. Retina Study Group, Tex. Med. Assn. (com. continuing edn. 1993—96, bd. dirs. TEXPAC 2000—02), So. Med. Assn. (vice-chmn. sec. ophthalmology 1995—96, chmn. sec. ophthalmology 1996—97), Christian Med. Assn., Assn. Rsch. Vision and Ophthalmology (pub. rels. com. 1997—2000), Am. Acad. Ophthalmology (bylaws and rules com. 1990—95, com. internat. ophthalmology 1991—95), Am. Legion, Sigma Xi (sec. Tex. Tech. chpt. 1990—91, v.p., pres.-elect 1999—2000, pres. 2000—01). Republican. Lutheran. Avocations: travel, photography, bicycling, hiking. Home: PO Box 1678 Lubbock TX 79408-1678 *If we are to survive as a free society, we must each accept responsibility. The individual must function on the premise that personal rewards come with the investment of hard, honest work and not as a right mediated by government at the expense of others. Our legislative bodies must enact laws for the common good and not for individual self-interest. Our judicial systems must provide for the just enforcement of our laws. Our leadership must be the watchdog to ensure the indvdual has the opportunity to life without unreasonable danger, the freedom to follow one's dreams, and the ability to pursue happiness through individual achievement. Security comes with the contribution of all who are able.*

**MAY, EDGAR,** former state legislator; b. Zurich, Switzerland, June 27, 1929; arrived in U.S., 1940, naturalized, 1954; s. Ferdinand and Renee (Bloch) May. B.J. with highest distinction, Northwestern U., 1957. Reporter, acting editor Bellows Falls (Vt.) Times, 1951-53; reporter Fitchburg (Mass.) Sentinel, 1953; part time reporter Chgo. Tribune, 1955-57; reporter Buffalo Evening News, 1958-61; dir. pub. welfare projects State Charities Aid Assn., 1962-64; mem. President's Task Force on War Against Poverty, 1964; spl. asst. to dir., asst. dir. Office Econ. Opportunity, 1964; spl. adviser to Ambassador Sargent Shriver, 1968-70; cons. Ford Found., 1970-75; mem. Vt. Ho. of Reps., 1975-82, Vt. Senate, 1983-91, chmn. com. appropriations; project dir. Vt. Jud. Mgmt. Study, 1992; COO Spl. Olympics Internat., Washington, 1993-96; cons. New Eng. Culinary Inst., 1996—2001; chmn. So. Vt. Recreation Ctr. Found., 1998—. Author: The Wasted Americans, 1964. With AUS, 1953-55. Recipient Page One award Buffalo Newspaper Guild, 1959, Walter O. Bingham award, 1959, Pulitzer prize for local reporting, 1961, Merit award Northwestern U. Alumni Assn., 1962; named Citizen of Yr., C. of C., 2003.

**MAY, ELAINE,** actress, theatre and film director; b. Phila., Apr. 21, 1932; d. Jack Berlin; m. Marvin May (div.); 1 child, Jeannie Berlin; m. Sheldon Harnick, Mar. 25, 1962 (div. May 1963). Studied Stanislavski method of acting with Marie Ouspenskaya. Stage and radio appearances as child actor; performed with Playwright's Theatre, in student performance Miss Julie, U. Chgo.; appeared with improvisational theatre group in night club The Compass, Chgo., 1954-1957, (with Mike Nichols) named N.Y. supper clubs, Village Vanguard, Blue Angel, also night clubs other cities; TV debut on Jack Paar Show, 1957; also appeared in Omnibus, 1958, Dinah Shore Show, Perry Como Show, Laugh Line, Laugh-In, TV spls.; comedy albums include Improvisations to Music, An Evening with Mike Nichols and Elaine May, Mike Nichols and Elaine May Examine Doctors; weekly appearance NBC radio show Nightline; appeared (with Mike Nichols) NBC radio show, N.Y. Town Hall, 1959, An Evening with Mike Nichols and Elaine May, Golden Theatre, N.Y.C., 1960-61; theater appearances include The Office, N.Y.C., 1966, Who's Afraid of Virginia Woolf?, Long Wharf Theatre, New Haven, Conn., 1980; dir. plays The Third Ear, N.Y.C., 1964, The Goodbye People, Berkshire Theater Festival, Stockbridge, Mass., 1971, various plays at Goodman Theatre, Chgo., 1983; dir., author screenplay, actress film A New Leaf, 1972; dir. films The Heartbreak Kid, 1973, Mikey and Nicky, 1976 (writer, dir. remake 1981), Ishtar, 1987 (also writer); appeared in films Luv, 1967, California Suite, 1978 (Acad. award Best Supporting Actress 1978), In The Spirit, 1990; co-author screenplay Heaven Can Wait, 1978, Birdcage, 1996, Primary Colors, 1998; author plays A Matter of Position, 1962, Not Enough Rope, 1962, Adaptation, 1969, Hot Line, 1983, Better Part of Valor, 1983, Mr. Gogol and Mr. Preen, 1991, (one act) Death Defying Acts, 1995, After the Night and the Music, 2005; stage revue: (with Mike Nichols) Telephone, 1984; co-recipient (with Mike Nichols) Grammy award for comedy performance, Nat. Acad. Recording Arts & Scis., 1961; actress (film) Small Time Crooks, 2000.

**MAY, ELEANOR GODDARD,** retired business administration educator; b. Groton, Mass., Sept. 26, 1925; d. Robert Morse and Virginia Ames (Woods) M. BS in Math. magna cum laude, Tufts Coll., 1947; postgrad., Am. U., 1966-68; MBA in Mktg., George Wash. U., 1971. Actuarial trainee group annuity dept. John Hancock Mut. Life Ins. Co., Boston, 1947-48; mem. staff Bur. Bus. Rsch. Harvard U. Grad. Sch. Bus. Administrn., Boston, 1948-51, asst. exec. sec., 1951-55, asst. and assoc. staff rschr., 1955-62; asst. dir., then dir. rsch. Woodward & Lothrop, Inc., Washington, 1962-70; lectr., then asst. prof. bus. administrn. U. Va. Darden Grad. Sch. Bus. Administrn., Charlottesvville, 1970-74, assoc. prof., 1974-78, prof., 1978-90, prof. emerita, 1990—, dir. Bus. Studies Ctr., Tayloe Murphy Inst., 1970-86. Staff cons. Menswear Retailers Am., 1972-77; faculty assoc. Mgmt. Analysis Ctr., Inc., 1979-86; rschr. Mktg. Sci. Inst., 1970-85; vol. exec. Internat. Exec. Svc. Corps, 1995; adv. com. Retail Rsch. Inst., 1964-65, dir., 1966-70; retail store stats. subcom. Retail Bur., Met. Washington Bd. Trade, 1964-66; presenter, expert witness, cons. in field Mem. editorial bd. Jour. Retailing, 1979-90, Jour. Mktg. Channels, 1989—; contbr. articles to profl. jours. Founding mem. bd. dirs. Cmty. Meals on Wheels, Charlottesville, 1978-88; bd. dirs. Adventure Bound Sch., Charlottesville, 1986-93, pres., 1990-93; bd. dirs. Elk Hill Farm, Goochland, Va., 1992—; bd. trustees Thomas Jefferson Meml. Unitarian Universalist Ch., 1997-2003, pres. 1999-2001; bd. dirs., treas. On Our Own Inc., 2004-05 Mem. Am. Collegiate Retailing Assn., Acad. Mktg. Sci., Ret. Faculty Assn. (bd. dirs., 1992-2002, v.p. 1992-99, pres. 1999-2001), Colonial Dames Am. (bd. dirs., treas. 1993-94), Contemporary Club (bd. dirs. 1994-96), Sigma Pi Sigma Unitarian Universalist Ch. Avocations: hiking, travel, reading. Home: 2933 Mill Grove Ln North Garden VA 22959-1621 Personal E-mail: emay@mindspring.com.

**MAY, ERNEST DEWEY,** academic administrator, musician; b. Jersey City, May 8, 1942; s. Ernest Max and Harriet Elizabeth (Dewey) M.; m. Eileen Marie Mayhew, Jan. 29, 1963 (div. 1984); children: Ernest Jr., Elizabeth May Goodell, Katherine May Waite, Caroline, Christopher, Abigail May Robles, Deirdre; m. Mary L. Milkey, June 29, 1985. AB, Harvard U., 1964; MFA, Princeton U., 1968, PhD, 1975. Asst. prof. music Amherst (Mass.) Coll., 1969-75; from asst. prof. to prof. music dept. music and dance U. Mass., Amherst, 1976-88, prof. music, chmn. dept. music and dance, 1988-2000, presiding officer faculty senate, 1997-2000, sec. faculty senate, 2000—. Faculty rep. bd. trustees U. Mass., 1988-97; chair Intercampus Faculty Coun., 2001—; organist, dir. mus. South Congl. Ch., Springfield, Mass., 1983-95. Rec.: Music for Trumpet and Organ, 1979, 2001; co-editor: J.S. Bach: Neve Ausgabe Samtlicher Werke Vol. I/20, 1986, J.S. Bach as Organist, 1986; contbr. New Harvard Dictionary of Music, 1986. Mem.: Am. Musicological Soc. (pres. New Eng. chpt. 1988—90), Am. Guild Organists, Am. Assn. Higher Edn. Home: 44 Amherst Rd Pelham MA 01002-9700 Office: U Mass Faculty Senate Amherst MA 01003 Business E-Mail: secretary@acad.umass.edu.

**MAY, FRANK BRENDAN, JR.,** lawyer; b. Bronx, NY, Oct. 17, 1945; s. Frank Brendan and Margaret May; m. Mary Frances Fitzsimmons, June 19, 1976; children: David Brendan, Brian Christopher. BA in Econs., NYU, 1973, postgrad., 1973-75; JD, John Marshall Law Sch., Chgo., 1978. Bar: Ill. 1979, U.S. Dist. Ct. (no. dist.) Ill. 1979, U.S. Ct. Appeals (7th cir.) 1979, U.S. Supreme Ct. 1995, Ill. real estate broker 1994. Legal intern criminal div. Cook County State's Atty.'s Office, Chgo., 1977-78; legal intern juvenile div. DuPage County State's Atty.'s Office, Wheaton, Ill., 1978; sr. assoc. atty. Lillig, Kemp & Thorness, Ltd., Oak Brook, Ill., 1978-81; v.p., gen. counsel Coldwell Banker, Oak Brook, 1981-90, Prudential Preferred Properties, Des Plaines, Ill., 1991-98, Law Offices, Frank B. May, Jr., Wheaton, Ill., 1999-2001; sr. corp. atty., asst. sec. Budget Rent a Car Corp., Lisle, Ill., 2001—03; sr. v.p., gen. coun. Coldwell Banker Primus Realty, Oswego, Ill., 2003—. Arbitrator 18th Jud. Cir. Ct., DuPage County, Ill., 1993—. Dir. Ray Graham Found. for People with Disabilities, 1999-2004. Sgt. USAF, 1963-67. NYU Coun. scholar, 1971-73; David Davis Meml. scholar, 1970-71. Mem. DuPage County Bar Assn., Medinah Country Club (mem. clubhouse com. 1995-96, mem. legal, bylaws com. 1996, membership com. 1997—, chmn. PGA credentials com. 1999, nominating com. 2004, chmn. 2006 PGA on-site transp. com.), Ill. Assn. Realtors (mem. large brokers com. 1996-98, exec. com., fin. com. 1998-1999, lic. law rewrite task force, nominating com. 1998-99, broker-lawyer com., 2006, chair ancillary svcs., 2006), Realtor Assn. Western Suburbs (legal counsel 1999-2000). Avocations: golf, music, gourmet cooking, wine collector. Home: 2064 Stonebridge Ct Wheaton IL 60187-7177 Office: Coldwell Banker Primus Realty 15 W Merchants Dr Oswego IL 60543 Business E-Mail: fmay@cbprimus.com. E-mail: frankbmayerjr@comcast.net.

**MAY, GEORGIANA,** biologist, educator; PhD, U. Calif., Berkeley, 1987. Assoc. prof. dept. plant biology U. Minn., St. Paul. Contbr. articles to profl. jours. Recipient Alexopoulos prize Mycological Soc. Am., 1997. Achievements include research on the interactions of fungi with plants, evolution of fungal populations and their interactions with other organisms, evolution of gene structure and function in mating compatibility loci, determining the genetic basis of smut resistance in maize, the impact of agricultural practice on host/pathogen interactions. Office: U Minn Dept Plant Biology 220 Biological Sci Ctr 1445 Gortner Ave Saint Paul MN 55108 Fax: 612-625-1738. E-mail: gmay@maroon.tc.umn.edu.

**MAY, GITA,** literature educator; b. Brussels, Sept. 16, 1929; came to U.S., 1947, naturalized, 1950; d. Albert and Blima (Sieradska) Jochimek; m. Irving May, Dec. 21, 1947. BA magna cum laude, CUNY-Hunter Coll., 1953; MA, Columbia U., 1954, PhD, 1957. Lectr. French CUNY-Hunter Coll., 1953—56; from instr. to assoc. prof. Columbia U., N.Y.C., 1956—68, prof., 1968—, chmn., 1983—93, mem. senate 1979—83, 1986—88, chmn. Seminar on 18th Century Culture 1986—89. Lecture tour English univs., 1965. Author: Diderot et Baudelaire, critiques d'art, 1957, De Jean-Jacques Rousseau à Madame Roland: essai sur la sensibilité préromantique et révolutionnaire, 1964, Madame Roland and the Age of Revolution, 1970 (Van Amringe Disting. Book award), Stendhal and the Age of Napoleon, 1977, French Women Writers, 1991, Encyclopedia of Aesthetics, 1998, Dictionnaire de Diderot, 1999, The Feminist Encyclopedia of French Literature, 1999, Elisabeth Vigée Le Brun: The Odyssey of an Artist in an Age of Revolution, 2005; co-editor: Diderot Studies III, 1961; mem. editl. bd. Romanic Rev., 1959—, 18th Century Studies, 1975—86, French Rev., 1975—86, 1998—, Women in French Studies, 2000—; contbg. editor: Oeuvres complètes de Diderot, 1984—, 1995—; gen. editor The Age of Revolution and Romanticism: Interdisciplinary Studies, 1990—, extensive essays on Diderot and George Sand in European Writers, 1984, 1985, and on Rebecca West, Anita Brookner and Graham Swift in British Writers, 1996, 1997, 1999, Bayle, Fontenelle and Fénelon in Dictionary of Literary Biography, 2003, Voltaire's Candide (in Barnes and Noble Classics), 2003; contbr. articles and revs. to

profl. jours. Decorated chevalier and officier Ordre des Palmes Acad.; recipient award Am. Coun. Learned Socs., 1961, award for outstanding achievement CUNY-Hunter Coll., 1963; Fulbright rsch. grantee, 1964-65; Guggenheim fellow, 1964-65, NEH fellow, 1971-72. Mem. AAUP, MLA (del. assembly 1973-75, com. rsch. activities 1975-78, exec. coun. 1980-83), Am. Assn. Tchrs. French, Am. Soc. 18th Century Studies (pres. 1985-86, 2d v.p. 1983-84, 1st v.p. 1984-85, One of Gt. Tchrs. award 1999), Soc. Française d'Etude du Dix-Huitième Siècle, Soc. Diderot, Am. Soc. French Acad. Palms, Soc. des Etudes Staëliennes, N.Am. Soc. for Study of Jean-Jacques Rousseau, Soc. des Professeurs Français et Francophones d'Amérique, Phi Beta Kappa. Office: Columbia U Dept French/Romance Philol 516 Philosophy Hall MC4918 New York NY 10027 Business E-Mail: gm9@columbia.edu.

**MAY, HAROLD LOUIS,** retired surgeon, not-for-profit developer; s. Arthur Earnest and Margaret Jestina May; m. Agnes Martens, Apr. 26, 1960; children: Jeannette Elizabeth, Alison Gabrielle, Margaret May Jenkins. Grad., Harvard U., Cambridge, Mass., 1947, MD, 1951, MPH, 1974. Lic. physician Mass., 1959, diplomate Am. Bd. of Surgery, 1965. Med. intern U. Minn. Hosps., Mpls., 1951—52; med. asst. resident Boston City Hosp., 1952—53; surg. resident Mass. Gen. Hosp., Boston, 1953—59; chief of surgery Albert Schweitzer Hosp., Deschapelles, Haiti, 1960—70; dir. Divsn. Cmty. Health and Med. Care Peter Bent Brigham Hosp., Boston, 1960—70; assoc. surgery Peter Bent Brigham Hosp. and Brigham and Women's Hosp., Boston, 1970—94; asst. prof. surgery Harvard Med. Sch., 1970—94; dir. med. svcs. Wrentham (Mass.) Devel. Svcs., 1975—94, ret., 1994. Exec. com. Boston-Brookline (Mass.) Health Resources Orgn., 1970—73; chmn. Region VI Emergency Med. Svcs. Com., Mass., 1972—74. Editor (author): Emergency Medicine, 1984; editor: Emergency Procedures, 1984; editor in chief: Emergency Medicine, 2d edit., 1992. Founder and pres. FAMILY, Inc. (Fathers and Mothers, Infants, elders, and Youth), Boston, 1997—2006; co-founder Ecole La Providence Primary Sch., Deschapelles, Haiti, 1960—62. Aviation cadet US Army Air Corps, 1945. Recipient Excellence in Tchg. Faculty prize, Harvard Med. Sch., 1987, 1992. Fellow: ACS; mem.: Boston Surg. Soc. Avocations: music, painting. Home and Office: FAMILY Inc 80 Waban Hill Road Newton MA 02467 Office Phone: 617-969-1454. Business E-Mail: haroldmay@familysystem.net.

**MAY, HENRY STRATFORD, JR.,** lawyer; b. Greensboro, NC, May 12, 1947; s. Henry Stratford and Doris (Richardson) May. BA, U. Tex., 1969, JD, 1971. Bar: Tex. 1972, US Ct. Appeals (DC cir.) 1974, US Supreme Ct. 1977 US Ct. Appeals (5th and 11th cirs.) 1981, US Dist. Ct. (so. dist.) Tex. 1985. Law clk. to judge U.S. Ct. Appeals (D.C. cir.), Washington, 1972-73; assoc. Vinson & Elkins LLP, Houston, 1973-79, ptnr., 1979—, head energy sect., 1990—. Mem. ABA, Tex. Bar Assn. E-mail: hmay@velaw.com.

**MAY, INGRID BARBARA,** elementary school educator; d. Pedro B. and Maria B. Luna; m. Fred L. May, Aug. 13, 1977; 1 child, Rebecca S. BA, Oklahoma City U., 1972; MA, So. Nazarene U., Bethany, Okla., 1975. Reading cert. Okla., 1972; nat. bd. cert. Nat. Bd. for Profl. Tchg. Stds., 2005. Educator, third grade Overholser Elementary Sch., Oklahoma City, 1972—; mem. Putnam City Sch. District Reading Com., 1974—, Putnam City Sch. Reading Coun., Oklahoma City, 1972—82, treas., 1974—79, pres., 1974—79; chmn. Overholser Reading Com. Bethany, 1980—, Overholser Social Studies Com., 1999—2005; mem. Title I, Bethany, 2004—, Overholser Prin.'s Adv. Comm., 2005—. Accompanist Silver Strings of Putnam City, Oklahoma City, 2000—05. Dir. Adopt-a-Grandparent Project, Bethany, 2004—. Named Tchr. of Yr., Overholser Elem. Sch., 1980—81, 2005—06; scholar Nat. Bd. Certification, Edn. Leadership Okla., 2005, Gt. Expectations, Okla. State Reading Orgn., 2006. Mem.: NEA (assoc.), Putnam City Assn. Classroom Tchrs. (assoc.), Okla. Edn. Assn. (assoc.). Republican. Nazarene. Avocations: handbell choir, piano, singing, gardening, sewing. Office Phone: 405-789-7913.

**MAY, JAMES HARVEY,** communications educator; s. Rhoudy and Ruby Mae May; m. Margit Röder, June 10, 1967; children: James Richard, Anika Nikol; 1 child, Tanja Babette Youngs. BS, Stanford U., 1958; MBA, Harvard U., 1964; certificate in radio and TV, NYU, 1966; DLS, Columbia U., 1973—78, advanced certificate in librarianship, 1977. Econ. engr. Gilbert Associates, Inc., NYC, 1964—67; v.p., treas. Pandex, Macmillan Info. Corp., NYC, 1967—72; dir., ctr. comm. and info. rsch. U. Denver, 1972—74; assoc. libr. dir., acting libr. dir. Sonoma State U., Rohnert Pk., Calif., 1974—83; vice provost info. resources Calif. State U., Chico, 1983—94; prof. comm. sci. and tech. Calif. State U. Monterey Bay, Seaside, 1994—, founding dean instrn., 1994—96, asst. to the pres., 1996—98. Ofcl. historian, bd. mem. Soc. Computer Simulation, 1991—97; panelist with US v.p. Al Gore Unity '99, Seattle, 1999; treas. Calif. Faculty Assn., 1999—2003, chpt. pres., 1998—2001, 2004—; ednl. effectiveness panel Am. Distance Edn. Consortium, 2000—; keynote spkr. Open Learning 2000, Brisbane, Queensland, Australia, 2000; bd. dir. Am. Indian Sci. and Engring. Soc., 2002—; co-chair, vice chair, bd. mem. Native Am. Pub. Telecom.; bd. mem. Native Am. TV. Contbr. articles to jour. and chpt. to books. Lt. JG USN, 1959—62, Las Vegas and No. Ireland. Recipient outstanding leadership in libr. services for Am. Indian People and founding the Am. Indian Libr. Assn., Am. Indian Libr. Alumni Assn., 1995, Union Mem. Yr., Monterey Ctrl. Labor Coun., AFL-CIO, 2000, Trade Unionist Yr., Monterey Bay Ctrl. Labor Coun., AFL-CIO, 2002. Mem.: Am. Indian Sci. and Engring. Soc. (life; bd.dir. 2002—, Ely S. Parker Medal 2000), United Keetoowah Band of Cherokee Indians (life). Achievements include created first computerized bibliographic database. Office: Calif State Univ Monterey Bay 100 Campus Ctr Seaside CA Home: 3704 Clubside Ln Sacramento CA 95835 E-mail: jameshmay@yahoo.com.

**MAY, JAMES M.,** medical educator, researcher; b. Oklahoma City, Aug. 20, 1947; married; 2 children. BS, Yale Coll., 1969; MD, Vanderbilt U., 1973. Diplomate Am. Bd. Internal Medicine, Am. Bd. Endocrinology and Metabolism. Intern Vanderbilt U., Nashville, 1973—74; resident in medicine Johns Hopkins Hosp., Balt., 1974—75; fellow in endocrinology U. Wash., Seattle, 1975—78; asst. prof. medicine Med. Coll. Va., Richmond, 1978—83, assoc. prof. medicine, 1983—86; assoc. prof. to prof. medicine Vanderbilt U., Nashville, 1986—, assoc. prof. to prof. molecular physiology and biophysics, 1993—. Mem. awards com. dept. medicine Vanderbilt U., 1992—; mem. awards com. Summer Diabetes Program Diabetes Rsch. and Tng. Ctr., 1994—. Mem. editl. bd.: Metabolism, 1996—; contbr. articles to profl. jours. Recipient Nat. Rsch. Svc. award, NIH, 1975—78, Poncin Fund award, 1975—78; grantee, NIH, 1993, 1995. Mem.: Southern Soc. Clin. Investigation, Am. Soc. Clin. Investigation, Am. Fedn. Clin. Rsch. (sec.-treas. Southern sect. 1983—86, nat. councilor 1983—88, pres.-elect and pres. 1986—88), Am. Diabetes Assn. (pres. Va. affiliate 1985—86, chmn. rsch. com. Tenn. affiliate 1990—92, Rsch. award 1996), Alpha Omega Alpha. Home: 44 Concord Park E Nashville TN 37205-4705 Office: Vanderbilt U Med Ctr Divsn Endocrinology & Diabetes 2220 Pierce Ave Bldg 2 Nashville TN 37232-0001

**MAY, JANET SUE,** playwright, lyricist; b. Bloomington, Ill., Dec. 24, 1946; d. James Woolston and Josephine Elisabeth (Ferguson) Grubb; children: John, Darbi, Heather, Brandy. Student, Lincoln Coll., 1965, Wabash Coll., 1965, St. Joseph's Hosp., 1966, Indian River C.C., 1983, Bloomington Sch. Practical Nursing, 1984; cert. in food svc. sanitation, Ill. State U., 1988. Chem. lab. tech. Eureka Williams, Bloomington, 1966; histology tech. St. Joseph's Hosp., Bloomington, 1966—67; activity dir. McLean County Nursing Home, Normal, Ill., 1968—70; rsch. asst. U. Fla. Med. Entomology Lab., Vero Beach, Fla., 1974—85; asst. libr. condemned unit Pontiac Prison, Ill., 1984—87; activity dir., meal supr. Bloomington Housing Authority, 1987—89; pub. rels. mgr. Miracle Ear, Peoria, Ill., 1990—92. Author: (children's poetry books) Winston-Smythe Worm, Prissy Penelope Grasshopper Presents, (children's books) Four Little Creatures; co-author (with James Kitzmiller): Patronymics of Mosquitoes, 2d edit., 1986; playwright: More

Than Just A Man, 2001; songwriter: Ice Age. Achievements include co-inventor, tissue vacuum pump; invention of jeweled perfumed hair tie; blinking hair tie. Avocations: art, poetry, singing. Home: 1281 Millpoint Rd East Peoria IL 61611

**MAY, JOHN T.,** college president; m. Shelly May. BS, U.S. Air Force Acad.; MS in Physics, PhD in Physics, N.C. State U. Prof. physics, head dept. Air Force Acad., 1980-84, vice dean faculty, chmn. basic sci. divsn., 1984-86; vis. prof. physics N.C. State U., 1987-88; dean spl. and career curriculum Atlantic Cape C.C., 1988, dean academics, 1989-94, pres., 1994—. Officer USAF, 1962-68, Vietnam. Address: 5100 Black Horse Pike Mays Landing NJ 08330-2623

**MAY, JOSEPH LESERMAN (JACK MAY),** retired lawyer; b. Nashville, May 27, 1929; s. Daniel and Dorothy (Fishel) M.; m. Natalie McCuaig, Apr. 12, 1957 (dec. May 1990); children: Benjamin, Andrew, Joshua, Maria; m. Lynn Hewes Lance, June 10, 1994. BA, Yale U., 1951; JD, NYU, 1958; postgrad., Harvard Bus. Sch., 1969. Bar: Tenn. 1959. Prodr. Candied Yam Jackson Show, 1947-51; with CIA, 1951-55; pres. Nuweave Socks, Inc., N.Y.C., 1955-59, May Hosiery Mills, Nashville, 1960-83, Athens Hosiery Mills, Tenn., 1966-83; v.p. Wayne-Gossard Corp., Chattanooga, 1972-83; dir. pvt. practice law Nashville, 1984—; ret., 2004. Dir. Merrill Lynch Investment Mgmt., 1987—2002; mem. adv. bd. Asian Strategies Group, 1994; chmn. Guardianship and Trust Corp., 1994—96; founding dir. Nashville Bank and Trust Co., 2003. Bd. dirs. Vanderbilt Cancer Ctr., 1994-99; chmn. Tarbox Ctr., 1969; chmn. Campus for Human Devel., 2000-02; mem. Collectors Cir., Frist Art Mus., 2004—; mem. AAA panel of neutrals, With USN, 1947-53, U.S. Army, 1954. Mem. Tenn. Bar Assn., Nashville Bar Assn., Am. Arbitration Assn. Panel of Neutrals, Tenn. Hist. Soc. (trustee, pres. 2002-04), Eagle Scout Assn., Belle Meade Country Club, Shamus Club, Old Oak Club, Old Goats, Zodiac, Yale Club N.Y., Rotary (pres. Nashville 1971). Republican. Jewish. Home: 133 Abbottsford Nashville TN 37215-2442

**MAY, KENNETH AUSTIN,** consumer products company executive; b. Memphis, Nov. 14, 1960; s. Forrest Sherman and Elizabeth (Austin) M. Degree in real estate, Memphis State U., 1983; MBA, U. Tenn., 1994. Supr. United Parcel Svc., Memphis, 1979-82; sr. mgr. Federal Express Corp., Memphis, 1982-90, mng. dir. Miami, 1990-96, v.p. Memphis, 1996—2004; exec. v.p., CEO FedEx Kinko's Inc., Dallas, 2004—06, pres., CEO, 2006—. Trustee March of Dimes Birth Defects Found., White Plains, NY. Republican. Baptist. Avocations: water-skiing, skiing, basketball, golf, fishing. Office: FedEx Kinkos Inc 3 Galleria Tower Ste 1600 13155 Noel Rd Dallas TX 75240 Office Phone: 214-550-7000. Office Fax: 214-550-7001.*

**MAY, KENNETH NATHANIEL,** retired nutrition consultant; b. Livingston, La., Dec. 24, 1930; s. Robert William and Mary Hulda (Caraway) M.; m. Patsy Jean Farr, Aug. 4, 1953; children: Sherry Alison (dec.), Nathan Elliott. BS in Poultry Sci., La. State U., 1952, MS in Poultry Sci., 1955; PhD in Food Tech., Purdue U., 1959, DAgr, 1988. Asst. prof. U. Ga., Athens, 1958-64, assoc. prof., 1964-67, prof., 1967-68, Miss. State U., State College, 1968-70; dir. rsch. Holly Farms Poultry, Wilkesboro, N.C., 1970-73, v.p., 1973-85, pres., 1985-88, chmn., CEO, 1989—2005, ret., 2005. Adj. prof. N.C. State U., 1975. Contbr. over 60 articles to profl. jours.; patentee treatment of cooked poultry. Bd. trustees Appalachian State U., 1987-94, chmn., 1989-90. Recipient Industry Service award Poultry and Egg Inst. Am., 1971, Meritorious Service award, Ga. Egg Commn., 1964, Disting. Service award Agribus. N.C., 1986; named to Am. Poultry Hall of Fame, 1992. Fellow Poultry Sci. Assn.; mem. Nat. Poultry Hist. Soc. (bd. dirs. 1982-83), Inst. Food Technologists. Methodist. Avocations: reading, stained glass. Office: 113 La Maison Belle Dr Denham Springs LA 70726 Personal E-mail: drknmay@aol.com.

**MAY, LINDA KAREN CARDIFF,** occupational health nurse, safety engineer, consultant; b. San Mateo, Calif., Oct. 26, 1948; d. Leon Davis and Jane Vivian (Gallow) Cardiff; m. Donald William May, Dec. 7, 1969 (div. Feb. 1988); children: Charles David, Andrew William. At, So. Ill. U., 1969; post grad., Ill. Wesleyan U., 1989; AAS, Parkland Coll., 1977; BS in Pub. Health and Safety Engring. with honors, U. Ill., Urbana, 1987; BSN, Lakeview Coll., 1990. RN Ill., Ind., Mo., N.Mex., Tex., Wis., registered profl. nurse; nat. registered EMT Ill., accredited instr. constrn. safety and health OSHA. Indsl. nurse C.S. Johnson Co., Champaign, Ill., 1979—84; safety engr. Clinton Nuclear Power Plant Ill. Power Co., 1984—86; occupl. nurse and health specialist Danville Vet.'s Med. Ctr., 1986—. With LKM Health and Safety Cons., Inc., Champaign, Ill. Active Mercy Hosp. Aux., Covenant Hosp Aux., 1977—, Champaign County Task Force on Arson, 1981—; alumni assn. liason Parkland Coll. Found. Bd., 1993; mem. Champaign County Crime Prevention Coun., 1978—83, bd. dir., 1980—82. Ill. State Gen. Assembly scholar, 1967. Mem.: APHA (occpl. health and safety sect.), AACN, Lakeview Coll. Nursing Alumni Assn., N.Y. Acad. Sci., Ill. EMTs Assn., Pre-Hosp. Care Providers Ill., Associated Ill. Milk, Food and Environ. Sanitarians, Ill. Soc. Pub. Health Educators, Ill. Environ. Health Assn., Nat. Registry EMT, Am. Assn. Occupational Health Nurses, Am. Nuc. Assn. (mem. biology and medicine divsn., mem. radiopharm. and isotope product stds. com.), Am. Soc. Safety Engrs. (vice chair Ctrl. Ill. sect. 1985—86), Ill. Wesleyan U. Alumni Assn., U. Ill. Alumni Assn. (life), Parkland Coll. Alumni Assn. (life; bd. dir. 1987—), v.p. 1992—), Eta Sigma Gamma. Methodist. Home: PO Box 3954 Champaign IL 61826-3954 Personal E-mail: lmay4111@aol.com.

**MAY, MISTY,** Olympic athlete; b. July 30, 1977; Majored in Kinesiology & Physical Ed., Long Beach State U. Mem. U.S. National Indoor Team, 1998, 1999; beach volleyball player Team USA, Sydney Olympic Games, 2000, Team USA, Athens Olympic Games, 2004. Named BVA Rookie of the Yr., 2000, AVP Team of the Yr. (with Kerri Walsh), 2003. Achievements include member of NCAA national championship team, 1998; one of only three players to be named a two-time AVCA National Player of the Year, 1997, 1998; winning FIVB Tour with teammate Kerri Walsh, 2002, 2003; winning a gold medal at Athens Olympic Games, beach volleyball, 2004. Office: c/o USOC One Olympic Plz Colorado Springs CO 80909

**MAY, PETER ALAN,** biology educator; b. Anderson, Ind., June 6, 1951; s. Ralph Fredrick and Mildred Eleen May; m. Debra May, June 16, 1978; children: Kimberly, Ted. BS in Natural Resources and Biology, Ball State U., Muncie, Ind., 1976, MA in Biology and Secondary Edn., 1987. Cert. profl. secondary edn. biology, earth sci. and phys. sci. Wyo. Auto worker Delco Rumy divsn. GM Corp., Anderson, 1969—78; biology tchr. Oreg.-Davis Sch. Corp., Hamlet, Ind., 1978—79; Sheridan (Wyo.) Sch. Dist. #2, 1979—. Ednl. lobbyist Sheridan Sch. Dist. #2, 2000—. State rep. candidate Dem. Party, Sheridan, 2000. With USAF, 1971. Recipient Floy Hurlbert award, Ball State U. Geography Dept., 1987, Chef's award, US Forest Svc., 2002. Mem.: NEA (legis. rep.), Wyo. Edn. Assn. (legis. rep.), Sheridan Ctrl. Edn. Assn. (v.p., pres. 1996—98, legis. rep.). Avocation: white-water rafting. Office: Sheridan HS 1056 Long Dr Sheridan WY 82801

**MAY, PETER WILLIAM,** business executive; b. NYC, Dec. 11, 1942; s. Samuel D. and Isabel (Meyer) M.; m. Leni Finkelstein, Aug. 16, 1964; children: Jonathan Paul, Leslie Ann. AB, U. Chgo., 1964, MBA, 1965. CPA, N.Y. Mgr. Peat, Marwick, Mitchell & Co., NYC, 1965-72; exec. v.p. Flagstaff Corp., NYC, 1972-78; pres., chief operating officer Trian Group. L.P. (formerly Triangle Industries, Inc.), NYC, 1979—93; also bd. dirs.; pres., COO Triarc Cos., Inc., NYC, 1993—; Bd. dirs. Encore Capital Group Inc., 1998—; Trustee Mt. Sinai Hosp., N.Y.C., exec. com., founding mem. Laura Rosenberg Meml. Fund for Pediatric Leukemia Rsch.; alumni dir. U. Chgo. Grad. Sch. Bus.; bd. dirs. 92d St. YMCA, United Jewish Appeal, Operation Exodus campaign. Mem. Am. Inst. CPA's, N.Y. Soc. of CPA's. Office: Triarc 280 Park Ave New York NY 10017*

**MAY, PHILIPALAN,** sociologist, educator; b. Bethesda, Md., Nov. 6, 1947; s. Everette Lee and Marie (Lee) M.; m. Doreen Ann Garcia, Sept. 5, 1972; children: Katrina Ruth, Marie Ann. BA in Sociology, Catawba Coll., 1969;

MA in Sociology, Wake Forest U., 1971; PhD in Sociology, U. Mont., 1976. NIMH predoctoral fellow U. Mont., Missoula, 1973-76; dir. health stats. and rsch. Navajo Health Authority, Window Rock, Ariz., 1976-78; from asst. prof. to prof. U. N.Mex., Albuquerque, 1978—89, prof., 1989—, from dir. Ctr. on Alcoholism, Substance abuse and Addictions to sr. rsch. scientist, 1990—2000, sr. rsch. scientist Ctr. on Alcoholism, Substance abuse and Addictions, 2000—, assoc. dir. Ctr. on Alcoholism, Substance abuse and Addictions, 2002—04, interim dir. Ctr. on Alcoholism, Substance abuse and Addictions, 2004. Fetal alcohol syndrome study com. Inst. Medicine of NAS, 1994-96; dir. Nat. Indian Fetal Alcohol Syndrome Prevention Program, Albuquerque, 1979-85; advy. bd. Nat. Orgn. on Fetal Alcohol Syndrome, Washington, 1990—; rsch. assoc. Nat. Ctr. for Am. Indian and Alaska Native Mental Health Rsch., 1986—; mem. U.S. Surgeon Gens. Task Force on Drunk Driving, 1988-89; prin. investigator fetal alcohol syndrome epidemiology rsch. in South Africa, 1991—; com. on pathophysiology and prevention of adolescent and adult suicide Inst. Medicine of NRC, NAS, 2000-02; cons. in field. Contbr. chpts. to books, articles to profl. jours. V.p. Bd. Edn., Laguna Pueblo, N.Mex., 1998—2002, pres., 2002—. Lt. (s.g.) USPHS, 1970—73. Recipient Spl. Recognition award U.S. Indian Health Svc., 1992, award Navajo Tribe and U.S. Indian Health Svc., 1992, Human Rights Promotion award UN Assn., 1994, Program award for Contbns. to Mental Health of Am. Indians, U.S. Indian Health Svc., 1996, O.B. Michael Outstanding Alumnus award Catawba Coll., 2000. Mem. APHA, Am. Sociol. Assn., Am. Assn. Suicidology, Population Ref. Bur., Coll. on Problems of Drug Dependence, Rsch. Soc. Alcoholism. Methodist. Home: 4610 Idlewilde Ln SE Albuquerque NM 87108-3422 Office: U NMex CASAA 2650 Yale Blvd Albuquerque NM 87106-3202 Office Phone: 505-925-2307. Business E-Mail: pmay@unm.edu.

**MAY, PHYLLIS JEAN,** financial executive; b. Flint, Mich., May 31, 1932; d. Bert A. and Alice C. (Rushton) Irvine; m. John May, Apr. 24, 1971 (dec. 1997). Grad., Dorsey Sch. Bus., 1957; cert., Internat. Corr. Schs., 1959; MBA, Mich. U., 1970; cert., Nat. Tax Inst., 1978. Registered real estate agt; lic. rife, auto and home ins. agt. Office mgr. Comml. Constrn. Co., Flint, 1962-68; bus. mgr. new and used car dealership Flint, 1968-70; contr. various corps., 1970-75; fiscal dir. Rubicon Odyssey Inc., Detroit, 1976-87, Wayne County Treas.'s Office, 1987-93; exec. fin. office Grosse Pointe Meml. Ch., Mich., 1993—. Acad. cons. acctg. Detroit Inst. Commerce, 1980-81; pres. small bus. specializing in adminstrv. cons. and acctg., 1982—; supr. mobile svc. stat., upholstery and home improvement businesses; owner retail bus. Pieces and Things. Pres. PTA Westwood Heights Schs., 1972; vol. Fedn. of Blind, 1974-76. Probate Ct., 1974-76; mem. citizens adv. bd. Northville Regional Psychiat. Hosp., 1988, sec., 1989-90; pres. La Renaissance Condominium Assn., Atlantic City, 1996-2000, sec., 2000-02, treas., 2004—. Recipient Meritorious Svc. award Genesee County for Youth, 1976, Excellent Performance and High Achievement award Odyssey Inc., 1981. Mem. NAFE (bd. dirs.), Am. Bus. Women's Assn. (treas. 1981, rec. sec. 1982, v.p. 1982-83, Woman of Yr. 1982), Womens Assn. Dearborn Orch. Soc., Dearborn Cmty. Art Ctr., Mich. Mental Health Assn., Internat. Platform Assn., Guild of Carillonneurs in N.Am., Pi Omicron (officer 1984-85, treas. 2002-05, state treas. 2004, dist. treas. 2005) Presbyterian. Office Phone: 313-882-5330. Business E-Mail: pmay@gpmchurch.org.

**MAY, RICHARD B.,** psychology professor; b. Seattle, Dec. 20, 1938; s. Louie B. and Ruby J. (Simmons) M.; m. Marjorie Ann Stevenson, Aug. 25, 1962; children: Robert Tobyn, Richard Forrest. BA, Whitman Coll., 1961; MA, Claremont Grad. Sch., 1963, PhD, 1966. Asst. prof. U. Victoria, B.C., Can., 1966-71, assoc. prof. B.C., 1971-81, prof. psychology, 1981-96, prof. emeritus, 1996—; rsch. assoc. Oxford U., England, 1972-73; vis. scholar U. Utah, Salt Lake City, 1995—96. Cons. Victoria Sch. Dist., 1971-72, Dept. Human Resources, Victoria, 1974-75. Author: Application of Statistics in Behavioral Research, 1990; contbr. articles to profl. jours., chpt. to book. Mem. foster care rev. bd. State of Utah, 1997-2001; gen. mgr. RMAY Investments LLC, 2001—. Fellow Social Scis. and Humanities Rsch. Coun., 1972-73, 79-80, 86-87, USPHS, 1962-66; rsch. grantee Nat. Sci. and Engrig. Coun. Rsch., 1969-71, 71-74, 74-77. Avocations: investing, reading, internet, card games. Home: 2072 S Parkwood Cir Spokane WA 99223-5037 Personal E-mail: rb.may@comcast.net.

**MAY, RICHARD WARREN,** writer; b. Marlboro, Mass., Mar. 1, 1944; s. Richard and Lavinia (Crane) M. BS in Psychology, U. Mass., 1968; MA in Humanities and Philosophy, Calif. State U., Dominguez Hills, 1991. Lic. real estate broker. Tchr. Boston Pub. Schs., 1970-89; pres., founder The Aleph (formerly Promethean Pastimes), Boston, 1975—. Adv. bd. mem. and rsch. assoc. Point One Adv. Group, Inc., Madisonville, Ky. Author: (games of strategy) Game of the Gods, 1984, Trihex, 1985, Aliens and Amazons, The Game of Tetra, 1994; contbr. (anthology) Thinking on the Edge, 1993; patentee game bd. and pieces TriHex, 1988. Mem. Assn. Advance Ethical Hypnosis, West Orange, NJ, 1974-75, Boston Tchrs. Union, 1984-89, Point One Adv. Group. Fellow Internat. Soc. Philos. Enquiry (asst. historian 1981-82, diplomate); mem. Nat. Coalition of Ind. Scholars, Prometheus Soc. (past first jour. editor, ombudsman 1984-94, pres. 1991-98), Hoeflin Rsch. Group, The Mega Soc., One-in-Million Soc., Triple Nine Soc. (membership officer 1983-84, regent 1987-90), Mensa, Intertel, Am. Acad. Religion, Internat. Acad. Philosophy (bd. dirs., founder Found.), The Jewish Geneal. Soc., Omega Soc. Office: Point One Adv Group PO Box 1111 Madisonville KY 42431-0022 Personal E-mail: ferdlilac@yahoo.com.

**MAY, ROBERT GEORGE,** dean, accounting educator; b. Detroit, Nov. 11, 1943; s. George Joseph and Winifred Marie (Donnelly) M.; m. Carol Ann Rogers, June 18, 1965; children: Gregory Charles, Lynn Marie. BBA, Mich. State U., 1965, PhD, 1970. Asst. prof. U. Wash., Seattle, 1970-73, assoc. prof., 1973-79; prof. acctg. U. Tex., Austin, 1979—, chmn. dept. acctg., 1988-92, assoc. dean, 1992-95, interim dean, 1995-2001, dean McCombs Sch. Bus., 2001—. Vis. asst. prof. Stanford U., 1972-73; dir. Fedn. Schs. Accountancy, Athens, Ga., 1982. Co-author: Accounting, 1995, Financial Accounting, 1995, Managerial Accounting, 1995, Corporate Financial Accounting, 1995; assoc. editor the Accounting Review Recipient Notable Contbn. to acctg. Lit. award AICPAs, 1976; named Outstanding Alumnus, Mich. State U. Dept. Acctg., 1995. Mem. Am. Acctg. Assn. (chmn. audit sect. 1988-89, pres., adminstrs. of acctg. programs 1993-94, Innovation in Acctg. Edn. award 1991, 93). Office: McCombs Sch Bus U Tex Deans Office 21st and Speedway GSB2 104 Austin TX 78712*

**MAY, ROBERT MCCREDIE (LORD MAY OF OXFORD),** biology educator; b. Sydney, Australia, Jan. 8, 1936; s. Henry W. and Kathleen (McCredie) M.; m. Judith Feiner, Aug. 3, 1962; 1 child, Naomi Felicity. BSc, Sydney U., 1956, PhD, 1959; DSc (hon.), City U. London, 1989, Uppsala U., 1990, Yale U., 1993, Heriot-Watt U., 1994, U. Edinburgh, 1994; DSC (hon.), U. Sydney, 1995. Gordon Mackay lectr. applied math Harvard U., Cambridge, Mass., 1959—61, mem. vis. faculty, 1966; theoretical physics lectr. Sydney U., 1962—64, reader, 1964—69, personal chair, 1969—73; prof. biology Princeton U., NJ, 1973—88; Royal Soc. rsch. prof. U. Oxford, England, 1989—, fellow Merton Coll., 1989—. Vis. faculty Calif. Inst. Tech., 1967; vis. prof. UKAEA Culham Lab., 1971, Magdalen Coll., 1971, Imperial Coll. England, 1975—2000; chief sci. adviser to U.K. Govt., head U.K. Office Sci. and Tech., 1995—2000. Editor: Stability and Complexity in Model Ecosystems, 1973, Population Biology of Infectious Diseases, 1982, Theoretical Ecology: Principles and Applications, 1976, Perspectives in Ecological Theory, 1989, Infectious Diseases of Humans: Dynamics and Control, 1991, Extinction Rates, 1995. Trustee Nuffield Found., Cambridge U. Gates Trust; chmn. emeritus bd. trustees Natural History Museum; bd. mem. UK Sport Institute. Decorated Order of Australia, Knighthood; recipient MacArthur award, 1984, Linnean Medal, Linnean Soc., 1991, Christian Marsh prize, 1992, Frink medal, 1995, Crafoord prize, Royal Swedish Acad. Scis., 1996, Balzan prize, 1998, Blue Planet prize, Asahi Glass Found., 2001, Life Peerage, Ho. of Lords Appointments Commn., 2001, Order of Merit, 2002. Fellow Royal Soc. (pres. 2000-2005), Am. Acad. Arts and Scis.; mem. NAS, Athenaeum Club. Office: The Royal Society 6-9 Carlton House Terrace SW1Y 5AG London England E-mail: robert.may@zoo.ox.ac.uk.

**MAY, ROBERT P.,** energy executive; b. May 1949; married; 5 children. Student, Harvard U. Former CEO Intelogistics divsn. Intelligence Electronics; former COO Towne Air Freight; sr. exec. FedEx Corp., 1973—94; COO, dir. Cablevision Sys. Corp., 1997—99; pres., CEO PNV Inc., 1999—2000; pvt. investor, strategic cons. for telecom. and logistics cos.; interim CEO HealthSouth Corp., Birmingham, Ala., 2003—04, non exec. chmn., 2004—05; acting pres., CEO Charter Communications Inc., St. Louis, 2005; CEO Calpine Corp., San Jose, Calif., 2005—. Bd. dirs. HealthSouth Corp., 2002—03, Charter Communications, Inc., 2004—. With USMC. Office: Calpine Corp 50 W San Fernando St San Jose CA 95113*

**MAY, RONALD ALAN,** lawyer; b. Waterloo, Iowa, Sept. 8, 1928; s. John W. and Elsie (Finlayson) M.; m. Naomi Gray, Aug. 18, 1950 (div. Feb. 1974); children: Sarah, Jonathan, Andrew, Rachel; m. Susan East Gray, May 9, 1975. BA, U. Iowa, 1950; LL.B., Vanderbilt U., 1953. Bar: Ark. 1953. Atty. Daggett & Daggett, Marianna, 1953-57, Wright, Lindsey & Jennings LLP, Little Rock, 1957-84, sr. ptnr., 1984-96; of counsel Wright, Lindsey & Jennings, LLP, 1996—. Editor: Automated Law Research, 1972, Sense and Systems in Automated Law Research, 1975; contbg. editor Fifty State Construction Lien and Bond Law, 1992, Fifty State Public Construction Contracting, 1994, assoc. editor Jour. Irreproducible Results. Pres. Spl. Com. on Pub. Edn., Ark. Assn. for Mental Health, Friends of Library, Central Ark. Radiation Therapy Inst.; chmn. Ark. Cancer Research Ctr., 1990-92; bd. dirs. Nat. Assn. for Mental Health, Ark. State Hosp., Gaines House, State Bd. Architects; bd. dirs. State Bd. Bar Examiners, chmn. 1987-88, Ark. ethics com., 1991-93; trustee Mus. Sci. and Natural History, Little Rock, chmn., 1973; mem. profl. adv. bd. sch. architecture U. Ark., 1990-96, mem. profl. adv. bd. sch. urban studies and design, 1993—; mem. instl. rev. bd. U. Ark. for Med. Scis., 2000—. Served with AUS, 1946-47. Mem. ABA (chmn. sci. and tech. sect. 1975-76), Ark., Pulaski County Bar Assns., Internat. Assn. Def. Counsel, Am. Inns of Ct. (Master of the Bench), Assn. for Computing Machinery, Chamber Music Soc. (bd. Little Rock 2006-), Order of Coif, Phi Beta Kappa. Episcopalian. Home: 821 Ash St Little Rock AR 72205-2051 Office: Wright Lindsey & Jennings LLP 200 W Capitol Ave Ste 2300 Little Rock AR 72201-3699 Office Phone: 501-371-0808. Business E-Mail: rmay@wlj.com.

**MAY, STEPHEN,** writer, federal official, historian; b. Rochester, NY, July 30, 1931; s. Arthur J. and Hilda (Jones) M. Grad., Wesleyan U., 1953; LLB, Georgetown U., 1961. Bar: NY 1963. Exec. asst. to Rep. and Senator Kenneth B. Keating, 1955-64; assoc., mem., then ptnr. Branch, Turner & Wise, Rochester, 1965-81; city councilman-at-large Rochester, 1966-73; mayor, 1970-73; chmn. and commr. N.Y. State Bd. Elections, Albany, 1975-79; asst. sec. for legis. and Congl. rels. Dept. Housing and Urban Devel., 1981-88; ind. historian, writer, lectr. for mags. and newspapers, 1988—. Vice chmn. Temporary State Commn. on Powers of Local Govt., 1970-73; mem. 20th Century Fund Task Force on Future of N.Y.C., 1979, Nat. Adv. Commn. Higher Edn. for Police Officers, 1977-79, Joint Com. Assn. Bar City N.Y. and Drug Abuse Coun. on N.Y. Drug Law Evaluation, 1977-78; chmn. Rochester Interfaith Com. on racial, 1973-81; del.-at-large Rep. Nat. Conv., 1972; mem. N.Y. State Crime Control Planning Bd., 1970-73; historian, writer and lectr. on art, culture, historic preservation and travels, 1988—. Bd. dirs. Police Found., 1970-81, Nat. Com. for Labor Israel, 1977-81, Empire State Report, 1974-81, Inst. Mediation and Conflict Resolution, 1973-81. Served with U.S. Army, 1953-55. Mem. Phi Beta Kappa. Home and Office: 4101 Cathedral Ave NW Washington DC 20016-3585 also: 270 Mt Pleasant Rd Union ME 04862-3003 Office Phone: 202-362-2399, 207-785-4178. Personal E-mail: stephenmay4@yahoo.com.

**MAY, STERLING RANDOLPH,** biology professor, department chairman; b. Muskogee, Okla., Dec. 27, 1946; s. William Sterling and Mary Catherine (Griffith) May. BA with honors, U. Kans., 1968; MS, U. Mich., 1969, PhD, 1977; M in Bus., Johns Hopkins U., 1995, MBA, 2000. Coord. Skin Bank St. Agnes Med. Ctr., Phila., 1977-79, assoc. dir. Burn Rsch., 1980, dir. Burn Rsch., 1981-83; dir. Southeastern Burn Rsch. Inst., Augusta, Ga., 1983-87; v.p. LifeCell Corp., The Woodlands, Tex., 1987-91; chief oper. officer ARC Nat. Hdqs., Arlington, Va., 1991-2000; pres. Health Care Rsch., Arlington, 2000—04; chmn. Dept. Math. and Sci. Brenau U., Gainsville, Ga., 2004—, assoc. prof. biology and genetics, 2004—. Rsch. asst. professor Hahnemann U. Sch. Medicine, Phila., 1979-82, rsch. assoc. prof., 1983; assoc. clin. prof. Med. Coll. Ga., 1984-87; adj. prof. U. Tex. Med. Sch., Houston, 1987-91. Editor: Care of the Burn Wound, 1985; author 84 published articles in biomed. lit., 1974—; mem. editorial bd. Jour. Burn Care and Rehab., 1982-90, Burns, 1985-92, Cryobiology, 1987-93. Mem. Soc. for Cryobiology (pres. 1989-91, chmn. 23d ann. meeting 1986), Am. Burn Assn. (chmn. rsch. com. 1998-2000), Internat. Soc. For Burn Injuries (mem. gen. coun. 1982-90), Am. Assn. Tissue Banks (sec. 1991-93, v.p. 1993-95, pres. 1995-97, bd. govs. 1989-93). Avocations: antique furniture, music. Home: 2318 River Cliff Dr Gainesville GA 30501-1685 Office: Dept Math and Sci Brenau Univ 500 Washington St NE Gainesville GA 30501 Office Phone: 770-534-6278. Business E-Mail: rmay@brenau.edu.

**MAY, THOMAS J.,** electric company executive; BS, Stonehill Coll.; MS in Fin., Bentley Coll. Various positions Boston Edison Co., 1976-90, exec. v.p., 1990-93, pres., CEO, 1993-94, chmn., CEO, 1994-99, NStar, Boston, 1999—. Office: NStar MSC P 1600 800 Boylston St Boston MA 02199

**MAY, TIMOTHY JAMES,** lawyer; b. Denver, Aug. 3, 1932; s. Thomas Henry and Helen Frances (O'Conner) M.; m. Monica Anita Gross, Aug. 24, 1957; children: Stephanie, Maureen, Cynthia, Timothy, Anthony. BA, Cath. U. Am., 1954; LLB, Georgetown U., 1957, LLM, 1960. Bar: D.C. 1957, US Ct. Appeals (Armed Forces, DC, 2d, 3d cir.), U.S. Supreme Ct. 1961. Law clk. to judge U.S. Ct. Appeals, D.C. Cir., 1957-58; assoc. Covington & Burling, Washington, 1958-61; cons. Exec. Office of Pres. U.S., Washington, 1961-62; chief counsel subcom. on antitrust Armed Svcs. Com., U.S. Senate, Washington, 1962-63; mng. dir. Fed. Maritime Commn., Washington, 1963-66; gen. counsel U.S. Post Office Dept., Washington, 1966-69; ptnr., Postal Policy & Regulation, Legis. Affairs practices, Patton Boggs LLP, Washington, 1969—, mem. exec. com. Bd. dirs. Legal Aid Soc. DC, 1984—; pres. Holy Family of Bethlehem Found., 1997-99, Coun. for Ct. Excellence, Washington, 1999-2005, Marine Corps Law Enforcement Found., 1996-2003; chmn. Bd. regents Cath. U. Am., 1988-93, trustee, 1993-2005, trustee emeritus, 2005—. Recipient Servant of Justice award Legal Aid Soc. D.C. 1997, St. Elizabeth Ann Seton award SOAR!, 1998, Caritas award Archdiocese D.C., 1998, Presdl. Award for Pub. Adminstrn., Jump Mem. Award. Fellow Am. Bar Found. (life); mem. ABA (House of Dels.), Fed. Bar Assn., Bar Assn. of DC (pres. 1991-92, Lawyer of Yr. award 1999), Congl. Country Club (bd. govs. 1992-98, sec. 1994-97), Nat. Christian Leadership Conf. for Israel (exec. com. 1992-2003), Met. Club, Indian Creek Country Club (bd. dirs. 1999—, pres. 2005—), Fed. City Coun., Econ. Club DC (bd. dirs. 2001—), Knight of Malta, Constantinian Order St. George (knight). Democrat. Roman Catholic. Home: 3828 52nd St NW Washington DC 20016-1924 Office: Patton Boggs LLP 2550 M St NW Washington DC 20037-1350 Home (Winter): 286 Bal Bay Dr Miami FL 33154 Office Phone: 202-457-6050. Office Fax: 202-457-6315. Business E-Mail: tmay@pattonboggs.com.

**MAY, WILLIAM FREDERICK,** manufacturing executive; b. Chgo., Oct. 25, 1915; s. Arthur W. and Florence (Hartwick) M.; m. Kathleen Thompson, June 14, 1947; children: Katherine Hartwick (Mrs. Edward W. Bickford), Elizabeth Shaw. BS, U. Rochester, 1937; grad. Advanced Mgmt. Program, Harvard U., 1950; D in Engring., Clarkson U.; LLD, Okla. Christian Coll.; LHD, Livingstone U.; LLD, Lafayette U. Rsch. worker E.I. Du Pont de Nemours Co., 1937-38; with Am. Can Co., Greenwich, Conn., 1940-80, mgr., 1957-58, v.p., 1958-64, exec. v.p., 1964-65, vice chmn. bd. dirs., 1965, chmn. bd. dirs., CEO, 1965-80, mem. exec. com.—. Dean Grad. Sch. Bus. Adminstrn., NYU, 1980-84; chmn. and CEO Statue of Liberty Found., 1984—. Bd. dirs. Lincoln Ctr.; trustee Am. Ditchley Found., Am. Mus. Natural History, Columbia-Presbyn. Hosp., U. Rochester; mem. corp. Poly. Inst. N.Y.; chmn. pub. policy coun. Advt. Coun. Mem. Nat. Order of Merit (France, officier), Econ. Club, Round Hill Club, Megunticook Golf Club,

Indian Harbor Yacht Club, Camden Yacht Club, Phi Beta Kappa, Alpha Delta Phi. Episcopalian. Home: 84 Indian Harbor Dr Greenwich CT 06830-7148 Office: Statue of Liberty Found 292 Madison Ave New York NY 10017-7769 Personal E-mail: wkmay@aol.com.

**MAY, WILLIAM HATHAWAY,** lawyer; BSME, Va. Poly. Inst., 1964; MS, U. So. Calif., 1970; LLB, U. Va., 1972. Bar: Calif. 1973. Assoc. Fowler Knobbe & Martens, 1972-76; div. staff atty. Beckman Coulter, Inc. (formerly Beckman Instruments, Inc.), Fullerton, Calif., 1976-79; sr. div. staff atty. 1979-82, litigation counsel, 1982-83, counsel litigation and corp. affairs, 1983-84, gen. counsel, sec., 1984-85, v.p., gen. counsel, sec., 1985—. Trustee Santa Ana Sch. Dist., 1982-83; mem. Santa Ana Pers. Bd., 1973-76, 81-82. Capt. USAF, 1966-70. Mem. L.A. Patent Law Assn. (chmn. corp. practice sect. 1977-78, bd. dirs. securities 1978-80). Office: Beckman Coulter Inc 2500 N Harbor Blvd Fullerton CA 92835-2601.

**MAYARAM, KARTIKEYA,** electrical engineer, educator; arrived in U.S., 1981; m. Namita Gandhi. BS in Engring. with honors, Birla Inst. Tech. and Sci., 1981; MS, SUNY, 1982; PhD, U. Calif., Berkeley, 1988. Mem. tech. staff Tex. Instruments Inc., Dallas, 1988—92, Bell Labs., Allentown, Pa., 1992—96; assoc. prof. Wash. State U., Pullman, Wash., 1996—99, Oreg. State U., Corvallis, Oreg., 2000—03, prof., 2003—. Cons. Mentor Graphics Corp., Wilsonville, Oreg., 1998—2001, Lucent Bell Labs., Allentown, Pa., 1996—98, Fairchild Semiconductor, San Jose, Calif., 2000—01; tech. advisor Berkeley Design Automation, Santa Clara, Calif., 2003—. Co-author: Analog Integrated Circuits for Communication: Principles, Simulation and Design. Grantee Career award, NSF, 1997—2001. Fellow: IEEE (fellow 2005). Office Phone: 541-737-2972. Business E-Mail: karti@eecs.oregonstate.edu.

**MAYDEN, BARBARA MENDEL,** lawyer; b. Chattanooga, Sept. 18, 1951; d. Eugene Lester Mendel and Blanche (Krugman) Rosenberg; m. Martin Ted Mayden, Sept. 14, 1986. AB, Ind. U., 1973; JD, U. Ga., 1976. Bar: Ga. 1976, N.Y. 1980. Assoc. King & Spalding, Atlanta, 1976-79, Willkie Farr & Gallagher, N.Y.C., 1980, Morgan Lewis & Bockius, N.Y.C., 1982-83, White & Case, N.Y.C., 1982-89; spl. counsel Skadden, Arps, Slate, Meagher & Flom, N.Y.C., 1989-95; mem. Bass, Berry & Sims PLC, Nashville, 1996—; lectr. Vanderbilt U. Sch. Law, Nashville, 1995-97. Mem. editl. bd.: mag. Business Law Today; editor: Business Lawyer; chair sect. bus. law:, 2004—05. Mem. bd. visitors U. Ga. Sch. Law, Athens, 1986—89; mem. Leadership Nashville, 1999—2000; mem. adv. bd. Women's Fund of the Cmty. Found. of Mid. Tenn., 2001—; bd. dirs. YWCA, 2001—, Jewish Cmty. Ctr., 2001—02. Fellow Am. Bar Found. (life); mem. ABA (chair young lawyers divsn. 1985-86, ho. of dels. 1986—2004, commn. on women 1987-91, commn. opportunities for minorities in profession 1986-87, select com. of the house 1989-91, chmn. assembly resolutions com. 1990-91, membership com. of the house 1991-92, bd. govs. 1991-94, chair com. on rules and calendar 1996-98, chair bd. govs. ops. com., exec. com. 1993-94, task force long range fin. planning 1993-94, com. scope correlation of work 1998-2003, chair 2001-02, sec. bus. law sect. 2001-02, vice-chair 2002-03, chair-elect 2003-04, chair 2004—05), Nat. Assn. Bond Lawyers (bd. dirs. 1985-86), Bond Attys.' Workshop (chmn. 1986), N.Y. State Bar Assn. (ho. of dels. 1993-95), Assn. Bar City N.Y. (internat. human rights com. 1986-89, 2d century com. 1986-90, com. women in the profession, 1989-92), N.Y. County Lawyers Assn. (com. spl. projects, chair com. rels with other bars), Am. Law Inst., Tenn. Bar Assn. (com. chair), Am. Bar Ins. Plans Cons., Inc. (bd. dirs., treas.). Democrat. Jewish. Home: 4414 Herbert Pl Nashville TN 37215-4544 Office: Bass Berry & Sims PLC AmSouth Center 315 Deaderick St Ste 2700 Nashville TN 37238-3001 Office Phone: 615-742-6208. Business E-Mail: bmayden@bassberry.com.

**MAYEAUX, ANNE RUSSELL,** education educator; b. Meridian, Miss., Aug. 27, 1943; d. Constant Hyacinth and Laura Archer Mayeaux. BA, St. Xavier U., 1961—65; PhD, Emory U., 1968—75. Dir. World Peace Ctr., Chgo., 1967—68; postdoctoral fellow and adj. faculty Candler Sch. of Theology, Atlanta, 1975—81. Exec. dir. Ga. Endowment for the Humanities, 1979—81; faculty and pres. Aquinas Ctr. of Theology at Emory U., Atlanta, 1983—90; vis. scholar in ethics and soc. Harvard Div. Sch., Cambridge, Mass., 1990—91; assoc. prof. Siena Heights U., Adrian, Mich., 1991—96; rschr. Inst. for Social Rsch., U. of Mich., 1996—99; chair, theology dept., and faculty St. Joseph, Madison, Miss., 1999—; adj. faculty Hinds C.C., Jackson, Miss., 2000—. Contbr. articles to jours. Pres. Las Casas, Nat. Ministry among the Native Americans, Clinton, Okla., 1989—93; bd. dirs. Nat. Assembly of Religious Women, Chgo., 1991—94; sec./treas. Internat. Found. for Scholarly Exch., Atlanta, 1988—94. Recipient Human Rights Citation, Dominican Justice Promoters of N.Am., 1991, Outstanding Tchg. of the Yr., Siena Heights U., 1992—93, Internat. Del. of Scholars to Russia and the Ukraine, People to People and Am. Acad. of Religion, 1993, Outstanding Tchg., Archdiocese of Atlanta, 1983—84, Catharine of Siena award, St. Catharine's Dominican Congregation, 1990, Citation for Courage for Human Rights Work in Gulf War, U.S. Dominican Leadership Conf., 1991; Catherine McAuley scholar, St. Xavier U., 1965, Raskob Found. grant, Raskob Found., 1992—94, N.E.H. Landmarks of Am. History: Summer Inst., Nat. Endowment for the Humanities, 2004, grant, 2002, Fulbright Scholar, U. of Tuebingen, German, Fulbright Commn., 1966—67. Mem.: AAUP (v.p., siena heights u. chpt. 1995), Am. Acad. of Religion (chair, program sect., s.e. region 1975—91). Democrat-Npl- Roman Catholic. Home: 217 Melrose Dr Jackson MS 39211

**MAYER, ALLAN,** communications consultant, writer; b. N.Y.C., Mar. 15, 1950; s. Theodore H. and Phyllis (Zwick) M. BA, Cornell U., 1971. Staff reporter Wall Street Jour., N.Y.C., 1972-73; fgn. corr. London, 1977-80, sr. editor Newsweek mag., N.Y.C., 1973-77, fgn. corr. London, 1977-80, sr. editor N.Y.C., 1980-82; editl. dir. Arbor House Pub., N.Y.C. 1986-88; sr. editor Simon & Schuster, N.Y.C., 1988-89; editor-in-chief Buzz mag., L.A. 1990-95, editor-in-chief, pub., 1996; sr. prnr. Sitrick and Co., L.A., 1997—2004, mng. dir., 2004—. Author: Madam Prime Minister, 1980, Gaston's War, 1987; co-author: Spin, 1998. Recipient award Overseas Press Club, 1974, Nat. Mag. award Am. Soc. Mag. Editors, 1978, William Allen White award City and Regional Mag. Assn., 1995-96. Mem. Writers Guild Am. Office Phone: 310-788-2850. E-mail: allan_mayer@sitrick.com.

**MAYER, ANTHONY JOHN,** investment company executive; b. Milw., Apr. 21, 1936; s. Anton J. and Mary (Plensk) Mayer. BS in Bus., Marquette U., 1958, advanced degree in Bus., 1965. Registered investment adv., 1994; cert. nutritionist. Ins. claims exec., 1962—65; adminstrv. mgr. Marquette U., 1960—63; founder Fixed Income Mutual Fund, Milw., 1968—; motel exec., 1968—80; pres. Anthony J. Mayer, Inc., Milw., 1994—; v.p. Banc One Investment Mgmt. Group, Chgo., 2001—. Chmn. Westridge Investors, 1998—, New Berlin Investors, 1998—, Millionaire Investor Entities Guidance.Com, 2000—, Hungarian Investors Com., 2003; country music seminar host, 1995. Anthony J. Mayer Investment Parables, 1995, Anthony J. Mayer Investment Advisory Book, 2003; author, editor, newsletter: Anthony J. Mayer Investment Bible, 1995:; columnist: Alaska newspapers, 1959—60; contbr. articles to profl. jours.; investment radio personality, 1990—93; prodr.: (plays) Surviving Without Love, 2001. Mem. Am. Red Cross, Hmls 1961-62; trustee Anthony J. Mayer Trust, 1991-2004; Jesuit Ptnrs., 1998—; active Ignatius Loyola Inner Circle, 1999-; pres. Pub. Lands Decor Classics, 2000-; bd. dirs. West Allis Food for Milw., First Mcpl. Credit Union, 1996-2001, Mukwonago State Bank, Wis., 2006-; del. Adv. Coun. Nat. Rep. Congl. Com., 2001-; mem. Rep. Nat. Com., 2005-; chmn. adv. bd. Nat. Rep. Party, 2004-; hon. sponsor Pres. Bush victory dinner, 2001; grassroots leader Rep. Campaign, 2004. With U.S. Army, 1958-60. Named Successful Investor of Yr., Sta. WGN, 1996, Notable Pulaskian, Milw. Pub. Sch. Sys., 1999; recipient VIP award, Speedway-Super Am., 1995, 2000, Cleve. Meadows Achievement award, 1998, Commendation cert., State of Wis., 2002, Animal Stewardship award, 2002, Cmty. Svc. award, Jerusalem Christian, 2003. Mem.: N.Am. Investors Alliance (founder, chmn. 1993), Rep. Govs. Assn., Aircraft Owners Assn., Acad. Country Music, Country Music Assn., KC. Roman Catholic. Avocation: reading. Office Phone: 414-321-7126.

**MAYER, CARL JOSEPH,** prosecutor, lawyer; b. Boston, Apr. 23, 1959; s. Arno Joseph and Nancy Sue (Grant) M. AB magna cum laude, Princeton U., 1981; JD, U. of Chgo., 1986; LLM, Harvard U., 1988. Bar: N.J. 1986, Mass. 1988, N.Y. 1989, D.C. 1989. Writer for Ralph Nader, Washington, 1981-83; law clk. to presiding justice U.S. Dist. Ct., Wilmington, Del., 1986-87; law assoc., prof. Hofstra Law Sch., Hempstead, N.Y., 1989-94; atty. Milberg, Weiss, Bershad, Hynes and Lerach, N.Y.C., 1995-96; spl. counsel N.Y. State Atty. Gen.'s Office, N.Y.C., 1999—2000; pvt. practice Mayer Law Group, 2000—. Cons. U.S. Senate Com., Washington, 1988-89. Author: Shakedown, 1998; co-author: Public Domain, Private Dominion, 1985; contbr. articles to profl. jours. Town committeeman, Princeton, N.J., 1995-98. NYU fellow, 1988-89. Mem. ABA, N.Y. Bar Assn., N.J. Bar Assn., Mass. Bar Assn. Avocations: running, squash, tennis. Home: 58 Battle Rd Princeton NJ 08540-4902 Office: Mayer Law Group 1040 Ave of Americas Ste 2400 New York NY 10018 Office Phone: 212-382-4686. E-mail: cyberesquire@aol.com.

**MAYER, CHRISTOPHER,** lawyer; b. Phila., Feb. 21, 1946; BA, Princeton U., 1968; JD, Columbia U., 1974. Bar: N.Y. 1975. Assoc. Davis Polk & Wardell, N.Y.C., 1974—82, ptnr., 1982—, mem. firm mgmt. com., 1992—2005. Mem. ABA, N.Y. State Bar Assn., Assn. of Bar of City of N.Y. Office: Davis Polk & Wardwell 450 Lexington Ave New York NY 10017-3982 Office Phone: 212-450-4338. Office Fax: 212-450-3338. Business E-Mail: chris.mayer@dpw.com.

**MAYER, FREDERICK RICKARD,** oil industry executive; b. Youngstown, Ohio, Jan. 25, 1928; s. Frederick Miller and Mildred Kathryn (Rickard) M.; m. Jan MacCasler Perry, Nov. 1, 1958; children: Frederick MacCasler, Anthony Rickard, Perry Ellen. BA, Yale U., 1950. Founder, pres. Exeter Drilling Co., Dallas and Denver, 1953-70, chmn. bd., chief exec. officer, 1970-80. Chmn. bd., dir. Exeter Drilling No., Inc., Denver, Exeter Drilling So., Inc., New Orleans, until 1982 Chmn. Wallace Village for Children, 1971-74; trustee Graland Country Day Sch., 1973-79; mem. arts adv. com. Phillips Exeter Acad., 1974—, trustee, 1980—; trustee Denver Art Museum, 1970-, v.p., 1971-75, chmn. bd. trustees, 1975-79, interim chmn. bd. trustees, 1980-81; trustee Am. Fedn. Arts, 1977-81, Nat. Gallery, 1983—; founder JFM Foundation, Denver. Served with U.S. Army, 1950-52. Named one of Top 200 Collectors, ARTnews Mag., 2004, 2006. Mem. Ind. Petroleum Assn. Am. (exec. com.), Chief Execs. Forum, Metro Denver Exec. Club, Am. Petroleum Inst. (bd. dirs.), Ind. Petroleum Assn. Mountain States (Rocky Mountain Wildcatter of Yr. award 1983), 25 Yr. Club of Petroleum Industry, Nat. Petroleum Council, Inst. Nautical Archaeology (bd. dirs. 1981-85, chmn. bd. 1985—). Clubs: Cherry Hills Country, Univ. of Denver, Garden of Gods, Castle Pines Golf, Denver and Dallas Petroleum, N.Y. Yacht. Avocation: Collector of Colonial and Latin American art. Home: PO Box 481150 Denver CO 80248-1150 Office: Exeter Drilling Co PO Box 5083 Denver CO 80217-5083 also: 1700 Lincoln St Suite 5000 Denver CO 80203*

**MAYER, GEORGE ROY,** education educator; b. National City, Calif, Aug. 28, 1940; s. George Eberly and Helen Janet (Knight) M.; m. Barbara Ann Fife, Sept. 9, 1964 (div. June 1986); children: Kevin Roy, Debbie Rae Ann; m. Jocelyn Volk Finn, Aug. 3, 1986 (div. July 2003); m. Mary Rossetti, Sept. 22, 2005 BA, San Diego State U., 1962; MA, Ind. U., 1965, EdD, 1966. Cert. sch. psychologist; bd.-cert. behavior analyst. Sch. counselor, psychologist Ind. U., Bloomington, 1964-66; asst. prof. guidance and ednl. psychology So. Ill. U., Carbondale, 1966-90; prof. edn. Calif. State U., L.A., 1966—. Cons. in field; adv. bd. Dept. Spl. Edn., L.A., 1986-90, Jay Nolan Ctr. for Autism, Newhall, Calif., 1975-86; lectr. in field; study group on youth violence prevention Nat. Ctr. for Injury Prevention and Control, Divsn. Violence Prevention of the Ctrs. for Disease Control and Prevention, 1998. Author: Classroom Mgmt.: A Calif. Resource Guide, 2000, Teaching Alternative Behaviors Schoolwide: Preventing Schoolwide Behavior Problems, 2003, Gang Prevention, 2006; co-author: Behavior Analysis for Lasting Change, 1991; contbr. articles to profl. jour. Recipient Outstanding Prof. award Calif. State U-L.A., 1988; U.S. Dept. Edn. grantee, 1996—. Mem. Assn. for Behavior Analysis, Nat. Assn. Sch. Psychologists, Calif. Assn. Behavior Analysis (hon. life, pres., conf. chmn.. Outstanding Contbr. to Behavior Analysis award 1997), Cambridge Ctr. for Behavioral Studies (adv. bd.), Calif. Assn. Sch. Psychologists (chmn. practitioners conf. 1994—). Avocations: horseback riding, fishing, swimming. Home: 10735 Frank Daniels Way San Diego CA 92131- Office Phone: 858-361-1993. Personal E-mail: grmayer@aol.com.

**MAYER, GERARD J.,** physician; b. Buenos Aires, Nov. 8, 1942; Came to the U.S., 1968. s. Ludwig and Yvonne (Moritz) M.; m. Nicole Paulette Wolf, July 23, 1971; children: Daniella, Marc. BA, Saint Andrews Scots Sch., Olivos, Argentina, 1960; MD, U. Buenos Aires, 1967. Diplomate Am. Bd. Pediatrics. Intern pediatrics Michael Reese Hosp., Chgo., 1968-69, resident in pediatrics, 1969-70, Montefiore Med. Ctr., Bronx, NY, 1970-71, Strong Meml. Hosp., U. of Rochester, NY, 1971-72; fellow in pediatrics St. Christopher's Hosp. for Children, Phila., 1972-74; attending physician Montefiore Hosp., Bronx, 1974—, North Central, Bronx, 1976-98; pvt. practice Yorktown Heights, NY, 1985—; head pediatric emergency Montefiore-NCB, Bronx, 1978-83; head pediatric primary care North Central Bronx Hosp., 1978-85; attending physician No. Westchester Hosp., Mount Kisco, NY, 1986—. Fellow Am. Acad. Pediatrics. Home: 60 Old Aspetong Rd Katonah NY 10536-3845 Office: 1880 Commerce St Yorktown Heights NY 10598 Office Phone: 914-962-5556.

**MAYER, HALDANE ROBERT,** federal judge; b. Buffalo, Feb. 21, 1941; s. Haldane Rupert and Myrtle Kathleen Mayer; m. Mary Anne McCurdy, Aug. 13, 1966; children: Anne Christian, Rebecca Paige. BS, U.S. Mil. Acad., 1963; JD, Coll. William and Mary, 1971. Bar: Va. 1971, D.C. 1980, U.S. Ct. Appeals (4th cir.) 1972, U.S. Dist. Ct. (ea. dist.) Va. 1972, U.S. Ct. Mil. Appeals 1973, U.S. Supreme Ct. 1977, U.S. Ct. Claims 1984. Law clk. U.S. Ct. Appeals (4th cir.), Richmond, Va., 1971—72; atty. McGuire Woods & Battle, Charlottesville, Va., 1975—77; spl. asst. to chief justice U.S. Supreme Ct., Washington, 1977—80; atty. Baker & McKenzie, Washington, 1980—81; acting spl. counsel U.S. Merit Systems Protection Bd., Washington, 1981—82; judge U.S. Claims Ct., Washington, 1982—87, U.S. Ct. Appeals (Fed. cir.), Washington, 1987—, chief judge, 1997—2004. Adj. prof. U. Va. Sch. Law, 1975—77, 1992—96, George Washington U. Law Sch., 1992—96. Bd. dirs. William and Mary Law Sch. Assn., 1979—85. Maj. U.S. Army, 1963—75, ret. lt. col. USAR. Decorated Bronze Star. Mem.: West Point Soc. D.C., Army Athletic Assn., West Point Assn. Grads., Omicron Delta Kappa. Office: US Ct Appeals for Fed Cir 717 Madison Pl NW Washington DC 20439-0002 Office Phone: 202-633-6556.*

**MAYER, IRA EDWARD,** gastroenterologist; b. Bklyn., July 31, 1951; s. Elias M. and Mollie (Taxerman) M.; m. Celeste Ann Sivak, Mar. 13, 1976; children: Madelaine Rose, Amanda Beth. BS, Bklyn. Coll., 1972; MD, N.Y. Med. Coll., 1975. Diplomate Am. Bd. Internal Medicine, Am. Bd. Gastroenterology, Nat. Bd. Med. Examiners. Asst. resident in internal medicine N.Y. Med. Coll./Met. Hosp. Ctr., N.Y.C., 1975-76, resident in internal medicine, 1976-78; fellow digestive diseases divsn. Emory U., Atlanta, 1978-80; attending gastroenterologist Maimonides Med. Ctr., Bklyn., 1980—, pres. med. staff, 2005—; clin. instr. medicine SUNY Health Sci. Ctr., Bklyn., 1980-81, instr. medicine, 1981-83, clin. asst. prof. medicine, 1983—2002, chmn. patient care com., 1984-99; clin. asst. prof. medicine Mt. Sinai Sch. Medicine, 2003—. Author: (with others) Digestive Diseases, 1983, Medicine, 1983; contbr. articles to profl. jours. Fellow ACP, Am. Coll. Gastroenterology; mem. Am. Gastroent. Assn., Am. Soc. for Gastrointestinal Endoscopy, N.Y. Acad. Scis., N.Y. Acad. Gastroenterolgy, N.Y. Soc. for Gastrointestinal Endoscopy, Med. Soc. for the State of N.Y. Jewish. Office: 2560 Ocean Ave Brooklyn NY 11229-4521 Office Phone: 718-891-0100.

**MAYER, JAMES HOCK,** lawyer, mediator; b. Neptune City, NJ, Nov. 1, 1935; s. J. Kenneth and Marie Ruth (Hock) M.; m. Carol I. Keating, Sept. 20, 1958 (div. Feb. 1981); children: Craig, Jeffrey; m. Patrisha Renk, Mar. 28, 1981 (div. July 2001); m. Judith Courtemanche, Mar. 23, 2004. AB with distinction, Dartmouth Coll., 1957; JD, Harvard U., 1964. Bar: Calif. 1965,

U.S. Dist. Ct (no. dist., so. dist.) Calif. 1965, U.S. Ct. Appeals (9th cir.) 1965, U.S. Supreme Ct. 1974. Assoc. Pillsbury, Madison & Sutro, San Francisco, 1964—72, ptnr., 1973—; ind. mediator, 1992—. Mem. Chancellor's Assocs. U. Calif. San Diego. Rear adm. USNR, 1957-93. Rufus Choate scholar Dartmouth Coll., 1956-57. Mem. Newcomen Soc., Navy League, Naval Order of U.S., Harvard Club, La Jolla Country Club, La Jolla Beach and Tennis Club. Office: Mayer Mediation Svcs 7924 Ivanhoe Ave Ste 3 La Jolla CA 92037 Home: 2370 Avenida de La Playa La Jolla CA 92037 Office Phone: 858-551-5525. Business E-Mail: just-results@msn.com.

**MAYER, JAMES JOSEPH,** retired corporate lawyer; b. Cin., Nov. 27, 1938; s. Cletus Joseph and Berna Mae (Schroeder) M.; m. Margaret Ann Hobbs, Oct. 24, 1964; children: Kimberly, Susanne, Terri. BEE, U. Cin., 1961; JD, No. Ky. U., 1969. Registered profl. engr., Ohio. Bar: Ohio 1969, Ky. 1975. Engr. Cin. Gas & Electric Co., 1961-69, atty., 1969-85, gen. counsel, 1986-91, v.p., gen. counsel, 1991-95, ret., 1995; of counsel Taft, Stettinius & Hollister, Cin., 1995—. With USAFR, 1961-64. Mem. Ohio Bar Assn., Ky. Bar Assn., Cin. Bar Assn., Terrace Park Country Club. Republican. Roman Catholic. Avocations: home remodeling, sports, golf. Office Phone: 513-381-2838. Business E-Mail: mayer@taftlaw.com.

**MAYER, JODY LYNN (JODY LYNN NOEL),** exercise physiologist; b. Hanover, Pa., Feb. 21, 1978; d. Henry T. and Cynthia M. Noel; m. Adam Joseph Moyer, Apr. 29, 2006. BA magna cum laude in Health and Exercise Sci., Gettysburg Coll., Pa., 2000; MS in Exercise Physiology, Ithaca Coll., NY, 2001. Cert. athletic trainer Nat. Athletic Trainer's Assn., 2000, personal trainer Am. Coun. Exercise, 1999, strength and conditioning specialist Nat. Strength and Conditioning Assn., 2001, health and fitness instr. Am. Coll. Sports Medicine, 2001. Exercise physiologist and athletic trainer Hanover Hosp., Pa., 2001—. Mem.: Amercian Coun. Exercise, Nat. Strength & Conditioning Assn., Amercian Coll. Sports Medicine, Nat. Athletic Trainer's Assn., Phi Beta Kappa. Roman Catholic. Avocations: exercise, fitness, health & wellness, sports medicine. Home: 38 Bonnie Field Cir Gettysburg PA 17325 Office: Hanover Hosp Med Fitness Ctr Ste 100 250 Fame Ave Hanover PA 17331 Office Phone: 717-633-8869. Office Fax: 717-633-8868. E-mail: meyerj@hanoverhospital.org.

**MAYER, JOHN,** musician; b. Bridgeport, Conn., Oct. 16, 1977; Student, Berklee Coll. Music. Singer: (albums) Inside Wants Out, 1999, Room for Squares, 2001 (Grammy award Best Male Pop Vocal Performance for song "Your Body is A Wonderland", 2002), Any Given Thursday, 2003, Heavier Things, 2003, As/is, 2004, Continuum, 2006; singer: (with John Mayer Trio) Try! John Mayer Trio Live In Concert, 2005; composer: (films) Serendipity, 2001, Vanilla Sky, 2001, How to Deal, 2003, Win a Date with Tad Hamilton!, 2004; exec. prodr.: (TV series) John Mayer Has a TV Show, 2004; monthly columnist Esquire mag., 2004—. Recipient Grammy Award for Song of the Yr. (Daughters), 2005. Office: Mick Mgmt c/o Michael McDonald 157 Chambers St 12th Fl New York NY 10007 also: Creative Artists Agy c/o Scott Clayton 3310 West End Ave 5th Fl Nashville TN 37203

**MAYER, JOHN ANTON, JR.,** bank executive; b. Phila., Mar. 8, 1940; BA, Princeton U., 1962; MBA, Harvard U., 1964. Head, securities subsidiary J.P. Morgan & Co., London, 1979—86, sr. v.p., mergers and acquisitions group N.Y.C., 1986—90, head, global investment banking, 1990—95, CFO, 1995—99; CEO J.P. Morgan Capital Corp., N.Y.C., 1999—2002; ptnr. Cove Harbor Partners. Bd. dirs. T.W. Phillips Gas and Oil Co. Bd. dirs. Ewing Marion Kauffman Found., 1994—, chair, bd. dirs., 2003—. Avocations: golf, tennis, skiing. Office: Cove Harbor Partners 1 Dock St Ste 400 Stamford CT 06901*

**MAYER, JOYCE HARRIS,** artist; b. N.Y.C., May 7, 1935; d. Harold and Dorothy Harris; m. Thomas Charles Mayer, Mar. 15, 1969; 1 child, Robert Charles. AAS, Inst. of Applied Art and Sci., N.Y.C., 1957. Sketcher Merrylen Cartooning Studio, 1952. Client contact, layout artist, Haire Publ., N.Y.C., 1957-59; art dir., Real Estate Forum, N.Y.C., 1959-60; Denhard and Stewart, N.Y.C., 1960-67; Herb Lubalin Graphic Art Award, 1964; self employed N.Y.C., 1967-71; co curator, New Orleans Mus. of Art, 1985. Among first women to have work pub. in Art Direction, 1964, exhibitions include N.Y. Inst. of Applied Arts and Sci., New Orleans Mus. of Art, 2003, Horizon Gallery, Royal Typographers, N.Y., Nat. Arts Club, Tulane Univ., Dominican Coll., Robinson Gallery, Mario Villa and Arthur Roger, New Orleans, TWEED Gallery, Plainfield, N.J., Barbara Gillman Gallery, Miami, Contemporary Art Ctr., New Orleans, Bruce Mus., Conn., Historic New Orleans Collection, N.C. Mus. Art, LBI Found. Arts and Sci. N.J., Cheltenham Art Ctr., Pa., Long Beach Island Nat. Exhbn., 2004, NJ Print Coun. Traveling Internat. Competition, 2005, AIR Gallery, Chelsea, N.Y., 2006, Spring Bull Gallery, Newport, R.I., 2006, Represented in permanent collections paintings, mono prints, and digital art in numerous collections in Europe and. U.S., Digital La., Contemporary Art Ctr., New Orleans, 2002, Biennale Internazionale dell Arte Contemporanea, Florence, Italy, 2003, N.C. Mus. Art, numerous others. Mem. Bd. Edn., Greenwich, Conn., 1978; art advisor Freeport McMoRan Art Collection, New Orleans, 1985; curator Mario Villa Gallery, New Orleans, 1989; juror Arts Coun., New Orleans, 1990. Recipient Chiam Gross sculpture award, 1967, N.Y. Graphic Soc. award, 1976, medal in photography, Florence Biennale, 2003, Otis B. Morse Meml. award, Am. Coll., Pa., 2005. Mem. Medici Coll. Art Assn., Am. Color Print Soc., The Print Ctr. Avocations: reading, theater, ballet, birdwatching. Studio: 8 Golf-view Dr Medford NJ 08055 Office Phone: 609-953-2390. E-mail: joycehmayer@aol.com.

**MAYER, MARISSA ANN,** information technology executive; b. Wausau, Wis., May 30, 1975; BS with honors in Symbolic Sys., Stanford U., MS in Computer Sci. With UBS rsch. lab, Zurich, Switzerland, SRI Internat., Menlo Park, Calif.; programmer, software engr. Google Inc., 1999, dir. consumer web products Mountain View, v.p. search products & user experience. Tchr. computer programming Stanford U. Named one of 25 Masters of Innovation, BusinessWeek, 2006; recipient Centennial Teaching Award, Stanford U., Forsythe Award. Office: Google Inc 1600 Amphitheatre Pky Mountain View CA 94043 Office Phone: 650-253-0000. Office Fax: 650-253-0001.*

**MAYER, MARTIN PRAGER,** writer; b. N.Y.C., Jan. 14, 1928; s. Henry and Ruby (Prager) M.; m. Ellen Moers, June 23, 1949 (dec. Aug. 1979); children: Thomas, James; m. Karin Lissakers, Oct. 25, 1980; children: Fredrica, Henry. AB, Harvard U., 1947; D.Litt. (hon.), Wake Forest U., 1977, Adelphi U., 1981. Reporter, N.Y. Jour. Commerce, 1947-48; asst. editor Labor and Nation, 1948-49; editor Hillman Periodicals, 1949-51; assoc. editor Esquire mag., 1951-54, record critic, 1952-75; freelance writer, 1954—; N.Y. critic Opera Mag. (Eng.), 1985—2004; columnist American Banker, 1987-89. Rsch. dir. study of internat. secondary edn. Twentieth Century Fund, 1965-66; cons. Am. Council Learned Socs., 1961-63, Twentieth Century Fund, Carnegie Found., Ford Found., Sloan Found., Kettering Found. Author: (novel) The Experts, 1955; Wall Street, Men and Money, 2d edit., 1960, Madison Avenue, USA, 1958, (novel) A Voice That Fills the House, 1959, The Schools, 1961, Where, When and Why, Social Studies in American Schools, 1963, The Lawyers, 1967, Emory Buckner, 1968, Diploma, 1968, (with Cornell Capa) New Breed on Wall Street, 1969, Bricks, Mortar and the Performing Arts, 1970, All You Know Is Facts, 1970, The Teachers Strike, 1970, About Television, 1972, The Bankers, 1975, Conflicts of Interest: Broker-Dealer Firms, 1975, Today and Tomorrow in America, 1976, The Builders, 1978, (novel) Trigger Points, 1979, The Fate of the Dollar, 1980, The Met: One Hundred Years of Grand Opera, 1983, The Diplomats, 1983, The Money Bazaars, 1984, (with G. Fitzgerald) Grandissimo Pavarotti, 1986, Making News, 1987, Markets, 1988, The Greatest Ever Bank Robbery, 1990, Whatever Happened to Madison Avenue?, 1991, Stealing the Market, 1992, Nightmare on Wall Street, 1993, (with Elizabeth Luessenhop) Risky Business, 1995, The Bankers: The Next Generation, 1997, Risk Reduction in the Federal Financial Architecture, 1999, The Fed, 2001. Mem. Pres.'s Panel on Ednl. Research and Devel., 1961-66; mem. edn. com. Music Critics Assn., 1978-82; chmn. N.Y. Local Sch. Bd., 1962-67; commr. Nat. Commn. on Reform Secondary Edn., 1972-73; bd. visitors Wake

Forest U., 1972-87; mem. Pres.'s Commn. on Housing, 1981-82. Guest scholar Brookings Instn., 1993—. Mem.: Century (N.Y.C.); Gardiner's Bay (Shelter Island, N.Y.). Democrat. Jewish. Address: PO Box 478 Shelter Island NY 11964-0478 Office Phone: 631-749-0610. Personal E-mail: mmayer2A1@netscape.net.

**MAYER, MICHEL,** computer company executive; b. France; Ingenieur, Ecole Superieure d'Electricite, Paris. Engring. & mgmt. positions through gen. mgr. IBM, 1984—2001, mem. worldwide mgmt. council: gen. mgr. IBM Microelectronics, 2001—04; chmn., CEO Freescale Semiconductor Inc., Austin, Tex., 2004—. Bd. dir. Semiconductor Ind. Assn. Office: Freescale Semiconductor 6501 William Cannon Dr W Austin TX 78735*

**MAYER, MORRIS LEHMAN,** marketing educator; b. Demopolis, Ala., Dec. 14, 1925; s. Lehman M. and Anne (Rochotsh) M.; m. Judith Marian Morton, Dec. 22, 1957; children: Susan Morton, Elizabeth Anne. BS in Bus. Adminstrn, U. Ala., 1949, DHL (hon.), 1994; MS in Retailing, N.Y. U., 1950; PhD in Bus. Orgn, Ohio State U., 1961. Buyer Goldblatts Dept. Store, Chgo., 1951-55; mem. faculty U. Ala., 1955—, prof., 1960—, chmn. dept. mktg., 1969-74, dir. Hess Inst. Retailing, 1985-92, Bruno prof. mktg., 1986-92; Bruno prof. mktg. emeritus, 1992—; instr. Ohio State U., Columbus, 1956-60. Cons. Mgmt. Horizons Co., Columbus, 1966-70, N.C.R. Co., Dayton, Ohio, 1967-75. Co-author: Modern Retailing, 1978, 6th edit., 1993, Retailing, 1981, 5th edit., 1993. With AUS, 1944-46, 50-51. Recipient Teaching Excellence award Burlington No. Found., 1986, Distinctive Image award Jewish Childrens Regional Svc. Bd., 1997, Circle of Honor award Direct Selling Edn. Found., 1997; Ford Found. fellow, 1962-63, So. Mktg. fellow, 1986; named to U. Ala. Bus. Faculty Hall of Fame, 1995, Retail Patronage Acad. Hall of Fame, 1995; Morris Mayer Endowed scholarship established 1992; Morris L. Mayer award established U. Ala., 1993; Morris L. Mayer Outstanding Sudtent award established Sales and Mktg. Execs., 1993, others. Mem. Am. Mktg. Assn. (Morris L. Mayer Outstanding Mem. award estab. Birmingham chpt. 1993), So. Mktg. Assn. (pres.), Ala. Retail Assn. (bd. dirs.), Am. Coll. Retail Assn. (pres., Hall of Fame 1992, Mortar Bd., Beta Gamma Sigma, Eta Mu Pi, Pi Sigma Epsilon, Omicron Delta Kappa, Zeta Beta Tau (chpt. trustee). Jewish. Home: 1321 Montclair Cir Tuscaloosa AL 35404-4241 Office: U Ala PO Box 870225 Tuscaloosa AL 35487-0154

**MAYER, RAYMOND RICHARD,** business administration educator; b. Chgo., Aug. 31, 1924; s. Adam and Mary (Bogdala) M.; m. Helen Lakowski, Jan. 30, 1954; children: Mark, John, Mary, Jane. BS, Ill. Inst. Tech., 1948, MS, 1954, PhD, 1957. Indsl. engr. Standard Oil Co., Whiting, Ind., 1948-51; orgn. analyst Ford Motor Co., Chgo., 1951-53; instr. Ill. Inst. Tech., Chgo., 1953-56, asso. prof., 1958-60; asst. prof. U. Chgo., 1956-58; Walter F. Mullady prof. bus. adminstrn. Loyola U., Chgo., 1960—. Author: Financial Analysis of Investment Alternatives, 1966, Production Management, 1962, rev. edit., 1968, Production and Operations Management, 1975, rev. edit., 1982, Capital Expenditure Analysis, 1978. Served with USNR, 1944-46. Ingersoll Found. fellow, 1955-56; Machinery and Allied Products Inst. fellow, 1954-55; Ford Found. fellow, 1962 Mem. Acad. Mgmt., Am. Econ. Assn., Am. Statis. Assn., Am. Inst. for Decision Scis., Nat. Assn. Purchasing Mgmt., Polish Inst. Arts and Scis. in Am., Alpha Iota Delta, Alpha Kappa Psi, Beta Gamma Sigma. Home: 730 Green Bay Rd Winnetka IL 60093-1912 Office: 820 N Michigan Ave Chicago IL 60611-2147

**MAYER, RICHARD EDWIN,** psychology professor; b. Chgo., Feb. 8, 1947; s. James S. and Bernis (Lowy) M.; m. Beverly Linn Pastor, Dec. 19, 1971; children: Kenneth Michael, David Mark, Sarah Ann. BA with honors, Miami U., Oxford, Ohio, 1969; MS in Psychology, U. Mich., 1971, PhD in Psychology, 1973. Vis. assist. prof. Ind. U., Bloomington, 1973-75; assist. prof. psychology U. Calif., Santa Barbara, 1975-80, assoc. prof., 1980-85, prof., 1985—, pres., chmn. dept., 1987-90. Vis. scholar Learning Rsch. and Devel. Ctr., U. Pitts., 1979, Ctr. for Study of Reading, U. Ill., 1984. Author: Foundations of Learning and Memory, 1979, The Promise of Cognitive Psychology, 1981, Thinking, Problem Solving, Cognition, 1983, 2d edit., 1992, BASIC: A Short Course, 1985, Educational Psychology, 1987, The Critical Thinker, 1990, 2d edit., 1995, The Promise of Educational Psychology, Vol. I, 1999, Vol. II, 2002, Multimedia Learning, 2001, Learning and Instruction, 2003, (with R. Clark) E-Learning and the Science of Instruction, 2004, Cambridge Handbook of Multimedia Learning, 2005; editor: Human Reasoning, 1980, Teaching and Learning Computer Programming, 1988; editor jours. Instructional Sci., 1983-87, Educational Psychologist, 1983-89. Sch. bd. officer Goleta (Calif.) Union Sch. Dist., 1981—. Grantee, NSF, 1975—88, 1991—. Fellow APA (divsn. 15 officer 1987—, G Stanley Hall lectr. 1988), Am. Psychol. Soc.; mem. Am. Ednl. Rsch. Assn. (divsn. C officer 1986-88), Psychonomic Soc. Democrat. Jewish. Avocations: computers, hiking, bicycling, reading, sports. Office: U Calif Dept Of Psychology Santa Barbara CA 93016 Business E-Mail: mayer@psych.ucsb.edu.

**MAYER, ROBERT ANTHONY,** retired college president; b. N.Y.C., Oct. 30, 1933; s. Ernest John and Theresa Margaret (Mazura) M.; m. Laura Wiley Christ, Apr. 30, 1960. BA magna cum laude, Fairleigh Dickinson U., 1955; MA, NYU, 1967. With N.J. Bank and Trust Co., Paterson, 1955-61, mgr. advt. dept., 1959-61; program supr. advt. dept. Mobil Oil Co., N.Y.C., 1961-62; asst. to dir. Latin Am. program Ford Found., N.Y.C., 1963-65, asst. rep. Brazil, 1965-67; asst. to v.p. adminstrn., 1967-73; officer in charge logistical services Ford Found. 1968-73; asst. dir. programs N.Y. Community Trust, 1973-76; exec. dir. N.Y. State Council on the Arts, N.Y.C., 1976-79; mgmt. cons. N.Y.C., 1979-80; dir. Internat. Mus. Photography George Eastman House, Rochester, NY, 1980-89, mgmt. cons., 1989-90; pres. Cleve. Inst. of Art, 1990-97; ret., 1997. Author: (plays) La Borgia, 1971, Alijandru, 1971, They'll Grow No Roses, 1975; mem. editl. adv. bd. Grants mag., 1978—80, exhibited profl. photography, 1993—. Mem. state program adv. panel NEA, 1977—80; mem. Mayor's Com. Cultural Policy, N.Y.C., 1974—75; mem. pres.'s adv. com. Bklyn. campus L.I. U., 1978—79; bd. dirs. Fedn. Protestant Welfare Agys., N.Y.C., 1977—79, Arts Greater Rochester, 1981—83, Garth Fagan's Dance Theatre, 1982—86; trustee Internat. Mus. Photography, 1981—89, Lacoste Sch. Arts, France, 1991—96, sec., 1994—96; mem. dean's adv. com. Grad. Sch. Social Welfare, Fordham U., 1976; mem. N.Y. State Motion Picture, TV Devel. Adv. Bd., 1984—87, N.Y. State Martin Luther King Jr. Commn., 1985—90, Cleve. Coun. Cultural Affairs, 1992—94; chmn. Greater Cleve. Regional Transit Authority Arts in Transit Com., 1992—95; bd. dirs. Friends Ariz. State U. Ctr. Latin Am. Studies, 1997—99, Villa Solana Townhouse Assn., 2001—06, pres., 2000; bd. dirs. Mesa Art Ctr. Found., 2004—. Recipient Nat. award on advocacy for girls Girls Clubs Am., 1976 Mem. Nat. Assembly State Art Agys. (bd. dirs. 1977-79, 1st vice chmn. 1978-79), Alliance Ind. Colls. Art (bd. dirs. 1983-91, vice chmn. 1986-87, sec. 1987-89), N.Y. State Assn. Museums (bd. councilors 1983-86, pres. 1986-89), Assn. Ind. Colls. Art and Design (bd. dirs 1991-97, exec. com. 1991-93, 96-97).

**MAYER, ROSEMARY,** artist; b. Ridgewood, N.Y., Feb. 27, 1943; d. Theodore Albert and Marie Anne (Stumpf) M. AB magna cum laude, U. Iowa, 1964; postgrad., Bklyn. Mus. Art Sch. Vis. Visual Arts, N.Y.C., 1967—69. Model Raphael Soyer, N.Y.C., 1968—74; writer Arts Mag., N.Y.C., 1972—75. Art in Am., N.Y.C., 1974—75. Vis. artist many schs. including Hartwick Coll., Oneonta, N.Y., 1976, Art Inst., Chgo., 1974; guest artist Nat. Endowment Workshop, Tyler Sch. Art, Phila., Mpls. Acad. Art and Design, 1981; adj. lectr. La Guardia C.C., CUNY, 1991—; adj. prof. L.I. U., 1988—; writer, speaker A.I.R. Gallery, N.Y.C., 1972-74. Translator: Pontormo's Diary 1983; author: Swatches, 1969, Surroundings, 1977. Grantee numerous orgns. including NEA, CAPS, 1976—. Democrat. Home: 55 Leonard St New York NY 10013-2928

**MAYER, STEVEN T.,** chemical engineer; BSChemE, SUNY, Buffalo, 1983; MSChemE, U. Calif., Berkeley, 1985, PhD in Chem. Engring., 1989. Sr. staff scientist Lawrence Livermore (Calif.) Nat. Labs., 1989—94; chief tech. officer Polystar Corp., Dublin and Livermore, 1994—98; prin. engr. Novellus Sys., Tualatin, Oreg., 1998—. Achievements include patents in field.

**MAYER, SUSAN MARTIN,** art educator; b. Atlanta, Oct. 25, 1931; d. Paul McKeen and Ione (Garrett) Martin; m. Arthur James Mayer, Aug. 9, 1953; 1 child, Melinda Marilyn. Student, Am. U., 1949-50; BA, U. N.C., Greensboro, 1953; postgrad., U. Del., 1956-58; MA, Ariz. State U., 1966. Artist-in-residence Armed Forces Staff Coll., Norfolk, Va., 1968-69; mem. art faculty U. Tex., Austin, 1971—2003. Co-editor: Museum Education: History, Theory and Practice, 1989; author various mus. publs.; contbr. articles to profl. jours. Recipient award Austin Ind. Sch. Bd., 1983. Mem. Art Edn. Assn. (bd. dirs. 1983-87, award 1987, 91), Tex. Art Edn. Assn. (mus. edn. chair 1982-83, Mus. Educator of Yr. 1986), Tex. Assn. Mus. (mus. edn. chair), Austin Visual Arts Assn., Am. Assn. Mus.

**MAYER, THEODORE V.H.,** lawyer; b. Waltham, Mass., Sept. 30, 1952; s. Jean and Elizabeth (Van Huysen) M.; m. Margery Weil, Dec. 28, 1975; children: Lily, Henry. BA, Yale U., 1974; JD, Harvard U., 1977. Bar: NY 1978, Mass. 1989, US Ct. Appeals 2nd, 3rd, 7th, Fed. Circuits, US Dist. Ct. So., Ea., We. Districts NY, US Dist. Ct. Dist. Ariz. Assoc. Hughes, Hubbard & Reed LLP, NYC, 1978-85, ptnr., 1985—. Co-author (with Robb Patryk): Product Liability, 1998; contbr. articles to profl. jours. Mem. New Media Repertory Co., NYC, 1991—. Mem. ABA (co-chair subcom. internat. environ. litig. of com. environ. litig. 1993-95), Assn. Bar City NY (chair com. product liability 2002-05). Office: Hughes Hubbard & Reed LLP One Battery Pk Plz New York NY 10004-1482 Office Phone: 212-837-6888. Office Fax: 212-422-4726. E-mail: mayer@hugheshubbard.com.

**MAYER, TOM G.,** orthopedist, researcher; b. N.Y.C., May 31, 1943; s. Eric Theodore and Lisa Margareta Mayer; m. Susan Hollingsworth Rollings, Nov. 30, 1968; children: Eric Auty, Margareta Makalani. BA, Harvard Coll., Cambridge, Mass., 1964; MD, Columbia U., N.Y.C., 1968. Diplomate Nat. Bd. Med. Examiners, 1968, lic. Tex., Colo., N.M. Hawaii, Calif., diplomate Am. Bd. Orthop. Surgeons. Orthop. surgeon Tom G. Mayer, M.D., PC, Los Alamos, Calif., 1976—81; med. dir. Productive Rehab. Inst. of Dallas for Ergonomics (PRIDE), Dallas, 1983—; founding editor-in-chief The Spine Jour., Chgo., 1999—2004; founding med. dir. Neuro-Rehab Unit Med. City Hosp. of Dallas, 1986—88; rsch. dir. Divsn. of Ortho Surgery, U. of TX Southwestern Med. Ctr., Dallas, 1981—88. Mem., bd. of assoc. editors Spine, Dartmouth, NH, 1989—; clin. prof. Dept. of Orthop Surgery, U. of TX Southwestern Med. Ctr., Dallas, 1988—; discussant/reviewer NAS Reporton Work-Related MSIs, Washington, 1999—99; coms. Tex. State Legislature Spl. Com. on Work Comp Reform, Austin, 1988—90; cons. injury task force Union Pacific RR, 1986—90. Editor (author): (book) Interventional Spine, (Co-Editor T Mayer with C. Slipman, S. Simeone, R. Derby), Elsevier Press, London, UK and Philadephia, PA (In Press), Occupational Musculoskeletal Disorders, (Eds. T. Mayer, R. Gatchel, P. Polatin), Lippincott, Williams & Wilkins, Philadelphia, PA, 1999, Contemporary Care for Painful Spinal Disorders: Concepts, Diagnosis & Treatment, (Eds. Mayer T, Mooney V, Gatchel R), Lea & Febiger, Philadelphia, PA, 1991, Functional Restoration for Spinal Disorders: The Sports Medicine Approach, Mayer T, Gatchel R; Lea & Febiger, Philadelphia, PA, 1988; contbr. over 150 articles to profl. jours. Bd. of trustees Dallas Opera Assn., 1989; mem./interviewer Radcliffe Schools Com., Dallas, 1987—92; exec. coun. Med. Quality Rev. Bd., Tex. Workers' Compensation Commn. Divsn., Dallas, 2002; chmn., parents coun. and dir. of med. ctr. fund (nursing) Georgetown U., Washington, 1994—2002. Lt. USNR, 1970—72. Named Resident, Western Orthop. Assn., 1974. Fellow: Am. Acad. of Orthop. Surgeons, ACS, Am. Orthop. Assn., Internat. Soc. for the Study of the Lumbar Spine; mem.: Tex. Orthop. Assn., Tex. Med. Assn., North Am. Spine Soc. (treas/vice pres. 1983, Henry Farfan award 1997, David Selby Disting Svc. award 2004), The Back Letter. Office: Pride 5701 Maple Ave #100 Dallas TX 75235 Office Phone: 214-351-6600. Office Fax: 214-351-6958. E-mail: tgmayer@pridedallas.com.

**MAYER, VICTOR JAMES,** geologist, educator; b. Mayville, Wis., Mar. 25, 1933; s. Victor Charles and Phyllis (Bachhuber) M.; m. Mary Jo Anne White, Nov. 25, 1965; children: Gregory, Maribeth. BS Geology, U. Wis., 1956; MS Geology, U. Colo., 1960, PhD Sci. Edn., 1966. Tchr. Colo. Pub. Schs., 1961—85; asst. prof. SUNY, Oneonta, 1965—67, Ohio State U., Columbus, 1967—70, assoc. prof., 1970—75, prof. edul. studies, geol. scis. and natural resources, 1975—95, prof. emeritus, 1995—; affiliate prof. U. Northern Colo., 2005. Co-organizer symposa 29th and 31st Internat. Geol. Congresses; internat. sci. edn. assistance to individuals and orgns. in Japan, Korea, Taiwan, Russia, and Venezuela; dir. NSF Insts., program for leadership Earth Sys. Edn., 1990-95; dir. Korean Sci. Tchrs. Insts., 1986-88, 95, 2005-06; co-convenor Second Internat. conf. Geosci. Edn., Hilo, Hawaii, 1997; disting. vis. prof. SUNY, Plattsburg, 1994; vis. rsch. scholar Hyogo U., Japan, 1996; sr. Fulbright rschr. Shizuoka U., Japan, 1998; vis. prof. Korea Nat. U. Edn., 2000; Fulbright prof. Pusan Nat. U. Korea, 2003-04, spkr. in field. Contbr. articles to profl. jours. Served with USAR Recipient Lifetime Disting. Svc. award Internat. Earth Sci. Edn. Cmty., 1997; named Disting. Investigator Ohio Sea Grant Program, 1983 Fellow AAAS (chmn. edn. 1988-89), Ohio Acad. Sci. (v.p. 1978-79, exec. com. 1993-94, Outstanding univ. educator 1995); mem. NSTA (bd. dirs. 1984-86), Sci. Edn. Coun. Ohio (pres. 1987-88), Sigma Xi, Phi Delta Kappa Roman Catholic. Avocation: photography. Home and Office: 8483 Sand Dollar Dr Windsor CO 80528 E-mail: mayer.4@osu.edu.

**MAYER, WILLIAM EMILIO,** investor; b. NYC, May 7, 1940; s. Emilio and Marie Mayer; m. Katherine Mayer, May 16, 1964; children: Elizabeth, William Franz. BS, U. Md., 1966, MBA, 1967. Pres., CEO First Boston Corp., N.Y.C., 1967-91; dean Coll. Bus. and Mgmt. U. Md., College Park, 1992-96; ptnr. Devel. Capital, 1996-99, Park Ave. Equity Ptnrs., 1999—. Bd. dirs. Lee Enterprises, Inc., Columbia Fund Group, Readers Digest Corp. Chmn. bd. U. Md.; chmn. Aspen Inst. Itt USAF, 1961—65. Mem. Annapolis Yacht Club, Manhasset Bay Club (N.Y.), Wilson Cove Yacht Club, Univ. Club (N.Y.C.), Mashomack Fish and Game Club, Met. Club (Washington). Home: 172 Long Neck Point Rd Darien CT 06820-5816 Office: 399 Park Av Fl 3204 New York NY 10022-1606

**MAYER, WILLIAM P.,** lawyer; AB summa cum laude, Dartmouth Coll., 1973; MS, Univ. Dar es Salaam, Tanzania, 1974; JD, Va. Law Sch., 1977. Bar: DC 1978, Mass. 1984. Law clerk, Hon. William H. Timbers US Ct. Appeals (2nd cir.), 1977—78; ptnr., bus. law dept., mem. fin. svcs. dept. Goodwin Procter LLP, Boston. Editor: Va. Law Rev.; lectr. in field. Bd. adv. Morin Ctr. Banking and Fin. Law Studies, Boston Univ. Office: Goodwin Procter LLP Exchange Pl 53 State St Boston MA 02109 Office Phone: 617-570-1534. Office Fax: 617-523-1231. Business E-Mail: wmayer@goodwinprocter.com.

**MAYERS, DANIEL KRIEGSMAN,** lawyer; b. Scarsdale, N.Y., July 10, 1934; s. Chauncey Maurice and Helen P. (Kriegsman) M.; m. Karen E. Silverman, Sept. 30, 1956, children: Peter D., Leslie H. Shroyer. AB, Harvard U., 1955, LLB, 1960. Bar: D.C. 1961, U.S. Supreme Ct. 1961. Law clk. to Justice Felix Frankfurter, U.S. Supreme Ct., Washington, 1960-61; spl. asst. U.S. Dept. Justice, Washington, 1961-62; assoc. Wilmer Cutler & Pickering, Washington, 1962-65, ptnr., 1967-99, of counsel, 2000—; exec. asst. to undersec. U.S. State Dept., Washington, 1965-66. Vis. com. Harvard Law Sch., Cambridge, Mass., 1982-89, chmn., 1986-89; chmn. Legal Action Ctr., N.Y.C., 1998—. Washington Ednl. TV Assn., 1993-97, Survivors Fund for Pentagon Victims, 2001—; bd. dirs. Hypres Corp., Netscan, Inc. Pres. Nat. Symphony Orch., Washington, 1987-89; chmn. Sidwell Friends Sch., Washington, 1979-81; mem. Ams. for Peace Now, 1991—, Fed. City Coun., Washington, 1991—; counsel, dir. Ctr. for Nat. Policy, Washington, 1984-93. With U.S. Army, 1955-57. Recipient Sears prize Harvard Law Sch., 1959 Mem. ABA, Met. Club, Burning Tree Woodstock Country Club. Democrat. Jewish. Avocations: tennis, fishing. Home: 3222 Woodland Dr NW Washington DC 20008-3547

**MAYERS, STANLEY PENROSE, JR.,** public health service officer, educator; b. Phila., Nov. 9, 1926; s. Stanley Penrose and Margaret Amelia (Thorpe) M.; m. Virginia Lee Lytle, Aug. 25, 1951 (dec. Oct. 1990); children: Douglas Lytle, Kenneth Stanley, Daniel John, Andrew William; m. Patricia Ann Harne Hulsey, Mar. 6, 1993. BA, U. Pa., 1949, MD, 1953; MPH, Johns Hopkins U., 1958. Diplomate Am. Bd. Preventive Medicine. Intern Phila. Gen. Hosp., 1953-54; resident Arlington County Health Dept., Va., 1954-55; health dir. Henry-Martinsville-Patrick Health Dist., Martinsville, Va., 1955-57; regional dir. Va. State Health Dept., Richmond, 1958-59; dist. state health officer N.J. State Dept. of Health, Trenton, 1959-62; asst. prof. and asst. dean Johns Hopkins Sch. Hygiene and Pub. Health, Balt., 1962-65; dir. Arlington County Dept. of Human Resources, Arlington, Va., 1965-71; prof. health policy and adminstrn. Pa. State U., University Park, 1971-97, prof. emeritus, 1997—, chmn., 1979-88, assoc. dean undergrad. studies Coll. Health and Human Devel., 1989-92, assoc. dean acad. studies Coll. Health and Human Devel., 1992-95, assoc. dean emeritus, 1997—. Interim dir. internat. edn. programs and studies Pa. State U., 2000-2001; faculty assoc. Johns Hopkins U. Sch. Hygiene and Pub. Health, Balt., 1965-75; clin. assoc. prof. Georgetown U. Sch. Medicine, Washington, 1965-71; cons. VA, 1985—. Contbr. articles to profl. jours. Pres. Arlington Optimist Club, 1970-71; bd. dirs. Centre County Family Planning Svcs., Bellefonte, Pa., 1972-79, vice chmn., Ctr. County Hosp. Commn., 2005-; With USN, 1945-46. Recipient Outstanding Achievement award Dept. Community Medicine, Georgetown U. Sch. Medicine, 1968, Saubel award Coll. of Human Devel., Pa. State U., 1985, Pioneer Achievement award Frankford H.S., Phila., 1999. Fellow Am. Coll. Preventive Med., APHA (chmn. membership com. health officer's sect. 1968-70, mem. nominating com. health adminstrn. sect. 1970-72, chmn. com. to draft a statement on local health agy. responsibilities 1973-74); mem. AMA, Arlington County Med. Soc. (Wellborn award 1971), Centre County Med. Soc. (pres. 1978), Med. Soc. Va., Met. Washington Health Officers Assn. (sec. 1967-71), Am. Assn. Pub. Health Physicians (pres. Va. chpt. 1970-71), Pa. Med. Soc. (mem. Ho. of Dels. for Centre County 1974-76, 81-97, treas. 1973-74, 85—, sec. 1974-76, v.p. 1976, pres. elect 1977, pres. 1978), Mt. Nittany Soc., Univ. Club (State College, Pa.), Phi Beta Kappa. Episcopalian. Avocations: fishing, boating, hiking. Home: 648 Wiltshire Dr State College PA 16803-1450 Office: Pa State U Human Devel Bldg Rm 115 University Park PA 16802 Business E-Mail: spm1@psu.edu. *Never attempt to promote something or someone that you do not believe in yourself.*

**MAYERSON, HY,** lawyer; b. Phila., June 29, 1937; s. Henry and Gertrude Mayerson; m. June 13, 1964 (div. 1973); children: Merrie Joy, Benjamin, Erin Megan, Stephnie Dawn; m. Colleen Koos. BS, Temple U., 1958, JD, 1961. Bar: Pa. 1961, Phila. Ct. Common Pleas 1962, Pa. Supreme Ct. 1968, U.S. Ct. Appeals (3d cir.) 1980, U.S. Ct. Appeals (4th cir.) 1986, U.S. Dist. Ct. (ea. dist.) Pa. Pvt. practice, Phila., 1961-65; sr. ptnr. Hy Mayerson Law Offices, 1965-81, Mayerson, Schniper & Gerasimowicz, Spring City, Pa., 1981-87, Mayerson, Gerasimowicz & Munsing, Spring City, 1987-91, Mayerson, Munsing, Corchin & Rosato, P.C., Spring City, 1991-95; pvt. practice The Mayerson Law Offices, P.C., Spring City, 1995—. Coord. Nat. Forklift Litigation, 1978-91; lead counsel Agent Orange Product Liability Litigation. Contbr. articles to profl. jours. Mem. ATLA (emeritus chair sect. on Indsl. & Agrl. Eqipment, Product Liability adv.bd.), Pa. Trial Lawyers Assn. Home: Sky Farm Birchrunville PA 19421 Office: Rt 724 Spring City PA 19475 E-mail: hy@mayerson.com.

**MAYERSON, PHILIP,** classics educator; b. N.Y.C., May 20, 1918; s. Theodore and Clara (Fader) M.; m. Joy Gottesman Ungerleider, Nov. 25, 1976 (dec. Sept. 9, 1995); children: Miriam Mayerson, Clare Mayerson. AB, NYU, 1947, PhD, 1956. With Puritan Fed. Clothing Stores, N.Y.C., 1935-42; instr. NYU, 1948-56, asst. prof., 1956-60, assoc. prof., 1960-66, prof. classics, 1966—, vice dean, 1969-71, acting dean, 1971-73, dean Washington Sq. and U. Coll. Arts and Scis., 1973-78. Author: The Ancient Agricultural Regime of Nessana and the Central Negeb, 1961, Classical Mythology in Literature, Art and Music, 1971, Monks, Martyrs, Soldiers and Saracens, 1994; contbr. articles in field of papyrology to profl. jours. Served with USN, 1942-45. Rockefeller Found. grantee, 1956-57; Am. Coun. of Learned Socs. fellow, 1961-62. Mem. Am. Philol. Assn., Am. Schs. of Oriental Rsch. Home: 720 Walton Ave Mamaroneck NY 10543-4437 Office: NYU Dept Classics 25 Waverly Pl New York NY 10003 Business E-Mail: pm2@nyu.edu.

**MAYERSON, SANDRA ELAINE,** lawyer; b. Dayton, Ohio, Feb. 8, 1952; d. Manuel David and Florence Louise (Tepper) M.; m. Scott Burns, May 29, 1977 (div. Oct. 1978); 1 child, Amy Jay. BA cum laude, Yale U., 1973; JD, Northwestern U., 1976. Bar: Ill. 1976, N.Y. 1997, U.S. Ct. Appeals (7th cir.) 1976, U.S. Dist. Ct. (no. dist.) Ill. 1977, U.S. Dist. Ct. Md. 1989, U.S. Ct. Appeals (5th cir.) 1994, U.S. Dist. Ct. (so. and ea. dists.) N.Y. 1997, U.S. Ct. Appeals (2nd Cir.) 1997, U.S. Dist. Ct. (ea. dist.) Mich. 2000. Assoc. gen. counsel JMB Realty Corp., Chgo., 1979-80; assoc. Chatz, Sugarman, Abrams et al, Chgo., 1980-81; ptnr. Pollack, Mayerson & Berman, Chgo., 1981-83; dep. gen. counsel AM Internat., Inc., Chgo., 1983-85; ptnr. Kirkland & Ellis, Chgo., 1985-87; ptnr., chmn. bankruptcy group Kelley Drye & Warren, N.Y.C., 1987-93; ptnr., chmn. N.Y. bankruptcy group McDermott, Will & Emery, N.Y.C., 1993-99; ptnr., bankruptcy nat. practice group leader Holland and Knight, N.Y.C., 1999—. Examiner Interco chpt. 11, 1991. Contbr. articles to profl. jours. Bd. dirs. Jr. Med. Rsch. Inst. coun. Michael Reese Hosp., Chgo., 1981-86, Self Help Inc., 2000-; met. divsn. Jewish Guild for Blind, 1990-92; nat. legal affairs com. Anti-Defamation League, 1990-91; lawyers' exec. com. United Jewish Appeal; chair Holland & Knight Nat. Bankruptcy & Creditors Rights Group, 2001-. Named one of Top 50 Women Litigators, Nat. Law Jour., 2001; assoc. fellow, Branford Coll., Yale U., 1993—. Mem. ABA (bus. bankruptcy com. 1976—, sec. 1990-93, chair avoiding powers subcom. 1993-96, chair claims trading subcom. 1997-2000, chair strategic planning subcom., 2000-), Ill. State Bar Assn. (governing council corp. and securities sect. 1983-86), Chgo. Bar Assn. (current events chmn. corp. sect. 1980-81), 7th Cir. Bar Assn., Yale Club (N.Y.C.). Democrat. Jewish. Office: Holland and Knight 195 Broadway Fl 24 New York NY 10007-3100 Business E-Mail; sandy.mayerson@hklaw.com

**MAYES, ALVA LOUIE,** physician, pediatrician; b. Appling, Ga., Feb. 19, 1931; a. Alva Louie Sr. and Pierce Avis (Morris) M.; m. Dora Lou Hawkins, Dec. 28, 1956; children: Pamela Jane, Patricia Ann, Alva Jeffrey, Joseph Pierce, Margaret Louise. BS in Chemistry, U. Ga., 1952; MD, Med. Coll. Ga. 1956. Diplomate Am. Bd. Pediats. Intern Macon (Ga.) Hosp., 1956-57; comd. lt. USN, 1957, physician Camp Lejeune, N.C., 1957-58; advanced through grades to lt. comdr., 1962; resident in pediats. U.S. Naval Hosp. and Children's Hosp., Phila., 1958-60; pediatrician U.S. Naval Hosp., Beaufort, S.C., 1960-63; pvt. practice Macon, 1963—. Bd. dirs. MAG Mut. Ins. Co., Atlanta, Med. Cen Found., Macon. Mem. AMA (del.), Med. Assn. Ga. (pres. 1995-96, chair coun. legis. 1996—), Am. Acad. Pediats. (bd. dirs. 1991-93). Democrat. Methodist. Office: 550 Professional Dr Macon GA 31201-1441

**MAYES, MICHAEL RICHARD,** research and development company executive, architect; b. Norristown, Pa., June 22, 1977; s. Richard Loraine and Susan White Mayes; m. Caroline Ashley Cundiff, Aug. 7, 2004. BArch, U. Va., Charlottesville, 1995—99. Project mgr. Capital One, Richmond, Va., 1999—2003; dir. TIAA-CREF, NYC, 2003—04; sr. mgr. Gerson Lehrman Grp., NYC, 2004—; pres. Circaviso, NYC, 2004—. Exhibitions include, Coney Island Visitor Ctr., 2005. Participant Civic Alliance, NYC, 2005, Regional Plan Assn., NYC, 2005, Ctrl. Village Block Assn., NYC, 2005. Mem.: ACLU, Am. Mus. Natural History (assoc.), Sierra Club, Sigma Phi Epsilon. Progressive. Achievements include research in Yanomami indian dwellings. Avocations: travel, architecture. Personal E-mail: mm@circaviso.com

**MAYES, MICHELE COLEMAN,** lawyer; b. LA, July 9, 1949; BA, U. Mich., 1971, JD, 1974. Bar: Mich. 1974, U.S. Dist. Ct. 1974, Ea. Dist. of Mich. 1976, Ill. 1980, U.S. Supreme Ct. 1988, Pa. 1988. Adj. prof. Wayne State U., 1981—87; in-house counsel Colgate-Palmolive, 1992—2003; sr. v.p., gen. counsel Pitney Bowes Inc., 2003—. Mem.: ABA (mem. commn. women in the profession 1992, co-chair, arbitration com. 1990—92). Office: Pitney Bowes Inc World Hdqs 1 Elmcroft Rd, Mail Stop MSC 6411 Stamford CT 06926-0700

**MAYES, PAUL EUGENE,** engineering educator, consultant; b. Frederick, Okla., Dec. 21, 1928; s. Robert Franklin and Bertha Ellen (Walter) M.; m. Lola Mae Davis, June 4, 1950; children: Gwynne Ellen, Linda Kay, Stuart Franklin, Patricia Gail, Steven Lee, David Thomas. BS in Elec. Engring., U. Okla., 1950; MS in Elec. Engring., Northwestern U., 1952, PhD, 1955. Rsch. asst. Northwestern U., Evanston, Ill., 1950-54; asst. prof. U. Ill., Urbana, 1954-58, assoc. prof., 1958-63, prof., 1963-93, prof. emeritus, 1994—. Tech. cons. Author: Electromagnetics for Engineers, 1965; contbr. articles to profl. jours.; inventor in field. Fellow IEEE. Avocations: woodworking, hiking, model railroading. Home: 1508 Waverly Dr Champaign IL 61821-5002 Office: U Ill 1406 W Green St Urbana IL 61801-2918 E-mail: p.mayes@insightbb.com.

**MAYES, WENDELL WISE, JR.,** former broadcasting company executive; b. San Antonio, Mar. 2, 1924; s. Wendell Wise and Dorothy Lydia (Evans) M.; m. Mary Jane King, May 11, 1946; children: Cathey, Sarah, Wendell Wise, III. Student, Schreiner Inst., 1941-42, U. Tex., 1942, Daniel Baker Coll., 1946; BS, Tex. Tech. Coll., 1949; BA summa cum laude, St. Edward's U., 2002, MLA, 2005, MBA, 2006. Program dir., sta. mgr. Sta. KBWD, Brownwood, Tex., 1949-57; mgr. Sta. KCRS, Midland, Tex., 1957-63, pres., 1965-84, chmn., 1984-96; pres. Sta. KNOW, Austin, Tex., 1970-81, Stas. KVIC and KAMG, Victoria, Tex., 1970-84, chmn., 1984-98, Sta. KCRS-FM, Midland, 1984-96; pres. Sta. KCSW, San Marcos, 1976-81; sec.-treas. Sta. KSNY-AM-FM, Snyder, 1952-94; mem. bd. mgrs. Stas. KLBJ/KHHT-AM-FM, Austin, 1991-97. Lectr. Coll. Communications, U. Tex., Austin, 1978-81. Chmn. bd. Am. Diabetes Assn., 1974—77; mem. Nat. Diabetes Adv. Bd., 1977—84; v.p. Internat. Diabetes Fedn., 1992-95, pres.-elect, 1988—91, pres., 1991—94, hon. pres., 1997—; pres. Tex. Broadcast Edn. Found., 1973—76, dir., 2002—; mem. Tex. Diabetes Coun., 1983—86, chmn., 1983—86, exec. dir., 1999; bd. regents Tex. Tech U., 1985—91, chmn., 1987—88; bd. dirs., treas. Writer's League Tex., 2005—. With USNR, 1943—46. Recipient Addison B. Scoville award Am. Diabetes Assn., 1977, first Wendell Mayes Jr. award, 1986, Josiah K. Lilly award, 1991, Harold Rifkin award, 1994, Masaji Takeda medal Kobe, Japan Colloquium Med. Sci., 1994; named to Tex. Tech. Mass Comm. Hall of Fame, 1978, Hall of Fame Tex. affiliate Am. Diabetes Assn., 1994; named Disting. Alumnus Tex. Tech. U., 1981, Disting. Engr., 1985. Mem. Tex. Assn. Broadcasters (pres. 1964, named Pioneer Broadcaster of Year 1978), Nat. Assn. Broadcasters (dir. 1969-72), Am. Council on Edn. in Journalism (dir. 1977-80), Broadcast Edn. Assn. (dir. 1973-77), AP Broadcasters (bd. dirs. 1988-91), Tex. Tech. Elec. Engring. Acad. Episcopalian (vestryman 1966-69, 86-88; sr. warden 1988). Home: 2834 Montebello Rd Apt 1 Austin TX 78746-6820 Office: 1907 N Lamar Blvd Austin TX 78705-4992 Office Phone: 512-477-6866. E-mail: wmayes@swbell.net.

**MAYEUX, RICHARD,** hospital administrator, neurologist; b. New Orleans, 1946; MD, U. Okla., 1972. Diplomate Am. Bd. Psychiatry and Neurology. Intern Boston City Hosp., 1972—73; resident in internal medicine, 1973—74; resident in neurology Columbia Presbyn. Med. Ctr., N.Y.C., 1974—77; fellow in neurology Boston U., 1977—78; neurologist Sergievsky Ctr., N.Y.C.; staff neurologist Columbia Presbyn. Med. Ctr., N.Y.C.; prof. Columbia Coll. Physicians and Surgeons, N.Y.C.; dir. Taub Inst., N.Y.C.; Gertrude H. Sergievsky prof. neurology, psychiatry & epidemiology Columbia Univ., dir. Gertrude H. Sergievsky Ctr.; mem. aging Rev. Com. NIH, mem. Epidemiology of Chronic Disorders Com.; med. & scientific adv. bd. Alzheimer's Assn. Robert Aird visiting prof. U. Calif. San Francisco; Emanuel Goldberg visiting prof. U. Rochester; J.L. Silversides visiting prof. U. Toronto. Recipient Leadership & Excellence in Alzheimer's Disease award, Nat. Inst. Aging, 1992, MERIT award, 2004, Dean's Disting. Clin. Scientist award, Columbia U., Rita Hayworth award, Alzheimer's Assn. Fellow: Am. Acad. Neurology; mem.: AAP, Soc. for Neuroscience, Soc. Epidemiologic Rsch. Am. Neurological Assn., NY Acad. Sci., Am. Epidemiological Soc., Assn. Rsch. Nervous & Mental Disease (ARNMD), Inst. of Medicine of NAS. Office: 622 W 168th St New York NY 10032 Office Phone: 212-305-2391. Office Fax: 212-305-2518, 212-305-2391. E-mail: rpm2@columbia.edu.*

**MAYFIELD, JEREMY,** race car driver; b. Owensboro, Ky., May 27, 1969; m. Shana Mayfield. Profl. race care driver NASCAR Winston Cup, 1993—. Raced go-karts, OWensboro, 1982—86. Named Rookie of Yr. and Most Improved Driver, Ky. Motor Speedway, 1986, Rookie of Yr., ARCA, 1993, winner, Pocono 500, 1998, NAPA Auto Parts 500, 2000. Office: Evernham Motorsports 320 Aviation Dr Statesville NC 28677 Address: PO Box 3998 Mooresville NC 28117

**MAYFIELD, MAX,** meteorologist; b. 1948; married; 3 children. BS in Math., U. Okla., 1970; MS in Meterology, Fla. St. U., 1987. With NOAA/Nat. Weather Svc., Miami, 1972—, dir. Tropical Prediction Ctr., Nat. Hurricane Ctr., 2000—. Chmn. regional assn. IV hurricane com. World Meterological Orgn.; chmn. office of fed. coord. Meteorology Working Group on Hurricanes; spkr. in field. Contbr. articles to profl. jours. Recipient Francis W. Reichelderfer award, Am. Meterological Soc., 1996, Outstanding Achievement award, Nat. Hurricane Ctr., 2000, Richard Hagemeyer award, Interdepartmental Hurricane Conf., 2004, NOAA Bronze medal, US Dept. Commerce. Mem.: Nat. Weather Assn., Am. Meteorological Soc. Office: NOAA Nat Weather Svc Nat Centers for Environ Prediction 11691 SW 17th St Miami FL 33165-2149

**MAYFIELD, ROBERT CHARLES,** academic administrator, geographer, educator; b. Abilene, Tex., Oct. 15, 1928; s. Percy Anderson and Fay (Hicks) M.; m. Loraine Poindexter, Sept. 3, 1952; children: Julie Barnes, Jennifer Manley, Mark Stanley, Malcolm Randall. BA, Tex. Christian U., 1952; MS, Ind. U., 1955; PhD, U. Wash., 1961. Chmn. geography dept. Tex. Christian U., Ft. Worth, 1960-64, U. Tex., Austin, 1968—71, Boston U., 1971—84, acad. v.p. external programs, 1977-83 provost, 1979-84 Coun. Coun. for Econ. Action, Boston, 1980—; adj. prof. U. Tex., Austin, 1987—; lectr. U.S. Info. Svc., Bangladesh, 1994; seminar dir. U. Tex. Seminars for Adult Growth and Enrichment, 1995—; mem. faculty rev. bd. Bangladesh U. Engring. and Tech., Dacca, 1996—. Editor, contbg. author: Man, Environment and Space, 1972. With USAF, 1946-49. Rsch. fellow Nat. Acad. Sci. No. India, 1957-58, Fulbright-Hays fellow Office Edn., Bangalore, Mysore, India, 1966-67; Rsch. grant Agrl. Devel. Coun., 1968. Mem. Assn. Am. Geographers. Business E-Mail: rmayfield@mail.utexas.edu.

**MAYFIELD, T. BRIENT, IV,** media and computer executive; b. Athens, Tenn., Mar. 31, 1947; s. Thomas Brient III and Alma Ruth (Bolton) M.; m. Katherine Rodgers, Dec. 7, 1974 (div. Mar. 1984); children: Brittany Alexander, Blair Ashton, Katherine Thomas; m. Margaret L. Reeves, Oct. 3, 1987 (div. Feb. 1998). BS, U. Tenn., 1969. Project mgr. Mayfield Dairy Farms, Athens, 1969-70; v.p. fin. 13-30 Corp., Knoxville, Tenn., 1970-72; exec. v.p. Computer Concepts Corp., Knoxville, 1970-77, pres., 1977-85, Resource Optimization Inc., Knoxville, 1986—; co-founder Whittle Communications LP, Knoxville, 1970, v.p., pub., 1987-92. Bd. dirs. Results Edn. Fund, Washington, 1990—. Republican. Avocations: flying, tennis, music. Address: PO Box 436 Knoxville TN 37901 Office: Resource Optimization PO Box 2747 Knoxville TN 37901-2747

**MAYGARDEN, JERRY LOUIS,** health care foundation executive; b. Pensacola, Fla., Dec. 22, 1948; s. Louis Ameal and Jean (Saxon) Maygarden; m. Rhonda Delene Fosha, June 25, 1977; children: Louis Ameal III, Morgan Lora. AA in Liberal Arts, Pensacola Jr. Coll., 1972; BA in Communications Arts, U. West Fla., 1974, MA in Communication, 1975. V.p. U. West Fla., Pensacola, 1980-83; exec. v.p. Sacred Heart Found., Pensacola, 1983-89; pres. Bapt. Health Care Found., Pensacola, 1989—. Bd. dirs. Bank of Pensacola; mem. Fla. House of Reps., 1994—. City councilman Pensacola City Coun., 1985-92, mayor pro tem, 1989-91, mayor, 1991-94; bd. dirs. C. of C. Com. 100, Pensacola, 1989—. With USN, 1968-74, Viet Nam. Recipient George Washington Honor medal, Freedoms Found. of Valley Forge, 1992, Paul Harris fellow, Rotary Found Internat., 1993; named Cmty. Leader of Yr. C. of C., Pensacola, 1988, Outstanding Young Man Am. U.S. Jaycees, 1977, Nat. Soc. Fund Raising Execs., Assn. for Health Care

Philanthropy, Rotary Internat. Mem. Fla. League Cities, Nat. League Cities, Nat. Soc. Fund Raising Execs., Assn. for Health Care Philanthropy, Rotary Internat. Democrat. Methodist. Avocations: tennis, sailing, hiking, biking, fishing. Office: Bapt Health Care Found PO Box 17500 Pensacola FL 32522-7500 Home: 516 E Zarragossa St Pensacola FL 32502-6155

**MAYHAR, ARDATH FRANCES (FRANK CANNON, JOHN KILLDEER, FRANCES HURST),** writer; b. 1930; Ind. book cons., 1979—; dairyman, 1947—57; prin. East Tex. Bookstore, Nacogdoches, 1958—62; proofreader Capital Jour., Salem, Oreg., 1968—75; chicken farmer, 1976—78; proofreader Daily Sentinel, Nacogdoches, 1979—82; writer, 1982—; co-mgr. View From Orbit Bookstore, Nacogdoches, 1984—99; writing instr. Writer's Digest, 1982—2005. Author: How the Gods Wove in Kyrannon, 1979, The Seekers of Shar Nuhn, 1980, Soul Singer of Tyrnos, 1981, Warlock's Gift, 1982, Khi to Freedom, 1982, Runes of the Lyre, 1982, Golden Dream, 1983, Lords of the Triple Moons, 1983, Exile on Vlahil, 1984, The Saga of Grittel Sundotha, 1985, The World Ends in Hickory Hollow, 1985, Medicine Walk, 1985, Carrots and Miggle, 1986, The Wall, 1987, Makra Choria, 1987, Feud at Sweetwater Creek (as Frank Cannon), 1988, A Place of Silver Silence, 1988; (collaboration with Marylois Dunn) The Absolutely Perfect Horse, 1983; (collaboration with Ron Fortier) Trail of the Seahawks, 1987, Monkey Station, TSR, 1989; (as John Killdeer) Wild Country, The Untamed, Wilderness Rendezvous, Blood Kin, People of the Mesa, 1992, Island in the Lake, 1993, Towers of the Earth, 1994, Passage West, 1994, Far Horizons, 1994, Hunters of the Plains, 1995, (as Frances Hurst) High Mountain Winter, 1996, Riddles and Dreams, 2003, elec. edits., 2004-05. Mem.: Sci. Fiction/Fantasy Writers Am. Home: 533 CR 486 Chireno TX 75937 Office Phone: 936-362-2913. E-mail: ardathm@netdot.com.

**MAYHEW, AUBREY,** music industry executive; b. Washington, Oct. 2, 1927; s. Aubrey and Verna June (Hall) M.; m. Carol de Onis, May 10, 1962 (div. 1971); children: Lawrence Aubrey, Michael Aubrey, Parris Mitchell, Casey Aran. Student, Wilson Tchs. Coll., 1948. Dir. WWVA, Wheeling, W.Va., 1947-54, WCOP, Boston, 1954-56; asst. to pres. MGM Records, N.Y.C., 1957-58; v.p. mktg. Capitol Records, LA, 1958-60; prodr., dir. KCAM-TV Prodns., Nashville, 1981—. Pres., founder John F. Kennedy Meml. Ctr., 1968; authority on John F. Kennedy life and memorabilia. Author: (books) Commandants Marine Corps, 1953, World Tribute to John F. Kennedy, 1965; composer (music) Touch My Heart, 1966 (Broadcast Music, Inc. award, 1967); record producer, artist mgmt., 1947—; music pub., 1954—; developed careers numerous entertainers including Johnny Paycheck, Jeannie C. Riley, Bobby Helms. Served to cpl. U.S. Army Signal Corps, 1945-48. Named Govs. Aide, Nashville, 1978. Mem. Country Music Assn., Broadcast Music Inc., Manuscript Soc., N.Y. Numismatic Soc., Gospel Music Assn. Republican. Episcopalian. Avocations: collector, historian, author. Office: Amcorp Music Group 827 Meridian St Nashville TN 37207-5856

**MAYHEW, DAVID RAYMOND,** political science professor; b. Putnam, Conn., May 18, 1937; s. Raymond William and Jeanie (Nicholson) M. BA, Amherst Coll., 1958; PhD, Harvard U., 1964. Tchg. fellow Harvard U., 1961-63; from instr. to asst. prof. polit. sci. U. Mass., Amherst, 1963-67; vis. asst. prof. Amherst Coll., 1965-66; faculty Yale U., 1968-77; prof. polit. sci., 1977—, chmn. dept., 1979-82, Alfred Cowles prof. govt., 1982-98, Sterling prof. polit. sci., 1998—. Olin vis. prof. Am. govt. Nuffield Coll., Oxford (Eng.) U., 2000-01. Author: Party Loyalty Among Congressmen, 1966, Congress: The Electoral Connection, 1974 (Washington Monthly ann. polit. book award 1974), Placing Parties in American Politics, 1986, Divided We Govern, 1991, America's Congress, 2000, Electoral Realignments, 2002. Recipient Richard E. Neustadt prize 1992, James Madison award, 2002, Yale Grad. Student Mentor award, 2002, Samuel J. Eldersveld award, 2004; Woodrow Wilson fellow, 1958-59, vis. fellow Nuffield Coll., Oxford, 1978, Guggenheim fellow, 1978-79, Hoover Nat. fellow, 1978-79, Sherman Fairchild fellow, 1990-91, fellow Ctr. for Advanced Study in Behavioral Scis., 1995-96. Fellow Am. Acad. Arts and Scis.; mem. Am. Polit. Sci. Assn. (nat. council 1976-78, Congl. fellow 1967-68), So. Polit. Sci. Assn., New Eng. Polit. Sci. Assn. Home: 100 York St Apt 5C New Haven CT 06511-5611 Office: Yale U Polit Sci Dept Box 208301 New Haven CT 06520-8301 Office Phone: 203-432-5237. Business E-Mail: david.mayhew@yale.edu.

**MAYHEW, ERIC GEORGE,** medical researcher, educator, consultant; b. London, June 22, 1938; came to U.S., 1964; s. George James and Doris Ivy (Tipping) M.; m. Barbara Doe, Sept. 28, 1966 (div. 1976); 1 child, Miles; m. Karen Caruana, Apr. 1, 1978 (div. 1994); children: Ian, Andrea; m. Ludmila Khatchatrian, June 29, 1995. BS, U. London, 1960, MS, 1963, PhD, 1967, DSc, 1993. Rsch. asst. Chester Beatty Rsch. Inst., London, 1960—64; cancer rsch. scientist Roswell Pk. Meml. Inst., Buffalo, 1964—68, sr. cancer rsch. scientist, 1968—72, assoc. cancer rsch. scientist, 1979—83, dep. dir. exptl. pathology, 1988—93; prin. scientist The Liposome Co., Princeton, NJ, 1993—99, May Pharm Consulting, 2000—. Assoc. rsch. prof. SUNY, Buffalo, 1979-93; ad-hoc mem. NIH study sects., 1982-94; cons. to industry, 2000-. Editor jour. Selective Cancer Therapeutics, 1989-91; contbr. articles to Jour. Nat. Cancer Inst., Cancer Rsch. and many other profl. jours. Grantee NIH, Am. Heart Assn., and pvt. industry, 1972-93. Mem. Am. Assn. Cancer Rsch., N.Y. Acad. Sci. Achievements include development of liposomes for drug delivery and patents for new chemical entities and liposome delivery. Office: May Pharm Consulting 1782 S Seaview Ave Coupeville WA 98239 Personal E-mail: eailkmay@aol.com.

**MAYHEW, KENNETH EDWIN, JR.,** retired transportation executive; b. Shelby, NC, Sept. 27, 1934; s. Kenneth Edwin and Evelyn Lee (Dellinger) M.; m. Frances Elaine Craft, Apr. 7, 1957 (dec. 2005); m. Darlene Burgess Randall, Jan. 7, 2006; 1 dau., Catherine Lynn Prince. AB, Duke U., 1956. CPA NC. Sr. auditor Arthur Andersen & Co., Atlanta, 1956-58, 60-63; controller Trendline, Inc. Hickory, NC, 1963-66; with Carolina Freight Corp., Cherryville, 1966-93, treas., 1969-74; v.p. Carolina Freight Carriers Corp., Cherryville, 1971-72, exec. v.p., 1972-85, pres., COO, 1985-89, dir., 1968-93, chmn., pres., CEO, 1989-93; ret. 1993. Pres., dir. Robo Auto Wash Shelby Inc., 1967-73, Robo Auto Wash Cherryville, Inc., 1968-73; dir. Cherryville Nat. Bank, Kenmar Bus. Group, Inc. Mem. Bus. Adv. Bd., Fuqua Sch. Bus., Duke U.; bd. dirs., vice-chmn. Gaston Meml. Hosp.; trustee Pfeiffer U. With AUS, 1958-60. Mem. AICPA, Am. Trucking Assn. (dir., v.p.), N.C. Trucking Assn. (dir., chmn.), Gaston County C. of C. (v.p. pub. affairs) Lions (pres. Cherryville 1972-73), Phi Beta Kappa, Omicron Delta Kappa, Phi Eta Sigma. Methodist. Home: 507 Spring St Cherryville NC 28021-3540

**MAYHUE, RICHARD LEE,** dean, minister, writer; b. Takoma Park, Md., Aug. 31, 1944; s. J. Richard Mayhue and Myrtle Lorraine (Beasall) Lee; m. Lois Elaine Nettleingham, June 18, 1966; children: Lee, Wade. BS, Ohio State U., 1966; MDiv, Grace Theol. Seminary, 1974, ThM, 1977; ThD, Grace Theol. Seminary, Winona Lake, Ind., 1981. Ordained pastor. Asst. pastor Grace Brethren Ch. of Columbus, Ohio, 1975—77; asst. prof. New Testament and Greek, Grace Theol. Seminary, Winona Lake, Ind., 1977—80; assoc. pastor Grace Cmty. Ch., Sun Valley, Calif., 1980—84, 1989—2004; sr. pastor Grace Brethren Ch., Long Beach, Calif., 1984—89; sr. v.p., dean, prof. systematic theology and pastoral mins. The Master's Seminary, Sun Valley, 1989—; sr. v.p., provost The Master's Coll., Santa Clarita, Calif., 2000—. Bd. dirs. Grace Theol. Sem., 1987-89. Author: The Biblical Pattern for Divine Healing, 1979, 2002, Snatched Before the Storm, 1980, 2002, Divine Healing Today, 1983, How to Interpret the Bible for Yourself, 1986, A Christian's Survival Guide, 1987, Unmasking Satan, 1988, 2d edit., 2001, Spiritual Intimacy, 1990, Spiritual Maturity, 1992, The Healing Promise, 1994, What Would Jesus Say About Your Church?, 1995, 2d edit., 2001, Fight the Good Fight, 1999, 2d edit., 2006, 1 and 2 Thessalonians, 1999, Seeking God, 2000, Practicing Proverbs, 2003; contbr., co-editor: Rediscovering Expository Preaching, 1992, rev. edit., 2005, Rediscovering Pastoral Ministry, 1994, rev. edit., 2005, The Master's Perspective on Pastoral Ministry, 2002, The Master's Perspective on Biblical Prophecy, 2002; contbr., assoc. editor MacArthur Study Bible, 1997, Think Biblically!, 2003; editor MacArthur

Bible Commentary, 2005, assoc. editor: Counseling: How to Counsel Biblically, 2005; contbr. articles to profl. jours., chpts. to books. Bd. dirs. Capitol Ministries, 1996-2005, Slavic Gospel Assn, 1993-2002; bd. elders Grace Cmty. Ch., 1989-2004; mem. bd. of ref. Coun. on Bibl. Manhood and Womanhood, 1991—. Recipient Bronze Star with Combat V USN, 1969. Mem. Evang. Theol. Soc., Nat. Fellowship Grace Brethren Ministers (pres. 1988), Far West Region Evang. Theol. Soc. (pres. 1995), Evang. Homiletics Soc. Avocations: n-gauge model railroading, U.S. stamp collecting. Office: The Master's Seminary 13248 Roscoe Blvd Sun Valley CA 91352-3739 also: The Master's Coll 21726 Placerita Canyon Rd Santa Clarita CA 91321-1200 Business E-Mail: rmayhue@tms.edu.

**MAYLAND, KENNETH THEODORE,** economist; b. Miami, Fla., Nov. 17, 1951; s. Herbert and Vera (Bob) M; m. Gail Fern Bassok, Apr. 14, 1984. BS, MIT, 1973; MS, U. Pa., 1976, PhD, 1979. Cons. economist Data Resources, Inc., Lexington, Mass., 1973; economist, then chief economist First Pa. Bank, Phila., 1973-89; sr. v.p., chief economist Soc. Nat. Bank, Cleve., 1989-94; sr. v.p., chief fin. economist Key Corp., Cleve., 1994-96, sr. v.p., chief economist, 1996-2000; pres. ClearView Econs., LLC, 2000—. Econs. instr., Chartered Fin. Aanalysts Assn., Phila, 1984—; econ. adv. com. Phila. Econ. Devel. Coalition, 1984-86; chmn. econ. adv. com. Pa. Bankers Assn., Harrisburg, 1982-84; mem. Gov.'s Econ. Adv. Com., Ohio, 1989—. Contbr. semi-monthly periodical Money Markets, 1981-85, quar. periodical Regional Report, 1980-89, EconViewpoint/KeyViewpoint biweekly periodical, 1989-2000, Regional Rev. quar. periodical, 1989-94, ClearView on the Economy, 2000—. Mem. curriculum adv. com. Widener U., 1986-89. Named 2d Best Forecaster 1st Quarter 2003, USA Today survey panel, Top Forecaster mid-2003 to mid-2004, Bloomberg Mag., 2004. Mem. Am. Bankers Assn. (econ. adv. com. 1990-93), Internat. Econ. Roundtable (vice chmn. 1987-88, chmn. 1988-90), Nat. Assn. Bus. Economists (New Face for the Eighties award 1979), Phila. Coun. Bus. Economists (pres. 1982-84), Cleve. Bus. Economist Club (sec.-treas. 1990-91, v.p. 1991-92, pres. 1992-93). Avocations: fishing, badminton, gardening, camping. Office: 3237 Fox Hollow Dr Cleveland OH 44124-5426 Office Phone: 216-595-9931.

**MAYLE, JANE,** apparel designer; d. Peter Mayle. Owner, designer Mayle, NYC. Office: Mayle 242 Elizabeth St New York NY 10021*

**MAYNARD, CHARLES DOUGLAS,** radiologist; b. Atlantic City, Sept. 11, 1934; m. Mary Anne Satterwhite; children: Charles D., Deanne, David. BS, Wake Forest U., 1955, MD, 1959. Diplomate Am. Bd. Radiology (trustee 1987-99, sec.-treas., v.p. 1992-94, pres. 1994-96, staff examiner). Intern U.S. Army Hosp., Honolulu, 1959—60; resident N.C. Baptist Hosp., 1963—66; dir. Nuclear Medicine Lab., 1966—77; asst. dean admissions Bowman Gray Sch. Medicine, 1966—71, assoc. dean student affairs, 1971—75, prof. radiology, chmn. dept., 1977—2000. Mem. Am. Bd. Med. Specialists; acting dean Wake Forest U. Sch. Medicine, 2001—02. Author: Clinical Nuclear Medicine, 1969; mem. editl. bd.: Yearbook of Diagnostic Radiology, Contemporary Diagnostic Radiology. Mem. Leadership Winston-Salem, Triad Leadership Network; bd. dirs. Downtown Devel. Corp., 1995—2000, Winston-Salem Bus., Inc., 1995—99, Forsyth Tech. CC, 1997—2005, pres., 2004—05; bd. dirs. Va. Tech. Coll. Engring., 2002—06, Wake Forest U. Health Scis. 2003—. Mem.: AMA, Greater Winston-Salem C. of C. (bd. dirs.), Acad. Radiology Rsch. (pres. 1999—2001), Soc. Chairmen Radiology Depts. (past pres.), Assn. Univ. Radiologists, Radiol. Soc. N.Am. Rsch. and Edn. Found. (chmn. bd. 1999), Radiol. Soc. N.Am. (pres. 1999—2000), Am. Coll. Radiology (past bd. chancellors, past chmn. commn. on nuc. medicine), Soc. Nuc. Medicine (past pres.). Office: Wake Forest U Sch Medicine Dept Radiology Medical Center Blvd Winston Salem NC 27157-1088 Business E-Mail: dmaynard@wfubmc.edu.

**MAYNARD, ELLIOTT E.,** state supreme court justice; b. Williamson, W.Va., Dec. 8, 1942; BS in Psychology, Fla. So. Coll., 1967; JD, W.Va. U., 1974. Atty. priv. practice, Williamson, W.Va., 1974—81; prosecuting atty. Mingo County, 1976—81; judge W.Va. Cir. Ct. 30th Jud. Cir., 1982-97; justice W.Va. Supreme Ct. Appeals, Charleston, 1997—, chief justice, 2000, 2004. Mng. dir. Tug Valley C. of C., 1968-70; active Boy Scouts Am.; dist. chmn. Mingo-Pike Dist., Chief Cornstalk Dist.; bd. dirs. Buckskin Coun. With USAF, 1961—66. Recipient Silver Beaver award Boy Scouts Am. Mem.: ABA, W.Va. Bar Assn., Am. Judicature Soc., Am. Judge's Assn. Office: State Capital State Ct Appeals Bldg 1 Rm E306 Charleston WV 25305*

**MAYNARD, ESTELLE L.,** pre-school educator, director; b. St.'Croix, May 1, 1966; d. Earl and Edith Maynard; 1 child, De'Von K. E. BA, Usapa Coll., East Orange, N.J., 1988; MA, Kean U., Union, N.J., 2002; student, Essex County Coll. N.J. Tchr. Newark Pub. Sch., 2001—, Tender Loving Care, East Orange, NJ; supr. Newark Pre-Sch. Coun., head tchr.; youth counselor, weekend supr. Tillmas House, East Orange. Office: Boylan Street Sch Apt 6 144 Elm St Orange NJ 07050-4055 E-mail: elmaynard@comcast.net.

**MAYNARD, JOHN RALPH,** lawyer; b. Mar. 5, 1942; s. John R. Maynard and Frances Jane (Mitchell) Maynard Kendryk; m. Meridee J. Sagadin, Oct. 11, 1995; children: Bryce James, Pamela Ann. BA, U. Wash., 1964; JD, Calif. Western U., San Diego, 1972; LLM, Harvard U., 1973. Bar: Calif. 1972, Wis. 1973. Assoc. Whyte & Hirschboeck, Milw., 1973-78, Minahan & Peterson, Milw., 1979-91, Quarles & Brady, Milw., 1991-2000, Davis & Kuelthau, Milw., 2000—05, Maynard, McIlnay, Schmitt & Button, Grafton, Wis., 2005—. Bd. dirs. Transitional Living Svcs., Inc., 1999—2003; pres. Milw. Chamber Orch., 2000—02; mem. Wis. Adv. Coun. to U.S. SBA, 1987—89; bd. dirs. Am. Heart Assn., 1979—82, Found. Internal Medicine Exchange, 2004—, Bel Canto Chorus, 2004—. Mem.: ABA, Milw. Yacht Club, Harvard Club (Wis.). Home: 809 E Lake Forest Ave Milwaukee WI 53217-5377 Office: Maynard McIlnay Schmitt & Button 1150 Washington St Grafton WI 53024 Office Phone: 262-376-1287. Business E-Mail: jrm@legalmms.com.

**MAYNARD, JOHN ROGERS,** language educator; b. Williamsville, N.Y., Oct. 6, 1941; s. Atherton Rogers and Olive (Fisher) M.; m. Florence Michelson, July 1, 1967 (div. 1980); 1 child, Alex Stevens; m. Ursula Krammer, Oct. 17, 1992 (div. 1995). BA, Harvard U., 1963, PhD, 1970. Asst. prof. Harvard U., Cambridge, Mass., 1969-74, NYU, N.Y.C., 1974-76, assoc. prof., 1976-84, prof. English dept., 1983-89. Chmn. English dept., 1983-89. Faculty Council NYU, 1983-84; vis. prof. U. Venice, Italy, 1991; co-dir. Biography Seminar, 2004—. Author: Brownings Youth, 1977 (Wilson prize 1977), Charlotte Bronte and Sexuality, 1984, Victorian Discourses on Sexuality and Religion, 1993, Browning Re-Viewed, 1998; editor: Literature and Sexuality, 1991-2004; series of books on sexuality and lit.; editor: (with Lockridge and Stone) Nineteenth Century Lives, 1989, (with Bloom) Shankman's Anne Thackeray Ritchie: Journals and Letters, (with Munich) Victorian Literature and Culture, 1991—, Tennyson: Poetry for Young People. Organizer Concord Sq. Assn., Boston, 1972—74. NEH grantee, 1972-73; Guggenheim fellow, 1979-80. Mem. IAUPE, MLA, PEN, Browning Inst. (bd. dirs.), Signet Soc., Tavern Club (Boston), Aroha Club (pres. 1983-84), Brooklyn Heights Assn. Democrat. Avocation: bicycling. Office: NYU Dept of English 5th Fl 19 University Pl New York NY 10003-4556

**MAYNARD, KENNETH DOUGLAS,** architect; b. Hackensack, NJ, Aug. 16, 1931; s. Douglas Harry and Eva (Whiting) M.; m. Myrna Myrtle James, Feb. 4, 1956; children: Colin, Vivien Noll. Cert. in Architecture, U. Natal, Durban, Republic of South Africa, 1958. Registered arch. Alaska State Bd. Registration Archs., Engrs., and Land Surveyors, 2004. Draftsman Morross & Graff, Johannesburg, Republic of South Africa, 1950-51, Anglo-Am. Corp. Johannesburg, Republic of South Africa, 1951-54, Moir & Llewellyn, Empangeni, Zululand, Republic of South Africa, 1955-57; architect Pearse Aneck-Hahn & Bristol, Johannesburg, 1957-60, Manley & Mayer, Anchorage, 1960-61, FAA, Anchorage, 1961-62, Crittenden Cassetta Wirum & Jacobs, Anchorage, 1962-65; prin. Schultz & Maynard, Anchorage, 1965-68, Kenneth Maynard Assocs., Anchorage, 1968-78; pres. Maynard & Partch, Anchorage, 1978-96; prin. USKH, Inc., Anchorage, 1996—. Active Western

Alaska Coun. Boy Scouts. Am., Anchorage, 1965-84; bd. dirs. Salvation Army Adv. Bd., Anchorage, 1981-87, Anchorage Mus. Assn., 1969-86, Anchorage Opera Co., 1983-90; chmn. Mayor's Comprehensive Homeless Program Strategy Group, 1992-94. Fellow AIA (pres. Alaska chpt. 1969, N.W. regional rep. for nat. com. on design 1976-89, nat. bd. mem. 1999-2001); mem. Constrn. Specification Inst. (pres. Cook Inlet chpt. 1993-94), Soc. Am. Mil. Engrs. Republican. Avocations: tennis, reading, travel. Home: 2237 Forest Park Dr Anchorage AK 99517-1324 Office: USKH 2515 A St Anchorage AK 99503-2776

**MAYNARD, KENNETH IRWIN,** pharmaceutical executive, medical educator, researcher; b. San Fernando, Trinidad, Jan. 17, 1963; Student, Howard U., 1982; BSc with honors, Univ. Coll. London, 1986, MSc, 1987, PhD, 1991. Cert. design and conduct of clin. trials. Postdoctoral rsch. assistantship Univ. Coll., London, 1991; postdoctoral rsch. fellow Stroke Rsch. Lab. Neurosurg. Svc. Mass. Gen. Hosp., Harvard Med. Sch., Boston, 1991—93, postdoctoral rsch. fellow neurophysiology lab. Neurosurg. Svc., 1993—97; tchg. fellow dept. neurobiology Harvard Med. Sch., Boston, 1992, instr. in surgery, 1995—98, asst. prof., 1998—2001; asst. neuroscientist Mass. Gen. Hosp., 1998—2001; section head, cerebrovascular disorders Aventis Pharms., Inc., 2000—02, prin. sci., 2002—04; project dir. Sanofi-Aventis, Inc., 2005—. Ad hoc reviewer Jour. Vascular Rsch., 1991, Neurosci. Letters, 1995, Vision Rsch., 1996, Neurosurgery, 1998, others; presenter in field; tutor dept. of neurobiology, 1998—2000; asst. prof. surgery, 1998; steering com. Boston Area Neurosci. Group, 1998—2000; ad hoc reviewer Ministry of Health, Internal Grant Agy., Czech Republic, 1998; med. rsch. grant program Jewish Hosp. Found., 2000; cons. neurosurgery Mass. Gen. Hosp., 2001—02; lectr. Harvard U. Med. Sch., 2001—02. Contbr. articles to med. jours. including Neurosci. Letters, articles to med. jours. including Stroke, articles to med. jours. including Exptl. Neurology, articles to med. jours. including Jour. Neurol. Rsch. Mem. parish pastoral coun. St. Joseph's Cath. Ch., Boston, 1992—95, chmn. stewardship commn., 1997; advisor regional com. ctrl. region on stewardship Archdiocese of Boston, 1995—97. Recipient Travel fellowship for minority neuroscientists, Nat. Inst. Neurol. Disease and Stroke, 1995, travel award, FASEB MARC, 1998; scholar, Autumn Sch. Caen France, 1996, Tokyo, 1998. Fellow: Am. Heart Assn. (minority scientist devel. award 1996, nat. affiliate brain/stroke study sect. 1999—, stroke coun. 2002, minority affairs com.); mem.: AAAS, Internat. Soc. Cerebral Blood Flow and Metabolism (Young Scientist Bursary award 1993), Congress of Neurosurg. Surgeons, Am. Assn. Neurosurg. Surgeons (adj. assoc. mem. joint sect. on cerebrovascular surgery 1995), Soc. for Neurosci. (minority edn., tng. and profl. advancement com. 2000—03, minority neurosci. fellowship program 2000—02, membership com. 2002—), N.Y. Acad. Sci., Am. Stroke Assn. (affiliate brain rsch. peer rev. group 1999—2003). Roman Catholic. Office: Sanofi Aventis Inc 200 Crossing Blvd BX2-306A Bridgewater NJ 08807 Office Phone: 908-304-6352. Business E-Mail: kenneth.maynard@sanofi-aventis.com.

**MAYNARD, MICHAEL,** librarian; b. Yuma, Ariz., July 8, 1955; s. Ernest Ray and Refugio (Guerrero) M. AAS in Electronic Tech., Phoenix Coll., 1986; BA in German, Ariz. State U., 1989; postgrad., U. Leipzig, 1990, Eberhard-Karls U., Tubingen, Germany, 1990—91; MLS, U. Ariz., 1992; cert. in computer applications, Rio Salado Coll., 2004. Electronics technician USN, 1977-83; asst. libr. Chapel Libr., Venice, Fla., 1983-84; security officer Anderson Agy., Phoenix, 1984-89; grad. asst. U. Ariz., Tuscon, 1989-90, libr. asst. main libr. acquisitions dept., 1992; asst. libr. Internat. Bapt. Coll., Tempe, Ariz., 1992-94; head libr. Velda Rose Ch. Fitch Libr., Mesa, Ariz., 1994-97; libr. II Ariz. Dept. Corrections, Douglas, 1997-2000, Goodyear, 2000—, instr. Latin, Greek, Hebrew, Russian, German, French, and Spanish, 2003—06. Author: History of the Debate Over I John 5:7-8, 1995. With USN, 1977—83. Scholar U. Ariz., 1989-90, Herman Weinel scholar, 1990. Mem.: Ariz. Road Racers. Baptist. Avocations: foreign languages, lexicology, philology, nutrition, New Testament studies. Home and Office: Comma Publs PO Box 1625 Tempe AZ 85280-1625 E-mail: receptus@sprynet.com.

**MAYNARD, MICHELINE ANN,** journalist, writer; b. Ann Arbor, Mich., Aug. 5, 1958; d. Frank Henry and Bernice Genevieve Maynard. BA in Humanities, Mich. State U., 1979; MA in Journalism, Columbia U., 1990. Legis. corr. United Press Internat., Lansing, Mich.; intern White House Press Office; assoc. editor US News & World Report, Washington, 1984-86; sr. bus. writer Newsday, NYC, 1986-88; bur. chief Reuters News Svc., Detroit, 1988-90; bus. journalist USA Today, Arlington, Va., 1999; freelance journalist, 1999—2003; bus. day reporter NY Times, Detroit, 2004—. Lectr. U. Mich. Sch. Bus. Adminstrn., 2000—03, U. Mich. Sch. Pub. Policy, 2004—. Author: Collision Course: Inside the Battle for General Motors, 1995, The Global Manufacturing Vanguard, 1998, The End of Detroit, 2003. Knight-Bagehot fellow, bus. and economics journalism, Columbia U., 1989—90, Knight Wallace fellow, U. Mich., 1999—2000, media fellow, Japan Soc. of NY, 2002. Mem.: Authors Guild, Univ. Musical Soc. Avocations: antiques, gardening, classical music, yoga, contemporary film. Office: NY Times 229 West 43rd St New York NY 10036 Office Phone: 212-556-1474. Office Fax: 212-556-1448. Business E-Mail: mickimay@nytimes.com. E-mail: Micheline@MichelineMaynard.com.

**MAYNARD, OLIVIA P.,** foundation administrator; m. S. Olof Karlstrom. BA, George Washington U., 1959; MSW, U. Mich., 1971. Dir. Mich. Office Svcs. to Aging, 1983—90; tchr. Sch. Social Work U. Mich., Mich. State U.; tchr. Ctr. for Aging Edn. Lansing (Mich.) C.C.; pres. Mich. Prospect for Renewed Citizenship, Flint, Mich., 1992—. Del. White House Conf. on Aging, 1995. Regent U. Mich., Ann Arbor; chmn. Mich. Dem. Party, 1973—82; candidate Lt. Gov. of Mich., 1990; trustee Charles Stewart Mott Found.; bd. dirs. Nature Conservancy of Mich., McLaren Regional Medical Ctr., Council of Mich. Found. Democrat. Office: Northbank Ctr Ste 406 432 N Saginaw St Flint MI 48502 also: Mich Prospect 2248 Mt Hope Rd Ste 101 Okemos MI 48864*

**MAYNARD, ROBERT HOWELL,** retired lawyer; b. San Antonio, Feb. 15, 1938; s. William Simpson Sr. and Lillian Isabel (Tappan) M.; m. Joan Marie Pearson, Jan. 6, 1962; children: Gregory Scott, Patricia Kathryn, Alicia Joan, Elizabeth Simms. BA, Baylor U., 1959, LLB, 1961; LLM, Georgetown U., 1965. Bar: Tex. 1961, D.C. 1969, Ohio 1973. Trial atty. gen. litigation sect. lands div. U.S. Dept. Justice, Washington, 1964-65; spl. asst. to solicitor U.S. Dept. Interior, Washington, 1965-69; legis. asst. U.S. Senate, Washington, 1969-73; ptnr., dept. head Smith & Schnacke, Dayton, Ohio, 1973-83; dir. Ohio EPA, Columbus, Ohio, 1983-85; ptnr., environ. policy and strategy devel., tech. law Vorys, Sater, Seymour and Pease, Columbus, 1985-2000; ret., 2000; pres. Tappan Woods LLC, 2001—. Trustee Ohio Found. for Entrepreneurial Edn., Bus. Tech. Ctr., 1994-2000, Episcopal Cmty. Svcs. Found., 1990-96, Columbus Technology Coun., 1992-2001, Johnson's Island Preservation Soc. USNR, 1962-65. Episcopalian.

**MAYNARD, TERRELL DENNIS,** minister; b. Paducah, Ky., Dec. 10, 1944; s. Claude and Euda (Finley) M.; m. Mary Jacqueline Chappell, Sept. 3, 1965; children: Terrell Geoffrey, Christopher Dennis. BA, Bethel Coll., 1966; MDiv, Memphis Theol. Sem., 1969. Pastor Cumberland Presbyn. Ch., Searcy, Ark., 1969-72, Hohenwald, Tenn., 1972-76, Swan Cumberland Presbyn. Ch., Centerville, Tenn., 1972-76, Elliottsville Presbyn. Ch., Alabaster, Ala., 1976-94, 1st Cumberland Presbyn. Ch., Jackson, Tenn., 1994—2002, Clarksville (Tenn.) Cumberland Presbyn. Ch., 2002—. Pres. Bd. Christian Edn., Memphis, 1976-85; chair Gen. Assembly's Exec. Com. Memphis, 1987-93. Bd. dirs., pres. Shelby Emergency Assistance, Montevallo, Ala., 1990-94; bd. dirs. Developing Ala. Youth Found., Alabaster, 1989-94, Shelby County Hosp. Authority, Alabaster, 1993-94, Area Relief Ministry, Jackson, 1996-2002; mem. adv. coun. PCC Tenn.-Clarksville, 2003—. Recipient Disting. Alumni award Bethel Coll., McKenzie, Tenn., 1992; named Outstanding Vol. Shelby County Chpt. ARC, Alabaster, 1989. Mem. Assn. Cumberland Presbyn. Ch. Educators. Presbyterian. Avocations: tennis, reading, golf, huntung, reading, college basketball. Home: 154 Village Way Clarksville TN 37043 Office: Cumberland Presbyn Ch 1410 Golf Club Ln Clarksville TN 37040 Office Phone: 931-648-0817. Personal E-mail: clkscpmaynard@bellsouth.net.

**MAYNARD, VIRGINIA MADDEN,** foundation administrator; b. New London, Conn., Jan. 29, 1924; d. Raymond and Edna Sarah (Madden) Maynard. BS, U. Conn., 1945; postgrad., Am. Inst. Banking, 1964—66, Cornell U., 1975. With Nat. City Bank (now Citibank), N.Y.C., 1954—79, asst. cashier, 1965—69, asst. v.p., 1969-74, v.p. internat. banking group, 1974-76, comptroller's div., 1976-79; v.p. First Women's Bank, N.Y.C., 1979-80; rep. Internat. Fedn. Univ. Women UN, 1982—2003. Trustee fellowships endowment fund AAUW Ednl. Found., Washington, 1977—80, Va. Gildersleeve Internat. Fund Univ. Women, inc., pres., 1987—93, bd. dirs. 1994—2000, rep. UN, 1997—; bd. dirs. (conf. Nongovtl. Orgns. Found., Inc., 1997—, treas., 1999—. Mem.: AAUW: fin. chmn. N.Y.C. br. 1976—79, bylaws chmn. 1979—83, adminstr. Meml. Fund 1983—92, 2000—, bd. dirs. 1992—94, 1996—99, Woman of Achievement 1976). Republican. Congregationalist. Home: 601 E 20th St New York NY 10010-7622

**MAYNE, KENNY,** sports anchor; b. Sept. 1, 1959; Student, Wenatchee (Wash.) Valley C.C.; BA in Broadcasting, U. Nev.-Las Vegas, 1982. Reporter Sta. KLVX-TV, Las Vegas, 1982, Sta. KSTW-TV, Tacoma/Seattle, 1982-89, prodn. asst., 1982-83, news writer, 1983-86, weekend sports anchor, news reporter, 1986-89; freelance reporter, field prodr. SportsCenter ESPN, 1990-94, SportSmash anchor, 1994, SportsNight reporter, 1994, anchor Sports-Center, 1994—; host RPM 2Night ESPN2, 1994. Football player, free agt. Seattle Seahawks, 1982 Guest appearance Dancing with the Stars, ABC, 2006. Office: c/o ESPN ESPN Plaza Bristol CT 06010*

**MAYNE, LUCILLE STRINGER,** finance educator; b. Washington, June 6, 1924; d. Henry Edmond and Hattie Benham (Benson) Stringer; children: Pat A., Christine Gail, Barbara Marie. BS, U. Md., College Park, 1946; MBA, Ohio State U., Columbus, 1949; PhD, Northwestern U., Evanston, Ill., 1966. Instr. fin. Utica Coll., 1949-50; lectr. fin. Roosevelt U., 1961-64, Pa. State U., 1965-66, asst. prof., 1966-69, assoc. prof., 1969-70; assoc. prof. banking and fin. Case-Western Res. U., 1971-76, prof., 1976-94, prof. emerita, 1994—, grad. dean Sch. Grad. Studies, 1980-84. Sr. economist, cons. FDIC, 1977-78; cons. Nat. Commn. Electronic Fund Transfer Sys., 1976; rsch. cons. Am. Bankers Assn., 1975, Fed. Res. Bank of Cleve., 1968-70, 73; cons. Pres.'s Commn. Fin. Structure and Regulation, 1971, staff economist, 1970-71; analytical statistician Air Materiel Command, Dayton, Ohio, 1950-52; asst. to promotion mgr. NBC, Washington, 1946-48; expert witness cases involving fin. instns. Assoc. editor: Jour. Money, Credit and Banking, 1980-83, Bus. Econs., 1980-85; contbr. articles to profl. jours. Vol. Cleve. Soc. for Blind, 1979-2004, Benjamin Rose Inst., 1995-2005; mem. policyholders nominating com. Tchrs. Ins. and Annuity Assn./Coll. Retirement Equities Fund, 1982-84, chair com., 1984; bd. dirs. Women's Cmty. Found., 1994-96. Grad. scholar, Ohio State U., 1949, doctoral fellow, Northwestern U., 1963—65. Mem. LWV (bd. dirs. Shaker Heights chpt. 1999-), Midwest Fin. Assn. (pres. 1991-92, bd. dirs. 1975-79, officer 1988-93), Phi Kappa Phi, Beta Gamma Sigma. Episcopalian. Home: 3723 Normandy Rd Cleveland OH 44120-5246 Office: Case Western Res U Weatherhead Sch Mgmt U Circle Cleveland OH 44106-7235 Business E-Mail: lucille.mayne@case.edu.

**MAYNE, THOM,** architect; b. Waterbury, Conn., Jan. 19, 1944; s. Walter and Bernice (Gornall) M.; m. Susan Burnham, Sept. 10, 1964 (div. 1970); 1 child, Richard; m. Blythe Alison Mayne, Aug. 8, 1981; children: Sam, Cooper. BArch, U. So. Calif., 1968; MArch, Harvard U., 1978. Mem. faculty UCLA Sch. Art and Architecture, Santa Monica, Calif., 1972—; bd. dirs. So. Calif. Inst. Architecture, Santa Monica, Calif., 1983—; architect Morphosis, Santa Monica, Calif. Adj. prof. UCLA, 1993; mem. vis. faculty Calif. State Coll., Pomona, 1971, Miami U., Ohio, 1982, Washington U., St. Louis, 1984, U. Tex., Austin, 1984, U. Pa., 1985, Columbia U., N.Y.C., 1986, Harvard U., 1988, Clemson U., 1991, Yale U., 1991, UCLA, 1986, 92, U. Ill., Urbana-Champaign, 1992-93, Tech. U., Vienna, Austria, 1993, Berlage Inst., Amsterdam, 1993, Hochschule für Andgewandt Kunst, Vienna, 1991, 93; lectr. in field; adjudicator numerous awards. Archtl. one-man exhbns. include 2 AES Gallery, San Francisco, 1988, Cheney Cowles Mus., Spokane, Wash., 1989, Walker Arts Ctr., Mpls., 1989, Gallery of Architecture, L.A., 1989, Contemporary Arts Ctr., Cin., 1989, San Francisco Mus. Modern Art, 1990, Graham Found., Chgo., 1990, Aedes Galerie and Architecture Forum, Berlin, 1990, Fenster Architekturgalerie, Frankfurt, Germany, 1990, Gallery MA, Tokyo, 1990, Laguna (Calif.) Art Mus., 1991, G201 Gallery, Ohio, 1991, 1-Space Gallery, Chgo., 1992, Sadock & Uzzan Galerie, Paris, 1992, Diane Farris Gallery, 1993; group exhbns. include Umwelt Galerie, Stuttgart, Germany, 1978, The Archtl. Gallery, Venice, Calif., 1979, La Jolla (Calif.) Mus. of Contemporary Art, 1982, Inst. Contemporary Arts, London, 1983, Archtl. Assn., London, 1983, NAD, N.Y.C., 1983, 88, Mus. Modern Art, San Francisco, 1983, Calif. Mus. Sci. and Industry, 1984, G.A. Gallery, Tokyo, 1985, 87, 90, Max Protech Gallery, N.Y.C., 1985, 86, I.D.C., N.Y.C., 1986, Axis Gallery, Tokyo, Milan, Paris, 1988, Pacific Design Ctr., L.A., 1988, Australia Ctr. for Contemporary Arts, Victoria, 1988, Cooper-Hewitt Mus., N.Y.C., 1988, Aedes Galerie für Architektur und Raum, Berlin, 1988, Kirsten Kiser Gallery, 1988, 89, Visual Arts Ontario, Toronto, 1988, Gallery Functional Art, Santa Monica, Calif., 1989, Deutsches Architektur Mus., Frankfurt, 1989, USIA, Moscow, 1989-90, Lameier Sculpture Park, St. Louis, 1989, Gwenda Jay Gallery, Chgo., 1990, Sadock & Uzzan Galerie, 1991, Bannatyne Gallery, Santa Monica, 1991, ROM Galleri for Arkitektur, Oslo, 1992, 65 Thompson Street Gallery, N.Y.C., 1992; archtl. projects include Sequoyah Edn. and Rsch. Ctr., Santa Monica, 1977 (Progressive Architecture award 1974), Flores Residence, 1979 (Progressive Architecture award 1980), Sedlak Residence, 1980 (AIA award 1981), Western Melrose Office Bldg. 1981 (Progressive Architecture award 1982), Hermosa Beach Ctrl. Bus. Dist. (Progressive Architecture award 1984), 72 Market Street Restaurant, 1983 (AIA award 1985, CCAIA award 1986), Bergren Residence, 1984 (AIA award 1985, CCAIA award 1986, Nat. AIA award 1986), Cedar Sinai Comprehensive Cancer Ctr., L.A., 1988 (Progressive Architecture award 1987, AIA award 1988, CCAIA award 1989), Arts Park Performing Pavilion, 1988, (Progressive Architecture award 1989), Leon Max Showroom, L.A., 1988 (CCAIA award 1990, Archtl. Record Interior award 1990), Club Post Nulear, Laguna Beach, Calif., 1988, Berlin Wall Competition, 1988, Expo '90 Folly, Osaka, Japan, 1989, The Emery Ctr. Performing Arts, 1989, Temple U. CCC, Phila., 1989, Politix, 1990 (AIA award 1990), Salick Health Care Corp. Hdqs., 1990 (AIA award 1992, CCAIA award 1993), Visual Performing Arts Sch. at Thomas More Coll., Crestview, N.Y., 1990, MTV Studios, L.A., 1990, Higashi Azabu Tower, Tokyo, 1991, Yuzen Vintage Car Mus., L.A., 1991 (AIA award 1993), Disney Inst. and Town Ctr. Competition, Orlando, Fla., 1991, Cranbrook Acad. Gatehouse Competition (Pilkington Planar prize 1993), Spreebogen Master Plan, Berlin, 1993, Check Point Charlie Office Bldg., Berlin, 1993; contbr. articles to profl. jours. Rome Prize fellow Am. Acad. Rome, 1987; recipient Architecture award Am. Acad. Arts and Letters, 1992, Pritzker Architecture prize, 2005. Mem. AIA, Am. Acad. Design. Democrat. Avocations: skiing, travel. Office: Morphosis Architecture 2041 Colorado Ave Santa Monica CA 90404-3415 Office Phone: 310-570-0123. Business E-Mail: t.mayne@morphosis.net.

**MAYNE, WILEY EDWARD,** lawyer; b. Sanborn, Iowa, Jan. 19, 1917; s. Earl W. and Gladys (Wiley) M.; m. Elizabeth Dodson, Jan. 5, 1942; children— Martha (Mrs. F.K. Smith), Wiley Edward, John. S.B. cum laude, Harvard, 1938; JD, State U. Iowa, 1941. Bar: Iowa 1941, US Supreme Ct. 1950. Practiced in Sioux City, 1946-66, 75—; mem. Shull, Marshall, Mayne, Marks & Vizintos, 1946-66, Mayne and Berenstein, 1975-87, Mayne & Mayne, 1988-99, Mayne, Marks and Madsen, Sioux City, 1999—. Spl. agt. FBI, 1941-43; Mem. 90th-93d Congresses, 6th Dist. Iowa; mem. judiciary com., agr. com. Commr. from Iowa Nat. Conf. Commrs. Uniform State Laws, 1956-60; chmn. grievance commn. Iowa Supreme Ct., 1964-66; del. FAO, 1973; chmn. Woodbury County Compensation Bd., 1975-80 Chmn. Midwest Rhodes Scholar Selection Com., 1964-66; pres. Sioux City Symphony Orch. Assn., 1947-54, Sioux City Concert Course, 1947-54; vice-chmn. Young Republican Nat. Fedn., 1948-50; bd. dirs. Iowa Bar Found., 1962-68. Lt. (j.g.) USNR, 1943-46. Fellow Am. Coll. Trial Lawyers; mem. ABA (ho. of dels. 1966-68), Iowa Bar Assn. (pres. 1963-64), Sioux City Bar Assn., Internat. Assn. Def. Counsel (exec. com. 1961-64), Harvard Club (N.Y.C.), Sioux City

Country Club, Masons (Scottish Rite/33 deg.). Office: Pioneer Bank Bldg 701 Pierce St Ste 405 Sioux City IA 51101 Home: 2525 Nebraska St Apt 115 Sioux City IA 51104-3509 Fax: 712-252-1535. Office Phone: 712-252-3220. E-mail: jmayne@maynelaw.com.

**MAYNES, CHARLES WILLIAM,** foundation executive; b. Huron, S.D., Dec. 8, 1938; s. Charles William and Almira Rose (Summers) M.; m. Gretchen Schiele, July 17, 1965; children: Stacy Kathryn, Charles William. BA, Harvard U., 1960; MA, Oxford U., Eng., 1962. UN polit. affairs ofcl. Dept. State, Washington, 1962-65; chief monetary economist AID, Laos, 1965-67; econ. officer Am. Embassy, Moscow, 1968-70; sec. Carnegie Endowment Internat. Peace, 1971-76; sr. legis. asst. to Sen. Fred R. Harris, 1972; mem. issues Sargent Shriver's Vice-Presdl. campaign, 1972; mem. Carter-Mondale Transition team, 1976-77; asst. sec. for internat. orgn. affairs Dept. State, 1977-80; editor Fgn. Policy mag., 1980-97; mem. Clinton-Gore Transition team, 1992-93, 96-97; pres. Eurasia Found., Washington, 1997—. Mem. Coun. Fgn. Rels., Washington Inst. Fgn. Affairs, UN Assn., Nat. Acad. Pub. Adminstrn., Internat. Inst. Strategic Studies. Contbr. articles to profl. jours. Recipient Meritorious Service award Dept. State; congl. fellow Rep. F. Bradford Morse, 1971, Sen. Fred R. Harris, 1971; Rhodes scholar. Mem. Phi Beta Kappa. Democrat. Office: Eurasia Found 10th Fl 1350 Connecticut Ave NW Washington DC 20036-1722 Home: 3914 Leland St Chevy Chase MD 20815-5036 E-mail: bmaynes@eurasia.org.

**MAYO, CLYDE CALVIN,** psychologist, educator; b. Robstown, Tex., Feb. 2, 1940; s. Clyde Culberson and Velma (Oxford) Mayo; m. Jeanne Lynn McCain, Aug. 24, 1963; children: Brady Scott, Amber Camille. BA, Rice U., Houston, 1961; BS, U. Houston, 1964, PhD, 1972; MS, Trinity U., 1966. Lic. psychologist Tex., La. Mgmt. engr. LWFW, Inc., Houston, 1966-72, sr. cons., 1972-78, prin., 1978-81; ptnr. Mayo, Thompson, Bigby, Houston, 1981-83; founder Mgmt. and Pers. Systems, Houston, 1983—. Counselor Interface Counseling Ctr., Houston, 1976—79; dir. Mental Health HMO Group, 1985—87; instr. St. Thomas U., Houston, 1979—90, U. Houston Downtown Sch., 1972, 2002—06, U. Houston, Clear Lake, 1983—88, U. Houston-Ctrl. Campus, 1984—; dir. mgmt. devel. insts. U. Houston Woodlands and West Houston, 1986—91; adj. prof. U. Houston, 1991—. Author: LWFW Annual Survey of Manufacturers, 1966—81, Bi/Polar Inventory of Strengths, 1978. Coach, mgr. Meryerland Little League, 1974—78, So. Belles Softball, 1979—80, S.W. Colt Baseball, 1982—83, Friends of Fondren Libr. Rice U., 1988—; charter mem. Holocaust Mus. Mem.: APA, Houston Area Indsl. Orgnl. Psychologists (bd. dirs. 1989—92), Am. Psychol. Soc., Tex. Psychol. Assn., Houston Psychol. Assn. (membership dir. 1978, sec. 1984), Tex. Indsl. Orgnl. Psychologists (founder, bd. dirs. 1995—, pres. 1999—2002), Soc. Indsl. Orgn. Psychologists, Found. Contemporary Theology (bd. dirs. 2005—), Meyerland Club (bd. dirs. 1988—92, pres. 1991), Forum Club. Home: 8723 Ferris Dr Houston TX 77096-1409 Office: Mgmt and Personnel Systems 4545 Bissonnet St Bellaire TX 77401-3121 Office Phone: 713-667-9251. Personal E-mail: mpsmayo@aol.com.

**MAYO, CYNTHIA GOULD,** music educator; d. Robert Hamilton and Mabel Dean Gould; m. Walter Stephen Mayo, Aug. 16, 1986; children: Megan, Melora. MusB in Edn., SUNY, Fredonia, 1974; MusM in Music Edn., Ithaca Coll., 1975. Cert. Permanent Tchg. NY. Music tchr. Orchard Pk. (NY) Mid. Sch., 1976—. Recipient Excellence in Music Edn. award, Buffalo Philharm. Orch., Erie County Coun. Music Coord., 2003. Mem.: Erie County Music Educator's Assn. (dir 2000—06), Buffalo Philharm. Chorus. Avocations: singing, african and caribbean drumming, travel. Home: 1316 Wis Rd Derby NY 14047 Office: Orchard Park Mid Sch 60 S Lincoln Ave Orchard Park NY 14127 Office Phone: 719-209-6220.

**MAYO, DAVID WAYNE,** sportswriter; b. San Diego, Dec. 28, 1960; s. Derwood Crandle and Shirley Ann (Jester) M. BA, Henderson State U., 1982. Sportswriter The Amarillo (Tex.) Globe-News, 1982-85, The Grand Rapids (Mich.) Press, 1985-87, sports columnist, 1989—; baseball beat writer Detroit Tigers Newhouse/Booth Newspapers, Lansing, Mich., 1987-89. Heisman Trophy elector, 1996—; Boxing Hall of Fame elector, 2003—. Contbg. writer: Ring Mag., 1999—. Recipient first place Mich. Sustained Sports Coverage, Mich. AP, Detroit, 1989; named Mich. Sports Feature of the Yr., Mich. Press Assn., Detroit, 1994, 95, 98, Sports Columnist of Yr., Mich. Press Assn., 1998. Mem. Football Writers Assn. Am., Basketball Writers Assn. Am., Boxing Writers Assn. Am. (Best Investigative award 2003), Phi Sigma Kappa. Democrat. Baptist. Office: The Grand Rapids Press 155 Michigan St NW Grand Rapids MI 49503-2353 Office Phone: 616-222-5477. E-mail: davidwmayo@yahoo.com.

**MAYO, GEORGE WASHINGTON, JR.,** lawyer; b. Waycross, Ga., Dec. 23, 1946; s. George Washington and Perrie R. (Ling) M.; m. Katherine Louise Boland, Nov. 15, 1977; children: Regan L.B., Taylor L.B. BA, Emory U., 1967; JD, U. Va., 1973. Bar: Va. 1973, DC 1974. Assoc. Hogan & Hartson, Washington, 1973—80, ptnr., 1980—, mng. ptnr.-ops. Contbr. articles. Bd. dirs. Vietnam Vets Meml. Fund, Inc., 1978—, Earth Conservation Corps, 1990—; bd. dirs. coll. coun. advisors Emory U., 1994—; bd. dirs. Deafness Rsch. Found., 1997—2001. 1st lt. U.S. Army, 1969—71, Vietnam. Mem.: ABA, DC Bar Assn., Congl. Country Club (Washington), City Club (Washington), Met. Club (Washington), Order of the Coif. Democrat. Methodist. Home: 26 Holly Leaf Ct Bethesda MD 20817-2652 Office: Hogan & Hartson 555 13th St NW Ste 800E Washington DC 20004-1161 Office Phone: 202-637-5679. Office Fax: 202-637-5910. Business E-Mail: gwmayo@hhlaw.com.

**MAYO, JOHN W.,** finance educator; BA in economics, Hendrix Coll.; MA in economics, PhD in economics, Washington U. St. Louis. Chief economist US Senate Small Bus. Com.; mem. faculty Washington U., U. Tenn., Va. Tech.; prof. McDonough Sch. Bus., Georgetown U., 1997—, sr. assoc. dean, 1999—2001, acting dean, 2002—04. Adv., cons. pub. and pvt. agys. including U.S. Dept. Justice, Fed. Trade Commn., Tenn. Valley Authority, U.S. Dept. Energy, Oak Ridge Nat. Lab.; former chief economist U.S. Senate Small Bus. Com. Co-author (with David L. Kaserman): Government and Business: The Economics of Antitrust and Regulation, 1995; contbr. numerous articles to profl. jours. Zaeslin Fellowship in law and econs., U. Basel, Switzerland. Mem.: Antitrust Law and Economics Assn., Am. Econ. Assn., So. Econ. Assn., Am. Econ. Assn. Office: Georgetown U McDonough Sch Bus 37th and O Sts NW Washington DC 20057 Office Phone: 202-687-6972. Business E-Mail: mayoj@georgetown.edu.*

**MAYO, LOUIS ALLEN,** diversified financial services company executive; b. Durham, NC, Nov. 27, 1928; s. Louis Allen and Amy Earl (Overton) M.; m. Emma Jean Minshew, Oct. 31, 1953 (div.); children: Louis Allen III, Robert Lawrence, Carolyn Jean; m. Myrna Ann Smith, Feb. 16, 1980 (div.). Student, Calif. State Poly. Coll., 1948—50; BA in Criminology, Calif. State Coll., Fresno, 1952; MA in Pub. Adminstrn., Am. U., 1960, PhD in Pub. Adminstrn., 1983; postgrad., U. So. Calif., 1960—62. Spl. agt. U.S. Secret Svc., Treasury Dept., LA, 1956-58, 60-63, White House, Washington, 1958-60, 63-66; program mgr. law enforcement Office Law Enforcement Assistance, Justice Dept., 1967-68; acting chief Rsch. Ctr., rsch. program mgr. Nat. Inst. Law Enforcement and Criminal Justice, 1968-74; alternate assoc. mem. Fed. Coun. on Sci. and Tech., White House, 1973-74; dir. tng. and testing divsn. Nat. Inst. Justice, 1975-87; pres. Mayo, Mayo & Assocs., Alexandria, Va., 1987—. Lectr. criminology Armed Forces Inst. Tech., 1954-55; professorial lectr. Am. U., 1974-82; adj. prof. August Vollmer U., 1990-95. 2d lt. to 1st lt. USAF, 1952-56. Mem. Police Assn. Coll. Edn. (exec. dir., founder), Internat. Assn. Chiefs of Police, ASPA (nat. chmn. sect. on criminal justice adminstrn. 1975-76), Am. Soc. for Law Enfocement Tng., Acad. Criminal Justice Scis., Police Exec. Rsch. Forum, Soc. Police Futurists Internat., Pi Sigma Alpha. Methodist. Home: 63 Lake Forest Dr Mineral VA 23117 Office Phone: 540-894-8781. E-mail: loumayo@police-association.org.

**MAYO, MARTI,** museum director, curator; b. Bluefield, W.Va., Oct. 17, 1945; d. Robert J. and Kathryn Ann (Kearns) Kirkwood; m. Edward K. Mayo, May 13, 1974 (div. 1983); 1 child, Nesta. BA, Am. U., 1970, MFA, 1974. Asst. dir. Jefferson Place Gallery, Washington, 1973-74; coord. exhbns. Corcoran Gallery Art, Washington, 1974-80; curator Contemporary Arts Mus., Houston, 1980-86; dir. Blaffer Gallery U., Houston, 1986—94; dir., chief curator Contemporary Arts Museum, Houston, 1994—. Mem. review panel, Inst. of Museum & Library Services; panelist Nat. Endowment for Arts, Texas Commn. on Arts. Author: Robert Morris Selected Works; 1970-80, 1981, Other Realities: Installations for Performance, 1981, Arbitrary Order: Paintings by Pat Steir, 1983, (with others) Robert Rauschenberg, Work from Four Series: A Sesquicentennial Exhibition, 1985, Joseph Glasco 1948-86: A Sesquicentennial Exhibition, 1986, Six Artists/Six Idioms, 1988. V.p. Cultural Arts Council of Houston/Harris County. Mem. Am. Assn. Mus., Coll. Art·Assn.; bd. dirs. Houston Museum District Assn. (vice pres. 1998-99, pres. 2001-02), bd. trustees Am. Federation of Arts, Assn. of Art Museum Directors. Office: Contemporary Arts Museum 5216 Montrose Blvd Houston TX 77006-6598

**MAYO, MARY E.,** music educator, conductor; b. Olean, NY, May 29, 1964; d. F. York and Elizabeth O. Mayo; children: Richard, Brooke. B Music Edn. in Voice, Ithaca Coll., 1986, M Music Edn., 1989. Cert. tchr. NY. Vocal music tchr. Morrisville (NY)-Eaton Jr./Sr. HS, 1986—89, Norwich (NY) HS, 1990—. Min. music 1st Congl. United Ch. of Christ, Norwich, 2003—; asst. dir. Catskill Choral Soc., Oneonta, NY, 2005—. Mem.: NEA, Music Educators Nat. Conf., Am. Choral Dirs. Assn., Sigma Alpha Iota. Office: Norwich HS Midland Dr Norwich NY 13815

**MAYO, ROBERT N.,** computer science researcher; b. Washington, Aug. 23, 1959; s. Robert P. and Marian A. Mayo. BS in Computer Sci., Washington U., St. Louis, 1981; MS in Computer Sci., U. Calif., Berkeley, 1983, PhD of Computer Sci., 1987. Asst. prof. U. Wis., Madison, 1988; staff Digital Equipment Corp./Compaq Computer/Hewlett Packard, Palo Alto, Calif., 1989—. Mem. IEEE, Assn. Computer Machinery. Home: 407 W Dana St Mountain View CA 94041-1337 Office: Hewlett Packard 1501 Page Mill Rd MS 1146 Palo Alto CA 94304 Business E-Mail: tech-ww@bobmayo.com.

**MAYO, ROBERT RAYMOND,** university librarian; Assoc. dir. rsch. libraries Rensselaer Poly. Inst., Troy, NY, 2001—06, acting dir. rsch. libraries, 2006—. Office: Rsch Libraries Rensselaer Poly Inst 110 8th St Troy NY 12180 Office Phone: 518-276-8303. Office Fax: 518-276-2044. Business E-Mail: mayor@rpi.edu.*

**MAYO, STEPHEN L.,** biochemist; BS in Chemistry, Pa. State U., 1983; PhD in Chemistry, Calif. Inst. Tech., 1987; postdoctoral study, U. Calif., Berkeley, 1988—89. Co-founder Molecular Simulations, Inc., 1984, v.p. bio. scis., 1989—90; sr. rsch. fellow Calif. Inst. Tech., 1991—92, asst. prof. biology, 1992—98, assoc. prof., 1998—2001, assoc. prof. biology and chemistry, 2001—; asst. investigator Howard Hughes Med. Inst., 1994—2000, assoc. investigator, 2000—. Adj. asst. prof. U. So. Calif. Sch. Medicine, 1994—. Recipient Scholar award, Rita Allen Found., 1993—98, Searle, 1994—97, prize, Johnson Found., 1997; fellow, Packard Found., 1993—98; Miller Rsch. fellowship, 1988—89. Mem.: NAS. Office: Calif Inst Tech Divsn Biology Mail Code 114-96 Pasadena CA 91125 Business E-Mail: steve@mayo.caltech.edu.

**MAYO, THOMAS WILLIAM,** law educator; b. Bangor, Maine, Sept. 7, 1949; s. Harvey William and Marilyn Louise (Chase) M.; m. Jane King Pollard, July 31, 1971; children: David William, Jeffrey Robert, Andrew Chase. BA Philosophy, Amherst Coll., 1971; JD magna cum laude, Syracuse U., 1977. Bar: N.Y. 1978, U.S. Ct. Appeals (D.C. cir.) 1979, D.C. 1980, U.S. Ct. Mil. Appeals 1980, U.S. Ct. Appeals (2nd cir.) 1981, U.S. Supreme Ct. 1981, U.S. Ct. Appeals (11th cir.) 1983. Assoc. Nixon, Hargrave, Devans & Doyle, Rochester, N.Y., 1977-79; law clk. U.S. Ct. Appeals (D.C. cir.), Washington, 1979-80; assoc. Covington & Burling, Washington, 1980-84; assoc. prof. Sch. Law So. Meth. U., Dallas, 1990—2004, asst. prof. Sch. Law, 1984-90, asst. prof., 2004—; assoc. dean acad. affairs 1992-95; adj. assoc. prof., Dept. Internal Med. Univ. of Tex. So. Western Med. Sch., Dallas, 1994—; counsel Haynes & Boone LLP, Dallas, 1989—. Of counsel Haynes and Boone, Dallas, 1989—; adv. coun. Susan G. Komen Found., 1999—. Contbr. articles to profl. jours. Co-founder, advisor Dallas Legal Hospice, 1988. With U.S. Army, 1971-74.Member, Institutional Ethics Comm.; Parkland Mem. Hosp. Dallas, 1989, co-chair 1992—; Baylor Univ. Med. Ctr., 1991—; RHD Mem. Hosp. Dallas, 1994—, Children's Med. Ctr., Dallas, 2001-; Adv. Comm. Program in Ethics in Sci & Med. Univ. of Tex. Southwestern Med. Ctr., 1998; Community Oversight Comm. Xenotransplantation Proj. Baylor Inst. of Transplantation Sciences, 1997—; Poetry columnist, Dallas Morning News, 1998—. Mem. ABA (health law sect.), Am. Coll. Legal Medicine, Am. Soc. Law and Medicine, Am. Acad. Hosp. Attys., Am. Health Lawyers Assn. (bd. dirs. 1997—), Order of Coif, Maguire Ctr. Ethics & Pub. Responsibility, Tex. Bar Assoc., Am. Coll. Health Care Execs., Nat. Bd. of Advisors Bureau of Nat. Affairs (Health Law reporter), Bd of Editors Matthew Bender's Health Care Law Monthly, Healthcare Financial Mgmt. Assoc., Dallas-Ft Worth Hosp. Coun., State Bar Tex. (health law sect. coun.). Democrat. Episcopalian. Office: So Meth U PO Box 750116 Dallas TX 75275-0116 E-mail: tmayo@mail.smu.edu.

**MAYO-JOHNSTON, JULIA A.,** psychiatry professor, psychotherapist; b. Phila., Aug. 16, 1926; d. Henry Mayo and Mamie Clark; 1 child, Wilvena Gordon. BA in Sociology with honors, U. Pa., Phila., 1947, PhD in Social Rsch., Social Work and Adminstrn., 1958; MS in Social Rsch., Bryn Mawr Coll., Pa., 1949. ACSW NY State Dept. Edn., bd. cert. diplomate clin. social work Am. Acad. Experts in Traumatic Stress, diplomate, master therapist Am. Psychotherapy Assn.; cert. in individual and group psychotherapy, supervision and adminstrn. Wash. Sch. Psychiatry, 1963. Probation officer Family Ct., Wilmington, Del., 1949—52; psychiatric social worker intern Embreeville State Hosp., Pa., 1952—53; psychiatric social worker Vets. Adminstrn. Hosp., Lyons, NJ, 1953—54, asst. chief, outpatient clinic Wilmington, 1954—61, chief social worker, dept. psychiatry, 1954—61; chief clin. social worker and psychosocial rsch. clin. studies CNRC, NIMH, NIH, Washington, 1961—66; chief clin. sociologist, chief evaluation unit/preventive treatment program, dept. psychiatry, 1972—75, chief clin. studies, dept. psychiatry, 1975—96, clin. supr. group and individual psychotherapy, chmn. clin. studies group, 1980—96, mem. various committees; assoc. prof. clin. psychiatry and behavioral sci. NY Med. Coll., Valhalla, 1978—92, clin. prof. psychiatry, 1993, clin. prof. psychiatry emeritus, 1996. Field work supr. for grad. students various schs., 1958—88; rsch. com. I.R.B. St. Vincent's Hosp. and Med. Ctr., 1974—76; adj. prof. med. anthropology New Sch. Social Rsch., 1978; mem. editl. bd. Comprehensive Psychiatry, 1975—, Group Psychotherapy Glossary, Clin. Sociology Review; cons. in field; pvt. practice, 1958—; alumni secondary sch. com. U. Pa. Undergraduate Admissions, 1981; bd. mem. Nat. Assn. D.M.D.A., 1992; lectr. and presenter in field. Contbr. articles to jour., chapters to books. Recipient Outstanding Performance award, Vets. Adminstrn. Hosp., Wilmington, 1959, Commendation/Meritorious Svc., 1961, Outstanding Tchr. of Yr. award, Dept. Psychiatry, St. Vincent's Hosp. and Med. Ctr., NY, 1989, 1992, Cert. of Commendation, John Templeton Spirituality and Medicine award, Award for Excellent Contbn., 2003; grantee, Karp Found., 1987, 1989; John F. Creed grant for rsch., 1985. Fellow: APPA, Am. Assn. Family and Marriage Counselors, Am. Group Psychotherapy Assn., Am. Psychopathological Assn. (life); mem.: APGA, AAAS, Nat. Inst. Healthcare Rsch., Am. Assoc. Social Work and Rsch., Am. Assn. Profl. Hypnotherapists, Am. Assn. Behavioral Therapists, Internat. Soc. Psychologists, Internat. Acad. Counseling and Psychotherapy, NY Acad. Scis., Internat. Coun. Sex Edn. and Parenthood, Assn. Profl. Responsibility in Medicine and Rsch., Am. Acad. Psychotherapists, Met. Med. Anthropology Assn., Soc. Study Social Biology, Am. Assn. Clin. Psychosocial Rsch., Acad. Cert. Social Workers, Ea. Sociol. Assn., Clin. Sociology Assn. (bd. mem. at large, Disting. Career in Clin. Sociology award 1986). Am. Sociol. Assn. Democrat. Episcopalian. Avocations: travel, music, theater, dance. Home and Office: 205 W End Ave 24J New York NY 10023 Office Phone: 212-787-6524.

**MAYOPOULOS, TIMOTHY J.,** lawyer; b. Reading, Pa., Mar. 7, 1959; s. Harry B. and Eleanor Ida (Raifsnider) M.; m. Amy F. Lefkof, Apr. 28, 1990; 1 child, Philip Alexander. AB with distinction, Cornell U., 1980; JD cum laude, NYU, 1984. Bar: N.Y. 1985, U.S. Dist. Ct. (so. and ea. dists.) N.Y. 1987, U.S. Ct. Appeals (2d cir.) 1993, Supreme Ct., 1993, U.S. Dist. Ct. (ea. we. dists.) Ark., 1994, U.S. Ct. Appeals (8th cir.), 1995. Law clerk Hon. William F. Conner, U.S. Dist. Ct. (so. dist.) N.Y., NYC, 1984-86; assoc. Davis, Polk & Wardwell, NYC, 1986—94; assoc. ind. counsel Office Ind. Couns. Kenneth Starr, 1994—96; assoc. gen. counsel Donaldson Lufkin & Jenrette, 1996; mng. dir., sr. dep. gen. counsel, Americas Credit Suisse First Boston; mng. dir., gen. counsel, corp. investment bank, Americas Deutsche Bank AG, 2002—04; exec. v.p., gen. counsel Bank of America, Charlotte, NC, 2004—. Mem. Fed. Bar Coun., Assn. of Bar of City of N.Y., N.Y. State Bar Assn., Securities Indust. Assn., Order of the Coif. Office: Bank of Am Bank of America Plz 101 S Tryon St NC1-002-29-01 Charlotte NC 28225

**MAYOR, HEATHER DONALD,** molecular biology educator; b. Melbourne, Victoria, Australia, July 6, 1930; d. Joseph A. L. and Elizabeth Emily (Boyd) Donald; m. Richard Blair Mayor, May 28, 1956; children: Diana Boyd (Mrs. Russell Hawkins), Philip Hastings. BS, U. Melbourne, Australia, 1949; MS, U. Melbourne, 1951, DSc, 1970; PhD, U. London, 1954. Electron microscopist Nat. Inst. for Med. Research, London, 1952-55; postdoctoral fellow Walter and Eliza Hall Inst., Melbourne, 1955-56; post doctoral fellow Harvard U. Med. Sch., Boston, 1956-60; from asst. prof. to prof. Baylor Coll. Medicine, Houston, 1960—, prof., 1970-96, prof. emeritus, 1996—. Cons. AEC, Washington, 1971—, Nat. Cancer Inst., Bethesda, Md., 1975—, U. Tex. Med. Sch., Houston, 1975—. Contbr. articles and papers to profl. jours.; artist, coordinator Life Shapes, Contemporary Arts Mus. Houston, Tex. art exhibs., 1974. Recipient Disting. award Ctr. for Interaction Man-Sci.-Soc., Houston, 1973, Sir Hiram Maxim award, 1990; named Scientist of Yr., Ency. Britannica, 1992; scholar in residence Rockefeller Inst. and Found., Bellagio, Italy, 1983. Mem. Am. Assn. Immunologists, Biophysical Soc. (program chmn.), Am. Soc. for Cell Biology (program chmn.), Houstonian Club, Houston Harpsichord Soc. (bd. dirs.). Anglican. Avocations: piano, harpsichord. Home: 6 N West Oak Dr Houston TX 77056-2120 Personal E-mail: hdmayor@bcm.tmc.edu. Office and Business E-Mail: hmayor@bcm.tmc.edu.

**MAYORA-ALVARADO, EDUARDO RENE,** lawyer, law educator; b. Guatemala, Apr. 20, 1957; s. Eduardo Alfredo Mayora-Dawe and Adelaida (Alvarado) De Mayora; m. Alicia Bascunana, June 18, 1983; children: Javier Eduardo, Santiago, Jose Andres, Sebastian. JD, U. Rafael Landivar, Guatemala, 1980; LLM, Georgetown U., U.S.A., 1982; Diploma (2) in Principles Econ. Sci., U. Francisco Marroquin, Guatemala, 1991, LLD, 1997; D in Pluralist, Pub. and Pvt. Law, M in Pluralist, Pub. and Pvt. Law, U. Autonoma Barcelona, 2004. Bar: Guatemala, 1980; cert. notary. Assoc. Mayora & Mayora, Guatemala, 1980-81, ptnr., 1982—, mem. tax adminstrn. bd., 1998-2000; prof. bus. and principles of law U. Francisco Marroquin, Guatemala, 1984-87, prof. bus. law and principles of law Sch. of Econs., 1986-88, prof. constitutional law, dean Sch. of Law, 1989-2000, prof. principles of pvt. and pub. law, 1993; bd. dirs. Financiera de Inversion, S.A., Guatemala, 1988-96. Alt. dir. Seguros Alianza S.A., Guatemala, 1988-94; trustee U. Francisco Marroquin, 1989—; vis. prof. Pontificia U. Catolica, Porto Alegre, Brazil, 1994, Montpellier U. Sch. Law, France, 1995. Coauthor: El Desafio Neoliberal, 1992; author: Teoría Constitucional para una sociedad libre Fundación República para una nueva generación, 1997, El Imperio Del Derecho Y El Contencioso Administrativo En El Derecho Guatemalteco Comparado, 2005; (essay) El Drama De La Arena Movedisa, 1993 (Charles Stillman award 1993); contbr. to profl. jours. Mem. Guatemala Bar Assn. (author articles Bar Law Jour. 1990—m v.p. ethics bd. 1985-86), Assn. De Amigos Del Pais, Fundacion Para La Cultura (v.p. 1994), Inst. Guatemalteco De Derecho Notarial, Phi Delta Phi, Guatemala Country Club. Roman Catholic. Avocations: reading, sailing, golf. Office: Mayora & Mayora15 Calle 1-04 Plz Centrica 3er Nivel #301 Zona 10 Guatemala City Guatemala also: PO Box 661447 Miami FL 33266-1447 Office Phone: 502-236-625-31. E-mail: emayoraa@mayora-mayora.com.

**MAYORAS, DONALD EUGENE,** corporate executive, writer, consultant, educator; b. Danville, Ill., Aug. 25, 1939; s. Andrew John and Katherine Ann (Shelato) M.; m. JoAnna Marie Kacmer, June 9, 1962; children: D. Tyler, Stacie J. BS in Edn., Purdue U., 1962; postgrad., Northwestern U., 1968-71; MBA, So. Ill. U., 1977. Regional mgr. Pacific Intermountain Express, Akron, Ohio, 1972-74; v.p. United Van Lines, Fenton, Mo., 1974-78; pres. Bekins Van Lines, L.A., 1978-83; pres., CEO Sun Carriers, Inc., Holliston, Mass., 1983-90, chmn. bd. dirs.; vice-chmn., CEO Builders Transport, Camden, S.C., 1990-91. Chmn., CEO Truckload Holding Inc., Chester, N.Y., 1995-97, Cloverleaf Transp., Inc., Chester, 1997—; spkr. in field. Trustee Ross Ade Found., West Lafayette, Ind., 1962—. Capt. U.S. Army, 1962-68; Europe, Vietnam. Decorated Bronze Star. Mem. Am. Trucking Assn. (v.p. 1983—, trustee Found. 1983-91), Nat. Spkrs. Assn., Nat. Coun. Logistics, Nat. Pvt. Truck Coun., Purdue U. Alumni Assn., Nat. Def. Transp. Assn., Aronomink Golf Club (Newton Sq., Pa.), Orange County Golf Club, Delta Nu Alpha, Beta Gamma Sigma, Omicron Delta Kappa. Republican. Roman Catholic. Avocations: golf, antiques, classic automobiles. E-mail: clor@aol.com, dmayoras@cloverleaftransport.com.

**MAYORKAS, ALEJANDRO,** lawyer, former prosecutor; b. Cuba; With Patterson, Belknap, Webb & Tyler, L.A., 1986-89; asst. U.S. atty., 1989-99; chief office's gen. crimes sect., 1996-98; U.S. atty. cen. dist. Calif. U.S. Dept. Justice, 1999—2001; ptnr. O'Melveny & Myers, L.A., 2001—. Tchr. trial advocacy Loyola Law Sch., 1997-98. Office: O'Melveny & Myers 400 S Hope St Los Angeles CA 90071-2899 Office Phone: 213-430-6363. Business E-Mail: amayorkas@omm.com.

**MAYPOLE, JOHN FLOYD,** real estate company executive; b. Chgo., May 17, 1939; s. John James and Althea Floyd M.; m. Anne White, 1961; children: Cynthia, John, Kimberly. BA in Econs., Yale U., 1961. With Arthur Andersen & Co., 1961-62-65-66; mgr. corp. acctg. Interpace Corp., 1966, asst. treas., 1967-68, treas., 1968-70, treas., controller, 1970-73, v.p. fin., 1973-77, sr. v.p., 1977-80, exec. v.p., 1980-81, pres., 1981-83; pres. chief operating officer Clevepak Corp., 1983-84; mng. ptnr. Peach State Real Estate Holding Co., Toccoa, Ga., 1984—. Bd. dirs. Knoll, Inc., Mass. Mut. Fin. Group, Nat. Captioning Inst., Inc. Bd. adjustment Borough of Mountain Lakes, N.J., 1971-81, chmn., 1980-81. Served with USMC, 1962-65. Mem. Yale Club, Ivy League Club (Sarasota), Rockaway River Country Club, Laurel Oak Country Club. Republican. Office: PO Box 1223 Toccoa GA 30577-1421

**MAYRO, KARL R.,** realtor; b. Drexel Hill, Pa., Apr. 13, 1966; s. Allan Dale and Patricia Mayro. BA in Econs., St. Joseph's U., 1988. Realtor Prudential Fox & Roach, Newtown Square, Pa., 1988—. Bd. mgrs. The Episcopal Acad., Merion, Pa., 2002—. Mem.: Suburban West Realtors Assn., Pa. Assn. Realtors, Nat. Assn. Realtors, World Affairs Coun. Phila., Phila. Mus. Art, Pa. Hort. Soc. Avocations: gardening, classic Cadillacs, golf, photography.

**MAYRON, LEWIS WALTER,** clinical ecology consultant; b. Chgo., Sept. 20, 1932; s. Max and Florence Minette (Brody) M.; married; children: Leslie Hope Mayron Coff, Eric Brian. BS in Chemistry, Roosevelt U., 1954; MS in Biol. Chemistry, U. Ill., 1955, PhD in Biol. Chemistry, 1959. Rsch. assoc. dept. biochemistry and nutrition U. So. Calif., L.A., 1959-61; instr. biochem. dept. biochemistry Presbyn.-St. Luke's Hosp., Chgo., 1961-62; instr. dept. biol. chemistry U. Ill., Chgo., 1961-62; biochemistry group leader Tardanbek Labs., Chgo., 1962-63; sr. devel. chemist Abbott Labs., Chgo., 1963-64; asst. attending physician, mem. spl. staff Michael Reese Hosp. and Med. Ctr., Chgo., 1964-66, rsch. assoc. Dept. Allergy Rsch., 1964-66; asst. prof. in biochemistry and physiology Sch. Dentistry Loyola U., Chgo., 1968-71; guest

investigator Argonne (Ill.) Nat. Lab., 1973-79; rsch. chemist V.A. Hosp., Hines, Ill., 1968-79; chief clin. radiobiochemist nuclear medicine svc. V.A. Wadsworth Hosp. Ctr., L.A., 1979-83; cons. in clin. ecology, 1980—. Contbr. articles to profl. jours. Mem. AAAS, Am. Assn. Clin. Chemists, Soc. for Exptl. Biology and Medicine, Sigma Xi. Home: 823 S 1850 West Cedar City UT 84720-8237

**MAYS, GEORGE WALTER, JR.,** educational technology educator; b. Decatur, Ill., July 1, 1926; s. George Walter Sr. and Ida May (Lookabaugh) M.; children: Richard, Steven, John, James. BS in Edn., U. Ill., Champaign, 1950, MS in Edn., 1952; BSEE, U. md., 1960; cert., Calif. State U., Carson, 1987. Tchr. math. and physics Mahomet (Ill.) High Sch., 1950-52, prin., 1952-55; br. chief engring studies Nat. Security Agy., Ft. Meade, Md., 1955-62; sr. engr. Jet Propulsion Lab., Pasadena, Calif., 1962-71; tchr. math.-sci., chair Aviation High Sch., Redondo Beach, Calif. 1971-82; tchr. math. and physics, dept. chair Redondo Union High Sch., 1982-89; cons. ednl. tech. Apple Valley, Calif., 1989—; math. coord. Sci. and Tech. Ctr., Apple Valley, Calif., 1990—. Part-time instr. electronics Pasadena City Coll., 1963-72, Pepperdine U., 1975-76, math. Victor Valley Coll., 1991-97; instr. math. Acad. for Acad. Excellence, Apply Valley, 1998—. Author: Educational Technology Application Notes, 1989-90. With USN, 1944-46. Recipient Appollo Achievement award NASA, 1969. Mem. IEEE (life), Calif. Tchrs. Assn. (WHO award 1988-89), Nat. Coun. Tchrs. of Math., Computer Using Educators, Apple Valley Country Club, Victor Valley Aero Club. Avocations: reading, sports, computer usage, flying.

**MAYS, J. C.,** automotive executive; b. 1955; Grad., Art Ctr. Coll. of Design, 1980. Worked for BMW, Calif.; chief designer Volkswagon of Am., Simi Valley, Calif., 1989—93; v.p. design devel. SHR Perceptual Mgmt., Scottsdale, 1995—97; cons. Ford Motor Co., group v.p. design, 1997—. Office: Ford Motor Co One American Rd Dearborn MI 48126-1899

**MAYS, JANICE ANN,** lawyer; b. Waycross, Ga., Nov. 21, 1951; d. William H. and Jean (Bagley) M. AB (hon.), Wesleyan Coll., Macon, Ga., 1973; JD, U. Ga., 1975; LLM in Taxation, U. Georgetown, 1980. Bar: Ga. 1976. Tax counsel com. on ways and means U.S. Ho. Reps., Washington, 1975-88, chief tax counsel com. on ways and means, staff dir. subcom. select revenue measures, 1988-93, chief counsel, staff dir. com. on ways and means, 1993-95, minority chief counsel, staff dir. com. on ways and means, 1995—. Recipient Disting. Achievement in Profession Alumnae award Wesleyan Coll., 1998. Mem. Tax Coalition (past chair). Office: Ways & Means Com 1106 Longworth Office Bldg Washington DC 20515-0001

**MAYS, JEFFERSON,** actor; BA, Yale U.; MFA, UCSD. Actor: (TV series) Dynaman, 1988; (TV miniseries) Liberty! The American Revolution, 1997; (films) The Killing Box, 1993, Some Folks Call It a Sling Blade, 1994, The Low Life, 1995, Hudson River Blues, 1997, Cousin Bette, 1998, The Big Brass Ring, 1999, (regional theater) Rosencrantz & Guildenstern Are Dead, Misalliance, The Importance of Being Earnest, The Beauty Part, Not Suitable for Children, The Cherry Orchard, The Winter's Tale, She Stoops to Conquer, Servant of Two Masters, Macbeth, Miss Julie, Private Lives; (Broadway plays) I Am My Own Wife, 2003— (Theater World award, 2004, Drama Desk award outstanding solo performance, 2004, Obie award oustanding performance, 2004, Tony award best actor in a play, 2004, Joseph Jefferson award for actor in a principal role (play), 2005), Of Thee I Sing, 2006.*

**MAYS, JILL DUNCAN,** social services administrator, counselor; b. Louisville, Apr. 17, 1966; d. Charles Henry Sr. and Ruth Ella (Bohannon) Duncan; m. Samuel Aaron Mays Sr., Dec. 28, 1991; children: Shelby Amaris, Samuel Aaron Jr., Jayce Allan. BA in Psychology, Emory U., 1988; MS in Cmty. Counseling, Ga. State U., 1992. Lic. profl. counselor, Ga.; master addiction counselor, Nat. Cert. Counselor Nat. Bd. Cert. Counselors, Inc., 2003. Rsch. interviewer Emory U. Sch. Pub. Health, Atlanta, 1990-92; evening outpatient coord. Decatur (Ga.) Hosp., 1992-94; counselor The Atlanta Union Mission, 1992-94, dir. women and children's svcs., 1994—, Atlanta City Mission, 2000—05. Cons. Intracultural Comm., Decatur, 1993-95, DeKalb County Dept. Youth Svcs., Decatur, 1993; comm. mem. Atlanta Summit Against Poverty, 1997; bd. dirs. Zion Hill Cmty. Devel. Corp.; mem. com. DeKalb County Bd. Health/Divsn. Health Assessment and Promotion, 2002-03; mem. Atlanta Regional Commn. Homelessness Women and Children's Coun., 2004-. Olympic Force coord. Atlanta Com. for the Olympic Games, 1995—96; min. New Piney Grove Bapt. Ch., 2003—. Recipient Women Making a Mark award, Atlanta Mag., 2002. Mem.: Coun. Vol. Adminstrs., Assn. Gospel Rescue Missions, Am. Assn. Christian Counselors, Alpha Kappa Alpha Sorority, Inc. Democrat. Baptist. Avocations: singing, reading, acting/playwriting. Office Phone: 404-532-1929. E-mail: jill.mays@myaum.org.

**MAYS, K. J.,** writer, musician; b. Lake Station, Ind. m. Lee Mays; 1 child, Mitchell. AA, Harold Washington, Chgo. Author, editor: Cinder Road Tales, 1998; composer: (songs) Plan, Call, Stand Up, 1999. Mem.: Golden Key. Achievements include invention of K.J. Mallet for cymbal, timpani, vibraphone, bells, bass drum, xylophone. Office: JLM Enterprises PO Box 79 West Brooklyn IL 61378-0079

**MAYS, L(ESTER) LOWRY,** broadcast executive; b. Houston, July 24, 1935; s. Lester T. and Virginia (Lowry) M.; m. Peggy Pitman, July 29, 1959; children: Kathryn Mays Johnson, Linda Mays McCaul, Mark P., Randall T. BS in Petroleum Engring., Tex. A&M U., 1959; MBA, Harvard U., 1962. Comml. recorder, San Antonio; with Sta. KTTU-TV, Tucson, Sta. KOKI/KTFO-TV, Tulsa, Sta. WMPI/WJTC-TV, Mobile and Pensacola, Okla., Sta. WAWS-TV, Jacksonville, Fla., Sta. KSAS-TV, Wichita, Kans., Sta. KLRT/KASN-TV, Little Rock, Sta. WFTC-TV, Mpls., Sta. WFTC-TV, WLMT/WMTU-TV, Memphis, Sta. WXXA, Albany, Sta. WQUE-AM-FM, New Orleans, Clear Channel Sports, Des Moines, Okla. News Network, Oklahoma City, Va. News Network, Stas. KJYO and KTOK, Oklahoma City, Sta. KEBC, Oklahoma City, Sta. WELI, New Haven, Sta. WKCI-WAVZ, New Haven, Sta. KPEZ, Austin, Tex., Stas. KHYS, KALO, KBXX, KMJQ, KPRC, KSEV and KYOK, Houston and Point Arthur, Tex., KMOD & KAKC, Tulsa, KTAM & KORA, Bryan and College Station, Tex., WHAS & WAMZ, Louisville; with radio and TV broadcasting WOAI, KQXT, and KAJA, San Antonio; chmn., CEO Clear Channel Comms., Inc., San Antonio, 1975—. Past chmn. bd. CBS Radio Affiliates Bd. Bd. dirs., trustee Tex. Rsch. Pk.; bd. dirs., mem. exec. com. United Way; chmn. United Way San Antonio and Bexar County, 1995; regent emeritus Tex. A&M U. Sys.; trustee Tex. Rsch. and Tech. Found.; mem. deve. bd. U. Tex. Health Sci. Ctr.; adv. dir. Permanent Univ. Fund Tex. Mem. Nat. Assn. Broadcasters (past chmn. joint bd.), Greater San Antonio C. of C. (past chmn.), Rotary. Home: 400 Geneseo Rd San Antonio TX 78209-6127 Office: Clear Channel Comms Inc PO Box 659512 San Antonio TX 78265-9512*

**MAYS, LINDA,** performing arts association administrator; Pres. Am. Guild Musical Artists, N.Y.C. Office: Am Guild Musical Artists 14th Fl 1430 Broadway New York NY 10018

**MAYS, MARK PITMAN,** communication company executive; b. San Antonio, Aug. 2, 1963; BA in Econs. and Math., Vanderbilt U.; MBA, Columbia U. V.p., treas. Clear Channel Comms., San Antonio, sr. v.p. ops., 1993—96, pres., COO, 1996—2004, interim CEO, 2004, pres., CEO, 2004—06, CEO, 2006—. Bd. dirs. NAB Radio Bd. Bd. dirs. Jr. Achievement San Antonio Chap., Alamo Area Coun. Boy Scouts Am., United Way San Antonio, SW Found. Biomedical Rsch. Office: Clear Channel Comms 200 E Basse Rd San Antonio TX 78209-8328 Fax: 210-822-2299.*

**MAYS, QUINCY,** art educator; b. Jinmachi, Japan, July 21, 1949; s. Joseph Roles and Edna Eileen Mays; 1 child from previous marriage, Isaac Marshall. B in Mil. Sci., Cameron U., 1971, BA in Math. 1971, BS in Elem. Edn., 1981, BFA, 1984; MEd, U. Okla., 1979. Tchr. Indiahoma (Okla.) HS, 1974—75, Brockland Elem., Lawton, Okla., 1976—81; tchr. art Whittier

Elem., Lawton, 1982—93, Pat Henry Elem., Lawton, 1994—97, Lawton HS, 1998—. Adj. prof. Cameron U., Lawton, 1984—96; coach cross country/tennis Lawton HS, 1998—, cmin. curriculum fine arts dept., 1999—; artist-in-residence kindergarten acad. Lawton Pub. Schs., 2002—; instr. Goddard Youth Camp Gifted/Talented, Lake of Arbuckles, Sulpher, 1981—2001; coach cross country MacArthur H.S., Lawton, 2005—. Mem. Arts and Humanities Coun., Lawton, 1995—. Capt. U.S. Army, 1970—74. Recipient numerous Best of Show awards for Visual Art; grantee, Coll. Bd., 1999. Mem.: Okla. Secondary Schs. Activities Assn., Phi Theta Kappa. Republican. Avocations: running, fishing, art, guitar, tennis. Home: 1702 NW Liberty Lawton OK 73507 Office: Lawton HS 601 NW Fort Sill Blvd Lawton OK 73507

**MAYS, RANDALL T.,** communications company executive; b. 1966; married. BA with honors, Univ. Tex., Austin, Tex.; MBA, Harvard Bus. Sch. With Trammell Crow Co. Real Estate Firm, Goldman, Sachs & Co., NY; v.p., treas. Clear Channel Commn., San Antonio, 1993—97, CFO, exec. v.p., 1997—2006, CFO, pres., 2006—; chmn. CCE SpinCo, Inc. Bd. dirs. XM Satelitte Radio. Adv. coun. Univ. Tex McCombs Bus. Sch. Mem.: Broadcast Cable Fin. Mgmt. Assn. (CFO of the Yr. 2002), Nat. Assn. of Broadcasters. Office: CCE Spinco Inc 2000 W Loop South Ste 1300 Houston TX 77027*

**MAYS, VICKIE M.,** psychology professor; BA in Psychology, Philosophy, Loyola U. Chgo., 1972, MA in Clin. Psychology, 1973; PhD in Clin. Psychology, U. Mass., 1979. Instr., dorm counselor Upward Bound program U. Mass., Amherst, 1974; lectr. devel. of Black child SW Residential Coll., U. Mass., Amherst, 1974; instr. career planning continuing edn. for women divsn. George Washington U., Washington, 1975—76; clin. supr. psychol. svcs. clinic U. Mass., Amherst, 1976—77, acting intake coord./clin. supr. psychol. svcs. clinic, 1977; asst. prof. clin. psychology UCLA, 1979—87, assoc. prof. clin. psychology, 1987—. Fellow/vis. scholar Nat. Survey Black Am. Program NIMH, 1981; cons. cmty. rels. divsn. George Washington U., 1975-76, Everywoman's Ctr. U. Mass., Amherst, 1977-78; psychol. cons. com. for collegiate edn. of Black students U. Mass., Amherst, 1978-79; consultation, edn. and prevention specialist Didi Hirsch Cmty. Mental Health Ctr., Culver City, Calif., 1980-81; psychologist Calif. Heatlh news program Sta. KCBS, L.A., 1986-87; dir. UCLA Ctr. on Rsch., Edn., Tng. and Strategic Comm. on Minority Health Disparities, 2003—; presenter in field. Assoc. editor Psychology of Women Quar., 1986-88; mem. editl. bd. Clin. Psychology of Women, AIDS Edn. and Prevention, Jour. of Homosexuality; guest editor Am. Psychologist; ad hoc reviewer Jour. Health and Social Behavior, Jour. Consulting and Clin. Psychology, Jour. Personality and Social Psychology, Milbank Quar., Profl. Psychology, Psychol. Bull. Pub. Health Reports, Sex Roles. NIMH Predoctoral fellow, 1973-74, fellow Nat. Ctr. for Health Svcs. Rsch. Award RAND/UCLA Health Studies Ctr., 1987-89; recipient NIMH New Investigator Rsch. award, 1983-85; named Outstanding Young Woman of Yr., Bd. Outstanding Young Women, Montgomery, Ala., 1984, 86. Mem. APA (chair com. on Black women's concerns divsn. 35, 1984, coun. of reps. 1986-89, chair women's caucus sec. 1988-89, publ. and comm. bd. task force on ethnic bias in lang. in publ. 1985, edn. and tng. com. on ethnic minority human resources devel. 1985-87, task force on AIDS 1986—), APHA (Black caucus health workers program com. 1991), We. Psychol. Assn., Acad. Behavioral Medicine Rsch. Office: UCLA Dept Psych 1285 Franz Hall PO Box 951563 Los Angeles CA 90095-1563 Office Phone: 310-206-5159.

**MAYS, WILLIAM G.,** chemical company executive; MBA, Ind. U. Test chemist Linkbelt Facility, Indpls.; acct. mgr. Procter & Gamble; market planning Eli Lilly and Co.; asst. to pres. Cummins Engine Co.; founder, pres. Mays Chem. Co., Indpls., 1980—. Bd. dirs. NBD-Inc. Mem. exec. com., bd. dirs. United Way Ctrl. Ind., Ind. Conv. and Visitors Assn.; bd. dirs. Associated Group, Corp. Cmty. Coun., Ind. Univ. Found., Cmty. Leaders Allied for Superior Schs.; mem. dean's adv. coun. Ind. U. Sch. Bus.; mem. pres.'s coun. Ind. U.; co-chmn. Coca-Cola Circle City Classic; elder Witherspoon Presbyn. Ch. Recipient Man of Yr. award B'Nai B'Rith Isidora Feibleman award, 1990, Elder Watson Diggs Achievement award Kappa Alpha Psi, 1991, Ind. Minority Small Bus. Advocate of Yr. award, 1991, Sagamore of Wabash award Gov. Ind., 1991, Ind. Enterprise award, 1992, Ind. Christian Leadership Conf. Businessman of Yr. award, 1992, Disting. Hooser, 1992, 13th in Black Enterprise Mag. Top 100 Indsl./Svc Cos., 'Above and Beyond' award Ind. Black Expo, 1992, Pres.'s award Black Pres.'s Roundtable Assn., 1992, Vol. Fund Raiser award, 1992, Anti-Defamation League Americanizm award, 1993, Charles Whistler award, 1993, Indpls. Edn. Assn.'s Human Rights award, 1994, Ind. State Conf. NAACP Labor and Industry award, 1994, Robert W. Briggs Humanitarian award, 1995, and numerous others; carried Olympic flame during trip through Indpls., 1995. Mem. Ind. C. of C. (bd. dirs.), Indpls. C. of C. (exec. com., bd. dirs.). Office: Mays Chemical Co Inc PO Box 50915 Indianapolis IN 46250-0915

**MAYS, WILLIAM GAY, II,** lawyer, real estate developer; b. Washington, Mo., Apr. 8, 1947; s. Frank G. and Geneva Pauline (Brookhart) M.; 1 son, Daniel Brookhart. AB, U. Mo., 1969, JD, 1972. Bar: Mo. 1972, U.S. Dist. Ct. (we. dist.) Mo. 1972. Legis. rschr. State of Mo., 1972; pub. defender 13th Jud. Cir. Mo., 1973-77; ptnr. Holt, Mays & Brady, Columbia, 1977-98; ptnr. and gen. counsel comml. real devel. firm. Mem. Jud. Planning Commn., Mo., 1977. Served to capt. USAFR, 1969-82. Named Outstanding Young Man of Am., 1974. Mem. Mo. Bar Assn., Boone and Callaway County Bar Assn., Mo. Trial Lawyers Assn., Mo. Pub. Defender Assn. (pres. 1976-77), Beta Theta Pi. Republican. Office: The Mays Bldg PO Box 10013 Columbia MO 65205-4001

**MAYS, WILLIE HOWARD, JR., (SAY HEY KID),** former professional baseball player; b. Westfield, Ala., May 6, 1931; s. William Howard and Ann M.; m. Margherite Wendell Chapman, 1956 (div. 1961), 1 adopted son, Michael; m. Mae Louise Allen, Nov. 27, 1971 LHD (hon.), Yale Univ., 2004. Baseball player Birmingham Black Barons, 1948-50, Trenton Inter-State League, 1950-51, Mpls. Millers, Am. Assn., 1951, N.Y. Giants, 1951-57, San Francisco Giants, 1958-72, N.Y. Mets, 1972-73; with Bally's Park Place, Atlantic City, 1980—; pub. rels. exec. San Francisco Giants, 1986-98, retired, 1998. Author: Willie Mays: My Life In and Out of Baseball, 1966, Say Hey: The Autobiography of Willie Mays, 1988. Served with AUS, 1952-54. Named Most Valuable Player Nat. League, 1954, 65; named Player of Yr. Sporting News, 1954, Baseball Player of Decade Sporting News, 1970, Male Athlete of Yr. AP, 1954, NL Rookie of Yr., 1951, Sporting News Player of the Year award, 1954, All-Star Game, 1954-73; recipient Hickok belt, 1954, Golden Bat award to commemorate 600 home runs, Gold Glove award (12 times), 1st Commissioner's award, 1970, Golden Plate awarded to America's Captains of Achievement by Am. Acad. Achievement, 1976, Spirit of Life award City of Hope, 1988, Sportsman of Decade, Cong. Racial Equality, 1991, Legendary Star award HBO Video; inducted into Ala. Sports Hall of Fame, Baseball Hall of Fame, 1979, Black Hall of Fame, 1973, Calif. Sports Hall of Fame. Achievements include being the holder of 4th place in major league homeruns (660); lifetime batting average of .302; signed lifetime pub. rels. contract with San Francisco Giants, 1993. Office: Baseball Hall of Fame PO Box 590 Cooperstown NY 13326-0590

**MAYSILLES, ELIZABETH,** speech communication professional, educator; b. Sleepy Creek, W.Va. d. Evers and Rose (Scott) M. AB, W.Va. U.; MA, Hunter Coll., N.Y.C., 1963; PhD, NYU, 1980. Announcer Radio Sta. WAJR, Morgantown, W.Va.; broadcaster Radio Sta. WGHF-FM, Rural Radio Network, N.Y.C.; group leader GMAC, N.Y.C.; instr. NYU, N.Y.C.; adj. prof. speech comm. Pace U., N.Y.C., 1978—2002; exec. adminstr. Am.-Scottish Found., N.Y.C., 1980-90; adminstrv. asst. Brit. Schs. and Univs. Found., Inc. Personal investment portfolio mgmt.; numerous radio and television appearances; lectr. in field; cons. Vol. counselor Help Line, N.Y.C., 1971-75. Recipient Disting. Svc. award NYU Grad. Dept., 1970-71. Mem. Internat. Platform Assn. (bd. govs. 1980—), N.Y. Acad. Scis., Caledonian Club N.Y. (bd. dirs. 1994-96, 2004—, chieftain 2001-02). Avocations: reading, swimming, gardening, travel in England and Scotland. Home: 155 E 77th St Apt 6F New York NY 10021

**MAYSLES, ALBERT H.,** filmmaker; b. Boston, Nov. 26, 1926; s. Philip and Ethel (Epstein) M.; m. Gillian Walker, Sept. 14, 1976; children: Rebekah, Philip, Sara. BA, Syracuse U., 1949; MA, Boston U., 1953. Rsch. fellow in anesthesia Mass. Gen. Hosp., Boston, 1951-52; instr. social rels. Boston U., 1953-55; pres. Maysles Films, Inc., N.Y.C., 1962—. Filmmaker, prodr. Psychiatry in Russia, 1955, (with others) Primary, 1960, Showman, 1963, What's Happening: The Beatles in the USA, 1964, Salesman, 1967, Gimme Shelter, 1970, Christo's Valley Curtain, 1974, (Blue Ribbon award 1975, Acad. award nomination), Grey Gardens, 1976, Running Fence, 1978 (Blue Ribbon award 1978), Ozawa, 1985, Vladimir Horowitz: The Last Romantic, 1985, Islands, 1986 (Blue Ribbon award, Emmy award), Horowitz Plays Mozart, 1987, Christo in Paris, 1990, Soldiers of Music: Rostropovitch Returns to Russia, 1990 (Emmy award), Abortion: Desparate Choices, 1995 (Peabody award), Letting Go, A Hospice Journey, 1996 (Ace Cable award), Concert of Wills: The Making of the Getty Art Center, 1997; LaLee's Kin, 2000, The Reales of Grey Gardens, 2006. Served as pvt. U.S. Army, 1944-46. Named one of 100 World's Finest Cinematographers, Eastman Kodak, 1999; recipient Career Achievement award, Internat. Documentary Assn., 1994, John Grierson award for Documentary, SMPTE, 1997, Pres.'s award, Am. Soc. Cinematographers, 1998, Vision award, The Boston Film and Video Found., 1998, The Doubletake Career Achievement award, 1998, Lifetime Achievement award, Toronto's Hot Docs, 1999, Flaherty award, 1999, award for documentaries, Sundance Film Festival Cinematography, 2001, Dupont award, 2004; Guggenheim fellow, 1968. Mem. The Reality Club. Office: 250 W 54th St New York NY 10019-5515 Home: 21 W 122nd St New York NY 10027-5602 Office Phone: 212-582-6050. E-mail: amaysles@mayslesfilms.com.

**MAYUGA, KENNETH A.,** cardiologist, researcher; s. Ruperto D. and Amelita A. Mayuga. BA, Northwestern U., Evanston, Ill., 1996—99, MD, U. Ill., Chgo.-Rockford, 2001—05. Vis. predoctoral fellow Feinberg Cardiovasc. Rsch. Inst., Northwestern U., Chgo., 2001—02; physician in residency Cleve. Clinic Found., Ohio, 2005—. Rschr., cardiology/cardiac electrophysiology Northwestern U. Med. Sch., 1999—2002. Contbr. articles and papers to profl. jours. and pubs. Recipient Eagle Scout, Boy Scouts Am., 1996; grantee Nat. Merit scholarship, 1996. Achievements include research in evaluation of autonomic and non-autonomic components of cardiac repolarization.

**MAZANKOWSKI, DONALD FRANK,** Canadian government official; b. Viking, Alta., Can., July 27, 1935; s. Frank and Dora (Lonowski) M.; m. Lorraine Poleschuk, Sept. 6, 1958; children: Gregory, Roger, Donald. Student, pub. schs., 1987; PhD in Engring (hon.), N.S. Inst. Tech.; LLD (hon.), U. Alta., 1993. MP Ho. of Commons, 1968—, chmn. com. transp., 1972-74, mem. com. govt. ops., 1976-77, mem. com. trans. and communication, 1977-79; min. of transp., min. responsible for Can. Wheat Bd. Govt. of Can., 1979-80, min. of transp. (re-drafted Nat. Transp. Act), 1984-86, dep. prime min., 1986—, govt. house leader, 1986-88, pres. Privy Coun., 1986-91, pres. Treas. Bd., 1987-88, min. responsible for privatization and regulatory affairs, 1988-91, min. of agriculture, 1988-91, min. of fin., 1991-93; former chmn. Inst. Health Econs. Former mem. bd. govs. U. Alta; bd. dirs. Power Corp. Can., Power Fin. Corp., Great West Life Assurance, The Investors Group, Shaw Comms. Inc., Weyerhauser Can., Can. Oilsands Trust, ATCO Ltd., London Life Ins., Yellow Pages Group; former chmn. Can. Genetic Diseases Network; sr. advisor Gowlings Lafleur Henderson, LLP. Apptd. chmn. Premier's Adv. Coun. on Health. Decorated officer Order of Can., Alta. Order of Excellence; recipient Alta. Centennial medal, 2005; Paul Harris fellow Rotary Internat., 2002; honoree Pub. Policy Forum Can., 2003; named one of Alta.'s 50 Most Influential People, 2002. Mem. Royal Can. Legion (life). Clubs: Vegreville Rotary (past dir.). Lodges: KC. Roman Catholic. E-mail: donmaz@shaw.ca.

**MAZANY, TERRY,** foundation administrator; BA in Anthropology, MA in Anthropology, MBA, U. Ariz. Positions in public sch. adminstrn. Mich. Sch. Dist.; former assoc. superintendent for curriculum and instruction Oakland Unified Sch. Dist., Calif.; former dir. orgnl. learning and devel. Calif. Sch. Leadership Acad.; dir., sr. prog. officer for ed. initiative Chgo. Comty. Trust, 2001—03, COO, 2003—04, pres., CEO, 2004—. Office: Chgo Cmty Trust 111 E Wacker Dr Ste 1400 Chicago IL 60601*

**MAZAR, DEBI,** actress; b. Queens, NY, Aug. 15, 1964; m. Gabriele Corcos, Mar. 16, 2002; children: Evelina Maria Mazar Corcos, Giulia Isabel Mazar Corcos. Actor: (films) Goodfellas, 1990, The Doors, 1991, Jungle Fever, 1991, Little Man Tate, 1991, In the Soup, 1992, Inside Monkey Zetterland, 1992, Singles, 1992, Malcolm X, 1992, Toys, 1992, So I Married an Axe Murderer, 1993, Love Is Like That, 1993, Money for Nothing, 1993, Beethoven's 2nd, 1993, Bullets Over Broadway, 1994, Batman Forever, 1995, Empire Records, 1995, Girl 6, 1996, Trees Lounge, 1996, Red Ribbon Blues, 1996, Things I Never Told You, 1996, Space Truckers, 1996, Meet Wally Sparks, 1997, Nowhere, 1997, She's So Lovely, 1997, Trouble on the Corner, 1997, The Deli, 1997, Frogs for Snakes, 1998, Hush, 1998, There's No Fish Food in Heaven, 1998, The Insider, 1999, More Dogs Than Bones, 2000, Held for Ransom, 2000, Ten Tiny Love Stories, 2001, Deception, 2001, The Tuxedo, 2002, Who Killed the Idea?, 2003, Return to Babylon, 2004, Goodnight, Joseph Parker, 2004, Collateral, 2004, My Tiny Universe, 2004, Be Cool, 2005, Edmond, 2005, Wait, 2005, The Alibi, 2006; (TV series) Civil Wars, 1991—93, L.A. Law, 1993—94, Temporarily Yours, 1997, Working, 1998—99, That's Life, 2000, Entourage, 2004—; (TV films) Witch Hunt, 1994, Musical Shorts, 1996, Casper: A Spirited Beginning, 1997, Witness to the Mob, 1998, David and Lisa, 1998, The Sissy Duckling (voice), 1999, The Groovenians (voice), 2002; guest appearances (TV series) Burke's Law, 1995, Providence, 1999, Get Real, 2000, Wanda at Large, 2002, Friends, 2002, 7th Heaven, 2003—04, All of Us, 2004, The Practice, 2004, CSI: Miami, 2004, NYPD Blue, 2005, Living with Fran, 2005—06. Office: c/o Creative Artists Agy 9830 Wilshire Blvd Beverly Hills CA 90212*

**MAZEK, WARREN F(ELIX),** dean, economics professor; b. Pitts., Oct. 14, 1938; s. Felix Frank and Josephine Catherine (Sethner) M.; m. Nancy Lee Metcalfe, June 18, 1960 (div. Jan. 1982); children: Thomas W., Erika A., Laura J., Michael M.; m. Susan Chapman, Apr. 24, 1982; 1 child, Marissa C. AB in Econs., Washington and Jefferson Coll., 1960; MA in Econs., Ind. U., 1962; PhD in Econs., U. Pitts., 1965. Asst. prof. econs. Coll. Wooster, 1965—67; asst. prof. Fla. State U., 1967—70, assoc. prof., 1970—75, prof., 1975—86, dean coll. Social Scis., 1973—86; academic dean, prof. econs. U.S. Mcht. Marine Acad., Kings Point, NY, 1986—. Cons. on econ. loss to legal firms, 1974—; vestryman Christ Ch., Manhasset, 1991-99; chmn. Big Bend chpt. March of Dimes, Tallahassee, 1981-83. Recipient faculty rsch. award Fla., Fla. State U., 1973—74, Disting. Exec. Award, N.Y. Fed. Exec. Bd., 1997, Presdl. Rank Award, 2001; Resources of the Future dissertation fellow, 1964, Richard K. Mellon fellow, Am. Coun. for Edn., 1975. Mem. Am. Assn. Higher Edn., Am. Econs. Assn., Regional Sci. Assn., Conf. Fed. Degree Granting Insts., Assn. Acad. Affairs Adminstrs. Episcopalian. Office: Office Acad Dean US Merchant Marine Acad 300 Steamboat Rd Kings Point NY 11024 Home: PO Box 4113 Great Neck NY 11023

**MAZER, MIKE,** cardiologist, retired nephrologist, artist; b. Boston, May 17, 1936; s. Louis and Belle Mazer; m. Marilyn Wood, Feb. 26, 1987; children: Mark, Pamela. BS cum laude, Boston U., Mass., 1958; MD, Univ Cin., 1962. Diplomate in internal medicine Am. Bd. Internal Medicine, 1970, in nephrology Am. Bd. Nephrology, 1978, in cardiology Am. Bd. Cardiology, 1979. Fellow GI Disease U. Cin., 1962—64; fellow renal and metabolic studies Med. Ctr. Boston (Mass.) U., 1964—65; fellow cardiovascular disease West Roxbury VA Hosp., Boston, 1967—68; dir. acute hemodialysis Goddard Meml. Hosp., Stoughton, Mass., 1968—90, chief Echocardiography and Noninvasive Vascular Lab, 1977—94, chief cardiology, 1968—94; chief of nephrology Cardinal Cushing Hosp., Brockton, Mass., 1968—94; pvt. practice Bridgewater Goddard Pk. Med. Assocs., Mass., 1968—98; co-dir. Brockton- Goddard Hemodialysis Unit, Brockton, 1992—97; chief cardiology Good Samaritan Med. Ctr., Brockton, 1994—97, chief Echocardiography and Noninvasive Vascular Lab, 1994—97; med. dir. Pk. Cardiographics, Taunton, Mass.; dir. Cardiac Ultrasonography and Transtelephonic Monitor-

ing Nat. Med. Co, Taunton; dir. Cardiac Rehab. Ctr. Striar Jewish Cmty. Ctr., Stoughton, 1994—97; artist Mattapoisett, Mass., 1997—. Splash 9: Tips and Techniques, 2006, Contemporary American Marine Art, 2003—04; co-author: Principles of Interpretation in Echocardiography, 1985; editor: Journal of Diagnostic Medical Sonography, 1985—87; over 200 exhbns. Recipient Top Money Water Media award, Am. Artists Profl. League, Grand Nat. Exhibitions, 1999, 2004, Best in Show award, Stoughton Art Assn., 2002, 2004, Miss. Grand Nat. Exhbn., 2003. Fellow: Am. Artists Profl. League; mem.: Phila. Watercolor Soc., New Eng. Watercolor Soc. (pres. 2004—), Canton (Mass.) Art Assn. (dir. edn. 1997—), Ea. Wash. Watercolor Soc., Coast Guard Artist Program, Cape Cod Art Assn., Audubon Artists, Inc, Allied Artists of Am., Academic Artists Assn., Am. Soc. of Marine Artists, R.I. Watercolor Soc. (Best in Show award 2004), North Shore Arts Assn., Phila. North East Watercolor Soc., Tex. Watercolor Soc., Pa. Watercolor Soc., Nat. Soc. of Artists, Mo. Watercolor Soc., Internat. Guild of Realism (assoc.), Miss. Watercolor Soc., Mont. Watercolor Soc., Internat. Soc. of Marine Painters, Hudson Valley Art Assn., Ga. Watercolor Soc., The Salmagundi Club, Alpha Omega Alpha, Watercolor U.S.A. Honor Soc. Achievements include development of the first acute hemodialysis on the South Shore of Massachusetts, 1968; discovery of a Left Ventricular Myxoma by ultra sonography, 1984. Home: 7 Holly Woods Rd Mattapoisett MA 02739

**MAZIAR, CHRISTINE M.,** academic administrator; BSEE, MSEE, Purdue U., PhD in Elec. Engring. Mem. faculty U. Tex., 1987—98, vice provost, 1995—98; faculty mem. U. Minn., Mpls., 1998—, v.p. for rsch., dean Grad. Sch., 1998—2002, exec. v.p., provost, 2002—04; mem. faculty U. Notre Dame, Ind., 2004—. Contbr. articles to profl. jours. Recipient Presdl. Young Investigator award, NSF, 1990, Tech. Excellence award, Semiconductor Rsch. Corp., 1992. Home: Office of Provost 800 Main Blvd Notre Dame IN 46556

**MAZLEN, ROGER GEOFFREY,** ophthalmologist, pharmacologist; b. Bklyn., Nov. 23, 1937; s. Henry Gershwin and Ann Kurland (Shapero) M.; m. Sandra Phyllis Kuritzky, Aug. 7, 1960; children: James Edward, Vivien Gayle. BS in Biology, Rensselaer Poly. Inst., 1959; MD, SUNY, Bklyn., 1963. Intern maimonides Med. Ctr., Bklyn., 1963-64, resident in medicine, 1964-65; rsch. assoc. NIH, Bethesda, Md., 1965-67; resident in med. ophthalmology Mt. Sinai Med. Ctr., N.Y.C., 1967-69; assoc. med. dir. Pfizer Inc., N.Y.C., 1970-71; asst. dir. clin. rsch. Ayerst Labs., N.Y.C., 1971-75; assoc. dir. clin. rsch. Schering Corp., Bloomfield, NJ, 1975-78; adj. assoc. prof. medicine N.Y. Med. Coll.; sr. clin. asst. prof. Mt. Sinai Sch. Medicine; sr. faculty, sr. attending div. endocrinology and metabolism Mt. Sinai Med. Ctr. Mem. cons. Profl. Children's Sch.; cons. in clin. nutrition and metabolism South Oaks Hosp; chief sci. officer Biomelecular Sci., Inc., 2000-. Author: A New Manifesto for Middle America, 1972; author: (with others) Nutrition and Health Care; contbr. (chpt.) Quick Reference to Clinical Nutrition, mem. editl. staff Jour. of the Chiropractic Coun. on Nutrition. Founder, chmn. Queens County (N.Y.) Common Cause, 1972—75, vice chmn. for N.Y. State, 1974—75; bd. dirs. Bayside Hills Civic Assn., 1970—80; adv. mem. bd. dirs. U.S.A., Inc., 1970—72; chmn. hyperalimentation com. Astoria (N.Y.) Gen. Hosp.; former dir. Clin. Rsch. N. Am. Immunatee Ltd., Montreal; nutrition dir. Cernitin Am. Nutritional, 1983—88, also mem. eating disorder adv. bd. With USPHS, 1965—67. Fellow: Am. Coll. Nutrition (chmn. coun. on nutrition and cardiovasc. diseases 1976—85, sec.-treas.); mem.: N.Y. State Soc. Internal Medicine, Soc. for Natural Immunity, Am. Coll. Cardiology (constituent mem. N.Y. State chpt.), Am. Soc. Clin. Pharmacology and Therapeutics, Muhammad Ali Internat. Sport Youth Athletic Found. Inc. (bd. dirs.). Republican. Office: 30 Middledeck Rd Roslyn NY 11576 Office Phone: 516-869-0717. E-mail: rgm1@aol.com.

**MAZLISH, BRUCE,** historian, educator; b. NYC, Sept. 15, 1923; s. Louis and Lee (Reuben) M.; m. Neva Goodwin, Nov. 22, 1988; children from previous marriage: Cordelia, Peter, Anthony, Jared. BA, Columbia U., 1944, MA, 1947, PhD, 1955. Instr. history U. Maine, 1946-48, Columbia U., 1949-50, Mass. Inst Tech., 1950-53; dir. Am. Sch. in Madrid, Spain, 1953-55; from mem. faculty to prof. emeritus Mass. Inst. Tech., 1955—2004, prof. emeritus, 2004—. Vis. prof. Harvard U., Cambridge, Mass., 2001—02; scholars coun. Libr. of Congress, 2001—04. Author: (with J. Bronowski) The Western Intellectual Tradition, 1960, The Riddle of History, 1966, In Search of Nixon, 1972, James and John Stuart Mill: Father and Son in the 19th Century, 1975, 2d edition, 1988, The Revolutionary Ascetic, 1976, Kissinger, The European Mind in American Policy, 1976, The Meaning of Karl Marx, 1984, A New Science: The Breakdown of Connections and the Birth of Sociology, 1989, The Leader, the Led and the Psyche, 1990, The Fourth Discontinuity: The Co-Evolution of Humans and Machines, 1993, The Uncertain Sciences, 1998, Civilization and Its Contents, 2004, (with Alfred Chandler) Leviathans, The Multinational Corporations and New Global History, 2005, (with Akira Iriya) The Global History Reader, 2005; Editor: Psychoanalysis and History, 1963, rev. edit., 1971, The Railroad and the Space Program: An Exploration in Historical Analogy, 1965, (with Ralph Bueltjens) Conceptualizing Global History, 1993, (with Leo Marx) Progress: Fact or Illusion, 1996; contbr. articles to profl. jours. Bd. dirs. Rockefeller Family Fund, 1987-97; v.p. Mount Desert Festival of Chamber Music, 1985—; bd. dirs. Toynbee Prize Found., 1992—, pres., 1997—; mem. gov. bd. Rockefeller Archives Ctr., 1999—. Served with inf. and OSS, AUS, 1943-45. Recipient Toynbee prize, 1986-87. Fellow Am. Acad. Arts and Scis. Clubs: Cambridge Tennis, Badminton and Tennis; Harbor (Seal Harbor, Maine). Home: 11 Lowell St Cambridge MA 02138-4725 Office: MIT 77 Massachusetts Ave Cambridge MA 02139-4307

**MAZO, MARK ELLIOTT,** lawyer; b. Phila., Jan. 12, 1950; s. Earl and Rita (Vane) M.; m. Fern Rosalyn Litman, Aug. 19, 1973; children: Samantha Lauren, Dana Suzanne, Ross Elliott, Courtney Litman. AB, Princeton U., 1971; JD, Harvard U., 1974. Bar: DC 1975, US Dist. Ct. DC 1975, US Claims Ct. 1975, US Ct. Appeals (DC cir.) 1976, US Supreme Ct, 1979. Ptnr Hogan & Hartson, L.L.P., Washington and Paris, 1990—. Contbr. articles to profl. jours. White House intern Exec. Office of Pres., Washington, 1972. Capt. USAR, 1971-79. Mem. ABA, Harvard Law Sch. Assn., DC Bar Assn., Columbia Country Club, Princeton Club (NYC), Colonial Club, City Club, Nassau Club, Timbers Club, Phi Beta Kappa. Republican. Home: 3719 Cardiff Rd Chevy Chase MD 20815-5943 Office: Hogan & Hartson LLP 555 13th St NW Washington DC 20004 also: Hogan & Hartson MNP 69 Ave Franklin Roosevelt 75008 Paris France Office Phone: 202-637-5673, (33)(0)1 55 73 23 00. Business E-Mail: memazo@hhlaw.com.

**MAZO, ROBERT MARC,** retired chemistry professor; b. Bklyn., Oct. 3, 1930; s. Nathan and Rose Marion (Mazo) M.; m. Joan Ruth Spector, Sept. 5, 1954; children: Ruth, Jeffrey, Daniel. BA, Harvard U., 1952; MS, Yale U., 1953, PhD, 1955. Rsch. assoc. U. Chgo., 1956-58; asst. prof. Calif. Inst. Tech., 1958-62; assoc. prof. U. Oreg., Eugene, 1962-65, prof. chemistry, 1965-95, prof. emeritus, 1996, head chemistry dept., 1978-81, dir. Inst. Theoretical Sci., 1964-67, 84-87, assoc. dean Grad. Sch., 1967-71; program dir. NSF, 1977-78. Alfred P. Sloan fellow, NSF Sr. Postdoctoral fellow, vis. prof. U. Libre de Bruxelles, Belgium, 1968-69; vis. prof. Technische Hochschule Aachen, Weizmann Inst., Rehovoth, Israel, 1981-82, U. New South Wales, Australia, 1989. Author: Statistical Mechanical Theories of Transport Processes, 1967, Brownian Motion, 2002, also rsch. articles. NSF Postdoctoral fellow U. Amsterdam, Netherlands, 1955-56. Fellow Am. Phys. Soc. Home: 2460 Charnelton St Eugene OR 97405-3214 Office: U Oreg Inst Theoretical Sci Eugene OR 97403 Office Phone: 541-346-5224. Business E-Mail: mazo@uoregon.edu.

**MAZON, MARGARET FAUSOLD,** language educator; b. Windber, Pa., Dec. 26, 1946; d. George McLelland and Ann (Shank) Fausold; m. José Antonio Mazón, Apr. 21, 1973 (div. June 1985); children: David José Mazón, Daniel Eladio Mazón. Student, U. Valladolid, 1967; BS in Spanish Edn., Ind. U. Pa., 1968; MA in Spanish, W.Va. U., 1973, EdD, 1992. Tchr. Spanish McGuffey St. Jr.-Sr. H.S., Claysville, Pa. Tchr. ESL Briam Inst., Madrid, 1970—71; adj. prof., asst. prof. St. Bonaventure U., Olean, NY, 1979—2002, assoc. prof., Dept. Chair, 2002—06, assoc. prof., 2006—. Contbr. articles to profl. jours.; translator: Olean Gen. Hosp., 2000—. Vol.

Interfaith Caregivers, Olean, 1999—. Mem.: Modern Lang. Assn. Democrat. Presbyterian. Avocations: swimming, bicycling, cooking, gardening. Office: Modern Lang Dept St Bonaventure Univ Saint Bonaventure NY 14778 Office Phone: 716-375-2468. Business E-Mail: mmazon@sbu.edu.

**MAZRUI, ALI AL'AMIN,** political science professor, researcher; b. Mombasa, Kenya, Feb. 24, 1933; came to U.S., 1960; s. Al'Amin Ali and Safia (Suleiman) M.; m. Molly Vickerman, 1962 (div. 1982); children: Jamal, Al'Amin, Kim Abubakar; m. Pauline Uti, Oct. 1991; children: Farid Chenmy, Harith Ekenechukwu. BA with distinction, U. Manchester, Eng., 1960; MA, Columbia U., 1961; DPhil, Oxford U., 1966. Lectr. Makerere U., Kampala, Uganda, 1963-65, prof. polit. sci., head dept. polit. sci., 1965-73; dean faculty social scis. Faculty Social Scis., Makerere U., Kampala, Uganda, 1967-69; prof. polit. sci., Ann Arbor, 1974-91, prof. Ctr. Afroam. and African Studies, dept. polit. sci., 1974-91; Andrew D. White prof.-at-large Cornell U., Ithaca, 1986-92; research prof. polit. sci. U. Jos, Nigeria, 1981-86; Albert Schweitzer prof. humanities SUNY, Binghamton, 1989—; Albert Luthuli prof.-at-large U. Jos (Nigeria), 1991—; sr. scholar, Andrew D. White prof.-at-large emeritus Cornell U, Ithaca, 1992—; dir. Inst. Global Cultural Studies SUNY, Binghamton, 1991—; chancellor Jomo Kenyatta Univ. Agrl. and Tech., Kenya, 2003—. Ibn Khaldun prof.-at-large Sch. Islamic and Social Scis., Leesburg, Va., 1997-2000; Reith lectr. BBC, London, 1979; vis. prof. various univs. including U. London, U. Chgo., Oxford U., U. Pa., Ohio State U., Manchester U., Harvard U., Nairobi U., UCLA, Northwestern U., U. Singapore, Colgate Coll., U. Australia, Stanford U., U. Cairo, Sussex U., U. Leeds, Internat. Islamic U., Malaysia, 1965—; mem. bank's coun. African advisers, World Bank, Washington, 1988-91; Walter Rodney disting. prof. U. Guyana, Georgetown, 1997-98. Author: Towards A Pax Africana: A Study of Ideology and Ambition, 1967, The Anglo-African Commonwealth: Political Friction and Cultural Fusion, 1967, On Heroes and Uhuru-Worship: Essays on Independent Africa, 1967, Violence and Thought: Essays on Social Tensions in Africa, 1969, Cultural Engineering and Nation-Building in East Africa, 1972, World Culture and the Black Experience, 1974, The Political Sociology of the English Language: An African Perspective, 1975, Soldiers and Kinsmen in Uganda: The Making of a Military Ethnocracy, 1975; co-editor: (with Robert I. Rotberg) Protest and Power in Black Africa, 1970, (with Hasu Patel) Africa in World Affairs: The Next Thirty Years, 1973; editor: The Warrior Tradition in Modern Africa, 1978, Africa since 1935 Volume III Unesco General History of Africa, 1973-93, (with Alamin M. Mazrui) The Political Culture of Language: Swahili, Society and the State, 1996—99, (with Alamin M. Mazrui) The Power of Babel: Language and Governance in Africa's Experience, 1998; sr. editor: (with T.K. Levine) The Africans: A Reader, 1986; author: The Trial of Christopher Okigbo, 1971, A World Federation of Cultures: An African Perspective, 1976; Africa's International Relations: The Diplomacy of Dependency and Change, 1977, Political Values and the Educated Class in Africa, 1978, The African Condition: A Political Diagnosis, 1980, (with Michael Tidy) Nationalism and New States in Africa, From About 1935 to the Present, 1984; narrator, presenter: The Africans: A Triple Heritage, 1986, Cultural Forces in World Politics, 1990; mem. editl. bd. various profl. jours., 1963—; contbr. articles to profl. publs. Fellow Ctr for Advanced Study in Behavioral Scis., Palo Alto, Calif., 1972-73; sr. fellow Hoover Instn. on War, Revolution and Peace, Stanford, Calif., 1973-74, Mich. Soc. Fellows, 1973-82. Fellow Internat. Assn. Mid. Ea. Studies, Ghana Acad. Arts and Scis. (hon.); mem. African Studies Assn. (exec. bd. 1975-80, pres. 1978-79, Disting. Africans award 1995), Internat. Congress African Studies (v.p. 1978-85), Internat. Polit. Sci. Assn. (v.p. 1970-73), World Order Models Project (dir. African sect. 1968-83), Royal African Soc. (v.p.), Royal Commonwealth Soc., United Kenya Club (Nairobi), Athenaeum Club (London). Office: SUNY Inst Global Cultural Studies Off Schweitzer Chair PO Box 6000 Binghamton NY 13902-6000 Office Phone: 607-777-4494. E-mail: amazrui@binghamton.edu.

**MAZUMDER, BIJOY SINGHA,** mathematician, educator, researcher; b. Nandail, Mymensingh, Bangladesh, Oct. 31, 1946; s. Khagendra Jiban and Bidyut Prova Mazumder; m. Madhusri Ray, Dec. 30, 1959; children: Rahul, Ayan. MSc, Indian Inst. Tech., Kharagpur, India, D of Info. Tech., PhD in Applied Math. Assoc. prof. of applied math. Indian Statis. Inst., Kolkata, West Bengal, India, 1987—91, prof. of applied math., 1991—. Vis. scientist U. Western Ont., London, 1984; vis. rsch. scientist Ill. State Water Survey, Champaign, Ill., 1989—91; vis. prof. U. Karlsruhe, Germany, 1994; guest prof. Tsinghua U., Beijing, 2000; chairperson numerous confs., India; sci. advisor numerous nat. and internat. confs., India. Contbr. over 50 articles to profl. jours. Expert in selection coms., reviewer jours., reviewer rsch. grants Indian Statis. Inst., Kolkata, West Bengal, india, 1991. Grantee, CSIR, INSA, Dept. Sci. and Tech., New Delhi, 1974, 1981, 2001. Mem.: Internat. Assn. Hydraulic Rsch., Calcutta Math. Soc. (life), Indian Soc. Theoretical and Applied Mechanics (life). Achievements include research in fluid mechanics related to sediment transport, diffusion processes, environmental fluid mechanics, navigation hydraulics, MHD flow and heat transfer. Home: 16 Tanupukur Rd West Bengal Kolkata 700 031 India Office: Indian Statis Inst 203 B T R Rd West Bengal Kolkata 700 108 India Office Phone: 0091-33-577-2088, 3033. Office Fax: 0091-33-577-3026. E-mail: bijoy@isical.ac.in.

**MAZUR, BARRY CHARLES,** mathematician, educator; b. NYC, Dec. 19, 1937; 1 child. PhD in Math. Princeton U., 1959; DSc (hon.), Colby Coll., 2004. Jr. fellow Harvard U., Cambridge, Mass., 1959—62, asst. prof. to prof., 1962—82, William Petschek prof. math., 1982—98, Gerhardt Gade Univ. prof., 1998—. Author: Imagining Numbers, 2002. Recipient Veblen prize in Geometry, Am. Math. Soc., 1966, Cole prize in Number Theory, 1982, Steele Prize, 1999, Chauvenet prize, Math. Assn. Am., 1994. Mem.: AAAS, NAS, American Philol. Soc. Office: Harvard U FAS Math Dept / Sci Ctr 1 Oxford St Cambridge MA 02138-2901 E-mail: mazur@math.harvard.edu.

**MAZUR, DENNIS JOHN,** internal medicine physician, educator, features editor; b. Kittanning, Pa. MD, Stanford U., 1979, PhD, 1983. Diplomate Am. Bd. Internal Medicine. Prof. medicine Oreg. Health Scis. U., Portland, 1986—; chmn. VISN 20 NW Health Network IRB, Dept. VA, Portland, 2003—; feature editor Med. Decision Making, Phila., 1997—. Author: (textbooks) Medical Risk and the Right to an Informed Consent, Shared Decision Making in the Patient-Physician Relationship, The New Medical Conversation. Office: Med Svc VAMC 3710 SW US Veterans Hospital Road Portland OR 97201 Office Phone: 503-220-8262. E-mail: dennis.mazur@med.va.gov.

**MAZUR, EDWARD JOHN, JR.,** financial planner; b. Lowell, Mass., Mar. 5, 1948; s. Edward John Sr. and Mary Annette (Terry) M.; m. Sheila MacDonald, Dec. 13, 1969 (div. Nov. 1984); 1 child, Kristen Leigh; m. Anna Maria Maia, May 18, 1985; children: Edward John III, Kara Maria Mazur. BA in History, U. Mass., 1969. CLU, Chartered Fin. Cons., Life Underwriters Tng. Coun. Fellow. From agt. to dir. agys. John Hancock Mut. Life Ins. Co., Boston, 1973—84, gen. agt. Hartford, 1984-89; founder Mazur Fin., Farmington, Conn., 1990—2000, Profl. Investors Exch., LLC, Farmington, 2000—05, Profl. Investor's Life and Annuity LLC, 2005—. Team coord. Team Conn., 1998—. Recipient Raymond T. Wilbur award, Mass. Jaycees, 1982-83; named President of Yr., Mass. Jaycees, 1982-83, Outstanding Young Men of Am., Mass. Jaycees, 1984. Mem. Million Dollar Round Table, Nat. Assn. Ins. and Fin. Advisors (pres. chpt. 2000-01), Hartford Life Underwriters Assn. (pres. 1995-97), US-Racquetball Assn. (pres. jr. coun. 2005—), Conn. Racquetball Assn. (pres. 1985-94). Avocations: racquetball, coaching, hiking. Home: 48 Knollwood Ln Avon CT 06001-2701 Office Phone: 860-678-7806. E-mail: mazurfin@aol.com.

**MAZUR, LEONARD L.,** pharmaceutical company executive; b. Ansbach, Germany, Jan. 23, 1945; came to U.S., 1949; s. Walter and Maria (Zatwarnitsky) M.; m. Helena Maria Olijnyk, Nov. 1966; children: Maria, Michael, Irene. BA, Temple U., 1968, MBA, 1975. Mktg. mgr. Cooper Labs., Inc., Fairfield, N.J. and Palo Alto, Calif., 1971—81; dir. product mgmt. Knoll Pharm. Corp. divsn. BASF, Whippany, NJ, 1981—84; v.p. ICN Pharm. Corp., Costa Mesa, Calif., 1984—88; pres., COO Chantal Pharm. Corp., L.A.,

1988—89; exec. v.p. Medicis Pharm. Corp., N.Y.C., 1989—93; vice chmn. Cabot Labs., Inc., N.Y.C., 1994—96; chmn., CEO Genesis Pharm., Inc., Parsippany, NJ, 1996—2006; COO Triax Pharms., LLC, Cranford, NJ, 2006—. Ptnr. Mazier Ptnrs. LLC, Morristown, NJ, 1995-2005. Mem. adv. bd. Manor Coll., Jenkintown, Pa., 1972-78, trustee, 2000—; ind. observer Referendum for Independence, Ukraine, 1991. Roman Catholic. Achievements include patents in field. Office: Triax Pharms LLC 20 Commerce Dr Cranford NJ 07016

**MAZUR, MICHAEL,** artist; b. N.Y.C., Nov. 2, 1935; s. Burton Boris and Helen (Isaacs) M.; m. Gail Lewis Beckwith, Dec. 28, 1958; children: Daniel Isaac, Kathe Elizabeth. BA, Amherst Coll., 1958; BFA, Yale U., 1959, MFA, 1961; degree (hon.), Lesley U./Art Inst. Boston, 2000, Coll. Creative Studies, Detroit, 2005. Asst. prof. fine arts Brandeis U., Waltham, Mass., 1965-76; instr. RISD, 1962-65. Vis. prof. Yale U. Sch. Art and Arch., 1972, 81, Queens Coll., CUNY, 1973, U. Calif., Santa Barbara, 1974-75, Boston U., 1982, Mass. Coll. Art, 1994, 95; lectr. Mus. Fine Arts, Boston, Brown U., U. Calif., Berkeley, New Sch. for Social Rsch., Bennington Coll., U. Iowa, Boston U., 1994-95, Katonah Mus., N.Y. Studio Sch., 1994; vis. lectr. Carpenter Ctr., Harvard U., 1976, 78, 89, 92, 94, 95, 97, others; illustrator Fleur du Mal, 1984, The Inferno of Dante, Farrar, Strans & Giroux, 1994, Genesis, 1996; co-chair bd. Fine Arts Work Ctr., Provincetown, Mass., 1996—. Exhibited in one-man shows at Kornblee Gallery, N.Y.C., 1960, 63, 66, Boris Mirski, Boston, 1963, 65, Phila. Print Club, 1964, Silvermine Guild, 1964, Fla. State U., 1966, Shoemaker Gallery Juniata Coll., 1966, Alpha Gallery, Boston, 1967, 68, 74, OGL Gallery, Los Angeles, Calif., 1968, Rose Art Mus., Brandeis U., 1969, A.A.A. Gallery, 1969, Inst. Contemporary Art, Boston, 1970, Terry Dintenfass, N.Y.C., 1974, 76, Picker Gallery, Colgate U., 1973, Trinity Coll., 1976, Ohio State U., 1975, Robert Miller Gallery, N.Y.C., 1977, 80, Harkus-Krakow, Boston, 1977, 79, 80, Pace Gallery, N.Y.C., 1980, John Stoller, Mpls., 1981, 85, 88, 91, William and Mary Coll., 1981, Ronald Greenberg, St. Louis, 1981, Janus Gallery, L.A., 1982, 84, 88, Barbara Mathes Gallery, N.Y.C., 1986, 88, Barbara Krakow Gallery, Boston, 1984, 86, 89, 91, 93, 95, 97, 98, 2000, Art Club Chgo., 1985, Beaver Coll., 1985, Joe Fawbush, N.Y., 1987, 88, Jan Turner Gallery, L.A., 1988, Butler Gallery, Houston, 1989, Mary Ryan Gallery, N.Y.C., 1990, 94, 95, 96, 97, 98, 99, 2000, Mus. Fine Arts, Boston, 2000, Cantor Ctr.-Stanford U., 2000, Zimmerli Art Mus., New Brunswick, N.J., 2000, Mus. di Castelvecchio, Verona, Italy, 2000, Am. Acad. Rome, 2000—; exhibited group shows at, Mus. Modern Art, 1964, 75, Bklyn. Mus., 1960, 62, 64, 66, 76, 80, 84, 86, Fogg Art Mus., 1966, 76, 94, Art. Inst. Chgo., 1964, Pa. Acad., 1966, 93, Phila. Mus., 1966, 88, Boston Mus. Fine Arts., 1967, 68, 76, 77, 80, 88, 90-91, 92, DeCordova Mus. Lincoln, Mass., 1965-67, 75, 86, 87, Whitney Mus. Am. Art, 1965, 81, 90, 92, Nat. Inst. Arts and Letters, 1965, 74, 80, 86, Sivermine Guild, 1965, Print Biennial of Americas, Santiago, Chile, 1965, Paris Biennale, 1969, Venice Biennale, 1970, Finch Coll. Mus., 1971-72, 2d and 3d Biennial Graphic Art, Cali, Colombia, N.A.D. Ann., 1974, Butler Inst., Youngstown, Ohio, 1974, Ball State U., 1974, America-1976, Sense of Place, Met. Mus., N.Y.C., 1979, 80, Montreal Mus. Fine Arts, 1977, Palais Royale, Brussels, 1979, Claude Bernard, Paris, 1980, Alan Frumkin, N.Y., 1981, 82, Madison Art Ctr., 1989, Nat. Gallery of Art, Washington, 1990, Pratt Mus., N.Y.C., 1990, Nat. Mus. Am. Art, 1997; traveling exhbns. include, Bicentennial Exhbn., 1976, State Arts Councils, Iowa, Kans., Mo., Nebr., 1973, Am. Monotypes, Smithsonian Instn., 1977; represented in permanent collections, Met. Mus., N.Y.C., Mus. Modern Art, Smith Coll. Art Mus., Library Congress, Fogg Art Mus., Art Inst. Chgo., Whitney Mus., Los Angeles County Art Mus., Mus. R.I. Sch. Design, Oreg. Art Mus., U. Maine, Mpls. Inst., Pa. State U., Toledo Art Mus., Phila. Art Mus., U. Ohio Westminster Found., Boston Mus. Fine Arts, Boston Pub. Library, Bklyn. Mus., Addison Gallery, Andover Acad., Yale Art Gallery, Montreal Mus. Fine Arts; commd. Fed. Res. Bank, Boston, 1998, USB-Warburg-Dillon, Stanford, Conn., 1999; (Recipient 2d prize Soc. Am. Graphic Artists 1963, Nat. Inst. Arts and Letters award 1965). Cofounder Artists Against Racism and the War, 1968; bd. dirs. Artists Found., co-chair, 1995—; bd. dirs. Fine Arts Work Ctr., Provincetown, Mass.; mem. Mass. Coun. on Arts and Humanities; mem. Pennell com. Libr. of Congress, 1983-93; founder, dir. Art for Nuc. Weapons Freeze, 1983-84, New Provincetown Print Project, 1990-95; chmn. bd. Provincetown Fine Arts Work Ctr.; overseer Mus. Fine Arts, Boston. Grantee Tiffany Found., 1964, Tamarind Lithography Workshop, 1968; Guggenheim Found. fellow, 1964-65; winner numerous purchase awards; recipient Disting. Svc. "Printworks Emeritus", So. Graphics Coun., 2005. Home: 5 Walnut Ave Cambridge MA 02140-2706

**MAZUR, PETER,** physiologist, cryobiologist; b. N.Y.C., Mar. 3, 1928; s. Paul M. and Adolphia (Kaske) M.; m. Drusilla Stevens, May 28, 1953 (dec. May 1982); 1 child, Timothy Stevens; m. Sara Jo Bolling, June 16, 1984 (dec. Apr. 2003). AB magna cum laude, Harvard U., 1949, PhD, 1953; DSc (hon.), Wilson Coll., 1998. NSF postdoctoral fellow Princeton (N.J.) U., 1957-59; rsch. staff biology divsn. Oak Ridge Nat. Lab., 1959-98. Group leader fundamental and applied cryobiology Oak Ridge Nat. Lab., 1966-98, sci. dir. biophysics and cell physiology, biology div., 1974-75, corporate fellow, 1985; chmn. ORNL Corp. Fellows Coun., 1985-86; mem. vis. com. biology Harvard U. Bd. Overseers 1972-77; rsch. prof. dept. biochem. and cellular and molecular biology U. Tenn., 1998—; mem. Space Sci. Bd. of Nat. Acad., 1975-77; Sigma Xi nat. lectr., 1980. Trustee Wilson Coll., Pa., 1984-93, trustee emeritus, 2003; bd. dirs. Meth. Hosp. Found., Oak Ridge, 1997—2003. Capt. USAF, 1953-57. Recipient Author of Yr. award, Martin-Marietta Energy Sys., 1985, Disting. Svc. award, Am. Assn. Tissue Banks, 1993, R&D 100 award, R&D Mag., 1993, Disting. Achievement award, Am. Soc. Reproductive Medicine, 2000; Labor fellow, Harvard U., 1952, John Harvard fellow, 1951. Fellow AAAS, Soc. Cryobiology (pres. 1973-74, bd. govs. 1979-96), mem. Rotary Club Oak Ridge, Phi Beta Kappa, Cosmos Club (Washington) Current work includes cryobiology and the mechanisms of freezing injury in living cells and tissues. Subspecialties are cell biology and biophysics. Home: 125 Westlook Cir Oak Ridge TN 37830-3856 Office: Dept Biochemistry and Cellular and Molecular Biology M407 Walters Life Sci Bldg Knoxville TN 37996-0001 Office Phone: 865-974-9960. E-mail: pmazur@utk.edu.

**MAZUR, RHODA HIMMEL,** community volunteer; b. Bklyn., July 4, 1929; d. Morris and Gussie (Nadler) Himmel; m. Marvin Irwin Mazur, June 7, 1952; children: Jody, Amy, Leslie, Eric. Student, CCNY, CUNY. Bd. dirs. Newport News Social Svcs. Adv. Bd., 1979-84; Gov.'s Commn. Status Women, Richmond, 1981-84, Coun. Jewish Fedns., NYC, 1985-87, Nat. Coun. Christians and Jews, 1985-89, Rodef Sholom Brotherhood Com., 1996—, Peninsula Jewish Hist. Soc., 1998—; v.p. Anti-Defamation League Regional Bd., Richmond, 1983-85, bd. dirs., 1985-98; pres. Newport News Hadassah, 1984-85, United Jewish Cmty. Va. Peninsula Inc., Newport News, 1985-88, Rodef Sholom Sisterhood, 1997-98; active Newport News Task Force on Emergency Housing, 1984-85; chair fin. com. Peninsula Peace Edn. Ctr., Newport News, 1984-85; adv. bd. Friends of the Homeless, Inc., 1987-00, pres., 1993-98, v.p. 1998-99; adv. bd. Associated Marine Inst., 1988-92; mem. social svcs. com. United Jewish Cmty. Va. Peninsula, 1995—, mem. campaign coun., 1999-. Jewish Hist. Soc. Va. Peninsula, 1995-; chair social action com. Rodef Sholom Temple, 1993-96, endowment com., 1998—; cmty. activist; bd. dirs., Peninsula Campy Fund, 2001—, Fed. Emergency Mgmt. Agy., 2001. Recipient Young Leadership award Jewish Fedn. Newport News, 1968, Brotherhood citation Nat. Conf. Christians and Jews, 1984, Anti-Defamation Leadership award, 1997. Democrat. Avocations: hand crafts, reading, music, photography. Home: 114 James River Dr Newport News VA 23601-3604

**MAZUR, THOMAS A.,** music educator; b. Newark, Nov. 10, 1945; s. Richard C. and Leocada Mazur; m. Faith Frankel, Mar. 29, 1975; 1 child, Joy; m. Jacqueline Mazur, Dec. 30, 2004. BA in Music, Rutgers U., 1989; M in Music Edn., NJCU, 2004. Vocal music tchr. Long Branch (N.J.) H.S., 1990—95, Roosevelt Mid. Sch., West Orange, NJ, 1995—. Recipient Excellence in Tchg. award, N.J. Symphony Orch., Newark, 1996—97. Mem. Kappa Delta Pi. Avocation: mountain climbing. Home: 708 Buckland Ct Denville NJ 07834 Office: Roosevelt Mid Sch 36 Gilbert Pl West Orange NJ 07052 Personal E-mail: tmazur@woboe.org.

**MAZUREK, JOSEPH P.,** lawyer, former state legislator; b. San Diego, July 27, 1948; m. Patty Mazurek; 3 children. BA, U. Mont., 1970, JD, 1975. Bar: Mont. 1975. Atty. Gough, Shanahan, Johnson, and Waterman, Helena, Mont., 1975—93; mem. Mont. Senate from 23d Dist., 1981—92, pres., 1991—92; atty. gen. State of Mont., 1993—2000; ptnr. Crowley, Haughey, Hanson, Toole & Dietrich, PLLP, Helena, Mont., 2000—. Mem. Revenue Oversight Com., 1983—92; chmn. Senate Judiciary Com. Mem. editl. bd.: Mont. Law Rev., 1974—75. With U.S. Army, 1970—72. Mem.: ABA, Phi Delta Theta, Phi Delta Phi, Beta Gamma Sigma. Democrat. Office: 100 N Park Ave Helena MT 59601-6263

**MAZZA, DAVID S.,** pediatrician; b. Burlington, Vt., Dec. 10, 1947; s. Frank, Jr. and Margret Alice (Fuller) M. B.A., U. Vt., 1969, M.A. in Math., 1971, M.D., 1977. Diplomate Am. Bd. Pediatrics. Resident in pediatrics NYU-Bellevue Hosp., N.Y.C., 1977-80, fellow in ambulatory pediatrics, 1980-82; attending staff emergency service Bellevue Hosp., 1982—; dir. pediatric ambulatory services Booth Meml. Med. Ctr., N.Y.C., 1982—; dir. fellowship program, 1985; attending staff North Shore U. Hosp., N.Y., 1985—, Cornell U., 1985—; instr. NYU, 1982-84. City Council campaign vol., N.Y.C., 1985. Mem. Am. Acad. Pediatrics, AAAS, N.Y. Acad. Sci., Sierra Club, Defenders of Wildlife, Nature Conservancy Group. Democrat. Avocations: swimming; bicycling; travel.

**MAZZAFERRI, ERNEST LOUIS,** endocrinologist, educator; b. Cleve., Sept. 27, 1936; s. Joseph and Nanetta (Marinelli) M.; m. Florence Mildred Marolt, Nov. 23, 1957; children: Patricia Marie Atchison, Michael Louis, Sharon Lynne Brown, Ernest Louis. BS cum laude, John Carroll U., 1958; MD, Ohio State U., 1962. Diplomate Am. Bd. Internal Medicine. Intern Ohio State U. Hosps., Columbus, 1962-63, resident, 1963-64, 66-68; asst. prof. medicine Ohio State U., 1968-70, assoc. prof., 1973-76, prof., 1976-79, dir. div. endocrinology and metabolism, 1975-78; acting dean U. Nev., Reno, 1979-81, prof., chmn. dept. medicine, 1978-84, prof. physiology, 1982-84; prof., chmn. dept. medicine, prof. physiology Ohio State U., Columbus, 1984-99, prof. emeritus, 1999—; pres. Dept. of Medicine Found., 1986-99; chmn. bd. Ohio State Practice Group, 1996-99; clin. prof. medicine U. Fla., Gainesville, 2001—. Bd. dirs. The Ohio State U. Hosps., 1997—99; mem. com. on exposure of Am. people to I-131 from Nev. atomic bomb tests Nat. Acad. Sci. Inst. of Medicine, 1997—99; mem. com. on health effects assoc. with exposures experienced during the Gulf War, 1999—2000; mem. com. guidelines for thyroid cancer screening Inst. Medicine, 1997—99; chmn. Nat. Cancer Ctr. Network Com. on Thyroid Cancer Guidelines; mem. com. on health effects associated with exposures during the Gulf War Inst. of Medicine Nat. Academies of Sci., 1999—2000. Author: Endocrinology Case Studies, 3d edit., 1985, Internal Medicine Pearls, 1993; editor: Textbook of Endocrinology, 3d edit., 1986, Contemporary Internal Medicine, 1988, 3d edit., 1990, Advances in Endocrinology and Metabolism, Vol. 6, 1995, Endocrine Tumors, 1993, Morning Report, 1999, Yearbook of Endocrinology, 1999—; Endocrine editor Yearbook of Medicine, 1999—; editor: Practical Management of Thyroid Cancer: A Medical Disciplinary Approach, 2005, Essentials of Thyroid Cancer Management, Kluwer Acad. Publishers, 2005-; mem. sci. adv. bd. Western Jour. Medicine, 1993; mem. editl. bd. Jour. Lab. Clin. Medicine, 1987-97, Hosp. Practice, Jour. of Clin. Endocrinology and Metabolism, Thyroid, 1999—; contbr. articles to profl. jours. Chmn. Gov.'s Com. on Radiation Fallout in Nev., 1980-84, hosp. ethics com. Ohio State U., 1994-98; mem. Sec. of Energy Dose Assessment Adv. Com., 1980-84, Agy. for Health Care Policy, Rsch. Cataract Guideline Com., 1991-92, Inst. of Medicine Guideline for Thyroid Cancer Screening com., 1997-99; mem. rsch. coun. com. on exposure of Am. People to I-131 from Nev. Atomic Bomb Tests: Implications for Public Health, 1997-99. Capt. USAF, 1964, maj. USAF, 1968, lt. col. USAF, 1968—73, col. USAR, 1984—91. Recipient Earl N. Metz Disting. Physician award, Ohio State U., 1998, Light of Life award, Light of Life Found. N.Y., 1999, Graves' award, Thyroid Soc. for Rsch. and Edn., 2001. Master: ACP (gov. for Nev. 1984—85, chmn. clin. efficacy assessment program com. 1992—95, edn. policy com. 1992—95, mem. health and pub. policy com.); mem.: AMA, Am. Coll. Clin. Endocrinology (bd. dis. 1995—96, Disting. Clinician award 2002), Ctrl. Soc. Clin. Rsch., Am. Clin. and Climatol. Assn., Endocrine Soc. (Disting. Educator award 2005), Am. Diabetes Assn. (pres. Ohio affiliate 1988—89), Am. Thyroid Assn. (pres.-elect 2004—05, pres. 2005—, Paul Star award), Am. Bd. Internal Medicine (chmn. Endocronology and Metabolism 1999—2003, bd. dirs. 1999—2003, cert. in endocrinology and metabolism, gen. internal medicine, cert. in geriatrics, continuous profl. devel.), Alpha Omega Alpha. Roman Catholic. Achievements include research in thyroid cancer. Home: 4020 SW 93rd Dr Gainesville FL 32608-4653 Office Phone: 352-846-2749. Personal E-mail: mazz01@bellsouth.net. E-mail: emazzaferri@cox.net. *Success, like every other human experience, is relative, measured against shifting standards and subject to the scrutiny of time. One must strike a fine balance— self certainty against external review— that permits the full expression of new ideas enriched by the best and time-worn thoughts of others.*

**MAZZAFERRO, JAMES JOSEPH,** music educator; b. San Francisco, Calif., Apr. 19, 1956; s. James John and Marilyn Jean Mazzaferro; m. Anita Marie Piccone, Nov. 27, 1976; children: Cherylyn, Joseph, Jeanette. Bachelors Music Edn., San Francisco State U., San Francisco, CA, 1978; Masters in Music Conducting, Calif. State U., Sacramento, 1995. San Francisco Archdiocese Archbishop Riordan HS, San Francisco, 1979—89; tchr. music Florin H.S. Elk Grove Unified, Sacramento, 1989—; tchr. music Elk Grove Unified, Sacramento, 1997—2001, Sheldon HS Elk Grove Unified, Sacramento, 1997—; Cosumnes River Coll. Los Rios CC, Sacramento, 1999—. Bd. directors Cazadero Performing Arts, Cazadero, Calif., 1995—2001, Calif. Band Directors, Fresno, Calif., 1999—2001. Mem.: Calif. Music Educators Assn. (band rep. 1994—98), Musician's Union Local 6, Music Educators Nat. Conf., Phi Kappa Lambada (hon.), Phi Kappa Phi (hon.). D-Liberal. Avocation: music performance. Home: 9068 Shetland Court Elk Grove CA 95624 Office: Sheldon High School 8333 Kingsbridge Drive Sacramento CA 95829 Office Phone: 916-681-7500. Personal E-mail: jmazz1@surewest.net.

**MAZZARELLA, DAVID,** editor; b. 1938; With AP, Lisbon, N.Y.C., Rome, 1962—70, Daily American, Rome, 1971—75, Gannett News, Washington, 1976—77, The Bridgewater, Bridgewater, NJ, 1977—83; editor USA Today, Arlington, Va., sr. v.p., 1999—. Office: USA Today 7950 Jones Branch Dr Mc Lean VA 22108-0001

**MAZZARELLA, JAMES KEVIN,** business administration educator; b. Phila., Sept. 22, 1955; s. Samuel Charles and Rosemary C. (Queenan) M. BA, St. Joseph's U., 1977; MBA, La Salle U., 1981; cert., 2001; MA, Temple U., 1987; PhD, Columbia-Pacific U., 1987; DBA, Pacific-Western U., 1988; cert. in acctg., Thomas Edison State Coll., 1996; cert. in e-Bus. & e-Commerce, U. Ill., 2003; cert. human rels. and law, Cornell U., 2004. Cert. mgmt. acct.; cert. in fin. mgmt. Asst. mgr. Olney Oil & Burner Co., Phila., 1977-80; data processing Craig Fuel Co., Phila., 1980-84; supr. M. Kelley Son's Inc., Phila., 1984-86; adj. instr. Holy Family Coll., Phila., 1987-88, instr., 1989, asst. prof., 1989—. Adj. instr. (Pa.) Coll. Textiles, 1984-86, La Salle U., Phila., 1985—, Rosemont (Pa.) Coll., 1988-91. Mem. Acad. Fin. Svcs., Am. Econs. Assn., Am. Fin. Assn., Am. Statis. Assn., Nat. Assn. Bus. Econs., Am. Risk and Ins. Assn., Inst. Mgmt. Accts., Math. Assn. Am., Fin. Mgmt. Assn., Prodn. and Ops. Mgmt. Soc., Midwest Fin. Assn., Western Econs. Assn. Internat., Ea. Econ. Assn., Ea. Fin. Assn., Am. Mgmt. Assn., So. Fin. Assn., Multinat. Fin. Soc., Am. Math. Soc., Am. Law and Econs. Assn., Nat. Coun. Tchrs. Math. Roman Catholic. Home: 5101 N Fairhill St Philadelphia PA 19120-3126 Office: Holy Family College Grant & Frankford Ave Philadelphia PA 19114

**MAZZARELLI, DEBRA JEAN,** real estate broker; b. Suffolk County, N.Y. d. Edward and Jean Werner; m. Gary Mazzarelli; children: Jessica, Kristy, Tori. Student, Boston U.; BA, St. Joseph's Coll., Patchogue, N.Y. Eaten County Legislator Ed Romaine, N.Y.; staff mem. Assemblyman John Cochrane, Albany, N.Y.; coord. Regional Fair Housing Conf.; writer Main Street Express, Patchogue, N.Y.; real estate broker Patchoque; assemblywoman N.Y.

State Assembly, Albany, 1995—2001. Mem. edn., tourism, small bus., environ. conservation coms.; mem. legis. task force on women's issues; mem. vol. firefighter subcom. Mem. N.Y. State Bd. Realtors, South Ocean PTA, Concerned Taxpayers of Patchoque, Patchoque C. of C., Bus. and Profl. Women (pres. Brookhaven chpt.), Nat. Women's Polit. Caucus. Democrat.

**MAZZE, EDWARD MARK,** marketing educator, consultant; b. NYC, Feb. 14, 1941; s. Harry Alan and Mollie (Schneider) M.; m. Sharon Sue Hastings, Sept. 9, 1967; children: Candace, Thomas. BBA, City U. NY, 1961, MBA, 1962; PhD, Pa. State U., 1966. Lectr. bus. adminstrn. CCNY, 1961-62; bus. cons., 1961—; instr. bus. Pa. State U., 1963-66; assoc. prof. mktg. U. Detroit, 1966-68; assoc. prof., dir. spl. programs W.Va. U., 1968-70; prof. bus. adminstrn., coordinator mktg. program Va. Poly. Inst. and State U., Blacksburg, 1970-75; v.p. adminstrv. services, dean Sch. Bus., Seton Hall U., South Orange, NJ, 1975-79; dean sch. bus. adminstrn. Temple U., Phila., 1979-86, prof. mktg. and internat. bus., 1979-93; dean Belk Coll. Bus. Adminstrn., prof. mktg. U. NC, Charlotte, 1993-98, co.-dir. Frank Hawkins Kenan Inst. Pvt. Enterprise, 1997—98; dean Coll. Bus. Adminstrn., Alfred J. Verrecchia-Hasbro Inc. Leadership chair in bus. U. RI, Kingston, 1998—2006, disting. univ. prof. bus. adminstrn., 2006—. Chmn. bd. William Penn Bank, Phila., 1985-87; bd. dirs. Technitrol, Inc., Washington Trust Bancorp, Inc., Barrett Growth Fund, Ocean State Bus. Devel. Authority; mem. state export coun. US Dept. Commerce, 1978-80, 83-93; mem. panel chpt. 7 trustees US Dept. Justice, 1984-96, 2005; adv. bd. McGettigan Ptrns., 1997-99, Radiator Specialty Co., 1997-99, Piedmont Venture Ptrns., 1997-98; mem. faculty cert. spl. studies in adminstrn. and mgmt. program Harvard U., 2003. Author: International Business: Articles and Essays, 1963, Readings in Organization and Management, 1963, Marketing in Action, 1963, Case Histories in Sales Management, 1965, Sales Management: Theory and Practice, 1965, International Marketing Adminstration, 1967, Introduction to Marketing, 1970, Marketing in Turbulent Times: The Challenges and the Opportunities, 1975, Personal Selling: Choice Against Chance, 1976, The Food Marketing Wars: Marketing Triumphs and Blunders, 1998, Specialty Retails: Marketing Triumphs and Blunders, 2001, Lifestyle Marketing: Reaching the New American Consumer, 2003, The Affluent Consumer: Marketing and Selling the Luxury Lifestyle, 2006; mem. editl. bd. Jour. Econs. and Bus., 1976-80, Indsl. Mktg. Mgmt., 1977-2003, Jour. Internat. Bus. Studies, 1978-82, Jour. Acad. Mktg. Sci., 1980-91, Jour. Mktg. Edn., 1985-94, Jour. Global Mktg., 1987—; contbr. articles to profl. jours. Trustee Phila. Home Care, 1984-89, Manor Coll., 1985-92, Thomas A. Edison State Coll. Found., 1987-89, Delaware Valley Coll. Sci. and Agr., 1991-97, Pa. Inst. Tech., 1992-93; chmn. econ. devel. adv. com. Village South Orange, 1977-80; mem., vice-chmn. Bd. Suprs. Doylestown Twp., 1980-81. Ford. Found. fellow, 1962-63 Mem. Am. Mktg. Assn., Acad. Internat. Bus., Nat. Assn. Corp. Dirs., Acad. Mktg. Sci., Beta Gamma Sigma, Pi Kappa Alpha. Home: 52 Horizon Dr Saunderstown RI 02874-2402 Office: U RI Coll of Business 350 Ballentine Hall Kingston RI 02881 Office Phone: 401-874-4308. Personal E-mail: emazze@cox.net. Business E-mail: emazze@uri.edu.

**MAZZEO, ANTHONY R.,** chemist; b. Buffalo, May 2, 1958; s. George J. and Louise C. M.; m. Darlene Van Eseltine, May 21, 1988; children: Victoria, Seth. BS, SUNY, Brockport, 1980; PhD, Syracuse U., 1991. Chemist DuPont, Aiken, SC, 1980—84; rsch'r, tchg. asst. Syracuse U., NY, 1984—88; mgr. quality assurance/tech. support New Methods Rsch., Syracuse, 1988—93; quality assurance scientist Bayer Corp., Spokane, Wash., 1993—99; sr. quality assurance scientist Hollister-Stier Labs., Spokane, 1999—2000; mgr. R&D stability DuPont Pharm. Co., Wilmington, Del., 2000—02; sr. prin. scientist Pfizer Global R&D, Ann Arbor, Mich., 2002—. Contbr. articles to profl. jours. Mem. Am. Chem. Soc. (chair Inland N.W. sect. 1998-2000, sec. treas. 1996), Am. Assn. Pharm. Scientists (pharmaceutical rsch. and manufacturers assn. stability expert team). Home: 25395 Crown Point Ct Farmington Hills MI 48335 Office: Pfizer Global Rsch and Devel 2800 Plymouth Rd Ann Arbor MI 48105

**MAZZEO, DANIEL PATRICK,** aerospace engineer, consultant; b. NYC, Apr. 18, 1949; s. Gennaro and Marie Grace (Mazzei) M.; m. Belva Faye Musick, Sept. 10, 1977; children: Daniel Jr., Jina Marie. BS in Aerospace Engring., Poly. U. NY, 1971; grad. in Aviation Safety, U.S. Naval Postgrad. Sch., Monterey, Calif., 1981. Commd. ensign USN, 1969, advanced through grades to comdr., 1982, aviator, 1969-91; aviation program mgr. BDI Engring., Pensacola, Fla., 1991-95; aviation project mgr. DH Engrs., Sarasota, Fla., 1995-99; pres., CEO Aerocomm Group, Pensacola, Fla., 1999—; sr. project mgr. Banks Engring., Naples, Fla., 2004—06. Airline transport pilot rating FAA, 1979; mem. State Aviation Planning Process, Fla., 1990—; completed over 150 major airport improvement projects; instr. civil engring. and engring. graphics Pensacola Tech. Acad., 2003-05; head Dept. Constrn. Tech. Triangle Tech. Inst., 2005—. Contbr. articles to profl. jours. Tech. advisor in aviation County Govt., Escambia, Fla., 1985, Santa Rosa, Fla., 1987, Tallahassee, Fla., 1994. Decorated Navy commendation medal, Navy expdn. medal, Navy Mertourous Citation Ribbon (four bronze stars), Navy Battle Ribbon (battle E), Navy Sea Svc. Ribbon (one bronze star), Navy Expert Pistol Ribbon, Def. Svc. medal with one bronze star; recipient Sci. grant N.Y.C., 1965, 68, Innovative Environmental award FAA, 1997, Airport of the Year award Fla. Dept. Transp., 1997. Mem. ASCE (section pres.), AIAA (sect. vice-chmn.), Soc. Am. Mil. Engrs., Aircraft Owners and Pilots Assn. (advisor 1997). Achievements include invention of electrophotographic imaging machine and invention of the respirograph employed in medical research. Home: PO Box 614 Gulf Breeze FL 32562-0614 Office: Aerocomm Group Pensacola FL 32502 Personal E-mail: onegoodengineer@aol.com, aerocomm@aol.com.

**MAZZETTI, ROBERT F.,** real estate manager, retired orthopedic surgeon; b. San Francisco, Sept. 29, 1930; children: Mark, Robert Alan, Michelle. BA, U. Calif., San Francisco, 1952, MD, 1955. Diplomate Am. Bd. Orthop. Surgery. Pvt. practice orth. surgeon, Santa Barbara, Calif., 1962-98; owner, pres. Mazat (Real Estate Mgmt. Co.) LLC, 2000—; owner Brushy Creek, Ltd., 1998. Mem.: Abbott Orthopedic Soc. (emeritus), Calif. Orthopedic Assn. (emeritus), Western Orthopedic Assn. (emeritus), Am. Acad. Orthopedic Surgeons (emeritus). Office: 11615 Angus Rd Ste 104 Austin TX 78759-4064 Office Phone: 512-343-1888. Personal E-mail: olmazz@aol.com.

**MAZZILLI, LEE,** professional baseball manager; b. N.Y., Mar. 25, 1955; Baseball player N.Y. Mets, 1976—81, Tex. Rangers, 1982, N.Y. Yankees, 1982, Pitts. (Pa.) Pirates, 1983—86, N.Y. Mets, 1986—89, Toronto (Can.) Blue Jays, 1990; coach Tampa (Fla.) Yankees, 1997—98, Norwich (Conn.) Yankees, 1998—2000; assist. coach N.Y. Yankees, 2000—03; mgr. Balt. (Md.) Orioles, 2004—05; bench coach New York Yankees, 2005—. Named to All Star Game, 1979. Office: New York Yankees 161st St and Rver Bronx NY 10451*

**MAZZIO-MOORE, JOAN L.,** retired radiology educator, physician; b. Belmont, Mass., Oct. 26, 1935; d. Frank Joseph and Maria L. Mazzio; children: James Thomas Moore, Edwin Stuart Moore. BA in Chemistry and Theology, Emmanuel Coll., 1957; MA in Genetics and Physiology, Mass. Wellesley Coll., 1961; PhD in Genetics, Bryn Mawr (Pa.) Coll., 1964; MD, Phila. Coll. Of Medicine, 1977, MSc in Radiology, 1981. Instr. in biochemistry Gwynedd Mercy Coll., Springhouse, Pa., 1963—65; instr. in anatomy Holy Family Coll., Phila., 1965—66; instr. in anatomy Phila. Coll. of Medicine, 1971—77, instr., 1973—77, asst. prof., 1977—84; prof. W.Va. Sch. of Medicine, 1984—2003, ret.; rotating intern Phila. Coll. of Medicine Hosp., 1977—78, resident in radiology and radiation therapy, 1978—81; advanced through grades to lt. col. USAR, 1984—2002; med. dir. 91W transition program U.S. Army Med. Corps Reserves, divsn. surgeon, 80th divsn. (IT) Richmond, Va., ret., 2004. Author (with Dr. DiVirgilito): Essentials of Neuropathology, 1974. Treas. Hist. Soc. of Frankford, Phila., 1968—75, Sch. Mother's Assn., Devon, Pa., 1980—81; vol. mentor. Ct. Appts. Spl. Adv. for Children; parlamentarian Greenbrier Com. on Aging; bd. trustees Lake Erie Coll. Medicine and Pharmacy, Erie, Pa.; organist Ch. of Incarnation, W.Va., St. Charles Borromeo Ch., White Sulphur Springs, W.Va., 2001—; lector St. Ann's Cath. Ch., Phoenixville, Pa., 1981—84. Lt. col. M.C. U.S. Army,

1992—2003. Mem. AAUP, Am. Acad. Family Physicians, Am. Assn. Women Radiologists, Am. Med. Women's Assn., Am. Osteo. Coll. of Radiology (life), Am. Soc. Clin. Oncology, Am. Soc. Therapeutic Readiologists, Hist. Soc. of Lewisburg (life), Pa. Osteo. Med. Assn., Pa. Osteo. Gen. Practitioner's Soc., Radiol. Soc. N.Am., Radiation Rsch. Soc., Res. Officers Assn. (life), W.Va. Soc. Osteo. Medicine, Greenbrier River Hike and Bike Trail. Home: PO Box 97 Frankford WV 24938 Home Fax: 304-497-2752. Personal E-mail: drjoanlmoore@frontiernet.net.

**MAZZO, KAY,** ballet dancer, educator; b. Evanston, Ill., Jan. 17, 1946; d. Frank Alfred and Catherine M. (Hengel) M.; m. Albert C. Bellas, 1978; children: Andrew, Kathryn. Student, Sch. Am. Ballet, 1959-61. Co-chair faculty Sch. Am. Ballet. Profl. debut in ballets U.S.A. 1961, touring Europe with co., performing for Pres. Kennedy at White House, 1961, joined N.Y.C. Ballet, 1962-80, soloist, 1965-69, prin. ballerina, 1969-80, prin. roles in world premiere of ballets including Tschaikowsky Suite No. #3, 1970, PAMTGG, 1971, Stravinsky Violin Concerto, 1972, Scherzo A La Russe, 1972, Duo Concertant, 1972, Sheherazade, 1975, Union Jack, 1976, Vienna Waltzes, 1977, Davidsbundlertanze, 1980; ballet tchr. Sch. Am. Ballet, 1980—; appeared as guest artist in leading roles with numerous cos. including Boston Ballet, Washington Ballet, Berlin Ballet, Geneva Ballet; appeared on TV in U.S., Can., Fed. Republic Germany. Recipient Mademoiselle Merit award 1970 Office: Sch Am Ballet 70 Lincoln Center Plz New York NY 10023-6548

**MAZZOCCO, ANGELO,** language educator, historian, linguist; b. Cerreto di Vastogirardi, Isernia, Italy, May 13, 1936; arrived in U.S.A., 1954; naturalized, 1957; s. Giuseppe and Ida (Rotolo) M.; m. Elizabeth (Hunt-Davis), Oct. 7, 1990; children: Michael Ray, Marco Angelo. BS, BA, Ohio State U., 1959, MA, 1963; PhD in Romance Lang. and Lit., U. Calif., Berkeley, 1973. Instr. Spanish John Carroll U., Cleve., 1962—65; teaching asst. Italian U. Calif., Berkeley, 1966—69; asst. prof. Italian No. Ill. U., DeKalb, 1970—75; asst. prof. Spanish and Italian Mt. Holyoke Coll., South Hadley, Mass., 1975—78, assoc. prof., 1978—83, prof., 1983—2003, emeritus prof., 2003—, chair dept., 1981—84, 1993—96, chair Romance langs. and lits., 1989—93, 1999—2002. Assoc. Columbia U. Renaissance Seminar, 1981-90, 2005; fellow-in-residence Inst. for Advanced Study, Ind. U., Bloomington, 1998; mem. editl. adv. bd. Renaissance Quart.; interviewer NPR, 2000. Author: Linguistic Theories in Dante/Humanists, 1993; contbr. numerous chapters to books, articles and reviews to profl. journals. Travel grantee Am. Coun. Learned Societies, 1985, Gladys Krieble Delmas Found. Rsch. grantee, 1993-94, 96-97; Italian, Am. traveling fellow U. Calif., 1969-70, NEH Italian Humanism summer sem. fellow, 1984, NEH/NSF Award, 1995-98. Mem. MLA (exec. com. Medieval and Renaissance Italian Lit. 1981-85, assembly del. 1985-87), Am. Assn. Teachers Italian, Dante Soc. Am. (coun. assoc. 1985-90, coun. 1994-97), Medieval Acad., Renaissance Soc. Am. (discipline rep. Italian lit., 2000—, mem. nominating com. 2003, 2005, chmn. Nelson Prize com. 2003, mem. Gordan Prize com. 2004), Internat. Assn. Neo-Latin Studies, N.Am. History Lang. Soc., Assn. Internat. Studi di Lingua e Letteratura Italiana, Internat. Soc. Classical Tradition, Am. Boccaccio Assn. (v.p. 1982-83), Am. Assn. Italian Studies, Nat. Assn. Scholars, Nat. Ital. Am. Found. Office: Mt Holyoke Coll Dept Spanish and Italian South Hadley MA 01075 Business E-Mail: amazzocc@mtholyoke.edu.

**MAZZOLA, ANTHONY THOMAS,** editor, graphics designer, consultant; b. Passaic, N.J., June 13, 1923; s. Thomas and Jennie (Failla) M.; m. Michele Morgan, Nov. 18, 1967; children: Anthony Thomas II, Marc Eden, Alisa Morgan. Grad., Cooper Union Art Sch., N.Y.C., 1948. Art dir. Street & Smith Publs., N.Y.C., 1948, Town and Country mag. (pub. by Hearst Corp.), N.Y.C., 1948-65, editor-in-chief, 1965-72, Harpers Bazaar, 1972-92; editor-in-chief, pres. Anthony Mazzola Design Corp., N.Y.C., 1963—; creative cons. Hearst Corp., 1992—. Editl. dir. 125 Great Moments of Harper's Bazaar, 1991—94, Town & Country 150th Anniversary, 1994—; curator fine arts Hearst Corp., 2001—; cons. designer UN Childrens' Fund, Assn. Jr. Leagues Am., Columbia Pictures Corp., Sells Spltys., Gen. Foods, Paramount Pictures, Princess Marcella Borghese, Inc., Huntington Hartford Ltd., NY World's Fair, 1965 Exhibited, Art Dirs. Club NY, ann. exhbns., 1948—. Exhibited, Art Dirs. Club. N.Y., ann. exhbns., 1948—. Served with AUS, 1943-46. Decorated Bronze Star, Knight Officer of Order of Merit Italy; recipient Cert. of Merit awards N.Y. Art Dirs. Club; medal Art Dirs. Club N.Y.C., 1955. Office: Hearst Corp 300 W 57th St New York NY 10019

**MAZZOLA, JOHN WILLIAM,** retired performing company executive, consultant; b. Bayonne, NJ, Jan. 20, 1928; s. Roy Stephen and Eleanor Burton (Davis) M.; m. Sylvia Drulie, Mar. 7, 1959; children: Alison, Amy. AB, Tufts U., 1949; LLD, Fordham U., 1952. Bar: N.Y. 1956. Mem. firm Milbank, Tweed, Hadley & McCloy, N.Y.C., 1952-64; sec., exec. v.p Lincoln Center for Performing Arts, N.Y.C., 1964-68, gen. mgr., chief exec. officer, 1970-77, mng. dir., chief exec. officer, 1970-77, pres., chief exec. officer, 1977-84; exec. v.p Embassy Pictures, 1984—86. Cons. performing arts ctrs. in U.S. and abroad; also motion pictures, non-profit orgns. Bd. dirs. various charitable orgns.; mem. adv. bd. Santa Fe Symphony. With CIC U.S. Army, 1953—55. Decorated cavaliere ufficiale Ordine al Merito della Repubblica Italiana; Ordre des Arts et des Lettres France; Benjamin Franklin fellow Royal Soc. Arts. Mem. Watch Hill Yacht Club, Misquamicut Club (R.I.). Episcopalian. Home: 12 Beekman Pl New York NY 10022-8059 Office Phone: 212-755-5117. Personal E-mail: johnwmazzola@aol.com.

**MAZZOLA, MARIO,** computer company executive; married; 3 children. MSEE, Bologna U., Italy. Co-founder, v.p. engring. David Systems (stands for Distributed Architecture, Voice, Image, and Data), 1982—90; co-founder, pres., CEO Crescendo (acquired by Cisco, renamed the Workgroup Business Unit), 1990—93; v.p. gen. mgr. Workgroup Business Unit, 1993, v.p., gen. mgr. Workgroup Bus. Unit (formerly Crescendo) Cisco Systems, Inc., San Jose, Calif., 1993—97, sr. v.p. new bus. ventures, sr. v.p. Enterprise Line of Bus., 1997—2001, sr. v.p., chief devel. officer, 1998—2005. Achievements include holding several patents on networking related technologies.

**MAZZOLA, MICHAEL,** lighting designer; Resident lighting designer Oreg. Ballet Theatre, 1986—. Lighting designer Bebe Miller Co., N.Y.C. Improvisational Festival. Recipient Bessie Ward award, 2002. Office: 4931 NE 36th Ave Portland OR 97211-7621

**MAZZONE, PETER,** physician; s. Philip and Norma Mazzone; m. Kimberly Paolucci, Sept. 13, 2003. MD, U. of Western Ont., London, Can., 1994. Staff physician Cleve. Clinic Found., 2001—. Office: Cleve Clinic Found 9500 Euclide Ave A90 Cleveland OH 44195 Office Phone: 216-445-4812.

**MAZZOTTA, GIUSEPPE FRANCESCO,** literature and language professor; b. Curinga, Calabria, Italy, Jan. 1, 1942; s. Pasquale and Rosa (Anania) M.; m. Carol Carlson, Mar. 2, 1972; children: Rosanna, Antony, Paula. BA, U. Toronto, Can., 1965, MA, 1966; PhD, Cornell U., 1969. Asst. prof. dept. romance studies Cornell U., Ithaca, NY, 1969-70, assoc. prof. dept. romance studies, 1973-78, prof. romance langs., 1978-83; asst. prof. dept. romance studies Yale U., New Haven, 1970-72, prof. Italian lang. and lit., 1983—; assoc. prof. Medieval Inst. U. Toronto, 1972-73. Author: Dante, Poet of the Desert: History and Allegory in the Divine Comedy, 1979, 2d edit., 1987, The World of Play: A Study of Boccaccio's Decameron, 1986, Dante's Vision and the Circle of Knowledge, 1993, The Worlds of Petrarch, 1993, The New Map of the World: The Poetic Philosophy of G.B. Vico, 1999, Cosmopoiesis: The Renaissance Experiment, 2001; mem. editl. bd. Yale Italian Studies, Dante Studies, Yale Jour. Criticism, Yale Jour. Law and Humanities. NEH Fellow Cornell U., 1977, Guggenheim Found. fellow Yale U., 1986-87. Fellow Am. Coun. Learned Soc., Soc. for the Humanities; mem. Dante Soc. Am. (pres., Silone prize). Roman Catholic. Avocation: basketball. Office: Yale U 82-90 Wall St Fl 4 New Haven CT 06520 Home: 148 Peck Hill Rd Woodbridge CT 06525-1009 Office Phone: 203-432-0595. Business E-Mail: giuseppemazzotta@yale.edu.

**MAZZUCATO, CARLA CARLI,** artist; b. Appiano, Bolzano, Italy, Nov. 2, 1935; came to U.S., 1962; d. Vigilio Gili and Anna (Bella) Carli; m. Giuseppe Mazzucato, June 16, 1962; children: Anna Virginia, Paolo Vigilio, Daniela Maria. BA, Wayne State U., 1983, MFA, 1985. Dir., owner Alpha Art Gallery, Gross Ile, Mich., 1982—90. Docent Detroit Inst. Arts, 1990-98. Author: Paintings and Poems, 1988, New Horizons, 1994, Heimkehr-Homecoming, 2001; Represented in permanent collections Mich. Opera Theatre, Detroit, Ch. Corpus Domini, BZ Italy, Appiano Art Mus., Italy. Trustee Downriver Coun. Arts, Detroit, 1985-90. Avocations: travel, music, gardening. Home: 10102 Kellams Ave Tustin CA 92782-1455 Office Fax: 714-505-1714. Personal E-mail: carla@mazzucato.org.

**MAZZUCELLI, COLETTE GRACE CELIA,** author, educator; b. Bklyn., Nov. 26, 1962; d. Silvio Anthony and Adeline Marie De Ponte. BA, U. Scranton, 1983; MALD in Law and Diplomacy, Fletcher Sch., Tufts U., 1987; PhD, Georgetown U., 1996; post grad., Columbia U., 2003—. Asst. ratification process Treaty European Union German Fgn. Ministry, 1992—93; lectr. U.S. Info. Svc. Spkrs. Program, Europe, 1994; dir. internat. programs and lectr. Budapest Inst. Grad. Internat. and Diplomatic Studies, 1995—97; instr. in-ho. tng. negotiations Hungarian Fgn. Ministry, 1996—97; del. to NATO accession talks Hungarian Ministry Def., 1997; advisor to bd. dirs. Transatlantic Info. Exch. Svc., 1997—98; founding dir., internat. peace and conflict resolution grad. program, asst. prof. polit. sci. Arcadia U., 1998—2000; chair Transatlantic internet multimedia seminar S.E. Europe (TIMSSE) ScPo, Paris, 2000—03; fellow EastWest Inst., 2001; program officer, internat. rep. NGO rep. UN Carnegie Coun. Ethics and Internat. Affairs, 2001—02; program devel. assoc. Tchrs. Coll. Columbia U., 2002—04; faculty John C. Whitehead Sch. Diplomacy and Internat. Rels. Seton Hall U., 2005—06; asst. prof. dept. history and polit. sci. Molloy Coll., Rockville Centre, 2006—. Rsch. fellow Inst. Europaeische Politik, Deutsche Gesellschaft Auswaertige Politik, Bonn, Deutsch-Franzoesisches Inst., Ludwigsburg; instr. Georgetown U., Washington, 1990, 96; adj. asst. prof. MS program global affairs Sch. Continuing and Profl. Studies NYU, 2005—; rsch. fellow Inst. Europaeische Politik Deutsche Gesellschaft Auswaertige Politik. Author: France and Germany at Maastricht Politics and Negotiations to Create the European Union, 1997, paperback 2d edit., 1999; asst. editor: The Evolution of an International Actor: Western Europe's New Assertiveness, 1990; author: Monnet Case Studies in European Affairs, 1995; co-editor: Ethics and Global Politics: The Active Learning Sourcebook, 2004, Leadership in the Big Bangs of European Integration, 2006; contbr.: Dimensions of German Unification, 1994, Redefining European Security, 1999, United Nations Chronicle, 2001, 40th Anniversary vol. commemorating Treaty of Friendship between France and Germany, 2005; contbr. articles to profl. jours. Mem. founding cabinet World Peace and Diplomacy Forum, 2003—. Grantee Swiss U., 1984-85, Profl. Devel. grant NYU, 2006; scholar Pi Gamma Mu, 1985, Rotary grad. scholar, 1987-88, Fulbright scholar, 1991; fellow Jean Monnet Coun., 1991, European Commn., 1992, Robert Bosch Found., 1992-93, Salzburg Seminar, 1997, 21st Century Trust fellow Merton Coll., Oxford (Eng.) U., 2001, Bosch Pub. Policy fellow Am. Acad., Berlin, Aspen Inst., Berlin, 2001; Da Vinci Laureate, 2004; named Internat. Educator of Yr., 2003, Pirate of Yr., 2006; recipient citation Nat. Women's Conf., 2006. Mem.: AAUW, Phi Alpha Theta, Fgn. Policy Assn., Robert Bosch Found. Alumni Assn. (mem. exec. com. 1994—96, 1997—98, co-pres. 1999—2000), European Union Studies Assn., Am. Coun. Germany, Am. Assn. Advancement Slavic Studies, Am. Polit. Sci. Assn., Rotary Club Metro N.Y., The Fletcher Club of N.Y. (v.p. 1998), Delta Tau Kappa, Alpha Mu Gamma, Pi Sigma Alpha, Phi Sigma Tau (founder Scranton chpt.), Pi Gamma Mu (chpt. sec. 1982—84, Frank C. Brown scholarship medal 1984), Alpha Sigma Nu (student pres. 1984). Avocations: chess, swimming, creative writing, astrology, Tae Kwon Do. Home: 1864 74th St Brooklyn NY 11204-5752 Office: Molloy Coll PO Box 5002 1000 Hempstead Ave Rockville Centre NY 11571 Office Phone: 646-372-4396. Business E-Mail: cgm7@nyu.edu, cmazzucelli@molloy.edu.

**MBADUGHA, LORETTA NKEIRUKA AKOSA,** social services administrator, consultant; b. Onitsha, Anambara, Nigeria, Dec. 10, 1957; d. James and Sylvia O. (Asika) Akosa; m. Christian Mbadugha; children: Kristen Ogechi, Kyle Kelechi, Kelsey Odinaka. Assoc., Langham Secretarial Coll., London, 1978; BS, Tex. So. U., Houston, 1981, MS, 1982; PhD, U. New Orleans, 2000, PhD in Higher Edn. Adminstrn., 2001. Program analyst Tex. So. U., Houston, 1982-84; sanitarian City of Houston Health Dept., 1984-85; adj. faculty So. U., New Orleans, 1981-90; asst. to exec. dir. YWCA, New Orleans, 1984-93; family rep. Jefferson Parish Human Svcs. Authority, New Orleans, 1993—2001; CEO Profl. Family Support Svcs., New Orleans, 1994—. Cons., founder, bd. mem. Camelot Providers, New Orleans, 1987—; bd. mem. United Svcs. AIDS Found., 1990-92; trainer Coun. for Early Childhood Profl. Recognition, 1987—; cons., trainer on child devel. State of La., 1987-89; exec. dir. Gilbert Acad.; asst. prof. edn. Dillard U. Sec. Chapel of Praise, 1997. Recipient Mayoral Cert. of Merit, New Orleans, 1991; Grace Hodge fellow YWCA, 1992. Mem. ACA, Nigeria Ebony Club for Women (pres. 1995). Office: 7041 Real Ln New Orleans LA 70127

**MBANEFO, ARTHUR CHRISTOPHER IZUEGBUNAN,** diplomat; b. Onitsha, Nigeria, June 11, 1930; With Chater, Knight & Co., Brighton, England, 1955—61, Coopers & Lybrand, London, 1961—65, Lybrand, Ross Bros. & Montgomery, Detroit, 1965—66, Price Waterhouse & Co., London, 1970—71; ptnr. Akintola Williams & Co., Lagos, Nigeria, 1962—99; amb. from Nigeria UN, N.Y.C., NY, 1999—. Fellow: Inst. Chartered Accts. England, Inst. Chartered Accts. Nigeria; mem.: Nigerian Assn. Mgmt. Cons. (coun. 1976—86, pres. 1986—89), Assn. Accountancy Bodies (coun. 1983—91, pres. 1987). Office: NY Permanent Mission 828 2d Ave New York NY 10017

**MCABEE, SONJA LOUISE,** library administrator; b. Anniston, Ala., Mar. 17, 1955; d. Ralph J. and Thelma Louise Sherman; m. Kenneth Blair McAbee, July 15, 1978; children: Megan Elizabeth, Patrick Ryan. BA in Polit. Sci. Jacksonville State U., 1975; MLS, U. Ala., 1988. Acquisitions libr. Jacksonville (Ala.) State U., 1990-96, head libr. svcs., 1996—. Contbr. articles to profl. jours. Mem. Ala. Libr. Assn. Democrat. Avocations: gardening, reading, home improvement projects. Home: 1837 Noah Valley Rd Jacksonville AL 36265 Office: Jacksonville State U 700 Pelham Rd North Jacksonville AL 36265 Office Phone: 256-782-5757. Office Fax: 256-782-5872. Business E-Mail: smcabee@jsu.edu.

**MCABEE, THOMAS ALLEN,** psychologist; b. Spartanburg, S.C., Mar. 31, 1949; s. Thomas Walker and Doris Lee (Gillespie) McA. Student, Ga. Inst. Tech., 1967-69; BA, Furman U., 1971; MA, U.S.C., 1975, PhD, 1979. Clin. counselor Adolescent Svc. William S. Hall Psychiat. Inst., Columbia, S.C., 1971-73; counselor children's therapeutic camp Columbia Area Mental Health Ctr., 1974; co-dir. cmty. problems survey Eau Claire Cmty. Project, Columbia, 1975; asst. aging svcs. planner Ctrl. Midlands Regional Planning Coun., Columbia, 1976; instr. U.S.C., 1976; NSF intern S.C. State Legislature, 1978; rsch. dir. S.C. Legis. Gov.'s Com. Mental Health and Mental Retardation, Columbia, 1979-80; co-dir. TV project "Feelings Just Are" Columbia Area Mental Health Ctr., 1980-89; psychologist S.C. Dept. Mental Retardation, 1982-93, S.C. Dept. Disabilities and Spl. Needs, 1993—2003, S.C. Vocat. Rehab. Dept., 2004—. Cons. S.C. Protection and Advocacy System for Handicapped Citizens, 1980, 81, S.C. Dept. Mental Health, 1981; mem. deinstitutionalization task force S.C. Developmental Disabilities Coun., 1979-80; mem. subcom. State Commr.'s Ad Hoc Com. to Study and Develop Work/Lodge System for S.C., S.C. Dept. Mental Health, 1979-80; mem. Media Task Force of Gov.'s Adv. Com. on Early Childhood Devel. and Edn., 1980-81; chmn. primary prevention public media com. S.C. Dept. Mental Health, 1979-81; adj. faculty U. S.C., Spartanburg, 2003. Recipient Palmetto Pictures Photography award, 1977; NIMH fellow, 1976-77. Mem. APA, S.C. Psychol. Assn. Home: 310 Snow St Greer SC 29651-4006 Office Phone: 864-585-3693. Business E-Mail: tmcabee@scvrd.state.sc.us.

**MCADAM, PAUL EDWARD,** retired library administrator; b. Balt., Jan. 30, 1934; s. Joseph Francis Jr. and Irene Cecile (Heineck) McA. BA in Romance Langs., Johns Hopkins U., Balt., 1955, MA, 1956; MLS, Drexel U., Phila., 1970. Libr. Free Libr. Phila., 1969-81; br. mgr. Phila. City. Inst. Libr., 1974-81; dir. Am. Libr., Paris, 1981-85; libr. collection devel., libr. tech. svcs. Catonsville C.C., Md., 1986-89; assoc. v.p. learning resources Carroll C.C., Westminster, Md., 1989-99, assoc. v.p. emeritus, 1999—; adj. libr. C.C. of Baltimore County, Catonsville, Md., 1999—2002, instr. continuing edn., 2003—04; adj. libr. Balt. Internat. Coll., 2000—; rschr. Transform, Inc., Columbia, Md., 2003—04. Mem. adv. bd. Coop. Librs. Ctrl. Md., Annapolis, 1992-96, State Libr. Resource Ctr., Balt., 1994-95; bd. dirs. Renew, 1995-2003; del. Internat. Fedn. Libr. Assn., 1993, 95. Vol. MPT, 1989-2000, Walters Art Mus., 1991—, Md. Fine Arts Festival, 1991-97 AIRS, 1999-2005, Drexel U., 2002—, Johns Hopkins U., 2004-05. 1st lt. U.S. Army, 1956-58. Mem. ALA (membership com. 1996-98), Coll. Air Consortium, Congress Acad. Libr. Dirs. (treas. 1998-2000), Md. Libr. Assn. (hon. mem., chair 1993-96 awards chair 1996-97, 1999-2000, treas. 1997-99, chair fundraising task force 2001-02), Consortium Md. C.C. Libr. Dirs. (treas. 1998-2000), Beta Phi Mu. Democrat. Home: 524 Academy Rd Baltimore MD 21228-1814 Personal E-mail: PaulMcAd@aol.com.

**MCADAM, WILL,** electronics executive, consultant; b. Wheeling, W.Va., Oct. 22, 1921; s. Will and Elizabeth Margaret (Wickham) McA.; m. Evelyn Virginia Warren, Sept. 12, 1945; children: Elizabeth Ruth, Margaret Evelyn. BSEE, Case Sch. Applied Sci., 1942; MSEE, U. Pa., 1959. Rsch. technologist Leeds & Northrup Co., Phila., 1945-57, head elec. sect. R&D dept. North Wales, Pa., 1957-68, assoc. dir. rsch. ops., 1968-76, mgr. devel. and engring. adv. devel., 1977-79, prin. scientist rsch. dept., 1979-82, ret., 1982; cons. in electronics, 1982—. Contbr. articles to profl. jours., chpts. to handbooks; 30 patents in field. 1st lt. AUS, 1942-45, ETO. Decorated Bronze Star. Fellow IEEE (life, chmn. subcom. on elec. and high frequency measurements 1957-59, com. indsl. electronic and control instruments 1961-65, Prize Paper award 1958), Eta Kappa Nu, Tau Beta Pi. Republican. Presbyterian. Avocations: amateur radio, woodworking/cabinetmaking. Home: 3321 Twin Silo Dr Blue Bell PA 19422

**MCADAMS, FRANK JOSEPH, III,** communications educator; b. Chgo., Nov. 18, 1940; s. Frank Joseph Jr. and Mary Irene (Geary) McA.; m. Patty Ann Rafferty, Dec. 27, 1966. BS, Loyola U., Chgo., 1967; MFA, UCLA, 1979. Instr. UCLA, 1981—, U. Calif., Irvine, 1989—. Adj. prof. Sch. of Cinema, U. So. Calif., L.A., 1991—; mem. judging panel Diane Thomas Awards, UCLA, 1986—; vis. lectr. screenplay structure U. Navarra, Pamplona, Spain, 1990; vis. lectr. Southampton Coll., L.I. U., 1997; mem. screenwriting adv. bd. U. Calif.-Irvine Extension, 1995—. Screenwriter California Rain, 1978, Stagecoach Bravo, 1979; author: The American War Film: History and Hollywood, 2002; co-author: Final Affair, 2002. Capt. USMC, 1966—72. Decorated Armed Forces Expeditionary medal (Laos), Vietnam Svc. medal, Rep. of Vietnam Campaign medal, Navy-Marine Corps medal, Navy Comm. medal with combat V, Presdl. Unit citation, Navy Unit citation, Meritorius Unit commendation; recipient award for best newspaper col. Orange County Press Club, 1974, HM for Best Series, 1974, Sam Goldwyn Screenwriting award Sam Goldwyn Found., 1978, 79. Mem. 1st Marine Divsn. Assn., VFW, Writers Guild Am. West, UCLA Theater Arts Alumni Assn., PEN Ctr. USA West. Democrat. Roman Catholic. Office: MAGLA PO Box 1511 Hollywood CA 90078-1511 Office Phone: 818-244-2144. Business E-Mail: rushact@cox.net.

**MCADAMS, JOHN POPE,** lawyer; b. Phila., June 5, 1949; s. Eugene P. and Mary (Miller) McA.; m. Anne Christina Connelly, Sept. 5, 1970; children: Emily Lane, Anne Connelly. BA, U. N.C., 1971; JD, Wake Forest U., 1976. Bar: Fla. 1976, N.C. 1976, U.S. Dist. Ct. (mid. dist.) Fla. 1977. Assoc. Carlton Fields, Tampa, Fla., 1976-82, ptnr., 1982—. Contbg. editor: The Developing Labor Law, 1983, Employee Duty of Loyalty, 1995; contbr. articles to profl. jours. Pres. Hillsborough Cmty. Mental Health Ctr., Tampa, 1983; trustee City of Temple Terrace (Fla.) Pension Plan, 1985-89; pres. Hyde Park Preservation, Inc., Tampa, 1993; bd. dirs., pres. Child Abuse Coun., Inc., Tampa Lighthouse for the Blind. Mem. ABA, ABA Equal Rights & Responsibilities Com., Fla. Bar Assn. (exec. coun. labor sect. 1987-89). Republican. Episcopalian. Home: 820 S Delaware Ave Tampa FL 33606-2915 Office: Carlton Fields PO Box 3239 Tampa FL 33601-3239 Office Phone: 813-223-7000. Business E-Mail: jmcadams@carltonfields.com.

**MCADAMS, MELINDA JEANNE,** copy editor; b. York, Pa., July 23, 1959; d. William Arthur and Jeanne Elaine (Sipe) McAdams. BA in Journalism, Pa. State U., 1981; MA in Media Studies, New Sch. Social Research, NYC, 1993. Copy editor Dell Pub. Co., Inc., N.Y.C., 1982-84, MIS Week, Fairchild Publs., N.Y.C., 1984-88; copy chief, 1987-88; copy editor Time Mag./Time Warner Inc., N.Y.C., 1988-93; freelance producer Prodigy Svcs. Co., White Plains, N.Y., 1991-92; copy editor The Washington Post, Washington, 1993-94, content developer Digital Ink, Co., 1994—. Pres. assoc. Am. Go Assn., N.Y.C., 1987-91; lectr. NYU, N.Y.C., 1992-93. Vol. Big sister, Big Sisters Inc., N.Y.C., 1984-85; tutor vol. Sch. Vol. Program N.Y.C., 1990-91. Mem. Soc. Profl. Journalists (new techs. com.). Democrat. Avocation: go (wei-chi). Address: 121 Dublin St N Apt A Guelph ON Canada N1H 4N8 Office: The Washington Post Digital Ink Co 1150 15th St NW Washington DC 20071-0002

**MCADAMS, RACHEL,** actress; b. London, Ont., Can., Oct. 7, 1976; d. Lance and Sandy McAdams. BFA with honors, NYU. Actor: (films) My Name is Tanino, 2002, Perfect Pie, 2002, The Hot Chick, 2002, Mean Girls, 2004, The Notebook, 2004, Wedding Crashers, 2005, Red-Eye, 2005, The Family Stone, 2005; (TV films) Guilt by Association, 2002; (TV series) Shotgun Love Dolls, 2001, Slings and Arrows, 2003. Named Choice Movie Actress: Comedy, Teen Choice awards, 2006. Office: The Gersh Agy 232 N Canon Dr Beverly Hills CA 90210 Office Phone: 310-274-6611.

**MCADARAGH, RAYMON MICHAEL,** aerospace engineer, researcher; b. Springfield, Ohio, Feb. 19, 1951; s. Bernard E. and Joan Patricia McAdaragh; m. Carol Ann Reese, Jan. 23, 1988; children: Jeffrey, Eric; 1 child from previous marriage, Sandra. BS, Christopher New Port U., 1980; BS in Aerospace Tech., Thomas A. Edison State Coll., 1990; M in Aerospace, Embry/Riddle Aero. U., 1994; PhD, U. Fla., 1999. Electrician Newport News (Va.) Ship Bldg. Co., 1974—78; wastewater treatment plant operator Hampton Rds. Sanitation Dist., Williamsburg, Va., 1980, lab. technician, 1981; air traffic control specialist FAA, Williamsport, Pa., 1982—88, Gainesville, Fla., 1988—99, aero. engring. rsch. psychologist Hampton, Va., 1999—. Cons., rschr. NASA, Hampton, 1999—2004; initiator, dir. human factors rsch. coordination NASA/FAA, Hampton, 2002—04, mem. weather tech. integration team, Washington, 2005—, mem. vision team, 2005. Writer, musician, singer: albums Midnight on the Water, 2001, East Virginia Bound, 2001, New World Destiny, 2005. Vol. curriculum devel. team Paquoson (Va.) Sch. Bd. 2001. With U.S. Army, 1969—74. Recipient 1st degree black belt, Shorin-Ken Karate, brown belt, Shorin-Ryu Karate, orange belt, Judo, Outstanding Contbns. to Aviation Weather Info. Rsch. NASA, 2002, Avaiation Safety Program award, 2004. Mem.: Tidewater Human Factors and Ergonomic Soc., Aerospace Human Factors Assn., Aerospace Med. Assn., Theosophical Soc. Am., Masons (3d degree, 32d degree Scottish Rite). Avocations: fishing, boating. Home: 40 Lodge Rd Poquoson VA 23662 Office: FAA NASA Langley Rsch Ctr Hampton VA 23681 Office Phone: 757-864-1941. Business E-Mail: raymon.mcadaragh@nasa.gov.

**MCAFEE, DIANA MAE,** media specialist, music educator; b. Charlestown, Ind., Oct. 24, 1951; d. Robert E. and Dorothy N. Williams; m. John J. McAfee, May 27, 1972; children: Michelle Renee McAfee Logan, Jennifer Melynne. B in Music Edn., Evangel U., Springfield, Mo., 1973; MusM, Pittsburg State U., Kans., 1977. Libr. cert. Mo. Piano instr. Evangel U., Springfield, 1971—73; piano tchr., judge Nat. Piano Guild, Carthage, Mo., 1975—; tchr. Carthage R-9 Schs., 1986—94, libr. media coord., 1995—99, libr. media specialist, 1999—. Adj. prof. Crowder Coll., Neosho, Mo., 1995—97; chairperson Career Ladder Carthage Schs., 2003—05. Choir dir.

1st Assembly God, Carthage, 1974—94. Mem.: Mo. Assn. Sch. Librs., Mo. State Tchrs. Assn. Avocations: travel, reading, movies. Home: 17184 Hawthorne Rd Carthage MO 64836 Office: Fairview Elem Sch 1201 E Fairview Carthage MO 64836 Business E-Mail: mcafeed@carthage.k12.mo.us.

**MCAFEE, LARRY W.**, chemistry educator; b. Oklahoma City, Okla., Oct. 20, 1946; s. Mv and Margaret McAfee; m. Donna Sigwart, Aug. 7, 1971; children: Joy Kiser, Hope Morgan. BA, U. N.C., Charlotte, 1965—69, MA, 1975—80. Chemistry tchr. South Cobb HS, Austell, Ga., 1969—71; sci. tchr. Coulwood Jr. HS, Charlotte, NC, 1971—74; chemistry tchr. East Mecklenburg HS, Charlotte, 1974—. Cross country/track coach South Cobb HS, 1969—71; track coach Coulwood Jr. HS, 1971—74; cross country/track coach East Mecklenburg HS, 1974—2003. State meet dir., cross country N.C. HS Athletic Assn., Charlotte, 1980—2001, state meet dir., indoor track Chapel Hill, 1990—2000; asst. regional coord. Foot Locker Cross Country Championships, Charlotte, 1982—2006; asst. coord. Foot Locker Nat. Cross Country Championships, San Diego, Calif., 1982—2006. Recipient County Achievement award, Nat. Assn. Counties, Wash. D.C., 1981, Outstanding Achievement, N.C. HS Athletic Assn., 1992, N.C. Chemistry Tchr. of Yr., Ciba Chem., N.C. State U., 1993, Star Tchr. award, Time-Warner, 1991, Oustanding Svc., N.C. HS Athletic Assn., 1999, Track Coach of Yr., 2000, Merit award, Foot Locker Cross Country Championships, 2005; grantee Summer Tchr. Rsch. Program, Hoechst Celanese, 1992, Sandoz Chem., 1994. Mem.: State Employees Assn. N.C. Avocations: photography, travel. Office: E Mecklenburg HS 6800 Monroe Rd Charlotte NC 28212 Office Phone: 980-343-6430.

**MC AFEE, MARGARET ANNE**, retired art educator; b. Denver, May 14, 1929; d. Abe I. and Anne M. Blomquist; m. George Lafayette Finn McAfee, July 22, 1972. AA, UCLA, 1947, BA, 1951; MA in Edn., Calif. State Coll. 1967. Cert. tchr. Calif. State Bd. Of Edn., 1955. Tng. tchr. UCLA, USC & Mt. St. Mary's Coll., 1955—66; art tchr. and dept. chmn. Hamilton Sr. HS, LA, 1952—69; tchr. and prof. of art emeritus LA (Calif.) C.C. Dist., 1969—89; assoc. tchr. art Saddleback C.C., Mission Viejo, Calif., 1990—2003. Cons. in field. Dir.: (TV series) How to Design, Make and Use Mosaic Projects In and Around the Home, 1961—66; contbr. articles to newspapers. Troop leader Girl Scouts Am., LA, 1949—50. Mem.: AAUW, Assn. Ret. Tchrs., The Enamelist Soc., Am. Fedn. Tchrs. Emeritus, Nat. Art Edn. Assn., Calif. Art Edn. Assn., Calif. Tchr.'s Assn., Phi Kappa Phi (hon.), Pi Lambda Theta (hon.). Avocations: gardening, drawing, cooking, reading, travel. Home: 27826 Torroba Mission Viejo CA 92692-2131 Personal E-mail: mgmcafee@cox.net.

**MCAFEE, NOELLE CLAIRE**, philosopher, educator; b. Tagiura, Libya, Nov. 25, 1960; d. Horatio Paul and Marika Chaniotakis McAfee; m. David G Armstrong, Aug. 8, 1992; children: Guthrie McAfee Armstrong, Eliza Dorothy Armstrong. BA in hist., U. of Tex. at Austin, 1986; MA in pub. policy, Duke U., 1987; MA in Philosophy, U. of Wis. at Madison, 1990; PhD, U. of Tex. at Austin, 1998. Lectr. in polit. theory U. Tex., Dept. of Govt., 1998—99; asst. prof. philosophy U. Mass., 1999—2003, assoc. prof. philosophy, 2003—. Dir. honors program U. Mass., 2004—; vis. prof. philosophy Brandeis U., Waltham, Mass., 2004. Assoc. editor Kettering Review, 1991—; author; Julia Kristeva, 2003, Habermas, Kristeva and Citizenship, 2000; editor: Standing with the Public, 1997; contbr. chapters to books, articles to profl. jours. Office: Dept of Philosophy, U Mass Lowell One University Ave Lowell MA 01854 Office Phone: 978-934-3912.

**MC AFEE, WILLIAM**, government official; b. Port Royal, Jan. 25, 1910; s. French and Willietta (Anderson) McA. BA, Coll. of Wooster, 1932; MA in Am. History, Pa. State U., 1941; student, Oxford, Eng., summer 1937. Wooster in India rep. on faculty Ewing Christian Coll., Allahabad, India, 1932-35; tchr. pub. high schs. and prep. sch. Pa., 1935-42; joined State Dept., 1946; country specialist (Office Chinese Affairs), 1946-50; coordinator current intelligence (Bur. Intelligence and Research), 1950-56, spl. asst. to dir., 1956-60, dir. ops. staff, 1960-66, asst. dep. dir. coordination, 1966-72, dep. dir. coordination, 1972-80, dep. asst. sec. intelligence coordination, 1980—; dir. (Office of Intelligence Liaison), 1981-86, ret. Adviser Griffin Econ. Aid Mission to S.E. Asia, 1950 Served to lt. col. AUS, 1942-46, CBI. Decorated Legion of Merit; Order Brit. Empire; Precious Tripod Chinese Nationalist Govt.; recipient Superior Honor award State Dept., 1964, Disting. Honor award, 1980 Mem. Am. Fgn. Service Assn., Delta Sigma Rho. Home: 4433 Brandywine St NW Washington DC 20016-4419

**MCALEESE, ALICE S.**, music educator; b. East Patchogue, N.Y., Apr. 23, 1960; d. Bernhard A. and Ilse A. Behnke; m. Sam W. McAleese; children: Kenneth, Kyle, Kane. AS, Suffolk C.C., Belden, N.Y., 1981; BA, St. Joseph's Coll., Patchogue, N.Y., 1984; MA, SUNY, Stony Brook, 1989. Cert. elem. edn., music K-12 tchr. N.Y. Elem tchr. Patchogue-Medford Sch. Dist., NY, 1984—85; tchr. music South Country Sch. Dist., Bellport, NY, 1985. Choir dir. Emanuel Luth. Ch., Patchogue, NY, 1979—90, Sayville Meth. Ch., NY, 1979—90; profl. voice Periphonica Corp., Bohemia, NY, 1980—93; dir. South Country Singers, Bellport, NY, 1986—. Dir., vocal dir., prodr.: musicals Mid. Sch., 1986—. Mem.: Am. Choral Dirs. Assn., Suffolk County Music Educators Assn. Lutheran. Home: 84 S Dunton Ave East Patchogue NY 11772 Office: South Country Ctrl Sch Dist Dunton Ave East Patchogue NY 11772 Office Phone: 631-730-1626. E-mail: mc5clan@optonline.net.

**MCALEESE DUBE, EILEEN MARIE**, retired secondary school educator; b. May 23, 1937; d. Patrick Leo and Hazel May (Dishon) McAleese; m. Darrell Eugene Dube, Sept. 17, 1960; 1 child, Brent Alexander. BA English, U. Akron, 1959. Tchr. Buchtel H.S. Akron Pub. Schs., Ohio, 1959—60, tchr. Ctrl.-Hower H.S., 1965—73; tchr. sr. advanced placement English East H.S., 1973—94; ret., 1994. Advisor Yr. Book East H.S., 1973—88. Contbr. Scholar, Jennings Found., 1982—83. Mem.: Ohio Coun. Tchrs. Eng. and Lang. Arts, Akron Edn. Assn., Greater Akron Tchrs. Eng., Nat. Coun.Tchrs. Eng., Ancient Order Hibernians Am., Friends Children's Hosp., Akron Fraternal Order Police Aux., Fairlawn City Women's Club, Phi Mu. Republican. Roman Catholic.

**MCALISTER, MICHAEL H.**, architect; b. Calif. s. Doyle R. and Mary E. McAlister. AA, Bakersfield Coll.; BArch, Calif. Poly. U. Planning technician Bakersfield (Calif.) City Hall, 1963; carpenter Del Webb Corp., Kern City, Calif., 1964; archtl. draftsman Goss & Choy Archs., Bakersfield, 1965-67; arch., v.p. D.G.C. & Assocs., Bakersfield, 1971-80; dir. architecture, v.p. N.B.A. & Assocs., Archs., Bakersfield, 1980-83; arch. Michael H. McAlister, A.I.A., Bakersfield, 1983—. Nephrology design cons. for various treatment groups and hosps., 1987—. Commr., archtl. advisor Hist. Preservation Commn., Bakersfield, 1986-87; bd. dirs. Camp Fire Coun., Kern County, Calif., 1980-84 Recipient Archtl. Pub. Bldg. Hist. award Beautiful Bakersfield Com., City of Bakersfield's City Coun. and Hist. Preservation Commn., 1985, 87, Exterior Environ. Design Excellence Bakersfield C. of C., 1988, Comml. Design Excellence award, 1984, Design Excellence and Beautification award City of Taft, Calif., 1989, Design Excellence award State of Nev., 1992, Beautiful Bakersfield Archtl. Comml. Remodel award, 2003 Mem. AIA (Calif. Coun., Golden Empire chpt.). Avocation: religious architecture and art. Office: 1302 Ironstone Dr Studio 201 Bakersfield Ca 93312-4668

**MCALISTER, SHEILA ANNE**, archivist; b. Belfast, Ireland, Oct. 24, 1969; d. Donald Beaton McAlister and Regina Ross; m. James Payne, Oct. 28, 2000. BS in French, Georgetown U., 1991; MA in Medieval Byzantine Studies, Cath. U. Am., 1995; MLIS, U. S.C., 2005. Electronic access coord. Richard B. Russell Libr. for Polit. Rsch. and Studies, U. Ga., Athens, 1999—2001; project mgr., digital metadata coord. Digital Libr. Ga., U. Ga. Libr., Athens, 2001—. Mem.: Acad. Cert. Archivists (cert.), Soc. Ga. Archivists (pres. 2004—05), Soc. Am. Archivists (chair preservation sect. 2004—05). Home: 380 Boulevard Athens GA 30601 Office: Univ Ga Libr Digital Libr Ga Athens GA 30602-1641 Office Phone: 706-542-5418. Office Fax: 706-542-4144. Business E-Mail: mcalists@uga.edu.

**MCALLISTER, BRUCE RICHARD**, art educator; b. Stanford, Calif., Feb. 25, 1964; s. Mark Marion McAllister and Ruth Cannon Lee; m. Katherine Reed, Apr. 10, 1993; children: Cameron Dale, Eric Reed. BFA, U. Calif., Irvine, 1989; MFA, Calif. Coll. of the Arts, 1993—95. Art instr. Pacific Art League, Palo Alto, Calif., 1991; adj. art instr. City Coll. of San Francisco, 1998; art instr. Antelope Valley Coll., Lancaster, Calif., 2000—, LA Pierce Coll., Woodland Hills, Calif., 2001—; adj. art instr. Glendale C.C., Calif., 2003—; art instr. Moorpark Coll., Calif., 2004—. Muralist, prop designer, builder Ahrens Studios, Novato, Calif., 1995—97, Club Ed, Lancaster, 1999—2002; creator storyboard for film The Big E Oaf Prodns., Glendale, Calif., 1999; web site developer Strategic Internet Sollutions, Lancaster, 1999—2001, bkmdesign.com, Quartz Hill, Calif., 2001—; juror Antelope Valley Union HS Dist. Art Show, Lancaster City Gallery and Mus., 2001. One-man shows include Pamela Skinner Gallery, Sacramento, 2004, 2005 (Critic's Pick, Sacramento Bee, 2005), 2006, B. Sakata Garo Gallery, Sacramento, 2004 (Critic's Pick, Sacramento Bee, 2004), exhibited in group shows at Fed. Bldg. Towers, Oakland, Calif., 1994, Palo Alto Cmty. Ctr., 1995, Andrea Schwartz Gallery, San Francisco, 1995, Weintraub Thomas Gallery, Sacramento, 1997, Lancaster (Calif.) City Gallery and Mus., 2001, Julie Baker Fine Art Gallery, Grass Valley, Calif., 2003—04, O'Hanlon Ctr., Calif., 2004, Solaris Gallery, West Hollywood, Calif., 2005, Pierce Coll., Woodland Hills, Calif., 2005, contemporaryquarterly.com, 2006, Roshambo Winery Gallery, Healdsburg, Calif., 2006, Pamela Skinner Gallery, 2006, represented in numerous pvt. collections. Recipient Gold Key Nat. Honor Soc., U. of Calif. at Irvine, 1988. Home: 4776 West Ave L-12 Quartz Hill CA 93536 Office Phone: 661-722-3060. Personal E-mail: bruce@brucemcallister.com.

**MC ALLISTER, GERALD NICHOLAS**, retired bishop, minister; b. San Antonio, Feb. 23, 1923; s. Walter Williams and Leonora Elizabeth (Alexander) McA.; m. Helen Earle Black, Oct. 2, 1953; children— Michael Lee, David Alexander, Stephen Williams, Elizabeth. Student, U. Tex., 1939-42, Va. Theol. Sem., 1948-51, DD (hon.), 1977. Ordained to ministry Episcopal Ch. as deacon, 1953, as priest, 1954. Rancher, 1946-48; deacon, priest Ch. of Epiphany, Raymondville, Ch. of Incarnation, Corpus Christi, St. Francis Ch., Victoria, Tex., 1951-63; 1st canon Diocese of West Tex., 1963-70; rector St. David's Ch., San Antonio, 1970-76; consecreated Episcopal bishop of Okla., Oklahoma City, 1977-89, ret., 1989; bishop-in-residence Episcopal Theol. Sem., Austin, Tex., 1990-93. Trustee Episcopal Theol. Sem. of S.W., 1961-2000, adv. bd., 1974—; mem. Cause Commn. Bd. for Theol. Edn., 1981-82; pres. Tex. Council Chs., 1966-68, Okla. Conf. Chs., 1980-83; bd. dirs. Presiding Bishop's Fund for World Relief, 1972-77, Ch. Hist. Soc., 1976—; chmn. Nat. and World Mission Program Group, 1973-76; mem. Structure of Ch. Standing Commn., 1979, mem. standing com. on Stewardship/Devel., 1979-85; founder Chaplaincy Program, Bexar County Jail, 1968; mem. governing bd. nat. council Ch. of Christ, 1982-85; chmn. standing commn. on stewardship Episcopal Ch., 1983-85; v.p., trustee The Episc., Episc. Theol. Sem. of Southwest, 1987-93, chmn. bd. trustees, 1993-97. Author: What We Learned from What You Said, 1973, This Fragile Earth Our Island Home, 1980. Bd. dirs. Econ. Opportunity Devel. Corp., San Antonio, 1968-69; mem. exec. com. United Way, 1968-70, vice-chmn., 1970. With U.S. Mcht. Marines, 1942; to 1st lt. USAAF, 1942-45. Recipient Agudas Achim Brotherhood award, 1968. Mem.: Alumni Coun. Va. Theol. Sem. Episcopalian. Address: 507 Bluffestates San Antonio TX 78216-7930

**MCALLISTER, KENNETH WAYNE**, lawyer; b. High Point, N.C., Jan. 3, 1949; s. John Calhoun and Ruth Welch (Buie) McA.; children: Katherine Owen, Kenneth Grey. BA, U. N.C., 1971; JD, Duke U., 1974. Bar: N.C. 1974, U.S. Dist. Ct. for Middle dist. N.C. 1974, U.S. Ct. Appeals for 4th circuit 1980, U.S. Supreme Ct. 1980. Ptnr. Fisher, Fisher & McAllister, High Point, 1974—81; U.S. atty. (middle dist.) N.C. U.S. Dept. Justice, Greensboro, 1981—86; sr. exec. v.p., gen. counsel Wachovia Corp., Winston-Salem, NC, 1988—2001; mem. McAllister & Hanks PLLC. Bd. dirs, Culp Inc., 2002-; bd. visitors Wake Forest U. Sch. of Law, 1988-96, U. N.C. at Chapel Hill, 1989-93, Duke U. Law Sch., 1996—; bd. advisors, U. N.C.Sch. Law Banking Inst., 1998-2002. Pres. High Point Drug Action Coun., 1977-78; chmn. High Point Rep.Com., 1976-78, 88-89; mem. adv. bd. Salvation Army, High Point, 197-79; bd. dirs. Sch. of Nursing Found., U. N.C., Chapel Hill, 1993-99; vice chair Attys. Gen. Adv. Com. U. S Atty., 1985-86; govs. commn. Bus. Laws and the Economy, 1994—; bd. govs. Presbyn. Homes, 1997—, chmn. 2000—; permanent mem. Fourth Cir. Jud. Conf. John Motley Morehead scholar Morehead Found., 1967; Arthur Priest scholar Phi Delta Theta, 1971 Fellow Am. Bar Found.; mem. N.C. Bar Assn. (bd. govs. 2000-03), Piedmont Triad Airport Authority (bd. dirs. 1998-2001), High Point Country Club, Phi Beta Kappa. Republican. Presbyterian. Office: McAllister & Hanks PLLC 201 Neal Pl PO Box 5006 High Point NC 27262 Office Phone: 336-882-4300. Business E-Mail: kmcallister@mcallisterhanks.com.

**MC ALLISTER, LESTER BELDEN**, economics professor; b. Chgo., Feb. 21, 1921; s. Lester Belden and Bertha (Wulpi) McA.; m. Elaine Schneider, Feb. 17, 1945; 1 child, Margaret. BA, Coe Coll., 1942; MA, Northwestern U., 1947; PhD (Carnegie fellow 1950-52), U. Oreg., 1953. Instr. econs. Coe Coll., 1947-50, Oreg. State Coll., 1952-53; mem. faculty Beloit Coll., 1953-91, prof. econs., 1959-91, prof. emeritus, 1991—, chmn. dept. econs. and bus., 1960-74. Cons.-examiner, 1974-91; vis. prof. econs. U. Wis., 1968; prof. fgn. affairs Nat. War Coll., 1961-62; mem. Wis. Banking Rev. Bd., 1974-79, Beloit Bd. Edn., 1955-58 Author articles, essays. Served to maj. USAAF, 1942-46. Ford Found. fellow U. Wis., 1957 Mem. Phi Beta Kappa. Home: 1400 N Drake Rd Apt 255 Kalamazoo MI 49006-3918

**MCALLISTER, SINGLETON BERYL**, lawyer; b. Balt., Mar. 25, 1952; d. James Winfred and Ann (Hughes) McAllister. BA, U. Md., 1975; JD, Howard U., 1984. Bar: Pa., 1985, DC, 1986, US Supreme Ct. Legis. asst. Congressman Parren J. Mitchell, Washington, 1975-78; asst. dir. Trans-Africa, Washington, 1978-79; legis. dir. Congressman William H. Gray III, Washington, 1979-81; spl. asst. Congressman Mickey Leland, Washington, 1981-83; law clk. to Judge Jack E. Tanner US Dist. Ct. We. Dist. Wash., Tacoma, 1984-86; sr. counsel US Ho. of Reps. Com. on the Budget, Washington, 1986-88; ptnr. Reed, Smith, Shaw & McClay, Washington, 1988—92; counsel Shaw Pittman Potts & Trowbridge, Washington, 1992—96; gen. counsel US Agy. for Internat. Devel., 1996—2001; ptnr. Patton Boggs LLP, 2001—03; ptnr., pub. law & policy strategies group Sonnenschein Nath & Rosenthal LLP, Washington, 2003, chair firm Corp. Diversity Counseling Group, 2003—05; ptnr. Mintz Lewin, 2005—. Past mem. adv. bd. African Devel. Found., Washington; counsel to Nat. Dem. Platform Drafting Com., 1988. Bd. dirs. Nat. Women's Bus. Ctr., Washington. Mem. ABA, Nat. Bar Assn., Delta Theta Phi. Avocations: aerobics, horseback riding.

**MCALLISTER, STEPHEN ROBERT**, dean, law educator; b. Lawrence, Kans., Nov. 27, 1962; s. Stephen Ray and Rhoda Alice (Bening) McA.; m. Suzanne Carey McAllister, Feb. 26, 2004. BA in Econs., U. Kans., 1985, JD, 1988. Bar: Ill. 1989, U.S. Ct. Appeals (7th cir.) 1989. Law clk. to Hon. Richard Posner U.S. Ct. Appeals (7th cir.), Chgo., 1988-89; law clk. to Hon. Byron R. White U.S. Supreme Ct., Washington, 1989—91; assoc. Gibson, Dunn & Crutcher, Washington, 1992—93; vis. assoc. prof. U. Kans. Sch. Law, 1993—95, assoc. prof., 1995—98, prof., 1999—, assoc. dean Academic Affairs, 1999—2000, dean, 2000—05. Interim dir. Dole Inst. Politics, 2003—04. Recipient Dean Frederick J. Moreau Award, 1997; grantee W.T. Kemper Fellowship, 1999. Fellow: Am. Bar Found.; mem.: Supreme Ct. Hist. Soc. (trustee), Order of Coif. Office: U Kans Sch Law 1535 W 15th St Lawrence KS 66045 E-mail: stever@ku.edu.

**MCALLISTER, WILLIAM HOWARD, III**, newspaper reporter, columnist, public affairs consultant; b. Durham, NC, Nov. 6, 1941; s. William Howard, Jr. and Dorothy Fisk (Tillett) McA.; m. Rena Catherine Farrell, June 13, 1965; children: William Howard IV, Christopher F., Jonathan T., Benjamin J. BA in Polit. Sci, U. NC, Chapel Hill, 1964, MA in Journalism, 1966. Cecil Prince research asst. U. NC, 1965; reporter The Virginian-Pilot, Norfolk, 1964-67; reporter, city editor Virginian-Pilot, 1972-75; reporter Wall St. Jour., San Francisco, 1968-72, Washington Post, 1975-78, Va. editor

1978-86, nat. reporter, 1986-99, columnist stamp and coin sect., 1987-99, lobbying columnist, 1997-99; Washington bur. chief Denver Post and MediaNews Newspapers, 1999—2003; Washington corr. Linn's Stamp News, 1997—. TV cons. Ford Found., 1969-72; cons. The Newseum, Arlington, Va., 2003—. Capt. USNR, 1966-93. Decorated Navy Commendation medal, Meritorious Svc. medal, Gold Star; recipient Lidman prize for philatelic writing, 1990. Mem. Am. Soc. Newspaper Editors, Kappa Tau Alpha, Nat. Press Club. Presbyterian. Home and Office: Linn's Stamp News 10121 Ratcliffe Manor Dr Fairfax VA 22030-2427 Personal E-mail: bmcallister@cox.net.

**MCALOON, NOREEN MARIE**, elementary school educator; b. Rockville Centre, N.Y., June 17, 1954; d. Frederick Edward and Dorothy Ann (Ryan) Watson; m. Dennis Robert McAloon, Nov. 29, 1975; children: Christopher Dennis, Elizabeth Dorothy. BS in Edn., St. John's U., 1975; MS in Reading, L.I. U., 1980; postgrad., Argosy U., 2002—; cert. in advanced grad. studies, Plymouth State U., 2002. Cert. reading specialist, N.H., elem. tchr., N.H., reading tchr., N.Y., 1982, elem. tchr., N.Y., 1980, adminstr. N.H., 2001, Mass., 2005. Elem. tchr. St. Patrick's Sch., Smithtown, N.Y., 1980, Christ the King Sch., Commack, N.Y., 1980-83, St. Catherine Sch., Manchester, N.H., 1984-85; adult educator Manchester Skill Ctr., 1986-87; reading specialist Goffstown (N.H.) Jr./Sr. H.S., 1985-87, McKelvie Mid. Sch., Bedford, NH, 1987—2002; assist. prin. Pelham Meml. Sch., 2002—. Adj. prof. NHCTC 2005. Contbr. articles to profl. jours. Mem. ASCD, Internat. Reading Assn. Nat. Coun. Tchrs. of English, N.H. Coun. Tchrs. of English (bd. dirs.) Republican. Roman Catholic. Home: 6 Olde English Rd Bedford NH 03110-5619 Office: Pelham Mid Sch 59 Marsh Rd Pelham NH 03076-3134

**MCALPIN, KIRK MARTIN**, lawyer; b. Newark, Sept. 14, 1923; s. Aaron Champion and Margaret (Martin) McAlpin; m. Sarah Frances Morgan, Dec. 14, 1951; children: Kirk Martin Jr., Philip Morgan, Margaret Champion Margeson. LLB, U. Ga., 1948; postgrad., Columbia U., 1949. Bar: Ga. 1949. Asst. solicitor gen. Ea. Jud. Cir. Ct. Ga., 1951; assoc. Bouhan, Lawrence, Williams, Levy & McAlpin, Savannah, Ga., 1952-53, ptnr., 1954-63; sr. ptnr. King & Spalding, Atlanta, 1963-86; pvt. practice Savannah, 1987—97, Atlanta, 1998—. Chmn. Inst. Continuing Legal Edn., 1980-81, Inst. Continuing Jud. Edn. in Ga., 1981-84, Jud. Council Ga., 1979-82. Pres. Atlanta Legal Aid Soc., 1971. Fellow Am. Bar Found., Am. Law Inst., Am. Coll. Trial Lawyers, Internat. Acad. Trial Lawyers, Internat. Soc. Barristers; mem. ABA (Jr. Bar Conf. chmn. 1958-59, chmn. gen. practice sect. 1972-73, chmn. sr. lawyers div. 1986-87, ho. of dels. 1960-90, state del. 1970-90, bd. govs. 1973-76), State Bar Ga. Assn. (chmn. Young Lawyers 1953-54, bd. govs. 1953-63, pres. 1979-80), Atlanta Bar Assn., Savannah Bar Assn. (v.p. 1960-61), Nat. Conf. Bar Pres. (exec. com. 1981-83), Ga. Def. Lawyers Assn., Fed. Bar Assn., Am. Judicature Soc., Assn. R.R. Trial Counsel, Soc. of Cin., Sons Colonial Wars, St. Andrews Soc., Capital City Club, Piedmont Driving Club, Oglethorpe Club, Phi Delta Phi, Sigma Alpha Epsilon. Episcopalian. Office: The Paces 352 77 E Andrews Dr NW Atlanta GA 30305-1392 Office Phone: 404-467-8307. Office Fax: 404-467-0619. Personal E-mail: kmcasratty@mindspring.com.

**MCALPINE, DONALD EUGENE**, physician; b. Milaca, Minn., Dec. 12, 1949; s. Donald Eugene and Katherine Elizabeth McAlpine; m. Mary Lois Dorr, Nov. 11, 1950; children: Megan Erin Osterlund, David Aaron. MD, U. Minn., Mpls., 1979. Diplomate Am. Bd. Psychiatry and Neurology, 1984. Cons. in psychiatry Mayo Clinic Coll. Medicine, Rochester, Minn., 1983—. Faculty Christian Med. and Dental Assn. Avocations: fishing. hunting. Office: Mayo Clinic Coll Medicine 200 SW 1st St Rochester MN 55905 Office Phone: 507-284-2511. Office Fax: 507-284-4158. Personal E-mail: donmcalpine@chartermi.net. Business E-Mail: mcalpine.donald@mayo.edu.

**MCALWEE, MARTIN FREDERICK**, lawyer; b. Washington, Oct. 4, 1943; s. Robert Walter and Norma Jean McAlwee; m. Maryann Sharma Siuda, Apr. 21, 2000; children from previous marriage: Gerald Steven, Jennifer Anne, Geoffrey Patrick. BA in Govt. and Polit., U. Md., Coll. Pk., 1966; JD, Cath. U., Washington, 1969; MSc in Acquistion and Contract Mgmt., Fla. Inst. Tech., 1982. Bar: DC 1969, Fla. 1982, Fla. Supreme Ct., U.S. Ct. Appeals (D.C. cir.), 1983. Dist. Ct. D.C. Judge advocate USAF, 1970—74; trial atty. Fed. Maritime Commn., Washington, 1974—79; contract mgmt. position Harris Corp., 1979—88; atty. advisor Office Staff Advocate 45th Space Wing, Patrick AFB, Fla., 1988—. Adj. prof. AF Inst. Tech., Wright-Patterson AFB, Ohio. Leader Boy Scouts Am. Ret. col. USAFR, 1999. Decorated Legion of Merit medal USAF, Bronze Star medal, Civil Svc. Meritorious Svc. medal; recipient James O. Wrightson award, 2000, Outstanding Civilian Atty., USAF Space Command, 1994, AF Space Command, 1998. Fellow: Nat. Contract Mgmt. Assn.; mem.: ABA, DC Bar Assn., Fla. Bar Assn. Avocations: golf, fishing. Office: 45th Space Wing Office Staff Judge Advocate 642 O Malley Rd Patrick Afb FL 32925-3329

**MCAMIS, EDWIN EARL**, lawyer; b. Cape Girardeau, Mo., Aug. 8, 1934; s. Zenas Earl and Anna Louise (Miller) McAmis; m. Malin Eklof, May 31, 1959 (div. 1979); 1 child, Andrew Bruce; life ptnr. Gerson Gonzalez. AB magna cum laude, Harvard U., 1956, LLB, 1959. Bar: N.Y. 1960, U.S. Dist. Ct. (so. dist.) N.Y. 1962, U.S. Supreme Ct. 1965, U.S. Ct. Appeals (2d and 3d cirs.) 1964, U.S. Ct. Appeals (D.C. cir.) 1981. Assoc. law firm Webster, Sheffield & Chrystie, N.Y.C., 1959-61, Regan Goldfarb Powell & Quinn, N.Y.C., 1962-65, Lovejoy, Wasson, Lundgren & Ashton, N.Y.C., 1965-69, ptnr., 1969-77, Skadden, Arps, Slate, Meagher & Flom, N.Y.C., 1977-90, spl. ptnr., pro bono, 1990-93; adj. prof. law Fordham U., 1984-85, Benjamin N. Cardozo Sch. Law, N.Y.C., 1985-90. Mem. Lambda Legal and Edn. Fund, 1991—95; bd. dirs Aston Magna Found. Music, Inc., 1982—93, Cmty. Rsch. Initiative N.Y., 1988—89. With U.S. Army, 1961—62. Mem.: ABA, Selden Soc. Personal E-mail: edwinmcamis1@comcast.net.

**MCANARNEY, ELIZABETH R.**, pediatrician, educator; b. NYC, May 7, 1940; d. Henry Kellers and Kathryn (Blaney) McA. AB, Vassar Coll., 1962; MD, SUNY, Syracuse, 1966. Diplomate Am. Bd. Pediatrics in pediatrics and adolescent medicine. Intern, resident SUNY Upstate Med. Ctr., Syracuse, NY, 1966-68; fellow in behavioral pediatrics U. Rochester (N.Y.) Med. Ctr., 1968-70, sr. instr. pediatrics, 1969-71, asst. prof. pediatrics, 1971-77, assoc. prof. pediatrics, 1977-85, chair pediatrics dept., 1993—. Adv. com. Fertility and Maternal Health FDA, Bethesda, Md, 1987-92; mem. program adv. bd. Robert Wood Johnson Clin. Scholars Program, Princeton, N.J., 1995—. Editor: (books) Premature Adolescent Pregnancy, 1983, Identifying Social/ Psychological Antecedents of Adolescent Pregnancy, 1984, Textbook of Adolescent Medicine, 1992; co-author of nearly 200 papers, chpts., and comm. Recipient McNeil Outstanding Achievement award Soc. for Adolescent Medicine, 1989, Job Lewis Smith award Cmty. Pediat., Am. Acad. Pediat., 1990; named to Alumni Honor Roll, SUNY, 1998. Fellow AAAS; mem. Soc. for Pediatric Rsch., Am. Pediatric Soc. (mem. exec. coun. 1998—, pres. 2004-2005), Assn. for Med. Sch. Pediatric Chairs (pres. 1999), Inst. Medicine, Nat. Acad. Sci. Achievements include determination of relationship between young maternal age and maternal/neonatal outcomes. Office: U Rochester Med Ctr Dept Pediatrics 601 Elmwood Ave Box 777 Rochester NY 14642-0001 E-mail: carole_berger@urmc.rochester.edu.*

**MCANDREW, MARK S.**, insurance company executive; Mgmt. positions with Torchmark Corp., McKinney, Tex., 1980—; pres. Globe Life & Accident Ins. Co., 1991—2005, CEO, 1999—2005; pres. United Am. Ins. Co., 1991—2004, CEO, 1999—2004; pres., CEO Am. Income Life Ins. Co., 1999—2003; bd. dir. Torchmark Corp., 1998—, exec. v.p.; 1999—2003, chmn. ins. ops., 2003—05, CEO, 2005—06, chmn., CEO, 2006—. Office: Torchmark Corp 3700 S Stonebridge Dr PO Box 8080 Mc Kinney TX 75070-8080*

**MCANDREW, THOMAS JOSEPH**, lawyer; b. Providence, Oct. 19, 1945; s. Joseph L. and Amelia L. (Bonhotel) McA.; children: John Maxwell, Mercedes, Hope, Marya, Cornelia. BA, Providence Coll., 1968; JD, Georgetown U.-Am. U.-George Washington U., 1971; LLM, Georgetown U., 1973. Bar: R.I., 1971, U.S. Dist. Ct. R.I., 1972, D.C. 1972, U.S. Ct. Claims, 1972, U.S. Tax Ct., 1971, U.S. Custom and Patent Ct., 1971, U.S. Ct. Mil. Appeals, 1971, U.S. Ct. Appeals (1st cir.), 1971, U.S. Ct. Appeals (D.C.), 1971, U.S. Supreme Ct., 1974, Comm. of Mass., 1985. Trial atty. Civil Aeros. Bd., Washington, 1971-72; legal asst. to John H. Fanning NLRB, Washington, 1972-73; labor rels. officer dept. edn. State of R.I., Providence, 1973-74, dep. asst. commr. edn., 1974-79, administr. labor rels., 1979-80; ptnr. Powers & McAndrew, Inc., Providence, 1980-87; pvt. practice Thomas J. McAndrew & Assocs., Providence, 1987—. Mem. Providence Com. on Fgn. Rels., Providence, 1974—; mem. Providence Com. on Fgn. Rels., Providence. Mem. ABA (com. on labor law) FBA, ATLA, Am. Arbitration Assn. (adv. coun.). Avocations: golf, tennis, walking. Home: 6 Wingate Rd Providence RI 02906-4910 Office: Ste 205 One Turks Head Place Providence RI 02903 Fax: 401-455-0882. Office Phone: 401-455-0350. Business E-Mail: tmcandrew@tjmcandrewlaw.com.

**MCANDREWS, JAMES PATRICK,** lawyer; b. Carbondale, Pa., May 11, 1929; s. James Patrick and Mary Agnes (Walsh) McA.; m. Mona Marie Steinke, Sept. 4, 1954; children: James P., George A., Catherine McAndrews Hazel, Joseph M., Anne Marie, Michael P., Edward R., Daniel P. BS, U. Scranton, 1949; LL.B., Fordham U., 1952; grad., Real Estate Inst., NYU, 1972. Bar: N.Y. 1953, Ohio 1974. Assoc. James F. McManus, Levittown, NY, 1955; atty. Emigrant Savs. Bank, N.Y.C., 1955-68; counsel Tchrs. Ins. and Annuity Assn., 1968-73; assoc. Thompson, Hine & Flory, 1973-74, ptnr. Cleve., 1974-84, Benesch, Friedlander, Coplan & Aronoff, Cleve., 1984-94. Mem. law faculty Am. Inst. Banking, N.Y.C., 1968-69; mem. faculty Lakeland C.C., 1995-97. Author Commercial Real Estate Law Practice Manual with Forms, 2001. 1st It. USAF, 1952-54. Fellow Am. Bar Found. (life); mem. Am. Coll. Real Estate Lawyers (gov. 1983-86, treas. 1986-88, chmn. membership devel. com. 1985-87), Ohio Land Title Assn. (life, trustee 1985-88), Bar Assn. Greater Cleve. (life; past chmn. real estate sect.), Ohio State Bar Assn. (hon. life). Roman Catholic. Home: Marine Towers West 12540 Edgewater Dr Ste 311 Lakewood OH 44107-1614 Office Phone: 216-363-4427. Personal E-mail: jpmlake@sbcglobal.net.

**MCANENY, DEBORAH H.,** insurance company executive; b. 1960; Staff John Hancock Life Ins. Co., Boston, 1985—98, v.p., 1998—2000; sr. v.p. John Hancock Fin. Svcs., Inc. & John Hancock Life Ins. Co., Boston, 2000—02; dir. and CEO John Hancock Natural Resource Group, Boston, 2001—; exec. v.p. John Hancock Fin. Svcs., Inc. & John Hancock Life Ins. Co., Boston, 2002—; also bd. dirs. John Hancock Subsidiaries, Boston, 2002—.

**MCANIFF, EDWARD JOHN,** lawyer; b. NYC, June 29, 1934; s. John Edward and Josephine (Toomey) m. Jane Reiss, June 11, 1960; children: John E., Maura T, Anne T. Annick, Jane A., Peter J., Kathleen A. AB magna cum laude, Holy Cross Coll., 1956; LLB cum laude, NYU, 1961. Bar: N.Y. 1962, Calif. 1963, D.C. 1976. Law clk. to Justice A.T. Goodwin Supreme Ct. Oreg., Salem, 1961-62; ptnr., of counsel O'Melveny & Myers, L.A., 1962—. Adj. prof. Sch. Law Stanford U., 1974-75, 94-98, Boalt Hall Law Sch. 1992-95, UCLA Law Sch., 1996—; vis. prof. U. Oreg. Law Sch., 1999—; fgn. law counsel Freehill, Hollingdale & Page, Sydney, 1981-82; bd. dirs. Mellon Fin. Corp. Bd. dirs. L.A. Master Chorale, 1979-81, 87—, chmn., 1996—; dir., exec. com. Perf. Art Ctr. Los Angeles County, 1992—; bd. dirs. Music Ctr. Found., 1992—. Capt. USNR, 1956-87. Republican. Office: O Melveny & Myers 400 S Hope St Ste 1717 Los Angeles CA 90071-2899 E-mail: tmcaniff@omm.com.

**MCANIFF, NORA P.,** publishing executive; b. NY, 1958; BA, Baruch Coll. From mktg. info. mgr. to pres. People Mag. Time Inc., NYC, 1982—98, pres. People Mag., 1998—2002, pub. Life Mag., 1992—93, pub. Teen People, 1997—98, exec. v.p., women's entertainment & luxury group, 2002—, and co-COO, 2005—. Dir. Saks Inc., 2002—; bd. dir. Michael J. Fox Found. for Parkinson's Rsch. Office: Time Inc 1271 Avenue of the Americas New York NY 10020-1300*

**MCANINCH, JACK WELDON,** urological surgeon, educator; b. Merkel, Tex., Mar. 17, 1936; s. Weldon Thomas and Margaret (Canon) McA.; m. Barbara B. Buchanan, Dec. 29, 1960 (div. Aug. 1972); m. Burnet B. Sumner, Dec. 29, 1987; children: David A., Todd G., Brendan J. BS, Tex. Tech U., 1958; MS, U. Idaho, 1960; MD, U. Tex., 1964. Diplomate Am. Bd. Urology (trustee 1991-97, pres. 1996-97). Commd. capt. U.S. Army, 1964-66, advanced through grades to col., 1977, ret., 1977; col. USAR; intern then resident Letterman Army Med. Ctr., San Francisco, 1964-69; chief urol. surgery San Francisco Gen. Hosp., 1977—; prof. urol. surgery U. Calif., San Francisco, 1977—. Editor: Urogenital Trauma, 1985, Urologic Clinics of North America, 1989, Smith's General Urology, 1995; section editor: Early Care of the Injured Patient, 1990, Traumatic and Reconstructive Urology, 1996. Col. US Army, 1964-72. Recipient Disting. Alumnus award Tex. Tech U., 1994; named Disting. Alumnus U. Idaho, 1997. Fellow ACS (gov. 1992-97, regent 1998—); mem. Am. Urol. Assn. (pres. we. sect. 1992-93, bd. dirs. 1990—, pres. 1996-97), Genitourinary Reconstructive Surgeons (pres.), Am. Assn. Surgery Trauma (v.p.), Soc. Univ. Urologists, Am. Bd. Urology (pres. 1996-97). Office: San Francisco Gen Hosp Dept Urology 1001 Potrero Ave San Francisco CA 94110-3594 Office Phone: 415-476-3372.

**MCANUFF, DES,** artistic director; b. Princeton, Ill., June 19, 1952; s. John Nelson and Ellen Boyd; m. Susan Berman, Jan. 1, 1984; 1 child, Julia Violet. Artistic dir. La Jolla Playhouse, until 1994. Founding mem. Dodger Prodns.; former faculty Julliard Sch.; now adj. prof. theatre U. Calif. San Diego. Dir.: (Broadway prodns.) Big River (Tony award 1985), A Walk in the Woods (San Diego Critics Circle award), Tommy (Tony award 1993), How to Succeed in Business Without Really Trying (Tony nomination 1995), 700 Sundays, 2004, Jersey Boys, 2005, Zhivago, 2006, The Wiz, 2006; (off-Broadway prodns.) Gimme Shelter (Soho Arts award 1979), The Crazy Locomotive, Chelsea Theatre Ctr., Mary Stuart, How It All Began, Henry IV Part One, The Death of Von Richthofen as Witnessed from Earth (Villager award 1982), NY Shakespeare Festival, A Mad World My Masters, Romeo & Juliet, As You Like It (San Diego Critics Circle award), The Sea Gull, Shout Up A Morning, Gillette, The Matchmaker, Two Rooms, 80 Days, Down The Road, Macbeth, The Three Sisters, A Funny Thing Happened on the Way to the Forum, Twelfth Night, La Jolla Playhouse, Macbeth, Stratford Festival Can., Palm Beach: The Screwball Musical, 2005; others; prodr.: A Walk in the Woods, My Children! My Africa!; playwright Leave it to Beaver is Dead (Soho Arts award), The Death of Von Richthofen as Witnessed from Earth (Villager and Bay Area Critic Circle awards), Troll, A Lime in the Morning, Silent Edward; contbg. editor Am. Theatre Mag. Can. Council grantee, Rockefeller grantee. Mem. Theatre Communications Group (past bd. dirs.), Soc. of Stage Dirs. and Choreographers.*

**MCANULTY, WILLIAM E., JR.,** state supreme court justice; m. Kristi W. McAnulty; 4 children. Grad., Ind. U.; MAT, JD, U. Louisville. With Jefferson County Juvenile Ct., 1975—83; judge Jefferson Dist. Ct., 1978—83, Jefferson Circuit Ct., 1984—90; atty., priv. practice Ind., 1990—93; judge Jefferson Circuit Ct., 1993—98, chief judge, 1998; judge Ky. Ct. of Appeals, 1998—2006; justice Ky. Supreme Ct., 2006—. Recipient Thomas C. Simons Disting. Leadership award, Leadership Louisville Foundation. Mem.: Ky. Trial Attorneys Assn. (Henry V. Pennington Outstanding Judge of Yr. 1997), Ky. Bar Assn., Louisville Bar Assn. Office: Ky Supreme Ct Jefferson Cty Judicial Ctr 700 W Jefferson St Ste 1000 Louisville KY 40202*

**MCARDLE, RICHARD JOSEPH,** retired academic administrator; b. Omaha, Mar. 10, 1934; s. William James and Abby Marie (Menzies) McA.; m. Katherine Ann McAndrew, Dec. 27, 1958; children: Bernard, Constance, Nancy, Susan, Richard. BA, Creighton U., 1955, MA, 1961; PhD, U. Nebr., 1969. Tchr. pub. high schs., Nebr., 1955-65; grad. asst. romance langs. U. Nebr., 1965-66, instr. fgn. lang. methods, 1966-69; chmn. dept. Cleve.

State U., 1969-70; chmn. dept. elem. and secondary edn. U. North Fla., 1971-75; dean Coll. Edn. Cleve. State U., 1975-87, prof. edn., 1987-89, spl. asst. to pres. for campus planning, 1991-92, acting provost, v.p. for acad. affairs, 1992-94, vice provost for strategic planning, 1994-96, prof. edn., 1996-2001, ret., 2001. Cons. in field. Author articles related to issues in tchr. edn. Mem. Assn. Higher Edn. Office: CASAL Dept Cleve State U Cleveland OH 44115 Office Phone: 216-687-4613. Business E-Mail: r.mcardle@csuohio.edu.

**MCARTHUR, ELDON DURANT,** geneticist, researcher; b. Hurricane, Utah, Mar. 12, 1941; s. Eldon and Denise (Dalton) McA.; m. Virginia Johnson, Dec. 20, 1963; children: Curtis D., Monica McArthur Bennion, Denise McArthur Johnson, Ted O. AS with high honors, Dixie Coll., 1963; BS cum laude, U. Utah, 1965, MS, 1967, PhD, 1970. Postdoctoral rsch. fellow, dept. demonstrator Agrl. Rsch. Coun. Gt. Britain, Leeds, Eng., 1970-71; rsch. geneticist Intermountain Rsch. Sta. USDA Forest Svc., Ephraim, Utah, 1972-75, rsch. geneticist Shrub Scis. Lab., Intermountain Rsch. Sta. Provo, Utah, 1975-83, project leader, chief rsch. geneticist, 1983-97, Rocky Mountain Rsch. Sta., USDA Forest Svc., Provo, Utah, 1997—. Adj. prof. Integrative Biology Dept. Brigham Young U., Provo, 1976—. Author more than 400 rsch. papers; contbr. chpts. to books; editor symposium procs. Named USDA Forest Svc. Superior Scientist, 1990, Disting. Scientist, 1996; Sigma Xi grantee, 1970, NSF grantee, 1981, 85, 96, Coop. State Rsch., Svc. grantee, 1986, 91; recipient Eminent Sci. Publ. award Rocky Mtn. Rsch. Station, 2001, New Century of Svc. award 2002. Mem. Soc. Range Mgmt. (pres. Utah sect. 1987, Outstanding Achievement award 1992, Utah sect. Range Mgr. of Yr. 2004), Botan. Soc. Am., Soc. Study Evolution, Am. Genetic Assn., Shrub Rsch. Consortium (chmn. 1983—, Disting. Svc. award 2002), Intermountain Consortium for Aridlands Rsch (pres. 1991—). Mem. Lds Ch. Avocations: hiking, bicycling, basketball. Home: 555 N 1200 E Orem UT 84097-4350 Office: USDA Forest Svc Shrub Scis Lab 735 N 500 E Provo UT 84606-1856 Office Phone: 801-356-5112. Personal E-mail: edmdixie@aol.com. Business E-Mail: dmcarthur@fs.fed.us.

**MC ARTHUR, GEORGE,** journalist; b. Valdosta, Ga., July 15, 1924; s. George and Ann (Johnson) McA.; m. Eva Kim, Sept. 17, 1979. BA in Journalism, U. Ga., 1948. With AP, 1948-69, corr. Korea, 1950-54, Paris, 1954-60, bur. chief Cairo, 1960-63, Manila, 1963-65, corr. Saigon, 1966-68, bur. chief, 1968-69; with Los Angeles Times, 1969-83, bur. chief Saigon, 1970-75, corr. for Southeast Asia Bangkok, 1975-79; diplomatic corr. U.S. News & World Report, 1983-85. Served with USNR, 1943-45. Recipient citation for fgn. reporting Overseas Press Club, 1973 Mem. Sigma Delta Chi. Clubs: Fgn. Corrs. (Hong Kong); Glen Arven Country (Thomasville, Ga.); River Bend Country (Gt. Falls, Va.). Address: 506 E Creek Ct Vienna VA 22180-3578 E-mail: kimparkcho@aol.com.

**MCARTHUR, JOHN HECTOR,** business educator; b. Vancouver, B.C., Can., Mar. 31, 1934; came to U.S., 1957; s. Hector and Elizabeth Lee (Whyte) McA.; m. Netilia Ewasiuk, Sept. 15, 1956; children: Jocelyn Natasha, Susan Patricia. B in Commerce, U. B.C., 1957, LLD (hon.), 1995; MBA, Harvard U., 1959, DBA, 1962; LLD (hon.), Simon Fraser U., 1982, Queens U., 1985, Middlebury Coll., 1988, U. Navarra, Spain, 1989, U. Western Ont., 1992. Prof. bus. adminstrn. Harvard U., Cambridge, Mass., 1962—79, Sylvan C. Coleman prof. fin. mgmt., 1972—80, George F. Baker prof. bus. adminstrn., 1980—96; dean Harvard Bus. Sch., 1980-96; sr. advisor to pres. World Bank Group, Washington, 1995—2005. Bd. dirs., chmn. Asia Pacific Found. Can. AES Corp., Bell Can., Bell Can. Enterprises, Inc., Cabot Corp., Duke U. Health System, HCA Inc., KOC Holdings A.S., Nat. Healthcare Coalition, Reuters Founders Share Co. Ltd., Telsat Can., Devel. Gateway Found.; cons. numerous cos. and govt. agys. in Can., Europe, Asia and U.S. Named Hon. Citizen, Hermanville, France; recipient Harvard Statesman award, HBS Club, NYC, Mgmt. Achievement award, McGill U., Can. Bus. Leadership award, HBS Clubs of Can.; John and Natty McArthur Univ. chair established at Harvard U., 1997, McArthur Hall named in his honor, Harvard Bus. Sch., 1999, John H. McArthur Can. Fellowship program, created at Harvard Bus. Sch., 2002. Mem. Harvard Club, Links Club, Comml. Club, Somerset Club, Willowbend Club, Varsity Club. Home: 140 Old Connecticut Path Wayland MA 01778-3202 Office: Harvard Univ Sch Bus Adminstrn Boston MA 02163

**MCARTHUR, JOHN R.,** utilities executive, lawyer; b. Rock Hill, SC, Jan. 5, 1956; BA cum laude, Davidson Coll., 1977; JD with honors, Univ. So. Carolina, 1981. Bar: NC 1982. Law clk. Judge Sam J. Ervin III, US Ct. Appeals, 4th cir., 1981—82; assoc. to ptnr. Hunton & Williams, Raleigh, NC, 1982—92; chief counsel NC Atty. Gen. Office, NC, 1993—97; sr. advisor NC Gov., Mike Easley, NC, 1998—2001; v.p., pub. affairs Progress Energy Inc., Raleigh, NC, 2001—02, v.p., corp. rels., 2002—, gen. counsel, corp. sec., 2004—. Editor Law Rev. U.S.C.; law clerk Hon. Sam J. Ervin III US Ct. Appeals Fourth Cir. Mem.: NC Bar Assn., Order of the Coif, Raleigh NC Wig & Robe. Mailing: Progress Energy Inc PO Box 1551 Raleigh NC 27602-1551 Office Phone: 919-546-4070. Business E-Mail: john.mcarthur@pgnmail.com.

**MCARTHUR, LISA R.,** music educator, musician; d. Tremaine James and Judith Hammon McArthur. PhD in Music Theory, U. of Ky., Lexington, Kentucky, 1995—99; MA in Music Theory, Kent State U., Kent, Ohio, 1990—94, MusM in performance, 1990—93; MusB in Music Edn., SUNY Potsdam Coll., Crane Sch. of Music, Potsdam, New York, 1986—90. Grad. asst. Kent State U., Kent, Ohio, 1990—92; orch. dir., grades 4-12 Akron Pub. Schools, Akron, Ohio, 1993—95; grad. tchg. asst. U. of Ky., Lexington, Ky., 1995—98; assoc. prof. Campbellsville U., Campbellsville, Ky., 1998—. Clinician Emerson Flutes, Elkhart, Ind., 2000—; dir. flute ensemble Campbellsville (Ky.) U., 1998—; presenter in field. Musician: (albums) Something Old, Something New, Something Borrowed, Something Blue, 2004; arranger: for flute ensemble Symphony No. 1, for flute solo and flute ensemble accompaniment Scherzino by Andersen and Concerto in D Maj by Mozart Named Coll/U. Educator of the Yr., Ky. Music Educators Assn., 2001; recipient Performer's cert., Crane Sch. of Music, 1990. Mem.: Nat. Assn. of Coll. Wind and Percussion Instructors, Nat. Flute Assn., Soc. for Music Theory, Coll. Music Soc., Music Educators Nat. Conf. (coll. chpt. advisor 1998—, state chpt. advisor 2003—05), Ky. Music Educators Assn., Flute Soc. of Ky. (pres. 2000—), Pi Kappa Lambda, Sigma Alpha Iota (life). Office: Campbellsville University UPO 922 Campbellsville KY 42718 E-mail: lrmcarthur@campbellsville.edu.

**MCARTHUR, WILLIAM SURLES, JR.,** astronaut, retired military officer; b. Laurinburg, N.C., July 26, 1951; s. William S. and Edith P. (Avant) McArthur; m. Cynthia Catherine Lovin; 2 children. BS in Applied Scis. and Engring., U.S. Mil. Acad., West Point, N.Y., 1973; MS in Aerospace Engring., Ga. Inst. Tech., 1983; DSc (hon.), U.N.C., Pembroke. Commd. 2d lt. U.S. Army, 1973, advamced through grades to Col., retired, 2001; 2d lt. U.S. Airborne Divsn., Fort Bragg, 1973—75; student U.S. Army Aviation Sch., 1975—76; aeroscout team leader, brigade aviation sect. commdr. US Army 2nd Infantry Divsn, Republic of Korea, 1976—78; company commdr., platoon leader, ops. officer 24th Combat Aviation Battalion, Savanna, Ga.; asst. prof. dept. mechs. U.S. Mil. Acad., West Point, 1983—86; student pilot USN Test Pilot Sch., 1986—87; exptl. test pilot U.S. Army, 1987—91; space shuttle vehicle integration test engr. NASA Johnson Space Ctr., Houston, 1987—91, astronaut, 1991—, held various assignments in the astronaut office, 1991—. Crew mem. STS-58 Columbia launched from Kennedy Space Ctr., Fla.; landed at Edwards AFB, Calif., 1993; crew mem. STS-74 Atlantis Kennedy Space Ctr., Fla.; crew mem. STS-92 Discovery launched from Kennedy Space Ctr., Fla.; landed Edwards Air Force Base, Calif., 2000; crew mem. ISS mission, 05. Named vis. Green Hons. Prof., Dept. Sci. and Engring. Tex. Christian U., 1997; recipient Order of the Long Leaf Pine, NC, Ellis Island Medal of Honor, Disting. Svc. medal, Def. Superior Svc. medal, Def. Meritorious Svc. medal (First Oak Leaf Cluster), Meritorious Svc. Medal (First Oak Leaf Cluster), Army Commendation medal, NASA Space Flight medal, NASA Exceptional Svc. medal, Ga. Tech Acad. Disting. Alumni, Flight Achievement award, Am. Astronautical Soc., 1996, Korolev Diploma, Fedn. Aeronautique Internat., 2000. Mem.: MENSA, AIAA, Assn. Space Explorers, U.S. Mil. Acad. Assn. Grads., United States Army, Army

Aviation Assn. Am. (Order of St. Michael (Silver award) 2000, Robert M. Leich award 2000), West Point Soc. Greater Houston, Phi Kappa Phi. Avocations: basketball, running, working with personal computers. Office: NASA Johnson Space Ctr Houston TX 77058*

**MCATEE, DARIN P.,** lawyer; b. Hays, Kans., Dec. 16, 1965; BA with highest distinction, Univ. Kans., 1988; JD magna cum laude, Harvard Univ., 1991. Bar: NY 1993. Law clk., Hon. Stanley F. Birch, Jr. US Ct. of Appeals, 11th Cir.; assoc. Cravath Swaine & Moore LLP, NYC, 1992—2004, ptnr., litig., 2004—. Articles related to issues in law. Office: Cravath Swaine & Moore LLP Worldwide Plz 825 Eighth Ave New York NY 10019-7475 Office Phone: 212-474-1480. Office Fax: 212-474-3700. Business E-Mail: dmcatee@cravath.com.

**MCATEE, DAVID RAY,** lawyer; b. Rosebud, Tex., Nov. 20, 1941; s. Lee Ray and Florine (Davis) McAtee; m. Carole Kay Pendergraft, Jan. 28, 1967; children: David Ray, Kristin Carole. BBA with honors, Baylor U., 1964; LLB, U. Tex., 1967. Bar: Tex. 1967, U.S. Dist. Ct. (no. dist.) Tex. 1968, U.S. Dist. Ct. (so. dist.) Tex. 1994, U.S. Dist. Ct. (ea. dist.) Tex. 1996, US Ct. Appeals (5th cir.) 1969, US Ct. Appeals (11th cir.) 1981, US Tax Ct. 1993, US Dist. Ct. (ea. dist.) 1996. Briefing atty. Supreme Ct. Tex., Austin, 1967—68; ptnr. Thompson & Knight, Dallas, 1968—90, Gibson, Dunn & Crutcher, Dallas, 1990—95; with Akin Gump Strauss Hauer & Feld LLP, Dallas, 1995; chmn. bd. dirs. Dallas Area Rapid Transit, 1992. Mem. City of Dallas Plan Commn., 1979—83, vice chmn., 1981—83; chmn. City of Dallas Thoroughfare Com., 1979—81; mem. City of Dallas Citizens Safety Adv. Com., Goals for Dallas Com.; bd. dirs. Friends of the Katy Trail, 2005—06; founder, bd. dirs. No. Hills. Neighborhood Assn., 1974—76; pres., bd. dirs. Montessori Sch. of Park Cities, 1975—76. Mem.: Tex. Bar Found. (trustee 2005—), ABA (antitrust sect.), Tex. Bar Assn. (legal ethics com. 1975—81), Dallas Bar Assn. (legal ethics com. 1979—81), U. Tex. Law Alumni Assn. (exec. com. 2003—06). Democrat. Methodist. Office: Akin Gump Strauss Hauer & Feld LLP 1700 Pacific Ave Ste 4100 Dallas TX 75201-4675

**MCAULEY, THOMAS H.,** real estate executive; Chmn. CEO, Ewing S.E. Realty, Inc., Atlanta, 1988-93; regional ptnr. Faison Assocs., Inc. (acquired Ewing S.E. Realty, Inc.), Charlotte, N.C., 1993-95; pres. IRT Property Co., Atlanta, 1995—, CEO, 1997—, chmn., 1998—. Office: Equity One Realty & Management SE IN 1275 Powers Ferry Rd SE #100 Marietta GA 30067-9490

**MCAULIFFE, ROSEMARY,** lawyer; b. New Rochelle, N.Y., May 24, 1927; d. William J. and Rose B. (Payne) McA. BA, Regis Coll., 1949; JD, New Eng. Sch. Law, 1954; MEd, Boston State Coll., 1971, Cert. advanced grad studies, 1981; LLD (hon.), New Eng. Sch. Law, Boston, 2002. Bar: Mass. 1956, U.S. Dist. Ct. Mass. 1957, U.S. Supreme Ct. 1961. Pvt. practice law, Boston, 1956—. Tchr. City of Boston, 1973-88. Prodr. (weekly TV show) The Legal Line, Boston Pub. Access Answer Channel. Active World Affairs Coun., Boston, 1980-95; sec. Italian Hist. Assn. Mass., 1988—. Mem. Mass. Bar Assn., Am. Acad. Trial Lawyers, Mass. Women Lawyers. Home and Office: 61 Prince St Boston MA 02113-1829

**MCAULIFFE, STEVEN JAMES,** federal judge; b. 1948; BA, Va. Mil. Inst., 1970; JD, Georgetown U., 1973. Capt. appellate coun. US Army JAGC, 1973-77; asst. atty. gen. Office NH Atty. Gen., 1977-80; prtnr. Gallagher, Callahan, Gartrell, P.A., Concord, NH, 1980-92; fed. judge US Dist. Ct. (NH dist.), Concord, 1992—2005, chief judge, 2005. Chair Rhodes Scholarship Selection Com. NH, 1998—2004. Trustee Univ. Sys. of NH, 1986-94; bd. dirs. NH Med. Malpractice Stabilization Res. Fund Trust, 1987-92, Office Pub. Guardian, 1980-92, Challenger Ctr. for Space Sci. Edn.; active NH Dem. Leadership Coun., 1988-92. Capt. US Army, 1970-77, USAR, 1977-80, NH Army NG, 1980-88. Decorated US Army Commendation medal. Fellow NH Bar Found.; mem. ABA, NH Bar Assn. (pres. 1991-92, pres.-elect 1990-91, v.p. 1989-90, mem. ex-officio NH Supreme Ct. com. profl. conduct 1989-90, mem. ethics com. 1984-86), Nat. Conf. Bar Pres., Merrimack County Bar Assn., DC Bar Assn., US Supreme Ct. Hist. Soc., NH Jud. Coun. (vice-chmn. 1991-92), Aircraft Owners and Pilots Assn., Concord Country Club. Office: US Dist Ct 55 Pleasant St Room 416 Concord NH 03301-3904

**MCAULIFFE, TERRY (TERENCE RICHARD MCAULIFFE),** former political organization administrator; b. Syracuse, N.Y., 1957; s. Jack and Millie McAuliffe; m. Dorothy Swann, 1988; children: Dori, Jack, Mary, Sally, Peter. BA in Polit. Sci., Cath. U., 1979; JD, Georgetown U., 1984. Fin. chmn. Gephardt for Pres. Campaign Com., 1988; amb., commr. gen. Internat. Expo., 1993; chmn. Dem. Bus. Coun., 1993; fin. chmn. Dem. Nat. Com., 1994, Bill Clinton/Al Gore Election Campaign, 1996; co-chair Presdl. Inaugural Com., 1997; chmn. Dem. Nat. Conv., L.A., 2000, Dem. Nat. Com., 2001—05.

**MCAUSLAND, RANDOLPH MELVILLE NEAL,** writer, art consultant; b. Phila., Oct. 9, 1934; s. John Randolph and Helen (Neal) McA.; m. Marilynn Kemp, July 10, 1965 (div. 1976); children: Andrew, Sean; m. Jan E. Tribbey, May 9, 1986 AB, Princeton U., 1957. Copy editor Wall Street Jour., N.Y.C., 1960—61; editor, pub. Stowe Reporter, 1961—63; consulting editor Interpub. Group Cos., 1963—67; creative dir. The Progress Group, N.Y.C., 1967—70, gen. mgr., 1970—75; dir. mktg. Billboard Pubs., N.Y.C., 1975—77; asst. to pres. Macmillan Mag., Stamford, Conn., 1977—80; editor The New Satirist, New Canaan, Conn., 1980—82; pres. Design Pubs. Inc., N.Y.C., 1983—89; dir. Design Arts Program, NEA, Washington, 1989—90; dep. chmn. NEA, Washington, 1990—93; writer, arts cons. Richmond, Va., 1993—94. Founder, dir. Design History Found., N.Y.C., NY, 1987—89. Author: Supermarkets: History of an American Institution, 1980; contbr. articles to profl. jours Bd. dirs. Hand Workshop, Richmond, 1993-94, Richmond Choral Soc., 1994, Worldesign Found., 1994-97, Fla. Friends Librs., 1995-99, Cin. Chamber Orch., 2002-04, Fla. Ctr. for the Book, Broward County Vision Com., Catacoustic Consort, dep. exec. dir., 2002—. With U.S. Army, 1957-60. Recipient Commendation N.Y.C. Police Dept., 1971, Pres. Cup Am. Comedy Club N.Y., N.Y.C., 1974, Bronze Apple award Indsl. Design Soc., 1987, Disting. Svc. award NEA, 1991-92 Mem. Am. Ctr. For Design (hon.), Coalition Ind. Scholars, Ivy Club Home: 7405 Fair Oaks Dr Cincinnati OH 45237-2925 Office Phone: 513-315-9678. E-mail: RandyMCA@cinci.rr.com.

**MCAVENEY, MARY SUSAN,** marketing executive; b. Perth Amboy, N.J., Jan. 1, 1960; d. Catherine Geraldine and Charles Joseph McAveney; m. David Clifford Briggs, Sept. 27, 1997; children: Alexander Patrick Briggs, Colin Andrew Briggs. BA, Coll. of NJ., 1989. Writer The Herald, Wall Township, NJ, 1984—88; mktg. assoc. Graphis US, Inc., N.Y.C., 1989—92; mktg. mgr. Harry N. Abrams, Inc., N.Y.C., 1992—98; mktg. dir. HarperCollins Children's Books, N.Y.C., 1998—. Spkr. Internat. Quality and Productivity Coun. Kid Power XChange, Fla., 2003, Internat. Quality and Productivity Coun.; Kid Power XChange, Fla., 2005—. Contbr. poetry. Sec. Sch. Leadership Team Pub. Sch. 58, Bklyn., 2004—05; mem. Curriculum Com., Pub. Sch. 58, Bklyn., 2004—05, Women's Dem. Com., Washington, 2004—05; mem. fundraiser Nat. Dem. Com., Washington, 2004—05; mem. Families First, Family Ctr., Bklyn., 2000—03. Garden State scholarship, State of N.J., 1983. Mem.: Promotion, Advt., and Mktg. Assn., Children's Book Coun. Democrat-Npl. Avocations: travel, photography, writing, cooking. Office: HarperCollins Children's Books 1350 Avenue of Americas New York NY 10019 Office Phone: 212-307-3623. Office Fax: 212-261-6785. Business E-Mail: mary.mcaveney@harpercollins.com.

**MCAVITY, JOHN GILLIS,** museum director, association executive, museologist; b. St. John, N.B., Can., Oct. 30, 1950; s. J. Patrick H. and Catharine A. (McNeill) McA. BA, U. N.B. 1972. Cert. assn. exec. Asst. curator Kings Landing Mus., Fredericton, N.B., 1972-73; provincial mus. adviser N.B. Mus., St. John, Can., 1973-76; exec. dir. Ont. Mus. Assn., Toronto, Can. 1976-81, Can. Mus. Assn. Ottawa, Ont. Can., 1981—. Bd. dirs. internat. mus. Mgmt. Com., Internat. Coun. Mus., Can. Com. of the Decorative Arts; sec. treas. Intercom, 2001—. Editor INTERCOM News, 1997—. V.p. St. John Heritage Trust, 1974-76; exec. com. Can. Club, St. John, 1975, English Speaking Union, St. John, 1974-76; vol. fundraiser Kidney Found., Can.; bd.

dirs. Centretown Citizens Corp.; founding dir. Mus. Found. Can., 1994—. Recipient Queen's Jubilee medal, 2002. Mem.: Internat. Coun. Museums (task force, legal affairs com. 2002—), Shefford Heritage Co-op (membership chair 1992—95, 2000—), Can. Art Mus. Dirs. Orgn., Can. Soc. Assn. Execs. (bd. dirs. 1993—96, Long Svc. Achievement award 2002), Can. Soc. Copyright Consumers, Ont. Assn. Art Galleries (bd. dirs. 1986—90), Nat. Mus. Assn. (chair internat. com. 2000—), Assn. Museums N.B. (founding), Tourism Industry Assn. Can. (bd. dirs.), Quaco Hist. and Libr. Soc. (hon. life), Assn. Cultural Execs. (bd. dirs. 1988—92, apptd. to senate 1995), Inst. Assn. Execs. (chmn. postal com., cert., bd. dirs. Ottawa chpt.), Mus. Found. Can. (founding dir. 1994—), Am. Assn. State and Local History (awards com. 1981—84, nominations com. 1985), Am. Assn. Museums. Anglican. Home: 300 Cooper St Apt 41 Ottawa ON Canada K2P 0G7 Home (Summer): 29 Kingshurst Ln Rothesay NB Canada E2H 1T3 E-mail: jmcavity@museums.ca.

**MCAVOY, BRUCE RONALD,** engineer, consultant; b. Jamestown, N.Y., Jan. 30, 1933; s. George Harold and Agda Amelia (Martinson) McA. BS in Physics, U. Rochester, 1954. Jr. engr. Westinghouse Air Arm Div., Balt., 1956-57, assoc. engr., 1957-58; rsch. engr. Westinghouse Rsch. Ctr., Pitts., 1958-69; sr. rsch. engr. Westinghouse R & D Ctr., Pitts., 1969-78, fellow engr., 1978-84, adv. scientist, 1984—. Mem. adv. bd. Nat. Ctr. Phys. Acoustics, U. Miss., 1987—88; lectr. elect. engring. dept. Carnegie Mellon U., 1968—70. Editor spl. issue IEEE Trans. Microwave Theory Tech., Ultrasonics Symposium procs., 1976-96; mem. editl. bd. jour. Microwave and Guided Wave Letters, 1990. With U.S. Army, 1954-56. Fellow IEEE (life, awards and recognition com. 1989—, def. R&D policy com. 1989-91, Centennial medal 1984, tech. program com. Internat. Microwave Symposium 1986-99); mem. DAV (life), Ultrasonic, Ferroelectric and Frequency Control Soc. of IEEE (pres. 1986-87, Disting. Svc. award 1999), Electromagnetics Acad., Microwave Theory and Techniques Soc. (chmn. microwave acoustics tech. com. 1988-99). Republican. Lutheran. Home: 926 Ivy St Pittsburgh PA 15232-2651 Office Phone: 412-621-2791. E-mail: brmcavoy@comcast.net.

**MCAVOY, JOHN JOSEPH,** lawyer; b. Worley, Idaho, June 28, 1933; s. Earl Francis and Florence Jewel (Mitchell) McA.; m. Joan Marjorie Zeldon, Sept. 20, 1964; children: Jason, Jon. BA, U. Idaho, 1954, LLB, 1958; LLM, Yale U., 1959. Bar: Idaho 1958, U.S. Supreme Ct. 1962, N.Y. 1963, U.S. Tax Ct. 1960, D.C. 1976. Asst. prof. law George Washington U., Washington, 1959-62; staff atty. stockpile investigating subcom. Armed Forces Com. U.S. Senate, Washington, 1962; assoc. White & Case, N.Y.C., 1963-71, ptnr., 1972-95; of counsel Lukas, Nace, Gutierrez & Sachs, Washington, 1995—. Adj. prof. Washington Coll. Law, Am. U., Washington, 1990; mem. D.C. com. on grievances U.S. Dist. Ct., 2003-. Bd. dirs. N.Y. Civil Liberties Union, 1975-77, commr. Uniform State Laws, 2001—; chmn. due process com. ACLU, 1975-73. With U.S. Army, 1954-56. Mem. DC Bar Assn. (ethics com. 1982-88, vice chmn. 1986-87, chmn. 1987-88), Phi Beta Kappa, Phi Alpha Delta. Democrat. Avocations: swimming, bicycling, foreign travel. Personal E-mail: mcavoylaw@aol.com.

**MCBEE, MARY LOUISE,** retired state legislator, retired academic administrator; b. Strawberry Plains, Tenn., June 15, 1924; d. John Wallace and Nina Aileen (Umbarger) McB. BS, East Tenn. State U., 1946; MA, Columbia U., 1951; PhD, Ohio State U., 1961. Tchr. East Tenn. State U., Johnson City, 1947-51; asst. dean of women, 1952-56, 57-60; dean of women, 1961-63, U. Ga., Athens, 1963-67; world campus afloat adminstr., 1966-67; assoc. dean of students, 1967-72; dean of students, 1972-74; asst. v.p. acad. affairs, 1974-76; assoc. v.p. acad. affairs, 1976-86; v.p. acad. affairs, 1986-88; ret., 1988; state rep. Clarke County Ga. Gen. Assembly, 1991—2004. Author: College Responsibility for Values, 1980; co-author: The American Woman: Who Will She Be?, 1974, Essays, 1979, 2d edit. 1981. Bd. dirs. Salvation Army, Athens, 1978—, United Way, Athens. Fulbright scholar, The Netherlands, 1956-57. Mem. Athens C. of C. (bd. dirs.). Democrat. Methodist. Avocations: gardening, tennis, hiking. Home: 145 Pine Valley Pl Athens GA 30606-4031 Personal E-mail: louisemcbee@charter.com. Business E-Mail: lmcbee@legis.state.ga.us.

**MCBEE, SUSANNA BARNES,** retired journalist; b. Santa Fe, N.Mex., Mar. 28, 1935; d. Jess Stephen and Sybil Elizabeth (Barnes) McBee; m. Paul H. Recer, July 2, 1983. AB, U. So. Calif., 1956; MA, U. Chgo., 1962. Staff writer Washington Post, 1957-65, 73-74, 77-79, asst. nat. editor, 1974-77; asst. sec. pub. affairs HEW, 1979; articles editor Washingtonian mag., 1980-81; assoc. editor U.S. News & World Report, 1981-86; news editor Washington Bur., Hearst Newspapers, 1987-89, asst. bur. chief, 1990—2003, ret., 2003; Washington corr. Life mag., 1965—69; Washington editor McCall's mag., 1970—72. Bd. dirs. Washington Press Club Found., 1992-95. Recipient Penney-Missouri mag. award, 1969, Hall of Fame award, Nat. Press Club. Profl. Journalists, 1996, Sigma Delta Chi Pub. Svc. award, 1969, Hearst Eagle award, 1994. Mem. Nat. Press Club, Cosmos Club. Home: 5190 Watson St NW Washington DC 20016-5329

**MCBRIDE, ANGELA BARRON,** nursing educator; b. Balt., Jan. 16, 1941; d. John Stanley and Mary C. (Szczepanska) Barron; m. William Leon McBride, June 12, 1965; children: Catherine, Kara. BS in Nursing, Georgetown U., 1962; MS in Nursing, Yale U., 1964; doctorate of Pub. Svc. (hon.), U. Cin., 1983; LittD (hon.), Purdue U., 1998; LLD (hon.), Ea. Ky. U., 1991; LHD (hon.), Georgetown U., 1993; DSc (hon.), Med. Coll. Ohio, 1995; LHD (hon.), U. Akron, 1997. Asst. prof., rsch. asst. inst. Yale U., New Haven, 1964-73; assoc. prof., chairperson Ind. U. Sch. Nursing, Indpls., 1978-81, 80-84, prof., 1981-92, assoc. dean rsch., 1985—91, interim dean, 1991—92, univ. dean, 1992—2003, disting. prof., 1992—2005, disting. prof., univ. dean emerita, 2006—; sr. v.p. acad. affairs, nursing Clarian Health Ptnrs., 1997—2003; Am. Acad. Nursing, Am. Nurses Found. scholar-in-residence Inst. Medicine, 2003—04. Mem. Nat. Adv. Mental Health Coun., 1987—91; adv. com. NIH Office of Women's Health Rsch., 1997—2001, NIH Office of Women's Health Rsch. Specialized Ctrs. Rsch. on Sex and Gender Factors, 2003—; coun. mem. Yale U., 1999—2005; ext. acad. advisor Sch. Nursing, Hong Kong Polytechnic U., 2000—; adv. bd. Meth. Health Found., 2000—; advisor U. Hong Kong, 2004—, Hong Kong Acad. Nursing, 2004—; Helen Denn Schulte vis. prof. U. Wis. Madison, 2006. Author: The Growth and Development of Mothers, 1973 (Best Book award 1973), Living with Contradictions, A Married Feminist, 1976, How to Enjoy A Good Life With Your Teenager, 1987; editor: Psychiatric-Mental Health Nursing: Integrating the Behavioral and Biological Sciences, 1996 (Best Book award 1996); compiler: Nursing and Philanthropy, 2000. Adv. bd. Women's Fund Indpls., 2000—05; bd. dirs. United Way of Ctrl. Ind. 2002—06, Clarian Health Ptnrs., 2004—, chair quality and patient care com. Recipient Disting. Alumna award Yale U., Disting. Alumna award Purdue U., Univ. Medallion, U. San Francisco, 2003, Hoosier Heritage award, 2000, Disting. Nurse Educator award Coll. Mt. St. Joseph, Cin., 2000, Ross Pioneering Spirit award Am. Assoc. Critical-Care Nurses, 2004, Lifetime Achievement award Assn. Fundraising Profls., Ind., 2005, Woman of Achievement award, Ball State U., 2005 Torchbearer award Ind. Commn. for Women, 2005, Melva Jo Hendrix Leadership award Internat. Soc. Psychiat. Nursing, 2006; named Influential Woman in Indpls., Indpls. Bus. Jour./Ind. Lawyer, 1999, HealthCare Hero Indpls. Bus. Jour., 2003, Adele Herwitz Disting. scholar Commn. Fgn. Nursing Schs., 2005; Kellogg nat. fellow; Am. Nurses Found. scholar, Salute to Women award Indpls. YMCA, 1999, Sagamore of Wabash, 1999. Fellow: Nat. Acads. Practice, Am. Acad. Nursing (dir. leadership devel. bldg. acad. capacity program 2000—, past pres.), Living Legend 2006), APA (Nursing and Health Psychology award divsn. 38 1995); mem.: Nat. Acad. Scis., Inst. of Medicine (mem. bd. health policy ednl. programs and fellowships 2006—), Soc. for Rsch. in Child Devel., Midwest Nursing Rsch. Soc. (Disting. Rsch. award 1985), Sigma Theta Tau (past pres., Mentor award 1993, disting. lectr 1995—99, Melanie Dreher award for contbns. as a dean 2001), Chi Eta Phi (hon.). Home: 744 Cherokee Ave Lafayette IN 47905-1872 Office Phone: 317-278-9076. Business E-Mail: amcbride@iupui.edu.

**MCBRIDE, BRIAN,** professional soccer player; b. Arlington Heights, Ill., June 19, 1972; m. Dina McBride; 2 children. Attended, St. Louis Univ. Forward Vfl Wolfsburg, Germany, 1994—95, Columbus Crew, 1996—2001, Preston North End, England, 2000—01, Columbus Crew, 2002, Everton FC, England, 2003, Columbus Crew, 2003—04, Fulham FC, England, 2004—. 92 caps; 30 goals U.S. Nat. Soccer Team, 1993—; mem. U.S. World Cup Team, 1998, 2002, 06. Spokesperson Ctrl. Ohio Diabetes Assn. Named to, Ea. Conf. All Star Team, 1996, 1997; recipient Gold Ball MVP award & Gold Boot top scorer award, CONCACAF Gold Cup, 2002.*

**MCBRIDE, CAROL BAILEY,** science educator, consultant; b. Clinton, S.C., Oct. 7, 1956; d. William Jerome and Bernest Lark Bailey; m. Clifford Duncan McBride, July 13, 1982; children: Andrew Bailey, Austin Leigh. BS in Home Econs. Edn., Winthrop Coll., Rock Hill, S.C., 1976; MEd, Clemson U., SC, 1983. Home economics tchr. Whitten Ctr. Hallett Sch., Clinton, SC, 1977—80; ld resource tchr. Woodruff (S.C.) Elem., 1981—85; sci. tchr. Mabry Jr. HS, Inman, SC, 1985—. Sci. cons. S.C. Upstate Hub, Spartanburg, 1997; horizon's adv. bd. Spartanburg (S.C.) Sch. Dist. 6, 1995. Named Tchr. of The Yr., Mabry Jr. HS, 1998; recipient Tchrs. Leading Tchr.'s Program, S.C. Dept. Edn., 1998, Sci. Plus Inst., Roper Mountain Ctr., 2001; grantee, Spartanburg Jr. League, 1995; EIA Unit grantee, S.C. Dept. Edn., 1998. Mem.: S.C. Sci. Coun., S.C. Mid. Sch. Assn., S.C. Jr. Beta Club (club advisor 1985—2006). Office Phone: 864-472-8402.

**MCBRIDE, CRAIG PATRICK,** mathematics professor; b. Newport Beach, Calif., Mar. 16, 1971; s. Cliff McBride; m. Susan Lee McDevitt, Mar. 5, 1969. MA in Math., U. Colo., Boulder, 2001. Math instr. U. Colo., Boulder, 1999—2002; math prof. Holy Cross Coll., Worcester, Mass., 2002—03; math instr. Clackamas (Oreg.) C.C., 2003—04; math edn. rsch. asst. U. Melbourne, Victoria, Australia, 2004—05; math prof. Silver Lake Coll., Manitowoc, Wis., 2005—. Lead instr., co-organizer Wis. Summer Tchg. Inst., Manitowoc, 2006—. Office: Silver Lake College 2406 S Alverno Rd Manitowoc WI 54220-9319 Office Phone: 920-686-6165. Business E-Mail: cmcbride@silver.sl.edu.

**MCBRIDE, DARL,** information technology executive; BS, Brigham Young U.; MS, U. Ill. at Urbana-Champaign. Networking leader Novell, 1988—96, v.p., gen. mgr., embedded systems divsn.; sr. v.p. IKON Office Solutions; founder, chmn., CEO SBI and Co.; CEO PointServe; pres. Franklin Covey; pres., CEO SCO Group, Inc., Lindon, Utah. Office: SCO Group Inc 355 S 520 West Ste 100 Lindon UT 84042-1911 Office Phone: 801-765-4999. Office Fax: 801-765-1313.

**MCBRIDE, EARLE F.,** geologist, educator; PhD, John Hopkins, 1960. Prof. and J. Nalle Gregory Chair in sedimentary geology U. Tex., Austin. Recipient Pettijon Sedimentology medal Soc. Sedimentaty Geology, 1995. Office: U Tex at Austin Geol Sci Dept 1 University Station C1100 Office 4 138 Austin TX 78712-0254 Office Phone: 512-471-1905. Office Fax: 512-471-9425. Business E-Mail: efmcbride@mail.utexas.edu.

**MCBRIDE, ELIZABETH ANNE WILMORE,** writer; b. Charlotte, N.C., Nov. 10, 1942; d. John Henry and Frances (Cox) Wilmore; divorced; children: John and Laura. BA in English, Rice U., 1964; MA in English & Creative Writing, U. Houston, 1982; student, Edward Albee Workshops, 1989-92. Instr. U. Houston, 1979—81, 1985—88; editor Lit. Mag., Houston, 1982-83, Domestic Crude, Houston, 1983-84; contbr. editor, columnist Artscene, 1989; editor rsch. papers for Naomi Kraus, U. Tex., Houston, 1990. Reader Houston Festival; judge Southwest Writers' Conf., 1984; bd. dirs. Lawndale Art and Performance Ctr.; panel mem. Seminar on Hispanic Art, U. Ariz., 1987-88. Guest curator Rice U., Houston, 1988, Glassel Sch., Houston, 1993, Houston Art League, 1997; contbr. author: (short stories) Her Work, Common Bonds, The Whole Story, Texas Short Stories II; reviewer The Houston Chronicle, 1980, ARTspace Mag., 1987-92, ARTnews, 1990-95, 2000, Pub. News, 1988-94, Sculpture Mag., 1989-90, Artscene Mag., 1984, Chelsea Mag., N.Y., and numerous others; poems: Vapor Trails, 1981, Diversions, 1982, Biloxi 1945, 1982, South Pacific Stars and Stripes, 1982, Kwajalein, 1983, Deep Sea Fishing With My Father, 1984, Everyday Places, 1985, Linguistics, 1987, Moctezuma's Headdress, 1992, I Bury My Father, 1993, Corazal, 1993, Inca Doves, 1993, O Corporeal, 1997; editor Ctr. for Big Bend Studies, Bosque Bonito, 2002; contbr. articles and short stories to profl. jours. and mags.; exhibited in group shows at Treebeards, 1995, The New Gallery, 1995, Lawndale Art Ctr., 1995, Diverse Works Alternative Space, 1996, Sally Sprout Gallery, 1996, Houston Pottery Guild and Gallery, 1997, 2000; one woman shows at Westenberg Gallery, Marfa, 2000, Big Bend Sentinel, Marfa, 2000, Devin Borden Hiram Butler Gallery, Houston, 2002, Terlingua Ho. Projects, Alpine, Tex., 2002, Highland Gallery, Marfa, 2003; represented in numerous pvt. collections, S.I. Assocs., Houston, Playwright, Long Island; writer-in-residence Chinati Found, 1995-96, art critic ArtLies Mag., Houston Tex. Vol. tchg. Hartman Jr. High, Roberts Elem. Sch., Valley of Peace, Belize, Marfa Tex. Libr.; mem. literacy events bd. Houston Festival, chmn. lit. arts panel, 1986; bd. dirs. lit. and humanities panel Cultural Arts Coun. Houston, 1987-88; mem. lit. panel Tex. Commn. Arts, 1988-89. Recipient Brazos for fiction prize, 1984; fellow MacDowell Colony, 1986, Edward Albee Found., 1990. Mem. Poets and Writers, League Women Voters (chmn. voters svc.); founding bd. mem. Zocalo Theater. Home: 610 W Avenue B Alpine TX 79830-4528

**MCBRIDE, GUY THORNTON, JR.,** college president emeritus; b. Austin, Tex., Dec. 12, 1919; s. Guy Thornton and Imogene (Thrasher) McB.; m. Rebekah Jane Bush, Sept. 2, 1942 (dec. Aug. 1998); children: Rebekah Ann, William Howard, Ellen M. Alsobrooks; m. Cordelia D. Rush, Aug. 7, 1999. BS in Chem. Engring., U. Tex., 1940; Sc.D., MIT, 1948; D.P.S. (hon.), Regis Coll., 1979; D.Engring. (hon.), Colo. Sch. Mines, 1984. Registered profl. engr., Tex. La., N.Y., Colo. Instr. chem. engring. Mass. Inst. Tech., 1942-44, research assoc., 1946-48; job engr. Standard Oil Co. Calif., 1944-46; asst. prof. chem. engring Rice Inst., 1948-55, assoc. dean students, 1950-57, dean, 1957-58, assoc. prof., 1955-58; cons. Tex. Gulf Sulphur Co., 1950-58, asst. mgr. research dept., 1958-59, mgr., 1959-60, v.p., mgr. research, 1960-63; v.p. Tex. Gulf Sulphur Co. (Phosphate div.), 1963-70, gen. mgr., 1966-70; pres. Colo. Sch. Mines, Golden, 1970-84; ret. Dir. Halliburton Co., Kerr-McGee Corp., Hercules, Inc.; hon. dir. Texasgulf Inc. Fellow Am. Inst. Chem. Engrs.; mem. Am. Chem. Soc., Nat. Soc. Profl. Engrs., Sigma Xi, Phi Lambda Upsilon, Tau Beta Pi. Clubs: Mile High (Denver). Home: 2615 Oak Dr Apt 13 Lakewood CO 80215-7182

**MCBRIDE, JAMES M.,** school system administrator; m. Sandi McBride; children: Jim, Monique. MBA, La. Tech. U., 1981; EdD, U. NC, 1983. Tchr. Caesar Rodney Jr. HS, Dover, Del., Air Force Acad.; sr. pres. CC of Air Force (CCAF), 1996—2001; supt. schs. Bennett, Colo., 2001—03; tech. adminstr. Wyo. Dept. Edn., 2003—05, supt. pub. instrn., 2005—. Mem. Coun. Chief State Sch. Officers, Mid-continent Rsch. for Edn. and Learning. Mem. Montgomery Trust Fund for Visually Impaired, Wyo. Higher Edn. Assistance Authority, Wyo. Early Childhood Coun., Wyo. Workforce Develop. Coun., Wyo. Edn. Planning and Coord. Coun. With USAF, 1975—2001. Office: Wyo Dept Edn Hathaway Bldg, 2nd Fl 2300 Capitol Ave Cheyenne WY 82002-0050 Office Phone: 303-777-7675. Business E-Mail: jmcbri@educ.state.wy.us.

**MCBRIDE, JOHN P.,** state commissioner; b. Buffalo, Wyo., Mar. 23, 1951; Grad., U. Wyo., 1973, law school grad. 1976. Lawyer Jones, Vines and Hunkins, Wheatland, Wyo., 1981-89; staff atty. to dep. commr. State of Wyo. Ins. Dept., Cheyenne, 1989-92, ins. commr., 1992. U.S. Army Judge Advocate Gen. Corps, 1977-81.

**MCBRIDE, JONATHAN EVANS,** management consultant, director; b. Wash., June 16, 1942; s. Gordon Williams and Martha Alice (Evans) McBride; m. Emilie Evans Dean, Sept. 5, 1970; children: Webster Dean, Morley Evans. BA, Yale U., 1964. Account exec. Merrill Lynch & Co., Washington, 1968—72; v.p. dept. mgr. Lionel D. Edie & Co., NYC,

1972—76; v.p. and exec. search cons. Simmons Assoc., Inc., Washington, 1976—79; pres. McBride Assoc., 1979—. Bd. dir. Yale U. Alumni Fund, 1974—79; trustee Sidwell Friends Sch., Washington, 1996—2004, vice chair, 2002—04. To lt. USNR, 1964—68. Mem.: Chevy Chase (Md.) Club, Met. Club (Washington), Yale Club (NYC). Office: 1700 Pennsylvania Ave NW Ste 400 Washington DC 20006 Office Phone: 202-349-3663. Personal E-mail: hearthunt@aol.com.

**MCBRIDE, JONICA HELENE,** mathematics professor; b. Charleston, Ill., July 16, 1977; d. John M. and Joyce H. Craft; m. Michael Lee McBride, July 31, 1999; children: Ethan Pierce children: Michaela Joy, Makenna Cait. BA in Math.; MA in Pure Math., Ea. Ill. U., Charleston, 2005; postgrad., Ind. State U., 2006—. Math. instr. Lake Land Coll., Mattoon, Ill., 2002—, Ea. Ill. U., Charleston, 2005—. Deaconess Charleston Cmty. Ch., 2003—05. Recipient Dulgar Math Grad. Student-Assts. award, The Family of Lee Dulgar, 2004—05. Mem.: U. Profls. Ill. Home: 6867 Knollcrest Dr Charleston IL 61920 Office: Eastern Illinois Univ Math Dept 600 Lincoln Ave Charleston IL 61920 Office Fax: 217-581-6284.

**MCBRIDE, MARTINA,** vocalist; b. Medicine Lodge, Kans., July 29, 1966; d. Daryl and Jeanne Schiff; m. John McBride, May 15, 1988; children: Delaney Katherine, Emma Justine, Ava Rose Kathleen. Vocalist Schiffters, 1975-86, assorted bands, Wichita, Kans.; represented by RCA Records, 1991—; backup singer Garth Brooks, 1992—93, European tour, 1994. Singer: (albums) The Time Has Come, 1992, The Way That I Am, 1993 (Platinum), Wild Angels, 1995 (Platinum), Evolution, 1997 (Triple Platinum), Martina McBride Christmas, 1998, Emotion, 1999 (Platinum), White Christmas, 1999 (Platinum), (various artists) Girls Night Out, 1999, (Group recording) Safe In The Arms Of Love, 2000, Greatest Hits, 2001 (Dounble Platinum), Martina, 2003 (Gold), (songs) (Runaway Bride soundtrack) I Love You, 1999, (Backstage at the Grand Ole Opry) Wrong Again, 2000, (Where The Heart Is soundtrack) There You Are, 2000, (The Mercy Project) You'll Get Through This, 2000; performer: (tv appearances co-star Pat Benatar) CMT Crossroads, 2003, (tv appearances) Nat. Anthem, NBA All Star Game, 2003, (presenter of award) CMT Flameworthy Awards, 2003, (tv biography) Lifetime Intimate portrait, 2002. Nominee Best Country Song for "Independence Day", Grammy, 1994, Video Yr. for "Independence Day", Acad. Country Music, 1994, Best Country Collaboration with Vocals for "Own My Own" with Reba McEntire, Linda Davis, and Trisha Yearwood, Grammy, 1995, Vocal Event Yr. for "On My Own" with Reba McEntire, Linda Davis, and Trisha Yearwood., Country Music Assn., 1996, Album Yr. for "Wild Angels", 1996, Best Country Female Vocal Performance for "Safe In The Arms of Love", Grammy, 1995, Vocal Event Yr. for "Still Holding On" with Clint Black, Country Music Assn., 1997, Best Country Collaboration with Vocals for "Still Holding On" with Clint Black, Grammy, 1997, Video Yr. for "A Broken Wing", Country Music Assn., 1998, Single Yr. for "A Broken Wing", 1998, Acad. Country Music, 1999, Song Yr. for "A Broken Wing", 1999, Video Yr. for "A Broken Wing", 1999, Best Country Female Vocal Performance for "I Love You", Grammy, 1999, Single Yr. for "Blessed", Country Music Assn., 2002, Best Female Country Vocal Performance for "Blessed", Grammy, 2002, Video Yr. for "Concrete Angel", Country Music Assn., 2003, Top Female Vocalist, Acad. Country Music, 1993, 1998, 2000, 2001, Horizon award, Country Music Assn., 1994, Female Vocalist Yr., 1996, 1998, 1999, 2001, Am. Music Awards, 2003; recipient Breakthrough Artist Video for "My Baby Loves Me", Music Row Ind. Summit Award, 1994, Music Video Yr. for "Independence Day", Country Music Assn. Awards, 1994, Best Video Yr. for "Independence Day", Gt. Brit. Music Awards, 1994, Video Yr. for "Independence Day", Nashville Music Awards, 1995, TNN Music City News Award, 1995, Gold Clio for Country Music Video Yr. for "Independence Day", Clio Awards, 1995, Best Southern Gospel, Country Gospel or Bluegrass Gospel for "Amazing Grace - A Country Salute To Gospel", Grammy Awards, 1995, Country Album Yr. for "Wild Angels", Nashville Music Awards, 1996, Video Yr. for "Safe In The Arms of Love", 1996, Female Video Yr. for "Blessed", CMT Flameworthy Awards, 2002, Female Video Yr. for "Concrete Angel", CMT Flameworthy Award, 2003, Top Female Vocalist, Acad. Country Music, 2002, Acad. Country Music award, 2003, 2004, Female Vocalist Yr., Country Music Assn. Award, 2002, Female Vocalist Yr. award, Country Music Assn., 2003, 2004, Country Female Artist Yr., Billboard Music Award, 2002, Best Female Artist, Country Radio Music Awards, 1996, Favorite Female Artist, Country, Am. Music Awards, 2003, Favorite Female Artist, Country Weekly, 2003. Address: RCA Records 1400 18th Ave S Nashville TN 37212-2809*

**MCBRIDE, MICHAEL FLYNN,** lawyer; b. Milw., Mar. 27, 1951; s. Raymond Edward and Marian Dunne (McBride); m. Kerin Ann (O'Brien), Mar. 23, 1991; children: Raymond Erin, Barbara Marian. BS in Chemistry and Biology, U. Wis., 1972, JD, 1976; MS in Environ. Engring. Sci., Calif. Inst. Tech., 1973. Bar: Wis. 1976, DC 1976. Assoc. LeBoeuf, Lamb, Greene, & MacRae LLP, Washington, 1976—84, ptnr., 1985—, chmn. Transp. Practice Group. Mem. Assn. Transp. Law Profls. (v.p., law inst. com. 1990, exec. com. 1990-, pres. 1994-95, 2004-, chmn. program com. 1998-99), Chantilly Nat. Golf and Country Club, Congl. Country Club. Avocations: golf, reading, travel. Office: LeBoeuf Lamb Greene & MacRae LLP 1875 Connecticut Ave NW Washington DC 20009-5728 Office Phone: 202-986-8050. Office Fax: 202-986-8102. Business E-Mail: michael.mcbride@llgm.com.

**MCBRIDE, MILDRED MAYLEA,** retired elementary school educator; b. Bowerston, Ohio, Oct. 7, 1922; d. Harry Scott and Mary McGary (Mowl) McB.; 1 adopted child, Marjorie Mi Sang McBride. BS in Music, Baldwin-Wallace Coll., 1944; MA, Columbia U., N.Y.C., 1949. Cert. Ohio, Hawaii. Traveling music tchr. Tuscarawas County Sch., 1944-45; tchr. elem. music Parma (Ohio) Schs., 1945-48, tchr. jr. h.s. music, 1946-48; tchr. h.s. gen. music, chorus Kamehameha Sch. for Girls, Honolulu, 1949-59; tchr. elem. music Tempe (Ariz.) Schs., 1959-60, Hawaii Pub. Sch., 1960-86, ret., 1986. Co-founder Elem., Intermediate, Gen. Music Interest Group, Honolulu, 1969-79. Author: (biography) Mele!, 1996, Three Women of Kintail, 2001, (hist. novels) Lady Janet, Genny MacKenzie and Her Bairns, The Troubled Child, Angus and Margaret Meira, Two Brothers, Travels with MiSang, Trouble in Paradise, Alexander and Margaret; writer mus. plays. Helper Bowerston Pub. Libr., 1939, 48, 97—; bd. dirs.; mem. Honolulu Symphony Chorus; soup kitchen, vol. Harris United Meth. Ch., Honolulu, 1990-96, mem. choir, 1975-96. Avocations: golf, travel, singing, cooking, enjoying daughter.

**MCBRIDE, MILFORD LAWRENCE, JR.,** lawyer; b. Grove City, Pa., July 16, 1923; s. Milford Lawrence and Elizabeth B. (Douthett) McB.; m. Madeleine Coulter, Aug. 6, 1947; children: Marta, Brenda, Trip, Randy, Barry. AB, Grove City Coll., 1944; BS, NYU, 1944; JD, U. Pa., 1949. Bar: Pa. 1949, U.S. Dist. Ct. (we dist.) Pa. U.S. Supreme Ct. Ptnr., McBride & McBride, Grove City, 1949-77, sr. ptnr., 1992—; ptnr. McBride and Mc-Nickle, Grove City, 1977-92; dir. Integra Fin. Corp., 1988-93; trustee Grove City Coll., 1995—. 1st lt. USAAF, 1943-46. Mem. Mercer County Bar Assn. (state treas. 1970-77), ABA, Am. Bar Found., Oakmont Country Club, Univ. Club (Pitts.). Republican Office: 211 S Center St Grove City PA 16127-1508

**MCBRIDE, PATRICK EDWARD,** medical educator, dean; b. Milw., Oct. 3, 1953; s. Raymond Edward and Marian Dunne McBride; m. Kimberly S. Schappe, June 8, 1980; children: Sean Gallagher, Gabrielle Kearnes. B in Gen. Curriculum, U. Wis., Milw., 1976; MD, U. Wis., Madison, 1980; MPH, U. SC, Columbia, 1983. Diplomate Am. Bd. Family Practice, cert. Exercise program dir. Am. Coll. Sports Medicine. Prof. family medicine U. Wis. Med. Sch., Madison, 1984—; prof. medicine U. Wis. Sch. Medicine and Pub. Health, Madison, 1997—, assoc. dean for students, 2004—; co-dir. preventive cardiology program U. Wis. Hosp. and Clinics, Madison, 1997—. Author: Contemporary Diagnosis and Management in Preventive Cardiology. Recipient nat. award for innovation in family medicine edn., Soc. Tchrs. of Family Medicine, 1992, Tchg. Acad. Lifetime Recognition, U. Wis., 1996, Van Hise Disting. Tchg. award, 2000, Disting. Physician Alumni award, U. SC Sch. Medicine, 2002. Fellow: Am. Coll. Cardiology, Am. Soc. Clin. Nutrition (life), Am. Heart Assn. (life); mem.: Am. Acad. Family Physicians, Am. Soc. Preventive Cardiology (pres. 1992—94). Office: U Wis Med Sch 750 Highland Ave Rm 2150 HSLC Madison WI 53705-2221 Office Phone: 608-263-4920. Office Fax: 608-263-1187.

**MCBRIDE, ROBERT ALBERT,** training services executive; b. Woonsocket, R.I., Mar. 9, 1960; s. Albert and Leonora Anna McB.; m. Kathryn Moore, June 14, 1998; 1 child, Jordan. BA in Psychology, Providence Coll., 1982; MBA in Mgmt., Bryant Coll., 1994. Commd. ensign USN, 1985, advanced through grades to capt.; sales rep. Aventis Pharms., Providence, 1991—96, regional trainer New England region, 1996—99, area mgr. Pa., 1999—2002; dir. global tng. Genzyme Corp., 2002—. Mem. adv. bd. Boy's & Girl's Club, Cumberland, R.I., 1995-99; instr. Literacy Vols. Am., Woonsocket, R.I., 1997-99. Decorated Navy & Marine Corp Commendation medal, Navy Achievement medal; recipient Global War on Terrorism Svc. medal. Mem. World Affairs Coun., U.S. Naval Res. Assn., Naval Inst. Roman Catholic. Avocations: golf, biking, reading, basketball. Home: 10 Cathedral Ct Cumberland RI 02864 Office: Genzyme Corp 500 Kendall St Cambridge MA 02142 Office Phone: 401-658-5320. E-mail: bob.mcbride@genzyme.com.

**MCBRIDE, TAMERA SHAWN DEW,** geologist; d. Lawrence Bernard Dew, Jr. and Daris Virginia Hutchinson Dew; m. William Scott McBride, June 6, 1998; children: Roger, Rastus. BA cum laude, Rollins Coll., 1993; MS, U. So. Fla., 1995. Cert. radon measurement technician Fla. Dept. Health, Divsn. Environ. Health, 1997, profl. geologist Fla. Dept. Bus. and Profl. Regulation, 2002. Phys. sci. technician U.S. Geol. Survey, Ocala, Fla., 1991—94; scientist Environ. Resources Mgmt., Inc., Tampa, Fla., 1995—2000; planner S.W. Fla. Water Mgmt. Dist., Brooksville, Fla., 2000—04, profl. geologist, 2004—. Acting ex-officio mem. Ctrl. Fla. Regional Planning Coun., Bartow, Fla., 2000—04. Soloist St. Catherine (Fla.) United Meth. Ch., 1975—, mem. choir, 2001—, vice chair com. lay leadership, 2005; asst. sec. S.W. Fla. Water Mgmt. Dist. Employee Com., 2003—04, vice-chair, 2004—. Mem.: U. South Fla. Geology Alumni Soc. (bd. dirs. 1998—2000), Fla. Assn. Profl. Geologists, Chronic Fatigue and Immune Dysfunction Syndrome Assn. of Am., Phi Eta Sigma. Avocations: fishing, travel, dance. Home: PO Box 1223 Bushnell FL 33513 Office: Southwest Florida Water Mgmt Dist 2379 Broad St Brooksville FL 34604 Office Phone: 352-796-7211. Personal E-mail: dewfish@aol.com. E-mail: tamera.mcbride@swfwmd.state.fl.us.

**MCBRIDE, THOMAS DWAYNE,** management consultant; b. Brownwood, Tex., Feb. 13, 1947; s. Thomas Alfred and Eula Faye (Harvey) McB.; m. Peggy Anne Kimbrough McBride, Oct. 14, 1967; children: Jeffery Dwayne, Stacy Anne. AS, Crowder Coll., Neosho, Mo., 1967; BS in Mech. Engring., U. Mo., Rolla, 1970; MBA in Mgmt., U. Akron, 1978. Registered profl. engr., Ohio. Engring. supr. Babcock & Wilcox, Barberton, Ohio, 1972-79; mgr. engring. Bendix Corp., South Beloit, Ill., 1979-83; mgr. sales engring. Bendix/Warner & Swasey, Worcester, Mass., 1983-84, mgr. Product Engring., 1984-86; program mgr. Design Tech. Corp., Billerica, Mass., 1986-87; mgr. engring. Netco, Inc., Haverhill, Mass., 1987-88; dir. engring. The Nelmor Co., North Uxbridge, Mass., 1988-95; tech. mgr. Lawrence (Mass.) Pumps Inc., 1995-96, ops. mgr., 1996-2000; pres. Ptnrs. for Creative Solutions, Inc. Shrewsbury, Mass., 2000—. Tech. and bus. cons. Micromation, Inc., Altoona, Pa., 1988-90. Inventor: Granulator Knife, 1991, 94, Bin Deflector, 1991; author: Society of Manufacturing Engineers, 1992, M&A Today, 2000. Mem. Trinity Ch. 1st lt. U.S. Army, 1971—72. Recipient Curator's scholarship, U. Mo., 1967. Mem.: Soc. Mfg. Engrs., Assn. Mfg. Excellence, Corridor 9 C. of C., Phi Theta Kappa (chpt. pres. 1966—67). Avocations: golf, bicycling, genealogy, religious history, hiking. Personal E-mail: tmcbride@pcs-info.com.

**MCBRIDE, WILLIAM HOWARD, JR.,** lawyer; b. Belleville, Ill., May 10, 1945; s. William Howard McBride and Patricia (Sullivan) Sweat; m. Adelaide Alexander Sink, July 10, 1986; children: William Albert, Cheryle Alexander. BA, U. Fla., 1967, JD, 1975. Bar: Fla. 1976, D.C. 1978. With Holland & Knight, Tampa, Fla., 1975—2001, mng. ptnr., 1992—2001; ptnr. Barnett, Bolt, Kirkwood, Long & McBride, Tampa, 2004. Bd. dirs. Lawyers Com. for Civil Rights Under Law. Chmn. United Way Campaign, Tampa, 1991, Community Needs Assessment, Tampa, 1990; pres. Hillsborough County Bar Assn., Tampa, 1983-84. Capt. USMC, 1968-71, Vietnam. Fellow Am. Bar Found.; mem. ABA, Am. Law Inst. Democrat. Avocations: fishing, history, science fiction. Home: PO Box 219 Thonotosassa FL 33592-0219 Office: Barnett Bolt et al 601 Bayshore Blvd Ste 700 Tampa FL 33606 Office Phone: 813-253-2020. E-mail: bmcbride@barnettbolt.com.

**MC BRIDE, WILLIAM LEON,** philosopher, educator; b. NYC, Jan. 19, 1938; s. William Joseph and Irene May (Choffin) McB.; m. Angela Barron, July 12, 1965; children: Catherine, Kara. AB, Georgetown U., 1959; postgrad. (Fulbright fellow), U. Lille, 1959-60; MA (Woodrow Wilson fellow), Yale U., 1962, PhD (Social Sci. Rsch. Coun. fellow), 1964. Instr. philosophy Yale U., New Haven, 1964-66, asst. prof., 1966-70, assoc. prof., 1970-73; lectr. Northwestern U., Evanston, Ill., summer 1972; assoc. prof. Purdue U., West Lafayette, Ind., 1973-76, prof., 1976-2001, Arthur G. Hansen disting. prof., 2001—. Senate chmn. Purdue U. 2004-05; lectr. Korcula Summer Sch., Yugoslavia, 1971, 73; Fulbright lectr. Sofia U., Bulgaria, 1997. Author: Fundamental Change in Law and Society, 1970, The Philosophy of Marx, 1977, Social Theory at a Crossroads, 1980, (with R.A. Dahl) Demokrati og Autoritet, 1980, Sartre's Political Theory, 1991, Social and Political Philosophy, 1994, Philosophical Reflections on the Changes in Eastern Europe, 1999, From Yugoslav Praxis to Global Pathos, 2001; editor: (with C.O. Schrag) Phenomenology in a Pluralistic Context, 1983, Sartre and Existentialism, 8 vols., 1997, (with M.B. Matustik) Calvin O. Schrag and the Task of Philosophy after Postmodernity, 2002, The Idea of Values, 2003. Decorated chevalier Ordre des Palmes Académiques. Mem. AAUP (pres. Purdue chpt 1983-86, pres. ind. conf. 1988-89), Am. Philos. Assn. (chmn. com. on internat. coop. 1992-95, bd. dirs. 1992-95), N.Am. Soc. for Social Philosophy (v.p. 1997-2000, pres. 2000-05), Am. Soc. Polit. and Legal Philosophy, Soc. Phenemonology and Existential Philosophy (exec. co-sec. 1977-80), Sartre Soc. N.Am. (pres. dirs. 1985-88, 91-93), Am. Soc. Philosophy in the French Lang. (pres. 1994-96), Fed. Internat. Soc. Philosophie (steering com. 1998—, sec. gen. 2003—). Home: 744 Cherokee Ave Lafayette IN 47905-1872 Office: Purdue U Dept Philosophy 100 N Univ St West Lafayette IN 47907-2098 Office Phone: 765-494-4285. Business E-mail: wmcbride@purdue.edu.

**MCBROOM, THOMAS WILLIAM, SR.,** aviation consultant; b. Atlanta, Mar. 29, 1963; s. William Ralph and Ethel Irene (Bradley) McB.; m. Susan H.; 1 child, Thomas William Jr. B in Mech. Engring., Ga. Inst. Tech., 1985, MS in Mech. Engring., 1987; JD, MBA, Ga. State U., 1992; postgrad., Embry-Riddle Aero. U. Registered profl. engr., Ga.; cert. ins. agt.-life, accident and sickness, property, casualty & surety Ga.; bar: Ga. 1993, D.C. 1994, U.S. Tax Ct. 1993, U.S. Supreme Ct. 1996; lic. commal. pilot and flight instr., registered mediator and arbitrator Ga. Mfg. engr. AT & T Techs., Norcross, Ga., 1985-86; energy systems engr. Atlanta Gas Light Co., 1987-89, sales engr., 1989-90, dir. power systems markets, 1991-94, sr. corp. planning analyst, 1994-95, mgr. major accounts, 1995-97, dir. major accts., 1997-99; atty., cons. Newnan, Ga., 1999—; pilot ground instr. Delta Air Lines, Atlanta, 2000—01; project mgr. Aviation Consulting, AIR, Inc., Atlanta, 2001—. Mem. Grad. Leadership Coweta, 1996, Grad. Coverdell Rep. Leadership Inst., 1997. With USAR, 1997—, capt. JAGC. Mem.: Ga. Bar Assn., Coverdell Leadership Inst., Phi Delta Phi (exchequer 1991). Home: 15 Culpepper Way Newnan GA 30265-2217 E-mail: tmcbroom@charter.net.

**MCBRYDE, CECILIA COLLINS,** secondary school educator; d. John and Naomi Collins; m. Johnnie E. McBryde, Jan. 7, 1967; children: Donna Marie McBryde-Hardy, Edward. Nursing Degree, Phila., 1974; B in Sociology summa cum laude, Fayetteville State U., 1989, M in Sociology, 1996. RN Pa., 1974, N.C., 1974. RN, oper. rm. nurse Phila. Grad. Hosp., 1974; RN Phila. Health Dept., 1974—77; RN intensive care unit Cape Fear Valley Hosp., Fayetteville, NC, 1978—81; home health nurse Cumberland County, Fay-

etteville, 1979—81; RN intensive care unit Wake Med. Ctr., Raleigh, NC, 1981—89; instr. Fayetteville Tech. C.C., 1991—; health occupations instr. Cumberland County Schs., Fayetteville, 1993—. CPR and first aid instr. AHA and ARC, Fayetteville, 1984—; presenter in field. Blood dr. organizer ARC, Fayetteville, 1993—. Howard Hughes grantee, 2002. Mem.: NCHOETA (treas., sec. 2003—04), S.E. region Program Area Leadership Coun. liaison person), NCACTE (ways and means com., newspaper com. 2003—04), ACTE (mem. region II conf. profl. devel. planning com.), N.C. Leadership Inst. for Vocat. Educators, Health Occupations Students Am., Health Occupations Educators (sec./treas. 2002, 2003, 2005), Alpha Kappa Delta, Kappa Delta Pi. Avocations: reading, sports, travel. Office: South View High Sch Hope Mills NC

**MCBRYDE, JOHN HENRY,** federal judge; b. Jackson, Oct. 9, 1931; m. Betty Vinson; children: Rebecca, Jennifer, John Blake. BS in Commerce, Tex. Christian U., 1953; LLB, U. Tex., 1956. Bar: Tex. 1956, U.S. Ct. Appeals (5th cir.) 1958, U.S. Dist. Ct. (no. dist.) 1958, U.S. Dist. Ct. (ea. dist.) 1989, U.S. Supreme Ct. 1972. Assoc. Cantey, Hanger, Johnson, Scarborough & Gooch, Ft. Worth, 1956-62; ptnr. Cantey & Hanger and predecessor firm, Ft. Worth, 1962-69, McBryde, Bennett and predecessor firms, Ft. Worth, 1969-90; judge U.S. Dist. Ct. (no. dist.) Tex., Ft. Worth, 1990—. Fellow Am. Bar Found. (life), Tex. Bar Found. (life), Am. Coll. Trial Lawyers. Office: US Dist Ct US Courthouse 501 W 10th St Ste 401 Fort Worth TX 76102-3642 Office Phone: 817-850-6650.

**MCBRYDE, NEILL GREGORY,** lawyer; b. Durham, NC, Jan. 11, 1944; s. Angus M. and Priscilla (Gregory) McBryde; m. Margaret McPherson, Aug. 1, 1970; children: Margaret Courtauld McBryde Young, Neill Gregory Jr. AB cum laude, Davidson Coll., 1966; JD with high honors, U. N.C., 1969. Bar: N.C. 1969., Ga. 1972. Assoc. King & Spalding, Atlanta, 1971-76; ptnr. Fleming, Robinson, Bradshaw & Hinson, Charlotte, NC, 1977-81, Helms, Mulliss & Johnston, Charlotte, 1981-86, Smith Helms Mulliss & Moore, Charlotte, 1986-90, Moore & Van Allen PLLC, Charlotte, 1990—. Lectr. in field; condr. workshops in field. Author, editor: First Union National Bank of North Carolina Will Book, 1986; contbr. articles to profl. jours. Elder and Deacon Myers Park Presbyn. Ch., Charlotte, 1980-86, 92-95, 2001-04, 05—; bd. dirs., sec. Presbyn. Home for Aged, Charlotte, 1978-82; trustee Charlotte Latins Schs., Inc., 1980-86, 87-93; past chmn., past trustee Mint Mus. Charlotte. Fellow Am. Coll. Trust and Estate Counsel (past mem. bd. regents, past pres.), Am. Coll. Tax Counsel; mem. ABA, Ga. Bar Assn., NC Bar Assn. (probate and fiduciary law sect.), So. Fed. Tax Inst. (trustee 1999, pres. 2005-06), Order of Coif, Phi Beta Kappa, Omicron Delta Kappa. Republican. Avocations: tennis, golf, fishing. Office: Moore & Van Allen PLLC Bank of Am Corp Ctr 100 N Tryon St Fl 47 Charlotte NC 28202-4003 Office Phone: 704-331-1094.

**MCBURNEY, CHARLES WALKER, JR.,** lawyer; b. Orlando, Fla., June 6, 1957; s. Charles Walker McBurney and Jeane (Brown) Chappell. BA, U. Fla., 1979, JD, 1982. Bar: Fla. 1982, U.S. Dist. Ct. (mid. dist.) Fla. 1983, U.S. Ct. Appeals (11th cir.) 1984. Assoc. Mathews, Osborne, McNatt, Gobelman & Cobb, Jacksonville, Fla., 1982-84; asst. state's atty. State's Atty.'s Office, Jacksonville, 1984-90, civil atty., 1987-88, sr. trial atty., 1988-90; ptnr. Fischette, Owen, Held & McBurney, Jacksonville, 1990—2004; pvt. practice Law Office Charles W. McBurney Jr., Jacksonville, 2004—. Dir. Serious or Habitual Juvenile Offender Program, 1986. Mem. adv. coun. Mandarin Oaks Elem. Sch., vice chmn., 2003—04, chmn., 2004—; mem. Mayor's Bicentennial Constnl. Commn., 1989—91; chmn. com. congl. campaigns Jacksonville, 1982, 1984, 1988; deacon South Jacksonville Presbyn. Ch., 2003—; bd. dirs. Civic Round Table, 1988—92, treas., 1988—89, pres., 1989—90; dir. Internat. Devel. Commn. for Jacksonville, 1993—2003, treas., 1995—97; chmn. S.E. Citizens Planning Adv. Com., 2005—; bd. dirs. Am. Heart Assn. N.E. Fla., 1990—92. Mem.: ABA, Comml. Law League (So. region exec. coun. 1998—, treas. 2000—), Jacksonville Bankruptcy Bar Assn. (bd. dirs. 1999—2004, treas. 2000—04), Jacksonville Bar Assn. (chmn. bankruptcy sect. 1998—2000, 2002—03), Duval County Rep. Club (treas. 2002—), Jacksonville Hist. Soc., First Coast Tiger Bay Forum (bd. dirs. 2001—, Leadership award 2004), Jacksonville C. of C. (bd. govs. 1987, govtl. affairs com. 1998—), Fla. Jaycees (legal counsel 1987—88, Most Outstanding Local Pres. award 1987), Jacksonville Jaycees (pres. 1986, Jaycee of yr. 1984), Summit Civitan (judge adv. 1991—93, 2001—02), James Madison Inst., Southside Bus. Men's Club (v.p. 2003—04, parliamentarian 2006—), Bull Snort Club (pres. 1995—96, chmn. bd. 1996—99, pres. 1999—2000), Masons, N.E. Fla. Phi Beta Kappa Alumni Assn. (v.p. 1998—2000, 2003—04). Republican. Presbyterian. Home: 6326 Christopher Creek Rd E Jacksonville FL 32217-2485 Office: Ste 590 76 S Laura St Jacksonville FL 32202 Personal E-mail: cmcburney@bellsouth.net.

**MCBURNEY, ELIZABETH INNES,** dermatologist, physician, educator; b. Lake Charles, La., Dec. 24, 1944; d. Theodore John and Martha (Caldwell) Innes; divorced, 1980; children: Leanne Marie, Susan Eleanor. BS, U. Southwestern La., 1965; MD, La. State U., 1969. Diplomate Am. Bd. Internal Medicine, Am. Bd. Dermatology. Intern Pensacola (Fla.) Edn. Program, 1969-70; resident in internal medicine Boston U. and Carney Hosps., 1970-72; resident in dermatology Charity Hosp., New Orleans, 1972-74; staff physician Ochsner Hosp., New Orleans, 1974-80; assoc. head of dermatology Ochsner Clinic, New Orleans, 1974-80; clin. asst. prof. La. Health Scis., New Orleans, 1976-79, clin. assoc. prof., 1979-90, clin. prof., 1990—; clin. asst. prof. Tulane Health Scis., New Orleans, 1976-88, clin. assoc. prof., 1988-91, clin. prof., 1991—. Mem. courtesy staff Northshore Regional Med. Ctr., Slidell, La., 1985—; mem. staff Slidell Meml. Hosp., 1988—, chmn. CME courses, 1988—, pres.-elect med. staff, 2000-01, pres., 2001—02; regional dir. Mycosis Fungoides Study Group, Balt., 1974-94; pres.-elect Women's Dermatologic Soc., 2005. Contbr. articles to profl. jours. Bd. dirs. Slidell Art Coun., 1988—, Camp Fire, New Orleans, 1979-80, Cancer Assn. New Orleans, 1978-83; juror Art in Pub. Places, Slidell, 1989; councilman St. Tammany Art Coun., 2003-06. Recipient Disting. Woman Physician award AMA, 1999, Thomas Pearson edn. meml. award, 2004. Fellow ACP; mem. Am. Soc. Dermatologic Surgery (treas. 1991-94, bd. dirs. 1988-91, pres. elect 1995-96, pres. 1996-97), Women's Dermatol. Soc. (pres. 2006, Samuel Stegman award 2000, Pub. Svc. award, 2001), Am. Acad. Dermatology (bd. dirs. 1994-98), Am. Bd. Laser Medicine and Surgery (bd. dirs. 1991-96), La. Dermatologic Soc. (pres. 1989-90), St. Tammany Med. Soc. (pres. 1988), Phi Kappa Phi, Alpha Omega Alpha. Avocations: reading, gardening, fine art, music, films. Office: 1051 Gause Blvd Ste 460 Slidell LA 70458-2985 Office Phone: 985-649-5880.

**MCBURNEY, MARGOT B.,** retired librarian; b. Lethbridge, Alta., Can. d. Ronald Laurence Maness and R. Blanche (Lott) Hart; children: Margot Elisabeth McBurney Lane, James Ronald Gordon. BA with honours, Principia Coll., 1953; M.Sc. in L.S, U. Ill., 1966. Sec. Marshall Brooks Library, Principia Coll., Elsah, Ill., 1966-69, reference librarian, 1969-70; systems analyst trainee in library systems U. Alta. Library, Edmonton, 1970-71, undergrad. reference librarian, 1971-72, editor periodicals holdings list, 1972-73, serials cataloguer, 1973-74, head acquisitions div., 1974-77; chief librarian Queen's U. Library, Kingston, Ont., Canada, 1977-90; distrbr. Pharmanex, 2005—06. Editor: Am. Soc. Info. Sci. Western Can. chpt. Proceedings, 1975, 76. Mem. Am. Soc. Info. Sci. (councilor-at-large 1976-79, past chmn. chpt.), Assn. Research Libraries (dir. 1978-81, chmn. task force on library edn. 1980-83), Can. Assn. Rsch. Libs., Can. Assn. Research Libraries, Can. Library Assn., Council on Library Resources (PETREL com. 1981-84), Phi Alpha Eta, Beta Phi Mu. E-mail: mbm33@sympatico.ca.

**MCCABE, BROOKS FLEMING, JR.,** state legislator; b. Charleston, W.Va., Jan. 19, 1949; s. Brooks F. Sr. and Jane (Mason) McC.; m. Barbara Given McCabe; 1 child, Katherine Jane. BS in Mgmt. Engring., MEd in Adminstrn., U. Vt., 1972; EdD in Adminstrn., W.Va. U., 1975. Asst. to dir. Gov.'s Office Fed. and State Rels., Gov.'s Office Fed. and State Rels., Charleston, 1975-77; gov.'s housing coord. State of W.Va., Charleston, 1977-79; comml. real estate salesperson Home Finders, Inc., Charleston, 1979-80; mem. W.Va. Senate, Charleston, 1998—. Bd. dirs Charleston

Renaissance Corp.; pres., bd. dirs. Silver Creek Properties, Inc., Slaty Fork, W.Va., 1988-92. Pres. Cmty. Coun. of Kanawha Valley, Charleston, 1987-89; campaign chmn. United Way of Kanawha Valley, Charleston, 1988; trustee U. Vt., Burlington, 1976-82, The Gow Sch., South Wales, N.Y., 1988-97, W.Va. Wesleyan Coll., Buchanon, 2000—02; bd. dirs. W.Va. State Coll. Found., Inc., Charleston Area Med. Ctr. Found., 1992—98, Greater Kanawha Valley Found., 1988-91. Named Vol. of the Yr., United Way of Kanawha Valley, 1986-87. Mem. Am. Inst. Cert. Planners, W.Va. Planning Assn., Kanawha Valley Bd. Realtors, W.Va. Assn. Realtors, Urban Land Inst., Nat. Trust Hist. Preservation, W.Va. Roundtable. Democrat. Episcopalian. Avocations: reading, history, skiing. Office: McCabe Henley LP 107 Capitol St Charleston WV 25301-2609 Address: WV State Senate 1900 Kanawha Blvd E Rm 441M Charleston WV 25305-0009 Office Phone: 304-347-7500.

**MCCABE, CLARE,** chemical engineer, educator; BS in Chemistry, U. Sheffield, England, 1995, PhD, 1999. Assst. prof. Colo. Sch. Mines, Golden, 2002—04, Vanderbilt U., Nashville, 2004—. Mem.: AIChE, Soc. Women Engrs., Am. Soc. Engring. Edn., Royal Soc. Chemistry, Am. Chem. Soc., Sigma Xi. Office: Vanderbilt U Dept Chem Engring Nashville TN 37235-1604 Office Phone: 615-322-6853. Business E-mail: c.mccabe@vanderbilt.edu.

**MCCABE, DAVID J.,** lawyer; b. New Rochelle, NY, Aug. 16, 1958; BA, Iona Coll., 1980; JD, Fordham U., 1983. Bar: NY 1984. Sr. ptnr. Pvt. Clients Group Willkie Farr & Gallagher LLP, NYC. Mem. estate planning and taxation com. Trusts and Estates Mag.; lectr. in field. Co-author: New York Limited Liability Companies: A Guide to Law and Practice, 1995; contbr. articles for mags. Co-founder Huguenot Children's Libr., pres., 1993—98, dir., 1993—2002; mem. adv. bd City Harvest, Inc., 1989—93, bd. dirs., 1993—96, mem. exec. com., sec., 1994—96; mem. Profl. Adv. Com. Mus. Arts and Design, NYC, 2003—; mem. Profl. Adv. Coun. Lincoln Ctr. for Performing Arts, NYC, 2003—; bd. dirs., v.p., co-counsel Boys and Girls Club, New Rochelle, 2002—; bd. dirs. New Rochelle Humane Soc., New Rochelle, 2002—05, Ursuline Sch., 2004—. Fellow: Am. Coll. Trusts and Estate Counsel; mem.: Assn. Bar City NY (chair com. trusts, estates and surrogate cts. 2005—, judiciary com. 2005—), NY State Bar Assn. (trusts and estates law sect., vice chmn. com. estate and trust adminstrn. 1996—99, ad hoc com. liaison to legis. adv. com.). Office: Willkie Farr & Gallagher LLP 787 Seventh Ave New York NY 10019 Office Phone: 212-728-8723. Office Fax: 212-728-9723. E-mail: dmccabe@willkie.com.

**MCCABE, EDWARD AENEAS,** lawyer; b. County Monaghan, Ireland, Mar. 4, 1917; came to U.S., 1928; naturalized, 1931; s. Patrick and Alice (McDonnell) McC.; m. Janet Isabel Stevens, Nov. 17, 1951, (dec. Oct. 1981); children: Thomas, Michael, Patrick, Barbara; m. Verna Ann Peterson, June 27, 1985 LLB, Columbus U., 1946; LHD (hon.), Johnson & Wales U., 1977; LLD (hon.), Allentown Coll., 1992. Bar: D.C. 1946, U.S. Supreme Ct. 1950. Exec. asst. Joint Congl. Com. Labor Mgmt. Rels., 1947-48; atty. labor rels. and trade assn. matters Washington, 1949-52; gen. counsel com. on edn. and labor Ho. of Reps., 1953-55; assoc., White House counsel to Pres. Eisenhower, 1956-58, adminstrv. asst. Washington, 1958-61; ptnr. Hamel, Morgan, Park & Saunders, Washington, 1961-71, Hamel, Park, McCabe & Saunders, Washington, 1971-82; of counsel Foley & Lardner, 1982—. Chmn. bd. dirs. USA GROUP, Inc., Indpls.; bd. dirs. First Am. Bank, Washington; chmn. bd. Student Loan Mktg. Assn.; White House cons. Presdl. transition, 1974-75, advisor, 1980-81; mem. D.C. Criminal Justice Coordinating Bd. Trustee Pub. Defender Svc. D.C., Immaculata Coll., Washington, 1965-78, Allentown Coll., Center Valley, Pa., 1969-75; bd. govs. USO; bd. advisers DeSales Sch. Theology, Washington; bd. dirs. Community Found. Greater Washington; bd. dirs., pres. Eisenhower World Affairs Inst., Washington; mem. cardinal's com. laity Archdiocese of Washington, com. for deferred gifts for Archdiocese; exec. cabinet Cath. Charities USA; founding chmn. Lumina Found. With U.S. Army, 1941—45. Mem. ABA, Fed. Bar Assn., D.C. Bar Assn., Jud. Conf. D.C. Cir., Capitol Hill Club, Met. Club (Washington), Burning Tree Club (Bethesda, Md.), Kenwood Golf and Country Club (Bethesda). Republican. Roman Catholic. Office: Foley & Lardner 3000 K St NW Washington DC 20007*

**MCCABE, EDWARD R. B.,** hospital administrator, educator, physician; b. Balt., Mar. 26, 1946; BA in Biology, Johns Hopkins U., 1967; PhD in Pharmacology, U. So. Calif., 1972, MD, 1974. Diplomate Am. Bd. Pediatrics. Resident in pediatrics U. Minn. Hosps., Mpls., 1974-76; pediatric metabolism fellow Sch. Medicine U. Colo., Denver, 1976—78, instr., asst. prof., assoc. prof. pediatrics Sch. Medicine, 1978—86; from assoc. prof. to prof. genetics, pediatrics Baylor Coll. Medicine, Houston, 1986—94; exec. prof., chmn. dept. pediatrics David Geffen Sch. Medicine UCLA, 1994—. Physician-in-chief Mattel Children's Hosp. UCLA, 1995—; mem. med. genetics residency rev. com. Accreditation Coun. Grad. MEd. Edn., 1993—97; chmn. conf. gaucher disease NIH, Bethesda, Md., 1994—96; mem. NICHD Coun., 1995—99. Editor: Biochem. and Molecular Medicine, 1990—97, Molecular Genetics and Metabolism, 1998—. Chair sci. adv. bd. HEreditary Disease Found., L.A., 1998—99; chmn. Basil O'Connor award March Dimes, White Plains, NY, 1997—99. Mem.: Inst. Medicine, Soc. Pediatric Rsch. (E. Mead Johnson award 1993), Am. Coll. Med. Genetics (chair sec.'s adv. com. genetics, health and society 2002—, maternal and child health bur. 1999—2000, pres. 2001—02, co-chair newborn screening screening task force), Am. Soc. Biochem. and Molecular Biology, Am. Pediatric Soc., Am. Fedn. Clin. Rsch., Am. Soc. Human Genetics, Am. Bd. Med. Genetics (bd. dirs. 1992—97, pres. Bethesda 1995—96, diplomate), Am. Acad. Pediatrics (chmn. com. genetics Elk Grove Village, Ill. 1987—91, co-founder, chmn. sect. genetics Elk Grove Village 1990, 1993—95), Alpha Omega Alpha, Sigma Xi, Phi Kappa Phi. Achievements include First to describe the Continguous Gene Syndrome Complex Glycerol Kinase Deficiency; first to extract DNA from blood in newborn screening blotters; first to set up molecular genetic diagonosis for sickle cell disease as part of newborn screening; development of concept of molecular genetic triage of bacterial infection. Office: UCLA Pediatrics Box 951752 22-412 MDCC Los Angeles CA 90095 Office Phone: 310-825-5095. E-mail: emccabe@mednet.ucla.edu.*

**MC CABE, GERARD BENEDICT,** retired library administrator; b. N.Y.C., Jan. 22, 1930; s. Patrick Joseph and Margaret Irene (McDonald) McC.; m. Jacqueline L. Maloney, Aug. 3, 1963 (dec. 1987); children: Theresa Marie, Rebecca Mary. BA in English, Manhattan Coll., 1952; A.M. in Library Sci. (scholar), U. Mich., 1954; MA in English, Mich. State U., 1959. Asst. acquisitions dept. U. Nebr. Library, Lincoln, 1954-56; chief bibliog. acquisitions dept. Mich. State U. Library, East Lansing, 1956-58; librarian Inst. Community Devel. and Service, Mich. State U., 1958-59; acquisitions librarian U. S. Fla., Tampa, 1959-66, asst. dir. planning and devel., 1967-70; assoc. dir. U. Ark. Library, Fayetteville, 1966-67; dir. univ. libraries Va. Commonwealth U., Richmond, 1970-82; dir. libraries Clarion U. of Pa., 1982-95; ret. 1995; libr. cons., Wilmington, NC, 1995—. Editor: The Smaller Academic Library: A Management Handbook, 1988, Operations Handbook for Small Academic Library, 1989, Academic Libraries in Urban and Metropolitan Areas, 1992; co-editor ann. pub. Advances in Libr. Adminstrn. and Orgn., vols. 1-12, Insider's Guide to Libr. Automation: Essays of Practical Experience, 1993, Acad. Librs.: Their Rationale and Role in Am. Higher Edn., 1995, Introducing and Managing Academic Library Automation Projects, 1996, Leadership for Academic Librarians, 1998, Planning for a New Generation of Public Library Buildings, 2000, Planning the Modern Public Library Building, 2003, It's All About Student Learning, 2006; contbr. articles to profl. jours. Mem. ALA, Southeastern Libr. Assn. Home and Office: 201 Crain Hwy N Apt 3B Glen Burnie MD 21061-3375 E-mail: bldlib@comcast.net. *Consideration for others is a guiding principle for my personal and professional behavior. I, as a librarian, must have concern for those I serve. Their needs are my first and only interest, not success, not notoriety, only their service and their satisfaction.*

**MCCABE, JIM,** publishing executive; BA in Polit. Sci., Hartwick Coll. Rsch. analyst Ogilvy & Mather Advertising; mgr. mktg. sales Forbes; with The New Republic; pub. Worth mag., Fast Company mag.; publ., v.p. Fast

Company mag. and Inc. mag.; v.p., pub. PC mag., 2005—. Office: PC Mag 28 East 28th St New York NY 10016 Office Phone: 212-503-3500. Office Fax: 212-503-5799. E-mail: jim_mccabe@ziffdavis.com.*

**MCCABE, JOHN CORDELL,** surgeon; b. Urbana, Ill., Jan. 29, 1941; s. Louis Cordell and Catherine (Hesselschwerdt) McC.; m. Monique Thomas, July 14, 1977 (div. 1982); children: Timothy, Valerie. AB, U. N.C., 1963; MD, George Washington U., 1967. Diplomate Am. Bd. Surgery, Am. Bd. Thoracic Surgery. Intern N.Y. Hosp.-Cornell Med. Ctr., 1967-68, resident, 1970-76; asst. prof. surgery Cornell Med. Ctr., N.Y.C., 1976-82, assoc. prof. surgery, 1982—; attending surgeon N.Y. Hosp., N.Y.C., 1976—; asst. chief divsn. thoracic surgery Lenox Hill Hosp., N.Y.C., 1987—2004, dir. cardiothoracics, 2005—. Contbg. author: Principles of Trauma Care, 1982, Patent Ductus; contbr. articles to profl. jours. With USNR, 1969-70, Vietnam. Decorated Naval Commendation medal with Combat "V." Mem. numerous profl. orgns. in field. Home: 140 Riverside Dr New York NY 10024-2605 Office: 130 E 77th St Fl 4 New York NY 10021-1851

**MCCABE, JOHN L.,** lawyer; b. Chgo., Oct. 17, 1941; BA, U. Notre Dame, 1963; LLB, Harvard U., 1966. Bar: Ill. 1967, Colo. 1967. Ptnr. Davis Graham & Stubbs LLP, Denver. Office: Davis Graham & Stubbs LLP 1550 Seventeenth St Ste 500 Denver CO 80202 Office Phone: 303-892-9400. E-mail: john.mccabe@dgslaw.com.

**MCCABE, JOSEPH, JR.,** telecommunications industry executive; B in Mgmt., St. John's U., MBA in Quantitative Analysis, MBA in Acctg. With NY Tele.; from contr. to internat. v.p. AT&T Bus. Comm. Sys.; v.p., CFO strategy and new svcs. innovation divsn. AT&T, 1996—99, exec. v.p., CFO Redmond, Wash., 1999—.

**MCCABE, LOUISE BEACHBOARD,** language educator; b. NYC, Apr. 11, 1941; d. Walter William and Harriet Wood (Colby) Beachboard; m. James Laws McCabe, June 8, 1974; children: Sarah Beachboard, William Laws. BA, Smith Coll., 1963; MAT, Yale U., 1966; PhD, Harvard U., 1978. Instr. Italian, Harvard U., 1969-70, Harvard U., 1971-72, Yale U., New Haven, 1974-75, Tyler Art Sch. Temple U., Elkins Park, Pa., 1984-87, Villanova U., Pa., 1987-91; Latin tchr. Roxbury Latin Sch., Mass., 1970-71; tchr. ESOL, Sch. Dist. Phila., 1992-93, Inst. Italian and French Holy Family Coll., 1999-2002, Ctrl. HS, Phila., 2002-04; adj. prof. Italian, St. Joseph's U., Phila., 1993; instr. Pa. State U., 2003-06. Asst. editor Chilton Books, Phila., 1963-65. Contbr. articles to profl. jours. Founding mem. Somerville Police Cmty. Rels. Com., Mass., 1973. Mem. Colonial Dames Am., Internat. Womens Club Phila., Acorn Club (Phila.), Smith Coll. Club (bd. dirs. 1989-91). Republican. Episcopalian. Avocation: genealogy Home: 701 Williamson Rd Bryn Mawr PA 19010-1830 E-mail: whatisthis@erols.com.

**MCCABE, MARY F.,** marketing professional; d. Frank Camarda and Inez Cunningham; children: Vincent Joseph Papile, Kristin Julia Papile. BA, Smith Coll., 1982, MA, 1983; MFA, Yale U., 1994. Co-founder, mng. dir. Children's Theatre of Mass., Springfield, 1980—91; assoc. mng. dir. Yale Repertory Theatre; mng. dir. Nat. Playwrights Conf., O'Neill Ctr., 1994—2001; assoc. mktg. solution Lehman Bros., 2001—. Strategic planning com. O'Neill Theater Ctr., 1997—2000, transition com. to identify exec. dir., 1999—2000. Edn. task force Springfield Schs., 1987—99; liaison for Yale Repertory Theatre Spl. Olympic World Games, 1993; mem. Coast Guard Auxiliary, 1997—; bd. advisors Seven Devils Playwrights Festival, Boise, Idaho, 2000—. Recipient regional award for artistic achievement, New England Theater Conf. (NETC), 1990. Democrat. Roman Catholic. Home: 95 Cabrini Blvd Apt 3-L New York NY 10033 Office: Lehman Bros 745 7th Ave 30th Fl New York NY 10033 Office Phone: 212-526-8272. Personal E-mail: acthuman@aol.com. Business E-mail: mmccabe@lehman.com.

**MCCABE, MICHAEL J. (MICK),** insurance executive, lawyer; b. Denver, June 19, 1945; s. Joseph J. and Mary J. (Kane) McC.; m. Catherine Corrine Marquette, July 21, 1978; children: Brian Michael, Shannon Marquette. BS, U. No. Colo., 1967; JD, Cath. U. Am., 1971. Bar: D.C. Air transport econ. analyst U.S. Civil Aeronautics Bd., Washington, 1967-71; Washington counsel Allstate Ins. Co., Northbrook, Ill., 1971-74, of counsel, law and regulation office, 1974-82, asst. v.p. bus. planning, 1982-84, v.p. corp. planning, 1984-89, group v.p., gen. atty. 1989-95, v.p., property-casualty claim svc., 1995—97, sr. v.p., mktg., brand devel., 1997—99; v.p., gen. counsel Allstate Corp., Northbrook, Ill., 1999—; and sr. v.p., gen. counsel Allstate Ins. Co., Northbrook, Ill., 1999—. Bd. advisors No. Ill. U. Sch. Bus., DeKalb, 1986—. Chmn. Gateway Found. Mem. ABA, Fed. Bar Assn., D.C. Bar Assn., Planning Forum, Sigma Chi, Pi Alpha Delta. Democrat. Roman Catholic. Office: Allstate Ins Co 2775 Sanders Rd Northbrook IL 60062

**MCCABE, PAUL CHRISTOPHER,** psychologist, educator; b. Norfolk, Va., Dec. 1, 1970; s. Paul Patrick and Ellen Thompson McCabe; life ptnr. Daniel P. McOlvin. AA Early Childhood Edn., Cazenovia Coll., 1990; BA Psychology, U. Rochester, 1992; PhD Clin. & Sch. Psychology, Hofstra U., 1998. Lic. psychologist NY, cert. sch. psychologist. Asst. prof. Rochester (NY) Inst. Tech., 1997—2004; assoc. prof. Bklyn Coll. CUNY, 2004—. Cons. in field. Pres. Sch. Psychology Educators Coun. NY State, Bklyn., 2004—06. Rsch. grant, CUNY, 2005. Mem.: NASP, APA. Avocations: travel, photography, aviation. Office: Bklyn Coll CUNY Sch Edn 2900 Bedford Ave Brooklyn NY 11210 Office Phone: 718-951-5876. Business E-mail: paulmc@brooklyn.cuny.edu.

**MCCABE, ROBERT HOWARD,** college president; b. Dec. 23, 1929; s. Joseph A. and Kathryn (Greer) McC.; m. Arva Moore Parks, June 1992. BEd, U. Miami, 1952, LLD (hon.), 1992; MS, Appalachian State U., Boone, N.C., 1959; PhD, U. Tex., 1963; LLD (hon.), Barry U., 1986, Fla. Internat. U., 1990. Asst. to pres. Miami Dade C. of C., Fla., 1963-65, v.p. Fla., 1965-67, exec. v.p. Fla., 1967—80, pres. Fla., 1980—95, Essex County Coll., Newark, 1967-69; sr. fellow League for Innovation in the C.C., 1995—; Disting. fellow Edn. Commn. of the States, 2000—. Exec. com. So. Regional Edn. Bd., Atlanta, 1981-83; trustee Coll. Bd., Princeton, 1988-90; vice chair The Miami Coalition for a Drug-Free Cmty., 1989-94, chair, 1991—; exec. dir. Nat. Alliance of Cmty. and Tech. Colls., 2005-; dir. The Bridge Partnership, 2002—; exec. dir. Nat. Alliance Cmty. and Tech. Colls., 2005-. Author: Man and Environment, 1971, No One to Waste, 2000, Yes We Can, 2002, several monographs; editor: Jour. Environ. Edn.; cons. editor Change Mag., 1980—; contbr. articles to profl. jours. Bd. dirs. Nat. Ctr. Pub. Policy and Higher Edn., 1998—. Recipient Disting. Svc. award Fla. Congl. Del., 1983, Spirit of Excellence award The Miami Herald, 1988, Harold W. McGraw Jr. prize in Edn., 1991, The Coll. Bd. medal, 1995; named Outstanding Grad., Coll. Edn., U. Tex., 1982, named one of the 18 Most Effective Chief Exec. Officers in C.C. (sr. fellow, dir. exec. com. 1985—, Disting. Svc. award 1995); mem. Am. Assn. C.C. (bd. dirs. 1991—, Disting. Svc. award 1995), Am. Assn. Higher Edn. (dir. on Higher Edn. Issues, Higher Edn. Consortium), Am. Coun. Edn. (dir. 1973-75), Am. Assn. for Environ. Edn. (pres. 1970-73), Am. Coun. on Edn. (bd. dirs. 1983-85, 92—), Southeast Fla. Edn. Consortium (chmn. bd. 1981-83). Episcopalian. Home: 1601 S Miami Ave South FL 33129-1103 Office Phone: 305-854-4428. E-mail: rmccabe@bellsouth.net.

**MCCAFFERTY, BARBARA JEAN (BJ MCCAFFERTY),** sales executive; b. Lincoln, Nebr., Dec. 6, 1940; d. Russell Rowley and Ruth Alice (Williams) Wightman; m. Eriks Zeltins, Dec. 29, 1962 (div. 1976); 1 child, Brian K. Zeltins; m. Charles F. McCafferty Jr., Oct. 3, 1981 (div. July 1986). Student, Drexel U., 1958—61; BS magna cum laude, Del. Valley Coll. Sci. and Agri., Doylestown, Pa., 1984; MBA in Mktg., LaSalle U., 1998, MBA in Fin., 2002. Dept. mgr. Strawbridge & Clothier, Neshaminy, Pa., 1968-73, asst. buyer Phila., 1973-76; office administr. Am. Protein Products, Croydon, Pa., 1976-78; tech. librarian Honeywell Power Sources Ctr., Horsham, Pa., 1978-85; sales dir. Colonial Life and Accident Ins., Wayne, Pa.,

1985-86; adminstrn. mgr. Mobi Systems, Inc., Ft. Washington, Pa., 1986-88; spl. rep. Universal Mktg. Corp., Southampton, Pa., 1988-89; ind. contractor McCafferty Ins. Svcs., Doylestown, Pa., 1989—; bus. rsch. asst. Merck & Co., Inc., West Point, Pa., 1991—. Alumni recruitment connection Delaware Valley Coll. Sci. and Agr Mem. NAFE, Nat. Assn. Profl. Saleswomen, Options, Inc., Franklin Mint Collectors Soc., Optomists, Lenox Collections Republican. Presbyterian. Avocations: aerobics, walking, reading, yoga, bicycling. Home: 224 Hastings Ct Doylestown PA 18901-2506 Business E-Mail: barbara_mccafferty@merck.com.

**MCCAFFERTY, EILEEN PATRICIA,** elementary school educator; b. Phila., June 9, 1953; d. Thomas Patrick and Frances Catherine (Friel) McC. BS in Elem. Edn., St. Joseph's U., 1990; cert. religious studies, St. Charles Sem., Phila., 1978. Cert. tchr., Pa. Tchr. 2d grade Our Lady of Loreto, Phila., 1972—2000, Mary Mother of Peace, Phila., 2000—. Fellow Nat. Cath. Edn. Assn. Avocations: bicycling, gardening, ceramics. Office: Mary Mother of Peace 64th & Buist Ave Philadelphia PA 19142

**MCCAFFERTY, LEO RAYMOND,** plastic surgeon; b. Pitts., Nov. 24, 1953; s. Leo Garvey and Virginia Catherine (Ballard) McC.; m. Susan Mary Kimball, July 31, 1992; children: Leo Thomas, Kristin Rae, Kimberly Lynn. BS, Pa. State U., 1975; MD, Temple U., 1981. Diplomate Am. Bd. Plastic Surgery. Resident in gen. surgery Cedars-Sinai Med. Ctr., L.A., 1981-85; resident in plastic surgery Jackson Meml. Hosp. U. Miami (Fla.), 1985-87, asst. prof. plastic surgery, 1987-90; pvt. practice, vol. asst. prof. Plastic Surgery U. Pitts., Pitts., 1990—. Asst. clin. prof. Plastic Surgery U. Pitts. Sch. Medicine, Pitts., 1990—. Contbr. articles to profl. jours. Med. practitioner Govt. Jamaica, Jamaica, 1987. State Sen. scholar Temple U., 1977-78, Measey scholar Temple U., 1977-78. Mem. Am. Soc. Plastic Surgeons, Am. Soc. Maxillofacial Surgeons, Am. Cleft Palate Assn., Am. Burn Assn., Greater Pitts. Plastic Surgery Soc. Avocations: athletics, art, music. Office: Plastic Surgery 211532 S Aiken Ave Pittsburgh PA 15232

**MCCAFFERY, LAURA BELLE,** retired librarian; b. Bourbon, Ind., Sept. 3, 1932; d. Glasgow Lavern and Fern Isabel (Meek) Hibbets; m. Ralph William McCaffery, May 25, 1928 (Dec.); children: Michael William, Steven William. BS, Ind. U., 1953. Lang. arts tchr. Hammond Pub. Schs., Ind., 1953-56; lib. br. mgr. Hammond (Ind.) Pub. Lib., 1956-59; young adult librarian Allen County Pub. Lib., Fort Wayne, Ind., 1959-82, readers svcs. librarian, 1982—2004; cmty. vol., 2004—. Supr. display materials Readers Svcs. Allen County Pub. Libr., Ft. Wayne, Ind., 1983—; libr. Non-profit Resource Ctr., 2001-04 Author: Book Reviews Fort Wayne News Sentinel 1959-70; editor: Column in Focus on Indiana Libraries, 1984; author: Move Books Not Furniture 1987, Building An ESL Collection For Young Adults, 1998. Mem. adv. bd. Horizons Coun. for the Gifted and Talented, Fort Wayne Cmty. Schs., Ind., 1982—; bd. dirs. 3 Rivers Literacy Alliance, Ind., 1985—, Allen County-Fort Wayne Hist. Soc., 2006—. Named Dist. Hoosier, Ind. Gov. Joe Kernan, 2004. Mem. Ind. Libr. Assn., Pub. Libr. Assn., ALA, Intellectual Freedom Roundtable, Internat. Reading Assn., Three Rivers Literacy Alliance, Friends of the Libr., Rainbow Girl Lodge, Alpha Delta Pi. Episcopalian. Avocations: gardening, music, cooking. Office: Allen County Readers Svcs 900 Webster St Fort Wayne IN 46802-3602 E-mail: lb_mccaffery@msn.com.

**MCCAFFREY, BARRY RICHARD,** retired military officer; b. Taunton, Mass., Nov. 17, 1942; s. William Joseph and Mary Veronica (Curtin) McC.; m. Jill Ann Faulkner, June 8, 1964; children: Sean, Tara, Amy. BS, U.S. Mil. Acad., 1964; MA, Am. U., 1971; postgrad., Command and Gen. Staff Coll., Ft. Leavenworth, Kans., 1976, Army War Coll., Carlisle Barracks, Pa., 1982. Commd. 2d lt. U.S. Army, 1964, advanced through grades to gen., 1994; ret. 1996; co. comdr. 7th Cav. Div., Vietnam, 1968-69; assoc. prof. dept. social sci. U.S. Mil. Acad., West Point, NY, 1972-75; from chief ops. br. to comdr. 2d battalion 3d Inf. Div., Germany, 1976-81; from chief staff to comdr. 3d brigade 9th Inf. Div., Ft. Lewis, Wash., 1982-86, comdr. 3d brigade, 1984-86; asst. comdt. U.S. Army Inf. Sch., Ft. Benning, Ga., 1986-88; dep. U.S. mil. rep. NATO, Brussels, 1988-89; div. comdr. 24th Inf. Div., Ft. Stewart, Ga., 1990-92; asst. to Chmn. Joint Chiefs of Staff The Pentagon, Washington, 1992-93; dir. strategic plans and policy directory The Joint Staff, Washington, 1993-94; comdr. in chief U.S. So. Commd., Quarry Heights, Panama, 1994-96; dir. White Ho. Office Nat. Drug Control Policy, Washington, 1996—2001; Olin disting. prof. nat. security studies U.S. Mil. Acad., 2001—05; pres. B.R. McCaffrey Assocs., LLC, Alexandria, Va., 2001—; mil. analyst NBC News. Contbr. articles to mil. publs. Decorated D.S.C. with oak leaf cluster, D.M.S. with oak leaf cluster, Silver Star with oak leaf cluster, Def. Superior Svc. medal, Purple Heart with two oak leaf clusters. Mem. NAACP, Assn. of U.S. Army, Coun. of Fgn. Rels., Inter-Am. Dialogue, Legion of Valor of U.S. Independent. Avocations: hunting, reading military history. Office: Br Mccaffrey Associates Llc 2900 S Quincy St Arlington VA 22206-2231

**MCCAFFREY, CARLYN SUNDBERG,** lawyer; b. NYC, Jan. 7, 1942; d. Carl Andrew Lawrence and Evelyn (Back) Sundberg; m. John P. McCaffrey, May 24, 1967; children: John C., Patrick, Jennifer, Kathleen. Student, Barnard Coll., 1963; AB in Econs., George Washington U., 1963; LLB cum laude, NYU, 1967, LLM in Taxation, 1970. Bar: NY 1974, US Tax Ct. 1975. Law clk. to C. J. Traynor Calif. Supreme Ct., 1967-68; teaching fellow law NYU, NYC, 1968-70, asst. prof. law, 1970-74; assoc. Weil, Gotshal & Manges LLP, NYC, 1974-80, ptnr., 1980—, co-head trust and estate dept. Prof. in residence Rubin Hall NYU, 1971-75; asst. prof. law 1970-74, adj. assoc. prof. law 1975-79, adj. prof. law 1979-, NYU Sch. Law; adj. prof. law U. Miami, 1979-81; lectr. in field; mem. adv. bd. Tax Analysts, mem. adv. com. Philip E. Heckerling Inst. on Estate Planning, U. Miami, 1978-. Co-author Structuring the Tax Consequences of Marriage and Divorce; Contbr. articles to profl. jours. Mem. bd. trustee Blythedale; bd. dirs. Breast Cancer Rsch. Fund, Children's Hosp.; mem. NY Archdiocese Planned Gifts Bequests com.; mem., sec. bd. dirs. Catholic Communal Fund; chair Central Park Profl. Adv. Com.; mem. planning giving adv. com. Mus. Modern Art; mem. profl. advisors coun. com. Lincoln Ctr. for the Performing Arts, Inc. Mem. ABA (chmn. and vice-chmn. com. on generation-skipping transfer tax com. 1979-81, 93—, mem. coun. real property probate and trust law sect.), NY State Bar Assn. (com. com. tax sect. 1979-80, co-chmn. estate and gift taxation com. 1976-78, 85—88, chmn. life ins. com. trusts and estates and tax sects. 1983-85, former co-chair com. income taxation of trusts and estates 1988-89, co-chmn. estates and trusts com. 1995-), Assn. of Bar of City of NY (matrimonial law com., chmn. tax subcom. 1984-86, Am. College Trusts & Estates Counsel (fellow, bd. regents 1992-97, mem. exec. com. 1995-97, past pres. 2002), Internat. Acad. Trust & Estate Counsel (mem., v.p.); fellow Am. Coll. Tax Counsel. Home: PO Box 232 Waccabuc NY 10597-0232 Office: Weil Gotshal & Manges LLP 767 5th Ave New York NY 10153 Office Phone: 212-310-8136. Office Fax: 212-310-8007. E-mail: carlyn.mccaffrey@weil.com.

**MCCAFFREY, CINDY,** information technology executive; BA in journalism, U. Nebr. Former reporter, editor publ. including Omaha World-Herald, Springfield (Mo.) Leader & Press, Kansas City Bus. Jour., Contra Costa Times, Macintosh Today; former comm. dir./mgr. co. including Apple Computer, E*TRADE, 3DO Co., and Smart Force; current v.p. corp. mktg. Google Inc., Mountain View, Calif.

**MCCAFFREY, JUDITH ELIZABETH,** lawyer; b. Providence, Apr. 26, 1944; d. Charles V. and Isadore Frances (Langford) McC.; m. Martin D. Minsker, Dec. 31, 1969 (div. May 1981); children: Ethan Hart Minsker, Natasha Langford Minsker. BA, Tufts U., 1966; JD, Boston U., 1970. Bar: Mass. 1970, D.C. 1972, Fla. 1991. Assoc. Sullivan & Worcester, Washington, 1970-76; atty. FDIC, Washington, 1976-78; assoc. Dechert, Price & Rhoads, Washington, 1978-82, McKenna, Conner & Cuneo, Washington, 1982-83; gen. counsel, corp. sec. Perpetual Savs. Bank, FSB, Alexandria, Va., 1983-91; ptnr. Powell, Goldstein, Frazer & Murphy, Washington, 1991-92, McCaffrey P.A., 1992—. Contbr. articles to profl. jours. Mem. Leadership Collier, 1998. Mem. ABA (chair subcom. thrift instns. 1985-90), D.C. Bar Assn. (bd. govs. 1981-85), Fla. Bar Assn. (chmn. fin. svcs. com. 1999-2000, exec. coun. bus.

law sect. 1998-), Women's Bar Assn. D.C. (pres. 1980-81), Collier County Women's Bar Assn. (pres. 1997-98), Gulf Coast Venture Forum (pres. 2001-03). Episcopalian. Avocations: travel, reading, martial arts, Spanish. Office: McCaffrey PA 568 9th St S Ste 255 Naples FL 34102-6620 Home: 3801 Portar SP NW Washington DC 20016

**MCCAFFREY, ROBERT HENRY, JR.,** retired manufacturing company executive; b. Syracuse, N.Y., Jan. 20, 1927; s. Robert Henry and May Ann (McGuire) McC.; m. Dorothy Anne Evers, Sept. 22, 1956; children: Michael Robert, Kathleen Mary. BS, Syracuse U., 1949. Sales asst. Sealright Corp., Fulton, NY, 1949-50; with TEK Hughes div. Johnson & Johnson, Metuchen, NJ, 1950-67, gen. sales mgr., 1958-59, v.p. sales, 1959-62, pres., 1962-67; gen. mgr. med. div. Howmet Corp., N.Y.C., 1967-70; group v.p. Howmedica, Inc., 1970-73, sr. v.p., 1973-74, exec. v.p., also bd. dirs., 1974-76; pres., CEO C.R. Bard, Inc., Murray Hill, NJ, 1976-78, chmn. bd. dirs., CEO, 1978-89, chmn. bd., 1989-91, also bd. dirs., chmn. exec. com., 1991—99. Bd. dirs. Summit and Elizabeth Trust, Summit Bancorp, Thomas & Betts Corp. Trustee Found. for Univ. Medicine and Dentistry N.J., 1987-90, Syracuse U., 1979-04, chmn. corp. adv. council, 1974-75. With AUS, 1945-46. Mem. Orthopedic Surg. Mfrs. Assn., Health Industry Mfrs. Assn. (bd. dir., chmn. 1982-83), N.Y. Sales Execs. Club, Sigma Chi. Republican. Roman Catholic. Avocations: reading, skiing, golf. Office: C R Bard Inc 730 Central Ave New Providence NJ 07974

**MCCAGHY, CHARLES HENRY,** retired social sciences educator; b. Eau Claire, Wis., Apr. 29, 1934; s. Elmer and Anna Josephine (Soha) McC.; m. M. Dawn Ysebaert, June 10, 1961 BBA, U. Wis., 1956, MS, 1962, PhD, 1966. Instr. sociology U. Conn., 1964-66; asst. prof. sociology Case Western Res. U., Cleve., 1966-70; assoc. prof. sociology Bowling Green State U., Ohio, 1970-76, prof. Ohio, 1976-94, prof. emeritus Ohio, 1994—; ret., 1994. Vis. scholar Australian Inst. Criminology, 1984 Author: Deviant Behavior: Crime, Conflict and Interest Groups, 1976, 7th edit., 2006, Crime in American Society, 1980, 2d edit., 1987. Lt. (j.g.) USN, 1956-59 Mem. Am. Soc. Criminology (treas. 1978-82). Home: 221 Williams St Bowling Green OH 43402-3259

**MCCAIG, JEFFREY JAMES,** transportation company executive; b. Moose Jaw, Sask., July 5, 1951; s. John Robert and Anne Shorrocks (Glass) McC.; m. Marilyn Graves, July 7, 1983; children: Robbert Angus, Scott Thomas, Christa Mae. Student, Can. Jr. Coll. Lausanne, Switzerland, 1970; AB, Harvard Coll., 1973; LLB, Osgoode Hall Law Sch., Can., 1976; MSc in Mgmt., Leland Stanford Jr. U., 1984. Assoc. MacKimmie Matthews, 1976-81; owner, sr. officer Jeffrey J. McCaig Profl. Corp., 1981-83; v.p. planning and corp. devel. Trimac, Calgary, Alta., Canada, 1983—87, exec. v.p., 1987—90, pres., 1990—94, pres., CEO, 1994—. Bd. dirs. Trimac Corp., Potash Corp. of Sask, EnerVest Group, Orbus Pharma Inc., Stoneham Drilling. Mem.: World Presidents' Orgn., Law Soc. Alta., Glencoe Club, Calgary Golf and Country Club.

**MCCAIN, BETTY LANDON RAY (MRS. JOHN LEWIS MCCAIN),** political party official, state official; b. Feb. 23, 1931; d. Horace Truman and Mary Howell (Perrett) Ray; m. John Lewis McCain, Nov. 19, 1955; children: Paul Pressly III, Mary Eloise. Student, St. Mary's Jr. Coll., Raleigh, N.C., 1948—50; AB in Music, U. N.C., Chapel Hill, 1952, LLD (hon.), 1998; MA, Columbia U., N.Y.C., 1953; LittD (hon.), U. N.C. Wilmington, 1997; HHD (hon.), Wake Forest U., Winston-Salem, N.C., 1999; LLD (hon.), Barton Coll., Wilson, N.C., 1999. Courier, European tour guide Ednl. Travel Assocs., Plainfield, NJ, 1952-54; asst. dir. YWCA, U. N.C., Chapel Hill, 1953-55; chmn. N.C. Dem. Exec. Com., 1976-79; mem. Dem. Nat. Com. 1971-72, 76-79, 80-85, chmn. sustaining fund NC, 1981, 88-91, mem. com. on presdl. nominations (Hunt Commn.), 1981-82, mem. rules com., 1982-85, mem. cabinet Gov. James B. Hunt, Jr., 1993-2001, sec. dept. cultural resources, 1993-2001; mem. State Dem. Exec. Com., 1971—99, 2001—. Mem. Winograd Commn., 1977-78; pres. Dem. Women of N.C., 1971-72, dist. dir., 1969-72; pres. Wilson County Dem. Women, 1966-67; precinct chmn., 1972-76; del. Dem. Nat. Conv., 1972, 88; mem. Dem. Mid-Term Confs., 1974, 78, mem. jud. coun. Dem. Nat. Com., 1985-89; dir. Carolina Tel. & Tel. Co. (now Embarq), 1981-97 (1st woman); bd. trustees U. N.C.-TV, 2002-06, vice chmn., 2006—; interim chair McCain Internat. Empowerment Project, 2001—. Contbg. editor: History of N.C. Med. Soc. Treas. Wilson on the Move, 1990—92; mem. Coun. on State Goals and Policy, 1970—72, Gov.'s Task Force on Child Advocacy, 1975—78; chmn. Wilson-Greene Morehead scholarship com., 1986—89; mem. career and personal counseling svc. adv. bd. St. Andrews Coll.; charter mem. Wilson Bch. Devel. Coun.; active Arts Coun. of Wilson, 1980—; pres. Wilson County Mental Health Assn. bd. dirs., legis. chmn.; bd. govs. U. N.C., 1975—81, 1985—93, pers. and tenure com., 1985—91, chmn. budget and fin. com., 1991—93; bd. regents Barium Springs Home for Children, chair Founds. com. Capital Campaign, 2003—; bd. dirs. N.C. Mus. History Assocs., 1982—83, pres., 1982—83, membership chair, 1987—88; co-chmn. Com. to Elect Jim Hunt Gov., 1976, 1980, co-chmn. senatorial campaign, 1984; mem. N.C. Adv. Budget Com. (1st woman), 1981—85; chmn. State Employees Combined Campaign N.C., 1993; bd. visitors Peace Coll., Wake Forest U. Sch. Law, 1980—83, U. N.C., Chapel Hill; co-chmn. fund dr. Wilson Cmty. Theater; v.p. Wilson County Hist. Assn., 2004—; chmn. devel. com., bd. visitors Lineberger Comprehensive Cancer Clinic, 2006—; chmn. centennial Am. Lung Assn., NC; Sunday sch. tchr. 1st Presbyn. Ch., Wilson, 1970—71, 1986—88, 1990—92, mem. chancel choir, 1985—, deacon, 1986—92, mem. fin. com., 1990—91, chair, 1992—93, elder, 1992—98, 2006—; state bd. dirs. N.C., Am. Lung Assn., 1985—88; bd. dirs. Roanoke Island Commn.; mem. battleship commn. USS/NC, 1993—2001; bd. dirs. Wilson Rose Garden, 2002—. Recipient state awards N.C. Heart Assn., 1967, Easter Seal Soc., 1967, Cmty. Svc. award Wilson Downtown Bus. Assocs., 1977, award N.C. Jaycees, 1979, 85, Women in Govt. award N.C. and U.S. Jaycettes, 1985, Alumni Disting. Svc. award U. N.C., Chapel Hill, 1993, Flora Mac Donald Scottish Heritage award, 1995, Carpathian award N.C. Equity, 1995, Pinnacle award, 1997, 1st winner Holderness-Weaver award U. N.C., Greensboro, 1999, Citizen of Yr. award Wilson C. of C., 2001, Ruth Coltrane Cannon award for hist. preservation Preservation N.C., 2000, N.C. State U. Sch. of Design award, 2000, The North Caroliniana award, 2006; named Dem. Woman of Yr., N.C., 1976, Internat. Founders award Eta State Delta Kappa Gamma Soc., 2005; named Outstanding Wilson Citizen of Yr., Wilson Red Cross, 2004. Mem.: DAR (historian John W. Dunham chpt.), Rotary Internat. (Paul Harris fellow 2003), N.C. Inst. Medicine (bd. dirs. 1993—2005), N.C. Sch. Arts (trustee 1993—2001), N.C. Equity (bd. dirs.), N.C. Soc. Internal Medicine Aux. (pres.), N.C. Symphony (trustee 1993—2001, 2002—05), Info. Resources Mgmt. Commn. N.C. Bd. dirs. 1993—2001), N.C. Agy. Pub. Telecom. (bd. dirs. 1993—2001), N.C. Found. for Nursing (bd. dirs. 1989—92), St. Mary's Alumni Assn. (regional v.p., Most Disting. Alumna 2005), U. N.C. Chapel Hill Alumni Assn. (chmn. 2001—02, dir.), Nat. Soc. Colonial Dames Am. NC (sec. local com. program co-chmn.), AMA Alliance (dir., nat. vol. health svcs. chmn., aux. liaison rep. AMA Coun. on Mental Health, aux. rep. Coun. on Vol. Health Orgns.), N.C. Art Soc., N.C. Lit. and Hist. Assn., Wilson Country Club, Little Book Club, The Book Club (pres.), Pi Beta Phi. Home: 1134 Woodland Dr NW Wilson NC 27893-2122

**MCCAIN, DANIEL,** retired agronomist; b. Delphi, Ind., Nov. 11, 1940; s. Thomas Clayton and Roseland Mary McCain; m. Virginia Arlene Waymire (div.); 1 child, Nicole Diane. BS in Agronomy, Purdue U., 1962. Soil conservationist USDA Soil Conservation Svc., Portland, Ind., 1962—63, Lafayette, Ind., 1963—64, dist. conservationist Williamsport, Ind., 1964—69, Ft. Wayne, Ind., 1969—87; nat. conservation tillage specialist Conservation Tech. Info. Ctr., Lafayette, Ind., 1987—94; ret., 1994. Cons. in field, 1994—2001. Author, compiler: nat. collection Conservation Tillage Survey By County, 1987—94. Vol. Earth Team, Delphi, 1994—; chmn. Delphi Hist. Trails, 1989—; bd. dirs. Ind. State Mus. Found., Indpls., 1998—2004. Recipient Sagamore of the Wabash award, Gov. of Ind., 2004, Samuel Milroy award, Delphi C. of C., 2001. Mem.: Am. Canal Soc. (bd. dirs. 2004—), Canal Soc. Ind. (bd. dirs. 1992—), Soil and Water Conservation Soc. (life), Lewis and

Clark Trail Assn., Wabash and Erie Canal Assn. (life; pres. 1999—2006). Avocation: camping. Home: 3198 N 700 W Delphi IN 46923 Office: Carroll County Wabash & Erie Canal Assn 1030 W Washington St Delphi IN 46923

**MCCAIN, DAVID B.,** lawyer; b. 1961; AB, Brown U., 1983; JD, U. Miami, 1986. Bar: Fla., 1986. V.p. Lennar Corp., Miami, Fla.; pres., CEO Lennar Fin. Svcs. LLC, Miami, 2005—. Mem. ABA. Office: Lennar Financial Svcs LLC 700 NW 107th Ave Ste 300 Miami FL 33172-3154 Business E-Mail: davidmccain@lfsi.com.

**MCCAIN, JOHN SIDNEY, III,** senator; b. Canal Zone, Panama, Aug. 29, 1936; s. John Sidney and Roberta (Wright) McCain; m. Carol, 1965 (div. 1980); 1 child Sidney Ann; m. Cindy Hensley, May 17, 1980; children: Doug, Andrew, Sidney, Meghan, Jack, Jimmy, Bridget. Grad. U.S. Naval Acad., 1958; grad., Nat. War Coll., 1973-74; degree (hon.), Johns Hopkins U., 1999, Colgate U., 2000; U. Penn., 2001, Wake Forest U., 2002; U. So. Calif., 2004. Dir. Navy Senate Liaison Office, Washington, 1977-81; mem. U.S. Ho. Reps. 98th-99th Congress from 1st Ariz. Dist., 1983—86; US Senator from Ariz., 1987—; mem. armed svcs. com. US Senate, chmn. commerce, sci. and transp. com., 1997—2001, 2001, 2003, chmn. Indian affairs com. Chmn. Internat. Republican Inst., 1993—; Republican candidate for presidential nomination, 2000; mem. Commn. on the Intelligence Capabilities of the US Regarding Weapons of Mass Destruction, 2004; speaker Republican Nat. Convention, NYC, 2004. Author (with Mark Salter): (nonfiction) Faith of My Fathers, 1999, Worth the Fighting For: What I Learned from Mavericks, Heroes, and Politics, 2002, Why Courage Matters: The Way to a Braver Life, 2004; author: (with Mark Salter) Character is Destiny, 2005. Served in USN, 1958—81, prisoner of war, 1967—73, Vietnam, became captain USN, 1977. Excellence in Pub. Svc. award, Am. Acad. of Pediatrics, 1999, Friendship award, League of Latin Am. Citizens, 1999, Intrepid Freedom award, Intrepid Museum Found., 1999, Profile in Courage award, John F. Kennedy Library Found., 1999, Paul H. Douglas Ethics in Govt. award, Institute of Govt. & Pub. Affairs, U. Il, 2000, William Penn Mott Jr. Park Leadership award, Nat. Parks Conservation Assn., 2001, Citizen Patriot award Citizen Patriot Orgn., 2003, Arthur T. Marix Congresional Leadership award Mil. Officers Assn. Am., 2004, Cancer Survivor of Yr. Cancer Rsch. and Treatment Fund, 2004, Econ. Patriot award The Concord Coalition, 2004, Evelyn F. Burkey award Writers Guild Am. East, 2004, Disting. Leadership award Am. Ireland Fund, 2005; Decorated Legion of Merit, Silver Star, Bronze Star, Purple Heart, Disting. Flying Cross, Vietnamese Legion of Honor; named on of the 25 Most Influential People in Am., Time mag., 1997, 100 Most Influential People, Time mag. 2006. Mem., Am. Legion, Society of the Cincinnati, VFW; bd. dirs. Community Assistance League, Phoenix, 1981-, Internat. Rep. Inst., 1993-, Nixon Ctr. for Peace and Freedom. Republican. Episcopalian. Office: US Senate 241 Russell Office Bldg Washington DC 20510 also: District Office Ste 105 5353 North 16th St Phoenix AZ 85016-3282 Office Phone: 202-224-2235, 602-952-2410. Office Fax: 202-228-2862, 602-952-8702.*

**MCCALEB, ANNETTE WATTS,** executive secretary; b. Darbfork, Ky., Dec. 11, 1931; d. Benjamin Taylor and Suzanna Elizabeth (White) Watts; m. John Henry McCaleb, Oct. 23, 1962; children: Jonathan Jeffrey, Suzanna Elizabeth McCaleb Woodhead, Sarah Leslie McCaleb Kaza. BS, U. Ky., 1954. Med. technologist Good Samaritan, Lexington, Ky., 1953-54; lab. supr. Charleston (W.Va.) Meml., 1954-58; chief med. technologist Meml. Hosp., Indpls., 1958-63; assoc. prof. UAMC, Little Rock, 1963-66; sec., treas., co-owner John H. McCaleb Constrn., Inc., Little Rock, 1966—. Justice of the peace Pulaski County Quorum Ct., Ark., 1989—; state bd. dirs. F.L.A.G., 1989-. Mem. S.W. Kiwanis (pres. 1997-99), Pulaski County Property Owners Assn. (pres. 1990-2000). Democrat. Baptist. Avocations: reading, crossword puzzles, gardening, sewing, swimming. Home and Office: 3900 Annette Ln Little Rock AR 72206-5357 Office Phone: 501-888-4253. Personal E-mail: annmccaleb@sbcglobal.net.

**MCCALEB, GARY DAY,** university official; b. Anson, Tex., Nov. 2, 1941; s. Victor Earl and Vivian (Day) McC.; m. Sylvia Ravanelli, June 5, 1964; children: Cara Lee Cranford, Bryan Day. BA, Abilene Christian Coll., 1964; MBA, Tex. A&M U., 1975, PhD, 1979. Asst. dir. alumni rels. Abilene (Tex.) Christian U., 1964-65, dir. alumni rels., 1965-69, dir. coll. rels., 1969-73, asst. acad. dean, 1978-80, v.p. pub. rels., 1980-83, v.p., dean campus life, 1983-91, v.p., 1991—, exec. dir. Ctr. for Bldg. Cmty., 1999—; asst. dir. devel Tex. A&M U., Bryan, 1973-75. Leader internat. travel and goodwill groups; U.S. rep. to world exec. com. Internat. Union Local Authorities, 1996-99. Author: Community, The Gift of Community. Coun. mem. City of Abilene, 1985-90, mayor, 1990-99; bd. dirs. Taylor County Am. Cancer Soc., 1972-73; mem. adv. bd. United Way of Abilene, 1979-83, dir. pub. svc. divsn., 1987, chmn. consortium on drug and alcohol abuse, 1989; bd. dirs. Civic Abilene, Inc., 1981-83; treas. Abilene Task Force on Drug and Alcohol Abuse, 1984-86; active March of Dimes; mem. Tex. Sci. and Tech. Coun., 1997-2000. Recipient Polit. Courage award John Ben Shepperd Pub. Leadership Forum, Austin, Tex., 1993, Tex. Urban Leadersip award U. Tex.-Arlington Sch. Urban and Pub. Affairs, 1995. Mem. Nat. League Cities (nat. steering com. on fin., adminstrn. and intergovtl. rels. 1989-90, adv. bd. 1994, bd. dirs. 1992-94), U.S. Conf. Mayors, Internat. Mcpl. Consortium (chmn. 1994-95), Tex. Mcpl. League (legis. policy com. Houston 1986, resolutions com. Dallas 1988, v.p. region 6 1988-89, bd. dirs. 1989-90, pres. 1992), Abilene C. of C. (aviation com. 1981, 94). Republican. Mem. Ch. of Christ. Avocations: art, baseball, jogging. Office: Abilene Christian Univ PO Box 29136 Abilene TX 79699-0001 E-mail: mccalebg@acu.edu.

**MCCALEB, MALCOLM, JR.,** lawyer; b. Evanston, Ill., June 4, 1945; BA, Colgate U., 1967; JD, Northwestern U., 1971. Bar: Ill. 1971. Atty. McCaleb, Lucas & Brugman, Chgo., 1970—85; ptnr. Keck, Mahin & Cate, Chgo., 1985—95, Foley & Lardner, Chgo., 1995—2000, Barack Ferrazzano Kirschbaum Perlman & Nagelberg, LLP, Chgo., 2000—. Chmn. Northfield (Ill.) Village Caucus, 1981-82, active, 1977-82, Northfield Zoning Commn., 1985-88; pres. bd. dirs. Vols. Am., 1977-79; active Northfield Sch. and Park Bd. Caucus, 1980-87. Mem. Chgo. Bar Assn., Bar Assn. 7th Fed. Cir., Patent Law Assn. Chgo., Internat. Trademark Assn. Office: Barack Ferrazzano Kirschbaum Perlman & Nagelberg LLC 333 W Wacker Dr Chicago IL 60606 Office Phone: 312-984-3100. Business E-Mail: mac.mccaleb@bfkpn.com.

**MCCALEB, NEAL A.,** former federal agency administrator; b. Oklahoma City; m. Georgann McCaleb; 4 children. BS in Civil Engring., Okla. State U. Sec. transp. Dept. Transp., Okla., 1987—91, Okla., 1995—2001; asst. sec. Bur. Indian Affairs, U.S. Dept. Interior, Washington, 2001—03. Mem. Okla. Ho. of Reps., minority floor leader, 1978.

**MCCALL, ANTHONY,** filmmaker; Founder Anthony McCall Associates, 1979; founder & mng. ptnr. Narrative Rooms LLC, 1996. Flim, Line Describing a Cone, 1973; author: (article) Visitors Online: Designing a Virtual Art Mus., 1996; Represented in permanent collections. Mus. Modern Art, NY, Whitney Mus. Am. Art, Centres Georges Pompidou, exhibited in group shows, Edinburgh International Film Festival, Carnegie Mus. Art, Pitts., Australian Nat. Gallery, Whitney Biennial, Whitney Mus. Am. Art. Office: Narrative Rooms 5130 NW 114 Pl Miami FL 33178

**MCCALL, BRENDAN,** dancer, educator; b. San Francisco, Calif., Apr. 24, 1972; s. Edwin McCall and Sarah Cracraft Roberts. Degree in Massage Therapy, Swedish Inst., NY, 1997; BFA with honors in Acting, NYU, 1993; MFA in Dance, Bennington Coll., Vt., 2003. Mem. faculty NYU, 1997—2001; mem. dance faculty Danshögskolan, Stockholm, 2002—06; mem. faculty movement Yale Sch. Drama, Conn., 2006—. Mem. faculty movement Atlantic Acting Sch., N.Y., 1997, 2004—05, Am. Acad. Dance, N.Y.C., 2000—02; mem. faculty NYU 2004; lectr. in field. Vol. Quantum Leap, Bennington, Vt., 2003, St. Vincent's Psychiat., N.Y., 2004. Recipient Dance Performance award, Danza Italia, 2000; grantee, Polli Talu, 2004,

Wilson Coll., Chambersburg, Pa., 2000, 2002, 2006. Mem.: Stage Dir.'s Choreographers Found., Actors Equity Assn. Mem. Soc. Of Friends. Avocations: comic book collecting, literature, films, travel, yoga. Home: 212 West 22d St 1N New York NY 10011

**MCCALL, CHARLES BARNARD,** health facility administrator, educator; b. Memphis, Nov. 2, 1928; s. John W. and Lizette (Kimbrough) McCall; m. Carolyn Jean Rosselot, June 9, 1951 (dec. Feb. 2002); children: Linda, Kim, Betsy, Cathy; m. Ernestine Mann, Jan. 5, 2004. BA, Vanderbilt U., 1950, MD, 1953. Diplomate Am. Bd. Internal Medicine, Am. Bd. Pulmonary Diseases. Intern Vanderbilt U. Hosp., Nashville, 1953-54; clin. assoc., sr. asst. surgeon USPHS, Nat. Cancer Inst., NIH, 1954-56; sr. asst. resident in medicine U. Ala. Hosp., 1956-57, chief resident, 1958-59; fellow chest diseases Nat. Acad. Scis.-NRC, 1957-58; instr. U. Ala. Med. Sch., 1958-59; from asst. prof. to assoc. prof. medicine U. Tenn. Med. Sch., 1959-69, chief pulmonary diseases, 1964-69; mem. faculty U. Tex. Sys., Galveston, 1969-75, prof. med. br., 1971-73; assoc. prof. medicine Health Sci. Ctr., Southwestern Med. Sch., Dallas, 1973-75, also assoc. dean clin. programs, 1973-75; dir. Office Grants Mgmt. and Devel., 1973-75; dean, prof. medicine U. Tenn. Coll. Medicine, 1975-77, Oral Roberts U. Sch. Medicine, Tulsa, 1977-78; interim assoc. dean U. Okla. Tulsa Med. Coll., 1978-79; clin. prof. medicine U. Colo. Med. Sch., Denver, 1979-80; prof. medicine, assoc. dean U. Okla. Med. Sch., 1980-82; exec. dean and dean U. Okla. Coll. Medicine, 1982-85; v.p. patient affairs, prof. medicine U. Tex. M. D. Anderson Cancer Ctr., 1985-94; chief of staff VA Med. Ctr., Oklahoma City, 1980-82; ret., 2004. Exec. dir. Worldwide Healthcare Svcs., Inc., Waco, Tex., 1998—2002; clinic dir. Claremore Family Medicine, 2002—04, cons. 2002; bd. dirs. Amigos Internacionales, Inc. Contbr. articles to med. jours. Fellow: ACP, Am. Coll. Chest Physicians; mem.: AMA, Am. Fedn. Clin. Rsch., So. Thoracic Soc. (pres. 1968—69), Am. Thoracic Soc., Sigma Xi, Alpha Omega Alpha. Baptist. Home: 225 Whitetail Dr Walnut Shade MO 65771 Personal E-mail: mccallcharles@centurytel.net.

**MCCALL, GENE WILLIAM,** conservator, sculptor, artist, furniture designer; s. Joseph Frederick and Verna Irene McCall; m. Sandra Ann Andreassi, Apr. 21, 1982; children: Kate, Taylor. Student, Keystone Coll., 1969—71, Elizabethtown Coll., 1971—73, Nat. Acad. Design/Sch. Fine Arts, 1981—82, SUNY, Purchase, 1983—84. Restorer/furniture maker Brumble's Antiques, Richmond, Va., 1973—75; owner McCall's Antiques, Richmond, 1975—78; conservator/furniture designer Reese's Antique Co., Richmond, 1978—79, Antique Furniture Workroom (formerly Stair & Co.), N.Y.C., 1979—82; owner McCall & Co., Mahopac, NY, 1983—91; pres. Gene McCall Conservation & Restoration Inc., Englewood, Fla., 1991—. Instr. wood sculpture Ringling Sch. Art and Design, Sarasota, Fla., 1992—93; judge fine furniture competition Fla. State Fair, Tampa, 1995—2003; guest expert Antiques Roadshow (PBS), Tampa, 1999; spkr. in field; cons. in field. Author: Best of Fine Woodworking (Tables and Chairs), 1995; sculpture, City of Joy (Best of Show, 1993), exhibitions include Ringling Mus. Art, 1998, Kristofer Lindsay Gallery; prodr.: (video series (episode 1) The Art of Gold Leafing with Gene McCall, 2004. Co-founder/bd. mem. Englewood (Fla.) Cmty. Alliance, 2004—05; pres. bd. Olde Englewood Village Assn., 2005. Recipient Outstanding Achievement award, Tampa/Hillsborough Planning Commn., 1999; fellow Conservation grantee, Hillsborough County Pub. Arts Commn., 2004. Mem.: Nat. Sculpture Soc., Am. Inst. for Conservation Hist. and Artistic Works (assoc.). Achievements include patents for new type of extensible furniture. Avocations: photography, kayaking. Office: Conservation & Restoration Inc 860-D South River Rd Englewood FL 34223 Office Phone: 941-473-1348. Home Fax: 941-473-2444; Office Fax: 941-473-2444. Personal E-mail: gmccall@ewol.com.

**MCCALL, H. CARL,** financial services executive, former state comptroller; b. Boston, Oct. 17, 1935; m. Joyce Brown; 1 child, Marci. BA, Dartmouth Coll., 1958; student, Andover Newton Theol. Sch., U. Edinburgh. Senator upper Manhattan dist. N.Y. State Senate, 1975—79; v.p. Citicorp/Citibank, 1984—93; pres. N.Y.C. Bd Edn., 1991—93; comptroller State of N.Y., 1993—2003; vice chmn., mng. dir. HealthPoint, LLC, 2003—. Bd. dirs. NY Stock Exch., 1999—2003, Tyco Internat. Ltd., 2003—. Amb. to UN; commr. Port Authority N.Y. and N.J.; commr. N.Y. State Divsn. Human Rights, 1983-85; mem. Coun. Fgn. Rels., Coun. Am. Ambs.; past. bd. dirs. N.Y. State Commn. State and Local Fin., Harlem Internat. Trade Ctr. Corp. Recipient Nelson A. Rockefeller Disting. Public Service award, 2002. Office: Healthpoint LLC 505 Park Ave 12th Fl New York NY 10022*

**MCCALL, JENNIFER JORDAN,** lawyer; b. NYC, Feb. 15, 1956; m. James W. McCall; children: Caroline, Hillary. BA cum laude in English Lit., Princeton U., 1978; JD, U. Va. Sch. Law, 1982; LLM in Taxation, NYU, 1988. Bar: N.Y. 1983, Calif. 2002. Assoc. Lord Day & Lord, NYC, 1982-92; ptnr. Lord Day & Lord, Barrett Smith, NYC, 1992-94; ptnr. Pvt. Client Group Cadwalader, Wickersham & Taft, NYC, 1994—2003; ptnr. Pillsbury Winthrop, LLP, NYC & Palo Alto, Calif., 2003—05; ptnr., co-chmn. Wealth Mgmt. & Individual Client practice Pillsbury Winthrop Shaw Pittman, NYC & Palo Alto, Calif., 2005—. Trustee Charitable Founds. and Trusts and advisor to numerous high net worth individuals; spkr. in field on estate and tax planning and adminstrn. Co-author: Estate Planning for Authors and Artists, 1998; contbr. chpt. to Estate Tax Techniques. Steering com., Planned Giving Adv. Com., The Mus. of Modern Art; mem. Proffl. Advisor's Coun., Lincoln Ctr., Inc.; trustee League for the Hard of Hearing, N.Y.C., 1992-2003, East Side House Settlement, Bronx, N.Y., 1995-2002, Chapin Sch., N.Y.C., 1998-2001; chairperson Ethel Gray Stringfellow Art Case Com., N.Y.C.; bd. trustees San Francisco Ballet. Fellow Am. Coll. Trust and Estate Counsel; mem. ABA (real property, probate and trust law sects.). N.Y. State Bar Assn. (com. on trusts and estates adminstrn.; chairperson subcom. on proposed legislation on executor's commns.), Calif. State Bar Assn. Office: Pillsbury Winthrop Shaw Pittman 2470 Hanover St Palo Alto CA 94304-1114 also: Pillsbury Winthrop Shaw Pittman 1540 Broadway New York NY 10036 Office Phone: 650-233-4020. Office Fax: 650-233-4545. Business E-Mail: jenniferjordan.mccall@pillsburylaw.com.

**MC CALL, JERRY CHALMERS,** retired federal official; b. Oxford, Miss., June 30, 1927; s. E. Forrest and Mariada (Huffaker) McC.; m. Margaret Denton, Nov. 28, 1952; children: Betsy, Lynn, Kim. BA, MA, U. Miss., 1951; MS, U. Ill., 1956, PhD, 1959. Tchg. asst. dept. math. U. Miss., 1950-51, instr. math., 1952-53, prof. math., 1973-76, exec. vice chancellor, 1973-76; rsch. assoc. U. Ill., 1953-57; applied sci. rep. IBM, Springfield, Ill., 1957-58, mgr. Bethesda, Md., 1966-68, Huntsville, Ala., 1968-71, Owego, N.Y., 1971-72; exec. v.p. Midwest Computer Service, Inc., Decatur, Ill., 1958-59; mem. sci. staff computation lab. Army Ballistic Missile Agy., Huntsville, 1959-60; asst. to dir. Marshall Space Flight Ctr., NASA, Huntsville, 1960-63; dep. dir. rsch. and devel. ops. Marshall Space Flight Ctr. NASA, Huntsville, 1963-66, dir. info. rsch. NASA Miss. Test Facility Bay St. Louis, 1972-73; pres. 1st State Bank and Trust Co., Gulfport, Miss., 1976-77; dir. Nat. Data Buoy Ctr., Miss., 1977-99; pres. McKool, Inc., Gulfport, Miss., 1982-94, Am. Mini Storage, Gulfport, 1985—, Am Crane Rentals, Inc., 1985-89, Cool-Power, Inc., 1988-93; ret., 1999; cons. EG & G Corp. 1999—2000; pres. Greentree Apts., 1999—2005. Head math. dept. St. Bernard Coll., Cullman, Ala., part-time, 1960-65; assoc. prof. math. U. Ala., Huntsville, 1960-62; pub. speaker, 1960-63; chmn. incorporators First State Bank & Trust Co., Gulfport, Miss., 1973-76; tech. cons. Gen. Electric Co., 1974-75 Editor: (with Ernst Stuhlinger) Astronautical Engineering and Science, 1963, From Peenemunde to Outer Space, 1963. Mem. Miss. Criminal Justice Standards Commn., 1974-75; mem. Miss. Marine Resources Council, 1974-76; bd. dirs. S. Miss. Found.; bd. advisers Sch. Engring., U. Miss., 1965-73; mem. indsl. advisors U. New Orleans; chmn. founders U. Ala. Research Inst., Huntsville, 1960-62. Mem. U.S. Dept. Commerce Sr. Exec. Assn. (bd. dirs.), Am. Judicature Soc. (lay mem.), U. Miss. Alumni Assn. (dir. 1963-74) Home: 19630Chanticleer Ct Baton Rouge LA 70809 Office Phone: 228-864-1004.

**MCCALL, JOHN PATRICK,** college president, educator; b. Yonkers, NY, July 17, 1927; s. Ambrose V. and Vera E. (Rush) McC.; m. Mary-Berenice Morris, June 15, 1957; children: Claire, Anne, Ambrose, Peter. AB, Coll. of Holy Cross, 1949; MA, Princeton U., 1952, PhD, 1955; DHL, Knox Coll.,

Galesburg, Ill., 1993. Instr. Georgetown U., 1955-57, asst. prof. English, 1957-62, assoc. prof., 1962-66; prof. U. Cin., 1966-82, head dept. English, 1970-76, sr. v.p., provost, 1976-82; pres. Knox Coll., 1982-93, pres. emeritus and prof. emeritus English, 1993—; vol. Peace Corps, Turkmenistan, 1993-95. Vis. prof. Turkmen State U., 1994-95; vice chmn. Gov.'s Task Force on Rural Ill., 1986; pres. Associated Colls. Ill. 1986-88; chmn. Associated Colls. of M.W., 1991-92; mem. edn. com. Ill. Bd. Higher Edn., 1985, 90; mem. rural libr. panel, State of Ill., 1992. Author: Chaucer Among the Gods: the Poetics of Classical Myth, 1979; contbr. articles to proffl. jours.; research in medieval lit. and Chaucer's poetry. Exec.-in-residence Xavier U. La., 1997—. With Signal Corps, U.S. Army, 1952-54. Am. Coun. Learned Socs. fellow, 1962-63; John Simon Guggenheim Meml. Found. fellow, 1975; Fulbright grantee, 1962. Mem. Medieval Acad. Am., MLA, AAUP, World Affairs Coun. New Orleans, Order of St. Louis, Archdiocese of New Orleans. Democrat. Roman Catholic. Home: 1750 St Charles Ave #317 New Orleans LA 70130 Office Phone: 504-520-6795. Business E-Mail: jmccall@xuba.edu.

**MCCALL, JOHN RICHARD,** lawyer; b. New Orleans, Sept. 18, 1943; s. Duke Kimbrough and Marguerite (Mullinnix) McC.; m. Sara Boykin Ferris, July 13, 1945; children: Sara Marguerite, Katherine Kimbrough, John Mathews. BA, Vanderbilt U., 1965, JD, 1967. Bar: Ky. 1967, U.S. Dist. Ct. (ea. and we. dists.) Ky. 1967, U.S. Dist. Ct. (so dist.) Ohio 1981, U.S. Dist. Ct. Colo. 1981, U.S. Ct. Appeals (6th and 10th cirs.) 1981. Assoc. Middleton, Seelbach, Wolford, Willis & Cochran, 1970-72; ptnr. Middleton & Reutlinger, Louisville, 1972-83, chmn. mgmt. com., 1979-82; ptnr. Brown, Todd & Heyburn, Louisville, 1983-99, chmn. litigation dept.; exec. v.p., gen. counsel and corp. sec. LG&E Energy Corp., Louisville, 1994—. Dir., sec. Ky. Wood Floors, Inc., Louisville. Mem. exec. com. So. Bapt. Conv.; chmn. Citizens for Better Judges; chmn. bd. Metro United Way, 1982-83. Served to lt. USNR, 1967-70. Mem. ABA, Def. Rsch. Inst., Ky. Def. Counsel, Louisville Bar Assn. Clubs: Country, Law Jefferson (Louisville). Democrat. Baptist. Office: LG & E Energy Corp 15th Fl 220 W Main St Louisville KY 40202-1377 E-mail: john.mccall@lgeenergy.com.

**MC CALL, JULIEN LACHICOTTE,** banker; b. Florence, S.C., Apr. 1, 1921; s. Arthur M. and Julia (Lachicotte) McC.; m. Janet Jones, Sept. 30, 1950; children: Melissa, Alison Gregg, Julien Lachicotte Jr. BS, Davidson Coll., 1942, LLD (hon.), 1983; MBA, Harvard U., 1947. With First Nat. City Bank, N.Y.C., 1948-71, asst. mgr. bond dept., 1952-53, asst. cashier, 1953-55, asst. v.ps., 1955-57, v.p., 1957-71; 1st v.p. Nat. City Bank, Cleve., 1971-72, pres., 1972-79, chmn., 1979-85, chief exec. officer, from 1979, also bd. dirs.; pres. Nat. City Corp.; 1983-90, chmn., chief exec. officer, 1980-86, also bd. dirs., cons. Mem. fed. adv. coun. Fed. Res. Bd., 1984-87. Trustee St. Luke's Found., United Way Services, Boy Scouts Am., Playhouse Sq. Found., Cleve. Mus. Natural History. To 1st lt. Ordinance Corps U.S. Army, 1942—46, Africa, ETO. Mem. Pepper Pike Club, Chagrin Valley Hunt Club, Mountain Lake Club (Lake Wales, Fla.), Rolling Rock Club (Ligonier, Pa.). Episcopalian. Home: Arrowhead 115 Quail Ln Chagrin Falls OH 44022 Office: 30195 Chagrin Blvd Ste 104W Pepper Pike OH 44124-5703

**MCCALL, JUNIETTA BAKER,** psychotherapist, minister; d. Cecil Stanford and Katherine Violet Baker; m. John Cornwall Pearson; children: Jonathan Seth, Jeremiah Brierly. BA, Beloit Coll., 1968; MDiv, Andover Newton Theol. Sch., Newton Centre, Mass., 1985, D of Ministry, 1991. Ordained min. United Ch. of Christ, 1983; cert. pastoral psychotherapist N.H., diplomate Am. Assn. Pastoral Counselors. Assoc. pastor South Congl. Ch., Concord, NH, 1980—85; dir. pastoral svcs. N.H. Hosp., Concord, 1985—. Dir. tng. Journeys Pastoral Counseling Ctr., Durham, NH, 1993—96; adj. faculty Andover Newton Theol. Sch., 1993—96. Author: Grief Education for Caregivers of the Elderly, 1999, A Practical Guide to Hospital Ministry, 2002, Bereavement Counseling, 2004. Avocations: quilting, gardening, antiques and collectibles. Office: NH Hosp 36 Clinton St Concord NH 03301 Office Phone: 603-271-5413. Business E-Mail: jmccall@dhhs.state.nh.us.

**MCCALL, ROBERT THE,** artist; b. Columbus, Ohio, Dec. 23, 1919; s. Harry and Lena (Storch) M. Student, Columbus (Ohio) Fine Art Sch., 1938-39; PhD in Graphics and Visual Arts (hon.), Columbus Coll. Art and Design, 1998. Freelance artist, Chgo., 1939-42, 45-49, N.Y.C. 1949-71, Paradise Valley, Ariz., 1971—. Mem. space commn. Gov. McCall, Ariz. Executed murals Spirit of Arizona, Phoenix, 1987, The Spirit of Aerospace Research, NASA Dryden Flight Rsch. Ctr., Calif., Smithsonian Air and Space Mus., Washington, Johnson Space Ctr., Houston, Udvar Hazy Ctr., Va.; (stained glass windows) The Light of the Universe, Valley Presbyn. Ch., Ariz.; (painting) Opening the Space Frontier—The Next Giant Step, Johnson Space Ctr., others; one-man shows include Smithsonian Air and Space Mus., 1984, Meadows Art Mus., Shreveport, La., 1995, Space Port, Houston, 1995, Space and Rocket Ctr., Huntsville, Ala., 1996, Cosi, Columbus, Ohio, 1997; co-author: Our World in Space, 1973, Vision of the Future, 1983; subject of book The Art of Robert McCall, 1992; mural NASA Dryden Flight Rsch. Ctr., 2005. With USAF, 1942-45. Named to Illustrators Hall of Fame, 1988, Ariz. Aviation Hall Fame, 2001; recipient Ariz. History-maker award Ariz. Hist. Soc., 1999, Yuri Gagarin medal Russia, 1988, Elder Statesman of Aviation award Nat. Aeronautic Assn., 2002, Douglas S. Morrow Pub. Outreach award The Space Found., 2003; honoree 24th Annual Govs. Arts award dinner, 2005. Mem. Am. Soc. Aviation Artists (founder), Rotary. Republican. Presbyterian. Home: 4816 E Moonlight Way Paradise Valley AZ 85253-2926 Office Phone: 480-991-0385. E-mail: robtmccall@cox.net.

**MCCALLISTER, MICHAEL B.,** insurance company executive; b. Indianapolis, May 27, 1952; m. Charlene Gray, 1985; children: Megan, Ryan. BA, La. Tech. U., 1974; MBA, Pepperdine U., 1983. Fin. specialist Humana Inc., Louisville, 1974—75, exec. dir. fin. Cmty. Hosp. Springhill, La., 1975; exec. dir. Humana Hosps. in Huntington and West Anaheim, Calif., 1978—85, Humana Hosp. West Hills, Canoga Park, Calif., 1985—88; pres. Humana Hosp. Phoenix, 1988—89; v.p. Humana Health Care Plans, Phoenix, 1989—92, San Antonio, 1992—96, pres. divsn. 1 with responsibility for Tex., Fla. and P.R., 1996—97; sr. v.p. health sys. mgmt. Humana Inc., Louisville, 1997—99, sr. v.p. office chmn, 1999—2000, pres., CEO, 2000—. Recipient Tower Medallian Award, La. Tech., 2003. Mem.: Am. Assn. Health Plans (bd. dirs.). Office: Humana Inc 500 W Main St Ste 300 Louisville KY 40202-4268*

**MCCALLISTER, RICHARD ANTHONY,** business consulting company executive; b. Newark, Ohio, Apr. 10, 1937; s. Ward C. and LeDema Mc.; m. Trina D. Gordon, Sept. 1, 1979; children: Todd. Mark. BS. Ill. State U., 1960; postgrad., U. So. Calif., 1960-62. Indsl. cons. Sci. Rsch. Assocs., 1964-66; v.p. Mgmt. Psychologists, Inc., Chgo., 1966-68; dir. Price Waterhouse & Co., Chgo., 1968-75; pres. William H. Clark Assocs., Inc., Chgo., 1975-89; sr. v.p., dir. Boyden Internat., Chgo., 1989-91; mng. dir. Boyden Midwest, Chgo., 1991—. Chmn. bd. DH2O, 2004—; chmn. WHCA Ptnrs., 1986—; bd. dir. Spirian Techs., Boyden World Corp.; mng. dir.; bd. dir. Mid Am., sec., treas.; mem. adv. bd. Fiduciary Management, Inc., Lionheart Trust Co., 1988—93. Former pres. Dist. 113 Bd. Edn., Deerfield, Ill.; bd. dirs., exec. com. Grant Hosp., Chgo., House of Vision, 1975-82. Mem. Glen View Club, Racquet Club, Chgo. Club, Mid-Am. Club Bd. dirs. pres. Home: 5 (res. 1995—). Office: 180 N Stetson Ave Chicago IL 60601-6710 Office Phone: 312-565-1300.

**MCCALL-RODRIGUEZ, LEONOR,** healthcare services company executive, entrepreneur; b. Chgo., Feb. 21, 1958; d. Sixto Rodriguez Hernandez and Dolores Leonor Jimenez de Rodriguez; m. Dean W. McCall, July 14, 2002; stepchildren: Samantha Lynn McCall, Christopher Dean McCall. Licenciatura in Econs., Universidad Nacional Autónoma de México, Mexico City, 1982; MBA, Universidad de Las Americas, Mexico City, 1998. Lic. economist Secretaría de Educación Publica, Mexico. Mktg. mgr. Casa Pedro Domecq, Mexico City, 1984—90, Braun divsn. Gillette, Mexico City, 1990—91, PepsiCo-Frito Lay, Mexico City, 1991—97, La Opinion, L.A., 1999—2000; pres. Bus. and Mktg. Solutions, Mexico City, 1997—99; v.p. Face to Face Mktg., Inc., Pasadena, Calif., 2000—03; gen. mgr. Walker Advt., Inc., San Pedro, Calif., 2000; pres. founder Mira Promo, Inc., Redondo Beach, Calif.,

2003—04, Latino Speakers Bur., Redondo Beach, 2003—; v.p., emerging mkts. WellPoint Inc., Indianapolis, Ind., 2004—. Adj. prof. econs. Universidad Nacional Autónoma de México, Mexico City, 1982—84. Author: (short stories) Cuentos de Juanita La Ranita, 2004; editor, translator: novel La Quileña, 2004. Vol. art tchr. 1736 Family Crisis Ctr., L.A., 2000—03; nat. bus. adv. coun. Rainbow Push Coalition. Named Corp. Leader of the Yr., Nat. Latina Bus. Women Assn., 2006. Mem.: Mexican Am. Nat. Assn. (assoc.), Women's Bus. Entrepreneurs Nat. Coun. (assoc.), Nat. Assn. Women Bus. Owners (assoc.), Latin Bus. Assn. (assoc.). Democrat. Roman Catholic. Avocations: writing, reef aquaria, travel. Office: WellPoint Inc 120 Monument Cir Indianapolis IN 46204

**MC CALLUM, CHARLES ALEXANDER,** academic administrator; b. North Adams, Mass., Nov. 1, 1925; s. Charles Alexander and Mabel Helen (Cassidy) McC.; m. Alice Rebecca Lasseter, Dec. 17, 1955; children: Scott Alan, Charles Alexander III, Philip Warren, Christopher Jay. Student, Dartmouth Coll., 1943-44, Wesleyan U., Middletown, Conn., 1946-47; DMD, Tufts U., 1951; MD, Med. Coll. Ala., 1957; DSc (hon.), U. Ala., 1975, Georgetown U., 1982, Tufts U., 1988, Chulalongkorn U., Thailand, 1993, U. Medicine and Dentistry, N.J., 1993. Diplomate Am. Bd. Oral Surgery (pres. 1970). Intern oral surgery Univ. Hosp., Birmingham, Ala., 1951-52, resident oral surgery, 1952-54, intern medicine, 1957-58; mem. faculty U. Ala. Sch. Dentistry, 1956-96, prof., chmn. dept. oral surgery, 1959-65, dean sch., 1962-77; prof., dept. surgery U. Ala. Sch. of Medicine, 1965-96; v.p. for health affairs, dir. U. Ala. Med. Center, Birmingham, 1977-87; pres. U. Ala., Birmingham, 1987-93, chief sect. oral surgery Sch. Dentistry, 1958-65, 68-69; prof., 1959-93; disting. prof., 1992-2000; disting. prof. emeritus, dean emeritus, 2000—. Mem. nat. adv. dental rsch. coun. NIH, 1968-72; mem. Joint Commn. on Accreditation of Hosps., 1980-91, vice chmn., 1985, chmn., 1986-88. Fellow Am. Coll. Dentists, Internat. Coll. Dentists; mem. ADA (council on dental edn. 1970-76), Am. Assn. Dental Schs. (pres. 1969), Ala. Acad. of Honor, AMA, Am. Soc. Oral Surgeons (trustee 1972-73, pres. 1975-76), Southeastern Soc. Oral Surgeons (pres. 1970), Inst. of Medicine of Nat. Acad. of Scis., Am. Acad. of Health Ctrs. (chmn. bd. dirs. 1984-85), Omicron Kappa Upsilon, Phi Beta Pi. Home: 2328 Garland Dr Birmingham AL 35216-3002 Office: Univ Ala Birmingham 120 Sdb Birmingham AL 35294-0001

**MCCALLUM, CHARLES EDWARD,** lawyer; b. Memphis, Mar. 13, 1939; s. Edward Payson and India Raimelle (Musick) McC.; m. Lois Ann Gowell Temple, Nov. 30, 1985; children: Florence Andrea, Florella Kye, Chandler Ward, Sabra Nicole Temple. BS in Math., MIT, 1960; JD, Vanderbilt U., 1964. Bar: Mich., Tenn. 1964. Assoc. Warner Norcross & Judd LLP, Grand Rapids, Mich., 1964-69, ptnr., 1969—, mng. ptnr., 1992-97. Rep. assemblyman State Bar Mich., 1973-78; chmn. Rsch. and Tech. Inst. West Mich., 1989-91; lectr. continuing legal edn. programs; mem. West Mich. World Trade Week Com. 1998-99, chmn., 1990-91; mem. Mich. Dist. Export Coun., 1990-99, chmn., 1992-97, TerraLex, 2006-. Chmn. Grand Rapids Area Transit Authority, 1976-79, mem., 1972-79; regional v.p. Nat. Mcpl. League, 1978-86, mem. coun., 1971-78; pres. Grand Rapids Art Mus., 1979-81, 96-98, trustee, 1976-83, 94-99; chmn. Butterworth Hosp., 1979-87, trustee, 1977-87; chmn. Butterworth Health Corp., 1982-89, dir., 1982-97, vice chmn., 1989-91, sec., 1991-97; chmn. Priority Health, 1995-2004, bd. dirs., 1995—. Woodrow Wilson fellow, 1960-61; Fulbright scholar U. Manchester, Eng., 1960-61. Fellow Coll. Law Practice Mgmt.; mem. ABA (chair-elect bus. law sect. 2006-, chair standing com. on ethics and profl. responsibility 2004-05, com. on multijurisdictional practice 2000-02, task force on corp. responsibility, 2001-03, task force on tax shelter ethical responsibilities, 2004-2005, editor-in-chief Bus. Lawyer 2005-06), Am. Bar Found., Am. Law Inst., Tenn. Bar Assn., Mich. Bar Assn. (common. bus. law sect. 1983-89, sect. chmn. 1988-89), Grand Rapids Bar Assn., Internat. Bar Assn., Grand Rapids C. of C. (pres. 1975, bd. dirs. 1970—), Univ. Club, Order of Coif, Sigma Xi. Home: 5410 Forest Bend DR SE Ada MI 49301-9005 Office Phone: 616-752-2104. E-mail: mccallce@wnj.com.

**MCCALLUM, GERALD CHRISTOPHER,** clinical psychologist; s. William Robert and Helen Frances (Kaullen) McCallum. BS in Psychology, U. Ill., Champaign, 1984; MS in Clin. Psychology, U. Memphis, 1991, PhD in Clin. Psychology, 1992. Lic. clin. psychologist Ill. Technician Forest Hosp., Des Plaines, Ill., 1983—86; clin. therapist, rsch. instr. U. Memphis, 1986—91; clin. intern Ark. Children's Hosp., U. Ark. Med. Scis., Little Rock, 1991—92; postdoctoral fellow U. Tenn., Memphis, 1992—93; clin. psychologist, program coord. Alexian Bros. Med. Ctr., Elk Grove, Ill., 1993—98; instr. Chgo. Sch. Profl. Psychology, 1995; clin. psychologist DuPage Psychol. Assocs., Naperville, Ill., 1995—. Mem.: APA, Ill. Psychol. Assn., Nat. Register Health Svc. Providers in Psychology. Roman Catholic. Avocations: reading, gardening, woodworking, travel, running. Home: PO Box 4345 Naperville IL 60567 Office: DuPage Psychol Assocs 1112 S Washington St Ste 217 Naperville IL 60540 Office Phone: 630-355-4070. E-mail: drgeraldmccallum@yahoo.com.

**MCCALLUM, JOHN,** Canadian government official; b. Montreal, Que., Can., Apr. 9, 1950; m. Nancy Lim; 3 children. BA, U. Cambridge, 1971; diplôme d'études supérieures, U. Paris, 1973; PhD in econ., McGill U., 1977. Asst. prof. econ. U. Manitoba, 1976—78; prof. econ. Simon Fraser U., 1978—82, U. Québec, 1982—87, McGill U., 1987—94, dean, faculty of arts, 1992—94; sr. v.p., chief economist Royal Bank of Can., 1994—2000; mem. Parliament, 2000—; parliamentary sec. to the min. finance, 2001—02; sec. of state (internat. fin. instn.), 2002; min. nat. def., 2002—03; min. vet. affairs, 2003—04; min. of nat. revenue, 2004—. Mem. Treasury Bd., Cabinet Com. on Econ. Union, Cabinet Com. on Pub. Safety and Anti-Terrorism. Office: Hon John McCallum Min of Nat Revenue 5th Fl 555 MacKenzie Ave Ottawa ON Canada K1A 0L5

**MCCALLUM, JOHN STUART,** finance educator, columnist; b. Prescott, Ont., Can., Feb. 2, 1944; s. Donald Robinson and Margaret Louise (Hoeschen) McC.; m. Deborah Jean Howe, Nov. 7, 1985; children: Pamela Anne, James Andrew. BS, U. Montreal, Que., Can., 1965, BA, 1968; MBA, Queen's U., 1968; PhD, U. Toronto, Ont., Can., 1973. With Bank of Montreal, 1965-68; sr. analyst Shell Can., Toronto, 1968-70; prof. fin. U. Man. Can., 1973—. Vice chmn. Man. Hydro, 1988-91, chmn., 1991—; bd. dirs. Toromont Industries Ltd., Man. Energy Authority, 1988—, Acctg. Rsch. Adv. Bd., 1988—; com. various Can. cos., 1977—; advisor Fed. Minister of Fin., 1984-2001. Columnist Bus. Quar, 1978—, Fin. Post., 1979—; author: The Term Structure of Interest Rates, 1974, The Canadian Chartered Banks and the Bond Market, 1976, The Changing Face of Canadian Finance, 1980, Canadian Finance and the Federal Bullt, 1983, Canada and Technological Change, 1985. Recipient Touche Ross Bus. Writing award, 1985, 86, 87. Mem. Am. Fin. Assn., Adminstrv. Studies Assn. Can. (v.p. 1975-79). Roman Catholic. Avocations: reading, jogging, minor hockey. Home: 26 Lake Lindero Rd Winnipeg MB Canada R3T 4P3

**MCCALLUM, LAURIE RIACH,** state government lawyer; b. Virginia, Minn., Aug. 19, 1950; d. Keith Kelvin and Maybelle Louella (Hanson) Riach; m. J. Scott McCallum, June 19, 1979; children: Zachary, Rory, Cara. BA, U. Ariz., 1972; JD, So. Meth. U., 1977. Bar: Wis. 1977. Consumer atty. Office of Commr. of Ins., Madison, Wis., 1977-79; asst. legal counsel Gov. of Wis., Madison, Wis., 1979-82; mng. ptnr. Petri and McCallum Law Firm, Fond du Lac, Wis., 1979-80; exec. dir. Wis. Coun. on Criminal Justice, Madison, 1981-82; commr. Wis. Pers. Commn., Madison, 1982—2002, chairperson 1988—2002; commr. Wis. Labor and Industry Rev. Commn., 2002—03, sr. rev. atty., 2003—. Mem. gov.'s jud. selection com. Supreme Ct, 1979. Dir. State Bar Labor Law Sect., Madison, 1989-91; faculty U. Wis. Law Sch., Madison, 1992, 93. Dir. Prevent Blindness Wis., Madison Symphony Orch., Wis. Women in Govt. Republican. Office: LIRC PO Box 8126 Madison WI 53708-8126 Office Phone: 608-266-9850. Business E-Mail: mccalla@dwd.state.wi.us.

**MCCALLUM, RICHARD WARWICK,** medical researcher, clinician, educator; b. Brisbane, Australia, Jan. 21, 1945; came to U.S., 1969; MD, BS, Queensland U., Australia, 1968. Rotating intern Charity Hosp. La., New Orleans, 1969-70; resident in internal medicine Barnes Hosp., Washington, 1970-72; fellow in gastroenterology Wadsworth VA Hosp., L.A., 1972-74, chief endoscopic unit, dept gastroenterology, 1974-76; dir. gastrointestinal diagnostic svcs. Yale-New Haven Med. Ctr., New Haven, 1979-85; asst. prof. medicine UCLA, 1974-76, Yale U., New Haven, 1977-82, assoc. prof., 1982-85; prof., chief div. gastroenterology, hepatology and nutrition U. Va., Charlottesville, 1985-95; dir. GI Motility Ctr. U. Va. Health Sci. Ctr., Charlottesville, 1990-96; Paul Janssen prof. medicine U. Va., Charlottesville, 1987-96; prof. medicine and physiology U. Kans. Med. Ctr., Kansas City, 1996—, chief div. gastroenterology and hepatology, 1996—, dir. Ctr. for Gastrointestinal, Nerve and Muscle Function and Motility Disorders, 1996—. Patentee catheter for esophageal perfusion, gastrointestinal pacemaker using-phased multipoint stimulation, esophageal protection by mastication. Fellow ACP, Am. Coll. Gastroenterology (pres. Kans. 1998—), Royal Australasian Coll. Physicians, Royal Australian Coll. Surgeons; mem. Australian Gastroenterology Soc., Am. Fedn. Clin. Rsch., Am. Assn. Study Liver Diseases, Am. Soc. Gastrointestinal Endoscopy, Am. Assn. for Clin. Investigation, Am. Gastroenterology Assn., Am. Motility Soc. (host-organizer 11th biennial meeting Kansas City 2000), So. Soc. for Clin. Investigation (pres. 1997-98), Internat. Electrogastrography Soc. (pres. 1998-2000), So. Med. Assn. (chmn. gastrointestinal 1996-97). Office: U Kans Med Ctr Dept Internal Medicine 3901 Rainbow Blvd Kansas City KS 66160-0001 Office Phone: 913-588-3842. Business E-Mail: rmccallu@kumc.edu.

**MCCALLUM, ROBERT DAVIS, JR.,** ambassador, former federal agency administrator; b. Jan. 30, 1946; s. Robert D. McCallum Sr. and Virginia Blackwell Jeff McCallum; m. Mary W. McCallum. BA, Yale U., 1968, JD, 1973; MA, Oxford U., 1971. Spl. asst. atty gen. State of GA, Atlanta, 1979—87; assoc. Alston & Bird LLP, Atlanta, 1973—79, ptnr., 1973—2001; asst. atty. gen. civil divsn. US Dept. Justice, Washington, 2001—03, assoc. atty. gen., 2003—06, acting dep. atty. gen., 2003—06; US amb. to Australia US Dept. State, Canberra, 2006—. Scholar Rhodes scholar, 1971. Office: US Embassy 7800 Canberra Pl Washington DC 20521*

**MCCALLY, CHARLES RICHARD,** construction company executive, consultant, mathematician, educator; b. Dallas, Oct. 5, 1958; s. Richard Holt and Elizabeth Ann (Webster) McC.; m. Shirley Elizabeth Avant, Aug. 18, 1979 (div.); children: Charles Richard Jr., Meredith Holt; m. Judy Lynn Tackett, June 24, 1993. BSME, So. Meth. U., 1981; MS in Higher Edn. and Math. summa cum laude, Tex. A&M U., 2003. Engr. McCally Co., Dallas, 1977-83; owner, v.p. DRT Mech. Corp., Dallas, 1983-95; owner McCally Svc. Co., Inc., Dallas, 1995-97; pres. C.R. McCally & Assocs., Inc., Dallas, 1997—. Prof. math. Navarro Coll., Corsicana, Tex., 1999—; cons. McCally Group, Inc., Lewisville, Tex., 2002—05; mech. group mgr. Hidalgo Internat. Svcs., Inc., 2005—. Active Young Reps., Dallas, 1980—. Mem. NSPE, ASME, ASHRAE, Am. Soc. Plumbing Engrs. (membership com. 1983-89), Tex. Soc. Profl. Engrs., So. Meth. U. Alumni Assn., SMU Mustang Club, Bent Tree Country Club (Dallas), Oaktree Country Club (Garland, Tex.) (bd. dirs. 1986-89), Sigma Chi. Avocations: tennis, boating, travel, camping. Home: 203 Chinaberry Way Coppell TX 75019-2961 E-mail: rick@mccally.com, rmccally@hidalgoindustrial.com.

**MCCAMBRIDGE, JOHN JAMES,** civil engineer; b. Bklyn., Oct. 27, 1933; s. John Joseph and Florence Josita (McDonnell) McC.; m. Dorothy Antoinette Cook, Mar. 17, 1962; children: Sharon J., John S., Patrick J., Kathleen C. BCE, Manhattan Coll., 1955; MS, Vanderbilt U., 1958; postgrad., UCLA, 1961—66. Civil engr. Raymond Concrete Pile Co., NYC, 1955; commd. 2d lt. USAF, 1955, advanced through grades to col., 1972; exec. sec. Def. Com. On Rsch., Washington, 1971-73, DOD-NASA Supportive Rsch. Tech. Panel, Washington, 1972-74; asst. dir. Def. Rsch. and Engring. (for Environ. and Life Scis.) Office Sec. Def., Washington, 1974-75; dir. Air Force Life Support Systems Program Office, Wright Patterson AFB, Ohio, 1975-79; ret. USAF, 1979; prin. Booz, Allen & Hamilton, Inc., Bethesda, Md., 1979-86; v.p. Espey, Huston & Assoc., Inc., Falls Church, Va., 1986-90; mng. prin. JMC Cons. Group, McLean, Va., 1990—2005. Chmn. air panel on NBC Def., NATO, Evere, Belgium, 1970-71; def. dept. rep. to physics survey com., NAS, Washington, 1971. Contbr. articles to profl. jours. Decorated Legion of Merit with oak leaf cluster. Fellow Aerospace Med. Assn. (exec. coun. 1972-73), Inst. Hazardous Materials Mgmt. (Disting. Diplomate, Diplomate 1984—2005, chmn. 1988-94, Lifetime Achievement award 2005, Founding Father award 2005); mem. Coun. Engring. and Sci. Splty. Bds. (dir., exec. com. 1995—2005, v.p. 2000, pres. 2001), Acad. Cert. Hazardous Materials Mgrs. (pres. 1984-86), Survival and Flight Equipment Assn. (nat. sec. 1977-78), Air Force Ret. Officers' Cmty. (dir. 1997-2003), The Washington Assembly (treas. 2002-03, vice chmn. 2003-05, chmn. 2005—), Black Tie Club (treas. 2002-03, v.p. 2003-04, pres. 2004-05), Dwight D. Eisenhower Soc. (trustee 2006-), Tower Club, KC, Sigma Xi, Chi Epsilon. Republican. Roman Catholic. Office: JMC Cons Group 9200 Falls Run Rd Mc Lean VA 22102-1028 E-mail: jjmccambridge@earthlink.net.

**MC CAMERON, FRITZ ALLEN,** retired university administrator; b. Nacogdoches, Tex., Oct. 8, 1929; s. Leland Allen and Gladys (Turner) Mc C.; m. Jeannine Young, June 11, 1957; 1 child, Mary Hartley. BBA, Stephen F. Austin State Coll., 1950, MA, 1951; PhD, U. Ala., 1954. C.P.A., La. Assoc. prof. La. State U., 1959-62, prof., 1962-67, chmn. dept. accounting, 1967-71, asst. vice chancellor, 1971-73, dean continuing edn., 1973-95; ret., 1995. Cons. in field. Author: FORTRAN Logic and Programming, 1968, Cobol Logic and Programming, rev. edit, 1970, 5th edit., 1985, FORTRAN IV, 1970, rev. edit., 1974, 3d edit., 1979. Mem. numerous civic and charitable bds. including Salvation Army, Womens Hosp., Computer Rehab. Tng. and others. Mem. Am. Inst. C.P.A.'s, La. Soc. C.P.A.'s, Am. Accounting Assn. Home: 930 Rodney Dr Baton Rouge LA 70808-5867

**MCCAMMON, JAMES ANDREW,** chemistry professor; b. Lafayette, Ind., Feb. 8, 1947; s. Lewis Brown and Jean Ann (McClintock) McC.; m. Anne Elizabeth Woltmann, June 6, 1969. BA magna cum laude, Pomona Coll., 1969; MA, Harvard U., 1970, PhD, 1976. NSF/NIH postdoctoral research fellow Harvard U., Cambridge, Mass., 1976-78; asst. prof. chemistry U. Houston, 1978-81, full prof., 1981, M.D. Anderson prof. chemistry, 1981-94, dir. Inst. for Molecular Design, 1987-94; prof. biochemistry, 1989-94; Joseph E. Mayer chair theoretical chemistry U. Calif. San Diego, 1995—; prof. pharmacology U. Calif. San Diego Sch. Medicine, 1995—; investigator Howard Hughes Med. Inst., 2000—. Adj. prof. molecular physiology and biophysics Baylor Coll. Medicine, Houston, 1986-94, adj. prof. biochemistry, 1992-94; cons. to Sterling-Winthrop Pharma., Stardent Computers, Rhone-Poulenc, Accelrys, Kimberly-Clark, DuPont-Merck Pharm., Merck — Co., and Bristol-Myers Squibb; mem. adv. bd. NAS, NSF, NIH and other agencies. Author: Dynamics of Proteins and Nucleic Acids, 1987; contbr. articles to profl. jours. Recipient Tchr.-scholar award Camille and Henry Dreyfus Found., 1982-87, NIH Rsch. Career Develop. award, 1980-85, George H. Hitchings award for Innovative Methods in Drug Design, Burroughs-Wellcome Fund, 1987, Smithsonian award for Breakthrough Computational Sci., 1995, Chancellor's Associates award for Rsch., 2002; named Alfred P. Sloan Rsch. fellow, 1980-84, Centennial lectr., U. Chgo., 1991 Fellow AAAS, Am. Phys. Soc., Biophys. Soc., Am. Acad. Arts & Sciences; mem. Am. Chem. Soc., Protein Soc., Phi Beta Kappa. Achievements include development of the molecular dynamics simulation method for proteins and nucleic acids, of the thermodynamic cycle perturbation method for studying molecular recognition, and of the Brownian dynamics method for simulating diffusion-controlled reactions. Office: U Calif San Diego Dept Chemistry La Jolla CA 92093-0365 E-mail: jmccammon@ucsd.edu.*

**MCCAMPBELL, ROBERT GARNER,** lawyer, former prosecutor; b. Oklahoma City, Nov. 23, 1957; s. Stanley Reid and Joan Fontane (Garner) McC. BA in History with honors, Vanderbilt U., 1980; JD, Yale U., 1983. Bar: Okla. 1983. Assoc. Crowe & Dunlevy, Oklahoma City, 1983-87, dir., 1994—2001, 2005—; asst. US atty. (we. dist.) Okla. US Dept. Justice,

1987-94, chief fin. fraud unit (we. dist.) Okla., 1990-94, Us atty. (we. dist.) Okla., 2001—05. Dir. Ctr. for Advancement of Sci. and Tech., 1995, chmn. 1999—2001; chmn. sub-com. sentencing Atty. Gen., 2004—05. Mem. ABA, Nat. Assn. Former U.S. Attys., Phi Beta Kappa. Republican. Episcopalian. Office: Crowe & Dunlevy 20 N Broadway Ste 1800 Oklahoma City OK 73102 Office Phone: 405-235-7700. Business E-Mail: mccampbr@crowedunlevy.com.*

**MCCAMY, SHARON GROVE,** English educator; b. Fredericksburg, Va., May 31, 1961; d. Howard E. and Vivian R. Grove; m. Michael D. McCamy, Jan. 10, 1986; 1 child, Katherine Howard. BA in English, Mary Washington Coll., 1983; MA in English, George Mason U., 1994. Devel. asst. Corcoran Gallery of Art, Washington, 1983-84; coord. individual giving Nat. Parks Conservation Assn., Washington, 1984-87; dir. devel. Piedmont Environ. Coun., Warrenton, Va., 1991-94; lectr. in English Mary Washington Coll., Fredericksburg, Va., 1996-99; head Divsn Arts and Scis. No. Va. Campus ECPI Coll. Tech., 2005—, dir. edn. No. Va. Campus, 2006—. Mem. Fauquier County Bd. Suprs., 2000—03; mem. bd. Fauquier County Water and Sewer Authority, 2000—03; mem. com. Fauquier Rep. Com., 1997—; bd. dirs. Fauquier County Pub. Libr., Warrenton, 1996—2000, Libr. Va., 1998—2003, Libr. Va. Found., 1999—2003, Va. Ctr. Book, 2000—03. Mem.: Piedmont Rep. Women's Club (sec. 1998—2000, v.p. 2004—). Home: PO Box 10 Sumerduck VA 22742 Personal E-mail: sharonmccamy@direcway.com

**MCCAN, JAMES LAWTON,** education educator; b. Plymouth, Ind., Aug. 10, 1952; s.Jean F. and Mildred P. (Hayn) McC.; m. Carolyn G. Splain, Jan. 16, 1971; children: Kendra, Brittany. B of Phys. Edn., Purdue U., 1974; MS in Edn., 1981, PhD, 1983. Tchr. reading and English Waynetown (Ind.) Mid. Sch., 1974-75, Yorkville (Ill.) H.S., 1979-80; reading specialist Purdue U., West Lafayette, Ind., 1983-89; program chair Basic Skills Advancement Ind. Voc-Tech. Coll., Lafayette, 1989-91; asst. prof., coord. student teaching Hillsdale (Mich.) Coll., 1991-95; dir. Student Achievement Zone, South Bend, Ind., 1995-96; assoc. prof. Nova Southeastern U., Ft. Lauderdale, Fla., 1996—. Contbr. articles and poetry to jours. Mem. Internat. Reading Assn., Fla. Reading Assn. Avocations: reading, music. Home: 1024 St Croix Ave Apopka FL 32703 Office: Nova Southeastern U Dept Edn Fort Lauderdale FL 33314

**MCCANDLESS, BRUCE, II,** aerospace engineer, retired astronaut; b. Boston, June 8, 1937; s. Bruce and Sue McCandless; m. Alfreda Bernice Doyle, Aug. 6, 1960; children: Bruce III, Tracy. BS, U.S. Naval Acad., 1958; MSEE, Stanford U., 1965; MBA, U. Houston, Clear Lake, 1987. Commd. ensign USN, 1958, advanced through grades to capt., 1979, naval aviator, 1960, with Fighter Squadron 102, 1960-64; astronaut Johnson Space Ctr., NASA, Houston, 1966-90; mem. Skylab 1 backup crew Johnson Space Center, NASA, Houston, mem. STS-11 shuttle crew, mem. STS-31 Hubble Space Telescope deployment crew; ret. USN, 1990; prin. staff engr. Lockheed Martin Astronautics, Denver, 1990-97, chief scientist Advanced Space Transp. Sys. Co., 1997—2005, prin. staff scientist civil space, 2005—. Mem. Hubble salvage strategy panel NASA. Decorated Legion of Merit; recipient Def. Superior Service medal, NASA Exceptional Service medal, NASA Spaceflight medal, NASA Exceptional Engring. Achievement medal, Collier Trophy, 1985, Haley Space Flight award AIAA, 1991; named to Astronomy Hall Fame, 2005. Fellow Am. Astron. Soc.; mem. U.S. Naval Inst., Nat. Audubon Soc., Houston Audubon Soc. (past pres.). Episcopalian. Achievements include executing 1st untethered free flight in space using Manned Maneuvering Unit. Home: 21852 Pleasant Park Rd Conifer CO 80433-6802 Office: Lockheed Martin Space Sys Co Civil Space Product Area PO Box 179 Denver CO 80201-0179 Office Phone: 303-971-6308. Personal E-mail: bruce2mc@logcabin.com.

**MCCANDLESS, CAROLYN KELLER,** retired human resources specialist; b. Patuxent River, Md., June 6, 1945; d. Stevens Henry and Betty Jane (Bethune) Keller; m. Stephen Porter McCandless, Apr. 22, 1972; children: Peter Keller, Deborah Marion. BA, Stanford U., Calif., 1967; MBA, Harvard U., Cambridge, Mass., 1969. Fin. analyst Time Inc., N.Y.C., 1969-72, mgr. budgets and fin. analysis, 1972-78, asst. sec., dir. internat. adminstrn., 1978-85, v.p., dir. employee benefits, 1985-90; v.p human resources and adminstrn. Time Warner, Inc., N.Y.C., 1990—2001; ret., 2001. Bd. dirs., treas. Friends and Relatives Institutionalized Aged; bd. dirs., mem. exec. com. Svc. Program Older People, Inc., Annie Eaton Soc.; adv. bd. Booker T. Washington Learning Ctr. and Preserve Coun. Nat. Pub. Radio; bd. dirs. Time-Life Alumni Soc. Democrat. Unitarian.

**MCCANDLESS, MICHAEL J.,** theater educator, director; s. Ernest E. and Eleanor V. McCandless; children: Christopher M., Katie M., Mary C. BA, Creighton U., Omaha, 1978; MA, U. Nebr., Omaha, 1993. Actor/tchr. Omaha Children's Theatre, 1979—80; actor Boston Shakepeare Co., 1980—81; adj. theatre faculty Creighton U., Omaha, 1989—; theatre dir. Creighton Prep. Sch., Omaha, 1994—. Prodn. dir. Marian H.S., Omaha, 2006—. Actor: Gross Indecencies: The Three Trials of Oscar Wilde (Theatre Arts Guild Best Supporting Actor, 2000), Art (Barbara Ford award for Outstanding Supporting Actor, 2000), Noises Off (Barbara Ford award for Outstanding Supporting Actor, 2004); author: (plays) Cursing Mummies, Gone the Rainbow, Return the Dove: Letters of War, Words of Peace. Instr. acting workshops Omaha Cath. & Pub. Schs., 1982—2006; acting instr. Omaha Symphony's Celebrate Creativity, 2002—06; tech. support Hope Ctr. Theatre Prodns., Omaha, 2003—06. Conservative. Roman Catholic. Avocations: writing, backpacking, bicycling, travel, reading. Office: Creighton Univ Fine Arts 2500 California Plz Omaha NE 68178 Office Phone: 402-280-2498. Office Fax: 402-280-2320. Business E-Mail: mjmcc@creighton.edu.

**MCCANLESS, ROSS WILLIAM,** lawyer, retail executive; b. 1957; BS in Acctg., Univ. N.C., 1979; JD cum laude, Wake Forest Univ., 1982. CPA. Pvt. practice, 1982—89; various positions, CEO, vice chmn. FoodLion, Delhaize Am., Inc., 1989—2003—. Mem.: Am. Corp. Counsel Assn., Rowan County Bar Assn., Am. Bar Assn., N.C. State Bar Assn. Office: SVP & General Counsel Lowe's Companies Inc 1000 Lowe's Blvd Mooresville NC 28117 Office Phone: 704-758-1000.

**MCCANN, BARRY JOHN,** music educator; b. Teaneck, NJ, Sept. 2, 1963; s. William James and Edith Jane McCann; m. Maria Herrera, Apr. 4, 1992; children: Jennifer Herrera, Kathryne Herrera. BA, Montclair State U., Upper Montclair, NJ, 1986; MA, Columbia U., NYC, 1991. Music tchr. K-12 NJ. Dept. Edn., 1986, Teacher of music K-12 NY State Dept. of Edn., 1991. Music tchr. North Bergen Sch. Dist., NJ, 1986—87; dir. Gloria Concert Band, North Haledon, NJ, 1985—87; dir. music Boonton H.S., NJ, 1987—90; dir. bands Irvington H.S., NJ, 1991—97, Bogota Jr. Sr. H.S., NJ, 1997—; dept. fine and performing arts coord., 2005—. Recipient Tchr. of Yr., Bogota Bd. of Edn., PTO, 2005—. Mem.: Music Educators Bergen County, Music Educators Nat. Conf. Office: Bogota Bd Edn 1 Henry C Luthin Pl Bogota NJ 07603 Office Phone: 201-441-4808.

**MCCANN, CLARENCE DAVID, JR.,** curator, artist; b. Mobile, Ala., Apr. 30, 1948; s. Clarence David and Theresa (Pope) McC.; m. Brenda Clemens (div. 1979); 1 child, Nathan; m. Robin Chiavaroli, 1980; children: Angela, John. BFA, U. South Ala., 1970; MFA, U. Cin., 1972; grad. cert., Mus. Mgmt. Inst., Berkeley, Calif., 1982. Art instr. Spring Hill Coll., Mobile, 1972-73, U. South Ala., Mobile, 1975-76; mem. staff, asst. registrar Fine Arts Mus. of South, Mobile, 1977-78, registrar, 1978-81, curator collection, 1981-84, asst. dir., 1985-86, 88-91, acting dir., 1986-88, mus. curator, 1988-91; asst. mgr. spl. events coord. City of Mobile, 1991—2003; ret. Adj. lectr. U.S. Ala., 1990-91, adj. lectr. Bishop State Community Coll., 1991-2000, 2002—; adj. art instr. U. South Ala., 1999—. Author: (catalogues) The Ripening of American Art: Duveneck and Chase, 1979, The Artists of Barbizon: The Boone Collection, 1983, Ensiled Visions: The Southern Nontraditional Folk Artist, 1987, The Acquisitive Eye: Selections From The Collection of James M. Younger, 1990. Pres. Contemporary Artists Consortium of Mobile,

1979—81, Mobile Art Assn., 2002—04; co-chair art adv. bd. Ctr. for the Living Arts Space 301, Mobile, 2003—; bd. dirs. Very Spl. Arts, Ala., 1997—2003. Recipient various painting awards Allied Arts Coun., Mobile, 1974; U. Cin. fellow, 1972. Mem. Am. Assn. Mus., Ala. Mus. Assn., Southeastern Mus. Assn. Democrat. Home: 9080 Rawhide Ct Semmes AL 36575-7275 E-mail: cdmccann@gmail.com.

**MCCANN, CLIFTON EVERETT,** lawyer; b. Des Moines, July 11, 1950; s. George Lockhart and Evelyn Elizabeth (Miller) McC.; m. Marcia Ellen Morrow, Feb. 19, 1984; children: Gregory Lockhart, Jeanna Lauren. BA in Psychology, No. Ill. U., 1972; JD, Columbus Sch. Law, 1977; LLM in Intellectual Property, George Washington U., 1985. Bar: Va. 1978, U.S. Patent Office 1980, U.S. Ct. Appeals (fed. cir.) 1982, U.S. Supreme Ct. 1983, D.C. 1984. Assoc. Beveridge, DeGrandi & Kline, Washington, 1978-83; ptnr. Lane, Aitken & McCann, Washington, 1983-2000; ptnr., intellectual property litig. Venable LLP, Washington, 2000—. Counsel intellectual property Am. Mensa, Ltd., Fort Worth, 1984—. Mem.: Am. Intellectual Prperty Law Assn., Bar Assn. D.C. (mem. steering com. patent, trademark, copyright sect. 1984—, chair 1996—97), D.C. Bar Assn. (chmn. trademark com. of the patent, trademark and copyright sect. 1985—89), Va. Bar Assn., ABA (chair fed. litigation sub-com. on patent claim interpretation 1996—99, chair com. on intellectual property litigation 1999—2001), Patent Lawyers Club (Washington), Delta Theta Phi. Office: Venable LLP 575 7th St NW Washington DC 20004

**MCCANN, DIANA RAE,** secondary school educator; b. Huron, S.D., Nov. 16, 1948; d. Ralph Henry and Rosina Agnes (Rowen) Yager; m. Gregory Charles McCann, 1974; children: Grant Christopher, Holly Ann. BS, S.D. State U., 1972. Tchr. Bon Homme 4-2, Tyndall, SD, 1972—74, 1976—, Avon (S.D.) Sch., 1975—76. Math. curriculum adv. bd., SD, 1992—; coord. Presdl. awards in math., SD, 1998—. Leader 4-H Club, 1986—; sec.-treas. 4-H Leaders Assn., 1992—2000; tournament coord. Bon Homme Youth Wrestling Club, 1986—93. Recipient Elem. Math. Presdl. award for Excellence in Math. Tchgs., NSF, 1993, Disting. Svc. award for Math. in S.D., 2003, Bon Homme Outstanding Tchr. award, 2005. Mem.: S.D. Coun. Tchrs. Math. (pres.-elect 1990—92, pres. 1992—94, treas. 1999—), Nat. Coun. Tchrs. Math. Avocation: gardening. Personal E-mail: dm57062@valyou.net.

**MCCANN, ELIZABETH IRELAND,** theater producer, television producer, motion picture producer; b. NYC, Mar. 29, 1931; d. Patrick and Rebecca (Henry) McC. BA, Manhattanville Coll., 1952, PhD hon., 1983; MA, Columbia U., 1954; LLD, Fordham U., 1966; ArtsD (hon.), Manhattanville Coll., 1987; LitD (hon.), Marymount Coll., 1993. Bar: N.Y. 1966. Assoc. firm Paul, Weiss, Rifkind, Wharton & Garrison, N.Y.C., 1965-66; assoc. numerous theater mgmts. Robert Joffrey, Hal Prince, Saint Suber, Maurice Evans, 1956-68; mng. dir. Nederlander Orgn., N.Y.C., 1968-76; pres. McCann & Nugent Prodns., Inc., N.Y.C., 1976-86; mng. prodr. Tony Awards, N.Y.C., 2001—. Bd. dirs. City Ctr. Music and Dance, Marymount Coll. Prodr.: (play) My Fat Friend, 1975, Dracula (Tony award for most innovative prodn. revival, 1978), The Elephant Man, 1978 (Tony award for best play, 1979, Drama Critics award, 1978, Drama Desk award, 1978, Outer Critics Circle award 1978, Obie award 1978), Night and Day, 1979, Home, 1980 (Adelco award, 1980), Morning's at Seven, 1980 (Tony award for reproduction play/musical, 1980), Amadeus, 1980 (Tony award for best play, 1981, Drama Desk award, 1980), The Philadelphia Story, 1980, Piaf, 1981, Rose, 1981, The Dresser, 1981, Mass Appeal, 1981, Macbeth, 1981, The Floating Light Bulb, 1981, The Life and Adventures of Nicholas Nickleby, 1981 (Tony award for best play, 1982, Drama Critics Circle award, 1981), Good, 1982, All's Well That Ends Well, 1983, The Glass Menagerie, 1983, Total Abandon, 1983, Painting Churches, 1983, The Lady and the Clarinet, 1983, Cyrano de Bergerac/Much Ado About Nothing, 1984, Pacific Overtures, 1984, Leader of the Pack, 1985, Les Liaisons Dangereuses, 1987 (Drama Critics Circle award, 1987), Stepping Out, 1987, Orpheus Descending, 1989, Nick & Nora, 1991, Three Tall Women, 1995, A Midsummer Night's Dream, 1995, In the West End with Robert Fox, Ltd., 1996, Who's Afraid of Virginia Woolf?, 1996, A Delicate Balance, 1997, A View from the Bridge, 1998 (Tony award for best revival play, 1998), The Unexpected Man, 1998, A View from the Bridge (Tony award), 1998, Copenhagen, 2000 (Tony award for best play, 2000), Cobb, 2000, The Play About the Baby, 2001, Tuesdays with Morrie, 2002, The Goat, or Who is Sylvia?, 2002 (Tony award for best play, 2002), The Smell of the Kill, 2002, Beckee/Albee, 2003, Well–, 2005, Who's Afraid of Virginia Woolf?, 2005; TV show Piaf, 1981, Morning's at Seven, 1982, Pilobolus Dance Theatre, 1982; assoc. prodr. Orpheus Descending, 1990. Recipient Entrepreneurial Woman award Women Bus. Owners of N.Y., 1981, 82, James J. and Jame Hoey award for Interracial Justice, 1981, Spl Drama League award for co-producing the Life and Adventures of Nicholas Nickleby on Broadway, 1982, Dr Louis M. Spadero award Fordham Grad. Sch. Bus., 1982 E-mail: liz@weproduce.biz.

**MCCANN, EVELYN LOUISE JOHNSON,** retired minister, retired counselor; b. Hawkins, Tex., Aug. 17, 1941; d. Saron and Alberta Johnson; m. Lovorn McCann, Aug. 1, 1960; children: Everett Stephon, Marcus Darwin. Cert. in Stenography, Tyler Comml. Coll., Tex., 1972; cert. in leadership and devel., Dallas Theol. Sem., 1984; cert. completion, Phillip Sch. Theology, Atlanta, 1998. Ordained to ministry Tex., 1976, ordained to chaplain/counselor Tex., 1999. Utility operator/tng. new employees Sewing Rm., Mineola, Tex., 1966—75; seamstry Fashion Clothing, Mineola, Tex., 1975—76; pastor Gladewater, Tex., 1980—84, Lindale, Tex., 1984—87, Wills Point, Tex., 1987—2000; ret., 2000. Instr. Hawkins, Tex., 1976—84. Dir. workshops, Mineola, 2000. Methodist. Avocations: travel, ministering/counseling, cooking, shopping. Home: PO Box 232 309 McDaniel St Mineola TX 75773 Personal E-mail: evemccann@phoneco1.net.

**MCCANN, FRANCIS (FRANK) DANIEL (FRANK MCCANN),** historian, educator; b. Lackawanna, N.Y., Dec. 15, 1938; s. Francis Daniel McCann and Catherine Louise Moran; m. Sankis Diane Marie, Aug. 18, 1962; children: Teresa B., Katherine D. AB cum laude, Niagara U., 1960; MA, Kent State U., 1962; PhD, Ind. U., 1967. Asst. prof. history U. Wis., River Falls, 1966-68; asst. prof. social scis. U.S. Mil. Acad., West Point, NY, 1968-70; rsch. fellow Princeton U., NJ, 1970-71; from asst. to prof. history U. N.H., Durham, 1971—; Fulbright prof. U. de Brasilia, Brazil, 1976—77, U. Fed. do Rio de Janeiro, 1991—92. Vis. prof. history U. de Brasilia, Brazil, 1976—77, NYU, 1979—80, U. N. Mex., Albuquerque, 1983, U. Fed. do Rio de Janeiro, 1991—92. Author: Brazilian-American Alliance, 1937-45, 1973, A Nasao Armada: Ensaios Sobre a Historia de Exercito Brasileira, 1982, Solders of the Pátria:History Brazilian Army 1889-1937, 2004; editor: Modern Brazil, 1989. Founding dir. Ctr. for Internat. Edn., U. NH, 1982—90; pres. New Eng. Coun., 1975—76, Northeast Assn. Brailianists, 1989—91. Capt. U.S. Army, 1968—70. Decorated cmdr. Order of Rio Branco Brazil; recipient Pacificador medal, Brazilian Min. of Army, 1995; Fulbright fellow, Brazil, 1965—66, 1974. Mem.: Latin Am. Studies Assn., Brazilian Studies Assn., Am. Hist. Assn. Democrat. Roman Catholic. Avocations: Indian lore, photography, canoeing. Office: Dept History U NH Durham NH 03824 Office Phone: 603-862-3028. Business E-Mail: fdm@cisunix.unh.edu.

**MCCANN, GAIL ELIZABETH,** lawyer; b. Boston, Aug. 25, 1953; d. Joseph and Ruth E. (Lagerquist) McC.; m. Stanley J. Lukasiewicz. AB, Brown U., 1975; JD, U. Pa., Phila., 1978. Bar: RI 1978, Mass. 1984, US Dist. Ct. RI 1978, US Dist. Ct. Mass. 1990. Ptnr. Edwards Angell Palmer & Dodge LLP, Providence, 1978—. Bd. dirs. Caritas House, Inc.; RI adv. coun. New Eng. Legal Found. Mem.: Am. Coll. Mortgage Attys. (RI state chair), RI Bar Assn., Brown U. Alumni Assn. (past pres.). Avocations: hiking, travel, yoga. Office: Edwards Angell Palmer & Dodge LLP 2800 Financial Plz Providence RI 02903 Office Phone: 401-274-9200.

**MCCANN, JEAN FRIEDRICHS,** artist, educator; b. NYC, Dec. 6, 1937; d. Herbert Joseph and Catherine Brady (Ward) Friedrichs; m. William Joseph McCann, May 14, 1960; children: Kevin, Brian, Maureen McCann Breslin, William, James, Denis Gerard, Kathleen. Student, Caton-Rose Inst. Fine Arts, 1955—57; AAS, SUNY, Farmingdale, 1959; BS, SUNY-Empire State Coll.,

Binghamton, 1986; MA summa cum laude, Marywood Coll., 1987, MFA in Art summa cum laude, 1989; completed Kellogg Leadership Program, Sch. Mgmt., SUNY, Binghamton, 1992; PhD, Nova Coll., 1995. Designer Patton Corp., N.Y.C., 1959—66; sub. art tchr. Owego-Apalachin Sch. Dist., 1968—88; tutor, evaluator Empire State Coll. SUNY, 1987—; dir. ArtSpace Gallery, Owego, NY, 1991—92, 1994—94. V.p. bd. dirs. Tioga County Coun. on Arts, 1990—91, pres., 1992—95; demonstrator for various schs., ednl. TV and county museums. One-woman shows include IBM, Owego, 1972, Tioga Hist. Soc. Mus., 1975, Nat. Hist. Ct. House, 1982, Visual Arts Ctr., Scranton, Pa., 1989—90, ArtSpace, Owego, N.Y., 1991, MacDonald Art Gallery, Coll. Misericordia, Dallas, Pa., 1992, Plaza Gallery, Binghamton, 1992, Krembs Gallery, 1993, 2000, 2003, Wilson Gallery, Johnson City, N.Y., 1994, 2001, 2003, Countryside Gallery, Owego, N.Y., 1996, 2002, Meml. Gallery, SUNY, Farmingdale, 1998, juried groups show, Roberson Mus., Binghamton, N.Y., 1972, Arnot Art Mus., Elmira, N.Y., 1974, 1989, 1992, Arena Nat. Exhibits, Binghamton, 1974—76, Pennino's Gallery, Burlington, Vt., 1975—77, Riise Gallery, St. Thomas, 1975—78, Grand Concourse Gallery, Albany, 1987, Schweinfurth Meml. Art Ctr., Auburn, N.Y., 2002, numerous pvt. and pub. collections. Bd. dirs. Birthright of Owego, 1991—2003. Recipient N.Y. State Artisans award, 1982, Nat. Strathmore award, 1989, 1st pl. in Graphic Arts award Jericho Arts Coun., 1994. Mem. Nat. Mus. Women in Arts (charter), Kappa Pi (pres. Zeta Omicron chpt. 1987-89, life), Artists Guild. Avocations: travel, reading. Home (Winter): 1776 Atwater Ct Kissimmee FL 34746-3588 Home: 6403 Roberts Dr Victor NY 14564

**MCCANN, JIM (JAMES F. MCCANN),** consumer products company executive; b. July 28, 1951; married; 3 children. BS in Psychology, John Jay Coll., 1974. Creator chain of 14 flower shops, N.Y.C.; chmn., CEO 1-800-FLOWERS.COM, 1987— Bd. dirs. Gateway 2000, OfficeMax, Inc., PETCO, Inc., Nat. Retail Fedn., Very Spl. Arts., Gtech Holdings, Boyd's Bears, Nat. Retail Federation. Author: Stop and Sell the Roses, 1998. Bd. dirs. Hofstra U., Winthrop-Univ. Hosp. Named Entrepreneur of Yr., Merrill Lynch and Inc. Mag., Retailer of Yr., Ernst & Young and L.I. Assn., one of top 100 Bus. Men, Irish Am. Mag., Direct Marketer of Yr., Direct Mktg. Day N.Y., 1996, Outstanding Bus. Spkr., Toastmaster Internat., 1997. Office: 1 800 Flowers com Inc 1600 Stewart Ave Westbury NY 11590-6696*

**MCCANN, JUNE VIVIAN,** retired physical education educator; b. Mpls., June 11, 1911; d. William H. and Lillian (Varco) McCann. BA in Edn., UCLA, 1932; MS, U. So. Calif., LA, 1952, EdD, 1954. Cert. secondary tchr., adminstr. Calif. Playground dir., evening sch. tchr. LA City Schs., 1932—37; tchr. Christ Jr. HS, LA, 1937, San Pedro HS, LA, 1937—42, East LA Jr. Coll., 1947—54; prof. UCLA, 1954—57; prof., dept. chmn. San Jose State U. 1957—76, mem. bd. athletics, 1968—78. Com. mem. Calif. Commn. on Children and Youth, 1959—60. Co-author: Exploring Physical Education, 1962; contbr. articles to profl. jours. Charter mem. San Jose City Sports Commn., 1964—73; pres. women's golf assn. Villages Golf and Country Club, 1986—87, chmn. rules com., 1988—89, 1992—96, bd. dirs., 1989—90. Lt. USNR, 1942—46. Recipient Cert. of Recognition for Outstanding Svc., Villages Women's Golf Assn., 1999, 2001. Mem.: Calif. Tchrs. Assn. (life), Calif. Assn. Health, Phys. Edn., Recreation and Dance (life; pres. 1957, Verne Landroth award 1971), Western Soc. for Phys. Edn. of Coll. Women (life; bd. dirs., life honor award), US Golf Assn., US Tennis Assn., WAVES Nat., Soroptimist (life; pres. 1965, SW dist. scholarship chmn. 1970, pres. 1972). Congregationalist. Avocations: bridge, music, sports.

**MCCANN, KIM LOU M.,** theater educator, director; b. Joplin, Mo., Dec. 8, 1954; d. James Cleland McCann and Mary Earline (Campbell) Kelley; m. Mark A. Lawson, Sr., Feb. 15, 2003. AA in Drama, Diablo Valley Coll., 1974; BA in Theater, Calif. State U., 1976; MFA in Drama, U. Calif., Davis, 1981. Artist, instr., asst. program dir. Short Ctr. South, Sacramento, 1982—; theater, film lectr., resident dir. Sacramento City Coll., City Theatre and Sacramento Shakespeare Festival, 1984—. Pres theatre alumni chpt. bd. Calif. State U., Sacramento. Dir. Twelfth Night, Love's Labour's Lost, Hamlet, Cyrano DeBergerac, Measure for Measure, Midsummer Night's Dream, Three Musketeers, Much Ado About Nothing, Twelfth Night, Shrew, Equus, As You LIke It, Blood Wedding, and 60 others; actor in over 100 prodns. including Mother Courage, Top Girls, Dancing at Lughnasa, Our Town, Hay Fever, Midsummer Night's Dream, The Matchmaker, Merry Wives, Winter's Tale, others. Chmn. bd. dirs. City Theater, 1985—. Avocations: pets, music, reading. Office: Sacramento City College ACTH 3 3835 Freeport Blvd Sacramento CA 95822-1386 Business E-Mail: mccannk@scc.losrios.edu.

**MCCANN, MARGARET ANN,** sister, educator; b. Port Arthur, Tex., June 3, 1953; d. Donald Joseph and Elizabeth Ann McCann. BA, Coll. of St. Elizabeth, 1996; MA, Montclair State U., 2002; postgrad., Marquette U., 2003—04. Cert. bereavement counselor Archdiocese of Newark, 2001; secondary edn. tchr. N.J., 1996. Tchr. H.S. English, Marylawn Acad. of the Oranges, South Orange, NJ, 1996—97, Acad. of Sacred Heart, Hoboken, NJ, 1997—98; adj. instr. English, Montclair State U., NJ, 1998—2002; instr. English composition, intro. to lit. Coll. of St. Elizabeth, Convent Station, NJ, 2001—02; tchr. H.S. English, Marylawn Acad. of the Oranges, South Orange, NJ, 2002—03. Panelist, presenter Mid-Atlantic Popular/Am. Culture Assn., Syracuse, NY, 1995, 17th Ann. Nat. Conf. of Peer Tutoring in Writing, Merrimack Coll., North Andover, Mass., 2000, 9th Ann. Meeting of the Group for Early Mod. Cultural Studies, Phila., Ctrl. NY Conf. on Lang. and Lit., SUNY, Cortland, 2002; moderator of panel 11th Ann. Conf.: Women's Studies Program: Women and Creativity, 2005; presenter in field. Presenter (paper) Women Addressing Male Hierarchies, Thirteenth ann. 18th and 19th Century British Women Writers Conf., 2005, Money Matters in Jane Austen's Sense and Sensibilty, 2005. Sister of charity, tchr. Sisters of Charity of St. Elizabeth, Convent Station, NJ, 1990—2004; mem. catechetical team Gesu Roman Cath. Ch., Milw., 2003—04. Grad. assistantship, Montclair State U., 1998-2000. Mem.: Womens Writers Assn., Nat. Coun. Tchrs of English, Kappa Gamma Pi (assoc.). Republican. Roman Catholic. Avocations: teaching, writing, poetry, travel, films. Personal E-mail: sistermccann@hotmail.com.

**MCCANN, MARGARET HAZEL,** artist, educator; b. Cleve., Feb. 15, 1957; d. George Frederick McCann and Juanita Jean Wilson. Student, Yale U., Norfolk, Conn., 1978; BFA, Washington U., St. Louis, 1979; student, N.Y. Studio Sch., N.Y.C., 1982—83; MFA, Yale U., New Haven, Conn., 1985. Lectr. R.I. Sch. Design European Honors Program, Rome, 1985—87, John Cabot U., Rome, 1987—93, St. Mary's Coll. Rome Program, Rome, 1987—93; lectr. art Trinity Coll. Rome Program, Rome, 1987—93; instr. Internat. Sch. Drawing and Painting, Todi/Monecastello, Italy, 2002, 2003; asst. prof. art Boston U. CFA, 1994—2004. Art critic Art New Eng., Boston, 2005—, Wire Newspaper, Portsmouth, NH, 2004—, columnist Woman on the Street, 2004—; resident Cite Internationale des Arts, Paris, 1998, Paris, 2003, Ragdale Art Colony, Millay Art Colony, 1990. One-woman shows include, Milan, Italy, 1997, N.H., 2002, Spartanburg (S.C.) County Mus., 1999. Vol. Wes Clark Presdl. Campaign, Portsmouth, NH, 2004. Recipient Blanche E. Coleman award, Mellon Trust, 2001, Ingram-Merrill grant, 1989, Fulbright-Hays grant, 1985. Mem.: AAUW, Coll. Art Assn. Democrat. Home: 14 Sheafe St Portsmouth NH 03801

**MCCANN, PETER PAUL,** biology researcher, educator; s. Peter F. and Kathleen (Burnett) McC.; m. Danielle Soury, July 31, 1971. AB in Zoology, Columbia U., 1965; PhD, Syracuse U., 1970. Fellow NIH, Bethesda, Md., 1970-73; sr. scientist Ctr. of Rsch. Merrell Internat., Strasbourg, France, 1973-79; sr. biochemist Merrell Dow Rsch. Inst., Cin., 1979-82; rsch. assoc. scientist Merrell Dow Rsch. Inst., Cin., 1982-84, dir. scientific and acad. liason, 1984-90, dir. sci. adminstrn., 1988-90; profl. U. Cin. Coll. Medicine 1981—; sr. dir., ctr. Marion Merrell Dow Inc., Indpls., 1990-93; pres. Brit. Biotech Inc., Annapolis, Md., 1993-98; interim pres. U. Md. Biotech. Inst., College Park, Md., 1998-99; pres., CEO Oncostasis, Inc., 1999—2001, Mymetics Corp., 2001—03; GG; ptnr. Profl. Fin. Advisor., 2004—. Co-vice chmn. Gordon Rsch. Conf. on Polyamines, 1987, co-chmn., 1989. Chief editor, co-author Inhibition of Polyamine Metabolism, 1987; co-editor, co-author Enzymes as Targets for Drug Design, 1989; contbr. articles to

profl. jours. Mem. Am. Soc. Cell Biology, Am. Soc. Tropical Medicine and Hygiene, Am. Soc. Biochemistry and Molecular Biology, Biochem. Soc. (editl. adv. bd. 1986-92, editor 1992-99), Soc. Protozoologists (editl. bd. reviewers 1989-95), Am. Philat. Congress, Inc. (pres. 1990-95), Am. Philat. Soc. (v.p. 1995-99, pres. 1999-2003, Fédération Internat. De Philatélie (v.p. 2004—). Achievements include patents for method of inhibiting the growth of protozoa, method of controlling phytopathogenic fungus. Personal E-mail: p103226706@cs.com.

**MCCANN, RENETTA,** advertising executive; married; 2 children. BS in Speech, Northwestern U., 1978. Client svc. trainee Starcom, 1978, v.p., 1988, media dir., 1989, sr. v.p., 1995; CEO Starcom N.Am., Chgo., 1999—2004; CEO Americas Starcom MediaVest Group, 2004—. Bd. mem. Audit Bur. Circulations Northwestern U., mem. adv. bd. Media Mgmt. Ctr.; bd. mem. Chgo. United. Named Media Maven, Advt. Age, 2001, Corp. Exec. of Yr., Black Enterprise, 2002, Advt. Woman of Yr., Women's Advt. Club Chgo., 2002; named one of 50 Women Who Are Changing the World, Essence, 2003, 50 Women to Watch, Wall Street Journal, 2005, Most Influential Black Americans, Ebony mag., 2006; recipient Outstanding Women in Comm. award, Ebony, Vanguard award, Chgo. Mags. Assn., Media Strategies award, Bus. Week, Matrix award for advertising, NY Women in Comm. Inc., 2006. Mem.: Am. Advt. Fedn. (mem. multicultural bus. practices leadership coun.), Am. Assn. Advt. Agys. (chair media policy com.). Office: Starcom NAm 35 W Wacker Dr Chicago IL 60601*

**MCCANN, RICHARD EUGENE,** lawyer; b. Billings, Mont., Aug. 14, 1939; s. Oakey O. and Edith May (Miller) McC.; children: Tami, Todd (dec.), Jennifer. BA magna cum laude, Rocky Mountain Coll., 1965; JD with highest honors, U. Mont., 1972. Bar: Mont. 1972, Washington 1977, Alaska 1982. Law clk. to Judge W. Jameson U.S. Dist. Ct., Billings, 1972-73; assoc. Crowley, Haughey, Hansen, Toole & Dietrich, Billings, 1973-77, Perkins Coie, Seattle, 1977-80, ptnr., 1981—2002, sr. counsel, 2003—. Contbr. articles to profl. jours. Trustee Rocky Mountain Coll., Billings., 1973-77. Served with USMC, 1957-61. Mem. ABA, Mont. Bar Assn., Wash. Bar Assn., Alaska Bar Assn. Office: Perkins Coie 1201 3rd Ave Fl 40 Seattle WA 98101-3029 Office Phone: 206-359-8616. Business E-Mail: rmccann@perkinscoie.com.

**MCCANN, RICHARD STEPHEN,** lawyer; b. Wilmington, Del., Dec. 26, 1938; s. Francis E.B. and Naomi H. (Riley) McC.; m. Gloria M. Bauin (div. 1973); 1 child, Heather Marie; m. Sharon R. Cannon. BA, Georgetown U., 1960, JD, 1963; MA in City Planning, U. Pa., 1965. Bar: Del. 1964. Alderman City of Newark, Newark, 1964-66, pvt. practice law, 1970—; city planner Dover, Del., 1966-70. Atty. Del. Police Chief's Coun., Dover, 1971—, Del. Police Chief's Found., Dover, 1983—. Atty. Aetna Hose, Hook & Ladder Co., Newark, 1975—. Mem. ABA, Del. Bar Assn. Avocations: skiing, gardening, cannons. Home: 2500 Wrangle Hill Rd Ste 210 Bear DE 19701-3838 Office Phone: 302-368-2543. E-mail: rsmccannesq@aol.com.

**MCCANN, ROBERT J.,** investment company executive; m. Cindy McCann; 2 children. BA, Bethany Coll.; MBA, Tex. Christian U.; grad. from advanced mgmt. prog., Harvard Bus. Sch. Assoc. MBA sales and trading prog. Merrill Lynch & Co., 1982, head US Equities, 1995—98, COO corp. and instl. client group (now global markets and investment banking), 2000—01, head global securities rsch. and econs., 2001—03, exec. v.p., vice chmn. wealth mgmt. group, 2003—05, exec. v.p., vice chmn. and pres. global pvt. client grp., 2005—. Bd. dirs. Am. Ireland Fund. Recipient Annie Moore award, Irish Am. Cultural Inst. Office: Merrill Lynch 4 World Fin Ctr 250 Vesey St New York NY 10080

**MCCANN, VONYA B.,** federal agency administrator, telecommunications industry executive; BA, U. Calif., L.A., 1976; MA in Pub. Policy, U. Calif., Berkeley, 1979, JD, 1980. Bar: D.C. 1980. Law clk. Commr. Tyrone Brown, Fed. Comm. Commn.; policy analyst Nat. Telecommunications and Info. Adminstrn. Dept. Commerce; ptnr. Arent, Fox, Kintner, Plotkin and Kahn; amb., dep. asst. sec. internat. comm. & info. policy Dept. State, 1994—99, prin. dep. asst. sec. of state for econ. and bus. affairs, 1997—99; sr. v.p., fed. external affairs Sprint Corp., Overland, Kans., 1999—2005; v.p. govt. affairs Sprint Nextel Corp., Overland, 2005—. Office: Sprint World Hdqrs 6200 Sprint Pkwy Overland Park KS 66251

**MCCANNON, TRICIA ANN,** multi-media specialist, writer, photographer, educator; b. Detroit, Dec. 26, 1953; d. John R. McCannon and Carolyn Hayes. BA, Fla. State, Tallahassee, 1975. Multi-media specialist Fla. Dept. of Human Resources, 1976—78; photographer and art dir. Haus Publs., Atlanta, 1978—80; pres. Horizons Unlimited Prodns., Inc., Atlanta, 1980—. Prof. art South Ea. Ctr. Arts, Atlanta, 1987—90; master of ceremonies and headliner Whole Life Expo, L.A., 1991—96; appearances on radio and TV including Unsolved Mysteries and Strange Universe; keynote spkr. in internat. venues and confs. Author: Dialogues with the Angels, 1996, Landscape of the Inner Planes, 1997, UFO's in Am., 1997, Beyond This World, Blue Print of the Soul, Claiming the Power Within, Angels and Extra Trerestrials, The Healing Power of Past Lives, Earth Revolutions: Secrets of the Ages, 2006. Bd. dir. Atlanta Writers Guild, 1985—87; pres. bd. dir. Atlanta UFO Forum, 1988—96. Named a Bishop, Madonna Ministries/L.A., 1998, Priestess, The Iseum of the Eagle and the Dove/Ireland, 1999. Mem.: Assn. of Past Life Therapies, Lightstreamers, Theosophical Soc. Unitarian-Universalist. Avocation: animals. Office: Horizons Unlimited Inc Ste E 2135 Defoors Hills Rd Atlanta GA 30318 Office Phone: 404-355-2211. Personal E-mail: tmccannon@charter.net

**MCCARBERG, BILL HAROLD,** physician; b. Seattle, Apr. 4, 1948; s. Harold Carl and Elizabeth Ann Mehlberg; m. Peggy J. McCarthy McCarberg. BA summa cum laude, U. Calif., Berkeley, 1972; MD, Northwestern U., 1976. Diplomate Am. Bd. Family Practice, Am. Coll. Pain Medicine; cert. in geriatrics. Residency Highland Hosp., Rochester, NY, 1979; physician in charge Kaiser Permanente, Escondido, Calif., 1982—2003; asst. clin. prof. U. Calif. Sch. Medicine, San Diego, 1983—; coord. pain svcs Kaiser Permanent, San Diego, 1974—2002; dir. chronic pain mgmt. program, 1984—2003; founding mem. managed care task force Am. Pain Soc., 1990—. Adv. bd. Knoll Pharma,-Olive Mt., N.J., 1998—. Author: (monograph) Chronic Pain Management: Perspective for Primary Care Physicians, 1998, (book chpt.) A Sample of Existing Managed Care Organizations Pain Programs, 1999; contbr. articles to profl. jours. Recipient K Star for Outstanding Svc., Kaiser Permanente, San Diego, 1985, 92, Award of Excellence Southern Calif. Cancer Pain Initiative, L.A., 1999. Mem. Am. Acad. Pain Medicine, Am. Pain Soc. (chair managed care com. 2000—, bd. dirs., Elizabeth Narcessian award 2003), Western Pain Soc. (chair program 1999—, pres.), Appraisal Physician Svcs., Phi Beta Kappa. Avocations: running, guitar, golf. Office: Kaiser Permanente 732 N Broadway Escondido CA 92025

**MCCARDELL, JAMES ELTON,** retired naval officer; b. Daytona Beach, Fla., Jan. 22, 1931; s. J. Elton and Margaret Almira (Payne) McC.; m. Nancy Ann Chandler, July 9, 1955; children: Jenise, Patrick. Student, U. Fla., 1948-50; BA, U.S. Naval Postgrad. Sch., 1965. Commd. ensign U.S. Navy, 1952, advanced through grades to rear adm., 1980; exec. officer USS Forrestal, 1972-73; dep. chief of staff Air Readiness Staff, Chief Naval Res., New Orleans, 1973-76; comdg. officer NAS, Key West, Fla., 1976-78; chief of staff Staff of Chief Naval Res., New Orleans, 1978-80; def. and naval attache U.S. Embassy, Brasilia, Brazil, 1981-83; dir. Inter-Am. Def. Coll., Fort L.J. McNair, Washington, 1983-85; ret., 1985. Decorated Legion of Merit with cluster, Bronze Star medal, Air medal with 12 clusters, Def. Disting. Service medal, Def. Superior Performance medal Republican. Roman Catholic. Home: PO Box 719 Pass Christian MS 39571-0719 *The absolute measure of successful leadership has always been reflected by performance of subordinates in the achievement of unit goals.*

**MCCARDELL, JOHN MALCOLM, JR.,** history professor, academic administrator; b. Frederick, Md., June 17, 1949; s. John Malcolm and Susan (Lane) McCardell; m. Bonnie Greenwald, Dec. 30, 1976; children: John Malcolm III, James Benjamin Lee. AB, Washington and Lee U., 1971; postgrad., John Hopkins U., 1972-73; PhD, Harvard U., 1976; LittD (hon.), Washington and Lee U., 1997; LHD (hon.), St. Michael's Coll., 2004. From asst. prof. history to prof. Middlebury (Vt.) Coll., 1976—87, prof. history, 1987—, dean faculty, 1988-89, provost, v.p for academic affairs, 1989-91, acting pres., 1991-92, pres., 1992—2004, pres. emeritus, 2004—; sr. rsch fellow U. S.C., Columbia, 1980-81, 96. Bd. dirs. Nat. Bank Middlebury, Comm. fin. Svcs. Group; vice chmn. bd. trustees Episc. H.S., 2004—. Author: The Idea of a Southern Nation, 1979 (Allan Nevins award, 1977); editor: A Master's Due, 1985. Bd. trustees Am. Civil War Ctr., Tredegar, Va. Sgt. USAR, 1971—77. Recipient Algernon Sydney Sullivan prize, Washington and Lee U., 1971, Charles Eliot medal, Eliot House Harvard U., 1976; fellow, NEH, 1980, Am. Philosophical Soc., 1979. Mem.: Vt. Hist. Soc., S.C. History Soc., So. Hist. Assn., Orgn. Am. Historians, Am. Hist. Assn., Lambda Chi Alpha, Phi Beta Kappa, Omicron Delta Kappa.

**MCCARL, DAVID,** costume designer, educator; b. Maryville, Mo., Apr. 21, 1954; MFA, Ind. U., Bloomington, 1980. Costume designer/faculty mem. U. Denver, 1980—85, Minn. State U., Mankato, 1985—. Author: (jour. article) Theatre Design & Technology, The Cutter's Rsch. Jour.; costume designer 106 prodns. at Minn. State U. (Meritorious Achievement, KCACTF, 6 awards). Mem.: US Inst. for Theatre Tech. Office: Minn State Univ Dept of Theatre and Dance Mankato MN 56001 Office Phone: 507-389-1421. Office Fax: 507-389-2922. Personal E-Mail: scotbeardm@yahoo.com. Business E-Mail: david.mccarl@mnsu.edu.

**MCCARL, HENRY NEWTON,** economist, geologist, consultant, venture capitalist; b. Balt., Jan. 24, 1941; s. Fred Henderson and Mary Y. McCarl; m. Louise Becker Rys, June 8, 1963 (div. 1985); children: Katherine Lynne(dec.), Patricia Louise, Fredrick James; m. Mary Frederica Rhinelander, Jan. 31, 1987; 1 stepchild, Francesca C. Morgan. BS in Earth Sci., Harvard U., 1963; MS in Geology, Pa. State U., 1964, PhD in Mineral Econ., 1969. Lic. profl. geologist Ala., N.H. Market rsch. analyst Vulcan Materials Co., 1966-69; asst. prof. econ., asst. prof. geology U. Ala., Birmingham, 1969-72; assoc. prof. econ., 1973-77, assoc. prof. econ. and geology, 1978-91, prof. econs. and geology, 1991-95, prof. econ., edn. and geology, 1995-2001, prof. emeritus, 2001—, dir. Ctr. for Econ. Edn., Sch. Bus., 1987-2001; chief econ. div. Ala. Energy Mgmt. Bd., Montgomery, 1973-74; sr. lectr. in energy econs. Fulbright-Hays Program, Bucharest, Romania, 1977-78; ret., 2001. Mng. dir. McCarl & Assocs., Gloucester, Mass., 1969—; vis. fellow Grad. Sch. Arts and Scis. Harvard U., Cambridge, Mass., 1987; v.p., prin. Economagic, 1999—. Co-author: Energy Conservation Economics, 1986, Introduction to Energy Conservation, 1987; contrib. articles to profl. jours. Mem. Birmingham Planning Commn., 1974—86, chmn., 1980—86; dist. commr. Boy Scouts Am., Birmingham, 1988—94, asst. coun. Com. Greater Ala. Coun., 1999—2001; mem. Glouster Planning Bd., 2002—; mem. edn. coun. MIT, 1974—. Recipient George B. Morgan award, MIT Alumni Assn., 1999. Mem.: SAR (life; nat. trustee 1996—97, 2004—, treas. gen. 2000—03, sec. gen. 2003—04, pres. gen. 2004—05, chmn. found. bd. 2004—05), Nat. Gavel Soc., Ala. Geol. Soc., Mineral Econ. and Mgmt. Soc. (pres. 1992—93), Am. Inst. Profl. Geologists (sect. pres. 1981—83, registered profl. geologist), Soc. Mining Engr. of AIME (bd. dirs. 1978—80, Disting. Mem. award 2000), St. Andrews Soc. Mid-South (life; sec. 1996—97), Sovereign Mil. Order the Temple Jerusalem. Republican. Episcopalian. Avocations: amateur radio, woodworking, beekeeping, model railroading. Home: 28 Old Nugent Farm Rd Gloucester MA 01930-3167 Office: 112 Eastern Ave Gloucester MA 01930 Office Phone: 978-283-6344. Business E-Mail: hmccarl@alum.mit.edu.

**MCCARLIE, V. WALLACE,** dentist, researcher; b. Las Vegas, Nev., Oct. 27, 1975; s. Van and Susan McCarlie. BA, Brigham Young U., Provo, Utah, 2002, MA, 2003; DMD, U. Nev.-Las Vegas, 2007. Sr. rsch. asst. dept chemistry and biochemistry Coll. Phys. and Math. Sci. Brigham Young U., Provo, Utah, 1998—2003, lab asst. in human physiology dept. physiology and devel. biology Coll. Biology and Agr., 2000, grad. rsch. asst. dept. pub. policy dept. polit. sci., 2001—02, grad. tchg. asst. in biology dept. plant and animal sci. Coll. of Biology and Agr., 2002, grad. rsch. asst. dept. ancient scripture Coll. Religious Edn., 2002—03; rsch. asst. dept. biomed. sci. Dental Medicine U. Nev., Las Vegas, 2005—. Nat. editl. bd., contbg editor Am. Student Dental Assn., Chgo., 2005—; editor-in-chief ASDA Impressions, Las Vegas, Nev., 2005—; lectr. in field. Editor: (publications) Globalization and the Information Technology Revolution; contbr. articles to profl. jours., chapters to books. Vol. Boys and Girls Club, Las Vegas, 2005; tchr.; ecclesiastical. leader LDS Ch., Las Vegas, 2003—. Recipient Leadership award for design excellence, Am. Student Dental Assn., 2005; fellow Religious Studies Ctr. fellow, Brigham Young U., 2003; grantee Inst. for the Study and Preservation of Ancient Religious Texts fellow, 2003, U. Nev. -Las Vegas Tchg. and Learning Ctr., 2006. Mem.: Internat. Assn. for Dental Rsch., History of Sci. Soc., Am. Student Dental Assn. (contbg editor, nat. editl. bd. 2005—), Am. Hist. Assn., Am. Dental Edn. Assn., ADA, Am. Assn. for Dental Rsch. (grantee 2006), AAAS. Avocations: golf, tennis, basketball, reading, travel.

**MCCARRICK, EDWARD R.,** magazine publisher; married; 2 children. Degree, Manhattan (N.Y.) Coll., 1971. From sales trainee to pub. Time Mag., NYC, 1973—99, pub., 1999—, and worldwide pres., 2005—; sales dir. Life Mag., NYC, 1988—91, pub., 1993—99. Vol. Cath. Charities; bd. dir. YMCA/YWCA. Avocations: golf, squash, tennis. Office: Time Inc 1271 Avenue of the Americas New York NY 10020-1300 Office Phone: 212-522-3273. E-mail: ed_mccarrick@timeinc.com.*

**MCCARRICK, JOHN F.,** lawyer; b. Bronx, NY, Mar. 18, 1959; BA, Manhattan Coll., 1981; JD, Georgetown U., 1985. Bar: NY 1986, Ohio 1992, US Dist. Ct. Ea., No. & We. Districts NY, Supreme Ct. Ohio. Assoc. Wilson, Elser, Moskowitz, Edelman & Dicker, NYC, 1985—90, Arter & Hadden, Columbus, Ohio, 1990—93, ptnr., 1993, McCarrick & Mayer, P.C., NYC, 1993—2000, Duane Morris LLP, Briarcliff Manor, NY, 2000—, chair firm ins. & fin. products group, 2000—, mng. ptnr. Westchester office. Mem.: ABA, Profl. Liability Underwriting Soc., Assn. of the Bar of the City of NY.

**MCCARRICK, THEODORE CARDINAL,** archbishop emeritus; b. NYC, July 7, 1930; s. Theodore Egan and Margaret (McLaughlin) McCarrick. AB, St. Joseph's Sem., 1954, AM, 1958; MA, Cath. U., 1960, PhD, 1963. Ordained priest Roman Cath. Ch., 1958, Episcopal ordination 1977. Asst. chaplain Cath. U. Am., Washington, 1959—61; dean students, 1961—63; asst. to rector, dir. devel., 1963—65, instr. dept. sociology, 1961—65; domestic prelate, 1965; pres. Cath. U. PR, 1965—69; assoc. dir. edn. Archdiocese of NY, 1969—71; sec. to Cardinal-Archbishop NY, 1971—77; aux. bishop, 1977—81; titular bishop of Rusibisir, 1977—81; apptd. first bishop Diocese of Metuchen, NJ, 1981, first bishop, 1982—86; apptd. archbishop Archdiocese of Newark, 1986, archbishop, 1986—2000, Archdiocese of Washington, 2001—06, archbishop emeritus, 2006; creator Cardinal titular ch. Saints Nereus & Archilleus, 2001. Mem. Fed. Commn. for Study of Migration and Econ. Devel., 1989; policy bd. Washington Consortium, Peace Corps, 1962—63, Pontifical Commn. for Migrants and Refugees, 1987; chmn. U.S. Bishops Com. on Migration, 1986—89, 1992—95, Gov.'s Commn. for Higher Edn. in P.R., 1968, P.R. Adv. Coun. on Tech. and Vocat. Edn., 1968—69; with US Sec. of State's Adv. Com. on Religious Freedom Abroad, 1996—99, US Com. Internat. Religious Freedom, 1999—2001, Synod for Am. and Post Synod Coun.; Episcopal promoter Apostleship of the Sea, 1989—92; chmn. Com. Aid to Ch. in Ctrl. and Ea. Europe, U.S. Conf. of Cath. Bishops, 1992—96, chmn. internat. policy com., 1996—99, chmn. domestic policy com., 2002—05. Sec.-treas. Papal Found., 1988—96, pres., 1997—. Decorated officer, knight grand cross Holy Sepulchre, Order of Cedars of Lebanon. Mem.: Knights Malta (chaplain 1978—82). Roman Catholic.

**MCCARRON, DOUGLAS J.,** labor union administrator; b. LA, Sept. 23, 1950; V.p., sec.-treas. LA County Dist. Coun. of Carpenters, pres., 1983; mem. Local 1506 United Brotherhood of Carpenters, LA, 1968, v.p., 1994—95; pres. United Brotherhood of Carpenters and Joiners Am., Washington, 1995—. Former bd. mem. ULLICO Inc.; mem. S. Calif. Council of Carpenters; trustee S. Calif. Pension Fund; pres. So. Calif. Conf. Carpenters, 1982. Office: United Brotherhood of Carpenters and Joiners 101 Constitution Ave NW Washington DC 20001-2133 also: 1221 Massachusetts Ave Washington DC 20005 Office Phone: 202-546-6206.*

**MCCARRON, JOHN FRANCIS,** editor; b. Providence, Jan. 20, 1949; s. Hugh Francis and Katherine Anne (Brooks) McC.; m. Janet Ann Velsor, Sept. 3, 1971; children: Veronica, Catherine. BS in Journalism, Northwestern U., 1970, MS in Journalism, 1973. Gen. assignment reporter Chgo. Tribune, 1973-80, urban affairs writer, 1980-91, fin. editor, 1991-92, editorial bd. columnist, 1992-2000; v.p. strategy and comms. Met. Planning Coun. Chgo., 2000—02; adj. prof. Medill Sch. Journalism Northwestern U., 2002—. Contbr. to Planning mag., World Book Ency., Preservation mag. Lt. USNR, 1970-72. Recipient Editors award AP, 1983, 84, Ann. Journalism award Am. Planning Assn., 1983, Heywood Broun award Am. Newspaper Guild, Washington, 1989, Peter Lisagor award Soc. Profl. Journalists, 1994. Home: 1425 Noyes St Evanston IL 60201-2639 E-mail: j.mccarron@att.net.

**MC CARTAN, PATRICK FRANCIS,** lawyer; b. Cleve., Aug. 3, 1934; s. Patrick Francis and Stella Mercedes (Ashton) Mc Cartan; m. Lois Ann Buchman, Aug. 30, 1958; children: M. Karen, Patrick Francis III. AB magna cum laude, U. Notre Dame, 1956, JD, 1959. Bar: Ohio 1960, U.S. Ct. Appeals (6th cir.) 1961, U.S. Ct. Appeals (3rd cir.) 1965, U.S. Ct. Appeals (DC cir.) 1980, U.S. Ct. Appeals (5th cir.) 1981, U.S. Ct. Appeals (4th cir.) 1989, U.S. Ct. Appeals (7th cir.) 1992, U.S. Supreme Ct. 1970. Law clk. to Hon. Charles Evans Whittaker, U.S. Supreme Ct., 1959; assoc. Jones Day, Cleve., 1961—65, ptnr., 1966—93, mng. ptnr., 1993—2002, sr. ptnr., 2003—. Trustee U. Notre Dame, 1989—, chair, 2000—; trustee Cleve. Clinic Found.; mem. standing com. on rules of practice and procedure Jud. Conf. of U.S. Fellow: Internat. Acad. Trial Lawyers, Am. Coll. Trial Lawyers; mem.: ABA, Bar Assn. Greater Cleve. (pres. 1977—78), Ohio Bar Assn., 6th Cir. Jud. Conf. (life), U.S.-Japan Bus. Coun., Coun. on Fgn. Rels., Greater Cleve. Growth Assn. (chmn. 1997—2000). Roman Catholic. Office: Jones Day North Point 901 Lakeside Ave E Cleveland OH 44114-1190 Office Phone: 216-586-3939, 216-586-7272. Business E-Mail: pmccartan@jonesday.com.

**MCCARTER, CHARLES CHASE,** lawyer; b. Pleasanton, Kans., Mar. 17, 1926; s. Charles Nelson and Donna (Chase) McC.; m. Clarice Blanchard, June 25, 1950; children: Charles Kevin, Cheryl Ann. BA, Principia Coll., 1950; JD, Washburn U., 1953; LLM, Yale U., 1954. Bar: Kans. 1953, U.S. Supreme Ct. 1962, Mo. 1968. Asst. atty. gen. State of Kans., 1954-57; lectr. law sch. Washburn U., 1956-57; appellate counsel FCC, Washington, 1957-58; assoc. Weigand, Curfman, Brainerd, Harris & Kaufman, Wichita, 1958-61; gen. counsel Kans. Corp. Commn., 1961-63; ptnr. McCarter, Frizzel & Wettig, Wichita, 1963-68, McCarter & Badger, Wichita, 1968-73; pvt. practice law St. Louis, 1968-76; ptnr. McCarter & Greenley, St. Louis, 1976-85; mng. ptnr. Gage & Tucker, St. Louis, 1985-87; Husch and Eppenberger, St. Louis, 1987-89, McCarter & Greenley, LLC, St. Louis, 1990—. Prof. law, assoc. dir. law sch. Nat. Energy Law and Policy Inst. Tulsa U., 1977-79; prof. law, coach nat. moot ct. coll. of law Stetson U. Coll., St. Petersburg, Fla., 1980-84; mem. govtl. adv. coun. Gulf Oil Corp., 1977-81; legal coun. Interstate Oil Compact Commn.; mem. adv. bd. Allegiant Bank, 1997—. Co-author: Missouri Lawyers Guide; assoc. editor Washburn U. Law Rev., 1952-53; contbr. articles to profl. jours. Chmn. Wichita Human Rels. Devel. Adv. Bd., 1967-68; bd. dirs. Peace Haven Assn.; active St. Louis Estate Planning Coun., 1987—; mem. bequests and endowment com. Salvation Army, 1995—; mem. YMCA endowment com., 1996—; mem. gifts and endowment bd. TV Channel 9, KETC, St. Louis, 2004—. With USNR, 1944-46. Recipient Excellent Prof. award U. Tulsa, 1979; vis. scholar Yale U., 1980 Mem. ABA (sect. real property, probate and trust law, bus. law sect.), Kans. Bar Assn., Mo. Bar Assn. (probate and trust com., tax com.), Am. Legion, VFW, Native Sons and Daus. Kans (pres. 1957-58), Kappa Sigma, Delta Theta Phi, Principia Dads Club (bd. dirs.) Republican. Office: One Metropolitan Sq Ste 2100 Saint Louis MO 63102-2751 Office Phone: 314-436-2100. E-mail: cmccarter@mccartergreenley.com.

**MC CARTER, JOHN WILBUR, JR.,** museum executive; b. Oak Park, Ill., Mar. 2, 1938; s. John Wilbur and Ruth Rebecca McC.; m. Judith Field West, May 1, 1965; children: James Philip, Jeffrey John, Katherine Field. AB, Princeton U., 1960; postgrad., London Sch. Econs., 1961; MBA, Harvard U., 1963. Cons., assoc., v.p. Booz Allen and Hamilton, Inc., Chgo., 1963-69; White House fellow Washington, 1966-67; dir. Bur. Budget and Dept. Fin., State of Ill., Springfield, 1969-73; v.p. DeKalb AgResearch, Ill., 1973-78, dir. Ill., 1975-86, exec. v.p. Ill., 1978-80, pres. Ill., 1981-82; pres., chief exec. officer DeKalb-Pfizer Genetics, 1982-86; pres. DeKalb Corp., 1985-86; sr. v.p. Booz Allen & Hamilton Inc., 1987-97; pres., CEO Field Mus., Chgo., 1996—. Bd. dirs Divergence Inc., W.W. Grainger, Inc., Janus. Trustee Chgo. Pub. Television, 1973—, chmn., 1989-96, trustee Princeton U., 1983-87, U. Chgo., 1993—. Office: Field Museum 1400 S Lake Shore Dr Chicago IL 60605-2496

**MCCARTER, LOUIS EUGENE,** lawyer; b. Enid, Okla., Mar. 15, 1940; s. Louis Eugene and Bertha Marguerite (Krittenbrink) McC.; m. Janet Ann Korn, May 25, 1968; children: Scott Louis, Kathryn Nicole. B.A., U. Okla., 1962; LL.M., U. Tex., 1965. Bar: Tex. 1965, U.S. Dist. Ct. (ea. and so. dists.) Tex. 1975, U.S. Ct. Mil. Appeals 1966. Assoc., Vinson & Elkins, Houston, 1968-75, ptnr., 1975—. Served to capt. JAGC, U.S. Army, 1965-68; Vietnam. Decorated Bronze Star, Army Commendation medal. Mem. ABA, Tex. Bar Assn., Tex. Bd. Legal Specialization, Am. Bd. Trial Advs., Internat. Assn. Def. Counsel, Ctr. Club, Houston Country Club. E-mail: lmccarter@velaw.com. Office: Vinson & Elkins 3300 First City Tower 1001 Fannin St Ste 3300 Houston TX 77002-6706 Office Phone: 713-758-2530. Business E-Mail: mccarter@velaw.com.

**MCCARTER, MARTIN D.,** surgeon, researcher; b. Dearborn, Mich., Feb. 16, 1965; s. Lowell Harold McCarter and Mary Ann Dalton; m. Lauren Anne Arnold, June 10, 1994; 1 child, Megan Anne McCarter-Arnold. AB, Dartmouth Coll., 1987; MD, U. Vt., 1992. Diplomate Am. Bd. Surgery. Resident in surgery N.Y. Hosp.-Cornell U., N.Y.C., 1992—99; fellow in surg. oncology Meml.-Sloan-Kettering Cancer Ctr., N.Y.C., 1999—2001; asst. prof. surgery U. Colo., Denver, 2001—. Author: (book chpt.) Carcinoma of the Colon in Surgical Decision Making, 2004; contbr. articles to med. jours. Recipient Golden Apple Tchg. award, U. Colo. Health Scis. Ctr., 2002, K-12 Career Devel. award in oncology, NIH, 2002. Fellow: ACS (physician liaison to com. on cancer 2002—); mem.: Surg. Oncology Soc., Soc. Univ. Surgeons, Colo. Am. Cancer Soc. (mem. colorectal task force 2001—). Avocations: running, hiking, skiing, bicycling. Office: U Colo Health Scis Ctr Box C-311 4200 9th Ave Denver CO 80220

**MCCARTER, THOMAS NESBITT, III,** investment company executive, consultant; b. NYC, Dec. 16, 1929; s. Thomas N. Jr. and Suzanne M. (Pierson) McCarter. Student, Princeton U., 1948-51. Chartered investment counselor. Sales exec. Mack Trucks, Inc., NYC, 1952—59; ptnr. Kelly, McCarter, D-Arcy Investment Counsel, NYC, 1959—62; v.p., sec., dir. D-Arcy McCarter & Chew, NYC, 1962—66; v.p., dir. Thruston, Wortham & Co., Inc., NYC, 1967—71, exec. v.p., 1971—75; chmn. bd., dir. Island Security Bank Ltd., 1976—78; pres. Knottingham Ltd., NYC, 1976—84; gen. ptnr. W.P. Miles Timber Properties, New Orleans, 1977—92; v.p. Yorke McCarter Owen & Bartles, Inc., NYC, 1985—89. Cons. Laidlaw Holdings, Inc., 1990—92; pres. Mentor Mgmt. Group, Inc., NYC, 1986—90; chmn. bd. dirs. Ramapo Land Co., Sloatsburg, NY, 1990—, Stillrock Mgmt., Inc., NYC, 1992—96, Pendragon Tech., 1996—98, Dir Anker Coal Group Inc., Hyseq Inc., Nuvelo, Inc.; bd. advisors Knowledge Delivery Sys. Inc.; vice chair Runnymede Capital Mgmt., Inc.; bd. dirs. Inst. Scientific Investment and Governance KCK Tokyo, So. Union Co. Chmn. bd. trustees Christodora

Found., Inc., NYC, 1970-93; charter trustee Dalton Sch., NYC, 1969-76, v.p., 1972-76; pres., trustee Civil War Libr. and Mus., Phila., 1985-92; chmn. bd. trustees ASPCA, 1984-95; chmn. loyal Legion Found., NYC; trustee Children's Aid Soc. NYC, 1973-94, Joffrey Ballet, Found. for Am. Dance, 1973-77; trustee NYC Marble Cemetery Assn., 1990-2002; mem. Nat. Com. for Preservation of US Treasury Bldg., 1988-92; trustee Nat. Symphony Orch., Washington, 1990-94; chmn. Gibralter Am. Coun., 1998-2002; bd. assocs. Whitehead Inst., Cambridge, Mass., 2000—. Mem. Loyal Legion US (comdr. NY State 1964-66, nat. comdr. in chief 1977-81); Racquet and Tennis Club, Brook Club, Links Club, River Club, St. Nicholas Soc., Pilgrims of US (NYC), Meadow Club (Southampton, NY), Ivy Club (Princeton, NJ). Republican. Home and Office: PO Box 2380 Palm Beach FL 33480

**MCCARTHY, ANN PRICE,** lawyer; b. LA, Jan. 30, 1947; d. Frank Judson and Marianna (Chase) Price; 1 child, Sundae Jan Cloe; m. Joseph Stephen McCarthy, Dec. 15, 1974; 1 child, Caitlin Price. BA, Old Coll., Reno, 1983; JD, Nev. Sch. Law, 1987. Bar: Nev. 1987, 1988, U.S. Dist. Ct. (no. dist.) Calif. 1988, U.S. Ct. Appeals (9th cir.) 1989. Legal asst. Aebi, FitzSimmons & Lambrose, Carson City, Nev., 1981-84; ind. legal researcher Reno, 1985; law clk. Martin H. Wiener, Esquire, Reno, 1985-87, Hon. Robin C. Wright, Reno, 1987-88, Hon. John C. Mowbray, Carson City, 1988; ptnr. Eck & McCarthy, Carson City, 1988-90; pvt. practice Ann Price McCarthy, Ltd., Carson City, 1990-91; ptnr. Aebi & McCarthy, Carson City, 1991—. Lectr. Nat. Bus. Inst., Reno, 1992, 93; instr. Juvenile Drug and Alcohol Edn. Program, Carson City, 1992. Bd. dirs., sec. Brewery Arts Ctr., Carson City, 1992, bd. dirs., pres., 1993-95. Mem. Am. Trial Lawyers Assn., Nev. Trial Lawyers Assn., Washoe County Bar Assn., First Jud. Dist. Bar Assn. (pres. 1991-92, 92-93), State Bar of Nev. (pres. 2004). Address: Ann Price McCarthy & Assoc 777 E William St Ste 201 Carson City NV 89701 Office: Aebi and McCarthy Ste 201 777 E William St Carson City NV 89701-4058

**MCCARTHY, BEVERLY FITCH,** retired civic leader, educator; b. St. Louis, Aug. 10, 1933; d. Clyde and Elsie (Graf) Fitch; children: Michael, Elizabeth; m. John Linley McCarthy, Mar. 17, 1973. AA, L.A. City Coll., 1953; BA in Social Scis., U. Calif., Berkeley, 1955; MA in Edn., Stanford U., Calif., 1957; adminstrv. credential, U. Pacific, Stockton, Calif., 1980. Mem. faculty Monterey (Calif.) Peninsula Coll., 1957-58, Santa Barbara (Calif.) City Coll., 1958-59, San Jose (Calif.) City Coll., 1959-60; tchr. Bret Harte High Sch., Angels Camp, Calif., 1960-62; instr. psychology San Joaquin Delta Coll., Stockton, Calif., 1962-85; dir. reentry program for women and men, 1974-85; mem. Stockton City Coun., Calif., 1990-92; ret., 1990—. Pres. Sunflower Presents, Inc., 1990-96; dir. Stockton Record Cmty. Found., 1994-95. Pres. Assistance League Stockton, 1969-71, Dem. Women's Club San Joaquin County, 1987, San Joaquin chpt. Nat. Women's Polit. Caucus, 1982, Stockton Symphony Assn., 1973-77, 2006—, Stockton Opera Guild, 1977-78, 87-89, 94-96, Stockton Civic Theatre League, 1981-82, San Joaquin County Child Abuse Prevention Coun. Aux., 1989-90; chmn. Stockton Redevel. Commn., 1986, San Joaquin County Commn. on Status Women, 1974-82, 93-95, 1999-2004, San Joaquin Family Resource and Referral Employer-Assisted Child Care Coalition, 1986-89, Stockton Opera Assn., 2001-03; elected Jr. Aid Stockton, 1993-2003; dir.-treas. Children's Mus. Stockton, 1994-96; travel aux. pres. Haggin Mus., 2003-06. Recipient Woman of Yr. award Soroptimist Club, Stockton, 1970, 74, Arts Recognition award Stockton Arts Commn., 1978, Women of Achievement award San Joaquin County Commn. on Status Women, 1983; Rosalie M. Stern award U. Calif.-Berkeley Alumni Assn., 1976, Alumni citation, 1985. Mem. AAUW (named gift Ednl. Found. 1977-78), Women Execs. Stockton (founder), Cal Club San Joaquin County (founder, pres. 1981-82), Stanford Women's Club San Joaquin County (founder, pres. 1974-76, 2002-05), Philanthropic Edn. Orgn., Friends of the Fox (bd.-elected 2004), Stockton Beautiful (bd. 1993-2006), Mortar Bd., Prytanean Soc., Gavel and Quill, North Stockton Rotary Club, Philomathean Club (pres. 2000-01), Nu Sigma Psi, Delta Psi Omega, Pi Lambda Theta, Phi Delta Kappa, Delta Kappa Gamma. Democrat. Avocation: gardening. Home: 215 W Stadium Dr Stockton CA 95204-3136 E-mail: linley17@comcast.net.

**MCCARTHY, BRIAN NELSON,** real estate developer; b. Detroit, May 24, 1945; s. Andrew Nelson and Ruth Elizabeth (Hill) McC.; children: Amanda Lang, Kelly Elizabeth, Meghan Virginia, Connor Michael; m. Valerie Reiheld, 1997. BS in Engring. Sci., Oakland U., 1966; MBA, Harvard U., 1972. Engr. Gen. Motors Corp., Pontiac, Mich., 1965-67; co-owner Sound Wave Systems, Costa Mesa, Calif., 1971-78; CFO, controller A&W Gershenson Co., Farmington, Mich., 1972-75; pres. Devel. Group, Inc., Southfield, Mich., 1975—81; CEO Brichard & Co., San Francisco, 1982-87; pres. Watermark Corp., Sausalito, Calif., 1987—92, Indian Wells Water Co., Inc., Sausalito, 1993—2000; dir. Co-Investor Group, Sonoma, Calif., 2000—01; chmn., pres. Southfork Devel. Group, El Dorado Hills, Calif., 2002—. Rear adm. USNR, 1966-96, res. Recipient Navy Achievement medal, Navy Commendation medal with gold star, Joint Commendation medal, Navy Meritorious Svc. medal with 2 gold stars, Joint Meritorious Svc. medal with oak leaf cluster, others. Mem. Navy Supply Corps Assn. (bd. dirs. 1987-96). Republican. Office: Southfork Devel Group PO Box 778 Camino CA 95762

**MCCARTHY, CAROLYN,** congresswoman; b. Bklyn., Jan. 5, 1944; m. Dennis McCarthy (dec. Dec. 1993); 1 child. LPN, Glen Cove Nursing Sch., NY, 1964. LPN St. Francis and Winthrop Hosp., 1964—93; gun safety activist, 1994—97; mem. US Congress from 4th NY dist., 1997—. Mem. edn. and the workforce com., US Congress, mem. fin. svcs. com. Recipient numerous awards, including being named one of Newsday's 100 LI Influentials, Congl. Quarterly's 50 Most Effective Legislators in Congress, one of nine Redbook Mag.'s "Mothers and Shakers", Ladies' Home Jour. list of America's 100 Most Important Women, and Advertising Age's list of Most Impact by Women in 1999; also honored by US Women's Soccer Team and Oprah Winfrey. Mem.: New Yorkers Against Gun Violence, NYC Stop the Violence Campaign, Guns for Goods, Ams. Against Gun Violence (hon.). Democrat. Roman Catholic. Office: US Ho Reps 106 Cannon Ho Office Bldg Washington DC 20515-3204 Office Phone: 202-225-5516.*

**MCCARTHY, CARRIE ANN,** secondary school educator, director; b. Cleve., Sept. 10, 1975; d. Calvin Paul and Linda Marie Corsi; m. Thomas Alexis McCarthy, Dec. 29, 2001. M. John Carroll U., University Heights, Ohio, 2004. Tchr. Cleve. Heights H.S., Ohio, 1997—2000; tchr., dept. head Normandy H.S., Parma, 2000—. Advisor student govt. Normandy H.S., 2002—. Mem.: Nat. Coun. Social Studies (assoc.). Roman Catholic. Home: 1135 Valley Parkway Broadview Heights OH 44147 Office: Normandy High School 2500 West Pleasant Valley Road Parma OH 44134 Office Phone: 440-885-2400. Office Fax: 440-885-2402. Personal E-mail: cacorsi@hotmail.com. E-mail: carriemcca@parma.k12.oh.us.

**MCCARTHY, CONNIE KEARNS,** university librarian; BA, Rosary Coll., Ill., 1968; MSLS, Catholic U., 1972. Past cataloger Folger U. Shakespeare Libr.; asst. univ. libr. for collections George Washingtn U.; assoc. univ. libr. William R. Perkins Libr. Duke U.; now dean univ. libr. Coll. William and Mary, 1997—. Chair steering com. Virtual Libr. of Va.; chair edtl. bd. CHOICE jour. Mem.: ALA. Office: Earl Gregg Swem Libr Coll William and Mary PO Box 8794 Williamsburg VA 23187-8794 Office Phone: 757-221-3055. Office Fax: 757-221-2635. E-mail: ckmcca@wm.edu.*

**MCCARTHY, CORMAC (CHARLES JOSEPH MCCARTHY),** writer; b. Providence, R.I., July 20, 1933; s. Charles Joseph and Gladys (McGrail) McC.; m. Lee Holleman, 1961 (div.); 1 child, Cullen; m. Anne deLisle, 1967 (div.), m. Jennifer, 1 child. Author: (novels) The Orchard Keeper, 1965 (William Faulkner Found. award 1965), Outer Dark, 1968, Child of God, 1974, Suttree, 1979, Blood Meridian, or The Evening Redness in the West, 1985, All the Pretty Horses 1992 (Nat. Book award for fiction 1992, Nat. Book Critics Circle award for fiction 1993), The Crossing, 1994, Cities of the Plain, 1998, No Country for Old Men, 2005, The Road, 2006; (teplays) The Gardner's Son, 1977; (plays) The Stonemason: A Play in Five Acts, 1994. With USAF, 1953—57. Ingram-Merrill Found. creative writing grantee, 1960, Am. Acad. Arts and Letter traveling fellow, 1965-66, Rockefeller

Found. grantee, 1966, Guggenheim fellow, 1976, MacArthur Found. grantee, 1981; recipient Jean Stein award Am. Acad. and Inst. Arts and Letters, 1991. Mailing: c/o Amanda Urban ICM 40 W 57th St New York NY 10019

**MCCARTHY, DANIEL WILLIAM,** management consultant; b. Syracuse, N.Y., Apr. 15, 1952; s. William Cornelius and Ruth Francis (Geller) McC.; m. Mary Coleen Kisil, Jan. 17, 1987; children: Katherine M., Kevin D., Patrick W. BA in Polit. Sci., SUNY, Geneseo, 1974; MBA, NYU, 1982. Asst. buyer Abraham & Straus, Bklyn., 1976—78; buyer Lord & Taylor, NYC, 1978—80; cons. Touche Ross, Newark, 1982—87; sr. mgr. Deloitte & Touche, NYC, 1987—93; dir. Coach Leatherware, NYC, 1993—94; prin. Greenvale Consulting Group, Poughkeepsie, NY, 1994—2000; pres. Retex Cons. Group, NYC, 2000—02; Greenvale Cons. Group, LLC, NY, 2002—03; dir. spl. projects Island Pacific, Inc., 2003—06; prin. Greenvale Cons. Group, 2006—. Author: Point of Sale - Current Trends and Beyond, 1986; contrb. articles to profl. jours. Mem. Town of Poughkeepsie Hist. Planning Commn. Named Open Foil Champion, North Atlantic Veterans, 2000, 2001, 2004. Mem. Nat. Retail Fedn., Inst. Mgmt. Cons. Roman Catholic. Avocations: wine collecting, ballet, fencing, architecture, investing. E-mail: danmed@msn.com.

**MC CARTHY, FRANK MARTIN,** oral surgeon, educator; b. Olean, NY, Aug. 27, 1924; s. Frank Michael and Joan (Quinn) McC.; m. Julia Richmond, Nov. 24, 1949; children: Robert Lee, Joan Lee. BS, U. Pitts., 1943, DDS, 1945, MD, 1949; MS in Oral Surgery, Georgetown U., 1954; ScD (hon.), St. Bonaventure U., 1956. Med. intern Mercy Hosp., Pitts., 1949-50; practice oral surgery L.A., 1954-75; tchg. fellow Georgetown U., 1952-53; rsch. fellow NIH, 1953-54; prof. oral surgery U. So. Calif. Sch. Dentistry, 1966-75, prof., sect. anesthesia and medicine, 1975-90, prof. emeritus, 1990—, chmn. dept. surg. scis., 1979-84, assoc. dean adminstrv. affairs, 1977-79, asst. dean hosp. affairs, 1979-84. Dir. anesthesiology U.So. Calif. oral surgery sect. L.A. County Hosp., 1958-89; clin. supr., lectr. dental hygiene program Pasadena City Coll., 1992—; sr. exam. Am. Dental Bd. Anesthesiology, 1984-89; lectr. in field; mem. adv. panel on dentistry sect. anesthesizing agts. Nat. Fire Protection Assn., 1971-79; mem. Am. Nat. Stds. Com., 1974-86, 95—; cons. in field. Author: Emergencies in Dental Practice, 1967, rev., 1972, 79, Medical Emergencies in Dentistry, 1982, Safe Treatment of the Medically Compromised Patient, 1987, Essentials of Safe Dentistry for the Medically Compromised Patient, 1989; mem. editorial bd.: Calif. Dental Assn. Jour; contrb. articles to profl. publs. Bd. councilors Sch. Dentistry, U. So. Calif., 1972-75. Served as lt., M.C. USNR, 1950-52. Recipient Lifetime Achievement award, So. Calif. Orofacial Acad., Palm Springs, Calif., 2006. Fellow Internat. Assn. Oral Surgeons (founder), Am. Coll. Dentists, Internat. Coll. Dentists; mem. ADA (editl. bd. jour.), Am. Dental Soc. Anesthesiology (Heidbrink award 1977), Am. Assn. Oral-Max Surgeons (chmn. anesthesia com. 1971), So. Calif. Soc. Oral Surgeons (pres. 1974), Calif., L.A. County Dental Assns., Delta Tau Delta, Phi Kappa, Phi Rho Sigma, Omicron Kappa Upsilon. Home and Office: 480 S Orange Grove Blvd Apt 11 Pasadena CA 91105-1720

**MCCARTHY, G. DANIEL,** lawyer; b. Butte, Mont., Mar. 23, 1949; s. George Denis and Mary Agnes (Kiely) McC.; m. Carolyn M. Scully, June 19, 1976; children: Brendan, Katie, Kelly, Sean. BA, U. Dayton, 1971; JD, U. Notre Dame, 1974; AMP, Harvard U., 1994. Bar: Md. 1974, D.C. 1975, U.S. Ct. Appeals (D.C. cir.) 1976, Pa. 1977, N.Y. 1985, U.S. Ct. Appeals (10th cir.) 1985. Assoc. Bilger & Blair, Washington, 1974-77, 79-80; asst. U.S. atty. U.S. Dist. Ct. (ea. dist.) Pa., Phila., 1977-78; assoc. Abourezk, Shack & Mendenhall, Washington, 1980-83; atty. AT&T, N.Y.C., 1983-85; v.p., gen. counsel and sec. AT&T Credit Corp., Morristown, NJ, 1985-89; sr. v.p., gen. counsel, sec., chief risk mgmt. officer. AT&T Capital Corp., Morristown, NJ, 1990-96; v.p., gen. counsel, sec. Compaq Fin. Svcs. Corp., Murray Hill, NJ, 1996—2002; v.p. govt. affairs, dep. gen. counsel Compaq Computer Corp., Houston, 2001—02; v.p., gen. counsel, sec. Hewlett-Packard Fin. Svcs. Co., Murray Hill, NJ, 2002—. Vis. lectr. Marymount Coll., Arlington, Va., 1979-83; mem. adv. coun. U. Dayton, Coll. of Arts and Scis., 1993-97, chmn., 1994-96; bd. dirs. Compaq Fin. Svcs. Europe, LLC, Tandem Computers Credit Corp., Hewlett-Packard Internat. Bank PLC. Mem.: DC Bar Assn., Fairmount Country Club (Chatham, NJ) (bd. dirs. 2002—). Avocations: golf, fly fishing. Office: HP Fin Svcs Co 420 Mountain Ave New Providence NJ 07974-0006 Office Phone: 908-898-4003. Business E-mail: dan.mccarthy@hp.com.

**MCCARTHY, GLORIA M,** insurance company executive; Various leadership positions Empire Blue Cross Blue Shield, 1974—97; sr. v.p. Empire Blue Cross Blue Shield (WellChoice, Inc became the parent holding co. in 2002), 1997—2002, WellChoice, Inc., 2002, sr. v.p. ops., managed care and medicare services, 2002—03, exec. v.p., COO, 2003—. Office: WellChoice 11 West 42nd St New York NY 10036

**MCCARTHY, HAROLD CHARLES,** retired insurance company executive; b. Madelia, Minn., Dec. 5, 1926; s. Charles and Merle (Humphry) McC.; m. Barbara Kaercher, June 24, 1949; children: David, Susan. BA, Carleton Coll., Northfield, Minn., 1950; postgrad. With Federated Mut. Ins. Co., Owatonna, Minn., 1950-67; with Meridian Mut. Ins. Co., Indpls., 1967-91, exec. v.p., then exec. v.p., gen. mgr., 1972-75, pres., 1975-90, bd. dirs., past chmn. bd., 1990-91; past pres. North Meridian Bus. Group; past pres., chmn. bd. Meridian Ins. Group, Inc. Chmn. bd., dir. Meridian Life Ins. Co.; past chmn., exec. com., bd. dirs. Ind. Ins. Inst.; mem. adv. bd. Harbor Fed. Savs. Bank. Former mem. Met. Devel. Comm., Corp. Cmty. Coun.; bd. dirs. Meth. Health Found., Family Services Assn., Boy Scouts Am., Indian River Symphony Assn.; trustee Butler U. With USNR, 1944-46. Named Sagamore of the Wabash. Mem. Skyline Club (Indpls.), Indian River Golf Club. Republican. Office: 2955 N Meridian St Indianapolis IN 46208-4714

**MCCARTHY, IAN J.,** construction executive; BS, City U., London. With Kier Ltd., 1980—81; pres., CEO Beazer Homes USA Inc., Atlanta, 1989—. Dir. Beazer Far East, 1981—91. Chmn. HomeAid's Nat. Adv. Bd.; bd. dir. Metro Atlanta Chamber; trustee Woodruff Arts Ctr., Atlanta. Office: Beazer Homes 1000 Abernathy Rd Ne Atlanta GA 30328-5606*

**MCCARTHY, J. THOMAS,** lawyer, educator; b. Detroit, July 2, 1937; s. John E. and Virginia M. (Hanlon) McC.; m. Nancy Irene Orrell, July 10, 1976 BS, U. Detroit, 1960; JD, U. Mich., 1963. Bar: Calif. 1964. Assoc. Julian Caplan, San Francisco, 1963—66; prof. law U. San Francisco, 1966—; counsel Morrison and Foerster, 2001—. Founding dir. McCarthy Inst. Intellectual Property and Tech. Law; mem. Trademark Rev. Commn., 1986—88; cons. in field. Author: McCarthy on Trademarks and Unfair Competition, 6 vols., 4th edit., 1996, McCarthy on Rights of Publicity and Privacy, 1987, 2d edit., 2000, McCarthy's Desk Encyclopedia of Intellectual Property, 3d edit., 2004. Recipient Jefferson medal N.J. Intellectual Property Assn., 1994, Ladas award Brand Names Ednl. Found., 1997, Pattishall medal Brand Names Found., 2000, Pres.'s award Internat. Trademark Assn., 2003. Mem. IEEE, Am. Intellectual Property Law Assn. (Watson award 1965, Centennial award in Trademark law 1997), Internat. Assn. for Advancement of Tchg. and Rsch. in Intellectual Property, Am. Law Inst. (adv. com. on restatement of law of unfair competition).

**MCCARTHY, JENNY,** actress; b. Chgo., Nov. 1, 1972; m. John Mallory Asher, Sept. 11, 1999, 1 child, Evan Joseph Asher. Student Sch. Nursing, So. Ill. U. Spokeswoman Jose Cuervo Tequila. Appeared in films Things to Do in Denver When You're Dead, 1995, The Stupids, 1996, BASEketball, 1998, Diamonds, 1999, Scream 3, 2000, Dirty Love, 2005, John Tucker Must Die, 2006; TV shows The Jenny McCarthy Show, 1997, Jenny, 1997-98, The Bad Girl's Guide, 2005; host game show Singled Out, MTV, 1995-96, Party @ the Palms, 2005; featured photographs in Playboy mag., 1993-96, 98, 05, including as Miss Oct. 1993, then as Playmate of Yr., 1994; author Jen-X, 1997, Belly Laughs: The Naked Truth About Pregnancy and Childbirth, 2004 (NY Times Bestseller list, 2004), Baby Laughs: The Naked Truth About

First Year of Mommyhood, 2005 (NY Times Bestseller list, 2005). Named one of 50 most beautiful people in the world, People mag., 1996. Avocation: kickboxing. Address: c/o United Talent Agy 9560 Wilshire Blvd Ste 500 Beverly Hills CA 90212-2427*

**MCCARTHY, JOHN,** computer scientist, educator; b. Boston, Sept. 4, 1927; s. Patrick Joseph and Ida McCarthy; children: Susan Joanne, Sarah Kathleen, Timothy Talcott. BS in Math., Calif. Inst. Tech., 1948; PhD in Math., Princeton U., 1951; Degree (hon.), Linkoping U., Sweden, Polytechnic U., Madrid, Colby Coll., Dublin and Concordia U., Montreal. Procter Fellow Princeton U., 1950—51, Higgins Rsch. instr. in math., 1951—53; acting asst. prof. math. Stanford U., 1953—55; asst. prof. math. Dartmouth Coll., 1955—58; asst. prof. comm. sciences MIT, Cambridge, 1958—61, assoc. prof. comm. sciences, 1961—62; prof. computer sci. Stanford U., 1962—2001, Charles M. Pigott prof. Sch. Engring., 1987—94, prof. emeritus computer scis., 2001—. Academic advisor Nat. Legal Ctr. for Pub. Info., 1976—80; fellow Ctr. for Advanced Study in the Behavioral Sciences, 1979—80; Bobby R. Inman prof. computer sci. U. Tex., 1987; bd. dir. Info. Internat., Inc., 1962—95, Inference Corp., 1983—91, Mad Intelligent Systems, 1987—91. Contbr. articles to profl. jours.; mem. editl. bd. Artificial Intelligence Jour., 1975—. Served with AUS, 1945-46. Named Disting. Alumnus, Calif. Inst. Tech.; recipient First Rsch. Excellence award, Internat. Joint Conf. on Artificial Intelligence, 1985, Kyoto prize, Inamori Found., 1988, Nat. Medal of Sci., NSF, 1990, Fellow award, Computer History Mus., 1999; Sloan Fellow in Phy. Sci., 1957—59. Fellow: Am. Assn. Artificial Intelligence (pres. 1983—84); mem.: NAE, NAS, AAAS, Am. Math. Soc., Assn. for Computing Machinery (A.M. Turing award 1971), Am. Acad. Arts and Scis., Sigma Xi. Achievements include invention of LISP programming language in 1958; circumscription method of non-monotonic reasoning in 1978; coined the term Artifical Intelligence in 1955. Home: 885 Allardice Way Stanford CA 94305-1050 Office: Stanford U Rm 208 Gates Bldg 2A Computer Sci Dept Stanford CA 94305-9020 Office Phone: 650-723-4430. Office Fax: 650-725-7411. Business E-Mail: jmc@cs.stanford.edu. E-mail: mccarthy@stanford.edu.

**MC CARTHY, JOSEPH MICHAEL,** historian, educator; b. Lynn, Mass., Oct. 2, 1940; s. Joseph Donald and Johanna (Downing) Mc C.; m. Kathleen Theresa Wright, July 30, 1966; children: Joanna, Kristenmarie, Erika, Joseph Michael. AB, St. Johns Sem., 1961, postgrad., 1961-63; AM, Boston Coll., 1968, PhD, 1972. Tchr. Bishop Fenwick H.S., Peabody, Mass., 1964-67; fin. adminstr. Boston Coll., 1967-71, lectr. edn., 1971-74; prof. edn.; dir. leadership programs Suffolk U., Boston, 1973—2006, prof. emeritus, 2006—. Vis. prof. Boston Coll., 1990; adj. lectr. Merrimack Coll., 1975, Boston U., 1973; prin. Ednl. Mgmt. Svcs., 1976—; gen. editor Garland Pub., 1979-92; bd. dirs. Inst. for Study of Academia, 1992-94. Author: An International List of Articles on the History of Education, 1977, Guinea-Bissau and Cape Verde Islands, 1977, Humanistic Emphases in the Educational Thought of Vincent of Beauvais, 1976, Pierre Teilhard de Chardin, 1981; mem. editl. bd. The Urban and Social Change Rev., 1969-72, The Bureaucrat, Inc., 1974-76; contbr. articles to profl. jours. Pres. N.E. region Popular Culture Assn./Am. Culture Assn., 1999-99. Hearn scholar, 1959-61, fellow, 1961-63. Mem. Am. Cath. Hist. Assn., Soc. for Medieval and Renaissance Philosophy, Soc. Romanian Historians, Soc. Mil. History, East European Rsch. Inst., Phi Alpha Theta, Phi Delta Kappa. Home: Knockglen Farm 103 Fuller St Middleboro MA 02346-1700 Office: Suffolk U Beacon Hill Boston MA 02114 Office Phone: 617-573-8262. Business E-Mail: jmccarth@suffolk.edu.

**MCCARTHY, KAREN P.,** former congresswoman, former state legislator; b. Mass., Mar. 18, 1947; BS in English, Biology, U. Kans., 1969, MBA, 1985; MEd in English, U. Mo., Kansas City, 1976. Tchr. Shawnee Mission (Kans.) South High Sch., 1969-75, The Sunset Hill (Kans.) Sch., 1975-76; mem. Mo. House of Reps., Jefferson City, 1977-94; cons. govt. affairs Marion Labs., Kansas City, Mo., 1986-93; mem. U.S. Congress from 5th Mo. dist., Washington, 1995—2005; mem. commerce com.; mem. Ho. Select Com. on Homeland Security. Rsch. analyst pub. fin. dept. Stearn Bros. & Co., 1984-85, Kansas City, Mo.; rsch. analyst Midwest Rsch. Inst., econs. and mgmt. scis. dept., Kansas City, 1985-86. Del. Dem. Nat. Conv., 1992, Dem. Nat. Party Conf., 1982, Dem. Nat. Policy Com. Policy Commn., 1985-86; mem. Ho. Commerce Com. Energy and Power, Telecom., Trade and Consumer Protection; co-chair Dem. Caucus Task Health Care Reform. Recipient Outstanding Young Woman Am. award, 1977, Outstanding Woman Mo. award Phi Chi Theta, Woman of Achievement award Mid-Continent Coun. Girl Scouts U.S., 1983, 87, Annie Baxter Leadership award, 1993; named Conservation Legislator of Yr., Conservation Fed. Mo., 1987. Fellow Inst. of Politics; mem. Nat. Inst. of Politics; mem. Nat. Conf. on State Legis. (del. on trade and econ. devel. to Fed. Republic of Germany, Bulgaria, Japan, France and Italy, mem. energy com. 1978-84, fed. taxation, trade and econ. devel. com. 1986, chmn. fed. budget and taxation com. 1987, vice chmn. state fed. assembly 1988, pres.-elect 1993, pres. 1994), Nat. Dem. Inst. for Internat. Affairs (instr. No. Ireland 1988, Baltic Republics 1992, Hungary 1993). Democrat.

**MCCARTHY, KEVIN,** state representative; b. Bakersfield, Calif., Jan. 26, 1965; m. Judy McCarthy; children: Connor, Meghan. BS in Bus. Adminstrn., Calif. State U., Bakersfield, 1989, MBA, 1994. Owner Bakersfield Batting Range, Kevin O's Deli; dist. dir. Rep. Bill Thomas; mem. Calif. Assembly, 2002—. Bd. dirs. Kern Econ. Opportunity Corp. Trustee dist. bd. Kern C.C., 2000—; exec. dir. McCarthy Found., 2000—; coach YMCA, 1999—; mem. Kern County Rep. Ctrl. Com., 1992—; bd. dirs. First Book, 2001—, Head Start, Kern County Food Bank. Mem.: Rotary. Republican. Office: PO Box 942849 Sacramento CA 94249 Address: 4900 California Ave Ste 140-A Bakersfield CA 93309

**MCCARTHY, MARK FRANCIS,** lawyer; b. Boston, July 8, 1951; s. William Alfred and Martha Louise (Blodgett) McC.; m. Karen Marie Umerley; children: Kevin Francis, Daniel Henry. AB in Theology, Georgetown U., 1973, JD, 1976. Bar: Ohio 1976. Assoc. Sweeney, Mahon, & Vlad, Cleve., 1976-80; ptnr. Tucker Ellis & West LLP, Cleve. Atty. asst. to bd. pres. Bd. Cuyahoga County Commrs., Cleve., 1976-80; adj. prof. Case Western Reserve Law Ctr., Cleve., 1986-2004. Active Greater Cleve. Growth Assn. Leadership Cleve., 1979-80; trustee Parmadale, Parma, Ohio, Western Res. Hist. Soc., 1978-80, Cath. Charities Found.; chmn. Cath. Charities Svcs. Corp.; trustee, sec. Caritas Connection; founder, sec., gen. counsel St. Martin De Porres H.S., Cleve., Inc. Mem. Ohio Assn. Civil Trial Attys.; chmn. product liability sect. 1989—), Fedn. Ins. & Corp. Counsel, Ct. of Nisi Prius, Rowfant Club. Democrat. Roman Catholic. Avocations: book collecting, fly fishing, upland shooting. Home: 363 Britannia Pky Avon Lake OH 44012-2180 Office: Tucker Ellis & West LLP 1150 Huntington Bldg 925 Euclid Ave Cleveland OH 44115-1475 Office Phone: 216-696-3290. Business E-Mail: Mark.McCarthy@tuckerellis.com.

**MCCARTHY, MARY ELIZABETH (BETH) CONSTANCE,** conductor, music educator; b. Chgo., Apr. 8, 1961; d. Thomas Joseph and Loretta Ann McCarthy. BA, North Ctrl. Coll., 1983; postgrad., Goethe Inst., 1991, Ea. Ill. U., 1993; MusM in Choral and Instrumental Edn. and Cognition and Vocal Performance, Northwestern U., 1999. Profl. cantor Joliet/Rockford Dioceses, Ill., 1979—; assoc. condr. Chorus Orch. Band Ill. Math. and Sci. Acad. at Ea. Ill. U., Charleston, 1990—95; soloist Lincoln Opera Co., Chgo., 1991—94; chmn. Dept. Fine Arts Rosary H.S., Aurora, 1993—; dept. chair music Aurora U., 1995—; condr., artistic dir. Fox Valley Festival Chorus, Aurora, 1999—. Profl. role coach pvt. students, Ill., 1989—; condr., avocation: dinner theatres, summer stock, Ill., 1990—; artistic cons. oratory and recitals, Ill., 1993—; adjudicator orchs., chorus, bands, Ill., 1993—; cons. to critique Nat. Stds. for the Arts, Ill., 1994; master class clinician various choral orgns., Ill., 1995—; guest condr. fine arts festivals, Ill., 2001—; host Cath. Conf. Fine Arts Festival Rosary H.S., Aurora, 2002. Contbr. rsch. articles to profl. publs.; author original scripts; music arranger:. Soc. The Beta Fine. Group, Sycamore, Ill., 1995—2002; conservation mem. Salmon Unlimited-Ill. chpt., 1997; religious edn. tchr. St. Peter and Paul Ch., Naperville, Ill., 1980—; cantor 1976—, Rite of Christian Initiation for Adults sponsor, 1995.

Recipient Internat. Bel-Canto Vocal Competition Opera award, Bel-Canto Found., 1995; fellow Richter fellow for internat. rsch./study, North Ctrl. Coll., 1982. Mem.: ASCD, AAUW, Lyric Opera Chgo., Ill. Music Educators' Assn. Music Educators' Nat. Conf., Fox Valley Music Educators' Assn., North Ctrl. Coll. Alumni Assn., Northwestern U. Music Sch. Alumni Assn. (bd. dirs. 1998—2001), Northwestern Club Chgo., Alpha Psi Omega, Beta Beta Beta, Phi Alpha Theta. Avocations: art, travel, running, boating, reading. Office: Aurora Univ Music Dept 347 S Gladstone Aurora IL 60506

**MCCARTHY, MAURA,** critic, editor; Visual arts critic and editor WashingtonPost.com. Office: Washington Post 1150 15th St NW Washington DC 20071

**MCCARTHY, MICHAEL S.,** lawyer; b. Springfield, Ill., 1950; Student, St. Louis U.; AB, U. Mich., 1971; JD, U. Colo., 1975. Bar: Colo. 1975. Ptnr. Faegre & Benson LLP, Denver. Comments editor: U. Colo. Law Review 1974-75. Office: Faegre & Benson LLP 3200 Wells Fargo Ctr 1700 Lincoln St Denver CO 80203 Office Phone: 303-607-3500. Office Fax: 303-607-3600.*

**MCCARTHY, MICHAEL SHAWN,** health care company executive, lawyer; b. Evergreen Park, Ill., May 16, 1953; s. Martin J. and Margaret Anne (McNeill) McC.; m. Jane F. Alberding, Oct. 28, 1988; children: Caroline Margaret, Nicholas Michael, Claire Patricia. BA, Georgetown U., 1975; MS, U. Ill., 1976; JD, Loyola U., 1980. Bar: Ill. 1980, U.S. Dist. Ct. (no. dist.) Ill. 1980. V.p., sec., gen. counsel Luth. Gen. Health Care System, Park Ridge, Ill., 1980-85, sr. v.p., sec., gen. counsel, 1985-91, sr. v.p. corp. svcs., sec., gen. counsel, 1990-93; chmn., CEO Parkside Sr. Svcs., LLC, Skokie, Ill., 1993—. Life trustee Lake Forest Acad.; mem. coun. of regents Loyola U., Chgo., Ill. Mem. ABA, ASHA (exec. bd.), Ill. Hosp. Assn., Ill. Pub. Health Assn., Chgo. Bar Assn., ALFA Leadership Coun. Roman Catholic. Avocations: golf, travel. Home: 1026 Pine St Winnetka IL 60093-2024 Office: Parkside Sr Svcs LLC 5215 Old Orchard Rd Skokie IL 60077-1035 E-mail: McCarthy@parkside-sr.com.

**MCCARTHY, MIKE,** professional football coach; b. Pitts., Pa., Oct. 10, 1963; Grad., Baker U., 1986. Grad. asst. Fort Hays State, 1987—88; quarterbacks, wide receivers coach U. Pitts., 1989—92; offensive asst. Kans. City Chiefs, 1993—94, quarterbacks coach, 1995—98, Green Bay Packers, 1999, head coach, 2006—; offensive coord. New Orleans Saints, 2000—04, San Francisco 49ers, 2005. Recipient NFC Asst. Coach Yr., 2000. Office: Green Bay Packers Lambeau Field 1265 Lombardi Ave Green Bay WI 54307*

**MCCARTHY, NOBU,** actress, performing company executive, educator; Adj. prof. Calif. State U. Artistic dir.: East West Players in Los Angeles, As The Crow Flies (Drama-Logue award), Sarcophagus, Come Back Little Sheba; dir. The Chairman's Wife, Webster Street Blues, And the Soul Shall Dance, (TV) China Beach, Island Son, Magnum P.I., Quincy, Farell to Manzanar, Playhouse 90, (feature films) Geisha Boy, Wake Me When It's Over, Karate Kid II, Pacific Heights.

**MCCARTHY, PAMELA MAFFEI,** magazine editor; b. NYC, May 28, 1952; d. Rudolph Paul Maffei and Mary Frances Maresca; m. Joseph Matthews McCarthy, Sept. 16, 1978; 2 children. Student, Trinity Coll., Dublin, Ireland, 1972-73; BA, Mt. Holyoke Coll., 1974. Copy staff Esquire mag., N.Y.C., 1974-76. Copy editor, 1976-79, exec. editor, 1978-84; mng. editor Vanity Fair mag., N.Y.C., 1984-92, The New Yorker, N.Y.C., 1992-95, 1995—, dep. editor. Mem. Am. Soc. Mag. Editors Office: The New Yorker Advance Publications Inc 4 Times Sq New York NY 10036-6561

**MCCARTHY, PATRICIA ANNE,** reading educator; d. John Donald and Ruth Catherine McCarthy; m. Moses Samuel Schanfield, Aug. 16, 1998; children from previous marriage: Stephanie Anne Murdock, Karin Joann Plotkin. BS, Le Moyne Coll., 1969; MA, Marquette U., 1971, PhD, 1999. Adj. asst. prof. Cardinal Stritch U., Milw., 1988—98; dir. Early Literacy Intervention Program, Wauwatosa, Wis., 1988—98; asst. prof. SUNY, Geneseo, 1999—2002, Hood Coll., 2003—04, Loyola Coll. in Md., Balt., 2004—. Scholar Milw. Area Tchrs. Assn., 1988—98, Marquette U. Edn. Dept., 1994—95. Mem.: ASCD, Nat. Reading Conf., Internat. Reading Assn., Phi Delta Kappa. Avocations: travel, art collecting, reading, walking. Office: Loyola Coll in Md 4501 N Charles St Baltimore MD 21210 Office Phone: 401-617-2459. Personal E-mail: pamccarthy@loyola.edu.

**MCCARTHY, PATRICK,** publishing executive; Joined Women's Wear Daily, 1977, reporter Washington, bur. chief London, Paris, editor N.Y.C., 1985-88, exec. editor, 1988-92; editor W, N.Y.C., 1985-88, exec. editor, 1988-92; exec. v.p. Fairchild Publs., N.Y.C., 1992-97; chmn., editl. dir., 1997—. Recipient Eugenia Sheppard award for fashion journalism CFDA, 1994. Office: Conde Nast Publs 750 Third Ave New York NY 10017

**MCCARTHY, PAUL,** artist; b. 1945; Attended, U. Utah, 1966—68; BFA, San Francisco Art Inst., 1969; MFA, U. Southern Calif., 1973. Luhring Augustine Gallery, 1997—98, 2002, New Mus. Contemporary Art, NY, 2000, Mus. Contemporary Art, LA, 2000, The Garden, Deitch Projects, 2000—01, Galerie Hauser & Wirth, Zurich, 2001, Tate Modern, London, 2003. Mailing: c/o 1301PE 6150 Wilshire Blvd 8 Los Angeles CA 90048

**MCCARTHY, PAUL FENTON,** aerospace transportation executive, retired military officer; b. Boston, Mar. 3, 1934; s. Paul Fenton and Jane Gertrude (O'Connor) McC., m. Sandra Williams, June 13, 1959; children: Paul Fenton III, Susan Stacy. BS in Marine and Elec. Engring., Mass. Maritime Acad., 1954; MS in Mgmt., U.S. Naval Postgrad. Sch., 1964; D of Pub. Adminstrn. (hon.), Mass. Maritime Acad., 1987. Commd. ensign U.S. Navy, 1954, advanced through grades to vice adm., 1985; 7 command tours have included Aircraft Carrier USS Constellation, Carrier Group One, Task Force Seventy-seven; commdr. U.S. 7th Fleet, 1980-82; dir. R & D USN, Washington, 1980-83; negotiator Naval Air, Incidents at Sea Agreement, Moscow, 1980; ret., 1990; cons. in field Alexandria, Va., 1990-92; pres. McCarthy and McCarthy, Ltd.; v.p., chief engr., dep. gen.mgr. McDonnell Douglas Aerospace/Boeing, St. Louis, 1992-95; v.p. processes and sys. integration McDonnell Douglas Aerospace, St. Louis, 1995-97, dir. naval systems integration, 1997-2000; vis. disting. prof. Peter Conrad chair Naval Post Grad. Sch., 2000-02; sr. ptnr. McCarthy and McCarthy, LLC, 2002—; sr. lectr. grad. studies U. San Diego, 2005—. Bd. visitors Mass. Maritime Acad. 1993. Decorated D.S.M., Legion of Merit, D.F.C., also by govts. of South Vietnam, Korea, Japan. Mem.: Mass. Maritime Acad. Alumni Assn. Episcopalian. Avocations: development and acquisition, aircraft and missile systems, financial management. Office Phone: 619-922-9494. E-mail: mcandmc@aol.com.

**MCCARTHY, ROGER LEE,** mechanical engineer; AB in Philosophy with high distinction, U. Mich., 1972, BS in Mech. Engring. summa cum laude, 1972; MS in Mech. Engring., MIT, 1973, D in Mech. Engring., 1975, PhD in Mech. Engring., 1977. Registered profl. engr., Calif., Ga., Ariz. Project engr. machine design and devel. engring. divsn. Proctor & Gamble, Inc., Cin., 1973-74; program mgr. Spl. Machinery Group Foster-Miller Assocs., Inc., Waltham, Mass., 1976-78; prin. design engr. Failure Analysis Assocs., Inc. (became Exponent Failure Analysis Assocs., Inc. in 1998), Menlo Park, Calif., 1978—, chmn. bd. dirs. 1988—; mem. emeritus Failure Analysis Assocs., Inc., Menlo Park, 2005—; CEO The Failure Group, Inc., Menlo Park, 1988-96, chief tech. officer, 1996-98; chmn. Exponent Failure Analysis Assocs., Inc., Menlo Park, 1998—. Co-contbr. numerous articles to profl. jours. Mem. Pres.' Commn. on Nat. Medal of Sci., 1992-94. Recipient Outstanding Civilian Svc. Gold medal U.S. Army, 1990; NSF fellow, 1972-75. Mem. ASME, ASHRAE, ASTM, NAE, Am. Soc. Metals, Soc. Automotive Engrs., Am. Welding Soc., Human Factors Soc., Nat. Fire

Protection Assn., Phi Beta Kappa, Sigma Xi (James B. Angell scholar). Office: Exponent Failure Analysis Assn Inc 149 Commonwealth Dr Menlo Park CA 94025 Office Phone: 650-688-7100. Office Fax: 650-688-7366. E-mail: sfrlm@exponent.com.*

**MCCARTHY, THOMAS EDWARD,** retired telecommunications executive; b. Sacramento, July 18, 1925; s. James Daniel and Lorene Margaret McCarthy; m. Joyce Elaine Reilly, June 28, 1952 (dec. Nov. 1987); children: Thomas E. Jr., Sharon E., Lisa A. McCarthy Harding; m. Gloria Adair Radford, Dec. 30, 1989. BS in Journalism with distinction, Northwestern U., Evanston, Ill., 1950. Cert. Pub. Rels. Soc. Am. Reporter UP, San Francisco, 1951-54, Wall St. Jour., N.Y.C., 1954-56; pub. rels. project mgr. Sylvania Electric, N.Y.C., 1956-62; mgr. pub. info. GTE Corp., N.Y.C., 1962-72, dir. pub. relns. Stamford, Conn., 1972-80, v.p. pub. affairs, 1980-86; ret., 1986. Cons. in field. Author: The History of GTE Corp., 1990 (Assn. Bus. Comms. award 1991). Irish Jubilee, 1997. With USAAC, 1943-46. Mem. Sigma Delta Chi, Kappa Tau Alpha, Zeta Psi. Roman Catholic. Avocations: reading, writing, travel, walking, history. Home: 9885 Mill Station Rd Sebastopol CA 95472-9662 Office Phone: 707-823-4151. Personal E-mail: tgmccart@somic.net.

**MCCARTHY, THOMAS JAMES, JR.,** lawyer; b. Pulaski, Va., Nov. 24, 1943; s. Thomas James and Jane (Osborne) McC.; m. Sally Stockdale, July 25, 1987. BA in Econs., Washington and Lee U., 1967; JD, U. Va., 1970. Bar: Va. 1970, U.S. Dist. Ct. (we. dist.) Va. 1974, U.S. Supreme Ct. 2000. Asoc. Gilmer, Sadler, Ingram Sutherland & Hutton, Pulaski, 1970-75, ptnr., 1975—; county atty. Pulaski County, Pulaski, 1983—. Adminstrv. hearings officer Commonwealth of Va., 1983—; commr. of accts. Pulaski County, 1989—. Bd. dir. Coun. Sch. Attys., 2005—, New River C.C. 1980-88, 96-2004, vice-chair, 1981-88, 2002-2005, chair 2002-04, found. bd., 1989-91, 2004-. Col. JAGC, U.S. Army Res., ret., 1997. Decorated Legion of Merit, Meritorious Svc. medal, Army Commendation medal. Mem. Va. Bar Assn., 27th Jud. Cir. Bar Assn. (pres. 1978-81), Pulaski County Bar Assn.; fellow Va. Law Found., Sigma Chi, Phi Alpha Delta. Democrat. Episcopalian. Home: PO Box 818 Pulaski VA 24301-0818 Office: Gilmer Sadler et al 65 E Main St Pulaski VA 24301-5013 Office Phone: 540-980-1360 x33.

**MCCARTHY, VINCENT PAUL,** lawyer; b. Boston, Sept. 25, 1940; s. John Patrick and Marion (Buckley) McC.; children: Vincent, Sybil, Hope. AB, Boston Coll., 1962; JD, Harvard U., 1965. Bar: Mass. 1965. Ptnr. Hale and Dorr LLP, Boston, 1965—; sr. ptnr. Hale and Dorr, Boston, 1976—2003; counsel Wilmer Cutler Pickering Hale & Dorr LLP, 2004—. Co-founder, bd. dirs., sec. Robert F. Kennedy Action Corps, Inc.; mem. Mass. Gov.'s Adv. Coun. on Alcoholism, Boston, 1984-94, Gov.'s Jud. Nominating Com., 1991-96; chmn. Mass. Housing Partnership Fund, 1991-2003; past chmn. Boston Ctr. for Arts; mem. adv. coun. Harvard Internat. AIDS Inst.; trustee, sec. Franklin Square Found.; past pres. Mass. Assn. for Mental Health; bd. dirs., past sec.-treas. Human Rights Campaign Found.; chmn. Gov.'s Commn. on Gay and Lesbian Youth, 2001-2003. Recipient Vols. of Am. Outstanding Svc. award, 1989. Mem.: ABA (Pro Bono Publico award 1987), Boston Bar Assn. (Pub. Svc. award 1995), Mass. Bar Assn. Office Phone: 617-526-6933. Business E-Mail: vincent.mccarthy@wilmerhale.com.

**MC CARTHY, WALTER JOHN, JR.,** retired utilities executive; b. N.Y.C., Apr. 20, 1925; s. Walter John and Irene (Trumbl) McC.; m. Linda Lyon, May 6, 1988; children by previous marriage: Walter, David, Sharon, James, William. B.M.E., Cornell U., 1949; grad. Oak Ridge Sch. Reactor Tech., 1952; D.Eng. (hon.), Lawrence Inst. Tech., 1981; D.Sc. (hon.), Eastern Mich. U., 1983; LHD, Wayne State U., 1984; LLD, Alma Coll., Mich., 1985. Engr. Public Service Electric & Gas Co., Newark, 1949-56; sect. head Atomic Power Devel. Assos., Detroit, 1956-61; gen. mgr. Power Reactor Devel. Co. Detroit, 1961-68; with Detroit Edison Co., 1968-90, exec. v.p. ops., 1975-77, exec. v.p. divs., 1977-79, pres., chief operating officer, 1979-81, chmn., chief exec. officer, 1981-90. Author papers in field. Past chmn., bd. dirs. Inst. Nuclear Power Ops.; past pres. Monterey County Symphony Orch. Fellow Am. Nuc. Soc., Engring. Soc. Detroit; mem. ASME, NAE. Methodist.

**MCCARTHY, WILLIAM JOSEPH,** lawyer, financial service executive; b. Bklyn., Feb. 13, 1923; s. William Joseph and Louise Ann (Malonson) M.; m. Carol E. Martin, Jan. 22, 1949 (dec. Jan. 1987); children: Christian, Mark, Margaret, Kelley, Mary. BS, Georgetown U., 1944, LLB, 1947; MBA, N.Y.U., 1965. Bar: D.C. 1947, U.S. Ct. Appeals (2d cir.) 1948, N.Y. 1947. Assoc., Hill, Rivkins & Middleton, 1947-49, Sullivan, Donovan, Heenehan & Hanrahan, 1949-52, Hawkins, Delafield & Wood, 1952-56; dep. U.S. mem. Validation Bd. for German Dollar Bond, 1956-60; mcpl. analyst Shearson, Hammill & Co., N.Y.C., 1960-62; sr. analyst, 1962-68, v.p., 1970, dir. new issue svc., 1962-72; mcpl. bond rsch. div., Moody's Investors Svcs., Inc., N.Y.C. 1972-75; v.p., mgr. mcpl. rsch. Blyth, Eastman, Dillon & Co., NYC, 1975-80; v.p. pub. finance Fitch Investors Svc., Inc., N.Y.C., 1980-90; cons., 1990-97. Active North East Yonkers Taxpayers Assn. (pres. 1970-71), Mohegan Heights Homeowners Assn. Mem. Soc. Mcpl. Analysts (pres. 1983), Assn. for Mcpl. Leasing & Fin. (dir. 1982-83), N.Y. Mcpl. Analysts (chmn. 1967-68), The Money Marketeers, Mun. Forum of N.Y., Met. Econ. Assn., Mcpl. Bond Club, KC. Republican. Roman Catholic. Home: 36 Shawnee Ave Yonkers NY 10710-5121

**MCCARTHY-ALLEN, MARY FRANCES,** medical foundation adminstrator, not-for-profit fundraiser, consultant; b. Washington, Apr. 16, 1937; d. Joseph Francis and Frances (Oddi) McGowan; m. Charles M. Sappenfield, Dec. 14, 1963 (div. June 1990); children: Charles Ross, Sarah Kathleen; m. Daniel Fendrich McCarthy, Jr., Aug. 25, 1990 (dec. Apr. 1999); m. Cary Walter Allen, Nov. 30, 2002. BA, Trinity Coll., Washington, 1958; cert. in bus. adminstrn., Harvard U.-Radcliffe Coll., 1959; MA, Ball State U., Muncie, Ind., 1984. Systems engr. IBM, Cambridge, Mass., 1959-61; editl. asst. Kiplinger Washington Editors, 1961-63; feature writer pub. info. dept. Ball State U., 1984-85, coll. editor Coll. Bus., 1985-86, coord. alumni and devel., 1986-88, dir. major gift clubs and donor rels., 1988-90; dir. devel. Sweet Briar (Va.) Coll., 1990-91; adminstr. St. Mary's Hosp. and Med. Ctr. Found., Grand Junction, Colo., 1991—. Editor: A History of Maxon Corporation, 1986, Managing Change, 1986, Indiana's Investment Banker, 1987; assoc. editor Mid-Am. Jour. Bus., 1985-86. Participant Leadership Lynchburg, 1990, Jr. League; regional dir. IX Assn. for Healthcare Philanthropy, 1996—98, found. bd., 1997—; bd. dirs. Sr. Companions, Grand Junction, 1992—; mem. steering com. Mesa County Health Cmtys., 1992—; bd. dirs. Grand Junction Musical Arts, 1997—; trustee Women's Found. of Colo., 2000—; bd. dirs. Grand Valley Hospice, 2002—; mem. Mesa County Health Assessment, 1994—. Recipient Golden Broom award Muncie Clean City, 1989; svc. of distinction award Ball State U. Coll. Bus., 1990. Mem. Coun. for Advancement and Support of Edn., Assn. of Healthcare Philanthropy (regional 9 cabinet 1992—; bd. dirs. 1997—), Nat. Soc. Fundraising Execs. (cert., Colo. chpt. bd. dirs. 1994—), Rotary. Republican. Avocations: biking, walking, cross country skiing, gardening.

**MCCARTNEY, CHAD EDWARD,** music educator; b. Gettysburg, Pa., June 22, 1972; s. Edward Berlin and Marjorie Ann McCartney; m. Andrea Michelle Mickey, Oct. 9, 1999. BS in Music Edn., Pa. State U., 2000, MS in Music Edn., 2004. Cert. tchr. Pa. Tchr. Littlestown Bands, Pa., 1995—96; dir. band Upper Dauphin Area Schs., Elizabethville, Pa., 1996. Performer Fink's Constant, Harrisburg, Pa., performer, composer, 2000—; performer Westernwomen Drum and Bugle Corps, 1996—, Black Horse Brass Quintet, 2002—; tchr. No. York High Sch. Marching Band, 2002—. Composer: (songs) I Can't Complain, 2001, One Day, 2002, Seuss, 2002, Be Not Afraid, 2004, Rush Hour, 2005. Mem.: Nat. Judges Assn. (judge 1999—), individual analysis music judge), Music Educators Nat. Conf. (sec. 1997—99), Pa. Music Educators Assn., Masons (life). Office: Upper Dauphin Area High School 220 North Church Street Elizabethville PA 17023 Home: 228 Shell St Harrisburg PA 17109-4731 Personal E-mail: mccartneychad@aol.com.

**MCCARTNEY, CHARLES PRICE,** retired obstetrician, retired gynecologist; b. Barnesville, Ohio, Aug. 18, 1912; s. Jesse Thomas and Carrie (Price) McC.; m. Phyllis Helen Graybill, Sept. 27, 1940; children— Marilyn B., Ann E. BS, U. Chgo., 1942, MD, 1943. Diplomate: Am. Bd. Obstetricians and Gynecologists. Intern U. Chgo. Clinics, 1943-44, resident, 1947-50; mem. faculty U. Chgo. Med. Sch., 1950-71, prof. obstetrics and gynecology, 1960-71, Mary Campeau Ryerson prof., 1967-71; clin. prof. obstetrics and gynecology U. Ill., 1971-80, prof. emeritus, 1980—. Attending gynecologist and obstetrician Chgo. Lying-In Hosp., 1950— Mem. Cook County Com. Maternal Welfare, 1965—. Served to maj., M.C. AUS, 1944-46. Fellow Am. Gynecol. Soc.; mem. Am. Gynecol. and Obstetrical Soc., Chgo. Gynecol. Soc. (pres. 1967), Chgo. Med. Soc. (councillor 1960—, pres. 1973, chmn. bd. trustees 1973), Am. Coll. Obstetricians and Gynecologists (chmn. Ill. sect. 1965—), Cen. Assn. Obstetricians and Gynecologists. Home: 200 Wyndemere Cir W-218 Wheaton IL 60187-2445

**MCCARTNEY, DAVID FARNHAM,** archivist, educator; b. Charles City, Iowa, May 29, 1956; s. Ralph Farnham and Rhoda Mae Huxsol McCartney; life ptnr. James Anthony Petersen. BA, U. Wis., 1979; MA, MLS, U. Md., 1998. Cert. Acad. Cert. Archivists, 2000. Archives technician Nat. Archives and Records Adminstrn., College Park, Md., 1994—98; records officer IMF, Washington, 1998—99; archives asst. Nat. Pub. Broadcasting Archives, College Park, 1995—2000; archives cons. History Assoc., Inc., Rockville, Md., 1999—2000; archivist U. Iowa, Iowa City, 2001—, adj. prof., 2002—. Nat. adv. bd. Iowa Broadcasting Archives, Waverly, Iowa, 2004—; bd. dirs. Nat. Collaborative for Women's History Sites, Chgo., 2004—. Contbr. chapters to books. Donor, scholarship fund Midwest Archives Conf., Milw., 2005; donor, vol. web mgr. Floyd County Hist. Soc., Charles City, 1998; donor Englert Civic Theater, Iowa City, 2002. Fellow, Richard Eaton Found., 1996—98; grantee, Nat. Film Preservation Found., 2002, 2003, 2005, Nat. TV and Video Preservation Found., 2004; scholar, H.W. Wilson Co., U. Md., 1996; Frank G. Burke fellow in Archives Studies, U. Md., 1998. Mem.: Soc. Am. Archivists (steering com. coll. and u. archives sect. 2004—, donor scholarship fund), Midwest Archives Conf., Iowa Conservation and Preservation Consortium, Consortium Iowa Archivists, Com. Instl. Coop. U. Archivists Group, Assn. Moving Image Archivists, Nat. 19th Amendment Soc. (adv. bd. 1991—), Nat. Collaborative for Women's History Sites, Beta Phi Mu. Avocations: reading, bicycling, hiking. Home: 1302 Muscatine Ave Iowa City IA 52240 Office: Dept Special Collections 100 Main Library Iowa City IA 52242-1420 Office Phone: 319-335-5921. Office Fax: 319-335-5900. Personal E-mail: dfmcc@yahoo.com. E-mail: david-mccartney@uiowa.edu.

**MCCARTNEY, KATHLEEN,** dean, education educator; m. William Hagen; children: Pres, Sam, Kaitlin, Kimberly. BA summa cum laude, Tufts Univ.; MS psychology, PhD psychology, Yale Univ. Asst. prof. psychology dept. Harvard U., 1982—87, mem. faculty edn., 2000—, Gerald S. Lesser prof. early childhood edn., academic dean, 2004—05, acting dean Grad. Sch. Edn., 2005—06, dean Grad. Sch. Edn., 2006—; dir. Child Study and Development Ctr. U. NH; prin. investigator Nat. Inst. Child Health & Human Devel. Vis. rsch. scholar Ctr. for Rsch. on Women, Wellesley Coll. Editl. bd. Child Devel. Jour., Devel. Psychology; contbr. articles tp profl. jours. Grantee Am. Psychological Soc., Bush Fellow, Yale Univ. Fellow: Am. Psychological Soc.; mem.: Soc. Research Child Devel. (co-chmn.). Office: Harvard U Human Devel & Psychology 7th Fl Larsen Hall Cambridge MA 02138 Office Phone: 617-495-3401. Office Fax: 617-496-1182. E-mail: kathleen_mccartney@gse.harvard.edu.*

**MCCARTNEY, N. L.,** investment banker; b. Jameson, Mo., Oct. 12, 1923; m. Helen M. Walsh, Feb. 11, 1950; children: Patricia, Deborah, Patrick. BS, U. Md., 1956; MBA, Syracuse U., 1959; MPA, George Washington U., 1963. Enlisted U.S. Army, 1944, advanced through grades to col., ret., 1972; dir. S.W. Mo. Health Care Foun., Springfield, 1974-88; pres. Resource Mgmt. Co., Springfield, 1988-96; exec. v.p. Spencer and Assocs., Springfield, 1990-94, Mo. Adv. Capital, 1995-99; pres. DMS, Inc., 1999—, CEO, 2001—. Instr. S.W. Mo. State U., Springfield, 1972-82. Pres. S.W. Mo. Adv. Coun. Govts., Ozarks Crime Prevention Coun., 1983-93, Vis. Nurse Assn.; mayor of Springfield, 1993-95. Mem. Rotary. Methodist. Home: 1233 E Loren St Springfield MO 65804-0041 Office: 330 N Jefferson Springfield MO 65806 Office Phone: 417-863-9992.

**MCCARTNEY, SIR PAUL (JAMES PAUL MCCARTNEY),** musician; b. Liverpool, Eng., June 18, 1942; s. James and Mary Patricia (Mohin) McC.; m. Linda Eastman, Mar. 12, 1969 (dec. April 17, 1998); children, James, Stella, Mary, Heather; m. Heather Mills, June 11, 2002 (separated May 17, 2006); 1 child, Beatrice. Degree, Univ. Sussex, Brighton, 1988. With John Lennon and George Harrison in groups Quarrymen, Johnny and the Moondogs, Silver Beatles, 1956-62, with John Lennon, George Harrison and Ringo Starr in group The Beatles, 1962-70,with group Wings, 1970-80; solo performer, 1970-; (albums with The Beatles) Meet the Beatles, 1964, The Beatles '65, 1964, Hard Day's Night, 1964, Help!, 1965, Rubber Soul, 1965, Revolver, 1966, Sgt. Pepper's Lonely Hearts Club Band, 1967, Magical Mystery Tour, 1967, The Beatles (The White Album), 1968, Yellow Submarine, 1969, Abbey Road, 1969, Hey Jude, 1970, Let It Be, 1970; (solo albums) McCartney, 1970, Ram, 1971, Red Rose Speedway, 1973, Band on the Run, 1973, Venus and Mars, 1975, Wings Over America, 1975, Wings at the Speed of Sound, 1976, London Town, 1978, Wings Greatest, 1978, Back to the Egg, 1979, McCartney II, 1980, Tug of War, 1982, Press to Play, 1986, All the Best, 1987, Flowers in the Dirt, 1989, Jet, 1989, Tripping the Live Fantastic, 1990, Unplugged/The Official Bootleg, 1991, Off the Ground, 1993, Paul is Live, 1993, Flaming Pie, 1997, Run Devil Run, 1999, Driving Rain, 2001, Chaos and Creation in the Backyard, 2005; composer numerous songs (with John Lennon) including Please Please Me, I Want To Hold Your Hand, All My Loving, Can't Buy Me Love, I Saw Her Standing There, Love Me Do, Yesterday, Michelle, She's a Woman, Here, There and Everywhere, Good Day Sunshine, Penny Lane, She's Leaving Home, Fool on the Hill, Back in the USSR, Martha My Dear, Blackbird, Helter Skelter, Hey Jude, Let It Be, The Long and Winding Road, Get Back; (solo) Maybe I'm Amazed, My Love, Live and Let Die, Band on the Run, Silly Love Songs, Another Day, No More Lonely Nights, With a Little Luck; composer The Liverpool Oratorio, 1991; animator, composer Paul McCartney: The Music and Animation Collection, 2004; film appearances include: A Hard Day's Night, 1964, Help!, 1965, Let It Be, 1970, Give My Regards to Broad Street, 1984, Get Back, 1991; TV appearances include Doctor Who, 1965, Magical Mystery Tour, 1967, The Morecambe & Wise Show, 1968, Frost on Sunday, 1968, James Paul McCartney, 1973, Wings Over the World, 1979, Bread, 1986, (voice) The Simpsons, 1995, Saturday Night Live, 1998, V.I.P., 2000; videos include The Beatles: The First U.S. Visit, 1994, Paul McCartney: In the World Tonight, 1997, Twentieth Century Blues: The Songs of Noel Coward, 1998; producer animated film The Oriental Nightfish, 1978; author, Each One Believing: Paul McCartney On Stage, Off Stage, and Backstage, 2004; (children's book) High in the Clouds, 2005. Decorated Order of Brit. Empire, 1965, Knight Comdr., 1997; recipient Acad. award (with Beatles) for Best Original Song Score, Let It Be, 1970, 5 Grammy awards with Beatles, 2 solo, 1 with Wings, Ivor Novello award for outstanding services to Brit. music, 1989, (with Linda McCartney) Lifetime Achievement award People for the Ethical Treatment of Animals, 1996; named to Rock and Roll Hall of Fame, 1988, Lifetime Achievement award, 1990. Fellow Royal Coll. Music.*

**MC CARTNEY, RALPH FARNHAM,** lawyer; b. Charles City, Iowa, Dec. 11, 1924; s. Ralph C. and Helen (Farnham) McC.; m. Rhoda Mae Huxsol, June 25, 1950; children: Ralph, Julia, David. JD, U. Mich., 1950; B. Sci., Iowa State U., 1972. Bar: Iowa 1950. Mem. firm Miller, Heuber & Miller, Des Moines, 1950-52, Frye & McCartney, Charles City, 1952-73, McCartney & Erb, Charles City, 1973-78; judge Dist. Ct. Iowa, Charles City, 1978-87; chief judge 2d Judicial Dist., 1987-92; sr. judge Ct. Appeals, 1992—. Mem. jud. coordinating com. Iowa Supreme Ct. Chmn. Supreme Ct. Adv. Com. on Adminstrn. of Clks. Offices; mem. Iowa Ho. of Reps., 1967-70, majority floor leader, 1969-70; mem. Iowa Senate, 1973-74. Bd. regents U. Iowa, Iowa State U., U. No. Iowa, Iowa Sch. for Deaf, Iowa Braille and Sight Saving Sch. Served with AUS, 1942-45. Mem.: Iowa Judges Assn. Home: 1828 Cedar View Dr Charles City IA 50616-9129

**MCCARTNEY, ROBERT CHARLES,** retired lawyer; b. Pitts., May 3, 1934; s. Nathaniel Hugh and Esther Mary (Smith) McC.; m. Janet Carolyn Moore, June 16, 1956; children: Ronald K., Sharon S., Carole J. AB, Princeton U., 1956; JD, Harvard U., 1959. Bar: D.C. 1959, Pa. 1960, U.S. Dist. Ct. (we. dist.) Pa. 1960, U.S. Ct. Appeals (3d dist.) 1960, U.S. Supreme Ct. 1966. Assoc. Eckert Seamans Cherin & Mellott, LLC, Pitts., 1959—64, ptnr., 1965—93, mem. exec. com., 1991—93, of counsel, 1993—. Sec., gen. counsel Ryan Homes, Inc., 1969-93; bd. dirs. United Meth. Found. of Western Pa., 1971— v.p., 1981-85, chmn., 1985-86; sec., gen. counsel Rimoldi of Am., Inc., 1989-99. Solicitor North Pitts. Cmty. Devel. Corp., 1968-76, alt. dir., 1968-80; mem. McCandless Twp. Govt. Study Commn., 1973-74, Princeton U. Leadership Devel. Coun., 2002—; solicitor, asst. sec. McCandless Indsl. Devel. Authority, 1972-98; exec. com. Princeton U. Alumni Coun., 1966-70, 76-85, vice-chmn., 1981-83, chmn., 1983-85, co-chair spl. com. 250th Anniversary Princeton U., 1994-97, nat chmn. class planned giving program, 2002—, mem. planned giving adv. com., 2002-, mem. steardship adv. coun., 2004—; trustee Otterbein Coll., 1975-83, Pa. S.W. Assn., 1992-96, Pitts. Cultural Trust, 1992-99; chmn. com.-wide endowment program United Meth. Conf. We. Pa., 1985-87; bd. dirs. Pitts. Civic Light Opera Assn., 1984—, v.p., 1987-92, pres., 1992-99; dir. The Ireland Inst. Pitts., 1991-2004, vice-chmn., 1996-2004; mem. No. Ireland Partnership, 1991—; bd. dirs. Pitts. Concert Chorale, 1997-2003, Pitts. Irish and Classical Theater, 2000-05. Princeton fellow Harvard U., 1956-59. Mem. Princeton U. Alumni Assn. West Pa. (pres. 1976-78), Duquesne Club, Nassau Club. Republican. Home: 9843 Woodland Rd N Pittsburgh PA 15237-4347 Office: Eckert Seamans 600 Grant St Ste 44th Fl Pittsburgh PA 15219-2703 Office Phone: 412-566-6025.

**MCCARTOR, SHEILA SMITH,** secondary school educator; b. Raymondville, Tex., May 4, 1941; d. M.D. Smith and Mae (Sansom) Jessie; m. Gary Don McCartor, July 20, 1999; m. Ira Yale Levanthal, Aug. 5, 1966; 1 child, Adam Yale. BS, N. Tex. State U., 1963, MEd, 1965; postgrad., Nova U., 1972, MIT, 1979. Elem. tchr. Grapevine (Tex.) Pub. Schs., 1963—65; tchr., team leader Lamplighter Sch., Dallas, 1965—. Task force for diversity Lamplighter Sch., 2002, mem. steering com., computer staff, 1979—84, sci. com., 1990—, chair, sci. com., 1993—94; presenter Internat. Conf. Tech. in Edn., U. London, 1994; pub. Internat. Conf. Tech. in Edn., 1993—94; staff Ind. Sch. Assn. of S.W. Beginning Tchr. Inst., 1993—94; presenter Internat. Coop. Learning Conf., Columbus, Ohio, 1996; pub. Dallas Opera Instrl. Series. Staff mem. Episc. Sch. Spirituality, Dallas, 1983, dir., 1989—. Mem.: Women of St. Francis (v.p. Dallas 1983, mem. task force diversity 2002). Office: Lamplighter Sch 11611 Inwood Rd Dallas TX 75229-3098

**MCCARTY, DARREN,** professional hockey player; b. British Columbia, Canada, Apr. 1, 1972; Mem. Detroit Red Wings, 1993—2005, Calgary Flames, 2005—. Achievements include member of Stanely Cup Champion Detroit Red Wings, 1997, 1998, 2002. Office: c/o Calgary Flames PO Box 1540 Stn M T2P 3B9 Calgary AL Canada

**MCCARTY, DORAN CHESTER,** religious organization administrator; b. Bolivar, Mo., Feb. 3, 1931; s. Bartie Lee and Donta Marian (Russell) McC.; m. Gloria Jean Laffoon, June 14, 1952; children: Gaye, Risë, Marletta, Leslie. AA, Southwest Bapt. Coll., 1950; AB, William Jewell Coll., 1952; BD, So. Bapt. Theol. Sem, 1956, PhD, 1963. Pastor 1st Bapt. Ch., Switz City, Ind., 1956-62, Pleasant Hill, Mo., 1962-65, Susquehanna Bapt. Ch., Independence, Mo., 1965-67; prof. Midwestern Bapt. Theol. Sem., Kansas City, Mo., 1967-81, Golden Gate Bapt. Theol. Sem., Mill Valley, Calif., 1981-87; coord. Northeastern Bapt. Sch. Ministry, Nyack, N.Y., 1987-94; exec. dir. Sem. Ext. Nashville, 1988-94; pres. McCarty Svcs., Nashville, 1994—. Cons. Bapt. Home Mission Bd., 1981—; assoc. dean So. Bapt. Theol. Sem., Louisville, 1989; pres. McCarty Svcs., St. Augustine. Author: Rightly Dividing trhe Word, 1973, Teilhard de Chardin, 1976, The Supervision of Ministry Students, 1978, The Supervision of Mission Personnel, 1983, The Inner Heart of Ministry, 1985, Working With People, 1987, Leading the Small Church, 1991, Supervision: Developing and Directing People on Mission, 1994, Making the Most of Your Time, 1996, Making the Most of Conflict, 1997, Making the Most of Change, 1998, Making the Most if Empowerment, 1999, Making the Most of Coping, 2000, Making the Most of Pastoral Leadership, 2002, Hallowed Be Thy Name, 2002; editor: Key Resources, 5 vols., Broadman Leadership Series, 16 vols., The Practice of Ministry: A Sourcebook, 1995. Recipient Life Service award Southwest Bapt. U., Bolivar, 1973, William Jewell Coll. Achievement citation, 1987. Mem. Assn. for Theol. Field Edn. (chairperson 1979-81), Inst. Theol. Reflection (exec. dir. 1978-86), Fellowship In Service Guidance Dirs. (pres. 1986-87, Lewis Newman award 1988). Home: 116 Village Del Lago Ln Saint Augustine FL 32080 E-mail: doranmccarty@bellsouth.net, doran@ang.com. *As I have experienced life, grace affords priviledge, priviledge calls forth duty, duty depends on transcendence, and transcendence provides enrichment.*

**MCCARTY, FREDERICK BRIGGS,** electrical engineer, consultant; b. Dilley, Tex., Aug. 11, 1926; s. John Frederick Briggs and Olive Ruth (Snell) Briggs McCarty; m. Doris Mary Cox, May 3, 1950 (div. 1970); children: Mark Frederick, David Lambuth, Jackson Clare; m. Nina Lucile Butman, Aug. 17, 1973. BSEE, U. Tex., 1949. Registered profl. engr., Calif. Design engr. GE, Schenectady, NY, 1949-51; sr. design engr. Convair, Ft. Worth, 1951-55; sr. engr. Aerojet Gen., Azusa, Calif., 1955-61; sr. engring. specialist Garrett Corp., Torrance, Calif., 1961-91; v.p., founder Patio Pacific, Inc., Torrance, 1973-84; owner, operator Textiger Co., Torrance, 1980-91; cons., 1991—. With USNR, 1944—46, PTO. Mem.: IEEE (sr.), Eta Kappa Nu, Tau Beta Pi. Democrat. Achievements include patents in field; design of superconducting acyclic motor for USN and high speed elec. machines for aerospace and transp. Home and Office: 1366 Stonewood Ct San Pedro CA 90732-1550

**MCCARTY, JOHN ALBERT,** management educator; b. Nashville, May 28, 1951; s. Justin Hunter and Emily Lavinder (Lacy) McC. BA, Vanderbilt U., 1973; MA, U. Ill., 1979, PhD, 1986; MA, U. Chgo., 1981. Rsch. assoc. Needham Harper Worldwide Advt., Chgo., 1983-85; asst. prof. dept. advt. and bus. adminstrn. U. Ill., Urbana, 1986-93; asst. prof. dept. mktg. Am. U., Washington, 1993—98, George Mason U., Fairfax, Va., 1998—2001; asst. prof. sch. bus. The Coll. NJ, Ewing, 2001—. Vis. sect. dept. advt. U. Ill., 1985-86. Contbr. chpts. in books: Advances in Non Profit Marketing, 1990, Global and Multi-National Advertising, 1994, Marketing and Consumer Research in the Public Interest, 1996, Integrated Communication: Synergy of Persuasive Voices, 1996, Values, Lifestyles and Psychographics, 1997, The Psychology of Entertainment Media, 2004, Marketing Communications: New Approaches, Technologies and Styles, 2005; contbr. articles to profl. jours.; reviewer Jour. of Advt., 1988—. Lt. (j.g.) USN, 1973-76. Mem. Am. Mktg. Assn. (workshop coord. 1987-88), Assn. for Consumer Rsch., Am. Acad. Advt., Am. Assn. Pub. Opinion Rsch. Office: The College of New Jersey 2000 Pennington Rd Ewing NJ 08628 Office Phone: 609-771-3220. Business E-Mail: mccarty@tcnj.edu.

**MCCARTY, MARGARET JANE,** retired elementary school educator; b. Quitman, Miss., July 16, 1945; d. Jack Crane Sr. and Sammie Margaret McCarty. BS, William Carey Coll., 1968, postgrad. Cert. elem. tchr. Miss. Tchr. 2d grade Ocean Springs (Miss.) Sch. Dist., 1969—95; ret., 1995. Mem. Magnolia Park Elem. Sch. PTO. Mem. Mt. Maurepas Reading Coun., Miss. Reading Assn., Kappa Kappa Iota. Home: 2242 County Rd 311 Enterprise MS 39330-9364

**MCCARTY, PERRY LEE,** civil and environmental engineering educator; b. Grosse Pointe, Mich., Oct. 29, 1931; m. Martha Davis Collins, Sept. 5, 1953; children: Perry Lee, Cara L., Susan A., Kathleen R. BSCE, Wayne State U.,

1953; MS in San. Engring., MIT, 1957, ScD, 1959; DEng (hon.), Colo. Sch. Mines, 1992. Field engr. Edwin Orr Co., Dearborn, Mich., 1951-52; engr. Pate & Hirn, Detroit, 1952-53; field engr. Hubbell, Roth & Clark, Detroit, 1953; instr. civil engring. Wayne State U., 1953-54; field engr. George Jerome & Co., Detroit, 1954; engr. Civil Engrs., Inc., Detroit, 1956; assoc. Rolf Eliassen Assocs., Winchester, Mass., 1958-61; asst. prof. san. engring. MIT, 1958-62; faculty Stanford (Calif.) U., 1962—, prof. civil engring., 1967-75, Silas H. Palmer prof., 1975-99, Silas H. Palmer prof. emeritus, 1999—, chmn. dept. civil engring., 1980-85; chair prof. environ. sci. and engring. Tsinghua U., 2004—. Chmn. Gordon Rsch. Conf. Environ. Scis., 1972; vice chmn. environ. studies bd. NRC-NAS, 1976-80, mem. com. on phys. scis., math. and resources, 1985-88, bd. on radioactive waste mgmt., 1989-96, mem. com. geoscis., environment, resources, 1994-97. Co-author: Chemistry for Environmental Engineering and Science, 5th edit., 2003, Environmental Biotechnology Principles and Applications, 2001. Recipient Tyler Prize for Environ. Achievement, 1992, Clarke Prize Outstanding Achievement Water Sci. and Tech., 1997; NSF faculty fellow, 1968-69. Fellow AAAS, Am. Acad. Microbiology, Am. Acad. Arts and Scis.; mem. ASCE (Walter L. Huber Rsch. prize 1964, Simon W. Freese Environ. Engring. award 1979, James R. Croes medal 1995), NAE, Am. Water Works Assn. (hon., life, chmn. water quality divsn. 1972-73, trustee rsch. divsn. 1980-85, Best Paper award 1985, A.P. Black Rsch. award 1989), Am. Soc. for Microbiology, Water Environment Fedn. (hon. 1989, Harrison P. Eddy award 1962, 77, Thomas Camp award 1995), Assn. Environ. Engring. Sci. Profs. (Disting. Faculty award 1966, Oustanding Publ. award 1985, 88, 98, 2003, Founders award 1992), Am. Soc. Engring. Edn.(vice-chmn. environ. engring. divsn. 1968-69), Sigma Xi, Tau Beta Pi (fellow 1957-58). Home: 823 Sonoma Ter Stanford CA 94305-1024 Office: Stanford U Civil Environ Engring Dept Stanford CA 94305-4020 Business E-Mail: pmccarty@stanford.edu.

**MCCARTY, RICHARD CHARLES,** psychology professor, dean; b. Portsmouth, Va., July 12, 1947; s. Constantine Ambrose and Helen Marie (Householder) McC.; m. Sheila Adair Miltier, July 15, 1965; children: Christopher Charles, Lorraine Marie, Ryan Lester, Patrick James. BS in Biology, Old Dominion U., 1970, MS in Zoology, 1972; PhD in Pathobiology, Johns Hopkins U., 1976. Rsch. assoc. NIMH, Bethesda, Md., 1976-78; asst. prof. U. Va., Charlottesville, 1978-84, assoc. prof., 1984-88, prof., 1988-2001, chair psychology, 1990-98, chair Coun. of Grad. Depts. Psychology, 1996-97; exec. dir. sci. directorate APA, Washington, 1998-2001; dean arts and sci. Vanderbilt U., Nashville, 2001—. Mem. editl. bd. Behavioral and Neural Biology, 1985—90, Physiology and Behavior, 1989—, editor-in-chief Stress, 1995—99; editor: Am. Psychologist, 2000—01. Lt. comdr. USPHS, 1976—78. Recipient Rsch. Scientist Devel. award, NIMH, 1985—90; sr. fellow, Nat. Heart Lung Blood Inst., NIH, 1984—85. Fellow AAAS, APA, Soc. Behavioral Medicine, Am. Psychol. Soc., Coun. for High Blood Pressure Rsch., Am. Heart Assn.; mem. Internat. Soc. for Investigation of Stress (exec. bd. 1996-2001). Roman Catholic. Office: Office of the Dean Vanderbilt U Coll Arts and Sci 301 Kirkland Hall Nashville TN 37240 Business E-Mail: richard.mccarty@vanderbilt.edu.

**MCCARTY, ROBERT CLARKE,** mathematician; b. Mountain View, Calif., Apr. 29, 1922; s. John Emmet and Eldora Lydia (Freeman) McC.; m. Netta Cassen, July 29, 1945 (div. Oct. 1968) 1 child, Stephanie Ann; m. Rita Ransier, July 29, 1969; children: Michael Wayne, Teresa Kay, Kathleen Gail. BA in Math., San Jose State U., 1950; MS in Math. and Statistics, U. Wash., 1957; PhD in Math., Pacific Western U., 1990. Staff mathematician Boeing Rsch. Labs., Seattle, 1952-59; rsch. mathematician Stanford Rsch. Inst., Menlo Park, Calif., 1959-70; pres., cons. McCarty and Assocs., Gilroy, Calif., 1976—; sr. staff scientist ESL-TRW Corp., Sunnyvale, Calif., 1984-87; prin. staff scientist ARGO Systems, Sunnyvale, 1987-93. Sci. advisor to Congresswoman Zoe Lofgren, sci. com. US Congress, 1994—; rsch. proxy for Prof. A.S. Paulraj, Dept. Elec. Engring., Info. Scis., Stanford U., 1993-95; sr. rsch. mathematician Ares Corp., Arlington, Va., 1994-96; cons. in field. Contbr. articles to profl. jours. Lt. USCGR, 1941—52, WWII, European and Pacific, ret. lt. USCGR, 1951—52, Korean War, Ctrl. and North Pacific. Mem. Sigma Xi. Avocations: amateur radio, rifle and pistol marksmanship, swimming. Home and Office: 9425 Marcella Ave Gilroy CA 95020-9085

**MCCARTY, SHIRLEY CAROLYN,** consumer products company executive; b. Minot, N.D., May 2, 1934; d. Harry and Cecelia Marie (Engene) Wolhowe; m. John Myron McCarty, Apr. 3, 1958. BS in Bus. Adminstrn., U. N.D., Grand Forks, 1958. Mem. tech. staff Douglas Aircraft, El Segundo, Calif., 1960-62, The Aerospace Corp., El Segundo, 1962-72, mgr., 1972-73, dir., 1973-79, prin. dir., 1979-89, gen. mgr., 1989—96; ret., 1996; pres. Shamrock Consulting, 1996—. Mem. adv. coun. Calif. State U., Northridge, 1979—2001, chmn., 1984-86; mem. indsl. adv. bd. Purdue U. Soc. Women Engrs., West Lafayette, Ind., 1979-82, 1985—; apptd. mem. aerospace safety adv. panel NASA, 1998, chair, 2002-03; spkr. in field. Named Woman of Yr. The Aerospace Corp., 1976, Pres.'s award, 1987; named to Hall of Fame Women in Tech. Internat., 2003; recipient Spl. Judges Award for Leadership, Los Angeles YWCA, 1977, Sioux Alumni Award, U. N.D. 1982, Achievement award Los Angeles County Commn. for Women, 1987. Fellow Soc. Women Engrs.; mem. IEEE, Assn. for Computing Machinery, Soc. Women Engrs., Bus. and Profl. Women (Woman of Achievement 1984, Golden Nike award 1985), Women in Bus.(corp. achievement award, 1987), Women in Computing (founding mem., bd. dirs.). Avocations: raising and training siberian huskies, travel, writing, architecture. Home: 357 Valley St El Segundo CA 90245-2932 Office Phone: 310-336-1781. E-mail: mccartys@earthlink.net.

**MCCARTY, THOMAS JOSEPH,** publishing executive; b. Waltham, Mass., June 10, 1938; s. Raymond Anthony and Mary Agatha (Riley) McC; m. Colette Ann Koechley, Aug. 3, 1963; children: Matthew Thomas, Brendan James, Sarah Katherine. BA, Holy Cross Coll., 1960; cert., Harvard U., 1961. Various mgmt. positions Oxford U. Press, N.Y.C., 1960-71, mgr. ops., 1971 79, dir. distrbn., 1980 81, v.p. distrbn., 1982-84, v.p. distrbn. and info. systems, 1985-88, sr. v.p., 1988-90; sr. v.p. gen. mgr. Oxford U. Press, Cary, N.C. ops., 1990-98, spl. cons. to pres., 1998-2000. Chmn., bd. advs. Carolina Pub. Inst. U. N.C., Chapel Hill, 1995-98. Trustee N.C. Symphony Found., v.p., 1998—; mem. adv. bd. Sch. Info. and L.S., U. N.C., Chapel Hill; mem. City of Cary Unified Devel. Ordinance Adv. Commn., 1999—; mem. bd. advisors Open Mind Publ. Group, 2000; mem. N.C. Mus. Art; bd. dirs. Shakti for Children Found., 1994—98, English Speaking Union of Research Triangle, pres., 1998—2002. Mem.: Exec. Svc. Corps., Fine Arts League Cary, Am. Mgmt. Assn., Svc. Corps Ret. Execs., Am. Assn. Pubs., U. N.C. Faculty Club (Chapel Hill), McGregor Downs Country Club (Cary). Personal E-mail: tjm2@mindspring.com.

**MCCARTY, V. K.,** publishing executive, chaplain, librarian; b. Boston, June 26, 1948; d. Charles Osner and Dorothy June (McAlister) Long. BM, Mich. State U., 1969; MM, U. Louisville, 1972; cert. in theatre arts, U. London, 1972; intern in clin. pastoral edn., St. Luke's Roosevelt Hosp., 1998, resident in clin. pastoral edn., 1995; student, Congreg. Devel. Inst. Tng., Diocese of Newark, 2003. Advt. asst. Lansing (Mich.) State Jour., 1968-69; market rsch. cons. Sta. WKLO, Louisville, 1969-70; libr. Louisville Free Pub. Libr., 1970-72; v.p. assoc. pub. Gen. Media Inc., N.Y.C., 1979-2000; acquisitions libr. Gen. Theol. Sem. St. Mark's Libr., N.Y.C., 2000—; part-time acquisitions libr. Union Theol. Sem. Burke Libr., N.Y.C., 2001—02; dir. Christian Formation, St. Paul's Ch., Chatham, NJ, 2002—03. Bd. dirs. B.F.T., Inc., N.Y.C. Dance editor Saturday Review Mag. Online, 1993-95. Master of ceremonies St. Ignatius of Antioch, N.Y.C., 1984-98; chaplaincy coord. St. Luke's Roosevelt Hosp., N.Y.C. Mem. N.Y. Liturgical Music Found. (steering com. 1982-84), N.Y. Ch. Club. Avocations: Biblical languages, riding, ballet, preservation of Benedictine monasticism, Byzantine art. Office: Gen Theol Sem St Mark's Libr 175 9th Ave New York NY 10011-4977

**MCCARUS, ERNEST NASSEPH,** retired language educator; b. Charleston, W.Va., Sept. 10, 1922; s. Nasseph Mitchell and Della (Saad) McC.; m. Adele Najib Haddad, Sept. 10, 1955; children: Peter Kevin, Carol Ann. Student, Morris Harvey Coll., 1939-40; AB, U. Mich., 1945, MA, 1949, PhD, 1956. Translation team capt. Allied Translators and Interpreters' Service, Allied

Hqrs., Tokyo, Japan, 1946-47; mem. English Lang. Inst. staff U. Mich., 1948-52, mem. univ. expdn. to Near East, 1951, instr. univ., 1952-56, asst. prof. Arabic, 1956-61; dir. Fgn. Service Inst., Field Sch. Arabic Lang. and Area Study, U.S. Dept. State, Beirut, 1958-60; assoc. prof. dept. Near Ea. studies U. Mich., 1961-67, prof., 1967-95, chmn. dept., 1969-77, dir. Ctr. for Arabic Study Abroad, 1974-83, dir. U. Mich. Center for Near Eastern and North African Studies, 1983-92, assoc. dir. Ctr for Mid. Ea. and North African Studies, 1995-97, prof. emeritus, 1995—. Author: Grammar of Kurdish of Sulaimania, Iraq, 1958, (with H. Hoenigswald, R. Noss, J. Yamagiwa) A Survey of Intensive Programs in the Uncommon Languages, 1962, (with A. Yacoub) Elements of Contemporary Arabic, 1962, 3d edn., 1966, (with Raji Rammuny) First Level Arabic: Elementary Literary Arabic for Secondary Schools, 1964, Teacher's Manual to Accompany First Level Arabic, 1964, (with Jamal J. Abdullah) Kurdish Basic Course - Dialect of Sulaimania, Iraq, 1967, Kurdish Readers, Vol. I Newspaper Kurdish, Vol. II. Kurdish Essays, Vol. III Kurdish Short Stories, 1967, A Kurdish-English Dictionary, 1967, (with P. Abboud) Elementary Modern Standard Arabic, 1968, (with R. Rammuny) Word Count of Elementary Modern Literary Arabic Textbooks, 1969, (with P. Abboud, E.T. Abdel-Massih, S. Altoma, W. Erwin, R. Rammuny) Modern Standard Arabic Intermediate Level, 1971, (with R. Rammuny) A Programmed Course in Modern Literary Arabic Phonology and Script, 1974; editor: Language Learning, Vol. VII, 1956-57, Language Learning, Vol. XIII, 1963, An-Nashra, 1967-74, Contemporary Arabic Readers, Vols. I-V, 1962-66, The Development of Arab-American Identity, 1994; contbr. articles to scholastic jours. Served with AUS, 1942-46. Recipient Bacharach Svc. award, 2005; Rockefeller fellow, 1951. Mem. Mich. Linguistic Soc. (pres. 1962-63), Am. Assn. Tchrs. Arabic (pres. 1973, exec. coun. 1979-81, 89-92), Middle East Studies Assn. (bd. dirs. 1973-75), Linguistic Soc. Am., Am. Oriental Soc., Linguistic Circle N.Y., Arabic Linguistic Soc. (pres. 1992). Home: 1400 Beechwood Dr Ann Arbor MI 48103-2940 E-mail: enm@umich.edu.

**MCCASH, JUNE HALL,** writer, retired language educator; b. Newberry, SC, June 8, 1938; d. James DeLeon and Williemaye Stone Hall; m. Marvin Hampton Martin (div. June 1971); children: Michael Hall Martin, Christopher Brenden Martin; m. William Barton McCash, July 3, 1974 (dec. Feb. 1991); m. Richard Douglas Gleaves, Jr., May 21, 1994. BA, Agnes Scott Coll., 1960; MA, Emory U., 1963, PhD, 1967. Instr. dept. romance langs. Emory U., Atlanta, 1964—66; from asst. to assoc. prof. Mid. Tenn. State U., Murfreesboro, 1967—75, from assoc prof. to prof., 1966—70, founding dir. honors program, 1973—80, prof. dept. fgn. langs., 1975—2004, chair dept. fgn. langs., 1980—92, grad. dir. dept. fgn. langs. and lits., 1996—2004, prof. emerita, 2004—. Presenter in field; fellow Am. Coun. Edn., 1986—87; elderhostel instr. W. Ga. Coll., Ga., 1992; interpreter for vis. French del. C. of C., Murfreesboro, 1992; exec. bd. Tenn. Humanities Coun., 1987—89, chair grant program com., 1987—88, vice-chair, 1988—89, chair, 1990—96, So. Humanities Media Fund, 1989—91, Tenn. Humanities Coun., 1989—91, exec. bd., 1991—92; local coord. ESL Inst. Tenn. Dept. Edn., 1992; coord. various profl. workshops. Author: Love's Fools: Aucassin, Troilus, Calisto and the Parody of the Courtly Lover, 1972, The Jekyll Island Cottage Colony, 1998, Jekyll Island's Early Years: From Prehistory through Reconstruction, 2005; co-author: Jekyll Island Club Historic District 100 Years, The Jekyll Island Club: Southern Haven for America's Millionaires, 1989; editor: The Cultural Patronage of Medieval Women, 1996; contbr. articles to profl. jours.; mem. editl. bd. Le Cygne: A Jour. on Marie de France. Hon. life mem. Jekyll Island Mus. Assocs., Friends of Linebaugh; trustee Jekyll Island Found., 2000—; layreader St. Paul's Episcopal Ch., Murfreesboro; chair adv. bd. So. Festival Books, 1988—92, mem. author's com., 1988—94. Recipient awrds for poetry, novel and juvenile fiction, Southeastern Writers Assn., 2006; Young Humanists fellow, NEH, 1975, Mellon grantee for workshop on medieval culture, Vanderbilt U., 1982, Am. Coun. Edn. fellow, 1986—87. Mem.: AAUP (chair com. on status of women 1969—70, sec. MTSU chpt. 1970—71, mem. exec. com. 1970—74, v.p. 1971—72), Medieval Acad. Am., Internat. Marie de France Soc. (mem. exec. bd. 1993—95, mem. adv. coun. 2001—), Southeastern Medieval Assn. (mem. exec. coun. 1991—94, v.p. 1995—97, pres. 1997—99,), Internat. Courtly Lit. Soc. (internat. treas. 1980—86, v.p N.Am. br. 1990—92, pres. N.Am. br. 1992—95, internat. v.p. 2001—04, internat. pres. 2004—), Soc. Rencesvals, Phi Sigma Iota, Phi Kappa Phi (pres. elect 1997—98, pres. 1998—99, MTSU chpt.), Alpha Mu Gamma. Democrat. Avocations: painting, photography, reading.

**MCCASKEY, MICHAEL B.,** professional football team executive; b. Lancaster, Pa., Dec. 11, 1943; s. Edward B. and Virginia (Halas) McCaskey; m. Nancy McCaskey; children: John, Kathryn. Grad., Yale U., 1965; PhD, Case Western Res. U. Tchr. UCLA, 1972-75, Harvard U. Sch. Bus., Cambridge, Mass., 1975-82; pres., chief exec. officer Chgo. Bears (NFL), 1983-99, chmn. bd., 1999—. Author: The Executive Challenge: Managing Change and Ambiguity. Named Exec. of Yr. Sporting News, 1987. Office: 1000 Football Dr Lake Forest IL 60045-4829

**MCCASKEY, RAYMOND F.,** insurance company executive; b. 1944; m. Judy McCaskey. With Continental Assurance Co., Chgo., 1963-73; asst v.p. Health Care Service Corp., 1973—79, chief actuary, 1979—82, CFO, 1982—91, pres., COO, 1991—98, pres., CEO, 1998—. Former bd. chmn. Lincoln Found. for Bus. Excellence. Office: Health Care Service Corp 300 E Randolph St Chicago IL 60601-5014 Office Phone: 312-938-6000.*

**MCCASKILL, CLAIRE,** auditor; b. Houston, July 25, 1953; Auditor State of Mo., Jefferson City, 1999—. Democrat. Office: Mo State Auditors Off PO Box 869 Jefferson City MO 65102-0869 Fax: 573-751-6539.

**MCCASLIN, DAVID E.,** hotel executive; BS in Hotel Mgmt., U. Mo., 1979. Gen. mgr. Lincoln Hotels, Dallas; hotel gen. mgr. CapStar, 1987-88, v.p. ops., COO, 1988; pres. MeriStar Hotels & Resorts Inc. Office: 4501 Fairfax DR #800 Arlington VA 22203-1656 Fax: 202-995-2187.

**MCCASLIN, LATANYA,** art educator; d. Frank and Eloise McCaslin. Student, U. Ala., Birmingham, 1987—92. Art lectr., Birmingham, 1992—; cultural arts dir. Sparkle Arts and Computers, Fairfield, Ala., 1992—. Active Dem. Nat. Com., Washington, Dem. Congl. Campaign Com., Washington. Home: 113 60th St Fairfield AL 35064

**MCCASLIN, RICHARD BRYAN,** history educator; b. Atlanta, Feb. 21, 1961; s. Jerry L. and Ann Elizabeth (Sharman) McC.; m. Jana Dawn Maryovich, Apr. 5, 1979; 1 child, Christina Michele. BA, Delta State U., 1982; MA, La. State U., 1983; PhD, U. Tex., 1988. Tchg. asst. La. State U., 1982-83, grad. asst. La. Bus. Rev., 1983; tchg. asst. U. Tex., Austin, 1983-87, rsch. assoc., 1984-87; rsch. assoc. U. Tenn., Knoxville, 1988-90; asst. prof. history High Point U., 1990-94, assoc. prof., 1994-2000, 2000—04; assoc. prof. U. North Tex., 2004—. Instr. Pellissippi State C.C., 1988-89, Roane State C.C., 1989; adj. prof. Corpus Christi (Tex.) State U., 1989, Hawaii Pacific U., 2003—; lectr. East Tenn. Hist. Soc., 1990; rsch. cons. Tex. Senate, 1986-89, Nat. Pk. Svc., 1989-90, Tex. State Historical Assn., 2000—; assoc. historian Futurepast: History Co., Spokane, Wash., 1987-89; presenter Southwestern Social Sci. Assn., AAAS, Soc. for Mil. History. Author: (with Earnest F. Gloyna) Commitment to Excellence: One Hundred Years of Engineering Education at The University of Texas at Austin, 1986, Andrew Johnson: A Bibliography, 1992, Portraits of Conflict: A Photographic History of South Carolina in the Civil War, 1994, Tainted Breeze: The Great Hanging at Gainesville, Texas, October 1862, 1994 (Tullis prize Tex. State Hist. Assn., commendation Am. Assn. for State and Local History), Remembered Be Thy Blessings: High Point University—The College Years, 1924-1991, 1995, Portraits of Conflict: A Photographic History of North Carolina in the Civil War, 1997 (Slatten award Va. Hist. Soc., Laney prize Austin Civil War Roundtable), Lee in the Shadow of Washington, 2001, The Last Stronghold: The Fort Fisher Campaign, 2003; contbr. chpt. to: 100 Years of Science and Technology in Texas: A Sigma Xi Centennial Volume, 1986; columnist Greensboro News and Record, 1993-94; reviewer Southwestern Hist. Quar., La. State U. Press, U. Nebr. Press, U.S.C. Press, Tex. A&M U. Press, U. North Tex. Press; asst. editor, then assoc. editor Papers of Andrew

Johnson, U. Tenn., 1988-90; contbr. articles and book revs. to various profl. publ. U. Tex. dissertation fellow, 1987-88, Clara H. Driscoll fellow in Tex. history Daus. of Republic of Tex., 1985-87; James H. and Minnie M. Edmonds Ednl. Found. scholar, 1983-85, Colonial Dames Am. grad. scholar, 1987. Fellow Tex. State Hist. Assn. (presenter); mem. So. Hist. Assn. (presenter), Soc. Civil War Historians (presenter), East Tex. Hist. Soc. (presenter). Episcopalian. Home: 1321 East Windsor Dr Denton TX 76209 Office: Univ North Tex Dept History PO Box 310650 Denton TX 76203-0650 Office Phone: 940-565-4207. E-mail: mccaslin@unt.edu.

**MCCASLIN, TERESA EVE,** human resources specialist; b. Jersey City, Nov. 22, 1949; d. Felix F. and Ann E. (Golaszewski) Hrynkiewicz; m. Gary A. McCue. BA, Marymount Coll., 1971; MBA, L.I. U., 1981. Adminstrv. officer Civil Service Commn., Fed. Republic Germany, 1972-76; personnel dir. Oceanroutes, Inc., Palo Alto, Calif., 1976-78; mgr., coll. relations Continental Grain Co., N.Y.C., 1978-79, corp. personnel mgr., 1979-81, dir. bus. redesign, internal cons., 1981-84; dir., human resources Grow Group, Inc., N.Y.C., 1984-85, v.p. human resources, 1985-86, v.p. adminstrn., 1986-89; corp. v.p. human resources Avery Dennison Corp., Pasadena, Calif., 1989-94; v.p. human resources Monsanto Co., St. Louis, 1994-97; sr. v.p. human resources, mem. mgmt. com. Conti Group Cos. (formerly Continental Grain Co.), N.Y.C., 1997—; exec. v.p. human resources & info. tech., 1999. Mem. global adv. bd. Am. Grad. Sch. Internat. Mgmt.; bd. dirs. Am. Arbitrator Assn., 2005. Mem. Am. Mgmt. Assn. (chair bd. trustees, fin. and exec. com.), Human Resources Coun. Roman Catholic. Avocations: travel, music, golf. Office: Conti Group Cos 277 Park Ave New York NY 10172-0003 Business E-Mail: teri.mccaslin@conti.com.

**MCCAUGHEY ROSS, ELIZABETH P. (BETSY MCCAUGHEY),** former lieutenant governor; b. Oct. 20, 1948; d. Albert Peterkin; m. Thomas McCaughey, 1972 (div. 1994); children: Amanda, Caroline, Diana. BA, Vassar Coll., 1970; MA, Columbia Univ., 1972, PhD, 1976. Public policy expert Manhattan Inst., N.Y.C.; lt. gov. State of N.Y., 1995—99. Asst. prof. Vassar Coll., 1979, Columbia U., 1980-84; chmn. Governor's Medicaid Task Force, 1994. Author: From Loyalist to Founding Father, 1980, Government By Choice, 1987; also articles including an article in The New Republic (Nat. Mag. award for Pub. Policy 1995). Recipient Bancroft Dissertation award, Richard B. Morris prize; Woodrow Wilson fellow, Herbert H. Lehman fellow, Honorary Vassar fellow, John Jay fellow, Post Doctoral Rsch. fellow NEH, 1984, John M. Olin fellow Manhattan Inst., 1993, sr. fellow Ctr. Study of the Presidency. Republican.

**MCCAUL, ELIZABETH,** investment advisor, former state agency administrator; BA in econ., Boston U., 1985; postgrad., Georgetown U. Congl. intern, 1981; investment banker, v.p. Goldman, Sachs & Co., 1985—95; chief of staff N.Y. State Banking Dept., 1995—96, first dep. supt. banks, 1996—97, acting supt. banks, 1997-2000, supt. banks, 2000—03; ptnr. Promontory Fin. Group, 2003—. Dir. Empire State Devel. Corp., State N.Y. Mortgage Agy., N.Y. State Job Devel. Authority, Harlem Cmty. Devel. Corp.; statutory mem. Cmty. Facilities Project Guarantee Fund. Scholar European Econ. Cmty., Inst. European Studies, Freiburg, Germany. Mem. Conf. State Bank Suprs. (bd. dirs., supervisory commn., 2001-02, internat. bankers adv. bd.), Fed. Fin. Inst. Examination Coun., 2002-03. Office: Promotory Fin Group 1201 Pennsylvania Ave NW Ste 617 Washington DC 20004

**MCCAUL, MICHAEL T.,** congressman; b. Dallas, Tex., Jan. 14, 1962; m. Linda McCaul; children: Caroline, Jewell, Lauren, Michael, Avery. BS, Trinity U., 1984; JD, St. Mary's U., 1987; sr. exec. fellow, Harvard U. John F. Kennedy Sch. Govt. Asst. atty. gen., Austin, Tex., 1987—90; atty. US Dept. Justice Criminal divsn., Washington, 1990—99; spl. asst. atty. gen. State of Tex., 1999—2000, dep. atty. gen. for criminal justice, 2000—02; chief Terrorism & Nat. Security sect. US Dept. Justice, U.S. Atty. we. dist. Tex., 2002; mem. US Congress from 10th Tex. dist., 2005—, mem. homeland security com., chmn. investigations subcommittee, mem. internat. rels. com., mem. sci. com. Republican. Roman Catholic. Office: US Ho Reps 415 Cannon Ho Office Bldg Washington DC 20515-4310 Office Phone: 202-225-2401.*

**MCCAULEY, BRUCE GORDON,** financial consultant; b. St. Louis; s. William Maurice and Evylin Adele (Halbert) McC.; m. Barbara Allen Stevens, Mar. 16, 1945 (dec.); children: David S., Sharon; m. Gwen Crumpton Cummings, Nov. 25, 1967. Student, U. Mo., 1939-41, Yale U., 1944; BS in Engring., U. Calif., Berkeley, 1948, MBA, 1949, MS in Indsl. Engring., 1952. Registered profl. engr., N.Y., Calif., Hawaii. Asst. purchasing agt. Curtis Mfg. Co., St. Louis, 1941—43; teaching asst. U. Calif., Berkeley, 1948—49, asst. prof. mech. engring., 1950—56, chmn. indsl. engring. inst., 1954—55; design engr. Standard Oil Co. of Calif., 1949—50; engr. McCauley & Dunmire, San Francisco, 1952—56; v.p. Shand & Jurs Co., Berkeley, 1956—58, exec. v.p. 1958—60; asst. to pres. Honolulu Star-Bulletin, 1960—62; gen. mgr. Christian Sci. Pub. Soc., Boston, 1962—69; gen. mgr., sec. N.Y. Daily News Inc., N.Y.C., 1969—74, v.p., 1971—73, sr. v.p., 1973—75, asst. to pres., 1974—77; dir., 1971—75; v.p. Daseke & Co. Inc., Westport, Conn., 1975—77, sr. v.p. 1977—80; mgr. West Coast office, 1978—86; vis. scholar Principia Coll., Elsah, Ill., 1988—91; pres. Rossmoor Mut. 48 Corp., Walnut Creek, 1994—97. Bd. dirs. Better Bus. Bur., N.Y.C., 1973-77, N.Y.C. Conv. and Visitors Bur., 1974-77, Albert Baker Found., 1979-90, Asher Found., 1983-93, Sopac Energy Corp., 1986-92. Capt. USAAF, 1943-46, PTO. Mem. ASME (life), NSPE (life), Am. Inst. Indsl. Engrs. (life), Nat. Assn. Accts. (life), U. Calif. Alumni Assn., Principia Alumni Assn., Rossmoor Golf Club, Masons (32 degree), Kiwanis, Sigma Xi, Tau Beta Pi, Beta Gamma Sigma, Pi Mu Epsilon. Christian Scientist. Home: 3266 Ptarmigan Dr Apt 3B Walnut Creek CA 94595-3149

**MCCAULEY, DAN PAUL,** dentist; b. Pittsburg, Tex., Nov. 13, 1949; s. Loyd Cecil McCauley and Claudia Aletha Moore; m. Sandra Scott Kraemer, Sept. 14, 1974; children: Jennifer, Rebecca, Crissy. BA in Psychology, So. Meth. U., 1974; DDS, U. Tex., 1977. Pvt. practice, Mt. Pleasant, Tex., 1977—. Sec. N.E. Tex. CC, 1994—2001. Active Boy Scouts Am., 1977—; trustee N.E. Tex. C.C., 1989—, pres., 1989—2001, pres. found., 1994—2005; bd. dirs. Red River Girl Scouts, 1986—89; chmn. Titus county Reps., Mt. Pleasant, 1980; deacon First Bapt. Ch., Mt. Pleasant, 1977—; bd. dirs. N.E. Tex. C.C., 1989—. Named Tex. Dentist of the Yr., Tex. Acad. General Dentistry, 2004; named one of Am. Top Dentists, Rsch. Coun. Am.; recipient Fraternal Achievement award, Psi Omega Dental Fraternity, 1976, Sandy Niforus Humanitarian award, Ralph Waller Lifetime Achievement award, Optimist Internat. 2004. Fellow: Am. Acad. Gen. Dentistry, Internat. Coll. Dentists, Am. Coll. Dentists, Pierre Fauchard Soc.; mem.: ADA, Acad. Gen. Dentistry (state dir. 2005—06), 1st Dist. Dental Soc. (pres. 1986—87, 2001—02, v.p. 2002, dir. 2002—), Tex. Dental Assn. (del. 1995—, 2002—, sr. dir. 2003—04, v.p. 2004—), N.E. Tex. Optimists (gov. 1985—86, Optimist Lifetime Achievement 1995). Republican. Baptist. Avocations: tennis, travel, skiing. Home: 1403 S Florey Ave Mount Pleasant TX 75455-5813 Office: 1603 N Jefferson Ave Mount Pleasant TX 75455-2366 Office Phone: 903-572-3981. Personal E-mail: drdansmu@hotmail.com.

**MCCAULEY, GERARD FRANCIS,** literary agent; b. Pitts., Apr. 9, 1934; s. John Edward and Beatrice (McNally) McCauley; m. Kerstin E. Borg, Apr. 24, 1965; children: Peter, Brian. BA, U. Pitts., 1956. Editor Alfred A. Knopf Publishing, N.Y.C., 1961—62, Little Brown, Boston, 1962—63; literary agt. Curtis Brown Ltd., N.Y.C., 1964—70, Gerard McCauley Agy., Katonah, NY, 1970—2003. Editor: (book) Playing Around, 1973. Petty officer 3d class USN, 1956—58, Key West, Fla. Mem.: Orgn. of Am. Historians, Assn. of Authors Reps., Dutch Treat Club. Democrat. Episcopalian. Home: 7 Outpost Rd Katonah NY 10536

**MCCAULEY, JANE REYNOLDS,** journalist; b. Wilmington, Del., Oct. 22, 1947; d. John Thomas and Helen (Campbell) McC. BA, Guilford Coll., 1969. Editor, sr. writer Nat. Geographic Soc., Washington, 1970-90; freelance writer, editor, artist, 1990-96; exec. editor AM Quilter's Soc., 1996-97;

freelance editor, writer, 1997—. Former owner Unique Native Crafts; tropical bird specialist. Author of 15 children's books; co-author award-winning travel books, art revs. Mem.: Children's Book Soc. E-mail: ritstuff4u@juno.com.

**MCCAULEY, KRISTINA AKEMI,** project coordinator; b. Willows, Calif., May 8, 1974; d. David Michael and Mildred Midori McCauley. AA in Liberal Studies, Diablo Valley Coll., Pleasant Hill, Calif., 1999; BA in Women's Studies, San Diego State U., 2002; MPhil in Internat. Peace Studies, U. Dublin, Ireland, 2005. Vet. technician VCA Angel Animal Clinic, San Diego, 2000—01; asst. editor Entheos Jour., San Diego, 2001—03; freelance massage therapist Pleasant Hill, Calif., 2003—04; NGO project coord. Catherine McAuley Centre, Dublin, 2005—. Intern San Diego Hist. Soc., 2001; cmty. svc. learning project vol. Women's History Mus., San Diego, 2001—02. Mem.: AAUW, Nat. Women's Studies Assn. Buddhist. Home: 520 Monti Cir Pleasant Hill CA 94523 Office: Catherine McAuley Ctr 23 Herbert St Dublin Dublin 2 Ireland Office Phone: 011 353 1 638 7500. Personal E-mail: kmccauley74@hotmail.com. Business E-mail: cmcauley@indigo.ie.

**MCCAULEY, MATTHEW K.,** apparel executive; b. 1973; BBA, Brigham Young U. Planning mgr. GAP Inc., 2000—01, mgr. bus. solutions, 2001; dir. allocation Gymboree Corp., 2001—03, v.p. planning and allocation, 2003—05, sr. v.p., gen. mgr., 2005, pres., 2005—, CEO, 2006—, chmn., 2006—. Office: Gymboree Corp 500 Howard Street San Francisco CA 94105 Office Phone: 415-278-7000. Office Fax: 415-278-7100.*

**MC CAULEY, R. PAUL,** criminologist, educator; b. Highspire, Pa., Jan. 13, 1943; s. Paul Herbert and Frances Vaden (Harper) McC.; m. Gail Lee Gummo, Jan. 30, 1965; 1 child, Brent Clayton. A.S., Harrisburg Area Community Coll., 1968; BS, Va. Commonwealth U., 1969; MS, Eastern Ky. U., 1971; PhD (fellow), Sam Houston U., 1973; certificate Home Office Detective Tng. Course, Eng., 1967. Diplomate Am. Coll. Forensic Examiners, Am. Bd. Law Enforcement Experts. Police officer Highspire Police, 1964-69; adminstr. Burns Internat. Security Services Inc., 1969-71; prof. police sci. and adminstrn., dir. grad. studies in adminstrn. of justice U. Louisville, 1973-82; prof., chmn. dept. criminology Indiana U. of Pa., 1982—; co-founder Sempas Security and Safety Technologies, 1980; advisor Reagan Presdl./Congressional Task Force on Criminal Justice, 1980; mem. staff So. Police Inst., 1973-82, Nat. Crime Prevention Inst., 1973-82. Researcher, pmr. McShan Assocs., 1974-85; cons. U.S. Congress Com. on Emergency Communications, 1967. Co-author: The Criminal Justice System, 1976, 3d edit., 1984; co-founder, editor: Criminal Justice Policy Rev., 1984-86; contbr. chpts. to books, articles to profl. jours.; patents. Active Metro Child Abuse Program, Crime Clinic of Greater Harrisburg, 1965-74; mem. Lower Swatara Twp. Police Civil Service Commn., 1967-69. Served with USMC, 1962-66 Recipient Mayor's Citation, City of Louisville, 1982, Gold medal Educator of the 1980's; honoree Silliman Coll., Yale U., 1984; Fulbright scholar, lectr., Australia, 1987. Mem. Acad. Criminal Justice Scis. (exec. bd. 1980-83, pres. 1985), Navy League (award for disting. community service) Home: 4620 Lucerne Rd Indiana PA 15701-6003 Office: Indiana U of Pa G-1 McElhaney Hall Indiana PA 15705-0001 Office Phone: 724-349-9676. Business E-mail: mccauley@iup.edu. *One's philosophy, spirit, and drive contributes more to his relative success than do economic resources, social position, planning, or timing.*

**MCCAUSLAND, MARGARET A.,** lawyer, educator; b. Bryn Mawr, Pa., Feb. 2, 1950; d. Joseph Edward and Margaret Mary O'Donnell; m. Paul Joseph McCausland, June 22, 1968; children: Patricia, Joseph. BS summa cum laude, St. Joseph's U., Phila., 1984; JD cum laude, Villanova U., 1987. Bar: Pa. 1987, U.S. Dist. Ct. (ea. dist.) Pa. 1987, U.S. Dist. Ct. (we. dist.) Mich. 1995, U.S. Ct. Appeals (3d cir.) 1997, U.S. Supreme Ct. 2002. Sec. Bankers Life, Bala Cynwyd, Pa., 1968-70, 1975—77, Frederick Brown & Assoc., Newton Square, Pa., 1977—84; assoc. Dechert LLP, Phila., 1987—93, Blank Rome LLP, Phila., 1993—97, ptnr., 1997—2006; atty. Law Offices of Margaret A. McCausland, LLC, 2006—. Adj. faculty Villanova (Pa.) U. Law Sch., 1999—, mem. bd. advisors 2001—04. Vol. atty. Support Ctr. Child Advs., Phila., 1987—; tutor Phila. Reads, 2001—; mem. bd. advisors Archbishop Prendergast HS Girls, Phila., 2001—05; bd. dirs., v.p. Robin's Nest, Inc., Glassboro, NJ, 1995—; pres., bd. dirs. CeaseFire Pa., Phila., 2002—. Named Disting. Adv., Support Ctr. Child Advs., 1996, Woman of Distinction, Phila. Bus. Jour., 2001, Pa. Super Lawyer, Law and Politics Mag., 2004, 2005, 2006; recipient Citizens Pro Bono award, Phila. (Pa.) Bar Found., 2004. Mem.: ABA, AAUW, Pa. Bar Assn., J. Willard O'Brien Inn Ct., Phila. Bar Assn. (bd. dirs.), Forum Exec. Women, Order of the Coif. Office: Blank Rome LLP One Logan Sq Philadelphia PA 19103 Business E-mail: mccausland@blankrome.com.

**MCCAUSLAND, PETER,** technology company executive; b. 1950; BA, U. S.C.; JD, Boston U. Bar: Pa. 1974. Gen. counsel MG Industries, Inc.; founder, chmn., CEO Airgas, Inc., Radnor, Pa., 1982—. Bd. dirs. Metrocall, Inc. Dir. Fox Chase Cancer Center, Independence Seaport Museum, Internat. Oxygen Manufacturers Assoc., Inc. Fax: 610-687-1052.

**MCCAUSLAND, THOMAS JAMES, JR.,** retired brokerage house executive; b. Cleve., Nov. 27, 1934; s. Thomas James and Jean Anna (Hanna) McC.; m. Kathryn Margaret Schacht, Feb. 9, 1957; children: Thomas James III, Andrew John, Theodore Scott. BA in Econs., Beloit (Wis.) Coll., 1956. V.p. A.G. Becker & Co., Inc., Chgo., 1959-74; v.p. The Chgo. Corp., 1974-76, sr. v.p., dir., 1976-83, exec. v.p., 1983-90, vice chmn., 1991-96; pres. The Chgo. Corp. Internat., 1990-96; ret., 2000. Treas. The LaSalle St. Coun., Chgo., 1990-93. V.p. Hospice the North Shore, Evanston, Ill., 1986-90; bd. dirs. McCormick Theol. Sem., Chgo., 1971-79, Presbyn. Home, Evanston, 1968-74; trustee Beloit Coll., 1987-90. Lt. USN, 1956-59. Mem. Union League, United Presbyn. Found. (trustee, vice-chmn. 1980-86), Skokie Country Club (bd. dirs. 1983-85, pres. 1993), Pelican Bay Club (Naples, Fla.)(chmn. 2001-03), Forum Club of Naples (bd. dirs.), Royal Poinciana Golf Club (Naples), Old Elm Club (Ill.). Republican. Avocations: travel, golf, history.

**MCCAW, CRAIG O.,** communications executive; b. Centralia, Wash., Aug. 11, 1949; s. John Elroy and Marion McCaw. Grad., Stanford U., 1973. Pilot; chmn., CEO McCaw Comm., 1968-88; chmn. bd. dirs., CEO McCaw Cellular Comm., Inc. (acquired MCI's cellular and paging ops. in 1986 sold to AT&T in 1994), Kirkland, Wash., 1982-94; chmn., CEO Lin Broadcasting Co. 1990—; founder, chief, co-exec. officer Teledesic Corp., Kirkland, 1990—; chmn., CEO NEXTLINK Comm. Inc. (now XO Comm.), 1994—2002, Eagle River Inc., Clearwire, 2003—, co-CEO, 2006—; acquired NextNet Wireless Inc, Minneapolis, 2004—. Bd. dirs. RadioFrame Networks, Inc., China Unicom Ltd., China, 2000—, non-exec. dir., 2002—; mem. Nat. Security Telecom. Adv. Com. Named one of 400 Richest Ams., Forbes mag., 2006; named to Gallery of Achievers Hall of Bus., 1989, Horatio Alger Assn. of Disting. Ams., 1999. Avocation: boating. Office: Clearwire 5808 Lake Washington Blvd NE Ste 300 Kirkland WA 98033*

**MCCAW, JOHN E., JR.,** investment company executive, professional sports team executive; b. John Elroy McCaw; married; 4 children. Grad., U. Wash. Co-founder McCaw Cable Vision, McCaw Cellular Comm., Orca Bay Ptnrs., Vancouver, BC; chmn. Orca Bay Sports and Entertainment, Orca Bay Capital Corp.; chmn., gov. Vancouver Canucks; owner, bd. dirs. Seattle Mariners, 1992; co-founder Tahoma Fund. Bd. dirs. Kistler Aerospace Corp. Bd. mem. Conservation Internat. Office: Vancouver Canucks 800 Griffiths Way Vancouver BC Canada V6B 6G1 also: Orca Bay Ptnrs 1301 First Ave Seattle WA 98101*

**MCCAW, ROBERT BRUCE,** lawyer; b. Durham, N.C., Dec. 24, 1943; s. Robert Hall and Patricia Louise (McKean) McC.; m. Susan Leland Wood, June 15, 1968 (dec. June 2002); children: Anne Meredith, Benjamin Hugo. BS in Math., Georgetown U., 1965; JD, U. Va., 1970. Bar: Va. 1970, U.S. Dist. Ct. D.C. 1971, U.S. Ct. Appeals (10th cir.) 1974, U.S. Supreme Ct. 1974, U.S. Ct. Appeals (7th cir.) 1987. Law clk. to assoc. justice Hugo L. Black U.S.

Supreme Ct., Washington, 1970-71; assoc. Wilmer, Cutler & Pickering, Washington, 1971-78, ptnr., 1978—2004; ptnr., co-chmn. Securities dept., office sr. ptnr. Wilmer Cutler Pickering Hale & Dorr, NYC, 2004—. Adj. prof., lectr. securities regulation George Washington U., Washington, 1980-83. Editor-in-chief Va. Law Rev., 1969-70; contbr. articles to profl. jours. 1st lt. U.S. Army, 1965-67. Mem. Order of Coif. Presbyterian. Office: Wilmer Cutler Pickering Hale & Dorr LLP 399 Park Ave New York NY 10022 Office Phone: 212-230-8810. Office Fax: 212-230-8888. Business E-mail: robert.mccaw@wilmerhale.com.

**MCCAW, SUSAN RASINSKI,** ambassador; b. Orange City, Calif. m. Craig McCaw; 3 children. BA, Stanford U.; MBA, Harvard U., 1988. Bus. analyst McKinsey & Co., NY, Hong Kong; assoc. Robertson Stephens' Venture Capital Group; principal Robertson Stephens & Co., San Francisco; pres. COM Investments, Wash.; mng. ptnr. Eagle Creek Capital; US amb. to Austria U.S. Dept. State, Vienna, 2005—. Mem. exec. bd. Stanford Alumni Assn. Office: US Dept State 9900 Vienna Pl Washington DC 20521-9900*

**MCCAW, WENDY PETRAK,** publishing executive; b. 1952; m. Craig Oliver McCaw, Aug. 18, 1974 (div. 1997). BA, Stanford U., 1973. Co-owner Cellular One Comm., Wash.; founder, CEO Ampersand Holdings LLC, Santa Barbara, Calif., 1998—; owner & CEO Santa Barbara (Calif.) News-Press, 2000—, co-publisher, 2006—. Pres. Wendy P. McCaw Found. (formerly Craig & Wendy McCaw Found.), Santa Barbara, Calif. Named one of America's Richest People, Forbes, 1999, World's Richest People, 2000. Avocations: environmentalism, vegetarianism. Mailing: Santa Barbara News-Press PO Box 1359 Santa Barbara CA 93102 Office: Santa Barbara News-Press 715 Anacapa St Santa Barbara CA 93101 Office Phone: 805-564-5200. Office Fax: 805-966-6258. E-mail: wmccaw@newspress.com.*

**MCCHESNEY, FRED S.,** law educator; b. Washington, DC, Nov. 19, 1948; AB magna cum laude, Holy Cross Coll., 1970; JD cum laude, U. Miami, 1978; PhD in Econs., U. Va., 1982. Law clk. to Judge Alfred T. Goodwin US Ct. Appeals (9th cir.), 1978—79; assoc. Steptoe & Johnson, 1979—81; assoc. dir. policy and evaluation FTC, 1981—83; asst. prof. Emory U. Sch. Law, 1983—85, assoc. prof., 1985—87, Robert T. Thompson prof. law and bus., 1987—97; prof. econs. Emory U., 1987—97; prof. Cornell U. Law Sch., 1997—99; Class of 1967 James B. Haddad prof. law Northwestern U. Sch. Law, Chgo. Vis. prof. Centro di Formazione e Studi, Naples, Italy, 1992; lectr. Am. Law Ctr., Moscow, 1994; John M. Olin vis. fellow in law and econs. Cornell U. Law Sch., 1994. Co-author: Causes and Consequences of Antitrust: The Public Choice Perspective, 1995, Antitrust Law: Interpretation and Implementation, 1998, Property Rights: Cooperation, Conflict and Law, 2003; author: Teacher's Manual to Antitrust Law: Interpretation and Implementation, 1998, 2002; editor: Economic Inputs, Legal Outputs: The Role of Economists in Modern Antitrust, 1997; contbr. articles to profl. jours. Vis. scholar Internat. Centre for Econ. Rsch., Turin, Italy, 1994. Office: Northwestern U Sch Law 357 E Chicago Ave Chicago IL 60611 Office Phone: 312-503-2277. Office Fax: 312-503-5950. E-mail: f-mcchesney@northwestern.edu.

**MCCHESNEY, MICHAEL C.,** computer company executive; b. Atlanta; BSBA magna cum laude, Vanderbilt U.; MBA in Fin. and Multinat. Corp. U. Pa. Sr. assoc. Investments Orange Nassau, Boston; v.p. corp. devel Lantech Sys., Inc., Dallas; co-founder, CEO SecureWare, Security First Techs. (formerly Five Paces and SecureWare), Atlanta, 1995-2000; chmn. Security First Network Bank, Atlanta, 1995-96; founder Webtone, Atlanta, 2000—. Office: Webtone Technologies 3535 Piedmont Rd Ne #800 Atlanta GA 30305-4535

**MCCHESNEY, ROBERT MICHAEL, SR.,** academic administrator; b. Effingham, Ill., Oct. 5, 1942; s. J.D. and Helen Grace (Russell) McC.; m. Laraine Freeman, Aug. 28, 1965; children: Robert M. Jr., Todd Patrick, Jennifer Laraine, Grant Russell, Brent Steven. BA, U. La., Lafayette, 1964; MA, U. Va., 1967, PhD, 1969. Asst. instr. U. Va., Charlottesville, 1967-68; chmn. dept. polit. sci. U. Ctrl. Ark., Conway, 1971-76, dean coll. scis. and humanities, 1976-82, v.p. for acad. affairs, 1982-89, disting. prof., 1989-90; provost U. Montevallo, Ala., 1990-92, pres., 1992—2006. V.p. Survey Rsch., Inc., Conway, 1989-92; spl. cons. U. Ark. System, Little Rock, 1989. Mem. Carmichael Found., Conway, 1975-79; exec. bd. Quapaw coun. Boy Scouts Am., Little Rock, 1982-88; Greater Ala. Area Coun., 1995—; chair Ala. Higher Edn. Partnership, Pres. Adv. Coun., 1999-2001. Capt. Med. Svc. Corps U.S. Army, 1968-71. Granite, State Justice Inst./Adminstrv. Office of Cts., Ark., 1989. Mem. Ala. Coun. Univ. and Coll. Pres. (chmn. 1993-95, vice chmn. 2005-), So. Com. Colls. and Schs. (exec. coun. 1996-99), Birmingham C. of C., Montevall C. of C., Rotary (pres. Conway Club 1987-88, Paul Harris fellow 1986), Phi Beta Kappa, Phi Kappa Phi, Alpha Chi, Golden Key, Phi Alpha Theta, Phi Eta Sigma, Blue Key. Mem. Lds Ch. Avocations: hunting, fishing, golf. Office: U Montevallo Station 6001 Montevallo AL 35115 Office Phone: 205-665-6001. Personal E-mail: rmcchesney@prodigy.net.

**MCCHESNEY, ROBERT PEARSON,** artist; b. Marshall, Mo., Jan. 16, 1913; s. John and Ruby (Pearson) McC.; m. Mary Ellen Fuller, Dec. 17, 1949. Student, Sch. Fine Arts, Washington U., 1931-34, Otis Art Inst., Los Angeles, 1936-37. Represented by Annex Galleries, Santa Rosa, Calif., Robert Green Fine Arts, Mill Valley, Calif., Thomas McCormick Gallery, Chgo., Claire Carlevaro Art Exchange, San Francisco, Michael Rosenfeld Gallery, NYC, Quicksilver, Forestville, Calif. Instr. art Calif. Sch. Fine Arts, San Francisco, 1949-51, Santa Rosa Jr. Coll., 1957-58; trustee San Francisco Art Inst., 1965-67. One-man shows include San Francisco Mus. Modern Art, 1949, 53, San Francisco Art Inst., 1957, 20th Century West, 1965, Bolles Gallery, N.Y., 1962, Nev. Mus., 1994, San Jose (Calif.) Mus., 2005, Quicksilver Mine, Calif., 2005, others; one-man retrospective Fresno (Calif.) Mus. Art, 1996, 2006, Calif. State U., Fresno. 1999, City Visions Gallery, Santa Rosa, Calif., 2000, Art Exch., San Francisco, 2002; group shows include Art Inst. Chgo., 1947, 3d Biennial Sao Paulo, Brazil, 1955, Whitney Annual, 1955, Corcoran, 1957, Provincetown, 1957, Chgo., 1959, Osaka, Japan, 1970, Whitney, 1980, Robert Green Fine Arts, Mill Valley, Calif., Natsoulas Gallery, Davis, Calif., others; represented in permanent collections, Fresno Art Mus., Art Inst. Chgo., Worcester (Mass.) Art Mus., Whitney Mus., N.Y., San Francisco Mus. Modern Art, Utah State Mus., Nev. Art Mus., Laguna Beach Art Mus., Cleve. Art Mus., San Jose Mus. Art, others; executed mural San Francisco Social Svcs. Bldg., 1978; (photo biography) Robert McChesney-An American Painter, 1996. Mailing: 2955 Sonoma Mountain Rd Petaluma CA 94954-9559 Address: c/o Dennis Calabi 7731 Elphick Rd Sebastopol CA 95462 Office Phone: 707-795-4612. *The desert wilderness, which I truly love to be in as much as possible, has influenced me a great deal. Of course, the artist is no different than anyone else in that he is influenced by everything around him visually and psychologically, but he has the ability to digest this, you might say, and then transform it into art.*

**MCCLAIN, BRENDA C.,** pain management physician; b. Wilson, NC, July 17, 1954; MD, U. NC, Chapel Hill, 1984. Cert. Pain Mgmt., Am. Bd. Anesthesiology, diplomate Am. Bd. Pain Medicine. Intern, anesthesia John Hopkins Hosp., Baltimore, Md., 1984—85, resident, anesthesiology and critical care medicine, 1985—87; fellow pediatric anesthesiology Children's Hosp. Pitts., 1987—88; asst. prof. Med. Coll. Ga., Augusta; dir. pediatric pain Vanderbilt U.; dir., pediatric pain mgmt. services, attending physician pediatric anesthesiology Yale-New Haven Hosp.; assoc. prof., anesthesiology and pediatrics Yale U., 1998—. Chairperson Yale New Haven Hosp. Sedation Analgesia Coun.; mem. examination coun. Am. Bd. Pain Medicine; spkr. in field. Contbr. articles to profl. jours., chapters to books; mem. several editl. boards. Mem.: Am. Pain Soc. (mem. pediatric pain pre-conference prog. com.), Am. Cancer Soc., Am. Acad. Pain Medicine. Office: Yale U 333 Cedar St TMP3 PO Box 208051 New Haven CT 06520-8051 Office Fax: 203-785-2802, 203-785-6664. Business E-mail: brenda.mcclain@yale.edu.*

**MCCLAIN, CINDY DUNSTAN,** music educator; d. Kenneth Warren and Janet Lou Dunstan; children: Melinda Wrye Washington, John Michael Kritos. MusB in Vocal and Instrumental Edn. K-12, Lincoln U. of Mo., Jefferson City, 1977; MA in Piano performance, U. Mo. State U., 1995. Dir., coord. music, adjudicator State Fair Coll., Sedalia, Mo., 1988—2003; dir. music, coord. fine arts Westminster Coll., Fulton, Mo., 2003—. Dir. Jefferson City (Mo.) Cantorum. Recipient Governor's award for excellence in tchg., State of Mo., 2000. Mem.: Mo. Assn. Dept. Schs. of Music, Mo. C.C. Assn., Music Educators Nat. Conf., Choral Dirs. Assn. Office: Westminster Coll 501 Westminster Ave Fulton MO 65251 Office Phone: 573-592-5214. Personal E-mail: cmcclain@socket.net. E-mail: mcclaic@westminster-mo.edu.

**MCCLAIN, DAVID STANLEY,** academic administrator, business and management professor; b. St. Joseph, Mo., Nov. 11, 1946; s. Stanley Russell and Veletta Mabel (Willis) McC.; m. Gayla Sue Webb, Dec. 30, 1967 (div. 1978); 1 child. BA, U. Kans., 1968; PhD, MIT, 1974. Dir. internat. econs. Data Resources, Inc., Lexington, Mass., 1974-78; sr. staff economist U.S. Pres.'s Council Econ. Advisers, Washington, 1979-80; assoc. prof. Sch. Mgmt., Boston U., 1983—, asst. prof., 1978-83, chmn. Fin. and Econs. Dept., 1985—91; Henry A. Walker Jr. Disting. Prof. Univ. Hawaii, Manoa, 1991—2000, dean Coll. Bus. & 1st Hawaiian Bank Disting. Prof. Mgmt., 2000—03; v.p. academic affairs Univ. Hawaii Sys., Honolulu, 2003—04, interim pres., 2004—. Econ. advisor Babson-United Investment Advisors, Boston, 1984—; cons. various cos.; head U.S. delegation Oppr. for Econ. Cooperation and Devel. Working Party on Short-Term Econ. Outlook, Paris, 1979-80. Author Apocalypse on Wall Street; contbr. On the Money tv series, 1984-85, articles to profl. jours. Vice chmn., trustee Acton (Mass.) Congl. Ch., 1987; chmn. stewardship Meml. Congl. Ch., Sudbury, Mass., 1983-84; mem. alumni mentor program MIT Dept. Econs., Cambridge, 1986-87; coach Acton-Boxboro Youth Soccer, 1987. Served to 1st lt. U.S. Army, 1968-71, Vietnam. Recipient Broderick Teaching prize Sch. Mgmt. Boston U., 1986; Woodrow Wilson fellow, NSF fellow. Mem. Am. Econ. Assn., Phi Beta Kappa, Sigma Chi, Beta Gamma Sigma. Democrat. Avocations: tennis, basketball. Office: University of Hawaii Bachman 204 2444 Dole St Honolulu HI 96822

**MCCLAIN, EDWARD FIFER, JR.,** retired physicist; b. Carrolton, Mo., Aug. 22, 1921; s. Edward Fifer and Corrine Carrie (Rahmoeller) McC.; m. Louise Cherry Shelby, Dec. 9, 1943; children: Deanna Louise, William Edward, Robert Jay. BSEE, George Washington U., 1950. With Naval Rsch. Lab., Washington, 1942-68, head radio astronomy br., 1956-68; ret., 1968. Past chmn. commn. radio astronomy Internat. Scientific Radio Union; past adv. com. Nat. Radio Astronomy Obs.; cons. Nat. Acad. Sci., Interdept. Radio Adv. Com., Nat. Radio Astronomy Obs.; astronomy panel NSF. Contbr. articles to profl. jours.; patentee in field. Fellow AAAS, Washington Acad. Scis.; mem. IEEE (sr., life), Internat. Astron. Union, Am. Astron. Soc., Scientific Rsch. Soc. Am., Sigma Tau. Achievements include conducting sea trials ST periscope radar in submarine; designed AN/APN67 self-contained doppler automatic navigator for aircraft; determined correct distance to radio source Cass A using galactic hydrogen absorption. Home: 4133 Maple Rd Suitland MD 20746-3514

**MCCLAIN, GREGORY DAVID,** chaplain; b. Anderson, SC, June 6, 1957; s. Lemuel David and Mary Josephine (Hawkins) McC.; m. Anne Leigh (Blackwell), May 21, 1983; children: Jonathan David and Sean Gregory. AS, Anderson Coll., 1977; BA, Erskine Coll., 1979; MDiv, Southeastern Bapt. Theol. Sem., Wake Forrest, N.C., 1982; D of Ministry, Wesley Theol. Sem., Washington, 1996. ordained Boulevard Bapt. Ch., 1983; cert. assoc. chaplain, Assn. of Profl. Chaplains, 2004. Chaplain extern Bapt. Med. Ctr., Columbia, SC, 1982; assoc. pastor First Bapt. Ch., South Boston, Va., 1983-86; min. Corrottoman Bapt. Ch., Lancaster, Va., 1986-93, Colonial Beach Bapt. Ch., 1993-98, Neill's Creek Bapt. Ch., Angier, NC, 1998—2001; CCR tchr. Harnett Ctrl. Mid. Sch., 2001—02; chaplain Duke U. Med. Ctr., Durham, NC, 2002—03, Wake Med, Raleigh, NC, 2003—04, N.C. Dept. Corrections, Lillington, 2004—05, Johnston Meml. Hosp., Smithfield, NC, 2005—. Pres. Dan River Bapt. Pastors, Halifax, Va., 1984-85; preacher jr. high weekend Va. Bapt. Gen. Assn., 1986, faculty youth week, 1984-88; v.p. Lancaster Ministerial Assn., 1987-88; v.p. Little River Bapt. Pastor's Conf., Lillington, N.C., 2000. Active CROP walk, South Boston, Va., 1984-85; coach youth soccer, South Boston, 1985, Westmoreland County, Va., 1995-97, Buics Creek, N.C., 1998; merit badge counselor Boy Scouts Am., Lancaster, 1990-93; mem. Lancaster Ednl. Task Force, 1988. Mem. Ruritan Club (chaplain 1990-93). Office: Johnston Meml Hosp PO Box 1376 Smithfield NC 27577 Business E-mail: gmcclain@johnstonmemorial.org. *The Kingdom of God exists wherever God is king.*

**MCCLAIN, LENA ALEXANDRIA,** protective services official; b. Toledo, Ohio, Aug. 15, 1966; d. Lee Earl McClain, Mattie May Roberts-McClain; m. David Angelo Neyland, Aug. 4, 1990 (div. July 1995). AAS in Criminal Justice Adminstrn., Pikes Peak C.C., Colorado Springs, Colo., 1994; post-grad., U. Colo., 1994—95; BS in Criminology, U. So. Colo., 1996; postgrad., Spring Arbor U., Mich., 2001—02; postgrad. in Social Work, Lourdes Coll., Toledo, OH, 2003—. Corrections officer Colo. Dept. Corrections, Colorado Springs, 1994—96, sgt., 1996—97, case mgr./lt., 1997—99; sr. resident specialist coord. N.W. Cmty. Corrections Ctr., Bowling Green, Ohio, 1999—2000; shift supr. Lucas County Dept. Wk. Release, Toledo, 2000—. Employee counsel, bd. dirs. Delta Correctional Ctr., 1998—99. Mem. Colo. Grievance Team, 1998; trio mem. Townsend Learning Ctr.; bd. dirs. Pub. Arts Commn., Delta, Colo., 1998; bd. dirs. liaison Nat. Assn. Blacks in Criminal Justice, Delta, 1998. With U.S. Army, 1987—90. Mem.: Am. Correctional Assn., Correctional Peace Officers Found., Social Work Nat. Honor Soc., Phi Theta Kappa. Democrat. Avocations: golf, basketball, softball, chess, writing. E-mail: breatis37@aol.com, brealis@toast.net.

**MCCLAIN, MICHAEL H.,** writer; b. Middletown, Ohio, Aug. 30, 1940; s. Thomas H. and Blanche (Hamilton) McC. BA in History, U. Miami, Ohio, 1962; MA in History, U. Granada, Spain, 1973. Staff columnist El Correo Gallego, Santiago de Compostela, Spain, 1974-84. Spkr. in field. *In 1984, Mr. McClain was invited to attend a conference on Buddhism in New Delhi, India. During his time in India, gave a conference on Muslim Spain at the tomb of the Sufi holy man, Nizam al-Din Auliya, in Delhi where he was honored with leis made of marigolds in 1993. Mr. McClain received a letter of thanks and congratulations from the Vatican for his research of 16th century Spanish poet and Mystic, St. John of the Cross, who inspired the priestly vocation of Pope John Paul II; he was the subject of John Paul II's doctoral thesis.* Contbr. articles to profl. jours. With U.S. Army, 1963-67. Mem. Nat. Assn. Scholars, Nat. Alumni Forum, Art History, Clubs. United for the Faith (sec. Dayton chpt. 1990—), Coun. of Shia Islamic Orgn., Valaam Soc. Am., Ameer Khusro Soc. Am., Assn. Literary Scholars and Critics, Great War Soc., Am. Tradition Family and Property, The 1745 Assn., Order of the White Rose, Archconfraternité du Archange St. Michel, Comunión Tradicionalista, Mensa, Alliance for Separation Sch. and State, NRA, Cardinal Newman Soc., Islamic Soc. N.Am., Miami Alumni Assn., Kateri Tekakawitha League, Sierra Club, Islamic Soc. N.Am., Sons Confederate Vets., Civil War Preservation Trust. Avocations: hunting, fishing, travel. Home: 4518 Bonita Dr Apt 130 Middletown OH 45044-6759 Office Phone: 513-423-8862.

**MCCLAIN, PAULA DENICE,** political scientist, educator; b. Louisville, Jan. 3, 1950; d. Robert Landis and Mabel (Molock) McC.; stepdau. of Annette Williams McClain; m. Paul C. Jacobson, Jan. 30, 1988; children: Kristina L., Jessica A. BA, Howard U., Washington, 1972; MA, Howard U., 1974, PhD, 1977; postgrad., U. Pa., 1981—82. Asst. prof. dept. polit. sci. U. Wis., Milw., 1977-82; assoc. prof. and prof. pub. affairs Ariz. State U., Tempe, 1982-91; prof. govt. and fgn. affairs U. Va., Charlottesville 1991-2000, chair govt. and fgn. affairs, 1994-97; prof. dept. polit. sci. Duke U., Durham, NC, 2000—. Co-author: Can We All Get Along? Racial and Ethnic Minorities in American Politics, 1995, 4th edit. 2005, Race, Place and Risk: Black Homicide in Urban America, 990; editor: Minority Group Influence, 1993; co-editor: Urban

Minority Administrators, 1988. Mem. Nat. Conf. Black Polit. Scientists (pres. 1989-90), Am. Polit. Sci. Assn. (exec. coun. 1985-87, v.p. 1993-94), So. Polit. Sci. Assn. (exec. coun. 1992-95, v.p. 2002-03, pres. elect 2004, pres. 2005), Internat. Polit. Sci. Assn. (exec. com. 1997-2003, v.p. 1997-2003), Midwest Polit. Sci. Assn. (v.p. 2002-04). Office: Duke U Dept Polit Sci Perkins Libr PO Box 90204 Durham NC 27708-0204 Office Phone: 919-660-4303. E-mail: pmcclain@duke.edu.

**MCCLAIN, SHAWN,** chef; Grad., U. Miami Ohio, School of Culinary Arts Kendall Coll., 1988—90. Chef Les Plumes, Prairie Restaurant, Boulevard Restaurant, Hotel Intercontinental, Chgo., sous chef; line cook Trio, Evanston, Ill., 1993, sous chef, exec. chef; owner, exec. chef Spring Restaurant, Chgo., 2000—. Named Rising Star Chef of Yr., Jean Banchet Awards for Culinary Excellence, 2002; recipient Chef of Yr. award, Esquire Mag., Best chef; Midwest award, James Beard Found., 2006. Office: Spring Restaurant 2039 W N Ave Chicago IL 60647*

**MCCLAIN, THOMAS EMERSON,** retired communications executive; b. East Liverpool, Ohio, July 26, 1950; s. Thomas E. and Helen Marie (Polinski) McC. BA, Case Western Reserve, Cleve., 1972; MA, Kans. State U., 1973. With intergovtl. rels. Ohio EPA, Columbus, 1974-77; legis. liaison Ohio Consumers Counsel, Columbus, 1977-80, dep. dir., 1980-81; press sec. Ohio Atty. Gen., Columbus, 1982-83; asst. dir. Pub. Utilities Commn., Columbus, 1983; with instnl. rels. dept. Battelle Project Mgmt. Div., Chgo., 1983-84, mgr. instl. rels., 1984-86; mgr. comms. Battelle, Columbus, 1986-88, dir. corp. comms., 1989-95, v.p. corp. comms., 1995—2006; ret., 2006. Sec. devel. bd. Children's Hosp., Columbus, 1990-91; adj. prof. Franklin U., Columbus, Ohio, 2006—. Vol. Ohio Youth Commn., Columbus, 1975-76; active ARC-Cen. Ohio chpt., 1986-87; mem. design rev. com. Ohio State U. Sci. and Tech. Park. Mem. Rotary (clmn. program com. 1991-93, bd. dirs. 1994-95, 2d v.p. 1996-97). Roman Catholic. Avocations: basketball, golf. Home: 2607 Wexford Rd Columbus OH 43221-3215 Office: Battelle 505 King Ave Columbus OH 43201-2693

**MCCLAIN, TIM S.,** lawyer; b. 1948; m. Lynn Hollyfield; children: Scott, Brendan. Grad., U.S. Naval Acad., 1970; JD, Calif. We. Sch. Law, San Diego, 1978. Bar: Calif., DC, US Supreme Ct. Commd. Navy JAG Corps USN, ret., 1990, mil. def. counsel Navy Legal Svc. Office San Diego, head claims officer Navy Legal Svc. Office, head legal assistance officer Navy Legal Svc. Office, staff judge adv. for the commanding officer Naval Air Station Miramar, 1981—83, dept. head, instr. Naval Justice Sch. Newport, RI, 1981—86, gen. court-martial mil. judge Navy-Marine Trial Judiciary, S.W., 1986—90; with litigation law firm, San Diego, 1990—96; joined internat. mgmt. cons. firm, dir. opers., 1996—99; pvt. practice Principi and McClain, La Jolla, Calif., 1999—2001; gen. counsel US Dept. Veterans Affairs, Washington, 2001—06, acting asst. sec. for human resources and adminstrn., 2004.

**MCCLAIN, WILLIAM ANDREW,** lawyer; b. Sanford, N.C., Jan. 11, 1913; s. Frank and Blanche (Leslie) McClain; m. Roberta White, Nov. 11, 1944. AB, Wittenberg U., 1934; JD, U. Mich., 1937; LLD (hon.), Wilberforce U., 1963, U. Cin., 1971; LHD, Wittenberg U., 1972. Bar: Ohio 1938, U.S. Dist. Ct. (so. dist.) Ohio 1940, U.S. Ct. Appeals (6th cir.) 1946, U.S. Supreme Ct. 1946. Mem. Berry, McClain & White, 1937—58; dep. solicitor City of Cin., 1957—63, solicitor, 1963—72; mem. Keating, Muething & Klekamp, Cin., 1972—73; gen. counsel Cin. br. SBA, 1973—75; judge Hamilton County Common Pleas Ct., 1975—76, Mcpl. Ct., 1976—80; of counsel Manley, burke, Lipton & Cook, Cin., 1980—. Adj. prof. U. Cin., 1963—72, Salmon P. Chase Law Sch., 1965—72. Mem. exec. com. ARC, Cin., 1978—; bd. dirs. NCCJ, 1975—. 1st lt. JAG U.S. Army, 1943—46. Decorated Army Commendation medal; recipient Nat. Layman award, A.M.E. Ch., 1943, Alumni award, Wittenberg U., 1966, Nat. Inst. Mcpl. Law Officers award, 1971, Ellis Island Medal of Honor, 1997. Fellow: Am. Bar Found.; mem.: ABA, Nat. Bar Assn., Ohio Bar Assn., Cin. Bar Assn., Am. Judicature Soc., Fed. Bar Assn., Bankers Club, Friendly Sons St. Patrick, Masons (32d degree), Sigma Pi Phi, Alpha Phi Alpha. Republican. Methodist. Home: 2101 Grandin Rd Apt 904 Cincinnati OH 45208-3346 Office Phone: 513-721-5525.

**MCCLANAHAN, DAVID M.,** energy executive; B in Math., U. Tex.; MBA, U. Houston. Various exec. capacities Reliant Energy, 1986—; pres., COO electric utility divsn. Reliant Energy HL&P, 1997—99; pres., COO delivery group Reliant Energy, 1999—2000, vice-chmn., 2000—02; pres., CEO, dir. CenterPoint Energy, Houston, 2002—. Chmn. bd. dirs. ERCOT; bd. dirs. Edison Electric Inst., Am. Gas Assn., Interstate Natural Gas Assn. Am. Chmn. bd. Univ. St. Thomas. Office: CenterPoint Energy PO Box 4567 Houston TX 77210-4567*

**MCCLANAHAN, HARRY ALLEN, III,** management consultant; b. Ypsilanti, Mich., Mar. 30, 1949; s. Harry Allen and Ann Mary (Micheletti) McC.; m. JoAnn Shroyer, Nov. 15, 1969 (div. 1981); children: Peter Jason, Claire Marie; m. Naomi Ruth Johnson, May 10, 1984 (div. 2003); 1 child, Briana Michelle. BA, St. Mary's Coll., Winona, Minn., 1971. Tchr. St. Bede Acad., Peru, Ill., 1972-78, Ind. Sch. Dist. 719, Prior Lake, Minn., 1978-83; tng. coordinator Lawson Assocs., Mpls., 1983-85; sr. tng. cons. Lawson Profl. Svcs., Mpls., 1985-86; tng. mgr. IDS Fin. Svcs., Mpls., 1986-87; pres. Pragmatic Solutions, Inc. St. Louis Park, Minn., 1987—. Contbr. articles to profl. jours. Mem.: NAt. Spkrs. Assn. - MN. Nat. Spkrs. Assn. (treas 2002—03, v.p. 2002—03, pres.-elect 2003—04, treas. 2003—04, pres. 2004—05). Democrat. Roman Catholic. Avocations: writing, cooking, amateur radio, music, reading. Office: Pragmatic Solutions Inc 3053 Cavell Ave S Minneapolis MN 55426-2915 Office Phone: 952-933-6092. E-mail: harrym@pragmaticsolutions.com.

**MCCLANAHAN, LELAND,** university director; b. Hammond, Ind., Mar. 14, 1931; s. Alonzo Leland and Eva (Hermanson) McC.; m. Lavaughn Adell Meyier, June 3, 1954; children: Lindel, Loren. Diploma. Ctrl. Bible Coll., 1954; PhBB, Nat. Postgrad. Bible Acad., 1969; BA, Southwestern Coll., 1973; MA, Fla. State Christian Coll., 1964, ThD, 1990; PhD, Faith Bible Coll. and Sem., Ft. Lauderdale, Fla. and Marina, Lagos, Nigeria, 1969; MA, Bapt. Christian U., 1988; PhD, Freedom U., 1989; ThD, Bapt. Christian U., 1989, DLitt (hon.), 1990, PsyD, 1991; PhD, Hawaii U., 1995; DEd, Bapt. Christian U., 1992, D in Bus. Adminstrn., 1993; DD (hon.), Internat. Evangelism Crusades, 1969, Trinity Union Coll. 1991; LLD, La. Bapt. U., 1994; StD, PhD, Trinity Internat. U., 1994; HHD (hon.), La. Bapt. U., 1995; LittD (hon.), Cambridge Theol. Sem., 1996; PhD, LittD, PsyD, DBA, LLD, EdD, U. Hawaii, 1995; LittD (hon.), Messianic Coll. Rabbinical Studies; MA, Am. Bible Coll. & Sem., 1998; MDiv, Chapel Christian U., 1991; PhD, Midwestern U., 1998; D in Min., Am. Bible Coll. and Sem., 1999; PhD, Gulf Coast Coll. and Seminary, 2005. Diplomate Nat. Bd. Christian Clin. Therapists; ordained pastor, Christian Ch., 1950. Founder, pastor Evangel Temple, Griffith, Ind., 1954-73; Abundant Life Temple, Cocoa, Fla., 1974-77; mgr. ins. divsn. United Agys., Cocoa, Fla., 1979-81; assoc. pastor Merritt Assembly of God, Merritt Island, Fla., 1982-85, Palm Chapel, Merritt Island, 1987-89, 1990-93; founder Hawaii U., Merritt Island Offices, Merritt Island, Fla., 1990-97; chancellor Hawaii U. Merritt Island Offices, 1995-97; dir. Fla. Hawaii U. Schs., 1994-97; dir., founder Chapel Christian U., Merritt Island, Fla., 1990—; founder People's Ch. Internat., Inc., 2000—. Founder, dir. Griffith Youth Ctr., 1960-70, Todd Nursery Sch., Griffith, 1971-73; founder, chancellor Ind. Bible Coll., Griffith, 1971-73; dir. Chapel Counseling Ctr., Merritt Island, 1990-94; nat. accreditation com. Hawaii U.; founder, pres. Brevard Humanity City, Inc., 2002; founder Mini Job Link, 2002, Adult Edn. 2003. Author: Is Divine Healing For Today?, 1989, Truths From the Gospel of St. John, 1991, An Outline of the Revelation, 1993, Numbers in the Bible, 1994, An Outline of the Acts of the Apostle, 1995, An Outline of the Book of Proverbs, 2000, How to Feel Better and Live Longer, 2006; author 144 book courses and books. Recipient Disting. Svc. award US Jaycees, 1966, Govs.'s Points of Light award, Fla., 2003, Congl. Order of Merit award, 2004, 06; named Hon. Lt. Col., Gov. Guy Hunt, 1988, Archbishop, Hierarchical Christ Ch., 2000, Rep. Presdl. Honor Roll, 2005, Nat. Congl. Com., 2005. Fellow Am. Biog. Inst. (life); mem. Internat. Platform Assn., Order of Internat. Fellowship (life), Am. Inst. Clin. Psychotherapists, Am. Assn. christian

Counselors, Nat. Christian Counseling Assn. (assoc., lic.), Internat. Assn. Pastoral Psychologists (lic.), Order of St. John, Knight of Malta (comdr. 1990), Angel Soc. Republican. Avocations: reading, walking, watching sports, watching television adventures, weightlifting. Office: Chapel Christian Univ 870 Australian St Merritt Island FL 32953-4676 Office Phone: 321-452-0135, 321-455-6605. Personal E-mail: sxrlelpeopl@pc.com.

**MCCLANAHAN, RUE (EDDI-RUE MCCLANAHAN),** actress; b. Healdton, Okla., Feb. 21, 1934; d. William Edwin and Dreda Rheua-Nell (Medaris) McC.; m. Tom Bish, 1958; 1 child, Mark Thomas Bish; m. Norman Hartweg; m. Peter DeMaio; m. Gus Fisher, 1976; m. Tom Keel, 1984 (div. 1985); m. Morrow Wilson, 1997. BA in German & Theatre Arts cum laude, U. Tulsa, 1956. Appearances include (theatre) Lottice and Lovage, Vienna, 1993, Harvey (London); (Broadway) Jimmy Shine, 1968-69, Sticks and Bones, 1972, California Suite, 1977, After-Play, 1995, The Women, 2002, Wicked, 2005—; (TV series) Maude, 1973-78, Apple Pie, 1978, Mama's Family, 1982-84, Golden Girls, 1985-92, Golden Palace, 1992-93, Safe Harbor, 1999; (TV movies) Having Babies III, 1978, Sgt. Matlowch vs. the U.S. Air Force, 1978, Rainbow, 1978, Topper, 1979, The Great American Traffic Jam, 1980, Word of Honor, 1981, The Day the Bubble Burst, 1982, The Little Match Girl, 1987, Liberace, 1988, Take My Daughters Please, 1988, Let Me Hear You Whisper, 1988, To the Heroes, 1989, After the Shock, 1990, Children of the Bride, 1990, To My Daughter, 1990, The Dreamer of Oz, 1990, Baby of the Bride, 1991, Mother of the Bride, 1993, Danielle Steele's Message from Nam, 1993, Burning Passion: The Margaret Mitchell Story, 1994, Nunsense, 1995, A Holiday to Remember, 1995, Columbo: Ashes to Ashes, 1998; (films) The People Next Door, 1970, They Might Be Giants, 1971, The Pursuit of Happiness, 1971, Modern Love, 1990, This World, Then the Fireworks, 1996, Dear God, 1996, Out to Sea, 1997, Rusty: A Dog's Tale, 1997, Starship Troopers, 1997, Border to Border, 1998, Columbo: Ashes to Ashes, 1998, A Saintly Switch, 1999, The Moving of Sophia Miles, 2000, (off-Broadway prodn.) The Vagina Monologues, 2001, (mini-series) Innocent Victims, 1995. Recipient Obie award for leading off-Broadway role in Who's Happy Now, 1970; Emmy award Best Actress in a comedy, 1987; named Woman of Yr., Pasadena Playhouse, 1986; Spl. scholar Pasadena (Calif.) Playhouse, 1959, Phi Beta Gamma scholar, 1955. Mem. Actors Studio, Actors Equity Assn., AFTRA, Screen Actors Guild. Office Phone: 212-372-1270.

**MCCLANE, ROBERT SANFORD,** entrepreneur, bank executive; b. Kenedy, Tex., May 5, 1939; s. Norris Robert and Ella Addie (Stockton) McC.; m. Sue Nitschke, Mar. 31, 1968; children: Len Stokes McClane Brown, Norris Robert. BS in Bus. Adminstrn., Trinity U., San Antonio, 1961. With Ford Motor Co., Detroit, 1961-62; with Frost Nat. Bank, San Antonio, 1962-97, mem. staff, 1962-68, v.p. 1968-78; exec. v.p. Cullen/Frost Bankers, Inc., 1976—85, pres., 1985-97, dir., 1985—. Benefit Planners, Inc., 1997-2001; advisor, dir. Ellison Grandchildren Trust, 1996—; pres., owner Mc-Clane Ptnrs., LLC, 1997—; dir., vice chmn. Tobin Internat., 1998—2003. Bd. dirs. Frost Nat. Bank, San Antonio, Princeton eCom., CCI Telecom, Inc., CareNet, 2005—. Crusade chmn. Bexar County chpt. Am. Cancer Soc., 1974; bd. dirs. Bexar County ARC, 1969-72; sr. warden St. Luke's Episopal Ch., San Antonio, 1980; trustee Alamo Pub. Telecomms. Coun., San Antonio, 1981-88; chmn. San Antonio Econ. Devel. Found., 1987-89, exec. com. 1985-91; bd. trustees Trinity U., 1990—, chmn., 2001-04 Mem. Greater San Antonio C. of C. (chmn. leadership San Antonio 1975-76, bd. dirs. exec. com. 1994-97, chmn. 1996), Trinity U. Alumni Assn. (pres. 1968-69, disting. alumnus 1987), Free Trade Alliance San Antonio (bd. dirs., 1997—, chmn. 1998-2000), Southwest Rsch. Inst. (trustee 1997—), San Antonio German Club, Order Alamo, Tex. Cavaliers, Argyle Club, Club Giraud, Plaza Club (bd. dirs. 1973-92). Episcopalian. Office: 1616 Frost Bank Tower 100 W Houston St San Antonio TX 78205-1435 Office Phone: 210-220-5353. E-mail: bob@mcclanellc.com.

**MCCLARD, JACK EDWARD,** lawyer; b. Lafayette, La., May 13, 1946; s. Lee Franklin and Mercedes Cecile (Landry) McClard; m. Marilyn Kay O'Gorman, June 3, 1972; 1 child, Lauren Minton. BA in History, Rice U., 1968; JD, U. Tex., 1974. Bar: Va. 1974, U.S. Dist. Ct. (ea. and we. dists.) Va. 1974, U.S. Ct. Appeals (4th cir.) 1978, DC 1981, U.S. Dist. Ct. DC 1981, U.S. Ct. Appeals (DC cir.) 1981, N.Y. 1985, U.S. Dist. Ct. (so. and ea. dists.) N.Y. 1985, U.S. Ct. Appeals (5th cir.) 1993, Tex. 1996, U.S. Dist. Ct. (ea. dist.) Tex. 1998, U.S. Ct. Appeals (7th cir.) 2001. Assoc. Hunton & Williams, Richmond, Va., 1974-81, ptnr., 1981—. Contbr. articles to profl. jours., chapters to books. Served to lt. (j.g.) USN, 1968—71. Mem.: ABA, Nat. Assn. R.R. Trial Ct., Lewis F. Powell, Jr. Inns Ct. (exec. com.), 5th Cir. Bar, Richmond Bar Assn., Va. Bar Assn. Democrat. Episcopalian. Avocations: bridge, gardening, wine. Home: 100 Trowbridge Rd Richmond VA 23238 Office: Hunton and Williams Riverfront Plz E Tower 951 E Byrd St Richmond VA 23219-4074 Office Phone: 804-788-8490. Business E-Mail: jmcclard@hunton.com.

**MCCLARY, GLEN DAVID,** education educator; b. Lackawanna, NY, Apr. 10, 1945; 1 child, David Henry. EdD, U. at Buffalo, NY, 1962—78. Biology, chem., physics, social studies and bus. NY State, 1974. Tchr. Buffalo Pub. Schs., 1970—2000; assist. prof. edn. D'Youville Coll., Buffalo, 1989—. Volleyball coach, Buffalo, 1977—99. Mem.: NSTA (assoc.), Sci. Tchrs. Assn. NY (assoc.), NY State Social Studies Assn. (assoc.), Nat. Assn. Tchr. Educators (assoc.). Home: 4825 Tonawanda Ck Rd N North Tonawanda NY 14120 Office: D'Youville Coll 320 Porter Ave Buffalo NY 14201 Office Phone: 716-829-7748. Personal E-mail: vbdoc@adelphia.net. Business E-Mail: mcclary@dyc.edu.

**MCCLARY, GRACIE BRANCH,** bank executive; b. Lumberton, NC, May 3, 1959; d. Robert E. and Audrey J. Branch; m. David K. McClary, Nov. 19, 1989; m. Mark A. Floyd, Oct. 9, 1977 (div. Jan. 15, 1986); children: Sara G., Dustin S. Floyd. Cert. Regulatory Compliance Mgr. Inst. Cert. Bankers Wash., DC, 1997. V.p., compliance officer Waccamaw Bank, Whiteville, NC, 1998—; v.p., sec., treas. McClary Designs, Inc. Whiteville, 1998—. Roman Catholic. Home: PO Box 1772 Whiteville NC 28472 Office: Waccamaw Bank 110 N Powell Blvd Whiteville NC 28472 Home Fax: 910-641-0595; Office Fax: 910-641-0595.

**MCCLARY, LORETTA MARY,** accountant; b. Boston, July 18, 1957; d. Loretto J. and Mary L. (Rufo) Salvucci; m. Richard E. McClary, May 17, 1980 (dec. Apr. 1997); children: Loretta, Robert, Gina. BA, Regis Coll., 1979; MA, Boston U. 1980; MBA, Suffolk U., 1984; MS in Taxation, advanced taxation cert., Bentley Coll., 1990; postgrad., Suffolk U. Law Sch. CPA, Mass. With fin. dept. GSA, Boston, 1979-84; acct. Feeley & Driscoll PC, Boston, 1986-97; prof. acctg. LaSell Coll., Newton, Mass., 1996—2000; sole practice Waltham, Mass., 1999—. Mem. fin. com. Our Lady's Parish, Waltham, Mass., 1999—. Mem. AICPA, Mass. Soc. CPA's. Avocation: golf. Home: 438 Main St Waltham MA 02452-6129 Office: 520 Main St Waltham MA 02452

**MCCLASKEY, MICHAEL KEITH,** information technology executive; b. Kirksville, Mo., June 8, 1963; s. Billy Keith and Martha Lee (Jones) McC.; m. Janet Sue Yearns, June 20, 1987. BA and BS in English, Truman State Univ., 1985; MA in English Lit., U. Mo., 1987. Teaching asst. U. Mo., Columbia, 1985-87; coord., tech. svcs. Mo. Sch. Bds. Assn., Columbia, 1987-90, dir., tech. svcs. 1990—95; leader US tech. svc. practice, bus. develop. group Perot Sys., Plano, Tex., 1995—2002, v.p. infrastructure solutions & chief info. officer, 2002—. Named one of Premier 100 IT Leaders, Computerworld, 2004. Baptist. Office: Perot Sys Corp 2300 W Plano Pkwy Plano TX 75075-8499*

**MCCLATCHY, J. D.,** editor, writer, educator; b. Bryn Mawr, Pa., Aug. 12, 1945; s. J. Donald and Mary Jane (Hayden) McC. BA summa cum laude, Georgetown U., 1967; PhD, Yale U., 1974. Instr. English dept. LaSalle Coll., Phila., 1968-71; asst. prof. English dept. Yale U., New Haven, 1974-81, lectr. English dept., 1983, 86-87; writer-in-residence CCNY, 1982; writer-in-residence Poetry Ctr. 92d St. YMCA, N.Y.C., 1983-84, workshop leader Poetry Ctr., 1982-91; lectr. Creative Writing program, English dept. Princeton

U., 1981-87, 89-93; editor The Yale Rev., New Haven, 1991—; prof. English Yale U., 2001—. Poet-in-residence Southampton Writers Conf., 1988; lectr. MFA Parsons/New Sch., 1989, English dept. Rutgers U., 1989, writing divsn. Columbia U., 1989, 92; vis. prof. English dept. UCLA, 1990, 92; selection com. Conn. Poetry Cir. Author: (poetry) Scenes from Another Life, 1981, (London 1983), Lantskip, Platan, Creatures Ramp'd, 1983, Stars Principal, 1986, Kilim, 1987, The Rest of the Way, 1990, Ten Commandments, 1998, Hazmat, 2002; librettist: A Question of Taste, 1989, Mario and the Magician, 1994, Orpheus Decending, 1994, Emmeline, 1996, revised edition, 2005; editor: The Yale Review, 1991—, (books) Anne Sexton: The Artist and Her Critics, 1978, For James Merrill: A Birthday Tribute, 1986, Recitative: Prose by James Merrill, 1986, Poets on Painters: Essays on the Art of Painting by Twentieth Century Poets, 1988, The Vintage Book of Contemporary American Poetry, 1990, Woman in White: Selected Poems of Emily Dickinson, 1991, The Vintage Book of Contemporary World Poetry, 1996, Twenty Questions, 1998, Christmas Poems, 1999, On Wings of Song, 2000, The Magic Flute (translation) 2000, Longfellow, Selected Poetry and Prose, 2000, Poems of the Sea, 2001, Love Speaks its Name, 2001, Bright Pages: Yale Writers, 1701-2001, 2001, James Merrill: Collected Poems, 2001, James Merrill: Collected Novels and Plays, 2002, Horace: The Odes, 2002, Division of Spoils, 2002, James Merrill Collected Prose, 2004, Poets of the Civil War, 2005; translator Carmen, 2001; assoc. editor Four Quarters, 1968-71; contbg. editor Am. Poetry Review; poetry editor The Yale Review, 1981-91; trans. articles, contbr. poems, stories, articles, reviews to various jours. Fellow Am. Acad. Arts and Scis., 1998—; mem. Am. Acad. and Ltrs., 1999—; bd. dirs. Ingram Merrill Found., 1986-99; chancellor The Acad. of Am. Poets, 1996—. Recipient gold medal Vergilian Acad., 1967, O. Henry award, 1972, prize Am. Acad. Poets,1972, Chase Going Woodhouse Poetry prize, 1976, Michener award, 1982, Gordon Barber Meml. award Poetry Soc. Am., 1984, Eunice Tietjens Meml. prize Poetry Mag., 1985, Witter Bynner Poetry prize Am. Acad. and Inst. Arts and Letters, 1985, award in lit., 1991, Oscar Blumenthal prize Poetry Mag., 1988, Levinson prize, 1990, Melville Cane award Poetry Soc. Am., 1991, Literary Lion N.Y. Pub. Libr., 1992; grantee Ingram Merrill Found., 1979, Conn. Commn. Arts, 1981; fellow NEA, 1987, John Simon Guggenheim Meml. Found., 1988; fellow lit. Acad. Am. Poets, 1991; artist resident Djerassi Found., 1988; Woodrow Wilson fellow 1967-68; Yale U. fellow, 1971-72; Ethel Boise Morgan fellow, 1972-74; artist's fellow N.Y. Found. Arts, 1986; artist resident Yaddo, 1991, MacDowell Colony, 1991. Mem. Acad. Am. Poets (chancellor 1996-2003, bd. dirs. 2003-), Phi Beta Kappa, Alpha Sigma Nu. Home: 15 Grand St Stonington CT 06378-1340 Office: The Yale Review Yale Univ PO Box 208243 New Haven CT 06520-8243

**MCCLATCHY, KEVIN S.,** professional sports team executive; b. Sacramento, Jan. 13, 1963; Diploma in Polit. Sci., U. Calif., Santa Barbara. Sport producer WPLG-TV, Miami; mktg. profl. Knight-Ridder Newspapers; nat. sales mgr. Newspaper Network (subs. McClatchy Newspapers); CEO, mng. gen. ptnr., owner Pittsburgh Pirates, 1996—; bus. opers. mgr. Amador Ledger-Dispatch, Calif., 1990. Co-owner Modesto A's, Oakland Athletics. Trustee Trinity-Pawling H.S., Pawling, N.Y., U. Calif. Santa Barbara; active United Way, Roberto Clemente Found., Extra Mile Found., U. Pitts. Cancer Inst., also Catholic charities. Office: Pittsburgh Pirates 115 Federal St Pittsburgh PA 15212*

**MCCLAUGHLIN, (PATRICIA) TRICIA MARIE,** education educator, artist; d. Gerard Martin McLaughlin and Bernadette Ward; m. Patricio Dia Aguiane (div.). BFA, Syracuse U., NY, 1986; MFA, Hunter Coll., NY, 2000. Asst. prof. Hunter Coll., N.Y.C., 2002—05, SUNY Coll., Old Westbury, NY, 2001—. Pub. art animation, Virginia Beach Aquatecture, 2006. Media Arts Grant, Jerome Found., 2004, Video fellowship, N.Y. Found., 2004, Fellowship, Guggenheim Found., 2005. Home: 241 Dewe St Brooklyn NY 11211

**MCCLAVE, DONALD SILSBEE,** academic administrator; b. Cleve., May 7, 1941; s. Charles Green and Anne Elizabeth (Oakley) McC.; m. Christine Phyllis Mary Tomkins, Feb. 19, 1966; children: Andrew Green, Susan Elizabeth (dec.). BA, Denison U., 1963. Mktg. rsch. officer Bank of Calif., San Francisco, 1968-70; v.p. Cen. Nat. Bank, Chgo., 1970-75, First Interstate Bank, Portland, Oreg., 1975-77; sr. v.p., 1977-79, exec. v.p., 1979-86; pres., CEO Portland Met. C. of C., 1987—2002; asst. to pres. Portland State U., 2002—. Instr. Pacific Coast Sch. Banking, Seattle, 1976-78, Grad. Sch. Mktg. and Strategic Planning, Athens, Ga., 1982-84; dir., mem. exec. com. Bank Mktg. Assn., 1976-82; bd. mem. Oreg. Nanosci. and Microtechs. Inst., 2003, dir. and chair fin. com. Pres. Oreg. Episc. Sch. Bd., Portland, 1983-84; pres. Assn. Oreg. Industries Found., Salem, 1984-85; pres., co-chmn. Japan-Am. Conf. Mayors and C. of C., Portland, 1985, trustee, 1991-98, exec. com., 1992-97; trustee YMCA of Columbia-Willamette, 1990-92, Portland Student Svcs. Corp., 1991-93; mem. METRO Urban Growth Mgmt. Adv. Com., 1989-92; mem. adv. com. Downtown Housing Preservation Partnership Adv. Com., 1989-94; mem. City of Portland Mayoral Transition Team, 1992, Mayor's Bus. Roundtable, 1993—; bd. dirs. Oreg. Trail chpt. ARC, 1994-95, Tri-Met, 1994—, chair fin. com., 1995—, United Way Columbia Willamette, 1978-83, 2000-01, Urban League Portland, 2000-01, Oreg. Nanoscience and Microtechnologies Inst., 2003-. Capt. USAF, 1963-68. Mem. Oreg. Chamber Execs. Assn. (pres. 1998). Avocations: reading, travel, golf, model building. Office: Portland State U PO Box 751 Portland OR 97207-0751

**MCCLEAN, LENORA JAMES,** nursing educator, dean; b. Jesup, Ga., Mar. 22, 1937; d. Ealey and Mary (Howard) Hayes; m. Robert William McClean, July 13, 1963; children: Anne-Marie St. John, Sharman Danielle, Tara Lauren, Marshall Hayes. Asst. prof. nursing Fla. State U., Tallahassee, 1963-64; asst. prof. nursing Tchrs. Coll. Columbia U., N.Y.C., 1964-73; clinician Bronx Psychiat. Center, 1966-73; asst. prof., dean graduate studies Sch. Nursing Health Scis. Ctr., Stony Brook, 1973-79, prof., 1979—, assoc. dean academic affairs 1979-80, acting dean, 1981; chief nursing officer U. Med. Ctr. Cons. in field; chair subcom. alternative healthcare delivery patterns Cmty. Health Plan Suffolk, 1977; mem. search com. for chmn. OB/GYN Nassau County Med. Ctr., 1977-78, for chief of nursing V.A. Hosp., Northport, N.Y., 1983, planning com. rsch. and edn. Stony Brook, 1983-86; planning group L.I. State Vets. Home, 1986-91, adv. group multidisciplinary opers., 1992; nursing adv. com. N.Y. State pub. svc. tng. program, 1988; faculty Comparative Health Care clin. study tour, U.S.-Morocco, 1990, Comparative Health Sys. Sino-Am. clin. study tour, China, 1982-91, Pediatric Nursing Soviet-Am. clin. study tour, 1981; researcher, presenter in field. Author: (with Dorothy Anderson) Identifying Suicide Potential, 1976; contbg. author: Comprehensive Psychiatric Nursing, 1979, 2d edit., 1982; contbr. numerous articles to profl. jours. Bd. dirs. Response Suffolk County, 1973-76; mem. cmty. adv. bd. transitional svcs., 1977, profl. adv. bd. chpt. Nat. Found.-March of Dimes Birth Defects, L.I. chpt., 1978-84, Blue Ribbon panel Suffolk County Infirmary, chair patient care subcom., 1989-90. Vis. fellow Sturt Coll. Advanced Edn., Bedford Park, South Australia, 1981-82; grantee. Mem. Am. Assn. Colls. Nursing (chair spl. interest group academic health sci. ctrs. 1990-93), Nat. League Nursing (coun. baccalaureate and higher degree programs), N.Y. State Nurses Assn. (v.p. 1980-82, reelected 1982, chair edn. com. 1985-87, N.Y. Nurses Assn. Coun. Deans of Nursing, Sr. Colls. and Univs. N.Y. State (-res. 1992), Sigma Theta Tau (Kappa Gamma chpt. 1988—). Democrat. Episcopalian.

**MCCLEAN, MURRAY R.,** metal products executive; Mng. dir. Commercial Metals Co., Sydney, Australia, 1985—93, pres. internat. div., 1993—99, pres. mktg. & dist. segment Irving, Tex., 1999—2004, exec. v.p., COO, 2004—06, pres. COO, 2006, pres., CEO, 2006—. Office: Commercial Metals Co Ste 800 6565 N MacArthur Blvd Irving TX 75039*

**MCCLEARY, BENJAMIN WARD,** investment banker; b. Washington, July 9, 1944; s. George William and Nancy (Grim) McCleary; m. Deirdre Marsters, May 6, 1967 (div. 1977); children: Benjamin, Katherine; m. Jean Muchmore, Oct. 15, 1983. AB, Princeton U., 1966. With Chemical Bank, N.Y.C., 1969-81, trainee, asst. sec., asst. v.p. v.p. Lehman Bros. Kuhn Loeb, N.Y.C., 1981-83; mng. dir. Shearson Lehman Bros., 1983-87, Shearson Lehman Hutton Internat., London, 1987-88, Shearson Lehman Hutton, Inc., N.Y.C., 1988-89; ptnr. McFarland Dewey & Co., LLC, N.Y.C., 1989—2005.

Bd. dirs. Detrex Corp., Harvel Plastics; mem. Seaview Capital LLC, Providence, 2005. Lt. (j.g.) USN, 1966—69. Office: Sea View Capital LLC 30 Kennedy Plaza Ste 400 Providence RI 02903 also: McFarland Dewey & Co LLC 420 Lexington Ave Ste 2650 New York NY 10170 Office Phone: 401-490-4845.

**MCCLEARY, LLOYD E(VERALD),** education educator; b. Bradley, Ill., May 10, 1924; s. Hal and Pearl McC.; m. Iva Dene Carter, June 13, 1971; children: Joan Kay, Victoria Lea, Karen Ann. Student, Kans. U., 1941—42; BS, U. Ill., 1948, MS, 1950, EdD, 1956; postgrad, Sorbonne U., Paris, 1946. Tchr., asst. prin. Portland (Oreg.) Pub. Schs., 1949-51; asst. prin. Univ. H.S., Urbana, Ill., 1951-52, prin., 1953-56; asst. supt. Evanston Twp. (Ill.) H.S., 1956-60; assoc. Roosevelt U., 1957-69; mem. faculty U. Mich., summers, 1958-59; prof. ednl. adminstrn. U. Utah, 1969—, chmn. dept., 1969-74. Assoc. CFK Ltd. Found., 1971-76; dir. projects in L.Am. for AID, World Bank, Ford Found., Bolivian Govt.; dir. Nat. Sch. Prin. Study, 1976-79, 86-89, res. project Families in Edn., 1992-94; edn. rep. to Utah People to People Program; keynoter Asian Conf. Edn., 1985; edn. adviser Office of the Queen, Jordan, 1985-86; advisor Nat. Commn. on Stds. in the Principalship; U.S. del. Conf. on Status Children, Senegal, 1992, Yr. of the Family, Malta, 1993; J. Lloyd Trump lectr., New Orleans, 1994. Author: Organizational Analysis X-Change, 1975, Politics and Power in Education, 1976, The Senior High School Principalship, 1980, Educational Administration, Today, 1984, High School Leaders and Their Schools, vols. 1 and 2, 1990, Leadership, 1996; editor Western Hemisphere Edn. Sch. Orgn., 1989—. Served with inf. AUS, 1941-46. Decorated Bronze Star with oak leaf cluster, Army Commendation medal; S.D. Shankland fellow, 1956; grantee Ford Found., 1968, 72, AID, 1966, 67, 70, 72, 74, 76, CFK Ltd., 1970-74, Rockefeller Family Found., 1979-80, U.S. Dept. State, 1981, 86-87, U.S. Dept. Def., 1986—; recipient Hatch Prize, 1988-89. Mem. Nat. Assn. Secondary Sch. Prins. (cert. of merit 1978, scholar-in-residence fall 1989, grantee 1969, 77, 86—), Assn. Supervision and Curriculum Devel., Nat. Assn. Elem. Sch. Prins., Phi Delta Kappa, Kappa Delta Pi. Methodist. Home: 1470 Wilton Way Salt Lake City UT 84108-2549 Office: U Utah 339 MBH Salt Lake City UT 84112 E-mail: www.birdsphoto@aol.com.

**MCCLEERY, WINSTON THEODORE,** information technology executive; b. Mobile, Ala., Sept. 6, 1935; s. Robert Alton and Theadora K. (Kiebel) McC.; m. Sandra Thoss, Dec. 28, 1958; children: Winston T., Jacqueline McCleery McNeely. BS, Springhill Coll., 1957; postgrad., U. Ala., 1957-58. Logic design engr. Autonetics N.Am. Aviation, Anaheim, Calif., 1960—65; dir. info. sys. Litton Industries, L.A., 1965—69; founder, owner Winston T. McCleery, Cons., 1969—; pres., CEO Mgmt. Software Systems, Inc., Mobile, 1979—. Patentee in field. With U.S. Army, 1958-60. Recipient Cert. for Heroism, Boy Scouts Am. 1949, Collifontanum award, Spring Hill Coll., 2006. Mem. Data Processing Mgmt. Assn., Assn. Computer Machinery, Am. Mgmt. Assn., Ind. Computer Cons.'s Assn., Optimists (pres. 1972). Republican. Achievements include contributions to the design and development of the U.S. Army Field Artillery's first digital fire direction computer; member of design team of the centaur missile's guidance system that made the first soft landing on the moon; design and development of seamless, integrated, on-line and instant-time computer application system for main frame class computers; inventor computer power and temperature enviroment control system, development of automatic documentation system used to document computer programs written in the Cobol language. Home: 5213 Janekyn Dr Mobile AL 36693-4142 Office: PO Box 9365 Mobile AL 36691-0365 Office Phone: 251-345-9960.

**MCCLEESTER, FRANK RAYMOND,** music educator; b. Windber, Pa., May 21, 1946; s. Raymond Earl and Eva McCleester; m. Joyce Marie Opdenhoff, June 26, 1971; children: Frank Raymond Jr., Melody Joy. MusB Edn, Evangel U., Springfield, Mo., 1968; MA, Indiana U. Pa., 1991; cert. adminstr., St. Francis U., Loretta, Pa., 2000. Cert. Instrnl. II tchr. Pa. Dir. band, tchr. music Bishop Carroll H.S., Ebensburg, Pa., 1968—76; various jobs Johnstown, Pa., 1976—81; substitute tchr., 1981—82, 1984—86; dir. band and chorus Ferndale Area Jr./Sr. H.S., Johnstown, 1986—. Interim dir. band U. Pitts. Johnstown 1986, 94; mem. Johnstown Civic Band, 1974—. Dir. choir Grace Assembly God, Johnstown, 1968—2000, 2006, exec. sec., 1970—. Named to Who's Who Among Am. Tchrs. Mem.: Pa. Music Educators Assn., Internat. Trumpet Guild, Phi Mu Alpha. Republican. Avocations: golf, gardening. Home: 1896 Frankstown Rd Johnstown PA 15902

**MC CLELLAN, CATHARINE,** anthropologist, educator; b. York, Pa., Mar. 1, 1921; d. William Smith and Josephine (Niles) McClellan; m. John Thayer Hitchcock, June 6, 1974. AB magna cum laude in Classical Archaeology, Bryn Mawr Coll., 1942; PhD (Anthropology fellow), U. Calif. at Berkeley, 1950. Vis. asst. prof. U. Mo. at Columbia, 1952; asst. prof. anthropology U. Wash., Seattle, 1952-56; anthrop. cons. USPHS, Arctic Health Research Center, Alaska, 1956; asst. prof. anthropology, chmn. dept. anthropology Barnard Coll., Columbia U., 1956-61; assoc. prof. anthropology U. Wis. at Madison, 1961-65, prof., 1965-83, prof. emeritus, 1983—, John Bascom prof., 1973. Vis. lectr. Bryn Mawr (Pa.) Coll., 1954; vis. prof. U. Alaska, 1973, 87. Assoc. editor: Arctic Anthropology, 1961; editor, 1975-82; assoc. editor: The Western Canadian Jour. of Anthropology, 1970-73. Served to lt. WAVES, 1942-46. Margaret Snell fellow AAUW, 1950-51; Am. Acad. Arts and Scis. grantee, 1963-64, Nat. Mus. Can. grantee, 1948-74 Fellow Am. Anthrop. Assn., Royal Anthrop. Inst. Gt. Britain and Ireland, AAAS, Arctic Inst. N.Am.; mem. Am. Ethnol. Soc. (sec.-treas. 1958-59, v.p. 1964, pres. 1965), Kroeber Anthrop. Soc., Am. Folklore Soc., Am. Soc. Ethnohistory (exec. com. 1968-71), Sigma Xi. Achievements include research in archaeological and ethnographic field investigations in Alaska and Yukon Territory in Canada.

**MCCLELLAN, CRAIG RENE,** lawyer; b. Portland, Oreg., June 28, 1947; s. Charles Russell and Annette Irene (Benedict) McC.; m. Susan Armistead Nash, June 7, 1975; children: Ryan Alexander, Shannon Lea. BS in Econs., U. Oreg., 1969; JD magna cum laude, Calif. We. U., 1976. Bar: Calif. 1976, U.S. Dist. Ct. (so. dist.) Calif. 1976, U.S. Dist. Ct. (ea., ctrl., no. dists.) Calif. 1991, U.S. Supreme Ct. 1991. Compliance specialist Cost of Living Coun. and Price Commn., Washington, 1972—73, dir. Oil Policy subcom., 1973; ptnr. Luce, Forward, Hamilton & Scripps, San Diego, 1976—87; owner McClellan Law Firm, San Diego, 1987—. Chmn. annual fundraising auction KPBS, 1984. Capt. USMC, 1969-72. Fellow Am. Coll. Trial Lawyers; mem. Inner Circle of Advs., Assn. Trial Lawyers Am., Am. Bd. Trial Advocates, Am. Inns of Ct. (master), Calif. State Bar Assn., San Diego County Bar Assn., Calif. Trial Lawyers Assn. (bd. govs. 1985-87), San Diego Trial Lawyers Assn. (bd. dirs. 1983-90), Nat. Forensics League, Phi Gamma Delta, Phi Alpha Delta. Presbyterian. Avocations: reading, running, tennis, chess, civic activities. Office: McClellan Law Firm 1144 State St San Diego CA 92101-3529 Office Phone: 619-231-0505. E-mail: craig@mcclellanlaw.com.

**MCCLELLAN, EDWIN,** literature educator; b. Kobe, Japan, Oct. 24, 1925; came to U.S., 1952; s. Andrew and Teru (Yokobori) McC.; m. Rachel Elizabeth Port, May 28, 1955; children: Andrew Lockwood, Sarah Rose. MA, U. St. Andrews, Scotland, 1952; PhD, U. Chgo., 1957. Instr. English, U. Chgo., 1957-59, asst. prof. Japanese lang. and lit., 1959-63, assoc. prof., 1963-65, prof., 1965-70, Carl Darling Buck prof., 1970-72, chmn. dept. Far Eastern langs. and civilizations, 1966-72; prof. Japanese lit. Yale U., New Haven, 1972-79, Sumitomo prof. Japanese studies, 1979-98, Sterling prof. Japanese lit., 1998-2000, Sterling prof. emeritus Japanese lit., 2000—, chmn. dept. East Asian langs. and lits. New Haven, 1973-82, 88-91, chmn. council humanities, 1975-77, chmn. council East Asian studies, 1979-82. Vis. lectr. Far Eastern langs. Harvard U., spring 1965; mem. adv. coun. Oriental studies Princeton U., 1966-71; mem. Com. to Visit East Asian Studies, Harvard U., 1982-88; mem. Am. adv. coun. Japan Found., 1985-95; mem. bd. Coun. for Internat. Exch. Scholars, 1981-84. Translator: Kokoro (Natsume Soseki), 1957, Grass on the Wayside (Soseki), 1969, A Dark Night's Passing (Naoya Shiga), 1976, Fragments of a Past (Eiji Yoshikawa), 1992; author: Two Japanese Novelists: Soseki and Toson, 1969, Woman in the Crested

Kimono, 1985; mem. bd. editors Jour. Japanese Studies, 1986-99; contbr. articles to profl. jours. Liason intelligence officer Royal Air Force, Washington, 1945-47; bd. trustees Society Japanese Studies U. Wash., 1992-99. With Royal Air Force, 1944—48. Recipient Kikuchi Kan prize for contbn. to study of Japanese lit., Tokyo, 1994, Noma Lit. Translation prize, 1995, Order of the Rising Sun, Gold Rays with Neck Ribbon, Japanese Govt., 1998, Dist. Contributions to Asian Studies award Assn. Asian Studies, 2005 Fellow Am. Acad. Arts and Scis. Home: 641 Ridge Rd Hamden CT 06517-2516

**MCCLELLAN, LARRY ALLEN,** minister, educator; b. Buffalo, Nov. 3, 1944; s. Edward Lurelle McClellan and Helen (Denison) Greenlee; m. Diane Eunice Bonfoey, Aug. 19, 1973; children: Kara E., Seth C. Student, U. Ghana, 1964-65; BA in Psychology, Occidental Coll., 1966; MTh, U. Chgo., 1969, D Ministry, 1970. Ordained to ministry Presbyn. Ch. (U.S.A.), 1970. Prof. of sociology and community studies Govs. State U., University Park, Ill., 1970-86; interim pastor Presbyn. Ch. (U.S.A.), Chgo. area, 1980-86; sr. pastor St. Paul Community Ch., Homewood, Ill., 1986-96; adj. prof. Govs. State U., University Park, Ill., 1987-96; dir. South Met. Regional Leadership Tr., Govs. State U., University Park, Ill., 1996—2001; cmty. rels. dir. Northeastern Ill. Planning Commn., 2001—05; pastor First Christian Ch. (Disciples), Chicago Heights, Ill., 2003—. Newspaper columnist Star Pubs. Chgo., 1993-2004; trustee Internat. Coun. Community Chs., 1989-91, pres., 1991-93. Author: Local History South of Chicago, 1988; developer social simulation games; contbr. articles to profl. publs. Mayor Village of Park Forest South (name now University Park), Ill., 1975-79; co-organizer S. Region Habitat for Humanity, Chgo. area, 1989; pres. S. Suburban Heritage Assn., Chgo. area, 1988-91. Fellow Layne Found., 1966-70, NEH, 1979. Mem. Am. Assn. State and Local History, Ill. State Hist. Soc. (Spl. Achievement award 1989). Office Phone: 708-754-3792. E-mail: larryamcclel@msn.com.

**MCCLELLAN, MARK B.,** former federal agency administrator; b. Austin, Tex., June 26, 1963; m. Stephanie McClellan; 2 children. BA, BS, U. Tex., Austin, 1985; MA, MPA, Harvard U., 1991, MD, 1992; PhD in economics, MIT, 1993. Resident in internal medicine Brigham and Women's Hosp., Boston; cons. The Rand Corp., Santa Monica, Calif., 1989—91; rsch. assoc. Harvard Med. Sch. Dept. of Health Care Policy, Boston, 1991—95; attending physician Stanford U. Health Services; assoc. prof. economics Stanford U., 1995—99; assoc. prof. medicine Stanford Med. Sch., dir. program on health outcomes rsch.; dep. asst. sec. for econ. policy US Dept. Treasury, Washington, 1998—99; mem. Coun. Econ. Advisors Exec. Office of the Pres., Washington, 2001—02; commr. FDA, Rockville, Md., 2002—04; adminstr. Centers for Medicare & Medicaid Services US Dept. Health & Human Services, Washington, 2004—06. Mem.: Inst. Medicine.*

**MCCLELLAN, MARY ANN,** pediatric nurse practitioner; b. Mar. 29, 1942; BS, Tex. Woman's U., 1964; MN, U. Wash., 1968-69; cert., U. Tex., Arlington, 1997. Cert. family life educator, CPNP, pediatric nurse practitioner; advanced RN practitioner, Okla. Charge nurse Baylor U. Med. Ctr., Dallas, 1964—65; pub. health staff nurse Dallas County Health Dept., Dallas, 1965—68; supervising nurse Okla. State Dept. Health, Oklahoma City, 1969—70, maternal-child health nurse cons., 1971; asst. prof. U. Okla. Coll. Nursing, Oklahoma City, 1971—72; from instr. to asst. prof. Harris Coll. Nursing Tex. Christian U., Ft. Worth, 1972—75; asst. prof. continuing edn. U. Okla. Coll. Nursing, Oklahoma City, 1976—79, asst. prof. baccalaureate program, 1979—96, mem. grad. faculty, 1991—. Cons. and lectr. in field. Contbr. chpts. to books, articles to profl. jours. Mem. Nat. Coun. on Family Rels., Okla. Family Resources Coalition, Nat. Assn. Pediatric Nurse Assocs. and Practitioners (Okla. chpt.), Assn. Faculty of Pediat. Nurse Practitioner Programs, So. Early Childhood Assn., Okla. Coun. on Family Rels., Okla. Early Childhood Assn., Sigma Theta Tau., Phi Kappa Phi. Office: U Okla Coll Nursing PO Box 26901 Oklahoma City OK 73126-0901

**MCCLELLAN, RICHARD AUGUSTUS,** retired small business owner; b. Gainesville, Fla., Sept. 13, 1930; s. Marion Theodore Sr. and Cornelia (Hampton) McC.; m. Thelma Watson, May 19, 1947 (dec. Mar. 1980); children: Richard A., Wayne Theodore, Viola Patricia, Michael Ray; m. Betty Lee Snow, Dec. 12, 1980 (div. July 1991); children: Claranell Y., Juanita F., Johnnie C.; m. Geraldine C. Williams, Aug. 14, 1993. Diploma, Nat. Inst. Drycleaning, 0075, Napoleon Hill Found., 1994. Drycleaner S & S Cleaners, Gainesville, 1958-97; ret., 1997. Mem. Am. Soc. Notaries (govt. rels. com. 1984, pub. rels. com. 1989), Notary Pub. Assn. State Fla., Nat. Notary Assn., Internat. Order St. Luke the Physician. Democrat. Mem. United Methodist Ch. Avocations: reading, radio, jazz music. Home and Office: 625 SE 15th St Gainesville FL 32641-3123

**MCCLELLAN, ROBERT EDWARD,** civil engineer; b. Atlanta, Feb. 27, 1922; s. Robert Edward and Maria Elizabeth (Ameln) McC.; m. Mary Margaret Billetter, Oct. 21, 1944; children: Kathleen Mary, Mary Elizabeth, Patricia Maura, Eileen Mary, Robert Edward III, Mary Margaret, Thomas Francis. BCE, U. So. Calif., 1947, MSCE, 1956, PhD in Engring., 1970. Registered profl. civil and structural engr., Calif. Gen. supt. design Rocketdyne, Canoga Park, Calif., 1959-62; mem. tech. staff The Aerospace Corp., El Segundo, Calif., 1962-69, mgr. strategic studies, 1980-85; chief tech. staff The Ralph M. Parsons Co., Pasadena, Calif., 1969-80; v.p. research and devel. Apollo Systems Tech., Canyon Country, Calif., 1985-88, also bd. dirs. Served to lt. (j.g.) USN, 1943-46, PTO. Recipient Outstanding Civil Engring. Grad. award U. So. Calif., 1977. Mem. AIAA, Am. Def. Preparedness Assn., AAAS, N.Y. Acad. Scis., L.A. Athletic Club, Sigma Xi, Tau Beta Pi, Chi Epsilon. Republican. Roman Catholic.

**MCCLELLAN, ROGER ORVILLE,** toxicologist; b. Tracy, Minn., Jan. 5, 1937; s. Orville and Gladys (Paulson) McC.; m. Kathleen May Dunagan, June 23, 1962; children: Eric John, Elizabeth Christine, Katherine Ruth. DVM with highest honors, Wash. State U., 1960; M of Mgmt., U. N.Mex., 1980; DSc (hon.), Ohio State U., 2005. Diplomate Am. Bd. Vet. Toxicology, Am. Bd. Toxicology. From biol. scientist to sr. scientist Gen. Electric Co., Richland, Wash., 1957-64; sr. scientist biology dept. Pacific N.W. Labs., Richland, Wash., 1965; scientist inst. rsch. dir. divsn. biology and medicine AEC, Washington, 1965-66; asst. dir. rsch., dir. fission product inhalation program Lovelace Found. Med. Edn. and Rsch., Albuquerque, 1966-73; v.p., dir. rsch. adminstrn., dir. Lovelace Inhalation Toxicology Rsch. Inst., Albuquerque, 1973-76, pres., dir., 1976-88; chmn. bd. dirs. Lovelace Biomed. and Environ. Rsch. Inst., Albuquerque, 1988-96; pres., CEO Chem. Industry Inst. Toxicology Rsch., Triangle Park, NC, 1988-99, pres. emeritus, 1999—; pvt. advisor Toxicology and Human Health Risk Analysis, 1999—. Mem. rsch. com. Health Effects Inst., 1981-92, mem. future techs. com., 2000—; bd. dirs. Toxicology Lab. Accreditation Bd., 1982-90, treas., 1984-90; adj. prof. Wash. State U., 1980-95, U. Ark., 1980-88; clin. assoc. U. N.Mex., 1971-85, adj. prof. toxicology, 1985—; adj. prof. toxicology and occupl. and environ. medicine Duke U., 1988—; adj. prof. toxicology U. N.C., Chapel Hill, 1989-2000; adj. prof. toxicology N.C. State U., 1991—; cons. faculty Colo. State U., 2002—; regents lectr. UCLA, 1999-2000; mem. dose assessment adv. group U.S. Dept. Energy, 1980-87, mem. health and environ. rsch. adv. com., 1984-85, 1999-2004; mem. exec. com. sci. adv. bd. EPA, 1974-95, mem. environ. health com., 1980-83, chmn., 1982-83, chmn. radionuclide emissions rev. com., 1984-85, chmn. Clean Air Sci. Adv. Com., 1987-92, Diesel Exhaust Panel, 1996-2001, chmn. rsch. strategies com., 1992-94, mem. Particulate Matter Panel, 1993-97, 99—; mem. com. on toxicology NAS-NRC, 1979-87, chmn., 1980-87; mem. com. risk assessment methodology for hazardous air pollution NAS-NRC, 1991-94, com. biol. effects of Radon NAS NRC, 1994-98, com. rsch. priorities for airborne particulate matter, 1998-2004; mem. Environ. Roundtable, Inst. Medicine, 1998-2002; mem. com. on environ. justice Inst. of Medicine, 1996-99, trustee toxicology excellence in risk assessment, 2000—, chmn. bd. trustees, 2002-04, mem. Bd. Vet. Toxicology 1970-73; mem. adv. coun. Ctr. for Risk Mgmt., Resources for the Future, 1987-2001; mem. Nat. Coun. for Radiation Protection 1970-2001, hon. mem., 2002—; bd. dirs. N.C. Assn. Biomed. Rsch., 1989-91, N.C. Vet. Med. Found., 1990-95, pres., 1993-94; bd. govs. Rsch. Triangle Inst., 1994-2001; mem. adv. com. alternative toxicol. methods Interagy. Ctr.

Evaluation Alternative Methods, Health and Human Svcs., 1998-2001; mem. sci. adv. bd. strategic environ. rsch. strategies program Dept. Def./Dept. Energy/EPA, 1997-99; mem. adv. com. Ctr. for Environ. Health, Agy. for Toxic Substances and Disease Registry, CDC, 2002-04, lunar dust toxicity panel NASA, 2005—; mem. bd. sci. counselors Ctr. for Environ. Health/Agy. for Toxic Substances Disease Registry, 2004—. Jour. Toxicology, 1984—89, assoc. dir., 1987—89; editor: Critical Revs. in Toxicology, 1987—; mem. edtl bd.: Regulatory Toxicology and Pharmacology, 1993—, Risk Analysis, 1998—, Ullman's Ency. of Indsl. Chemistry, 1999—, Non-Linearity in Biology-Toxicology-Medicine, 2003—; contbr. articles to profl. jours. Trustee Wash. State U. Found., 2001—; mem. bd. of vis. Wash. State Univ., Coll. and Sci., 2002—; mem. dean's adv. coun. Coll. Vet. Medicine Wash. State U., 2003—, chair dean's adv. coun., 2003—05. Recipient Herbert E. Stokinger award Am. Conf. Govtl. Indsl. Hygienists, 1985, Alumni Achievement award Wash. State U., 1987, Disting. Assoc. award Dept. Energy, 1987, 88, Arnold Lehman award Soc. Toxicology, 1992; co-recipient Frank R. Blood award Soc. Toxicology, 1989, Merit award Soc. Toxicology, 2005; Internat. Aerosol fellow Internat. Aerosol Rsch. Assembly, 1998; named Disting. Vet. Medicine Alumnus Wash. State U., 1999, Robert Leader Meml. lectr. Mich. State U., 1999; named to Hall of Fame Robert O. Anderson Schs. of Mgmt., U. N.Mex., 2002. Fellow: AAAS, Acad. Toxicol. Sci., Gesellschaft fur Zerosol Forschung, Health Physics Soc. (chmn. program com. 1972, Elda E. Anderson award 1974), Am. Acad. Vet. and Comparative Toxicology, Soc. Risk Analysis; mem.: Am. Vet. Med. Assn., Internat. Soc. Aerosols in Medicine (Thomas Mercer Joint prize for Aerosol Rsch. 1997), Am. Assn. Aerosol Rsch. (bd. dirs. 1982—94, treas. 1986—90, v.p. to pres. 1990—93), Toxicology Edn. Found. (founding pres. 1990—91), Internat. Congress Toxicology VII (treas. 1995), Soc.Toxicology (chmn. 1983—85, inhalation splty. sect. v.p. to pres. 1983—86, bd. publs. 1983—86, v.p.-elect to pres. 1987—90, Amb.mid-Atlantic chpt. 1995), Am. Conf. Govtl. Indsl. Hygienists, Internat. Regulatory Pharmacology and Toxicology (Internat. Achievement award 1999), Am. Assn. Cancer Rsch., Am. Thoracic Soc., Radiation Rsch. Soc. (chmn. fin. com. 1979—82, sec.-treas. 1982—84), Inst. Medicine (elected 1990, chair other health professions sect. 1999—2001), Am. Chem. Soc., Phi Zeta, Phi Kappa Phi, Sigma Xi. Republican. Lutheran. E-mail: roger.o.mcclellan@att.net.

**MCCLELLAN, SCOTT K.,** former White House press secretary; b. Austin, Tex., Feb. 14, 1968; s. Barr McClellan and Carole Keeton Strayhorn; m. Jill Martinez, Nov. 2003. BA, U. Tex., Austin, 1991. Campaign mgr. for Carole Keeton Strayhorn Tex. Comptroller, 1998; dep. comm. dir. to Gov. George W. Bush State of Tex., 1999—2000; traveling press sec. Bush-Cheney Presdl. Campaign, 2000; dep. press sec. The White House, Washington, DC, 2001—03, asst. to Pres., press sec., 2003—06. Republican.

**MC CLELLAN, WILLIAM MONSON,** retired library director; b. Groton, Mass., Jan. 7, 1934; s. James Lewis and Ruth Caldwell (Monson) McC.; m. Jane Muir, Sept. 3, 1955; children— Jennifer, Anne, Margaret, Amy. BA, Colo. Coll., 1956, MA, 1961; A.M. in L.S, U. Mich., Ann Arbor, 1959. Music librarian U. Colo., Boulder, 1959-65; dir. Music Library, U. Ill., Urbana, 1965-97. Cons. music library resources and services to colls. and univs.; co-dir. Inst. Music Librarianship, Kent State U., 1969 Editor: Music Library Assn. Notes, 1977-82; Contbr. articles to profl. jours. Council on Library Resources fellow, 1976-77 Mem. Internat. Assn. Music Librs., Music. Libr. Assn. (pres. 1971-73, conf. panelist, chmn. stats. subcom. 1990-93). Home: 1212 Raintree Dr Apt I175 Fort Collins CO 80526 Personal E-mail: muirmack@frii.com. *To commit myself daily to giving and opening myself to others in all professional and other contexts.*

**MCCLELLAND, CRAIG ALEXANDER,** architect, educator, business owner; b. Renton, Wash., Nov. 3, 1962; s. James Richard and Carol Anne (Hawkins) McC.; m. Kamilla Kuroda, June 25, 1989. BArch, U. Wash.; MArch, U. Ill. Lic. architect. Technician III, Wash. State Dept. Transportation, Seattle, 1985; project mgr. Van Horne and Van Horne, Seattle, 1986-87, Alexander Sasonoff, Seattle, 1989-91; arch. James and Scherer, Olympia, Wash., 1991-96; owner, arch. Alexander Archs., Olympia, 1996—2001, ow comml. project mgr.; residential project mgr.; lectr. instr. South Sound C.C., Olympia, 1998—. Comml. project mgr. Ambia, Olympia, 1997—. Amb. Olympia C. of C., 1997, Shelton C. of C., 1997. Mem. AIA. Avocations: mountain climbing, construction, reading, writing. Home and Office: 724 Columbia St NW Ste 400 Olympia WA 98501

**MCCLELLAND, HELEN,** music educator; b. Chgo., Dec. 5, 1951; d. Leon Leroy and Willie Jo (Darnell) McC.; (div. Sept. 1981); 1 child, Tasha Renee. Diploma in arts, Kennedy-King Coll., 1971; cert. in voice, Sherwood Music Coll., 1971-73; BS, Chgo. State U., 1975, MA in Adminstrn., 1983; D in Adminstrn. and Supervision, U. Calif., 1993. Tchr. Faulkner Sch., Chgo., 1975-78; tchr. music Harvey (Ill.) Pub. Sch. Dist. 152, 1978—. Dir. music Pleasant Green Missionary Bapt. Ch., Chgo., 1971—; mem. sch. bd. New World Christian Acad., Chgo. 1988—; bd. dirs. South Shore Drill Team, Chgo. Author: operetta So You Want to Be a Star, 1987. Cmty. worker People United to Save Humanity, Chgo., 1973, Harold Washington Orgn., Chgo., 1987; cmty. educator Chgo. Planned Parenthood, 1988; cmty. counselor Lincoln Cmty. Ctr., Chgo., 1975; mem. sch. bd. Dist. 160, 1994, now v.p.; mem. Ill. State Sch. Bd., 1997-98; bd. dirs. Operation P.U.S.H.; vice chmn. Ill. Assn. Sch. Bds., Ill. State Assn. Sch. Bd.; bd. dirs. Ill. State Assn. Sch. Bd., So. Cook Div., 2003-; v.p. Sch. Dist. #160;; mem. Grace M.B. Ch. Named Tchr. of the Yr., Faulkner Sch., 1976; recipient Nat. Sch. Bd. award for Disting. Svc., Ill. State Assn. Bd., 2003. Mem. Ill. Edn. Assn., NEA, Harvey Edn. Assn., Tennis Club, Traveling Club, Phi Delta Kappa, Pi Lambda Theta. Democrat. Baptist. Avocations: singing, bowling, piano. Home: 18029 Ravisloe Ter Country Club Hills IL 60478-5169

**MCCLELLAND, JAMES LLOYD,** psychologist, educator, cognitive neuroscientist; b. Cambridge, Mass., Dec. 1, 1948; s. Walter Moore and Frances (Shaffer) McClelland; m. Heidi Marsha Feldman, May 6, 1978; children: Mollie S., Heather Ann. BA in Psychology, Columbia U., 1970; PhD in Cognitive Psychology, U. Pa., 1975. Asst. prof. dept. psychology U. California, San Diego, 1974-80, assoc. prof., 1980-84, Carnegie-Mellon U., Pitts., 1984-85, prof. psychology, 1985—, prof. computer sci., 1987—, acting head psychology, 1989-90, co-dir. Ctr. for Neural Basis of Cognition, 1994—, univ. prof., 2001—, Walter Van Dyke Bingham chair in psychology and cognitive neurosci., 2002—. Adj. prof. neurosci. U. Pitts., 1995—; vis. scientist dept. psychology and Ctr. Cognitive Sci., MIT, 1982-84; vis. scholar dept. psychology Harvard U., 1982-84; rev. panel for cognition, emotion and personality NIMH, 1983-87, Cognitive Functional Neurosci., 1995—, chair 1997—; mem. Nat. Adv. Mental Health Coun., 2000-2003, Assoc. Neuroscience Rsch. Program. Author: (with others) Parallel Distributed Processing: Explorations in the Microstructure of Cognition, Vols. I, II, 1986; co-author: A Handbook of Models, Programs, and Exercises, 1988, Semantic Cognition: A Parallel-Distributed Processing Approach, 2004; contbr. numerous articles, reports, book chpts. to profl. publs.; sr. editor Cognitive Sci., 1988-91; sect. editor (Cognitive Neuroscience), Internat. Ency. of The Social and Behavioral Sciences; mem. numerous jour. edit. bds. Co-recipient Grawemeyer prize in psychology, 2002; recipient William W. Cumming prize, Columbia U., 1970, Rsch. Scientist Career Devel. award, NIMH, 1981—86, 1987—97; fellow, NSF, 1970—73; grantee, 1976—79, 1980-84, 1986—87, 1988—; Office Naval Rsch., 1982—87. Fellow: APA (Disting. Sci. Contbn. award 1996), AAAS, Am. Psychol. Soc. (William James Fellow award 2003—04); mem.: NAS, Soc. Exptl. Psychologists (Warren medal 1993), Internat. Assn. for Study Attention and Performance (lectr. 1986, governing bd. 1986—94), Psychonomics Soc., Cognitive Sci. Soc. (governing bd. 1988—93, chmn. 1991), Phi Beta Kappa. Office: Ctr Neural Basis of Cognition 115 Mellon Inst 4400 5th Ave Pittsburgh PA 15213-2617 E-mail: jlm@cnbc.cmu.edu.

**MCCLELLAND, PATRICIA G.,** minister; b. Warsaw, Mo., July 12, 1944; d. Gail Raymond and Martha Carolyn (Lewis) Easton; m. Lester E. McClelland, Aug. 18, 1974; 1 child, Melody. BS, U. Mo., 1968; MA, Drury Coll., 1972. Cert. tchr., Mo., Kans., U.; lic. counselor; ordained to ministry Unity Ch., 1986. Instr. U. Mo., Kansas City, 1968, 71-74, Park Coll.,

Parkville, Mo., 1968-70; spl. cons. Kansas City Pub. Schs., 1970-71; author edn. materials, 1975-78; instr. U. Wis., 1978-79; min. Milw., 1979-81; instr. Sem. Unity Sch. Christianity, 1983-85; co-min. Unity Ch. Pitts., 1985-86; sr. min. Unity Ch., Anderson, Ind., 1986-87; sr. minister Warren, Ohio, 1987-88, Massillon, Ohio, 1988-90; dir. housing Southwestern Coll., Winfield, Kans., 1990-91; min. specializing in ministry to women, cons., Lincoln, Nebr., 1991-93; co-min. Lindenwood Union Ch., Rockford, Ill., 1993—. Founding min. Council Bluffs Unity Ch.; tchr. pub. schs., Rochelle, Ill., 1994—2000; instr. Rockford (Ill.) Coll.; tchr., facilitator Skylight grad. program Rock Valley Coll., Janesville, Wis., 2001—03; tchr. Belvidere Pub. Schs., 2002—, St. Xavier U., 2002—. Mem. NAFE, ASCD, TESOL, Nat. Assn. Self-Employed, Internat. New Thought Alliance, Internat. Platform Assn. Methodist/Unity. Home and Office: 7399 Bermuda Dr Rockford IL 61108-4486 E-mail: revpatmcc@yahoo.com. *Our inheritance as Children of God is a world where everything necessary is available for every human being to live a happy, healthy, peaceful, abundant life. The choice to do so, as well as the work to fulfill that choice, is up to us both individually and collectively.*

**MCCLELLAND, RICHARD LEE,** dentist; b. Pitts., May 18, 1927; s. William Noble and Pauline Elizabeth (Lee) McC.; m. Elizabeth Anne Michon, Dec. 6, 1958; children: Richard Scott, William Alfred, Robert Craig. BA, Princeton U., 1950; DDS, U. Pa., 1954. Pvt. practice, Princeton, NJ, 1958-92. Clin. instr. U. Pa. Dental Sch., Phila., 1958-62; mem. exec. com. Med. Ctr. Princeton, 1971-72, past chmn. dental dept.; elected Nat. Dental Surgeon Res. Officers Assn. of U.S., 1972-73. With USN, 1945-46, WWII, lt. Dental Corps, USNR, 1954-57, capt., ret. Fellow: Acad. Gen. Dentistry, Internat. Coll. Dentists, Am. Coll. Dentists; mem.: ADA, Fedn. Dentaire Internat., Princeton Officers' Soc., Res. Officers Assn., Princeton Club (N.Y.C.), Princeton Nassau Club, Rotary (pres. Princeton 1978—79). Republican, Episcopalian. Avocations: sailing, photography. Home. 2606 Emmy Lane Charlotte NC 28226-3853

**MC CLELLAND, ROBERT NELSON,** surgeon, educator; b. Gilmer, Tex., Nov. 20, 1929; s. Robert Hilton and Verna Louise (Nelson) McC.; m. Connie Logan, May 5, 1958; children: Robert Christopher, Alison, Julie. BA, U. Tex., Austin, 1952; MD, U. Tex., Galveston, 1954. Diplomate Am. Bd. Surgery. Rotating intern U. Kans. Med. center, 1954-55; resident in gen. surgery Parkland Hosp., Dallas, 1957-59, 60-62; instr. surgery Southwestern Med. Sch., U. Tex., Dallas, 1962-63, asst. prof., 1963-67, asso. prof., 1967-71, prof., 1971—, Alvin Baldwin prof. surgery, 1977—. Examiner Nat. Bd. Med. Examiners Editor Audio Jour. Rev. Gen. Surgery, 1971-82, Selected Readings in Gen. Surgery, 1974—; contbr. numerous articles to profl. jours., chpts. to books. Served to capt. M.C. USAF, 1955-57. Fellow ACS (mem. grad. edn. com.); mem. AMA, Am. Surg. Assn., Western Surg. Assn., Soc. Surgery of Alimentary Tract, Am. Gastroent. Assn., Southwestern Surg. Soc., So. Surg. Assn., Dallas Soc. Gen. Surgery (pres. 1987-88), Tex. Surg. Soc., Tex. Med. Assn., Dallas Country Med. Soc., Soc. Internatale de Chirurgie (bd. dirs. Am. chpt.), Phi Beta Kappa, Alpha Omega Alpha. Republican. Methodist. Home: 3601 Potomac Ave Dallas TX 75205-2110 Office: 5323 Harry Hines Blvd Dallas TX 75390-7208

**MCCLELLAND, SHEARWOOD JUNIOR,** orthopaedic surgeon; s. Shearwood and Zenobia McClelland; m. Yvonne Shirley Thornton, 1974; children: Shearwood III, Kimberly. AB, Princeton U., 1969; MD, Columbia U., 1974, MPH, 1996. Diplomate Am. Bd. Orthopaedic Surgery. Intern St. Luke's Hosp., N.Y.C., 1974—75; resident St. Luke's Hosp., 1975—76; asst. resident in orthop. surgery N.Y. Orthop. Hosp., 1976—79; lt. comdr. USNR, 1979—82; staff orthop. surgeon Nat. Naval Med. Ctr., Bethesda, Md., 1979—82; asst. prof. surgery Uniformed Svcs. U. Health Scis., 1980—82; acting chief orthop. surgery Harlem Hosp. Ctr., 1983—84, assoc. dir. orthop. surgery, 1985—92, acting dir., 1992—94, dir., 1994—; asst. prof. clin. orthop. surgery Columbia U., 1983—94, assoc. prof. clinic, 1994—. Oral examiner Am. Bd. Othopaedic Surgery, 1993—; mem. N.Y. State Bd. of Profl. Med. Conduct, 1989-98. Annie C. Kane fellow in orthopaedic surgery, 1978-79; fellow in total joint implant surgery Ohio State U., 1982. Recipient Alumni Fedn. medal, Columbia U., 2005; fellow, Nat. Assn. Pub. Hosps., 2005. Fellow ACS, AMA, Am. Acad. Orthop. Surgeons, N.Y. Acad. Medicine, Nat. Assn. Pub. Hosps.; mem. Assn. Mil. Surgeons U.S., Am. Coll. Phys. Execs., N.Y. Orthop. Hosp. Alumni Assn., Mensa, No. N.J. Princeton Alumni Assn., Columbia P&S Alumni Assoc. (pres. 2002-04, Alumni Fedn. medal 2005) Office: Harlem Hosp Ctr Dept Orthopaedic Surgery 506 Lenox Ave New York NY 10037-1802 Office Phone: 212-939-3510. E-mail: sjm2@columbia.edu.

**MCCLELLAND, W. CARTER,** bank executive; BS in Aero. Engring., Stanford U., 1967, MBA, 1973. Engr. NASA-Jet Propulsion Lab., Calif.; various positions including dir. corp. fin. Morgan Stanley, chief administrv. officer, mem. oper. com., 1993—95; pres., CEO Deutsche Bank N.Am., 1995—98, also bd. dirs.; sr. mng. dir., co-dir. investment banking Nations-Banc Montgomery Securities LLC (now Banc of Am. Securities LLC), San Francisco, 1998—; head banking and equities Banc of Am. Securities LLC, 2001—, pres., 2001—; mng. dir. Bank of Am. Corp., market pres. NY, 2003—. Bd. dirs. United Way N.Y., Nat. Coun. on Econ. Edn., NYC2012. Office: Bank Am Securities LLC 9 W 57th St New York NY 10019

**MCCLENAHAN, JOHN LORIMER,** retired radiologist; b. Assiut, Egypt, Apr. 25, 1915; arrived in U.S., 1927; s. Robert Stewart and Janet Wallace McClenahan; m. Mary Tyler Cheek (dec. Jan. 16, 2005); children: John Spencer, Susan Starrett Stockdale. BA, Yale U., 1937; MD, U. Pa., 1941. Diplomate Am. Bd. Radiology. Intern Pa. Hosp., Phila., 1941—42; ward officer Walter Reed Gen. Hosp., 1942—43; rschr. in physiology Trudeau Sanatorium, NY, 1946—47; ship surgeon The Grace Line, NY, 1947; residen in radiology N.Y. Hosp.-Cornell Med. Ctr., N.Y.C., 1950—55; asst. attending radiologist N.Y. Hosp., N.Y.C., 1952—55; asst. in radiology Presbyn. Hosp., Phila., 1956—57; vis. radiologist Hosp. of U. Pa., 1957—68; clin. assoc. prof. radiology Thomas Jefferson Hosp., 1968—79, ret. 1979. Author: Radiology As an Art, 1968, On Going a Journey, 2002. 1st lt. MC, AUS, 1942—45. Recipient Cert. of Merit, Am. Roentgen Ray Soc., 1955. Mem.: Med. Soc. Va., Coll. Physicians. Phila. (Disting. Svc. medal). Democrat. Episcopalian. Avocation: writing. Home: 413 Stuart Cir Richmond VA 23220

**MCCLENDON, AUBREY K.,** energy executive; m. Kathleen Byrns. Graduate, Trinity Coll. Duke Univ., 1981. Independent producer of oil & gas, 1982—89; co-founder, chmn., CEO Chesapeake Energy Corp., Okla. City, 1989—. Mem. bd. vis. Fuqua Sch. Bus., Duke Univ., Fuqua Sch. Bus. Duke Univ. Named one of Forbes' Richest Americans, 2006. Office: Chesapeake Energy Corp PO Box 18496 Oklahoma City OK 73154-0496

**MCCLENDON, FRED VERNON,** real estate professional, consultant, equity and realty appraiser, financial consultant; b. Vernon, Tex. s. Guy C. and Lexie M. (Johnson) Mc C.; m. Dorothy J. Seibert, June 1943 (div. 1953); children: Cathy, Kent, Tracy; m. Ethel R. Cherry, Sept. 15, 1959; children: Tess, Rob, J.T. Assoc. in Commerce, Hannibal La Grange Coll., 1947; BBA, Baylor U., 1949; MBA, Harvard U., 1951, postgrad. in law, 1951; postgrad. in banking, Colo. U., 1951—52; postgrad., Denver U., 1951—52. Lic. ins. agt., Tenn.; cert. real estate broker, Tenn.; cert. internat. financier. Asst. cashier U.S. Nat. Bank, Denver, 1951; gen. mgr. Nat. Paper Band Co., Denver, 1952—53; mgr. ins. Houston Fire & Casualty Co., Ft. Worth, 1954—56; mgr. gen. sales City Lincoln/Mercury, Dallas, 1957—58; owner INS-Bank Pers. Agy., Dallas, 1959—61; mng. prtnr. Allen & Mc Clendon Ins., Dallas, 1959—63; owner, broker Mc Clendon Real Estate, Dallas, 1959—63; pres. Mc Clendon Realty Co., Hampton, Tenn., 1961—2001; gen. mgr. Eagle Nest Ranch, Roan Mountain, Tenn., 1963—88, Mile High Ranch, Roan Mountain, 1988—99; pres. FMV Appraisal Co., Hampton, 1988—99, Amerifund Ventures, Internat., Tex., 2000—. Cons. Gen. Adjustments Bur., 1981—, Debourdieux Corp., 1985—, Wachesaw Corp., 1985—, Hidden Lakes Devel. Corp., various ins. cos. and law firms in U.S. and Can., IRS, U.S. Marshals Svc., U.S. Customs, 1993—, Heartland Presbyn. Chur., 1985—. El Dorado Ranch, 1991-98; lectr. to lodges and assns.; gen. ptnr. Flexnet Investments, Ltd., Dallas, 1988-91; pres. Bus. Realty Internat. Cons., Hillsboro, Tex., 2000—; exec. v.p. OmniVue, Inc., S.C., 1992-95; chmn. AmeriFund Ventures,

Internat., Tex., 1995-99, Tex., 2000—; pres. U.S. Med-Am. Bus. Svcs., 1995—. Contbr. articles to profl. jours. Recipient W.T. Grant fellow Harvard U., 1950-51. Mem. Am. Quarter Horse Assn. (life), Australian Appaloosa Assn., Appaloosa Horse Club U.S., Tenn. Walking Horse Breeders Assn., Am. Paint Horse Assn., Am. Soc. Equine Appraisers, Am. Horse Coun., Am. Soc. Appraisers (Accredited sr. appraiser, bd. examiners 1990—), Internat. Real Estate Inst., Nat. Assn. Real Estate Appraisers, Environ. Assessment Assoc. (cert. insp. 1991—), Appraisers Assn. Am. (cert. sr. appraiser), Internat. Soc. Financiers (cert. internat. financier). Republican. Mem. Seventh Day Adventists. Avocations: boating, travel, fishing, swimming. Home: Eagle Nest West Ranch 1580 Hwy 77 N Hillsboro TX 76645 Office: Amerifund Ventures Internat PO 1209 Hillsboro TX 76645-1209 Office Phone: 254-632-4441. E-mail: fredmcclendon@hillsboro.net.

**MCCLENDON, IRVIN LEE, SR.,** business owner, editor; b. Waco, Tex., June 12, 1945; s. Irvin Nicholas and Evelyn Lucile (Maycumber) McC.; divorced; children: Michael Boyd, Irvin Lee Jr., Laura Ann, Paul Nicholas, Richard Lester. Student, El Camino Coll., 1961-63, U. So. Calif., 1962-66; BA in Math., Calif. State U., Fullerton, 1970, postgrad. in bus. administrn., 1971-76; cert. nat. security mgmt., Indsl. Coll. Armed Forces, 1974; postgrad. in religion, Summit Sch. Theology, 1982-84; student, Fullerton Coll., 1998, 2004-. Engring. lab. asst. Rockwell Internat. Corp., Anaheim, Calif., 1967-68, test data analyst, 1968-70, mem. tech. staff, 1970-82; sys. programmer A-Auto-trol Tech. Corp., Denver, 1982-84; sr. tech. writer, editor Colo. Data Systems, Inc., Englewood, Colo., 1986-87; engring. writer III CalComp subs. Lockheed Co., Hudson, NH, 1987; sr. tech. writer CDI Corp., Arvada, Colo., 1987-88; staff cons. CAP GEMINI AM., Englewood, 1989; sr. tech./instrnl. writer & editor TTS Inc., Aurora, Colo., 1990-96, sr. multimedia developer, 1996-97; gen. mgr., chief editor The Berkeley Group, LLC, Denver, 1997-99; writer Am. Resume Ctr., Northglenn, Colo., 1997-98; info. processing technician County of Orange, Health Care Agy., Santa Ana, Calif., 1998—2002; vol. The David Bohnett Cyber Ctr., The Ctr. Orange County, Garden Grove, Calif., 2002—04; copy editor The Orange County and Long Beach Blade, Laguna Beach, Calif., 2003—04; owner, gen. mgr., writer, editor, proofreader, tutor McClendon Profl. Svcs., Garden Grove, Calif., 2004—; tutor Fullerton Coll. Disability Support Svcs., 2004. Sec. governing bd. Yorba Linda Libr. Dist., 1973-78; mem. First United Meth. Ch. of Orange, 1998—; mem. Men Alive, The Orange County Gay Men's Chorus, 2004—; trustee Ch. of God (Seventh Day), Bloomington, Calif., 1979-81, treas., 1980-81, mem. Calif. State U. and Coll. Statewide Alumni Coun., 1976-77; 2d v.p. Orange County chpt. Calif. Spl. Dists. Assn., 1976, pres., 1977; mem. Adams County Rep. Ctrl. Com., 1984-90, Denver County Rep. Ctrl. Com., 1992-95; mem. Scouting for All, Petaluma, Calif. 1998—, vol., copy editor, 1998—, asst. southwestern regional dir.; grassroots organizer, Garden Grove (Calif.) Alliance for Human Rights, 2003—; tech. support adviser to chmn. Colo. Rep. Com., 1997-98, mem. Soulforce Orange County, 2004—; vol. Orange County chpt. Parents, Families and Friends of Lesbians and Gays, 1988-; sec., bd. dirs The Friendly Ctr., Inc., 2005-. With USAFR, 1967-71 USAF Nat. Merit scholar, 1963-67. Mem. Calif. Assn. Libr. Trustees and Commrs. (exec. bd., So. Calif. rep. 1976-78), Nat. Eagle Scout Assn. (life), Bible Sabbath Assn. (life), Calif. State U.-Fullerton Alumni Assn. (dir. 1975-77). Republican. Office Phone: 714-554-2195. Personal E-mail: leeinGG2@yahoo.com. Business E-Mail: McClendonSr@scoutingforall.org.

**MCCLENDON, MICHELE ROSALIND,** literature educator; BS in English Edn., Ind. U. Pa., 1970; M in Edn. Reading Specialist, Duquesne U., 1992. Cert. Elem. Edn. Duquesne U., Pa., 1994, Reading Supervision Edn. Duquesne U., Pa., 2005. Reading tchr. Hill Ho. Assn. Pitts. in Partnership with Parents, 1990—92, 1990—92, addnl. coord., 1992, 1992; reading specialist Pitts. Pub. Sch., 1992—95, 1992—95; English tchr. Pitts. Pub. Sch., Langley HS, 1995—2001; secondary literacy coach Pitts. Pub. Sch., Allderdice HS, Langley HS, 2001—05; secondary literacy coach, testing coord. Pitts. Pub. Sch., Allderdice HS, 2005—. Reading com. mem. Pa. Dept. Edn., Harrisburg; summer seminar participation profl. devel. Pitts. Health Career Initiative, 1997—2001; rep. Pitts. Tchrs. Inst., 1999—98; tech. team Langley HS Pitts. Pub. Sch., 1998—2001; cons. Partners Edn. Consortium, 1999. Mem.: ASCD (assoc.), Nat. Coun. Tchrs.English (assoc.), Internat. Reading Assn. (assoc.). Avocations: piano, cooking. Office: Pitts Public Sch Allderdice HS 2409 Shady Ave Pittsburgh PA 15219

**MC CLENDON, WILLIAM HUTCHINSON, III,** retired lawyer; b. New Orleans, La, Feb. 19, 1933; s. William H. and Eleanor (Eaton) McC.; m. Eugenia Mills Slaughter, Feb. 6, 1960; children: William Hutchinson, IV, Virginia Morris, Eleanor Eaton, Bryan Slaughter. BA, Tulane U., 1956, LLB, 1958. Bar: La. 1958, US Supreme Ct. 1964. Atty. Humble Oil & Refining Co., 1958-60; with firm Taylor, Porter, Brooks & Phillips, Baton Rouge, 1960—, ptnr., 1966-2001, mem. exec. com., 1987-2001; mediator, assoc. Mediation Arbitration Profl. Sys., Inc., 1999—2001. Instr. comml. law and negotiable instruments Am. Inst. Banking, 1963-74; lectr. movable Property La. Bar Assn. Bridging the Gap Inst., 1965; lectr. La. State U. LAw Sch. and Real Estate Seminar chmn., 1972, 74, 76, 80, 82, 85, 87, 95, La. Soc. of Profl. Surveying, 1989, La. Soc. CPA's, 1991, Banking Seminar, 1995; adj. prof. La. State U. Legal Negotiation, 1983-2003, U. Tenn., 2003-, Western Carolina U., 2003-; mem. faculty Profl. Edn. Group, Inc. Contbr. articles to legal jour. Bd. dir. Cancer Soc. Baton Rouge, 1968-71; trustee Episcopal HS, 1976-78; mem. Dean's council Tulane U. Law Sch., 1984-88. Served to capt. AUS. Recipient Preservation award Found. for Hist. La., 1997. Mem. ABA, Am. Judicature Soc., La. Bar Assn. (chmn. sect. trust estates, probate and immovable property law 1969-70, Meml. award article 1987), Baton Rouge Bar Assn. (chmn. title standards com. 1968-69), Tulane Alumni Assn. Greater Baton Rouge (pres. 1968-69), Baton Rouge Green (bd. dir. 1991-93), Hilltop Aboretum (bd. dir. 1993-95), La. Civil Svc. League (pres. 1992-94), La. Tulane Law Alumni (treas., 2d v.p. 1964-65), Baton Rouge Assembly (treas. 1983, ball chmn. 1997, chmn. 1999), Toastmasters (pres. 1970) Baton Rouge Country Club, Camelot Club, Pickwick Club, Rotary (bd. dir. Baton Rouge club 1972), Kappa Alpha, Baton Rouge Symphony (bd. dir. 2001-02). Republican. Episcopalian (vestry, sr. warden 1975, 81, 84, diocesan standing com. 1985-89). E-mail: wh.mcclendon@verizon.net.

**MCCLENNEN, MIRIAM J.,** former state official; b. Seattle, Sept. 16, 1923; d. Phillip and Frieda (Golub) Jacobs; m. Louis McClennen, Apr. 25, 1969; stepchildren: Adams Peter, James C.A., Helen, Persis, Crane, Emery. BA, U. Wash., 1945; MBA, Northwestern U., 1947. Exec. trainee Marshall Field & Co., Chgo., 1945-47; buyer Frederick & Nelson (subs. of Marshall Field), 1949-57, Goldwaters, Phoenix, 1963—67; administrv. asst. to pres. Ariz. State Senate, Phoenix, 1973-76; dir. publs. Office of Sec. of State, Phoenix, 1976-87. Chairwoman legis. subcom. administrv. procedure Ariz. State Legislature, Phoenix, 1984-85. Original compiler, codifier, editor publ. Ariz. Adminstrv. Code, 1973-87, Ariz. Adminstrv. Register, 1976-87. Bd. dirs., mem. Phoenix Art Mus. League, 1972—90; bd. dirs., mem. exec. bd. Phoenix Symphony Guild, 1969—88; bd. dirs., sec. Combined Met. Phoenix Arts and Scis., 1974—90, mem. adv. bd., 1990—95; bd. dirs. Phoenix Art Coun., 1973—78, Master Apprentice Programs, 1980—83; bd. dirs., mem. exec. bd. Heard Mus., 1982—88, 1990—; mem. adv. bd. Ariz. State Hist. Records, 1987—90, Ariz. Commn. on Arts, 1989—96, Phoenix Art Mus., 1966—; bd. dirs. Arizonans for Cultural Devel., 1996—2002; mem. Cape Mus. Fine Arts, 1996—. Recipient Disting. Svc. award Atty. Gen. Ariz., 1987, Outstanding Svc. to People, Ariz. State Senate, 1987, Nat. Assn. Secs. of State award, 1987. Mem.: Univ. Club, Ariz. Club, Phoenix Country Club, Charter 100 (bd. dirs. 1981—85). Personal E-mail: mjmlm@earthlink.net.

**MC CLENNEY, BYRON NELSON,** community college administrator; b. San Antonio, Dec. 14, 1939; s. Thomas B. and Lorene Holley McC.; children: Mark Nelson, Don Alan; m. Kay McCullough, May 17, 1986. BS, U. Tex., 1961, MEd, 1963, EdD, 1969. Asst. dean evening divsn. San Antonio Coll., 1966-68; dean instrn. McLennan C.C., Waco, Tex., 1968-70, Eastfield Coll. Dallas County, Tex., 1970-71, pres., 1971-78, Parkersburg (W.Va.) C.C., 1978-81, San Antonio C.C. Dist., 1981; chancellor Alamo C.C. Dist., 1982-86; pres. C.C. Denver, 1986-2000, Kingsborough C.C., 2000—. Author: Management for Productivity, 1980. Mem. steering com. Pres. Clinton's Am.

Reads Challenge, 1997-2000. Recipient PBS O'Banion prize, 2002; NDEA fellow, 1965-66; recipient Disting. Alumni award U. Tex. Coll. Edn., 1982-83, Thomas J. Peters Nat. Leadership award League for Innovation, 1989. Mem. Am. Assn. Cmty. and Jr. Colls. (chmn. pres.'s acad. 1983-84, mem. urban comm. 1987-90), Commn. on Instns. of Higher Edn. Clubs: Rotary (past dist. gov.). Presbyterian. Office: 2001 Oriental Blvd Brooklyn NY 11235

**MCCLENNY, PATSY See FAIRCHILD, MORGAN**

**MCCLENON, JOHN RAYMOND,** retired chemistry professor; b. Grinnell, Iowa, May 1, 1937; s. Raymond Benedict and Erika (Weber) McC.; m. Mary Alice Thornton, June 7, 1959; children: Anne Jeanette, Marca Kay, Maureen. BA, Grinnell Coll., 1959; PhD, UCLA, 1964. Asst. prof. chemistry Sweet Briar (Va.) Coll., 1965-72, assoc. prof., 1972-76, prof., 1976-82, Charles A. Dana prof., 1982—2002. Head FBN Microcomputing, Lynchburg, Va., 1980—, Johnny McClenon Big Band, Lynchburg, Va., 1978—Editor: (newsletter) Macintosh User's Group, Sweet Briar Coll. Chmn. ACLU local chpt., 1966-75; prin. clarinettist Lynchburg Symphony, Va., 1976—. Mem. AAUP (chmn. Sweet Briar chpt. 1982-83) Democrat. Unitarian Universalist. Home: 712 Riverside Dr Lynchburg VA 24503-1327 E-mail: mcclenon@cstone.net.

**MCCLIMON, TIMOTHY JOHN,** lawyer; b. Clinton, Iowa, July 17, 1953; s. Leonard James and Celeste Margaret (Borman) McC.; m. Suzanne Berman, Jan. 30, 1994. BA magna cum laude, Luther Coll., 1975; MS, St. Cloud State U., 1976; JD, Georgetown U., 1986. Bar: N.Y. 1987. Asst. dir. student activities St. Cloud State U., Minn., 1975-76; performing arts coordinator Western Ill. U., Macomb, 1976-79; program specialist Nat. Endowment for the Arts, Washington, 1979-82, program administr., 1982-86, law clk., 1985-86; assoc. Webster and Sheffield, N.Y.C., 1986-88; v.p. AT&T Found., 1988-96, exec. dir., 1996—2003, Second Stage Theatre, 2003—06; pres. Am. Express Found., N.Y., 2006—. Adj. prof. NYU, 1990—; bd. dirs. Second Stage Theatre, N.Y.C., BBB Found., N.Y.C., Times Square Alliance, N.Y.C., Field Papers, Inc., N.Y.C.; spkr. confs. on arts mgmt., fundraising and nonprofit mgmt., 1979—; cons. NEA, Washington, 1986—; mem. mayor's cultural affairs adv. commn. City of N.Y.C., 1992-94. Author: (textbook chpt.) Audiences and the Arts, 1981; contbr. articles to Jour. of Law and the Arts, 1986, other publs., 1989—. Recipient Eagle Scout award Boy Scouts Am., 1967, Faculty award Blue Key Nat. Honor Frat., 1979. Mem. N.Y.C. Bar Assn. (com. mem. 1987-92), ABA (com. mem. 1986-88), N.Y. State Bar Assn., Vol. Lawyers for the Arts. Avocations: photography, bicycling, travel, reading. Home: 222 Riverside Dr Apt 14A New York NY 10025-6809 Office: American Express 200 Vesey St New York NY 10284 Personal E-mail: mcclimon1@verizon.net. Business E-Mail: timothy.j.mcclimon@aexp.com.

**MCCLINTIC, JAMES A.,** lab administrator; BS in Mktg., Calif. State U., San Diego. From sales rep to v.p., mktg. & planning to v.p., sales Bristol Myers Squibb; pres. SciCor Inc.; regional pres., eastern opers. Corning MetPath, Teterboro, NJ; pres., CEO Esoterix Inc., Austin, Tex., 1999—. Office: Esoterix Inc 4509 Freidrich Ln Bldg 1 Ste 100 Austin TX 78744

**MCCLINTOCK, DONALD WILLIAM, III,** lawyer; b. Sapporo, Japan, Feb. 10, 1954; came to U.S., 1956; s. Donald William McClintock and Kazuko (Uchida) Inman; m. Barbara Joan Cleary, Aug. 9, 1980; children: Kime, Daniel. AB, Stanford U., 1976; JD, Harvard U., 1980. Bar: Calif. 1980, Alaska 1981, U.S. Dist. Ct. Alaska 1982, U.S. Ct. Appeals (9th cir.) 1987, U.S. Supreme Ct. 1988. Law clk. to justice Alaska Supreme Ct., Anchorage, 1980-81; asst. atty. gen. Alaska State Dept. Law, Anchorage, 1981-83; pres. Ashburn & Mason, Anchorage, 1983—. Bd. dirs. Family Resource Ctr. Anchorage, 1984-88, Alaska Youth and Parent Found., 1984-90; bd. dirs. Anchorage Cmty. Mental Health Assocs., 1994—, pres., 1996-98. Recipient Pro Bono award, Robert E. Hickerson, 2006. Mem.Alaska Bar Assn. Office: Ashburn & Mason 1130 W 6th Ave Anchorage AK 99501-5914 Office Phone: 907-276-4331. E-mail: dwm@anchorlaw.com.

**MCCLINTOCK, JESSICA,** fashion designer; b. Frenchville, Maine, June 19, 1930; d. Rene Gagnon and Verna Hedrich; m. Frank Staples (dec. 1964); 1 child Scott. BA, San Jose State U. 1963. Elem. sch. tchr., Marblehead, Mass., 1966-68, Long Island, N.Y., 1968, Sunnyvale, Calif., 1964-65, 68-69; fashion designer Jessica McClintock, Inc., San Francisco, 1969—. Active donor, AIDS and Homeless programs; scholarship sponsor Fashion Inst. Design and Merchandising. Recipient Merit award Design, 1989, Dallas Fashion award, 1988, Tommy award, 1986, Pres. Appreciation award, 1986, Best Interior Store Design, 1986, Calif. Designer award, 1985, Karma award, 1981, numerous others. Mem. Coun. Fashion Designers of Am., Fashion Inst. Design & Merchandising (adv. bd. 1979—), San Francisco Fashion Industry (pres. 1976-78, bd. dirs. 1989). Office: Jessica McClintock Inc 1400 16th St San Francisco CA 94103-5181*

**MCCLINTOCK, MARTHA K.,** biologist, educator; AB, Wellesley College, 1969; MA in Psychology, U. Penn., 1972, PhD in Psychology, 1974. With U. Chgo., 1976—, asst. prof., psychology and human devel., 1976, David Lee Shillinglaw Distinguished Svc. Prof. Psychology, dir., Inst. Mind & Biology; co-dir. Ctr. Interdisciplinary Health Disparities Rsch. Chmn. biopsychology com., 1986—99; mem. neurobiology com., evolutionary biology com., human develop. com. Contbr. articles to profl. jours. Recipient Disting. Sci. Award for Early Career Contbn. to Psychology, APA, 1982, MERIT Award, NIMH, 1992, Edith Krieger Wolf Disting. Vis. Prof., Northwestern Univ., 2000, Henry G. Walter Sense of Smell Award, Sense of Smell Inst., 2001. elected mem., Inst. of Medicine, 1999, Acad. of Arts and Sciences, 1999. Office: U Chgo 5730 S Woodlawn Ave Chicago IL 60637

**MCCLINTOCK, RICHARD POLSON,** dermatologist; b. Lancaster, N.H., Dec. 16, 1933; s. Richard P. and Dorothy Grace McClintock; m. Barbara Wyatt, June 1959 (div. Mar. 1970); children: Peter, Pamela; m. Mary Joy Fitzgerald, Mar. 21, 1970; children: Wayne, Patrick. BA, Dartmouth Coll., 1956; MD, Harvard U., 1960. Diplomate Am. Bd. Dermatology, Am. Bd. Dermatopathology. Intern in medicine U. N.C., Chapel Hill, 1960-61; resident in dermatology Stanford U., Palo Alto, Calif., 1964-67; pvt. practice Ukiah, Calif., 1967—; clin. instr. dermatology Stanford U., Palo Alto, 1967-78, clin. asst. prof., 1978-86, assoc. clin. prof., 1986-92, lectr., 1992-98, assoc. clin. prof., 1998—. Mem. hosp. staff Ukiah Valley Med. Ctr., chief of staff, 1974; bd. dirs. IPA and Found. Med. Care Mendocino and Lake Counties. Contbr. articles to profl. jours. Trustee Found. for Med. Care for Mendocino and Lake Counties, 1990-94, pres., 1992-94. Lt. Med. Corps, USN, 1961-64. Mem. San Francisco Dermatol. Soc. (Practitioner of Yr. 2004), Pacific Dermatol. Assn., Am. Acad. Dermatology, Calif. Med. Soc., Mendocino Lake County Med. Soc., Internat. Soc. Dermatology. Home: 723 S Dora St Ukiah CA 95482-5335 E-mail: fitzmac@pacific.net.

**MCCLINTOCK, WILLIAM THOMAS,** health care administrator; b. Pittsfield, Mass., Oct. 23, 1934; s. Ernest William and Helen Elizabeth (Clum) M.; m. Wendolyn Hope Eckerman, June 22, 1963; children: Anne Elizabeth, Carol Jean, Thomas Daniel. BA, St. Lawrence U., Canton, NY, 1956; MBA, U. Chgo., 1959, MHA, 1962. Prodn. planner Corning (NY) Glass, 1959-60; adminstrv. asst. Univ. Hosps. of Cleve., 1962-65; asst. adminstr. Presbyn. Hosp., Whittier, Calif., 1965-68; regional asst. Kaiser Found. Hosps., Oakland, 1968-70; assoc. dir., exec. dir. Conn. Hosp. Planning Commn., New Haven, 1970-75; project dir., lectr. sch. health studies U. N.H., Durham, 1975-77; regional mgr. Tex. Reg. Found., Austin, 1977-81; administr. Schick Shadel Hosp., Ft. Worth, 1981-87; mgmt. cons. George S. May Internat. Co., Park Ridge, Ill., 1987-88; mgr. Nat. Ctr. Rsch. Programs Am. Heart Assn., Dallas, 1988-89; administr. Ambulatory Svcs. Health Care of Tex., Ft. Worth, 1990-92; CEO Boundary Cmty. Hosp., Bonners Ferry, Idaho, 1992-2000; healthcare cons., 2000—02; exec. dir. Oceanview Convalescent Ctr., Long Beach, Wash., 2002—06, Gilroy Healthcare and Rehab. Ctr., Calif., 2006—. 1st lt. U.S. Army, 1957. Fellow Am. Coll. Health Care Execs. (life, Sr.-Level

Healthcare Exec. Regent's award 2000); mem. Am. Hosp. Assn. (life), Am. Heart Assn. (bd. dirs. Idaho/Mont. affiliate 1993-95), Idaho Hosp. Assn. (bd. dirs. 1995-2000, sec.-treas. 1998, chmn.-elect 1998, chmn. bd. dirs. 1999, Recognition of Retirement award 2000), Masons (Unity Lodge No. 9). Avocations: book collections, gardening, photography, fly fishing. Address: County Rd 62C PO Box 1226 Bonners Ferry ID 83805 Office Phone: 408-842-9311. E-mail: wtmcclintock@charter.net.

**MCCLINTON, DAVID ANTHONY,** performing company executive; s. Tyrone McClinton and Delores Marlene Rosebrook. BA, U. Denver, 1988. Data analyst Internat. Bus. Svc./Source One Mgmt., Lakewood/Denver, 1984—89; actor Denver Theatre & Media, 1991—; photographer, publicist Denver Theatre Venues, 1997—, dir., 1997—, playwright, 1997—; spl. places ops. supr. U.S. Census Bur., Denver, 1999—2000; artistic dir. Temple Events Ctr., Denver, 2001—, Brooks Ctr. Arts, Denver, 2006—. Founder, artistic dir. Temple Theatre Co., Denver, 2001—, Temple Arts Cmty., Denver, 2001, Temple Theatre Project, Denver, 2001, N.Y.C. Stage West Theatre Prodns., Denver, 2004—, Brooks Ctr. Arts' Play Showcase Festival, Denver, 2006. Author: (plays) Sybil's Others, 1998, (screenplays) Weirding Ways, 1998, (plays) Sisters in Blood, 2004, poetry. Named Semi Finalist Playwright, Moondance Internat. Film Festival, 2002, Quarter Finalist Screenwriter, The Writer's Network, 2003, 2004. Avocations: sailing, tennis, bicycling, hiking, dance. Office: Brooks Ctr Arts 1400 Williams St Denver CO 80210 Office Phone: 303-322-7738. E-mail: agogus1@yahoo.com.

**MCCLINTON, DONALD GEORGE,** retired diversified holding company executive; b. Pitts., June 30, 1933; s. Donald K. and Ethel M. McC.; m. Jane Ann Knoebel, Apr. 12, 1958; children: Catherine, D. Scott. BS, Miami U., Oxford, Ohio, 1955. Audit mgr. Arthur Andersen & Co., Cleve., 1955-62; mgr. accounting E. Ohio Gas Co., Cleve., 1962-66; exec. v.p. Nat. Industries, Inc., Louisville, 1966-79; pres. Yellow Cab Co., Louisville, 1979-94; owner, chmn. bd. Interlock Industries, Inc., 1982-94; pres. Skylight Thoroughbred Tng. Ctr., Inc., 1994—2002. Bd. dirs. Almost Framily, Clifton Ctr., MidAm. Bancorp, 1980—2002; trustee Jewish Hosp. Health Care Systems, Inc., 1983—2004, 2006—. mem. Louisville-Jefferson County Bicentennial Commn., 1976-77; mem. coun., treas. Old Kentucky Home. coun. Boy Scouts Am., 1976-94; mem. Citizens at Large Jefferson County Budget Com., 1978-84; bd. overseers Bellarmine Coll., 1978-84; bd. dirs. Ky. Derby Festival, 1978—, Jewish Hosp., Louisville, 1978-83; trustee Spalding U., 1985-91. Mem.; Fin. Execs. Inst. E-mail: dmcclinton@insight.bb.com.

**MCCLINTON, JAMES LEROY,** city administrator; b. Longview, Wash., Oct. 14, 1949; s. James Delmer and Norma Jean (Ammons) McC.; m. Carmen Lassaphine Amador, Nov. 7, 1983; children: James Andrew, Ian Tyler, Kevin Riley. AA, SUNY, Albany, 1973; BA, Upper Iowa U., 1974; MA, Calif. State U., Carson, 1984; PhD, Calif. Coast U., 1985. Cert. mgr. Inst. Cert. Profl. Mgrs. With USCG, 1967-83, commd. officer, 1981-83, advanced through grades to comdr., 1987, ret., 1989; bur. mgr. adminstrv. svcs. Charleston (S.C.) County Sheriff's Office, 1989—2003; chief dep. clk. of ct. Berkeley County, SC, 2003—. Spkr. pro tem S.C. Criminal Justice Acad., Columbia, 1989—; mem. auditor selection com. Charleston County Govt., 1989—; computer users action com., 1989—; mem. various coms. County Govt. and Sheriff's Office, Charleston, 1989—; chief dep. clerk of ct. Berkeley County, S.C., 2003-. Editor: (newsletter) The Badge, 1989—; author: Pawprints in Heaven, —; contbr. articles to profl. jours. and mags.; newspaper columnist. Mem. Charleston Police Pipes and Drums, 1994—; grad. Leadership S.C. 1993, Leadership Charleston, 1997. Recipient Achievement award Nat. Assn. Counties, Washington, 1993, 96, Golden Pen award The Post and Courier Newspaper, Charleston, 1996. Mem. ASPA, S.C. Law Enforcement Officers Assn., Rotary Internat. (bd. dirs. North Charleston), Nat. Assn. Count Mgrs. Republican. Avocations: bagpipes, writing. Office Phone: 843-719-4508. Personal E-mail: ag4nm@comcast.net. Business E-Mail: jmcclinton@co.berkeley.sc.us.

**MCCLISTER, MICHAEL,** writer; b. Bristol, Va., July 9, 1941; s. Cecil McClister and Pauline McNeil; divorced; children: Porter, Jennifer. BA, U. N.C., Chapel Hill, 1962; MA, Rutgers U., New Brunswick, N.J., 1963. Author: Campaign Manual Series -- Democratic National Committee, 1976, Grassroots Campaigning -- National Education Association, 1981, Victim's Choice, 1999, Double Deal, 2000. Home: PO Box 3279 Placida FL 33946-3279 Office Phone: 941-716-0273. Home Fax: 941-697-1868. Personal E-mail: mcclister123@comcast.net.

**MCCLOSKEY, DEIRDRE NANSEN,** economics and history educator; b. Ann Arbor, Mich., Sept. 11, 1942; s. Robert Green and Helen (Stueland) McC.; m. J. Comi, June 19, 1965 (div. 1995); children: Daniel Robert, Margaret Anne. BA, Harvard U., 1964, PhD, 1970. Mem. faculty U. Chgo., 1968-80, assoc. prof. econs., 1973-80, assoc. prof. history, 1979-80; prof. econs. and history U. Iowa, Iowa City, 1980-99; Disting. Prof. Econs., History and English U. Ill., Chgo., 1999—. Vis. prof. Erasmus U. Rotterdam, Stanford U., Australian Nat. U., U. York, U. Manchester, U. London. Author: Economic Maturity and Entrepreneurial Decline, 1973, Enterprise and Trade in Victorian Britain, 1981, The Applied Theory of Price, 1986, The Rhetoric of Economics, 1986, If You're So Smart, 1990, Knowledge and Persuasion in Economics, 1994, The Vices of Economists, 1996, Crossing: A Memoir, 1999, How to Be Human Though an Economist, 2001; editor: Jour. Econ. History, 1980-85. Fellow Guggenheim, 1983, Inst. for Advanced Study-Princeton, N.J., 1983-84 Mem. Am. Econ. History Assn. (pres. 1996-97), Social Sci. History Assn. (pres.), Midwest Econ. Assn. (pres. 1992), Ea. Econ. Assn. (pres. 2003). Home: 720 S Dearborn St Apt 206 Chicago IL 60605-1820 Office: Dept Economics U Ill 601 S Morgan 210UH M/C 144 Chicago IL 60607 Office Phone: 312-996-3913. Office Fax: 312-996-3344. E-mail: deirdre2@uic.edu.*

**MCCLOSKEY, J(OHN) MICHAEL,** retired environmental services administrator; b. Eugene, Oreg., Apr. 26, 1934; s. John Clement and Agnes Margaret (Studer) McC.; m. Maxine Mugg Johnson, June 17, 1965 (dec. 2006); stepchildren: Claire, Laura, James, Rosemary Johnson. BA, Harvard U., 1956; JD, U. Oreg., 1961. N.W. rep. Sierra Club, Eugene, 1961-65, asst. to pres. San Francisco, 1965-66, conservation dir., 1966-69, exec. dir., 1969-85, chmn. Washington, 1985-99, acting exec. dir., 1986-87; vice-chmn. Commn. on Environ. Law and Policy (Internat. Union for Conservation of Nature), Gland, Switzerland, 1978-88; mem. Pres.'s Commn. on Agenda for 1980's, Washington, 1979-80; co-chmn. OSHA-Environ. Conf., Washington, 1983-87; vice chmn. Am. Com. on Internat. Conservation, 1988-90; mem. Internat. Union Conservation of Nature World Commn. Protected Areas, 1988—; ret.; with urban forestry commn. City of Portland, 2005—. Mem. adj. faculty Sch. Natural Resources, U. Mich., 1988—2000; chmn. Mineral Policy Ctr., 1998-2001, Nat. Resources Coun. of Am., 1992-93; co-chmn. environ. policy task force Pres.'s Coun. Sustainable Devel., 1997-99; pres. Fedn. of Western Outdoor Clubs, 2000-03. Contbr. articles to profl. jours. Bd. dirs. Nat. Resources Coun. Am., 1988-94, vice chmn., 1989-91, chmn., 1992-93, chmn. Advocacy Forum, 1989-91; bd. dirs. Ind. Sector, 1990-96, Mineral Policy Ctr., 1988-2001, Coalition for Environmentally Responsible Economies, 1989-99, OMB Watch, 1998-2004; bd. trustees Sierra Club Found., 2000—; mem. steering com. Blueprint for Environ., 1987-88; nominated candidate Oreg. Ho. of Reps., 1962. Recipient award Calif. Conservation Coun., 1969, John Muir award Sierra Club, 1979, UN Environ. Program Global 500 award, 1992, Lifetime Achievement award Wild Found., 1998, Honor award Natural Resources Coun. Am., 1999, Packard award Internat. Union for Conservation of Nature Parks Commn., 2003, Conservation award Fedn. of Western Outdoor Clubs, 2004, Lifetime Achievement award Pub. Land Law Conf., 2006. Mem. Univ. Club (Portland, Oreg.), Explorers Club (N.Y.C.). Democrat. Office Phone: 503-245-9338. Personal E-mail: jmmccloskey@aol.com.

**MCCLOSKEY, KATHY ANN,** psychologist; b. Brookville, Ohio, Jan. 31, 1958; s. James W. McCloskey and Mary Ann Surrel; m. Catherine A. Marchal, July 17, 1994; 1 child, Sydney. BS in Psychology, Wright State U., 1983, MA in Human Factors, 1986; PhD, Exptl. Psychology, San Rafael,

Calif., 1991; D in Psychology, Wright State U., 1998. Lic. psychologist, Ohio, Ind. Civilian rsch. scientist USAF, Ohio, 1984-94; clin. psychologist Wright State U., Dayton, Ohio, 1998—. Co-author: Innovations in Clinical Practice, 1999; contbr. articles to profl. jours. Clin. dir. Preventing Abuse Home, Dayton; rsch. scientist Montgomery County Domestic Violence Rsch. Group, Dayton; adviser Montgomery County Criminal Justice Coun., Dayton, Montgomery County Batterers'. Treatment Domestic Violence Task Force, Dayton. Recipient Psychol. Dimensions Peacework award Psychologists Social Responsibility, 1998. Mem. APA, AAAS, Human Factors and Ergonomics Soc. (char test and evaluation tech. group 1993). Democrat. Avocations: reading, alternative health care approaches, computers, bike riding. Office: Wright State U Sch Profl Psychology 9 N Edwin C Moses Blvd Dayton OH 45407-2837 Fax: 937-775-4323.

**MCCLOSKEY, MICHAEL,** social sciences educator; AB with honors, U. Scranton, Pa., 1965; MA, Loyola U., Chgo., 1969, PhD, 1974; MDiv, Cath. Theol. Union Chgo., 1987. Asst. prof. Benedictine U., Lisle, Ill., 1970—74; prof. Harry S. Truman City Coll., Chgo., 1974—. Recipient Grad. medal, Loyola U. Chgo., 1970, Centennial medallion, 1970; Arthur J. Schmitt scholar, Schmitt Found., 1969—70. Mem.: Religious Rsch. Assn. (mng. editor 1972—78), Assn. for Sociology Religion, Am. Sociol. Assn. Office: Harry S Truman City College 1145 W Wilson Ave Chicago IL 60640-6063

**MCCLOUD, MELODY THERESA,** obstetrician-gynecologist, surgeon; BA, Boston U., 1977, MD, 1981. Intern Emory U. Affiliated Hosps., Atlanta, 1981-82, resident in ob-gyn., 1982-85; pres., founder, CEO Atlanta Women's Health Care, 1985—. Bd. dirs. Vis. Nurses Health Sys., Atlanta; med. cons. Greeley Co., Wis., 1994—; spkr. Nat. Dental Assn.-Atlanta Bus. League, 1995, Women-On-Tour Conf., Nat. Coalition 100 Black Women, Congl. Black Caucus-Women, others; cons. health WXIA-TV, Atlanta, 1995, 99. Author: Medical Bloopers!! Amusing, Amazing Stories, 1994, The Health Diary for Women, 1999, Blessed Health, 2003, Melodies of the Heart, 2004; med. advisor Body and Soul, 1994; health columnist: Women Looking Ahead, 1995—. Med. support group Com. Olympic Games, Atlanta, 1996; chair selection com. YWCA Acad., Atlanta, 1999 Inductee Leadership Atlanta, 1992, YWCA Acad. for Women Achievers, 1992; named Bus. Woman of Yr. Am. Bus. Women's Assn., 1994, Atlanta's Top 100 Black Women of Influence Atlanta Bus. League, 2003; recipient Cmty. Health Svc. award Black Pages. Mem. Med. Assn. Ga., Ga. Ob-Gyn Soc., Med. Assn. Atlanta, Atlanta Med. Assn., Soc. Laparoendoscopic Surgeons. Baptist. Avocations: tennis, bowling, water sports, theater, travel. Office: Melody T McCloud MD PO Box 344 Roswell GA 30077-0344 Office Phone: 770-921-6038. E-mail: mtm@drmccloud.com.

**MCCLOUD, SAMUEL ALFRED,** lawyer; b. Chgo., Feb. 24, 1943; s. Walter Hall and Jeraldine Mae McCloud; children: Eric, Daniel, Christina, Amber, Samantha, Cassondra, Cheyenne, Rockel, Travis, Johnna. JD, Wm. Mitchell Coll. Law, 1977. Pvt. practice, Shakopee, Minn. With USAF, 1962—66. Mem.: Nat. Assn. Criminal Def. Lawyers. Office: PO Box 216 Shakopee MN 55379 Office Phone: 952-445-8805.

**MCCLOY, ELIZABETH K.,** lawyer; b. 1959; BA, Dartmouth Coll., 1981, JD, Northwestern U., 1984. Bar: Ill. 1984. With Sidley Austin Brown & Wood, Chgo., 1984—, ptnr., 1993—. Office: Sidley Austin Brown and Wood Bank One Plz 10 S Dearborn St Chicago IL 60603

**MCCLUGGAGE, KERRY,** film and television executive; Studied broadcasting and film, U. So. Calif., 1976; MBA, Harvard U., 1978. With MCA/Universal, 1979—90; chmn. Paramount TV Group, Viacom, 1991—2002; founder, independent prodr., CEO Craftsman Films, 2002—; acquired with Jeff Sagansky, also co-chmn. Ardustry Home Entertainment, Woodland Hills, Calif., 2005—. Co-founder UPN Network, 1995. Supervised and developed programs such as: The A-Team, Coach, Deadwood, The Equalizer, Frasier, JAG, Northern Exposure, Law & Order, Miami Vice, Murder She Wrote, Quantum Leap and a few Star Trek Series. Address: Ardustry Home Entertainment 21250 Califa St Ste 102 Woodland Hills CA 91367

**MCCLUNG, A(LEXANDER) KEITH, JR.,** retired lawyer; b. Gallipolis, Ohio, Sept. 13, 1931; s. Alexander Keith and Florence (Juhling) McC.; m. Sandra B. Foley, Aug. 17, 1957; children: Alexander Keith III, Martha E. AB, W.Va. U., 1956; JD, Harvard U., 1959. Bar: W.Va. 1959, Md. 1970, Mich. 1972. Assoc. Jackson, Kelly, Holt & O'Farrell, Charleston, W.Va., 1959-69; assoc. counsel Comml. Credit Corp., Balt., 1969-70; v.p.; counsel McCullagh Leasing, Inc., Roseville, Mich., 1970-73, Comml. Credit Corp., Balt., 1973-82, gen. atty., 1982-85; sr. gen. atty. Comml. Credit Co., Balt., 1985-89, sr. v.p., gen. counsel, 1989-98. Bd. dirs. Travelers Bank; trustee Roland Park Found.; mem. adv. coun. Coll. Arts and Sci., W.Va. U. Capt. USAR. Mem. ABA (subcom. uniform comml. code, com. equipment leasing), Soc. Colonial Wars in the State of Md., St. George Soc. Md. Democrat. Home: 13 Devon Hill Rd Baltimore MD 21210-1044 E-mail: campussandy@aol.com.

**MCCLUNG, GWENDOLYN,** soil microbiologist; b. Takoma Park, Md., Sept. 5, 1956; d. Lowell Neal and Margaret May (Whaley) McC.; m. Guy Alan Athey; children: John Carl, Elaine Ashley Athey. BS in Agronomy, U. Md., 1977, MS in Soil Microbiology, 1981; PhD in Soil Microbiology, U. Calif., Riverside, 1986. Student lab. technician dept. agronomy U. Md., College Park, 1974-77, faculty rsch. asst., 1977-81; grad. rsch. and tchg. asst. dept. soil and environ. scis. U. Calif., Riverside, 1981-86; postdoctoral fellow dept. agronomy Ohio State U., Wooster, 1987-88; postdoctoral fellow Belts Agrl. Rsch. Ctr., USDA, Beltsville, Md., 1988-90; microbiologist, ecol. hazard assessor, risk assessor of genetically engineered microorganisms U.S. EPA, Washington, 1990—. Guest lectr. U. Md., College Park, 1991, 95. Contbr. articles to profl. jours. Pres. postdoctoral fellow Ohio State U., Wooster, 1986-87, Kinney postdoctoral fellow Beltsville Agrl. Rsch. Ctr., USDA, 1988-90. Mem. Am. Soc. Microbiology, Am. Soc. Agronomy, Soil Sci. Soc. Am. Achievements include research on plants and soil science and microbiology. Office: US EPA 1200 Pennsylvania Ave NW Washington DC 20460-0002 Office Phone: 202-564-8911. E-mail: mcclung.gwendolyn@epa.gov.

**MCCLUNG, HUGO JUHLING,** pediatrician, educator; b. Gallipolis, Ohio, Feb. 27, 1941; s. A. Keith and Florence E. (Juhling) McC.; m. Helen K. Peters, Aug. 22, 1964; children: William J., Andrew P., Matthew A. BA, W. Va. U., 1963, MD, 1967. Diplomate Am. Bd. Pediatrics in Gen. Pediatrics, Pediatric Gastroenterology. Intern, then resident U. Wis.; rsch. fellow Hosp. for Sick Children, Toronto, Ont., Canada, 1972—74; chief pediatric gastroenterology Ohio State U., Columbus, Ohio, 1974—; assoc. med. dir. Columbus Children's Hosp., 1985—2000; prof. pediatrics Ohio State U., Columbus, 1992—. Med. dir. Children's Homecare Svcs., 1992—. Elder Presbyn. Ch., Blacklick, Ohio. Maj. US Army, 1969-72. Mem. Am. Gastroenterology Assn., N. Am. Soc. Pediat. Gastroenterology and Nutrition, Pediat. Acad. Assn. (pres. 1992-99). Avocation: genealogy. Home: 6470 Havens Rd Blacklick OH 43004-9671 Office: Columbus Children's Hosp 700 Childrens Dr Columbus OH 43205-2664 Office Phone: 614-722-3450.

**MCCLUNG, KENNETH AUSTIN, JR.,** training executive, performance consultant; b. Decatur, Ga., Apr. 11, 1947; s. Kenneth Austin Sr. and Marianne (Conklin) McC.; m. Christina June Palensar, Mar. 21, 1975. BA, North Ga. Coll., 1969; MS, EdD, U. So. Calif., 1976. Commd. 2d lt. U.S. Army, 1969, advanced through grades to maj., 1980; col. USAR; sr. ptnr. Instrl. Design Group, Inc., Morristown, N.J., 1981-99; v.p., nat. learning dir. Jack Morton Worldwide, 1999-2000, nat. learning dir., 2000—02; ptnr. McClung, McClung & Assoc., Hertford, NC, 2002—. Bd. dirs. Nat. Productivity Ctr., Boulder, Colo., Price Waterhouse Learning Bd.; author/mgr. over 150 mgmt., sales, and tech. tng. programs; cons. in field. Author: Microcomputers for Medical Professionals, 1984, Microcomputers for Legal Professionals, 1984, Microcomputers for Investment Professionals, 1984, Microcomputers for Insurance Professionals, 1984, Personal Computers for Executives, 1984,

French edit. 1985; co-author: Sales Training Handbook, 1989. Mem. ASTD, Internat. Soc. for Performance Improvement (pres. N.J. chpt. 1986-88, N.E. regional cons. 1989-90, nat. nomination chmn. 1990-91, nat. emerging tech. chmn. 1991-92). Avocations: sailing, tennis, bicycling, running, skiing. Home: 128 Back Creek Dr Hertford NC 27944 Office: McClung McClung & Assoc 128 Back Creek Dr Hertford NC 27944

**MCCLUNG, SAMUEL BRENTON,** music educator, consultant; b. Parkersburg, W.Va., Feb. 2, 1954; s. Asa Maples (Stepfather) and Dorothy Faith Reece; life ptnr. Margarita Maria Vera; m. Julie Ann Illingworth, Aug. 16, 1975 (div. Oct. 2, 2002); children: Catherine Faith McClung - Smith, Leta Marie Mcclung. MusB, Stetson U., 1976; MusM, Mich. State Univ., 1979, PhD, 1981. Cert. tchr. Am. Orff-Schulwerk Assn., MN, 1998. Instr. Mich. State U., East Lansing, Mich., 1980—81; music dir. Dade County Pub. Schs., Miami, Fla., 1982—84, Cedar Grove HS, Atlanta, 1984—85; music specialist Gwinnett County Pub. Schs., Norcross, Ga., 1985—. Cons. Ga. State Univ., Atlanta, 1999—. Composer: (songs) God With Us. Fellow: AOSA (life; pres. 1994—96, Hon. Six). Liberal. Roman Catholic. Avocations: squash, reading, swimming, folk instr.'s, poetry. Home: 3501 Grovewood Lane Duluth GA 30096 Personal E-mail: levelbor@bellsouth.net.

**MCCLURE, A. GLENN,** education educator, department chairman; b. Norristown, Pa., Aug. 10, 1939; EdD, Nova Southeastern U., Ft. Laudedale, Fla., 2002. Edn. dept. chair Valley Forge Christian Coll., Phoenixville, Pa., 1997—. Office: Valley Forge Christian Coll 1401 Charlestown Rd Phoenixville PA 19460 Office Phone: 610-917-1453. E-mail: agmcclure@vfcc.edu.

**MCCLURE, BROOKS,** management consultant; b. NYC, Mar. 8, 1919; s. Walter Harsha and Angelica (Mendoza) McClure; m. Olga Beatrice Gallik, Oct. 15, 1949; 1 child, Karen (dec.). AB summa cum laude, U. Md.; disting. grad., U.S. Naval War Coll. N.Y. corr. Western Press Ltd., Australia, 1939-42; copy editor Washington Eve. Star, 1946-51; joined State Dept. Fgn. Service, 1951; information officer, attache embassy Copenhagen, 1951-53; press attache embassy Vienna, 1953-55; information officer, attache embassy Cairo, 1956—57, Seoul, 1957-60, Bonn, 1960-63; policy officer Europe USIA, 1963-66; pub. affairs officer 1st sec. embassy, Copenhagen, 1967-72; spl. asst. policy plans and nat. security council affairs, internat. security affairs Dept. Def., 1972-76; internat. security adviser USIA, 1976-77; program coordinator Crisis Assessment Staff, Dept. Commerce, 1977-78; dir. ops. Internat. Mgmt. Analysis and Resources Corp., 1978-81, v.p., 1982—; sec. Cross-Continent Assocs. Ltd., 1994-99. Various spl. assignments Europe, Mid. East, Asia, Africa; detailed to Vietnam, 1967, 70; mem. working group Cabinet Com. to Combat Terrorism, 1973—77; lectr. FBI Acad., Fgn. Svc. Inst., Inter-Am. Def. Coll., Army War Coll., Navy War Coll., NJ Police Acad., NY State Police Acad. Contbg. author: book Modern Guerrilla Warfare, 1962, International Terrorism in Contemporary World, 1978, Corporate Vulnerability and How to Assess it: Political Terrorism and Business, 1979, Business and the Middle East, 1981, Political Terrorism and Energy, 1981; author (treatise) Dynamics of Terrorism, 1977; contbr. articles to profl. jours.; author: report to Senate Judiciary Com. on internat. terrorism and hostage def. measures; testifier on internat. security, hostage behavior, def. of Alaskan pipeline, FBI charter U.S. Senate, 1975—79. With AUS, 1942—46, ETO. Recipient Presdl. medal, Slovak Republic, 2002. Mem.: DACOR, Nat. Press Club, Assn. Diplomatic Studies, Am. Fgn. Svc. Assn., Alpha Sigma Lambda, Phi Kappa Phi. Home: 6204 Rockhurst Rd Bethesda MD 20817-1756 Office: IMAR Corp PO Box 34528 Bethesda MD 20827-0528 E-mail: imarmgtsvcs@mindspring.com, b-kmcclure@mindspring.com.

**MCCLURE, CALEB J.,** associate principal; b. Muleshoe, Tex., Dec. 18, 1960; s. Carl Herman and Helen Joyce McClure; m. Kimberly Kay McClure, July 15, 2000; 1 child, Xander Cole. BBA in Fin., Tex. Tech. U., 1984, MEd, 1997. Cert. tchr. prin. Tex. Tchr., basketball coach Olton (Tex.) Ind. Sch. Dist., 1986—90, Lubbock (Tex.)-Cooper Ind. Sch. Dist., 1990—98, Whitharral (Tex.) Ind. Sch. Dist., 1998—99, Lubbock H.S., 1999—2000; tchr. Randall H.S., Amarillo, Tex., 2000—02, asst. prin. curriculum and instrn., 2004—05, assoc. prin., 2005—. Named Educator of Yr., Lubbock-Cooper HS, 1994; recipient Excellence in Edn. award, 1998, Tchr. Excellence award, Randall HS, 2001. Mem.: Tex. Assn. Secondary Sch. Prin. (Region 16 Asst. Prin. of Yr. 2005—06). Baptist. Home: 6210 Bowie Amarillo TX 79118 Office: Randall HS 5800 Attebury Amarillo TX 79118

**MCCLURE, CHARLES G.,** automotive executive; BS in Mech. Engring., Cornell U.; MBA, U. Mich. Heavy truck sales engr., product engr. Ford Motor Co.; v.p., gen. mgr. automotive sys. groups for the Ams. Johnson Controls, Inc., pres.; Detroit Diesel Corp., 1997—2003, CEO, 1999—2003; CEO, pres. Federal-Mogul Corp., 2003—04; chmn., pres., CEO ArvinMeritor Inc., Troy, Mich., 2004—. Mem. Bus. Roundtable; bd. dir. NAM, R.L. Polk and Co., Intermet Corp., Motor & Equip. Mfr. Assn. Bd. dir. Detroit Renaissance, Detroit Regional C. of C., Horizons Upward Bound; mem. exec. com. A World in Motion. Lt. (j.g.) USN, 1975—79. Office: ArvinMeritor Inc 2135 W Maple Rd Troy MI 48084*

**MCCLURE, DANIEL M.,** lawyer; b. Enid, Okla., Feb. 5, 1952; s. Larry M. and Marie Dolores (Sarver) McC.; m. Judy Lynn Pinson, Jan. 3, 1976; children: Andrew Mead, Mark William, Kathleen Claire. BA with highest hons., U. Okla., 1974; JD cum laude, Harvard U., 1978. Bar: Tex. 1978, U.S. Dist. Ct. (so. dist., ea. dist.) Tex. 1979, U.S. Ct. Appeals (5th cir., 10th cir., 11th cir.) 1981, U.S. Supreme Ct., 2003. Assoc. Fulbright & Jaworski, LLP, Houston, 1978-86, ptnr., 1986—. Fellow Tex. Bar Found.; mem. ABA, Nat. Health Lawyers Assn., Nat. Assn. R.R. Trial Counsel, Tex. Bar Assn., Houston Bar Assn. (cert. civil trial law), Am. Inns of Ct., Harvard Law Sch. Assn. Avocation: tennis. Home: 2 Long Timbers Ln Houston TX 77024-5445 Office: Fulbright & Jaworski LLP 1301 McKinney St Houston TX 77010-3031 Office Phone: 713-651-5151. E-mail: dmcclure@fulbright.com.

**MCCLURE, DONALD STUART,** physical chemist, educator; b. Yonkers, N.Y., Aug. 27, 1920; s. Robert Hirt and Helen (Campbell) McC.; m. Laura Lee Thompson, July 9, 1949; children: Edward, Katherine, Kevin. BChem, U. Minn., 1942; PhD, U. Calif., Berkeley, 1948. With war rsch. divsn. Columbia U., 1942-46; mem. faculty U. Calif., Berkeley, 1948-55; group leader, mem. profl. staff RCA Labs., 1955-62; prof. chemistry U. Chgo., 1962-67, Princeton (N.J.) U., 1967-91, prof. emeritus, 1991—, vis. lectr. various univs.; cons. to govt. and industry. Author: Electronic Spectra of Molecules and Ions in Crystals, 1959; co-author: Some Aspects of Crystal Field Theory, 1964; also articles. Guggenheim fellow Oxford (Eng.) U., 1972-73; Humboldt fellow, 1980; recipient Irving Langmuir prize, 1979 Fellow Am. Acad. Arts and Scis., Nat. Acad. Scis., Am. Phys. Soc.; mem. Am. Chem. Soc. Home: 23 Hemlock Cir Princeton NJ 08540-5405 Office Phone: 609-258-4980. E-mail: d.s.mcclure@att.net, dmcclure@princeton.edu.

**MCCLURE, FREDERICK DONALD,** lawyer; b. Ft. Worth, Feb. 2, 1954; s. Foster Donald and Mayme Nell (Barnett) McClure; m. Harriet Elizabeth Jackson, Dec. 17, 1977; children: Lauren Elizabeth, Frederick Donald. BS in Agrl. Economics, summa cum laude, Tex. A&M U., 1976; JD, Baylor U., 1981. Bar: Tex., 1981, DC, US Dist. Ct. So. Dist. Tex., 1982, US Ct. Appeals 5th Cir., 1982. Agrl. asst. to US Senator John Tower, Washington, 1977-79, legis. dir., 1983; assoc. Reynolds, Allen & Cook, Houston, 1981-83; assoc. dep. atty. gen. US Dept. Justice, Washington, 1984-85; spl. asst. for legis. affairs to Pres. Ronald Reagan, Washington, 1985-86; v.p. govt. affairs Tex. Air. Corp. 1986—89; asst. for legis. affairs to Pres. George H.W. Bush, Washington, 1989-92; mng. dir. First S.W. Co., Dallas, 1992-94, Pub. Strategies, Inc., 1995—2001; mng. shareholder Winstead Sechrest & Minick, Washington, 2001—04; ptnr., pub. law & policy strategies group Sonnenschein Nath & Rosenthal LLP, Washington, 2004—. Mem. State of Tex. Inaugural Com., 1994, Bush-Cheney Transition Com., 2001; mem. transition com. Gov. Rick Perry, Tex.; mem. Energy Adv. Bd.; bd. dirs. Alex Lee, Inc. Mem. bd. visitors US Naval Acad., 1992-95, chmn., 1994; bd regents Tex A&M U. Sys., 1995-2001. Named a Tex. A&M Disting. Alumni, Assn. Former Students & Tex. A&M U., 1991; named Disting. Alumnus,

Baylor U., 1991; named one of Am.'s 50 most promising leaders age 40 and under, Time mag., 1994; recipient Jimmy Williams Disting. Svc. Award, Dallas A&M Club, 2002. Mem. State Bar Tex., Former Students Assn. of Tex. A&M (v.p. 1985-89, 93-95), Future Farmers Am. (nat. sec. 1973-74), Tex. Future Farmers Am. (state pres. 1972-73), Cotton Bowl Athletic Assn. (chmn. 1998—2002), Phi Alpha Delta, Phi Kappa Phi, Alpha Zeta (dir. 1985-93), Alpha Gamma Rho. Republican. Baptist. Office: Sonnenschein Nath & Rosenthal LLP Ste 600, E Tower 1301 K St NW Washington DC 20005 Office Phone: 202-408-3235. Office Fax: 202-408-6399. Business E-Mail: fmcclure@sonnenschein.com.

**MCCLURE, GROVER BENJAMIN,** management consultant; b. Houstonia, Mo., Oct. 15, 1918; s. Grover B. and Sue F. (Cook) McC. BA, U. Richmond, 1939. Pres. internat. div. Richardson-Merrell, N.Y.C., 1954-62; pres. Europe and Africa divs. Paris, 1960-81; exec. v.p., dir. Richardson-Vicks, Inc., Wilton, Conn., 1981-85; cons. New Canaan, Conn., 1985—. Bd. dirs., chmn. emeritus Silvermine Art Guild. Served to lt. comdr. USNR, 1941-46. Mem. Silver Springs Club (Ridgefield, Conn.). Republican. Presbyterian. Avocations: tennis, golf, travel, yachting. Home: 1321 Meadow Ridge Redding CT 06896

**MCCLURE, HAL H.,** film producer; b. Indpls. s. Harold Alonzo and Betty (Zemah Hays) McClure; m. Dorothea Vernell Millar, Jan. 15, 1949 (dec. 1994). AA, L.A. City Coll., 1941. Journalist various newspapers, Calif., 1949-56; newsman AP, L.A., 1956-58, N.Y.C., 1959-60, fgn. corr. S.E. Asia and Mid. East, 1961-76, bur. chief N.J. Newark, 1976-77; prin., travel film prodr. Hal McClure Prodns., Laguna Woods, Calif., 1978—. Adj. asst. prof. journalism Seton Hall U., South Orange, NJ, 1976—77. Co-author: (book) Lighting Out of Israel, 1967; co-editor: Fire Over Suez, 1971; prodr.: (films) Istanbul-Travels in Turkey, 1990, Land of Legend-England Scotland and Wales, 1993, Adventure Holland, 1994, Mystery Tales of Europe, 1996, Dracula-Travels in Transylvania, 1997, Story Book England, 1999, Magic of Malaysia, 2001, Casablanca-Travels in Morocco, 2003, Echo of Hoofbeats - the Pony Express Story, 2005; editor, co-owner Travel Adventure Cinema mag., 1978—, leader in move to digital prodn. travel film field. Capt. USAFR, 1942—56. Named to Travelogue Hall of Fame, 1994; recipient Rising Star award, 1978; Ogden Reid Found. fellow, 1959. Mem.: Travel Adventure Cinema Soc. Home and Office: 686 Avenida Sevilla # C Laguna Woods CA 92637-3838

**MCCLURE, HOWARD JEAN, JR.,** advocate; b. High Point, NC, June 15, 1959; s. Howard Jean McClure Sr. and Mary Elizabeth McClure. Author: Conflict Of Interest, 1999. Chmn. polit. action com. Carolina Advocates for Legal Reform, Charlotte, NC, 2001—02; v.p., 2001—02; active Charlotte Mecklenburg Cmty. Rels. Com., 2002—; chmn. membership and cmty. rels. com. Western Region NC Black Leadership Caucus, 2003—05; active Black Polit. Caucus Charlotte-Mecklenburg, 1998—2004, Robert F. Kennedy Meml., 2005; founder Citizens Coun. for Equal Opportunity, 2003; mem. Nat. Campaing Tolerance; vice chair 29th precinct Mecklenburg County Dem. Party, 2004. Recipient Outstanding Svc. award, Black Polit. Caucus of Charlotte Mecklenburg, 2003, Appreciation award, 2004, Chmn.'s Dem. of Month award, Mecklenburg County Dem. Party, 2004, Advocacy award, Nat. Assn. Human Rights Workers, 2005. Mem.: NAACP (mem. legal redress com. 1999—, edn. com. 2001—, labor & industry com. 2003—). Conservative. Avocations: music, writing, fishing, travel, football. Home: 3621 B Central Ave Charlotte NC 28205 Office: Citizens Coun Equal Opportunity PO Box 18812 Charlotte NC 28218 Office Phone: 704-531-3543. Personal E-mail: theebonysaint@webtv.net. E-mail: theebonysaint2@msn.com.

**MCCLURE, JACK B.,** retired thoracic surgeon; b. Gilman, Colo., Sept. 1, 1922; s. Frank Gilmore and Bethel Sarah McClure; m. Patricia Ann Nolan, June 15, 1963. BS, U. Chgo., 1948, MD, 1950. Diplomate Am. Bd. Surgery, Am. Bd. Thoracic Surgery. Intern Good Samaritan Hosp., Portland, Oreg., 1950—51; resident in gen. surgery U. Kans., Kansas City, 1951—55; pvt. practice Myrtle Creek (Oreg.) Clinic, 1955—56; commd. 2d lt. U.S. Army, 1957, advanced through grades to col., advanced resch. grants 1956—74; chief surg. svc. VA Med. Ctr., Roseburg, Oreg., 1974—80; field rep. Joint Commn. Accreditation of Hosps., Chgo., 1980—85. Prof. health sci. Baylor U., Waco, Tex., 1971—92; clin. prof. surgery U. Tex., San Antonio, 1989—92. Decorated Legion of Merit U.S. Army, Soldiers Medal, various others. Fellow: Am. Coll. Surgeons. Republican. Episcopalian. Avocations: golf, writing.

**MCCLURE, JAMES FOCHT, JR.,** federal judge; b. Danville, Pa., Apr. 6, 1931; s. James Focht and Florence Kathryn (Fowler) McC.; m. Elizabeth Louise Barber, June 14, 1952; children: Holly McClure Kerwin, Kimberly Ann Pacala, Jamee McClure Sealy, Mary Elizabeth Hudec, Margaret McClure Persing. AB, Amherst Coll., 1952; JD, U. Pa., 1957. Bar: D.C. 1957, Pa. 1958, U.S. Dist. Ct. D.C. 1957, U.S. Dist. Ct. (ea. and mid. dist.) Pa. 1958, U.S. Ct. Appeals (3d cir.) 1959. Atty., advisor Dept. State, Washington, 1957-58; assoc. Morgan, Lewis & Bockius, Phila., 1958-61; atty. Merck & Co., Inc., N.Y.C., 1961-65; prtnr. McClure & McClure, Lewisburg, Pa., 1965-77, McClure & Light, Lewisburg, 1978-84; pres., judge Ct. Common Pleas, 17th Jud. Dist. Pa., Lewisburg, 1984-90; sr. dist. judge U.S. Dist. Ct. (mid. dist.) Pa., Williamsport, Pa., 1990—. Dist. atty. Union County, Lewisburg, 1974-75. Pres. bd. sch. dirs. Lewisburg Area Sch. Dist., 1969-74. Cpl. U.S. Army, 1952-54. Mem. Pa. Bar Assn., Union County Bar Assn., Bucknell U. Golf Club, Susquehanna Valley Chorale, Order of Coif, Phi Beta Kappa. Republican. Presbyterian. Office: US Dist Ct 240 W 3rd St Ste 320 Williamsport PA 17701-6466 Office Phone: 570-323-9772.

**MCCLURE, JAMES JULIUS, JR.,** lawyer, former city official; b. Oak Park, Ill., Sept. 23, 1920; s. James J. and Ada Leslie (Baker) McC.; m. Margaret Carolyn Phelps, Apr. 9, 1949; children: John Phelps, Julia Jean, Donald Stewart. BA, U. Chgo., 1942, JD, 1949. Bar: Ill. 1950. Ptnr. Gardner, Carton & Douglas, Chgo., 1962-91, of counsel, 1991—; mem. Oak Park Plan Commn., 1966-77, Northeastern Ill. Planning Commn., 1973-77, pres., 1975-77, Village of Oak Park, 1973-81, Oak Park Exch. Congress Inc., 1978—2002. Mem. Bus. Leaders for Transp., 1998—. Pres. United Christian Cmty. Svcs., 1967-69, 71-73, Erie Neighborhood House, 1953-55, Oak Park-River Forest Cmty. Chest, 1967; moderator Presbytery Chgo., 1969; mem. Gov.'s Spl. Com. on MPO, 1978-79; bd. dirs. Leadership Coun. of Met. Open Cmtys., 1981-2002, sec., 1990-98; bd. dirs. Met. Planning Coun., 1982-93, hon. dir., 1993—; bd. dirs. Cmty. Renewal Soc., 1982-91, v.p., 1984-88, treas. 1988-91; bd. dirs. Christian Century Found., 1972—, chmn., 1981—; trustee McCormick Theol. Sem., 1981—, chmn. bd. 1987-90. hon. trustee, 1990—; mem. vocation agy., 1973-82; mem. ch. vocations unit, 1987-92, vice chair 1990; mem. gen. assembly coun. Presbyn. Ch. U.S.A., 1987-90, mem. gen. assembly Permanent Jud. Commn., 1997-2003; bd. dirs. Oak Park Edn. Found., 1991-96, Oak Park River Forest Cmty. Found., 1991-2002; mem. Vision 2000 (Oak Park) Coordinating Com., 1995. With USNR, 1942-46. Recipient Disting. Citizen award Oak Park, 1976; Silver Beaver award; Disting. Eagle Scout award Boy Scouts Am., Carl Winters Cmty. Svc. award Oak Park Rotary Club, 1996, William Staczak award Oak Park Edn. Found., 1997, Rita Johnson award Oak Park Family Svc. and Mental Health Ctr., 1997, Public Svc. award U. Chgo. Alumni Assn., 1997, Tradition of Excellence award Oak Pk. River Forest H.S., 1998, Alumni Svc. medal, Chgo. Alumni Assn., 2003, Gutenberg Award Chgo. Bible Soc., 2003; named one of 100 distinguished. Oak Parkers for Millenium, Wed Jour., 2002. Mem. ABA, Am. Coll. Trust and Estate Counsel, Ill. State Bar Assn., Chgo. Bar Assn., Am. Law Inst., Order of the Coif, Lambda Alpha. Clubs: Univ. (Chgo.). Office: Gardner Carton & Douglas 191 N Wacker Dr Chicago IL 60606-4719 *Love of God, love of family, awareness of both the uniqueness and the contribution of every other human being, a sense of the wholeness of life with my religious faith, my profession of law, my family and my community service each playing an important part and complimenting each other.*

**MCCLURE, JEFFREY B.,** lawyer; b. Columbus, Ohio, 1952; BA, Miami U., 1974; JD summa cum laude, Ohio State U., 1977. Bar: 1978, Calif. 1978, US Ct Appeals (5th Cir.), US Dist. Ct. (No. Dist.) Tex., US Dist. Ct. (So. Dist.) Tex., US Dist. Ct. (Ea. Dist.) Tex., US Dist. Ct. (We. Dist.) Tex.

---

Law clk. to Hon. John V. Singleton US Dist. Ct. (So. Dist.) Tex., 1977-78; atty. Butler & Binion, Houston; ptnr., Health Care Litig. Andrews Kurth LLP, Houston, mem. mgmt. com. Spkr. in field. Mem.: Def. Rsch. Inst., Nat. Health Lawyers Assn., Greater Houston Soc. Healthcare Risk Mgmt., Houston Bar Assn., State Bar Calif., Tex. Assn. Def. Counsel, State Bar Tex., Am. Soc. Healthcare Risk Mgmt., Order of Coif. Office: Andrews Kurth LLP 600 Travis St Ste 4200 Houston TX 77001-3090 Office Phone: 713-220-4772. Office Fax: 713-238-7403. Business E-Mail: jeffmcclure@andrewskurth.com.

**MCCLURE, LEE,** musician, composer, educator; b. Danville, Ky., 1947; s. Arnold Bruce Come, Sr. and Elizabeth Come. Studied Arnold Schoenberg's Harmonielehre, Turtle Bay Music Sch., 1973—76; BS in Music Composition, CUNY, 1979. Founder, artistic dir. Eclectix Chamber Orch., N.Y.C., 1985—; founder Eclectix Dance Co., 2006—. Leader Lee McClure Band, N.Y., 2004—; adj. instr. Touro Coll., Bklyn., 1998—2000. Composer: (orchestral) Symphony No.1 For Orchestra And Jazz Drummer, 1988, Cerulean Narrows, 1985, Hiatus, 1986, (chamber music) Heartbreak Phase III, 1975, Express and Local, 1978, (choral) Litany To The Holy Spirit, 1988, (Operas) Mother And Child, 1990, Voice, 1992, (songs) Lullabye/Anatonia, 1991, (albums) Lee McClure Electric Flute, 1998, (string quartet) Night Shifts, 2002, (piano) Suite From The Voyage, 1991, Twice My Muse was Real, 2005, (fusion quartet) Rock Adagio, 1994, Bolero Acid Glide, 2005. Grantee, ASCAP, 1983—2005. Mem.: Am. Music Ctr. (Margaret Jory grant 1988). Achievements include design of electric flute using 10 processors and sampler to present live music creating Grand Canyon echoes, shimmering highs, profound bass, in contrapuntal lines. Avocation: tennis. Home and Office: Eclectix Chamber Orchestra Inc 105 Duane St 14-C New York NY 10007 Office Phone: 212-566-2217. Personal E-mail: eclectix@earthlink.net.

**MCCLURE, RICHARD H.,** transportation executive; m. Sharon McClure; children: Ryan, Lindsay. Degree in Mgmt., Southwest Mo. State U.; MPA, U. Syracuse. Chief of staff Gov. Mo., John Ashcroft, 1985—92; in corp. svcs. Ctrl. Bancompany; various pos., to group exec. v.p. corp. fin. svcs. UniGroup, Inc., St. Louis, pres., COO, 2002—; also COO United Van Lines and UniGroup WorldWide. Office: UniGroup Inc 1 Premier Dr Fenton MO 63026*

**MCCLURE, TERI PLUMMER,** lawyer; b. Kansas City, Kans., Dec. 31, 1963; m. Roderick McClure; 2 children. BS, BA, Washington U., 1985; JD, Emory U., 1988. Bar: Ga. 1988. Employment counsel United Parcel Svc Inc., 1995—98, coord. labor and practice group, 1998—2003, mgr. ctrl. Fla. dist., 2003—05, gen. counsel, sr. v.p., mgmt. com. mem., 2005—. Bd. dirs. Jr. Achievement Ga., Anne E. Casey Found., UPS Found., Ctr. for Working Families. Mem.: Nat. Employment Law Counsel (mem. coord. com.), State Bar Ga. (mem. labor and employment law sect.), Am. Corp. Counsel Assn., Atlanta Bar Assn. Office: United Parcel Svc Inc 55 Glenlake Pkwy NE Atlanta GA 30328*

**MCCLURE, WILLIAM PENDLETON,** lawyer; b. Washington, May 25, 1925; s. John Elmer and Helen Newsome (Pendleton) McC.; children: Marilyn Alexander, Helen Pendleton, Elizabeth Ruffin, Melinda Geoghagan. BS, U. Pa., 1949; JD, George Washington U., 1951, LLM, 1954; postgrad., The Hague Acad. Internat. Law, Netherlands, 1952. Bar: D.C. 1951. Sr. ptnr. McClure & Trotter, Washington, 1952-91, McClure, Trotter & Mentz, Washington, 1991-93, McClure, Trotter & Mentz, chartered, Washington, 1993-95; of counsel White & Case, Washington, 1995—. Chmn. D.C. div. Crusade Against Cancer, Am. Cancer Soc., 1966, 67. Served from pvt. to 1st lt., inf. U.S. Army, 1943-46, PTO. Mem. Am. Bar Assn., Am. Bar Assn. D.C., Am. Judicature Soc., Order of Coif, Phi Delta Phi, Phi Delta Theta. Clubs: Metropolitan (Washington), Columbia Country (Washington). Office: 701 13t St NW Washington DC 20005

**MCCLUSKEY, FRANK BRYCE,** director; b. Orange, N.J., July 28, 1949; s. Frank Bryce and Angela McCluskey; life ptnr. Marguerite Walker; children: Brandon Albert McCLuskey, Kelly Bryce. BA in Philosophy, Bloomfield Coll., NJ, 1972; PhD in Philosophy, New Sch. U., N.Y.C., 1977. Prof. philosophy Mercy Coll., Dobbs Ferry, NY, 1977—, dean of online learning, 2000—; postdoctoral fellow Yale U., New Haven, 1978. Cons. Am. Mgmt. Assn., N.Y.C., 1994—2001; spkr. in field. Author: Thoughts on Fire; Life Lessons of a Volunteer Firefighter (Readers Choice award Writers Advantage, 2003), Burning for Success; contbr. articles to profl. jours. V.p. Putnam County Fire Chiefs, Carmel, NY, 1995—2004. Named Firefighter of Yr., Mahopac Falls (N.Y.) Vol. Fire Dept., 1990; fellow, NEH, 1978. Mem.: Internat. Assn. Fire Chiefs, Nat. Assn. Vol. Firefighters, N.Y. State Assn. Fire Chiefs. Republican. Roman Catholic. Avocation: travel. Home: 456 N Lake Blvd Mahopac NY 10541 Office: Mercy Coll 555 Broadway Mahopac NY 10522 E-mail: fmcckuskey@mercy.edu.

**MCCLUSKEY, NEIL GERARD,** gerontologist, educator, literary agent; b. Seattle, Dec. 15, 1920; s. Patrick John and Mary Genevieve (Casey) McC.; m. Elaine Lituchy, June 5, 1977. AB, Gonzaga U., 1944, MA, 1945; Lic. in Sacred Theology, Gen. Theol. Union, Berkeley, 1952; PhD, Columbia U., 1957. Assoc. editor Am. (Nat. Cath. Weekly), N.Y.C., 1955-60; dean sch. edn. Gonzaga U., Spokane, 1960-62, dir. hon. program, 1963-65, v.p. acad., 1963-66; prof. U. Notre Dame, South Bend, Ind., 1966-71, dean, dir. Inst. Studies in Edn., 1968-71; prof., dean profl. studies Lehman Coll. CUNY, 1971-75; dir. Ctr. Gerontol. Studies CUNY Grad. Sch., 1975-81; exec. dir. BHRAGS Social Svcs. Ctr., Bklyn., 1981-84; sr. cons. Retirement Advisors, Inc., N.Y.C., 1985—. Pres. Westchester Lit. Agy., 1991—. Author: Public Schools and Moral Education, 1958, Catholic Viewpoint on Education, 1959, Catholic Education Faces Its Future, 1969; author, editor: Aging and Society, 1980, Aging and Retirement, 1981. Bd. dirs. Cath. Big Bros. N.Y., 1985—. Home: 5144 NE 18th Terr Fort Lauderdale FL 33308 Personal E-mail: neilagency@adelphia.net.

**MCCLUSKY, DUNCAN KEMP,** librarian; b. San Francisco, Dec. 31, 1954; BS in Fisheries, Humboldt State U., 1978; cert. in Secondary Sch. Tchg., No. Ariz. U., 1987; MLS, U. Ky., 1990. Lab. technician Lake County Mosquito Abatement Dist., Lakeport, Calif., 1979—80; fisheries vol. Peace Corps, Democratic Republic of Congo, 1980—83; prodn. mgr. Valley Fish Farm, Brawley, Calif., 1985—86; reference libr. Auburn (Ala.) U., 1990—96; br. libr. U. Ga., Tifton, Ga., 1996—. Contbr. articles to mags. Asst. del. leader Internat. Spl. Olympics, Raleigh, NC, 1999—99; vol. Internat. Paralympics, Atlanta, 1996—96; chmn. adv. bd. Keep Tift Beautiful, 2005—. Named a Hometown Hero, Keep Ga. Beautiful and State of Ga., 1998; recipient Svc. to Rsch. award, Sigma Si, 2001, Recognition award, Dixie Wheelchair Athletic Assn., 2002, Environmentalist citation, Woodmen of World, 2003. Mem.: U.S. Agrl. Info. Network, Coun. Bot. and Hort. Librs., Internat. Assn. Aquatic and Marine Scis. Librs. and Info. Ctrs., Spl. Libraries Assn. Environment and Resource Mgmt. Divsn. (membership chair 1991—93, chair 1994—95, discussion list mgr. 1995—, pub. rels. chair 1997—2002, Outstanding Mem. 1997, Spl. Recognition Award 2001), Civitan Club Auburn (pres. 1994—95, honor key 1994, named Civitan of Yr. 1992), Cir. K Internat. (hon.; regional adminstr. Ga. dist. 2001, project planning com. 2002—03), Kiwanis Club of Tifton (historian 1998—, sec. 2005—), Kiwanian of the Yr. 1996-1997, 1997-1998, Kiwanian of the Decade 1998-1999). Avocations: community service, photography. Home: 811 East 46th Street Tifton GA 31794 Office: University of Georgia 4601 Research Way Tifton GA 31793 E-mail: mcclusky@uga.edu.

**MCCLUSKY, LORNA S.,** lawyer; d. Elbert Brooks and Virginia (Wyatt) Sullivan; children: Candice, Bridget, Joseph, Aaron. BA, Memphis State U., 1991; JD, Cecil C. Humphreys Sch. Law, 1994. Assoc. Law Office of Roscoe Field, Memphis, 1994—98, Law Office of William D. Massey, Memphis, 1994—2000; ptnr. Law Office of Massey McClusky, Memphis, 2000—. Author: Memphis State U. Law Rev., 1993. Recipient Faculty's Choice award, Memphis State U., 1991, Luyani Barrett award, Tenn. Assn. Criminal Def. Attys., 2001, Death Penalty Achievement award, Bob Richie Svc. award, 2004. Mem.: Nat. Assn. Criminal Def. Lawyers, Tenn. Assn. Criminal Def.

---

Lawyers (bd. dirs.). Avocations: sailing, pottery. Office: Law Office of Massey McClusky 3074 E St Memphis TN 38128 Office Phone: 901-384-4004. Office Fax: 901-937-8004. Personal E-mail: lsmdefend@aol.com.

**MCCOBB, ALLAN PAUL,** not-for-profit organization executive; b. Russell, Kans. s. Boyden and Doris Marie (Marsh) McC.; m. Ursula Seubert Fox, June 25, 1983 (div. Sept. 1991). BS in Phys. Edn., Kans. State U., 1967, BS in Bus. and Acctg., 1971; MS in Exercise Sci., Ft. Hays State U., 1986. Staff acct. Arthur Young & Co., Kansas City, 1972-74; gen. mgr., part owner McCobb Inc., Russell, Kans., 1974-80; grants mgr. N.W. Kans. Area Agy. on Aging, Hays, 1980-81; exec. dir. S.W. Kans. Area Agy. on Aging, Dodge City, Kans., 1981-85; grants mgr. N.W Area Agy. on Aging, Hays, 1985-86; exec. dir. United Way of Enid and N.W. Okla., Enid, 1990—. Exec. dir. Wheatbelt Girl Scout Coun., Hutchinson, Kans., 1987-90; presenter, group facilitator Meth. Divorce Support Group and Workshop, Enid, 1993—; youth coord. Enid Cmty. Children's Choir, 1994—; mem. initial bd. Enid Cmty. Free Health Clinic, Enid, 1996-99, Enid Cmty. Found., 1998—, Gar. County Child Advocacy Coun., 1997-2002; small claims mediator N.W. Okla. Early Settlement, Fairview, 1998—. With U.S. Army, 1968-70, Vietnam. Decorated Bronze Star U.S. Army, 1970; inductee Lake Atwood 10 Mile Hall of Fame, 1984. Mem. Garfield County Area C. of C., Enid Rotary Club. Methodist. Avocations: running, genealogy, youth work. Home: PO Box 771 Enid OK 73702-0771 Office: United Way Enid NW Okla 321 W Cherokee Ave Ste C Enid OK 73701-5603

**MCCOID, DONALD JAMES,** bishop; b. Wheeling, W.Va., Dec. 31, 1943; s. Roy Conrad and Alberta Virginia (Sturm) McC.; m. Saundra Ernette Piisila, Oct. 20, 1973; children: Kimberly, Elizabeth. AB, West Liberty (W.Va.) State Coll., 1965; MDiv, Luth. Theol. Sem., Phila., 1968; DD (hon.), Thiel Coll., 1983. Ordained to ministry Evang. Luth. Ch. in Am., 1968. Pastor St. Luke's Luth. Ch., Monessen, Pa., 1968-72; assoc. pastor St. John's Luth. Ch. Highland, Pitts., 1972-74; area Luth. coord. Western Pa.—W.Va. synod, Luth. Ch. Am., Clarksburg, W.Va., 1974-77; sr. pastor Trinity Luth. Ch., Latrobe, Pa., 1977-87; bishop Southwestern Pa. synod, Evang. Luth. Ch. in Am., Pitts., 1987—. Chmn. Pa. Coun. Chs., Harrisburg, Inst. for Mission, 1997-2002; co-chmn. Luth.-Orthodox Nat. Dialogue, 1997—, Internat. Dialogue, 2004—; del. Luth. World Fedn. Assembly, 1997, Luth. Sem. at Gettysburg, 2003—, chair bd. 2005-; bd. dir. Faith and Order Conf. Bd. dirs. Religious Leadership Forum, Pitts., 1988—, Luth. Svcs. in Am., 1997-2003; exec. com. Christian Assocs. S.W. Pa., Pitts., 1988—; chair coun., 1994-96, vice chair, 2005-; chair Conf. Bishops, Evangel. Luth. Ch. Am., 1999-2003. Lutheran. Office: Evang Luth Ch in Am SW Pa Synod 9625 Perry Hwy Pittsburgh PA 15237-5555 Office Phone: 412-367-8222. Business E-Mail: donald.mccoid@ecunet.org.

**MC COIN, JOHN MACK,** social worker; b. Sparta, NC, Jan. 21, 1931; s. Robert Avery and Ollie (Osborne) McC. BS, Appalachian State Tchrs. Coll., Boone, NC, 1960; MS in Social Work, Richmond Profl. Inst., Va., 1962; postgrad., U. NC, 1959—60; PhD, U. Minn., 1977. Lic. master social worker; cert. social worker, N.Y. Social svc. worker Broughton State Hosp., Morganton, NC, 1958-59, John Unstead State Hosp., Butner, NC, 1960-61; clin. social worker Dorothea Dix State Hosp., Raleigh, NC, 1962-63; child welfare case worker Wake County Welfare Dept., Raleigh, 1963-64; psychiat. social worker Toledo Mental Hygiene Clinic, 1964-66; sr. psychiat. social worker N.Y. Hosp.-Cornell U. Med. Ctr. Westchester divsn., White Plains, 1966-68; social worker VA Hosp., Montrose, NY, 1968-73; also vol. mental health worker Westchester County Mental Health Assn. and Mental Health Bd., White Plains; seminar instr. Grad. Sch. Social Work U. Minn., Mpls., 1973-74; social worker F.D.R. VA Health Care Facility, Montrose, 1975-77; asst. prof. social work U. Wis., Oshkosh, 1977-79, chmn. dept. cmty. liaison com., 1979-83; assoc. prof. social work Grand Valley State Colls., Allendale, Mich., 1979-81; social worker VA Med. Ctr., Battle Creek, Mich., 1981-83, supr. social worker dept. Leavenworth, Kans., 1983-94. Cons. 44th Gen. Hosp., USAR, Menasha, Wis., 1978-79, 5540th Support Command, USAR, Grand Rapids, Mich., 1979-83; cons. in field; adj. faculty mem. social scis. dept. Kansas City C.C., 1985-89, St. Mary Coll., 1984, Kellogg C.C., Battle Creek, 1981-83; adj. faculty mem. sch. social welfare U. Kans., Lawrence, 1992; presenter in field. Author: Adult Foster Homes: Their Managers and Residents, 1983; founder (with Human Scis. Press), editor Adult Foster Care Jour., 1987-88, Adult Resdl. Care Jour., 1989-91, indl. jour., 1992-96; contbr. articles to profl. jours. With USMC, 1948-52, USMCR, 1957-72; lt. col. USAR, 1972-91. Recipient Outstanding Performance award VA, 1971, 83, Superior Performance award, 1982; grantee NIMH, 1974. Mem. NASW (social action com. West Mich. br. 1980-81), Alpha Delta Mu. Democrat. Baptist. Avocations: golf, jogging, genealogy, military history. Home and Office: 4913 Colonial Way Lawrence KS 66049-3599

**MCCOLGAN, ELLYN,** investment company executive; b. Jersey City; BA in Psychology, Montclair State Coll., NJ; MBA, Harvard Bus. Sch. With Shearson Lehman Bros., NYC, 1983, Bank of New Eng., Fidelity Brokerage Co., 1990—, pres. fin. fidelity intermediary svcs., pres., 2002—. Mem. bd. dir. Securities Industry Assn. Trustee Babson Coll. Office: Fidelity Investments 82 Devonshire Boston MA 02109 Office Phone: 617-563-7000. Office Fax: 617-476-6152.*

**MCCOLLAM, CRAIG A.,** manufacturing executive; b. 1960; Dir. fin., corp. controller Dionex Corp, Sunnyvale, Calif., 1993-99, v.p. fin. & adminstrn., CFO, 1999—. Office: PO Box 3603 1228 Titan Way Sunnyvale CA 94085-4015 Office Phone: 408-481-4107. Business E-Mail: craig.mccollam@dionex.com.

**MCCOLLAM, MARION ANDRUS,** consulting firm executive, educator; b. New Orleans, Feb. 8, 1931; d. Gerald Louis and Lucile Gordon (Isacks) Andrus; m. Andrew McCollam, Jr., Jan. 29, 1955 (div. 1978); children: Andrew III, Gerald Andrus, Marion Cage. BA, Tulane U., 1952; M. Urban and Reg. Planning, U. New Orleans, 1978. Human affairs coord. Office of the Mayor, City of New Orleans, 1978, arts coord., 1978-80; dir. planning, prin. cons. Duncan Plaza Design Project, New Orleans, 1978-80; dir. planning Downtown Devel. Dist., New Orleans, 1980-81; pres. Andrus and Roberts Inc., Phoenix, New Orleans, 1980-84; exec. dir. Arts Coun. New Orleans, 1981-90, Cultural Arts Coun. of Houston and Harris County, 1991-98; pres. McCollam Cons., LLC, 1998—. Adj. lectr. in arts adminstrn. Goucher Coll., 1998—2004; mem. nat. adv. com., 2005—; cons. in field. Mem. nat. adv. com. Working Capital Fund, Mpls., 1995-99, Nat. Arts Stabilization, Balt., 1998—; adv. panel design Nat. Endowment for the Arts, Washington, 1995, adv. and chair local arts agencies, 1992-94; bd. dirs., sr. fellow Am. Leadership Forum, Houston, 1994-2000; mem. cmty. assessment com. United Way of Tex. Gulf Coast, 1995-99; bd. dirs. Urban League of New Orleans, 1984-89; pres. Jr. League of New Orleans, 1969-70. Recipient Arts Adminstr. of Yr. award Arts Mgmt. Inst./Nat. News Svc., 1987, Award for Sustained Mgmt. Excellence, Greater New Orleans Found., 1989. Mem. Am. Inst. Cert. Planners, AIA (hon.), U.S. Urban Arts Fedn. (pres. 1988), Nat. Assembly of Local Arts Agencies (vice chair 1988-94, Chairman's award 1992). Avocations: music, art, reading, travel. Office: 1914 Bissonnet St Houston TX 77005-1645

**MCCOLLAM, SHARON L.,** retail executive; BS in Acctg. CPA. Former acctg. Ernst and Young; divisional v.p., CFO Dole Food Co., Inc., 1993—2000; v.p. fin. Williams-Sonoma, Inc., San Francisco, 2000—01, sr. v.p., CFO, 2001—03, exec. v.p., CFO, 2003—. Office: Williams-Sonoma Inc 3250 Van Ness Ave San Francisco CA 94109

**MCCOLLAM, WILLIAM, JR.,** utilities executive; b. New Orleans, Mar. 15, 1925; s. William and Marie (Mason) McC.; m. Hope Flower Joffrion, Apr. 20, 1947; children: Ellendale McCollam Hoffman, William Cage, Stephen Mason. BS, La. State U., 1943; BS in Engring., U.S. Mil. Acad., 1946; MS in Civil Engring., MIT, 1954. Registered profl. engr., N.Y. Commd. 2d lt. U.S. Army, 1946; advanced through grades to lt. col. U.S Army; resigned U.S. Army, 1961; with Ark. Power and Light Co., Little Rock, 1961-70, exec. asst. 1961-64; v.p. Ark Power and Light Co., Little Rock, 1964-68; sr. v.p. Ark.

Power and Light Co., Little Rock, 1968-70; exec. v.p. New Orleans Pub. Service, 1970-71, pres., 1971-78, Edison Electric Inst., Washington, 1978-90, pres. emeritus, 1990—. Cons. energy mgmt., Washington, 1990—. Chmn. Burns and Roe Group, Inc., Oradell, NJ; trustee Thomas Alva Edison Found., Detroit, 1978—89; past chmn. S.W. Power Pool, Little Rock, 1973—74, Nat. Elec. Reliability Coun., Princeton, NJ, 1975—78; bd. dirs., exec. com. U.S. Mem. Com., World Energy Coun., Washington, 1978—94; bd. dirs. McDermott Internat., Inc., 1990—99. Past pres. Greater New Orleans area C. of C., 1974-75; former dir. Loyola U., New Orleans, 1975-78; pres.'s council Tulane U., 1982-86. Named to La. State U. Alumni Hall of Distinction, 1985; recipient U.S. Energy award in recognition of outstanding contbn. to world energy coun., 1991. Mem. La. Soc. Profl. Engrs. (A.B. Paterson award 1975) Clubs: Chevy Chase, Metropolitan (Washington); Boston, New Orleans Country. Republican. Episcopalian. Office: Edison Electric Inst 701 Pennsylvania Ave NW Fl 3 Washington DC 20004-2696 Home: 4563 Powers Ferry Rd Nw Atlanta GA 30327-3424

**MCCOLLEY, ROBERT MCNAIR,** historian, educator; b. Salina, Kans., Feb. 2, 1933; s. Grant and Alice Elizabeth (McNair) McC.; m. Diane Laurene Kelsey, Aug. 30, 1958; children: Rebecca, Susanna, Teresa, Margaret, Carolyn, Robert Lauren. BA, Harvard U., 1954, MA, 1955; PhD, U Calif.-Berkeley, 1960. Instr. to prof. history U. Ill., Urbana, 1960—97. Mem. Com. for Advanced Placement Test in Am. History, 1987-90, chmn. 1988-90. Author: Slavery and Jeffersonian Virginia, 1964 (Dickerson award 1964); editor: Federalists, Republicans and Foreign Entanglements, 1969; editor: Henry Adams, John Randolph, 1995; co-editor: Refracting America, 1993; mem. editorial bd. Jour. Early Republic, 1981-85, Va. Mag. of History and Biography, 1994-98; editor Jour. Ill. State Hist. Soc., 1998-2002, editl. bd., 2002—; classical recs. reviewer Fanfare mag., 1989—. Mem. Soc. Historians of Early Republic (pres. 1982), Orgn. Am. Historians, Va. Hist. Soc., Ill. Hist. Soc. (bd. dirs. 1978-81, 92-95, pres. 1997-99), Chgo. Hist. Soc., Cliff Dwellers. Home: 503 W Illinois St Urbana IL 61801-3927 Office: U Ill Dept History 810 S Wright St Urbana IL 61801-3644 E-mail: rmccolle@uiuc.edu.

**MC COLLISTER, JOHN CHARLES,** writer, minister, educator; b. Pitts., June 1, 1935; s. John Charles and Caroline Jesse (Hall) Mc C.; m. Beverly Ann Chase, Aug. 6, 1960; children: Beth Ann, Amy Susan, Michael John. BA, Capital U., 1957; MDiv, Luth. Theol. Sem., Columbus, Ohio, 1961; PhD, Mich. State U., 1969. Ordained to ministry Luth. Ch., 1961. Pastor Zion Luth. Ch., Freeland, Mich., 1961-65, Bethlehem Luth. Ch., Lansing, Mich., 1965-71; prof. religion and Greek Olivet (Mich.) Coll., 1970-74; prof. religion and philosophy Bethune-Cookman Coll., Daytona Beach, Fla., 1974-76, Embry-Riddle Aero. U., 1976-82, dir. profl. programs, 1979-80, cons. to pres., 1980-82. Pres. Wright Advt. Co., Daytona Beach, 1975-76; CEO New Arran Prodns., Inc., Daytona Beach, 1993—, Yongestreet Prodns., Ormond Beach, Fla., 1986; arbitrator Fed. Mediation and Conciliation Svc., 1978; spl. master Fla. Pub. Employees Rels. Comm., 1975—; mgmt. cons. Hoover Ball and Bearing, Charlotte, Mich.; pres. Am. Writers Inst., 1982—. Host Open Phone Forum, radio sta. WROD, Daytona Beach, 1974—76; author: A Philosophy of Flight, 1981, So Help Me, God, 1981, The Christian Book of Why, 1983; Problem Solving for Executives, 1984; author: The Sky is Home, 1986; co-author: The Sunshine Book, 1979, Day by Day, 1990; editor and compiler A Child is Born, 1972, Portraits of the Christ, 1974, Writing for Dollars, 1995, The Story of the Pittsburgh Pirates, 1998, The Tigers and Their Den, 1999, The Best Baseball Games Ever Played, 2002, Tales from the Pirates Dugout, 2003, Tales from the Cockpit, 2003, Echoes from the Smithsonian, 2004; editor and compiler: Tales From the 1979 Pittsburgh Pirates, 2005, God and the Oval Office, 2005; contbr. articles to various mags. Vol. probation officer, Mich., 1961-71, hearing officer, 1970-74; commr. Mich. Dept. Commerce, 1969-72; speaker Nat. Lincoln Day Observance, Washington, 1982; internat. adviser Han Nam U., Taejon, Republic of Korea, 1989. Recipient Outstanding Am. award Daytona Beach Jaycees, 1974. Mem. Am. Arbitration Assn. Home and Office: 26 Lazy Eight Dr Daytona Beach FL 32128-6775 Office Phone: 386-767-9999. E-mail: writerdoc@aol.com.

**MCCOLLOUGH, JACK,** apparel designer; b. Montclair, NJ; Attended, San Francisco Art Inst.; BA, Parsons Sch. of Design, 2002. Former intern Marc Jacobs; designer, co-founder, co-owner (with Lazaro Hernandez) Proenza Schouler, 2003—. Work featured in Women's Wear Daily, People, Town & Country and New York mag. Named Designers of the Yr., Parsons Benefit and Fashion Show. Office: c/o PR Consulting 42 Bond St 6 Fl New York NY 10012*

**MCCOLLOUGH, NEWTON CLARK, III,** orthopaedic surgeon; b. Butler, Pa., July 17, 1934; s. Newton C. and Margaret Elizabeth (Mattocks) McC.; m. Mary Eva Semanski, Feb. 22, 1968; children: Peter Scott, Amy Marie. BA, Duke U., 1956; MD, U. Pa., 1959. Diplomate: Am. Bd. Orthopaedic Surgery. Intern Jackson Meml. Hosp., Miami, Fla., 1959-60, resident in orthopaedic surgery, 1960-64; dir. orthopaedic resident edn. Orange Meml. Hosp., Orlando, Fla., 1965-66; asst. prof. orthopaedics and rehab. U. Miami Sch. Medicine, 1968-72, assoc. prof., 1972-76, prof., vice chmn. dept., 1976-78, prof., chmn. dept., 1978-86; dir. rehab. Jackson Meml. Hosp., Miami, 1972-82, chief orthopedics and rehab., 1978-86; dir. med. affairs Internat. Shriners Hosps. Children, Tampa, Fla., 1986-2001, 2001—, mem. med. adv. bd., 2001—, dir. med. affairs emeritus 2001—, med. adv. bd., 2001—. Dir. Am. Bd. for Certification in Prosthetics/Orthotics, 1974-77; mem. Health Planning Council So. Fla. Task Force on Long Term Patient Care, 1974-77; asst. med. dir. Div. of Children's Med. Services, State of Fla., 1975-86; chmn. Statewide Com. for Spinal Cord Injury, 1976-78 Trustee Jour. Bone and Joint Surgery, 1992-98, vice chmn., 1996-98; contbr. articles to med. jours. Served to lt. comdr. M.C. USNR, 1966-68. Decorated Legion of Merit. Mem. ACS, AMA, Am. Acad. Orthopaedic Surgeons (bd. dirs. 1978-79, 87-92, 2d v.p. 1987-88, 1st v.p. 1988-89, pres. 1989-90), Am. Burn Assn. (Disting. Achievement award 2001), Fla. Orthopaedic Soc. (mem. exec. com. 1978-79), Miami Orthopaedic Soc. (v.p. 1978-79), Am. Acad. Orthotists and Prosthetists (hon.), Fla. Med. Soc. Hillsborough County Med. Assn., Am. Congress Rehab. Medicine, Nat. Rehab. Assn., Scoliosos Rsch. Soc., Internat. Soc. Prosthetics and Orthotics, Am. Orthopaedic Assn., Orthopaedic Rsch. and Edn. Found. (trustee 1991-97, sec. 1995-97), Internat. Soc. Prosthetics and Orthotics (dir. 1980-83), Assn. Children's Prosthetic and Orthotic Clinics (pres. 1983-84), Rehab. Engring. Soc. N.Am. (dir. 1980-83), Am. Spinal Injury Assn., Internat. Med. Soc. Paraplegia, Pediatric Orthopaedic Soc. (dir. 1983-84, pres. 1984-85, Disting. Achievement award 2000), 20th Century Orthopaedic Assn. (treas. 1984-89), Am. Acad. Pediatrics, Phi Beta Kappa, Alpha Omega. Republican. Lutheran. Office: 602 Juan Anasco Dr Longboat Key FL 34228 Office Phone: 941-383-6146. Personal E-mail: newt3md@aol.com.

**MCCOLLUM, BETTY,** congresswoman; b. Mpls., July 12, 1954; m. Douglas McCollum; 2 children. BS in Edn., Coll. St. Catherine, 1987. Retail store mgr., Minn.; mem. Minn. Ho. Reps., 1992-2000, mem. com. environ. and natural resources com., mem. gen. legis. com., vet. affairs and elections com., mem. transportation and transit com., asst. majority leader, chair legis. commn. on econ. status of women, mem. rules and adminstrv. legis. com.; mem. U.S. Congress from Minn. 4th Dist., Washington, 2001—; mem. edn. and workforce com., resources com.; mem. Com. on Internat. Relations. Mem. St. Croix Valley Coun. Girl Scouts. Mem.: Am. Legion Aux., VFW Aux. Democrat. Office: US Ho Reps 1029 Longworth Ho Office Bldg Washington DC 20515-2304

**MCCOLLUM, CLIFFORD GLENN,** college dean emeritus; b. South Gifford, Mo., May 12, 1919; s. William Henry and Aultie V. (Westfall) McC.; m. Alice Elizabeth Erickson, Aug. 18, 1940; children: Eric Edward, Lisa Buren. Student, Central Coll., 1935-37; BS, U. Mo., 1939, MA, 1947, EdD, 1949. Tchr. pub. schs., Monett, Mo., 1938-39, Poplar Bluff, Mo., 1939-41, Boonville, Mo., 1941-42; asst. prof. sci. U. No. Iowa, 1949-55, assoc. prof., 1956-59, prof., 1959-84, prof. emeritus, 1984—, head dept. sci., 1957-68; dean U. No. Iowa (Coll. Natural Scis.), 1968-84, dean emeritus, 1984—. Prof. State U. N.Y. at Oneonta, 1955-56; Dir., instl. rep. Central States Univs., Inc.; cons. Coronet Instrnl. Films; cons. on sci. curricula to pub. schs. and colls.;

---

speaker in field. Contbr. articles to profl. jours. Served with USAAF, 1943-46. Fellow AAAS (nat. committeeman 1964-67), Iowa Acad. Sci. (pres. 1979-80); mem. Am. Inst. Biol. Scis., Nat. Assn. Biology Tchrs. (regional dir. 1963-65), Nat. Assn. Research in Sci. Teaching, Nat. Sci. Tchrs. Assn., Sigma Xi, Phi Delta Kappa. Home: 6511 N Revere Ave Kansas City MO 64151-3989 E-mail: cmccollum1@kc.rr.com. *My personal response to the philosophical conditions in which we live today is one of preparing to live rather consistently with crises. It is my conviction that the mood of our time is toward a growing pessimism, and much of this is associated with the concomitants of a galloping technology. Yet we are not willing at this point to give up our human condition to the natural evolution that would result from basic environmental mechanisms. We will still try to condition that destiny.*

**MC COLLUM, IRA WILLIAM, JR., (BILL MC COLLUM),** former congressman; b. Brooksville, Fla., July 12, 1944; s. Ira William and Arline Gray (Lockhart) McC.; m. Ingrid Mary Seebohm, Sept. 25, 1971; children: Douglas Michael, Justin Randolph, Andrew Lockhart. BA, U. Fla., 1965, JD, 1968. Bar: Fla. 1968, D.C. 2001. Ptnr. Pitts, Eubanks & Ross (P.A.), Orlando, Fla., 1973-80; mem. 97th-102nd Congresses from 5th Dist. Fla., 1981-92, 103d-106th Congresses from 8th Dist. Fla., 1993-2001; former vice chmn. banking/fin. svcs. com.; former chmn. judiciary subcom. on crime; former mem. select com. on intelligence; ptnr. Baker & Hostetler LLP, Orlando, Fla. and Washington, D.C. 2001—. Vice chair House Rep. Conf. 101st-103d Congresses. Chmn. Rep. Exec. Com. Seminole County, Fla., 1976-80; county chmn.'s rep. 5th Dist. Fla. State Rep. Exec. Com., 1977-80; co-chmn. rep. platform com., 1992. With USN, 1969-72. Mem. Fla. Bar, Naval Res. Assn., Res. Officers Assn., Orange County Bar Assn. (exec. coun. 1975-79), Am. Legion, Mil. Order World Wars, Fla. Blue Key, Phi Delta Phi, Omicron Delta Kappa, Kiwanis. Republican. Episcopalian.

**MCCOLLUM, JAMES FOUNTAIN,** lawyer; b. Reidsville, NC, Mar. 24, 1946; s. James F. and Dell (Frazier) McC.; m. Susan Shasek, Apr. 26, 1969; children: Audra Lynne, Amy Elizabeth. BS, Fla. Atlantic U., 1968; JD, Fla. State U., 1972. Bar: U.S. Ct. Appeals (5th cir.) 1973, Fla. 1972, U.S. Ct. Appeals (11th cir.) 1982, U.S. Supreme Ct. 2006. Assoc. Kennedy & McCollum, 1972-73; prin. McCollum & Rinaldo, P.A., 1973-77, McCollum & Oberhausen, P.A., 1977-80, McCollum, Oberhausen & Tuck, L.L.P. (and predecessor firm), Sebring, Fla., 1977—. Bd. dirs. Comml. Bancorp, Inc., Comml. Bank Highlands County; pres. Highlands Devel. Concepts, Inc., Sebring, 1982—; sec. Focus Broadcast Comm., Inc., Sebring, 1982-87; mng. ptnr. Highlands Investment Service; pres. Am. Svc. Title & Escrow, Inc., 2001— Treas. Highlands County chpt. ARC, 1973-76; vestryman St. Agnes Episcopal Ch., 1973—, chancellor, 1978—; mem. Fla. Sch. Bd. Atty.'s Assn., 1974-2001, bd. dirs., 1989-97, pres., 1995-96; mem. Com. 100 of Highlands County, 1975-83, bd. dirs., 1985-87, chmn., 1991-92; chmn. Highlands County High Speed Rail Task Force; chmn. bd., treas. Ctrl. Fla. Racing Assn., 1976-78; chmn. Leadership Sebring: life mem., past pres. Highlands Little Theatre, Inc.; bd. dirs. Palms of Sebring Nursing Home, 1988-90, Palms Estate Mobile Home Park, Sebring Airport Authority, 1988-90, treas., 1988, chmn. indsl. com., 1988, vice-chmn., 1989-90, chmn., 1990-91, Highlands County High Speed Rail Task Force, 1986-89, Highlands County Family YMCA, 1985-93, pres. Sebring br., 1992-93, chmn. bldg. com., 1992-94, Good Shepherd Hospice, Inc., v.p., 2000—, chmn. bd. dirs., 2003—, Primal Connection, Inc., 2006—; commr. Sebring Redevel. Agy., 2006—; campaign chmn. Jeb Bush for Gov., Highlands County, 1998, 2002, George W. Bush for President, 2000, 04. Recipient ARC citation, 1974, Presdl. award of appreciation Fla. Jaycees, 1980-82, 85, Outstanding Svc. award Highlands Coun. of 100, 1988, Most Valuable Player award Highlands Little Theatre, Inc., 1986, Zenon Significant Achievement award, 1991, Best Set award, 2002; named Jaycee of Year, Sebring Jaycees, 1981, Outstanding Local Chpt. Pres., U.S. Jaycees, 1977, Citizen of Yr., United Way Ctrl. Fla., 2004, Highlands Counties Best Lawyer, Highlands Today and News Sun newspapers, 2003, 05, 06. Mem. ABA, ATLA, Comml. Law League Am., Am. Arbitration Assn. (comml. arbitration panel), Nat. Assn. Retail Credit Attys., Fla. Bar (jour. com.), Highlands County Bar Assn. (past chmn. legal aid com.), Fla. Sch. Bd. Attys. Assn. (bd. dirs. 1989-97, v.p. 1993-94, pres. 1994-95), Greater Sebring C. of C. (dir. 1982-89, pres. 1986-87, chmn. transp. com. 1986—, Most Valuable Dir. award 1986-87), Fla. Jaycees (life, internat. senate 1977—), Lions (bd. dirs. 1972-73, v.p. 1994-95, Disting. award 1984). Republican. Episcopalian. Office: 129 S Commerce Ave Sebring FL 33870-3602 Office Phone: 863-385-5188. Personal E-mail: jimmccollum@earthlink.net.

**MCCOLLUM, JEAN HUBBLE,** medical technician; b. Peoria, Ill., Oct. 21, 1934; d. Claude Ambrose and Josephine Mildred (Beiter) Hubble; m. Everett Monroe Patton, Sept. 4, 1960 (div. Jan. 1969); 1 child, Linda Joanne; m. James Ward McCollum, Jan. 2, 1971; 1 child, Steven Ward. Student, Bradley U., Ill. Cen. Coll. Stenographer Caterpillar Tractor Co., Peoria, 1952-53, supr. stenographer pool, 1953-55, adminstrv. sec., treas., 1955-60, sec., asst. dept. mgr., 1969-71; med. staff sec. Proctor Cmty. Hosp., Peoria, 1978-82; med. asst. Drs. Taylor, Fox and Morgan, Peoria, 1982-84; freelance med. asst. Meth. Hosp. and numerous physicians, Peoria, 1984-89; office mgr. bus. office Dr. Danehower, McLelland and Stone, Peoria, 1989—. Vol. tutor Northmoor Sch., Peoria, 1974-78; bd. dirs., mem. exec. com., chmn. patient rels. com., com. chmn. Planned Parenthood, Peoria, 1990-92; judge Region 2 Ill. State History Fair, Bradley U., 2004, 05; hon. mem. scholarship com. Am. Indian Edn. Found. Recipient Outstanding Performance award Proctor Hosp., 1981, also various awards for svc. to schs., ch. and hosps. for mentally ill. Mem. Nat. Wildlife Fedn., Mensa Internat. (publs. officer, scholarship com., editor 1987-89, cshoolar com. 1993), Mothers League (treas. 1977), Willow Knolls Country Club (social com. 1989-90), Nature Conservancy (Seasons of the River event com. 2000—), World Wildlife Fund, Forest Park Found., Nat. Trust for Historic Preservation, Natural Resources Def. Coun., Religious Coalition for Reproductive Rights, USO, Am. Indian Educators Found. (hon., scholar com. 2004). Methodist. Avocations: reading, travel, theater, yoga. Home: 6501 N Brookwood Ln Peoria IL 61614-2401

**MCCOLLUM, JOHN MORRIS,** tenor; b. Coalinga, Calif., Feb. 21, 1922; s. Fay James and Ingabord Telette (Mason) McC.; m. Mary Margaret Wilson, Jan. 23, 1944; children: Kristi Elizabeth, Timothy James. Student, Coalinga Coll., 1939-40; BA in Journalism, U. Calif. at Berkeley, 1947; student voice and acting, Am. Theatre Wing, 1951-53. Reporter, city editor Coalinga Record, 1947-50; editor agrl. news U. Calif. Coll. Agr., 1950-51. Prof. music and chmn. voice faculty U. Mich.; dir. U. Mich. div. Nat. Music Camp; faculty Aspen Music Festival and School, 1963-76 Concert and opera singer, 1951—, soloist, Fifth Ave. Presbyn. Ch., N.Y.C., 1953-56, debut, Town Hall, N.Y.C., 1952, with Boston Symphony Orchestra, Tanglewood, Mass., summer 1952, engagements with Symphony Orchestras in N.Y.C., Chgo., Phila., San Francisco, Cleve., Washington, St. Louis, Boston, New Orleans, Toronto, London, Mexico; with opera companies of Boston, Washington, Toronto, Ft. Worth, Central City, Colo., also, NBC-TV, music festivals and oratorio societies, European debut, Festival of Two Worlds, Spoleto, Italy, summer 1958, Santa Fe Opera Co., leading tenor, N.Y.C. Opera Co., performing mem., Music Assos. of Aspen. Recipient award Atwater Kent Auditions 1950, Am. Theatre Wing award 1952). Mem. Rep. Ctrl. Com., Fresno County, Calif., 1950; pres. Ann Arbor Civic Theatre, 1987-88; mem. Sarasota County Rep. exec. com.; bd. dirs. Sarasota Concert Assn.; bd. dirs. Univ. Mich. Alumni Club. Served with U.S. Navy, 1942-49. Mem. U. Calif. Alumni Assn., Nat. Assn. Tchrs. Singing, Am. Acad. Tchrs. Singing, Alpha Tau Omega, Sigma Delta Chi, Pi Kappa Lambda. Episcopalian (lay reader). Clubs: Rotary (pres. 1977, Paul Harris fellow), Ann Arbor Golf and Outing (pres. 1979), The Meadows Country Club (Sarasota, Fla.). Home: 3380 W Chelmsford Ct Sarasota FL 34235-0947

**MCCOLLUM, ROBERT WAYNE,** epidemiologist, educator; b. Waco, Tex., Jan. 29, 1925; s. Robert Wayne and Minnie (Brown) McC.; m. Audrey Talmage, Oct. 16, 1954; children: Cynthia, Douglas Scott. AB, Baylor U., 1945; MD, Johns Hopkins, 1948; DPH, London Sch. Hygiene and Tropical Medicine, 1958; MA (hon.), Yale U., 1965, Dartmouth Coll., 1985. Intern in pathology Columbia-Presbyn. Med. Center, N.Y.C., 1948-49; intern in internal medicine Vanderbilt Hosp., Nashville, 1949-50; asst. resident in

---

internal medicine Yale-New Haven Med. Center, 1950-51; faculty Yale Sch. Medicine, 1951-81, prof. epidemiology, 1965-81, chmn. dept. epidemiology and public health, 1969-81; dean Sch. Medicine Dartmouth Coll., Hanover, NH, 1982-90, prof. epidemiology, 1982-95, dean emeritus, 1990—; prof. emeritus, 1995—. Assoc. physician Yale-New Haven Hosp., from 1954; v.p. Dartmouth-Hitchcock Med. Ctr., 1983-90, acting v.p. for devel., 1999; cons. WHO, 1962-79; surgeon gen. U.S. Army, from 1960. Contbr. articles on epidemiology and control infectious diseases to profl. jours. Bd. sci. advisers Merck Inst., 1981-85; trustee Mary Hitchcock Meml. Hosp., Hanover, 1982-90. Capt. M.C., AUS, 1952-54. Mem. Assn. Tchrs. Preventive Medicine, Am. Epidemiological Soc., Internat. Epidemiological Assn., Infectious Diseases Soc. Am., Conn. Acad. Sci. and Engring., Am. Coll. Epidemiology Office: Dartmouth Med Sch Dartmouth-Hitchcock Med Ctr Lebanon NH 03756

**MCCOMAS, DAVID JOHN,** science administrator, space physicist; b. Milw., May 22, 1958; s. Harrold James and Hazelyn (Melconian) McC.; m. Richelle Wolff, May 30, 1981; children: Random A., Koan I., Orion G. BS in Physics, MIT, 1980; MS in Geophysics and Space Physics, UCLA, 1985, PhD in Geophysics and Space Physics, 1986. Mem. staff Los Alamos (N.Mex.) Nat. Lab., 1980-91, sect. leader space plasma and planetary physics, 1991-92, group leader for space and atmospheric scis., 1992-98, founding dir. Ctr. for Space Sci. and Exploration, NASA program, 1998—2000; exec. dir. space sci. and engring. divsn. S.W. Rsch. Inst., San Antonio, 2000—03, sr. exec. dir., 2004—. Strategic planning com. earth and space scis. divsn. Los Alamos Nat. Lab, 1986; advanced composition explorer phase A study team NASA, 1988-89, space physics data system steering com., 1990-91, inner magnetosphere imaging study team, 1991-94, prin. investigator Interstellar Boundary Explorer, Ulysses Solar Wind Observations Over the Poles of the Sun Experiment, Two Wide-Angle Imaging Neutral-Atom Spectrometers, Explorer Mission-of-Opportunity, Solar Wind Electron Proton Alpha Monitor (instrument on the Advanced Composition Explorer, co-investigator Medium Energy Neutral Atom instrument on IMAGE Midsized Discovery Mission, plasma instrument for Cassini mission to Saturn, GENESIS Discovery mission, ISTP Polar Spacecraft's Thermal Ion Dynamics Experiment, Cluster plasma electron instrument, team New Millennium Plasma Experiment for Planetary Exploration, Space Sci. Adv. Com., chmn. Sun-Earth Connections Adv. Subcom., Solar Probe Sci. and Tech. Definition Team, 2004-05; com. solar-terrestrial rsch. Nat. Rsch. Coun., 1991-94, com. space sci. tech. planning Aeronautics and Space Engring. Bd./space studies bd., 1992, task group rsch. prioritization future space sci. space studies bd., 1994—; former prin. investigator series of 10 magnetospheric plasma analyzer instruments at geosynchronous orbit Dept. Energy; com. mem., panelist Nat. Acad. Sci.'s Nat. Rsch. Coun., U. Calif., State of N.Mex., others. Assoc. editor Jour. Geophys. Rsch.-Space Physics, 1993-94; contbr. over 300 articles to profl. jours. Grad. fellow Inst. Geophysics and Planetary Physics, 1983-84. Fellow Am. Geophys. Union (James B. Macelwane award 1993). Achievements include patents in field. Office: SW Rsch Inst PO Drawer 28510 San Antonio TX 78228-0510

**MCCOMB, DAVID GLENDINNING,** history professor; b. Kokomo, Ind., Oct. 26, 1934; s. John Floyd and Jennie (Glendinning) McC.; m. Mary Alice Collier, Sept. 6, 1957; children: Katherine, Susan, Joseph. BA, So. Meth. U., 1956; MBA, Stanford U., 1958; MA, Rice U., 1962; PhD, U. Tex., 1968. Purchasing agt. McRan Co., Houston, 1958-60; instr. South Tex. Jr. Coll., Houston, 1962, U. Houston, 1966-68; asst. prof. San Antonio Coll., 1962-66; rsch. assoc. U. Tex., Austin, 1968-69; assoc. prof. history Colo. State U., Ft. Collins, 1969-72, assoc. prof., 1972-77, prof., 1977—2002, chmn. dept., 1975—80, emeritus prof., 2002—. Interviewer, dir. Oral History of Colo. Project, 1973—77, Big Thompson Disaster Oral History, 1976—78, Olympic Tng. Ctr. Oral History, 1983—87. Author: Houston, a History, 1969; rev. edit., 1981 (Tullis award 1969), Galveston, a History, 1986 (Tex. history 1987), Texas, a Modern History, 1989, Texas, an Illustrated History, 1995, Historic Seacoast of Texas, 1999, Travels with Joe, 2001, Sports in World History, 2004, also others; editor: World History Ann. Edits., 1987, 89, 92, 96, 98, 2000, 01; contbr. articles to hist. jours. Recipient award of merit Am. Assn. for State and Local History, 1980, Disting. Svc. award Colo. State U., 1986; Danforth Found. grantee, 1978, Sigma Xi, 2001, also others, 1966-85. Fellow Tex. Hist. Assn.; mem. Oral History Assn. (program chmn. 1980), N.Am. Assn. for Sports History, World History Assn. (exec. coun. 1997-99), Western History Assn. (program chmn. 1979), Rocky Mountain World History Assn. (chmn. 1988-92). Democrat. Unitarian Universalist. Avocation: master swimming competition. Office: Colo State U Dept History Fort Collins CO 80523-0001 Business E-Mail: david.mccomb@colostate.edu.

**MCCOMBS, BILLY JOE (RED MCCOMBS),** professional football team executive; m. Charlene McCombs; 3 daughters. Founder, dir. Clear Channel Communications, Inc, 1972—; former owner, chmn. bd. Denver Nuggets, 1982—86, San Antonio Spurs; chair. bd of trustees Southwestern Univ.; owner, chair., pres. Minnesota Vikings, Eden Prairie, 1998—2005. Film appearances: The Longest Yard, 2005. Chmn. bd. trustees Southwestern U.; former chmn. United Way of San Antonio, HemisFair World's Fair '68. Named to Bus. Hall of Fame; named one of Forbes Richest Americans, 2006. Mem. San Antonio C. of C. (former chmn.), Nat. Ford Dealers, U. Tex. Longhorn Club. Office: Winter Pk Admin Office 9520 Viking Dr Eden Prairie MN 55344-3898

**MCCOMBS, DAVID LOUIS,** lawyer; b. Gloucester, Mass., July 5, 1959; s. H.L. and Joan (Vasek) McCombs. BS in Physics, Denison U., 1981; JD, U. Miami, Fla., 1984. Bar: Tex. 1988, admitted to practice: US Dist. Ct. (No. Dist.) Tex. 1985, US Ct. Appeals (Fed. Cir.) 1985, US Ct. Appeals (5th Cir.) 1986, US Patent and Trademark Office. Assoc. Hubbard, Thurman, Turner & Tucker, Dallas, 1984—; prtnr. Haynes & Boone LLP, Dallas. Exec. bd. mem. Richardson Symphony Orchestra; rsch. adv. bd. U. Tex., Dallas; adv. bd. mem., Metroplex Tech. Bus. Council Richardson C. of C.; bd. mem. Trolley For Toys. Mem.: Computer Law Assn., Inst. Elec. and Electronics Engrings., Am. Electronics Assn., State Bar Tex., Dallas-Fort Worth Patent Law Assn. (pres. 1994), Nat. Assn. Mfrs., Am. Trial Lawyers Am., Am. Intellectual Property Law Assn., ABA (antitrust, litig., patents trademarks and copyrights sects.), Sigma Pi Sigma. Office: Haynes & Boone LLP 901 Main St Ste 3100 Dallas TX 75202-3789 Office Phone: 214-651-5533. Office Fax: 214-651-5940. Business E-Mail: david.mccombs@haynesboone.com.

**MCCONAUGHEY, MATTHEW,** actor; b. Uvalde, Tex., Nov. 4, 1969; Grad., U. Tex., Austin, 1993. Represented by William Morris Agy., Beverly Hills, Calif., 1993—. Appearances in films include: My Boyfriend's Back, 1993, Dazed and Confused, 1993, The Return of the Chainsaw Massacre, 1994, Angels in the Outfield, 1994, Boys Submission, 1995, Judgement, 1995, Boys on the Side, 1995, Lone Star, 1996, A Time to Kill, 1996, Larger than Life, 1996, Glory Daze, 1996, Scorpion Spring, 1997, Amistad, 1997, Contact, 1997, The Rebel, 1998 (also writer, dir.), The Newton Boys, 1998, Making Sandwiches, 1998, South Beach, 1999, Last Flight of the Raven, 1999, Edtv, 1999, U-571, 2000, The Wedding Planner, 2001, Thirteen Conversations About One Thing, 2001, Frailty, 2001, Reign of Fire, 2002, How To Lose a Guy in 10 Days, 2003, Tiptoes, 2003, Two for the Money, 2005, Failure to Launch, 2006; actor, exec. prodr.: Sahara, 2005; TV films Absolute Evel: The Evel Knievel Story, 2005; TV appearances include Unsolved Mysteries, 1992, (voice) King of the Hill, 1999, Sex and the City, 2000. Named Sexiest Man Alive, People mag., 2005; recipient Favorite Male Action Star, People's Choice Award, 2006. Address: care Horowitz Zoron McMahon Ste 1015 1888 Century Park East Los Angeles CA 90067 also: William Morris Agy 151 El Camino Dr Beverly Hills CA 90212*

**MCCONKEY, JAMES RODNEY,** literature and language educator, writer; b. Lakewood, Ohio, Sept. 2, 1921; s. Clayton Delano and Grace (Baird) McC.; m. Gladys Jean Voorhees, May 6, 1944; children: Lawrence Clark, John Crispin, James Clayton. BA, Cleve. Coll. 1943; MA, Western Res. U. 1946; PhD, U. Iowa, 1953. Teaching fellow, instr. Cleve. Coll., 1945-46; teaching asst. U. Iowa, Iowa City, 1949-50; asst. prof. Morehead State Coll. Ky., 1950-54, assoc. prof. Ky., 1954-56; asst. prof. Cornell U., Ithaca, N.Y.,

1956-62, assoc. prof., 1962-67, prof., 1967-87, Goldwin Smith prof. English lit., 1987-92; Goldwin Smith prof. emeritus, 1992—. Dir. Morehead Writers Workshop, 1951-56, Antioch Seminar in Writing and Pub., Yellow Springs, Ohio, 1957-59 Author: The Novels of E.M. Forster, 1957, Night Stand, 1965, Crossroads, 1968, Journey to Sahalin, 1971, The Tree House Confessions, 1979, Court of Memory, 1983, To a Distant Island, 1984, Kayo: The Authentic and Annotated Autobiographical Novel From Outer Space, 1987, Rowan's Progress, 1992, Stories From My Life With the Other Animals, 1993, The Telescope in the Parlor, 2004; editor: The Structure of Prose, 1963, Chekhov and Our Age, 1984, The Anatomy of Memory, 1996. Served with U.S. Army, 1943-45. Guggenheim fellow, 1970; Eugene Saxton Meml. Trust Fund fellow, 1962; recipient Nat. Endowment of Arts essay award, 1968, Am. Acad. and Inst. Arts and Letters award in lit., 1979 Democrat. Home: 402 Aiken Rd Trumansburg NY 14886-9733 Office: Cornell Univ Goldwin Smith Hall Dept English Ithaca NY 14853 E-mail: jrm9@cornell.edu.

**MCCONKIE, GEORGE WILSON,** education educator; b. Holden, Utah, July 15, 1937; s. G. Wilson and Mabel (Stephenson) McC.; m. Orlene Carol Johnson, Sept. 6, 1962; children: Lynnette Mooth, Heather Usevitch, April Rhiner, Faline Coffelt, George Wilson, Bryce Johnson, Camille Howard, Elissa, Esther Ostler, Bryna Fisher, Ruth Olson, Anna May Cox, Cynthia, Thomas Oscar. AA, Dixie Jr. Coll., 1957; BS, Brigham Young U., 1960, MS, 1961; PhD, Stanford U., 1966. Missionary LDS Ch., 1957-59; asst. prof. edn. Cornell U., 1964-70, asso. prof., 1970-75, prof., 1975-78, chmn. dept. edn., 1977-78; prof. U. Ill., Champaign, 1978—2003, chmn. dept. ednl. psychology, 1993-94, 95-97, prof. emeritus, 2003—. Sr. scientist Ctr. for Study of Reading, 1978-95, Beckman Inst., 1989-2004; rsch. fellow Cath. U. Louvain, Belgium, 1991-92; vis. prof. Nat. Yang Ming U., Taiwan, 1998, Beijing Normal U., 1999. Contbr. articles to profl. jours. Recipient Outstanding Sci. Contbn. award Soc. for Sci. Study of Reading, 1995; NIMH spl. fellow, 1971-72, NIH Fogarty Internat. fellow, 1991-92; grantee U.S. Office Edn., 1970-73, Nat. Inst. Edn. 1974-77, NIMH, 1974-84, NICHHD, 1983-89, 91-95, AT&T, 1986-89, NSF, 1989-91, 2000-03, CIA, 1991-97, Army Rsch. Lab., 1996-2001, Yamaha Motor Corp., 1997-99, GM, 2002-04; Fulbright scholar, Taiwan, 1998, Sr. scholar Chiang Chung Kuo Found., 1998-99. Mem. Lds Ch. Home: 2605 Berniece Dr Champaign IL 61822-7225 Office: Coll Education Dept Educational Psych 1310 S Sixth St Champaign IL 61820 Business E-Mail: gmcconk@uiuc.edu.

**MCCONNAUGHAY, PHILIP J.,** dean, law educator; BA, Ill. U., 1975, JD, 1982. Bar: Ill. 1978, Calif. 1979, DC 1983. Clk. to Hon. A.Y. Kirkland US Dist. Ct., No. Dist., Ill., 1978—79; assoc. Morrison & Foerster, San Francisco, 1979—83, ptnr. Washington, DC, Tokyo, Hong Kong, 1985—95; spl. dep. gen. counsel EEOC, Washington, DC, 1983—84; assoc. prof. U. Ill. Coll. Law, 1996—2001, prof., 2001—02; dean, Donald J. Farage Prof. Law Pa. State U., Dickinson Sch. Law, Carlisle, Pa., 2002—. Office: Dickinson Sch Law Pa State U 150 S Coll St Carlisle PA 17013 Office Phone: 717-240-5272. E-mail: pjm30@psu.edu.

**MCCONNAUGHEY, GEORGE CARLTON, JR.,** retired lawyer; b. Hillsboro, Ohio, Aug. 9, 1925; s. George Carlton and Nelle (Morse) McC.; m. Carolyn Schlieper, June 16, 1951; children: Elizabeth, Susan, Nancy. BA, Denison U., 1949; LLB, Ohio State U., 1951, JD, 1967. Bar: Ohio 1951. Sole practice, Columbus; ptnr. McConnaughey & McConnaughey, 1954-57, McConnaughey, McConnaughey & Stradley, 1957-62, Laylin, McConnaughey & Stradley, 1962-67, George, Greek, King, McMahon & McConnaughey, 1967-79, McConnaughey, Stradley, Mone & Moul, 1979-81, Thompson, Hine & Flory (merger McConnaughey, Stradley, Mone & Moul with Thompson, Hine & Flory), 1981—92, ret. ptnr., 1992—. Bd. dirs. N.Am. Broadcasting Co. (Sta. WMNI, WBZX and WTDA Radio); asst. atty. gen. State of Ohio, 1951-54. Pres. Upper Arlington (Ohio) Bd. Edn., 1967-69, Columbus Town Meeting Assn., 1974-76; chmn. Ohio Young Reps., 1956; U.S. presdl. elector, 1956; trustee Buckeye Boys Ranch, Columbus, 1967-73, 75-81, Upper Arlington Edn. Found., 1987-93; elder Covenant Presbyn. Ch., Columbus. With U.S. Army, 1943-45, ETO. Fellow Am. Bar Found., Ohio Bar Found., Columbus Bar Found.; mem. ABA, Ohio State Bar Assn., Columbus Bar Assn., Am. Judicature Soc., Scioto Country Club, Athletic Club, Rotary, Masons. Home: 1993 Collingswood Rd Columbus OH 43221-3741 Office: Thompson Hine LLP One Columbus 10 W Broad St Ste 700 Columbus OH 43215-3435 Office Phone: 614-469-3224.

**MCCONNELL, W. BRUCE,** lawyer; b. Pitts., 1943; AB cum laude, Princeton Univ., 1965; JD, Univ. Pa., 1970. Bar: Pa. 1971. Atty., gen. counsel's office to legal asst. to Commr. Richard Smith SEC, 1970—73; assoc. Drinker Biddle & Reath LLP, Phila., 1973—77, ptnr., 1977—2002, mng. ptnr., 2002—, chmn., investment mgmt. group and mem., mgmt. com. Office: Drinker Biddle & Reath LLP One Logan Sq 18th & Cherry Sts Philadelphia PA 19103-6996 Office Phone: 215-988-2817. Office Fax: 215-988-2757. Business E-Mail: bruce.mcconnel@dbr.com.

**MCCONNELL, ALBERT LYNN,** director; b. Springfield, Ohio, Oct. 20, 1946; s. Jack Pershing and Betty Ann (Venema) McConnell; m. Rannette Oledge, Dec. 21, 2001; 1 child, Ciara Lynn 1 stepchild, Joshua Hooper. BA, Ctrl. State U., 1969; MA, Webster U., 1983; MS, USACGSC, 1984. Commd. 2d. lt. U.S. Army, 1969, advanced through grades. to maj., 1980; ret., 1989; served as inf. bn. intelligence officer Schofield Barracks, Hawaii, 1970-71; inf. co. comdr., asst. ops. officer, inf. bn., 1971; intelligence analyst and briefer U.S. Mil. Assistance Command, Schofield Barracks, 1972-73; instr. U.S. Army Intelligence Sch., Ft Huachuca, Ariz., 1973-77; served in 3rd Armored Div., Frankfurt, Germany, 1980-81; project officer Combined Arms Ctr., Ft. Leavenworth, Kans., 1981-83, comdr. spl. security detachment, 1981-83; dir. intelligence, asst. chief staff for intelligence U.S. Army South Ft. Clayton, Panama, 1984-85, mng. exec. officer Ft. Davis, Panama, 1985-86; tactical intelligence officer, chief adminstrv. svcs. U.S. Army Air Def. Arty. Sch., Ft. Bliss, Tex., 1986-87, dep. directorate chief, 1987-88, sr. intelligence officer, dept. divsn. chief, 1988-89; ops. analyst RAM Inc., Sierra Vista, Ariz., 1989-92; prof. bus. adminstrn. and mgmt. So. Ohio Coll., Columbus, 1992, Bliss Coll., Columbus, 1993; store mgr. Circle K Corp., Yuma, Ariz., 1993-94; tchr. Glendale (Ariz.) Union HS, 1994-95; mgr. Dexter Book Store, 1995-96; dean students Ariz. Inst. Bus. and Tech., Phoenix, 1996-98, 2002—04, campus dir. Mesa, Ariz., 1998-2000; prof. Phoenix, 2002—03; dir. edn. High Tech Inst., Phoenix, 2000—02; dean students Internat. Inst. Ams., Phoenix, 2003—05, campus dir., 2005—. Met. Coll., Phoenix, 2005. Adj. prof. Chapman U., Sierra Vista, 1990—92; tax preparer H&R Block, Sierra Vista, 1990—92; br. mgr. Jackson Hewitt Tax Svc. Met. Ctr., Phoenix, 2002—. Voter registration ofcl. Maricopa County, Ariz., 2001—02; treas. Antioch Missionary Bapt. Ch., Huachuca City, Ariz., 1991—92. Decorated Bronze Star. Mem.: Assn. Old Crows, Ret. Officers Assn., Assn. U.S. Army, Air Force Assn., Scabbard and Blade, Iota Beta Sigma, Phi Alpha Theta. Republican. Baptist. Avocations: photography, reading, coaching youth football and baseball. Office: IIA 6049 N 43rd Ave Phoenix AZ 85019-1600 Office Phone: 602-242-6265 210. Personal E-mail: azlynnmac@hotmail.com. Business E-Mail: lmcconnell@iia.edu.

**MCCONNELL, BRUCE WILLIAM,** information technology executive; b. Washington, Oct. 26, 1949; s. John Paul McConnell and Sally Dean McConnell Breul; m. Margaret Reagan Anderson. BS, Stanford U., 1971; MPA, U. Wash., 1985. Registered professional engr., Wash. Engr. Austin-Mac, Inc., Seattle, 1980-83; analyst U.S. Office of Mgmt. and Budget, Washington, 1985—92, chief info. policy and tech., 1992—99; dir. Internat. Y2K Cooperation Ctr., Washington, 1999—2000; co-chair encryption policy com. U.S. Nat. Security Coun., Washington, 1996—2000; mem. Dispute Resolution Panel WIPO ICANN, 2000—. Mem. bd. visitors RH Smith Sch. of Bus., U. Md., College Park, 2000—; mem. policy group on network-enabled svcs. and govt. Harvard U. Kennedy Sch. Government, Cambridge, Mass., 1997—. Bd. trustees Charles Babbage Found., 2003—; tenor Vocal Express, Washington, 2003—. Recipient Eagle award, Fed. Computer Week, 2000, Elmer B. Staats award for accountability in govt., Am. Soc. Pub. Administrn.,

2000. Mem.: Nat. Press Club. Office: McConnell Internat LLC 1301 K St NW Ste 450 W Washington DC 20005 Business E-Mail: mcconnell@mcconnellinternational.com.

**MCCONNELL, CHARLES PRESCOTT,** retired science educator; b. Wayne, Nebr., Mar. 3, 1942; s. Charlie Irving and Truma McConnell; m. Cathie Dianne Harris, Aug. 22, 1964; children: Stefanie Michele, John Edward. BS, U. Nebr., 1964, MS, 1967. Tchr. Fresno Unified Sch. Dist., Calif., 1967—2001. Active Boy Scouts Am. Recipient Silver Beaver award. Mem. NEA (life), Calif. Tchr. Assn., Fresno Tchr. Assn. (life), Calif. Retired Tchr. Assn., Quarter Century Wireless Assn. (life), Am. Radio Relay League (life, sect. mgr. 1976-89, 2002-, vice dir. Pacific div. 1988-90, dir. 1990-93), Sigma Xi (assoc.). Republican. Lutheran. Avocation: amateur radio. Home: 1658 W Mesa Ave Fresno CA 93711-1944 E-mail: w6dpd@arrl.org.

**MCCONNELL, DANA RAE,** psychologist; b. Jan. 3, 1977; d. Bernard John and Marlyce Joan Konter; m. Scott Patrick McConnell, July 5, 2003. BS, U. Wis., Eau Claire, 1999; MS in Edn., U. Wis., Menominie, 2000, cert. edn. specialization in sch. psychology, 2002. Nat. cert. sch. psychologist. Sch. psychologist Indepedence (Wis.) Sch. Dist., 2001—03, Eau Claire Area Sch. Dist., 2003—. Adj. prof. U. Wis., Menomonie, 2005. Contbg. author Childhood Disorders: Diagnostic Desk Reference, 2003. Recipient Cooperative Rsch. Achievement award, U. Wis., Menomonie, 2003. Mem.: Nat. Assn. Sch. Psychologists. Avocations: hiking, camping, fishing, hunting, geocaching. Business E-Mail: dmcconnell@ecasd.k12.wi.us.

**MCCONNELL, DAVID KELSO,** lawyer; b. NYC, July 12, 1932; s. David and Caroline Hanna (Kelso) McC.; m. Alice Schmitt, Dec. 26, 1953; children: Elissa Anne McConnell Henebry, Kathleen Anne, David Willet. BCE, CCNY, 1954; LLB, Yale U., 1962. Bar: Conn. 1962, U.S. Dist. Ct. Conn. 1963, U.S. Ct. Appeals (2d cir.) 1964, U.S. Ct. Appeals (3d cir.) 1966, U.S. Sup. Ct. 1970, U.S. Dist. Ct. (ea. dist.) Pa. 1971, Pa. 1975, N.Y. 1986. Asst. counsel N.Y.N.H. & H.R.R. New Haven, 1962-65, counsel, 1966-68; asst. atty. gen. U.S. V.I., 1965-66; asst. gen. atty. Pa. Cen. Transp. Co., New Haven, 1969-70, asst. gen. counsel Phila., 1970-71, sr. reorganization atty., 1971, adminstrv. officer, spl. counsel to trustees, 1971-76, gen. atty., 1977-78; asst. to chmn., CEO The Penn Cen. Corp., N.Y.C., 1979-80, corp. sec., 1980-82; v.p., gen. counsel Gen. Cable Co., Greenwich, Conn., 1982-85; pvt. practice Stamford, Conn., 1985-86, Pelham, N.Y., 1989-91, Greenwich, Conn., 1991-98. Of counsel McCarthy, Fingar, Donovan, Drazen & Smith, White Plains, N.Y., 1986-89. Dep. supr., councilman Town of Pelham, NY, 1986—90, budget officer; dep. mayor, trustee Village of Pelham, 1992—95, village atty., 1995—96; clk. of session, elder, trustee, deacon Huguenot Meml. Ch., Pelham; pres., bd. dirs. Newport Rotary Charities Fund, 2005—. With USN, 1954—59, with USNR, 1959—79. Mem.: Mil. Officers Assn., Navy League, Yale Law Sch. Assn. (exec. com. 1988—91, dir. New Eng. 2001—), Assn. Bar City NY, NY Bar Assn., Conn. Bar Assn., Quindecim, The Corinthians (mem. afterguard, dir. The Corinthians Assn., fleet capt. New Eng. fleet, trustee, pres., treas., sec. The Corinthians Endowment Fund), St. Andrews Soc. NY (bd. mgrs. 1986—89, chmn. bd. mgrs. 1988—89, bd. mgrs. 1996—99), Little Ship Club, Newport Sail and Power Squadron, Rotary Club of Newport RI (dir. 2001—), Rotary Club of The Pelhams NY (pres. 1993—94). Home: 68 1/2 Roseneath Ave Newport RI 02840-3849 E-mail: david.mcconnell.law.62@aya.yale.edu.

**MCCONNELL, E. HOY, II,** advertising and public policy executive; b. Syracuse, NY, May 14, 1941; s. E. Hoy and Dorothy R. (Schmitt) McC.; m. Patricia Irwin, June 26, 1965; children: E. Hoy, III, Courtney. BA in Am. Studies magna cum laude with high honors, Yale U., 1963; MBA in Mktg, Harvard Bus. Sch., 1965. With Foote, Cone & Belding, Chgo., 1965-76, v.p. account supr., 1971—76; with D'Arcy-MacManus & Masius, Chgo., 1976-85, sr. v.p. dir. client services, then vice chmn., 1978-80, pres., 1980-84, chmn., 1984-85; mng. dir. D'Arcy Masius Benton & Bowles, Chgo., 1986-96, also bd. dirs.; sr. v.p., account dir. Leo Burnett Co., Chgo., 1996-98; exec. dir. Bus. and Profl. People for the Pub. Interest, 1999—. Bd. dirs. Evanston (Ill.) United Way, 1980-83, Evanston Youth Hockey Assn., 1980-89, pres. 1981-83; bd. dirs. Off-the-Street Club, 1980-90, Bus. Profl. People for Pub. Interest, 1981-, v.p. 1984-89, pres. 1990-95; co-chair Housing Ill., 2002-; bd. dirs. Harvard Bus. Sch. Club, 1990-92; bd. dirs. The Cradle Soc., 2000—, mem. exec com., 2004-, sec, 2004-05, treas., 2005-; mem. Chgo. Coun. on Fgn. Rels., 1989-95, Wayfarers Club, 2001-. Mem. Am. Assn. Advt. Agys. (gov.-at-large Chgo. coun. 1984, sec. 1986, vice chmn. 1987, chmn. 1988-89), Glen View Country Club (bd. dirs. 1992-96), Dairymen's Country Club, Yale Club Chgo. (bd. dirs. 1996-99). Democrat. Unitarian Universalist. Home: 2703 Colfax St Evanston IL 60201-2035 Office: BPI 25 E Washington St Ste 1515 Chicago IL 60602-1804 Office Phone: 312-759-8259. Business E-Mail: hmcconnell@bpichicago.org.

**MCCONNELL, EDWARD BOSWORTH,** legal association administrator, lawyer; b. Greenwich, Conn., Apr. 3, 1920; s. Raymond Arnott and Anna Bell (Lee) McC.; m. Jeanne M. Rotton (dec. 1984); children: Annalee, Marilyn, Edward (dec. 1994), Barbara, William; m. Florence M. Leonard, (dec. 1991); stepchildren: Susan L. Little, William R. Leonard, Molly M. Leonard. AB, U. Nebr., 1941, LLB, 1947; MBA with distinction, Harvard U., 1943. Bar: Nebr. 1947, NJ 1950. Mem. faculty Rutgers U. Sch. Bus. Adminstrn., Newark, 1947-53; assoc. firm Toner, Speakman and Crowley, Newark, 1949-50; adminstrv. asst. and law sec. to Chief Justice of NJ, 1950-53; adminstrv. dir. Cts. of NJ, Trenton, 1953-73; also standing master Supreme Ct., 1953-73; pres. Nat. Center for State Cts., Williamsburg, 1973-90, bd. dirs., 1980-90, pres. emeritus, 1990—, cons. on ct. mgmt., 1990—. Mem. US Dept. Justice Coun. on Role of Cts. in Am. Soc., 1978-83; mem. adv. com. Dispute Resolution Policy Study, Social Sci. Rsch. Inst., U. So. Calif., 1975-79, Civil Litigation Rsch. Project, U. Wis. and U. So. Calif., 1979-83, nat. judge edn. program to promote equality for men and women in the cts., 1980—; mem. Nat. Crim. Justice Task Force, Urban Consortium, 1979-83; participant Access To Justice Colloquium, European Univ. Inst., Florence, Italy, 1979; nat. adv. coun. Ct. Adminstrn. Justice, Wayne State U., 1973-76; nat. project com. State Jud. Info. Sys. Project SEARCH Group, 1973-76; lectr. Inst. of Local and State Govt. Wharton Sch. U. Pa., 1955-65, Appellate Judges Seminar, Inst. Jud. Adminstrn., NYU, 1962-75; vis. expert UN Asia and Far East Inst., Tokyo, 1971; mem. Cts. Task Force Nat. Adv. Commn. Criminal Justice Standards and Goals, 1971-73; nat. adv. com. DC Ct. Mgmt. Project, 1966-70; trustee Inst. Ct. Mgmt., 1969-73, 84-86; chmn. Nat. Conf. Ct. Adminstrv. Officers, 1956; mem. nat. task force on gender bias in cts. Nat. Assn. Women Judge's 1985-90; mem. adv. bd. Nat. Ctr. for Citizen Participation in Adminstrn. of Justice, 1984-90; mem. Common. Trial Ct. Performance Standards, 1991-95. Mem. adv. com. on article III Commn. on the Bicentennial of the Constitution, 1989-91; adv. com. Judicary Leadership Coun., 1990-95. Maj. C.E., AUS, 1943-46, European Theater, 1944-46. Decorated Bronze Star medal; recipient Warren E. Burger award for greatest contbn. to improvement of ct. adminstrn. Inst. for Ct. Mgmt., 1975, Herbert Lincoln Harley award for efficient adminstrn. justice Am. Judicature Soc., 1973, Glenn R. Winters award for outstanding service in jud. adminstrn. Am. Judges Assn., 1974, Tom C. Clark award for outstanding contbns. to field of ct. adminstrn. Nat. Conf. Met. Cts., 1983, Award of Merit Nat. Assn. Ct. Mgmt., 1987, Spl. award, Nat. Assn. Women Judges, 1989, Paul E. Reardon award for disting. svc. Nat. Ctr. for State Cts., 1991, Alumni Achievement award U. Nebr., 1991, Robert B. Yegge award ABA Jud. Divsn. Lawyers Conf., 1997. Fellow Nat. Acad. Pub. Adminstrn. (mem. panel on evaluation budget decentralization project of fed. cts. 1989-91, mem. panel long range planning in fed. cts. 1991-92, mem. panel on study of fed. trial ct. adminstrv. structure 1995-96); mem. ABA (fellow-at-large, coun. members 1960-66, 71-80, house of dels., 1977-80, chmn. com. on oversight and goals 1975-76, chmn. com. on jud. compensation jud. adminstrn. div. 1984-89, chmn. jud. adminstrn. div. 1976-77, sect. of litigation jud. adminstrn. div. 1986-88, task force on reduction of litigation cost and delay, jud. adminstrn. div. 1984-94, chmn. 1991-94, mem. long range planning com. 1989-94), N.J. Bar Assn., Nebr. Bar Assn., Fellows of Am. Bar Found. (life), Warren E.

Burger Soc., Kingsmill (Va.) Golf Club, Kingsmill Tennis Club (pres. 2001), Kingsmill Yacht Club, Order of Coif (hon.), Delta Upsilon, Sigma Delta Phi, Phi Delta Phi. Office Phone: 757-220-3012. Personal E-mail: ebm80@aol.com.

**MCCONNELL, GLENN F.,** state legislator, lawyer, art gallery director; b. Charleston, S.C., Dec. 11, 1947; s. Samuel W. and Evelyn (McDaniel) McConnell. BS, Coll. of Charleston, 1969; JD, U. S.C., 1972. Bar: S.C. 1972. Pres. CSA Galleries, Inc., Charleston; mem. S.C. Senate, Columbia, 1981—, pres. pro tempore, 2001—, chmn. judiciary com., mem. banking and ins. com., ethics com., judiciary com., labor, commerce and industry com., rules com., fish, game and forestry com., interstate coop. Bd. dirs. Neighborhood Legal Assistance Program, 1977—80, S.C. Battle Ground Preservation Trust, Inc.; mem. Am. Legis. Exch. Coun.; chair African Am. History Monument Commn.; chmn. Hunley Commn.; del. Rep. Nat. Conv., 1980, 1984, 1988; chmn. Charleston County Rep. Com., 1978—82. Recipient Outstanding Achievement award, S.C. Rep. Com., 1980. Mem.: SCV, 19th Ind. Vols., 27th S.C. Eutaw Vols., Palmetto Bn., Scottish Soc. Charleston, Pi Kappa Phi. Episcopalian. Office: 101 Gressette Bldg PO Box 142 Columbia SC 29202 Office Phone: 803-212-6610. Business E-Mail: sjv@scsenate.org.

**MCCONNELL, J. DANIEL,** marketing and public relations professional; b. Noblesville, Ind., Oct. 5, 1944; s. John Worley and Nadine Lillian (McFarlin) McC.; m. Jane Brantlinger, June 29, 1968. AB in English/Journalism, Ind. U., 1966, MS in Bus. 1968. Asst. to pres. Ind. U. Found., Bloomington, 1966-67; legis. liaison Dept. HEW, Washington, 1968; dir. pub. rels. Cummins Engine Co., Columbus, Ind., 1970-72, dir investor comm., 1972-75, dir. exec. recruiting, 1975-77; prin., CEO The McConnell Co. Pub. Rels., Seattle, 1977-93; sr. v.p., group dir. Elgin DDB, Seattle, 1993-96, sr. v.p., mng. dir., 1997—. Founder The Mountain Summit Internat. Symposium, 1987—; co-founder Coll. Baseball Classic Found., 1990-95; bd. dirs. Great Adventures Ltd., Jersey, U.K. Bd. dirs. Child Haven, Seattle, 1985-91, Internat. Snow Leopard Trust, Seattle, 1991-95, Pacific Crest Outward Bound Sch., Portland, Oreg., 1992-2001; trustee Seattle Ctrl. C.C., 1992—, bd. pres., 1997—; mem. adv. bd. pub. rels. cert. program U. Wash., 1990—, instr., 1991—. Capt. U.S. Army, 1968-70. Mem. Pub. Rels. Soc. (Hoosier chpt. bd. dirs. 1975-77, Puget Sound bd. dirs. 1995-98). Avocations: skiing, mountain climbing, racquetball, sailing. Office: DDB Seattle 1000 2nd Ave #1000 Seattle WA 98104-1094 E-mail: dan.mcconnell@sea.ddb.com.

**MCCONNELL, JACK BAYLOR,** retired corporate executive, physician; b. Crumpler, W.Va., Feb. 1, 1925; s. Enoch L. and Mattie (Davidson) McC.; m. Mary Ellen Rhodes, Nov. 29, 1958; children: Steven Rhodes, Katherine Marie, Page Samuel. Student, U. Va., 1943-45, U. Miss., 1945-47; MD, U. Tenn., 1949; postgrad., Columbia U., 1963, Harvard U., 1972; DSc (hon.), Emory & Henry Coll., 1982; HHD (hon.), Presbyn. Coll. of SC, 1998. Dir. clin. investigation Lederle Labs., Pearl River, NY, 1953-61; v.p. comml. devel. McNeil Labs., Ft. Washington, Pa., 1961-68; corp. dir. advanced tech. Johnson & Johnson, New Brunseick, NJ, 1968—89. Trustee Morristown (N.J.) Meml. Hosp., 1977-87; bd. dirs. African Med. and Rsch. Found., NYC. Author: The Story of the Volunteers in Medicine Clinic, 1998. Mem. Bd. Health, Basking Ridge, N.J., 1972-74; cons. U.S. Senate, Washington, 1987—. With USN, 1943-46; founder, chmn. emeritus, Vols. in Medicine Clinic, Hilton Head, SC., 1994-, Vols. in Medicine Inst. Recipient Disting. Scientist award Tenn. Tech. Found., 1985, Disting. Svc. to State Govt. award Nat. Govs.' Assn., 1993, Outstanding Svc. award Hilton Head Chpt. NAACP, 1993, award of Achievement, Gleitsman Found., 1994, Cmty. Svc. award SC Hosp. Assn., 1994, Citizen of Yr. award Presbyn. Men's Club of Hilton Head, 1995, Nat. Assn. Cmty. Health Ctrs. award, 1997, Disting. Svc. Award, SC Rural Health, 1999, Humanitarian award Watson Clinic Found., Lakeland, Fla., 2000, Pride in Profession award AMA Found., 2004; named Humanitarian of Yr., Kidney Found. of NJ, 1988, Disting. Alumnus of Yr., U. Tenn. Coll. Medicine, 1990, Physician of Yr., Nat. Assn. Hospice and Home Care, 1995; named one of 200 Disting. Grads., U. Tenn., 1994; named to Order of the Palmetto, State of SC, 1999. Mem. AMA. Avocations: sports, jazz, travel, bridge.

**MCCONNELL, JOHN,** environmental activist, founder of Earth Day; b. Davis City, Iowa, Mar. 22, 1915; Founder & v.p. Nobell Rsch. Found., LA, 1939; publisher Toe Valley View, NC, 1956, Mountain View, Calif., 1959; dir. No. Calif. Meals for Millions, 1962; founder Minute for Peace, 1963, World Equality Inc., 1968; proposed & organized Earth Day, 1969; founder Earth Soc., 1973. Author: Earth Charter, 1979, 77 Theses on the Care of Earth, 1985, Earth Magna Carta, 1995. Mailing: Earth Trustees Inc 4924 E Kentucky Circle Denver CO 80246 E-mail: trusteeone@aol.com.

**MCCONNELL, JOHN EDWARD,** retired electrical engineering company executive; b. Minot, ND, July 28, 1931; s. Lloyd Waldorf and Sarah McConnell; m. Carol Claire Myers, July 4, 1952 (dec. Feb. 1989); children: Kathleen Anne, James, Amy Lynn; m. Heidi Banziger, Sept. 29, 1990. BSME, U. Pitts., 1952; MS, Drexel Inst. Tech., 1958. Registered profl. engr., Pa. With mktg. and design depts. for turbomachinery Westinghouse Electric Corp., Lester, Pa., 1954-60, 63-67, Pitts., 1960-63; mgr. power generation equipment activities in U.S. ASEA Inc., White Plains, NY, 1967-79, regional mgr. power equipment activities Middle Atlantic and Southeastern U.S. regions, 1967-79, mgr. turbine generator dept., 1979-83, mgr. internat. ops. Power Sys. divsn., 1983-84, mgr. transmission substas. dept., 1984-85; mgr. Ea. U.S. ops. ASEA Power Sys., Inc., 1985-86, mgr. ea. ops. measurement divsn. GEC, 1986-91; mgr. ea. region Protection and Control divsn. GEC Alsthom T&D Inc., 1991 98; prin. JEMTECH, 1998—2003, v.p. ATG Exodus, 2000—02. Adviser U.S. Congress 1968-74; spkr. in field Contbr. articles on energy and electric power to profl. jours. 1st lt. C.E., U.S. Army, 1952-54. Mem. IEEE (life, sr., energy com., past chmn. subcom. energy conservation and cogeneration, hon. mem. power sys. relay com.), IEEE Power Engring. Soc. (sr., past chmn. chpts. pub. affairs subcom.). Republican. Achievements include development of analytical techniques for power systems performance characteristics and economics of cogeneration sys. Home: 173 Remington Rd Ridgefield CT 06877-4324 Office: JEMTECH PO Box 229 Ridgefield CT 06877-0229 Personal E-mail: j.e.mcconnell@ieee.org. Business E-Mail: mcconnell173@cs.com. *1) If it doesn't produce revenue, is it worthwhile? 2) Problem solving begins with careful listening. 3) Keep people informed. If they don't know, they'll assume the worst. 4) The truth is the most credible explanation you'll find.*

**MCCONNELL, JOHN HOWARD,** personnel management consultant, writer; b. Highland Park, Mich., June 18, 1933; s. Melvin William and Dorothy Marie (Miller) McC.; m. Dolores Ann Cooper, Oct. 29, 1955; children: Keith Ernest, Brian Howard, Eric William. BS, Wayne State U., 1957, MEd, 1963. Tchr. Detroit Bd. Edn., 1957-59, Highland Park Bd. Edn., 1959-60; personnel mgr. Wolverine Tube Co., Allen Park, Mich., 1960-69; personnel dir. Garan, Inc., N.Y.C., 1970-71; cons. Morristown, N.J. 1971-74; cons. human resource mgmt., pres. McConnell, Simmons & Co., Inc., Morristown, 1974—. Bd. dirs. Circus Royale, Inc. Morristown. Author: How To Audit, 8 vols., 1974-85, Introduction to Human Resources, 1982, A Ring, A Horse and A Clown, 1994, Shrine Circus, 1998, Hunting Heads, 1999, Auditing the Human Resources Department, 2000, How to Identify Training Needs, 2002, How to Design, Implement and Interpret an Employee Survey, 2003, How to Develop Essential HR Policies and Procedures, 2004; prodr. Player's Theater in Concert, 1989, 90, London Follies, 1994, 96; contbr. articles to various publs. Pres. Morristown Civic Assn., 1980. Mem. Am. Psychol. Assn., Am. Mgmt. Assn., Acad. Magical Arts, Magic Castle Club (L.A.), Circus Hist. Soc. (bd. dirs.), Masons. Democrat. Methodist. Avocation: producing entertainment events. Home: 1 Skyline Dr Morristown NJ 07960-5146 Office: 73 E Hanover Ave Morristown NJ 07960-3161 Office Phone: 201-859-5514. Business E-Mail: john@mcconnell-simmons.com.

**MCCONNELL, JOHN P.,** metal products executive; With Worthington Industries, Columbus, Ohio, 1975—, v.p.: gen. mgr., 1985, dir., 1990—, vice chmn., 1992—96, CEO, 1993—, chmn., 1996—. Bd. dir. Alltel Corp., The Wilds. Office: Worthington Industries 200 Old Wilson Bridge Rd Columbus OH 43085

**MCCONNELL, JOHN THOMAS,** publishing executive; b. Peoria, Ill., May 1, 1945; s. Golden A. and Margaret (Lyon) McC.; 1 child, Justin. BA, U. Ariz., 1967. Mgr. Fast Printing Co., Peoria, 1970-71; mgmt. trainee Quad-Cities Times, Davenport, Iowa, 1972-73; asst. mgr., then v.p., gen. mgr. Peoria Jour. Star, 1973-81, pub., 1981—, pres., 1987—; v.p. The Copley Press, Inc., Peoria, 1997—. Bd. dirs. Peoria Downtown Devel. Council, Peoria Devel. Corp.; past trustee Methodist Hosp., Peoria. Served with USAR, 1967-69. Named Young Man of Year Peoria Jaycees, 1979 Mem. Peoria Advt. and Selling Club, Peoria C. of C. Clubs: Peoria Country, Mt. Hawley C.C. Congregationalist. Office: Peoria Jour Star Inc 1 News Plz Peoria IL 61643-0001 Business E-Mail: mac@pjstar.com

**MCCONNELL, JOHN WILLIAM, JR.,** lawyer; b. Bessemer, Ala., Apr. 17, 1921; s. John W. and Elizabeth (Sheridan) McC.; m. Margaret B. Snider, Jan. 7, 1944; children—Margaret E. (Mrs. John Evans), Rebecca L. (Mrs. A.D. Braden), Catherine L., John W. III. AB, U. Ala., 1942, MA, 1946; LL.B., Yale, 1948. Bar: Ala. 1948, D.C. 1977. Atty. Inge, Twitty, Armbrecht & Jackson, Mobile, Ala., 1948-56, Armbrecht, Jackson, McConnell & DeMouy, 1956-65; dir. U.S. Peace Corps, Nigeria, 1965-68; v.p. legal Sea-Land Service, Inc., Menlo Park, NJ, 1968-76; also dir., of counsel Haight, Gardner, Poor & Havens, Washington, 1977-94. Atty. for Reynolds v. Sims on legislative reapportionment, U.S. Supreme Ct., 1963-64 Mem. Ala. Dem. Exec. Com., 1963-65. Served to capt. AUS, 1943-46, 50-52, maj. ret., 1957. Mem. ABA, Ala. Bar Assn., D.C. Bar Assn., Maritime Law Assn.

**MCCONNELL, LORELEI CATHERINE,** retired library director; b. Port Jefferson, NY, Dec. 5, 1938; d. Alvin and Mary (McConnell) Philibert; m. Thomas McConnell, Jan. 20, 1962; children: Catherine, Michael. BA, Drew U., 1960; MLS, Rutgers U., 1963. Reference libr. Irvington (N.J.) Pub. Libr., 1963-90, dir., 1990-98; founder Irvington Literacy Program, 1986, dir., 1986-90; ret., 1999; cons., 2000—. Mem. exec. bd. Infolink, 1998-99. Mem. ALA, N.J. Libr. Assn. (mem. exec. bd. 1990-93, N.J. Libr. of Yr. 1993-94), Irvington (N.J.) C. of C. (exec. bd. 1992—), Civic award 1996), Beta Phi Mu. Home: 563 Park St Montclair NJ 07043-2027 *The world would be a better place if we could find ways to reward and honor every single person who works hard and does the right thing.*

**MCCONNELL, MARY PATRICIA,** lawyer; b. Mpls., Sept. 30, 1952; BS, U. Minn., 1978; JD, William Mitchell Coll. Law, St. Paul, 1984. Bar: Minn. 1988. Sr. biologist C.E., U.S. Army, St. Paul, 1979-84; asst. county atty. Dakota County, Hastings, Minn., 1985—92; ptnr. Lindquist & Vennum, Mpls., 1992—95; from v.p. environ. and regulatory affairs to sr. v.p., gen. counsel, sec. Genmar Holdings, Inc., 1995—2002; gen. counsel control products divsn. Honeywell, 2002—03; v.p., gen. counsel Polaris Industries, Inc., Medinia, Minn., 2003—. Master gardener U. Minn. Ext., St. Paul, 1992—. Contbr. articles to profl. jours. Dir. Wetlands Forum, Mpls., 1990—. Mem. Minn. Bar Assn. (governing coun. environ. and natural resources 1990—, law sect.), Mpls. C. of C. (Leadership Mpls. 1992). Office: Polaris Industries Inc 2100 Highway 55 Medina MN 55340 Office Phone: 763-542-0500. Office Fax: 763-542-0599. E-mail: mary.mcconnell@polarisind.com.

**MCCONNELL, MATTHEW STEPHEN,** composer; b. North Adams, Mass., Dec. 1, 1980; s. Stephen Earl and Patricia Ann McConnell. BA in Music, Bennington Coll., 2003; MusM in Composition, New England Conservatory, 2005. Organist St. Andrew's Episcopal Chapel, North Adams, Mass., 1996—2003; choir dir. 1st Bapt. Ch., Cheshire, 1998—99; asst. instr. composition Bennington Coll., Vt., 2002; music copyist Ricky Ian Gordon, 2002—04. Pvt. tutor, Boston, 2003—; freelance organist, 2003—; co-founder, performer The Toyland Band, Boston, 2004—. Composer: Sonata for Solo Viola, 2003, Piano Trio No. 1, 2004, Concerto for Toy Piano & Chamber Orch., 2004. Benefit concert organist Salvation Army, North Adams, Mass., 1999, Berkshire Food Project, 2000, C.O.D.Y. Youth Project, 2001. Grantee, Wolley Fund Composition, 2003; scholar, Berkshire AGO, 1993—94, The Conducting Inst., 2001. Mem.: Am. Guild Organists. Episcopalian. Home: 39 Williams St North Adams MA 01247

**MCCONNELL, MICHAEL,** art educator; b. 1944; Prof. art U. NH, chmn. art dept. Office: Dept Art & Art History University N H 30 College Rd Durham NH 03824-3538 Office Fax: 603-862-2190. E-mail: michael.mcconnell@unh.edu.

**MCCONNELL, MICHAEL ARTHUR,** lawyer; b. Ft. Worth, Jan. 15, 1947; BA, Loyola U., New Orleans, 1969; JD, U. Tex., 1972. Bar: Tex. 1976, U.S. Dist. Ct. (no. dist.) Tex. 1976, U.S. Dist. Ct. (ea. dist.) Tex. 1981, U.S. Dist. Ct. (we. dist.) Tex. 1982, U.S. Dist. Ct. (so. dist.) Tex. 1989, U.S. Ct. Appeals (5th cir.) Tex. 1980, U.S. Ct. Appeals (10th cir.) 1987. Briefing atty. U.S. Dist. Ct. Hon. Eldon B. Mahon, Ft. Worth, 1976-77; assoc. atty. Cantey, Hanger, Gooch, Munn and Collins, Ft. Worth, 1977-81, ptnr., 1981-83; judge no. dist. U.S. Bankruptcy Ct., Ft. Worth, 1983-86; ptnr. Jackson Walker LLP, Ft. Worth, 1988—95, McConnell & Assocs., Ft. Worth, 1995—2000, Winstead Sechrest & Miniak P.C., Ft. Worth, 2000—06, Kelly Hart & Hallman LLP, Ft. Worth, 2006—. Sgt. USAF, 1969-73. Mem. Nat. Conf. Bankruptcy Judges. Office: Kelly Hart & Hallman LLP 201 Main St Ste 2500 Fort Worth TX 76102 Office Phone: 817-332-2500. Business E-Mail: michael.mcconnell@khh.com.

**MCCONNELL, MICHAEL THEODORE,** lawyer; b. San Francisco, June 18, 1954; s. Lawrence V. and Ann McConnell. BS, U. Oreg., 1977; JD, U. Denver, 1980. Bar: Colo., Wyo., U.S. Dist. Ct. Colo., U.S. Ct. Appeals (10th cir.), U.S. Supreme Ct., U.S. Dist. Ct. Wyo 1980-84; v.p. COO Guidant Corp., Indpls., Ill., 1998—. Bd. dir. Global Healthcare Exchange, Vesalius Ventures. Former chmn. Children's Mus. of Indpls., Am. Red Cross of Greater Indpls., Red Cross of Conner Prairie; former bd. mem. Acordia Personal Ins. Svcs.; hon. trustee Children's Mus. of Indpls.; bd. gov. Nat. Am. Red Cross; chmn. bd. trustee Trustee Leadership Development; bd. mem., info. tech. com. Cmty. Hosp. of Indpls., Inc., Ind. U. Info. Tech. Advancement Coun. Office: Guidant Corp 111 Monument Cir 2900 Indianapolis IN 46204-5129 Mailing: Guidant Corp PO Box 44906 Indianapolis IN 46244*

**MCCONNELL, MICHAEL V.,** medical educator, researcher; b. NYC; SB, MIT, 1983, SM in Elec. Engring., 1985; MD, Stanford U., 1990. Intern medicine Brigham and Women's Hosp., Boston, 1990-91, jr. asst. resident in internal medicine, 1991-92, cardiology fellow, 1992-96, assoc. physician medicine, 1996—; cardiovasc. imaging fellow Brigham and Women's Hosp., Beth Israel Hosp., Boston, 1995-96; clin. fellow in medicine Harvard Med. Sch., Boston, 1990-93, rsch. fellow in medicine, 1993-96, instr. medicine, 1996—. Tech. intern pacing rsch. divsn. Medtronic, Inc., 1982, 83; bioengring. apprentice Micro-Med, Paris, 1985. Contbr. articles to profl. jours. Recipient Undergrad. Rsch. award Uniroyal, 1981, Individual Nat. Rsch. Svc. award NHLBI, 1994, fellowship award for rsch. in cardiac imaging Bracco Diagnostics, Inc.-Soc. for Cardiac Angiography and Interventions, 1995. Mem. Am. Cardiology, Am. Heart Assn. Coun. Clin. Cardiology (student rsch. fellow 1987, clinician scientist award 1996), Internat. Soc. Magnetic Resonance Medicine, Mass. Med. Soc., Eta Kappa Nu, Sigma Xi, Tau Beta Pi. Achievements include research in magnetic resonance angiography of coronary artery disease, magnetic resonance imaging of atherosclerotic plaque.

**MC CONNELL, MICHAEL W.,** federal judge, law educator; b. Louisville, Ky., May 18, 1955; m. Mary Cargill Norton McConnell; 3 children. BA, Mich. State U., 1976; JD, U. Chgo., 1979. Bar: D.C. 1981. Law clk. to Hon. J. Skelly Wright U.S. Ct. Appeals (DC cir.), 1979-80; law clk. to Hon. William J. Brennan Jr. U.S. Supreme Ct., Washington, 1980-81; asst. gen. counsel U.S. Office of Mgmt. and Budget, Washington, 1981-83; asst. to the solicitor gen. U.S. Dept. Justice, Washington, 1983-85; asst. prof. U. Chgo.,

1984-89, prof., 1989—92, William Graham prof. law, 1992—96; Presdl. prof. U. Utah Coll. Law, 1997—2002; vis. prof. Harvard Law School, 1999; special consultant Mayer, Brown & Platt, 1989—2002; judge U.S. Ct. Appeals (10th Cir.), 2002—. Mem. Am. Acad. Arts and Scis., Order of Coif, Phi Beta Kappa, Phi Kappa Phi. Office: 10th Circuit Ct Appeals 125 S State St # 6404 Salt Lake City UT 84138*

**MCCONNELL, MITCHELL, JR., (ADDISON MITCHELL MCCONNELL JR.),** senator, lawyer; b. Tuscambia, Ala., Feb. 20, 1942; s. Addison Mitchell and Julia (Shockley) McC.; m. Elaine Chao, Feb. 6, 1993; children: Eleanor Hayes, Claire Redmon, Marion Porter. BA with honors, U. Louisville, 1964; JD, U. Ky., 1967. Bar: Ky. 1967. Chief legis. asst. to Senator Marlow Cook, Washington, 1968-70; sole practice Louisville, 1970-74; dep. asst. U.S. atty. gen. Washington, 1974-75; judge Jefferson County, Louisville, 1978-85; US Senator from Ky., 1985—; asst. majority leader, 2002—; chmn. Nat. Republican Senatorial Com. 105th and 106th Congress. Com. agr., nutrition, and forestry US Senate, com. appropriations, com. rules and adminstrn. Chmn. Jefferson County Republican Com., 1973-74; co-chmn. Nat. Child Tragedies Coalition, 1981; chmn., founder Ky. Task Force on Exploited and Missing Children, 1982; mem. Pres.'s Partnership on Child Safety. Recipient commendation Nat. Trust on Hist. Preservation in U.S., 1982, Conservationist of Yr. award League Ky. Sportsmen, 1983, cert. of appreciation Am. Correctional Assn., 1985, Golden Plow award, Am. Farm Bur. Fedn., 1996, Freedom award Nat. Coun. Union Burma, 1999, Sam Rainsy Pary Freedom award, 2002, Ky. Warbler Migratory Songbird Conservation award US Fish and Wildlife Svc., Ky. Dept. Fish and Wildlife Resources, 2002, Defender of Freedom award James Madison Ctr. Freedom Speech, 2002, Disting. Svc. award Am. Farm Bur., 2002. Mem. Ky. Assn. County Judge Execs. (pres. 1982), Nat. Inst. Justice (adv. bd. 1982-84) Republican. Baptist. Avocations: fishing, cooking. Office: US Senate 361-A Russell Office Bldg Washington DC 20510-0001 also: Gene Snyder US Courthouse Rm 630 601 West Broadway Louisville KY 40202-2228 Office Phone: 202-224-2541, 502-582-6304. Office Fax: 202-224-2499, 502-582-5326.*

**MCCONNELL, NICHOLAS STILLWELL,** lawyer; b. Chgo., May 25, 1946; s. James Millholland and Emily (Robinson) McC.; m. Nancy Haines Fifield, Dec. 14, 1968; children: Abigail Haven, Rebecca Fifield. BA, Bowdoin Coll., 1968; JD, George Wash. U., 1972. Bar: Va. Supreme Ct. 1972, U.S. Supreme Ct. 1973, U.S. Ct. Appeals D.C. 1973, D.C. Ct. Appeals 1973, U.S. Dist. Ct. D.C. 1973, Md. Ct. Appeals 1978, US Ct. Claims, 1991, US Ct. Appeals (11th cir), US Dist. Ct., Md., 2001. Assoc. Jackson, Gray & Laskey, Washington, 1972-78; prin. Jackson & Campbell, P.C., Washington, 1978—. Mem. faculty Nat. Inst. Trial Advocacy, South Bend, Ind., 1984-95; dir. Sauls Lithograph Co., Inc., Washington, 1986—; Am. Hospice Found. 1997-2003. Pres., dir. Combined Health Appeal Nat. Capital Area, Washington, 1980-93; dir. Combined Health Appeal Am., Atlanta, 1993-94; pres. Albert L. and Elizabeth T. Tucker Found, 1996—; dir. Am. Hospice Found. 1997-2003. With U.S. Army, 1969-71. Recipient Young Lawyer of Yr. award Bar Assn. D.C., 1982. Fellow Am. Coll. Trial Lawyers; mem. Am. Health Lawyers Assn., D.C. Def. Lawyers, Def. Rsch. Inst., Barristers (pres. 1998), Counsellors, Bar Assn. D.C. (pres.-elect 2002-03, pres. 2003-04), Am. Bar Assn. (house of dels., 2003-2004)9+, Cosmos Club, Lawyers Club Congregationalist. Avocations: tennis, squash, golf, sailing. Home: 5004 Warren St NW Washington DC 20016-4370 Office: Jackson & Campbell PC 1 Lafayette Ctr 300 S Tower 1120 20th St NW Washington DC 20036-3437 Office Phone: 202-457-1628. E-mail: nmcconnell@jackscamp.com.

**MCCONNELL, SUSAN K.,** neuroscientist; AB summa cum laude in Biology, Harvard and Radcliffe Colls., Mass., 1980; PhD in Neurobiology, Harvard U., Mass., 1987. Postdoctoral fellow dept. neurobiology Stanford U. Sch. Medicine, Calif., 1987—89, prof. neurology and neurol. scis., 2002—; asst. prof. biol. scis. Stanford U., 1989—95, assoc. prof., 1995—2000, prof., 2000—; Susan B. Ford prof. Stanford U. Sch. Humanities and Scis., 2003—. Mem. sci. adv. bd. Hereditary Disease Found., 1992—96, Cure Autism Now, 1997—2001, James S. McDonnell Found. Prog. in Brain Cancer Rsch., 2003—; mem. nat. adv. bd. Pew Scholars Prog. in Biomedical Scis., 1999—2005; mem. adv. com. Nat. Inst. Neurol. Disorders and Stroke Gene Expression Nervous Sys. Atlas, 2003—; mem. external adv. com. Rose F. Kennedy Ctr. Rsch. in Mental Retardation and Devel. Disabilities, Albert Einstein Coll. Medicine, 2004—; mem. external adv. bd. Alaskan Basic Neuroscience Prog. U. Alaska, Fairbanks, 2004—; mem. sci. adv. com. Studies to Advance Autism Rsch. and Treatment and Collaborative Progs. of Excellence in Autism Ctrs., 2004—. Contbr. articles to profl. jours.; ad hoc reviewer: Science, 1989—, mem. bd. reviewing editors:, 1996—2001, ad hoc reviewer: Neuron, 1989—, mem. editl. bd.:, 1995—, ad hoc reviewer: Cell, 1989—, Development, 1989—, mem. editl. adv. bd.:, 1999—2002, ad hoc reviewer: Devel. Biology, 1989—, European Jour. Neuroscience, 1989—, Jour. Neuroscience, 1989—, assoc. editor:, 1992—98, 2005—, mem. publs. com.: Soc. Neuroscience, 1993—96, mem. editl. bd.: Jour. Neurobiology, 1995—, Molecular and Cellular Biology, 1995—2002, reviewing editor: Molecular and Cellular Neuroscience, 2002—, mem. editl. com.: Ann. Rev. Cell and Devel. Biology, 1999—2004; co-editor: Fundamental Neuroscience, 2002. Named Pew Scholar, Biomedical Scis., 1989—94, McKnight Scholar, 1993—96, McKnight Investigator, 1997—99; recipient Nat. Rsch. Svc. award, Nat. Eye Inst., 1987—89, Searle Scholars award, 1989—92, Marcus Singer award, 1990, Presdl. Young Investigator award, NSF, 1991—93, Hoagland prize, Undergraduate Tchg., 1997; grantee Presdl. Faculty fellowship, NSF, 1993—96, Alfred P. Sloan Rsch. fellowship, 1991—93. Fellow: Am. Acad. Arts & Scis.; mem.: Soc. Devel. Biology, AAAS, Soc. Neuroscience (Young Investigator award 1995), Phi Beta Kappa. Office: Dept Biol Scis Stanford U Stanford CA 94305-5020 E-mail: suemcc@stanford.edu.*

**MCCONNELL, WILLIAM F., JR.,** medical products executive; b. LaGrange, Ill. BS in sys. analysis, Miami U., Oxford, Ohio, 1971. CPA. Staff mem. Arthur Andersen LLP, Indpls., 1971—75, mgr., 1975—81, ptnr., 1981—83, mng. ptnr., bus. cons., 1983—89, rejoined, 1997; CFO Resort Condo. Internat., 1989—90, COO, 1990—96, info. officer, worldwide, 1996—97; v.p., COO Guidant Corp., Indpls., Ill., 1998—. Bd. dir. Global Healthcare Exchange, Vesalius Ventures. Former chmn. Children's Mus. of Indpls., Am. Red Cross of Greater Indpls., Red Cross of Conner Prairie; former bd. mem. Acordia Personal Ins. Svcs.; hon. trustee Children's Mus. of Indpls.; bd. gov. Nat. Am. Red Cross; chmn. bd. trustee Trustee Leadership Development; bd. mem., info. tech. com. Cmty. Hosp. of Indpls., Inc., Ind. U. Info. Tech. Advancement Coun. Office: Guidant Corp 111 Monument Cir 2900 Indianapolis IN 46204-5129 Mailing: Guidant Corp PO Box 44906 Indianapolis IN 46244*

**MCCONNELL, WILLIAM STEWART,** application developer; b. Munich, June 30, 1955; s. William Marion and Mary Catherine McConnell; m. Lisa Ann Fuller, July 17, 2004; children: Ashley Marie Fuller, Brian Daniel Fuller, Caleb Matthew Fuller WhiteSide. AS in Aerospace Control Sys., CC. USAF, 1983; AS in Computer Info. Sys., George C. Wallace State C.C., 1995; BS in Computer Info. Sys., Troy State U., 1998; MS in Computer Info. Sys., U. Phoenix, 2005. Commd. lt. USAF, 1974, advanced through grades to MSGT, 1974—87, non-commissioned officer various assignments, 1977—93, ret., 1994; warehouse mgr. The Barn, Ozark, Ala., 1993—98; software designer Grossman and Assocs., Savoy, Ill., 1998—. Dist. leader Boy Scouts Am., Del Rio, Tex., 1989—92. Decorated Commendation medal USAF, Meritorious Svc. medal, Achievement medal. Avocations: music, ballroom dancing. Home: 1353 Abram Dr Rantoul IL 61866 Office: Grossman and Assocs 5 Dunlap Ct Savoy IL 61840 Office Phone: 217-398-1986. Personal E-mail: stew_mcconnell@hotmail.com. Business E-Mail: smcconnell@gman.com.

**MCCONNELL, WILLIAM THOMPSON,** bank executive; b. Zanesville, Ohio, Aug. 8, 1933; s. William Gerald and Mary Gladys McC.; m. Jane Charlotte Cook, Aug. 25, 1956; children: Jennifer Wynne, William Gerald. BA, Denison U., 1955; MBA, Northwestern U., 1959. Pres. Park Nat. Bank, Newark, Ohio, 1979-83, pres., chief exec. officer, 1983-93, chmn., chief exec. officer, 1993-98, also bd. dirs., chmn., 1999—2004; pres., chief exec. officer

Park Nat. Corp., Newark, 1987-94, chmn., CEO, 1994-98, chmn., 1999—2004, chmn. exec. com., 2005—. Mem. Newark Area C. of C. (past pres., dir. 1977-83), Ohio Bankers Assn. (pres., chmn. 1981-83), Am. Bankers Assn. (pres. 1997-98). Office: Park Nat Bank PO Box 3500 Newark OH 43058-3500

**MCCONNELL, III, BRIGHT,** orthopaedic surgeon; b. Augusta, Ga., Mar. 3, 1953; s. Bright McConnell, Jr. and Elizabeth Custer McConnell; m. Pam Hollings, Oct. 14, 1978; children: Elizabeth Anne McConnell, Bright McConnell, IV, Ian Deryck McConnell. BS, Davidson Coll., NC, 1971—75; MD, Med. Coll. Ga., Augusta, 1975—79. Lic. orthopaedic surgeon Am. Bd. Orthopaedic Surgery, 1987, cert. clin. densitometrist Internat. Soc. Clin. Densitometry, 2001. Residency in orthopaedic surgery U. Fla., 1984; fellowship in sports medicine Kerlan-Jobe Orthopaedic Clinic & Nat. Athletic Health Inst., 1985; orthopaedic surgeon, ptnr. Orthopaedic Specialists of Charleston, SC, 1985—2002; CEO Prevecare, Charleston, 2002—05; pvt. practice Daniel Island, SC, 2005—. Mem. Internat. Ctr. Birds of Prey, Awendaw, SC, 2005—. Named to Best Doctors in Am., 2006. Fellow: Am. Acad. Orthopaedic Surgery; mem.: Charleston County Med. Soc., Am. Orthopaedic Soc. Sports Medicine, Aircraft Owners & Pilots Assn. Avocations: aerobatics, fishing, flying. Home: 8863 Hwy 17N McClellanville SC 29458 Office: Ste 100 234 Seven Farms Dr Daniel Island SC 29492 Office Fax: 843-284-5201. Personal E-mail: makaira1@aol.com. Business E-Mail: drbrightmcconnell@yahoo.com

**MCCONNELL SERIO, SUZIE THERESA,** former professional basketball player, professional basketball coach; b. Pitts., July 29, 1966; married; 4 children. BA, Pa. State U., 1988. Coach Oakland Cath. High Sch., Pitts.; guard Cleve. Rockers, WNBA, 1998—2000; head coach Oakland Cath. H.S., 1990—2003, Minn. Lynx, WNBA, 2003—. Recipient Gold medal Olympic Games, Barcelona, 1988, Bronze medal Olympic Games, Seoul, 1992, Sportsmanship award WNBA, 1998, 1999, Newcomer award, 1998; named to All-WNBA 1st team, 1988. Office: Minn Lynx 600 First Ave North Minneapolis MN 55403

**MCCONNEY, MARY E.,** information technology executive; BA in physics & Environ. Studies, Whitman Coll., 1976; M in Econ., U. Pa., 1979, M in Urban Planning, 1980, PhD in Spatial Econ., 1983. Applied statistician U. Wash., 1977—85, U. Pa., 1977—85; applied statistician & database design NAS, 1985—88; pres. HiroSoft Internat. Corp., 1988—; CFO Sunhawk.com, Seattle, 1992—99, treas., 1999—; with Freehand Systems, Inc. Contbr. articles to profl. jours. Office: Freehand Music Inc 1463 E Republican St Seattle WA 98112-4517

**MCCONVILLE, EDWARD PATRICK,** lawyer; b. Albany, N.Y., Nov. 5, 1932; s. Edward Patrick McConville and Anne Dolores Leonard; m. Lois Anne Bessette, June 30, 1956 (div. Aug. 1982); 1 child, Stephen Patrick; m. Michelle Cristin Coderre, Mar. 17, 1984; 1 child, Collin William. BA, U. Notre Dame, 1954; JD, Union U., 1956. Bar: N.Y., INd., D.C., U.S. Supreme Ct. Investigator U.S. Civil Svc. Commn., N.Y.C., 1958—59; asst. divsn. counsel bowling divsn. Am. Machine and Foundry Co., N.Y.C., 1959—63; asst. counsel Lincoln Nat. Life Ins. Co., Ft. Wayne, Ind., 1963—66; asst. chief counsel U.S. Dept. Commerce, Econ. Devel. Adminstrn., Portland, Maine, 1966—67, Washington, 1967—68; v.p. First Nat. Bank, Washington, 1968—70, sr. v.p., 1970—73, exec. v.p., 1973, Cmty. State Bank, Albany, NY, 1973—75, Union Nat. Bank, Albany, 1975—77; sr. v.p. Maney McConville & Liccardi, P.C., East Greenbush, NY, 1977—; ptnr. Valatie, NY, 1977—; pres. People Comml. Bank, Albany, 1984—86; hearing officer N.Y.S. Dept. Agr. and Markets, 2006—. Instr. Hudson Valley C.C., 1978—85, 1992; lectr. fin. Siena Coll., 1989; instr. bus. law and internat. bus. St. Rose Coll., 1991—99; chmn. bd. Evergreen Bank, Albany, NY, 1991—92. Vol. probation officer Albany County Probation Dept., 1981; dir. Cath. Youth Orgn., Washington, 1971—73, dir. adv. Model Cities Econ. Devel. Corp., Washington, 1972—73. With U.S. Army, 1956—58, with USAR, 1958—60. Mem.: N.Am. Currach Assn. (pres. 1988—89), Old Chatham Hunt Club (pres. 1981—85), Albany Currach Rowing Club (dir. 1987—), Ft. Orange Club. Democrat. Roman Catholic. Avocations: rowing, horseback riding. Home: 55 Fordham Rd Valatie NY 12184 Office: Maney McConville and Liccari 22 Troy Rd East Greenbush NY 12061 Office Phone: 518-758-6296. E-mail: edmcconville@berk.un.

**MCCONVILLE, JUDY ALLEN,** social studies educator; d. Edwin Frederick and Bertha Herdegen Allen; m. James McConville, June 25, 1978; children: Catherine Margarethe, Elizabeth Allen. BA in History, Randolph-Macon Woman's Coll., Lynchburg, Va., 1968; MA in Tchg. Govt., U. Va., Charlottesville, 1972. Tchr. Alexandria City Pub. Schools, Va., 1971—98, curriculum specialist for social studies, 1998—. Chmn. Va. Conf. for Social Studies Educators, Norfolk, 2004, World History Stds. of Learning Revision Com., Richmond, Va., 2000—01; mem. Mgmt. Com. History and Social Sci. Stds. of Learning, Richmond, Va., 2000—01. Edn. com., sub com. co-chair coll. student outreach Annandale United Meth. Ch., Va., 1998—2004. Mem.: NEA, Nat. Social Studies Suprs. Assn., Nat. Coun. for the Social Studies, Va. Conf. for Social Studies Educators (treas. 2005—), Va. Consortium of Social Studies Specialists and Coll. Educators (pres. 2003—04), Nat. Coun. for History Edn., Va. Edn. Assn., Edn. Assn. Alexandria, Alpha Delta Kappa (pres. 1988—90, mem. chpt. 1996—98). Methodist. Avocations: reading, needlecrafts. Office: Alexandria City Pub Schools 2000 N Beauregard St Alexandria VA Office Phone: 703-461-4043. Office Fax: 703-370-7704. E-mail: jmcconvi@acps.k12.va.us.

**MCCOOK, KATHLEEN DE LA PEÑA,** librarian, educator; b. Chgo. d. Frank Eugene and Margaret L. (de la Peña) McEntee; m. Philip G. Heim, Mar. 20, 1972 (div.); 1 child, Margaret Marie; m. William Woodrow Lee McCook, Oct. 12, 1991; stepchildren: Cecilia, Billie Jean, Nicole. BA, U. Ill., Chgo.; MA, Marquette U., U. Chgo.; PhD, U. Wis.-Madison. Reference librarian Elmhurst Coll. Libr., Ill.; dir. pub. svcs. Dominican U., River Forest, Ill.; lectr. U. Wis., Madison; asst. prof. library sci. U. Ill., Urbana; dean, prof. La. State U. Sch. Libr. and Info. Sci., Baton Rouge; dean grad. sch. La. State U.; dir. Sch. Libr. and Info. Sci., U. South Fla., 1993-99, prof.; 1993—, coord. cmty. outreach, 2000—02, disting. univ. prof., 2002—; McCusker lectr. Dominican U., 2003— Author: (with K. Weibel) Role of Women in Librarianship, 1978, (with L. Estabrook) Career Profiles, 1983, (with William E. Moen) Occupational Entry, 1989, Adult Services, 1990, (with Gary O. Rolstad) Developing Readers' Advisory Services, 1993, Toward a Just and Productive Soc., 1994, Opportunities in Library and Information Science, 1997, (with B. Ford) Global Reach: Local Touch, 1998, Women of Color in Librarianship, 1998, (with B. Immroth) Library Services to Youth of Hispanic Heritage, 2000, A Place at the Table, 2000, Introduction To Public Libraries, 2004; mem. editl. bd. Cath. Lib. World Jour., 2005—; contbr. essays to books, articles to profl. jours. Chmn. Equal Rights Amendment Task Force, Ill., 1977-79, South Count Coalition for Cmty. Concerns, 1996—; active Eugene McCarthy campaign, U. Ill., Chgo., 1968, Bill Clinton campaign, 1992, 96, Al Gore campaign, 2000, Bill McBride campaign, Fla., 2002, Betty Castor campaign, 2004; John F. Kerry campaign, 2004; mem. La. Gov.'s Commn.for Women, 1985-88; bd. dirs. La. Endowment for Humanities, 1991-92; mem. exec. bd. Rural Social Svcs. Partnership, Hillsborough County, 1998-2001; mem. dem. exec. com., Hillsborough County, 2001-04; dem. del. Fla. State Convention, 2002-03; Ruskin Neigborhood Adv. Com., Fla., 2003-, Hillsborough County, Citizen's Action Bd., 2004—; mem. collective bargaining com. United Faculty Fla., 2003-; mem. Cmty. Action Bd., 2004—. Recipient Disting. Alumnus award U. Wis., 1991, award of merit Trejo Foster Found., 1999; named Bradshaw scholar Tex. Woman's Univ., 1994; named scholar in residence Oklahoma U., 2003. Mem.ALA (com. chmn. 1980—, editor RQ jour. 1982-88, Pub. Librs. Jour. 1989-90, Am. Librs. adv. com. 1994-96, contbg. editor Am. Librs. 1999-2001, column editor RUSQ 2000-06, Notable Books Coun. 2001-06), Progressive Librs. Guild. (coord. com., editl. bd., 2005—), REFORMA (bd. dirs. 1997-98, Latino Libr. of Yr. 2002, Equality award 1987, Monroe Adult Svc. award 1991, Futas Catalyst for Change award 1998, Achievement in Diversity Rsch. award 2004), Assn. for Libr. and Info. Sci. Edn. (com. chmn. 1981—; pres. 1987-88, Pres. award 1997), Fla.

Libr. Assn. (bd. dirs. 1995-98, Transformer award 1996), Tampa Bay Libr. Consortium (bd. dirs. 1994-97), Women Libr. Workers, Ruskin Civic Assn. (sec. 1997-99), Ill. Libr. Assn. (treas. 1981-83), Progressive LIbrarians Guild (coord. com. 2004-06), Beta Phi Mu (50th Anniversary Disting. Mem. 1999, Dist. Lectr. award 2002, Disting. Svc. to Edn. for Librarianship 2003), Cath. Libr. Assn. (Brubaker award for Outstanding Article 2003). Democrat. Roman Catholic. Avocation: reading. Office: U South Fla Sch Libr and Info Sci 4202 E Fowler Ave Stop CIS1040 Tampa FL 33620-7800 Personal E-mail: kmccook@tampabay.rr.com.

**MCCOOK, RICHARD PAUL,** grocery chain financial executive; b. Miami, Fla., Mar. 15, 1953; s. Leon Ennis and Ruth Erminor (Davenport) McC.; m. Anne Thackerson, Mar. 22, 1975; children: Ryan Wesley, Kelly Lauren. BS in Acctg., Fla. State U., 1975, M in Accountancy, 1976. CPA, Fla. Sr. audit mgr. Peat, Marwick, Mitchell & Co., Jacksonville, Fla., 1976-84; fin. v.p., CFO Winn-Dixie Stores, Inc., 1984—, sr. v.p., CFO. Participant Leadership Jacksonville, 1986-87. Mem. Am. Inst. CPA's, Fla. Inst. CPA's, Fin. Execs. Inst. Clubs: River (Jacksonville). Democrat. Methodist. Avocations: hunting, fishing, tennis. Office: Winn-Dixie Stores Inc 5050 Edgewood Ct Jacksonville FL 32254-3601

**MCCOOL, COURTNEY,** Olympic athlete; b. Kansas City, Apr. 1, 1988; Mem. U.S. Nat. Gymnastics Team, 2002—; gymnast Team USA, Athens Olympic Games, 2004. Achievements include mem. U.S. Championship Team, Pan Am. Games, 2003; invention of Athens Test Event, 1st in all-around, 2004; Silver medal, Olympics. Office: c/o USOC One Olympic Plz Colorado Springs CO 80909

**MCCORD, GUYTE PIERCE, JR.,** retired judge; b. Tallahassee, Sept. 23, 1914; s. Guyte Pierce and Jean (Patterson) McC.; m. Laura Elizabeth Mack, Dec. 1, 1939 (dec. Oct. 8, 2000); children: Florence Elizabeth, Guyte Pierce III, Edward LeRoy; m. Elizabeth Rogers Green, May 24, 2002. Student, Davidson Coll., 1933-34; BA, JD, U. Fla., 1940. Bar: Fla. 1940. Summer ranger Yosemite Nat. Park, 1936-39; rsch. aide Fla. Supreme Ct., summer 1940; pvt. practice Tallahassee, 1940-48; dep. commr. Fla. Indsl. Commn., 1946-47; pros. atty. Leon County, 1947-48; asst. gen. counsel Fla. Pub. Svc. Commn., 1949-60; judge 2d Jud. Cir. Fla., Tallahasee, 1960-74, Ct. Appeals 1st Dist. Fla., 1974-83, chief judge, 1977-79. Mem. Fla. Senate Pres.'s Council on Criminal Justice 1972; mem. appellate ct. rules com. Fla. Supreme Ct., 1977-78, mem. appellate ct. structure commn. 1978-79. Pres. Murat House Assn., Inc., 1967-69; bd. dirs. Fla. Heritage Found., 1969-70, mem. exec. com., 1965-69; mem. Andrew Jackson staff of Springtime Tallahassee, 1973-74, 84-86, Andrew Jackson, 1987. Commdr. USNR, 1942—64, WWII, Korea. Mem. ABA, Mil. Officers Assn. Am., Fla. Bar, Fla. Conf. Cir. Judges (sec.-treas. 1970, chmn. 1972), Fla. State U. Pres. Club, Kiwanis (dir. 1958-59). Presbyterian (elder 1960—, ch. trustee 1981-86). Home: 2718 Timbertrail Cir Tallahassee FL 32308-5745

**MC CORD, JOHN HARRISON,** lawyer, educator; b. Oceanside, N.Y., Dec. 22, 1934; s. John Francis and Elsie (Powers) McC.; m. Maureen Ursula Maclean, Dec. 30, 1961; children: John F.X., Paul V., David G., Maureen E. AB, Fordham Coll., 1957; JD magna cum laude, St. John's U., 1960; LLM, U. Ill., 1965. Bar: N.Y. 1960, Ill. 1964. Atty. U.S. Dept. Justice, Washington, 1960-61; mem. faculty U. Ill. Coll. Law, Champaign, 1964—, prof. law, 1965—99, prof. law emeritus, 1999—, assoc. dean for acad. affairs., 1990-92; of counsel Meyer Capel PC, 1998—2004; auditor/notary Cath. Diocese of Peoria, 2000—. Acad. coun. Ill. Inst. Continuing Legal Edn., 1968-72; vis. prof. law U. N.C., 1975, U. Hawaii, 1976 Author: (with Keeton and O'Connell) Crisis in Car Insurance, 1967, Buying and Selling Small Businesses, 1969, (with O'Byrne) Deskbook for Illinois Estate Planners, 1969, Closely Held Corporations, 1971, (with O'Neill, Pearlman and Stroud) Buying, Selling and Merging Businesses, 1975, (with Lowndes and Kramer) Estate and Gift Taxes, 3d edit, 1974, (with McKee) Federal Income Taxation-A Summary Analysis, 1975, (with Kramer) Problems for Federal Estate and Gift Taxes, 1976, Estate and Gift Tax Reform, 1977, Estate and Gift Tax Summary, 15th edit. 1993, Estate, Gift and Generation-Skipping Taxes, 1999; editor: Dimensions and Academic Freedom, 1969, With All Deliberate Speed: Civil Rights Theory and Reality, 1969, Ill. Law Forum, 1965-69; contbr. articles to profl. jours.; author computer programs for estate planning, 1984— Served to capt. JAGC, USAF, 1961-64. St. Thomas More fellow St. John's U., 1960. Fellow Am. Coll. Trust and Estate Counsel; mem. ABA (com. CLE and chief reporter for study outline on buying, selling and merging businesses sect. Real Estate tax 1969-73, com. estate and gift taxes 1973-84, chmn. subcom. gross estate issues 1976-78, subcom. tax reform 1978-84), Ill. Bar Assn. (exec. coun. fed. tax sect. 1966-73, chmn. sect. 1971-72, exec. coun. bus. planning sect. 86-91), Champaign County Bar Assn., Am. Arbitration Assn. (nat. panel arbitrators 1969-90), Eastern Ill. Estate Planning Coun. (pres. 1970-71), U. Miami Inst. Estate Planning (adv. coun. 1978-97), Assn. Am. Law Schs. (fed. taxation roundtable coun. 1969-72), Ill. Inst. CLE (bd. dirs. 1991-2000, estate planning adv. com. 1978-84), U.S. Navy League. Order of Coif. Home: 104 E Sherwin Dr Urbana IL 61802-7133 Office: U Ill Coll Law 504 E Pennsylvania Ave Champaign IL 61820 Business E-Mail: jhmccord@law.uiuc.edu.

**MCCORD, JULIE ANN,** retired conductor; b. Chgo., Oct. 5, 1970; d. Michael Henry Schrage and Barbara Jeanne Schrage (Kosac); m. Ronald Andrew McCord, Jan. 21, 1995; children: Ryan Michael, Jason Daniel. MusB, No. Ill. U., DeKalb, 1993; MusM Edn., Vandercook Coll. Music, Chgo., 2002. Cert. tchr. Ill. Band and chorus dir. grades 5-12 Tampico Unit Dist., Tampico, Ill., 1993—94; band and chorus dir./music dept. chairperson Rock Falls H.S. Dist. #301, Rock Falls, Ill., 1994—2005. Gen. chair conf. music dirs. North Ctrl. Ill. Conf. of H.S., Ill., 2002—05. Composer: (instrumental band music) Illinois Institute of Technology School Song. Pianist Sauk Valley Prodns., Dixon, Ill., 2002—04, St. John's Luth. Ch., Sterling, Ill., 2004—05. Mem.: NEA (assoc.), Rock Falls H.S. Fdn. Assn. (mem. bldg. rep. 1998, 2002, sec. 2003—04), Ill. Music Educators Assn. (assoc.), Music Educators Nat. Conf. (assoc.). Home: 1827 2nd Ave Sterling IL 61081 Personal E-mail: ramjam@insightbb.com.

**MCCORISON, MARCUS ALLEN,** librarian, cultural organization administrator; b. Lancaster, Wis., July 17, 1926; s. Joseph Lyle and Ruth (Mink) McCorison; m. Janet Buckbee Knop, June 10, 1950 (dec. 1998); children: Marcus Allen II, Judith McCorison Gove, Andrew Buckbee, Mary McCorison Rosenbloom(dec.), James Rice, Peter Gardner; life ptnr. Carolyn K. Dik. AB, Ripon Coll., 1950; MA, U. Vt., 1951, LittD (hon.), 1992; MS, Columbia U., 1954; LHD (hon.), Assumption Coll., Worcester, Mass., 1987, Coll. of the Holy Cross, 1992; LittD (hon.), Clark U., 1992. Librarian Kellogg-Hubbard Library, Montpelier, Vt., 1954-55; chief of rare books dept. Dartmouth Coll. Library, Hanover, NH, 1955-59; head spl. collections dept. State U. Iowa Libraries, 1959-60; libr. Am. Antiquarian Soc. Worcester, Mass., 1960-91, editor Procs., 1960-67, dir., 1967-89, pres., 1989-92, pres. emeritus, 1993—; cons. Christie, Manson & Woods, Internat., 1993-96, N.Y. Hist. Soc., 1994-95, Libr. Congress, Hist. Soc. of Pa., U. Kans., 1998-99. Mem. N.Am. steering com. 18th Century Short Title Catalogue, 1977—; mem. Com. for a New Eng. Bibliography, 1970-79; meas., 1970-77; mem. adv. com. Eleutherian Mills-Hagley Found., 1971-74, 87-89; chmn. Ind. Rsch. Librs. Assn., 1972-73, 78-80; mem. adv. coun. Princeton U. Libr., 1988-92; bd. govs. Hist. Librs. Group, 1980-91, chmn. preservation com., 1989-91, chmn. Writings of James Fenimore Cooper, 1991-2002. Author: Vermont Imprints 1778-1820, 1963, The 1764 Catalogue of the Redwood Library, 1965; contbr.: The Pursuit of Knowledge in the Early American Republic, 1976, Publishing and Readership in Revolutionary France and America, 1993; editor: History of Printing in America by Isaiah Thomas, 1970. Trustee Fruitlands Mus., 1978-89, Old Sturbridge Village, 1981-92, Hist. Deerfield, Inc., 1991—2002; mem. bd. mgrs. Lewis Walpole Libr., Yale U., 1995—; nat. trustee Newberry Libr., 1995—; mem. Cultural Commn. City Worcester, Mass., 1999-2004, Mass. Hist. Commn., 1999—; mem. com. of mgmt. Wm. L. Clements Libr., U. Mich., 2001—. Recipient Samuel Pepys medal Ephemera Soc., London, 1980, Disting. Alumni award Ripon Coll., 1989, Columbia U. Sch. Libr. Svc., 1992. Rickards medal Ephemera Soc. Am., 2000. Mem. Am. Antiquarian Soc., Coll. and Rsch. Librs. Assn. (chmn. rare books sect. 1965-66), Bibliog. Soc. Am. (pres. 1980-84, del. to ACLS 1985—2002), Am. Printing Hist. Assn. (trustee 1998—2004, laureate 1998), Vt. Hist. Soc. (trustee 1956-66), Worcester Hist. Mus. (exec. com. 1967-80), Ctr. for Rsch. on Vt. (assoc.), N.E. Am. Soc. 18th Century Studies (pres. 1978-79), Colonial Soc. Mass., Club of Odd Vols., Grolier Club (councillor 1979-82, 83-84), Zamorano Club (hon.), Roxburghe Club, Century Assn. Democrat. Home and Office: 101 Greenwich Ct Worcester MA 01609-1159

**MCCORKINDALE, DOUGLAS HAMILTON,** publishing executive; b. N.Y.C., June 14, 1939; s. William Douglas and Kathleen (Miles) McC.; m. Nancy Walsh, Dec. 24, 1991; children by previous marriage: Laura Ann, Heather Jean. BA, Columbia U., 1961, LLB cum laude (Harlan Fiske Stone scholar), 1964. Bar: N.Y. 1964. Assoc. Thacher Proffitt & Wood, N.Y.C., 1964-70, ptnr., 1970-71; gen. counsel, sec. Gannett Co., Inc., Arlington, Va., 1971-72, v.p., gen. counsel, sec., 1972-77, sr. v.p. fin. and law, 1977-79, sr. v.p., chief fin. officer, 1979-83, pres. diversified media div., 1980-83, exec. v.p., 1983, vice chmn., 1985—2001, CFO, 1985—97, chief adminstrv. officer, 1986—97, pres., 1997—2005, CEO, 2000—05, chmn., 2005—06. Bd. dirs. AP, Continental Airlines Inc., Lockheed Martin Corp., Mut. Ins. Co. Ltd. Mem. ABA, Newspaper Assn. Am., Pine Valley Golf Club, Mid Ocean Club, Burning Tree Club. Office: Gannett Co Inc 7950 Jones Branch Dr Mc Lean VA 22102*

**MCCORKLE, LEON MARSHALL, JR.,** lawyer, educator; b. Alliance, Ohio, Mar. 2, 1941; s. Leon Marshall and Mary Carrington McC.; m. Patricia McCorkle Dec. 28, 1964 (div. Oct. 1982); children: Catherine Shapiro, Molly Carrington McCorkle; m. Virginia Marie Brotherton Trethewey, Nov. 28, 1986; children: Kyle, John Marshall. AB, Harvard Coll., Cambridge, Mass., 1964; JD, The Ohio State U. Coll. Law, Columbus, 1972. Bar: Supreme Ct. Ohio, 1972, U.S. Ct. (so. dist.), 1990. Sr. ptnr. Vorys, Sater, Seymour & Pease, LLP, Columbus, Ohio, 1972-98; adj. prof. Ohio State U. Coll. Law, Columbus, 1991-92, 95—; sr. v.p., gen. counsel Wendy's Internat., Inc., Dublin, Ohio, 1998—. Commr. Nat. Conf. Commissioners on Uniform State Laws, Chgo., 1988—; Editor in chief The Ohio State U. Law Jour., 1971-72. Lt. USN, 1963-69. Trustee Columbus Symphony Orchestra, Columbus, 1997-98, Columbus Bar Svcs., Inc., 1999; mem. bd. dirs. ACCA, Columbus, 1999. Fellow Columbus Bar Found.; mem. ABA, Ohio State Bar Found., Columbus Bar Found., Put-in-Bay Yacht Club, Am. Law Inst., Order of the Coif. Avocations: boating, weather instructor U.S. Power Squadrons, my children. Office: Wendys Internat Inc PO Box 256 Dublin OH 43017-0256

**MCCORKLE, PAMELA LOVERIDGE,** elementary school educator; b. Augusta, Ga., Feb. 16, 1959; d. David Roger Loveridge, Sr. and Lucille Lucky Loveridge; m. Michael Wayne McCorkle; 1 stepchild, Jered 1 child, Caleb Stovall. B of Music Edn., Augusta State U., 1998. Cert. tchr. Pk-12 Ga. Music tchr. Columbia County Bd. Edn., Appling, Ga., 1998—2000, Harlem, Ga., 2000—. Recipient 1st pl. award, Nat. Assn. Tchrs. Singing, 1997, Louise Proctor Character Acting award, Augusta Players, 1989, Best Actress award, Augusta Players, 1993. Home: 4546 Glennwood Dr Evans GA 30809 Business E-Mail: pmccorkle@ccboe.net.

**MCCORKLE, ROBERT ELLSWORTH,** agribusiness educator; b. Salinas, Calif., Apr. 3, 1938; s. Stanley Harold and Muriel Eugenia (Vosti) McC.; m. Mary E. McCorkle, June 26, 1965; children: Bonnie Kathleen, Robyn Krystyna. BSc in Farm Mgmt., Calif. Poly. State U., San Luis Obispo, 1960; MSc in Agrl. Econs., U. Calif., Davis, 1962; postgrad., U. Wis., 1969, Oreg. State U., 1966. Rsch. statistician U. Calif., Davis, 1960-62; asst. prof. agrl. bus. Calif. Poly. State U., San Luis Obispo, 1962-66, dir. internat. edn., 1970-74, assoc. prof. agrl. mgmt., 1969-76, prof. agribus., 1976—; chief farm mgmt. officer Ministry Agr., Lusaka, Zambia, 1967-69; dir., owner McCorkle Farms, Inc., Wilsona, Calif., 1970—. Vis. prof. Mich. State U., U.S. AID, Washington, 1984-85; dir., owner McCorkle Trucking, Glenn, Calif., 1988—; agrl. economist U.S. AID-Redso ESA, Nairobi, Kenya, 1984-85. Author: Guide for Farming in Zambia, 1968. Pres. Cabrillo Property Owners Assn., Los Osos, Calif., 1976-78; vol. Atty. Gen.'s Adv. Com., Calif., 1972-74. U.S. Peace Corps strategy grantee, Washington, 1976-2006. Mem. Am. Agrl. Econs. Assn., Am. Soc. Farm Mgrs. and Rural Appraisers, Western Agrl. Econs. Assn., Calif. Poly. Farm Mgmt. Club, Calif. Poly. Alumni Assn., Blue Key, Alpha Zeta (founding mem., sr. advisor Delta chpt., nat. high coun. chronicler, sec.-treas., bd. dirs.), Nat. Alpha Zeta Found. (bd. dirs.), Golden Key. Republican. Episcopalian. Avocations: hunting, fishing. Office: Calif Poly State U San Luis Obispo CA 93407 Office Phone: 805-756-5024. Business E-Mail: rmccorkl@calpoly.edu.

**MCCORKLE, RUTH,** oncological nurse, educator, researcher; BS, U. Md., 1968; MA, U. Iowa, 1972, PhD, 1975. Staff nurse CCU Vanvouver (Wash.) Med. Hosp., 1968-69; oncological clin. nurse specialist U. Iowa Hosps. and Clinics, Iowa City, 1971-73; instr. psychiat. nursing and oncological nursing Sch. Nursing, U. Iowa, Iowa City, 1974-75; from asst. prof. to prof. dept. cmty. health care sys. U. Wash., Seattle, 1975-85; prof. adult health and illness divsn. Sch. Nursing, U. Pa., Phila., 1986—98, chairperson, 1988-89, dir. Ctr. Advancing Care in Serious Illness, 1989—98, dir. cancer control Cancer Comprehensive Ctr., 1990-98; prof. nursing, chmn. doc program, dir. Ctr. Chronic Illness Sch. Yale U., New Haven, 1998—. Mem. nursing sci. rev. com. Nat. Ctr. Nursing Rsch., 1988-92. Contbr. articles to profl. jours. Fellow Am. Acad. Nursing; mem. ANA, NAS, Internat. Soc. Nurses Cancer Care (dir-at-large 1983-89), Am. Assn. Cancer Edn., Am. Psychosocial Oncology Soc. (charter mem., dir.-at-large 1998-), Oncology Nursing Soc. (charter mem., mem. rsch. com. 1981-82, dir.-at-large 1983-85). Office: Yale U 100 Church St S PO Box 9740 New Haven CT 06536-0740 Business E-Mail: ruth.mccorkle@yale.edu.

**MC CORMAC, JOHN WAVERLY,** judge; b. Zanesville, Ohio, Feb. 8, 1926; s. Samuel D. and Phyllis (Murray) McC.; m. Martha Ann Cunningham, June 22, 1952; children: Michael Paul, John Mark, James Samuel. BS, Muskingum Coll., 1951; JD, Capital U., 1961. Bar: Ohio 1961. Fire protection engr. Ohio Insp. Bur., 1951—60; pvt. practice Columbus, 1961—65; prof. law Capital U., Columbus, 1965-66, 71-74, dean Law Sch., 1966—71; judge 10th Dist. Ct. Appeals, 1975—92; prof. law Ohio State U., Columbus, 1993—2001. Mem. staff coms. rules adv. com. Supreme Ct. Ohio; chmn. adv. bd. Vols. in Probation, 1972-74; chmn. ohio Jud. Conf., 1982-84; commr. Ohio Dispute Resolution Com., 1989-96, chmn., 1993-95; chief justice Ohio Ct. Appeals Assn., 1989-91. Author: Ohio Civil Rules Practice, 1970, 2nd edit., 1992, Anderson's Ohio Civil Practice, Vol. 1, 1971, Vol. 2, 1976, Vol. 3, 1977, Wrongful Death in Ohio, 1982. Served with USNR, 1943-46. Fellow Ohio Bar Assn. Found.; mem. League Ohio Law Schs. (pres. 1969-70), ABA, Ohio Bar Assn. (council of dels. 1973-77), Columbus Bar Assn. (bd. govs. 1968-72, sec.-treas. 1973-74, pres. 1975-76), Am. Judicature Soc., Phi Alpha Delta. Clubs: Masons (33 deg.). Republican. Home: 395 Longfellow Ave Columbus OH 43085-3024 E-mail: johnmccormac46@hotmail.com.

**MCCORMACK, DONALD PAUL,** newspaper consultant; b. Brockton, Mass., Jan. 15, 1926; s. Everett G. and Esther (Lufkin) McC.; m. Petronella Ruth Seger, Apr. 28, 1951; 1 son, Christopher Paul. BA, U. Pitts., 1949. Corr. U.P.I., 1949-52; asst. city editor Pitts. Sun-Telegraph, 1952-56; pub. relations exec., 1956-64; copy reader N.Y. News, 1964-67, editorial writer, 1967-72, chief editorial writer, 1972-82; cons., 1982—. With USAAF, 1944-46, Pa. N.G., 1952-57. Home and Office: PO Box 3539 Westport CT 06880-8539

**MCCORMACK, DOUGLAS P.,** lawyer; b. 1968; s. BA in Polit. Sci., U. So. Calif., 1992; JD, Am. U. 1998. Bar: Md. 2000. With Arent Fox Kintner Plotkin & Kahn, Washington; ptnr., pub. law & policy strategies group Sonnenschein Nath & Rosenthal LLP, Washington, Office: Sonnenschein Nath & Rosenthal LLP Ste 600, E Tower 1301 K St NW Washington DC 20005 Office Phone: 202-408-9138. Office Fax: 202-408-6399. Business E-Mail: dmccormack@sonnenschein.com.

**MCCORMACK, ERIC,** actor; b. Toronto, Ont., Can., Apr. 18, 1963; currently holds dual citizenship in Am. and Can. s. James Keith and Doris McCormack; m. Janet Holden, Aug. 1, 1997; 1 child, Finnigan Holden. Grad., Ryerson U. Sch. Theatre, Toronto. Mem. Stratford Shakespearean Festival, Canada, 1985—89. Actor: (plays) A Midsummer Night's Dream, Henry V, The Three Sisters, Some Girl(s), 2006; (TV films) The Boys From Syracuse, 1986, Much Ado About Nothing, 1987, Relentless: Mind of a Killer, 1993, Family of Strangers, 1993, Miracle on Interstate 880, 1993, Call of the Wild, 1993, Double, Double, Toil and Trouble, 1993, Island City, 1994, The Man Who Wouldn't Die, 1994, Townies, 1996, Night Visitors, 1996, Borrowed Hearts, 1997, The Audrey Hepburn Story, 2000, Dead Like Me, 2004, In From the Night, 2005; (TV series) Street Justice, 1992—93, Lonesome Dove: The Series, 1994, Lonesome Dove: The Outlaw Years, 1995, Will & Grace, 1998—2006 (Emmy award, outstanding lead actor in a comedy, 2001); (TV miniseries) A Will of Their Own, 1998; (films) The Lost World, 1992, Return to the Lost World, 1992, Giant Steps, 1992, Exception to the Rule, 1997, Free Enterprise, 1998, Holy Man, 1998, Here's to Life, 2000, Break a Leg, 2005, The Sisters, 2006; (Broadway plays) The Music Man, 2001; writer/dir. (films) Pirates, 2003. Mailing: Will & Grace NBC 100 Universal City Plaza Universal City CA 91608 also: c/o Hyler Mgmt 20 Ocean Park Blvd Ste 25 Santa Monica CA 90405*

**MC CORMACK, FRANCIS XAVIER,** lawyer, former oil company executive; b. Bklyn., July 9, 1929; s. Joseph and Blanche V. (Dengel) McC.; m. Margaret V. Hynes, Apr. 24, 1954; children: Marguerite, Francis Xavier, Sean Michael, Keith John, Cecelia Blanche, Christopher Thomas. AB cum laude, St. Francis Coll., Bklyn., 1951; LLB, Columbia U., 1954. Bar: N.Y. 1955, Mich. 1963, Calif. 1974. Pa. 1975. Assoc. Cravath, Swaine & Moore, N.Y., 1956-62; sr. atty Ford Motor Co., 1962 64, asst. gen. counsel, 1970-72; v.p., gen. counsel, sec. Philco-Ford Corp., 1964-72; v.p., gen. counsel Atlantic Richfield Co., 1972-73, sr. v.p., gen. counsel, 1973-94. Editor Columbia U. Law Rev., 1954. Decorated commendatore Ordine al Merito (Italy); Stone scholar Columbia U., 1954. Mem. Calif. Club, Chancery Club, Annandale Golf Club.

**MCCORMACK, GRACE LYNETTE,** retired civil engineer; b. Dallas, Nov. 2; d. Audley and Janice Meredith (Metcalf) McC. Tech. degree, Durham's Coll., 1958; grad. in civil engring., El Centro Coll., 1972; grad. in advanced surveying, Eastfield, 1975. Cert. sr. engr. technician. Contract design technician various engring firms, Dallas, 1958-70; sr. design engr. technician City of Dallas Survey Div., 1970-80, street light div., 1980-95, ret. 1995. Mem. Unity Ch. Avocations: numerology, astrology, metaphysics, Egyptian-Arabian horses, lighting and designing black and white portrait photography. Home: 1428 Meadowbrook Ln Irving TX 75061-4435

**MCCORMACK, JOHN JOSEPH, JR.,** insurance company executive; b. Morristown, NJ, Aug. 22, 1944; s. John Joseph and Marion Loretta (Smith) McC.; m. Judith Gail Harvey, July 20, 1968; children: Brendan, Matthew, Margaret. BBA, St. Bonaventure U., 1966. From group underwriter to exec. v.p. Tchrs. Ins. and Annuity Assn.-Coll. Retirement Equities Fund, N.Y.C., 1966-98; pres. TIAA-CREF Enterprises, 1998-99, group pres., 1999-2001; chmn. McCormack's Retirement and Fin. Svcs. Cons., 2001—. Trustee Am. Psychol. Assn. Ins. Trust, Washington, 1980-90, chmn., 1985-86, trustee investment com., 1990-98, 2001—; trustee Employee Benefit Rsch. Inst., Washington, 1983—, treas., 1986-90, vice-chmn., 1997-98, chmn., 1999-2001; mem. adv. bd. Andrew W. Mellon Found., N.Y.C., 1997-2001. Pres.'s coun. St. Bonaventure U., 1986—, chmn., 1986-89, trustee, 1996—, chmn. investment com., 1999-2003, vice chmn. bd. trustees, 2003—; bd. visitors Ctr. for Study Future Mgmt. U. Md., 1987-92; trustee Coll. and Univ. Pers. Assn. Found., 1992-94; bd. govs. Investment Co. Inst., 1994-2000; trustee Fenimore Asset Mgmt. Funds, 2004-. Roman Catholic. Office: PO Box 432 New Vernon NJ 07976-0432 Office Phone: 908-415-0104. E-mail: jmccsbu@aol.com.

**MCCORMACK, LOWELL RAY,** oil industry executive, corporate financial executive, consultant; b. Ladonia, Tex., Oct. 26, 1925; d. Lowell and Orianna (McDonnold) Cooney; m. Paul H. McCormack, June 4, 1948; children: Sharron Ann, Lowell Henry. At, Rutherford Met. Coll., Dallas, 1962, U. Tex., Arlington and Dallas, Eastfield Coll., Dallas, Cooke County Coll., Gainesville, Tex., 1989—; AA, Wm. Alexander Art, 1991. Master graphoanalyst Internat. Graphoanalysis Soc. Bookeeper Jot-Em-Down Gin Corp., Pecan Gap, Tex., 1947, Shedd-Bartush Foods, Dallas, 1948—52; v.p. and sec.-treas. Safari Oil Co., 1954—88, pres., 1989—; acct. and credit mgr. J. P. Ashcraft Co., Inc., 1956—65; v.p., sec.-treas. and CFO Dallas Title Co., 1965—83; treas. First Nat. Bank, Cooper, Tex., 1986—87; pres. Scorpio Oil Co., 1987—. Treas. Butterfield Stage, Gainesville, Tex.; acctg. cons. to atty.; lectr. in field. Author: Stories of Growing Up in the Coney Family, 2005; featured writer Tex. State Hist. Assn. Web Site, 2005. Troop leader Girl Scouts USA, 1955—65; founder Yarn Spinners, Gainesville, Tex., 1988; mem. Newcomers Club, 1986—, pres., 1989—; columnist Cooke County Leader, 1988; founding mem. Gainesville Area Visual Arts; mem. Baptist Choir, Centennial Cir. Mem.: Internat. Platform Assn., North Tex. Oil and Gas Assn., Internat. Graphoanalysis Soc. (life; v.p. Tex. chpt. 1978, pres. 1979, Graphoanalyst of Yr. 1987, keynote spkr. 1987, Okla. seminar leader 1990), Red Hat. Soc., Crosstimbers Geneal. Soc., MENSA, Gainesville C. of C., Cooke County Heritage Soc., Kiwanis (one of 1st women mems. Gainesville chpt. 1988, v.p. 1990—91, pres. 1991—92), Zonta Club (co-chmn. fin. com. 1982, dir. and 2d v.p. 1983—84), Soroptimist Club, Toastmistress (pres. 1981, com. chmn. internat. conv 1984), Phi Theta Kappa (pres. Psi Iota chpt. 1990, acad. all-Am. 3d team for cmty. tech. and jr. colls. 1992). Baptist. Home: 631 S Lindsay St Gainesville TX 76240-5336 Personal E-mail: l.r.mccormack@sbcglobal.net.

**MCCORMACK, MICHAEL,** state supreme court justice; b. Omaha, July 20, 1939; JD, Creighton U., 1963. Asst. pub. defender, Douglas County, Nebr., 1963-66; pvt. practice Omaha, 1966-97; justice Nebr. Supreme Ct., 1997—. Fellow: Internat. Soc. Barristers; mem.: Sarpy County Bar Assn., Omaha Bar Assn., Colo. Bar Assn. Office: State Supreme Ct Office Capitol Bldg Rm 2218 Lincoln NE 68509 also: PO Box 98910 Lincoln NE 68509*

**MCCORMACK, RICHARD THOMAS FOX,** diversified financial services company executive, former ambassador; b. Bradford, Pa., Mar. 6, 1941; s. C.H. and Ruth N. (Fox) McC.; m. Karen L. Hagstrom, Oct. 18, 1980; children: Charlotte Louise, Justin Randall, Elizabeth Caroline. BA, Georgetown U., 1963; PhD, U. Fribourg, Switzerland, 1966. With Peace Corps, 1966-67; sr. staff mem. Pres.' Adv. Council on Exec. Orgn., White House, Washington, 1969-71; with Am. Enterprise Inst., 1975-77; dep. asst. sec. for internat. econ. affairs US Dept. Treasury, 1974; mem. staff U.S. Senate, 1979-81; asst. sec. state for econ. and bus. affairs U.S. Dept. State, Washington, 1982-85, US amb. to OAS, 1985-89, under sec. for econ. affairs, 1989-91; sr. advisor Ctr. Strategic Internat. Studies, Washington, 2004—06; vice chmn. Merrill Lynch & Co., NYC, 2006—. Candidate in primary elections for U.S. Congress, 1972, 74; cons. Office Telecommunications Policy, 1971, Coun. on Internat. Econ. Policy, 1972, Office Spl. Trade Rep., 1975, Exec. Office of the Pres., White House, Washington; guest scholar Woodrow Wilson Ctr. Smithsonian Instn., Washington, 1991-92; bus. advisor Am. companies, cons. U.S. Govt. on Internat. Econ. Affairs, 1992-2005. Author: Asians in Kenya, 1971, The Twilight War, 1979, Microeconomic Reforms for Israel, 1991, Managing Japan's Financial Crisis, 1992, Vulnerabilities in the Global Economy: Looking Forward in War Time, 2005. Recipient Superior Honor award Dept. State, 1987, Sec. of State's Disting. Svc. award, 1991; decorated Legion of Honor (France). Mem. Internat. Inst. Strategic Studies, Econ. Club NY, Coun. Am. Ambassadors, Coun. Fgn. Relations. Republican. Office: Merrill Lynch & Co Inc 4 Financial World Ctr New York NY 10080

**MCCORMACK, ROBERT CORNELIUS,** investment banker; b. N.Y.C., Nov. 7, 1939; m. Mary Lester, Dec. 14, 1963; children: Robert Cornelius Jr., Walter, Scott. BA, U. N.C., 1962; MBA, U. Chgo., 1968. V.p. Dillon Read & Co. Inc., 1968-81; mng. dir. Morgan Stanley & Co., Inc., Chgo., 1981-87;

dep. asst sec. def. prodn. support U.S. Dept. Def., Washington, 1987-88, dep. under sec. def. indsl. and internat. programs, 1988-89, acting dep. under sec. of def. acquisition, 1989-90, asst. sec. Navy fin. mgmt. Washington, 1990-93; founding ptnr. Trident Capital L.P., Chgo., 1993—. Served to lt. USNR, 1963-66. Office: 277 83RD St #B2 Burr Ridge IL 60527-5846

MCCORMACK, SEAN IAN, federal agency administrator; B in Economics, Colby Coll., 1986; MA, U. Md., 1990. Analyst Meridian Corp.; with Fgn. Svc., 1995—99; Farsi-speaking officer consular sect. U.S. Embassy, Ankara, 1996—98, econ. reporter on consular issues Algiers, 1998—99; with ops. ctr. US Dept. State, Washington, 1999, with exec. secretariat staff; dep. press sec. for fgn. policy The White House, Washington; spl. asst. to Pres., spokesman NSC, Washington, 2001—05; asst. sec. pub. affairs, dept. spokesman US Dept. State, Washington, 2005—. Office: US Dept State Harry S Truman Bldg 2201 C St NW Rm 6800 Washington DC 20520 Office Phone: 202-647-6607.

MCCORMACK, STANLEY EUGENE, financial consultant; b. Olney, Ill., Oct. 15, 1949; s. Donald Eugene and Patricia Louise (Dickerson) McC.; m. Janis Eileen Bush; m. Jeffrey Daniel, Erin Louise, Evan Stuart. Student, DePauw U., 1967-68, Ohio State U., 1968-71; MS in Fin. Svc., The Am. Coll., 1991, MS in Mgmt., 1996. CLU; chartered fin. cons, cert. sr. advisor, 2005. Ins. agt. Art Holtzman Assocs., Rochester, NY, 1973-75, ins. sales mgr., 1975-82; fin. cons., pres. Assoc. Fin. Cons., Rochester, 1983—. Instr. Am. Coll., Rochester, 1988, Empire State Coll. Moderator Webster (N.Y.) Bapt. Ch., 1985-88; mem. fin. com. Webster Swim Assn., 1993-95, treas., 1989-91. Mem.: Estate Planning Coun. Rochester, Internal Assn. Fin. Planners (bd. dirs. 1989—95, v.p. chmn. symposium 1990, pres. 1993—94, pres. adv. bd. 1994—96), Am. Soc. Chartered Life Underwriters and Chartered Fin. Cons., Phi Delta Theta (pres. Beta West 1999—2001). Avocations: voice, bridge. Home: 622 Fairmont Dr Webster NY 14580-8967 Office Phone: 585-381-5820. E-mail: smccorm123@aol.com.

MCCORMACK, THOMAS JOSEPH, retired publishing executive, playwright; b. Boston, Jan. 5, 1932; s. Thomas Joseph and Lena Carolyn (Allen) McC.; m. Sandra Harriet Danenberg, Aug. 21, 1964; children: Daniel Aaron, Jed Charles (dec.), Jessie Ann. Student, U. Conn., 1950-51; AB summa cum laude (James Manning scholar), Brown U., 1954; postgrad. (G.H. Palmer scholar), Woodrow Wilson fellow), Harvard U., 1956. Writer radio news WSTC, Stamford, Conn., 1957-59; editor Doubleday & Co., Inc., N.Y.C., 1959-64, Harper & Row, N.Y.C., 1964-67; edin. editor New Am. Library, N.Y.C., 1967-69; dir. trade dept. St. Martin's Press, N.Y.C., 1969-70, pres., 1970-87, chief exec. officer, editorial dir., 1970-96, chmn., 1987-97. Pres., chmn. bd. St. James Press, Ltd., London, 1973-79; v.p., treas. Sandra D. McCormack, Inc. (Interior Designer.); chmn., chief exec. officer Tor Books, N.Y.C., 1987-96; exec. com. Holtzbrinck GmbH, Stuttgart, Germany, 1995-97. Author: Afterwords, Novelists on Their Novels, 1969, The Fiction Editor, the Novel and the Novelist, (plays) American Roulette, 1969, Endpapers, 2002; columnist: The Cheerful Skeptic, 1997—99. Mem. Play Devel. Coun., Manhattan Theater Club, 1995-2001, Dramatists Gild, 1997—. With AUS. 1954-56. Mem. Assn. Am. Pubs. (dir. 1973-76, freedom to read com. 1974-77, Curtis Benjamin award 1997, LMP Lifetime Achievement award 1997), Phi Beta Kappa. Clubs: The Players (N.Y.C.), Century Assn. (N.Y.C.). Home: 50 Central Park W New York NY 10023-6028 E-mail: cheerskep@aol.com.

MCCORMACK, WILLIAM F., lawyer; b. Washington, Dec. 27, 1946; BS, Va. Poly. Univ., 1968; JD, Catholic Univ., Washington, 1971; LLM, Univ. Va., 1972. Bar: Va. 1971, N.Y. 1973. Ptnr. Reboul MacMurray Hewitt & Maynard; ptnr. corp. dept. & co-head private equity practice group Ropes & Gray, N.Y.C., 2003—. Mem.: ABA, N.Y. State Bar Assn., Va. Bar Assn. Office: Ropes & Gray 45 Rockefeller Plz New York NY 10111-0087 Office Phone: 212-841-0627. Office Fax: 212-841-5725. Business E-Mail: william.mccormack@ropesgray.com.

MCCORMALLY, KEVIN JAY, editor; b. Boston, Mar. 13, 1950; s. John Patrick and Marguerite Louise (Wichert) McC.; m. Anne Louise Long, May 27, 1972; children: Niamh Anna, Patrick Henry. BA with honors, U. Iowa, 1972. Area editor Burlington (Iowa) Hawk Eye, 1969-70; city editor Daily Iowan, Iowa City, 1971-72; press sec. U.S. Rep. Edward Mezvinsky, Washington, 1972-77; assoc. editor Changing Times Mag., Washington, 1977-85, sr. editor, 1985-90; exec. editor Kiplinger's Personal Fin. Mag. (formerly Changing Times), Washington, 1991-2000; editl. dir. Kiplinger's Personal Fin. mag., 2000—05, Kiplinger Washington Editors, 2005—. Commentator Nightly Bus. Report PBS and ABC Radio. Author: Successful Tax Planning, 1988, Sure Ways to Cut Your Taxes, 1989-94, Cut Your Taxes, 1996, 97, 98, 99; co-author: A Term to Remember, 1977; editor: Get More for Your Money, 1981. Mem. Nat. Press Club (best consumer journalism award 1986, 88), Sigma Delta Chi. Democrat. Roman Catholic. Avocation: photography. Home: 161 D St SE Washington DC 20003-1809 Office: Kiplingers Washington Editors 1729 H St NW Washington DC 20006-3925 Business E-Mail: kmccormally@kiplinger.com.

MCCORMICK, BARNES WARNOCK, aerospace engineering educator; b. Waycross, Ga., July 15, 1926; s. Barnes Warnock and Edwina (Brogdon) McC.; m. Emily Joan Hess, Aug 18, 1946; 1 dau., Cynthia Joan. BS in Aero. Engring. Pa. State U., 1948, MS, 1949, PhD, 1954. Research assoc. Pa. State U., University Park, 1949-54, assoc. prof., 1954-55, prof. aero. engring., 1959-92, Boeing prof. aero. engring., 1985-92, prof. emeritus, cons., 1992—, head dept. aerospace engring., 1969-85. Assoc. prof., chmn. aero. dept. Wichita U., 1958-59; chief aerodynamics Vertol Helicopter Co., 1955-58; mem. Congl. Adv. Com. Aeros., 1984-86; U.S. coord. flight vehicle integration panel Adv. Group for Aerospace R&D, 1988—; cons. to industry. Author: Aerodynamics of V/Stol Flight, 1967, Aerodynamics, Aeronautics and Flight Mechanics, 1979, 2d edit., 1995; co-author: (with M.P. Papadakis) Aircraft Accident Reconstruction and Litigation, 1996; contbr. articles to profl. jours.; patentee in field. Served with USNR, 1944-46. Recipient joint award for achievement in aerospace edn. Am. Soc. Engring. Edn.-Am. Inst. Aeros. and Astronautics, 1976 Fellow Am. Inst. Aeros. and Astronautics; mem. ASEE, Am. Helicopter Soc. (hon. fellow), Sigma Xi, Sigma Gamma Tau, Tau Beta Pi. Clubs: Masons. Home: 611 Glenn Rd State College PA 16803-3475 Office: Pa State U Coll Engring University Park PA 16802 Office Phone: 814-863-0602. E-mail: bwmaer@engr.psu.edu.

MCCORMICK, CAROLYN, actress; b. Midland, Tex., Sept. 19, 1959; BFA with honors, Williams Coll.; MFA, Am. Conservatory Theatre; student, Ctr. d'Etudes Francais, Avignon, France. Actress Am. Conservatory Theatre Co., 1983-85, Denver Ctr. Theatre Co., 1989-90; newscaster Channel 39 News, Houston, 1976—77. Appearances include (films) Enemy Mine, 1985, Rain Without Thunder, 1993, A Simple Twist of Fate, 1994, Loverboy, 2004, Spectropia, 2004, (TV series) Spenser: For Hire, 1986-87, Law and Order, 1991-2006, Cracker, 1997, (TV movies) Victim of Rage, 1994, The Osiris Chronicles, (TV episodes) Star Trek: The Next Generation, 1988, 90, Homocide: Life on The Street, 1996, (stage) In Perpetuality Throughout the Universe, 1988-89, There's One in Every Marriage, 1988, The Importance of Being Earnest, 1988-89, Much Ado About Nothing, 1990-91, Dinner Party, 1999, Dinner with Friends, 1999, Evolution, 2004, Privilege, 2005, Celebration, 2005. Office: Bresler Kelly & Assocs 11500 W Olympic Blvd Ste 510 Los Angeles CA 90064-1578

MCCORMICK, CORI, marketing executive, vocalist, community leader; d. Jelte and Cornelia Lanting; m. Roy McCormick, Apr. 6, 1991; children: Sarah, Hayden. BA, U. So. Calif., LA, 1986; MA, Calif. State U., Fullerton, 1991. Cert. educator Calif. Mktg. svcs. mgr. MITI, Long Beach, Calif., 1994—96; mktg. comm. mgr Sage Software, Irvine, Calif., 1996—2000; dir. advt. and brand mktg. Delta Faucet Co., Indpls., 2000—05; dir. mktg. comm. Holt, Rinehart & Winston, Austin, Tex., 2006—. Singer (Broadway cast reunion) Company; actor: Into the Woods, The Student Prince, A Funny Thing Happened on the Way to the Forum, (world stage premiere and tour) State

Fair; contbr. Trojan Family Mag. Troop leader Girl Scouts; vol. Humane Soc., Keep Austin Beautiful; vocalist, comm. team Grace Cmty. Ch.; team leader Destination Imagination. Recipient Team award, Sage Software, 1999; vocal scholar, U. So. Calif. Mem.: NAGC, Actors Equity Assn., Pub. Rels. Soc. Am., Am. Mktg. Assn., U. So.Calif. Alumni Club, Alpha Chi Omega (life).

MCCORMICK, DALE, state official; b. N.Y., Jan. 17, 1947; BA, U. Iowa, 1970. Mem. Maine State Senate from 18th dist, 1991-96; treas. State of Maine, Augusta, 1997—2004; dir. State Housing Aithority, Maine, 2004—. Author: Against the Grain, a Carpentry Manual for Women, 1977. Office: Maine State Housing Authority 353 Water St Augusta ME 04330-4633

MCCORMICK, DAVID ARTHUR, lawyer; b. McKeesport, Pa., Oct. 26, 1946; s. Arthur Paul and Eleanor Irene (Gibson) McC. BA, Westminster Coll. 1967; JD, Duquesne U., 1973, U. Pa., 1975. Bar: Pa. 1973, D.C. 1978, U.S. Ct. Appeals (3d cir.) 1977, U.S. Ct. Appeals (4th and D.C. cirs.) 1980, U.S. Supreme Ct. 1980. Asst. commerce counsel Penn Crtl. R.R., Phila., 1973—76; assoc. labor counsel Consol. Rail Corp., Phila., 1976—78; atty. Dept. Army, Washington, 1978—. Author: various geneal. and hist. works; contbr. articles to profl. jours. Mem. ATLA, Pa. Bar Assn., Phila. Bar Assn., DC Bar Assn., Assn. Transp. Law Profls., Soc. Petroleum Engrs., Soc. Cin. (Del. chpt.), SAR (Pitts. chpt.), Am. Legion, Res. Officers Assn., Masons, Phi Alpha Delta, Theta Chi Presbyterian.

MCCORMICK, DAVID H., federal agency administrator; BA, West Point; MS, PhD, Princeton U. Mgmt. cons. McKinsey & Co., Inc.; gen. mgr. core bus. markets FreeMarkets, Inc., 1999—2001, exec. v.p., 1999—2000, sr. v.p., 2000—01, exec. v.p., 2001—02, pres., 2002—04, CEO, 2003—04; pres., dir. Ariba, Inc., 2004—05; under sec. for industry & security U.S. Dept. Commerce, 2005—. Office: US Dept Commerce Herbert Clark Hoover Bldg 14th St and Constitution Ave NW Rm 3898 Washington DC 20230 Office Phone: 202-482-1455. Office Fax: 202-482-2387.*

MCCORMICK, DAVID HAROLD, government agency administrator; b. Washington, Pa., Aug. 17, 1965; s. James Harold and Maryan (Garner) McCormick; m. Amy Frances Richardson, May 30, 1999; children: Elizabeth Cora, Tess Ann, Ava Garner. BS, U.S. Mil. Acad., 1987; M in Pub. Affairs, Princeton U., 1994, PhD in Internat. and Pub. Affairs, 1996. Officer U.S. Army, Fort Bragg, NC, 1987—92; tchg. asst./grad. student Princeton U., NJ, 1992—96; cons. McKinsey & Co., Inc., Pitts., 1996—99; v.p./s.v.p./e.v.p. FreeMarkets, Inc., Pitts., 1999—2002, pres./CEO/dir., 2002—04; pres./dir. Ariba, Inc., Sunnyvale, Calif., 2004—05; under sec. Bur. Industry and Security Dept. Commerce, Washington, 2005—. Bd. mem. Pitts. Tech. Coun., 2004—05, Allegheny Conf. on Cmty. Devel., 2004—05. Author: (chapt.) From Peacekeeping to Peacebuilding: Restructuring Military and Policy Institutions in El Salvador in Keeping the Peace: Multidimensional UN Operations, (book) The Downsized Warrior: America's Army in Transition. Bd. mem. Pitts. Parks Conservancy, 2001—05, Manchester Bidwell Corp., Pitts., 2000—05. Capt. U.S. Army, 1987—92. Decorated Bronze Star; recipient Young Leader award, French-Am. Found., 1999; fellow, Earhart Found., 1996; Henry Crown Fellow, Aspen Inst., 2003.

MCCORMICK, DONALD BRUCE, retired biochemist, educator; b. Front Royal, Va., July 15, 1932; s. Jesse Allen and Elizabeth (Hord) McC.; m. Norma Jean Dunn, June 6, 1955; children: Susan Lynn, Donald Bruce, Michael Allen. BA, Vanderbilt U., Nashville, Tenn., 1953, PhD, 1958. Postdoctoral fellow U. Calif., Berkeley, 1958—60; asst. prof. Cornell U., 1960-63, assoc. prof., 1963-69, prof. nutrition, biochemistry and molecular biology, biol. scis., 1969-79, Liberty Hyde Bailey prof. nutritional biochemistry, 1978-79; chmn. dept. biochemistry Emory U., Atlanta, 1979-94, Fuller E. Callaway prof. biochemistry, 1979-99, prof. emeritus, 1999—; exec. assoc. dean sci. Emory U. Sch. Medicine, 1985-89. Vis. lectr. U. Ill, 1963; Wellcome vis. prof. U. Fla., 1986, Med. Coll. Pa., 1989; Hurley lectr. U. Calif., Davis, 1992; O'Dell lectr. U. Mo., Columbia, 1993; biochem. cons. Interdepartmental Com. on Nutrition for Nat. Def., Spain, 1958; mem. and chmn. nutrition study sect. NIH, 1977-81; mem. diet and health com., dietary guidelines implementation com., vice chmn. food and nutrition bd. NRC, Inst. Medicine of NAS; exec. com., chmn. dept. med. biochemistry, Coun. Acad. Soc., Am. Assn. Med. Colls., 1984-87; mem. biology panel U.S. Civilian R&D Found., 1998-2001. Author: (with others) Spain: Nutrition Survey of the Armed Forces, 1958, Molecular Associations in Biology, 1968, Flavins and Flavin Enzymes, 1968, Flavins and Flavoproteins, 1980, 82, 84, 88, 89, 91, Comprehensive Biochemistry, Vol. 21, 1971, Riboflavin, 1974, Metal Ions in Biological Systems, Vol. 1, 1974, Present Knowledge in Nutrition, 1976, 84, 90, 2001, Natural Sulphur Compounds, 1979, Vitamin B6, Metabolism and Role in Growth, 1980, Ann. Rev. of Nutrition, Vol. 1, 1981, Vol. 9, 1989, Vol. 24, 2004, Mechanisms of Enzymatic Reactions: Stereochemistry, 1986, Chemical and Biological Aspects of Vitamin B6 Catalysis, Part A, 1984, Biochemistry of Vitamin B6, 1987, Biochemistry and Molecular Biology of Vitamin B6 and PQQ-Dependent Proteins, 2000, Tietz Textbook of Clinical Chemistry, 1986, 94, 99, Fundamentals of Clinical Chemistry, 1987, 95, 2000, Vitamins and Biofactors in Life Science, 1992, Encyclopedia of Food Science, 1993, 2003, Encyclopedia of Life Sciences, 1999, Encyclopedia of Molecular, Biology and Molecular Medicine, 1996, 97, 2003, Modern Nutrition in Health and Disease, 1988, 94, 99, New Trends in Biological Chemistry, 1990, Chemistry and Biochemistry of Flavins, 1991, Encyclopedia of Human Biology, 1991, 97, Liver, 1994, Molecular Biology and Biotechnology, 1995, Biochemical and Physiological Bases of Human Nutrition, 2000, Nutrition in Space Flight and Weightlessness Models, 1999, Encyclopedia of Dietary Supplements, 2005; editor: Vitamins and Hormones, Vitamins and Coenzymes, Ann. Rev. of Nutrition, Handbook of Vitamins. Recipient award Bausch and Lomb, 1950, award Mead Johnson, 1970, award Osborne and Mendel, 1978, award Ga. Nutrition Coun., 1989, award Bristol-Myers Squibb/Mead Johnson, 1999; Westinghouse Sci. scholar, 1950; fellow NIH, 1957-58, 58-60; Guggenheim fellow, 1966-67. Fellow AAAS, Am. Inst. Nutrition (now Am. Soc. Nutrition, pres. 1991); mem. Am. Soc. Biochemistry and Molecular Biology, Soc. Exptl. Biology and Medicine, Am. Chem. Soc., Am. Inst. Nutrition, Am. Dietetic Assn., Fedn. Am. Socs. Exptl. Biology (bd. dirs., LSRO sci. steering group), Microbiol. Soc., Photobiol. Soc., N.Y. Acad. Sci., Protein Soc., Sigma Xi. Office Phone: 770-270-5508. Business E-Mail: biocdbm@emory.edu.

MCCORMICK, FRANK, research scientist; BSc in biochemistry, U. Birmingham, 1972; PhD in biochemistry, U. Cambridge, 1975; postdoctoral fellow, SUNY, Stony Brook, 1975—78, Imperial Cancer Rsch. Fund, 1978—81. Dir. molecular biology Cetus Corp., 1981—90, v.p. rsch., 1990—91, Chiron Corp., 1991—92; founder and chief sci. officer Onyx Pharm., 1992—96; dir. Comprehensive Cancer Ctr. and Cancer Rsch. Inst. U. Calif., San Francisco, 1997—, mem. Biomedical Sci. Program, 1997—, mem. Herbert Boyer Program in Bio. Sci., 1997, David A. Wood endowed chair in tumor biology and cancer rsch., 1997—. Mem. sci. adv. bd. Iconix Pharm. Recipient AACR-GHA Clowes Meml. award, 2002; fellow, Royal Soc., 1996. Mem.: Inst. Medicine. Office: Comprehensive Cancer Ctr Univ Calif San Francisco 2340 Sutter St Box 0128 San Francisco CA 94143 also: Comprehensive Rsch Ctr Univ Calif San Francisco Box 0128 San Francisco CA 94143-0128*

MCCORMICK, HAROLD J., music educator; b. Dover, N.J., Sept. 22, 1954; s. Harold Joseph and Dorothy McCormick; m. Patricia Anne McCormick, Oct. 4, 1980; children: Harold J. IV, Timothy Vincent, Caroline Constance, Cecilia James. B in Music Edn., Kean U., 1979. Band dir. Red Bank (N.J.) Cath. H.S., 1981—83, Jackson (N.J.) Twp. Meml. H.S. 1984—. Adjudicator Drum Corps Assocs., Monmouth Beach, NJ, 1987—, Music Showcase Festivals, 1994—; drum corps arranger; marching band music arranger. Active Jackson Coun. of the Arts, 2000—02. Mem.: Ga. Marching Band Assn., U.S. Scholastic Band Assn., Music Educators Nat. Conf. Office: Jackson Meml HS 101 Don Connor Blvd Jackson NJ 08527 Office Phone: 732-833-4600.

MCCORMICK, HUGH THOMAS, lawyer; b. McAlester, Okla., Nov. 24, 1944; s. Hugh O. and Lois (McGucken) McC.; m. Suzanna G. Weingarten, Dec. 5, 1975; 1 child, John B. BA, U. Mich., 1968; JD, Rutgers U., 1977; LLM in Taxation, Georgetown U., 1980. Bar: N.Y. 1977, D.C. 1979, Maine 1981. Atty. office chief counsel interpretative divsn. IRS, Washington, 1977-81; assoc. Perkins, Thompson, Hinkley & Keddy, Portland, Maine, 1981-83, LeBoeuf, Lamb, Leiby & MacRae, N.Y.C., 1983-88, counsel, 1989-91; ptnr. LeBoeuf, Lamb, Greene & MacRae, L.L.P., N.Y.C., 1992—2005; exec. v.p. Scottish Re Group, Ltd., Hamilton, Bermuda, 2005—. Dir. Ins. Tax. Conf., 1993-04, pres., 2002-04. Mem. bd. contbrs. and advisors Jour. of Taxation of Investments; contbr. articles to profl. jours. Trustee U.S. Team Handball Found., N.J., 1985-95. Fellow Am. Bar Found.; mem. ABA (chmn. com. on taxation of ins. cos. 1989, chmn. subcom. sect. of taxation 1989-96, mem. torts and ins. practice sect., sect. on taxation), D.C. Bar Assn. Democrat. Home: 7132 Seton House Ln Charlotte NC 28277 Office: Scottish Re Group Ltd Crown House 4 Par La Ville Rd 3rd Flr Hamilton HM MX Bermuda Office Phone: 441 298 4397. Business E-Mail: hugh.mccormick@scottishre.com.

MCCORMICK, JAMES HAROLD, academic administrator; b. Ind., Pa., Nov. 11, 1938; s. Harold Clark and Mary Blanche (Truby) McCormick; m. Maryan Kough Garner, June 7, 1963; children: David Harold, Douglas Paul. BS, Indiana U. of Pa., 1959; MEd, U. Pitts., 1961, EdD, 1963, postdoctoral, 1966, Columbia U., U. Mich., 1966-67, Harvard U., 1982. Tchr. Punxsutawney (Pa.) Area Joint Sch. Dist., 1959-61; adminstr. Baldwin-Whitehall Schs., Pitts., 1961-64; grad. asst. U. Pitts., 1962-63; asst. supt. instrn. Washington (Pa.) City Schs., 1964-65; prof. dept. edn. and psychology, asst. dean acad. affairs, acting dean acad. affairs, acting dean tchr. edn., asst. to pres., v.p. adminstrn. and fin. Shippensburg (Pa.) U., 1965-73; pres. Bloomsburg (Pa.) U., 1973-83, pres. emeritus, 1983—; founding chancellor Pa. State System Higher Edn., Harrisburg, 1983—2001; chancellor Minn. State Colls. and Univs., 2001—. Falk intern in politics, 1959; mem. adv. bd. Pa. Ednl. Policy Seminar; mem. Gov.'s Econ. Devel. Partnership Bd.; mem. higher edn. adv. coun. Pa. State Bd. Edn.; past commr. Edn. Commn. of the States; chmn. Midwestern Higher Edn. Compact; bd. mem. Great North Alliance, Minn. Job Skills Partnership; founder, mem. Minn. P-16 Edn. Partnership; active Govs. Edn. Coun.; mem. postsecondary edn. and workforce devel. adv. com. ECS. Contbr. articles profl. jours. Named One of 10 Outstanding Young Men of Yr., Pa. Jr. C. of C.; recipient Young Leader in Edn. award Phi Delta Kappa, 1981, Disting. Alumnus award Indiana U. Pa., 1981, Outstanding Alumni award Bloomsburg U., 1984, Outstanding Alumnus award U. Pitts., 1985, Adler award Pa. Edn. Assn., 1992; selected CIVITAS Prague mission, 1995, Presdl. Lectures, Kuwait U., 1993, Svc. award Coll. and Univ. Pub. Rels., Assn. Pa., 1999, Distig. Svc. award Pa. Assn. Couns. of Trustees, 1998, Alumni Assn. Leadership award Bloomsburg U., 1999; McCormick Human Svcs. Ctr. named in his honor Bloomsburg U., 1983; McCormick House named in his honor Dixon U., 1994. Mem. Am. Assn. State Colls. and Univs. (Pa. state rep. 1988-93, former chmn. acad. and student pers. com., mem. com. on state rels. and task force on ednl. equity, chmn. policies and purposes com. 1996), Am. Coun. on Edn. (commn. on women in higher edn.), Nat. Assn. Sys. Heads, (exec. com., past pres.), Commn. State Colls. and Univs. (mem. and past chmn. govt. rels. and student rels. coms.), Assn. Governing Bds. (adv. coun.), Am. Assn. for Affirmative Action, Am. Assn. Higher Edn., Am. Assn. Sch. Adminstrs., Am. Assn. Univ. Adminstrs. (Tosney Leadership award 1993), Pa. Assn. Colls. and Univs. (bd. dirs., chair 1982), Natl. Ctr. for the Study of Sport in Soc., Pa. Black Conf. on Higher Edn., State Higher Edn. Ofcrs. (exec. com.), Pers. Assn., Bloomsburg Area C. of C. (pres. 1983), Harrisburg Rotary (bd. dirs. to 1992), St. Paul Rotary, Phi Delta Kappa. Office: Wells Fargo Pl 30 7th St East Ste 350 Saint Paul MN 55101 Home: 10560 Pinnacle Way Woodbury MN 55129 Office Phone: 651-296-7971.

MCCORMICK, JAMES K., application developer; BS in Acctg. summa cum laude, Fla. State U., 1984. CPA, Ga., 1985. Sr. auditor emerging bus. divsn. Arthyr Andersen & Co., Atlanta, 1984-89; cons. mgr. strategic svcs. divsn. Andersen Cons., Melbourne, Australia, 1989-91; dir. fin. Am. Sign & Mktg. Svcs., Inc., 1991-92; corp. controller, treas. United Dairy Farmers, Inc., 1992-97; mgr. acctg., fin. MIS & human resources depts. Knology, 1997-99; chief fin. officer Harbinger Corp., Atlanta, 1999—. Office: Harbinger Corp 11720 Amberpark Dr Ste 100 Alpharetta GA 30004-2271

MCCORMICK, JAMES THOMAS, surgeon, researcher; s. James Nagel and Jean C McCormick; m. Tricia Kuhar McCormick, July 22, 1994; children: Marnie children: Moira, Clara. BA in Biology, Canisius Coll., Buffalo, 1992; DO, Lake Erie Coll. of Osteo. Medicine, Erie, Pa, 1998. Gen. surgery resident Temple U. Sch. Medicine Clin. Campus Western Pa. Hosp., Pitts., 1998—, chief adminstry. resident, 2003—; colorectal surgery residency U. Tex., Dallas. Curriculum com. rep. Lake Erie Coll. Osteo. Medicine, Erie, Pa., 1994—98; co-founder and coord. Bridging the Gaps/Erie Cmty. Health Internship, Pa., 1995; founder and pres. Erie Med. Student Sect. AMA, Pa., 1995; grad. med. edn. com. rep. The Western Pa. Hosp., Pitts., 1999—, resident rep. gov.'s bd., 2003—, mem. surg. exec. com., 2003—. Contbr. articles to internat. jours. in surg. scis., including Annals of Thoracic Surgery, Burns, Am. Jour. Surgery, Surg. Endoscopy, Abdominal Surgery. Recipient Laparoscopic Achievement award, Soc. for Laparoendoscopic Surgery, 2001; scholar, NY State Bd. of Regents, 1987, Pa. Osteo. Med. Assn. Found., 1996. Mem.: ACS, Am. Soc. Gen. Surgeons, Soc. Am. Gastrointestinal Endoscopic Surgeons, Am. Soc. Colon and Rectal Surgeons, Psi Sigma Alpha. Achievements include research in the use of routine chest x-ray films after chest tube removal in postoperative cardiac patients; effect of diagnosis and treatment of sinusitis in critically ill burn victims; laparoscopic revision of failed open bariatric procedures; laparoscopic management of complications following laparoscopic Roux-en-Y gastric bypass for morbid obesity; fine needle aspiration biopsy of the thyroid: an outcome study at a community hospital; management of a complex enterocutaneous fistula using cadaver skin; prospective study to determine if orocecal transit time can be used as a prognosticator of weight reduction in patients undergoing Roux-en-Y gastric bypass for morbid obesity; effect of gum chewing on bowel function and hospital stay after laparoscopic and open colestomy: rectal prolapse, preoperative evaluation for colorectal cancer. Avocations: exercise, sailing. Office: West Penn Hosp Dept Surgery 4800 Friendship Ave Pittsburgh PA 15224 Office Phone: 412-578-6880.

MCCORMICK, JOHN HOYLE, lawyer; b. Pensacola, Fla., July 30, 1933; s. Clyde Hoyle and Orrie Brooks (Frink) McC.; m. Patricia McCall, Dec. 27, 1974. BS, U. Fla., 1955; JD, Stetson U., 1958. Bar: Fla. 1958. Ptnr. McCormick, Drury & Scaff, Jasper, Fla., 1958-74; county atty., 1973—; sr. ptnr. McCormick, Drury & Scaff, Jasper, 1974-91; pvt. practice Jasper, 1991—. County judge, Hamilton County, Fla., 1960-72; local counsel So. Ry. System, 1968—, CSX, Ry., 1972—; atty. Hamilton County Devel. Authority, 1970-91; bd. dirs. 1st Fed. Savs. Bank Fla.; bd. dirs., v.p., atty. Hamilton County Bank. Mayor City of White Springs, Fla., 1959; pres. Hamilton County C. of C., Jasper, 1961. Mem.: Masons, Phi Delta Phi. Democrat. Methodist. Avocations: gardening, motorhome camping, college football. Home: 403 2nd Ave NW Jasper FL 32052-6687 Office: 215 2nd St NE Jasper FL 32052-6616 Address: PO Drawer O Jasper FL 32052-0695

MCCORMICK, JOHN OWEN, retired comparative literature educator; b. Thief River Falls, Minn., Sept. 20, 1918; s. Owen Charles and Marie Antoinette Beauchemin (Smith) McC.; m. Helen Manuel, 1942; m. Mairi Clare MacInnes, 1954; children: Jonathan, Peter, Antoinette, Fergus. BA magna cum laude, U. Minn., 1941; MA, Harvard U., 1947, PhD, 1951. Dean, lectr. Salzburg Seminar in Am. Studies, 1951-52; lectr., prof. Free U., Berlin, 1952-59; prof. comparative lit. Rutgers U., 1959-87, prof. emeritus, 1987—. Vis. prof. Nat. U. Mexico, 1961-62, Hachioji (Tokyo) seminar, 1979; Christian Gauss Seminar lectr. Princeton, 1969; resident fellow Sch. Letters of Ind. U., 1970 Author: The Middle Distance: A Comparative History of American Imaginative Literature, 1919-32, 1971, The Complete Aficionado, 1967, 2d edit., 1998, (with Mairi MacInnes McCormick) Versions of Censorship, 1962, Der moderne amerikanische Roman, 1960, Amerikanische Lyrik, 1957, Catastrophe and Imagination, 1957, 2d edit., 1998, Fiction as

Knowledge, 1975, 2d edit., 1999, George Santayana: A Biography, 1987, 2003, Wolfe, Malraux, Hesse, 1987, American and European Literary Imagination: 1919-1932, 2000; editor: (with G. Core) Sallies of the Mind: Essays of Francis Fergusson, 1998, Seagoing: Essay-Memoirs, 2000. With USNR, 1941-46. Recipient prize for non-fiction Longview Found., 1960, Am. Acad. and Inst. Arts and Letters award, 1988; Guggenheim fellow, 1964-65, 79-80, Bruern fellow Leeds (Eng.) U., 1975-76, NEH fellow, 1983-84, hon. fellow U. York, 1992. Mem. Taurino Club (London), Harvard Club (NYC), Authors League

**MCCORMICK, KAREN LOUISE,** savings and loan association executive; b. San Jose, Calif., Nov. 22, 1954; d. Clifford Kaye Jr. and Margaret Elizabeth (Bigler) McC.; children: Crystal DeAnne, Sheralyn Rose McCormick. Grad. high sch., Mountain View, Calif., 1973; cert. Inst. Fin. Edn., Ariz. State U., 1987. Cashier, loan officer Santa Clara County Employees' Credit Union, San Jose, 1973-77; teller, loan officer First Fed. Savs. & Loan Assn. Port Angeles, Wash., 1977-83, v.p., br. mgr., 1983-87, v.p., adminstr. loan prodn., 1987-89, v.p., ass. dir. lending, 1989-90, sr. v.p., dir. lending, 1990—97, pres., CEO, 1997—. Bd. dirs., chair opns. com. Wash. Community Reinvestment Assn., Seattle, 1992-95.; mem. Wash. Savs. League Affordable Housing com., 1991; vice chair Wash. Fin. League, 2003-; chair bd. dirs. WFL Services (subsid. corp. of Wash. Fin. League), 2003-; past bd. mem. & pres. Thrift Inst. Adv. Coun. Contbr. articles to newspapers, 1989-91. Bd. dirs Clallam County YMCA, 1992-95, Diversified Industries, Inc., Port Angeles, 1985-87, Port Angeles C of C; mem. Queen of Angels sch. bd., 1988-90; co-founder Olympic Peninsula Housing Coalition, 1992—; treas. Peninsula Coll. Found., past pres. Nor'Wester Rotary Club of Port Angeles. Named one of The Top 25 Most Powerful Women in Banking, US Banker mag., 2003. Mem.: America's Cmty. Bankers (pres. 2003). Avocations: creative writing, reading, music, travel. Office: First Fed Savs Port Angeles PO Box 351 Port Angeles WA 98362-0055

**MCCORMICK, KATHLEEN,** archivist, educator; d. Harold Edward and Nancy Anne McCormick. BA, Emory U., Atlanta, 1996; MA, Boston Coll., 2001; MLS, Simmons Coll., Boston, 2005. Asst. dir. Gaelic Roots Irish Music Summer Sch. and Festival Boston Coll., 2000—02, libr. assist. Irish Music Ctr., 2003—05; reference archivist U. N.C., Charlotte, 2005—, coord. Oral History Program, 2005—. Instr. Norfolk County Correctional Facility, Dedham, Mass., 2003—05; lectr. Quincy (Mass.) Coll., 2001—03; bd. dirs. N.C. Preservation Consortium, NC. Participant South by South Africa Dialogue Group, Charlotte, 2006., Boston Coll. fellow, 2000—01. Mem.: ALA, Soc. N.C. Archivists, Oral History Assn., Soc. Am. Archivists, Beta Phi Mu. Avocations: travel, hiking, bicycling, swimming, reading.

**MCCORMICK, KATHLEEN ANN KRYM,** geriatrics nurse, computer information specialist, federal agency administrator; b. Manchester, N.H., June 27, 1947; BSN, Barry Coll., 1969; MSN, Boston U., 1971; MS, U. Wis., 1975, PhD, 1978. Capt. nurse officer USPHS, COSTEP nurse Staten Island, NY, 1968, staff nurse, instr. Brighton, Mass., 1970; staff nurse Mercy Hosp., Miami, 1969, St. Elizabeth's Hosp., Brighton 1970—71; clin. nurse special-ist Boston U. Hosp., 1970—71; clin. nurse specialist, instr. U. Wis., Madison, 1971—72; assist. rsch. to chief nursing clin. ctr., dept. Nursing NIH, Bethesda, 1978—83; nurse, co-dir. inpatient geriatric continence project, Lab. Behavioral Scis., Gerontology Rsch. Ctr. Nat. Inst. Aging, Balt., 1983—88, dir. nursing rsch., 1988—91; dir. office forum quality and effectiveness health care Agy. Health Care Policy and Rsch., Rockville, Md., 1991—93, sr. sci. adviser, 1993—. Adj. asst. prof. Cath. U., Washington, 1979, Washington, 82; faculty assoc. U. Md., Balt., 1979—81; ad hoc reviewer biomed. rsch. grants NIH, 1979—80, divns. nursing rsch. and tng. HRA, 1979—82; instr. Found. Advanced Edn. in Scis., 1981—82; exec. com. Reg. Nursing Liaison Ctr. Nursing Rsch., 1986—91; Surgeon Gen.'s rep. Sec. Alzheimer's Task Force19089, 1989—; Surgeon Gen. alt. to Bd. Regents Nat. Libr. Medicine, 1989—; co-chair panel guidelines for urinary incontinence in adult, 1990—91; spkr. in field. Editor: Nursing Outlook, 1988—90; mem. editl. staff: Mil. Medicine, 1985—93, assoc. editor: Internat. Jour. Tech. and Aging, 1985—87. Recipient award, Jour. Acad. Sci., 1965, travel award, NSF, 1973, J.D. Lane Jr. Investigator award, USPHS Profl. Assn., 1979, Excellence in Writing award, Nat. League Nursing/Humana, 1983, award Spl. Recognition Rsch., U. Pa. Sch. Nursing, 1986, Fed. Svc. Nursing award, 1987, Surgeon Gen.'s medallion, 1989; grantee, U. Wis. Grad. Sch., 1977, Upjohn Co., 1977; scholar Queen's Vis. scholar, Royal Adelaide (Australia) Hosp., 1990. Fellow: NAS Inst. Medicine, Gerontologic Soc. Am. (clin. med. sect., computer program coord. 1985—87, clin. medicine rep. publs. com., Nurse of Yr. 1992), Coll. Am. Med. Informatics, Royal Coll. Nursing (Australia), Am. Acad. Nursing; mem.: AACN (strategic planning com. 1987—89, Disting. Rsch. award 1986), ANA (editor newsletter coun. nurse rschrs. 1980—85, vice chairperson exec. com. coun. computer applications in nursing 1984—86, sec.), Md. Lung Assn. (awards and grants subcom. 1978, 1992, v.p. exec. bd. dirs. 1980—87), Met. Area Nursing Rsch. Consortium, Commd. Officers Assn., Assn. Mil. Surgeons (Sustaining Mem. award 1982), Internat. Med. Informatics Assn. (working group 8, program com. 1984—), Acad. Medicine, Am. Med. Informatics Assn. (bd. dirs.), Am. Lung Assn./Am. Thoracic Soc. (chairperson 1983—84, nominating com. 1989, nat. rsch. rev. com., cert. appreciation mid.-Md. chpt. 1982, 1983, 1984), Capital Spkrs. Club (10M), Am. News Women's Club, Sigma Theta Tau (grantee 1976), Sigma Delta Epsilon (Eloise Gerry grant-in-aid fellow 1979—80), Lambda Sigma. Office: 540 Gaither RD Rockville MD 20850-6649

**MCCORMICK, MARIE CLARE,** pediatrician, educator; b. Winchester, Mass., Jan. 7, 1946; d. Richard John and Clare Bernadine (Keleher) McC.; m. Robert Jay Blendon, Dec. 30, 1977. BA magna cum laude, Emmanuel Coll., 1967, LHD (hon.), 2006; MD, Johns Hopkins U., 1971, ScD, 1978; MA, Harvard U., 1991. Diplomate Am. Bd. Pediat. Pediatric resident, fellow Johns Hopkins Hosp., Balt., 1971-75, rsch. fellow, 1972-75; asst. prof. U. Ill. Schs. Medicine & Pub. Health, Chgo. 1975-76; pediat. instr. Johns Hopkins Med Sch., Balt., 1976-78; asst. prof. healthcare orgn. Johns Hopkins Sch. Hygiene & Pub. Health, 1978-81; asst. prof. pediat. U. Pa., Phila., 1981-86, assoc. prof. pediat., 1986-87, Harvard Med. Sch., Boston, 1987-91, prof. pediat., 1992—, 1st Sumner and Esther Feldberg prof. maternal/child health, 1996—; prof. Harvard Sch. Pub. Health, Boston, 1992—2003, chair maternal and child health, 1992—2003, prof. Soc., Human Devel. and Health, 2003—. Adj. assoc. prof. pediat. U. Pa., 1987-92; active attending physician, Johns Hopkins Hosp., 1976-81, physician Children's Hosp. Phila., 1981-84, assoc. physician, 1984-86, sr. physician, 1986-87, assoc. pediatrician Brigham & Women's Hosp., 1987—; sr. assoc. in medicine Children's Hosp., 1987—; sr. assoc. in pediat. Beth Israel Deaconess Med. Ctr., 1987—; vis. prof. Wash. U., St. Louis, 1993; editl. bds. Health Svcs. Rsch., 1985-94, Pediat. in Rev., 1986-91, Pediat., 1993-99; assoc. editor Jour. Ambulatory Pediatric Assn., 1990—; adv. coun. Ctr. Perinatal & Family Health Brigham & Women's Hosp., 1991—; cons. to numerous coms., orgns. and bds. Contbr. articles to profl. jours. Adv. The David and Lucile Packard Found., 1993-95; bd. dirs. Family Planning Coun. S.E. Pa., 1984-87; chair com. child health Mayor's Commn. Phila., 1982-83. Named Henry Strong Denison scholar, Johns Hopkins Sch. Medicine, 1971, Leonard Davis Inst.; recipient Johns Hopkins U. Soc. Scholars award, 1995, award, Nat. Assn. of Nat. Acads., 2001, David Rall award, Inst. Medicine, 2005; Health Econs. fellow, U. Pa., 1984. Fellow: Am. Acad. Pediat.; mem. AAAS, Inst. Medicine of NAS, Ambulatory Pediat. Assn. (Rsch. award 1996), Soc. Pediatric Rsch. (sr., Douglas K. Richardson award 2006), Am. Pediatric Soc., Am. Pub. Health Assn., Internat. Epidemiol. Assn., Assn. Health Svcs. Rsch., Ea. Soc. Pediatric Rsch., Soc. Pediatric Epidemiologic Rsch., Assn. Tchrs. Maternal and Child Health, Mass. Med. Soc., Norfolk Dist. Med. Soc., Mass. Pub. Health Assn., Johns Hopkins U. Soc. Scholars. Office: Harvard Sch Pub Health 677 Huntington Ave Boston MA 02115-6096 Business E-Mail: mmccormi@hsph.harvard.edu.

**MCCORMICK, PAULA SHURLING,** elementary school educator; b. Macon, Ga., Sept. 28, 1951; d. Harley Frank and Lucile Devariant (Thaxton) Shurling; m. John Douglas McCormick, June 24, 1973; children: John, Jason, Josh, Justin. BSHE, U. Ga., 1973; MED, Ga. So. U., 1983, EdS, 1987. nat. bd.

cert. tchr., Ga., 2003. Tchr. Blackwell Jr. High Sch., Elberton, Ga., 1973, Willow Hill, Portal, Ga., 1973—74, Southeast Bulloch Jr. High Sch., Brooklet, Ga., 1974-76, Brooklet Elem. Sch., 1986—. Life mem. supt.'s coun. Statesboro, Ga. Mem. Ga. Coun. Tchrs. Math., Profl. Assn. Ga. Educators. Methodist. Avocations: needlecrafts, crocheting, reading. Home: 902 Rushing Rd Brooklet GA 30415-6372 Office: Brooklet Elem Sch 600 West Lane St Brooklet GA 30415-6216

**MCCORMICK, RICHARD LEVIS,** academic administrator; b. New Brunswick, N.J., Dec. 26, 1947; s. Richard Patrick and Katheryne Crook (Levis) McCormick; m. Joan C. Barry, July 22, 2006; children: Elizabeth, Michael. BA in Am. Studies, Amherst Coll., 1969; PhD in History, Yale U., 1976. From asst. prof. to prof. Rutgers U., New Brunswick, NJ, 1976—92, dean Faculty Arts and Scis., 1989—92; exec. vice chancellor, provost, vice chancellor acad. affair U. N.C., Chapel Hill, 1992—95; pres. U. Wash., Seattle, 1995—2002, Rutgers U., New Brunswick, NJ, 2002—. Author: From Realignment to Reform: Political Change in New York State 1893-1910, 1981, The Party Period and Public Policy: American Politics from the Age of Jackson to the Progressive Era, 1986. Fellow, Am. Coun. Learned Socs., 1978—79, John Simon Guggenheim Meml. Found., 1985. Mem.: Phi Beta Kappa. Office: Rutgers Univ New Brunswick NJ 08901 Office Phone: 732-932-7454. E-mail: rlm@rutgers.edu.

**MCCORMICK, ROBERT JUNIOR,** former federal agency administrator; b. Boone, Iowa, Aug. 1, 1929; s. Ivyl Robert and Darlene Adel (Bowes) McC.; m. Shirley May Zerbe, Dec. 24, 1950; children: Elaine McCormick Newland, Kathleen, Michael, Tara McCormick Wieting, Tammy McCormick Kirby. Grad., Flying Sch., Williams Field, Ariz., 1951, Parachute Jump Sch., 1964, Armed Forces Staff Coll., Norfolk, Va., 1966, Def. Systems Mgmt. Coll., Ft. Belvoir, Va., 1975; BS in Mech. Engring., Tex. Tech. U., 1963; cert., Harvard U. Def. Studies Program, 1984. Served as enlisted man USAF, 1948—51, commd. 2d lt., 1951, advanced through grades to col., 1971, pilot U.S., Japan, Europe, Vietnam, fighter pilot Korean War, 1951—52; exec. officer to asst. sec. George Brown 7th Air Force, Saigon, Vietnam, 1969—70; mil. asst. to asst. sec. of Air Force for research and devel. USAF, Washington, 1970—74, ret., 1975; exec. officer NASA, Washington, 1976—80; adminstrv. asst. to sec. of Air Force USAF, Washington, 1980—94; mem. U.S. Sr. Exec. Service, 1979—94; pres. McG, Ltd., Fairfax, Va. Mem. Pres.'s transition team Dept. of Def., 2001. Decorated Air Force Legion of Merit, Bronze star, Air medal, Meritorious Svc. medal, Air Force Exceptional Civilian Svc. medal, NASA Exceptional Svc. medal, 1980; recipient Presdl. Meritorious Rank, 1989, Disting. Civilian Svc. medal Dept. Def., 1994, Commendation medal State of Calif., 2001. Mem. ASME, DAV, Air Force Assn., Nat. Def. Indsl. Assn., Order of Daedalians, St. Andrews Soc. Washington, Mil. Order of Carabao, Chevaliers du Testevin. Clubs: Army-Navy Country (Fairfax, Va.). E-mail: mcgltd1@aol.com.

**MCCORMICK, STEVEN D.,** lawyer; b. Waterloo, Iowa, Apr. 24, 1946; AB, U. Notre Dame, 1968; JD, Northwestern U., 1971. Bar: Ill. 1972. Ptnr. Kirkland & Ellis LLP, Chgo., 1977—, head in-house trial advocacy program, 1993—. Lectr. Nat. Inst. Trial Advocacy, Chgo., Boulder, Colo., 1989—98; adj. prof. law Northwestern U., 1997—. Named one of Top 10 Trial Lawyers in Am., Nat. Law Jour., 2006. Office: Kirkland & Ellis LLP 200 E Randolph St Fl 54 Chicago IL 60601-6636 E-mail: smccormick@kirkland.com.*

**MCCORMICK, STEVEN THOMAS,** insurance company executive; b. Phila., Dec. 18, 1955; s. Howard C. and Ruth Marion (Stahl) McC.; m. Helene Mary Trommler, Nov. 21, 1981; children: Matthew Thomas, Bria Helene. BBA, U. Ky., 1978; gen. ins cert., Ins. Inst. Am., 1980; MBA, Sullivan U., 2006. Cert. adminstrv. mgr., purchasing mgr., ins. agt., Ky., 1980. Supr. trainee Ky. Farm Bur. Ins. Cos., Louisville, 1978-79, supr. micrographics dept., 1979-83, supr. adminstrv. svcs., 1983-85, mgr. adminstrv. svcs., 1985-89, asst. v.p. ops., 1989—, dir. adminstrv. svcs., 2005—. Bd. dirs. Ky. Athletic Hall of Fame, 2005—. Named to Hon. Order Ky. Cols., Outstanding Employee of Yr. Nat. Assn. of Mut. Ins. Cos., 1986; recipient Cert. of Excellence, Jefferson County Bd. Edn. Mem. Adminstrv. Mgmt. Soc. (internat. top recruiter 1985, chpt. pres. 1988, internat. dir. area 7 1990-91, internat. v.p. profl. devel. 1992-93), Acad. Adminstrv. Mgmt. (mem. bd. regents 1991-92, internat. v.p. 1992-93, internat. pres. 1993-94), U. Ky. Alumni Assn., Sigma Nu. Republican. Home: 706 Elsmere Cir Louisville KY 40223-2764 Office: Ky Farm Bur Ins Cos PO Box 20700 Louisville KY 40250-0700

**MCCORMICK, SUSAN KONN,** retired publishing executive; b. Cleve., Dec. 13, 1953; d. Frank Andrew and Mary Lou (Dunn) Konn; m. Michael F. McCormick, May 25, 1985; children: Amanda, James. BS, Ind. U., 1976; MBA, Stanford U., 1983. CPA, N.Y. Acct. Deloitte Haskins & Sells, Indpls., 1975-77; fin. analyst GM, N.Y.C., 1977-83; exec. Brown Bros. Harriman, N.Y.C., 1983-84; v.p. Bankers Trust Co., N.Y.C., 1984-85; treas. Scholastic, Inc., N.Y.C., 1985-94; now ret., 1994. Mem. AICPA, N.Y. State Soc. CPA's, Risk Mgmt. Soc., Stanford U. Alumni Assn., N.Y. Treas.'s Club. E-mail: mccormsk@aol.com.

**MCCORMICK, WALTER BERNARD, JR.,** trade association administrator; b. Kansas City, Mo., Feb. 8, 1954; s. Walter Bernard and Dorothy Ann (Power) M.; m. Mary Lou Edlefsen, Jan. 3, 1987; children: Walter Patrick, Megan Boutin. Student, Georgetown U., 1975; BJ, U. Mo., 1976, JD, 1979. Bar: Mo. 1979, DC 1980. Assoc. Leighton, Conklin, Lemov & Jacobs, Washington, 1980-81, Pepper, Hamilton & Scheetz, Washington, 1981-82; legis. asst. US Senate, Washington, 1982-84; gen. counsel US Senate Com. Commerce, Sci. and Transp., Washington, 1985-87, minority chief counsel, staff dir., 1988-92; gen. counsel US Dept. Transp., Washington, 1992-93; ptnr. Bryan Cave LLP, Washington, 1993—98; pres., CEO Am. Trucking Assns., 1998—2001, US Telecom Assn., 2001—. Mem. City Club, Washington, 1993—. Republican. Roman Catholic. Office: US Telecom Assn 607 14th St NW Ste 400 Washington DC 20005 Office Phone: 202-326-7300.

**MCCORMICK, WILLIAM PAUL,** ambassador; b. Providence, Aug. 18, 1939; m. Gail McCormick; 6 children. Attended, Roger Williams Jr. Coll., Boston U. With Conn. Gen. Life Ins. Co., San Francisco 1963—65; co-owner Refectory Internat. Inc.; co-founder, pres. McCormick & Schmick's Seafood Restaurants, Inc., 1972—94, chmn., 2003—04, chmn. emeritus, 2004—05; U.S. amb. to New Zealand and Samoa US Dept. State, Wellington, 2005—. Served with Army Reserve Military Police. Recipient Secretary's award, US Dept. Veteran's Affairs. Office: 4360 Wellington Pl Washington DC 20521*

**MCCORMICK, WILLIAM THOMAS, JR.,** electric and gas company executive; b. Washington, Sept. 12, 1944; s. William Thomas and Lucy Valentine (Offutt) McCormick; m. Ann Loretta du Mais, June 13, 1969; children: Christopher, Patrick. BS, Cornell U., 1966; PhD, M.I.T., 1969. Mem. staff Inst. for Def. Analysis, Arlington, Va., 1969—72; mem. staff Office of Sci. and Tech.; Exec. office of the Pres., Washington, 1972—73; sr. staff mem. Energy Policy Office, The White House, 1973—74; chief sci. and energy tech. br. Office Mgmt. and Budget, Exec. Office of the Pres., 1974—75; dir. commercialization U.S. Energy Rsch. and Devel. Adminstrn., 1975—76; v.p. policy and govt. relations Am. Gas Assn., 1976—78; v.p., asst. to chmn. Am. Natural Resources Co., Detroit, 1978—80; exec. v.p. Mich. Wis. Pipeline Co., Am. Natural Resources System, Detroit, 1980—82; pres. Am. Natural Resources Co., Detroit, 1982—85; chmn., chief exec. officer Consumers Power Co., Jackson, Mich., 1985—92, chmn., 1992—2002; chmn., CEO CMS Energy Corp., 1985—2002. Bd. dirs. Bank One Corp., Rockwell Inst.; Schlumberger Ltd. Prin. author, editor Commercialization of Synthetic Fuels in the U.S., 1975. Bd. dirs. McGregor Fund, St. John Hosp. Alfred P. Sloan scholar, 1962—66. Mem.: Detroit Club, Country Club Detroit, Detroit Athletic Club, Econ. Club Detroit (bd. dirs.). Roman Catholic.

**MCCOSHAM, JOYCE L.,** secondary school educator; b. Norwood, Ohio, Dec. 25, 1927; d. Stanley James and Mary Emily Chambers; m. William Duncan McCosham, June 12, 1948 (dec.); children: Lynn Colleen Hamberg,

Kyle Maureen Hellman. BS in Edn., U. Cin., 1948, MEd, 1972. Lic. profl. counselor Ohio, 1986. Instr. water safety, cmty. ctr. leader Cin. Recreation Commn., 1948—74; tchr. phys. edn., health, coach North College Hill Schs., 1948—52; tchr. phys. edn., health, coach, athletic dir., counselor, asst. prin. Mother of Mercy High Sch. and Acad., 1952—92; instr., tchr. edn. Edgecliff Coll., 1959—74; counselor Oak Hills High Sch., 1992—99; ret. Elder Mt. Auburn Presbyb. Ch., Cin., 1974—, recreation program, 1965—70. Named Disting. Alumni, U. Cin. Coll. Edn., 1998, in her honor Joyce McCosham Day, Mayor Roxanne Qualls, Cin., 1999; named to Ath. Hall Fame, Mother of Mercy HS, 1987; recipient cert. of Merit, Ohio Counseling Assn., 1999. Mem.: Mother of Mercy Athletic Hall of Fame, Oak Hills Ret. Tchrs. Assn., Mercy Ret. Tchrs. Assn., Ohio Edn. Assn., Nat. Retd. Assn., Hamilton County Ret. Tchrs. Assn., Greater Cin. Counseling Assn. (pres., v.p., sec.-treas. 1972—, Mary Corre Foster award 1994), Nat. Hole-in-One Assn., U. Cin. Golden Bearcat Club, Kappa Delta Pi Nat. Hon. Avocations: boating, water-skiing, golf, bowling, travel.

**MCCOTTER, THADDEUS GEORGE,** congressman; b. Livonia, Mich., Aug. 22, 1965; s. Dennis and Joan McCotter; m. Rita Michel; children: George, Timothy, Emilia. BA in Polit. Sci., summa cum laude, U. Detroit, 1987, JD, 1990. Bar: Mich. 1991. Trustee Schoolcraft C.C., 1989; commr. Wayne County, Mich., 1992-98; mem. 9th dist. Mich. Senate, Lansing, 1998—2002; mem. US Congress from 3rd Mich. dist., 2003—. Mem. com. budget US Congress, com. internat. relations, com. small bus. Rep. precinct del., 1986; chair Wayne County Rep. com. Recipient Outstanding Michigan-der award, Mich. Jaycees, 2001, Legis. of Yr., Police Officers Assn. of Mich., 2002. Republican. Roman Catholic. Office: District Office 17197 N Laurel Pk Dr Ste 533 Livonia MI 48152-7908 also: US Congress 1632 LHOB Washington DC 20515-2211 Office Phone: 202-225-8171, 734-632-0314. Office Fax: 202-225-2667, 734-632-0373.*

**MCCOURT, FRANK (FRANCIS MCCOURT),** writer; b. Bklyn., Aug. 19, 1931; s. Malachy and Angela McCourt; m. Ellen McCourt. Bachelors, Masters, NYU. Tchr. McKee Vocat. and Tech. Sch., Peter Stuyvesant H.S., N.Y.C. Author: Angela's Ashes, 1996 (National Book Critics Circle award 1997, Pulitzer prize 1997), Tis: A memoir, 2000, Through Irish Eyes: Visual Companion to Angela in Court's Ireland, 2001, Brotherhood, 2001, Teacher Man, 2005; (films) The McCourts of Limerick, 1998, The McCourts of NY, 1999. Address: Simon & Schuster Trade Division 1230 Avenue Of The Americas New York NY 10020-1513

**MCCOWEN, ALEC,** actor; b. Tunbridge Wells, May 26, 1925; s. Duncan and Mary (Walkden) McC., Ed. Skinners Sch., Tunbridge Wells, and Royal Acad. Dramatic Art. Appeared as Touchstone, Ford, Richard II, Mercutio, Malvolio, Oberon at Old Vic Theatre, 1959-60; appeared with R.S.C. as Fool in King Lear, 1964, Hadrian VII, 1968, The Philanthropist, 1970, The Misanthrope, 1972, as Dr. Dysart in Equus, 1972, as Henry Higgins in Pygmalion, 1974, as Ben in The Family Dance, 1976, Someone Who'll Watch Over Me, 1992, as Prospero in The Tempest, 1994, as Gaev in The Cherry Orchard, 1995; appeared with Prospect Co. as Antony in Antony and Cleopatra, 1977, in solo performance of St. Mark's Gospel, 1978, 81, as Frank in Tishoo, 1979, as Malvolio in Twelfth Night (TV), 1980, of Kipling, 1984, as Reilly in The Cocktail Party, 1986, as Nicolai in Fathers and Sons, 1987, as Vladimir in Waiting for Godot, 1987; appeared with Nat. Theatre and Abbey Dublin as Jack in Dancing at Cughnasa, 1990; appeared with Nat. Theatre as Crocker-Harris in The Browning Version, Arthur in Harlequinade, Capt. Corcoran in H.M.S. Pinafore, 1981, Adolf Hitler in The Portage to San Cristobal of AH, PTO, 1982, Reginald, in 2000 Quartet; films: Frenzy, 1971, Travels with My Aunt, 1973, Stevie, 1978, Personal Services, Cry Freedom, 1987, The Age of Innocence, 1992, Gangs of New York, 2000; TV: Private Lives, 1976; author: Young Gemini,1979, Double Bill, 1980, Personal Mark, 1984. Named Best Actor, Evening Standard (now New Standard), 1968, 73, 82, Variety Club Stage Actor, 1970. Office: care Conway Van Gelder 18-21 Jermyn St London SW1 Y6HB England

**MCCOWN, HALE,** retired judge; b. Kansas, Ill., Jan. 19, 1914; s. Ross S. and Pauline (Collins) McC.; m. Helen Lanier, July 15, 1938; children: Robert B., William L., Mary Lynn. AB, Hastings Coll., 1935; LLB, Duke U., 1937. Bar: Oreg. 1937, Nebr. 1942. With firm Carey, Hart, Spence & McCulloch, Portland, 1937-42; pvt. practice Beatrice, Nebr., 1942-65; ptnr. McCown, Baumfalk & Dalke; justice Supreme Court Nebr., 1965-83. Author articles in legal jours. Served to lt. USNR, 1943-45. Recipient Disting. Alumnus award Hastings Coll., 1981, Charles S. Murphy award Duke U., 1986, Legal Pioneer award Nebr. Bar Found., 1996, Alumni Appreciation award Duke U. 1981. Fellow Am. Coll. Trial Lawyers, Am. Coll. Trust and Estate Counsel; mem. ABA (legal ethics com. 1957-62), Nebr. Bar Assn. (chmn. ho. dels. 1955-56, pres. 1960-61), Am. Law Inst. (mem. council 1969—2000, emeritus 2000—), Am. Judicature Soc. Presbyterian.

**MCCOY, ANN,** artist; b. Boulder, Colo., July 8, 1946; d. Abram Armstrong McC. and Ruthanna (Eames) Evans. B.F.A., U. Colo., 1969; MA, UCLA, 1972. Instr. dept. art history Barnard Coll., N.Y.C., 1980—. One-woman shows include Fourcade, Droll Inc., N.Y.C., 1974, Inst. Contemporary Art, Boston, 1977, Mus. Loabnig, Cologne, Germany, 1977, Portland (Oreg.) Ctr. for the Visual Arts, 1979, The Arts Club, Chgo., 1979, Margo Leavin Gallery, L.A., 1979, Brooke Alexander, Inc., 1979, 81, 82, 84, 85, Met. Mus. Art, N.Y.C., 1982, Galerie Kornfeld, Bern, Switzerland, 1983, Greenville (S.C.) County Mus. Art, 1984, Eugene Binder Gallery, Dallas, 1986, A.C.A., N.Y.C., 1988, Arnold Herstand Gallery, N.Y.C., 1990, The Contemporary Mus., Honolulu, 1991, Ctrl. Fine Arts, N.Y.C., 1998; exhibited in group shows at Oberlin Coll., 1973, Whitney Mus. Am. Art, 1973, 79, The N.Y. Cultural Ctr., 1974, Indpls. Mus. Art, 1974, The Contemporary Art Ctr., Cin., 1974, Corcoran Gallery of Art, 1976, Crysler Mus., 1982, L.A. County Mus., 1983, P.S. 1, N.Y.C. 1986, San Francisco Mus. Art, 1986, Venice (Italy) Biennale, 1986, Nat. Mus. Am. Art, Washington, 1989, La Jolla (Calif.) Mus. Contemporary Art, 1989, High Mus. Art, Atlanta, 1989, M. Gutierrez Fine Arts, Miami, Fla., 1993, Mus. Contemporary Religious Art, St. Louis, 1993, New Orleans Mus. Art, 1995, Nuberger Mus. Art, Purchase, 1995, The Equitable Gallery, N.Y.C., 1996, A.C.A. Gallery, N.Y.C., 1997, Z Gallery, N.Y.C., 1997; represented in permanent collections at Hirshorn Mus., Met. Mus., Dallas Art Mus., Honolulu Acad. Arts, Indpls. Mus. Art, L.A. County Mus. Art, Mus. Modern Art, Whitney Mus., Newberger Mus., Des Moines Art Ctr., Nat. Gallery Australia, Powis Gallery, Lannan Found., San Francisco Mus. Modern Art, New Orleans Mus. Recipient Contemporary Art Council Mew Talent award Los Angeles County Mus. Art, 1972, EA award, 1978, award in visual arts Prix de Rome, NEA, E.D. Found., 1989, Alice Baber award, 1990, Pollock Krasner award, 1993, 98; grantee Adolph and Esther Gottlieb Found., 1996. Address: PO Box 1907 Long Island City NY 11101 Office Phone: 646-249-5937. Business E-Mail: annartistmccoy@earthlink.net.

**MCCOY, DEBRA MARLENE BLACK,** sales executive; b. Pitts., Nov. 6, 1953; d. Donald T. and Doris A. (Porter) B.; m. Edward B. McCoy, Aug. 8, 1998. BA, Ky. Wesleyan Coll., 1975; MA, Western Ky. U., 1983. Cert. elem. tchr., kindergarten endorsement, Ky. Tchr. kindergarten Owensboro (Ky.) Ind. Schs., 1975-79, Owensboro-Daviess County Child Care, 1987-88; elem. tchr. Ohio County Bd. Edn., Hartford, Ky., 1979-80; substitute tchr. Owensboro Ind. Schs., 1980-86; tchr. kindergarten Daviess County Bd. Edn., Owensboro, 1988-91; preschool tchr. Mary Mitchell Preschool, Owensboro, 1992—96; sales assoc. Bacons Dept. Stores, 1991—98; area sales mgr. Famous Barr divsn. May Co., Owensboro, Ky., 1998—. Named Area Sales Mgr. of Yr., 2003, 2006. Mem. Beta Sigma Phi (chpt. pres. 1988-91, Woman of Yr. award 1990). Republican. Presbyterian. Avocations: reading, cross stitch, sewing. E-mail: demccoy@bellsouth.net.

**MCCOY, DOROTHY ELOISE,** writer, educator; b. Houston, Sept. 4, 1916; d. Robert Major and Evie Letha (Grimes) Morgan; m. Roy McCoy, May 22, 1942; children: Roy Jr., Robert Nicholas (dec.). BA, Rice U., 1938; MA, Tex. A&I U., 1968; postgrad., Ind. U., 1971, U. Calif., Berkeley, 1972, U. Calif., Santa Cruz, 1977. Cert. secondary tchr. BA Corpus Christi (Tex.) Independent Schs., 1958-84, MA, 1985; freelance writer Corpus Christi, 1987—; co-owner United Iron and Machine Works, Corpus Christi, 1946-82. Freelance lectr.; master tchr. Nat. Coun. Tchrs. English, 1971, Nat. Humanities Faculty, Concord Mass., 1977-78; mem. steering com. Edn. Summit, Corpus Christi, 1990-91, mem. summit update, 1991. Author: A Teacher Talks Back, 1990, Let's Restructure the Schools, 1992; contbr. articles and columns to profl. jours. Sr. advisor to U.S. Congress, Washington, 1982-85; trustee Corpus Christi Librs., 1987-90; mem. Corpus Christi Mus.; mem. Friends Corpus Christi Librs., chmn. publicity com., 1988; participant Walk to Emmaus Group, 1990, UPDATE, U. Tex., 1978-92; com. Libr. Bd. Democracy competition Am. 2000; sec. adminstrv. bd. First United Meth. Ch., 1992-93. Recipient Teacher of Yr. Paul Caplan Humanitarian award, 1981, Advanced Senior Option Program award, 1968. Mem. AAUW, LWV, Phi Beta Kappa. Avocations: gardening, writing. Office Phone: 361-852-0726.

**MCCOY, DUSTAN ELWOOD,** manufacturing executive, lawyer; b. Ashland, Ky., July 16, 1949; s. Elwood and Mary Anna (Mullins) McC.; m. Rebecca Lancashire, Feb. 28, 1970; children: Dustan Chad, Drew Christopher. BA, Eastern Ky., 1971; JD, No. Ky. U., 1978. Bar: Ky. 1978. Atty. Ashland Oil Inc., Ky., 1973-83, sr. atty. Ky., 1983-85, gen. atty. Ky., 1985, assoc. gen. counsel Ky.; sr. v.p., gen. counsel, corp. sec., exec. v.p. Witco Corp.; v.p., gen. counsel Brunswick Corp., 1999—2000, pres. Brunswick boat group, 2000—05, chmn., CEO, 2005—. Bd. dirs. La.-Pacific Corp. Local bd. mem. U.S. SSS, 1987; mem. law bd. visitors No. Ky. U. Mem. ABA, Ky. Bar Assn. Avocations: jogging, hunting, fishing. Office: Brunswick Corp 1 N Field Ct Lake Forest IL 60045-4811 Office Phone: 847-735-4700. Office Fax: 847-735-4765.*

**MCCOY, FREDERICK JOHN,** retired plastic surgeon; b. McPherson, Kans., Jan. 17, 1916; s. Merle D. and Mae (Tennis) McC.; m. Mary Bock, May 17, 1972; children: Judith, Frederick John, Patricia, Melissa, Steven. BS, U. Kans., 1938, MD, 1942. Diplomate Am. Bd. Plastic Surgery (dir. 1973-79, chmn. 1979). Intern Lucas County Hosp., Toledo, 1942-43; resident in plastic surgery U. Tex. Med. Sch., Galveston, 1946; preceptorship in surgery Grand Rapids, Mich., 1947-50; practice medicine specializing in plastic and reconstructive surgery Kansas City, Mo., 1950-83; staff St. Mary's Hosp., 1950-83, St. Joseph's Hosp., 1950—, N. Kansas City Meml. Hosp., 1955—; mem. staff, chief plastic surgery Kansas City Gen. Hosp. and Med. Center, 1952-72, Children's Mercy Hosp., 1954-93, Research Hosp., 1950—, St. Luke's Hosp., 1951—, Baptist Hosp., 1958—, Menorah Hosp., 1950—; chief div. plastic surgery Truman Med. Ctr., 1972-91; chmn. maxillo-facial surgery U. Kansas City Sch. Dentistry, 1950-57; assoc. prof. surgery U. Mo. Med. Sch., Kansas City, 1964-69, clin. prof. surgery, 1969—; pres. McCoy Enterprises, Kansas City, Mo. Author: articles to profl. jours.; editor: Year Book of Plastic and Reconstructive Surgery, 1971-88. Bd. govs. Kansas City Mus., 1959-93, pres., 1973-74. Served to maj. M.C. U.S. Army, 1943-46. Mem. ACS (pres. Mo. chpt. 1973), AMA, Am. Acad. Pediatrics, Am. Soc. Plastic and Reconstructive Surgeons (sec. 1969-73, dir. 1973-76, pres. 1976, chmn. bd. 1977, Spl. Achievement award 1988), Am. Soc. Pediat. Plastic Surgeons, Pan Pacific Surg. Soc., Singleton Surg. Soc. (v.p. 1965), Am. Assn. Plastic Surgeons (founder plastic surgery rsch. coun.), Internat. Soc. Aesthetic Plastic Surgery, Am. Soc. Aesthetic Plastic Surgery, Jackson County Med. Soc. (pres. 1964-65), Kansas City Southwest Clin. Soc. (pres. 1971), Mo. Med. Assn. (v.p. 1975), Internat. Coll. Surgeons (v.p. 1969), Royal Soc. Medicine (London), U. Tex. Sys. Chancellors Coun., Kansas City C. of C., Conservation Fedn. Mo., Natural Sci. Soc. (founder, chmn. 1973), Citizens Assn. Kansas City, Explorer's Club, Mission Hills Country Club, Boone and Crocket Club, Phi Delta Theta, Nu Sigma Nu. Republican. Mem. Christian Ch.

**MCCOY, JEANIE SHEARER,** analytical chemist, consultant; b. Mancelona, Mich., May 27, 1921; d. Theophil R. and Goldie Margaret (Halladay) Schroeder; m. Theodore R. Shearer, June 14, 1958 (div. 1964); 1 child, Blair Barnett; m. George Altha McCoy, July 23, 1966. AA, North Park Coll., 1941; BS, Northwestern U., 1944; MS, No. Ill. U., 1970. Jr. analytical chemist Buick Motor divsn. GM, Melrose Park, Ill., 1944—45; asst. rsch. chemist Hodson Oil Corp., Chgo., 1945—47; asst. analytical chemist Internat. Harvester Co., Melrose Park, 1947—49, analytical chemist, 1949—60, prin. chemist, 1961—74, supr. metal process control, 1974—82; cons. cutting fluid mgmt. divsn. JMT, Inc., Lombard, Ill., 1983—2003; cons. Jeanie McCoy Cutting Fluid Mgmt. Co., Lombard, 2004—. Editor: Lubrication Engring. Mag., 1979—2000; contbr. chpt. to book. Fellow: Soc. Tribologists and Lubrication Engrs. (Allan Mantafel award Chgo sect. 1987, P. M. KU award 1991, Internat. award 2000); mem.: AAUW, Soc. Mfg. Engrs., Abrasive Engring. Soc., Am. Chem. Soc., Soc. Automotive Engrs. Avocations: seashell collecting, stamp collecting/philately, fitness activities. Home and Office: 654 N West Rd Lombard IL 60148-1547 Office Phone: 630-627-2721. Personal E-mail: j10mccoy@aol.com.

**MCCOY, JEANNE M.,** principal; b. Hastings, Minn. d. Robert J. and Rosella M. McCoy. BA in Math Edn., Mt. Mary Coll., Milw., 1977; MA in Pvt. Sch. Adminstrn., U. San Francisco, 1985; MA in Pastoral Studies, U. St. Thomas, St. Paul, 2002. Cert. tchr., adminstr. Wis., 1977. Tchr. St. Mary Sch., New England, ND, 1977—78, Xavier H.S., Appleton, Wis., 1978—87; elem. prin. Sacred Heart Sch., Appleton, Wis., 1987—89; mid. sch. prin. Seton Cath. Mid. Sch., Menasha, Wis., 1989—91; elem. sch. princpal St. Francis Sch., Ellsworth, Wis., 1991—. Office: St Francis Sch PO Box 250 244 W Woodworth St Ellsworth WI 54011-0250 Office Phone: 715-273-4391.

**MCCOY, JENNIFER,** artistic collaborator, educator; b. Sacramento, Calif., 1968; Attended Critical Studies Film Program with CIEE, U. Paris III, Paris, France, 1990; BA in Theater Arts, Cornell U., Ithaca, 1990; MFA in Electronic Arts, Rensselaer Polytechnic Inst., Troy, NY, 1994. Asst. prof. computer graphics Brooklyn Coll. Artistic collaborator with Kevin McCoy (making a wide range of video, installation, new media and performance works dealing with the cultural manifestations of technology in the world); (solo exhibitions) We Like to Watch, Postmasters Gallery, NYC, 2002, Love and Terror, Butler Art Inst., Youngstown, Ohio, 2002, We Like to Watch, Van Laere Contemporary Art Gallery, Antwerp, Belgium, 2002, Stardust, San Jose State U. Art Gallery, Calif., 2003, Soft Rains, FACT (catalog), Liverpool, UK, 2003, Galerie Guy Bartschi, Geneva, Switzerland, 2003, Soft Rains, Postmasters Gallery, NY, 2004, Learning to Watch, Sala Rekalde, Bilbao (catalog), 2004, (video screening) Cluster Images, Werkleitz Geselschaft, Tornitz, Germany, 1996, Video Room Video Festival, Brooklyn, NY, 1998, (web project-solo exhibition) Maintenance/Web, The Thing, NYC, 1997, (web project) Airworld, Walker Art Ctr., Mpls., MN, 1999, (interactive video installation) Tomorrow's Homes Today, Mus. of Sci. and Industry, Manchester, Eng., 1998, (interactive installation) Viper Internat. Media Festival, Lucerne, Switzerland, 1999, Toys and Noise, OK Ctr. for Contemporary Art, Linz, Austria, 1999, (electronic sculpture) Subject to Sound, The Rotunda Gallery, Brooklyn, NY, 2000, (performance) Verbal 3, The Kitchen, NYC, 2000, (screening) Video Viewpoints, Mus. of Modern Art, 2001, Robert Flaherty Film Seminar, Durham, NC, 1999, (group shows) New Acquisitions, Dept. of Photographs, Mus. of Modern Art, 2002, American Dream, Ronald Feldman Gallery, NY, 2002, Tag Team, White Box, 2003, Game Show, James Cohan Gallery, 2004, Open House: Working in Brooklyn, Brooklyn Mus., 2004, Our Grotesque, curated by Rob Storr, 5th Internat. Biennial, SITE Santa Fe, NMex., 2004, and several others. Co-recipient Rave award in Art, WIRED Mag., 2005. Address: c/o Postmaster Gallery 459 W 19th St at 10th Ave New York NY 10001

**MCCOY, JOHN DENNY,** artist; b. Columbus, Ohio, Dec. 13, 1945; s. Robert William and Dorothy Louise (Denny) McC.; children: Melinda Rene and Nathan Robert. Cert. of Grad., Columbus Coll. Art and Design, 1967; MFA, Washington U., St. Louis, 1969. Instr. Columbus Coll. Art and Design, Ohio, 1969—73; program dir. Presidio of Monterey, Calif., 1975—78; gallery dir. Richard Danskin Gallery, Carmel, Calif., 1978—79, Bleich Gallery West, Carmel, Calif., 1979—80. One-man shows include Brunswick Gallery, Columbus, 1973, Seaside, Calif. City Hall, 1978, Bleich Gallery, Carmel, Calif., 1980, Angles Gallery, Santa Monica, Calif., 1987, Hagger Gallery, Dallas, 1999, Flatbed Gallery, Austin, Tex., 2000, O2 Gallery, Austin, Tex.,

2004, d. berman Gallery, Austin, Tex., 2005; exhibited in group shows at Columbus Mus. Art, 1965, Laclede Town Gallery, St. Louis, 1967, Merton Boyd Gallery, Columbus, 1970, Changing Scene Gallery, 1971-72, Gallery Five, Columbus, 1972, Monterey Peninsula Mus. Art, 1976-77, Angles Gallery, Santa Monica, 1989, Richard Bennett Gallery, L.A., 1991, Arlington Mus. Art, 1998, Meridian Internat. Ctr., Washington, Vietnam, China, Singapore, Indonesia, 1999-2000, Haggerty Gallery, Dallas, 2000, d. berman Gallery, Austin, Tex., 2002, 04. Columbus Coll. Art and Design scholar, 1963; Ford Found. grantee, 1966; Washington U. fellow, 1968-69. Home: PO Box 989 Wimberley TX 78676-0989

**MCCOY, JOHN JOSEPH,** lawyer; b. Cin., Mar. 15, 1952; s. Raymond F. and Margaret T. (Hohmann) McC. BS in Math. summa cum laude, Xavier U., 1974; JD, U. Chgo., 1977. Bar: Ohio 1977, D.C. 1980. Ptnr. Taft, Stettinius & Hollister, Cin., 1977—, exec. com., 2002—. Lectr. Greater Cin. C. of C., 1984. Pro bono rep. Jr. Achievement Greater Cin., 1978; fund raiser Dan Beard coun. Boy Scouts Am., 1983; fund raising team leader Cin. Regatta, Cin. Ctr. Devel. Disorders, 1983; account mgr. United Appeal, Cin., 1984; mem. green areas trust adv. com. Village of Indian Hill, 1994-98. Named to Ohio Super Lawyers, 2006, Best Lawyers in Am. Mem. ABA, Ohio State Bar Assn. (banking, comml. and bankruptcy law com., corp. law com., fed. ct. practice com.), Cin. Bar Assn. (fed. cts., common pleas cts. and negligence law coms., trustee Vol. Lawyers for the Poor Found. 1994—, chmn. 1996-97), Cin. Inn. of Ct. (barrister 1984-86), Cin. Athletic Club (pres. bd. trustees 1986-89, nominating com. 1989—), Rhodesian Ridgeback Club of the U.S. (bd. dirs. 2000—).

**MCCOY, JOHN V.,** lawyer; b. Waukesha, Wis., June 7, 1958; BS, U. Wis., Oshkosh, 1980; JD, Drake U., 1984. Bar: Wis. 1988, Iowa 1984, US Dist. Ct. (Ea. & We. Dist.), Wis. Ptnr. McCoy & Hofbauer, Waukesha, Wis. Pres. Propane Gas Defense Assn., 1994—95; chair & founding mem. Self-Insurance Inst. of Am., Wis. div., 1998; mem. Civil Trial Counsel of Wis., Defense Rsch. Inst., Federation of Defense and Corp. Counsel. Pres. & founding mem. Wis. Clean Cities-Southeast Area, Inc., 1994—; bd. dirs. Ctr. for Deaf and Hard of Hearing, 1990—96, 1999—. Mem.: Waukesha County Bar Assn., Milwaukee County Bar Assn., Wis. Bar Assn. Office: McCoy & Hofbauer Riverwood Corp Ctr N19 W24200 Riverwood Dr Ste 125 Waukesha WI 53188 Office Phone: 262-522-7000. Office Fax: 252-522-7020. Business E-Mail: jmccoy@mh-law.us.

**MCCOY, KEVIN,** artistic collaborator, educator; b. Seattle, 1967; BA in Philosophy, Whitman Coll., Walla Walla, WA, 1989; attended, U. Paris III, Dept. Cinema and Audio-Visual Studies, Paris, France, 1990; MFA in Electronic Arts, Rensselaer Polytechnic Inst., Troy, NY, 1994. Asst. prof. multimedia, art dept. City Coll. NY. Artistic collaborator with Jennifer McCoy (making a wide range of video, installation, new media and performance works dealing with the cultural manifestations of technology in the world), (solo exhibitions) We Like to Watch, Postmasters Gallery, NYC, 2002, Love and Terror, Butler Art Inst., Youngstown, Ohio, 2002, We Like to Watch, Van Laere Contemporary Art Gallery, Antwerp, Belgium, 2002, Stardust, San Jose State U. Art Gallery, Calif., 2003, Soft Rains (FACT catalog), Liverpool, UK, 2003, Galerie Guy Bartschi, Geneva, Switzerland, 2003, Soft Rains, Postmasters Gallery, NY, 2004, Learning to Watch, Sala Redkalde, Bilbao (catalog), 2004, (video screening) Cluster Images, Werkleitz Geselschaft, Tornitz, Germany, 1996, Video Room Video Festival, Brooklyn, NY, 1998, (web project-solo exhibition) Maintenance/Web, The Thing, NYC, 1997, (web project) Airworld, Walker Art Ctr., Mpls., MN, 1999, (interactive video installation) Tomorrow's Homes Today, Mus. of Sci. and Industry, Manchester, Eng., 1998, (interactive installation) Viper Internat. Media Festival, Lucerne, Switzerland, 1999, Toys and Noise, OK Ctr. for Contemporary Art, Linz, Austria, 1999, (electronic sculpture) Subject to Sound, The Rotunda Gallery, Brooklyn, NY, 2000, (performance) Verbal 3, The Kitchen, NYC, 2000, (screening) Video Viewpoints, Mus. of Modern Art, 2001, Robert Flaherty Film Seminar, Durham, NC, 1999, (group shows) New Acquisitions, Dept. of Photographs, Mus. of Modern Art, 2002, American Dream, Ronald Feldman Gallery, NY, 2002, Tag Team, White Box, 2003, Game Show, James Cohan Gallery, 2004, Open House: Working in Brooklyn, Brooklyn Mus., 2004, Our Grotesque, curated by Rob Storr, 5th Internat. Biennial, SITE Santa Fe, NMex., 2004, and several others. Co-recipient Rave award in Art, WIRED Mag., 2005. Address: c/o Postmaster Gallery 459 W 19th St at 10th Ave New York NY 10001

**MCCOY, LOIS CLARK,** retired social services administrator, retired county official, editor; b. New Haven, Oct. 1, 1920; m. Herbert Irving McCoy, Oct. 17, 1943; children: Whitney, Kevin, Marianne, Tori, Debra, Sally, Daniel. BS, Skidmore Coll., 1942; student, Nat. Search and Rescue Sch., 1974. Asst. buyer R.H. Macy & Co., N.Y.C., 1942-44; assoc. buyer, 1944-48; instr. Mountain Medicine & Survival, U. Calif., San Diego, 1973-74; cons. editor Search & Rescue Mag., 1975, Rescue Mag., 1988-97, editor, 1992-94, Press On Newsletter, 1992—2000. Coord. San Diego Mountain Rescue Team, La Jolla, Calif., 1973-75; exec. sec. Nat. Assn. for Search and Rescue, Inc., Nashville, La Jolla, 1975-80, comptr., 1980-82; disaster officer San Diego County, 1980-86, Santa Barbara County, 1985-91, ret.; pres. Nat. Inst. Urban Search & Rescue, Inc., 1987—; assoc. dir. Armed Forces Commns. and Electronics Assn., 2003—; mem. project info. techs. to enhance disaster mgmt., NAS, 2005, group using info. tech. to enhance crisis preparedness and response, Nat. Rsch. Coun., 2005; lectr. in field. Author: Search and Rescue Glossary, 1974, The Last Desperado, 2005, Kiss, Shoot, Aim, 2006; contbr. editor Rescue Mag., 1989-97; editor-in-chief Response! mag., 1982-86; editor Press On! Electronic mag., 1994—; mem. adv. bd. Hazard Monthly, 1991-99; contbr. articles to profl. jours. Cons. law enforcement divsn. Calif. Office Emergency Svcs., 1976-77; pres. San Diego Com. for L.A. Philharm. Orch., 1957-58; bd. dirs. Search and Rescue of the Californias, 1976-77, Nat. Assn. for Search and Rescue, Inc., 1980-87, pres., 1985-87, trustee, 1987-90, mem. Calif. OES strategic com., 1992-96; CEO Nat. Inst. for Urban Search, 1989—; mem. Gov.'s Task Force on Earthquakes, 1981-82, Earthquake Preparedness Task Force, Seismic Safety Commn., 1982-85, Army Sci. and Tech. Commn., 2003; mem. adv. coun. Nat. Meml. Inst. for the Protection from Terrorism; named to NSF Project "Info. Tech. to Enhance Disaster Mgmt.", 2005. Recipient Hall Foss Outstanding Svc. to Search and Rescue award, 1982, Diamond Safety award, 1996, Superior Performance award AFCEA, 2004, Rep. Senatorial Freedom medal, 2004, Congl. Order merit Rep. Congl. Del., 2005; named to The Fed. 100, 2002. Mem.: IEEE, Armed Forces Comm. and Electronics Assn. (named to Army Sci. and Tech. com. for Homeland Def. 2003—04, bd. dirs. 2003—), San Diego Mountain Rescue (life), Nat. Assn. Search and Rescue (life Svc. award 1985, 2002), Santa Barbara Amateur Radio Club. Episcopalian. Office: PO Box 91648 Santa Barbara CA 93190-1648 Office Phone: 800-767-0093. Personal E-mail: niusr@cox.net.

**MCCOY, MARY JANE,** retired principal; d. Albert Louis Haley and Della Muriel (Haley-Skinner) Smith; m. Edgar Allen McCoy, Aug. 31, 1957; children: Kim Michelle, Shelley Anne. AA, San Bernardino Valley Jr. Coll., Calif., 1965; BA, Calif. State U., San Bernardino, 1967; MS, Pepperdine U., 1976. Tchg. credential Calif., Wash. adminstrv. credential Calif., Wash. Tchr. San Bernardino Unified, 1968—76, resource reading specialist, 1972—76, elem. vice prin., 1976—78, elem. prin., 1978—92; tchr. Dist. 81, Spokane, Wash., 1992—95. Mem.: NAACP (life), Spokane Women's Coalition, The Links, Inc. (1st v.p. Spokane chpt. 2004—, pres. Spokane chpt. 2000—04, v.p.), Soroptimists, Delta Sigma Theta (sec. 2002—), Phi Delta Kappa (regional dir. far west 1994—95, pres. 1995—, pres. perpetual scholarship found. 1995—). Avocations: reading, crafts, sewing, cross stitch.

**MCCOY, MICHAEL D.,** lawyer; b. Joliet, Ill., Apr. 8, 1950; BSEE with honors, U. Ill., 1972; JD with honors, Chgo.-Kent Coll. Law, 1975. Bar: Ill. 1975, N.C. 1983, U.S. Patent and Trademark Office. Ptnr. and coord. intellectual property law practice Alston & Bird LLP, Charlotte, NC. Mem. panel patent dispute arbitrators Am. Arbitration Assn., Internat. Anticounterfeiting Coalition, 1984—. Contbr. articles to profl. jours. Named one of Best

Lawyers in Am., 2005. Mem.: ABA, Licensing Exec. Soc. Office: Alston & Bird LLP Bank of Am Plz Ste 4000 101 S Tryon St Charlotte NC 28280-4000 Office Phone: 704-444-1011. Office Fax: 704-444-1111. Business E-Mail: mmccoy@alston.com.

**MCCOY, STUART SHERMAN,** manufacturing executive; b. Little Rock, Dec. 16, 1958; s. Gene Guy and Idella Maria Theresa (Brown) McC.; m. Juliet Kathryn Goens, Sept. 9, 1977 (div. Apr. 1986); children: Ashley Nicole, Christopher Sean. Student, U. Ark., Little Rock, 1976, 78. Various positions Ad Craft Ark., Inc., Little Rock, 1976-80, prodn. supr., 1980-82, v.p. prodn., 1982-86, v.p. ops., 1986-93, exec. v.p., 1993—. Bd. dirs. Subiaco Acad. Alumni Assn. Photojournalist. Team mgr. Red Elk Motorsports, 1990-93, pres., 1991—; v.p. Ark. Dirt Riders, 1991-92, pres., 1992-93. Mem. Am. Advt. Fedn. (10th dist Addy award com. 1989-96, 10th dist. student competition com. 1994—, Nat. Addy com., 1994-96, constrn. and bylaws com. 1991—), Screen Print Assn. Internat., Ark. Advt. Fedn. (bd. dirs. 1992—), Jaycees (state dist. bd. dirs. Ark. 1983, state bd. dirs. pub. rels. com. 1984-85), Masons., Sabiaco Acad. Alumni Assn. (bd. dirs. 1991-95). Republican. Episcopalian. Avocations: sports, computers, photography, writing short stories, camping, hunting, motorcycle riding. Home: 11940 Southridge Dr Little Rock AR 72212-1740 Office: Ad Craft Ark Inc 1122 W 3rd St Little Rock AR 72201-2008

**MCCOY, THOMAS,** information technology executive; BA, Stanford U.; JD, U. So. Calif. Assoc., ptnr. O'Melveny and Meyers, 1977—95; gen. counsel Advanced Micro Devices, Sunnyvale, Calif., 1993—95, sec., 1995—2003, sr. v.p., gen. counsel, 1998—2003, exec. v.p., gen. adminstrv. officer, 2003—. Office: Advanced Micro Devices One AMD Pl PO Box 3453 Sunnyvale CA 94088-3453

**MC COY, TIDAL WINDHAM,** former government official; b. Gainesville, Fla., Apr. 25, 1945; Grad., U.S. Mil. Acad., 1967; MA in Bus. Fin, George Washington U., 1975. Officer U.S. Army, 1967-72; mem. long-range planning and net assessment group Office of Sec. Def., Washington, 1972-73; mem. staff Nat. Security Council, 1973; staff asst. and then dep. asst. to Sec. Def., 1973-77; sci. asst. to asst. sec. for research, engring. and systems Dept. Navy, 1977-78; dir. policy research, office of under sec. for policy Dept. Def., 1978-79; asst. for nat. security affairs to Sen. Jake Garn, 1979-81; asst. sec. for manpower, res. affairs and installations Dept. Air Force, Washington, 1981-87; asst. sec. for readiness support USAF, Washington, 1987-88, acting sec. and undersec., 1981-88; sr. assoc. Hecht, Spencer & Assocs., 1988-89; v.p. govt. rels. Thiokol Corp., 1989—2002; chmn., CEO Washington Capital Ptnrs., 1998—. Chmn. Washington Capital Ptnrs., 1998—. Recipient DOD Outstanding Civil Svc. medal, USAF Exceptional Civilian Svc. medal. Mem. Space Transp. Assn. U.S.A. (dir., chmn. 1996—), Def. Forum Found. (vice-chmn.).

**MCCOY, WESLEY LAWRENCE,** musician, educator, conductor; b. Memphis, Jan. 27, 1935; s. Harlan Eftin and Gladys (Coggin) McCoy; m. Carolyn June Noble, Aug. 26, 1960; children: Jill Laurene McCoy Kurtz, Scott Edward. B of Music Edn., La. State U., 1957, PhD, 1970; M of Music Edn., U. Louisville, 1958; M of Sacred Music, So. Bapt. Theol. Sem., 1960. Min. of music Beechmont Bapt. Ch., Louisville, 1959-62; also instr. music So. Bapt. Theol. Sem., Louisville; asst. prof. music dir. bands Carson Newman Coll., Jefferson City, Tenn., 1962-67; asst. prof. music U. S.C., Columbia, 1969-72; assoc. prof. music U. Ark., Little Rock, 1972-77, prof., 1977-80, asst. dean for pub. svc. Coll. Fine Arts, 1978-79; condr. Wind Ensemble, River City Cmty. Band, 1972-80. Oklahoma City Youth Symphony, 1985-89; chmn. dept. music Phillips U., Enid, Okla., 1980-82, chmn. fine arts divsn., 1982-84; music tchr. Bishop Sullivan H.S., 2003—04; supr. Baton Rouge Recreation Dept., 2004—. Min. music 1st United Meth. Ch., Edmond, Okla., 1983-2000; owner WJ Travel, Oklahoma City, 1985-2002. French horn player, Knoxville (Tenn.) Symphony Orch., 1962-67, Columbia Philharm. Orch., 1969-72, Ark. Symphony Orch., 1972-80, Enid-Phillips Symphony, 1980-84; contbr. to Ch. Musician, 1974-76, 85-86. Co-chmn. Jefferson County (Tenn.) Com. for Goldwater for Pres., 1962; mem. Pulaski County (Ark.) Rep. Com., 1977-81; mem. Oklahoma County Rep. exec. Com., 1995-97; pres. Ctrl. Okla. La. State U. Alumni, 1997-98; choir dir. First United Meth. Ch., Hammond, La., 2004—. Mem. S.C. Music Educators Assn. (pres. coll. divsn. 1971-73), Ark. Music Edn. Assn. (chmn. rsch. 1975-80), Phi Mu Alpha, Pi Kappa Lambda, Phi Delta Kappa, Alpha Tau Omega. Republican. Baptist. Home and Office: 8548 Kaylynn Ave Baton Rouge LA 70810 Personal E-mail: wesleymccoy@yahoo.com

**MCCRABB, DONALD RAYMOND,** pastoral field educator; m. Barbara Humphrey; children: Andrew Thomas, Jacob Creighton, Martin Joseph. BA in Religion, BA in Polit. Sci., Wright State U., 1975; MA in Theology, U. Dayton, 1978; DMin, United Theol. Sem., 1998. Cert. catechetical leader, Roman Cath. Ch. Campus min. Newman Ctr., Wright State U., Dayton, Ohio, 1975-76; pastoral assoc. U. Dayton, 1976-78; pastoral assoc. St. Raphael Cath. Ch., Springfield, Ohio, 1978-82; Cath. campus min. Cen. State U., Wilberforce U., 1982-85; exec. dir. Cath. Campus Ministry Assn., 1985-98; dir. devel. Sojourners, Washington, 1998-99; dir. pastoral field edn. Dominican House of Studies, Washington, 1999—; dir. adminstrn. Mem. planning com. Cath. Edn. Futures Project, 1985-88; bd. dirs., site visitor Commn. on Cert. and Accreditation, U.S. Cath. Conf., 1986-92. Office: Dominican House of Studies 487 Michigan Ave NE Washington DC 20017-1585 Office Phone: 202-529-5300. Business E-Mail: dmccrabb@dhs.edu.

**MCCRACKEN, EDWARD R.,** electronics executive; b. Fairfield, Iowa, 1943; children: Kathi, David. BSEE, Iowa State U., 1966; MBA, Stanford U., 1968. With Hewlett Packard Co.; pres., CEO Silicon Graphics, Inc., 1984—98, chmn., CEO, 1994—98. Bd. dirs. Digital Rsch., Inc.; chmn. bd. The PRASAD Project, 1992—; dir. Nat. Semiconductor Corp., Tularik, Inc., Acumen Internat. Recipient Disting. Info. Scis. award, Data Processing Mgmt. Assn., 1994, Nat. Tech. medal, 1995, Exec. of Yr., R&D Mag., 1995, Disting. Achievement award, Iowa State Alumni Assn., 1995.

**MCCRACKEN, HARRY,** journalist; b. Boston; s. Samuel and Natalie (Jacobson) McC. BA in History, Boston U., 1986. Editor Animato Mag., Cambridge, Mass., 1987-91; sr. editor CorpTech, Woburn, Mass., 1987-91; reviews editor Computer Buying World Mag., Wakefield, Mass., 1991-92; features editor Infoworld Direct mag., Boston, 1992-94; sr. assoc. editor PC World mag. and pcworld.com, 1994—2000, exec. features editor, 2000—02, editor, 2002—04, editor-in-chief, 2004—; Contbg. editor: Multimedia World Mag., San Francisco, 1994-96; mem. editl. bd. Am. Bus. Media; contbr. articles to profl. jours. Office: PC World Communications 501 Second Street San Francisco CA 94107

**MC CRACKEN, PAUL WINSTON,** retired economist, business educator; b. Richland, Iowa, Dec. 29, 1915; s. Sumner and Mary (Coffin) McC.; m. Emily Ruth Siler, May 27, 1942; children— Linda Jo, Paula Jeanne. Student, William Penn Coll., 1937; MA, Harvard U., 1942, PhD, 1948. Faculty Found. Sch., Berea Coll., Ky., 1937-40; economist Dept. Commerce, Washington, 1942-43; fin. economist, dir. research Fed. Res. Bank of Mpls., 1943-48; assoc. prof. Sch. Bus. Adminstrn., U. Mich., 1948-50, prof., 1950-66, Edmund Ezra Day Univ. prof. bus. adminstrn., 1966-86, prof. emeritus, 1986—, ret. Dir. emeritus Nat. Bur. Econ. Rsch. Author: monographs Can Capitalism Survive?; articles on financial, econ. subjects. Fellow Am. Statis. Assn.; mem. Am. Econ. Assn., Royal Econ. Soc., Harvard Grad. Soc. (coun.). Clubs: Cosmos (Washington); Harvard (N.Y.C.). Presbyterian. Home: 2564 Hawthorne Rd Ann Arbor MI 48104-4032

**MC CRACKEN, PHILIP TRAFTON,** sculptor; b. Bellingham, Wash., Nov. 14, 1928; s. William Franklin and Maude (Trafton) McC.; m. Anne MacFetridge, Aug. 14, 1954; children— Timothy, Robert, Daniel. BA in Sculpture, U. Wash., 1954. Asst. to Henry Moore, England, 1954. One-man shows: Willard Gallery, N.Y.C., 1960, 65, 68, 70, Seattle Art Mus., 1961, Wash. State Capitol Mus., Olympia, 1964, Art Gallery of Greater Victoria,

B.C., 1964, LaJolla (Calif.) Mus. Art, 1970, Anchorage Hist. and Fine Arts Mus., 1970, Tacoma Art Mus., 1980, Kennedy Galleries, N.Y.C., 1985, Lynn McAllister Gallery, Seattle, 1986, 89, Valley Mus. N.W. Art, La Conner, Wash., 1993, Whatcom Mus., Bellingham, Wash., 1994, Schneider Mus. Art, 1994, So. Oreg. State Coll., 1994, Monterey Mus. Art, 1999, Mus. N.W. Art, La Conner, 2004, others; group shows include: Mus. Art, Ogunquit, Maine, 1957, Chgo. Art Inst., 1958, Detroit Inst. Arts, 1958, Pa. Acad. Fine Arts, 1958, Contemporary Art Gallery, Houston, 1958, DeYoung Meml. Mus., San Francisco, 1960, Los Angeles Mcpl. Art Mus., 1960, Galerie Claude Bernard, Paris, 1960, Phillips Gallery, Washington, 1966, Corcoran Gallery, 1966, Mus. Art, Akron, 1967, Finch Coll., N.Y.C., 1968, Rutgers U., 1968, Whitney Mus. Art, 1978, Portland Art Mus., 1976, Mont. State U., Bozeman, 1979, Brigham Young U., 1980, Bellvue (Wash.) Art Mus., 1986, Lynn McAllister Gallery, 1986, Am. Acad. Arts and Letters, N.Y.C., 1986, Schmidt Bingham Gallery, 1987, Wash. State Capital Mus., 1987, 89, Cheney-Cowles Mus., Spokane, Wash., 1988, Smithsonian Instn., 1991—, Nat. Mus., Ottawa, Can., 1991-92, Gallery Three-Zero, N.Y.C., 1993, Seattle Art Mus., 1994, SA Gallery Christ Ch., New Zealand, 1996, Art and Cultural Ctr., Fallbrook, Calif., 2002, others; sculptures represented: Norton Bldg., Seattle, Kankakee (Ill.) State Hosp., Swinomish Indian Tribal Center, LaConner, UN Assn., N.Y.C., King County King Dome, Seattle, City Hall, Everett, Wash., Bartlett Square, Tulsa, OK, 2005, others. (Recipient numerous prizes, awards). Address: 5029 Guemes Island Rd Anacortes WA 98221-9039

**MCCRACKEN, STEVEN CARL,** lawyer; b. Artesia, Calif., Oct. 29, 1950; s. Glenn A. and Helen V. (Fears) McCracken; m. Susan Lee Waggener, July 29, 1979; children: Casey James, Scott Kevin. BA magna cum laude, U. Calif., Irvine, 1972; JD, U. Va., 1975. Bar: Calif. 1975, U.S. Dist. Ct. (cen. dist.) Calif. 1975, U.S. Ct. Appeals (9th cir.) 1976, U.S. Dist. Ct. (no. dist.) Calif. 1977, D.C. 1979, U.S. Supreme Ct. 1985, U.S. Dist. Ct. (so. dist.) Calif. 1990. Assoc. Gibson, Dunn & Crutcher, L.A., 1975-82, ptnr. Irvine, Calif., 1983-94; v.p., sec. and gen. counsel Callaway Golf Co., Carlsbad, Calif., 1994-96, exec. v.p., gen. counsel and sec., 1996-97, exec. v.p. licensing, chief legal officer, sec., 1997-2000, sr. exec. v.p., chief legal officer, sec., 2000—. Lawyer rep. Ninth Cir. Jud. Conf., 1989-91. Editor Va. Law Rev., 1973-75, mng. ed. 1974-75, bd. editors The Computer Lawyer, 1984-96. Mem. ABA (antitrust sect.), Orange County Bar Assn. (bd. dirs. 1988-90, chmn. fed. ct. com. 1988-89, chmn. bus. litigation sect. 1990, sec. 1991, treas. 1992, pres.-elect 1993, pres. 1994). Democrat. Office: Callaway Golf Co 2180 Rutherford Rd Carlsbad CA 92008-8815

**MCCRACKEN, STEVEN R.,** textiles executive; b. Tacoma, Wash., 1953; m. Judy McCracken; children: Morgan, Kelsey. BS in Mech. Engring., Rose-Hulman Inst. Tech. Field engr. DuPont, Nonwovens-Tyvek, 1978—79, fin. mgr., 1981—84, mktg. dir. apparel, 1984—89; mng. dir. Lycra, Geneva, 1989—93, DuPont Corian, 1993—97, v.p., gen. mgr., 1997—2001; group v.p., gen. mgr. DuPont Apparel & Textile Scis., 2001—02; group v.p. DuPont Textiles & Interiors, Wilmington, Del., 2002—03; pres. Invista Inc. (formerly Dupont Textiles & Interiors), Wilmington, Del., 2003—04; CEO Invista Inc. 2003, COO, 2003—04; pres., CEO, chmn. Owens-Illinois, Inc., Toledo, 2004—. Office: Owens-Illinois Inc One Seagate Toledo OH 43666*

**MCCRACKEN, THOMAS JAMES, JR.,** lawyer; b. Chgo., Oct. 27, 1952; s. Thomas J. Sr. and Eileen (Brophy) McC.; children: Catherine, Michael, Amanda, Quinn. BA, Marquette U., 1974; JD, Loyola U., 1977. Bar: Ill. 1977, U.S. Dist. Ct. (no. dist.) Ill., U.S. Ct. Appeals (7th cir.) 1984. Asst. state's atty. DuPage County State's Atty.'s Office, Wheaton, Ill., 1977—81; assoc. atty. McCracken & Walsh, Chgo., 1981—84; ptnr. McCracken, Walsh & deLaVan, Chgo., 1984—. Commr. Nat. Conf. of Commns. on Uniform State Laws, 1989—; bd. dirs. Oak Trust and Savs. Bank, Chgo. Contbr. articles to profl. jours. State rep. Ill. Gen. Assembly, Springfield, Ill., 1983-93, state senator, 1993; chmn. Regional Trans. Authority, Chgo., 1993-2004. Named Top Ten Legislators Chgo. Mag., 1990. Mem.: Chgo. Bar Assn., Ill. State Bar Assn. Avocations: skiing, fishing, hunting, coaching children's sports. Office: McCracken Walsh & deLaVan 134 N La Salle St Ste 600 Chicago IL 60602-1079 Office Phone: 312-346-7700. Business E-Mail: tjm@mcc-w.com.

**MCCRACKEN, WILLIAM HENRY,** retired mining executive; b. Johnstown, Pa., Dec. 3, 1923; s. William Henry and Bernice (Johnson) McCracken; m. Juana Edelmira Pascarella, Oct. 3, 1959; children: William Henry, Derek James, David Andrew, Susan Linda. BS in Mining Engring., Pa. State U., 1944, MS in Mining Engring., 1947. Profl. engr. Pa. Field engr. Harbison-Walker Refractories Co., Pitts., 1947-57; mng. dir. Refractarios Peruanos SA, Lima, Peru, 1957-72; mgr. raw materials Harbison-Walker Refractories Co., Pitts., 1972—85; tech. dir. minerals and ores F&S Internat., Inc., Pitts., 1985-98; ret., 1998. Lt. (j.g.) USNR, 1944—46. Fellow: Am. Ceramic Soc.; mem.: AIME (legion of honor mem.), ALAFAR (hon.), UNITECR (life), Pa. Ceramic Assn. (dir. emeritus). Home: 2219 Alnwick Dr Duluth GA 30096-2212

**MCCRADY, BARBARA SACHS,** psychologist, educator; b. Evanston, Ill., May 7, 1949; d. James Frederick and Margaret Maxine (Miller) Sachs; m. Dennis D. McCrady, June 13, 1969; 1 child, Eric Paul. BS, Purdue U., 1969; PhD, U. R.I., 1975. Lic. clin. psychologist. Clin. project evaluator Butler Hosp., Providence, 1974-75, chief psychol. assessment program, 1975-76, chief problem drinkers' project, 1976-83; assoc. prof. psychology Rutgers U., Piscataway, NJ, 1983-89, prof. psychology, 1989-2000, prof. II, 2000—. From instr. to assoc. prof. psychiatry Brown U., Providence, 1975—83; acting dir. Rutgers Ctr. Alcohol Studies, Piscataway, 1990—92, dir. clin. tng. dept. psychology, 1993—2005, chair dept. psychology, 2005—; reviewer Nat. Inst. on Alcohol Abuse and Alcoholism, Washington, 1979—82, extramural sci. adv. bd., 1989—93, mem. State Medicine, Washington, 1988—89. Author; The Alcoholic Marriage, 1977; editor: Marriage and Marital Therapy, 1978, Directions in Alcohol Abuse Treatment Research, 1985, Research on Alcoholics Anonymous: Opportunities and Alternatives, 1993, Addictions: A Comprehensive Guidebook, 1999. Grantee Nat. Inst. on Alcohol Abuse and Alcoholism, 1979-83, 1988—. Fellow Am. Psychol. Assn. (past pres. divsn. addictions); mem. Assn. for Advancement Behavior Therapy, Rsch. Soc. on Alcoholism (bd. dirs., 1999-2003). Avocations: horseback riding, skiing, piano. Office: Rutgers U Ctr Alcohol Studies 607 Allison Rd Piscataway NJ 08854-8001 Office Phone: 732-445-0667. E-mail: bmccrady@rci.rutgers.edu.

**MCCRADY, JAMES DAVID,** veterinarian, educator; b. Beaumont, Tex., June 26, 1930; s. James Homer and Lucyle (Ward) McCrady; m. Mary Elizabeth MacDougald, Sept. 8, 1951; children: David, Diane, Darla. BS, Tex. A&M U., 1952, DVM, 1958; PhD, Baylor U., 1965. From instr. to asst. prof. Tex. A&M U., 1958- 62, mem. faculty, 1964—, prof., head dept. vet. physiology and pharmacology, 1966-90, prof., dir. spl. programs, 1990—; dir. animal rsch., instr. Baylor U. Coll. Medicine, 1962-64. Dir. Russian-Am. Tng. Partnership, 1995—; adj. prof. Baylor Coll. Medicine, M.D. Anderson Hosp., Tumor Inst. With USAF, 1952—54. Mem.: AVMA, Am. Physiol. Soc., Tex. Acad. Sci., Sigma Xi, Phi Zeta, Phi Kappa Phi. Achievements include research in comparative cardiovascular and respiratory physiology. Home: 511 Olive St Bryan TX 77801-3506 Office: Tex A&M U College Station TX 77843-0001 Office Phone: 979-845-7261. Business E-Mail: jd-mccrady@tamu.edu.

**MCCRAE, JOCELYN DIANE,** psychologist; b. Elizabeth, NJ, Dec. 19, 1957; d. John Christopher and Edna Mae McCrae. BA, Temple U., 1980; MSc, Villanova U., 1987; PhD, Wayne State U., 1996. Lic. Psychologist Mich., 2000. Clin. psychologist Children's Hosp. Mich., Detroit, 1993—. Bd. mem., cmty. mental health bd. Phila. Cmty. Coun., 1978—79. Contbr. articles to profl. jours. Tel. crisis counselor Contact Teleministries, Phila., 1986—87. Recipient Legion Honor award, Chapel Four Chaplains, 1983, Recognition cert., Contact Teleministries, 1986; fellow, Wayne State U., 1991—92; Thomas C. Rumble Grad. fellow, 1988—89, Rsch. grant, 1994, Martin Luther King, Jr.-Cesar Chavez-Rosa Parks fellow, 1991—92. Mem.: APA, Soc. Pediatric Psychology. Methodist. Achievements include facilitating the for-

mation of a martial arts support group for children with sickle cell disease. Office: Childrens Hosp Michigan 3901 Beaubien Blvd Detroit MI 48201 Personal E-mail: jocelynmccrae@netscape.net.

**MCCRAE, KEITH R.,** medical educator, researcher; b. Springfield, Mass., Dec. 4, 1956; m. Jo Ann McCrae; children: Brett, Kristen Ann. BA in Biochemistry summa cum laude, Dartmouth Coll., 1978; MD, Duke U., 1982. Diplomate Am. Bd. Internal Medicine, Am. Bd. Med. Oncology, Am. Bd. Hematology. Resident in internal medicine Duke U. Med. Ctr., Durham, 1982—85; fellow in hematology and oncology U. Pa., Phila., 1985—89, postdoctoral fellow, 1986—88, co-dir. clin. coagulation lab., 1991-93, dir. clin. coagulation course, 1992—93; rsch. assoc. U. Pa. Sch. Medicine, 1989, lectr. bridge curriculum, 1989—93, asst. prof. medicine, 1990—93, asst. prof. pathology and lab. medicine, 1991—93; lectr. basic curriculum U. Pa. Dental Sch., 1989—92; attending physician Hosp. of U. Pa., 1989—93, Phila. VA Hosp., 1990—93, Temple U. Hosp., 1993—; asst. prof. medicine Temple U. Sch. Medicine, 1993—96, lectr. bridge curriculum, 1993—, assoc. prof. medicine, 1996—. Tchg. attending hematology consult svc. U. Pa., 1989—93, tchg. attending hematology oncology inpatient unit, 1992—93; with hematology/oncology outpatient clinic, 1989—93; attending staff mem. hematology consult svc. Temple U. Sch. Medicine, 1993—, attending staff mem. hematology sickle cell outpatient clinic, 1993—, attending staff mem. gen. internal medicine svc., 1993; lectr. in field. Co-author (with M.D. Feldman): Blood: Hemostasis, Transfusion and Alternatives in the Perioperative Period, 1995; jour. reviewer: Blood, 1990—, Thrombosis and Haemostasis, 1991—, Annals of Internal Medicine, 1991—, Jour. Biol. Chem., 1992—, Placenta, 1992—, Jour. Exptl. Medicine, 1992—, Platelets, 1992—, Jour. Allergy and Clin. Immunology, 1992—, Cancer Rsch., 1993—, Am. Jour. Hematology, 1993—, Jour. Clin. Oncology, 1994—, Jour. Histochemistry and Cytochemistry, 1994—, Am. Jour. Physiol., 1995—, Thrombosis Rsch., 1995—; contbr. articles to profl. jours., chpts. to books. Mem.: AAAS, Am. Fedn. Clin. Rsch., Am. Soc. Hematology, Am. Heart Assn. (mem. thrombosis coun. 1994—, mem. arteriosclerosclerosis coun. 1994—, mem. southeastern Pa. peer rev. com. B 1995—), Phi Beta Kappa. Office: Case Western Res U Sch Med 2109 Adelbert Rd Cleveland OH 44106-2624

**MCCRAIN, MICHAEL WILLIAM,** accountant, financial planner; b. Bklyn., Apr. 25, 1952; s. William Joseph Sr. and Penelope (Malarios) McC.; m. Kathleen Jean O'Donnell, June 9, 1974; children: Michael Walter, Kevin O'Donnell, Christopher William. AS in Computer Sci. with honors, Suffolk County C.C., Selden, N.Y., 1973; BBA in Pub. Acctg. cum laude, Hofstra U., 1975; MS in Bus., Columbia U., 1988. CPA, N.Y. Supervising sr. acct. Peat, Marwick, Mitchell Co., Jericho, N.Y., 1974-79; corp. acctg. mgr. Pall Corp., Glen Gove, N.Y., 1979-81; v.p. CFO North Atlantic Industries, Inc., Hauppauge, N.Y., 1981-88; v.p. fin. Loral Fairchild Sys., Syosset, N.Y., 1988-89; pres. MKC Assocs., Inc., Islandia, NY, 1989—. Trustee Sachem Schs. Dist., Lake Ronkonkuma, N.Y., 1992-93; v.p. Sachem Athletic Booster Club, Lake Ronkonkuma, 1993-94, pres., 1994-95; vice chairperson Sachem Cmty. Adv. Coun., Lake Ronkonkuma, 1994-95, chairperson, 1995-97. Mem. AICPA, N.Y. Soc. CPAs, Beta Gamma Sigma. Avocations: racquetball, skiing, golf, computers, coaching lacrosse. Office: 1747 Veterans Hwy Ste 12 Central Islip NY 11749-1537

**MCCRANK, LAWRENCE J.,** dean, school librarian; b. Fargo, N.D., Apr. 17, 1945; s. James F. McCrank and Florence Kloeckner; m. Ruth D. Madson; children: Kirstin L., Jaime L. BA, Minn. State U., Moorhead, 1967; MA, U. Kans., 1969; PhD, U. Va., 1974; MLS, U. Oregon, 1975. Asst. prof. libr. and info. sci. U. Md., College Park, 1976—82; dept. head rare books and spl. collections Ind. State U., Terre Haute, 1982—84; dean librs. Auburn U., Montgomery, Ala., 1984—88, Ferris State U., Big Rapids, Mich., 1988—95; dir. librs. ITT Tech. I, Grand Rapids, Mich., 1996—97, Davenport U., Grand Rapids, Mich., 1998—99; dean libr. and instrn. svcs. Chgo. State U., 2000—. Author: Historical Information Science, 2002, History Under Debate, 2004; contbr. articles to profl. jours. Fellow: Royal Archeol. Soc. Tarragona, Soc. Am. Archivists. Avocations: medieval history, frontier studies. Office: Chgo State Univ 9501 S King Dr Chicago IL 60628-1598 Office Phone: 773-995-2253. Office Fax: 773-995-3772. Business E-Mail: lj-McCrank@csu.edu.*

**MCCRARY, BRIAN FOUNTAIN,** physician; b. Lake City, Iowa, Mar. 1, 1958; s. Warren Ashton and Marilyn Maree McCrary; m. Hamidah Ahmad, Feb. 28, 1986; children: Nicolai, Julian. BS in Psychology, Ariz. State U., 1981; MPH, U. Ariz., 1993; DO, U. Osteo. Med. and Health Sci., Des Moines, 1985. Diplomate Am. Bd. Preventive Occupational Medicine, Am. Bd. Preventive Medicine, Am. Bd. Profl. Disability Consultants, Am. Bd. Forensic Examiners, Am. Bd. Ind. Med. Examiners. Intern U. N.Mex. Hosps., Albuquerque, 1985-86; resident in occupl. medicine U. Ariz. Health Sci. Ctr., Tucson, 1986-88; med. dir. Tucson Med. Assoc., 1988-90; divsn. med. dir. Lockheed Martin Astronautics Divsn., Denver, 1993-94; dir. occupl. health svcs. U.S. Army, Seoul, 1990-93; regional med. dir. Liberty Mutual Ins. Co., Phoenix, 1996-98; med. dir. HealthOne Occupl. Med. and Rehab., Englewood, Colo., 1998—. Adj. faculty The Rocky Mountain Poison Ctr., Denver, 1994—. Contbr. articles to profl. jours. Vol. physician Denver Rescue Mission Clinic, 1993-94; EMT instr. Nev. Test Site, 1998; med. team leader USNG, 1994. Comdr. USN, 1994-99. Fellow Am. Coll. Occupl. and Environ. Medicine, Am. Coll. Preventive Medicine; mem. Am. Acad. Paint Mngt., Phi Kappa Phi. Baha'I. Avocations: painting, martial arts, weightlifting, religious studies. Office: HealthOne Occupl Med and Rehab 125 E Hampton Ave Englewood CO 80110 E-mail: mccrarymia@aol.com.

**MCCRARY, EUGENIA LESTER (MRS. DENNIS DAUGHTRY MC-CRARY),** civic worker, writer; b. Annapolis, Md., Mar. 23, 1929; d. John Campbell and Eugenia (Potts) Lester; m. John Campbell Howard, July 15, 1955 (dec. Sept. 1965); m. Dennis Daughtry McCrary, June 28, 1969; 1 child, Dennis Campbell. AB cum laude, Radcliffe Coll.-Harvard U., 1950; MA, Johns Hopkins U., 1952; postgrad., Harvard U., 1953, Pa. State U., 1953—54, Drew U., 1957—58, Inst. Study of USSR, Munich, 1964. Grad. asst. dept. Romance langs. Pa. State U., 1953—54; tchr. dept. math. The Brearley Sch., N.Y.C., 1954—57; dir. Sch. Langs., Inc., Summit, NJ, 1958—69, trustee, 1960—69. Co-author: Nom de Plume: Eugenia Campbell Lester, (with Allegra Branson) Frontiers Aflame, 1987; film script adaptation (with John Gallagher) Frontier, 1998. Dist. dir. Ea. Pa. and NJ auditions Met. Opera Nat. Coun., NYC, 1960-66, dist. dir. publicity, 1966-67, nat. vice chmn. publicity, 1967-71, nat. chmn. public rels., 1972-75, hon. nat. chmn. pub. rels., 1976-99; bd. govs., chmn. Van Cortlandt House Mus., 1985-90 Mem. Nat. Soc. Colonial Dames Am. (bd. mgrs. NY 1985-90), Met. Opera Nat. Coun., Soc. Mayflower Descs. (former bd. dirs. NY soc., chmn. house com. 1986-89), Soc. Daus. Holland Dames (bd. dirs. 1982-87, 96—, 3d directress gen. 1987-92, directress gen. 1992-96), L'Eglise du St.-Esprit (vestry 1985-88, sr. warden 1988-90), Huguenot Soc. Am. (governing coun. 1984-90, 2000-03, 2004-05, asst. treas., 1990-91, sec. 1990-91, 2d v.p. 1995-2000), Colonial Dames Am., Daus. of Cin., Colony Club (bd. govs. 1988-96), Causeries du Lundi, The Acorn Found. (bd. mem.), The Hereditary Order Descendants of Colonial Govs. Republican. Episcopalian. Home: 24 Central Park S New York NY 10019-1629 Personal E-mail: elmccrary@aol.com.

**MCCRAW, EARL C., JR.,** textiles executive; b. Edna McCraw; m. Joan M. McGuire, May 11, 1979; children: Karen Robertson, Edna. BS in Profl. Chemistry, Wofford Coll., Spartanburg, SC, 1974—78; PhD in Synthetic Organic Chemistry, Ga. Inst. Tech., Atlanta, 1978—83. Rsch. scientist CIBA Vision Corp., Atlanta, 1984—85, rsch. mgr., 1986—89, rsch. dir. materials sci., 1990—92; dir. new textile materials 1993—94; rsch. dir. surface sci. Kimberly-Clark Corp., Roswell, Ga., 1994—97, bus. dir. digital textile printing, 1998—. Achievements include patents in field; patents pending in field. Office: Kimberly-Clark Corp 1400 Holcomb Bridge Rd Roswell GA 30076 Office Phone: 678-352-6370.

**MCCRAW, MICHAEL K.,** construction executive; CFO Pacific USA, Plano, Tex., 1989—.

**MCCRAW, THOMAS KINCAID,** business history educator, editor, writer; b. Corinth, Miss., Sept. 11, 1940; s. John Carey and Eugenia Olive (Kincaid) McC.; m. Susan Morehead, Sept. 22, 1962; children: Elizabeth, Thomas Kincaid Jr. BA, U. Miss., 1962; MA, U. Wis., 1968, PhD, 1970; MA (hon.), Harvard U., 1978. Tchg. asst. U. Wis., Madison, 1968-69; asst. prof. U. Tex., Austin, 1970-74, assoc. prof., 1974-78; vis. assoc. prof. Bus. Sch., Harvard U., Boston, 1976-78, prof., 1978-89, Straus prof. bus. history, 1989—, dir. research, 1985-87, co-chmn. bus. govt. and internat. economy unit, 1986-97. Ednl. cons. to cos., U.S., Japan, 1977-95. Author: Morgan versus Lilienthal, 1970, TVA and the Power Fight, 1971, Prophets of Regulation, 1984, American Business, 1920-2000: How it Worked, 2000; co-author, editor: Management Past and Present, 1996, Creating Modern Capitalism, 1997; editor: Regulation in Perspective, 1981, America Versus Japan, 1986, The Essential Alfred Chandler, 1988; editor: Bus. History Rev., 1994—; co-editor: The Intellectual Venture Capitalist, 1999; contbr. numerous articles to various publs., chpts. to books. Trustee Bus. History Conf., 1986-95, pres., 1989; mem. coun. Mass. Hist. Soc., 1989-92. Lt. USN, 1962-66. Recipient Lyons Master's Essay award Loyola U., Chgo., 1969, Younger Humanist award NEH, 1975, Pulitzer prize in history Columbia U., 1985, Thomas Newcomen Book award, 1986; Woodrow Wilson fellow, 1966-67; named to Alumni Hall of Fame, U. Miss., 1986; Newcomen fellowship Harvard U., 1973-74. Mem. Orgn. Am. Historians, Econ. Hist. Assn., Am. Econ. Assn. Democrat. Roman Catholic. Office: Harvard U Bus Sch Soldiers Fld Boston MA 02163-1317

**MCCRAW, WILLIAM GARY,** music educator, director, musician; b. Spartanburg, SC, July 7, 1955; s. William Charles and Annie Rollins McCraw; m. Julie Karen McAlhany, Apr. 17, 1982; 1 child, Collins William. AA, Spartanburg Meth. Coll., 1975; BSc, Wofford Coll., 1977; MusM, U. SC, 1996. Instr. piano Case Bros. and Brasington Ho. Music, 1977—86; dir. music ministry Westminster Presbyn. Ch., Spartanburg, SC, 1986—; asst. prof., dir. of music Wofford Coll., 2000—. Pianist: Spartanburg Little Theatre; musician: (cd recording) Hymns to Him, Christmas Memories; composer: Song of Dedication. Mem.: Alpha Psi Omega. R-Conservative. Presbyterian. Avocations: travel, reading. Home: 134 Mabry Rd Spartanburg SC 29307-4438 Office: Wofford Coll 429 N Church St Spartanburg SC 29303-3663 Office Phone: 864-597-4597. Office Fax: 864-597-4595. Personal E-mail: gmac1@charter.net. Business E-Mail: mccrawwg@wofford.edu.

**MCCRAY, ALEXA T.,** health science association administrator, director; PhD, Georgetown U., Washington, 1981. Faculty Georgetown U., Washington, 1981—84; rsch. staff mem. IBM T.J. Watson Rsch. Ctr., 1984—86; with Lister Hill Nat. Ctr. for Biomed. Comms., a divsn. Nat. Libr. of Medicine, NIH, Bethesda, Md., 1986—, dir. Contbr. articles to profl. jours.; co-editor-in-chief Methods of Information in Medicine, mem. editl. bd. Jour. Am. Med. Informatics Assn. Fellow: AAAS, Am. Coll. Med. Informatics; mem.: Internat. Med. Informatics Assn., Am. Med. Informatics Assn. (bd. dirs.), Inst. Medicine of NAS. Achievements include research in medical informatics. Office: Nat Library Medicine 8600 Rockville Pike Bethesda MD 20894

**MCCRAY, CURTIS LEE,** academic administrator; b. Wheatland, Ind., Jan. 29, 1938; s. Bert and Susan McCray; m. Mary Joyce Macdonald, Sept. 10, 1960; children: Leslie, Jennifer, Meredith. BA in psychology, Knox Coll., Galesburg, Ill., 1960; postgrad., U. Pa., 1960-61; PhD in English, U. Nebr., 1968. Mem. faculty Saginaw Valley Coll., Univ. Ctr., Mich., 1968—77, chmn. dept. English, 1972-73, dean arts and scis., 1973-75, v.p. acad. affairs, 1975-77; provost, v.p. acad. affairs Govs. State U., Chgo., 1977-82; pres. U. North Fla., Jacksonville, 1982-88, Calif. State U., Long Beach, 1988-93, Millikin U., Decatur, Ill., 1993-98, Nat.-Louis U., Chgo., 1998—. Chmn. high tech and industry coun., SUS, 1986-88; mem. state rels. and undergrad. edn. com., Am. Assn. State Colleges and Universities, 1985-88. Bd. dirs. Jacksonville United Way, 1982-88, campaign chmn., 1987; bd. dirs. Sta. WJCT Channel 7 and Stereo 90, Jacksonville, 1982-88, Jacksonville Art Mus., 1983-88, Meml. Med. Ctr. Jacksonville, 1983-88, Jacksonville Cmty. Coun. Inc., 1982-88, Arts Assembly Jacksonville, 1984-88, Jacksonville Urban League, 1985-88; hon. dir. Jacksonville Symphony Assn., 1983; mem. Dame Point Bridge Commn., Jacksonville, 1982; mem. Jacksonville High Tech. Task Force, 1982. George F. Baker scholar, 1956; Woodrow Wilson fellow, 1960-61; Johnson fellow, 1966; Ford Found. grantee, 1969; recipient Landee award for excellence in tchg. Saginaw State Coll., 1972. Mem. AAUP, Torch Club. Office: Nat-Louis U 122 S Michigan Ave Chicago IL 60603-6191

**MCCRAY, DORIS RAINES,** minister; b. Petersburg, Va., July 1, 1940; d. Linwood and Florence Raines; m. John McCray, Aug. 29, 1958; children: Ronald, Deborah Ramsey, Wayne, Donald. Student, Va. State U., 1980; BA, Richmond Va. Sem., 1986, MDiv, 1988. Notary pub. Va. Assoc. min. Met. Ch., Petersburg, Va., 1982—84, 1990—2000; assoc. pastor Good Shepherd Ch., 1985—86, asst. pastor, 1986—87; interim pastor, 1987—90; assoc. pastor Olive Br. Ch., Dinwiddie, 2000—. Counselor Southside Mental Health, Petersburg, 1984—90, Southside Area Family Counseling, 1984—90; chaplain Southside Regional Hosp., 1983—95. Sr. citizen mem. Sr. Adv. Com., Richmond, Va., 2002; ct. apptd. spl. advocate, 2001—; counselor Contact Tri-City Teleministry, 1978—87; mem. Am. Baptist Churches, 1983—91, Min. Coun., 1989, Petersburg Area Clergy, 1982—2004, pres., 1989; founder, advisor Cmty. Out-Reach Mighty Ministerial Advocacy, 2000—04. Mem.: AARP, Nat. Notary Assn., Nat. Women's History Mus. (charter mem.), U. Va. Alumni Assn. (assoc.). Democrat. Baptist. Avocations: reading, travel. Home: 1712 W Clara Dr Petersburg VA 23803 Office: Olive Br Ch 11119 Bovdton Plank Rd Dinwiddie VA 23841 Personal E-mail: preacherdot@hotmail.com.

**MCCRAY, LORA,** real estate developer; b. Donalsonville, Ga., Nov. 5, 1963; d. Robert and Eula Mae McCray. BA in Polit. Sci., U. Ga., 1985; JD, U. Wash., 1988; MA in Applied Anthropology, U. Memphis, 1998. Bar: Md. 1988. Sr. case supr. DSZ & Assocs., Arlington, Va., 1990—96; rsch. assoc. Cu. Urbun Rsch. and Dev. Inst., Memphis, 1996—98; bus. developer Fannie Mae, Washington, 1998—2002; sr. devel. assoc. McAuley Inst., Silver Spring, Md., 2002—. Dir. Lamont Productions, Washington, 1996—; leadership awards com. mem. Washington Area Women's Found., 2002—03. Literacy tutor Washington Literacy Coun., Washington, 1999—2002. Fellow, U. Wash., 1985—88; scholar, Nat. Merit Scholar Program, 1981—85. Mem.: ABA, Am. Anthrop. Assn., Md. State Bar Assn. (licentiate), Phi Kapp Phi. Avocations: travel, reading, literature. Office: Mcauley Institute 8380 Colesville Rd Ste 300 Silver Spring MD 20910-6264 Personal E-mail: java2jo@aol.com. E-mail: lmccray@mcauley.org.

**MCCRAY, RONALD DAVID,** lawyer; b. Bronx, NY, July 2, 1957; s. Sylvester David and Vivian Marie (Bethea) McCray; m. Monica Ann Simon, Sept. 28, 1985; children: Morgan Marie, Adriane Michelle, Jordan Ellyse. BA, Cornell U., 1979; JD, Harvard U., 1983. Bar: NY 1984, Tex. 1989. Assoc. Weil, Gotshal & Manges, NYC, 1983-85, Jones, Day, Reavis & Pogue, Dallas, 1985-87; sr. atty. Kimberly-Clark Corp., Dallas, 1987—93, sr. counsel, 1993—94, v.p., chief counsel, 1996—99, v.p., sec., 1999—2001, v.p., assoc. gen. counsel, sec., 2001—03, sr. v.p. law and govt. affairs, 2003—. Bd. dirs. Knight-Ridder Inc., 2003—. Editor: Pattern Discovery: Anti-Trust, 1982, Harvard CR/CL Law Review, 1981-82. Trustee The Hockaday Sch., Dallas. Mem. ABA (wire payment systems subcom. 1988—), NY Bar Assn., Tex. Bar Assn. (comml. code com. 1989-93), Dallas Bar Assn., Tex. Bus. Law Found. (bd. dirs. 1990-93), Nat. Assn. of Securities Profls., Am. Corp. Counsel Assn., Coun. Fgn. Rels. Roman Catholic. Avocations: reading, sports, music. Office: Kimberly-Clark Corp 351 Phelps Dr Irving TX 75038

**MCCREADY, GUY MICHAEL,** lawyer; b. Tulsa, Okla., Mar. 21, 1960; s. John McCready and Patsy Ann (Xander) Ryman; children: Sean, Loren. BA, Ft. Hays State U., 1984; JD, Washburn Law Sch., 1987; diploma, Nat. Inst. for Trial Advocacy, 1992. Bar: Colo. 1987, U.S. Dist. Ct. Colo. 1989, U.S. Ct. Appeals (10th cir.) 1990. Pvt. practice, Colorado Springs 1987—; prin. founder Affordable Legal Svcs., 2004. Prof. ethics U. So. Colo., Colorado Springs, 1991; mem. jud. com. to reform juvenile ct. procedure, 2000. Author: Manitou, 2002; author: (asst.) Hierarch of School Law, 1987; contbr. articles to profl. jours. Vol. Pikes Peak Legal Svcs., Colorado Springs, 1987—. Mem. Assn. Trial Lawyers Am., Colo. Trial Lawyers Assn., Colo. Bar Assn., El Paso

County Bar Assn., Order of Barristers. Avocations: skiing, hiking, jogging. Office: Ste 1100 102 S Tejon Colorado Springs CO 80903 Home: 3308 W Bijou Colorado Springs CO 80904 Office Phone: 719-578-3301.

**MCCREADY, KENNETH FRANK,** former electric utility executive; b. Edmonton, Alta., Can., Oct. 9, 1939; s. Ralph and Lilian McCready; children: John, Janet, Brian. BSc, U. Alta., 1963. Supr. data processing and systems Calgary (Alta.) Power Ltd., 1965-67, supr. rates and contracts, 1967-68, adminstrv. asst. to exec. v.p., 1968-72, asst. mgr. mgmt. coms. div., 1972-75; mgr. mgmt. systems dept., gen. mgr. Montreal Engring. Co., Calgary, 1975-76; v.p. adminstrn. Calgary (Alta.) Power Ltd., 1976-80; sr. v.p. ops. TransAlta Utilities, Calgary, 1980-85, pres., COO, 1985-89, also bd. dirs. 1988-96; pres., CEO TransAlta Corp., 1989-96; CEO TransAlta Energy Corp., 1989-96; pres. K. F. McCready & Assocs. Ltd., Calgary, 1996—. Bd. dirs. Encana Corp., Calgary, Biosphere Technologies, Inc., Edmonton, Canada, Computer Modelling Group, Calgary, Can. Environ. Tech. Advancement Corp., Calgary, Nexterra Energy Corp., Vancouver, Naikun Wind Devel. Inc., Vancouver, Canada, NABEST, Innovest Strategic Value Advisors Inc., N.Y., Minister's Adv. Coun. on Sci. and Tech., Ottawa; sr. policy advisor Energy Coun. Can., Ottawa; past chmn. Conf. Bd. Can.; past chmn. bd. Advanced Computing Techs., Inc.; past adv. bd. Tata Energy Rsch. Inst., Washington, Internat. Inst. for Sustainable Devel., Airborne Techs. Inc., Calgary; past moderator Premier's Forum, Govt. of Alta.; past environ. adv. bd. ABB Asea Brown Boveri, Zurich. Past dep. chmn. bd. govs. So. Alta. Inst. Tech.; past chair Alta. Round Table on Environment and Econ.; past mem. com. on trade and environment Govt. Can. Internat. Trade Adv.; past pres. Western Electric Power and Light Assn.; past chair environ. task force Bus. Coun. Nat. Issues. Mem. Assn. Profl. Engrs., Geologists and Geophysicists of Alta., Ranchmen's Club. Avocations: computers, bicycling, photography. E-mail: ken.mccready@telus.net.

**MCCREADY, SAM,** theater educator, actor, theater director; b. Belfast, No. Ireland, Nov. 22, 1936; s. David James and Sarah Elizabeth (Howlett) McC.; m. Joan Carslake, Mar. 16, 1962; children: Marcus Diarmuid Julian, Richard Alastair. MA, U. N. Wales, U.K., 1976. Advt. mgr. Berkshire Internat., Ireland, 1961-63; head dept. theatre Orangefield Boys Sch., Belfast, Ireland, 1963-67, head English dept., 1967-69; lectr. U. North Wales, Bangor, England, 1969-78; artistic dir. Lyric Theatre, Belfast, Ireland, 1980-81; head dept. theatre Stranmillis Coll., Belfast, Ireland, 1978-83; assoc. prof. theatre U. Md., Catonsville, 1984-99, prof., 1999—2001; artistic dir. Shakespeare On Wheels, 1985-96. Examiner Guildhall Sch. Music and Drama, London, 1969—; trustee Lyric Theatre, Belfast, 1978-82; adjudicator Mid Ulster Speech and Drama Festival, 1980, 84, 87, 93, 96, 2001, 04, 06; actor Tartuffe, Md. Stage Co., Ctr. Stage, Balt., 1997, 98, Serebriakov, Round House Theatre, Washington, 1997, Songs of Wandering Aengus, NYC, Sligo, Ireland, 1999, 2000, Krapp's Last Tape, Trinity Coll., Hartford, Conn., 1999, That Time, 2000, Early Memories, NY, 2001; The Great Yeats, 2002, Elizabeth the Queen, 2003, Folger Theatre, Washington, 2003; Heartbreak House, Roundhouse, DC, 2003; Irish Studies Internat. Summer Sch., Sligo, Ireland, 1998, 99, 2000, 03, 04, 05, 06. Author: Theatre in the North of Ireland, 1969-99, 2000, Lucille Lortel: The Queen of Off-Broadway, 1993, Yeats Encyclopedia, 1997, Coole Lady, 2005; adaptor, dir. play: Spring's Awakening, 1987 (Best Dir. award 1987), No Country for Old Men, 1985, Picture of Dorian Gray, 1988, Salome, 1989, The Tutor, 1992, The Widening Gyre, 1994, The Shadow of a Gunman, 1995, Diary of a Scoundrel, 1996 (Best Dir. award 1997), On the Verge, 1997, Deirdre, 1997, What the Butler Saw, 1998, Yerma, 2000, Macbeth, 2001, The Belfast Carmen, 2002, Death of Cuchulain, Sligo, 2003, Coole Lady (Irish tour), 2004, (off Broadway) Sword Against the Sea (Terre Haute and Irish tour), 2005, Two By Yeats, 2006; contbr. articles to profl. jour. Named Outstanding Dir. Am. Coll. Theatre Festival, 1986, 87, 93, 97. Mem. Brit. Actors Equity, Am. Actors Equity, East Ctrl. Theatre Conf., Am. Conf. Irish Studies, Phi Kappa Phi. Episcopalian. Avocations: painting, music, photography, reading, gardening. Personal E-mail: akwadux@yahoo.com.

**MCCREARY, FRANK E., III,** lawyer; b. Santa Monica, Calif., Mar. 25, 1943; s. Frank Elijah and Irma (Holland) McC.; m. Jacqueline Moehlman, Feb. 15, 1969; children: Jennifer Claire, Frank Ward. BA, Cornell U., 1965; LLB with honors, U. Tex., 1968. Bar: Tex. 1968. Ptnr. Vinson & Elkins, Houston, 1970—. Trustee United Way of Tex. Gulf Coast, Houston, 1988-90; bd. dirs. Vol. Ctr. Houston, 1987-99. Capt. US Army, 1968-70, Vietnam. Mem. Nat. Assn. Bond Lawyers, Tex. Law Rev. Assn., Houston Bar Found. Office: Vinson & Elkins Ste 2500 First City Tower 1001 Fannin St Houston TX 77002-6760 Office Phone: 713-758-2440. Office Fax: 713-615-5256. E-mail: fmccreary@velaw.com.

**MC CREARY, JAMES FRANKLIN,** lawyer, mediator; b. Farmington, Mo., June 15, 1942; s. Frank J. and Bernice E. (Dugal) McCreary; m. Martha Jean Tucker, June 30, 1962; children: James Franklin, III, Jason Tucker, Josh Adam. BSBA, U. Evansville, 1964; JD, Nashville Law Sch., 1969; MBA, Vanderbilt U., 1980. Bar: Tenn. 1969, rule 31 listed mediator: Tenn. With Old Nat. Bank, Evansville, Ind., 1960-64; with First Am. Corp., Nashville, 1972-80, exec. v.p., corp. sec., gen. counsel, 1974-80; with First Am. Nat. Bank Nashville (N.A.), 1964-72, 80-86, exec. v.p., 1980-86; ptnr. Borod & Huggins Attys., Memphis, 1986-87, Gerrish McCreary Smith PC, Memphis, 1988, of counsel, 1988—92, dir., 1993—. Pres. Met. Fed. Bank, 1988-91; vis. prof. bus. law David Lipscomb U., 1975-77; instr. law and banking Am. Inst. Banking, 1969-75. Mem. Beta Gamma Sigma Mem. Ch. of Christ. Office: Gerrish McCreary Smith PC 5214 Maryland Way Brentwood TN 37027 E-mail: fmccreary@gerrish.com.

**MCCREDIE, JAMES ROBERT,** fine arts educator; b. Chgo., Dec. 31, 1935; s. William and Mareta (Black) McC.; m. Marian Lucille Miles, Sept. 3, 1960; children: Miles William, Meredeth Black Winter. AB in History and Literature summa cum laude, Harvard U., 1958, AM, 1961, PhD, 1963; student, Am. Sch. Classical Studies, Athens, Greece, 1958-59, 61-62; LittD (hon.), U. Athens, 2004. Instr. NYU, 1963-64, asst. prof., 1965-66, assoc. prof., 1967-70, prof., 1970, 78-88, Sherman Fairchild prof. fine arts, 1988—2002, Sherman Fairchild prof. emeritus fine arts, 2002—, dep. dir. Inst. Fine Arts, 1967-69, acting dir., 1982-83, dir., 1983—2002, trustee, 2003—, asst. field dir. Excavations in Samothrace, 1962, field dir., 1963-65, dir. excavations, 1966—. Dir. Am. Sch. Classical Studies at Athens, Greece, 1969—77, chmn. mng. com., 1980—90, trustee, 1980—, pres., 2001—; vis. mem. Inst. Advanced Study, Princeton, NJ, 1977—78; mem. vis. com. dept. classical and Near East. archaeology Bryn Mawr Coll., 1982; mem. vis. com. dept. European paintings Met. Mus. Art, 1983—2003; mem. vis. com. Ctr. Old World Archaeology and Art Brown U., Providence, 1985; mem. adv. bd. Alexander S. Onassis Ctr. for Hellenic Studies NYU, 1990—97; cons. in field. Author: Fortified Military Camps in Attica, Hesperia, 1966, Samothrace, 7, The Rotunda of Arsinoe, 1992; mem. adv. bd. Am. Jour. Archaeology, 1969-81; contbr. articles to prof. jours. Bd. dirs. Hellenic-Am. Union, Athens, 1973-77, vice chmn., 1974-77, U.S. Ednl. Found., Greece, 1969-75; active Pres. Adv. Com. on Cultural Property, 1992-95. Charles Norton fellow, 1961-62; named hon. citizen Community of Samothrace, 1976. Mem. Am. Philos. Soc., Archaeol. Inst. Am. (life, trustee 1972-75, mem. exec. com. 1978-81), Archaeol. Soc. Athens (hon.), Deutsches archaeologisches Inst. (corr.). Home: 30 Battle Rd Princeton NJ 08540-4902 also: Palaiopolis GR-680 02 Samothrace Greece Office: NYU Inst Fine Arts 1 E 78th St New York NY 10021-0119 Business E-mail: jrm1@nyu.edu.

**MCCREE, DONALD HANNA, III,** diversified financial services company executive; Grad., U. Vt. Co-head Investment Banking Europe J.P. Morgan Chase & Co., co-head North Am. Credit Markets Grp., mng. dir. Mem. exec. com. J.P. Morgan Chase & Co., mem. investment bank mgmt. com., mem. exec. risk com. Bd. trustees Westchester Arts Coun. Office: JP Morgan Chase & Co 270 Park Ave New York NY 10017-2070*

**MCCREE, PAUL WILLIAM, JR.,** systems design and engineering company executive; b. St. Louis, Oct. 27, 1926; s. Paul William and Hazel Elfrieda (Wilson) McC.; m. Carolyn Williams, Sept. 7, 1955; children: Brian,

Paula, Ross. BS in Biochem. Scis., Harvard U., 1950. Mem. tech. staff System Devel. Corp., Santa Monica, Calif., 1956-62, Mitre Corp., Bedford, Mass., 1966-67; prin. engr. equipment divsn. Raytheon Co., Sudbury, Mass., 1963-66, 67-72; mem. tech. staff MIT Lincoln Labs., Lexington, Mass., 1972-76; mgr. Aerospace Systems divsn. Input Output, Waltham, Mass., 1976-79, tech. dir., 1979-80; mem. tech. staff Mitre Corp., Bedford, Mass., 1980-82; founder, pres. BPR Co., Profl. Cons. Svcs., 1981—. Sr. mem. tech. staff, mgr. subsystem design and devel. dept. GTE Strategic Systems Divsn., 1982-84; tech. dir. HH Aerospace and Design Co. Inc., Bedford, 1984-85; prin. engr., mem. tech. staff Raytheon equipment divsn. Software Sys. Lab., Sudbury, 1985-86; v.p. HH Aerospace and Design Co. Inc., Bedford, 1986-91. Mem. NAACP, Urban League. Served with U.S. Army, 1944. Recipient Black Achiever award, Greater Boston YMCA, 1977. Mem. AAAS, IEEE, Math. Assn. Am., Am. Math. Soc., N.Y. Acad. Scis., Harvard Inst. Learning in Retirement. Democrat. Home: 173 Goodman's Hill Rd PO Box 77 Sudbury MA 01776-0077 Office Phone: 978-440-9268. Personal E-mail: pmccree@att.net.

**MCCREEDY, EDWIN JAMES,** lawyer; b. Atlanta, Dec. 29, 1939; m. Linda Jandora, Mar. 20, 1965; children: James M., Matthew B. BA, Columbia Coll., 1961; JD, Fordham U., 1968. Bar: N.J. 1968, U.S. Supreme Ct. 1982, cert. civil trial atty. N.J. Supreme Ct. 1982. Ptnr. McCreedy & Cox, Cranford, NJ, 1984—. Pres. Richard J. Hughes Inn of Court, 1991-92; mem. civil practice com. Supreme Ct. N.J., 1985-96. Capt. USMC, 1961—65. Fellow ABA, Internat. Soc. Barristers, Internat. Acad. Trial Lawyers, Am. Coll. Trial Lawyers (chair state com. 1995-97); mem. N.J. State Bar Assn. (trustee 1997-2001, chmn. jud. adminstrn. com. Trial Assn. 1994-96, treas. 2001, 1st v.p. 2002, pres. elect 2002-03, pres. 2004-), Trial Attys. N.J. (trustee), Union County Bar Assn. (pres. 1987). Avocations: golf, travel. Office: McCreedy & Cox 6 Commerce Dr Ste 13 Cranford NJ 07016-3551 Office Phone: 908-709-0400. Personal E-mail: edjmccr@aol.com.

**MCCREERY, JEAN TERRELL,** retired draftsman, editor; b. Troy, Ohio, Apr. 28, 1924; d. Ivan Dewitt and Marguerite G. Terrell; m. Earl H. Moreo, Jr., 1945 (dec. 1983); children: Martha T. Fischer, Earl Moreo III, William Moreo, Emily K. Friend, Mary Farrell, Clara L. Bowser, Joseph Moreo, Matt Moreo, Maude E. Clemons, Robert Moreo; m. John W. McCreery, 1990 (dec. 1996). Grad., Troy H.S. Civil engring. draftsman City of Dayton, Ohio, 1971—73, Kraft, Shaw, Weiss, Dayton, 1973—77, Cole, Layer Trumble, Dayton, 1977—79, City of Vandalia, Ohio, 1979—84, Burgess & Niple Inc., Columbus, Ohio, 1985—94, Washington County, Marietta, Ohio, 1994—99. Editor: WASP Class Book, 1996, WASP News, 1998—2004. With Women's Air Svc. Pilots USAF, 1944, WWII. Mem.: LWV, Internat. Women's Air and Space Assn., Women in Aviation Inc., Women in Mil. Aviation, Womens Air Svc. Pilots WWII (sec. 2004—06), Am. Legion (comdr. 1993), Daedalians Soc., Ohio State Hist. Soc., Washington County Hist. Soc. Democrat. Roman Catholic. Avocations: writing, swimming, flying. Home: 309 Wooster St Marietta OH 45750

**MCCREIGHT, JOANN OAKLEY,** retired librarian; b. Suffern, N.Y., Sept. 3, 1937; d. Leslie S. and A. Mildred (Roland) Oakley; m. John C. McCreight Jr., June 25, 1961; children: JoMargaret, Jennifer C. Madlem, Leslie Ann. BS in Edn., SUNY, New Paltz, 1959; MLS, SUNY, Albany, 1983. Tchr. jr. high social studies Goshen Ctrl. Sch., NY, 1959-63; tchr. Hartford Ctrl. Sch., 1966-67; elem. tchr. Catskill Ctrl. Sch., 1973-75; clk. Pub. Libr., 1980-83; pub. libr. dir. Saugerties Pub. Libr., NY, 1983-85; evening libr. Columbia Greene C.C., Hudson, 1985—87; A-V libr. Marist Coll., Poughkeepsie, NY, 1986—88; reference libr. Hudson Valley C.C., Troy, 1989; libr. dir. Fulton Montgomery C.C., Johnstown, 1990-94; ret., 1994. Avocations: bird watching, travel, genealogy, needlecrafts. Home: 10 Orchard Dr Kinderhook NY 12106-1810

**MCCREIGHT, LOUIS RALPH,** retired materials scientist; b. Nov. 26, 1922; s. Ralph B. and Phronia (Benckendorf) McC.; m. Malvina Eloris Smith, Oct. 15, 1949; children: Brian R., Barbara L. BS in Ceramic Engring., U. Ill., 1946, MS, 1949. Rsch. asst., rsch. assoc. U. Chgo. and MIT Ceramic Group for Manhattan Project, 1944—45, U. Ill., Urbana, 1945-49; ceramic engr. Knolls Atomic Power Lab., Schenectady, NY, 1949-55; mgr. materials rsch. and devel. Gen. Electric Missiles and Space Divsn., Phila., 1955-81; dir. materials sci. lab. Aerospace Corp., El Segundo, Calif., 1981-84; sr. engr., engring. divsn., 1984-92, ret., 1992. Mem. rsch. adv. com. on materials NASA, Washington, 1959-69, chmn., 1965-67; mem. Nat. Materials Adv. Bd., NRC, 1966-70. Co-author: Ceramic and Graphite Fibers and Whiskers, 1965, 2d edit., 1968; contbr. articles to profl. jours.; patentee in field. Pres. Chester County coun. Boy Scouts Am., 1979-81; v.p. Upper Main Line YMCA, 1973-81. Fellow Am. Ceramic Soc. (officer); mem. ASTM (rsch. com. 1963-70), Materials Rsch. Soc. Republican. Presbyterian. Home: 101 Cresta Verde Dr Rolling Hills Estates CA 90274-5477 E-mail: malovmc@hotmail.com.

**MCCRERY, JAMES (JIM MCCRERY),** congressman; b. Shreveport, La., Sept. 18, 1949; m. Johnette Hawkins, Aug. 3, 1991; children: Claiborne Scott, Otis Clark. BA, La. Tech. U., 1971; JD, La. State U. 1975. Bar: La. 1975. Pvt. practice, Leesville, La., 1975-78; asst. city atty. City of Shreveport, 1979-80; staff U.S. Rep. Buddy Roemer, 1981-84; regional mgr. Ga.-Pacific Corp., 1984-88; mem. U.S. Congress from 4th La. dist., 1988-93, 97—, U.S. Congress from 5th La. dist., 1993-97; mem. ways and means com. Republican. Office: US Ho Reps 2104 Rayburn Ho Office Bldg Washington DC 20515-1804

**MCCRIE, ROBERT DELBERT,** editor, educator; b. Sarnia, Ont., Can., Oct. 8, 1938; s. Robert Newton and Evelyn May (Johnston) McC.; m. Fulvia Madia, Dec. 22, 1965; children: Carla Alexandra, Mara Elizabeth. BA, Ohio Wesleyan U., 1960; MS, U. Toledo, 1966; postgrad., U. Chgo., 1962-63; MA, Hunter Coll., 1994; MPhil, CUNY, 1994, PhD, 1995. Cert. protection profl. Researcher Connective Tissues Research Lab., Copenhagen, 1963; copywriter numerous advt. agys., 1965-70; owner, editor Security Letter, N.Y.C., 1970—; editor, pub. HBJ Publs., N.Y.C., 1973-76; pres. Mags. for Medicine, Inc., N.Y.C., 1972-81. Faculty John Jay Coll. Criminal Justice, 1985—, adj. to full prof., chair Law, Police Sci. and Criminal Justice Adminstrn., 1997—2003; cons. in field; stpts. at numerous meetings. Author: Security Operations Management, 2001, rev. edit., 2006, Readings in Security Management, 2002; editor: Security Letter Source Book, 1983—, Behavioral Medicine, 1978—81, Security Jour., 1989—98; contbr. books and articles on security and urban crime and policing. Mem.: AAUP, Accolade, Internat. Assn. Profl. Security Cons. Disting. Svc., Internat. Security Mgmt. Assn. (Brennan award 1993), Nat. Coun. Investigation and Security Svcs. (Duffy Meml. Achievement award 1992), ASIS Internat. (pres.'s cert. of merit 1990) Correctional Edn. Assn., Urban History Assn. (life), Union League Club, Pi Delta Epsilon, Delta Sigma Rho, Alpha Tau Omega. Presbyterian. Home: 49 E 96th St New York NY 10128-0782 Office: 166 E 96th St New York NY 10128-2565 also: John Jay Coll Criminal Justice 899 10th Ave New York NY 10019-1069 Office Phone: 212-237-8386. Personal E-mail: rmccrie@verizon.net. Business E-mail: rmccrie@jjay.cuny.edu.

**MCCRIMMON, BARBARA SMITH,** writer, librarian; b. Anoka, Minn., May 3, 1918; d. Webster Roy and Jessie (Sargeant) Smith; m. James McNab McCrimmon, June 10, 1939; Children: Kevin Mor, John Marshall. BA, U. Minn., 1939; MSLS., U. Ill., 1961; PhD, Fla. State U., 1973. Asst. librarian Ill. State Nat. Hist. Survey, Champaign, Ill., 1961-62; research assoc. Bur. Community Planning, U. Ill., Champaign, 1962-63; librarian Ill. Water Survey, Champaign, 1964-65, Am. Meterol. Soc., Boston, 1965-67; edit. asst. Jour. Library History, Tallahassee, 1967-69, 73-74. Adj. asst. prof. Sch. Library Sci., Fla. State U., Tallahassee, 1976-77. Author: Power, Politics and Print, 1981, Richard Garnett: The Scholar as Librarian, 1989; editor: American Library Philosophy, 1975; contbr. articles to profl. jours. Mem. ALA, Pvt. Libraries Assn., Beta Phi Mu, Manuscript Soc. Democrat. Home: The Colonnades C30 2600 Barracks Rd Charlottesville VA 22901

**MCCRONE, ALISTAIR WILLIAM,** retired academic administrator; b. Regina, Can., Oct. 7, 1931; BA, U. Sask., 1953; MSc, U. Nebr., 1955; PhD, U. Kans., 1961. Instr. geology NYU, 1959-61, asst. prof., 1961-64, assoc. prof., 1964-69, prof., 1969-70, supr. Rsch. Ship Sea Owl on L.I. Sound, 1959-64, asst. dir. univ. program at Sterling Forest, 1965-66, resident master Rubin Internat. Residence Hall, 1966-69, chmn. dept. geology, 1966-69, assoc. dean Grad. Sch. Arts and Scis., 1969-70; prof. geology, acad. v.p. U. Pacific, 1970-74, acting pres., 1971; prof. geology, pres. Calif. State U. Sys. Humboldt State U., Arcata, 1974—2002. Exec. coun. Calif. State U. Sys., 1974-2002, acad. senate Humboldt State U., 1974-2002, mem. chancellor's com. on innovative programs, 1974-76, trustees' task force on off-campus instrn., 1975-76, exec. coun. Chancellor's Coun. of Pres., 1976-79, Calif. state del. Am. Assn. State Coll. and Univ., 1977-80; mem. Commn. on Ednl. Telecomm., 1983-86; chair Calif. State U. Statewide Task Force on Earthquake and Emergency preparedness, 1985-88, 95-97; chmn., mem. accreditation teams Western Assn. Sch. and Coll.; chair com. on energy and environ. Am. Assn. State Coll. and Univ., 1980-84; chair program com. Western Coll. Assn., 1983-84, panelist, 1983; chair. bd. dirs Assn. Am. Coll., 1992-93. Contbr. articles to profl. jour.; lectr. on geology Sunrise Semester program CBS Nat. Network, 1969-70; various appearances on local TV stas. Bd. trustees Presbyn. Hosp.-Pacific Med. Ctr., San Francisco, 1971-74; mem. Calif. Coun. for Humanities, 1977-82; mem. local campaign bd. United Way, 1977-83; mem. Am. Friends Wilton Park, 1980—; bd. dirs. Humboldt Convention and Visitors Bur., 1980-87, Redwood Empire Assn., 1983-87; bd. dirs. Calif. State Automobile Assn., 1988—, Am. Automobile Assn., 1990-93; bd. trustees Calif. State Parks Found., 1994-2000. Recipient Erasmus Haworth Disting. Alumnus award U. Kans., 2000; Shell fellow in geology U. Nebr., 1954-55; Danforth assoc. NYU, 1964. Fellow Calif. Acad. Sci.; mem. AAAS, Geol. Soc. Am., Am. Assn. U. Adminstrs. (nat. bd. 1986-89, 96-99, 2001-2002), St. Andrews Soc. NY (life), Rotary, Sigma Xi (pres. NYU chpt. 1967-69), Phi Kappa Phi. Avocation: golf. Office: Humboldt State U Univ Campus Arcata CA 95521 Business E-Mail: mccrone@humboldt.edu.

**MCCRORY, JOHN BROOKS,** retired lawyer; b. St. Cloud, Minn., Oct. 23, 1925; s. John Raymond and Mary Lee (Rutter) McC.; m. Margaret Joan Dickson, Sept. 4, 1954 (dec. Apr. 1957); 1 child, William B.; m. Elizabeth Ann Quick, June 27, 1959; children: John B., Ann Elizabeth. BA, Swarthmore Coll., Pa., 1948; JD, U. Pa., 1951. Bar: N.Y. 1952, D.C. 1985. Assoc. Donovan, Leisure, Newton, Lumbard & Irvine, N.Y.C., 1951-52, Nixon, Hargrave, Devans & Doyle, Rochester, NY, 1952-62, ptnr., 1963-92; ret., 1992. Author: Constitutional Privilege in Libel Law, 1977-90. Served to lt. comdr. USNR, 1943—47, PTO. Fellow Am. Coll. Trial Lawyers; mem. ABA, Monroe County Bar Assn., N.Y. State Bar Assn., D.C. Bar Assn. Democrat. Quaker. Address: 25 Kendal Dr Kennett Square PA 19348-2321 Office: Nixon Peabody LLP Clinton Sq PO Box 31051 Rochester NY 14603-1051 Office Phone: 585-263-1000.

**MCCRORY, MICHAEL KEITH,** lawyer; b. Bloomington, Ind., Feb. 4, 1954; s. Charles Keith and Carol Ann McCrory; m. Patricia Polis, July 18, 1981; 2 children. BS cum laude, Ind. State U., 1976; JD cum laude, Ind. U. Sch. Law, 1979. Bar: Supreme Ct. Ind. 1979, U.S. Dist. Ct., so. and no. dists., Ind. 1980, U.S. Ct. Appeals (7th cir.) 1980, D.C. 1992. Law clk. Hon. James E. Noland, U.S. Dist. Ct., Indpls., 1979—81; atty. Bloxham, Carr & Meyer, Indpls., 1981—87; ptnr. Barnes & Thornburg, LLP, Indpls., 1987—. Author numerous articles on a variety of topics including protecting the rights of secured lenders and lessors in bankruptcy, foreclosure and repossessions, fraudulent transfers, and the treatment of personal property leases under Article 2A of the Uniform Comml. Code. V.p., exec. bd. Crossroads Coun., Boy Scouts Am., Indpls., 2002—; bd. govs. Indpls. Mus. Art, 2003—; chmn.-elect, bd. dirs. Am. Heart Assmn., Indpls., 2004. Fellow: Ind. Bar Found., Ind. Bar Assn. (chair corp. banking and bus. law sect. 1986—87); mem.: D.C. Bar Assn., ABA, (bankruptcy liaison 2003—), ABA, Indpls. Bar Assn. (chair comml. and bankruptcy law sect. 1996—97, fin. com. 2002—). Office: Barnes & Thornburg LLP 11 S Meridian St Indianapolis IN 46204 Office Phone: 317-231-7267. Office Fax: 317-231-7433. Business E-Mail: michael.mccrory@btlaw.com.

**MCCRORY, PATRICK,** mayor; b. Columbus, Oct. 17, 1956; m. Ann Gordon McCrory. BA in Polit. Sci. and Edn., Catawba Coll., 1978, doctorate (hon.), 2001. With Duke Energy Corp., NC, 1978—, now mgr. bus. rels. NC, Charlotte City Coun., NC, 1989—95, mayor protem NC, 1993-95, mayor NC, 1995—. Co-chmn. Charlotte's Fighting Back Commn.; mem. Children Svcs. Network; hon. chmn. Cystic Fibrosis Found., Arthritis Found.; former chmn. United Way Corp. Campaign; former mem. U. NC-Charlotte Bus. Adv. Com., Charlotte Bond Campaign, ARC Pers. Recruitment Com.; HS basketball ofcl.; former bd. dirs. Drug Free Workplace Alliance Com.; founder Uptown Crime Prevention Coun., Mayor's Mentoring Alliance, 1995; leader Homeland Security; mem. adv. coun. President's Homeland Security; pres. Republican Mayors and Local Ofcls.; bd. dir. US Conf. of Mayors, chair, Hosing and Cmty. Develop. Com.; chair NC Metropolitan Coalition; hon. chair Charlotte chpts., Alzheimer Found., Cystic Fibrosis Found., Arthritis Found. Recipient Governor's Outstanding Local Ofcl. award, 2001. Mem.: Mayor's Mentoring Alliance (founder 1995), Republican Mayors and Local Ofcls. Orgn. (pres.), U.S. Conf. Mayors. Office: Office of the Mayor Govt Ctr 600 E 4th St Charlotte NC 28202-2816 Business E-Mail: mayor@ci.charlotte.nc.us.*

**MC CRORY, WALLACE WILLARD,** pediatrician, educator; b. Racine, Wis., Jan. 19, 1920; s. Willard L. and Beulah (St. Clair) McC.; m. Sylvia E. Hogben, Feb. 6, 1943; children— Pamela, Michael, Christine. BS, U. Wis., 1941, MD, 1944. Diplomate: Am. Bd. Pediatrics. Rotating intern Phila. Gen. Hosp., 1944-45; resident pediatrics Children's Hosp., Phila., 1945-46, chief resident physician, 1948-49; asso. pediatrician, 1953-55, sr. pediatrician, 1955-58; provisional asst. pediatrician to out-patients, Lewis Cass Ledyard, Jr. fellow pediatrics N.Y. Hosp., 1949-50, pediatrician-in-chief, 1961-80, sr. pediatrician, chief pediatric nephrology, 1980—. Chief pediatric service Univ. Hosp., Iowa City, 1958-61; instr. pathology U. Wis. Med. Sch., 1942-43; instr. pediatrics U. Pa. Sch. Medicine, 1948-49, instr., research fellow pediatrics, 1950-53, asst. prof., 1953-55, asso. prof., 1955-58; prof. pediatrics, chmn. dept. State U. Iowa Coll. Medicine, 1958-61; prof. pediatrics Cornell U. Med. Coll., 1961— Pres. Nat. Kidney Found., 1964-66. Served to capt., M.C. AUS, 1946-48. Fellow N.Y. Acad. Medicine, Royal Soc. Medicine; mem. Am. Pediatric Soc., Am. Acad. Pediatrics, Soc. Pediatric Research, Am. Soc. Nephrology, Am. Soc. Pediatric Nephrology, AAAS, Sigma Xi, Alpha Omega Alpha. Home: 61 Carrs Tavern Rd Clarksburg NJ 08510-1506 Office: NY Hosp Cornell Med Ctr 525 E 68th St New York NY 10021-4885 Personal E-mail: wallacemccrory@msn.com.

**MCCRYSTAL, JENNIFER CROSS,** elementary school educator; b. Sarasota, Fla., Dec. 11, 1970; d. J. Walter and Frances Marie Cross; m. Michael John McCrystal, Mar. 12, 1994; children: Mary Kathryn, Benjamin Thomas. BS, Fla. So. Coll., Lakeland, 1992; M in Ednl. Leadership, U. South Fla., Tampa, 2006. Cert. profl. educator Fla., 2004. Tchr. Valrico (Fla.) Elem. Sch. Author: (character edn. program) Captain Character (What's Right with Tampa Bay, 1999), The Friendship Company (Drum Maj. in Edn. Award Nominee, 1992); contbr. chapters to books. Coord. donations The Friendship Co., Valrico, 1998—2006; vol. First United Meth. Music Ministry, Brandon, Fla., 1995—2006, First United Meth. Student Ministry, Brandon, 1998—2006; sec. United Meth. Women/Daughters of the Son, Brandon, 1999—2003. Methodist. Avocations: reading, travel, cooking, scrapbooks. Office: Valrico Elementary School 609 South Miller Rd Valrico FL 33594 Office Phone: 813-744-6777. Personal E-mail: jennifer@mccrystalimage.com. Business E-Mail: jennifer.mccrystal@sdhc.k12.fl.us.

**MCCUAN, WILLIAM PATRICK,** real estate company executive; b. Muskogee, Okla., Oct. 28, 1941; s. Lee L. and LaRee A. (Beverage) McC.; m. Jill Pamela Thomas, May 5, 1982; children: Lee Megan Student, U. Tulsa, 1961—62; BA Psychology, Baylor U., 1965; MRE, So. Sem., Louisville, 1967; MS, U. Louisville, 1969; postgrad., U. Md., 1971—73. Prof., asst. dean grad. sch. U. Md., Balt., 1969—73; lobbyist and cons. Washington,

1973—76; CEO KMS Group, Inc., Columbia, Md., 1976—84, MDG Cos. Md., 1994—, MDG-Capital Corp., Naples, Fla., 1992—, MDG Cos. W.Va., Berkeley Springs 1991—, McCuan Family Found., McCuan Farms, LLC, 2005—. Adj. prof. Cmty. Coll., Balt., 1969-72, U. Md. College Park, 1969-71; lectr. Univ. Coll.-U. Md., Balt., 1970-71, Howard C.C., Columbia, 1987-88; CEO Pet Holiday, Inc., Toledo, 1973-94; CEO Uniglobe Columbia Travel Ctr., 1986-94; non-lawyer mem. Atty. Grievance Commn., Md., 1990-96 Contbr. to numerous publs Chmn., bd. dir. Concert Soc. Md., 1988-98; chmn. United Way, Howard County, Md., 1984, Am. Presdl. Inaugural Com., Md., 1988, 2004, Howard County Cmty. Partnerships; fin. chmn. Rep. Ctrl. Com., Howard County, 1988-92; trustee Columbia Found.; mem. Pres.'s Commn. on Food, Nutrition and Health, Washington, 1970, Howard County Environ. Affairs Bd.; mem. bus. adv. coun. Howard C.C.; bd. dir. Congl. Commn. on Mental Health of Children, Washington, 1973-75, Human Svcs. Inst. Children and Families; pres., chmn. & trustee McCuan Family Found., 1997—; active Nat. Rep. Com. Eagles, Team 100, 2002—; bd. govs. St Margaret's Sch., 2003— Recipient Alumni Fellows award, U. Louisville, 1996. Mem. Nat. Assn. Home Builders (bd. dir. 1979-87, fed. govt. affairs com.), Md. Builders Assn. (pres. 1981-82), Home Builders Assn. Md. (bd. dir. 1977-82, Award of Honor 1979, Award of Excellence 1980, Presdl. award 1982), Howard County Home Builders Assn. (pres. 1978-80), Howard County C. of C. (pres. bd. dir. 1984-86) Home: 4256 Snowberry Ln Naples FL 34119-8513 Office: MDG Corp Ctr I Ste 400 8850 Columbia 100 Pky Columbia MD 21045 Business E-Mail: pmccuan@mdgcompanies.com.

**MCCUBBIN, SHARON A.,** elementary school educator; b. Fullerton, Calif., Nov. 20, 1948; children: Julie, Adrian, Matthew; m. Robert Patrick McCubbin BA, U. Calif., 1973; MEd, Cleve. State U., 1993; MEd in Early Childhood Psychology, Loyola Coll., Balt., 2006. Cert. mid. childhood generalist NBCT, 2000, early childhood generalist NBCT, 2003, English as a new lang. NBCT, 2002, literacy, reading and lang. arts NBCT, 2005. Clear crosscultural, lang. and acad. devel. tchr. Primanti Montessori, Orange, Calif., 1977—81; tchr., adminstr. Montessori of Orange, 1981-83, Tustin Hills Montessori, Santa Ana, Calif., 1983-89; tchr., cons. for Montessori programs Irvine (Calif.) Unified Sch. Dist., 1990—; Montessori elem. mentor tchr., 1990—. Founding found. legacy tchr. Irvine Pub. Sch. Asst. Jr. Disabled Programs, Orange, 1988—; bd. mem. Orange Co. Children's Therapeutic Arts Ctr., 2004—06. SBD fellow Johns Hopkins U., 1999. Mem. ASCD, AAUW, Assn. Montessori Internat., Assn. Montessori Internat./U.S.A., Assn. Montessori Internat. Elem. Alumni Assn., N.Am. Montessori Tchrs. Assn., Pvt. Sch. Adminstrs., Calif. Tchrs. Assn., Irvine Tchrs. Assn., Nat. Coun. Tchrs. Math., Nat. Assn. Edn. of Young Children, Educateurs sans Frontieres, U. Calif.-Irvine Alumni Assn., Pi Lamda Theta. Home: PO Box 616 Tustin CA 92781-0616 Office: Irvine Unified Sch Dist 5050 Barranca Pkwy Irvine CA 92604-4698 also: Springbrook Elem Sch 655 N Springbrook Irvine CA 92614 E-mail: smccubbi@iusd.org.

**MCCUE, ARTHUR HARRY,** artist, educator; b. NYC, Sept. 27, 1944; s. Raymond Noel and Alice (Cassidy) McC.; m. Lorraine Havel Bingham, Nov. 18, 1989. BFA, Pratt Inst., N.Y.C., 1967; MFA, U. Colo., Boulder, 1969. Instr. art SUNY, Geneseo, 1969-72; instr. printmaking and drawing Ithaca Coll., N.Y., 1973-77, assoc. prof., 1987-2001, chmn. dept. art, 1977—, prof., 2001—. Guest speaker sch. supt.'s seminar Ithaca Coll., 1990; guest artist N.Y. State Pastel Artists Assn., Cooperstown, 1990, 92, Schweinfurth Meml. Art Ctr., 1990; cons., interpreter on wheelwrighting Onondaga County Parks, Salt Mus., Liverpool, N.Y., 1989-90; guest lectr. dept. art Tompkins Cortland Community Coll., 1987. One-man shows include Univ. Club, Boulder, Colo., 1968, David Gallery, Rochester, NY, 1973, Ithaca Coll., 1977, 79, 97, Art Gallery Adelphi U., Garden City, NY, 1980, Ithaca House Gallery, 1984, 85, Schwein Furth Meml. Mus., Auburn, NY, 1986, Johnson Mus. Art, Ithaca, 1987, Upstairs Gallery, Ithaca, 1992, Lamoreaux Landing Wine Cellars Gallery, Lodi, NY, 1993, 97, 99, Trumanburg Conservatory Fine Arts, 1993, Wells Coll., Aurora, NY, 1995; exhibited in two-person shows at Harry McCue/David Smyth, Ithaca House, 1980, Hackworth/McCue, U. Pa., Edinboro, Grippi/McCue, Handwerker Gallery, Ithaca, McCue/Licht, Upstairs Gallery, Ithaca, McCue/Weisend, Handwerker Gallery,Ithaca 2004; exhibited in group shows at Internat. Gallery, Denver, 1969, Double U. Gallery, NYC, 1977, Handwerker Gallery, 1980, 82, 84-87, 89-95, 97-2000, 2003, Upstairs Gallery, 1983-2006, Everson Mus., Syracuse (2d prize printmaking 1987), New Visions Gallery, Ithaca, 1987-90, Elmira Coll., 1991, Cazenovia Coll., 1993, Cooperstown Nat., 1993, 96-97, 01, Old Park Gallery Art Assn., 1992, West End Gallery, Corning, NY, 1996-97, 2001-06; nat. exhibitions: Galeria Mesa, Ariz., 1998, Wright State U., Dayton, Ohio, 2000, Wichita (Kans.) Ctr. for Arts, 2001, 04, Purdue U., Lafayette, Ind., 2004, U. Wis., Parkside, Wis., 2003; Fall River Art Show, Mass., 1973-74, 76, Marietta (Ohio) Coll., 1974, 76, Arnot Mus., Elmira, NY, 1977, 96, 2001, Ft. Hays State U., 1984, 2003, U. Maine, 1985, 92-93, 96-99, Everson Mus., 1985, 2006; included in book The American History Supply Catalogue, 1983, NY Art Rev., 3d edit.; invited spl. guest at Christie's Auction House, NYC, 1984, Roch Meml. Art Gallery, 1991; commd. by Cornell U./Statler Hotel to design art work for hotel, 1988; paintings on loan to Sen. Hillary Rodham Clinton for office in Senate Russell Office Bldg., Washington, 2004-06; represented in permanent collection at Wichita Ctr. for Arts. Lodestar grantee, 1984; recipient: Juror's award, Galleria Mesa, Mesa Art Ctr., Ariz., 1998, Made in New York honor award, Schweinfurth Meml. Art Ctr., Auburn, NY, 1999, merit purchase award, Maine Maritime Provinces Exhibition, U. Maine, 1996, purchase award, Wichita Art Ctr., Kans., 2004. Home: 2423 Skinner Rd Lodi NY 14860-9739 Office: Ithaca Coll Dept Art Danby Rd Ithaca NY 14850-5736 Business E-Mail: hmccue@ithaca.edu.

**MCCUE, DAVID J.,** information systems specialist, entrepreneur; b. Phila., Mar. 28, 1956; s. Earl E. and A. Kathleen McCue; m. Nicole E. Schumacher, Aug. 16, 1981; 1 child, Christopher D. BSc, Rider U., 1978; MBA, NYU, 1980. Cons. Human Sys. Inc., New Vernon, NJ, 1980-81; from cons. to regional dir. tech. Andersen Consulting, NJ, 1981-93; chief info. and resource officer Am. Practice Mgmt., Inc., N.Y.C., 1993-96; chief info. officer Computer Scis. Corp., N.Y.C., 1996-2001; corp. dir. global applications Computer Scis. Corp. Worldwide, N.Y.C., 2001—03; v.p. applications portfolio mgmt. Computer Scis. Corp., Falls Church, Va., 2003—. Mem. adv. bd. Coll. Edn., Rider U., Lawrenceville, N.J., 1997-99. Mgr. Somerset County 4-H Fair, 1998—99; mem. Air Safety Found.; bd. dirs. Rider U. Alumni Assn., 1984—. Mem. Inst. Mgmt. Cons. (cert.), Assn. MBA Execs., Am. Prodn. and Inventory Control Soc. (cert. prodn. and inventory mgr.), Am. Soc. Indsl. Security, Aircraft Owners and Pilots Assn., Exptl. Aircraft Assn., NRA, NRCC (bus. adv. coun.). Republican. Roman Catholic. Avocations: commercial aviation pilot, equestrian sports. Home: PO Box 909 21580 Lower Woodchuck Rd Florence MT 59833-0909 Office: CSC Corp Office VTC-C 630 MC 320 3170 Fairview Park Dr Falls Church VA 22042 Office Phone: 706-641-3076. Business E-Mail: djmccue@mccue.org.

**MCCUE, DENNIS MICHAEL,** management consultant; b. Pitts., July 28, 1952; s. Stephen J. and Mary (Maddalan) McC. BA, U. Dayton, 1974. Dist. exec. Allegheny Trails Coun., Boy Scouts Am. Pitts., 1974-77; area mgr. The Nestle Co., Pitts., 1977-79; account mgr. So. Pacific Communications, Pitts., 1979-82; dir. sales and mktg. Amertel Co., Pitts., 1982-84, ITT Bu. Communications, Newport Beach, Calif., 1985-86; dir. mktg. Damac Products, Santa Fe Springs, Calif., 1986-87; ptnr. Hunter-McCue Mgmt. Cons., Newport Beach, Calif., 1987-89; pres. Dynamic Firm Mgmt., Newport Beach, Calif., 1989—. Instr. computer info. sys. Cerritos Coll., Norwalk, Calif., 1996-2000. Contbr. articles to profl. jours. Grad. Leadership Tng., 1998, program chmn., bd. dirs., 1993-95. Mem. Nat. Assn. Corp. Dirs., Nat. Bur. Profl. Mgmt. Cons. (cert.), Inst. Mgmt. Cons. (cert., bd. dirs., pres. 2004-06), Profl. Network Group (group leader), Assn. Profl. Cons., L.A. County Bar Assn. (exec. com. practice mgmt. sect. 2004—), Lew Epstein Men's Club (mgr. 1986-90). Avocations: travel, pc computing, dogs. Office: Dynamic Firm Mgmt 4570 Campus Dr Ste 60 Newport Beach CA 92660

**MCCUE, HOWARD MCDOWELL, III,** lawyer, educator; b. Sumter, S.C., Jan. 4, 1946; s. Howard McDowell and Carolyn Hartwell (Moore) McC.; m. Judith Weiss, Apr. 3, 1972; children— Howard McDowell IV, Leigh AB,

Princeton U., 1968; JD, Harvard U., 1971. Bar: Mass. 1971, Ill. 1975, U.S. Tax Ct. 1977. Assoc. Hale and Dorr, Boston, 1971-72, Mayer Brown Rowe & Maw LLP, Chgo., 1975-77, ptnr., 1977—. Adj. prof. law master in tax program Chgo. Kent Coll. Law, 1981— Author: (with others) Drafting Wills and Trust Agreements, 1979, 82, 85, 87, 90; mem. editorial adv. bd. Trusts and Estates mag., 1981-2000; contbr. articles to profl. jours. Bd. dirs. Art Inst. Chgo., Arts Club Chgo.; former chmn. bd. govs. Northwestern U. Libr. Coun.; past vice-chmn. Ravinia Festival Assn.; chmn. Lloyd A. Fry Found. Lt. USN, 1972-75. Princeton U. scholar, 1965 Mem. ABA, Chgo. Bar Assn. (fed. tax com., past chmn., exec. coun.), Chgo. Bar Found. (past pres.), Am. Coll. Tax Counsel, Am. Coll. Trust and Estate Counsel (regent, chair charitable planning and exempt orgns. com.), Harvard Law Soc. Ill., Internat. Acad. Estate and Trust Law, Phi Beta Kappa.

**MCCUE, JUDITH W.,** lawyer; b. Phila., Apr. 7, 1948; d. Emanuel Leo and Rebecca (Raffel) Weiss; m. Howard M. McCue III, Apr. 3, 1971; children: Howard, Leigh. BA cum laude, U. Pa., 1969; JD, Harvard U., 1972. Bar: Ill. 1972, U.S. Tax Ct. 1984. Ptnr. McDermott Will & Emery LLP, Chgo., 1995—. Dir. Schawk, Inc., Des Plaines, Ill.; past pres. Chgo. Estate Planning Coun. Trustee Chgo. Symphony Orch., 1995—, vice chmn., 1998—2001, 2005—. Mem.: Chgo. Bar Assn. (chmn. probate practice com. 1984—85, chmn. estate and gift tax divsn. of fed. tax com. 1988—89), Am. Coll. Trust and Estate Counsel (com. chmn. 1991—94, regent 1993—2000, com. chmn. 1998—2001, pres. 2005—06, immediate past pres. 2006—). Office: McDermott Will & Emery LLP 227 W Monroe St Ste 3100 Chicago IL 60606-5096 E-mail: jmccue@mwe.com.

**MCCUEN, JOHN,** finance and tooling company executive, columnist, educator; b. Washington, Mar. 30, 1926; s. Joseph Raymond and Josephine (Joachim) McCuen; m. Gloria Joyce Seidel, June 16, 1949; children: John Joachim Jr., Les Seidel. BS, U.S. Mil. Acad., 1948; M of Internat. Affairs, Columbia U., 1961; grad., U.S. Army War Coll., 1968. Commd. 2d. lt. U.S. Army, 1948, advanced through grades to col.; dir. internal def. and devel. U.S. Army War Coll., Carlisle Barracks, Pa., 1969—72; chief U.S. Def. Liaison Group, Jakarta, Indonesia, 1972—74; chief field survey office U.S. Army Tng. and Doctrine Command, Ft. Monroe, Va., 1974—76; ret. U.S. Army, 1976; mgr. tng. Chrysler Def., Center Line, Mich., 1977—82; mgr. modification ctr. Land Sys. divsn. Gen. Dynamics, Sterling Heights, Mich., 1982—83, mgr. field ops. Warren, Mich., 1983—94; pres. Mich. Econ. Devel. Corp., Birmingham, Mich., 1994—, The Magic Christmas Tree, Inc., Birmingham, 1994—; pres., CEO Laminar, Inc., Southfield, Mich., 1996—; owner Adventure and Exotic Travel Outfitters, Inc., Birmingham, 1995—; past pres. First Internat. Corp., Birmingham, 1995—97; chmn., CEO Multi-Nat. Tooling LLC, Birmingham, 2005—. Ptnr. East West Connection, Birmingham; past pres. Energy Resource Mgmt. Sys., Inc., Birmingham; armor advisor 3d Royal Thai Army, 1957—58; U.S. rep. users' com. NATO Missile Firing Installation Crete, Paris, 1964—66; advisor Vietnamese Nat. Def. Coll., Saigon, 1968—69; spkr., writer terrorism and counter insurgency; lectr. in field. Author: The Art of Counter Revolutionary War-The Strategy of Counter Insurgency, Faber, 1966, Stackpole, 1967, Circulo Militar, 1967; columnist: Army Times, 2002—. Bd. dirs. Troy and Mt. Clemens (Mich.) Cmty. Concert Assn., 1982—2006, pres., 1985—2006; past pres. Mich. Oriental Art Soc., Birmingham; pres. Grander View Found. Sr. Housing and Nursing, Milford, Mich., 1984—89; past chmn. region VI N.E. unit Detroit United Way Campaign; 1st reader First Ch. of Christ Scientist, Birmingham, 1989—92, chmn. bd. dirs., 2000—01. Mem.: Nat. Mgmt. Assn., Soc. Logistics Engrs., Oriental Art Assn. Am. U.S. Army. Republican. Avocations: oriental antiques, writing. Home: 1530 Northlawn Blvd Birmingham MI 48009 Office: Multi-Nat Tooling LLC 999 Haynes Ste 235 Birmingham MI 48009 Office Phone: 248-644-3485. Personal E-mail: jjmccuen@aol.com.

**MCCUEN, JOHN FRANCIS, JR.,** lawyer; b. N.Y.C., Mar. 11, 1944; s. John Francis and Elizabeth Agnes McCuen; m. Christine McCuen; children: Sarah, Mary, John. AB, U. Notre Dame, 1966; JD, U. Detroit, 1969. Bar: Mich. 1970, Fla. 1970, Ohio 1978. Legal counsel Kelsey-Hayes Co., Romulus, Mich., 1970-77; corp. counsel Sheller-Globe Corp., Toledo, 1977-79; v.p. gen. counsel, 1979-86, sec., 1982-87, sr. v.p. gen. counsel, 1986-89; ptnr. Marshall & Melhorn, Toledo, 1989-92; pvt. practice Law Offices John F. McCuen, Toledo, 1992-93; counsel Butzel Long, Ann Arbor, Mich., 1993—94; v.p. legal Kelsey Hayes Co., Livonia, Mich., 1994-98, v.p., gen. counsel, 1998-99; of counsel Butzel Long, 1999—2001. Trustee Kidney Found. N.W. Ohio, 1979-88, pres., 1984-86. Mem. Mich. Bar, Forest Lake Country Club. Home: 1668 Trading Post Ln Bloomfield Hills MI 48302-1868

**MCCUEN, MAUREEN E.,** history educator; b. Fairfax, Va., July 24, 1972; d. John M. and Mary Anne McGovern; m. Jeffrey P. McCuen, Apr. 25, 1998; children: Elizabeth K., Patrick R. BA, James Madison U., Harrisonburg, Va., 1989—93. Cert. Secondary Composite Social Studies Tchr. Tex. Bd. Edn., 1998. Social studies tchr. Potomac Sr. HS, Prince William County Pub. Schs., Dumfries, Va., 1995—98, Travis Jr. HS, Paris Ind. Sch. Dist., Tex., 1998—2002; ap/honors. U.S. history tchr. Paris HS, Paris Ind. Sch. Dist., 2002—. Academic decathlon coach Paris HS, 2003—. Mem.: Assn. Supervision and Curriculum Devel. Avocations: camping, running, violin, theater. Office: Paris HS 2400 Jefferson Rd Paris TX 75462 Office Phone: 903-737-7400. Business E-Mail: mmccuen@parisisd.net

**MCCUISTION, PEG OREM,** retired health facility administrator; b. Houston, July 28, 1930; d. William Darby and Dorothy Mildred (Beckett) Orem; m. Palmer Day McCuistion, Sept. 4, 1949 (div. 1960); 1 child, Leeanne E. BBA, Southwest Tex. State, 1963; MBA, George Washington U., 1968; EdD, Wayne State U., 1989. Patient care adminstr. Holy Cross Hosp., Silver Spring, Md., 1968-79; exec. dir. Hospice of S.E. Mich., Southfield, 1979-86, Hospice Austin, Tex., 1987-94; CEO EMBI, Inc., Arlington, Tex., 1994—98; gen. mgr. Hospice Home Care, San Antonio, 2001—04; ret., 2004. Bd. dirs. Cmty. Home for the Elderly, Austin, 1989-92. Fellow Am. Coll. Health Care Execs. (membership com.); mem. Internat. Hospice Inst. (assoc.), Nat. Hospice Orgn. (chair standards and accreditation com.), Tex. Hospice Orgn. (pres. 1993-94), exec. com., standards and ethics com., edn. com., chair legis. com.), Mich. Hospice Orgn. (chair edn. com., bd. dirs.). Personal E-mail: pegomc@wimberley-tx.com.

**MCCUISTION, ROBERT WILEY,** hospital administrator, management consultant, lawyer; b. Wilson, Ark., June 15, 1927; s. Ed Talmadge and Ruth Wiley (Bassett) McC.; m. Martha Virginia Golden, June 11, 1949 (dec. Nov. 1991); children: Beth, Dan, Jed.; m. Sudola M. Getz, Feb. 12, 1994. AB in History, Hendrix Coll., Conway, Ark., 1949; JD, U. Ark., 1952. Bar: Ark. 1952, U.S. Dist. Ct. (we. dist.) Ark. 1953. Practice in Dermott, Ark., 1952-57; dep. pros. atty. 10th Jud. Dist. Ark., 1952-57; bus. mgr. St. Mary's Hosp., Dermott, 1953-56, asst. adminstr., 1956-57; adminstr. Stuttgart (Ark.) Meml. Hosp., 1957-60, Forrest Meml. Hosp., Forrest City, Ark., 1960-68; assoc. adminstr. St. Edward Mercy Hosp., Ft. Smith, Ark., 1968-70; pres. Meml. Med Center, Corpus Christi, Tex., 1970-79; adminstr. Methodist Hosp., Mitchell, SD, 1979-85, cons., 1985-86; mgmt. cons., owner Creative Leadership Concepts, Denton, Tex., 1985—; adminstr. Cen. United Meth. Ch., Fayetteville, 1986-91. Sec. Ark. Hosp. Adminstrs. Forum, 1958-59, pres., 1959-60; pres. Ark. Hosp. Assn., 1964-65, Areawide Health Planning, 1970; pres. Ark. Conf. Cath. Hosps., 1970; chmn. Twin City Hosp. Coun. West Ark., 1968; v.p. Ark. Assn. Mental Health, 1966-70. Div. chmn. Forrest City United Cmty.Svcs., 1961, Corpus Christi United Way Cmty. Svcs., 1972, DeSoto coun. Boy Scouts Am., Explorer advisor, 1954-57; vice chmn., sec. ofcl. bd. Meth. Ch., 1957, lay del. S.D. ann. conf., 1980-85, cert. lay spkr., 1960—; trustee Midwest Hosp. Coun., Corpus Christi, Mo., 1966-68. With USAAF, World War II. Recipient Eminent Leadership award DeSoto Area council Boy Scouts Am., 1956 Mem. Am. Assn. Hosp. Accts. (pres. Ark. chpt. 1957), S.D. Hosp. Assn. (dist. chmn. 1980-81), Mid-West Hosp. Assn. (trustee 1963-65), Am. Coll. Health Execs. (life), Rotary (pres. Forrest City 1964-65). Home and Office: 2401 St Gregory St Arlington TX 76013

**MCCULLAGH, GRANT GIBSON,** retired architect; b. Cleve., Apr. 18, 1951; s. Robert Ernest and Barbara Louise (Grant) McC.; m. Suzanne Dewar Folds, Sept. 13, 1975; children: Charles Weston Folds, Grant Gibson Jr. BArch, U. Ill., 1973; MArch, U. Pa., 1975; MBA, U. Chgo., 1979. Registered architect, Ill. Dir. mktg. The Austin Co., Chgo., 1977-83, asst. dist. mgr., 1983-84, dist. mgr., 1984-88, v.p., 1987-88; chmn., CEO McClier Corp., Chgo., 1988—98; chmn. Holmes & Narver, Orange, Calif., 1997-2001; exec. v.p. AECOM, L.A., 2000—03, vice chmn., 2003—04; chmn., CEO Global Integrated Bus. Solutions, Inc., 2004—; CEO The Facility Group, 2005—. Contbr. articles to various indsl. publs. Trustee Newberry Libr., Brookfield Zoo/Chgo. Zool. Soc., 2004—, Chgo. Pub. Libr. Found.; council trustee Nat. Trust for Historic Preservation. Fellow: AIA; mem.: Design/Build Inst. Am., Calif. Club, Comml. Club, Indian Hill Country Club, Univ. Club, Casino Club, Chgo. Club, Econ. Club. Republican. Episcopalian. Home: 43 Locust Rd Winnetka IL 60093-3725 Office: 181 W Madison St Ste 3900 Chicago IL 60602 E-mail: grant.mccullagh@gibscorp.com.

**MCCULLAGH, JAMES CHARLES,** publishing executive; b. London, Oct. 22, 1941; s. James Christopher and Violet Anne (Smith) McCullagh; children: Declan, Deidre. BS, Ind. U. Pa., 1968; MA, Lehigh U., 1970, PhD, 1974. Tchr. Holidaysburg (Pa.) Area H.S., 1968; teaching asst. Lehigh U., Bethlehem, Pa., 1968-71, doctoral fellow, 1971-73; vis. poet Pa. Coun. Arts, Harrisburg, 1974-78; editor Rodale Press Inc., Emaus, Pa., 1979-83, pub., editor dir., group v.p., 1984—; pub. Novii Fermer, USSR, 1991—; pub. dir. Scuba Diving, 1992; sr. v.p. Internat. Mag. Devel.; mng. dir. Rodale Press, Inc., Russia, 1996—, DeSilva & Phillips, 1997—; dir. acquisitions Hachette Filipacchi Mags., N.Y.C., 1998-99; v.p. corp. strategy, 1999—; mng. dir. Sci. Am., N.Y.C., 2000—. Author: (book) Bicycle Fitness Book, 1984, Bicycling for Health and Fitness, 1995, Cycling for Health, Fitness and Well-Being, 1995, The Mad Cow Culture Book, 1999, (poetry) That Kingdom Coming Business, 1984, Magazines and Culture, 2005; pub.: Mountain Bike, 1994; editor: Pedal Power, 1978, Ways to Play, 1978, The Solar Greenhouse Book, 2003. With USN, 1960—64. Recipient Man of the Yr. award, Bicycle Mfrs. Assn. Am., 1983. Mem.: Bicycle Inst. Am. (pres. 1993—), Bicycle Fedn. (bd. dirs. 1980—), Mag. Pubs. Assn., Am. Assn. Mag. Editors. Democrat. Roman Catholic. Home: 16 Germonds Rd New City NY 10956-2857 Office Phone: 212-872-3770. E-mail: cmccullagh@magazine.com.

**MCCULLEN, JOSEPH T., JR.,** venture capitalist; b. Phila., Mar. 15, 1935; s. Joseph Thomas and Sara Ellen (Berryman) McC.; m. Eleanor Joan Houder, July 5, 1958; children: Geoffrey, Jennifer, Justin. BA, Villanova U., 1957, PhD (hon.), 1976. Mgr. planning & acquisitions Merck & Co., Inc., Rahway, NJ, 1961-65; sr. v.p. ptnr. Spencer Stuart & Assocs., N.Y.C., 1965-71; spl. asst. to Pres. Richard M. Nixon, Washington, 1971-73; asst. sec. The Navy, Washington, 1973-77, acting sec., 1977; sr. v.p. sec. New Eng. Mut. Life, Boston, 1977-80; pres. McCullen Ptnrs. Inc., Boston, 1980—; mng. dir. OneLiberty Ventures, Boston, 1986-99, Whitney & Co., Boston, 1999—2002; chmn. McCullen Capital, 2002—. Bd. dirs. MetroPCS, Inc., Dallas, EXTRAPRISE Group, Boston, Atlantis Wireless, Inc., Washington, TeleCorp WCS Inc., Washington; advisor Heritage Capital, Atlanta, 2001—, Carrott Capital, N.Y.C., 2001—; chmn. transition team Mass. Port Authority, 2002—03; sr. advisor Key Prin. Ptnrs., Cleve., 2001—, Key Venture Ptnrs., Waltham, Mass., 2003—. Mem. selection com. White House Fellows Program, 1979-96; bd. dirs. World Affairs Coun., 1977-95, Boston Ballet, 1978-85, chmn., 1980-85; bd. trustees Goodwill Industries, 1979-95, Boston Biomed. Rsch. Inst., 1989-95; assoc. dir. Pres. Reagan Transition Team, 1980; advisor Pres. Bush Transition Team, 1988, Presdl. Bus. Commn., 2003—; bd. mem. Internat. Ctr. for Rel. and Diplomacy, 2004-, dir. 2005-, bd. mem. Serving Our Seniors, Boston, 2004—. Served with U.S. Navy, 1952-53; lt. U.S. Army, 1958-61. Recipient Disting. Pub. Svc. medals Exec. Office of Pres., 1973, U.S. Dept. Def., 1977. Home: 97 Essex Rd Chestnut Hill MA 02467-1316 Office: One Liberty Sq 12th Fl Boston MA 02109-4825 Business E-Mail: jt@mccullencapital.com.

**MCCULLEY, JAMES PARKER,** ophthalmologist, educator; MD, Washington U., St. Louis, 1968. Diplomate Am. Bd. Ophthalmology, 1968. Prof., chmn. dept. ophthalmology U. Tex. Southwestern Med. Sch., Dallas, 1980—; assoc. prof. Stanford U. Med. Sch., Palo Alto, Calif., 1976—80. Spkr. alliance Alcon Labs., Inc., Fort Worth, 1980—; med. consultants panel, Soflens divsn. Bausch & Lomb, 1978—80; med. dir. Stanford Eye Bank, Palo Alto, 1976—80; chair rsch. sect. com. ARVO, 1979—82; mem. adv. bd. Ctr. for Alternatives to Animal Testing Johns Hopkins U., Balt., 1981—2003; mem. adv. coun. State Commn. for the Blind, Austin, Tex., 1982—; med. adv. bd. Corneal Dystrophy Found., 1982—; exec. com. Cornea Soc., 1984—. Contbr. scientific papers more than 350 articles to profl. jours. Sci. adv. bd. Alcon Labs., Inc., Fort Worth, 2002—03; chmn. FDA Ophthalmic Device Panel, Washington, 1998—2002. Lt. comdr. M.C. USN, 1974—76. Grantee, NEI, 1978—, Alcon Labs., 2003—, Santen Pharm., 2001—. Achievements include research in chronic blepharitis, lipid layer of tear film, acanthamoeba keratitis. Office: Univ Texas Southwestern Med Sch Dept Ophthalmology 5323 Harry Hines Blvd Dallas TX 75390-9057 Office Phone: 214-648-2020. E-mail: james.mcculley@utsouthwestern.edu.

**MCCULLEY, TIMOTHY J.,** ophthalmologist, surgeon, educator; b. Boston, Sept. 26, 1968; s. James P. and Mary Ann McCulley; m. Lynda Van. BA, Pitzer Coll. of the Claremont (Calif.) Colls., 1991; MD, Washington U., St. Louis, 1995. Dir. ophthalmic plastic and reconstructive surgery and neuro-ophthalmology Stanford U. Sch. of Medicine, Calif., 2003—06; dir. ophthalmic plastic and reconstructive surgery U. Calif. San Francisco. Sch. Medicine, 2006—. Presenter in field; vis. prof. numerous profl. socs. and univ.-based continuing edn. courses, 2000—06. Contbr. articles to profl. jours. Named to Guide to Am.'s Top Ophthalmologists, Consumers Rsch. Coun. Am., 2006; recipient Carl F. and Gerty T. Cory awards for superior scholarship in biochemistry, Washington U. Sch. Medicine, 1996, award for best case series, TEI Pfizer, 2003, Ophthalmology Tchg. award, Joint Commn. of Allied Health Profls., 2004. Fellow: Am. Soc. Ophthalmic Plastic and Reconstructive Surgery, Am. Acad. Ophthalmology (editl. com. basic and clin. sci. course 2001—06); mem.: Peninsula Eye Soc. (incumbent pres. 2006—), N.Am. Neuro-Ophthalmology Soc. (patient edn. com. 2001—06), Assn. Rsch. in Vision and Ophthalmology. Avocations: scuba diving, surfing, hiking, soccer. Office: U Calif San Francisco Sch Medicine 10 Koret Way Campus Box 0730 San Francisco CA 94143 Office Phone: 415-476-3321. Office Fax: 415-476-0336.

**MC CULLOCH, ERNEST ARMSTRONG,** internist, educator; b. Toronto, Ont., Can., Apr. 27, 1926; s. Albert E. and Letitia (Riddell) McC.; m. Ona Mary Morganty, 1953; children: James A., Michael E., Robert E., Cecelia E., Paul A. MD with honors, U. Toronto, 1948, DSc (hon.), 2004. Intern Toronto Gen. Hosp., 1949-50, sr. intern, 1951-52; NRC fellow dept. pathology U. Toronto, 1950-51; asst. resident Sunnybrook Hosp., Toronto, 1952-53; pvt. practice specializing in internal medicine Toronto, 1954-67; clin. tchr. dept. medicine U. Toronto, Toronto, 1954-64, asst. prof. dept. med. biophysics, 1959-64, assoc. prof., 1964-66, prof., 1966, asst. prof. dept. medicine, 1967-68, assoc. prof., 1968-70, prof., 1970—, Univ. prof., 1982-91, Univ. prof. emeritus, 1991—; mem. grad. faculty U. Toronto (Inst. Med. Sci.), 1968—, chm., 1975-79; asst. dean Sch. Grad. Studies U. Toronto, 1979-82. Physician Toronto Gen. Hosp., 1960-67; sr. scientist, sr. physician Ont. Cancer Inst., 1957-91, head divsn. biol. rsch., 1982-89, head divsn. cell and molecular biology, 1989-91, sr. scientist emeritus, 1991-93; vis. prof. U. Tex. Med. Ctr. Anderson Cancer Ctr., Houston, 1992-93, adj. prof., 1993-98; cons. Nat. Cancer Plan, 1972—; mem. standing com. on health rsch. and devel. Ont. Coun. Health, 1974-82. Author numerous articles on rsch. in hematology; mem. editl. bd.: Blood, 1969-80, Biomedicine, 1973, Clin. Immunology and Immunopathology, 1972-76; assoc. editor: Jour. Cellular Physiology, 1966-68; editor, 1968-74. Trustee Banting Rsch. Found., 1975-84, hon. sec.-treas., 1958-74, v.p., 1977-79. Decorated officer Order of Can., 1988; recipient William Goldie prize U. Toronto, 1964, Gairdner Award Internat. Gairdner Found., 1969, Starr Medallist award Dept. Anatomy U. Toronto, 1957; Thomas W. Eadie Medal, 1991, Royal Soc. Canada, Nat. Cancer Inst. Can. fellow, 1954-57, Albert Lasker award for Basic Med. Rsch., Lasker

Found., 2005; named to Can. Med. Hall of Fame, 2004. Fellow Royal Soc. Can. (pres. Nat. Acad. Sci. 1987-90, Thomas W. Eadie Medal 1991, Golden Jubilee Medal), Royal Coll. Physicians and Surgeons Can., Royal Soc. London, Can. Acad. Sci.; mem. Am. Soc. Exptl. Pathology, Am. Assn. Cancer Rsch., Can. Soc. Cell Biology, Can. Soc. Clin. Investigation, Am., Internat. Socs. Hematology, Internat. Soc. Exptl. Hematology, Inst. Acad. Medicine (charter mem.), Badminton Club, Racquet Club. Home: 480 Summerhill Ave Toronto ON Canada M4W 2E4 Office: Princess Margaret Hosp 9th Fl Rm 112 610 University Ave Toronto ON Canada M5G 2M9 Office Phone: 416-340-4800 x2957. E-mail: mcculloch@uhnres.utoronto.ca. *Research success depends on associating with agreeable and talented people.*

**MCCULLOCH, KENNETH JOHN,** lawyer; b. NYC, July 22, 1943; s. John K. and Muriel A. (Gallagher) McCulloch; m. Carmen Otero, Aug. 9, 1970; children— Kenneth Erik, Paul David. BA, Columbia U., 1965; JD, Fordham U., 1968. Bar: NY 1968, DC 1975, Pa. 1975, US Dist. Cts., PR. Asst. dist. atty. NY County, 1968-71; NY regional counsel EEOC, 1971-73, supervisory atty. Phila. Litigation Ctr., 1973-75; pvt. practice law, NYC, 1975-77; of counsel Ballard, Rosenberg, Golper & Savitt, LLP, NYC, 1977—. Bd. advisors NY Employment Law & Practice. Mem. NY State Bar Assn. (labor and EEO com.), Assn. of Bar of City of NY (labor and social security com.). Author: Selecting Employees Safely Under the Law, 1981, Termination of Employment, 1991; contbg. author: Winning an Equal Employment Opportunity Case, 1974; Title VII and Collective Bargaining, 1976; contbr. articles to profl. jours. Home: 2 Tudor City Pl New York NY 10017-6800 Office: Ballard Rosenberg Golper 516 Fifth Ave, 12th Fl New York NY 10036-7501 Office Phone: 212-398-9500. E-mail: kmcculloh@brgslaw.com.*

**MCCULLOCH, LINDA,** school system administrator; b. Mont., Dec. 21, 1954; m. Bill McCulloch, 1978. BA in Elem. Edn., U. Mont., 1982, MA in Elem. Edn., 1990. Tchr. Pub. Schs., Mont., Ashland, Missoula, Bonner, 1978—95; rep. Mont. Ho. of Reps., 1995—2001; supt. pub. instrn. Mont., 2002—. Mem. juvenile justice, mental health, judiciary, Indian Affairs coms. Mont. Ho. Reps., 1997; minority caucus leader Ho. Reps., Helena, Mont., 1999; vice chair edn. com. Mont. Ho. Reps., 1999. Mem., officer PTA Assn. Helena, 1985—; bd. dirs Missoula Developmental Svcs. Corp.; mem. adv. com. Missoula Youth Homes Foster Care. Recipient Mike and Maureen Mansfield Libr. scholaship, 1981, J.C. Penny Vol. Program award, 1998. Mem.: AAUW, LWV, Five Valleys Reading Assn., Mont. State Reading Coun., Mont. Fedn. Tchrs., Mont. Ednl. Assn., Mont. Libr. Assn. (Legislator of Yr. award 1997), Mont. Family Union, Montana Dem. Womens Club. Office: Mont Office Pub Instruction PO box 202501 1227 11th Ave Helena MT 59620-2501 Office Fax: 406-444-5658. Business E-mail: opisupt@mt.gov.

**MCCULLOCH, RACHEL,** economist, educator; b. 1942; m. Gary Edward Chamberlain; children: Laura Chamberlain Gehl, Neil Dudley Chamberlain BA, U. Pa., 1962; MA in Teaching, U. Chgo., 1965, MA, 1971, PhD, 1973; student, MIT, 1966-67. Economist Cabinet Task Force on Oil Import Control, Washington, 1969; instr., then asst. prof. Grad. Sch. Bus. U. Chgo., 1971-73; asst. prof., then assoc. prof. econs. Harvard U., Cambridge, Mass., 1973-79; assoc. prof., then prof. econs. U. Wis., Madison, 1979-87; prof. Brandeis U., Waltham, Mass., 1987—, Rosen Family prof., 1989—, dir. Lemberg Program in Internat. Econs. and Fin., 1990-91, dir. PhD program Grad. Sch. Internat. Econs. and Fin., 1994—2001, chair dept. econs., 2006—. Mem. Pres.'s Commn. on Indsl. Competitiveness, 1983-84; mem. adv. coun. Office Tech. Assessment, U.S. Congress, 1979-88; cons. World Bank, Washington, 1984-86, 2004-05; mem. com. on internat. rels. studies with People's Republic of China, 1984-91; rsch. assoc. Nat. Bur. Econ. Rsch., Cambridge, 1985-93; mem. adv. com. for Internat. Econs., Washington, 1987—; faculty Advanced Mgmt. Network, La Jolla, Calif., 1985-92; mem. com. examiners econs. test Grad. Record Exam. Ednl. Testing Svc., 1990-96, chair, 1992-96; mem. discipline adv. com. for Fulbright scholar awards in econs. Coun. Internat. Exch. Scholars, 1991-93, chair, 1992-93; mem. adv. com. for Fulbright Chairs Program, 1997; cons. Global Economy Project, Edn. Film Ctr., 1993-94; mem. study group on pvt. capital flows to developing and transitional economies Coun. Fgn. Rels., 1995-96, acad. adv. panel, Fed. Reserve Bank of Boston, 1999—; faculty assoc. Harvard Inst. for Internat. Devel., 1997-2000; fellow Internat. Leadership Forum, 2001-; AGIP prof. internat. econs. Sch. Advanced Internat. Studies, Bologna Ctr., Johns Hopkins U., 2004-05. Author: Research and Development as a Determinant of U.S. International Competitiveness, 1978; contbr. articles to profl. jours. and books. Grantee NSF, 1975-79, Hoover Inst., 1984-85, German Marshall Fund of U.S., 1985, Ford Found., 1985-88, U.S. Dept. Edn., 1990-91, Schulhof Found., 2001-02. Mem. Am. Econ. Assn. (dir. summer program for minority students 1983-84, mem. executive com., 1997-2000), Internat. Trade and Fin. Assn. (bd. dirs 1993-95). Office: Brandeis U Dept Econs MS 021 PO Box 549110 Waltham MA 02454-9110 Business E-mail: mcculloch@brandeis.edu.

**MC CULLOCH, SAMUEL CLYDE,** history professor; b. Ararat, Australia, Sept. 3, 1916; came to U.S., 1936, naturalized, 1944; s. Samuel and Agnes Almond (Clyde) McC.; m. Sara Ellen Rand, Feb. 19, 1944; children: Ellen (Mrs. William Henry Meyer III), David Rand, Malcolm Clyde. AB with highest honors in History, UCLA, 1940, MA (grad. fellow history), 1942; PhD, U. Cal. at Los Angeles, 1944. Asst. U. Calif. at Los Angeles, 1941-44; instr. Oberlin Coll., 1944-45; asst. prof. Amherst Coll., 1945-46; vis. asst. prof. U. Mich., 1946-47; mem. faculty Rutgers U., 1947-60, prof. history, assoc. dean arts and scis., 1958-60; dean coll., prof. history San Francisco State Coll., 1960-63; dean humanities, prof. history U. Calif. at Irvine, 1963-70, prof., 1970-87, prof. emeritus, 1987—, coordinator Edn. Abroad Program, 1975-85, dir. Australian Study Ctr., 1986, 87. Vis. summer prof. Oberlin Coll., 1945, 46, U. Calif. at Los Angeles, 1947, U. Del., 1949; Fulbright Research prof. Monash U., Melbourne (Australia) U., 1970; Am. Philos. Soc. grantee, 1970 Author: British Humanitarianism, 1950, George Gipps, 1966, River King: The Mc Culloch Carrying Company and Echura, 1865-1898, 1986, Instant University: A History of U.C.I., 1957-1993, 1995, William McCulloch, 1932-1909, 1997, A Collection of Book Reviews, 1948-93, 2000; contbr. numerous articles, revs. to profl. jours.; assoc. editor Jour. Brit. Studies, 1960-68, bd. advisors, 1968-70; bd. corrs. Hist. Studies: Australia and New Zealand, 1949-83. Mem. Calif. Curriculum Commn., 1961-67, Highland Park (N.J.) Bd. Edn., 1959-60. Grantee Am. Philos. Soc., Social Sci. Rsch. Coun. and Rutgers U. Rsch. Coun. to Australia, 1951; Fulbright rsch. fellow U. Sydney, Australia, 1954-55; grantee Social Sci. Rsch. Coun. to Eng., summer 1955 Fellow Royal Hist. Soc.; mem. Am. Hist. Assn., Church, Royal Australian hist. socs., A.A.U.P., Conf. Brit. Studies (exec. sec. 1968-73, pres. 1975-77), English Speaking Union (pres. New Brunswick 1957-59), Phi Beta Kappa, Pi Gamma Mu. Episcopalian (vestry). Home: 2121 Windward Ln Newport Beach CA 92660-3820

**MCCULLOH, JUDITH MARIE,** editor; b. Spring Valley, Ill., Aug. 16, 1935; d. Henry A. and Edna Mae (Traub) Binkele; m. Leon Royce McCulloh, Aug. 26, 1961. BA, Ohio Wesleyan U., 1956; MA, Ohio State U., 1957; PhD, Ind. U., 1970. Asst. to dir. Archives of Traditional Music, Bloomington, Ind., 1964-65; asst. editor U. Ill. Press, Champaign, 1972-77, assoc. editor, 1977-82, sr. editor, 1982-85, exec. editor, 1985—, dir. devel., 1992—2003; asst. dir., 1997—. Advisor John Edwards Meml. Forum, LA, 1973—. Mem. Editorial Bd. Am. Music, 1980-89, Jour. Am. Folklore, 1986-90; co-editor Stars of Country Music, 1975; editor (LP) Green Fields of Ill., 1963, (LP) Hell-Bound Train, 1964, Ethnic Recordings in America, 1982; gen. editor Music in American Life series. Trustee Am. Folklife Ctr., Libr. of Congress, Washington, 1986—2004, chair, 1990—92, 1996—98, trustee emerita, 2004—. Fulbright grantee, 1958-59; NDEA grantee, 1961, 62-63; grantee Nat. Endowment for the Humanities, 1978; recipient Disting. Achievement citation Ohio Wesleyan U. Alumni Assn., Disting. Svc. award Soc. for Am. Music, Lifetime Achievement award Belmont U. Curb Music Industry, Disting. Achievement award Internat. Bluegrass Music Assn. Fellow: Am. Folklore Soc. (exec. bd. 1974—79, pres. 1986—87, exec. bd. 2001—03); mem.: Am. Musicological Soc. (mem. coun. 2005—), Am.

Anthropol. Assn., Soc. Ethnomusicology (hon.; treas. 1982—86), Soc. Am. Music (1st v.p. 1989—93, coun. 2005—). Democrat. Office: U Ill Press 1325 S Oak St Champaign IL 61820-6903 Business E-Mail: jmmccull@uillinois.edu.

**MCCULLOH, THAYNE MARTIN,** university administrator, consultant; b. L.A., Aug. 20, 1964; m. Julie Ann Lopach, July24, 1993; children: Kathryne Angela, Anne Elizabeth, Emily Clara. BA in Psychology, Gonzaga U., 1989; PhD in Exptl. Social Psychology, Oxford U., 1998. Test administr. Pearn Kandola Downs Occupl. Psychologists, Oxford, England, 1989—90; coord. residence life Gonzaga U., Spokane, 1990—92, dir. housing, 1993—95, asst. dean students, 1995—96, dean student acad. svcs., 1996—98, dean student fin. svcs., 1998—2002, assoc. acad. v.p., 2002—04, v.p. adminstrn. and planning, 2004— Tutor in social psychology Oxford U., England, 1989—93; accreditation evaluator N.W. Commn. Coll. and U., Redmond, Wash. 1997—; cons. enrollment mgmt. and fin. aid, Spokane, 2000—. Mem. Human Rights Commn., Spokane, 2005—06. Sgt. U.S. Army, 1983—86. Decorated Army Achievement medal U.S. Army, Army Commendation medal; recipient Sr. award, Gonzaga U. Alumni Assn., 1989; scholar, Chancellors and Prin., U.K., 1989—93. Mem.: APA, Citibank Ednl. Leadership Financing Coun., Nat. Assn. Student Fin. Aid Adminstrs., Nat. Assn. Student Pers. Adminstrs. (New Profl. of Yr., region V 1995). Roman Catholic. Achievements include research in mentoring and its relationship to leadership succession planning. Home: 1208 S Wall St Spokane WA 99204-3748 Office: Gonzaga Univ 502 E Boone Ave Spokane WA 99258-0086 Office Phone: 509-323-6289. Office Fax: 509-323-6288.

**MCCULLOUGH, COLLEEN,** author; b. Wellington, N.S.W., Australia, June 1, 1937; m. Ric Robinson, Apr. 13, 1984. Student, U. Sydney, Australia, London U.; LittD (hon.), Macquarie U., Sydney, 1993. Neurophysiologist Sydney, London, Yale U. Sch. Medicine, 1967-77. Author: Tim, 1974, The Thorn Birds, 1977, An Indecent Obsession, 1981, Cooking with Colleen McCullough and Jean Easthope, 1982, A Creed for the Third Millennium, 1985, The Ladies of Missalonghi, 1987, The First Man in Rome, 1990, The Grass Crown, 1991, Fortune's Favorites, 1993, Caesar's Women, 1996, Caesar, 1997, The Song of Troy, 1998, Roden Cutler, V.C. (The Biography), 1998, Morgan's Run, 2000, The October Horse, 2002, The Touch, 2003, Angel Puss, 2004. Office: PO Box 333 Norfolk Island Australia Fax: (6723) 23313.

**MCCULLOUGH, DAVID,** writer, educator; b. Pitts., July 7, 1933; s. Christian Hax and Ruth (Rankin) McC.; m. Rosalee Ingram Barnes, Dec. 18, 1954; children: Melissa, David, William Barnes, Geoffrey Barnes, Doreen Kane. BA, Yale U., 1955; LHD, Skidmore Coll., 1983, Rensselaer Poly. Inst., 1983; LHD (hon.), Wesleyan U., Middletown, Conn., 1984, Colo. Coll., 1985, U. N.H., 1993, Chatham Coll., 1994, Beloit Coll., 1996, Georgetown U., 1995, Coll. William and Mary, 1996, Grinnell Coll., 1997, Dickinson Coll., 1998, Northeastern U., 2002, Brandeis U., 2003, OH State U., 2003; DEng (hon.), Villanova U., 1984; doctorate (hon.), Worcester Poly. Inst., 1984, U. Miami, 1996, Grand Valley State U., 1997, Yale U., 1998, Brown U., 2000, Tufts U., 2001, U. Del., 2001; LittD (hon.), Allegheny Coll., 1984, Middlebury Coll., 1986, Indiana U. at Pa., 1991, U. S.C., 1993, U. Pitts., 1994, Union Coll., 1994, Washington Coll., 1994, Hamilton Coll., 1996, SUNY, 1999, U. Conn., 1999, U. Vt., 2002, Dartmouth Coll., 2003; LLD (hon.), Lafayette Coll., 1995, U. Mass., 1998, Wheaton Coll., 2002. Writer, editor Time, Inc., N.Y.C., 1956-61, USIA, Washington, 1961-64; Am. Heritage Pub. Co., N.Y.C., 1964-70; sr. contbg. editor Am. Heritage mag.; free-lance author, 1970—. Newman vis. prof. American civilization, Cornell U., fall 1989; mem. Bennington (Vt.) Coll. Writers Workshop, 1978-79; scholar-in-residence U. N. Mex., 1979, Wesleyan U. Writers Conf., 1982, 83; mem. adv. bd. Ctr. for the Book, Libr. of Congress; past vis. prof. Dartmouth Coll., Wesleyan U.; spkr. and lectr. in field. Author: The Great Bridge, 1972, The Path Between the Seas, 1977, The Johnstown Flood, 1968, Mornings on Horseback, 1981, Brave Companions, 1992, Truman, 1992 (Pulitzer Prize for biography 1993), John Adams, 2001 (Pulitzer prize for biography 2002), 1776, 2005 (Quills award for best history/current events/politics, 2005, #1 on Publishers Weekly Bestseller list, 2005); host TV series: Smithsonian World, 1984-88, The American Experience, 1988—; narrator numerous TV documentaries including The Civil War, Napoleon, 2000, Abraham & Mary Lincoln: A House Divided, 2001. Mem. Harry S. Truman Centennial Commn.; trustee Nat. Trust Hist. Preservation, Harry S. Truman Libr. Inst., Hist. Soc. Western Pa., Jefferson Meml. Found., Boston Pub. Libr.; hon. trustee Carnegie Inst.; founding mem. Protect Hist. Am. Guggenheim fellow, 1986; recipient N.Y. Diamond Jubilee award, 1973, cert. of merit Mcpl. Art Soc. N.Y., 1973, Nat. Book award for history, 1978, Francis Parkman prize, 1978, 93, Samuel Eliot Morison award, 1978, Cornelius Ryan award, 1978, Civil Engring. History and Heritage award, 1978, L.A. Times prize for biography, 1981, Am. Book award for biography, 1982, Harry S. Truman Pub. Svc. award, 1993, St. Louis Lit. award, 1993, Pa. Gov.'s award for excellence, 1993, Pa. Soc. Gold Medal award, 1994, Charles Frankel prize contributions to humanities Endowment Humanities U.S. Govt., 1995, Disting. Contbns. to Am. Letters award. Nat. Book Found., Lit. Lion award N.Y. Pub. Libr., 1981, Emmy award for work in pub. TV, 1985, Gold medal Pa. Soc., Carl Sandburg Lit. award, 2000, Am. Revolution Round Table Book award, 2001, LA Pub. Libr. Lit. award, 2002, William Bradford award, Pilgrim Soc., 2002, Christopher award, 2002, Robin Winks award, Nat. Pks. Conservation Assn., 2003. Fellow Soc. Am. Historians (pres.); mem. ASCE (hon.), Am. Acad. Arts and Scis., Am. Acad. Arts and Letters, Soc. Am. Historians (pres. 1991—). Avocations: travel, reader, landscape painter, sunday night spaghetti chef. Office: Janklow & Nesbit Associates 445 Park Ave # 13th New York NY 10022-2606*

**MCCULLOUGH, DAVID LEGARDE,** urologist; b. Chattanooga, 1938; MD, Bowman Gray, 1964. Intern U. Hosps. Case Western Res. U., Cleve., 1964-65, resident in surgery, 1965-66; fellow urology Baylor U. Coll. Medicine, Houston, 1968-69; resident in urology Mass. Gen. Hosp., Boston, 1969-72; chief urologist N.C. Bapt. Hosp., Winston-Salem, 1983—; prof., former chmn. urology Wake Forest U. Coll. Medicine, Winston-Salem. Past pres. Am. Bd. Urology. Mem. ACS, AMA, Am. Urol. Assn. (past pres. southeastern sect., past pres., bd. dirs., chair for edn.), Am. Assn. Genitourinary Surgeons (past pres.), Clin. Soc. Urol. Surgeons, Halsted Soc. Office Phone: 336-716-4131.

**MCCULLOUGH, EDWARD L.,** artist, educator; b. Danville, Ill., Sept. 18, 1934; s. Fred and Helen McCullough; m. Gale Carter Carter, Dec. 15, 1954; children: Scott, Reggie Johnson, Allison McClendon. BS, Ill. State U., 1962, MA, 1966. Assoc. prof. of art Ill. Wesleyan U., Bloomington, 1966—80; adj. prof. of art Columbia Coll., Chgo., 1990—. Sculpture, Meridian Vii, Chgo. Pub. Art Program, 2001, sculpture, Meridian Viii, Dominican U., River Forest, Ill., 2005, sculpture, Meridian Vi Ctrl. Ill. Regional Airport, Bloomington, Ill., 2001, Meridian Iii, Ea. Ill. U., 1997, VISION, Fed. Bank Res. of Chgo., 1998. With USN, 1955—59. Fellow Artist in Residence Program, Nat. Endowment of the Arts, 1980, 1981; Project Completion grant, Ill. Arts Coun., 1985. Mem.: Chgo. Sculpture Soc., Internat. Sculpture Soc., Chgo. Artists Coalition (assoc.). Home: 421 N First St Cissna Park IL 60924-9789 Home Fax: 815-457-3010.

**MCCULLOUGH, EILEEN (EILEEN MCCULLOUGH LEPAGE, ELLI MCCULLOUGH),** financial consultant, writer, editor, educator; b. Phila., Oct. 16, 1946; d. Charles Norman and Marie Teresa (Inglesby) McCullough; m. Clifford Bennett LePage Jr., Mar. 6, 1970; children: Clifford Bennett III, Alexander Pierce. BA in English and Secondary Edn., George Washington U., Washington, D.C., 1969; MEd in Spl. Edn., Temple U., Phila., 1972. Cert. secondary sch. tchr.; registered securities rep. Record-keeper child growth and devel. program Children's Hosp. of Phila., 1965; with advt. dept. Phila. Inquirer, 1966-67; with ops. control U.S. Civil Svc. Commn., Washington, 1967-69; mgr. N.J. Bell Telephone, Trenton, 1969; rschr. Temple U., Phila, 1969-71; tchr. Wyomissing, Pa., 1972-77; fin. cons. various orgns., 1984-93; cons. EMLC, Reading, 1994—. Adj. instr. Reading (Pa.) Area C.C., 1978-81; lectr. English Albright Coll., Reading, 1981-84; founding mem. Common

Cents Investment Club, 1983-93; founding and mng. ptnr. Klein LePage McCullough Partnership, Ocean City, N.J., 1982-96; presenter in field. Author: The Clue in the Cavern, 1959; editor: 1st Complete Pocket Guide to Atlantic City Casinos, 1984, The Autobiography of Capt. Michael Kevolic, 1986; photographer Cherry Hill Mtg. Bd. dirs. Nat. Found. March of Dimes, Reading, 1969-75, chmn., 1974-75; bd. sch. dirs. Wyomissing Area Sch. Dist., 1984-92; bd. dirs. Wyomissing Pub. Libr., Reading, 1980-85; asst. chmn Region 8 Pa. Sch. Bds. Assn., 1989-91; dir. Saturday Morning Sch., Assn. for Children with Learning Disabilities, Reading, 1970; acting sec. Berks County Commn. for Women, Reading, 1993; active Reading Community Players, 1980; past bd. mem. Berks Ballet Theatre; past vol. Berks C. of C.; vol. mus. guide Reading Pub. Mus. and Art Gallery, 1999-2002, Berks County Chpt Am. Red Cross, 1997; presenter Green Circle, Reading Berks Human Rels. coun., Reading Pub. Schs., 1998-99. Fellow Pa. writing project; mem. AAUW (life; topic chmn.), Am. Assn. Individual Investors (life), Internat. Platform Soc., Women's Internat. Fedn. for World Peace. Avocations: dance, singing. Home and Office: EMLC 10 Phoebe Dr Reading PA 19610-2857 E-mail: emlco@comcast.net.

**MCCULLOUGH, FRANK WITCHER, III,** lawyer; b. New Orleans, Dec. 13, 1945; s. Frank Witcher, Jr. and Kathleen Elizabeth (Van Pelt) McCullough; m. Barry Jean Bock, Mar. 7, 1981; children: William David Oat, Frank Witcher IV, Elizabeth Layton. BA, Stetson U., 1967; JD, W.Va. U., 1970. Bar: W.Va. 1970, Tex. 1970, U.S. Dist. Ct. (so. dist.) W.Va. 1970, U.S. Dist. Ct. (so. dist.) Tex. 1972, U.S. Ct. Appeals (5th cir.) 1972, U.S. Supreme Ct. 1980, U.S. Dist. Ct. (no. dist.) Calif. 1983, U.S. Dist. Ct. (we. dist.) Tex. 1987, U.S. Dist. Ct. (ea. dist.) Tex. 1993. Indsl. rels. specialist Continental Oil Co., Houston, 1970-72; asst. U.S. atty.'s Office, Houston, 1972-75; assoc. Baker & Botts, Houston, 1975-76, Austin, Tex., 1985-89; ptnr. Weiner Strother & Lamkin, Houston, 1983-85; regional counsel GATX Leasing Corp., Houston, 1976-78; ptnr. Walsh Squires Tompkins & McCullough, Houston, 1978-82; shareholder Sheinfeld, Maley & Kay, Austin, 1989-2001, Diamond McCarthy Taylor & Finley, Austin, 2001—04, Haynes and Boone, LLP, Austin, 2004—. Spl. commr. Harris County, Houston, 1982; mem. Bellaire (Tex.) Bd. Adjustments, 1982; bd. dirs. Big Bros. and Big Sisters Austin, 1991—94. Mem.: SAR, State Bar Tex. (mem. grievance com. 1979—87, chmn. unauthorized practice law com. 1984—87, mem. grievance com. 1995—2001, panel chair 2000—01), Stetson U. Alumni Assn. (bd. dirs 2006—), Austin Country Club. Republican. Episcopalian. Home: 6707 Bridge Hill Cv Austin TX 78746-1338 Office: Haynes and Boone LLP 600 Congress Ave Ste 1300 Austin TX 78701 *Notable cases include: Univ. Savs. Assn. vs. Springwood Shopping Ctr., 1982, in which the Tex. Supreme Ct. created significant exception to the rule of law that the terms and provisions of deed of trust must be strictly followed in foreclosure proceeding.*

**MCCULLOUGH, GLENN L., JR.,** electric power industry executive; b. Tupelo, Miss. m. Laura White; children: Vance, Glenn Thomas. Degree in agrl. econ., Miss. State U., 1977. Dir. Appalachian Regional Commn. (ARC), Miss., 1992—97; mayor Tupelo, Miss., 1997—99; chmn., bd. dirs. Tenn. Valley Authority 1999—. Mem. Nat. Electric Adv. Bd., Dept. Energy; mem. bd. Miss. Partnership Econ. Devel., Econ. Devel. Partnership, Ala.; mem. governing bd. Electric Power Rsch. Inst., Inst. Nuc. Power Ops., Nuc. Energy Inst. Governing bd. United Way; mem. Big Bros./Big Sisters Orgn.; governing bd. Cmty. Devel. Found., Commn. Future Northeast Miss. Recipient All-Am. City award, Nat. Civic League, 1999. Office: Tenn Valley Authority 400 W Summit Hill Dr Knoxville TN 37902-1499 Office Phone: 865-632-2600. Business E-Mail: tvaineot@va.gov.

**MC CULLOUGH, J. LEE,** industrial psychologist; b. Bryn Mawr, Pa., Oct. 3, 1945; s. Leo Francis and Margaret Mary (Hart) McC.; m. Bonnie R. Goldberg, Jan. 14, 1979. AB, Villanova U., 1967; MA, Ohio State U., 1968, PhD, 1971. Tchg. asst. Ohio State U., 1967-68, rsch. assoc., 1968-69; assoc. O.P.S. Assocs., Columbus, 1970-71; assoc., sr. assoc., sr. prin., v.p Hay Group, N.Y.C., 1971-90, v.p., dir. fin. svcs. cons., 1990-94; prin. William M. Mercer, Inc., N.Y.C., 1994—2006; fin. cons. Towers Perrin, Inc., N.Y.C., 2006—. Adj. prof. Fordham U. Grad. Sch. Bus., 1984-89. Served with AUS, 1972. NSF fellow, 1969; NDEA Title IV fellow, 1970; Univ. Dissertation Year fellow, 1971. Mem. Am. Psychol. Soc., Met. Psychol. Assn. Home: 6 Hereford Dr Princeton Junction NJ 08550-1514 Office: Towers Perrin Inc 21st Fl 335 Madison Ave New York NY 10017-4605 Office Phone: 212-345-7844, 212-309-3712. Personal E-mail: LeeMcCull@comcast.net. Business E-Mail: lee.mccullough@mercer.com, lee.mccullough@towersperrin.com.

**MCCULLOUGH, JAMES,** composer, writer, retired art association administrator, writer; b. Richmond, Va., Feb. 2, 1939; s. William J. McCullough and Maggie McMoore. BS Mus. Edn., Va. State U.; grad., New Eng. Conservatory Music. Head Curriculum Rsch. Ctr. Boston State Coll. (now U. Mass.), 1967—95; sr. arts administr. music, lit. & folk life Mass. Coun. Arts, Humanities & Scis. (now Mass. Cultural Coun.), 1996—2002; ret., 2003. Dir. music publs. Amarilli Press, Boston, 1965—90; soloist, composer-in-residence Old South Ch., Boston, 1971—82; lit. cons. Adult Literacy Resource Inst., Boston, 1990—95. Stage dir.: Cambridge Opera Co., 1965—67. Panel mem. music theater and opera Nat. Endowment Arts, Washington, 1992; chorus bd. Handel & Haydn Soc., Boston, 1970—73; bd. dirs. Strand Theatre, Boston, 1995—98. Recipient Pride in Performance award, Gov. Mass., 1998. Mem.: Am. Choral Dirs. Assn., Am. Soc. Composers, Authors and Pubs., Alpha Phi Alpha, Phi Mu Alpha. Avocation: collecting books, CDs, DVDs of choral and chamber music. Home: 4400 Killiam Ct Glen Allen VA 23060-6486

**MCCULLOUGH, JOHN PHILLIP,** management consultant, educator; b. Lincoln, Ill., Feb. 2, 1945; s. Phillip and Lucile Ethel (Ornellas) McC.; m. Barbara Elaine Carley, Nov. 29, 1968; children: Carley Jo, Ryan Phillip. BS, Ill. State U., 1967, MS, 1968; PhD, U. N.D., 1971. Adminstrv. mgr. McCullough Ins. Agy., Atlanta, Ill., 1963-68; ops. supr. Stetson China Co., Lincoln, 1967; asst. mgr. Brandtville Svc., Inc., Bloomington, Ill., 1968; instr. in bus. Ill. Ctrl. Coll., 1968-69; rsch. assist. U. N.D., Grand Forks, 1969-71; assoc. prof. mgmt. West Liberty State Coll., 1971-74, prof., 1974—. Chmn. dept. mgmt., West Liberty State Coll., 1974-82, dir. Sch. Bus., 1982-86, dean, 1986—, provost, 1998—; instr. mgmt., 2001, dir. Small Bus. Inst., 1978—; mgmt. cons., Triadelphia, W.Va., 1971—; instr. Am. Inst. Banking, 1971—; lectr. W.Va. U., 1971—; adj. prof. MBA program Wheeling Coll., 1972—, U. Steubenville, 1982—; lectr. Ohio U., 1982—; profl. assoc. Inst. Mgmt. and Human Behavior, 1975—; v.p. West Liberty State Coll. Fed. Credit Union, 1976—; rep. W.Va. Bd. Regents Adv. Coun. of Faculty. Author: (with Howard Fryette) Primer in Supervisory Management, 1973; contbr. articles to profl. jours. Team leader Wheeling divsn. Am. Cancer Soc.; coord. Upper Ohio Valley United Fund, 1972-74; instr. AFL-CIO Cmty. Svcs. Program, Wheeling; project dir. Ctr. for Edn. and Rsch. with Industry; bd. dirs. Family Svc.-Upper Ohio Valley, Ohio Valley Indsl. and Bus. Devel. Corp., Inc., Labor Mgmt. Inst. Wheeling Salvation Army, Progress, Inc., Ohio Valley Health Svcs. and Edn. Corp. Recipient Svc. award Bank Adminstrn. Inst., 1974, United Fund, 1973, Acad. Achievement award Harris-Casals Found., 1971. Mem. Soc. Humanistic Mgmt. (nat. chmn.), ORgn. Planning Mgmt. Assn. (exec. com.), Spl. Interest Group for Dcrt. Bus. Educators (nat. dir.), Soc. Advancement Mgmt. (chpt. advisor), Acad. Mgmt., Adminstrv. Mgmt. Soc. (cert.), Am. Soc. Pers. Adminstrn. (cert.), Nat. Bus. Honor Soc. (Excellence in Tchg. award 1976, dir. 1974—), Alpha Kappa Psi (Dist. Svc. award 1973, Civic award 1977, chpt. advisor 1971—), Merit Found. W.Va. (Ednl. Excellence award), Delta Mu Delta, Delta Pi Epsilon, Delta Tau Kappa, Phi Gamma Nu, Phi Theta Pi, Pi Gamma Mu, Pi Omega Pi, Omicron Delta Epsilon. Home: 68 Elm Dr Triadelphia WV 26059-9620 Office Phone: 304-336-8004. Business E-Mail: mccullljp@ulsc.edu.

**MCCULLOUGH, JOHN PRICE,** retired oil company executive; b. Dallas, May 10, 1925; s. John A. and Alta (McGee) McC.; m. Mary Ann Calvert, Aug. 5, 1946; children: Sherri, Cathryn, Patricia. Student U. Denver, 1942-43; BS in Chem. Engring. U. Okla. 1945; MS, Oreg. State U., 1948, PhD in Chemistry, 1949. With U.S. Bur. Mines, Bartlesville, Okla., 1949-63, phys. chemist, 1949-57, chief thermodynamics br., 1958-63; mgr. central research div. Mobil Oil Corp., Princeton, NJ, 1963-69, mgr. applied research and devel. Paulsboro, NJ, 1969-71; gen. mgr. research and devel. Mobil Chem. Co., Edison, NJ, 1971-78; v.p. environ. health and safety Mobil Research & Devel. Corp., Princeton, NJ, 1978-89. Adj. prof. chemistry Okla. State U., Stillwater, 1961-63; vis. fellow Woodrow Wilson Found., 1991-95; dir. Internat. Petroleum Industry Environ. Conservation Assn., 1983-89, chmn., 1985-88; dir. Mobil Found., Inc., 1987-89. Co-author: (with Donald Scott) Experimental Thermodynamics, Volume I: Calorimetry of Non-reacting Systems, 1968; contbr. 90 articles on thermodynamics, molecular structure and energetics, environ. and health policy to profl. jours. Mem. adv. com. Mercer County (N.J.) C.C., 1968-69; bd. dirs. Chem. Industry Inst. Toxicology, 1977-89, chmn., 1986-88; bd. dirs. United Cmty. Fund, Princeton, 1963-69, Middlesex-Somerset-Mercer Regional Study Coun., 1968-69, 86-89, World Environ. Ctr., 1986-89; mem. adv. bd. Georgetown U. Inst. Health Policy Analysis, 1986-89; trustee Stony Brook-Millstone Watershed Assn., 1989-95, vice chmn., 1991-93, adv. bd., 1996-99; trustee Friends of Art Mus. Princeton U., 1994-2000, treas., 1997-2001; elder Nassau Presbyn. Ch. Lt. (j.g.) USNR, 1943-54. Recipient Meritorious Svc. award U.S. Dept. Interior, 1959, Disting. Svc. award, 1962; DuPont fellow, 1947-48. Mem. AAAS, Gordon Rsch. Conf. (trustee, chmn. bd. trustees, mem. coun.), Am. Chem. Soc. (editl. bd. Jour. Chem. and Engring. Data, Jour. Phys. Chemistry, mem. coun. com. on chemistry and pub. affairs 1984-92, chmn. 1987-89, award for petroleum chemistry 1963, Chemtech. award 1977), Internat. Calorimetry Conf. (chmn. 1970, S.C. Study Sentencing), Am. Inst. Chemists, Sigma Xi. Home: 7 Fringe Tree Ct Princeton NJ 08540-5061 E-mail: jmccullough55@comcast.net.

**MCCULLOUGH, JOSEPH,** retired academic administrator; b. Pitts., July 6, 1922; s. Joseph Phillip and Margaret (List) McC.; m. Elizabeth Cramer, Mar. 31, 1945; children— Marjorie Ann, Warren BFA, Yale U., 1949-50, MFA, 1951; Diploma, Cleve. Sch. Art, 1948; DFA (hon.), U. Evansville, Ind. 1980; DA (hon.), Cleve. Inst. Art, 1996. Instr. San Jose State Coll., Calif., 1948-49; asst. instr. Yale U., New Haven, 1949-51; asst. dir. Cleve. Inst. Art, 1952-54, dir., 1954-74, pres., 1974-88. Artist paintings, nat. regional and local exhbns., 1948— Chmn. Fine Arts Adv. Com., Cleve. Planning Commn., 1963-91; trustee Mpls. Coll. of Art and Design, 1988-98, Sculpture Ctr. Cleve., 1990-98; trustee, sec. Access to the Arts, Cleve., 1991-95. Capt. USAAF, 1943-46, ETO. Recipient Cleve. Arts prize Women's City Club, 1971, Centennial medal John Carroll U., 1987, medal for excellence Cleve. Inst. of Art, 1997. Mem.: Coll. Art Assn. ((past dir.)). Home: 20101 North Park Blvd Cleveland OH 44118-5006

**MCCULLOUGH, M. BRUCE,** judge; b. Princeton, N.J., July 26, 1944; s. Malcolm S. and Ruth S. (Strandness) McC.; m. Kathleen M. Ryan, Apr. 12, 1985. BA in Polit. Sci. and Econs., Whitworth Coll., 1966; JD, U. Mich., 1969. Bar: Pa., Fla., D.C. Ptnr. Buchanan Ingersoll P.C., Pitts., 1969-95; judge U.S. Bankruptcy Ct., Pitts., 1995—. Chmn. ARC (southwest Pa., 1994-96). With USAR, 1969-75. Mem. Chartiers Country Club, Duquesne Club. Avocations: golf, boating, hunting. Office: US Bankruptcy Ct 600 Grant St Pittsburgh PA 15219-2702

**MCCULLOUGH, RALPH CLAYTON, II,** law educator; b. Daytona Beach, Fla., Mar. 28, 1941; s. Ralph C. and Doris (Johnson) McCullough; m. Elizabeth Grier Henderson, Apr. 5, 1986; children: Melissa Wells, Clayton Baldwin. Ba, Erskine Coll., 1962; JD, Tulane U., 1965. Bar: La. 1965, SC 1974. Assoc. Gelhaus, Haspel, Maloney, Rainold and Meyer, New Orleans, 1965-68; from asst. prof. law to prof. U. SC, 1968—2002, disting. prof., 2002—03, provost Charleston Sch. Law, 2005—; adj. prof. medicine Med. U. SC, 1984—; of counsel Finkel & Altman, 1978—. Adj. prof. pathology Med. U. SC 1985—; asst. dean U. SC Sch. Law 1970-75, Disting. prof. law, 2001, Disting. prof. law emeritus, 2003—; mem. adv. com. rules and procedures US Ct. Appeals (4th cir.), 2001—, chair, 2006—; bd. vis. Med. U. SC. Author: (with J.L. Underwood) The Civil Trial Manual, 1974, 7th supplement, 1987, The Civil Trial Manual II, 1984, 87, (with Myers and Felix) New Directions in Legal Education, 1970, (with Finkel) S.C. Torts II, 1986, III, 1990, IV, 1995; co-reporter S.C. Criminal Code, 1977, S.C. Study Sentencing, 1977. Mem. ATLA, ABA, La. Bar Assn., SC Bar (sec. 1975-76, exec. dir. 1972-76, award of service 1978), New Orleans Bar Assn., Am. Law Inst. (life), Am. Coll. Trial Lawyers, Southeastern Assn. Am. Law Schs. (pres.), SC Trial Lawyers Assn. (bd. govs. 1984-88), Forest Lake Club, Phi Alpha Delta. Republican. Episcopalian. Home: PO Box 939 Charleston SC 29402 Office: 440 King St Charleston SC 29402 Office Phone: 843-329-1000 ext. 2426. Business E-mail: rmccullough@charlestonlaw.org.

**MCCULLOUGH, RICHARD LAWRENCE,** advertising executive; b. Chgo., Dec. 1, 1937; s. Francis John and Sadie Beatrice McCullough; m. Julia Louise Kreimer, May 6, 1961; children: Stephen, Jeffrey, Julie. BS, Marquette U., 1959. Commd. U.S. Army, 1959, advance through grades to sgt., 1966; account exec. Edward H. Weiss Advt., Chgo., 1960-66; account supr. Doyle Dane Bernbach, N.Y.C., 1966-68; sr. v.p. J. Walter Thompson Co., Chgo., 1969-86; pres. E.H. Brown Advt., Chgo., 1986-97; exec. v.p. Space-Time Media Mgmt., Chgo., 1997—; ptnr. Callahan Group, Chgo., 2000—. Developer Mktg. with Country Music nat. seminar, 1996. Author: Building Country Radio, 1986, A New Look at Country Music Audiences, 1988, (video) Country Music Marketing, 1989. Bd. dirs. Gateway Found., Chgo., 1976—, chmn., 1988-91; bd. dirs., chmn. mktg. com. Cath. Charities, Chgo. Recipient Nat. Cmty. Svc. award, Gateway Found., 2002, Dennis Kelly Honor award, Cath. Charities, 2002. Mem. Country Music Assn. (Nashville bd. dirs. 1979—, pres. 1983-85, Pres.'s award 1987, elector Country Music Hall of Fame), NARAS (Nashville chpt.), North Shore Country Club (Glenview, Ill.), Dairymen's Country Club (Boulder Junction, Wis.), Quail Creek Country Club (Naples, Fla.). Roman Catholic. Home: 2720 Lincoln St Evanston IL 60201-2043 Office: Space-Time Media Mgmt Inc 35 E Wacker Dr Chicago IL 60601-2103 Home: 2720 Lincoln St Evanston IL 60201-2043 E-mail: dick@spacetimemedia.com, relchar@aol.com.

**MCCULLOUGH, ROBERT DALE, II,** osteopath; b. Tulsa, June 2, 1937; s. Robert Dale and Roberta Maud (Purdy) McC.; m. Lindell Arlene Wilcox, Sept. 28, 1963; children: Robert Mark, Lori Lindell. Student, Wheaton (Ill.) Coll., 1955-57; BS, N.E. Mo. State U., 1958; DO, Kansas City (Mo.) Coll. Osteopathy, 1958-62. Diplomate in internal medicine and med. oncology Am. Osteo. Bd. Internal Medicine. Gen. practice McCullough Clinic, Tulsa, 1963-68; internal medicine resident Detroit Osteo. Hosp., 1968-71; internal medicine Baker-Todd-McCullough-Sutton, Tulsa, 1971-74; fellow med. oncology M.D. Anderson Hosp., Houston, 1974-75; internal medicine-med. oncology Baker-Todd-McCullough-Sutton, Tulsa, 1975-90; pvt. practice Tulsa, 1990-93; attending staff mem. VA Outpatient Clinic, Tulsa, 1993-94; assoc. med. dir. Blue Cross/Blue Shield of Okla., Tulsa, 1994—2005. Trustee Tulsa Regional Med. Cttr., 1983-88, 90-93; bd. dirs. Okla. Blue Cross Blue Shield, Tulsa, 1983-92, vice chmn., 1991-92; mem. adv. coun. Okla. State U. Coll. Osteo. Medicine, 1988-94, chmn. 1988-90; part-time worker VA and Indian Health Svc. Mem. bd. editors Patient Care Magazine, Montvale, N.J., 1988-93. Mem. Okla. State Bd. Health, Oklahoma City, 1983—87, Tulsa City/County Bd. Health, 1988—95, chmn., 1993; bd. mem. Cmty. Health Found., 1997—, chmn., 2003—05. Mem. Nat. Osteo. Found. (trustee 1993-00, treas. 1998-00), Am. Osteo. Assn. (vice speaker Ho. of Dels. 1986-92, trustee 1993-00), Am. Coll. Osteo. Internists, Okla. Osteo. Assn. (pres. 1982-83), Tulsa Downtown Lions Club, Soc. for Preservation and Encouragement of Barbershop Quartet Singing in Am. Republican. Southern Baptist. Avocation: barbershop quartets. Home: 5803 E 75th Pl Tulsa OK 74136-7255 Personal E-mail: RMccull207@aol.com.

**MCCULLOUGH, ROSS A., JR.,** delivery service executive; b. Decatur, Ill., Mar. 18, 1966; s. Ross A. and Laura K. McCullough; m. Cindy E. Mullinax, June 11, 1992; children: Ross III, Gracie. MBA, Emory U., 1996; BS in Indsl. Tech., Ga. Inst. Tech., 1987. Mgr. strategic planning UPS, Atlanta, 1994—96, v.p. electronic commerce, 1996—2001, v.p. corp. strategy Brussels, 2001—03, v.p. mktg. supply chain solutions Alpharetta, Ga., 2004—. Mem.: Coun. Logistics Mgmt. Office: UPS Supply Chain Solutions 12380 Morris Rd Alpharetta GA 30005

**MCCULLOUGH, V. BETH,** pharmacist, educator; b. Harrison, Ark., May 15, 1953; d. A. G. and Willene L. (McLain) McC.; m. David Mark Pearson, Oct. 25, 1980; children: Colin McCullough-Pearson, Emily McCullough-Pearson. BS in Edn. cum laude, S.W. Mo. State U., 1976; BS in Pharmacy, U. Mo., 1981. Registered Pharmacist, Mo. Chief pharmacist Mt. Vernon Park Pharmacy, Springfield, Mo., 1981-89; dir. pharmacy Foster Health Care Group, Springfield, 1989-96; chief pharmacy ops. Balanced Care Corp./Foster Health Care Group, Springfield, 1996-97; cons. pharmacist Managed Healthcare Pharmacy divsn. Omnicare Corp., Springfield, 1997-2001; owner Med. Park Pharmacy, Eureka Springs, Ark., 2001—. Long term care pharmacy cons. Foster Health Care Group, Springfield, 1981-83, Managed Healthcare Pharmacy, Springfield, 1997-2001. Mem. NOW, Springfield, 1982—, assoc. mem. Animal Shelter League of the Ozarks, Nixa, Mo. Mem. Am. Soc. Cons. Pharmacists, Southwest Mo. Humane Soc., Mo. Equine Coun., Mo. Pharmacy Assn., Long Term Care Acad., Biokinetics (instnl. rev. bd. 1999-2001). Avocations: watercolor painting, jewelry making, horse breeding and showing. Office: 146 Passion Play Rd Eureka Springs AR 72632-9495 Home: 146 CR 238 Berryville AR 72616 Office Phone: 479-253-9751. E-mail: medparkpharm@aol.com.

**MCCULLY, EMILY ARNOLD,** illustrator, writer; b. Galesburg, Ill., 1939; d. Wade E. and Kathryn (Maher) Arnold; m. George E. McCully, 1961 (div. 1975); children: Nathaniel, Tad. BA, Brown U., 1961; MA, Columbia U., 1964; LittD (hon.), Brown U., 2002. Author: How's Your Vacuum Cleaner Working? O'Henry Collection, 1977, A Craving, 1982, (novel) Picnic, 1984 (Christopher award), First Snow, 1985, (novel) Life Drawing, 1986, The Show Must Go On, 1987, School, 1987, You Lucky Duck!, 1988, New Baby, 1988, Grandma's at the Lake, 1990, The Evil Spell, 1990, Speak Up, Blanche!, 1991, Mirette on the Highwire, 1992 (Caldecott medal 1992), Grandma's at Bat, 1993, The Amazing Felix, 1994, My Real Family, 1994, Crossing The New Bridge, 1994, Little Kit, or: The Industrious Flea Circus Girl, 1995, The Pirate Queen, 1995, The Ballot Box Battle, 1996, The Bobbin Girl, 1996, Popcorn at the Palace, 1997, Starring Mirette and Bellini, 1997, an Outlaw Thanksgiving, 1998, Beautiful Warrior, 1998, Mouse Practice, 1999, Monk Camps Out, 2000, The Orphan Singer, 2001, Four Hungry Kittens, 2001, Squirrel and John Muir, 2004; illustrator: Sea Beach Express, 1966, The Seventeenth Street Gang, 1966, Rex, 1967, Luigi of the Streets, 1967, That Mean Man, 1968, Gooney, 1968, Journey From Peppermint Street, 1968 (Nat. Book award 1969), The Mouse and the Elephant, 1969, The Fisherman, 1969, Tales from the Rue Brocca, 1969, Here I Am, 1969, Twin Spell, 1969, Hobo Toad and the Motorcycle Gang, 1970, Slip! Slop! Gobble!, 1970, Friday Night is Papa Night, 1970, Maxie, 1970, Steffie and Me, 1970, The Cat and the Parrot, 1970, Gertrude's Pocket, 1970, Go and Hush the Baby, 1971, Finders Keepers, 1971, Ma n Da La, 1971 (Bklyn. Mus. award 1976, N.Y. Pub. Libr. award 1976), Hurray for Captain Jane!, 1971, Michael Is Brave, 1971, Finding Out With Your Senses, 1971, Henry's Pennies, 1972, Jane's Blanket, 1972, Grandpa's Long Red Underwear, 1972, Girls Can Too!, 1972, The Boyhood of Grace Jones, 1972, Black Is Brown Is Tan, 1973, Isabelle the Itch, 1973, When Violet Died, 1973, That New Boy, 1973, How To Eat Fried Worms, 1973, Jenny's Revenge, 1974, Her Majesty, Grace Jones, 1974, Tree House Town, 1974, I Want Mama, 1974, Amanda, the Panda and the Redhead, 1975, The Bed Book, 1976, My Street's A Morning Cool Street, 1976, Professor Coconut and the Thief, 1977, Martha's Mad Dog, 1977, That's Mine, 1977, Where Wild Willie, 1978, No Help At All, 1978, Partners, 1978, The Twenty-Elephant Restaurant, 1978, What I Did Last Summer, 1978, The Highest Hit, 1978, I and Spraggy, 1978, Edward Troy and the Witch Cat, 1978, My Island Grandma, 1979, Whatever Happened to Beverly Bigler's Birthday?, 1979, Last Look, 1979, Ookie-Spooky, 1979, The Black Dog Who Went Into the Woods, 1980, How I Found Myself at the Fair, 1980, How We Got Our First Cat, 1980, Oliver and Allison's Week, 1980, Pajama Walking, 1981, The Golly Fowl, 1981, I Dance in My Red Pajamas, 1982, The Halloween Candy Mystery, 1982, Go and Mush the Baby, 1982, Mitzi and the Terrible Tyrannosaurus Rex, 1983, Best Friend Insurance, 1983, Mail-Order Wings, 1984, Gertrude's Pocket, 1984, Fifth Grade Magic, 1984, The Ghastly Glasses, 1985, Fourth of July, 1985, The Explorer of Barkham Street, 1985, Wheels, 1986, Lulu and the Witch Baby, 1986, Richard and the Vratch, 1987, Molly, 1987, Molly Goes Hiking, 1987, Jam Day, 1987, The Boston Coffee Party, 1988, The Take-Along Dog, 1989, Selene Goes Home, 1989, The Magic Mean Machine, 1989, It Always Happens to Leona, 1989, The Grandpa Days, 1989, Dinah's Mad, Bad Wishes, 1989, Stepbrother Sabotage, 1990, Lulu Goes to Witch School, 1990, The Day Chubby Became Charles, 1990, The Christmas Present Mystery, 1990, Bad Guys to White Cat, 1991, Meatball, 1991, Leona and Ike, 1991, The Butterfly Birthday, 1991, Yankee Doodle Drumsticks, 1992, One Very Best Valentine's Day, 1992, Meet the Lincoln Lions Band, 1992, Jingle Bells Jam, 1992, In My Tent, 1992, Anne Flies the Birthday Bike, 1993, Amzat and His Brothers, 1993, Leo the Magnificent, 1996, Old Home Day, 1996, The Divide, 1997, Rabbit Pirates, 1999, Sing a Song of Piglets: A Calender in Verse, 2002, One, Two, ILove You, 2004.

**MCCULLY, THOMAS RICHARDSON,** lawyer; b. Rushville, Ind., Mar. 10, 1941; s. Kenneth Brody and Frances (Richardson) McCully; m. Susan C. McCully, Dec. 5, 1998; children: Julie A., Thomas R. II, Michael G. stepchildren: Keith W. Long, Thomas Long. BA Polit. Sci., Philosophy, Wabash Coll., Crawfordsville, Ind., 1963; JD with distinction, Ind. U., Bloomington, 1966. Bar: Ind. 1966, U.S. Dist. Ct. (So. Dist.) Ind. 1966, U.S. Dist. Ct. (No. Dist.) Ind 1968, U.S. Ct. Appeals (7th cir.) 1973, U.S. Supreme Ct. 1973. Assoc. Stuart & Branigin, LLP, Lafayette, Ind., 1966—71, ptnr., 1971—. Guest lectr. Purdue U. Lafayette, Ind.; frequent speaker, author Ind. Continuing Legal Edn. Forum, Lohrman Bus. Ctr. Lafayette; speaker Greater Lafayette Small Bus. Devel. Ctr.; bd. dirs. LSB Fin. Corp. and Lafayette Savings Bank, Ind., 1999—. Pres. Highland Sch. PTA; exec. com. Gus Macker, Lafayette, 1997—2001; Elder Ctrl. Presbyn. Ch., Lafayette; bd. dirs Ctrl. Presbyn Found., Lafayette, Legal Aid Corp., Tippecanoe County, Ind., 1974—96, pres., 1987—89; bd. visitors Ind. U. Sch. Law, Bloomington, Ind., 1994—; bd. dirs. Jr. Achievement of Greater Lafayette, 1994—, Harrison Trails and Sagamore Couns., Boy Scouts Am. (past), Lafayette, Vol. Bur. Tippecanoe County (past). Named one of Best Lawyers in Am., 1987—; recipient Pro Bono Publico award, Ind. Bar Found., 1995. Master: Ind. Bar Found. (fellow); mem.: ABA, Am. Health Lawyers Assn., Ind. State Bar Assn. (mem. spl. com. to revise Ind. Zoning Laws 1982—88, chmn. land use and zoning sect. 1992—94), Tippecanoe County Bar Assn., John Purdue Club, Lafayette Country Club (legal counsel 1977—), Ind. U. Varsity Club, Elks Lodge 143, Phi Delta Phi. Office: Stuart & Branigin LLP 300 Main St Ste 900 Lafayette IN 47902 Office Phone: 765-423-1561. Office Fax: 765-742-8125. Business E-mail: trm@stuartlaw.com.

**MC CUNE, BARRON PATTERSON,** retired federal judge; b. West Newton, Pa., Feb. 19, 1915; s. James Patterson and Lyda Barron (Hammond) McC.; m. Edna Flannery Markey, Dec. 23, 1943; children: Edward M., James H., Barron Patterson. AB, Washington and Jefferson Coll., 1935; LLB, U. Pa., 1938. Bar: Pa. bar 1939. Practiced in, Washington, Pa., 1939-62; judge 27th Jud. Dist. Ct. Common Pleas, Washington, Pa., 1964-71, U.S. Dist. Ct., Western Dist. Pa., Pitts., 1971-95, sr. fed. judge; ret., 1995. Trustee emeritus Washington and Jefferson Coll.; bd. dirs. emeritus Washington (Pa.) Hosp. Served with USNR, 1942-45. Home: 144 Lemoyne Ave Washington PA 15301-3636

**MCCUNE, JOSEPH MIKE,** epidemiologist, educator, researcher; AB in biochemistry, Harvard Univ.; PhD, Rockefeller U., 1981; MD in cell biology/immunology, Cornell Med. Coll., 1982. Diplomate in internal medicine 1987. Resident in internal medicine U. Calif., San Francisco, 1982—84, infectious disease fellow, 1984—86, assoc. prof. medicine, 1995—; postdoctoral fellow, dept. pathology Stanford U. Sch. Medicine, 1985—88; physician U. Calif., AIDS Clinic, San Francisco Gen. Hosp., 1987—; sci. dir. SyStemix, Inc., 1988—91, founder, v.p. New Enterprise Rsch. Divsn., 1991—94; assoc. investigator Gladstone Inst. Virology and Immunology, 1995—99, sr. investigator, 1999—; assoc. dir. Gen. Clin. Rsch. Ctr. San Francisco Gen. Hosp., 1995—. Dir. SyStemix-Sandoz Antiviral Project & SyStemix-Sandoz HIV

Gene Therapy Joint Venture (Progenesys, Inc.), 1993—94; founder Progenesys. Contbr. over 120 articles to profl. jour. Recipient Scientist award, Elizabeth Glaser Pedia. AIDS Found., 1996—2000, Clin. Scientist award in Translational Rsch., Burroughs Wellcome Fund, 2000, MERIT award, NIH, 2001, Pioneer award, 2004. Mem.: Am. Assn. Physicians, Am. Soc. Clin. Investigation. Achievements include research in HIV effects on the producton of disease-fighting white blood cellsin patients with HIV disease; 20 patents in field. Office: U Calif Gladstone Inst Virology and Immunology SFGH Bldg 3 Box 1234 San Francisco CA 94143 Office Phone: 415-695-3828. Office Fax: 415-826-8449. Business E-Mail: mmccune@gladstone.ucsf.edu.

**MCCUNE, PHILIP SPEAR,** lawyer; b. Spokane, Wash., Sept. 14, 1965; s. Calmar A. McCune and Katrina Y. Spear; m. Patricia Ann Ryan; children: Emma Sophia, Jackson Spear. BA magna cum laude, Dartmouth Coll., 1987; JD cum laude, U. Mich., 1991. Bar: Wash. 1991, U.S. Dist. Ct. (we. dist.) Wash. 1991, U.S. Dist. Ct. (ea. dist.) Wash. 1996, U.S. Ct. Appeals (9th cir.) 1991, U.S. Dist. Ct. (no. dist.) Utah 1996, U.S. Supreme Ct. 2004. Law clk. Hon. John C. Coughenour chief judge U.S. Dist. Ct. (we. dist.) Wash., Seattle, 1991—93; with Heller, Ehrman, White and Maculiffe, Seattle, 1993—97; ptnr., founder Summit Law Group, Seattle, 1997—. Author: The Forest Practices Act, Washington Environmental Law and Practice; sr. editor U. Mich. Jour. Law Reform; contbr. articles to profl. jours. Bd. dirs. Friends of Ind. Schs. and Better Edn., Seattle Repertory Theater, Am. Friends St. Michael's U. Sch. Recipient Rising Star and Super Lawyer awards, Wash. Law and Politics Mag. Mem. ABA, Wash. State Bar Assn., King County Bar Assn., Wash. Athletic Club, U. Mich. Law Sch. Barristers. Avocations: hiking, running. Office: Summit Law Group 315 Fifth Ave S Ste 1000 Seattle WA 98104-2682 Office Phone: 206-676-7038. E-mail: philm@summitlaw.com.

**MCCUNE, THOMAS ROBERT,** nephrologist, medical educator; b. Ft. Lauderdale, Fla., Oct. 29, 1960; s. James Naber and Gale Linda Ann McCune; m. Mollie Wolcott; children: James Francis Naber, Victoria Katharine Power. BS in Biology, The Va. Mil. Inst., 1982; MD, Ea. Va. Med. Sch., 1985. Diplomate Am. Bd. Internal Medicine, Am. Bd. Nephrology. Fellow Vanderbilt U. Med. Ctr., Nashville, 1988-91; ptnr. Nephrology Assocs. of Tidewater, Norfolk, Va., 1991—; asst. prof. dept. internal medicine Ea. Va. Med. Sch., Norfolk, 1991-2000, assoc. prof. dept. internal medicine, 2000—, chair divsn. nephrology; med. dir. renal and pancreas transplant program Sentara Norfolk Gen. Hosp., 1998—. Contbr. chpts. to books. Sec., treas., pres. South Ea. Organ-Procurement Found., Richmond, Va., 1996-98, pres., 2000-01; rep. UNOS, 1998—; founder Living Organ Donor Soc. Am. Lt. col. Va. N.G. Decorated Bronze Star, comdr. Order of St. Lazarus of Jerusalem. Fellow ACP; mem. Am. Soc. Transp. (patient care and edn. com., co-chair, chair 1999-01), Alpha Omega Alpha, Phi Kappa Phi. Democrat. Roman Catholic. Achievements include co-developer of Living Organ Donor Network; research in kidney transplantation. Avocation: travel. Office: Nephrology Assocs Tidewater 907 Medical Tower Norfolk VA 23507-1970

**MCCUNNEY, ROBERT JOSEPH,** physician; b. July 4, 1948; s. Robert H. McCunney; m. Marilyn Stanton, Nov. 7, 1987; children: Robby, Kelsey. BSCE, Drexel U., 1971; MS in Environ. Health, U. Minn., 1972; MD, Jefferson Med. Coll., 1976; MPH in Occupl. Health, Harvard U., 1981. Intern, resident Northwestern U. Med. Ctr., Chgo., 1976-78; occupl. medicine fellow Harvard Sch. Pub. Health, Boston, 1979-81; emergency rm. physician Choate Meml. Hosp., Woburn, Mass., 1978-80, Sancra Maria Hosp., Cambridge, Mass., 1979-80; med. dir. occupl. health svc. Sturdy Meml. Hosp., Attleboro, Mass., 1981-83; med. dir. Goddard Occupl. Health Svcs., Stoughton, Mass., 1982-90; chief occupl. & environ. medicine, dir. occupl. med. residency program Boston U. Med. Ctr., 1983-94; corp. med. dir. Cabot Corp., Boston, 1983—; dir. environ. med. svc. med. dept. MIT, Cambridge, 1994—. Instr. anatomy Thomas Jefferson U., 1973; instr. medicine Brown U., Providence, 1982-85; adj. asst. prof. pub. health Boston U., 1983—; clin. asst. prof. Med. Coll. Wis., Milw., 1989—; lectr. medicine Harvard Med. Sch., Boston; staff physician Mass. Gen. Hosp., Boston. Editor: Handbook of Occupational Medicine, 1988, A Practical Approach to Occupational and Environmental Medicine, 1994, A Manager's Guide to Occupational Health Services, 1995, Occupl. & Environ. Medicine Report, Medical Center Occupational Health and Safety, 1999, Occupational and Environmental Medicine Self Assessment Guide, 1998; co-editor Health & Safety Manual, 1992; contbr. chpts. to books and articles to profl. jours. Fellow Am. Occupl. Medicine Assn., Am. Coll. Preventive Medicine; mem. AMA, APHA, Am. Conf. Govtl. Indsl. Hygienists, Am. Coll. Occupl. & Environ. Medicine (dir. 1991-94, 95—, chair pubs. com. 1985-88, house dels. 1983-89, govt. affairs com. 1989-93, past pres. New Eng. chpt. 1984-86, dir. residency sect. 1988-93), Tau Beta Pi, Phi Beta Upsilon. Roman Catholic. Avocations: athletics, photography, boating. Office: MIT Dept Biol Engring 77 Massachusetts Ave 16-771 Cambridge MA 02139-4307 Office Phone: 617-258-5650. E-mail: mccunney@mit.edu.

**MCCURDY, DAVID KEITH,** trade association administrator, former congressman; b. Canadian, Tex., Mar. 30, 1950; s. Thomas L. and Aileen (Geis) McC.; m. Pamela Mary Plumb, Aug. 14, 1971; children: Josh, Cydney, Shannon. BA, U. Okla., 1972, JD, 1975; postgrad., U. Edinburgh, Scotland, 1977-78. Bar: Okla. 1975. Asst. atty. gen. State of Okla., 1975-77; assoc. Luttrell, Pendarvis & Rawlinson, Norman, Okla., 1978-79; pvt. practice Norman, 1979-80; mem. 96th-103rd Congresses from 4th Okla. dist., Washington, 1981—95; mem. armed svcs. com., sci., space and tech. com.; chmn., CEO McCurdy Group L.L.C.; pres. Electronic Industries Alliance, Arlington, Va., 1998—. Chmn. Nat. Dem. Leadership Coun. Fellow Internat. Rotary Club; recipient Disting. Svc. award U. Okla., 1991. Mem. Okla. State Bar Assn., Assn. of C., Omicron Delta Kappa, Rotary. Office: Electronic Industries Alliance 2500 Wilson Blvd Arlington VA 22201

**MCCURDY, HARRY WARD,** otolaryngologist; b. Branchton, Pa., Aug. 15, 1918; s. Adam Oscar and Sarah Fern (Hindman) McC.; m. Joan Jacqueline Talty, Dec. 10, 1955; children: Bridget Elizabeth, Peter Adam. AB, Allegheny Coll., 1940; MD, U. Pa., 1943. Diplomate Am. Bd. Otolaryngology. Intern Geisinger Meml. Hosp., Danville, Pa., 1944, resident in otolaryngology, 1944-45, 48-49; resident in pathology Hamot Hosp., Erie, Pa., 1945-48; mem. staff Geisinger Med. Center, Danville, 1948-50; commd. 2d lt. U.S. Army, 1945, advanced through grades to col., 1962-74; mil. cons. Surgeon Gen., U.S. Army, 1964-74; ret., 1974; exec. v.p. Am. Soc. Otolaryngology-Head and Neck Surgery, Washington, 1974-84; mem. staff Walter Reed Army Hosp. Mem. resources council Gallaudet Coll., 1975-80; mem. nat. adv. council Sertoma Found., 1976-84; chmn. FDA Panel on Otolaryngologic Med. Devices, 1974-78, cons., 1978-84 Mem. ACS, AMA, Royal Soc. Medicine (U.K.), Am. Acad. Otolaryngology, Mil. Surgeons Assn., Am. Soc. Assn. Execs., Soc. Med. Consultants to Armed Forces, AAAS, Am. Soc. Facial Plastic Surgery, Soc. Mil. Otolaryngologists, Am. Acad. Facial Plastic and Reconstructive Surgery, Am. Laryngol., Rhinol. and Otol. Soc., Anglo-Am. Med. Soc., Am. Audiology Soc., Royal Soc. Health, Osler Med. Soc., Acad. Medicine, Univ. Otolaryngologists, Am. Council Otolaryngology, Pan-Am. Soc. Bronchoesophagology., Internat. Fedn. Otolaryngol. Socs. (sec. gen. 1981—), Soc. Mil. Cons. to Armed Forces (sec. 1993—). Clubs: Army Navy, Press, Mil. Attaches of London, Les Chevaliers du Tastevin. Republican. Methodist. Home and Office: 6006 Dellwood Pl Bethesda MD 20817-3812 Office Phone: 301-229-5388.

**MCCURDY, LARRY WAYNE,** automotive parts company executive; b. Commerce, Texas, July 1, 1935; s. Weldon Lee and Eula Bell (Quinn) McC.; m. Anna Jean Ogle, June 2, 1956; children: Michael, Kimberly, Laurie. BBA, Tex. A&M U., 1957. Jr. acct. Tenneco Inc., Houston, 1958-60; sr. acct. Tenneco Oil Co., Houston, 1960-64; acctg. supr. Tenneco Chems., Houston, 1964-69, from divsn. controller to v.p. fin. Saddle Brook, NJ, 1970-78; sr. v.p. fin. Tenneco Automotive, Deerfield, Ill., 1978-80; pres. Walker Mfg. Co., Racine, Wis., 1980-81; exec. v.p. N.Am. ops. Tenneco Automotive, Deerfield, 1981-82; v.p. fin. Echlin Inc., Branford, Conn., 1983; pres., COO Echlin, Inc., Branford, Conn., 1983-85, pres., 1997—; pres., CEO Moog Automotive Inc., St. Louis, 1985-94; exec. v.p. ops. Cooper Industries, Houston, 1994-97; chmn. bd., pres., CEO Echlin, Inc., Branford, Conn., 1997-98; pres. Dana

Automotive Aftermarket Group, 1998-2000; ret., 2000. Bd. dirs. Lear Corp., Mohawk Industries, Inc., Gen. Parts, Inc., Affinia Group Inc. Trustee Somerset County Coll., Somerville, N.J., 1974-78, Millikin U., Decatur, Ill., 1991-97, St. Raphaels's Hosp., New Haven, Conn., 2002—; former mem. bd. dirs. Jr. Achievement, Chgo.; bd. dirs. Sam Houston coun. Boy Scouts Am., 1995-97; mem. adv. coun. Tex. A&M U. Engring. Sch., 1995-97; dir. New Haven Symphony Orch., 2002—. Mem. Fin. Execs. Inst., Nat. Assn. Accts., Motor Equipment Mfrs. Assn. (chmn. bd. dirs. 1989). Personal E-mail: larrywmccurdy@aol.com.

**MCCURDY, LAYTON,** medical educator; b. Florence, SC, Aug. 20, 1935; m. Gwendolyn A. McCurdy, 1958; children: Robert Jr., David Barclay. BS, U. NC, 1956; MD, Med. U. SC, 1960. Resident in psychiatry NC Meml. Hosp., Chapel Hill, 1961—66; with psychiatry tng. br. NIMH, Bethesda, Md., 1964—66; asst. prof. dept. psychiatry Sch. Medicine Emory U., Atlanta, 1966—68; prof., chmn. dept. psychiatry and behavioral scis. Med. U. SC, 1968—82, v.p. med. affairs, dean, 1990—2001, dean emeritus, disting. prof., 2001—; prof. psychiatry Sch. Medicine U. Pa., Phila., 1982—90; psychiatrist-in-chief Inst. of Pa. Hosp., Phila., 1982—90. Vis. colleague Inst. Psychiatry, U. London, 1974—75; nat. adv. mental health coun. NIMH, 1980—83; apptd. Pa. Adv. Com. for Mental Health and Mental Retardation, 1984—87. Recipient Disting. Alumnus award, Med. U. SC, 1988, George C. Ham. Soc., 1990. Fellow: Am. Coll. Psychiatrists (bd. regents 1987—90, v.p. 1990—93, pres. 1993—94, Bowis award 1997); mem.: SC Commn. on Higher Edn. (chmn. 2005—), Royal Coll. Psychiatrists (U.K.), Waring Libr. Soc. (pres. 1979—80, exec. com. 1991—99), Am. Psychiat. Assn. (joint commn. pub. affairs 1981—84, chmn. com. on diagnosis and assessment 1988—94), VA CARES Commn., Cosmos Club (Washington), Alpha Omega Alpha. Office: Med Univ SC Inst Psychiatry PO Box 250861 Charleston SC 29425 Office Phone: 843-792-2084. Business E-mail: mccurdy@musc.edu.

**MCCURDY, MICHAEL CHARLES,** illustrator, author; b. NYC, Feb. 17, 1942; s. Charles Errett and Beatrice (Beatson) McC.; m. Deborah Lamb, Sept. 7, 1968; children: Heather, Mark. BFA, Tufts U., 1964, MFA, 1971. Dir. Penmaen Press, Lincoln, Mass., 1968-85; instr. Concord (Mass.) Acad., 1972-75, Wellesley (Mass.) Coll., 1976. Illustrator: The Man Who Planted Trees, 1985, American Tall Tales, 1991, American Buffalo, 1992, The Way West: Journal of a Pioneer Woman, 1993, Giants in the Land, 1993, The Gettysburg Address, 1995, The Seasons Sewn, 1996; author, illustrator: Hannah's Farm, 1988, Trapped by the Ice, 1997, The Sailor's Alphabet, 1998, An Algonquian Year: The Year According to the Full Moon, 2000; editor, illustrator: Escape From Slavery: The Boyhood of Frederick Douglass in His Own Words, 1994, American Fairy Tales, 1996, War and the Pity of War, 1998, Tarzan, 1999, The Wizard of Oz, 1999, Iron Horses, 1999, The Signers: The 56 Stories Behind the Declaration of Independence, 2002, Walden by H.D. Thoreau, 2004. Mem. Great Barrington (Mass.) Housing Authority, 1990-93. Small press grantee Nat. Endowment Arts, 1978, Mass. Arts and Humanities, 1978. Mem. Soc. Printers, St. Botolph Club. Democrat. Episcopalian. Personal E-mail: mccurdy@michaelmccurdy.com.

**MC CURDY, PATRICK PIERRE,** editor; b. Angers, France, Sept. 14, 1928; s. Joseph Alexander and Constance Yolande (Hillairet de Boisferon) McC.; m. Eiko Yamada, May 30, 1953; children: Alan J., Wendy C., Alec J., Jeffrey R. BS in Chem. Engring., Carnegie Inst. Tech., 1949. Chem. engr. tech. service dept. Humble Oil & Refining Co., Baytown, Tex., 1949-50; chem. engr. Calery Chem. Co., Pa., 1954-56; sr. chem. engr. U.S. Army Engr. R & D Labs., Ft. Belvoir, Va., 1956-60; asst. editor Chem. & Engring. News, Washington, 1960-61, N.Y.C., 1961-62, bur. head Frankfurt, Germany, 1962-64, Tokyo, 1964-67, mng. editor Washington, 1967-69, editor, 1969-73; editor in chief Chemical Week, 1973-80, 84-87, editor-in-chief, assoc. pub., 1987-88; dir. communications Am. Chem. Soc., 1988-91, dir. industry rels., 1991-93, founding editor Today's Chemist at Work, 1989-97; cons. American Chemical Soc., 1993-97; pub. issues mgr. Dow Chem. Co., Midland, Mich., 1980-82, dir. tech. communications, 1982-84. Cons. in field, 1997—; editl. cons. Chem. Heritage mag., 1997—. Served U.S. Coast Guard, Great Lakes, 1945, first lt. C.E. AUS, 1950-54. Recipient Jesse H. Neal award, 1979, finalist 1985; recipient Carnegie Mellon Univ. Alumni Merit award, 1988. Mem.: Societe de Chimie Industrielle (past pres. Am. sect.), Chemists Club, Fgn. Corrs. Club Japan, Am. Chem. Soc., Tokyo Am. Club, Tau Beta Pi, Phi Kappa, Theta Tau, Phi Kappa Phi. Home and Office: 11717 Chauncey Ln Mason Neck VA 22079-4140 Personal E-mail: mccurdypp@aol.com.

**MCCURLEY, MARY JOHANNA,** lawyer; b. Baton Rouge, La., Oct. 3, 1953; d. William Edward and Leora Elizabeth (Block) Trice; m. Carl Michael McCurley, June 6, 1983; 1 stepchild, Melissa Reneé McCurley. BA, Centenary Coll., 1975; JD, St. Mary's U., 1979. Bar: Tex. 1979; cert. family law. Assoc. Martin, Withers & Box, Dallas, 1979-82, Raggio & Raggio, Inc., Dallas, 1982-83; ptnr. Bruner, McColl, McColloch & McCurley, Dallas, 1983-87; assoc., ptnr. Selligson & Douglass, Dallas, 1987-90; jr. ptnr. Koons, Fuller, McCurley & VanderEykel, Dallas, 1990-92; ptnr. McCurley, Orsinger, McCurley,. Nelson & Downing, Dallas, 1992—. Contbr. articles to profl. jours. Adv. Women's Service League, Dallas, 1993—. Master: Annette Stewart Am. Inn. Ct. (sec.-treas. 2003—04); mem.: Dallas Bar Assn., Tex. Acad. Family Law Specialist, Tex. State Bar Assn. (sec. 2001, vice-chair 2001, treas. 2001, chair 2003—, family law coun.), Dallas Bar Assn. (chair family law sect. 1985), Am. Acad. Matrimonial Lawyers (treas. Tex. chpt. 1993—95, sec. 1995—96, pres. 1997, pres. Tex. chpt. 1997—98, bd. govs. 2000, nat. sec. 2000—02, nat. v.p. 2002—, nat. bd. dirs.). Methodist. Avocations: golf, travel, jogging, horseback riding. Home: 4176 Hanover Ave Dallas TX 75225-7009 Office: McCurley Orsinger McCurley Nelson & Downing LLP 5950 Sherry Ln Ste 800 Dallas TX 75225-6533 Office Phone: 214-273-2400.

**MCCURLEY, ROBERT LEE, JR.,** lawyer, educator; b. Gadsden, Ala., Sept. 7, 1941; s. Robert Lee and Nellie Ruth McC.; m. Barbara; 1 child, Allison Leah. BS, U. Ala., 1963, JD, 1966. Bar: Ala. 1966, D.C. 1973, U.S. Ct. Mil. Appeals 1966, U.S. Supreme Ct. 1970, U.S. Ct. Appeals (5th cir.) 1972, U.S. Ct. Appeals (11th cir.) 1973, U.S. Ct. Appeals (fed. cir.) 1981. Asst. to dir. Fed. Savs. & Loan Ins. Corp., Washington, 1966-67; partner firm Rains, Rains, McCurley & Wilson, Gadsden, Ala., 1967-75; city judge Southside, Ala., 1970-75; dir. Ala. Law Inst., 1975—; assoc. dir. U. Ala. Center Public Law and Service, 1981-82; asst. dean Sch. Law U. Ala. 1978-81. Panelist White House Conf. on Volunteerism; pres. Gadsden Jaycees, 1972; mem. White House Fifty States Project; Henry Toll fellow Coun. State Govt., 1992. Editor: Divorce, Alimony and Child Support Custody, 4th edit., 2005, Land Laws of Alabama, 8th edit. rev., 2006, The Legislative Process, 8th edit., 2003, Alabama Law Office Practice Deskbook, 9th edit., 2001, Federally Mandated State Legislation, 1990, Alabama Legislation, Cases and Statutes, 5th edit., 2003, Alabama Election Handbook, 12th edit., 2006. Pres. Gadsden Boys Club, 1971, Kiwanis Internat. Found., 1998—2000; mem. Nat. Dem. Charter Commn., 1974. Recipient Svc. award, Ala. Bar Commn., 2004, Guin award, Ala. State Bar, 2000, Bar Commnrs. award, 2004, Roger Sayers Disting. Svc. award, U. Ala., 2005. Fellow ABA, Ala. Bar Assn.; mem. Am. Law Inst. (life), Order of Coif, Scribes, Farrah Law Soc., Commn. Uniform State Laws, Kiwanis (pres. Tuscaloosa club 1976, gov. Ala. dist. 1984, 91-92, v.p. 1998-2000, Internat. Found. 2005—), Indian Hills County Club, Univ. Club. Baptist. Office Phone: 205-348-7411.

**MCCURLEY, THOMAS W.,** manufacturing executive; V.p. info. services Hardware and Home Improvement Group, Black & Decker Corp., Lake Forest, Calif. Named one of Premier 100 IT Leaders, Computerworld, 2005. Office: Black & Decker Hardware and Home Improvement Group 19701 DaVinci Lake Forest CA 92610-2622*

**MCCURN, NEAL PETERS,** federal judge; b. Syracuse, NY, Apr. 6, 1926; LL.B., Syracuse U., 1952, JD, 1960. Bar: N.Y. 1952. Ptnr. Mackenzie Smith Lewis Mitchell & Hughes, Syracuse, 1957-79; judge U.S. Dist. Ct. (no. dist.) N.Y., 1979-88; chief judge U.S. Dist. Ct. (no. dist.), NY, 1988-93; sr. judge, 1993—. Del. N.Y. State Constl. Conv., 1976; mem. 2d Cir. Jud. Council, 1987-93. Pres. Syracuse Common Coun., 1970-78. Mem. ABA, N.Y. State

---

Bar Assn. (chmn. state constn. com.), Onondaga County Bar Assn. (past pres.), Am. Coll. Trial Lawyers, Am. Judicature Soc. (bd. dirs. 1980-84). Office: US Dist Ct 100 S Clinton St Rm 344 Syracuse NY 13261-6100 Office Phone: 315-234-8590. Business E-mail: juwest@nynd.uscourts.gov.

**MCCURRY, MARGARET IRENE,** architect, educator, furniture designer, interior designer; b. Chgo., Sept. 26, 1942; d. Paul D. and Irene B. McC.; m. Stanley Tigerman, Mar. 17, 1979. BA, Vassar Coll., 1964. Registered architect, Ill., Mass., Mich., Tex., Wis., Pa., Ind., Fla.; registered interior designer, Ill. Design coord. Quaker Oats Co., Chgo., 1964-66; sr. interior designer Skidmore, Owings & Merrill, Chgo., 1966-77; pvt. practice architect Margaret I., Chgo., 1977-82; ptnr. Tigerman, McCurry, Chgo., 1982—. Vis. studio critic Art Inst. Chgo., 1985-86, 88, 98, lectr., 1988, 98; vis. studio critic U. Ill., Chgo., Miami U., Oxford, Ohio, 1990; juror Internat. furniture awards Progressive Architecture mag., N.Y.C., 1986, advt. awards, 1988; juror design grants Nat. Endowment for Arts, Washington, 1983; NEA Challenge Design Rev., 1992; peer reviewer design excellence program Gen. Svcs. Administrn., 1992—; juror, Wis., Minn., Calif., Va., Washington, Pitts., Ky., Ga. Conn. Soc. Architects, Detroit, N.Y.C., Memphis, Austin, L.A., Toledo, Jacksonville chpts. AIA, Am. Wood Coun., AIA Students Design Competition, 1993. Author: Margaret McCurry: Constructing 25 Short Stories, 2000; contbr. Chgo. Archtl. Club Jour.; designer, contbr. archtl. exhibit Art Inst. Chgo., 1983-85, 93, 99, 2005, Chgo. Hist. Soc., 1984, Gulbenkian Found., Lisbon Portugal, 1989, Chgo. Athenaeum, 1990, Gwenda Jay Gallery, 1992, Women of Design Traveling Exhbn., 1992-96; archtl. drawings and models in permanent collection Art Inst. Chgo. and Deutsches Architektur Mus., Frankfurt, Germ. Furniture sect. fundraising auction Sta. WTTW-TV, PBS, Chgo., 1975-76; mem. Chgo. Beautiful Com., 1968-70; pres. alumni coun. Grad. Sch. Design, Harvard U., 1997-2000; bd. dirs. Architecture and Design Soc. Art Inst. Chgo., 1988-97, mem. textile adv. bd. Loeb fellow Harvard U., 1986-87; recipient Builders Choice Grand award Builders Mag., 1985, Interior Design award Interiors Mag., 1983, Dean of Architecture award Chgo. Design Source and the Merchandise Mart, 1989, Designer of Distinction award ASID, 2002; named a Dean of Design, Archtl. Digest, 2005; inducted into Interior Design Hall of Fame, Interior Design Mag., 1990, ASID Design Excellence Residential III Chptr award, 2005, Hist. Preservation award, 2005, Corp. Office award, 2005 Fellow AIA (mem. coll. fellows, v.p. bd. dirs. Chgo. chpt. 1984-89, chair 1993, nat. design com., lectr. Colo. chpt. 1985, nat. conv. 1988, 97-98, Monterey Design Conf. 1989, Washington Design Ctr. 1989, Nat. Honor award 1984, Nat. Interior Architecture award 1992, 98, Disting. Bldg. award Chgo. chpt. 1984, 86, 91, 94, 99-2000, Disting. Interior Architecture award 1981, 83, 88, 91, 97, product display Neocon award 1985, 88, Gold award best of Neocon 1998, Associated Licensed Archs. Silver Medal Design award 2003), Internat. Interior Design Assn., Chgo. Network, Am. Soc. Interior Designers (v.p. bd. dirs. Chgo. chpt., Nat. Design award 1992, 94, Ill. chpt. Design award 1994, 2005, Ill. chpt. Merit award 1994, Designer Distinction award 2002, Ill. chpt. Design Excellence award in hist. preservation, 2005, in corp. interiors 2005), Chgo. Archtl. Club, Arts Club Chgo., Harvard Alumni Assn. (dir. 2000—, v.p. Chgo.), Episcopalian. Avocations: drawing, writing, travel, golf, gardening. Office: Tigerman McCurry Archs 444 N Wells St Chicago IL 60610-4501 Office Phone: 312-644-5880. Business E-Mail: mimccurry@tigerman-mccurry.com.

**MCCUSKER, THOMAS J.,** lawyer, insurance company executive; b. South Bend, Ind., 1943; BA, U. Notre Dame, 1965, JD cum laude, 1969. Bar: NY 1970, Nebr. 1973, US Tax Ct. 1971. Exec. v.p. gen. counsel Mutual of Omaha Ins. Co. Mem.: ABA, Nebr. Bar Assn., Omaha Bar Assn. Office: Mutual of Omaha Ins Co Mutual Of Omaha Plz Omaha NE 68175-1008

**MCCUSKEY, JOHN F.,** lawyer; b. Clarksburg, W.Va., Nov. 7, 1947; BS, W.Va. Wesleyan Coll., 1969; BSEE, U. Pa., 1970; JD, W.Va. U., 1973. Bar: W.Va. 1974, U.S. Dist. Ct. (no. dist.) W.Va., U.S. Dist. Ct. (so. dist.) W.Va., U.S. Ct. Appeals (4th cir.). Mem. W.Va. Ho. of Dels., 1972—76, 1978—82; justice Supreme Ct. Appeals W.Va., 1998; atty. Shuman, McCuskey & Slicea, Charleston, W.Va. Capt. USAR, 1974—80. Recipient Disting. Faculty award, Def. Trial Counsel of W.Va. Mem.: ABA, W.Va. State Bar, Kanawha County Bar Assn., W.Va. Bar Assn. (pres.-elect 2003), Omicron Delta Kappa. Office: Shuman McCuskey and Slicea Va Ctr 1411 Virginia St E PO Box 3953 Charleston WV 25339

**MCCUTCHAN, GORDON EUGENE,** retired lawyer, insurance company executive; b. Buffalo, Sept. 30, 1935; s. George Lawrence and Mary Esther (De Puy) McC.; m. Linda Brown; children: Lindsey, Elizabeth. BA, Cornell U., 1956, MBA, 1958, LLB, 1959. Bar: N.Y. 1959, Ohio 1964. Pvt. practice, Rome, NY, 1959-61; atty., advisor SEC, Washington, 1961-64; ptnr. Mc-Cutchan, Druen, Maynard, Rath & Dietrich, 1964-94; mem. office of gen. counsel Nationwide Mut. Ins. Co., Columbus, Ohio, 1964-94, sr. v.p., gen. counsel, 1982-89, exec. v.p., gen. counsel, 1989-94; exec. v.p. Law and Corp. Svcs., Nationwide Ins. Enterprise, 1994-98; ret., 1998. Trustee, bd. govs. Franklin U., 1992-97; trustee Ohio Tuition Trust Authority, 1992-97. Mem. Columbus Bar Assn., Ohio Bar Assn., Am. Corp. Counsel Assn., Assn. Life Inst. Counsel (bd. govs. 1990-94), Fedn. Ins. and Corp. Counsel, Am. Coun. Life Ins. (chair legal sect. 1992-93). Home: 2376 Oxford Rd Columbus OH 43221-4011 E-mail: tunkpa@columbus.rr.com.

**MCCUTCHEN, TAMMY DEE,** federal agency administrator; b. Kewanee, Ill., Oct. 20, 1965; BA, Western Ill. U.; JD, Northwestern U. Clk. U.S. Ct. Appeals (7th cir.), 1991—92; assoc. Skadden, Arps, Slate, Meagher and Flom, Chgo., 1992—95, Matkov, Salzman, Madoff and Gunn, 1995—99; sr. counsel Hershey Foods Corp., 1999—2001; administr. wage and hour divsn. U.S. Dept. Labor, Washington, 2001—. Office: US Dept Labor 200 Constitution Ave NW Washington DC 20210

**MCCUTCHEN, THOMAS ENGLISH, JR.,** lawyer; b. Bishopville, SC, June 20, 1919; s. Thomas English and Cornelia (Lavender) McC.; m. Jane Perry McCutchen, Sept. 25, 1943; children: English, Jane Perry, Grace. AB (magna cum laude), U. SC, 1940, LLB, 1946. Bar: S.C., 1941, U.S. Supreme Ct., 1955. Ptnr. McCutchen, Blanton, et. al., Columbia, S.C. Instr. U. S.C. Law Sch., 1949-50. Major USAF, 1941-45. Recipient Compleat Lawyer award U. S.C. Law Sch., 1991. Mem. ABA, S.C. Bar Assn., Richland County Bar Assn. (pres. 1970), Am. Coll. Trial Lawyers. Office: McCutchen Blanton Johnson & Barnette LLP 1414 Lady St Columbia SC 29201-3304 Office Phone: 803-799-9791.

**MCCUTCHEN, WILLIAM WALTER, JR.,** management educator; b. Hamlet, N.C., Aug. 26, 1940; s. William Walter and Edith Wall (Rucker) McC.; m. Irene Katherine Lilly, June 16, 1962; 1 child, William Walter III. BS in Civil Engring., Duke U., 1962; MBA, Harvard U., 1967; PhD, Ind. U., 1988. Sales rep. Eli Lilly and Co., San Francisco, 1967-69, analyst econ. studies Indpls., 1969-70, mgr. econ. studies, 1970-72, mgr. personnel (mktg.), 1972-73; dir. nat. sales Elizabeth Arden, N.Y.C., 1973-76; mng. dir. Lilly Industries Pty. Ltd., Sidney, Australia, 1976-79; dir. corp. communications Eli Lilly & Co., Indpls., 1980-83; assoc. prof. mgmt. Zicklin Sch. of Bus., Baruch Coll., CUNY, N.Y.C., 1988—, dep. chmn. dept. mgmt., 1995—. Capt. USMC, 1962-65. Mem. Acad. Mgmt., Am. Econ. Assn., Woodstock Club, Univ. Club, Shorehaven Golf Club, Phi Delta Theta, Beta Gamma Sigma. Congregationalist. Office: CUNY Baruch Coll Zicklin Sch of Bus 17 Lexington Ave New York NY 10010-5518 Office Phone: 646-312-3633. Business E-Mail: william_mccutchen@baruch.cuny.edu.

**MCCUTCHEON, ALLAN LEE,** sociology educator; b. Clarinda, Iowa, Mar. 15, 1950; s. Merle Marvin and Margaret Lucille (Larabee) McC.; m. Nancy Ann Cooper, June 13, 1970 (div. May 1975); 1 child, Jennifer; m. Elisabeth Jean Crockett, May 25, 1985. BS, Iowa State U., 1972, MA, U. Chgo., 1977, PhD, 1982. Asst. prof. sociology U. Del., Newark, 1982-88, assoc. prof. sociology, 1988-96, assoc. chair dept. sociology, 1989-95; Donald O. Clifton disting. prof. survey rsch. U. Nebr., Lincoln, 1996—, dir. Gallup Rsch. Ctr., 1996—; sr. scientist Gallup Orgn., 1996—. Cons. Disaster Rsch.

---

Ctr., Newark, 1986-88; vis. scientist Max Planck Inst., Freiburg, Germany, 1988-89; dozent U. Cologne (Germany), 1989, 96, 2001; instr. European Consortium for Polit. Rsch. U. Essex (Eng.), 1990—; mem. sci. adv. coun. German Ctr. for Survey Rsch. and Methodology, 1998-2004. Author (book) Latent Class Analysis, 1987; editor (with J. Hagenaars): (book) Applied Latent Class Analysis, 2002 (newsletter) States and Societies, 1988-95; contbr. articles to profl. jours. Resource cons. Leadership Del. United Way, Wilmington, 1991-92. U. Chgo. rsch. fellow, 1974-77; Deutscher Akademischer Austauschdienst scholar, 1990; Fulbright scholar, The Netherlands, 1995-96. Fellow Am. Statis. Assn.; mem. World Assn. for Pub. Opinion Rsch. (sec.-treas. 2000-2004, gen. sec. 2004—), Coun. for European Studies, Am. Assn. for Pub. Opinion Rsch., Midwest Assn. for Pub. Opinion Rsch. (v.p. 2002-2003, pres. 2003-2004), Am. Sociol. Assn., Sigma Xi. Avocations: German culture, literature. Office: U Nebr Gallup Rsch Ctr 200 N 11th St Lincoln NE 68508-1406 E-mail: AMcCutcheon1@unl.edu.

**MCCUTCHEON, JOHN TINNEY, JR.,** retired journalist; b. Chgo., Nov. 8, 1917; s. John Tinney and Evelyn (Shaw) McC.; m. Susan Dart, Feb. 1, 1943; children: Anne McCutcheon Lewis, Mary, John Tinney III. BS, Harvard U., 1939. Reporter City News Bur., Chgo., 1939-40, Chgo. Tribune, 1940-51, editor column A Line O' Type or Two, 1951-57, editorial writer, 1957-71, editor editorial page, 1971-82, columnist, 1967-70. Pres. Lake Forest (Ill.) Libr., 1970—72. With USNR, 1941—46. Mem. Soc. Midland Authors, Am. Soc. Newspaper Editors, Nat. Conf. Editorial Writers, Geog. Soc. Chgo. (pres. 1955-57), Chgo. Zool. Soc. (hon. trustee), Chgo. Hist. Soc. (life trustee), Inter Am. Press Assn. (dir. freedom of press com. 1978-87), Wayfarers Club (Chgo.), Tryon (N.C.) Country Club, Sigma Delta Chi. Home: 10 Fox Paw Ln Saluda NC 28773-9527

**MCCUTCHEON, STEVEN CLIFTON,** ecological and environmental engineer, hydrologist; b. Decatur, Ala., Oct. 29, 1952; s. Bernard Clifton and Rosa May (Askenbury) McC.; m. Sherry Lynn Sharp; children: Michael Ian, Alexander Tavis. BS, Auburn U., 1975; MS, Vanderbilt U., 1977, PhD, 1979. Hydrologist U.S. Geol. Survey, Bay St. Louis, Miss., 1977-86; sr. environ. engr. U.S. EPA, Athens, Ga., 1986—. Adj. asst. prof. Tulane U., New Orleans, 1984-85; panel mem. Nat. Rsch. Coun., Washington, 1989-92; adj. prof. forestry, mem. faculty engring., U. Ga., Athens, 1993—; asst. prof. Clemson (S.C.) U., 1990-97; program evaluator Accreditation Bd. Engring. & Tech., 1992—. Author: Water Quality Modeling, vol. 1, 1989, Water Quality, Handbook of Hydrology, 1993; editor and author (with others): Manual for Performing Estuarine Waste Load Allocations, 1990, Hydrodynamics and Transport for Water Quality Modeling, 1999, editor and author: Phytoremediation, 2003; editor Jour. Environ. Engring., 1992—94, mem. editl. bd. Ecol. Engring., 1995—, Internat. Jour. Phytoremediation, 2000—, Hazardous Toxic and Radioactive Waste Mgmt., 1996—97, co-editor Environ. Sci. and Pollution Rsch., 2003—05, adv. editor, 2006—; contbr. chapters to books, articles to profl. jours. Mem. Zoning Commn., St. Tammany Parish, La., 1984-85; vice-chmn. Planning Adv. Bd., St. Tammany Parish, 1985; asst. den leader Cub Scouts Am., Athens, pack 83, 1991-92, pack 96, 1998-99, den leader, 1999-2001. Co-recipient EPA Sci. Achievement award in waste mgmt., Air and Waste Mgmt. Assn., 1995, EPA Sci. Achievement award in Chemistry, Am. Chem. Soc., 1997, Sci. and Tech. Achievement award, EPA, 1999, Bronze medal, 2001, 2002; recipient medal and plaque, Korea Soc. Water Pollution Rsch. and Control, Seoul, 1986, Engr. of Yr. award in EPA, NSPE, 1992, Engr. of Yr. in Govt. award, Ga. Engr. Week Com., 2004, Sci. and Tech Achievement award, II, 2006. Mem.: ASCE (br. pres. 1983—84, sect. dir. 1984—85, 1995—2001, sect. v.p. 2001—03, sect. pres.-elect 2003—04, rep. Dist. 14 coun. 2003—04, sect. pres. 2004—05, pres. 2004—05, nat. dir. Dist. 14 2004—07, Young Civil Engr. of Yr. award 1984, Richard R. Torrens award 1994, Govt. Civil Engr. of Yr. award 2004, Outstanding Membership Chair 2004), Am. Acad. Water Resources Engrs. (elected charter diplomate 2005), Water Environ. Fedn., Internat. Assn. Hydrologic Scis., Internat. Water Assn., Internat. Soc. Environ. Ethics (charter), Am. Geophys. Union, Am. Ecol. Engring. Soc. (chair com. registration and certification 2001—04, v.p., pres.-elect 2004—05, pres. 2005—06, past pres. 2006—, charter), Phi Theta Kappa, Phi Kappa Phi, Sigma Xi (chpt. sec. 1982—84, membership com. 1984—85). Achievements include research in phytoremediation and ecological engring. to clean up federal facilities and response to Exxon Valdez oil spill. Home: 147 Spalding Ct Athens GA 30605-3716 Office: U Ga Faculty of Engring Driftmier Engring Ctr Athens GA 30602 Office Phone: 706-542-1455. Business E-Mail: StevenMc@uga.edu. E-mail: EnvironHyd@aol.com.

**MCDADE, HERBERT H., III,** investment company executive; m. Martha McDade, 1989. BA, Duke U.; MBA, U. Mich., 1983. Corp. bond trader Lehman Brothers Holdings Inc., 1983—91, head, corp. bond dept., 1991—95, head, high grade credit bus., 1995—98, global head, debt capital markets, 1998—2000, co-global head, fixed income divsn., 2000—02, head, global fixed income divsn., 2002—05, mng. dir., mem. exec. com., global head equities, 2005—. Mem. nat. adv. council Fannie Mae. Mem.: Bond Market Assn. (v. chmn.), Winged Foot Golf Club (bd. govs.). Office: Lehman Brothers Holdings Inc 745 Seventh Ave New York NY 10019*

**MCDADE, JAMES RUSSELL,** management consultant; b. Dallas, Jan. 15, 1925; s. Marion W. and Jeannette (Reneau) McD.; m. Elaine Bushey, Sep. 10, 1955. BSEE, So. Meth. U., Dallas, 1947; MBA, Northwestern U., Evanston, Ill., 1950. Asst. to pres. Davidson Corp., Chgo., 1951-52, Mergenthaler Linotype Co., Bklyn., 1952-53, comml. works mgr., 1953-56; chief indsl. engr. Tex. Instruments, Inc., Dallas, 1956-57, product gen. mgr., 1958-60, v.p., 1961-64; chmn. bd. McDade Properties Co., Aspen (Colo.), Denver, Dallas, 1964—. Bd. dirs. Pitkin County Bank, Aspen, chmn. bd. dirs. Harley-Davidson Tex., Westec Security of Aspen, Aspen Security, Inc. Founding mem. Aspen Art Mus., 1980; mem. Ballet Aspen, 1980—; pres. club Aspen Valley Hosp., 1984—. Served to 1st lt. USAF, 1943-46. Mem.: Presidents Assn., Am. Mgmt. Assn., Rep. Senatorial Inner Circle. Avocations: skiing, horseback riding, camping, swimming. Personal E-mail: jrmco@jrmco.com.

**MCDADE, MARK,** biotechnology company executive; BS, Dartmouth Coll.; MBA, Harvard U. With Sandoz Ltd.; COO Boehringer Mannheim Therapeutics, divsn. of Corange Ltd.; co-founder, exec. v.p., COO Corixa pres., COO, 1999—2000; CEO Signature BioSci., Inc., Hayward, Calif., 2000—. Bd. dirs. Corixa Corp., Valentis Inc.

**MCDADE, SANDY D.,** manufacturing executive; BA, Whitman Coll., 1974; JD cum laude, Seattle U., 1979. Mem. law dept., gen. counsel Weyerhaeuser Co., 1980—2000, corp. sec., 1993—2000, v.p. strategic planning, 2000—03, sr. v.p. Can., 2003—. Mem. camping svcs. bd. Seattle Met. YMCA; mem. Wash. State Corp. Act Revision Com. Mem.: Wash. State Bar Assn. (past chmn. corp. law dept. sect.), Am. Soc. Corp. Secs. Office: Weyerhaeuser Co 33663 Weyerhaeuser Way S Federal Way WA 98063-9777

**MCDAID, JENNIFER DAVIS,** archivist; b. Norfolk, Va., Apr. 18, 1965; m. Christopher Ludden McDaid, Oct. 5, 2001; 1 child, Katharine Ludden. MA, Coll. William and Mary, 1990. Asst. editor Va. Cavalcade Univ. of Va., Richmond, 1996—99, archives rsch. coord., 1999—. Dep. coord. State Hist. Records Adv. Bd., Richmond, 1996—. Contbr. Mem.: So. Assn. Women Historians (Listserv co-editor 1997—2006). Office: Libr of Virginia 800 E Broad St Richmond VA 23219 Office Phone: 804-692-3648.

**MCDANIEL, BRUCE ALAN,** economist, educator; b. Warsaw, Ind., June 12, 1946; s. Maurice M. and Hattie M. (Stidham) McD.; m. Darcy L. Stouder, Dec. 29, 1972; children: Rachel L., Nathan A., Jordan J. BS, Manchester Coll., 1968; MA, Ball State U., Muncie, Ind., 1972; PhD, Colo. State U., 1979. Instr. Colo. State U., Fort Collins, 1975-79; asst. prof. Ind. U., Indpls., 1979-82, Marquette U., Milw., 1982-85; pres., owner Prairieland, Atwood, Ind., 1985—; prof. U. No. Colo., Greeley, 1992—; owner Prairieland, Inc. Loveland, Colo. Contbr. articles to profl. jours. Sam M. Walton fellow, U. No. Colo., 2000-06. Mem. Assn. for Social Econs. (midwest regional dir.

1986-92, exec. coun. 1983-92, Helen Potter award 1983), Assn. for Evolutionary Econ., Assn. for pvt. Entrepereuship Edn., Am. Soc. Bus. and Behavorial Sci., Phi Kappa Phi, Omicron Delta Epsilon. Office: U No Colo Dept Econs Greeley CO 80639-0001 Office Phone: 970-351-1163. Business E-Mail: bruce.mcdaniel@unco.edu.

**MCDANIEL, CHARLES-GENE,** journalism educator, writer; b. Luxora, Ark., Jan. 11, 1931; s. Charles Waite and Edith Estelle (Kelly) McD. BS, Northwestern U., 1954, MS in Journalism, 1955. Reporter Gazette and Daily, York, Pa., 1955-58; sci. writer Chgo. bur. A.P., 1958-79; assoc. prof. journalism dept. Roosevelt U., Chgo., 1979-83, prof., 1984-96, chmn. dept., 1979-93, head faculty of journalism and communication studies, 1993-95, prof. emeritus, 1996—. Contbg. editor Libido; contbr. to anthologies, poems, Ency. Britannica, World Book Ency.; contbr. articles to profl. jours.; Chgo. corr. The Med. Post, Toronto, 1979-2000; columnist www.libidomag.com. Trustee Roosevelt U., 1985-94; bd. dirs. Internat. Press Ctr. Chgo., 1993-96. Recipient writing awards Erikson Inst. for Early Edn., 1972, writing award AMA, 1974, writing awards Chgo. Inst. for Psychoanalysis, 1971, 73, writing awards Ill. Med Soc., 1972, 73, writing awards ADA, 1975, Am. Psychol. Assn., 1982. Mem. ACLU, Fellowship of Reconciliation, War Registers League, Art Inst. Chgo. (life), Mus. Contemporary Art (charter), Ill. Arts Alliance, Handgun Control Inc., Hemlock Soc., Ptnrship in Caring. Home and Office: 5109 S Cornell Ave Chicago IL 60615-4215 *That which we achieve for ourselves is for naught unless we have at the same time contributed to a world in which peace and justice prevail.*

**MCDANIEL, DAVID HENRY,** physician; b. Clarksburg, W.Va., May 12, 1952; s. Hubert Harold and Ada Virginia (Ann) McD.; m. Sheila Marie Travis, Sept. 17, 1994. BS in Chemistry cum laude, W.Va. U., Morgantown, 1974, MD, 1978. Diplomate Am. Bd. Dermatology, 1983. Emergency physician Monongalia Gen. Hosp., Morgantown, 1979—82; dir. Laser Skin and Vein Ctr. of Va., Virginia Beach, Va., 1982—; asst. prof. clin. dermatology Ea. Va. Med. Sch., Norfolk, 1991—, asst. prof. clin. plastic surgery, 1992—; command cons. dept. plastic surgery Naval Med. Ctr., Portsmouth, Va., 1994—; dir. rsch. and innovation Light BioSci., LLC, 2002—. Adj. asst. prof. dept. biol. scis. Old Dominion U., 2001—; pres. The Ctr. for Disfigurement, Virginia Beach, 1993—; adv. coun. mem. Disfigurement Guidance Ctr., Scotland, 1994—; pres. David H. McDaniel Cons., Internat., Virginia Beach, 1995—. Contbr. numerous articles to sci. jours. Fellow Am. Acad. Dermatology, Am. Soc. Laser Medicine and Surgery, Am. Soc. Dermatologic Surgery (com. practice mktg. and pub. rels. 1993-96, chair 1996), Internat. Soc. Dermatologic Surgery; mem. Tidewater Dermatology Soc. (pres. 1987-88), Space Dermatology Found. (founding), Va. Space Bus. Roundtable (charter), Phi Lambda Upsilon. Avocations: nature and wildlife photography, bicycling, gardening, hiking, church and charitable activities. Office: Laser Skin & Vein Ctr Va 933 First Colonial Rd Ste 113 Virginia Beach VA 23454-3172 Office Phone: 757-437-8900. Business E-Mail: mjohnson@lsvcv.com.

**MCDANIEL, FLOYD DELBERT, SR.,** physics professor, researcher; b. Memphis, Aug. 27, 1942; s. Floyd McDaniel and Trudy (Crume) Culver; m. Linda Marie Houston, 1985; children: Floyd Delbert Jr., Todd, Kimberly, Chad, Derek. BS, Memphis State U., 1966; MS, U. Ga., Athens, 1968, PhD, 1971. Asst. prof. U. North Tex., Denton, 1975-79, assoc. prof., 1979-84, prof., 1984—2002, Regents prof. physics and material sci. and enrging., 2003—, chair physics, 2003—. Vis. scientist Hahn Meitner Inst., Berling, 1989; vis. asst. prof. U. Ky., Lexington, 1971-74; cons. Tex. Instruments, Dallas, 1980—, S.W. Rsch. Inst., San Antonio, 1980—, Tex. Utilities Electric, Dallas, 1988—; appointee faculty rsch. com. Oak Ridge (Tenn.) Nat. Lab., 1979, 80. Contbr. numerous articles to profl. jours. Me. City of Denton Land Use Commn., 1979-80. With USMC, 1960-61. Grantee NSF, Office of Naval Rsch. Mem. AAAS, IEEE, Am. Phys. Soc., Materials Rsch. Soc., Kiwanis (pres. Denton chpt. 1985-86), Phi Kappa Phi, Sigma Pi Sigma, Sigma Xi. Achievements include research in use of atomic and nuclear physics techniques to study/analyze materials accelerator mass spectrometry to determine trace impurities in semiconductor materials at sensitivities of one part in a trillion. Home: PO Box 2982 Denton TX 76202-2982 Office: U North Tex Dept of Physics PO Box 311427 Denton TX 76203 Office Phone: 940-565-3251. Business E-Mail: mcdaniel@unt.edu.

**MCDANIEL, JAMES ARTHUR,** educational association administrator; b. Cameron, Tex., Apr. 8, 1945; s. Arthur Talmadge McDaniel and Ruby Lee Offield; m. Brenda Lea Law, Nov. 20, 1967; children: Meredith Elise Millard, Paige Elizabeth Ross. MS, Ctrl. Mich. U., 1979. Mil. commd. officer US Army, Washington, 1967—89; dir. adminstrv. svcs. Nat. Cath. Ednl. Assn., Washington, 1989—. Br. chief, army officer edn. mgmt. US Army Mil. Pers. Ctr., Alexandria, Va., 1982—86. Lt. col. US Army, 1967—89, various locations. Office: Nat Catholic Educational Assn 1077 30th St NW Washington DC 20007-3852 Office Phone: 202-337-6232. Personal E-mail: jmcdaniel22@verizon.net.

**MCDANIEL, JAMES EDWIN,** lawyer; b. Dexter, Mo., Nov. 22, 1931; s. William H. and Gertie M. (Woods) McD.; m. Mary Jane Crawford, Jan. 22, 1955; children: John William, Barbara Anne. AB, Washington U., St. Louis, 1957, JD, 1959. Bar: Mo. 1959. Assoc. firm Walther, Barnard, Cloyd & Timm, 1959—60, McDonald, Barnard, Wright & Timm, 1960—63, ptnr., 1963—65, Barnard, Timm & McDaniel, St. Louis, 1965—73, Barnard & Baer, St. Louis, 1973—82, Lashly & Baer, St. Louis, 1982—2002, of counsel, 2002—; pros. atty. Glendale, Mo., 1968—. City atty. City of Glendale, Mo., 1996—; bd. dirs. Eden. Theol. Sem.; lectr. Latvian U., Riga, Inst. Fgn. Rels., Banking in Am., 1992-93. Leader legal del. Chinese-Am. Comparative Law Study, China, 1988, Russian-Am. Comparative Law Study, Russia, 1990; trustee, past chmn., past treas. 1st Congl. Ch. St. Louis. With USAF, 1951-55. Fellow Am. Bar Found. (life); St. Louis Bar Found. (life; bd. dirs. 2005); mem. ABA (bd. govs. 1997-2000, ho. of dels. 1976-80, 84-92, 97-2000, state del. 1986-92, chmn. lawyers conf., jud. adminstrn. divsn. 1992-95, 8th cir. rep. standing com. on fed. jud 1995-98, mem. standing com on jud qualification, tenure and compensation 1996-97, adv. com. law and nat. security 1999-), The Mo. Bar (pres. 1981-82, bd. govs. 1974-83), Mo. Assn. Def. Counsel, Bar Assn. Met. St. Louis (pres. 1972), Internat. Assn. Ins. Counsel, Assn. Def. Counsel St. Louis (past pres.), Phi Delta Phi. Home: 767 Elmwood Ave Saint Louis MO 63122-3216 Office: Lashly & Baer 714 Locust St Saint Louis MO 63101-1699 Office Phone: 314-621-2939. Personal E-mail: jemglendale@earthlink.net.

**MCDANIEL, JAMES MARK, JR.,** health care executive; b. Harrisonburg, Va., Mar. 18, 1953; s. James Mark and Mary (Jones) McD.; m. Lynne Stewart, Mar. 21, 1981; children: Diane Marie, Laura Elizabeth. BA, U. N.C., Greensboro, 1975. Pres. Rock-O-Lawn Mfrs., High Point, N.C., 1976-81; ins. exec. R.P.M. Assocs., Raleigh, N.C., 1981-84; adminstr. White Eye Clinic, Greenville, N.C., 1984-85; pres. S.I.S.I., Greensboro, N.C., 1988—; chief exec. officer Southeastern Eye Ctr., Greensboro, N.C., 1985—. Pres. Salem Optical Co., Winston-Salem, N.C., 1988—. Football coach Lewisville (N.C.) Titans Athletic Assn., 1982-83, 85-87, Pfafftown (N.C.) Packers Football Assn., 1988—; basketball coach Clemmons (N.C.) Basketball Assn., 1981-84; elder Community in Christ Presbyn. Chr., Forest Oaks, N.C., 1976. Republican. Avocation: coaching football and basketball. Office: Southeastern Eye Ctr 3312 Battleground Ave Greensboro NC 27410-2400 also: 146 Sycamore Ridge Dr Advance NC 27006-7476

**MCDANIEL, JARREL DAVE,** lawyer; b. Clovis, N. Mex., Oct. 17, 1930; s. Raymond Earl and Blanch (Booth) McD.; m. Anne Louise McAllister; children: Jarrel Dave Jr., Julia Anne. AA, Riverside Coll., 1951; BA, U. Tex. 1956, LLB, 1957. Bar: Tex. 1957. Assoc. Vinson & Elkins, Houston, 1957-69, ptnr., 1969-96; of counsel Sheinfeld, Maley & Kay, Houston, 1997-2001; sr. counsel Akin Gump Strauss Hauer & Feld L.L.P., Houston, 2001—. Author, lectr. in field. Served with USAF, 1950-54. Mem.: ABA, Am. Bankruptcy Inst., State Bar Tex., Am. Coll. Bankruptcy, Houston Bankruptcy Club. Roman Catholic. Home: 1217 Potomac Dr Houston TX 77057-1919 Office: Akin Gump Strauss Hauer & Feld LLP 1111 Louisana St 44th Fl Houston TX 77002 Office Phone: 713-220-5838. Business E-Mail: jmcdaniel@akingump.com.

**MCDANIEL, JOANAVA B.,** nurse; b. Belmont Land, Barbados, May 22, 1948; d. Charles Herbert and Etheline Odessa Griffith; 1 child, Shelley Johnson. AA in Liberal Arts with honors, Delaware County C.C., Media, Pa., 1986; BA in Orgnl. Mgmt. with honors, Ea. U., St. Davids, Pa., 1993. Cert. health mgmt. nurse, Barbados, pub. health nurse, W.I. Sch. Pub. Health, midwife, Tercentenary Sch. Nursing, Barbados, RN Eng. Staff nurse Ministry of Health, Barbados, 1972—77, pub. health nurse, 1977—83; pvt. duty nurse Lansdale Agy., Newtown Square, Pa., 1984—88; pvt. duty and vis. nurse PRN Health Care Svcs., Inc., Ardmore, Pa., 1986—88, dir. profl. svcs., 1988—91; asst. dir. clin. svcs. Home Nurse, Inc., Wayne, Pa., 1992—2001; clin. support specialist Bayada Nurses, Moorestown, NJ, 2001—. Missionary nurse Project Word Found., Inc., Pa., 1995—, pres. Wayne, Pa., 2000—; bd. dirs. Life Bible Inst., Ardmore, 2002. Avocations: reading, sewing, cooking, gardening, Scrabble. Office: Bayada Nurses 286 Chester Ave Moorestown NJ 08057 Office Phone: 856-778-5300.

**MCDANIEL, MYRA ATWELL,** lawyer, former state official; b. Phila., Dec. 13, 1932; d. Eva Lucinda (Yores) Atwell; m. Reuben Roosevelt McDaniel Jr., Feb. 20, 1955; children: Diane Lorraine, Reuben Roosevelt III. BA, U. Pa., 1954; JD, U. Tex., 1975; LLD, Huston-Tillotson Coll., 1984, Jarvis Christian Coll., 1986. Bar: Tex. 1975, U.S. Dist. Ct. (we. dist.) Tex. 1977, U.S. Dist. Ct. (so. and no. dists.) Tex. 1978, U.S. Ct. Appeals (5th cir.) 1978, U.S. Supreme Ct. 1978, U.S. Dist. Ct. (ea. dist.) Tex. 1979. Asst atty. gen. State of Tex., Austin, 1975-81, chief taxation div., 1979-81, gen. counsel to gov., 1983-84, sec. of state, 1984-87; asst. gen. counsel Tex. R.R. Commn., Austin, 1981-82; gen. counsel Wilson Cos., San Antonio and Midland, Tex., 1982; assoc. Bickerstaff, Heath & Smiley, Austin, 1984, ptnr., 1987-96; mng. ptnr. Bickerstaff, Heath, Smiley, Pollan, Kever & McDaniel, Austin, Tex., 1996—2000, of counsel, 2003. Mem. asset. mgmt. adv. com. State Treasury, Austin, 1984-96; mem. legal affairs com. Criminal Justice Policy Coun., Austin, 1984-8, Inter-State Oil Compact, Oklahoma City, 1984-86; bd. dirs. Austin Cons. Group, 1983-86; mem. Jud. Efficiency Coun., Austin, 1995-96; lectr. in field. Contbr. articles to profl. jours., chpts. to books Del. Tex. Conf. on Librs. and Info. Sci., Austin, 1978, White House Conf. on Librs. and Info. Scis., Washington, 1979; mem. Libr. Svcs. and Constrn. Act Adv. Coun., 1980-84, chmn., 1983-84; mem. long range plan task force Brackenridge Hosp., Austin, 1981; clk. vestry bd. St. James Episcopal Ch., Austin, 1981-83, 89-90; bd. visitors U. Tex. Law Sch., 1983-87, vice chmn., 1983-85; bd. dirs. Friends of Ronald McDonald House Ctrl. Tex., Women's Advocacy, Inc., Capital Area Rehab. Ctr.; trustee Episcopal Found. Tex., 1986-89, St. Edward's U., Austin, 1986—, chmn. acad. com., 1988-2002, vice chair, 2002-04, chmn. 2004—; chmn. divsn. capital area campaign United Way, 1986; active nat. adv. bd. Leadership Am.; trustee Episcopal Sem. S.W., 1990-96, Assn. Governing Bds. Univs. and Colls., Leadership Edn. Arts Program, 1995-2004; adv. bd. mem. Women Basketball Coaches Assn., 1996-99; bd. dirs. U.Tex. Law Sch. Found., 1997-98, Wells Fargo Cmty. Bd., Ctrl. Tex., 2000-03; trustee Episcopal Health Charities, 1997—. Recipient Tribute to 28 Black Women award Concepts Unltd., 1983; Focus on women honoree Serwa Yetu chpt. Mt. Olive grand chpt. Order of Eastern Star, 1979, Woman of Yr. Longview Metro C. of C., 1985, Woman of Yr. Austin chpt. Internat. Tng. in Communication, 1985, Citizen of Yr. Epsilon Iona chpt. Omega Psi Phi, Lone Star Girl Scout Coun. Women of Distinction, 1997, Profiles in Power Austin Bus. Jour., 1999, Silent Samaritan award Samaritan Counseling Ctr., 2000. Master Inns of Ct.; mem. ABA, Am. Bar Found., Tex. Bar Found. (trustee 1986-89), Travis County Bar Assn., Travis County Women Lawyers' Assn., Austin Black Lawyers Assn., State Bar Tex. (chmn. Profl. Efficiency & Econ. Rsch. subcom. 1976-84), Golden Key Nat. Honor Soc., Longhorn Assocs. for Excellence in Women's Athletes (adv. coun. 1988—), Order of Coif (hon. mem.), Omicron Delta Kappa, Delta Phi Alpha. Democrat. Office: Bickerstaff Heath Smiley Pollan Keever & McDaniels 1700 First Bank Plz 816 Congress Ave Austin TX 78701-2443 Office Phone: 512-472-8021. Business E-Mail: mmcdaniel@bickerstaff.com.

**MCDANIEL, NORWOOD ALLAN,** insurance agent; b. Pitts., Dec. 16, 1928; children: Norwood Jr., Cherie Suzanne, Thomas Cavin. Student, Washington and Lee U., 1948-50; PhD (hon.), C.C. Allegheny County. Gen. ins. broker, Pitts., 1949—. Adv. bd. Union Nat. Bank, Pitts. Asst. treas. C.C. Allegheny County, 1980-90. Recipient citation Pa. Senate, 1987, Pa. Ho. of Reps., 1987, tribute Congl. Record, Pres. Ronald Reagan, 1987; inducted into Pa. Sports Hall of Fame, 1973. Mem. Fellows Club (pres.), City Club, Ins. Club Pitts., Profl. Ins. Agts. Assn., Amen Corner (pres.), Masons, Shriners (potentate Syria Temple Shrine 1978), Variety Club (chief barker), The Shrine Treas. Assn. N.Am. (sec.-treas. 1985-98). Home and Office: 26319 Feathersound Dr Punta Gorda FL 33955

**MCDANIEL, RAYMOND W., JR.,** financial information company executive; BS in polit. sci., Colgate U.; JD, Emory U., 1983. Bar: NY 1984. Joined Moody's Corp., 1987, sr. analyst asset securitization dept., mng. dir. internat., 1996—2000, sr. v.p. internat., 2000—01, sr. v.p. global ratings and rsch., 2001—03, exec. v.p. global ratings and rsch., 2003—04, bd. dirs., 2003—, COO, 2004—05, pres., 2004—05, chmn., CEO, 2005—; sr. mng. dir. global ratings and rsch. Moody's Investors Svc., 2001, pres., 2001—05. Bd. dirs. John Wiley & Sons, Inc., 2005—, Nat. Coun. Econ. Edn. Mem.: Fixed Income Analysts Soc. Office: Moodys Corp 99 Church St New York NY 10007 Office Phone: 212-553-0300. Office Fax: 212-553-7194.*

**MCDANIEL, RODERICK ROGERS,** petroleum engineer, consultant; b. High River, Alta., Can., 1926; s. Dorsey Patton and Daisy (Rogers) McD.; m. Trudy Ethier, Apr. 15, 2000; children: Nancy, Leslie. BS, U. Okla., 1947. Petroleum reservoir engr. Creole Petroleum Corp., 1947, Imperial Oil Ltd., 1948-52, chief reservoir engr., 1952-55; founder McDaniel Cons., Calgary, Canada, 1955—; chmn. Can. Airlines Ltd., Calgary, 1974-91, Can. Regional Airlines, Calgary, 1991-92. Hon. dir. Calgary Exhbn. and Stampede, 1979-88, hon. bd. dirs., 1988—; dir. Calgary Stampeder Football Team, 1988. Mem. Assn. Profl. Engrs. Alta. (hon. life), Can. C. of C (bd. dirs 1973), Calgary C of C. (past pres.), Calgary Petroleum Club (past pres.), Calgary Highlanders (hon. col. ret.), Calgary Golf and Country Club, Outrigger Club (Honolulu), Mission Hills Country Club. Home: # 2200 255 5 Ave SW Calgary AB Canada T2P 3G6 Office: McDaniel & Assoc 2200 255 5th Ave SW Calgary AB Canada T2P 3G6

**MCDANIEL, SARA SHERWOOD (SALLY MCDANIEL),** trainer, consultant; b. St. Louis, Apr. 24, 1943; d. Edward Leighton and Dolores Edic (Pitts) Sherwood; m. Allen Polk McDaniel, Dec. 29, 1967; children: James Polk, Fontaine Maury. AA, Mt. Vernon Coll., 1963; BS, Vanderbilt U., 1965. Tchr. Kanawha Valley Schools, Charleston, W.Va., 1965-66, Fulton County Schools, Atlanta, 1966-68, Trinity Sch., 1969-71; tournament dir. Atlanta Classic, 1972-77; dir. alumni affairs Leadership Atlanta, 1988-89; pvt. practice cons., trainer Atlanta, 1988—. Bd. dirs. AID Atlanta, The High Mus. Art, Leadership Coun. Kennedy Ctr. of Vanderbilt U., UNICEF-Atlanta, The Atlanta Women's Found., Leadership Atlanta. Bd. dirs. Girl Scouts U.S., Ga., High Mus. Art, Atlanta Opera, UNICEF Atlanta, Aid Atlanta, Fine Art Collectors; active Com. on Women and Minorities for 1996 Olympics; mem. exec. com. Leadership Atlanta, Jr. League; mem. Friends of Spelman; trustee Mt. Vernon Coll.; bd. chair Atlanta Women's Fund; bd. dirs. Pub. Leadership Edn. Network, Ga. Women of Achievement. Mem. Am. Soc. Trainers and Dirs., Atlanta Women's Network (bd. dirs., pres.), Vanderbilt U. Alumni Assn., Alumni Assn. Peabody Coll., The Atlanta Girls Sch. Presbyterian.

**MCDANIEL, SHARON TOLIVER,** social welfare administrator, foundation administrator; BA, Penn. State U.; MPA, U. Pitts.; Cert. in Non-Profit Mgmt., Heinz Sch. Public Policy, Carnegie-Mellon U.; D.Ed., NOVA Southeastern U. Former caseworker, supervisor and court liaison Allegheny County Children Youth and Family Svc.; former caseworker and program dir. Black Adoption Svc. Program of Three Rivers Adoption Council; pres., CEO, founder A Second Chance Inc., 1994—. Co-chair Task Force of Kinship Care; co-facilitator Allegheny County Foster Care and Kinship Initiative; bd. mem. Black Administrators in Child Welfare; adv. Children's Defense Fund. Co-investigator, author Subsidized Legal Guardianship: A Permanency Planning Option Study for Children Placed in Kinship Care, Subsidized Legal Guardianship Update. Trustee Casey Family Programs, 2005—. Recipient Nubabian Queen Mother award, Girl Scouts of Southwestern Pa. award. Office: A Second Chance Inc 204 N Highland Ave Pittsburgh PA 15206*

**MCDANIEL, SUE POWELL,** writer; b. Jefferson City, Mo., Mar. 13, 1946; d. Ernest Gayle and Ruth Angeline (Raithel) Powell; m. Walter Lee Zimmerman, Aug. 14, 1966 (div. 1980); m. Olin Cleve McDaniel, June 23, 1985 (div. 2002). BS in Edn., U. Mo., 1968, MEd in Edn., 1977, EdS, 1980, PhD, 1985. Cert. tchr., Mo. Tchr. Jefferson City Pub. Schs., 1968-80; fiscal assoc. Mo. Coordinating Bd. for Higher Edn., Jefferson City, 1980-90; exec. dir. Mo. Women's Coun., Jefferson City, 1990-99; exec. dir. Skillpath Seminars, 2000—03; pres. Alternatives, Jefferson City, Mo., 1999—; dir. Heisinger Hope Found., 2004. Author: (with C. Dixon) Learning, Changing, Leading: Keep to Success in the 21st Century, 1998, Missouri Women Today, 1993, Status of the Women, 1994, I.M. Heart, 2006. Mem. Zonta Internat. Avocations: reading, music, drawing, flower garden, photography. Home: 1600 Stadium Blvd Jefferson City MO 65109-2418

**MCDANIEL, THOMAS R.,** utilities executive; BS in Civil Engring., UCLA; postgrad., Calif. State U., L.A., U. So. Calif. Joined So. Calif. Edison, 1971; CEO, dir. Edison Capital, 1987—2005; CEO, pres. Edison Mission Energy, Irvine, Calif., 2002—05, chmn., 2003—05; exec. v.p., CFO, treas. Edison Internat., Rosemead, Calif., 2005—. Active Huntington Youth Shelter; dir. Sr. Care Action Network. Office: Edison Internat 2244 Walnut Grove Ave Rosemead CA 91770-0800*

**MCDANIEL, WAYNE ALLEN,** transportation executive, consultant; b. Lynwood, Calif., Aug. 8, 1947; s. Allen and Audyne McDaniel; m. Ellen O. Jacob, Nov. 5, 1976; children: Julia Lathrop, Jennifer Russo, Josh Lathrop, Matthew. BA in Econs., U. Calif., L.A., Calif., 1969, MA in Urban Planning, 1971. Cert. planner Am. Inst. Cert. Planners, 2004. Planner Md. Dept. Transp., Silver Spring, 1971—78; chief transp. planning City of Long Beach, Long Beach, Calif., 1978—80; exec. asst. Md. Gov.'s Office, Annapolis, Md., 1980—86; dir. ops. Md. Transp. Authority, Balt., 1986—91; dep. dir. gen. Internat. Rd. Fedn., Washington, 1993—99; cons. PB Consult, Balt., 1999—. Mem.: Am. Planning Assn. Avocations: bridge, kayaking. Office: PB Consult 100 S Charles St Baltimore MD 21201 Office Phone: 410-385-4157. Business E-Mail: mcdaniel@pbworld.com.

**MCDANIELS, AUDREY EVELYN,** microbiologist; b. Grants Pass, Oreg., Feb. 11, 1928; d. Charles Pixley and Ruby Clark Best; divorced; 1 child, David Douglas. BS in Microbiology, Oreg. State U., 1950; BS in Edn., U. Wash., 1964; MS in Gen. Scis., Oreg. State U., 1965; PhD in Environ. Sci., U. Mich., 1980. Jr. scientist GE, Hanford, Wash., 1950-53; microbiologist City of Seattle, 1954-57, Wash. State Pub. Health, Seattle, 1957-60; 4th grade tchr. Amity (Oreg.) Elem., 1965-68; biology tchr. Rainier (Oreg.) H.S., 1968-72; microbiologist EPA, Cin., 1980—. Home: 1029 Fashion Ave Cincinnati OH 45238 Office: US EPA 26 W Martin Luther King Dr Cincinnati OH 45268 Office Phone: 513-569-7332. Business E-Mail: mcdaniels.audrey@epa.gov.

**MCDANIELS, WILLIAM E.,** lawyer; b. Needham, Mass., July 1, 1941; BA, Williams Coll., 1963; JD, Georgetown U., 1966. Bar: D.C. 1967, Md. 1983. Grad. fellow criminal law, litigation U. Pa., Phila., 1966-68; pub. defender Phila. Pub. Defender's Office, 1966-68; adj. prof. evidence, criminal law, advanced criminal procedure Georgetown U. Law Ctr., Washington, 1970-87; mem. Williams & Connolly LLP, Washington, 1968—. Instr. Nat. Inst. Trial Advocacy, 1975—. Fellow Am. Coll. Trial Lawyers; mem. ABA, Md. State Bar Assn, D.C. Bar. Office: Williams & Connolly LLP 725 12th St NW Washington DC 20005-5901 Office Phone: 202-434-5055. Business E-Mail: wmcdaniels@wc.com.

**MCDARRAH, FRED WILLIAM,** photographer, editor, writer; b. Bklyn., Nov. 5, 1926; s. Howard Arthur and Elizabeth (Swahn) McD.; m. Gloria Schoffel, Nov. 5, 1960; children: Timothy Swann, Patrick James. BA in Journalism, NYU, 1954. Mem. staff Village Voice Newspaper, N.Y.C., 1959—, picture editor, 1971—; book reviewer ASMP Infinity Mag., 1972-73, Photo Dist. News, 1985-88, The Picture Profl., 1990—2002. Exhibited in Soho Photo Gallery, 1973, Whitney Mus., 1974, 76-77, Dallas Mus. Art, 1974, San Francisco Mus. Art, 1975, Wadsworth Atheneum, 1975, Sidney Janis Gallery, 1976, Basel (Switzerland) Art Fair, 1976, Alfred Stieglitz Gallery, 1976, Empire State Mus., Albany, N.Y., 1978, Lightworks Gallery, Syracuse, N.Y., 1981, Cape Cod Gallery, Provincetown Mass., 1982, Galleria di Franca Mancini, Pesaro, Italy, 1983, Musée du Quebec, 1987, Anita Shapolsky Gallery, N.Y.C., 1988, Hartnett Gallery U. Rochester, N.Y., 1989, G. Ray Hawkins Gallery, L.A., 1989, Read Gallery Antioch (Ohio) Coll., 1989, Mus. Art/Sci./Industry, Bridgeport, Conn., 1989, N.Y.C. Gallery Queens Mus., 1989, Ctr. Photography, Woodstock, 1989, Frumkin/Adams Gallery, 1990, Musée d'Art Moderne De La Ville de Paris, 1990, Musée d'Art Contemporain, Montreal, 1990, Pollack-Krasner Mus., East Hampton, N.Y., 1990, Found. Cartier, Paris, 1990, Marty Carey Pictures Gallery, Woodstock, N.Y., 1992, Galerie Gilles Ringuet, Belfort, France, 1992, Galerie Contre Jour, Belfort, France, 1992, Galleria La Pescheria, Cesena, Italy, 1994, Whitney Mus. Am. Art, 1995—, Nat. Portrait Gallery, 1996, Candice Perich Gallery, 1996; exhbns. include Jack Kerouac Visions of the Road, Les Rencontres D'Arles, Arles, France, 1991, Jack Kerouac Travelling Writers, Saint-Malo (France) Internat. Festival, 1991, 97, Images of Greenwich Village N.Y. Camera Club, 1992, Walker Art Ctr., Mpls., 1996, M.H. de Young Meml. Mus., San Francisco, 1996, Whitney Mus. Am. Art, 1997-98, New York Stories, Chiostro del Bramante, Rome, 1999, Detroit Inst. Arts, 2000, Great Modern Pictures, N.Y., 2000, MOCA, Wexner Ctr., Parrish Mus., 2000, Mus. Nat. Modern Art 2001, Gallerie Comunale d'Arte Moderna, Rome, 2001, Mus. City of N.Y., 2001, Centro Pompidou, 2001, Albright-Knox Art Gallery, 2002, Mus. Contemporary Art, L.A., 2002, Fahey/Klein Gallery, L.A., 2002, Grimaldi Forum, Monaco, 2003, Snap Galleries, Birmingham, Eng, 2004, Castello di Rivoli, Turin, 2004, Triennale di Milano, 2004, Provd Galleries, 2005, others; author: The Beat Scene, 1960, The Artist's World in Pictures, 1961, rev. edit. 1988, Greenwich Village, 1963, New York, New York, 1964, Sculpture in Environment, 1967, Museums in New York, 1973, French edit., 1979, 5th edit., 1994, Photography Marketplace, 2d edit., 1977, Stock Photo and Assignment Source Book, 1977, 2d edit., 1984, Gay Pride: Photographs from Stonewall to Today, 1994, Frommer's Virginia Guide, 2d edit., 1994, Fodor's Cancun, Cozumel, Yucatan Peninsula, 1996, Kerouac and Friends: A Beat Generation Album, 1984, Japanese edit, 1990, 2nd edit, 2002, Frommer's Atlantic City and Cape May, 4th edit., 1991, 5th edit., 1993, New York Stories, 2001, Anarchy, Protest & Rebellion & the Counter Culture that Changed America, 2003; co-author: The New Bohemia, 1967, 2d edit., 1990, Guide for Ecumenical Discussion, 1970, Greenwich Village Guide, 1992, Frommer's Virginia, 1992, 2d edit. 1994; author: (with Timothy S. LA Pop Art Negli Anni '60 Chiostro del Bram Ante, 1999; author: (with Gloria S. McDarrah) Beat Generation: Glory Days in Greenwich Village, 1998; The Beat Generation: Glory Days in Greenwich Village, edito., 1996; editor: (with Gloria S. McDarrah and Timothy S. McDarrah) The Photography Encyclopedia, 1999; author: (with Gloria S. McDarrah) The Artist's World in Pictures, 2d edit., 1988; Saturday Rev. Executive Desk Diary, 1962-64; photographer: Personality Posters, Fotofolio (post cards) (polit. and social figures); contbr. articles, picture features to various pubs. including N.Y. Mag., Vanity Fair. Paratrooper U.S. Army, 1944-47. Recipient numerous photography awards including 1st place spot news photo award N.Y. Press Assn., 1964, 68; recipient 1st place feature photo award N.Y. Press Assn., 1967, 1st place picture story award N.Y. Press Assn., 1969, 2nd place spot news photo award N.Y. Press Assn., 1967, 70, 3d place spot news photo award N.Y. Press Assn., 1965, 3d place feature photo award N.Y. Press Assn., 1965, 3d place picture story award N.Y. Press Assn., 1970, 1st place Best Pictorial Series Nat. Newspaper Assn., 1966, Page One award Newspaper Guild N.Y., 1971, 80; Guggenheim fellow in photography, 1972. Mem. N.Y. Press Photographers Assn., Authors Guild, N.Y. Press Club, Am. Soc. Picture Profls. Office: 36 Cooper Sq New York NY 10003-7118 Office Fax: 212-254-5547.

**MCDARRAH, GLORIA SCHOFFEL,** editor, writer; b. Bronx, N.Y., June 22, 1932; d. Louis and Rose Schoffel; m. Fred W. McDarrah, Nov. 5, 1960; children: Timothy, Patrick. BA in French, Pa. State U., 1953; MA in French, NYU, 1966. Editorial asst. Crowell-Collier, N.Y.C., 1957-59; exec. asst. to pub. Time Inc., N.Y.C., 1959-61; libr., tchr. N.Y.C. Pub. Schs. and St. Luke's Sch., 1972-76; exec. asst. to pres. Capital Cities Communications Inc., N.Y.C., 1972-76; analyst N.Y.C. Landmarks Preservation Commn., 1976-79; project editor Grosset & Dunlap Inc., N.Y.C., 1979-80; sr. editor Prentice Hall trade div. Simon & Schuster Inc., N.Y.C., 1980-88; pres. McDarrah Media Assocs., N.Y.C., 1988—. Editor book rev. The Picture Profl., 1989—; book reviewer Pub.'s Weekly, 1994—. Author: Frommer's Guide to Va., 1992, Frommer's Guide to Va. 2d edit., 1994—95, Frommer's Atlantic City and Cape May, 1984, Frommer's Atlantic City and Cape May 4th edit., 1991, Frommer's Atlantic City and Cape May 5th edit., 1993—95, The Artist's World 2d edit., 1988, Photography Encyclopedia, 1999; co-author: Museums in N.Y. 5th edit., 1990, Photography Marketplace, 1975, The Beat Generation: Glory Days in Greenwich Village, 1996, Anarchy, Protest and Rebellion and the Counter-Culture That Changed Am., 2003; co-editor: Exec. Desk Diary Saturday Rev., 1962—64; contbg. editor (quar.): Dollarwise Traveler, Fodor's Cancun, Cozumel, Yucatan Peninsula, Fodor's Ariz.

**MCDAVID, DOUGLAS WARREN,** executive research consultant; b. San Francisco, Feb. 25, 1947; s. James Etheridge and Elizabeth Rae (Warren) McD.; m. Nancy Kathleen Somers, June 1968 (div. 1982); 1 child, Amy Kemp; m. Carleen Ann Richmond, Feb. 14, 1987; 1 child, Amanda Claire. BA in Sociology, U. Calif., Santa Cruz, 1969; MA in Libr. Sci., San Jose State U., 1972. Libr. Palo Alto (Calif.) City Libr., 1969-81; systems analyst Tymnet (Tymshare), Cupertino, Calif., 1981-84; mgr. systems architecture Tymnet McDonnell Douglas, San Jose, Calif., 1984-86; data modeling cons. Fireman's Fund Ins., Terra Linda, Calif., 1986-87, Bank of Calif., San Francisco, 1988; systems cons. Pacific Bell, San Ramon, Calif., 1989-93; prin. Integrated Info., 1993—; exec. cons. IBM Global Svcs., 1995—, IBM Almaden Rsch Ctr., 2002—. Mem. IBM Acad. Tech., 2000—; spkr. Entity/Relationship Conf. Internat., Burlingame, Calif., 1991, DAMA Internat. Conf., 1994—; sr. cons. in bus. semantic modeling for object oriented applications IBM Corp., 1994—; 1996 spkr. Bus. Rules Conf. OOPSLA, IBM Object Technology Conf., Ind. Labor & Mgmt. Coun.; cons. IBM, 1994-98, mgr. knowledge devel., 1999—; spkr. in field. Assoc. editor: Handbook of Object Technology. Mem. IEEE, Assn. for Computing Machinery, Data Adminstrn. Mgmt. Assn. (San Francisco bd. dirs. 1987-91, Sacramento bd. dirs. 1992, speaker 1991, 92), Data Processing Mgmt. Assn. (speaker 1992), Am. Assn. Artificial Intelligence (speaker 1993), Internat. Soc. Sys. Sci. (speaker 1999). Avocations: golf, gardening, creative writing, investing, swimming. Home and Office: 8611 Kingslynn Ct Elk Grove CA 95624-3135 Office Phone: 916-549-4600. Business E-Mail: mcdavid@us.ibm.com.

**MCDAVID, GEORGE EUGENE (GENE MC DAVID),** retired newspaper executive; b. McComb, Miss., June 30, 1930; s. O. C. and Inez S. McDavid; m. Betty Ernestine Tinsley, Sept. 24, 1949; children: Carol, Martha Gene Newman. BBA cum laude, U. Houston, 1965. Owner, pub. Wilk Amite Record, Gloster, Miss., 1949-58; with Houston Chronicle, 1958—, prodn. mgr., 1967-74, v.p. ops., 1974-85, v.p., gen. mgr., 1985-90, pres., 1990-98, ret., 1998. Mem. adv. bd. Am. Press Inst.; past pres., bd. dirs. S.W. Wch. Printing Mgmt. Chmn. Greater Houston chpt. ARC, 1st vice-chmn.; pres.'s counsel Houston Bapt. U; vice-chmn. Sam Houston Boy Scouts Am., United Negro Coll. Fund, Asia Soc. Goodwill Industries, YMCA; chmn. Houston Forum, Houston region Am. Cancer Soc., bd. regents, 1997—; bd. deacon Second Bapt. Ch., Houston.; bd. dirs. Nat. Conf. Christians and Jews; nat. bd. govs. Greater Houston chpt. ARC; bd. dirs. Greater Houston Partnership; bd. dirs., pres. Houston Symphony; bd. dirs., v.p. Books of the World; vice-chmn. devel. bd. U. Houston, chair bd. regents, 2003. Recipient Franklin award, U. Houston, 1961, Disting. Alumnus award, 1990, 1997, Taggart award, Tex. Newspaper, 1992, Man of Yr. award, NCCJ, 1993, named Outstanding Ex-Citizen Gloster, 1973, Hon. Father of Yr., 1996, named to Miss. Jour. Hall of Fame, 2002. Mem.: So. Newspaper Pubs. Assn. (pres.), Am. Newspaper Pubs. Assn. (chmn. tech. com.), Pine Forest Country Club, Houston C. of C. (Houston Citizen's Cmty. Svc. award 1993, named Houston Cultural Leader of Yr. 1998), Tex. Daily Newspaper Assn. (pres.), Crown Colony Country Club, Beta Gamma Sigma, Phi Kappa Phi. Address: 4 Hunters Park Ln Houston TX 77024-5438 Personal E-mail: gene.mcdavid@chron.com.

**MCDAVID, JANET LOUISE,** lawyer; b. Mpls., Jan. 24, 1950; d. Robert Matthew and Lois May (Bratt) Kurzeka; m. John Gary McDavid, June 9, 1973; 1 child, Matthew Collins McDavid. BA, Northwestern U., 1971; JD, Georgetown U., 1974. Bar D.C. 1975, U.S. Ct. Appeals (fed. cir.) 1975 (D.C. cir. 1976), U.S. Supreme Ct. 1980, U.S. Ct. Appeals (5th cir.) 1983, (9th cir.) 1986. Assoc. Hogan & Harston, Washington, 1974-83, ptnr., 1984—. Gen. counsel ERAmerica, 1977-83; mem. antitrust task force Dept. Defense, 1993-94, 96-97; mem. antitrust coun. U.S. C. of C., 1994—; advisor Bush adminstrn. transition team, 2001. Contbr. articles to profl. jours. Participant Clinton and Bush adminstrn. transition team FTC. Mem. ABA (antitrust sect., vice chmn. civil practice com. 1986-89, sect. 2 com. 1989-90, chmn. franchising com. 1990-91, coun. mem. 1991-94, program officer 1994-97, vice chair 1997-98, chair-elect 1998-99, chair 1999-2000, immediate past chair, governing com. of forum on franchising 1991-97), ACLU, U.S.C. of C. (antitrust coun. 1995—), Washington Coun. Lawyers, D.C. Bar Assn., Fed. Bar Assn., Women Legal Def. fund. Democrat. Office: Hogan & Hartson 555 13th St NW Washington DC 20004-1109 Office Phone: 202-637-8780. Business E-Mail: jlmcdavid@hhlaw.com.

**MCDAVID, JO COLLINS,** library manager; b. Kingsport, Tenn., Sept. 12, 1953; d. Joe E. and Estal Price Collins; 1 child, Christopher Lynn. AS, North East State, Blountville. Tenn., 1990; BSc, ETSU, Johnson City, Tenn., 1999. Cert. Pub. Libr. Mgr. Univ. Tenn., 1997. Br. mgr. Sullivan County Libr., Blountville, Tenn., 1991—; tech support SPS, Gray, Ind., 1994—97. Pres. Sullivan Band Boosters. Kingsport, Tenn., 1993—94; bd. mem. ACES, Blountville, Tenn., 2002—. Mem.: Tenn. Libr. Assn. (chairperson 1998—2000). Office: Colonial Heights Br Libr 149 Pactolus Rd Kingsport TN 37664 Business E-Mail: jmcdavid@wrlibrary.org.

**MCDAVID, JOHN SANFORD,** lawyer; b. New Orleans, June 19, 1958; s. John Land and Sylvia (Sanford) McD.; m. Mary Beth Waggener, July 31, 1982; children: Patrick Sanford, Jason Harkins. BBA in Mgmt., U. Miss., 1981, JD, 1984. Bar: Miss. 1984. La. 1984. Ptnr. McDavid Noblin & West PLLC, Jackson, Miss., 1984—2003, Young Williams PA, 2003—. Mem. ABA, La. State Bar, Miss. Bar (chmn. sect. real property 2000-01), Miss. Oil and Gas Lawyers Assn. (pres. 1999-2000), Tri-County Real Attys. Assn. (pres. 1998-99), Hinds County Bar Assn., Univ. Club. Office: 210 E Capitol St 20th Fl Jackson MS 39201-2505 Home: 112 Woodbury Park Madison MS 39110 Office Phone: 601-360-9014. Business E-Mail: jmcdavid@youngwilliams.com.

**MCDAVID, SARA JUNE,** librarian; b. Atlanta, Dec. 21, 1945; d. William Harvey and June (Threadgill) McRae; m. Michael Wright McDavid, Mar. 20, 1971. BA, Mercer U., 1967; MLS, Emory U., 1969. Head librarian Fernbank Sci. Ctr., Atlanta, 1969-77; dir. rsch. libr. Fed. Res. Bank of Atlanta, 1977-81; mgr. mem. services SOLINET, Atlanta, 1981-82; media specialist Parkview High Sch., Atlanta, 1982-84; ptnr. Intercontinental Travel, Atlanta, 1984-85; librarian Wesleyan Day Sch., Atlanta, 1985-86; mgr. info. svcs. Internat. Assn. Fin. Planning, Atlanta, 1986-90; dir. rsch. Korn Ferry Internat., Atlanta, 1990-95; clinical rsch. coord. Lamalie Amrop Internat., Atlanta, 1995-98; dir. practice splty. teams LAI Ward Howell, 1998; prin. McDavid Rsch. Assocs., Atlanta, 1998-99; lead rsch'r. The Boston Consulting Group, Atlanta, 1999—. Bd. dirs. Southeastern Library Network, Atlanta, 1977-80, vice chmn. bd., 1979-80. Contbr. articles to profl. jours. Pres., mem. exec. com. Atlanta Humane Soc., 1985-86, bd. dirs. aux., 1978-90. Mem. Ga. Libr. Assn. (v.p. 1981-83), Spl. Librs. Assn. (treas. 1994, mem. dir. divsn. 1998-2000, editor Libr.

Mgmt. Quar. 1996-98, 2002). Home: 1535 Knob Hill Dr NE Atlanta GA 30329-3206 Office: Boston Consulting Group Inc 600 Peachtree St NE Ste 3800 Atlanta GA 30308-2218 Office Phone: 404-877-5200. Business E-Mail: mcdavid.sara@bcg.com.

**MCDAVID, WILLIAM HENRY,** lawyer; b. NYC, May 10, 1946; m. Sylvia Noin, Dec. 21, 1984; children: Andrew, Madeline, William, Flora. AB, Columbia Coll., NYC, 1968; JD, Yale U., 1972. Assoc. Debevoise & Plimpton, NYC, 1972-81; asst. gen. counsel Bankers Trust Co., NYC, 1981-83, assoc. gen. counsel, 1983-84, v.p., 1984-85, v.p., counsel, 1986-88; gen. counsel J.P. Morgan & Co., NYC, 1988—2000, J.P. Morgan Chase & Co., NYC, 2000—03, chief legal officer, 2003—04; legal officer Bank One Corp (merged with J.P. Morgan Chase & Co.), 2004—. Office: JP Morgan Chase & Co Office Gen Coun 270 Park Ave Fl 8 New York NY 10017-2014

**MCDAVIS, RODERICK J.,** academic administrator; b. Dayton, Ohio, Oct. 17, 1948; m. Deborah Moses; children: Ryan, Tony. BS in Social Scis. in Secondary Edn., Ohio U., 1970; MS in Student Pers. Adminstrn., U. Dayton, 1971; PhD in Counselor Edn., U. Toledo, 1974. Asst. prof. edn. grad. divsn. Siena Heights Coll., Adrian, Mich., 1973—74; asst. prof. edn. dept. counselor edn. Coll. Edn. U. Fla., Gainesville, 1974—79, assoc. prof. edn. dept. counselor edn. Coll. Edn., 1979—82, prof. edn. dept. counselor edn. Coll. Edn., 1982—89, acting asst. dean for grad. studies Grad. Sch., 1984—85, assoc. dean Grad. Sch. and Minority Programs Grad. Sch., 1986—89, prof. edn. dept. counselor edn. Coll. Edn., 1994—99, dean Coll. Edn., 1994—99; prof. counselor edn. dept. edn. leadership, counseling and founds. Coll. Edn. U. Ark., Fayetteville, 1989—94, dean Coll. Edn., 1989—94; prof. edn. divsn. ednl. studies Sch. Edn. Va. Commonwealth U., Richmond, 1999—2004, provost, v.p. acad. affairs, 1999—2004; pres. Ohio U., Athens, 2004—. Vis. prof. edn. dept. counselor edn. and human svcs. Grad. Sch. Edn. U. Dayton, 1979—83, 1992. Named Person of Yr. in Edn., The Gainesville Sun, 1995; recipient Disting. Svc. award for cmty. outreach through TV media, Fla. Assn. for Counselor Edn. and Supervision, 1978, Key to the City, City Commn., Gainesville, 1995, Outstanding Alumnus award, Ohio U. Coll. Edn., 1996, Black Achiever's award in edn., Fla. Conf. Black State Legislators, Tallahassee, 1997. Mem.: Nat. Alliance Black Sch. Educators, Am. Coll. Pers. Assn., Phi Kappa Phi, Phi Delta Kappa (Post-secondary Outstanding Educator award North Ctrl. Fla. chpt. 1996). Office: Office of the Pres 108 Cutler Hall Athens OH 45701 Office Phone: 740-593-1804. E-mail: mcdavis@ohio.edu.*

**MCDEMMOND, MARIE VALENTINE,** academic administrator, consultant; b. New Orleans, Feb. 4, 1946; d. George Graham and Marie Valentine (Prudeaux) McD.; m. Louis Saulny, June 15, 1966 (div. 1972); children: Alan Peter, Eric W. Reid; m. Roy Russell Mouton, Sept. 18, 1987. BA, Xavier U., 1968; MEd, U. New Orleans, 1971; postgrad, SUNY, Albany; EdD, U. Mass., 1985. Tchr. Kohn Jr. High Sch., New Orleans, 1968-70; dir. Community Leadership Program, New Rochelle, N.Y., 1970-72, Community Leadership Consortium, Westchester County, N.Y., 1973-73; assoc. Higher Edn. Opportunity Program Office, Albany, N.Y., 1973-74; instr. dept. edn. Ithaca (N.Y.) Coll., 1974; with bus. office, dept. acctg. Bronx (N.Y.) Phychiatric Ctr., 1974-77; assoc. higher edn. N.Y. State Bd. Regents, Albany, 1977-78; dir. fin. Mass. Bd. Regional Community Colls., Boston, 1979-80; assoc. vice chancellor U. Mass., Amherst, 1980-84; v.p. budget & fin. Atlantic U., 1984-85; asst. v.p. for fin. Emory U., Atlanta, 1985-86; pres. McDemmond & Assoc., Boca Raton, Fla., 1986-89; asst. prof. edn. U. New Orleans, 1987-88; asst. v.p. adminstrn. & fin. Fla. Atlantic U., Boca Raton, 1988-89; v.p. adminstrn. & fin., 1990-96; pres. Norfolk (Va.) State U., 1996—. Adj. asst. prof. Coll. New Rochelle, N.Y., 1971-73; adj. prof. edn. U. Mass., Amherst, 1984; hostess Sta. WTCC, Springfield, Mass., 1983-84; lectr. in economic redevel., 1989; adv. bd. mem. Historically Black Coll. and U. Author tng. course. Civil svc. examiner State N.Y., Albany, 1976-78; precinct coord. Democrats for Jackson, Amherst, 1984; advisor Palm Beach Judicial Bldg., West Palm Beach, Fla., 1991; bd. dirs. Lumina Found., United Way, Urban League, Hampton Roads. Named Fla. Woman Who Makes a Difference Nat. Assn. Women Bus. Owners, 1990, Adminstr. of Yr. Va. Assn. Ed. Office Profl.; recipient Pioneer award Outstanding Profl. Women of Hampton Roads. Mem. Bus. and Profl. Women's Club Am. (Woman of Achievement award 1991), New England Minority Women (pres. 1982-84), So. Assn. Coll. and Bus. Officers (exec. com. 1991—), Nat. Assn. Coll. and Univ. Bus. Officers, Coun. Minority Edn. (pres. 1982-84). Roman Catholic. Avocations: gardening, reading. Office: Norfolk State U 700 Park Ave Norfolk VA 23504-8090*

**MCDERMID, MARGARET E.,** information technology executive, engineer; B in bus., Mary Baldwin Coll.; MBA, U. Richmond. With Stone and Webster Engring. Corp.; joined Va. Power, 1982, various positions engring. & construction dept., 1982—86, dir. adminstrv. svcs., 1986—98; v.p. info. tech., CIO Dominion Resources Inc., 1998—2000; sr. v.p. info. tech., CIO, 2000—. Mem. apptd. by Gov. Gilmore CIO Adv. Bd., 2000. Active with United Way, Big Brothers, Big Sisters; bd. trustees Mary Baldwin Coll.; found. bd. J. Sargeant Reynolds Cmty. Coll.; bd. dirs. Greater Richmond Tech. Coun., Children's Mus. Richmond Bus. Com., CIO Forum; mem. Va. Rsch. and Tech. Adv. Coun. Achievements include first woman to enter the Apprentice Program at Newport News Shipyard where she completed the Patternmaker's program. Office: Dominion Resources Inc 120 Tredegar St Richmond VA 23219 Office Phone: 804-819-2000.

**MCDERMOTT, AGNES CHARLENE SENAPE,** philosophy educator; b. Hazelton, Pa., Mar. 11, 1937; d. Charles G. and Conjetta (Ranieri) Senape; children: Robert C., Lisa G., Jamie C. BA, U. Pa., 1956, PhD, 1964; postgrad., U. Calif.-Berkeley, 1960—61, U. Amsterdam, Netherlands, 1965, U. Wis., 1967—69. Instr. math. Drexel Inst. Tech., Phila., 1962-63; asst. prof. philosophy SUNY-Buffalo, 1964-65, Hampton Inst., Va., 1966-67; asst. prof. U. Wis.-Milw., 1967-70; assoc. prof. philosophy U. N.Mex.-Albuquerque, 1970-80, prof., dean grad. studies. 1981-86; dean in residence Coun. of Grad. Schs., Washington, 1985-86; provost, v.p. acad. affairs CUNY, 1986-89, prof. philosophy, 1986-91; dean for acad. and student affairs, cons. Albuquerque Acad., 1991-93; ind. cons. Corrales, N.Mex., 1993—. Vis. assoc. prof. U. Wash., Seattle, 1974, U. Calif.-Berkeley, 1973-74, U. Hawaii, Honolulu, 1975; vis. prof. U. Calif.-Berkeley, 1980; vis. prof. Semester at Sea, U. Pitts., fall 1994; bd. dir. Juvenile Diabetes Rsch. Found.; lectr., panelist in field. Author: An Eleventh Century Buddhist Logic of 'Exists', 1969, Boethius' Treatise on the Modes of Signifying, 1980; compiler, editor anthology: Comparative Philosophy: Selected Essays, 1983; rev. editor Phil. East West, 1986—; contbr. articles and stories to profl. and literary jours. Active Albuquerque Care Alliance, 1988—2000; state leader Juvenile Diabetes Rsch. Found., N.Mex. AAUW postdoctoral fellow, 1965-66; NEH Younger Humanist fellow, 1971-72; faculty rsch. fellow U. N.Mex., 1978, 79, 80; U. Pa. grad. fellow, 1961-62; S. Fels Found. fellow, 1963-64; U. Pa. tuition scholar; Pa. Hist. Soc. scholar Mem. N.Y. Acad. Scis., Am. Philos. Soc., Am. Philos. Assn. (exec. com. 1977-80), Assn. Asian Studies (exec. com. 1977-80), Am. Oriental Soc., Western Assn. Grad. Schs. (pres. 1986-87), Phi Beta Kappa, Pi Mu Epsilon. Democrat. Avocations: skiing, fly fishing. Personal E-mail: mcdcott@netzero.net.

**MCDERMOTT, ALICE,** writer; b. Bklyn., June 27, 1953; married; 3 children. BA, SUNY, Oswego, 1975; MA, U. N.H., 1978. Instr. U. Calif., San Diego, Am. U., Washington; lectr. in English U. N.H.; writer-in-residence Lynchburg Coll., Va.; Hollins Coll., Va.; Johns Hopkins U., Balt. Author: A Bigamist's Daughter, 1982, That Night, 1987 (Pulitzer Prize finalist, Nat. Book Award finalist, L.A. Times Book Prize finalist), At Weddings and Wakes, 1992, Charming Billy, 1998 (Nat. Book Award), After This, 2006; contbr. short stories to numerous profl. publs. Recipient Whiting Writers award. Office: Farrar Straus and Giroux 19 Union Sq W New York NY 10003

**MCDERMOTT, ANN ELIZABETH,** chemistry professor; b. Enumclan, Wash., Oct. 12, 1960; d. Andrew Oliver and Lila Anne (Diemert) McD. BS, Harvey Mudd Coll., 1981; PhD, U. Calif., Berkeley, 1987. Postdoctoral rschr. MIT Nat. Magnet Lab., Cambridge, Mass., 1988-89, U.C.L. an dC.P.,

Brussels, 1990-91; asst. prof. Columbia U., NYC, 1991-96, assoc. prof., 1997, prof., 1998—. Contbr. articles to sci. jours. Recipient ACS award in pure chemistry, 1996. Mem.: NAS. Office: Columbia U Chemistry Dept New York NY 10027

**MCDERMOTT, DENNIS MICHAEL,** trade association executive; b. Akron, Ohio, Jan. 9, 1947; s. Gerard Joseph and Irene Cathryn McDermott; m. Margaret Mary Hayden, Dec. 14, 1968 (div. July 1981); children: Martin Jerome, Kathleen Marie; m. Margaret Amberg Egan, Apr. 30, 1983; 1 stepson, Michael Amberg. BS in Journalism, Kent (Ohio) State U., 1969; postgrad. in edn., Chapman Coll., 1972; postgrad. in pub. rels., Kent (Ohio) State U., 1975. Reporter Akron Beacon Jour., 1967-69; conv. mgr. Am. Sch. of Health, Kent, 1973-74, asst. exec. dir., 1974-77; exec. dir. Emergency Dept. Nurses Assn., Chgo., 1977-80; exec. v.p. Oakland (Calif.) Bd. Realtors, 1980-83; v.p. Calif. Assn. of Realtors, L.A., 1983-87; exec. v.p. Mo. Assn. of Realtors, Columbia, 1988—. Vis. lectr. journalism Kent State U., 1973-77; cons. 30 trade assns., 1977-87. Contbg. editor Jour. of Sch. Health, 1973-77; exec. editor Jour. of Emergency Nursing, 1977-80, Oakland Realtor mag., 1980-83, Missouri Realtor mag., 1988—. Life mem. Realtors Polit. Action Com., Washington, 1984—. Sgt. USAF, 1969-73. Scholar Knight Found., 1969-73. Mem. Am. Soc. of Assn. Execs., Pub. Rels. Soc. of Am. Avocations: travel, photography. Home: 3812 Barrington Dr Columbia MO 65203-4453 Office: Mo Assn of Realtors PO Box 1327 Columbia MO 65205-1327

**MCDERMOTT, DYLAN,** actor; b. Waterbury, Conn., Oct. 26, 1961; s. Richard "Mac" and Diane McDermott; m. Shiva Afshar, Nov. 19, 1995; children: Colette, Charlotte Rose. BA in Drama, Fordham U., 1983. Appeared in films: Hamburger Hill, 1987, Twister, 1988, Steel Manolias, 1989, In The Line Of Fire, 1993, The Cowboy Way, 1994, Miracle on 34th Street, 1994, Destiny Turns On The Radio, 1995, Home For The Holidays, 1995, 'Til There Was You, 1996, Texas Rangers, 2000, Three to Tango, 1999, Party Monster, 2003, Wonderland, 2003, The Tenants, 2005, Edison, 2005; TV series: The Practice, 1997-2003, The Grid, 2004, dir. 1997; TV guest appearances Ally MacBeal, 1997, Tales from the Crypt, Will & Grace, 2003; stage The Treatment, 2006. Recipient Golden Globe award, 1999. Address: William Morris Agy 151 El Camino Dr Beverly Hills CA 90212*

**MCDERMOTT, FRANCIS OWEN,** retired lawyer; b. Denver, Feb. 25, 1933; s. Paul Harkins and Agnes (Clark) McD.; divorced; children: Diana, Daniel, Christopher, Anthony, Justine; m. Estella Marina Idiaquez, June 6, 1986; stepchildren: Bernard, Michael, Nicole, Marie, Steven. JD, Am. U., 1960. Bar: D.C. 1960, U.S. Dist. Ct. D.C., 1960, U.S. Ct. Appeals (D.C. cir.) 1960, u.S. Tax Ct. 1961, U.S. Supreme Ct. 1964. Trial atty. office regional counsel IRS, Washington, 1961-65; mem. profl. staff com. on fin. U.S. Senate, Washington, 1965-68; tax counsel Assn. Am. R.R.s, Washington, 1968-73; assoc. Hopkins & Sutter, Washington, 1973-76, ptnr., 1976-98, ret., 1999; ret. ptnr. Foley & Lardner, Washington, 2001—02. gen. counsel Inst. Ill., Washington, 1987-96. Mem. ABA, Fed. Bar Assn., Nat. Def. Transp. Assn. (v.p., gen. counsel 1974—). Roman Catholic. Avocation: tennis. Home: 1 S Montague St Arlington VA 22204-1007 Office Phone: 202-945-6092. E-mail: fmcdermott@foley.com.

**MCDERMOTT, JAMES A.,** congressman, psychiatrist; b. Chicago, Dec. 28, 1936; m. Therese Hansen; 2 children. BS, Wheaton Coll., Ill., 1958; MD, U. Ill. Med. Sch., Chgo., 1963. Intern Buffalo Gen. Hosp., 1963-64; resident adult psychiatry U. Ill. Hosps., Chgo., 1964-66; resident child psychiatry U. Wash. Hosps., Seattle, 1966-68; asst. clin. prof. dept. psychiatry U. Wash., Seattle, 1970-83; mem. Wash. State Ho. Reps. from 43rd Dist., 1971-72, Wash. State Senate, 1975-87; regional med. officer U.S. Fgn. Svc., 1987-88; mem. US Congress from 7th Wash. dist., 1989—, mem. ways and means com., ranking minority mem. human resources subcommittee. Mem. exec. and edn. com. Nat. Conf. State Legislatures, chair ethics com.; co-chmn. Congl. task force internat. HIV/AIDS, Congl. Caucus on India and Indian Ams., Africa Trade and Investment Caucus, Congl. Kidney Caucus. Mem. Wash. State Arts Commn., Wash. Coun. for Prevention Child Abuse and Neglect; Dem. nominee for gov., 1980. Lt. comdr. M.C. USN, 1968—70. Mem. Am. Psychiat. Assn., Wash. State Med. Assn., King County Med. Soc. Democrat. Episcopalian. Office: US Ho Reps 1035 Longworth Ho Office Bldg Washington DC 20515 Office Phone: 202-225-3106.*

**MC DERMOTT, JOHN FRANCIS,** psychiatrist, physician; b. Hartford, Conn., Dec. 12, 1929; s. John Francis and Camilla R. (Cavanaugh) McD.; m. Sarah N. Schemm, Dec. 27, 1958; children: Elizabeth C., John Francis III. AB, Cornell U., 1951; MD, N.Y. Med. Coll., 1955. Diplomate in psychiatry and child psychiatry Am. Bd. Psychiatry and Neurology. Intern Henry Ford Hosp., Detroit, 1955-56; resident in psychiatry U. Mich. Med. Center, 1956-58, resident in child psychiatry, 1960-62; practice medicine, specializing in psychiatry and child and adolescent psychiatry Honolulu, 1966-95; instr., asst. prof., asso. prof. psychiatry U. Mich. Sch. Medicine, 1962-69; prof., chmn. dept. psychiatry U. Hawaii Sch. Medicine, 1969-95, prof. emeritus, 1995—; scholar-in-residence Rockefeller Found. Study Ctr., Bellagio, Italy, 1985, 92. Chmn. com. cert. in child psychiatry Am. Bd. Psychiatry and Neurology, 1974-78, bd. dirs., 1983-91, chmn. R&D com., 1985-91; sr. vis. scientist dept. exptl. psychology Oxford (Eng.) U., 1993; sr. vis. fellow Inst. Criminology Cambridge U., Eng., 1998, 2000; vis. prof. numerous univs.; cons. numerous mental health clinics and orgns. Author: Psychiatry for the Pediatrician, 1970, Childhood Psychopathology, 1972, Mental Health Education in New Medical Schools, 1973, Roles and Functions of Child Psychiatrists, 1976, Psychiatric Treatment of the Child, 1977, New Directions in Childhood Psychopathology, vol. I, 1980, vol. II, 1982, Raising Cain (and Abel Too), 1980; People and Cultures of Hawaii, 1980, Culture Mind and Therapy: An Introduction to Cultural Psychiatry, 1982, Japanese edit., 1984, The Complete Book on Sibling Rivalry, 1987, German edit., 1991; editor Jour. Am. Acad. Child and Adolescent Psychiatry, 1987-97; contbr. over 150 articles to profl. jours.; mem. editorial bds. numerous psychiat. jours. Served with USN, 1958-60. Named Disting. Alumnus N.Y. Med. Coll., 1976; life mem. Clare Hall, Cambridge (Eng.) U. Fellow Am. Psychiat. Assn. (disting. life, Agnes Purcell McGavin award 1984), Am. Orthopsychiat. Assn. (life), Am. Acad. Child and Adolescent Psychiatry (life), Am. Coll. Psychiatrists, World Psychiat. Assn. (chmn. child and adolescent psychiatry 1977-89), Benjamin Rush Soc. (sec.-treas. 2000-02, v.p. 2002-04, pres. 2004-06), Cosmos Club. Outrigger Canoe Club. Home: 330 Willow Rd Winnetka IL 60093-4130 Office: McDermott Will & Emery 227 W Monroe St Ste 3100 Chicago IL 60606-5096 Office Phone: 312-984-7562. Personal E-mail: mcdermott330@cs.com.

**MCDERMOTT, JOHN HENRY,** lawyer; b. Evanston, Ill., June 23, 1931; s. Edward Henry and Goldie Lucile (Boso) McD.; m. Ann Elizabeth Pickard, Feb. 19, 1966; children: Elizabeth A., Mary L., Edward H. BA, Williams Coll., 1953; JD, U. Mich., 1956. Bar: Mich. 1955, Ill. 1956. Assoc. McDermott, Will & Emery, Chgo., 1958-64, ptnr., 1964-99, of counsel, 2000—. Bd. dirs. Patrick Industries Inc. 1st lt. USAF, 1956-58. Mem. ABA, Chgo. Bar Assn. Clubs: Commerical of Chgo., Econ. of Chgo., Legal Chgo. (pres. 1981-82), Law Chgo. (pres. 1986-87). Home: 330 Willow Rd Winnetka IL 60093-4130 Office: McDermott Will & Emery 227 W Monroe St Ste 3100 Chicago IL 60606-5096 Office Phone: 312-984-7562. Personal E-mail: mcdermott330@cs.com.

**MCDERMOTT, KATHLEEN E.,** lawyer; b. 1949; BS in fgn. svc., Georgetown U., JD. Bar: 1975. Assoc. Collier, Shannon, Rill & Scott, Washington, 1975—81, ptnr., 1981—93; exec. v.p., chief legal officer Am. Stores Inc. (now Albertson's Inc.), Salt Lake City, 1993—99; ptnr. Collier Shannon Scott PLLC, Washington; sr. v.p., gen. counsel Nash Finch Inc., Mpls., 2002—. Mem.: ABA (vice chair corp. counseling com. antitrust sect.). Office: Nash Finch Co 7600 France Ave S Minneapolis MN 55440-0355

**MCDERMOTT, KEVIN R.,** lawyer; b. Youngstown, Ohio, Jan. 26, 1952; s. Robert J. and Marion D. (McKeown) McD.; m. Cindy J. Darling, Dec. 11, 1976; children: Ciara, Kelly. AB, Miami U., Oxford, Ohio, 1974; JD, Ohio State U., 1977. Bar: Ohio 1977, U.S. Dist. Ct. (so. dist.) Ohio 1978, U.S. Dist. Ct. (no. dist.) Ohio 1988, U.S. Dist. Ct. (we. dist.) Mich. 1993, U.S. Supreme

Ct. 1990, U.S. Ct. Appeals (3rd cir.) 1996, U.S. Ct. Appeals (6th cir.) 1988. Assoc. ptnr. Murphey Young & Smith, Columbus, Ohio, 1977-88; ptnr. Squire Sanders & Dempsey, Columbus, Ohio, 1988-90, Schottenstein Zox & Dunn, Columbus, Ohio, 1990—. Adv. bd. mem. Capital U. Legal Asst. Program, Columbus, Ohio, 1988—. Bd. pres. Easter Seal Soc. Ctrl. Ohio, Columbus, 1992-94, bd. mem. 1988-92; pres. Upper Arlington Civic Svc. Commn., Columbus, Ohio, 1988-93. Office: Schottenstein Zox & Dunn 250 West St Columbus OH 43215 Office Phone: 614-462-5001.

**MCDERMOTT, PATRICIA (TRICIA MCDERMOTT),** theater director, educator; b. Hempstead, NY, June 6, 1965; d. Patrick Joseph McDermott and Gertrude Bisco-McDermott. BA in Theatre, Fla. State U., 1987; MFA in Directing, Ill. State U., 1997. Founder, producing artistic dir. Airmid Theatre Co., L.I., NY, 2000—; exec. dir. Shakespeare Globe Ctr. USA, N.Y.C., 2001—04. Adj. prof. various univs., L.I. and N.Y.C., 1997—2001. Dir. founder Door Mouse Theatre for Young Audiences. Mem.: Shakespeare Theatre Assn. Am. (assoc.), Zonta Club of Suffolk County Area (bd. dirs. 2003—). Office Phone: 631-704-2888. E-mail: airmidtheatre@hotmail.com.

**MCDERMOTT, ROBERT J.,** commissioner; b. Bklyn., Sept. 5, 1944; AB, Georgetown U., 1966; JD cum laude, NYU, 1970, LLM in Taxation, 1974. Bar: NY 1971. Ptnr. Dewey Ballantine, N.Y.C.; commr. tax appeals tribunal NY State, 2005—. Mem. ABA, NY State Bar Assn. (exec. com., tax sect. 1980-91), Assn. of Bar of City of NY, Order Coif. NY State Bar Found. (life fellow), NYU Law Alumni Assn. (pres. 1989-91) Office: Divsn Tax Appeals Riverfront Pro Tower 500 Federal St Troy NY 12180 Office Phone: 518-266-3000. Office Fax: 518-272-5178.*

**MCDERMOTT, SANDRA,** national park administrator; d. Joseph McDermott and Julia Ferrari; children: Jennifer Faulkner, Benjamin Faulkner. BA in Psychology, U. Alaska, 1975, BA in History, 1980; MA in History, U. Oreg., 1984. Grad. tchg. fellow U. Oreg., 1982—84; adj. faculty U. Alaska, 1984—97; hist. preservation program mgr. Nat. Pk. Service, Anchorage, 1987—92, regional historian, 1992—2004; dep. assoc. regional dir. intermountain region Nat. Pk. Svc., Santa Fe, 2004—; acting asst. supt. Joshua Tree Nat. Pk., Twenty-Nine Palms, Calif., 2004. Nat. mgmt. coun. for cultural resource stewardship & partnership Nat. Pk. Svc., Office of the Assoc. Dir., Washington, 2000—; instr., Alaska nat. interest conservation act US Dept. of Interior U., 2003; spkr. Alaska Humanities Forum Speakers Bur., 1996—98. Book reviewer (professional journal) Journal of Public History; contbr. articles to profl. jours. Co-chair Alaska at War Internat. Conf., 1993; pres. Nat. History Day in Alaska, 1989—2004, Alaska Hist. Soc., 1992—98; chair, publs. com. Cook Inlet Hist. Soc., Anchorage, 1997—2000; mem. program com. Western Mus. Assn., Alaska, 1997—98. Recipient President's award, Alaska Hist. Soc., 1989, Fed. Employee of the Yr., Team Leader award, Fed. Employees Assn., 1996, Spl. Svc. Act award, Nat. Pk. Svc., 1997, Nat. Partnership award, Hon. Mention, Nat. Pk. Found., 2001, Cert. of Appreciation, Nat. Coun. for History Edn., 2003, Spl. award for Contributions to Alaska History, Alaska Hist. Soc., 2004, Cert. of Merit in Hist. Preservation, Alaska State Hist. Preservation Office, 2004, Lifetime Achievement award, Nat. History Day in Alaska, 2004, STAR award, NPS-Cultural Resource Adv. Coun., 2004. Mem.: Am. Hist. Assn. (assoc.). Avocation: music. Office: Nat Pk Svc PO Box 728 Santa Fe NM 87504-0728 Office Phone: 505-988-6773. Office Fax: 505-988-6876. E-mail: sande_mcdermott@nps.gov.

**MCDERMOTT, SUSANNE FINCKH,** fisheries biologist; d. Martin and Valentina Finckh; m. Barry Arthur McDermott, May 1, 1994; children: Leina Celeste, Martin Orion, Mira Moon. PhD, U. of Wash., Seattle, 2003. Biol. observer Nat. Marine Fisheries Svc., Seattle, 1990—91; fisheries biologist U. of Wash., Seattle, 1994—2003. Rsch. fisheries biologist Nat. Marine Fisheries Svc., Alaska Fisheries Sci. Ctr., Seattle, 2003—. Contbr. articles to profl.jours. Mem.: Oceanography Soc. Liberal. Achievements include research in fefundity and population estimation of Atka mackerel in the Aleutian Islands. Avocations: swimming, horseback riding. Office: NOAA/NMFS/Alaska Fisheries Science Cente 7600 Sandpoint Way NE Seattle WA 98115-6349 Office Phone: 206-526-4417. Office Fax: 206-526-6723. E-mail: susanne.mcdermott@noaa.gov.

**MCDERMOTT, THOMAS JOHN, JR.,** lawyer; b. Santa Monica, Calif., Mar. 23, 1931; s. Thomas J. Sr. and Etha Irene (Cook) McD.; m. Yolanda Amante Jatap; children: Jodi Friedman, Kimberly E., Kish S. BA, UCLA, 1953, JD, 1958. Bar: Calif. 1959. Ptnr. Gray, Binkley and Pfaelzer, L.A., 1964-67, Kadison, Pfaelzer, Woodward, Quinn and Rossi, L.A., 1967-87, Rogers & Wells, L.A., 1987-93, Bryan Cave, L.A., 1993-95, Manatt, Phelps & Phillips, LLP, L.A., 1995-99, Shanks and Herbert, San Diego, 1999—2003. Served with U.S. Army, 1953-56, Korea, 1999-2003. Fellow Am. Coll. Trial Lawyers; mem. ABA, Assn. Bus. Trial Lawyers (pres. 1980-81, mem. exec. com. 9th cir. jud. conf. 1993—, chair 1997), State Bar Calif. (chair litigation sect. 1993-94), UCLA Law Alumni Assn. (pres. 1961-62), Order of Coif. Office: McDermott & DeLauteur LLP 74-770 Highway 111 Ste 201 Indian Wells CA 92210 Office Phone: 760-346-8200. E-mail: tmcdermottjr@earthlink.net.

**MCDEVITT, CHARLES FRANCIS,** retired judge, lawyer; b. Pocatello, Idaho, Jan. 5, 1932; s. Bernard A. and Margaret (Hermann) McDevitt; m. Virginia L. Heller, Aug. 14, 1954; children: Eileen A., Kathryn A., Brian A., Sheila A., Terrence A., Neil A., Kendal A. LLB, U. Idaho, 1956. Bar: Idaho 1956. Ptnr. Richards, Haga & Eberle, Boise, 1956-62; gen. counsel, asst. sec. Boise Cascade Corp., 1962—68; mem. Idaho State Legislature, 1963-66; sec., gen. counsel Boise Cascade Corp., 1965-67, v.p. sec., 1967-68; pres. Beck Industries, 1968-70; group v.p. Singer Co., N.Y.C., 1970-72, exec. v.p., 1973-76; pub. defender Ada County, Boise, 1976-78; co-founder Givens, McDevitt Pursley & Webb, Boise, 1978-89; justice Idaho Supreme Ct., Boise, 1989-97, chief justice, 1993-97; ptnr., founder McDevitt & Miller, LLP, Boise, 1997—. Served on Gov.'s Select Com. on Taxation, Boise, 1988-89; mem. State Select Com. on Campaign Ethics and Campaign Finances, State Select Com. on Legis. Compensation. Chair Idaho Jud. Coun., 1993-97, Cts. Advisors Coun., 1994-98; mem. Multi-State Tax Com. Recipient Legal Merit award, Univ. of Idaho, 2002, Professionalism award, Idaho State Bar, 2005. Home: 4940 Boise River Ln Boise ID 83716-8816 Office: MC McDevitt Miller 420 W Bannock Boise ID 83702-6034 Office Phone: 208-343-7500. Business E-mail: chas@McDevitt-Miller.com.

**MCDEVITT, HUGH O'NEILL,** immunologist, educator; b. Cin., Aug. 26, 1930; MD, Harvard U., 1955. Diplomate: Am. Bd. Internal Medicine. Intern Peter Bent Brigham Hosp., Boston, 1955-56, sr. asst. resident in medicine, 1961-62; asst. resident Bell Hosp., 1956-57; research fellow dept. bacteriology and immunology Harvard U., 1959-61; USPHS spl. fellow Nat. Inst. Med. Research, Mill Hill, London, 1962-64; physician Stanford U. Hosp., Calif., 1966—; assoc. prof. Stanford U. Sch. Medicine, Calif., 1969-72, prof. med. immunology Calif., 1972—; prof. med. microbiology Calif., 1980—2001, Burt and Marian Avery Prof. Immunology Calif., 1988—2001. Cons. physician VA Hosp., Palo Alto, Calif., 1968— Served as capt. M.C., AUS, 1957-59. Recipient Abbott Lab. award in Clin. and Diagnostic Immunology, Am. Soc. Microbiology, 2003. Mem. NAS, AAAS, Am. Fedn. Clin. Rsch., Am. Soc. Clin. Investigation, Am. Assn. Immunologists, Transplantation Soc., Inst. Medicine, Royal Soc. (fgn.). Office: Sherman Fairchild Bldg Stanford U Sch of Medicine 299 Campus Dr MC5124 Stanford CA 94305-5124 Business E-mail: hughmcd@stanford.edu.

**MCDEVITT, JAMES A.,** prosecutor, lawyer; b. July 1943; Bachelor, U. Wash.; MBA, JD, Gonzaga U. Asst. atty. gen. State of Wash., Office of Atty. Gen., 1975—77; from sr. atty. to mng. ptnr. Reed & Geisa, Spokane, Wash., 1977—94; ptnr. Preston, Gates & Ellis, Spokane, Wash., 1994—2002; US atty. (ea. dist.) Wash. US Dept. Justice, 2002—. With USAF, 1965—71, brig. gen. Wash. Air Nat. Guard, ret. Office: US Attys Office PO Box 1494 Spokane WA 99210*

**MCDEVITT, JERRY S.,** lawyer; BS cum laude, U. Pa., 1973; JD cum laude, Duquesne U. Sch. Law, 1980. Bar: Pa. 1980, US Dist. Ct., Western Dist. Pa. 1980, Pa. Supreme Ct. 1980, US Ct. of Appeals, 3rd Cir. 1985, US Court Appeals, 2nd Cir. 1992, US Supreme Ct. 1994, US Ct. Appeals, 8th Cir. 1994, US Dist. Ct. (ea. dist Wis.) 2003, US. Ct. Appeals 11th Cir. 2004, Numerous pro hac vice admissions in various State and Fed. Cts. Ptnr. Kirkpatrick & Lockhart Nicholson Graham, LLP, Pitts. Exec. recent decisions editor Duquesne Law Review. Officer USMC, 1973—76. Named one of Top 10 Litigators, Nat. Law Jour., 2003. Mem.: Pa. Bar Assn., ABA, Allegheny County Bar Assn. (Pro Bono award for Representation of Death Row Inmate 1990). Office: Kirkpatrick & Lockhart Nicholson Graham LLP Henry W Oliver Bldg 535 Smithfield St Pittsburgh PA 15222-2312 Office Phone: 412-355-8608. Office Fax: 412-355-6501. Business E-mail: jmcdevitt@klng.com.

**MCDEVITT, JOHN,** delivery service executive; b. Upper Darby, Pa., Aug. 15, 1958; m. Lori McDevitt; children: Kelly, Tara, Shannon, John. BS in Polit. Sci., Rutgers U., 1980; grad., U. Mich., 1999. Part-time loader UPS, Edison, NJ, 1976—77, part-time supr. Bound Brook, 1977—80, package car driver, 1980—81, supr., 1981—84, mgr. Parsippany, 1984—87, divsn. mgr. Meadowlands, 1987—92, dist. mgr. East Long Island, NY, 1992—94, West Long Island, 1994—96, v.p. corp. compliance Atlanta, 1996—98, mgr. corp. labor rels., 1998—99, v.p. air ops., 1999—2003, sr. v.p. strategic integration, 2003—. Office: UPS 55 Glenlake Kwy NE Atlanta GA 30328

**MCDEVITT, SHEILA MARIE,** lawyer, energy executive; b. St. Petersburg, Fla., Jan. 15, 1947; d. Frank Davis and Marie (Barfield) McD. AA, St. Petersburg Jr. Coll., 1966; BA in Govt., Fla. State U., 1968, JD, 1978. Bar: Fla. 1978. Research assoc. Fla. Legis. Reference Bur., Tallahassee, 1968-69; adminstr., research assoc. Constitution Revision Commn. Ga. Gen. Assembly, Atlanta, 1969-70; adminstrv. asst., analyst Fla. State Sen., Tallahassee, Tampa, 1970-79; assoc. McClain, Walkley & Stuart, P.A., Tampa, Seminole, Fla., 1979-81; govtl. affairs counsel Tampa Electric Co., 1981-82, corp. counsel, 1982-86; sr. corp. counsel TECO Energy, Inc., Tampa, 1986-89, asst. v.p., 1989-92, v.p., asst. gen. counsel, 1992-99, corp. compliance officer, 1993-99, v.p., gen. counsel Tampa, 1999—2001, sr. v.p., gen. counsel, chief legal officer, 2001—. Mem. Worker's Compensation adv. coun. Fla. Dept. Labor, Tallahassee, 1984-86; trustee St. Leo U., 1999—, vice chair, 2001-2005, chair 2005; mem. bd. visitors Fla. State U. Coll. Law, 1996—, chmn., 2003-2005; mem. bd. advisors The Centre for Women, 1998—, Met. Ministries, 1996—; mem. ethics adv. bd. U. Tampa Ctr. for Ethics, 1997-99; mem. jud. nominating commn. 13th Jud. Cir., 2001-2003; mem. Fla. bd. govs. State Univ. sys., 2004. Bd. dirs. Vol. Ctr. Hillsborough County, Tampa, 1984-85, Fla. Aquarium, 1999-2000; bd. dirs. Lowry Park Zoo Soc., 1999-2004, chmn., trustee, 1986-94, also legal advisor; bd. dirs. Hillsborough County Easter Seal Soc., 1994-95; mem. Fla. Rep. Exec. Com., Tallahassee, 1974-75, Hillsborough County Rep. Exec. Com., 1974-75; mem. transition team for Fla. Gov. Bob Martinez, 1986-87; mem. Fed. Jud. Adv. Commn., 1989-93; mem. Fla. Humanities Coun., 2000-2004; mem. WW Women's Leadership, 2004—; bd. trustees Fla. Orch., 2004—. Mem ABA, Fla. Bar (vice chmn., then chmn. energy law com. 1984-87, jud. nominating procedures com. 1986-91, jud. adminstrn. selection and tenure com. 1991-93), Hillsborough Bar Found. (trustee 2002-), Hillsborough County Bar Assn. (chmn. law week com. 1990, corp. counsel com. 1986-87, internat. law com. 1994-95) corporate counsel of the yr. award, 2001-02, Am. Corp. Counsel Assn. (bd. dirs. Ctrl. Fla. chpt. 1986-87), Hillsborough County Bar Found., Tampa Club, Tiger Bay Club, Tampa Yacht and Country Club. Roman Catholic. Avocations: photography, bicycling, reading, boating. Office: TECO Energy Inc PO Box 111 702 N Franklin St Fl 5 Tampa FL 33602-4440 Business E-mail: smmcdevitt@tecoenergy.com.

**MCDIARMID, BRUCE W.,** lawyer; b. San Jose, Calif., June 27, 1947; AB, U. Calif., Berkeley, 1968; JD magna cum laude, Harvard U., 1974. Bar: Calif. 1974. Ptnr. Pillsbury Madison & Sutro, San Francisco; (Pillsbury Madison & Sutro merged with Winthrop, Stimson, Putnam, 2001); ptnr., chmn. mktg., distribution & franchising practice group Pillsbury Winthrop LLP, San Francisco, 2001—05; (Pillsbury Winthrop LLP merged with Shaw Pittman LLP, 2005); ptnr., chmn. mktg., distribution & franchising practice group Pillsbury Winthrop Shaw Pittman LLP, San Francisco, 2005—. Mem.: ABA (mem. antitrust section, mem. forum on franchising). Office: Pillsbury Winthrop Shaw Pittman LLP 50 Fremont St San Francisco CA 94105 Office Phone: 415-983-1043. Office Fax: 415-983-1200.

**MCDIARMID, DIANE,** education educator, researcher; d. Dana Webb; m. George McDiarmid, Jan. 31, 1966; children: Michelle Husted, Debbie, Michael. BSW, Washburn U., Topeka, Kans., 1994; MSW, U. Kans., Lawrence, 1995. Dir. tng. and tech. assistance U. Kans. Sch. Social Welfare, Lawrence, 1994—98, dir. supported edn. rsch. and tng., 1998—. Dir. social work adminstrn. Consumers as Provider program. Author: Social Work, Pathways to Recovery, 2004. Bd. dirs. Mar. of Dimes, Lawrence, 1999—99; sec. bd. dirs. Topeka Rowing Assn. Recipient Tom Wernert Behavioral Health Innovation award, 2004, Unity award, Kans. Recovery Conf., 2003. Mem.: US Rowing Assn. (assoc.), Masters Rowing Assn. (assoc.). Avocations: rowing, travel. Office: U Kans 2706 Iowa Lawrence KS 66046 Office Phone: 877-458-6804. Business E-mail: dianem@ku.edu.

**MCDIARMID, IAN,** actor, film director; b. Tayside, Scotland, Apr. 17, 1944; Student, Royal Scottish Acad. Music and Drama, 1968. With Royal Shakespeare Co., 1974; co-founder Almeida Theatre Co., 1986, joint artistic dir., 1990—2001. Actor: (films) Star Wars: Return of the Jedi, 1983, Dirty Rotten Scoundrels, 1988, Star Wars: Episode I - The Phantom Menace, 1999, Sleepy Hollow, 1999, Star Wars: Episode II Attack of the Clones, 2002, Star Wars: Episode III Revenge of the Sith, 2005; (plays) They Put Handcuffs on the Flowers, 1973, The Likely Lads, 1976, Ivanov, Tartuffe, School for Wives, Creditors, Henry V, Merchant of Venice, The Party, The War Plays, Crimes in Hot Countries, Hated Nightfall, Love of a Good Man, Raft of the Medusa, The Country Wife, The Black Prince, Peer Gynt, Mephisto; (Broadway plays) Faith Healer, 2006 (Theatre World award, 2006, Tony award, best performance by featured actor in a play, 2006); (TV films) Macbeth, 1979, Chernobyl: The Final Warning, 1991, Heart of Darkness, 1994, Annie: A Royal Adventure, 1995, Hillsborough, 1996, Rebecca, 1997, All the King's Men, 1999; (TV miniseries) Cold Lazarus, 1996, Karaoke, 1996, Touching Evil, 1997, Crime and Punishment, 2002, Charles II: The Power & the Passion, 2003. Office: c/o Almeida Theatre Almeida St London N1 1TA England*

**MCDIARMID, LUCY,** literature educator, writer; b. Louisville, Mar. 29, 1947; BA, Swarthmore (Pa.) Coll., 1968; MA, Harvard U., 1969, PhD, 1972. Asst. prof. Boston U., 1972-74; from asst. prof. to assoc. prof. Swarthmore Coll., 1974-81; asst. prof. U. Md. Baltimore County, Balt., 1982-84; prof. Villanova (Pa.) U., 1984—. Vis. prof. English Princeton U., 1995; Carole and Gordon Segal vis. chair Irish lit. Northwestern U., 2005; mem. exec. com. Am. Conf. for Irish Studies, 1987-91, v.p., 1995-97, pres., 1997-99, past pres., internat. rep., 1999—2001. Author: Saving Civilization: Yeats, Eliot and Auden Between the Wars, 1984, Auden's Apologies for Poetry, 1990, The Irish Art of Controversy, 2005; co-editor: Selected Writings of Lady Gregory, 1995, High and Low Moderns: Literature and Culture, 1889-1939, 1996; contbr. articles to profl. jours. ACLS grantee, 1976; NEH fellow, 1981-82, Bunting Inst. fellow, 1981-82, Guggenheim fellow, 1993-94, vis. fellow N.Y. Inst. Humanities, 1993-95, fellow Dorothy and Louis B. Cullman Ctr. Scholars and Writers, NY Pub. Libr., 2005-06. Mem. MLA (exec. coun. Twentieth Century Lit. divsn.), Internat. Assn. for Study Anglo-Irish Lit. (Am. sec.-treas. 1994-96), Phi Beta Kappa. Home: 1931 Panama St Philadelphia PA 19103-6609

**MCDIARMID, ROBERT CAMPBELL,** lawyer; b. N.Y.C., July 13, 1937; s. Norman Hugh and Dorothy (Shoemaker) McD.; m. Ruth Sussman, 1963 (div. 1996); children: Jennifer, Alexander Samuel; m. Frances Enseki Francis, 1996. BS in Mech. Engring., Swarthmore Coll., 1958; MS in Engring. Physics, Cornell U., 1960; LLB, Harvard U., 1963. Bar: D.C. 1964, Va. 1964,

U.S. Supreme Ct. 1967, U.S. Ct. Appeals (4th, 6th and 9th cirs.) 1965, U.S. Ct. Appeals (3d, 5th and 10th cirs.) 1966, U.S. Ct. Appeals (7th, 8th and D.C. cirs.) 1967, U.S. Ct. Appeals (2d cir.) 1970, U.S. Ct. Appeals (1st cir.) 1979, U.S. Ct. Appeals (11th cir.) 1981. Assoc. Weaver & Glassie, Washington, 1963-64; trial atty. civil divsn. appellate sect. Dept. Justice, Washington, 1964-68; asst. to gen. counsel Fed. Power Commn., Washington, 1968-70; assoc. Law Office of George Spiegel, Washington, 1970-73; ptnr. Spiegel & McDiarmid, Washington, 1973—. Mem. alumni coun. Swarthmore Coll., 1986-89. Mem. ABA, Va. State Bar, Bar Assn. D.C., D.C. Bar, Energy Bar Assn. (exec. com. 1982-83, bd. dirs. 1997-2000). Democrat. Mem. Soc. Of Friends. Home: 3625 Fulton St NW Washington DC 20007-1452 Office: Spiegel & McDiarmid 1333 New Hampshire Ave NW Washington DC 20036 Office Phone: 202-879-4040. Business E-mail: robert.mcdiarmid@spiegelmcd.com.

**MCDOLE, SYDNEY BOSWORTH,** lawyer; b. Chgo., 1947; BA summa cum laude, Vassar Coll., 1970; MA, Middlebury Coll., 1971; JD magna cum laude, Northwestern Univ., 1974. Bar: Ill. 1974, Tex. 1986, admitted to practice: US Fed. Courts 1974, US Supreme Ct. 1983. Ptnr., gen. litigation and energy issues Jones Day, Chgo., now ptnr., gen. litigation and energy issues Dallas. Coord., new associates group Jones Day. Editor-in-chief Law Rev., Harvard Univ., 1974. Mem.: Ill. State Bar Assn., State Bar of Tex., Order of Coif, Phi Beta Kappa. Office: Jones Day 2727 N Harwood St Dallas TX 75201-1515 Office Phone: 214-969-3785. Office Fax: 214-969-5100.

**MCDONAGH, STEVE,** chef; life ptnr. Dan Smith; 1 adopted child, Nate. Co-founder, bus. mgr. The Hearty Boys catering co., Chgo.; co-founder The Cafe at Hearty Boys, Lakeview, Ill., 2003—. HB restaurant, The Cafe at Hearty Boys, Lakeview, Ill., 2005—. Co-host Party Line with the Hearty Boys; co-author: Solving the Run of the Mill; featured in Chgo. Mag., guest appearances ABC, NBC, CBS, FOX, CLTV. Achievements include appearing on several radio shows, TV commercials, and the Chgo. stage; co-winning The Next Food Network Star with ptnr. Dan Smith, 2005. Office: The Hearty Boys Caterers 3404 N Halsted Chicago IL 60657 Office Phone: 773-244-9866. Office Fax: 773-244-8088.*

**MCDONALD, ALAN ANGUS,** federal judge; b. Harrah, Wash., Dec. 13, 1927; s. Angus and Nell (Britt) McD.; m. Ruby K., Aug. 22, 1949; children: Janelle Jo, Saralee Sue, Stacy. BS, U. Wash., 1950, LLB, 1952. Dep. pros. atty. Yakima County, Wash., 1952—54; ptnr. Halverson, Applegate & McDonald, Yakima, 1954—85; judge U.S. Dist. Ct. (ea. dist.) Wash., Yakima, 1985—95, sr. judge, 1995—. Fellow Am. Coll. Trial Lawyers; mem. Yakima Country Club, Royal Duck Club (Yakima). Office: US Dist Ct PO Box 2706 Yakima WA 98907-2706

**MCDONALD, ANGUS WHEELER,** farmer; b. Washington, Apr. 21, 1927; s. John Yates and Dorothy Helen (Bosworth) McD.; m. Mary Joan Montgomery, May 8, 1952 (div. Sept. 1958); children: Mary Ann Hetzer, Paul Yates. BA, Columbia Union Coll., 1974. Farmer, owner Pleasant View Farm, Charles Town, W.Va., 1953—. Presdl. candidate Democratic Party, 1987-88, 92, 2000. With U.S. Army, 1946-47. Mem. AARP, Jefferson County Farm Bur., W.Va. State Hort. Soc., No. W.Va. Automobile Club, Am. Legion, The Moose. Avocations: photography, travel, attending historical events. Home and Office: Pleasant View Farm 2225 Flowing Springs Rd Charles Town WV 25414-9413 Office Phone: 304-725-7238.

**MCDONALD, APRIL D.,** writer; b. Arlington County, Va., May 29, 1981; d. Butler Cassell William, Jr. and Veronica Denise McDonald. Degree in Journalism, No. Va. Coll., 2003. Cert. A+ NOVA, 2001. CEO ADM Publishing LLC, Norcross, Ga. Author: Sex, Lies & Consequences, 2005. Mentor Big Sister program, Atlanta, 2005—. Independent. Avocations: travel, jet skiing, writing, public speaking. Business E-mail: aprilmcdonaldinc@yahoo.com.

**MCDONALD, AUDRA ANN,** actress, vocalist; b. Berlin, July 3, 1970; d. Stanley and Kathryn McDonald; m. Peter Donovan, Sept. 10, 2000; 1 child, Zoe Madeline Donovan. BFA in Voice, Juilliard Sch., 1993; attended, Sch. Arts., Calif. Stage appearances include (regional) Man of La Mancha, Evita, The Wiz, A Chorus Line, Grease, Anything Goes, The Real Inspector Hound, Anyone Can Whistle, 2005;(Broadway) The Secret Garden, Man of La Mancha, 1989, Carousel, 1994 (Tony award best featured actress in a musical, 1994), Outer Critics Circle award outstanding actress in a musical, 1994), Master Class, 1995-97 (Tony award best featured actress in a musical, 1996, LA Ovation award best featured actress in a musical, 1996), Ragtime, 1998-99 (Tony award best featured actress in a musical, 1998), Sweeney Todd, 2000, A Raisin in the Sun, 2004 (Tony award best featured actress in a play, 2004, Drama Desk award best featured actress in a play, 2004), See What I Wanna See (formerly titled R Shomon), 2005; (TV series) Bill Cosby pilot, 1996, Mister Sterling, 2003; (TV Movies) Having Our Say: The Delaney Sisters' First 100 Years, 1999, Annie, 1999, The Last Debate, 2000, Wit, 2001 (Emmy award nom. best supporting actress, 2001); (films) Seven Servants, 1996, The Object of My Affection, 1998, Cradle Will Rock, 1999, It Runs in the Family, 2003, The Best Thief in the World, 2004; concert performances include S'Wonderful, Some Enchanted Evening, Christa Ludwig and James Levine Recital, Revelation in Courthouse Park, Requiem Canticles; singer: (albums) Leonard Bernstien's New York, 1996, Sings Rodgers & Hart, 1996, George & Ira Gershwin: Standards & Gems, 1998, George Gershwin: 100th Birthday Celebration, 1998, Broadway in Love, 2000, Marie Christine: A New Musical, 2000, Broadway Cares: Home for the Holidays, 2001, Dreamgirls in Concert, 2002, (solo albums) Way Back to Paradise, 1998, How Glory Goes, 2000, Happy Songs, 2002, Build a Bridge, 2006. Recipient Theatre World award, 1994, Drama League award distinguished achievement in musical theatre, 2000. Office: Gersh Agency Inc 41 Madison Ave Fl 33 New York NY 10010-2210

**MCDONALD, BERNARD ROBERT,** retired federal agency administrator; b. Kansas City, Kans., Nov. 17, 1940; s. Bernard Luther and Mabel McD.; m. Jean Graves, June 7, 1963 (div. 1996); children: Aaron Michael, Elizabeth Kathleen; m. Joann Huffaker, Aug. 2, 1997. BA, Park Coll., Parkville, Mo., 1962; MA, Kans. State U., 1964; PhD, Mich. State U., 1968. Prof. math. U. Okla., Norman, 1968-83, chmn. math. dept., 1981-83; program dir. div. math. scis. NSF, Washington, 1983-86, program dir. spl. projects, 1986-88, dep. dir. div. math. scis., 1988—2004; ret. Author: R-linear Endomorphism, 1983, Geometric Algebra, 1976, Finite Rings, 1974, Ring Theory III, 1980. Mem. AAAS, Am. Math. Soc., Math. Assn. Am., Soc. Ind. and Applied Math., Assn. Women Math., Sigma Xi. Home: 5016 35th St N Arlington VA 22207-2816 E-mail: math1940@aol.com.

**MCDONALD, BRADLEY G.,** lawyer; m. Ann Gilbert, Sept. 3, 1964; 1 child, Perry. BA, U. Okla.; JD, Georgetown U., 1961. Bar: D.C. 1961, U.S. Ct. Appeals (D.C., 11th and 4th cirs.), U.S. Supreme Ct. With McDonald & Karl, Washington. Guest lectr. Wash. Coll. of Law, Am. Univ., Washington. Mem. nat. alumni adv. coun. U. Okla; mem. Arlington Com. of 100; bd. dirs. Washington Montessori Sch. of McLean. 1st lt. USMC, 1956-58. Recipient 1st Regent's Alumni award U. Okla. Mem. Sigma Nu (trustee Ednl. Found.). Office Phone: 202-293-3200. Personal E-mail: abmcdonal7@aol.com.

**MCDONALD, BRENNA CATHLEEN,** psychologist; d. Daniel Ford and George Marie McDonald. BA, Williams Coll., Williamstown, Mass., 1994; MA, Widener U., Chester, Pa., 1998; Psy.D., MBA, Widener U., 2000. Lic. psychologist N.H., 2002, cert. sch. psychologist N.H., 2005, Pa., 1999. Clin. psychologist N.H., 2002, cert. sch. psychologist N.H., 2005, Pa., 1999. Clin. and instr. Dartmouth Med. Sch., Hanover, NH, 2002—04, asst. prof. of psychiatry, 2004—. Recipient Student Loan Repayment award, NIH, 2003—05; grantee Rsch. grantee, Partnership for Pediatric Epilepsy Rsch., 2004—06. Mem.: Am. Neuropsychiat. Assn., Phila. Neuropsychology Soc.,

Nat. Acad. of Neuropsychology, Internat. Neuropsychol. Soc., APA. Office: DMS Dept of Psychiatry DHMC One Medical Center Dr Lebanon NH 03756-0001 Office Phone: 603-650-5824. Office Fax: 603-650-5842. E-mail: brenna.c.mcdonald@dartmouth.edu.

**MCDONALD, CAPERS WALTER,** biomedical engineer, manufacturing executive, entrepreneur, educator; b. Georgetown, SC, Nov. 29, 1951; s. WalBern and Cecilia (Lockwood) McD.; m. Marion E. Kiper, Aug. 23, 1975; 1 child, Adam Capers. BS in Engring. magna cum laude, Duke U., 1974; MS in Mech. Engring., MIT, 1976; MBA, Harvard Bus. Sch., 1983. Dir. mktg. Becton Dickinson Co., Sunnyvale, Calif., 1978-81; cons. Booz, Allen & Hamilton, San Francisco, 1982-84; v.p. Siegen Corp., Mountain View, Calif., 1984, HP Genenchem, South San Francisco, Calif., 1984-87; bio-analytic systems mgr. Hewlett-Packard Co., Palo Alto, Calif., 1986—87; v.p. Orion Instruments, Inc., Redwood City, Calif., 1987-89, Spectroscopy Imaging Systems Corp., Fremont, Calif., 1989-90, pres., bd. dirs., 1991—92; pres., CEO, bd. dirs. BioReliance Corp., Rockville, Md., 1992—2004; pres., CEO MAGENTA Corp., Rockville, 1993—2000; chmn., dir. MAGENTA Svcs., Ltd., Stirling, Scotland, 1994-2000; dir. BioReliance Holdings GmbH, Heidelberg, Germany, 1996—2004, Q-One Biotech Group Ltd., Glasgow, Scotland, 2003—04; exec. in residence, faculty mem. Johns Hopkins U., 2004—. Bd. dirs. Expion, Inc., Olney, Md., 1999—, Md. Health Care Product Devel. Corp., 2000—, chmn., 2004-05; co-founder, chmn. Md. Biosci. Alliance, 1995-98; bd. visitors U. Md. Biotech. Inst., 1996-00, Duke U. Sch. Engring., 2001—, chmn. student affairs com., 2005—; bd. advisors Md. Partnership for Workforce Quality, 1996-98, Washington Bus. Jour., 2003-05; vice chmn. High Tech. Coun., 1998-01; chmn. Tech. Coun. Md., 2001-04; mem. industry adv. bd. Chesapeake Bay Area chpt. ISPE, 1998-00; lectr. in field. Contbr. chpts. to books; patentee flow microfluorometer; contbr. articles to profl. jours. Asst. scoutmaster Boy Scouts Am., Georgetown, SC, 1965-66; trustee Bethesda Acad. Performing Arts, 1998-01; oversight bd. advanced tech. consortium Montgomery Coll., 1998-01; steering com. Biotech. Industry Orgn., 2003 Ann. Meeting, 2002-03; econ. adv. coun. Montgomery County, 1998-05; founding exec. bd. Greater Washington Regional Partnership, 1998-01; mem. leadership coun. Treatment and Learning Ctrs., 1998-2000; mem. advanced tech. bus. devel. commn., Md., 2003, MBA Capstone Co., Johns Hopkins U., 2003-04; state planning com. for postsecondary edn. Md. Higher Edn. Commn., 2004; chmn. Md. Adv. Tech. del. to Peoples Republic China, 2004; chmn. Eagle Career Day, Greater Washington, 2002-03. Duke U. scholar, 1970-74, MIT scholar, 1974-76; hon. fellow NSF, 1974; recipient Leadership in Tech. award Md. High Tech. Coun., 1996, Employer of Yr. award Md. Pvt. Industry Coun., 1996, Region's Most Admired Bosses award Washington Techway Mag., 2000, Good Scout award Nat. Capital Area Coun., 2000, Nat. Disting. Eagle Scout award Boy Scouts Am., 2001, Export award Scottish Coun. Devel. and Industry, 2001, Nat. Gemstone award, 2002, award Capstone Co. Johns Hopkins U., 2004, Stevie award Am. Bus. Awards, 2003, Disting. Alumnus award Pratt Sch. Engring., Duke U., 2005; Endowed Ann. awards excellence in tchg. and rsch. and excellence mentoring and advising, 2005—; named Greater Washington Entrepreneur of Yr. in Life Scis., 2002; named one of Forbes 200 Entrepreneurial Hot Shots, 2003. Mem. AAAS, ASME, Acad. Mgmt., Biomed. Engring. Soc., NC Acad. Sci., Md. C. of C. (bd. dirs. 1996-00), Harvard U. Alumni Assn., Duke U. Alumni Assn., MIT Alumni Assn., Johns Hopkins Club, Iron Dukes, Congl. Country Club, Sigma Xi, Tau Beta Pi (chpt. pres. 1973-74; endowed nat. ann. award), Phi Eta Sigma, Pi Mu Epsilon. Methodist. Avocations: fishing, travel. Office: Johns Hopkins Univ 9601 Med Ctr Dr Rockville MD 20850 Office Phone: 301-294-7269. Business E-mail: capersmcd@jhu.edu.

**MC DONALD, CHARLES J.,** dermatologist, educator; b. Tampa, Fla., Dec. 6, 1931; s. George B. and Bertha C. (Harbin) McDonald; m. Maureen McDonald; children: Marc S. McDonald, Maureen D. McDonald, Eric S McDonald. BS magna cum laude, A and T Coll. NC, 1951; MS, U. Mich., 1952; MD with highest honors, Howard U., 1960. Diplomate Am. Bd. Dermatology. Rotating intern Hosp. St. Raphael, New Haven, 1960-61, asst. resident in medicine, 1961-63; asst. resident, dermatology Yale U., 1963-65, spl. USPHS rsch. fellow, chief resident dermatology, 1965-66, instr. medicine, pharmacology, 1966-67, asst. prof. medicine, pharmacology, 1967-68; asst. prof. med. sci. Brown U., Providence, 1968-69, assoc. prof., 1969-74, prof., 1974—; dir. dermatology program, 1970-74, head subsect. dermatology, 1974-82, dir. divsn. dermatology, 1982—96, chair dept. dermatology, 1996—; dir. dermatology Roger Williams Gen. Hosp., 1968-97; physician in chief, dept. dermatology RI Hosp., 1989—. Mem. com., task force, chmn. task force minority affairs Am. Acad. Dermatology, 1975—80; mem. dermatology adv. panel Fed. Drug Administrn., 1975—78, cons., 1978—; chmn. com. pub. edn., v.p. RI divsn. Am. Cancer Soc., 1978—80, pres., 1980—83, bd. dir. nat. soc., 1983—, nat. dir. at large, 1990—95, mem. nat. exec. com., 1991—99, nat. officer, 1995—2001, pres. elect, 1997—98, pres., 1998—99; mem. pharm. scis. rev. commn. NIH, 1979—83; mem. residency rev. com. dermatology ACGME, 1992—97; vice chmn. RRC dermatology, 1996—97; mem. adv. com. Arthritis, Muscular, Skeletal, Skin Disease Inst., NIH, 1993—95; bd. dirs. Lifespan RI. Editor: Post Grad. Med. Jour., 1970—85; contbr. numerous articles to med. publs. Trustee Howard U., 1993—, chair health affairs com., 1994—98, mem. exec. com., 1994—98; chair adv. bd. Howard U. Cancer Ctr., 2005—; chair bd. advisors Sch. Medicine, 1998—2005; founding mem. bd. dirs. Providence Health Care Found., chmn. mem. adv. com., 1976—87; bd. dirs. Providence Fund for Edn., Providence Pub. Libr., 1987—2000, sec., 1991—96; mem. R.I. Statist Bd. Edn., 1970—72; bd. dirs. R.I. Cancer Coun., 1999—2001. Maj. USAF, 1952—56. Recipient Disting. Svc. award, Hosp. Assn., RI, 1971, Disting. Alumni award, Howard U. Coll. Medicine, 1983, St. George medal, Nat. Divsn. award, Am. Cancer Soc., 1992, Candle award, Morehouse Coll., 2005, Disting. Alumni award for medicine and cmty. affairs, Howard U., 2005, Cmty. Svc. and Medicine award, RI Black Heritage Soc., 2005. Mem.: Assn. Profs. Dermatology (bd. dirs. 1991—94), Dermatology Found. (chmn. sci. com. 1972—76), New Eng. Dermatology Soc., Am. Soc. Clin. Oncology, Nat. Med. Assn. (chmn. sect. dermatology 1973—75), Am. Acad. Dermatology (bd. dirs. 1987—91), Am. Fedn. Clin. Rsch., Soc. Investigative Dermatology, Noah Worcester Dermatol. Assn. (bd. dirs. 1983—86), RI Dermatol. Assn., New Eng. Cancer Soc., New Eng. Dermatol. Soc. (v.p. 1983—84, pres. 1984—85), Am. Dermatol. Assn. (bd. dirs. 1995, pres elect 2002, pres. 2003—04), AAAS, Beta Kappa Chi, Alpha Kappa Mu, Alpha Omega Alpha, Sigma Xi. Democrat. Office: RI Hosp Dept Dermatology 593 Eddy St Providence RI 02903-4971 Office Phone: 401-444-7137. E-mail: charles_mcdonald@brown.edu.

**MCDONALD, CHRISTIE ANNE,** literature and language professor, writer; b. NYC, May 4, 1942; d. John Denis and Dorothy (Eisner) McD.; m. Eugene Augustus Vance, June 11, 1965 (div. June 1986); children: Adam Vance, Jacob Vance; m. Michael David Rosengarten, Dec. 4, 1987. AB, Mt. Holyoke Coll., 1964; PhD, Yale U., 1969; MA (hon.), Harvard Coll., 1994. Acting instr. Yale U., New Haven, 1968-69; asst. prof. French U. Montreal, Que., Canada, 1969-77, assoc. prof. French Que., 1977-83, prof. Que., 1983, 86-93; prof. modern langs. Emory U., Atlanta, 1984-86; prof. romance langs. and. lits. Harvard U., Cambridge, Mass., 1994—, chmn. romance langs. and lits., 2000—. Author: The Dialogue of Writing, 1985, Dispositions, 1986, The Proustian Fabric, 1991; editor: The Ear of the Other, 1988, Transpositions, 1994, Images of Congo, 2005. Decorated chevalier Order Palmes Academiques; recipient Clifford prize Am. Assn. 18th-Century Studies, 1994-95. Mem.: Royal Soc. Can. Office: Harvard U 431 Boylston Hall Cambridge MA 02138 Office Phone: 617-497-0826.

**MCDONALD, CRAYDON DEAN,** psychologist; b. Denver, Dec. 22, 1946; s. Donald B. and Irene (Dunlavy) McDonald; children: Ian, Brendan, Tavis, Morgynne. BFA, Parsons Sch. Design, N.Y.C., 1970; MDiv cum laude, St. Paul Sch. Theology, Kansas City, Mo., 1979; D of Ministry, Wesley Theol. Sem., Washington, 1982; PhD, Boston U., 1987. Diplomate Am. Bd. Profl. Psychology, lic. psychologist Mass., Wis., Ill., Ariz., approved supr. Am. Assn. Marriage and Family Therapy; ordained to ministry United Meth. Ch., 1982. Psychologist Worcester (Mass.) Pastoral Counseling Ctr., 1982-87;

chief psychologist Dr. McDonald & Assocs., Inc., 1982—; assoc. prof., asst. program dir. Loyola U., Chgo., 1987-88; clin. psychologist Lake Geneva, Wis., 1987-93; psychology faculty No. Ariz. U., 1993—. Examiner Am. Bd. Profl. Psychology. Author: Personality and Cognitive Theology, 1982, Type A Coronary Prone Behavior and Narcissism, 1987. Fellow: Acad. Family Psychology; mem.: APA (mem. program com. divsn. 43), Am. Assn. Pastoral Counselors, Human Factors Soc. Democrat. Office: 1100 N San Francisco St Ste C Flagstaff AZ 86001-3260 Office Phone: 928-774-1100. *I have seldom found what a person does to be as significant as the motivation for doing it.*

**MCDONALD, DAVID EUGENE,** transportation operator; b. Decatur, Ill., July 6, 1956; s. Robert Alexander McDonald and Ida Jane (Varvil) Crowell; m. Lynda Jean Christensen McDonald, Apr. 23, 1983; children: Melanie Ann, Joshua Glen and Jordan David (twins). BS in History, Ill. State U., Normal; student, Parkland C.C., Champaign, Chgo., 1978-81; mgr. Gen. Cinema Corp., Decatur, Champaign, Chgo., 1978-81; mgr. Classic Cinemas, Elmhurst, Ill., 1981-83, World Mgmt. Inc., Downers Grove, Ill., 1983-87; driver UPS, Addison, Ill., 1987—. Active Jr. Achievement, 1971-75, Dupage County Rep., Wheaton, Ill., 1993-2002; treas. Local Luth. Laymans League, 2000—. Named Mr. Exec. Jr. Achievement, Decatur, Ill., 1975; recipient Internat. Literary award Manuscripts Internat., Dayton, Wash., 1988. Republican. Lutheran. Avocations: politics, photography, reading, writing. Home: 841 Prospect Ave Elmhurst IL 60126-4862 Office: UPS 150 S Lombard Rd Addison IL 60101-3020

**MCDONALD, DORCAS,** psychologist, educator; b. Glasgow, Scotland, July 10, 1939; came to U.S., 1940; d. John Robert Harrison and Dorcas (Hutcheson) McD.; m. Lee William Johnson, Feb. 23, 1965 (div. 1972); children: Lee Johnson, Dorcas Anne Johnson. BA English, Cornell U., 1961; MA Clin. Psychology, Fielding Inst., 1985, EdD Human Devel., 1991. Dir. Resource for Divorcing Parents, Princeton, NJ, 1991—91; founder, dir. Learning for Living, Boulder, Colo., 1991—. Tchr., trainer The Focusing Inst., Chgo., 1989-97. Mem. numerous environ. groups. Mem.: Boulder C. of C. Avocations: architecture, music, hiking, environmental causes. Office: Learning for Living 1030 13th St Ste 305 Boulder CO 80302-7092 E-mail: dorcasmcdonald@yahoo.com.

**MCDONALD, DOUGLAS ROBERT,** non profit agency executive; b. San Francisco, May 27, 1949; s. Robert Angus and Shirley Anne (Beine) McD.; m. Karen Bachanas, June 24, 1978; children: Jennifer, Cameron. AB, Stanford Univ., 1971; MBA, Santa Clara Univ., 1974. Dist. exec. Boy Scouts Am. San Mateo, Calif., 1971-74, exec. Palo Alto, Calif., 1974-76; regional sales mgr. Baron Data Systems, San Leandro, Calif., 1976-81; field dir., COO Boy Scouts Am., San Mateo, Calif., 1981-86, assoc. reg. dir. Sunnyvale, Calif., 1986-88, scout exec., CEO Stockton, Calif., 1988-92, San Jose, Calif., 1992-99, Sacramento, 1999—2003, scout exec., COO Redlands, Calif., 2003—. Active 1910 Soc. Boy Scouts Am. Recipient Paul Harris fellow Rotary Internat., 1990, St. George award Roman Cath. Diocese of Sacramento, 2000; James E. West fellow Boy Scouts Am., 1993. Mem. Am. Fundraising Profs., Sigma Alpha Epsilon, Alpha Phi Omega, Silicon Valley Planned Giving Coun., Rotary Internat., Scouting Heritage Soc., KC. Republican. Roman Catholic. Avocations: travel, computers, investments. Personal E-mail: drmcdon@aol.com.

**MCDONALD, FRANCES D.,** government official, editor, lawyer; b. Washington, July 6, 1949; BA, U. Va., 1971; JD, Cath. U. Am., 1981. Bar: Va. 1982. Legal publs. specialist Office Fed. Register. Nat. Archives and Records Adminstrn., Washington, 1980-82, atty., 1982-86, dir. legal svcs., 1986-91, dir. presdl. and legis. divsn., 1991-96, mng. editor, 1996—. Mem. Pi Gamma Mu. Office: Office Fed Registr Nat Archives-Recs Adminstrn 800 N Capitol St Rm 700 Washington DC 20408-0001 Office Phone: 202-741-6002. Business E-mail: frances.mcdonald@nara.gov.

**MCDONALD, FRANCIS MICHAEL,** judge trial referee, retired state supreme court justice; b. Waterbury, Conn., Jan. 22, 1931; s. M. Francis and Margaret (Kelly) McD.; m. Mary Kelly, Jan. 28, 1956; children: Michael, Mary Ann, John K. AB, Holy Cross Coll., 1953; LLB, Yale U., 1956. Bar: Conn. 1956. Spl. agt. FBI, Washington, 1956-57; asst. U.S. atty. Dist. of Conn., New Haven, 1958-60; asst. prosecutor Cir. Ct., Waterbury, 1961-68; state's atty. Waterbury, 1968-84; judge Superior Ct., Waterbury, 1984-96; assoc. justice Conn. Supreme Ct., Hartford, 1996-99, chief justice, 1999-2001, judge trial referee Conn., 2001—. Avocations: fishing, skiing, fly tying. Home: 257 Christian Rd Middlebury CT 06762-2908 Office: Superior Ct 400 Grand St Waterbury CT 06702-1900

**MC DONALD, GAIL FABER,** musician, educator; b. Jersey City, Oct. 24, 1917; d. Samuel and Jennie (Weiss) Faber; m. George Walther, Nov. 17, 2000; children from previous marriage: Lora McDonald Ferguson, Charles McDonald, Henry McDonald. Diploma, Mannes Music Sch., N.Y.C., 1938; BA, U. Md., 1962; MusM, Cath. U., 1968; DMus Arts, U. Md., 1977. Legis. asst. Capitol Hill, 1943-46; pvt. tchr. piano and music theory Washington and Md., 1950—. Piano soloist Nat. Gallery Art, 1977; rec. artist Educo Records; lectr., performer Bach Sinfonias and Mendelssohn's Complete Songs Without Words; recorded complete solo piano works of Daniel Gregory Mason. Author: Muzio Clementi and the Gradus Ad Parnassum, 1968. Mem. D.C. Music Tchrs. Assn., Md. Music Tchrs. Assn. (pres. 1977-1981), D.C. Fedn. Music Clubs, Nat. Guild Piano Tchrs. (adjudicator 1972-2005), Friday Morning Music Club (performing mem.). Address: 801 N Monroe St Apt 602 Arlington VA 22201-2372 E-mail: gailmcdonald@comcast.net.

**MCDONALD, GREGORY CHRISTOPHER,** author; b. Shrewsbury, Mass., Feb. 15, 1937; s. Irving Thomas and Mae (Haggerty) M.; m. Susan Aiken, Jan. 12, 1963 (div. Oct. 1990); children: Christopher Gregory, Douglas Gregory; m. Cheryle Higgins, May 25, 2001. BA, Harvard U., 1958. Bd. dirs. Camaldon Corp. Author: (novels) Running Scared, 1964, Fletch, 1974, Confess, Fletch, 1976, Flynn, 1977, Love Among the Mashed Potatoes, 1978, Fletch's Fortune, 1978, Fletch Forever, 1978, Who Took Toby Rinaldi, 1980, Fletch and the Widow Bradley, 1981, The Buck Passes Flynn, 1981, Fletch's Moxie, 1982, Fletch and the Man Who, 1983, Carioca Fletch, Flynn's In, 1984, Fletch Won, Safekeeping, 1985, Fletch, Too, 1986, (non-fiction) The Education of Gregory Mcdonald, 1985, Fletch Chronicle, Vol. 1, (drama) Bull's Eye, 1986, A World Too Wide, 1987, Exits and Entrances, 1988; Fletch Chronicle, Vol. 3, 1988, Merely Players, 1988, The Brave, 1991, Son of Fletch, 1993, Fletch Reflected, 1994, Skylar in Yankeeland, 1997, Flynn's World, 2003; editor: Last Laughs, 1986; dir.: Bach Cantata Singers, 1973—80; author: (stage play) CDI pour SDF, 2003. Mem. vis. com. Boston Mus. Fine Arts, 1970-73, 85—; mem. Lincoln Recreation Com., 1977, 78; mem. Winthrop House Sr. Commons Harvard Coll. 1982—. Recipient Humanitarian of Yr. award Tenn. Assn. Fed. Execs., 1989, Citizen of Yr. award Nat. Assn. Social Workers, 1990, Roger William Straus award NCCJ, 1990, Alex Haley award, 1992. Mem. Authors Guild, Dramatists Guild, Mystery Writers Am. (dir. 1977—, pres. 1985-86, Poe award 1975, 77), Crime Writers Eng., Writers Guild Am., Mass. Chiefs Police Assn., Giles Countians United, Mid-Tenn. Harvard-Radcliffe Assn. Clubs: Harvard (Boston); Overseas Press (N.Y.C.); Hillcrest Country (Pulaski, Tenn.). Office: care Arthur Greene Esq 101 Park Ave New York NY 10178-0002

**MCDONALD, JACKSON,** ambassador; b. Fla., Jan. 1956; married; 3 children. Grad., Georgetown U., Inst. d'Etudes Politiques, Paris, Ecole Nat. d'Adminstrn. 3rd sec., vice consul Am. Embassy Dhaka Dept. of State, Bangladesh, 1980—82, country officer for Bangladesh, 1982—84, 2nd sec. for polit. affairs Am. Embassy Beirut, 1984—86, 1st sec. for polit. affairs Am. Embassy Paris, 1987—89, 1st sec. for polit. affairs Am. Embassy Moscow, 1990—91, from chargé d' affaires to dep. chief of mission Am. Embassy Almaty Kazakhstan, 1992—94, consul gen. Marseille, France, 1994—97, dep. chief of mission Am. Embassy Abidjan Cote d'Ivoire, 1998—2001, U.S. amb. to Gambia, 2001—04, U.S. amb. to Guinea, 2004—.

**MCDONALD, JAMES FRANCIS,** electronics company executive; b. Louisville, Feb. 17, 1940; s. Matthew Joseph and Eileen Frances (Schmidt) McD.; m. Paula S. Smith; children: Jimmie L., Susan J., Ashley K. BSEE, U. Ky., 1962, MSEE, 1964. Mgr. prodn. engring. IBM Corp., Boulder, Colo., 1974-75, mgr. devel. lab., 1975-76, mgr. task force, 1976-77, mgr. bus. planning and product planning office products, 1977, systems mgr. copier products, 1977-78, lab. dir. office parts, 1978-80, gen. mgr. mfg. systems products Boca Raton, Fla., 1980-84; pres., chief operating officer Gould, Inc., Rolling Meadows, Ill., 1984-86, chief operating officer, 1984, chmn., chief exec. officer, 1986-88; pres., chief exec. officer J.H. Whitney & Co., 1989-91, gen. partner, 1991-93; pres. and CEO Scientific-Atlantic, Inc., Norcross, Ga., 1993—. Mem. Robot Inst. Am., (bd. dirs.), United Telecommunications, Inc. (bd. dirs. 1986—). Office: Scientific Atlanta 5030 Sugarloaf Pkwy Lawrenceville GA 30044-2869

**MCDONALD, JAMES S.,** investment company executive; b. Titirangi, New Zealand, 1953; arrived in U.S., 1960; AB, Harvard Coll., 1974; JD, U. Va., 1977. With Choate, Hall & Stewart, 1977—86, Boston Harbor Trust Co., N.A. (now Pell Rudman), 1988—; pres. Boston Harbor Trust N.A. (formerly Pell Rudman Trust Co. N.A.), 1988; COO Pell Rudman Trust Co., N.A., 1993—98, CEO, 1998—2000, Rockefeller & Co., Inc., N.Y.C., 2000—. Bd. dirs. NY Stock Exch., NYC, 2003—06, NYSE Group, Inc., 2006—. Office: Rockefeller & Co Inc 30 Rockefeller Plaza New York NY 10112 also: NYSE Group Inc c/o Corp Sec 11 Wall St New York NY 10005*

**MCDONALD, JOHN CLIFTON,** surgeon; b. Baldwin, Miss., July 25, 1930; s. Edgar Hone and Ethel (Knight) McD.; m. Martha Dennis, Sept. 9, 1956; children: Melissa Lee, Karen Ann, Martha Knight. BS, Miss. Coll., 1951; MD, Tulane U., 1955. Diplomate Am. Bd. Surgery. Intern Confederate Meml. Med. Ctr., Shreveport, La., 1955-56; asst. resident Meyer Meml. Hosp., Buffalo, 1958-62, resident, 1962-63; from asst. attending surgeon to attending surgeon, 1963-68, assoc. dir. surg. research lab., 1965-68; from asst. attending surgeon to attending surgeon Deaconess Hosp., Buffalo, 1965-69, head sect. transplantation, 1966-68; dir. transplantation Charity Hosp. of La., New Orleans, 1969-77, vis. surgeon, 1969-77; clin. asst. surgeon Touro Infirmary, New Orleans, 1969-77; med. staff So. Bapt. Hosp., New Orleans, 1969-77; assoc. dept. surgery Hotel Dieu Hosp., 1969-77; surgeon in chief La. State U. Med. Ctr., Shreveport, 1977-2000, prof., chmn. dept. surgery, 1977-2000, chancellor, dean, 2000—. Buswell rsch. fellow in immunology SUNY-Buffalo, 1963-65, instr. surger, 1963-65, assoc. prof., 1965-68; asst. prof. surgery SUNY-Buffalo, 1965-68; cons. surgeon various La. Hosps., 1969-77; dir. La. Organ Procurement Program, 1971-77; cons. N.W. La. Emergency Med. Services, 1977—; assoc. prof. surgery Tulane U. Sch. Medicine, 1969-72, prof., 1972-77, assoc. prof. microbiology and immunology, 1969-77, dir. surg. research labs., 1969-77, dir. transplantation labs., 1969-77, dir. Med. Ctr. Histocampatability Testing Lab., 1969-77. Contbr. articles to med. jours. Served to capt. USAF, 1956-58. Recipient Owl Club award for outstanding teaching Tulane U., 1977; grantee Kidney Found., 1966-67, NIH, 1969—; Schlieder Found., 1970-73, Cancer Assn. Greater New Orleans, 1971-72, La. Regional Med. Program, 1971-73. Mem. AMA, ACS, Am. Assn. Clin. Histocompatability Testing (founding), Am. Assn. Immunologists, Am. Soc. for Artificial Internal Organs, Am. Soc. Transplant Surgeons (founding, pres. 1987), Buffalo Surg. Soc. (sec. 1968, Roswell Pk. medal 2002), So. Surg. Assn. (Arthur H. Shipley award 1972, treas. 1988-91, sec. 1991-3, pres. 1993-94), Surg. Assn. La. (dir. 1977—, pres. 1983), Am. Assn. for Surgery of Trauma, Transplantation Soc., Southeastern Surg. Congress, Am. Surg. Assn., Halsted Soc. (pres. 1991), Soc. U. Surgeons, La. Med. Soc., Shreveport Med. Soc., United Network for Organ Sharing (pres. 1986-88), Am. Endocrine Surgeons, Am. Hepato-Pancreato-Biliary Assn., Internat. Liver Transplantation Soc., Soc. Critical Car Medicine, Soc. Laparoendoscopic Surgeons. Office: La State U Health Scis Ctr Shreveport Office of Chancellor Shreveport LA 71130 E-mail: jmcdon@isuhsc.edu.

**MCDONALD, JOHN FRANCIS PATRICK,** electrical engineering educator; b. Narberth, Pa., Jan. 14, 1942; s. Frank Patrick and Lulu Ann (Hegedus) McD.; m. Karen Marie Knapp, May 26, 1979. BSEE, MIT, 1963; MS in Engring., Yale U., 1965, PhD, 1969. Instr. Yale U., New Haven, 1968-69; asst. prof., 1969-74; assoc. prof. Rensselaer Poly. Inst., Troy, NY, 1974-86, prof., 1986—. Founder Rensselaer Ctr. for Integrated Electronics, 1980—. Contbr. more than 276 articles to profl. publs.; patentee in field. Recipient numerous grants, 1974—. Mem. ACM, IEEE (sr., assoc. editor Transactions on VSLI Design 1995—), Optical Soc., Acoustical Soc., Vacuum Soc., Materials Rsch. Soc. Office: Rensselaer Poly Inst Ctr for Integrated Electronics Troy NY 12181 Office Phone: 518-276-2919. Business E-mail: mcdonald@unix.cie.rpi.edu.

**MCDONALD, JOHN GREGORY,** financial investment educator; b. Stockton, Calif., 1937; m. Melody McDonald. BS, Stanford U., 1960, MBA, 1962, PhD, 1967. Mem. faculty Grad. Sch. Bus. Stanford U., Calif., 1968—, now The Stanford Investors prof. fin. Grad. Sch. Bus. Vis. prof. U. Paris, 1972, Columbia Bus. Sch., 1975, Harvard Bus. Sch., 1986; gov., vice-chmn., bd. govs. NASD/NASDAQ Stock Market, 1987—90; mem. adv. bd. InterWest Venture Capital; bd. dirs. Growth Fund of Am., New Perspective Fund, Inc., Plum Creek Timber Co., Scholastic Corp., EuroPacific Growth Fund. Contbr. articles to profl. jours. Bd. overseers vis. com. Harvard U. Bus. Sch., Cambridge, Mass., 1994-2000. Fulbright scholar, France, 1986-98. Office: Stanford U Grad Sch Bus 518 Memorial Way Stanford CA 94305

**MCDONALD, JOHN J., JR.,** lawyer; b. St. Paul, Minn., Dec. 12, 1954; BA, Univ. St. Thomas, 1977; JD, Creighton Univ., 1981. Bar: Minn. 1982, Wis., US Dist. Ct. (Minn., Wis., ND dist.), US Ct. Appeals (1st, 7th, 8th cir.), US Supreme Ct. Ptnr., comml. litigation, mem. mgmt. com. Meagher & Geer PLLP, Mpls. Named a Minn. Super Lawyer, Minn. Law & Politics, 2000—04. Mem.: ABA, Am. Bd. Trial Advocates, Internat. Assn. Def. Counsel, Def. Rsch. Inst., Minn. State Bar Assn., Wis. State Bar Assn. Office: Meagher & Geer PLLP Suite 4200 33 S 6th St Minneapolis MN 55402 Office Phone: 612-347-9120. Office Fax: 612-338-8384. Business E-Mail: jmcdonald@meagher.com.

**MCDONALD, JOHN JOSEPH,** electronics executive; b. N.Y.C., Apr. 18, 1930; s. John J. and Margaret (Shanley) McD.; m. Tessa de R. Greenfield, Aug. 22, 1956; children: Kathryn, Elizabeth, Andrew. BA, Bklyn. Coll., 1951. With Sperry Rand Corp., Blue Bell, Pa., 1954-75, v.p., 1972-75; mng. dir. Casio Electronics Inc., London, 1975-78, pres. Casio Europe, 1975-78; pres., CEO Casio Inc., Dover, NJ, 1978-99, also bd. dirs.; chmn. Casio Can. Ltd., 1988—99; pres., CEO McDonald Assoc., Dover, NJ, 1999—, Electric Fuel Corp. (Instant Power subs.), 2002. Mem. exec. com. Electronic Ind. Found., 1994—. Chmn. Electronics Industries Found., 1997-98; trustee Bklyn. Coll., CUNY, 1997—. Served with US Army, 1952-54. Mem. Electronic Industries Assn. (bd. gov.), Electronic Industries Found. (trustee 1987—), Consumer Electronics Assn.(dir.). Home and Office: PO Box 322 Hope NJ 07844-0322 Office Phone: 908-459-5386. E-mail: johnmac@nac.net.

**MC DONALD, JOHN RICHARD,** lawyer; b. Connersville, Ind., Aug. 8, 1933; s. Vernon Louis and Thelma (Venham) McD.; m. Mary Alice Boyd, Aug. 17, 1957; children: Anne Elizabeth, John Richard, Colleen Lynn. BA, U. Ariz., 1957, LL.B., 1960. Bar: Ariz. 1960. Since practiced in, Tucson; assoc. Richard N. Roylston, 1961-62; pvt. practice, 1963-65; ptnr. McDonald & Rykken, 1965-68, DeConcini & McDonald (now DeConcini, McDonald, Yetwin, Lacy, and Richardson P.C.), 1968—. Mem. adv. bd. Dependable Nurses, Inc., 1994—. Mem. Ariz. Law Rev. Pres., bd. dirs. emeritus Comstock Children's Hosp. Found.; v.p. Ariz. Sch. Bds. Assn., 1979, pres., 1981; v.p. All Ariz. Sch. Bd., 1981; v.p. bd. dirs. Tucson Assn. for Blind, 1966-86; trustee Catalina Foothills Sch. Dist., 1976-82; bd. dirs. Tucson Unified Sch. Dist. Ednl. Enrichment Found., 1994-2003, Ariz. Acad., 1981-89, Tucson Symphony Soc., 1997-2003, Catalina Foothills Sch. Dist. Found., 1998-2004, Grand Canyon Music Festival, 2003—. Mem. Ariz. Bar Assn. Ariz. Law Rev. Assn. (pres. 1994), Pima County Bar Assn. (pres. 1978-86, pres. 1984-85), Nat. Coun. Sch. Attys. (dir. 1992-96), Delta Chi. Independent. Presbyterian. Home: 6151 N Camino Almonte Tucson AZ 85718-3729 Office:

2525 E Broadway Blvd Tucson AZ 85716-5398 Office Phone: 520-322-5000. Personal E-mail: mjm85718@aol.com. Business E-Mail: jmcdonald@dmyl.com. E-mail: mjm@aol.com.

**MC DONALD, JOHN WARLICK,** diplomat; b. Coblenz, Germany, Feb. 18, 1922; s. John Warlick and Ethel Mae (Raynor) McD.; m. Barbara Jane Stewart, Oct. 23, 1943 (div.); children: Marilyn Ruth, James Stewart, Kathleen Ethel, Laura Ellen; m. Christel Meyer, Oct. 24, 1970. AB, U. Ill., 1943, JD, 1946; PhD (hon.), Mt. Mercy Coll., 1989, Teikyo Marycrest U., 1991, Salisbury State U., 1993. Bar: Ill. 1946, U.S. Supreme Ct. 1951. With legal div. Office Mil Govt., Berlin, 1947; asst. dist. atty. U.S. Mil. Govt. Cts., Frankfort, Germany, 1947-50; with Allied High Commn., Bonn, Germany, 1950-52; U.S. mission to NATO and OEEC, Paris, 1952-54; fgn. affairs officer Dept. State, Washington, 1954-55; exec. sec. to dir. ICA, Washington, 1955-59; U.S. econ. coord. for CENTO affairs Ankara, Turkey, 1959-63; chief econ. and comml. sect. Am. Embassy, Cairo, 1963-66; student Nat. War Coll., Washington, 1966-67; dep. dir. office econ. and social affairs Bur. Internat. Orgn. Affairs, Dept. State, 1967-68, dir., 1968-71; coord. UN Multilateral Devel. Programs, Dept. State, 1971-74, acting dep. asst. sec. econ. and social affairs, 1971, 73; dep. dir. gen. ILO, Geneva, 1974-78; pres. INTELSAT Conf. Privileges and Immunities, 1978; U.S. coord. Tech. Coop. among Developing Countries, 1978; rep. with rank of amb. to UN Conf., 1978—. Sec. gen. 27th Colombo Plan Ministerial Meeting, 1978; U.S. coord. UN Decade on Drinking Water and Sanitation, 1979; U.S. coord., amb. Third World Conf. on Indsl. Devel., 1979, World Assembly on Aging, 1980-82; chmn. fed. inter-agy. com. Internat. Yr. of Disabled Persons, 1980-81; U.S. rep. Internat. Youth Yr., 1981-83; coord. multilateral affairs Ctr. Study of Fgn. Affairs, 1983-87; profl. lectr. in law George Washington U. Nat. Law Ctr., 1987-88, lectr. in conflict resolution, multilateral diplomacy and art of negotiation; pres. Iowa Peace Inst., Grinnell, 1988-92; prof. polit. sci. Grinnell Coll., 1989-92, Disting. vis. prof. George Mason U., Fairfax, Va., 1992-93; chmn., CEO Inst. for Multi-Track Diplomacy, Washington, 1992—; mem. Fgn. Affairs Res. Cons., 1993—; adj. prof. Union Inst., 1993-94, 97-98; adj. prof. conflict resolution, 1998-01, 05-06. Author: The North-South Dialogue and the UN, 1982, How to Be a Delegate, 1984, 2nd edit., 1994; co-editor: International Negotiation, 1985, Perspectives on Negotiation, 1986, Conflict Resolution: Track Two Diplomacy, 1987, 2nd edit., 1995, U.S. Soviet Summitry, 1987, US Bases Overseas: Negotiations with Spain, Greece and The Philippines, 1990, Multi-Track Diplomacy, 1991, Chinese edit., 2006, Defining A U.S. Negotiating Sytle, 1996; contbr. articles on aging, terrorism, water and conflict resolution; featured in exhibit Va. Hist. Soc., 2006. Bd. dirs. Global Water, 1982-, chair, 1982—; Touchstone Theatre, 1982-88, World Com.-UN Decade of Disabled Persons, 1987—, Countdown 2001, 1987-93, People-to-People Com. on Disability, 1987—2003, Am. Impact Found., 1987-89, chmn. bd., 1988-89; dir. Am. Assoc. Retired Persons, 1983—2003, chmn., 1983—2003; v.p. nat. capital area UN Assn., 1993-98, mem., 1978—. Recipient Superior Honor award, State Dept., 1972, Presdl. Meritorious Svc. award, State Dept., 1984, Peace Builders award Search for Common Ground Internat., 2005, Alumni Achievement award U. Ill. Sch. Liberal Arts and Sci., 2004, 06; named Patriot of Yr., Kansas City, 1987; nominee Nobel Peace prize, 1994. Mem. ABA, Am. Fgn. Svc. Assn., U.S. Assn. for Club of Rome (chair 2002-05), People to People Internat. (bd. trustees 2003-), Soc. Profls. in Dispute Resolution, Consortium of Peace Rsch., Edn. and Devel., Va. Hist. Soc., USA Club Rome (Donella Meadows award 2006), Cosmos Club, Delta Kappa Upsilon, Phi Delta Phi. Office: IMTD 1901 Fort Myer Drive Ste 405 Arlington VA 22209 Office Phone: 703-528-3863. Business E-Mail: jmcdonald@imtd.org.

**MCDONALD, JOSEPH VALENTINE,** neurosurgeon; b. N.Y.C., June 7, 1925; m. Carolyn Alice Patricia Petersen, Apr. 30, 1955; 5 children. AB, Coll. Holy Cross, 1946; MD, U. Pitts., 1949. Intern St. Vincent's Hosp. N.Y.C., 1949-50; rsch. fellow neuroanatomy Vanderbilt U., 1950-51; gen. surgery asst. resident Cushing VA Hosp., Boston, 1951-52; neurology extern Lenox Hill Hosp., 1952; asst. resident neurosurgery Johns Hopkins Hosp., 1953-55, resident neurosurgeon, 1955-56; practice medicine specializing in neurol. surgery Rochester, NY, 1956—; emeritus prof. neurosurgery U. Rochester Med. Sch. Mem. Soc. Neurol. Surgeons, A.C.S., Am. Assn. Neurol. Surgeons, Congress Neurosurgeons. Home: 800 Allens Creek Rd Rochester NY 14618-3412

**MCDONALD, KARIS JEANINE,** elementary school educator, adult education educator; b. Newport News, Va., July 22, 1975; d. Isaac L. and Ann K. McDonald. BA in Elem. Edn., N.C. Ctrl. U., 1997; MA in Reading, Lang., and Literacy, The Coll. William & Mary, 2002. Tchr. Newport News (Va.) Pub. Schs., 1997—2001, adult edn. tchr., 1998—, reading specialist, 2001—. Grantee, Va. Power, 2000; scholar, Target Found., 2001. Mem.: NEA (grantee 2000), Va. State Reading Coun., Internat. Reading Assn., Tidewater Assn. N.C. Ctrl. U. Alumni Assn. (life; rec. sec. 1998—2004, chaplin 1998—2004). Democrat. Avocations: travel, piano, swimming. Home: 14 Tillerson Drive Newport News VA 23602 Office Phone: 757-591-4500. Personal E-mail: krsjmc@yahoo.com.

**MCDONALD, KIRK,** publishing executive; b. LaJolla, Calif. m. Kathleen McDonald; 1 child, Meghan. Sports reporter The Blade Tribune, 1974—76, asst. sports editor, 1976—79, dir. retail advt., 1985—87; pub. The Citizen, 1979—84; retail advt. mgr. San Antonio Light, 1987—88, display advt. dir., 1988—89; advt. dir. Denver Post, 1989, v.p. advt., 1989—93, sr. v.p. sales and mktg., 1993—95, exec. v.p., mag. 1995—98; v.p. newspapers Hearst Newspapers, 1998—2000; pres., CEO Denver Newspaper Agy., 2000—. Active Legatus; bd. mem. Regis U., Webb-Waring Inst., Denver Metro C. of C. Office: Denver Newspaper Agy 400 W Colfax Ave Denver CO 80204

**MCDONALD, LINDA L.,** massage therapist; b. Morgantown, W.Va., Dec. 18, 1946; d. Bonita Viola Wittebort; children from previous marriage: Tatiana Denning, Leo Konchesky, Chad. BSc in Psychology, Davis Elkins Coll., 1995; diplom in Therapeutic Massage, Cayce/Reilly Sch. of Masseotherapy, 1999. Cert. massage therapist, colon therapist, hypnotherapist 2005. Lab. asst. Monogahela Gen. Hosp., Morgantown, W.Va., 1965—66; doctor's aide Meml. Gen. Hosp., Elkins, W.Va., 1977—81; direct care provider Immediate Crisis Intervention Ctr., Elkins, 1995—96; massage therapist Cayce/Reilly Sch. of Masseotherapy, Va. Beach, Va., 1999—; pvt. practice Va. Beach, 1999—. Hospice vol. Elkins, W.Va., 1995—; vol. Adult Literacy Coun., Fairbanks, Ala., 1996—, Chrysler Ctr., Va. Beach, 1999—, Options Self-Actualizing Ctr., Shefield, Mass., 2001. Author: Song's On The Wind, 1997, Shadow Walker, 1999. Vol. Adult Literacy Coun., Fairbanks, Alaska, 1996, Hospice, Elkins, W.Va., 1995. Mem.: Internat. Massage Therapist Assn. Avocations: painting, writing, travel, nutrition/alternative medicine, reading. Office: Heritage Holistic Ctr 314 Laskin Rd Virginia Beach VA 23457 Home: 315 33rd St Apt 6 Virginia Beach VA 23451-2945 Personal E-mail: dolphynspirit@yahoo.com.

**MCDONALD, MACKEY J.,** apparel executive; With VF Corp., Greensboro, NC, 1983—, pres. 1993—2006, CEO, 1996—, chmn., 1998—. Bd. dirs. Hershey Foods Corp., 1st Union Corp., Tyco Internat. Ltd. Trustee Davidson Coll. Mem.: Am. Apparel Mfrs. Assn. (bd. dirs.). Mailing: VF Corp PO Box 21488 Greensboro NC 27420-1488 Office: VF Corp 105 Corporate Ctr Blvd Greensboro NC 27408*

**MCDONALD, MARIANNE,** classicist; b. Chgo., Jan. 2, 1937; d. Eugene Francis and Inez (Riddle) McD.; children: Eugene, James, Bryan, Bridget, Kirstie (dec.), Hiroshi. BA magna cum laude, Bryn Mawr Coll., 1958; MA, U. Chgo., 1960; PhD, U. Calif., Irvine, 1975; doctorate (hon.), Am. Coll. Greece, 1988; diploma (hon.), Am. Archaeol. Assn.; DLitt (hon.), U. Athens, 1994, U. Dublin, 1994, Aristotle U., 1997, U. Thessalonika, 1997, Nat. U. Ireland, 2001. Instr. Greek, Latin, English, mythology, cinema U. Calif. Irvine, 1975-79; founder, rsch. fellow Thesaurus Linguae Graecae Project, 1975-97. Tchg. asst. U. Calif., Irvine, 1972-74; vis. prof. U. Ulster, Ireland, 1997, U. Dublin, 1990—, Univ. Coll. Dublin, 1999, 2002, U. Cork, 1999-; adj. prof. theatre U. Calif., San Diego, 1992-94, prof. theatre and classics, 1994—; bd. dirs Centrum. Author: (novels) Semilemmatized Concordances to Euripides' Alcestis, 1977, Semilemmatized Concordance to Euripides Cyclops, 1978, Terms for Happiness in Euripides, 1978, Cyclops, Andromache, Medea, 1978, Heraclidae, Hippolytus, 1979, Hecuba, 1984, (play) And Then He Met A Woodcutter, 2005 (San Diego Critics Cir. award for best play, 2005), (critical works) Hercules Furens, 1984, Electra, 1984, Ion, 1985, Trojan Women, 1988, Iphigenia in Taurus, 1988, Andromache, 2001, The Heart Made Visible, 1983, The Living Art of Greek Tragedy, 2003; translator: The Cost of Kindness and Other Fabulous Tales (Shinichi Hoshi), 1986, Views of Clytemnestra, Ancient and Modern, 1990, Classics and Cinema, 1990, Modern Critical Theory and Classical Literature, 1994, A Challenge to Democracy, 1994, Ancient Sun/Modern Light: Greek Drama on the Modern Stage, 1990, Star Myths: Tales of the Constellations, 1996, Sole Antico Luce Moderna, 1999, Mythology of the Zodiac: Tales of the Constellations, 2000, Antigone by Sophocles, 2000, Mythology of the Zodiac, 2000, Sing Sorrow: Classics, History, Heroines in Opera, 2001; translator: (with Michael Walton) Euripides Andromache, 2001; translator: Euripides' Electra, 2004, Euripides' Hecuba, 2005; editor (with M. McDonald and Michael Walton): Six Greek Tragedies, 2002; editor: (with Michael Walton) Amid Our Troubles: Irish Versions of Greek Tragedy, 2002, Canta la tua Pena, 2002; contbr. chapters to books, articles in field to profl. jours., reviews. Bd. dirs. Am. Coll. of Greece, 1981-90, Scripps Hosp., 1981, Am. Sch. Classical Studies, 1986-; mem. bd. overseers U. Calif., San Diego, 1985-; nat. bd. advisors Am. Biog. Inst., 1982—; pres. Soc. for the Preservation of the Greek Heritage, 1990-, Asian Am. Repertory Theatre, 2003; founder Hajime Mori Chair for Japanese Studies, U. Calif., San Diego, 1985, McDonald Ctr. for Alcohol and Substance Abuse, 1984, Thesaurus Linguarum Hiberniae, 1991-, Hiroshi McDonald Mori Performing Arts Ctr. Recipient Ellen Browning Scripps Humanitarian award, 1975, Disting. Svc. award U. Calif., Irvine, 1982, 2001, Irvine medal, 1987; named one of the Cmty. Leaders Am., 1979-80, Philanthropist of Yr., 1985, Headliner San Diego Press Club, 1985, Philanthropist of Yr. Honorary Nat. Conf. Christians and Jews, 1986, Woman of Yr. AHEPA, 1988, San Diego Woman of Distinction, 1990, Woman of Yr. AXIOS, 1991; recipient Bravissimo gold medal San Diego Opera, 1990, Gold Medal Soc. Internationalization of Greek Lang., 1990, Athens medal, 1991, Piraeus medal, 1991, award Desmoi, 1992, award Hellenic Assn. of Univ. Women, 1992, Acad. of Achievement award AHEPA, 1992, Woman of Delphi award European Cultural Ctr. Delphi, 1992, Civis Universitatis award U. Calif., San Diego, 1993, Hypatia award Hellenic U. Women, 1993, Am.-Ireland Fund Heritage award, 1994, Contbn. to Greek Letters award Aristotle U. Thessaloniki, 1994, Mirabella Mag. Readers Choice One of 1000 Women for the Nineties, 1994, citations from U.S. Congress and Calif. Senate, Alexander the Gt. award Hellenic Cultural Soc., 1995, made hon. citizen of Delphi and gold medal of the Amphiktuonon, Del. Bus. award for Fine Arts San Diego Bus. Jour., 1995, Vol. of Decade Women's Internat. Ctr., 1994, 96, Gold Star award San Diego Arts League, 1997, Golden Aeschylus award Inst. Nat. Drama Antkg. Siracusa, 1998, Women Who Mean Bus., Fine Arts award San Diego Bus. Jour., 1998, Fulbright award, 1999, Ellis Island award, 1999, Spirit of Scripps award 1999; Theatre Excellence award KPBS Patte, 2001, Laud and Laurels, U. Calif. Disting. Alumni award Hellenic Cultural Soc. San Diego, 2003, Sledgehammer Theatre award, 2003, New Path award, 2003, Egeria award Women's Internat. Ctr., 2004, Billie award, 2004, Patté award, 2004. Mem. MLA, AAUP, Am. Philol. Assn. (disting. svc. award 1999), Soc. for the Preservation of the Greek Heritage (pres.), Libr. of Am., Am. Classical League, Philol. Assn. Pacific Coast, Am. Comparative Lit. Assn., Modern and Classical Lang. Assn. So. Calif., Hellenic Soc. (coun. award 2000), Calif. Fgn. Lang. Tchrs. Assn., Internat. Platform Assn., Royal Irish Acad., Greece's Order of the Phoenix (comdr. 1994), KPBS Prodrs. Club, Hellenic Univ. Club (bd. dirs.). Avocations: Karate, harp (medieval), skiing, diving. Home: PO Box 929 Rancho Santa Fe CA 92067-0929 Office: U Calif at San Diego Dept Theatre La Jolla CA 92093 Office Phone: 858-481-0107. E-mail: mmcdonald@ucsd.edu.

**MCDONALD, MARILYN A.,** academic assistant; b. Des Moines, Nov. 7, 1932; d. Edmund and Alice Groomes; m. Thomas Edwin McDonald, Feb. 12, 1955 (dec. June 1991); children: Deborah Sue, Thomas Groomes, Sarah Alice, Janet Louise. BS, Iowa State U., 1954. Instr. Sch. Home Econs. Iowa State U., Ames, 1955; tchr. civics and English Evanston Twp. H.S., Evanston, 1956; home economist Pub. Sve. Co., Northbrook, Ill., 1957; substitute tchr. Ft. Worth Ind. Sch. Dist., 1973—76, mid. sch. tchr., 1976—92; exec. asst. dept. neurosurgery U. Tex. Med. Sch., Houston, 1994—. Founding mem., mem. issues com. Save Our ER, Houston, 2001; mem., discussion leader Bible Study Fellowship, Ft. Worth and Houston, 1983—2000; elder First Presbyn. Ch., Houston. Mem.: Mortar Bd., Omicron Nu, Phi Kappa Phi. Avocations: tennis, reading, travel. Office: U Tex Med Sch Dept Neurosurgery 6431 Fannin Ste 7 148 Houston TX 77030

**MCDONALD, MARK DOUGLAS,** electrical engineer; b. Princeton, NJ Aug. 3, 1958; s. James Douglas and Jacquelyn (Milligan) McD.; m. Patricia Joann Watson, Sept. 12, 1980. BSE, Duke U.; MS, N.C. State U. Product engr. Exide Electronics, Raleigh, NC, 1981—84; rsch. asst. N.C. State U., Raleigh, 1985—86; tech. staff Avantek (Hewlett Packard), Newark, Calif., 1987—90; prin. engr. Nat. Semiconductor, Santa Clara, Calif., 1990—92, engring. project mgr., 1992—95; design engring. mgr. Linear Tech. Corp., Milpitas, Calif., 1995—2001; dir. RF/Analog Bermai Inc, Palo Alto, Calif., 2001—02; dir. McDonald Watson and Assocs., Campbell, Calif., 2002—; v.p. hardware devel. Altierre Corp., San Jose, 2003—. Session chmn. Wireless Symposium, Santa Clara, 1993-2002, RF and Microwave Applications Conf., Santa Clara, 1992; mem. com. Symposium on VLSI Circuits Program, 1995-97. Contbr. articles to profl. jours. Precinct capt. various polit. campaigns, Fremont, Calif., 1988. Mem. IEEE (sr.), Cairn Terrier Club of No. Calif. (asst. chair 1995, splty. show chair 1994-97, bd. govs. 1996-99), Cairn Terrier Club Am., Sacramento Valley Cairn Terrier Club, No. Calif. Terrier Assn. (bd. govs. 2002—). Achievements include U.S. and foreign patents in area of high-speed analog circuits; designed front-end integrated circuits in first wireless digital European cordless telecom. transceiver (DECT) for voice comm.; design of first selective frequency trip circuit for parallel uninterruptible power supplies. Personal E-mail: markm@altierre.com.

**MCDONALD, MARY FRANCES,** language educator; b. Dallas, Apr. 26, 1948; d. John Brenton and Dorothy Frances (Cobler) McD.; m. David Ralph Abbott, Jr., Jan. 26, 1985; 1 child, Jessica McDonald Leak. Student, U. Tex., Arlington, 1966-67; BA in English, Phillips U., Enid, Okla., 1967-69,71; student, Columbia U., N.Y.C., 1969-70; MA in English, U. Ctrl. Okla., 2003. Cert. tchr., Okla.; cert. Nat. advanced placement English cons., Coll. Bd., 1996. Lang. arts tchr. Waukomis (Okla.) Pub. Schs., 1971-75; composition tchr. Enid Pub. Schs., 1975-76; lang. arts tchr. Garber (Okla.) Pub. Schs., 1976-80; tchr. advanced placement English and Shakespeare Enid Pub. Schs., 1980—. Drama coach, teen improvement for teen problems Youth and Family Svcs., Enid, Okla., 1989-92, 94-99; reader AP English exam, 1995—. Bd. dirs., pres. Gaslight Theatre, Enid, 1984, 92-94, 2005—; cmty. prodr. P.E.G.A.S.Y.S., Enid, 1990-95; com. chair Ambucs, Enid, 1992-93. Recipient Tchr. of Yr. award, Enid Pub. Schs., 2000, Enid H.S. Tchr. of Yr. award, 2006. Mem. Enid Edn. Assn., Okla. Edn. Assn., NEA, Nat. Coun. Tchrs. English, Delta Kappa Gamma. Democrat. Mem. Disciple of Christ. Avocations: theatre-acting, directing, reading, gardening. Office Phone: 580-234-2404.

**MCDONALD, MARY HELEN,** special education educator; b. Killeen, Tex., Jan. 21, 1953; d. Eugene W. and Shirley A. (Clem) Toifl; m. Randy C. McDonald, Feb. 26, 1972; children: Brent McDonald, Mistie McDonald Boyle. BA, U. Tex. San Antonio, 1980; MA, Incarnate Word U., 1990. Cert. tchr. spl. edn. administrn., Tex. Tchr. Concordia Luth. San Antonio, 1980-88; tchr., administr. Northside Ind. Sch. Dist., San Antonio, 1989-97; spl. edn. adminstrn. N.E. Ind. Sch. Dist., San Antonio, 1997—, asst. prin., 1998—, coord. spl. edn. program, 1999—, spl. edn. administr., 1999—. Vol. Conservation Soc. San Antonio, 1985—. Mem. Zonta (mem. chair 1995—), Phi Delta Kappa. Republican. Lutheran. Avocations: walking, reading, boating, fishing. Home: 820 CR 262 Mico TX 78056 E-mail: mmcdon@neisd.net.

**MC DONALD, MEG,** public relations executive; b. Santa Monica, Calif., Oct. 11, 1948; Dir. radio & TV svcs. Fran Hynds Pub. Rels., 1969-75; owner, CEO Mc Donald Media Svcs., 1975—. Recipient Buccaneer award PI-RATES, 1980, 82, Prisms award Pub. Rels. Soc. Am., 1981, Pro awards Publicity Clubs of L.A. Mem. Pub. Rels. Soc. Am. (sec. 1985), Radio ane TV News Assn. of So. Calif. (mem. bd. dirs. 1973-78), Publicity Club of L.A. (pres. 1979-80), L.A. Advt. Women (v.p. 1984-85), Print Interactive Radio and TV Ednl. Soc. (pres. 1998-00), Radio and TV News Assn. Office: Mc Donald Media Svcs 11076 Fruitland Dr Studio City CA 91604-3541 Business E-Mail: mcdmedia@earthlink.net.

**MCDONALD, MICHAEL PERRY,** retired transportation engineer, musician; b. Boston, Apr. 26, 1940; adopted s. Francis C. and Olive C. McDonald; m. Alma Adriana Maria de Guadalupe Tovar-Velazquez, Apr. 22, 1967; children: Miguel Kevin McDonald-Tovar, Adriana Maria Kathleen Reguera, Rafael Neal McDonald-Tovar. BA, Harvard Coll., 1963; MusB, U. Mich., 1977. Commd. lt. USAF, 1963, advanced through grades to capt., 1967; telecom coord. Nat. Steel Co., Ecorse, Mich., 1978—83; telecom. analyst NYNEX Info. Resources Co., Lynn, Mass., 1984—86; electronics engr. Volpe Nat. Transp. Systems Ctr. U.S. Dept. Transp., Cambridge, Mass., 1986—2005; ret., 2005. Composer: (songs) The Prayer of Humble Access, Duo Seraphim. Mem.: Am. Musicological Soc., Convivium Musicum, Inc. (treas. 1996—2001), Sports Car Club Am. Republican. Episcopalian. Avocations: singing, musical composition, auto sports. Home: 14 Mansfield St Peabody MA 01960-4856

**MCDONALD, PATRICK ALLEN,** lawyer, educator, arbitrator; b. Detroit, May 11, 1936; s. Lawrence John and Estelle (Maks) Mc D.; m. Margaret Mercier, Aug. 10, 1963; children: Michael Lawrence, Colleen Marie, Patrick Joseph, Timothy, Margaret, Thomas, Maureen. PhB cum laude, U. Detroit, 1958, JD magna cum laude, 1961; LLM (E. Barrett Prettyman Trial scholar, Hugh J. Fegan fellow), Georgetown U., 1962. Bar: D.C. 1961, Mich. 1961, Colo. 1993. Case worker Dept. Pub. Welfare, Detroit, 1958; field examiner NLRB, Detroit, 1961; practiced in Washington, 1961-62; trial cons. NIH, Bethesda, Md., 1962; staff judge adv. USAF, France, 1962-65; ptnr. Monagham, LoPrete, Mc Donald, Yakima & Grenke, Detroit, 1965—. Bd. dirs., past chmn. Delta Dental Plan Mich.; past chmn. Delta Dental Plan Ohio; bd. dirs., v.p. Guest House, Lake Orion, Mich., Rochester, Minn., Detroit Athletic Club, Brighton Hosp.; instr. polit. sci. and law U. Md., 1963-65, U. Detroit Law Sch., adj. prof., 1965-2004; adj. prof. Ave Maria Law Sch., 2003—. Co-author: Law and Tactics in Federal Criminal Cases, 1963; author magnet plans for schs., Detroit, Boston. Mem. Detroit Bd. Edn., 1966-76, pres.; sec., trustee Mt. Elliott Cemetary Assn.; mem. U. Detroit Sports Hall of Fame; mem. adv. bd. Providence Hosp., Southfield, Mich.; exec. bd. U. Detroit Pres.'s Cabinet. Named one of Five Outstanding Young Men of Mich., Outstanding Young Man of Detroit. Mem. ABA, Detroit Bar Assn., State Bar Mich. (commr.), U. Detroit Alumni Assn. (bd. dirs.), Mensa, Blue Key, Alpha Phi Omega (pres. Eta Pi chpt. 1955), Alpha Sigma Nu (v.p. 1960). Home: 13066 Lashbrook Ln E Brighton MI 48114-6002 Office: 40700 Woodward Ave Bloomfield Hills MI 48304-2211 Fax: 248-642-9460. Office Phone: 810-220-3444. *In the field of law, as an attorney, professor and arbitrator, I have prayed and attempted to be able in argument, accurate in analysis, correct in conclusion, candid with clients, honest with adversaries, and responsible for obligations assigned to me. I have advocated moderation in all things with the exception of my love for Him who created me.*

**MCDONALD, PETER D,** airline executive; m. Diane McDonald; children: Megan, Katie. B. Judson Coll., 1976. Various positions United Airlines Corp., 1969—, v.p., op. svcs., 1999—2001, sr. v.p. airport ops., 2001—02, exec. v.p. ops., 2002—.

**MCDONALD, PEYTON DEAN,** brokerage house executive; b. Kansas City, Kans., Feb. 6, 1936; s. Charles H. and Myra (Miller) McD.; m. Frances B. Beighley, June 14, 1958; children: Peyton D., Todd B. BS, Bucknell U., 1958. Sales rep. Sprout Waldron and Co., Inc., Muncy, Pa., 1958-67; v.p. Blair & Co., Williamsport, Pa., 1967-69; v.p., mgr. Hugh Johnson, Williamsport, 1969-77, E.F. Hutton & Co. Inc., Williamsport 1977-87; sr. v.p. Smith Barney, Williamsport, 1987—. Mem. N.Y. Stock Exchange; pres. Hope Enterprizes. Pres. United Way, Williamsport, 1977-80, Pa. Coll. Found., 1985-86; campaign chmn. Heinz for Senator, Lycoming County, Pa., 1978, 96; bd. dirs., treas. Divine Providence Hosp., 1984—, chmn.; mem. Susquehanna Health Care Bd. 1st lt. U.S. Army, 1958-59. Mem. Ross Club, Williamsport Country Club, Farmington Country Club, Masons. Republican. Presbyterian. Avocation: golf. Home: 1545 Grampian Blvd Williamsport PA 17701-1917

**MCDONALD, R. BRUCE,** corporate financial executive; B Commerce, McMaster Univ., Hamilton, Ont. With Lucas Varity plc; v.p., fin. TRW Inc.; v.p., corp. controller Johnson Controls Inc., Milw., 2001—04, v.p., asst. CFO, 2004—05, v.p., CFO, 2005—. Office: Johnson Controls Inc 5757 N Green Bay Ave Milwaukee WI 53201*

**MCDONALD, REGINALD ADRIAN,** musician, educator; b. Columbus, Ohio, Mar. 16, 1968; s. Charlie Alf McDonald, Jr. and Muriel Paulette McDonald; m. Coretta Craddock, July 14, 2000; m. Mia Rochelle Bell, Sept. 7, 1991 (div. Sept. 22, 1995). BA Music Ed., Ala. State Univ., Montgomery, AL, 1991; M. Music, State Univ. West Ga., Carrollton, GA, 1997. Cert. Education Specialist Clark Atlanta Univ., 2002. Band dir. McNair Mid. Sch., College Park, Ga., 1991—96; band dir./music dept. chair SW DeKalb H.S., Decatur, 1996—2001; assoc. dir. of bands/asst. music prof. Tenn. State Univ., Nashville, 2001. Saxophone/clarinet clinician Precision Camp, Inc., Atlanta, 1996—2001; band cons. Milestone, Inc., Atlanta, 1996—2001; band adjudicator/clinician Ga. Music Educators Assn., Atlanta, 1995—; assoc. condr. Tenn. State Univ., Nashville, 2002—. Pres. student govt. Alabama State Univ., Montgomery, Ala., 1990; saxophonist/mem. Ga. Afro-American All-Star Band, Atlanta, Ga., 1994—99. Recipient Tchr. of the Yr., McNair Mid. Sch., Coll. Pk., GA, 1996-1997. Expert Tchr. Citation, Fulton County Bd. of Edn., Atlanta, GA, 1996, Medal of Excellence, Coll. Pk. Bus. Cmty. Mem.: Alpha Phi Alpha, Inc., Music Educators Nat. Conf., Phi Mu Alpha Sinfonia (pres. delta beta 1988—90). Democrat-Npl. Methodist. Avocations: golf, golf. Office: Tennessee State Univ 3500 John A Merritt Blvd Nashville TN 37209 Home: 5600 Cedar Rock Dr Nashville TN 37211-6731 Personal E-mail: mcdonaldreginald@hotmail.com.

**MCDONALD, ROBERT ALAN (BOB MCDONALD),** manufacturing executive; b. Gary, Ind., June 20, 1953; s. Ray Wellington and Froso (Manolios) McD.; m. Diane Janine Murphy, Dec. 31, 1977; children: Jennifer Elizabeth, Robert Wade. BS in Engring., U.S. Mil. Acad., 1975; MBA, U. Utah, 1978. Asst. Solo brand Procter & Gamble, Cin., 1980-81, asst. mgr. Dawn brand, 1981-82, asst. mgr. Cascade brand, 1982-83, mgr. Cascade brand, 1983-84, mgr. Tide brand, 1984—86, assoc. advt. mgr., 1986—89, mgr. laundry prod. P&G Canada, 1989—91, gen. mgr. P&G Far East, 1991—94, v.p., gen. mgr. P&G Far East, 1994—96, regional v.p. Japan, P&G Asia, 1996—99, v.p. NE Asia, 1999, pres. NE Asia, 1999—2001, pres. global fabric care & home care, 2001—04, vice chmn. global ops., 2004—. Instr. econs. Meth. Coll., Golden Gate U., Campbell U., Fayetteville, N.C., 1979-80; bd. dirs. Xerox Corp., GS1. Deacon Knox Presbyn. Ch., Cin., 1982-85, Mt. Washington Presbyn. Ch., Cin., 1985-89; trustee No. Ky. Univ. Sch. Bus., Duke Univ.; mem. bd. adv. Northwestern Integrated Mktg. Communications. Advanced through grades to capt. U.S. Army, 1975—80. Fellow Royal Soc. of Arts of London (Silver medal 1975); mem. Phi Kappa Phi, Beta Gamma Sigma, Commonwealth Club. Republican. Avocations: reading, running, painting. Office: Procter & Gamble 1 Procter And Gamble Plz Cincinnati OH 45202-3393 Mailing: Procter & Gamble PO Box 599 Cincinnati OH 45201-0599*

**MCDONALD, SALLY J.,** lawyer; b. Ind., 1964; d. Homer C. and Esteleen M. McD.; m. Richard M. Levin, Oct. 16, 1993. BS, Ind. U., 1986; JD, Duke U., 1990. Bar: Ill. 1990, Ill. Supreme Ct., US Dist. Ct. (no. dist. Ill.), US Ct. Appeals (7th cir.), Fed. Trial Bar. Assoc. Bell, Boyd & Lloyd, Chgo., 1990-92,

Piper Rudnick, Chgo., 1992-98, hiring ptnr., 1998—99; ptnr., labor, employment group, co-nat. hiring ptnr. Piper Rudnick (now DLA Piper Rudnick Gray Cary), 1999—. Gen. counsel Gtr. Chgo. Food Depository, 1995-99. Contbr. chpt. to book. Bd. mem. Pub. Interest Law Initiative; pres. bd. dir. CARPLS; outside counsel Greater Chgo. Food Depository. Mem. ABA, Chgo. Bar Assn. (bd. mgrs. 1998-2000, chair Young Lawyers sect. 1996-97, Maurice Weigle award 1994), Chgo. Bar Found. (bd. dir., treas.), Women's Bar Assn. Office: DLA Piper Rudnick Gray Cary Suite 1900 203 N LaSalle St Chicago IL 60601-1293 Office Phone: 312-368-8927. Office Fax: 312-236-7516. Business E-Mail: sally.mcdonald@dlapiper.com.

MCDONALD, STEPHEN DOUGLAS, banker; b. Cambridge, Ontario, Can., Oct. 17, 1956; came to U.S., 1984; s. William C. and Evelyn V. (Dakin) McD.; m. Donna Eva Dauneckas, Sept. 28, 1984. LLB, U. Western Ont., London, Ont., Can., 1980, MBA, 1983. Real estate lending officer Toronto Dominion Bank, Atlanta, 1984-86, dir. N.Y.C., 1986-87, mng. dir. communications fin., 1987-90; pres. Toronto Dominion Securities (USA), Inc. (now TD Waterhouse), 1991—98; CEO TD Waterhouse Group, N.Y.C., 1998—2002; vice-chmn., corp. TD Bank Fin. Group, 2002—. Office: TD Waterhouse Group 100 Wall St New York NY 10005-3701

MCDONALD, SUSAN, publishing executive; V.p., CFO San Jose (Calif.) Mercury News. Office: San Jose Mercury News 750 Ridder Park Dr San Jose CA 95190-0001

MCDONALD, THERESA BEATRICE PIERCE (MRS. OLLIE MCDONALD), church official, minister; b. Vicksburg, Miss., Apr. 11, 1929; d. Leonard C. Pierce and Ernestine Morris Templeton Pierce; m. Ollie McDonald, Apr. 23, 1966. Student, Tougaloo Coll., 1946-47, U. Chgo. Indsl. Rels. Ctr., 1963-64; BA in Sociology with deptl. honors, Roosevelt U., 1997; student, Chgo. Theol. Sem., 1997—. Ordained to Gospel Ministry, 1997. Vol. rep. Liberty Bapt. Ch., Am. Legion Aux., VA West Side Hosp., 1971-73; nat. instr. ushers dept. Prog. Nat. Bapt. Conv. Inc., Washington, 1973-75, nat. sec. ushers dept., 1975-76, v.p. at large, 1980-82, chmn. pers. com., 1982-84; mem. faculty Congress of Christian Edn., 1978-85; mem. pub. rels. staff Liberty Bapt. Ch., Chgo., 1973-79, trustee, 1987-91; asst. Christian edn. dir. Maryland Ave. Bapt. Ch., Chgo., 1995-99; assoc. min. Md. Ave. Bapt. Ch., Chgo., 1997—; Tchr. Tng. Instr., 1998, 2000; dir. Christian edn. Md. Ave. Bapt. Ch., Chgo., 2000—02. Cons., lectr. in field; Sunday ch. sch. tchr.; bible class instr.; guest speaker TV and radio programs. Participant White House Regional Confs., 1961. Recipient Christian Svc. award Prog. Nat. Bapt. Conv. Inc., 1986, 92, 94, Disting. Svc. award, 1990-94, Dedicated Svc. award, 1998. Mem. VFW (life mem. Hunt aux. 2024), Bethlehem Bapt. Dist. Assn. Chgo. (asst. sec. 1982-84), Ch. Women United in Greater Chgo. (Ecumenical Actions com. 1981-83), Am. Legion (Outstanding Svc. award 1972, 73), Bapt. State Conv. Ill. (life), Order Ea. Star. Address: 9810 S Calumet Ave Chicago IL 60628-1432

MCDONALD, THOMAS ALEXANDER, lawyer; b. Chgo., Aug. 20, 1942; s. Owen Gerard and Lois (Gray) McD.; m. Sharon Diane Hirk, Nov. 25, 1967; children: Cristin, Katie, Courtney, Thomas F. and Rebecca J. BA in (eng.), Georgetown U., 1965; JD, Loyola U., Chgo., 1968. Bar: Ill. 1969, U.S. Dist. Ct. (no. dist.) Ill. 1969. Ptnr. Clausen Miller, PC, Chgo., 1969—2001, McDonald & McCabe, LLC, Chgo., 2001—. Mem.: ABA, Chgo. Bar Assn., Ill. Bar Assn. Office: McDonald & McCabe LLC 300 S Wacker Dr Ste 1600 Chicago IL 60606 Office Phone: 312-845-5199. Business E-Mail: tmcdonald@mcdonaldmccabe.com.

MCDONALD, TRACY KATHLEEN, science educator; b. Oak Lawn, Ill., June 29, 1972; d. Robert Thomas and Karen Therese McDonald; m. Michael Thomas Marcuccilli, Nov. 20, 1999; children: Michael Lee, David Arthur. BS in Biology, Loyola U., Chgo., 1995. Cert. tchr. Ill. Tchr. chemistry and biology South H.S. Hinsdale Pub. Sch. Dist. 86, Darien, Ill. Mem. sci. curriculum task force Hinsdale Pub. Sch. Dist 86, Darien, Ill. Mem. Ret. Greyhounds as Pets (REGAP), Ill. Mem.: Nat. Sci. Tchrs. Assn., Nat. Wildlife Fedn. Roman Catholic.

MCDONALD, VIVIAN, minister; b. Gainesville, Fla., June 26, 1949; d. Preston and Pearl Williams; m. Frankie McDonald (dec.); children: Tilwanna Renee Brown, Anita Tyese Mann; adopted children: Cassandra Abbott, Calvin LaMar Abbott, Isaiah K. Phillips. Degree in ministerial enrichment, Bible Inst., 1982. ETA approved tchr. Evangelical Tng. Assn., 1997. Ministerial intern Ch. of God, Tifton, Ga., 1992—93, pastor Dawson, Ga., 1993—. Recipient Women Making Magic, Southwest Ga. Living, 2004. Mem.: Black Ministries. Avocations: sewing, reading, puzzles. Personal E-mail: ladymackie@aol.com.

MCDONALD, WARREN GEORGE, accountant, consultant, mortgage company executive, savings and loan association executive; b. Oakland, Calif., Feb. 14, 1939; s. George Daniel and Barbara (Sainsot) McD.; m. Roberta Anne Peterson, Apr. 27, 1968; children: Edward Bruce, Deborah Lynn. BA, San Francisco State Coll., 1962. CPA, Calif. Ptnr. Main Lafrentz & Co., CPAs, San Francisco, 1969-74; v.p., treas. Imperial Corp. Am., San Diego, 1975-80; v.p. fin. No. Calif. Savs. & Loan, Palo Alto, 1980-82; sr. v.p. fin. Unified Mortgage Co., Santa Clara, Calif., 1982-85; pres. Saratoga Savs., 1985-89; pvt. practice cons. San Francisco, 1989—2003; ret., 2003. Co-author: Power Above The Law, 1990. Served to capt. USCGR. Mem. AICPA, Calif. Soc. CPAs, Inst. Mgmt. Accts., Res. Officers Assn., Naval Inst., Navy League, Mil. Officers Assn. Am. (nat. bd. dirs. 2004—). Home: 1430 Wendy Way Menlo Park CA 94025-6022 Personal E-mail: mcdcpa@earthlink.net. E-mail: mcdcpa@gmail.com.

MCDONALD, WESLEY S., retail executive; b. 1962; Bachelor Degree cum laude, Bucknell U.; MBA, Wharton. Various fin. positions Target Corp., 1988—2000; CFO Abercrombie & Fitch, 2000—03; exec. v.p., CFO Kohl's, 2003—. Office: Kohls Corp N56 W17000 Ridgewood Dr Menomonee Falls WI 53051-5660*

MCDONALD, WILLIAM BRICE, educational association administrator; b. Greenville, Ky., June 16, 1957; s. James Marlin and Joyce Rudale (Cox) M. BS in Polit. Sci., Loyola U., Chgo., 1976, MA in Internat. Rels., 1973; MA in Media, Northeastern U., Chgo., 1985; postgrad., Northwestern U., 1993; DD, St. Johns, Saskatchewan. 1995. Tchr. Chgo. Pub. Schs., 1967-69, libr., 1969-85; coordinator Edn. Service Ctr. 6, 1986-92; coord. Bur. of Librs. Chgo. Pub. Schs., 1992—; CEO Pax Vobiscum, Inc., 1993—. Cons. bd. examiners Chgo. Pub. Schs., 1987; judge, participant Ill. Young Authors, Chgo., 1987-99; advisor Chgo. Tchrs. Libr. Assn., 1988; advisor High Sch. Libr. Media Assn., 1988, treas., 1992—; treas. Chgo. Libr. Club, 1992—; bd. dirs. No. Ill. U. Children's Lit. Inst., 1992-99; edn. cons., 2001—. Author: Alliance for Progress, 1981, Library Networking, 1985, Illinois School Library Media Program Guidelines, 1992. Del. Chgo. Schs. Union, 1968-81; bd. dirs. McDonald Charitable Trust, 2002—. George M. Pullman Found. scholar, Chgo., 1966, Kiwanis- Internat. scholar, Chgo., 1974, State of Ill. scholar, Chgo., 1978; grantee Northeastern U., Chgo., 1984. Mem. Oriental Inst. Chgo., Breasted Soc., Am. Rsch. Ctr. Egypt (life), Citizens Sch. Com., Friends Chgo. Pub. Libr., Newberry Libr. Assocs., Soc. Sch. Librs. Internat. (nominating com.), Ill. Libr. Assn. (bd. dirs. 1990-92, north cen. evaluation team 1992), Ill. Coalition Libr. Advisors, Assn. Supervision and Curriculum Devel. (Midwest authors selection com. 1993, Chgo. Pub. Libre-Chgo. Pub. Schs. task force com. 1992—), Children's Reading Roundtable (bd. dirs. 1992—). Avocations: aviation, bibliophile, archeology, stamp collecting/philately. Home: 3750 N Lake Shore Dr Apt 9D Chicago IL 60613-4233 Office: CPS Bur Libr 1819 W Pershing Rd Chicago IL 60609-2300 also: Pax Vobiscum Inc 1820 Campbell La Salle IL 61301

MCDONALD, WILLIAM HENRY, manufacturing executive; b. Ottawa, Ont., Can., Sept. 8, 1924; s. Joseph and Constance Mary (Gordon) McD.; m. D. Gwen Selkirk, July 8, 1950; 1 child, Barbara Elaine. Grad. high sch. Credit and operating mgr. B.F. Goodrich Co., Winnipeg, Man., Canada, 1945-49; fin. admnstrn. officer Govt. Can., Ottawa, 1949-55; asst. gen. mgr. mortgages

Bank of N.S., 1955-66; mng. dir. Boyd Stott & McDonald Ltd., Toronto, Ont., 1966-79; exec. v.p., dir. Morguard Trust Co., 1966-74; chmn. bd. Can. Comml. Bank, Toronto, 1976-81, chmn. exec. com., 1981-84; chmn. bd. Can. Comml. Bank Mortgage Investment Corp., 1983-84; pres., CEO, dir. Boyd Stott and McDonald Techs., Ltd., 1984—2003. Pres. Thornton McDonald Assocs., Inc. Mem. bd. govs. J. Douglas Ferguson Hist. Research Found., 1971—. Served with RCNVR, 1943-45. Mem. Can. Paper Money Soc. (hon. pres.), Internat. Bank Note Soc. (life), Can. Credit Inst., Classical & Medieval Numismatic Soc. (exec. sec.). Conservative. Anglican. E-mail: billmcdo@idirect.com.

MCDONALD, WILLIAM HENRY, lawyer; b. Niangua, Mo., Feb. 27, 1946; s. Milburn and Fannie M. McDonald; m. Janice E. Robinson, July 13, 1968; children: Melissa L., Meghan M. BS in Pub. Adminstrn., Southwest Mo. State U., 1968; JD, U. Mo., 1971. Bar: Mo. 1971, U.S. Dist. Ct. (we. dist.) Mo. 1973, U.S. Supreme Ct. 1978, U.S. Ct. Appeals (8th cir.) 1982. Ptnr., pres. Woolsey, Fisher, Whiteaker & McDonald, PC, 1973-95; pres. William H. McDonald & Assocs., PC, Springfield, Mo., 1995—. Chmn. blue ribbon task force on Delivery of Mental Health Services to Southwest Mo., Mo. Commn. Continuing Legal Edn.; pres. Tan Oaks Homeowners Assn.; mem. fin. com. Child Adv. Council, Rep. Nat. Com., Mo. Rep. Com., Greene County Nat. Com.; active various Southwest Mo. State U. Clubs; bd. dirs. Greene County div. Am. Heart Assn., Ozarks regional Am. Athletic Union Jr. Olympics; pres., bd. dirs. Springfield Little Theatre; v.p. pub. affairs Springfield Area C. of C., bd. dirs., 1995-98. Capt. U.S. Army, 1971-73. Named one of Outstanding Young Men Am., 1978, 81, Outstanding Young Men Springfield, 1980. Fellow ABA (life, antitrust and litigation and torts and ins. sects.); mem. ATLA, Fed. Bar Assn., Mo. Bar Assn. (chmn. spol. com. on mandatory continuing edn., various coms., Pres.'s award 1986), Mo. Assn. Trial Attys. (bd. govs. 1998-2001), Springfield Met. Bar Assn. (bd. dirs., chmn. pub. edn. speakers bur.), Met. Bar Assn. St. Louis, Def. Rsch. Inst., Am. Judicature Soc., Am. Bd. Trial Advs. (state coord.), Nat. Bd. Trial Advs., Am. Coll. Barristers, Million Dollar Forum, 31st Jud. Cir. Bar Com. (chmn.), Supreme Ct. Hist. Soc., U. Mo.-Kansas City Sch. Law Found., Springfield Claims Assn. (pres.), U.S. Cavalry Assn. (life), Am. Legion, 1st Inf. Divsn. Soc., K.T., Beta Omega Tau, Kappa Epsilon. Presbyterian. Home: 4857 E Royal Dr Springfield MO 65809-2425

MCDONALD-WEST, SANDI MACLEAN, director, consultant; b. Lowell, Mass., May 8, 1930; d. Walter Allan and Celina Louise (Lalime) MacLean; m. Thomas D. McDonald, Sept. 8, 1951 (div.); children: Todd F., Brooke Goodfriend, Ned M., Reid A., Heather McDonald McLean. BA, DePauw U., 1951; MA, Fairleigh Dickinson U., 1966; MEd, North Tex. State U., 1980. Cert. in Montessori teaching. Tchr., adminstr. Hudson (Ohio) Montessori Sch., 1966-68, Berea (Ohio) Montessori Sch., 1968-70, Creative Learning Ctr., Dallas, 1970-71; tchr., head of lower sch. The Selwyn Sch., Denton, Tex., 1971-83; tchr., headmaster Cimarron Sch., Enid, Okla., 1983-87; cons. Corpus Christi (Tex.) Montessori Sch., 1987-89, Azlann-Eren Horn Montessori Sch., Denton, 1989-95, Highland Meadow Montessori Acad., Southlake, Tex., 1994-2001, various pub. and pvt. Montessori Schs., 1999—. Ednl. dir., pres. Southwestern Montessori Tchg. Ctr., Inc., Denton, 1974—; adj. prof. North Tex. State U., Denton, 1979-80; cons., lectr. Am. Montessori Soc., N.Y.C., 1970—, Japanese Montessori Soc., 1978—, also pub. and pvt. schs., 1972—; chair commn. for accreditation Montessori Accreditation Coun. Tchr. Edn., 1991-97, chair emerita, 1997—; cons. Public Montessori Programs, 1995-. Developer various Montessori materials; contbr. articles to profl. jours. Mem. AAUW, No. Ohio Montessori Assn. (pres. 1968-70), Assn. Montessori Internat., N.Am. Montessori Tchrs. Assn Avocations: ecology, golf, reading, travel. Home: 2005 Marshall Rd Denton TX 76207-3316 Personal E-mail: swest4smtc@aol.com.

MCDONELL, HORACE GEORGE, JR., instrument company executive; b. N.Y.C., Sept. 23, 1928; s. Horace Gustave and Anabel (Armstrong) McD.; m. Eileen Romar, Sept. 6, 1952; children: Victoria (dec.), Diane, Horace. AB, Adelphi Coll., 1952; postgrad., Harvard U., 1962; DHL, Adelphi Coll., 2002. Engr. Sperry Gyroscope Co., N.Y.C., 1952; with Perkin-Elmer Corp., Norwalk, Conn., 1963—, mgr. instrument group, 1967-77, v.p., 1966-69, sr. v.p., 1969-77, exec. v.p., 1977-80, pres., 1980-85, chmn., 1985-90, ret., 1990. Bd. dirs. Perkin Elmer, Ltd., U.K. UniRoyal, Inc., Perkin Elmer Internat., Inc., Harvey Hubbell, Inc., Ethan Allen Inc.; Mem. adv. task force on export controls U.S. Def. Sci. Bd., 1975—, chmn. instrumentation subcom.; 1975— Mem. Bd. Edn., Ridgefield, Conn., 1969; Bd. dirs. Conn. Sci. Fair.; Trustee, bd. dirs. Danbury (Conn.) Hosp.; trustee Adelphi U.; bd. dirs. Danbury Health Svcs. With AUS, 1946-48. Mem. Sci. Apparatus Maker Assn. (dir., chmn. analytical instrument sect.), Am. Inst. Physics, AAAS, Instrument Soc. Am., Am. Electronics Assn. (bd. dirs. 1984-89, chmn. 1987) E-mail: chatham28@aol.com.

MCDONELL, ROBERT TERRY, magazine editor, novelist; b. Norfolk, Va., Aug. 1, 1944; s. Robert Meinard and Irma Sophronia (Nelson) McD.; m. Joan Raffeld Hitzig, June 15, 1981; Robert Nicholas Campbell, Thomas Hunter Campbell. Student, U. Calif., Berkeley, 1962-63, San Jose State U., 1963-64; BA in Art, U. Calif., Irvine, 1967. With AP, N.Y.C., 1970-72; reporter Los Angeles Weekly, 1972-73; assoc. editor San Francisco mag., 1974-76, City mag., San Francisco, 1976-77; sr. editor San Francisco mag., 1977, Outside mag., San Francisco, 1978-79; founding editor Rocky Mountain mag., Denver, 1979-80; mng. editor Rolling Stone mag., N.Y.C., 1980-83; asst. mng. editor Newsweek Mag., N.Y.C., 1983-86; founder Smart mag., N.Y.C., 1986-90; editor-in-chief Esquire mag., N.Y.C., 1990-93; editor-in-chief, pub. Sports Afield Mag., N.Y.C., 1994-97; editor Men's Journal, 1997-99; v.p. Wenner Media, 1997—; editor-in-chief US Weekly, N.Y.C., 2000—02; mng. editor Sports Illustrated, N.Y.C., 2002—. Author: California Bloodstock, 1980, paperback edit., 1989; screenwriter: Miami Vice, China Beach. Office: US Weekly 1290 Avenue Of The Americas Fl 2 New York NY 10104-0298

MCDONELL, TERRY, publishing executive, writer, editor; b. Santa Cruz, Calif.; m. Joanie McDonell; children: Robert Nicholas, Thomas Hunter. Attended, U. Calif. at Berkeley and Irvine. Worked on film in Tehran, Iran; began career in journalism as freelance photographer with writer, photographer NY Associated Press, 1971; founder, writer, editor Outside, 1977, Rocky Mountain, 1979; mng. editor Rolling Stone, 1981—83; asst. mng. editor Newsweek, 1983—88; founder, pres., editor Smart, 1988—90; editor-in-chief Esquire, 1990—93; editor-in-chief, publishing editor Sports Afield, 1993—97, publishing/editorial dir., 1997; editor Men's Jour., 1997—99, editor-in-chief, 1999—2000, US Weekly, 2000—; mng. editor Sports Illustrated, 2002—. Author: California Bloodstock, 1980; screenwriter: TV series Miami Vice, China Beach. Avocations: painting, surfing. Office: Sports Illustrated 1271 Avenue of the Americas New York NY 10020 Office Phone: 212-522-1650. Office Fax: 212-522-7117. E-mail: Terry_McDonell@simail.com.*

MCDONNELL, BARBARA, lawyer; B, Univ. Ill.; M, Univ. Iowa; JD magna cum laude, Univ. Pa. Law Sch. With Sherman & Howard, 1982-87; staff atty. Colo. Ct. Appeals, 1988-89; law clerk Phila.; legal adv. Gov. Romer, dep. dir. policy and rsch., 1989-90; exec. dir. Colo. Dept. Human Svcs., 1991-99; chief dep. atty. gen. Office of Atty. Gen., Denver, 1999—. Rep. Nursing Adv. bd., team leader Policy Acad. Team on Families & Children At Risk.

MCDONNELL, BOB (ROBERT FRANCIS MCDONNELL), state attorney general, former state legislator; b. Phila., June 15, 1954; m. Maureen Patricia Gardner; children: Jeanine, Cailin, Rachel, Robert, Sean. BBA in Mgmt., U. Notre Dame, 1976; MBA, Boston U., 1980; MA, JD, Regent U., 1989. Various positions Am. Hosp. Supply Corp., 1981—85; policy intern, Rep. Policy Com. US Ho. of Reps, 1988; law clk. Office Commonwealth's Atty., Chesapeake, 1989, asst. Commonwealth atty. Virginia Beach, 1990—91; mem. Va. State Legis., 1992—2006, asst. majority leader, 2002—06, mem. cts. of justice com., mem. edn. com., mem. health welfare & insts. com. Chesapeake and its tributaries com.; ptnr. Huff, Poole &

Mahoney, P.C., Virginia Beach, 1992—2006; atty. gen. State of Va., Richmond, 2006—. Served in U.S. Army, 1976—81 USAR, 1981—97. Named Legislator of the Yr., Network of Victims of Crime, 1996, Family Found., 1998, 2001, Nat. Legislator of the Yr., Nat. Child Support Enforcement Assn., 1998, Legislator of the Yr., Va Sheriff's Assn., 2005. Republican. Roman Catholic. Office: Office Atty General 900 E Main St Richmond VA 23219 Office Fax: 804-786-2071.*

MCDONNELL, DAVID CROFT, diversified financial services company executive; Nat. mng. ptnr. Grant Thornton Internat. (UK office), 1989—2001; global CEO Grant Thornton Internat., 2001—. Office: Grant Thornton Internat 175 W Jackson Blvd Chicago IL 60604*

MCDONNELL, MICHAEL R., communications executive; With Pricewaterhouse, 1986—89; mgr. high-tech. group, 1989—96; ptnr. Pricewaterhouse-Coopers LLP, 1996—2000; sr. v.p., CFO EchoStar Comms., Littleton, Colo., 2000—. Office: EchoStar Communications 5701 South Santa Fe Drive Littleton CO 80120

MCDONNELL, SANFORD NOYES, air transportation executive; b. Little Rock, Oct. 12, 1922; s. William Archie and Carolyn (Cherry) McD.; m. Priscilla Robb, Sept. 3, 1946; children: Robbin McDonnell MacVittie, William Randall. BA in Econs., Princeton U., 1945; BS in Mech. Engring., U. Colo., 1948; MS in Applied Mechanics, Washington U., St. Louis, 1954. With McDonnell Douglas Corp. (formerly McDonnell Aircraft Corp.), St. Louis, 1948—, v.p., 1959-66, pres. McDonnell Aircraft div., 1966-71, corp. exec. v.p., 1971, corp. pres., from 1971, chief exec. officer, from 1972, chmn., 1980-88, chmn. emeritus, 1988—. Active St. Louis United Way; mem. exec. bd. St. Louis and nat. councils Boy Scouts Am.; trustee, elder Presbyn. Ch.; chmn. bd. Character Edn. Partnership, Washington, 1993-2005, chmn. emeritus, 2005—. Fellow AIAA; mem. Newcomen Soc. (life), Tau Beta Pi Office: McDonnell Douglas Corp PO Box 516 Saint Louis MO 63166-0516

MCDONNELL, THOMAS A., information technology executive; b. Kansas City, Mo. BSBA in Acctg., Rockhurst Univ., 1966; MBA, Univ. Pa., 1968. With DST Systems, Inc., 1969—, pres., 1973—84, 1987—, treas., 1973—95, vice chmn., 1984—95, CEO, 1984—. Bd. dir. DST Systems Inc., 1971—, BHA Group Holdings Inc., Blue Valley Ban Corp., Commerce Bancshares Inc., Computer Sci. Corp., Euronet Worldwide Inc., Garmin Ltd., Janus Capital Corp., Ascential Software Inc., Asurion. Trustee Ewing Marion Kauffman Found., 2003—; chmn. Greater Kansas City C. of C., 1994, Civic Coun. Greater Kansas City, 1999—2001; bd. dir. Greater Kansas City Cmty. Found., Midwest Rsch. Inst., Harry S Truman Libr. Inst.; trustee Rockhurst Univ. Office: DST Systems 333 W 11th St Kansas City MO 64105 Office Phone: 816-435-1000.*

MCDONNELL, TIMOTHY ANTHONY, bishop; b. N.Y., Dec. 23, 1937; Ordained priest N.Y., ordained bishop 2001. Aux. bishop, N.Y.C., 2001; titular bishop of Semina, 2001; bishop Diocese of Springfield, 2004—. Office: Diocese Of Springfield 65 Elliot St Springfield MA 01105-1713

MCDONOUGH, ANN PATRICE, ice skater; b. Korea, May 29, 1985; Grad. high sch. Figure skater competing numerous events including State Farm U.S. Championships, 1999—; Jr. Grand Prix, Norway, Mex., 2000, World Jr. Championships, 2001—02, Four Continents Championships, 2002—03, Campbell's Classic, 2002—03, Smart Ones Skate Am., 2002, ABC Sports Internat. Figure Skating Challenge, 2003, Cup of China, 2003, numerous other competitions. Recipient numerous 1st place awards including, Gardena Spring Trophy, Southwestern Sectional, Midwestern Sectional, Jr. Grand Prix Final, Southwestern Regional, World Jr. Championships, numerous 2d place awards including, Jr. GLlrand Prix Norway, World Jr. Championships, Nebelhorn Trophy, Campbell's Class., Smart Ones Skate Am. Office: US Figure Skating Hdqrs 20 First St Colorado Springs CO 80906

MCDONOUGH, BRIDGET ANN, music theatre company director; b. Milw., June 19, 1956; d. James and Lois (Hunzinger) McD.; m. Gregory Paul Opelka, Sept. 20, 1986 (div. Aug. 1993); m. Robert Markey, Feb. 29, 2000. BS, Northwestern U., 1978. Bus. mgr. Organic Theater Co., Chgo., 1979-80; mng. dir., founder Light Opera Works, Evanston, Ill., 1980—. U.S. rep. European Congress Musical Theatre, 1995. Founder, mem. Chgo. Music Alliance, 1984—, pres., 1995-98; mem. Ill. Arts Alliance; bd. dirs., Nat. Alliance for Musical Theatre, 2001-2005, sec., 2001—04; bd. dirs. Evanston Convention Visitors Bur., 1999-2002; mem. alumni adv. bd. Northwestern U. Sch. Speech, 1999-2002; bd. dirs. Around the Coyote Arts Festival, 2002—. Recipient Women on the Move award Evanston YWCA, 1991. Mem. Evanston C. of C. (bd. dirs., 1993-99), North Shore Internat. Network, Rotary (pres. Evanston chpt. 1999-00), Union League Club. Avocation: birdwatching. Office: Light Opera Works 927 Noyes St Evanston IL 60201-6206

MCDONOUGH, GERALD CLYDE, transportation leasing company executive; b. Cleve., 1928. B.B.A., Case Western Res. U., 1953. Treas. Molded Fiberglass Co., 1964-69, Rexnord Inc., 1969-74; v.p. and treas. Reliance Electric Co., 1974-79; exec. v.p., dir. Leaseway Transp. Corp., Cleve., 1979-82, chmn. and chief exec. officer, 1982-88, acting pres., chief operating officer, 1985, chmn., York Internat. Corp., York, Pa., 1999-2005; dir. AmeriTrust Corp., Brush Wellman Inc., York Internat. Corp. 1988-2005. *

MCDONOUGH, JEROME PATRICK, librarian; b. Inglewood, Calif., May 23, 1963; s. Arthur Henry and Francine Christine McDonough; m. Lori Sue Kendall. MLS, U. Calif., 1992, PhD, 2000. Programmer, analyst U. Calif., Berkeley, 1998—2000; digital libr. devel. team leader NYU, NYC, 2000—05; asst. prof. U. Ill. Urbana-Champaign, Champaign, 2005—. Mem. NISO Standards Devel. Com., Washington, 2004—. Mem.: ALA, Assn. Computing Machinery, Am. Soc. Info. Sci. and Tech., Beta Phi Mu. Achievements include development of Metadata Encoding & Transmission Standard. Office: U Ill Urbana Champaign GSLIS 501 E Daniel St MC-493 Champaign IL 61820 Office Phone: 212-998-2425. E-mail: jerome@nyu.edu.

MCDONOUGH, JOHN MICHAEL, lawyer; b. Evanston, Ill., Dec. 30, 1944; s. John Justin and Anne Elizabeth (O'Brien) McD.; m. Susan J. Moran, Sept. 19, 1981; children: John E., Catherine Anne. AB, Princeton U., 1966; LLB, Yale U., 1969. Bar: Ill. 1969, Fla. 1991. Assoc. Sidley & Austin, Chgo., 1969-75, ptnr., 1975—. Bd. dirs. Met. Planning Coun., 1978—, pres., 1982-84; bd. dirs. Ctr. Am. Archeology, 1980-85, chmn., 1982-84; bd. dirs. Leadership Greater Chgo., 1984-90, sec.-treas., 1987-90; bd. dis. Brian Rsch. Found., 1985—, pres., 1989-94, chmn. 1999-. Mem. with JAGC, USAR, 1969-75. Mem. ABA, Racquet Club, Saddle & Cycle Club, Commonwealth Club, Phi Beta Kappa. Democrat. Episcopalian. Home: 1407 N Dearborn St Chicago IL 60610-1505

MCDONOUGH, PATRICK DENNIS, academic administrator; b. Virginia, Minn., Jan. 30, 1942; s. James Morris and Vivian S. McDonough; children: Jeffrey, Anne; m. Karen Howe, June 27, 1981. BA cum laude, Moorhead State U., 1964; MA, U. Kans., 1969; PhD, U. Minn., 1972. Asst. prof. theatre Emporia (Kans.) State U., 1968-70; dir. sales, mktg. Guthrie Theater, Mpls., 1971, 72; asst. prof. speech, dir. of forensics Moorhead (Minn.) State U., 1972-73; assoc. prof., mng. dir., chair Marshall Performing Arts Ctr. U. Minn., Duluth, 1973-76; dean fine arts, prof. U. Evansville (Ind.), 1976-81; vice chancellor, prof. U. Wis., Stevens Point, 1981-84; program dir. (edn. and leadership) W.K. Kellogg Found., Battle Creek, Mich., 1984-89; 15th pres., prof. theatre and mgmt. Marietta (Ohio) Coll., 1989-95, exec. dir. McDonough Ctr. for Leadership and Bus.; assoc. vice chancellor planning and analysis Calif. State U. Sys., Long Beach, 1995-97; prof. theatre Calif. State U., Long Beach, 1997—; exec. v.p. higher edn. practice The Charitable Resources Group, Pitts., 1997—; sr. fellow James MacGregor Burns Acad. of Leadership U. Md., 2001—. Pres. Emporia chpt. AAUP, 1969; cons. Lexington (Ky.) Children's Theatre, 1979; festival evaluator Am. Coll. Theatre Festival, 4 states, 1975-76; mem. theatre panel Ind. Arts Commn., Indpls., 1977-79; arts orgn. panel Mich. Arts Bd., Detroit, 1985-89; presenter in field. Producer, dir. 100 plays and musicals, 1964-84; contbr. articles to profl. jours. Bd. visitors U. Wis., Stevens Point, 1988-90; dist. organizer Eugene McCarthy Presdl. Campaign, Emporia, 1968; mem. leadership commn. Am. Coun. Edn., 1989-94; mem. exec. com. Campus Compact, 1990-95; bd. dirs. numerous civic and arts orgns., 1973-90; chmn. govs. adv. com. on vol. svc., Ohio, 1990-93; mem. leadership studies project U. Md., 1994—. Recipient Disting. Alumnus award Moorhead State U., 1989; grantee Minn. Arts Bd., 1974-76, Ind. Arts Commn., 1976-79. Mem. Am. Assn. Higher Edn., Univ. and Coll. Theatre Assn. (v.p. 1982-83), Marietta Country Club, Stevens Point Country Club, Athletic Club of Columbus. Democrat. Episcopalian. Avocations: travel, international relations, arts. Office Phone: 562-985-2262. E-mail: mcdonou@verizon.net.

**MCDONOUGH, RICHARD MICHAEL,** philosophy educator; b. Pitts., Jan. 29, 1950; s. Walter and Marilyn (Duman) McD.; m. Mary Lau, July 26, 1991. BA summa cum laude, U. Pitts., 1971; MA, Cornell U., 1974, PhD, 1975. Asst. prof. philosophy Bates Coll., Lewiston, Maine, 1975-82; sr. lectr. Nat. U. Singapore, 1982-91; asst. prof. philosophy U. Tulsa, 1991—; assoc. prof. philosophy, psychology U. Putra Malaysia, Selangor, 1997-98; prof. philosophy Overseas Family School: The College, Republic of Singapore, 1999—, lectr., 1999—. Editor Wittgenstein and cognitive sci. spl. issue Idealistic Studies, 1999. Author: The Argument of the Tractatus, 1986, Martin Heidegger's Being and Time, 2006; contbr. articles to profl. jours. Woodrow Wilson fellow, 1971-72, NSF fellow, 1971-74; postdoctoral rsch. grantee NEH, Ind. U., 1980-81. Mem. Australasian Debating Fedn. (hon. life, adjudicator 1991—), Phi Kappa Phi. Achievements include prodn. of original interpretation of Wittgenstein's logical-metaphys. sys., original application Kantian Copernican Revolution to philosophy of lang.; significant interdisciplinary work logic, linguistics, psychology & philosophy. E-mail: richmary@pacific.net.sg, the_philosopher1950@yahoo.com, richard_mcdonough@ofs.edu.sg.

**MCDONOUGH, RUSSELL CHARLES,** retired state supreme court justice; b. Glendive, Mont., Dec. 7, 1924; s. Roy James and Elsie Marie (Johnson) McD.; m. Dora Jean Bidwell, Mar. 17, 1946; children: Ann Remmich, Michael, Kay Jensen, Kevin, Daniel, Mary Garfield. JD, George Washington U., 1949. Bar: Mont. 1950. Pvt. practice, Glendive, Mont., 1950-83; judge Gen. Jurisdiction State of Montana, Glendive, 1983-87; justice Mont. Supreme Ct., Helena, 1987-93, ret., 1993. City atty. City of Glendive, 1953-57; county atty. Dawson County, Mont., 1957-63; del. Mont. Constl. Conv., Helena, 1972. 1st lt. USAAF, 1943-45, ETO. Decorated DFC. Mem. Mont. Bar Assn. Roman Catholic. Home: 210 Gresham St Glendive MT 59330 Personal E-mail: swedemc@yahoo.com.

**MCDONOUGH, THOMAS P.,** health facility administrator; BBA, Northeastern U. COO Jardine Group Svcs. Corp., 1988—93; pres. Harrington Svcs. Corp., 1993—95; sr. v.p. claim svcs. United HealthCare, Inc., 1995—97, exec. v.p. customer svc. group, 1997, CEO Uniprise, 1997—98; exec. v.p., COO Coventry Health Care, Bethesda, Md., 1998—2005, pres., 2005—. Bd. dir. FireLogic Homes. Office: Coventry Health Care 6705 Rockleged Drive Bethesda MD 20817*

**MCDONOUGH, WILLIAM ANDREWS,** architect; b. Tokyo, Feb. 20, 1951; s. James Edwin and Sara (Andrews) McD.; m. Elizabeth Demetriades, May 30, 1981. A.B., Dartmouth Coll., 1973; postgrad. in art Yale U., 1973-76, M.Arch., 1976. Registered architect, N.Y. Photographer, Kilkenny Design Workshop (Ireland), 1974; architect, builder William A. McDonough, Cork, Ireland, 1974-77; architect Davis, Brody & Assocs., N.Y.C., 1977-81; prin. Mad River Hydro, Warren, Vt., 1981—; prin. McDonough, Rainey Architects, N.Y.C., 1981-85, McDonough Nouri Rainey & Assocs., Inc., N.Y.C., 1985—; founding ptnr., William McDonough & Ptnrs.; dean sch. architecture, U. Va., Charlottesville, 1994-99, founder, McDonough Braungart Design Chemistry, 1995—; cons. Inst. for Indsl. Research and Standards, Dublin, Ireland, 1975-77; dir. North Wind Power Co., Inc., Moretown, Vt., 1982—; dir. Am. Residential Architecture Found., N.Y.C., 1983—. Founder Solar Energy Soc. Ireland, Dublin, 1976. Mem AIA. Club: Yale (N.Y.C.). Author: (with Michael Braungart) Hannover Principles: Design for Sustainability, 1992, Cradle to Cradle: Remaking the Way We Make Things, 2002; Recipient: Presdl. award for Sustainable Devel., 1996, Design of the Year award, Bus. Week & Archtl. Record mags., 1997, Presdl. Green Chemistry award, 2003, Nat. Design award, 2004; Office: 700 E Jefferson St Charlottesville VA 22902

**MCDONOUGH, WILLIAM J.,** diversified financial services company executive; b. Chgo., 1934; married. BS, Coll. of Holy Cross, 1956; MA, Georgetown U., 1962. With Dept. of State, 1961-67; 1st Nat. Bank of Chgo., 1967-89, asst. v.p. internat. banking dept., 1967-70, v.p., gen. mgr. Paris, 1970-72, area head, Europe, Mid. East and Africa, 1972-73, sr. v.p., head internat. banking dept., 1973-75, exec. v.p., 1975-86, CFO, 1982-89, chmn. asset and liability mgmt. com., until 1989; vice chmn. 1st Chgo. Corp. and 1st Nat. Bank Chgo., 1986-89; exec. v.p., head markets group Fed. Res. Bank of N.Y., N.Y.C., 1992-93, pres., CEO, 1993—2003; chmn. Pub. Co. Acctg. Oversight Bd., Washington, 2003—05; vice chmn. Merrill Lynch & Co., Inc., NYC, 2006—. Bd. dirs. N.Y. Philharm. Orch.; chmn. investments com. joint staff pension fund UN. Office Phone: 312-449-0871. Business E-Mail: william_mcdonoughw@ml.com.

**MCDORMAND, FRANCES,** actress; b. Chgo., June 23, 1957; m. Joel Coen, 1984; 2 children. BA, Bethany Coll., 1979; MFA, Yale U. Sch. Drama, 1982. Stage appearances include Awake and Sing!, N.Y.C., 1984, Painting Churches, N.Y.C., 1984, The Three Sisters, Mpls., 1985, N.J., 1991, All My Sons, New Haven, 1986, A Streetcar Named Desire, N.Y.C., 1988, Moon for the Misbegotten, 1992, Sisters Rosensweig, N.Y.C., 1993, The Swan, N.Y.C., 1993, To You, the Birdie!, 2002, Far Away, 2002; TV appearances include The Twilight Zone, The Equalizer, Spenser: For Hire, Hill Street Blues, (series) Hunter, 1984, Legwork, 1986-87, Twilight Zone, 1986, State of Grace, 2001; film appearances include Blood Simple, 1984, Crime Wave, 1986, Raising Arizona, 1987, Mississippi Burning, 1988 (Academy award nominee), Chattahoochee, 1990, Darkman, 1990, Miller's Crossing, 1990, Hidden Agenda, 1990, The Butcher's Wife, 1991, Passed Away, 1992, Short Cuts, 1993, Beyond Rangoon, 1995, Plain Pleasures, 1996, Fargo, 1996 (Academy award for Best Actress in a Leading Role, 1997), Lone Star, 1996, Primal Fear, 1996, Palookaville, 1996, Paradise Road, 1997, Johnny Skidmarks, 1998, Madeline, 1998, Talk of Angels, 1998, Wonder Boys, 1999, Almost Famous (Academy award nominee, Brit. Acad. award nominee, Golden Globe nominee, SAG nominee), Man Who Wasn't There, 2001, City by the Sea, 2002, Something's Gotta Give, 2003, Last Night, 2004, North Country, 2005, Aeon Flux, 2005, Friends With Money, 2006, (TV movies) Scandal Sheet, 1985, Vengeance: The Story of Tony Cimo, 1986, Crazy In Love, 1992, Good Old Boys, 1995, Hidden in America, 1996, (narrator) Precinct Hollywood, 2005.*

**MCDOUGAL, STUART YEATMAN,** comparative literature educator, author; b. L.A., Apr. 10, 1942; s. Murray and Marian (Yeatman) McDougal; m. Menakka Weerasinghe, Apr. 29, 1967 (div. 1977); children: Dyanthe Rose, Gavin Rohan; m. Nora Gunneng, Aug. 4, 1979; children: Angus Gunneng, Tobias Yeatman. BA, Haverford Coll., 1964; MA, U. Pa., 1965, PhD, 1970. Lectr. U. Lausanne, Switzerland, 1965-66; asst. prof. Mich. State U., East Lansing, 1970-72; from asst. prof. to prof. English, comparative lit. and film /video U. Mich., Ann Arbor, 1972-85; dir. program in comparative lit. U. Mich., Ann Arbor, 1981-97, asst. to dean spl. projects, 1997-98; Dewitt Wallace prof. English, chair English Dept. Macalester Coll., St. Paul, 1998—2005; vis. scholar Cornell U., 2006—. Vis. prof. film Aegean Inst. Greece, 1994; vis. scholar Senapulli, Brazil, 1996. Author: Ezra Pound and the Troubadour Tradition, 1972 (Bredvold prize 1973), 1973; Made into Movies: From Literature to Film, 1985, Korean Art, 2002; editor: Dante Among the Moderns, 1985; co-editor: Play It Again, Sam: Retakes on Remakes, 1998; editor: Stanley Kubrick's A Clockwork Orange, 2003; contbr. articles to profl. jours. Am. Council of Learned Socs. fellow, 1974-75; U. Mich. Rackham Research grantee, 1975-76; Fulbright Assn. sr. lectr., Italy,

1978; recipient Faculty Recognition award, U. Mich., 1987. Fellow Dirs. Guild Am. (summr workshop, 1993); mem. MLA, Am. Comparative Lit. Assn. (sec.-treas. 1983-89, v.p. 1989-91, pres. 1991-93), Internat. Comparative Lit. Assn., Soc. Cinema Studies. Democrat. Office: Cornell U English Dept Ithaca NY 14850 Business E-Mail: mcdougal@macalester.edu, sym23@cornell.edu.

**MCDOUGAL, WILLIAM SCOTT,** urology educator; b. Grand Rapids, Mich., 1942; s. William Julian and Verna Wilma (Pasma) McD.; m. Mary Stuart Logan, Sept. 19, 1992; 1 child, Molly Katherine. AB, Dartmouth Coll., 1964; MD, Cornell U., 1968. Intern in surgery U. Hosps., Cleve., 1968-69, resident in surgery, 1969-75, attending urologist, 1977-80; postdoctoral fellow in physiology Yale U., New Haven, 1971-72; postdoctoral fellow in surgery Case-Western Res. U., Cleve., 1972-75; chief, burn study div. Inst. Surg. Rsch. Brooke Army Med. Ctr., Ft. Sam Houston, 1975-77; instr. surgery U. Tex., San Antonio, 1975-77; asst. prof. urology Case Western Res. U., Cleve., 1977-78, assoc. prof., 1978-80, Dartmouth Coll., Hanover, NH, 1980-84, chmn. dept. urology, 1982-84; prof., chmn. dept. urology Vanderbilt U., Nashville, 1984-90; Walter S. Kerr Jr. prof. urology Harvard Med. Sch., 1990—; chief urology Mass. Gen. Hosp., Boston, 1990—. Office: Mass Gen Hosp Dept Urology Fruit St Boston MA 02114 Office Phone: 617-726-3010.

**MCDOUGALL, DONALD BLAKE,** retired provincial official, librarian; BA, BEd, U. Sask., 1966; BLS, U. Toronto, 1969; MLS, U. Alta., 1983, cert. pub. adminstrn., 1990. Classroom tchr. Regina Bd. Edn., Sask., 1960-63, vice prin. Sask., 1963-68; asst. chief libr. Stratford Pub. Libr., Ont., Canada, 1969, chief libr. Ont., 1970-72; supr. info. svcs. Edmonton Pub. Libr., Alta., Canada, 1972, head pub. svcs. Alta., 1973-74; legislature libr. Province of Alta., Edmonton, Can., 1974-87; asst. dep. min., legis. libr. Legis. Assembly Alta. 1987—93; ret., 1993. Editor microfilm: Alberta Scrapbook Hansard, 1906-1964, 1976; editor: A History of the Legislature Library, 1979; author: Princess Louise Caroline Alberta, 1988, Premiers of the Northwest Territories and Alberta, 1876-1991, 1991; co-author, editor: Lieutenant-Governors of the Northwest Territories and Alberta, 1876-1991; (pamphlet) Canadian Parliamentary Libraries, 1989. Govt. Sask. scholar, 1965; recipient Queen's Silver Jubilee medal Govt. Can., 1977; named Hon. Clk.-At-The-Table, Legis. Assembly Alberta, 1987-93. Mem. Alta. Govt. Librs. Coun. (chmn 1975), Assn. Parliamentary Librs. in Can. (pres. 1980-82), Edmonton Libr. Assn., Hist. Soc. Alta. (v.p. Edmonton chpt. 1987), Libr. Assn. Alta., Can. Libr. Assn., Edmonton Jaguar Drivers Club, Edmonton Scottish Soc., Can. Vintage Motorcycle Assn., Beta Phi Mu. Presbyterian.

**MC DOUGALL, DUGALD STEWART,** retired lawyer; b. Indpls., May 15, 1916; s. George and Effie (Barclay) McD.; m. Carol Brueggeman, Aug. 1938; children: George, Duncan, Walter, Robert; m. Judith Stephen, Dec. 1967. AB, U. Chgo., 1935, JD, 1937. Bar: Ill. 1937. Since practiced in, Chgo.; sr. ptnr. McDougall, Hersh & Scott, 1961-87. Sec., dir. Aladdin Industries, Inc. Served with USNR, 1942-46. Fellow Am. Coll. Trial Lawyers; mem. ABA, Am. Patent Law Assn., Patent Law Assn. Chgo., Law Club Chgo., Union League (Chgo.). Clubs: Union League (Chgo.); Olympia Fields (Ill.) Country. Office: 25 Pine Forest Ln Haines City FL 33844-9675

**MCDOUGALL, GAY,** lawyer; b. Atlanta, Aug. 13, 1947; BA, Bennington Coll., 1969; JD, Yale U., 1972; LLM, London Sch. Econs., 1978. Bar: Court Appeals State NY 1974, US Dist. Ct. So. Dist. NY 1977, US Supreme Ct. 1979, DC 1994. Assoc. Debevoise, Plimton, Lyons and Gates, NYC, 1972—74; gen. counsel Nat. Conf. Black Lawyers, NYC, 1975—76; staff atty. minimum standards unit Bd. Corrections, NYC, 1976—77; assoc. counsel Office Dep. Mayor Criminal Justice, NYC, 1979—80; dir. So. Africa project The Lawyer's Com. Civil Rights Under the Law, Washington, 1980—94; exec. dir. Global Rights (formerly Internat. Human Rights Law Group), Washington, 1994—2006; ind. expert on minority issues UN, 2005—. Dir. So. Africa Project, Lawyers' Com. for Civil Rights Under Law, 1980-94; mem. Ind. Electoral Commn. South African Elections, 1994. Founder Commn. Independence for Namibia; mem. com. on elimination of racial discrimination UN, spl. rapporteur on systematic rape and sexual slavery in armed conflict, sub commn. on human rights, 1997-2000; mem. sub-Commission prevention discrimination and protection minorities human rights commn., UN, 1995-2000; ind. expert treaty body that oversees the internat. convention elimination of all forms racial discrimination, UN, 1997-2001; Bd. dirs. Global Fund for Women, 2005-, Africare, 2005-, CARE USA, CARE Internat., Robert F. Kennedy Meml. Found., internat. human rights coun., Jimmy Carter Presidential Ctr. Fellow MacArthur Found., 1999. Mem.: Am. Soc. Internat. Law (president's advisory panel, Judges Panel three major Honors and Medals 2003—), Coun. Fgn. Relations (Africa Program Advisory Panel Ctr. Preventive Action). Office: Palais des Nations CH-1211 Geneva Switzerland*

**MCDOUGALL, IAIN ROSS,** nuclear medicine educator; b. Glasgow, Scotland, Dec. 18, 1943; came to U.S., 1976; s. Archibald McDougall and Jean Cairns; m. Elizabeth Wilson, Sept. 6, 1968; children: Shona, Stewart. MB, ChB, U. Glasgow, 1967, PhD, 1973. Diplomate Am. Bd. Nuclear Medicine (chmn 1985-87), Am. Bd. Internal Medicine (gov. 1984-86). Lectr. in medicine U. Glasgow, 1969-76; fellow Harkness-Stanford Med. Ctr., 1972-74; assoc. prof. radiology and medicine Stanford U., Calif., 1976-84, prof. radiology and medicine, 1985—. Contbr. numerous articles to sci. jours. Fellow Royal Coll. Physicians (Glasgow), Am. Coll. Physicians; mem. Am. Thyroid Assn., Soc. Nuclear Medicine, Western Assn. for Clin. Research. Office: Stanford U Med Ctr Divsn Nuclear Medicine Stanford CA 94305 Business E-Mail: rossmcdougall@stanford.edu.

**MCDOUGALL, RODERICK GREGORY,** lawyer; BBA in Econs., U. Ariz., JD. Bar: Ariz. 1965, U.S. Ct. Claims 1965, U.S. Supreme Ct. 1970, U.S. Dist. Ct. Ariz. 1972, U.S. Ct. Appeals (9th cir.) 1972. Law clk. Ariz. Supreme Ct., 1964, Ariz. Ct. Appeals, 1965; dep. county atty. Maricopa County, 1965-67; staff atty. Ariz. State Senate, 1967; asst. atty. gen., 1967-74; chief asst. Atty. Gen., Ariz., 1974-84; city atty. City of Phoenix, 1984-2000; pvt. practice, 2000—. Advisor Ariz. Supreme Ct. Mem. ABA, Internat. Mcpl. Lawyers Assn. (bd. dirs. 1994-2000), Ariz. Bar Assn., Maricopa County Bar Assn. E-mail: rodmcdougall@cox.net.

**MCDOUGALL, RONALD ALEXANDER,** restaurant executive; b. Chgo., Aug. 12, 1942; s. John A. and Doris E. (Sengstock) McD.; m. Dale O. Ryser, Feb. 1, 1964 (div. July 1969); children: Timothy, Jonathan; m. Carolyn Kay Conley, Aug. 9, 1979; 1 child, Matthew. BA, U. Wis., 1964, MBA, 1965. With Procter & Gamble, Cin., 1967-68, Sara Lee, Deerfield, Ill., 1969-72, The Pillsbury Co., Mpls., 1972-74, S&A Restaurant Corp., Dallas, 1974-82, Burger King, Miami, Fla., 1982-83; pres., CEO,& COO Brinker Internat., Dallas, 1983—. Bd. dirs. Brinker Internat., Excel Comm. Inc. With U.S. Army, 1965-67. Mem. Nat. Restaurant Assn., Am. Mgmt. Assn., Bent Tree Country Club, Aerobics Activity Ctr., Employment Policies Inst. Republican. Presbyterian. Avocations: running, bicycling, golf.

**MC DOW, JOHN JETT,** biosystems engineering educator; b. Covington, Tenn., Jan. 6, 1925; s. Robert Simpson and Lucy Ann (Cocke) McD.; m. Dorothy Virginia Glass, Dec. 22, 1946 (dec. 2004); children: Ronald Allan, Jane Virginia. Student, Franklin and Marshall Coll., 1944-45; BS, U. Tenn., 1948; MS, Mich. State U., 1949, PhD, 1957. Registered profl. engr., Tenn., La. Instr. Mich. State U., 1949, Okla. State U., 1949-51, asst. prof. agrl. engring., 1951; assoc. prof. La. Poly. U., 1951-57, prof., 1957-62, head agrl. dept., 1953-62; prof., head dept. biosys. engring. U. Tenn., Knoxville, 1962-73, dean admissions and records, 1973-83, prof. agrl. engring., 1983-92, prof. emeritus, 1992—. Cons., coordinator Agrl. Research Service, US Dept. Agr., 1970-76; leader Rotary Internat. Found. Group Study Exchange Team to Philippines, 1984; mem. scholarship selection com. N.Am. Philips Corp., 1976-88. Contbr. articles to profl. jours. Mem. La. Engring. Coun., 1955-56; bd. dirs. Tenn.-Venezuela-Amazonas Partners, 1977-80; vol. Internat. Centennial Olympic Summer Games, Atlanta, 1996. With USN, 1943—46, comdr. USNR, to 1977. So. Fellowship grantee, 1957. Mem. Am.

Soc. Agrl. Engring. (dir. 1973-75), Am. Soc. Engring. Edn. (sec. agrl. engring. div. 1971-72, vice chmn. 1972-73, chmn. 1973-74), Sigma Xi, Tau Beta Pi, Pi Mu Epsilon, Omicron Delta Kappa, Gamma Sigma Delta, Phi Kappa Phi (v.p. 1971-77, nat. pres. elect 1977-80, pres. 1980-83, pres. found. 1974-78). Lodges: Rotary (pres. 1989-90, chmn. dist. scholarship selection com., 1982-87, 88-91). Presbyterian. Home: 2008 Walnut Hills Dr Knoxville TN 37920-2946

**MCDOWELL, CHARLES EAGER,** lawyer, retired military officer; b. Manchester, N.H., Sept. 9, 1923; s. Joseph Curry and Mildred (Eager) McD.; m. Carolyn A. Gibbons, June 21, 1947; children— Robin, Patricia. AB, Dartmouth Coll., 1947; JD, U. Va., 1950. Bar: Tex. 1950, Va. 1981, D.C. 1981. With land div. Shell Oil Co., Houston, 1950; commd. lt. (j.g.) USN, 1951, advanced through grades to rear adm., 1976; staff legal officer Comdr. Service Force, U.S. Pacific Fleet; staff judge adv., head internat. law div. Naval War Coll., 1963-66; staff legal officer, comdr. 7th Fleet, 1966-68; sr. Navy mem. ad hoc com., dep. asst. judge adv. gen. Office Judge Adv. Gen. Dept. Def., Washington, 1968-72; staff judge adv. on staff comdr. in chief U.S. Naval Forces, Europe, London, 1972-75; comdg. officer Naval Justice Sch., Newport, RI, 1975-76; dep. judge adv. gen. Navy Dept., Washington, 1976-78, judge adv. gen., 1978-80; pvt. practice Dumfries, Va., 1981-96. Served to 2d lt. AUS, 1943-46. Decorated D.S.M., Bronze Star, Joint Service Commendation medal, Navy Commendation medal with Combat V, Purple Heart, Combat Inf. badge. Mem. FBA, Tex. Bar Assn., Va. Bar Assn., Judge Advs. Assn., Order of Coif, Chi Phi, Square Dancer Club. Methodist. Home: 1106 Croton Dr Alexandria VA 22308-2008

**MCDOWELL, CHARLES LINDSAY,** orthopedist, surgeon; b. Charlotte, NC, July 20, 1933; s. Roy Hendrix and Kathryn (Bowers) McDowell; m. Virginia Carter Donnan McDowell, Aug. 17, 1957. BS, Wake Forest U., NC, 1955; MD, Jefferson Med. Coll., Phila., 1959. Cert. orthop. surgeon FACS, 1966. Intern Jefferson Hosp., Phila., 1959—60, orthop. resident, 1960—64; hand surgery fellow Columbia Presbyn. Med. Ctr., NYC, 1964—65; pvt. practice Richmond, Va., 1965—99; vets. adminstrr. Vets. Adminstrn., 1999—. Clin. prof. of orthop. surgery Va. Commonwealth Med. Sch., Richmond, 1965—; chief of surgery Richmond Children's Hosp., Richmond, 1965—88; disting. educator Va. Commonwealth U., 2005; vis. prof. Harvard U., 1988. Contbr. chapters to books. Mem., pres. Richmond Br. Arthritis Found., 1980—2000. Recipient Orthop. prize, Jefferson Med. Coll., 1959. Mem.: Am. Acad. for Surgery of Hand, Am. Acad. of Orthop. Surgeons, Am. Orthop. Assn. Avocations: sailing, fishing, hiking.

**MCDOWELL, CHARLES S.,** lawyer; b. Norfolk, Va., June 20, 1945; AB cum laude, Princeton U., 1967; JD, U. Va., 1974. Bar: Del. 1975. Ptnr. Potter Anderson & Corroon LLP, Wilmington, Del. Counsel Del. Health Facilities Authority. Dir. WHYY, Inc. (Delaware Valley Pub. TV and Radio); mem. com. LPGA Urban Youth Golf Program. Mem.: ABA, Nat. Assn. Bond Lawyers, Del. State Bar Assn. (pres.-elect 2003, pres. 2003). Office: Potter Anderson and Corroon LLP Hercules Plz PO Box 951 1313 N Market St Wilmington DE 19899-0951

**MCDOWELL, DAVID J.,** psychology professor; PhD in Psychology, U. Calif., Riverside, 2001. Asst. prof. psychology U. Rochester, NY, 2002—. Com. chairperson Cub Scouts, Rochester, 2003—06. Mem.: Soc. for Rsch. in Child Devel. Office: Univ Rochester RC Box 270266 Rochester NY 14627-0266 Office Phone: 585-275-8711. Office Fax: 585-273-1100.

**MCDOWELL, DAVID MICHAEL,** psychiatrist, educator, researcher; b. Middletown, Conn., Mar. 16, 1963; s. Arthur Vanall and Jacqueline Larson McDowell. MD, Columbia Coll. Physicians and Surgeons, 1989. Bd. cert. psychiatry Am. Bd. Psychiatry and Neurology, 1993, cert. addiction psychiatry Am. Bd. Psychiatry and Neurology, 1996. Fellow in addiction psychiatry NYU Med. Ctr., N.Y.C., 1993—95; instr. psychiatry Bellevue Hosp./NYU Med. Ctr., N.Y.C., 1995—; asst. prof. clin. psychiatry Columbia U. Coll. Physicians and Surgeons, N.Y.C., 1995—; dir. buprenorphine program Columbia U.; founder, med. dir. STARS the Substance Treatment and Rsch. Svc. Columbia U., N.Y.C., 1997—. Cons. Malinckrodt Pharmaceuticals, St. Louis, 2002—; cons. psychiatrist The Actors Fund. Author: (textbook) Substance Abuse: From Principles to Practice; contbr. chapters to books, articles to profl. jours. Bd. mem. The Three Dollar Bill Theater Co., N.Y.C., 1995—99. Grantee, NIH/Nat. Inst. on Drug Abuse, 2000—. Fellow: Am. Psychiat. Assn. (disting.) (vice chair sci. program com. 2000—, disting. life fellow); mem.: The Charaka Club. Achievements include Advisor for Creative work including the Golden Globe Award winning film Quills, and other plays and film scripts. Avocations: cooking, singing. Office: Stars 3 East 65th St New York NY 10019 Home: 160 W 86th St # 6 B New York NY 10024 Office Phone: 212-570-4166, Personal E-mail: drdave@bway.net.

**MCDOWELL, DONNA SCHULTZ,** lawyer, educator; b. Cin., Apr. 23, 1946; d. Robert Joseph and Harriet (Parronchi) Schultz; m. Dennis Lon McDowell, June 20, 1970; children: Dawn Megan, Donnelly Lon. BA in English with honors, Brandeis U., 1968; MEd, Am. U., 1972; C.A.S. with honors in Reading, Johns Hopkins U., 1979; JD with honors, U. Md., 1982; MS, Hood Coll., 1995; postgrad., U. Md. Bar: Md. 1982; cert. tchr. reading K-12, D.C.; advanced profl. cert. in English, Biology and Reading, Md. Instr. Anne Arundel & Prince George's C.C., Severna Park and Largo, Md., 1977-78; coll. adminstr. Bowie State Coll., Md., 1978—79; assoc. Miller & Bortner, Lanham, Md., 1982-83; sole practice Lanham, 1983-87, Gaithersburg, Md., 1987—; sci. tchr. DC Pub. Schs., Washington, 1999-2000; chair dept. English Montgomery County Pub. Schs., Ala., 2000—, English lit. tchr., 2002—03, lit. lead tchr. 2003—05, instrnl. specialist 2005—06, lit. lead, 2006—. Ednl. cons.; presenter in field. Chmn. Housing Hearing Com., Bowie, 1981-83; trustee Unitarian-Universalist Ch., Silver Spring, Md., 1979-83; bd. dirs. New Ventures, Bowie, 1983, Second Mile (Runaway House), Hyattsville, Md., 1983; officer Greater Laytonsville Civic Assn., 1989; founding mem. People to Preserve, Laytonsville; mem. Solid Waste Adv. Com., Montgomery County, Md.; election judge; presenter in field. Recipient Am. Jurisprudence award U. Md., 1981; Michael Jordan grantee, 2000, D.C. Pub. Schs. grantee. Mem. Phi Kappa Phi. Democrat. Avocations: gardening, reading, bluebirds, movies. Home: 24308 Hipsley Mill Rd Gaithersburg MD 20882-3132 Office Phone: 301-517-5844. Personal E-mail: DonnaSMcD@aol.com.

**MCDOWELL, ELAINE,** retired federal government executive, educator; b. Balt., June 28, 1942; d. McKinley and Lena (Blue) McDowell; children: Nathan H. Jr. Murphy, Michael W. Murphy. BA, Morgan State U., Balt., 1965; MSW, U. Md., 1971, PhD, 1988. Drug abuse adminstr., acting regional dir. State Md. Drug Abuse Adminstrn., Balt., 1971-72; social sci. analyst, pub. health advisor Nat. Inst. Drug Abuse, Rockville, MD, 1972-76; dep. dir., dir. div. communicable assistance, 1976-82, dep. assoc. dir. for policy devel., 1981-82, div. dir. prevention and communications, 1982-85; exec. asst. to adminstr. Alcohol, Drug Abuse & Mental Health Adminstrn., Rockville, Md., 1985; dep. dir. Nat. Inst. on Drug Abuse, Rockville, MD, 1985-88; dir. Ctr. for Substance Abuse Prevention, 1988-96; acting adminstr. Alcohol, Drug Abuse and Mental Health Adminstrn., Rockville, Md., 1992, Substance Abuse and Mental Health Svcs. Adminstrn., Rockville, Md., 1992-94. Expert cons. in substance abuse, treatment, and mental health field; prof. Morgan State U., Balt. Chmn. non-alcoholic internat. gen. svc. bd. Alcoholics Anonymous, 2001—05, trustee emeritus, 2005—; active Presbyn. Ch. U.S.A., Balt., 1998—; bd. dirs. Rosalynn Carter Inst. for Human Devel. Recipient Outstanding Leadership in Improving Health Care in Black Cmty. award Nat. Med. Assn., 1989, Sec.'s commendation HHS, 1989, Disting. Svc. award, 1990, Nat. Coun. on Alcoholism and Drug Dependence Ind., Pres. award for outstanding fed. leadership, 1991, Presdl. Meritorious Exec. Rank award, 1991, Presdl. Meritorious Disting. Rank award, 1993, Clyde Bailey, Sr. Meml. award Nat. African Am. Drug Policy Coalition, 2006. Mem.: NASW, Sr. Execs. Assn. Personal E-mail: JLuvenia@aol.com.

**MCDOWELL, ELIZABETH MARY,** retired pathology educator; b. Kew Gardens, Surrey, Eng., Mar. 30, 1940; arrived in U.S., 1971; d. Arthur and Peggy (Bryant) McD. B Vet. Medicine, Royal Vet. Coll., London, 1963; BA, Cambridge U., 1968, PhD, 1971. Gen. practice vet. medicine, 1964-66; Nuffield Found. tng. scholar Cambridge (Eng.) U., 1966-71; instr. dept. pathology U. Md., Balt., 1971-73, asst. prof., 1973-76, assoc. prof., 1976-80, prof., 1980-96, ret., 1996. Co-author: Biopsy Pathology of the Bronchi, 1987; editor: Lung Carcinomas, 1987; contbr. over 120 articles to sci. jours., chpts. to books. Rsch. grantee, NIH, 1979—92. Avocations: conservation education, gardening, swimming.

**MCDOWELL, EUGENE CHARLES,** systems analyst, bioethicist; b. Washington, Jan. 13, 1940; s. Charles Jacob and Voilet Marie (Brown) McD.; m. Jill Perry Huntley, May 4, 1986 (dec. 1989); m. Hendrika Maria Ram, Mar. 21, 1992. BA, Am. U., 1962; MA, U. Chgo., 1966, 76; adv. cert. in Pub. Adminstrn., U.S. Dept. of Agr. Grad. Sch., 1973; grad. cert. Mastery U., 1995. Rsch. asst. ops. rsch. office Johns Hopkins U., Bethesda, Md., 1958-61; rsch. asst. Rsch. Analysis Corp., McLean, Va., 1961-66, ops. rsch. analyst, 1966-71, Nat. Bur. Standards, Gaithersburg, Md., 1971-80, mgmt. analyst, 1980-82; ops. rsch. analyst NOAA, Rockville, Md., 1982-87, computer systems analyst, 1987—2005; mem. bioethics com. and policy subcom. Washington Hosp. Ctr., Washington, 1996—; guest rschr. Nat. Inst. Stds. and Tech., Gaithersburg, Md., 2005—. Mem. U.S. Fed. pub. key infrastructure steering com., 1999-2003, U.S. Fed. Identity Credentialing Com., 2003—, mem. legal/policy working group, 1999—, chmn., 2001—, mem. tech. working group, 2000—, others; convenor Symposium on Legis. for Physician-Assisted Suicide, Bethesda, Md., 1996; mem. bioethics adv. panel Superior Ct. of D.C., 1997—; mem. rsch. working group Md. Atty. Gen., 1997-98. Student condr. Nat. Symphony Orch., Washington, 1960. Pres. Hemlock Soc. Nat. Capital Area, Washington, 1991-93, mem. bd. dirs. 1990-97, Nuclear Free Am., Balt., 1991-94, mem. bd. dirs. 1995—, Garrett Park (Md.) Citizens Assn., 1982-84; originator nuclear-free zone movement in U.S., Garrett Park, Md., 1982; auditor North Bethesda Congress of Citizens Assn., 1982-84; mem. U. Chgo. Profl. Achievement Award Com., Washington, 1977—, chmn. 1982-84. Recipient Spl. Svc. citation Nat. Oceanic and Atmospheric Adminstrn., 1991, U.S. Dept. of Commerce Bronze medal, 1995, Govt. Computer News citation, 1995. Mem. Hemlock Soc. USA (life), AAAS (life), Philos. Soc. Washington (life, bd. dirs. 1996-98), Azalea Soc. Am., Metropolitan Washington Bioethics Network (bd. dirs. 1996—), Standards Engring. Soc. (chmn. bd. govs. 1983-84, sr. 1982). Democrat. Unitarian Universalist. Avocations: gardening, reading. Home: 901 Mill Pond Rd Frederick MD 21701-9312

**MCDOWELL, HEATHER L.,** lawyer; b. Pitts., Apr. 12, 1965; BS with distinction, State Univ., 1987; JD, George Washington Univ., 1990. Bar: Md. 1990, Va. 1991, DC 1993. Ptnr., adv., mktg., new media communications Venable LLP, Washington, 2000—. Mem. FTC, 1991—94, FCC, 1994—96. Office: Venable LLP 575 Seventh St NW Washington DC 20004 Office Phone: 202-344-4897. Office Fax: 202-344-8300. Business E-Mail: hlmcdowell@venable.com.

**MCDOWELL, JEFFEREY THOMAS,** information technology educator; b. Minot, ND, May 27, 1963; s. Dennis Cly and Beverly May McDowell; 1 child, Roy Dennis. AA in Computer Sci., ND State Coll. Sci., Wahpeton; BS in Vocat. And Tech. Edn., Valley City State U., ND; BS in Mgmt., Minot State U.; M in Mgmt., Info. Tech., U. Mary, Bismarck, ND; diploma radio and TV broadcasting, Brown Inst., Mpls. Cert. internet web master designer cert. instr. Prosoft Learning, Inc., 2005, A+, Network+, iNet+ CompTIA, 2000, preinstallation specialist Microsoft, 2000, info. tech. career And tech. credential N.D. Career And Tech. Edn., 2000; cert. workplace safety N.D. Safety Coun. Inc., 2004. Computer info. tech. dept. chair, instr. United Tribes Tech. Coll., Bismarck, ND, 2000—. Mem.: The Collaboration (assoc.), Computing Tech. Industry Assn., Inc. (assoc.; N.D. tech. prep com. mem.), Skills USA - VICA (assoc.; student advisor 2001—05, Outstanding Svc. award 2003—04, Cisco Networking Acad. Outstanding Instr. award for Relevance 2006). Office: United Tribes Tech Coll 3315 University Dr Bismarck ND 58504 Office Phone: 701-255-3285. E-mail: jmcdowell@uttc.edu.

**MCDOWELL, JENNIFER,** sociologist, composer, playwright; b. Albuquerque; d. Willard A. and Margaret Frances (Garrison) McD.; m. Milton Loventhal, July 2, 1973. BA, U. Calif., 1957; MA, San Diego State U., 1958; postgrad., Sorbonne, Paris, 1959; MLS, U. Calif., 1963; PhD, U. Oreg., 1973. Tchr. English Abraham Lincoln H.S., San Jose, Calif., 1960-61; free-lance editor Soviet field, Berkeley, Calif., 1961-63; editor, pub. Merlin Papers, San Jose, 1969-80, Merlin Press, San Jose, 1973—; rsch. cons. sociology San Jose, 1973—; music pub. Lipstick and Toy Balloons Pub. Co., San Jose, 1978—, Abbie & Dolley Records, 2003—; composer Paramount Pictures, 1982-88. Tchr. writing workshops; poetry readings, 1969-73; co-producer radio show lit. and culture Sta. KALX, Berkeley, 1971-72. Author: (with Milton Loventhal) Black Politics: A Study and Annotated Bibliography of the Mississippi Freedom Democratic Party, 1971 (Smithsonian Inst. 1992), Contemporary Women Poets, 1977; co-author: (plays off-off Broadway) Betsy and Phyllis, 1986, Mack the Knife Your Friendly Dentist, 1986, The Estrogen Party To End War, 1986, The Oatmeal Party Comes to Order, 1986, (plays) Betsy Meets the Wacky Iraqi, 1991, Bella and Phyllis, 1994; author numerous poems; writer: (songs) Money Makes a Woman Free!, 1976, 2004, 3 songs featured in Parade of Am. Music, 1976-77; co-creator mus. comedy Russia's Secret Plot To Take Back Alaska, 1988, (Cassingle) Intern Girl, 1998, Smithsonian, 2002; (CDs) Our Women Are Strong, 2000, 02, The Wearing of the Green Burkas, 2003; (musical revs. CD) She, A Tapestry of Women's Lives, 2004. Recipient 8 awards Am. Song Festival, 1976-79, Service to Poetry award, 1977, Bill Casey award in Letters (Soviet Studies), 1980, SHE award, Calif. State U.-ERFA Found., 2004, collected by Nobel Inst. for 2003 Nobel Peace Prize laureate Shirin Ebadi; doctoral fellow AAUW, 1971-73; grantee Calif. Arts Coun., 1976-77. Mem. AAUW, Am. Assn. for Advancement of Slavic Studies, Soc. Sci. Study of Religion, Am. Sociol. Assn., Dramatists Guild, Phi Beta Kappa, Sigma Alpha Iota, Beta Phi Mu, Kappa Kappa Gamma. Democrat. Office: care Abbie and Dolley Records PO Box 5602 San Jose CA 95150-5602 Personal E-mail: jeditorphd@earthlink.net.

**MC DOWELL, JOHN B.,** bishop; b. New Castle, Pa, July 17, 1921; s. Bernard A. and Louise M. (Hannon) McD. BA, St. Vincent Coll., 1942, MA, 1944, Catholic U. Am., 1950, PhD, 1952; Litt.D. (hon.), Duquesne U., 1962; grad., St. Vincent Sem., Latrobe, Pa. Ordained priest Roman Cath. Ch., 1945, consecrated as titular bishop of Tamazuca and aux. bishop of Pitts., 1966—; asst. pastor St. Irenaeus Ch., Oakmont, 1945-49; asst. supt. schs. Diocese of Pitts., 1952-55, supt. schs., 1955-70, vicar for edn., 1973-83; vicar gen.; pastor Epiphany Parish, Pitts., 1969-96; ret., 1996. Papal chamberlain to Pope Pius XII, 1956, to Pope John XXIII, 1958; domestic prelate to Pope Paul VI, 1964; chmn. ad hoc com. on moral values in our soc. Nat. Conf. Cath. Bishops, from 1973, Bishops Com. for Pastoral on Moral Values, from 1975; mem. Internat. Council for Catechesis, from 1975 Author: Water, Death and Grace: The Life of Hugh C. Boyle, 6th Bishop of Diocese of Pittsburgh, 1999, Catholic Schools, Public Education, and American Culture, 2000, Giants Were On the Earth in Those Days, The Life of John Francis Regis Canevin, 5th Bishop, Diocese of Pittsburgh, 2000, Blessed Are the Poor in Spirit, For Theirs is the Kingdom of Heaven, the Life of Vincent Martin Leonard, the 9th Bishop of Diocese of Pitts, 2001, I Am Going To Tell You A Mystery, the life of the fourth Bishop, Diocese of Pitts., 2002, To Dwell in the House of the Lord All the Days of My Life, the life of Father Charles Bonaventure Maguire, O.F.M., 2003, Reflections on the Life of John Cardinal Wright, S.T.D. Eighth Bishop of Pittsburgh, 2003; co-author elem. sch. religion series, JHS lit. series, elem. sci. series and elem. reading series; contbr. ednl. articles to various pubs.; former editor: Cath. Educator Mag. Bd. dir. Allegheny County Community Coll.; bd. dir. Western Pa. Safety Council, Duquesne U. Named Man of Yr. in Religion Pitts., 1970, 93, Educator of Yr.,

United Pvt. Acad. Schs. Assn., 1978, Man of Yr., Pitts. chpt. KC, 1989. Mem. Nat. Cath. Ednl. Assn., Cath. Ednl. Assn. Pa., Omicron Delta Kappa Gamma Circle (hon.) Roman Catholic. Address: Chancery Office 111 Blvd Of The Allies Pittsburgh PA 15222-1613

**MCDOWELL, JOHN HENRY, JR.,** lawyer; b. Las Cruces, N.Mex., June 1, 1957; s. John H. and Jacqueline (O'Sullivan) McD.; 1 child, Michal Jillian. BA in Econs., Stanford U., 1979; JD, U. Va., 1982. Bar: Tex. 1983, U.S. Dist. Ct. (no. dist.) Tex. 1983, U.S. Dist. Ct. (ea. dist.) Tex. 1985, U.S. Dist. Ct. (we. dist.) Tex. 1987, U.S. Dist. Ct. (so. dist.) Tex. 1995. Ptnr. Hughes & Luce LLP, Dallas. Spkr. in field. Named one of Best Lawyers in Dallas, D Mag., 2005. Fellow: Dallas Bar Found., Tex. Bar Found., Dallas Assn. Young Lawyers Found. (life; chair fellows program 2004); mem.: Am. Intellectual Property Law Assn. (antitrust com.), Dallas Assn. Young Lawyers (pres. 1991), Tex. State Bar Assn. (long range planning com. 1990—91), Tex. Young Lawyers Assn. (bd. dir. 1991—93, Award of Achievement 1990), Dallas Bar Assn. (bd. dir. 1990—91), ABA (antitrust com. litig. sect., litig. and antitrust sect. Award of Achievement 1990). Office Phone: 214-939-5413. Office Fax: 214-939-5849. E-mail: john.mcdowell@hughesluce.com.

**MCDOWELL, LAURA ONEITA,** secondary school educator; b. Erick, Okla., Jan. 21, 1929; d. Roy Marion and Sybil Faye (Tapley) Carr; m. Billy Gene McDowell, Aug. 15, 1954; children: Darwin, Deonn, Dwila, Donnette, Deylan, Devin. Student, Jacksonville (Tex.) Bapt. U., 1948-49; BA, Wayland Bapt. U., Plainview, Tex., 1950-54; MA, West Tex. U., 1954-57; postgrad., U. Ariz. Cert. tchr., Ariz; lic. minister Assembly of God Ch. English tchr. Kress (Tex.) Ind. Sch. Dist., 1954-60, Ea. Ariz. Coll., Clifton, 1965-72; substitute English tchr. various high schs., Clifton, Morenci, Ariz., 1973-78; English and typing tchr. Bowie (Ariz.) High Sch., 1979-80; bus. and publs. tchr. San Simon (Ariz.) High Sch., 1980-87; English and Spanish tchr. San Simeon (Ariz.) High Sch., 1987—92; pastor Oakwood Assembly of God, Oakwood, Tex., 1995—99; adult Sunday sch. tchr. Buffalo Assembly of God, Buffalo, Tex., 1999—2002; adult Sunday sch. tchr. Chapel of the Hills, Centerville, Tex., 2002—05. Evaluator computer software Ariz. State Dept. Edn., Phoenix, 1984-86. Author: Your Identity in Christ, 2002. Vol. Clifton Pub. Schs., 1972-73; adult sunday sch. tchr. Assembly of God Ch., Willcox, Ariz., 1980-92. Mem. Delta Kappa Gamma Soc. Internat. (pres. alpha lambda chpt. 1984-86, sec. 1982-84, newsletter editor 1984-86). Mem. Pentecostal Church. Avocations: reading, studying theology, cooking, poetry, bowling.

**MCDOWELL, MALCOLM,** actor; b. Leeds, Eng., June 13, 1943; m. Mary Steenburgen, 1980 (div.); 2 children; m. Kelley Kuhr, 1991; 1 child, Beckett Taylor; m. Margot Dullea (div.). Began career with: Royal Shakespeare Co., Stratford, Eng., 1965-66; early TV appearances include: role of Dixon of Dock Green in Z Cars, British TV; other TV appearances: Little Red Riding Hood, Faerie Tale Theatre, Showtime TV, 1983, Gulag, HBO, 1985, Our Friends in the North, 1996, Lexx: The Dark Zone, 1996, The Great War, 1996, Captain Simian and The Space Monkeys, 1996, The Little Riders, 1996, Pearl, 1996-97, Nazis: The Occult Conspiracy, 1998, Beings, 1998; stage appearance: Look Back in Anger, N.Y. Stage, 1980, In Celebration, N.Y.C., 1984, Hunting Cockroaches, L.A. Stage, 1987, Another Time - Stage, 1993; films include: Poor Cow, 1967, If..., 1969, Figures in a Landscape, 1970, The Raging Moon, 1971, A Clockwork Orange, 1971, O Lucky Man, 1973, Royal Flash, 1975, Aces High, 1976, Voyage of the Damned, 1977, Caligula, 1977, The Passage, 1978, Time After Time, 1979, Cat People, 1981, Britannia Hospital, 1984, Blue Thunder, 1983, Get Crazy, 1983, Cross Creek, 1983, Sunset, 1987, Buy and Cell, 1989, Class of 1999, 1989, Assassin of the Tsar, 1990, Bopha!, 1993, Milk Money, 1994, The Caller, Star Trek: Generations, 1997, Tank Girl, 1995, Yesterday's Target, 1996, Where Truth Lies, 1996, Asylum, 1996, Superman, 1996, Mr. Magoo, 1997, Hugo Pool, 1997, 2103 The Deadly Wake, 1997, The Gardener, 1998, Beings, 1998, World of Moss, 1998, Y2K, 1999, Southern Cross, 1999, My Life So Far, 1999, Love Lies Bleeding, 1999, Gangster #1, 2000, Island of the Dead, 2000, Just Visiting, 2001, Dorian, 2001, Tempo, 2003, The Company, 2003, Red Roses and Petrol, 2003, Bobby Jones, Stroke of Genius, 2004, (voice) Pinocchio 3000, 2004, (voice) Dinotopia: Curse of the Ruby Sunstone, 2004; TV guest appearances Tales From the Crypt, 1989, Spider-Man, 1995, Superman, 1996, Ruby, 1999, (voice) South Park, 2000, numerous others.

**MCDOWELL, RICHARD WILLIAM,** academic administrator; b. McDonald, Pa., Aug. 20, 1936; s. William Murdock and Cora Josephine (Brackman) McD.; m. Ann Brammer, May 27, 1961; children: Susan, Kathleen, Karen. BS, Indiana U. of Pa., 1960, MEd, 1962; MS, Purdue U., 1967, PhD, 1969. Cert. tchr., Pa. Tchr. Penn Hills Sch. Dist., Pa., 1960-67; divsn. chmn. Cmty. Coll. Allegheny County, West Mifflin, Pa., 1969-71; dean, acting pres. C.C. Beaver County, Monaca, Pa., 1971-72; exec. dean C.C. Allegheny County, Monroeville, Pa., 1972-80, v.p. strategic planning Pitts., 1980-81; pres. Schoolcraft Coll., Livonia, Mich., 1981—. Mgmt. cons., Pa. and Ill., 1975-80; chmn., mem. evaluation team Middle States Assn., Phila., 1972-80; trainer workshop leaders Higher Edn. Mgmt. Inst., Washington, 1976-77. With USMC, 1954-56. Recipient Outstanding Tchr. award Spectroscopy Soc., Pitts., 1966, Edn. award Plymouth C. of C., Mich., 1982. Mem. Am. Assn. Cmty. and Jr. Colls., Mich. C.C. Assn. (bd. dirs. exec. com.), W.E. Mich. League C.C. (chmn.), North Central Assn., Assn. C.C. Trustees. Office: Schoolcraft Coll 18600 Haggerty Rd Livonia MI 48152-3932

**MCDOWELL, ROBERT M.,** commissioner; b. 1963; m. Jennifer McDowell; 2 children. AB cum laude, Duke U., 1985; JD, Coll. William and Mary. Bar: Va. 1990, U.S. Dist. Ct. (ea. dist.) Va., U.S. Ct. Appeals DC (1st, 4th and 5th cir.), U.S. Supreme Ct. Chief legis. aide Va. Ho. of Delegates; with Arter & Hadden, Washington; exec. v.p., gen. coun. Am. Carriers Telecomm. Assn.; sr. v.p., asst. gen. counsel COMPTEL, 1999—2006; commr. FCC, 2006—. Mem. North Am. Numbering Coun. Inc. Mem. North Am. Numbering Plan Billing and Collection, Inc. Mem. gov.'s advisory bd. Safe and Drug-Free Va. Va. Bd. Contractors; chmn. bd. McLean Project for Arts; counsel Bush-Cheney Fla. Recount Team, 2000. Office: FCC 445 12th St SW Washington DC 20554*

**MCDOWELL, WILBUR BENEDICT,** retired chemist consultant; b. Omaha, Feb. 27, 1920; s. Samuel Brownlee and Rose Gwendolen (Benedict) McDowell; m. Jean Erskine Clapp, Aug. 9, 1947 (dec. Aug. 1996); children: Linda Jane, Wendy Sue, Bruce Benedict. BSc, Ohio State U., 1941, MSc, 1942, PhD, 1944. Asst. Ohio State U., Columbus, 1942—43, tchg. fellow, 1943—44; rsch. assoc. The Squibb Inst., New Brunswick, NJ, 1944—52, section head, 1953—58, sr. rsch. assoc., 1958—66; mgr. prof. svc. dept. Squibb Corp., N.Y.C., 1966—69, Princeton, NJ, 1970—85; ret., 1985. Cons., archivist Squibb Corp., 1985—89, Bristol-Myers Squibb Co., Princeton, 1989—99, New Brunswick, NJ, 2000—. Mem., v.p., pres. BOE, East Brunswick, NJ, 1957—65. Fellow: AAAS; mem.: Soc. Nuclear Medicine, Am. Chem. Soc. Achievements include 8 patents in field of manufacturing processes for pharmaceuticals. Home: 4 Fairview Ave East Brunswick NJ 08816 E-mail: benmcdowell@prodigy.net.

**MCDOWELL-CRAIG, VANESSA DENNISE,** supervisor, consultant; b. Washington, Dec. 9, 1954; d. John David and Ossie Ola McDowell; m. John Maurice Craig, May 19, 1984. BS, U. DC, 1995; MEd, Trinity U., Washington, 2000; postgrad., Gallaudet U., 2001—. Cert. mgmt. change leadership Gallaudet U., elem. edn. DC, emerging leaders program DC, ednl. rsch. and dissemination program Am. Fedn. Tchrs. Tng. instr. Blue Cross - Blue Shield, Washington, 1980—87; claims supr. Mut. Omaha, Washington, 1987—88, Health Plus, Riverdale, Md., 1988—89; supr., team mgr. Humana Group Health Plan, Washington, 1989—93; elem. tchr. grades 1-6 DC Pub. Sch. Sys., 1993—2001, instrnl. facilitator, supr., 2002—, sch. edn. coord., supr., cons. Cons. TechAgility LLC, Washington, 2004—. Mem.: ASCD (assoc.), Assn. Childhood Edn. Internat. (assoc.), Internat. Reading Assn. (assoc.; corr. sec. DC reading coun. 1999—2002), Delta Sigma Theta (life). Democrat. African Methodist Episcopal. Avocations: travel, reading, bicycling, singing, dance. Home: 7134 Marbury Court District Heights MD 20747 Office: DC

Pub Sch Sys Turner Elem Sch 3264 Staton Rd SE Washington DC 20020 Office Phone: 202-698-1167. Home Fax: 301-736-2365; Office Fax: 202-698-1166. Personal E-mail: vannettie@aol.com. Business E-Mail: vanessa.craig@k12.dc.us.

**MCDUFFIE, KEITH A.,** literature educator; b. Spokane, Wash., Feb. 12, 1932; s. Clair L. and Helen Marie (Yaeger) McD.; m. Helen E. Ferry, June 5, 1965 (div. July 1995); children: Anne Leslie, Andrew Keith; m. Pamela Philips Bacarisse, Aug. 10, 1995 (dec. Mar. 1996). BA in English, Gonzaga U., Spokane, 1954; MA in Spanish, Middlebury (Vt.) Coll., 1960. Univ. Complutense, Madrid, Spain, 1960; PhD in Hispanic Lit., U. Pitts., 1969. Prof. U. Mont., 1969-74; Mellon postdoctoral fellow U. Pitts., 1974, prof., chair dept. Hispanic lit., 1975-92, prof. Hispanic lit., 1975-99, ret., 1999. Editor Revista Iberoamericana, Pitts., 1991-96; pres. Univ. Senate, 1995-97. Co-author: Co-Textes: Digit Editor: Texto y Contexto-Actas 19 Congreso del IILI, 1980, En Este Aire de America: Homenaje a Alfredo Roggiano, 1990. With U.S. Army Security Agy., 1954-56. Mellon Predoctoral fellow U. Pitts., 1965, Title VI fellow U.S. Govt., 1966; Spanish Govt. scholar Spanish Govt., 1959-60. Mem. Instituto Internacional de Literatura Iberoamericana (contbg., bd. dirs. 1991-96, exec. dir. 1991-96). Democrat. Home: 220 N Dithridge St Apt 1001 Pittsburgh PA 15213-1425 E-mail: kamcd@pitt.edu.

**MC DUFFIE, MALCOLM,** oil industry executive; b. San Francisco, Nov. 14, 1915; s. William Chester and Mary (Skaife) McD.; m. Mary Sutherland de Surville, Dec. 8, 1951; children: Cynthia de Surville, Duncan de Surville. AB in Econs, Stanford U., 1940. With O.C. Field Gasoline Corp., 1940-41, Wilmington Gasoline Corp., 1941-42; with Mohawk Petroleum Corp., 1945-80, pres., 1969-80; dir. Res. Oil & Gas Co., 1973-80, sr. v.p., 1977-80; sp. asst. to pres. Getty Oil Co., Los Angeles, 1980-82. Bd. overseers Huntington Library, Art Gallery and Bot. Gardens, 1972-98; bd. dirs. Calif. Inst. Tech. Assocs., 1976-82. Mem. Nat. Petroleum Refiners Assn. (Dir. 1970-80), Ind. Refiners Assn. Calif. (pres. 1967-69, 77-78, dir. 1950-80), Rancheros Visitadores. Clubs: California (Los Angeles); Bohemian (San Francisco); Valley Hunt (Pasadena, Calif.), Annandale Golf (Pasadena, Calif.); Birnam Wood (Santa Barbara, Calif.), Valley (Montecito, Calif.). Republican. Episcopalian. Home and Office: 457 Eastgate Ln Santa Barbara CA 93108-2249

**MCDYESS, ANTONIO,** professional basketball player; b. Quitman, Miss. Forward Denver Nuggets, 1995-97, 1998—2002, Phoenix Suns, 1997—98, N.Y. Knicks, 2003—04, Phoenix Suns, 2004, Detroit Pistons 2004—. Named to NBA All-Rookie First Team, 1995—96, All-NBA Third Team, 1998—99. Avocations: bowling, rhythm and blues. Office: c/o Detroit Pistons Palace of Auburn Hills 2 Championship Dr Auburn Hills MI 48326

**MCEACHEN, RICHARD EDWARD,** banker, lawyer; b. Omaha, Sept. 24, 1933; s. Howard D. and Ada Carolyn Helen (Baumann) McE.; m. Judith Ann Gray, June 28, 1969; children: Mark E., Neil H. BS, U. Kans., Lawrence, 1955; JD, U. Mich., 1961. Bar: Mo. 1961, Kans. 1982. Assoc. Hillix, Hall, Hasburgh, Brown & Hoffhaus, Kansas City, Mo., 1961-62; sr. v.p. First Nat. Bank, Kansas City, Mo., 1962-75; exec. v.p. Commerce Bank Kansas City, Mo., 1975-85, Centerre Bank of Kansas City N.A., 1985-87, Security Bank Kansas City, Kans., 1987-88; exec. v.p., trust officer UMB Overland Park Bank, 1988-93; atty. Ferree, Bunn, O'Grady & Rundberg, Chartered, Overland Park, 1994—. Gov. Am. Royal Assn., Kansas City, Mo., 1970-2002, amb., 1980-2004, com. mem., 1995—2005; bd. dirs. Harry S Truman Med. Ctr., Kansas City, 1974-86, mem. fin. com., 1975-86, treas., 1979-84, bd. govs., 1986-2002, mem. bldg. and grounds com., 1993-2002, mem. pension com., 1976-93, 96-2000; trustee Clearinghouse for Midcontinent Founds., 1980-87; bd. dirs. Greater Kansas City Mental Health Found., 1963-69, treas., 1964-69, v.p., 1967-69; adv. bd. urban svcs. YMCA, Kansas City, 1976-83; cubmaster Kanza dist. Boy Scouts Am., 1982-83, dist. vice chmn., 1982-83, troop com., 1983-90, treas., 1986-88; bd. dirs. Scout Booster Club, Inc., 1989-94; mem. planned gift com. William Rockhill Nelson Gallery Art, Children's Mercy Hosp. Planned Gift Coun., 1991—2005; mem. adv. com. Legal Assistance Program Avila Coll., 1978-80, adv. coun. Future Farmers Am., 1972-82; mgr. Oppenstein Bros. Found., 1979-85; trustee Village Presbyn. Ch., 1987-90, chmn., 1989-90, elder, 1994-97; found. com. Am. Royal Charitable Found., 1995—; bd. dirs. Village Presbyn. Ch. Found., 1987-89, 94-97, chmn., 1996-97, mem. adv. bd., 1997-2001; bd. dirs. Estate Planning Coun., 1984-86; mem. Kansas City Fed. Estate Planning Symposium Com., 1992-98; bd. dirs. Shawnee Mission Med. Ctr. Found., 1988—, fin. com., 1989-92, 2002—, mem. planned giving com., 1996-, mem. investment com., 2000—; mem. adv. coun. Shawnee Mission Edn. Found., 2003. Mem. Nat. Assn. Securities Dealers Inc. (bd. arbitrators 1994—2004), Am. Arbitration Assn. (panel arbitrators 1994-96), Estate Planning Soc. Kansas City, Mo. Bar Assn., Kans. Bar Assn., Johnson County Bar Assn., Estate Planning Assn. (pres. 1974-75), Kansas City Jr. C. of C. (v.p. 1964-66), Ea. Kans. Estate Planning Coun., 40-Yrs. Ago Column Club (program com. 1999-2000, pres. 2001, trustee 2001-04), Indian Hills Club, Delta Tau Delta Alumni (v.p. Kansas City chpt. 1978-80). Republican. Home: 9100 El Monte St Shawnee Mission KS 66207-2627 Office: One Glenwood Pl 9300 Metcalf Ave Ste 300 Shawnee Mission KS 66212-6319

**MCEACHERN, ALLAN,** lawyer; b. Vancouver, BC, Can., May 20, 1926; s. John A. and Blanche L. (Roadhouse) McE.; m. Gloria, July 17, 1953 (dec. Sept. 1997); children: Jean Williams, Joanne Evans; m. Mary Victoria Newbury. BA, U. B.C., Vancouver, 1949, LLB, 1950, LLM (hon.), 1990. Assoc., sr. ptnr., barrister, solicitor Messrs. Russell & DuMoulin, Vancouver, 1950-78; chief justice Supreme Ct. B.C., Vancouver, 1979-88, Ct. Appeals B.C., Vancouver, 1988—2001; assoc. counsel Faskin Martineau, Vancouver, 2001—; chancellor U. B.C., 2002—. Pres. Kats Rugby Club, Vancouver, 1953-64, B.C. Lions Football Club, Vancouver, 1967, 68, 69, We. Football Conf., 1964, Can. Football League, 1967-68, commr. 1967-68. Mem. Can. Bar Assn. (bd. dirs.), Vancouver Bar Assn. (bd. dirs.), Legal Aid Soc. (pres. 1977-78), Law Soc. B.C. (bencher 1971-79). Avocations: sailing, gardening, walking. Office: Faskin Martineau 1075 W George St Vancouver BC V6E 3G2 Canada Office Phone: 604-631-4955. Business E-Mail: amceachern@van.fasken.com.

**MCEACHERN, STEPHEN MATHEW,** accountant; b. Nacogooches, Tex., Oct. 18, 1948; s. Maxie Neil and Exa Julia (Stephenson) McE.; m. Rebecca Brookshire, Dec. 29, 1968 (div. Sept. 1973); 1 child, Mathew Clayton; m. Sherry Jane Fears, Sept. 1, 1974; 1 child, Stephene Lee. BBA in Acctg., Tex. A&M U., 1971. CPA, Tex. Staff acct. Ernst & Whinney, Houston, 1971-75; sr. acct. Fitts, Roberts & Co., Houston, 1975—77, ptnr., 1977—97, pres., mng. ptnr., 1997—. Deacon, chmn. personnel and bldg. fin. com. Met. Bapt. Ch., Houston, 1984-86; committeeman Houston Livestock Show and Rodeo., 1983—. Mem. AICPA (auditing standards bd., 1995-98, tech. standards com., 2000-02, chair, 2002-05) Am. CPA's Tex. Soc. CPA's (bd. dirs., Houston chpt. 1985—), Houston CPA Soc. (pres. 2004-05) Lodges: Rotary (sec. 1985—). Republican. Office: Fitts Roberts & Co Inc 3707 Fm 1960 Rd W Houston TX 77068-3526 Home: 16710 Saddle Ridge Pass Cypress TX 77433

**MCELDOWNEY, NANCY,** ambassador; b. Fla. m. Tim Hayes; 1 child, Jessica. BA, New Coll.; grad., Columbia U., Nat. Def. U. With Office of Sec. Def. Pentagon; Office of Soviet Affairs US Dept. State, Office of European Security Affairs, Front Office, European Bur., Office of Dep. Sec.; dir. European Affairs, Nat. Security Coun. White House; dep. chief of mission, US Embassy in Baku US Dept. State, Azerbaijan, dep. chief US Mission to Turkey Ankara, 2005—, chargé d'affaires in Turkey. Recipient Disting. Writing award, Nat. War Coll., Sinclair Linguistic award, Superior Honor award, US Dept. State. Mailing: 7000 Ankara Pl Washington DC 20521-7000*

**MC ELHANEY, JOHN HESS,** lawyer; b. Milw., Apr. 16, 1934; s. Lewis Keck and Sara Jane (Hess) McE.; m. Jacquelyn Masur, Aug. 4, 1962; children— Scott, Victoria. BBA, So. Meth. U., 1956, JD, 1958. Bar: Tex. bar 1958. Pvt. practice law, Dallas, 1958—; pntr. Locke, Liddell & Sapp, L.L.C., Dallas, 1976—. Lectr. law So. Meth. U., 1967-76 Contbr. articles to legal jours. Trustee St. Mark's Sch. Tex., 1980-86. Fellow Am. Coll. Trial Lawyers; mem. Am. Bd. Trial Advs., ABA, Tex. Bar Assn., So. Meth. U. Law Alumni Assn. (pres. 1972-73, dir. 1970-73), Town and Gown Club (pres. 1981-82). Presbyterian. Home: 5340 Tanbark Dr Dallas TX 75229-5555 Office: Locke Liddell & Sapp 2200 Ross Ave Ste 2200 Dallas TX 75201-6776 Office Phone: 214-740-8000.

**MCELHATTON, JERRY,** credit card company executive; m. Jane McElhatton. B degree in Indsl. Mgmt., Franklin U.; attended graduate degree program, Western Michigan U. Held exec. mgmt. positions in ops. and tech. Ameritrust, Cleve.; Banl One, Columbus, Ohio; pres., CEO First Republic Bank Svcs. Corp., Payment Systems Tech. & Consulting, Inc.; Dallas; sr. exec. v.p., global tech. and ops Mastercard Internat., O'Fallen, Mo., 1994—. Bd. advisors BMC; bd. dir. Mascon. Mem. bd. trustee Nat. Coun. of the Washington U. Olin Sch. Bus., St. Louis U.; bd. dir. St Louis Sci. Ctr., United Way, St. Louis Variety Club, Rainbow Village. Avocation: model trains. Office: Mastercard Internat 2200 Mastercard Blvd O Fallon MO 63366

**MCELHENY, JOSIAH G.,** sculptor; b. Boston, 1966; BFA, Rhode Island Sch. Design, 1989. Apprentice to master glassblower Jan-Erik Ritzman, 1989—91, Sven-Ake Carlsson, 1989—91, Lino Tagliapietra, 1992—97; artist-in-residence Isabella Stewart Gardner Mus., 1998, U. Nev., Las Vegas, 2000; vis. critic Yale U. Sch. Art, 2001—03. Spkr. in field. One-man shows include Henry Art Gallery, Seattle, Isabella Stewart Gardner Mus., Boston, 1999, Johnson County CC, Overland Park, Kans., 2001, Art Inst. Chgo., Centro Galego de Arte Contemporanea, Spain, 2002, Brent Sikkema, NYC, 2000, 2003, Donald Young Gallery, Chgo., 1995, 1997, 2000, 2004, others, exhibited in group shows at Site Santa Fe, N.Mex., Whitney Biennial, Whitney Mus. Am. Art NYC, 2000, The Saatchi Gallery, London, Nordic Inst. Contemporary Art. Recipient award, Louis Comfort Tiffany Found., 1995, Bagley Wright Fund award, Seattle, 1998, 15th Rakow Commission, Corning Mus. Glass, Corning, NY, 2000; MacArthur Fellow, John D. and Catherine T. MacArthur Found., 2006. Office: c/o Donald Young Gallery 933 W Washington Blvd Chicago IL 60607*

**MCELHINNEY, JAMES LANCEL,** artist, educator; b. Abington, Pa., Feb. 3, 1952; s. James and Joan Howland (Carpenter) McE.; m. Victoria Maria Dávila, Sept. 12, 1981 (div.), m. M.L. Burnell Shively, May 14, 2003 (div. 2006). Scholarship student, Skowhegan (Maine) Sch. of Art, 1973; BFA, Temple U., 1974; MFA, Yale U., 1976. Asst. prof. Moore Coll. Art, Phila., 1977-78, Skidmore Coll., Saratoga Springs, NY, 1979-87; adj. instr. UCLA, 1983, Moore Coll. Art, 1983, Tyler Sch. Art, Phila., 1983-86, U. of Arts, Phila., 1985-89; instr. Milw. Inst. Art and Design, 1991-93; vis. artist East Carolina U., Greenville, NC, 1994-98; head painting and drawing program visual arts dept. U. Colo., Denver, 1998—2003; dir. study abroad program Feltre, Veneto, Italy, 2000—02; vis. asst. prof. Pratt Inst., NYC, 2004—; faculty Art Students League of NY, 2005—. Artist in residence Harper's Ferry Nat. Hist. Park, 1999; lectr. USAF Acad., 2001. One-man shows include Peninsula Ctr. for the Fine Arts, Newport News, Va., 1993, Danville (Va.) Mus., 1993, Second Street Gallery, Charlottesville, Va., 1995, F.A.N. Gallery, Phila., 1995, 1998, Greenville (N.C.) Mus. Art, 1996, Lee Hansley Gallery, Raleigh, N.C., 1996, 1998, 1999, Asheville (N.C.) Art Mus., 1996, William Havu Gallery, Denver, 2001—02, Mus. of the S.W., Midland, Tex., 2003, Letterkenny Arts Ctr., Donegal, Ireland, 2003, William Havu Gallery, 2001, Mus of Southwest, Midland, Tex., 2003, Letterkenny Arts Ctr., Donegal, Ireland, 2003, The Painting Ctr., NYC, 2005, exhibited in group shows at Chrysler Mus., Norfolk, Va., 1999, Allen Sheppard Gallery, N.Y.C., 1999, Ucross Found., 2000, Nicolayseu Mus., 2000, Newarts Gallery, Litchfield, Conn., 2005, Kent Gallery, Conn., 2005, Represented in permanent collections Chrysler Mus. Art, Denver Art Mus., Asheville Art Mus.; contbr. articles to various profl. mag., to profl. jours.; prin. works include multiple venues, 2003; author: (Manual) The Instruction of Civil War Pioneer Troops, 2004. Vol. Richmond (Va.) Nat. Battlefield Park, 1991—, Frontier Army Living History Corps of Discovery, U.S. Army C.E. Lewis and Clark Bicentennial, Topog. eng. 1st Divsn. Staff, Hdqs. A.N.V (U.S.C.W.). Grantee painting, NEA, 1987—88, Ptnrs. in Arts, Richmond Arts Coun., 1995; rsch. grant, U. Colo., 2000, Faculty Devel. grant, 2003. Mem. Coll. Art Assn., SAR, Civil War Preservation Trust, Frontier Army L.H. Assoc.,Foote Family Assoc. Home: 241 Warren St Hudson NY 12534 Office: Art Students League of NY 215 W 57th New York NY 10019 Office Phone: 518-929-6295. Personal E-mail: mcelhinney@aol.com

**MCELHINNY, HAROLD JOHN,** lawyer; b. San Francisco, Jan. 5, 1947; s. Harold James and Margaret I. (Mahoney) McE.; m. Mary Ellen McElhinny, June 22, 1968; children: Hannah, Jennifer, William. BA in Polit. Sci., U. Santa Clara, 1970; JD, U. Calif., Berkeley, 1975. Bar: Calif. 1976, U.S. Supreme Ct. 1983. Vol. Peace Corps., Tripoli, Libya, 1968-69; juvenile counselor Santa Clara County (Calif.) Juvenile Hall, 1969-72; law clk. U.S. Dist. Ct., Hartford, Conn., 1975-76; ptnr. Morrison & Foerster, San Francisco, 1976—. Mem. ABA, Calif. Bar Assn., State Bar Calif. (rev. dept. 1986-89, chmn. 1988), San Francisco Bar Assn., Am. Intellectual Property Law Assn., Assn. Bus. Trial Lawyers (bd. govs. 1992-97, pres. 1997). Democrat. Roman Catholic. Office: Morrison & Foerster 425 Market St Fl 34 San Francisco CA 94105-2482 Office Phone: 415-268-7265. E-mail: hmcelhinny@mofo.com.

**MCELHINNY, WILSON DUNBAR,** banker; b. Detroit, July 27, 1929; s. William Dunbar and Elizabeth (Wilson) McE.; m. Barbara Cheney Watkins, June 6, 1952 (dec.); children: David Ashton, Ward Cheney, Edward Wilson, William Dunbar; m. Lisa Lesher Mar. 27, 1993, BA, Yale U, 1953. With Union and New Haven Trust Co., 1952-63, Reading Trust Co., Pa., 1963-68, pres., 1968-70, Nat. Ctrl. Bank (formerly Reading Trust Co.), Pa., 1970-79, CEO, 1975-79; chmn. bd. dirs., pres., CEO Hamilton Bank (formerly Nat. Ctrl. Bank), Lancaster, Pa., 1979-81, chmn. bd. dirs., CEO, 1981-83, chmn. bd. dirs., 1981-90; pres. CoreStates Fin. Corp., Phila., 1983-86, vice chmn., 1986-90; pres., chmn. Hamilton Bank, Lancaster, 1988-90. Bd. dirs. Reading Eagle Co., 1st Bank Idaho, SIGCO, Portland, Maine. Mem. St. Luke's Wood River Found. Mem. Pa. C. of C. (chmn. 1990-92), Yale Club N.Y., The Valley Club. Home and office: PO Box 3070 Ketchum ID 83340-3070

**MCELIGOT, ARCHANA JAISWAL,** epidemiologist, educator; d. Indravadan Jayaswal and Jyotsna Jaiswal; m. Jeremy McEligot, July 20, 1996; children: Lee, Rohan. BS, MS, U. Calif., San Diego, PhD, 2001. Asst. prof. U. Calif., Irvine, 2002—; assoc. prof. Calif. State U., 2006—. Grantee, Tobacco Related Disease Rsch. Program, 2004; U. Calif. Irvine, 2003—04, Nat. Cancer Inst., 2005—. Mem.: Cancer Family Registry (co-chair 2002—03), Am. Soc. Nutrition. Office: University of California Irvine/CSUF 224 Irvine Hall Irvine CA 92697-7555 Office Phone: 949-824-4358. Business E-Mail: mceligot@uci.edu.

**MCELLIGOTT, JAMES PATRICK, JR.,** lawyer; b. Chgo., Jan. 11, 1948; s. James Patrick and Helen Cecelia (Hogan) McE.; children: Michael Sean, Andrew David; m. Trina Reff, Aug. 25, 1985. BA, U. Ill., Urbana, 1970; JD, Harvard U., 1973. Bar: Va. 1974, U.S. Dist. Ct. (ea. and we. dists.) Va. 1974, U.S. Ct. Appeals (4th cir.) 1974, U.S. Supreme Ct. 1979. Research asst. U. Ill., 1970; assoc. McGuire, Woods & Battle, Richmond, 1973-79; ptnr. McGuire Woods, Richmond, 1979—. Mem. exec. com. Va. Home for Boys, 1976-92, pres. bd. govs., 1981-83; mem. Leadership Metro Richmond-Met. C. of C., 1984-85; bd. dirs. ARC Greater Richmond Chpt., 1990-96, chmn., 1994-95. Recipient Clara Barton award ARC Richmond Chpt., 1997. Mem. ABA, Va. Bar Assn. (exec. com., chmn. pub. rels. com. 1978-82, producer pub. svc. message 1973, Hot Spot award 1973), Coll. of Labor and Employment Lawyers, Richmond Bar Assn., Fed. Bar Assn. (pres. Richmond chpt. 1986), Nat. Sch. Bds. Assn., Coun. of Sch. Attys., Coll. Labor and Employment Lawyers, Phi Beta Kappa, Phi Kappa Phi, Omicron Delta Epsilon. Home: 203 Cyril Ln Richmond VA 23229-7740 Office: McGuire Woods LLP One James Ctr Richmond VA 23219-3229 E-mail: jmcelligot@mcguirewoods.com.

**MC ELRATH, RICHARD ELSWORTH,** retired insurance company executive; b. Thompsontown, Pa., Oct. 11, 1932; s. Clayton Ellsworth and Jane Elizabeth (Shoop) McE.; m. Donna Gail Booher, Aug. 18, 1952; children: Leslie Jo, Jennifer Jo, Josie Arlene Elizabeth, Rebekah Clare. BS cum laude, Elizabethtown Coll., Pa., 1955; MBA cum laude, Harvard U., 1961. Research asst. Harvard U., 1961-62; asst. to pres. Callaway Mills Co., LaGrange, Ga., 1963-65; with Irving Trust Co., N.Y.C., 1965-73, v.p., 1969-73; treas. Tchrs. Ins. Annuity Assn. and Coll. Retirement Equities Fund, 1973-81; v.p. Met. Life Ins. Co., 1982-95. Pres., dir. MetLife Funding, Inc., MetLife Credit, Inc., 1984-95. Author articles, case studies. Trustee Elizabethtown Coll.; mem. Society Valley Hosp., Ridgewood, N.J.; mem. Boston Rep. Com., 1961-63, Troup County (Ga.) Rep. Com., 1964-65; bd. dirs Family Counseling Svc., Ridgewood, 1986-92. Lt. comdr. USNR, 1956-59. Mem. Assn. Gov. Bds. Univs. and Colls. Clubs: Harvard (N.Y.C.). Methodist. Home: 17 Cedar St Glen Rock NJ 07452-1608

**MCELROY, EDWARD J.,** labor union administrator; b. Providence, Mar. 17, 1941; s. Edward J. Sr. and Clara (Angelone) McE.; m. Edwina Barbara Ricci, Apr. 20, 1963; children: Kathleen, Mary, Stephen, Elizabeth. AB, Providence Coll., 1962. Cert. tchr. Tchr. Lockwood Jr. High Sch., Warwick, R.I., 1962-72; pres. Warwick Tchrs. Union, Warwick, R.I., 1967-69, R.I. Fed. Tchrs., Am. Fed. Tchrs., Providence, 1971-92, R.I. AFL-CIO, Providence, 1977-92; v.p. Am. Fed. Tchrs., AFL-CIO, Providence, 1974-92, sec. treas. Washington, 1992 2004, pres., 2004—. Exec. com. R.I. Democratic State Com., Providence, 1976-92; sec. exec. com. United Way So. New England, Providence, 1978-92; devel. commn. R.I. State, 1984-85, mem. Workforce 2000, 1987-92. Recipient Quirk Inst. award Providence Coll., 1980. Mem. Aurora Civic Assn. bd. dirs., Voices for Working Families, Amalgamated Bank of Chgo. Democrat. Roman Catholic. Avocations: golf, photography, reading. Office: Am Fed Tchrs AFL CIO 555 New Jersey Ave NW Washington DC 20001-2029

**MC ELROY, JOHN HARLEY,** electrical and industrial engineering educator; b. Marion, Ohio, June 27, 1936; s. Francis and Alice Marie McElroy; m. Eleonore Hildegard Schmidt, Mar. 18, 1957. BS in Elec. Engring, U. Tex., Austin, 1966; M.E.E., Cath. U. Am., 1973, PhD, 1978. Instr. guided missles Air Defense Sch. U.S. Army, 1957-63; rsch. asst. Quantum Electronics rsch. Lab U. Texas, Austin, 1963-66; staff Goddard Flight Ctr., Greenbelt, Md., 1966-79, 80-82, chief comms. tech. div., 1978-79, dep. dir. ctr., 1980-82; dir. comms. programs NASA Hdqrs., Washington, 1979-80; asst. administr. NOAA, Washington, 1982-85; dir. spl. projects Hughes Aircraft Co., Los Angeles, 1985-86; v.p. tech. Hughes Comms., Inc., 1986-87; dean Coll. Engring., prof. elec. engring U. Tex., Arlington, 1987-96, vice provost for rsch. and grad. studies, 1996-97, prof. elec. and indsl. engring., 1997-2000, dean emeritus Coll. Engring.; chair space studies bd. Nat. Rsch. Coun., 2000—03. Coms. satellite communications and earth observations. Contbr. articles to profl. jours. Served with AUS, 1954-63. Recipient Apollo Achievement award NASA, 1969, Applications Tech. Satellite award, 1975, Earth Resources Satellite award, 1973, Internat. Coop. in Space Sci. medal AIAA, 1997, Pub. Svc. medal NASA, 2003; named Wernher von Braun Meml. Lectr. Smithsonian Instn., Disting. Hon. Alumnus U. Tex., Arlington, 1998. Fellow AIAA, IEEE, Washington Acad. Scis.; mem. Nat. Acad. Engring. Home: 5687 Wild Olive St Las Vegas NV 89118-1956 Personal E-mail: jhmcelroy@worldnet.att.net.

**MCELROY, KATHLEEN O.,** dining editor; b. 1961; BA, Texas A&M, 1981. Editor Austin American-Statesman, Newsday; sr. editor, nat. copy chief The National; copy editor, asst. sports editor, dep. sports ed. NY Times, 1991—2002, assoc. mng. editor for weekends, 2002—04, dining editor, 2004—. Co-recipient Am. Copy Editors Soc. headline contest, 2004. Mem.: Nat. Assn. Black Journalists, Culinary Historians NY (co-editor 2001, assoc. editor 2002). Office: NY Times Dining Sect 229 W 43rd St New York NY 10036 Office Phone: 212-556-1435. Office Fax: 212-556-1481. E-mail: mcelroy@nytimes.com.*

**MCELROY, MICHAEL ROBERT,** lawyer; b. Providence, Feb. 7, 1951; s. Gerald Robert and Jeannette (Belanger) McE.; m. Christine Anne O'Donnell, June 5, 1976; children: Brian Robert, Dianne Elizabeth, Erin Christine. BA with highest distinction, U. R.I., 1973; JD cum laude, Boston U., 1976; MS in Taxation cum laude, Bryant Coll., 1987. Bar: Tenn. 1976, Mass. 1985, U.S. Dist. Ct. (ea. dist.) Tenn. 1977, U.S. Ct. Appeals (5th cir.) 1977, U.S. Supreme Ct. 1979, U.S. Ct. Appeals (6th cir.) 1980, R.I. 1981, U.S. Dist. Ct. R.I. 1981, U.S. Ct. Appeals (1st cir.) 1981, U.S. Dist. Ct. Mass. 2000. Trial atty. TVA, Knoxville, 1976-81; counsel R.I. Pub. Utilities Commn., Providence, 1982-83; spl. asst. atty. gen. Office Atty. Gen., Providence, 1982-83; ptnr. O'Leary & McElroy, Providence, 1981-85; sole practice Providence, 1985-87; ptnr. Schacht & McElroy, Providence, 1987—. Pres. Utility Cons., Inc., Providence, 1983; ptnr. McElroy, Lawrence, Edge & Assocs., Providence, 1983-85. Legal counsel for candidate Congl. campaign, Providence, 1982; chief speech writer for candidate gubernatorial campaign, R.I., 1984; chief legal counsel for candidate gubernatorial campaign, R.I., 1988, Gov. Bruce Sundlun's successful gubernatorial campaign, 1990; legal counsel to R.I. Pers. Appeal Bd., 1991—; arbitrator Superior Ct. R.I., 1992—; spl. master/commr., 1993—; mediator Superior Ct., 1999—; spl. legal counsel to R.I. Ethics Commn., 2000-02. Danforth Found. hon. fellow, 1973; Rhodes scholar nominee, 1973; honoree for life-saving CPR, TVA, 1980; nominated for judgeship Jud. Nom. Commn. Superior Ct., 1994. Mem.: ATLA, Million Dollar Advs. Forum, Assn. Trial Lawyers R.I., R.I. Bar Assn. (chmn. Superior Ct. Bench/Bar com. 2003—, mem. Supreme Ct. com., fed. ct. and superior ct. Bench/Bar coms.). Roman Catholic. Office: PO Box 6721 Providence RI 02940-6721 Office Phone: 401-351-4100. E-mail: mcelroymik@aol.com.

**MCELVAIN, DAVID PLOWMAN,** retired manufacturing executive, finance company executive; b. Chgo., Oct. 16, 1937; s. Carl R. and Ruth P. (Plowman) McE.; m. Mary Rosalind Hysong, Dec. 20, 1961; children: Jana, Jodi. BBA, U. Ariz., 1961, MBA, 1962. Cert. mgmt. acct. Consolidation acct., exec. divsn. Dresser Industries, Inc., Dallas, 1962-67, corp. fin. controller, 1973-76, dir. fin. svcs., 1976-78, staff v.p. fin. svc. and risk mgmt., 1978-82, exec. v.p. fin. svcs. group, 1982-83, pres. fin. svcs. group, 1984-86, v.p. fin., CFO, 1987-93; owner McElvain Oil Co., Dallas, 1993—. Controller crane, hoist & tower div., Muskegon, Mich., 1967-73. Mem. Nat. Assn. Accts., Beta Gamma Sigma, Phi Delta Theta. Episcopalian. Home: 14828 Bellbrook Dr Dallas TX 75254-7647 Personal E-mail: mcelvaincl@msn.com.

**MCELVAINE, ROBERT STUART,** writer, educator; b. East Brunswick, N.J., Jan. 24, 1947; s. Edward and Ruth Ludewig McElvaine; m. Anne Therese Lee, Aug. 24, 1968; children: Kerri Anne, Lauren Lee Itzkowitz, Allison Therese, Brett Edward. BA, Rutgers U., 1968; MA in History, SUNY, Binghamton, 1971; PhD, SUNY, 1974. Asst. prof. history Millsaps Coll., Jackson, Miss., 1973—79, assoc. prof. history, 1979—84, prof. history, 1984—, Elizabeth Chisholm prof. arts & letters, 1988—. Cons. PBS series, Blackside Productions, Boston, 1991—93; assoc. editor, Am. Nat. Biography Oxford U. Press, N.Y.C., 1997—2001; editor-in-chief, The Ency. of the Great Depression Macmillan Reference USA, 1999—2004. Author: The Great Depression: America, 1929-1941, The End of the Conservative Era: Liberalism After Reagan, Mario Cuomo: A Biography, What's Left? - A New Democratic Vision for America, Eve's Seed: Biology, the Sexes and the Course of History, Franklin Delano Roosevelt; editor: Down and Out in the Great Depression: Letters from the Forgotten Man, The Depression and New Deal: A History in Documents, The Encyclopedia of the Great Depression. Recipient Silver medal, Nat. Prof. of the Yr., Coun. Advancement & Support Edn., 1988, Miss. Prof. Yr., Carnegie Endowment Edn., 2002. Mem.: AAUP, Orgn. Am. Historians, Am. Hist. Assn. Liberal. Roman Catholic. Avocations: travel, sports, music, movies, photography. Home: 201 Concord Drive Clinton MS 39056 Office: Millsaps College 1701 N State Street Jackson MS 39210 Office Phone: 601-974-1291. Personal E-mail: mcelvrs@millsaps.edu.

**MCELVEEN, JOSEPH JAMES, JR.,** journalist, writer, newscaster, educator; b. Sanford, Fla., Feb. 23, 1939; s. Joseph James Sr. and Genevieve (Stoll) McE.; m. Mary Louise Young, Aug. 18, 1979; 1 child, Ryan Leighton. BA, Furman U., 1961; MA, U. S.C., 1968. Editor, pub. West Ashley News, Charleston, S.C, 1951-57; reporter, photographer Charleston Post, 1955-57; tchr. English and journalism St. Andrew's Parish High Sch., Charleston, 1961-65; dir. info., prof. journalism Columbia Coll., S.C, 1965-68; prof. journalism U. S.C., Columbia, 1968-79; sr. pub. affairs specialist FCC, Washington, 1979-81; dir. pub. affairs adminstrn. Nat. Cable TV Assn., Washington, 1981-87; dir. internal communications Corp. for Pub. Broadcasting, Washington, 1987-92, dir. program adminstrn., 1992-96, sr. program officer, 1996-99; media/comms. cons. Vienna, Va., 1999—; tchr. English, Fairfax County Pub. Schs., Vienna, Va., 2002—. Ombudsman, columnist Alexandria Gazette, Va., 1981—88; pres. McElveen Seminars, Vienna, 2000—. Author: Introduction to Creative Writing, 1963, Modern Communications, 1964; contbr. chpt. to Dictionary of Literary Biography (Mencken), 1986, Words, Words, Words: A Journalist's Memoir, 1997, Effective Writing and Editing, 2000, 1940s: Decade on the Threshold, 2000. Mem. Orgn. of News Ombudsmen, Soc. Profl. Journalists, Mencken Soc. Episcopalian. Avocations: photography, reading, desktop pub. Office: 1807 Hursley Ct Vienna VA 22182-2105 Personal E-mail: jjmcelveen@aol.com.

**MCELVEEN, JUNIUS CARLISLE, JR.,** lawyer; b. Rogersville, Tenn., Feb 17, 1947; s. Junius Carlisle and Martha Kathleen (Harrison) McE.; m. Mary Wallace Pyles, Sept. 22, 1973; children: Kathryn Carlisle, Sarah Elizabeth. BA cum laude, U. Va., 1969, JD, 1972. Bar: Va. 1972, Calif. 1975, U.S. Dist. Ct. (ea. dist.) Va. 1976, D.C. 1978, U.S. Ct. Appeals (4th cir.) 1978, U.S. Ct. Appeals (Fed. cir.) 1986, U.S. Ct. Appeals (11th cir.) 1990. Rsch. assoc. Atlantic Richfield, Washington, 1972; assoc. Pender & Coward, Norfolk, Va., 1976-77; from assoc. to ptnr. Seyfarth, Shaw, Washington, 1977—83; ptnr. Jones Day, Washington, 1983—. Mem. adv. com., reproductive hazards in the workplace Office of Tech. Assessment, Washington, 1984-86; mem. adv. council Ctr. Environ. Health, U. Conn., 1986-95; mem. editorial bd. The Occupational and Environ. Medicine Report, 1986—, Human and Ecol. Risk Assessment, 1998—. Contbr. articles to legal jours. Elder Kirkwood Presbyn. Ch., Springfield, Va., 1984-86. Served as lt. USN, 1972-75. Mem. ABA, Va. State Bar, State Bar Calif., Phi Beta Kappa, Phi Delta Phi (sec. local chpt. 1971-72, Outstanding Grad. award 1972). Home: 2121/2 S Pitt St Alexandria VA 22314 Office: Jones Day 51 Louisana Ave NW Washington DC 20001 Office Phone: 202-879-3726. Business E-Mail: jcmcelveen@jonesday.com.

**MCELVEEN, WILLIAM LINDSAY,** broadcasting executive, lecturer; b. Columbia, S.C., Sept. 20, 1950; s. Henry Moody and Dorothy Butler (Sligh) McE.; m. Laurie Wells Boyle, Sept. 8, 1969 (div. 1976); 1 child, Earle Sligh; m. Catharine Elizabeth McCaslin, Aug. 13, 1992; 1 child, Kerry Elizabeth McCaslin. BA in English, U. of South, 1972. Acct. exec. Sta. WNOK-FM, Columbia, SC, 1972-73, mng. dir., 1973-79; v.p., gen. mgr. Stas. WNOK-AM-FM, Columbia, 1979-84; pres. Audubon Broadcasting Co., Columbia, 1984-89, Radio South Carolina, Columbia, 1989—. Exec. dir. Bloomington Broadcasting Corp., 1998-2000; lectr. Internat. Media Fund, Washington, 1993—; v.p. s.e. region Citadel Broadcasting, 2000—. Chmn. bd. dirs. Columbia Urban League, 1983-85; bd. dirs. Crimestoppers of Midlands, 1984-88, S.C Law Inst., Columbia, 1985-88, Helpline of Midlands, 1986-90, U. S.C. Coll. Journalism Partnership, 1996—, Greater Columbia C. of C., 2002-04, Children's Hosp. SC, 2006—; gen. campaign chair United Negro Coll. Fund, Columbia, 1985-86; mem. exec. com. United Way of Midlands, Columbia, 1987-88. Mem. Nat. Assn. Broadcasters (bd. dirs. 1988-92, 96—2000, v.p. 1997-98, chmn 1998-2000), S.C Broadcasters Assn. (exec. com., bd. dirs. 1980-87, pres. 1985-86, Hall of Fame inductee 1996), Columbia Advt. Fedn. (pres. 1980-81), Media Club of Columbia (bd. dirs., pres. 1983-84). Presbyterian. Avocations: golf, tennis, travel. Home: 263 Tombee Ln Columbia SC 29209-0804 Office: Radio SC 1801 Charleston Hwy Cayce SC 29033-2019 E-mail: bill.mcelveen@citcomm.com.

**MCELVEEN-HUNTER, BONNIE,** international relief organization executive; b. SC, Jan. 1945; m. Bynum Merritt Hunter, Sr.; 1 child, Bynum Merritt Hunter Jr. Pres., CEO, owner Pace Comm., Inc.; US amb. to Finland Dept. of State, Helsinki, 2001—03; chair Am. Red Cross, Washington, 2004—. Chmn. Alexis de Tocqueville Soc., United Way Greater Greensboro, NC; bd. mem. United Way Am., chair nat. women's leadership giving campaign; chair Women in Philanthropy Summit, Washington; internat. bd. mem. Habitat for Humanity; bd. mem. Internat. Women Build Habitat for Humanity, Habitat for Humanity First Ladies Build. Named Comdr. Grand Cross Order of Lion, Pres. of Finland; recipient Dr. Carl-Christian Rosenbröijer award. Office: American Red Cross National Headquarters 2025 E St NW Washington DC 20006 Office Phone: 202-737-8300.*

**MCELVY, JAMES DOUGLAS,** lawyer; BS, Univ. Ala., JD, 1971; student, St. Bernard Coll. Cert.: mediator, Am. Acad. of Atty. Mediators. Of counsel Azar & Azar LLC, Montomery, Ala. Bd. dir. Univ. Ala. Law Sch. Found.; trustee Ala. Law Found.; former chmn. Tuscaloosa Coalition for Character; former adj. prof. of law Univ. Ala. Sch. of Law; former prof., alternative dispute resolution Oak Brook Coll. of Law and Govt. Policy. Christian Legal Soc.; former deacon First Baptist Ch. of Tuscaloosa; former v.p. bd. dir. YMCA Metro. Mem.: Ala. State Bar Assn. (mem. bd. of bar commrs.-3 terms, exec. com.-4 terms, v.p. 2002 03, pres.-elect 2003 04, pres. 2004—05), Tuscaloosa County Bar Assn. (sec. treas. 1989, pres.-elect 1990, pres. 1990—91, exec. com.). Office: Azar & Azar LLC 260 Washington Ave PO Box 2028 Montgomery AL 36102-2028

**MCELWAINE, JAMES WILLIAM,** music educator; b. Galveston, Tex., May 18, 1947; s. James Murrell and Kathryn Rhea McElwaine; m. Molly Ann Murphy, 1967 (div. 1970); life ptnr. Katherine Davenny, 1970 (separated 1973); m. Theresa Weedy, 1989; 1 child, Gabriel. MusB, North Tex. State U., 1969; MusM, Yale U., 1971. Instr. San Francisco (Calif.) Conservatory, 1971—72; prof. music Hampshire Coll., Amherst, Mass., 1972—76, Purchase (NY) Coll. - SUNY, 1978—; instr. Nassau CC, Garden City, NY, 1982—84. V.p., exec. com. mem. U. Faculty Senate, Albany, NY, 2000—; guest lectr. Amherst Coll., Smith Coll., Mt. Holyoke, CUNY, SUNY, Brockport, U. Albany, U. Tenn., Cal Tech., U. Tex., U. Calif., Berkeley, Berklee Sch. Orchestrator Starmites (6 TONY nominations); contbr. chapters to books Scribners Encyclopedia of American Lives; composer (orchestrator, conductor, dir.): American Stage Festival, Criterion Times Square Theater, Vineyard Theater, Truck and Warehouse Theater, Collonades Theater, American Place Theater, Asheville Blues Festival, Internat. Ragtime Festival; musician (programmer): Jim Henson's Muppet Babies; Smithsonian Institute, Bar Harbor Festival, Prairie Home Companion, 1984 Olympics; composer (arranger): The Slow Drag, Der Ring Gott Farblonjet (6 Obie nominations); musical dir. Lenny and the Heartbreakers, orchestrator Goblin Market (Critic's Inner Cir. award, 1983); musician (conductor, co-founder): (chamber music ensemble) Musical Elements; musician: (co-founder) New York Quintet; composer (performer, producer, arranger): Warner Bros., SONY-Columbia, Tropique, Importe-12, Pye, Eurodance, Shanachie, Rhino, Carrere, Seven Arts, Tommy Boy, Ariola, Melodia, Country Music Heritage; composer: (condr.) Charles Ludlam's Ridiculous Theater. Mem.: ASCAP, Am. Fedn. Mus., United U. Professions. Achievements include design of innovative univ. curriculum (BFA, MFA, BMus, MMus) for composition; development of innovative univ. curriculum (BA) for new media studies; innovative univ. curriculum (BFA) for music production. Office: Conservatory Music Purchase Coll 735 Anderson Hill Rd Purchase NY 10577 Office Phone: 914-251-6730. Office Fax: 914-251-6739. Business E-Mail: jim.mcelwaine@purchase.edu.

**MCELWEE, DENNIS JOHN,** lawyer, former pharmaceutical company executive; b. New Orleans, July 30, 1947; s. John Joseph and Audrey (Nunez) McE. BS, Tulane U., New Orleans, 1970; JD, U. Denver, 1992. Clean room and quality control analyst Sci. Enterprises Inc., Broomfield, Colo., 1975-76; analytical chemist in toxicology Poisonlab. Inc., Denver, 1977; analytical chemist, then dir. quality control program Colo. Sch. Mines Rsch. Inst., 1977-79; dir. quality control, then dir. compliance Benedict Nuclear Pharms. Co., Golden, Colo., 1979-84; pres. MC Projections Inc., Morrison, Colo., 1985-86; dir. regulatory affairs Electromedics Inc., Englewood, Colo., 1986-89; pvt. practice Denver, 1992—. Author: Mineral Research Chemicals, Toxic Properties and Proper Handling, 2d edit., 1979; mem. editl. bd. CF Network Mag.; contbr. articles to profl. jours. Bd. dirs. Denver chpt. Cystic Fibrosis Found., 1996, Assn. of Vols. for Children's Hosp., Denver, 1999, hon. lifetime mem., 2004. Recipient Sutton prize in internat. law U. Denver Sch. Law, 1991, Finest award Denver Charities, 1999; named first lifetime hon. bd. mem. of bd. dirs., Assn. Vols. Childrens Hosp. Mem. Colo. Bar Assn., 1st Jud. Dist. Bar Assn. Office: 7475 W 5th Ave # 315 Lakewood CO 80226 Office Phone: 303-274-2021.

**MCELWREATH, SALLY CHIN,** corporate communications executive; b. N.Y.C., Oct. 15, 1940; d. Toon Guey and Jean B. (Wong) Chin; m. Joseph F. Callo, Mar. 17, 1979; 1 child, R.J. McElwreath III. BA, Pace Coll., 1963; MBA, Pace U., 1969. Copywriter O.E. McIntyre, N.Y.C., 1963-65; editl. asst. Sinclair Oil Corp., N.Y.C., 1966-70; account exec. Muller, Jordan & Herrick, N.Y.C., 1970-71; regional mgr. pub. rels. United Airlines, N.Y.C., 1971-79; dir. corp. comm. Trans World Airlines, N.Y.C., 1979-86; v.p. pub. rels. TWA Mktg. Svcs., Inc. The Travel Ch. Direct, N.Y.C., 1986-88; ptnr. The Comm. Group, N.Y.C., 1988-90; gen. mgr. corp. comm. Ofcl. Airline Guides, 1990-91; v.p. corp. comm. Macmillan, Inc., 1991-93; cons. N.Y.C., 1993-94; sr. v.p. corp. comm. Aquila Inc., 1994—2005. Pub. affairs officer USNR, 1973-2000. Ret. Capt. Named Woman of Yr., YWCA, 1980, Alumnus of Yr., Pace U., 1976. Mem. N.Am. Pub. Rels. Assn. (vice chair 2003-05), Wings Club (N.Y.C.). Avocations: sailing, skiing, harpsichord.

**MCELYEA, JACQUELYN SUZANNE,** accountant, real estate consultant; b. Dallas, July 19, 1958; d. Owen Clyde and Mary Lou (Cockerill) Harvey; m. James E. McElyea, June 11, 1983. BBS, Tex. A&M U., 1980. CPA, Tex. Acctg. mgr. Oxford Tex. Devel., Dallas, 1980-81; staff to dir. PriceWaterhouseCoopers, Dallas, 1981—. Pres. Nat. Assn. Corp. Real Estate, Dallas. Co-author: Real Estate Accounting Reporting, 1995. Bd. dirs. Am. Diabetes Assn., Dallas, 1996-97. Mem. AICPA, Nat. Assn. Real Estate Cos., Tex. Soc. CPAs. Presbyterian. Avocations: animals, cooking. Office: Price Waterhouse Coopers Llp 350 S Grand Ave Ste 4500 Los Angeles CA 90071-3477 E-mail: smcelyea@home.com.

**MCENROE, JOHN PATRICK, JR.,** professional tennis player; b. Wiesbaden, Fed. Republic Germany, Feb. 16, 1959; s. John Patrick and Kathy McEnroe; m. Tatum O'Neil, Aug. 1, 1986 (div. 1994); children: Kevin, Sean, Emily; m. Patty Smyth, 1997; children: Anna, Ava 1 stepchild, Ruby. Grad. Trinity Sch., N.Y.C., 1977; student, Stanford U. Winner numerous U.S. jr. singles and doubles titles; winner jr. titles French Mixed Doubles, 1977, French Jr. Singles, 1977; winner Nat. Coll. Athletic Assn. Intercollegiate U.S. Men's Singles title, 1978; professional tennis player, 1978-93; played on victorious U.S. Davis Cup Team, 1978, 79, 81, 82, 92; winner Grand Prix Masters Tournament, N.Y.C., 1979, U.S. Open Men's Singles Championship, 1979, 80, 81, 84, World Championship Tennis Championship, 1979, 83, Wimbledon Singles, 1981, 83, 84, Tournament of Champions, 1981, 83, Wimbledon Doubles, 1992; winner (with Jonas Bjorkman) Doubles Title SAP Open, 2006; tennis sportscaster USA Network, 1993; host The Chair, 2002, McEnroe, 2004. Owner John McEnroe Gallery. Co-author (with James Kaplan): (autobiography) You Cannot Be Serious, 2000; author: Serious, 2003. Inducted, Tennis Hall of Fame, 1999. Mem. Men's Seniors' Tour Circuit, 1994. Achievements include winner 21 Singles Titles, Sr. Champions Tour, 1998-2005.*

**MCENROE, KATE,** broadcast executive; BA in Advt., U. Colo.; MBA, NYU. Past mktg. dir., new product devel. mgr. Outward Bound Sch.; past gen. mgr., exec. v.p. Am. Movie Classics Rainbow Programming Holdings, Inc., from mktg. dir. to pres. Am. Movie Classics Woodbury, NY, 1981—. Recipient Pres.'s award for contbns. to prosoc. and ednl. programming, NATAS. Mem.: NAFE, CTAM, Women in Cable. Office: Rainbow Media Svc Holdings Inc 111 Stewart Ave Bethpage NY 11714-5310

**MCENROE, MICHAEL LOUIS,** lawyer; b. July 31, 1951; s. C. Louis and Mary C. (Cain) McEnroe. BA magna cum laude, Loras Coll., 1973; JD, Creighton U., 1976. Bar: Ill. 1976, Iowa 1977, U.S. Dist. Ct. (no. dist.) Iowa 1977, U.S. Dist. Ct. (so. dist.) Iowa 1988, U.S. Supreme Ct. 1992. Assoc. McMahon & Cassel, Algona, Iowa, 1977-78; ptnr. McMahon, Cassel, McMahon, McEnroe & MacDonald, Algona, Iowa, 1979—88; judicial magistrate 3rd Judicial Dist. State of Iowa, Algona, 1981-89; ptnr. Cook, Gotsdiner, McEnroe & McCarthy, Des Moines, 1988—98; shareholder McEnroe, McCarthy & Gotsdiner PC, West Des Moines, Iowa, 1998—2004, McEnroe, Gotsdiner, Brewer, Burdette, Steinbach PC, West Des Moines, Iowa, 2005—; mem.: Polk County Bar Assn., Iowa Assn. Trial Lawyers, Iowa State Bar Assn. (mem. exec. coun. young lawyers sect. 1986—88, mem. agrl. law com. 1986—90, mem. gen. practice com. 2000—03, bd. govs. 2004—), Ill. State Bar Assn., Delta Epsilon Sigma. Democrat. Roman Catholic. Home: 700 S 32nd Ct West Des Moines IA 50265-5701 Office: McEnroe Gotsdiner Brewer Burdette and Steinbach PC 1701 48th St Ste 100 West Des Moines IA 50266-6723 E-mail: mmcenroe@mcenroelaw.com.

**MCENROE, PATRICK,** former professional tennis player, sports commentator; b. Manhasset, N.Y., July 1, 1966; s. John Patrick Sr. and Katy McEnroe. Grad., Stanford Univ. Doubles winner French Open, 1989; winner ATP tournament, Sydney, Australia, 1995. Mem. US Davis Cup team, 1993, 94, 96, captain, 2001—04; commentator CBS Sports and ESPN, 1998—; bd. dir. US Tennis Assn. 1999—2000; player, partial owner NY Sportimes, World Team Tennis; US Olympics Men's Tennis coach, Athens, Greece, 2004. Author: (books) Tennis for Dummies, 1998. Achievements include ranked 12th, US Tennis Assn.; 1991; ranked 664th, 1999. Office: Sportime at Harbor Island PO Box 783 Mamaroneck NY 10543

**MCENTEE, CHRISTINE W.,** architecture association administrator, former medical association administrator; married; 2 children. BS in Nursing, Georgetown Univ., 1977; MS in Health Adminstrn., George Washington U., 1982; student adv. exec. program, Kellogg Sch. Mgmt., Northwestern Univ. Dir., office constituency rels. Am. Hosp. Assn., 1986—90, v.p., dep. dir., fed. rels., 1990—94, exec. v.p., 1994—98; CEO Am. Coll. Cardiology, Bethesda, Md., 1998—2005; exec. v.p., CEO Am. Inst. Architects, Washington, 2006—. Named an Under 40 Mover and Shaker, Crain's Chgo. Bus., 1994; recipient Annual Achievement in Health Care Mgmt. award, Women Health Execs. Network, 1997. Mem.: Greater Washington Soc. Assn. Execs., European Soc. Cardiology (nurse fellow). Office: Am Inst Architects 1735 New York Ave NW Washington DC 20006 Office Phone: 301-897-5400.

**MCENTEE, GERALD W.,** labor union administrator; b. Phila., Jan. 11, 1935; four children. B in Econs., LaSalle Coll., 1956; postgrad., Temple U., Harvard U. With Am. Fedn. State County and Mcpl. Employees, 1973—; former leader Dist. Coun. 13 Harrisburg, Pa., union internat. v.p., mem. exec. bd., since 1974, internat. pres. Washington, 1981—; v.p., mem. exec. coun., chair polit. com. AFL-CIO. Office: AFSCME 1625 L St NW Washington DC 20036-5687

**MCENTEE, BETTY,** health facility administrator; Exec. dir. Am. SIDS Inst., Marietta, Ga. Lectr. in field. Contbr. to articles in profl. jours. Office: Am SIDS Inst 509 Augusta Dr SE Marietta GA 30067-8205 Office Phone: 770-426-8746. Office Fax: 770-426-1369.

**MCENTIRE, REBA NELL,** musician, actress; b. McAlester, Okla., Mar. 28, 1955; d. Clark Vincent and Jacqueline (Smith) McE.; m. Charlie Battles June 21, 1976 (div. 1987); m. Narvel Blackstock, 1989; 1 child, Shelby Steven McEntire Blackstock; 3 stepchildren. Student elem. edn., music, Southeastern State U., Durant, Okla., 1976. Rec. artist Mercury Records, 1978-83, MCA Records, 1984—. Achievements include Whoever's in New England (Gold award), 1986, What Am I Gonna Do About You (Gold award), 1987, Greatest Hits (Gold award, Platinum award, U.S., Can.), 1987, Merry Christmas To You, 1987, The Last One To Know (Gold award), 1988, Reba (Gold award 1988), Sweet 16 (Gold award 1989, U.S.), Rumor Has It (Gold award 1991, Platinum award 1992, Double Platinum 1992), Reba Live (Gold award 1990, Gold award 1991, Platinum award 1991), For My Broken Heart, 1991, Forever in Your Eyes, 1992, It's Your Call, 1992, Read My Mind, 1994, Starting Over, 1995, What If It's You, 1996, If You See Him, 1998, Forever Reba, 1998, Star Profile, 1999, So Good Together, 1999, I'll Be, 2001, Room to Breathe, 2003; Reba compilation video (Gold award, Platinum award 1992), Reba Live (video), 1995, What If It's You, 1996, Celebrating 20 Years (video), 1996; author: (with Tom Carter) Reba: My Story, 1994; actress: (stage) South Pacific, 2005, (films) Tremors, 1990, The Little Rascals, 1994, North, 1994, One Night at McCool's, 2000, (TV films) The Gambler Returns: The Luck of the Draw, 1991, The Man From Left Field, 1993, Is There Life Out There?, 1994, Forever Love, 1998, Secret of Giving, 1999; (TV series) Disney's Hercules, 1998, A Salute to Dustin Hoffman, 1999, Reba (also prodr.), 2001-; other TV appearances include Country Gold, 1982, Bob Hope Winterfest Christmas Show, 1987, (video) Wrestlemania VIII, 1992; appeared on TV series Evening Shade, 1993, Frasier, 1994, The Roseanne Show, 1998, One Life to Live; (host) Acad. Country Music awards, 2004. Spokesperson Middle Tenn. United Way, 1988, Nat. and State 4-H Alumni, Bob Hope's Hope for a Drug Free Am.; Nat. spokesperson Am. Lung Assn., 1990-91. Recipient numerous awards in Country music including Disting. Alumni award Southeastern State U., Female vocalist award Country Music Assn., 1984, 85, 86, 87, Grammy award for Best Country Vocal Performance, 1987, 2 Grammy nominations, 1994, Grammy award, Best Country Vocal Collaboration for "Does He Love You" with Linda Davis, 1994, Entertainer of Yr. award Country Radio Awards, 1994, Female Vocalist award, 1994; named Entertainer of Yr., Country Music Assn., 1986, Female Vocalist of Yr. Acad. Country Music, 1984, 85, 86, 87, 92, Top Female Vocalist, 1984, 85, 86, 87, 1991, 94, Am. Music award favorite female country singer, 1988, 90, 91, 92, 93, Am. Music award, 1989, 90, 91, 92, Best Album, 1991, Favorite Female Vocalist, 1994, Favorite Female Vocalist, Peoples Choice Award, 1992, Favorite Female Country Vocalist, 1992, 93, Favorite Female Vocalist, TNN Viewer's Choice Awards, 1993, Favorite Female Country Artist, Billboard, 1994, Favorite Country Album award Am. Music Awards, 1995, Favorite Female Country Vocalist, 1995, Favorite Female Artist-Country, 2004, Favorite Female Vocalist award People's Choice Awards, 1995, Top Female Vocalist of Yr. award Acad. Country Music, 1995, Entertainer of Yr. award Acad. Country Music, 1995, Favorite Female Vocalist award TNN Viewer's Choice Awards, 1995, Star on the Walk of Fame, 1999. Mem. Country Music Assn., Acad. County Music, Nat. Acad. Rec. Arts and Scis., Grand Ol' Opry, AFTRA, Nashville Songwriters Assn. Inc. Avocations: golf, shopping, being with narvel and shelby, horse racing, raising horses.

**MCEVOY, FRANCES JANE COMAN,** writer, editor; b. Phoenix, May 11, 1929; d. James Lindley Coman and Pearl Catherine Bruns; m. Joseph Francis McEvoy, Nov. 10, 1956 (dec. Oct. 1997); children: David L., Stephen C., Anne G. BA, Ariz. State U., 1951; postgrad., Boston U., 1959—60. Editor Helios Lit. Mag. Ariz. State U., Tempe, 1948—50; editor Am. Acad. Arts and Scis., Boston, 1951—52; reporter Waltham News Tribune Dailey, Mass., 1952—54, State House News Svc., Boston, 1952—55; press sec. Senator Leslie B. Cutler, Boston, 1954—55; asst. dir. publicity Boston U., 1955—56; writer features Boston Herald, 1975—80; writer, contbr. Dell Horoscope Astrologers Newsletter, 1980—98; editor Geocosmic Mag. Nat. Coun. Geocosmic Rsch., 1984—. Author: Power of Yod & Quincuux, 1998, Out of Bounds Moon and Planets, 2002; contbr. articles to jours.; portrait artist, 1970—2002. Mem. pub. rels. com. Greater Boston Com., 1954, Rep. State Com., Boston, 1955. Mem.: Women's Edn. and Ind. Union, De Cordova Mus. (Lincoln, Mass.), Boston Mus. Fine Arts, Bostonian Soc., DAR, Tenn. Hist. Soc., New Eng. Hist. and Geneal. Soc., Daus. Colonial Wars. Avocations: painting, writing, historic research. Home and Office: 209 Common St Belmont MA 02478

**MCEVOY, LORRAINE KATHERINE,** oncology nurse; b. S.I., N.Y., Mar. 24, 1950; d. Edward Donald and Josephine (Boyle) McMahon; children: Kelly Ann, Kevin Michael. RN, St. Vincent's Sch. Nursing, 1970; BSN, Seton Hall U., 1994; MSN, Kean U. N.J., 1997. RN, N.J. Staff nurse St. Joseph's Hosp. and Med. Ctr., Paterson, N.J., 1981-88, nurse mgr. oncology, bone marrow transplant, 1988—, cons., educator devel. bone marrow, stem cell and cord blood transplant programs, 1995-98. Adj. prof. Kean U., 1997-98. Recipient Disting. Alumni award Kean U., 1999; Susan G. Komen Breast Cancer Found. grantee, 1997, 98, 99. Mem. Oncology Nursing Soc., Transcultural Nursing Soc., Tri-State Bone Marrow Transplant Nurses Assn., Breast Cancer Connection, Sigma Theta Tau.

**MCEVOY, MICHAEL JOSEPH,** economist; b. Cork, Ireland, Feb. 16, 1963; came to U.S., 1991. s. Patrick Joseph and Pauline (Heffernan) McE. BA, Univ. Coll., Cork, Ireland, 1984, M in Econ. Sci., 1987; MBA, U. Penn., 1996. Rsch. economist Irish Export Bd., Dublin, 1986-87; sr. analyst economist Fixpoint Ltd., London, 1987-91; rsch. assoc. Micra, Inc., Washington, 1991-92; chief economist Embassy of France, Washington, 1992-96; dir. The Tower Group, Boston, 1996—2002; CEO Nechtain LLC, Boston, 2002—. Dir. Fixpoint Ltd., 1989-91. Co-author: (quarterly pub.) European Business: Forecasts, Strategies, Tactics, 1989-91. Sponsor and supporter animal and environ. concerns. Mem.: Nat. Economists Club, Nat. Assn. Bus. Economists, U.S. Holocaust Mem. Mus. Roman Catholic. Office Phone: 617-243-9500. Business E-Mail: mmce@nechtain.com.

**MCEVOY, SHARLENE ANN,** law educator; b. Derby, Conn., July 6, 1950; d. Peter Henry Jr. and Madaline Elizabeth (McCabe) McE. BA magna cum laude, Albertus Magnus Coll., 1972; JD, U. Conn., West Hartford, 1975; MA, Trinity Coll., Hartford, 1980, UCLA, 1982, PhD, 1985. Bar: Conn., 1975. Pvt. practice, Derby, 1984—; asst. prof. bus. law Fairfield (Conn.) U. Sch. Bus., 1986—92; adj. prof. bus. law, polit. sci. Albertus Magnus Coll., New Haven, 1978-80, U. Conn., Stamford, 1984-86; acting chmn. polit. sci. dept. Albertus Magnus Coll., 1980; assoc. prof. law Fairfield U., 1992-98, prof. bus. law, 1998—. Chmn. Women's Resource Ctr., Fairfield U., 1989-91. Staff editor Jour. Legal Studies Edn., 1989-94; reviewer Am. Bus. Law Assn. jour., 1988—, staff editor, 1995—; sr. articles editor N.E. Jour. Legal Studies in Bus., 1995-96; editor-in-chief N.E. Jour. Legal Studies, 2003—. Active Derby Tercentennial Commn., 1973—74; justice of the peace City of Derby, 1975—83; alt. mem. Parks and Recreation Commn., Woodbury, 1995—99; v.p. N.E. Acad. Legal Studies in Bus., 2001—04, pres-elect., program chair, 2003, pres., 2003—04; treas. Woodbury Dem. Town Com., 1995—96, corr. sec., 1996—98; bd. dirs. Valley Transit Dist., Derby, 1975—77. Recipient Best Paper award N.E. Regional Bus. Law Assn., 1990, Best Paper award Tri-State Regional Bus. Law Assn., 1991; Fairfield U. Sch. Bus. rsch. grantee 1989, 91, 92, Fairfield U. rsch. grantee, 1994. Mem. ABA, Conn. Bar Assn., Acad. Legal Studies in Bus., Mensa (coord. SINISTRAL spl. interest group 1977—). Democrat. Roman Catholic. Avocations: sailing, tennis, swimming. Office: 198 Emmett Ave Derby CT 06418-1258 Office Phone: 203-254-4000 ext. 2836. Business E-Mail: samcevoy@mail.fairfield.edu.

**MCEWEN, ADAM,** artist; b. 1965; BA in English Lit., Oxford U., Christ Church Coll., 1987; attended, Calif. Inst. Arts. 1991. One-man shows include Much Better, 17 Rosebery Avenue, London, 2002, Sleeper, Edinburgh, Scotland, 2002, Alessandra Bonomo Gallery, Rome, 2003, The Wrong Gallery, NY, 2003, The McAllister Inst., NY, 2003, History is a Perpetual Virgin..., Nicole Klagsrun Gallery, NY, 2004, Jack Hanley Gallery, San Francisco, 2006, exhibited in group shows at Grapeshot Bullseye Harvest, Attache Gallery, London, 2001, Free Coke, Greene Naftali Gallery, NY, 2001, Art Transplant, British Consulate in NY, 2001, Yes We're Excerpts, Andrew Kreps Gallery, NY, 2002, Happy Birthday newspaper project, Gavin Brown's Enterprise, NY, 2002, I See A Darkness, Blum & Poe, LA, 2003, Melvins, Anton Kern Gallery, NY, 2003, A Matter of Facts, Nicole Klagsbrun Gallery, NY, 2003, I Love Music, Creative Growth Gallery, Calif., 2004, The Chaim Soutine: Tattoo Project, Frieze Art Fair, London, 2004, I'll Be Your Mirror: Hotel Project at Frieze Art Fair, 2004, Situational Prosthetics, New Langton Ctr. for Arts, San Francisco, 2005, Post Notes, ICA, London, 2005, in words and pictures, Murray Guy, NY, 2005, OK/OKAY, Swiss Inst. Contemporary Art, NY, 2005, Take it Furthur, Andrew Mummery Gallery, London, 2005, Bridge Freezes Before Road, Barbara Gladstone Gallery, NY, 2005, Drunk vs. Stoned 2, Gavin Brown Enterprise, 2005, Star Star: toward the center of attention, CAC Contemporary Arts Ctr., Cin., 2005, Superstars, Kunsthalle Wien, Vienna, Austria, 2005; curator A Fete Worse Than Death, 2004, Couldn't Get Ahead, Independent Art Space, London, 2004, Power, Corruption and Lies, Roth Horowitz, NY, 2004, Interstate, Nicole Klagsbrun Gallery, NY, 2005. Mailing: c/o Nicole Klagsbrun 526 West 26th St Room 213 New York NY 10001*

**MCEWEN, ALEXANDER CAMPBELL,** legal association administrator, consultant, cadastral studies educator, former Canadian government official, land use planner; b. Ryde, Isle of Wight, Eng., Aug. 22, 1926; emigrated to Can., 1949; s. Walter Scott and Florence Lilian (Goodall) McE.; m. Patricia Stuart Richards, July 27, 1956 (div. 1988); m. Sherry Lee Wilson, June 13, 1993; children: Ann Florence, Sheila Jean, Laura Susan. LL.B., U. London, 1966, PhD, 1979; LL.M., U. East Africa, 1970. Survey adviser Govt. Can., Jesselton, 1954-56; tech. expert UN, Victoria, Seychelles, 1958-61; sr. surveyor H. Wheeler Assocs., Toronto, Ont., Can., 1961-62; sec. treas. Assn. Ont. Land Surveyors, Toronto, 1963-64; prin. Survey Tng. Centre, Dar es Salaam, Tanzania, 1964-70; survey cons. Ottawa, Ont., Can., 1970-72; dir. lands and surveys Govt. Nfld., St. John's, 1972-76; commr. Internat. Boundary Commn., Ottawa, Ont., 1976-90; survey adviser Govt. Can., Lagos, Nigeria, 1980-90; prof. cadastral studies dept. geomatics engring. U. Calgary, Alta., Canada, 1991—96; survey cons. Can. Exec. Svc. Orgn., La Paz, Bolivia, 2002—03; pvt. practice Calgary, Canada, 2004—. Cons. in field. Author: International Boundaries of East Africa, 1971 In Search of the Highlands, 1988; contbr. articles to profl. jours. Served with Royal Armoured Corp. Mem. Can. Inst. Geomatics (mem. coun. 1977-81, 97-2002, Jim Jones award 1967, 83, 90, 99, Presdl. citation 1981), Western Can. Bd. Examiners for Land Surveyors (registrar, bd. dirs. 1991-96), Assn. Ont. Land Surveyors (sec.-treas. 1963-64), Assn. Nfld. Land Surveyors (bd. examiners 1975-76). Home: 2129 2d Ave NW Calgary AB Canada T2N OG8 Office Phone: 403-283-9087. Personal E-mail: amcewen@telusplanet.net.

**MCEWEN, BRUCE SHERMAN,** neuroscientist, educator; b. Jan. 17, 1938; AB summa cum laude, Oberlin Coll., 1959; PhD in Cell Biology, Rockefeller U., 1964. Postdoctoral fellow Inst. of Neurobiology, Goteborg, Sweden, 1964—65; asst. prof. Dept. Zoology, U. Minn., 1966, Rockefeller U., NYC, 1966—71, assoc. prof., 1971—73; prof., head Harold & Margaret Milliken Hatch Lab. of Neuroendocrinology, 1981—; assoc. dean grad. and post-grad. studies, 1985—91, 1993—94, dean, 1991—93, faculty chair Sci. Outreach Program, 1992—; Alfred E. Mirsky prof., 1999—. Mem. MacArthur Found. Socioeconomic Status and Health Rsch. Network, 1996—. Co-author: The Hostage Brain, 1994; contbr. articles to profl. jours.; mem. editl. bd. Brain Rsch., 1972—, Jour. of Neuroendocrinology, 1989—95, assoc. editor Jour. of Neuroscience, 1989—98. Recipient Jacob Javits Award, MERIT Award. Fellow: AAAS, NY Acad. Scis., Am. Acad. Arts and Scis.; mem.: NAS, Internat. Soc. for Psychoneuroendocrinology, Internat. Soc. for Neurochemistry, Internat. Brain Rsch. Orgn., Endocrine Soc., Am. Soc. for Neurochemistry, Am. Assn. of Biological Chemists, Inst. Medicine, Internat. Soc. of Neuroendocrinology (pres. 1992—95), Soc. for Neuroscience (pres. 1996—97, pres.-elect, pres., past pres. 1996—99), Sigma Xi, Phi Beta Kappa. Office: Rockefeller U Lab Neuroendocrinology 1230 York Ave New York NY 10021-6399                Office                Fax:                212-327-8634.                E-mail: mcewen@mail.rockefeller.edu.

**MCEWEN, CRAIG A.,** dean; AB, Oberlin Coll.; MA, PhD, Harvard U. Mem. faculty Bowdoin Coll., Brunswick, Maine, 1975—, Daniel B. Fayerweather prof. polit. economy and sociology; dean acad. affairs. Mediator Ct. Mediaton Svc., Maine. Author (with Nancy Rogers): Mediation: Law, Policy and Practice. Home: 15 Baxter Ln Brunswick ME 04011 Office: Bowdoin Coll 5800 College Sta Brunswick ME 04011-8449

**MCEWEN, LAURA,** publishing executive; m. James McEwen; 1 child, Sean. BA. Fordham U. Pub. New Woman, Snow Country Mag.; sr. pub. Harpers Bazaar, Family Circle; pub. YM Mag., 2000—03; v.p., pub. dir. Readers Digest Mag., 2003—. Mem., planning com. Mag. Pub. of Am., 2003. Mem.: Fragrance Found., N.Y. Advt. Club, Advt. Women of N.Y., Fashion Group Internat. (bd. dirs.), Cosmetic Exec. Women (bd. dirs.). Office: Readers Digest Mag Box 200 Pleasantville NY 10572-0200 Office Fax: 914-244-7599, 212-850-7275, 914-238-4559. E-mail: laura_mcewen@rd.com.*

**MCFADDEN, CORI ERIN,** psychotherapist, educator; b. Woodbury, N.J., Feb. 25, 1975; d. John Thomas and Linnea Maska McFadden; m. Paul Edward McMahon, June 14, 2003. MA in clin. Counseling Psychology, La Salle U., Phila., 2001; PsyD in Clin. Psychology, La Salle U., 3Phila., 2003. Staff clinician, psychotherapist Cmty. Treatment Solutions, Moorestown, NJ, 2003—05, interim dir., 2005; psychotherapist Friends Hosp., Phila., 2005; psychology prof. - part time La Salle U., Phila., 2002—; adj. faculty psychology. Assessment lab coord.; admissions counselor. Mem. Rebuilding Together of Gloucester County, NJ; alumni coun. chairperson Friends Sch., Mullica Hill, NJ, 2004—06. Recipient Grad. Student of the Yr., La Salle U. Dept. of Grad. Psychology, 2001. Mem.: APA (assoc.), Pa. Psychol. Assn. (assoc.), Assn. for Behavior and Cognitive Therapy (assoc.), Rotary Internat. Wooddbury Breakfast Club, Psi Chi (life). Independent. Avocations: travel, art museums, bicycling. Office: La Salle University 1900 West Olney Ave Philadelphia PA 19141 Office Phone: 215-951-1270. Personal E-mail: coridoc@aol.com. E-mail: mcfadden@lasalle.edu.

**MCFADDEN, CYNTHIA GRAHAM,** news correspondent, journalist; b. Lewiston, Maine, May 27, 1956; d. Warren Graham and Arlene McFadden; m. James Hoge (div.); 1 child; m. Michael Davies, 1998 (div.). BA summa cum laude, Bowdoin Coll., 1978; JD, Columbia U., 1984. Exec. prodr. Media and Soc. Columbia U., NYC, 1984-90; sr. prodr., anchor Court TV, NYC, 1990-94; legal corr. ABC News, NYC, 1994—96, sr. legal corr., 1996—, corr. PrimeTime Live, 1996—2004, co-anchor PrimeTime, 2004—, co-anchor Nightline, 2005—. Mem. gov. bd. dirs. Bowdoin Coll., Brunswick, Maine, 1989-95. Recipient Woman of Distinction award Crohns and Colitis Found. Am., 1997, George Foster Peabody award, six CINE Golden Eagle awards, Ohio State award, two Silver Gavel awards ABA, 1987-88, Grand award N.Y. Film Festival, Blue Ribbon Am. Film Festival, Dupont Award, 2001-02, Emmy, Fgn. Press Club award Mem.: Phi Beta Kappa. Office: ABC News 147 Columbus Ave New York NY 10023-5999

**MCFADDEN, DANIEL LITTLE,** economist, educator; b. Raleigh, NC, July 29, 1937; s. Robert S. and Alice (Little) McFadden; m. Beverlee Tito Simboli, Dec. 15, 1962; children: Nina, Robert, Raymond. BS in physics, U. Minn., 1957, PhD in econs., 1962; LLD, U. Chgo., 1992; degree (hon.), U. Coll. London, 2003; PhD in Sci. (hon.), No. Carolina St. Univ., 2006. Asst. prof. econs. U. Pitts., 1962-63, U. Calif., Berkeley, 1963—66, assoc. prof. econs, 1966—66, prof., 1968—79, E. Morris Cox Chair, prof. econs. Coll. Letters & Sci., 1991—, dir. Econometrics Lab., 1991—95, 1996—, chmn. dept. of econ., 1995—96; vis. assoc. prof. U. Chgo., 1966—67; Irving Fisher research prof. Yale U., New Haven, 1977—78; prof. econs. MIT, Cambridge, Mass., 1978—91; James R. Killian Chair, 1984—91, dir. Stats. Rsch. Ctr. Cambridge, Mass., 1986—88; Sherman Fairchild Prosthetics, Scholar Calif. Inst. Tech., 1990. Mem. econs. adv. panel NSF, 1969—71, Univs. Nat. Bur., 1974—77; chmn. NSF-NBER Conf. Econs. of Uncertainty, 1970—; bd. dirs. Nat. Bur. Econ. Rsch., 1976—77, 1980—83; mem. book com. Sloan Found., 1977—79; mem. rev. com. Calif. Energy Com. Forecasts, 1979; chmn. awards com. AEA, 1981—84. Editor: Jour. Statis. Physics, 1968—70,

Econmeteric Soc. monographs, 1980—83; mem. bd. editors Am. Econ. Rev., 1971—74, Jour. Math. Econs., 1973—77, Transp. Rsch., 1978—80; assoc. editor: Jour. Econometrics, 1977—78; adv. com. Jour. Applied Econs. 1996—; co-editor: Essays on Economic Behavior Under Uncertainty, 1974, Production Economics, Vols. I and II, 1978, Structural Analysis of Discrete Data with Econometric Applications, 1981, Preferences, Uncertainty, and Optimality, 1990, Handbook of Econometrics Vol. IV, 1994; co-author: Urban Travel Demand: A Behavioral Analysis, 1975, Microeconomic Modeling and Policy Analysis, 1984. Mem. adv. com. Transp. Models Project, Met. Transp. Commn., 1975, City of Berkeley Coordinated Transit Project, 1975—76. Recipient Outstanding Tchr. Award, MIT, 1981, Nobel Prize in Econs., 2000, Nemmers prize in Econs., Northwestern U., 2000, Richard Stone prize in Applied Econs., Jour. Applied Econmtrics, 2000—01; Ford Found. Behavioral Sci. Fellow, 1958—62, Earhart Fellow, 1960—61, Mellon Post-Doctoral Fellow, 1962—63, Ford Faculty Rsch. Fellow, 1966—67. Mem.: NAS (mem. com. basic rsch. social scis. 1982—87, mem. com. energy demand modelling 1983—84, mem. commn. behavioral and social scis. and edn. 1989—94, mem. commn. sci. engring., pub. policy 1995—), chair sect. 54 econ. scis. 2003—, chair com. forecasting demand/supply of doctoral scientists and engrs. 1997—2000), Am. Phil. Soc., Transp. Rsch. Bd. (mem. exec. com. 1975—78), Math. Assn. Am., Am. Statis. Assn., Econometrics Soc. (Fisher-Schultz lectr. 1979, mem. exec. com. 1983—86, v.p. 1984, pres. 1985, fellow 1969, Frisch Medal 1986), Am. Econ. Assn. (mem. exec. com. 1985—87, v.p. 1994, pres.-elect 2004, John Bates Clark Medal 1975), Am. Acad. Arts and Scis. Democrat. Avocations: bicycling, tennis, squash, sailing, skiing. Office: U Calif Berkeley Dept Econs 549 Evans Hall # 3880 Berkeley CA 94720-3880 Office Phone: 510-643-8428. Office Fax: 510-642-0638. Business E-Mail: mcfadden@econ.berkeley.edu.*

**MCFADDEN, DAVID MICHAEL,** music educator, director; b. Corbin, Ky., Dec. 10, 1969; s. Arnold Gale and Carolyn McFadden. MusB in Edn., Ea. Ky. U., 1994, MusM, 1998, MA in Ednl. Adminstrn., 2004. Cert. Music Edn. Tchr. (kindergarten through twelfth grade) Ky., 1994. Band dir. Bell County HS, Pineville, Ky., 1994—96, Casey County Schs., Liberty, Ky., 1996—2001, North Laurel HS, London, Ky., 2001—. Pres. Bluegrass All-Regional Band, Ky., 2006. Named a Ky. Col., Ky. Gov., 1999; recipient Golden Apple awards, Ashland Oil, Inc, 1998; Am. Legacies fellow, Ky. Hist. Soc., 2002—. Mem.: Ky. Music Educators Assn. (dist. pres. 2004—, mem. festival commn. 2005—). Home: 78 Catalpa Ct London KY 40744 Office: North Laurel High Sch 1300 E Hal Rogers Pky London KY 40741 Home Fax: 606-862-4702; Office Fax: 606-862-4702. Personal E-mail: neonconductor@adelphia.net. Business E-Mail: david.mcfadden@laurel.kyschools.us.

**MCFADDEN, DENNIS,** psychologist, educator; b. Oakland, Calif., Oct. 2, 1940; s. Samuel John and Evelyn (Dinnerson) McF.; m. Nancy L. Wilson, Dec. 28, 1960; children: Tracie Ann, Devin James. BA, Sacramento State Coll., 1962; PhD, Ind U., 1967. Asst. prof. U. Tex., Austin, 1967-72, assoc. prof., 1972-77, prof., 1977—, Piper prof., 1987, Ashbel Smith prof., 1998—. Contbr. articles to profl. jours. Recipient Jacob K. Javits Neurosci. Investigator award, NIH, 1984-89, Claude Pepper award of Excellence, 1989-91; NIH grantee. Fellow AAAS, Acoustical Soc. Am., Am. Psychol. Soc.; mem. Assn. for Rsch. in Otolaryngology, Com. Hearing, Bioacoustics and Biomechanics (NAS-NRC com. on hearing, bioacoustics and biomechanics), Soc. Neurosci., Soc. for Behavioral Neuroendocrinology, Internat. Acad. for Sex Rsch., Orgn. for Study of Sex Differences. Avocations: jogging, bicycling, birdwatching, travel. Office: U Tex Dept Psychology 1 University Station Seay Bldg A 8000 Austin TX 78712-0187 Business E-Mail: mcfadden@psy.utexas.edu.

**MCFADDEN, FRANK HAMPTON,** lawyer, former judge; b. Oxford, Miss., Nov. 20, 1925; s. John Angus and Ruby (Roy) McF.; m. Jane Porter Nabers, Sept. 30, 1960; children— Frank Hampton, Angus Nabers, Jane Porter. BA, U. Miss., 1950; LL.B., Yale U., 1955. Bar: N.Y. 1956, Ala. 1959. Assoc. firm Lord, Day & Lord, N.Y.C., 1955-58, Bradley, Arant, Rose & White, Birmingham, Ala., 1958-63, partner, 1963-69; judge U.S. Dist. Ct. No. Dist. Ala., Birmingham, 1969-73, chief judge, 1973-81; sr. v.p., gen. counsel Blount. Inc., Montgomery, Ala., 1982-91, exec. v.p. adminstrn. and govt. affairs, 1991, exec. v.p. legal affairs, 1991-93, exec. v.p., gen. counsel, 1993-95; mem. Capell & Howard, P.C., Montgomery, 1995—. Chmn. Blount Energy Resource Corp., Montgomery, 1983-88. Mem. jud. panel CPR Inst. for Dispute Resolution, 1985—. Served from ensign to lt. USNR, 1944-49, 51-53. Fellow Am. Coll. Constrn. Lawyers; mem. Am. Corp. Counsel Assn. (bd. dirs. 1984-93, chmn. 1989). Office: Capell & Howard PC 150 S Perry St Montgomery AL 36104-4227 Office Phone: 334-241-8041. Business E-Mail: fhm@chlaw.com.

**MC FADDEN, GEORGE LINUS,** retired army officer; b. Sharon, Pa., Oct. 16, 1927; s. George Linus and Frances Jane (Byrne) McF.; m. Floretta Theresa McFadden, Nov. 20, 1948; children: Kenneth William, Mark Edward (dec.), Mary Kathleen, Robert Bernard, George Linus, William. BE, U. Omaha, Nebr., 1961; MS, George Washington U., Washington, 1967; grad., Advanced Mgmt. Program Harvard U., Cambridge, Mass., 1971. Pvt. U.S. Army, 1946, advanced through grades to maj. gen., 1976; comdg. officer (7th inf. div. arty.), Korea, 1969-70; dep. comdg. gen. U.S. Army Security Agy., Arlington, Va., 1972-74; dep. dir. for field mgmt. and evaluation, dep. chief central security service Fort George G. Meade, Md., 1975-78; dep. dir. ops. Nat. Security Agy., 1978-79; comdg. gen. U.S. Army So. European Task Force, Vicenza, Italy, 1979-82; comp. v.p. CompDyne Corp., 1986-89; sr. v.p. The Abbott Group, Inc., Annapolis, Md., 1989-90; dir. Washington Studies and Analysis Group McDonnell Douglas Corp., 1985-86; dir. security affairs Dept. Energy, 1990-97, cons., 1999—. Pres., chmn. bd. Met. Washington chpt. Arthritis Found., 1986-95. Decorated D.F.C., D.S.M., Silver Star, Bronze Star, Purple Heart, others. Roman Catholic. Personal E-mail: mcfaddengl@verizon.net.

**MC FADDEN, JOSEPH MICHAEL,** historian, educator; b. Joliet, Ill., Feb. 12, 1932; s. Francis Joseph and Lucille (Allen) McF.; m. Theresa Cardwell, Oct. 11, 1958; children: Timothy Joseph, Mary Colleen, Jonathan Andrew. BA, Lewis Coll., 1954; MA, U. Chgo., 1961; PhD, No. Ill. U., 1968. Tchr. history Joliet Cath. High Sch., 1957-60; mem. faculty history dept. Lewis Coll., Lockport, Ill., 1960-70, assoc. prof., 1967-70, v.p. acad. affairs, 1968-70; prof. history, dean sch. Nat. and Social Sci., Kearney (Nebr.) State Coll., 1970-74; prof. history, dean Sch. Social and Behavioral Scis., Slippery Rock (Pa.) State Coll., 1974-77; pres. No. State Coll., Aberdeen, SD, 1977-82, U. S.D., Vermillion, 1982-88, U. St. Thomas, Houston, 1988-97, pres. emeritus, prof. history, 1997—. Served with USNR, 1954-56. Roman Catholic. Office: U St Thomas Office of Pres 3812 Montrose Blvd Houston TX 77006-4626 Office Phone: 713-942-5905. Business E-Mail: mcfadden@stthom.edu.

**MCFADDEN, LEE VERNON,** religious organization administrator; b. Manning, S.C., Jan. 5, 1968; s. Daisy Rena and Aaron McFadden; m. Landa LaYota Montgomery, July 22, 2001; children: Ricky Antonio Montgomery-McFadden, Lee Vernon Jr., Aliaya Chanell, Destiny Le'anda. B in Bus. Adminstrn., Trinity U., Sioux Falls, S.D., 1999. Founder, CEO Youth Ministry Tng. Corps, Sumter, SC, 1996—. Prodr.(composer,singer,choreographer): Testimony. Musician St. Mark Bapt. Ch., Silver, SC, 2006—06. Recipient Dedication and Leadership to Youths award, 2005. Mem.: Alpha Phi Omega. Office: Youth Ministry Tng Corps 2245 Stadium Rd Sumter SC 29154 Office Phone: 803-481-4882. Personal E-mail: flevmcfadden@yahoo.com.

**MCFADDEN, MARY JOSEPHINE,** fashion industry executive; b. NYC, Oct. 1, 1938; d. Alexander Bloomfield and Mary Josephine (Cutting) McF.; m. Philip Harari; 1 child, Justine. Student, Sorbonne, Paris, Traphagen Sch. Design, 1957, Columbia, 1959-62; DFA, Internat. Fine Arts Coll., 1984. Pub. rels. dir. Christian Dior, N.Y.C., 1962—64; merchandising editor Vogue South Africa, 1964—65, editor, 1965—69; polit. and travel columnist Rand (South Africa) Daily Mail, 1965—68; founder sculptural workshop Vukutu, Zimbabwe, 1968—70; spl. projects editor Vogue U.S.A., 1973; pres. Mary McFadden, Inc., N.Y.C., 1976—; ptnr. MMcF Collection by Mary McFadden.

1991—. Bd. dirs., advisor Sch. Design and Merchandising Kent State U., Eugene O'Neill Meml. Theatre Ctr.; mem. profl. com. Cooper-Hewitt Mus., Smithsonian Inst., Nat. Mus. of Design; designer Collection by Mary McFadden, 2000, Mary McFadden Collection, 2003, Earth-BOUND, N.Y.C., 2003; lectr. U. Phila., 2004, Dept. Ancient Near Eastern Art, Met. Mus. Art, 2004, Sackler Mus., Japan Soc., 2004, U. Archeology and Anthropology, Pa., 2005, Newark Mus., 2005, Freer Gallery, 2006, RMA, N.Y., 2006, Parrish Mus., 2006, CUNY Grad. Sch., 2006, Phipps Westbury Gardens, 2006, Rubin Mus., Queens Coll., NYC, others. Fashion and jewelry designer, 1973—; maj. retrospective of fashion, textiles and jewels at Allentown (Pa.) Art Mus., 2004; author introduction Mary McFadden High Priestess of High Fashion, 2004; artist (exhbn.) Dixon Mus. and Garden, Memphis, 2005. Advisor Nat. Endowment for Arts; active local Police Athletic League, We Care About N.Y., CFDA-Vogue Breast Cancer Initiative, Beth Israel Hosp., The Chemotherapy Found.; curator emeritus Lannan Found., 1973-85; founding trustee Robert Redford's Sundance Inst., 1978-83; trustee Devi Ahilya Bai Holkal Meml. Charitable Trust, Maheshwar, Indore, India. Recipient Am. Fashion Critics award-Coty award, 1976, 78, 79, Audemars Piguet Fashion award, 1976, Rex award, 1977, award More Coll. Art, 1977, Pa. Gov.'s award, 1977, Roscoe award, 1978, Pres.'s Fellows award RISD, 1979, Neiman-Marcus award of excellence, 1979, Design Excellence award Pratt Inst., 1993, award N.Y. Landmarks Conservancy, 1994, NU Breed Fashion award, 1996, Marymount Coll. Fashion award, 1996, Legends award N.Y., 2001, Lifetime Achievement award South Am. Press Assn., Miami, Fla., 2002, Pratt Legions award, 2002, Spirit of Design award Phila. U., 2004; named to Fashion Hall of Fame, 1979; fellow RISD. Mem. Fashion Group (bd. dirs. 1981-82), Council of Fashion Designers Am. (past pres., I Can award). Office: Mary McFadden Inc 525 E 72nd St New York NY 10021 E-mail: mcfcouture@aol.com.

**MCFADDEN, NANCY ELIZABETH,** lawyer; b. Wilmington, Del., Oct. 20, 1958; d. William P. and Mary Elizabeth (Adams) McF. BA, San Jose State U., 1984; JD, U. Va., 1987. Judicial clk. Hon. John P. Wiese U.S. Claims Ct., Washington, 1987-88; atty. O'Melveny & Myers, Washington, 1988-91; deputy communications dir. Office of Pres.-Elect, Washington, 1992-93; asst. atty. gen. U.S. Dept. Justice, Washington, 1993, prin. deputy assoc. atty. gen., 1993-95; gen. counsel Dept. Transp., Washington, 1996—. Nat. deputy polit. dir. Clinton for Pres. Campaign, 1992, nat. surrogate dir. Clinton-Gore for Pres. Campaign, 1992.

**MCFADDEN, P. MICHAEL,** physician, surgeon; b. Hobbs, N.Mex., June 16, 1946; s. Paul Marion and Venita Lenora (Bowen) McF.; m. Jennifer Marie James, Apr. 8, 1990; children: Heather Anne, Jennifer Suzanne, Bryn Ellen, Callan Michael. BS, La. State U., 1968; MD, Tulane U., 1974. Diplomate Am. Bd. Surgery, Am. Bd. Thoracic Surgery. Surg. intern, resident Tulane U. Sch. Medicine, New Orleans, 1974-79, instr. surgery, 1974-79; resident in thoracic surgery Ochsner Clinic, New Orleans, 1979-81; cardiovascular and thoracic surgeon Stanford (Calif.) U. Hosp., 1981-91; chief cardiovascular surgery Palo Alto (Calif.) Med. Clinic, 1983-91; cardiovascular and thoracic surgeon Ochsner Clinic, 1991—, surg. dir. lung transplantation, 1991—, dir. thoracic surgery program, 1998—; clin. prof. surgery Tulane U. Sch. Medicine, 1991—. Contbr. articles to profl. jours. Bd. dirs. YMCA, Palo Alto area, 1988-91; bd. dirs. U. Tulane Health Svcs., 2006—. Capt USNR, 1984-94. Fellow ACS, Am. Coll. Cardiology, Am. Coll. Chest Physicians; mem. AMA, Alton Ochsner Surg. Soc., Am. Assn. for Thoracic Surgery, Am. Soc. Vascular Surgery, Am. Heart Assn. (coun. on cardiovascular surgery), Assn. Mil. Surgeons U.S., Internat. Soc. for Cardiovascular Surgery, Internat. Soc. for Heart and Lung Transplantation, New Orleans Surg. Soc., Norman E. Shumway Surg. Soc., Orleans Parish Med. Soc., Pacific Coast Surg. Assn., So. Surg. Assn., So. Thoracic Surg. Assn., Southeastern Surg. Congress, So. Med. Assn., Surg. Assn. La., Thoracic Surgery Found., Tulane Surg. Soc., Tulane U. Med. Alumni Assn., Western Thoracic Surg. Assn., Alpha Omega Alpha, Alpha Epsilon Delta, Nu Sigma Nu, Kappa Alpha. Republican. Presbyterian. Office: Ochsner Clinic Dept Surgery Divsn Cardiothoracic Surg 1514 Jefferson Hwy New Orleans LA 70121-2483 Home: 9 Blanc Pl New Orleans LA 70115-4102 Office Phone: 504-842-4251. E-mail: mmcfadden@ochsner.org.

**MCFADDEN, PETER WILLIAM,** retired mechanical engineering educator; b. Stamford, Conn., Aug. 2, 1932; s. Kenneth E. and Marie (Gleason) McF.; children: Peter, Kathleen, Mary. BSME, U. Conn., 1954, MS, 1956; PhD, Purdue U., 1959. Registered profl. engr., Ind. Asst. instr. U. Conn., 1954-56, prof. mech. engring., 1971-98, dean Sch. Engring., 1971-85, dir. devel., 1985-88, provost, v.p., 1988, exec. asst. to pres., exec. sec. to bd. trustees, 1989-98; mem. faculty Purdue U., 1956-71; prof. mech. engring., head Purdue U. (Sch. Mech. Engring.), 1965-71; postdoctoral research Swiss Fed. Inst., Zurich, 1960-61. Cons. to industry, 1959-98. Achievements include research in cryogenics, heat transfer, mass transfer.

**MCFADDEN, ROBBYN KILBANE,** interior designer, public policy specialist, artist, advocate; b. Chgo., Oct. 5, 1951; d. Robert Harrison and Adrienne Fay (Seyring) Kilbane; m. James E. McFadden Jr., Dec. 20, 1975; 1 child, Ryan James. BFA, U. Ill., 1969-74; Diploma in Interior Design, Harper Coll., Chgo., 1976. Designer Euromarket Designs, 1978-83; project cons. Volo Interiors, 1983-90; educator, art and design dept. Coll. of Lake County, 1981-83; owner, prin. Design Perspectives, 1983—. Design cons. Law Offices of Patricia Hogan, Monadnock Bldg., Chgo., 1989; project designer retail space Historic Harbor House, Waukegan, Ill., 1988, others. Pub. design commns. include Hunterdon Art Ctr. Archival Print System, 1994, Cleve. Edn. Fund. Historic Dallas Bldg., 1998, Kids First Festival, Lake County, Ill., 1998, numerous others; pvt. commns. include residences in Ill., N.J., Ohio, Calif. & England. Mem. adv. com. to internat. programs LWV USA, Washington, 1994—; nat. bd. dirs. UNIFEM/UN Devel. Fund for Women, N.Y.C., 1999-2004; fundraiser, pub. policy advocate Ctr. for the Humanities and Environment, Jackson Hole, Wyo., 1992-95; adv. mem., cons. Com. for Pub. Art, Cleve., 1995-97; vis. svcs. cons. Art Inst. Chgo., 2003—; specialist advisor Lake County Women's Coalition Arts, 2003—; mem. women's bd. Hist. Genesee Theater, Lake County, Ill. Recipient Carrie Chapman Catt award LWV, Cleve., 1998. Mem. LWV (bd. dirs., Ill. chpt., Lake County pres. 2003-05), Consultive Delegate UN Conf. on Status of Women, 2005, Am. Soc. Interior Designers (allied) Interior Design Soc. Nat. Home Furnishings Assn., PEO, Lake County Dem. Women (bd. mem., 2006). Avocations: painting, golf. Personal E-mail: indezyn@aol.com.

**MCFADDEN, ROBERT DENNIS,** reporter; b. Milw., Feb. 11, 1937; s. Francis Joseph and Violet (Charleston) McF.; m. Judith Marian Silverman, June 20, 1971; 1 son, Nolan Seth. BS cum laude, U. Wis., 1960. Reporter Wis. Rapids Daily Tribune, 1957-58, Wis. State Jour., Madison, 1958-59, Cin. Enquirer, 1960-61; sr. writer, reporter N.Y. Times, 1961—. Mem. adv. coun. St. John's U. dept journalism, 1996—. Co-author: No Hiding Place, 1981, Outrage: The Story Behind the Tawana Brawley Hoax, 1990. With U.S. Army, 1960—61, with USAR, 1968—. Recipient Pulitzer Prize for Spot News Reporting (N.Y. Times team), 1996; (individual) 1996; Byline award N.Y. Press Club, 1973, 74, 80, 87, 89, 92, Page One award Newspaper Guild N.Y., 1978, Spot News award Uniformed Firemen's Assn., 1967, Spot News award L.I. Press Club, 1984, 95, Chancellor's award for Disting. Svc. U. Wis., 1987, Man of Yr. award Alumni N.Y., 1997, Excellence in Local Reporting award N.Y. Newpaper Publishers Assn., 1988, Spot News award N.Y. Newspaper Publishers Assn., 1988, Spot News award N.Y. State Associated Press, 1989, 91, Continuing Coverage award, 1995, 99, In Depth Reporting award, 1989, 91, Feature Writing award, 1996, Ochs Prize in Journalism, 1989, Best News/Feature Story award Internat. Assn. Fire Fighters, 1991, Nat. Spot News award Asian-Am. Journalists Assn., 1994, Comprehensive Reporting award, N.Y. Uniformed Fire Officers Assn., 1995. Mem. N.Y. Soc. Silurians (Spot News Story award 1977, 2001, Peter Kihss award 1987, Investigative reporting award 1989, Excellence in Journalism award 1994, President's award, 2006, gov. 1988—). Office: NY Times 229 W 43rd St New York NY 10036-3959

**MCFADDEN, THOMAS,** academic administrator; b. NYC, Nov. 12, 1935; m. Monica A. Dowdall; children: Monica, David. BA, Cathedral Coll., 1957; STL, Gregorian U., 1961; STD, Cath. U., 1963. Asst. prof. St. Joseph's Coll., Bklyn., 1963-66; chmn. theology dept. Cathedral Coll., Douglaston, NY, 1966-68; asst. prof. Loyola Coll., Balt., 1968-69; prof. St. Joseph's U., Phila., 1970-82, dean Coll. Arts & Scis., 1982-87; acad. v.p. St. John Fisher Coll., Rochester, NY, 1987-92; pres. Marymount Coll., Calif., 1992—. Vis. prof. Cath. U., Washington, 1967-68, LaSalle U., Phila., summer 1974-76. Author, editor: New Cath. Ency., 1974, 79l editor: Dictionary of Religion, 3 vols., 1979, Liberation, Revolution and Freedom, 1975, America in Theological PErspective, 1976. Recipient Disting. Teaching award Lindback, 1978, N.Y. State Excelsior award Bd. Examiners, 1991; HEW grantee, 1972, CAPHE grantee, 1985. Mem. AAUP, Coll. Theology Soc. (chmn. pubs. com. 1973-77). Democrat. Roman Catholic. Office: Marymount Coll 30800 Palos Verdes Dr E Rancho Palos Verdes CA 90275-6273 Business E-Mail: tmcfadden@marymountpv.edu.

**MCFADIN, HELEN LOZETTA,** retired elementary school educator; b. Tucumcari, N.Mex., Sept. 7, 1923; d. Henry J. and LaRue Altha (Ford) Stockton; m. John Reece McFadin, July 3, 1946; 1 child, Janice Lynn McFadin Koenig. AB in Edn./Psychology, Highlands U., Las Vegas, N.Mex., 1956; MA in Teaching, N.Mex. State U., 1968; postgrad., U. N.D., 1965, St. Leo's Coll., St. Leo, Fla., 1970. Cert. tchr., K-12 reading/psychology specialist, N.Mex. Tchr. 1st and 2d grades Grant County Schs., Bayard, N.Mex., 1943-44; tchr. 4th grade Durango (Colo.) Pub. Schs., 1946-48; tchr. 2d grade Artesia Pub. Schs., Loco Hills, N.Mex., 1955; tchr. 3d grade Alamogordo (N.Mex.) Pub. Schs., 1957-66, h.s. reading specialist, 1966-72, elem. reading specialist, 1972-77, tchr. 4th grade, 1977-82, reading tchr. 7th grade, dept. chair, 1982-87; ret, N.Mex State U., Alamogordo, 1987, instr. edn., 1987-90. Organizer reading labs. h.s., elem. schs., Alamogordo, 1966-77, designer programs and curriculum, 1957-89; presenter/cons. in field; cons. Mary Kay Cosmetics; rep. Excel Telecomms., Inc. Contbr. articles to profl. jours. Local and dist. judge spelling bees and sci. fairs Alamogordo Pub. Schs., 1987-98. Recipient Literacy award Otero County Reading Coun., 1986; named to Women's Hall of Fame, Alamogordo Women's Clubs, 1989. Mem. Am. Bus. Women's Assn. (pres. 1986-87, v.p. local chpt. 1999-00, named Woman of the Yr. 1988, 2003), NEA (del. 1957-87, Dedicated Svc. award 1987), N.Mex. Edn. Assn., Internat. Reading Assn. (mem. Spl. League of the Honored 1985, pres. 1975-76), N.Mex. Reading Assn. (bd. dirs. 1988-94, del. to 1st Russian reading conf. 1992, Dedicated Svc. award 1994), Tularosa Basin Hist. Soc., Beta Sigma Phi (pres. local chpt. 1998-99, formed new master chpt. 1999, Golden Cir. Anniversary award 2002), Kappa Kappa Iota (local pres. Kappa Conclave 1998-00, state officer, nat. com., co-chair nat. conv. 2000-02, Disting. Educator Emeritus Cert. of Merit 1988, VIP award 2000, 2002). Republican. Baptist. Avocations: reading, fashion modeling. Home: 2364 Union Ave Alamogordo NM 88310-3848

**MCFALL, CATHERINE GARDNER,** poet, critic, educator; b. Jacksonville, Fla., July 10, 1952; d. Albert Dodge and Joan (Livingston) McF.; m. Peter Forbes Olberg, Oct. 21, 1978; 1 child, Amanda Olberg. Baccalaureat, U. Paris, 1973; AB magna cum laude, Wheaton Coll., Norton, Mass., 1974; MA, Johns Hopkins U., 1975; PhD, NYU, 1990. Editl. asst., short story editor Ladies' Home Jour., N.Y.C., 1975-77; adminstrv. dir. Poetry Soc. Am., N.Y.C., 1981-83; instr. writing NYU, N.Y.C., 1983-87, asst. dir. Poetics Inst., 1984-86; asst. prof. humanities Cooper Union, N.Y.C., 1990-98. Adj. asst. prof. English, Hunter Coll., N.Y.C. Author: Jonathan's Cloud, 1986, Discovery, 1989 (Nation award), Naming the Animals, 1994, The Pilot's Daughter, 1996; editor: Made with Words, 1998; contbr. poetry and revs. to mags. including Paris Rev., Atlantic Monthly, N.Y. Times, others. Bd. dirs. Yaddo, 2003—. MacDowell Colony fellow, 1980, 86, Yaddo fellow, 1981, 84, 91, 93, 97, 99, Nat. Arts Club Poetry scholar Bread Loaf Writers Conf., 1983. Mem. MLA, Poets and Writers, Poetry Soc. Am.

**MCFALL, DONALD BEURY,** lawyer; b. Charleston, W.Va., Aug. 2, 1941; s. Henry Tucker and Elizabeth Katharine (Beury) McF.; m. Donna Glenn Binion, May 27, 1972; children: Katharine Atkinson, Mary Crawford. BA, Washington and Lee U., 1964, JD, 1969. Bar: Va. 1969, Tex. 1969, U.S. Supreme Ct. 1979, U.S. Dist. Ct. (we., no., so, and ea. dists.) Tex. 1969. Asst. U.S. atty. U.S. Dept. Justice, Houston, 1970-71; assoc. Butler & Binion, Houston, 1971-77, ptnr., 1977-85, McFall, Sherwood & Sheehy, Houston, 1985-2000; shareholder McFall, Sherwood & Breitbeil, P.C., Houston, 2000—. Trustee Humana Hosp.-Sharpstown, Houston, 1984—85, Southmore Med. Ctr., Houston, 1994—98; bd. dirs. Planned Parenthood Houston and S.E. Tex., 1978—87; trustee Woodberry Forest Sch., Orange, Va., 1984—90, Washington and Lee U., 1997—2006. Lt. U.S. Army, 1964—66. Named Super Lawyer, Tex. Monthly Mag., 2003—, Houston's Top Lawyers, Tex. Mag., 2004. Fellow: Internat. Soc. Barristers, Am. Coll. Trial Lawyers, Houston Bar Found., Tex. Bar Found.; mem.: Tex. Assn. Def. Counsel, Am. Judicature Soc., Am. Bd. Trial Advocates (advocate, nat. bd. dirs. 1996—2000), Fedn. Def. and Corp. Counsel, Tex. State Bar Assn., Va. State Bar Assn., Internat. Assn. Def. Counsel, Garland Walker Inn, Am. Inns of Ct. Office: McFall Sherwood & Breitbeil PC 1250 Four Houston Ctr 1331 Lamar St Houston TX 77010-3027 Office Phone: 713-590-9300. Personal E-mail: dbmcf@aol.com. Business E-Mail: dmcfall@mcfall-law.com.

**MCFALL, JOHN,** artistic director; b. Kansas City, Mo. Studies with Tatiana Dokoudovska, Conservatory of Music; student, San Francisco Ballet Sch., 1964-65. Formerly with San Francisco Ballet, prin. dancer, 1969; artistic dir. BalletMet, Columbus, Ohio, 1984; artistic dir., CEO Atlanta Ballet Co., 1994—. Choreographer Nat. Ballet Can., Am. Ballet Theatre, Dance Theatre Harlem, San Francisco, Hubbard St. Dance Co., Atlanta Ballet, for other artists, including Mikhail Baryshnikov, Cynthia Gregory. Choreographer Commd. 2 world premieres for 1996 Olympic Arts Festival; recently staged: 10 Atlanta prodns., including The Nutcracker. Ford Found. scholar, Nat. Francis Dallas Sch., 1984, Nat. Endowment for Arts fellow, 1978, 1980, 1985. Office: Atlanta Ballet 1400 W Peachtree St Atlanta GA 30309-2906 E-mail: jmcfall@atlantaballet.com.

**MCFARLAN, FRANKLIN WARREN,** business administration educator; b. Boston, Oct. 18, 1937; s. Ronald Lyman and Ethel Warren (White) McF.; m. Margaret Karen Nelson, Dec. 17, 1971; children: Andrew, Clarissa, Elizabeth. AB, Harvard Coll., 1959, MBA, 1961, D.BA, 1965. Asst. prof. Harvard Bus. Sch., Boston, 1964-68, assoc. prof., 1968-73, prof. bus. adminstrn., 1973—, prof. emeritus bus. adminstrn., sr. assoc. dean, dir. rsch. Boston, 1991-95, sr. assoc. dean external rels. 1995-2000, sr. assoc. dean, dir. Asia Pacific, 2000—. Dir. Providian Fin. Corp., San Franciso, Li and Fung Corp., HOng Kong, Computer Sci. Corp., L.A. Author: (with Richard Nolan) Information Systems Administration, 1973; (with Linda Applegate and Robert Austin) Corporate Information Management, 6th edit., 2003, (with Linda Applegate and Robert Austin) Creating Business Advantages in Information Age, 2002, (with Cathleen Benko) Connecting the Dots, 2003; editor: (with Richard Nolan) Information Systems Handbook, 1973, Information Systems Research Challenge, 1984; sr. editor MIS Quar., 1984-88. Bd. dirs., pres. Belmont (Mass.) Day Sch., 1982-86; bd. dirs. Dana Hall Sch., Wellesley, Mass., 1982-94, chmn. 1993; trustee Mt. Auburn Hosp., 1991-99, ch mn. bd., 1995-98, trustee care group, 1996—; trustee Winsor Sch., 1994-2000, Milton Acad., 2001—. 1st lt. U.S. Army, 1962-67. Mem.: The Country (Brookline, Mass.). Republican. Episcopalian. Office: Harvard Bus Sch Morgan Hall 131 Harvard Way Boston MA 02163-1317 Office Phone: 617-495-6402. E-mail: fmcfarlan@hbs.edu.

**MCFARLAND, ALAN ROBERTS,** investment banker; b. Washington, Oct. 4, 1942; s. Alan Roberts and Elizabeth (Mathieu) McF.; m. Ellen Michel, Aug. 6, 1966 (div. 1984); children: Andrew Roberts, Gavin Richards; m. Kathleen Troia, Jan. 12, 1985; children: Fiona Fuller, Lucas Haskell Sawyer, Camilla Collins. BA, Yale U., 1964, LLB, 1967. Law clk. U.S. Ct. Appeals, 3d Cir., Phila., 1967-68; assoc. Drinker Biddle & Reath, Phila., 1968-69; v.p. Donaldson Lufkin & Jenrette, N.Y.C., 1969-73; mng. dir. Lehman Bros., N.Y.C., 1973-78; gen.ptnr. Lazard Freres & Co., N.Y.C., 1978-89, McFarland Dewey & Co., N.Y.C., 1989—. Bd. dirs. Placer Dome Inc., Vancouver, B.C.,

Can., Foxboro Co. Mass., 1990, Premdor Inc., Willowdale, Ont., Can. Trustee Children's Aid Soc., N.Y.C., 1978—; bd. dirs. World Resources Inst., Washington, 1980-94. Republican. Episcopalian. Office: Mcfarland Dewey Securities Co 420 Lexington Ave Suite 2650 New York NY 10170-2699*

**MC FARLAND, H. RICHARD,** food products executive; b. Hoopeston, Ill., Aug. 19, 1930; s. Arthur Bryan and Jennie (Wilkey) McF.; m. Sarah Forney, Dec. 30, 1967. BS, U. Ill., 1952. With Campbell Soup Co., Camden, NJ, 1957-67, mgr. purchasing, 1961-67; dir. procurement Keebler Co., Elmhurst, Ill., 1967-69; v.p. purchasing and distbn. Ky. Fried Chicken Corp., Louisville, 1969-74, v.p. food svcs., sales and distbn., 1974-75; pres., dir. Mcfarland Carton Co., Louisville, 1974-75, Ky. Fried Chicken Mfg. Corp.. Nashville, 1974-75; owner, pres., dir. McFarland Foods Corp., Indpls., 1975—. Chmn. processed foods com. World's Poultry Congress, 1974; mem. exec. coun., nat. franchise coun. Ky. Fried Chicken, 1979-85; dir. nat. advt. coun. Ky. Fried Chicken, 1985-91, exec. com., 1988-90, chmn., 1989-90; mem. devel. com. U. Ill., 1989—. Mem. U. Ill. Found., 1992—; bd. dirs., 1993-05, life bd. dirs., 2005—, vice chmn., 2001-05, bd. U. President's Cir., 2005-; chmn. U. Ill. Nat. Advocates, 1992-2001; life pres. U. Ill. Sr. Class of '52; bd. dirs. Ind. Fedn. Children and Youth, 1983-84; Ind. bd. dirs. Fellowship Christian Athletes, 1997-98, Ind. bd. advisors, 1998—; chmn. campaign Ind. Ky. Fried Chicken March of Dimes, 1978-87; nat. trustee McCormick Theol. Sem., 1993-97, mem. adv. coun., 1998-2002; trustee Hanover Coll., 2004—; life trustee Indpls. Mus. Art, 2005—; bd. dirs. U. Ind. Cancer Ctr. Devel., 2004—, Ind. Ovarian Cancer Orgn., 2003—. 1st lt. USAF, 1952-54, Korea. Recipient Award of Merit U. Ill. Coll. Agr., 1988, Achievement award U. Ill. Alumni Assn., 1996. Mem. Ky. Restaurant Assn. (bd. dirs. 1970-75), Nat. Broiler Coun. (bd. dirs. 1971-74), Ind. Restaurant Assn., Am. Shorthorn Breeders Assn., Great Lakes Ky. Fried Chicken Franchise Assn. (bd. dirs. 1975-91, 1st v.p. 1978-79, pres. 1979-80), Delta Upsilon. Clubs: Main Line Ski (Phila.) (pres. 1964); Hillcrest Country. Presbyterian. Home: 10720 Compass Ct Indianapolis IN 46256-9532

**MC FARLAND, JAMES JOSEPH,** cardiothoracic surgeon; b. Paterson, N.J., Sept. 25, 1942; s. James Edward and Elizabeth Mc Farland. BS, Upsala Coll., 1964; MS, Seton Hall U., 1966; MD, U. Bologna, 1976; sabatical studies, 1988-90. Diplomate Am. Bd. Surgery, Am. Bd. Thoracic Surgery; lic. Calif., La., Maine, Mich., N.J., N.Y., Pa., Tenn., Tex., Ind. Extern in medicine and surgery St. Joseph's Hosp., Paterson, NJ, 1969; extern in pathology Beth Israel Med. Ctr., 1973; extern in internal medicine, thoracic and vascular surgery U. Bologna, 1973-76, intern in rotating medicine and surgery, 1976; intern in gen. surgery and medicine, resident gen. surgery N.Y. Med. Coll. 1976-77, 77-78; resident in gen. surgery Bridgeport Hosp., 1978-81; resident in thoracic and cardiovascular surgery Tulane U. and Wayne State U., 1982-84, 84-85; fellow in thoracic and cardiovascular surgery St. Thomas Hosp., Nashville, 1985-86; fellow in cardiac surgery Wilkes-Barre (Pa.) Gen. Hosp., 1987-88; assoc. attending surgeon in pvt. practice of cardiothoracic and vascular surgery Scranton, Pa., 1990-92; fellow in cardiothoracic surgery Hosp. of Univ. Pa., Phila., 1992-93; clin. instr. surgery divsn. cardiothoracic surgery U. Pa. Sch. Medicine, Phila., 1992-93; fellow in pediatric cardiothoracic surgery Children's Hosp., Phila., 1992-93; fellow in cardiothoracic surgery Med. Coll. of Pa., Phila., 1993-94; clin. instr. surgery divsn. cardiothoracic surgery Med. Coll. Pa., Phila., 1993-94. Clin. asst., prof. surgery divsn. cardiothoracic surgery Ohio State U., 1999—2000; chief cardiothoracic surgery Heart Hosp., Midland, Tex., 2003. Contbr. articles to profl. med. jours. Recipient First prize in Resident Paper Competition in Trauma, ACS and Am. Bd. Surgery, 1979, Outstanding Achievement in Am. Bd. Surgery In-Tng., 1981, Competitive Rsch. grant CABG, 1987; Advanced Clin. fellow in MInimally Invasive Cariothoracic Surgery, Ohio State U. Med. Ctr., 1999-2000. Mem. AMA, Lake County Med. Soc., Ind. Med. Soc., Internat. Soc. Minimally Invasive Cardiothoracic Surgeons. Roman Catholic. Avocations: jogging, hiking, camping, swimming, tennis. Home and Office: 8610 Durbin Ln Crown Point IN 46307-1536

**MCFARLAND, JAMES W.,** finance educator; BA, Texas A&M U., 1967, PhD, 1971. Instr. Inst. Stats. Texas A&M U., 1970—71; econometrician Nat. Water Commn., 1971; asst. prof. dept. math. U. La., Lafayette, 1971—73; asst. prof. dept. resource econs. U. RI, 1973—75; adj. prof. Robert O. Anderson Sch. Mgmt., U. N. Mex., 1975—76; staff mem. stats. and energy systems analysis Los Alamos Nat. Lab. U. Calif., 1975—76, vis. staff. mem., 1976—85; assoc. prof. Coll. Bus. Adminstrn., U. Houston, 1976—79, chmn. mgmt. scis., 1977—79, assoc. dean, 1979—85, prof., 1983—88, dean, 1985—88; dean and J.F. Jr. Seinsheimer chair bus. A.B. Freeman Sch. Bus., Tulane U., New Orleans, 1988—2005, now mem. faculty. Bd. dirs. Am. Indemnity Fin. Corp., 1994—99, Petroleum Helicopters, Inc., 1996—2001, Sizeler Property Investors, Inc., 1994—, Stewart Enterprises, Inc., 1995—. Bd. dirs. New Orleans World Trade Ctr., 1990—. Recipient Disting. Svc. Award, Nat. Water Commn., 1971, Disting. Faculty Mem. Award, Coll. Bus. Adminstrn., U. Houston, 1983, Disting. Svc. Award, U. Houston Alumni Assn., 1988. Office: AB Freeman Sch Bus Tulane U 440 Goldring/Woldenberg New Orleans LA 70118-5669*

**MCFARLAND, JAMES WILLIAM,** real estate company executive, consultant; b. Montgomery, Ala., Sept. 7, 1948; s. Ward Wharton and Frances Adelia (Morrow) McFarland; m. Miriam Melinda Webster, Feb. 20, 1971; children: James William, Mimi Morrow. BS, U. Ala., 1971. Dir. real estate Ky., Ind. and Tenn. Winn-Dixie Stores, Inc., Louisville, 1970—72; v.p. Ward McFarland, Inc., Tuscaloosa, Ala., 1972—. Dir. Ward McFarland, Inc., Tuscaloosa, Ala.; charter investor chair of real estate U. Ala. Mem. Coun. Devel. of French in La., 1976—, Friends of Libr., 1975—; commr. Dept. Mental Health, Ala., 1987—89; Rep. nominee U.S. Congress Ala. 7th Dist., 1986; chmn. Ala. Rapid Rail Transit Commn.; vice chmn. U.S. La.-Miss.-Ala. Rapid Rail Transit Commn., 1983—84, chmn., 1984; state advisor Congl. Adv. Com., Am. Security Coun.; mem. Rep. State Exec. Com., 1991—; chmn. Tuscaloosa County Reps., 1991—; young churchmen adviser Episcopal Diocese Ala., 1976, conv. del.; sr. warden Christ Episc. Ch., 1984; bd. dir. Tuscaloosa Kidney Found. Named hon. citizen of Mobile and New Orleans, hon. mem. mayor's staff, Mobile, Ala. Mem.: Nat. Small Bus. Assn., Tuscaloosa Bd. Realtors, Nat. Assn. Realtors, USCG Aux. (flotilla comdr. and dist. pub. affairs officer 1997, flotilla staff officer 1994—, dist. staff officer 1997—), U. Ala. Alumni Assn., U. Ala. Commerce Execs. Soc., Ala. Assn. R.R. Passengers (pres. 1982, 1990, 1991), Nat. Assn. R.R. Passengers, Kiwanis (Greater Tuscaloosa chpt.), North River Yacht Club, Delta Sigma Pi. Home: 8714 Forrestal Dr NE Tuscaloosa AL 35406-3404 Office: 325 Skyland Blvd E Tuscaloosa AL 35405-4030 Office Phone: 205-759-5161.

**MCFARLAND, JAMES WILLIAM, JR.,** real estate manager; b. Tuscaloosa, Ala., Sept. 8, 1979; s. James William McFarland, Sr. and Miriam Melinda (Webster) McFarland. Diploma, Tuscaloosa Acad., Ala., 1987—98. Cert. notary public Ala. Internship US Ho. Reps., DC, 2003; found., managing mem. Buffex LLC, 2004—; mgr., Skyland Apts. Ward McGarland Inc., 2005—. Author: (biography) Ward Wharton McFarland: Veteran, Attorney, Public Servant, Businessman. Mem. Friends Tuscaloosa Pub. Libr., 2003—05; jr. patron Birmingham Mus. Art, 2004—05; vol. Friends Bryce Hosp., Tuscaloosa; mem. Ala. World Trade Assn., Montgomery; founding mem. US Dept. Homeland Security, 2002; hon. col. appointed by Gov. George C. Wallace State Ala., Montgomery, 1987; del. campaign mgr. Lisa T. Wallace for Ala. State Treas., 2002; exec. com. mem. Ala. Rep. Party, Birminghamn, 2003—04; founding chmn. Tuscaloosa Young Reps., 2003—04; del. Rep. Nat. Conv., NYC, 2004, 2006—; mem. St. Jude League. Chgo., 1998—2005. Staff officer US Coast Guard Aux. Named Hon. Capitol Hill Historian, US Capitol Hill Hist. Soc., 2003, Hon. Citizen, State of Ohio, Gov. Bob Taft, Hon. Citizen, City of New Orleans, City Coun., Mayor Ernest Morial, Hon. Citizen, Father Flanagan's Boys and Girls Town, Nebr., 2006; recipient cert. of recognition, Ala. Gov. Bob Riley, Montgomery, 2003. Republican. Roman Catholic. Avocations: travel, writing, photography. Office: Ward McFarland Inc 325 Skyland Blvd E Tuscaloosa AL 35405 Mailing: Buffex LLC 130 Wildwood Pky Ste 108 Birmingham AL 35209

**MCFARLAND, KATHLEEN TROIA (KT MCFARLAND),** government defense consultant; b. Madison, Wis., July 22, 1951; d. August Joseph and Edith (Fuller) Troia; m. Alan Roberts McFarland, Jr., Jan. 12, 1985; 5 children. BA, George Washington U., 1973; MA, Oxford U., Eng., 1978; postgrad., MIT, 1978-81. Research asst. to Dr. H. A. Kissinger Nat. Security Council, Washington, 1970-73; staff mem. Senate Armed Services Com., Washington, 1981-82; asst. to sec. def. Dept. Def., Washington, 1982-83, dep. asst. sec. def., 1983-84, cons., 1985. Campaign for US Senate NY, 2006—. Student trustee George Washington U., 1971-73 Fellow Ford Found., 1979-81, Arms Control and Disarmament Agy., 1980-81, Inst. for Study World Politics, 1980-81 Mem. Council on Fgn. Relations Republican. Episcopalian. Office: KT McFarland for Senate 954 Lexington Ave Box 135 New York NY 10021*

**MCFARLAND, KAY ELEANOR,** state supreme court chief justice; b. Coffeyville, Kans., July 20, 1935; d. Kenneth W. and Margaret E. (Thrall) McF BA in English & History, Washburn U., Topeka, 1957, JD, 1964. Bar: Kans. 1964. Sole practice, Topeka, 1964-71; probate and juvenile judge Shawnee County, Topeka, 1971-73; dist. judge Topeka, 1973-77; assoc. justice Kans. Supreme Ct., 1977-95, chief justice, 1995—. Mem. Kans. Bar Assn., Women Attys. Assn. Topeka., Topeka Bar Assn First woman appointed justice of Kans. Supreme Ct. Office: Kans Supreme Ct Kans Jud Ctr 301 SW 10th Ave Topeka KS 66612-1507 Fax: (785) 291-3274.

**MCFARLAND, KEVIN JOHN,** foundation administrator; b. Mt. Clement, Mich., Mar. 18, 1958; s. Chuck Paul and Myrna (Bell) McFarland; m. Betty Ann Bolton, Nov. 26, 1976; children: Michelle, Michael, Melinda. BS in Bibl. Studies magna cum laude, Abilene Christian U., Tex., 1980; postgrad., Tex. Tech. U., 1980-81, Stanford U., 1982-83. Resident asst. Abilene (Tex.) State Sch., 1976-78; pvt. landscaping bus. Abilene, 1978-80; research assoc., home and family life dept. Tex. Tech. U., Lubbock, 1980-81; youth and family min. Redwood Ch., 1981-84; pres. Manna Internat. Relief and Devel. Corp., Redwood City, 1984—. Mem. Amnexty Internat., Bread for the World; bd. dirs. Am. Coun. Voluntary Internat. Action. Mem.: Internat. Devel. Network, Acad. Polit. Sci., Inst. Cultural Affairs, Inst. Coop. Interant. Devel. (bd. dirs., founder, exec. dir.), Soc. Internat. Devel. Global Affairs Coun., Evang. for Social Action, Cultural Survival, Nat. Assn. Scholars, Nat. Honor Soc., Alpha Chi. Home: PO Box 70 Sacramento CA 95812 also: 903 Madison Ave Redwood City CA 94061-1540

**MCFARLAND, MICHAEL C.,** academic administrator; b. Boston, 1948; AB in Physics, Cornell U., 1969; M in Elec. Engring., Carnegie M in Elec. Engring., PhD in Elec. Engring., Carnegie Mellon U.; MDiv, Weston Sch. Theology, ThM in Social Ethics. Ordained to ministry Jesuits, 1984. Cons. AT&T Bell Labs., 1985—86; assoc. prof. computer sci. Boston Coll., 1986—96, dept. chair; prof. computer sci., dean Coll. Arts and Scis. Gonzaga U., Spokane, 1996—2000; pres. Coll. of the Holy Cross, Worcester, Mass., 2000—. Bd. dir. Worcester Mcpl. Rsch. Bur., Worcester Cath. Charities; bd. dirs. U. Scranton. Avocation: running. Office: Coll of the Holy Cross 1 College St Worcester MA 01610-2395 Office Phone: 508-793-2525.*

**MC FARLAND, NORMAN FRANCIS,** bishop; b. Martinez, Calif., Feb. 21, 1922; Student, St. Patrick's Sem. Ordained to ministry Cath. Ch., 1946, consecrated bishop Cath. Ch., 1970. Auxilliary bishop, San Francisco, 1970—74; apostolic adminstr. Diocese of Reno, 1974—76; bishop Diocese of Reno-Las Vegas, 1976—87, Diocese of Orange, Calif., 1987—98. Office: 200 W La Veta Ave Orange CA 92866-1936

**MC FARLAND, PHILIP JAMES,** secondary school educator, writer; b. Birmingham, Ala., June 20, 1930; s. Thomas Alfred McFarland and Alice Lucile Sylvester; m. Patricia Katherin Connors, July 23, 1960; children: Philip James Jr., Joseph Thomas. BA, Oberlin Coll., 1951; MA, Cambridge U., 1957. Editor textbooks Houghton Mifflin Co., Boston, 1958—64; tchr. English Concord Acad., Mass., 1965—95. Author: A House Full of Women, 1960, Sojourners, 1979, Seasons of Fear, 1984, Sea Dangers, 1985, A History of Concord Acad. 2 vols., 1986, 2000, The Brave Bostonians, 1998, Hawthorne in Concord, 2004; sr. editor: Houghton Mifflin Literature Series, 6 vols., 1972, Focus on Literature, 7 vols., 1978; editor: Composition: Models and Exercises, 5 vols., 2d edit., 1971. Lt. j.g. USN, 1951-55. Fellow Mass. Hist. Soc. Democrat. Avocations: bicycling, trekking. Home: 18 Independence Ave Lexington MA 02421-5939 E-mail: pmcf@rcn.com.

**MCFARLAND, RICHARD MACKLIN,** retired journalist; b. Blockton, Iowa, Mar. 27, 1922; s. William Harold McFarland and Elsie (Sisson) McFarland Chavannes; m. Jacquelyn Jean Folske, Mar. 22, 1955; children: Bethany Rose, Scott Macklin, Elizabeth Ann McFarland Heyda, Kathryn Belle. BA, U. Iowa, 1944. Newsman UPI, Des Moines, 1944, Chgo., 1945, 46-47, bur. mgr. Bismarck, ND, 1944-45, Herrin, Ill., 1945, Sioux Falls, SD, 1947-49, Milw., 1949-51, regls. reporter Des Moines, 1947, Denver, SD, 1949, Iowa mgr. Des Moines, 1951-54, NW mgr. Mpls., 1954-55, Wis. mgr. Milw. 1956-57, regional exec. sales, 1958-59, bur. mgr. Chgo., 1960-61, Minn. mgr. Mpls., 1961-69, Mich. editor Detroit, 1969-71, Minn. editor Mpls., 1971-84, bur. mgr.-capitol reporter St. Paul, 1985-89; ret., 1989. Former deacon Advent Luth. Ch., Roseville, Minn.; coun. mem. Redeemer Luth. Ch., Bradenton, Fla., 1996—98, pres. coun., 1998—99, coun. mem., 2001—05. With USN, 1943—44. Avocations: reading, music, fishing, backpacking, golf. Home: 7312 5th Ave NW Bradenton FL 34209-1522 Personal E-mail: rmcf@aol.com.

**MCFARLAND, ROBERT BRUCE,** physician; b. Ames, Iowa, Sept. 18, 1929; s. Julian Ecwart and Winnie Florence (Goering) McF.; m. Zoë Euphrosyne Bucuvalas, June 1, 1958; children: Laura Ann, Bruce Damon. BA, Kenton Coll., 1950; MD, U. Iowa, 1954. Intern San Francisco Gen. Hosp., 1955; house officer Mass. Gen. Hosp., Boston, 1957-59; asst. resident U. Colo. Med. Ctr., Denver, 1959-61; physician pvt. practice, Boulder, Colo., 1961-76, 78-93; prof. U. Mo.-Kansas City, 1976-78. Contbg. editor Jour. Psychohistory, 1996—; contbr. articles to profl. jours. Vestryman St. John's Episcopal Ch., Boulder, 1966-69; jail physician Boulder County, Kansas City, 1972-75, 76-78; co-founder Parenting Place, Boulder, 1984-2001; cons., bd. health No. Cheyenne Tribe, Lame Deer, Mont., 1976-84. Comdr. USNR-R, 1955-78. Avocations: hiking, reading. Home: 2300 Kalmia Ave Boulder CO 80304-1931 E-mail: mcfarland73@msn.com.

**MC FARLAND, ROBERT HAROLD,** retired physicist; b. Severy, Kans., Jan. 10, 1918; s. Robert Eugene and Georgia (Simpson) McF.; m. Twilah Mae Seefeld, aug. 28, 1940; children: Robert Alan, Rodney Jon. BS and BA, Kans. State Tchrs. Coll., Emporia, 1940; Ph.M. (Mendenhall fellow), U. Wis., 1943, PhD, 1947. Sic. instr., coach high sch., Chase, Kans., 1940-41; instr. navy radio sch. U. Wis., Madison, 1943-44; sr. engr. Sylvania Elec. Corp., 1944-46; faculty Kans. State U., 1947-60, prof. physics, 1954-60, dir. nuclear lab., 1958-60; physicist Lawrence Livermore Radiation Lab. U. Calif., 1960—69; dean Grad. Sch., U. Mo., Rolla, 1969-79, dir. instnl. analysis and planning, 1979-82; prof. physics U. Mo., Rolla, 1969-84, prof. emeritus physics dept., 1985—; v.p. acad. affairs U. Mo. System, 1974-75; Intergovtl. Personnel Act appointee Dept. Energy, Washington, 1982-84; vis. prof. U. Calif., Berkeley, 1980-81. Mem. Grad. Record Exams. Bd., 1971-75, chmn. steering com., 1972-73; cons. Well Surveys, Inc., Tulsa, 1953-54, Argonne Nat. Lab., Chgo., 1955-59, Kans. Dept. Pub. Health, 1956-57, cons. in residence Lawrence Livermore Radiation Lab., U. Calif., 1957, 58, 59, med. physics U. Okla. Med. Sch., 1971, grad. schs., PhD physics program, Utah State U., 1972; physicist, regional counselor Office Ordnance Research, Durham, N.C., 1955. Author: (with T. McFarland) McFarland Collections, 1985, Simpson Connections, 1987; co-author two family geneacl. books; contbr. over 113 articles to profl. jours.; patentee in field of light prodn., vacuum prodn., controlled thermonuclear reactions. Active Boy Scouts Am., 1952—, mem. exec. bd. San Francisco Bay Area council, 1964-68, Ozark Council, 1986—; chmn. Livermore (Calif.) Library Bond drive, 1964. Mem. Kans. N.G., 1936-40. Recipient Silver Beaver award Boy Scouts Am., 1968, Community Service award C. of C., 1965, Disting. Alumnus award Kans.

State Tchrs. Coll., 1969. Fellow AAAS, Am. Phys. Soc., Kiwanis Internat.; mem. AAUP (chpt. pres. 1956-57), Am. Assn. Physics Tchrs., Mo. Acad. Sci., Mo. Assn. Phys. Sci. Tchrs., Am. Soc. Engring. Edn., Kiwanis (lt. gov. Mo.-Ark. dist. 1984-85, internat. accredited rep. 1985-92. Disting. Lt. Gov. 1985, Tablet of honor award 1997, 50 Yr. Perfect Attendance pin 2003), Sigma Xi, Lambda Delta Lambda, Xi Phi, Kappa Mu Epsilon, Kappa Delta Pi, Pi Mu Epsilon, Gamma Sigma Delta, Phi Kappa Phi. Home: 416 W Spring St Apt 3 Neosho MO 64850-1777 Office: U Mo Dept Physics Rolla MO 65401 Business E-Mail: robmcf@umr.edu. *Continuation of the last hundred years of major progress in the quality of life for the human race will not only require the best of our educational systems and technological talents but a sincere interest in all of us to contribute positively toward our collective well-being.*

**MCFARLAND, SAMUEL P., JR.,** psychologist; b. Atlanta, Oct. 16, 1957; s. Samuel P. and Gladys Blake (Pepper) McF. BA in Psychology, Mercer U., 1983; MA in Gen. and Exptl. Psychology, Fla. Atlantic U., 1987; MS in Clin. Psychology, Nova U., 1993; PhD in Clin. Psychology, Nova Southeastern U., 1998. Store mgr. Reeds Drugs Inc., Atlanta, 1973—81; mental health technician C.P.C. Parkwood Hosp., Atlanta, 1982—84; mental health asst. C.P.C. Ft. Lauderdale Hosp., Fla., 1985, N.M.E. Fair Oaks Hosp., Delray Beach, 1985-87; peer acad. advisor Fla. Atlantic U., Boca Raton, 1986-87; clin. counselor/supr. Henderson Mental Health Ctr./New Vistas, Ft. Lauderdale, 1987-88; adj. faculty instr. Art Inst. Ft. Lauderdale, 1992-93; case mgr., psychologist Bradley Ctr. of St. Francis, Columbus, Ga., 1993—. Therapist Biofeedback Clinic/Nova Clinic, Davie, Fla., 1992, The Family Ctr./Nova U., 1991-92, Child & Adolescent Anxiety Disorders Clinic/Nova Clinic, Coral Springs, 1988-89. Co-sponsor Al-Ateen Group, Atlanta, 1975-76. Mem. APA (nat. treas. 1988-90, mem. divsns. 12 and 37 1994—), Am. Psychol. Assn. Gread. Students (nat. treas. 1988-90), Am. Psychol. Soc., Columbus Psychol. Assn. Office: Bradley Ctr St Francis 2000 16th Ave Columbus GA 31901 Office Phone: 706-320-3766. E-mail: wolf444@charter.net.

**MCFARLAND, WALTER GERARD,** management consultant; b. Chicago Heights, Ill., June 28, 1952; s. Walter Louden and Rosemary (Voelker) McF. BA in Psychology, So. Ill. U., 1976, MPA, 1978; MA in Nat. Security, Georgetown U., 1991; EdD in Human Resource Devel., George Washington U., 1999. Program analyst USAF, San Antonio, 1978-82; program monitor CIA, Washington, 1982-85; spl. asst. to sec. of def. Dept. of Def., Washington, 1985-88; mgmt. cons. Hay Mgmt. Consultants, Washington, 1988-97; prin. rsch. scientist Am. Insts. Rsch., Washington, 1997—. Guest lectr. CIA, 1985-88, Georgetown U., 1995, Johns-Hopkins U., Washington, 1996. Elder Great Falls (Va.) Bible Ch., 1988-90; mem. Wakefield H.S. PTA, Arlington, Va., 1992-96. Mem. ASPA (nat. chpt. head 1985-86, chpt. dir. 1987), Acad. Mgmt. Republican. Baptist. Home: 4050 40th St N Arlington VA 22207-4608

**MCFARLAND, WILLIAM JOSEPH (JOE MCFARLAND),** academic administrator; b. Sterling, Kans., July 25, 1929; s. Armour James and Sylvia Jane Louise (Hutcheson) McF.; m. Mary Roberta Dill, Dec. 21, 1951; children: William Joseph, Kathryn Ann, Matthew Curtis. BA, Sterling Coll., 1951; MA, U. No. Colo., 1957; EdD, Ind. U., 1966; PhD (hon.), Sterling Coll., 1992, Geneva Coll., 2001. Cert. tchr. and adminstr., pilot. Elem. prin., coach, tchr., supt. schs. Turon Pub. Schs., Kans., 1953-59; assoc. prof. edn., dir. student teaching, head elem. dept. Emporia State U., Kans., 1959-68; assoc. exec. sec. Kans. NEA, Topeka, 1968-71; dir. acad. affairs Kans. Bd. Regents, Topeka, 1971-84; pres. Geneva Coll., Beaver Falls, Pa., 1984-92; cons., scholar in residence Christs Coll., Taipei, Taiwan, 1992—2002; headmaster Am. Acad. Nicosia, Cyprus, 2002—. Chmn. scholarship selection com. Beech Aircraft Co., Wichita, Kans., 1979-84; pres. coun. Nat. Assn. Intercollegiate Athletics, Kansas City, Kans., 1984-92. Contbr. articles to profl. jours. Pres. Topeka Fellowship, Inc., 1977-84; mem. exec. coun., v.p. Boy Scouts Am., Emporia and Topeka, 1963-83; legis. liason person NEA, Topeka, 1968-71; chmn. Kans. Commn. on Aerospace Edn., 1971-83, Gov's. Commn. on Sch. to Work, 1995-2001; trustee Sterling Coll., Kans., 1971-84, Geneva Coll., 1973-84; sec. Pa. Found. Ind. Colls.; bd. dirs. United Way, Beaver County, Pa., 1985-92, ARC of Beaver County, 1985-92, Beaver Valley C. of C., 1985-88; mem. Christian Coll. Coalition, 1984-92. With U.S. Army, 1951-53, Korea. Recipient Lieber Meml. Teaching award Ind. U., Bloomington, 1966; Disting. Service award Sterling Coll., 1983; VIP award Sta. WREN, Topeka, 1971. Mem. Assn. Governing Bds. (exec. com.), Pa. Assn. Colls. and Univs., Nat. Assn. Ind. Colls. and Univs., Beaver Valley C. of C., ARC (pres. local chpt.), Knife and Fork Club (bd. dirs. 1979-84, Rotary (life, pres. 1986-87, Paul Harris fellow 1988, chmn. scholarship selection com. Rotary Found.), Phi Delta Kappa (v.p. 1969-73) Republican. Presbyterian. Avocations: flying, football officiating, golf, hunting. Home and Office: 2709 SW Boswell Ave Topeka KS 66611-1604 E-mail: joromcf@sbcglobal.net.

**MCFARLANE, BETH LUCETTA TROESTER,** retired mayor; b. Osterdock, Iowa, Mar. 9, 1918; d. Francis Charles and Ella Carrie (Moser) Troester; m. George Evert McFarlane, June 20, 1943 (dec. May 1972); children: Douglas, Steven(dec.), Susan, George. EdB, U. No. Iowa, Cedar Falls, 1962, MEd, 1971. Cert. tchr. Tchr. rural and elem. schs., Iowa, 1936-50, 55-56; elem. tchr. Oelwein Cmty. Schs., Iowa, 1956-64, jr. high reading tchr., 1964—71, 1983; city council Oelwein, 1981-82; mayor of Oelwein, 1982-89; ret. Evaluator N. Ctrl. Accreditation Assn. Ednl. Programs; mem. planning team confs. Iowa cities N.E. Iowa, 1985; v.p. N.E. Iowa Regional Coun. Econ. Devel., 1986—89; mem. area econ. devel. com. N.E. Iowa, 1985, mem. legis. interim study com. rural devel., 1987—88; mem. policy com. Iowa League Municipalities, 1987—88. V.p. Fayette County Tourism Coun., 1987—88; mem. Iowa State steering com. road use tax financing, 1988—89; chmn. bd. govs. Oelwein Cmty. Ctr., 1990—94, bd. govs., 2001—; chmn. bldg. and fin. com. Reorganized LDS/Cmty. Christ Ch. Bldg., 1980—, dist. ch. fin. com., 1992—2001, dist. ch. revolving loan com., 1982—2000. Named Iowa Reading Tchr. of Yr., Internat. Reading Assn. Iowa, 1978; recipient Outstanding Contbn. to Reading Coun. Acitivities award, Internat. Reading Assn. N.E. Iowa, 1978, State of Iowa's Gov.'s Leadership award, 1988. Mem.: Oelwein Bus. and Profl. Women (Woman of Yr. 1983), MacDowell Music and Arts Orgn. (pres. 1978—80), N.E. Iowa Reading Coun. (pres. 1975—77), Area Univ. Women (pres. 1999—2000), Oelwein Area Ret. Sch. Pers. (pres. 1994—96), Oelwein Area C. of C. (bd. dirs. 1986—89, Humanitarian award 1987), Delta Kappa Gamma (pres. 1980—82). Reorganized Mem. Cmty. Of Christ Ch. Avocations: hiking, refinishing antiques, gardening, walking, creative sewing. Home: 512 7th Ave NE Oelwein IA 50662-1326

**MCFARLANE, DONOVAN ANTHONY,** finance educator, poet, researcher; b. Manchester, Jamaica, Apr. 19, 1978; came to U.S., 1997; s. Merceline Agatha Wright. Cert., deCarteret Coll., Jamaica, 1995, Church Tchrs. Coll., 1997; PhD in Parapsychic Sci., Am. Inst. Theology, 2003; diploma in fitness and nutrition, Harcourt Learning Direct, Scranton, Pa., 1999; diploma in mgmt. reconstr. and hotel, Profl. Career Devel. Inst. Atlanta, 2000; diploma in bus. mgmt. with highest honor, Stratford Career Inst., Washington, 2000; diploma in small bus. mgmt., Lifetime Career Sch., Archbald, Pa., 2000; BS in Geog. Sci., Bernadean U., North Hollywood, Calif., 2000; PhD in Metaphysics, Am. Coll. Metaphy. Theology, Golden Valley, Minn., 2000, PhD in Comparative Religion, 2002; cert. in paralegal studies, Blackstone Sch., 2002; BS in Parapsychic Sci., Am. Inst. Holistic Theology, 2003, MS in Parapsychic Sci., 2002; MBA, Frederick Taylor U., 2002; MBA in Mgmt., Barrington U., 2003; BSBA, Nova Southeastern U., Fla., 2003; diploma in writing, Inst. Childrens Lit., 2003; B in Metaphys. sci., U. Metaphysics, Calif., 2003; diploma, U. Metaphysics, 2003; cert. metaphysical practitioner, U. Metaphysics Sem., 2003; MBA, Nova Southeastern U., 2005. Bd. cert. holistic health practitioner Am. Assn. Drugless Practitioners, 2005, bd. cert. alternative med. practitioner Am. Alternative Med. Assn., 2005; cert. in secondary edn. Tchr. trainee in Spanish and social studies Comprehensive H.S., Jamaica, 1997; tutor gen. sci. Church Tchrs. Coll., Jamaica; curriculum planner pvt. orgn., Fla., essayist Fla., cons. Lauderdale Lakes, Fla., 1998—; clk. Phillips and Phillips, Ft. Lauderdale, Fla., 1997—98; supr. inventory and warehouse Lord's Supermarket, Oakland, Fla., 1999; with Corp. Edu. Rsch., 2001—; prof. bus. studies U. Ft. Lauderdale,

2005—, City Coll. Ft. Lauderdale, 2005. Adj. instr. bus. studies City Coll., Ft. Lauderdale, Fla., 2005—; founder, chief preceptor, chancellor Donovan Soc., LLC, Ft. Lauderdale, 2006. Author: numerous poems; contbr. scientific papers to profl. jours. Recipient cert. excellence in Spanish, social studies, geography, math., history, cert. diligence in spanish, religious edn., cert. outstanding achievement in social studies, cert. outstanding achievement in Spanish, Internat. Poet of Merit award, 2002, Outstanding Achievement in Poetry Silver award, 2003, Commemorative award, 2003; named hon. alumni Oglata Lakota Coll., S.D., 2000. Mem.: Internat. Libr. Poetry (laureate cert. 2002), Internat. Soc. Poets (Editor's Choice award 1998), Nat. Libr. Poetry (Disting. Membership cert. and plaque 1998), Sigma Beta Delta (Outstanding Scholastic Achievement 2005). Avocations: dance, oratory, martial arts, singing, writing.

**MCFARLANE, SETH,** animator, director; b. Kent, Conn., Oct. 26, 1973; s. Ron and Perry McFarlane. Grad., RI Sch. Design. Animator Hanna-Barbera Prodns. (now Cartoon Network Studios); writer Walt Disney Animation, Fox Broadcasting Co. Writer, dir. (TV series) Shnookums and Meat Funny Cartoon Show, 1993, writer, dir., actor The Life of Larry, 1995, Larry & Steve, 1996, writer Dexter's Laboratory, 1996—, Jungle Cubs, 1996—98, Ace Ventura: Pet Detective, 1996, Cow and Chicken, 1997—2001, Johnny Bravo, 1997—, writer, dir. Zoomates, 1998, exec. prodr., writer, creator, actor Family Guy, 1999—, cons. prodr. The Pitts, 2003, exec. prodr., writer, dir., actor American Dad!, 2005—. Office: Fox Broadcasting Co 10201 West Pico Blvd Los Angeles CA 90035

**MCFARLANE, WALTER ALEXANDER,** lawyer, educator; b. Richlands, Va., May 4, 1940; s. James Albert and Frances Mae (Padbury) McF.; m. Judith Louise Copenhaver, Aug. 31, 1962. BA, Emory and Henry Coll., 1962; JD, U. Richmond, 1966. Bar: Ba. 1966, U.S. Supreme Ct. 1970, U.S. Ct Appeals (4th cir.) 1973, U.S. Ct. Appeals (D.C. Cir.) 1977, U.S. Dist. Ct. (ea. dist.) Va. 1973. Asst. atty. gen. Office Va. Atty. Gen., Richmond, 1969-73, dep. atty. gen., 1973-90; exec. asst., chief counsel, dir. policy Gov.'s Office Commonwealth of Va., 1990-94, supt. Dept Correctional Edn., 1994—. Acting dir. Dept. Juvenile Justice, 1997, State Bd. Dept. Criminal Justice Svcs., 1994—; prof. adj. staff U. Richmond, 1978—, A.L.Philpott disting. prof. T.C. Williams Sch. Law, 2003; chmn. transp. law com. Transp. Rsch. Bd., Nat. Rsch. Bd. Nat. Acads. Sci. and Engring., Washington, 1977-85, 88-94, chmn. legal affairs com., 1978-85, chmn. environ., archeol. and hist. com., 1985-90; mem. State Water Commn., 1994-96, mem., Coun. of State Govts. Henry Toll Fell., 1988, Legal Task Force, 1988-2002. Contbr. articles to profl. jours. Mem. exec. com., bd. govs. Emory and Henry Coll., 1985-98, Gen Assembly, Am. Correctional Assn., 2002—; pres. Windsor Forest Civic Assn., Midlothian, Va., 1975-76; bd. dirs. Greater Midlothian Civic League, 1980-86, v.p., 1980; instr. water safety ARC, 1962-87; chmn. bldg. com. Mt. Pisgah United Meth. Ch., 1980-85, pres. men's club, 1980-81; bd. dirs. ctrl. Va. chpt. Epilepsy Assn., Va., 1988-91, Woodland Pond Club Assn.; pres.-elect Va. Correctional Assn., 2004—. Capt. JAGC, USAF, 1966-69. Recipient J.D. Buscher Disting. Atty. award Am. Assn. State Hwy. and Transp. Ofcls., 1983, John C. Vance legal writing award Nat. Acads. Sci. and Engring., 4th ann. outstanding evening lectr. award Student Body, U. Richmond, 1980, Lifetime Achievement award Va. Correctional Assn., 2004. Mem. Chesterfield Bar Assn., Richmond Bar Assn. (bd. dir. 1989-93), Richmond Scottish Soc. (bd. dirs. 1980-82), Va. Correctional Assn. (pres.-elect 2004-, lifetime achievement award 2004), Am. Correctional Assn. (mem. gen. assembly 2002-), Emory and Henry Coll. Alumni Assn. (chpt. pres. 1971-73, regional v.p. 1974-77, pres. 1981-83), Meadowbrook Country Club (bd. dir. 2001-04). Home: 9001 Widgeon Way Chesterfield VA 23838-5274 Office: 101 N 14th St Richmond VA 23219-3684 Business E-Mail: wamcfarlane@dce.state.va.us.

**MCFARLANE, WILLIS MCKEE,** buffalo company executive; b. Cleve., May 27, 1933; BA in Econs. cum laude, Amherst Coll., 1955. Exec. Northwestern Mut. Life Ins., 1955-60; ptnr. life ins. co. Files, Cristal, and McFarlane, 1956—; founder AIRCOA, Cleve., 1968-79, Denver, 1979-90; co-owner Denver Buffalo Mktg. Co., 1990—, Buffalo Bar, Idaho Springs, 1995—. Chmn. bd. dirs. Colo. Symphony Orch.; bd. dirs. Colo. Wildlife Heritage Found. Mem. Cherry Hills Country Club. Office: Denver Buffalo Co 5800 Franklin St Ste 101 Denver CO 80216-1249

**MCFARLIN, BRIAN KEITH,** medical educator, researcher; b. Richardson, Tex., Oct. 2, 1975; s. Keith L. and Debbie Mayer McFarlin; m. Meredith Ann Lewis, Dec. 9, 1977; 1 child, Michael Keith. PhD, Purdue U., West Lafayette, Ind., 2003. Postdoctoral fellow Purdue U., West Lafayette, 2003—04; asst. prof. U. of Houston, 2004—. Recipient GEAR award, U. Houston Rsch. Coun., 2005—06. Mem.: Am. Coll. of Sports Medicine (assoc.). Republican. United Methodist. Avocation: running. Office: U Houston 3855 Holman St Pearland TX 77584-2015 Office Phone: 713-743-9860. Office Fax: 713-743-9860. E-mail: bmcfarlin@uh.edu.

**MCFARLIN, DIANE HOOTEN,** publisher; b. Lake Wales, Fla., July 10, 1954; d. Ruffie Denton Hooten and Anna Loraine (Peeples) Huff; m. Henry Briggs McFarlin, Aug. 28, 1976 (div. 1993). BS, U. Fla., 1976. Reporter Sarasota (Fla.) Jour., 1976-77, asst. news editor, 1977-78, city editor, 1978-82; asst. mng. editor Sarasota (Fla.) Herald Tribune, 1983-84, mng. editor, 1985-87; exec. editor Gainesville (Fla.) Sun, 1987-90; from exec. editor to assoc. publ. Sarasota Herald-Tribune, 1990-99, publ., 1999—. Adv. bd. U. Fla. Coll. Journalism and Comm., 1987—; Pulitzer juror Columbia U., 1995-96, 2001-02. Mem. accrediting coun. Edn. in Journalism and Mass Comms., 1994-96. Recipient Alumna of Distinction award U. Fla., 1999. Mem. Am. Soc. Newspaper Editors (com. chair 1992, 94, 96, 2000, bd. dirs. 1994—, treas., v.p. 2001, pres. 2002), Fla. Soc. Newspaper Editors (sec.-treas. 1993, v.p. 1994, pres. 1995). Office: Sarasota Herald-Tribune PO Box 1719 Sarasota FL 34230-1719 also: 801 S Tamiami Trail Sarasota FL 34236-7824

**MCFARLIN, RICHARD FRANCIS,** retired industrial chemist, researcher; b. Oklahoma City, Oct. 12, 1929; s. Loy Lester and Julie Mae (Collins) McF.; m. Clare Jane Burroughs, Apr. 4, 1953; children: Robin Sue McFarlin Godwin, Richard Prescott, Rebecca Lynn McFarlin Bray, Roger Whitsitt. BS, Va. Mil. Inst., 1951; MS, Purdue U., 1953, PhD, 1956. Rsch. chemist Monsanto Chem. Co., St. Louis, 1956-60; supr. inorganic rsch. Internat. Minerals and Chems., Mulberry, Fla., 1961; mgr. Agr. Rsch. Ctr. Armour Agrl. Chem. Co., Atlanta, 1962; v.p. rsch., ops., devel. & adminstrn. div agri-chems. U.S. Steel, Atlanta, 1986; tech. dir. Lester Labs. Inc., Atlanta, 1986-88; exec. dir. Fla. Inst. Phosphate Rsch., Bartow, 1988-96; ret., 1996. Mem. bd. advisors engring. coun. U. South Fla., Lakeland, 1990—, U. Fla., Gainesville, 1991—; mem. bd. advisors Inst. Recyclable Materials La. State U., Baton Rouge, 1990—. Capt. USAR, 1951-61. M. M. Cohn Found. scholar, 1947, L. D. Wall scholar, 1949, O. M. Baldinger scholar, 1950. Presbyterian. Achievements include eight U.S. and foreign patents for selective organic reducing agents, fertilizer processes and selective biocides. Home: 3239 Bridgefield Dr Lakeland FL 33803-7903 E-mail: rmcf203@msn.com.

**MCFARLIN, SHANNON DIANNE,** writer, researcher; b. St. Louis, Mo., May 26, 1954; d. Marion Amos and Dolores Jeannette McFarlin; m. David Lamar Maywhoor, Mar. 17, 1973 (div.). BA cum laude, Murray State U., Murray, Ky., 2002; MA in Pub. History, Murray State U., 2004. Newspaper reporter Daily Std., Celina, Ohio, 1973—96, Wapakoneta Daily News, Wapakoneta, Ohio, 1996—96. Writer Bowling Green State U. Pub. Rels. Office, Bowling Green, Ohio, 1997—99, Paris Post-Intelligencer, Paris, 2003—05; contbg. editor Paris Mag., 2005—; featured spkr. on vanished black communities for Black History Month Ohio State Univ., Lima, Ohio, 1999; panelist The Journal, WBGU-TV, Bowling Green, 1999; featured spkr. Ohio Valley History Conf., Murray, Ky., 2006; writer The Henry Countian Com., 2006—. Sec. Henry County Dem. Women, Paris, Tenn., 2000—03. Nominee Pulitzer Prize, 1991; recipient Winner, Hellman/Hammett Award, Human Rights Watch, 2000, First Pl., Investigative Reporting, Ohio AP, 1991, Hon. Mention, Writer's Digest Writing Competition, 2005; grantee Vanished

Black Communities Project, The Ohio Hist. Preservation Soc., 1980. Mem.: Alpha Sigma Lambda, Alpha Chi, Pi Sigma Alpha, Phi Alpha Theta. D-Liberal. Achievements include research in vanished black communities in pre and post Civil War era, funded by Ohio Historical Preservation Society; Frances Wright and her experimental community in Nashoba, Tennessee. Avocation: writing. Home: 713 Park St Paris TN 38242 Personal E-mail: shannonmcfarlin@hotmail.com

**MCFARLING, USHA LEE,** newswriter; BA, Brown U., 1988; MA, U. Calif. Berkeley, 1998. With Boston Globe, San Antonio Light; science writer planetary and earth sciences L.A. Times. Mem. sci. and soc. journalism awards com. Nat. Assn. Sci. Writers, Inc.; mem. judging com. Wistar Inst., 2004—; spkr. in field. Recipient award, Wistar Inst., 2004; fellow Knight Sci. Journalism, MIT, 1992—93. Office: LA Times 202 W First St Los Angeles CA 90012 Office Fax: 213-237-4712. Business E-Mail: usha.mcfarling@latimes.com.*

**MCFARREN, FREDDY E.,** military career officer; b. Cleburne, Tex., Oct. 13, 1943; s. Aubrey McFarren; children: Preston, William. BS, U.S. Mil. Acad., 1966; MEd, Duke U.; grad., Armed Forces Staff Coll., U.S. Army War Coll. Commd. 2d lt. US Army, 1966, advanced through grades to maj. gen., various positions, comdr. 18th Field Artillary Brigade, XVIII Airborne Corps, bn. comdr. 1st Bn. 319th Airborne Field Artillery 82d Divsn., exec. officer 155mm bn. 8th Inf. Divsn. Europe, advisor to Vietnamese Rangers Vietnam, field arty. battery comdr. XVIII Airborne Corps Arty., asst. chief staff ops. G3 XVIII Airborne Corps Ft. Bragg, NC, asst. divsn. comdr. 24th Inf. Divsn. (Mechanized) Ft. Stewart, Ga., dir. tng. Office of the Dep. Chief Staff for Ops. and Plans Washington, chief Office Mil. Cooperation Cairo, commdg. gen. 24th Inf. Divsn. (Mechanized) Ft. Riley, Kans., 1998—2000, commdg. gen., 5th US Army Fort Sam, Tex., 2000—; tactical officer US Mil. Acad., comdt. of cadets West Point, NY. Decorated Silver Star, Def. Superior Svc. medal, Legion of Merit with four oak leaf clusters, Bronze Star with V device and three oak leaf clusters, Purple Heart, Meritorious Svc. medal with two oak leaf clusters, Air medal, Army Commendation medal with oak leaf cluster, French Croix de Guerre with Gold Star, The Republic of Vietnam Cross of Gallantry with two Palms and the Honor medal first class.

**MCFARREN, NAZA,** artist; b. Santa Cruz do Piaui, Brazil, Apr. 19, 1955; d. Jose Cortez and Guiomar Maia Rufino; m. Stuart McFarren, June 22, 1984 (div. Aug. 1991); children: Daniel, Guiomar Silva. Tchr. art Fayetteville (N.C.) Mus. Art, 1990-93; owner, pres. Naza Art Studio, Boca Raton, Fla., 1993—. Exhibited in Sao Paulo Mus. Art, Fayetteville (N.C.) Mus. Art, Cornell Mus. Art and History, Delray, Fla., Parish Gallery, Washington, Ardel Gallery, Washington, Vila Riso Gallery, Rio de Janeiro, Patrimony Gallery, Recife, Brazil, Arte Maior Gallery, Recife, Galerie J.L.T., Paris, Gallery Two, Wooster, 93 South Art Gallery, Nyack, N.Y.; represented in permanent collections West Point Acad., Pres. Clinton, Pres. Fernando H. Cardoso, Ivana Trump, Brigite Bardot, Airton Senna Found., also pvt. collections. Recipient Merit award Fayetteville Mus. Art, 1991; decorated Croix d'Argent, Le Merite et Devouement Francaise (France), Comenda Renacenca-Piaui (Brazil); N.C. Arts Coun. Emerging Artist grantee, 1991. Mem. Women in Visual Arts, Profl. Artists Guild, Boca Raton Mus. Art, Soroptimists Internat. (Woman of Distinction). E-mail: naza@naza.com.

**MCFATE, KENNETH LEVERNE,** trade association administrator; b. LeClaire, Iowa, Feb. 5, 1924; s. Samuel Albert and Margaret (Spear) McF.; m. Imogene Grace Kness, Jan. 27, 1951; children: Daniel Elliott (dec.), Kathryn Margaret, Sharon Ann. BS in Agrl. Engring., Iowa State U., 1950; MS in Agrl. Engring., U. Mo., 1959. Registered profl. engr. Mo. Agrl. sales engr. Ill. No. Utility Co., Aledo, 1950-51; extension agrl. engr. Iowa State U., Ames, 1951-53, rsch. agrl. engr., 1953-56; prof. agrl. engr. U. Mo., Columbia, 1956-86, prof. emeritus, 1986; dir. Mo. Farm Electric Coun., Columbia, 1956-75; exec. mgr. Nat. Farm Electric Coun., Columbia, 1975-86; pres. Nat. Food and Energy Coun., Columbia, 1986-91, pres. emeritus, 1991; mgr. Electrotechnology Rsch., 1991-93. Bd. dirs. Internat. Congress Agrl. Engrs., Brussels, 1989—94. Editor, author: (with others) Handbook for Elsevier Science, Electrical Energy in World Agriculture, 1989; mem. editl. bd. Energy in Agriculture for Elsevier Sci., Amsterdam, The Netherlands, 1981-88. With USAAF, 1943—45, 2d lt. USAAF, 1945. Recipient Outstanding Svc. awards Nat. Safety Coun., 1975, MOFEC, 1976, Nat. 4-H Coun., 1982, Nat. Hon. Extension Frat., 1984, Hon. Am. Future Farmers Assn. degree, 1991. Fellow Am. Soc. Agrl. Engrs. (George Kable elec. award 1974, Spl. Svc. award, 2000); mem. Alpha Epsilon, Gamma Sigma Delta. Republican. Presbyterian. Avocations: technical writing, gardening, woodworking.

**MCFATE, PATRICIA ANN,** foundation executive, science educator; b. Detroit, Mar. 19, 1936; d. John Earle and Mary Louise (Bliss) McF.; m. Sidney Norman Graybeal, Sept. 10, 1988. BA (Alumni scholar), Mich. State U., 1954; MA, Northwestern U., 1956, PhD, 1965; MA (hon.), U. Pa., 1977. Assoc. prof. English, asst. dean liberal arts and scis. U. Ill., Chgo., 1967-74, assoc. prof. English, assoc. vice chancellor acad. affairs, 1974-75; assoc. prof. folklore Faculty Arts and Scis., U. Pa., Phila., 1975-81; prof. tech. and soc. Coll. Engring. and Applied Sci., 1975-81, vice provost, 1975-78; dep. chmn. Nat. Endowment for Humanities, Washington, 1978-81; exec. v.p. Am.-Scandinavian Found., N.Y.C., 1981-82, pres., 1982-88; sr. scientist Sci. Applications Internat. Corp., Mc Lean, Va., 1988—, program dir. Ctr. for Nat. Security Negotiations, 1988—; cons. UN, 1994-95. Vis. assoc. prof. dept. medicine Rush U., Chgo., 1970-73; bd. dirs. First Union Corp.; mem. sr. adv. panel Dept. Def., 1998—. Author: The Writings of James Stephens, 1979, Uncollected Prose of James Stephens, 1983; exec. producer Northern Stars, 1985, Diego Rivera: I Paint What I See, 1989, The Bear in the Skies, 1998; contbr. articles in fields of sci. policy and lit. to various jours. Mem. Arms Control and Non-Proliferation Adv. Bd., Dept. of State, 1995-2001; mem. disting. adv. panel Sandia Nat. Labs.; bd. dirs. Raoul Wallenberg Com. of U.S., Swedish Coun. Am., Santa Fe Cmty. Found., Santa Fe Opera, Lensic Performing Arts Ctr. Decorated officer Order of Leopold II Belgium, comdr. Order Icelandic Falcon, comdr. Royal Order of Polar Star (Sweden), comdr. Order of Lion (Finland), comdr. Royal Norwegian Order Merit, Knight 1st class Royal Order Dannebrog (Denmark); U. Ill. Grad. Coll. faculty fellow, 1968; Swedish Bicentennial Fund grantee, 1981 Fellow N.Y. Acad. Scis.; mem. AAAS (chmn. com. on sci., engring. and pub. policy 1984-87, com. on sci. and internat. security 1976-78, 89-93), Coun. on Fgn. Rels., Acad. Scis. Phila. (founding mem., corr. sec. 1977-79), Theta Alpha Phi, Omega Beta Pi, Delta Delta Delta. E-mail: patricia.a.mcfate@saic.com.

**MCFAYDEN, SHANNON W.,** bank holding company executive; b. Sept. 21, 1960; BA in psychology, Davidson Coll. Head human resources Fla. Bank (merged with Wachovia); with Wachovia Corp., 1982—, dir. human resources client svc., 1998—2001, dir. cmty. affairs, 2001—04, sr. v.p., 2004—, head corp. and cmty. affairs, 2004—. Mem. steering com. Bus. Strengthening Am. Bd. dirs. United Way Capital Campaign Planning, KinderMourn, Cmty. Sch. Arts and Child Care Resources, Charlotte -Mecklenburg Pub. Schs. Found. Mem.: Davidson Coll. Alumni Assn. Office: Wachovia Corp 1 Wachovia Ctr Charlotte NC 28288 E-mail: shannon.mcfayden@wachovia.com.

**MCFEATTERS, ANN CAREY,** journalist; b. Colorado Springs, Colo., June 27, 1944; d. Norman Cromer and Mildred Harriet Carey; m. Dale B. McFeatters, Sept. 27, 1969; children: Dale C., Matthew C., Kirsten C. BA, Marquette U., 1966. Reporter Evansville (Ind.) Press, 1966-68, Pitts. Press, 1969, Washington Daily News, 1969-70, Scripps Howard News Svc., Washington, 1970-99; Washington bur. chief The Pitts. Post-Gazette and The Toledo Blade, Washington, 1999—. Author: Sunday Day O'Connor: Justice In The Balance, 2006. Named to Hall of Fame Soc. Profl. Journalists, 1998; recipient Disting. Svc. award Scripps Howard News Svc., 1999. Mem. Nat. Press Found. (chmn. 1996-98), Washington Press Club (pres. 1980-81), The Gridiron Club. Office: Block News Alliance 529 14th St NW Ste 955 Washington DC 20045 E-mail: amcfeatters@nationalpress.com.

**MCFEE, ARTHUR STORER,** physician; b. Portland, Maine, May 1, 1932; s. Arthur Stewart and Helen Knight (Dresser) McF.; m. Iris Goeschel, May 13, 1967. BA cum laude, Harvard U., 1953, MD, 1957; MS, U. Minn., 1966, PhD, 1967. Diplomate: Am. Bd. Surgery. Intern U. Minn. Hosp., 1957-58, resident in surgery, 1958-65; asst. prof. surgery U. Tex. Med. Sch., San Antonio, 1967-70, asso. prof., 1970-74, prof., 1974-2001, ret., 2001, prof. emeritus, 2001—. With Univ. Health Sys., Bexar County, 1968-2003; spl. cons. on emergency med. care text to AAOS. Contbr. articles to profl. jours. Served with USNR, 1955-67. Fellow ACS; mem. AMA, Am. Assn. History of Medicine, Assn. Acad. Surgery, Tex. Med. Assn., Bexar County Med. Soc., Tex. Surg. Soc., Western Surg. Assn., San Antonio Surg. Soc., Soc. Surgery Alimentary Tract, So. Med. Assn., N.Y. Acad. Scis., Royal Soc. Medicine, So. Surg. Assn., Internat. Surg. Soc., Halsted Soc., J. Bradley Aust Surg. Soc., Am. Surg. Assn. Home: 131 Brittany Dr San Antonio TX 78212-1721 Office: MC 7842 7703 Floyd Curl Dr San Antonio TX 78229-3900 Office Phone: 210-567-2164. Business E-Mail: mcfee@uthscsa.edu. *Most of my life has been spent in training surgeons. It has been an informative experience.*

**MCFEE, RICHARD,** electrical engineer, physicist; b. Pitts., Jan. 24, 1925; s. William and Beatrice (Allender) McF.; m. Anne Stauffer, June 26, 1947 (div. 1960); m. 2d., Joanellen Lewis, Dec. 31, 1974. BEE, Yale U., 1947; MS in Physics, Syracuse U., 1949; PhDEE, U. Mich., 1955. Rsch. asst. Syracuse U. Med. Sch., 1947-48; instr. Syracuse U. elec. engring. dept., 1948-49; rsch. assoc. U. Mich. Med. Sch., 1949-51; engr. Electro-Mech. Rsch. Inc., Ridgefield, Conn., 1951-52; mem. tech. staff Bell Tel. Labs., Whippany, NJ, 1952-57; prof. elec. engring. Syracuse U., 1957-82; ind. rschr. Union Springs, NY, 1982—86, Hawi, Hawaii, 1986—. Contbr. articles on electronics, electrocardiography, magnetocardiography, superconductivity, circuit theory, thermodynamics, elec. measurements; patentee in field. Sgt. U.S. Army, 1943-46. Sci. Faculty fellowship NSF, Stanford U., 1970. Fellow IEEE; mem. AAAS, Sigma Xi. Home and Office: PO Box 989 Kapaau HI 96755-0989 Office Phone: 808-889-5778.

**MCFEELY, WILLIAM DRAKE,** publishing company executive; b. Port Chester, NY, July 15, 1954; s. William Shield and Mary (Drake) McF.; m. Karen Gail Eliason, Aug. 12, 1978; children: Matthew Bensen, Eric Daniel, Laura Mae. BA cum laude, Amherst Coll., 1976. Coll. traveler W.W. Norton & Co., Inc., N.Y.C., 1976-80, asst. sales mgr., 1980-82, editor, 1982—, v.p., 1990-94, bd. dirs., 1990—, pres., 1994—, chmn., 2000—. Dir. W.W. Norton & Co., Ltd.; trustee Princeton Univ. Press, chmn., 2004-, Ithaka Harbors, Inc. Mem. Pubs. Lunch Club (pres. 1998-99), Seven Bridges Field Club (pres. 1989). Home: 106 Seven Bridges Rd Chappaqua NY 10514-1121 Office: WW Norton & Co 500 5th Ave Fl 6 New York NY 10110-0054

**MC FEELY, WILLIAM SHIELD,** historian, writer; b. NYC, Sept. 25, 1930; s. William C. and Marguerite (Shield) Mc F.; m. Mary Drake, Sept. 13, 1952; children: William Drake, Eliza, Jennifer. BA, Amherst Coll., 1952, LHD, 1982; MA, Yale U., 1962, PhD, 1966; LD, Washington Coll., 1986. Asst. prof. history and Am. studies Yale U., 1966-69, assoc. prof., 1969-70; dean faculty Mount Holyoke Coll., 1970-73, prof. history, 1970-80, Rodman prof. history, 1980-82, Andrew W. Mellon prof. humanities, 1982-86; Richard B. Russell prof. Am. history U. Ga., Athens, 1986-94, Abraham Baldwin prof. humanities, 1994-97, prof. emeritus, 1997—; Cardozo vis. prof. history Yale U., 2001—. Tchr. Yale-Harvard-Columbia intensive summer studies program, 1967-69; vis. prof. history Univ. Coll. London, 1978-79, Amherst Coll., 1980-81, U. Mass., 1984-85, John J. McCloy prof., 1988-89; cons. to com. on judiciary U.S. Ho. of Reps., 1974 Author: Yankee Stepfather: Gen. O.O. Howard and the Freedmen, 1968, Grant: A Biography, 1981, Frederick Douglass, 1991, Sapelo's People, 1994, Proximity to Death, 1999, Ulysses S. Grant: An Album, 2004, Portrait: The Life of Thomas Eakins, 2006. Recipient Pulitzer Prize in biography, 1982, Francis Parkman prize, 1982, Lincoln prize, 1992, Avery O. Craven award, 1992; Morse fellow, 1968-69, fellow Am. Coun. Learned Socs., 1974-75, Huntington Library, 1976, 83, Guggenheim fellow, 1982-83, assoc. fellow Charles Warren Ctr., 1991-91, fellow Libr. Co. of Phila., 2002-03, Radcliff Instn. Advanced Study, 2006-, vis. scholar W.E.B. Du Bois Inst., Harvard U., 1992—; NEH grantee, 1986-87 Mem. Am. Hist. Assn., So. Hist. Assn., Soc. of Am. Historians, Orgn. Am. Historians, PEN Ctr., Century Assn., Authors Guild. Home: 35 Mill Hill Rd Wellfleet MA 02667-7441

**MC FERON, DEAN EARL,** mechanical engineer, educator; b. Portland, Oreg., Dec. 24, 1923; s. Wallace Suitor and Ruth Carolyn (Fessler) McF.; m. Phyllis Grace Ehlers, Nov. 10, 1945; children: David Alan, Phyllis Ann, Douglas Dean, Donald Brooks. Student, Oreg. State Coll., 1942-43; BSME with spl. honors, U. Colo., 1945, MSME, 1948; PhD, U. Ill., 1956. Instr. U. Colo., Boulder, 1946-48; assoc. prof. U. Ill., 1948-58; rsch. assoc. Argonne (Ill.) Nat. Lab., 1957-58; prof. mech. engring., assoc. dean U. Wash., Seattle, 1958-82, prof. emeritus, 1983—. Cons. to industry, 1959-80 Served with USNR, 1942-46; to comdr. Res., 1946-72. Co-recipient Outstanding Tech. Applications Paper award ASHRAE, 1974; Endl. Achievement award Soc. Mfg. Engrs., 1970; NSF faculty fellow, 1967-68 Mem. ASME, Am. Soc. Engring. Edn., U.S. Naval Inst. Life); Sigma Xi (nat. dir. 1974-78, pres. 1978), Tau Beta Pi, Sigma Tau, Pi Tau Sigma. Home: 4008 NE 40th St Seattle WA 98105-5422 Office: U Wash Dept Mech Engring Seattle WA 98195-0001 *What matters most in life is what you can do for others.*

**MCFERREN, MARTHA DEAN,** writer, librarian; b. Henderson, Tex., Apr. 25, 1947; d. Manley Edward McFerren and Emma Lou Turner; m. Dennis Scott Wall, May 22, 1977. BS, North Tex. State U., 1969, M of Libr. Scs., 1971; MFA, Warren Wilson Coll., 1988. Cert. secondary tchr., Tex. Libr. San Jacinto Coll., Pasadena, Tex., 1971-70, Jefferson Parish Libns., Metairie, La., 1976-81, New Orleans Schs., 1984-85; instr. Dillard U., New Orleans, 1991. Poetry instr. Slidell (La.) Pub. Schs., 1989. Author: Delusions of a Popular Mind, 1983, Get Me Out of Here!, 1984, Contours for Ritual, 1988, Women in Cars, 1992 (Marianne Moore prize 1992); assoc. editor New Laurel Rev., 1980-88. Recipient Moore prize Helicon Nine, 1992, Poetry prize Deep South Conf., 1985, creative writing fellowship Yaddo Colony, 1985, writer's fellowship NEA, 1991, Artist fellowship La. Endowment for the Arts, 1985. Mem. New Orleans Poetry Forum (publicity dir. 1976-90), Poetry Soc. of Am. Home: 2679 Verbena St New Orleans LA 70122-6037 Office Phone: 504-944-2707. E-mail: martha1dennis@aol.com.

**MCFERREN, TINA JOANN,** secondary school educator; b. Zanesville, Ohio, July 13, 1963; d. James Lester and Betsy Eileen McFerren; 1 child, Joshua James. BA, Muskingum Coll., New Concord, Ohio, 1986. Cert. Tchr. Edn. Fla., 1986, Nat. Bd. Cert. Tchrs., 2003. Tchr. Lyman HS, Longwood, Fla., 1986—87, Loch Lowe Prep. Sch., Lake Mary, Fla., 1989—89, Oak Ridge HS, Orlando, 1990—, 1990—. Spkr. Fla. State Conf. at Risk Students, 1995; social studies benchmark devel. team Orange County Pub. Schs., Orlando, 2003. HS sponsor BETA Club, Orlando, 2004—06. Mem.: NEA. Conservative. Methodist. Avocation: travel. Home: 2672 Susanday Dr Orlando FL 32812 Office: Oak Ridge HS 6000 S Winegard Orlando FL 32809 Office Phone: 407-852-3200. Office Fax: 407-850-5152. Business E-Mail: mcferrt@ocps.net.

**MCGAAN, ANDREW RAYMOND,** lawyer; b. Highland Park, Ill., Oct. 15, 1961; s. Dean Bailey and Nancy Eva (Acheson) M. AB with honors, Cornell U., 1983, JD magna cum laude, 1986. Bar: Conn. 1986, Ill. 1991, U.S. Dist. Ct. Conn. 1987, U.S. Dist. Ct. So. & Ea. N.Y. 1988, No. & Ctrl. Ill., U.S. Ct. Appeals 2nd, 7th, 9th & 11th cir. Press. sec. Com. to Elect Congressman Stewart B. McKinney, Fairfield, Conn., 1986; law clk. to Judge Warren W. Eginton U.S. Dist. Ct. Conn., Bridgeport, 1987-88; assoc. Cummings & Lockwood, Stamford, Conn., 1988—90; ptnr. Kirkland & Ellis, Chgo., 1990—. Counsel rep. Forum, Stamford, chmn. polit. action com.; rep. Republican Town Com., Stamford; elder, trustee First Presbyn. Ch. Chgo. Mem. ABA, Conn. Bar Assn., Order of the Coif. Presbyterian. Office: Kirkland & Ellis 200 E Randolph Dr Chicago IL 60601

**MCGAFFEY, JERE D.,** retired lawyer; b. Lincoln, Nebr., Oct. 6, 1935; s. Don Larsen and Doris McG.; m. Ruth S. Michelsen, Aug. 19, 1956; children: Beth, Karen. BA, BSc with high distinction, U. Nebr., 1957; LLB magna cum laude, Harvard U., 1961. Bar: Wis. 1961. Mem. firm Foley & Lardner LLP, Milw., 1961—2004, ptnr., 1968—2004. Dir. Wis. Gas Co., 1978-00, Smith Investment Co., Northwestern Mut. Trust Co., 2000-06, Lord Balt. Corp.; mem. take-over adv. com., Gov. Wis., 1988-89, commn on state/local partnerships 21st century 2000-01. Author works in field. Chmn. bd. dirs. Helen Bader Found.; former vice chmn. legis. Milw. Met. Assn. Commerce, 1984—2003; former chmn. Wis. Taxpayers Alliance, sec.-treas., 1994—; bd. dirs. Aurora Health Care, 1986—, chmn., 1986—90, dir., 1987—; chmn. bd. advisors U. Wis. Nursing Sch., Milw. Mem. ABA (chmn. tax sect. 1990-91, ho. dels. 1995-2000, Sect. Taxation Disting. Svc. award 2005), AICPA, Wis. Bar Assn., Wis. Inst. CPAs, Am. Coll. Tax Counsel (chmn. 1996-98), Am. Coll. Trust and Estate Counsel (chmn. bus. planning com. 1994-97, regent 2000-06), Am. Law Inst., Univ. Club, Milw. Country Club, Harvard Club, Phi Beta Kappa, Beta Gamma Sigma, Delta Sigma Rho. Home: 12852 NW Shoreland Dr Mequon WI 53097-2304 Office: Foley & Lardner 777 E Wisconsin Ave Ste 3600 Milwaukee WI 53202-5302 Business E-Mail: jmcgaffey@foleylaw.com.

**MCGAFFIGAN, EDWARD, JR.,** commissioner; b. Boston, Dec. 8, 1948; s. Edward McGaffigan and Margaret (O'Brien); m. Peggy Weeks, 1982 (dec. 2000); children: Edward Francis, Margaret Ruth. AB in Physics summa cum laude, Harvard U., 1970; MS in Physics, Calif. Inst. Tech., 1974; M in Pub. Policy, Harvard Kennedy Sch. Govt., 1976. Cons. RAND Corp, 1974—75; with Arms Control and Disarmament Agy., Washington, 1975; fgn. svc. officer US Dept. State, 1976—83; sci. attache US Embassy, Moscow, 1978-80; sr. policy analyst, asst. dir. Office Sci. and Tech. Policy The White House, Washington, 1981-83; staff mem. NSC, Washington, 1982-83; legis. asst. to Senator Jeff Bingman, US Senate, Washington, 1983—88, legis. dir., 1989—92, sr. policy adv., 1993—96; commr. US Nuclear Regulatory Commn., Rockville, 1996—2005, 2005—. Harvard Nat. scholar; Sheldon Traveling fellow, NSF fellow, Woodrow Wilson Found. fellow, Millikan fellow, Harvard Nat. Grad. fellow.; recipient NM Medal of Merit, 1986, Nat. Guard Bur. Eagle award, 1996 Mem.: Am. Physics Soc. Roman Catholic. Office: US Nuclear Regulatory Commn One White Flint N Bldg 11555 Rockville Pike Rm 18G1 Rockville MD 20852-2738 Office Phone: 301-415-1800. Business E-Mail: exm@nrc.gov.

**MCGAGH, WILLIAM GILBERT,** financial consultant; b. Boston, May 29, 1929; s. Thomas A. and Mary M. (McDonough) McG.; m. Sarah Ann McQuigg, Sept. 23, 1961; children: Margaret Ellen, Sarah Elizabeth. BSBA, Boston Coll., 1950; MBA, Harvard U., 1952; MS, MIT, 1965. Fin. analyst Ford Motor Co., Dearborn, Mich., 1953-55; mem. staff treas. office Daimler-Chrysler, Detroit, 1955-64, compt. treas. Canadian divsn. Windsor, 1965-67, staff exec.-fin. Latin Am. ops. Detroit, 1967-68, asst. treas., 1968-75, treas., 1975-76, v.p., treas., 1976-80; sr. v.p. fin., dir. Northrop Grumman Corp., L.A., 1980-88; owner McGagh Assocs., Beverly Hills, Calif., 1988—. Mem. adv. bd. Santa Monica-UCLA and Orthopaedic Hosp. Mem. bd. regents Mt. St. Mary's Coll.; bd. dirs. L.A. Orthop. Hosp.; chmn. bd. dirs. John Tracy Clinic. Sloan fellow MIT, 1965. Mem. Fin. Execs. Inst. (pres. Detroit chpt. 1979-80), Harvard Club (N.Y.C. and Boston), Beach Club (Santa Monica, Calif.), L.A. Country Club, Calif. Club (L.A.), Eastward Ho Country Club (Chatham, Mass.). Office: McGagh Assocs 9601 Wilshire Blvd Ste 560 Beverly Hills CA 90210-5208 Home: 2189 Century Hill Los Angeles CA 90067 Office Phone: 310-248-4395. Personal E-Mail: wgm9601@aol.com.

**MCGAHA, CINDY,** education educator; b. Donald McGaha and Thelma Baxter; 1 child, Marietta. PhD, U. NC, Greensboro, 1997. Asst. prof. East Carolina U., Greenville, NC, 1997—2000; assoc. prof. Appalachian State U., Boone, NC, 2000—. Contbr. articles to profl. jours. V.p. NC Assn. for the Edn. of Young Children, 2002—05; sec. Intermountain Head Start, Spruce Pine, NC, 2003—05. Frances Finnell Vandiver fellow, Berea Coll., 1991, Josie Nance fellow, U. NC, 1996. Mem.: Coun. for Exceptional Children, Nat. Assn. for the Edn. of Young Children (life; v.p. pub. awareness 2003—05), Phi Kappa Phi. Office: Appalachian State Univ Boone NC 28608 Office Phone: 828-262-2632. Home Fax: 828-265-8620; Office Fax: 828-265-8620. Business E-Mail: mcgahac@appstate.edu.

**MCGAHEE, WILLIS,** professional football player; b. Miami, Fl, Oct. 20, 1981; Student, U. of Miami. Player Buffalo Bills, 2004—. Office: c/o Buffalo Bills 1 Bllls Dr Orchard Park NY 14127*

**MCGANN, CHRISTOPHER JOHN,** cardiologist, educator; b. New Haven, Conn., May 30, 1965; s. Jerome John and Anne Patricia McGann; m. Margaret Niver, Aug. 7, 1994; children: Fiona Baird, Owen Jerome. MD, U. Va., Charlottesville, 1990—94. Lic. cardiologist Am. Bd. Internal Medicine, 2000. Asst. prof. medicine U. Utah Health Scis. Ctr., Salt Lake City, 2000—. Dir., cardiovascular MRI U. Utah Health Scis. Ctr., 2003—. Contbr. articles to profl. jours. Independent. Unitarian Universalist. Achievements include patents for newt limb regeneration extract. Office: Univ Utah Health Scis Ctr 50 N Medical Dr Salt Lake City UT 84132 Office Fax: 801-581-7735. Business E-Mail: chris.mcgann@hsc.utah.edu.

**MCGANN, JEROME JOHN,** language educator; b. N.Y.C., July 22, 1937; s. John Joseph and Marie Violet (Lecouffe) McG.; m. Anne Patricia Lanni, July 26, 1969; children: Geoffrey, Christopher, Jennifer. BS, Le Moyne Coll., 1959; MA, Syracuse U., 1962; PhD, Yale U., 1966; LHD (hon.), U. Chgo., 1996. From asst. prof. to prof. U. Chgo., 1966-75; prof. Johns Hopkins U., Balt., 1975-80; Dreyfuss prof. humanities Calif. Inst. Tech., Pasadena, 1980-86; John Stewart Bryan univ. prof. U. Va., Charlottesville, 1987—. Author: Swinburne: An Experiment in Criticism, 1972 (Melville Cane award 1972), The Romantic Ideology, 1983, The Beauty of Inflections, 1985, Social Values and Poetic Acts, 1987, Towards a Literature of Knowledge, 1989, The Textual Condition, 1991, Black Riders: The Visible Language of Modernism, 1993; editor: The New Oxford Book of Romantic Period Verse, 1993, Poetics of Sensibility: A Revolution in Literary Style, 1996, Byron: Complete Poetical Works, 7 vols., 1980-93, Dante Gabriel Rossetti and the Game That Must Be Lost, 2000, The Complete Writings and Pictures of Dante Gabriel Rossetti: A Hypermedia Research Archive, 2000—, Radiant Textuality, Literature after the World Wide Web, 2001, Byron and Romanticism, 2002, D.G. Rosetti. Collected Poetry and Prose, 2003, Swinburne, Selected Poetry and Prose, 2004, The Scholar's Art: Literary Studies in a Managed World, 2006; author, editor 25 scholarly books and 4 poetry books. Recipient Mellon Achievement award, 2003, Richard Lyman award, 2002, James Russell Lowell award, 2002; Fulbright fellow, Fels Found. fellow, Eng., 1965-66; Guggenheim fellow, Eng., 1970-71, 74-75; NEH fellow, Eng. and Europe, 1975-76, 87-88, 2003—. Fellow: Am. Acad. Arts and Scis.; mem.: MLA. Address: English Department Bryan Hall 1 VA Charlottesville VA 22903 Office Phone: 434-924-4064. Business E-Mail: jjm2f@virginia.edu.

**MCGANN, LISA B. NAPOLI,** language educator; b. West Hartford, Conn., Sept. 07; d. James Napoli; m. Edward Harrison McGann, Jr. BA, Vassar Coll., 1980; MA, Columbia U., 1983, postgrad., 1991-95; MA, Middlebury Coll., 1987. Cert. tchr. French, ESL and Italian, Conn. Cmty. English program coord. Tchrs. Coll. Columbia U., N.Y.C., 1982-83; mgr. English tchg. com. Jr. League N.Y., 1983-84; asst. dir. ESL Fordham U., N.Y.C., 1988-89; ESL instr. Laguardia C.C., CUNY, Long Island City, NY, 1983—; Columbia U., 1983-96. ESL instr. Yale U., 1988, 89; ESL specialist, tchr. UN, N.Y.C., 1990. Big sister Highland Hts., New Haven, 1976-77; ESL tchr. Boys and Girls Club, Astoria, N.Y., 1992. Recipient awards and scholarships. Mem. Nat. TESOL Soc., Am. Assn. Tchrs. Italian, Italian-Am. Hist. Soc., Nat. Italian Am. Found. (coun.), The Statue of Liberty-Ellis Island Found., Inc. Roman Catholic. Avocations: ballet, reading, travel, real estate, tennis.

**MCGANNEY, THOMAS,** lawyer; b. San Mateo, Calif., Mar. 12, 1938; s. Daniel James and Mary Irene (West) McGanney; m. Mildred Kalik McGanney; children: Jennifer, Abigail, Melanie, Juliana. BA, Stanford U., 1959;

LLB, Harvard U., 1962. Bar: N.Y. 1963, U.S. Dist. Ct. (so. and ea. dists.) N.Y. 1965, U.S. Ct. Appeals (2d cir.) 1966, U.S. Ct. Appeals (3d cir.) 1969, U.S. Ct. Appeals (10th cir.) 1970, U.S. Supreme Ct. 1971, U.S. Ct. Appeals (9th cir.) 1990. Law clk. U.S. Dist. Ct., So. Dist. N.Y., 1962—64; assoc. White & Case, N.Y.C., 1964—72, ptnr., 1973—. Adj. prof. NYU Law Sch., 1984—86. Mem.: ABA, Assn. Bar City of N.Y., Fed. Bar Coun., N.Y. State Bar Assn., Am. Coll. Trial Lawyers. Office: White & Case Bldg Ll 1155 Avenue Of The Americas New York NY 10036-2787 E-mail: tmcganney@whitecase.com.

**MCGAREL-WARKOCKI, LYNN M.,** history educator; b. Evergreen Park, Ill., Jan. 12, 1966; d. Owen F. McGarel and Lillian Levri-McGarel; m. Robert J. Warkocki, June 23, 1990; children: Elizabeth Lynn Warkocki, Ana Jo Warkocki. Bachelor's, U. Ill., Chgo., 1989; Master's, St. Xavier U., Chgo., 2000. Tchr. social studies Jerling Jr. HS, Orland Park, Ill., 1990—91; tchr. history Amos Alonzo Stagg HS, Palos Hills, Ill., 1991—. Dir. Dist. 230 Age Group Gymnastics, Palos Hills, 1991—97. Mem.: NEA, Nat. Coun. for Social Studies, Sports Car Club of Am., Phi Alpha Theta (founder, sponsor Dist. 230 chpt. 2004—). Avocations: reading, exercise. Office: Amos Alonzo Stagg HS 111th & Roberts Rd Palos Hills IL 60465 E-mail: lmcgarel@d230.org.

**MCGARR, ARTHUR FRANCIS,** geophysicist; b. San Francisco, Calif., May 24, 1940; s. Arthur Francis and Elizabeth (Radius) McGarr; m. Annette Bilger McGarr, Feb. 9, 1971; children: Philip, Timothy. BS, Calif. Inst. Tech., 1962, MS, 1963; PhD, Columbia U., 1968. Sr. rsch. fellow U. Witwatersrand, Johannesburg, 1968—70, sr. rsch. officer, 1970—77; geophysicist U.S. Geol. Survey, Menlo Pk., Calif., 1977—. Assoc. editor: Jour. Geophys. Rsch., 1983—85, author, editor: Induced Seismicity, 1993. Scoutmaster Boy Scouts Am. Troop 52, Palo Alto, Calif., 1987—93. Mem.: AAAS, Seismological Soc. Am. (assoc. editor bulletin 1994—), Am. Geophys. Union. Avocations: rock climbing, tennis, windsurfing. Office: US Geological Survey MS 977 345 Middlefield Rd Menlo Park CA 94025

**MCGARR, FRANK JAMES,** retired federal judge, consultant; b. Feb. 25, 1921; married; 6 children. BA cum laude, Loyola U., Chgo., 1942, JD, 1950, degree (hon.), 2002. Bar: Ill. 1950. Assoc. Dallstream Schiff Stern & Hardin, Chgo., 1952—54; asst. U.S. atty., chief criminal divsn. No. dist. of Ill., 1954—55, first asst. U.S. atty., 1955—58; ptnr. McKay Solum & McGarr, Chgo., 1958—68; first asst. atty. gen. State of Ill., 1969—70; judge U.S. Dist. Ct. for No. Ill., 1970—88, chief judge, 1981—86, sr. judge, 1986—88; of counsel Phelan Cahill & Quinlan, Chgo., 1988—96, Foley & Lardner, Chgo., 1996—2001; arbitration and mediation pvt. practice, 2001—. Instr. Eng. and pub. speaking Loyola U., 1946—48, administrv. asst. to pres., 1948—52; instr. law Loyola U. Law Sch., 1950—52, instr. criminal law, 1953—57, prof. admiralty and maritime law, 1953—57; instr. legal ethics John Marshal Law Sch., 1985—86. Chmn. law observance com. Chgo. Crime Comm., v.p., bd. dirs.; chmn. Law Enforcement Week Com.; pres. Constl. Rights Found., 1994; chmn. Ill Gov.'s Comm. on Death Penalty, 2000. With USN, 1942—45, Pacific Fleet. Named Man of Yr., Cath. Lawyers Guild Chgo., 1985; recipient Alumni Medal of Excellence, Loyola Law Alumni, 1964, Mother Cabrini award, Columbus-Cuneo-Cabrini Med. Ctr., 1978, Dei Gloriam award, St. Ignatius Coll. Prep, 1984, Disting. Jurist award, Loyola U. Law Sch., Chgo. Fellow: Am. Coll. Trial Lawyers; mem.: Soc. Trial Lawyers, Chgo. Bar Assn., Fed. Bar Assn. (pres. chgo. chpt. 1962—63, mem. exec. com.), 7th Cir. Bar Assn. Office: 4146 Venard Rd Downers Grove IL 60515-1908 Office Phone: 630-960-4655.

**MCGARRELL, JAMES,** artist, educator; b. Indpls., Feb. 22, 1930; s. James and Gretchen (Heermann) McG.; m. Anna (Harris), June 24, 1955; children: Andrew Rider, Flora Raven. BA, Ind. U., 1953; MA, U. Calif. at Los Angles, 1955. Artist in residence Reed Coll., Portland, Oreg., 1956—59; prof. fine arts, dir. grad. painting Ind. U., Bloomington, Ind., 1959—80; prof. emeritus, 1993—; artist in residence Dartmouth Coll., 1993, Roswell, N. Mex. Found., 1999. Exhibitions include Frumkin, Adams Gallery, N.Y.C., 1961, 1964, 1966, Gallery Claude Bernard, Paris, 1967, Gallery Il Fante de Spade, Rome and Milan, 1967, Frumkin, Adams Gallery, N.Y.C., 1968, Gallery Claude Bernard, Paris, 1970, Gallery Il Fante de Spade, Rome and Milan, 1971, Frumkin, Adams Gallery, N.Y.C., 1971, Gallery Il Fante de Spade, Rome and Milan, 1972, Utah Mus. Art, Salt Lake City, 1972, Frumkin, Adams Gallery, N.Y.C., 1973, Gallery Il Fante de Spade, Rome and Milan, 1974, Gallery Claude Bernard, Paris, 1974, Gallery Il Fante de Spade, Rome and Milan, 1976, Frumkin, Adams Gallery, N.Y.C., 1977, Gallery Il Fante de Spade, Rome and Milan, 1979, Frumkin, Adams Gallery, N.Y.C., 1980, Galeria Gian Ferrari, Milan, 1981, Art Mus. Univ. N.Mex., Albuquerque, 1982, Gallery Gian Ferrari, Milan, 1983, Frumkin, Adams Gallery, N.Y.C., 1984, St. Louis Art Mus., 1985, Frumkin, Adams Gallery, N.Y.C., 1986, More Gallery, Phila., 1987, Frumkin, Adams Gallery, N.Y.C., 1988, Struve Gallery, Chgo., 1988, Frumkin, Adams Gallery, N.Y.C., 1989, Gallery Simonne Stern, New Orleans, 1989, Frumkin, Adams Gallery, N.Y.C., 1989, More Gallery, Phila., 1989, Frumkin, Adams Gallery, N.Y.C., 1990, Struve Gallery, Chgo., 1990, Printworks Gallery, 1990, Gallery Simonne Stern, New Orleans, 1991, Frumkin, Adams Gallery, N.Y.C., 1991, 1993, More Gallery, Phila., 1994, Gallery Simonne Stern, New Orleans, 1994, Frumkin, Adams Gallery, N.Y.C., 1995, Gallery Simonne Stern, New Orleans, 1995, George Adams Gallery, N.Y.C., 1997, Gallery Simonne Stern, New Orleans, 1998, The Art Gallery Univ. N.H., Durham, 1998, Art Mus. U. Ariz., Tucson, 1998, Printworks Gallery, Chgo., 1999, Gallery Simonne Stern, New Orleans, 2000, George Adams Gallery, N.Y.C., 2000, Sonia Zaks Gallery, Chgo., 2001, 2003, Heriard Cimino Gallery, New Orleans, 2003, Represented in permanent collections Mus. Modern Art, N.Y.C., Met. Mus. Art, Whitney Mus. Am. Art, Pa. Acad., Phila., Santa Barbara Mus. Art, Calif., San Francisco Art Mus., Art Inst., Chgo., Joseph Hirshborn Mus., Washington, St. Louis Art Mus., Hamburg Mus. Art, Germany, Centre Georges Pompidou, Paris, Rose Art Mus., Brandeis U. Bd. gov. Skowhegan Sch. Painting and Sculpture. Recipient Am. Acad. Arts and Letters Lifetime Achievement Award, 1995; Fulbright Fellow, 1955-56; Guggenheim Found. Fellow, 1965; Nat. Endowment for Arts grantee, 1967, 85; Bogliasco Found. Fellow, 2003; Rockerfeller Found. Bellagio Ctr. Fellow Mem. Coll. Art Assn. (bd. dir. 1969-73), Academie des Beaux Arts de L'Institut de France, Nat. Acad. Design. Home: PO Box 39 Newbury VT 05051-0039 Office Phone: 802-866-5447. E-mail: bluedeuce@charter.net.

**MCGARRIGLE, THOMAS J.,** lawyer; b. Phila., Aug. 4, 1953; BS in acctg., Villanova U., 1975, JD, 1978. Bar: Pa. 1978, US Ct. Appeals 3rd Cir., US Dist. Ct. Ea. Dist. Pa., US Dist. Ct. Dist. Ariz., Supreme Ct. Pa. 3rd. dist. atty., Phila., 1978—85; assoc. Reed Smith LLP, Phila., 1985—90, ptnr., 1990—, Phila./Wilmington practice group leader litig. group. Mem. Phila. Assn. Def. Counsel, Phila. Bar Assn. Office: Reed Smith LLP 2500 One Liberty Pl 1650 Market St Philadelphia PA 19103 Office Phone: 215-851-8220. Office Fax: 215-851-1420. Business E-Mail: tmcgarrigle@reedsmith.com.

**MCGARRY, DOROTHY,** librarian; b. Omaha, May 1, 1929; d. Moore and Ruth (Gorelick) Lasher. AB, UCLA, 1949, MLS, 1971. Catalog libr. UCLA, 1971-76, head cataloging divsn. phys. sci. and tech. libr., 1976-93, emerita, 1993—. Mem. vocabulary task force for revision GeoRef Thesaurus 4th edit. Am. Geol. Inst. Fellow Spl. Libr. Assn. (chair commn. on cataloging 1983-89, 97-99, 2002-05, rep. CIP adv. group 1983-88, rep. Internat. Fedn. Libr. Assns. and Instns. sect. on classification and indexing 1988-95, 2003—, rep. to sect. on cataloging 1995-2003, chair physics astronomy-math. divsn. 1982-83, chair sci.-tech. divsn. 1991-92, rep. of the SLA geography and map divsn. Anglo-Am. Cataloging com. for Cartographic Materials, 1988—, internat. rels. com. 1989-97, bd. dirs. 1995-97, SLA del. to the Internat. Fedn. of Libr. Assns. and Instns. 1993-97, treas So. Calif. chpt. 1991-93, pres. So. Calif. Chpt. 1994-95, SLA John Cotton Dana award 1991, chair by-laws com. 2000-2002, Hall of Fame 2003—); mem. AAAS, ALA (resources and tech. svcs. divsn., catalog form and function com. 1986-90), Assn. for Libr. Collections and Tech. Svc. (orgn./by-law com., 1999-2001, cataloging and classification sect. chair com.

on cataloging desc. and access 1985-86, mem., 2001-05, policy and rsch. com. 1988-92, subject analysis com. 1993-96, mem.-at-large cataloging and classification sect. 1993-96, chair cataloging and classification sect. 1997-98, Margaret Mann Citation, 2005), Map and Geography Round Table (cataloging and classification com., 1999—; honors award 2003), Am. Math. Soc. (libr. com. 1989-98), Am. Phys. Soc., Am. Soc. for Info. Sci. (L.A. chpt., chair by-laws com. 1989-89, 99-2001, sec. 1987-88, Outstanding Mem. Yr. award 1990, 94, other coms.), Assn. Coll. Rsch. Librs. (sci.-tech. sect., chair ad hoc com. designing conf. proc. style sheet 1984-87, other coms.), Calif. Acad. and Rsch. Libr., Calif. Libr. Assn., Geosci. Info. Soc., Internat. Fedn. Libr. Assns. and Instns. (chair com. on classification and indexing 1989-93, sec. 1993-95, mem., 2003-07, sect. cataloging 1995-2003), Math. Assn. Am., N.Am. Serials Interest Group, Online Audiovisual Catalogers, South Calif. Tech. Processes Group, ISBD (review group, 1997-). Office: UCLA Sci & Engring Libr 8251 Boelter Hl Los Angeles CA 90095-1598 E-mail: dmcgarry@ucla.edu.

**MCGARRY, JOHN EVERETT,** lawyer; b. Madison, Wis., May 11, 1939; s. Daniel E. and Margaret A. (Haas) McG.; m. Kate Wickman, Aug. 26, 1961; children: John Eric, Andrew Lawrence. BA, Lehigh U., 1961, BS in Metall. Engring., 1962; LLB, Georgetown U., 1966. Bar: Okla. 1966, Mich. 1968. Atty. Phillips Petroleum Co., Bartlesville, Okla., 1966-67, Price, Heneveld, Huizenga & Cooper, Grand Rapids, Mich., 1967-70; pvt. practice, Grand Rapids, 1970-72; ptnr. McGarry & Waters, Grand Rapids, 1972-78, Varnum Riddering Wierengo & Christenson, Grand Rapids, 1979-84, Varnum Riddering Schmidt & Howlett, Grand Rapids, 1984-97, Rader Fishman & Grauer, PLLC, Grand Rapids, 1997—2001; chmn. McGarry Bair, PC, Grand Rapids, 2001—. Mem. Opera Grand Rapids, 1984-92, pres., 1991. Mem. Am. Intellectual Property Law Assn. (chmn. harmonization com. 1993-95, chmn. alternate dispute resolution com. 2002-04). Office: McGarry Bair PC 171 Monroe Ave NW Ste 600 Grand Rapids MI 49503-2634 Office Phone: 616-742-3500. Business E-Mail: jem@mcgarrybair.com.

**MCGARRY, LISA COUGHLIN,** language educator; b. Phila., June 10, 1963; d. Neil G. and Nancy V. Coughlin; m. Patrick J. McGarry, Apr. 5, 1986; 1 child, Neil Patrick. BA in English, Temple U., 1986; MA, Villanova U., 1992; PhD, Lehigh U., 2002. V.p. mktg. Universal Svc. Agy., Fort Washington, Pa., 1987—91; lectr. Gwynedd-Mercy Coll., Gwynedd Valley, Pa., 1992—98, dir. acad. resource ctr., 1998—2002, asst. prof., dir., 2002—03, asst. prof., writing program coord., 2003—. Co-chair mission and values com. Gwynedd-Mercy Coll., Pa., 2000—02, mem. strategic planning steering com., 2003—05; mem. faculty-student com. Gwynedd-Mercy Coll. Middle States Self-Study Work Group, 2004—, chair faculty-student com., 2006—, chair middle states self-study workgroup, 2004—06, co-chair, FYE Task Force, 2005—06. Mem.: MLA, Internat. Va. Woolf Soc., Nat. Coun. Tchrs. English, Lambda Iota Tau, Kappa Delta Pi (hon.). Office: Gwynedd-Mercy Coll 1325 Sumneytown Pike Gwynedd Valley PA 19437 E-mail: mcgarry.l@gmc.edu.

**MCGARRY, ROBERT ALAN,** university administrator; b. Passaic, N.J., Dec. 23, 1965; s. Thomas R. and Irene (Crawford) McG. MusB, Bucknell U., 1988; M. Music Edn., Hartt Sch. Music, Hartford, Conn., 1990. Cert. tchr. music. Assoc. dir. student affairs The Juilliard Sch., N.Y.C., 1993—. Mem. Mid Atlantic Assn. Coll. and Univ. Housing Officers (presenter 1992), Am. Coll. Pers. Assn. (presenter 1990—). Avocation: solo singing. Home and Office: The Juilliard Sch Office of Student Affairs 60 Lincoln Center Plz New York NY 10023-6500

**MCGARVIE-MUNN, IAIN LACHLAN,** curator, writer, agent; b. NYC, Dec. 24, 1949; m. Juliet van Otteren, Jan. 12, 1996. Dir. restoration, curator Chateau d'Entrecasteaux, France, 1974—95; freelance curator-coord. Hon. vice consul of Guatemala, Marseille, France, 1982—92; pres. Rt. Historique des Hauts Lieux de Provence, France, 1982—92. Recipient prize, Assn. Vielles Maisons Francaise, 1972, Diplome d'Honneur, Assn. Vielles Maisons Francaises, 1990, Prix des Chefs d'Oeuvre en Peril, French Ministry of Culture, 1977, Obelisque du Conseil de l'Europe, European Coun./La Demeure Historique, 1980, Prix de La Fondation Am., Versailles Found., 1986, Label du Meilleur Accueil dans les Musees, Ministry of Culture, 1988, Qualite Var Accueil, State Dept. Tourism, 1994, Marc de Beauvau Craon, La Demeure Historique/Ministry of Tourism, 1994, Grand Prix des Depliants Touristiques, Ministry of Tourism, 1995, Tourism medal. Achievements include founding of the association of historical monuments open to the public in Var Goute, France; founding of the Festival International de Musique d'Entrecasteaux, France. Personal E-Mail: iainmunn@earthlink.net.

**MCGAUGHEY, CHARLES GILBERT,** retired biochemist; b. San Diego, Sept. 8, 1925; s. Gilbert Arthur and Louisa Ellen (Inskeep) McG. BA, U. Calif., Berkeley, 1950; MA, U. So. Calif., 1952. Diplomate Am. Inst. Oral Biology. Scientist radiol. hazards evaluation U.S. Naval Radiol. Def. Lab., San Francisco, 1952; rsch. biochemist VA Med. Ctr., Long Beach, Calif., 1953-81; prin. investigator studied dental caries, plaque and oral cancer Oral Diseases Rsch. Lab., 1978-81. Contbr. articles to profl. jours. Grantee Nat. Inst. Dental Rsch., 1965. Mem. AAAS. Home: 337 N Winnipeg Pl Long Beach CA 90814-2564

**MCGAVICK, MICHAEL S.,** former insurance and financial services company executive; b. Seattle, Feb. 7, 1958; BA, U. Wash., 1983. V.p. The Rockey Comp., Wash. Round Table, 1986—88; chief of staff for Sen. Slade Gorton, 1989—91; ptnr. The Gallatin Group, Seattle, 1991—92; dir. Superfund Improvement Project, Am. Insurance Assn., 1992—95; pres. & COO CNA Fin. Corp., Chicago, 1995—2001; CEO, pres. SAFECO Corp., 2001—05, chmn., 2001—05.*

**MCGAVRAN, FREDERICK JAEGER,** lawyer; b. Columbus, Ohio, Apr. 24, 1943; s. James Holt and Marion (Jaeger) McG.; m. Elizabeth Dowlig, Jan. 5, 1980; children: Sarah Ann, Marian Katherine. BA, Kenyon Coll., 1965; JD, Harvard U., 1972. Bar: Ohio 1972, U.S. Supreme Ct. 1984, Ky. 1992. Assoc. Kyte, Conlan, Wulsin & Vogeler, Cin., 1972-78, Frost & Jacobs, Cin., 1978-2000, Frost, Brown & Todd, LLC, Cin., 2000—. Editor-in-chief Sixth Circuit Federal Practice Manual, 1999. Lt. USN, 1965-69. Mem. Fed. Bar Assn. (cin. chpt. 1984-85, mem. exec. com. Cin. chpt. 1985—), Ohio State Bar Assn. (chmn. com. on fed. cts. 1982-85), Univ. Club of Cin., The Literary Club (trustee). Home: 3528 Traskwood Cir Cincinnati OH 45208 Office: Frost Brown & Todd LLC 2200 PNC Ctr Cincinnati OH 45202 Office Phone: 513-651-6940. E-mail: fmcgavran@fbtlaw.com, fmcgavran@fuse.net.

**MCGEADY, PAUL JOSEPH,** lawyer; b. Jersey City, Nov. 12, 1920; BS, St. Peters Coll., 1942; LLD, Fordham U., 1948. Bar: N.Y. 1949, U.S. Ct. Appeals D.C. 1989, U.S. Supreme Ct. 1988. Asst. v.p., counsel Continental Can, N.Y.C., 1950-78; gen. counsel Morality in Media, N.Y.C., 1978—; dir. Nat. Obscenity Law Ctr., N.Y.C., 1978—. Author: Rise and Fall of the ACA, 1972, ABC Statutes and Regulations, 1977; editor: Obscenity Law Reporter, 2986. Bd. dirs. Morality in Media, Inc.; chmn. & pub. Served to 1st lt. USAAF, 1943-45, MTO. Decorated Air medal, knight Holy Sepulchre. Mem. KC. Republican. Roman Catholic. Office: Morality in Media Inc 475 Riverside Dr Ste 239 New York NY 10115-0056 Business E-Mail: paul@moralityinmedia.org.

**MCGEE, BRUCE D.,** evangelist; b. Lenoir, NC, Nov. 29, 1943; s. Julian B. and Lorece M. McGee (Stepmother), Dorothy I. McGee; m. Ann E. Saxon, Nov. 29, 1945; children: Robert L., Melissa A. Flow. BA, U. La., Monroe, 1974. Pastor Columbia Heights Bapt., Columbia, La., 1997—, Good Hope Bapt., West Monroe, La., 1988—97, Ctr. Point Bapt., West Monroe, 1981—88; store mgr. Safeway Stores, Inc., Texarkana, Ark., 1974—78; asst. mgr. Safeway Stores Inc., West Monroe, 1968—74. Chaplain Caldwell Sheriff's Dept., Columbia, La., 2000—; exec. bd. mem. La. Bapt. Conv., Columbia, La.; pastoral ministries dir. Caldwell Bapt. Assn. Columbia, La., 1999—. Composer (writer): (book) Born To Grow In Jesus, Sealed In His

Spirit. Bd. dirs. Crossover Ministries, Columbia, La., 1999—2003. Sgt. USAF, 1963—67. R-Conservative. Christian. Avocation: golf. Home: 205 Adams Columbia LA 71418 Personal E-mail: mcge3582@bellsouth.net.

**MCGEE, HAROLD JAMES,** writer; b. Cambridge, Mass., Oct. 3, 1951; s. Charles Gilbert and Louise (Hanney) McG.; m. Sharon Rugel Long, July 7, 1979; children: John, Florence. BS, Calif. Inst. Tech., 1973; PhD, Yale U., 1978. Co-founder Senomyx, Inc., La Jolla, Calif., 1999. Author: On Food and Cooking, 1984 (André Simon award 1985) 2nd edit., 2004, The Curious Book, 1990; contbr. articles to profl. jours. Recipient André Simon award André Simon Meml. Fund, Pioneer award Chefs Assn.

**MCGEE, HAROLD JOHNSTON,** former academic administrator; b. Portsmouth, Va., Apr. 13, 1937; s. Harold Valentine McGee and Clara Mae (Johnston) Webber; m. Mary Frances Eure, Mar. 22, 1959; children: Harold Johnston, Mary Margaret, Matthew Hayden; m. Linda Gayle Stevens, Apr. 3, 1976; 1 child, Andrew Meade. BS, Old Dominion U., 1959; MEd, U. Va., 1962, EdD, 1968; HumD, James Madison U., 1999. Tchr. Falls Church (Va.) City Schs., 1959-62; asst. dean, then dean of admissions Old Dominion U., Norfolk, Va., 1962-65; field rep., program officer, sr. program officer U.S. Office Edn. Bur. Higher Edn., Charlottesville, 1965-70; provost Tidewater Community Coll., Portsmouth, 1970-71; founding pres. Piedmont Va. Community Coll., Charlottesville, 1971-75; various offices including dean grad. sch., asst. to pres., v.p. student affairs, v.p. adminstrv. affairs, sec. bd. visitors James Madison U., Harrisonburg, Va., 1975-86; pres. Jacksonville (Ala.) State U., 1986-99, pres. emeritus, 1999—. Bd. dirs. Gulf South Conf., chmn., 1990—92, Ala. Coun. Univ. Pres., 1991—92; bd. dirs. Trans America Athletic Conf., chmn., 1998—99. Author: Impact of Federal Support, 1968, The Virginia Project, 1976. Mem. United Way Calhoun County Ala., 1986—92, Leadership Ala.; bd. dir. Ala. 529 Fund Savs. Bd., 2004—, Ala. Prepaid Coll. Tuition Bd., 2004—. Mem.: NCAA (coun. 1991—95), Phi Delta Kappa. Episcopalian.

**MCGEE, HENRY ALEXANDER, JR.,** academic administrator; b. Atlanta, Sept. 12, 1929; s. Henry Alexander and Arrie Mae (Mallory) McG.; m. Betty Rose Herndon, July 29, 1951; children: Henry Alexander, Charles Nelson, Kathy Nan. BChemE, Ga. Inst. Tech., 1951, PhD, 1955; postgrad., U. Wis., 1955-56. Rsch. scientist Army Rocket and Guided Missile Agy. and NASA, Huntsville, Ala., 1956-59; from assoc. prof. to prof. chem. engring. Ga. Inst. Tech., Atlanta, 1959-71; prof. Va. Poly. Inst. and State U., Blacksburg, 1971-94, head dept. chem. engring., 1971-82; assoc. provost for engring. Va. Commonwealth U., Richmond, 1994-95, founding dean engring., 1995-99, founding dean emeritus, prof. chem. engring., 1999—2006; asst. dean engring. and mfg. techs. J. Sargeant Reynolds C.C., 2006—. Vis. prof. Calif. Inst. Tech., 1984; dir. chem. and transport sys. div. NSF, Washington, 1990-93; cons. in field. Author: Molecular Engineering, 1991; editorial adv. bd.: Chemical Abstracts; contbr. numerous articles to profl. publs. Bd. dirs. Greater Richmond Tech. Coun. Recipient Cmty. Svc. award Richmond Joint Engrs. Coun., 2000, Leadership award Greater Richmond Tech. Coun., 2002; various rsch. grants NSF, NASA, Air Force Office Sci. Rsch.; named one of five Outstanding Young Men of Yr. Atlanta, 1964, Acad. Disting. Engring. Alumni, Ga. Tech., 1994; Danforth assoc.; named to Hall of Fame, Ga. Tech., 2006. Fellow AIChE (chmn. nat. program com., mem. editl. bd. jour); AAAS (chmn. sect. on engring. 1985-86); mem. Am. Chem. Soc.; mem. Sigma Xi. Republican. Home: 6 River Court Ln Richmond VA 23238-5581 Office: Va Commonwealth U Richmond VA 23284 Office Phone: 804-754-5576. Business E-mail: hmcgee@vcu.edu.

**MCGEE, HUGH E., III,** investment company executive; BS summa cum laude, Princeton Univ., 1981; JD with honors, Univ. Tex., 1984. With Lehman Bros. Holdings, NYC, 1993—, mng. dir., mem. exec. com., head investment banking div., 2002—. Office: Lehman Bros Holdings 745 Seventh Ave New York NY 10019 Office Phone: 212-526-2863. Business E-mail: hmcgee@lehman.com.*

**MCGEE, HUMPHREY GLENN,** retired architect; b. June 26, 1937; s. James Gladney and Elizabeth Adams (Williams) McG. BArch, Clemson U., 1960. Designer Clark, McCall & Leach, Hartsville-Kingstree, S.C., 1961; designer prodn. A. G. Odell & Assocs., Charlotte, N.C., 1962; chief designer Clark, McCall & Leach, Hartsville-Kingstree, 1963; sr. designer LBC & W, Inc., Columbia, SC, 1965—76, sr. v.p. client svcs. and design, 1976; pres. CEDA, Inc., Columbia, S.C., 1976-86; pres., treas. McGee-Howle & Assocs., Vero Beach, Fla., 1986—2002; pvt. practice Indian River Shores, Fla., 2002—05, Chattanooga, 2002—05; ret., 2005. Pub.: Who's Who in Interior Design, 1993-95; cited in 100 Designer's Favorite Rooms, 1993, 94, 95. With USAR, 1961-67. Mem. AIA, Nat. Soc. Interior Designers (award 1972), Am. Soc. Interior Designers (chmn. S.C. chpt. com. on Found. Interior Design Edn. and Rsch. 1976). Personal E-mail: hglennmcgee@aol.com.

**MCGEE, JAMES M.,** federal agency administrator; Pres. Nat. Alliance Postal and Fed. Employees. Named one of Most Influential Black Americans, Ebony mag., 2006. Office: Nat Alliance Postal Federal Employees 1628 11th St NW Washington DC 20001 Office Phone: 202-939-6325. E-mail: JMcGee@NAPFE.ORG.*

**MCGEE, JAMES SEARS,** historian, educator; b. Houston, July 12, 1942; s. William Sears and Mary Elizabeth (Peterson) McG.; m. Mary Arnall Broach, Aug. 20, 1966; children: Elizabeth, Claude. BA, Rice U., 1964; MA, Yale U., 1966, M in Philosophy, 1968, PhD, 1971. Asst. prof. Ga. So. Coll., Statesboro, 1969-71; asst. prof. history U. Calif., Santa Barbara, 1971-78, assoc. prof., 1978-84, prof., 1984—, chmn. dept., 1990-95. Pres. Pacific Coast Conf. on Brit. Studies, 1998-2000. Author: The Godly Man in Stuart England, 1976; co-author: The West Transformed, 2000; editor: The Miscellaneous Works of John Bunyan, Vol. 3, 1987. Named Disting. Tchr. in Soc. Scis., U. Calif., Santa Barbara, 1989; fellow Abraham Found., 1962 63, Woodrow Wilson fellow, 1964-65, recipient summer stipend NEH, 1975. Fellow Royal Hist. Soc.; mem. Am. Soc. Ch. History, Am. Hist. Assn., N.Am. Conf. on Brit. Studies. Democrat. Episcopalian. Avocation: gardening. Office: U Calif Dept History Santa Barbara CA 93106

**MC GEE, JOHN FRAMPTON,** communications company executive; b. Charleston, SC, Jan. 9, 1923; s. Hall Thomas and Gertrude (Frampton) McG.; m. Ruth Bouknight Smedley, June 19, 1971; children: Beverly C. McGee Kinder, Catharine F. McGee Mebane, Charles V. Smedley. BS in Bus. and Polit. Sci., Davidson Coll., 1943. With Charleston Post-News and Courier, 1946-62; asst. gen. mgr. State-Rcords Newspapers, Columbia, S.C., 1962-64, gen. mgr., pres., co-pub., 1964-69; gen. exec. Knight Newspaper, Inc., Miami, Fla., 1969-70; pres., assoc. pub. Charleston (W.Va.) Daily Mail, 1970-87, pub., 1987-90; gen. ptnr. McGee Enterprises, Charleston, 1991—. Pres. Clay Comms., Inc. parent co Charleston Daily Mail, Raleigh Register, Post-Herald, Beckley, W.Va., Enquirer-Jour., Monroe, NC, Shelby (NC) Daily Star, Sta. WWAY-TV, NC, others; bd. dirs., exec. com. AP, NYC; bd. dirs. Thomson Newspapers, Inc., NYC and Toronto, United Nat. Bank, Charleston, W.Va.; adv. bd. Sch. Journalism, W.Va. U.; vis. prof. Grad. Sch. Journalism, U. Nairobi, Kenya, 1992, 93, Harare Zimbabwe, 1993-94; vis. lectr. media matters USIS Wind Hook Namibia, 1994; print media counselor, Namibia and Botswana, 1995. Vice chmn. Charleston Area Med. Ctr.; U. Charleston; chmn. bd. visitors, trustee Davidson (NC) Coll.; co-chmn. McGee Found.; bd. dirs. Coun. for Cmty. and Economic Devel. W.Va.; gen. exec. bd Presbyn. Ch. U.S.A., 1974-76; active SC Commn. for Higher Edn., 1966-69, Capt. inf. U.S. Army, 1943-45. Decorated Purple Heart with oak leaf cluster, Bronze Star with three oak lead clusters, Combat Inf. badge, Croix de Guerre with palm (France and Belgium); recipient Presdl. Merit citation Knight Found., 1995. Fellow Internat. Press Inst. (bd. dirs. Am. com., mem. UNESCO commn. for free press during South African elections 1994); mem. So. Newspaper Pubs. Assn. (bd. dirs. 1967-69, W.Va. Press Assn. (pres. 1977-78, New Eng. Soc. S.C., Cosmos Club (Charleston), Edgewood Country Club of W.Va. Office: McGee Enterprises Bank One Ctr Ste 312 Charleston WV 25301 E-mail: jfm@citynet.net.

**MCGEE, LIAM E.,** bank executive; Grad., U. San Diego; MBA, Pepperdine U.; JD, Loyola Marymount U. Law Sch. With Wells Fargo and Co., Security Pacific Corpn.; mem. staff Bank Am. Corpn., 1990, pres. So. Calif., 1998—2000, pres. Calif., 2000—01, pres. global consumer banking, 2001—04, pres. global consumer and small bus. banking, 2004—. Dir. Fed. Res. Bank, San Francisco; mem. risk and capital com. Bank Am. Corpn., mem. mgmt. operating com. Bd. trustees Nat. Urban League; bd. dirs. Arts and Sci. Coun., Charlotte, NC; chmn. bd. trustees U. San Diego; chmn. United Way Greater LA. Office: Bank Am Corp Ctr 100 N Tryon St Fl 58 Charlotte NC 28255-0001*

**MCGEE, LINDA MACE,** judge, lawyer; b. Marion, NC, Mar. 20, 1949; d. Cecil Adam and Norma Jean (Hogan) Mace; m. B. Gary McGee, Dec. 19, 1970; children: Scott Adam, Jeffrey Sean. BA, U. N.C., 1971, JD, 1973. Bar: N.C. 1973. Exec. dir. N.C. Acad. Trial Lawyers, Raleigh, 1973-78; assoc. Finger, Watson & di Santi, Boone, NC, 1978-80; ptnr. Finger, Watson, di Santi & McGee, Boone, 1980-89, di Santi, Watson & McGee, Boone, 1989-95; judge N.C. Ct. of Appeals, 1995—. Mem. trustee panel U.S. Bankruptcy Ct., Greensboro, N.C., 1980-82; bd. dirs. Legal Services of N.C., Raleigh, 1980-84; mem. N.C. Bd. Law Examiners, 1986-93. Vice-chairperson Watauga County Coun. on Status of Women, Boone, 1979-82; trustee Caldwell C.C. and Tech. Inst., Hudson, N.C., 1980-89; mem. exec. bd. N.C. Assn. C.C. Trustees, 1983-85; trustee Caldwell C.C., 1981-89; mem. Pub. Edn. Commn., 2000—. Mem. ABA, ATLA, AAUW, LWV, ABA Found.; Am. Law Inst., N.C. Assn. Women Attys. (charter, treas. 1980-84, chair jud. divsn. 1997, Gwyneth B. Davis award 1997, Outstanding Judge of Yr. award 1999), N.C. Bar Assn. (bd. govs. 1983-86, co-chair lawyers in schs. com., Pro Bono Svc. award, 1992, jud. divsn. Outstanding Judge of Yr. award 1999), N.C. Acad. Trial Lawyers (bd. govs. 1993-95), N.C. State Bar, Boone C. of C. (bd. dirs. 1982-85), N.C. Bus. and Profl. Womens Clubs (chair polit. action com. 1982-83, Young Career Woman 1980), Boone Bus. and Profl. Women's Club (Woman of Yr. 1980), N.C. Women's Forum. Democrat. Presbyterian. Home: PO Box 508 Corolla NC 27927 Office: PO Box 888 Raleigh NC 27602-0888

**MCGEE, MICHAEL JAY,** protective services official, educator; b. Ft. Worth, June 9, 1952; s. Cecil Carl McGee and Helen Ruth (Peeples) McGee-Furrh; m. Carol Lee Garbarino, Sept. 18, 1982; children: Megan Rose, John Michael, Molly Caitlin. Student, U. Tex., 1970-73, Western Oreg. State U., 1983; AAS in Fire Protection Tech., Colo. Mountain Coll., 1990. Lic. fire suppression systems insp., Colo., vocat. educator, Colo.; cert. hazardous materials technician, Colo., 1992, EMT, Colo.; cert. fire investigator, 2002, fire safety hazardous materials insp., evaluator. Driver Massengale Co., Austin, Tex., 1970-73; gen. mgr. Sundae Palace, Austin, 1973-74; staff mem. Young Life, Colorado Springs, Colo., 1970-75; mgr. Broadmoor Mgmt. Co., Vail, Colo., 1974-76; technician Vail Cable Communications, 1976-77; dep. chief, fire marshal Vail Fire Dept., 1977—, fire sci. coord., 1995—, emergency med. program coord., 1996—2002; 2000v.p. HAZPRO (Hazardous Materials and Fire Safety Consulting Firm), 1996; pres. Fire Protection Tng. & Consulting, Inc., 1999; v.p. OTB, LLC, 2002—; joint ptnr. OTB, Colo., 2004—. Dist. rep. Joint Coun. Fire Dist. Colo., 1983-85; co-chmn. Eagle County Hazardous Materials, 1984-85, mem. planning com., 1987-90; mem. accountability com. Eagle County Sch. Dist., 1991-96, mem. budget rev. com., 1991-93, vice chair accountability com. 1992-93, chmn. accountability com., 1993-96; mem. policy rev. com., 1993-96, bldg. coord., team coach Odyssey of the Mind at Eaglewalle Elem. Sch., 1995; invited dir. workshops Colo. Dept. Edn. Dist. Accountability Convention, Colo. Springs, 1995; pres. Fire Protection Tng. and Cons., Inc.; instr., trainer EMP Am. Inc. Chmn. Eagle County chpt. ARC, 1980-83, disaster chmn., 1977-80; tng. officer Eagle Vol. Fire Dept., 1988-90; mem. parish coun. St. Mary's Parish, Eagle County, 1989-90; mem. citizen's adv. com. Colo. Mountain Coll., 1990-91, bd. dirs. 1990; bldg. coord., team coach Odessey of the Mind, Eagle Valley Elem. Sch., 1994-95, 97-98, 98-99, coach Destination Imagination, 1999-2000; mem. facilities master planning com. Engle County Sch. Dist. 1996-97; mem. planning com. 1999 World Alpine Ski Championships; program coord. Eagle County Driver's Edn. Named Alumnus of the year, Co. Mountain Coll., 2001. Mem.: KC (trustee 2003—, charter Grand Knight, Eagle Count chpt.), Nat. Inst. Cert. Engring. Tech. Cert., Glendale Fire Safety Inst., Colo. State Fire Chiefs Assn., Colo. State Fire Marshals Assn., Nat. Fire Protection Assn., Internat. Assn. Home Builders (Colo. chpt.), Internat. Platform Assn. Office: Vail Fire Dept 42 W Meadow Dr Vail CO 81657-5000 Office Phone: 970-479-2135. Business E-mail: mmcgee@vailgov.com.

**MCGEE, MICHAEL VANHOOK,** writer, playwright; b. Ft. Smith, Ark., July 23, 1928; s. Lillard Harold Weatherman and Hila VanHook McGee; m. Evelyn Elizabeth Weber; children: Michael VanHook Jr.(dec.), Patricia Lynn McGee Gunderson, Sarah Valerie McGee Cannon. AB polit. sci., Univ. of the South, 1950; LLB, Southern Law U., 1957; MFA, U. Alaska, Fairbanks, 1982. Clk. and announcer Radio Sta. WMPS, Memphis, 1948; bank clk. Union Planters Bank, Memphis, 1950—51, bank teller, 1953—56; real estate ins. sales Galbreath Co., Memphis, 1956—62; writer, 1979—. Contbr. articles publ. to profl. jour. 2nd lt. USAF, 1951—53, ret. as maj. USAF, 1962—79. Mem.: Fairbanks Arts Assn. (bd. dirs. 1981—94, pres. 1994), Shriners, Masons. Anglican. Avocations: fishing, camping, painting. Home: PO Box 56116 North Pole AK 99705 Office Phone: 907-488-3326.

**MCGEE, PATRICK EDGAR,** postal service clerk; b. Chgo., Jan. 13, 1944; s. Ralph and Minnie Odelia (Crutcher) McG. Machine clk. U.S. Postal Svc., Chgo., 1977—. Author of poems. Mem. The Art Inst. Chgo., Mus. Sci. & Industry, Chgo. Mem. Internat. Soc. Poets. Democrat. Roman Catholic. Avocations: painting, jazz, walking, jogging.

**MCGEE, ROBERT MERRILL,** oil industry executive; b. Laramie, Wyo., Dec. 15, 1946; s. Gale William and Loraine (Baker) McG., m. Mary Louise Lehman, July 26, 1969; children: Kirk Lehman, Scott Baker. BA in Polit. Sci., Allegheny Coll., 1969. Bus. assoc. B.F. Goodrich Co., Akron, Ohio, 1969-70; dir. of info. Nat. Petroleum Coun., Washington, 1970-73; asst. dir. pub. rels. Occidental Internat. Corp., Washington, 1973-74, exec. asst. to pres., 1974-76, v.p., 1976-78, exec. v.p., 1978-82, sr. exec. v.p., 1982-91, pres., 1991—; v.p. Occidental Petroleum Corp., 1994—. Mem. Pres.'s Commn. on White House Fellowships, Washington, 1993—2000, Meridian Internat. Ctr., Washington, 1994—98; mem. bd. advisors Pan Am. Devel. Found., Washington, 1985, pres., 1991—93; bd. govs. Ford's Theatre, Washington, 1991—; bd. govs. Karl Landegger Program in internat. bus. diplomacy Sch. Fgn. Svc., Georgetown U., Washington, 1991—2000; bd. dirs. Decatur House, Washington, 1998, vice chmn. bd., 2000, chmn. bd. dirs., 2001—04. Mem. The Econ. Club of Washington, Met. Club Washington, Nat. Press Club. Office: Occidental Internat Corp Ste 400 1717 Pennsylvania Ave NW Washington DC 20006-4614

**MCGEE, WILLIAM HOWARD JOHN,** library director; b. Rochester, N.Y., May 15, 1942; s. William Peter and Cecilia Matilda (Kuhn) McG.; m. Sheila Anne Drumm, Sept. 4, 1965; children: Kathleen Moira, Margaret Frances. BA with honors, U. Toronto, Ont., Can., 1965; MEd, U. Toronto, 1973; MLS, U. Western Ont., London, 1980. Tchr. Mimico (Ont.) High Sch., 1966-67; tchr., libr. Applewood Secondary Sch., Mississauga, Ont., 1967-71; libr. Crestwood Secondary Sch., Peterborough, Ont., 1971-74; libr. Cayman Islands Edn. Dept., Grand Cayman, B.W.I., 1975-79; adminstrv. asst. Lake Erie Regional Libr., London, Ont., 1980-83; chief libr. Ft. Erie (Ont.) Pub. Libr., 1983-86; asst. dir. McAllen (Tex.) Pub. Libr., 1986-89; coord. Hidalgo County Libr. System, McAllen, 1989—2001; libr. mgr. Lark Cmty. Ctr. Library, McAllen, 2001—. Cons. Grand Ct. Libr., Grand Cayman, 1974-79; mem. Tex. State Libr. Task Force, Austin, 1993—93; adv. coun. Libr. Svcs. Tech. Act, Austin, 1993—. Editor InTraLogue jour., 1980-83; assoc. editor Can. Jour. Info. Sci., 1980. Bd. dirs. C-ME-CU Credit Union, 1994-99, chmn., 1999. Mem. ALA, Ont. Libr. Assn., Tex. Libr. Assn. (chmn. dist. 4 1994-95, 96-97, intellectual freedom com. 1995-96, profl. rights, responsiblities, and recruitment, 1996—, centennial celebration com. 2000—), Bibliothecaires Francophones Internat. Roman Catholic. Avocations: gourmet cooking, music, travel, reading. Office: Lark Community Center P R PO Box 220 Mcallen TX 78505-0220 Office Phone: 956-688-3320. Personal E-mail: magee.bill@gmail.com. Business E-mail: billmcgee@mcallen.lib.tx.us.

**MCGEE, WILLIAM TOBIN,** surgeon; b. Port Chester, NY, May 23, 1957; s. James R. and Mary (Delzotto) McG.; m. Sarah McGrath; children: Erin, Kelly, Mary, Kate. BA in Physics, Dartmouth Coll., 1979; MD, N.Y. Med. Coll., 1983; M in Health Adminstrn., Clark U., 1997. Diplomate Am. Bd. Internal Medicine with spl. qualifications in Critical Care. Resident in internal medicine Baystate Med. Ctr., Springfield, Mass., 1983-86, intensivist, actg. dir. surg. ICU, 1990-95; fellow in critical care St. Louis U/St. John's Mercy Med. Ctr., St. Louis, 1986-88; intensivist critical care divsn. Baystate Med. Ctr., Springfield, Mass., 1990-98, dir. ICU quality improvement, 1998—; DeWitt Wallace fellow rehab. medicine Rusk Inst. NYU Med. Ctr. Fellow Coll. Chest Physicians (Cecile Lehman Mayer award 1993); mem. AMA, Soc. Critical Care Medicine (presdl. citation 2000, internal medicine specialty award 2000), Am. Soc. Parenteral and Enteral Nutrition. Roman Catholic. Avocations: skiing, biking, hiking, sailing, windsurfing. Office: Baystate Med Ctr 759 Chestnut St Springfield MA 01199-1001

**MCGEENEY, JOHN STEPHEN,** lawyer; b. Manhasset, N.Y., Dec. 22, 1934; s. John Joseph and Marion Alice (Morse) McG.; m. Diane Tyler; children: Michael Morse, Luke Stephen. AB, Amherst Coll., 1956; LLB, Harvard U., 1959. Bar: Conn., U.S. Supreme Ct. 1961, U.S. Supreme Ct. 1965, U.S. Dist Ct. (ea. dist.) Va. 1967, U.S. Ct. Appeals (2d cir.) 1969, U.S. Ct. Appeals (4th cir.) 1971, U.S. Dist. Ct. (so. dist.) N.Y. 1980, U.S. Dist. Ct. Mont. 1987. Assoc. Cummings & Lockwood, Stamford, Conn., 1959-68, ptnr., 1968-89, Paul, Hastings, Janofsky & Walker, Stamford, 1989—, chmn., 1994—, mem. policy com. Bd. dirs. Dorr-Oliver Inc., Milford, 1989—. Fellow Am. Coll. Trial Lawyers; mem. ABA, Fed. Bar Coun., Conn. Bar Assn. (Fed. Practice com.). Officer: Paul Hastings Janofsky & Walker 1055 Washington Blvd Stamford CT 06901-2216 Office Phone: 203-961-7402. Office Fax: 203-358-8705. Business E-mail: stevenmcgeeney@paulhastings.com

**MCGEER, EDITH GRAEF,** retired neurological science educator; b. N.Y.C., Nov. 18, 1923; d. Charles and Charlotte Annie (Ruhl) Graef; m. Patrick L. McGeer, Apr. 15, 1954; children: Patrick Charles, Brian Theodore, Victoria Lynn. BA, Swarthmore Coll., 1944; PhD, U. Va., 1946; DSc (hon.), U. Victoria, 1987, U. B.C., 2000. Rsch. chemist E.I. DuPont de Nemours & Co., Wilmington, Va., 1946—54; rsch. assoc. divsn. neurol. sci. U. B.C., Vancouver, Canada, 1954-74, assoc. prof., 1974—76, prof., acting head, 1976—83, prof., head, 1983—89, prof. emerita, 1989—. Author: (with others) Molecular Neurobiology of the Mammalian Brain, 1978, 2d edit., 1987; editor: (with others) Kainic Acid as a Tool in Neurobiology, 1978, Glutamine, Glutamate, and GABA, 1983; contbr. articles to profl. jours. Decorated officer Order of B.C., Order of Can.; recipient citation, Am. Chem. Soc., 1958, Rsch. award, Clarke Inst., 1992, Lifetime Achievement award, Sci. Coun. B.C., 1995, Hon. Alumnus award, 1996, cert., Internat. Sci. Inst., 2001, medal of svc., Dr. Cam Coady Found., 2003, Lifetime Achievement award, U. B.C. Med. Faculty, 2006. Fellow Can. Coll. Neuropsychopharmacology, Royal Soc. Can.; mem. Can. Biochem. Soc., Internat. Brain Rsch. Orgn., Internat. Soc. Neurochemistry, Soc. Neurosci., Am. Neurochem. Soc. (councilor 1979-83), North Pacific Soc. Neurology and Psychiatry (hon. fellow), Lychnos Soc., Sigma Xi, Phi Beta Kappa. Office: U BC Divsn Neurol Sci 2255 Wesbrook Mall Vancouver BC Canada V6T 1Z3 Office Phone: 604-822-7380. Business E-mail: mcgeer@interchange.ubc.ca.

**MCGEGAN, NICHOLAS,** music director; b. Eng. Student, Cambridge U., Oxford U. Music dir. San Francisco's Phila. Baroque Orch., 1985—, Irish Chamber Orch.; artistic dir. Göttingen Handel Festival, Germany, 1990, Killaloe Festival; prin. guest condr. Scottish Opera, 1992-98; prin. condr. Drottningholm Ct. Theatre, 1993-95; founder, dir., harpsichordist The Arcadian Acad. Guest condr. San Francisco, St. Louis, Houston, Detroit, Indpls., Minn., Nat. Symphony orchs., City of Birmingham Symphony Orch., Halle Orch., Acad. of St. Martin-in-the-Fields in Breat Britain, Montreal Symphony, Nat. Arts Ctr. Orch., Ottawa, Orchestra de la Suisse Romande, Jerusalem Symphony, NY Philharm., Phila. Orch.; condr. Hanover Band, Freiburg Baroque Orch., Orch. of the Age of Enlightment; artist-in-residence, Mills U. Symphony Orch.; condr. over 40 operas in Europe and U.S. Condr. (Operas) Mostly Mozart Festival, NYC, 2003. Office: The St Paul Chamber Orchestra Third Fl of the Hamm Bldg 408 St Peter St Saint Paul MN 55102-1497*

**MC GEHEE, H(ARRY) COLEMAN, JR.,** retired bishop; b. Richmond, Va., July 7, 1923; s. Harry Coleman and Ann Lee (Cheatwood) McG.; m. June Stewart, Feb. 1, 1946; children: Lesley, Alexander, Harry III, Donald, Cary. BS, Va. Poly. Inst., 1947; JD, U. Richmond, 1949; MDiv, Va. Theol. Sem., 1957, DD, 1973. Bar: Va. 1949, U.S. Supreme Ct. 1954; ordained to ministry Episcopal Ch., 1957. Spl. counsel dept. hwys. State of Va., 1949-51, gen. counsel employment svc., 1951, asst. atty. gen., 1951-54; rector Emmanuel Ch.-on-the-Hill, Va. Sem., 1960-71; bishop Diocese of Mich.. Detroit, 1971-90. Adv. bd. Nicaraguan Network, Ctr. for Peace and Conflict Studies, Wayne State U.; bd. dirs. Mich. Religious Coalition for Abortion Rights, 1976-84; trustee Va. Theol. Sem., 1978-93; mem. Episc. Ch. Pub. Co., 1978-85. Columnist Detroit News, 1979—85, weekly commentator pub. radio sta. WDET-AM, Detroit, 1984—90. Mem. Gov.'s Commn. on Status of Women, 1965-66, Mayor's Civic Com., Alexandria, 1967-68; sponsor Nat. Assn. for ERA, 1977-85; pres. Alexandria Legal Aid Soc., 1969-71; bd. dirs. No. Va. Fairhousing Corp., 1963-67; pres. Mich. Coalition for Human Rights, 1980-89 (Humanitarian award 2001); chmn. Citizens' Com. for Justice in Mich., 1983-84; sponsor Farm Labor Orgn. for Children, 1983-85; bd. dirs. Pub. Benefit Corp., Detroit 1988-90, Mich. Citizens for Personal Freedom, 1989-92, Poverty and Social Reform Inst., Detroit, 1989—, Bread for the World, 1990-94, Ams. United for Separation of Ch. and State, 1990, ACLU Oakland County, Mich., 1991-94; co-chair Lesbian-Gay Found. Mich., 1991— 1st lt. C.E., U.S. Army, 1943-46. Named Feminist of Yr., Detroit NOW, 1978, Person of Yr., Econ. Justice Commn. Mich., 1997; recipient Humanitarian award Detroit ACLU, 1984, Phillip Hart medal Mich. Women's Studies Assn., 1984, Sayre award for justice and peace Episc. Peace Fellowship, 1988, Spirit of Detroit award, 1989, Archbishop Romero award Mich. Labor Com., 1990, Brotherhood award AME Ch., Detroit, 1993, Ira Jayne award Detroit br. NAACP, 1993, Martin Luther King, Jr. award United Ch. of Christ, 1995, William Scarlett award Episc. Ch. Pub. Co., 1997, Humanitarian award Mich. Coalition for Human Rights, 2001. Mem.: Detroit Econ. Club (bd. dirs.). Episcopalian. Home: 1496 Ashover Dr Bloomfield Hills MI 48304-1215

**MCGEHEE, LARRY THOMAS,** retired academic administrator; b. Paris, Tenn., May 18, 1936; s. George Eugene and Margaret Elizabeth (Thomas) McG.; m. Elizabeth Hathhorn Boden, Aug. 26, 1961; children: Elizabeth Hathhorn, Margaret Thomas. BA, Transylvania Univ., 1958; BD, Yale U., 1963, MA, 1964, PhD, 1969. Dir., asst. v.p. for univ. relations U. Ala., 1966-68, exec. assoc. to pres., 1968-69, exec. v.p., 1969-71; lectr., assoc. prof. dept. Am. studies, 1969-71, acad. v.p.; 1971; chancellor U. Tenn., Martin, 1971-79; spl. asst. to pres. U. Tenn. Sys., Knoxville, 1979-82; v.p. coll., prof. religion Wofford Coll., Spartanburg, SC, 1982—2005; emeritus prof. religion, 2005—. Syndicated columnist Southern Seen, 1982—. Danforth fellow Yale U., 1960-66. Home: 1047 Woodburn Rd Spartanburg SC 29302-2867 Office: Wofford Coll 429 N Church St Spartanburg SC 29303-3663 Office Phone: 864-597-4197. E-mail: mcgeheelt@wofford.edu.

**MCGEHEE, ROBERT B.,** energy executive; Grad., Nuclear Power Sch. and Submarine Sch., U.S. Naval Acad.; law degree, U. Tex. Atty. Wise Carter Child & Caraway, Jackson, Miss.; sr. v.p., gen. counsel Carolina Power & Light Co., 1997—99, exec. v.p., gen. counsel, chief adminstrv. officer, 1999—2000; pres. CEO Progress Energy Svc. Co., LLC, 2000—02; exec. v.p. Carolina Power & Light Co. and Fla. Progress Corp., 2000—, Progress Energy, Inc., Raleigh, NC, 2000—02, pres., COO, 2002—04, chmn., CEO,

2004—. Mem. exec. com., past vice-chmn. Nuclear Energy Inst. Lt. USN. Office: Progress Energy PO Box 1551 411 S Wilmington St Raleigh NC 27601-1748 E-mail: bob.mcgehee@pgnmail.com.*

MCGEHEE, SHARON, school system administrator; Tchr. Ramona Elem. Sch.; prin. Berlyn Elem. Sch., Lehigh Elem. Sch.; with personnel svcs. Ontario-Montclair Sch. Dist., Calif., dir. certificated personnel and staff devel., asst. supt., dep. supt., 1998—2000, supt., 2000—. Office: Ont-Montclair Sch Dist 950 W D St Ontario CA 91762

MCGEORGE, DON W., retail executive; Joined Kroger Co., Cin., 1977, sr. v.p., 1997—2000, former pres., Tex. Divsn., exec. v.p. 2000—03, pres., COO, 2003—. Office: Kroger Co 1014 Vice St Cincinnati OH 45202-1100*

MCGETTIGAN, CHARLES CARROLL, JR., investment banker; b. San Francisco, Mar. 28, 1945; s. Charles Carroll McGettigan and Molly (Fay) McGettigan Pedley; m. Katharine Havard King, Nov. 1, 1975 (div. 1981); m. Meriwether Lewis Stovall, Aug. 6, 1983; 1 child, Meriwether Lewis Fay. AB in Govt., Georgetown U., 1966; MBA in Fin., U. Pa., 1969. Assoc., asst. v.p., v.p. Blyth Eastman Dillon, N.Y.C., 1970-75, 1st v.p., 1975-78, sr. v.p. San Francisco, 1978-80, Dillon, Read & Co., San Francisco, 1980-83; gen. ptnr. Woodman Kirkpatrick & Gilbreath, San Francisco, 1983-84; prin. corp. fin. Hambrecht & Quist, Inc., San Francisco, 1984-88; mng. dir., founder McGettigan, Wick & Co., Inc., San Francisco, 1988—; gen. ptnr., founder Proactive Ptnrs., L.P., San Francisco, 1990—, Proactive Investment Mgrs., L.P., San Francisco, 1991—. Gen. ptnr. Fremont Proactive Ptnrs., 1991—2001; bd. dirs. Cuisine Solutions, Inc., Alexandria, Va.; chmn. Modtech, Inc., Perris, Calif.; Onsite Energy Corp., Carlsbad, Calif.; Tanknology, Inc., Austin, Tex.; adv. dir. Chesapeake Ventures, Balt., 1984—94. Trustee St. Francis Meml. Hosp., San Francisco, 1980-86; mem. United San Francisco Rep. fin. coun., 1983—, steering coun., 1986—; adv. bd. dirs. Leavey Sch. Bus. Administrn., Santa Clara U., Calif., 1984-90. With USN, 1966. Mem. The Brook, Racquet and Tennis Club (N.Y.), The Pacific Union Club, Bohemian Club (San Francisco), San Francisco Golf Club, Burlingame Country Club (Hillsborough, Calif.), Boston (New Orleans), White's (London). Republican. Roman Catholic. Home: 3375 Clay St San Francisco CA 94118-2006 Office: McGettigan Wick & Co Inc 50 Osgood Pl San Francisco CA 94133-4622 Office Phone: 415-986-4433. E-mail: Chas@McGettigan-Wick.com.

MCGHEE, CARLA RENEE, professional basketball player; b. Peoria, Ill., Mar. 6, 1968; Degree in Sports Mgmt. with honors, U. Tenn., 1990. Basketball player USA Women's Nat. Team Olympics, 1996; profl. basketball player Orlando (Fla.) Miracle, 1999—.

MCGHEE, DIANE BAUMANN, dance instructor, consultant; b. Salem, NJ, 1954; d. Nelson Paul and Alice Elizabeth Baumann; children: Christine, Jonathan, Michael Porcaro. BS, Madison Coll., 1972—76; MS, James Madison U., 1976—78. Phys. edn. and dance instr. Salisbury State Coll., Md., 1978—82; resident choreographer; booking and tour mgr. Mandala Folk Ensemble, Boston, 1984—88; dir. of sch. outreach programs and tchr. MJT Dance Co., Boston, 1988—94; sr. tchr. Boston Renaissance/Edison Project Partnership Sch., 1994—97; dir. SE Ctr. for Dance Edn., Columbia Coll., 1997—2000; assoc. prof. Dept. of Theatre and Dance, Winthrop U., Rock Hill, SC, 2000—02; dir., arts for children interdisciplinary program; assoc. prof. of dance SUNY Coll. at Brockport, Brockport, NY, 2002—. Steering and coordinating committees Arts in Basic Curriculum Project, cons., arts edn. leadership inst.; adv. bd. and cons. Am. Dance Legacy Inst.; edn. cons. NY State Summer Sch. of the Arts Sch. of Dance; dir. Etudes Ednl. Project; exec. bd. Project U.N.I.Q.U.E., arts learning lab; art edn. roundtable Greater Rochester Arts and Cultural Coun. Author: (dance education lesson studies) Roots & Branches: Exploring an Evolving Dance Legacy, (dance unit of study) Civil War to Civil Rights: A Lesson in Humanity, Making Connections: Technology, Education, and Dance, American Indian Dance; A Celebration of Survival and Adaptation, Structuring Time and Space: A Dance Hypothesis. Recipient Presdl. Leadership award in Dance, SC. Dance Assn., 1998, Contbn. to Dance Edn., Fidelity Investments (Am. Ballet Gala, Boston), 1999, Artistic Vision, Comittment to Children, Dedication to Dance Edn., MJT Dance Co., 1994. Mem.: Internat. Assn. for Health, Phys. Edn., Recreation, Sport and Dance, SC Dept. Edn. (co-chair, arts tech. standards com., mem. task force, visual and performing arts curricular standards, arts report card task force, SAT improvement com.), Nat. Dance Edn. Org. (exec. bd. and charter mem.). Office: SUNY Brockport 350 New Campus Dr Brockport NY 14420 Office Phone: 585-395-5304. Business E-Mail: dmcghee@brockport.edu.

MCGHEE, GEORGE RUFUS, paleobiologist, educator; b. Henderson, NC, Sept. 25, 1951; m. Marae Paschall, Nov. 25, 1971. BS, NC State U., 1973; MS, U. NC, 1975; PhD, U. Rochester, 1978. Asst. prof. Rutgers U., New Brunswick, NJ, 1978—83, assoc. prof., 1983—93, prof., 1993—2006, disting. prof., 2006—. Vis. scientist Field Mus. of Natural History, Chgo., 1981; guest lectr. U. Tuebingen, Germany, 1982, 83, guest prof., 84; fellow Konrad Lorenz Inst. for Evolution and Cognition Rsch., Altenberg, Austria, 2005—. Author: The Late Devonian Mass Extinction, 1996, Theoretical Morphology: the Concept and Its Applications, 1999; contbr. articles to profl. publs. Peace activist Religious Soc. of Friends, Princeton, NJ. Rsch. grantee, NSF, Petroleum Rsch. Fund. Fellow: Geol. Soc. Am.; mem.: Brit. Palaeontological Assn., Internat. Palaeontological Assn., Die Palaeontologische Gesellschaft, Paleontol. Soc. Am. Fellow. Office: Rutgers U Dept Geol Scis 610 Taylor Rd Piscataway NJ 08854 Office Phone: 732-445-3832.

MCGIBBON, PHYLLIS ISABEL, art educator, artist; b. Madison, Wis., Jan. 9, 1961; d. W. Henry and G. Louise McGibbon. BFA, U. Wis., 1983, MFA, 1988. Luther Gregg Sullivan vis. artist Wesleyan U., Middletown, Conn., 1989-91; asst. prof. art Pomona Coll., Claremont, Calif., 1991-94, Wellesley (Mass.) Coll., 1994-97, assoc. prof., 1997—. Artist residency Bemis Ctr. for Contemporary Art, Omaha, 1995, Millay Colony, Austerlitz, N.Y., 1996, Va. Ctr. Creative Arts, Sweet Briar, 1997. Solo art installations include Davison Art Ctr., Middletown, Conn., 1990, Orange County Ctr. for Contemporary Art, Santa Ana, Calif., 1992, Sushi Performance and Visual Art, Inc., San Diego, 1994, Davis Mus. and Cultural Ctr., Wellesley, 1996, John Michael Kohler Arts Ctr., Sheboygan, Wis., 1998. Recipient award Elizabeth Greenshields Found., Montreal, Can., 1991, award Western States Arts Found. NEA, 1992, award Art Matters, Inc., N.Y.C., 1994; fellow Kala Inst., Berkeley, Calif., 1992-93, individual artist fellow Nat. Endowment for Arts 1995. Mem. Coll. Art Assn., Am. Print Alliance. Office: Wellesley Coll Dept of Art Jewett Arts Ctr Wellesley MA 02481

MCGIFFERT, MICHAEL, retired historian; b. Chgo., Oct. 5, 1928; s. Arthur Cushman and Elisabeth (Eliot) McG.; m. Genevieve White Mischel, Aug. 13, 1960; m. Elizabeth Eastman, June 19, 1949 (div. 1960). BA, Harvard Coll., 1949; B.D., Yale U., 1952, PhD, 1958; postgrad., Union Theol. Sem., N.Y.C., 1949-50. Instr. history Colgate U., Hamilton, NY, 1954-55, 56-60, U. Md., College Park, 1955-56; asst. prof. history U. Denver, 1960-64, assoc. prof., 1964-69, prof. history, 1969-74; editor William and Mary Quar., Inst. Early Am. History and Culture, prof. history, Coll. William and Mary, Williamsburg, Va., 1972-97; ret. Author: The Higher learning in Colorado, 1964; editor: The Character of Americans, 1964 (rev. edit.), 1969, Puritanism and the American Experience, 1969, (with Robert A. Skotheim) American Social Thought, 1972, God's Plot: The Paradoxes of Puritan Piety, 1972, God's Plot: Puritan Spirituality in Thomas Shepard's Cambridge, 1994. Faculty rsch. grantee U. Denver, 1970, Coll. William and Mary, 1981-82, 89; rsch. fellow NEH, 1977-78. Mem. com. Am. Hist. Assn., Orgn. Am. Historians, Confr. of Hist. Jours. (pres.1987-89), Am. Antiquarian Soc., Mass. Hist. Soc. Home: 102 Old Glory Ct Williamsburg VA 23185-4914 Personal E-mail: mcgiff@widomaker.com

MCGILL, CARLA ANN, language educator; b. Fontana, Calif., Feb. 13, 1955; d. Robert Coldiron and Ruth Marie Peavy; m. David William McGill, Jul. 26, 1980. BA English, Calif. State U., San Bernardino, 1986; MA English, U. Calif., Riverside, 1988, PhD English, 1993. Tchg. asst. U. Calif., Riverside, 1988-91; sr. lectr. Biola U., La Mirada, Calif., 1993-97; instr. Biola BOLD Prog., La Mirada, Calif., 1995-97; sr. lectr. Azusa Pacific U., Azusa, Calif., 1998—2000; lectr. Calif. State U., San Bernadino, 1999—2001, U. Calif., Riverside, 1999—2001; instr. Corinthian Colls., Santa Ana, 2003—05; lectr. U. Redlands, Redlands, Calif., 2005—. Author: Thomas Shepard's "Confessions" dissertation, 1993; contr. book reviews, poems, articles to mags. Mem. Live Poets' Soc. at the Huntington Libr. Michael J. Connell Foun. Fellow, Huntington Libr., 1993. Mem. Am. Lit. Assn., Modern Lang. Assn., Soc. Early Americanists, Colloquium for Study of Amer. Culture. Avocations: poetry, fiction, screenwriting. E-mail: cmcgill215@aol.com.

MCGILL, DAN MAYS, insurance business educator; b. Greenback, Tenn., Sept. 27, 1919; s. John Burton and Jane (Mays) McG.; m. Elaine Kem, June 22, 1952; children: Douglas Russell, Melanie Mays BA, Maryville Coll., 1940, LLD (hon.), 1982; MA, Vanderbilt U., 1941; PhD, U. Pa., 1947. Assoc. prof. fin. U. Tenn., Knoxville, 1947-48; Julian Price assoc. prof. ins. U. N.C., Chapel Hill, 1948-51; assoc. prof. ins. U. Pa., Phila., 1952-56, Frederick H. Ecker prof. life ins., 1959-90, chmn. ins. dept., 1965—89. Trustee N.W. Mut. Life Ins. Co., Milw., 1978-90; bd. dirs. NRG Life Reassurance Corp., Phila., 1984-94, Phila. Reins. Corp., 1990—, Independence Blue Cross, 1990—; exec. dir. S.S. Huebner Found., 1954-75, 78-86, chmn., 1965-94; dir. rsch. Pension Rsch. Coun., 1952-90; chmn., mem. governing bd. Leonard Davis Inst. Health Econs., 1967-90; 1st chmn. adv. commn. Pension Benefit Guaranty Corp., 1975-78, mem. 1978-81. Author: An Analysis of Government Life Insurance, 1949, The Fundamentals of Private Pensions, 8th edit., 2005, Legal Aspects of Life Insurance, 1959, Fulfilling Pension Expectations, 1962, Life Insurance, 1967, Preservation of Pension Benefit Rights, 1972, others; editor: (with others) World Insurance Trends, 1959, others. Trustee Presbyn. Med. Ctr., Phila., 1987—96; chmn. Boettner Inst. Fin. Gerontology, 1993—2002; mem. retirement bd. Mass. Bay Transp. Authority, 1980—96; chmn. bd. pensions Presbyn. Ch. U.S.A., 1977—88; trustee Presbyn. Found. for Phila., 1996—2001. Maj. USAF, 1942—46, Maj. USAF, 1951—52. Recipient Disting. Alumni award Maryville Coll., 1962, Huebner Gold medal award Am. Coll., 1977, Gold medal Internat. Ins. Soc., 1987. Mem.: Am. Risk and Ins. Assn. (pres. 1959, Elizur Wright award 1955, 1981), Merion Cricket Club, Union League. Republican. Presbyterian. Avocations: music, travel, sports. Home: 50 Belmont Ave Bala Cynwyd PA 19004-2437

MCGILL, HENRY COLEMAN, JR., pathologist, educator, researcher; b. Nashville, Oct. 1, 1921; s. Henry Coleman and Thursa (Lowry) McG.; m. Cloace Laurite Ferguson, Sept. 12, 1945; children: Margaret Ann, Laurilynn, Elizabeth Gail. BA, Vanderbilt U., 1943, MD, 1946. Intern Vanderbilt Hosp., Nashville, 1946-47; asst. prof. pathology La. State U. Med. Ctr., New Orleans, 1950-55, assoc. prof., 1955-61, prof., chmn. dept., 1961-66; prof. pathology U. Tex. Health Sci. Ctr., San Antonio, 1966-72, chmn. dept., 1966-72; sci. dir. S.W. Found. for Biomed. Rsch., San Antonio, 1978-92, sr. scientist, 1992-96, sr. scientist emeritus, 1996—. Contbr. articles to med. jours. Capt. M.C., U.S. Army, 1948-50. Mem. Phi Beta Kappa, Sigma Xi, Alpha Omega Alpha. Home: 4102 Fawnridge Dr San Antonio TX 78229-4212 Office: PO Box 760549 San Antonio TX 78245-0549 Office Phone: 210-258-9408. Business E-Mail: hmcgill@icarus.sfbr.org.

MCGILL, JAY, magazine publisher; With Hearst Magazines, 1979—; pub. Country Living, NYC, 1993—97; v.p. pub. Popular Mechanics, 1997—2003; dir., digital integration Hearst Corp., 2001—03; senior v.p. and pub. SmartMoney, NYC, 2003, now pres., pub. Office: Attn Jay McGill Hearst Mags 224 W 57th St New York NY 10019-3212 also: SmartMoney Mag 1755 Broadway New York NY 10019 Business E-Mail: jmcgill@hearst.com.*

MCGILL, KENNETH, JR., mental health services professional; b. Paterson, NJ, Aug. 22, 1965; s. Kenneth and Shirley A. McG.;m. Barbara Joan, Dec. 27, 1989; children: Megan Elizabeth, Shannon Eileen BA, William Paterson Coll., 1989; MA in Edn., Seton Hall U., 1995; Ednl. Specialist, 1999. Social Worker N.J.; cert. Hypnotherapist Am. Bd. Clin. Hypnotherapy, lic. Marriage and Family Therapist. Mental health worker Wayne (N.J.) Gen. Hosp., 1989-90; case supr. N.J. Superior Ct. Essex County, Newark, 1990-95; adj. prof. psychology William Paterson U., Wayne, 1995—; asst. dir. admissions, evalns., 1996-99; marriage and family therapist St. Mary's Counseling Svcs., Pompton Lakes, N.J., 1998—; owner, pres., therapist Bergen-Passaic Psychol. Assocs., LLC, North Haledon, N.J., 1999—. Bd. dirs. Apraxia Network Bergen County, Paramus, N.J., 2000—. Reviewer books. Asst. soccer coach North Haledon Soccer Assn., 2000. Mem. APA, ACA, Am. Assn Marriage and Family Counselors, Mental Health Assn. Passaic County (bd. dirs. 1995-96, 2000—), Assn. Christian Counselors, KC (1st, 2nd degree 1995, 3rd degree 1996, Knight of the Month 1997), Ancient Order Hibernians, Psi Chi. Democrat. Roman Catholic. Avocations: mountain biking, hiking, sketching, writing. Office: Bergen Passaic Psychological 851 Franklin Lakes Rd Ste 33 Franklin Lakes NJ 07417-2266 E-mail: mcgillkb@bellatlantic.net.

MCGILL, LEONARD JOHN, lawyer; b. Edinburgh, Scotland, Oct. 26, 1957; s. Alexander and Mary (Thomson) McG.; m. Nancy Ann Fasulo, Sept. 29, 1981. LLB with honors, U. Edinburgh, 1979; JD magna cum laude, Georgetown U., 1985. Bar: D.C. 1986, Calif. 1988. Assoc. Skadden, Arps, Slate, Meagher & Flom, Washington, 1986-87, Gibson, Dunn & Crutcher, L.A., 1987—2002; v.p., dep. gen. counsel Fleetwood Enterprises, Inc., 2002—03; sr. v.p., corp. fin. & chief governance officer, 2003—. Mem. ABA (internat. law and practice sect. 1986—, bus. law sect. 1986—), Masons. Democrat. Presbyterian. Avocations: golf, football. Office: Fleetwood Enterprises Inc 3125 Myers St Riverside CA 92503

MCGILL, MAURICE LEON, corporate financial executive; b. Malden, Mo., Aug. 22, 1936; s. William Howard and Iris (Phillips) McG.; m. Wanda Coral Wirt, Feb. 2, 1957; children— Melany, Melinda, William Shannon BS, U. Mo., 1958, MA, 1959. C.P.A., Mo., Iowa, Ariz. Mgr. Touche, Ross, Bailey & Smart, Kansas City, Mo., 1959-64; fin. v.p., treas. Iowa Beef Packers, Inc., Dakota City, Nebr., 1964-69; exec. v.p., treas. Spencer Foods, Inc., Iowa, 1969-71, also dir. Iowa; sr. v.p. Diamond Reo Trucks, Inc., Lansing, Mich., 1971-72; fin. v.p. Ariz. Colo. Land & Cattle Co., Phoenix, 1972-75; ptnr. Touche Ross & Co., Phoenix, 1975-81; exec. v.p. fin. and adminstrn., treas., bd. dirs. IBP, Inc., Dakota City, Nebr., 1981-89; pres., bd. dirs. Wirmac Corp., Garland, Tex., 1989—. Bd. dirs. Premium Std. Farms, Kansas City, Mo. Mem.: AICPA. Home: 6909 Aberdeen Dr Garland TX 75044-1314 E-mail: mandwmcgill@msn.com.

MCGILL, STUART R., oil industry executive; b. Australia; BAChemE, DSChemE, Sydney U., Australia. Engr. prodn. dept. Esso Australia Ltd., 1969, engr. Melbourne, Longford, Long I. Point, Australia, Exxon Co. USA, Exxon Prodn. Rsch., Houston; mng. dir. Esso Prodn. Malaysia, Kuala Lumpur, 1980; dir. Esso Australia Ltd., 1983, chmn. and mng. dir., 1985; v.p. Exxon Co. Internat., 1988; CEO Esso Holding Co. Holland Inc., 1991, Esso B.V., 1991; exec. v.p. Exxon Co. Internat., 1994—2003, pres., 1998; v.p. ExxonMobil Corp., 1999—2003. Office: ExxonMobil Corp 800 Bell St Houston TX 77002

MCGILL, THOMAS CONLEY, physics educator; b. Port Arthur, Tex., Mar. 20, 1942; s. Thomas Conley and Susie Elizabeth (Collins) McG.; m. Toby Elizabeth Cone, Dec. 27, 1966; children: Angela Elizabeth, Sara Elizabeth. BS in Math., Lamar State Coll., 1963, BEE, 1964; MEE, Calif. Inst. Tech., 1965, PhD, 1969. NATO postdoctoral fellow U. Bristol, Eng., 1969-70; NRC postdoctoral fellow Princeton (N.J.) U., 1970-71; from asst. to assoc. prof. applied physics Calif. Inst. Tech., Pasadena, 1971-77, prof., 1977—. Cons. United Techs. Corp., 1988-95, Advance Projects Agy./Def. Sci. Rsch. Coun., Arlington, Va., 1979—; chief Naval Ops. Exec. Panel, 1995-2000; mem. Semiconductor Tech. Coun., 1995-98; mem. adv. bd. Sematech

U., 1992-95. Alfred P. Sloan Found. fellow, 1974. Fellow Am. Physical Soc.; mem. AAAS, IEEE, Am. Vacuum Soc., Sigma Xi. Office: Calif Inst Tech Mail Code 128 # 95 Pasadena CA 91125-0001

MCGILL, WILLIAM JAMES, JR., academic administrator, writer; b. St. Louis, Mar. 25, 1936; s. William James Sr. and Ethel (Williams) McG.; m. Ellen Buck, June 18, 1960; children: Sara Louise, Susan Elizabeth, Alison Marcia. BA, Trinity Coll., 1957; MA, Harvard U., 1958, PhD, 1961, grad. Inst. Ednl. Mgmt., 1989; LHD (hon.), Lebanon Valley Coll., 1998. Instr. history Western Md. Coll., Westminster, 1960-62; asst. prof. history Alma (Mich.) Coll., 1962-68, assoc. prof., 1968-72; dean of coll. Washington & Jefferson Coll., Washington, Pa., 1972-75, prof. history, 1972-84; asst. dir., div. edn. programs NEH, Washington, 1984-86; v.p., dean faculty Lebanon Valley Coll., Annville, Pa., 1986-98, acting pres., 1987-88. Author: Maria Theresa, 1972, The Rock Springs Chronicles, 1999, George Herbert, R.S. Thomas and the Argument with God, 2003; contbr. 72 articles to profl. jours., 53 book revs., 20 short stories, numerous poems; poetry editor Spitball Mag., 1993—, mng. editor, 2000—. Assoc. to rector St. Luke's Episc. Ch., Lebanon, Pa., 1986-98; priest-in-charge St. George's Episc. Ch., Waynesburg, Pa., 1974-83; actor Washington Theater Wing, 1984-86, Gretna Playhouse, Mt. Gretna, Pa., 1987-90; bd. dirs. Lebanon County United Way, 1987-95, Gretna Prodns., Mt. Gretna, 1986-90, 91-92, Concertante, 1999-01; trustee Penn Coll. Art and Design, 1992-06. Mem. Phi Beta Kappa. Avocations: sailing, writing, acting. Home and Office: PO Box 333 Annville PA 17003-0333 E-mail: wjmcgill@earthlink.net.

MCGILLICUDDY, JOAN MARIE, psychotherapist, consultant; b. Chgo., June 23, 1952; d. James Neal and Muriel (Joy) McG. BA, U. Ariz., 1974, MS, 1976; PhD, Walden U., 1996. Cert. nat. counselor. Counselor ACTION, Tucson, 1976; counselor, clin. supr. Behavioral Health Agy. Ctr. Ariz., Casa Grande, 1976-81; instr. psychology Cen. Ariz. Coll., Casa Grande, 1978-83; therapist, co-dir. Helping Assocs., Inc., Casa Grande, 1982—, v.p., sec., 1982—; cert. instr. Silva Method Mind Devel., Tucson, 1986—. Active Mayor's Com. for Handicapped, Casa Grande, 1989-90, Human Svcs. Planning, Casa Grande, 1985-95, Pinal Gila Sr. Coun. Found., 2005—. Named Outstanding Am. Lectr. Silva Mind Internat., 1988-99. Mem. ACA. Avocations: jogging, singing. Office: Helping Assocs Inc 1901 N Trekell Rd Casa Grande AZ 85222-1706 Office Phone: 520-836-1029. E-mail: haicg@c212.com.

MC GILLICUDDY, JOHN FRANCIS, retired banker; b. Harrison, N.Y., Dec. 30, 1930; s. Michael J. and Anna (Munro) McG.; m. Constance Burtis, Sept. 9, 1954; children: Michael Sean, Faith Burtis Benoit, Constance Erin Mc Gillicuddy Mills, Brian Munro, John Walsh. AB, Princeton, 1952; LL.B., Harvard, 1955. With Mfrs. Hanover Trust Co. subs. Mfrs. Hanover Corp., N.Y.C., 1958-91, v.p., 1962-66, sr. v.p., 1966-69, exec. v.p., asst. to chmn., 1969-70, vice chmn., dir., 1970, pres., 1971-79, chmn., chief exec. officer, 1979-91; chmn. bd., chief exec. officer Chem. Banking Corp., N.Y.C., 1992-93, ret., 1994. Bd. dirs. Kelso, Inc. Bd. dirs. life trustee, chmn. emeritus N.Y. Presbyn. Hosp.; trustee emeritus Princeton U.; pres. Boy Scouts Am.; Greater N.Y. Couns. Lt. (j.g.) USNR, 1955—58. Mem. Westchester Country Club (Rye, N.Y.), Blind Brook Club (Port Chester, N.Y.), Princeton Club (N.Y.C.), Augusta Nat. Golf Club (Ga.), Pine Valley Golf Club (N.J.), Laurel Valley Golf Club (Ligonier, Pa.), Seminole Golf Club (north Palm Beach, Fla.), Links Club (N.Y.C.). Roman Catholic. Office: JP Morgan Chase Corp 270 Park Ave New York NY 10017-2014

MC GIMSEY, CHARLES ROBERT, III, anthropologist; b. Dallas, June 18, 1925; s. Charles Robert, Jr. and Ellen Randolph (Parks) McG.; m. Mary Elizabeth Conger, Dec. 20, 1949; children— Charles Robert, Brian Keith, Mark Douglass. Student, Vanderbilt U., 1942-43, U. of South, 1943-44; BA, U. N.Mex., 1949; MA, Harvard U., 1954, PhD, 1958. Instr. U. Ark., Fayetteville, 1957, assoc. prof., 1958-62, assoc. prof., 1962-67, prof. anthropology, 1967-90, prof. emeritus, 1990—, chmn. dept., 1969-72; asst. curator U. Ark. Mus., 1957-59, dir., 1959-83, Ark. Archeol. Survey, 1967-90, dir. emeritus, 1990—. Cons. archeology U.S. GAO, 1979-87, U.S.-Internat. Com. on Monuments and Sites; Rep. to Internat. Com. on Archeol. Heritage Mgmt., 1988-95. Author: (with G.R. Willey) Monagrillo Culture of Panama, 1954, Mariana Mesa, 1980, Indians of Arkansas, 1969, Public Archeology, 1972, Archeology and Archeological Resources, 1973, (with H.A. Davis) The Management of Archeological Resources, 1977, CRM on CRM, 2004; assoc. editor Am. Antiquity, 1972-80; Co-editor (with H. A. Davis) Southeastern Museums Conf., 1964-73; Contbr. articles to profl. jours. Mem. Ark. Rev. Com., Historic Preservation Program, 1968-76; collaborator Nat. Park Service, 1971-74, adviser, 1974-77; mem. Com. on Recovery Archeol. Remains, 1971-78; mem. adv. bd. dirs. Red River Mus., 1975-76; mem. adv. bd. Am. Indian Archeol. Inst., 1975-80, Am. Natural and Cultural Heritage Dept., 1976-90. Served to lt. (j.g.) USNR, 1943-47. Recipient Cert. Recognition State of Ark., 1990; rsch. grantee Am. Philos. Soc., Am. Acad. Arts and Scis., Andean Rsch. Inst., Nat. Park Service, NSF, Smithsonian Instn., Wenner-Gren Found.; rsch. fellow dept. archaeology U. Cambridge, 1985-86, assoc. mem. Darwin Coll., 1985— Fellow: Am. Anthrop. Assn.; mem.: Archeol. Inst. Am. (Conservation and Heritage Mgmt. award 2006), Register Profl. Arch., Am. Assn. State and Local History (award of merit 1985), Am. Assn. Mus., Soc. Profl. Archaeologists (founder, bd. dirs. 1976—79, pres. 1983—84, emeritus, life, Seiberling 1989, presidential recognition award 1997), Am. Soc. Conserv. Archeology (founding, outstanding contrib. 1980), Southeastern Mus. Conf. (coun. 1962—71, editor 1964—77), Ark. Archeol. Soc. (editor 1960—83, Preservationist 1989), Soc. Am. Archeology (pres. 1974—75, Distinguished Serv. 1975, excellence in cultural resource mgt. 1995), Register of Profl. Archeologists (Disting. Svc. award 2003). Home: 435 W Hawthorn St Fayetteville AR 72701-1935 Office: Ark Archeol Survey 2475 N Hatch Ave Fayetteville AR 72704-5590

MCGINLEY, PAUL ANTHONY, JR., lawyer; b. Allentown, Pa., Apr. 24, 1948; s. Paul A. Sr. and Mary (McGurl) McG.; children: Paige, Laura, Paul Anthony III, Jonathan. AB, Princeton U., 1970; JD, Georgetown U., 1974. Bar: Pa. 1974, U.S. Dist. Ct. (ea. dist.) Pa. 1974, U.S. Supreme Ct. 1987. Assoc. Gross & Brown, Allentown, 1974-76; asst. pub. defender Lehigh County, Allentown, 1976-77, asst. county solicitor, 1977-78; ptnr. Gross, McGinley & McGinley, Allentown, 1978-83; Gross, McGinley, McGinley & LaBarre, Allentown, 1983-86, Gross, McGinley & LaBarre, Allentown, 1986-87, Gross, McGinley, LaBarre & Eaton, Allentown, 1987—. Mem. legal affairs com. Mag. Pubs. Am., 1994—; chmn. hearing com. disciplinary bd. Supreme Ct. of Pa., 1986-90, 1997-2003; co-chmn. bd. dirs. Rodale Inst., 2005—; asst. sec. Rodale Inc., 1999—, gen. counsel, 2000—; dir., sec. Velodrome Fund, 1995— Bd. dirs. Swain Sch., Allentown, 1984-89, Cedar Crest Coll. Bd. Assocs., Allentown, 1986-88; trustee Allentown YWCA, 1985-88. Mem. ABA, Pa. Bar Assn., Lehigh County Bar Assn. (bd. dirs. 1978-84, pres. 1987), Pa. Trial Lawyers Assn., Allentown-Lehigh County C. of C., Princeton Quadrangle Club (bd. dirs.) Democrat. Roman Catholic. Avocations: skiing, tennis. Office: Gross McGinley LaBarre & Eaton 33 S 7th St Allentown PA 18101-2436 Office Phone: 610-820-5450. Business E-Mail: pmcginley@gmle.com.

MCGINLY, WILLIAM C., healthcare association executive; PhD in Adminstrn., Am. U. Cert. Assn. Exec. (CAE). Pres., CEO Assn. for Healthcare Philanthropy (AHP) Found. and Hosp. Devel. and Ednl. Fund of Can. Bd. dirs. Ctr. on Philanthropy at Ind. U., Indpls., eTapestry, e-PhilanthropyFoundation; tchr. Am. U., Mt. St. Mary's Coll.; spkr. in field. Fellow: I/D/E/A/; mem.: Am. Soc. of Assn. Execs., Greater Washington Soc. Assn. Execs. Office: Assn for Healthcare Philanthropy Ste 400 313 Park Ave Falls Church VA 22046 Office Phone: 703-532-6243. Office Fax: 703-532-7170. Business E-Mail: bill@ahp.org.

MCGINN, KATHLEEN M., mathematics educator; d. Ronald E. and Annette F. Dietl; m. Jeffrey H. McGinn, Dec. 28, 1983; 1 child, Kaitlin A. BA, D'Youville Coll., Buffalo, NY, 1980. Cert. profl. educator Fla., 2009. Math. tchr. Eau Gallie H.S., Melbourne, Fla., 1999—, math. dept. chairperson. Mem. math. leadership team Brevard County Pub. Schs., Viera, Fla. Choir mem. Holy Name of Jesus Cath. Ch., Indialantic, Fla., 2003–06. Mem.: Brevard Coun. Tchrs. Math., Fla. Coun. Tchrs. Math., Nat. Coun. Tchrs. Math. Roman Catholic. Avocations: reading, puzzles and games, quilting. Office Phone: 321-242-6400.

**MCGINN, RICHARD A.,** telecommunications company executive; Bachelor's degree, Grinnell Coll. With Ill. Bell, 1969; exec. positions internat. and computer sys. groups AT&T, 1978, CEO network sys.; CEO, pres. Lucent Techs., chmn., CEO, 1997-2000. Bd. dirs. Lucent Techs., Oracle Corp., Am. Express Co. Bus. Coun.

**MCGINN, TIMOTHY J.,** lawyer; b. NYC, Dec. 12, 1950; BA, Fordham U., 1972, JD, 1976. Bar: NY 1977, US Dist. Ct. Ea. Dist. NY, US Dist. Ct. So. Dist. NY, US Ct. Appeals 2nd Cir. Asst. dist. atty., Bronx County, NY, 1976—81; ptnr. Wilson, Elser, Moskowitz, Edelman & Dicker LLP, NYC. Mem.: ABA (medicine & law com.), Assn. of the Bar of the City of NY, NY State Bar Assn. Office: Wilson Elser Moskowitz Edelman & Dicker LLP 23rd Fl 150 E 42nd St New York NY 10017-5639 Office Phone: 212-490-3000 ext. 2779. Office Fax: 212-490-3038. Business E-Mail: mcginnt@wemed.com.

**MCGINNIS, BARRY EUGENE,** music educator, musician; s. Calvin G. and Martha S. McGinnis; m. Amy McGinnis. BS, Towson State U., Md., 1984—91; MusM - Woodwind Specialist, East Carolina U., Greenville, N.C., 1991—93; D of Musical Arts - Saxophone Performance, U. Ga., Athens, 1993—2002. Instr. of music Ga. Coll. & State U., Milledgeville, Ga., 1995—97; instr., music Piedmont Coll., Demorest, Ga., 1997—2000; vis. asst. prof., music Adams State Coll., 2000—01, instr., music, 2001—02; asst. prof., music, dir. woodwinds, dir. jazz combo Newberry Coll., SC, 2002—. Author: (profl. journal articles) Nat. Assn. of Coll. Wind and Percussion Instructors. Mem.: S.C. Band Dirs. Assn., S.C. Music Educators Assn., Music Educators Nat. Conf., College Music Soc., Nat. Assn. of Coll. Wind and Percussion Instructors, Internat. Clarinet Assn., North Am. Saxophone Alliance, Delta Omicron, Pi Kappa Lambda, Kappa Kappa Psi. Office: Newberry College Music Department 2100 College St Newberry SC 29108 Home: 2317 College St Newberry SC 29108 Office Phone: 803-321-5178. Personal E-mail: barry.mcginnis@newberry.edu.

**MCGINNIS, DAVE,** former professional football coach; b. Independence, Kansas, Aug. 9, 1951; Attended, Tex. Christian U. Freshmen coach Tex. Christian U., 1973—74, defensive backfield coach, 1982; grad. asst. Missouri U., 1975, def. backs coach, 1976—77; secondary coach Ind. State U., 1978; defensive ends, linebackers coach Kansas State U., 1983—85; linebackers coach Chgo. Bears, 1986—95; defense coord. Ariz. Cardinals, 1996—2000, coach, 2000—03. Avocations: travel, golf, jazz, reading.

**MCGINNIS, JAMES LANDON,** lawyer; b. St. Louis, May 10, 1954; s. Robert Delmar (Stepfather) and Rosalind Appel Ritchie; children: Lorna Rose, Rowan Grace. BA in History, Yale U., 1976; JD, U. Calif.-Berkeley, 1979. Bar: Pa. 1979, Calif. 1980. Assoc. Morgan, Lewis & Bockius, Phila., 1979—80, Jackson, Tufts, Cole & Black, San Francisco, 1980—84; asst. atty. Ea. and Ctrl. Districts of Calif., Fresno, L.A., 1984—88; ptnr. Morgenstein & Jubelirer, San Francisco, 1988—2002, Sheppard, Mullin, Richter & Hampton, San Francisco, 2002—. Author: (article-Nat. Law Jour.) The Impact of Booker on Sentencing in Criminal Antitrust Cases. Mem.: San Francisco Bar Assn., Calif. Bar Assn., ABA. Avocations: weightlifting, tennis, guitar. Home: 23 Sycamore Ave Mill Valley CA 94941 Office: Sheppard Mullin 17th Fl Four Embarcadero Ctr San Francisco CA 94111 Office Phone: 415-774-3294. Office Fax: 415-434-3947. Business E-Mail: jmcginnis@sheppardmullin.com.

**MCGINNIS, JAMES MICHAEL,** physician; b. Columbia, Mo., July 12, 1944; s. Leland Glenn and Lillian Ruth (Mackler) McG.; m. Patricia Anne Gwaltney, Aug. 4, 1978; children— Brian, Katherine AB, U. Calif., Berkeley, 1966; MA, MD, UCLA, 1971; M.P.P., Harvard U., 1977. House officer in internal medicine Boston City Hosp., 1971-72; internat. med. officer HEW, 1972-74; dir. Office for Asia and Western Pacific, 1974-75; state coordinator smallpox eradication program WHO, India, 1974-75; fellow Harvard Center for Community Health and Med. Care, Boston, 1976-77; cons. to sec. HEW, Washington, 1977, dep. asst. sec. for health, dir. office disease prevention, 1977-95, asst. surgeon gen., 1980-95, acting dir. office of rsch. integrity, 1992-93; scholar-in-residence NAS, Washington, 1995-99; sr. cons. Robert Wood Johnson Found., Princeton, 1996—99; sr. v.p. dir. Health Grp., 1999—2004, counselor to pres., 2004—05; sr. scholar, Inst. Medicine NAS, 2005—. Instr. medicine George Washington U. Med. Sch., 1973-75; adj. prof. pub. policy Duke U., 1979-81, 99—; chair, task force on smoking and health; chair exec. com. HHS Environ. Health Policy Com.; mem. U.S. Japan Leadership program; chair World Bank/European Commn. Task Force on Reconstrn. of Health Sector, Bosnia, 1996-97; sr. scholar Assn. of Acad. Health Ctrs., 1997-99. Mem. editl. bd. Jour. Med. Edn., 1975-78, Jour. Preventive Medicine, 1987—; Jour. Health Promotion, 1992-98; editor-in-chief; Healthy People, Healthy People 2000, Surgeon General's Report on Nutrition and Health, Determining Risks to Health, Food Marketing to Children and Youth. Bd. dirs. United Way of Nat. Capital, Nemours Found. With USPHS, 1972—75, with USPHS, 1977—95. Recipient Arthur S. Flemming Pub. Svc. award, 1979, USPHS Disting. Svc. medal, 1989, Surgeon Gen.'s medallion, 1995, Fed. Profile in Leadership award, 1989, Wilbur Cohen award, 1995, award for excellence APHA, 1995, Health Leader of Yr. award, 1996. Fellow Am. Coll. Epidemiology, Am. Coll. Preventive Medicine; mem. Inst. Medicine/NAS. Office: 500 5th St NW Washington DC 20001 Office Phone: 202-334-3963. Business E-Mail: mcginnis@nas.edu.

**MCGINNIS, MARCY ANN,** broadcast executive; b. Long Branch, N.J., Apr. 9, 1950; d. Joseph Arthur and Ruth (Thomas) McG. AAS, Marymount U., 1970, PhD (hon.), Hofstra U. Exec. sec. news Sta. CBS News, N.Y.C., 1970-71; adminstrv. asst. Sta. CBS TV, N.Y.C., 1971-73; asst. producer, 1973-76, assoc. producer 1976 82, producer, 1982 83, sr. producer, 1983-89, exec. producer, 1989-92; dep. bur. chief London, dir. CBS NEWSNET Europe, 1992-95, TV news exec. prodr., v.p. and London bur. chief, 1995—97; v.p. news coverage CBS News, 1997—2001, sr. v.p. news coverage, 2001—05. Bd. dirs. Internat. Women's Media Found., La. State U. Manship Sch. Mass. Comm. Mem. NATAS, NAFE, TV and Radio Working Press Assn. Roman Catholic.*

**MCGINNIS, PATRICIA GWALTNEY,** non-profit organization executive; b. Goldsboro, N.C., July 19, 1947; d. Thomas McKim Gwaltney and Patricia Anne (Watkins) Schools; m. James Michael McGinnis, Aug. 4, 1978; children: J. Brian, Katherine B. BA, Mary Washington Coll., 1969; MPA, Harvard U., 1975. Dir. spl. studies U.S. Dept. Commerce, Washington, 1975-76; profl. staff mem. U.S. Senate Budget Com., Washington, 1976-77; dep. assoc. dir. U.S. Office Mgmt. and Budget, Washington, 1977-81; sr. cons. Cresap, McCormick and Paget, Inc., Washington, 1981-82; prin. The FMR Group, Inc., Washington, 1982-94; pres., CEO Coun. for Excellence in Govt., Washington, 1994—. Mem. exec. alumni coun. Kennedy Sch. Govt., Harvard U., Cambridge, Mass., 1992-96; dir. Primark Corp., Waltham, Mass., 1995-2000; mem. assoc. coun. George Washington Sch. Bus. and Pub. Adminstrn., 1996-99; bd. dirs. Brown Shoe Co., St. Louis, Imagitas, Inc., Newton, Mass.; bd. visitors U. Md. Sch. Pub. Affairs; dir. Logistics Mgmt. Inst., McLean, Va. Contbr. articles to profl. jours. Fellow: Nat. Acad. Pub. Adminstrn. Office: Coun for Excellence in Govt 1301 K St NW Ste 450W Washington DC 20005-3397

**MCGINNIS, ROBERT EARL,** lawyer; b. Caldwell, Ohio, May 1, 1931; s. Earl Peregoy and Mary Ethel (Richner) McG.; m. Jane Ann Lindenmeyer, Sept. 12, 1953; children: Sharon Ann. David E. BA, Ohio Wesleyan U., 1952; JD summa cum laude, Ohio State U., 1954. Bar: Ohio 1954, Calif. 1956. Asst. judge advocate USAF, 1954-56; sr. atty. Puce, Forward, Hamilton & Scripps, San Diego, 1956—. Counsel to pub. utilities, pub. agys., savs. and loan instns., ins. cos. and contractors. Trustee Wesley Meth. Ch., San Diego, Fine Arts Soc., First Meth. Ch., La Mesa, Calif.; counsel Kensington Community

Ch.; dir. San Diego Opera Assn., corp. sec., v.p. Mem. Order of Coif. Republican. Mem. United Ch. Christ. United Ch.Of Christ. Office: Luce Forward Hamilton & Scripps 600 W Broadway Ste 2600 San Diego CA 92101-3372 Office Phone: 619-699-2441. Business E-Mail: rmcginnis@luce.com

**MCGINNIS, W. PATRICK,** diversified company executive; BA in Political Science, Univ. Denver, 1970; MBA, Washington Univ. St. Louis, 1972. With Ralston Purina (now Nestle Purina), St. Louis, 1972—; dir. mktg, cons. prod. Ralston Purina Internat., 1978—80; exec. v.p., dir., grocery products Canadian div. Ralston Purina Co., Ontario, Canada, 1980—83, div. v.p. dir. mktg., grocery products St. Louis, Mo., 1983—84; pres., COO, grocery products group Ralston Purina, St. Louis, 1989—92; pres., CEO, grocery products group Ralston Purina Co., St. Louis, 1992—99, pres., CEO, 1999—2001, Nestle Purina, St. Louis, 2001—; corp. v.p., exec. v.p Ralston Purina, St. Louis, 1984—89. Bd. dir Brown Shoe Co. Recipient Disting. Alumni Award, Olin Sch Bus., Washington Univ., 1993. Office: Nestle Purina Co Checkerboard Sq Saint Louis MO 63164-0001

**MCGINNITY, MAUREEN ANNELL,** lawyer; b. Monroe, Wis., Apr. 6, 1956; d. James Arthur and Marie Beatrice (Novak) McG.; m. Richard W. Ziervogel, July 17, 1982; 1 child, Brigitte Kathleen. BS, U. Wis., Milw., 1977; JD, U. Wis., 1982. Bar: Wis. 1982, U.S. Dist. Ct. (ea. and we. dists.) Wis. 1982, U.S. Ct. Appeals (7th cir.) 1989, U.S. Ct. Appeals (1st cir.) 1991, U.S. Tax Ct. 1995, U.S. Supreme Ct. 1991. Assoc. Foley & Lardner LLP, Milw., 1982-91, ptnr., 1991—, chairperson tax valuation & fiduciary litig. practice group. Mem. Wis. Supreme Ct. Planning and Policy Adv. Com., Madison, 1991-94; adv. bd. Domestic Violence Legal Clinic, Milw., 1991—. Treas. Waukesha (Wis.) Food Pantry, 1988-94; trustee Boys & Girls Club Greater Milw., 1991—; bd. dirs. Task Force on Battered Women & Children, Inc., 1994-2006. Recipient Outstanding Svc. award Legal Action Wis., Milw., 1984, 93 Outstanding Fundraising awards Boys & Girls Club Greater Milw., 1987-92, Cert. Recognition, Common Coun. Task Force on Sexual Assault & Domestic Violence, Milw., 1991, Cert. Appreciation, Wis. Equal Justice Task Force, Madison, 1991, Cmty. Svc. award Wis. Law Found., 1995. Mem. ABA, State Bar Wis. (bd. govs. 1992-96, Pro Bono award 1990, chair 1993-94), Assn. for Women Lawyers (various offices, pres. 1992-93), Milw. Young Lawyers Assn. (bd. dirs. 1987-92, pres. 1990-91, Pres.' award 1991), Profl. Dimensions. Office: Foley & Lardner LLP 777 E Wisconsin Ave Ste 3800 Milwaukee WI 53202-5367 Office Phone: 414-297-5510. Office Fax: 414-297-4900. Business E-Mail: mmcginnity@foley.com.

**MC GINTY, JOHN MILTON,** architect, consultant; b. Houston, Apr. 24, 1935; s. Milton Bowles and Ruth Louise (Dreaper) McG.; m. Juanita Jones, May 4, 1957; children: Christopher Harold, Jacqueline Ruth McGinty Carlson. BS, Rice U., 1957; M.F.A., Princeton U., 1961. With archtl. firm Barnes, Landes & Goodman, Austin, Tex., 1957-58, Ingram & Harris, Beaumont, Tex., 1958-59; prin. McGinty Partnership, Architects, Inc., Houston, 1961-89, City Assos., Inc., 1979-91, Bovay-McGinty, Inc., engrs. & architects, Houston, 1989-91; founder, pres. Am. Constrn. Investigations Inc., Houston, 1991-2000, McGinty Archtl. Consultants, LLP, Houston, 2001—. Instr. archtl. design U. Houston, 1965-67; White House fellow, asst. to Sec. of Interior, 1967-68; vis. prof. architecture Rice U., 1969-70 Named Disting. Alumnus Rice U., 1986. Fellow AIA (mem. U.S. delegation to USSR 1972, pres. Houston chpt. 1973, nat. pres. 1977) Office: McGinty Archtl Cons LLP 602 Sawyer St Ste 740 Houston TX 77007 Home: 3614 Montrose Blvd #607 Houston TX 77006 Office Phone: 713-868-7021. Personal E-mail: jmginty@arch.com.

**MCGIRR, DAVID WILLIAM JOHN,** pharmaceutical executive; b. Glasgow, Scotland, May 19, 1954; arrived in US, 1991, naturalized, 2004; s. Edward McCombie and Diane Curzon (Woods) McG.; m. Margaret Joslin Richardson, May 9, 1981; children: William David, Katherine Joslin, Lucy Ann, Elizabeth Margaret. BSc (hon.), U. Glasgow, 1976; MBA, U. Pa., 1978. Assoc. S.G. Warburg & Co. Ltd., London, 1978—80, exec. dir., 1981—86; mng. dir. S.G. Warburg & Co. Inc., NYC, 1991—95, CFO, 1992—95; assoc. Warburg Paribas Becker Inc., N.Y.C., 1980—81; exec. dir. S.G. Warburg Securities, London, 1986—87; CEO S.G. Warburg Securities Ltd., Toronto, Ont., Canada, 1987—89; COO, CFO Bunting Warburg Inc., Toronto, 1989—91; pres. GAB Robins North Am. Inc., Parsippany, NJ, 1996—99, CEO, 1997—99; COO hippo, Inc., New Haven, 1999—2002, pres., 2001—02; sr. v.p., CFO Cubist Pharm., Inc., Lexington, Mass., 2002—, treas., 2002—03. Selection com. Thouron Scholarship. Bd. dirs. Friends of Glasgow U., Inc., 2003—. Thouron scholar, 1976-78. Mem. Apawamis Club (Rye, N.Y.). Avocations: collecting cars, golf, classic wooden boats. Office: 65 Hayden Ave Lexington MA 02421 Office Phone: 781-860-8526. Business E-Mail: david.mcgirr@cubist.com.

**MCGIVERIN, ARTHUR A.,** former state supreme court chief justice; b. Iowa City, Iowa, Nov. 10, 1928; s. Joseph J. and Mary B. McG.; m. Mary Joan McGiverin, Apr. 20, 1951; children: Teresa, Thomas, Bruce, Nancy. BSc with high honors, U. Iowa, 1951, JD, 1956. Bar: Iowa 1956. Pvt. practice law, Ottumwa, Iowa, 1956; alt. mcpl. judge, 1960-65; judge Iowa Dist. Ct. 8th Jud. Dist., 1965-78; assoc. justice Iowa Supreme Ct., Des Moines, 1978-87, chief justice, 1987-2000; sr. judge, 2000—. Mem. Iowa Supreme Ct. Commn. on Continuing Legal Edn., 1975. Served to 1st lt. U.S. Army, 1946-48, 51-53. Mem. Iowa State Bar Assn., Am. Law Inst. Roman Catholic. Avocation: golf. Office: Iowa Supreme Court State Capitol Building Des Moines IA 50319-0001

**MCGIVNEY, JOHN JOSEPH,** lawyer; b. Boston, Oct. 31, 1956; s. William A. and Margaret (Wall) McG. AB magna cum laude, Boston Coll., 1978, JD cum laude, 1981. Bar: Mass. 1981, U.S. Dist. Ct. Mass. 1982, U.S. Ct. Appeals (1st cir.) 1983, U.S. Supreme Ct. 1990. Assoc. Burns & Levinson, Boston, 1981-87, ptnr., chief appellate dept., 1988-96, ptnr. Rubin and Rudman, Boston, 1997—. Sec. Lynnfield (Mass.) Dem. Town Com., 1974-75, chmn., 1976-77. Mem. Mass. Acad. Trial Attys., Mass. Def. Lawyers Assn. (bd. dirs.), Algonquin Club of Boston. Home: 47 Doncaster Cir Lynnfield MA 01940-2255

**MCGLAMERY, BARBARA ELLEN,** librarian; d. Jimmie Lee and Barbara Ann McGlamery; m. Adam Perlmutter, May 16, 1998; 1 child, Lorenzo Aaron James Perlmutter. M of Libr. and Info. Sci., L.I. U., Brookville, N.Y., 1998. Data libr. Entertainment Weekly, N.Y.C., 2000—04; sr. libr. for ontology devel. Time Inc. Interactive, N.Y.C., 2005—. Bd. dirs Greenpoint Waterfront Assn. for Parks and Development, Bklyn., 2000—06; pres. Huron St. Block Assn., Bklyn., 2003—06. Recipient Pres.' award, Time Inc, 2003. Mem.: ALA (assoc.), Am. Soc. for Info. Sci. and Tech. (assoc.), Spl. Librs. Assn. (assoc.). Office: Time Inc Interactive 1271 Ave of the Americas New York NY 10020 Office Phone: 212-522-9198. E-mail: barbara_mcglamery@timeinc.com.

**MC GLAMERY, MARSHAL DEAN,** agronomist, educator, weed scientist; b. Mooreland, Okla., July 29, 1932; s. Walter Gaiford and Bernice (Gardner) McG.; m. Marilyn Hudson, June 2, 1957; children: Paul, Steve. BS, Okla. State U., 1956, MS, 1958; PhD, U. Ill., 1965. Instr. Panhandle A. and M. Coll., 1958-60; agronomist Agribus. Co., Lawrence, Kans., 1960-61; teaching asst. U. Ill., 1961-63, research fellow, 1963-65, asst. prof. weed sci., 1965-70, assoc. prof., 1970-76, prof., 1976-2000, prof. emeritus, 2002—; ext. crop scientist, 1965-2000, ret., 2000. Served with U.S. Army, 1953-55. NSF fellow, 1963 Mem. Weed Sci. Soc. Am., Coun. Agr. and Tech. Baptist. Home: 35 Lange Ave Savoy IL 61874-9705 Office: 1102 S Goodwin Ave Urbana IL 61801-4730 Business E-Mail: mmcglame@uiuc.edu

**MCGLAMRY, MAX REGINALD,** retired lawyer; b. Wilcox County, Ga., Sept. 12, 1928; s. Edgar Lee and Allie Bea (Faircloth) McGlamry; m. Jean Louise Hilyer, Dec. 28, 1950; children: Sharon Kay McGlamry Christopher, Michael Lee. BS, Auburn U., 1948; LLB cum laude, Mercer U., 1952, JD cum laude, 1970. Bar: Ga. 1953, U.S. Dist. Ct. (mid. dist.) Ga. 1954, U.S. Ct. Appeals (5th cir.) 1964, U.S. Supreme Ct. 1972, U.S. Ct. Appeals (11th cir.)

1981, U.S. Ct. Appeals (4th cir.) 1985, U.S. Dist. Ct. (no. dist.) Calif. 1988, U.S. Dist. Ct. (no. dist.) Ga. 1989. Pvt. practice, Columbus, Ga., 1953-64; from ptnr. to officer Swift, Pease, Davidson & Chapman (name changed to Page, Scrantom, Harris, McGlamry & Chapman, P.C.), Columbus, 1964-85; ptnr. Pope, Kellogg, McGlamry, Kilpatrick & Morrison, Columbus, 1985-90, Pope, McGlamry, Kilpatrick & Morrison, LLP, Columbus, 1990-2000; pres. Max R. McGlamry, P.C., Columbus, 2000—04. Exec. com. Muscogee County Dem. Orgn., Columbus, 1956-60; bd. dirs. Columbus Jr. C. of C. Ens. USN, 1948—49, Ens. USNR, 1949—59. Am. Coll. Trust & Estate Counsel fellow, 1973, Lawyers Found. Ga. fellow, 1983. Mem. ABA, State Bar Ga. (emeritus), Ga. Trial Lawyers Assn., Ga. Sr. Golfers Assn., Valley Sr.'s Golf Assn. (pres. 2003), Urban League of Greater Columbus, Inc., Columbus Lawyers Club (pres. 1964-65), Lions (Columbus chpt. pres. 1967-68), Green Island Country Club, Phi Kappa Phi, Alpha Epsilon Delta, Phi Alpha Delta, Pi Kappa Alpha. Democrat. Methodist. Avocations: golf, fishing. Home: 6941 Wethersfield Rd Columbus GA 31904-3317

**MCGLASHAN, THOMAS HAMEL,** psychiatrist, educator; b. Rochester, N.Y., Oct. 20, 1941; m. Patricia L. Gwiazdowski, 1964; children: Lara, Jennifer. BA in Chemistry magna cum laude, Yale U., 1963; MD, U. Pa., 1967. Diplomate in psychiatry Am. Bd. Psychiatry and Neurology. Intern Mary Hitchcock Meml. Hosp., Hanover, NH, 1967-68; resident, chief resident psychiatry Mass. Mental Health Ctr., 1968-71; officer in psychiatry, sr. asst. surgeon USPHS, 1971-73; chief clin. rsch. unit psychiat. assessment sect. NIMH, Adult Psychiatry Br., Bethesda, Md., 1973-75; staff psychiatrist Chestnut Lodge, Rockville, Md., 1975-90, dir. adult studies Rsch. Inst., 1977-81, dir. rsch., 1982-90; prof. dept. psychiatry Yale U. Sch. Medicine, 1990—; exec. dir. Yale Psychiat. Inst., New Haven, 1990-2000. Spl. and invited faculty, supr. Washington Sch. Psychiatry, 1978, 81, 82, 83; instr. Washington Psychoanalytic Inst., 1982-89, Western New Eng. Psychoanalytic Inst., 1992-93; clin. assoc. prof. dept. psychiatry Uniformed Svcs. U. of the Health Scis., 1983-88, clin. prof. dept. psychiatry, 1988-90; rsch. prof. dept. psychiatry U. Md. Sch. Medicine, 1986-90; bd. dirs. Parents Found. for Transitional Living, 1991-97; cons. and grant cons. in field; presenter in field; many others. Author: The Documentation of Clinical Psychotropic Drug Trials, 1973, The Borderline: Current Empirical Research, 1985, Schizophrenia: Treatment, Process and Outcome, 1989. Early Intervention in Psychosis, 2001, A Developmental Model of Borderline Personality Disorder, 2003; editl. cons.: Schizophrenia Bull., 1980-82, 84—, Archives of Gen. Psychiatry, 1982—, Am. Jour. Psychiatry, 1982—, Hosp. and Cmty. Psychiatry, 1984—, Jour. Personality Disorders, 1987—, Schizophrenia Rsch., 1987—, Acta Psychiatrica Scand., 1999—, Jour. Abnormal Psychology, 1988, Psychiatry Rsch., 1988—, others; mem. editl. bd.: Jour. Personality Disorders, 1989—, Schizophrenia Bull., 1989—; contbr. chpts. to books, over 200 articles to profl. jours. Recipient Gary Morris Rsch. award Washington Psychoanalytic Soc., 1980, Presdl. award for rsch. Nat. Assn. Pvt. Psychiat. Hosps., 1988, Silvano Arieti award Am. Acad. Psychoanalysis, 1990, Psychiat. Inst. Am. Found. award for rsch. devel. in hosp. psychiatry, 1990, Alexander Granlick award Am. Psychiat. Found., 1997, Established Investigator award Nat. Alliance Rsch. Schizophrenia & Depression, 1997-98; grantee Fund for Psychoanalytic Rsch. Am. Psychoanalytic Assn., 1978, 79, NIMH, 1996—, Norwegian Rsch. Coun., 1997—. Fellow Am. Psychiat. Assn., Am. Psychopathol. Assn.; mem. Western New Eng. Psychoanalytic Inst. and Soc., Soc. for Psychotherapy Rsch., Assn. for Clin. Psychosocial Rsch., Psychiat. Rsch. Soc., Internat. Study Personality Disorders, Internat. Early Psychosis Assn. Business E-Mail: thomas.mcglashan@yale.edu.

**MCGLATHERY, JAMES MELVILLE,** retired foreign language educator; b. New Orleans, Nov. 22, 1936; s. Samuel Lyon and Mary Jackson (Garrott) McG.; m. Nancy Judith Beyer, June 1, 1939; children: Samuel Lyon, Daniel Beyer, Andrew James, Benjamin Kim. AB, Princeton U., 1958; AM, Yale U., 1959, PhD, 1964. Instr. German Phillips Andover (Mass.) Acad., 1959-60; lectr. German Harvard U., 1963-64, instr. German, 1964-65; from asst. prof. to assoc. prof. U. Ill. at Urbana-Champaign, 1965-84, prof. German, 1984-2000, prof. emeritus, 2000—, acting dept. head, spring 1985, dept. head, 1985-95. Instr. Colby Coll. Summer Lang. Sch., 1964, Harvard U. Summer Lang. Sch., 1965-66, 70, U. Ill., Urbana-Champaign, 1972, 74, 76, 78, 80, 82, 87, 90, U. Göttingen, Germany, 1993-94, 2001; lectr., presenter in field. Author: Mysticism and Sexuality: E. T. A. Hoffmann, Part One: Hoffmann and His Sources, 1981, Desire's Sway: The Plays and Stories of Heinrich von Kleist, 1983, Mysticism and Sexuality: E. T. A. Hoffmann, Part Two: Interpretations of the Tales, 1985, Fairy Tale Romance: The Grimms, Basile, Perrault, 1991, Grimms' Fairy Tales: A History of Criticism on a Popular Classic, 1993, E.T.A. Hoffmann, 1997, Wagner's Operas and Desire, 1998; editor: German Source Readings in the Arts and Sciences, 1974, Journal of English and Germanic Philology, 1976, The Brothers Grimm and Folktale, 1988, 91, Music and German Literature: Their Relationship since the Middle Ages, 1992; contbg. author: Reader in German Literature, 1969, Fairy Tales as Ways of Knowing: Essays on Märchen in Psychology, Society, and Literature, 1981, Reflection and Action: Essays on the Bildungsroman, 1991, A Companion to the Nibelungenlied, 1998, A Companion to Wagner's Parsifal, 2005; mng. editor: Jour. English and Germanic Philology, 1972-00; contbr. articles and book revs. to profl. jours. Princeton U. scholar, 1954-58; undergrad. rsch. assistantship Princeton U., 1956-58; Woodrow Wilson Nat. fellow Yale U., 1958-59, Jr. Sterling fellow Yale U., 1960-61, Nat. Def. Edn. Act fellow in Russian, Yale U., 1961-63; grad. rsch. bd. grantee U. Ill. Urbana-Champaign, 1975, 79-80, 86, 89, 92. Mem.: N.Am. Heine Soc., E.T.A. Hoffmann Assn. Home: 1204 Thomas Dr Champaign IL 61821-1632 Business E-Mail: mcg@uiuc.edu.

**MCGLAUCHLIN, TOM,** artist; b. Turtle, Wis., Sept. 14, 1934; s. Charles Orion and Frances Lenore McGlauchlin; m. Patricia Ann Smith, Aug. 5, 1961; children: Christopher, Jennifer (dec.), Jeffrey. BS in Art, U. Wis., Madison, MS in Art, 1960; studied pottery with James McKinnell, 1962. Instr. dept. art and art edn. U. Wis., Madison, 1960-61; instr. art dept. Cornell Coll., Mt. Vernon, Iowa, 1961-64, asst. prof. art dept., 1964-68, assoc. prof., chmn. art dept., 1968-71; instr. Toledo Mus. Art, 1971-82, prof., dir. glass program, 1982-84. One-man exhbns. include Habatat Gallery, Dearborn, Mich., 1979, Glass Art Gallery, Toronto, 1981, 85, Glass Gallery, Bethesda, Md., 1981, 85, 87, 91, Heller Gallery, N.Y.C., 1983, B.Z. Wagman Gallery, St. Louis, 1983, Running Ridge Gallery, Santa Fe, 1990; selected group exhbns. include Toledo Mus. Art, 1972, 88, Glasmuseum Frauenau, Franenau, Germany, 1977, Habatat Gallery, 1980, 84, The Hand and the Spirit Gallery, Scottsdale, Ariz., 1980, Gallery of Contemporary Crafts, Detroit, 1980, The Naples (Fla.) Art Gallery, 1981, The Craftsman's Gallery, Scarsdale, N.Y., 1981, 84, The Nat. Mus. Modern Art, Kyoto and Tokyo, 1981, Perception Gallery, Houston, 1985, The AirLoft Gallery, Honolulu, 1986, The Corning (N.Y.) Mus. Glass, 1987; selected competitive exhbns. include Everson Mus. Art, Syracuse, N.Y., 1961, 62, Mus. Contemporary Crafts, N.Y.C., 1962, Corning Glass Mus., Met. Mus. Art, N.Y.C., Victoria and Albert Mus., London, Musee Ars Decoratif, Paris; public collections include Toledo Mus. Art, The Smithsonian Collection, Washington, Portland (Oreg.) Art Mus., New Orleans Mus. Art, Mus. Contemporary Crafts, Musee des arts decoratifs de la Ville de Lausanne, Switzerland, Minn. Mus. Art, St. Paul, Kunstmuseum, Dusseldorf, Germany, Corning Glass Mus. Grantee Associated Colls. Midwest, 1966-67; recipient First Jury award Toledo Glass Nat. II, 1968. Mem. Am. Crafts Coun., Internat. Sculpture Soc., Ohio Designer-Craftsmen, Glass Art Soc. Office: The Glass Studio 1940 W Central Ave Toledo OH 43606-3944 Office Phone: 419-461-4097. Business E-Mail: tom@mcglauchlin.com.

**MCGLAUGHLIN, THOMAS HOWARD,** publishing executive, retired military officer; b. Cin., Jan. 12, 1928; s. George Godden and Cordelia (Herrlinger) McG.; m. Moana Maharam-Stone, Jan. 4, 1984. BS in Elec. Engring., U.S. Naval Acad., 1950. Lic. master mariner. Commd. ensign U.S. Navy, 1950, advanced through grades to capt., 1970; White House aide to Pres. John F. Kennedy, Washington, 1960-63; exec. officer USS Prichett, Long Beach, Calif., 1963-65; comdg. officer USS Maddox, Long Beach, 1965-67; exec. officer USS Boston, Boston, 1967-70; chief naval ops. Comdr.-in-Chief, Pacific, Honolulu, 1970-74; chief of staff Mil. Sealift

Command, N.Y.C., 1974-79; ret. U.S. Navy, 1979; pres. Falmouth Press, Honolulu, 1983—. Marine surveyor R.W. Dickieson Internat., Inc., Honolulu, 1982—; master Motor Vessel Rella Mae, Honolulu, 1981-90, Royal Taipan, Cebu, Philippines, 1990. Hon. police chief Boston Police Dept., 1969. Decorated Bronze Star, Navy commendation medal with combat "v", combat action ribbon, Vietnamese Disting. Svc. order; recipient medal for Outstanding Svc., Am. Legion, Pitts., 1942. Mem. Nat. Def. Transp. Assn., VFW (life), U.S. Naval Acad. Alumni Assn. (life), The Mil. Officers Assn. Republican. Presbyterian. Avocations: flying, scuba diving, tennis, golf. Home: 118 Kiionioni Pl Honolulu HI 96816-4248 Office: RW Dickieson Internat Inc 46-208 Kahuhipa St Kaneohe HI 96744-3905

**MCGLONE, GERARD J.,** psychology professor; s. Stephen Andrew and Margaret Mary McGlone. MDiv, Weston Sch. Theology, Cambridge, Mass., 1987; MA in Counseling Psychology, Boston Coll., Mass., 1990; MA in Clin. Psychology, Calif. Sch. Profl. Psychology, San Diego, 1992, PhD in Clin. Psychology, 2001. Clin. and rsch. fellow John Hopkins U., Balt., 2001—04; asst. prof. Georgetown Sch. Medicine, Washington; adj. prof. Loyola Coll., Balt.; v.p. for mission St. Joseph's U., Phila. Author: (book) Creating Safe and Sacred Spaces. Roman Catholic. Office: St Josephs Univ 5600 City Ave Wolfington Philadelphia PA 19131 Office Phone: 610-660-3290. Office Fax: 610-660-1042. E-mail: gmcglone@sju.edu.

**MCGLONE, MICHAEL ANTHONY,** lawyer; b. New Orleans, Jan. 6, 1951; s. James Godfrey and Dorothy (Barta) McG.; m. Suzanne Blanchard, Nov. 27, 1976; children: Kevin, Kathleen, Meghan. BBA cum laude, Loyola U., New Orleans, 1972, JD, 1975. Bar: La. 1975, U.S. Dist. Ct. (ea. dist.) La. 1975, U.S. Ct. Appeals (5th and 11 cirs.) 1975, U.S. Dist. Ct. (we. dist.) La. 1978, U.S. Dist. Ct. (mid. dist.) La. 1979, U.S. Supreme Ct. 1981. Law clk. to Hon. Herbert W. Christenberry U.S. Dist. Ct., New Orleans, 1975-76; ptnr. Kean Miller, 1976—. Fellow Am. Coll. Trial Lawyers; mem. ABA, ALA, FBA (bd. dirs. New Orleans chpt. 1986—, pres. 1995-96), La. Bar Assn., Southeastern Admiralty Law Inst., New Orleans Bar Assn., Maritime Law Assn., St. Thomas More Inn of Ct. (master barrister), Alpha Sigma Nu, Beta Gamma Sigma. Democrat. Roman Catholic. Home: 4708 N Turnbull Dr Metairie LA 70002-1447 Office: Kean Miller 601 Poydras St New Orleans LA 70130-6029 Office Phone: 504-885-6333. Personal E-Mail: biocyc@aol.com. Business E-Mail: mike.mcglone@keanmiller.com.

**MCGLOTHEN, STEVEN RAYMOND,** motion picture producer; b. Stockton, Calif., Oct. 3, 1951; MA, Brooks Inst., 1973. Work in films and TV includes Cracking Up, 1975, The Hughes Mystery, 1976, Happy Birthday, 1980, A Family Tree, 1980, Hoboken Chicken Emergency, 1984, Contract for Life, 1985, Lena, My Hundred Children, 1987, Daddy, 1987, Glitz, 1988, Desperate for Love, 1988, The Image, 1989, Max and Helen, 1990, The Amnesty Files, 1990, The Marla Hanson Story, 1991, Battling for Baby, 1992, Deliver Them from Evil: The Taking of Alta View, 1992, Lady Boss, 1992, Sugar Hill, 1994, Against the Wall, 1994, Silver Strand, 1995, 2 Harts in 3/4 Time, 1995, A Family Divided, 1995, Broken Trust, 1995, Hart to Hart: Harts in High Season, 1996, The Christmas Tree, 1996, Moby Dick, 1998, David and Lisa, 1998, Rip Girls, 2000, When Good Ghouls Go Bad, 2001, Big Shot: Confessions of a Campus Bookie, 2002, I, Robot, 2004, Aquamarine, 2006. Mem. Dirs. Guild Am.*

**MCGLOTHLEN, JOHN M.,** librarian; s. Gary and Barbara (Myers) McGlothlen; m. Angela Wells, Aug. 17, 1991; children: Emily, Ethan. BS, Charter Oak State Coll., 1995; MA, U. Iowa, 1998. Assoc. libr. Iowa Wesleyan Coll., Mount Pleasant, Iowa, 1998—2000; electronic svcs. libr. Sioux City Pub. Libr., Sioux City, Iowa, 2000—01; libr. The Gazette, Cedar Rapids, Iowa, 2001—. Editor: (web site) The Bible as Music (http://bibleasmusic.com). Mem.: SLA. Avocation: music. Office Phone: 319-398-8328.

**MCGLOTHLIN, MICHAEL GORDON,** lawyer; b. Richlands, Va., Oct. 31, 1951; s. Woodrow Wilson and Sally Ann (Cook) McG.; m. Sandra Lee Keen, Oct. 1, 1983; children: Michael Alexander, Robert Aaron. BA, U. Va., 1974; JD, Coll. William and Mary, 1976. Bar: Va. 1977, U.S. Dist. Ct. (we. dist.) Va. 1978. Ptnr. McGlothlin, McGlothlin & McGlothlin, Grundy, Va., 1977-79; commonwealth atty. Buchanan County, Grundy, 1980-83; ptnr. McGlothlin & Wife, Grundy, 1984—; atty.for Buchanan County 1984-89; bd. dirs. Gt. Southwest Home Commn., vice chmn., 1983—. Mem. adv. bd. Clinch Valley Coll.; sec. Buchanan County Dem. Party. Mem. ABA, Va. State Bar Assn., Buchanan County Bar Assn. (pres. 1984), Kiwanis (sec. Buchanan County Dem. Com.), Phi Alpha Delta, Phi Sigma Kappa. Presbyterian. Home and Office: PO Box 810 Grundy VA 24614-0810

**MCGLYNN, ELIZABETH A.,** health policy analyst; PhD, RAND Grad. Sch.; MMP, U. Mich. Assoc. dir. RAND Health, Santa Monica, Calif.; dir. Ctr. Rsch. on Quality in Health Care, Santa Monica, Calif. Adv. com. Nat. Com. for Quality Assurance (NCQA), Nat. Quality Forum (NQF), Coun. Accountable Physician Practices, Am. Med. Group Assn.; editorial bd. Health Svcs. Rsch., Milbank Meml. Fund Quarterly. Mem.: Inst. Medicine. Achievements include development of QA Tools. Office: RAND Health Communications PO Box 2138 1776 Main St Santa Monica CA 90407-2138*

**MCGLYNN, JAMES FRANCIS,** chemistry educator, chemical engineer; b. Hazleton, Pa., Apr. 28, 1961; s. John Francis and Rosemary McGlynn; m. Beth Ann Shaefbook; children: Jessica, Ryan, Patrick. BSChemE, Pa. State U., State College, 1987; cert. tchr., Hood Coll. Frederick, Md., 1999. Chem. engr. DuPont, Aiken, SC, 1988—89, Westinghouse, Aiken, 1989—94, Sci. Applications Internat. Corp., Gaithersburg, Md., 1999—2002; chem. tchr. Penn Manor Sch. Dist., Millersville, Pa., 2000—. Home: 391 Squire Ln Lititz PA 17543 Personal E-mail: james.mcglynn@pennmanor.net.

**MCGLYNN, MARGARET G.,** pharmaceutical executive; BS in Pharmacy, SUNY, Buffalo, 1982, MBA in Mktg., 1983. Profl. rep. Merck & Co., Inc., Whitehouse Sta., NJ, 1983—84, mktg. analyst, 1985—86, promotion mgr., 1986, product mgr., 1987—89, dir. bus. devel., 1987—89, 1989—90, sr. dir. mkt. planning, 1990—91, exec., dir. nat. consumer mktg. U.S. human health, 1991—93, v.p. bus. mgmt. and devel. U.S. human health, 1993, sr. v.p. managed care U.S. human health, 1994—95, sr. v.p. bus. planning proposals and analysis Merck-Medco Managed Care, 1994, sr. v.p. health and utilization mgmt., Merck-Medco Managed Care L.L.C., Whitehouse Sta, 1995—98, sr. v.p. world wide human health mktg., 1998—2001, exec. v.p. customer mktg. and sales U.S. human health, 2001—02, pres. U.S. human health, 2003—05; pres. Merck Vaccines, 2005—. Bd. dir. Air Products and Chemicals. Corp. exec. bd. Phila. Mus. Art; mem. dean's adv. coun. U. Buffalo Sch. Mgmt. Office: Merck & Co Inc One Merck Dr PO Box 100 Whitehouse Station NJ 08889-0100*

**MCGLYNN, SEAN,** secondary school educator; b. Syracuse, N.Y., Mar. 14, 1965; s. Edward and Phyllis Jean McGlynn; m. Sheila McGlynn, Nov. 22, 1997; 1 child, Casey. BS in Biology, Binghamton U., NY, 1987; MS in Environ. and Forest Biology, SUNY, Syracuse N.Y., 1990; MS in Sci. Edn., Syracuse U., NY, 1990. Cert. tchr. N.Y. State Edn. Dept., 1990. Tchr. sci. East Syracuse-Minoa (N.Y.) Ctrl. Schs., 1990—. Home: 316 Albert Rd Syracuse NY 13214 Office: East Syracuse-Minoa Central Schools 6400 Fremont Road East Syracuse NY 13057 Office Phone: 315-656-7242. Personal E-mail: smcg24@hotmail.com. Business E-Mail: smcglynn@esmschools.org.

**MC GLYNN, SEAN PATRICK,** physical chemist, educator; b. Dungloe, Ireland, Mar. 8, 1931; arrived in U.S., 1952, naturalized, 1957; s. Daniel and Catherine (Brennan) Mc Glynn; m. Helen Magdalena Salacz-von Dohnanyi, Apr. 11, 1955 (div.); children: Sean Ernst, Daniel Julian, Brian Charles, Sheila Ann, Alan Patrick; m. Maureen G. Potts, Oct. 23, 1985; children: Shane Joseph, Brennan John, Colin Michael. BS, Nat. U. Ireland, 1951, MS, 1952; PhD, Fla. State U., 1956. Fellow Fla. State U., 1956, U. Wash., 1956-57; mem. faculty La. State U., 1957—, prof. chemistry, 1964—, Boyd prof. chemistry, 1967—, dean Grad. Sch., 1981-82, vice chancellor rsch., 1981-91.

Assoc. prof. biophysics Yale U., 1961; Humboldt prof. physics U. Bonn, Germany, 1979—80; cons. to pvt. cos. Author (with others): (book) Molecular Spectroscopy of the Triplet State, 1969, Introduction to Applied Quantum Chemistry, 1971, Photophysics and Photochemistry in the Vacuum Ultraviolet, 1985, The Geometry of Genetics, 1988; editor: Wiley-Interscience Monographs in Chem. Physics; contbr. articles to profl. jours., chapters to books. Recipient award, Baton Rouge Coun. Engring. and Sci. Socs., 1962—63, Sr. Scientist award, Alexander von Humboldt Found., 1979, Disting. Rsch. medal, U. Bologna, Italy, 1979; fellow, Rsch. Corp., 1960—63; Sloan fellow, 1964—68. Mem.: AAAS, Am. Phys. Soc., Am. Chem. Soc. (S.W. Regional award 1967, Fla. sect. award 1970, Coates award 1977). Achievements include research in molecular electronic spectroscopy; electronic structure; energy transfer; molecular genetics; bioenergetics; mathematical biology; optoacoustics; optogalvanics. Home: 12048 Pecan Grove Ct Baton Rouge LA 70810-4835 Office Phone: 225-578-3392. Business E-Mail: chspm@lsu.edu. E-mail: maureenpotts@cox.net.

**MCGLYNN, WILLIAM CHARLES,** brokerage house executive; b. Hazelton, Pa., Apr. 4, 1944; s. William Charles and Mary McGlynn; m. Phyllis Marie Fotia, May 28, 1967; children: William Jason, Devon Laura, Robert Ryan, Kirsten Ann. BS in Bus. Mgmt., Farleigh Dickenson U., Madison, N.J., 1968, postgrad. studies in Fin. and Econs., 1968-69. V.p. William D. Witter, Inc., N.Y.C., 1970-75, Dillon Read & Co., Inc., N.Y.C., 1975-79, Tucker Anthony R. L. Day, N.Y.C., 1979-81; mng. dir. L.F. Rothschild, Inc., N.Y.C., 1982-88, Bear, Stearns & Co., Inc., N.Y.C., 1988—2002, sr. mng. dir., 2002—. Fundraiser Wall St. Charity Fund, N.Y.C., 1971—75; benefits com. Cath. Charities Home Bur., N.Y.C., 1980—90; trustee, exec. com. mem. Oak Knoll Sch. Holy Child, Summit, NJ, 1989—; fundraiser, mem. Fathers and Friends Delbarton Sch., 1993—98, Morristown Bearcd Sch. Assn., 1998—99; advisor, mem. Oak Knoll Fathers Bd., 1989—; trustee, chmn. fin. com. Chubb Found., 2001—. Republican. Roman Catholic. Avocations: skiing, tennis, boating, reading. Office: Bear Sterns & Co Inc 245 Park Ave New York NY 10167-0002

**MCGOLDRICK, JOHN LEWIS,** lawyer; b. Plainfield, N.J., Mar. 2, 1941; s. John Leslie and Sarah (Walker) McGoldrick; m. Ann Chapman Puffer, Oct. 1, 1966; children: Scott Runyon, Jennifer Winslow. BA cum laude, Harvard U., 1963, LLB, 1966. Bar: N.J. 1966, N.Y. 1985. Assoc. McCarter & English, Newark, 1966-73, ptnr., 1974-95; sr. v.p., gen. counsel Bristol-Myers Squibb Co., NYC, 1995—98, sr. v.p., gen. counsel, pres., Med. Devices Group, 1998—2000, exec. v.p., 1995—, gen. counsel, 2001— Vice-chmn., bd. dirs. N.J. Transit Corp., Newark, 1979—2005; bd. dirs. Bristol-Myers Squibb Found., Zimmer Holdings, Inc., HealthCare Inst. N.J., Regional Plan Assn., N.J. Network Found. Trustee Essex-Newark Found. Legal Svcs. N.J. Montclair State U.; mem. com. to visit The Coll., mem. com. to visit Sch. Pub. Health Harvard U.; mem. Harvard Malaria Initiative Adv. Coun. Fellow: Am. Acad. Appellate Lawyers, Am. Bar Found., Am. Coll. Trial Lawyers; mem.: ABA, Am. Arbitration Assn., Nat. Panel Arbitrators, Coun. Fgn. Rels., Aspen Inst. World Economy, CPR Inst. Dispute Resolution (mem. exec. com.), Coun. Chief Legal Officers (Conf. Bd. Inc.), Assn. Gen. Counsel, Am. Law Inst., Assn. Fed. Bar N.J. (former pres.), Assn. Bar City of N.Y., N.Y. Bar Assn., N.J. Bar Assn., Legal Svcs. N.J. (bd. dirs.), World Econ. Forum, Coun. U.S. and Italy, Harvard Law Sch. Assn., N.J. (former pres.). Office: Bristol-Myers Squibb Co 345 Park Ave New York NY 10154-0004 Office Phone: 212-546-4460.

**MCGOLDRIK, MONICA,** marriage and family therapist, researcher; b. N.Y.C., July 23, 1943; d. Joseph Daniel and Helen Cahalane McGoldrick; m. Sophocles Orfanidis, May 16, 1970; 1 child, John Orfanidis. BA, Brown U., Providence, RI, 1960—64; MSW; MA, Yale U., New Haven, CT, 1964—66; MSW, Smith Coll. Sch. for Social Work, Northampton, MA, 1967—68, PhD (hon.), 1991. Lic. LCSW NJ, 1976; Marriage Counseling NJ, 1978. Staff social worker St Raphael's Hosp., New Haven, Conn., 1969—72; dir. family therapy tng. U. of Medicine and Dentistry of N.J., Piscataway; dir. Multicultural Family Inst., Highland park, 1991—; vis. faculty Sch. Social Wk. Fordham U., N.Y.C., 1993—2003. Assoc. prof. of clin. psychiatry U. of Medicine and Dentistry of N.J., Piscataway. Author: The Expanded Family Life Cycle: Individual, Family, and Social Perspectives, (book) Ethnicity and Family Therapy, Genograms: Assessment and Intervention, You Can Go Home Again: Understanding your Family Relationships, Living Beyond Loss: Death & the Family, (professional book) Revisioning Family Therapy: Race, Culture and Gender in Family Therapy, Women in Families. Recipient Disting. Contbn. to Family Therapy Theory and Practice, Am. Family Therapy Acad., 1994. Office: Multicultural Family Institute 328 Denison St Highland Park NJ 08904 Office Phone: 732-565-9010. Home Fax: 732-565-0703; Office Fax: 732-565-0703. E-mail: mmcgoldrick@mindspring.com.

**MCGONAGLE, DUNCAN FRANCIS,** mental health nurse, substance abuse counselor; b. Bklyn., May 6, 1939; s. John and Kathleen (Rooney) McGonagle; m. Gloria Maria Carrubba, Dec. 5. 1987. AA, Allan Hancock, 1964; AAS in Nursing, CUNY, 1992. Cert. psychiat. and mental health nurse, addictions RN. Substance abuse counselor Pritikin Longevity Ctr., Santa Monica, Calif., 1978-84; paramedic N.Y.C. Emergency Med. Svc., 1987-92; psychiatric nurse Bellevue Hosp. Ctr., N.Y.C., 1992-99; adminstr. Methadone Maintenance Treatment Program, St. Barnabas Hosp., Bronx, NY, 1999—2001; nurse mgr. Methadone Maintenance Treatment Program, Beth Israel Med. Ctr., N.Y.C., 2001—. Founder Methadone Anonymous, N.Y. Aux. police officer N.Y.C. Police Dept., 1985—. With USN, 1956-60, 1961-62, Vietnam. Recipient Nat. award for Clin. Excellence in Nursing, Nat. Nurses Soc. on Addictions, 1995. Mem. Blue Knights, Knights of Life, Rolls Royce Owners Club, Harley Owners Group. Roman Catholic. Avocations: computers, sailing, motorcycling, antique autos. Home: 73 Verona St Brooklyn NY 11231-1612 Office: Beth Israel Med Ctr 160 Water St New York NY 10038-4922 Office Phone: 212-256-2595. E-mail: duncan73@aol.com.

**MCGONIGLE, JAMES GREGORY,** financial consultant; b. Bklyn., Nov. 17, 1945; s. William John and Helen Bernadette (Dennin) McG.; m. Francine Anne Falango, May 27, 1972; children: MarieElena, Lauren Anne. AAS in Acctg., CUNY, 1972; BS in Fin. summa cum laude, L.I. U., 1980. Cert. fin. planner Internat. Bd. Cert. Fin. Planners. Account exec. Coburn Credit Corp., Rockville Centre, NY, 1965-66; asst. credit mgr. UNI-CARD, Greatneck, NY, 1966-68; accounts receivable mgr. Granite Leasing Corp., Garden City, NY, 1968-73; v.p. Citicorp., N.Y.C., 1973-88; cons. O/E Learning, Inc., Detroit, 1988-90; regional dir. Ednl. Techs., Inc., Troy, Mich., 1989—. Adj. faculty Coll. for Fin. Planning, Denver. Vol. Family Svc. Assn., Nassau, N.Y., 1981-84, Better Bus. Bur., Farmingdale, N.Y., 1987—; vol., career advisor L.I. U., Brookville, N.Y., 1990—; treas. W. Tresper Clarke Friends of Arts, 1988-89. Mem. ABA (assoc.), Fin. Mgmt. Assn., Internat. Assn. Fin. Planning, Adelphi Soc. Cert. Fin. Planners, Internat. Assn. Registered Fin. Planners (speaker's bur.), Nat. Assn. Life Underwriters, Nat. Panel Consumer Arbitrators, Nat. Ctr. for Fin. Edn., Inst. Cert. Fin. Planners (bd. dirs. L.I 1989-92), N.Y. State Assn. Cert. Fin. Planners, Delta Mu Delta. Republican. Roman Catholic. Avocations: bicycling, public speaking, travel, writing, gardening. Home: 2167 Plum Tree Rd N Westbury NY 11590-6029 Office: 33 Willis Ave Mineola NY 11501-4423

**MCGONIGLE, TERRY L.,** theater educator, consultant; b. Wichita, Kans., Aug. 17, 1951; s. Arthur Glen and Betty Ruth McGonigle; 1 child, Tiffani Dawn Black. MA, Emporia State U., Kans., 1974. Cert. tchr. Ga., 1974. Theatre arts tchr. Forsyth County Schs., Cumming, Ga., 2002—04; tchr. tech. theatre studies Grayson Sch. Tech., Loganville, 2004—. Costume designer: Ragtime. Maj. contbr. Broadway Cares / Equity Fights AIDS, 2000. Named to Hall of Fame, Kans. Thespian Soc., 2005. Mem.: Ednl. Theatre Assn. (life; internat. student officer adult liaison 2006). Home: 1365 Stoney Field Pl Lawrenceville GA 30043 Office: Grayson HS 50 Hope Hollow Rd Loganville GA 30052 Office Phone: 770-554-7089. E-mail: terry_mcgonigle@gwinnett.k12.ga.us.

**MCGOUGH, BRIAN EDWARD,** investment banker, lawyer; b. NYC, Feb. 18, 1964; s. George V. McGough Sr. and Mary Elizabeth (Keaveny) Covell; m. Tamra Ann Pearce, Aug. 1, 1987; children: Michael Christopher, Christopher Thomas, Matthew Steven. BS, Bradley U., 1986; JD, No. Ill. U., 1990. Bar: Ill. 1991, U.S. Dist. Ct. (no. dist.) Ill. 1990, U.S. Tax Ct. 1993, U.S. Ct. Appeals (7th cir.) 1991, U.S. Supreme Ct. 1993. Assoc. Katten Muchin & Zavis, Chgo., 1990-96; v.p. JP Morgan & Co., Chgo., 1996-98; sr. mng. dir. Bank One Capital Markets, Chgo., 1998—2003; mng. dir. RBC Dain Rauscher, Inc., Chgo., 2003—. Spl. asst. atty. gen. State Ill., Chgo., 1992-96. Bd. dirs. Naperville (Ill.) Cmty. Outreach, 1990—; trustee No. Ill. U., DeKalb, 1993, mem. law sch. adv. bd., 1993. Recipient Disting. Alumnae award No. Ill. U., DeKalb, 1998.

**MCGOUGH, DUANE THEODORE,** economist, consultant, retired federal official; b. Rice Lake, Wis., Aug. 3, 1932; s. James Patrick and Josephine Margaret (Huerth) McG.; m. Donna Mae Jones, June 13, 1959 Student, Wis. State Coll., Eau Claire, 1950-52, U. Wis., 1952-54, 56-60, BS in Light Constrn. Industry, 1959, MBA in Urban Land Econs., 1962; postgrad., U. So. Calif., 1968-69. Housing mgmt. officer Pub. Housing Adminstrn. Atlanta, 1960-62; program planning analyst Pub. Housing Adminstrn. Phila., 1962-67; program analyst HUD, Washington, 1967-68, 69-70, industry economist, 1970-73, supervisory economist, 1973-77, dir. housing and demographic analysis, 1977-97, govt. tech. rep. ann. housing survey, 1977-83; govt. tech. rep. Am. Housing Survey, 1984-97; acting dep. asst. sec. for econ. affairs (chief economist) HUD, Washington, 1977, 82, 84-85, ret., 1997. US rep housing subcom. UN Econ. Commn. for Europe, Geneva, 1976, 79, Madrid, 1982; HUD rep. Interagy. Com. on Population Rsch., 1978-97, Interagy. Forum on Aging-Related Stats., 1986-97; mem. Fed. Task Force on Household Survey Redesign, 1988-97; mem. policy com. Year 2000 Census; coord. PRSC Ctr. U.S./Mex. Sem. Housing Stats., Mexico City, 1997. Editor: President's Report on Housing Goals, 1974-78, Nat. Housing Prodn. Report, 1980, 82; U.S. Housing Market Conditions Report, 1994-97, FEMA National Emergency Management Program, 1967-97, Housing Consultant, 1997—; tenor, Washington Choral Ensemble, 2002-. With U.S. Army, 1954-56; saxophonist 7th Army Band. Fellow Nat. Inst. Pub. Affairs, 1969; recipient Outstanding Performance award Pub. Housing Adminstrn., Phila., 1966, HUD, 1984, 92, 97, Career Edn. award Nat. Inst. Pub. Affairs, 1968-69, Cert. Spl. Achievement, HUD, 1978, 83, 84, 96, Cert. Superior Svc., HUD, 1988, 95, Cert. Appreciation, Bur. Census, 1990. Mem. Lambda Alpha Internat. (v.p. programs 1987-89, chmn. real estate and fin. com. George Washington chpt. 1990-92, dir.-at-large 1992-93), Lambda Chi Alpha. Avocations: music, gardening, rockhounding, web-surfing. Personal E-mail: duanetm@aol.com.

**MCGOUGH, WALTER THOMAS, JR.,** lawyer; b. Pitts., Nov. 7, 1953; s. Walter Thomas and Jane (Fitzpatrick) McGough; m. Rebecca Gai Frazier, June 24, 1978; children: Emily Ann, Walter Thomas III. BA, Princeton U., 1975; JD, U. Va., 1978. Bar: Pa., 1978, DC, US Dist. Ct. We. Dist. Pa. 1980, US Ct. Appeals 3rd cir., 1983, US Ct. Appeals, 6th cir. 1984, Pa. Supreme Ct. 1978, US Supreme Ct., 1983. Law clk. to Hon. Collins J. Seitz U.S. Ct. Appeals 3rd cir., Wilmington, Del., 1978-79; law clk. to Hon. William H. Rehnquist US Supreme Ct., Washington, 1979-80; asst. US atty. We. Dist. Pa., 1980-82; assoc. Reed Smith LLP, Pitts., 1982-86, ptnr., 1987—, head of litigation dept., 1998—, mem. exec. com. Assoc. counsel, Sen. Select Com. on Secret Mil. Assistance to Iran and the Nicaraguan Opposition, Washington, 1987; mem. lawyers adv. com. US Ct. Appeals 3d cir., 1987-89, chmn., 1989; mem. appellate rules com. US Jud. Conf., 1998-2005. Co-author: Fed. Appellate Procedure, 3rd Cir., 1996; contbr. articles to profl. jours. Trustee Sta. WQED, Pitts., 1996-2002, vice chmn, 1997-99, chmn., 1999-2002; mem. 3d Cir. Task Force on Rule 11, 1987-89. Fellow Am. Coll. Trial Lawyers, Am. Acad. Appellate Lawyers; mem. Allegheny County Bar Assn. (ethics com. 1983-86, bd. govs. 1994-2001, pres. 1999-2000), Allegheny County Acad. Trial Lawyers, Duquesne Club, Ross Mountain Club. Office: Reed Smith LLP 435 6th Ave Pittsburgh PA 15219-1886 Office Phone: 412-288-3088. Office Fax: 412-288-3063. Business E-Mail: wmcgough@reedsmith.com.

**MCGOVERN, ELIZABETH,** actress; b. Evanston, Ill., July 18, 1961; Student, Juilliard Sch. Music. Actress: (stage prodns.) To Be Young, Gifted and Black, 1981, Hotel Play, My Sister in this House, 1981-82 (Theatre World award 1981-82), Major Barbara, 1982, Painting Churches, 1983-84, Twelfth Night, 1984, The Hitch-hiker, 1985, A Map of the World, 1985, Hamlet, As You Like It, A Midsummer Night's Dream, Three Sisters, Ring Round the Moon, The Misanthrope, Hurly Burly, Three Days of Rain, Dinner with Friends, Maids of Honour, (feature films) Ordinary People, Ragtime, 1981, Lovesick, 1983, Racing with the Moon, 1984, Once Upon a Time in America, 1984, The Bedroom Window, 1987, Native Son, 1987, She's Having a Baby, 1987, Wings of Courage, 1995, The Wings of a Dove, 1997, Johnny Handsome, The Handmaid's Tale, A Shock to the System, House of Mirth, The Misadventures of Margaret, The Man with Rain in His Shoes, Tune in Tomorrow, Manila, 2000, House of Mirth, 2000, Buffalo Soldiers, 2001, The Truth, 2006, (TV) The Scarlet Pimpernel, 1998, If Not for You, Flamingo Rising, 2001, The Summer of Ben Tyler, Clover, Hawkins, Tales from Hollywood, Broken Glass, Broken Trust, The Changeling, Thursday the Twelfth, Tante Twelve, Hawk, Three Moons Over Milford, 2006. Office: AMG Ste 212 9465 Wilshire Blvd Beverly Hills CA 31027-6173*

**MCGOVERN, GEORGE STANLEY,** former senator; b. Avon, SD, July 19, 1922; s. Joseph C. and Frances (McLean) McG.; m. Eleanor Stegeberg, Oct. 31, 1943; children: Ann, Susan, Teresa (dec.), Steven, Mary. BA, Dakota Wesleyan U., 1945; MA, Northwestern U., 1949, PhD, 1953. Prof. history and polit. sci. Dakota Wesleyan U., 1949-53; exec. sec. S.D. Dem. Party, 1953-55; mem. 85th-86th Congresses, 1st Dist. S.D.; spl. asst. to Pres., dir. Food for Peace, 1961-62; U.S. senator from S.D., 1963-81; chmn. senate select com. on nutrition and human needs; pres. Middle East Policy Coun.; amb. to U.S. Mission UN Agys., Rome, Italy, 1998—. Chmn. Ams. for Common Sense, Washington, 1981-82; guest lectr. Northwestern U., Evanston, Ill., Duke U., Columbia U., Cornell U., Munich. Berlin, and numerous others in U.S. and Europe, from 1981 Author: The Colorado Coal Strike, 1913-14, 1953, War Against Want, 1964, Agricultural Thought in the Twentieth Century, 1967, A Time of War, A Time of Peace, 1968, (with Leonard Guttridge) The Great Coalfield War, 1972, An American Journey, 1974, Grassroots, 1978, Terry: My Daughter's Life and Death Struggle with Alcoholism, 1996, The Third Freedom: Ending Hunger in Our Time, 2001; co-author (with Bob Dole, Donald Messer): Ending Hunger Now: A Challenge to Persons of Faith, 2005. Democratic nominee for Pres. U.S., 1972; candidate for presdl. nomination of Dem. Party, 1984; Served as pilot USAAF, World War II. Decorated D.F.C.; recipient Presdl. Medal of Freedom, 2000, Food for Life award World Food Program, 2000. Mem. Am. Hist. Assn.; Clubs: Mason (33 deg., Shriner), Elk, Kiwanian. Methodist. E-mail: jedelhoff@usaid.gov.

**MCGOVERN, JAMES P.,** congressman; b. Worcester, Mass., Nov. 20, 1959; m. Lisa Murray; children: Patrick George, Molly Ginette. BA, Am. U., 1981, MA in Pub. Administration, 1984. Aide U.S. Senator George McGovern (Dem. South Dakota); spokesman, legis. dir., sr. aide U.S. Congressman Joe Moakley (Dem. South Boston); mem. U.S. Congress from 3rd Mass dist., 1997—; elected regional whip, mem. transp. & infrastructure com., house rules com. Mgr. George McGovern for Pres., 1984; delivered McGovern presdl. nomination speech Dem. Nat. Convention, San Francisco, 1984; leader Congressional Investigation on El Salvador, 1989 Candidate for U.S. Congress, 1996; vol. Mt. Carmel House; bd. dirs. Jesuit Internat. Mission. Democrat. Roman Catholic. Office: Ho Reps 430 Cannon Ho Office Bldg Washington DC 20515-2103 Home: 34 Mechanic St Worcester MA 01608-2424

**MCGOVERN, LORE HARP,** communications executive, philanthropist; m. Patrick J. McGovern. Undergrad., Calif. State Univ.; MBA, Pepperdine Univ. Co-founder Vector Graphics Inc., 1976; founder Pacific Tech. Venture Fund, San Francisco, 1981, dir., 1983—85; founder Aplex Corp., 1985—89; CEO Good Morning Teacher! Pub., 1990—99; mem. bd. dir. Internat. Data Group. Chmn. bd. assoc. Whitehead Inst. MIT; mem. bd. advisors Women.com, Blue

Pumpkin Software, Skillsville.com. Named one of 50 Most Generous Philanthropists, Fortune Mag., 2005; recipient Entrepreneur Yr., 1983. Mem.: Am. Elec. Assn. (former dir.). Office: IDG One Exeter Plz Boston MA 02116 Office Fax: 617-423-0240.*

**MCGOVERN, MARK EDWARD,** pharmaceutical company executive, researcher; s. Donald Harry McGovern and Barbara Ann Bickford. BA, Princeton U., NJ, 1975; MD, U. Vt., Burlington, 1980. Diplomate cardiology Am. Bd. Internal Medicine, 1987, internal medicine Am. Bd. Internal Medicine, 1983. Exec. dir., heart failure, atherosclerosis, clin. rschr. Bristol-Myers Squibb, Princeton, NJ, 1986—97; chief med. officer, clin. rschr. Kos Pharm., Weston, Fla., 1997—. Contbr. scientific papers. Fellow: ACP, Am. Coll. Cardiology; mem.: American Atherosclerosis Soc., Am. Heart Assn. D-Liberal. Achievements include research in prevention of heart attack and stroke by drugs affecting lipid metabolism. Office: Kos Pharm 2100 N Commerce Pkwy Weston FL 33326 Office Phone: 954-331-3730. Business E-Mail: mmcgovern@kospharm.com.

**MCGOVERN, MICHAEL,** lawyer; b. NYC, Mar. 6, 1947; s. Michael Malachy and Annette (Barbot) McG.; m. Christine Anne Beaudet, Sept. 2, 1972; children: Kathleen, Ellen, Maura. AB, Georgetown U., 1969, JD, 1972; LLM in Taxation, George Washington U., 1987. Bar: D.C. 1973, Md. 1978. From assoc. to ptnr. Wilkes & Artis, Washington, 1973-79; sole practice Washington, 1980, 84-87; ptnr. Lambert, Griffin & McGovern, Washington, 1981-84, Venable, Baetjer, Howard & Civiletti, Washington, 1987-93, Montedonico, Hamilton & Altman, Washington, 1994-98, Hanson & Molloy, Washington, 1998—. Bd. dirs. Hist. Soc. Washington, 1984-93, Montgomery County Hist. Soc., 1997—; co-founder, vice-chair, bd. dirs. mem. Greater Bethesda-Chevy Chase Coalition Inc., 1986—; pres. Westmoreland Citizens Assn. Inc., 1988-90; mem. Leadership Washington, 1987—, Washington Estate Planning Coun. Served to capt. USAFR, 1969—82. Recipient Disting. Svc. award, Fed. Bar Assn., 1978. Mem. Columbia Country Club (Chevy Chase), Met. Club (Washington), Barristers, John Carroll Soc. Republican. Home: 5414 Albemarle St Bethesda MD 20816-1825 Office: Hanson & Molloy 1320 19th St NW Ste 300 Washington DC 20036 Office Phone: 202-833-9300. Business E-Mail: mcgovern@hanson-molloy.com.

**MCGOVERN, PATRICK J.,** communications executive; m. Lore Harp. BA in Physics, M.I.T., 1959. Founder Internat. Data Corp., Framingham, Mass., 1964, chmn., 1976—; founder IDG Comm. Inc., Framingham, 1987, CEO, 1999. Trustee Mass. Inst. Tech., Whitehead Inst. RecipientThe Bus. Pub. of the Year award Delaney Report, The Communicator of the Year award N.Y. Chpt. Bus. Profl. Advertisers Assn., The Entrepreneur of the Year award Ernst & Young, Lifetime Achievement award, Am. Soc. Bus. Publ. Editors, 2004; Lifetime Achievement award, Mag. Publishers of Am., 2005; Named one of 50 Most Generous Philanthropists, Fortune Mag., 2005, Richest Americans, Forbes, 2000-, World's Richest People, 2001-. Achievements include providing a $350 mil. endowment to M.I.T. Office: Internat Data Group 1 Exeter Plz Fl 15 Boston MA 02116-2848*

**MCGOVERN, PETER JOHN,** law educator; b. N.Y.C., Dec. 6, 1938; s. John Phillip and Helen Marie (Gaisser) McG.; m. Catherine Bigley, Aug. 31, 1963; children: Brian Peter, Sean Daniel. AB, Notre Dame U., 1961; JD, Fordham U., 1964; EdD, S.D.U., 1980. Bar: N.Y. 1964, S.D. 1972, Ind. 1983, Ill. 1990, U.S. Supreme Ct. 1968. Atty. criminal divsn. Dept. Justice, 1971-72; prof. law U. S.D., Vermillion, 1972-83; from asst. dean to assoc. dean U. S.D. Sch. Law, Vermillion, 1972-77, dir. programs and planning, 1979-83; dean Valparaiso (Ind.) U. Sch. Law, 1983-85, St. Thomas U. Sch. Law, Fla., 1985-87, John Marshall Law Sch., Chgo., 1987-90, prof. law, 1990—. Dir. Ctr. for Internat. Bus. and Trade Law, 2000; dir. continuing legal edn. State Bar S.D., 1972-83; past chmn. S.D. Family Law Coun.; bd. dirs. Legal Svcs. of Greater Gary Inc. Past pres. Vermillion Area Arts Coun., Nat. Anti-Vivisection Soc.; bd. dirs. Lawyer for Creative Arts, 1990-92. Lt. comdr. JAGC, USN, 1965-71. Recipient Legal Writing award Fed. Bar Assn., 1969. Fellow Ind. Bar Found.; mem. ABA, bd. dirs., mediator, arbitrator, Internat. Acad. Dispute Resolution Democrat. Roman Catholic. Office: John Marshall Law Sch 315 S Plymouth Ct Chicago IL 60604-3968 Home: 204 Benedictine Ln Yankton SD 57078-6878 Office Phone: 312-987-2369. Business E-Mail: 7mcgover@jmls.edu.

**MCGOWAN, ANGELA KAY,** government agency administrator, researcher; b. Decatur, Ga., Sept. 6, 1970; d. John E. McGowan, Jr. and Linda Kay (Hudson) McGowan. BA, Coll. William & Mary, 1992; JD, Vanderbilt U., 1995; MPH, Emory U., 1998. Bar: Ga. 1995. Atty. Troutman Sanders, LLP, Atlanta, 1996—97; legal svcs. officer Disvn. Pub. Health Ga. Dept. Human Resources, Atlanta, 1999—2002; epidemic intelligence svc. officer Ctrs. for Disease Control & Prevention, Atlanta, 2002—04, pub. health law analyst, 2004—. Pres. Atlanta chpt. William & Mary Alumni Club, 1999—2000; alumni bd. govs. Robinson Sch. Pub. Health, Emory U., Atlanta, 2004—. Mem.: Ga. Bar Assn., Pub. Health Law Assn., Am. Pub. Health Assn. Office: Centers for Disease Control & Prevention 4770 Buford Hwy K-40 Atlanta GA 30341 Office Phone: 770-488-8210. Personal E-mail: angiemcgowan@cs.com. Business E-Mail: amcgowan@cdc.gov.

**MCGOWAN, BERNARD WAYNE (BERNIE MCGOWAN),** venture capitalist, writer; b. Stonington, Colo., May 22, 1925; s. Neal and Lena Elton (Dean) McGowan; m. Betty B. Neill, Apr. 2, 1944; children: Wava K. Morris, Darwin L., Marla G. Grad., Walsh H.S., Colo., 1943. Farmer, rancher, Walsh, 1943—50; rancher Cotopaxi, Colo., 1951—61; owner, auto, farm equip. dealer Cotopaxi Garage, Cotopaxi, Colo., 1953—60; ptnr. Paul & McGowan Constrn. Co., Cotopaxi, 1955—62; owner Auto/Aircraft Financing & Leasing, Denver, 1962—66; founder, pres. Aircraft Appraisal Assn., 1967—82; pres. pub. Aircraft Bluebook Price Digest, Oklahoma City, 1967—86; mgr. v.p. Insured Aircraft Title Svc., Oklahoma City, 1970—74; ptnr. McGowan Investment Co., Oklahoma City, 1986—2001; pres. TIVY Math Games Inc., Oklahoma City, 1991—2000. Past editor, pub.: Jour. Aviation Finance. With USAF, 1944—45. Mem.: Okla. Auctioneers Assn., Nat. Auctioneers Assn., Aircraft Fin. Assn., Internat. Flying Bankers Assn., Aviation Writers Assn. Achievements include several copyrights and patents for two math games. Home: 8205 Brownsville Ln Bethany OK 73008-3038 Personal E-mail: bmcgowan2@cox.net.

**MCGOWAN, GERALD S.,** diplomat; b. Birmingham, Mich., 1946; married Susan Anne Brophy; seven children. BSBA, Georgetown U., 1968, JD, 1974. Bar: D.C.; U.S. Ct. Appeals (D.C.), U.S. Dist. Ct. D.C., U.S. Supreme Ct. Founding prin. Lukas, McGowan, Nace & Gutierrez, Washington; amb. to Portugal U.S. Dept. of State, 1998—. Founder Integrated North Coast, Inc; developer cellular system ea. Ohio, 1992; bd. dirs. Overseas Pvt. Investment Corp. lst lt. U.S. Army, Vietnam, 1970-71. Mem. D.C. Bar, Fed. Comms. Bar Assn.

**MCGOWAN, MICHAEL JEREMY,** lawyer; b. Evanston, Ill., Aug. 28, 1961; s. Melvin Joseph and Lydia Judith McGowan; m. Karen Jean Palmer; children: Genevieve, Quinn, Grace. BA, U. Notre Dame, 1983; JD, Layola U., 1988. Bar: Ill. States atty. Lake County, Ill. States Atty. Office, Waukegan 1988—89; assoc. Querrey & Harrow, Ltd., Waukegan, 1989—95, non-equity ptnr. Chgo., 1995—97, O'Hagen, Smith and Amundsen, LLC, Chgo., 1997—2000, equity ptnr., 2000—. Trustee St. Martin de Porres HS, Waukegan, 2003—; mem. Defense Rsch. Inst., Chgo., 2005—, Ill. Ann. Defense Counsel, Chgo., 1995—, U.S. Law Network, 2002—. Mem., dir. U. Notre Dame Club, Lake County, 2001—. Named Highest Rated Lawyer, Martindale-Hubbell, 2003, Ill. Super Lawyer, 2006, Top Law Student, Loyola U., Sch. Law, 1985—86. Republican. Roman Cath. Avocations: history, football, carpentry, skiing, travel. Home: 410 E Onwentsia Rd Lake Forest IL 60045 Office: OHagan Smith and Amundsen LLC 150 N Mich Ave Ste 3300 Chicago IL 60601

**MCGOWAN, MICHELE PATRICE,** advertising executive; b. Balt., Feb. 27, 1956; d. William Clayton and Dolores Louise (Stull) McG. AA in Retailing, Harcum Jr. Coll., 1976; BS in Mktg., Seton Hall U., 1979. Account exec. Investors Diversified Services, Parsippany, N.J., 1977-78; asst. mgr. Bamberger's, Livingston, N.J., 1978-79; media dir. Lewis Advt., Newark, 1979-81; sr. media buyer, planner Gianettino & Meredith Advt., Short Hills, N.J., 1981-85; media dir. Gillespie Advt., Inc., Princeton, N.J., 1985—. Chmn. mag., promotion coms. Princeton Area C. of C., 1987. Mem. N. Jersey Advt. Club, Communications and Mktg. Assn. Republican. Presbyterian. Avocations: antiques, crafts, decorating, skiing.

**MCGOWAN, PATRICK FRANCIS,** lawyer; b. N.Y.C., July 23, 1940; s. Francis Patrick and Sonia Veronica (Koslow) M.; m. Patricia Neil, June 6, 1964; children: Susan Claire, Kathleen Anne. BA, Rice U., 1962; JD, U. Tex., Austin, 1965. Bar: Tex. 1965, U.S. Ct. Appeals (5th cir.) 1969, U.S. Tax Ct. 1972, U.S. Supreme Ct. 1970, U.S. Ct. Appeals (11th cir.) 1981, U.S. Ct. Appeals (fed. cir.) 1993. Briefing atty. Tex. Supreme Ct., Austin, 1965—66; ptnr. Strasburger & Price, Dallas, 1966—98, Akin, Gump, Strauss, Hauer & Feld, Dallas, 1998—. Pres., chmn. bd. Tex Lex, Inc., 1991-98. Contbr. numerous articles on internet, trademark, copyright and franchise law. Bd. advisors Dallas Ft. Worth Sch. Law. Fellow Coll. State Bar Tex. (faculty Franchising Inst. 1987, Intellectual Property Inst. 1992, S.W. Legal Found. Patent Law Inst. 1992, Practising Law Inst. 1996, Ctr. for Am. and Internat. Law I.P. Inst. 2001-04); mem. ABA (alt. dispute resolution, forum com. on franchising, trademark and unfair competition com., patent, trademark and copyright law sect., chair ADR survey com. 2004—), State Bar Tex. (alt. dispute resolution, intellectual property sect., com. CLE, chair ADR com. 2002—), Dallas Bar Assn. (dir. intellectual property law sect. 1994—, chmn. basics seminar 1999, sect. vice chmn. 2001, chmn. 2002), Internat, Anti-Counterfeiting Assn., Inst. Law and Tech., Tex. Law Rev. Editors Assn., Phi Delta Phi. Office: Akin Gump 1700 Pacific Ave Ste 4100 Dallas TX 75201-4675 Office Phone: 214-969-2800. Business E-Mail: pmcgowan@akingump.com.

**MCGOWAN, RODGER ALAN,** administrative assistant; b. St. Louis, Mo., Mar. 2, 1954; s. Neil Bryan and Norma Marie McGowan. BSc cum laude, Southeast Mo. State U., 1976, MA in Am. History, 1979. Records clk. Mo. Dept. Revenue, Jefferson City, 1989—95; sales assoc. Famous Barr Co., St. Louis, 1996—97; office asst. IV Kans. State U., Manhattan, 2000, office asst. III, 2000; vol., liaison Kansans for Shallenberger, Topeka, 2002; staff asst. U. Kans., 2002. Book reviewer. Recipient Grambling scholarship, Southeast Mo. State U., 1975—76. Mem.: Southern Hist. Assn., Phi Alpha Theta. Republican. Home: 2405 E 27th Terrace Lawrence KS 66046

**MCGOWAN, ROSE,** actress; b. Florence, Italy, Sept. 5, 1973; Actor: (films) Encino Man, 1992, The Doom Generation, 1995, Bio-Dome, 1996, Kiss & Tell, 1996, Scream, 1996, Going All The Way, 1997, Nowhere, 1997, Lewis & Clark & George, 1997, Seed, 1997, Phantoms, 1998, Southie, 1998, Devil in the Flesh, 1998, Jawbreaker, 1999, Sleeping Beauties, 1999, Ready to Rumble, 2000, The Last Stop, 2000, Monkeybone, 2001, Strange Hearts, 2001, Vacuums, 2002, The Black Dahlia, 2006; (TV films) God Is In the T.V., 1999, The Killing Yard, 2001, Elvis, 2005; (TV series) Charmed, 2001—06, (TV appearances) True Colors, 1990, What About Joan, 2001.*

**MCGOWAN, STEPHEN T.,** corporate financial executive; BS, Northeastern Univ.; MBA, Loyola Univ. Chgo. With Sun Microsystems Inc., Santa Clara, Calif., 1992—; v.p. fin. No. Am. & Australia field ops, 1992—94, worldwide fin. ops., 1994—98, computer sys., 1998—2000; v.p. staff ops. global sales ops., 2000—01, v.p. fin. global services, 2001—02, v.p., CFO corp. resources, 2002—. Office: Sun Microsystems 4150 Network Circle Santa Clara CA 95054*

**MCGOWAN, SUSAN,** gifted and talented educator; b. Alameda, Calif., May 12, 1959; d. Thomas and Gladys Mae (Prutzman) McG.; m. Warren Howard Jones, Oct. 31, 1980 (div.); children: Kelly Hardcastle, Reilly James; m. Barry William McLaughlin, May 22, 2004 AS in Edn., No. Va. Community Coll., 1988; BA in Russian Area Studies, George Mason U., 1991; MEd, Marymount U., 1994; postgrad., Coll. William & Mary, 2003—. Cert. tchr. Va. Data processor Tracor, Inc., Virginia Beach, Va., 1982-83; computer operator Hughes, Bendix, Holmes and Narver, Virginia Beach, 1983-84; data analyst Tracor, Inc., Virginia Beach, 1984; systems analyst Advanced Tech., Inc., Virginia Beach, 1984-85, computer programmer Reston, Va., 1986-87; tech. writer Swiger Group, Reston, 1987; tchr. 3rd grade Loudoun Country Day Sch., Leesburg, Va., 1991-93; tchr. 4th and 5th grade Loudoun County Pub. Schs., 1994—2000, Va. Beach City Pub. Sch., 2001—. Master tchr. Nat. Tech. Tchr. Inst., WNVT, Fairfax, 1998-99; translation cons. Systems Ctr., Inc., Reston, 1990— Recipient Presdl. award, Va. Gov.'s Sch., 2005. Mem. ASCD, World Affairs Coun., Golden Key, Phi Theta Kappa, Alpha Chi. Personal E-mail: smjones59@aol.com. Business E-Mail: smmcgo@wm.edu.

**MCGOWAN, THOMAS RANDOLPH,** retired religious organization administrator; b. Balt., Apr. 19, 1926; s. Robert and Mary (Miller) McGowan; m. Bernice A. Bernard, May 20, 1967 (dec. Nov. 1981); children: Howard, James, Terry; m. Roedean Olivia Oden, Feb. 9, 1985; children: Karen White, Kevin, Kurt. AA, Oakland Jr. Coll., 1964; postgrad., San Francisco State Coll., 1964-68; BS, U. Md., 1978. Lt. security police Oakland (Calif.) Army Base, 1955-60; chief motor pool San Francisco Procurement Agy., Oakland, 1960-64, contract specialist, 1964-68, Harry Diamond Labs., Washington, 1968-79, br. chief procurement divsn., 1972-79; chief procurement directorate Yuma (Ariz.) Proving Ground, 1979-82; dir. ecumenism Roman Cath. Diocese of Oakland, 1983—; dir. African Am. Cath. Pastoral Ctr., 1991— Bd. dirs. Columbia (Md.) Found., 1972—74, chmn., 1975—79; convenor Interreligious Coun. Oakland, 1988—; trustee Greater Oakland Interfaith Network, 1989—92; bd. dirs. Thea Bowman Manor, Oakland 1989—, St. Mary's Ctr. mem. T. Oakland Renewal Task Force, 1990—; div. Bd. Coms., Graymoor, NY, 1990—. With U.S. Army, 1944—46. Mem.: Rotary, Knights Peter Claver. Democrat. Avocations: tennis, woodworking. Home: 139 Pinto Dr Vallejo CA 94591-8451 E-mail: ThomDean@pacbell.net.

**MCGOWEN, GERALD ELLIS,** biologist; b. Muskegon, Mich., Dec. 27, 1946; s. Gerald Edward and Helen Lorraine McGowen. BS in Biology, San Diego State U., 1970, MS in Biology, 1977; PhD in Biology, U. So. Calif., L.A., 1987. Assoc. environ. specialist Occidental Coll., L.A., 1974-78; rsch. assoc. U. So. Calif., L.A., 1978-80; asst. rsch. curator Natural History Mus. L.A. County, 1978-92; lectr. Calif. State U., Long Beach, 1990; water biologist environ. monitoring divsn. City of LA, 1992—2001, water biologist regulatory affairs divsn., 2001—03, environ. supr., environ. affairs dept., 2003—05, lab. mgr. environ. monitoring divsn., 2005—. Cons. Tenera, San Francisco, 1996-2000. Author: (book chpts.) Ontogeny and Systematics of Fishes, 1984; contbr. articles to books and profl. jours. Mem. Soc. Environ. Toxicologists and Chemists (mem., bd. dirs. So. Calif. chpt. 1999-2002), So. Calif. acad. Scis., So. Calif. Toxicity Assessment Group. Avocations: fishing, hiking, camping, diving, pool. Office: City of LA Environ Monitoring Divsn 12000 Vista del Mar Marina Del Rey CA 90293 E-mail: gem1440@adelphia.net, gem@san.lacity.org.

**MCGOWEN, LORRAINE S.,** lawyer; b. Phila., 1960; m. Gailon McGowen; 4 children. BS, Georgetown U., 1983; JD, Columbia U., 1986. Bar: N.Y. 1987, U.S. Dist. Ct., So. Dist. N.Y. 1988, U.S. Dist. Ct., Ea. Dist. N.Y. 1988, D.C. 1994, U.S. Ct. Appeals, Second Cir. 1994. Ptnr. Orrick, Herrington & Sutcliffe LLP, NYC, co-chair Bankruptcy and Debt Restructuring Group. Mem.: Am. Coll. Investment Counsel, Am. Bankruptcy Inst., DC Bar, Assn. Bar City NY, ABA (bus. law com.). Office: Orrick Herrington & Sutcliffe LLP 666 Fifth Ave New York NY 10103 Office Phone: 212-506-5114. Office Fax: 212-506-5151. Business E-Mail: lmcgowen@orrick.com.

**MC GOWIN, WILLIAM EDWARD,** artist; b. Hattiesburg, Miss., June 2, 1938; s. William Edward and Emily (Ratliff) Mc G.; m. Claudia DeMonte, May 28, 1977; children: Leah, Jill. BS, U. So. Miss., 1961; MA, U. Ala.,

1964. Prof. art SUNY, Old Westbury, 1978—. Coll. Old Westbury; mem. faculty Corcoran Gallery Art, 1966-77, head sculpture dept., 1967-74; lectr. in field. One-man shows include Corcoran Gallery Art, Washington, 1962, 71, 75, Martha Jackson Gallery, N.Y.C., 1968, Am. Cultural Ctr., Paris, 1974, Mus. Modern Art, Paris, 1978, Brooks Jackson Gallery, Iolas, N.Y.C., 1978-80, Fendrick Gallery, Washington, 1977-80, U. Colo., New Orleans Contemporary Art Ctr., 1982, Project Studios 1, L.I., N.Y., Cranbrook Acad., Bloomfield Hills, Mich., 1983, Art Park, Lewiston, N.Y., 1984, Gracie Mansion Gallery, N.Y.C., 1985, 86, 89, Mus. Fine Arts, Miami, Jones, Troyer Gallery, Washington, 1987, 89, 91, Boca Raton (Fla.) Mus., 1991, Margulis-Taplin Gallery, Miami, 1993, Paris-N.Y.-Bangkok Gallery, Bangkok, Thailand, 1994, Grey Art Gallery, NYU, 1995, Siipakorn U., Bangkok, 1997, Genkan Gallery, Tokyo, 1997, Miss. Mus. Art, 2000, Osuna Art, Bethesda, Md., 2005, Mobile Mus. Art., Ala., 2006, PS1 Mus. Modern Art, L.I., N.Y., 2006; group shows include Contemporary Mus., Houston, Miss. Mus. Art, Whitney Mus., N.Y.C., Detroit Inst. Art, Washington Mus., Speed Mus., Ky., Cologne (Germany) Art Fair, Zurich Art Fair; represented in permanent collections Phillips Collection, Washington, Indpls. Mus. Art, Addison Mus. Art, Andover, Mass, Corcoran Gallery Art, Nat. Collection Fine Arts, Washington, New Orleans Mus. Art, Whitney Mus. Am. Art, N.Y.C., Guggenheim Mus., Hirshorn Gallery and Sculpture Garden, Ogden Mus. New Orleans; permanent commn. U.S. Gen. Svc. Adminstrn., 1979, VA, Indpls., 1985, Percent for Art, N.Y.C., 1992, City of Jubai, Saudi Arabia, 1993, Dallas Rapid Transit Authority, 1994, Queens County N.Y. Supreme Ct., 1996, Art in Pub. Places, Socorro, N.Mex., 1997, Met. Transit Authority State of N.Y., Bayside, 1998, Inst. for Internat. Econs., Washington, 2000, St. Marks Gates, Plan de Grass, France, 2002, U. Iowa, Cedar Falls, 2003, Clarette Group, N.Y.C., 2004, N.Mex. Arts Sculpture, Santa Rosa, 2004, 2005, Broward County (Fla.) Pub. Art Commn., 2006, Ft. Lauderdale Fire Rescue, 2006. Recipient Oscar for painting, 1977, Painting prize 9th Internat. Painting Festival, Cagnes-sur-Mer, France, 1977, Miss. Arts and Letters award for visual arts, 1980, Art Commn. Design award N.Y.C., 1998; Nat. Endowment for Arts grantee, 1967-68, 79-80, pub. outdoor sculpture grantee, 1977, Cassandra Found. grantee. Home and Office: 96 Grand St New York NY 10013-2633 Office Phone: 212-966-4496. Personal E-mail: edmcgowin@aol.com.

**MCGOWN, JOHN, JR.,** lawyer; b. Bowling Green, Ky., June 15, 1949; s. John Stanley and Margaret (Deatherage) McG.; m. Mary Grunewald, Apr. 20, 1978; children: Erin Margaret, Brenna Kathryn. BS, U. Ky., 1971; JD, U. Colo., 1974; LLM in Taxation, U. Denver, 1981. Bar: Colo. 1975, U.S. Tax Ct. 1981, Idaho 1982; cert. mediator tax disputes Multistate Tax Commn., 1998. Dep. dist. atty. Weld County, Colo., 1974-78; assoc. Montgomery, Little, Young, Campbell & McGrew, Denver, 1979-80; rschr. appellate divsn. IRS, Denver, 1980-81; mem. staff tax dept. Price Waterhouse, Denver, 1981-82; ptnr. Hawley Troxell Ennis & Hawley, LLP, Boise, Idaho, 1982-99, of counsel, 2000—. Adj. prof. Boise State U., 1983, assoc. prof., 2000-02; guest lecturer U. Idaho Coll. Law, Moscow, 1990, 2003, 04, 05; guest speaker various tax seminars, 1983— Contbr. over 90 articles to profl. jours. Bd. dirs. Assn. for Retarded Citizens Ada County, Inc., 1987-93, pres. 1991-92, Assoc. Taxpayers Idaho, Inc., 1993-2002, exec. com. 1995-2002; audit review panel United Way Ada County, 1986-91; IRS vol. tax asst. program 1982, 87. Fellow Am. Coll. of Trust and Estate Counsel; mem. ABA (taxation sect.), Idaho State Bar Assn. (founding mem., taxation probate and trust law sect.), Idaho Soc. CPAs (tax and estate taxation com. 1984-89, bus. legis. com. 1989-91, pers. fin. com. 2000—), Boise Bar Assn., Toastmasters (pres. 1991), Beta Gamma Sigma, Sigma Chi (pioneer). Home: 282 S Mobley Ln Boise ID 83712-8329 Office: Hawley Troxell Ennis & Hawley LLP 877 Main St Ste 1000 Boise ID 83702-5883

**MCGRADY, ANGELE VIAL,** psychophysiologist; b. New Rochelle, N.Y., Dec. 31, 1941; d. Fernand Louis and Santina (Cosentino) Vial; m. Patrick McGrady, June 29, 1968; children: Michele, Kevin. BS, Chestnut Hill Coll., Phila., 1963; MS, Mich. State U., 1965; PhD, U. Toledo, 1972, MEd, 1984. Lic. counselor, 1986. Instr. Wash. State U., Pullman, 1965-66; rsch. assoc. Kresge Eye Inst., Wayne State U., Detroit, 1966-68; instr. Med. Coll. Ohio, Physiology, Toledo, 1968-72, asst. prof. physiology, 1972-79, faculty dept. psychiatry, 1982—, assoc. prof. physiology, 1979—; prof. psychiatry, adj. prof. physiology, 1995—. Contbr. articles to profl. jours.; reviewer various jours. Recipient Rsch. Recognition, Biofeedback Soc. Am., 1988, Tchg. Excellence award Med. U. Ohio, 1997. Mem. Biofeedback Soc. Ohio (pres. 1985-86), Assn. Applied Psychophysiology and Biofeedback (exec. bd. 1989-92, pres. 1995-96). Office: Medical U Ohio 3120 Glendale Ave Toledo OH 43614-5809 Office Phone: 419-383-5695.

**MCGRADY, PHYLLIS,** television producer; Exec. prodr. PrimeTime Live, N.Y.C., Turning Point; with ABC, 1977—; v.p. and exec. prodr. spl. programming ABC News, 1998—2000; exec.-in-charge Good Morning Am., 1999—; sr. v.p. primetime, early morning and news program devel. ABC News, 2000—. Office: PrimeTime Live 147 Columbus Ave Fl 3D New York NY 10023-5900

**MCGRADY, TRACY,** professional basketball player; b. May 24, 1979; Forward Toronto Raptors, 1997—2000, Orlando Magic, 2000—04, Houston Rockets, 2004—. Active NBA's Reading Time-Out program. Named to NBA All-Star Game, 2000—05, All-NBA First Team, 2002, 2003. Achievements include holds the record for NBA scoring champion, 2003. Office: c/o Houston Rockets 1510 Polk St Houston TX 77002 Office Phone: 407 89M AGIC.*

**MCGRAIL, JEANE KATHRYN,** artist; b. Mpls., May 1, 1947; d. Robert Vern and Mary Virginia (Kees) McGrail. BS, U. Wis.-River Falls, 1970; MFA, Cranbrook Acad. Art, 1972; postgrad., Sch. of Art Inst. of Chgo., 1983, Ill. Inst. Tech., 1993. Tchr. Inst. Contemporary Art. Group exhbn. include Saginaw Art Mus., Mich., 1972, Met. Mus. Art, Miami, Fla., 1974, Lowe Mus. Art, Coral Gables, Fla., 1974, 76, Miller Galleries, Coconut Grove, Fla., 1978, 80, Cicchinelli Gallery, NYC, 1980-82, Harper Coll., 1984, Contemporary Art Ctr. Arlington, Arlington Heights, Ill., 1984, 85, 86, 94, Evanston Art Ctr., 1985, South Shore Cultural Ctr., Chgo., 1990, N.A.M.E. Gallery, 1990, Artemisia Gallery, Chgo., 1991, 92, 93, 94, North Lakeside Art Ctr., Chgo., 1991, 94, 95, Ceres Gallery, NYC, 1992, Harper Coll., Ill., 1993, Environ. Concerns, Chgo., 1993, North Pk. Coll., Chgo., 1993, Franklin Square Gallery, Chgo., 1994, 95, 96, Space 900 Gallery, Chgo., 1994, 95, 96, 97, 98, 99, Chuck Levitan Gallery, NYC, 1995, Riverwest Art Ctr., Milw., 1995, Nat. Mus. Women in the Arts, Wash., 1996, Gallery 1040, 1997-, "Red", Chgo., 1998, Ashton Coll. Gallery, Ill., 1999-, Women's Works, Woodstock, Ill., 1999, "Paint It Siver", ARC Gallery, Chgo., 1999, Past/Present, Chgo., 1999, "Blue", Northeastern Ill. U.,Chgo., 2000, Then and Now, Chgo., 1999, Norris Cultural Ctr., St. Charles, Ill., 1999, others; represented in permanent collections at Chgo. Mus. Sci. and Industry, U. Chgo., Mus. Photography, Chgo., Miami-Dade Pub. Libr., U. Wis.-River Falls, MacGregor Found., Printmakers Workshop, NYC, Norman R. Eppnik Art Gallery Emporia State U., Kans., 2000, Mini Print Internat. Exhbn., Binghamton, NY, 2000, Yale U. Med. Libr., 2000, Columbia U. Med. Ctr., 2000, 06, Mini Print Internat. of Cadaques, Spain, Macy Gallery, Providence, RI, 2000, Brickton Gallery, Pk. Ridge, Fla., 2001, Mini Print Internat. of Cadaques, Spain, 2001—, Last of Primaries, Coll. of Lake Co., 2003-, Ukrainian Mus. Contemporary Art, Chgo., 2003, Chautauqua Nat. Exhbn., N.Y., 2004, others; solo exhbn. include Gallery at the Commons, Chgo., 1982, Truman Coll. Gallery, Chgo., 1991, C.G. Jung Inst., Evanston, Ill., 1992, Carlson Tower Gallery, Chgo., 1994, Olcott Ctr. Gallery, Theosophical Soc. Am., Wheaton, Ill., 2001; pub. "Mosaic", 1992, The Best of Printmaking, 1997; contbr. to profl. jour. Cranbrook Acad. Art scholar, 1971; CAAP grantee Dept. Cultural Affairs City Chgo, 1992; recipient Poster Competition award Vizcaya Mus., 1974; Print award Auction WPBT, 1979. Tchr. Inst. Contemporary Art, Art Inst. Chgo., 2004. Mem. Coll. Art Assn., Chgo. Women's Caucus for Art (bd. dirs. 1992-95, sec.), Chgo. Artists Coalition. Independent. Studio: 1040 W Huron St LL5 Chicago IL 60622-6591 Office Phone: 312-882-8512. E-mail: whoswho@jeanemcgrail.com.

**MCGRANE, MILES A., III,** lawyer; b. Oct. 3, 1947; m. Patricia Lea McGrane; children: Miles IV, Ashley, Blake. AS in Bus. Adminstrn., Jr. Coll. Broward County, 1968; BS in Bus. Adminstrn., Fla. Atlantic U., 1970; JD, Samford U., 1975. Bar: Fla. 1975, D.C. 1982, U.S. Dist. Ct. (so. dist.) Fla. 1976, U.S. Dist. Ct. (so. dist. trial bar) Fla. 1976, U.S. Ct. Appeals (5th cir.) 1976, U.S. Tax Ct. 1977, U.S. Supreme Ct. 1979. Assoc. Adams, George, Wood, Lee & Schulte, 1975—78, George & Thompson, P.A., 1978—80; ptnr. Kubicki, Draper, Gallagher & Magrane PA, 1980—93, McGrane & Nosick, P.A., Miami, Fla., 1993, McGrane, Nosich and Ganz PA, Miami, Fla. Adj. prof. trial program sch. law U. Miami, 1980—; mem. Judicial Nominating Comsn., 11th Cir., 1990-1994. Bd. govs. Fla. Med. Malpractice Joint Underwriting Assn., 1982-85, 88-90, 90-92, 1992-2002; bd. dirs. Legal Svcs. Greater Miami, Inc., 1984-90, v.p., 1987-88, pres., 1988-90; mem. bldg. com. U. Miami Law Sch., com. of 100; bldg. com. St. Thomas Episcopal Parish Sch. Recipient Leadership Award, Legal Svcs. Greater Miami Inc., 2001, Dist. Alumni Award, Broward Community Coll., 2002. Mem. Am. Coll. Legal Medicine, Am. Soc. Law and Medicine, Am. Acad. Hospital Attys., Internat. Assn. Def. Counsel (legal malpractice com. 1994-96, med. malpractice com. 1994-96, casualty insurance com. 1994-96), Fla. Def. Lawyers Assn., The Fla. Bar (pres. 2002-03, various coms. and positions), D.C. Bar, Dade County Bar Assn. (various coms. and positions), Dade County Def. Bar Assn.; diplomate Am. Bd. Trial Advocates (exec. com. Miami chpt. 1994-2000, treas. 1999, sec. 2000, v.p. 2001, pres. 2002, Nat. Bd. mem 1994-96.) Office: McGrane Nosich and Ganz PA 2801 Ponce de Leon Blvd 12th Fl Coral Gables FL 33134

**MCGRATH, CAMPBELL,** poet, educator; b. Chgo., Jan. 26, 1962; BA, U. Chgo., 1984; MFA, Columbia U., 1988. Part-time tchr. U. Chgo.; assoc. prof. creative writing, head poetry program Fla. Internat. U. Author: (poetry) Capitalism, 1990, American Noise, 1994, Spring Comes to Chicago, 1996 (Kingsley Tufts award 1997), Road Atlas, 1999, Florida's Poems, 2002, Pax Atomica, 2004; contbr. to numerous jours. Recipient Acad. Am. Poets prize, 1984; Guggenheim fellow, 1998. Office: Fla Internat Univ Creative Writing Program 3000 NE 151st St North Miami FL 33181-3605

**MCGRATH, DENNIS MICHAEL,** secondary school educator; b. Dover, Ohio, Nov. 15, 1962; s. Samuel Chester and Vera Marie McGrath; m. Kathy Jean Mutton, Mar. 11, 1988; 1 child, None. BA, Muskingum Coll., New Concord, Ohio, 1985; MA, Salem Internat., W.Va., 2005. Cert. Ohio Dept. Edn., 1985. Tchr. Steubenville City Sch., Ohio, 1985—. Mem.: B.P.O.E., Kappa Sigma. Home: 180 Keagler Dr Steubenville OH 43953 Office: Steubenville City Sch 932 N 5th St Steubenville OH 43952 Office Phone: 740-282-3481. Personal E-mail: dmcgrath@steubenville.k12.oh.us.

**MCGRATH, DOMINIC VINCENT,** chemistry professor; b. N.Y., Aug. 26, 1965; s. Martin Joseph and Mary Anna McGrath; m. Lisa Marie Dollinger; children: Liam Matthew, Lily Michele. BS in Chemistry, Yale U., New Haven, Conn., 1988; PhD in Chemistry, Calif. Inst. Tech., Pasadena, Calif., 1992. Postdoctoral assoc. The Scripps Rsch. Inst., La Jolla, Calif., 1992—94, Calif. Inst. Tech., 1994; asst. prof. U. Conn., Storrs, Conn., 1994—98, U. Ariz., Tucson, 1998—2001, assoc. prof., 2001—. Grantee, NSF, 1997—2002; scholar, Camille and Henry Dreyfus Found., 1999—2004; Cottrell scholar, Rsch. Corp., 1997. Achievements include research in synthesis and characterization of organic materials (e.g. polymers, dendrimers) for electronic, photonic, and photomechanical applications. Office: University of Arizona PO Box 210041 Tucson AZ 85721 Office Phone: 520-626-4690.

**MCGRATH, DON JOHN,** bank executive; b. Springfield, Ill., June 15, 1948; s. Donald John and Wilma P. (Beck) McG.; m. Patriaia Ratti, May 7, 1983. BS in Mktg., U. Ill., 1970; MBA, Boston U., 1973. Investment officer Banque Nationale de Paris, San Francisco, 1975-76, treas. San Francisco and L.A., 1976-78, v.p., treas., 1978-80, Bank of the West, San Francisco, 1980, v.p., CFO, 1980-81, sr. v.p., CFO, 1981-84, sr. exec. v.p., CFO, 1984-87, sr. exec. v.p., COO, 1987-91, pres., COO, 1991-95, pres., CEO, 1996—, chmn., CEO, 2005, pres., COO, dir. BancWest Corp., 1998—2004, pres., CEO, dir. 2005—. Bd. dirs. Commonwealth Club Calif., Nature Conservancy Calif. Dominican Univ. San Rafael, Calif.; bd. govs. Pacific Exch. Mem. Calif. Bankers Assn., Univ. Club, St. Francis Yacht Club (San Francisco), Diablo (Calif.) Country Club. Office: BancWest Corp 180 Montgomery St 25th Fl San Francisco CA 94104 Office Phone: 415-765-4823.

**MCGRATH, ELEANOR BURNS,** editor, writer; b. Gloucester, Mass., July 28, 1952; d. Edward James and Julia Ann (Holloran) McG.; m. Paul Allen Witteman, May 5, 1984; 1 child, Katharine McGrath Witteman. AB magna cum laude, Mt. Holyoke Coll., 1974. Rschr. Time-Life Books, N.Y.C., 1974-76; reporter, staff writer, edn. rschr Time Mag., N.Y.C., 1976-86; sr. editor Women's Sports and Fitness Mag., San Francisco, 1986-87; spl. corr. Time Mag., San Francisco, 1988; sr. editor, articles editor Self Mag., N.Y.C., 1991-98; editor Time Mag./Princeton Rev. Coll. Guide, 2000—02; editor and pub. McWitty Press, 2000—. Journalist-in-residence U. Mich., Ann Arbor, 1984-85. Author: My One and Only: The Special Experience of the Only Child, 1989; editor: One Earth, 1990. Trustee Mt. Holyoke Coll., South Hadley, Mass., 1976-79; pres. Greater N.Y. Athletic Assn., N.Y.C. 1980-84. Time fellow, Duke U., 1981. Mem. N.Y. Rd. Runners Club. Home: 110 Riverside Dr New York NY 10024-3715 Personal E-mail: mcwittypress@aol.com.

**MCGRATH, EUGENE R.,** utility company executive; b. NYC, 1942; BSME, Manhattan Coll., 1963; MBA, Iona Coll., 1980. With Consol. Edison Co. N.Y., NYC, 1963—, v.p., 1978-82, exec. v.p., 1982-89, pres., 1990—98, chmn., pres., CEO, 1998—2005, chmn., 2005—06. Mem. NAE. Office: Consol Edison Co NY Inc 4 Irving Pl New York NY 10003*

**MCGRATH, J. PAUL,** lawyer; b. Rochester, N.Y., Sept. 9, 1940; s. Thomas E. and Evelyn R. McG.; m. Eileen Robinson, Aug. 29, 1964; children: John P., Patricia, David R., Robyn. AB, Coll. of the Holy Cross, 1962; LL.B., Harvard U., 1965. Mem. firm Dewey, Ballantine, Bushby, Palmer and Wood, N.Y.C., 1965-73, ptnr., 1973-81, 85-92; asst. atty. gen. civil div. Dept. Justice, Washington, 1981-83, asst. atty. gen. antitrust div., 1983-85; v.p., gen. counsel Allied-Signal Inc., 1992—96; sr. v.p., gen. counsel FMC Corp., Chgo., 1996—2000; sr. v.p., gen. counsel, sec. Am. Standard Cos. Inc., Piscataway, 2000—. Fellow Am. Coll. Trial Lawyers. Clubs: Montclair Golf. Republican. Roman Catholic.

**MCGRATH, JAMES THOMAS,** real estate investment company executive; b. N.Y.C., Nov. 10, 1942; s. Thomas James and Mary Ita (Finnegan) McG.; m. Paulette L. Franck, Aug. 16, 1980; 1 child, Tara (dec.). BS in Acctg., Providence Coll., 1964. CPA, N.Y.; lic. gen. contractor, N.C., 2006. Sr. auditor Coopers & Lybrand, N.Y., 1968-72, mgmt. cons., 1972-74; group contr. IU Internat. Corp., Phila., 1974-77; v.p. fin. Taylor Engring. Corp. subs. IU Internat., Detroit, 1977-78; controller Pool Co. subs. Enserch Corp., Houston, 1978-85; sr. v.p. fin., treas. Lone Star Gas Co. subs. Enserch Corp., Dallas, 1985-91; pres. McGrath & Assocs., Inc., Dallas, 1991—. Lt. Cmdr. USN, 1964-68. Mem. AICPA, Dallas Athletic Club, St. Vincent de Paul Soc. Libertarian. Roman Catholic. Avocations: golf, cooking, skiing, scuba diving, sailing. Home and Office: 2838 Colleen Dr Garland TX 75043-1215 Office Phone: 972-271-5803. Personal E-mail: pjmcgrath2@comcast.net.

**MCGRATH, JOSEPH W.,** computer services company executive; Bachelor's, Rutgers U. V.p. and svc. dir. Gartner Group, worldwide info. tech. cons. firm; with Xerox Corp., 1989—98, v.p. N.Am. sys. sales, v.p. mktg., integrated sys. ops., v.p. strategy and mktg. Xerox Prodn. Sys. Group, v.p. and gen. mgr. Xerox Prodn. Color Sys.; joined Unisys Corp., 1999, sr. v.p. maj. accounts sales and chief mktg. officer, 1999—2000, exec. v.p. and pres. Global Industries, 2002, exec. v.p. and pres Enterprise Transformation Svcs., 2002—04, pres. and COO, 2004—05, pres. & CEO, 2005—. Office: Unisys Corp Unisys Way Blue Bell PA 19424*

**MCGRATH, JUDY (JUDITH ANN MCGRATH),** broadcast executive; b. Scranton, Pa., July 2, 1952; d. Charles and Ann McGrath; m. Michael Corbett; 1 child, Anna. BA in English Literature, Cedar Crest Coll. Copy chief Glamour mag.; sr. writer Mademoiselle; copywriter Nat. Advt., Phila.; copywriter, on-air promotion Warner Amex Satellite Entertainment Corp. (predecessor to MTV), 1981; editl. dir. MTV, sr. v.p., creative dir., 1988—92, exec. v.p., creative dir., 1992—93, co-pres., creative dir., 1993—94, pres. 1994—96, MTV, MTV2, 1996—2000, pres. MTV Group, chmn. Interactive Music, 2000—02; pres. MTV Networks Music Group, 2002—04, chmn., CEO, 2004—. Hon. chair Cable Positive. Trustee emeritus Nat. Campaign to Prevent Teen Pregnancy; bd. dirs. Rock the Vote. Named Humanitarian of Yr., T.J. Martell Found. Leukemia, Cancer and AIDS Rsch., 2003; named one of 100 Most Powerful Women in Entertainment, Hollywood Reporter, 2004, 2005, Most Powerful Women in Bus., Fortune mag., 2005, 100 Most Powerful Women, Forbes Mag., 2006; recipient Cable Ace Award, 1993, Founders award, Rock the Vote, 2001, Friend of the Children award, Harlem Children's Zone, 2001. Office: MTV 1515 Broadway Fl 28 New York NY 10036-8901

**MCGRATH, KATHRYN BRADLEY,** lawyer; b. Norfolk, Va., Sept. 2, 1944; d. James Pierce and Kathryn (Hoyle) Bradley; children: Ian M., James D. AB, Mt. Holyoke Coll., 1966; JD, Georgetown U., 1969. Ptnr. Gardner, Carton & Douglas, Washington, 1979-83; dir. div. investment mgmt. SEC, Washington, 1983-90; ptnr. Morgan Lewis, Washington, 1990—2002, Crowell & Moring, LLP, Washington, 2002—05, Mayer, Brown, Rowe & Maw LLP, Washington, 2005—. Named Disting. Exec., Pres. Reagan, 1987. Mem. Fed. Bar Assn. (exec. council securities law com.). Office: Mayer Brown Rowe & Maw LLP 1909 K St NW Washington DC 20006 Office Phone: 202-263-3374. Business E-Mail: kmcgrath@mayerbrownrowe.com.

**MCGRATH, KEVIN GARY,** library science educator; b. Newton, Mass., July 19, 1972; s. Gary Harris and Carol Lillian McGrath; m. Cynthia Varlan Cox, July 13, 1969; 1 child, Connor Scott. BA in English, U. Vt., 1994; MS in Libr. Sci., Simmons Coll., Boston, 1996. Cert. tchr. Mass. Libr. media specialist Beverly HS, Mass., 1998—2004; libr. tchr. Newton North HS, Newtonville, Mass., 2004—. Tchr., webmaster Primary Rsch., Beverly, Mass., 1999—; close-up tchr. Newton North HS, 2004—. Children's book illustrator, Leonard Beetle's Sole Ride; contbr. articles to profl. jours. Bd. mem. Beverly Cultural Coun., Mass., 1998—2001; mem. ednl. steering com. Mass. Civil Liberties Union, Boston, 1998. Recipient Prince Saunders award, Nat. Pk. Svc., 2005, Disting. Secondary Educator award, Mass. Dept. of Edn., 2003; grant, Inst. of Mus. and Libr. Services, 2002, NE Mass. Regional Libr. Sys., 2002, Mass. Hist. Records Adv. Bd., 2000. Avocation: guitar, surf casting, bocce. Office Phone: 617-559-6290. Personal E-mail: mcgrath@primaryresearch.org. E-mail: kevin_mcgrath@newton.mec.edu.

**MCGRATH, KIMBERLY KAY,** music educator; d. Roger Allen and Joan Beth Turner; m. Michael Paul McGrath, July 23, 1999; 1 child, Connor. B of Music Edn., Ariz. State U., 1990; MusM and Choral Conducting, Temple U., 1992. Choir tchr., dept. chair Basic H.S., Henderson, Nev., 1993—99, Foothill H.S., Henderson, 1999—. Named Tchr. of Yr., Henderson C. of C., 2001. Mem.: Music Educators Nat. Conf., Nev. Music Educators Assn. (chair all-state choir 2002—04), Am. Choral Dirs. Assn. (Nev. state pres. 2003—05). Avocations: hiking, travel, singing, playing piano.

**MCGRATH, MARY HELENA,** plastic surgeon, educator; b. NYC, Apr. 12, 1945; d. Vincent J. and Mary M. (Manning) McG.; children: Margaret E. Simon, Richard M. Simon. BA, Coll. New Rochelle, 1966; MD, St. Louis U., 1970; MPH, George Washington U., 1994. Diplomate Am. Bd. Surgery, Am. Bd. Plastic Surgery, lic. physician Calif. Resident in surg. pathology U. Colo. Med. Ctr., Denver, 1970-71, intern in gen. surgery, 1971-72, resident in gen. surgery, 1971-75, chief resident in gen. surgery, 1975-76; resident in plastic and reconstructive surgery Yale U. Sch. Medicine, New Haven, 1976-77, chief resident plastic and reconstructive surgery, 1977-78; fellow in hand surgery U. Conn.-Yale U., New Haven, 1978; instr. in surgery divsn. plastic and reconstructive surgery Yale U. Sch. Medicine, New Haven, 1977-78, asst. prof. plastic surgery, 1978 80; attending in plastic and reconstructive surgery Yale-New Haven Hosp., 1978-80, Columbia-Presbyn. Hosp., N.Y.C., 1980-84, George Washington U. Med. Ctr., Washington, 1984-2000, Children's Nat. Med. Ctr., Washington, 1985-2000, Loyola U. Med. Ctr., 2000—02, Hines VA Hosp., 2001—02, U. Calif., San Francisco, 2003—, San Francisco VA Ctr., 2003—, San Francisco Gen. Hosp., 2003—; asst. prof. plastic surgery Columbia U., N.Y.C., 1980-84; assoc. prof. plastic surgery Sch. Medicine, George Washington U., Washington, 1984-87, prof. plastic surgery, 1987-2000, Loyola U. Med. Ctr., 2000—02, U. Calif., San Francisco, 2003—. Bd. dirs. Am. Bd. Plastic Surgery, 1989-95, historian, 1991-95; examiner certifying exam., 1986—; mem. Residency Rev. Com. Plastic Surgery, 2006—; senator med. faculty senate George Washington U., bd. govs. Med. Faculty Assocs.; presenter, cons. in field. Co-editor: (with M.L. Turner) Dermatology for Plastic Surgeons, 1993; assoc. editor: The Jour. of Hand Surgery, 1984-89, Annals of Plastic Surgery, 1984-87, Plastic and Reconstructive Surgery, 1989-95, Contemporary Surgery, 1999-2006, Archives of Surgery, 2004—; advt. editor Plastic and Reconstructive Surgery, 2003—; guest reviewer numerous jours.; contbr. chpts. to books and articles to profl. jours Recipient numerous rsch. grants, 1978—; Fellow ACS (D.C. chpt. program ann. meeting chmn., 1992, pres. 1994-95, bd. govs. 1995-98, exec. com. 1996-97, chmn. adv. coun. plastic surgery 1995-98, regent 1997—, vice-chair bd. regents 2005-06); mem. AAAS, Am. Surg. Assn., Am. Assn. Hand Surgery, Am. Assn. Plastic Surgeons (trustee 1997-00), Am. Burn Assn., Am. Soc. for Aesthetic Plastic Surgery, Am. Soc. Maxillofacial Surgeons, Am. Soc. Plastic and Reconstructive Surgery (chmn. ethics com. 1985-87, chmn. device/tech. evaluation com. 1993-94, chmn. workforce task force 1997-00, bd. dirs. 1994-96, chmn. endowment bd. dirs. 2000-04, trustee 2004—, ednl. found. bd. dirs. 1985-96, treas. 1989-92, v.p. 1992-93, pres.-elect 1993-94, pres 1994-95), Am. Soc. Reconstructive Microsurgery (edn. com. 1992-94), Am. Soc. Surgery of Hand (chmn. 1987 ann. residents' and fellows conf. 1986-87, rsch. com. 1988-90), Assn. Acad. Chmn. Plastic Surgery (bd. dirs. 1999—), Assn. Acad. Surgery, Chgo. Soc. Plastic Surgeons (treas. 2001-02), Calif. Soc. Plastic Surgeons, San Francisco Surg. Soc., Chgo. Surg. Soc., Internat. Soc. Reconstructive Surgery, Met. D.C. Soc. Surgery Hand (pres. 1995-97), N.Y. Surg. Soc., Northeastern Soc. Plastic Surgeons (treas. 1993-96, pres. 1997-98), Pacific Coast Surg. Assn., Plastic Surgery Rsch. Coun. (chmn. 1990), Surg. Biology Club III, The Wound Healing Soc Office Phone: 415-353-4389. Business E-Mail: mcgrathm@surgery.ucsf.edu.

**MCGRATH, MICHAEL G.,** finance company executive; CFO, mng. ptnr. Accenture, Chgo. Office: Accenture 161 N Clark St Fl 11 Chicago IL 60601-3362

**MCGRATH, MIKE,** state attorney general; b. Aug. 22, 1947; BS, U. Mont., 1970; JD, Gonzaga U., 1975. Bar: Wash. 75, Mont. 77, U.S. Ct. Appeals (9th cir.) 80, U.S. Supreme Ct. 80. Reginald Heber Smith cmty. lawyer fellow; atty. Washoe County Legal Svcs., Reno, 1975—76; asst. atty. gen. State of Mont., Helena, 1977—82, atty. gen., 2001—; county atty. Lewis and Clark County, Helena, 1983—2001. Bd. dirs. Mont. Legal Svcs. Assn., 1980—2003, pres., 1984—85, 1995—96; bd. dirs. Mountain chpt. Nat. Com. for Prevention of Child Abuse, 1985—90, Big Bros. Sisters, Helena, 1977—83, Friendship Ctr. Helena, 1989—, pres., 1995—97; chmn. Conf. We. Atty. Gens., 2003—04. With USAF, 1970—72. Mem.: Mont. County Attys. Assn. (pres. 1996—97), Nat. Dist. Attys. Assn., Mont. Bar Assn., Rock Mountain Elk Found. Democrat. Home: 514 Hayes Ave Helena MT 59601-6106 Office: Office of Atty General Justice Bldg 215 N Sanders PO Box 201401 Helena MT 59620 Office Phone: 406-444-2026.

**MCGRATH, PATRICK,** writer; b. London, Feb. 7, 1950; s. Patrick and Helen (O'Brien) McG; m. Maria Aitken. BA with honors, U. London, 1971; student, Simon Fraser U. Mng. editor Speech Tech. mag. Media Dimensions, NYC, 1982-87; freelance writer; with Broadmoor Hosp., England; tchr. BC, Canada. Author: The Lewis and Clark Expedition, 1985, Blood and Water and

Other Tales, 1988 (Bram Stoker best collection nominee, 1989), The Grotesque, 1989, Spider, 1990 (screenplay 2002), Dr. Haggard's Disease, 1993, Asylum, 1996 (Whitbread award nominee, Brit. Fantasy award nominee), Matha Peake, 2000, Port Mungo, 2004, Ghost Town, 2005; editor: (with Bradford Morrow) The New Gothic: A Collection of Contemporary Gothic Fiction, 1991, Picador Book of the New Gothic, 1992; contbg. editor Bomb mag., Conjunctions mag. Mailing: c/o Deborah Rogers Rogers Coleridge & White 20 Powis Mews London W11 1JN England Home: NYC & London England

**MCGRATH, RICHARD,** lawyer; b. Chgo., Aug. 10, 1929; s. John Francis and Helen Leone (Hoyer) M.; m. Luisa Sacco y Artze, Aug. 12, 1956; children: Lisa, Deborah, Holly. BA magna cum laude, Georgetown U., 1951; JD cum laude, Harvard U., 1954. Bar: D.C. 1954, N.Y. 1955, Mass. 1957, Conn. 1960, U.S. Supreme Ct. 1965. Assoc. Hughes, Hubbard, Blair and Reed, 1954-57; corp. counsel Raytheon Co., 1957-60; assoc. Cummings & Lockwood, Stamford, Conn., 1960-63, ptnr., 1963—2003; counsel Murtha Cullina, LLP, New Haven, 2004—. Gen. counsel, corp. sec. Internat. Exec. Svc. Corps, 1990—. Mem. editl. bd. Harvard Law Rev., 1952-54; contbr. articles to profl. jours.; panelist law seminars. Past pres. Fairfield County Coun. Boy Scouts Am. Mem.: Conn. Bar Assn. (chmn. corp. law com. 1984—86, fee disputes arbitration com. 1980—84), Woodway Country Club (Darien, Conn.) (bd. govs., sec. 1983—91, chmn. nominating com. 2000), Stamford Rotary Club (past pres.), Gold Key Soc., Eta Sigma Phi, Pi Gamma Mu. Avocations: golf, trap, chess. Office: Murtha Cullina LLP 177 Broad St Stamford CT 06901 Office Phone: 203-653-5412. Business E-Mail: rmcgrath@murthalaw.com.

**MCGRATH, THOMAS JOHN,** retired lawyer, writer, film producer; b. NYC, Oct. 8, 1932; children: Maura Lee, J. Connell; m. Diahn W. McGrath, Sept. 28, 1974; 1 child, Courtney C. BA, NYU, 1956, JD, 1960. Bar: NY 1960. Assoc. Milbank, Tweed, Hadley & McCloy, N.Y.C., 1960-69; ptnr. Simpson, Thacher & Bartlett, N.Y.C., 1970-95; retired, 1995. Lectr., writer Practicing Law Inst., 1976—, Am. Law Inst. ABA, 1976-81. Author: Carryover Basis Under Tax Reform Act, 1977; contbg. author: Estate and Gift Tax After ERTA, 1982; producer: (film) Deadly Hero, 1977. Bd. dirs. N.Y. Philharm.; pres. Am. Austrian Found. With U.S. Army, 1953-54, Korea. Fellow Am. Coll. Trust and Estate Coun.; mem. ABA, N.Y. State Bar Assn., Assn. Bar City N.Y. Office: Simpson Thacher & Bartlett 425 Lexington Ave New York NY 10017-3954 Office Phone: 212-355-2232. Personal E-mail: mcgrathtwf@aol.com.

**MCGRATH, WILLIAM JOSEPH,** lawyer; b. Cleve., July 6, 1943; s. William Peter and Marie Agnes (Wolf) McG.; m. Mary Ann Ostrenga; children: William Peter, Geoffrey Walton, Megan Joy. ABcl, John Carroll U., 1965; MA, Loyola U., 1967; JD, Harvard U., 1970. Bar: Ill. 1970. Assoc. McDermott, Will & Emery, Chgo., 1970-75, ptnr, 1976—, mem. mgmt. com., 1993-98, mem. exec. com., 1994-97. Vice chmn. investment com. Glencoe Capital LLC, 1997-2000, vice chmn., mng. dir., 2000—; bd. dirs. Tomy Am., Inc., Torrance, Calif. Trustee Boys and Girls Club Found., 1983; bd. dirs. Ctr. for Econ. Policy and Analysis, 1989—. Mem. ABA, Evanston Golf Club, Union League (Chgo.), Chgo. Club, Met. Club. Chgo. Democrat. Roman Catholic. Home: 943 Edgemere Ct Evanston IL 60202-1428 Office: Glencoe Capital LLC 222 W Adams St Chicago IL 60606

**MCGRATTAN, MARY K.,** state legislator; b. NYC; married; 6 children. RN, St. Catherine's Hosp. Sch. of Nursing. RN NY, Conn.; cert. notary pub., justice of the peace. Mem. town coun. Town of Ledyard, Conn., 1977-83, mayor, 1983—91; pres. Conn. Conf. of Municipalities, 1990-91; mem. Conn. Ho. of Reps., Hartford, 1993—2002; cons. Ledyard Obesity Prevention Project, 2003; coord. Faith in Action Network, 2003—. Vol. Ledyard Fair, Our Lady of Lourdes Festival; event coord. Crop Walk for Hunger; chair Ledyard HEart Fund Charity Dr.; mem. Ledyard Dem. Town Com. Named Legislator of Yr., Conn. Nurses Assn.; recipient cert. of appreciation, C. of C., Breath of Life award, Am. Lung Assn., award of appreciation, Conn. Assn. Optometrists, Nightingale award for excellence in nursing, 2003; Paul Harris fellow, Rotary. Mem.: Avalonia Land Conservancy, Ledyard Libr. Friends, Ledyard Hist. Soc., Rotary. Avocations: reading, sewing, cooking. Address: 13 Lynn Dr Ledyard CT 06339-1312 Office Phone: 860-442-0733. E-mail: mary@community-partnerships.com.

**MC GRAW, DARRELL VIVIAN, JR.,** state attorney general; b. Mullens, W.Va., Nov. 8, 1936; s. Darrell Vivian and Julia (ZeKany) Mc Graw; m. Jorea Marple; children: Elizabeth, Sarah, Darrell, Elliott. AB, W.Va. U., 1961, JD, 1964, MA, 1977. Bar: W.Va. 1964. Gen. atty. Fgn. Claims Settlement Commn., U.S. Dept. State, 1964; counsel to gov. State of W.Va.; 1965—68; pvt. practice Charleston, Shepherdstown and Morgantown, 1968—76; judge W.Va. Supreme Ct. Appeals, Charleston, 1977—88, chief justice, 1982—83; atty. gen. State of W.Va., Charleston, 1993—. With U.S. Army, 1954—57. Fellow, W.Va. U., Nat. Ctr. Edn. in Politics/Ford Found. Mem. Am. Polit. Sci. Assn., Rotary. Democrat. Office: Office of Atty Gen 1900 Kanawha Blvd E Rm E-26 Charleston WV 25305-0009 Office Phone: 304-558-2021.

**MCGRAW, DONALD JESSE,** biologist, science historian, writer; b. Altadena, Calif., Oct. 27, 1943; s. Jesse E. and Mary L. (Hajostek) McG.; m. Laura Lee Hansen, July 13, 1968; children: Adrienne, Holly, Rachel. BS in Biol. Scis., Calif. State Poly. Coll., 1965; MS, Utah State U., 1967; PhD, Oreg. State U., 1976. Registered microbiologist Am. Acad. Microbiology. Research asst. microbiology Utah State U., 1965-66, teaching asst. food and aquatic microbiology, 1966-67; grad. teaching asst. gen. biology Oreg. State U., 1970-72, instr., 1972-73; tchr. phys. and biol. scis. U.S. Bur. Indian Affairs Boarding Sch., Shonto, Ariz., 1974-75; asst. prof. biology Franklin Coll., Ind., 1975-78; adj. asst. prof. biology Ind. Central U., Indpls., 1977-78; adj. asst. prof. Ind. U.-Purdue U., Columbus, 1978; mem. faculty Yavapai C.C., Prescott, Ariz., 1978-79; assoc. dir. Ute Research Lab., Ft. Duchesne, Utah, 1980-81, dir., 1981-82; asst. prof. biology Coll. St. Thomas, Minn., 1985-87; assoc. provost U. San Diego, 1988—2004, prof., 2001—04. Summer ranger/naturalist U.S. Nat. Park Svc., 1970—79, 1983—86; vis. prof. Bard Coll., N.Y., 1984. Author: Andrew Ellicott Douglass and the Role of the Giant Sequoia in the Development of Dendrochonology, 2001, Edmund Schulman and the Living Ruins: Bristlecone Pines, Tree Rings and Radiocarbon Dating, 2006; contbr. articles to profl. jours. Commr. San Diego County Columbian Quincentenary Commn., 1990-93, chmn. edn. com., 1990-93; mem. pres.'s adv. com. San Diego Zool. Soc., 1995-97; trustee Quail Bot. Gardens Found., 1995-98. Capt. (0-6) USPHS Res. Recipient Disting. Alumnus award, Calif. State Poly. U., 1991, Monrovia H.S., 1991, Meritorious Pub. Svc. award USN, 2003; Eli Lilly doctoral grantee Oreg. State U., 1972, NSF grantee, 1998. Mem. AAAS, Cabrillo Hist. Assn. (bd. dirs. 1989-94, vice chair 1992, chair 1993, 94), History of Sci. Soc., Tree Ring Soc., Alpha Scholastic Honor Soc. of Franklin Coll. (pres. 1976-78), Sigma Xi (sec. San Diego chpt. 1996-97, v.p. 1997-98, pres. 1999-2000, assoc. dir. S.W. region 2000-02, bd. dirs. 2004—. Silver medal of achievement San Diego (Calif.) chpt. 2002), Beta Beta Beta. Office Phone: 619-216-4650. Personal E-Mail: granttree@yahoo.com.

**MCGRAW, GARY,** computer scientist, writer; m. Amy Barley; children: Jack, Eli. BA in Philosophy, U. Va.; PhD in Computer Sci. and Cognitive Sci., Ind. U. Chief technology officer Cigital, Inc. (formerly Reliable Software Technologies), Dulles, Va.; also bd. dir. Co-founder, software security group Cigital, Inc., 1999—; cons. with major software producers and consumers on software and application security; prin. investigator on grants from Air Force Research Labs, DARPA, Nat. Sci. Found., and NIST's Advanced Technology Program; mem. adv. bd. Authentica, Counterpane, Fortify Software, Indigo Security, Cenzic, Finjan, Necrotainty, Tovaris; advises computer sci. dept. U. Davis. Co-author (with Ed Felten): Java Security: Hostile Applets, Holes, and Antidotes, 1996; co-author: (with Jeffrey Voas) Software Fault Injection: Inoculating Programs Against Errors, 1997; co-author: (with Ed Felten) Securing Java: Getting Down to Business with Mobile Code, 1999; co-author: (with John Viega) Building Secure Software: How To Avoid Security Problem the Right Way, 2001; co-author: Exploiting Software, 2004; written over 60 peer-reviewed tech. publs.; contbr. articles to popular trade publs.; quoted in nat. press articles. Avocation: musician. Office: Cigital Inc 21351 Ridgetop Cir Ste 400 Dulles VA 20166-6503 Office Phone: 703-404-9293. Office Fax: 703-404-9295. Business E-Mail: gem@cigital.com.

**MCGRAW, HAROLD W., III, (TERRY MCGRAW),** information company executive; b. Summit, N.J., Aug. 30, 1948; s. Harold W. McGraw Jr.; m. Nancy Goodrich, Sept. 22, 1973; children: Harold W. IV, Megan G. BA, Tufts U., 1972; MBA, U. Pa., 1976. Fin. mgmt. staff GTE; asst. v.p. pension investment GTE Mgmt. Corp., McGraw-Hill, Inc., NYC, 1980-83, dir. corp. planning systems, 1983-84, v.p. corp. planning, 1984-85; group v.p., pub. transp. group McGraw-Hill Publs. Co., NYC, 1985-86, group v.p., pub. transp., aerospace and def. group, 1986-87, pres., 1987-88, McGraw-Hill Fin. Svcs. Co., NYC, 1988-89; exec. v.p. McGraw-Hill Cos., NYC, 1989-93, pres., COO, 1993-98, pres., CEO, 1998—, chmn., 1999—. Chmn., Bus. Roundtable, 2006-; bd. dirs. Mag. Publ. Am., Am. Bus. Press. Bd. dirs. Hartley House, N.Y.C., 1983—, Prep for Prep, Black Execs. Exchange Program, Nat. Actors Theatre; co-chmn. Carnegie Hall's Corp. Fund. Mem. Assn. Am. Publ. (bd. dirs.). Office: The McGraw Hill Companies Ste C3A 49th Fl 1221 Ave Americas New York NY 10020-1095*

**MCGRAW, HAROLD WHITTLESEY, JR.,** publishing executive; b. Bklyn., Jan. 10, 1918; s. Harold Whittlesey and Louise (Higgins) McG.; m. Anne Per-Lee, Nov. 30, 1940; children: Suzanne, Harold Whittlesey III, Thomas Per-Lee, Robert Pearce. AB, Princeton U., 1940. With G.M. Basford (advt. agy.), N.Y.C., 1940-41, Brentano's Bookstores, Inc., 1946; with McGraw-Hill Book Co., Inc., N.Y.C., 1947—, successively promotion mgr., dir. co. advt. and trade sales, 1947-55, dir., v.p. charge trade book, indsl. and bus. book depts., co. advt., 1955-61, sr. v.p., 1961-68, pres., 1968-74, McGraw-Hill, Inc., 1974-81, CEO, 1975-83, chmn., 1976-88, chairman emeritus, 1988—. Bd. dirs. McGraw Hill, Inc., 1954-88. Founder, pres., bd. dirs. Bus. Council Effective Literacy and Bus. Press Ednl. Found. Served as capt. USAAF, 1941-45. Mem.: Wee Burn Club (Darien, Conn.), Blind Brook Club (Purchase, N.Y.). Home: Watch Tower Rd Darien CT 06820 Office: The McGraw-Hill Cos 1221 Avenue Of The Americas New York NY 10020-1095

**MCGRAW, JACK WILSON,** federal agency administrator; b. Balt., May 19, 1943; s. P.W. and Nina (Gwinn) McG.; m. Nancy F. Foster, Aug. 31, 1974; children— David, Mark BA, Morris Harvey Coll., 1964; B.Div., Tex. Christian U., 1967. Ordained minister Christian Ch. (Disciples of Christ). Dir. temporary housing HUD, Washington, 1979-82; asst. assoc. dir. Fed. Emergency Mgmt. Agy., Washington, 1982, dep. asst. dir., 1982-83; dep. asst. adminstr. EPA Office Solid Waste and Emergency Response, Washington, 1983-88, acting asst. adminstr.; dep. regional adminstr. EPA Regional Office, Denver, 1988—2005, ret. 2005; prin., owner Jack McGraw and Assocs. LLC, Englewood, Colo., 2005—. Nominee William H. Jump award HUD, 1972; recipient Presdl. Meritorious award, Presdl. Disting. Exec. award. Presbyterian. Home: 8074 S Oneida Ct Englewood CO 80112-3128 Office: EPA Regional Office 8074 S Oneida Ct Englewood CO 80112

**MCGRAW, LAVINIA MORGAN,** retired rental company executive; b. Detroit, Feb. 26, 1924; d. Will Curtis and Margaret Coulter (Oliphant) McG. AB, Radcliffe Coll., 1945. Mem. Phi Beta Kappa.

**MCGRAW, PHILLIP CALVIN See DR. PHIL**

**MCGRAW, SUSAN CATHERINE,** interior designer; b. Long Beach, Calif., Apr. 16, 1945; d. Thomas Printiss and Mary Ruth (Reese) Gregg; m. Don George McGraw, Nov. 21, 1964; children: DeAnna Coulombe, Katrina Daymude. Dental assistant diploma, Career Tng. Inst., 1964. Cert. interior designer, 1993. Ptnr., buyer The Corner, Garden Grove, Calif., 1971-79; interior designer Kris Noel & Assoc., Huntington Beach, Calif., 1980-85; owner, designer A.I. Designs, Huntington Beach, Calif., 1986-94; ptnr., designer Ross-McGraw Studio, Huntington Beach, Calif., 1994—, owner, designer, 1994—. Pres., ptnr. Red Tee Golf, Huntington Beach, 1998-2001. Bd. dirs. Parent Help USA, Huntington Beach, 1992; sec. Seaclift Home Owners Assn., Huntington Beach, 1992-93; v.p. ways and means Friends of Huntington Youth Guild, Huntington Beach, 1994-96, pres., 1996-98; v.p. ways and means com. Friends of Huntington Youth Shelter, 2003-2004. Mem. Am. Soc. Interior Design (profl. mem.). Office Phone: 714-840-1779. Business E-Mail: suemcgraw@socal.rr.com.

**MCGRAW, TIM,** country music singer; b. Delhi, La., May 1, 1967; s. Tug McGraw; m. Faith Hill; children: Gracie Katherine, Maggie Elizabeth, Audrey Caroline. Musician: (albums) Tim McGraw, 1993, Not a Moment Too Soon, 1994 (triple-platinum, Album of Yr., Acad. County Music, 1994), All I Want, 1995, Everywhere, 1997 (Album of Yr., Country Music Assn., 1998), A Place in the Sun, 1999 (Album of Yr., Country Music Assn., 1999), Tim McGraw Greatest Hits, 2000, Set the Circus Down, 2001 (Best Country Album, Am. Music Awards, 2002), Tim McGraw and the Dancehall Doctors, 2002, Live Like You Were Dying, 2004 (Most Inspiring Video of Yr., Country Music Television Music award, 2005, Single Record of Yr., Acad. Country Music Awards, 2005, Am. Music Awards Favorite Country Album, 2005), Tim McGraw Reflected Greatest Hits Vol. 2, 2006, (single) Welcome to the Club, 1992, It's Your Love, 1997 (Single & Song of Yr., Acad. Country Music, 1998), Grown Men, 2001 (Single & Song of Yr., Radio Music Assn., 2001), Live Like You Were Dying, 2004 (Single & Song of Yr., Country Music Assn., 2004, Song of Yr., Acad. Country Music Awards, 2005), (with Nelly) Over and Over, 2004; vocal collaboration (with Faith Hill) Let's Make Love, 2001 (Grammy award, 2001); actor: (films) Black Cloud, 2004, Friday Night Lights, 2004. Recipient Favorite New Artist, Am. Music Awards, 1995, Favorite Male Country Artist, 2002, 2001, 2003, 2005, Top Male Vocalist, Acad. Country Music, 1994, 1999, 1998, Vocal Event of Yr., 1997, 1998, Country Music Assn., 1997, Male Vocalist of Yr., 1999, 2000, Entertainer of Yr., 2001, Male Artist of Yr., TNN/Music City News, 1999, Favorite Male Artist, Blockbuster Award, 2001, Country Male Artist, Radio Music Awards, 2003, Favorite Male Musical Performer, People's Choice Awards, 2004, Favorite Male Performer, 2006, Best Country Collaboration With Vocals (with Faith Hill), 2006. Office: care Curb Records 3907 W Alameda Ave Burbank CA 91505-4332*

**MCGREAL, JOSEPH A., JR.,** publishing executive; b. Bklyn., Mar. 6, 1935; s. Joseph A. and Aresta (Noon) McG.; m. Margaret A. Molloy, June 6, 1959; children— Patrick, Pegeen, Joseph. BBA, St. Francis Coll., 1962. Pres. Med./Pharm. Pub. Co., Inc., Spring Lake Heights, NJ, 1986-2001. Served with U.S. Army, 1955-57. Home and Office: 71 Willow Ln Spring Lake NJ 07762-2188

**MCGREEVEY, JIM (JAMES EDWARD MCGREEVEY),** former governor; b. Jersey City, N.J., Aug. 6, 1957; s. Jack and Veronica McGreevey; m. Karen J. Schutz, 1991 (div. 1997); 1 child, Morag Veronica; m. Dina Matos, 2000 (separated); 1 child, Jacqueline Matos; life ptnr. Mark O'Donnell. BA, Columbia U., 1978; JD, Georgetown U., 1981; MEd, Harvard U., 1982; LLD (hon.), Rutgers U., 1992. Mem. NJ State Assembly (19th dist), Middlesex, 1990—91; mayor City of Woodbridge, NJ, 1992-2001; mem. NJ State Senate (19th dist.), 1994—97; gov. State of NJ, Trenton, 2002—04; ptnr. Weiner Lesniak LLP, Parsippany, NJ, 2004—05. Atty., regional mgr. Merck & Co., Rahway, NJ, 1987-91. Author: (polit. memoir) The Confession, 2006. Campaign com. vol. State Legis. Campaigns, 1983, 85, 87; campaign vol. Middlesex County Freeholder reelection campaigns, 1983-88; atty., policy counsel Assembly Dem. Majority Conf., 1983-84; campaign vol. speaker for Congressman Bernard J. Dwyer, 1984, 86, 88, Senator Frank R. Lautenberg, 1988, 94; former chmn. Ctrl. Jersey chpt. ARC. Mem. Nat. Conf. Christians and Jews (former chmn.), Middlesex County Cult and Heritage Commn. (former chmn.), N.J. League Nursing (former trustee), Diocese of Metuchen Cath. Lawyers Guild (past pres.). Democrat.*

**MCGREEVEY, LISA S.,** investment company executive; BA, So. Methodist U. Spl. asst. to Pres. for polit. & intergovernmental affairs The White House, Washington; sr. legis. mgr. US Dept. Treasury, Washington, 1988—92; with Conf. State Bank Supervisors, 1992—99; exec. v.p. for external affairs, pres. Govt. Affairs Coun. The Fin. Services Roundtable, Washington, 1999—2006; exec. v.p., COO Managed Funds Assn., Washington, 2006—. Named one of The Top 40 Lobbyists, The Hill, 2004, The Most Powerful Women in Washington, US Banker, 2005. Office: Managed Funds Assn 2025 M st NW Ste 800 Washington DC 20036*

**MCGREGOR, DOUGLAS A.,** real estate company executive; Exec. v.p., dir. devel. & ops. The Rouse Co., Columbia, Md., 1989—. Office: The Rouse Co 10275 Little Patuxent Pkwy Columbia MD 21044-3455

**MCGREGOR, DOUGLAS HUGH,** pathologist, educator; b. Temple, Tex., Aug. 28, 1939; s. Harleigh Heath and Joyce Ellen (Lambert) McG.; m. Mizuki Kitani, July 6, 1969; children: Michelle Sakuya, David Kenji. BA, Duke U., 1961, MD, 1966; postgrad., U. Edinburgh, Scotland, 1961-62. Diplomate Am. Bd. Pathology. Intern, chief resident in pathology UCLA Med. Ctr., 1966-68; surgeon, lt. comdr. Atomic Bomb Casualty Commn., Hiroshima, Japan, 1968-71; chief resident in pathology Queens Med. Ctr., Honolulu, 1971-73; asst., assoc. prof. pathology U. Kans. Med. Ctr., Kansas City, 1973-82, prof., 1982—. Dir. anat. pathology VA Med. Ctr., Kansas City, Mo., 1975-94, chief pathology and lab. medicine, 1994-2003, dir. surg. pathology, 2003—. Contbr. numerous articles to profl. jours., chpts. to books. Leader YMCA Indian Princess Program, Overland Park, Kans., 1977-79, Indian Guide Program, 1978-80, Cub Scout Am., Overland Park, 1980-82, Boy Scouts Am., Leawood, Kans., 1982—. Lt. comdr. USPHS, 1968-71, Japan. Grantee Merck, Sharp and Dohme, 1980. Fellow Coll. Am. Pathologists, Am. Soc. Clin. Pathologists; mem. Am. Assn. Pathologists, Internat. Acad. Pathologists, Soc. Exptl. Biology and Medicine, N.Y. Acad. Scis., AAAS, Kansas City Soc. Pathologists (sec.-treas. 1982-83, pres. 1983-84), Leawood Country Club. Achievements include research in ultrastructure and pathobiology of neoplasms, radiation carcinogenesis, and morphogenesis of atherosclerosis. Home: 9400 Lee Blvd Shawnee Mission KS 66206-1826 Office: VA Med Ctr 4801 E Linwood Blvd Kansas City MO 64128-2226 Business E-Mail: douglas.mcgregor@med.va.gov.

**MCGREGOR, EWAN GORDON,** actor; b. Crieff, Perthshire, Scotland, Mar. 31, 1971; s. James and Carol McGregor; m. Eve Mavrakis, July 22, 1995; children: Clara Mathilde, Esther Rose; 1 adopted child. LLD, U. Ulster, 2001. Motion picture actor; stage actor; co-founder (with John Lee Miller, Sean Pertwee, Jude Law, Sadie Frost) Natural Nylon (prodn. co.). Actor: (films) Being Human, 1993, Shallow Grave, 1994, The Pillow Book, 1994, Blue Juice, 1995, Emma, 1996, Trainspotting, 1996 (Brit. Actor of Yr., 1996), Brassed Off, 1996, A Life Less Ordinary, 1997, Velvet Goldmine, 1998, Little Voice, 1998, Nora, 1999, Eye of the Beholder, 1999, Star Wars: Episode I-The Phantom Menace, 1999, Moulin Rouge, 2001 (European Film award for Achievement in World Cinema, 2001, Film Actor Award, The Variety Club Showbusiness Awards, 2002), Black Hawk Down, 2001, Star Wars: Episode II-Attack of the Clones, 2002, Down With Love, 2003, Young Adam, 2003, Big Fish, 2003, Star Wars: Episode III-Revenge of the Sith, 2005, The Island, 2005; voice (films) Robots, 2005, Valiant, 2005; actor (films) Stay, 2005; others, (TV films) Lipstick on Your Collar, 1993, Doggin' Around, 1994, TV guest appearances include Tales from the Crypt, 1989, ER, 1994, Kavanagh QC, 1994; (plays) Guys and Dolls, 2005. Named No. 36 on the list, "100 Top Movie Stars of All Time", Empire mag. (UK), 1997, No. 4 on the list, "British Culture's Top 50 Movers and Shakers", BBC 3, 2004; recipient ALFS award, 1997. Office: care Lindy King Drury House 34-43 Russell St Peters etc London WC2B 5HA England*

**MCGREGOR, JUDITH ANN,** education educator; b. Pitts., Aug. 24, 1954; d. William James and Jeanne Harris McGregor. BS in Elem. Edn., Fla. State U., 1976, MS in Elem. Edn. with honors, 1977, PhD in Elem. Edn. with honors, 1992. Instr. Devel. Rsch. Sch., Fla. State U., Tallahassee, 1976—77; asst. prof. St. Petersburg Jr. Coll., Clearwater, 1978—80; instr. Fla. State U., 1981—82; asst. prof. Calif. State U., Long Beach, 1983—87, instr. Fullerton, 1990—91, asst. prof., supr. field work Dominguez Hills, 1992—. Pres. Jean Harris Entertainment, LA, 2006—; cons. in field of children and family TV and film. Author: Occupational Protrayal in Television: A Comparative Study of Children and Family Programs, 1993, (children's TV series) Whispie and Company, 1994. Mem.: NOW, NEA, AAUW, AAUP, Fla. State U. Alumni Assn. Avocations: skiing, rollerblading, kayaking, golf. Office: Brentwood Village 149 S Barrington Ave Ste 182 Los Angeles CA 90049 Office Phone: 310-650-0774.

**MCGREGOR, RUTH VAN ROEKEL,** state supreme court justice; b. Le Mars, Iowa, Apr. 4, 1943; d. Bernard and Marie Frances (Janssen) Van Roekel; m. Robert James McGregor, Aug. 15, 1965. BA summa cum laude, U. Iowa, 1964, MA, 1965; JD summa cum laude, Ariz. State U., 1974; LLM, U. Va., 1998. Bar: Ariz. 1974, U.S. Dist. Ct. Ariz. 1974, U.S. Ct. Appeals (9th cir.), U.S. Supreme Ct. 1984. Assoc. Fennemore, Craig, von Ammon, Udall & Powers, Phoenix, 1974-79, ptnr., 1980-81, 82-89; law clk. to justice Sandra Day O'Connor U.S. Supreme Ct., Washington, 1981-82; judge Ariz. Ct. Appeals, 1989-98, vice chief judge, 1993-95, chief judge, 1995-98; justice Ariz. Supreme Ct., 1998—, vice chief justice, 2002—05, chief justice, 2005—. Mem. disciplinary commn. Ariz. Supreme Ct., 1984-89, City of Mesa jud. adv. bd., 1997. Mem., newsletter editor Charter 100, Phoenix, 1981—; bd. dirs. mem. Ctr. for Law in Pub. Interest, Phoenix, 1977-80. Named Dwight D. Operman award for Top Judge in the Nation, Am. Judicature Soc., 2005. Mem. ABA (chmn. state memberships 1985-89: named fellow) Ariz. Bar Assn. (disciplinary com. 1984-89), Ariz. Judges Assn. (exec. com. 1990-98, sec. 1991-92, v.p. 1992-93, pres. 1993-94), Nat. Assn. Women Judges (chair first time attendees com. 1990-91, 1994 conv. com.; exec. com. 1995—), Ariz. Woman Lawyers Assn., 1975-. Democrat. Lutheran. Office: Ariz Supreme Ct 1501 W Washington St Phoenix AZ 85007-3231*

**MCGREGOR, SCOTT A.,** electronics company executive; BS, MS, Stanford Univ. Dir., interactive intelligence group Microsoft; sr. mgmt. Digital Equip. Corp., 1985—90; sr. v.p. & gen. mgr. Santa Cruz Ops., 1990—98; pres. & CEO, semiconductor div. Royal Philips Electronics, 2001—04; pres., CEO, dir. Broadcom Co., Irvine, Calif., 2005—. Office: Broadcom Co 16215 Alton Pkwy Irvine CA 92618*

**MCGRIFF, CHERYL RENEE,** medical products executive; d. Herb Hightower and Georgie Luvern Burnett, Julius Burnett (Stepfather) and Mai Bach Hightower (Stepmother); children: Georgina Janelle Greene, Christina Marie Grayson, Felicia Renee Holley, Dorian Gerard, Destinee Gerard, Delilah Grayson. BA in Bus., Eckerd Coll., St. Petersburg, 1998; BSN, Rockville U., 2004, MS in Healthcare Adminstrn., 2004, PhD in Pub. Health, 2004. Indsl. nurse, safety mgr. Lykes Pasco, Inc., Tampa, Fla., 1991—95; COO Global Internat. Med. and Safety Supply, Tampa, 2004—. Minority bus. coun. mem. Lakeland C. of C., 1999—2000; cmty. svc. chair Imperial Assn. of Life Underwriters, Lakeland, 1999—2000. Mem.: Am. Bus. Women's Assn., Gamma Sigma Sigma, Kappa Epsilon (life). Office Phone: 813-382-5967. Office Fax: 813-931-8881. Business E-Mail: globalmedsafety@aol.com.

**MCGRUDER, AARON,** cartoonist; b. Chgo., May 29, 1974; Diploma, U. Md., 1997. Cartoonist; creator The Boondocks cartoon strip, 1996—. Co-author (with Reginald Hudlin): (novels) Birth of a Nation, 2004. Recipient Chmn.'s award, NAACP Image Awards, 2002. Office: The Boondocks Universal Press Syndicate 4520 Main St Kansas City MO 64111 Office Phone: 800-255-6734.*

**MCGUAN, KATHLEEN H.,** lawyer; b. May 9, 1954; BA, Am. U., 1975; MA in hist. musicology, U. Pa., 1978; JD, Cath. U., 1981. Bar: DC. Joined Reed Smith LLP, Washington, 1991, ptnr., 1994—. Office: Reed Smith LLP 1301 K St NW, Ste 1100 - East Tower Washington DC 20005 Office Phone: 202-414-9230. Office Fax: 202-414-9299. Business E-Mail: kmcguan@reedsmith.com.

**MCGUCKIN, JOHN HUGH, JR.,** lawyer; b. Bryn Mawr, Pa., Nov. 8, 1946; AB magna cum laude, Harvard Coll., 1968, JD, 1971. Bar: Mass. 1971, Calif. 1973. Assoc. Orrick, Herrington, Rowley & Sutcliffe, 1972-79; sr. counsel legal divsn. Bank Am., 1979-81; exec. v.p., gen. counsel, corp. sec. Union-BanCal Corp./Union Bank Calif., N.A., San Francisco, 1981—. Adj. instr. Hastings Coll. Law U. Calif., 1980-82; judge pro tem San Francisco Superior Ct. Contbr. articles to profl. jours. Mem. ABA, State Bar Calif. (v.p., treas., bd. govs., chmn. subcom. duties and liabilities trustees probate and trust law sect. 1985-86, legal svcs. trust fund comm. 1989-90, minimum CLE com.), Assn. Corp. Coun. (chmn. 2003-04), Phi Beta Kappa. Office: Union Bank Calif NA 16th Fl 400 California St San Francisco CA 94104-1320

**MCGUINN, BRENDA BECK,** mathematics educator; b. Lexington, NC, Nov. 11, 1957; d. Charles Calvin and Sue Thompson Beck; m. Richard Eugene McGuinn, Aug. 21, 1977; 1 child, Jennifer Leigh. BS in Mid. Grades Edn., U. NC, Greensboro, 1993. Lic. tchr. NC. Prodn./inventory clk. Duracell Battery Inc, Lexington, 1978—86; prodn. worker Kimberly Clark, Lexington, 1986—87; counselor Kids Only Daycare, Lexington, 1987—93; store clk. Jai-Lynn's Restaurant, Lexington, 1989—90; sch. bus driver Davidson County Schs., Lexington, 1989—91; tchr. 6th grade math. and social studies Tyro Mid. Sch., Lexington, 1996—, tchr. 8th grade math. and algebra I, 1998—. Summer camp dir. Tarheel Triad Girl Scout Coun., Greensboro, NC, 1993—94. Troop leader Tarheel Triad Girl Scout Coun., Lexington, 1988—98; coach Math Counts, Lexington, 2000, Jr. Solar Sprint Team, Lexington, 2003; coach academic competition team Tyro Mid. Sch., 2003, score keeper softball team, 2003, videographer basketball team, 2003. Named Tyro Tchr. of Yr., 2003—04. Mem.: NCAE (assoc.).

**MCGUINN, EDWIN J.,** chemicals executive; b. 1953; BA in Math. and Econ., Colgate U.; MA in Acctg., N.Y. U. cert. CPA. Mng. dir. Lehman Brothers; mgmt. Mabon Securities, Rodman & Renshaw Capital Group, Inc.; exec. v.p., head ops. InterVest Securities, Inc.; pres., CEP Automated Trading Sys., Inc, eLot, Inc., Milford, Conn., 2000—.

**MCGUINN, MARTIN GREGORY,** retired bank executive, lawyer; b. Phila., Sept. 9, 1942; s. Martin G. and Rita (Horgan) McG.; m. Ann M. Muldoon, Sept. 17, 1977; children: Patrick J., Christopher M. AB, Villanova U., 1964, JD, 1967. Bar: Pa. 1967, N.Y. 1970. Assoc. Sullivan & Cromwell, N.Y.C., 1970-77; mng. counsel The Singer Co., Stamford, Conn., 1977-80; chmn., CEO Mellon Bank, Pitts., 1998—2006; CEO, chmn. Mellon Fin. Corp, Pitts., 1999—2006. Bd. consultors Villanova Law Sch., 1972—, chmn. 1985-87; bd. dirs. U.S.-Japan Bus. Coun., Inc., Allegheny Conf. on Cmty. Devel. Editor in chief Villanova Law Rev., Vol. 12, 1966-67. Bd. dirs. UPMC Health Sys.; trustee Carnegie Mus. of Pitts.; chmn. Hist. Soc. Western Pa. Mem. ABA, N.Y. State Bar Assn., Pa. Bar Assn., Allegheny County Bar Assn., Am. Law Inst., The Fin. Svcs. Roundtable, Am. Soc. Corp. Secs. (chmn. 1990-91).*

**MCGUIRE, EDWARD DAVID, JR.,** lawyer; b. Waynesboro, Va., Apr. 11, 1948; s. Edward David and Mary Estelle (Angus) McG.; m. Karen Elizabeth Jacobson, Dec. 31, 2005; children: Matthew Edward, Kathryn Anne, Georgia Gail. BS in Commerce, U. Va., 1970; JD, Coll. William and Mary, 1973. Bar: Va. 1973, D.C. 1974, Md. 1990, Pa. 1995, U.S. Dist. Ct. (ea. dist.) Va. 1974, U.S. Dist. Ct. D.C. 1974, U.S. Dist. Ct. Md. 1990, U.S. Ct. Appeals (4th cir.) 1974, U.S. Ct. Appeals (D.C. cir.) 1974, U.S. Supreme Ct. 1993. Assoc. Wilkes and Artis, Washington, 1973-78; gen. corp. counsel Mark Winkler Mgmt., Alexandria, Va., 1978-80; sr. contracts officer Amtrak, Washington, 1980-81; sr. real estate atty., asst. corp. sec. Peoples Drug Stores, Inc., Alexandria, 1981-88; of counsel Cowles, Rinaldi & Arnold, Ltd., Fairfax, Va., 1989-91; sr. assoc. Radigan, Rosenberg & Holmes, Arlington, Va., 1991; pvt. practice Annandale, Va., 1992-97, 2000—05; sr. assoc. Stein, Sperling, Bennett, DeJong, Driscoll, Greenfeig Metro, Rockville, Md., 1997-99; of counsel Hodes, Ulman, Pessin & Katz, P.A., Annandale, 1999-2000; mng. dir., personal trust adminstr. Riggs Bank, N.A., Washington, 2000—03; mng. dir., gen. counsel MFB Holdings, LLC, 2004—. Co-author: Legacy: Plan, Protect and Preserve Your Estate, 1995, Generations: Planning Your Legacy, 1998. Bd. dirs. Dist. XVI Va. Student Aid Found., 1978-85, George Washington dist. Boy Scouts Am., 1986; active William and Mary Law Sch. Assn., bd. dirs., 1983-96, pres., 1987-88, treas., 1990-91. Capt. JAGC, USANG, 1973-79. Mem. ABA, Va. Bar Assn., DC Bar, Md. State Bar Assn., Pa. Bar, William and Mary Alumni Soc. (bd. dirs. D.C. chpt. treas. 1992-94), U. Va. Club of Washington (schs. com. chmn. 1995—, v.p. outreach 1997-99, pres.-elect 1998-99, dir. 1996-99), Rotary (treas. Springfield chpt. 1985-86, sec. 1986-87, pres.-elect 1987, chmn. World Affairs Conf. 1985-88, bd. dirs. 1984-88, 96-97, Dist. 7610 youth leadership awards chmn. 1994-97, Outstanding Rotarian award 1985). Greek Orthodox. Avocations: racquetball, coaching youth sports. Home and Office: MFB Holdings LLC 14533 Bluebird Park Rd Windermere FL 34786 Office Phone: 407-456-3304, 202-246-6370. Personal E-mail: edwmcg31@aol.com.

**MCGUIRE, GARRY K., SR.,** communications executive; b. Rochester, N.Y. BS in Econs., U. Dayton; student in Exec. Edn. Program, U. Pa. With Detroit (Mich.) Bank & Trust Co., 1969—83; from dir. ops. and adminstrn. to v.p. strategic planning No. Telecom Fin. Corp., 1983—90; v.p. strategic planning No. Telecom Inc., 1991—95; pres. NORTEL Comms. Sys. Inc., 1995—2002; sr. v.p. Avaya, Basking Ridge NJ, 2002, CFO, 2002—, pres., CFO William Comms. Solutions LLC. Bd. dir. Globespan Virata, Inc., chmn. audit com.; bd. trustees U. Dayton. With USAF. Office: Avaya 211 Mount Airy Rd Basking Ridge NJ 07920

**MCGUIRE, JOHN ALBERT,** dentist; b. Warren, Ohio, June 20, 1950; s. Bernard Leo and Lucille Ann (Guarnieri) McG.; m. Pamela Kay Muter, May 30, 1969; children: John, Jessica. BS, Ohio State U., 1972, DDS, 1975. Dentist, capt. USAF, Bellevue, Nebr., 1975-77; dentist pvt. practice Dayton, Tenn., 1977-83, Knoxville, Tenn., 1983—. Author: (short story) Stirs, 1990, (screenplay) Sonspot, 2000. Mem. Sertoma Club, Knoxville, 1983-88, Jaycees, Dayton, 1978-81; vol. United Meth. Ch., Tilaran, Costa Rica, 1985. Recipient Scholarship, Fred M. Roddy Found., 1990. Mem. Phi Kappa Phi. Avocations: fly fishing, photography, bicycling, music, writing. Home: 301 Grandeur Dr Knoxville TN 37920-6325 Office: 529 E Gov John Sevier Hwy Knoxville TN 37920-5932

**MCGUIRE, JOHN F.,** international relief organization executive; BS in Chemistry, Iona Coll.; MBA, Harvard U. With DuPont; mng. dir. UK and Belgium Johnson & Johnson Ortho Diagnostics Inc.; pres. & CEO Hemasure Inc., 1997—2001; pres. Waltman PLC N.Am.; exec. v.p. biomedical services Am. Red Cross, 2004—; interim pres. and CEO, 2005—. Capt. USMC. Avocations: golf, fly fishing. Office: American Red Cross National Headquarters 2025 E St NW Washington DC 20006 Office Phone: 202-303-5646.*

**MCGUIRE, JOHN LAWRENCE,** pharmaceutical executive; b. Kittanning, Pa., Nov. 3, 1942; s. Lawrence F. and Florence G. (Jones) McG.; m. Pamela Hale, Aug. 2, 1969; children: Megan L., Christa H. BS, Butler U., 1965; MA, Princeton U., 1968, PhD, 1969; postgrad., Columbia Sch. Bus., 1981. Asst. in instrn. Princeton U., 1967-69; pharmacologist Ortho Pharm. Corp., Raritan, NJ, 1969-72, sect. head molecular biology, 1972-75, exec. dir. rsch., 1975-80, v.p. preclin. R&D, 1980-88, bd. dirs., 1988—92; v.p. global rsch. and devel., pharm./diagnostics group Johnson & Johnson, New Brunswick, NJ, 1992—2004; pres. Ferring Rsch. Insts., Lausanne, Switzerland, 2004—; exec. com. Ferring Pharm. Corp., Lausanne, 2004—; bd. dirs. Ferring Holding SA, St. Prex, Switzerland, 2005—. Adj. assoc. prof. dept. medicine

M.S. Hershey Sch. Medicine Pa. State U., 1978—; adj. prof. dept. animal sci. Rutgers U., 1983-92, ob-gyn. East Va. Med. Sch., 1987—, ob-gyn. and reproductive endocrinology U. Medicine and Dentistry of NJ, 1988—; cons. NASA, 1985-87; cons. Nat. Tech. Transfer Ctr., 1997-2000; bd. dirs. MDAdvantage Ins. Co., Lawrenceville, N.J. Mem. editl. bd. Ullman's Ency. Indsl. Chemistry, 1987—; editor numerous books; contbr. articles to profl. jours.; patentee in field. Trustee Hunterdon Med. Ctr. Found., 1986—, chmn., 2002—; trustee NJ State Hosp. Assn., 2002—, NJ State Theater, New Brunswick, 2002—06, August Found., 1997—, pres., 1997—; trustee Raritan Valley CC, North Branch, NJ, 1986—, vice chmn., 1990—2005, chmn., 2005—; trustee Hunterdon Med. Ctr., Flemington, NJ, 1978—2002, vice chmn., 1984—86, chmn., 1988—98; trustee Hunterdon Health Care Sys., Flemington, NJ, 1986—, chmn., 1989—2002; trustee Atlantic Health Sys., Morristown, NJ, 1991—93, vice chmn., 1992—93; trustee The Pennington Sch., NJ, 1995—, pres., CEO, 1996—; exec. bd. Keystone Area coun. Boy Scouts Am., Harrisburg, Pa., exec. bd. George Washington coun. Trenton, NJ, 1980—86, 1995—99, exec. bd. Ctrl. N.J. coun. Princeton, 1999—, pres., 2000—05, mem. N.E. Region bd., 2004—; bd. dirs. United Way of Hunterdon County, NJ, 1983—97, pres. NJ, 1985—87; bd. dirs. Tri-State United Way, NY, 1987—94, Hunterdon County YMCA, NJ, 1982—87, Mid Jersey Health Corp., 1986—88, chmn., 1986—88; bd. visitors Butler U., Indpls., 2004—. Named NJ Hosp. Trustee of Yr., 2001; recipient Silver Beaver award, Boy Scouts Am., 1984, Disting. Eagle Scout award, 2000, Silver Antelope award, 2006, Johnson medal for rsch. and devel., 1990; Population Coun. fellow, 1969. Mem. Am. Soc. Pharmacology and Exptl. Therapeutics, Am. Exptl. Biology and Medicine, Am. Physiol. Soc., Endocrine Soc., Am. Coll. Ob-Gyn, Am. Soc. Clin. Pharmacology and Therapeutics, Soc. Gynecol. Investigation, Licensing Execs. Soc., Biochemistry Soc. Great Britain, Royal Soc. Medicine (UK), Am. Chem. Soc. Clubs: Princeton (NYC). Home: 10 Club House Dr Whitehouse Station NJ 08889-3378 Personal E-mail: John.McGuire@Ferring.com.

**MCGUIRE, JOHN W., SR.,** advertising executive, marketing professional, writer; b. Chgo., May 12, 1952; s. Eugene H. Sr. and Marjorie (Bolger) McG.; m. Mary Sue Roper, June 17, 1972 (div. 1977); 1 child, John William Jr.; m. Lynn L. Rembos, June 21, 1984 (div. April 1991); children: Kelly Lynn, Ryan Michael. AA, Chgo. City Colls., 1972; BA, Northeastern Ill. Chgo., 1974. Janitor Bd. of Edn., Chgo., 1970-74; sales rep. Motorola Comms., Inc., Schaumburg, Ill., 1974-76, Pattis Group, Chgo., 1976-77; midwest sales mgr. Harcourt Brace Jovanovich Pub. Co., N.Y.C., 1977-79; account sales mgr. Cosmopolitan Mag. Hearst Pub. Co., N.Y.C., 1979-81; midwest acct. mgr. Psychology Today Mag. Ziff-Davis Pub. Co., N.Y.C., 1981-82; midwest regional mgr. Pennwell Pub. Co., Tulsa, Okla., 1982-84; western regional sales mgr. Nursing Mgmt. Mag. SN Pub. Co., West Dundee, Ill., 1984-91; western regional sales mgr. U.S. Pharmacist Mag. Jobson Pub. Co., N.Y.C., 1991-98; v.p. SK&A Info. Svcs., Irvine, Calif., 1998-99; assoc. pub. Health Mgmt. Technology Mag. Nelson Pub., Nokomis, Fla., 1999; pres., CEO Blossom Pub. Co., Wasco, Ill., 2000—. Author: (book) One Man's Life: A Poetic Review, 1995; co-author: (with Scott Mennie) The Original Parent and Family Logbook, 2002; singer (cassette tapes), designer (creative posters) with USN, 1970. Mem. VFW, Midwest Healthcare Mktg., Arlington Poetry Project. Republican. Roman Catholic. Avocations: writing, scuba diving, horseback riding, travel, skydiving.

**MCGUIRE, JOSEPH,** Canadian government official; b. Morell, Can. s. Louis and Etta McGuire; m. Mary Cain; children: Moira, Matthew. Student, Prince Wales Coll. Tchrs. Tng., U. N.B.; BA, St. Dunstans U., 1968. Tchr. Tracadie (Prince Edward Island) Sch.; vice prin. Sioux Lookout (Ont.) Elem. Sch.; with Cmty. Employment Strategy, O'Leary Svc. Ctr., George Henderson, MP, Egmont Constituency Office; asst. to Joe Ghiz Office of Premier of Prince Edward Island; asst. campaign mgr. George Henderson for Mem. Parliament campaign, 1980, campaign mgr., 1984; mem. parliament for Egmont Can. House of Commons, 1988—, mem. standing com. Fisheries, Oceans and Natural Resources; chair standing com. Fisheries and Oceans; chair standing com. Agr.; vice-chair Atlantic Caucus; parliamentary sec. to minister of agr. and agri-food, 1998-2000; mem. standing com. human resources devel./ disabled persons, 2000—; mem. Atlantic Can. opportunities agy. Govt. Can., Ottawa, 2003—. Bd. dirs. West Prince Forestry, Tyne Valley Sports Ctr.; mem. St. Patrick's Parish Coun., Grand River. Avocations: sports, historical novels, golf, hiking. Office: House of Commons 807 Confederation Bldg Ottawa ON Canada K1A 0A6 E-mail: mcguij@parligc.ca.

**MCGUIRE, KATHLEEN ALISON,** conductor; b. Melbourne, Australia, May 22, 1965; d. Frank Leonard McGuire and Jeanette Mary Tilson; life ptnr. Stephanie Lynne Smith. MusB, U. Melbourne, 1987; grad. diploma arts in music, Victorian Coll. Arts, U. Melbourne, 1990; grad. diploma in edn., Monash U., Melbourne, 1992; MusM with Distinction, U. Surrey, Guildford, UK, 1995; Dr. in Mus. Arts, U. Colo., 2000. Cert. preparing future faculty U. of Colo. at Boulder, 2000, grad. tchr. cert. U. Colo., Boulder, 2000. Music educator Sacre Coeur Girls' Sch., Melbourne, Victoria, Australia, 1983—86; educator Our Lady of Mercy Coll., 1986; music dir. Mentone Old Time Theatre Soc., Melbourne, Victoria, Australia, 1985—88; educator Killester Coll., Melbourne, Victoria, Australia, 1987; music educator Sacred Heart Regional Girls' Coll., Melbourne, Victoria, Australia, 1988; educator Mentone Girls' Secondary Coll., Melbourne, Victoria, Australia, 1988—89; music tchr. McKinnon Secondary Coll., Melbourne, Victoria, Australia, 1988—90, Mentone Girls' Grammar Sch., Melbourne, Victoria, Australia, 1990—94; dir. of music Sandringham East Primary Sch., Melbourne, Victoria, Australia, 1988—89; condr. Musical Theatre Soc., U. Surrey, Guildford, Sussex, England, 1994—95; asst. condr. Symphony Orch., U. Surrey, Guildford, Sussex, England, 1994—95; condr. Wind Symphony, U. of Surrey, Guildford, Sussex, 1994—95; educator Parkdale Secondary Coll., Melbourne, Victoria, Australia, 1995; music dir. St. Aidan's Episcopal Ch., Boulder, Colo., 1996—2000; asst. condr. U. of Colo. at Boulder Symphony Orch., Boulder, Colo., 1996—2000; assoc. condr. Lakewood Symphony Orch., Denver, 1996—2000; artistic dir./condr. The Rainbow Chorus, Fort Collins, Colo., 1997—2000; asst. condr. Lyric Theatre, U. Colo., Boulder, Colo., 1997—2000; assoc. condr. New Music Ensemble, U. of Colo., Boulder, Colo., 1998—2000; lead grad. tchr. U. of Colo. at Boulder, 1999—2000; assoc. condr. Boulder Youth Symphony, Boulder, Colo., 1999—2000; artistic dir., condr. San Francisco Gay Men's Chorus, 2000—; condr. Opera By the Bay, Marin, Calif., 2001, Cmty. Women's Orch., San Francisco, 2005—; music tchr. Convent of the Sacred Heart H.S., San Francisco, 2004—; music dir. Melbourne U. Choral Soc., Melbourne, Victoria, Australia, Mordialloc Light Opera Co., Melbourne, Victoria, Australia, Nova Theatre, Melbourne, Victoria, Australia, Whitehorse Mus. Theatre, Melbourne, Victoria, Australia; condr., founder Victorian Women's Orch., Melbourne, Victoria, Australia; condr. Kew Philharm. Orch., Melbourne, Victoria, Australia, Steamboat Springs Cmty. Orch.; music dir. Festival Theatre Co., Melbourne, Victoria, Australia, Renaissance Opera Co., Melbourne, Victoria, Australia, Viola Operatic Soc., Melbourne, Victoria, Australia, Melbourne Opera Co., Melbourne, Victoria, Australia, Melbourne Dancers Co., Melbourne, Victoria, Australia, CLOC Musical Theatre, Melbourne, Victoria, Australia, Gilbert and Sullivan Soc., Melbourne, Victoria, Australia, Melbourne U. Gilbert and Sullivan Soc., Melbourne, Victoria, Australia; asst. condr. St. Aidan's Anglican Ch., Melbourne, Victoria, Australia; music dir. Altona City Theatre, Melbourne, Victoria, Australia, Lyric Opera, Melbourne, Victoria, Australia. Instrumentalist Marie Wilson Band, Melbourne, Victoria, Australia, 1992—94; guest condr. for lighting Guildford Philharm., Guildford, Surrey, England, 1995; guest condr. Rocky Mountain Ctr. Mus. Arts, Boulder, Colo., 1996, Boulder Philharm., Boulder, 1996; condr. & founder Colo. Quilt Chorus, Denver, 1997; guest condr. Golden Gate Opera, San Francisco, 2001, Women's Philharm., San Francisco, 2001—02, Sacramento Ballet & Empyrean Ensemble, Sacramento, 2002, Gay Games & Cultural Festival, Sydney, New South Wales, Australia, 2002, Goat Hall Prodns., San Francisco, 2002, Cmty. Women's Orch., San Francisco, 2005, Victorian Music Theatre Guild Awards, Melbourne, Victoria, Australia, Royal Women's Hosp. Fundraiser, Melbourne, Fairfield Hosp. Fundraiser, Melbourne, Ann. AIDS Requiem Svcs., Melbourne; asst. condr. Byrd-Cage Singers, Melbourne; cantor Toorak Uniting Ch. Choir, Melbourne; condr. Malvern City Coun. - ann. fundraiser,

Melbourne; instrumentalist Frankston City Band, Melbourne, Mordialloc City Band, Melbourne, Moomba Youth Band, Melbourne, Victoria, Australia; asst. condr. Intervarsity Choral Festival, Melbourne; instrumentalist Yamaha Youth Music Festival, Melbourne. Arranger (choral music concert suite) SFGMC Does Queen, (choral music) We Shall Overcome, Turn the World Around by Harry Belafonte, Every Time I Feel the Spirit, Harriet Tubman, Silent Night, Land of the Free, Peace Like a River; editor: (choral music) (by Gareth Valentine) Requiem in Memory of Those Who Have Died of AIDS; contbr. article to profl. jour., CD insert, ednl. pubs., electronic newsletter; prodr.: (comml. compact disc recording) Home for the Holidays (winner, OutMusic award, Outstanding New Choral Recording, 2006), Oh, Happy Day! (finalist OutMusic awards, Outstanding New Recording, choir or chorus, 2005), Closer Than Ever (winner, OutMusic Awards, Outstanding New Recording, choir or chorus, 2005); prodr.(and arranger): (comml. compact disc recording) Divas' Revenge; prodr.(and arranger): (comml. compact disc recording) SFGMC Does Queen (finalist, Outstanding new choral rec., OutMusic awards, 2002); contbr. comml. compact disc recording (Wash. Area Music award and finalist, Outstanding New Rec., OutMusic awards, 2001); composer: (choral music) Magnificat, On Love, May God Shield You, Don't Ask, Don't Tell; music dir. (comml. compact disc recordings) Beginnings, Five Years for Freedom, St. Aidan's Prayer for Lindisfarne. Mem. Bay Area Cmty. Women, San Francisco; grand marshal San Francisco Pride, 2006; musician City of Refuge United Ch. Christ, San Francisco, 2004—; bd. mem. Gay and Lesbian Assn. Choruses, Washington, 2002—03; ex-officio bd. mem. Golden Gate Performing Arts, Inc., San Francisco, 2004—. Fellow Enrollment Enhancement fellowship, U. of Colo., Coll. of Music, 1996 - 1997; Ambassadorial fellow, Rotary Internat., 1994 - 1995, Writing fellow, Choral Jour., Florence Bradford scholar, U. Melbourne, 1991, Ivy-Hay Pendlebury scholar, 1985. Mem.: ASCAP, Coll. Music Soc., Am. Choral Dirs. Assn., Gay and Lesbian Assn. Choruses, Inc., Am. Symphony Orch. League, Conductors Guild, Vancouver Men's Chorus, Lesbian/Gay Chorus of San Francisco, Seattle Men's Chorus, San Diego Men's Chorus, Atlanta Gay Men's Chorus, Buffalo Gay Men's Chorus, Coun. Oaks Men's Chorale, Houston Men's Chorus, Oakland East Bay Gay Men's Chorus, Rochester Gay Men's Chorus, Philadelphia Gay Men's Chorus, Triad Men's Chorus, Twin Cities Gay Men's Chorus, Pi Kappa Lambda. Achievements include first appointed woman conductor and artistic director of the world's oldest and largest openly gay men's chorus (founded 1978); along with life partner, was one of the same-sex couples married at San Francisco City Hall, February 23, 2004; conducted the U.S. and Australian premieres of the rock opera, Metropolis; conducted the U.S. and Australian premieres of the world's first AIDS Requiem (by Gareth Valentine - composed in 1991); conducted the Australian premiere of The Apple Tree by Jerry Bock; arranged for men's chorus and conducted John Rutter's renowned Gloria in honor of the work's 30th anniversary (December, 2004); founder of Australia's first women's orchestra; conducted performances at Carnegie Hall (NY), Kennedy Center (DC), Davies Symphony Hall (San Francisco), Salle Wilfrid Pelletier (Montreal, Canada), Grace Cathedral (San Francisco); conducted the Sacramento Ballet and the Empyrean Ensemble at the inaugural season of the Mondavi Center, Sacramento, CA; conducted a choir of 560 voices at the Sydney Opera House (Australia) for Gay Games VI (November, 2002); opening ceremonies Chgo. Gay Games VII (July 2006); performed with many celebrities, including: Carol Channing, Sir Ian McKellen, Alan Cumming, Joanna Gleason, Sharon Gless, B.D. Wong, Armistead Maupin, Nichelle Nichols, Julie Newmar, Cris Williamson; arranged music that has been performed by premier artists, including: Turtle Creek Chorale, Pot Pourri, Les Ms, Boston Gay Men's Chorus, Men Alive, Metropolitan Community Church Choir of San Francisco; arranged music performed by artists including: San Diego Men's Chorus, Atlanta Gay Men's Chorus, Buffalo Gay Men's Chorus, Seattle Men's Chorus, Houston Gay Men's Chorus, Twin Cities Gay Men's Chorus; arranged mucic performed by artists including: Lesbian/Gay Chorus San Francisco, Oakland Eastbay Gay Men's Chorus, Phila. Gay Men's Chorus, Rochester Gay Men's Chorus, Vancouver Men's Chorus; conducted a choir of 80 at Rosie O'Donnell's wedding at San Francisco City Hall, February 2004; completed AIDS Life Cycle V 585 mile bicycle ride from San Francisco to Los Angeles June 2006. Avocations: travel, culinary arts, outdoor sports, crossword puzzles. Office: Golden Gate Performing Arts Inc 1800 Market St PMB 1000 San Francisco CA 94102 Office Phone: 415-865-3650. Office Fax: 415-865-3655.

**MCGUIRE, KEVEN JAMES,** hydrologist, educator; b. Abington, Pa., Jan. 28, 1975; s. James Patrick and Carol Joan McGuire; m. Dana Friedman, June 10, 2000; 1 child, Brayden Charles. BS in Environ. Sci., Susquehanna U., Selinsgrove, Pa., 1997; MS in Forest Resources, Pa. State U., U. Pk., Pa., 1997; PhD in Forest Engring., Oreg. State U., Corvallis, Oreg., 2004. Grad. asst. Pa. State U., 1997-99; grad. asst. Oreg. State, 2000—04; post doctoral fellow Ga. Tech., Atlanta, 2004—05; asst. prof. Plymouth State U., NH, 2005—. Rsch. hydrologist Forest Svc. USDA, Durham, NH, 2005—. Mem.: Nat. Assn. Geoscience Tchrs., Am. Geophysical Union, Am. Water Resources Assn. Office: Ctr Environ Plymouth State Univ 17 High St MSC 63 Plymouth NH 03264

**MCGUIRE, LESIL L.,** state representative; b. Portland, Oreg., Jan. 22, 1971; Degree in Speech Comm. and Polit. Sci., Willamette U., 1993, JD, 1998. Legis. and press aide U.S. Senator Ted Stevens, 1993—95; legal intern U.S. Atty., 1996; law clk. Oreg. Dept. Justice, 1996—98; mem. Alaska Ho. of Reps., 2000—, judiciary com. Vol. Habitat for Humanity; mentor Bush Elem. Sch. Mentor Program; vol. Salem's Women's Crisis Ctr. Mem.: Young Rep., Anchorage Rep. Women's Club, Am. Diabetes Assn. Republican. Avocations: fishing, skiing, flying, scuba diving, reading. Office: Rm 118 State Capitol Juneau AK 99801-1182 Address: 716 W 4th Ave Ste 430 Anchorage AK 99501-2133 Office Phone: 907-269-0250. E-mail: lesilmcguire@yahoo.com.

**MCGUIRE, LILLIAN HILL (LILLIAN ELIZABETH HILL MCGUIRE),** historian, researcher, retired education educator, writer; b. Middlesex County, Va., 1928; d. Howard Garfield Hill, Sr. and Malissie O'Neal (Carter) Hill; m. Charles Edward McGuire, Aug. 11, 1957 (dec. July 30, 1997); children: Brenda Colette, Gina Renae, Laura Jane Fortune Battle. Student, Hampton Inst., 1946—48; BS, Morgan State U., 1951. Primary and Secondary Tchg. Cert. Va. Dept. of Edn. Classroom tchr. Richmond County Sch. Sys., Warsaw, Va., 1951—65, Essex County Sch. Sys., Tappahannock, Va., 1965—88; adult edn. tchr. Rappahannock C.C., Warsaw, Va., 1989—94; adult edn. tchr. Essex County Sch. Sys., Tappahannock, 1989—94. Pres. Essex Edn. Assn., Tappahannock, 1982—86, editor-news letter, 1982—88; historian Va. Ret. Tchrs. Assn., Blacksburg, 1995—97. Author: (book) The Vista of a Century: History of the Southside Rappahannock Baptist Association and Allied Bodies, 1977, Our Spiritual Heritage: History of First Baptist Church Tappahannock, VA, 1993, Uprooted & Transplanted: From Africa to America; Focus on African Americans in Essex County, VA, 2000, In Retrospect, 2005; contbr. poetry to Twilight Musings. Charter mem. Mid. Peninsula African-Am. Geneal. and Hist. Soc. Va., 2005—, Essex County Mus., Tappahannock, 1996—2006; mem. adv. coun. Essex County Mus. Hist. Soc., Tappahannock, 2006—; mem. NAACP Essex County Br., Tappahannock, 1950. Named Outstanding Elem. Sch. Tchr. of Am., Bd. of Advisors, Washington, 1974; recipient Honor award, Essex Edn. Assn., Tappahannock, 1977, Disting. Svc. award, 1982. Mem.: Internat. Soc. Poets, Mid. Peninsula Geneal. and Hist. Soc. Va. (charter mem.), Rappahannock Indsl. Acad. Alumni assn. (historian 1975), Morgan State U. Nat. Alumni Assn., Dist. A of Va. Ret. Tchrs. (life; historian 1988). Bapt. Avocations: writing, puzzles, travel, exercise. Home: 445 Marsh St PO Box 143 Tappahannock VA 22560

**MCGUIRE, MICHAEL FRANCIS,** plastic surgeon; b. St. Louis, Oct. 4, 1946; s. Arthur Patrick and Virginia Claribel (Gannon) McG. BA, Columbia U., 1968, MD, 1972. Diplomate Am. Bd. Surgery, Am. Bd. Plastic Surgery. Intern UCLA, 1972-73, resident in gen. surgery, 1973-77, resident in plastic surgery, 1978-80; fellow in plastic surgery rsch. Stanford (Calif.) U., 1977-78; traveling fellow in plastic surgery Gt. Britain, 1980; chief plastic surgery L.A. County-Olive View Med. Ctr., Sylmar, Calif., 1980-85; pvt. practice Santa Monica, Calif., 1980—; chief plastic surgery St. John's Health Ctr., 1990—; asst. clin. prof. surgery UCLA, 1980-97, assoc. clin. prof., 1998—. Bd. dirs. Calif. Med. Rev., Inc., sec-treas., 1997, v.p., 1997-99, chmn. bd. dirs.

1999—2003; chmn. surg. rev. St. Johns Health Ctr., 1996-98; pres. Pacific Coast Plastic Surgery Ctr., 1988—. Charter patron L.A. Music Ctr. Opera, 1983—; sponsoring patron Los Angeles County Art Mus., 1986—2005; patron Colleague Helpers in Philanthropic Svc., Bel Air, Calif., 1987, 93, 95; pres. Found. for Surg. Reconstrn., 1996—; bd. dirs., pres. Surg. Facilities Resource Inc., 2005—. Fellow ACS, Royal Soc. Medicine; mem. Am. Soc. Plastic Surgeons (membership chmn. 1997-2000, bd. dirs. 2002-05, sec. 2005—, chmn. leadership devel. com. 2004-), Am. Soc. Aesthetic Plastic Surgery (ethics chmn. 1998-99, bd. dirs. 2004—, pub. edn. chmn. 2004-05, commr. comm. 2005-), Am. Health Quality Assn. (bd. dirs. 1999—2005), L.A. County Med. Assn. (v.p. 1995-97, sec.-treas. 1997-99), Calif. Med. Assn. (del., exec. com., splty. delegation 1994-99), Calif. Soc. Plastic Surgery (exec. com., auditor 1988-89, program chmn. 1990, exec. coun. 1991-94, treas. 1994-97, v.p. 1997-98, acting pres. 1997, pres.-elect 1998-99, pres. 1999-2000, nominating com. chmn. 2000-01, strategic planning com. chmn. 2001—), Am. Assn. Accreditation of Ambulatory Surgery Facilities (ops. com. 1995-96, bd. dirs. 1996-2006, treas. 1996-98, sec. 1998-2000, v.p. 2000-02, pres. 2002-04), Alpha Omega Alpha. Avocations: golf, travel, collecting antique glass, opera, art. Office: 1301 20th St Ste 460 Santa Monica CA 90404-2054 Office Phone: 310-315-0121. Business E-Mail: mmcguire@ucla.edu.

**MCGUIRE, MICHAEL JOHN,** environmental engineer; b. San Antonio, June 29, 1947; s. James Brendan and Opal Mary (Brady) McG.; m. Deborah Marrow, June 19, 1971; children: David, Anna. BS in Civil Engring., U. Pa., 1969; MS in Environ. Engring., Drexel U., 1972, PhD in Environ. Engring., 1977. Diplomate Am. Acad. Environ. Engring.; registered profl. engr., Pa., N.J., Calif., Ariz., Tex. San. engr. Phila. Water Dept., 1969-73; rsch. assoc. Drexel U., Phila., 1976-77; prin. engr. Brown & Caldwell Cons. Engrs., Pasadena, Calif., 1977-79; water quality engr. Met. Water Dist. of So. Calif., L.A., 1979-84, water quality mgr., 1984-86, dir. water quality, 1986-90, asst. gen. mgr., 1990-92; pres. McGuire Environ. Cons., Inc., Santa Monica, Calif., 1992—2005; v.p. McGuire Malcolm Pirnie, Inc., Santa Monica, 2005—. Cons. to subcom. on adsorbents, safe drinking water com. Nat. Acad. Scis., 1978-79, NRC, Drinking Water Contaminants (comm. mem., 1999); cons. mem. Techs. Workgroup U.S. EPA, DBP Reg. Neg., 1992-93, 97, 98-2000. Editor: (with I.H. Suffet) Activated Carbon Adsorption of Organics from the Aqueous Phase, 2 vols., 1980, Treatment of Water by Granular Activated Carbon, 1983, (with J.L. McLain and A. Obolensky) Information Collection Rule Data Analysis, 2003; contbr. articles to profl. jours. Mem. ASCE, Internat. Water Assn. (specialist group on taste and odor control 1982—, chmn. organizing com. 1991, off-flavor symposium 1987-91), Internat. Ozone Assn. (internat. bd. dirs. 1992-95), Am. Water Works Assn. (hon., Calif.-Nev. sect. chmn. water quality and resources divsn. 1982-83, governing bd. 1984-87, 89-96, exec. com. 1989-96, chmn. 1991-92, nat. edn. divsn. chmn. 1982-83, 1994-96, chair taste and odor com. 1993-98, exec. com. 1994-96, water quality and tech. divsn. trustee 2004—, Acad. Achievement award 1978, Fuller award 1994, Publs. award 2001, George A. Elliot award 2005, Hon. Membership award 2006), Am. Chem. Soc., Sigma Xi, Sigma Nu, Sigma Tau. Office: McGuire Malcolm Pirnie Inc # 200 1919 Santa Monica Blvd Santa Monica CA 90404-1954

**MCGUIRE, RAYMOND J.,** investment banker; b. Dayton, Ohio; AB cum laude, Harvard Coll., 1979; MBA, Harvard Bus. Sch., 1984; JD, Harvard Law Sch., 1984. With Mergers & Acquisitions Group First Boston Corp., 1984—88; joined Wasserstein Perella & Co., 1988, ptnr., mng. dir., 1991—94; mng. dir. Mergers & Acquisitions Group Merrill Lynch, 1994—2000, Morgan Stanley, NYC, 2000—05; co-head Global Investment Banking Citigroup, 2005—. Pres. bd. trustees Internat. Ctr. Photography; trustee Whitney Mus. Art, mem. investment com.; trustee NY Presbyterian Hosp., Enterprise Found.; chmn. Studio Mus. Harlem, bd. dir.; chmn. De LaSalle Acad., bd. dir., The Enterprise Found., Joseph & Claire Flom Found., Howard Gilman Found.; mem. overseers, dirs. nominating com. Harvard U. Recipient Rotary Fellowship, U. of Nice, France, 1980. Office: Citigroup 388 Greenwich St New York NY 10013

**MCGUIRE, SANDRA LYNN,** nursing educator; b. Jan. 28, 1947; d. Donald Armstrong and Mary Lue (Harvey) Johnson; m. Joseph L. McGuire, Mar. 6, 1976; children: Matthew, Kelly, Kerry. BSN, U. Mich., 1969, MPH, 1973, EdD, 1988, MSN, 1997. Staff nurse Univ. Hosp., Ann Arbor, Mich., 1969; pub. health nurse Wayne County Health Dept., Eloise, Mich., 1969—72; instr. Madonna Coll., Livonia, Mich., 1973; pub. health coord. Plymouth Ctr. for Human devel., Northville, Mich., 1974—75; asst. prof. cmty. health nursing U. Mich., Ann Arbor, 1975—83; asst. prof. U. Tenn., Knoxville 1983—88, assoc. prof., 1990—, coord. gerontol. nurse practitioners program, 1998—, chair MSN program Coll. Nursing. Dir. Kids Are Tomorrow's Srs. Program, 1988—; resource person Gov.'s Com. Unification of Mental Health Svcs. in Mich.; spkr. profl. assns. and workshops. Author (with S. Clemen-Stone and D. Eigsti)): Comprehensive Community Health Nursing, 1981, Comprehensive Community Health Nursing, 5th edit., 1998, Comprehensive Community Health Nursing, 6th edit., 2002. Bd. dirs. Ctr. Understanding Aging, 1987-93, v.p., 1995; bd. dirs. Mich. chpt. ARC, 1980-83, Knoxville chpt., 1984-85; founder Knoxville Intergenerational Network, 1989. Recipient John W. Runyan, Jr. Cmty. Health Nursing award U. Tenn. Memphis, 2002, Outstanding Svc. award U. Tenn. Knoxville Libr. Friends, 2004; USPHS fellow, 1972-73, Robert Woodruff fellow Emory U., 1996-97, Hewlett Innovative Tech. fellow U. Tenn., Knoxville, 1999-00, Profl. Devel. awardee U. Tenn. Knoxville, 1996-97, 99-2000. Mem. ANA, AARP Nat. Policy Coun., Tenn. Nurses Assn., Soc. Gerontological Soc. Am., Assn. Gerontology, Nat. Conf. Gerontol. Nurse Practitioners, Nat. Gerontol. Nursing Assn., Mich. Pub. Health Assn. (chmn. mental health sect. 1976, dir., co-chmn. residential svcs. com. 1976-79, chmn. health svcs. 1979-82), Nat. Assn. Retarded Citizens, Mich. Assn. Retarded Citizens, Nat. Coun. on Aging, Ctr. for Understanding Aging (v.p. 1994-95), Plymouth (chmn. residential svcs. com. 1975-77), Tenn. Assn. Retarded Citizens, So. Nursing Rsch. Soc., Sigma Theta Tau, Pi Lambda Theta, Phi Kappa Phi. Home: 11008 Crosswind Dr Knoxville TN 37934 Office: 1200 Volunteer Blvd Knoxville TN 37996 Office Phone: 865-974-7589. Business E-Mail: smcguire@utk.edu.

**MCGUIRE, THOMAS PETER,** show boat captain, secondary school educator; b. N.Y.C., Apr. 27, 1945; s. Thomas Edward and Susan Rose (Cafarelli) McG. BA, Calif. State U., 1979, postgrad., 1979-83, MA in English CUNY, 1993. co. mgr. Vaudeville Driftwood Floating Theatre, 1963-75; Tchr., St. Philip's Sch., Pasadena, Calif., 1981-83; prodr. Driftwood Floating Theatre, 1968-75; owner, capt. Driftwood ShowBoat, Kingston, N.Y., 1983-98; pres. Driftwood ShowBoat Co., 1983—; tchr. English John F. Kennedy H.S., N.Y.C., 1986-2003; mem. faculty, founding mem. adv. com. Bronx Theatre H.S., 2003-; guest lectr. Hayden Planetarium, N.Y.C., 1960-64. Contbr. articles to profl. jours. Activist in human rights and equal rights. Served with USN, 1966-68. Mem. Am. Guild Variety Artists, Soc. Am. Magicians, Lesbian and Gay Tchrs. Assn. N.Y.C. (pres. 1998—). Roman Catholic. Avocations: writing, ballooning, astronomy. Home and Office: Driftwood Showboat PO Box 1032 Kingston NY 12402-1032

**MCGUIRE, TIM,** editor; Mng. editor Star Tribune, Mpls., 1979—92, editor, sr. v.p., 1992—2002; syndicated columnist United Media, 2002—. Juror Pulitzer Prize, 2002; prof. Washington & Lee U., Lexington, Va., Davidson Coll. Sch. Journalism & Pub. Policy, NC. Author: (weekly column) More Than Work, 2002—. Mem.: Am. Soc. Newspaper Editors (pres. 2001—02). Roman Catholic. Office: Star Tribune 425 Portland Ave Minneapolis MN 55488-0002*

**MCGUIRE, TIMOTHY JAMES,** lawyer, editor, columnist; b. Mount Pleasant, Mich., Mar. 24, 1949; s. James Edward and Anita Matilda (Starr) McGuire; m. T. Jean Fannin, May 10, 1975; children: Tracy, Jason, Jeffrey. BA, Aquinas Coll., Grand Rapids, Mich., 1971; JD cum laude, William Mitchell Coll. Law, St. Paul, 1987. Bar: Minn. 1987. Mng. editor Ypsilanti Press, Mich., 1973—75, Corpus Christi Caller, Tex. 1975—77, Lakeland Ledger, Fla., 1977—79, Mpls. Star, 1979—82; mng. editor features and sports Mpls. Star and Tribune, 1982—84, mng. editor, 1984—91, exec. editor,

1991—93, editor, sr. v.p., 1993—2002; syndicated columnist, spkr. on workplace spirituality, ethics and values. Pulitzer Prize juror, 1988—89, 1995—2002. Lay preacher at St. Joseph Roman Cath. Ch., Mpls., 1995—. Mem.: Minn. State Bar Assn., Am. Soc. Newspaper Editors (bd. dirs. 1992—, chmn. change com. 1994—95, chmn. program com. 1996—97, treas. 1998—99, sec. 1999—2000, v.p. 2000—01, pres. 2001—02). Roman Catholic.

**MCGUIRE, TIMOTHY WILLIAM,** economics and management educator, dean; b. Englewood, NJ, Nov. 30, 1938; s. Charles James and Marie (McCarthy) McG.; children: Timothy William Jr., Gretchen Elizabeth, Michael Joseph; m. Nancy Paule Melone, 1991. BS in Indsl. Mgmt., Carnegie Inst. Tech., 1960, MS in Econs., 1961; PhD in Econs., Stanford U., 1968. Staff mem. Coun. Econ. Advisors, 1963—64; rsch. assoc. econs. Grad. Sch. Indsl. Administrn. Carnegie Mellon U., Pitts., 1964—66, asst. prof. econs. Grad. Sch. Indsl. Administrn., 1966—69, assoc. prof. Grad. Sch. Indsl. Administrn., 1969—75, prof. Grad. Sch. Indsl. Administrn., 1975—79, prof. mgmt. and econs. Grad. Sch. Indsl. Administrn., 1982—, dep. dean Grad. Sch. Indsl. Administrn., 1983—90, prof. social scis. and econs. Dept. Social Scis., 1981—82; prof. econs., chmn. dept. U. Iowa, Iowa City, 1979—80; dean, Harry B. Miller prof. bus. Charles H. Lundquist Coll. Bus. U. Oreg., Eugene, 1994—98; COO, sr. exec. v.p. Mgmt. Sci. Assocs., Inc., Pitts., 1998—2005, chmn.; sr. exec. v.p., 2005—. Sr. visitor U. Cambridge, England, 1970; bd. dirs. Mgmt. Sci. Assocs., Inc., Pitts.; bd. visitors Joseph M. Katz Grad. Sch. Bus., U. Pitts. Contbr. articles to profl. jours. Bd. trustees Point Park Coll.; chmn. corp. adv. bd. Pitts.(Pa.) Ctr. Sports, Arts and Entertainment Mgmt. Fellow, Ford Found., 1962—63, 1970—71; Woodrow Wilson Nat. Hon. fellow, Carnegie Inst. Tech., 1960—61, Stanford U. fellow, 1961—62. Mem.: Soc. Judgment and Decision Making, Omicron Delta Kappa, Tau Beta Pi. Home: 118 Lakeland Dr Mars PA 16046-2114 Office: Mgmt Sci Assocs Inc 6565 Penn Ave Pittsburgh PA 15206-4490 Office Phone: 412-362-2000. Business E-Mail: tmcguire@msa.com.

**MCGUIRE, WALTER F.,** library director; BA, Earlham Coll.; MLS, U. Ky. Joined St. Louis Pub. Libr., 1989, dep. dir., 1994—2004, exec. dir., 2004—. Office: St Louis Pub Libr 1301 Olive St Saint Louis MO 63103 Office Phone: 314-241-2288. Office Fax: 314-539-0393.*

**MCGUIRE, WILLIAM,** civil engineer, educator; b. S.I., N.Y., Dec. 17, 1920; s. Edward Joseph and Phoebe (Sellman) McG.; m. Barbara Weld, Feb. 5, 1944; children: Robert Weld, Thomas Rhodes. BSCE, Bucknell U., 1942; MSCE, Cornell U., 1947. Structural designer Jackson & Moreland (engrs.), Boston, 1947-49; faculty Cornell U., Ithaca, 1949—, prof. civil engring., 1960-90, prof. emeritus of civil engring., 1990—; dir. Cornell U. (Sch. Civil Engring.), 1966-68; vis. prof. civil engring. Asian Inst. Tech., Bangkok, Thailand, 1968-70. Vis. research engr. Nat. Bur. Standards, 1972; Gledden vis. sr. fellow U. Western Australia, 1973; cons. structural engr., 1951—; vis. prof. U. Tokyo, 1979, U. Strathclyde, 1986 Author: Steel Structures, 1967; author: (with R.H. Gallagher and R.D. Ziemian) Matrix Structural Analysis, 1979, 2d edit., 2000. Served to lt. USNR, 1942-45. Recipient Naval Letter of Commendation, award for Outstanding Achievement, Bucknell U., 1987, T.R. Higgins Lectureship award Am. Inst. Steel Constrn., 1992, G. Haaijer awrd Am. Inst. Steel Constrn., 2000, L. Beedle award Structural Stability Rsch. Coun., 2005. Fellow ASCE (pres. Ithaca 1964, Norman medal 1962, 94, Hardesty award 1992, honorary mem. 1994); mem. Internat. Assn. Bridge and Structural Engring., Nat. Acad. Engring., Sigma Xi, Chi Epsilon, Kappa Delta Rho. Congregationalist. Home: 121 Simsbury Dr Ithaca NY 14850-1728 Business E-Mail: wm20@cornell.edu.

**MCGUIRE, WILLIAM ALBERT,** humanities educator; b. St. Louis, Mar. 18, 1944; s. William Albert and Virginia Marie (Grant) McGuire. BA, St. Louis U., 1966; MA, San Francisco State U., 1976. Instr. De Andreas H.S., St. Louis, 1966—69, Presentation H.S., San Francisco, 1977—91, U. San Francisco, 1992—97, San Francisco State U., 1995, City Coll. of San Francisco, 1975—. Coord. humanities City Coll. of San Francisco, 1998—. Mem. Soc. for the Preservation of San Francisco Archl. Heritage, 1986—, E-5 U.S. Army, 1969—71. Mem.: C.C. Humanities Assn., Calif. Humanities Assn., ACLU, UNICEF, Friends of Urban Forest, Amnesty Internat., Vets. for Peace, Sierra Club. Democrat. Roman Catholic. Avocations: music, gardening, cooking, writing. Office: City Coll of San Francisco 50 Phelan Ave San Francisco CA 94112 Office Phone: 415-452-7257. Business E-Mail: wmcguire@ccsf.edu.

**MCGUIRE, WILLIAM B(ENEDICT),** lawyer; b. Newark, Feb. 14, 1929; children: Joan Ellen, Ralph R., James C., Keith P., Grant W. BS, Fordham U., 1950; JD, Seton Hall U., 1958; LLM in Taxation, NYU, 1963. Bar: N.J. 1958, U.S. Dist. Ct. N.J. 1958, U.S. Supreme Ct. 1971, U.S. Ct. Appeals (3d cir.) 1980, N.Y. 1982. Chief acct. Hanover Fire Ins. Co., N.Y.C., 1950-58; sr. ptnr. Lum, Blunno & Tompkins, Newark, 1958-83, Tompkins McGuire Wachenfeld & Barry LLP, Newark, 1984—, mng. ptnr. Asst. prosecutor Essex County, N.J., 1964-65; trustee St. Barnabas Corp., St. Barnabas Med. Ctr. and Irvington Gen. Hosp.; mem. Essex County Ethics Com., 1974-77; chair bd. visitors Seton Hall U., Sch. Law, 2005— Fellow Am. Coll. Trial Lawyers, Am. Bar Found. (state chmn. 1990-95), Am. Bd. Trial Advocates, Internat. Acad. Trial Lawyers, Internat. Soc. Barristers; mem. ABA, N.J. State Bar Assn. (trustee 1982-89, sec. 1989-90, treas. 1990-91, 2d v.p. 1991-92, 1st v.p. 1992-93, pres.-elect 1993-94, pres. 1994-95), N.J. State Bar Found. (pres. 1988-89), Essex County Bar Assn. (pres. 1975-76), Internat. Assn. Ins. Counsel, Fedn. Ins. Counsel, Def. Rsch. Inst., Maritime Law Assn., Trial Attys. N.J., Assn. Fed. Bar N.J. (pres. 1985-88), Essex County Country Club (pres. 1983), Newark Club. Roman Catholic. Office: Tompkins McGuire Wachenfeld & Barry LLP 4 Gateway Ctr 100 Mulberry St Newark NJ 07102-4007 Office Phone: 973-622-3000. Office Fax: 973-623-7780. Business E-Mail: wmcguire@tompkinsmcguire.com.

**MCGUIRE, WILLIAM DENNIS,** healthcare consultant; b. Glen Ridge, NJ, Sept. 24, 1943; s. John William and Kathleen Mary (Sexton) McG.; m. Nancy Katherine Hoyne, Aug. 13, 1966; children: Kathleen Anne, Colleen Dempsey. BA, U. Notre Dame, 1965; M.H.A., U. Mich., 1968. Asst. administr. U. Wis. Hosps., Madison, 1971-74; administr. Children's Hosp. Ctr. Dayton, Ohio, 1974-79; COO Mercy Cath. Med. Ctr., Phila., 1979-80; CEO Wills Eye Hosp., Phila., 1980-85; pres., CEO Mercy Health Care Sys., Scranton, Pa., 1985-89, Mt. Carmel Health, Columbus, Ohio, 1989-92, Incarnate Word Health Svcs., San Antonio, 1992-95, Cath. Med. Ctrs. of Bklyn. and Queens, N.Y.C., 1996—2000, Kaleida Health, Buffalo, 2002—06; health care cons., 2000—. Adj. faculty dept. health care Trinity U., 1992-95, Harvard Bus. Sch. Club, 2003-06; asst. prof. Ohio State U., 1990-92; asst. clin. prof. Wright State U. Sch. medicine, Dayton, Ohio, 1978-79; instr. U. Wis. Madison, 1972-73; mem. Wilkes Coll. Health Administrn. Adv. Com, 1988-89; bd. dirs. Coll. Misericordia Health Care Task Force, 1988-89; bd. govs. League Vol. Hosps., 1996-2000, sec., 1997-2000; mem. bd. govs. Fidelis Care N.Y., 1996-2000, Queensbrook Ins. Ltd., 1996-2000, vice chmn., 1996-97, chmn., 1997-2000; trustee Cmty. Blood Ctr., 1977-79; trustee Cath. Social Svcs., 1976-79, pres. 1978-79; bd. dirs. Coop. Purchasing Coun., 1974-79; mem. Dayton Pub. Schs. Lay Adv. Com. on Vocat. Edn., 1974-79; pres. Dayton Area Young Administrs. Group, 1977; pres. elect Greater Dayton Area Hosp. Assn., 1979; mem. allied health techs. adv. com. Sinclair C.C., 1974-79. Bd. dirs. Covenant Health Svcs., 1992-2003, chmn. fin. com. 2001-03, Fletcher Allen Health Care, 2002-03, Consol. Cath. Risk Retention Group, 1992-95, Cath. Charities, 1996-2000, Primary Care Devel. Corp., 1997-2000. Buffalo Niagara Partnership, 2002—06, D'Youville Coll., 2004—06; active Health Policy Forum, United Hosp. Fund, United Way, ARC. Mem. Am. Coll. Healthcare Execs., Acad. for Cath. Health Care Leadership, Mercy Leadership Group. nat. commn. Cath. health care ministry), Maj. Cath. Health Alliance (sec. 1990-95, chmn. 1997-99), Health Care Fin. Mgmt. Assn., Am. Assn. Univ. Profs. Ophthalmology, Am. Soc. Law and Medicine, Am. Hosp. Assn., Am. Assn. Eye and Ear Hosps. (pres.-elect 1984-85), Health Mgmt. Edn. Assn. (mem. 1987-88), Hosp. Assn. N.Y. State (bd. dirs. 1998-2000, 02-05), Greater N.Y. Hosp. Assn. (mem. bd. govs. 1997-2000, 02-06), Tex. Hosp. Assn., We. N.Y. Hosp. Assn. (bd. dirs. 2002-05), Ohio Hosp. Assn.,

Hosp. Assn. Pa., Cath. Health Assn., Am. Pub. Health Assn., Pa. Pub. Health Assn., Del. Valley Hosp. Council, Pa. Emergency Health Svcs. Coun., Del. County Emergency Health Svcs. Coun., Nat. Union Hosp. and Health Care Employees (plan trustee), Pa. Hosps. Ins. Co. Adv. Coun., 1988-89. C. of C., U. Notre Dame Alumni Assn., U. Mich. Alumni Assn., U. Wis. Med. Sch. Alumni Assn., Wills Eye Soc., Sorin Soc., Badin Guild, Notre Dame Club (pres. 1971, v.p. 1983-84), Dominion Country Club. Office: 6 Clubhouse Green San Antonio TX 78257 Home: 6 Clubhouse Grn San Antonio TX 78257-1295 Office Phone: 716-698-6543. Personal E-mail: billmcg@together.net.

**MCGUIRE, WILLIAM JAMES,** psychologist, educator; b. N.Y.C., Feb. 17, 1925; s. James William and Anne M. (Mitchell) McG.; m. Claire Vernick, Dec. 29, 1954; children: James William, Anne Maureen, Steven Thomas. BA, Fordham U., 1949, MA, 1950; PhD, Yale U., 1954; PhD (hon.), Eötvös U., Budapest, Hungary, 1990, U. Bologna, Italy, 2005. Postdoctoral fellow U. Minn., 1954-55; assoc. prof. psychology U. Ill., 1958-61; prof. Columbia U., 1961-67, U. Calif., San Diego, 1967-70; vis. prof. London Sch. Econs., 1970-71; asst. prof. Yale U., New Haven, 1955-58, prof., 1970—, chmn. dept. psychology, 1971-73. Mem. adv. panel for sociology and social psychology NSF, 1963-65; mem. review panel for social scis. NIMH, 1968-72, cons. 1974-95. Author: Content and Processes in the Experience of Self, 1988, A Perspectivist Approach to Strategic Planning, 1989, Structure of Attitudes and Attitude Systems, 1989, The Content, Structure, and Operation of Thought Systems, 1991, Explorations in Political Psychology, 1993, Creative Hypothesis Generating in Psychology, 1997, Constructing Social Psychology: Creative and Critical Processes, 1999, After a Half Century of Election Studies: Whence, Where and Whither, 2001; contbr. to Ency. Brit.; editor Jour. Personality and Social Psychology, 1967-70; cons. editor European Jour. Social Psychology, 1978—, Jour. Applied Social Psychology, 1983—, Jour. Exptl. Social Psychology, 1994—, Comm. Rsch., 1988—, Human Comm. Rsch., 2001—, Jour. Commn., 2002—, Applied Psychology in Hungary, 2002—; contbr. Ency. Psychology. With AUS, 1943-46. Recipient Am. Social Psychology award AAAS, 1964, Gen. Electric Found. awards, 1963, 64, 66, Disting. Scientist award Soc. Exptl. Social Psychology, 1992, Disting. Sci. award Internat. Soc. Political Psychology, 1999; grantee NSF, 1960-79, NIH, 1979-99; Fulbright fellow Louvain (Belgium) U., 1950-51, Ctr. for Advanced Study in Behavioral Scis. fellow, 1965-66, Guggenheim fellow, 1970-71, William James fellow Am. Psychol. Soc., 1989—. Fellow APA (pres. divsn. personality and social psychology 1973-74, Disting. Sci. Contbn. award 1988), Am. Acad. Arts and Scis.; mem. Am. Sociol. Assn., Am. Assn. Pub. Opinion Rsch., Sigma Xi. Home: 225 St Ronan St New Haven CT 06511-2313 Office: Yale U Dept Psychology PO Box 208205 New Haven CT 06520-8205 Office Phone: 203-432-4535. Business E-Mail: william.mcguire@yale.edu.

**MCGUIRE, WILLIAM W.,** health insurance company executive; b. Troy, NY, 1948; m. Nadine McGuire; 2 children. BA, U. Tex., 1970, MD, 1974. Internal med. resident, chief resident & pulmonary fellow U. Tex. Health Sci. Ctr., San Antonio, 1974—78; rschr. Scripps Clinic & Rsch. Found., La Jolla, Calif., 1978—80; practicing physician Colo. Springs, 1980—85; v.p. health systems Peak Health Plan, 1985—86, med. dir., Coastguard, 1985—86, pres., COO, 1985—88; exec. v.p. United Healthcare Corpn., Minnetonka, Minn., 1988—89, pres., 1989—91, CEO, chmn., 1991—98, UnitedHealth Grp., Inc., Minnetonka, 1998—; founder William W. McGuire & Nadine M. McGuire Family Found. Chmn. Colo. Found. for Med. Care, Region 111, 1984—85; bd. dirs. UnitedHealth Grp. Inc. (formerly United HealthCare Corp.), 1989—, Minn. Bus. Partnership. Trustee Mpls. Inst. Arts; dir. Minn. Orch. Assn. Named one of Forbes' Richest Americans, 2006. Mem.: NIH Nat. Cancer Policy Bd. Office: UnitedHealth Group Inc PO Box 1459 Minneapolis MN 55440*

**MCGUIRE-RIGGS, SHEILA,** Democratic party chairman; Chmn. Iowa Democrat Party, Iowa. Democrat. Mailing: 5661 Fleur Dr Des Moines IA 50321 E-mail: smriggs@iowademocrats.org.

**MCGUIRK, RONALD CHARLES,** retired bank executive, economic advisor; b. Balt., Dec. 9, 1938; s. Charles F. and Grace E. (Delcher) McG.; m. Katherine Sauer, Oct. 1, 1960; children: Frank D., Ann E. Student, St. John's Coll., Annapolis, Md., 1956-59. Sr. data processing officer 1st Nat. Bank, Balt., 1966-72, v.p. data processing, 1972-76, v.p. mktg., 1976-80, sr. v.p. mktg., 1980-90, sr. v.p. corp. plan, chief of staff to CEO, 1990-94; sr. v.p., corp. sec. 1st Md. Bancorp, Balt., 1995-99; sr. econ. advisor Anne Arundel County, Md., 1999—. Bd. dirs., v.p., treas. Balto-Washington Med. Ctr., Glen Burnie, Md., 1974—, v.p., 1999—; bd. dirs., treas. Internet Inc., 1990-95, Glen Burnie Town Ctr. Com., 1995—, AACO Conf. and Vis. Bd., 1999—, Annapolis Symphony, 1991-92; trustee Mt. Washington Pediat. Hosp., 1997—2004; mem. adv. bd. Hist. Annapolis Found., 1982-85, pres. 1985-90; chmn. Annapolis Boundary Commn., 1983-84; mem. Anne Arundel County Coun., 1974-82, Anne Arundel County Libr. Bd., 1974-84; pres. Anne Arundel County Scholarship for Scholars/Bd. Edn., 1983-85, treas., 1985-88; mem. Anne Arundel County Charter Rev. Commn., 1986, Anne Arundel County Govt. Salary Commn., 1985, 89; chmn. Anne Arundel County Impact Fee Study Task Force, 1987; pres. Anne Arundel County YMCA, 1987-89, bd. dirs., 1982-87, 89-90; mem. Commn. for Ednl. Excellence, 1988-90; vice chmn. Ft. Meade Coordinating Coun., 1989-91; mem. Exec. Com. Md. Bus.-Industry PAC, 1991-99, Anne Arundel County Charter and Orgn. Transition Group, 1991; corp. ptnr. Sch. Bus. and Mgmt. Morgan State U. 1991-92; trustee Md. Hist. Soc., 1995-96; co-chair Anne Arundel County transition fin. com., 1998-99; chair adhoc Fire Dept. Com., 2003-04. Mem. Ctr. Club. Democrat. Roman Catholic. Office: Arundel Ctr Calvert St Annapolis MD 21401 Office Phone: 410-222-1821. Personal E-mail: rm21061@aol.com. Business E-Mail: rmcguirk@aacounty.org.

**MCGUIRK, TERRENCE,** former broadcasting company executive; b. Bklyn., Apr. 2, 1925; s. William Edward and Loretta Beatrice (Lanigan) McG.; m. Gloria Helen Geoghan, June 17, 1950; children: Terence F., Sara McGuirk Duncan, Susan McGuirk Blank, Elizabeth McGuirk Magee, Melissa McGuirk Bowman, Bryan, Michelle McGuirk O'Connor. BS, Fordham U., 1950. Nat. sales mgr. St. WAGA-TV, Atlanta, 1966-68; mgr. Sta. WAGA-TV, Atlanta, 1970-75; eastern sales mgr. Storer TV Sales, N.Y.C., 1968-70; pres., gen. mgr. Sta. WTEN-TV, Albany, NY, 1976-82; pres. Knight-Ridder Broadcasting, Inc., 1982-85; ret. Assoc. trustee Siena Coll., Loudonville, N.Y., 1979-83; trustee Meml. Hosp. Found., 1980-83; dir. Albany chpt. ARC, 1987-91. Served with U.S. Army, 1943-46. Mem. Mariner Sands Country Club, Babylon Yacht Club (hon.).

**MCGUIRL, MARLENE DANA CALLIS,** law librarian, educator; b. Hammond, Ind., Mar. 22, 1938; d. Daniel David and Helen Elizabeth (Baludis) Callis; m. James Franklin McGuirl, Apr. 24, 1965. AB, Ind. U., 1959; JD, DePaul U., 1963; MALS, Rosary Coll., 1965; LLM, George Washington U., 1978; postgrad., Harvard U., 1985. Bar: Ill. 1963, Ind. 1964, D.C. 1972. Asst. DePaul Coll. of Law Libr., 1961-62, asst. law libr., 1962-65; ref. law librarian Boston Coll. Law Sch. Libr., 1965-66; libr. dir. D.C. Bar Libr., 1966-70; asst. chief Am.-Brit. Law Divsn. Libr. of Congress, Washington, 1970, chief, 1970-90, environ. cons., 1990—; counsel Cooter & Gell, 1992-93; administr. Washington Met. Transit Authority, 1994—2004. Libr. cons. Nat. Clearinghouse on Proverty Law, OEO, Washington, 1967-69, Northwestern U. Nat. Inst. Edn. in Law and Poverty, 1969, D.C. Office of Corp. Counsel, 1969-70; instr. law librarianship Grad. Sch. of Library U.S. Dept. of Agr., 1968-72; lectr. legal lit. Cath. U., 1972; adj. prof., 1973-91; assoc. prof. environ. law George Washington U., 1979—; judge Nat. and Internat. Law Moot Ct. Competition, 1976-78, 90—; pres. Hamburger Heaven, Inc., Palm Beach, Fla., 1981-91, L'Image de Marlene Ltd., 1986-92, Clinique de Beauté Inc., 1987-92, Heads & Heads Inc., 1987-92, Horizon Design & Mfg. Co., Inc., 1987—; dir. Stoneridge Farm Inc., Gt. Falls, Va., 1984—. Contbr. articles to profl. jours. Mem. Georgetown Citizens Assn.; trustee D.C. Law Students in Ct.; del. Ind. Democratic Conv., 1964. Recipient Meritorious Svc. award Libr. on Congress, 1974, letter of commendation Dirs. of Pers., 1976, cert. of appreciation, 1981-84. Mem. ABA (facilities law libr. Congress com.

1976-89), Fed. Bar Assn. (chpt. council 1972-76), Ill. Bar Assn., Women's Bar Assn. (pres. 1972-73, exec. bd. 1973-77, Outstanding Contbn. to Human Rights award 1975), D.C. Bar Assn., Am. Bar Found., Nat. Assn. Women Lawyers, Am. Assn. Law Libraries (exec. bd. 1973-77), Law Librarians Soc. of Washington (pres. 1971-73), Exec. Women in Govt. Home: 3416 P St NW Washington DC 20007-2705 Personal E-mail: marlenemcguirl@aol.com.

**MCGUNNIGLE, GEORGE FRANCIS,** lawyer, judge; b. Rochester, N.Y., Feb. 22, 1942; s. George Francis and Mary Elizabeth (Curran) McG.; m. Priscilla Ann Lappin, July 13, 1968; children: Cynthia A., Brian P. AB, Boston Coll., 1963; LLB, Georgetown U., 1966; LLM, George Wash. U., 1967. Bar: Conn. 1971, Minn. 1972, U.S. Dist. Ct. D.C. 1967, U.S. Dist. Ct. Conn. 1971, U.S. Dist. Ct. Minn. 1972, U.S. Ct. Appeals (2d cir.) 1971, U.S. Ct. Appeals (8th cir.) 1977, U.S. Supreme Ct. 1986. Asst. U.S. atty. Office of U.S. Atty., Bridgeport, Conn., 1971—72; assoc. Leonard, Street and Deinard, Mpls., 1972—73, ptnr., 1974—2000; judge Fourth Jud. Dist., Mpls., 2000—. Editor: Business Torts Litigation, 1992. Bd. dirs. Cath. Charities, 1997—2003, North Ctrl. chpt. Arthritis Found., Mpls., 1986-92, 94—2003, mem. exec. com., 1988-92, 2001—03. Lt. JAGC, USN, 1967-71. Recipient Nat. Vol. Svc. citation Arthritis Found., 1992. Mem. ABA (litigation sect., chmn. bus. torts litigation com. 1988-91, divsn. dir. 1991-92, 97-98, coun. 1992-95, sect. of dispute resolution coun. 2000-01). Avocation: reading. Office: Fourth Judicial Dist C-1251 Hennepin County Govt Ctr Minneapolis MN 55487-0422 Office Phone: 612-596-7730. E-mail: george.mcgunnigle@courts.state.mn.us.

**MCGURK, CHRISTOPHER J.,** former film company executive; b. 1957; BS, Syracuse U.; MBA, U. Chgo. Various positions including CFO Pepsico, 1982—88; sr. v.p. fin. Walt Disney Studios, 1988-90, exec. v.p., CFO, 1990—94, pres. motion pictures group, 1994—96; various positions including pres., CEO Universal Pictures, 1996—99; vice chmn., COO Metro-Goldwyn-Mayer Inc., 1999—2005; sr. advisor new ventures IDT Entertainment, 2006—. Exec. prodr.: (films) The Brothers Grimm, 2005. Office: IDT Entertainment 520 Broad St Newark NJ 07102 Fax: 310-264-8690.*

**MCGURK, MICHAEL R.,** lawyer; b. Abington, Pa., Feb. 11, 1960; BSChemE, U. Del., 1983; JD, George Washington U., 1988. Bar: Pa. 1988, NJ 1988, DC 1990, Mass. 2002, registered: US Patent & Trademark Office, lic.: US Ct. Appeals (Fed. Cir.) 1990, US Supreme Ct. 1993, US Ct. Appeals (9th Cir.) 2000. Examiner US Patent & Trademark Office, 1985—87; with Finnegan, Henderson, Farabow, Garrett & Dunner LLP, 1987—, ptnr., Chem./ Metall. Practice Group, leader, Interference Sect. Adj. prof. George Mason U., 1998—2000. Mem.: Am. Chem. Soc., Am. Intellectual Property Law Assn. (chmn. pub. info. com. 1996—98), ABA (Litig. Sect., Patent, Trademark & Copyright Law Sect.), Fed. Cir. Bar Assn., Pa. Bar Assn., DC Bar Assn. (Patent, Trademark & Copyright Law Sects.), Boston Patent Law Assn., Boston Bar Assn. Office: Finnegan Henderson Farabow Garrett & Dunner LLP 55 Cambridge Pky Cambridge MA 02142 Office Phone: 617-452-1600. Office Fax: 617-452-1666. Business E-Mail: michael.mcgurk@finnegan.com.

**MC GURN, BARRETT,** communications executive, writer; b. N.Y.C., Aug. 6, 1914; s. William Barrett and Alice (Schneider) McG.; m. Mary Elizabeth Johnson, May 30, 1942 (dec. Feb. 1960); children: William Barrett III, Elizabeth Hehn, Andrew; m. Janice Ann McLaughlin, June 19, 1962; children: Summers, Martin Barrett, Mark Barrett. AB, Fordham U., 1935, LittD (hon.), 1958. Editor-in-chief Fordham Ram, 1934-35; with N.Y. Herald Tribune, 1935-66, asst. corr. Rome, 1939, bur. chief, 1946-52, 55-62, reporting staff NY, 1935-42, 62-66, bur. chief Paris, 1952—55, acting chief bur. Moscow, 1958; with, assignments in Morocco, Algeria, Tunisia, Hungary (1956 revolution), Egypt, Greece, Yugoslavia, Poland, Cen. Africa, Gaza Strip.; press attache Am. Embassy, Rome, 1966-68, counselor for press affairs Saigon, 1968—69; U.S. consular officer, sec. appointed by Pres., 1969; dir. U.S. Govt. Press Ctr., Vietnam, 1968-69; White House and Pentagon liaison for State Dept. spokesman Washington, 1969-72; World Affairs commentator USIA, 1972-73; dir. pub. info. U.S. Supreme Ct., Washington, 1973-82; dir. communications Cath. Archdiocese of Washington, 1984-87; pres. Carroll Pub. Co. pub. Cath. Standard and El Pregonero, 1987-91; dir. Our Sunday Visitor Pub. Co., 1988-98. Mem. Italian-Am. com. to select Italian fellowship winners for study in U.S., 1950-52; mem. U.S. Nat. Cath. Com. on Comm. Policy, 1970-74, White House Com. on Drug Control Info., 1970-72; mem. interdept. com. on U.S. govt. press info. policy, 1970, interdept. U.S. govt. task force to rescue 100 Ams. kidnapped in Jordan, 1970, one-man U.S. Presdl. mission to Cambodia on media news problems, 1970; archivist John Carroll Soc., Washington, 1990-97. Author: Decade in Europe, 1959, A Reporter Looks at the Vatican, 1962, A Reporter Looks at American Catholicism, 1967, America's Court, The Supreme Court and The People, 1997, The Pilgrim's Guide to Rome, 1999, Yank, Reporting the Greatest Generation, 2004; contbg. author: The Best from Yank, 1945, Yank, the GI Story of the War, 1946, Combat, 1950, Highlights from Yank, 1953, Overseas Press Club Cook Book, 1962, I Can Tell it Now, 1964, U.S. Book of Facts, Statistics and Information, 1966, New Catholic Treasury of Wit and Humor, 1967, How I Got that Story, 1967, Heroes for Our Times, 1968, Newsbreak, 1975, Saints for all Seasons, 1978, Informing the People, 1981, The Courage to Grow Old, 1989, Am. Peoples Encyclopedia Yearbook, Close To Glory: Yank Correspondents Untold Stories of World War II, 1992; contbr. articles to profl. jours. Trustee Corrs. Fund, 1965-68; mem. bd. Anglo-Am. Charity Fund in Italy, 1967-68; v.p. Citizens Assn., Westmoreland Hills, Md., 1984-86. Sgt. AUS, 1942-45. Decorated Purple Heart; grand knight Italian Order of Merit; Vietnam Psychol. Warfare medal 1st class; recipient AIA pward for outstanding fgn. reporting L.I. U., 1956; named best press corr. abroad Overseas Press Club, 1957; recipient N.Y.C. Fire Dept. Daisy Silver Medal, 1924, N.Y. Times Oratorical Contest Bronze Medal, 1930; Christopher award for one of ten most inspiring books of year, 1959; named Man of Year Cath. Inst. Press, 1962, Fordham U. Alumnus of Year in communications, 1963; co-winner Am. Golden Typewriter award N.Y. Newspaper Reporters Assn., 1965, nominated by N.Y. Herald Tribune for Journalism Pulitzer Prize, 1965; outstanding pub. service award N.Y. chpt. Sigma Delta Chi, 1965; recipient Page One award N.Y. Newspaper Guild, 1966, Silurians award, 1966, award N.Y. Newspaper Reporters Assn., 1966, Citation for pub. service N.Y.C. Citizens Budget Commn., 1966, U.S. Army Gold medal for civilian svc. in Vietnam, 1969, pres. commendation for Cambodia mission on news problems, 1970, Meritorious Honor award Dept. State, 1972; Lifetime Achievement award Fordham U. Club, Washington, 1986. Mem. Fgn. Press Assn. Italy (v.p. 1951-52, pres. 1961-62), SHAPE Corrs. Assn. Paris (treas. 1955), Authors Guild, Am. Fgn. Svc. Assn., Pax Romana Soc. for Cath. Intellectuals, Overseas Press Club (pres. 1963-65), Nat. Press Club, Diplomats and Consular Officers, Ret., Kenwood Club, Cosmos Club, Fordham U. Club Washington (bd. govs. 1980—99). Roman Catholic. Home: 5229 Duvall Dr Bethesda MD 20816-1875 Office Phone: 301-229-7439. Personal E-mail: jmcgurn@erols.com. *Providing information to our democratic public has been the work of my life both as a foreign correspondent, as a government spokesman, and as a lecturer. The newsman and the person who speaks for government share the same objective of explaining government policy. The spokesman has an added responsibility— to help government policy succeed. The reporter and the spokesman sometimes are at war with one another, but it is a war in behalf of the same beneficiary: the people.*

**MCGURN, WILLIAM BARRETT, III,** lawyer; b. N.Y.C., Apr. 3, 1943; s. Barrett and Mary Elizabeth (Johnson) McGurn; m. Catherine Roche, June 17, 1972; children: Mary Anne, Edward Johnson. BA, Yale U., 1965; JD, Harvard U., 1972. Bar: DC 1973, Paris 1992. Ptnr. Cleary, Gottlieb, Steen & Hamilton LLP, Washington, Paris, Rome, 1972—. Gov. Am. Hosp. Paris, 1991—; chmn. Dem. Abroad, France, 1987—89; bd. dirs. Spl. Olympics Italy, 2005—. Lt. USNR, 1967—69. Mem.: ABA, Am. C. of C. France (bd. dirs. 1996—, v.p. 1998—2000, pres. 2000—02). Democrat. Home: via del Pié di Marmo 16 00186 Rome Italy Office: Cleary Gottlieb Steen and Hamilton LLP Piazza di Spagna 15 00187 Rome Italy

**MCGWIRE, MARK DAVID,** retired professional baseball player; b. Pomona, Calif., Oct. 1, 1963; s. John and Kathy McGwire; 1 child, Matthew. Student, U. So. Calif. With Oakland Athletics, Calif., 1984—97, St. Louis Cardinals, 1997—2001. Named Am. League Rookie of Yr., 1987, Male Athlete of Yr., AP, 1998; named to All-Star Team, 1987—92, 1995—2000, MLB All-Century Team, 1999; recipient Gold Glove award, 1990. Achievements include being a member of U.S. Olympic Baseball Team, 1984; mem. of World Series Championship Team, 1989; led Am. League in Home Runs, 1987 (49), 1996 (52); led Nat. League in Home Runs, 1998 (70), 1999 (65); led Nat. League in RBI's (147), 1999.

**MCHALE, EDWARD ROBERTSON,** retired lawyer; b. Chgo., Jan. 24, 1921; s. Edward F. and Martha (Robertson) McH.; m. Helen Louise Lindgren, Aug. 28, 1953; children: Nancy Ellen McHale Kaufman, Sally Jane McHale Cutler, John Robertson. BSS., Northwestern U., 1942; LL.B., Harvard U., 1948. Bar: Calif. 1949. Asst. U.S. atty. So. Dist. Calif., 1949—51, chief tax div., 1954—61; assoc. Mitchell, Silberberg & Knupp, Los Angeles, 1961—64, ptnr., 1965—86, mgr. litigation dept, 1978—82; pres. Edward R. McHale, P.C., 1979—86; ret., 1986. Lectr. U. So. Calif. Law Center, 1958-61 Co-author: Handling Federal Tax Litigation, 1961. Served to lt. USNR, 1943-46. Mem. Fed. Bar Assn. (past pres. Los Angeles chpt., past nat. v.p. for 9th Circuit), Assn. Bus. Trial Lawyers (bd. govs. 1981-83), State Bar Calif., Delta Sigma Rho. Clubs: South Hills Country (West Covina); Clan Donnachaidh Soc. Lutheran. Home: 1116 S Serena Dr West Covina CA 91791-3754 E-mail: casu8@earthlink.net.

**MC HALE, JOHN JOSEPH,** baseball club executive; b. Detroit, Sept. 21, 1921; s. John Michael and Catherine M. (Kelly) McH.; m. Patricia Anne Cameron, Feb. 15, 1947 (dec.); children: Patricia Cameron II, John Joseph, Jr., Kevin K., Anne F., Brian F., Mary M. AB cum laude, U. Notre Dame, 1947. Profl. baseball player, 1941-42, 45-47; asst. dir. minor league clubs Detroit Tigers Baseball Club, 1948, asst. farm dir., 1948-53, dir. minor league clubs, 1954-55, dir. player personnel, 1956-57, gen. mgr., 1957-58; v.p., gen. mgr. Milw. Braves Baseball Club (became Atlanta Braves Baseball Club 1961), 1957-61, pres., gen. mgr., 1961-67; dep. commr. N.Y.C., 1968—82; pres., gen. mgr. Montreal Expos Baseball Club, 1968-87, dep. chmn., CEO, 1987—; ret. Japan Sports Sys. Dir. Perini Corp. Ret. trustee emeritus, Intracoastal Hosp. Corp., West Palm Beach, Fla., 1986—; dir. emeritus Schwartz Investment Trust, now Maria Fund., 2001; bd. dirs. Nat. Baseball Hall of Fame and Mus.; mem. adv. bd. Hospice of Treasure Coast, Fla. Mem. Nat. Monogram Club (U. Notre Dame), Assn. Ret. Ball Players Am. (pres., dir.), Harbour Ridge Club. Address: Harbour Ridge 2014 NW Royal Fern Ct Palm City FL 34990-8025

**MCHALE, JUDITH A. (JUDITH OTTALLORAN),** broadcast executive, lawyer; b. N.Y.C., 1947; m. Michael McHale; 2 children. B in Politics, U. Nottingham, Eng.; JD, Fordham U.Law Sch., 1979. Atty. Battle, Fowler, N.Y.C.; gen. counsel MTV networks, Discovery Comm., Inc., 1987, sr. v.p., gen. counsel, exec. v.p., gen. counsel, pres., COO, 1995—2004, pres., CEO 2004—. Mem. Md. State Bd. of Edn., 1997—2001; bd. dirs. Polo Ralph Lauren, John Hancock Co., Potomac Electric Power Co., Host Marriott Corp., Cable in the Classroom, Vital Voices Global Partnership, Africa Soc., Africare, Sister-to-Sister Everyone Has a Heart Found. Office: Discovery Comm 7700 Wisconsin Ave Bethesda MD 20814*

**MCHALE, KEVIN EDWARD,** professional sports team executive, retired professional basketball player; b. Hibbing, Minn., Dec. 19, 1957; m. Lynn McHale; children: Kristyn, Michael. Student, U. Minn., 1976-80. Basketball player Boston Celtics, 1980-93; v.p. basketball ops. Minn. Timberwolves, 1995—, interim head coach, 2005—. Named to NBA All Rookie Team, 1981, NBA All-Defensive First Team, 1986-88, All-NBA First Team, 1987, NBA All-Star Game, 1984, 86-91; recipient NBA Sixth Man award, 1984, 85. Achievements include playing on NBA Championship Team, 1981, 84, 86. Office: Minn Timberwolves 600 1st Ave N Minneapolis MN 55403-1416

**MCHALE, MAUREEN BERNADETTE KENNY,** controller; b. Scranton, Pa., July 2, 1955; d. John Theodore and Ann Marie (Slowey) McH. BFA cum laude, Wilkes Coll., 1977; postgrad., Wilkes Coll., Rome, 1977; MBA in Acctg. with honors, U. Notre Dame, 1984; MST with honors, Kings Coll., 1995. Internal auditor Cen. Tax Bur., Forty Fort, Pa., 1977-82; placement coord. U. Notre Dame, South Bend, Ind., 1983-84; sr. acct. Laventhol and Horwath, Wilkes Barre, Pa., 1984-88; contr. Greco Holdings, Inc., Wilkes Barre, 1988-97; dir. fin. Mercy Health Care Ctr., Nanticoke, Pa., 1997—2000; CFO Little Flower Manor/St. Thérèse Residence, Wilkes-Barre, Pa., 2000—. Founder Entrepreneurship Lecture Series, U. Notre Dame, 1984. Leader Girl Scouts U.S., Forty Fort, 1977-82; chmn. County Children's Fingerprinting Program, Kingston, Pa., 1988; mem. exec. com., bd. dirs. Bishop O'Reilly H.S.; bd. dirs. Northeastern Pa. Choral Soc., 1996-2000, Mercy Ctr.; pres. bd. dirs. St. Michael's Sch U. Notre Dame Scholar, 1984. Mem. Jaycees (bd. dirs. 1987-88), U. Notre Dame Alumni Assn. (bd. dirs., pres. Scranton chpt.) Democrat. Roman Catholic. Avocations: walking, bicycling, football. Home: 31 Virginia Ter Forty Fort PA 18704-4929 Office: 200 S Meade St Wilkes Barre PA 18702-6221 Office Phone: 570-823-6131. E-mail: mmchale@lfmstr.com.

**MCHALE, PAUL F., JR.,** federal agency administrator, former congressman; b. Bethlehem, Pa., July 26, 1950; m. Katherine McHale; children: Matthew, Mary, Luke. BA in Govt. summa cum laude, Lehigh U., 1972; JD, Georgetown U. Law Sch., 1977. Atty., Bethlehem, 1977—82; mem. Pa. Ho. of Reps., 1983—92, US Congresses from 15th Pa. dist., 1993—99; former mem. nat. security com., mem. sci. com.; mem. Tallman, Hudders and Sorrentino, Allentown, Pa., 1999—2003; asst. sec. for homeland def. US Dept. Def., Washington, 2003—. Infantry officer USMC, 1972—74, Okinawa, Philippines, maj. USMCR, 1990—92, Persian Gulf. Decorated Navy Commendation medal; recipient Disting. Pub. Svc. medal, US Dept. Def., Frank M. Tejada Leadership award, Marine Corps. Reserve Officers Assn., 1997, Reserve Officers Assn. Minuteman of the Year award, 1998. Mem. Phi Beta Kappa. Democrat.

**MCHALE, VINCENT EDWARD,** political science professor; b. Jenkins Twp., Pa., Apr. 17, 1939; m. Ann Barbara Cotner, Nov. 8, 1963; 1 child, Patrick James. A.B., Wilkes Coll., 1964; M.A., Pa. State U., 1966, Ph.D. in Polit. Sci., 1969. Asst. prof. polit. sci. U. Pa., Phila., 1969-75; dir. grad. studies, 1971-73; assoc. prof. Case Western Res. U., Cleve., 1975-84, prof., 1984-03, chmn. dept. polit. sci., 1978-03; vis. lectr. John Carroll U., summer 1980, Beaver Coll., 1975; Marcus A. Hanna prof., 2006-. Author: (with A.P. Frognier and D. Paranzino) Vote, Clivages Socio-politiques et Developpement Regional en Belgique, 1974. Co-editor; contbr.: Evaluating Transnational Programs in Government and Business, 1980; Political Parties of Europe, 1983; edtl. adv. bd. Worldmark Ency. of Nations, 1994—. Contbr. chpts. to books, articles to profl. jours. Project cons. Council Econ Opportunity in Greater Cleve., 1978-81; mem. Morris Abrams Award Com., 1977—. Recipient Outstanding Prof. award Lux chpt. Mortar Bd., 1989, 90; named one of Most Interesting People of 1988, Cleve. Mag.; NSF grantee, 1971-72; HEW grantee, 1974-78; Woodrow Wilson fellow, 1968, Ruth Young Boucke fellow, 1967-68; All-Univ. fellow, 1967-68. Mem. Phi Kappa Phi. Home: 3070 Coleridge Rd Cleveland OH 44118-3556 Office: Case Western Res U Cleveland OH 44106 Office Phone: 216-368-2425. Business E-Mail: vem@case.edu.

**MCHARD, JAMES LORIN,** corporate financial executive, freelance/self-employed composer, writer; b. Bay City, Mich., June 23, 1942; s. James Alvah and Daisy Evelyn McHard; m. Jerilee Miles, June 6, 1964 (div. May 15, 1985); m. Alice Brallie Dekle, May 24, 1997; children: Maureen Day, Clair James Ian. B.S. U. Mich., 1964. Cert. secondary sch. tchr. Mich. Engring. fin. analyst Ford Motor Co., Livonia, Mich., 1964—97; pres. J & A Music Enterprises, Mich. Freelance composer, lectr., writer; lectr. music theory. Composer: Tremors, 1991, Virtuals, 1992; editor: Voice of Reason newsletter, 1980—82; author: The Future of Modern Music, 2001, Julio

Estrada, Five Years of ONCE, Pape: Cinema Texas, 2002; contbr. articles to profl. jours.; pub.: program notes for premiere of Estrada's opera ISCM New Music Festival. Mem.: Southern Poverty Law Ctr. (name included on Wall of Tolerance), Electronic Music Found., S.E. Mich. Horn Club (assoc.; sec. 1985—88). Home: 28860 Richland Livonia MI 48150 Office Phone: 734-525-6265. Personal E-mail: release10@sbcglobal.net.

**MC HARGUE, CARL JACK,** lab administrator; b. Jan. 30, 1926; s. John David and Virginia (Thomas) McH.; m. Edith Trovillion, Aug. 28, 1947; children: Anne Odell McHargue Diegel, Carol Virginia Hornberger, Margaret Katherine McHargue; m. Betty Ford, Sept. 30, 1960. BS in Metall. Engring., U. Ky., 1949, MS, 1951, PhD, 1953. Instr. U. Ky., Lexington, 1949-53; with Oak Ridge Nat. Lab., 1953-90, sect. head, 1960-80, program mgr. for materials scis., 1961-88, sr. rsch. staff, 1980-90; prof. materials sci. and engring. U. Tenn., Knoxville, 1991—. Vis. prof. U. Newcastle upon Tyne, Eng., 1987; adj. prof. Vanderbilt U., 1988—; bd. dirs. Accreditation Bd. for Engring. and Tech., 1998—; bd. dirs. The Minerals, Metals and Materials Soc. Contbr. numerous articles in field to profl. jours. 1944-46. Recipient Disting. Svc. award The Minerals, Metals and Materials Soc., 2001; named to Engring. Hall of Distinction, U. Ky., 1995. Fellow Metall. Soc. AIME, Am. Soc. for Metals; mem. Materials Rsch. Soc., Sigma Xi, Tau Beta Pi. Republican. Presbyterian. Home: 7201 Sheffield Dr Knoxville TN 37909-2414 Office: U Tenn 514 E Stadium Hill Knoxville TN 37996-0750 Office Phone: 865-974-7680. Business E-Mail: crl@utk.edu.

**MCHENRY, BARNABAS,** lawyer; b. Harrisburg, Pa., Oct. 30, 1929; s. William Cecil and Louise (Perkins) McH.; m. Marie Bannon Jones, Dec. 13, 1952; children: Thomas J.P., W.H. Davis, John W.H. AB, Princeton U., 1952; LLB, Columbia U., 1957. Bar: N.Y. 1957. Assoc. Lord, Day, & Lord, N.Y.C., 1957-62; gen. counsel The Reader's Digest Assn., Inc., N.Y.C., 1962-85; exec. dir. Wallace Funds, N.Y.C., 1985-86; chmn. N.Y. state orgns., 1986—. Trustee, pres. Boscobel Restoration, Inc., 1964; trustee Am. Conservation Assn., 1977; trustee emeritus Met. Mus. Art, 1980; coun. mem. Villa I Tatti, Harvard Sch. Renaissance Studies, 1982; regent emeritus Smithsonian Instn., 1985; commr. Palisades Interstate Park Commn., 1987; chmn. Hudson River Valley Greenway Coun., 1989; co-chair Hudson River Valley Nat. Heritage Assn., 1996. Home: 164 E 72nd St New York NY 10021-4363 Fax: 212-681-4552.

**MCHENRY, HENRY MALCOLM,** anthropologist, educator; b. LA, May 19, 1944; s. Dean Eugene and Emma Jane (Spindt) McH.; m. Linda Jean Conway, June 25, 1966; children: Lindsay Jean, Annalisa Jane. BA, U. Calif., Davis, 1966, MA, 1967; PhD, Harvard U., 1972. Asst. prof. anthropology U. Calif., Davis, 1971-76, assoc. prof. anthropology, 1976-81, prof. anthropology, 1981—, chmn. dept. anthropology, 1984-88. Fellow AAAS, Am. Anthrop. Assn., Calif. Acad. Sci.; mem. Am. Assn. Phys. Anthropologists (exec. com. 1981-85), Soc. Study Evolution, Soc. Vertebrate Paleontology, Phi Beta Kappa, Phi Kappa Phi. Democrat. Buddhist. Avocation: winemaker. Home: 330 11th St Davis CA 95616-2010 Office: U of Calif Davis Dept Of Anthropology Davis CA 95616 Business E-Mail: hmmchenry@ucdavis.edu.

**MCHENRY, JULIE,** communications executive; BJ, U. Mo.; MBA in Mktg., U. Portland. Adv. prog. supr. Tektronix, Inc., Beaverton, Oreg.; acct. exec. Regis McKenna Inc., Portland, Oreg.; co-founder, v.p. The Waggener Group; co-founder Global Tech. Comm., Wilson McHenry Co. Spkr. in field.

**MCHENRY, MARTIN CHRISTOPHER,** physician, educator; b. Feb. 9, 1932; s. Merl and Marcella (Bricca) McH.; m. Patricia Grace Hughes, Apr. 27, 1957; children: Michael, Christopher, Timothy, Mary Ann, Jeffrey, Paul, Kevin, William, Monica, Martin Christopher. Student, U. Santa Clara, 1950-53; MD, U. Cin., 1957; MS in Medicine, U. Minn., 1966. Diplomate Am. Bd. Internal Medicine. Intern Highland Alameda County (Calif.) Hosp., Oakland, 1957-58; resident, internal medicine fellow Mayo Clinic, Rochester, Minn., 1958-61, spl. appointee in infectious diseases, 1963-64; staff physician Henry Ford Hosp., Detroit, 1964-67, Cleve. Clinic, 1967-72, chmn. dept. infectious diseases, 1972-92, sr. physician infectious diseases, 1992-98. Cons. infectious diseases, 1998—; asst. clin. prof. Case Western Res. U., 1970-77, assoc. clin. prof. medicine, 1977-91, clin. prof. medicine, 1991—; assoc. vis. physician Cleve. Met. Gen. Hosp., 1970-00; cons. VA Hosp., Cleve., 1973-74. Contbr. more than 100 articles to profl. jours., also chpts. to books. Chmn. manpower com. Swine Influenza Program, Cleve., 1976. With USNR, 1961-63. Named Disting. Tchr. in Medicine, Cleve. Clinic, 1972, 90; recipient 1st ann. Bruce Hubbard Stewart award Cleve. Clinic Found. for Humanities in Medicine, 1985, Nightingale Physician Collaboration award Cleve. Clinic Found. Divsn. Nursing, 1995, Clinician of Yr. award Acad. Medicine of Cleve./No. Ohio Med. Assn., 2002. Fellow ACP, Infectious Diseases Soc. Am. (Clinician award 2000), Am. Coll. Chest Physicians (chmn. com. cardiopulmonary infections 1975-77, 81-83), Royal Soc. Medicine of Gt. Britain; mem. Am. Soc. Clin. Pharmacology and Therapeutics (chmn. sect. infectious diseases and antimicrobial agts. 1970-77, 80-85, dir.), Am. Thoracic Soc., Am. Soc. Clin. Pathologists, Am. Fedn. Clin. Rsch., Am. Soc. Tropical Medicine and Hygiene, Am. Soc. Microbiology, N.Y. Acad. Scis., Assn. for Profls. in Infection Control and Epidemiology, So. Med. Assn. Home: 2779 Belgrave Rd Pepper Pike OH 44124-4601 Office: 9500 Euclid Ave Cleveland OH 44195-0001

**MCHENRY, PATRICK TIMOTHY,** congressman; b. Mecklenburg, NC, Oct. 22, 1975; Attended, NC State U.; BA in Hist., Belmont Abbey Coll., 1999. Exec. DCI/New Media, Inc., Washington; owner & broker McHenry Real Estate, Gastonia, NC; spl. asst. to Sec. Elaine L. Chao US Dept. Labor, Washington, 2000; mem. NC State Ho. Reps., 2003—05, US Congress from 10th NC dist., 2005—. Mem. fin svcs. com. US Congress, 2005—, mem. budget com., mem. govt. reform com., vice chmn. Rep. conf. retirement security team, mem. exec. com. Nat. Rep. Congl. Com. Bd. dirs. United Success by Six Youth Prog. Named a Small Bus. Champion, Small Bus. and Entrepreneurship Coun., Hero of the Taxpayer, Ams. for Tax Reform, Protector of Property Rights, Property Rights Alliance; recipient Spirit of Enterprise award, US C. of C. Mem.: Gaston C. of C, NRA, Gastonia Rotary Club. Republican. Roman Catholic. Office: US Ho Reps 224 Cannon Ho Office Bldg Washington DC 20515-3310 Office Phone: 202-225-2576.*

**MC HENRY, POWELL,** lawyer; b. Cinn., May 14, 1926; s. L. See McHenry and Marguerite L. (Powell) Heinz; m. Venna Mae Guerrea, Aug. 27, 1948; children: Scott, Marshall, Jody Lee, Gale Lynn. AB, Yale U., 1947; LLB, Harvard U., 1951, JD, 1969. Bar: Ohio 1951, U.S. Ct. Appeals (6th cir.) 1964, U.S. Supreme Ct. 1966. Assoc. Dinsmore, Shohl, Sawyer & Dinsmore, Cinn., 1951-57; ptnr. Dinsmore, Shohl, Coates & Deupree (and predecessors), Cinn., 1958-75; gen. counsel Federated Dept. Stores, Inc., 1971-75; assoc. gen. counsel Procter & Gamble Co., 1975-76, v.p., gen. counsel, 1976-83, sr. v.p., gen. counsel, 1983-91; counsel Dinsmore & Shohl, Cin., 1991—; bd. dirs. Eagle Picher Industries, Inc., 1991-97. Mem. com. Hamilton County Pub. Defender, Cin., chmn., 1996-2000. With USNR, 1944-46. Recipient award of merit Ohio Legal Center Inst., 1969, Lifetime Achievement in Law award, Cin. Bar Found., 2004. Mem. ABA, Ohio Bar Assn., Cin. Bar Assn. (pres. 1979-80, exec. com. 1975-81), Harvard U. Law Sch. Assn. Cin. (pres. 1960-61), Am. Law Inst., Assn. Gen. Counsel (pres. 1986-88), Harvard Club, Western Hills Country Club (pres. 1964-70, sec. 1966-69, 87-89, treas. 1969-70, 89-90), Queen City Club, Commonwealth Club (pres. 1996-97). Republican. Methodist. Office: Dinsmore & Shohl 1900 Chemed Ctr 255 E 5th St Cincinnati OH 45202-4700 Office Phone: 513-977-8295.

**MCHOES, ANN MCIVER,** academic administrator, computer engineer; b. San Diego, June 17, 1950; d. Donald Anthony and Ann Mae McIver; children: A. Genevieve, Katherine Marie. BS in Math., U. Pitts., 1973, MS in Info. Sci., 1986. Tech. writer Westinghouse Electric Corp., Pitts., 1973—79; pres. McHoes & Assocs., Pitts., 1981—; dir. enrollment svcs. Chatham Coll., Pitts., 2002—. Mem. adj. faculty computer sci., Carlow Coll., Pitts., 1992—; Duquesne U., 1997-99; cons. Westinghouse Electric Corp., 1988-99, PNC Bank, Pitts., 1988—, CBS Corp., 1996-99, Intel, 1998—, McDonalds Corp.,

1998-2001, commonwealth of Pa. Healthy Women Project, 1998—; vis. lectr. Pa. State U., State College, 1990-91; judge Pa. Jr. Acad. Sci., Pitts., 1993—; vol. tutor Greater Pitts. Literacy Coun., 1996-98; webmaster NVR Mortgage, 1998-2000; bd. dirs. Pitts. Playback Theatre, 2000-2001. Co-author: Understanding Operating Systems, 1991, 2d edit., 1997, 3d edit., 2000 (used in colleges and univs., North Am., Europe, Africa, Asia and Australia); assoc. editor: (4-vol. ency.) Computer Science for Students, 2002. Recipient 2001 Texty Excellence award Text and Academic Authors Assn., 2001. Mem. IEEE Computer Soc., Assn. Computing Machinery, Info. Sys. Security Assn. (chpt. sec. 1991-94, v.p. 1995-96, membership chair 1994—), Pa. Mid. Sch. Assn. (conf. exhibit chair 1996-97). Avocations: travel, tennis, golf.

**MCHUGH, CARIL EISENSTEIN DREYFUSS,** art dealer, art gallery director, consultant; b. New Haven; d. Irving and Gertrude (Lax) Eisenstein; m. Barney Dreyfuss II (div.); children: Caryn, Barney III (Terry), Andrew, Evan; m. James Marshall McHugh Jr., Dec. 31, 1976. BA, Smith Coll. Libr. archivist, mem. staff art rental Washington Gallery of Modern Art, 1963-67; asst. to curator of prints and drawings Nat. Mus. Am. Art, Washington, 1967-69; dir. Studio Gallery, Washington, 1970-75; dir., ptnr. Parsons-Dreyfuss Gallery, N.Y.C., 1976-80; dir. Frank Marino Gallery, N.Y.C., 1981; Humphrey Fine Art, N.Y.C., 1988-90, Gregory Gallery, N.Y.C., 1995-96; freelance curator, adv. bd. Hugo de Pagano Gallery, 1997—2000; rschr. Barnett Newman Found., N.Y.C., 2001—. Art cons., writer, N.Y.C., 1982—; arranger exhbns. Nat. Mus. Am. Art, Washington, 1968-69, USIA, Washington, 1976, Automation House, N.Y.C., 1983; curator Creative Works Exhbn., Smith Coll., 2005. An Homage to Betty Parsons exhbn., 2000, Portraits by Tom Block/Amnesty Internat. Exhbn., 2002, essays to catalogs, articles to profl. mags. Bd. dirs. Women's Nat. Dem. Club, Washington, 1972-76, Friends of the Corcoran, Washington, 1972-76, Smith Club of Washington, 1974-76; Sophia Smith Assoc. Smith Coll., Northampton, Mass., 1985, 90, 95, 2000, 2005, Women in the Arts, 1995—. Avocations: reading, hiking, swimming, poetry. Home: 241 Central Park W Apt 9C New York NY 10024-4545 E-mail: carilmchugh@msn.com.

**MCHUGH, HEATHER,** poet; b. Calif., Aug. 20, 1948; BA, Radcliffe Coll., 1970; MA, U. Denver, 1972. Assoc. prof. English SUNY, Binghamton, 1976-82; prof. English, Milliman writer-in-residence U. Wash., Seattle, 1983—. Vis. prof. Columbia U., 1987; Holloway lectr. U. Calif., Berkeley, 1987; judge Nat. Poetry Series book award, 1986, 95. Author: (poetry) Dangers, 1977, A World of Difference, 1981, To the Quick, 1987, Shades, 1988, Hinge & Sign: Poems, 1968-93, 1994 (Nat. Book award nomination 1994), The Father of the Predicaments, 1999, Eyeshot, 2003, (essays) Broken English: Poetry and Partiality, 1993; translator: D'Apres Tout: Poems by Jean Follain, 1981; (with Nikolai Popov) Because the Sea Is Black: Poems by Blaga Dimitrova, 1989, (with Nikolai Popov) Glottal Stop: 101 Poems by Paul Celan, 2000, (with David Konstan) Cyclops of Euripides, 2000. Recipient Harvard U./Pollock prize, 1995, Lila Wallace/Reader's Digest Writer's award, 1996, PEN Voelcker prize, 2000. Mem. Acad. Am. Poets (chancellor 1999), Am. Acad. Arts and Scis. Office: U Washington Dept English Box 354330 Seattle WA 98195-4330

**MCHUGH, JAMES JOSEPH,** lawyer; b. Phila., Sept. 15, 1961; s. James Joseph and Helene Anne (Kiernan) McHugh; m. Colette Marie McHugh, May 20, 1989; children: Albert Taylor, James Joseph III, Cole Michael, Sophia Kiernan. BSME, Drexel U., 1985; JD magna cum laude, Villanova (Pa.) Law Sch., 1992. Bar: Pa. 1992, N.J. 1992, U.S. Dist. Ct. (ea. dist.) Pa., U.S. Dist. Ct. N.J. Ptnr. McHugh Plumbing & Heating, Phila., 1984-89; project mgr. Fluidics Mech Contractors, Phila., 1989-92; assoc. Pepper, Hamilton & Scheetz, Phila., 1992-94; ptnr. The Beasley Firm, LLC, Phila., 1994—. Author, editor case notes. Mem. adv. com. Penn Pub. Svc. Program, Sch. Law, U. Pa. Named to Order of the Coif, Villanova Law Sch., 1992. Mem. ATLA, Pa. Bar Assn., Phila. Bar Assn. Home: 65 Brooks Rd Moorestown NJ 08057-3855 Office: The Beasley Firm 1125 Walnut St Philadelphia PA 19107-4918 Office Phone: 215-592-1000. Business E-Mail: jjm@beasleyfirm.com.

**MCHUGH, JAMES LENAHAN, JR.,** lawyer; b. Pitts., June 28, 1937; s. James Lenahan and Annette (Dalton) McH.; m. Mary-Ann Curto, Feb. 16, 1963 (div. 1988); children: Angela Dalton Sherrill, Hillary Lenahan Clagett; m. Rosa Lamoreaux, Sept. 8, 1991. BA, Duquesne U., 1959; LLB, Villanova U., 1962. Bar: DC 1963. Law clk. U.S. Dist. Ct. (ea. dist.) Pa., Phila., 1962-63; law clk. to Assoc. Justice Tom C. Clark, U.S. Supreme Ct., Washington, 1963-64; assoc. Steptoe & Johnson, Washington, 1967-70, ptnr., 1970-94; gen. counsel APA, Washington, 1994—2001, sr. counsel, 2001—. Mem. bd. consultors Law Sch., Villanova U., 1973—; dir. Higher Achievement Program, Washington, 1984-87; coord. Washington Lawyers' Project, Robert F. Kennedy Meml. Found., Washington, 1972-75. Editor-in-chief Villanova Law Rev., Vol. VII, 1961-62; chmn. editl. adv. bd. Fed. Comm. Law Jour., 1981-84. Bd. dirs. Columbia Hosp. for Women's Found., Washington, 1985-96, Children's Radio Theatre, Washington, 1983-86, Cantate Chamber Singers, 2006-; chmn. exec. giving Archbishop's Appeal, Archdiocese of Washington, 1982-84; mem. bd. visitors Ctr. for Study of Orgns. and Mgmt., U. Md. Univ. Coll., 1987-92; bd. dirs. Human Resources Rsch. Orgn., Inc., 1978—; chmn. bd. dirs., 1991—; mem. adv. bd. Inst. for Conflict Analysis and Resolution, George Mason U., 1990-94. Capt. U.S. Army, 1964-67. Mem. ABA (sect. in labor law, tax, intellectual property and legal edn.), D.C. Bar Assn., Am. Soc. Assn. Execs. (chmn. Washington Legal Symposium 2002-04, vice chmn. legal sect. coun. 2003-04, chmn. 2004-05), Choral Arts Soc., Villanova Law Alumni Assn. (pres. Greater Balt./Washington area chpt. 2002—04), Order of Coif, Confrerie des Chevaliers du Tastevin. Home: 4112 Fessenden St NW Washington DC 20016-4227 Office: APA 750 1st St NE Washington DC 20002-4242 Office Phone: 202-336-6089. Business E-Mail: jmchugh@apa.org.

**MCHUGH, JOHN MICHAEL,** congressman; b. Watertown, NY, Sept. 29, 1948; s. Donald and Jane (O'Neill) McHugh. BA in Polit. Sci., Syracuse U. Utica Coll., 1970; MPA, SUNY Nelson A. Rockefeller Grad. Sch. Pub. Affairs, 1977. Asst. city mgr., Watertown, NY, 1968-75; confidential asst. to city mgr., 1971-76; chief rsch., liaison with local govts. Staff of NY State Senator H. Douglas Barclay, 1976-84; mem. NY State Senate, 1985—93, chmn. joint legis. commn. on dairy industry devel., 1987-92; mem. US Congress from 23rd NY dist., 1993—, mem. govt. reform com., mem. armed svcs. com., chair mil. pers. subcommittee, mem. permanent select com. on intelligence. Named Hon. First Citien, City of Watertown, NY, 1976; recipient Individual Achievement award, NY State Dept. Econ. Devel., George (Buck) Gillespie award, Blinded Am. Vets. Found., 1999, President's award, Nat. Newspaper Assn., 2000, Outstanding Legislator award, Assn. US Army, 2003, Friend of Zion award, Jerusalem Fund, 2004, Pub. Svc. award, Direct Mktg. Assn. Nonprofit Fedn., 2004, Bertrand H. Snell award, Clarkson U., 2005. Mem. Legis. on State Legislators (nat. conf. state legislators), Nat. Conf. State Legislators (vice chmn. agrl. and internat. trade com. State-Fed. Assembly), Am. Soc. Young Polit. Leaders. Republican. Roman Catholic. Avocations: boating, skiing, music. Office: US Ho Reps 2333 Rayburn Ho Office Bldg Washington DC 20515-3223 Office Phone: 202-225-4611.*

**MCHUGH, PAUL R.,** psychiatrist, neurologist, educator; b. Lawrence, Mass., May 21, 1931; s. Francis Paul and Mary Dorothea (Herlihy) McH.; m. Jean Barlow, Dec. 27, 1959; children: Clare Mary, Patrick Daniel, Denis Timothy. AB, Harvard U., 1952, MD, 1956. Diplomate: Am. Bd. Psychiatry and Neurology. Intern Peter Bent Brigham Hosp., Boston, 1956-57; resident in neurology Mass. Gen. Hosp., 1957-60, fellow in neuropathology, 1958-59; teaching fellow in neurology and neuropathology Harvard, 1957-60; clin. asst. psychiatry Maudsley Hosp., London, Eng., 1960-61; mem. neuropsychiatry div. Walter Reed Army Inst. Research, Washington, 1961-64; asst. prof. psychiatry and neurology Cornell U., N.Y.C., 1964-68, assoc. prof., 1968-71, prof., 1971; dir. electroencephalography N.Y. Hosp., 1964-68; founder, dir. N.Y. Hosp. Bourne Behavioral Rsch. Lab., 1964-68, clin. dir. supr. psychiat. edn., founder, dir. Westchester divsn. dept. psychiatry, 1968-73; prof., chmn. dept. psychiatry U. Oreg. Health Sci. Center, Portland, 1973-75; Henry Phipps prof. psychiatry Johns Hopkins, Balt., 1975—2001, chmn.

dept. psychiatry, 1975—2001, prof. dept. mental hygiene, 1976—; psychiatrist-in-chief Johns Hopkins Hosp., 1975—2001; dir. Blades Ctr. for Clin. Practice and Rsch. in Alcoholism Johns Hopkins Med. Inst., 1992—2001; chmn. med. staff Johns Hopkins Hosp., 1983-89, trustee, 1983—89. Author: The Perspectives of Psychiatry, 1983; (with Phillip R. Slavney) Psychiatric Polarities, 1987, Genes, Brain and Behavior, 1990, The Mind Has Mountains: Reflections on Society and Psychiatry, 2006; contbg. author: Cecil-Loeb Textbook of Medicine; mem. editl. bd. Am. Jour. Physiology, Jour. Nervous and Mental Disease, Comprehensive Psychiatry, Medicine, Psychol. Medicine, 1976—, Am. Scholar; contbr. articles to profl. jours. Mem. Md. Gov.'s Adv. Com., 1977—80, U.S. Conf. Cath. Bishops Nat. Rev. Bd. Office of Child and Youth Protection, 2002—, Pres.'s Coun. on Bioethics, 2001—. Grantee NIH, 1964-68, 67-70, 70-74, 75—; recipient William C. Menninger award ACP, 1987. Fellow: Am. Psychiat. Assn., Royal Coll. Psychiatry; mem.: Am. Coll. Psychiatrists (Disting. Svc. award 2002), Pavlovian Soc., Am. Psychopath. Assn. (Joseph Zubin award 1995), Am. Coll. Neuropsychopharmacology, Harvey Soc., Am. Physiol. Soc., Am. Neurol. Assn., Inst. Medicine-NAS, W Hamilton St. Club. Home: 3707 St Paul St Baltimore MD 21218-2403 Office: Johns Hopkins Med Insts Meyer 127 600 N Wolfe St Baltimore MD 21287 Office Phone: 410-502-3150. Business E-Mail: pmchugh1@jhmi.edu.

**MCHUGH, THOMAS EDWARD**, state supreme court justice; b. Charleston, W.Va., Mar. 26, 1936; s. Paul and Melba McHugh; m. Judith McHugh, Mar. 14, 1959; children: Karen, Cindy, James, John. AB, W.Va. U., 1958, LLB, 1964. Bar: W.Va. 1964. Pvt. practice law, Charleston, 1964-66, 69-74; law clk. to presiding judge Harlan Calhoun W.Va. Supreme Ct. of Appeals, 1966-68; chief judge Cir. Ct. (13th cir.) W.Va., Charleston, 1974-80; justice W.Va. Supreme Ct., Charleston, 1980-97; chief justice W. Va Supreme Ct, Charleston, 1984, 88, 92; mediation practice Allen Guthrie McHugh & Thomas, PLLC, Charleston, 1997—. Served to 1st lt. U.S. Army, 1958-61. Mem. W.Va. Jud. Assn., W.Va. Bar Assn., Order of the Coif. Democrat. Roman Catholic. Office: Allen Guthrie McHugh & Thomas PLLC PO Box 3394 500 Lee St E Charleston WV 25333-3394

**MCILQUHAM, DAVID J.**, consumer products company executive; Grad. with honors, Queens Univ. Mgmt. positions GE Canada; mgmt. positions through gen. mgr. Canadian ops. & v.p. mktg. Samsonite Corp.; v.p. mktg., corp. v.p. sales & mktg. Sealy Inc., Trinity, NC, 1990—2001, pres., COO, 2001—06, pres., CEO, 2006—. Office: Sealy Inc 1 Office Pkwy at Sealy Dr Trinity NC 27370*

**MCILROY, ALAN F.**, manufacturing executive; b. 1950; Internat. contr. Wheelabrator Corp., 1983-87; bus. unit contr. Gen. Chem., 1987-90; sr. v.p. Harris Chem.; head Greenock Group; CFO Dayton Superior Corp., Miamisburg, Ohio, 1997—. Office: Dayton Superior Corp Ste 130 7777 Washington Village Dr Dayton OH 45459

**MCILVAIN, ISABEL**, sculptor, art educator; b. 1943; BA, Smith Coll.; MFA, Pratt Inst. Asst. prof. & artist-in-residence Washington & Lee Univ., 1975—82; assoc. prof. Sch. Visual Arts, Boston Univ., 1982—. Vis. assoc. prof. Sweet Briar Coll., 1977. Exhibitions include Robert Schoelkopf Gallery, NYC, 1982-87, Moore Gallery, Phila., 1993, Arnot Art Mus., Elmira N.Y.; Numerous group exhibitions in N.Y., Pa. and Va.; JFK Commission 1989. Grantee Sculpture Fellowship award, Artists Found., Boston, 1984. Mem.: NAD (academician). Office: School of Visual Arts Room 552 855 Commonwealth Ave Boston MA 02215

**MCILVAINE, PATRICIA MORROW**, physician; b. Pitts., Feb. 4, 1947; d. James Morrow McIlvaine and Virginia Fuller Tucker. BS in Chemistry, Simmons Coll., 1969; MD, U. Utah, 1984. Rsch. technician Mass. Gen. Hosp., Boston, 1969-70, MIT, Cambridge, 1970-75, Utah State U., Logan, 1975-80; resident in internal medicine U. Mass. Hosp., Worcester, 1984-87; pvt. practice, Monson, Mass., 1987-2001; mem. grp. practice Walla Walla (Wash.) Clinic, 2002—. Staff physician Wing Meml. Hosp., Palmer, Mass., 1987-2001. Vol., mem IRBIS Enterprises, Mongolia, 1998-2004. NFS summer scholar, 1968, Helena Rubinstein scholar Simmons Coll., 1968-69. Mem. ACP/Am. Soc. Internal Medicine, Sigma Xi. Avocations: fiber crafts, international travel, hiking, gardening, sailing. Home: 913 Bonnie Brae Walla Walla WA 99362

**MCILVANE, EDWARD JAMES**, stained glass artist, educator; b. N.Y.C., July 5, 1947; s. Edward James Sr. and Irene (Logue) McI.; m. Rose F. Aloisi, 1970 (div. 1985); children: Jessica, Blake. BS in Edn. and Art Edn., St. John's U., N.Y.C., 1975; MFA, R.I. Sch. Design, 1978. Stained glass craftsman Claude Gaches Studio, L.I., 1969-71, The Lamb Studio, N.J., 1971-72, Greenland Studio, N.Y.C., 1972-75, Helmut-Schardt Studio, Northport, N.Y., 1975-78; freelance artist and designer Providence, 1978—. Guest artist Summrvail Workshop for Art, Vail, Colo., 1980, N.Y. Exptl. Glass Workshop, N.Y.C., 1980; program coord. Pilchuck Sch., Stanwood, Wash., 1979; instr. Haystack Mt. Sch. Crafts, Deer Isle, Maine, 1977. Prin. works include Johnson's Wax Co., Rancine, Wis., Temple Beth-El, Prov, R.I., Providence Coll., Bank of Boston, Joseph W. Martin, Jr. Inst. for Law and Soc. Stonehill Coll., North Easton, Mass., Licht residence, Little Compton, R.I., Vinyl Tech. Sch., Middletown, Conn., Presbyn. World Hdqs., Louisville, R.I. State Coun. on the Arts fellow, 1980, 86, Nat. Endowment for the Arts fellow, 1983. Mem. Glass Art Soc. Avocations: tai chi, angling. Home: 329 Pomfret Rd Brooklyn CT 06234 Office Phone: 860-774-4822. Personal E-mail: macdeverre@charter.net.

**MCILWAIN, HARRIS H.**, physician, researcher; s. Cordelia B. McILwain; m. Linda F. Fulghum, June 19, 1970; children: Laura E. McILwain, Kimberly L. McILwain, Michael Fulghum McILwain, Daniel E. McILwain, Virginia H. McILwain, Lisa Ann McILwain. MD, Emory U., Atlanta, GA, 1973. Diplomate Am. Bd. Internal Medicine, Am. Bd. Rheumatology, Am. Bd. Geriat. Intern in internal medicine Grady Meml. Hosp., Atlanta, 1973—74; resident in internal medicine Emory U., Atlanta, 1974—76, rheumatology fellow, 1976—78; physician Tampa Med. Group, Fla., 1978—. Med. dir. John Knox Village Retirement Ctr., Tampa, 1995—. Contbr. articles to profl. jours. Bd. dirs. Fla. Osteoporosis Bd., Tampa, 1998—2003. Named one of Top Physicians in the US, Town and Country Mag., 1997, Top 100 Physicians in the US, 1998. Mem.: AMA, ACP, Assoc. Prof. in Coll. Pub. Health, Am. Med. Directors Assn. (cert.), Fla. Med. Assn., Hillsborough County Med. Assn., Am. Coll. Rheumatology, Alpha Omega Alpha. Avocation: soccer. Office: Tampa Med Group 4700 Habana Ave Ste 303 Tampa FL 33614 Office Phone: 813-875-9742. Personal E-mail: hmcil@aol.com.

**MC ILWAIN, WILLIAM FRANKLIN**, newspaper editor, writer; b. Lancaster, S.C., Dec. 15, 1925; s. William Franklin and Docia (Higgins) McI.; m. Anne Dalton, Nov. 28, 1952 (div. 1973); children: Dalton, Nancy, William Franklin III; m. K. L. Brelsford, June 5, 1978 (div. 1983). BA, Wake Forest Coll., 1949; postgrad., Harvard, 1957-58. Various positions with Wilmington (N.C.) Star, 1943, Charlotte (N.C.) Observer, 1947, Jacksonville (Fla.) Jour., 1945, Winston-Salem (N.C.) Jour.-Sentinel, 1949-52, Richmond (Va.) Times-Dispatch, 1952-54; chief copy editor Newsday, Garden City, N.Y., 1954-57, day news editor, 1957-60, city editor, 1960-64, mng. editor, 1964-66, editor, 1967-70; writer-in-residence Wake Forest U., 1970-71; dorm leader Alcoholic Rehab. Ctr., Butner, N.C., 1971; dep. mng. editor Toronto Star, 1971-73; mng. editor The Record, Hackensack, N.J., 1973-77; editor Boston Herald Am., 1977-79; dep. editor Washington Star, 1979-81, exec. mng. editor, 1981; editor Ark. Gazette, 1981-82; founding editor N.Y. Newsday, 1982-84; exec. editor Sarasota (Fla.) Herald-Tribune, 1984-90; sr. editor N.Y. Times Regional Newspaper Group, 1991-92; chmn. Bill Mc Ilwain, Inc., 1993—. Author: The Glass Rooster, 1960, (with Walter Friedenberg) Legends of Baptist Hollow, 1949; collaborator: (with Newsday staff) Naked Came The Stranger, 1969, A Farewell to Alcohol, 1973; contbr. to: Reader's Digest, Harper's, Esquire, Atlantic Monthly; editor N.C. Writer's Workshop. Mem. Pres. Johnson's Commn. on Civil Rights; mem. adv. bd. Pulitzer Prize, 1982. With USMC, 1944. Named to N.C. Journalism Hall of Fame. Mem. Am. Soc.

Newspaper Editors, Soc. Nieman Fellows. Home and Office: 305 N Channel Dr Wrightsville Beach NC 28480-2723 E-mail: jacktbear@ec.rr.com. As Fats Waller said, "One never knows, do one?".

**MCILWAIN-MASSEY, NADINE**, retired foundation administrator; b. Canton, Ohio, July 29, 1943; d. Willie J. and Mabel W. (White) Williams; m. Albert H. McIlwain, Aug. 20, 1966 (dec. June 1989); children: Jeaneen J., Floyd R.; m. William P. Massey, July 4, 2002. BA, Malone Coll., Canton, Ohio, 1970; MA, U. Akron, Ohio, 1978; MEd, Ashland U., Ohio, 1990. Cert. tchr. social studies, sociology. Lab. asst. Canton City Health Dept., 1962—65; telephone operator Ohio Bell Telephone Co., 1965—71, svc. cons. Akron, 1970—71; tchr. Canton City Schs., Ohio, 1971—90, curriculum specialist, 1985—90; prin. Alliance (Ohio) City Schs., 1990—2002, Allen Classical Traditional Acad., Dayton, Ohio; program officer Sisters of Chairty Found., Canton, 2002—05; ret., 2005. Co-author: From Ghetto to God: The Incredible Journey of NFL Star Reggie Rucker, 2002, My Father's Child, 2006. Chair Stark Met. Housing Authority, Canton, 1992—; v.p. Alliance Symphony Assn., 1991—; mem. Canton City Coun., 1985-86; bd. dirs. Canton Players Guild; mem. minority outreach com. Canton Cultural Ctr.; v.p. Canton City Bd. Edn.; life mem. Alliance br. NAACP; active Canton Urban League, Alliance Area Farmworkers Housing Assn., Alliance Project Hope; mem. Canton City Sch. Bd. Edn., 2001-, pres., 2003-2005; elected Canton City Bd. Edn. 2006-. Named Woman of Yr., Canton Negro Oldtimers Athletic Assn., 1982, Am. Bus. Women's Assn., 1983, Aphesis Deliverence Christian Ch., 2003; recipient Black History award, Stark County African-Am. History Month Com., 1975, Polit. award, Nat. Black Women's Leadership Caucus, 1981, Liberty Bell award, Stark County chpt. ABA, 1989, Achievement award, Alliance br. NAACP, 1993, Nat. Educator award, Milken Family Found., 1993, Ohio Humanitarian award for Edn., State of Ohio of Adminstry. Svcs. Civil Rights Divsn. and Martin Luther King Jr. Holiday Commn., 1994, Golden Dove award, Multi-Devel. Assn., 2003. Mem. NEA, Nat. Alliance of Black Sch. Educators, Nat. Sociol. Hon. Soc., Ohio Mid. Sch. Assn., Ohio Coun. for Social Studies (exec. bd. dirs.), Ohio Edn. Assn. (Doris L. Allen minority caucus), Canton Profl. Educators Assn., Leila Green Alliance of Black Sch. Educators, Stark County African-Am. Fedn., Delta Sigma Theta. Home: 3409 Tradewinds Cove NW Canton OH 44708 Personal E-mail: retired6105@sbcglobal.net.

**MC INDOE, DARRELL WINFRED**, retired nuclear medicine physician; b. Wilkinsburg, Pa., Sept. 28, 1930; s. Clarence Wilbert and Dorothy Josephine (Morrow) McIndoe; m. Carole Jean McClain, Aug. 23, 1952; children: Sherri L. McIndoe, Wendy L. McIndoe, Darrell B. McIndoe, Ronald S. McIndoe, Holly B. McIndoe. BS, Allegheny Coll., 1952; MD, Temple U., 1956, MS, 1960. Commd. 2d lt. M.C. US Air Force, 1956, advanced through grades to col., 1971; intern Brooke Army Med. Ctr., San Antonio, 1956-57; resident in medicine Temple U. Med. Ctr., Phila., 1957-60; chief internal medicine and Hosp. svc. Norton AFB, 1960-64; dir. divsn. nuc. medicine St. Joseph Hosp., Towson, Md., 1992-2000; chief internal medicine and hosp. services 7520 U.S. Air Force Hosp., England, 1964-68; vis. rsch. fellow Royal Post Grad. Med. Sch., London, 1968-69; chief endocrinology svcs., chmn. dept. nuc. medicine USAF Med. Ctr., Keesler AFB, Miss., 1969-75; dep. dir. Armed Forces Radiobiology Rsch. Inst., Def. Nuc. Agy., Bethesda, Md., 1975-77, dir., 1977-79; staff physician nuc. medicine br., dept. radiology Nat. Naval Med. Ctr., Bethesda, Md., 1979-82; sr. lectr. mil. medicine Uniformed U. of Health Scis., Bethesda, Md., 1975-80; asst. prof. radiology/nuc. medicine and rsch. program coord. Uniformed U. of Health Sci., 1980-82; assoc. divsn. nuc. medicine St. Joseph Hosp., Towson, Md., 1982-91, dir. divsn. nuc. medicine 1991—2000; ret, 2000. Med. advisor Nev. ops. office Dept. Energy, Las Vegas; cons. in field. Fellow: Am. Coll. Nuc. Physicians (regent ea. USA), Fellow royal Soc. Medicine; mem.: AMA, Soc. Med. Cons.'s to Armed Forces, Assn. Mil. Surgeons U.S., Health Physics Soc. (dir. Balt.), Washington chpt.), Md. Soc. Nuc. Medicine (past pres.), Soc. Nuc. Medicine (ho. of dels.), Uniformed Svcs. Nuc. Medicine Assn. (pres. 1975), Air Force Soc. Physicians (bd. govs 1973—77), Alexander Graham Bell Soc. Home: 15510 Foxpaw Trail Woodbine MD 21797-8000

**MCINERNEY, JAMES EUGENE, JR.**, trade association executive; b. Springfield, Mass., Aug. 3, 1930; s. James Eugene and Rose Elizabeth (Adikes) McInerney; m. Mary Catherine Hill, July 17, 1963; children: Anne Elizabeth, James Eugene III. BS, U.S. Mil. Acad., 1952; MS in Engring., Princeton U., 1960; postgrad., Royal Air Force Staff Coll., 1964; MS in Internat. Affairs, George Washington U., 1970. Commd. 2d lt. USAF, 1952, advanced through grades to maj. gen., 1976, fighter pilot Republic of Korea, Japan and Germany, comdr. tactical fighter squadron S.E. Asia Thailand, 1967, tactical fighter wing Germany, 1971; sr. US adviser Turkish Air Force, 1973—75; dir. mil. assistance and sales Hdqrs. USAF, 1975-78; comdt. Indsl. Coll. Armed Forces, 1978-79; dir. programs Hdqrs. USAF, 1979-80, asst. dep. chief of staff for programs and evaluation, 1980; dir. legis. liaison McDonnell Douglas Corp., Washington, 1980-83, dir. internat. affairs, 1983-86; from v.p. to exec. v.p. Am. League for Exports and Security Assistance, 1986-92, exec. v.p., 1989-92; v.p. Am. Def. Preparedness Assn., 1992-97, Nat. Def. Indsl. Assn., 1997—. Decorated Air Force Cross, D.S.M. (2), Silver Star (3), D.F.C. (7), Bronze Star, Air medal (18), Meritorious Svc. medal (2), Air Force Commendation medal, Vietnamese Crosses of Gallantry with palm and star, Republic of Korea Cheongsu medal, comdr. Order of the Brit. Empire (CBE). Mem. Air Force Assn. (citation of honor 1968, Medal of Merit, 2002), Brit.-Am. Bus. Assn.-Washington (pres. 1982-94, chmn. 1994-96), Brit.-Am. Bus. Coun. (chmn. 1996-97), Am.-Air Mus. in Britain (exec. dir. 1984—), The Jefferson Islands Club, Capitol Hill Club, Congl. Country Club. Roman Catholic. Home: 1031 Delf Dr Mc Lean VA 22101-2009 Business E-Mail: jmcinerney@ndia.org.

**MCINERNEY, JAY**, writer; b. Hartford, Conn., Jan. 13, 1955; s. John Barrett and Marilyn Jean (Murphy) McI.; m. Linda Rositer, 1979 (div. 1979); m. Merry Reymond, June 7 1984 (dec.); m. Helen Bransford, Dec. 27, 1991 (separated). BA, Williams Coll., 1976; postgrad., Syracuse U. Reporter Hunterdon County Democrat, Flemington, NJ, 1977; textbook editor Time Life Pubs., Osaka, Japan, 1978-79; fact checker New Yorker, NYC, 1980; reader Random House Pubs., NYC, 1980-81; instr. English Syracuse U., 1983; writer, 1983—. Author: (novels) Bright Lights, Big City, 1984, Ransom, 1985, Story of My Life, 1988, Brightness Falls, 1992, The Last of the Savages, 1997, Model Behavior, 2000, How It Ended, 2001, Bacchus and Me: Adventures in the Wine Cellar, 2002, The Good Life, 2006; screenwriter: (films) Bright Lights, Big City, 1988; (TV movies) Gia, 1998; (TV series) Hotel Room, 1993; contbr. articles to profl. jours. Princeton in Asia fellow, 1977. Mem. Authors Guild, PEN, Writers Guild. Address: 1572 Old Hillsboro Rd Franklin TN 37069-9135 Office: care Amanda Urban Intl Creative Mgt 40 W 57th St New York NY 10019-4001 also: Apt 15B 455 W 23rd St New York NY 10011-2153*

**MCINERNY, RALPH MATTHEW**, philosopher, educator, writer; b. Mpls., Feb. 24, 1929; s. Austin Clifford and Vivian Gertrude (Rush) McI.; m. Constance Terrill Kunert, Jan. 3, 1953 (dec. May 2001); children: Cathleen, Mary, Anne, David, Elizabeth, Daniel. BA, St. Paul Sem., 1951; MA, U. Minn., 1952; PhD summa cum laude, Laval U., 1954; LittD (hon.), St. Benedict Coll., 1978, U. Steubenville, 1984; DHL (hon.), St. Francis Coll., Joliet, Ill., 1986; DHL, St. John Fisher Coll., 1994, St. Anselm Coll., 1995, Holy Cross Coll., New Orleans, 2001. Instr. Creighton U., 1954-55; prof. U. Notre Dame, Ind., 1955—, Michael P. Grace prof. medieval studies Ind., 1988—, dir. dept. Ind., 1978-85, dir. Jacques Martin Ctr., 1978-2005. Vis. prof. Cornell U., 1988, Cath. U., 1971, Louvain, 1983, 95; founder Internat. Cath. U.; disting. vis. prof. Truman State U., Mo., 1999; Joseph lectr., Rome, 2003; vis. lectr. Pontifical U. of Holy Cross, Rome, 2006, Ctr. of Applied Law, Cath. U. Chile, 2006. Author: The Logic of Analogy, 1961, History of Western Philosophy, vol. 1, 1963, vol. 2, 1968, Thomism in an Age of Renewal, 1966, Studies in Analogy, 1967, New Themes in Christian Philosophy, 1967, St. Thomas Aquinas, 1976, Ethica Thomistica, 1982, History of the Ambrosiana, 1983, Being and Predication, 1986, Miracles, 1986, Art and Prudence, 1988, A First Glance at St. Thomas: Handbook for Peeping Thomists, 1989, Boethius and Aquinas, 1989, Aquinas on Human Action,

1991, The Question of Christian Ethics, 1993, Aquinas Against the Averroists, 1993, The God of Philosophers, 1994, Aquinas and Analogy, 1996, Ethica Thomistica, 1997, Student Guide to Philosophy, 1999, Vernunftgemässes Leben, 2000, Characters in Search of Their Authors, 2001, Conversion of Edith Stein, 2001, John of St. Thomas, Summa Theologiae, 2001, Defamation of Pius XII, 2001, Very Rich Hours of Jacques Maritain, 2003, Aquinas, 2003; (novels) Jolly Rogerson, 1967, A Narrow Time, 1969, The Priest, 1973, Gate of Heaven, 1975, Rogerson at Bay, 1976, Her Death of Cold, 1977, The Seventh Station, 1977, Romanesque, 1977, Spinnaker, 1977, Quick as a Dodo, 1978, Bishop as Pawn, 1978, La Cavalcade Romaine, 1979, Lying Three, 1979, Abecedary, 1979, Second Vespers, 1980, Rhyme and Reason, 1981, Thicker than Water, 1981, A Loss of Patients, 1982, The Grass Widow, 1983, Connolly's Life, 1983, Getting Away with Murder, 1984, And Then There Were Nun, 1984, The Noonday Devil, 1985, Sine Qua Nun, 1986, Leave of Absence, 1986, Rest in Pieces, 1985, Cause and Effect, 1987, The Basket Case, 1987, Veil of Ignorance, 1988, Abracadaver, 1989, Body and Soil, 1989, Four on the Floor, 1989, Frigor Mortis, 1989, Savings and Loan, 1990, The Search Committee, 1991, The Nominative Case, 1991, Sister Hood, 1991, Judas Priest, 1991, Easeful Death, 1991, Infra Dig, 1992, Desert Sinner, 1992, Seed of Doubt, 1993, The Basket Case, 1993, Nun Plussed, 1993, Mom and Dead, 1994, The Cardinal Offense, Law and Ardor, 1995, Let's Read Latin, 1995, Aquinas and Analogy, 1996, The Tears of Things, 1995, Half Past Nun, 1997, On This Rockne, 1997, Penguin Classic Aquinas, 1997, The Red Hat, 1998, What Went Wrong With Vatican II, 1998, Lack of the Irish, 1998, Irish Tenure, 1999, Grave Undertakings, 1999, Heirs and Parents, 2000, Shakespearean Variations, 2000, Book of Kills, 2001, Triple Pursuit, 2001, Still Life, 2001, Sub Rosa, 2001, Emerald Aisle, 2001, John of St. Thomas, Summa Theologiae, 2001, Law and Ardor, 2001, As Good as Dead, 2002, Celt and Pepper, 2002, Prodigal Father, 2002, Last Things, 2002, Ablative Case, 2003, Irish Coffee, 2003, Requiem For A Realtor, 2004, Green Thumb, 2004, Blood Ties, 2005, Irish Gilt, 2005, Soul of Wit, 2005, (memoirs) Only I Have Escaped to Tell You, 2006, Prudence of the Ilesh, 2006; editor New Scholasticism, 1967-89; editor, pub. Crisis, 1982-96; pub. Catholic Dossier, 1995-2002, Fellowship of Cath. Scholars Quar., 2003—. Exec. dir. Wethersfield Inst., 1989-92; bd. govs. Thomas Aquinas Coll., Santa Paula, Calif., 1993-2001; bd. dirs. Southern Cross Found., 1999—; mem. Pres. Bush's Com. on the Arts and Humanities, 2002—. With USMC, 1946-47. Fulbright rsch. fellow, Belgium, 1959-60, NEH fellow, 1977-78, NEA fellow, 1983, Catholic Scholars fellow, 1992-95; Fulbright scholar, Argentina, 1986, 87, Outstanding Philosophical scholar Delta Epsilon Sigma, 1990; recipient Thomas Aquinas medal U. Dallas, 1990, Thomas Aquinas Coll., 1991, Maritain medal Am. Maritain Assn., 1994, P.G. Wodehouse award CRISIS Mag., 1995; Gifford lectr. Glasgow U., Scotland, 1999-2000, Joseph lectr. Pontifical Gregorian Inst., Rome, 2003. Fellow Pontifical Roman Acad. St. Thomas Aquinas; mem. Am. Philos. Assn., Am. Cath. Philos. Assn. (past pres., St. Thomas Aquinas medal 1993), Cath. Acad. Scis., Am. Metaphys. Soc. (pres. 1992), Am. Maritain Assn. (pres. 2004—), Internat. Soc. for Study Medieval Philosophy, Medieval Acad., Mystery Writers Am. (Lifetime Achievement award 1993), Authors Guild, Fellowship Cath. Scholars (pres. 1992-95, Cardinal Wright award 1996, Premio Roncevalles de Navarre 2002). Office: U of Notre Dame Jacques Maritain Ctr 714 Hesburgh Notre Dame IN 46556-5677

**MCINNES, DONALD GORDON**, rail transportation executive; b. Buffalo, Nov. 6, 1940; s. Milton Gordon and Blanche Mae (Clunk) McI.; m. Betsy Campbell, Mar. 18, 1967 (dec. Feb. 1995); children: Campbell Gordon, Cody Milton; m. Carol Anne Haverty, Oct. 12, 1996; stepchildren: Molly Carolina, Lawrence Joseph. BA, Denison U., 1963; MS, Northwestern U., 1965; Cert. in Transp., Yale U., 1965. Budget mgr. operating AT&F R.R. Co., Chgo., 1969-71; v.p., COO Burlington No. Santa Fe Corp., 1995—; from asst. trainmaster to sr. v.p., COO AT&SF R.R. Co., San Bernardino, Calif., 1971—94, sr. v.p., COO Chgo., 1994—95; COO Burlington No. Santa Fe Corp., 1995—2000. Bd. dirs. Nocona Athletic Goods Co., Global Logistics Acquisition Corp.; founding mem. Intermodal Assn. N.Am., 1st chmn., 1991-93. Trustee, vice chair Vt. Acad., Saxtons River; chmn. bd. Found. for Intermodal Rsch. and Edn., Washington; chair bd. Heritage Mus. and Gardens, Sandwich, Mass.; bd. dirs. Highfield Hall, Falmouth, Mass. Served to 2d lt. USAF, 1965-67; capt. U.S. Army, 1967-69. Decorated Bronze Star. Mem. Ballymeade Country Club (North Falmouth, Mass.), Falmouth Yacht Club. Home: 75 Waterside Ave Falmouth MA 02540-3825

**MC INNES, WILLIAM CHARLES**, priest, academic administrator; b. Boston, Jan. 20, 1923; s. William Charles and Mary (Byrne) Mc Innes. BS, Boston Coll., 1944, AB, 1950, MA, 1951; STL, Weston Coll., 1958; PhD, NYU, 1955; degree (hon.), U. Bridgeport, Sacred Heart U., Xavier U., Cin., U. Scranton, Loyola U., Chgo., Fairfield U. Joined Soc. of Jesus, 1946; ordained priest Roman Cath. Ch., 1957; prof. mktg. and bus. ethics Sch. Bus. Adminstrn. Boston Coll., 1959-63, assoc. dean Sch. Bus. Adminstrn., 1961-63, dir. honors program, 1963-64, mem. citizens seminar planning com., 1959-63, dir. Nat. Jesuit Honor Soc., 1997—2003; pres. Fairfield (Conn.) U., 1964-73, prof. urban problems, 1969-72; pres. U. San Francisco, 1972-77, Assn. Jesuit Colls. and Univs., 1977-89; campus min. U. Conn., Storrs, 1990-96. Vis. fellow Woodstock Theol. Ctr., 1990—91; adj. prof. bus. ethics Boston (Mass.) Coll., 1996—. Life mem. United Cerebral Palsy Assn. Fairfield County; mem. adv. com. Conn. Dept. Social Svcs., 1993—96; chaplain Boston Coll. Alumni Assn., 1997—; past pres. bd. dirs. ABCD (cmty. action agys.); bd. dirs. Nat. Better Bus. Bur.; past pres. Conn. Assn. Cmty. Action Programs; founder Fairfield County Cmty. Forum Conn. Charter Oak Coll.; vice chmn. Nat. Better Bus. Bur. Found.; chmn. Calif. Coun. Humanities. Served to capt. USAF, 1942—46, CBI. Mem.: Alpha Epsilon Delta, Phi Kappa Theta, Delta Sigma Pi, Alpha Sigma Nu, Beta Gamma Sigma. Home: Jesuit Cmty Boston Coll Chestnut Hill MA 02467 Business E-Mail: mcinnewi@bc.edu

**MCINNIS, ROBIN LYNN**, voice educator; b. Joplin, Mo., Apr. 28, 1969; d. Ralph Harrison and Nancy Kaye Williston; m. Mark Thomas Muetzel (div.); children: Zachary Thomas Muetzel, Hannah Marie Muetzel; m. Scott Allan McInnis, July 8, 2002. BA, Graceland U., Lamoni, Iowa, 1991. Vocal and instrumental music tchr. K-12 Osborn-R.O. Schs., Osborn, Mo., 1991—95; vocal and instrumental music tchr. 6-12 Lathrop Schs., Lathrop, Mo., 1995—98; vocal and gen. music tchr. K-12 North Platte Schs., Dearborn, Mo., 1998—. Singer Cantata Singing Ensemble, Platte County, 2003—. Mem.: Mo. State Tchrs. Assn., Music Educators Nat. Conf., Am. Choral Dirs. Assn. (gen. music v.p. 2001—05). Home: 23515 DD Hwy Dearborn MO 64439 Office: North Platte R-1 Schs 212 W 6th St Dearborn MO 64439

**MCINNIS, SCOTT STEVE**, lawyer, former congressman; b. Glenwood Springs, Colo., May 9, 1953; s. Kohler McInnis and Carol Kreir; m. Lori McInnis; children: Daxon, Tessa, Andrea. BA, Ft. Lewis Coll., 1975; JD, St. Mary's Law Sch., 1980. Atty. Delaney & Balcomb P.C., Glenwood Springs, Colo., 1981—93; mem. Colo. State Ho. of Reps., 1984-93, chmn. agrl. livestock and natural resources com., 1986-90, majority leader, 1990-92; mem. U.S. Ho. Congresses from 3rd Colo. dist., 1993—2005; mem. rules com. U.S. Ho. Reps., 1998, mem. house ways and means com., 2001—, chmn. resources subcom. on forests and forest health; ptnr. Hogan & Hartson LLP, Denver, 2005—. Recipient Florence Sabin award, 1984, Guardian of Small Bus. award Nat. Fed. Ind. Bus., 1990, Lee Atwater Leadership award, 1991, and various awards from United Vets. Commn.; named Legislator of Decade and Legislator of Yr by Colo. Ski Country and Colo. Wildlife Found. Mem. Elks, Rotary, Phi Delta Phi. Republican. Roman Catholic. Office: Hogan & Hartson LLP 1200 17th St Denver CO 80202 E-mail: smcinnis@hhlaw.com.

**MCINTIER, RUSSELL J.**, retired writer; s. Ralph E. and Caroline M. McIntier; m. Gladys F. VanZandt, Sept. 12, 1965; children: Debbra F. Burchett, Russell J.(dec.). Br. chief US ATSC, Corpus Christi Army Depot, Tex., 1988—94, site mgr. Ft. Sill, Okla., 1980—88; team leader US ACRC, Pueblo Army Depot, Colo., 1966—80; airman/sgt. USAF, McConnell AFB, 1955—64. Survey officer US ATSC, Corpus Christi Army Depot, Tex.,

1990—94. Author: (novel) Hardscrabble, (short story) The Denver City No Girls Club (Cert. Of Exellence, 1997), (book of short stories) Peace Officer: A Collection of Short Stories. Achievements include Caregiver.

**MCINTIRE, LARRY VERN,** biomedical engineering educator; b. St. Paul, June 28, 1943; s. James Lawrence and Lenore Vineal (Converse) McI.; m. Suzanne G. Eskin, June 27, 1997. BChemE, MS, Cornell U., 1966; MA, Princeton U., 1968, PhD, 1970. Registered profl. engr., Tex. Asst. prof. Rice U., Houston, 1970-74, assoc. prof., 1974-78, prof. chem. engring., 1978—2003, E.D. Butcher prof., 1983—2003, chmn. dept., 1981-91, chmn. Bioscis. and Bioengring. Inst., 1991—2003, chmn. rsch. coun., 1988-91, dir. biomed. engring. lab., 1980—99, chmn. dept. biomed. engring., 1997—2003, Wallace Coulter prof., 2003—. Adj. prof. medicine Baylor Coll. Medicine, Houston, 1982—, U. Tex. Med. Sch., Houston, 1982—, M.D. Anderson Cancer Ctr., 2001—; chmn. dept. biomed. engring. Ga. Tech., 2003—; chmn. blood/materials working group NIH. Bethesda, Md., 1982-85; surgery and bioengring. study sect. NIH, 1984-88, 99-2003; com. on bioprocessing NRC, 1991-94; chmn. rheology subcom. Nat. Coun. on Thrombosis and Hemostasis, 1985-89. Editor-in-chief: Annals of Biomed. Engring., 2002—; contbr. articles to profl. jours. Recipient Merit award NIH, 1989; NSF fellow Cornell U., Princeton U., 1965-69, NATO-NSF postdoctoral fellow Imperial Coll., London, 1976-77. Fellow AAAS, Am. Inst. Med. Biol. Engring. (sec., treas. 1993-96, pres. 1997-98), AICHE (officer local sect. 1980-81, 86, Food Pharm. and Bioengring. divsn. award 1992, divsn. chair 1998), Biomed. Engring. Soc. (bd. dirs. 1992-97, pres. 1995-96, Disting. lectr. 1992); mem. N.Am. Soc. Biorheology (v.p. 1992-94, pres. 1994-96), N.Y. Acad. Scis., Am. Heart Assn. (coun. on thrombosis, exec. com. 1994-98), Faculty Club Rice U. (bd. dirs., chmn. 1982-84), Sigma Xi (nat. lectr. 1993-96), Nat. Acad. Engring. (editor-in-chief Annak Biomed. Engring., 2002-). Presbyterian. Avocations: tennis, squash, classical music, hiking. Office: Ga Tech Dept Biomed Engring Atlanta GA 30332-0535 Office Phone: 404-894-5057. E-mail: larry.mcintire@bme.gatech.edu.

**MCINTIRE, MIKE,** journalist; BA in Polit. Sci., Hartwick Coll., NY. Investigations editor, reporter The Hartford Courant, 1990—2003; metro. reporter The New York Times, 2003—. Author: (articles) Dangerous Doctors, 2000, US Response to Storms Becomes Weapon for Democrats in NY Race, 2005. Recipient National Public Service Award, Scripps Howard Foundation, 1992, Nat. Press Found. award, 1997, Pulitzer Prize for Breaking News, 1999. Office: New York Times City Hall Rm 9 New York NY 10007 Office Phone: 212-556-1947.*

**MCINTOSH, ANITA JANE,** retired administrative assistant; b. Huntington, W.Va., Mar. 5, 1937; d. Harold Herbert and Edwinna Work (Barnhart) Boyd; m. Melvin Dwight McIntosh, June 21, 1958; children: Kevin Neal, Menita Lynn. Art and Illustration cert. Famous Artists Schs., Conn., 1965. Sec. Life Ins. Co. of Ga., Atlanta, 1955—59, adminstrv. asst. Charlotte, 1982—99; sec. Santee Sales, High Point, NC, 1968—73; tchrs. aide Burke County Dept. Social Svcs., Morganton, NC, 1974—82; art instr. Myers Pk. United Meth. Ch., Charlotte, NC, 1988, 2002, 2005. Author: (poem) Teacher in the Church Today, 1991, (devotions) Upper Room Devotional Book, 2002, (poetry and watercolors) Musings and Images, 2004. Mem.: Charlotte Mecklenburg Sr. Games (Gold award, Silver award, Bronze award), Watercolor Soc. N.C. United Methodist. Avocations: watercolors, water-skiing, swimming. Home: 2832 Morris Ln Denver NC 28037 Home Fax: 704-483-9270. E-mail: waterwood@charter.net.

**MCINTOSH, CAROLYN LEIGH,** lawyer; b. Boulder, Colo., Dec. 10, 1955; d. Glen Elvis and Alice Joy McIntosh; m. Roger Alan Bucholz, Oct. 4, 1980 (div. Dec. 1998); m. Leland Kioshi Marable, Dec. 11, 1998. BA cum laude, Middlebury Coll., 1978; JD, U. Colo., 1981. Bar: Colo. 1981, U.S. Dist. Ct. Colo. 1981, Mont. 1988 (specially admitted), U.S. Dist. Ct. Mont. 1989, U.S. Ct. Appeals 2000. Rsch. asst. Rocky Mountain Mineral Law Found., Boulder, 1979—80; assoc. Sisk, Foley, Hultin & Driver, Denver, 1981—83, Hultin, Driver & Spaanstra, Denver, 1983—85; asst. atty. gen. Colo. Dept. of Law, Denver, 1986—88; assoc. Cogswell & Wehrle, Denver, 1988—89, shareholder, 1989—90; spl. asst. atty. gen. State of Mont., 1988—90; sr. assoc. Patton, Boggs & Blow, Denver, 1990—92; ptnr. Patton Boggs, LLP, Denver, 1992—, mng. ptnr. Denver office, 1993—2002. Assoc. adj. prof. Colo. Sch. Mines, 1991—2000; mem., atty. program to provide legal svcs. to indigent, Denver, 1982—86. Mem. procedural rules subcom. Colo. Air Quality Control Commn., 1983-84; mem. Lafayette Planning Commn., 1986-87, 95-99, Lafayette City Coun., 1987-99, mayor pro tem, 1989-91, mayor, 1995-99; mem. bd. Denver Regional Coun. Govts., 1990-99; mem. Regional Air Quality Coun., 1992-99, mem. exec. com., 1996-99; mem. Colo. Water Conservation Bd., 2001-04, Urban Drainage and Flood Control Bd., 1995-99. Mem. ABA (natural resources sect.), Colo. Bar Assn., Denver Bar Assn. (legal fees arbitration com. 1983-84, 86-87), Alliance Profl. Women (bd. dirs. 1986-90), Internat. Inst. Environ. Risk Mgmt. (bd. govs. 1996—). Office: Patton Boggs 1660 Lincoln St Ste 1900 Denver CO 80264-1901 Office Phone: 303-894-6127. Business E-Mail: cmcintosh@pattonboggs.com. Notable cases include: Environ. Def. Fund vs. Colo. Dept. Health, 1986, defending against unsuccessful challenge to the State of Colo.'s prevention of significant deterioration air quality regulations; State of Colo. vs. Idarado Mine Co., 1989, prosecution of superfund clean up claims against Idarado; Denver vs. Adolph Coons Co., et al, superfund cost recovery action.

**MCINTOSH, DAVID M.,** former congressman; b. June 8, 1958; m. Ruthie McIntosh. Grad., Yale Coll., 1980, U. Chgo., 1983. Bar: Ind., U.S. Supreme Ct. Spl. asst. domestic affairs to Pres. Reagan; spl. asst. to Atty. Gen. Meese; liaison Pres.'s Commn. on Privatization; spl. asst. to V.P. Quayle, dep. legal counsel to Council Pres.'s Coun. on Competitiveness; sr. fellow Citizens for a Sound Economy; founder Federalist Soc. for Law & Pub. Policy, now co-chmn.; mem. U.S. Congress from Ind., Washington, 1995-2001; ptnr. Mayer, Brown, Rowe and Maw, 2002—; prof., dept of econ. Ball St. Univ. Sch. of Bus., 2002—. Mem. State Bar of Ind. Republican. Office: Mayer Brown Rowe and Maw 1909 K St NW Washington DC 20006 Home: 3432 N George Mason Dr Arlington VA 22207-1840 E-mail: dmcintosh@mayerbrown.com.

**MCINTOSH, DENNIS KEITH,** veterinarian, consultant; b. Glen Ridge, N.J., June 12, 1941; s. Sheldon Weeks and Enid Nicholson (Casey) McI.; children: Kevin, Jamie. BS in Animal Sci., Tex. A&M U., 1963, BS in Vet. Sci., 1967, DVM, 1968. Asst. county agrl. agt., Cleburne, Tex., 1963—65; owner, operator Park North Animal Hosp., San Antonio, 1970—75, El Dorado Animal Hosp., San Antonio, 1973—. Co-chmn. vet. tech. adv. coun. Palo Alto Coll., 1995—, tchr. Animal Health Tech., San Antonio Coll., 1985-95; pres., mgr. Bexar County Emergency Animal Clinic, Inc., 1978-81; cons. vet. practice mgmt., mlpk., client rels.; spkr. for vet. meetings, assns.; co-host Ask the Vet, Adopt a Pet, Sta. KENS-TV, 1980-93; vet. mem. Tex. Bd. Health, 1984-89, chmn. disease control com., pers. com.; mem. environ. health, hosps. com. Team capt. Alamo Roundup Club and Pres.' Club of San Antonio C. of C., 1970-75; mem. Guadalupe County Youth Fair Bd., 1978-80. Contbg. author: Mosby's Review Questions and Answers for Veterinary Boards, 1998, Chicken Soup for the Pet Lover's Soul, 1998; contbr. articles to profl. jours. With Vet. Corps, USAF, 1968-70. Recipient Alumnus award Guadalupe County 4-H Club, 1979, Outstanding Svc. award San Antonio Coll., 1988-87, Outstanding Bus. Ptnrs. award N.E. Ind. Sch. Dist., 1995-96. Mem. AVMA, Tex. Vet. Med. Assn. (pres., chmn. bd. dirs.), Tex. Acad. Vet. Practice (charter mem., pres.), San Antonio C. of C. (life), Tex. County Agrl. Agts. Assn. (4th v.p. 1964), Am. Legion, Tex. Old Time Fiddler's Assn., Delta Soc. (pres. San Antonio chpt. 1989-90), Alpha Zeta. Office: 13039 Nacogdoches Rd San Antonio TX 78217-1960 Office Phone: 210-656-1444.

**MCINTOSH, ELAINE VIRGINIA,** nutrition educator; b. Webster, S.D., Jan. 30, 1924; d. Louis James and Cora Boletta (Bakke) Nelson; m. Thomas Henry McIntosh, Aug. 28, 1955; children: James George, Ronald Thomas, Charles Nelson. BA magna cum laude, Augustana Coll., Sioux Falls, S.D., 1945; MA, U. S.D., 1949; PhD, Iowa State U., 1954. Instr., asst. prof. Sioux Falls Coll., 1945-48; instr. Iowa State U., Ames, 1949-53, rsch. assoc.,

1955-62; postdoctoral rsch. assoc. U. Ill., Urbana, 1954-55; asst. prof. human biology U. Wis., Green Bay, 1968-72, assoc. prof., 1972-85, prof., 1985-90, emeritus prof., 1990—, writer, cons., 1990—, chmn. human biology dept., 1975-80, asst. to vice chancellor, asst. to chancellor, 1974-76. Author 3 books including American Food Habits in Historical Perspective, 1995, Lewis and Clark: Food, Nutrition, and Health, 2003; contbr. numerous articles on bacterial metabolism, meat biochemistry and nutrition edn. to profl. jours. Fellow USPHS, 1948-49. Avocation: travel. Office: LS 455 Human Biology U Wis Green Bay 2420 Nicolet Dr Green Bay WI 54311-7001

**MC INTOSH, JAMES EUGENE, JR.,** interior designer; b. Dadeville, Ala., Nov. 13, 1938; s. James Eugene and Jessie (Latimer) McI. B.Interior Design, Auburn U., Ala., 1961. Designer contract div. Rich's Dept. Store, Atlanta, 1961-64; assoc. William Trapnell & Assocs., Atlanta, 1964-70; dir. Interior Concepts, Inc., Atlanta, 1970-72; dir. design comml. design div. Rich's Dept. Store, 1972-80; v.p. Comml. Interior Designs, Inc., 1980-82; exec. staff Rollins Inc., 1982—; pres. Gene Mc Intosh & Assocs., 1985—. Fellow Am. Soc. Interior Designers (Presdl. citation 1974); mem. Nat. Trust Hist. Preservation, Ala. Hist. Soc., High Mus. Art, Soc. Archtl. Historians. Home: Gene McIntosh & Assocs 130 Church St Decatur GA 30030 E-mail: cmeneg@earthlink.net.

**MCINTOSH, JON CHARLES,** illustrator, graphics designer, painter; b. Alliance, Ohio, Aug. 8, 1947; s. John Cowles and Lucile Tipple (Ketcham) McI.; 1 child, Forgan Cowles. Student, Hobart Coll., 1965-67; BFA, R.I. Sch. of Design, 1974. Pres. McIntosh Ink, Inc., Key West, Fla., 1971—. Bd. ov overseers New Eng. Conservatory of Music, Boston, 1989-95; bd. dirs. Sail Martha's Vineyard. Illustrator: (book) The Foolish Dinosaur Fiasco, 1978, The Mysterious Zetabet, 1980, The Doctor's Handbook, 1982, Witch Way to The Country, 1995, Witch Way to the Beach, 1997, The Longest Hair in the World, 1999; author, illustrator: Hooked On Golf, 1986, Fineart: Gingerbread Sq. Gallery, Grannary Gallery, Casa Vieja Gallery. Artwork contbr. Ducks Unltd; art for advt. Bose, Wang, Digital, NASA. Recipient Silver medal V.I. Internat. Film Festival, 1976, Gold medal Soc. of Newspaper Designers, 1985, First place Francis Hatch Advt. Awards, 1987, First place New Eng. Newspaper Awards, 1998, Silver award Soc. Newspaper Designers, 2000. Mem. Soc. of Illustrators (Silver Funny Bone 1991), The Country Club. Republican. Episcopalian. Avocations: musician, ski racing, tennis, fishing, skeet shooting. Office: McIntosh Ink Inc 813 Frances St Key West FL 33040 Office Phone: 305-295-8277.

**MCINTOSH, L(ORNE) WILLIAM,** research and development company executive; b. Kingston, Ont., Can., May 1, 1945; s. Jack Lorne and Lillian (Oaks) McI.; m. Siobhan McAfee, May 18, 1998. BSBA, Lehigh U., 1967, MBA, 1968. Asst. prof. Union Coll., Cranford, NJ, 1968-72; sr. market rsch. analyst Merck, Sharp & Dohme, West Point, Pa., 1972-75, advt. copywriter, 1975-77, product mgr., 1977-80, assoc. dir. advt., 1980-82, dir. licensing and acquisitions, 1982, sr. dir. mktg., 1983-86; exec. v.p. mktg. Medco Containment Svcs., Inc., Fair Lawn, NJ, 1987-88; v.p. mktg. and bus. devel. Boehringer Mannheim Pharms., Rockville, Md., 1988-92; chmn. bd., CEO Target Mktg. Systems, Inc., Blue Bell, Pa., 1992-93; sr. v.p. bus. devel. and com. ops. Zynaxis, Inc., Malvern, Pa., 1993—95; sr. cons. SmithKline Beecham, Phila., 1995—97; sr. v.p. bus. devel. and fin., CFO VIMRx Pharms. Inc., 1997—98; pres., CEO Nexell Therapeutics, 1998—2000; pres., chief bus. officer FASgen, Inc., Balt., 2001—03; CEO, Q-RNA, Inc., N.Y.C., 2004—. Mem. Am. Econ. Assn., Am. Mktg. Assn., Lic. Execs. Soc., Antique Automobile Club Am., Model A Ford Club Am., Vintage Chevrolet Club Am., Pontiac Oakland Owners Club, Beta Gamma Sigma. Avocations: antique automobiles, woodworking, antique furniture restoration, music. Home: 1711 Cannongate Rd Forest Hill MD 21050-2203 Office Phone: 410-420-7638. E-mail: mcamci@msn.com.

**MCINTOSH, ROBERT B.,** lawyer; BS in Finance, Va. Tech.; JD, Wash. and Lee U.; MBA, Emory U. With King & Spalding, Atlanta, 1987—95; v.p., gen. counsel, asst. sec. Rock-Tenn Co., Norcross, Ga., 1995—2000, sr. v.p., gen. counsel, sec., 2000—. Named to mgmt. com. Rock-Tenn Co., Norcross, Ga., 2000—. Mem.: Atlanta Bar Assn. Office: Rock-Tenn Co 504 Thrasher St Norcross GA 30071 Office Phone: 770-448-2193. Office Fax: 678-291-7666. E-mail: bmcintosh@rocktenn.com.

**MCINTOSH, TERRIE TUCKETT,** lawyer; b. Ft. Lewis, Wash., July 20, 1944; d. Robert LeRoy and Elda Tuckett; m. Clifton Dennis McIntosh, Oct. 13, 1969; children: Alison, John. BA, U. Utah, 1967; MA, U. Ill., 1970; JD, Harvard U., 1978. Bar: NY 1979, Utah 1980. Assoc. Hughes, Hubbard & Reed, N.Y.C., 1978-79, Fabian & Clendenin, Salt Lake City, 1979-84, shareholder, 1984-86; staff atty. Questar Corp., Salt Lake City, 1986-88, sr. atty., 1988-92, sr. corp. counsel, 1992—. Instr. philosophy Douglass Coll. Rutgers U., New Brunswick, N.J., 1971-72; mem. adv. com. civil procedure Utah Supreme Ct., Salt Lake City, 1987—, judge nominating com. 5th Cir. Ct., Salt Lake City, 1986-88. Mem. Utah State Bar (ethics and discipline screening panel 1989-96, vice chair ethics and discipline rev. com. 1996-99, 2006—, co-chair law related edn. 1985-86, bar examiner rev. com. 2005—), Women Lawyers of Utah (chair exec. com. 1986-87, Woman Lawyer of Yr. award 2005), Salt Lake Legal Aid Soc. (trustee 1999—), Harvard Alumni Assn. Utah (bd. dirs. 1987—), Phi Beta Kappa, Phi Kappa Phi Office: Office Phone: 801-324-5532.

**MCINTURFF, FLOYD M.,** retired state agency administrator; b. Greenback, Tenn., May 1, 1923; s. Samuel Floyd and Hazel Agnes (Vaden) M.; m. Merle Celeste Sosna, May 27, 1950; children: Judith Margaret, Laura Ellen, Melissa Ann. BS, U. Tenn., Knoxville, 1950. Asst. to the chief engr., missiles Rockwell Internat., Columbus, 1957-73; chief, targeted jobs tax credit program Ohio Bur. Employment Svcs., Columbus, 1974-88; ret., 1988. Commd. officer U.S. Army Signal Corps., 1942-46, 51-52. Mem. Opera Columbus, Columbus Astron. Soc., Am. Atheists, Sons of Revolution, First Families of Tenn. Avocations: music, astronomy, photography, elderhostel. Home: 4985 Beatrice Dr Columbus OH 43227-2114

**MCINTYRE, ANITA GRACE JORDAN,** lawyer; b. Louisville, Ky., Jan. 29, 1947; d. Blakely Gordan and Shirley Evans (Grubbs) Jordan; m. Kenneth James McIntyre, Oct. 11, 1969; children: Abigail, Jordan Kenneth. BA, Smith Coll., 1969; JD, U. Detroit, 1975. Bar: Mich. 1975, U.S. Dist. Ct. (ea. dist.) Mich. 1975, U.S. Dist. Ct. (we. dist.) Mich. 1979, U.S. Ct. Appeals (6th cir.) 1979. Rsch. Rollins White & Rollins, Detroit, 1975-79; vis. assoc. prof. Detroit Coll. Law, 1979-81; assoc. Tyler & Canham, Detroit, 1981-82; prin. Anita G. McIntyre, P.C., Grosse Pointe, Mich., 1982-87, 91—; of counsel Nederlander Dodge & Rollins, Detroit, 1987-90; assoc. Damm & Smith, P.C., Detroit, 1990-91. Hearing panel chmn. Atty. Discipline Bd., 1985—. Editor, author (case notes) U. Detroit Jour. Urban Law, 1975; contbr. articles to profl. jours. Sec. Berry Subdivsn. Assn., Detroit, 1975-77; pres. Smith Coll. Club Detroit, 1982-86; mem. parents bd. U. Liggett Sch., Grosse Pointe, Mich., 1991,95; vice chair state pub. affairs com. Mich. State Coun. Jr. Leagues, 1998-2000, chair, 2001-. Mem.: Wayne County Juvenile Trial Lawyers Assn., Wayne County (Mich.) Probate Bar Assn., State Bar Mich., Edgemont Park Assn. (sec.), Jr. League Detroit (chair pub.affairs com. 1998—2001, vice chair Mich. state pub. affairs com. 1999—2001, chair 2001—02). Episcopalian. Avocations: skiing, swimming, needle point. Office Phone: 313-881-4433. Personal E-mail: agmcintyr@cs.com.

**MCINTYRE, BRUCE HERBERT,** media consultant, marketing professional; b. Takoma Park, Md., Jan. 24, 1930; s. Orrin Raymond and Leila Hazel (Olmsted) McI.; m. Natalie Ann Wolff, Oct. 10, 1953; children: Douglas A., Elizabeth W., Emily O., Catherine N.; Jane A. Student, Gannon Coll., 1954-57, U. Akron, 1958-61. Reporter, city editor Erie (Pa.) Times and News, 1949-57; reporter, city editor, asst. to exec. editor Akron (Ohio) Beacon Jour., 1958-67; with Battle Creek (Mich.) Enquirer & News, 1967-71, asst. mng. editor, 1967-68, mng. editor, 1968-71; exec. v.p., editor Oakland Press, Pontiac, Mich., 1971-77, pub., 1977-95; v.p., pub. div. Capital Cities/ABC Inc., 1987-96; chmn. Great Lakes Media Inc., 1995-96; pres.

McIntyre Media LLC, West Bloomfield, Mich., 1997—; sec., dir. Clarkston Fin. Corp., Mich., 1998—; chair, dir. Huron Valley State Bank, 2005—; councilman City of Orchard Lake Village, Mich., 1998—2004, mayor, 2001—04. Lectr. Am. Press Inst., 1968—; journalism juror Pulitzer Prizes, 1972— Served with AUS, 1951-53; lt. col. Res. ret. Mem. Soc. Profl. Journalists, Pine Lake Country Club (Bloomfield, Mich.). Episcopalian. Personal E-mail: bhmcintyre@comcast.net.

**MCINTYRE, EDWARD PATRICK, JR.,** not-for-profit executive; b. Montgomery, Ala., Aug. 27, 1969; s. Edward Patrick McIntyre Sr. and Mary Kathryn Campbell; m. Ellen Maureen Bowden, Aug. 9, 2003. BA, U. Ala., 1992; MA, U. Miss., 1995. Cert. preservation leadership Nat. Trust Hist. Preservation. Endangered properties coord. Ala. Hist. Commn., Montgomery, 1999—2002; exec. dir. Tenn. Preservation Trust, Nashville, 2002—. Mem. Sec. Interior's Adv. Coun., Selma-Montgomery Nat. Hist. Trail, Montgomery, 1998—2000; bd. dirs. Preservation Action, Washington, 2004—06, Belmont Mansion Assn., Nashville, 2003—06, Ala. Preservation Alliance, Montgomery, 1997—2001; mem. adv. bd. Tenn. Civil War Preservation Assn., Nashville, 2005—06; bd. dirs. Tenn. Conservation Voters, Nashville, 2003—06. Named one of 40 Under 40, Tennessean Newspaper, Nashville, 2004; Group Study Exch. fellow, Rotary Found., 2001. Episcopalian. Avocations: travel, photography, antiques, art. Home: 313 Fairfax Ave Nashville TN 37212 Office: Tenn Preservation Trust Ste 119 315 10th Ave N Nashville TN 37203 Office Phone: 615-259-2289. E-mail: ellenbowde@aol.com.

**MCINTYRE, JAMES G.,** lawyer; b. 1933; 3 children. BS, Stephen F. Austin State U.; LLB, Miss. Coll. Sch. Law. Bar: 1964. Atty. McIntyre Law Firm, Jackson, Miss., 1964—. Achievements include defense atty. for former Neshoba County Sheriff Lawrence Rainey, who won acquittal in the 1967 federal trial; defense atty. for Edgar Ray Killen, convicted of the 1964 manslaughter of 3 civil rights workers, Andrew Goodman, James Chaney and Michael Schwerner in June 2005. Office: McIntyre Law Firm 828 N State St Jackson MS 39202 Office Phone: 601-355-2481.

**MCINTYRE, JAMES OWEN,** insurance executive; b. Cleve., July 21, 1958; s. Owen Eugene and Carole Diane (Saladin) McI.; m. Marina Zeccardi, Dec. 4, 1981 (div.); children: Antoinette, Owen, Helen, Robert; m. Enid Draviczky, Apr. 4, 1998. BS, Pa. State U., 1980, M of Mgmt., 1992. CLU. Sales rep. Liberty Mutual Ins. Co., Boston, 1982-89; sales mgr. Prudential Ins. Co., Blue Bell, Pa., 1989-94, adv. coun. agents Ft. Washington, Pa., 1989; mgr. Del. Valley Fin. Group (agy. of Provident Mutual), Radnor, Pa., 1994-96; sales support and competition cons. Provident Mut. Ins. Co., Valley Forge, Pa., 1996-97, dir. competition and sales support officer, 1997-99, regional v.p., 1999—. Author: Economic Effect of Banks Entering the Insurance and Financial Services Industry, 1992. Mgr. Hatfield Area Little League, Pa., 1991-97; den leader Boy Scouts of Am., Hatfield, Pa., 1994-96. Recipient Pa. Life Roundtable award Pa. Assn. Life Underwriters, 1991. Fellow Life Underwriting Tng. Coun.; mem. Nat. Assn. Life Underwriters, Am. Soc. CLU & ChFC, Gen. Agt. and Mgrs. Assn. Republican. Lutheran. Avocation: golf. Office: Provident Mut Ins Co 1000 Chesterbrook Blvd Berwyn PA 19312-2421 Home: 39 Guilford Pl Burlington NJ 08016-4186 E-mail: JamesMcIntyre@providentmutual.com.

**MCINTYRE, JENNIFER NOEL,** academic administrator; b. Houston, Dec. 21, 1971; d. James Hutzel and Gloria Gayle Sadler; m. George McIntyre; 1 child, Katelyn Grace. BS, Ctrl. Mo. State U., Warrensburg, Mo., 1990—95; MS, Nova Southeastern U., Ft. Lauderdale, Fla., 2001—03. Mktg. dir. New times Newspaper, Miami & Ft. Lauderdale, Fla., 1997—99; grad. student advisor Nova Southeastern U., 1999—2001, dir. distance edn., 2001—05, asst. dean online programs, 2005—. Com. mem. Students with Disabilities Nova Southeastern U., 2003—, com. mem. Assn. Student Svcs., 2004—. Avocations: running, yoga. Home: 9917 NW 2nd St Plantation FL 33324 Office: Nova Southeastern Univ 3305 College Ave Fort Lauderdale FL 33314 Business E-Mail: mcintyrej@nsu.law.nova.edu.

**MCINTYRE, JERILYN SUE,** academic administrator; b. June 24, 1942; d. Frank Otto and Maxine (Ward) McIntyre; m. W. David Smith. Student, Stanford U., Italy, 1962; AB in History with distinction, Stanford U., 1964, MA in Journalism, 1965, cert. Summer Radio-TV Inst., 1965, tchrs. cert., 1968; PhD in Comms., U. Washington, 1973; postgrad. Inst. Edml. Mgmt., Harvard U., 1993. Corr. World News Bureau McGraw-Hill Pub. Co., L.A., 1965-67; asst. prof. dept. mass comm. Chico (Calif.) State Coll., 1968-70; asst. prof. Sch. Journalism U. Iowa, Iowa City, 1973-77; assoc. prof. dept. comm. U. Utah, Salt Lake City, 1977-2000, assoc. dean Coll. Humanities, 1984-88, assoc. v.p. acad. affairs, 1988-90, interim pres., 1997, v.p. acad. affairs, 1990-98; pres. Ctrl. Wash. U., Ellensburg, 2000—. Dir. Wall St. Jour. Publs. Workshop, Chico State Coll., 1968; mem. edn. adv. bd. NFL, 1996; mem. exec. com. coun. acad. affairs Nat. Assn. State Univs. and Land Grant Coll., 1995—98, chair, 1997; mem. steering com. Utah Edn. Network, 1995—98. Editl. asst. Chemical Week Mag., 1965-66, World News Bureau, 1966-67; mem. editl. bd. Journalism History; co-author: Symbols & Society; contbr. articles to profl. jours., chpts. to books. Mem. Utah Women's Forum. Named a David P. Gardner fellow, 1984; recipient Yesterday's Girl Scout Today's Successful Woman, Utah Girl Scout Coun., 1996, Salt Lake City chpt. Disting. Woman, AAUW, 1994. Mem.: Assn. Edn. in Journalism and Mass Comm. Office: 400 E University Way Ellensburg WA 98926-7501 E-mail: mcintyrej@cwu.edu.

**MCINTYRE, JERRY L.,** lawyer; b. Atlantic City, July 1, 1941; AB, Columbia U., 1963; JD, Fordham U., 1969. Bar: N.Y. 1969, R.I. 1970. Mem. McIntyre, Tate & Lynch, Providence, 1993—. Pres. town coun., Town of Jamestown, R.I., 1983-89. Fellow Am. Acad. Matrimonial Lawyers; mem. ABA (sect. family law), N.Y. State Bar Assn. (sect. trusts and estates law), R.I. Bar Assn., R.I. Bar Found. Office: McIntyre Tate & Lynch 321 S Main St Providence RI 02903-7108 Office Phone: 401-351-7700. Business E-Mail: jlm@mtlhlaw.com.

**MCINTYRE, JOHN ARMIN,** physics professor; b. Seattle, June 2, 1920; s. Harry John and Florence (Armin) McI.; m. Madeleine Forsman, June 15, 1947; 1 son, John Forsman. BS, U. Wash., 1943; MA, Princeton U., 1948, PhD, 1950. Mem. faculty elec. engring. Carnegie Inst. Tech., Pitts., 1943; radio engr. Westinghouse Elec. Co., Balt., 1944; research assoc. Stanford, 1950-57; mem. faculty Yale, 1957-63, assoc. prof., 1960-63; prof. physics Tex. A&M U., College Station, 1963-95, emeritus prof., 1995—; assoc. dir. Cyclotron Inst., 1965-70. Mem. council Oak Ridge Asso. Univs., 1964-71 Contbr. articles to profl. jours. Fellow Am. Phys. Soc., Am. Sci. Affiliation (exec. council 1968-73); mem. AAAS. Presbyterian. Achievements include research and publs. on scintillation counters for gamma ray spectroscopy; determination of nuclear charge distbns. by electron scattering; study of nuclear structure by neutron transfer reactions; devel. variable energy gamma ray beams, gamma ray cameras. Home: 2316 Bristol St Bryan TX 77802-2405 E-mail: jmcintyre@physics.tamu.edu.

**MCINTYRE, JOHN GEORGE WALLACE,** real estate developer, management consultant; b. Toronto, Ont., Can., July 26, 1920; s. George Crerar and Gwendolyn Alberta (Wallace) McI.; m. Ruth Elizabeth Wilson, July 26, 1945 (dec.); children: Angus, Heather, Robert, Anne. B of Commerce, U. Toronto, 1941; MBA, Harvard U., 1947. Budget acct. Abitibi Paper Co. Toronto, 1947-51; budget mgr., asst. gen. mgr. Ford of Can., Windsor, Ont., 1951-58, gen. mgr. mfg. ops., 1963-65; asst. mng. dir., mng. dir. Ford of Australia, Melbourne, 1958-63; exec. v.p., pres. Columbia Cellulose Ltd., Vancouver, B.C., Canada, 1965-67; v.p. retail devel. and distbn. Hudson's Bay Co., Toronto, 1967-84; pres. Rupert's Land Tng. Co., Hudson's Bay Co. Devels. Ltd.; trustee Internat. Council of Shopping Ctrs., 1970-84; v.p., gen. mgr. Broadcast Ctr. Devel. Project Can. Broadcasting Corp., 1984-88; cons., 1988—. Chmn. Soldiers' Tower Com., U. Toronto, 1998-2004. Served to capt. Royal Can. Ordnance Corps., 1942-45, ETO. Address: Ste 412 Richview Residence 105 Clement Rd Etobicoke ON Canada M9R 4C2

**MCINTYRE, JOHN LAWRENCE,** lawyer; b. St. Paul, Apr. 25, 1942; s. John F. and Mary E. (Clancy) McI.; m. Mary E. Seifert, May 6, 1967; children: Matthew, Aimee, Brendan. BA in Philosophy, Coll. St. Thomas, 1963; LLB, U. Minn., 1966. Bar: Minn. 1966, U.S. Ct. Appeals (8th cir.) 1966, U.S. Supreme Ct. 1984. Law clk. to judge U.S. Ct. Appeals (8th cir.), 1966-67; mem. Doherty, Rumble and Butler, St. Paul and Mpls., 1967-93; gen. counsel, v.p., sec. The Toro Co., Mpls., 1993—. Mem. ABA (law and acctg. com. bus. law sect.), U.S. Club, Minn. Bar Assn., Hennepin City Bar Assn., Minn. Corp. Counsel Assn. (dir.), Order of Coif. Roman Catholic. Office: The Toro Co 8111 Lyndale Ave S Minneapolis MN 55420-1196 Office Phone: 952-887-8059. Office Fax: 952-887-8920. Business E-Mail: larry.mcintyre@toro.com.

**MCINTYRE, LAURA LEE,** psychology professor, consultant; d. Lee Allen and Shirley Marie McIntyre. BA in Developmental Psychology, La Sierra U.; PhD, U. Calif., 1998. Cert. Behavior Analyst Behavior Analyst Certification Bd., 2001, in Sch. Psychology Calif., 2001, NY, 2004, lic. Psychologist NY, 2005. Behavior therapist Ctr. Autism and Related Disorders, Encino, Calif., 1997—98; preschool assessment team mem., collaborative family study UCLA, 1998—2002; sch. psychologist, behavior specialist Jurupa Unified Sch. Dist., Calif., 2001—02; predoctoral intern, pediat. and behavioral psychology Johns Hopkins Sch. Medicine, Balt., 2002—03; asst. prof. psychology Syracuse U., NY, 2003—. Ednl., psychol. cons Oswego County Dept. Health, NY, 2004—; consulting psychologist Little Lukes Childcare Ctr., 2005—; adj. asst. prof. pediat. SUNY Upstate Med. U., Syracuse, 2005—. Contbr. articles to profl. jours. in field. Bd. mem. mental health subcommittee Head Start, Early Head Start, Syracuse, 2003—; bd. mem. Families for Effective Autism Treatment Ctrl. NY, Syracuse, 2004—, Autism Task Force Oswego County, 2005—. Child Health and Human Devel. Rsch. Grant, NIH, 2006—. Mem.: NASP, APA (member-at-large 2005—), Acad. Mental Retardation, Am. Assn. Mental Retardation, Internat. Assn. Sci. Study Intellectual Disability. Office: Syracuse Univ Dept Psychology 430 Huntington Hall Syracuse NY 13244 Office Phone: 315-443-2354. Office Fax: 315-443-4085. Business E-Mail: llmcinty@syr.edu.

**MCINTYRE, MICHAEL JOHN,** lawyer, educator; b. Attleboro, Mass., Mar. 12, 1942; sd. John W. and Margaret E. (McBrien) McI.; m. May Ping Soo Hoo; children: Devin J., Colin J. AB, Providence Coll., 1964; JD, Harvard U., 1969. Bar: Mass. 1969, D.C. 1970. Vol. Peace Corps, Bhopal, India, 1964-66; assoc. Ivins, Phillips and Barker, Washington, 1969-71; dir. tng. Internat. Tax Program, Harvard U., Cambridge, Mass., 1971-75; prof. law Wayne State U., Detroit, 1975—. Cons. govt. of Egypt, State of N.Y., Navajo Tribe, govts. of Spain, Australia, 1975—; cons. UN Group Experts Internat. Coop. Tax Masters. Author: Readings in Federal Taxation, 1983, International Income Tax Rules of United States, 2d edit., 2001, (with Arnold) International Tax Primer, 1995, 2d edit., 2002; editor-in-chief Tax Notes Internat., 1989-91; contbr. articles to numerous publs. Office: Wayne State Univ Law Sch Detroit MI 48202 Office Phone: 313-577-3944. E-mail: mcintyre@wayne.edu.

**MCINTYRE, MIKE (DOUGLAS CARMICHAEL MCINTYRE II),** congressman; b. Lumberton, NC, Aug. 6, 1956; s. Douglas Carmichael and Thelma Riley (Hedgpeth) McIntyre; m. Lola Denise Strickland, June 26, 1982; children: Joshua Carmichael, Stephen Christopher. BA, 1978, JD, 1981. Bar: NC 1981, US Dist. Ct. (ea. dist.) NC 1984, US Dist. Ct. (mid. dist.) NC 1985., US Ct. Appeals (4th cir.) 1987, US Supreme Ct., 1987. Assoc. Law Office Bruce Huggins, Lumberton, 1981-82, McLean, Stacy, Henry & McLean, Lumberton, 1982-86; ptnr. Price & McIntyre PA, Lumberton, 1987-89; prin. McIntyre Law Firm, PA, Lumberton, 1989-96; congressman US Congress from 7th NC dist., 1997—. Mem. law-focused edn. adv. com. NC Dept. Pub. Instrn., 1986-87; mem. US Ho. Com. on Agr., 1997—, Nat. Security Com., 1997—; co-chmn. Coalition Task Force on Edn., 1997-98, Congrl. Task Force on Promotion of Fatherhood, Rural Health Care Coalition, 1999-2002, Dem. Task Force on Children, 1999-2000, Coalition Task Force on Bus. and Tech., Spl. Forces Caucus, 2002—; mem. President's Summit on Am.'s Future, 1997. Del. Dem. Nat. Conv., NYC, 1980, NC Dems., Raleigh, 1974—; pres. Robeson County Young Dems., Lumberton, 1982; sec.-treas. 7th Congl. Dist. Young Dems., NC, 1983, chmn., 1984; 2nd vice chmn. 7th Congl. Dist. Dems. So. NC, 1986-89, 1st vice chmn., 1989; mem. state adv. bd. North Carolinians Against Drug and Alcohol Abuse, Raleigh, 1984-85; chmn. Morehead Scholarship Selection Com., Robeson County, 1985-94; deacon, elder, clk. of session Presbyn. Ch.; active Boy Scouts Am., Lumberton, 1983; mem. NC Commn. on Children and Youth, 1987-89, NC Commn. on the Family, 1989-91; mem. Young Life Lumberton com., 1987-89; chmn. Robeson County US Constn. Bicentennial com., 1986-87; mem. lawyers' adv. com. to NC Commn. on Bicentennial of US Constn., 1986-89; bd. dirs. Robeson County Grp. Home, Lumberton, 1984-87, Lumberton Econ. Advancement for Downtown, Inc., 1987-90, pres., 1988-89, 89-90; chmn. legis. affairs com. C. of C., 1991, 92, 93, bd. dirs., 1992-94; mem. NC Mus. Hist. Assocs., 1987-89; mem. regional selection com. Gov.'s Award for Excellence in Tchg. Social Studies, 1991. Morehead Found. scholar, 1974-78; named one of Outstanding Young Men in Am., 1981, 84, 85, 88; Outstanding Young Dem. Robeson County Young Dems., 1984-85; one of State's Outstanding Young Dems. Young Dems. NC, 1984-85; recipient Algernon Sydney Sullivan award U. NC, 1978, Outstanding Young North Carolinian award NC Jaycees, 1988, Outstanding Young North Carolinians, Heart Robeson Jaycees, 1988, Nat. Bicentennial Leadership award for Individual Achievement Coun. for Advancement of Citizenship and Ctr. for Civic Edn., Washington, 1987, Gov.'s Outstanding Vol. Svc. award, 1989, Thomas Jefferson award Food Distbrs. Internat., 1998, 2002, Guardian of Small Bus. award, Nat. Fedn. Ind. Bus., 1997-99, Nat. Rural Health Legis. award, 1999, 2003, Outstanding Health Svc. award Cmty. Ptnrs. Health Net, 2000, Spirit of Enterprise award, US C. of C., 1997-98, Super Hero award Nat. Assn. Cmty. Health Ctrs., 2001-03, Internat. Pub. Policy award Internat. Assn. Pers Employment, 2002, Law Enforcement award, NC Narcotics Officers Assn., 2002, Quality Pub. Svc./Pub. Health and Health Care award Am. Fedn. Tchrs., 2001, Charles Dick Medal of Merit Nat. Guard Assn., 2000, Disting. Svc. to Agr. award Robeson County Crop Promotion Assn., 2001, Congrl. Partnership award Nat. Assn. Devel. Orgns., 2002, Admiral's Ctr. award Nat. Mfrs. Assn., 2004, MVP award Sr. Citizens League, 2004, Disting. Christian Statesman award, 2006; named to Legis. Honor Roll So. Econ. Devel. Coun., 1997, 2001-04, Beach Preservationist of Yr., Oak Island Preservation Soc., 2005. Mem. ABA (exec. com. citizenship edn. com. 1985-87, nat. cmty. law week com. 1982-83), Internat. Platform Assn., NC Bar Assn. (chmn. youth edn. and constn. bicentennial com. 1986-87, youth edn. com., exec. coun. young lawyers divsn. 1986-87), Robeson County Bar Assn. (founder, chmn. citizenship edn. com. 1982-94, law day com.), 16th Jud. Dist. Bar Assn., NC Acad. Trial Lawyers, NC Coll. Advocacy, Christian Legal Soc. (state adv. bd. 1986-90, state pres. 1987), Lumberton C. of C. (bd. dirs. 1992-94), The Ret. Officers' Assn. (hon. life), Order of Old Well, Lumberton Rotary Club (bd. dirs. 1995-96), Phi Beta Kappa, Phi Eta Sigma. Democrat. Avocations: tennis, skiing, softball, dance, bible study. Office: US Ho Reps 2437 Rayburn Ho Office Bldg Washington DC 20515 Office Phone: 202-225-2731. E-mail: congmcintyre@mail.house.gov.

**MCINTYRE, NINA M.,** counseling administrator; b. Hot Springs, Ark., Dec. 12, 1947; d. Stanley L. and V. Edith Lewis; m. Jerry R. McIntyre, June 1, 1974; 1 child, Laura M. BA in Psychology, Henderson State U., 1971; MS in Sch. Psychology, U. Ctrl. Ark., 1976. Nat. cert. sch. psychol. sch. psychol. specialist, lic. psychol. examiner Ark. Personal sec. U.S. Army Infantry Staff Surgeon, Fort Benning, Ga., 1968—69; rsch. asst. Ctr. for Early Devel., Little Rock, 1974—76; psychologist II State Youth Svcs., Little Rock, 1976—78; sch. psychol. Sp. LPE Little Rock Schs., Little Rock, 1978—. Mem. Cmty. Mental Health Adv. Bd., Little Rock, 1978—79. Mem.: NEA, Ark. Edn. Assn., Ark. Sch. Psychol. Assn., Nat. Assn. Sch. Psychologists. Episcopalian. Avocations: reading, travel. Home: 3208 Foxcroft Rd Little Rock AR 72227 E-mail: ninamcintyre99@hotmail.com.

**MCINTYRE, OSWALD ROSS,** physician; b. Chgo., Feb. 13, 1932; m. Jean Geary, June 5, 1957; children— Margaret Jean, Archibald Ross, Elizabeth Geary. AB cum laude, Dartmouth Coll., 1953, postgrad, 1953-55; MD, Harvard U., 1957. Intern U. Pa. Hosp., 1957-58; resident in medicine Dartmouth Med. Sch. Affiliated Hosps., 1958-60; instr. medicine Dartmouth Coll., 1964-66, asst. prof. medicine, 1966-69, assoc. prof., 1969-75, prof., 1976—, James J. Carroll prof. oncology, 1980-95, dir. Norris Cotton Cancer Center, 1975-92, prof. emeritus, 1995—; attending physician VA Hosp., White River Junction, Vt., 1964. Cons. in hematology and oncology; acting chmn. dept. medicine Dartmouth-Hitchcock Med. Ctr., 1987-89; chmn. Cancer and Leukemia Group B.; 1990-95. Mem. Am. Soc. Hematology, Am. Assn. Cancer Rsch., Am. Soc. Clin. Oncology, Assn. Cancer Inst. (pres. 1988-89), New Eng. Cancer Soc. (pres. 1989-90). Home: 34 Lamphire Hill Ln Lyme NH 03768-3109

**MCINTYRE, PETER MASTIN,** physicist, researcher; b. Clewiston, Fla., Sept. 26, 1947; s. Peter Mastin and Ruby Eugenia (Richaud) McI.; m. Rebecca Biek, June 29, 1968; children: Peter B., Colin H., Jana M., Robert J. AB with honors, U. Chgo., 1967, MS, 1968, PhD, 1973. Asst. prof. Harvard U., Cambridge, Mass., 1975-80; group leader Fermilab, Batavia, Ill., 1978-80; assoc. prof. Tex. A&M U., College Station, 1980-84, prof. physics, 1985—, assoc. dean Coll. of Sci., 1990-92; pres. Accelerator Tech. Corp., Bryan, Tex., 1988—. Dir. Tex. Accelerator Ctr., The Woodlands, 1991—93. Recipient IR-100 award, Indsl. Rch. Mag., 1980; fellow, Sloan Found., 1976—78. Fellow: Am. Phys. Soc. (pres. Tex. sect. 1990—91); mem.: AAAS. Achievements include proton-antiproton colliding beams; E-beam assisted removal of mercury and sub-micron carbon particles from power plant exhausts; electronic pasteurization system for killing bacteria in food and removing organic contaminants in water; superconducting magnets for future hadron colliders; silicon microdevices for DNA sequencing; structured cable using high-temperature superconductors for practical coils; flux-coupled isochronous cyclotron driver for thorium-cycle nuclear fission power; creation of Visual Physics, a new laboratory/problem solving curriculum for first-year college physics; hybrid magnet technology for accelerating dipoles and spectroscopy solenoids to 25 Tesla; superconducting accelerator structures using YBCO high-temperature superconductor; a method by which to steer hurricanes; patents for continuous ionized tunneling system, gigatron high power microwave amplifier, microstrip chamber for medical imaging. Home: 611 Montclair Ave College Station TX 77840-2868 Office: Tex A&M U Dept Physics College Station TX 77843-0001 Office Phone: 979-845-7727. Business E-Mail: p-mcintyre@physics.tamu.edu.

**MCINTYRE, ROBERT WHEELER,** retired conservation organization executive; b. Chgo., Aug. 26, 1936; s. Henry Langenberg and Winifred (Wheeler) McI.; m. Emily Beardsley Taylor, Oct. 12, 1961 (div. 1985); children: W. Burley, Nancy T., Oliver W., Shanna L., Amanda K.; m. Miriam de Jesus Zarate, June 23, 1990 (div. 1998); m. Myung Sook Son, Jan. 6, 2001, 1 child Suzanne Felton. AB in Sociology, Stanford U., 1959; MBA, Harvard U., Cambridge, Mass., 1964. Loan analyst Wells Fargo Bank, San Francisco, 1964-65; supr. budget analysis Ford Aerospace, Palo Alto, Calif., 1965-69; controller Allied Life Scis., San Leandro, Calif., 1969-70; ptnr. Diplomat Mfg. Co., Palo Alto, 1970-71; staff cons. Opportunity Through Ownership, San Francisco, 1971-72; gen. mgr. Quality Metal Finishers, San Francisco, 1972-73; sr. v.p., chief fin. officer The Trust for Pub. Land, San Francisco, 1973—2003, ret., 2003. Adv. bd. Peninsula Open Space Trust, Menlo Park, 1978—, audit com., 2005—; adv. com. Marin Headlands, 1978—81; bd. dirs., treas. Robert C. Wheeler Found., Palo Alto, 1965—95; chair, bd. dirs. Families Adopting Interracially, San Jose, 1971—74; adv. Jr. Achievement, 1966; bd. dirs. Environ. Vols., Palo Alto, 1980—, diversity com., 2003—, chmn. fin. com., CFO, 2004—; bd. dirs. fin. com. Stanford U. Hist. Soc., 2005—; bd. dirs. Resource Renewal Inst., Sausalito, 1988—98, Water Heritage Trust, Sausalito, 1988—99, Dorothy Erskine Open Space Fund, San Francisco, 1978—, Sempervirens Fund, Mountain View, 2002—, treas., CFO, chmn. fin. com., 2003—, exec. com., 2003—. Lt. USN, 1959—62, hon. discharge USN, 1964. Recipient Presdl. Citation award Trust for Pub. Land, 1988, Spl. Svc. award Environ. Vols., 1989, Cert. of Recognition for Outstanding Svc. to Environ. Vols. Calif. State Senate, 2005. Mem. Harvard Club NY, Harvard Club Boston, San Francisco Tennis Club, Stanford Diamond Club, USS Coral Sea Assn., Palo Alto Tennis Club, Alpine Hills Tennis Club Portola Valley. Avocations: hiking, backpacking, tennis, travel. Home: 1061 Fulton St Palo Alto CA 94301-3313

**MCINTYRE, SARAH ELIZABETH,** vocalist; b. Jacksonville, N.C., Dec. 26, 1978; d. Luther Byron and Anne Elizabeth McIntyre. MusB, Samford U., Birmingham, Ala., 2001; MusM, Belmont U., Nashville, 2003. Pvt. voice tchr. Metropolis Sch. Performing Arts, Arlington Heights, Ill.; pvt. studio voice tchr. Fine Arts Voice, Chgo. Head voice dept. Metropolis Performing Arts Ctr., Arlington Heights; founder fine arts opera Fine Arts Voice, Chgo. Recipient Hon. Diploma, Minister of Culture, Russia, 2001; grantee Acting grantee, Victory Gardens Theatre, Chgo., 2004. Mem.: Nat. Assn. Tchrs. Singing. Office: Fine Arts Voice 410 S Michigan #616 Chicago IL 60605

**MCINTYRE, VIRGIE M.,** elementary school educator; b. Chesnee, SC, Feb. 27, 1923; d. Ed Lawson and Etta Rebecca (Jones) Mahaffey; m. Henry Bryson McIntyre, June 8, 1947; children: Teresa, Dawn. BA in edn., Berea Coll., 1945; M in supr. and adminstrn., Western Carolina U., 1964. Cert. advanced standing (reading) Syracuse U., 1968. Elem. tchr. Polk County Pub. Sch., Columbus, NC, 1945—53, 1957—65, Rutherfordton County, Spindale, NC, 1953—56; suprv. Polk County, 1965—67, reading cons., title 1 dir., 1968—70; reading ctr. prof. Western Carolina U., Cullowhee, NC, 1971—84; ret., 1984. Dir. reading conf. Western Carolina U., Cullowhee, NC, 1971—84, reading cons., 1971—84. Author: Reading Strategies and Enrichment Activities for Grades 4-9, Printing Spl. Level Christians, 1993; contbr. articles various profl. jours Vol. Outreach Min., Columbus, NC, 2000, Green Creek Computer Ctr., Tryon, NC, 2002; vol., dir, pianist Ch. Choir, Columbus, NC, 1984—99. Fellowship grant, Syracuse U., 1969. Mem.: Christian Writer's Group, NC Retired Employee Group. Independent. Avocations: painting, travel, swimming, music, volunteerism. Personal E-mail: tvtmacbd@alltel.com.

**MCINTYRE-IVY, JOAN CAROL,** data processing executive; b. Port Chester, N.Y., Mar. 1, 1939; d. John Henry and Molly Elizabeth (Gates) Daugherty; m. Stanley Donald McIntyre, Aug. 24, 1957 (div. Jan. 1986); children: Michael Stanley McIntyre, David John McIntyre, Sharon Lynne McIntyre; m. James Morrow Ivy IV, June 1, 1988. Student, Northwestern U., 1956-57, U. Ill., 1957-58. Assoc. editor Writer's Digest, Cin., 1966-68; instr. creative writing U. Ala., Huntsville, 1974-75; editor Strode Pubs., Huntsville, 1974-75; paralegal Smith, Huckaby & Graves (now Bradley, Arant, Rose & White), Huntsville, 1976-82; exec. v.p. Micro Craft, Inc., Huntsville, 1982-85, pres., 1985-89, ceo, chmn. bd., 1989—; also bd. dirs., co-owner. Author: numerous computer operating manuals for law office software, 1978—; co-author: Alabama and Federal Complaint Forms, 1979; editor: Alabama Law for the Layman, 1975; contbr. numerous articles to profl. jours and short stories to mags. and lit. mags. Hon. scholar Medill Sch. Journalism Northwestern U., 1956. Mem. Huntsville Literary Soc. (bd. dirs. 1976-77). Republican. Methodist. Office: 123 Fairington Rd NW Huntsville AL 35806-2429 Office Phone: 800-225-3147. Personal E-mail: verdictsales@aol.com.

**MCISAAC, CHRISTOPHER C.,** lawyer; b. Rochester, NY, 1959; BA with highest honors, U. NC, 1982; JD, U. Va., 1985. Bar: Va. 1985, DC 1986. Ptnr. Winston & Strawn LLP, Washington, 1995—. Adj. prof. law Georgetown U.; mem. power technologies subgroup U.S.-China Joint Commn. Commerce and Trade; spkr. in field. Contbr. articles to profl. jours. Bd. trustees Cmty. Preschool Palisades. Mem.: Va. State Bar Assn., DC Bar Assn., Phi Beta Kappa. Office: Winston & Strawn LLP 1400 L St NW Washington DC 20005-3502 Office Phone: 202-371-5971. Office Fax: 202-371-5950. E-mail: cmcisaac@winston.com.

**MCIVER, BARBARA BASORE,** language educator; b. Oklahoma City; d. George Milroy and Eleanor (Irvin) Basore; m. William Wood McIver. BA, U. Ark., 1968, MA, 1988, PhD, 1994. Tchr. St. Paul H.S., Ark., 1968—69, Ctrl. H.S., Kansas City, Mo., 1970—71; office mgr. AMC, Inc. Mech. Contractors, Fayetteville, Ark., 1972—85; grad. tchg. asst., lectr. U. Ark., Fayetteville, 1985—94; asst. prof., assoc. prof. Claflin U., Orangeburg, SC, 1994—, interim chair dept. English and fgn. langs., 2006—. Dir. Writing Ctr. Claflin U., Orangeburg, 2000—. Contbr. articles to profl. jours.; editor: Claflin Rev., 2003—. Faculty advisor Friends of Earth, Orangeburg, 1998—; Grantee, NEH, 2000—03. Mem.: S.C. Coun. on Langs., South Ctrl. Modern Lang. Assns., Phi Kappa Phi, Alpha Mu Gamma, Sigma Tau Delta. Office: Claflin Univ 400 Magnolia Orangeburg SC 29115 Office Phone: 803-535-5215. Business E-Mail: bmciver@claflin.edu.

**MCIVER, DEBORAH KAY,** tax specialist, entrepreneur, small business owner; b. Des Moines, Iowa, May 6, 1948; d. Floyd Malcolm and Nora Marguerite McIver. BS, N.Mex. Inst. Mining and Tech., 1970; MBA, Pepperdine U., 1981; postgrad., U. N.Mex., 1985—87. Chem. control technician McGaw Labs., Glendale, Calif., 1971—72; statistician Northrop Corp., Hawthorne, 1972—73; math. analyst TRW Sys. Group, Redondo Beach, 1973—76; sci. programmer ISS/Sperry Univac, Cupertino, 1976—77; mem. tech. staff TRW Sys. Group, Sunnyvale, 1977—78, ArgoSys., 1978—79; sr. sci. programmer Finnigan-MAT Corp., San Jose, 1979—82; software engr. Ford Aerospace Co., Sunnyvale, 1982—83; v.p. software ops. controller Askeri, Inc., Santa Clara, 1983; owner McIver Enterprises, 1983—86, Deborah K. McIver, MBA, EA, 1990—. Gen. contractor own home, 1994—95. Active Sea Scouts Am., L.A., 1975—76; friendly visitor United Way, L.A., 1977—79; judge Santa Clara County Sci. and Engring. Sci. Fair, 1980, 1982, 1984; instr., coord. AARP Tax-Aide, 1992—, Colo. state coord., 2006—. Mem.: Soc. Women Engrs. (v.p. San Francisco Bay Area sect. 1980—81, pres. 1981—82, sect. rep. 1982—83), N.Mex. Inst. Mining and Tech. Alumni Assn. (life; pres. No. Calif. chpt. 1980—81). Republican. Disciples Of Christ. Home and Office: PO Box 889 Monument CO 80132-0889 Office Phone: 719-488-3022.

**MCIVOR, DONALD KENNETH,** retired petroleum company executive; b. Winnipeg, Man., Can., Apr. 12, 1928; s. Kenneth MacIvor and Nellie Beatrice (Rutherford) McI.; children: Gordon, Deborah, Duncan, Donald, Daniel. BS with honors in Geology, U. Man., 1950; postgrad., Nat. Def. Coll., 1973. Geophysical trainee seismic crew Imperial Oil Ltd., Alta., 1950, various operational and rsch. positions in exploration Alta., 1950-58, held various positions including asst. to exploration mgr., suprv. exploration planning, mgr. exploration rsch. Calgary, 1958-68, with Jersey Prodn. Rsch. Co. Angola, France and Tulsa, Okla.; asst. mgr., mgr. corp. planning Toronto HO, 1968-69, mgr. exploration, 1970-72, sr. v.p., dir., 1973, exec. v.p., 1975; v.p. oil and gas exploration and prodn. Exxon Corp., 1977-81; dep. chmn., dir. Imperial Oil Ltd., 1981, chmn., chief exec. officer, 1982-85; dir. sr. v.p. Exxon Corp., Dallas, 1985-92; with John S. Herold Inc., 2006—. Bd. dirs. Nat. Coun. on Econ. Edn., Internat. Exec. Svc. Corps., N.W. Oil Co. Mem. Can. Soc. Petroleum Geologists, Am. Petroleum Inst. Home: 79 Lukes Wood Rd New Canaan CT 06840-2202 Personal E-mail: mcivordon@aol.com.

**MCJUNKIN, JOHN G.,** lawyer; b. Kingsport, Tenn., Jan. 5, 1962; s. John L. and Wanda (Goode) McJ.; m. Karen Russell, June 16, 1984. BA summa cum laude, Hamden-Sydney Coll., 1984; JD, U. Cin., 1987. Bar: N.C. 1987, D.C. 1989, Va. 1990. Md. 1993. Assoc. Moore & Van Allen, Raleigh, N.C., 1987-89, Taft, Stettinius & Hollister, Washington, 1989-90, Mays & Valentine, Arlington, Va.; ptnr. Bankruptcy & Bus. Reorganization practice, office mng. ptnr. DLA Piper Rudnick Gray Cary, Reston, Va. Active Vol. Lawyers Program, Raleigh, 1987-89; election advisor Rep. Nat. Com., Raleigh, 1988; law firm coord. United Way, Raleigh, 1988. Mem. ABA, N.C. Bar Assn., Va. Bar Assn., D.C. Bar, Arlington County Bar Assn., Order of Barristers, Phi Beta Kappa, Omicron Delta Kappa. Avocations: skiing, golf, tennis, fishing. Office: DLA Piper Rudnick Gray Cary Suite 400 1775 Wiehle Ave Reston VA 20190-5159 Office Phone: 703-773-4154. Office Fax: 703-773-6279. Business E-Mail: john.mcjunkin@dlapiper.com.

**MCKAGAN, DUFF (MICHAEL ANDREW MCKAGAN),** bassist; b. Seattle, Feb. 5, 1964; m. Amanda Brixx, May 28, 1988 (div. May 1, 1990); m. Linda Johnson, Sept. 1992 (div. Sept. 1995); m. Susan Holmes, Aug. 28, 1999; children: Grace, Mae Marie. Band mem. Fastbacks, 1980—81, The Fartz, 1981—82, 10 Minute Warning, 1982—84; bassist Guns n' Roses, 1985—97; re-formed 10 Minute Warning, 1998; bassist Velvet Revolver, 2002—. Albums: (with Guns n' Roses) Live Like a Suicide, 1986, Appetite for Destruction, 1987 (Am. Music awards Favorite Heavy Metal/Hard Rock Album, 1990, one of 100 Greatest Albums, VH1, 2001, #1, Spin mag.'s Greatest Metal Albums, 2002, one of 500 Greatest Albums of All Time, Rolling Stone, 2003), Guns n' Roses Lies, 1988, Use Your Illusion I, 1991, Use Your Illusion II, 1991, The Spaghetti Incident?, 1993, (solo album) Believe in Me, 1993, (with Velvet Revolver) Contraband, 2004; songs: (with Guns N' Roses) Welcome to the Jungle, 1987 (one of 500 Songs that Shaped Rock & Roll, Rock & Roll Hall of Fame, 1997, one of 100 Greatest Videos Ever Made, MTV, 1999), Sweet Child O' Mine, 1987, (Am. Music Awards Favorite Pop/Rock Single, 1989, MTV Video Music awards Best Heavy Metal Video, 1989, one of 100 Greatest Videos Ever Made, MTV, 1999, one of 100 Greatest Pop Songs, Rolling Stone & MTV, 2000, #3, VH1's 100 Best Songs of Past 25 Yrs., 2003), November Rain, 1991, (MTV Video Music awards Best Cinematography, 1992, one of 100 Greatest Videos Ever Made, MTV, 1999, one of 100 Greatest Videos, VH1, 2001); contbr.: (albums) Brick by Brick, by Iggy Pop, (films) The Dead Pool, 1988, Lean on Me, 1989, Interview with the Vampire, 1994, Grosse Point Blank, 1997, Hulk, 2003, (video games) Grand Theft Auto: San Andreas, 2004; actor: (TV series) Sliders, 1997. Named Best New Artist, MTV Video Music awards, 1988, Favorite Hard Rock Artist, Am. Music awards, 1990, 1992, World's Best Selling Hard Rock Artist of Yr., World Music awards, 1993; named one of 100 Greatest Artists of Hard Rock, VH1, 2000, Sexiest Artists, 2002, Top Pop Artists of Past 25 Yrs., 2004; recipient Video Vanguard award, MTV Video Music awards, 1992. Office: RCA Records 1540 Broadway New York NY 10036*

**MCKAGAN, MICHAEL ANDREW See MCKAGAN, DUFF**

**MCKANE, DAVID BENNETT,** business executive; b. Salem, Mass., July 10, 1945; s. Vernon Wilson and Barbara Inez (Bennett) McK.; m. Wilson Linebugh Baldwin, Apr. 16, 1977; adopted daughters, Taylor A., Lee and Paige Baldwin. BA, Dartmouth Coll., 1967; MBA, Amos Tuck Sch., 1969. Product mgr. Church & Dwight Co. Inc. (Arm and Hammer Products), NYC, 1969-72; v.p. NTA Inc. NYC, Nanuet, NY, 1972-75; v.p., exec. asst. to chmn. Schick Inc., Westport, Conn., 1975-77; v.p. Pruyn-77, COO, exec. v.p., 1979-84, treas., 1980-84; chmn., CEO A.I. Friedman, Inc., NYC, 1985-87; chmn. McKane Robbins & Co. Inc., NYC and Westport, 1986-96; mng. gen. ptnr. Riverland and Indian Sun, LC, Westport, 1996—. Bd. dirs. Oakhurst Dairy, Portland, Maine, Impax Corp., Westport. Bd. trustees Green Farms (Conn.) Acad., 1991—. Mem. New Eng. Soc. in City N.Y., Mass. Mayflower Soc., Union Club (N.Y.C.), Country Club Fairfield (Vero Beach, Fla.), RedStick Golf Club (Vero Beach, Fla.), Tucker's Point Club (Bermuda). Episcopalian. Home: 48 Owenoke Park Westport CT 06880-6833

**MCKAY, ALEXANDER GORDON,** classics educator; b. Toronto, Dec. 24, 1924; s. Alexander Lynn and Marjory Maude Redfern (Nicoll) McKay; m. Helen Jean Zulauf, Dec. 24, 1964; stepchildren: Julie Anne Stephanie Brott, Danae Helen Fraser. BA, U. Toronto, 1946; MA, Yale U., 1947, Princeton U., 1948, PhD, 1950; LLD (hon.), U. Man., 1986, Brock U., 1990, Queen's U., 1991; DLitt (hon.), McMaster U., 1992, U. Waterloo, 1993. Mem. faculty classics Wells Coll., 1949-50, U. Pa., 1950-51, U. Man., 1951-52, 55-57, Mt. Allison U., 1952-53, Waterloo Coll., 1953-55; mem. faculty McMaster U., 1957-90, prof., chmn. dept. classics, 1962-68, 76-79, dean humanities, 1968-73, mem. univ. senate, 1968-73, 85-87, prof. emeritus, 1990—; Disting. vis. prof. classics U. Colo., 1978; prof. in charge Intercollegiate Center for Classical Studies, Rome, 1975; vis. mem. Inst. Advanced Study, Princeton,

1979, 81. Vis. scholar U. Tex., Austin, 1987; Hardt, Vandoevres, Geneva, 88; vis. fellow Trinity Coll., Cambridge, 1988; adj. prof. humanities York U., 1990—96; Disting. vis. lectr. Concordia U., Montreal, 1992—93, prof. emeritus, 2001—; vis. scholar Rockefeller Study and Conf. Ctr., Bellagio (Como), Italy, 1993. Author: Naples and Campania: Texts and Illustrations, 1962, Roman Lyric Poetry: Catullus and Horace, 2d edit., 1974, Vergil's Italy, 1970, Cumae and the Phlegraean Fields, 1972, Naples and Coastal Campania, 1972, Houses, Villas and Palaces in the Roman World, 1975, reprint, 1998, Roman Satire, 1976, Vitruvius, Architect and Engineer, 1978, 2d edit., 1985, Römische Häuser, Villen und Paläste, 1980, Roma Antiqua: Latium and Etruria, 1986; co-author: Selections from Vergil, Aeneid I, IV and VI (Dido and Aeneas), 1988, Festschrift, The Two Worlds of the Poet: New Perspectives on Vergil, 1992, Tragedy, Love, and Change: Roman Poetic Themes and Variations, 1994, Arma Virumque: Heroes at War (Aeneid 10 and 12), 2 vols., 1998, Classics at McMaster (1890-2000), 2000, A Song of War: Readings from Vergil's Aeneid, 2003. Pres., bd. govs. Hamilton Philharm. Orch., 1967-96, Hamilton Chamber Music Soc., 1965-67, Hamilton br. Archtl. Conservancy Ont., 1965-67, Hamilton and Region Arts Coun., 1971-72; bd. dirs. Can. Fedn. Humanities, 1980-82; v.p., dir. Internat. Acad. Union, 1978-90; v.p. U. Bristol Inst. Greece, Rome and Classical Tradition, 1997—; trustee Hamilton Found., 1972-75; bd. govs. Art Gallery Hamilton; bd. govs., dir. Boris Brott Summer Music Festival, 1989-2000 (pres. 2001), Montreal Chamber Music Festival, 1997—; presdl. bd. trustees McMaster U. Art Gallery, 1985-91; pres. Sir Ernest MacMillan String Ensemble, 1988-90, pres. Nat. Acad. Orch., 2001—; mem. adv. bd. Inst. for Classical Tradition, Boston U., 1987-88; v.p., dir. Bach-Elgar Choral Soc., Hamilton, 1992-95. Decorated knight comdr. Order St. John of Jerusalem; officer Order of Can.; recipient Silver Jubilee medal Queen Elizabeth II, 1977, 125th Anniversary medal Can. Confedn., Golden Jubilee medal Queen Elizabeth II, 2002; Woodrow Wilson fellow, 1947-48, Can. Coun. fellow, 1973-74, Killam rsch. fellow, 1979-80, fellow Vanier Coll., York U., 1991—, vis. scholar, 1996—. Fellow Royal Soc. Can. (hon. editor 1970-83, pres. 1984-87, past pres. 1987-89, Centennial medal 1982); mem. Vergilian Soc. (pres. 1972-74, Hon. Pres. for Life 1988—, chmn. Villa Vergiliana mgmt. com. 1993—), Classical Assn. Mid. West and South (pres. 1972-73, award of merit com. 1989-91), Classical Assn. Can. (v.p. 1970-72, 76-78, pres. 1978-80), Ont. Classical Assn. (hon. pres. 1994—), Master Print and Drawing Soc. (Toronto) (v.p. 1998-2001, pres. 2001-05), Yale Club (N.Y.C.), Tamahaac Club (Ancaster), Arts and Letters Club (Toronto), X Club (Toronto), Univ. Club (McMaster). Home: 15 Inglewood Dr Hamilton ON Canada L8P 2T2 E-mail: ag.mckay@sympatico.ca.

**MC KAY, EMILY GANTZ**, civil rights and nonprofit professional; b. Columbus, Ohio, Mar. 13, 1945; d. Harry S. and Edwina (Bookwalter) Gantz; m. Jack Alexander McKay, July 3, 1965. BA, Stanford U., 1966, MA, 1967. From pub. info. specialist to rsch. assoc. Cmty. Action Pitts., 1967—70; freelance cons., 1969—70; pub. rels. and materials specialist Met. Cleve. JOBS Coun., 1971—72; rsch. and mgmt. cons. BLK Group, Inc., Washington, 1970—73; dir. tech. products Am. Tech. Assistance Corp., McLean, Va., 1973—74; rsch. and mgmt. cons. CONSAD Rsch. Corp., Pitts., 1974—76, v.p., 1976—78; spl. asst. to pres. for planning and eval. Nat. Coun. La Raza, Washington, 1978—82, v.p. rsch., advocacy & legislation, 1981—88, exec. v.p., 1983—88, cons. to pres., 1988—90, v.p. instl. devel., 1991—93, sr. v.p. instl. devel., 1993—94. Pres. Mosaica: Ctr. for Nonprofit Devel. and Pluralism, 1994—; cons. resource devel. New Israel Fund, 1989-91; cons. City of Cleve., Nat. Assn. Cmty. Devel., Nat. Coun. La Raza, 1975-78, Ford Found., 1989, Nat. AIDS Network, 1988-89, Am. Cultural Ctr., Israel, 1990, Nat. Hispana Leadership Inst., 1993; vol. orgnl. cons. SHATIL, Jerusalem and cmty. based groups in Israel, 1987—; guest faculty Union Inst. Grad. Sch., 1975-78; adj. faculty Sch. Internat. Svc. Am. U., Washington, 1995—; mem. faculty Salzburg (Austria) Seminar on Leadership, 2003. Author orgnl. devel. tng. materials and HIV/AIDS tech. assistance materials. Co-chmn. Citizens Adv. Com. to D.C. Bar, 1986-87; mem. Mayor's Commn. Coop. Econ. Devel., 1981-83; non-lawyer bd. govs. D.C. Bar, 1982-85; exec. com., bd. dirs. Indochina Resource Action Ctr., 1982-92; bd. dirs. exec. com. Southeast Asia Resource Action Ctr., 1993-97; co-chmn. Citizens Commn. Administrn. Justice, 1982-84; exec. com. Coalition on Human Needs, 1981-88; Washington area steering com. New Israel Fund, 1989-91; co-chmn. adv. com. to Washington dist. office dir. Immigration and Naturalization Svc., 1984-88; chair Refugee Women in Devel., 1987-90, vice-chair, 1990-94; nat. adv. bd. Project Blueprint United Way of Am., 1992-94, diversity com., 1994-96; vice-chair, treas. Fund for Future of Our Children, 1994—; sec. bd. dirs. New Bosnia Fund, 1995-99, U.S. vice-chair, 1997-99; bd. advisors Internat. Ctr. for Residential Edn., 1994-96; bd. dirs. Mary's Ctr. Maternal and Child Care, 1995-2000, treas., 1996-2000; treas., bd. dirs. AVODAH: The Jewish Svc. Corps., 1996-99; bd. dirs. Acad. of Hope, 2001—; bd. dirs. Nat. Hispana Leadership Inst., 1997-2003, treas., 1998-2003, Hispanic Link Journalism Found., Washington, D.C., 2004—; working group Memorandum of Understanding between HHS and Israeli Ministry of Labour and Social Welfare, 1990-94, chair subcom. Youth at Risk, 1992-94; adv. merit sel. panel Superior Ct. D.C., 1987-90; planning task force U.S.-Israel Women to Women, 2000-01. Recipient I. Pat Rios award Guadalupe Ctr., 1988, Milagro Beanfield award Ayuda, 2004; Ford Found. nat. honors fellow, 1966-67. Mem. NAACP, Nat. Coun. La Raza, Phi Beta Kappa. Democrat. Home: 3200 19th St NW Washington DC 20010-1006 Office: 1522 K St NW Ste 1130 Washington DC 20005-1225 Office Phone: 202-887-0620. Business E-Mail: Emily@mosaica.org.

**MCKAY, GEOFF**, private equity investor; b. Hope, B.C., Canada, Aug. 13, 1967; s. Gordon McKay and Sharon Ferguson. BA, U. Victoria, B.C., Can., 1990, MBA, U. Pa., 1997. Chartered acct., Can. Inst. Chartered Accts., 1994. Mgr. Ernst & Young, Victoria, 1990—95; assoc. Goldman Sachs, N.Y.C., 1997—99, London, 1999—2000, Forstmann Little & Co., N.Y.C., 2000—. Office: Forstmann Little & Co 767 Fifth Ave New York NY 10153 E-mail: gmckay@forstmannlittle.com.

**MCKAY, GRETCHEN KREAHLING**, dean, educator, director; d. Robert P. and Suzanne K. Kreahling; m. John H. McKay, Jr., July 15, 1995. PhD. U. Va., Charlottesville, Va. 1997. Asst. prof. art history Savannah (Ga.) Coll. Art and Design, 1997—2001; asst. prof. McDaniel Coll., Westminster, Md., 2001—06, dir. honors program, 2005—, assoc. prof., assoc. dean acad. affairs, 2006—. Curator Savannah Coll. Art and Design. Lectr. 48th Ann. Conf. Greek Orthodox Choirs, St. Louis; mem. renovation com. St. Paul's Greek Orthodox Ch., Savannah, 2000—01; lectr. St. Mark's Orthodox Ch., Bethesda, Md. Recipient Trumpeters award Most Inspiring Tchr., Trumpeters' Svc. Orgn., McDaniel Coll., 2005; summer fellow, Nat. Humanities Ctr., Durham, NC, 2004. Mem.: Internat. Ctr. Medieval Art, Byzantine Studies Conf. Avocations: painting, travel. Office: McDaniel Coll 2 College Hill Westminster MD 21157 Office Phone: 410-871-3388. Office Fax: 410-386-4657. Business E-Mail: gmckay@mcdaniel.edu.

**MCKAY, JOHN**, prosecutor, lawyer; b. Seattle, June 19, 1956; s. John Larkin and Kathleen (Tierney) M. BA, U. Wash., 1978; JD, Creighton U., 1982. Bar: Wash. 1982, U.S. Dist. Ct. (we. dist.) Wash. 1982, U.S. Supreme Ct. 1990, U.S. Ct. Appeals (9th cir.) 1990, D.C. 1999. Ptnr. Lane Powell Spears Lubersky, Seattle, 1982-92, Cairncross & Hempelmann, Seattle, 1992-97; pres. Legal Svcs. Corp., Washington, 1997—2001; US atty. (we. dist.) Wash. US Dept. Justice, 2001—. White House fellow, Washington, 1989-90. Mem. ABA (bd. govs. 1991-94), Wash. State Bar Assn. (pres. young lawyers divsn. 1988-89). Republican. Roman Catholic. Avocations: soccer, golf. Office: US Attys Office 700 Stewart St Ste 5220 Seattle WA 98101-1271 Office Fax: 206-553-0882.*

**MCKAY, JOHN PATRICK**, history professor; b. St. Louis, Aug. 27, 1938; s. John Price and Eleanor Jeffrey McKay; m. JoAnn Ott, Apr. 21, 1961; children: John Philip, Thomas Jeffrey. BA, Wesleyan U., Middletown, Conn., 1961; MA, Tufts U., 1962; PhD, U. Calif., Berkeley, 1968. From instr. to assoc. prof. history U. Ill., Urbana, 1966-76, prof., 1976-99, prof. emeritus, adj. tchg. prof., 1999—. Mem. author's adv. bd. Houghton Mifflin Co., Boston, 1992-94. Author: Pioneers for Profit: Foreign Entrepreneurship and

Russian Industrialization, 1885-1913, 1970 (Herbert Baxter Adams prize Am. Hist. Assn. 1970), Tramways and Trolleys: The Rise of Urban Mass Transit in Europe, 1976; co-author: (with B. Hill and J. Buckler) A History of Western Society, 1979, 8th edit., 2006, (with B. Hill, J. Buckler, P. Ebrey and R. Beck) A History of World Societies, 1983. Fellow for western Europe, Fgn. Area Program, 1964-66, John Simon Guggenheim fellow, 1970, Internat. Rsch. Exch. fellow, USSR, 1970, fellow NEH, 1984. Mem. Am. Hist. Assn., Econ. History Assn., Bus. History Conf., World History Assn., French Hist. Soc. Avocations: hiking, travel, gardening, cooking. Office: U Ill Dept History 810 S Wright St Urbana IL 61801 Business E-Mail: jpmckay@uiuc.edu.

**MCKAY, KENNETH GARDINER**, retired physicist, retired electronics company executive; b. Montreal, Quebec, Canada, Apr. 8, 1917; came to U.S., 1946, naturalized, 1954; s. James Gardiner and Margaret (Nicholas) McK.; m. Irene C. Smith, July 25, 1942; children— Margaret Craig, Kenneth Gardiner B.Sc., McGill U., 1938, M.Sc., 1939; Sc.D, MIT, 1941; D.Eng. (hon.), Stevens Inst. Tech., 1980. Research engr. Nat. Research Council Can., 1941-46; with Bell Telephone Labs., 1946-66, 73-80, dir. solid state device devel., 1957-59, v.p. systems engring., 1959-62, exec. v.p. systems engring., 1962-66, exec. v.p., 1973-80; v.p. engring AT&T, 1966-73; chmn. bd. Bellcomm Inc., 1966-73, Charles Stark Draper Lab., 1982-87; ret., 1987. Advisor Min. of Transp. and Comms., Republic of China, 1982-95. Trustee Stevens Inst. Tech., 1974-87; bd. govs. McGill U., 1972-77, N.Y. Coll. Osteo. Medicine, 1980-89; mem. vis. com. for engring. Stanford U., 1974-87; mem. sci. and acad. adv. com. U. Calif., 1980-88; mem. Sci. and Tech. Adv. Group, Republic of China, 1982-96. Fellow IEEE, Am. Phys. Soc., N.Y. Acad. Scis.; mem. NAS, NAE (councillor 1970-73), Century Assn. Home and Office: 200 E 66th St Apt A1901 New York NY 10021-9179

**MCKAY, MARGO MARQUITA**, federal agency administrator, lawyer; b. Baltimore, Md., Oct. 9, 1946; d. Gordon and Gary Venetia (Jones) M.; m. James Phillip Allen, Jr., June 10, 1978; children: Marja Allen, Eric Allen, Kaila Allen. BA, Fisk U., Nashville, Tenn., 1968; JD, Georgetown U., Washington, D.C., 1975. Bar: Penn. 1975, Va. 1982. Trial atty. US Dept. Justice, Washington, 1975-78; atty. Am. Legal Cons., 1979; br. chief Dept. Army US Dept. Def., 1980-81; mng. atty. Legal Serv. No. Va., Alexandria, 1982-83; exec. asst. to vice-chmn., sr. advisor, US Merit Systems Protection Bd., Washington, 1983-91; dep. dir. for ethics US Dept. Housing & Urban Devel., Washington, 1990; adminstrv. judge, temp. panel Office Employee Appeals, DC; dir. compliance, assoc. gen. counsel Fannie Mae; asst. sec. for civil rights USDA, Washington, 2006—. Author (high sch. textbook): Street Law, 1975. Recipient numerous employment awards, 1970—. Mem. ABA, Federal Circuit Bar Assoc. Office: USDA Jamie L Whitten Bldg 14th St & Independence Ave SW Rm 240-W Washington DC 20250*

**MCKAY, MARIE CONYERS**, librarian, writer; b. Brumley, Mo., Aug. 18, 1930; d. Raymond Harold Conyers and Nellie Mae Bunch; m. Julius S. McKay, Oct. 19, 1964; children: Michelle Leighanne O'Beirne, Rosemary Susan O'Hern. AA, S.W. Bapt. Coll., Bolivar, Mo., 1948; BA, Okla. Bapt. U., Shawnee, 1950; MA in Libr. Sci., George Peabody Coll. Tchrs. (now Vanderbilt U.), Nashville, 1951; M in Religious Edn., So. Bapt. Theol. Sem., Louisville, Ky., 1959. Libr. cataloger N.E. Mo. State Coll. (now Harry Truman State U.), Kirksville, 1951—53; libr. S.W. Bapt. Coll. (Now U.), Bolivar, Mo., 1953—57; dep. libr. Hong Kong Bapt. U., Kowloon, 1960—64; curator archive on the history of Christianity in China, 1996—98; libr. cataloger Miss. State U., Starkville, 1987—96. Contbr. articles to profl. jours. Missionary So. Bapt. Fgn. Mission Bd., Richmond, Va., 1959—64. Mem.: ALA. Baptist. Home: 108 Kyle Ct Gardendale AL 35071 Personal E-mail: mmckay@bellsouth.net.

**MCKAY, MELINDA**, hotel executive; b. Sydney, Australia, 1974; Corp. mktg. devel., rsch. svcs. Jones Lang LaSalle Hotels Asia Pacific; mktg. rsch. Jones Lang LaSalle Hotels, rsch. mgr. Chgo., 1997—99, sr. v.p., 2001—. Named one of 40 Under Forty, Crain's Chgo. Bus., 2005. Office: Jones Lang Lasalle Hotels 190 S LaSalle St Chicago IL 60603*

**MCKAY, MICHAEL WENDELL**, lawyer; b. Beaufort, SC, Dec. 14, 1949; s. John W. and Alice (Thornhill) M.; m. Leah H. McKay; children: Wendell, Slater, Watson, Harris. BA, La. State U., Baton Rouge, 1971, JD, 1974. Bar: La. 1974, U.S. Dist. Ct. (mid. dist.) La. 1974, U.S. Dist. Ct. (we. dist.) La. 1976, U.S. Dist. Ct. (ea. dist.) La. 1977, U.S. Ct. Appeals (5th cir.) 1977, U.S. Supreme Ct. 1977, U.S. Ct. Appeals (11th cir.) 1981. Assoc./ptnr. Brewer & McKay, Baton Rouge, 1974-80; ptnr. Roy, Kiesel, Patterson & McKay, Baton Rouge, 1980-84; pvt. practice Baton Rouge, 1984-88; dir. Hoffman Sutterfield, Baton Rouge, 1988-97; of counsel Shows, Cali & Burns, Baton Rouge, 1997-99; ptnr. McKay Williamson Lutgring & Cochran, LLC, Baton Rouge, 1999—2004, McKay Lutgring & Cochran, LLC, Baton Rouge, 2004—. Bd. dirs. Baton Rouge Area Found., 1994-97; treas., bd. dirs. Capital Area Legal Svcs. Corp., Baton Rouge, 1978-83. Mem. ABA, La. State Bar Assn. (bd. govs. 1995-98, treas. 1999-2000, pres., 2004-05, Pres.'s award 1997, Pro Bono Publico award 1994), Baton Rouge Bar Assn. (pres., sec., treas. 1989-93), La. Bar Found. (bd. dirs. 1998-2000), La. Assn. Def. Counsel (bd. dirs. 1999-2001), Am. Inns of Ct., La. Trial Lawyers Assn. (bd. govs. 1988-). Democrat. Episcopalian. Avocation: tennis. Home: 1558 Ingleside Dr Baton Rouge LA 70808-1200 Office: McKay Lutgring & Cochran 2431 S Acadian Thruway Ste 290 Baton Rouge LA 70808 Business E-Mail: mike@mlclawyers.com.

**MCKAY, MONROE GUNN**, federal judge; b. Huntsville, Utah, May 30, 1928; s. James Gunn and Elizabeth (Peterson) McK.; m. Lucile A. Kinnison, Aug. 6, 1954; children: Michele, Valanne, Margaret, James, Melanie, Nathan, Bruce, Lisa, Monroe. BS, Brigham Young U., 1957; JD, U. Chgo., 1960. Bar: Ariz. 1961. Law clk. Ariz. Supreme Ct., 1960-61; assoc. firm Lewis & Roca, Phoenix, 1961-66, ptnr., 1968-74; assoc. prof. Brigham Young U., 1974-76, prof., 1976-77; judge U.S. Ct. Appeals for 10th cir., Denver, 1977-91, chief judge, 1991-94, sr. judge, 1994—. Mem. Phoenix Community Council Juvenile Problems, 1968-74; pres. Ariz. Assn. for Health and Welfare, 1970-72; dir. Peace Corps, Malawi, Africa, 1966-68; bd. dirs. pres. Maricopa county Legal Aid Soc., 1972-74. Served with USMCR, 1946-48. Mem. Ariz. Bar Assn. Mem. Lds Ch. Office: US Ct Appeals 10th Cir Fed Bldg 125 S State St Ste 6012 Salt Lake City UT 84138-1181*

**MCKAY, PATRICIA A.**, corporate financial executive; CPA. V.p., fin., controller Dole Food Co., 1993—96; sr. v.p. fin. AutoNation Inc.; exec. v.p., CFO Restoration Hardware Inc., 2003—05, Office Depot, Delray Beach, Fla., 2005—. Bd. dir. Office Depot, 2004-05. Office: Office Depot 2200 Old germantown Rd Delray Beach FL 33445*

**MCKAY, RENEE**, artist; b. Montreal, Que., Can. came to U.S., 1946, naturalized, 1954; d. Frederick Garvin and Mildred Gladys (Higgins) Smith; m. Kenneth Gardiner McKay, July 25, 1942; children: Margaret Craig, Kenneth Gardiner. BA, McGill U., 1941. Tchr. art Peck Sch., Morristown, NJ, 1955-56. One woman shows include Pen and Brush Club, N.Y.C., 1955-58, Nat. Assn. Women Artists, Nat. Acad. Galleries, 1954-78, N.Y. World's Fair, 1964-65, Audubon Artists, N.Y.C., 1955-62, 74-79, N.Y. Soc. Women Artists, 1979-80, Provincetown (Mass.) Art Assn. and Mus., 1975-79; traveling shows in France, Belgium, Italy, Scotland, Can., Japan; represented in permanent collections: Slater Meml. Mus., Norwich, Conn., Norfolk (Va.) Mus., Butler Inst. Am. Art, Youngstown, Ohio, Lydia Drake Libr., Pembroke, Mass., Nat. Arts Club, N.Y.C., Provincetown Mus.- Mass., Provincetown, many pvt. collections. Recipient Jane Peterson prize in oils Nat. Assn. Women Artists, 1954, Famous Artists Sch. prize in watercolor, 1959, Grumbacher prize Watercolor award 1970, Solo award Pen and Brush, 1957, Sadie-Max Tesser award in watercolor Audubon Artists, 1975, Peterson prize in oils, 1980, Michael Engel prize Nat. Soc. Painters in Casein and Acrylic, 1983. Mem. Nat. Assn. Women Artists (2d v.p. 1969-70, adv. bd. 1974-76), Audubon Artists (pres. 1979, dir. oils 1986-88), Artist Equity (dir. 1977-79, v.p.

1979-81), N.Y. Soc. Women Artists, Pen and Brush, Nat. Soc. Painters in Casein and Acrylic M.J. Kaplan prize 1984, Nat. Arts Club, Provincetown Art Assn. and Mus., Key West Art Assn., Cosmopolitan Club.

**MCKAY, RICHARD JAMES**, professional sports team executive; b. Eugene, Oreg., Mar. 16, 1959; s. John H. and Nancy Jean (Hunter) McK.; m. Terrin Lea Few, May 19, 1984; children: K. Hunter, John Crosby. BA, Princeton U., 1981; JD, Stetson Coll. Law, St. Petersburg, Fla., 1984. Bar: Fla. 1984, U.S. Dist. Ct. (mid. dist.) Fla. 1984. Law clk. to Hon. William Terrell Hodges U.S. Dist. Ct. (middle dist. Fla.), Tampa, 1984-86; ptnr. Hill, Ward & Henderson, Tampa, Fla., 1986-92; gen. mgr. Tampa Bay Bucaneers, 1993—2003; pres., gen. mgr. Atlanta Falcons, 2003—. Adj. prof. Stetson Coll. Law, St. Petersburg, 1994—; co-chmn. NFL Competition Com., 1994—. Office: Atlanta Falcons 4400 Falcon Pkwy Flowery Branch GA 30542*

**MCKAY, RYAN THOMAS**, psychologist; b. Yarloop, Western Australia, Australia, Sept. 28, 1975; BSc in Psychology with honors, U. Western Australia, Perth, 1996; M in Psychology, Macquarie U., Sydney, NSW, Australia, 2004, PhD, 2004. Clin. neuropsychologist Nat. Hosp. for Neurology and Neurosurgery, London, 2004—05; rsch. assoc. Ctr. for Cognitive Studies, Tufts U., Medford, Mass., 2005—. Recipient Young Scientist's award, VII Internat. Symposium on Schizophrenia, 2005; Australian Postgraduate scholar, Australian Fed. Govt., 2000—03, Tng. fellow in Psychiat. Rsch., NSW Inst. Psychiatry, 2003, Postgraduate scholar for Schizophrenia Rsch., Neuroscience Inst. Schizophrenia and Allied Disorders, 2003—04. Mem.: Internat. Neuro-Psychoanalysis Soc., Cognitive Neuroscience Soc., Can. Soc. for Brain, Behaviour and Cognitive Sci., Soc. for the Study of Artificial Intelligence and the Simulation of Behaviour, Brit. Psychol. Soc. (assoc.). Office: Center for Cognitive Studies 111 Miner Hall Tufts Univ Medford MA 02155 Office Phone: +1 617 627 3297. Business E-Mail: ryan.mckay@tufts.edu.

**MCKAYLE, DONALD COHEN**, choreographer, director, writer, dance educator; b. NYC, July 6, 1930; s. Philip Augustus and Eva Wihelmina (Cohen) McKayle; m. Esta Beck, 1954; m. Leah Levin, 1965; children: Gabrielle, Liane, Guy Eylon. Student, CCNY. Mem. faculty Bennington Coll., Sarah Lawrence Coll., Conn. Coll., Bard Coll., Neighborhood Playhouse, Juilliard Sch., Martha Graham Sch., Am. Dance Festival; artistic dir. Calif. Inst. Arts, dean Sch. of Dance; prof. dance, artistic dir. U. Calif., Irvine, Claire Trevor prof. dance. Dancing debut, 1948; dir., 1964—; choreographer, 1950—, for cos. including, Alvin Ailey Am. Dance Theater, Batsheva Dance Co. Israel, Repertory Dance Theater, San Francisco Ballet, Cleve. San Jose Ballet, Dayton Cmtemporary Dance Co., Cleo Parker Robinson Dance Ensemble, Dallas Black Dance Theatre, L.A. Contemporary Dance Theatre, Am. Repertory Dance Co.; artistic mentor, resident choreographer Limón Dance Co., 1995; dir., choreographer stage prodns.: Free and Easy, 1961, Trumpets of the Lord, 1963 (Tony award nominee for best dir. and best choreographer 1975), Raisin, 1974 (Tony award nominee for best choreographer 1974), Dr. Jazz, 1975 (Tony award nominee for best choreographer 1975), The Last Minstrel Show, 1978, Evolution of the Blues, 1978-79, Sophisticated Ladies, 1981 (Best Choreographer award Outer Critics Cir. 1981, Tony award nominee for best choreographer 1981, NAACP Image award 1982); choreographer stage prodns.: The Tempest, 1963-64, Anthony and Cleopatra, 1963-64, As You Like It, 1963-64, Golden Boy, 1964 (Tony award nominee for Best Choreographer, 1965), A Time for Singing, 1966, The Four Musketeers, 1967, I'm Solomon, 1968, Mass., 1972; choreographer films: The Great White Hope, 1968, Bed Knobs and Broomsticks, 1970, Charlie and the Angel, 1972, The Jazz Singer, 1980; T.V. works include: Baseball Ballet, 1963, Amahl and the Night Visitors, 1963, Fan Fare, 1965, Jazz Dance, U.S.A., 1965, The Strolling Twenties, 1965, Ten Blocks of the Camino Real, 1966, The Ed Sullivan Show, 1966-67, The Bill Cosby Special, 1967, Soul, 1968, Soul, 1968, TCB, 1968, The Second Bill Cosby Special, 1968, The Sounds of Summer, 1969, The Leslie Uggams Show, 1969, Dick Van Dyke and the Other, 1969, And Beautiful, 1969, Yesterday, Today and Tomorrow, 1970, The Super Comedy Bowl, 1971, A Funny Thing Happened on the Way to a Special, 1972, The New Bill Cosby Show, 1972-73, Angelitos Negros, 1973, Free to Be You and Me, 1974, Good Times, 1974-78, The Minstrel Man, 1977 (Emmy nominee 1977), The Richard Pryor Special, 1977, Cindy, 1978; choreographer concert works: Games, 1951, Nocturne, 1952, Rainbow Round My Shoulder, 1959, Dist. Storyville, 1962, They Called Her Moses, Incantation, 1968, Migrations, 1972, Album Leaves, 1976, Blood Memories, 1976, and numerous others; (staged club acts and TV specials for Diana Ross, Ann-Margret, Harry Belafonte, Mary Tyler Moore and others; author (autobiography) Transcending Boundaries: My Dancing Life, 2002. Recipient Drama Logue Critics award Evolution of the Blues, Samuel H. Scripps Am. Dance Festival award, 1992, Capezio award, 1963, Lauds and Laurels profl. achievement award U. Calif. Irvine Alumni Assn., 1992, Disting. Faculty Lectureship award for rsch., 1997, Balasaraswati/Joy Ann Dewey Beinecke Endowed Chair for Disting. Tchg., 1997, Lifetime Achievement award Am. Dance Guild, 1994, Living Legend award Nat. Black Arts Festival, 1994, Balasaraswati, Joy Ann Dewey Beinecke Endowed chair for Disting. Teaching, Am. Dance Festival, 1997, Dance Mag. award, 2005; named One of America's Irreplaceable Dance Treasures: the first 100, Dance Heritage Coalition. Office: University California Irvine Arts Dance 300 Mesa Arts Irvine CA 92697-2775 Office Phone: 949-824-6798. Office Fax: 949-824-4563. E-mail: dmckayle@uci.edu.*

**MCKAY-WILKINSON, JULIE ANN**, minister, marriage and family therapist; b. Washington, D.C., Feb. 26, 1953; d. Charles William and Evelyn Loretta (Starr) McKay; m. Grover Gene Wilkinson, Jan. 13, 1990; 1 child, Angela Starr Gotti. AS, Camden County Coll., 1975; BA, Rowan U., 1978; grad., Unity Sch. Christianity, Lee's Summit, Mo., 1997. Cert. pastoral addictions counselor, and lic. addictions counselor, co-dependency counselor. Probation officer York County Probation, Pa., 1983—86; therapist pvt. practice, York, 1985—90, New Insights, York, 1985—87, Clare Ctr., York, 1987—90; founder, min., therapist Unity Christ Ch., Lubbock, Tex., 1997—2003. Editor: (monthly newsletter) Spiritual Sidelines, 1997—2003. Chairperson Christmas toy dr. Unity Christ Ch., 1997—2003, founder, Christmas bear dr., 2003—. Mem.: Lubbock Ecimenical Orgn. Democrat. Avocations: gardening, music, movies. Office: Christ Unity Church 7300 Mallard Creek Rd Charlotte NC 28262 Home: 2540 Pickway Dr Charlotte NC 28269 Office Phone: 704-599-1180. Personal E-mail: revjulie3@carolina.rr.com.

**MCKEACHNIE, GAYLE F.**, former lieutenant governor; b. Vernal, Utah, Jan. 26, 1943; s. Colton Orville and Helen (Fletcher) McK.; m. Kathlene Argyle, Dec. 15, 1967; children: Brett, Michelle, Jared, Ashley, Dana Marie, Jonathan, Jacob. BA, Coll. So. Utah, 1967; JD, U. Utah, 1970. Bar: Utah 1970, U.S. Dist. Ct. Utah 1970, U.S. Ct. Appeals (10th cir.) 1970, U.S. Tax Ct. 1985, U.S. Supreme Ct. 1985. Assoc. Senior & Senior, Salt Lake City, 1970-72; adj. faculty UT State U. 1972—2000; prin. Gayle F. McKeachnie & Assocs., Vernal, 1972-78; ptnr. McKeachnie & Allred, Vernal, 1978-81, Nielson & Senior, Vernal, 1981-89, pres., 1988-89, also bd. dirs.; adj. prof. BYU J. Reuben Clark Law School, 1996—2000; lt. gov. State of UT, Salt Lake City, 2003—05. Atty. Daggett County, Manila, Utah, 1974-79; dep. atty. Uintah County, Vernal, 1976-79; appointed to Utah Commn. on Adminstrn. Justice in the Dist. Cts. 1986; chmn. Utah Constl. Review Commn., 1989-01; mem. task force Mgmt. and Regulation of the Practice of Law, Utah Supreme Ct., 1990-92; bd. dirs. Utah Bar Commrs., 1990-94; adv., rural affairs advisor Utah Gov. Mem. Utah Ho. of Reps., Vernal, 1979-88; Utah Bd. State Lands and Forestry, 1992-94. Recipient Disting. Lawyer of Yr. award, Utah Bar Assn., 1997, Disting. Alumnus award, So. Utah U., 1995. Mem. Kiwanis (pres. 1977-78), Utah State U. (chmn., bd. trustees 1994-04), BYU J. Reuben Clark Law Sch. (bd. visitors 1998-00). Mem. Lds Ch. Office Phone: 435-789-4908. Business E-Mail: gmckeachnie@mckeachnie.com.

**MCKEAG, DOUGLAS BRUCE**, physician, educator; b. Berwyn, Ill., July 21, 1945; s. Diane (Dolan) McKeag; children: Heather, Kelly, Ian. BS in Zoology, Iowa State U., 1968; MS in Cardiov. Phys., Mich. State U., 1970,

MD, 1973. Diplomate Am. Bd. Family Practice. Intern Presbyn. Hosp., Pacific Med. Ctr., San Francisco, 1973-74; resident in family practice Grand Rapids Area Med. Edn. Ctr., Mich., 1974-76; fellow in family practice Mich. State U., East Lansing, 1976-77, fellow in adolescent medicine, 1976-77; team physician dept. intercollegiate athletics, 1977—95, assoc. dir., coordinator sports medicine, 1984—95, adj. assoc prof. sch. health edn., 1986—95; dir. Primary Care Sports Medicine. vice chmn. Dept. Family Medicine and Orthopedic Surgery U. Pitts., 1995—99, Arthur J. Rooney Sr. chair for sports medicine, 1996—99; chmn. Dept. Family Medicine Ind. U. Sch. Medicine, 1999—, OneAmerica prof. preventive health medicine, 1999—, dir. Ctr. Sports Medicine, 1999—. Mem. com. Nat. Bd. Med. Examiners, 1988—; mem. drug testing and drug edn. subcom. NCAA, 1988—; cons. Kuwait U. Faculty of Medicine, Walt Disney Ednl. Svcs., Puerto Rico Olympic Com.; presenter in field. Editor series Primary Care Sports Medicine, 1988—; Basketball (Handbook of Sports Medicine and Science), 2003; assoc. editor: Medicine and Science in Sports and Exercise, 1987; mem. editorial bd. various jours. in field; contbr. articles to profl. publs. Grantee Mich. Heat Assn., 1975-76, NIH, 1980-81, 81-82, 84, 85, Nat. Collegiate Athletic Assn., 1983, 88, Mich. Acad. Family Physicians, 1986; NIH fellow, 1968-70; named one of America's Top Doctors, 2005. Fellow Am. Coll. Sports Medicine (trustee 1987); Am. Acad. Family Physicians; mem. N.Am. Primary Care Rsch. Group, Soc. Tchrs. Family Medicine, Soc. Adolescent Medicine, Am. Medical Soc. for Sports Medicine, Am. Bd. of Family Practice, Am. Coll. Sports Medicine, Ind. Acad. Family Physicians. Office: Ind U Dept Family Medicine 1110 W Michigan St Indianapolis IN 46202 Office Phone: 317-278-0360. Business E-Mail: dmckeng@iupui.edu.

**MCKEAGE, ALICE JANE,** computer programmer; b. Saginaw, Mich., Mar. 27, 1948; d. Donald William and Genevieve Francis McK. BS in Edn., Ctrl. Mich. U., Mt. Pleasant, Mich., 1970. Tchr. Madison Dist. Pub. Schs., Madison Heights, Mich., 1970—79, computer programmer Retail Mgmt. Svcs., Birmingham, Mich., 1980—82, 3 PM, Livonia, Mich., 1982—85, Am. Fin. Cons. Co., Troy, Mich., 1985—87, Cats Co. Troy, 1988—90, Ford Motor Co., Dearborn, Mich., 1990—. Interviewee (TV show) Straight Talk About Gays in the Workplace, 2001. Co-founder gay, lesbian, bisexual transgender employee network Ford Motor Co., 1994; co-founder Race Matters, Detroit gay, lesbian, bisexual, transgender discussion group on racism and sexism, 2000; mem. human rights campaign Nat. Gay and Lesbian Task Force, Gay and Lesbian Alliance Against Defamation; mem. steering com. Main St. Pride, Royal Oak, Mich., 1996, outreach co-chair, 1997; bd. dirs. Affirmations Gay Lesbian Bisexual Transgender Cmty. Ctr., Ferndale, 2000—03. Recipient Cmty. Svc. award, Gay Lesbian Bisexual Transgender Pride, 1999, Spirit of Detroit award, Detroit City Coun., 2001, Unity award, Race Matters Day, Lesbian, Bisexual Transgender Pride award, 2002, Jan Stevenson award, Affirmations Gay and Lesbian Cmty. Center, 2004. Mem.: NOW, Out and Equal Workplace Advs. Democrat. Avocations: senior softball, gardening, hiking. Office: Ford Motor Co The American Rd Dearborn MI 48121

**MCKEAGUE, DAVID WILLIAM,** judge; b. Pitts., Nov. 5, 1946; s. Herbert William and Phyllis (Forsyth) McKeague; m. Nancy L. Palmer, May 20, 1989; children: Mike, Melissa, Sarah, Laura, Elizabeth, Adam. BBA, U. Mich., 1968, JD, 1971. Bar: Mich. 1971, US Dist. Ct. (we. dist.) Mich. 1972, US Dist. Ct. (ea. dist.) Mich. 1978, US Ct. Appeals (6th cir.) 1988. Assoc. Foster, Swift, Collins & Smith, Lansing, Mich., 1971-76, ptnr., 1976-92, sec.-treas., 1990-92; judge U.S. Dist. Ct., (we. dist.) Mich., Lansing, Mich., 1992—2005, US Ct. Appeals (6th cir.), 2005—. Adm. prof. Mich. State U. Coll. Law, 1998—. Mem. nat. com. U. Mich. Sch. Fund, 1980—92; gen. counsel Mich. Rep. Com., 1989—92; mem. adv. coun. Wharton Ctr. Mich. State U., 1996—2002; adv. bd. Corp. Supportive Housing, 2002—. With USAR, 1969—75. Mem.: FBA (bd. dirs. Western Mich. chpt. 1991—), Federalist Soc. Law and Pub. Studies (lawyers divsn. Mich. chpt. 1996—), Am. Inns Ct. (pres. Mich. State U. Coll. Law chpt. 1999—2001), Mich. Bar Assn., Country Club Lansing (bd. govs. 1988—92, 1995—2001). Roman Catholic. Office: US Ct Appeals 315 W Allegan Rm 119 Lansing MI 48933 Office Phone: 517-377-1563. E-mail: ca06-mckeague_chambers@ca6.uscourts.gov.

**MCKEAN, HOWARD CURTIS,** music educator, composer; b. New Orleans, La., Jan. 7, 1953; s. Raymond Lowell and Barbara Jean McKean; life ptnr. Kathleen Ann Wenz. MusB Edn., U. Nebr., Omaha, 1988. Cert. tchr. Nebr. Composer, freelance musician Omaha Arkestra, BlueHouse, Luigi Inc., 1970—; wholesale prerecorded music buyer Records and Tapes Inc., Omaha, 1977—84; tchr. Cathedral Arts Jazz Workshop, Omaha, 1998—2004; music tchr. Morton Mid. Sch., Omaha Pub. Schs., 1992—2004, Marrs Magnet Sch., Omaha Pub. Schs., 2004—. Artist-in-residence, schs. and cmtys. Nebr. Arts Coun., Omaha, 1992—. Composer, prodr.: jazz CD Fear Not, Luigi Inc.; composer: Distant Relatives, compositions for jazz sextet. Recipient Hon. Mention, Artist Fellowship Music Composition, Nebr. Arts Coun., 1991. Mem.: Omaha Edn. Assn. Home: 1906 S 33rd St Omaha NE 68105

**MC KEAN, JOHN ROSSEEL OVERTON,** university dean; b. Cortland, N.Y., July 31, 1928; s. Norman Dodge and Janet (Passage) McK.; m. Ruth MacDonald, July 2, 1955; children: Janet, Annalise. BA, Coll. William and Mary, 1951; M.Ed., Cornell U., 1956, Ed.D., 1961. Tchr. Landon Sch. for Boys, Washington, 1952-53; tchr. Central Sch., Homer, NY, 1953-55; asst. prof. history, dean students Allegheny Coll., 1957-67; headmaster Kingswood Sch. for Girls, Cranbrook, Bloomfield Hills, Mich., 1967-68; dean Hobart Coll., 1968-73; v.p. Coll. Kenyon Coll., Gambier, Ohio, 1973-77; dean arts and scis. State U. N.Y. at Canton, 1977-92. Mem. SUNY Coun. Deans Arts and Scis., Nat. Assn. Student Personnel Administrs. (pres. Pa. 1958-59), SUNY Coun. Two-Yr. Bus. Administrs., Nat. Assn. Student Personnel Administrs. (dir. 1959-61), Am. Assn. Higher Edn., C.C. Gen. Edn. Assn., Middle States Assn. Colls. and Secondary Schs., Direct Descs. Signers Declaration Independence (historian), St. Lawrence County Hist. Soc., Geneva Concerts Assn., (dir. 1969 72) Am Hist. Assn., Round Table, English-Speaking Union, St. Andrews Soc., Chapel Hill Tennis Club, Rotary, Phi Delta Kappa, Kappa Sigma. Home: 25 Flemington Rd Chapel Hill NC 27517-5638

**MCKEAN, KEVIN S.,** publishing executive, writer; b. Ann Arbor, Mich; BA in English cum laude, Yale U. Police reporter City New Bur. Chgo., 1974; gen. assignment writer, broadcast editor AP, Denver and New Orleans, 1975; nat. sci. writer NY, 1978; staff writer, sr. editor Discover mag., 1981—87; sr. editor, founding new media editor Money mag., 1987—97; asst. mng. editor for business and finance Time Inc. New Media; exec. editor Forbes.com; editl. dir., v.p. PC World mag., 2000—03; editorial dir., CEO InfoWorld Media Group, San Francisco, 2002—05; v.p. editl. dir. Consumers Union (consumer Reports). Spkr. in field. Sci. editor (3 hr. WGBH-produced pub. TV spl.) Living Against the Odds, 1991; contbr. chapters to books; appeared (TV programs) NBC'S Today show, CBS This Morning, CNN, CNBC, CNNfn. Named to Power Media 50, B2B Mag., 2005. Office: Consumers Union 101 Truman Ave Yonkers NY 10703-1057*

**MCKEAN, ROBERT JACKSON, JR.,** retired lawyer; b. N.Y.C., Dec. 21, 1925; s. Robert Jackson and Isabel (Murphy) McK.; m. Sally H. Ament; children from previous marriage: Katherine, Douglas, Lauren, Andrew. BA, Amherst Coll., 1950; LL.B., Harvard U., 1953. Bar: N.Y. 1954. Assoc. Simpson Thacher & Bartlett, N.Y.C., 1953-62, ptnr., 1962-85. Trustee Amherst Coll., Mass., Folger Shakespeare Library, Washington. Served with U.S. Army, 1944-46, ETO. Recipient medal for eminent service Amherst Coll., 1968 Mem. Phi Beta Kappa. Democrat.

**MCKEAN, THOMAS WAYNE,** dentist, retired military officer; b. Adams County, Ind., May 18, 1928; s. Gorman F. and Elmira B. (Staley) McK.; m. Marilyn Kimberlin, Aug. 9, 1952; children: Thomas Wayne, Randall K., Dana K. D.D.S., Ind. U., 1953; grad., Naval Dental Sch., 1963. Diplomate: Am. Bd. Oral Surgery. Commd. ensign Dental Corps USN, 1949, advanced through grades to rear adm., 1980; stationed at Naval Tng. Ctr., Great Lakes, Ill., 1953; dental officer U.S.S. Randall, 1953-56; head dental svc., asst. dental

officer U.S. Naval Acad./Naval Hosp., Annapolis, Md., 1956-59; dental officer FASRON III; asst. dental officer U.S. Naval Sta., Bermuda, 1959-63; postgrad. student Naval Dental Sch., Bethesda, Md., 1963-64; resident oral and maxillofacial surgery Naval Hosp., Great Lakes, Ill., 1964-66; dental officer U.S.S. America, 1966-68; chief oral surgery Naval Hosp., Orlando, Fla., 1968-70; dir. oral surgery and gen. practice residency tng. programs Naval Regional Med. Ctr., Great Lakes, 1970-74, chmn. dept. dentistry, 1970-74; cons., lectr. U.S. Army, Fort Sheridan, Ill., 1970-74; dir. oral surgery and gen. practice residency tng. programs Naval Regional Med. Ctr., Oakland, Calif., 1974-78, chmn., dept. dentistry, 1974-78; lectr. oral surgery Letterman Army Med. Ctr., San Francisco, 1974-78; clin. lectr. dept. oral surgery U. of Pacific Sch. Dentistry, San Francisco, 1974-78; comdg. officer Naval Regional Dental Ctr., Pensacola, Fla., 1978-80; lectr. oral surgery Pensacola (Fla.) Jr. Coll., 1978-80; cons., lectr. Dwight D. Eisenhower Army Regional Med. Ctr., Augusta, Ga., 1978-80; insp. gen. dental Bur. Medicine and Surgery, Dept. of Navy, Washington, 1980-81; comdg. officer Naval Regional Dental Ctr., San Diego, 1981-82; insp. gen. Naval Med. Command, Washington, 1983-85; ret. USN, 1985. Contbr. articles to profl. jours. Chmn. bd. trustees UMC, Winter Park, 1992, mem. bd. adminstrs. 1995-98; bd. dirs. Circle of Friends Fla. Hosp. Found., 1989-91, Fla. Hosp. Found., 1991—, chmn. bd., 1995-96; bd. dirs., chmn. Fla. Hosp. Found., 1991—; chmn. Fla. Hosp. Shares (Internat. Med. Missions), 1994—; mem. Fla. Hosp. Cmty. Benefits subcom., 1996—. Decorated Humanitarian Service medal, Legion of Merit with Gold Star, Meritorious Service medal, Nat. Def. Service medal with star, Vietnam Service medal, Republic of Vietnam Campaign medal with device, others; recipient Alumnus of Yr. award Ind. U. Sch.of Dentistry Alumnus Assn., 1988. Fellow Am. Dental Soc. of Anesthesiology, Internat. Coll. Dentists, Am. Coll. Dentists, Internat. Assn. Oral Surgeons; mem. Am. Assn Oral and Maxillofacial Surgeons, ADA, Western Soc. Oral Surgeons, Assn. Mil. Surgeons U.S. (medal), Fla. Soc. Oral Surgeons, Delta Sigma Delta, Sigma Chi (Significant Sig award 1983). Home: 1309 Temple Grove Ct Winter Park FL 32789-2716 Personal E-mail: tokinavy52@earthlink.net.

**MCKEAND, PATRICK JOSEPH,** newspaper publisher, educator; b. Anderson, Ind., June 10, 1941; s. William Dale and Iva Pearl (Shaw) McK. BA, Ind. U., 1963; MA, Ball State U., 1983. Staff writer The St. Petersburg (Fla.) Times, 1963; mng. editor The Anderson (Ind.) Herald, 1968-79; administr. analyst Ind. Medicaid Program, Indpls., 1980-81; assoc. prof. Defense Info. Sch., Ft. Ben Harrison, Ind., 1981-89; owner p.m. ink!, Indpls., 1989—. Pub. bd. dirs. Student Pub. at Ind. U., Purdue U. at Indpls., 1992—; bd. dirs. Miss Inds. Scholarship Pageant, Indpls., 2005—. Capt. U.S. Army, 1964-68. Recipient Ind.'s Sagamore of the Wabash award, 2003; decorated Bronze Star, Army Commendation medal with 1 oak leaf cluster. Mem. Soc. Profl. Journalists (bd. dirs.), Soc. Newspaper Design, Assn. Educators in Journalism and Mass Comm., Associated Press Mng. Editors Assn., Investigative Reporters and Editors, Ind. Collegiate Press Assn. (bd. dirs., exec. dir.), Coll. Media Advisors (Disting. Newspaper Adviser award 1998), Faculty Club IUPUI (bd. dirs. 2002—). Home: 4450 E 56th St Indianapolis IN 46220-5710 E-mail: pmckeand@iupui.edu.

**MCKEATING, THOMAS FRANCIS,** secondary school educator; b. Buffalo, N.Y., Feb. 13, 1948; s. Oliver Henry and Madelon Joan McKeating; m. Linda Josephine Varecka, May 19, 1972; children: Todd M., Colleen M. BS in Edn., SUNY, Buffalo, 1973, MS in Edn., 1976, MA in Econs., 1980. Tchr. Letchworth Ctrl., Gainesville, NY, 1973—74; Bishop Timon H.S., Buffalo, 1974—75; tchr., dept. chair West Seneca H.S., NY, 1975—2006. Mem. Buffalo Civil Rights Commn., 1975—78. Sgt. USAF, 1967—71, Ark., Germany. Mem.: N.Y. State United Tchrs. (editor 1986—2006, del. 1984—2003, 19 journalism awards 1986—2006). Democrat. Roman Catholic. Home: 7063 Brandywine Dr Derby NY 14047

**MCKEE, ADELE DIECKMANN,** retired church music director, educator; b. Atlanta, Oct. 29, 1928; d. Christian William and Emma Pope (Moss) D.; m. Dean Greer McKee, Nov. 14, 1972 (dec. July 1987). BA summa cum laude, Agnes Scott Coll., 1948; MA, Wellesley Coll., 1949; M in Sacred Music magna cum laude, Union Theol. Sem., N.Y.C., 1955. Tchr. Latin and music theory, chapel organist The Northfield Schs., East Northfield, Mass., 1949-53; tchr. Latin and English Westminster Schs., Atlanta, 1955-58; dir. music, organist Trinity Presbyn. Ch., Atlanta, 1955-83; asst. organist Cathedral St. Philip, Atlanta, 1984-85; organist, choir master St. Luke's Presbyn. Ch., Atlanta, 1985-89; ret., 1989. Dir. Montreat Conf. on Worship and Music, 1968; chmn. new music commns. Am. Guild of Organists Nat. Convention, Atlanta, 1992—. Choral reviewer The Am. Organist, 1967-71; contbr. articles to Reformed Liturgy mag., 1970—. Mem. City of Decatur Hist. Preservation Task Force, 1989-90. Fellow Am. Guild Organists (nat. councillor 1967-70, dean 1964-66, 76-78, program chmn. nat. conv. 1966, chmn. cert. work Atlanta chpt., mem. exec. com. 1999—); mem. Choristers Guild (nat. bd. dirs. 1976-79), Decatur Book Lovers' Club, Atlanta Young Singers, Young Singers Callanwolde (bd. dirs. 1993—, pres. bd. dirs. 1994-98.

**MCKEE, CATHERINE LYNCH,** lawyer, educator; b. Boston, June 7, 1962; d. Robert Emmett and Anne Gayle (Tanner) Lynch; m. Bert K. McKee Jr., Dec. 25, 1990; children: Timothy Kingston, Shannon Lancaster. BA in Biol. Sci., U. Calif. Berkeley, 1984; JD, U. San Diego, 1988. Bar: Calif. 1988, U.S. Dist. Ct. (cen., so. and ea. dists.) Calif. 1989, U.S. Ct. Appeals (9th cir.) 1989. Assoc. Parkinson, Wolf, Lazar & Leo, L.A., 1988—89, McCormick & Mitchell, San Diego, 1989—91; prof. Mt. San Antonio Coll., Walnut, Calif., 1994—, mock trial coach, 1994—2000, dir. paralegal program, 1999—2003, 2004—05. Cert. rev. hearing officer, Orange County, 1994-2004; legal counsel Imperial Valley Lumber Co., Valley Lumber and Truss Co., 1998—; coach nat. champion C.C. mock trial team, 2000; mem. acad. senate once. enun Mt San Antonio Coll., 1996-2000, chmn. campus equivalency com., 1999, chair paralegal program adv. com., 1999-2003, 04-05, verifier for cert. of online tchg., 2005—, adv. student club Paralegal Soc., 2006; mem. East San Gabriel Valley regional occupl. program adv. com., 2003—. Contbr. weekly newspaper column, 1993-99; prodr., star videos An Attorney's Guide to Legal Research on the Internet, 1998, 99; co-author: Jeff and Catherine's World's Best List of Legal (and Law-related) Internet Sites. Chair scholarship com. U. Calif. Alumni Assn., Berkeley, 1995—; capt. auction team SCATS Gymnastics, 2002—02. Named Cmty. Person of Yr., Diamond Bar C. of C., 1995. Mem. NEA, State Bar Calif. (probation monitor 1993—), Ea. Bar Assn. L.A. (trustee 2000—), Calif. Tchrs. Assn., Am. Inns of Ct., Calif. Assn. Lanterman-Petris-Short Hearing Officers. Avocations: weightlifting, photography, reading. Office: Mount San Antonio Coll 1100 N Grand Ave Walnut CA 91789-1341 Office Phone: 909-594-5611 ext. 4907. Business E-Mail: cmckee@mtsac.edu.

**MCKEE, CHRISTOPHER FULTON,** librarian, historian, educator; b. Bklyn., June 14, 1935; s. William Ralph and Frances McKee; m. Ann Adamczyk, 1993; children: Sharon, David. AB, U. St. Thomas, Houston, 1957; AMLS, U. Mich. 1960. Catalogue libr. Washington and Lee U., Lexington, Va., 1958-62; social sci. libr. So. Ill. U., Edwardsville, 1962-66, book selection officer, 1967-69, asst. dir., 1969-72; libr. of coll. Grinnell Coll., Iowa, 1972—2006, Samuel R. and Marie-Louise Rosenthal prof. Soc. of Navy rsch. chair naval history Naval Hist. Ctr., Washington, 1990—91; trustee Bibliog. Ctr. Rsch., Denver, 1984—88. Author: (book) Edward Preble, 1972, A Gentlemanly and Honorable Profession: The Creation of the U.S. Naval Officer Corps 1794-1815, 1991, Sober Men and True: Sailor Lives in the Royal Navy 1900-1945, 2002. Recipient U.S. Naval History prize, 1985, John Lyman Book award, N.Am. Soc. Oceanic History, 1991, Samuel Eliot Morison Disting. Svc. award, USS Constn. Mus., 1992; fellow NEH-Newberry Libr., 1978—79, Newberry Libr.-Brit. Acad., 1995—96. Mem.: U.S. Naval Inst., Soc. Historians Early Am. Republic, Orgn. Am. Historians, Soc. Mil. History, Navy Records Soc., Can. Nautical Rsch. Soc., Soc. Nautical Rsch. Home: 2382 Willowbrooke Ln Iowa City IA 52246-1834 Office: Grinnell Coll Burling Libr 1111 6th Ave Grinnell IA 50112-1690 Office Phone: 641-269-3351.

**MCKEE, CHRISTOPHER FULTON,** physicist, astronomer, educator; b. Washington, Sept. 6, 1942; m. Suzanne P. McKee; 3 children. AB in Physics summa cum laude, Harvard U., 1963; PhD in Physics, U. Calif., Berkeley, 1970. Physicist Lawrence Livermore (Calif.) Labs., 1969-70, cons., 1970—; rsch. fellow in astrophysics Calif. Inst. Tech., Pasadena, 1970-71; asst. prof. astronomy Harvard U., Cambridge, Mass., 1971-74; asst. prof. physics and astronomy U. Calif., Berkeley, 1974-77, assoc. prof., 1977-78, prof., 1978—; Miller Rsch. prof., 1984-85, 99, 2001, chair dept. physics, 2000—04; assoc. dir. Space Scis. Lab., Berkeley, 1978-83, acting dir., 1983-84, dir., 1985-98, Theoretical Astrophysics Ctr., Berkeley, 1985. Co-chair Astronomy and Astrophysics Survey com. NRC, 1998-2001. Fannie and John Hertz Found. fellow, 1963-69, Guggenheim fellow, 1998; Sherman Fairchild Disting. scholar, 1981, NAS, 1992. Fellow AAAS, Am. Phys. Soc. (exec. com. astrophysics divsn. 1986-88); mem. Am. Astron. Soc. (councillor 1981-84), Am. Acad. Arts and Scis., Internat. Astron. Union, Phi Beta Kappa. Office: U Calif Dept Physics Berkeley CA 94720-0001

**MCKEE, DAVID CHARLES,** neurologist; b. May 19, 1961; m. Marie-Laure Mazquiain, Dec. 29, 1984; children: Tyvand, Camille, Charlotte, Alexanne. BA in Chemistry, Macalaster Coll., 1983; MD, U. Wis., 1987. Diplomate Am. Bd. Psychiatry and Neurology, Am. Bd. Electrodiagnostic Medicine. Resident in neurology Oreg. Health Scis. U., 1987—91; Jeanne Timmins fellow Montreal Neurol. Inst., 1991—92; clin. neurologist Northland Neurology and Myology, Duluth, Minn., 1992—; chief sect. neurology St. Lukes Hosp. and Regional Trauma Ctr., Duluth, 1993—; assoc. prof. neurology Duluth Med. Sch. U. Minn., 1993—; pres. Northland Med. Assocs., 2000—02. Chmn. bd. dirs. Care North Health Sys., 2001—02. Comdr. USNR med. corp., 1998—. Fellow: Am. Assn. Electrodiagnostic Medicine; mem.: European Neurol. Soc., Am. Acad. Neurology, Alpha Omega Alpha, Phi Beta Kappa. Office: 1000 E 1st St Ste 202 Duluth MN 55805-2297 Home: 2215 E Superior St Duluth MN 55812

**MCKEE, DAVID LANNEN,** economics professor; b. St. John, N.B., Can., Apr. 18, 1936; arrived in U.S., 1961; s. Horace George and Mary K. (Lannen) McK.; m. Yosra A. Amara, Dec. 23, 1995. BA magna cum laude, St. Francis Xavier, 1958; MA, U. N.B., Fredericton, 1959; PhD, U. Notre Dame, 1966. Lectr. Ind. U., Ft. Wayne, 1965-66, asst. prof., 1966-67, Kent (Ohio) State U., 1967-69, assoc. prof., 1969-74, prof. econs., 1974—. Author: Growth, Development, and the Service Economy in the Third World, 1988, Schumpeter and the Political Economy of Change, 1991, Urban Environments in Emerging Economies, 1994; editor: Canadian American Economic Relations: Conflict and Cooperation on a Continental Scale, 1988, Hostile Takeovers: Issues in Public and Corporate Policy, 1989, Energy, the Environment and Public Policy, 1991, External Linkages and Growth in Small Economies, 1993; co-author: Developmental Issues in Small Island Economics, 1990, Accounting Services, the International Economy and Third World Development, 1992, Accounting Services, Growth, And Change in the Pacific Basin, 1996, Accounting Services and Growth in Small Economies, Evidence from the Caribbean Basin, 1998, Accounting Services, the Islamic Middle East and the Global Economy, 1999, Offshore Financial Centers, Accounting Serivces and the Global Economy, 2000, Crisis, Recovery, and the Role of Accounting Firms in the Pacific Basin, 2002, others; co-editor: Regional Economics: Theory and Practice, 1970, Spatial Economic Theory, 1970, Urban Economics: Theory Development and Planning, 1970, Structural Change in an Urban Industrial Region, 1987; contbr. articles to profl. jours. Mem. Internat. Acad. of Bus. Disciplines (pres. 2003-05), Am. Soc. for Competitiveness (adv. bd.), Am. Econ. Assn. Roman Catholic. Home: 616 Yacavona Dr Kent OH 44240-3318 Office: Kent State U Dept Econs Kent OH 44242-0001 Office Fax: 330-672-1096. Business E-Mail: dmckee@bsa3.kent.edu.

**MCKEE, DENISE MICHELLE,** history educator; b. Waynesboro, Pa., June 22, 1972; d. Dave and Margaret Brownlee; m. Virgil Dale McKee, June 10, 1997; children: August, Tyler, Raine. BS in Edn., Temple U., Phila., 1996. History tchr. Sch. Dist. of Phila., 1996—97, Duval County Schs., Jacksonville, Fla., 1997—99, Hawkins County Schs., Edison, Tenn., 2001—. Mario Fantini scholar, 1990. Home: 309 Bays Cove Trl Kingsport TN 37660

**MCKEE, ELLSWORTH R.,** food products executive; BA in Bus. and Econs., So. Adventist U., 1954; postgrad., Andrews U., 1987. Shipping/receiving clk. Jack's Cookie Co., Charlotte, NC, 1949-50; various positions McKee Foods, Collegedale, 1951-54, v.p. prodn. and fin., 1954-62, exec. v.p., treas., 1962-71, pres., CEO, 1971-96, also bd. dirs., 1954—, chmn. bd. dirs., 1997—. Bd. dirs. So. Adventist U., Collegedale, Andrews U., Berrien Springs, Mich., 1976—2000. Recipient Pvt. Sector Initiative Commendation, Pres. Ronald Reagan, 1988. Office: McKee Foods PO Box 750 Collegedale TN 37315-0750

**MCKEE, GEORGE MOFFITT, JR.,** civil engineer, consultant; b. Valparaiso, Nebr., Mar. 27, 1924; s. George Moffitt and Iva (Santrock) McK.; m. Mary Lee Taylor, Aug. 11, 1945; children: Michael Craig, Thomas Lee, Mary Kathleen, Marsha Coleen, Charlotte Anne. Student, Kans. State Coll. Agr. and Applied Sci., 1942—43, Bowling Green State U., Ohio, 1943; BS in Civil Engring., U. Mich., 1947. Registered profl. civil engr., Kans., Okla., land surveyor, Kans. Draftsman Jackson Constrn. Co., Colby, Kans., 1945-46; asst. engr. Thomas County, Colby, 1946; engr. Sherman County, Goodland, Kans., 1947-51; salesman Oehlert Tractor & Equipment Co., Colby, 1951-52; owner, operator George M. McKee, Jr.; cons. engrs. Colby, 1952-72; sr. v.p. engring. Contract Surety Cons., Wichita, Kans., 1974-2000; engring. cons. Wichita, 2000—. Adv. rep. Kans State U., Manhattan, 1957-62; adv. com. N.W. Kans. Area Vocat. Tech. Sch., Goodland, 1967-71; chmn. ofcl. bd. Meth. Ch., 1966-67. With USMCR, 1942-45. Mem. Kans. Soc. Profl. Engrs. (pres. N.W. profl. engrs. chpt. 1962-63, treas. cons. engrs. sect. 1961-63), Kans. County Engr's Assn (disp. v.p. 1950-51), N.W. Kans. Hwy. Ofcls. Assn. (sec. 1948-49), Nat. Soc. Profl. Engrs., Kans. State U. Alumni Assn. (life, pres. Thomas County 1956-57), Am. Legion (Goodland 1st vice comdr. 1948-49), Alumni Assn. U. Mich. (life), Colby C. of C. (v.p. 1963-64), Goodland Jr. C. of C. (pres. 1951-52), Masons (32 degree, Shriner), Order of the Ea. Star. Home: 3636 North Ridge Rd Apt 229 Wichita KS 67205-1219

**MCKEE, HARRY W.,** retired federal judge; b. 1940; PhB, U. N.D., 1963; LLB, George Washington U., 1966. Trial atty. US Dept. Justice, Washington, 1966-79, spl. asst., 1979, asst. US atty., 1979-82; apptd. magistrate judge ea. dist. US Dist. Ct. Tex., 1982—2006; ret., 2006. Mem. ABA, State Bar Tex., Smith County Bar Assn.

**MCKEE, JAMES LEE,** publisher, retail books executive, author, historian; b. Lincoln, Nebr., Dec. 12, 1940; s. Charlie and Charlotte Arline (Smith) McK.; m. Linda Lee Hillegass, June 9, 1978; 1 child, Laura Jane. B.A., B.S., U. Nebr., 1963. Pres., J & L Lee Corp., Lincoln, 1980—; corp. sec., treas. Bailey, Lewis & Assocs., Lincoln, 1969—; cons. Lincoln Pub. Schs., 1967—; prof. history Southeast Community Coll., Lincoln, 1972—; bd. dirs. KUCV Radio, 1986. Author: Nebraska Wildcat Banks, 1969, Lincoln: A Photo History, 1977, Lincoln The Prairie Capital, 1984. Contbr. articles on history to profl. jours. Organizer, Lincoln Host Family Assn., 1967, Lincoln, Lancaster Landmarks Soc., 1978; bd. dirs., treas. The Lincoln Found., 1975-81; bd. dirs. Lincoln, Lancaster Hist. Assn.; mem. Lincoln Hist. Preservation Commn., 1985; appointed to Mayor's Bicentennial of U.S. Constitution Com., 1986, bd. trustees, Nebr. State Hist. Soc., Served to sgt. U.S. Army, 1963-69. Recipient Numismatic Ambassador award Numismatic News, 1984. Mem. Nebr. Numismatic Assn. (life, editor 1955—); mem. Am. Booksellers Assn., Nebr. Writers Guild, Cen. States Numismatic Soc., Am. Numismatic Soc. Presbyterian. Clubs: Sertoma (bd. dirs.), Lincoln Coin (sec. 1958—). Avocations: numismatics; history; swimming; reading; book collecting. Home: 3425 Otoe St Lincoln NE 68506-3245

**MCKEE, JUDITH NELSON,** elementary school educator, educational consultant; b. Iowa Falls, Iowa, Nov. 8, 1939; d. Herbert and Emma (Czako) Nelson; m. Bernard B. McKee, Oct. 20, 1962; children: Susan Jennifer Ziegler, Blair David. BA, U. No. Iowa, 1961; MA, Roosevelt U., 1967;

postgrad., Ill. State U. Cert. tchr. K-9, learning disabilities K-12. Tchr. 2d grade Dist. 25 Pub. Schs., Arlington Heights, Ill., 1961-67; itinerant tchr. learning disabilities N.W. Suburban Spl. Edn. Dist., Palatine, Ill., 1968-72; tchr. Winnetka (Ill.) Pub. Sch. Nursery, 1974-75; tchr. spl. edn. North Suburban Spl. Edn. Dist., Glenview, Ill., 1975-76; tchr. gifted Worlds of Wisdom and Wonder, Evanston, Ill., 1985-87; instr. astronomy North Cook County Ednl. Svc. Ctr., Glenview, 1987; mem. faculty Nat. Louis U., Evanston, Ill., 1991—2004, DePaul U., Chgo., 2000—01; tchr. primary grades dist. 39 Wilmette, Ill., 1976—99; faculty U. No. Iowa, Cedar Falls, 2002—. Presenter, cons. state and internat. coms. Co-author: Integrating Instruction: Literacy and Science, 2005; author (with others): Physical Science Activities for Elementary and Middle School, 1987, Fact, Fiction, and Fantasy, 1995; contbr. articles to profl. jours. Named Ill. Honors Sci. Tchr. NSF, Ill. State. U., 1989-91. Mem. Internat. Reading Assn., Nat. Sci. Tchrs. Assn. (ret. adv. bd. 2000-03, chair 2002-03), Coun. Elem. Sci. Internat., Ill. Sci. Tchrs. Assn., Phi Delta Kappa. Presbyterian. Home: 315 Fairview Ave Winnetka IL 60093-4210

MCKEE, KEITH EARL, manufacturing technology executive; b. Chgo., Sept. 9, 1928; s. Charles Richard and Maude Alice (Hamlin) McK.; m. Lorraine Marie Celichowski, Oct. 26, 1951; children: Pamela Ann Houser, Paul Earl. BS, Ill. Inst. Tech., 1950, MS, 1956, PhD, 1962. Engr. Swift & Co., Chgo., 1953-54; rsch. engr. Armour Rsch. Found., Chgo., 1954-62; dir. design and product assurance Andrew Corp., Orland Park, Ill., 1962-67; dir. engring. Rsch. Ctr. Ill. Inst. Tech., Chgo., 1967-80, dir. mfg. prodn. ctr., 1977—. Prof. Ill. Inst. Tech., Chgo., 1979—, dir. indsl. programs, 1994—; coord. Nat. Conf. on Fluid Power, Chgo., 1983-88; mem. com. on materials and processing Dept. Def., Washington, 1986-92. Author: Productivity and Technology, 1988; co-author: Managing Technology Dependence Operation, 2004; editor: Automated Inspection and Process Control, 1987; co-editor: Manufacturing High Technology Handbook, 1987; mng. editor: Manufacturing Competitiveness Frontier, 1977-97. Capt. USMC, 1950-54. Recipient ounstanding presentation award Am. Soc. of Quality Control, Milw., 1983. Fellow World Acad. Productivity Scis.; mem. ASCE, Am. Def. Preparedness Assn. (pres. Chgo. chpt. 1972-95), Am. Assn. Engring. Soc. (Washington) (coor. com. on productivity 1978-88), Inst. of Indsl. Engrs., Soc. Mfg. Engrs. (Gold medal 1991), Am. Assn. for Artificial Intelligence, Robotic Industry Assn. (bd. dir. 1978-81), Assn. for Mfg. Excellence, Soc. for Computer Simulation. Democrat. Roman Catholic. Home: Ste 504 3115 S Michigan Ave Chicago IL 60616 Office: Illinois Inst Tech Mfg Productivity Ctr 3424 S State St Ste 4001 S Chicago IL 60616 Office Phone: 312-567-3650. Business E-Mail: mckee@iit.edu.

MCKEE, LYNN B., human resources specialist; B in Acctg., St. Joseph's U.; MBA, Drexel U. Various positions including dir. employee rels., dir. human resources and exec. devel. Aramark Corp., Phila., 1980—86, mgr. hqtrs. human resources, 1986—89, dir. human resources, 1989, v.p. exec. devel. and compensation, 1998—2001, sr. v.p. human resources, 2001—04, exec. v.p. human resources, 2004—. Mem. human resources roundtable group; mem. conf. bd. advisory coun. human resources mgmt. Office: Aramark Corp Aramark Tower 1101 Market St Philadelphia PA 19107-2988 Office Phone: 215-238-3000. Office Fax: 215-238-3333.

MCKEE, MARGARET JEAN, federal agency administrator; b. New Haven, June 20, 1929; d. Waldo McCutcheon and Elizabeth McKee. AB, Vassar Coll., 1951. Staff asst. United Rep. Fin. Com., N.Y.C., 1952, N.Y. Rep. State Com., N.Y.C., 1953—55, Crusade for Freedom (name later changed to Radio Free Europe Fund), N.Y.C., 1955—57; researcher Stricker & Henning Rsch. Assocs., Inc., N.Y.C., 1957—59; exec. sec. New Yorkers for Nixon (name later changed to N.Y. State Ind. Citizens for Nixon Lodge), N.Y.C., 1959—60; asst. to Raymond Moley, polit. columnist N.Y.C., 1961; asst. campaign com. Louis J. Lefkowitz for Mayor, N.Y.C., 1961; rsch. programmer, treas. Consensus, Inc., N.Y.C., 1962—67; spl. asst. to U. S. Senator Jacob K. Javits NY, 1967 —73; adminstr. asst. NY, 1973—75; dep. adminstr. Am. Revolution Bicentennial Adminstrn., 1976, acting adminstr., 1976—77; chief of staff Perry B. Duryea (minority leader) N.Y. State Assembly, 1978; pub. affairs cons., 1979—80; dir. govt. rels. Gen. Mills Restaurant Group, Inc., 1980—83; exec. dir. Fed. Mediation and Conciliation Svc., 1983—86; mem. Fed. Labor Rels. Authority, 1986—89, chmn., 1989—94; mem. Nat. Partnership Coun., 1993—94; chmn. adv. bd. Workplace Solutions, 1996—98. Mem. U.S. Adv.Commn. on Pub. Diplomacy, 1972—82; dir. scheduling and spkrs.' bur. N.Y. Com. to Re-elect the Pres., 1972; mem. bd. govs. Women's Nat. Rep. Club, N.Y.C., 1963—66; mem. N.Y. State Bingo Control Commn., 1965—72; pres. Bklyn. Heights Slope Young Rep. Club, 1955—56; co-chmn. Bklyn. Citizens for Eisenhower-Nixon, 1956; chmn. 2nd Jud. Dist. Assn. N.Y. State Young Rep. Clubs, Inc., 1957—58, vice chmn., mem. bd. govs., 1958—60, v.p., 1960—62, pres., 1962—64; mem. exec. com. Fedn. Women's Rep. Clubs N.Y. State, Inc., 1960—64; asst. campaign mgr. Kenneth B. Keating for Judge Ct. Appeals, NY, 1965; dir. scheduling Gov. Rockefeller campaign, 1966, Sen. Charles E. Goodell campaign, 1970; dir. planning and strategy Conn. Reagan-Bush campaign, Hartford, 1980; mem annual fund adv. com. Vassar Coll., 1992—96, chmn. 50th Reunion, 2001. Mem.: Conn. Olmsted Heritage Alliance (treas. 2005—), Nat. Assn. Olmsted Parks (trustee 2003—), New Eng. Hist. Geneal. Soc. (mem. adv. coun. 2001—03, trustee 2003—06, mem. adv. coun. 2006—), Nat. Women's Edn. Fund. (former mem. bd.), Exec. Women on Govt. (chmn. 1986), Nat. Soc. Colonial Dames, Vassar Club (past dir., Bklyn.), Am. Newspaper Women's Club, Jr. League of Bklyn. (past dir.). Republican. Episcopalian. Also: 3001 Veazey Ter NW Apt 1225 Washington DC 20008-5407 Address: 532 S Brooksvale Rd Cheshire CT 06410

MCKEE, RICHARD MILES, retired agricultural studies educator; b. Cottonwood Falls, Kans., Oct. 8, 1929; m. Marjorie Fisk, June 22, 1952; children: Dave, Richard, Annell, John. BS in Agriculture, Kans. State Coll. Agriculture and Applied Sci., 1951; MS in Animal Husbandry, Kans. State U., 1963; PhD in Animal Science, U. Ky., 1968. Herdsman Moxley Hall Hereford Ranch, Coun. Grove, Kans., 1951-52, 54-55, Luckhardt Farms, Tarkio, Mo., 1955-58; asst. mgr. L&J Crusoe Ranch, Cheboygan, Mich., 1958-59; asst. instr., cattle herdsman Kans. State U., Manhattan, 1959-65, from asst. prof. to assoc. prof., 1959-65, prof., departmental teaching coord., 1976-99; ret., 2005. Program participant and/or official judge numerous shows, field days including Kans. Jr. Hereford Field Day, Kans. Jr. Shorthorn Field Day, Better Livestock Day, Kans. Jr. Livestock Assn., Am. Jr. Hereford Assn. Field Day, Cheyenne, Wyo., 1973, Kans. Jr. Polled Hereford Field Day, Am. Jr. Shorthorn Assn., Kans. City, Mo., 1965, Am. Jr. Charolais Assn. Show, Lincoln, Nebr., 1976, Am. Royal 4-H Livestock Judging Contest, Kans. City, 1975, Jr. Livestock Activities various cattle breed assns. nationwide, 1977-81; served on many breed assn. coms.; judge County Fairs; official judge 14 different Nat. Beef Breed Shows U.S. and Can.; conducted 60 livestock judging and showmanship schs. at county level. Contbr. articles to profl. jours. Deacon 1st Presbyn. Ch., Manhattan, 1969-75, Sunday Sch. tchr., Chancel choir, elder; project leader com. mem. 4-H; foster parent Kans. State U. Football Program. Lt. USMC, 1952-54, Korea. Named Hon. State Farmer of Kans.; Hall of Merit Honoree for Edn. by Am. Polled Hereford Assn., 1985; NDEA scholar U. Ky., 1966-67; Miles McKee Student Enrichment Fund established at Kans. State U. Mem. Am. Soc. Animal Sci., Kans. Livestock Assn. (beef cattle improvement com. 1970-78, cow-calf clinic com. 1973, 74, 75, 76, 77, 78), Nat. Assn. Colls. and Tchrs. Agriculture, Block and Bridle Club, Am. Jr. Hereford Assn. (hon.), FarmHouse, Sigma Xi, Phi Kappa Phi, Alpha Zeta, Gamma Sigma Delta, Alpha Tau Alpha (hon.). Home: 901 Juniper Dr Manhattan KS 66502-3148 Office: Dept of Animal Scis & Industry Kansas State U Manhattan KS 66506 Office Phone: 785-532-1237.

MCKEE, ROGER A., lawyer; b. L.A., Aug. 24, 1943; s. Jerome F. and Florence A. McKee; 1 child, Andrew. BS, UCLA, 1965; JD, U. San Diego, 1969; diploma, Northwestern U., 1970. Bar: Colo. 1970, Calif. 1970, Ariz. 1971, U.S. Ct. Appeals (9th cir.) 1974, U.S. Supreme Ct. 1974. Legal advisor Ariz. Dept. Pub. Safety, Phoenix, 1970—71; dep. county atty. Maricopa County Atty., Phoenix, 1971—74; town atty. Town of Paradise Valley, Ariz.,

1974—78; pvt. practice Phoenix, 1978—. Mem.: State Bar Ariz. (chmn. sole practitioners sect. 1991—92, bd. govs. 1993—95). Office: 6544 N 7th Ave Unit 12 Phoenix AZ 85013-1155 Office Phone: 602-864-3369. Business E-Mail: rogerm@wb-law.com.

MCKEE, ROGER CURTIS, retired federal judge; b. Waterloo, Iowa, Feb. 11, 1931; s. James A. and Leonace (Burrell) McK.; m. Roberta Jeanne Orvis, Sept. 3, 1954; children: Andrea Jane, Brian Curtis, Paul Robert. BA, State Coll. of Iowa, 1955; MA, U. Ill., 1960; JD, U. San Diego, 1968. Bar: Calif. 1970, U.S. Dist. Ct. (so. dist.) Calif. 1969, U.S. Ct. Appeals (9th cir.) 1971. Telegrapher, agt. Ill. Cen. R.R., 1950-55; tng. asst. No. Ill. Gas Co., Aurora, 1959-60; with indsl. rels. dept. Convair div. Gen. Dynamics Corp., San Diego, 1960-68; contract adminstr. and supr. Datagraphix div. Gen. Dynamics Corp., San Diego, 1968-69, asst. counsel, 1969-70; ptnr. Powell & McKee, San Diego, 1970-75, Millsberg, Dickstein & McKee, San Diego, 1975-83; magistrate judge U.S. Dist. Ct. for So. Dist. Calif., San Diego, 1983-97; presiding magistrate judge, 1993-97. Bd. trustees So. Calif. Presbyn. Homes, L.A., 1979-81; moderator Presbytery of San Diego, 1980. Capt. USNR, 1949-85. Mem. Calif. Bar Assn., Fed. Magistrate Judges Assn., Navy League U.S., Naval Res. Officers Assn., Res. Officers Assn., Dixieland Jazz Soc. (bd. dirs. San Diego chpt. 1984—). Republican. Home Fax: 858-277-0444. Personal E-mail: rcmckee10@sbcglobal.net.

MCKEE, THEODORE A., federal judge; b. Rochester, NY, 1947; BA, SUNY, Cortland, 1969; JD magna cum laude, Syracuse U. Coll. of Law, 1975. Dir. of minority recruitment & admissions SUNY, Binghamton, 1969—72; atty. Wolf, Block, Schorr & Solis-Cohen, Phila., 1975—77; asst. U.S. atty., Eastern Dist. Pa., 1977—80; asst. U.S. atty., Eastern Dist. Gen. Crimes Unit, Narcotics and Firearms Unit, then Polit. Corruption Unit; lectr. Rutgers U. Coll. of Law, 1980—91; dep. city solicitor Law Dept., Phila., 1980—83; gen. counsel Phila. Parking Auth., 1983; judge Ct. of Common Pleas, 1st Jud. Dist, Pa., 1984—94, judge major felony program, 1986, judge orphans' ct. divsn., 1992; judge U.S. Ct. Appeals (3d cir.), Phila., 1994—. Bd. dirs. Diagnostic and Rehab. Ctr. of Phila. Trustee Edna McConnell Clark Found.; mem. adv. bd. City Yr. for Phila. Mem.: ABA, Pa. Bar Assoc., Phila. Bar Assoc., Temple Inn of Ct., Barristers' Assn. Phila., Am. Law Inst., Nat. Bar Assn., Crime Prevention Assn. (bd. dirs.). Office: 20614 US Courthouse 601 Market St Philadelphia PA 19106*

MCKEE, THOMAS FREDERICK, lawyer; b. Cleve., Oct. 27, 1948; s. Harry Wilbert and Virginia (Light) McK. BA with high distinction, U. Mich., 1970; JD with high distinction, Case Western Rs. U., 1975. Bar: Ohio 1975, U.S. Dist. Ct. (no. dist.) Ohio 1975, U.S. Supreme Ct. 1979. Assoc. firm Calfee, Halter & Griswold, Cleve., 1975-81, ptnr., 1982—, also vice-chmn. exec. com.; sec. McDonald & Co. Investments, Inc., Chart Industries, Inc., Signature Brands, Inc.; bd. dirs. Mr. Coffee, Inc., Longbow Rsch. Contbg. editor Going Public, 1985. Mem. ABA (com. fed. regulation securities law sect.), Bar Assn. Greater Cleve., Order of Coif., Union Club, Tavern Club, Country Club, 50 Club, Pepper Pike Club. Home: 210 Pheasant Run Dr Chagrin Falls OH 44022-2968 Office: Calfee Halter & Griswold 800 Superior Ave E Ste 1400 Cleveland OH 44114-2601

MCKEE, TIMOTHY CARLTON, taxation educator; b. South Bend, Ind., Mar. 9, 1944; s. Glenn Richard and Laura Louise (Niven) McK.; m. Linda Sykes Mizelle, Oct. 13, 1984; children: Brandon Richard. BS in Bus. Econs., Ind. U., 1970, MBA in Fin., 1973, JD, 1979; LLM in Taxation, DePaul U., 1980. Bar: Ill. 1980, U.S. Dist. Ct. (no. dist.) Ill. 1980; CPA, Va.; cert. govt. fin. mgr. Procedures analyst Assocs. Corp., South Bend, 1969-71; asst. dir. fin. Ind. U., Bloomington, 1971-79; sr. tax mgr. Peat Marwick Mitchell & Co., Chgo., Norfolk, Va., 1979-84; corp. counsel K & K Toys, Norfolk, 1984; assoc. prof. acctg. Old Dominion U., Norfolk, 1985-98, chmn. dept., 1994-95, chmn. acctg., fin. and law dept., 1995, univ. prof. dept. acctg., 1998—. Computer coord. Peat, Marwick, Mitchell & Co., 1982-84; micro computer cons. Old Dominion U., 1985-91. Contbr. articles to profl. jours. Active Friends of Music, Bloomington, 1978, Art Inst., Chgo., 1981; loan exec. United Way, Chgo., 1981; telethon chmn. Va. Orch. Group, Norfolk, 1983. Mem. Assn. Govt. Accts., Am. Acctg. Assn., Am. Assn. Atty. CPAs, Inc., Am. Tax Assn., Fin. Execs. Inst. (pres. 1995-96), Hampton Rds. Tax Forum, Inst. Internal Auditors, Beta Alpha Psi, Beta Gamma Sigma. Home: 412 Rio Dr Chesapeake VA 23322-7144 Office: Old Dominion U Constant Hall Rm 2153 Norfolk VA 23529

MCKEEN, ALEXANDER C., retired engineering executive, foundation administrator; b. Albion, Mich., Oct. 10, 1927; s. John Nisbet and Janet (Callander) McK.; m. Evelyn Mae Feldkamp, Aug. 18, 1951; Jeffrey, Brian, Andrew. BSME, U. Mich., 1950; MBA, Mich. State U., 1968. Registered profl. engr., Mich. From asst. supt. maintenance to supt. final assembly Cadillac Motor Car divsn. GM, Detroit, 1961-69; asst. dir. reliability cadillac motor car divsn. GM, Detroit, 1969-72, exec. engr. product assurance Warren, Mich., 1972-75, from asst. dir. to dir engring. analysis, 1975-87; pres., owner Engring. Analysis Assocs., Inc., Bingham Farms, Mich., 1987-99; cons. Detroit Exec. Svc. Corps, 1999—; pres. McKeen Found., 2002—. Pres. Dells of Bloomfield Home Owners Assn., Bloomfield Hills, Mich., 1987-88; trustee Kirk in Hills, Bloomfield Hills, 1990-93, 2003—, elder, 1995-97. Mem. Soc. Auto. Engrs., Am. Soc. Quality Control, Econ. Club Detroit, Detroit Athletic Club, Bloomfield (Mich.) Lions Club (pres. 2004—), Stonycroft Hills Golf Club, Pelican Nest Golf Club, Beta Gamma Sigma. Avocations: tennis, golf, photography, travel, gardening. Office: Detroit Executive Service Corps 16250 Northland Dr Ste 390 Southfield MI 48075

MC KEEN, CHESTER M., JR., retired manufacturing executive; b. Shelby, Ohio, Mar. 18, 1923; s. Chester Mancil and Nettie Augusta (Fox) McKeen; m. Alma Virginia Pierce, Mar. 1946 (dec. 1998); children: David Richard- (dec.), Karin, Thomas Kevin; m. Sally Ann Werst, Nov. 1999; 1 stepchild, Stephen Harry Werst. BS in Mil. Sci., U. Md., 1962; MBA, Babson Coll., Wellesley, Mass., 1962. Advanced through grades to maj. gen. U.S. Army, 1942-77; dir. logistics Bell Helicopter Internat., Tehran, Iran, 1977-79; v.p. procurement Bell Helicopter Textron, Ft. Worth, 1979-82, v.p. materiel, 1982-89; pres. Logistics Svcs. Internat., Arlington, Tex., 1990—2002; ret., 2002. Decorated D.S.M., Legion of Merit (3), Commendation medal (3); named to U.S. Army Ordnance Hall of Fame. Mem. Nat. Def. Indsl. Assn., Assn. U.S. Army, Ridglea Country Club, Rotary, Masons (33 degree), Shriners, Sojourners, Sigma Pi. Home: 2310 Woodsong Trail Arlington TX 76016-1037 Personal E-mail: cmmckeen@aol.com. To live for oneself is to pursue emptiness. To live for others is to insure fulfillment.

MCKEEVER, JOHN EUGENE, lawyer; b. Phila., Oct. 24, 1947; s. John James and Marie Julia (Supper) McKeever; m. Kathleen Marie Wynne, Dec. 9, 1995; children: John Joseph, Jeannine Marie. BA magna cum laude with distinction, U. Pa., 1969, JD magna cum laude, 1972. Bar: Pa. 1972, U.S. Dist. Ct. (ea. dist.) Pa. 1972, U.S. Dist. Ct. (mid. dist.) Pa. 1977, U.S. Ct. Appeals (3d cir.) 1979, U.S. Ct. Appeals (DC cir.) 1981, U.S. Supreme Ct. 1981. Assoc. Schnader, Harrison, Segal & Lewis, Phila., 1972-80, ptnr., 1980-98, DLA Piper Rudnick Gray Gary US LLP, Phila., 1998—. Trustee Lawyers Com. Civil Rights Under Law, Washington, 2002, dir., 2003—, mem. exec. com. 2005—. Mem. Bus. Leadership organized Cath. Schs., Phila., 1984—; co-chair Oblates St. Francis De Sales Capital Campaign, 1998—99; capt. spl. gifts com. Cath. Charities Appeal, Phila., 1986—91; bd. dir. Jr. Achievement, Phila., 1986—2006; mem. pres.'s coun. De Sales U., Center Valley, Pa., 1980—; mem. adv. coun. Camden Diocese Secondary Sch. Theology, Washington, trustee 1988—91. Mem.: Pro-Life Lawyers' Guild (bd. dir. 1983—84, chancellor 1984—86), Phila. Bar Assn., St. Thomas More Soc. (gov. 1979—91, pres. 1981—82), Phi Beta Kappa, Order of Coif, Pi Gamma Mu. Republican. Roman Catholic. Office: DLA Piper Rudnick Gray Cary US LLP One Liberty Pl 1650 Market St Ste 4900 Philadelphia PA 19103 Office Phone: 215-656-3310. E-mail: john.mckeever@dlapiper.com.

MCKEEVER, JOSEPH FRANCIS, III, lawyer; b. Weymouth, Mass., July 21, 1950; s. Joseph Francis Jr. and Virginia Agnes McK.; m. Janice Danielle Kearney, Oct. 17, 1970. BA, George Washington U., 1972, JD, 1978. Bar: D.C. 1978, U.S. Supreme Ct. 1989. Editor Congl. Rsch. Svc. Libr. Congress, Washington, 1974-78; law clk. Honorable Harry Wood U.S. Ct. Claims, Washington, 1978-79, Honorable Wilson Cowen U.S. Ct. Claims, Washington, 1979-80; atty. Sutherland, Asbill & Brennan, Washington, 1980-85; ptnr. Davis & Harman LLP, Washington, 1985—. Author, editor: Annuities Answer Book, 1999; contbr. articles to profl. jours. Mem. ABA (chair sect. on taxation com. on ins. cos. 2000-02); Nat. Assn. for Variable Annuities (chmn., 2002-2003) Avocations: gardening, bicycling. Home: 2812 34th Pl NW Washington DC 20007-1405 Office: Davis & Harman LLP Willard Office Bldg 1455 Pennsylvania Ave NW Washington DC 20004-1008 Office Phone: 202-347-2252.

MCKEEVER, KENT, library director, law librarian; b. Southampton, NY, Sept. 6, 1952; BA, SUNY, Oswego, 1974; MLS, JD, La. State U., 1980. Bar: La. 1980. Ref. libr. Fordham U. Sch. Law Libr., 1981—82; internat., fgn. and comparative law libr. Columbia U. Law Sch. Libr., NYC, 1982—83, assoc. law libr. head collection devel. and tech. svcs., 1983—93, acting law libr., 1994—95, dir. Diamond Law Libr., 1996—. Lectr. Fudan U., Shanghai, 1986, Columbia U. Sch. Libr. Svc., N.Y.C., 1986—91, Columbia Summer Program, Leiden, Netherlands, 1998—2000; cons. Beijing U., Dept. of Treaty and Law, China, MetaMetrics, Inc.; grant application evaluator NEH. Class of 1950 scholar, La. State U., Supr.'s scholar, Tullis-Herget scholar. Office: Diamond Law Libr 435 W 116th St New York NY 10027 Business E-Mail: mckeever@law.columbia.edu.

MCKEEVER, MICHAEL PIERCE, SR., economics and business educator; b. Glendale, Calif., Mar. 3, 1941; s. Samuel Pierce and Martha Frances (Darby) McK.; m. Jeanetta Ross, Oct. 20, 1964 (div. June 1970); 1 child, Nancy; m. Marjorie Alice McKean, Dec. 17, 1970; (div. March, 2004); children: Michael P. Jr., Johnathan Brooks; m. Yelena Udalova, Jan. 6, 2006. BA with honors, Whittier (Calif.) Coll., 1963; MS in Econs., London Sch. Econs., 1966. Life credential bus., econs., social sci. Calif. C.C. Owner Counseling Brokerage Group, Santa Rosa, Calif., 1980-84, Bus. Plan Workshop, Santa Rosa, 1980-95; asst. prof. econs. and bus. Armstrong U., Berkeley, Calif., 1995-97; founder McKeever Inst. Econ. Policy Analysis, Berkeley, 1995—. Instr. Vista Coll., Berkeley, Calif., 1998—2002; CFO Platform Tech. Computer Svcs., Oakland, Calif., 1999—2005; instr. City Coll. San Francisco, 2003—; CEO Licensing Capital LLC, San Francisco, 2005—. Author: How to Write a Business Plan, 1981, Conceptual Economics, 1993, Moral Economics, 2001. Dir. Inst. Small Bus. Dept. Sonoma State U., 1981; pres. We Care, Santa Rosa, 1984; chmn. adv. com. Suppression of Drug Abuse in Schs. Sonoma County, Santa Rosa, 1985. Recipient award Role Recognition-Downtown Devel., Santa Rosa City Coun., 1983; named Vol. of Yr. Santa Rosa City Schs., 1984. Avocation: baseball. Home and Office: 1627 47th Ave San Francisco CA 94122 E-mail: mpmckeever@earthlink.net.

MCKEIGHEN, RONALD EUGENE, physicist; b. Marion, Ill., Oct. 17, 1942; s. George A. and Aileen (Reach) McK.; m. Loretta M. Ward, Sept. 3, 1966; children: Kevin, Christy. BS in Engring. Physics, U. Ill., 1964, MS in Nuclear Engring., 1965, PhD in Physics, 1971. Postdoctoral in cancer rsch. and nuclear medicine Oak Ridge Nat. Lab., 1972-73; sr. rsch. scientist Searle/Siemens Ultrasound, Des Plaines, 1973-79; sr. R&D engr. KB-Aerotech, Lewistown, Pa., 1979-83; staff scientist Advanced Diagnostic Rsch., Tempe, Ariz., 1983-85; prin. staff engr. Motorola Space Elect, Scottsdale, Ariz., 1985-86; mgr. advanced devel. Advanced Tech. Labs., Bothel, Wash., 1986-93; dir. advanced devel. Acoustic Imaging Inc., Phoenix, 1993—2001; prin. rsch. engr. SAR signal processing Lockheed-Martin, Litchfield Park, Ariz., 2001—. Contbr. articles to profl. jours., chapters to books. Spl. fellow in nuclear enring. AEC. Mem. IEEE. Mem. Pentecostal Ch. Achievements include development of ultrasonic transducer arrays and sensors; patents for concept of digital beam former for ultrasonic phased array; research in synthetic aperture radar signal processing at Lockheed-Martin. Office: Lockheed-Martin Litchfield Park AZ Office Phone: 623-925-7178. E-mail: ronelori@cox.net.

MCKEITHEN, R.L. SMITH (SMITH MCKEITHEN), lawyer; b. NC, 1943; s. Lee McKeithen; m. Kathleen Danchuk; children: Emma, Wesley. BA in Eng., Davidson Coll., 1965; JD, Columbia Law Sch., 1971. Atty. Sherman & Sterling, NYC, 1971—74; counsel US House Judiacty Impeachment Com., 1974; atty. Howard Rice Nemerovski Canady Falk & Rabkin, San Francisco, 1974—83; gen. counsel Strategic Mapping Inc., Silicon Graphics Inc., Cooper Cos., Activision Inc.; sr. v.p., sec., gen. counsel Cadence Design Systems Corp., 1996—. Served in U.S. Army. Office: Cadence Design 2655 Seely Ave San Jose CA 95134 Office Fax: 408-943-0513.*

MCKELDIN, WILLIAM EVANS, management consultant; b. Richmond, Va., Aug. 14, 1927; s. Robert A.W. and Mary E. (Burk) McK.; children: William Evans, Roberts Evans; m. Phyllis Shellhase, Jan. 23, 1982. BSBA, Temple U., 1951, postgrad., 1951-53, U. Pitts., 1953-54. Various mgmt. positions Westinghouse Corp., Pitts., 1950-62, Farrel Corp., Rochester, NY, 1963-66, Gen. Signal Corp., Norwalk, Conn., and Watertown, N.Y., 1966-71, Copperweld Steel Co., Warren, Ohio, 1971-75, Tenn. Forging Steel, Knoxville, 1975-77, Val Bradley Assocs., West Chester, Pa., 1977-79; pres., owner McKeldin Assocs., West Chester, 1979-95; founder, co-owner McKeldin Group, Bala Cynwyd, Pa., 1995—. Contbr. articles to profl. jours. Bd. dirs. United Fund, YMCA, ARC, Rochester Inst. Tech., Jefferson C.C., Kent State U. With USAAF, 1945—47. Mem. Inst. Mgmt. Cons., Am. Soc. Safety Engrs., Am. Soc. Personnel Adminstrn., C. of C. (bd. dirs.), Masons, Rotary. Republican. Presbyterian. Office: The McKeldin Group 24 Timber Ln Hilton Head Island SC 29926-1002 Office Phone: 847-837-6565. Personal E-mail: mckeldin@webtv.net.

MCKELL, CYRUS M., retired dean, plant physiologist, consultant; b. Payson, Utah, Mar. 19, 1926; s. Robert D. and Mary C. (Ellsworth) McK.; m. Betty Johnson; children: Meredith Sue, Brian Marcus, John Cyrus. BS, U. Utah, 1949, MS, 1950; PhD, Oreg. State U., 1956; postgrad., U. Calif., Davis, 1957. Instr. botany Oreg. State U., Corvallis, 1955-56; range rsch. plant physiologist U. Calif. USDA-Agrl. Research Service, Davis, 1956—61; prof., dept. chmn. U. Calif., Riverside, 1961—69; prof. dept. head., dir. Utah State U., Logan, 1969-80; v.p. research NPI, Salt Lake City, 1980-88; dean Coll. of Sci. Weber State U., Ogden, Utah, 1988-94; pres., prin. Applied Ecol. Svcs. Inc., Logan, Utah, 1995—. Cons. Ford Found. 1968-72, Rockefeller Found., 1964-70, 89, UN, 1978, 90, NAS, 1980, 89, 91, 92, 93, USAID, 1972, UN Devel. Program, 1989; mem. faculty of sci. adv. bd. UAE Nat. U., 2000-02. Editor: Grass Biology and Utilization, 1971, Useful Wildland Shrubs, 1972, Rehabilitation of Western Wildlife Habitat, 1978, Paradoxes of Western Energy Development, 1984, Resource Inventory and Baseline Study Methods for Developing Countries, 1983, Shrub Biology and Utilization, 1989, Wilderness Issues, Arid Lands of the Western United States, 1992; contbr. over 230 articles to profl. jours. Chmn. Cache County Planning Commn., Logan, 1974-79; mem. Utah Energy Conservation and Devel. Coun., 1976-79, Gov.'s Sci. Adv. Coun., 1988-97, chmn., 1990-91, 96-97; mem. Commn. of the Californias, Riverside, 1965-68; mem. Holladay City Planning Commn., 2003—. Recipient Utah Gov.'s Sci. and Tech. medal, 1999, Gardner Prize in Sci., awarded by Utah Acad. Scis., Arts and Letters, 1999; Fulbright scholar Spain, 1967-68; World Travel grantee Rockefeller Found., 1964. Fellow: AAAS (com. chmn. 1979—89, sci. exchange to China grantee 1984—85, 1989, sci. panel U.S.-Chile 1987); mem.: Am. Soc. Agronomy, Soc. Range Mgmt. (pres. Calif. sect. 1965, pres. Utah sect. 1982). Mem. Lds Ch. Avocations: travel, photography, history. Home: 2248 E 4000 S Holladay UT 84124-1864 Business E-Mail: cmmc1@xmission.com.

MCKELLAR, DON, actor, screenwriter, filmmaker; b. Toronto, Can., Aug. 17, 1963; Founding mem. Child's Play Theatre, Toronto, Augusta Theatre Co., Toronto. Writer, actor (films) Roadkill, 1989, Highway 61, 1992, 32 Short Films About Glenn Gould, 1993, The Red Violin, 1998 (Jutra award for Best Screenplay, Genie award for Best Screenplay, 1999), Elimination Dance,

1998 (Best Short Narrative Film, Cinequest San Jose Festival, 2000), writer, actor, dir. Last Night, 1998 (Best Can. 1st Feature Film, Toronto Internat. Film Festival, Young Cinema award, Cannes Film Festival, 1998, Claude Jutra award, Fantasporto Dir.'s Week award, 1999, Canadian Comedy award for Film Directing, 2000), Childstar, 2004 (Best Actor & Best Dir., Vancouver Film Critics Cir., 2005), writer, dir. Blue, 1992 (Best Can. Short Film, Toronto Internat. Film Festival, 1992), dir. The Bloody Nose, 1992, writer, dir. A Word from the Management, 2000, writer, dir., cinematographer Phone Call from Imaginary Girlfriends, 2005; actor: (films) The Adjuster, 1991, Giant Steps, 1992, Coleslaw Warehouse, 1992, Arrowhead, 1994, Exotica, 1994 (Genie award, best supporting actor, 1994), Camilla, 1994, When Night is Falling, 1995, Joe's So Mean to Josephine, 1996, Never Met Picasso, 1996, Bach Cello Suite #4: Sarabande, 1997, The Herd, 1998, The Passion of Ayn Rand, 1999, eXistenZ, 1999, This Might Be Good, 2000, Vinyl, 2000, Waydowntown, 2000, The Art of Woo, 2001, Rub & Tug, 2002, The Event, 2003, Public Domain, 2003, Clean, 2004, Where the Truth Lies, 2005; (TV miniseries) I Was a Rat, 2001, Trudeau, 2002, Prairie Giant: The Tommy Douglas Story, 2006; (TV series) Slings & Arrows, 2003—, (voice) Odd Job Jack, 2003—; (TV films) In the Presence of Mine Enemies, 1997, Sea People, 1999, (TV episodes) Degrassi: The Next Generation, 2001; writer (TV series) Twitch City, 1998 (Writers Guild Can. award, 1999); author: (screenplays) Dance Me Outside, 1995; translator Clean, 2004; co-author (with Bob Martin): (Broadway plays) The Drowsy Chaperone (Tony award, best book of a musical, 2006, Drama Desk award, outstanding book of a musical, 2006). Office: Rhombus Media Inc Ste 600 99 Spadina Ave Toronto ON M5V 3P8 Canada also: Shadow Shows Inc 2nd Fl 18 Gloucester Lane Toronto ON M4Y 1L5 Canada also: Accent Entertainment 666B Queen St W Toronto ON M6J 1E5 Canada

**MCKELLEN, SIR IAN,** actor; b. Burnley, England, May 25, 1939; s. Denis Murray and Margery (Sutcliffe) McK.; life partner Sean Mathias. Grad., Cambridge U. Prof. Oxford U., 1990-91. First stage appearance as Roper in A Man for All Seasons, Belgrade Theatre, Coventry, Eng., 1961; numerous other parts include title roles in Henry V, Luther, Ipswich, 1962-63, Aufidius in Coriolanus, Arthur Seaton in Saturday Night and Sunday Morning, title role in Sir Thomas More, Nottingham Playhouse, 1963-64; London debut as Godfrey in A Scent of Flowers, 1964, Claudio in Much Ado About Nothing, Andrew Cobham in Their Very Own and Golden City, 1966; title part in O'Flaherty, V.C. and Bonapart in The Man of Destiny, 1966, (Broadway debut) Leonidik in the Promise, London, 1966-67, Richard II, Edward II, Hamlet, Prospect Theatre Co., 1968-71; Captain Plume in The Recruiting Officer; founder-mem. Actors' Co., Edinburgh Festival, 1972 and touring as Giovanni in Tis Pity She's a Whore, Faustus, Ruling the Roost, title role Wood Demon; debut with R.S.C. as Dr. Faustus, Edinburgh Festival, 1974; title role in The Marquis of Keith, Philip the Bastard in King John, 1974-75, Young Vic Colin in Ashes, 1975; Royal Shakespeare Co.: Burglar in Too True to be Good, Romeo, MacBeth, Leontes in the Winter's Tale, Face in the Alchemist, Bernick in Pillars of the Community, Langevin in Days of the Commune, 1976-78, Ivanov in Every Good Boy Deserves Favour, Toby Belch in Twelfth Night, Andrei in The Three Sisters, Max in Bent, 1979, Amadeus, N.Y.C., 1980, Iago in Othello, The Other Place, Stratford, 1989; European tour of one-man show Acting Shakespeare, 1983, also L.A., N.Y.C., 1984, one-man show A Knight Out at the Lyceum (devised especially for Gay Games I U.K. and South Africa tour), 1994, An Enemy of the People, 1997, Peter Pan, 1998, The Seagull, 1998, Present Laughter, 1998, The Tempest, 1999, Dance of Death, N.Y.C, 2001-02, London, 2003, Sydney, 2004; assoc. dir. Nat. Theatre, London, 1984-86; dir. first prodn. The Prime of Miss Jean Brodie, Liverpool Playhouse, 1969, A Private Matter, 1973, The Clandestine Marriage, 1975; plays include: All in Good Time, 1963, The Alchemist, 1977, Amadeus, 1980, Venice Preserved, Wild Honey (recipient, Laurence Olivier Theatre award for Best Actor in a Revival, 1985), Coriolanus, Duchess of Malfi, The Cherry Orchard, King Lear, Richard III (recipient Laurence Olivier Theatre award for Best Actor (Royal Nat. Theatre), 1991, Acting Shakespeare, Napoli Milionaria, Uncle Vanya, An Enemy of The People, Peter Pan, Aladdin, 2004, and several others; films include Alfred the Great, 1968, A Touch of Love/Thank You All Very Much, 1968, The Promise, 1969, The Keep, 1983, Zina, 1985, Plenty, 1986, Scandal, 1988, I'll Do Anything, 1992, The Ballad of Little Jo, 1992, Last Action Hero, 1993, Six Degrees of Separation, 1993,, The Shadow, 1994, Jack and Sarah, 1994, Restoration, 1995, Richard III, 1996 (also exec. prodr., writer), Surviving Friendly Fire, 1997, Bent, 1997, Swept From the Sea, 1997, Apt Pupil, 1998, Gods and Monsters, 1998, X-Men, 2000, Lord of the Rings: The Fellowship of the Ring, 2001 (Outstanding Performance by Male Actor in Supporting Role SAG award 2002, nominee Best Supporting Actor Acad. Award 2002, Best Supporting Actor Saturn award 2002; nominee Best Performance by Actor BAFTA Film award, Empire award, Golden Satellite award, MTV Movie award, and OFCS award 2002), Lord of the Rings: The Two Towers, 2002, X2: X-Men United, 2003, The Lord of the Rings: The Return of the King, 2003, Emile, 2004, The Lord of the Rings: The Third Age (voice), 2004, Eighteen (voice), 2004, The Lord of the Rings: The Battle for Middle-Earth (voice), 2004, Sprung!The Magic Roundabout (voice), 2005, Asylum, 2005, Coronation Street, 2005, Neverwas, 2005, Doogal (voice), 2006, X-Men: The Last Stand, 2006, The Da Vinci Code, 2006; TV appearances include: Sunday Out of Season, 1965, The Trial ans Torture of Sir John Rampayne, 1965, David Copperfield, 1966, Hay Fever, 1968, What If It's Just Green Cheese?, 1969, Ross, 1970, The Tragedy of King Richard II, 1970, Edward II, 1970, Keats, 1970, The Last Journey, 1971, Hamlet, 1972, The Recruiting Officer, 1973, Graceless Go I,1973, Hedda Gabler, 1974, Macbeth, 1979, Priest of Love, 1979, Every Good Boy Deserves Favour, 1978, Dying Day, 1980, Loving Walter, 1982, Acting Shakespeare, 1982, The Scarlet Pimpernel, 1982, Walter and June, 1983, Windmills of the Gods, 1988, Othello, 1988, Countdown to War, 1989, Sleepers, 1991 (TV mini series), Tales of the City, 1993 (TV mini series), And the Band Played On, 1993 (Emmy nomination, Supporting Actor, 1993), Cold Comfort Farm, 1994, Rasputin, 1996(Emmy nomination, Supporting Actor,1996) David Copperfield, 1999, The Simpsons: The Regina Monologues, 2003; (voice) To Die For, 1994, Cirque du Soleil Journey of Man, 2000. Recipient Clarence Derwent award, 1964, Variety and Plays and Players awards, 1966; Actor of Year, Plays and Players, 1976, Soc. of West End Theatres for Best Actor in Revival award, 1977, for Best Comedy Performance, 1978, for Best Actor in a New Play, 1979, Tony Award for Best Actor, Drama Desk award, Outer Critics Circle award, N.Y. Drama League award, 1981, Performer of the Yr. award Royal TV Soc., 1983, Soc. London Theatre Spl. award, 2006; decorated comdr. Order Brit. Empire, Knight Bachelor. Mem. Brit. Actors' Equity (coun. 1970-71). Office: ICM Oxford House 76 Oxford St London W1D 1BS England*

**MCKELVEY, ANDREW J.,** advertising executive; 1 son, Stuart J. McKelvey. BA, Westminster Coll. Chmn. bd. TMP Worldwide, Inc., NYC, 1967—; CEO TMP Worldwide, Inc. (now Monster Worldwide, Inc.), NYC, 1967—. bd. dirs. Yellow Pages Pubs. Mem. Assn. Director Mktg. (bd. dirs. 1994-96). Office: Monster Worldwide Inc 622 Third Ave 39th Fl New York NY 10017-6707 Business E-mail: andrew.mckelvey@monsterworldwide.com.

**MCKELVEY, CONNIE ELKINS,** lawyer; b. Salem, Oreg., July 23, 1957; d. Merlin Harold and Hollis Joy (Campbell) Elkins; m. Gregory Wayne McKelvey, Oct. 19, 1991; children: Toussaint, Gregory Robert. BS, U. Oreg., 1979; JD, Lewis & Clark Coll., 1983. Bar: Oreg. 1983, U.S. Dist. Ct. Oreg., 1983, U.S. Ct. Appeals (9th cir.) 1983. Assoc. Cooney & Crew, Portland, Oreg., 1983-94; ptnr. Hoffman Hart & Wagner, Portland, Oreg., 1994—. Frequent spkr. to profl. groups on health law issues; appointed to profl. Oreg. State Bar Bd. Govs. State Health Divsn. HIV/AIDS, 1988-90; appointed to Oreg. Coun. on Ct. Procedures, 1998—, chairan 2005. Contbr. articles to numerous health law publs., including Oregon Health Law Manual. Mem. alumni bd. Northwestern Sch. Law Lewis & Clark Coll., 1998-2005—. Mem. Oreg. State Bar Assn. (mem. exec. com. health law sect. 1990-97, chair 1994-95, chair joint professionalism com. with Oreg. Med. Assn. 1996-97), Oreg. Med. Assn. (med. legal task force on AIDS 1987—), Oreg. Acad. Health Law Attys. (exec. com. 1995-2000, sec./treas. 1996-98, pres. 2000), Def. Rsch. Inst., Oreg. Assn. Def. Counsel (chair profl. liability sect. 2001-03), Multnomah County Bar Assn. (court liaison com. 1990-93). Office: Hoffman Hart & Wagner 1000 SW Broadway Ste 2000 Portland OR 97205-3072 Office Phone: 503-222-4499. Business E-Mail: cem@hhiv.com.

**MCKELVEY, JAMES MORGAN,** chemical engineering educator, retired dean; b. St. Louis, Aug. 22, 1925; s. James Grey and Muriel (Morgan) McK.; m. Edith Rothbauer, Dec. 28, 1957; children: James, Robert; m. Judith Hood Forgotson, Sept. 4, 1992. BS, U. Mo.-Rolla, 1945; MS, Washington U., St. Louis, 1947, PhD, 1950. Research engr. E.I. DuPont de Nemours & Co., Inc., 1950-54; asst. prof. chem. engring. Johns Hopkins U., Balt., 1954-57; mem. faculty Washington U., St. Louis, 1957—, dean Sch. Engring. and Applied Sci., 1964-91, prof. chem. engring., 1991-98, sr. prof. chem. engring. 1998—. Recipient Disting. Educator award Soc. Plastics Engrs., 1979 Home: 9861 Copper Hill Rd Saint Louis MO 63124-1063 Office Phone: 314-935-4836. Personal E-mail: jmckelvey@aol.com.

**MCKELVY, MICHAEL JOHN,** chemist, research scientist; b. Berkeley, Calif., Apr. 19, 1954; s. Andy Milton and Dagmar Marie (Johnson) McK.; m. Margaret Knight Riddall, Aug. 2, 1975; children: Robin, Adam, Evan. BS in Chemistry, U. Calif., Berkeley, 1975; MS in Chemistry, Ariz. State U., 1981, PhD in Chemistry, 1985. Engr. crystal growing lab., ctr. solid state sci. Ariz. State U., Tempe, 1976-82, materials sci. engr. II, 1982-84, rsch. specialist, 1984-90, mgr. materials facility, 1986-94, assoc. rsch. scientist, 1990-99, affiliate assoc. prof. sci. & engring. of materials PhD program, 1993-99, dir. materials facility, 1994—2005, dir. Goldwater materials sci. labs., 1995—2005, acting dir. ctr. solid state sci., 1997, sr. rsch. scientist, 1999—, affiliate prof. sci. and engring. materials grad. program, 1999—, mgr. Goldwater materials facilities, 2006—. Invited asst. prof. Inst. des Matériaux de Nantes, U. Nantes, France, 1993; NRC sr. rsch. assoc. Albany (Oreg.) Rsch. Ctr., 2002; proposal reviewer Petroleum Rsch. Fund, Washington, 1992-94, U.S. Dept. Energy, 2000—. Contbr. articles to profl. jours.; manuscript reviewer Chemistry of Materials, 1994-2002, Jour. Physics and Chemistry of Solids, 1995, Jour. Solid State Chemistry, 1996—, Molecular Crystals and Liquid Crystals, 1997-98, Journal of American Chemical Society, 1998-2001, Journal of American Ceramic Society, 2001-02, Environmental Science and Technology, 2003—. Coach Chandler (Ariz.) Youth Baseball, 1988-95, Chandler Am. Little League, 1996-97; com. chmn. cub scouts Boy Scouts Am., Mesa, Ariz., 1992, mem. Boy Scout com., Chandler, 1993-95. Recipient Outstanding Cmty. Impact award, Acad. Cmty. Engagement Svcs., ASU, 2002; rsch. grantee NSF, 1986—, Petroleum Rsch. Fund, 1992-95, Dept. Energy, 1995—; NRC sr. rsch. assoc., 2002. Mem. Am. Chem. Soc., Materials Rsch. Soc., Minerals, Metals and Materials Soc. Democrat. Presbyterian. Achievements include patents for method for detection of chemical components, chemical switch and method for detection of chemical compounds, and chemical switch for detection of chemical components; co-development of atomic-level imaging of lamellar intercalation reaction processes using dynamic high-resolution transmission electron microscopy and scanning tunneling microscopy/spectroscopy; research in new materials synthesis, materials reaction mechanisms, carbon dioxide mineral sequestration, intercalation chemistry, thermal chemistry and analysis, materials sci. edn. Office: Ariz State U Ctr for Solid State Science Tempe AZ 85287-1704 Office Phone: 480-965-4535. Business E-Mail: mckelvy@asu.edu.

**MCKENDRICK, RYAN PARKER,** music educator, conductor; b. Charlotte, Aug. 10, 1982; s. Robert P and Vicki D McKendrick, Gregg Hardee (Stepfather) and Julie McKendrick (Stepmother). MusB, Furman U., 2005. Dir. music John Calvin Presbyn. Ch., Greenville, SC, 2003—05; choirmaster Rivercliff Luth. Ch., Atlanta, 2006—. Grad. asst. Ga. State U., Atlanta, 2005—. Fellow Music Theory, Furman U., 2003—05. Mem.: Am. Choral Dirs. Assn., MENC, Phi Mu Alpha Sinfonia (music dir. 2004—05). Republican. Lutheran. Avocations: reading, travel. Office Phone: 770-993-4316.

**MCKENDRY, JOHN H., JR.,** lawyer; b. Grand Rapids, Mich., Mar. 24, 1950; s. John H. and Lois R. (Brandel) McK.; m. Linda A. Schmalzer, Aug. 11, 1973; children: Heather Lynn, Shannon Dawn, Sean William. BA cum laude, Albion Coll., 1972; JD cum laude, U. Mich., 1975. Bar: Mich. 1975. Assoc., then ptnr. Landman, Latimer, Clink & Robb, Muskegon, Mich., 1976-85; ptnr. Warner, Norcross & Judd, Muskegon, 1985—. Dir. debate Mona Shores High Sch., Muskegon, 1979-90; adj. prof. of taxation (employee benefits), Grand Valley State U., 1988—; debate instr. Muskegon C.C., 1999-2001. Pres. local chpt. Am. Cancer Soc., 1979; bd. dirs. West Shore Symphony, 1993-00, v.p. 1995-97, pres., 1997-99; bd. dirs. Cath. Social Svcs., 1998-04; chair profl. divsn. United Way, 1994, 98; chair bd. dirs. Deaf Hard of Hearing Connection, 2003—; bd. dirs. Mona Lake Watershed Coun., 2003-05; chair Charter Commn. City of Norton Shores, 2003-06. Recipient Disting. Service award Muskegon Jaycees, 1981; named 1 of 5 Outstanding Young Men in Mich., Mich. Jaycees. 1982; named to Hall of Fame, Mich. Speech Coaches, 1986, Diamond Key Coach Nat. Forensic League, 1988. Mem. ABA, Mich. Bar Assn., Muskegon County Bar Assn. (dir. 1992-98, pres. 1996-97), Muskegon C of C. (bd. dirs. 1982-88), Mich. Interscholastic Forensic Assn. (treas. 1979-86), Optimists (pres. 1992). Republican. Roman Catholic. Home: 1575 Brookwood Dr Muskegon MI 49441-5276 Office: Warner Norcross & Judd LLP PO Box 900 400 Terrace Pla Muskegon MI 49443-0900 Office Phone: 231-727-2637. Business E-Mail: mckendjh@wnj.com.

**MCKENNA, ALVIN JAMES,** lawyer; b. New Orleans, Aug. 17, 1943; s. Dixon N. Sr. and Mabel (Duplantier) McK.; m. Carol Jean Windheim, 1963; children: Sara, Alvin James Jr., Martha, Andrea, Erin, Rebecca. AB, Canisius Coll., 1963; JD, Notre Dame U., 1966. Bar: N.Y. 1966, Ohio 1967, U.S. Dist. Ct. (so. dist.) Ohio 1968, U.S. Dist. Ct. (no. dist.) Ohio 1978, U.S. Ct. Appeals (6th cir.) 1984, U.S. Supreme Ct. 1977. Law clk. to judge of U.S. Dist. Ct. (so. dist.), Columbus, Ohio, 1966-68; asst. U.S. atty., 1968-70; ptnr. Porter, Wright, Morris & Arthur, 1970—. Mem. Gahanna (Ohio) City Coun., 1972-80, 82-84; chmn. Gahanna Charter Rev. Commn. 1981, 2006; pres. Cmty. Urban Redevel. Corp., Gahanna, 1984—2006. Named one of Ten Outstanding Young Persons in Columbus, Jaycees, 1974. Mem. ABA, Ohio Bar Assn., Fed. Bar Assn. (pres. Columbus chpt. 1973-74), Columbus Bar Assn. (chair fed. cts. com 1972-74). Home: 202 Academy Ct Columbus OH 43230-2104 Office: Porter Wright Morris & Arthur 41 S High St Ste 2800 Columbus OH 43215-6194 Office Phone: 614-227-1945. Business E-Mail: amckenna@porterwright.com.

**MCKENNA, ANDREW JAMES,** wholesale distribution executive, printing company executive, sports association executive; b. Chgo., Sept. 17, 1929; s. Andrew James and Anita (Fruin) McK.; m. Mary Joan Pickett, June 20, 1953; children: Suzanne, Karen, Andrew, William, Joan, Kathleen, Margaret. BS, U. Notre Dame, 1951; JD, DePaul U., 1954. Bar: Ill. Chmn. Schwarz Paper Co. (name now Schwarz), Morton Grove, Ill., 1964—; non-exec. chmn. McDonald's Corp., 2004—. Bd. dirs. Skyline Corp., AON Corp., Click Commerce, Inc., McDonald's Corp., 1991—. Chmn. trustees, emeritus U. Notre Dame; trustee Mus. Sci. and Industry, Chgo.; bd. dirs. Cath. Charities of Chgo., Children's Meml. Med. Ctr. Chgo.; founding chmn. Chgo. Metropolis 2020. Mem. Comml. Club Chgo., Econ. Club Chgo., Lyric Opera (bd. dirs.), Execs. Club Chgo., Glenview Golf Club, Old Elm Club, Merit Club, Casino Club, The Island Club. Home: 60 Locust Rd Winnetka IL 60093-3751 Office: Schwarz 8338 Austin Ave Morton Grove IL 60053-3288

**MCKENNA, ANN K.,** nutritionist, educator; d. Mary Giannavola and Joseph Peter Kupchak; m. Robert William McKenna, Aug. 10, 1963; children: Rodney William, Scot Robert, Stacy McKenna Brazil, Alison McKenna Rothwell, Cynthia McKenna Holmes. BS in Nutrition and Edn., Marywood Coll., Pa., 1959, MS in Nutrition and Dietetics, 1992. Registered Dietitian Am. Dietetic Assn., 1968, Cert.in Family and Consumer Sci. Am. Assn. of Family and Consumer Sci., 1985, lic. Dietitian, Nutritionist Pa., 2002. Adminstrv. dietitian Flower & Fifth Ave. Hosp., NYC, 1959—62; clin. dietitian Moses Taylor Hosp., Scranton, Pa., 1971—82; cons. dietitian, self employed in long term care facilities and home health orgns. Pa., 1982—; nutrition cons. Scranton Head Start Program, Scranton, 1984—; part-time faculty Marywood U., 1984—; clin. dietitian, educator Moses Taylor Hosp. Diabetes Edn. Program, 1998—2004. Bd. mem. NE Pa. Dietetic Assn., Scranton, Wilkes-Barre, Pa., 1995—; health adv. bd. mem. Scranton Lackawanna Head Start Program, Scranton, 1990—; coordinating cabinet mem. Marywood U. Nutrition and Dietetics Program, 1990—. Recipient Kappa Kappa Nu, Honor Soc. for Nutrition Grads. through Marywood Coll., 1992, Anita Owen award for Dietetic Profs., N.E. Pa. Dietetic Assn., 1998, Outstanding Dietetic Educator, Pa. Dietetic Assn., 1999, Dietetic Educators of Am. Dietetic Assn., 1999, Woman Yr. Head Start Program Scranton Lackawanna Human Devel. Agy., 2000. Mem.: Am. Assn. of Family and Consumer Sci. (assoc.), Am. Dietetic Assn. (assoc.), Pa. Dietetic Assn. (assoc.; bd. mem. 1999—2000), NE Pa. Dietetic Assn. (assoc.; career guidance, job referral chair 1996—2005). Avocations: fitness, gourmet cooking, reading. Home: 1329 Electric St Dunmore PA 18509 Office: Marywood Univ Adams Ave Scranton PA 18509 Office Phone: 570-346-6422. Home Fax: 570-346-6422. Personal E-mail: akmrd@aol.com.

**MCKENNA, FRANK JOSEPH,** ambassador, lawyer; b. Apohaqui, N.B., Can., Jan. 19, 1948; s. Durward and Olive (Moody) McK.; m. Julie Friel; children: Tobias John, Christine Alice, James Durward. BA with honors, St. Francis Xavier U., 1970; postgrad., Queen's U., 1970-71; LLB, U. N.B., 1974; DSc (hon.), Université de Moncton, Can., 1988; LLD (hon.), University of N.B., Can., 1988, Mt. Allison U., 1991. Spl. asst. to pres. Privy Council, 1971; rsch. asst. Constl. Law Unit, 1973-74; v.p. U. N.B. Faculty of Law Liberal Assn., Fredericton, 1974; ptnr. Martin, Lordon, McKenna & Bowes, Chatham, 1974-87; mem. N.B. Liberal Party, 1982, leader, 1985; premier Province of N.B., Fredericton, 1987-97; with McInnes Cooper, Moncton, 1998—2005; amb. to the US Govt. Can., Washington, 2005—, Counsel McInnes Cooper Firm, Olser Hoskin & Harcourt; appointee Security Intel. Review Com. Chair Can. Quality Month, 1994. Named Econ. Developer of Yr., Econ. Developer's Assn. Can., 1993; recipient Vanier award, 1988, Distinction award, Can. Advanced Tech. Assn., 1994. Mem.: N.B. Bar Assn., Can. Bar Assn. Liberal. Avocations: jogging, reading, golf. Office: Embassy Can 501 Pennsylvania Ave NW Washington DC 20001 Business E-Mail: frank.mckenna@mcinnescooper.com

**MCKENNA, GEORGE LAVERNE,** art museum curator; b. Detroit, Dec. 7, 1924; s. John LaVerne and Carolyn Georgia (Schwab) McK.; m. Janice Ballinger, July 22, 1966. Student, U. Oreg., 1943-44, U. Calif., Berkeley, 1948-49, U. Chgo., 1950; AB, Wayne State U., 1948, MA, 1951. Curator prints, drawings and photographs Nelson-Atkins Mus. Art, Kansas City, Mo., 1952-96, cons, 1997—. Cons. Hallmark Cards, Inc., Kansas City, 1974-76. Curator, author exhbn. and coll. catalogues. With U.S. Army, 1943-46. Mem. Am. Assn. Mus., Print Coun. Am. Office: Nelson-Atkins Mus Art 4525 Oak St Kansas City MO 64111-1873

**MCKENNA, JAMES RICHARD,** agronomy educator; b. Orange, N.J., Feb. 27, 1942; s. John Frances and Esther Hope (Rice) McK.; m. Judith Ann Morse, June 21, 1969 (div. Nov. 1979); children: Catherine Jean, Jennifer Lynn; m. Debra Lynn Morris, Mar. 22, 1980. BS, U. R.I., 1964; MS, U. Maine, 1970; PhD, Va. Poly. Inst. and State U., 1988. Tchr. sci. Patton Acad., Sch. Dist. 25, Patten, Maine, 1964-68; rsch. asst. Dept. Plant and Soil Sci., Orono, Maine, 1968-70; tchr. biology Houlton (Maine) High Sch., Sch. Dist. 29, 1970-78; extension agt. Maine Coop. Extension Svc., Houlton, 1978-79, Va. Coop. Extension Svc., Harrisonburg, 1979-84; instr. dept. crop and soil environ. sci. Va. Poly. Inst. and State U., Blacksburg, 1984-88, prof., 1988—. Ind. farmer, Houlton and Patten, 1964-78; cons. Mali (W. Africa) Farming Systems Rsch/Extension Project, U.S. AID, 1988-91. Assoc. editor: Jour. Natural Resources and Life Scis. Edn.; contbr. articles to profl. jours. Chmn. Town Planning Bd., Houlton, 1977; master of ceremonies Mountain Acad. Coun., Blacksburg, 1989. Recipient Young Scientist award Am. Forage and Grassland, Springfield, Ill., 1987, Excellence in Acad. Advising award Alumni Assn. of Va. Poly. Inst. and State U., 1991; Nat. Assn. of Coll. & Teachers of Agrl. Fellow, 1993, Diggs Tchg. scholar 1996. Fellow Am. Soc. Agronomy (chair crops com. 1991, Agronomic Resident Edn. award 1997); mem. Crop Sci. Soc. Am. (vice chair collegiate crops judging 1990), Nat. Assn. Colls. and Tchrs. of Agr. (ea. regional dir., 2002, v.p. 2002, presdl. nominee 2003), Va. Poly. Inst. and State U. Faculty Assn. (sec. faculty affairs com. 1991), Gamma Sigma Delta (teaching award of merit 1990). Mem. Ch. of Brethren. Achievements include development of global orientations for course and curriculum in deptartments of crops and soil environmental science, of undergraduate BS degree in Environmental Science, of practice of using prolific (multiple ear) corn as part of sustainable production, of recommendations for rock phosphate use on sorghum/cowpea association in Mali of system for establishment of warm-season grasses no-till in Virginia. Office: Va Poly Inst and State Univ 235 Smyth Hall Blacksburg VA 24061 Home: 5000 Whitethorne Rd Blacksburg VA 24060-0882

**MCKENNA, KEVIN PATRICK,** newspaper editor; BA, U. So. Calif., 1976; MS, Columbia, U., 1977. Reporter AP, Raleigh, NC, 1977-78; copy editor Internat. Herald Tribune, Paris, 1978-84; editorial staff The New York Times, N.Y.C., 1984-95; editorial dir. N.Y. Times Electronic Media Co., 1995-97; asst. to dep. mng. editor N.Y. Times, 1998, technology editor, 1999-2001, circuits sect. editor, 2001—. Knight Journalism fellow Stanford U., 1997-98. Mem. Am. Soc. Newspaper Editors. Office: NY Times 229 W 43rd St New York NY 10036-3959*

**MCKENNA, MARGARET ANNE,** academic administrator; b. RI, June 3, 1945; d. Joseph John and Mary (Burns) McK.; children: Michael Aaron McKenna Miller, David Christopher McKenna Miller. BA in Sociology, Emmanuel Coll., 1967; postgrad., Boston Coll. Law Sch., 1968; JD, So. Meth. U., 1971; LLD (hon.), U. Upsala, NJ, 1978, Fitchburg State Coll., Mass., 1979, Regis Coll., 1982; LLD (hon.), Emmanuel Coll., 2000, Episcopal Divinity Sch., 2003, Bari Ion. 1971, D.C. 1973. Atty. Dept. Justice, Washington, 1971-73; exec. dir. Internat. Assn. Ofcl. Human Rights Agys., Washington, 1973-74; mgmt. cons. Dept. Treasury, Washington, 1975-76; dep. council to Pres. White House, Washington, 1976-79; dep. undersec. Dept. Edn., Washington, 1979-81; dir. Mary Ingraham Bunting Inst., Radcliffe Coll., Cambridge, Mass., 1981-85; v.p. program planning Radcliffe Coll., Cambridge, 1982-85; pres. Lesley U., Cambridge, 1985—. Bd. dirs. Dominion Resources, Inc., Cisco Learning Inst. Bd. dirs. Am. Assn. Coll. for Tchr. Edn., Coun. for Higher Edn. Accreditation, Datatel Scholars Found.; chmn. higher edn. task force Clinton Transition, 1992-93; chmn. edn. task force Mayor Thomas Menino Transition Com., 1994; mem. Princeton Adv. Bd. ACE Policy Adv. Com., Campus Compact Policy Com., MassNetworks. Recipient Outstanding Contribution award Civil Rights Leadership Conf., 1978; named Woman of Yr. Women's Equity Action League, 1979, Outstanding Woman of Yr. Big Sister Assn., 1986, Pinnacle award for Lifetime Achievement, Lelia J. Robinson award Women's Bar Assn. Mass., 1996, Valeria Addams Knapp award, The Coll. Club, 2005; named Margaret A. McKenna Day, Gov. DePrete, R.I. Mem. Boys Scouts Am., Big Sisters Ass Boston, Y.W.C.A. Cambridge, Women's Equity Action League, Nat. Women's Polit. Conf., Nat. Assn. Official Human Rights Agencies. Democrat. Office: Lesley Univ Office of President 29 Everett St Cambridge MA 02138-2702

**MCKENNA, PATRICK JAMES,** management consultant; b. Edson, Alta., Can., Oct. 31, 1951; s. James Edward and Madeline (Watson) McKenna; m. Monique, 1 Child, David. CIM, Can. Inst. Mgmt., Toronto, Ont., 1979. P. Mgr., 1977, MBA, 1982, ICIA, 1985. Asst. div. mgr. Hudsons Bay Co., Edmonton, Alta., 1973-75; gen. mgr. Alta. C of C. Edmonton, 1975-78; mng. dir. QCTV Ltd., Edmonton, 1978-81; v.p. Achieve Enterprises Ltd., Edmonton, 1981-83; ptnr. Edge Intl., Edmonton, 1984. Can. Inst. Mgmt., 1981-85. Author: Building Business Abroad, 1985; co-author: Creating the Marketing Mindset, 1989; contrib. author: The Lawyer's Handbook, 3rd edit., 1992; co-author, Herding Cats, 1995, Beyond Knowing, 2000, First Among Equals, 2002 contbr. articles to profl. jours.; mem. publ. adv. bd. Partner-to-Partner Advisory, The Marcus Letter on Prof. Svcs. Mktg. Mem. ABA, Strategic Leadership Forum. Conservative. Home: 11226 60th St Edmonton AB Canada T5W 3Y8

**MCKENNA, PETER DENNIS**, lawyer; b. Amityville, N.Y., Aug. 15, 1937; s. John Paul and Margaret (Foley) McK.; children: Michael A., Suzanne E. AB cum laude, Coll. of the Holy Cross, Worchester, Mass., 1959; JD cum laude, N.Y.U., 1968. Bar: N.Y. 1968, U.S. Dist. Ct. (so. dist.) N.Y. 1970, U.S. Supreme Ct. 1973, U.S. Ct. Appeals (4th cir.) 1977, U.S. Ct. Appeals (7th cir.) 1979, U.S. Ct. Appeals (2nd cir.) 1983. Assoc. Wachtell, Lipton, Rosen & Katz, N.Y.C., 1968-71, ptnr., 1972-91, of counsel, 1992—2001. Mem. pres.'s coun. NYU, Weinfeld Ptnr. NYU Law Sch.; regent mem. pres.'s coun. Coll. Holy Cross. Editor-in-chief N.Y.U. Law Review, 1967-68; contbr. articles to profl. jours. Mem. Cmty. Sch. Bd. Dist. 26, Queens, N.Y., 1973-77; adv. bd. St. Aloyisius Sch. for Cen. Harlem Inner-City Children, 1992—, mem. exec. com., 1994-2001; founding dir. Ctrl. Harlem Initiative for Learning and Devel., 1994—; bd. dirs. Mt. St. Michael Acad., 1994-2001, mem. exec. com., 1994-99. Lt. USN 1959-65. MEM. ABA, Am. Arbitration Assn. (comml. and securities panels), Assn. of Bar of City of N.Y., Order of Coif. Democrat. Roman Catholic. Avocations: history, public affairs, travel, swimming, golf. Address: 21205 NE 37th Ave Apt 1607 Aventura FL 33180-4056 E-mail: ppeter68@aol.com.

**MCKENNA, ROB**, state attorney general, former councilman; b. Ft. Sam Houston, Tex., Oct. 1, 1962; m. Marilyn McKenna; children: Madeleine, Katie, Robert, Connor. BA in economics and internat. studies, 1985; JD, U. Chgo., 1988. Bar: Wash. 9th Cir. US Ct. Appeals. Atty. Perkins Cole, Bellevue, Wash., 1988—95; councilman King County, Wash., 1996—2004; atty. gen. State of Wash., 2005—. Co-founder, bd. mem. Eastside Human Services Forum; bd. mem. Econ. Devel. Coun. of Seattle & King County; mem. Sound Transit Bd., 1996—2001; chair Eastside Transp. Partnership, 1999—2001, Wash. State Transp. Improvement Bd., 2001—03. Mem. King County Open Space Citizens Oversight Com., 1990—94; founder, bd. dirs. Advance Bellevue, 1991—2001; past pres., bd. mem. Bellevue Schools Found., 1993—2002; mem. Bellevue Rotary, 1993—; bd. mem. King County Open Space Citizens Oversight Com., 1995—98; co-chair City of Hope Walk for Hope to Cure Breast Cancer, 1998, 1999; co-founder, bd. mem. Evergreen Forest Trust, 2000—; bd. mem. Bellevue CC Found., 2000—; mem. steering com. Citizens for Renton Schools, 2002—03; mem. exec. bd. Chief Seattle Coun. Boy Scouts Am., 2003—; mem. St. Louise Cath. Parish, 1977—; Eagle Scout. Named Elected Ofcl. of Yr., Nat. Assn. Indsl. and Office Properties, 1999; named one of The 25 Smartest People in Wash., Wash. Law & Politics, 2003; recipient Doug Mason Meml. Award, Mcpl. League King County, 1991, 40 under 40 Award, Puget Sound Bus. Jour., 2000, Advance Bellevue 10th Anniversary Legacy Award, 2003. Mem.: King County Bar Assn., Wash. State Bar Assn. Republican. Office: Office Atty Gen 1125 Washington St SE PO Box 40100 Olympia WA 98504 Office Phone: 360-753-6200. Business E-Mail: rob.mckenna@atg.wa.gov.

**MCKENNA, ROBERT JOSEPH, JR.**, thoracic surgeon; b. NYC, May 28, 1951; s. Robert Joseph and Madelyn (Dyer) McKenna; m. Kathy Polson, Jan. 1, 1982; children: Kelley, Rob, Kristen. MD, U. So. Calif., 77. Resident in surgery Stanford U., Palo Alto, Calif., 1982; resident in thoracic surgery MD Anderson Med. Ctr., Houston, 1983—87; resident in cardio-thoracic surgery U. So. Calif., LA, 1987—97; head thoracic surgery Cedars Sinai Med. Ctr., LA, 1997—, dir. fellowship, 2001—; prof. thoracic surgery UCLA, 1999—. Spkr., presenter in field. Contbr. more than 150 articles to med. jours., 29 chpts. to books. Mem.: ACS, Am. Assn. Thoracic Surgery, Soc. Thoracic Surgeons. Achievements include development of minimally invasive surgery for lung cancer. Avocations: travel, tennis. Office: 8635 W 3d Ste 975W Los Angeles CA 90048

**MCKENNA, TERENCE PATRICK**, retired insurance company executive; b. Oldham, Lancashire, Eng., Sept. 3, 1928; came to U.S., 1929, naturalized, 1939; s. Patrick A. and Mary F. McK.; m. Patricia Buckley, Sept. 22, 1973. Student, St. Thomas Coll., Bloomfield, Conn., 1946—48. With John Hancock Mut. Life Ins. Co., 1951-87, gen. agt. Cherry Hill, NJ, 1963-67, field v.p. gen. agy. dept. Atlanta, 1967-69, field v.p. dist. agy. dept. Boston, 1969-73, 2d v.p. mktg. ops. dept., 1973-74, v.p. dept., 1974-76, sr. v.p. dept., 1976-83, sr. v.p. gen. agy. sales dept., 1983-87, ret., 1987. V.p., also dir. John Hancock Variable Life Ins. Co.; chmn. bd. mgrs. I.V.A.; bd. dirs. John Hancock Distbrs. Inc., John Hancock Property and Casualty Ins. Co. Served with USMC, 1952-54. Mem.: Am. Soc. CLUs, Am. Coll. Life Underwriters, El Niguel Country Club (Laguna Niguel, Calif.), Woods Hole Golf Club (Falmouth, Mass.). Personal E-mail: tmckenna@bellsouth.net.

**MCKENNA, WILLIAM JOHN**, retired textile products executive; b. N.Y.C., Oct. 11, 1926; s. William T. and Florence (Valis) McK.; m. Jean T. McNulty, Aug. 27, 1949 (dec. Nov. 1984); children: Kevin, Marybeth, Peter, Dawn; m. Karen Lynne Hilgert, Aug. 6, 1988; children: Katherine Lynne, William John IV. BBA, Iona Coll., 1949; MS (Univ. Store Service scholar), NYU, 1950. V.p. Hat Corp. Am., N.Y.C., 1961-63, v.p. mktg., 1961-63, exec. v.p., 1963-67; pres. Manhattan Shirt Co. N.Y.C., 1967-74; pres., dir. Lee Co., Inc., Shawnee Mission, Kans., 1974-82, Kellwood Co., St. Louis, 1982—, chief exec. officer, 1984—, also bd. dirs., chmn. CEO, 1991-97, chmn., 1991-99, chmn. emeritus, 1999—. Dir. United Mo. Bank of St. Louis. Trustee emeritus St. Louis U., Boys Hope; permanent deacon Archdiocese St. Louis. With USN, 1944-46, PTO. Mem. Sovereign Mil. Order Malta, St. Louis Club, Bellerive Country Club. Roman Catholic. E-mail: william_mckenna@kellwood.com.

**MCKENNA, WILLIAM MICHAEL**, advertising executive; b. Washington, Apr. 4, 1951; s. William H. and Betty Ann (Cashin) McK.; m. Lynn Stevenson, Dec. 18, 1976; children: James Langdon, Lee Stevenson. BA, Wesleyan U., 1973; MS in Journalism, Boston U., 1978. V.p., creative dir. Ingalls Quinn & Johnson, Boston, 1981-88; sr. v.p., creative dir. Young & Rubicam, N.Y.C., 1988-94; chief creative officer, exec. v.p. AF GL Internat., N.Y.C., 1994-95; mng. dir., chief creative officer Citigate Albert Frank, N.Y.C., 1996-99; mng. dir., COO, Marstellar, N.Y.C., 1999-2000; pres., CEO Marsteller Advt., N.Y.C., 2000—. V.p. comm. Middlebury Coll., Vt., 2005—. Recipient CLIO, Hatch, N.Y. Film Soc. creative awards, 1982-95, Telly award. Office: Burson Marstellar 230 Park Ave S New York NY 10003-1513 Home: 869 James Rd Middlebury VT 05753-9538

**MCKENNON, KEITH ROBERT**, chemical company executive; b. Condon, Oreg., Dec. 25, 1933; s. Russel M. and Lois E. (Edgerton) McK.; m. Patricia Dragon, Sept. 30, 1961; children: Brian, Marc, Kevin. BS, Oreg. State U., 1955. Rsch. chemist Dow Chem. Co., Pittsburg, Calif., 1955—67, sales mgr. Houston, 1967, from research mgr. to exec. v.p. Midland, Mich., 1968—87, bd. dirs., 1982—92, 2003—, exec. v.p., 1987-92; pres. Dow USA, 1987-90; chmn., chief exec. officer Dow Corning Corp., 1992-94; also bd. dirs.; chmn. PacifiCorp, Portland, Oreg., 1994-99, CEO, 1998-99. Patentee. Recipient Chemical Industry medal Soc. of Chemical Industry, 1994 Republican. Presbyterian. E-mail: kmck96@aol.com.

**MCKENTY, PATRICK**, research scientist; b. Dearborn, Mich., Aug. 30, 1953; PhD, U. Ariz., Tucson, 1983. Sr. rsch. scientist Lab. for Laser Energetics, Rochester, NY, 1984—2006. Office: Lab for Laser Energetics 250 E River Rd Rochester NY 14623 Office Phone: 585-275-3865. Business E-Mail: pmck@lle.rochester.edu.

**MCKENZIE, BRIAN BRUCE**, finance educator; b. Kelowna, BC, Canada, Nov. 23, 1948; arrived in U.S., 2003; s. Rex Bruce and Dorothy McKenzie; m. Molly Kathleen Farrend, Mar. 21, 1970. BA, U. BC, Vancouver, Can., 1974; MBA, U. Victoria, Can., 1997, PhD, 2003. Cert. qualification - boatbuilding Province of BC, 1990. Pres. Brian McKenzie Boatbuilding, Inc, Victoria, Canada, 1982—97; lectr. U. Victoria, 1997—2002; asst. prof. U. Calif., East Bay, 2003—. Vis. instr. Worcester (Mass.) Poly. Inst., 1999—2000. Contbr. scientific papers, rsch. to profl. jours. Recipient Entrepreneurship Theory and Practice Best Conceptual Paper award, 2004. Fellow: Students Free Enterprise (Sam Walton Fellow 2005—06); mem.: Can. Anthrop. Assn., Small Bus. Inst., N.Am. Case Rsch. Assn., Acad. Mgmt. (chair nontraditional academics com.entrepreneurship divsn., Innovations in

Pedagogy award 1999), U.S. Assn. Small Bus. and Entrepreneurship (Model Undergraduate Program award 2000), Oral History Assn. Office: Calif State U 25800 Carlos Bee Blvd Hayward CA 94542 Office Phone: 510-885-2858. Personal E-mail: brian@brian-mckenzie.com. Business E-Mail: bmckenzie@csueastbay.edu

**MCKENZIE, DENISE**, religious organization administrator, academic administrator; b. Lackawanna, NY, Mar. 2, 1950; d. John Patrick and Dolores Marguerite McKenzie. AAS, Trocaire Coll., 1972; BA in Religious Studies, Canisius Coll., 1973, MA in Religious Studies, 1980. Religion tchr. Mt. Mercy Acad., Buffalo, 1973—89; prof. religious studies Trocaire Coll., Buffalo, 1984—89; dir. campus ministry D'Youville Coll., Buffalo, 1989—96, prof. religious studies, 1989—96; diocesan dir. of religious edn. Diocese of Buffalo, 1996—2002, sec. edn., 2002. Vocal cantor Nat. Shrine of Our Lady of Victory; mem. Fidelis health bd. Cath. Health Sys., Buffalo, 2002—; bd. mem. Cantilican Ctr. for Learning, Buffalo, 2002—; mem. bd. Cath. edn. Diocese of Buffalo, 1997—. Recipient Vol. of Yr., Mary Agnes Manor Nursing Home, 1992, Disting. Alumni, Trocaire Coll., 2003, Mt. Mercy Acad., 1998, Adminstr. of Yr., D'Youville Coll., 1992. Mem.: Nat. Conf. Cathechetical Leadership, Nat. Cath. Edn. Assn., Chief Administrators of Cath. Edn. Office: Diocese of Buffalo 795 Main St Buffalo NY 14203 Office Phone: 716-847-5520. Business E-Mail: dmckenzie@buffalodiocese.org.

**MCKENZIE, ELIZABETH MCDANIEL**, law librarian; b. Lexington, Ky., June 27, 1954; d. William E. and JoAnn E. (Harris) McDaniel; m. James A. McKenzie, May 20, 1978; children: Joseph D., E. Alexa. BA with distinction, Transylvania U., 1975; JD, U. Ky., 1981, MLS with distinction, 1984. Bar: Ky. 1981, U.S. Dist. Ct. (ea. dist.) Ky. 1981. Reginald Heber Smith community lawyer fellow Cen. Ky. Legal Svcs., Lexington, 1981-83; info. specialist Ky. Dept. for Environ. Protection, Frankfort, Ky., 1984-85; readers svcs. librarian St. Louis U. Law Library, 1986-96; dir. Suffolk U. Law Librr., Boston, 1996—. Owner, mgr. Juris Data Legal Rsch. Co., Lexington, 1985-86. Contbg. author: Libraries, Erotica and Pornography. Recipient Article of Yr. award Law Libr. Jour., 1999; Nat. Merit scholar Transylvania U., 1972-75. Mem. ABA, Ky. Bar Assn., Am. Assn. Law Libraries, Law Libraries New England, New England Law Library Consortium, Assn. Boston Law Libraries. Democrat. Roman Catholic. Office: Suffolk U Law Sch 120 Tremont St Boston MA 02108-4977 Business E-Mail: emckenzi@suffolk.edu.

**MCKENZIE, JAMES W., JR.**, lawyer; b. Oct. 3, 1959; AB, Dartmouth Coll., 1982; MBA, JD, U. Pa., 1987. Bar: Pa. 1987. Assoc. Morgan, Lewis & Bockius LLP, Phila., 1987—95, partner, 1995—2000, 2002—; exec. v.p., gen. counsel VerticalNet, Inc., 2002—02. Named one of 12 "Dealmakers of the Yr.", The American Lawyer, 2004. Office: Morgan Lewis & Bockius LLP 1701 Market St Philadelphia PA 19103-2903

**MCKENZIE, JOHN F.**, lawyer; b. Chgo., Sept. 28, 1947; s. John Cummings and Mary Jane (Manny) McK.; m. Lucy A. Roman, Jan. 14, 1978; children: Melissa Ann, Sean Cummings. BA magna cum laude, Williams Coll., 1969; JD cum laude, Harvard U., 1976. Bar: Calif. 1976, U.S. Dist. Ct. (No. Dist.) Calif. 1976, U.S. Ct. Appeals (10th Cir.) 1984, Ct. Internat. Trade. Assoc. Baker & McKenzie LLP, San Francisco, 1976-83, ptnr., 1983—. Spkr. in field. Contbg. author, editor Computers & Software, 4th edit., 1989; contbr. articles on export controls, anti-boycott regulations and software licensing to profl. publs.; articles editor Harvard Law Review, 1975-76. Mem. ABA (internat. law sect.), State Bar of Calif. (internat. sect.), Bar Assn. San Francisco, Santa Clara Valley World Trade Assn., Assn. Freight Forwarders and Customs Brokers (assoc. mem.), Am. Electronics Assn. (lawyers com.), Calif. Coun. on Internat. Trade (mem. legis. coun.), Dist. Export Coun. for Northern Calif., U.S. Dept. Commerce (no. Calif. dist. export coun.); Phi Beta Kappa (Magna Cum Laude) Home: 10 Mann Dr Kentfield CA 94904-1034 Office: Baker & McKenzie LLP 2 Embarcadero Ctr Ste 2400 San Francisco CA 94111-3909 also: Baker & McKenzie 1 Prudential Pla 130 E Randolph St Ste 3700 Chicago IL 60601-6316 Office Phone: 415-576-3033. Business E-Mail: john.f.mckenzie@bakernet.com.*

**MCKENZIE, KAY BRANCH**, public relations executive; b. Atlanta, Feb. 12, 1936; d. William Harllee and Katherine (Hunter) Branch; m. Harold Cantrell McKenzie, Jr., Apr. 11, 1958; children: Ansley, Katherine, Harold Cantrell III. Student, Sweet Briar Coll., 1955, Emory U., 1956-57. Account exec. Hill and Knowlton Inc., Atlanta, 1979-80, account supr./dir. S.E. govt. rels., 1981-83; ptnr. McKenzie, Gordon & Potter, Atlanta, 1983-85; pres. McKenzie & Assocs. Inc., Atlanta, 1986-89; sr. v.p. Manning Selvage & Lee, Atlanta, 1989-93; v.p. comm. and creative svcs. 1996 Atlanta Paralympic Games, 1993-96; v.p. comm. and devel. U.S. Disabled Athletes Fund, 1997—. Mem. Commn. on Future of South, 1974; co-chmn. John Lewis for Congress, Atlanta, 1986; regional bd. dirs. Inst. Internat. Edn., 1987-93 Fellow Soc. Internat. Bus. Fellows (bd. dirs. 1983-85, 92-93, v.p. 1986-88); mem. Pub. Rels. Soc. Am., Ga. C. of C. (bd. dirs. 1983-97), Leadership Atlanta, Ga. Internat. Horse Park Found. (bd. dirs. 1993-98). Democrat. Episcopalian. Office: 280 Interstate N Cir Ste 450 Atlanta GA 30339 Home: 670 Crossfire Ridge Marietta GA 30064 E-mail: kmckenzie@blazesports.com.

**MCKENZIE, KEVIN PATRICK**, artistic director; b. Burlington, Vt., Apr. 29, 1954; s. Raymond James and Ruth (Davison) McKenzie. Grad. high sch., Washington. Mem. corps de ballet Nat. Ballet of Washington, 1972-74; prin. Joffrey Ballet, NYC, 1974-78, Am. Ballet Theatre, NYC, 1979-91; artistic assoc. Washington Ballet, 1991-92; artistic dir. Am. Ballet Theatre, NYC, 1992—; assoc. artistic dir. New Amsterdam Ballet. Pres. bd. dirs. Am. Ballet Theatre Dancers Fund, Inc., 1982—89; assoc. dir. New Amsterdam Ballet, N.Y.C., 1984—; founding bd. mem. Kaatsbaan Internat. Dance Ctr., 1991—. Performer: (films) Unicorn, 1971; dancer Houston Ballet, 1978, Spoleto Festival, 1980, 1984, Theatre des Champs Elysees, Paris, 1981, Sadler's Wells Theatre, London, 1981, Asami Maki Ballet Co., Tokyo, 1983, Aspen Festival, 1982; prodr., dir. The Party of the Year, 1982; choreographer Groupo Zambaria Ballet, 1984, Liszt Etudes, 1991, Lucy and the Count, 1992, The Nutcracker, 1993; created roles Adrienne Dellos' The Blind Man's Daughter, Seoul, Korea, 1986, Amnon V'Tamar, S.P.E.B.S.Q.S.A., appeared with Martine Van Hamel Swan Lake, Nat. Ballet of Cuba, Havana, 1986, appeared with Merrill Ashley Tchaikowsky Pas de Deux, Bolshoi Theatre, Moscow, 1986; dancer La Bayadere, Carmen, Cinderella, Coppelia, Dim Lustre, Don Quixote, Giselle, The Garden of Villandry, Jardin aux lilas, The Leaves Are Fading, Pillar of Fire, Raymonda, Requiem, Rodeo, Romeo and Juliet, The Sleeping Beauty, Swan Lake, La Sylphide, Paquita, Sylvia Pas de Deux, Theme and Variations. Named Kevin McKenzie Day, City of Burlington, 1985; recipient Silver medal, Varna Internat. Ballet Competition, Bulgaria, 1972, Artistic Achievement medal, Dept. State, U.S. Govt., 1972, Mayor Burlington, Vt., 1984, Performing Arts award, Am. Ireland Fund, 1994. Office: Am Ballet Theatre 890 Broadway New York NY 10003-1211

**MCKENZIE, LAWRENCE J.**, composition educator; b. Cumberland, Md., Oct. 9, 1970; s. Lawrence J. McKenzie Sr. and Judith A. Crumbaugh-Erlewine. BA in Philosophy/Religion, U. Charleston, 1994; MA, Meth. Theol. Sch., Delaware, Ohio, 1998. Cert. candidate for ordination W.Va., 1993. Theol. intern/assoc. pastor St. Andrew United Meth. Ch., St. Albans, W.Va., 1993—96; assoc. pastor/cmty. youth dir. Ostrander United Meth. Ch., Ohio, 1994—96; pastor Hyatt's United Meth. Ch., Ohio, 1997—98; instr. of humanities U. Charleston, W.Va., 1998—2000; instrn. of composition/lit. W.Va. State Coll., Institute, 1998—2000; paralegal The Law Office, Parkersburg, W.Va., 2000—01; prof. of composition W.Va. U., Parkersburg, 2000—. Exec. bd. sec./acquisitions editor Mountain State Press, Charleston, W.Va., 2000—05; faculty senate rep. W.Va. U., Parkersburg, 2000—. Humanities Spkr. Series, Parkersburg, 2002—, W.Va. Assn. of Devel. Educators, Institute, 2002—; acquisitions editor W.Va. Writers Assn., Inc., Charleston, 2003—; asst. forensic coach W.Va. U., Parkersburg, 2003—; mem. W.Va. Consortium for Faculty and Course Devel. in Internat. Studies, Morgantown, 2004—. Pres. Cmty. Acres Homeowners Assn., Inc., Davisville,

W.Va., 2003—05; assoc./intern United Meth. Ch., Charleston, W.Va., 1987—89; mem. Order of St. Luke, Delaware, Ohio, 1994—98; interim pres. Cmty. Acres Homeowners Assn., Inc., Davisville, W.Va., 2002—03. Recipient Unsung Hero award, W.Va. U., 2003;, W.Va. Humanities Coun., 2002. Mem.: MLA, ASCD (hon.), W.Va. Assn. Devel. Educators, Nat. Coun. Tchrs. of English. Achievements include development of Erik J. Bitterbaum Pres.'s Award for Innovation in Tchg; Gear Up For Success (GUS) Innovation in Tchg. Avocations: fly fishing, national/international travel, fiction/non-fiction, academic writing. Office: WVa Univ 300 Campus Dr Parkersburg WV 26104 Office Phone: 304-424-8000. Office Fax: 304-424-8315. Business E-Mail: lawrence.mckenzie@mail.wvu.edu.

**MC KENZIE, LIONEL WILFRED**, economist, educator; b. Montezuma, Ga., Jan. 26, 1919; s. Lionel Wilfred and Lida (Rushin) McK.; m. Blanche Veron, Jan. 2, 1943 (dec. July 1999); children— Lionel Wilfred (dec.), Gwendolyn Veron (dec.), David Rushin. AB, Duke U., 1939; MA, Princeton U., 1946, PhD, 1956; BLitt, Oxford U., Eng., 1949; postgrad., U. Chgo., 1950-51, LLD (hon.), 1991; D of Econs. (hon.), Keio U., Japan, 1998; DPhil (hon.), Kyoto U., Japan, 2004. Asst. economist WPB, 1942; instr. Mass. Inst. Tech., 1946; from asst. prof. to assoc. prof. Duke, 1948-57; prof. econs. U. Rochester, 1957-64, John Munro prof. econs., 1964-67, Wilson prof. econs., 1967-89, Wilson prof. emeritus, 1989—, chmn. dept., 1957-66. Taussig research prof. Harvard U., 1980-81; Mem. math. divsn. NRC, 1960-63, mem. behavioral scis. divsn., 1964-70; mem. math., social scis. bd. Center for Advanced Study in Behavioral Scis., Palo Alto, Calif., 1964-70, chmn., 1969-70 Author: Classical General Equilibrium Theory, 2002; assoc. editor Internat. Econs. Rev., 1964-96, Jour. Econ. Theory, 1970-73, Jour. Internat. Econs., 1970-84, Econ. Theory, 1991-95; contbr. articles to profl. jours. Lt. (s.g.) USNR, 1943-45. Recipient Rising Sun award Japan, 1995; Rhodes scholar Oriel Coll. Oxford U., 1939; Guggenheim fellow, 1973-74, fellow Center for Advanced Study in Behavioral Scis., 1973-74. Fellow Econometric Soc. (coun. 1973-78, pres. 1977), Am. Acad. Arts and Scis., Am. Econ. Assn.; mem. NAS, Royal Econ. Soc., Am. Math. Soc., Am. Econ. Assn. (Disting. Fellow 1993), Phi Beta Kappa (chpt. v.p. 1968-70, chpt. pres. 1972-73). Home: 225 Dorchester Rd Rochester NY 14610-1322 Business E-Mail: mcke@mail.rochester.edu.

**MCKENZIE, MARY BETH**, artist; b. Cleve. d. William Jennings and Mary Elizabeth (McCray) McK.; m. Tony Mysak, May 8, 1974; children: Zsuzsa McKenzie Mysak, Maria McKenzie Mysak. Student, Mus. Fine Arts, Boston, 1964-65, Cooper Sch. Art, Cleve., 1965-67; diploma, NAD, N.Y.C., 1974. Painting instr. NAD, 1981—, Art Students League, 1995—. Author: A Painterly Approach, 1987; contbr. articles to profl. jours.; one-woman shows include Nat. Arts Club, N.Y.C., 1976, FAR Gallery, 1980, Perin and Sharpe Gallery, New Canaan, Conn., 1981, Frank Caro Gallery, N.Y.C., 1988—89, Joseph Keiffer Gallery, 1991, Union County Coll., 1998, exhibited in group shows at Sindin Gallery, N.Y.C., 1985—86, Ice Collection, 1995—96, Met. Mus. Art, 2001, Represented in permanent collections The Butler Mus. Am. Art, Met. Mus. Art, N.Y.C., Mus. City of N.Y., NAD, Art Students League of N.Y., Nat. Mus. Women in the Arts, Nat. Mus. Am. Art, Smithsonian Instn., Bklyn. Mus. Art, New Britain Mus. Am. Art, N.Y. Hist. Soc., Spanierman Gallery, N.Y.C., exhibitions include Met. Mus. Art, 2001. Recipient Nat. Scholastic award Mus. Fine Arts, Boston, numerous awards including Thomas B. Clark prize and the Isaac N. Maynard prize Nat. Acad. Design, Greenshields Found. grantee, Stacey Found. grantee. Mem. Nat. Acad. Design, Pastel Soc. Am. (Best In Show, Award of Exceptional Merit, Exhbn. Com. award), Allied Artists Am. (Gold medal, The Jane Peterson award, Grumbacher Cash award, Silver medal), Audubon Artists (Pastel Soc. Am. award). Home: 525 W 45th St New York NY 10036-3414 Personal E-mail: mckenzie525@netscape.com.

**MCKENZIE, RALPH NELSON**, mathematician, educator; b. Cisco, Tex., Oct. 20, 1941; s. Milton Woodrow and Annie Laurie (Rosenquest) McK.; m. Laura Kathryn Brown, May 19, 1961; children: Deborah, Kathryn Ann. BA, U. Colo., 1963, PhD, 1966. Instr. U. Calif., Berkeley, 1966, asst. prof., 1967—71, assoc. prof., 1971—78, prof., 1978—2004; disting. prof. Vanderbilt U., Nashville, 1994—, prof. emeritus, 1994—. Vis. asst. prof., U. Colo., 1970-71; mem. Inst. for Advanced Study, Princeton, 1971-72; vis. prof. U. Hawaii, 1983, U. Siena, Italy, 1984; vis. researcher, LaTrobe U., Melbourne, 1989; Ulam prof., U. Colo., 1990; chmn. Fulbright Adv. Com. for Math., 1991-94; invited lectr. in field. Co-author: Structure of Finite Algebras, 1987, Commatory Theory for Congrugace Moduler Varieties, 1984, Algebras, Lattices, Varieties, 1986; mem. editl. bd. Algebra Universelis, 1970-, Internat. Jour. Algebra & Composition, 1990-, Global Jour. Math. and Math. Sciences, 2004-, Internat. Jour. Pure and Applied Math. Sciences, 2004-; contbr. articles to profl. jours. NSF Grad. Fellow, 1963-66, NSF Postdoctoral Fellow, 1971-72, Alfred P. Sloan Found. fellow, 1973-75, Fulbright Sr. Scholar, Australia, 1989; Rsch. grantee NSF, 1980-92, 94-. Avocations: reading, fly-fishing, mountain climbing. Office: Vanderbilt Univ Math Dept 1326 Stevenson Ctr Nashville TN 37240-0001 Office Phone: 615-322-7456. Business E-Mail: m.mckenzie@vanderbilt.edu, ralph.n.mckenzie@vanderbilt.edu.*

**MCKENZIE, WALTER L.**, information technology executive, consultant; b. Boston, Mass., Oct. 31, 1960; s. Walter L. McKenzie and Mary D. Golden; m. Carleen R. Fisher; children: Christopher Michael, Mallory Elise. BS in Edn., Ohio State U., 1985; MEd in Instrnl. Tech., George Mason U., 2000. Tchr. Fredericksburg City Schs., Va., 1985—86; tchr./gifted coord. King George County Schs., Va., 1995—99; sr. tech. tng. specialist Advanced Tech. Sys., McLean, Va., 1999—2000; dept. chair, presenter, course developer Classroom Connect, El Segundo, Calif., 1999—2005; tech. coord. Arlington Pub. Schs., 2000—03; dir. info. sys. Salem Pub. Schs., Salem, Mass., 2003—. Webmaster, surfaquarium.com The One and Only Surfaquarium, Amesbury, Mass., 1995—2005, webmaster, multiple intelligence pages, 1996—2005; cons. Surfaquarium, Amesbury, Mass., 1997—2005; editor Innovative Tchg. Newsletter, Amesbury, Mass., 1998—2005; participant, the arts in every classroom Annenberg Project, Washington, 2001—02; participant, changing edn. through the arts Kennedy Ctr., Washington, 2002—03; editor Va. Soc. Tech. Educators Jour., Blacksburg, Va., 2002—05; dir. Mass. Computer Using Educators, Wellesley, Mass., 2004—05; editor Digital Dozen Newsletter, Amesbury, Mass., 2004—05. Contbr. articles to profl. jours.; author: (book) Multiple Intelligences and Instructional Technology: A Manual for Every Mind, Standards-Based Lessons for tech-Savvy Students: A Multiple Intelligences Approach; prodr.: (online collaborative project) eIditarod Project, Art & Architecture, Build a Better Mousetrap, 2004 National CyberConvention, The Presidents' Project; editor (contributing author): (book) NETS S Curriculum Series: Social Studies Units for Grades 9—12; editor: Va. Soc. Tech. Educators. Judge ThinkQuest, Mass., 1999; sponsor Am. Top Ten Online Educators Awards, Amesbury, Mass., 2003—05. Grantee Instrnl. Devel. Project, Va. Coun. Fine Arts, 2002. Mem.: ASCD, Internat. Soc. Tech. in Edn., MassCUE (dir., webmaster 2003—05). Achievements include development of surfaquarium digital communities of practice, 2004. Avocations: writing, music, reading, travel. Office: Salem Pub Schs 29 Highland Ave Salem MA 01970 Office Phone: 978-825-3608. Personal E-mail: walter@surfaquarium.com. E-mail: waltermckenzie@salem.k12.ma.us.

**MCKENZIE-SWARTS, MOLLY**, human resources specialist, hotel executive; b. Calif. U. So. Calif. Dir. human resources Berkhemer & Kline Pub. Rels., LA; various human resources positions in employment, facilities, adminstrn., compensation, benefits, and human resource info. systems Hilton Hotels Corp., Beverly Hills, Calif., sr. v.p. human resources, 1994—. Mem. Juniors of Social Svc., Nat. Charity League. Office: Hilton Hotels Corp 9336 Civic Center Dr Beverly Hills CA 90210 Office Phone: 310-278-4321. Office Fax: 310-205-7678.

**MCKEON, HOWARD PHILLIP (BUCK MCKEON)**, congressman, former mayor; b. LA, Sept. 9, 1938; m. Patricia Kunz; 6 children. BS, Brigham Young U., 1985. Mem. city coun. City of Santa Clarita, Calif., 1987-92, mayor, 1987—92; mem. U.S. Congress from 25th Calif. dist.,

1993—; mem. armed services com.; chmn. edn. and workforce com., 2006—. Founding dir., chmn. Valencia Nat. Bank, 1987-92; co-owner Howard & Phil's Western Wear, Inc., 1963-. Hon. chmn. Leukemia Soc. Celebrity program, 1990, Red Cross Community Support Campaign, 1992; active Dist. Com. Boy Scouts Am.; chmn., trustee William S. Hart Sch. dist., 1979-87; chmn.; dir. Henry Mayo Newhall Meml. Hosp., 1983-88; mem. Calif. Rep. State Ctrl. Com., 1988-92; bd. dirs. Santa Clarita Valley Sml. Bus. Devel. Ctr., 1990-92, Canyon Country C. of C., 1988-92. Named Newsmaker of the Yr. award, Santa Clarita Svc. Club, 1996; recipient Silver Spur award for Outstanding Community Svc., Coll. of the Canyons Found., 2000, Robert J. Collier award, Nat. Aeronautic Assn., 2001, Advocacy of Ind. Higher Edn. award, Nat. Assn. Ind. Colleges & Universities, 2002. Republican. Mormon. Office: US Ho Reps 2351 Rayburn Ho Office Bldg Washington DC 20515-0525 E-mail: tellbuck@mail.house.gov.

**MCKEON, JAMI WINTZ,** lawyer; b. Mar. 13, 1957; BA, Pa. State U., 1978; JD, Villanova U., 1981. Bar: Pa. 1981, U.S. Supreme Ct. 1984. Ptnr. Morgan, Lewis & Bockius LLP, San Francisco, chmn. firm bus. & corp. litig. practice, firm adv. com. Frequent instr. Nat. Inst. Trial Advocacy. Office: Morgan Lewis & Bockius LLP One Market Spear St Tower San Francisco CA 94105 Office Phone: 415-442-1001. Office Fax: 415-442-1405. Business E-Mail: jmckeon@morganlewis.com.

**MCKEON, JOHN C.,** publishing executive; BA in Polit. Sci., NYU, MBA. V.p. mktg. Times Mirror Nat. Mktg.; various advt. and mktg. positions Newsday, Melville, NY, 1986—98, retail advt. mgr., 1991—92, advt. dir., 1992—94, v.p. advt., 1994—98, sr. v.p. advt., chief innovation officer, 1998, exec. v.p., gen. mgr., 2004—; sr. v.p. advt. L.A. Times, 1998—2001; sr. v.p., gen. mgr. South Fla. Sun-Sentinel, 2001—04. Office: Newsday 235 Pinelawn Rd Melville NY 11747

**MCKEOUGH, WILLIAM DARCY,** supply company executive; b. Chatham, Ont., Can., Jan. 31, 1933; s. George Grant and Florence Sewell (Woodward) McK.; m. Margaret Joyce Walker, June 18, 1965; children: Walker Stewart, James Grant. BA, U. Western Ont., 1954; LLD (hon.), Wilfred Laurier U., 1980; DDiv, Huron Univ. Coll., 2003. Chmn. McKeough Supply Inc. Bd. dirs. Retirement Residential REIT, Can. Gen. Tower Ltd., CableServ Inc.; former chmn. Ridley Coll. Found., Huron Coll. Found. Former mem. exec. com. Anglican Diocese of Huron; former mem. Gen. Synod, Anglican Ch., Can.; mem. Chatham City Coun., 1960-63; also mem. Planning Bd. and Lower Thames Valley Conservation Authority; former mem. Chatham-Kent adv. bd. Can. Nat. Inst. of the Blind; former bd. dirs. Chatham YMCA, Chatham Little Theatre; former chmn. and pres. bd. govs. pres. Ridley Coll.; former bd. govs. Stratford Shakespearian Festival, Wilfrid Laurier U.; former mem. Can. group Trilateral Commn.; mem. Ont. Legislature, 1963-78, minister without portfolio, 1966, minister mcpl. affairs, 1967; treas. and minister of econs., also chmn. Treasury Bd., 1971-72, minister mcpl. affairs, 1972, treas. and minister of econs. and intergovtl. affairs, 1972, parliamentary asst. to premier Ont., 1973, minister of energy, 1973-75, treas. and minister econs. and intergovtl. affairs, 1975-78; former chmn. Ridley Coll. Found., Huron Coll. Found. Decorated officer of Order of Can. Home and Office: PO Box 940 Chatham ON Canada N7M 5L3 Office Phone: 519-352-7110.

**MCKEOWN, ALLAN JOHN,** television producer, theater producer; b. London, May 21, 1946; arrived in US, 1976; s. Albert Victor and Edith Mabel (Humphries) McKeown; m. Tracey Ullman, Dec. 27, 1983; children: Mabel, John. Mng. dir. James Garrett Ptnrs., England, 1970-72, Lion Internat. Prodns., England, 1972-74, Witzend Prodns., 1974-88; chief exec. officer Selectu PLC, 1988—. Exec. prodr.: (TV series) Porridge, 1979, The Other Arf, 1980, Astronauts, 1981, Auf Weidersehen Pet, 1983, Roll Over Beethoven, 1985, Mog, 1985, Legmen, 1986, Birds of a Feather, 1989, The Old Boy Network, 1991, So You Think You've Got Troubles, 1991, Love Hurts, 1992, Westbeach, 1993, Over the Rainbow, 1993, Goodnight Sweetheart, 1993, Pie in the Sky, 1994, Men of the World, 1994, Sometime, Never, 1995; (TV series, HBO) Tracey Takes On..., 1996, (TV special) The Best of Tracey Takes On..., 1996, Tracey Ullman in the Trailer Tails, 2003, Tracey Ullman: Live and Exposed, 2005, Jerry Springer: The Opera, 2004 (Olivier award, best musical, 2004); prodr.: (plays) The Last Night of the Poms, Anyone for Dennis; (Broadway plays) The Big Love, 1991, Lennon, 2005; writer, prodr. (HBO TV series) Tracey Takes On..., 1996. Mem'r British Acad. of Film and TV Arts, Royal TV Soc. Avocation: golf. Mailing: c/o Broadhurst Theatre 235 West 44th St New York NY 10036

**MCKEOWN, ASHLEY,** biological anthropologist, educator; PhD, U. Tenn., Knoxville, 2000. Biological anthropologist, faculty mem. U. Mont., Missoula, Mont. Office: Dept Anthropology U Mont 32 Campus Dr Missoula MT 59812 Office Phone: 406-243-2145. Business E-Mail: ashley.mckeown@umontana.edu.

**MCKEOWN, JAMES CHARLES,** finance educator, consultant; b. Cleve., Nov. 3, 1945; s. Charles Joseph and Dara Ferrol (Prew) McK.; m. Mary Alinda Park, Jan. 2, 1965 (div. May 1980); children—Jeffrey Charles, Pamela Lynn; m. 2d, Nancy Ann Stratton, Jan. 3, 1981 BS in Math. with high honors, Mich. State U., 1966, PhD in Bus. Adminstrn., 1969. Asst. prof. accountancy U. Ill., Urbana-Champaign, 1968-73, assoc. prof., 1973-76, prof., 1976-80, Weldon Powell prof. accountancy, 1980-83, A.C. Littleton prof. accountancy, 1983-89; disting. prof. acctg. Pa. State U., University Park, 1989-92, Ernst & Young prof. acctg., 1992-99. Mary Jean and Frank P. Smeal chaired prof. acctg., 1999—. Cons. research, computers; expert witness. Editor: Inflation and Current Value Accounting, 1979; author computer-delivered acctg. course PLATO for Elementary Accounting, 1978; contbr. numerous articles to acad. jours. Recipient Instructional award U. Ill., Urbana-Champaign, 1970, Weldon Powell award, 1973; Fred Roedgers Research award U. Ill., 1978; Ford Found. fellow, 1967-68 Mem. Am, Acctg Assn (Manuscript award 1970, Outstanding Acctg. Educator 2003), Am. Statis. Assn., Decision Scis. Inst. Republican. Office: Pa State U 314 Business Bldg University Park PA 16802 Business E-Mail: jcm@psu.edu.

**MCKEOWN, JAMES T.,** lawyer; b. Columbus, Ohio, Aug. 16, 1958; s. James J. and M. Eileen (O'Neill) McK.; m. Kathleen E. McKeown, Dec. 28, 1981; children: Bridget, Caitlin, Neil, Aislinn. BA in Econs., St. John's U., Collegeville, Minn., 1980; JD, U. Minn., 1984, MA in Pub. Affairs, 1985. Bar: Wis. 1984, U.S. Ct. Appeals (7th cir.) 1985, U.S. Dist. Ct. (ea. dist.) Wis. 1985, U.S. Supreme Ct. Law clk. Hon. Harlington Wood, Jr. U.S. Ct. Appeals for 7th Cir., Springfield, Ill., 1984-85; assoc. Foley & Lardner LLP, Milw., 1985-93, ptnr., 1993—, chmn. antitrust practice group. Adj. asst. prof. Marqueete U., 1993-95. Contbr. articles to profl. jours. Civil svc. commr. Village of Shorewood, Wis.; fin. com. chmn. St. Robert Parish, Shorewood, 1993-94. Mem. Milw. Young Lawyers Assn. (Svc. award 1991). Office: Foley & Lardner LLP 777 E Wisconsin Ave Ste 3800 Milwaukee WI 53202-5367 Office Phone: 414-297-5530. Business E-Mail: jtmckeown@foley.com.

**MCKEOWN, LORRAINE LAREDO,** travel company executive, writer; b. N.Y.C., Mar. 20, 1928; d. Frank A. and May (Collins) Laredo; m. William Taylor McKeown, July 9, 1964; children: Beth Ellison, Kate Taylor, Suzanne Harris. Talent agt. Carl Eastman, N.Y.C., 1960-65; cooking/travel columnist Camping Jour./Boating Jour., N.Y.C., 1968-70; travel agt. Beecher Travel, N.Y.C., 1968-70; founding ptnr. Computer Travel Info., N.Y.C., 1984, v.p., pres., 1985-90, CEO, 1990—. Contbr. articles to various publs. Bd. dirs. Chapin-Brearley Exch., N.Y.C., 1980, Howland Cultural Ctr., 2002—, Howland Cultural Ctr., 2002—. Mem. Freelance Assocs., Beacon Conservation Coun. Personal E-mail: mckeown@bestweb.net.

**MCKEOWN, MARY MARGARET,** federal judge; b. Casper, Wyo., May 11, 1951; d. Robert Mark and Evelyn Margaret (Lipsack) McKeown; m. Peter Francis Cowhey, June 29, 1985; 1 child, Megan Margaret. BA in Internat. Affairs and Spanish, U. Wyo., 1972; JD, Georgetown U., 1975. Bar: Wash. 1975, D.C. 1982. Assoc. Perkins Coie, Seattle, 1975—79, Washington, 1979—80; spl. asst. US Dept. Interior, Washington, 1980—81, The White House, Washington, 1980—81; ptnr., mem. exec. com. Perkins Coie, Seattle, 1981—98, mng. dir. strategic planning and client rels., 1990—95; judge US Ct. Appeals (9th Cir.), San Diego, 1998—. Trustee The Pub. Defender, Seattle, 1982—85; rep. 9th Cir. Judicial Conf., San Francisco, 1985—89; mem. gender bias task force, 1992—93; jud. conf. Com. on Codes of Conduct, 2001—; exec. com. 9th Cir., 2001—; lect. U. Wash. Law Sch., 2000—01; adj. prof. U. San Diego, 2003—; bd. dirs. RAND Inst. for Civil Justice, 2003—. Author: Girl Scout's Guide to New York, 1990; contbr. chpt. to book and articles to profl. jours. Nat. bd. dirs. Girl Scouts U.S., N.Y.C., 1976—87; mem. exec. com. Corp. Coun. for the Arts, Seattle, 1988—98; bd. gen. counsel Downtown Seattle Assn., 1986—89; mem. exec. com. Wash. Coun. Internat. Trade, 1994—; bd. dirs. YMCA Greater Seattle, 1998—, Family Svcs., Seattle, 1982—84. Named one of 100 Young Women of Promise, Good Housekeeping, 1985, Washington's Winningest Trial Lawyers, Washington Jour., 1992, Top 50 Women Lawyers, Nat. Law Jour., 1998; recipient Rising Stars of the 80's award, Legal Times Washington, 1983; fellow Japan leadership, 1992—93. Fellow: ABA (ho. of dels. 1990—, Jud. Adv. Com. to Standing Com. on Ethics 2000—, chair 2002—, Joint Commn. to Evaluate Code of Jud. Conduct 2003—); mem.: Louis M. Welsh Chpt. Am. Inns of Ct., Am. Judicature Soc. (bd. dirs. 2001—), Assn. Bus. Trial Lawyers (bd. dirs. 2003—), Am. Intellectual Property Law Assoc., Am. Law Institute, Nat. Assn. Iolta Programs (bd. dirs. 1989—91), Wash. Women Lawyers (bd. dirs., pres. 1978—79), Legal Found. Wash. (trustee, pres. 1989—90), Seattle-King County Bar Assn. (trustee, sec. 1984—85, Outstanding Lawyer award 1992), Wash. Bar Assn. (chmn. jud. recommendations 1989—90), Fed. Bar Assn. (trustee western dist. Wash. 1980—90), White House Fellows Found. (bd. dirs. 1998—, pres. 2000—01). Avocations: travel, classical piano, hiking, gourmet cooking, tennis. Office: US Ct Appeals 401 West A St Ste 2000 San Diego CA 92101-7908 E-mail: Judge_McKeown@ca9.uscourts.gov.*

**MCKEOWN, WILLIAM B.,** lawyer; b. Atlanta; m. Constance Coles; children: Sarah, Isaiah. B, Harvard U., 1967; MDiv, Union Theol. Sem., 1971; JD, Columbia Law Sch., 1974. Atty. Patterson, Beknap, Webb & Tyler, NY, 1974—98; gen. counsel Wildlife Conservation Soc., 1998—. Office: Wildlife Conservation Society 2300 Southern Blvd Bronx NY 10460 Office Phone: 718-220-5100.*

**MCKEOWN, WILLIAM P.,** retired lawyer; m. Elizabeth McKeown; 4 children. B Comm., McGill U., Montreal, Que., 1956; LLB, U. Toronto, 1959. Queen's counsel Ont. 1983. Counsel Dept. Health, Province Ont., Toronto, 1962-63, McMillan Binch, Toronto, 1963-64, Can. GE, Toronto, 1965-74; dep. dir. investigation and rsch. Bur. Competition Policy, Ottawa, Ont., 1974-77; ptnr. Stephens French McKeown, Toronto, 1977-86; judge Supreme Ct. Ont., Toronto, 1986-90; judge gen. divsn. Ont. Ct. Justice, Toronto, 1990—93; judge trial divsn. Fed. Ct. Can., Ottawa, Canada, 1993—2002; chmn. Competition Tribunal, Ottawa, 1993—2002; sr. counsel Fasken, Martineau, DuMoulin, LLP, Toronto, 2002—06; ret., 2006. Mem. Can. Bar Assn., Toronto Lawyers' Club. Office Phone: 416-868-3523. E-mail: mckeown41575@rogers.com.

**MC KEOWN, WILLIAM TAYLOR,** magazine editor, author; b. Ft. Collins, Colo., July 4, 1921; s. Stuart Ellison and Eunice Harris (Akin) Mc K.; m. Lorraine Laredo; children: Elizabeth Ellison, Katherine, Suzanne. AB, Bowdoin Coll., 1942; student, Columbia U. Grad. Sch., 1948. Editor Fawcett Library Series, 1953-56; founding editor True's Boating Yearbook, 1955-56, Popular Boating mag., 1956, editor-in-chief, 1956-62; CEO The Mc Keown Co., N.Y.C., 1993—; editl. dir. Computer Travel Info., 1994—. Travel editor Davis Publs.; outdoor/boating/travel editor Popular Mechanics, 1971-82; sr. editor Outdoor Life, 1983-93. Author weekly NEA syndicated newspaper column American Afloat, 1959-65; contbr. fiction, non-fiction to nat. mags., 1947—; author: Boating Handbook, 1956, Boating in America, 1960. Pilot USAAF, WW II, ETO. Mem. Am. Power Boat Assn., U.S. Power Squadrons, 357 FIghter Group Assn., N.Y. Yacht Club, Overseas Press Club, Royal Danish Yacht Club (Copenhagen), Turtles Internat. Avocation: international competitor in power and sail racing events. Office: The Mc Keown Co 52 Monell Pl Beacon NY 12508-1424

**MCKEOWN-MOAK, MARY PARK,** educational consultant; d. John Paton and Sophie Cichon Park; m. Lynn Martin Moak, Oct. 4, 1997; children: David Lynn Moak, Susan Marie Moak; m. James Charles McKeown, Jan. 2, 1965 (div.); children: Jeffrey Charles McKeown, Pamela Lynn McKeown. m. Kenneth Forbis Jordan, Jan. 2, 1982 (div. Sept. 1993). BA, MA, Mich. State U., East Lansing, 1966; PhD, U. Ill., Urbana-Champaign, 1974. Cert. tchr. Mich., 1966, real estate agent Ill., 1977. Bus. mgr. U. Ill. Found., Champaign, 1974—77; sch. fin. specialist, asst. prof. pub. adminstrn. Ill. Bd. Edn., Sangamon State U., Springfield, 1977—80; assoc. dir. fin. and facilities Md. State Bd. Higher Edn., Annapolis, 1980—87; dir. strategic planning Ariz. State U., Tempe, 1987—94; assoc. exec. dir., sr. fin. officer Ariz. Bd. Regents, Phoenix, 1994—98; ptnr. MGT Am., Inc., Austin, Tex., 1998—. Pres. Fiscal Issues Spl. Interest Group Am. Edn. Rsch. Assn., Washington, 1990—91, pres., chair Futures Planning Spl. Interest Group, 1992—93; pres. Am. Edn. Fin. Assn., Denver, 1996—97. Contbr. articles to profl. jours. Pres. coll. Bus. Faculty Wives, Champaign, 1971—73; troop leader Girl Scouts, Boy Scouts, Champaign, 1974—78; treas. Champaign-Urbana PTA Coun., 1978—80; pres. Alameda Estates Homeowners Assn., Tempe, Ariz., 1988—95, v.p., 1988—95, sec., 1988—95. Mem.: Travis Audubon Soc., Phi Delta Kappa (sec. Ariz. chpt. 1987—91). Avocations: gardening, travel, birdwatching. Home: 8800 Gallant Fox Road Austin TX 78737 Office: MGT Am Inc 502 E 11th Street Ste 300 Austin TX 78701 Office Phone: 512-476-4697. Business E-Mail: mmoak@mgtamer.com.

**MCKERLEY, ANNETTE ELIZABETH,** school system administrator; b. Nashville, Feb 8 1951; d. James and Dorothy Ann Shaub; m. Ronald Joseph McKerley, May 24, 1997; stepchildren: Marc, Michael, Keith. BS in Educable Mentally Retarded and Psychology, U. Tenn., 1973; MEd in Spl. Edn. and Rehab., U. Memphis, 1979. Cert. tchr. Tenn. Spl. edn. resource tchr. Alcorn County Schs., Cornith, Miss., 1974—76, Decatur County Schs., Decaturville, Tenn., 1977—86; spl. edn. comprehensive devel. class tchr. Harrison County Tng. Ctr. for Exceptional Children, Gulfport, Miss. 1976—77; program/complaince cons. divsn. spl. edn. Tenn. Dept. Edn., Nashville, 1987—92, dir. programs and svcs. divsn. spl. edn., 1993—2000, dir. mgmt. svcs., 2000—; edni. diagnostician Washington County Schs., Jonesborough, Tenn., 1992—93. Mem.: Delta Kappa Gamma (treas. Beta Mu chpt. 1982—84, pres. 1984—86). Office: Tenn Dept Edn Dvisn Spl Edn 710 James Robertson Pkwy 7th Fl Nashville TN 37243-0380 Fax: 615-532-9412.

**MCKERNS, CHARLES JOSEPH,** lawyer; b. Shenandoah, Pa., July 17, 1935; s. Charles Francis and Bridgett Ann (Barrett) McK.; m. Helen Patricia Nott, Feb. 13, 1960; children: Charles J. Jr., Michael H., Patricia B. BS, Georgetown U., 1957, JD, 1960. Bar: D.C. 1960, U.S. Ct. Appeals (D.C. cir.) 1961, U.S. Supreme Ct. 1971, Va. 1992. Law clk. to assoc. judge U.S. Ct. Appeals (D.C. cir), Washington, 1960—61; assoc. Dow, Lohnes & Albertson, Washington, 1961—65, ptnr., 1965—97, of counsel, 1991—95; ptnr. McKerns and McKerns, Heathsville, Va., 1991-96, of counsel, 1996—98. 1st lt. U.S. Army, 1957—59. Mem. ABA, University Club (Washington), Belle Haven Country Club (Alexandria, Va.), Indian Creek Yacht and Country Club (Kilmarnock, Va.). Republican. Roman Catholic. Avocations: hiking, reading, swimming. Home: Windy Blue PO Box 248 Ophelia VA 22530 Office: McKerns Law Office PO Box 220 Heathsville VA 22473-0220 also: Dow Lohnes & Albertson 1200 New Hampshire Ave NW Washington DC 20036-6802 Office Phone: 804-580-8225. Personal E-mail: cmckerns@yahoo.com.

**MC KETTA, JOHN J., JR.,** chemical engineering professor; b. Wyano, Pa., Oct. 17, 1915; s. John J. and Mary (Gelet) McK.; m. Helen Elisabeth Smith, Oct. 17, 1943; children: Charles William, John J. III, Robert Andrew, Mary Anne. BS, Tri-State Coll.; Angola, Ind., 1937; BSE., U. Mich., 1943, MS, 1944, PhD, 1946; D.Eng. (hon.), Tri-State Coll., 1965, Drexel U., 1977;

Sc.D., U. Toledo, 1973. Diplomate: registered profl. engr., Tex., Mich. Group leader tech. dept. Wyandotte Chem. Corp., Mich., 1937-40, asst. supt. caustic soda div., 1940-41; teaching fellow U. Mich., 1942-44, instr. chem. engring., 1944-45; faculty U. Tex., Austin, 1946—, successively asst. prof. chem. engring., assoc. prof., then prof. chem. engring., 1951-52, 54—, E.P. Schoch prof. chem. engring., 1970-81, Joe C. Walter chair, 1981-94, prof. emeritus, 1994—. Asst. dir. Tex. petroleum research ctr., 1951-52, 54-56, chmn. chem. engring. dept., mem. bd. regents, Tri State Univ, 56-, disting. service in truteeship, 2002, 1950-52, 55-63, dean Coll. Engring., 1963-69; exec. vice chancellor acad. affairs U. Tex. System, 1969-70; editorial dir. Petroleum Refiner, 1952-54; pres. Chemoil Cons., Inc., 1957-73; chmn. Tex. AEC, So. Interstate Nuclear Bd., 1963-70; mem. Tex. Radiation Adv. Bd., 1978-84; chmn. Nat. Energy Policy Com., 1970-72, Nat. Air Quality Control Com., 1972-85; mem. adv. bd. Carnegie-Mellon Inst. Research, 1978-84; pres. Reagans's rep. on U.S. Acid Precipitation Task Force, 1982-88; apptd. mem. Nuclear Waste Tech. Rev. Bd., 1992-97. Author: series Advances in Petroleum Chemistry and Refining (10 vols.); Chmn. editorial com.: series Petroleum Refiner; mem. adv. bd.: series Internat. Chem. Engring. mag.; exec. editor: series Ency. of Chem. Processing and Design (68 vols.). Recipient Bronze plaque Am. Inst. Chem. Engrs., 1952, Charles Schwab award Am. Steel Inst., 1973, Lamme award as outstanding U.S. educator, 1976, Joe J. King Profl. Engring. Achievement award U. Tex., 1976, Gen. Dynamics Teaching Excellence award, 1979, Triple E award for contbns. to nat. issues on energy, environment and econs. Nat. Environ. Devel. Assn., 1976, Boris Pregal Sci. and Tech. award NAS, 1978, Internat. Chem. Engring. award, Italy, 1984, Pres. Herbert Hoover award for advancing well-being of humanity and developing richer and more enduring civilization Joint Engring. Socs., 1989, Centennial award exceptional contbn. Am. Soc. Engring. Edn., 1993; named Disting. Alumnus U. Mich. Coll. Engring., 1953, Tri-State Coll., 1956; fellow Allied Chem. & Dye, 1945-46; named Disting. fellow Carnegie-Mellon U., 1978; Chem. Engring. Dept. at U. Tex. named The John J. McKetta Ctr. for Excellence in Chem. Engring. Edn. in his honor, 1995, Chem. Engring. Dept. at Tri State U. named The Dr. John J. McKetta Chem. Engring. Dept. in his honor, 1998. Mem. Am. Chem. Soc. (chmn. Central Tex. sect. 1950), Am. Inst. Chem. Engrs. (chmn. nat. membership com. 1955, regional exec. com., nat. dir., nat. v.p. 1961, pres. 1962, service to soc. award 1975), Am. Soc. Engring. Edn., Chem. Markets Research Assn., Am. Gas Assn. (adv. bd. chem. from gas 1954), Houston C. of C. (chmn. refining div. 1954, vice chmn. research and statistics com. 1954), Engrs. Joint Council (dir.), Engrs. Joint Countil Profl. Devel. (dir. 1963-85), Nat. Acad. Engring., Sigma Xi, Chi Epsilon, Alpha Chi Omega, Tau Omega, Phi Lambda Upsilon, Phi Kappa Phi, Iota Alpha, Omega Chi Epsilon, Tau Beta Pi, Omicron Delta Kappa. Home: 4100 Jackson Ave Apt 318 Austin TX 78731-6070 Office Phone: 512-471-5227. Business E-Mail: mcketta@che.utexas.edu.

**MCKETTA, JOHN J., III,** lawyer; b. Austin, Tex., May 5, 1948; s. John J. and Helen Elisabeth (Smith) McK.; m. Sallie Martin Sharp, Aug. 6, 1977; children: Elisabeth, Mary Elliott, Sarah John. BA, Harvard U., 1969; JD, U. Tex., Austin, 1977. Bar: Tex. 1977, D.C. 1978, U.S. Ct. Appeals (D.C. cir.) 1978, U.S. Dist. Ct. D.C. 1978, U.S. Ct. (we. dist.) Tex. 1982, U.S. Ct. Appeals (5th cir.) 1982. Assoc. Covington & Burling, Washington, 1977-82, Graves, Dougherty, Hearon & Moody, Austin, Tex., 1982-84, ptnr., 1984—, pres., 1998—. Fellow: Am. Coll. Trial Lawyers; mem.: Am. Law Inst. (coun. 1998—). Democrat. Episcopalian. Office: PO Box 98 Austin TX 78767-0098 Business E-Mail: mmcketta@gdhm.com.

**MCKIBBEN, HOWARD D.,** federal judge; b. Apr. 1, 1940; s. James D. and Bernice McKibben; m. Mary Ann McKibben, July 2, 1966; children: Mark, Susan. BS, Bradley U., 1962; MPA, U. Pitts., 1964; JD, U. Mich., 1967. Assoc. George W. Abbott Law Office, 1967-71; dep. dist. atty. Douglas County, Nev., 1969-71, dist. atty. Nev., 1971-77; dist. ct. judge State of Nev., 1977-84; judge U.S. Dist. Ct. Nev., Reno, 1984—. Mem. Nev. Bar Assn., Am. Inns of Ct. (pres. Am. Coll. Pres.). Methodist. Avocations: tennis, golf, racquetball. Home: PO Box 588 Verdi NV 89439-0588 Office: US Dist Ct 400 S Virginia St Ste 804 Reno NV 89501-2197

**MCKIBBIN, WILLIAM ALEX,** artist; b. Phila., May 7, 1940; s. William A. and Jane Harrison (Pippin) McK.; m. Dorothy K. McKibbin, Jan. 26, 1963; children: Erin P., William Alex IV. Student, Barnes Found., Merion, Pa., 1958-59, 60-61; BFA, Temple U., Phila., 1963; MFA, The Claremont Grad. Sch., 1965; postgrad., U. Hartford, Conn., 1967-68. Instr. Mt. Pleasant (Del.) Jr. High Sch., 1965-66, U. Hartford Coll. Basic Studies, 1966-68; instr. evening divsn. Cen. Conn. State Coll., 1967-68; instr. Aegean Sch. Fine Arts, Paros, Greece, summers 1967-68; asst. prof. Western Coll., 1968-74, acting chair, 1968, 69, 70-71; instr. Cin. Art Acad., 1972-74; asst. prof. Miami U. Oxford, Ohio, 1974-77, assoc. prof., 1977-84, full prof., 1984—. Juried various exhbns. throughout U.S. One-man shows at Evansville (Ind.) Mus. Arts and Scis., Main Artist Gallery, 1985, Museum of the Maya Culture, Chetumal, Q.R., Mex., 2002, Casa de la Cultura de Cancun, Mex., 2001; exhibited in over 200 exhbns. including group shows at East Carolina U., Greenville, N.C., 1981, Second Crossing Gallery, Valley City, N.D., 1981, 93, Okla. Art Ctr., Oklahoma City, 1981-82, U. N.D., Grand Forks, 1982, 85, Art Chgo. Internat. Art Expo, 1982-90, Trenton (N.J.) State Coll., 1983, Fort Hays (Kans.) State U., 1984, 88, Owensboro (Ky.) Mus. Fine Arts, 1984, Middletown (Ohio) Fine Arts Ctr., 1985, Cameron U., 1986, Springfield (Mo.) Art Mus., 1988-90, 94, 2003, La Fond Galleries, Inc., Pitts., 1994, numerous others; represented by Zaks Gallery, Chgo., The Art Exch., Columbus, Boody Fine Arts, Inc., St. Louis, Nancy Mulle Assocs., Cleve., Steinway Gallery, Chapel, N.C., Yvonne Rapp Gallery, Louisville, Orbe Gallery, Cancun, Mex., Gallery Henoch, N.Y.C.; pub. collections include Pomona Coll., Claremont, Calif., Thomas More Coll., Ft. Mitchell, Ky., The Springfield Mus., Ind. U. East, Richmond, Evansville (Ind.) Mus. Art and Sci., Art Ctr., Inc., South Bend, Ind. Cin. Art Mus., Grinnell (Iowa) Coll., Ft. Hays State U., Hays, Kans., Des Moines Art Ctr., Charles H. MacNider Mus., Mason City, Iowa, Ohio State U., Columbus, Clark State U., Springfield, Ohio, U. N.C., Chapel Hill, Ohio State U. Law Sch., So. Alleghenies Mus. of Art, Loretto, Pa., Blanden Meml. Art Mus., Ft. Dodge, Iowa, Ark. Arts Ctr., Little Rock, Taos Art Mus., Taos, N.Mex., Casa de la Cultura de Cancun, Mex., Fitton Ctr. for Creative Arts, Hamilton, Ohio; pvt. collections, 70 corporate collections; reprodns. of work appear in (books) Watercolor Bold and Free, 1980, Figure Drawing, 5th edit., 2000, The Watercolor Solution Book, 1988, Splash I, 1990, The Art of Responsive Drawing, 1992, Splash II, 1993, Watercolor Step-By-Step, 1993, Watercolor School, 1993, Collins' Artist's Manual, 1995, Splash IV, 1995, The Encyclopedia of Watercolour Landscape Techniques, 1996, Painting Shapes and Edges, 1996, North Light Illustrated Book of Watercolor Techniques, Splash VIII, 2004; (mags.) Artist's Mag., The Bull., Jiangsu Pictorial, China, Watercolor Magic, Tropo a la una, Cancun, Mex., Internat. Artist, 2000; work included as cover art on CDs Music for Winds, The Miami Wind Quintet, Vol. 1, 1995, Vol. 2, 1996. Recipient Cert. of Merit Tyler Sch. of Art Temple U., Gen. Alumni Assn., 1991, First State Bank award for watercolor Vechten-Lineberry, Taos Art Mus., 18 cash and purchase awards from various orgs. Studio: PO Box 31 77760 Akumal QR Mexico Office: 435 Tacoma Ave Buffalo NY 14216 Home: 199 Berkley Dr Villa Rica GA 30180-2400

**MCKIBBIN, WILLIAM JEFFREY,** management consultant; b. St. Louis, May 15, 1955; s. Ralph Eddowes McKibbin and Ida Mae Vessel; m. Cheryl Ann Jones, July 9, 1977 (div. Mar. 31, 1998); m. Sally Ruth Wolfe, May 1, 2001. AA, Valley Forge Mil. Acad., Wayne, Pa., 1973—75; BA, Temple U., Phila., 1975—77; MA, Georgetown U., DC, 1984—86; PhD, Capella U., Mpls., 2000—05. Infantry officer US Army, 1977—92; registered rep. & agt. First Command Fin. Svcs., Inc., Ft. Worth, 1992—98; registered investment advisor, prin. McKibbin Fin. Ptnrs., Hollidaysburg, Pa., 1998—2001; mgmt. cons., prin. McKibbinUSA, LLC, State College, Pa., 2001—. Mem. Pa. Chamber Bus. & Industry, Harrisburg, Chamber Bus. & Industry, State College, Pa. Maj. USAR, ret. USAR, 1997. Decorated medal 3rd Oak Leaf Cluster US Army, Army Commendation medal, Oak Leaf Cluster; recipient Order Anthony Wayne medal, Valley Forge Mil. Acad., 1975. Mem.: Ctr. Hills Country Club, Am. Legion Post 245. Libertarian. Office: McKibbinUSA LLC

210 W Hamilton Ave Box 369 State College PA 16801 Home: 455-3A Windmere Ave State College PA 16801 Office Phone: 814-238-3100. Office Fax: 814-689-7000. Business E-Mail: wjmc@mckibbinusa.com.

**MC KIE, TODD STODDARD,** artist; b. Boston, Apr. 25, 1944; s. Roy Albert and Lois E. (Barwood) McK.; m. Judy Anne Kensley, Apr. 10, 1967; 1 son, Jesse Simon. BFA, RISD, 1966. Vis. artist RISD, 1977, Mass. Coll. Art, 1977-78, Sch. Mus. Fine Arts, Boston, 1979; artist-in-residence Isabella Stewart Gardner Mus., Boston, 2000; lectr. schs. and museums. Exhibited in one-man shows Harcus Krakow Gallery, Boston, 1977, 79, 83, Aquavella Gallery, N.Y.C., 1978, 79, 81, Hokin-Kaufman Gallery, Chgo., 1983, Helander Gallery, N.Y.C., 1990, 92, Toale Gallery, Boston, 1994, Barbara Singer Gallery, Boston, 1996, Greenville (S.C.) Mus. of Art, 1997, Littlejohn Contemporary Art, 1999, Clark Gallery, Lincoln, Mass., 2001, Victoria Munroe Gallery, Boston, 2003, 04, Centre d'Art, Marnay-sur-Seine, France, 2003, Gallery Naga, Boston, 2005; exhibited in group shows including, Whitney Museum Am. Art, N.Y.C., 1975, Harcus Krakow Gallery, 1975, 78, Mus. Fine Arts, Boston, 1975, 77, 81, Acquavella Gallery, 1976, 78, 79, 81, Inst. Contemporary Art, Boston, 1979, Addison Gallery Am. Art, 1981; represented in permanent collections including Fogg Art Mus., Cambridge, Mass., M.I.T., Cambridge, Brockton (Mass.) Mus., Mus. Fine Arts, Boston, DeCordova Mus., Lincoln, Mass., Rose Art Mus. Brandeis U., Mus. of Modern Art, Fidelity Investments, Microsoft; also numerous pvt. collections. Recipient Blanch E. Colman award Colman Found., 1974; Artists fellowship Villa Montalvo, 1995; Artists Found. fellow Boston, 1975, 89. Home and Office: 82 Holworthy St Cambridge MA 02138-4579 Office Phone: 617-492-0471.

**MCKILLIP, PATRICIA CLAIRE,** operatic soloist; b. Milw., Apr. 28; d. Lester J. and Ruth J. (Lohneis) McK.; m. Mark Richard McKillip, June 16, 1990. BA in English-Drama, Creative Writing, Lit. Alverno Coll., 1980, MusB in Applied Music, 1981; postgrad., Wis. Conservatory of Mus., 1981-82; MS in Fine Arts Edn., U. Wis., Milw., 1996; postgrad., The Juilliard Sch., 1982-84, Am. Acad. Dramatic Arts, 1983-84, Adelphi U., 1984; MA in English-Creative Writing and Lit., U. Wis., Milw., 1997; postgrad., Milw. Inst. Art and Design, 2003—. Soloist Amadeus Opera Co.; instr. vocal music seminars various high schs., NY. Co-founder, co-dir. The Masque Consort, N.Y.C., 1990-91, exec. v.p., 1991; v.p., co-founder Creative Learning Assocs.; instr. Cardinal Stritch Coll., Milw., 1994—. Performer Florentine Opera Co., Music Under the Stars Prodns., Milw. Opera Co., Westchester Lyric Opera Co., Profl. Opera Workshop at Lincoln Ctr., Met. Opera Co., N.Y. Grand Opera Co., Monteverdi Opera Guild Prodns., Republic Opera Co., La Puma Opera Co., others; puppeteer, costumer, designer Puppet Art Troupe; author: (poetry and artwork) Springdrift, 2003; author numerous poems. Exec. v.p. Masque Consort, a multi-media theatrical orgn. Music dept. scholar Alverno U.; named Woman of Yr., Am. Biographical Inst. Bd. Internat. Rsch., 2003. Mem. AFTRA, SAG, Nat. Assn. Music Tchrs., Music Educators Nat. Conf. (treas.), Internat. Platform Assn., Wis. Fedn. Music Clubs, Music Clubs Am., Am. Guild Mus. Artists, Q'ahal-Liturgical Music Soc., Am. Poets, Milw. Artists Resource Network, Walker's Point Ctr. for Arts, Delta Omicron (v.p., chaplain, warden Gamma Gamma chpt., WMA State and Regional Vocal award 1978, Star of Delta Omicron award 1980, 40 music medals from state and dist. WSMA), Alpha Sigma Tau. Democrat. Roman Catholic. Avocations: dance, creative writing, art. Home: 4860 S 69th St Greenfield WI 53220-4452 Personal E-mail: celticdramaticsoprano@yahoo.com.

**MCKIM, PAUL ARTHUR,** management consultant, retired gas industry executive; b. Milford, Conn., Feb. 1, 1923; s. Arthur and Helen Agnes McK.; m. Daisy Flora Brown, June 18, 1943; 1 dau., Meredith Ann. Student, Lamar Inst. Tech., 1940-42; BS in Chem. Engring., La. State U., 1943, MS, 1947, PhD, 1949; grad. Advanced Mgmt. Program, Harvard, 1959; grad. Aspen Inst. Humanistic Studies Exec. Program, 1970. With Ethyl Corp., 1949-62, asst. gen. mgr. research and devel. operations, 1958-62; v.p., gen. mgr. rsch. and devel. Atlantic Refining Co., Phila., 1962-66; v.p. Atlantic Richfield Co., 1966-78; v.p. comml. devel. Arco Chem. Co., 1966-69, v.p. nuclear operations and comml. devel., 1969-73; exec. v.p. Sinclair Koppers Co., 1973; pres. Arco Polymers, Inc., 1974-78; asst. to pres. Tex. Eastern Corp., 1978-80, v.p., 1980-84, sr. v.p., 1985-88. Chmn. US Organizing com. for 12th World Petroleum Congress, Houston, 1987. Past chmn. bd. mgrs. Franklin Inst. Research Labs; past vice chmn. bd. mgrs. Spring Garden Coll., Phila. Coll. Art.; past vice chmn. World Affairs Council of Phila. Served to lt. (j.g.) USNR, 1944-46. Mem. AIChE, Houston Club, Shreveport (La.) Country Club, Alpha Chi Sigma, Omicron Delta Kappa, Tau Beta Pi, Phi Lambda Upsilon, Phi Kappa Phi, Delta Kappa Epsilon. Home: Sterling Glen of Darien 50 Ledge Rd Apt 252 Darien CT 06820

**MCKIM, RUTH ANN,** financial planner; b. Keokuk, Iowa, Nov. 26, 1932; d. Carl Edward and Ruby Irene (Martin) McKim; m. William James Ashbrook, Aug. 15, 1959 (div. 1974); children: Leslie, Diane Hodges. BS, U. Louisville, 1955, MS in Cmty. Devel., 1977. Dir. art therapy Ky. Bapt. Hosp., Louisville, 1955—56; co-dir. art therapy Norton-Children's Hosps. Inc., 1956—57; dir. art therapy NKC Hosps., 1957—59; rschr. Bd. Aldermen, 1976; pub. rels. staff Dept. Consumer Affairs, 1976—78; realtor assoc. Century 21, 1979—86; fin. planner Mut. Life Vt., 1986—. Tutor Ky. Assn. Specific Perceptual-Motor Disability, Louisville, 1970—74. Author: Banking Survey, 1977. Arts festival com., 1975—77; coord. Louisville Food Day, 1978; vol. and ednl PBS, 1985—88; voter registration canvasser, 1976, 1978, 1982; active Rep. Nat. Com., Rep. Presdl. Task Force, Nat. Rep. Senatorial Com., Nat. Rep. Congl. Com. Com.; sec., treas. St. Francis in the Fields Espicopal Ch., Louisville, 1975—76. Recipient Rep. Presdl. Legion of Merit medal, Order of Merit; scholar Allen R. Hite Art Inst., 1952—54; Bd. Realtors scholar, 1979—. Mem.: Inst. Community Devel. Assn., Ky. Artists and Craftsmen, Louisville Craftsmans Guild (life), U. Louisville Alumni Assn. Republican. Episcopalian. Avocation: oil and acrylic painting. Home: No 43 410 Mockingbird Valley Rd Louisville KY 40207-1318

**MCKIM, SAMUEL JOHN, III,** lawyer; b. Pitts., Dec. 31, 1938; s. Samuel John and Harriet Frieda (Roehl) McK; children: David Hunt, Andrew John; m. Eugenia A. Leverich. AA cum laude, Port Huron Jr. Coll., 1959; BA cum laude, U. Mich., 1961, JD cum laude, 1964. Bar: Mich. 1965, U.S. Dist. Ct. (so. dist.) Mich. 1965, U.S. Ct. Appeals (6th cir.) 1965, U.S. Supreme Ct. 1994. Assoc. Miller, Canfield, Paddock and Stone, PLC, Detroit, Bloomfield Hills, 1964-71, sr. mem., 1971—, head state and local tax sect., 1985—, chmn. tax dept., 1989-94, mng. ptnr., 1979-85, chmn., mng. ptnr., 1984-85. Mem. tax coun. State Bar Mich., 1981-94, chmn. state and local tax com. real property sect., 1982-90; adj. prof. law sch. Wayne State U., 1993-. Assoc. editor Mich. Law Rev. Bd. dirs., past chmn. Goodwill Industries of Greater Detroit, 1970-2000; dir. Goodwill Industries Found. 1982-95; Stevens min. commd. lay assoc. pastor First Presbyn. Ch., Lapeer, Mich. Fellow: Am. Coll. Tax Counsel; mem.: ABA, Barrister's Soc., Detroit Bar Assn., Mich. Bar Assn., Mariner Sands Country Club, Port Huron Golf Club, Nomads Club, Order of Coif, Phi Delta Phi. Home (Summer): 8351 Lakeshore Rd Lexington MI 48450 Home (Winter): 6403 SE Brandywine Ct # 124 Stuart FL 34994 Office: Miller Canfield Paddock & Stone 150 W Jefferson Ave Ste 2500 Detroit MI 48226-4416 Office Phone: 313-496-7546. Business E-Mail: mckim@millercanfield.com.

**MCKINLEY, CRAIG R.,** career military officer; BSBA, So. Meth. U., 1974; MS in Mgmt. and Econs., Webster Coll., 1979; postgrad., Squadron Officer Sch., 1984, Air Command and State Coll., 1990; postgrad. in Nat. Security Strategy, Nat. War Coll., 1995; postgrad., Nat. Security Mgmt. Course, Syracuse, N.Y., 1997, Capstone, Ft. Lesley J. McNair, Washington, 1998, Combined Forces Air Component Comdr. Course, Maxwell AFB, Ala., 2002, US-Russia Security Program, Harvard U., 2004. Commd. 2nd lt. USAF, 1974, advanced through grades to lt. gen., 2006, T-38 instr. pilot Craig AFB, Ala., 1975-77, comdr. air force mil. tng. ctr. Lackland AFB, Tex., 1977-78, T-38 instr. pilot Laughlin AFB, Tex., 1978-80, F-106 alert pilot 125th Fighter Interceptor Group Jacksonville, Fla., 1980-82, F-106 instr. pilot, chief of safety 125th Fighter Interceptor Group, 1982-87, F-16 instr. pilot, chief of standardization/evaluation 125th Fighter Interceptor Group, 1987-88, dep.

comdr. ops. 125th Fighter Interceptor Group, 1988-91, group comdr. 125th Fighter Interceptor Group, 1991-94, wing comdr. 125th Fighter Interceptor Wing, 1995-96, vice comdr. Southeast Air Def. Sector Tyndall AFB, Fla., 1996, comdr. Southeast Air Def. Sector, 1996-98; dep. dir. Air Nat. Guard, Arlington, Va., 1998—2001; comdr. Air Nat. Guard Readiness Ctr., Andrews AFB, Md., 1998—2001; dep. insp. gen. USAF, Washington, 2001—02, comdr. 1st Air Force, Air Combat Command, comdr. continental US NORAD region Tyndall, Fla., 2002—04; dir., mobilization & reserve affairs directorate US European Command, Stuttgart-Vaihingen, Germany, 2004—05; asst. dep. chief of staff for plans & programs USAF, Washington, 2005—06; dir. Air Nat. Guard, Arlington, Va., 2006—. Decorated Def. Disting. Svc. medal, Disting. Svc. medal with oak leaf cluster, Def. Superior Svc. medal, Legion of Merit, Meritorious Svc. medal with two oak leaf clusters, Air Force Tng. Ribbon, Armed Force Res. medal, Air Force Commendation medal with two oak leaf cluster, Air Force Achievement medal with two oak leaf clusters, Air Force Outstanding Unit award, Combat Readiness medal with four oak leaf clusters, Nat. Def. Svc. medal with bronze star, Global War on Terroris, Svc. medal, Humanitarian Svc. medal, Air Force Longvity Svc. award with silver oak leaf cluster, Armed Forces Reserve meal with silver hourglass; Recipient I.G. Brown trophy, 1993, Disting. Alumni award So. Methodist U., 2003, Office: Air Nat Guard 1411 Jefferson Davis Hwy Arlington VA 22202-3231*

**MCKINLEY, DOUGLAS WEBSTER (WEBB MCKINLEY),** consultant; b. Bay City, Mich., May 26, 1917; s. Frank and Amelia Ingraham (Webster) McK.; m. Martha Slade, July 12, 1945; children: Judith Anne, Martha Webster (Mrs. Duane Kissick), Mary Slade (Mrs. Joel Bingham), Jane Elizabeth; m. Roberta Baughman Burton, Nov. 25, 1994; m. Peggy Lighter. BA, Amherst Coll., 1939. Reporter Ann Arbor News, 1940-41, 46-47; staff AP, Detroit, 1947-53, Rome, 1953—60, chief Middle East services Beirut, 1960-65, news editor world services N.Y.C., 1965-82; cons. to agys. in developing nations Zimbabwe, Malaysia, Morocco, Tunisia, 1982—. Author: Trouble in the Middle East. Served to maj. AUS, 1941-45. Mem. Phi Kappa Psi. Home: 619 Old Plantation Rd Jekyll Island GA 31527-0723

**MCKINLEY, ELLEN BACON,** priest; b. Milw., June 9, 1929; d. Edward Alsted and Lorraine Goodrich (Graham) Bacon; m. Richard Smallbrook McKinley, III, June 16, 1951 (div. Oct. 1977); children: Richard, Ellen Graham, David Todd, Edward Bacon. BA cum laude, Bryn Mawr Coll., 1951; MDiv, Yale U., 1976; STM, Gen. Theol. Sem., N.Y.C., 1979; PhD, Union Theol. Sem., N.Y.C., 1988. Ordained deacon Episcopal Ch., 1980, as priest Episcopal Ch., 1981. Intern St. Francis Ch., Stamford, Conn., 1976-77; pastoral asst. St. Paul's Ch., Riverside, Conn., 1979-80, curate, 1980-81; asst. St. Saviour's Ch., Old Greenwich, Conn., 1982-90; interim asst. Trinity Ch., Princeton, NJ, 1990—91; priest assoc. All Saints Ch., Princeton, NJ, 1992—97, St. Christophers Ch., Chatham, Mass., 1997—. Episc. election com. Diocese of Conn., 1986—87, com. on human sexuality, 1987—90, donations and bequests com., 1987—90; major chpt. mem. Trinity Cathedral, Trenton, NJ, 1992—96; interim rector All Saints Ch., Princeton, NJ, 1993. Sec. Greenwich Com. Drugs, 1970—71; active Episcopal Women's Caucus; bd. dirs. Greenwich YWCA, 1971—72, Chatham Old Village Assn., 1998—2004. Mem.: Colonial Dames Am.

**MCKINLEY, JAMES FRANK, JR.,** retired manufacturing executive; b. Chgo., Feb. 17, 1943; s. James F. Sr. and Annabell I. (Williams) McK.; m. Sharon M., Dec. 7, 1968; children: James P., Scott J., Rebecca L. BS, Monmouth Coll., 1964; MS, Ill. Inst. Tech., 1966; MBA, Stanford U., 1987. Salesman Joseph T. Ryerson & Son, Chgo., 1961-66, Scot Forge Co., Cicero, Ill., 1966-71, v.p. sales, 1971-76, exec. v.p., 1976-85, pres., COO, 1985-92, pres., CEO, COO, 1992—; pres., bd. dirs. Ringmasters (formerly Ovaco Ajax), Wayne, Mich., 1996—; ptnr. N.Am. Forgemasters, 1997, vice-chmn., 2001, ret., 2002; owner Classic Electric Boats, 2004—. Fox Waterway Agy., state office, 1997—, chmn. 2000—. Capt. USCG Aux., Fox Lake, Ill., 1985—; dir. Allendale Sch., Lake Villa, Ill., 1983-96; regent Milw. Sch. Engring., 1995; McHenry County mem. Sheriff Merit Commn., 2000. Mem. Am. Soc. Metals, Forging Industry Rsch. Found., Forging Industry Assn. (bd. dirs. 1986—, gov. coun. 1990—, dir. 1998, v.p. 1999, pres. 2000—), Ill. St. Andrews Soc. (bd. govs., v.p. 1996-97), Profl. Capts. Assn., McHenry C. of C. (chmn. 1999). Republican. Avocations: boating, skiing, scuba diving, golf. Office Phone: 715-356-9483. Personal E-mail: jmkinleyjr@msn.com.

**MCKINLEY, JIMMIE JOE,** small business owner; b. Bertram, Tex., July 23, 1934; s. Joseph Crofford and Velma Anne (Barnett) McK. AA, Tarleton Coll., Tex., 1953; BJ, U. Tex., Austin, 1955; MS, U. Ky., Lexington, 1964. Asst. libr. Bethel Coll., McKenzie, Tenn., 1961—63, reference libr., 1966—70, acting head libr., 1970—71; owner, mgr. Longview Book Co., Tex., 1974—. Former mem., bd. dirs. Longview-Piney Woods chpt. ARC; trustee Bethel Coll., 1977-86. Mem. East Tex. Hist. Assn., Gregg County Hist. Soc., Burnet County Hist. Assn., History Club East Tex., East Tex. Oil Mus. Guild (pres. 1996-97), Kilgore Hist. Preservation Found., U.S. Lighthouse Soc. Presbyn. Office: PO Box 1748 Longview TX 75606-1748

**MCKINLEY, JOHN,** information technology executive; Grad., U. Pa., 1979. With Ernst & Young LLP, 1982—95, ptnr., 1992; sr. v.p., chief tech. and information officers GE Capital Corp., 1995; sr. v.p., chief tech. officer Merrill Lynch & Co., 1998, exec. v.p., head global technology and svcs.; chief tech. officer, pres. AOL Technologies AOL, Dulles, Va., 2003—04, pres. digital services bus., 2004—, interim chief tech. officer, 2006—. Office: AOL 22000 AOL Way Dulles VA 20166 Office Phone: 703-265-1000. Office Fax: 703-265-1101.

**MC KINLEY, JOHN KEY,** retired oil company executive; b. Tuscaloosa, Ala., Mar. 24, 1920; s. Virgil Parks and Mary Emma (Key) McK.; m. Helen Grace Heare, July 19, 1946; children: John Key Jr., Mark Charles. BS in Chem. Engring. U. Ala., 1940, MS in Organic Chemistry, 1941, LL.D. (hon.), 1972; grad., Advanced Mgmt. Program, Harvard U., 1962; LL.D. (hon.), Troy State U., 1974. Registered profl. engr., Tex. With Texaco Inc., 1941-86, asst. dir. research Beacon, NY, 1957-59, asst. to v.p., 1959-60, mgr. comml. devel., 1960, gen. mgr. petrochem. dept. N.Y.C., 1960-67, v.p. petrochem. dept., v.p. in charge supply and distbn., 1967-71, sr. v.p. worldwide refining, petrochems., also supply and distbn., 1971, pres., dir., 1971-80, pres., chief operating officer, chmn. exec. com., 1980, chmn. bd., pres., chief exec. officer, 1980-83, chmn. bd., chief exec. officer, 1983-86, ret., 1986. Bd. dirs. emeritus Federated Dept. Stores, Inc. Patentee for chem. processing. Hon. bd. dirs. Met. Opera Assocs.; nat. chmn. Met. Opera Centennial Fund, 1980; bd. dirs. The Ams. Soc.; mem. Bus. Coun. Maj. AUS, 1941-45, ETO. Decorated Bronze Star; recipient George Washington Honor medal Freedoms Found., 1972; Andrew Wellington Cordier fellow Columbia U.; named to Ala. Bus. Hall of Fame, 1982, Ala. Acad. Honor, 1983, State of Ala. Engring. Hall of Fame, 1992. Fellow Am. Inst. Chem. Engrs.; mem. Am. Petroleum Inst. (hon. dir.), Wee Burn Country Club, Links Club, Brook Club, Augusta Nat. Golf Club, Blind Brook Country Club, North River Yacht, Sigma Xi, Tau Beta Pi, Gamma Sigma Epsilon, Kappa Sigma. Office: 1 Canterbury Grn Stamford CT 06901-2032 Office Phone: 203-967-3000.

**MCKINLEY, LORI,** education educator; b. Tuscumbia, Mo., July 23, 1957; d. Luchin Lymoin and Lura Maxine McKinley; children: Dana Michelle Petrechko, Jonathan Lukas Petrechko, Daniel Ryan Petrechko. BA in Psychology, U. Mo., Columbia, 1979, MEd in Counseling, 1982, PhD, 2003. Program specialist Dept. Mental Health, Jefferson City, Mo., 1989—90; counselor U. Hosp. and Clinics, Columbia, Mo., 1990—93; adj. prof. Columbia Coll., 1995—96; project devel. specialist U. Mo., Columbia, 1997—2003, rsch. asst. prof., 2003—. Recipient Donald K. Anderson Tchg. award, U. Mo., 1996. Mem.: Rotary, Nat. Alliance for Mentally Ill (assoc.). Office: Univ Mo-Columbia 3 Hospital Dr Rm 135 Columbia MO 65211 Office Phone: 573-882-1498. Home Fax: 573-884-1010. Personal E-mail: mckinleyda@health.missouri.edu.

**MCKINLEY-HAAS, MARY,** artist; b. St. Louis; d. Lee Carrington and Florence (Dowden) McK.; m. Saul Haas; children: Christopher, Matthew. BA, Smith Coll.; student, Art Students League, 1973—74, Nat. Acad. Design, 1965—66, Studio and Forum Stage Design. Head costume design dept. ABC-TV, NYC, 1968-73. One-woman shows include Tarlowe Gallery, Westhampton Beach, N.Y., 1974, Fontbonne Gallery, St. Louis, 1977, Gallery Yssa, N.Y.C., 1979, Vered Gallery, East Hampton, N.Y. 1981, Netherlands Bank & Ludlow-Hyland Gallery, N.Y.C., 1981, U. Tex., Austin, 1988, RVS Fine Art, Southampton, N.Y., 1990, TSS Gallery, N.Y.C., 1992, U. Tex., Austin, 1992, TAI Gallery, N.Y.C., 1999; exhibited in group shows at Guild Hall, East Hampton, N.Y., 1974-76, 78, 81, 85, 96, Parrish Art Mus., Southampton, 1975-76, 78, 81, Water Mill Mus., 1983, 92, Vared Gallery, East Hampton, N.Y., 1985, Lincoln Ctr., N.Y.C., 1989-90, Queens Coll. Art Ctr., Flushing, N.Y., 1991, Dorothy Chandler Pavillion, L.A., Calif., 1993, Stony Brook U. Art Gallery, N.Y., 1994, Women in Art and Culture, Beijing, 1995, Elite Gallery, Moscow, 1995, Nat. Mus. Women in Arts, Washington, 1996, Soho 20 Gallery, N.Y.C., 1998—, Canajoharie (N.Y.) Libr. and Art Ctr., 2000, Weill Cornell Med. Libr., N.Y.C., 2002, Noho-N.Y. Art Walk, 2004-05, others; represented in permanent collections at Nat. Mus. Women in the Arts, Washington, Tari Women's Cultural Ctr., Papua, New Guinea, Fontbonne Coll., St. Louis, No. Trust Naples (Fla.); also pvt. collections; costume designer for Broadway and network TV shows, Harkness Ballet, Holiday on Ice, others. Mem. United Scenic Artists, Women in the Arts, N.Y. Artists Equity. Address: 280 Lafayette St Loft 5B New York NY 10012-3303

**MCKINNELL, HANK (HENRY A. MCKINNELL JR.),** pharmaceutical executive; b. Victoria, BC, Can., Feb. 23, 1943; 4 children. BA, U. BC, 1965; MBA, Stanford U., 1967, PhD in Bus. 1969. Joined Pfizer, Inc., Tokyo, 1971; pres. Pfizer Asia, Hong Kong; chief fin. officer, pres. med. technology group Pfizer, Inc., exec. v.p., 1992—99; pres. Pfizer Pharms. Group, prin. oper. divsn., 1997—2001; COO Pfizer, Inc., NYC, 1999—2000, pres., 1999—2001, chmn., CEO, 2001—06, chmn. 2006—. Mem. Presidential Advisory Council on HIV/AIDS; bd. dirs. ExxonMobil Corp., Moody's Corp., John Wiley & Sons, Inc., Trilateral Commn., Bus. Coun.; chmn. Bus. Roundtable, 2003—06; chmn. emeritus Pharm. Rsch. and Mfrs, of Am.; vice chmn. Com. Econ. Devel.; chmn. Food and Drug Law Inst. Bd. trustee NY Pub. Libr., NYC Police Found., Econ. Club of NY; chmn. Stanford U. Grad. Sch. of Bus. Adv. Coun.; chmn. emeritus, Bus.-Higher Edu. Forum. Fellow, NY Acad. of Medicine. Office: Pfizer Inc 235 E 42d St New York NY 10017-5755*

**MCKINNELL, ROBERT GILMORE,** retired zoologist, biology professor, geneticist; b. Springfield, Mo., Aug. 9, 1926; s. William Parks and Mary Catherine (Gilmore) McK.; m. Beverly Walton Kerr, Jan. 24, 1964; children: Nancy Elizabeth, Robert Gilmore, Susan Kerr. B in Naval Sci., U. Notre Dame, 1946; AB, U. Mo., 1948; BS, Drury Coll., 1949, DSc (hon.), 1993; PhD, U. Minn., 1959. Rsch. assoc. Fox Chase Cancer Ctr., Phila., 1958-61; asst. prof. biology Tulane U., New Orleans, 1961-65, assoc. prof., 1965-69, prof., 1969-70; prof. zoology U. Minn., Mpls., 1970—76, prof. genetics and cell biology St. Paul, 1976—99, prof. emeritus, 1999—. Vis. scientist Dow Chem. Co., Freeport, Tex., 1976; guest dept. zoology U. Calif., Berkeley, 1979; Royal Soc. guest rsch. fellow Nuffield dept. pathology John Radcliffe Hosp., Oxford U., 1981-82; NATO vis. scientist Akademisch Ziekenhuis, Ghent, Belgium, 1984; faculty rsch. assoc. Naval Med. Rsch. Inst., Bethesda, Md., 1988; secretariat Third Internat. Conf. Differentiation, 1978; organizer, secretariat 6th Internat. Conf. on Pathology of Reptiles and Amphibians, 2001; mem. amphibian com. Inst. Lab. Animal Resources, NRC, 1970-73, mem. adv. coun., 1974; mem. panel genetic and cellular resources program NIH, 1981-82, spl. study sect., Bethesda, 1990. Author: Cloning: Amphibian Nuclear Transplantation, 1978, Cloning, A Biologist Reports, 1979; sr. editor: Differentiation and Neoplasia, 1980, Cloning: Leben aus der Retorte, 1981, Cloning, of Frogs, Mice, and other Animals, 1985, (with others) The Biological Basis of Cancer, 1998, 2d edit., 2006, (with D.L. Carlson) Pathology of Reptiles and Amphibians, 2002, also symposium procs. in field; mem. editl. bd. Differentiation, 1973—; mem. bd. advisors Marquis Who's Who; contbr. articles to profl. jours. Served to lt. USNR, 1944-47, 51-53. Recipient Outstanding Teaching award Newcomb Coll., Tulane U., 1970; Disting. Alumni award Drury Coll., 1979, Morse Alumni Tchg. award U. Minn., 1992; Rsch. fellow Nat. Cancer Inst., 1956-58, Prince Hitachi award Japanese Found. Cancer Rsch., 1998; Sr. Sci. fellow NATO, 1974. Fellow AAAS, Linnean Soc. (London); mem. Am. Assn. Cancer Rsch. (emeritus), Am. Assn. Cancer Edn. (sr.), Am. Assn. History of Medicine, Indian Soc. Devel. Biology (lifetime emeritus), Internat. Soc. Differentiation (pres. 1994-96), Minn. Acad. Medicine, Gown-in-Town Club, Sigma Xi. Office: 140 Gortner Lab Biochemistry 1479 Gortner Ave Saint Paul MN 55108 Business E-Mail: mckin002@umn.edu.

**MCKINNEY, ALEXANDER STUART,** retired neurologist; b. N.Y.C., Feb. 3, 1933; s. John McDowell and Katherine Elizabeth (Morse) McK.; m. Carolyn Clifton Braman, Aug. 15, 1958 (div. July 1985); children: James, David, Mark; m. Susan Lowe Childress, July 30, 1985; children: Josephine, Mary, Jennifer. AB, Princeton U., 1955; MD, Columbia U., 1959. Diplomate Am. Bd. Neurology. Intern St. Luke's Hosp., N.Y.C., 1959-60; resident N.Y. Neurological Inst., 1960-63; prof. neurology Emory U., Atlanta, 1965-85; pvt. practice Mountain Med. Assocs., Clyde, N.C., 1985-95; chief of staff Haywood County Hosp., Clyde, N.C., 1989-90. Contbr. articles to profl. jours. Served to lt. comdr. USNR, 1963-65. Fellow Am. Acad. Neurology (sr.); mem. N.C. Neurol. Soc. (pres. 1992). Avocations: travel, gardening. Home: 9 Charles Wesley Dr Waynesville NC 28786-3066 E-mail: ssmck@charter.net.

**MCKINNEY, CAROLYN,** educational association administrator, educator; BS in Early Childhood Edn., U. N.C., Greensboro; M in Elem. Edn., Gardner-Webb U. Elem. sch. tchr. Winston-Salem/Forsyth County Schs.; elem. tchr. Sedge Garden Sch. Math. and Sci.; 2n and 3d gr. tchr. Kernersville Elem. Sch.; tchr. Gen. Greene Sch., Guilford County; pres. N.C. Assn. Educators, Raleigh, 2001—. Mem.: NEA (alt. dir. bd. dirs.), N.C. Assn. Educators (bd. dirs., Terry Sanford award for excellence in edn. 1997), Forsyth Assn. Classroom Tchrs. (pres.). Office: NC Assn Educators PO Box 27347 Raleigh NC 27611

**MCKINNEY, CYNTHIA ANN,** congresswoman; b. Atlanta, Ga., Mar. 17, 1955; d. Billy and Leola McKinney; 1 child, Coy Grandison. BA in internat. rels., U. So. Calif., 1978; MA, Tufts U. Fletcher Sch. Law & Diplomacy; postgrad., Ga. State U., U. Wis. Former instr. Clark Atlanta U., Atlanta Met. Coll.; mem. Ga. Ho. Reps., 1988-92, US Congress from 4th Ga. dist., 1993—2003, 2005—, mem. com. on armed svc., com. on budget. Mem. HIV Health Services Planning Coun., Atlanta, 1991—92; Frank H.T. Rhodes vis. prof. Cornell U., Ithaca, NY, 2003—04. Named a Diplomatic fellow, Spellman Coll., 1984; named one of Most Influential Black Americans, Ebony mag., 2006; recipient Edgar Wayburn award, Sierra Club, 1998, Outstanding Contribution award, Nat. Orgn. Sierra Leonians in N Am., 2000. Mem.: Progressive Caucus, Congl. Black Caucus, Agrl. Com., Sierra Club, Nat. Coun. Negro Women, Metro Atlanta, NAACP. Democrat. Roman Catholic. Achievements include the first African American woman elected to Congress from Georgia. Office: US Ho Reps 320 Cannon Ho Office Bldg Washington DC 20515-1004 also: N DeKalb Mall Ste D-46 2050 Lawerenceville Hwy Decatur GA 30033 Office Phone: 202-225-1605. Office Fax: 202-226-0691.*

**MCKINNEY, DAVID DUANE,** museum director, architectural historian; b. Danville, Va., Nov. 14, 1956; s. Lafayette Wadsworth and Katie Jones McKinney. AB in History, Coll. William & Mary, 1979; MA in Archtl. History, U. Va., 1984, PhD in Archtl. History, 1992. Architect, asst. curator Ash Lawn Coll. William & Mary, Charlottesville, 1981—84; reference staff Alderman Libr. U. Va., Charlottesville, 1984—91; dir. programming Very Spl. Arts, Washington, 1991—95; instrnl. designer, sr. scientist Human Resources Rsch. Orgn., Alexandria, Va., 1995—97; dir. statewide partnerships Va. Mus. Fine Arts, Richmond, 1997—2003; dir. U.S. Dept. of the Interior Mus., Washington, 2003—. Lectr. archtl. history Goucher Coll., Washington, 1996—97; bd. dirs. Va. Assn. Museums, Richmond, 1998—2005; lectr. art history Va. Commonwealth U., Richmond, 2000—01; mem. steering com. stds. learning devel. Va. State Bd. Edn., 2000—02, mem. governor's adv. bd. on gifted edn., 2001—02. Contbr. dictionary, exhibition catalogue, articles to profl. jours. Fellow Alumni Dissertation fellow, U. Va., 1990—91; scholar, Scottish Rite Order, 1977—79; Governor's scholar, Commonwealth Va., 1981—83, Dewey Lee Curtis scholar, Am. Decorative Arts Trust, 1988, Maverick fellow, Attingham Program, 1988, Resident scholar, Lewis Walpole Libr., Yale U., 1989, Va. Mus. fellow, Va. Mus. Fine Arts, 1989—90, Dumas Malone Meml. Traveling fellow, U. Va., 1989—90, Fiske Kimball Meml. fellow, 1990—91. Mem.: Va. Assn. Museums (dir. art 1998—2005, bd. dirs. 1998—), Am. Assn. Museums. Home: 1239 Vermont Ave NW #409 Washington DC 20005 Office: US Department of the Interior Museum Mail Stop 2266 1849 C Street NW Washington DC 20240 Office Phone: 202-208-7017. Office Fax: 202-208-1535. Business E-Mail: david_d_mckinney@nbc.gov.

**MC KINNEY, DAVID E(WING),** retired information processing products company executive, museum administrator; b. Harriman, Tenn., Nov. 28, 1934; s. David Lloyd and Mattie (Ewing) McK.; children: Mary, John, James, Mark; m. Nancy Coates Hale, Aug. 29, 1991. Student (Founders scholar), Vanderbilt U., 1952-53; BS in Mktg. (Gen. Electric scholar), U. Tenn., 1956. With IBM, 1956—, br. mgr. New Orleans, 1966-68, exec. asst. to chmn. bd. Armonk, N.Y., 1971-73, pres. info. records div. Princeton, N.J., 1975-76, v.p. office products div. Franklin Lakes, N.J., 1976-77, v.p. personnel Armonk, 1979-80; asst. group exec. IBM Gen. Bus. Group, White Plains, NY, 1980; v.p., asst. group exec. IBM Info. Systems Group, Rye, 1982; pres. IBM World Trade, Americas/Far East Corp., 1986, v.p. communications, sr. v.p. corp. ops. staff, mgmt. com., corp. mgmt. bd., 1987—89; pres., dir. gen. IBM Europe, Paris, 1989-91; sr. v.p. IBM Corp., Armonk, NY, 1991—92, ret., 1992. Pres. Met. Mus. of Art, NYC, 1999—2005; bd. dirs. Gen. Re. Corp., Paxar Corp. Mem. adv. bd. T. J. Watson Found.; Providence; bd. dirs., corp. mem. Brown U.; bd. dirs. Internat. Exec. Svc. Corps, N.Y. Philharmonic; trustee Am. U. Paris; elder 1st Presbyn. Ch., New Canaan, Conn. Served to lt. U.S. Army, 1957—58. Mem.: Country Club of New Canaan.

**MCKINNEY, DONALD LEE,** magazine editor; b. Evanston, Ill., July 12, 1923; s. Guy Doane and Cora Redfield (Brenton) McK.; m. Mary Frances Joyce, Dec. 14, 1958; children— Jennifer Joyce, Douglas Guy. AB, U. N.C., 1948. Salesman textbooks John Wiley & Sons, N.Y.C., 1949-52; freelance writer mostly comic books with some short articles and fiction, 1952-54; asst. mng. editor True mag., N.Y.C., 1955-62; editor articles Saturday Evening Post, 1962-69; spl. features editor N.Y. Daily News, 1969-70; mng. editor McCalls mag., N.Y.C., 1969-86; Gonzales prof. journalism U. S.C., Beaufort, 1986-90, prof. emeritus, 1990—. Author: Magazine Writing That Sells, 1994; reporter, book reviewer. Served with USNR, 1943-46. Democrat. Home: 10520 Shadowlawn Dr Raleigh NC 27614 *I learned early that it is important to speak up if you think you are being treated unfairly; sometimes it's true, and nobody else will complain if you don't. I also learned that in my business, and probably in most others, it is best to always say what you think. Truth is usually more helpful than any assortment of euphemisms, and it also saves a lot of worry over who you have lied to and just what you've said. Truth is not only the best policy— by all odds it's the easiest to keep track of.*

**MCKINNEY, E. KIRK, JR.,** retired insurance company executive; b. Indpls., Mar. 27, 1923; s. E. Kirk and Irene M. (Hurley) McK.; m. Alice Hollenbeck Greene, June 18, 1949; children: Kirk Ashley, Alan Brooks, Nora Claire McKinney Hiatt, Margot Knight. AB, U. Mich., 1948. Asst. treas. Jefferson Nat. Life Ins. Co., Indpls., 1949-52, asst. to pres., asst. treas., 1952-53, treas., asst. to pres., 1953-55, v.p., treas., 1955-59, pres., 1959-90, chmn. bd., 1970-90; vice chmn. bd. Somerset Group Inc., 1986-89; ret., 1990. Corp. rels. com. U. Mich.; former pres., former CEO, bd. govs., treas., bd. dirs., exec. com. Indpls. Mus. Art; past bd. dirs. (hon.) Greater Indpls. Progress Com.; former vice chmn. Indpls.-Marion County Bd. Ethics; former dir. Park Tudor Sch., Cmty. Svc. Coun. Indpls., Hosp. Devel. Corp., Ind. Repertory Theater; past adv. com. Indpls. Retirement Home; former bd. dirs., and pres. Episcopal Cmty. Svcs., Inc.; former vice chmn., life trustee Nature Conservancy; mem. adv. bd. Ind. U., Purdue U.; active Indpls. Symphony Orch.; former bd. dirs. Ind. Pub. Broadcasting Svc.; past adv. bd. Indpls. Civic Theater, 2001—, Athenaeum Found., 2000—. Mem. Life Office Mgmt. Assn. (bd. dirs. 1981-83), Am. Coun. Life Ins. (state v.p. 1973-75, dir., exec. com. 1976-79), Am. Council Life Ins. Cos. (pres. 1969-71), Indpls. C. of C., Sigma Chi. Clubs: Economic of Indpls. (bd. dirs.). Democrat. Home: 250 W 77th St Indianapolis IN 46260-3608 Office: 1330 W 38th St #100 Indianapolis IN 46208-4103 Office Phone: 317-925-2223. Personal E-mail: ekirkjr@sbcglobal.net.

**MCKINNEY, GEORGE HARRIS, JR.,** training systems analyst; b. Birmingham, Ala., Nov. 23, 1943; s. George Harris and Elizabeth Dickey (Fikes) McK.; m. Lynda Jeanne Ponder, June 26, 1965 (div. Aug. 18, 1992; children: Michael Thomas, Carol Elizabeth; m. Tambri Sue Hillis, Aug. 19, 1992. BS in Polit. Sci., U.S. Air Force Acad., 1965; MS in Psychology, Troy State U., 1977. Fighter pilot U.S. Air Force, worldwide, 1965-85, commd. 2d lt., 1965, advanced through grades to lt. col., 1981, ret., 1985; pvt. practice Milton, Fla., 1985—. Decorated D.F.C. (5), Air medal (26), Purple Heart, Meritorious Svc. medal (3). Mem. Order of Daedalians, USAFA Assn. Grads., Air Force, Assn., Am. Def. Preparedness Assn. Avocations: whitetail deer hunting, fishing. Home: 3101 Chippewa Dr Milton FL 32571-9603 Office Phone: 850-452-1001 ext 1730. Personal E-mail: geortamb@bellsouth.net.

**MCKINNEY, JANET KAY,** law librarian; b. Kansas City, Mo., Feb. 15, 1959; d. Charles Durward and Helen Jean (Bost) Freeman; m. Larry Emmett McKinney, July 11, 1981. BA, Avila Coll., 1981; MA in Libr. Sci., U. Mo., 1989; MA in Religious Studies, Ctrl. Bapt. Theol. Sem., 1997. Circulation libr. Midwestern Bapt. Theol. Sem., Kansas City, 1981-84, acquisitions libr., 1984-85, reference libr., 1985-90; environ. divsn. libr. Black & Veatch, Kansas City, 1990-91; dir. collection resources U. Mo. Leon E. Bloch Law Libr., Kansas City, 1991-2000; computer svc. Thl. Shook, Hardy & Bacon, Kansas City, 2000—. Mem. ALA, Am. Assn. Law Libns. (com. on rels. with info. vendors 1994-96, editl bd. Tech. Svcs. Law Libr. 1994-96, tech. svcs. spl. interest sect. chair 1999-2000, treas pvt. law librs. spl. interest sect. 2001—, index to fgn. legal periodicals adv. com. 2001—, cataloging and intranet access to electronic resources spl. com. 2002-03, program com. 2003-04), Mid-Am. Assn. Law Librs. (newsletter adv. mgr. 1993-94, treas. 1997-99, 2002-2003, v.p., pres.-elect 2003-04, pres. 2004—), Southwestern Assn. Law Librs., Spl. Librs. Assn. (chpt. employment com. chmn. 1990-91, chpt. treas. 1991-94, chpt. pres. 1995-96), Kansas City Assn. Law Librs. (v.p., pres. 2000). Office: Shook Hardy & Bacon LLP 2555 Grand Blvd Kansas City MO 64108 Business E-Mail: jmckinney@shb.com.

**MCKINNEY, JOHN ADAMS, JR.,** lawyer; b. Washington, Mar. 10, 1948; s. John A. and Cleo G. (Turner) McK.; m. Carol A. Cowen, Dec. 22, 1970; children: John III, Thomas. BA, Principia Coll., 1970; JD, Coll. William and Mary, 1973. Bar: N.J. 1973. Assoc. Mason, Griffin & Pierson, Princeton, NJ, 1973-77; gen. atty. Nabisco, Inc., East Hanover, NJ, 1977-79; asst. counsel Republic Steel Corp., Cleve., 1979-84; atty. and sr. atty. AT&T, Berkeley Heights, NJ, 1984-90; ptnr. McCarter & English LLP, Newark, 1990—2003; mem. Wolff & Samson PC, West Orange, NJ, 2003—. Adj. prof. Sch. of Law, Seton Hall U., 1997—; charter mem., program chair Justice Pollock Environ. Am. Inn of Ct., 2004-; mem. N.J. Historic Sites Coun., 2005-. Co-author: The RCRA Practice Manual, 2d edit., 2004; co-editor: CERCLA Enforcement, 1996. Mem. N.J. Hist. Sites Coun., 2005—; trustee Hackettstown (N.J.) Free Pub. Libr., 1998—2005, Drumthwacket Found., 2003—. Mem. ABA (vice-chair sect. natural resources energy and environ. law solid and hazardous waste com. 1990-98, chair, teleconf. programs 1994-97), N.J. Bar Assn. (dir. environ. law sect. 1992-96, chair 1996-97). Office: Wolff & Samson PC One Boland Dr West Orange NJ 07052-3698 Office Phone: 973-530-2036.

**MCKINNEY, JOHN PAUL,** performing company executive; b. Birmingham, Ala., Dec. 27, 1956; s. Clifford Littleton and Lisa Michelle (Lankford) McKinney; m. Pamela Elaine Whitaker (div.); 1 child, John Paul II. Cert. in radiological tech., C.C. of the Air Force, 1977; attended, Bethany Bible Coll.,

1990; D in biblical studies (hon.), Progressive Life Ch., 1993, D (hon.) in counseling, 1993. Cert. drug and alcohol counseling Alpha & Omega Inc. Pastor, CEO Trinity Cmty. Fellowship, Aptos, Calif., 1987—96; caregiver, adminstr. Trinity Ministries, So. San Francisco, Calif., 1996—2001; min., founder Prepare Ye the Way Ministries, Tuscaloosa, Ala., 2001—04; global relief outreach Solicitor Fund Raiser, Talladega, 2003; writer, dir. Full Moon Inst., Talladega, 2003—04. Pres., founder Trinity Ministries, So. San Francisco, Calif., 1996—2001, Prepare for the Way Ministries, Ala., 2001—04; pres. Full Moon Inst., Talladega, 2003—04. Sgt. USAF, 1976—80. Mem.: Full Moon Insight Soc. Democrat. Baptist. Avocations: chess, reading, golf, hiking. Home: 110 Coffee St Apt 1 1/2 Talladega AL 35160 Office: Alpha Omega Inc 110 Coffee St Talladega AL 35160

**MCKINNEY, JUDSON THAD,** broadcast executive; b. Sacramento, Aug. 21, 1941; s. Judson Bartlet and Mildred Eoline (Taylor) McK. Student, Sacramento State U., 1959-61, Western Bapt. Bible Coll., 1961-62, Am. River Coll., 1962-63. Prodn. dir. Sta. KEBR, Sacramento, 1962-65; prodn. dir. Sta. KEAR, Merced, Calif., 1965-68; sta. mgr. Sta. KAMB, 1968-75, Sta. KEAR, San Francisco, 1975-78, 79-88, WFME, Newark, 1978; western regional mgr. Family Stas. Inc., 1988—. Pres. Abounding Love Ministries, 2000-04; instr.for study of electronic Christian media Grad. Theol. Union. V.p. New Millennium Strings 2003—04, pres., 2005—; sec., treas. Trinity Lyric Opera 2005—; chmn. 1st. Bapt. Ch. San Francisco, 1985—91; recording engr. 1st Bapt. Ch. Los Altos, Calif. Mem. Gideons. Republican. Baptist. Office: Family Stations Inc 290 Hegenberger Rd Oakland CA 94621-1436 E-mail: thad@familyradio.com

**MCKINNEY, KAY GRIFFIN,** elementary school educator; b. Spartanburg, SC, Aug. 21, 1951; d. Ivan Lynn and Betty Ruth Griffin; m. Thomas Lewis McKinney, May 19, 1973; children: Robin Pope, Karen Edwards, Daniel. BA in Elem. Edn., Clemson U., 1973, MA in Elem. Edn., 1986. Nat. bd. cert. tchr. 5th grade tchr. Oconee County Schs., Seneca, SC, 1973—74, Chattanooga City Schs., 1974—75, 3d grade tchr., 1975—76, 2d grade tchr., 1976—78; learning disabilities resource tchr. Pickens County Schs., Easley, SC, 1989—90, 1st grade tchr., 1990—. Named Honor Roll Tchr. of Yr., Pickens County Sch. Dist., 2003.

**MCKINNEY, LARRY J.,** federal judge; b. South Bend, Ind., July 4, 1944; s. Lawrence E. and Helen (Byers) McK.; m. Carole Jean Marie Lyon, Aug. 19, 1966; children: Joshua E., Andrew G. BA, MacMurray Coll., Jacksonville, Ill., 1966; JD, Ind. U., 1969. Bar: Ind. 1970, U.S. Dist. Ct. (so. dist.) Ind. 1970. Law clk. to atty. gen. State of Ind., Indpls., 1969-70, dep. atty. gen., 1970-71; ptnr. Rodgers and McKinney, Edinburgh, Ind., 1971-75, James F.T. Sargent, Greenwood, Ind., 1975-79; judge Johnson County Cir. Ct., Franklin, Ind., 1979-87, U.S. Dist. Ct. (so. dist.) Ind., Indpls., 1987—, chief judge, 2001—. Presbyterian. Avocations: reading, jogging. Office: US Dist Ct 204 US Courthouse 46 E Ohio St Indianapolis IN 46204-1903

**MCKINNEY, MARK A.,** finance educator; b. Hampton, Va., Nov. 9, 1967; s. Thurman B. McKinney, Sr. and Gladys G. McKinney; m. JoAnn J. Collins, June 15, 2002; children: Mark A. McKinney, Jr., Anusha S. BA, U. Nev., 1996; MPA, Webster U., 1998, MA, 1999; PhD, Madison U., 2002, Capella U., 2005. Cert. nurse aide State Md., 2002. State trooper Nev. Hwy. Patrol, Las Vegas, 1990—94; asst. mgr. Prestige Stations, Inc., Las Vegas, 1995—96; paralegal asst. Jordan Enterprises. Ltd., San Bernardino, Calif., 1996—97; human resrouces sgt. U.S Army, 1997—2001; med. adminstrn. officer USAR 2002; project asst. Force 3 Corp., Crofton, Md., 2003—04; assoc. dean Aims C.C., Greeley, Colo., 2004—. Content evaluator Am. Coun. Edn., Washington, 2004—; instr. Strayer U., Millersville, Md., 2000—03, Nat. Am. U., Kans. City, Mo., 2003—04; instr. online Park U., Parkville, Mo., 2003—; cons. in field. Author: The Financial Workbook: An everyday guide to financial freedom for the average income individual., Healthcare Diversity: Addressing Professional and Societal Needs. Bd. dirs. Greeley (Colo.) Ctr. Independence, 2004; mem. Greeley (Colo.) Art Commn., 2004. Mem.: Assn. Mil. Surgeons U.S. (peer reviewer 2003—), Am. Health Info. Mgmt. Assn., Health Info. & Mgmt. Sys. Soc., Am. Soc. Pub. Adminstrn., Health Care Compliance Assn., Am. Coll. Healthcare Exec., Mil. Officers Assn. Am., Phi Beta Sigma Frat., Inc. Personal E-mail: mark_1914@yahoo.com. E-Mail: mark_mckinney@doh.state.fl.us.

**MC KINNEY, MICHAEL WHITNEY,** trade association executive; b. San Angelo, Tex., Aug. 23, 1946; s. Wallace Luster and Mitzi Randolph (Broome) McK.; m. Martha LaNan Hooker, Feb. 24, 1973; children: Wallace Blake, Lauren Brooke. BA in Govt., U. Tex., Austin, 1973. Adminstrv. asst. to lt. gov. State of Tex., Austin, 1968-69, adminstrv. asst. to gov., 1969-73; asst. to dir. Tex. Water Quality Bd., Austin, 1973-76; chief of staff Tex. Alcoholic Beverage Commn., 1976-83; v.p. for industry affairs Wholesale Beer Distbrs., Tex., 1984-88, exec. v.p., chief exec. officer Tex., 1989—. Bd. govs. Keep Tex. Beautiful, 1997—98; mem. Travis County Zoo Task Force, 1986, Senate Com. on Fees and Grants, 1982—83; bd. dirs. Friends of Gov.'s Mansion, 1993—97, Bob Bullock Tex. State History Mus. Found., 2002—. Recipient Bert Ford award Tex. Alcholic Beverage Commn., 1996, Pres. award for legis. excellence Nat. Beer Wholesalers Assn., 1998, F.X. Matt award Brewers Assn. Am., 2002. Mem.: Nat. Wholesale Beer Assn. Execs. (pres. 2001—02, chmn. 2002—, Industry Svc. award 2002), Austin Assembly, Sam. Houston Soc., Knights of the Symphony, Austin Club (bd. dirs. 1989—, exec. com. 1994—, Mem. of Yr. 1994), Austin Country Club, Masons (32 deg., K.T.), Phi Kappa Psi. Home: 1708 Intervail Dr Austin TX 78746-7630 Office: 823 Congress Ave Ste 1313 Austin TX 78701-2434

**MCKINNEY, RONALD W.,** lawyer; b. Greenville, S.C., Mar. 23, 1948; s. William R. and Doris (Chadwick) McK.; m. Kathleen Crum Jan 13, 1979; children: William Kathleen. BA, Furman U., 1970; MA, U. N.C., 1973; JD, U. S.C., 1978. Bar: S.C. 1978. Atty. S.C. Consumer Advocate's Office, Columbia, 1978-81; ptnr. Duggan, Reese & McKinney, Greer, SC, 1981-95; city atty. City of Greenville, SC, 1995—, interim city mgr., 2000. Chair Greenville County Transportation Com., 1994-95. Mem. ABA, S.C. Bar Assn., Internat. Mcpl. Lawyers Assn., S.C. Mcpl. Attys. Assn. (pres. 1997). Methodist. Avocations: travel, reading. Office: City of Greenville PO Box 2207 Greenville SC 29602-2207 E-mail: mckinnr@greatergreenville.com.

**MCKINNEY, ROSS ERWIN, SR.,** civil engineering educator; b. San Antonio, Aug. 2, 1926; s. Roy Earl and Beatrice (Saylor) McK.; m. Margaret McKinney Curtis, June 21, 1952; children: Ross Erwin, Margaret E., William S., Susanne E. BA, BSCE, So. Meth. U., 1948; SM, MIT, 1949, ScD, 1951. San. scientist S.W. Found. for Research and Edn., San Antonio, 1951-53; asst. prof. MIT, 1953-58, assoc. prof., 1958-60; prof. U. Kans., 1960-63, chmn. dept. civil engring., 1963-66, Parker prof. civil engring., 1966-76, N.T. Veatch prof. environ. engring., 1976-93, prof. emeritus 1993—. Adj. prof. Tongji U., Shanghai, Peoples Rep. China, 1985; v.p. Rolf Eliassen Assocs., Winchester, Mass., 1954-60; pres. Environ. Pollution Control Services, Lawrence, Kans., 1969-73; adj. prof. environ. engring. Duke U., 1997-2002. Author: Microbiology for Sanitary Engineers, 1962, Environmental Pollution Control Microbiology, 2004; editor: Nat. Conf. on Solid Waste Research, 1964, 2d Internat. Symposium for Waste Treatment Lagoons, 1970. Mem. Cambridge (Mass.) Water Bd., 1953-59, Lawrence-Douglas County Health Bd., 1969-76, Kans. Water Quality Council, 1965-76, Kans. Solid Waste Adv. Council, 1970-76, Kans. Environ. Adv. Bd., 1976-85. With AOM 3c, V6 & V12 USNR, 1943—46, appointed ensign USNR, 1947, with civil engring. corps. USNR, 1949, lt. CEC USNR, 1950—55. Recipient Harrison P. Eddy award, 1962, Rudolph Hering award, Water Pollution Control Fedn., 1964, U.S. Presdl. Commendation, 1971, Environ. Quality award, EPA Region VII, 1979, Chancellors Tchg. award, U. Kans., 1986, Lifetime Achievement award, Enviro-Water Resources Inst./ASCE, 2001. Mem.: AAAS, NAE, ASCE (hon.), Am. Soc. Microbiologists, Am. Chem. Soc., Water Pollution Control Fedn. (Thomas R. Camp medal 1982), Am. Water Works Assn., Kans. Water Pollution Control Assn. (hon. Gordon M. Fair medal 1991), Tau Beta Pi, Chi Epsilon, Kappa Mu Epsilon, Sigma Tau, Sigma Xi. Democrat.

Unitarian Universalist. Achievements include patent for water treatment process. Home: 750 Weaver Dairy Rd # 248 Chapel Hill NC 27514-1493 Office Phone: 919-918-2623. E-mail: remck@mindspring.com.

**MCKINNEY, SALLY VITKUS,** state official; b. Muncie, Ind., Aug. 6, 1944; d. Robert Brookins and Mary (Mann) Gooden; m. Alan George Vitkus (div. Jan. 1979); m. James Larry McKinney, Feb. 1, 1986. AA, William Woods U., 1964; BS, U. Ariz., 1966; postgrad., U. Nev., Las Vegas, 1966-68. Tchr. Las Vegas Day Sch., 1972—76; salesperson Globe Realty, Las Vegas, 1976—79; owner, pres. Realty West, Las Vegas, 1979—96; chief investigator State of Nev. Real Estate Divsn., 1996—2000; prin., owner McKinney Realty, Las Vegas, 2000—; corp. broker, dir. bus. and devel. Real Estate Temps, Las Vegas. Rec. sec. Clark County Rep. Cen. Com., Las Vegas, 1982, 1st vice chmn., 1985; vice-chmn. Nev. Rep. com., 1986, chmn., 1987-88; active Assistance League Las Vegas; state chmn. Nev. Rep. Party. Mem. Nat. Assn. Realtors, Nat. Assn. Home Builders, Las Vegas Bd. Realtors, Greater Las Vegas C. of C., Gen. Fedn. Womens Clubs (nominee Outstanding Young Woman Am. 1979, exec. bd. 1980-82), Jr. League Las Vegas (sustaining), Mesquite Club (chmn. pub. affairs com. 1986-87, past pres., secret witness exec. bd. 1994-96, vice chmn.). Presbyterian. Avocations: bridge, fly fishing. Home: 511 Mountain Dell Ave Henderson NV 89012-2509

**MCKINNEY, SUEANNE E.,** education educator; b. Portsmouth, Va., Dec. 10, 1959; d. Joseph Edward and Betty Ann McKinney. BA in Elem. Edn., U. NC, Wilmington, 1982; MEd in Adminstrn., Old Dominion U., Norfolk, Va., 1991, PhD in Urban Edn., 2000. Cert. mid. sch. tchr., prin. Va. Tchr. Norfolk Pub. Schs. 1983—97; grad. assist. Old Dominion U., 1998—2003, asst. prof., 2005—, U. NC, Charlotte, 2003—05. Contbr. articles to profl. jours. Named Tchr. of Yr., Norfolk Pub. Schs., 1996, Teletechnet Instr. of Yr., Old Dominion U., 2002. Mem.: Am. Educator Rsch. Assn., Assn. Tchr. Educators, Nat. Assn. Holms Scholars Alumni (membership chmn.). Office: Old Dominion U Hampton Blvd Norfolk VA 23529

**MCKINNEY, TIMOTHY RICHMOND,** music educator; b. Ft. Worth, Mar. 17, 1956; s. James Carroll and Elizabeth Richmond McKinney; m. Cynthia Lynn Cavender, Mar. 18, 1978; children: Erin Elizabeth, Brian Richmond. BS in Viola Performance, William Jewell Coll., 1978; MusM in Music Theory, Southwestern Bapt. Theol. Sem., 1981; PhD in Music Theory, U. North Tex., 1989. Asst. prof. music theory U. Tex., Arlington, 1989—95, assoc. prof. music theory, 1995—2002, assoc. dean Coll. Liberal Arts, 2001—02; assoc. prof. music theory Baylor U., Waco, Tex., 2002—. Fellow Mannes Inst. for Advanced Music Theory, N.Y.C., 2001. Contbr. articles to profl. jours. Children and youth choir leader Broadway Bapt. Ch., Ft. Worth, 1998—2002, ordained deacon, 2001; youth choir vol. asst. Seventh and James Bapt. Ch., Waco, 2003—; violist Ft. Worth Symphony Orch., 1975—76. Named Oustanding Alumnus, Coll. Music, U. North Tex., 2006. Mem.: South Ctrl. Soc. for Music Theory (archivist 1991—99), Am. Musicol. Soc., Soc. for Music Theory, Tex. Soc. for Music Theory (pres. 2003—06), Pi Kappa Lambda (pres. Iota Zeta chpt.), Phi Kappa Phi, Sigma Alpha Iota (hon.; nat. art assoc.). Office: Baylor Univ Sch Music One Bear Pl #97408 Waco TX 76798 Office Phone: 254-710-1417.

**MCKINNEY, WILLIAM T.,** psychiatrist, educator; b. Rome, Ga., Sept. 20, 1937; BA cum laude, Baylor U., 1959; MD, Vanderbilt U., 1963. Diplomate Nat. Bd. Med. Examiners (mem. psychiatry test com. 1982-87, chmn. 1984-87); cert. Am. Bd. Psychiatry and Neurology (sr. examiner 1979-90, bd. dirs. 1991—, mem. rsch. com., co-chair part I test com., chair added qualifications in geriatric psychiatry test com., mem. part II audio visual com., mem. disability accomodations com., rep. to residency rev. com.). Intern in medicine Bowman Gray Sch. Medicine, Wake Forest U., Winston-Salem, NC, 1963-64; resident dept. psychiatry Sch. Medicine, U. N.C., Chapel Hill, 1964-66, Sch. Medicine, Stanford (Calif.) U., 1966-67; clin. assoc. psychosomatic sect. adult psychiatry br., tng. specialist, asst. br. chief NIMH, Bethesda, Md., 1967-69; asst. prof. psychiatry dept. psychiatry Sch. Medicine, U. Wis., Madison, 1969-72, assoc. prof. psychiatry, 1972-74, prof. psychiatry, 1974-93; Asher prof. of psychiatry dept. psychiatry and behavioral scis., dir. Asher Ctr. for Study and Treatment of Depressive Disorders Med. Sch., Northwestern U., Chgo., 1993—. Part-time clin. pvt. practice, Bethesda, 1967-69; NIMH rsch. career investigator Sch. Medicine, U. Wis., Madison, 1970-75, rsch. psychiatrist Primate Lab., 1974-93, affiliate sci. Wis. Regional Primate Rsch. Ctr., 1974-93, affiliate prof. psychology dept. psychology, 1974-93, chmn. dept. psychiatry, 1975-80, dir. Wis. Psychiat. Rsch. Inst. Ctr. Health Scis., 1975-80; sr. staff psychiatrist William S. Middleton Meml. VA Hosp., Madison, Wis., 1974-93; rsch. sub dept. animal behaviour U. Cambridge, Eng., 1974; mem. rsch. rev. com. VA Behavioral Scis., 1976-79; Abbott Sigma XI Club lectr., 1976; Milw. Psychiat. Hosp. lectr., 1977; mem. program adv. com. and workshop chmn. Dahlem Found. Internat. Conf. on Depression, Berlin, 1982; U. Minn. lectr. at Festshrift, 1982; cons. grad. sch. U. Minn., 1982; fellow Ctr. Advanced Study in Behavioral Scis., Stanford, Calif., 1983-84; mem. external adv. bd. Clin. Rsch. Ctr. Depst. Psychiatry U. N.C., Chapel Hill, 1984—; cons., bd. advisors clin. rsch. fellow tng. program dept. psychology, 1988—; William F. Orr lectr. Vanderbilt U., 1985; vis. prof. dept. psychiatry U. Tex. Health Scis. Ctr., Dallas, 1986, U. Utah Sch. Medicine, Salt Lake City, 1987, U. Minn. Sch. Medicine, Mpls., 1988; cons. biol. scis. tng. br. divsn. manpower and tng. programs NIMH, 1975-76, mem. psychiatry spl. com. 1983, plenary lectr., Clearwater, Fla., 1987, co-chairperson Workshop on Non-Human Primate Models of Psychopathology, 1987, mem. biol. psychopathology spl. rev. com., 1992—; mem. sci. core group MacArthur Found. Mental Health Rsch. Network I: The Psychobiology of Depression and Other Affective Disorders, 1988-93; vis. spkr. So. Calif. Psychiat. Soc., L.A., 1988; plenary lectr. Soc. Biol. Psychiatry ann. meeting, Montreal, 1988; vis. prof. Dalhousie U. Sch. Medicine, N.S., 1989, UCA Riv in the Hosp., Chgo., 1989, U. Pa., Phila., 1991, U. N.Mex., Albuquerque, 1992, Northwestern U., Chgo., 1992; invited spkr. Animal Models in Psychopharmacology Symposium, Duphar, Amsterdam, 1990; vis. spkr., cons. CIBA-GEIGY, Basel, Switzerland, 1990; mem. minority instns. rsch. devel. rev. com. Alcohol, Drug Abuse and Mental Health Adminstrn., 1990; guest spkr. Inst. Pa. Hosp., Phila., 1991; reviewer Human Frontier Sci. Program, 1992—; external cons. dept. psychiatry Mental Health Clin. Rsch. Ctr. U. Tex. Southwestern Med. Ctr. Dallas, 1992—; presenter in field. Author: Animal Models of Mental Disorders: A New Comparative Psychiatry, 1988; co-author: Mood Disorders: Towards a New Psychobiology, 1984; mem. editl. bd. Archives of Psychiatry and Neurol. Scis., Contemporary Psychiatry, 1981-82, Ethology and Sociobiology, Experientia, 1982-89, Trends in Neurosciences, 1982-86, Neuropsychopharmacology, 1987-90; manuscript and book reviewer numerous sci. jours.; contbr. articles to profl. jours. USHPS fellow in biostats. Vanderbilt U., 1962; recipient Beauchamp award Vanderbilt U. Med. Sch., 1963, Rsch. Career Devel. award NIMH, 1975, Rsch. Leave award U. Wis., 1983-84, Am. Acad. Pediats. award, 1991. Fellow Am. Psychiat. Assn. (cons. psychiat. edn. consultation svc. 1983—), Am. Coll. Psychiatrists, Am. Coll. Neuropsychopharmacology (mem. consultation and rules com. 1985-87, mem. ethics com. 1987-89, mem. fin. com. 1990-92, panel chair San Juan, P.R. 1992, panel presenter 1992); mem. Am. Soc. Primatologists, Am. Psychosomatic Soc. (mem. program com. 1975-76), Internat. Primatology Soc., Internat. Coll. Neurobiology, Biol. Psychiatry and Psychopharmacology (lectr. Zurich 1985), Internat. Soc. Devel. Psychobiology, Internat. Soc. Ethological and Behavioral Pharmacology (bd. advisors 1983—), Collegium Internat. Neuro-Psychopharmacologicum, Psychiat. Rsch. Soc., Soc. Neuroscience, Wis. Psychiat. Assn. (chmn. program com. 1972, co-chairperson task force on sexual misconduct and membership edn. 1986-88, pres.-elect 1989-91, pres. 1991-93). Office: Northwestern U Med Sch Dept Psychiatry and Behavioral Scis 303 E Chicago Ave Bldg 9-721 Chicago IL 60611-3072

**MCKINNIS, MICHAEL B.,** lawyer; b. St. Louis, May 31, 1945; s. Bayard O. and Doris (Lammert) McK.; m. Patricia Butow, Aug. 24, 1968; children: Scott, Christopher, Elizabeth. BS, Drake U., 1967; JD, U. Mo., 1970. Bar: Mo. 1970, U.S. Dist. Ct. (ea. dist.) Mo. Ptnr. Bryan Cave LLP, St. Louis, leader firm litigation practice, mem. firm operating group. Editor U. Mo. Law

Rev., 1969-70. Mem. ABA, Mo. Bar Assn., Order of Coif, Phi Delta Phi. Office: Bryan Cave LLP One Metropolitan Square 211 N Broadway, Ste 3600 Saint Louis MO 63102-2733 Office Phone: 314-259-2000. E-mail: mbmckinnis@bryancavellp.com.

**MCKINNISH, RICHMOND D.,** manufacturing executive; From mem. staff to pres., CEO Carlisle Cos. Inc., Charlotte, NC, 1974—2001, pres., 2001—, CEO, 2001—. Bd. dirs. Carlisle Cos. Inc. Office: Carlisle Cos Inc 13925 Ballantyne Corp Place Charlotte NC 28277

**MCKINNON, ARNOLD BORDEN,** retired transportation company executive; b. Goldsboro, N.C., Aug. 13, 1927; s. Henry Alexander and Margaret (Borden) McK.; m. Oriana McArthur, July 19, 1950; children: Arnold Borden Jr., Colin McArthur, Henry Alexander. AB, Duke U., 1950, LLB, 1951; grad. Advanced Mgmt. Program, Harvard U., 1972. Bar: D.C. 1951, N.C. 1966. With Norfolk So. Corp. (formerly So. Ry. System), Norfolk, Va., 1951-2000, from v.p. law to chmn., 1971-92, chmn. exec. com., 1992-2000, ret., 2000. Bd. trustees Chrysler Mus. Art; active Mil. Civilian Liaison Group; bd. dirs. Norfolk Forum, Inc. With U.S. Army, 1946—47. Mem.: ABA, Am. Soc. Corp. Execs., D.C. Bar Assn., N.C. Bar Assn., Rotary, Norfolk German Club, Bonita Bay Club, Cedar Point Club, Met. Club, Chevy Chase Club, Norfolk Yacht and Country Club. Presbyterian. Home: 552 Mowbray Arch Norfolk VA 23507-2130 Office: Norfolk So Corp 3 Commercial Pl Norfolk VA 23510-2108

**MCKINNON, CAROLYN ANN,** child care center director; b. Bangor, Maine; d. Joseph Russell and Muriel Ann (Capen) Johnston; m. James Coolidge McKinnon, July 24, 1967; step-children: Michael, Ronald, Shaun, Jeannine; children: William, John. RN, D.C. Gen. Hosp., Washington. RN, N.Y., Colo., Maine. Nurse D.C. Gen. Hosp., Washington, Onondago Gen. Hosp., Syracuse, NY, Colo. Gen. Hosp., Denver, Bangor Mental Health Inst., Maine; dir. adminstr. A Small World Day Care Ctr., Bangor; ad copy writer Interactive Mktg. Group, Bangor. Spkr. TV and radio programs, 1997. Author: Insanity, Inc., 1996. Mem. PETA, ASCPA, HSUS, NHES, ALDF, IDA, IFAW, PCRM, others. Mem.: Physicians Com. for Responsible Medicine, Internat. Fund for Animal Welfare, In Def. of Animals, Animal Legal Def. Funds, Nat. Humane Edn. Soc., Humane Soc. US, People for Ethical Treatment Animals. Roman Catholic. Avocation: theater and musical organizations. Home: 287 Birch St Bangor ME 04401-4025 Office: A Small World Day Care Ctr 300 Forest Ave Bangor ME 04401-3947 also: Interactive Mktg Group 304 Hancock St Bangor ME 04401-5123

**MC KINNON, CLINTON DAN,** aerospace transportation executive; b. San Bernardino, Calif., Jan. 27, 1934; s. Clinton Dotson and Lucille V. McK.; m. Janice Bernard; children: Holly Jean, Sherri Lynn, Clinton Scott, Lisa Caroline BA, U. Mo., 1956; doctorate (hon.), Nat. U., 1987. Page U.S. Ho. of Reps., 1950-52; reporter, photographer, advt. salesman Sentinel Newspaper, San Diego, 1960-62; owner, pres. KSON Radio, San Diego, 1962-85, KSON-FM, San Diego, 1964-85; pub. La Jolla (Calif.) Light Jour., 1969-73; owner House of Hits (book and music pub.), San Diego, 1972—; co-owner KIll-TV, Corpus Christi, Tex., 1964—, KBMT-TV, Beaumont, Tex., 1976—, KUSI-TV, San Diego, 1992—; chmn. CAB, Washington, 1981-84; with spl. projects CIA, 1985-86; founder, chmn., pres. North Am. Airlines, Jamaica, NY, 1989—2005. Author: Bullseye--One Reactor (aka Bullseye Iraq), 1986, The Ten Second Message, 1994, Words of Honor, 1995, Rescue Pilot, 2002, Safe Air Travel Companion, 2002. Chmn. exec. com. Greater San Diego Billy Graham Crusade, 1976, commr., Nat. Guard and Reserves Commn., 2005-. Served as aviator USNR, 1956—60. Recipient Advt. Man of Year award San Diego Advt. and Sales Club, 1971; Radio Sta. Mgr. of Year award Billboard Mag., 1973; Internat. Pres.'s award Youth for Christ, 1975; Man of Distinction award Mexican-Am. Found., 1976; George Washington Honor medal Freedoms Found., 1976; Headliner of Yr. (govt.), San Diego Press Club, 1985; named to Country Radio Hall of Fame, 2003. Mem. Country Music Assn. (pres. 1977, Pres. award 1980), C. of C. (dir.), Nat. Assn. Broadcasters (bd. dirs. 1970-74), Calif. Broadcasters Assn. (dir.), Navy League (Media Man of Yr. 1980), Wings Club (bd. govs 1995-2003, pres. 2002-2003), San Diego Rotary. Achievements include setting Navy helicopter peacetime rescue record of 62 air/sea rescues, 1958; 1st person to close down fed. govt. regulatory agy., CAB, 1984. Office: 1125-101 Pacific Beach Dr San Diego CA 92109

**MCKINNON, FLOYD WINGFIELD,** textile executive; b. Columbus, Ga., Dec. 1, 1942; s. Malcolm Angus and Sarah C. (Bullock) McK.; m. Barbara Evans Roles, June 18, 1966; children: James Wingfield, Sarah Elizabeth, Robert Kent. AB, Washington and Lee U., 1964. Lic. airplane pilot. Pres. Cotswold Industries, Inc., N.Y.C., 1966—, also bd. dirs.; v.p., corp. sec. Cen. Textiles, Inc., S.C., 1984—, also bd. dirs. S.C. Arbitrator Am. Arbitration Assn., 1983-2001; bd. dirs. Scarsdale Leasing Corp. Pres. Berkley-in-Scarsdale Assn., 1980; admissions rep. Washington and Lee U., 1979-89, 93-99. Mem. Aircraft Owner's and Pilot's Assn., St. Andrews Soc. N.Y., Union League Club N.Y. (bd. govs. 1974-77, 88-91, 97—, sec. 1981-83, chmn. admissions com. 1996, pres. 2005—), Scarsdale Golf Club (bd. govs. 1983-91, pres. 1990-91) (Hartsdale, N.Y.), Bras Coupe Club (exec. com. 1980—) (Maniwaki, Can.). Republican. Episcopalian. Home: 26 Taunton Rd Scarsdale NY 10583-5610 Office: Cotswold Industries 10 E 40th St Rm 3410 New York NY 10016-0367 Business E-Mail: wink@cotswoldindustries.com. E-mail: wink85wm@optonline.net.

**MCKINNON, F(RANCIS) A(RTHUR) RICHARD,** utilities executive; b. Delburne, Alta., Can., Mar. 5, 1933; s. John Donald and Ruth Rebecca (Sundberg) McK.; m. Elma Lorraine Lebsack, June 1, 1957; children: Kenneth Richard, Stephen David, Karen Diane. B. Commerce, U. Alta., 1954; postgrad., Stanford Exec. Program, Stanford U., 1982. With Alta. Gas Trunk Line Co. Ltd., Calgary, 1966-75, treas., 1971-75; dir. fin. TransAlta Utilities Corp. (formerly Calgary Power Ltd.), 1975—, treas., 1976-81, v.p. fin., 1981—, Trans Alta Energy Corp., Trans Alta Corp.; pres. ELM FARMS CONS., INC., Calgary, 1996—. Bd. dirs. AEC Power Ltd. Past bd. dirs. Foothills Gen. Hosp., Calgary. Fellow Inst. Chartered Accts. of Alta.; mem. Can. Inst. Chartered Accts., Fin. Execs. Inst. Can. (past chmn., past pres., bd. dirs. Calgary chpt., v.p.), Fin. Execs. Inst. (bd. dirs.). Clubs: Calgary Petroleum, Canyon Meadows Golf and Country. Office: ELM FARM CONS INC 1412 Windsor St NW Calgary AB Canada T2N 3X3

**MCKINNON, JAMES BUCKNER,** real estate sales executive, writer, researcher; b. Tacoma, Dec. 5, 1916; s. James Mitchell and Rochelle Lenore (Buckner) McK.; m. Mary C. Corbitt, Dec. 1961 (div. June 1963); 1 child, James H.C.; m. Marylyn Adelle Coote, Mar. 12, 1967 (div. May 1977); 1 child, Michelyn; m. Martha Sackmann, June 12, 1977. BA in Internat. Studies, U. Wash., 1983, H.M. Jackson Sch. Police detective Los Angeles, 1946-50; bn. security officer 1st med. bn. 1st Marine div. Fleet Marine Force, 1950-53; owner, operator, mgr., dir. promotional sales The Saucy Dog Drive-In, Venice, Calif., 1953-63; salesman new car sales and leasing Burien Mercury, Seattle, 1963-66; real estate salesman and appraiser various firms Seattle, 1966—; instr., lectr. U.S. Naval Support Activity, Sandpoint, Wash., 1964-74. Mem., lectr. NRC 11-8, Naval Postgrad. Sch., Monterey, Calif., 1975-76; Burien Mercury announcer KOMO TV. Author: (poetry) On the Threshold of a Dream, Vol. III, 1992, Best Poems of the 90's, 1992; contbr. to anthologies: Where Words Haven't Spoken, 1993, Fire From Within, 1994; contbr. articles to various newspapers and mil. jours. Mem. br. advv. com. Wash. State YMCA, Seattle, 1994—, treas., 1986-94, 95, mem. so. dist. fin. bd., 1989-93, 94, 95-96. With USN, 1939-53, PTO, Korea. Recipient Wilmer Culver Meml. award Culver Alumni Fictioneers, Seattle, 1979, Silver Poet award World of Poetry Press, 1986, Golden Poet award, 1992, Best Poet of the 90's award Nat. Libr. of Poetry, 1992, First Place with Editor's Preference award Creative Arts and Scis. Enterprises, 1996; Occidental Coll. scholar, 1935; named to Honorable Order Ky. Cols., 1976; named One of Best New Poets, Am. Poetry Assn. Anthology, 1988; inducted into the Internat. Poetry Hall of Fame, 1996. Mem. Internat. Soc. Authors and Artists (1st place award for 1997 poem), Internat. Platform Assn., U.S. Naval Inst. (life), Internat. Soc. Poets (life), N.W. Writers Conf., Acad. Am. Poets, Ret. Officers

Assn. (life), Mensa, Acad. Am. Poets, KP, Masons. Republican. Home: PO Box 4774 Spanaway WA 98387-4051 *Personal philosophy: To realize one's greatest potential pursue goals that hold the greatest meaning in life.*

**MCKINNON, JOHN D.,** reporter; Fed. budget & econ. reporter Wall St. Jour., Washington, White House reporter. Co-recipient Robert Spiers Benjamin award, Overseas Press Club, 2006. Office: Wall Street Journal Washington Bur Ste 800 1025 Connecticut Ave NW Washington DC 20036 Office Phone: 202-862-9217. E-mail: john.mckinnon@wsj.com.*

**MCKINNON, KARL LUTHER,** museum director; b. Asheboro, N.C., Mar. 31, 1962; s. George F. and Barbara Ann (Johnson) McKinnon; m. Maribeth Bryan, Dec. 9, 1995. BA Biology, U. N.C., Greensboro, 1984. Zookeeper, docent Natural Sci. Ctr., Greensboro, NC, 1981—83; dir., head naturalist Dan Nichols Park Nature Ctr., Salisbury, NC, 1984—85; exec. dir. Rocky Mount Children's Mus., NC, 1985—95; dep. dir. Nat. Sci. Ctr., Greensboro, NC, 1995—2002; exec. dir. Dakota Sci. Ctr., Grand Forks, ND, 2002—03; exec. dir. Imagination Sci. Sci. Mus., Wilson, NC, 2003—. Chmn. fin. com. NC Grassroots Sci. Mus. Collaborative, 2000—02, bd. dirs., 2003—. Mem.: N.C. Mus. Assn., Summit Rotary Club (Greensboro, N.C.) (pres. elect 2002—, Rotarnet chmn. 1998—2000), All Am. Kiwanis Club (Wilson, N.C.) (bd. dirs., 2000—02, Kwwiet Kiwanian 2004, Pres. award 2004), Wilson Rotary Club (bd. dirs.). Office: Imagination Sta Sci Mus 224 E Nash St Wilson NC 27893 Office Phone: 252-291-5113. E-mail: kmckinnon@imaginescience.org.

**MCKINNON, RUSSELL F.,** professional society administrator; b. Springfield, Mass., Feb. 11, 1944; s. John McKinnon and Margret Louise Bates; m. Deborah Oplinger, July 11, 1987; 1 child, John. AB in History, Coll. Holy Cross, 1966; M in Mgmt., George Washington U., 1988. Pres. The Mackinnon Co., Alexandria, Va., 1972—; exec. Nat. Rural Electric Coop. Assn., Arlington, Va., 1994—; pres. Internat. Theos Found., Alexandria, 1998—. Photographer Parade Mag., 1989. Lt. USNR, 1966-72. Mem. Am. Soc. Assn. Execs. (cert.), Assn. Meeting Planners. Avocations: skiing, golf. Office: Nat Rural Electric Coop Assn 4301 Wilson Blvd Arlington VA 22203-1867 E-mail: md1995@erols.com.

**MCKINSEY, DAVID STEPHEN,** infectious diseases specialist; b. Dallas, Oct. 24, 1955; s. John Jerome and Jacqueline (Ronay) McK. BS cum laude, Tulane U., New Orleans, 1977; MD, U. Mo., 1981. Diplomate Am. Bd. Internal Medicine, Am. Bd. Infectious Diseases. Intern, then resident in internal medicine U. Iowa Hosps. and Clinics, Iowa City, 1981-84; fellow in infectious disease U. Tenn., Memphis, 1984-86; co-dir. dept. infectious disease Rsch. Med. Ctr., Kansas City, Mo., 1986—; clin. asst. prof. medicine U. Mo., Kansas City, 1986-90; clin. assoc. prof. medicine U. Kans., Kansas City, 1991—2002, clin. prof. medicine, 2002—; med. dir. Health Midwest Pharmacy, Kansas City, 1999—2002. Recipient Outstanding Young Physician award U. Mo., Columbia, 1999. Fellow ACP, Infectious Diseases Soc. Am. (Clinician of Yr. award 1998); mem. Am. Soc. Microbiology, Soc. Hosp. Epidemiologists Am., Kansas City S.W. Clin. Soc. (pres. 1992). Office: Ste 392 6400 Prospect Ave Kansas City MO 64132-1199

**MCKINZIE, CARL WAYNE,** lawyer; b. Lubbock, Tex., Dec. 3, 1939; s. J. Clyde and Flora (Cates) McK.; m. Rowena Ann Williams; children: Wayne, Clinton, Morgan (dec.). BBA, Tex. Tech U., 1962, MBA, 1963; JD, So. Meth. U., 1966. From assoc. to ptnr. Nossaman, Guthner, Knox & Elliot, L.A., 1966-80; prin. Riordan & McKinzie, L.A., 1980—2003; ptnr. Bingham McCutchen (merged with Riordan & McKinzie), 2003—. Bd. dirs., exec. com., Saint John's Health Ctr., Santa Monica, Calif., 2001—, vice chair, 2002-2003, chair, 2003-. Contbr. articles to law jours. Trustee Jaquish Found., 2000-04, Raymond Marshall Found., 1993-2003; bd. visitors Sch. Law So. Meth. U., Dallas, 1979-82, 90—, bd. dirs., 1970-73, 84-89, chmn. exec. com., 1996-98; bd. visitors Ariz State U. Coll. Law, 1990-98; bd. dirs. Riordan Found., 1992—, Rx for Reading, 1992—, The Welk Group, 2004—; bd. dirs., exec. com. Libr. Found. LA, 2002—, vice chair, 2003-04; bd. dirs., exec. coun. Pub. Counsel, 1996-99, Calif. Cmty. Found., 1994-98; bd. advisors Coll Law, U. Wyo., 1987-91, 2001—. Recipient disting. alumni award, So. Meth. U., Dallas, 1994. Mem. ABA (chmn. current devel. subcom., com. tax problems 1978-80), Nat. Assn. Real Estate Investment Trusts (bd. govs. 1986-89), Calif. Bar Assn., Los Angeles County Bar Assn., Jonathan Club, City Club on Bunker Hill, L.A. Country Club. Republican. Home: 527 21st Pl Santa Monica CA 90402-3047 Office: Bingham McCutchen 44th Fl 355 S Grand Ave Los Angeles CA 90071-3106 Office Phone: 213-229-8484. Business E-Mail: carl.mckinzie@bingham.com.

**MCKINZIE, JAMES S.,** librarian; b. Sweetwater, Tex., Dec. 15, 1951; s. John O. and Laverne McKinzie; m. Anna B. Baker; children: Amy, Jane, Jonathan, William. BA in History, Tex. A&M U., 1975; MA in History, E. Carolina U., Greenville, NC, 1982; MLS, Vanderbilt U., 1988. Social sci. libr. Dickinson Coll., Carlisle, Pa., 1988—; libr. dir. Catawa Coll., Salisbury, NC, 2006—. Contbr. articles and book revs. to profl. jours. Presbyterian.

**MCKIRAHAN, RICHARD DUNCAN,** classics and philosophy educator; b. Berkeley, Calif., July 27, 1945; s. Richard Duncan and Helen Marion (Hixson) McK.; m. Voula Tsouna, June 3, 1961; 1 child, Helen Hamilton. AB, U. Calif., Berkeley, 1966; BA, U. Oxford, Eng., 1969; MA, Oxford U., Eng., 1979; PhD, Harvard U., 1973. Teaching fellow, tutor Harvard U., Cambridge, Mass., 1971-73; asst. prof. classics and philosophy Pomona Coll., Claremont, Calif., 1973-79, assoc. prof., 1979-87, E.C. Norton prof. classics and philosophy, 1987—, chair dept. classics, 1992—. Author: Socrates and Plato, A Comprehensive Bibliography, 1958-1973, 1978, Plato's Meno, 1986, Principles and Proofs: Aristotle's Theory of Demonstrative Science, 1992, Philosophy Before Socrates, 1994, A Presocratics Reader, 1996, Cicero, De Natura Deorum I, 1997, Simplicius, On Aristotle's Physics, book 8, chpts. 6-10, 2001; contbr. articles on Greek philosophy, math. and scis. Marshall Aid Commemoration Commn. scholar, U. Oxford, 1966-69, Fulbright Sr. scholar, 1999, Overseas Vis. scholar St. John's Coll., Cambridge, 1999; Woodrow Wilson Found. fellow, 1966-67; NEH grantee, 1975, 85, 90, 98, 2004. Mem. Am. Philol. Assn., Soc. Ancient Greek Philosophy, Phi Beta Kappa. Office: Pomona Coll Dept Classics 140 W 6th St Claremont CA 91711-4301 Business E-Mail: rmckirahan@pomona.edu.

**MCKISSOCK, DAVID LEE,** retired manufacturing company executive; b. Boston, Mar. 27, 1933; s. Allan and Elizabeth (Lee) McK.; m. Diana Parish, Sept. 1, 1956; children: David Lee Jr., Christopher Lee. BA, Middlebury Coll., 1955. Salesman Am. Flange and Mfg. Co., N.Y.C., 1957-62, asst. to v.p. sales Linden, N.J., 1962-64, salesman rip cap closures, 1964-73, v.p. rip cap closures, 1973-89, also bd. dirs. With USNR, 1955-57. Mem. Rumson Country Club, Seabright Lawn Tennis and Cricket Club. Republican. Unitarian Universalist. Avocations: tennis, golf, platform tennis. Home: 20 Hance Rd Fair Haven NJ 07704-3210

**MCKITRICK, JAMES THOMAS,** retired retail executive; b. Cin., Sept. 14, 1945; s. Harry J. and L. May (Buck) McK.; m. Margaret J. Haynes, Sept. 6, 1975; children: Angela, Greg, Randal, Paul, Sheri, Richard, Mike. Student, Salem Coll., 1963-64. Dir. mdse. K Mart Corp., Troy, Mich., 1965-84; exec. v.p., gen. mgr. T.G. & Y. Stores, Oklahoma City, 1984-86, exec. v.p. merchandising and mktg., 1986; pres., chief exec. officer Warehouse Club, Skokie, Ill., 1986-87; pres., chief operating officer G.C. Murphy Co. subs. Ames, Rocky Hill, Conn., 1987-89; chmn. Zayre Discount, Rocky Hill, 1988-89; pres. & CEO Builders Emporium, Irvine, Calif., 1989-92, Quality Stores Inc. (formerly Central Tractor Farm & Country), Muskegon, Mich., 1992—2000. Republican. Methodist. Office: Quality Stores Inc PO Box 1002 Muskegon MI 49443-1002

**MCKITTRICK, WILLIAM WOOD,** lawyer; b. Mt. Carmel, Ill., July 11, 1915; s. Lafe E. and Mary Lynn (Wood) McK.; m. Carolyn Lenne Davis, Dec. 19, 1942; children: Lynn McKittrick Pond, Bruce W. AB, DePauw U., 1936; JD, Northwestern U., 1939. Bar: Ill. Assoc. Pope & Ballard, Chgo., 1939-48,

ptnr., 1948-52; atty. Office Gen. Counsel, Panama C.Z., 1942; ptnr. Vedder, Price, Kaufman & Kammholz, Chgo., 1952-95; lectr. on labor law Northwestern U. Sch. Law, Chgo., 1961-62. Case note editor, mem. editorial bd. Ill. Law Rev., 1938-39. Life trustee Orchestral Assn. of Chgo. Symphony Orch., 1980—, Chgo. Symphony Musicians Pension Trust, 1987-98; bd. dirs. Am. Symphony Orch. League, 1986-93, mem. exec. com., 1988-91; trustee Newberry Libr., Chgo., 1984-98, life trustee, 1998—, exec. com., 1989-98; vice chmn. exec. bd. Libr. Coun., Northwestern U., 1984-96; chmn. Friends of Ryerson & Burnham Librs., Art Inst. Chgo., 1988-90, mem. com. on librs., 1982—. Lt. USNR, 1943-45, PTO. Recipient Svc. award Northwestern U., 1968. Mem. ABA, Ill. Bar Assn., Chgo. Bar Assn. (lectr. various programs 1940-70, bd. mgrs. 1961-63), Lawyers Club of Chgo., Univ. Club (Chgo.), Michigan Shores Club, Skokie Country Club, Caxton Club of Chgo. (v.p. 1982-83, pres. 1983-85). Home: 232 Essex Rd Kenilworth IL 60043-1122

**MCKNIGHT, CARL PHILLIP,** psychologist; b. Bogota, Colombia, Jan. 20, 1969; (parents Am. citizens); s. Elwin D. and Elsa V. McKnight; m. Susan A. Kasparrow, July 18, 1998; 1 child, Angela. BS, Tex. A&M U., 1991; MA, Stephen F. Austin State U., 1995; PsyD, Pepperdine U., 2000. Lic. psychologist Calif. Bd. Psychology. Pediatric psychologist Children's Hosp. Orange (Calif.) County, 2001—06; project behavioral psychologist Med. Ctr. U. Calif., Irvine, 2003—06; clin. psychologist II L.A. County Dept. Mental Health, 2006—. Cons. St. Joseph's Hosp., Orange, 2005—06. Contbr. columns in mags. Mem. childhood obesity steering com. Children and Families Commn. Orange County, Irvine, Calif., 2002—04. Pediatric and Clin. Child Psychology fellow, Children's Hosp. L.A. and U. So. Calif. Sch. of Medicine, 1999—2001. Mem.: APA, Soc. Pediatric Psychology. Achievements include development of pilot psychological screening and treatment program for morbidly obese children and adolescents. Office: Los Angeles County DMH 921 E Compton Blvd Compton CA 90221-1683 Office Phone: 714-532-8482. Personal E-mail: 15225@msn.com.

**MCKNIGHT, FREDERICK L.,** lawyer; b. Kansas City, Mo., Nov. 28, 1947; s. Harry A. and Donna Ruth (Breining) McK.; m. Linda Jean McKnight, June 20, 1970; children: Justin Teague, Cristin Ruth. AB honors, Princeton U., 1969; JD, U. Calif., Berkeley, 1972. Bar: Calif. 1973, N.Y. 1973. Regional mng. ptnr. Jones Day Reavis & Pogue, LA, 1997; now ptnr.-in-charge LA office Jones Day. Adv. com. Jones, Day, Reavis & Pogue, Cleve. Bd. dirs. Econ. Devel. Corp., L.A., 1992—, St. Vincent Med. Ctr. Found., L.A., 1994—. Fellow Am. Coll. of Trial Lawyers; mem. Assn. Bus. Trial Lawyers. Office: Jones Day 555 S Flower St # 50 Los Angeles CA 90071-2300 Office Phone: 213-243-2777. Office Fax: 213-243-2539. Business E-Mail: fmcknight@jonesday.com.

**MCKNIGHT, GREGORY RICHARD,** research and development director; b. Sparta, NC, Feb. 18, 1968; s. James Richard and Carol Norman McknIght; life ptnr. Steven B. McGinnis, 1996. BA, Wake Forest U., Winston-Salem, NC, 1990. Rsch. analyst Wake Forest U. Health Scis., Winston-Salem, 1997—2000, dir. prospect rsch./mgmt., 2000—. Mem.: Carolina's Assn. Profl. Rschrs. for Advancement (dir., treas. 2002—). Moravian. Avocations: travel, motorcycling, bicycling. Office: Wake Forest U Health Scis Medical Center Blvd Winston Salem NC 27157-1021 Home: 225 Banner Ave Winston Salem NC 27127

**MCKNIGHT, JOSEPH WEBB,** lawyer, educator, historian; b. San Angelo, Tex., Feb. 17, 1925; s. John Banning and Helen Katherine (Webb) McK.; m. Julia Ann Dyer, July 20, 1957 (dec. Jan. 1972); children: John Banton, Joseph Adair; m. Mildred Katherine Virginia Payne. Aug. 9, 1975 BA, U. Tex., Austin, 1947; Oxford U. Eng., 1949, BCL, 1950, MA, 1954; LLM, Columbia U., N.Y.C., 1959. Bar: Tex. 1951, U.S. Ct. Appeals (5th cir.) 1982. Assoc. Cravath, Swaine & Moore, N.Y.C., 1951-55; asst. prof. So. Meth. U., Dallas, 1955-57, assoc. prof., 1957-63, prof. law, 1963—, acad. dean, 1977-80, Larry and Jane Harlan faculty fellow, 1991—. Vis. prof. various univs. Gen. editor Creditors' Rights in Texas, 1963, History of the Texas Supreme Court Project, 1998—; author: (with William A. Reppy, Jr.) Texas Matrimonial Property Law, 1983, 9th edit. 2006; contbr. articles to profl. jours. Pres., Tex. Old Missions and Forts Restoration Assn., 1977-79, 99-2001; bd. dirs. San Jacinto Mus. History Assn., 1976-99; mem. exec. coun. Tex. State Hist. Assn., 1988-91, fellow, 2004; bd. trustees Tex. Supreme Ct. His. Soc., 1990—; dir. Tex. Supreme Ct. Project, 1998-. Served to lt. USNR, 1942-47 Rhodes scholar, 1947-50; James Kent fellow Columbia Law Sch., 1958-59; Academico, Acad. Mexicana de Derecho Internat., 1988, Hall of Legends, State Bar of Texas Fam. Law Sec., 1997. Fellow, Soc. for Advanced Legal Studies (London), 1998; mem. ABA, State Bar Tex., Dallas Bar Assn., Tex. Bar Found. (v.p. 1959), Nat. Legal Aid and Defenders Assn. (bd. dirs. 1963-66), Selden Soc., Am. Soc. Legal History (v.p. 1967-68, bd. dirs. 1967-75), Inst. Texan Cultures (exec. bd. 1990-95), Oxford and Cambridge Club (London), Sigma Chi. Democrat. Episcopalian. Office: So Meth U Law Sch 3315 Daniel Ave Dallas TX 75275-0116 Office Phone: 214-768-2591, 214-768-3851. E-mail: jmcknigh@smu.edu.

**MCKNIGHT, KELLY MARIE,** psychologist; b. Greensburg, Pa., July 20, 1974; d. Nora Darlene and Jesse Wilson Adams (Stepfather); m. Shawn Edward McKnight, Aug. 8, 1998. BA, N.C. State U., 1996; MEd, Coll. of William and Mary, 1997, Ednl. Specialist, 1999. Accounts receivables clk. Penn Compression Moulding, Garner, NC, 1992—98; sch. psychologist Cumberland County Schs., Fayetteville, NC, 1998—. Mem.: NASP. Avocations: reading, travel. Office: Cumberland County Schs PO Box 2357 Fayetteville NC 28302 Office Phone: 910-678-2729.

**MCKNIGHT, MARK L.,** biology professor, researcher; b. Covina, Calif., Oct. 13, 1956; s. Donald Keith McKnight and Betty Eleanor McKnight (nee Temby). BS, Calif. State Poly. U., Pomona, 1978, MS, 2981; PhD, U. Ill., Urbana-Champaign, 1989. Fellow U. Calif., Davis, 1990—96; adj. prof. Am. River Coll., Carmichael, Calif., 1997—2002; asst. prof. Mo. State U., Springfield, 2002—. Contbr. articles to profl. jours. Mem.: Soc. Systematic Biologists (assoc.), Mo. Herpetological Assn. (assoc.), Soc. Study of Evolution (assoc.), Ctrl. Plains Soc. Mammalogists (life), Am. Soc. Mammalogists (life). Office: Mo State Univ 901 S National Ave Springfield MO 65897 Office Phone: 417-836-6289. E-mail: markmcknight@missouristate.edu.

**MCKNIGHT, MICHELYNN,** librarian; b. Monmouth, Ill., May 9, 1947; d. Roger Glenn and Jane Eleanor (Morgan) Smith; m. Curtis C. McKnight, Nov. 29, 1968. BA in Music Edn., Western Ill. U., 1969; M. Music, U. Ill., 1971, M.S. in Libr. and Info. Sci., 1981, PhD in Info. Sci., U. North Tex., 2004; cert. med. librarian. Tchr. band and music Fairmount (Ill.) Pub. Schs., 1970-72; dir. band, orch. Urbana (Ill.) Pub. Schs., 1972-75; orch. dir., tchr. music Champaign (Ill.) Pub. Schs., 1975-79; tchr. music, instrumental music Univ. High Sch., Urbana, Ill., 1979-81; adult svcs. librarian Shawnee (Okla.) Pub. Library, 1981-83; dir. health scis. library Norman (Okla.) Regional Hosp., 1983—2004; chmn. Greater Oklahoma City Area Health Scis. Library Consortium, 1984-85, asst. prof. La. State U. Sch. Libr. Info. Scis., Baton Rouge, 2004—, mem. Nat. Libr. Medicine Biomed. Libr. and Info. Rev. Com., 2001-05. Am. Soc. Info. Sci., Acad. Health Info. Profls. (disting.), Med. Libr. Assn. (bd. dirs. 2002-05), Beta Phi Mu, Mu Phi Epsilon. Democrat. Home: 2208 Whiteoak Cir Norman OK 73071-1029 Office: La State U 269 Coates Hall Baton Rouge LA 70808

**MCKNIGHT, PATRICIA GAYLE,** musician, artist, writer, educator; b. Rochester, Minn., Aug. 9, 1935; d. William Robert and Maxine Matilda (Hutchings) McK.; m. James Russell Grittner, Nov. 24, 1962; children: Leah Kristin, Rachel Anne. BS in Music, U. Wis., Superior, 1982, MA in Art, 1990, MA in Art History, 1993; postgrad. in Musicology, U. Iowa, 1982—83. Asst. MS editor Am. Acad. Ophthalmology and Otolaryngology, Rochester, Minn., 1958-63. Musician U. Iowa Symphony Orch., U. Iowa Opera Orch., U. of Iowa Small Ensembles, U. Wis. Superior Symphony Orch., Rochester Symphony Orch. Exhibited in group shows including Kruk Gallery, Rochester Cmty. Coll., Duluth Art Inst. Biennial, 1988, 90, Port Wing (Wis.) Gallery; author: Zenith City Arts newspaper. Mem. historic preservation com. City of Superior, 1996—. Avocations: playing cello, viola da gamba. Home: 2325 Hughitt Ave Superior WI 54880-4920

**MCKNIGHT, ROBERT B., JR.,** sporting goods manufacturing executive; BS, Univ. So. Calif. Co-founder, bd. dir. Quicksilver Inc., Huntington Beach, Calif., 1976—, pres., 1979—91, chmn., CEO, 1991—. Office: Quicksilver Inc 15202 Graham St Huntington Beach CA 92649*

**MCKNIGHT, STEVEN LANIER,** molecular biologist; b. El Paso, Tex., Aug. 27, 1949; s. Frank Gillespie and Sara Elise (Stevens) McK.; m. Jacquelynn Ann Zimmer, Sept. 16, 1978; children: Nell, Grace, Frances, John Stevens. BA summa cum laude, U. Tex., 1974; PhD, U.Va., 1977. Fellow U. Va., 1975—76; postdoctoral fellow Carnegie Instn. Washington, Balt. 1977—80, staff assoc., 1980—81, mem. staff, 1984-92; co-founder, dir., dir. rsch. Tularik Inc., San Francisco, 1992—; with U. Tex. Southwestern Med. Ctr., Dallas, 1996—, prof., chmn. biochemistry dept., 2000—, disting. chair Basic Biomed. Rsch. Dallas, Sam. G. Winstead and F. Andrew Bell disting. chair biochemistry. Prof., chmn. dept. biochemistry U. Tex. Southwestern Med. Ctr., 1995—; hon. prof. Johns Hopkins U., scientific rev. bd. Howard Hughes Med. Inst., 1997—; trustee Carnegie Inst., Washington, 2000. Mem. editl. bd. numerous peer-reviewed jours.; contbr. articles to jours. in field. With U.S. Army, 1969-71, Vietnam. Decorated ARCOM medal; recipient Eli Lilly award Am. Soc. Microbiology, 1987, Newcomb-Cleveland award, AAAS, 1989, NAS Molecular Biology award Nat. Acad. Sci., 1991, Pioneer award, NIH, 2004. Fellow Carnegie Inst. Washington (hon.), Am. Soc. Microbiology (hon.); mem. NAS (Monsanto award 1991), Am. Acad. Arts and Scis., Am. Soc. for Biochemistry and Molecular Biology, Am. Chem. Soc., Am. Soc. for Cell Biology, Japanese Biochem. Soc. (hon.), Inst. Medicine. Achievements include research in leading to the discovery of genes that control the body's internal clock and regulate processes such as sleep, wakefulness and hunger. Home: 3717 Euclid Ave Dallas TX 75205-3161 Office: U Tex Southwestern Med Ctr Dept Biochemistry 5323 Harry Hines Blvd Dallas TX 75390-7208 also: Tularik Inc Two Corp Dr South San Francisco CA 94080 Office Phone: 214-648-9152. Business E-Mail: steven.mcknight@utsouthwestern.edu.*

**MCKNIGHT, TERRANCE THALES,** music educator; s. Edward and Katie Mae McKnight; m. Chanda Leigh Bailey, May 31, 2003. BA in liberal arts, Morehouse Coll., 1990; MA in piano pedagogy, Ga. State U., 1998. Piano instr. Neighborhood Music Sch., Atlanta, 1994—99; adj. prof. of music Morehouse Coll., Atlanta, 1998—; resident prodr. Nat. Pub. Radio, Washington, 1999—2000; prodr./announcer Ga. Pub. Broadcasting, Atlanta, 2000—; music prodr. Ga. Pub. Radio, Atlanta, 2000—. Cons. Nat. Pub. Radio, Washington, 2000—01. Prodr.: (radio feature) Singing in the Oral Tradition (Best Use of Sound - NABJ, 2000), (radio program) Musically Reclined, Studio GPR. Scholar, Morehouse Coll., 1987-1990. Office: Georgia Pub Broadcasting 260 14th St Atlanta GA 30318 Personal E-mail: tmcknight@gpb.org.

**MCKNIGHT, THOMAS FREDERICK,** artist; b. Lawrence, Kans., Jan. 13, 1941; m. Renate Hödl. BA cum laude, Wesleyan U., Middletown, Conn., 1963; postgrad., Columbia U., 1963-64. One-man shows Basel (Switzerland) Art Fair, 1975-77, Tomic Galerie, Dusseldorf, Germany, 1976, Hartmann Gallery, Munich, 1977, Newport (R.I.) Art Assn., 1981, Kobe (Japan) Mcpl. Art Mus., 1993; R² Gallery, N.Y.C., 2002; exhibited in group shows Ljubljana, Yugoslavia, 1981, Tokyo, 1989, Davison Art Ctr., Wesleyan U., 1988, 98, numerous others; represented in permanent collections Davison Art Ctr., N.Y. State Mus., Albany, Smithsonian Instn., Washington, Met. Mus. Art, N.Y.C.; represented in Art in Embassies program; commns. include poster and print U.S. Constn. Bicentennial, 1989, prints Am.'s Cup, 1992, paintings and prints Urban Fair, Kobe, Japan, 1991, White House Christmas card, 1994, 95, 96; author: Thomas McKnight: Voyage to Arcadia, 1993, Thomas McKnight's Arcadia, 2006. Recipient Disting. Alumni award Wesleyan U., 1998. Office Phone: 860-618-5441. Personal E-mail: info@thomasmcknight.com.

**MCKOWEN, DOROTHY KEETON,** librarian, educator; b. Bonne Terre, Mo., Oct. 5, 1948; d. John Richard and Dorothy (Spoonhour) Keeton; m. Paul Edwin McKowen, Dec. 19, 1970; children: Richard James, Mark David. BS, Pacific Christian Coll., 1970; MLS, U. So. Calif., 1973; MA in English, Purdue U., 1985, PhD, 2003. Libr.-specialist Doheny Libr., U. So. Calif., L.A., 1973-74; asst. libr. Pacific Christian Coll., 1974-78; serials cataloger Purdue U. Librs., 1978-88; head children's and young adult svcs. Kokomo-Howard County Pub. Libr., Ind., 1988-89, coord. children's and tech. svcs. Ind., 1989-91; cataloger, network libr. Ind. Coop. Libr. Svcs. Authority, 1991-2001. Mem. adj. faculty Ivy Tech. C.C. of Ind., 2001—; lectr. Purdue U., 2003—. Mem. ALA, MLA, Soc. Early Americanists, Assn. for Libr. Collections and Tech. Svcs. (bd. dirs. 1986-90, 95-96, vice chair, chair-elect coun. of regional groups 1986-88, chair 1988-90, conf. program com. 1986-88, internat. rels. com. 1986-88, micropub. com. 1986-87, subject analysis com., membership com. 1988-90, planning and rsch. com. 1988-90, chair program initiatives com. 1991-93, orgn. and bylaws com. 1991-92, 99-2001), Network OCLC Svc. Mgrs. (MARC Task Force 2000-01), Ind. Coun. Libr. Automation (bibliog. stds. task force), Ind. Libr. Fedn. (chair tech. svcs. divsn. 1984-85), Ohio Valley Group Tech. Svcs. Libr. (chmn. 1985-86). Republican. Home: 7625 Summit Ln Lafayette IN 47905-9729 E-mail: mckowens2@yahoo.com.

**MCKOWN, CHARLES HENRY,** dean; b. Huntington, W.Va., Dec. 29, 1934; BS, W.Va. U., 1956; MD, Med. Coll. Va., 1960. Intern Med. Coll. Va., 1961; resident in radiology McGuire VA Hosp., 1961—62; fellow NIH, 1964—67; prof. radiology, chmn. dept. radiology Marshall U., Huntington, W.Va., 1975—88, v.p. health scis., dean Sch. Medicine, 1989—. Office: Marshall U Joan C Edwards Sch Medicine Ste 3400 1600 Medical Center Dr Huntington WV 25701 3655

**MC KOY, BASIL VINCENT CHARLES,** theoretical chemist, educator; b. Trinidad, W.I., Mar. 25, 1938; came to U.S., 1960, naturalized, 1973; s. Allan Cecil and Doris Augusta McK.; m. Anne Ellen Shannon, Mar. 18, 1967; 1 son, Christopher Allan. B.Chem. Eng., N.S. Tech. U., 1960; PhD in Chemistry (Univ. fellow), Yale U., 1964. Instr. chemistry Calif. Inst. Tech., 1964-66, asst. prof. chemistry, 1966-69, assoc. prof., 1969-75, prof. theoretical chemistry, 1975—, chmn. of faculty, 1985-87. Cons. Lawrence Livermore Lab., U. Calif., Livermore, 1974—, Inst. Def. Analysis, 1984—; vis. prof. Max Planck Inst., Munich, Ger., 1976—, U. Paris, 1968—, U. Campinas, Brazil, 1976—; lectr. Nobel Symposium, Goteborg, Sweden, 1979. Contbr. articles to Jour. Physics, London, chem. Physics Letters, Phys. Rev., Jour. Chem. Physics; bd. editors; Chem. Physics Jour., 1977-79, mem. adv. editorial bd., 1992—; co-editor: Electron-Molecule and Photon-Molecule Collisions, 1979, 83, Swarm Studies and Inelastic Electron-Molecule Collisions, 1986; co-author: Electron-Molecule Collisions and Photoionization Processes, 1982. Recipient medal Gov.-Gen. Can., 1960; Alfred P. Sloan Found. fellow, 1969-73; Guggenheim fellow, 1973-74 Fellow Am. Phys. Soc. Home: 3855 Keswick Rd La Canada Flintridge CA 91011-3945 Office: Calif Inst Tech Divsn Chemistry Pasadena CA 91125-0001 Office Phone: 626-395-6545. Business E-Mail: mckoy@caltech.edu.

**MCKUSICK, VICTOR ALMON,** geneticist, educator, physician; b. Parkman, Maine, Oct. 21, 1921; s. Carroll L. and Ethel M. (Buzzell) McK.; m. Anne Bishop, June 11, 1949; children: Carol Anne, Kenneth Andrew, Victor Wayne. Student, Tufts Coll., 1940-43; MD, Johns Hopkins U., 1946; DSc (hon.), N.Y. Med. Coll., 1974; MD (hon.), Liverpool U., 1976; DSc (hon.), U. Maine, 1978, Tufts U., 1978; U. Rochester, 1979, MemI. U., Nfld., 1979; DMCh (hon.), U. Helsinki, 1981; D Med. Sci. (hon.), Med. U. S.C., 1979; MD (hon.), Edinburgh U., 1984; DSc (hon.), Aberdeen U., 1988, Med. Coll. Ohio, 1988, Bates Coll., 1989; PhD (hon.), Tel Aviv U., 1989; MD (hon.), Zurich U., Switzerland, 1990; DSc (hon.), Colby Coll., 1991, U. Chgo., 1991, Mt. Sinai Sch. Medicine, 1992; DSc (hon.), Med. Coll. Wis., 1998, Rock-

efeller U., 2002. Diplomate Am. Bd. Internal Medicine. Tng. in clin. medicine, lab. rsch. Johns Hopkins U./USPHS, 1946-52; instr. medicine Johns Hopkins Sch. Medicine, 1951-54, asst. prof., 1954-57, assoc. prof., 1957-60, chief divsn. med. genetics, dept. medicine, 1957-73, prof. medicine, 1960-85, prof. epidemiology, biology, 1969-78, William Osler prof. medicine, 1978-85, chmn. dept. medicine, 1973-85; physician-in-chief Johns Hopkins Hosp., 1973-85, Univ. prof. medical genetics, 1985—, chief div. med. genetics, 1957-73, 85-89. Mem. rsch. adv. com. Nat. Found., 1959—78; mem. adv. bd. Howard Hughes Med. Inst., 1967—83; com. mapping and sequencing of human genome Nat. Acad. Sci., 1986-88; pres. Internat. Med. Congress, Ltd., 1972—78; mem. Nat. Adv. Rsch. Resources Coun., 1970—74; mem. bd. sci. advisors Roche Inst. Molecular Biology, 1967—71; trustee Jackson Lab., 1979—; founding mem. Am. Bd. Med. Genetics, 1979—82; pres. 8th Internat. Conf. Human Genetics, Washington, 1991; mem. human genome adv. com. NIH, 1988—92, NIH/DOE work group on ethical, legal and societal implications of human genome project, 1990—95; co-chmn. Centennial of Johns Hopkins Hosp., 1989—90; co-founder, co-dir. ann. short course in med. and exptl. mammalian genetics, Bar Harbor, Maine, 1960—, European Sch. Med. Genetics Sestri Levante and Bertinoro, 1988—; chmn. com. on DNA tech. in forensic sci. NRC/NAS, 1989—92, adv. update com., 1993—96; mem. sci. adv. bd. Celera Genomics, 1998—; founding fellow Am. Coll. Med. Genetics. Author: Heritable Disorders of Connective Tissue, 1956, 60, 66, 72, 93, Cardiovascular Sound in Health and Disease, 1958, Medical Genetics 1958-60, 1961, Human Genetics, 1964, 69, On the X Chromosome of Man, 1964, Mendelian Inheritance in Man, 1966, 68, 71, 75, 78, 83, 86, 88, 90, 92, 94, 98, Medical Genetics Self-Instruction Guide, 1993, (with others) Osler's Textbook Revisited, 1967, Genetics of Hand Malformations, 1978, Medical Genetic Studies of the Amish, 1978, A Model of its Kind, 1989, Osler's Legacy, 1990, A Century of Biomedical Science at Johns Hopkins, 1993; author, editor: Online Mendelian Inheritance in Man, 1985—; editor-in-chief Medicine jour., 1985—; founding co-editor-in-chief Genomics jour. 1987—; editor med. textbook. Named hon. citizen of Genoa, 1997; named to Internat. Pediat. Hall of Fame, 1987; recipient Disting. Achievement award, Modern Medicine, 1965, John Phillips award, ACP, 1972, Silver medal, U. Helsinki, 1974, Gairdner Internat. award, 1977, Premio Internazionale Sanremo per le Ricerche Genetiche, 1983, Col. Saunders award, March of Dimes, 1988, Disting. Alumnus award, Johns Hopkins U., 1983, Alumnus Svc. award, Johns Hopkins Med. Sch., 1989, Passano award, 1989, Disting. Svc. award, Miami Biotech. Winter Symposium, 1991, Frank Bradway Rogers Info. Advancement award, Med. Libr. Assn., 1991, Silver Columbus medal, Comune di Genova, 1992, Maine prize (with twin), 1993, Mendel medal, Villanova U., 1995, Big "M" award, Maine State Soc. Washington, D.C., 1995, Coriell medal, Coriell Inst., Camden, N.J., 1997, Lasker award for lifetime achievement in med. sci., 1997, City of Medicine award, Durham, N.C., 1997, James P. McGovern Compleat Physician award, 2000, Albert Lasker award for Special Achievement in Medicine, Lasker Found., 2000, Nat. medal of sci., 2002, Rsch. Achievement award, Am. Heart Assn., 2002. Fellow AAAS (chair med. scis. sect. 1991), Am. Acad. Orthopedic Surgeons (hon.), Royal Coll. Physicians (London), Hastings Ctr., Am. Coll. Med. Genetics (hon.); mem. Nat. Acad. Sci. (James Murray Luck award 1982), Am. Philos. Soc. (v.p. 1996—), Benjamin Franklin medal for disting. achievement in scis. 1996), Am. Soc. Human Genetics (pres. 1975, Wm. A. Allan award 1977), Assn. Am. Physicians (Kober medal 1990), Am. Soc. Clin. Investigation (v.p. 1967), Human Genome Orgn. (founder pres. 1988-89), Am. Acad. Arts and Sci., Little People of Am. (hon. life), Acad. Nat. Médecine (France; corr.), Phi Beta Kappa, Alpha Omega Alpha, Johns Hopkins Club, West Hamilton St. Club, St. Andrew's Soc. Balt. Presbyterian (elder). Office: Johns Hopkins Hosp Inst Genetic Medicine-Blalock 1007 600 N Wolfe St Baltimore MD 21287-4922 Home: 1055 W Joppa Rd Unit 528 Towson MD 21204-3747*

**MCKUSICK, VINCENT LEE,** retired judge, arbitrator, lawyer, mediator; b. Parkman, Maine, Oct. 21, 1921; s. Carroll Lee and Ethel (Buzzell) McK.; m. Nancy Elizabeth Green, June 23, 1951; children: Carroll McKusick Liscord, James Emory, Katherine McKusick Ralston, Anne Elizabeth. AB, Bates Coll., 1943; SB, SM, MIT, 1947; LLB, Harvard U., 1950; LLD, Colby Coll., 1976, Nasson Coll., 1978, Bates Coll., 1979, Bowdoin Coll., 1979, Suffolk U., 1983; LHD, U. So. Maine, 1978, Thomas Coll., 1981. Bar: Maine 1952. Law clk. to Chief Judge Learned Hand, 1950-51; to Justice Felix Frankfurter, 1951-52; partner Pierce, Atwood, Scribner, Allen & McKusick and predecessors, Portland, Maine, 1953-77; chief justice Maine Supreme Jud. Ct., 1977-92; of counsel to Pierce Atwood (formerly Pierce, Atwood, Scribner, Allen, Smith, & Lancaster), Portland, Maine, 1992—. Mem. adv. com. rules civil procedure Maine Supreme Jud. Ct., 1957-59, chmn., 1966-75, commr. uniform state laws, 1968-76, sec. nat. conf., 1975-77; mem. Conf. Chief Justices, 1977-92, bd. dirs., 1980-82, 91-92, pres.-elect, 1989-90, pres., 1990-91, standing com. past pres., 1992—; dir. Nat. Ctr. for State Cts., 1988-89, chmn.-elect, 1989-90, chmn., 1990-91; spl. master U.S. Supreme Ct. Conn. v. N.H., 1992-93, La. v. Miss., 1994-96, Kans. v. Nebr., 1999-2003; spl. master Mass. S.J.C. Liquidation Am. Mutual Liability Ins. Co., 1995-96; leader Am. League to Repub. of China, 1983, USSR, 1988, U.S. State Dept. Rule of Law Del. to Republic of Ga., 1992; mem. permanent com. Oliver Wendell Holmes Devise, 1993-2001. Author: Patent Policy of Educational Institutions, 1947, (with Richard H. Field) Maine Civil Practice, 1959, supplements, 1962, 67, (with Richard H. Field and L. Kinvin Wroth) 2d edit., 1970, supplements, 1972, 74, 77; also articles in legal publs. Trustee emeritus Bates Coll.; mem. adv. com. on pvt. internat. law U.S. State Dept., 1980-85, Fed.-State Jurisdiction com., Jud. Conf. of U.S., 1987-89. With AUS, 1943-46. Recipient The Maine prize U. Maine Sys., 1993, Benjamin E. Mays award Bates Coll., 1994, Big M award Maine State Soc. Washington, 1995, Paul C. Reardon award Nat. Ctr. for State Ctrs., 1999. Fellow Am. Bar Found. (bd. dirs. 1977-87), Am. Philos. Soc. (coun. 1990-96, 97-02, v.p. 2002—); mem. ABA (chmn. fed. rules com. 1966-71, bd. editors jour. 1971-80, chmn. 1976-77, mem. study group to China 1978, ho. dels. 1983-87, coun. sr. lawyers divsn. 1997-01), Maine Bar Assn., Cumberland County Bar Assn., Am. Arbitration Assn. (bd. dirs. 1994—), Am. Judicature Soc. (dir. 1976-78, 92-98), Am. Law Inst. (coun. 1968—), Maine Jud. Coun. (chmn. 1977-92), Inst. Jud. Administrn., Supreme Ct. Hist. Soc. (trustee 1994—), Rotary Club (hon., past pres. Portland club), Phi Beta Kappa, Sigma Xi, Tau Beta Pi. Republican. Unitarian Universalist. Home: 1152 Shore Rd Cape Elizabeth ME 04107-2115 Office: 1 Monument Sq Portland ME 04101-1110 Office Phone: 207-791-1100. Personal E-mail: judgemac@maine.rr.com. Business E-mail: vmckusick@pierceatwood.com.

**MCLACHLAN, SARAH,** musician, composer; b. Halifax, Nova Scotia, Jan. 28, 1968; m. Ashwin Sood, Feb. 7, 1997; 1 child, India. Founder, performer Lilith Fair. Albums include Touch, 1989, Solace, 1991, Live EP, 1992, Fumbling Towards Ecstasy, 1994, Freedom Sessions, 1995, Rarities, B-Sides, and Other Stuff, 1996, Surfacing, 1997, Mirrorball, 1999, Sarah McLachlan Remixed, 2001, Afterglow, 2003, Wintersong, 2006, Mirrorball: The Complete Concert, 2006; appearances include Gravity, 1991, Island of Circles: A Nettwork C, 1991, No Alternative, 1993, Christmas at Mountain Stage, 1994, Testimonial Dinner: the Songs of Xt, 1995, Memories of the Soul Shack Survivor, 1996, Heroine, 1996, Bloom, 2005; worked with Delerium, Donovan. Recipient Order of Canada, Best Female Pop Vocal Performance award Grammy, 1997, 1999, Best Pop Instrumental Performance award, 1997; nominated for Grammy for Best Female Pop Vocal Performance for "Fallen," 2003. Achievements include founding Lilith Fair, all-female performance concert tour, 1997-1999. Office: Nettwerk Mgmt 1650 W 2nd Ave Vancouver BC V6J 4R3 Canada

**MCLACHLIN, BEVERLEY,** Canadian supreme court chief justice; b. Pincher Creek, Alta., Can., Sept. 7, 1943; m. Roderick McLachlin (dec. 1988); 1 child, Angus; m. Frank E. McArdle, 1992. BA, U. Alta., MA in Philosophy, LLB, LLD (hon.), 1991, U. B.C., 1990, U. Toronto, 1995, York U., 1999, Law Soc. Upper Can., 2000, U. Ottawa, 2000, U. Calgary, 2000, Brock U., 2000, Simon Fraser U., 2000, U. Victoria, 2000, U. Alberta, 2000, U. Lethbridge, 2001, Bridgewater State Coll., 2001, Mt. St. Vincent U., 2002, U. PEI, 2002, U. Montreal, 2003, U. Man., 2004, Queen's U., Belfast, 2004, Dalhousie U., 2004, Carleton U., 2004, U. Ft. Kent, Maine, 2005. Bar: Alta.

1969, B.C. 1971. Assoc. Wood, Moir, Hyde and Ross, Edmonton, Alta., Canada, 1969—71, Thomas, Herdy, Mitchell & Co., Fort St. John, B.C., Canada, 1971—72, Bull, Housser and Tupper, Vancouver, 1972—75; from lectr. to prof. U. B.C., 1974—81; appointed to County Ct., Vancouver, 1981; justice Supreme Ct. of B.C., 1981—85, B.C. Ct. of Appeal, Canada, 1985—88; chief justice Supreme Ct. of B.C., Canada, 1988; justice Supreme Ct. Can., Ottawa, Ont., Canada, 1989—2000, chief justice Can., 2000—. Co-author: B.C. Supreme Court Practice, B.C. Court Forms, Canadian Law of Arch. and Engring.; contbr. articles to profl. jours. Office: Supreme Ct Bldg 301 Wellington St Ottawa ON Canada K1A 0J1 Office Phone: 613-992-6940.

**MCLAFFERTY, FRED WARREN,** chemist, educator; b. Evanston, Ill., May 11, 1923; s. Joel E. and Margaret E. (Keifer) McLafferty; m. Elizabeth E. Curley, Feb. 5, 1948; children: Sara L., Joel P., Martha A., Samuel A., Ann E. BS, U. Nebr., 1943, DSc (hon.), 1983, MS, 1947; PhD, Cornell U., 1950; DSc (hon.), U. Liege, Belgium, 1987, Purdue U., 1995. Fellow U. Iowa, 1949-50; rsch. chemist, divsn. leader Dow Chem. Co., 1950-56; dir. Eastern Rsch. Lab., 1956-64; prof. chemistry Purdue U., 1964-68, Cornell U., 1968-92, Peter J.W. Debye prof. chemistry emeritus, 1992—. Chem. sci. and tech. bd., numerical data adv. bd., bd. Army sci. tech., bd. radioactive waste mgmt. NRC; chem. co-chmn. World Bank's Chinese Univ. Devel. Project. Author: Mass Spectrometry of Organic Ions, 1963, Mass Spectral Correlations, 2d edit., 1981, Interpretation of Mass Spectra, 4th edit., 1993, Tandem Mass Spectrometry, 1983, Advances in Analytical Chemistry and Instrumentation; (with C.N. Reilley), Vols. 4-7, 1967-70, Index and Bibliography of Mass Spectrometry, (with J. Pinzelik), 1967, Atlas of Mass Spectral Data; (with E. Stenhagen and S. Abrahamsson), 1969, Registry of Mass Spectral Data, 1974; (with D.B. Stauffer) Wiley/NBS Registry of Mass Spectral Data, 1989, Important Peak Index of Mass Spectral Data, 1991; editor: Accounts of Chemical Research, 1986-94; co-editor: (with E. Stenhagen and S. Abrahamsson) Archives of Mass Spectral Data, 1969-72. With AUS, 1942-45, ETO. Decorated Purple Heart, Combat Inf. badge, Bronze Star with 4 oak leaf clusters, Presdl. Unit citation; recipient Pitts. Spectroscopy award Spectroscopy Soc. Pitts., 1975, Gold medal U. Naples, 1989, Robert Boyle Gold medal Royal Soc. Chemistry, 1992, Bijvoet medal U. Utrecht, 1997, W.L. Evans award Ohio State U., 1987, Jaroslav Heyrovsky Gold medal Czech Acad. Scis., 1999, Guilio Natta Gold medal Italian Chem. Soc., 2000, Torbern Bergman medal Swedish Chem. Soc., 2001, Lavoisier medal French Chem. Soc., 2004; John Simon Guggenheim fellow, 1972, Overseas fellow Churchill Coll., Cambridge (Eng.) U., 1979. Fellow: AAAS, NAS, Am. Acad. Arts and Scis., N.Y. Acad. Scis.; mem.: Internat. Assn. Protein Structure and Analytical Proteomics (Pehr Edman award 2006), Italian Nat. Acad. Scis. XL (fgn.), Am. Inst. Chemists (Chem. Pioneer award 1996), Am. Soc. Mass. Spectrometry (founder, sec. 1957—58, Disting. Contbn. in Mass Spectrometry award 2003), Assn. Analytical Chemists (Anachem award 1985), Internat. Spectrometry Orgn. (Sir J.J. Thomson gold medal 1985), Am. Chem. Soc. (chmn. analytical chem. divsn. 1969, chmn. Midland sect. 1956, Northeastern sect. 1964, award chem. instrumentation 1971, award analytical chemistry 1981, Nichols medal N.Y. sect. 1984, Oesper award Cin. sect. 1986, award mass spectrometry 1989), Soc. Analytical Chemists (Pitts. Analytical Chemist award 1987, Pioneer Analytical Instrumentation award 1994), Alpha Chi Sigma, Phi Lambda Upsilon, Sigma Xi. Home: 103 Needham Pl Ithaca NY 14850-2120 Office Phone: 607-255-4699. Business E-Mail: fwm5@cornell.edu.

**MCLAIN, PAUL KING,** systems analyst; b. Bremerton, Wash., June 10, 1946; s. Paul Shavor and Ramona Marilyn McLain; m. Maureen Elizabeth Miner, Aug. 23, 1969 (div. Dec. 16, 1986); children: Paul Joseph, Andrew John; m. Donna Joan Miller, Nov. 19, 1988. BA in Psychology, U. Wash., 1973, BA in History, 1975; cert. in bus. computing, North Seattle CC, 1979; MDiv, Seattle U., 2002. Ordained min. Universal Life Ch. Warehouse clk. Seattle Transfer and Storage, 1969—70; returns supr. Transcontinental Music Co., Seattle, 1970—71; entry mgr. A. L. Tokin Custom Ho. Broker, Seattle, 1973—74; import adminstr. Eckert Overseas Agy., Seattle, 1974—76; warehouse and container terminal clk. Port of Seattle, 1976—79; sys. analyst Boeing Co., Seattle, 1979—2001; point-of-sale clk. Sinnett's Market Pl., Longview, Wash., 2004—05; sys. analyst Longview Fibre Co., Wash., 2005—. Presenter in field; lectr. in field. Actor: (musical) The Fantastics. Del. Dem. State Conv., Tacoma, 2004; mem. Cowlite County Dem. Women's Club; treas. Aspire! for Unitarian Universalist Ministerial Candidates, Boston, 2000—01; pres. Saltwater Unitarian Universalist Ch., Kent, Wash., 1993—94; chpt. pres. Toastmasters Internat., Kent, Wash., 1988—89, area gov., 1989—90. With USN, 1965—69. Decorated Navy Unit Commendation (2) USN, Vietnam Svc. Medal (3), Republic of Vietnam Campaign medal Dept. of Def. Mem.: VFW, Am. Bus. Women's Assn., Mensa. Liberal. Unitarian Universalist. Achievements include reduction of time required for work center loading system; design of webpage timeline. Avocations: digital video, computing, music. Home: 136 Hi-Loch Ln Kelso WA 98626-9827 Personal E-mail: uuseeker@earthlink.net.

**MCLANE, FREDERICK BERG,** lawyer; b. Long Beach, Calif., July 24, 1941; s. Adrian B. and Arlie K. (Burrell) McL.; m. Lois C. Roberts, Jan. 28, 1967; children: Willard, Anita. BA, Stanford U., 1963; LLB, Yale U., 1966. Bar: Calif. 1967, U.S. Dist. Ct. (cen. dist.) Calif. 1967. Assoc. prof. law U. Miss., Oxford, 1966-68; assoc. O'Melveny & Myers LLP, LA, 1968-74, ptnr., 1975—2005, of counsel, 2005—. Lectr. in field. Pres., bd. dirs. Legal Aid Found., L.A., 1974-83; deacon Congl. Ch., Sherman Oaks, Calif., 1979-83; vice-chair L.A. Music Ctr., Unified Fund, 1992-94; bd. dirs. Calif. Sci. Ctr. Found., 1991-2000. Mem.: ABA (banking com., fed. regulation of securities com.), Calif. Bar Assn. (fin. insts. com., uniform commI. codes), Calif. Club (L.A.), L.A. Country Club (bd. dirs.), The Quarry at La Quinta, Order of Coif. Democrat. Avocations: golf, walking, reading. Office: O'Melveny & Myers LLP 1999 Ave of the Stars Los Angeles CA 90067-6035 Office Phone: 310-246-8554. Business E-Mail: fmclane@omm.com

**MCLANE, ROBERT DRAYTON, JR.,** food products company executive; b. Cameron, Tex., July 22, 1936; s. Robert Drayton and Gladys (Blaylock) McL.; m. Mary Elizabeth Cockrell, Feb. 2, 1972; children: Robert Drayton III, Denton. BBA, Baylor U., 1958; MS, Mich. State U., 1959. With McLane Co., Inc., Temple, Tex., 1957—, v.p., 1964-74, exec. v.p., sec.-treas., 1974-78, chief exec. officer, pres., 1978—, also bd. dirs. First Nat. Bank, Temple, Tex. Pres. United Way Campaign, Temple, 1985—; mem. Tex. State Bd. Mental Health and Mental Retardation, 1985—, exec. bd. Heart O'Tex. Council Boy Scouts Am., 1968—; bd. dirs. Scott and White Meml. Hosp., Temple, 1985—. Recipient Mgmt. Excellence and Achievement award Coll. Bus. Mgmt. U. Ga., 1986; named Entrepreneur of Yr. Arthur Young/Venture, Dallas, 1987; named one of Forbes' Richest Americans, 2006. Mem.: Am. Wholesale Grocers Assn. (chmn. 1986-88), Nat. Assn. Convenience Stores, Grocery Mfrs. Am., Tex. Food Industry Assn. Baptist. Avocation: tennis. Office: McLane Group PO Box 549 Temple TX 76503-0549*

**MCLANE, WILLIAM DELANO,** mechanical engineer; b. Ralls, Tex., Aug. 22, 1936; s. Clyde and Lillian Helen (Earp) McL.; m. Mary Ann Clark, Feb. 17, 1962; children: William Devin, Keri, Kristi, Mandy. BSME, Tex. Tech. U., 1961. Profl. engr. Tex. Engr. Texaco Inc., Tulsa, 1961-63; plant engring. mgr. Owens-Corning Fiberglas Corp., Toledo, 1963-72; pres., CEO Tucker-McLane Tire Corp., Waxahachie, Tex., 1972-89; commr. County of Ellis, Waxahachie, 1989-93; engr. Morrison Knudsen Corp., Dallas, 1993-94, MK-Ferguson, Albuquerque, 1994-95, Parsons Brinckerhoff, Dallas, 1995-96; quality control mgr. Sedalco, Inc., Ft. Worth, 1996-97; engring. mgr. Fortra Fiber-Cement, LLC, Waxahachie, Tex., 1997-2001; constrn. mgr. FWTA commuter rail project Parsons Brinckerhoff Constrn. Svcs., Inc., Dallas, 2001—02, sr. project mgr., Bush Internat. Airport Svcs. Improvement program Houston, 2002—05; constrn. mgr. Dallas County Cmty. Coll. Dist., Irving, Tex., 2005—. Mem. adv. bd. Guaranty Fed. Bank, Waxahachie, 1993—, Citizens Nat. Bank, Waxahachie, 1991-92, City of Waxahachie, 1990-91, Tex. State Tech. Coll., Inc., Waco, 1998—, Navarro Coll., Corsicana, 1998—, Portland Cement Assn., Skokie, Ill., 1998—, Sec. bd. Waxahachie Sch. Dist., 1979-88; vice chmn. Ctrl. Tex. Econ. Devel. Dist., Waco, 1989-93; mem. adv. com. Tex. State Tech. Coll., Waco, 1998—. Mem.

ASME, ASCE, NSPE, Tex. Soc. Profl. Engrs., So. Bldg. Code Congress Internat., Internat. Soc. Tribologists and Lubrication Engrs., Internat. Conf. Bldg. Officials, Waxahachie C. of C. (pres. 1977). Republican. Presbyterian. Avocations: civic and political volunteer work, golf, fishing, cooking. Home: 1612 Alexander Dr Waxahachie TX 75165-1902 Office: Parsons Brinckerhoff Constrn Svcs 2777 Stemmons Fwy Ste 1333 Dallas TX 75207 Personal E-mail: delmclane@sbcglobal.net.

**MCLAREN, RICHARD WELLINGTON, JR.,** lawyer; s. Richard Wellington and Edith (Gillett) McL.; m. Ann Lynn Zachrich, 1971; children: Christine, Richard, Charles. BA, Yale U., 1967; JD, Northwestern U., 1973. Bar: Ohio 1973, Ill. 1997, U.S. Dist. Ct. (no. dist.) Ohio 1973, U.S. Dist. Ct. (no. dist.) Ill. 1997, U.S. Ct. Appeals (6th cir.) 1978, U.S. Ct. Appeals (7th cir.) 1997, U.S. Ct. Appeals (fed. cir.) 1997, U.S. Supreme Ct. 1981. Assoc. Squire, Sanders & Dempsey, Cleve., 1973-82, ptnr., 1983-87; prin., counsel Ernst & Whinney, Cleve., 1988-89; assoc. gen. counsel Ernst & Young, Cleve., 1989-93; prin. counsel Centerior Energy Corp., Cleve., 1994-96; prin. Welsh & Katz, Ltd., Chgo., 1997—. 1st lt. U.S. Army, 1967-70. Mem. ABA (litigation, intellectual property and corp. law), FBA, Am. Judicature Soc., Ohio Bar Assn., Ill. Bar Assn. Home: 638 S Monroe St Hinsdale IL 60521-3926 Office: 120 S Riverside Plz Fl 22 Chicago IL 60606-3913 Office Phone: 312-655-1500. Business E-mail: rwmclaren@welshkatz.com.

**MCLARNEY, CHARLES PATRICK,** lawyer; b. Hemple, Mo., Mar. 28, 1942; s. Charles Joseph and Owatonna Mary (Sayles) McL.; m. Martina Borkowski, Aug. 28, 1965; children: Ellen, Megan, Michael. BS, St. Benedict's Coll., 1964; JD, U. Mo., 1968. Bar: Mo. 1968, U.S. Dist. Ct. (we. dist.) Mo. 1968, U.S. Ct. Appeals (8th cir.) U.S. Supreme Ct. 1968. Assoc. Shook, Hardy & Bacon LLP, Kansas City, Mo., 1968-72, ptnr., 1972-93, mng. ptnr., 1985-88, 91—, shareholder, pres., 1993-96, mng. ptnr., 1996. Active Friends of Art, Kans. City, 1980—; v.p. Civic Coun. Greater Kansas City. Named Outstanding Lawyer Kans. City Met. Bar Assn., 2004, Legal Leader of Yr. The Daily Record, 2005. Fellow Internat. Soc. Barristers (bd. dirs. 1989-94), Am. Coll. Trial Lawyers; mem. Kansas City Met. Bar, Lawyers Assn. Kansas City (pres. 1987-88), Mo. Bar (bd. govs., bd. dirs. 1991-94), Kansas City Soc. Fellows, Eight Twenty-Two Club, Kansas City Club, Plaza Bus. Breakfast Club (pres. 1983-84). Democrat. Roman Catholic. Avocations: tennis, golf, skiing. Office: Shook, Hardy & Bacon LLP 2555 Grand Blvd Kansas City MO 64108 Office Phone: 816-474-6550. Home Fax: 816-421-5547. Business E-Mail: pmclarney@shb.com.

**MCLARNON, MARY FRANCES,** neurologist; b. Montreal, Que., Canada, May 13, 1944; came to U.S., 1969; d. John Francis and Patricia Jessica (Dore) McL.; m. Malcolm Weiner, Dec. 21, 1975; m. Lawrence Zingesser, Oct. 12, 1982; children: Andrea, Eliza. BS, McGill U., 1965, MD, 1969. Intern St. Vincent's Hosp., N.Y.C., 1969-70; fellow seizure unit Boston Children's Hosp., 1970-71; resident in neurology Albert Einstein Coll. Medicine, Bronx, N.Y., 1971-73; resident in radiology N.Y. Hosp.-Cornell Med. Ctr., N.Y.C., 1973-76; pvt. practice. Home: 752 Cove Rd Mamaroneck NY 10543-4324 Office Phone: 917-856-8301. Personal E-mail: mmclmd@hotmail.com.

**MCLARTY, THOMAS F., III, (MACK MCLARTY),** former governement advisor, business executive; b. Hope, Ark., June 14, 1946; s. Thomas Franklin and Helen (Hesterly) McL.; m. Donna Kay Cochran, June 14, 1969; children: Mark Cochran, Franklin Hesterly BA, U. Arkansas, Fayetteville, 1968. Founder, pres. McLarty Leasing System Inc., Little Rock, 1969-79; pres. McLarty Cos., 1979-83; with Arkla Inc., Shreveport, from 1983, pres., CEO Arkla Gas divsn., 1983; pres., COO Arkla Gas divsn. Arkla, Inc., Shreveport, 1984, chmn. bd., pres., CEO, from 1985; chief of staff The White House, Washington, 1993-94, sr. adviser to President Clinton, 1994—, counselor to pres., spl. envoy for Ams.; vice chmn. Kissinger McLarty Assocs., Washington, D.C., 1998—. Chmn. Arkla Energy Mktg. Co., Shreveport, La., Arkla Chem. Corp., Shreveport, AER-Ark. Gas Transit Co., Shreveport; chmn., chief exec. officer, Miss. River Transmission Corp., St. Louis, MRT Energy Mktg. Co., St. Louis, Ark. La. Fin. Corp., Shreveport. Mem. Ark. Ho. of Reps., 1970-72; chmn. Ark. Dem. Com.; mem. Dem. Nat. Com., 1974-76; treas. David Pryor Gubernatorial Campaign, 1974, Gov. Bill Clinton campaign, 1978; bd. dirs. Hendrix Coll., Conway, Ark.; bd. visitors U. Ark., Little Rock; former chmn. United Negro Coll. Fund Campaign, fund-raising campaign Ark. Symphony Mem. Greater Little Rock C. of C. (pres. 1983) Office: Kissinger McLarty Assocs 1775 Pennsylvania Ave NW Washington DC 20006-4605 also: The McLarty Cos 425 W Capitol Ave Ste 3810 Little Rock AR 72201-3460

**MCLAUGHLIN, ALLAN D.,** information technology executive; BS in Math. and Computer Sci., W.Va. Wesleyan Coll.; MBA, U. Dayton. Joined LexisNexis, Miamisburg, Ohio, 1988; mng. dir. Reed Elsevier Tech. Group, Cambridge, Mass., 1997-2000; v.p. Reed Elsevier, Inc., Cambridge, 1997—2000; sr. v.p., CTO LexisNexis Group, Miamisburg, 2000—. Trustee Greater Dayton (Ohio) Info. Tech. Alliance, founder exec.-on-loan program, Va. Piedmont Tech. Coun., Charlottesville; mem. adv. bd. Write State U. Computer Sci. and Engring. Sch., Dayton; mem. CIO adv. bd. U. Dayton; mem. tech. task force City of Dayton, 2002—03. Office: LexisNexis 9443 Springboro Pike Miamisburg OH 45342

**MCLAUGHLIN, BARBARA LYN,** elementary school educator; b. Watseka, Ill., Jan. 18, 1950; d. LaVerne Melvin and Marian Barbara (Borchers) Reitz; m. Steven Joseph McLaughlin, Oct. 7, 1972; children: Laurie Lyn Peterson, Lisa Kay Kolavennu, Angela Marie. BS in Edn., Ea. Ill. U., 1971; MA in Edn., Olivet Nazarene U., 1999. Std.Spl. Tchg.K-12 Ill., 1971, Std. Elem. Tchg.K-9 Ill., 1971. Kindergarten tchr. Danville Elem. Schs., Ill., 1971—72; first grade tchr. Clifton Elem., Clifton, Ill., 1972—73; substitute tchr. Ctrl. Unit Sch. Dist. 4, 1973—78; spl. edn. tchr. Chebanse Elem., Chebanse, Ill., 1978—. Dept. chair Ctrl. Unit Sch. Dist. # 4 Spl. Edn. Dept., Clifton, Ill., 2000—05, mentor, Chebanse, Ill., 2004—05; mem. sch. improvement team Chebanse Elem., Ill., 1990—2002, 2005—06; guest tchr. Wash. U. On-line, 2004, 05, Chebanse Elem., Chebanse, 2003—. Contbr. chapters to books educational contribution to textbook. Supporter Spl. Olympics. Recipient Disney Am. Tchr. award Honoree, Walt Disney Co., 2002-2003, Disting. Educator award, Ea. Ill. U., 2004; First of Am. ednl. grantee, 2004, Ednl. scholar, Target, 1998. Mem.: Assn. Supervision and Curriculum Devel., Coun. for Exceptional Children (Appearance in CEC's Today 2004), Pi Lambda Theta, Kappa Delta Pi (hon.), Delta Kappa Gamma (hon.; sec. 2000—04). Lutheran. Avocations: reading, conservation of natural resources, gardening, sports. Home: 440 East 3200 North Rd Clifton IL 60927 Office: Chebanse Elem 475 School Street Chebanse IL 60922 Office Phone: 815-697-2642. Personal E-mail: grove@dlogue.com.

**MCLAUGHLIN, CALVIN STURGIS,** biochemistry professor; b. St. Joseph, Mo., May 29, 1936; s. Calvin Sturgis and Agnes Jane McLaughlin; m. Chin Helen Moy, Sept. 7, 1960; children: Heather Chin Chu, Christine Leng Oy, Andrew Calvin Moy. BS, King Coll., 1958; postgrad., Yale U., 1958-59; PhD, MIT, 1964. Postdoctoral fellow Institut de Biologie Physico-Chimique, Paris, 1964-66; prof. biochemistry U. Calif., Irvine, 1966—, dir. Cancer Rsch. Inst., 1981-83; vis. prof. Sch. Botany Oxford U., Eng., 1976, 80. Mem. peer rev. panels Am. Cancer Soc., NSF, NIH, VA Contbr. numerous articles to profl. jours.; mem. editl. bds. Jour. Bacteriology, 1975-80, Exptl. Mycology, 1980-86; reviewer profl. jours. Bd. dirs. Am. Cancer Soc., Orange County, 1980-89; mem. Traffic Affairs Com., Newport Beach, Calif., 1972-78. Named Outstanding Tchr. U. Calif.-Irvine, 1978, Gabriel Lester Meml. Lectr. Reed Coll., 1979; fellow Rockefeller Found., 1958-59, Upjohn Found., 1959-60, Nutrition Found., 1960-61, NIH, 1961-64, Am. Cancer Soc., 1964-66 Mem. Genetics Soc. Am., Am. Soc. Biochemistry and Molecular Biology, Am. Soc. Microbiology, Am. Soc. Mycology, Am. Soc. for Cell Biology, Yeast Genetics and Molecular Biology Soc. Am. (co-chair 1986-88), Electrophoresis Soc. Presbyterian. Office: U Calif Irvine Dept Biol Chemistry Irvine CA 92697-1700 Business E-Mail: cal@uci.edu.

**MCLAUGHLIN, CATHERINE G.,** healthcare educator; AB, Randolph-Macon Woman's Coll., 1971; MS in Econs., U. Wis., 1978, PhD in Econs., 1980. Prof. health mgmt. and policy U. Mich., 1983—, dir. Econ. Rsch. Initiative on the Uninsured, prof. dept. health mgmt. and policy, dir. Robert Wood Johnson Found. Scholars in Health Policy Rsch. Program. Dir. U. Mich. component Agy. for Healthcare Rsch. and Quality's Ctr. of Excellence on Managed Care Markets and Quality. Contbr. articles to profl. jours.; sr. assoc. editor Health Svcs. Rsch. Office: U Mich Dept Health Mgmt and Policy 109 S Observatory M3166 SPH II Ann Arbor MI 48109-2029 Business E-Mail: cmcl@umich.edu.

**MCLAUGHLIN, DAVID,** foundation administrator; Grad., M.B.A., Dartmouth Coll.; PhD (hon.), Colby-Sawyer Coll. Pres. Dartmouth College, 1981—87; chmn. Aspen Institute, 1987—88; chmn., CEO Orion Safety Products, 1988—; former chmn. CBS Corp., N.Y.C.; mem. bd. of gov. American Red Cross, 1998—, chmn., 2001—. Mem.: Ausbon Sargent Land Preservation Trust, Lake Sunapee Protective Assoc., Friends of the John Hay National Wildlife Refuge, Colby-Sawyer Coll. Bd. of Trustees. Office: Amer Red Cross 6900 Georgia Ave NW Washington DC 20307

**MCLAUGHLIN, DAVID,** academic administrator, mathematics professor, neural science educator; Asst. prof. math. NYU, N.Y.C., 1970, dir. Courant Inst. Math. Scis., 1994—2002, provost, 2002—; chmn. applied math. U. Ariz., 1974—89; dir. applied and computation math. Princeton U., 1989. Chmn. Bd. Mathematical Sci. & Their Applications. Editor: two books; contbr. articles to profl. jours. Recipient Lester Ford award, 1976, David Alcaraz Spinola award, 1995. Fellow: Am. Acad. Arts and Scis.; mem.: NAS, Soc. Indsl. and Applied Math. Office: NYU 70 Washington Sq South New York NY 10012

**MCLAUGHLIN, HARRY ROLL,** architect; b. Indpls., Nov. 29, 1922; s. William T. and Ruth E. (Roll) McL.; m. Linda Hamilton, Oct. 23, 1954. Registered Ind., Ohio, Ill., cert. Nat. Coun. Archtl. Registration Bds. Past pres. James Assocs. Inc., Indpls. Restorations include Old State Bank State Meml, Vincennes, Ind., Andrew Wylie House, Bloomington, Ind., Old Opera House State Meml, New Harmony, Ind., Old Morris-Butler House, Indpls. (Merit award 1972), Market St. Restoration and Maria Creek Baptist Ch., Vincennes, Benjamin Harrison House, Old James Ball Residence, Lafayette, Ind. (1st Design award 1972), Lockerbie Sq. Master Plan Park Sch., Indpls., Knox County Ct. House, Vincennes, 1972, J.K. Lilly House, Indpls., 1972, Waiting Station and Chapel, Crown Hill Cemetery, Indpls., 1972, Blackford-Condit House Ind. State U., Terre Haute, Indian houses Angel Mounds Archaeol. Site and Interpretative Ctr., Ind.; architect: Glenn A. Black Mus. Archaeology, Ind. U., Bloomington; Restoration Morgan County Ct. House, Indpls. City Market, Hist. Schofield House, Madison, Ind., Ernie Pyle Birthplace, Dana, Ind., Phi Kappa Psi Nat. Hdqrs, Indpls., 1980 (Design award), East Coll. Bldg, DePauw U., Greencastle, Ind., Pres.'s House Restoration, DePauw U., 1992; contbr. articles to profl. jours.; Illustrator: Harmonist Construction. Past chmn. bd., past pres., now chmn. emeritus Historic Landmarks Found., Ind.; bd. dirs., archtl. adviser, bd. advisers Historic Madison, Inc.; mem. adv. coun. Historic Am. Bldgs. Survey, Nat. Park Svc., 1967-73; past mem. nat. profl. rev. com. for Nat. Register nominations, 1967-81; past adv. bd. Conner Prarie Mus., Patrick Henry Sullivan Found.; past adviser Indpls. Historic Preservation Commn.; past mem. preservation com. Ind. U.; past mem. Meridian St. Preservation Commn., Indpls., 1971-2001; hon. mem. Ind. Bicentennial Commn.; bd. dirs. Park-Tudor Sch., 1972-85; past nat. bd. dirs. Preservation Action; life bd. dirs. Historic New Harmony; trustee Historic Masonic Heritage Found.; past bd. dirs. Ind. Masonic Home, 1984-91, Inpls. Pub. Libr. Found., treas. 1988, 95—, v.p. 1989, pres. 1990-97; past trustee Eiteljorg Mus. Western Art, mem. adv. and planning com., 1999; past mem. Hamilton County Tourism Commn., 1989-91. Recipient Gov.'s citation State of Ind., 1967, Sagamore of Wabash award, 1967, 80, 82; Mayor's citation City of Indpls., Sec.'s citation U.S. Dept. Interior, Design and Environ. citation, 1975, Disting. Achievement award Ball State U., 2004. Fellow AIA (nat. com. historic bldgs., chmn. historic resources com. 1970); mem. Ind. Soc. Architects (state preservation coord. 1960—, Biennial award 1972, Design award 1978), Nat. Trust Historic Preservation (past trustee, bd. advisers), Soc. Archtl. Historians (Wilbur D. Peat award Ctrl. Ind. chpt. outstanding contbns. to understanding and appreciation of archtl. heritage 1993, past bd. dirs., Disting. Achievement in Hist. Preservation award 2005), Ind. Com. for Preservation of Archtl. Records, Indpls. Mus. Art (trustee, chmn. bldgs. com., bd. govs. 1986-95), Zionsville C. of C. (hon. bd. dirs.), U.S. Capitol (hon. trustee), Ind. Hist. Soc. (pres. 1999, trustee, bldg. com.), Marion County Hist. Soc. (past v.p., bd. dirs.), Zionsville Hist. Soc. (hon. life), Navy League U.S. (life), Ind. State Mus. Soc. (life), English Speaking Union (past bd. dirs. Indpls.), Hamilton County Hist. Soc. (life), Woodstock Club (bd. dirs. 1982-86, pres. 1985, ex-officio 1986) Literary Club Found. (trustee), Amateur Movie Club, Skyline Club (life), Packard Club, Masons (33 deg.). Home and Office: 950 W 116th St Carmel IN 46032-8864

**MCLAUGHLIN, JAMES LEE,** musician, director; b. Hillsboro, Ohio, Mar. 27, 1946; s. Robert Barker McLaughlin and Virgie Lee Prine-McLaughlin. BFA, Ohio U., Athens, 1968. Cert. music dir. West Ohio Conf. United Meth. Ch., 1973. Organist Hillsboro Ch. Christ, Ohio, 1960—64, First Christian Ch., Athens, 1964—68; tchr. vocal music Zanesville City Schs., Zanesville, 1968—99; dept. chair vocal music, 1991—99; dir. music Faith United Meth. Ch., 1968—86, Ctrl. Trinity United Meth. Ch., 1986—. Founder and dir. Optimists Boys Club Choir, 1981—92; pres. Thursday Music Club, Zanesville, Ohio, 1984—86, 1994—96, 2002—04; dir. music and condr. Zanesville Civic Chorus, 1993—; mem. and asst. condr. Y-City Barbershop Chorus, 2000—; organ recitalist; coach voice, piano, organ; accompanist. Performer: Robert Shaw Chorus. Advisor Virgil Lee McLaughlin Fund of Found. for Appalachian Ohio, 2002—; bd. dirs. So. Ohio Symphony Orch., New Concord, Ohio, 1974—76, Zanesville Concert Assn., 1979—, pres., 1981—84, booking agt., 2006—; bd. dirs. Katherine B. Geis Scholarship, 1991—. Named an Outstanding Educator, Phi Delta Kappa, 1999; scholar, Stewart-Glapat Company, 1999, Matha Holden Jennings Found., 1982—83. Mem.: Am. Guild Organists, Fellowship of United Meth. Musicians, Ohio Music Edn. Assn. (adjudicator 1993—, dist. 9 chmn. 1988—90). Avocations: travel, philanthropy. Home: 413 Moore Ave Zanesville OH 43701-1234 Office: Ctrl Trinity United Meth Ch 62 S Seventh St Zanesville OH 43701 Office Phone: 740-453-1210.

**MCLAUGHLIN, JOHN EDWARD,** former federal agency administrator; b. McKeesport, PA, June 15, 1942; married; 2 children. BA, Wittenberg U., 1964; MA, Johns Hopkins U., 1966; postgrad., SAIS Ctr., Bologna, Italy. U. Pa. With CIA, 1972—2004, with US Dept. State, Bur. European & Can. Affairs, 1984—85, deputy dir. Office European Analysis, 1985—89, dir. European analysis, 1989, dir. Slavic and Eurasian analysis, 1989—95, acting chmn. Nat. Intelligence Coun., 1995—97, dep. dir. intelligence, 1997—2000, dep. dir. 2000—04, acting dir., 2004; non-resident sr. fellow Brooking Instn., Washington, 2005—; sr. fellow, Philip Merrill Ctr. for Strategic Studies John Hopkins U., Washington, 2005—. With U.S. Army, 1966—69

**MCLAUGHLIN, JOHN J.,** broadcast executive, television producer, journalist, political commentator; s. Augustus Hugh and Eva Philomena (Turcotte) McL.; m. Ann Dore Lauenstein, Aug. 23, 1975 (div. 1992); m. Cristina Vidal, Jun. 22, 1997. AB, Boston Coll., 1951, MA in Philosophy, 1952, BDiv, 1959, MA in English, 1961; PhD, Columbia U., 1967. Ordained priest Roman Catholic Ch., 1960. Mem. Jesuit Order, N.E., N.Y. and Washington; resigned order and active ministry, 1975; tchr., dir. communications Fairfield (Conn.) Univ. and Preparatory Sch., 1960-64; assoc. editor America Mag., N.Y.C., 1967-70; speech writer & dep. spl. asst. to Pres. Richard Nixon and Gerald Ford, Washington, 1971-74; pres. McLaughlin and Co. Pub. Policy Cons., Washington, 1975-79; radio talk-show host Sta. WRC-AM, Washington, 1979-82; pres., chmn. bd. dirs. Oliver Prodns., Inc., Washington, 1983—. Lectr. numerous univs., corps. and orgns. nationwide and abroad, 1963—; host various TV series, Sta. WJAR-TV, Providence, 1962-63, Sta. WNHC-TV, New Haven, 1963, Sta. WTIC-TV, Hartford, 1963, Sta. WOR-TV,

N.Y.C., 1964; host, exec. producer Biafra Today report ABC-TV Network, 1969; radio commentator Sta. WSTC, Stamford, Conn., 1964, CBS Network Radio, N.Y.C., 1964, Nat. Pub. Radio All Things Considered, Washington, 1981-85; dir. film insts. Yale U., Holy Cross Coll., Manhattanville Coll.; juror Am. Film Festival, 1969; congressional testimony pub. broadcasting and TV license renewal, Washington, 1967, 69. Author: Love Before Marriage, 1970; editor National Review, Washington, 1981-89, columnist From Washington Straight, 1982-89; TV host and exec. producer The McLaughlin Group NBC and PBS TV stas., 1982—; John McLaughlin's One on One, 1984—; McLaughlin CNBC cable system, 1989-94; TV appearances (host spl. episode) Cheers, 1990, (cameo) Murphy Brown, 1995, Lateline, 1998; Motion picture appearances: Dave, 1993, Mission Impossible, 1996, Independence Day, 1996, Murder at 1600, 1997, Bulworth, 1998. Rec. candidate U.S. Senate, R.I., 1970. Recipient Excellence in Journalism award Cath. Press Assn., 1969, News Media award VFW, 1984; nominee Nat. Acad. Cable Programming ACE award, 1989, 90, 91, 94; The McLaughlin Group named Best Polit. Talk Show, Washingtonian mag., 1997, George Mag., 1998. Mem. NATAS (Emmy award 1984), Am. Fedn. TV and Radio Artists, Screen Actors Guild. Office: 1717 Rhode Island Ave NW Ste 640 Washington DC 20036 E-mail: slucian@mclaughlin.com.

**MCLAUGHLIN, JOHN SHERMAN,** lawyer; b. Pitts., Apr. 1, 1932; s. John H. and Dorothy I. (Schrecongost) McL.; m. Suzanne Shaver, June 5, 1971; children: Dorothy, Sarah, Martha. AB, Harvard U., 1954, LLB, 1957. Bar: Pa. 1958, U.S. Supreme Ct. 1967. Assoc. Reed, Smith, Shaw & McClay, Pitts., 1957-71, ptnr., 1971—2002, of counsel, 2002—. Trustee Harmarville Rehab. Ctr., Inc., 1980-87; pres., trustee Western Pa. Sch. for the Deaf, 1985—; pres. Pa. NG Assn., 1976-78; justice of peace Borough of Edgewood, 1963-73; trustee Winchester Thurston Sch., 1987-2002; life trustee Carnegie Libr. of Pitts., Carnegie Inst., 1994—, Carnegie Mus. Art, 1997—; dir. Pitts. Symphony, 1985-95, adv. 1996-99; emeritus coun. mem. Scotch Irish Soc. USA. Lt. col. Air NG, 1957-79. Mem.: Am. Coll. Trust and Estate Counsel, Allegheny County Bar Assn., Am. Law Inst., Rolling Rock Club (Ligonier, Pa.), Duquesne Club. Office: Reed Smith LLP 435 6th Ave Pittsburgh PA 15219-1886 Business E-Mail: jmclaughlin@reedsmith.com.

**MCLAUGHLIN, JOSEPH,** lawyer; b. Newark, Aug. 1, 1941; s. Joseph Nicholas and Genevieve Veronica (Lardiere) McL.; m. Elisabeth Lippold, July 31, 1965; children: Elisabeth Rogers, Jessica Lierzer, Emilie McLaughlin AB, Columbia U., 1962, LLB, 1965. With Sullivan & Cromwell, NYC, 1968-76; v.p., gen. counsel Goldman, Sachs & Co., 1976-88, cons., 1988-90; ptnr. Sidley Austin LLP, NYC, 1993—. Adj. prof. law NYU Sch. Law, 1988-92; spkr., presenter in field. Author (with C.J. Johnson Jr.): Corporate Finance and the Securities Laws, 3d edit., 2004; contbr. articles to profl. jours. Trustee Greenwich (Conn.) Acad., 1988-2000; treas. Presbyn. Ch. Old Greenwich, 1988-91; bd. dirs. United Way, Greenwich, 1993-97; mem. Rep. Town com., Greenwich, 1993-96. Jervey fellow Parker Sch. Fgn. Comparative Law, Columbia Law Sch., U. Munich, 1966-68. Mem. ABA (sect. bus. law, fed. regulation securities com., subcom. broker-dealer matters 1985—, subcom. civil litigation and SEC enforcement matters 1989—, chair task force rule 10b-6 1995-97, co-chair task force sellers' due diligence and similar defenses under fed. securities laws 1989-92), Am. Law Inst., Assn. of Bar of City of NY (internat. law com. 1979-84, chair 1981-84, civil rights com. 1984-87, internat. arms control and security affairs com. 1988-90), NY Stock Exch. (legal adv. com. to bd. govs. 1985-88, subcom. corp. governance, subcom. internat. issues 1988—), Securities Industry Assn. (fed. regulations com. 1978-88, chair 1982-84), Nat. Assn. Securities Dealers, Inc. (corp. financing com. 1983-86), Am. Arbitration Assn. (dir. 1986-90). Republican. Congregationalist. Office Phone: 212-839-5312. Business E-Mail: jmclaughlin@sidley.com.

**MCLAUGHLIN, JOSEPH MICHAEL,** federal judge, law educator; b. Bklyn., Mar. 20, 1933; s. Joseph Michael and Mary Catherine (Flanagan) McLaughlin; m. Frances Elizabeth Lynch, Oct. 10, 1959; children: Joseph, Mary Jo, Matthew, Andrew. AB, Fordham Coll., 1954, LL.B., 1959; LL.M., NYU, 1964; LL.D., Mercy Coll., White Plains, N.Y., 1981; LLD, Fordham U., 1998. Bar: N.Y. 1959. Assoc. Cahill, Gordon, NYC, 1959—61; prof. law Fordham U., NYC, 1961—71, dean Sch. of Law, 1971—81, adj. prof., 1981—90; judge U.S. Dist. Ct. Eastern Dist. N.Y., Bklyn., 1981—90, U.S. Ct. Appeals (2nd Cir.), NYC, 1990—98, sr. judge, 1998—; editor-in-chief Fed. Practice Guide; adj. prof. St. John's Law Sch., N.Y.C., 1982—97; chmn. N.Y. Law Revision Commn., Albany, 1975—82. Author (with Peterfreund): New York Practice, 1964; author: Evidence, 1979, also articles. Capt. Corps of Engineers U.S. Army, 1955—57, Korea. Mem.: ABA, N.Y. State Bar Assn., Assn. of Bar of City of N.Y., Lotos Club. Roman Catholic. Office: US Courthouse US Ct Appeals 40 Foley Sq Rm 2402 New York NY 10007-1502*

**MCLAUGHLIN, JOSEPH THOMAS,** lawyer; b. Boston, Mar. 30, 1944; s. James Francis and Madeline Louise (Hickman) McL.; m. Christine E. Mullen, Sept. 2, 1967; children: Amy Melissa, Caitlin Christine, Ian Michael. BA magna cum laude, Boston Coll., 1965; JD, Cornell U., 1968. Bar: Mass. 1969, N.Y. State 1968, U.S. Supreme Ct. 1974. Research asst. Brit. Council of Archaeology, Winchester, Eng., 1964, site supr., 1966; legis. asst. Rep. Thomas P. O'Neill, Washington, 1967; research asst. Cornell U., 1967-68; law clk. to chief justice Mass. Superior Ct., 1968-69; assoc. Shearman & Sterling, NYC, 1969-76, ptnr., 1976-97; exec. v.p., legal and regulatory affairs Credit Suisse First Boston, 1997—2001; chmn. Credit Suisse First Boston Found. Trust, 2001—02; ptnr., chmn. Heller Ehrman LLP, NYC, 2002—. Adj. prof. Fordham Law Sch., 1981-88; vis. prof. Cornell Law Sch., 1995-96. Author: Federal Class Action Digests, 1974, 1976; contbr. articles to profl. jours. Exec. dir. Brooklyn Heights Draft Counseling Svc., 1970-74, Presbyn. Task Force for Justice Counseling Svc., 1973-75; v.p., bd. dirs. Brooklyn Heights Assn., 1973-77; bd. dirs. Willoughby Settlement House, Inc., Ingersoll-Willoughby Cmty. Ctr., Inc., 1970-75, United Neighborhood Houses, 1976-78, Good Shepherd Svcs., Resources for Children with Spl. Needs, Inc., Internat. House, Bklyn. Mus. Art; mem. CRR Inst. for Dispute Resolution. Mem. ABA, Assn. of Bar of City of N.Y. (mem. com. on profl. discord 1986—, mem. com. to promote diversity in the legal profession), N.Y. State Bar Assn. (chmn. com. on marijuana and drug abuse 1972-75), Am. Law Inst., Am. Arbitration Assn., N.Y. Lawyers for Pub. Interest (mem. bd. dirs.) ABAC (com. on promoting settlements), Heights Casino Club. Office: Heller Ehrman LLP Times Square Tower 7 Times Square New York NY 10036 Office Phone: 212-847-8789. Office Fax: 212-763-7600. Business E-Mail: joseph.mclaughlin@hellerehrman.com.

**MCLAUGHLIN, LEIGHTON BATES, II,** journalist, educator, retired reporter; b. Evanston, Ill., Apr. 10, 1930; s. Leighton Bates and Gwendolyn I. (Markle) McL.; m. Beverly Jean Jeske, May 5, 1962; children: Leighton Bates III, Jeffrey, Steven, Patrick. Student, Kenyon Coll., Gambier, Ohio, 1948-50, Northwestern U., 1951; BA in English Lit., UCLA, 1983; MA in Comms., Calif. State U. Fullerton, 1990. Copyboy, reporter, rewriteman City News Bur., Chgo., 1957-58; reporter, rewriteman Chgo. Sun-Times, 1958-62; rewriteman, asst. city editor Ariz. Jour., Phoenix, 1962; reporter Miami (Fla.) Herald, 1962-64; successively rewriteman, night city editor, 1st asst. city editor, telegraph editor Chgo. Sun-Times, 1964-74; dir. Chgo. Daily News/Sun-Times News Service, 1974-79; editorial coord. electronics newspaper div. Field Enterprises, 1975-79; adminstr. reference libr. and communications ctr. Field Newspapers, 1979; editor News Am. Syndicate, Irvine, Calif., 1979-85; mng. editor San Gabriel Valley Daily Tribune, 1986; assoc. prof. journalism Riverside (Calif.) C.C., 1987-96, chmn. performing arts and media dept., 1993-96, coll. publs. editor, ret., 1996-99; lectr. in journalism Calif. State U.-Fullerton, 1984-96. Copy editor The Press-Enterprise, Riverside, Calif., 1988-95; lectr., condr. seminars in field. Author articles in field. Served to 1st lt. USMC, 1951-54. Recipient Stick-o-Type award for best feature story Chgo. Newspaper Guild, 1961, Best News story award Ill. AP and UPI, 1967 Mem. Chgo. Journalists Assn., Verban Soc., Psi Upsilon. Office: Riverside CC 4800 Magnolia Ave Riverside CA 92506-1242 *Reporting the news is like any other intellectual activity in that it involves research, verification, organization, and clarity of presentation. But news reporting is unique in that all this is done on a dead run, in time for the day's editions.*

**MCLAUGHLIN, MARGARET BROWN,** adult education educator, writer; b. Miami Beach, Fla., Aug. 24, 1926; d. J. Clifford and Grace Lindsey (DuPre) Brown; m. Francis Edward McLaughlin, Oct. 30, 1982 (dec.). BA cum laude, U. Miami, 1946; MA, Duke U., Durham, N.C., 1949; PhD, Tulane U., New Orleans, 1976. Instr., lectr. in English U. Miami, Coral Gables, Fla., 1946-47, 56-61, 73-91, 2000; instr. Narimasu Am. Sch., Tokyo, 1963-65; asst. prof. Manchester Coll., North Manchester, Ind., 1965-67; instr. Miami-Dade C.C., 1977, 81; dir. writing workshop for fgn. students U. Miami Sch. Medicine, 1991-92; adj. prof. English, Asian and Liberal Studies and Acad. Lifelong Learning, Fla. Internat. U., Miami, Fla., 1997—; instr. humanities Barry U., Miami, 2004. Prodr. Dade County Cable TV series Caribbean Writers and Their Art, 1991; prodr., host cable tv series Haiti Cherie, 1993-94. Contbr. articles to popular Japanese and U.S. mags. and newspapers; contbr. play reviews to Internet pub. Trustee Mus. Sci., Miami, 1977-78. Mem. Am. Lit. Assn. (Henry Adams Soc.), Egyptology and Asian Civilizations Soc. Miami (bd. dirs., pres. 1976-78, 83-85), South Fla. Internat. Press Club (scholarship chmn. 2002—), South Fla. Writers' Assn. Avocations: writing, travel, editing. Home and Office: 1621 S Bayshore Dr Miami FL 33133-4201 Office Phone: 305-858-7224. Personal E-mail: mjmbjb711@aol.com.

**MCLAUGHLIN, MICHAEL JOHN,** retired insurance company executive; b. Cambridge, Mass., Feb. 14, 1944; s. Michael John and Evelyn Katherine (Quinn) McL. BA, Boston Coll., 1965; JD, N.Y. U., 1968. Bar: N.Y., Mass. With N.Y. Life Ins. Co., 1968—, sr. v.p. info. systems and services dept., 1982-88, sr. v.p., 1988-91, sr. v.p., dep. gen. counsel, 1991-95, sr. v.p., gen. counsel, 1995-2000. Mem. ABA, N.Y. State Bar Assn. Personal E-mail: mmclau2260@aol.com.

**MCLAUGHLIN, PATRICK J.,** lawyer; b. 1947; BA summa cum laude, Univ. Minn., 1971, JD magna cum laude, 1975. Bar: Minn. 1975. Ptnr., banking, trial practice groups, chair, corp. trust svcs. group Dorsey & Whitney LLP, Mpls. Gen. counsel Minn. Police Relief Assn. Lectr. in field. Office: Dorsey & Whitney LLP Ste 1500 50 S Sixth St Minneapolis MN 55402-1498 Office Phone: 612-340-2975. Office Fax: 612-340-2643. Business E-Mail: mclaughlin.patrick@dorsey.com.

**MCLAUGHLIN, PATRICK MICHAEL,** lawyer; b. Monahans, Tex., July 23, 1946; s. Patrick John and Ann (Donnelly) M.; m. Christine Manos, Aug. 21, 1970; children— Brian Patrick, Christopher Michael, Conor Andrew B Gen. Studies, Ohio U., 1972; JD, Case We. Res. U., 1976. Bar: Ohio 1976, U.S. Dist. Ct. (no. dist.) Ohio 1977, U.S. Ct. Appeals (6th cir.) 1979, U.S. Supreme Ct. 1980; U.S. Dist. Ct. (so. dist.) Ohio 1989, U.S. Ct. Appeals (5th cir.). Dir. wris. edn. project. Am. Assn. Cmty. and Jr. Colls., Washington, 1972—73; law clk. Common Pleas Ct., Cleve., 1976—77; law clk. to judge 8th Jud. Dist. Ct. of Appeals, Cleve., 1977—78; asst. U.S. atty. No. Dist. Ohio, Cleve., 1978—82, chief civil divsn., 1982—84, U.S. atty. Cleve., 1984—88; ptnr. Janik & McLaughlin, Cleve., 1988—89, Mansour, Gavin, Gerlack & Manos Co., LPA, Cleve., 1989—97; apptd ind. spl. prosecutor Ohio Attys. Gen., 1993—96; mng. ptnr. McLaughlin & McCaffrey, LLP, Cleve., 1997—. Cons. Nat. League of Cities, U.S. Conf. Mayors, 1971-72; co-creator Opportunity Fair for Veterans Concept, 1971 Editor-in-chief Case Western Res. Jour. Internat. Law, 1975-76 Chmn. North Ohio Drug Abuse Task Force, 1986-88; chmn. Law Enforcement Coordinating Commn., North Ohio, 1985-88; chmn. civil issues subcom. Atty. Gen.'s Adv. Commn., 1986-88; exec. v.p. Greater Cleve. Vets. Meml., Inc., 1993, pres., 1994—. Decorated Silver Star, Bronze Star, Purple Heart, Army Commendation medal, Vietnamese Cross of Gallantry with Silver and Bronze Stars; named to Ohio Vets. Hall of Fame, 2003, Ohio Mil.Hall of Fame for Valor, 2004. Fellow Am. Coll. Trial Lawyers; mem. ABA, FBA, Ohio Bar Assn., Cleve. Bar Assn., Nat. Assn. Former U.S. Attys., Soc. 1st Divsn., 18th Inf. Regiment Assn., Order of Ahepa, Vietnam Vets. Am., Nat. Vietnam Vets. Network (Disting. Vietnam Vet. award 1985), Nat. Assn. Concerned Vets. (nat. v.p. external affairs 1971-72, exec. dir. 1972-73), Cuyahoga County Vets. (award 1985), Nat. Soc. SAR (law enforcement commendation medal 1989). Republican. Roman Catholic. Office: McLaughlin & McCaffrey LLP Eaton Ctr 1111 Superior Ave Ste 1350 Cleveland OH 44114-2500 Office Phone: 216-623-0900. Business E-Mail: pmm@paladin-law.com.

**MCLAUGHLIN, PHILIP VANDOREN, JR.,** mechanical engineering educator, researcher, consultant; b. Elizabeth, NJ, Nov. 10, 1939; s. Philip VanDoren and Ruth Evans (Landis) McL.; m. Phoebe Ann Feeney, Aug. 19, 1961; children: Philip VanDoren III, Patrick Evans, Christi M. Barton. BSCE, U. Pa., 1961, MS in Engring. Mechanics, 1964, PhD in Engring. Mechanics, 1969. Assoc. engr. Boeing-Vertol, Morton, Pa., 1962-63, engr. II, 1963; rsch. engr. Scott Paper Co., Phila., 1963-65, rsch. project engr., 1965-69, sr. rsch. project engr., 1969; asst. prof. theoretical and applied mechanics U. Ill., Urbana, 1969-73, asst. dean engring., 1971-72; project mgr. Materials Scis. Corp., Blue Bell, Pa., 1973-76; assoc. prof. mech. engring. Villanova (Pa.) U., 1976-81, prof., 1981—2003, prof. emeritus, 2003—. Cons. Naval Air Engring. Ctr., Lakehurst, N.J., 1977-79, U.S. Steel Corp., Trenton, 1980-82, RCA Corp., Moorestown, N.J., 1986, Coal Tech Corp., Merion Station, Pa., Air Products and Chems., Allentown, Pa., 1988, Aircraft divsn. Naval Air Warfare Ctr., Patuxent River, Md., 1995-96, Christini Technologies, Phila., 1999—, Alpha Sci. Corp., Southeastern, Pa., 2000-01, Materials Rsch. & Design, Inc., Rosemont, Pa., 2002—, DETechs., King of Prussia, Pa., 2002—; vis. prof. dept. engring. U. Cambridge, Eng., 1990-91. Reviewer for sci. and tech. jours.; contbr. numerous articles to profl. jours. Rsch. grantee NSF, 1970-72, Naval Air Engring. Ctr., 1978-84, Lawrence Livermore Nat. Lab., 1979-81, Naval Air Devel. Ctr., 1985-86, RCA Corp., 1986-87; sr. rsch. assoc. NRC, Washington, 1983-84; USN-Am. Soc. for Engring. Edn. sr. faculty fellow, 1995. Mem.: ASME; chmn. applied mechanics divsn. Phila. sect. 1981—83, materials divsn. com. on composites 1992—2003), ASCE (life; chmn. engring. mechanics divsn. com. on inelastic behavior 1977—79, assoc. editor Jour. Engring. Mechanics Divsn. 1977—79, aero-space divsn. com on structures and materials 1986—), Am Soc, Composites, Am. flor Engring, Edn., Am. Acad. Mechanics, Sigma Xi. Achievements include research and consulting on composite materials and structures, structural analysis and design and inelastic behavior. Office: Villanova U Dept Mech Engring 800 Lancaster Ave Villanova PA 19085-1681 Office Phone: 610-291-2023. Business E-Mail: philip.mclaughlin@villanova.edu.

**MCLAUGHLIN, SALLY CRUMP,** elementary school educator; b. Farmville, Va., Sept. 24, 1953; d. James Lewis and Girleen Barnette Crump; m. Wayne Scott McLaughlin, Oct. 10, 1976. AA, Southside Va. C.C., Keysville, 1971—73; BS, Longwood Coll., Farmville, Va., 1973—75, MS, 1976—78. Cert. Reading Specialist Va. State Bd. Edn., 1979, in early education Va. State Bd. Edn., 1975. Kindergarten tchr. W. End Elem. Sch., Keysville, Va., 1975—76, Lunenburg Primary Sch., Victoria, Va., 1976—82, first grade tchr., 1982—92, Victoria Elem. Sch., Va., 1992—. Conservative. Baptist. Avocations: reading, gardening, walking. Home: 6623 Court House Rd Victoria VA 23974 Office: Victoria Elem Sch 1521 8th St Victoria VA 23974 Office Phone: 434-696-2163. Personal E-mail: sallymack@kerrlake.com.

**MCLAUGHLIN, SYLVIA CRANMER,** volunteer, environmentalist; b. Denver, Dec. 24, 1916; d. George Ernest and Jean Louise (Chappell) Cranmer; m. Donald Hamilton McLaughlin, Dec. 29, 1948; children: Jean Katherine McLaughlin Shaterian, George Cranmer McLaughlin. AB, Vassar Coll., 1939. Co-founder Save San Francisco Bay Assn., Berkeley-Oakland, Calif., 1961-99, pres., 1993-95. Bd. dirs. Ptnrs. for Liveable Cmtys., Washington, 1975-78; mem. waterfront adv. com. City of Berkeley, Calif., 1964-68; sec., bd. dirs. Resource Renewal Inst., 1980—, Citizens for East Shore State Parks, 1980—; founder, bd. dirs. Pub. Trust Group, Oakland, Calif., 1997—; mem. awards com. Berkeley Cmty. Fund, 1998—; mem. adv. bd. Greenbelt Alliance, San Francisco, 1982—; mem. nat. adv. coun. Trust for Pub. Land, San Francisco, 1986—, Ecocity Builders, Berkeley, 1990—. Mem. Nat. Audubon Soc. (bd. dirs. 1970-76), Nat. Recreation and Parks Assn. (bd. dirs. 1974-78), East Bay Conservation Corps (bd. dirs. 1985-97), Student Conservation Assn. (bd. dirs. 1979-84). Avocations: reading, travel, exercise. Home: 1450 Hawthorne Ter Berkeley CA 94708-1804

**MCLAUGHLIN, T. MARK,** lawyer; b. Salem, Mass., Apr. 20, 1953; s. Terrence E. and Mary E. (Donlon) McL.; m. Sandra L. Roman, Oct. 16, 1982; children: Daniel, Kathleen, Eileen. BA in Econs., U. Notre Dame, 1975, JD, 1978. Bar: Ill. 1978, U.S. Dist. Ct. (no. dist.) Ill. 1978, U.S. Dist. Ct. (cen. dist.) Ill. 1992, U.S. Dist. Ct. (ea. dist.) Wis. 1992, U.S. Ct. Appeals (7th cir.) 1982, U.S. Ct. Appeals (11th cir.) 1982, U.S. Ct. Appeals (8th cir.) 1998. Assoc. Mayer Brown Rowe & Maw LLP, Chgo., 1978-84, ptnr., 1985—. Adj. faculty law Loyola U., Chgo., 1983, 86-90. Bd. dirs. no. Ill. affiliate Am. Diabetes Assn., Chgo., 1985-94. Mem. ABA (franchising forum com. antitrust law sect.), Phi Beta Kappa. Office: Mayer Brown Rowe & Maw LLP 71 S Wacker Dr Chicago IL 60606-4637 Office Phone: 312-701-7066. E-mail: mmclaughlin@mayerbrownrowe.com.

**MCLAUGHLIN, THOMAS KEITH,** diversified financial services company executive; BS in Bus., Calif. State U., Northridge. CPA Grant Thornton, 1980—85; fin. analyst Countrywide Fin. Corp., Calabasas, Calif., 1986—87, treas. Countrywide Home Loans, 1989—96, mng. dir. fin., 1997—2000, CFO, 2000—, sr. mng. dir., 2001—. Office: Countrywide Fin Corp 4500 Park Granada Calabasas CA 91302-1613

**MCLAUGHLIN, WILLIAM IRVING,** space technical manager, writer; b. Oak Park, Ill., Mar. 6, 1935; s. William Lahey and Eileen (Irving) McL.; m. Karen Bjorneby, Aug. 20, 1960; children: William, Margot, Walter, Eileen. BS with highest honors, U. Calif., Berkeley, 1963, MA, 1966, PhD, 1968. Mem. tech. staff Bellcomm, Inc., 1968-71, Jet Propulsion Lab., Pasadena, Calif., 1971-99. Supr. terrestrial planets mission design group, 1981-83, mission design mgr. for Infrared Astron. Satellite, 1976-83, mgr. flight engring. office for Voyager/Uranus project, 1985-86; mgr. mission profile and sequencing sect 1986-92; dep. mgr. astrophysics and fundamental physics program office, 1992-96, mgr. mission and syss. architecture sect., 1996-99. Served with USMC, 1957-60. Recipient Apollo Achievement award, 1969, Pioneer 10 Mission Analysis Team Group Achievement award, 1974, Exceptional Svc. medal NASA, 1984, Outstanding Leadership medal NASA, 1986; asteroid 4838 Billmclaughlin named in his honor. Fellow Brit. Interplanetary Soc. (L.J. Carter Meml. lectr. London 2002, Space Achievement Bronze medal 1993); mem. Philosophy Sci. Assn., Internat. Acad. Astros., Phi Beta Kappa, Sigma Xi.

**MCLAURIN, HUGH MCFADDIN, III,** military officer, museum program director; b. Sumter, S.C., Jan. 30, 1936; s. Hugh McFaddin and Louise Mellette (Nettles) McL.; m. Virginia Anne Harvin, Aug. 22, 1958; children: Mary Louise, Virginia Harvin, Hugh IV. BS, Clemson U., 1959; grad. (hon.), Command & Gen. Staff Coll., Ft. Leavenworth, Kans., 1978. Commd. 2d lt. U.S. Army, 1958, advanced through grades to col., 1985; exec. officer 151st Field Arty. Brigade, Sumter, 1975-85; dir. pers. S.C. NG, Columbia, 1986-91, dir. logistics, 1991-95, rank of brig. gen., ret., 1996; owner McLaurin Farms, Wedgefield, SC, 1999—. Cons. S.C. Ednl. TV, Columbia, 1992-93; moderator Nat. Def. Seminar, Washington, 1978. Author: History of South Carolina National Guard and Militia, 1989. Elder, Presbyn. Ch., Wedgefield, 1961, moderator Presbytery Coun., 2001-04; v.p. Com. for Progress, Sumter, 1963; chmn. bd. dirs. S.C. NG Mus., Columbia, 1982-99; trustee Thornwell Home for Children and Sch. Fellow Coll. Mil. Historians; mem. Field Arty. Soc. S.C. (pres. 1987), SAR (historian) Sumter County Hist. Soc. (dir. 1996-99, pres. 2000), The Sumter Assembly (pres. 1991), Soc. of High Hills of Santee (steward 2002), Hon. Order St. Barbara, Fortnightly Club. Avocation: American Revolution research. Home: Stirling Plantation 6380 McLaurin Rd Wedgefield SC 29168-9393

**MCLAWHON, RONALD WILLIAM,** pathology educator, biochemist; b. Chgo., Sept. 10, 1957; s. William Columbus and Esther Shirley (Bukowski) McL. AB in Biol. Scis., U. Chgo., 1979, MS in Biochemistry, 1980, PhD in Biochemistry, 1982; MD, Rush Med. Coll., 1986. Diplomate Am. Bd. Pathology. Rsch. assoc. pediat. Joseph P. Kennedy Jr. Mental Retardation Rsch. Ctr., Chgo.; rsch. assoc. pediatrics U. Chgo. Pritzker Sch. Medicine, 1982-83; resident in pathology Rush-Presbyn.-St. Luke's Med. Ctr., Chgo., 1986-87, pathologist, 1987-88; instr. Rush Med. Coll., Chgo., 1986-87, asst. prof., 1987-88; resident in pathology U Chgo. Med. Ctr., 1988-90; asst. prof. U. Chgo. Pritzker Sch. Medicine, 1990-96, assoc. prof., 1996—; dir. clin. chemistry, attending physician U. Chgo. Med. Ctr., 1990—; dir. outreach and clin. support svcs. U. Chgo. Hosps. and Health Sys., 1997, dir. regional lab. svcs. and med. dir. of hosp. labs., 1998—. Contbr. articles to Jour. Biol. Chemistry, Molecular Pharmacology, Jour. Neurochemistry, Jour. Membrane Biology, Procs. of NAS, Am. Jour. Clin. Pathology, Clin. Chemistry. U.S. Pub. Health Predoctoral fellow NIH, 1981-82; James B. Herrick scholar Rush Med. Coll., 1986-87; recipient Young Investigator award Acad. Clin. Lab. Physicians and Scientists, 1990. Fellow: Am. Soc. Clin. Pathologists, Coll. Am. Pathologists, Nat. Acad. Clin. Biochemistry; mem.: AAAS, Am. Soc. Cell Biology, Am. Soc. Biochemistry and Molecular Biology, Am. Soc. Investigative Pathology, Am. Assn. Clin. Chemistry (chair Chgo. sect. 2005, Chgo. Chpt. Past Chmn. award 2006), Sigma Xi. Achievements include research in biochemistry of cell membrane receptors and signal transduction in the nervous system, molecular pharmacology of opiates and opioid peptides, regulation of complex carbohydrate and lipid metabolism, clinical laboratory automaton and robotics. Office: U Chgo Pritzker Sch Medicine Dept Pathology 5841 S Maryland Ave MC0004 Chicago IL 60637-1470 Office Phone: 773-702-1318. Business E-Mail: rm28@midway.uchicago.edu.

**MCLEAN, ARTHUR FREDERICK,** mechanical engineer; b. Bristol, Eng., Apr. 16, 1929; came to U.S., 1959; naturalized, 1966; s. Frederick Robert and Edith (Hawkins) McL.; m. Oriole R. Robinson, Aug. 30, 1952; children: Mark F., Peter A. Nat. and Higher Nat. degrees in Mech. Engring., Bristol Coll. Tech., 1952. Sr. engr. aircraft control sys. Bristol Aero-Out,Jla Engines Can., 1953-59; st. engr. power sys. tech. Bendix Corp., Southfield, Mich., 1959-61; supr. turbine sys. sect. Ford Motor Co., Dearborn, Mich., 1961-66, mgr. turbine R & D, 1967-78, mgr. ceramic materials rsch., 1979-86, mgr. materials engring., 1987-88; pvt. practice Oceanside, Calif., 1988—. Patentee in field; contbr. articles to profl. jours. With RAF, 1951-54. Recipient Soichiro Honda medal. Fellow ASME (past chmn. vehicular com., ceramics com.), Am. Ceramic Soc.; mem. Soc. Automotive Engrs. (past turbine com.), Inst. Mech. Engrs. Home: 3764 Southridge Way Oceanside CA 92056-5428 Office Phone: 760-724-3102. Personal E-mail: artmcl@cox.net.

**MCLEAN, CRAIG ELLIOTT,** retired non-commissioned officer; b. Muskegon, Mich., Dec. 12, 1950; s. Elliot Garber and Margaret Irene (Carlson) McL. Grad., Langley H.S., McLean, Va., 1969. Enlisted U.S. Army, 1971, advanced through ranks to sgt. first class; served in continental U.S., West Germany and West Berlin; ret., 1992. Contbr. short stories and poetry to profl. publs. Field rep. Law Enforcement Alliance Am., Falls Church, Va., 1998—; mem. Coun. Conservative Citizens, St. Louis, 1999—. Decorated French Commando Badge, French Army, 1981. Mem. DAV, Golden Key Nat. Honor Soc., U-Boot-Archiv (full friend), Sigma Tau Delta. Avocations: study of world war ii and u-boat history, writing.

**MCLEAN, DAVID J.,** lawyer; m. Tammy Lynne Ross, May 26, 1985; children: Emily, Michael. BA summa cum laude, Washington & Lee U., 1978; grad student, U. Edinburg, Scotland, 1979; JD magna cum laude, Georgetown U. Law Ctr., 1982. Bar: Calif. 1982, DC 1991, N.Y. 2004, (various others). Assoc. Latham & Watkins, LA, 1982—89; ptnr., litigation dept. Latham & Watkins LLP, LA, 1989—2003, ptnr. in charge of ltg., 1999—2002, office managing ptnr. Newark, 2000—03; exec. comm. CPR Inst. for Dispute Resolution, N.Y.C., 2003—. Trustee San Martino (Calif.) Schs. Found., 1999—2002. Mem.: ABTL (LA) (bd. of governors, alternative dispute resolution section), CPR Ctr. for Dispute Resolution (standing com. on dispute resolution), Chancery Club (litig. section). Office: Latham & Watkins LLP One Newark Ctr Newark NJ 07101 Office Phone: 973-639-1234. Business E-Mail: david.mclean@lw.com.

**MC LEAN, DON,** singer, instrumentalist, composer; b. New Rochelle, N.Y., Oct. 2, 1945; s. Donald and Elizabeth (Bucci) McL.; m. Patrisha Shnier, Mar., 1987. Student, Villanova U., 1964; BBA, Iona Coll., 1968. Pres., owner The Benny Bird Co., Inc., Fairfield, Conn.; recorded for United Artists, Artista Records, EMI Records. Star BBC-TV spls., 1973, 78, numerous concert appearances. Albums include Tapestry, 1972, American Pie, 1972, Don McLean, 1972, Playin' Favourites, 1973, Homeless Brother, 1974, Solo, 1976, Prime Time, 1987, Chain Lightning, 1979, Very Best of, 1980, Believers, 1982, Dominion, 1983, The Best of Don McLean, 1987, Don McLean's Greatest Hits Then & Now, 1987, Love Tracks, 1988, For the Memories, 1989, Don McLean's Greatest Hits Live, 1990, Headroom, 1991, Classics, 1992, The River of Love, 1995, Solo, 1995, Greatest Hits Live, 1997, Don McLean's Christmas Dreams, 1997; singles include American Pie, 1971, Vincent, 1971, Crying, 1980; wrote Perry Como hit And I Love You So, 1973; performances include America's Millenium, Washington, Starry Starry Night (TV special). Mem. bd. Hudson River Sloop Restoration, World Hunger Yr., Advs. for Arts; fund raiser Scenic Hudson, Hudson River Fisherman's Assn. Recipient more than 30 gold and platinum records worldwide, 5 grammy award nominations and others; Israel Cultural award, 1981. Mem. Coffee House Club. Office: Atlantic Records 1290 Avenue Of The Americas New York NY 10104-0184 also: PO Box 307 Camden ME 04843-0307

**MC LEAN, DONALD MILLIS,** microbiologist, educator, pathologist, pediatrician; b. Melbourne, Australia, July 26, 1926; s. Donald and Nellie (Millis) McL.; married. BSc, U. Melbourne, 1947, MB, 1950, MD, 1954. Fellow Rockefeller Found., N.Y.C. and Hamilton, Mont., 1955; vis. instr. bacteriology II Hmn., Mpls., 1957, med. officer Commonwealth Serum Labs., Melbourne, 1957; virologist Research Inst., Hosp. for Sick Children, Toronto, Ont., Canada, 1958-67; assoc. prof. microbiology, assoc. in pediatrics U. Toronto Med. Sch., 1962-67; prof. med. microbiology U. B.C. Med. Sch., Vancouver, Canada, 1967-91, prof. emeritus Pathology, 1991—. Author: Virology in Health Care, 1980, Immunological Investigation of Human Virus Disease, 1982, Same-Day Virus Diagnosis, 1984, Virological Infections, 1988, Medical Microbiology Synopsis, 1991, Acute Viral Infections, 1991; contbr. articles to profl. jours. Fellow Royal Coll. Physicians (Can.), Royal Coll. Pathologists; mem. Am. Epidemiological Soc., Am. Soc. Tropical Medicine, Can. Med. Assn., Am. Soc. Virology, Soc. for Vector Ecology, Soc. for Gen. Microbiology, Infectious Diseases Soc. Am. Home: 6-5885 Yew St Vancouver BC Canada V6M 3Y5 Office Phone: 604-263-9076.

**MCLEAN, JAMES ALBERT,** artist, educator; b. Gibsland, La., Nov. 25, 1928; s. Charles Edward and Lucille (Bowdon) McL.; m. Ocelia Jo Perkins, Nov. 27, 1954; 1 child: Gregory Scott. BA, Southwestern La. Inst., 1950; BD, So. Meth. U., 1953; MFA, Tulane U., 1961. Meth. student dir. Centenary Coll., Shreveport, La., 1957-59; head art dept. LaGrange (Ga.) Coll., 1964-66; assoc. prof. art Ga. State U., Atlanta, 1967-68, prof. art, 1968-95; ret., 1995. Exhibited in numerous group shows including Brooklyn Mus., 1976-77, Positive/Negative Exhbn., 1988, Siggraph Exhbn. 1988, 89, Clemson U. Nat. Print and Drawing Exhbn., 1989, Purdue U. Small Print Exhbn., 1990. Mem. Siggraph. Avocations: animation, puppetry. Home: 1256 Dunwoody Knoll Dr Atlanta GA 30338-3219 E-mail: mcle231@bellsouth.net.

**MCLEAN, R. BRUCE,** lawyer; b. NYC, Nov. 15, 1946; BS with honors, Ind. U., 1968, JD cum laude, 1971. Bar: Ind. 1971, DC 1974. Atty. appellate ct. br. Nat. Labor Rels. Bd., 1971—73; chair, litig. practice Akin, Gump, Strauss, Hauer & Feld L.L.P., Washington, 1982—94, now chmn. Bd. visitors Ind. U. Sch. Law, 1989—, vice chair, 1998—; bd. visitors Georgetown Law Ctr., 2002—. Mem. Fed. City Coun. Mem.: ABA, DC Bar, Fed. Bar Assn., Order of Coif, Phi Alpha Delta. Office: Akin Gump Strauss Hauer & Feld LLP Robert S Strauss Bldg 1333 New Hampshire Ave NW Washington DC 20036-1564 Office Phone: 202-887-4022. Office Fax: 202-887-4288. Business E-Mail: bmclean@akingump.com.

**MCLEAN, ROBERT JAMES CAMERON,** microbiologist, educator; b. Toronto, Sept. 18, 1956; came to U.S., 1993; m. Martha Elaine Law, May 21, 1988; children: Malcolm Albert Campbell, Alistair Ian Law. BSc, U. Guelph, Ont., Can., 1978; PhD, U. Calgary, Alta., Can., 1986. Asst. prof. Queens U., Kingston, Ont., 1988-93; from asst. prof. to prof. Tex. State U., San Marcos, 1993—. Cons. Kingston Techs., Trenton, N.J., 1991, Q-Life Systems, Inc., Kingston, 1992-93, ICET, Inc., Norwood, Mass., 1995, Sulzer Carbomedics Inc., Austin, Tex., 1999-2001. Author: (with I. A. Veliky) Immobilized Biosystems, 1994, (with A.W. Decho) Molecular Ecology of Biofilms, 2002; mem. editl. bd. Applied and Environ. Microbiology, 1999—, Bioresource Tech., 1997-2002, Geomicrobiology Jour., 1999—; contbr. articles to profl. jours. Recipient Pres. award Microscopical Soc. Can., 1986. Mem. Am. Soc. for Microbiology (pres. Tex. br. 2003-05), Can. Soc. Microbiologists (chmn. morphology and structure sect. 1994-96), Internat. Soc. Microbial Ecology, Sigma Xi. Presbyterian. Achievements include first experimental bacterial biofilm formation during space flight; recovery of bacteria from space shuttle Columbia wreckage; co-discovery of quorum sensing signal molecules in naturally occurring biofilms; research on gene expression including slow growth, starvation survival and quorum sensing genes in biofilm growth. Office: Tex State Univ Dept Biology 601 University Dr San Marcos TX 78666 Office Phone: 512-245-3365. E-mail: McLean@txstate.edu.

**MCLEAN, VINCENT RONALD,** former manufacturing company financial executive; b. Detroit, June 1, 1931; s. Frederick Ronald and Bernice Mary (Vincent) McL.; m. Joyce Adrienne Koch, July 23, 1960; children— Judith Adrienne, Bruce Ronald BBA, U. Mich., 1954, MBA, 1955. Fin. analyst Ford Motor Co., Detroit, 1954—55, Mobil Oil Corp., N.Y.C., 1958—69; treas. Mobil Chem. Co., N.Y.C., 1966—69; v.p. fin. treas. NL Industries, N Y C 1969—76, exec. v.p. fin. and planning, dir., 1976—82, exec. v.p., CFO, dir. Sperry Corp., N.Y.C., 1982—86; sr. advisor Wertheim Schroder & Co., N.Y.C., 1988—89. Bd. dirs. Legal and Gen. Am., Inc., William Penn Life Ins. Co. NY, Banner Life Ins. Co., Md. Served with U.S. Army, 1955-57 Mem. N.Y. Soc. Security Analysts, Econ. Club N.Y. Home: 702 Shackamaxon Dr Westfield NJ 07090-3408

**MCLEAN, WALTER FRANKLIN,** government agency administrator, business consultant, legislator, minister; b. Leamington, Ont., Can., Apr. 26, 1936; s. J.L.W. McL.; m. Barbara Muriel Scott, Aug. 19, 1961; children: Scott, Chima, Ian, Duncan BA, Victoria Coll., U. B.C., 1957; M.Div., Knox Coll., U. Toronto, 1960; LLD (hon.), Wilfrid Laurier U., 1995; DD (hon.), Knox Coll., 2002. Ordained to ministry, Presbyterian Ch. Min. Knox Presbyn. Ch., Waterloo, 1971-79; mem. House of Commons, Ottawa, Ont., Canada, 1979—93, Sec. of State of Can., 1984—85, sworn to Privy Coun., 1984, min. of immigration, 1985—86; min. responsible for status of women Govt. of Can., 1984-86. CUSO, Nigeria coord., 1962-67; chaplain U. Nigeria, 1962-67; dep. dir. Internat. Program Can. Centennial, 1967; exec. dir. Man. Assn. for World Devel., 1970; past chmn. World Concerns Commn. Canadian Coun. Chs.; Can. del. Gen. Assemblies UN, 1986-93; apptd. prime minister's spl. rep. Commonwealth and South African affairs, 1989-93; Can. rep. Africa Devel. Coordination Conf., 1987-93; del. Commonwealth Fgn. Mins. Against Apartheid, 1987-93, African Devel. Bank, 1990-91, Assn. West European Parliamentarians Against Apartheid, 1988-89; leader fact finding mission to Mozambique, 1987, Can. delegation UN Conf. on Women, Nairobi, 1985; led Parliamentary del. to observe the pre-election process and attended Namibian Indpedence, Mar. 21, 1990; chmn. paliamentary Com. on Devel. and Human Rights; Commonwealth observer South African and Sri Lanka elections 1994; pres. Franklin Cons. Ltd., 1993—; chair McLean and Assocs., 2004—; dir. TAB Internat. Energy Corp., 2005—; dir. Toronto Sch. Tech. Alderman City of Waterloo, Ont., 1976-79; co-founder UN based Parliamentarians Global Action; hon. consul of the Rep. of Namibia, 1994—; convenor Millenium Celebration Presbyn. Ch., 1998-00; prin. The Osborne Group, 2000—; mem. bd. dirs. Toronto Sch. Theology, 2005-; mem. adv. bd. Royal Rds. U., Victoria BC, 1995-. Chaplain 404 wing RCAF, 1976-03; mem. Cosl Criminal Injuries Compensation Bd., 2000-03. Recipient Can. U. Svcs. Overseas award, 1990, Can. Bur. Internat. Edn. award, 1994, Disting. Alumni award U. Victoria, 2002; Paul Harris fellow, 1984. Mem. UN Assn. Can. (chair human rights com.), Rotary. Progressive Conservative. Office Phone: 519-578-5932. E-mail: walter@mcleanandassociates.ca.

**MCLEAN, WILLIAM RONALD,** retired electrical engineer, consultant; b. Bklyn., Mar. 26, 1921; s. Harold W. and Helena Winifred (Farrell) McL.; m. Cecile L. Mills, Aug. 17, 1946 (div.); m. Evelyn Hupfer, Nov. 29, 1968. BA in Math., Bklyn. Coll., 1980, BS in Computational Math., 1981. Chief electrician U.S. Mcht. Marine, 1942-64, elect. designer, engr., 1965-76; sr. elect engr. M. Rosenblatt & Son, Inc., N.Y.C., 1976-86; cons., 1986-98; ret., 1996. Mem. AAAS, IEEE, Soc. Naval Archs. and Marine Engrs., Am. Soc. Naval Engrs. Home and Office: 1250 67th Street Brooklyn NY 11219 Office Phone: 718-331-6342. E-mail: mclnbill@aol.com.

**MCLEER, LAUREEN DOROTHY,** drug development and pharmaceutical professional; b. N.Y.C., Feb. 5, 1955; d. William Myers and Una Lee (Massey) McLeer. BS, Columbia U., 1977; MBA, U. London, 1981. RN N.Y., D.C., state reg. nurse, Eng., registered state nurse, Wales. Staff nurse NYU Med. Ctr., N.Y.C., 1977-78; charge nurse Scripps Clinic and Rsch. Found., La Jolla, Calif., 1979-80; clin. rschr. Ayerst Labs., N.Y.C., 1982; sales rep. Pfizer, Inc., N.Y.C., 1983-87; Cahners Pub. Co., N.Y.C., 1988-89; dir. bus. devel. Pro Clinica, N.Y.C., 1990-91; account supr. Salthouse Torre Norton, Inc., Rutherford, N.J., 1992-93; dir. bus. devel. Med. & Tech. Rsch. Assocs., Inc., Wellesley, Mass., 1993-94; sr. project dir. Quiltiles Inc., Arlington, Va., 1994-99; project mgr. product devel. and commercialization Aventis Pharms., Inc., Berwyn, Pa., 1999—2002; clin. trial mgmt. leader AstraZeneca, LP, Wilmington, Del., 2002—, assoc. dir., 2005—. Mem. com. for healthcare issues and legis. United Hosp. Fund, N.Y.C., 1992—94. Chmn. Help Our Neighbors Eat Yr. 'Round, N.Y.C., 1987—89; trustee Murray Hill Com., N.Y.C., 1988—90; bd. dirs. East Midtown Svcs. for Older People, 1987—94; vol. nurse Whitman Walker Clinic, 1995—99; bd. dirs. Cecil Land Trust, 2002—06, Eastern Shore Land Conservancy, 2003—, treas., exec. bd. dirs., 2005—. Named Md. Wildlife Farmer of Yr., Md. Dept. Natural Resources, 2004. Mem.: Drug Info. Assn., Regulatory Affairs Profl. Soc. Home: PO Box 681 Chesapeake City MD 21915 Office: AstraZeneca LP 1800 Concorde Pike Wilmington DE 19850-2034 Office Phone: 302-885-5213. Business E-Mail: laureen.mcleer@astrazeneca.com.

**MCLELLAN, A. ANNE,** Canadian government official; b. Hants County, N.S., Can., Aug. 31, 1950; d. Howard Gilmore and Joan Mary (Pullan) McL. BA, Dalhousie U., LLB, 1974; LLM, King's Coll., U. London, 1975. Bar: N.S., 1976. Asst. prof. law U. N.B., Can., 1976-80; assoc. prof. law U. Alta., Edmonton, Can., 1980-89, assoc. dean faculty of law, 1985-87, prof. law, 1989-93, acting dean, 1991-92; M.P. for Edmonton West Ho. of Commons, Can., 1993—; min. of nat. resources Govt. of Canada, Ottawa, 1993—97, min. of energy, mines and resources, 1993—95, min. of forestry, 1993—95, fed. interlocutor for metis and non-status Indians, 1993—97, min. justice and atty. gen. of Canada Ottawa, Canada, 1997—2002, min. of health, 2002—03, dep. prime min., 2003—, min. of public safety and emergency preparedness, 2003—. Commentator on Can. Charter of Rights and Freedoms and on human rights issues. Contbr. articles to profl. publs. Past bd. dirs. Can. Civil Liberties Assn., Alta. Legal Aid; past v.p. U. Alta. Faculty Assn. E-mail: McLellan.A@parloge.ca.

**MCLELLON, RICHARD STEVEN,** aerospace engineer, consultant; b. Lawton, Okla., May 28, 1952; s. Robert Nelson and Jane (Wariner) McL. BSME, Old Dominion U., 1979. Aerospace engr. Naval Engring. Support Office, Norfolk, Va., 1979-82, U.S. Army Aviation Systems Commd., Ft. Eustis, Va., 1982-86; mission lead dynamicist Astronautics Space Launch Sys., Lockheed Martin Corp., Denver, 1986—2005, stress analyst, loads analyst, Workshare, Tech. Ops., 2005—. Cons. Aircraft Devel., Inc., Littleton, Colo., 1991—.

**MCLEMORE, JOAN MEADOWS,** librarian, consultant; b. Bivens, Tex., Aug. 24, 1929; d. James Leon Jr. and Dell (Crawford) Meadows; m. Kenneth Lyons McLemore, May 6, 1950 (dec.); 1 child, Ken Malcolm. Student, Miss. State Coll. for Women, 1947-49; BS, U. So. Miss., 1976, MLS, 1983. Libr. Franklin County Pub. Libr., Meadville, Miss., 1976-90; libr. dir. Copiah-Lincoln C.C., Natchez, Miss., 1990—2003. Story teller, presenter conf. The Delta Kappa Gamma Soc. Internat., Louisville, 1991, Nashville, 1994; internat. spkr. Delta Kappa Soc., Red Deer, Can., 1994; mem. faculty Elderhostel, Natchez, Miss., 1990—; presenter Southeastern Regional Conf., Delta Kappa Gamma Soc. Internat., Charleston, S.C, 1997; pres. Franklinc Mus., 1999-2004, Franklin County Mus., Meadville, Miss., 2002—, Inst. Lng. in Retirement, 2003—. Contbr. articles to profl. jours. Libr. trustee Franklin County, Meadville, 1962-76, Lincoln-Lawrence-Franklin Regional Libr., Brookhaven, Miss., 1971-76; trustee Franklyn County Meml. Hosp., 1997-2001, jury com., 1998-2001; deacon Presbyn.Ch., 2003—; Miss. com. Humanities Spkrs. Roster, 2004—. Mem. Miss. Libr. Assn. (com. chair, exec. dir. libr. week activities 1989), Colonial Dames (gov. George Harlan chpt., 2nd v.p. 2002-05, parliamentarian 2005—), DAR (Homochitlo River chpt. 1979-1999, Natchez chpt. 2000—), Dames of the Ct. of Honor (treas. 2001—, chaplain 1999-2003), Mis. Soc. DAMES of the South, Daughters of Soc. of War of 1812, Natchez Garden Club, Natchez Hist. Soc. (trustee 2005—), Miss. Hist. Soc., Order of the First Families of Miss.: 1619-1817 (chaplain 2002-05, historian 2005—), First Families Twin Territories, Delta Kappa Gamma (pres. 1979-80, 1979-97 Rho chpt.), Delta Kappa Gamma Soc. Internat. (Alpha Omicron chpt.), Progressive Study Club (sec. 2006-), Natchez Women's Book Soc., Friends of Armstrong Libr., Rose Craft Club, Scottish Heritage Soc., Natchez Retriee Partnership. Avocations: genealogy, reading, baking, historial research, story telling. Home: Apt A 310 S Dr Ml King Jr St Natchez MS 39120-3533 E-mail: joanmcl1@bellsouth.net.

**MCLEMORE, LAURA LYONS,** archivist, history educator; b. Shreveport, La., July 21, 1950; d. Val Alexander and Bobbie Chennault Lyons; m. Jim Ray McLemore, June 7, 1975; children: Havard Roland, Austen Laurence, Ivy Elizabeth. BA, So. Meth. U., 1971; MA, Tex. A&M U., 1991; PhD, U. of North Tex., 1998. Coll. archivist Austin Coll., Sherman, Tex., 1987—2004; adj. instr. Grayson County Coll., Denison, Tex., 1998—; archivist La. State U., Shreveport. Author: (book) Inventing Texas: Early Historians of the Lone Star State. Mem. Hist. Preservation Adv. Bd., Denison, 2003—04; pres. Red River Hist. Mus., Sherman, 1996—97; mem. Shreveport Symphony Orch., 2005—. Named Outstanding Grad. Student in History, U. of North Tex., 1995—96; recipient Hatton W. Sumners Dissertation fellowship, 1996. Mem.: North La. Hist. Assn., La. Hist. Assn., Tex. State Hist. Assn. (John H. Jenkins Rsch. fellowship 1996), La. Archives and Manuscripts Assn., Acad. of Cert. Archivists (regent for outreach 2004—06), Soc. of S.W. Archivists (pres. 1998—99), Soc. of Am. Archivists, Phi Kappa Phi. Episcopalian. Avocations: choral singing, gardening, bridge, reading, tennis. Office: La State U One University Pl Shreveport LA 71115 Office Phone: 318-797-5378. Business E-Mail: lmclemore@lsus.edu.

**MCLEMORE-WHEELER, LINDA M.,** literature educator; b. Akron, Ohio, Oct. 26, 1970; d. Lee and Catherine White; m. William A. Wheeler, June 10; children: Elizabeth Wheeler, Jordan Wheeler, Austin Wheeler. BA in English, Jackson State U., Miss., 1988—92, MA in English, 1995—97. Computer instr. Johnson Elem., Jackson, Miss., 1992—96; English instr. Coahoma C.C., Clarksdale, Miss., 1998—2000, Jackson State U., Jackson, Miss., 2000—. Editor: (cookbook) Heart and Soul: Student Recipes for Everyday Living. Vol. Couples Ministry Outreach, Jackson, Miss., 2000—01. Mem.: Miss. Assn. for Devel. Edn., Nat. Coun. for the Teachers of English, Writer's Guild, Alpha Epsilon Lambda (sec. 1995), Phi Kappa Phi. Baptist. Avocations: piano, reading, singing, poetry. E-mail: linda.m.wheeler@jsums.edu.

**MCLENDON, MELBURNE DEKALB,** lawyer, arbitrator; b. Atlanta, Apr. 21, 1921; s. Jesse Martin and Elizabeth Lee (Sartain) McL.; m. Loyce Jacqueline Kirkland, Dec. 31, 1949; children: James Kirkland, Loyce Eloise McLendon Snyder. LLB, U. Ga., 1948. Bar: Ga. 1949, U.S. Dist. Ct. (no.

dist.) Ga. 1949, U.S. Ct. Appeals (5th cir.) 1965, U.S. Supreme Ct. 1973, U.S. Dist. Ct. (mid. dist.) Ga. 1985. Law clk. Fulton County Superior Ct., Atlanta, 1949-50; ptnr. Carter Ansley Smith & McLendon, Atlanta, 1950-86; dir. Amica Mutual Ins. Co., 1976-96; cons. U.S. VA Hosp., Decatur, Ga., 1996—; pro bono. Arbitrator N.Y. Stock Exch., 1980-88, U.S. Dist. Ct. (mid. dist.) Ga., Macon, 1988—. Scout master Boy Scouts Am., Atlanta, 1959-70; active pro bono work for war vets., 1998—. Staff sgt. USAAF, 1942-45, ETO. Recipient Disting. Svc. award U.Ga., 1996, Exceptional Performance citation def. Rsch. Inst., 1985. Mem. Ga. Def. Lawyers Assn. (pres. 1984), Atlanta Bar Assn., Lawyers Club of Atlanta, Univ. Yacht Club, Buckhead Men's Garden Club (pres. 2002), Masons (32 deg.), Phi Alpha Delta, Phi Delta Kappa, Blue Key. Republican. Methodist. Avocations: gardening, woodwork, travel, fishing, spectator sports. Personal E-mail: melburne@bellsouth.net.

**MCLENDON, RICHARD CHARLES,** music educator; b. Troy, Ala., July 9, 1953; s. Charles Elie and Doris Dean McLendon; m. Michelle Rene Buck, June 25, 1988 (div. July 2, 1996); children: Zachary, Ryan; m. Tatyana Klimentyevna Stepanova, June 4, 2003; 1 stepchild, Nikita. BS in Edn., Jacksonville State U., 1977; MusM, U. Southwestern La., 1979; Ednl. Specialist, Troy State U., 1997; EdD, Argosy U., Sarasota, 2004. Cert. tchr. Ga. Grad. asst. U. Southwestern La., Lafayette, 1977—79; band dir. Murray (Ky.) Ind. Sch. Sys., 1979—80; program coord. Pride of Cin., Inc., 1981—83; instr. of percussion Murray (Ky.) State U., 1981—82; band dir. Colquitt County Jr. H.S., Moultrie, Ga., 1984—93; dir. of bands Colquitt County H.S., Moultrie, Ga., 1993—2004, adminstrv. asst., 2002—04; asst. dir. band Lowndes H.S., Valdosta, Ga., 2004—. Assoc. condr. European tour US Collegiate Wind Band, 1998; creative & instrnl. staff tour of Ecuador and Colombia US All-Star Marching Band, 1978. Composer: Medigated Goo II (3rd Pl., 11th Internat. Percussion Composition Contest, Percussive Arts Soc., 1984). Mem.: Music Educators Nat. Conf., Nat. Band Assn., Comparative and Internat. Edn. Soc., Am. Assn. for the Advancement of Slavic Studies, Ga. Music Educators Assn. (dist. chmn. 2002—04), Kappa Delta Pi, Pi Kappa Lambda, Phi Mu Alpha Sinfonia. Avocations: swimming, bicycling, hiking, travel. Home: 3735 Kingston Ct Valdosta GA 31605 Office: Lowndes High Sch 1112 N St Augustine Rd Valdosta GA 31601 Personal E-mail: rcmclendon@bellsouth.net.     Business     E-Mail: rmclendon@lowndes.k12.ga.us.

**MCLENDON, ROGER EDWIN,** pathologist; b. Dawson, Ga., Jan. 7, 1957; s. Harold Edwin and Vivian Lucille (Woodall) McL.; m. Patti Jo Swain; children: Patrick Edwin, Erin Elizabeth, Ryan Hodges. AA, Oxford Coll., 1977; BA, Emory U., 1979; MD, Med. Coll. Ga., 1982. Diplomate Am. Bd. Pathology. Intern surgery Med. Ctr. Cen. Ga., Macon, 1983; resident anatomical pathology Duke Med. Ctr., Durham, N.C., 1983-87, neuropathology fellow, 1985-87; pathologist Tifton Path. Svcs., PC, Tifton, Ga., 1987-91; asst. prof. pathology Duke Med. Ctr., 1992-98, chief sect. neuropathology, 1994—, assoc. pathology, 1998—2001, prof. pathology, 2001—, dir. anat. pathology svc., 2001—. Asst. prof. Mercer U. Sch. Medicine, Macon, 1987—. Author: Pathology of Tumors of the Central Nervous System; editor: Russell and Rubinstein's Pathology of Tumors of the Nervous Sytem, 7th edit.; contbr. articles, abstracts and book chpts. to scientific publs. V.p. Tift County chpt. Am. Cancer Soc., 1991, bd. dirs. Ga. Div., 1990-91. Mem. Coll. Am. Pathology, Am. Assn. Neuropathology, U.S. Can. Assn. Pathology, Tift County Med. Soc. (pres. 1991), 2d Dist. Med. Assn. (pres. 1991), Am. Assn. Cancer Rsch., Phi Beta Kappa. Avocations: golf, gardening, reading, history.

**MCLENNAN, ANDREW M.,** economics professor; b. East Orange, N.J., Mar. 7, 1954; s. William Stewart and Janet McLennan; m. Shino Takayama, Apr. 28, 2003; m. Nita Krevans, Dec. 28, 1984 (div. Dec. 30, 2001); children: Sean, Martina Krevans. PhD, Princeton U., NJ, 1980. Asst. prof. U. Toronto, Ont., Canada, 1980—84, Cornell U., Ithaca, NY, 1984—87; assoc. prof. U. Minn., Mpls., 1987—2000, prof., 2000—05, U. Sydney, 2005—. Author: (software) Gambit. Mem.: Internat. Soc. Econ. Theory (co-editor jour.), Game Theory Soc. (assoc. editor jour. 2001—06), Econometric Soc. (assoc. editor Econometrica). Democrat. Avocations: reading, games. Home: 20/52 Shepherd St Chippendale 2008 Australia Office: U Sydney Economics Discipline H-04 Merewether Building Sydney 2006 Australia Office Phone: +61-2-9351-6607. Business E-Mail: a.mclennan@econ.usyd.edu.au.

**MCLENNAN, BARBARA NANCY,** tax specialist; b. NYC, Mar. 25, 1940; d. Sol and Gertrude (Rochkind) Miller; m. Kenneth McLennan, Aug. 14, 1962; children: Gordon, Laura. BA magna cum laude, CCNY, 1961; MS, U. Wis., 1962, PhD, 1965; JD, Georgetown U., 1983. Bar: DC 1983, U.S. Ct. Internat. Trade 1988, U.S. Ct. Appeals (DC cir.) 1988, U.S. Supreme Ct. 1988, Va. 1991; cert. accredited valuation analyst Nat. Assn. Cert. Valuation Analysts, 2004. From asst. prof. to assoc. prof. Temple U., Phila., 1965—78; budget analyst Com. Budget, U.S. Ho. of Reps., Washington, 1978—81; legis. asst. fin. and budget Senator Dan Quayle, Washington, 1981—84; internat. tax specialist IRS U.S. Dept. Treasury, Washington, 1984—89; dep. asst. sec. trade, info. and analysis U.S. Dept. Commerce, Washington, 1989—91; prin., atty.-at-law Bitonti and Wilhelm, PC., McLean, Va., 1991—93; staff v.p. govt.-legal affairs consumer electronics group Electronic Industries Assn., Washington, 1993—94, staff v.p. tech. policy, consumer electronics group, 1994—95; v.p. Van Scoyoc Assocs., Washington, 1995—96; cons. on tax related issues in U.S., former Soviet Union, and West Bank and Gaza McLean, Va., 1996—. Adj. prof. Coll. William and Mary, 2005—; sr. polit. scientist SRI-Internat., Arlington, Va., 1971—74; vis. prof. Am. Coll., Paris, 1975—76; cons. UNESCO, Paris, 1977—78. Author: (book) Comparative Political Systems, 1975; contbr. articles to profl. jours. Mem. parents adv. coun. Randolph-Macon Coll., Ashland, Va., 1990—93. Fellow NDEA, 1962—65. Mem.: ABA, Va. Bar Assn., Fed. Bar Assn., DC Bar Assn., Am. Soc. Assn. Execs., Phi Beta Kappa. Home: 1620 Harbor Rd Williamsburg VA 23185 E-mail: barb.mcl@cox.net.

**MCLENNAN, HAMISH,** advertising executive; Account mgr. George Patterson Bates, internat. client svcs. dir. Hong Kong, 1994, mng. dir. Melbourne, nat. mng. dir., 1999; chmn., CEO Young & Rubicam Brands, Australia, New Zealand, 2002—06; CEO Y&R Advt., NYC, 2006—. Office: Y&R Advt 285 Madison Ave New York NY 10017 Office Phone: 212-210-3000.*

**MCLEOD, CAROLYN LOUISE,** artist; b. Palo Alto, Calif., Sept. 26, 1946; d. James and Virginia McLeod; m. William Bailey, Nov. 19, 1965 (div. 1969); 1 child, William; m. Peter Johnson, Dec. 31, 1987 AA in Art with honors, Foothill Coll., 1972; postgrad., Sonoma State U., 1973-74; BA in Art with honors, San Jose State U., 1976, postgrad., 1976-77, Truckee Meadows C.C., 1995—. Sec. Stanford (Calif.) U., 1982-87, U.S. Geol. Survey, Menlo Park, Calif., 1988-92. One-woman shows include Hollister (Calif.) City Hall, 1983, King St. Gallery, Carson City, Nev., 1995, Nev. State Libr. & Archives, Carson City, 1997, Clay Nichols Gallery, Reno, 2006, McKinley Arts and Culture Ctr., 2006, exhibited in group shows at Sacramento Fine Arts Ctr., Carmichael, Calif., 1994 (Excellence award), Carl Cherry Ctr. for Arts, Carmel, Calif., 1994, Las Vegas (N.Mex.) Arts Coun., 1995, 1997, Poudre Valley Art League, Lincoln Ctr., Ft. Collins, Colo., 1995, River Gallery, Reno, 1995 (Best of Show), Nat. Assn. Women Artists, NYC, 1995—2005, Nat. Mus. Women Arts, Washington, 1996, China World Trade Ctr., Beijing, 1995, Sierra Arts, Reno, 1996, Artists' Atelier of Atlanta, 1999, Sierra Arts Ctr., Reno, 1999, Roswell Mus. and Art Ctr., N.Mex., 2000, Mus. of Fine Arts, St. Petersburg, Fla., 2000, Atelier 14, NYC, 2000, Paris Gibson Sq. Mus. Art, Gr. Falls, Mont., 2001, Binney Smith Gallery, Bethlehem, Pa., 2002, UN, NYC, 2002, Gulf Coast Mus. Art, Largo, Fla., 2003, Strathmore Hall Arts Ctr., North Bethesda, Md., 2004, Leepa-Rattner Mus. Art, Fla., 2004, Smithsonian Instn., Washington, 2004, Dunedin (Fla.) Fine Art Ctr., 2005, King St. Gallery, 2006 (2 1st pl. awards), Strathmore Hall Arts Ctr., Bethesda, Md. 2004, exhibited in group shows at Dunedin Fine Art Ctr., Fla., 2005. Dean's scholar San Jose State U., 1976. Mem.: Cider Painters Am., Miniature Art Soc. Fla., Sierra Watercolor Soc., Nev. Mus. Art, Sierra Arts Found., Nat.

Mus. Women in Arts, Nev. Artists Assn. (newsletter editor 1996—99, Recognition award 1997—98), Nat. Assn. Women Artists (Mary K. Karasick Meml. award 2001, Myra Bigger Staff award 2002). Home: 2512 Plumas St Reno NV 89509-4255

**MCLEOD, CHANSE L.,** lawyer; b. Dallas, 1965; BBA with honors in Fin., U. Tex., Austin, 1988; JD, Houston U., 1991. Bar: Tex. 1991. Ptnr., Real Estate Andrews Kurth LLP, Houston. Assoc. editor Houston Law Rev., 1989—91. Mem.: Houston Bar Found., Tex. Bar Found., Houston Bar Assn., Houston Young Lawyers Assn., State Bar Tex., Tex. Young Lawyers Assn., ABA, Phi Delta Phi. Office: Andrews Kurth LLP 600 Travis St Ste 4200 Houston TX 77002-3090 Office Phone: 713-238-7257, 713-220-4020. Business E-Mail: cmcleod@andrewskurth.com.

**MCLEOD, DAVID G.,** urologist, educator; BS, MD, U. N.C.; JD, No. Va. Law Sch. Dir. Ctr. Prostate Disease Rsch., Urologic Oncology Walter Reed Army Med. Ctr., Washington, 1984—. Prof. surgery Uniformed Svcs. U. of Health Scis., Bethesda, Md.; rsch. investigator Ctr. for Prostate Disease Rsch. Contbr. chpts. to books, articles to profl. jours. Decorated Legion of Merit award with 2 Oak Leaf Clusters, Bronze Star, Air medal, Combat Med. Badge. Mem.: Nat. Prostate Cancer Project, Soc. Univ. Urologists, Am. Urol. Assn. (pres. Mid-Atlantic sect.), Am. Found. Urol. Disease (pres. 1999—2004), Soc. Surg. Oncology, Am. Assn. Clin. Urologists, Soc. Urol. Oncology, Am. Soc. Clin. Urology. Office: Walter Reed Army Med Ctr Urology Svc 6900 Georgia Ave NW Washington DC 20307-5001 Address: Uniformed Svcs Univ 4301 Jones Bridge Rd Bethesda MD 20814

**MCLEOD, E. DOUGLAS,** real estate developer, lawyer; b. Galveston, Tex., Aug. 6, 1941; s. Vaughan Watkins McLeod and Dorothy (Milroy) Burton; m. Sarah Jackson Helms, Mar. 20, 1965 (div. 1979); children: Chanse, Alexandra, Lindsey; m. Joan Margaret Williams, Dec. 26, 1979; 1 child, Joanie stepchildren: Meg. Libbie. BBA, U. North Tex., 1965; postgrad., So. Meth. U., 1965-66; JD, South Tex. Coll. Law, 1992; LLM, U. Houston, 1993. Bar: Tex., U.S. Dist. Ct. (so. dist.) Tex.; lic. real estate broker. Pres., owner McLeod Properties & co., Galveston, 1967—; tchr. Galveston Ind. Sch. Dist., 1967-69, pres., trustee, 1969—73; banker W. L. Moody & Co., Galveston, 1969-72; developer, broker McLeod Properties/Builders, Galveston, 1972-82; developer Moody Found., Galveston, 1982—. Bd. dirs. Am. Nat. Ins. Co., Galveston, Nat. Western Life Ins. Co., Austin, Anrem Corp., Galveston, Colonel Inc., Galveston, Moody Gardens Inc., Galveston, chmn., 1984—. Mem. editl. bd.; Currents Internat. Trade Law Jour., 1992—. Mayor pro-tem, city coun. City of Galveston, 1973—76; state legislator Tex. Ho. Reps., Austin, 1976—83; bd. visitors South Tex. Coll. Law, 1990—96, bd. dirs. 2000—; mem. adv. bd. U. Houston, 1986—95; bd. dirs. STCL, Ronald McDonald House, 1986—93, Trinity Episcopal Sch., 1990—96, Galveston Econ. Devel. Partnership, 1998—2002; vestryman, sr. warden, chancellor Episc. Ch. With USMC, 1961—67. Mem.: ABA, Am. Judicature Soc., Galveston County Bar Assn., Tex. Bar Assn., Marine Corps League. Avocations: physical fitness advocate, legal history collector. Home: 53 Cedar Lawn Cir Galveston TX 77551-4631 Office: The Moody Found 2302 Post Office St Ste 704 Galveston TX 77550-1994 Office Phone: 409-797-1521. Business E-Mail: dmcleod@moodyf.org.

**MCLEOD, WALTON JAMES,** lawyer, state legislator; b. Walterboro, S.C., June 30, 1937; s. Walton James Jr. and Rhoda Lane (Brown) M.; m. Julie Edwina Hamiter, Feb. 15, 1969; 1 child, Walton James IV BA, Yale U., 1959; LLB, U. S.C., 1964. Bar: S.C. 1964, U.S. Supreme Ct. 1974. Law clk. to Chief Judge Clement Haynsworth U.S. Ct. Appeals (4th cir.), Richmond, Va., 1964-65; assoc. Pope and Schumpert, Newberry, SC, 1965-67; asst. U.S. Atty. Columbia, SC, 1967-68; gen. counsel S.C. Dept. Health & Environ. Ctrl., Columbia, 1968-94, spl. counsel, 1994-96; dep. S.C. atty. gen. Columbia, 1987-88. Magistrate Newberry County, Little Mountain, S.C., 1981-83; mcpl. judge Town of Little Mountain, 1981-83, mayor, 1983-89, 93-96; mem. S.C. Ho. of Reps., Columbia, 1996—. Author: Legal Perspectives of Environmental Health, 1973; co-author: Environmental Quality Law, 1975, Hospital Franchising Law and Regulation, 1979. Pres. Newberry (S.C.) Jaycees, 1967; bd. dirs. S.C. Housing Fin. & Devel. Authority, Columbia, 1977-96; chair Ctrl. Midlands Coun. Govts., Columbia, 1981-82, 2001—; trustee S.C. State Mus., Columbia, 1981-85. Lt. (j.g.) USN, 1959-61, served to Capt. USNR, 1961-92, ret. Recipient Outstanding Jaycee award Newberry Jaycees, 1967, Howell Excellence award Naval Res. Law Program, Washington, 1991; named Outstanding Freshman Rep. of Yr. Carolina Hist. Found. Soc., Inc., 1997. Fellow S.C. Bar Found.; mem. S.C. Magistrates Assn. (pres. 1976-77, Disting. Jud. Svc. award 1975, 77), Judge Advs. Assn. (nat. pres. 1991-92), S.C. Res. Officers Assn. (state pres. 1981-82, Res. Officer of Yr. 1998), S.C. Soc. (pres. 1990-93). Democrat. Luth. Avocations: jogging, reading. Home: 308 Pomaria St Little Mountain SC 29075-9003 Office: SC House of Reps PO Box 11867 Columbia SC 29211-1867 Fax: 803-345-0770.

**MCLESKEY, CHARLES HAMILTON,** anesthesiologist, educator, pharmaceutical executive; b. Phila., Nov. 8, 1946; s. W. Hamilton and Marion A. (Butts) McL.; m. Nanci S. Simmons, June 3, 1972; children: Travis, Heather. BA, Susquehanna U., 1968; MD, Wake Forest U., 1972. Diplomate Am. Bd. Anesthesiology. Intern Maine Med. Ctr., Portland, 1972-73; resident in anesthesiology U. Wash. Sch. Medicine, Seattle, 1973-76, NIH rsch. trainee, 1974-75; clin. teaching assoc. dept. anesthesiology U. Calif., San Francisco, 1976-78; asst. prof. anesthesiology Wake Forest U. Bowman Gray Sch. Medicine, Winston-Salem, NC, 1978-83, assoc. prof., 1983-84, U. Tex. Med. Br., Galveston, 1985-87; assoc. prof. anesthesiology U. Colo. Health Sci. Ctr., Denver, 1987-91, prof., 1991-93, dir. acad. affairs, 1987-93; prof., chmn. dept. anesthesiology Tex. A&M U., 1993-2000; chmn. dept. anesthesiology, med. dir. perioperative svcs. Scott and White Clin. and Meml. Hosp., Temple, Tex., 1993-2000; assoc. med. dir. Scott and White Health Plan, 1995-2000; sr. dir. clin. devel. Abbott Labs., Abbott Park, Ill., 2000—02, global med. dir., global mktg. dir. anesthesia and sedation, 2002—06; v.p. clin. affairs ZARS, Salt Lake City, 2006—. Cons., lectr. Janssen Pharmaceutica, Piscataway, N.J., 1980-98, Alza Corp., Palo Alto, Calif., 1986-99; cons. Glaxo-Wellcome Co., Research Triangle Park, N.C., Abbott Labs., Chgo., Hoechst, Marion, Roussel, Kansas City, Kans., Aspect Med., Natick, Mass., Baxter Labs., Chgo., Scott Labs., Lubbock, Tex.; lectr. to over 500 nat. and state med. orgns., 1982—; examiner Am. Bd. Anesthesiology; lectr. Ohmeda, Liberty Corner, N.J. Assoc. editor Anesthesiology Rev., Anesthesiology News, Pharmacy Practia News; editor Geriatric Anesthesiology, 1997; contbr. numerous articles to med. jours. Mem. choir Friendswood (Tex.) Meth. Ch., 1985-87; mem. Friendswood Fine Arts Commn., 1985-87; mem. Temple Chamber Arts Adv. Coun., 1997-99. Lt. comdr. M.C., USN, 1976-78. Woodruff-Fisher scholar, 1964-68. Mem.: Temple C. of C., Evergreen Newcomers, Soc. Acad. Anesthesia Chairs (councilman 1996—99), Soc. for Ambulatory Anesthesia (program chair 1996), Internat. Anesthesia Rsch. Soc., Colo. Soc. Anesthesiologists (past pres.), Soc. for Edn. in Anesthesiology (past v.p., past pres., SEA-Duke Edn. prize), Am. Soc. Anesthesiologists (del. 1983—85, 1988—90), Assn. U Anesthesiologists, Nat. Spkrs. Assn., Internat. Platform Assn., Mensa, Alpha Omega Alpha. Republican. Presbyterian. Avocations: running, fishing, racquetball, squash. Address: #1606 North 48 W Broadway Salt Lake City UT 84101 Office Phone: 801-350-0202. Personal E-mail: charles.mcleskey@comcast.net.

**MCLIN, RHINE LANA,** mayor, former state legislator; b. Dayton, Ohio, Oct. 3, 1948; d. C. Josef, Jr. and Bernice (Cottman) McL. BA in Sociology, Parsons Coll., 1969; MEd, Xavier U., 1972; postgrad. in law, U. Dayton, 1974-76; AA in Mortuary Sci., Cin. Coll., 1988. Lic. funeral dir. Tchr. Dayton Bd. Edn., 1970-72; divorce counselor Domestic Rels. Ct., Dayton, 1972-73; law clk. Montgomery Common Pleas Ct., Dayton, 1973-74; v.p., dir. embalmer McLin Funeral Homes, Dayton, 1972—; mem. Ohio Ho. of Reps. from 36th & 38th dists., Columbus, 1988-94, Ohio Senate from 5th dist., Columbus, 1994—2002; mem. Ways & Means Com.; controlling bd., ins. commerce comn. ranking mem.; state and local govt. com. Columbus; minority whip Ohio Senate, Columbus, 1994—2001; mayor City of Dayton, 2002—. Instr. Central State U., Wilberforce, Ohio, 1982-97; mem. Ohio Tuition Trust Authority. Mem. Dem. Nat. Com., Children's Def. Fund. Toll fellow; Paul Harris fellow; Flemming fellow; BLLD fellow; named Ohio Legislator of Yr., Ohio Social Workers Assn., 1999. Mem. Nat. Funeral Dirs. Assn., Ohio Funeral Dirs. Assn., Montgomery County Hist. Soc., NAACP (life), Nat. Coun. Negro Women (life), Delta Sigma Theta. Achievements include being first female mayor of Dayton. Office: City Hall 2nd Fl 101 W Third St Dayton OH 45402 Office Phone: 937-333-3653. Business E-Mail: Rhine.McLin@cityofDayton.org.

**MCLORIE, GORDON ARTHUR,** urologist, educator; b. St. John, New Brunswick, Can., May 2, 1945; arrived in U.S., 2003; m. Blair Hilton, Dec. 20, 1968; children: Scott, David, Graham, Megan. MD, U. Toronto, Can., 1969. Cert. Am. Bd. Urology, 1982. Intern Toronto Gen. Hosp., Canada, 1969; resident in urology and renal transplant U. Toronto, Canada, 1971—76; fellowship dept. urology UCLA, 1976—77; fellowship in pediatric urology Harvard U., Boston, 1981—82; chief pediatric urology Childrens Hosp. Mich., Detroit, 2002—; prof. pediatric urology Wayne State U., Detroit, 2002—. Fellow: Royal Coll. Physicians and Surgeons Can., Am. Acad. Pediat.; mem.: Am. Urology Assn., Can. Urology Assn. (pres.). Achievements include research in vesicourethral reflux, and reconstructive surgery of infants and children with congenital anomalies of the genitourinary system. Avocations: skiing, golf. Office: Childrens Hosp Mich 3901 Beaubien Detroit MI 48201 Office Phone: 313-745-5749. Office Fax: 313-993-8758. Personal E-mail: gmclorie@dmc.org.

**MCLUCAS, KATE,** magazine editor; Exec. editor, testing dir. Infoworld, San Mateo, Calif.

**MCLUCAS, WILLIAM ROBERT,** lawyer, former federal agency administrator; b. Altoona, Pa., Aug. 12, 1950; s. James Daniel and Ruth Virginia (Sweeney) McL. BA in Polit. Sci. with distinction, Pa. State U., 1972; JD, Temple U., 1975. Bar: Pa. 1975, DC 1998, NY 1999. Atty. Fed. Home Loan Bank Bd., 1975-77; staff atty. through assoc. dir. SEC, Washington, 1977—89, dir., div. of enforcement, 1989—98; ptnr., co-chmn. Securities dept. Wilmer Cutler Pickering Hale & Dorr, Washington. Rsch. editor Temple Law Quar., 1972-75; contbr. articles to profl. jours. Named a Leading Lawyer in securities & corp. governance, Legal Times, 2004; named one of Top 30 Lawyers in Washington, Washingtonian mag., 2004, 100 Most Influential Lawyers in Am., Nat. Law Jour., 1997; recipient Nat. Pub. Svc. award, Nat. Soc. Pub. Adminstrn., 1996, Tom C. Clark Outstanding Lawyer award, Fed. Bar Assn., 1997. Mem. Phi Beta Kappa. Office: Wilmer Cutler Pickering Hale & Dorr 2445 M St NW Washington DC 20037 Office Phone: 202-663-6622. Office Fax: 202-663-6363. Business E-Mail: william.mclucas@wilmerhale.com.

**MC LURE, CHARLES E., JR.,** economist, consultant; b. Sierra Blanca, Tex., Apr. 14, 1940; s. Charles E. and Dessie (Evans) McL.; m. Patsy Nell Carroll, Sept. 17, 1962. BA, U. Kans., 1962; MA, Princeton U., 1964, PhD, 1966. Asst. prof. econs. Rice U., Houston, 1965-69, assoc. prof., 1969-72, prof., 1972-79, Allyn R. and Gladys M. Cline prof. econs., 1973-79; exec. dir. for research Nat. Bur. Econ. Research, Cambridge, Mass., 1977-78, v.p., 1978-81; sr. fellow Hoover Instn., Stanford U., 1981—; dep. asst. sec. Dept. Treasury, 1983-85. Sr. staff economist Coun. Econ. Advisers, Washington, 1969-70; vis. lectr. U. Wyo., 1972; vis. prof. Stanford U., 1973; cons. U.S. Treasury Dept., Labor Dept., World Bank, UN, OAS, Interam. Devel. Bank, Tax Found., Com. Econ. Devel., IMF, Internat. Tax and Investment Ctr., govts. Can., Colombia, Malaysia, Panama, Jamaica, Bolivia, Indonesia, New Zealand, Brazil, Trinidad and Tobago, Venezuela, Guatemala, Peoples Republic China, Egypt, Malawi, Mex., Bulgaria, Brazil, Russia, Ukraine, Romania, Kazakhstan, South Africa, Vietnam, Chile, Argentina. Author: Fiscal Failure: Lessons of the Sixties, 1972, (with N. Ture) Value Added Tax: Two Views, 1972, (with M. Gillis) La Reforma Tributaria Colombiana de 1974, 1977, Must Corporate Income Be Taxed Twice?, 1979, Economic Perperspectives on State Taxation of Multijurisdictional Corporations, 1986, The Value Added Tax: Key to Deficit Reduction, 1987; co-author: Taxation of Income from Business and Capital in Colombia, 1989; also numerous articles on econs., tax law and public finance. Ford Found. faculty research fellow, 1967-68, Disting. Svc. medal, US Treas. Dept., 1985, Daniel M. Holland medal, Nat. Tax Assn., 2004. Mem. Am. Econ. Assn., Nat. Tax Assn., Beta Theta Pi. Home: 250 Yerba Santa Ave Los Altos CA 94022-1609 Office: Stanford U Hoover Instn Stanford CA 94305-6010 Office Phone: 650-723-2657. Business E-Mail: mclure@hoover.stanford.edu.

**MCLURE, JOHN DOUGLAS,** management consultant, former Canadian government official; b. Melita, Man., Can., July 10, 1942; s. Malcolm Alexander and Rachel (Simpson) McL.; m. Nicole Lafrance, Aug. 26, 1967. BSc, U. Man., Winnipeg, 1963; Ammunition Tech. Officer, Royal Mil. Coll. Sci., Wiltshire, Eng., 1964. Program analyst Treasury Bd. Secretariat, Ottawa, Canada, 1975-79, group chief industry and natural resources divsn., 1979-80, dir. industry and natural resources divsn., 1980-82, asst. sec. econ. devel., 1982-84; asst. dep. min. small bus. and spl. projects Dept. Regional Indsl. Expansion, Ottawa, 1984-85, asst. dep. min. crown investments and spl. projects, 1985-86, asst. dep. min. native econ. devel., 1986-87; asst. dep. min. fin., pers., adminstrn. Dept Industry, Sci. & Tech., Ottawa, 1987—95; asst. dep. min. Dept. Nat. Def., Ottawa, 1995—96, assoc. dep. min., 1996—97; dep. min. Dept. Western Econ. Diversification, Ottawa, 1997—2000; sr. v.p. Hill and Knowlton Can. Ltd., Ottawa, 2000—; pres., CEO JDM Consulting Inc., 2000—; sr. assoc. Hill and Knowlton Can. Ltd., Ottawa, 2001—. Chmn. bd. Def. Constrn. Can. Maj. Can. Land Forces, 1960-75. Recipient N.Am. Best Practice Recognition, Ctr. Creative Leadership, Greensboro, N.C., 1994. Mem. Assn. Profl. Execs. (Leadership award 1995), Club Link Le Fontainebleau Golf Club, Rideau Club. Avocations: golf, alpine skiing. Home: 35 Somerset St W Ottawa ON Canada K2P 0H3 Office: Hill and Knowlton Can Ltd 55 Metcalfe St Ste 1100 Ottawa ON Canada K1P 6L5 Business E-Mail: john.mclure@hillandknowlton.ca.

**MCLUSKIE, ED,** communications educator; s. Clarence Edward and Francis McLuskie, Irma McLuskie (Stepmother); m. Ariel Thomas Haney, Oct. 4, 2004; m. Mary Elizabeth Trapp, Aug. 11, 1974 (div. Jan. 11, 1986); 1 child, Melissa Davis. BA, Mont. State U., Billings, 1970; PhD, U. Iowa, Iowa City, 1974. Prof. U. Wis., Whitewater, 1974—78, Fla. Atlantic U., Boca Raton, 1978—80, Boise State U., 1981—; Fulbright prof. U. Vienna, 1996—97, guest prof., 2002; Fulbright prof. Tbilisi State U., Georgian Inst. Pub. Affairs, Georgia, 2004—05. Contbr. articles to profl. jours., chapters to books. Bd. mem. Snake River Alliance, Boise, 1987—88; keynote spkr. Leadership Boise, 2004. Fellow, NEH, 1979, Fulbright Commn., 1996—97, 2004—05; grantee, Can. Embassy, 1983. Mem.: Internat. Comm. Assn. (life). Office: Boise State Univ Dept Communication 1910 Univ Dr Boise ID 83725-1920 Office Phone: 208-426-1927. Personal E-mail: emclusk@bigfoot.com. Business E-Mail: emclusk@boisestate.edu.

**MCMACKIN, F. JOSEPH, III,** lawyer; b. N.Y.C., July 23, 1946; s. Frank Joseph and Mary Ann (Dunn) McM.; m. S. Elizabeth Simonton, Jan. 12, 1974; children: Frank Joseph IV, Ian Simonton, James Tyler. AB, Wesleyan U., 1968; JD, U. Miami, Fla., 1973. Bar: Fla. 1973, U.S. Dist. Ct. (so. dist.) Fla. 1973, U.S. Ct. Appeals (5th cir.) 1974, U.S. Ct. Appeals (D.C.) 1975, U.S. Tax Ct. 1981, U.S. Ct. Appeals (11th cir.) 1982, Wis. 1984. Practice law, Fla.; assoc. Spingler & Mackin, 1973-77; sole practice as F. Joseph McMackin III, Chartered, Fla., 1977-82; ptnr. Quarles & Brady, Naples, Fla., 1982—; mng. ptnr., 1982—; bd. dirs. Barnet Bank of Naples. Bd. dirs. Telford Found. Served to It. USN, 1968-70. Mem. Fla. Bar (20th jud. cir. grievance com. "B"), D.C. Bar Assn., Wis. Bar Assn. Republican. Office: Quarles & Brady 1395 Panther Ln 300 Naples FL 34109-7875

**MCMAHAN, JOHN WILLIAM,** real estate investment advisor; b. San Antonio, Aug. 4, 1937; s. John William and Lena Margaret (Coleman) McMahan; m. Jacqueline Mary Cardozo, Sept. 22, 1973; children: Justin, Vanessa;children from previous marriage: Cathy, Jason. AB, U. So. Calif., 1959; MBA, Harvard U., 1961. Dir. feasibility studies Charles Luckman Assoc., 1961—63; founder and prin. Devel. Rsch. Assoc., L.A., 1963-70;

v.p. real estate svcs. Booz, Allen & Hamilton, N.Y.C., 1970—73; mem. faculty Stanford U. Grad. Sch. Bus., 1974—; founder and prin. John McMahan Real Estate Advisors, Inc., San Francisco, 1976—90; pres. and CEO Mellan/McMahan Reed Estate Advisors, Inc., 1990—. Author: McGraw Hill Real Estate Pocket Guide, 1979, Property Development: Effective Decision Making in Uncertain Times, 1989; editor: Ency. of Urban Planning, 1973. Mem.: Jonathan Club (U.K.), Royal Town Planning Inst., Am. Inst. Planners, Am. Econ. Assn., Urban Land Inst., Soc. Real Estate Counsellors, Banker's Club (U.K.), Lambda Alpha.

**MCMAHON, CATHERINE DRISCOLL,** lawyer; b. Mineola, N.Y., Apr. 28, 1950; d. Matthew Joseph and Elizabeth (Driscoll) McM.; m. Gregory Arthur McGrath, Sept. 10, 1977 (div. 1991); children: Elizabeth Driscoll, Kerry Margaret, Michael Riley. BA, Simmons Coll., 1972; JD, Boston Coll., 1975; postgrad., Suffolk U., 1972-73; LLM, NYU, 1980. Bar: N.Y. 1976, D.C. 1979, U.S. Supreme Ct. 1980, U.S. Tax Ct. 1991. Tax atty. asst. Exxon Corp., N.Y.C., 1975-76, asst. tax atty., 1976-77; sr. tax atty., 1979-81; tax atty. Exxon Internat. Co., N.Y.C., 1977-79; sr. tax counsel Florham Park, NJ, 1990-92, Exxon Co. U.S.A., Houston, 1992—98, Exxon Coal and Minerals Co., Houston, 1998—2002, Exxon Mobil Corp., 2003—. Tax mgr. Exxon Rsch. & Engring. Co., Florham Park, 1981-90. Bd. dirs. S.E. Morris chpt. ARC, Madison, N.J., 1983. Recipient TWIN award YMCA, Plainfield/Westfield, N.J., 1983. Mem. ABA, N.Y. State Bar Assn., D.C. Bar Assn. Roman Catholic. Office: Exxon Mobil Corp 800 Bell St Houston TX 77002-7497 Business E-Mail: catherine.d.mcmahon@exxonmobil.com.

**MCMAHON, DALTON EDWARD,** history professor, social sciences educator, department chairman; b. Rapid City, S.D., Nov. 12, 1945; s. Dalton William and Rosemary Lucille McMahon, m. Annie Buendia McMahon, Apr. 28, 1972; children: Annie Christina Norman, Dalton Edward Jr. BS in Edn., U. S.D. 1967, MA, 1975; DA, U. N.D. 1986. Social sci. tchr. Newman Grove (Nebr.) H.S., Dept. Def. Overseas Schs., Subic Bay Naval Station, Philippines, 1969—74, Giessen, Germany, 1974—82; grad. tchg. asst. history U. N.D., Grand Forks, 1982—85, instr. history, 1985—86; asst. prof. history Marymount of Kans., Salina, 1986—89; prof. history/social sci. Mayville (N.D.) State U., 1989—, chair liberal arts divsn., 2003—. Mem. coun. coll. faculties N.D. U. Sys., Bismarck, 1991—98, v.p. coun. coll. faculties, pres. coun. coll. faculties, 1994—95; mem. faculty senate Mayville State U., 1994—95, pres. faculty assn., 1995—97; lectr. in field. Judge DAR Outstanding Am. History Tchr. Contest, ND, 2002—03, Voice of Democracy Contest, Mayville, 1997—99; trustee United Ch. of Christ, Mayville, 1999—2003. Named U. N.D.Outstanding Grad. Historian, Phi Alpha Theta, U. N.D., 1985, Outstanding Tchr., Mayville State U., 1996, I.A. O'Shaughnessy Disting. Prof. of Humanities, Marrymount Coll. Kans., 1988—89; Atlantic-Bridges fellow, 2006. Mem.: So. Hist. Assn., Phi Alpha Theta. Home: 605 State Ave Portland ND 58274 Office: Mayville State University 330 3rd St NE Mayville ND 58257 Office Phone: 701-788-4480.

**MCMAHON, DONALD AYLWARD,** investor, corporate director; b. N.Y.C., Feb. 20, 1931; s. William F. and Anne (Aylward) McM.; m. Nancy Lantz, Apr. 12, 1953; children: Gail, Brian, Lisa, Glenn, Anne, Carol, William, Douglas. MBA, Emory U., 1982. With Dime Savs. Bank, Bklyn., 1952; salesman Monroe Calculating Machine Co., Bklyn., 1952-55, asst. br. mgr. Pitts., 1955-56, br. mgr. Phila., 1956-63, asst. gen. sales mgr. Orange, N.J., 1963-64, Eastern regional gen. sales mgr., 1964-65, v.p. mktg., 1965-66; pres Monroe Calculator Co. div. Litton Industries, Inc., Orange, 1966-70; v.p. Litton Industries, 1967-70; pres., chief operating officer. dir. Baker Industries, Inc., Parsippany, N.J., 1970-74; pres., chief exec. officer, dir. Royal Crown Cos., Inc., Atlanta, 1975-85. Bd. dirs. Intelligent Systems Corp., Atlanta. Bd. dirs. Boys Clubs Metro Atlanta. Mem. Sovereign Order of Knights of Malta. Home: 1665 Winterthur Close NW Atlanta GA 30328-4688

**MCMAHON, ED,** television and radio personality; b. Detroit, Mar. 6, 1923; m. Pam Hurn; children: Claudia, Michael (dec.), Linda, Jeffrey, Katherine Mary; 1 stepson, Alexis. Student, Boston Coll.; BA, Cath. U. Am., 1949. Author: For Laughing Out Loud: My Life and Good Times, 1998, Here's Johnny!: My Memories of Johnny Carson, The Tonight Show, and 46 Years of Friendship, 2005; TV announcer: Tonight Show, 1962-92; appeared in films The Incident, 1967, Fun with Dick and Jane, 1975, Butterfly, 1982, Love Affair, 1994, (tv movie) The Kid from Left Field, 1979, The Great American Traffic Jam, 1980, (mini series) The Golden Moment, 1980, The Star Maker, 1981, Bewitched, 2005; host TV series The Kraft Music Hall, 1968, Whodunnit?, 1979, TV's Bloopers and Practical Jokes, Ed McMahon's Star Search; host TV specials: Thanksgiving Day Parade, (co-host) Jerry Lewis Labor Day Telethon; appeared on TV, The Tom Show, 1997; now host Lifestyles Live, USA Radio Network, Orlando; numerous other TV appearances; appeared on Broadway in The Impossible Years. Active Muscular Dystrophy Assn.; mem. bd. dirs. Horatio Alger Assn. With USMC, PTO; col. res., ret. Office: Lifestyles Live Bldg 22-A, Ste 245 1000 Universal Studios Plaza Orlando FL 32819 Office Phone: 407-224-3162. Office Fax: 407-224-3163.*

**MCMAHON, EDWARD RICHARD,** lawyer; b. Jersey City, June 7, 1949; s. Edward Barnawall and Jean (Sullivan) McM.; m. Ellen Mary Bosek; children: Meghan Jean, Kerry Eileen, Ryan Edward. AB, Colgate U., 1972; JD, Seton Hall U., 1975. Bar: N.J. 1975, U.S. Dist. Ct. N.J. 1975, U.S. Ct. of Appeals (3rd circ.) 1980. Law clk. to judge U.S. Dist. Ct., Newark, 1975-77; assoc. Lum, Biunno & Tompkins, Newark, 1977-83; ptnr. Lum, Danzis, Drasco & Positan, LLC, Roseland, NJ, 1983—. Mem. Essex County Chancery Ct. Mediation Prog., 1992—, Supreme Ct. of N.J. Dist. Ethics Com., 1994—97, Supreme Ct. of N.J. Dist. Fee Arbitration Com., 2005—; founding mem. and couns Morris & Essex Inn of Transactional Counsel, 2001—, U.S. Dist. Ct. Arbitration Prog., 2001—, New Jersey Ct. Approved Mediator, 2002—. Mem. Morris County Rep. Com., N.J., 1982-94; mem. Chatham (N.J.) Boro Rep. Com., 1982-94, chmn., 1986-94; bd. dirs. Madison area YMCA, 1989-95; bd. trustees Richard J. Hughes Found., 2001-; mem. N.J. State Rep. Com., 1994-. Mem.: ABA (litigation and banking sects.), Colgate U. Alumni Assn. (class rep. 1993—), 200 Club Morris County, Delbarton Sch. Alumni Assn. (class rep. 1984—), Essex County Bar Assn. (Essex County Chancery Ct. Mediation program 1992—, Supreme Ct. of N.J. dist. ethics com. 1994—97, Supreme Ct. of N.J. dist. fee arbitration com. 2000—, founding mem., counselor Morris & Essex Inn of Transactional Counsel 2001—, U.S. Dist. Ct. Arbitration program 2001—, N.J. Ct. approved mediator 2002—), Morris County Bar Assn., Am. Judicature Soc., Assn. Fed. Bar N.J., N.J. Bar Assn., Colgate (No. N.J.), Phi Alpha Delta, Delta Upsilon. Republican. Roman Catholic. Home: 150 Van Houton Ave Chatham NJ 07928-1239 Office: Lum Danzis Drasco & Positan LLC 103 Eisenhower Pky Roseland NJ 07068-1029 also: 325 Broadway New York NY 10007

**MCMAHON, GERALD LAWRENCE,** lawyer; b. Youngstown, Ohio, July 16, 1935; s. Lawrence J. and Lee Z. McM.; m. Donna Ghio, June 17, 1956; children: Maria, Michael, Mark, Matthew, Angela. BS cum laude, U. So. Calif., 1956; JD summa cum laude, U. San Diego, 1964. Bar: Calif. 1965, U.S. Dist. Ct. (so. dist. Calif.), U.S. Ct. Claims 1966, U.S. Ct. Appeals (9th cir.) 1966, U.S. Supreme Ct 1966. Chief of contracts Centaur space vehicle program Gen. Dynamics Astronautics, San Diego, 1960-64; from assoc. to chmn. & head litigation dept. Seltzer Caplan McMahon Vitek, San Diego, 1964—. Adj. prof. Univ. San Diego Sch. Law, 1969—72; lectr. Calif. Western Law Sch. Editor: San Diego Law Rev., 1963-64; frequent speaker & legal edn. panelist. Trustee, Sidney Kimmel Cancer Ctr.; chmn. bd. vis., U. San Diego Law Sch., 1979-80, 1996-98. Aviator with USN, 1956-59. Fellow Am. Coll. Trial Lawyers; mem. ABA, San Diego Bar Assn. (vp., dir. 1974-77), State Bar of Calif. (disciplinary referee pro tem 1977-84), Am. Judicature Soc., Am. Bd. Trial Advocates (pres. San Diego chpt. 1981), Calif. Trial Lawyers Assn., Am. Arbitration Assn., Am. Acad. Matrimonial Lawyers, San Diego Inn of Ct. (panelist 1975, dir. 1979), Phi Alpha Delta, Order of the Coif.

Republican. Roman Catholic. Avocations: tennis, skiing, lic. pvt. pilot. Office: Seltzer Caplan McMahon Vitek Symphony Towers 750 B St San Diego CA 92101 Office Phone: 619-685-3114. Office Fax: 619-702-6803. Business E-Mail: mcmahon@scmv.com.

**MCMAHON, JAMES BRISLIN,** medical researcher; b. Burlington, Vt., Oct. 9, 1950; s. James William and Margaret Joan (McGarry) McM.; m. Laurie Jean Hinds, Oct. 1, 1983; children: Megan, Michael. BA in Chemistry, U. Vt., 1972, PhD in Cell Biology, 1978. Scientist 1 Frederick Cancer Rsch. Ctr., Md., 1978-81, scientist 2, 1981-83; cancer expert Nat. Cancer Inst., Bethesda, Md., 1983-88, rsch. biologist, 1988-90; sr. rsch. biologist Frederick Cancer R&D Ctr., Nat. Cancer Inst., 1990; now dir. Molecular Targets Devel. Program Ctr. Cancer Rsch., Nat. Cancer Inst., Frederick. Contbr. articles to profl. jours.; patentee in field. Pres. Frederick County Alzheimer's Assn., 1987-89; mem. Sci. Curriculum Rev. Com., Frederick, 1990-91. Mem. Am. Chem. Soc., Tissue Culture Assn., N.Y. Acad. Scis., Am. Assn. for Cancer Rsch., Sigma Xi. Avocations: skiing, fishing, photography. Office: Nat Cancer Inst - Frederick Molecular Targets Devel Program PO Box B Bldg 1052 Rm 121 Frederick MD 21702-1201 Office Phone: 301-846-5391. Office Fax: 301-846-6919. E-mail: mcmahon@ncifcrf.gov.*

**MCMAHON, JAMES E.,** lawyer, former prosecutor; b. 1951; m. Kathy McMahon; 3 children. BS, Morningside U.; JD, U. S.D., 1977. Asst. atty. gen. State of SD, 1978—81; ptnr. Boyce, Murphy, McDowell & Greenfield, 1981—2002; pvt. practice Sioux Falls, SD, 2002—; US atty. Dist. SD US Dept. Justice, Sioux Falls, SD, 2002—05. Recipient Trial Lawyer of Yr. award, S.D. Trial Lawyers Assn., 2000.

**MCMAHON, JAMES PATRICK,** ecologist, consultant; b. Chgo., July 10, 1951; s. James Patrick and Helen Margaret (Walter) McM.; children: J. Emrys, Jacqueline Anne. BS in Ecology, U. Ill., 1974; postgrad., Cen. Wash. U., 1975-76, Naropa Inst., Boulder, 1993-94. Owner Seattle Recycling, Inc., 1976-79; program planner City of Seattle, 1979-80; divsn. mgr. Fibres Internat., Bellevue, Wash., 1980-85; owner Environ. Enhancement Group, Lynnwood, Wash., 1985-88; regional mgr. 20:20 Recycle Ctrs., Inc., L.A., 1987-88; nat. mktg. dir. May Mfg., Denver, 1990-94; ptnr. Agua Fria Enterprises, Prescott, Ariz., 1992-98; project dir. Nature Conservancy, 1994-98; dir. of Virgin River Programs Grand Canyon Trust, 1999—2002; active Sweetwater, LLC, 2002—. Sr. fellow Independence Inst., Golden, Colo., 1990-93; participant 50 for Colo. leadership program Colo. Assn. Commerce and Industry, 1993; condr. numerous bus. seminars; developer original recycling strategy City of Seattle; expatriot in Saint Martin, French West Indies, 1989. Exec. prodr. (video) Recycling in Washington State, 1985; contbr. many articles on Western pub. lands, natural resources, Philippine Eagle recovery, logging and men's issues to newspapers, mag. and other publs., U.S. and London; frequent radio commentator. Mem. survey and nat. conf. coms. Dept. Ecology, 1985-86; bd. dirs. Nat. Recycling Coalition, 1983-86. Mem. Greater Seattle C. of C., Rocky Mountain Angling Club, Trout Unltd. Avocations: skiing, fly fishing, scuba diving, hiking, camping. Home and Office: 375 Cedar Tree Dr Brookside UT 84782 Office Phone: 435-574-2711. E-mail: jim@jamespmcmahon.com.

**MCMAHON, JANET MANKIEWICH,** critical care nurse; b. Rockville Centre, N.Y., Apr. 23, 1957; d. Walter J. and Lois May (Johns) Mankiewich; m. Michael T. McMahon, July 12, 1985; children: Shannon and Sandy (twins), Patrick. BSN, Adelphi U., 1980. RN, N.Y., Va.; cert. BLS instr., ACLS. Nurse St. Francis Hosp., Roslyn, NY; charge nurse L.I. Jewish Hillside Med. Ctr., New Hyde Park, NY, Alexandria (Va.) Hosp., Mary Washington Hosp., Fredricksberg, Va., Mt. Vernon (Va.) Hosp., George Washington U. Hosp., Washington; nurse Potomac Hosp., Woodbridge, Va. Mem. AACCN. Home: 4803 Kempair Ct Woodbridge VA 22193-4631

**MCMAHON, JOHN ALEXANDER,** law educator; b. Monongahela, Pa., July 31, 1921; s. John Hamilton and Jean (Alexander) McMahon; m. Betty Wagner, Sept. 14, 1947 (div. Mar. 1977); children: Alexander Talpey, Sarah Francis, Elizabeth Wagner, Ann Wallace; m. Anne Fountain Willets, May 1, 1977 (dec. June 1996); m. Anne Hall Davis, Apr. 18, 1999. AB magna cum laude, Duke U., 1942; student, Harvard U. Bus. Sch., 1942—43; JD, Law Sch., 1948; LLD, Wake Forest U., 1978; DSc (hon.), Georgetown U. Sch. Medicine, 1985. Bar: N.C. 1950. Prof. pub. law and govt., asst. dir. Inst. Govt. U. N.C., 1948—59; gen. counsel, sec.-treas. N.C. Assn. County Commrs., Chapel Hill, 1959—65; v.p. spl. devel. Hosp. Saving Assn., Chapel Hill, NC, 1965—67; pres. N.C. Blue Cross and Blue Shield, Inc., Chapel Hill, 1968—72, Am. Hosp. Assn., Chgo., 1972—86; chmn. dept. health adminstrn. Duke U., Durham, NC, 1986—92, exec.-in-residence Fuqua Sch. Bus., 1992—. Mem. Chapel Hill bd. N.C. Nat. Bank, 1967—72; bd. govs. Blue Cross Assn., 1969—72; mem. Orange County Welfare Bd., 1956—63; chmn. N.C. Comprehensive Health Planning Coun., 1968—72, Health Planning Coun. of Ctrl. N.C., 1963—69; mem. Pres.'s Com. on Health Edn., 1971—72; mem. com. health svcs. industry and health industry adv. com. Econ. Stblzn. Program, 1971—74; mem. adv. coun. Kate Bitting Reynolds Health Care Trust, 1971—95, Northwestern U., 1973—86; mem. med. adv. com. VA, 1975—85; bd. dirs. The Forest at Duke, Durham, NC, 1994—2002, Exec. Svc. Corps of Greater Triangle, 1986—99, mem. adv. bd., 2000—. Author: North Carolina County Government, 1959, The North Carolina Local Government Commission, 1960; editor: N.C. County Yearbook, 1959—64, Proceedings of the Annual National Forum on Hospital and Health Affairs, 1993—2000. Chmn. bd. trustees Duke U., 1971—83, chmn. emeritus 1983—; bd. mgrs., mem. exec. com. Internat. Hosp. Fedn., London, 1975—85, pres., 1981—83; mem. Orange County Dem. Exec. Com., also chmn. Kings Mill Precinct, 1964—68; bd. dirs. Rsch. Triangle Found., 1971—83, 1992—, Nat. Ctr. for Health Edn., 1974—86. With USAF, 1942—46, col. Res., ret. Recipient Citation Disting. Svc. by Layman, AMA, 1978, Special award. Ill Hosp Assn, 1985, DollasFort Worth Hosp. Coun., 1985, many others. Mem.: Inst. Medicine of NAS (Disting. Svc. award 1979), N.C. State Bar, Duke Alumni Assn. (pres. 1968—70, Silver Medal award 1986), Dunes Golf and Beach Club (Myrtle Beach), Hope Valley Country Club (Durham). Republican. Presbyterian. Home: 181 Montrose Dr Durham NC 27707-3929 Office: Duke U Fuqua Sch Bus Durham NC 27708-0120 Office Phone: 919-660-7760.

**MCMAHON, JOHN E.,** marketing analyst, director; s. Robert K. and Ann L. McMahon; m. Michele M. Regnante, June 20, 1992. BA, Fordham U., 1991; MA, Clark U. Worcester, Mass., 1993; PhD, Clark U., 2004. Sr. rsch. analyst Drexel U., Phila., 1997—99, dir. of rsch., 1999—2001, asst. v.p. devel. rsch., 2002—03; mktg. analyst The Hartford Fin. Svcs. Group, Inc., Conn., 2004—06, territory mgr., 2006—. Dir. Assn. of Profl. Rschrs. for Advancement, Phila., 2002—03; cons. Assn. of Fundraising Profls., Phila. V.p. Cana Mission, Hancock, NH, 2001—. Recipient Grad. fellowship, Clark U., 1991—2004. Mem.: Coun. for the Advancement and Support of Edn., Assn. of Profl. Rschrs. for Advancement, Phi Alpha Theta. Home: 29 South Rd Marlborough CT 06447-1573 Office: The Hartford Fin Svcs Group Inc Hartford Plz HO-GL-19 Hartford CT 06115 Office Phone: 860-547-6388. Personal E-mail: jmcmahon29@comcast.net.

**MCMAHON, JOSEPH EINAR,** lawyer, consultant; b. Chgo., Aug. 26, 1940; s. Reynold Bernard and Dorothy Marie (Oftedahl) McM. BA cum laude, Denison U., 1962; JD, U. Mich., 1965. Bar: Mass. 1968, D.C. 1980. Asst. to Atty. Gen. and Senator Edward Brooke, Boston and Washington, 1965-67; exec. asst. Lt. Gov. Sargent of Mass., Boston, 1967-69; v.p. BedStuy D&S Corp. Restoration, Bklyn., 1969-74; dir. govt. regulations Westinghouse Electric Corp., Washington, 1974-78; v.p. corp. affairs Federated Dept. Stores, Cin., 1978-80; atty., cons. McMahon and Assocs., Washington, 1980—; v.p. pub. policy Covenant House, 2001—. Exec. dir. (part time), bd. dirs. The Get Ahead Found./USA, 1991-99. Life trustee Denison U.; visitor U. Mich. Law Sch.; 1st v.p. Boston Newc. Clubs, 1968-69; presdl. appointee Nat. Coun. Econ. Opportunity, 1975-76; exec. dir. Nat. Bus. for Reagan-Bush Com., 1980; dir. emeritus Luther Inst., Washington, Rodale Inst., Emmaus, Pa.; dir. Luth. Lesbian and Gay Min., San Francisco, 1994-2003; mem. outreach bd. Evang. Luth. Ch. in Am., 1995-2001. Mem. Capitol Hill Club, Phi Delta Phi, Pi

Sigma Alpha, Omicron Delta Kappa. Lutheran. Office: McMahon & Assocs 2031 Q St NW Washington DC 20009 also: 1125 Meridian Ave Miami Beach FL 33139 Office Phone: 202-293-6464. Personal E-mail: mcmahon@aol.com.

**MCMAHON, JULIAN,** actor; b. Sydney, Australia, July 27, 1968; s. William and Sonia McMahon; m. Dannii Minogue, Jan. 2, 1994 (div. 1995); m. Brooke Burns, Dec. 22, 1999 (div. 2001); 1 child, Madison. Attended, U. Sydney. Actor: (TV series) The Power, the Passion, 1989, Home and Away, 1989—91, Another World, 1992—96, Profiler, 1996—2000, Charmed, 2000—03, Nip/Tuck, 2003—; (TV films) Another Day, 2001; guest appearance (TV series) Will & Grace, 1998, Charmed, 2005; actor: (films) Wet and Wild Summer!, 1992, Magenta, 1996, In Quiet Night, 1998, Chasing Sleep, 2000, Fantastic Four, 2005, Prisoner, 2005; actor, exec. prodr.: Meet Market, 2004. Nominee Best Actor in a TV Series (Drama), 62nd Ann. Golden Globe Awards, 2005. Office: c/o MGM ROAR 2400 Broadway Santa Monica CA 90404

**MCMAHON, LINDA E.,** sports association executive; b. New Bern, N.C., Oct. 4, 1948; d. Henry and Evelyn Edwards; m. Vincent K. McMahon, Aug. 6, 1966; children: Shane, Stephanie. BA French, East Carolina U., 1969. Co-founder, bd. dirs. World Wrestling Entertainment, Inc., Stamford, Conn., 1980—, pres., 1993—2000, CEO, 1997—. Prodr.: (TV series) WWE: Raw is War, 1997—, WWE: Sunday Night Heat, 1998—, WWE: Smackdown!, 1999—; exec. prodr.: WWE Experience, 2004. Office: World Wrestling Entertainment Inc Titan Towers 1241 E Main St Stamford CT 06902

**MCMAHON, PAUL FRANCIS,** finance company executive; b. Malone, NY, Apr. 28, 1945; s. Philip Francis and Shirley (Roy) M.; m. Sheila Ann Lester, Nov. 30, 1963; children: Michael, Marsha BS, Syracuse U., 1968. CPA, N.Y., Oreg.; cert. mgmt. acct., mgmt. cons. With Ernst & Young, Syracuse, NY, 1968—79, mgr., 1975-79, ptnr. in charge of mgmt. cons. in Europe Brussels, 1979-84, vice-chmn. Cleve., 1984-87; exec. ptnr. Ernst & Young Internat., N.Y., 1987-93; chmn. Ernst & Young Ea. Europe, 1990-93; regional dir. Asia/Pacific Ernst & Young Internat., Singapore, 1994-96; contr. Coop. Mktg. Agy., Syracuse, 1973-75; COO Amrop Internat., Brussels, 1997-2001; ptnr. Network Journey, 2002—04. Treas. Chamber Music N.W.; chair lit. and hist. com. Arlington Club; bd. mem. Oreg. Coun. of Humanities; mem. adv. bd. Humanitnet; treas. Health Bridges Internat.; mem. adv. bd. Humanitnet. Mem.: AICPA, Nat. Acad. Scis., Coun. Consulting Orgns. (past chmn.), Assn. Mgmt. Consulting Firms (bd. dirs.), Inst. Mgmt. Acctg., N.Y. Soc. CPAs, Oreg. Soc. CPAs. Democrat. Roman Catholic. Avocations: sculpture, travel, gardening, biographies. Home: 1030 SW Jefferson St Apg 261 Portland OR 97201 Office Phone: 503-708-4336. Personal E-mail: pfmcmahon@earthlink.net.

**MCMAHON, ROBERT M.,** physician, lawyer; b. Chambersburg, Pa., Sept. 6, 1949; s. Robert James and Bernice G. (Moore) McM.; 1 child, Natalie Ann. BA, U. Calif., San Diego, 1971; JD, U. Calif., San Francisco, 1974; MD, Washington U., St. Louis, 1989. Bar: Mo., Calif., U.S. Supreme Ct.; diplomate Am. Bd. Internal Medicine, Am. Bd. Gastroenterology. Staff counsel State Bar of Calif., L.A., 1975-80; sole practice law Beverly Hills, Calif., 1980-85; physician Jewish Hosp., St. Louis, 1989-92, St. Joseph's Hosp., St. Charles, Mo., 1992-93, U. Ark., Little Rock, 1993-95; pvt. practice in gastroenterology Little Rock, 1995-97, St. Louis, 1997—. Judge pro tem Superior Ct., L.A., 1983-85. Dir. South Ctrl. Bar Assn., Compton, Calif., 1983-85. Fellow Am. Coll. Legal Medicine; mem. Am. Soc. Gastrointestinal Endoscopy, St. Louis Met. Med. Soc. (councillor 2000-03). Avocations: computer hobbyist, graphic arts, model aircraft. Office St Louis GE Cons PC 10012 Kennerly Rd Ste 101 Saint Louis MO 63128

**MCMAHON, SUSAN HENDERSON,** biology professor; d. Neil Finsher Hendeson and Kathleen Hill Henderson; m. John M. McMahon, June 13, 1980; children: Matthew, Jennifer. BS in Biology, East Tenn. State U., Johnson City, Tenn., 1974, MS in Biology, 1976; PhD in Microbiology, Pa. State U., Univ. Pk., Pa., 1980. Instr. Edinboro (Pa.) State Coll., 1976—77, 1986—87, Pa. State U., 1980—81, U. Pitts., 1983—85; adj. instr. Fullerton (Calif.) Coll., 1985—86; instr. U. Tenn., Knox, Tenn., 1987—92; from asst. prof. to prof. Pellissippi State C.C., Knox, 1993, prof., coord. Pre-nuring Edn. Bd. visitors Nursing Dept. Tenn. Weslayan/Ft. Saunders Hosp., Knoxville, Tenn., 2005—06; pres. S.W. Appalachian Sci. and Engring. Fair, Knoxville, 1994—96. Named Tchr. of Yr., Fullerton (Calif.) Coll. Student Union, 1986, Sci. Tchr. of Yr., Am. Women in Sci., 1992, Faculty of Yr., Students Pellissippi State C.C., 2002. Office: Pellissippi State Cmty Coll PO Box 22990 Knoxville TN 37933

**MCMAHON, THOMAS MICHAEL,** lawyer; b. Evanston, Ill., May 11, 1941; s. Robert C. and Kathryn D. McM.; m. M. Ann Kaufman, July 11, 1964; children— Michael, Patrick. Notre Dame, 1959-61; BA, Marquette U., 1963; JD magna cum laude, Northwestern U., 1970. Bar: Ill. 1970. Mgr. legal advs. sect. III. EPA, Springfield, 1970-72; assoc. Sidley & Austin, Chgo., 1972-75, ptnr., founder nat. environ. group, 1975-2000, sr. counsel, 2001—. Lectr. in field; mem. City of Evanston Environ. Control Bd., 1981-83. Author: The Superfund Handbook, 1989, International Environmental Law and Regulation, 1992, Legal Guide to Working with Environmental Consultants, 1992, The Environmental Manual, 1992. Lt. USN, 1963-67. Decorated Republic of Vietnam Campaign medal. Mem. ABA (chmn. environ. disclosures com., vice-chmn. alternative dispute resolution com., past vice-chmn. environ. quality com., environ. aspects of bus. trans. com., internat. environ. law com., lectr. confs., teleconfs. and satellite seminars), Order of Coif.

**MCMAHON, VINCE (VINCENT KENNEDY MCMAHON),** sports entertainment company executive; b. Pinehurst, NC, Aug. 24, 1945; s. Vincent James McMahon; m. Linda Edwards, Aug. 6, 1966; children: Shane, Stephanie. BS in Mktg., Ea. Carolina U. 1964. Announcer World Wrestling Fedn (formerly World Wide Wrestling Fedn.), 1971—82; acquired Capitol World Wrestling Corp., 1982; chmn. World Wrestling Entertainment Inc. (formerly World Wrestling Fedn.), Stamford, Conn., 1982—. Office: World Wrestling Entertainment Inc Titan Towers 1241 E Main St Stamford CT 06902-3521

**MCMAINS, DONALD PAUL,** education educator; b. Kennewick, Wash., Apr. 14, 1960; s. Paul and Shirley McMains; m. Tami Jo Gilmore, Apr. 1, 1995; children: Deven M. Kuoppala, JoEll L. Kuoppala, Elizabeth M., Melissa A. Michelle K. BA, Ctrl. Wash. U., Ellensburg; EdM in Guidance and Counseling, Ctrl. Wash. U., Renton, Wash. Cert. sch. counselor Wash. Tchr. Meridian Sch. Dist., Bellingham, Wash., 1984—. Mem.: Wash. Edn. Assn. Avocations: golf, gardening.

**MCMANAMAN, KENNETH CHARLES,** lawyer; b. Fairfield, Calif., Jan. 25, 1950; s. Charles James and Frances J. (Holys) McM.; m. Carol Ann Wilson, Apr. 15, 1972; children: Evan John, Kinsey Bridget, Klerin Rose. BA cum laude, S.E. Mo. State U., 1972; JD, U. Mo., Kansas City, 1974; grad., Naval Justice Sch., Newport, RI, 1975; MS in Bus. Mgmt. summa cum laude, Troy State U., Montgomery, Ala., 1978; LLM in Advanced Litigation, Nottingham-Trent U., 2004. Bar: Mo. 1975, US Dist. Ct. (we. dist.) Mo. 1975, Fla. 1976, US Dist. Ct. no. and mid. dists.) Fla. 1976, US Dist. Ct. Mil. Appeals 1977, US Ct. Appeals (5th and 8th cirs.) 1977, US Dist. Ct. (ea. dist.) Mo. 1978, US Supreme Ct. 1978, D.C. 1991; cert. mil. judge spl. 1996, gen. ct. martials 1998; diplomate Am. Bd. Forensic Examiners; cert. Homeland Security, Level III, Am. Coll. Forensic Examiners Internat.; qualified mil. judge gen. ct. martial, Navy-Marine Corps. Prof. bus. law Troy (Ala.) State U., 1976-78; pvt. practice; ptnr. O'Loughlin, O'Loughlin & McManaman, Cape Girardeau, Mo., 1978—2002, Kenneth C. McManaman, Esq., 2002—06, Kenneth C. McManaman, LLC, 2006—; prof. bus. law S.E. Mo. State U., Cape Girardeau, 1978-84, prof. criminal justice, 1998—; prof. leadership Sch. Law William Woods U., 1998—; prof. bus. mgmt. Sch. Law Nat. Inst. Trial Advocacy. Mem. Cape Girardeau County Coun. on Child Abuse, 1989—; membership dir. S.E. Mo. scouting coun. Boy Scouts Am.

---

1980—82; mem. Cape Girardeau County Mental Health Assn., 1982—92; sponsor drug edn./prevention program in schs.; sec., pres. Jackson Area Soccer Assn., 1987—93; mem. Jackson R-2 Alt. Sch. Bd., 1999—; mem. dept. acctg. and fin. adv. bd. S.E. Mo. State U., 2001—03; active local and state Dem. Party, del. Dem. Nat. Conv., San Francisco, 1984; mem. County Dem. Com., 1984—96; mem. 8th Congl. Dist. Dem. Com., 1984—86, 27th State Dem. Senatorial Com., 1980—90; ward committeeman Dem. Party, 1984—96; bd. dirs. Area-wide Task Force on Drug and Alcohol Abuse, 1984—87, Cape County chpt. Nat. Kidney Found., 1988—93, S.E. Mo. State Alumni Assn., 2006—. Capt. JAGC USNR, 1994—2003. Recipient Robert Chilton award City of Jackson for Leadership, Integrity and Responsibility, 1995-97; named One of Outstanding Young Men Am., 1981, 82, 84, 85, Outstanding Pub. Svc. award Cape Girardeau Police Dept. Mem. ABA (Mo. del. young lawyers divsn. 1982-83), Mo. Bar Assn. (chmn. trial advocacy task force 1983), Mo. Bar (young lawyers sect. coun. rep. dist. 13 1980-85), Fla. Bar Assn., Kansas City Bar Assn., Assn. Trial Lawyers Am., Fed. Bar Assn., Nat. Coll. Dist. Attys., Cape Girardeau County Bar Assn. (founder, pres. young lawyers sect. 1981-82), Cape County Bar Assn. (sec. 1999, treas. 2000, v.p. 2001), Naval Res. Assn. (v.p. S.E. Mo/So. Ill. chpt. 1980-85, 2001—), Grand Praetor So. Mo. Province, Order of Constantine, S.E. Mo. State U. Alumni Coun. (Merit award 2000-02), Sigma Chi (numerous awards), Sigma Tau Delta, Pi Delta Epsilon. Roman Catholic. Home: 1162 Trail Ridge Dr Jackson MO 63755-3507 Office: Blattner Bldg Ste One 1028A N Kings Hwy Cape Girardeau MO 63701 Office Phone: 573-335-8522. Personal E-mail: kenmcm@sbcglobal.net, kmcmanaman@charter.net.

**MCMANIGAL, SHIRLEY ANN,** retired dean; b. Deering, Mo., May 4, 1938; d. Jadie C. and Willie B. (Groves) Naile. BS, Ark. State U., 1971; MS, U. Okla., 1976, PhD, 1979. Med. technologist, 1958—75; chair dept. med. tech. U. So. Miss., Hattiesburg, 1979—83, Tex. Tech U. Health Scis. Ctr. Lubbock, 1983—87, dean Sch. Allied Health, 1987—97. Gov.'s appointee to statewide health coord. coun., 1994-97. Leadership Tex., 1992; Lt. Alumnae Regl. dir., 1994-97. Recipient Citation, State of Tex., 1988; named Woman of Yr., AAUW, Tex. divsn., 1990, Woman of Excellence in Edn. YWCA, Lubbock, 1990. Mem.: AAUW (Tex. bd. dirs. 1990—94, mem. ednl. found. internat. fellows panel 1994—98, chair 1998—2001), Tex. Soc. Med. Tech. (Educator of Yr. 1990), Tex. Soc. Allied Health Professions (pres. 1990—91), So. Assn. Allied Health Deans at Acad. Health Ctrs., Nat. Assn. Women in Edn., Am. Soc. Med. Tech., Clin. Lab. Mgmt. Assn. (chair edn. com. 1989, 1991), Phi Beta Delta, Alpha Eta. Home: 24633 Ivory Cane Dr 103 Bonita Springs FL 34134 E-mail: smcmanigal@comcast.net.

**MCMANIS, JAMES,** lawyer; b. Haverhill, Mass., May 28, 1943; s. Charles and Yvonne (Zinn) McM.; m. Sara Wigh, Mar. 30, 1968. BA, Stanford U., Palo Alto, Calif., 1964; JD, U. Calif., Berkeley, 1967. Bar: Calif. 1967, U.S. Dist. Ct. (no. dist.) Calif. 1967, U.S. Ct. Appeals (9th cir.) 1967, U.S. Supreme Ct. 1971. Dep. dist. atty. Santa Clara County Dist. Atty., 1968-71; mem. McManis, Faulkner & Morgan, San Jose, Calif., 1971—. Spl. master tech. equities litig., 1987-98; spl. examiner State Bar Calif., 1995-98; prof. law Lincoln U. Law Sch., San Jose, 1972-82; lectr. Calif. Continuing Edn. of Bar, 1989-90; instr. U. Calif. Law Sch., 1992-96, Stanford U. Sch. Law, 1994-99. Pres. Santa Clara County Bar Assn. Law Found., 1996, dir., 1987—. Fellow Am. Coll. Trial Lawyers, Internat. Acad. Trial Lawyers, Am. Bar Found.; mem. ABA, State Bar Calif., Calif. Trial Lawyers Assn., Santa Clara County Bar Assn., Boalt Hall Alumni Assn. Avocations: history, books, travel, running. Office: McManis Faulkner & Morgan 50 W San Fernando St 10th fl San Jose CA 95113 Fax: 408-279-3244. Office Phone: 408-279-8700. Business E-Mail: jmcmanis@mfmlaw.com.

**MCMANN, EDITH BROZAK (EDITH BROZAK),** performing and visual artist; b. Totowa, NJ, Mar. 26, 1929; d. Henry and Lena (Ulmer) Brozek; m. Frank Richard McMann, May 26, 1957; children: Robert, Stephen. Dance student, Sch. Am. Ballet, N.Y.C., 1945-57; student art, Westchester Art Workshop; student, Art Student's League, N.Y.C.; student art, SUNY, Purchase, NY, 1976—84; B in Profl. Studies in Dance and Visual Arts, SUNY, 1984; MS in Studio Art, Coll. of New Rochelle, 1989. Performing artist Alicia Alonso's Nat. Ballet Cuba tours, Mex., Ctrl. Am., S.Am., 1948-50, George Balanchine's N.Y.C. Ballet, 1950-57; visual artist N.Y.C., 1970—; intern Silvermine Coll. Art, 1989. Exhibitions include Depicting Dance in Art, Gutman Gallery, White Plains, 1990, Xavier Gallery, New Rochelle, NY, 1989—94, Mamaroneck Artist Guild Gallery, Larchmont, NY, 1990—, Beaux Arts Exhibits, 1991—94, Manhattanville Coll., Purchase, NY, 1991, Town Ctr. Gallery, Mamaroneck, 1993—, NYC Ballet, 1993—, Westbeth Gallery, NYC, 1994, Hammond Mus., Salem, NY, 1994, Town House Gallery, Stamford, Conn., 2000—, Tower Perrins, Stamford, 2000—02. Represented in permanent collections; represented in archives Libr. of Performing Arts, NYC, Lincoln Center, NYC Ballet Archives. Nat. Mus. for Women in Arts, Washington, Ohio State U.; Columbus, Harvard Theater Collection, Mass., San Francisco Performing Arts Libr. and Mus., others; dancer (ballets) Alicia Alonso's Nat. Ballet Cuba, Mex., Ctrl. Am., South Am., 1948—50, Apollo, Sleeping Beauty, Pas de Quatre, Ensayo Symphonica, George Balanchine N.Y.C. Ballet, US, Europe, Canada, 1950—57, Swan Lake, Symphony C, Con Amore, Nutcracker. Recipient Cert. of Merit U.S. Senator-N. Spano, 1989, U.S. State Assemblyman-R. Brodsky, 1989, Letter of Appreciation U.S. Senator Pat Moynihan, 1989, Letter of Congratulations U.S. Congressman -B. Gilman, 1989, others Mem. Allied Artist of Am., Hudson River Contemporary Artists, Nat. Mus. for Women in Art, Silvermine Guild of Artists, Scarsdale Art Soc., Stamford Art Assn., Mamaroneck Artists Guild (bd. dirs. assoc. rep. 1990-91, receiving com. 1992). Home: 10 Burkewood Rd Hartsdale NY 10530-2933 Personal E-mail: emcmann200@aol.com.

**MCMANUS, DECLAN PATRICK See COSTELLO, ELVIS**

**MC MANUS, EDWARD JOSEPH,** federal judge; b. Keokuk, Iowa, Feb. 9, 1920; s. Edward W. and Kathleen (O'Connor) McM.; m. Sally A. Hassett, June 30, 1948 (dec.); children: David P., Edward W., John N., Thomas J., Dennis Q.; m. Esther Y. Kanealy, Sept. 15, 1987. Student, St. Ambrose Coll., 1936-38; BA, U. Iowa, 1940, JD, 1942. Bar: Iowa 1941. Gen. practice of law. Keokuk, 1946-62; city atty., 1946-55; mem. Iowa Senate, 1955-59; lt. gov. Iowa, 1959-61; chief U.S. judge No. Dist. Iowa, 1962-85, sr. U.S. judge, 1985—. Del Democrat Nat. Conv., 1956, 60. Served as lt. AC USNR, 1942-46. Office: US Dist Ct 329 US Courthouse 101 1st St SE Cedar Rapids IA 52401-1202 Office Phone: 319-286-2350. Business E-Mail: edward_mcmanus@iand.uscourts.gov.

**MCMANUS, JAMES WILLIAM,** lawyer; b. Kansas City, Mo., Aug. 1, 1945; s. Gerald B. and Mary M. McManus. BA, Rockhurst Coll., 1967; JD, St. Louis U., 1971. Bar: Mo. 1971, U.S. Dist. Ct. (we. dist.) Mo. 1972, U.S. Ct. Appeals (8th cir.) 1974, U.S. Supreme Ct. 1979, U.S. Ct. Appeals (10th cir.) 1984, U.S. Dist. Ct. Kans., 1995. Law clk. to presiding justice U.S. Dist. Ct. (we. dist.) Mo., 1971-73; assoc. Shughart, Thomson & Kilroy, P.C., Kansas City, 1973-76, dir., 1977-94; counsel Dysart, Taylor, Lay, Cotter & McMonigle, P.C., Kansas City, 1994—2002, DeWitt & Zeldin, L.L.C., Kansas City, 2002—04, McManus Law Offices, Kansas City, 2005—. Course lectr. med. jurisprudence U. Health Scis., Coll. Osteo. Medicine, Kansas City, 1994; lectr. in field. Adv. coun. St. Joseph Health Ctr., 1989-2002. Named to Best of the Bar, Appeals and Trials, Kansas City Bus. Jour., 2003, 2005; recipient Congenial Counselor award, Kansas City Metro Bar Assn., 2003, Exceptional Trial and Appellate atty. award, Mo. Ho. Reps., 2003. Fellow Am. Bar Found.; mem. ABA, ATLA (membership com. 2003-), Mo. Bar Assn., Kansas City Lawyers Assn., Kansas City Met. Bar Assn. (chmn. alternate dispute resolution com. 1996-97, vice chmn. 1994-95, chmn. med. malpractice com. 1989, Congenial Counselor award 2003), Mo. Assn. Trial Attys., Nat. Lawyers Assn., St. Louis Alumni Assn. (pres. 1984-92), St. Louis U. Law Sch. Alumni Assn. Home: 6824 Valley Rd Kansas City MO 64113-1929 Office: McManus Law Offices 1111 Main St Ste 700 Kansas City MO 64105 Office Phone: 816-835-1850, 816-474-3018. Business E-Mail: jamesmcmanus@justice.com.

---

**MCMANUS, JASON DONALD,** retired editor-in-chief; b. Mission, Kans., Mar. 3, 1934; s. John Alan and Stella Frances (Gosney) McM.; m. Patricia Ann Paulson, Oct. 18, 1958 (div. Feb. 1966); 1 child, John Alan; m. Deborah Hall Murphy, Dec. 2, 1973; children: Sophie Eleanor, Mage Caroline. BA, Davidson Coll., 1956, Litt.D. (hon.), 1979; M.P.A., Princeton U., 1958; postgrad., Oxford U., 1958-59; LittD (hon.), Monmouth Coll., 1988, U. N.C. 1991, Loyola U., Balt., 1992. Common Market bur. chief Time Mag., Paris, 1962-64, assoc. editor N.Y.C., 1964-68, sr. editor, 1968-75, asst. mng. editor, 1975-78, exec. editor, 1978-83, mng. editor, 1985-87; corp. editor Time Inc., N.Y.C., 1983-85; editor-in-chief Time Warner Inc., N.Y.C., 1987-95; ret. Author: short stories Introduction, 1960. Mem. presdl. adv. commn. Internat. Edn. Exchange, 1982-83. Rhodes scholar, 1958-59. Mem.: Century Assn. (N.Y.C.).

**MCMANUS, JOANNA QUILALA,** medical device sales manager, physician assistant; d. Jimmy Ortanez and Filipina Caneda Quilala. BA in Chemistry, Calif. State U., Fullerton, 1994—2000; MS in Physician Asst. Studies, Western U. of Health Scis., Pomona, Calif., 2000—02. Field rschr., phlebotomist RAND, Santa Monica, Calif., 1998—2005; dist. mgr. Cook Med., Inc., 2005—. Physician asst. helper U. So. Calif./L.A. County Med. Ctr., 1997—2000. Allied Health Careers Scholarship, Kaiser Permanente, 2000—01. Mem.: Calif. Acad. Physician Assts. (assoc.), Western U. Alumni Assn. (life). Roman Catholic. Avocations: travel, dance, singing. Personal E-mail: qtkeylala@aol.com.

**MCMANUS, PATRICK FRANCIS,** editor, educator, writer; b. Sandpoint, Idaho, Aug. 25, 1933; s. Frances Edward McManus and Mabel Delana (Klaus) DeMers; m. Darlene Madge Keough, Feb. 3, 1954; children: Kelly C., Shannon M., Peggy F., Erin B. BA in English, Wash. State U., 1956, MA in English, 1962, postgrad., 1965-67. News reporter Daily Olympian, Olympia, Wash., 1956; editor Wash. State U., Pullman, 1956-59; with Ea. Wash. U., Cheney, 1959—; ret., 1983; news reporter Sta. KREM-TV, 1960-62; assoc. prof. Ea. Wash. U., Cheney, 1971-74, prof., 1974-83, prof. emeritus, 1983—. Author: A Fine and Pleasant Misery, 1978, Kid Camping from Aaaaiii! to Zip, 1979, They Shoot Canoes, Don't They?, 1981, Never Sniff a Gift Fish, 1983, The Grasshopper Trap, 1985, Rubber Legs & White Tail-Hairs, 1987, The Night The Bear Ate Goombaw, 1989, Whatchagot Stew, 1989, Real Ponies Don't Go Oink!, 1991, The Good Samaritan Strikes Again, 1992, How I Got This Way, 1994, Never Cry "Arp!" and Other Great Adventures, 1996, Into the Twilight, Endlessly Grousing, 1997, The Deer on a Bicycle, Excursions Into the Writing of Humor, 2000, The Bear in the Attic, 2002, The Blight Way, 2006; (stage play) A Fine and Pleasant Misery: The Humor of Patrick F. McManus, 1994, Misery II: McManus In Love, 1995, Pat McManus, Endlessly Grousing, 1997, Pott's Luck, 1999; assoc. editor Field & Stream mag., 1977-81; editor-at-large Outdoor Life, 1981—. Recipient Booksellers award P.N.W. Booksellers, 1983, Trustees medal EWU, 1984, Gov.'s award Wash. State Libr., 1985, Excellence in Craft award OWAA, 1986, Disting. Achievement award WSU, 1994, Founder's Day award EWU, 1994, Circle of Honor award The Outdoor Channel, 2004; named to Idaho's Hall of Fame, 1995, Legendary Communicator, Nat. Fresh Water Fishing Hall Fame, 2004. Mem.: Outdoor Writers Am. (bd. dirs. 1981—84, Excellence award 1986), Authors Guild. Roman Catholic. Avocations: outdoor sports, woodworking, travel. Home: PO Box 28216 Spokane WA 99228-8216

**MCMANUS, RICHARD PHILIP,** lawyer, agricultural products executive; b. Keokuk, Iowa, Oct. 20, 1929; s. Edward William and Kathleen (O'Connor) M.; m. Marjorie Theresa Mullaney, Nov. 5, 1955; children: Michael L., Mark J., Matthew A. BA, St. Ambrose U., Davenport, Iowa, 1949; JD, U. Mich., 1952; MBA, Roosevelt U., Chgo., 1965. Bar: Calif. 1982, Ill. 1958, Iowa 1952. Ptnr. McManus & McManus, Keokuk, 1953-63; div. counsel USN Facility Engring. Command, Great Lakes, Ill., 1963-66; v.p., dir. law Household Fin. Corp., Chgo., 1966-81; exec. v.p., sec. Security Pacific Fin. Svcs., Inc., San Diego, 1981-91; gen. counsel, 1981—91; exec. v.p./sec. Bank Am. Fin. Svcs., San Diego, 1991-92, gen. counsel, 1991—92; pres., chmn. bd. dirs. Mosamac Co., Inc., 1992—2006. Mem. gen. com. Conf. Consumer Fin. Law, Chgo., 1975-92; mem. adv. bd. Hostler Inst. Internat. Affairs, San Diego State U., 2005—. Contbr. articles to profl. jours. Bd. dir., trans., atty. Tijuana/San Diego Habitat for Humanity, Inc., 1992-95; trustee Village of Lake Bluff, Ill., 1974-78; bd. dir. Charles Hostler Inst. World Affairs, San Diego State U., 2004-. Recipient San Diego Vol. Lawyer Disting. Svc. award, 1995-2005, Pres. Calif. Bar Pro Bono Svs. award, 1998; named San Diego Pro Bono Atty. of Yr., 2005. Mem. Calif. Bar Assn., San Diego Bar Assn., Calif. Fin. Svcs. Assn. (chmn. law com. 1981-92), Am. Fin. Svcs. Assn. (chmn. law forum 1980-81, Disting. Svc. award 1990), Lions, Elks, KC, Beta Gamma Sigma. Democrat. Roman Catholic. Avocations: golf, flying, sailing, woodworking. E-mail: mcman1000@peoplepc.com.

**MCMANUS, ROBERT FRANCIS,** lawyer; b. Jamaica, N.Y., Dec. 8, 1959; s. Robert Gordon and Margaret Mary McManus; m. Frances Sica McManus, Apr. 27, 1985; children: Robert Alexander, Cassidy Frances. BA, Fordham U., 1981; JD, Thomas M. Cooley Law Sch., Lansing, Mich., 1985. Bar: N.Y. 1987. Prin. Law Office of Robert F. McManus, Warwick, NY, 1988—; pres., counsel Esquire Title Agy., Inc., Warwick, 1999—. Mem.: ABA, N.Y. State Land Title Assn., Am. Land Title Assn., Orange County Bar Assn., N.Y. State Bar Assn. Office: Law Offices of Robert F McManus 14 Oakland Ave Warwick NY 10990

**MCMANUS, SEAN JOSEPH,** broadcast executive; b. Feb. 16, 1955; s. James Kenneth and Margaret Dempsey McManus; m. Tracy Lynne Torre, May 23, 1998. BA in English & History, cum laude, Duke U., 1977. Prodn. asst. to assoc. prodr. ABC Sports, NYC, 1977—79; assoc. prodr. to prodr. NBC Sports, NYC, 1979—81, v.p. planning, prodr., 1981—87; sr. v.p. US TV sales, programming Trans World Internat. (TV divsn. IMG), NYC, 1987—96; pres. CBS Sports, NYC, 1996—, CBS News, NYC, 2005—. Dir. CBS SportsLine, 1997—.

**MCMANUS, WALTER LEONARD,** brokerage house executive; b. N.Y.C., Apr. 27, 1918; s. Charles E. and Eva M. (Olt) McM.; m. Lillian Ziegler, June 21, 1941; children: Walter Leonard, Peter David, Susan. Student, Harvard Bus. Sch.; BS in Fin. Sci., Georgetown U., 1940. With Crown Cork & Seal Co., Inc., Balt., 1940-60, became sec., 1945, v.p., 1949, sec.-treas., 1958-60. Pres., dir. Cem Securities Corp.; assoc. Castlewood Realty Co.; dir. Hospice of Martin County, Fla. Bd. dirs. Vols. of Medicine. Mem. Vols. in Medicine, Halifax River Yacht Club, Lighthouse Point Yacht Club, Cocoanut Point Yacht Club, Internat. Order of Blue Gavel. Home: 1766 NW Harbor Pl North River Shores Stuart FL 34994 Office: 204 E Joppa Rd Towson MD 21286-3183 Personal E-mail: crealtycom@aol.com

**MCMANUS, WILLIAM PAUL,** police chief; married; 3 children. Bachelor's degree, Villanova U.; MS, Johns Hopkins U. Police officer Met. Police Dept., Washington, asst. police chief, 1998—2001; police chief City of Dayton, Ohio, 2001—03, City of Mpls., 2004—06, City of San Antonio, 2006—. Office: Police Dept Office of City Mgr San Antonio TX 78201 Office Phone: 210-207-7360. Office Fax: 210-207-4377.*

**MCMARTIN, JOHN,** actor; b. Warsaw, Ind. children: Kathleen Alice, Susan Helen. Actor: (Broadway plays) The Conquering Hero, 1961, Blood, Sweat and Stanley Poole, 1961, Children From Their Games, 1963, A Rainy Day in Newark, 1963, Sweet Charity, 1966 (Tony award nomination best featured actor in a musical, 1966), Follies, 1971, The Great God Brown, 1972—73 (Drama Desk award outstanding performance, 1973), Don Juan, 1972 (Drama Desk award outstanding performance, 1973, Tony award nomination best featured actor in a play, 1973), Sondheim: A Musical Tribute, 1973, The Visit, 1973, Chemin de Fer, 1973—74, Love for Love, 1974, The Rules of the Game, 1974, Happy New Year, 1980, Solomon's Child, 1982, A Little Family Business, 1982, Artist Descending a Staircase, 1989, Show Boat, 1994 (Tony award nomination best actor in a musical, 1995), High Society, 1998 (Drama Desk award nomination outstanding featured actor in a musical, 1998, Tony award nomination best featured actor in a musical, 1995), Into the Woods,

2002 (Tony award nominaton best actor in a musical, 2002), Passion, 2004, (off-Broadway) Little Mary Sunshine, 1959—60 (Theatre World award, 1960), The Misanthrope, 1977, Too Much Johnson, 1985, Henry IV, 1985, Julius Caesar, 1988, Grey Gardens, 2006 (Drama Desk award nomination outstanding featured actor in a musical, 2006), Indian Blood, 2006; (films) A Thousand Clowns, 1965, What's So Bad About Feeling Good?, 1968, Sweet Charity, 1969, All the President's Men, 1976, Thieves, 1977, Brubaker, 1980, Blow Out, 1981, Pennies from Heaven, 1981, Dream Lover, 1986, Legal Eagles, 1986, Native Son, 1986, Who's That Girl?, 1987, Little Sweetheart, 1989, A Shock to the System, 1990, Three Businessmen, 1998, The Dish, 2000, Kinsey, 2004; (TV films) Ride with Terror, 1963, Out of the Blue, 1968, Ritual of Evil, 1970, God Bless Mr. Ferguson, 1971, The Rules of the Game, 1975, Fear on Trial, 1975, The Fatal Weakness, 1976, The Defection of Simas Kudirka, 1978, Butterflies, 1979, The Greatest Man in the World, 1980, Looking Back, 1981, Private Contentment, 1982, The Last Ninja, 1983, Concealed Enemies, 1984, Murrow, 1986, Lincoln, 1988, Roots: The Gift, 1988, Day One, 1989, Separate But Equal, 1991, Citizen Cohn, 1992, H.U.D., 2000. Mem.: The Players (N.Y.C.). Office: The Artists Agy 1000 Santa Monica Blvd North Hollywood CA 91601*

**MCMASTER, BELLE MILLER,** religious organization administrator; b. Atlanta, May 24, 1932; d. Patrick Dwight and Lila (Bonner) Miller; m. George R. McMaster, June 19, 1953; children: Lisa McMaster Stork, George Neel, Patrick Miller. BA, Agnes Scott Coll., 1953; MA, U. Louisville, 1970, PhD, 1974. Assoc. corp. witness Presbyn. Ch. USA, Atlanta, 1974-77, dir. corp. witness, 1977-81, dir. div. corp. and social mission, 1981-87, dir. social justice and peacemaking unit Louisville, 1987-93; acting dir. program women in theology and ministry Candler Sch. Theology Emory U., 1993-96, dir. advanced studies Candler Sch. Theology, 1995—2003. Vice-moderator chs. commn. internat. affairs World Coun. Chs., 1984-91, mem. justice, peace and creation commn., 1991-99; chair commn. internat. affairs Nat. Coun. Chs., NYC, 1986-89, v.p., 1990-95, exec. bd., 1986-2003, chair ch. world svc. and witness unit com., 1990-2003; chair fin. com. Ch. World Svc. and Witness Unit Com., NC, 1997-99, bd. dirs., 1995-2003. Author: Witnessing to the Kingdom, 1982, book columnist "What I Have Been Reading" in Church and Society Magazine, 1993-2001; contbr. articles to profl. jours. Pres. League of Women Voters, Greenville, S.C., 1963-64; bd. dirs. Interfaith Housing, Atlanta, 1975-81. Danforth fellow, 1969-74. Mem.: MLA, Soc. for Values in Higher Edn., Acad. Am. Religion, Phi Beta Kappa. Presbyterian. E-mail: bmcmast@emory.edu.

**MCMASTER, BRIAN JOHN,** artistic director; b. May 9, 1943; With internat. artists dept. EMI, 1968-73; contr. opera planning English Nat. Opera, 1973-76; mng. dir. Welsh Nat. Opera, Cardiff, 1976-91; dir. Edinburgh Internat. Festival, Scotland, 1991—2006; artistic dir. Vancouver Opera, BC, Canada, 1983-89. E-mail: brian.mcmaster@hotmail.com.

**MCMASTER, GLORIA (GLORIA BUGNI JUHN),** mezzo-soprano, educator; b. Montreal, Wis., Oct. 22, 1926; d. Anton George and Rose (Gatto) Bugni; m. Chester L. McMaster (dec. 1972); children— Chester Anthony, Raymond Dale, Brian Monroe, Maureen Anne, Heather Lynn; m. Martin Juhn, July 30, 1977. Student U. Minn.; B.S., Juilliard Sch. Music, N.Y.C.; postgrad. Columbia U., U. Detroit, SUNY-Brockport; Mus.M., Eastman Sch. Music, U. Rochester. Prin. voice instr. McMaster Music Studios, Rochester and Dansville, N.Y., 1987—. Performed in concert, oratorio, opera throughout U.S., including solo appearances with Juilliard Opera Theater, Chautauqua Opera Assn., Rochester Opera Theater; appeared as soloist with Mpls. Symphony, Rochester (N.Y.) Philharm. Buffalo Philharm. Music Theater of Rochester, Eastman Rochester Symphony, Rochester, Hornell (N.Y.) Symphony, Sarasota Opera, 2003—; recitals at Youngstown, Ohio, Ironwood, Mich., Hornell, Alfred U., and Rochester, N.Y.; concerts Nazareth Art Ctr., Nat. Opera Assns., New Orleans, Sarasota, Fla.; dir. Dansville Music Theater; asst. prof. Youngstown State U., State U. Coll., Geneseo, N.Y.; prof. Houghton (N.Y.) Coll; judge scholarship com. Sarasota Opera. Soloist Republican Nat. Convention, Miami; appeared in title role Nat. Edn. Television prodn. The Medium; appeared in plays by Phil Gelb, Sarasota, 1986-87. Mem. pres.'s leadership council U. Rochester. Mem. AAUW (past pres. Dansville area br.), AAUP (past chpt. exec. bd.), Nat. Opera Assns., Nat. Assn. Tchrs. Singing, Juilliard Alumni Assn., Eastman Alumni Assn., N.Y. Music Tchrs. Assn. Address: 3830 Glen Oaks Manor Dr Sarasota FL 34232 E-mail: gloriajuhn@comcast.net.

**MCMASTER, HENRY DARGAN,** state attorney general; b. Columbia, S.C., May 27, 1947; s. John Gregg and Ida Bacot (Dargan) McM.; m. Peggy Jean McAbee, Mar. 18, 1978 BA, U. S.C., 1969, JD, 1973. Bar: S.C., U.S. Dist. Ct. S.C., U.S. Ct. Claims, U.S. Ct. Appeals (4th cir.), U.S. Supreme Ct. Atty., legis. asst. U.S. Senator Strom Thurmond, Washington, 1973-74; ptnr. Tompkins & McMaster, Columbia, SC, 1974—81, 1985—2003; U.S. atty. Dist. SC, Columbia, 1981-85; atty. gen. State of SC, 2003—. Mem. U.S. Atty. Gen.'s adv. com. of U.S. Attys., Washington, 1981-83; chmn. Com. on Ct. Rules and Legislation, Washington, 1983-85. Contbr. articles to legal publs. Mem. region IV youth adv. bd. EPA, Atlanta, 1972; mem. S.C. Commn. on Higher Edcn., 1991-94; chmn. S.C. Rep. Party, 1993-2002; bd. dirs. S.C. Policy Coun., 1991-2003; atty. gen. S.C., 2003-. Mem. Richland County Bar Assn. (program com. 1978), S.C. Bar, ABA, Nat. Assn. R.R. Trial Counsel, Def. Rsch. Inst., Centurian Soc., Caroliniana Ball Club, St. Andrew's Soc. (Columbia), Phi Delta Phi, Blue Key, Kappa Alpha (dep. province comdr. 1974-75, province comdr. 1975-91). Republican. Presbyterian. Office: 1731 Senate St Columbia SC 29201 also: Office of Atty General Rembert C Dennis Office Bldg PO Box 11549 Columbia SC 29211-1549 Office Phone: 803-734-3970.*

**MCMASTER, JULIET SYLVIA,** English language educator; b. Kisumu, Kenya, Aug. 2, 1937; emigrated to Can., 1961, naturalized, 1976; d. Sydney Herbert and Sylvia (Hook) Fazan; m. Rowland McMaster, May 10, 1968; children: Rawdon, Lindsey. BA with honors, Oxford U., Eng., 1959; MA, U. Alta., Can., 1963, PhD, 1965. Asst. prof. English U. Alta., Edmonton, Canada, 1965—70, assoc. prof., 1970—76, prof. English, 1976—86, prof., 1986—2000, prof. emeritus, 2000—. Author: Thackeray: The Major Novels, 1971, Jane Austen on Love, 1978, Trollope's Palliser Novels, 1978; author: (with R.D. McMaster) The Novel from Sterne to James, 1981; author: Dickens the Designer, 1987, Jane Austen the Novelist, 1995, Reading the Body in the Eighteenth Century Novel, 2004, Woman Behind the Painter: The Diaries of Rosalie, Mrs. James Clarke-Hook, 2006; co-editor: Jane Austen's Business, 1996, Cambridge Companion to Jane Austen, 1997, The Child Writer From Austen to Woolf, 2005; gen. editor: Juvenilia Press, 1993—2002, illustrator/editor: children's picture book (by Jane Austen) The Beautifull Cassandra, 1993; contbr. articles to profl. jours. Fellow Can. Coun., 1969-70, Guggenheim Found., 1976-77, Killam Found., 1987-89; recipient Molson prize in Humanities for Outstanding Contbn. to Canadian Culture, 1994, Alberta Centennial medal, 2005. Fellow Royal Soc. Can.; mem. Victorian Studies Assn. Western Can. (founding pres. 1972), Assn. Can. Univ. Tchrs. English (pres. 1976-78), MLA, Jane Austen Soc. N.Am. (dir. 1980-91). Office Phone: 708-436-5284. Business E-Mail: juliet.mcmaster@ualberta.ca.

**MCMASTER, LEE P.,** chemicals executive; BSChemE, U. Del; PhD in Chem. Engring., MIT. Engr., project scientist chems. and plastics divsn. Union Carbide, Bound Brook, NJ, 1969—77, various bus. and mktg. positions, 1977—82, v.p., gen. mgr. specialty polymers and composites divsn., 1982—86, v.p., gen. mgr. polyolefins divsn., 1989—90, v.p., gen. mgr. unipol sys. divsn., 1990—92, pres. indsl. chems. divsn., 1992—93, corp. v.p., gen. mgr. ethylene/oxide glycol, 1993—98, corp. v.p., gen. mgr. specialty polymers and porducts, 1998—2000; v.p., gen. mgr. performance products bus. Amoco Chem., 1986—87, v.p. corp. planning and devel., 1987—89; bus. group pres. chems. bus. group Dow Chem. Co., Midland, Mich., 2000—. Mem.: Chlorine Chemistry Coun. (chmn. bd. dirs.), World Chlorine Coun. (vice chmn. bd. dirs.).

**MCMASTERS, KELLY MARC,** surgeon, educator; b. Camden, NJ, Jan. 29, 1961; m. Beth Hendrickson; children: Austin James, Steven Patrick, Owen Frederick. BA in Biology, Colgate U., Hamilton, NY, 1983; PhD, Rutgers U., New Brunswick, 1988; MD, U. Medicine and Dentistry NJ, Piscataway, 1989. Asst. prof. divsn. surg. oncology U. Louisville, 1996—2001, divsn. dir. surg. oncology dept. surgery, 2002—05, prof. dept. pharmacology & toxicology, 2004—06, prof., chmn. dept. surgery, 2005—; dir. multidisciplinary melanoma clinic James Graham Brown Cancer Ctr., 2000—06; assoc. dir. James Graham Brown Cancer Ctr., Ctr. Melanoma Programs, 2001—; chief surgery U. Louisville Hosp., 2005—. Recipient Hiram C. Polk, Jr. award Excellence Surg. Edn., U. Louisville, 2003, Disting. Alumni award, Alumni Assn. U. Medicine & Dentistry NJ, -Grad. Sch. Bioscis., 2006. Fellow: ACS; mem.: Southeastern Surg. Congress, Am. Assn. Cancer Rsch., Am. Soc. Clin. Oncology, Soc. Surg. Oncology, Assn. Acad. Surgery, Soc. U. Surgeons, Western Surg. Assn. (J. Bradley Aust award 2001), So. Surg. Assn. Home: 5707 Spring Bluff Dr Crestwood KY 40014 Office: U Louisville Dept Surgery 550 S Jackson St Louisville KY 40202 Office Phone: 502-852-5447. Home Fax: 502-241-8914; Office Fax: 502-852-1704. Business E-Mail: mcmasters@louisville.edu.

**MCMATH, ELIZABETH MOORE,** graphic artist; b. Iredell, Tex., Feb. 20, 1930; d. Fred William and Elizabeth Carol (Smith) Moore; m. Charles Wallis McMath, Jan. 16, 1978 (dec. Dec. 1990); children: Charles Wallis, John Seals. BA, BS in Advt. Design, Tex. Woman's U., Denton, 1951; grad. gemologist, Gemol. Inst. Am., L.A., 1977. Layout artist Leonard's Dept. Store, Ft. Worth, Tex., 1951-52; artist/bookkeeper Bud Biggs Studio, Dallas, 1953; sec./artist Squire Haskins Studio, Dallas, 1953-54; artist/art dir. Dowdell-Merrill, Inc., Dallas, 1954-58; owner/artist Moore Co., Dallas, 1958-90. Mem. Stemmons Corridor Bus. Assn. Dallas, 1988-89. Mem. Dallas/Ft. Worth Soc. Visual Comm. (founder), Tex. Woman's U. Nat. Alumnae Assn., Greater North Tex. Orchid Soc. (treas. 1987), Daylily Growers of Dallas (sec. 1989-90, 1st v.p. and program chmn. 1992), Internat. Bulb Soc., Native Plant Soc. Tex. (publicity chmn. Trinity Forks chpt. 1991-02, pres. 1998, sec. 1999-2003, Elm Fork chpt., master naturalist 2001—), Fort Worth Orchid Soc. Presbyterian. Avocations: ranching, horticulture, plant propagation, lost wax casting, gemstone cutting. Home: PO Box 1068 Denton TX 76202-1068 E-mail: elizabeth.mcmath@sbcglobal.net.

**MCMATH, LULA WRAY,** retired elementary school educator, realtor; b. Grenada, Miss., Apr. 27, 1933; d. Alva and Augusta McMath; m. Jesse C. Terry; 1 child, Damita. BS in Edn., Chgo. State U., 1971, MS in Urban Edn., 1972, MS in Corrections, 1974. Lic. realtor Chgo. (Ill.) Bd. Realtors, 1986. Seamstress Hart Schaffner and Marx, Chgo., 1952—65; tchr. Chgo. (Ill.) Bd. Edn., 1965—93; realtor Ronald Waters, Chgo., 1986—. Author: How 8th Grade Students View Discipline, 1973, Places I Have Visited, 1994, My Lovely Garden, 1994. Vol. gardener City of Chgo., 1989; vol. literacy educator Roosevelt U., Chgo., 1993; ballot giver Dem. Party, Chgo., 1988, poll watcher, 1984, judge, 1990, registrar, 1988. Recipient Valuable Svc. award, Faith Temple Ch., 1975, Meritorious award, United Negro Colls., 1991. Mem.: Am. Fedn., Ret. Tchrs. Avocations: gardening, singing, dance, interior decorating. Home: 10621 S Wood St Chicago IL 60643-2717

**MCMECHAN, GEORGE,** science educator; b. Vancouver, B.C., Canada, Aug. 21, 1947; BA in Applied Sci., U. of B.C., Vancouver, Can., 1970; MS, U. of Toronto, Ont., Can., 1971; BS, U. of Victoria, Can., 1983. Registered profl. engr., APEGBC, B.C., Can., 1976. Prof. of geosci. U. of Tex. at Dallas, Richardson, 1983—. Rsch. scientist Pacific Geosci. Ctr., Sidney, B.C., Canada, 1972—82; dir. Ctr. for Lithospheric Studies, U. of Tex. at Dallas, Richardson, 1985—. Contbr. over 200 articles to profl. jours. Mem.: Seismol. Soc. of Am., Am. Geophys. Union, Soc. of Exploration Geophysicists (Virgil Kauffman Gold medal 1997). Avocations: physical fitness, movies. Office: Univ of Tex at Dallas 2601 N Floyd Rd Richardson TX 75080 Office Phone: 972-883-2419. E-mail: mcmec@utdallas.edu.

**MCMEEKIN, DOROTHY,** botanist, plant pathologist, educator; b. Boston, Feb. 24, 1932; d. Thomas LeRoy and Vera (Crockatt) McM. BA, Wilson Coll., 1953; MA, Wellesley Coll., 1955; PhD, Cornell U., 1959. Asst. prof. Upsala Coll., East Orange, NJ, 1959-64, Bowling Green State U., Ohio, 1964-66; prof. natural sci. Mich. State U., East Lansing, 1966-89, prof. botany, plant pathology, 1989—. Author: Diego Rivera: Science and Creativity, 1985; contbr. articles to profl. jours. Mem. Am. Phytopath. Soc., Mycol. Soc. Am., Soc. Econ. Bot., Mich. Bot. Soc. (former bd. dirs.), Mich. Women's Studies Assn., Sigma Xi, Phi Kappa Phi. Avocations: gardening, sewing, travel, drawing. Home: 1055 Marigold Ave East Lansing MI 48823-5128 Office: Mich State U Dept Botany-Plant Pathology 100 N Kedzie Hall East Lansing MI 48824-1031 E-mail: mcmeekin@msu.edu.

**MCMEEKIN, THOMAS OWEN,** dermatologist; b. Shelby, Nebr., Apr. 17, 1945; s. Wallace Walton and Evajane (Taber) McM.; m. Dale Goodwin, 1999; children: Michele, Sean. BA with distinction, Stanford U., 1967; MD with honors, U. Rochester, 1971. Intern Beth Israel Hosp., Boston, 1971-72; resident U. Rochester (N.Y.), 1974-76, Mass. Gen. Hosp., Boston, 1976-78; clin. prof. depts. medicine, pediatrics, dermatology U. Rochester Sch. Medicine, 1978—; dermatologist pvt. practice, Rochester, 1978—; clin. asst. prof. SUNY, Buffalo, 1997—. Pres. Geneese Valley Laser Ctr., Rochester, 1990—. Capt. USPHS, 1972—74. Kohn fellow U. Rochester, 1980-81; recipient Doren J. Stephens Alumni award U. Rochester, 1971, Brian Flanagan Teaching Svc. award, 1995. Fellow Am. Acad. Dermatology (Svc. award 1993), Am. Bd. Internal Medicine, Am. Soc. LASer MEdicine (co-chmn. 1993-94), Am. Soc. Dermatologic Surgery (adm. com. 1983—); mem. N.Y. State Dermatological Soc. (v.p. 1993, treas. 1992), Buffalo Rochester Dermatological Soc. (pres. 1990), Rochester Dermatological Soc. (pres. 1988-89), Alpha Omega Alpha. Avocations: golf, tennis, computers. Office: 300 White Spruce Blvd Rochester NY 14623-1606 Office Phone: 585-424-6770. Personal E-mail: 041745@msn.com.

**MCMEEKING, ROBERT MAXWELL,** mechanical engineer, educator; b. Glasgow, Scotland, May 22, 1950; came to U.S., 1972; s. Robert Maxwell and Elizabeth Higginson (Craighead) McM.; m. Norah Ann Madigan, Sept. 4, 1976; children: Gavin Robert, Anne Catherine. BSc with 1st class honors, U. Glasgow, 1972; MS, Brown U., 1974, PhD, 1977. Acting asst. prof. Stanford (Calif.) U., 1976-78; asst. prof. U. Ill., Urbana, 1978-82, assoc. prof., 1982-85; prof. U. Calif., Santa Barbara, 1985—, chmn. mech. and environ. engring. Santa Barabara, 1992—95, 1999—2003. Cons. in field. Co-editor Intermetallic Matrix Composites, 1990; assoc. editor Jour. Applied Mechanics, 1987-93; editor Jour. Applied Mechanics, 2002—; contbr. articles to profl. jours. Recipient Alexander von Humboldt Rsch. award for Sr. U.S. Scientists, 2004; vis. fellow Cambridge U., 1983, 95-96. Fellow ASME, Am. Acad. Mechanics; mem. AAAS, NAE, Inst. Sci. Info. (Highly Cited Rschr. award) Sigma Xi. Office: U Calif Materials Dept Mech Engring Dept Santa Barbara CA 93106 Office Phone: 805-893-8434. Business E-Mail: rmcm@engineering.ucsb.edu.

**MC MEEL, JOHN PAUL,** newspaper syndicate and publishing executive; b. South Bend, Ind., Jan. 26, 1936; s. James E. and Naomi R. (Reilly) McM.; m. Susan S. Sykes, Apr. 16, 1966; children: Maureen, Suzanne, Bridget. BS, U. Notre Dame, 1957. Sales dir. Hall Syndicate, 1960-67; asst. gen. mgr., sales dir. Publishers-Hall Syndicate, 1968-70; co-founder Universal Press Syndicate, Kansas City, Mo., 1970; pres. Andrews McMeel Universal, 1970—. Chmn. bd. Andrews McMeel Pub., 1973—; mem. arts and letters U. Notre Dame. Co-founder Christmas in October, Kansas City, 1984—, James F. Andrews fellowship program, U. Notre Dame, 1981, adv. com. program in journalism; mem. The Civic Coun. Greater Kansas City. Mem. Fed. Assn. USA, Sovereign Mil. Order Malta. Home: Three Sunset Pl 5300 Sunset Dr Kansas City MO 64112-2358 Office: Andrews McMeel Universal 4520 Main St Kansas City MO 64111-1816 Office Phone: 816-932-6602. Business E-Mail: jmcmeel@amuniversal.com.

**MCMEEN, ELMER ELLSWORTH, III,** musician, retired lawyer; b. Lewistown, Pa., June 3, 1947; s. Elmer Ellsworth II and Frances Josephine McM.; m. Sheila Ann Taenzler, July 31, 1971; children: Jonathan Ellsworth, Daniel Biddle, James Cunningham and Mary Josephine (twins). BA cum laude, Harvard U., 1969; JD cum laude, U. Pa., 1972. Bar: 1973, U.S. Ct. Appeals (2nd cir.) 1973, U.S. Dist. Ct. (so.and ea. dists.) NY 1975. Assoc. Cravath, Swaine & Moore, N.Y.C., 1972-75, LeBoeuf, Lamb, Greene & MacRae, LLP, N.Y.C., 1975-78, ptnr., 1979-99, of counsel, 2000, retired, 2001. Lectr. Editor U. Pa. Law Rev., 1970-72. Author: numerous guitar books, Celtic Treasures for String Trio; musician: (solo instrnl. audio and DVD lessons and performance DVDs) Stefan Grossman's Guitar Workshop and Rounder Records; co-author: The Passion Dialogues, 2006, musician numerous solo guitar recordings; contbr. articles to legal jours. Chmn. N.Y.C. regional com. U. Pa. Law Sch., 1984-86; class sec. Northfield Mt. Hermon Sch. Class of 1965, Mass., 1984-91; pastoral staff vol. Andover Subacute and Rehab. Ctr., N.J. Named Internat. Musician of Yr., Internat. Biography Ctr., Cambridge, Eng., 2005. Mem.: Rockaway River Country Club. Office: 34 Angelo Dr Sparta NJ 07871 E-mail: elmcmeen@yahoo.com.

**MCMEEN, SHEILA TAENZLER,** retired lawyer; b. Morristown, N.J., Aug. 26, 1946; d. William Paul and Mary Cunningham Taenzler; m. E. Ellsworth McMeen, III, July 31, 1971; children: Jonathan, Daniel, James, Mary. AB summa cum laude, Muhlenberg Coll., Allentown, Pa., 1968; JD cum laude, U. Pa., 1971. Bar: N.Y. 1972, U.S. Supreme Ct. 1979. Assoc. Davis Polk & Wardwell, N.Y.C., 1971—80; ret. Editor: U. Pa. Law Rev. Pastoral care vol. staff Andover (N.J.) Rehab Ctr., 2004—; mem. Bd. of Edn. Mountain Lakes, NJ, 1993—2001, Sussex County Child Placement Rev. Bd., Newton, NJ, 2003—. Mem.: Phi Beta Kappa. Avocations· needlework, cryptic puzzles, reading. Home: 34 Angelo Dr Sparta NJ 07871 E-mail: elmcmeen@ptd.net.

**MCMENAMIN, JOHN ROBERT,** lawyer; b. Evanston, Ill., Sept. 30, 1946; BA, U. Notre Dame, 1968, JD, 1971. Bar: Ill. 1971. Law clk. to presiding judge U.S. Ct. Appeals (7th cir.), 1971-72; ptnr. Mayer, Brown & Platt, Chgo., 1978-89, McDermott, Will & Emery, Chgo., 1989—. Chmn. adv. bd. Holy Trinity High Sch., Chgo., 1986-88; pres. Lawyer's Club Chgo., 2003-04. Mem. ABA, Lawyers Club, U. Club, Econ. Club. Roman Catholic. Office: McDermott Will & Emery 227 W Monroe St Ste 3100 Chicago IL 60606-5096

**MCMENAMIN, RICHARD F.,** lawyer; b. Nov. 23, 1946; BA, St. Joseph's Coll., 1968; MA, Boston U., 1971; JD, Temple U., 1977. Bar: Pa. 1977. Ptnr. Morgan, Lewis & Bockius, Phila. Office: Morgan Lewis & Bockius 1701 Market St Philadelphia PA 19103-2903 Office Phone: 215-963-5596. Business E-Mail: rmcmenamin@morganlewis.com.

**MCMENAMIN, TERENCE MICHAEL,** economist; b. Meadowbrook, Pa., Sept. 4, 1970; s. John Patrick and Helen Marie McMenamin. BS, Pa. State U., University Park, 1997—2000; MA, Am. U., Washington, D.C., 2000—03. Economist U.S. Bur. Labor Stats., Washington, 2000—. Presenter in field. With U.S. Army, 1987—93. Home: 3112 River Bend Ct #H202 Laurel MD 20724 Personal E-mail: tmcmenamin88@hotmail.com.

**MCMENNAMIN, MICHAEL J.,** savings and loan executive, investment banker; b. Berlin, N.H., June 27, 1945; s. John Lester and Ruth Ellen (Donaldson) McM.; children: Kelly, Tricia. AB in Econs., Ohio U., 1967; MBA in Banking and Fin., Case Western Res. U., 1972. Exec. v.p. Nat. City Bank, Nat. City Corp., Cleve., 1968-81; vice chmn. Bank One Columbus (Ohio), NA, 1981-85; chief investment officer Banc One Corp., Columbus, 1981-85; ptnr., v.p. Meuse Rinker Chapman Endres & Brooks, Columbus, 1985-88; chmn. Midwest Savs. Bank, Degraff, Ohio, 1986-87; chmn., chief exec. officer Buckeye Fed. Savs. & Loan, Buckeye Fin. Corp., Columbus, 1988-90, Bank One, Columbus, 1990-95; exec. v.p. finance Banc One Corp., Columbus, 1995—. Lectr. Grad. Sch. Banking, U. Wis., Madison, 1975-80; mem. treasury and fed. agy. com. Pub. Securities Assn., 1977-81, 85; mem. exec. com. funds mgmt. div. Am. Bankers Assn., 1977-79. Author articles in field. Mem. The Golf Club (Columbus), The Capital Club (Columbus), The Athletic Club (Columbus), Wedgewood Country Club (Columbus), Pinehurst (N.C.) Nat. Golf Club, Pinehurst Country Club. Republican. Roman Catholic. Avocations: golf, squash, tennis, reading.

**MCMENNAMY, ROGER NEAL,** automotive executive; b. Amarillo, Tex., Oct. 9, 1942; s. Wilson Foch and Mildred Evelyn (Freudiger) McMennamy; m. Marilyn Kay Gibbons, Jan. 1, 1967; children: Timothy Neal, Traci Nicole. Student, Abilene Christian U., 1961-62; BBA in Mgmt. cum laude, U. Tex., Arlington, 1970; MBA in Fin., U. Tex., Austin, 1971. CPA Tex. Contr., treas. E. N. Wolcott Corp., Houston, 1971-73; mem. corp. staff ELPAC, Inc., Houston, 1973-74; gen. mgr. BS&B Mfg., Houston, 1974-75; gen. mgr. adminstrn. Gulf Interstate Co., Houston, 1975-77; exec. v.p., CFO NWS Supply Group, Houston, 1977-83; v.p., CFO Newpark Resources, Inc., Metairie, La., 1983-86; sr. v.p., CFO Gemcraft, Inc., 1986-88; exec. v.p., CFO Cooper Cmtys., Inc., Bella Vista, Ark., 1988-90, pres., CEO, 1990-97; pres., CEO, gen. mgr. Daryl Hickman Chevrolet, Inc., Siloam Springs, Ark., 1998—2005; pres., CEO Guaranteed Auto Fin., Inc., 2003—, SHAC, Inc., 2003—. With USMC, 1962—66, Vietnam. Avocations: travel, golf, waterfowl hunting. Office: Guaranteed Auto Fin Inc PO Box 730 Tontitown AR 72770 Office Phone: 479-361-4300.

**MCMICHAEL, DONALD EARL,** lawyer; b. Denver, Aug. 8, 1931; s. Earl L. and Charlotte F. McM.; m. Zeta Hammond, July 6, 1955; children: Lauren A. McMichael Burnett, Thomas D., Susan E. McMichael Markle. AB, Dartmouth Coll., 1953; LLB, U. Colo., 1956. Bar: Colo. 1956, U.S. Dist. Ct. Colo. 1956, U.S. Ct. Appeals (10th cir.) 1956. Assoc. Holme Roberts & Owen, 1956-58, pres. Corp. Ins. Assocs., 1958-70; dir. trust devel. Ctrl. Bank Denver, 1970-72; ptnr. Brenman, Sobol & Baum, Denver, 1972-74, McMichael, Benedict, Multz & Lipton, Denver, 1974—99; of counsel Schmidt & Horen, Denver, 2000—02; pvt. practice, 2002—. Chmn. Denver Ctrl. YMCA, 1971-73. Capt. USAR, 1956—64. Named Layman of Yr. Denver Ctrl. YMCA, 1973, named to Denver Metro YMCA Hall of Fame, 1989. Mem. Colo. Bar Assn., Denver Bar Assn., Denver Estate Planning Coun. (sec. 1971-73). Republican. Methodist. Office: 6325 W Mansfield Ave Unit 234 Denver CO 80235-3015 Office Phone: 303-716-8406. E-mail: dlmcmic@aol.com.

**MCMICHAEL, GUY H., III,** federal official; b. South Bend, Ind., Dec. 26, 1939; m. Nancy Moore. AB, Harvard U., 1962; JD, U. Mich., 1967. Pvt. practice, 1967—71; dept. prosecuting atty. State of Ind., 1967—71; gen. counsel com. vet. affairs U.S. Senate, Washington, 1971—77; gen. coun. Dept. Vet. Affairs (formerly VA), 1977—81; adminstrv. judge bd. contract appeals Dept. Vet. Affairs, 1981—90, chmn., chief adminstrv. judge, 1990—2003, acting chief staff, 2000—01, acting chief info. officer, 2001, acting under sec. benefits, 2000—02. With U.S. Army, 1962-64. Mem. ABA, Bds. Contract Appeals Judges Assn. (pres. 1989-90), Ind. Bar Assn., D.C. Bar Assn.

**MCMICHAEL, JESSICA LEIGH,** journalist, writer, poet; b. Nederland, Tex. d. James William and Jean Ann McMichael. B in English-Creative Writing, U. Houston, 2004. Promotions mgr. The Facts newspaper, Crute, Tex., 1997—. Contbr. articles to publs. Mem.: Golden Key Internat., Sigma Tau Delta, Phi Sigma Phi (pres. 2003—04). Republican.

**MCMICHAELS, SUSAN BISHOP WINSHIP,** writer, educator; b. Norwalk, Conn., Oct. 30, 1946; d. Paul Michelini and Susan Washburne (Reyburn) Winship; m. John William McMichaels, Oct. 21, 1967; children: Matthew Cogan, Susan Washburne. Bs, Smith Coll., 1968; MLA, U. N.C., Asheville, 1995. Cert. tchr., N.C. Tchr. Shenendehowa Ctrl., Elnora, N.Y., 1970-71, Blackwell Sch., Sheffield, Mass., 1974-76, Asheville Sch., 1976-77, Carolina Day Sch., Asheville, 1977-88, Asheville City Schs., 1988-97, The Mountain Cmty. Sch., Hendersonville, N.C., 1999—. Adj. instr. U. N.C.

Asheville, 1997—99; chair Asheville City Schs. Reading Recovery Site-Based Mgmt., 1995. Author: Journey Out of the Garden: St. Francis of Assisi and the Process of Individuation, 1997; contbr. biographies to Am. Nat. Biography, 1999. Mem. zoning com. Hoopers Creek, N.C., 1998-99. Asheville City Schs. Found. arts grantee, 1996-97; NEH grantee, 1994.

**MCMILLAN, CAMPBELL WHITE,** pediatrician, educator, hematologist; b. Soochow, China, Jan. 10, 1927; arrived in U.S., 1940; s. Henry Hudson and Leila McNeill (Memory) McM.; m. Florence Jean MacKenzie, June 11, 1955; children: Ian Johnson, Sally Hudson, Donna Jean, Andrew Duncan, Bridget White, Wendy McNeill. BS summa cum laude, Wake Forest Coll., 1948; MD, Bowman Gray Sch. Medicine, 1952. Diplomate Am. Bd. Pediatrics, Pediatric Hematology-Oncology. Intern Harvard Med. Service, Boston City Hosp., 1952-53; resident in pediatrics St. Mary's Hosp., London, 1955; pediatrician Nemazee Hosp., Shiraz, Iran, 1956-58; fellow in pediatric hematology Harvard U., 1958-60; instr. pediatrics, 1960-61; gen. practice pediatrics Laurinburg, NC, 1961-63; asst. prof. pediatrics U. N.C., Chapel Hill, 1963-68, asso. prof., 1968-72, prof., 1972-92, chief div. pediatric hematology, 1963-83, prof. emeritus, 1992—. Asso. dir. Clin. Research Center, U. N.C. 1966-78 Assoc. editor: Blood Diseases of Infancy and Childhood, 1978, 84; contbr. articles profl. jours., chpts. in books. Served with USNR, 1945-46. Recipient Lederle Med. Faculty award, 1964, Disting. Alumnus award Bowman Gray Sch. Medicine, 1972, Outstanding Career Achievement award Nat. Hemophilia Found., 1998. Fellow Am. Acad. Pediatrics; mem. Soc. Pediatric Rsch., Am. Pediatric Soc., Phi Beta Kappa, Alpha Omega Alpha. Democrat. Episcopalian. Home: 408 Ridgecrest Dr Chapel Hill NC 27514-2103 *It was my extremely good fortune to live and to work in a time of the most explosive growth medical knowledge had ever undergone.*

**MCMILLAN, CHARLES WILLIAM,** consulting company executive; b. Ft. Collins, Colo., Feb. 9, 1926; s. Charles and Margaret (Jennings) McM.; m. Jardell Hollier, Feb. 12, 1951; children: Brett W., Kurt C., Scott P. BS, Colo. State U., 1948. Asst. 4-H agt., Denver, 1948; county agrl. agt. LaJara, Colo., 1949-50, Julesburg, 1950-53; faculty Colo. State U., 1954; div. head, agrl. research dept. Swift & Co., 1954-59; exec. v.p. Am. Nat. Cattlemen's Assn., 1959-77; v.p. Nat. Cattlemen's Assn., 1977-81; asst. sec. for mktg. and inspection services USDA, Washington, 1981-85; pres. McMillan and Farrell Assocs., Inc., Washington, 1985-94, C.W. McMillan Co., Alexandria, Va., 1994—. Served to lt. (j.g.) USNR, World War II. Mem. Sigma Alpha Epsilon. Home: 4003 Pine Brook Rd Alexandria VA 22310-2144 Office: PO Box 10009 Alexandria VA 22310-0009

**MC MILLAN, GEORGE DUNCAN HASTIE, JR.,** lawyer, former state official; b. Greenville, Ala., Oct. 11, 1943; s. George Duncan Hastie and Jean (Autrey) McM.; m. Ann Dial, Nov. 20, 1971; children: George Duncan Hastie, III, Ann Dial. BA magna cum laude, Auburn U., 1966; LL.B. (Southeastern Regional scholar), U. Va., 1969. Bar: Ala. bar 1969. Research asst. dept. agronomy Auburn U., summers 1963-65; law clk. firm Lange, Simpson, Robinson & Somerville, Birmingham, Ala., summers 1967-68; law clk. to judge U.S. Dist. Ct. No. Dist. Ala., 1969-70; instr. U. Ala. Law Sch., 1969-70; individual practice law Birmingham, 1970-71; ptnr. firm McMillan & Spratling, Birmingham, 1971-86; of counsel Haskell, Slaughter, Young and Lewis, 1986; ptnr. McMillan, Jones and Assocs., 1987-90; pres. McMillan Assocs., 1990—; mem. Ala. Ho. of Reps., 1973, Ala. Senate, 1974-78; lt. gov. Ala., 1979-83. Vice-chmn. Nat. Conf. Lt. Govs., 1980-82; mem. Permanent Study Commn. on Ala.'s Jud. System, 1975-79 Chmn. Ala. Film Commn. 1976-83; mem. Arts Task Force, Nat. Conf. State Legislatures, 1978-80, Multi-State Transp. Adv. Bd., 1974-79; mem. exec. com. So. Growth Policies Bd., 1974-83, vice chmn., 1981-83; bd. dirs. Campfire, Inc., 1975-82, Met. YMCA, Birmingham, Boys and Girls Ranches, Ala., Positive Maturity, 1987—; chmn. bd., pres. Birmingham Cultural and Heritage Found., 1988—; pres., bd. dirs. Birmingham Repertory Theatre, 1989—; exec. prodr. City Stages, 2003—; vice chair Black Belt Cmty. Found. Served to lt. USAR, 1969. Recipient award Ala. Nurses Assn., 1975; named Legislator of Yr. Ala. Forestry Assn., 1978; Hardest Working Senator Capitol Press Corps, 1976; 1 of 4 Outstanding Young Men Ala. Jaycees, 1977; 1 of 10 Most Outstanding State Legislators Assn. Govtl. Employees, 1978; award Birmingham Emancipation Assn., 1977; award Ala. Hist. Commn., 1978; James Tingle award, 1979, Citizen of Yr. award City of Birmingham, 1990. Mem. Birmingham Bar Assn., Ala. Bar Assn., Am. Bar Assn., Birmingham Jaycees, Ala. Jaycees (dir. 1970-72), Birmingham Urban League, United Negro Coll. Fund. Democrat. Mem. Ch. of Christ. Club: Rotary (Birmingham). Office: Mc Millan Assocs Ste 900 1929 3rd Ave N Birmingham AL 35203 Office Phone: 205-324-6881. Business E-Mail: george@mcmillan-associates.com.

**MCMILLAN, JENNY HILL,** elementary school educator; d. Ralph Durwood and Rebekah Starling Hill; m. Huey Alexander, Nov. 23, 1985; children: Stephen Alexander, Jonathan Seth. BA in Edn. A. U., NC, Charlotte, 1985. Cert. tchr. of academically and intellectually gifted NC. 5th grade tchr. Belmont (NC) Ctrl. Elem. Sch., 1985—. Mem.: Profl. Educators NC. Personal E-mail: mcmillanj2002@yahoo.com.

**MCMILLAN, JULIA A.,** pediatrician; b. Pinehurst, N.C., July 10, 1946; MD, SUNY, Syracuse, 1976. Intern SUNY Upstate Med. Ctr., Syracuse, 1976-77, resident in pediatrics, 1977-78, 79-80, fellow in infectious diseases, 1979-81; mem. staff Johns Hopkins U. Hosp., Balt.; assoc. prof. Johns Hopkins U., Balt., dep. dir., residency program dir., prof., vice-chair med. edn., 1996—; chair. Am. Bd. of Pediatrics, Chapel Hill. Author: Oski's Pediatrics: Principles and Practice, 3d edit., 1999, The Best of the Whole Pediatrician Catalogs, I-III, 1984, The Whole Pediatrician Catalog: A Compendium of Clues to Diagnosis and Management, 1977. Mem. ASM, IDSA, Am. Acad. Pediatrics. Office: Johns Hopkins Hosp Dept Pediatrics 600 N Wolfe St Dept Baltimore MD 21287-0005

**MCMILLAN, LEE RICHARDS, II,** lawyer; b. New Orleans, Aug. 26, 1947; s. John H. and Phoebe (Skillman) McM.; m. Lynne Clark Potharst, June 27, 1970; children: Leslie Clark, Hillary Anne, Lee Richards III. BS in Commerce, Washington and Lee U., 1969; JD, Tulane U., 1972; LLM in Taxation, NYU, 1976. Bar: La. 1972. Assoc. Jones, Walker, Waechter, Poitevent, Carrere & Denegre, New Orleans, 1976-79, ptnr., 1979—, sect. head, corp. and securities sect., 1987—90, 1994—2002, exec. com., 1990—94, 1996—99, 2001—02, chmn. exec. com., 1991—94, 1996—98, 2001—02. Vice chmn. Mech. Equipment Co., Inc., New Orleans, 1980-86, chmn. bd., 1986—, pres., 1989—99; mem. The Bus. Coun. Greater New Orleans, 1998—, exec. com., 1999—; bd. dirs. The Chamber/New Orleans and the River Region, 1996—98; trustee Alton Ochsner Med. Found. 1995—2003. Trustee New Orleans Mus. Art., 1989-95; bd. dirs. Bur. Govtl. Rsch. New Orleans, 1987-93, Louise S. McGehee Sch., New Orleans, 1982-88, co-chmn. capital fund dr., 1984-86, pres. bd. dirs.; trustee, bd. govs. Isidore Newman Sch., New Orleans, 1991-95. Lt. JACG USNR, 1972-75. Mem. ABA (com. on negotiated acquisitions 1986-94), La. State Bar Assn. (chmn. corp. and bus. law sect. 1985-86, mem. com on bar admissions 1986-87), Young Pres. Orgn., Washington and Lee U. Alumni Assn. (bd. dirs. 1995-99). Republican. Episcopalian. Avocation: sailing. Office: Jones Walker Waechter Poitevent Carrere & Denegre 201 Saint Charles Ave Ste 5100 New Orleans LA 70170-5101

**MCMILLAN, M. SEAN,** lawyer; Diploma, U. Munich, 1963; cert., Internat. Sch., Copenhagen, Denmark, 1962; SB, U. So. Calif., 1967; JD, Harvard U., 1970. Bar: Calif. 1971. Spl. projects dir. Mass. Gen. Hosp., Boston, 1967-70; ptnr. Keatinge, Libbott, Bates & Loo, Los Angeles, 1970-74, Loo, Merideth & McMillan, Los Angeles, 1974-85, Bryan Cave LLP, Los Angeles/Santa Monica, 1986—2001, Greenberg Traurig LLP, L.A., 2001—. Editor: Harvard Internat. Law Jour., 1968-70. Mem. ABA, Am. Soc. Internat. Law. Office: Greenberg Traurig LLP 2450 Colorado Ave Ste 400E Santa Monica CA 90404 Office Phone: 310-586-7700. Business E-Mail: mcmillan@gtlaw.com.

**MCMILLAN, MARY BIGELOW,** retired minister, volunteer; b. St. Paul, July 30, 1919; d. Charles Henry and Allison (McKibbin) Bigelow; m. Richard McMillan, June 26, 1943; children: Richard Jr., Charles B., Douglas D., M. Allison, Anne E. BA, Vassar Coll., 1941; MDiv, United Theol. Sem. Twin Cities, 1978, DDiv (hon.), 1989. Ordained to ministry Presbyn. Ch., 1978. Asst. min. House of Hope Presbyn. Ch., St. Paul, 1978-82; interim pres. United Theol. Sem. Twin Cities, New Brighton, Minn., 1982-83, ret., 1987. Contbg. author The Good Steward, 1983. Regional dir. Assn. Jr. Leagues, N.Y.C., 1959—61, pres. St. Paul chpt., 1957—59; vice chair Ramsey County Welfare Bd., St. Paul, 1962—66, St. Paul Health and Welfare Planning Coun., 1964—70, F.R. Bigelow Found., St. Paul, 1988—95, also 1st vice chair; 1st vice chair, trustee Wilder Found., 1973—89; active Presbyn. Homes Found., 1996—; trustee Minn. Ch. Found., Mpls., 1984—99, United Theol. Sem. Twin Cities, 1977—89, also chmn. bd. trustees; bd. dirs. Inst. for Ecumenical and Cultural Rsch., Collegeville, Minn., 1982—2003. Recipient award for cmty. planning United Way, 1965, also for yr. round leadership, 1973, Leadership in Cmty. Svc. award YWCA, 1980, Sisterhood award NCCJ, Mpls., 1989, Outstanding Vol. Fundraiser award Minn., 2005; named Disting. Alumna, St. Paul Acad. and Summit Sch., 1988 Mem.: Univ. Club, New Century Club. Avocations: knitting, reading. Home: 2925 Lincoln Dr #713 Roseville MN 55113 Personal E-mail: mbmcmo@comcast.net.

**MCMILLAN, MICHAEL REID,** retired orthopedic surgeon; b. Conway, S.C., Aug. 28, 1941; s. Hoyt and Sara Best (Sherwood) McM.; B.S., The Citadel, 1963: M.D., Duke U., 1967. Diplomate Nat. Bd. Med. Examiners, Am. Bd. Orthopedic Surgery; lic. physician, 1971-01, S.C.; Intern in medicine Balt. City Hosps., 1967-68; fellow in medicine Johns Hopkins Hosp., Balt., 1967-68; resident in orthopedic surgery Greenville (S.C.) Hosp. Systems and Greenville Shriners Hosp., 1971-75; practice medicine specializing in orthopedic surgery, Conway, S.C., 1975—2000, ret. 2000. mem. staff Conway Hosp., 1975—00, chief of orthopedics, 1975-82; bd. dirs. Burroughs and Chapin Co., 1990-96, Burroughs Co., Snow Hill Co., Conway, S.C. Trustee Burroughs Found., Conway, 1979—. Served to lt. comdr. MC, USN, 3d marine divn., 1968-71; Vietnam. Mem. AMA, S.C. Med. Assn., S.C. Orthopedic Assn., Horry County Med. Soc., Citadel Alumni Assn., Stelling Soc. Bapt., Forest Landowners Assn., Pres.'s Club Heritage Found., Pres.'s Coun. Brookgreen Gardens, Nat. Trust, SC Hist. Soc., Found. Econ. Edn., Save-the-Redwoods-League, Am. Legion, Civil War Preservation Trust, Third Bn. Third Marines RVN Assn., Horry County Citadel. Republican. Home and Office: 1400 9th Ave Conway SC 29526-4106

**MCMILLAN, NATHANIEL (NATE MCMILLAN),** professional basketball coach; b. Raleigh, NC, Aug. 3, 1964; m. Michelle McMillan; children: Jamelle, Brittany Michelle. Student, Chowan Coll., 1982-84, N.C. State U., 1984-86. Guard Seattle SuperSonics, 1986—98, head coach, 2001—05, Portland Trail Blazers, 2005—. Dir. summer basketball camp. Holder NBA single-game rookie record assists; Seattle SuperSonics all-time leader steals, assists, single-game record assists, single-game playoff record assists; named Jr. Coll. All-Am., top 10 N.C. State list assists, 2d team All-NBA def., 1993-94, 94-95; Head Coach NBA Northwestern Div. championship team, 2004-2005. Avocation: football. Office: Seattle SuperSonics 351 Elliott Ave W Seattle WA 98119-4101*

**MC MILLAN, R(OBERT) BRUCE,** retired museum director, anthropologist; b. Springfield, Mo., Dec. 3, 1937; s. George Glassey and Winnie Mae (Booth) McM.; m. Virginia Kay Moore, Sept. 30, 1961; children: Robert Gregory, Michael David, Lynn Kathryn. BS in Edn, S.W. Mo. State U., 1950; MA in Anthropology, U. Mo., 1963; PhD in Anthropology, U. Colo., 1971. Rsch. assoc. in archaeology U. Mo., 1963-65, 68-69; assoc. curator anthropology Ill. State Mus., Springfield, 1969-72, curator anthropology, 1972-73, asst. mus. dir., 1973-76, mus. dir., 1977—2005; exec. sec. Ill. State Mus. Soc., 1977—2005; ret., 2005. Lectr. anthropology Northwestern U., 1973. Editor: (with W. Raymond Wood) Prehistoric Man and His Environments, 1976. Mem. Ill. Spl. Events Commn., 1977-79, program chmn., 1977-78; commr. Ill. and Mich. Canal Nat. Heritage Corridor Commn., 1988-96; bd. dirs. Found. Ill. Archaeology, 1978-83. Grantee NSF, 1971-72, 80, NEH, 1978. Fellow AAAS, Am. Anthrop. Assn.; mem. Am. Assn. Mus. (coun. 1982-86), Midwest Mus. Conf. (pres.), Soc. Am. Archaeology, Current Anthropology (assoc.), Am. Quaternary Assn., Sigma Xi. Office: Ill State Mus 502 S Spring St Springfield IL 62706-5000 also: Dickson Mounds Museum Lewistown IL 61542 Office Phone: 217-524-0498. Business E-Mail: mcmillan@museum.state.il.us.

**MCMILLAN, ROBERT RALPH,** lawyer; b. NYC, May 21, 1932; s. Harry and Vivian (Beatty) McM.; m. Phoebe Parker Bunn, Nov. 2, 1996; children: Robin, Karen, Kenneth. Student, Adelphi U., 1951-52, 55-56; JD, Bklyn. Law Sch., 1960. Bar: N.Y. 1960. Spl. asst. staff of Richard M. Nixon, NY, Washington, 1960, 64-65; counsel Senator Kenneth B. Keating, Washington, 1960-62; govt. rels. advisor Mobil Oil Co., NYC, 1962-63, 65-68; v.p. Avon Products, NYC, 1973-78, 79-85; sr. v.p. A&S Dept. Stores, NYC, 1978-79; counsel Rivkin, Radler, Bayh, Hart & Kremer, Uniondale, NY, 1986-91; ptnr. McMillan, Rather, Bennett & Farinoci, P.C., Melville, NY, 1991—2003, Fischbein Badillo Wagner Harding, Melville, 2003—05, Bee Ready Fishbein Hatter & Donovan LLP, Melville, 2005—. Chmn. Panama Canal Commn., 1993-94; mem. nat. adv. coun. FannieMae, 1998-2000, co-hosts Face-Off, PBS, NY. News commentator Sta. WLIW-TV, 1993—; columnist, Anton Community Newspapers, Long Island; occasional columnist for Newsday. Trustee Adelphi U., 1984-89; bd. dirs. L.I. (N.Y.) Assn.; chmn. L.I. Housing Partnership, 1988-2002. 1st lt. U.S. Army, 1952-54. Decorated Bronze Star; recipient Excellence in Leadership award, Helen Keller Services for the Blind, Humanitarian award, Alzheimer's Assn. Mem.: AMA (bd. trustees 2002—), Suffolk County Bar Assn., Nassau County Bar Assn. Republican. Avocations: golf, fishing. Office Phone: 516-746-5599. E-mail: mcmillanr@aol.com.

**MCMILLAN, ROBERT WALKER,** physicist, consultant; b. Sylacauga, Ala., Apr. 18, 1935; s. Robert Thomas and Alma (Bush) McM.; m. Ann Simmons, Sept. 11, 1955; children: Marisa Ann, Robert Murray, Natalie June. BS, Auburn U., 1957; MS, Rollins Coll., 1966; PhD, U. Fla., 1974. Engr. Westinghouse Electric, Balt., 1960-61; staff engr. Martin Marietta Aerospace, Orlando, Fla., 1961-76; prin. rsch. scientist Ga. Tech. Rsch. Inst., Atlanta, 1976—; with Rsch. Lab USAF, Rome, NY, 1995—98; sr. rsch. scientist U.S. Army Space and Missile Def. Commd., Huntsville, Ala., 1998—. Chmn. various confs.; cons. in field. Contbr. over 200 articles to profl. jours., conference digests. Lt. USAF, 1958—60. Recipient Meritorious Presdl. Rank award, 2005. Fellow IEEE; mem. Optical Soc. Am., Soc. Photo-Optical Instrumentation Engrs. Democrat. Baptist. Achievements include patents in field. Office Phone: 256-955-5418.

**MCMILLAN, TERRY L.,** writer, educator; b. Port Huron, Mich., Oct. 18, 1951; d. Edward McMillan and Madeline Washington Tillman; 1 child, Solomon Welch; m. Jonathan Plummer, 1998 (div. 2005). BA in Journalism, U. Calif., Berkeley, 1979; postgrad., Columbia Univ., N.Y.C., 1979. Instr. U. Wyoming, Laramie, 1987-88; prof. U. Ariz., Tucson, 1988-91. Author: Mama, 1987 (Nat. Book award Before Columbus Found.), Disappearing Acts, 1989, Waiting to Exhale, 1992, How Stella Got Her Groove Back, 1996, A Day Late & A Dollar Short, 2001, The Interruption of Everything, 2005 (NY Times and Publishers Weekly hardcover bestseller list); editor: Breaking Ice: An Anthology of Contemporary African-American Fiction, 1990; screenwriter (with Ron Bass) (movies) Waiting to Exhale, 1995, How Stella Got Her Groove Back, 1998. Recipient NY Found.for the Arts Fellowship, 1986, Nat.Endowment for the Arts fellowship, 1988, Doubleday/Columbia Univ. Lit. Fellowship, MacDowell Colony fellow, Yaddo Artist Colony fellow (three times).

**MCMILLAN, WILLIAM P.,** lawyer; b. Roanoke Rapids, NC, Mar. 22, 1960; BA with highest distinction, U. Va., 1982; JD with high honors, Duke U., 1985. Bar: Tex. 1985, NC 1994. Ptnr. real estate and creditor's rights Katten Muchin Zavis Rosenman, Charlotte, NC. Mem.: ABA, NC Bar Assn.,

Mecklenburg County Bar Assn. Office: Katten Muchin Zavis Rosenman 401 S Tryon St, Ste 2600 Charlotte NC 28202 Office Phone: 704-444-2030. Office Fax: 704-344-3065. E-mail: william.mcmillan@kmzr.com.

**MCMILLEN, ELIZABETH CASHIN,** artist; b. Chgo. d. James Blaine and Hortense (Fears) Cashin; m. John Stephen Jerabek; 1 child, Michael N. Student, Western Coll. for Women, 1961-63; BA, Bard Coll., 1965. Coord. com. and juror Spectra I, sponsor state exhbn. women artists Westbrook Coll., Portland, Maine, 1979; dir. Hancock County Auditorium Art Gallery, Ellsworth, Maine, 1984, 85. Exhibited at Frick Gallery, Belfast, Maine, 1993, 94, Maine Coast Artists Juried Show, Rockport, 1994, Portland Children's Mus., 1995, Lakes Gallery, Sebago, Maine, 1995—, Maine Coast Artists, Rockport, 1998, Portland Mus. Art, 1998, 2001, American Embassy Santiago Chili, 1998—, Maine Art Gallery, Wiscasset, 2001, Payson Gallery, Portland, 2002, June Fitzpatrick at MECA, Portland, 2004, U. Maine Mus. Art., Bangor, 2005, Ctr. for Maine Contemporary ARt, Rockport, 2005; one-person shows include Area Gallery, Portland, 1994, Frick Gallery, Belfast, Maine, 1995, Lakes Gallery, Sebago, Maine, 1997, June Fitzpatrick Alternative, Portland, 1999, June Fitzpatrick Gallery, Portland, 2001, 04; two persons show Maine Coast Artists, Rockport, 1996. Dem. chair Town of Lamoine, Maine, 1984-85, 86-87, 88-89; legislation coord. Amnesty Internat., Ellsworth, 1991-97. Democrat. Episcopalian. Avocations: writing, politics, teaching, African-American history.

**MCMILLEN, MARIETA LOUISE,** art educator; b. Kansas City, Kans., May 2, 1937; d. John Sanford and Dorothy Louise Spurgeon; adopted children: Jon Jason(dec.), Wayne Carey. EdB, Kans. U., 1964, M in Art Edn., 1964; postgrad., Art Inst., Kansas City, Mo., 1973—75. Artist Hallmark Cards, Kansas City, Mo., 1955—58; H.S. art tchr. Unified Sch. Dist. 500, Kansas City, Kans., 1962—65, elem. and secondary sch. art tchr., 1971—95; jr. and sr. H.S. art tchr. Unified Sch. Dist. 458, Basehor, Kans., 1966—71; adj. prof. Davis Coll., Johnson City, NY, 2001—. Infant and toddler tchr. U. Mo. Berkeley Ctr., Kansas City, 1960—99; asst. to phys. therapy Presbyn. Manor, Kansas City, Kans., 1971—72. Author: (novels) Death is Belligerent, 2004, Death is Compulsive, 2005. Adoptive parent Kansas City Kans. Black Adoption Agy., 1973, 1980; foster parent Kansas City Kans. S.S., 1985—95, acdtive fgn. exch. students Am. Field Svc., Kansas City, Kans., 1989—91; art tchr. Home Schoolers, Johnson City, 2004—06; active Bethel Bapt. Ch. Scholar, David Nance S. Found., 1958—62, Maude Ellsworth S. Found., 1961—62. Republican. Avocations: creative writing, camping, fishing, fossil records. Home: 32 Frederick St Johnson City NY 13790 Office: Davis College 400 Riverside Dr Johnson City NY 13790

**MCMILLEN, ROBERT STEWART,** lawyer; b. Yonkers, N.Y., Feb. 25, 1943; s. David Harry and Blodwyn Elizabeth (Evans) McM; m. Dorothea Anne Murray, July 2, 1966; children: Elissa London (Mrs. Elliott Aten), Tara Evans. BS, U. Rochester, 1964; JD cum laude, Albany Law Sch. Union U., 1969. Bar: N.Y. 1969, U.S. Dist. Ct. (no. dist.) N.Y. 1969. Assoc. Clark, Bartlett & Caffry, Glens Falls, NY, 1969-73; ptnr. Caffry, Pontiff, Stewart, Rhodes & Judge, Glens Falls, 1974-80; prin. Bartlett, Pontiff, Stewart & Rhodes, P.C., Glens Falls, 1981—. Sr. law examiner N.Y. State Bd. Law Examiners, Albany, 1986-2001, bd. mem. 2001—; bd. dirs. Cmty. Title Agy., Inc., Glens Falls, 1984—, pres., 1984-99 ; v.p., sec., 1999—. Editor-in-chief Albany Law Rev., 1968-69. Bd. dirs. officer Voluntary Action Ctr. of Warren County, Inc., Glens Falls, 1984-94; mem. Warren County Rep. Com., Queensbury, N.Y., 1979-2001; alt. or del. Rep. Jud. Nomination Com. 4th Jud. Dist. N.Y., 1977—. Recipient Disting. Svc. award Voluntary Action Ctr. of Glens Falls Area, Inc., 1990. Mem. ABA, Nat. Conf. Bar Examiners (mem. multistate performance test com. 2001-04, multistate essay examination com. 2005—), N.Y. State Bar Assn. (mem. com. profl. ethics 1990-99, 2000—), Warren County Bar Assn. (bd. dirs. 1979-82, treas. 2001—), Adirondack Regional C. of C. (bd. dirs. 1997-2000, vice chmn. 1999-2000, counsel 2000—), Rotary. Avocations: travel, downhill skiing, boating. Home: 147 Assembly Point Rd Lake George NY 12845-5201 Office: 1 Washington St Glens Falls NY 12801-2963 Office Phone: 518-792-2117. Business E-Mail: rsm@bpsrlaw.com.

**MCMILLIN, DAVID ROBERT,** chemistry professor; b. East St. Louis, Ill., Jan. 1, 1948; s. Robert Cecil and Clara Rose McMillin; m. Nicole Wilson, Nov. 3, 1974; children: Robert Stephen, Andrew Wilson. BA, Knox Coll., 1969; PhD. U. Ill., 1973. Postdoctoral fellow Calif. Inst. Tech., Pasadena, 1974; asst. prof. chemistry Purdue U., West Lafayette, In., 1975-80, assoc. prof., 1980-85, prof., 1985—. Contbr. articles to profl. jours. Recipient F.D. Martin Teaching award Purdue U., 1975. Mem. Am. Chem. Soc., Inter-Am. Photochem. Soc. (sec. 1986-90, v.p. 1994-96, pres. 1996-98), Phi Beta Kappa, Sigma Xi. Presbyterian. Avocations: sports, reading. Office: Purdue U Dept Chemistry 560 Oval Dr West Lafayette IN 47907-2084 E-mail: mcmillin@purdue.edu.

**MCMILLIN, JOAN AUSTIN,** social worker; b. Hartford, Conn., July 4, 1941; d. John Francis and Charlotte (Kilmer) Austin; m. J. Michael McMillin, May 9, 1970 (div. June 2002); children: John Andrew, Christy. BA, U. Conn., 1963; MSW, Boston Coll., 1966. Cert. social worker, Ill.; S.D. Social worker, student suor. Hamm Psychiat. Clinic, St. Paul, 1970-74; social worker Mass. Gen. Hosp., Boston, 1966-70, VA Hosp., Sioux Falls, S.D., 1980—; clin. social worker Charter Counseling Ctr., Sioux Falls, 1991-96; dir. social svcs. Great Plains Psychol. Svcs., Sioux Falls, 1996—99; sec. govt. affairs com. AARP of S.D., 2000—. Parent trainer S.D. Parent Connection, Sioux Falls, 1986-88; bd. dirs. Community Disabilities, 1990—93, bd. dirs. Coun. for Disability Rights, Chgo., 1988-89; del. United Cerebral Palsy Assn., N.Y.C., 1987, bd. dirs., pres. S.D. chpt., Sioux Falls, 1980-87; sec., bd. dirs. Vis. Nurses Assn., Sioux Falls, 1984-88. U.S. Dept. Vocat. Rehab. grantee, 1964-66; recipient T. Brown Community Svc. award Sioux Falls Masons, 1986. Mem. Nat. Assn. Social Workers (exec. dir. S.D. chpt., 2003), Am. Bd. Examiners in Clin. Social Work, Phi Beta Kappa, Phi Kappa Phi. Home: 4409 Yellowstone Ln Sioux Falls SD 57105-6756

**MCMILLIN, STEPHEN S.,** federal official; b. 1966; m. Dawn McMillin. BA, U. Tex. Legis. asst. to Sen. Phil Gramm U.S. Senate, fin. economist, legis. dir.; staff mem. com. on banking, housing and urban affairs US Senate; dep. asst. to Pres., advisor to chief of staff The White House, 2005—06; assoc. dir. gen. govt. programs Office Mgmt. & Budget, Exec. Office of the Pres., dep. dir. for budget, 2006. Office: Exec Office of Pres Eisenhower Exec Office Bldg 1650 Pennsylvania Ave NW Rm 252 Washington DC 20503*

**MCMILLION, CHARLES WAYNE,** economist, educator, consultant; b. Ft. Worth, June 20, 1948; s. Charles Wayne and Billie Ruth (Hickman) McM.; m. Marilyn Ruth Saks, Nov. 24, 1982. BA, U. Tex., Arlington, 1970; MA, So. Meth. U., 1972, Rutgers U., 1978, PhD, 1980. Market rsch. editor Curtis Mathes Sales Co., Dallas, 1970-71; Peace Corps tchr. Imperial Ethiopian Air Force Acad., Debre Zeit, 1972-73; fin. analyst Akin, Gump, Strauss, Hauer & Feld, Dallas, 1973-74; pres. MBG Info. Svcs., Washington, 1988—; assoc. dir. Inst. Policy Studies, assoc. prof. Johns Hopkins U., Balt., 1988—91. Staff chief economist U.S. Senate Dems. Working Group on Competitiveness, 1986; founder, exec. dir., policy dir., Congl. Econ. Leadership Inst., Washington, 1986-88; cons. in field Contbg. editor Harvard Bus. Rev., 1993-95; contbr. articles to profl. jours. V.p. Capitol Hill Restoration Soc., Washington. Sloan Found. fellow So. Meth. U., 1971, Porte World Peace Found. fellow Rutgers U., 1979-81, USIA Ampart fellow, Italy and Spain, 1988, Poland and India, 1989-90, Spain and Germany, 1993. Avocations: golf, photography. Home: 223 F St NE Washington DC 20002-4928 Office: MBG Info Svcs 223 F St NE Washington DC 20002-4928 Office Phone: 202-544-6490. Business E-Mail: cwm@mbginfosvcs.com.

**MCMILLION, MARGARET KIM,** foreign service officer; b. New Brighton, Pa., Nov. 4, 1951; d. Theodore M. and Margaret Jane (Houlette) McM. BA, Eisenhower Coll., 1973; MPIA, U. Pitts., 1975; cert., Nat. War Coll., 1990. Analyst, intern Gulf Oil Corp., Pitts., 1974; polit. and consular officer

U.S. Embassy, Kigali, Rwanda, 1975-77, consular officer Taipei, Taiwan, 1977-79; travel svcs. officer Am. Inst. in Taiwan, Taipei, 1979; desk officer Office of West African Affairs U.S. Dept. of State, Washington, 1979-81; with tng. dept. Fgn. Svc. Inst., Washington, 1981—82; polit. officer. U.S. Embassy, Pretoria, South Africa, 1982—85; with Thai lang. tng. dept., Washington, 1985-86; prin. officer U.S. Consulate, Udorn, Thailand, 1986—89; asst. dir. Office of Korean Affairs, Washington, 1990—91; spl. asst. under sec. for polit. affairs U.S. Dept. State, Washington, 1991—92; polit. counselor U.S. Embassy, Bangkok, 1992—95; dep. chief Mission in Vientiane, Laos, 1996—99; dir. Office for Analysis of Africa, Bur. Intelligence and Rsch., 1999—2001; U.S. amb. to Rwanda, 2001—04; dep. comdr. internat. affairs U.S. Army War Coll., 2004—06; ret. State Dept., 2006. Presbyterian. Achievements include speaks French, Afrikaans, Thai and Lao. Avocations: swimming, hiking, music, reading. Office: 191 Surawangse Rd Bangkok 10500 Thailand Office Phone: 717-245-3505. Business E-Mail: margaret.mcmillion@carlisle.army.mil.

**MCMILLON, DOUG,** retail executive; Degree in Acctg., U. Ark.; MBA in Fin., U. Tulsa. Buyer and merchandise mgr. various cos.; buyer trainee in sporting goods Wal-Mart Stores, Inc., 1984—91, v.p. and gen. merchandise mgr. Sam's Club Internat., sr. v.p. and gen. merchandise mgr., 1999—2002, exec. v.p. merchandising Sam's Club div., 2002—, pres., CEO Sam's Club div. Bentonville, Ark., 2005—. Office: Wal-Mart Stores Inc 702 SW Eighth St Bentonville AR 72716

**MCMINDES, ROY JAMES,** aggregate company executive; b. Essex, Md., July 12, 1923; s. Roy Preston and Edith S. (Sh) McMindes; m. Prudence Atsinger, June 8, 1946; children: Gail Karen, Joan Susan, James Lee. BS, U. Md., 1948. Pres. Sheridan Corp., Lebanon, Pa., 1951—, Grays Ferry Brick Co., Lebanon, 1971—2001, Waylite Co. Lebanon, 1976 88. Chmn. lxl. Peoples Nat. Bank, Lebanon, 1984—92, dir., 1965—92. Bd. dirs. Lebanon YMCA, 1964—86, Good Samaritan Hosp., Lebanon, 1970—93. With A.C. USN, 1943—46, with USNR, 1946—52. Recipient Founders Day award, Lebanon Valley Coll., 1987. Mem.: Lebanon Valley U. of C. (pres. 1973), Lebanon Country Group, Jesters, Shriners. Republican. Presbyterian. Office: 1212 W Maple St Lebanon PA 17046-2701

**MCMINN, J. B.,** retired philosophy educator, composer; b. Pt. Neches, Tex., Nov. 12, 1922; s. Joe Byron and Mary Thelma (Gray) McMinn; m. Dorothy Louise Smith, Aug. 31, 1944 (div. May 15, 1969); children: Jan Branton, Robert Errol. BA in English and religious studies, La. Coll., 1943; ThM in Hellenistic Greek, So. Sem., 1946; postgrad., La. State U., 1948; PhD in Hellenistic Greek, So. Sem., 1951; MA in Classical Greek and Philosophy, Tulane U., 1960, postgrad., 1968, U. Athens, 1970, postdoctoral in Modern Greek, 1979. Assoc. prof. English La. Coll., 1948—51; tchg. asst. in classics Newcomb Coll., 1951—52, Tulane U., 1952—54, asst. prof. classics, 1953—58; from asst. prof. philosophy to assoc. prof. to prof. philosophy U. Ala., 1960—87. Vis. prof. philosophy Miles Coll., 1990; vis. assoc. prof. philosophy and classics Tulane U., 1960, 61; spkr., lectr., presenter in field. Contbr. articles to profl. jours.; composer piano and vocal pieces; contbr. spirit song for Million Dollar Band of U. Ala. Fight On to Victory, 1987, poetry to anthologies: author: (book of poetry and songs) Une Petite Ménagerie, 1997, (plays) Waiting for Gotdough, 1995, (book) "Mythtaken"; Le Mot de L' Énigme, 2002. Rep. commr., New Orleans, 1956—60; mem. So. Soc. Christian Leadership Conf., New Orleans, 1954—60. Cadet officer USNR, 1941—42. Recipient Merit award, U. Ala. Band Assn., 1991, VIP award, Internat. Soc. Poets, 1996, grad. scholarship in classical langs., Tulane U., 1951—54, tchg. assistantship in classical langs., 1951, Fulbright Adj. Lectr. award, 1972, West Germany Lectr. award, 1973, tchg. and rsch. grants in field, Internat. Poet of Merit award, 1996. Mem.: ASCAP, Poetry Soc. Am., Acad. Am. Poets, Nat. Acad. Popular Music-Songwriters Hall of Fame, Internat. Soc. Poets (life), Eta Sigma Phi. Office: Rembrant Music Properties PO Drawer H Rusk TX 75785 Office Phone: 800-439-2149 22.

**MCMORRIS, CATHY,** congresswoman; b. Salem, Oreg., May 22, 1969; BA in Pre-Law, Pensacola Christian Coll., Fla., 1990; MBA, U. Wash., 2002. Mem. Wash. State Ho. Reps. from 7th Dist., 1994—2004; minority leader Wash. State Ho. Reps., 7th Dist., 2002—03; mem. US Congress 5th Wash. dist., 2005—; mem. armed svcs. com., mem. resources com., mem. edn. and the workforce com. Recipient Cornerstone award, Assn. Wash. Bus., 1995—96, Sentinal award, Wash. State Law Enforcement Assn., 1996, Guardian of Small Bus. award, Nat. Fedn. Ind. Bus., 1996, Gold Medal, Ind. Bus. Assn., 1996. Mem.: Wash. Women for Survival of Agr., Wash. Rural Health Assn., Wash. State Farm Bur. (Legislator of the Year 1997), Wash. State Cattlemen's Assn., N.E. Wash. Women in Timber. Republican. Office: US Ho Reps 1708 Longworth Ho Office Bldg Washington DC 20515-4705 Office Phone: 202-225-2006.*

**MCMORRIS, JERRY,** transportation company executive, sports team executive; Past CEO NW Transport Svc, Denver; chair, pres., CEO Colorado Rockies, Denver, 1993—. Office: 4765 Oakland St Denver CO 80239-2717

**MCMORROW, MARY ANN GROHWIN,** retired state supreme court justice; b. Chgo., Jan. 16, 1930; m. Emmett J. McMorrow, May 5, 1962; 1 dau., Mary Ann. Attended, Rosary Coll., 1948—50; JD, Loyola U. 1953. Bar: Ill. 1953, U.S. Dist. Ct. (7th dist.) Ill. 1960, U.S. Supreme Ct. 1976. Atty. Riordan & Linklater Law Offices, Chgo., 1954—56; asst. state's atty. Cook County, Chgo., 1956-63; sole practice Chgo., 1963-76; judge Cir. Ct. Cook County, 1976-85, Ill. Appellate Ct., 1985-92; justice Ill. Supreme Ct., 1992—2006, chief justice, 2002—2005; faculty adv. Nat. Jud. Coll., U. Nev., 1984. Contbr. articles to profl. jours. Mem. Chgo. Bar Assn., Ill. State Bar Assn., Women's Bar Assn. of Ill. (pres. 1975-76, bd. dirs. 1970-78), Am. Judicature Soc., Northwestern U. Assocs., Ill. Judges Assn., Nat. Assn. Women Judges, Advocates Soc., Northwest Suburban Bar Assn., West Suburban Bar Assn., Loyola Law Alumni Assn (bd. govt. 1985 ) 11 Judges Assn. (bd. dirs.), Cath. Lawyers Guild (v.p.), The Law Club of the City of Chgo., Inns of Ct.

**MCMORROW, WILLIAM J.,** finance company executive; b. LA; BA, MBA, U. So. Calif. Sr. v.p. Fidelity Bank, Pa.; exec. v.p., chmn. Credit Policy Com. Imperial Bank; then. Kennedy Wilson, Beverly Hills, Calif., 1988—, CEO, 1988—. Bd. dirs. Lusk Sch. Bus. U. So. Calif. Founder Donald F. Kennedy Youth Found., 1997—. Office: Kennedy Wilson 9601 Wilshire Blvd Ste 220 Beverly Hills CA 90210

**MCMULLAN, WILLIAM PATRICK, III,** investment banker; b. Newton, Miss., Dec. 29, 1952; s. William Patrick Jr. and Rosemary (Lyons) McM.; m. Rachel Smylie McPherson, Oct. 16, 1982. BA, Vanderbilt U., 1974; MBA, U. Pa., 1976. V.p. Lehman Bros. Kuhn Loeb, N.Y.C., 1976-82; assoc. dir. Prudential-Bache Securities, N.Y.C., 1982-85; mng. dir. Donaldson, Lufkin & Jenrette Securities Corp., N.Y.C., 1985-2000; mng. dir., chmn. global health care Credit Suisse First Boston, N.Y.C., 2000—03; sr. mng. dir., co-head global healthcare Bear, Stearns & Co., NYC, 2003—. Bd. dirs. Scenic Hudson, Gilda's Club Worldwide, Lar Lubovitch Dance Co., Project Reach Youth, Consolidated Corp. Fund, Lincoln Ctr., Good Dog Found. Mem. Met. Club, Mashomack Fish and Game Club, Confrerie des Chevaliers du Tastevin. Home: 607 6th St Brooklyn NY 11215-3701 Office: Bear Stearns & Co 383 Madison Ave New York NY 10179 Office Phone: 212-272-2392. Personal E-mail: pmcmullan@bear.com.

**MCMULLEN, CURTIS T.,** mathematics professor; b. May 21, 1958; BA, Williams Coll., 1980; PhD, Harvard U., 1985. Faculty MIT, Cambridge, Mass., 1985, MSRI, 1986, Inst. Advanced Study, Princeton NJ, 1986—87, Princeton U., NJ, 1987—90; prof. U. Calif., Berkeley, 1990—97, Harvard U., Cambridge, Mass., 1997—. Author: Logic Minimization Algorithms for VLSI Synthesis, 1984, Complex Dynamics and Renormalization, 1994, Renormalization and 3-Manifolds which Fiber over the Circle, 1996, (course notes) Riemann surfaces, dynamics and geometry, 1998, Hyperbolic manifolds, discrete groups and ergodic theory, 1996, Complex Manifolds, 1996, Com-

plex Analysis, 1993, 1995, Theichmuller Theory, 1993; contbr. articles to profl. jours. Recipient Fields medal, 1998; grantee Guggenheim Fellowship, 2004. Mem.: AAAS, Am. Acad. Arts & Sci. (elected mem. 1998). Office: Mathematics Dept Harvard U One Oxford St Cambridge MA 02138-2901

**MCMULLEN, SUSAN TAYLOR,** librarian; b. Oneida, N.Y., Mar. 7, 1956; d. Bert L. and Doris A. Taylor; m. John G. McMullen, June 4, 1977; children: Allison, Benjamin. BA, SUNY, Geneseo, 1977, MLS, 1978; MSc, Syracuse U., 2002. Head reference libr. Pawtucket Pub. Libr., RI, 1979—87; sr. reference/electronic info. libr. Seekonk Pub. Libr., Mass., 1987—95; libr. info. resources Roger Williams U., Bristol, RI, 1995—. Presenter in field. Contbr. articles to profl. jours. Mem.: NEA, ALA, Assn. Coll. and Rsch. Librs. Democrat. Episcopalian. Avocations: gardening, reading, weaving. Home: 10 Musket Rd Swansea MA 02777 Office: Roger Williams Univ One Old Ferry Rd Bristol RI 02809 Office Phone: 401-254-3086. Business E-Mail: smcmullen@rwu.edu.

**MCMULLEN, W. RODNEY,** financial officer; BS in Acctg., U. Ky., 1981, BBA in Fin., 1981, MS in Acctg., 1982. CPA. Fin. analyst The Kroger Co., Cin., 1985-88, asst. treas., 1988-90, v.p. planning and capital mgmt., 1990-93, v.p. fin. svcs. and control, 1993-95, group v.p., chief fin. officer, 1995-97, chief fin. officer, sr. v.p., 1997-2000, exec. v.p. strategy, planning and fin., 2000—03, vice chmn., 2003—. Dir. Cin. Fin. Corp. Office: The Kroger Co 1014 Vine St Cincinnati OH 45202-1100

**MCMULLIN, RUTH RONEY,** retired publishing executive; b. NYC, Feb. 9, 1942; d. Richard Thomas and Virginia (Goodwin) Roney; m. Thomas Ryan McMullin, Apr. 27, 1968; 1 child, David Patrick. BA, Conn. Coll., 1963; M Pub. and Pvt Mgmt., Yale U., 1979. Market rschr. Aviation Week Mag., McGraw-Hill Co., N.Y.C., 1962-64; assoc. editor, bus. mgr. Doubleday & Co., N.Y.C., 1964-66; mgr. Natural History Press, 1967-70; v.p., treas. Weston (Conn.) Woods, Inc., 1970-71; staff assoc. GE, Fairfield, Conn., 1979-82; mng. fin. analyst GECC Transp., Stamford, Conn., 1982—84; credit analyst corp. fin. dept. GECC, Stamford, Conn., 1984-85; sr. v.p. GECC Capital Markets Group, Inc., N.Y.C., 1985-87; exec. v.p., COO, CEO, John Wiley & Sons, N.Y.C., 1987—90, pres., CEO; CEO Harvard Bus. Sch. Pub. Corp., Boston, 1991-94; mem. chmn.'s com., acting CEO UNR Industries Inc., Chgo., 1991-92, also bd. dirs.; mgmt. fellow, vis. prof. Sch. Mgmt. Yale U., New Haven, 1994-95; chairperson trustees Eagle-Picher Personal Injury Settlement Trust, 1996—; chairperson Claims Procesing Facility, Inc., 1998—. Bd. dirs. Bausch & Lomb, Rochester, N.Y.; vis. prof. Sch. Mgmt., Yale U., New Haven, 1994-95. Mem. dean's adv. bd. Sch. Mgmt. Yale U., 1985—92; bd. dirs. Yale U. Alumni fund, 1986—92, Yale U. Press, 1988—99, Math. Scis. Edn. Bd., 1990—93; bd. dirs., treas. Mighty Eighth Air Force Heritage Mus., 2000—03; chmn. Mighty Eighth Found., 2003—; bd. dirs. Savannah Symphony, 1999—2003, The Landings Club, 2002—04. Mem. N.Y. Yacht Club, Stamford Yacht Club, Yale Club. Avocations: sailing, skiing, golf, tennis. Home: 8 Breckenridge Ln Savannah GA 31411-1701 Office: Eagle Picher Trust P O Box 206 652 Main St Cincinnati OH 45202-2542 Personal E-mail: rrmcmullin@aya.yale.edu. Business E-Mail: ruthmcmullin@direcway.com

**MCMURPHY, MICHAEL ALLEN,** energy company executive, lawyer; b. Dothan, Ala., Oct. 1, 1947; s. Allen L. and Mary Emily (Jacobs) McM.; m. Maureen Daly, Aug. 8, 1970; children: Matthew, Kevin, Patrick. BS, USAF Acad., 1969; MA, St. Mary's U., San Antonio, 1972; JD, U. Tex., 1975. Bar: Tex. 1975, U.S. Supreme Ct. 1977, U.S. Ct. Mil. Appeals, D.C. 1978, U.S. Ct. Appeals (fed. cir.) 1982. Commd. 2d lt. USAF, 1969, advanced through grades to capt.; instr. Air U., Ala., 1975-79; resigned USAF, 1979; atty., advisor Oak Ridge (Tenn.) ops. U.S. Dept. Energy, 1979-83; gen. counsel COGEMA, Inc., Washington, 1983-87, v.p., 1987-88, pres., CEO, Bethesda, Md., 1988—; pres. Areva T&D, Inc., 2005—. Pres., CEO Va. Fuels, Inc., Lynchburg, 1987-92; co-CEO AREVA Enterprises, Inc., Washington, DC, 2002-03, vice chmn., pres., 2003—; bd. dirs. Soc. Gen. Techs. Nouvelles, S.A., St. Quentin, France, Transnuclear, Inc., Columbia, Md., Canberra Industries, Meriden, Conn., Cogema Resources, Inc, Casper, Wyo., Numatec Hanford Co., Wash., Framatome-ANP, Inc., Lynchburg, Va. and Richland, Wash.; bd. govs. Duke Cogema Stone & Webster, LLC, Charlotte, N.C., 1998—; pres. Uranium Producers Am., 1991-92 Mem. editorial bd. Air Force Law Rev., l977-79. Lt. col. USAFR ret., 1992. Decorated chevalier Nat. Order of Merit (France). Avocation: skiing. Home: 9324 Garden Ct Potomac MD 20854 Office: COGEMA Inc 1 Bethesda Ctr 4800 Hampden Ln Ste 1100 Bethesda MD 20814 Business E-Mail: mcmurphy@cogema-inc.com.

**MCMURRAY, CLAUDIA ANNE,** federal agency administrator, lawyer; d. Raymond D. and Sally Kathryn (Martin) McM.; m. Donald V. Moorehead, June 6, 1987. AB with honors, Smith Coll., 1980; JD, Georgetown U., 1984. Bar: D.C. 1985. Legis. asst. to Rep. Bill Emerson US Ho. Reps, Washington, 1980-81; law clk. Office of Counsel to the Pres. The White House, Washington, 1983-84; atty. Patton, Boggs & Blow LLP, 1984-87, Kirkland & Ellis LLP, 1987-89; legis. counsel to Senator John W. Warner US Senate, 1989-90, minority counsel Com. on Environment and Pub. Works, 1991—95, gen. counsel to Senator Fred Thompson, 1996—98; v.p. Van Scovyoc Associates, Inc., 1998—2000; assoc. dep. adminstr. & chief of staff to dep. adminstr. EPA, 2000—03; dep. asst. sec for environ., Bur. Oceans & Internat. Environ. & Sci. Affairs US Dept. State, Washington, 2003—06, asst. sec. for oceans, internat. environ., & scientific affairs, 2006—. Editor The Tax Lawyer. Office: US Dept State Harry S Truman Bldg 2201 C St NW Rm 7831 Washington DC 20520*

**MCMURRAY, JAMIE,** race car driver; b. Joplin, Mo., June 3, 1976; Race car driver Brewco Motorsports, Central, Ky., Roush Racing. Film appearances: Talladega Nights: The Ballad of Ricky Bobby, 2006. Fundraiser Autism Soc. Am. Named Champion, Lebanon I 44 Speedway, 1997, Nascar Winston Cup Rookie of Yr., 2003. Achievements include won his first NASCAR cup race at Lowe's Motor Speedway in 2002, becoming the first race car driver in Winston/Nextel cup series history to win in his second career start.*

**MCMURRY, IDANELLE SAM,** educational consultant; b. Morganfield, Ky., Dec. 6, 1924; d. Sam Anderson and Aurelia Marie (Robertson) McM. BA, Vanderbilt U., 1945, MA, 1946. Tchr. English Abbot Acad., Andover, Mass., 1946-50, Hockaday Sch., Dallas, 1951-54, San Jacinto High Sch., Houston, 1954-55; dean of girls Kinkaid Sch., Houston, 1955-63; headmistress Harpeth Hall Sch., Nashville, 1963-79, Hockaday Sch., Dallas, 1979-89; ret.; now pvt. sch. cons. The Edn. Group, Dallas. Bd. dirs. Ednl. Records Bur., 1979-85, trustee, 1980-85. Bd. dirs. Tex. council Girl Scouts U.S., 1980-82, Town North YMCA; trustee Winston Sch., 1979-85, Spl. Care Sch., 1979-81, Asheville Sch., Manzano Day Sch. Mem. Nat. Study Sch. Evaluation (bd. dirs. 1979-83), Headmasters Assn., Nat. Assn. Ind. Schs. (bd. dirs. 1974-84, acad. com. 1974-79, sec. 1978-80, chmn. 1980-84), So. Assn. Ind. Schs. (pres. 1974-75), Tenn. Assn. Ind. Schs. (pres. 1967-68), Mid-South Assn. Ind. Schs. (pres. 1972-73), Nat. Assn. Prins. Schs. for Girls (sec. 1970-72, pres. 1975-77, coun. 1970-79), Nat. Assn. Secondary Sch. Prins., Country Day Sch. Headmasters Assn. (exe. com. 1984-87, v.p. 1988-89), So. Assn. Colls. and Schs. (adminstry. coun. 1974-77, ctrl. reviewing com. 1972-77, vice chmn. secondary commn. 1975-76, chmn. 1976-77, bd. dirs. 1976-81), Ladies Hermitage Assn., Vanderilt Aid Soc. (sec. 1971-73, pres. 1994-96), Ind. Edn. Svcs. (trustee 1980-88, chmn. 1986-88), Susan Komen Found. (adv. bd.), Belle Meade Club, Centennial Club, Phi Beta Kappa, Pi Beta Phi. Democrat. Presbyterian. Office: 5 Strawberry Hill Nashville TN 37215-4118

**MCMURRY, JAMES FINLEY, JR.,** endocrinologist, researcher; b. Sentinel, Okla., Aug. 25, 1940; s. James Finley and Anna Jo McMurry; m. Rebecca L. Lomax, May 21, 1987. MD, U. Okla., 1965. Diplomate Am. Bd. Internal Medicine. Chief, med. services USAF Hosp., Dover, Del., 1969—71; endocrinologist Scott and White Clinic, Temple, Tex., 1972—81; assoc prof. internal medicine Tex. A & M U., Temple, 1979—81; asst prof. internal

medicine U. Ky., Lexington, 1981—84, Georgetown U., Washington, 1984—87; pvt. practice Rockville, Md., 1984—. Editor: Jefferson, Callender and the SALLY Story, 2000; co-author: Anatomy of a Scandal: Thomas Jefferson and the SALLY Story, 2002. Capt. USAF, 1969—71. Fellow: ACP; mem.: Montgomery County Med. Assn., Md. (com. chmn. 1987—89), Am. Diabetes Assn. (pres. South Tex. chpt. 1980—81, pres. DC chpt. 1986—87, chmn. Ky. affiliate 1983—84), Endocrine Soc. Independent. Avocations: history, photography, gardening. Office: 11119 Rockville Pike Ste 409 Rockville MD 20852-3143 Office Phone: 301-468-1820.

**MCMURRY, JOHN EDWARD,** chemistry professor; b. N.Y.C., July 27, 1942; s. Edward and Marguerite Ann McMurry; m. Susan Elizabeth Sobuta, Sept. 4, 1964; children: Peter Michael, David Andrew, Paul Matthew. BA, Harvard U., 1964; MA, Columbia U., 1965, PhD, 1967. Prof. chemistry U. Calif., Santa Cruz, 1967-80, Cornell U., Ithaca, NY, 1980—. Author: textbooks; assoc. editor: Accounts of Chem. Rsch., 1975—95. Recipient Humboldt Sr. Sci. award, 1987; Sloan Found. fellow, 1969-71; Career awardee NIH, 1975-80. Fellow AAAS; mem. Am. Chem. Soc. Home: 625 Highland Rd Ithaca NY 14850-1411 Office: Cornell Univ Dept Chemistry Baker Lab Ithaca NY 14853 Office Phone: 607-255-4819. E-mail: jem24@cornell.edu.

**MCMURRY, GARY MICHAEL,** geochemist, educator; b. Upland, Calif., Feb. 25, 1950; s. James Samuel and Grace Marietta (Tomlinson) McM.; m. Francine Emy Yagawa, Mar. 3, 1976. BS with honors, U. Calif., Riverside, 1972; MS, U. Hawaii, 1975, PhD, 1979. Research geologist U. Calif., San Diego, 1979-80; asst. geochemist U. Hawaii, Honolulu, 1980-86, assoc. geochemist, 1986-88; sci. dir. Hawaii Undersea research Lab., Honolulu, 1983-88; grad. faculty mem. U. Hawaii, Honolulu, 1982—, assoc. prof. oceanography, 1988—. Cons. TRW Corp., Redondo Beach, Calif., 1979-80; assoc. dir. Electron Microscopy Lab., Honolulu, 1983-86; panelist Nat. Undersea research program NOAA, Washington, 1985—; guest scientist Los Alamos Nat. Lab., 1991-92; affiliate scientist Jet Propulsion Lab., Caltech, Pasadena, Calif., 1999-2000. Contbr. articles to profl. jours. Recipient Antarctic Service medal NSF, 1979. Mem. AAAS, Am. Geophys. Union, Hawaii Acad. Sci., Marine Tech. Soc., Soc. Econ. Paleontologists and Mineralogists, The Planetary Soc., Sigma Xi. Avocations: tennis, surfing, computing. Office: U Hawaii Sch Ocean & Earth Sci/Tech Dept Oceanography 1000 Pope Rd Honolulu HI 96822-2336 Office Phone: 808-956-6858. E-mail: garymc@soest.hawaii.edu.

**MC MURTRY, JAMES GILMER, III,** neurosurgeon; b. Houston, June 11, 1932; s. James Gilmer and Alberta Elizabeth (Matteson) McMurtry. Student, Rice U., Houston, 1950—53; MD cum laude, Baylor U., Houston, 1957. Intern Hosp. U. Pa., Phila., 1957—58; resident gen. surgery Baylor U. Affiliated Hosps., Houston, 1958—59; asst. neurol. surgery Coll. Physicians and Surgeons, Columbia U., N.Y.C., 1959—60; asst. resident neurol. surgery and neurology Neurol. Inst. N.Y., Columbia Presbyn. Med. Ctr., 1960—62, chief resident neurol. surgery, 1963—65, assoc., 1965—68, asst. prof. clin. neurol. surgery, 1968—73, assoc. prof., 1973—89, prof., 1989—2003, Herbert and Linda Gallen prof. neurol. surgery, 2003—05, Herbert and Linda Gallen prof. neurol. surgery emeritus, 2005—. Asst. attending neurol. surgeon Neurol. Inst. N.Y., N.Y.C., 1964—73, assoc. attending neurol. surgeon, 1973—89, attending neurol. surgeon, 1989—2005; chief neurol. surgery clinic Vanderbilt Clinic, Columbia Presbyn. Med. Ctr., N.Y.C., 1964—68; attending-in-charge neurosurgery Lenox Hill Hosp., N.Y.C., 1970—91; assoc. cons. neurol. surgery Englewood (N.J.) Hosp., 1964—70; asst. cons. neurol. surgery Harlem Hosp., N.Y.C., 1964—75; cons. neurol. surgery Bronx (N.Y.) VA Hosp., 1964—65; mem. NIH Parkinson Rsch. Group, Columbia U., 1965—70; mem. med. adv. bd. N.Y. State Athletic Commn. Author: Medical Examination Review Book-Neurological Surgery, 1970, rev. edit., 1975, Neurological Surgery Case Histories, 1975; contbr. articles to profl. jours. Trustee Glimmerglass Opera, Morris-Jumel, Opera Manhattan. Fellow Allen fellow dept. neurol. surgery, Columbia U., 1964—65; scholar Jesse H. Jones scholar, Baylor U. Coll. Medicine, 1953—57. Fellow: ACS, Linnean Soc. (London); mem.: AMA, AAAS, AAUP, The Med. Soc. of London, Med. Strollers, Baylor U. Coll. Medicine Alumni Assn., Osler Soc., N.Y. County Med. Soc., Med. Soc. State N.Y., N.Y. Neurosurg. Soc., N.Y. Acad. Sci., N.Y. State Neurosurgery Soc., N.Y. State Soc. Surgeons, Pan Am. Med. Assn., Am. Assn. Stereotaxic Surgeons, European Congress Pediatric Neurosurgery, Am. Assn. Neurol. Surgeons, The Harveian Soc., Norfolk Yacht and Country, Met. Opera (N.Y.C., dir. and v.p. 2002), The Gravik Club (London), The Union Club, The Atheneum (London), Alpha Omega Alpha. Home: 1 Cobb Ln Tarrytown NY 10591-3003

**MCMURTRY, LARRY JEFF,** author; b. Wichita Falls, Tex., June 3, 1936; s. William Jefferson and Hazel Ruth (McIver) McM.; m. Josephine Ballard, July 15, 1959 (div. 1966); 1 child, James. BA, N. Tex. State Coll., 1958; MA, Rice U., 1960. Instr. Tex. Christian U., Ft. Worth, 1961-62; lectr. in English and creative writing Rice U., Houston, 1963-69; co-owner Booked Up Book Store, Washington, from 1970. Vis. prof. George Mason Coll., 1970, Am. U., 1970-71. Author: (novels) Horseman, Pass By, 1961 (Jesse H. Jones award Texas Inst. of Letters 1962), Leaving Cheyenne, 1963, The Last Picture Show, 1966, Moving On, 1970, All My Friends Are Going to be Strangers, 1972, Terms of Endearment, 1975, Somebody's Darling, 1978, Cadillac Jack, 1982, The Desert Rose, 1983, Lonesome Dove, 1985 (Pulitzer prize for Fiction 1986), Texasville, 1987, Anything for Billy, 1988, Some Can Whistle, 1989, Buffalo Girls, 1990, The Evening Star, 1992, Streets of Laredo, 1993, The Late Child, 1995, Dead Man's Walk, 1995, Comanche Moon, 1997, Duane's Depressed, 1999, Boone's Lick, 2000, Sin Killer: The Berrybender Narratives Book One, 2002, The Wandering Hill: The Berrybender Narratives Book Two, 2003, By Sorrow's River: The Berrybender Narratives Book Three, 2003, Folly and Glory: The Berrybender Narratives Book Four, 2004, Loop Group, 2004, Telegraph Days, 2006; Co-author (with Diana Ossana) Zeke and Ned, 1997, Pretty Boy Floyd, 1994; Author (non-fiction) Walker Benjamin at Dairy Queen, 1999, Roads: Driving America's Great Highways, 2000, Paradise, 2000, Sacagawea's Nickname: Essays on the American West, 2001, The Colonel and Little Missie: Buffalo Bill, Annie Oakley, and the Beginnings of Superstardom in America, 2005, Oh What a Slaughter: Massacres in the American West: 1846-1890, 2005; (essays) In a Narrow Grave: Essays on Texas, 1968, It's Always We Rambled: An Essay on Rodeo, 1974, Film Flam: Essays on Hollywood, 1987; screenwriter: (with Peter Bogdanovich) The Last Picture Show, 1971 (Academy award nomination best adapted screenplay 1971), Texasville, 1990, Montana, 1990, Falling From Grace, 1992, (with Cybill Shepard) Memphis, 1992, Brokeback Mountain, 2005 (best screenplay-motion picture Hollywood Fgn. Press Assn., Golden Globe award, 2006, British Acad. Film & TV Arts award for adapted screenplay, 2006, Adapted Screenplay, Acad. Motion Pictures Arts & Sciences, 2006); also articles, essays, book revs. in N.Y. Times, Saturday Rev., Washington Post, Am. Film, others. Wallace Stegner fellow, 1960, Guggenheim fellow, 1964; recipient Barbara McCombs/Lon Tinkle award Texas Inst. of Letters, 1986. Mem. Tex. Inst. Letters (Jesse H. Jones award 1962). Mailing: Author Mail Simon & Schuster 1230 Ave of the Americas New York NY 10020-1586*

**MCMURTRY, R. ROY,** federal judge; b. Toronto, Ont., Can., May 31, 1932; s. Roland Roy and Doris Elizabeth (Belcher) McM.; m. Ria Jean Macrae, Apr. 18, 1957; children: Janet, James, Harry, Jeannie, Erin, Michael. BA with honors, U. Toronto, 1954; LLB, Osgoode Hall Law Sch., 1958; LLD (hon.), U. Ottawa, 1983, Leeds U., U.K., 1988, York U., 1991, U. Toronto, 1998. Bar: Called to bar 1958, created Queen's counsel 1970. Partner firm Benson, McMurtry, Percival and Brown; mem. Provincial Parliament for Eglinton, 1975-85; atty. gen. for Ont., 1975-85; solicitor gen. for Ont., 1978-82; high commnr. for Can. to Gt. Brit. and No. Ireland, 1985-88; ptnr. Blaney, McMurtry Stapells, Toronto, 1988-91; chmn. Can. Football League, 1989-91; assoc. chief justice Ont. Ct. Justice, Toronto, 1991-94, chief justice, 1994-96; chief justice of Ont. Ont. Ct. of Appeal, Toronto, 1996—. Freeman of City of London, 1986. Mem. United Ch. of Can. Office: Ont Ct of Appeal 130 Queen St W Toronto ON Canada M5H 2N5 Office Phone: 416-327-5803. Business E-Mail: cath.lanni@jus.gov.on.ca.

**MCNABB, CORRINE RADTKE,** librarian; b. Detroit, Dec. 18, 1956; d. Eugene R. and Dorothy A. (Dorosz) Radtke; children: Brynne Catherine, Kalen Daniel. BA, Aquinas Coll., 1978; MS, Drexel U., 1982, cert. advanced study, 1997. Cert. tchr. Pa., SC. Assoc. Nat. Libr. Medicine, Bethesda, Md., 1982-83; dir. libr. svcs. Carbondale (Pa.) Gen. Hosp., 1983-85; libr. dir. Interboro Libr., Peckville, Pa., 1985-86; reference libr. U. Scranton, Pa., 1986-87; libr. Cmty. Med. Ctr., Scranton, 1987-95; elem. libr. Carbondale Area Sch. Dist., 1995-96, Mountain View Sch. Dist., Kingsley, Pa., 1996—; adj. faculty Univ. Scranton, 2002—. Bd. dirs. Carbondale Pub. Libr., 1993—. Mem. ASCD, ALA, Pa. Sch. Librs. Assn. Roman Catholic. Avocations: reading, travel, walking. Home: 214 Stoney Creek Rd Clarks Summit PA 18411 Office: Mountain View Elem Libr RR 1 Box 339A Kingsley PA 18826-9778 Office Phone: 570-434-2181. Personal E-mail: santafe13@hotmail.com.

**MCNABB, DAVID E.,** business educator, writer; b. L.A., Nov. 29, 1932; s. Jay B. McNabb and Josephine P. Recagno; m. Janet C. Lagerquist, June 12, 1962; children: Meghan, Michael, Sara. BA, Calif. State Coll., Fullerton, 1965; MA, U. Wash., Seattle, 1968; PhD, Oreg. State U., Corvallis, 1980. Prof. Pacific Luth. U., Tacoma, 1979—; vis. prof. UMUC-Europe, Heidelberg, Germany, 1998—99, The Evergreen State Coll., Olympia, Wash., 1999—2000, Stockholm Sch. Econs., Riga, Latvia, 2000—03. Vis. scholar Thunderbird Internat. U., Phoenix, 1990. Author: Research Methods for Public Administration, 2002, Research Methods for Political Science, 2004, Public Utilities: Management Challenges, 2005, Knowledge Management In The Public Sector, 2006. Served with USN, 1952—54. Mem.: ASPA, Assn. for Rsch. on Nonprofit Orgns. and Vol. Action, Acad. Polit. Sci., Acad. Mgmt., Rotary. Home: 605 E Barbary Rd Shelton WA 98584 Office Phone: 253-535-8722. E-mail: mcnabbde@plu.edu.

**MCNABB, DIANNE LEIGH,** investment banker, accountant; b. Huntsville, Ala., Sept. 7, 1956; d. Walter David and Mary Josephine (Hawkins) McN.; m. William Roland Lantz, July 1, 1983; 1 child, Sarah Elizabeth. BS in Acctg., U. Ala., Tuscaloosa, 1976. CPA, Ga., Ala. Acct. Lilly Flagg Assocs. & Subsidiaries, Huntsville, 1977-78; mgr. Johnston, Joyce & Wigginton, CPA's, Huntsville, 1978-84; sr. mgr. KPMG Peat Marwick, CPA's, Atlanta, 1984-91; mng. dir. A.G. Edwards & Sons, Inc., Atlanta, 1991—. Mem. ways and means com. Atlanta Jr. League, 1991-98; instr., advisor Jr. Achievement, Atlanta, 1985-88; mem. hospitality com. Dem. Nat. Conv., Atlanta, 1988; vol. Ga. Spl. Olympics, Atlanta, 1989-91. Mem. AICPA, Govt. Fin. Officers Assn. (spl. rev. com. 1991-95), Ga. Soc. CPA (govtl. acctg. and auditing com. 1992), Assn. of Govt. Accts. (bd. dirs. Atlanta chpt. 1990-92), Ala. Soc. CPA (sec.-treas. 1984), Am. Soc. Women Accts. (pres. Huntsville chpt. 1983-84), U. Ala. Alumni Assn. (treas. 1983-84), Zeta Tau Alpha (advisor 1988-93, v.p. 1983, treas. 1987-89, pres. 1984, 89-91, panhellenic del. 1988-91, dist. pres. 1993-95, Cert. of Merit 1992, Zeta Lady award 1991, Alum Chum award 1991). Avocations: tennis, scuba. Home: 2530 Alpine Way Duluth GA 30096-4440 Office: A G Edwards 3399 Peachtree Rd NE Ste 1100 Atlanta GA 30326-1150 Office Phone: 404-995-8930.

**MCNABB, DONOVAN,** professional football player; b. Chgo., Nov. 25, 1976; s. Samuel and Wilma McNabb; m. Raquel Nurse, 2003. Degree in Speech Comm., Syracuse U., 1998. Backup quarterback Syracuse U. basketball team, 1995—96, 1996—97; quarterback Phila. Eagles, 1999—. Co-host (with Beasley Reece) The Donovan McNabb Show. Established own scholarship found.; mem. Life as a Rookie panel Rookie Symposium, 2000. Named NFL Player of Yr., CBS Radio, 2000; named to All Madden Team, 2000, Nat. Football Conf. Pro Bowl Team, 2000—04. Office: Phila Eagles NovaCare Way Philadelphia PA 19145*

**MCNAIR, EMMA LOUISE,** minister; b. Ellisville, Miss., Mar. 11, 1935; d. Will and Chanie Prince Bell; m. Willie Charles McNair Jr., Mar. 16, 1956 (dec. Dec. 1967); children: Ruth, Channie, Willie C. Jr., Victor D., Karen L., Yul L. AA in Edn., Prentiss Inst., Miss., 1974; BA in Social Work, Rust Coll., 1979; MDiv, Memphis Theol. Sem., 1983; cert., East Miss. State Hosp., 1991. Ordained deacon 1981, ordained elder 1993. Pastor Victor/Taylor Charge, Senatobia, Miss., 1981—83, Marion/Walhall Parish, Columbia, Miss., 1983—84, Enterprise (Miss.) Cir., Brookhaven (Miss.) Charge, 1988—89; staff chaplain East Miss. Hosp., Meridian, Meth. Med. Ctr., Jackson, Miss., 1991—2000. Address: 153 Dacetown Rd Ellisville MS 39437

**MCNAIR, JOHN WILLIAM, JR.,** civil engineer; b. Asheville, N.C., June 17, 1926; s. John William and Annie (Woody) McN.; m. June Clemens Kratz; children: Jeffry, Marsha, Cathy. BS in Forestry, Pa. State U., 1950; BSCE, Va. Poly Inst. State U., 1955; postgrad. in engring., U. Va., 1957—2004. Registered profl. engr., VA, NC, MD, WV, PA, NY, KY. Forester U.S. Forest Svc., Flagstaff, Ariz., 1950, U.S. Gypsum Co., Altavista, Va., 1951; mem. engring. faculty U. Va., Charlottesville, 1955-58; prin. John McNair & Assocs., Waynesboro, Va., 1958—; owner Brucheum Group, Waynesboro, 1983—; chmn., CEO Info. Systems Support, Inc., 1998—. With Va. Bd. Architects, Profl. Engrs. and Land Surveyors, 1969-79, v.p., 1977-78, pres., 1978-79. Author numerous engring. and land mgmt. study reports. Mem. Waynesboro City Coun., 1968-72, vice mayor, 1970-72; chmn. Waynesboro Indsl. Devel. Authority, 1984-2000. Capt. AUS, 1944-46, 51-53, France, Okinawa. Recipient Disting. Svc. cert. Va. Soc. Profl. Engrs., 1971. Fellow ASCE; mem. Acad. Environ. Engrs. (diplomate), Rotary, Rappahannock River Yacht Club (founding mem.). Republican. Presbyterian. Office Phone: 540-942-1161. Business E-Mail: jmcnair@brucheum.com.

**MCNAIR, ROBERT C.,** communications executive; BS, U. S.C., 1958. Chmn. Cypress Telecom. Corp., U.S. Telesys, Inc.; founder, CEO Cogen Techs. Energy Group, Houston; chmn., CEO Houston Texans, 2002. Chmn. bd. trustees McNair Found., Free Enterprise Inst.; bd. govs. Rice U. Bd. trustees Baylor Coll. Medicine, Houston; bd. dirs. Fed. Res. Bank Dallas; dir. Mosher, Inc.; spkr. in field. Pres. Houston Grand Opera Assn.; trustee Sigma Chi Found.; elder Meml. Drive Presbyn. Ch., Houston. Named one of Forbes' Richest Americans, 2006.

**MCNAIR, RUSSELL ARTHUR, JR.,** lawyer; b. Detroit, Dec. 2, 1934; s. Russell Arthur and Virla (Standish) McN.; m. Rosemary M. Chesbrough, Apr. 6, 1957; children: Julie McNair Schwerin, Russell Arthur III, Douglas S. AB in Econs. cum laude, Princeton U., 1956; JD with distinction, U. Mich., 1960. Bar: Mich. 1960, Fla. 2001. Assoc. Dickinson, Wright, Moon, Van Dusen & Freeman (now Dickinson Wright PLLC), Detroit, 1960-67, ptnr., 1968-98, chmn., 1994-98. Cons. Evans & Luptak, PLC, Boca Raton, 2000-; adj. prof. U. Detroit Sch. Law, 1968-72; mem. adv. bd. Fin. Transactions Inst., 1984-94; adj. prof. Wayne State U. Law Sch., 1994-96; spkr. in field. Trustee Children's Home, Detroit, 1975-95, pres. 1986-87, hon. trustee 1995—; mem. community leaders coun. United Way, 1994-98; dir. Mich. Jobs Commn., 1995-98, TED Ctr., Delray Beach, Fla., 2006—. Mem.: Mich. Bar Found., Am. Coll. Real Estate Lawyers, Am. Law Inst., Fla. Bar Assn., Mich. Bar Assn. Republican. Presbyterian. Avocations: golf, tennis, platform tennis. Home: 4383 Gleneagles Dr Boynton Beach FL 33436-4802 Office: Evans & Luptak 2201 NW Corporate Blvd Ste 104 Boca Raton FL 33431 Office Phone: 561-443-4343. Personal E-mail: mcnairs47@bellsouth.net. E-mail: rmcnair@evansluptak.com.

**MCNAIR, STEVE LATREAL,** professional football player; b. Mount Olive, Miss., Feb. 14, 1973; m. Mechelle McNair; 1 child, Tyler. Student, Mt. Olive H.S.; BA, Alcorn State U., 1994. Quarterback Houston Oilers, 1995—96, Tenn. Oilers, 1997—98, Tenn. Titans, 1999—2006, Baltimore Ravens, 2006—. Named NFL Co-MVP, AP, 2003; named to AFC Pro-Bowl Team, 2003, 2005. Office: Baltimore Ravens 1101 Russell St Baltimore MD 21230*

**MCNALL, SCOTT GRANT,** sociologist, educator, academic administrator; b. New Ulm, Minn., Jan. 16, 1941; s. Everett Herman and Dorothy Grant (Brown) McNall; m. Sally Anne Allen, Oct. 31, 1960; children: Miles Allen, Amy Ellen. BA, Portland State U., 1962; PhD, U. Oreg. 1965. Instr.

sociology U. Oreg., Eugene, 1964-65; asst. prof. U. Minn., Mpls., 1965-70; from assoc. prof. to prof. Ariz. State U., Tempe, 1970-76; prof., chmn. dept. sociology U. Kans., Lawrence, 1976-89, prof., chmn. dept. Am. studies, 1989-90; dean Coll. Arts and Scis. U. Toledo, 1990-94; provost Calif. State U., Chico, 1994—, interim pres., 2003—05. Fulbright lectr., Greece, 1968—69; vis. lectr. Mid-Am. State U. Assn., 1982—83. Author: (book) The Sociological Experience, 1969, 3d edit., 1974, The Greek Peasant, 1974, Social Problems Today, 1975, Career of a Radical Rightist, 1975; author: (with Sally A. McNall) Plains Families: Exploring Sociology Through Social History, 1983, The Road to Rebellion, 1988; editor: The Sociological Perspective, 1968, 4th edit., 1977, Theoretical Perspectives in Sociology, 1979, Current Perspectives in Social Theory, 1980, 6th edit., 1985, Political Economy: A Critique of American Society, 1981; editor: (with others) Studies in Historical Social Change, 1986—, The Road to Rebellion: Class Formation and Kansas Populism, 1865-1900, 1988; editor: (with Rhonda Levine) Bringing Class Back in, 1991; editor: (with Sally A. McNall) Sociology, 1992; editor: Current Perspectives in Social Theory, 1980—87; adv. editor: Sociol. Quar., 1969—72, assoc. editor: Am. Sociologist, 1975—78, Jour. Polit. and Mil. Sociology, 1982—; contbr. articles to profl. jours. East-West Ctr. Vis. fellow, 1978, Fulbright grantee, 1983. Mem.: Pacific Sociol. Soc., Am. Sociol. Assn. (chair Marxist sect. 1989—90), Midwest Sociol. Soc. (pres. 1982—83). Democrat. Congregationalist. Home: 520 Crestwood Dr Paradise CA 95969-3825 Office: Calif State U VPAA Office Chico CA 95929 Office Phone: 530-898-6101. Business E-Mail: smcnall@csuchico.edu.

**MCNALLEN, JAMES BERL,** federal agency administrator, marketing professional, educator; b. Heber Springs, Ark., Feb. 17, 1930; s. George Berl and Sally Lou (Brown) McNallen; m. Marianne Patricia Kakos, Mar. 4, 1952 (dec. Sept. 1990); children: James Lawrence, Marianne Victoria, Thomas Berl(dec.), John Kennedy. AB, Columbia U., 1951; MBA, N.Y. U., 1960, PhD, 1975. Mktg. asst. Am. Petroleum Inst., N.Y.C., 1954—67, coor. products mktg., 1967—69, asst. dir. divsn. fin. and acctg., 1969—70; corp. mgr. mktg. rsch. Atlantic Richfield Co., 1970—71; lectr. bus. adminstrn. Sch. Bus. Adminstrn. U. Conn., Storrs, 1972—75, asst. prof., 1975—76; mktg. rsch. specialist, market rsch. and mktg. divsn. Office Customer Service Support Fed. Supply Svc. GSA, Washington, 1976—78, mgr. mktg. rsch. Office of Requirements, 1978—82, mgr. forecasting and bus. analysis Office of Mgmt., 1982—84; mktg. specialist and tng. officer Ctrl. Supply Mgmt. Devel. project GSA Fed. Supply Svc., 1984—88, spl. asst. commr. Office of Customer Svc. and Mktg., 1991, chief program devel. and support Office Transp. Audits, 1992—93, dep. dir. regulations & program developing, 1993—. Mem. U.S. del. U.S.-Saudi Arabian Joint Econ. Commn., Riyadh, 1984—88; pres. McNallen Investment Co., Arlington, Va.; ptnr. McNallen Enterprise, Big Spring, Tex.; lectr. mktg. Va. Poly. Inst., Reston, Va., 1976—77, George Mason U., Fairfax, 1977—84, Georgetown U., Washington, 1978—80; adj. prof. mgmt. U. D.C., Washington, 1980—84. Contbr. articles to profl. jours. Mem. planning bd. Twp. of South Brunswick, 1966—67; bd. dir., vice chmn. and sec. South Brunswick Mcpl. Utilities Authority, 1966—68; pres. South Brunswick Library Assn., NJ, 1965—69; comdg. officer Naval Air Intelligence Res. Unit, Lakehurst, NJ, 1970—71, Naval Investigative Svc. HQ Res. Unit, Washington, 1978—79; inspector gen. Naval Res. Intelligence Area 19, 1981; dep. area comdr. Co. IVTU Dist. 19, 1982. To lt. (j.g.) USN, 1951—54, capt. USNR, 1976—87, ret. USNR, 1987. Recipient Gold medal, Am. Mktg. Assn., 1960. Mem.: U.S. Naval Inst. Res. Officers Assn. (exec. v.p. Washington D.C. Nat. Navy chpt. 1982—84), Mil. Order World Wars, Naval Order U.S., Ret. Officers Assn., Naval Res. Assn. (pres. Washington chpt. 1978—79, pres. 5th dist. 1979—81, mem. nat. exec. com. 1979—81), Jaycees (pres. South Brunswick chpt. 1964—65, state v.p. 1965—66), Kennedy Ctr. Friends, Wolf Trap Friends, Ancient Order Hibernians, Smithsonian Assocs., KC. Roman Catholic. Home: Apt 21W 2 Park Pl Hartford CT 06106-5007

**MCNALLY, ANDREW, IV,** publishing executive, director; b. Chgo., Nov. 11, 1939; s. Andrew and Margaret C. (MacMillin) McN.; m. Jeanine Sanchez, July 3, 1966; children: Andrew, Carrie, Ward. BA, U. N.C., 1963; MBA, U. Chgo., 1969. Bus. mgr. edn. divsn. Rand McNally & Co., Chgo., 1967-70, exec. v.p., sec., 1970-74, pres., 1974-97, CEO, 1978-97, also chmn. bd. dirs., 1993-97; ptnr. Hammond Kennedy Whitney, Chgo., 1998—. Bd. dirs. Hubbell Inc., Reinhold Industries, Seneca Inc., Effox, Boyt Harness, Qualis. Trustee Newberry Libr.; bd. dirs. Children's Meml. Hosp.; active vis. com. of libr. U. Chgo. With Air Force N.G., 1963-69. Mem. Chgo. Club, Saddle and Cycle Club, Commonwealth Club, Racquet Club, Links (N.Y.C.). Office: 333 N Michigan Ave Ste 2200 Chicago IL 60601-4104

**MCNALLY, CONNIE BENSON,** magazine editor, publisher, antiques dealer; b. Chgo. d. Peter D. and Joanna Agriostathes; m. Dick Benson, Nov. 19, 1955 (div. Mar. 1961); 1 child, Douglas; m. William C. McNally, July 27, 1975. Student, Univ. Wis., 1954-55; BA, Baylor, 1962. Midwest supr. Slenderella Internat., Chgo., 1955-59; dir. John Roberts Powers Sch., Dallas, 1960-62; backgammon tchr., profl. Racquet Club, Palm Springs, Calif., 1969-75, La Costa (Calif.) Resort, 1973-75; antique dealer Palm Springs, 1975—; ptnr. Carriage Trade Antiques, 1975-78; owner, mgr. McNally Co. Antiques, 1978—; editor, pub. Silver Mag., Inc., Rancho Santa Fe, Calif. 1993—. Mem. Am. Antique Dealers, Antique Dealers Assn. Calif., Country Firends (vol. chair 1985-87, area dir. 1988-89), publicity chair 1990-91, program chair 1992-93, exec. 1994-95, bd. dirs.), Social Svc. League La Jolla, Soc. Am. Silversmiths, Rancho Santa Fe Rep. Women's Club. Avocations: equestrian, gourmet cooking.

**MCNALLY, JAMES HENRY,** physicist, defense consultant; b. Orange, NJ, Dec. 18, 1936; s. James Osborne and Edith Maude (Jones) McN.; m. Nancy Lee Eudaley, July 4, 1976. B. in Engring. Physics, Cornell U., 1959; PhD in Physics, Calif. Inst. Tech., 1966. Staff mem. program mgr. Los Alamos (N.Mex.) Nat. Lab., 1965-74; asst. dir for laser and isotope separation tech. AEC/ERDA, Washington, 1974-75; assoc. div. leader, dep. for inertial fusion, asst. for nat. sec. issues Los Alamos Nat. Lab., 1975-86; dep. asst. dir Arms Control and Disarmament Agy., Washington, 1986-88; dir. office staff Los Alamos Nat. Lab., 1988-90; pvt. practice, 1990—96; cons. US Dept. of State, 2004—. U.S. del. Geneva Conf. on Disarmament, 1969, 73, 74, Threshold Test Ban Treaty, Moscow, 1974, Nuclear Testing Talks, Geneva, 1986-88. Bd. dirs. Wilson Mesa Met. Water Dist., 1976-88; mem., v.p., pres. Mountain Canine Corps, 1994-98. Recipient Meritorious Honor award Arms Control and Disarmament Agy., 1988, Superior Honor award Dept. of State, 2005. Mem. AAAS, Am. Phys. Soc., Internat. Inst. Strategic Studies. Home: 41 Bowen Rd Kittery ME 03904-1355

**MCNALLY, JAMES RAND (RANDY MCNALLY),** pharmacist, state legislator; BS, Memphis State U., 1967; postgrad., U. Tenn., 1969. Hosp. pharmacist Meth. Med. Ctr., Oak Ridge, Tenn., 1978—; mem. Tenn. Ho. of Reps. 91st-94th Gen. Assemblies, Tenn. Senate 95th-103d Gen. Assemblies, former vice chmn. fin., ways and means com., chmn. edn. com., Republican floor leader. Recipient Bill Bates award United Dem. League, 1994, MADD Outstanding Legislator, Disting. Svc. award Am. Coun. on Alcohol Problems, 1994, Common Cause Bird Dog award, 1994; named Rep. Legislator of the Yr., 1990, Sertoma Man of the Yr., 1991; Paul Harris fellow Rotary Internat., 1996. Republican. E-mail: sen.randy. Office: 302 War Memorial Bldg Nashville TN 37243 Fax: 615-253-0285. Business E-Mail: mcnally@legislature.state.tn.us.

**MCNALLY, RICHARD JAMES,** clinical psychologist, educator; b. Detroit, Apr. 17, 1954; s. George Vincent and Marjorie Frances (Tobin) McN.; m. Margaret Cain, Aug. 16, 1985 (div. 2005). BS in Psychology, Wayne State U., 1976; MA in Clin. Psychology, U. Ill., Chgo., 1980, PhD in Clin. Psychology, 1982. Clin. psychology intern dept. psychiatry Temple U. Med. Sch., Phila., 1982-83, postdoctoral fellow dept. psychiatry, 1983-84; from asst. prof. to assoc. prof. dept. psychology U. Health Scis., Chgo. Med. Sch., North Chicago, Ill., 1984-91; assoc. prof. dept. psychology Harvard U., Cambridge, Mass., 1991-95, prof., 1995—. Assoc. editor Behavior Therapy, 1992-95; author: Panic Disorder: A Critical Analysis, 1994, Remembering Trauma, 2003; contbr. articles to Psychol. Bull., Psychol. Rev. Recipient

Disting. Scientist award, Soc. for the Sci. of Clin. Psychology, 2005; rsch. grantee NIMH Mem. APA (mem. DSM-IV task force 1989-94), Assn. for Advancement of Behavior Therapy, Am. Psychol. Soc. Democrat. Office: Harvard U Dept Psychology 33 Kirkland St Cambridge MA 02138-2044 Business E-Mail: rjm@wjh.harvard.edu.

**MCNALLY, TERRENCE,** playwright; b. St. Petersburg, Fla., Nov. 3, 1939; s. Hubert Arthur and Dorothy Katharine (Rapp) McNally. BA, Columbia U., 1960. Stage mgr. Actors Studio, N.Y.C., 1961, tutor, 1961-62; film critic The Seventh Art, 1963-65; asst. editor Columbia Coll. Today, N.Y.C., 1965-66. Author: (plays) The Lady of the Camellias, 1963, And Things That Go Bump in the Night, 1964, Apple Pie and Last Gasps, 1966, Sweet Eros, Witness, Tour, Cuba Si!, Noon, 1968, Next, 1969, Where Has Tommy Flowers Gone?, Botticelli, Bringing It All Back Home, 1971, Bad Habits, 1971 (Obie award, 1971), Whiskey, 1973, The Tubs, 1974, The Ritz, 1975 (Obie award best play, 1974), The Golden Age, 1975, Broadway, Broadway, 1979, The Five Forty-Eight, 1974, It's Only a Play, 1982, The Rink, 1984, Frankie and Johnny in the Clair de Lune, 1988, The Lisbon Traviata, 1989, Up in Saratoga, 1990, Kiss of the Spider Woman, 1990 (Tony award best book of a musical, 1993), Andre's Mother, 1990 (Emmy award), Preludes, Fuges & Rifts, Lips Together, Teeth Apart, 1991, (screenplay) Frankie and Johnny, 1991, A Perfect Ganesh, 1993 (Pulitzer prize for drama nomination, 1994), Kiss of the Spiderwoman, 1993, Love! Valour! Compassion!, 1994 (Outer Critics' Circle award best Broadway play, 1995, N.Y. Drama Critics Best Am. play, Tony award for Best Play), Master Class, 1994, Ragtime, 1997 (Tony award Best Book of a Musical Corpus Christi, 1998), The Full Monty, 2000, The Visit, 2001, Frankie and Johnny in the Clair de Lune, 2002, Chita Rivera: The Dancer's Life, 2005. Recipient Dramatists Guild Hull-Warriner award, 1973, 1988, 1990; Guggenheim fellow, 1966—69. Mem.: Am. Acad. Arts and Letters, Dramatists Guild (v.p. 1981—98). Office: care Peter Franklin William Morris Agy 1325 Avenue Of The Americas New York NY 10019-6026

**MCNALLY, THOMAS CHARLES, III,** lawyer; b. San Francisco, Dec. 5, 1938; s. Thomas Charles and Claire Marie (Egan) McN.; m. Paula Ann Berger, Sept. 3, 1960; children: Megan, Martin, J. Tevis. BS, U. San Francisco, 1960; JD, U. Calif., San Francisco, 1963. Bar: Calif. 1964. Dep. atty. gen., Calif., 1964; assoc. firm Bohnert, Flowers & McCarthy, San Francisco, 1965-68; asst. sec., counsel DiGiorgio Corp., San Francisco, 1968-73, sec., counsel, 1974-75; sec., gen. counsel Consol. Fibres, Inc., San Francisco, 1975-88, v.p., 1981-88, also bd. dirs.; of counsel McInerney & Dillon, P.C., Oakland, Calif., 1989-91; pvt. practice San Francisco, 1991—. Lectr. McGeorge Bar Rev., 1964-65, Continuing Edn. of Bar, U. Calif., 1975-76; judge moot ct. U. San Francisco, 1974-84; arbitrator Am. Arbitration Assn., NASD, 1988—. Co-chmn. Mill Valley Citizens Adv. Com., 1974-76; mem. pub. affairs com. San Francisco Assn. Mental Health, 1965-69; commr. Mill Valley Park and Recreation Commn., 1988-93, chmn., 1990; commr. Larkspun Park & Recreation Commn., 2005-; lector Roman Cath. ch. Mem. ABA, State Bar Calif., San Francisco Bar Assn., Olympic Club (bd. dirs. 1999—, v.p. 2001), Scott Valley Tennis Club (founder, bd. dirs. 1971-76, 80-82, pres. 1980-82), World Trade Club. Republican. Home: 108 Hawthorne Ave Larkspur CA 94939 Office: 455 Market St Ste 1900 San Francisco CA 94105-2448 E-mail: tmcnally@lmi.net.

**MCNALLY, VINCENT JOSEPH,** historian, educator; b. Phila., Feb. 6, 1943; s. Joseph Edward and Dorothy Elizabeth (Connor) McNally. PhD, Univ. of Dublin, Trinity College, Dublin, Ireland, 1971—77. Prof. ch. history Sacred Heart Sch. of Theology, Hales Corners, Wis., 1992—; asst. prof. history Simon Fraser U., Burnaby, B.C., Canada, 1987—92. Author: (Book) Education Facsimiles 241-260: Catholic Emancipation, 1793-1829, 1976, A History of the Roman Catholic Diocese of Victoria, B.C., 1990, Reform, Revolution and Reaction: Archbishop John Thomas Troy and the Catholic Church in Ireland, 1787-1817, 1995, The Lord's Distant Vineyard: A History of the Oblates and the Catholic Community in British Columbia, 2000, "Hope for the Future: the Church's Challenges of the New Millennium", 2000, (book) Christianity and Native Cultures: Christian and Native Spiritualities in British Columbia: The Historic Struggle to Respect Diversity and Ambiguity, 2004, (Journal: Historical Studies) Challenging the Status Quo: An Examination of the History of Catholic Education in British Columbia, 1999, (Journal: Western Oblate Studies) "Fighting for a Foundation: Oblate Beginnings in Far Western Canada, 1847-1864, 1996, (Journal: Canadian Church Historical Soci) "Fighting City Hall: The Church Tax Exemption Battle Between the City and Roman Catholic Diocese of Victoria", 1992, (Journal of Church and State) "Church-State Relations and American Influence in British Columbia before Confederation", 1992, (Catholic Historical Review) "Archbishop John Thomas Troy and the Establishment of St. Patrick's, Maynooth, 1791-1795", 1981, (Research Project) Practicing What We Preach: Testing and Publishing a Guide for Implementing a Pastoral Theology of Acceptance and Reconciliation in Northern Ireland", 2001 (Assoc. of Theological Schools in US and Canada: Lilly Research Award, 2001), (Research Project:) "Challenging Prejudice: Creating a Theology of Acceptance and Reconciliation in the Schools of Northern Ireland, 2000 (Pew Charitable Trusts, 2000), (Research Award) Researching, Writing and Publishing of a survey history: Irish Catholics: The Catholic Church in Ireland from the Reformation to the Present, 1999 (Eli Lilly Fellowship, 1999), Developing Healthy Theological Imaginations, 1998 (Lilly Endowment Fellowship for Teaching and Learning in Theology and Religion, 1998), Challenging Ourselves: A Practical Guide for Moving Beyond Prejudice in the Schools of Northern Ireland, 2004. Recipient Rsch. award, NEH, 2004, fellowship U. Chgo., 2005.: American Catholic Historical Society (Peter Guilday Prize 1981). Avocations: drawing, harpsichord, painting, travel. Office: Sacred Heart School of Theology PO Box 429 Hales Corners WI 53130 Office Phone: 414-425-8300 7181. Office Fax: 414-529-6999. Business E-Mail: vmcnally@shst.edu.

**MCNAMARA, BRENDA NORMA,** retired secondary school educator; b. Blackpool, Lancashire, Eng., Aug. 8, 1945; arrived in U.S., 1946; d. Milford Hampson and Nola (Welsby) Jones; m. Michael James McNamara, July 19, 1969. BA in History, Calif. State U., Long Beach, 1967; postgrad., Calif. State U., various campuses, 1967—. Cert. secondary tchr. and lang. devel. specialist Calif. Tchr. history West HS, Torrance, Calif., 1968—, dept. chair, 1989-99, 2000—04; ret. 2004. Cons. Golden State Exam. in History Calif. State Dept. Edn., 1998; state del. NEA Annual Meeting, 2000, 02, local del., 03, 04; cons. in field. Co-author: (book) World History, 1988. Western Internat. Studies Consortium grantee, 1988. Mem.: NEA (retired 2004), Am. Hist. Assn., Nat. Coun. Social Studies, So. Calif. Coun. Social Studies, Torrance Tchrs. Assn. (bd. dirs. 1992—2004), Calif. Coun. Social Studies, Calif. Tchrs. Assn. (retired 2004). Avocations: travel, theater, mystery reading, gourmet cooking. E-mail: brenmcnamara@cox.net.

**MCNAMARA, DANIEL EDWARD,** geologist, seismologist; b. Lansing, Mich., July 13, 1964; s. Daniel Edward and Gail Elizabeth McNamara; m. Kristie Lane Mather, Oct. 22, 1974; children: Abigail Lane, Lilia Lane. BS, Ctrl. Mich. U., Mt. Pleasant, 1987; MS, U. Mo., Columbia, 1989; PhD, U. S.C., Columbia, 1995. Rschr. Lawrence Livermore Nat. Lab., Calif., 1995—97; rsch. seismologist Alaska Earthquake Info. Ctr., Fairbanks, 1997—99; seismologist U.S. Geol. Survey, Golden, Colo., 1999—. Grantee, NSF, 2004—05. Mem.: Seismological Soc. Am., Am. Geophys. Union. Independent. Avocations: mountaineering, music. Office Phone: 303-273-8550.

**MCNAMARA, FRANCIS JOSEPH, JR.,** retired foundation executive, lawyer; b. Boston, Nov. 30, 1927; s. Francis Joseph and Louise (English) McN.; m. Noreen E. O'Connor, June 18, 1953 (dec. Feb. 1984); children: Francis Joseph III, Moira Patricia (Mrs. Lance F. James), John Allen, Kathleen Louise (Mrs. Robert J. Hugin), Martha Jeanne (Mrs. James R. Bordewick), Mark Jeffrey; m. Lois L. Magner, Jan. 17, 1986. AB, Georgetown U., 1949, LLB, 1951; LLD, Fairfield U., 1983. Bar: Conn. 1952. Assoc. firm Pullman, Comley, Bradley & Reeves, 1953; asst. U.S. Atty., dist. Conn., 1953-57; assoc. firm Cummings & Lockwood, Stamford, Conn., 1957-59, ptnr., 1959-91. Guest lectr. Salzburg (Austria) Seminar, 1981; chmn. grievance com. U.S. Dist. Ct. Conn., 1983-89; mem. panel comml. arbitrators Am.

Arbitration Assn., Ctr. Dispute Resolution. Trustee Fairfield (Conn.) U., 1968-80, trustee emeritus, 1980—; trustee Charles E. Culpeper Trust, 1968-2001; chmn. bd. Charles E. Culpeper Found., 1968-99, pres., 1991-99. With USNR, 1946, 51-53. Fellow Am. Bar Found., Am. Coll. Trial Lawyers (state com. 1985-91, state chmn. 1989-90); mem. U.S. Supreme Ct. Hist. Soc. (Conn. state chmn. 1989-91, trustee 1992-2000), Navy League U.S., Knight of Holy Sepulchre, Knight of Malta, Knight of St. Gregory the Great, Wee Burn Country Club (Darien, Conn.), Orchid Island Golf and Beach Club (Vero Beach, Fla.). Republican. Roman Catholic. also: 110 Island Plantation Terrace Vero Beach FL 32963-5000 Office: 75 Bank St New Canaan CT 06840-6203

**MCNAMARA, J. DONALD (JOHN DONALD MCNAMARA),** retired lawyer, business executive; b. Bridgeport, Conn., Feb. 28, 1924; s. John T. and Agnes (Keating) McN.; m. Shirley Addison Holdridge, Nov. 5, 1960. BA, Dartmouth Coll., 1945; MA in Govt., Harvard U., 1947, LLB, 1950. Bar: N.Y. 1951, Conn. 1951. Assoc. Hall, Haywood, Patterson & Taylor, N.Y.C., 1951-53, 55-56; asst. U.S. Atty. So. Dist., N.Y., 1953-55; assoc. Wickes, Riddell, Bloomer, Jacobi & McGuire, N.Y.C., 1956-57; assoc., then ptnr. Nottingham & McEniry (and successor), N.Y.C., 1957-59; sec., gen. counsel Interpub. Group of Cos., Inc., N.Y.C., 1960-79, dir., 1965-85, sr. v.p., 1966-73, exec. v.p., 1973-79, pres., 1980-85; ret., 1985. Chmn. U.S. Nat. Tennis Championships, 1965. Served to lt. (j.g.) USNR, 1943-46 Mem. Am. Ceramic Cir., The Silver Soc. (London), River Club, Univ. Club, Met. Opera Club (bd. dirs. 1999-2006, pres. 2004-06), Ekwanok Country Club (bd. govs. Manchester, Vt. 1991-95), Dorset (Vt.) Field Club (bd. govs. 1996-99, pres. 1997-98), West Side Tennis Club (pres. Forest Hills, N.Y. 1964-66, 79-80) Home: 350 E 57th St New York NY 10022-2953 also: River Rd Manchester VT 05254

**MCNAMARA, JAMES M.,** broadcast executive; b. Republic of Panama; m. Lana McNamara; 3 children. B in Bus. Adminstrn. and Polit. Sci., Rollins Coll.; M, Am. Grad. Sch. of Internat. Mgmt. Sr. v.p., exec. v.p. and pres. New World Entertainment, Calif., 1986—91, CEO Calif., 1991—95; pres. Universal Television Enterprises, Calif., 1996—98, JMM Management, Calif., 1998—99; pres. & CEO Telemundo Network (subs. GE-NBC), Fla., 1999—2005. Bd. dir. Scandinavian Broadcasting Sys, S.A., Film Roman (animated programming).

**MCNAMARA, JAMES O.,** physician, scientist; b. Portage, Wis., Sept. 25, 1942; s. Louis Vincent and Lucille (O'Connell) McN.; m. Ann Marilyn Niebler, Aug. 15, 1964; children: Dennis, Brigid, James, Michael, Brian. AB in Philosophy, Marquette U., 1964; MD, U. Mich., 1968. Diplomate Am. Bd. Psychiatry and Neurology, 1976, Am. Bd. Clin. Neurophysiology, 1977. Neurologist U.S. Army Hosp., Fort Hood, Tex., 1971-73; dir. epilepsy ctr. VA Med. Ctr., Durham, NC, 1976-86, neurologist, 1986—; asst. prof. neurology Duke U. Med. Ctr., Durham, NC, 1975-80, assoc. prof. neurology, 1980-85, asst. prof. pharmacology, 1981-86, dir. Duke Ctr. for Adv. Study of Epilepsy, 1982—, prof. neurology, 1985—, assoc. prof. pharmacology, 1986—, prof. neurobiology, 1990—, Carl R. Deane prof. neuroscience, 1993—, chair neurobiology dept., 2002—. Mem. editl. bd., cons. to numerous jours.; mem. com. ad-hoc grant review; mem. Klingenstein Neuroscience Adv. Com., 1994—, Sandoz Pharmaceutical Duke Adv. Com. Contbr. articles to profl. jours. Maj. U.S. Army, 1971-73. Recipient grant NIH, 1980, 1994, Merit Review grantee Veterans Adminstrn., 1992-95, 95—; Postdoctoral fellow Nat. Multiple Sclerosis Soc.; CIBA-Geigy award for VA Coop. Study on Antiepilectic Drugs Internat. League Against Epilepsy, Epilepsy Rsch. award Am. Soc. Pharmacology & Exptl. Therapeutics, Rsch. Recognition award Am. Epilepsy Soc., 2 Jacog Javits Neuroscience Investigator awards, NIH. Mem. Am. Epilepsy Soc. (pres. 1993, Rsch. Recognition award 1994) Epilepsy Found. Am. (bd. dirs. 1987-92), N.C. Soc. Neuroscience (pres. 1990-91), Soc. Neuroscience (edn. com. 1993-96), Inst. Medicine. Roman Catholic. Achievements include discovery of an auto-immune cause of Rasmussen's encephalitis. Home: 403 Lakeshore Ln Chapel Hill NC 27514-1730 Office: Duke U Med Ctr Box 3676 401 Bryan Rsch Bldg Durham NC 27710-0001 E-mail: jmc@neuro.duke.edu.*

**MCNAMARA, JOHN J(OSEPH),** advertising executive, writer; b. Yonkers, NY, Mar. 7, 1934; m. Patricia A. Widmann, Sept. 14, 1963; children: Mary, John. BS, Yale U., 1956; MBA, NYU, 1963. Pres. Young & Rubicam Inc., from 1982; later pres. McCann Erickson Worldwide, ret., 1990. Cons. in field. Author: Advertising Agency Management, 1989; columnist: Gulf Stream mags. Pres. Pelham United Way, NY; chmn. Pelham Manor Planning Bd.; trustee Village of Pelham Manor, mayor, 1989—90; mem. Boys and Girls Club, Indian River County, Fla.; pres., bd. dirs. John's Island Property Owners Assn. Mem.: John's Island Club (bd. dirs.), Winged Foot Club, Pelham Country Club (pres.). Office: PO Box 8204 Vero Beach FL 32963-8204

**MCNAMARA, JOHN REGIS,** psychology educator; b. Binghamton, N.Y., May 27, 1941; s. Regis Charles and Jane (Bradley) McN.; m. Lucille J. Martel, Dec. 5, 1972; children: Brian, Paul. BA, U. Notre Dame, 1963; MA, Xavier U., 1967; PhD, U. Ga., 1972. Diplomate Am. Bd. Profl. Psychology. Asst. prof. psychology and medicine U. Mo., Kansas City, 1971-72; prof. clin. psychology Ohio U., Athens, 1972—. Cons. U.S. Army, Panama Canal Zone, 1972, U.S. Gen. Acctg. Office, Washington, 1977-81; trainer U.S. AID-Mideast, Athens, 1994. Author: Overcoming Dating Anxiety, 1991; editor: Behavioral Approaches to Medicine, 1979, Critical Issues, Developments and Trends in Professional Psychology, Vol. 1, 1982, Vol. 2, 1984, Vol. 3, 1987. Fellow APA, Sigma Xi. Home: 23 Coventry Ln Athens OH 45701-3718 Office: Ohio U Porter Hall Dept Psychology Athens OH 45701 Office Phone: 614-593-1707. Business E-Mail: mcnamara@ohio.edu.

**MCNAMARA, JOHN STEPHEN,** artist, educator; b. Cambridge, Mass., Feb. 16, 1950; s. John Stephen and Mary (Adams) McN. BFA in Painting, Mass. Coll. Art, Boston, 1971, MFA in Painting, 1977. Tchr. Mus. Fine Arts Sch., Boston, 1983, 90-92; undergrad. and grad. painting tchr. Mass. Coll. Art, Boston, 1988; undergrad. painting tchr. Boston Archtl. Ctr., Boston, 1987; color fundamentals tchr. Mass. Coll. Art, Boston, 1987, undergrad. drawing and painting, 1975-88. Vis. lectr. San Francisco Art Inst., 1992, 93, U. Calif., Berkeley, 1993—. One-man shows include The Exhbn. Space at 112 Greene St., N.Y.C., 1992, Stavaridis Gallery, Boston, 1983-85, 86-89, Bess Cutler Gallery, N.Y.C., 1984, 85, 86, 88, Mass. Coll. Art, 1986, Honolulu Acad. Fine Art, 1987, Nielsen Gallery, 1990, 92, Miller Block Gallery, Boston, 1995, Ebert Gallery, San Francisco, Clark Gallery, Lincoln, Mass., 2002, others; exhibited in group shows at Boston Collects, Mus. Fine Arts, Stavaridis Gallery, 1986, Bess Cutler Gallery, N.Y.C., 1987, Am. Painters and Sculptors, Met. Mus. Art, N.Y.C., 1988, Resonant Abstraciton, Fuller Mus. Art, Brockton, Mass., 1989-90, Tucson Mus. Fine Art, 1996, DeCordova Mus., Lincoln, Mass., 2002, Painting in Boston, 1950-2000. Recipient Outstanding Alumnus award, Mass. Coll. Art, 1986, Faculty Outstanding Mentorship award, Grad. Student Instrs., 2003; grantee, Equitable Life and the Rockefeller Found., 1980, 1982, 1983, 1986, 1989, Nat. Endowment Arts, 1981; McDowell Colony fellow, Peterborough, NH, 1985. Home: 1501 Park Ct Novato CA 94945-1472 Office Phone: 510-642-2582. Business E-Mail: namara@calmail.berkeley.edu.

**MC NAMARA, JOSEPH DONALD,** researcher, retired protective services official; b. N.Y.C., Dec. 16, 1934; s. Michael and Eleanor (Shepherd) McN.; divorced; children: Donald, Laura, Karen. BS, John Jay Coll., 1968; fellow, Harvard Law Sch., 1970; DPA (Littauer fellow), Harvard U., 1973. Served to dep. insp. Police Dept., N.Y.C., 1956-73; police chief Kansas City, Mo., 1973-76, San Jose, Calif., 1976-91; rsch. fellow Hoover Instn., Stanford U., 1991—. Adj. instr. Northeastern U., 1972, John Jay Coll., 1973, Rockhurst Coll., 1975-76, San Jose State U., 1980; cons. U.S. Civil Rights Commn., 1978; lectr., appearances on nat. TV; apptd. nat. adv. bd. U.S. Bur. Justice Stats., 1980, U.S. Drug Control Policy Office, 1993; commentator Pub. Broadcasting Radio. Author: (non-fiction) Safe and Sane, 1984, (novel) The First Directive Crown, 1985, Fatal Command, 1987, The Blue Mirage, 1990, Code 211 Blue, 1996; contbr. articles to profl. publs. Bd. dirs. Drug Policy

---

Found., Washington; active NCCJ. Served with U.S. Army, 1958-60. Named one of 200 Young Am. Leaders Time mag., 1975; recipient disting. alumni award John Jay Coll., 1979, Pres.'s award Western Soc. Criminology1979, Morrison Gitchoff award Western Soc. Criminology, 1992, H.B. Spear award Drug Policy Found., 1992; Kansas City police named Best in Country by Nat. Newspaper Enterprises, 1974, San Jose Police Dept. named Nat. Model U.S. Civil Rights Commn., 1980; named Law Enforcement Officer of Yr., Calif. Trial Lawyers Assn., 1991. Mem. Internat. Assn. Chiefs of Police, Calif. Police Chiefs Assn., Calif. Peace Officers Assn., Major Cities Police Chiefs Assn., Police Exec. Research Forum (dir.) Office: Hoover Instn Stanford CA 94305 Office Phone: 650-723-1475. E-mail: mcnamara@hoover.stanford.edu. *In our country, social mobility is possible for people from even the most humble backgrounds. Despite problems, our nation has provided more liberty and dignity for the common individual than any other civilization in history. Continuation of our free society depends upon how successful we are in teaching each new generation an appreciation of our precious freedoms and the patience to achieve progress within our democratic process.*

**MCNAMARA, JULIA MARY,** academic administrator, foreign language educator; b. N.Y.C., Dec. 13, 1941; d. John P. and Julia (Dowd) McNamara. BA in History and French, Ohio Dominican Coll., 1965; MA in French, Middlebury Coll., 1972; MPhil, Yale U., 1977, PhD in French Lang. and Lit., 1980; DHL (hon.), Sacred Heart U., Hamden, Conn., 1984. Mem. faculty St. William Sch., Pitts., 1963-64, Holy Spirit Sch., Columbus, Ohio, 1964-65, Newark (Ohio) Cath. High Sch., 1965-66, Northwest Cath. High Sch., West Hartford, Conn., 1966-69, St. Vincent Ferrer High Sch., N.Y.C., 1969-70, St. Mary's High Sch., New Haven, 1971-74; lectr. french Albertus Magnus Coll., New Haven, 1976-80, dean of students, 1980-82, acting pres., 1982-83, pres., 1983—, Prof. French Albertus Magnus Coll., 1981—; mem. Conn. Health and Edn. Facilities Authority, Hartford, 1983—; chair Conn. Conf. Ind. Colls., Hartford, 1990-92, sec.-treas. 1986—, chmn., 1990-92; lectr. in field; assoc. fellow Yale U., Morse Coll.; bd. dirs. New Haven Savs. Bank. Chairperson United Way Greater New Haven, 1987; bd. dirs. St. Mary's High Sch., New Haven, 1982-91, ARC, New Haven Savs. Bank, 1990—; trustee Yale-New Haven Hosp., 1984— (chair med. com., 1989-91 vice chair bd., 1991-), chair, Yale-New Haven Health Sys.; adv. bd. Bank of Boston-Conn., 1983-87; adv. com. Jr. League Greater New Haven, 1985; trustee Hartford Sem., 1985-91. Fulbright fellow, Paris, 1977-78; Yale U. fellow, 1974-78, Am. Council on Edn. fellow, 1981; recipient Disting. Woman in Leadership award New Haven YWCA, 1984, Veritas award Providence Coll., 1987, Greater New Haven Jr. Achievement Ann. award, 1990. Mem. Fulbright Alumni Assn., New Haven C. of C. (bd. dirs. 1984-90), New England Assn. Schs. and Colls. (appeals bd. 1986-88). Roman Catholic. Office: Albertus Magnus Coll Office of the President 700 Prospect St New Haven CT 06511-1224

**MCNAMARA, KEVIN JOHN,** museum administrator; b. Abington, Pa., Oct. 6, 1957; s. John Kerwin and Dolores Ann (Auchinleck) McNamara; m. Juliane Cary Roebuck, July 17, 1982 (div. Dec. 2005); children: Hilary Megan, Whitney Morgan. BA, Temple U., 1989; cert., U. Pa., 1994; MA, Temple U., 1995; cert., U. Va., 2000. Journalist Calkins Newspapers Inc., Doylestown, Pa., 1981-85; congl. aide U.S. Rep. R. Lawrence Coughlin, Washington, 1985-88; asst. dir. Fgn. Policy Rsch. Inst., Phila., 1988-93, rapporteur, 1990-93, adj. scholar, 1994—; dir. devel. Intercollegiate Studies Inst., Wilmington, Del., 1994—98; assoc. v.p. Drexel U., Phila., 2000—2004; v.p. Independence Seaport Mus., Phila., 2004—. Author: The Presidency, 2000; contbg. editor Directors and Boards, 1989-90. Orbis: A Jour. of World Affairs, 1990-93; contbr. articles to profl. jours. Vol. Sam Katz for Gov., 1994, Craig Snyder for Congress, 1992, George Bush for Pres. Com., 1987-88, Snyder for State Ho. Com., 1990; cons. Coughlin for Congress Com., 1986; bd. dirs. Abington Free Libr., 1992-93. Grantee, Tawani Found., 2004; Earhart Found. fellow, 2003—04. Mem. Phila. Com. Fgn. Rels., Assn. of Fundraising Profls. Republican. Avocations: reading, writing, gardening. Office: 211 S Columbus Blvd and Walnut St Philadelphia PA 19106-3199

**MCNAMARA, LAWRENCE JOHN,** lawyer; b. Evergreen Park, Ill., Aug. 10, 1950; s. William Francis and Florence M.; m. Martha Ann Sanchez, Jan. 7, 1992. BA cum laude, Ill. Coll.; JD, Vanderbilt U. Bar: Tex. 1976, D.C. 1988, U.S. Dist. Ct. (so. dist.) Tex. 1977, U.S. Dist. Ct. (ea. dist.) Tex. 1978, U.S. Dist. Ct. (no. dist.) Tex. 1985, U.S. Dist. Ct. (we. dist.) Tex. 1991, U.S. Ct. Appeals (5th cir.) 1976, U.S. Ct. Appeals (11th cir.) 1981, U.S. Ct. Appeals (7th cir.) 1989, U.S. Ct. Appeals (9th cir.) 1991, U.S. Ct. Appeals (8th cir.) 1994, U.S. Supreme Ct. 1979. Assoc. Baker & Botts, Houston, 1976-85; ptnr. Baker, Smith & Mills, Dallas, 1985-87; ptnr., shareholder Johnson & Gibbs, Dallas, 1987-95; ptnr. Locke Liddell & Sapp (and predecessor firm), Dallas, 1995—. Mem. ABA, Tex. Bd. Legal Specialization (cert.), Phi Beta Kappa. Roman Catholic. Avocations: golf, running. Office: Locke Liddell & Sapp 2200 Ross Ave Ste 2200 Dallas TX 75201-6776

**MCNAMARA, MARTIN BURR,** lawyer, former gas industry executive; b. Danbury, Conn., Sept. 10, 1947; s. William Joseph and Geraldine Margaret (Young) McN. BA in English, Providence Coll., 1969; JD, Yale U., 1972. Bar: NY 1973, US Dist. Ct. (so. and ea. dists.) NY 1973, US Dist. Ct. (no. dist.) Tex. 1993, US Dist. Ct. (so. dist.) Tex. 1994, US Ct. Appeals (2d cir.) 1973, Tex. 1980, US Ct. Appeals (5th and 11th cirs.) 1981. Assoc. Shea & Gould, NYC, 1972-76; asst. US atty. (so. dist.) NY, NYC, 1976-79; v.p., gen. counsel, sec. Tex. Oil & Gas Corp., Dallas, 1979-91; gen. counsel, sr. v.p. adminstrn. Delhi Gas Pipeline Corp., Dallas, 1979-91; ptnr. litig. and corp. securities Gibson, Dunn & Crutcher LLP, Dallas, 1991—, and ptnr.-in-charge Dallas office. Mem. exec. com. Gibson Dunn & Crutcher, bd. dirs. Transocean Sedco Foret, Inc.; lectr. State Bar Tex., Dallas Bar Assn., U. Tex. Corp. Counsel Inst., Okla. Bar Assn., U. Tex. Mem. exec. com. Yale Law Sch. Assn., 1983-86 Mem. State Bar of Tex. (chmn. 1988-89), Bar Assn. Fifth Fed. Cir., Assn. Bar. City of NY, NY State Bar Assn., Fed. Energy Bar Assn. Clubs: Petroleum. Republican. Roman Catholic. Office: Gibson Dunn & Crutcher LLP Ste 1100 2100 McKinney Ave Dallas TX 75201-6912 Office Phone: 214-698-3127. Office Fax: 214-571-2938. Business E-Mail: mmcnamara@gibsondunn.com.

**MCNAMARA, MARY ELLEN,** not-for-profit executive; b. Mpls., Dec. 18, 1943; d. Edward Emmanuel and Gladys Theresa (Mattson) Bjorklund; m. Peter Alexander McNamara II (div.); children: Peter Alexander III, Nathaniel Paul. BA, Carleton Coll., 1965; MDiv, Harvard U., 1968. Cert. fin. planner. Program dir. St. Peter's Ch., NYC, 1968-72; program dir., dep. exec., 1977-80; program dir. Ctr. Ch. on-the-Green, 1972-74; program developer Westminster Presbyn. Ch., Springfield, Ill., 1974-77; assoc. Gen. Assembly Coun. Presbyn. Ch. (USA), NYC, 1980—86; dir. not-for-profit sector City of NY, 1986—90; pres., exec. dir. Interchurch Ctr., NYC, 1990-99; interim pres. Union Theol. Sem., NYC, 1998—99, exec. v.p., 1999—; mem. exec. com. Assn. Theol. Schs., 2003—. V.p. Pathways for Youth, Bronx, NY, 1987—96; pres. Morningside Area Alliance, N.Y.C., 1991—98; parish assoc. Fifth Ave. Presbyn. Ch., 1998—2002. Moderator Presbyn. NYC, 1995—96, chair com. on ministry, 1992—95, chair implementation task force, 1996—98, chair nominating com., 2005—; chmn. bd. dirs. exec. com. Presbyn. Conf. Ctr., Stony Point, NY, 1996—2002, chmn. nominating com., 2005—; bd. dirs. Blanton/Peale Inst. on Religion and Health, 1994—2001, Wartburg Adult Care Cmty., 1999—, chair elect, 2001—03, chair, 2003—, chmn. pers. com., exec. com., 2001—03. Mem.: Assn. Theol. Seminaries (mem. exec. com. 2004—, bd. dirs. 2005—). Home: 99 Claremont Ave Apt 621 New York NY 10027-5711 Office: Union Theol Sem 3041 Broadway New York NY 10027-5710

**MCNAMARA, MICHAEL,** lighting designer, educator; b. Rockford, Ill., Aug. 25, 1966; s. Nancy Elaine Eliseo and Jack Edward McNamara. BS, Carroll Coll., Waukesha, Wis., 1989; MFA, Northwestern U., Evanston, Ill., 1993. Freelance lighting designer, Chgo., 1993—95; asst. lighting designer Wash. Nat. Opera, 1995—2003. Mem.: United Scenic Artists Local 829. Office: Univ Ariz PO Box 210003 Tucson AZ 85721

---

**MCNAMARA, MICHAEL,** electronics executive; BS, Univ. Cinn.; MBA, Santa Clara Univ. Prin. Pittiglio Rabin Todd & McGrath; v.p. mgr. ops. Anthem Electronics; v.p. No. Am. ops. Flextronics Internat., 1994—97, pres. Americas' ops., 1997—2001, COO Singapore, 2002—05, CEO, 2006—. Office: Flextronics Internat 2 Changri S Lane Singapore 486123 Singapore*

**MCNAMARA, MICHAEL T.,** lawyer; b. Kansas City, Mo., June 26, 1969; AB summa cum laude, Duke U., 1990; JD magna cum laude, Harvard U., 1996. Bar: Md. 1996, DC 1997. Economist US Dept. Commerce, Washington; with Arent Fox Kintner Plotkin & Kahn, Washington; ptnr. Sonnenschein Nath & Rosenthal LLP, Washington, 2002—. Office: Sonnenschein Nath & Rosenthal LLP Ste 600, E Tower 1301 K St NW Washington DC 20015 Office Phone: 202-408-6477. Office Fax: 202-408-6399. Business E-Mail: mmcnamara@sonnenschein.com.

**MC NAMARA, ROBERT A.,** construction company executive; b. 1953; BA in Econs., Brown U., 1975. Contracts mgr. Limbach Co., Woburn, Mass., 1975-78; v.p. sales and mktg. Marshall Contractors Inc., Rumford, RI, 1978-83; exec. v.p. to pres, COO Marshall Contractors Inc. (acquired by Fluor Corp.), Rumford, RI, 1983—96; various positions including sr. group pres. responsible for China Fluor Corp., 1996—2006; pres., CEO LVI Services Inc., 2006—. Office: LVI Services 80 Broad St 3rd fl New York NY 10004*

**MCNAMARA, ROBERT STRANGE,** former President of the World Bank, former Secretary of Defense; b. San Francisco, June 9, 1916; s. Robert James and Clara Nell (Strange) McN.; m. Margaret Craig, Aug. 13, 1940 (dec. Feb. 3, 1981); children: Margaret Elizabeth, Kathleen, Robert Craig; m. Diana Masieri Byfield, Sept. 16, 2004. AB, U. Calif., 1937, LLD (hon.); MBA, Harvard U., 1939, LLD (hon.), U. Mich., Columbia U., George Washington U., Princeton U., Amherst Coll., Williams Coll., U. Ala., Ohio State U., NYU, U. Notre Dame, U. Pa., U. St. Andrews, U. Philippines, Aberdeen U., Oxford U., U. SC. Asst. prof. bus. adminstrn. Harvard U., 1940-43; exec. Ford Motor Co., 1946-61, controller, 1949—53, asst. gen. mgr., Ford divsn., 1953—55, v.p., gen. mgr. Ford divsn., 1955—57, dir., group, v.p. car divsn., 1957-61, pres., 1960-61; sec. U.S. Dept. Def., 1961-68; pres. World Bank, 1968-81; ret., 1981. Mem., trustee pub. and pvt. instns. including Overseas Devel. Coun., Urban Inst., Enterprise Found., Brookings Inst., Royal Dutch Petroleum, 1981-87, Bank of Am., 1981-87, Corning, 1981-90, Washington Post Corp., 1981-89; spl. cons. War Dept., 1942. Author: The Essence of Security: Reflections in Office, 1968, One Hundred Countries-Two Billion People, 1973, The McNamara Years at the World Bank, 1981, Blundering Into Disaster, 1986, Out of the Cold: New Thinking for American Foreign and Defense Policy in the 21st Century, 1989, (with Brian Vandemark) In Retrospect: The Tragedy and Lessons of Vietnam, 1995, Argument Without End: In Search of Answers to the Vietnam Tragedy, 1999, Wilson's Ghost: Reducing the Risk of Conflict, Killing, and Catastrophe in the 21st Century, 2001; Film appearances: The Fog of War: Eleven Lessons from the Life of Robert S. McNamara, 2003; TV appearances: JFK Remembered, 1988, Cold War (mini-series), 1998, Vietnam: A Descent Into Hell, 1999. Served as lt. col. USAAF, 1943-46. Decorated Legion of Merit, D.S.M.; recipient Presdl. Medal of Freedom with distinction, 1968, Disting. Svc. medal, 1968, Christian A. Herter Meml. award, Albert Pick Jr. award U. Chgo., 1979, Albert Einstein Peace prize, 1983, Franklin D. Roosevelt Freedom from Want medal, 1983, Sidney Hillman Foundn. award, 1987, Olive Branch award for Outstanding Book on subject of World Peace, 1987, Onassis Athinai prize, 1988, Am. Assembly Svc. to Democracy award, Dag Hammarskjold Hon. medal, Entrepreneurial Excellence award, Yale Sch. Orgn. & Mgmt. Mem. Phi Beta Kappa. Office: 1350 I St NW Washington DC 20005-3305

**MCNAMARA, STEPHEN,** newspaper executive; b. Chgo., July 9, 1934; s. Robert Charles McNamara Jr. and Susan (Deuel) Shattuck; m. Anne Mogensen Petterson, Feb. 21, 1960 (div. Aug. 1970); children: Lise, Natalie, Kevin; m. Kay Copeland, June 10, 1978; children: Christopher, Morgan. AB in Am. History, Princeton U., 1955. Reporter Winston-Salem Jour., NC, 1955—57; sports writer Miami Herald, 1957—59; contbg. European editor Car & Driver, N.Y.C., 1960; asst. news editor, exec. sports editor, Sunday editor San Francisco Examiner, 1961—66; CEO, editor, pub. Pacific Sun, Mill Valley, Calif., 1966—2004; co-pub. The Ark, Tiburon, Calif., 1987—99; pres. Marin Sun Printing Co., Mill Valley, 1967—93; mng. gen. ptnr. Sunlight Investment Co., Mill Valley, 1980—. Vis. lectr. San Francisco State U., 1967; mem. innovation and planning commn. Calif. Dept. Edn., Sacramento, 1980; co-founder, pres. Marin Solar Village Corp., Mill Valley, 1976—, Marin Cmty. Video, Mill Valley, 1973-78. Mem. Soc. Profl. Journalists, Nat. Assn. Alternative Newsweeklies (pres. 1978-81), Calif. Assn. Alternative Newsweeklies (pres. 1990-92), Calif. Soc. Newspaper Editors (pres. 1985-86, bd. dirs. 1983-93), Calif. Newspaper Pubs. Assn. (bd. dirs. 1989-93), San Francisco Press Club (1st place newspaper writing award 1967, 3-2d place awards), Cap and Gown Club (Princeton U.). Democrat. Home: 2 Bradford Way Mill Valley CA 94941-1111 Personal E-mail: smcnamara@aol.com.

**MCNAMARA, TED (THOMAS EDMUND MCNAMARA),** federal official, former ambassador; b. New Haven, Sept. 16, 1940; s. Joseph Michael and Anne Marie (Meehan) McN.; m. Emma Julia Fonseca, June 11, 1966; children: David Fonseca, Michelle Anne. BA, Manhattan Coll., 1962; MA, Notre Dame U., 1964. Joined fgn. svc. State Dept., 1965; 2nd sec. Am. Embassy, Paris, 1967-69; BENELUX desk officer European bur. US Dept. State, 1969-71; consul Am. Consulate, Lubumbashi, Zaire, 1971-72, Bukavu, Zaire, 1972-73; with Armed Forces Staff Coll., Norfolk, Va., 1973-74; internat. affairs officer Arms Control & Disarmament Agy., 1974-75; chief external divsn., polit. sect. Am. Embassy, Moscow, 1976-78; office dir., polit.-mil. bur. US Dept. State, Washington, 1978-80; dep. chief of mission Am. Embassy, Kinshana, Democratic Republic of Congo, 1980-83, dept. asst. sec., bur. polit.-mil. affairs US Dept. State, Washington, 1983-86; sr. seminar Fgn. Svc. Inst., Washington, 1986-87; dir. counterterrorism and narcotics Nat. Security Coun., 1987-88; US amb. to Colombia US Dept. State, Bogota, 1988-91; special asst. to the Pres. for nat. security affairs The White House, Washington, 1991-92; coord. for counter-terrorism US Dept. State, Washington, 1992-93; prin. dep. asst. sec., bur. polit.-mil. affairs, 1993-94, asst. sec., bur. polit.-mil. affairs, 1994—98; pres., CEO Am. Soc. & Coun. Americas, NYC, 1998—2001; sr. adv. for counter-terrorism & homeland security US Dept. State, Washington, 2001—04; program mgt. Program Mgr. Info. Sharing Environ., Washington, 2006—. Adj. prof. Eliott Sch. Internat. Affairs George Washington U. Contbr. articles to profl. jours. Recipient Superior Honor award US Dept. State, 1980, 84, 86. Mem. Am. Fgn. Service Assn., Army-Navy Club.*

**MCNAMARA, TOM,** scientific consulting corporation executive; b. Battle Creek, Mich., May 23, 1944; s. George P. (Stepfather) and Mildred E. Lunt; m. Ellen K. LaRue, Sept. 24, 1977 (div. Dec. 2005); 1 child, George Lunt. Grad. in Chemistry, Mich., 1966; MBA, Northeastern U., 1970. With corp. planning dept. Reynolds Aluminum, Richmond, Va., 1970—72; sr. cons. Technomic Cons., Chgo., 1972—74; founder, pres. NUVENTURES Cons., Chgo. and San Diego, 1975—97. Spkr. trade convs. and confs. worldwide; frequent guest TV and radio talk shows; on water advisor Am.'s Cup, 1988, 91, 94. Author: Henry Lunt and The Ranger, 1991, Henry Lunt and The Spymaster, 1994; co-author: America's Changing Workforce, 1990; editor: George and The Pitching Machine, 1994; contbr. articles to profl. publs. Mem. various coms. United Fund and Chgo. Assn. Commerce and Industry, 1975—79; spokesman 200th Anniversary U.S. Bill of Rights tour, 1991; Rep. nominee Ill. Gen. Assembly, 1974, 1976. Recipient Presdl. Commendation for heroism, 1974, Commendation award, Chgo. Police Dept., 1974, Pulitzer Prize nomination, 1991. Mem.: Acacia, Sarasota Yacht Club, San Diego Tennis and Racquet Club, Bahia Corinthian Yacht Club. Personal E-mail: tommcnamara1944@earthlink.com, tomtheauthor@msn.com.

**MCNAMARA, WILLIAM P.,** retail executive; b. Newton, Mass. m. Patricia Ann McCole; 2 children. BS, Boston Coll. From exec. trainee to sr. v.p., gen. merch. mgr. Filene's divsn. May Dept. Stores Co., St. Louis, 1972—95, sr.

v.p., gen. merch. mgr. May merchandising divsn., 1995—97, pres., CEO Famous-Barr divsn., 1997—98, pres. May merchandising divsn., 1998—2000, vice-chmn., CEO 2000—. Office: May Dept Stores Co 611 Olive St Saint Louis MO 63101

**MCNAMEE, SISTER CATHERINE,** theology studies educator; b. Troy, N.Y., Nov. 13, 1931; d. Thomas Ignatius McNamee and Kathryn McNamee Marois. BA, Coll. of St. Rose, 1953, DHL (hon.), 1975; MEd, Boston Coll., 1955, MA, 1958; PhD, U. Madrid, 1967. Grad. asst. Boston Coll., 1954-55, asst. registrar Grad. Sch., 1955-57; mem. faculty Coll. St. Rose, Albany, NY, 1960-65, acad. v.p., 1968-75; dir. liberal arts Thomas Edison Coll., Trenton, 1975-76; pres. Trinity Coll., Burlington, Vt., 1976-79, Coll. St. Catherine, St. Paul, 1979-84; dean Dexter Hanley Coll., U. Scranton, Pa., 1984-86; pres. Nat. Cath. Ednl. Assn., Washington, 1986-96; sr. scholar Ctr. for Cath. Studies, U. St. Thomas, St. Paul, 1996-2000; prof. U. Catolica, Talca, Chile, 2000—. Bd. dirs. Am. Forum for Global Edn. Trustee assoc. Boston Coll. Spanish Govt. grantee, 1965-67; OAS grantee, 1967-68; Fulbright grantee, 1972-73 Mem. Inter-Am. Confedn. Cath. Edn., Internat. Orgn. Cath. Edn., Nat. Cath. Ednl. Assn., Internat. Fedn. Cath. Univs., Delta Epsilon Sigma. Roman Catholic. Home: 1880 Randolph Ave Saint Paul MN 55101 Personal E-mail: cmncsj@hotmail.com.

**MCNAMEE, JAMES M.,** lab administrator; With Hooper Holmes, Inc., Basking Ridge, NJ, 1968—79, officer, 1979—84, pres., CEO, 1984—, chmn., bd. dirs., 1996—. Mem., exec. com. and nom. com. Hooper Holmes, Inc., Basking Ridge, NJ. Office: Hooper Holmes Inc 170 Mt Airy Rd Basking Ridge NJ 07920

**MCNAMEE, LAWRENCE ROSS, JR.,** manufacturing executive; b. Gary, Ind., June 7, 1931; s. Lawrence Ross and Pearl Agnes (Heyburn) McNamee; m. Mary Ann Youlden, 1956; children: Lawrence R. III, Catherine Ann, John Charles. BA, Claremont McKenna Coll., 1957; MBA, Claremont Grad. U., 1958; postgrad., UCLA. Supr. Gen. Dynamics, Pomona, Calif., 1958-61; mem. staff Arthur D. Little, Inc., LA, 1961-65; dir. Booz Allen & Hamilton, LA, 1965-70; gen. mgr. Hydril Co., LA, 1970-76; pres. Diogenes Group, LA, 1976-91; chmn., CEO Radiant Tech. Corp., Fullerton, Calif., 1991-2005, GreenBridge Tech., Inc., Fullerton, 2006—. With U.S. Army, 1952-54. Mem.: Ops. Rsch. Soc. Am., Turn Around Mgmt. Assn., Semiconductor Equipment and Materials Internat., Malibu Orchid Soc. (pres. 2003), Getty Villa Coun., Calif. Yacht Club. Avocations: sailing, fishing, photography, art collecting. Office: GreenBridge Tech Inc 1335 S Acacia Ave Fullerton CA 92831-5315

**MCNAMEE, MARK,** academic administrator; BS in Chemistry, MIT, 1968; PhD, Stanford U., 1973. Postdoctoral assoc. Columbia U. Coll., 1973—75; asst. prof. U. Calif., Davis, 1975—85, prof., 1985, chair dept. biochemistry and biophysics, 1990—93, dean divsn. biol. scis., 1993—2001; provost, v.p. Va. Tech., Blacksburg, 2001—. Office: Va Tech Univ Provost and VP for Acad Affairs 210 Burruss Hall Blacksburg VA 24061

**MCNAMEE, REBECCA LANDES,** engineering educator, researcher; b. Pitts., Oct. 29, 1970; d. John David and Anne Ruth Landes; m. Kenneth McNamee, June 3, 1995; children: John Landes, Patrick Kenneth. PhD, U. Pitts., 1999. Prof./rsch. scientist U. Pitts., 1999—. Grantee, Nat. Inst. on Drug Abuse, 2002—. Mem.: IEEE (assoc.), Orgn. for Human Brain Mapping (assoc.), Tau Beta Pi (assoc.). Office: Univ Pitts 707 Salk Hall Pittsburgh PA 15261 Office Phone: 412-383-7324. Office Fax: 412-624-1929. Business E-Mail: bmcnamee@pitt.edu.

**MCNAMEE, ROGER B.,** venture capitalist, musician; BA, Yale Univ.; MBA, Tuck Sch. Bus., Dartmouth Coll. Portfolio mgr. T. Rowe Price Assoc., 1988—91; co-founder, gen. ptnr. Integral Capital Partners, Menlo Park, Calif., 1991—, Silver Lake Partners, 1999—, Elevation Partners, 2004—. Guitarist, lead vocalist Flying Other Brothers Band. Author: The New Normal, Penguin Books, 2004; panelist, Louis Rukeyser's Wall Street, CNBC; record albums: IPO, San Francisco Sounds Trustee Bryn Mawr Coll.; mem. bd. overseers Amos Tuck Sch. Bus, Dartmouth Coll.; dir. Rex Found. Office: Integral Capital Partners Bldg 3 Ste 240 3000 Sand Hill Rd Menlo Park CA 94025

**MCNAMEE, STEPHEN M.,** federal judge; b. 1942; BA, U. Cinn., 1964; MA, U. Ariz., 1967, JD, 1969. US atty. Dist. of Ariz., Phoenix, 1985-90; judge US Dist. Ct. Ariz., Phoenix, 1990—, chief judge, 1999—2006. Office: US Dist Judge Sandra Day O'Connor US Ct 401 W Washington St SPC 60 Phoenix AZ 85003-2158 Office Phone: 602-322-7555.

**MCNATT, GLENN,** art critic; With Time magazine; editl. writer, columnist Baltimore Sun, 1985—95, art columnist, 1995—99, art critic, 1999—. Office: Baltimore Sun Co 501 N Calvert St PO Box 1377 Baltimore MD 21278 Office Phone: 410-332-6051. Business E-Mail: glenn.mcnatt@baltsun.com.

**MCNAUGHT, WILLIAM P.,** museum director; b. Portland, Oreg., July 6, 1943; s. Robert Roland and Irene Plover McNaught. BA, Portland State U., 1966; MA, Oberlin Coll., Ohio, 1968; post grad., U. Pa., Phila., 1968—70. Lectr. Frick Collection, NYC, 1971—75; NY regional dir. Archives of Am. Art Smithsonian Instn., NYC, 1976—89; dir. Am. Mus. in Britain, Bath, England, 1989—2003, Oysterponds Hist. Soc., Orient, NY, 2003—. Pres. Am. Friends of Attingham Summer Sch., NYC, 1986—89; coun. mem. Attingham Summer Sch. Trust, London, 1995—; trustee Bath Preservation Trust, 1997—2003. Office: Oysterponds Hist Soc Village Ln Box 70 Orient NY 11957

**MCNAUGHTON, KENNETH JOHN,** former publisher; b. Melbourne, Australia, July 22, 1940; arrived in U.S., 1970, naturalized, 2005; s. Charles Dudley and Lilian May (Beard) McN.; m. Victoria Ann Yocum, Oct. 28, 1972 (div. Oct. 1982); children: Aurelius John, Candace Ann. B in Chem. Engring., U. Melbourne, 1961; M in Engring. Sci., Monash U., Clayton, Australia, 1964. Dir. comm. network Found. Faith, N.Y.C., 1966-77; asst. editor Chemical Engring., N.Y.C., 1978-81, assoc. editor, 1981-86; editor-in-chief Industrial Chemist, N.Y.C., 1986-89; dir. new publs. divsn. sci. and tech. Warren Gorham & Lamont, N.Y.C., 1989-90; mng. editor Physics Today, N.Y.C., 1991-94; assoc. pub. The Industrial Physicist, College Park, Md., 1995—2004. Pres. McNaughton Comms., N.Y., 1978—. Contbr. over 100 articles to profl. jours.; photo exhibitions, Ellicott City, Md., 2005. Mem. Friends of Benjamin Banneker Hist. Park, Oella, Md., 1996—; founder Campaign to Save the Trees, Roosevelt Island, N.Y., 1991; pres. PTA H.S. for the Humanities, N.Y., 1990-91; pres. bd. dirs. Greystone Condominiums, N.Y.C., 1998-2003; mem. Port Phillip Pioneers Group. Avocations: music, dance, films, swimming, walking. Home: 3778 College Ave Ellicott City MD 21043-4662 Office Phone: 410-418-9340. Personal E-mail: kjmcn@comcast.net.

**MCNAUGHTON, WILLIAM FRANK,** translator, educator; b. Westboro, Mo., May 21, 1933; s. Frank McNaughton and Ruth Ellen (Flanders) Francis; m. Margaret Orminski, Apr. 4, 1956 (div. 1971); children: John Ferenc, Dorothy Ellen; m. Li Ying, Apr. 8, 1990; 1 child, Andrea. Student, U. Mo., 1951-53; studied poetry and translation with Ezra Pound, 1953-56; student, Georgetown U., 1953-54; BA, Bklyn. Coll., 1961; PhD, Yale U., 1965. Asst. prof. Oberlin (Ohio) Coll., 1965-70; lectr. Exptl. Coll., Oberlin, 1970-71; vis. lectr. Bowling Green (Ohio) State U., 1972-74, Denison U., Granville, Ohio, 1972-78; prof. Program for Afloat Coll. Edn. (PACE) USN, Norfolk, Va., 1978-84; vis. prof. King Saud U., Abha, Saudi Arabia, 1984-85; sr. lectr. English, translation Cuny Poly. Hong Kong, 1986-89; prin. lectr. translation, 1989-94; univ. sr. lectr. City U., Hong Kong, 1994-95, assoc. prof., 1995-98; retired, 1998. Guest lectr., U. degli Studii, Venice, Italy, 1975; coord. Tri-Coll. Chinese program, Oberlin, Ohio, 1969-70; vis. lectr. Lakes Colls. Assoc., Ann Arbor, 1965-68; cons., Asian Lit. program Asia Soc., N.Y.C., 1967-80, Nat. Translation Ctr., Austin, Tex., 1965-68, Ballantine Books, N.Y.C., 1985, Princeton U. Press, 1965; presenter

papers at lit. confs. Author: Reading and Writing Chinese, 1979, rev. edit. 1999, Simplified Character Edit., 2005, Pound's Usura and the Islamic Concept of Riba, 1996; co-translator: Poem Without a Hero and Selected Poems of Anna Akhmatova, 1989, As Though Dreaming: The Tz'u...of Li Ch'ing-chao, 1977, A Gold Orchid: The Love Poems of Tzu Yeh, 1972; editor, translator: Light from the East, 1978, The Confucian Vision, 1974, The Book of Songs, 1971, The Taoist Vision, 1971, Guerilla War, 1971; contbr. articles to profl. publs., translations to various lit. mags.; editor-in-chief: City Univ. Bull., 1995-98; mem. editl. bd. City Univ. Press, 1996-98. Woodrow Wilson Found. fellow, 1961-62; modern fgn. lang. fellow, NDEA, 1962-65; grantee, Nat. Translation Ctr., Austin, 1967, Gt. Lakes Colls. Assn., Ann Arbor, 1965, 67-68, Asia Soc., N.Y.C., 1971-72, 74; Fulbright fellow, 1968-69. Avocations: sailing, music, venetian culture and history. Home and Office: Flat 20C Block 26 Baguio Villa 555 Victoria Pokfulam Hong Kong Office Phone: 852 2776 1426. Personal E-mail: wmcnaughton@netvigator.com.

**MCNAUGHTON, WILLIAM JOHN,** retired bishop; b. Lawrence, Mass., Dec. 7, 1926; s. William John Sr. and Ruth Irene (Howe) McN. BA, U. of State of N.Y., Ossining, 1948, B of Sacred Theology, 1953; M in Religious Edn., Maryknoll Sem., Ossining, 1953. Ordained Maryknoll priest, 1953; cert. in Korean Lang. Studies, Yale U., 1954. Pastor Pouk Moun Ro Cath. Ch., Chong Ju Diocese, Korea, 1955-57, Nae Duk Dong Cath. Ch., Chong Ju Diocese, Korea, 1957-60; consultor Chong Ju Diocese, 1958-59, vicar gen., 1959-60; consecrated bishop Inchon (Korea) Diocese, 1961—2002, ret., 2002. Roman Catholic. Address: 39 Woodburn Dr Methuen MA 01844-2812

**MCNEAL, BETTY JEAN,** librarian, writer; b. Houston, Pa., July 31, 1932; d. Eugene and Lyda Harper Dent; m. James W McNeal, Apr. 12, 1982; m. Coleman Lewis, June 5, 1958 (div.); 1 child, John Elliott Lewis. BS in Edn., Cheyney State Tchrs. Coll., 1955; MLS, We. Mich. U., 1976; JD, Cleve. State U., 1966. Bar: Ohio 1967. Tchr. Youngstown Pub. Schs., Ohio, 1955—58, Cleve. Pub. Schs., 1958—61; libr. Wash. State U., Pullman, 1976—84; dir. pub. svcs. Gonzaga U. Law Libr., Spokane, Wash., 1984—86; dir. Nev. State Data Ctr., Carson City, 1988—94; dir. info. svcs. Internat. Gaming Inst. U. Nev., Las Vegas, 1997—. Author: Amazing Plan for Total Success, 2000. Trustee East Cleve. Pub. Libr., 1970—71. Recipient Excellence in Jurisprudence, Lawyers Coop. Pub. Co.; Thurgood Marshall fellow, We. Mich. U., 1975—76. Mem.: Thoreau Soc. Achievements include design of Truth/Character/Wealth Power Plan for life renewal. Office: University of Nevada Las Vegas 4505 Maryland Parkway Las Vegas NV 89154

**MCNEAL, JAMES E.,** music educator; b. Greeley, Colo., June 12, 1941; s. Wayne and Olive V. McNeal; m. Priscilla R. Stolarczyk, June 12, 1965; children: Michael, Nancy. BA, U. No. Colo., Greeley; MA, Colo. State U., Ft. Collins. Dir. orchs. St. Vrain Valley Schs., Longmont, Colo., 1967—72, Poutre Sch. Dist., Ft. Collins, 1972—2005.

**MCNEAL, JANE ERSKINE,** music educator, musician; b. Somers Point, NJ, Oct. 29, 1958; d. James Kelley and Jane Emma McNeal. BA Psychology, Stockton State Coll., 1983; music studies, Wheaton Coll., Ill., 1976—78; Kindermusik Cert., Westminster Choir Coll., Princeton, NJ, 1997; Crescendo Music Cert., Acad. Cmty. Music, Ft. Washington, Pa., 2005. Choir dir., NJ, 1991—95; piano instr. NJ, 1975—; vocal instr. Vineland, NJ, 1999—; profl. accompanist NJ, 1976—; ch. and synagogue organist NJ, 1983—; organ and piano recitalist NJ, 1989—. Advocate for mentally ill. Scholar music scholarship, Wheaton Coll., 1976, Nat. Merit Corp. Scholarship, Sun Shipbuilding, Chester, Pa., 1976—78. Mem.: Local Musicians Union, Am. Guild Organists, Nat. Guild Piano Tchrs., Psi Chi. Avocations: walking, classical music, jazz, reading. Home: 529 Sassafras St Millville NJ 08332 Office: St Bernadette Cath Ch 1421 New Rd Northfield NJ 08225 Office Phone: 609-646-5611.

**MCNEAL, LYLE GLEN,** science educator, rancher, consultant; b. Glendale, Calif., May 16, 1942; s. Darrell Glenn and Elizabeth Bessie McNeal; m. Nancy Coles Wilkie, Aug. 10, 1962; children: Tamara A., Sean E., Joshua M., Travis G., Susannah R., Jenny L., Ian B., Ilene L. BS in Animal Husbandry, Cal Poly Coll., 1964; MS in Animal Breeding, U. Nev., 1966; PhD in Reproductive Physiology, Utah State U., 1978. Shepherd Cal Poly Coll., Pomona, 1962—64; prof. animal sci. Cal Poly State U., San Luis Obispo, Calif., 1969—79; grad. rsch. asst. U. Nev., Reno, 1964—66, extension agt. Minden, 1966—69; rsch. scientist U.S. Sheep Experiment Sta., Dubois, Idaho, 1972—77; founder, exec. dir. Navajo Sheep Project, Logan, Utah, 1977—2002; prof. animal sci. Utah State U., Logan, 1979—. Ranch hand Bar Lazy B Ranch, Ronan, Mont., 1959—61; asst. ranch mgr. Hidden Trails Ranch, Agoura, Calif., 1960—61; Arabian horse showman Kellogg Arabian Horse Ranch, Pomona. Author: Small Ruminant Production Medicine, 2002; contbr. chapters to books. 1st lt. USAF, 1959—61, Norton AFB. Named Tchr. of Yr, U.S.D.A., 1990—94; recipient award, NHL, 1994, Nat. Camptender award, Am. Sheep Industry Assn. Mem.: Am. Livestock Breeds Conservancy (Conservation Breeder of Yr. 1996), Soc. Range Mgmt., Am. Soc. Animal Sci. (mem. tchg. com. 1972—77, Nat. Tchr. of Yr. 1996), Am. Sheep Ctr. (mem. founding bd. 1999—), Navajo-Churro Sheep Assn. (life; hon. 1986—), Dine' be'iina (life; hon. 1991—). Achievements include rescued from extinction the first domestic sheep brought to North America by the Spanish conquistadores; saved and bred back this famous Navajo-Churro sheep for the benefit of Navajo and Hispanic cultures, 1977-2002. Avocations: horseback riding, fly fishing, piloting aircraft, history, reading. Home: 85 Quarter Circle Dr Logan UT 84321 Office: Animal & Vet Dept Utah State U 4815 Old Main Hill Logan UT 84322-4815 E-mail: sheepman@cc.usu.edu.

**MCNEAL, PHYLLIS PAULETTE,** parole agent; d. Earline Brown. BA in Psychology, Calif. State U., Long Beach, 1982; MSW, Calif. State U., San Bernardino, 2003. Mental health intern Jenesse Domestic Violence Ctr., LA, 2001—01, Los Padrinos Juvenile Hall, Downey, Calif., 2002—03; group supr. Calif. Youth Authority, Norwalk, 1981—84, youth counselor Ontario, 1984—89; parole agt. I parole and cmty. svcs. divsn. Calif. Dept. Corrections, Inglewood, 1989—99, asst. unit supr. LA, 1999—. Sponsor Calif. Youth Authoity, Ontario, 1986—89; small group tng. instr. Calif. Youth Authority, Onartio, 1986—89; founder, CEO Straight Talk Program, Inc., Corona, Calif., 1990—; coll. internship coord. parole and cmty. svcs. divsn. Calif. Dept. Corrections, Ingelwood, 1990—98, defensive tactics instr., LA, 1991—99. Author: Corrections in America an Introduction, 9th edit. (Correctional Champions, 2001); editor: Corrections Today Mag. (Best in the Bus., 1998). Prison min. Abundant Living Family Ch., Rancho Cucamonga, Calif., 2003—05; prison com. mem. Nat. Assn. Equal Justice in Am., Compton, Calif., 2002—05; bd. dirs. Cornerstone Accelerated Learning Acad., LA, 2001—05. Named Parole Agt. of the Yr., Calif. Probation, Parole, and Correctional Assn., 1998, Citizen of the Week, KNX Newsradio 1265, 1998, Hero Of the Week, UPN Channel 13, 1998; recipient Cmty. Stars award, Staples, 1999, award, Freedom Jour., 2000, Trailblazer Award, First AME Ch., 2004, amb. of Progress, Blackwall St., 2005, Local Heroes Neighborhood Excellence award, Bank of Am., 2005. Mem.: Save Our Sons (assoc.; publicity com. mem. 2000—05), Black Women's Network (assoc.), Delta Sigma Theta (life; dean pledge 1980). Office: Straight Talk Program Inc PO Box 5693 Norco CA 92860 Business E-Mail: straighttalkprogram@charter.net.

**MCNEALEY, ERNEST,** college president; m. Earnestine Green; children: Ernest II, David. BS, Ala. State U.; MAT, Ind. U.; PhD, Ohio State U. V.p. acad. affairs undergrad. acad. affairs Claflin (S.C.) U.; assoc. provost, dean of undergrad. acad. affairs SUNY, Stony Brook; pres. Stillman Coll., Tuscaloosa, Ala., 1997—. Office: Stillman Coll PO Box 1430 Tuscaloosa AL 35403-1430 E-mail: emcnealey@stillman.edu.*

**MCNEALY, SCOTT GLENN,** information technology executive; b. Columbus, Ind., Nov. 13, 1954; s. Raymond William and Marmaline McNealy; m. Susan Ingemanson, 1994; 4 children. BA, Harvard U., 1976; MBA, Stanford U., 1980. With Rockwell Internat. Corp., Troy, Mich., 1976-78, sales engr.; staff engr. FMC Corp., Chgo., 1980-81; dir. ops. Onyx Systems, San

Jose, Calif., 1981-82; co-founder Sun Microsystems, Inc., Santa Clara, Calif., 1982, v.p. ops., 1982—84, COO, 1984, pres., 1984—99, 2002—04, CEO 1984—2006, chmn., 1984—. Bd. dirs. Sun Microsystems, Inc., 1982—. Named one of World's Richest People, Forbes Mag., 400 Richest Americans, America's Most Powerful People. Avocation: hockey. Office: Sun Microsystems Inc 4150 Network Cir Santa Clara CA 95054*

**MCNEANEY, LEE ANNE,** physical education educator; b. Worcester, Mass., Aug. 15, 1953; d. Richard C. and Barbara M. Bogart; m. David R. McNeaney, Aug. 20, 1977; 1 child, Brian D. BS, Bridgewater State Coll., Mass., 1975. Cert. K-12 health and phys. edn. Mass. Gymnastic dir. Worcester Girls Club, 1975—80; health/phys. edn. tchr. North Brookfield (Mass.) Pub. Schs., 1980—. Health Protection grantee, Mass. Dept. Edn., Safe Schs. for Gay/Lesbian Teens grantee, Safe and Drug Free Schs. grantee, Fed. Govt. Mem.: AAHPERD, Mass. Assn. for Health, Phys. Edn., Recreation and Dance. Avocations: boating, skiing, bicycling, tennis. Home: 5 Point Rd North Brookfield MA 01535 Office: North Brookfield Elem Sch 10 High School Dr North Brookfield MA 01535-2095

**MCNEELY, JAMES LEE,** lawyer; b. Shelbyville, Ind., May 4, 1940; s. Carl R. and Elizabeth J. (Orebaugh) McN.; m. Rose M. Wisker, Sept. 5, 1977; children: Angela, Susan, Meg, Matt. AB, Wabash Coll., 1962; JD, Ind. U., 1965. Bar: Ind. 1965, U.S. Dist. Ct. (so. dist.) Ind. 1965, U.S. Ct. Appeals (7th cir.) 1970. Assoc. Pell & Mitchell, Shelbyville, 1965-70; ptnr. Matchett & McNeely, Shelbyville, 1970-74; sole practice Shelbyville, 1974-76; sr. ptnr. McNeely & Sanders, Shelbyville, 1976-86, McNeely, Sanders & Stephenson, Shelbyville, 1986-89, McNeely, Sanders, Stephenson & Thopy, Shelbyville, 1989-96, McNeely, Stephenson, Thopy & Harrold, Shelbyville, 1997—. Guest lectr. Franklin Coll., Ind., 1965-72; judge Shelbyville City Ct., 1967-71. Chmn. Shelbyville County Rep. Cen. Com., 1968-88; bd. dirs. Ind. Lung Assn., 1972-75, Crossroads Council Boy Scouts Am., 1982; bd. dirs., pres. Shelbyville Girls Club. Named Sagamore of the Wabash, Gov. Ed Whitcomb, 1971, Gov. Otis Bowen, 1977, Gov. Robert Orr, 1986, 88, Gov. Evan Bayh, 1996, Gov. Frank O'Bannon, 1999. Fellow Ind. Bar Found. (patron, sec. 1999-2000, chair elect 2000-01, chmn. 2002-03); mem. ABA, Ind. Bar Assn. (sec. 1985-87, bd. dirs. 1976-78, chair-elect Ho. Dels. 1994-95, chair 1995-96, v.p. 1996-97, pres.-elect 1997-98, pres. 1998-99), Shelby County Bar Assn. (pres. 1975), Ind. Lawyers Commn. (pres., dir.), Fed. Merit Selection Commn. (adv. mem. 1988-92, chmn. 2001—), Shelbyville Jaycees (Distinguished Service award 1969, Good Govt. award 1970), Wabash Coll. Nat. Assn. Wabash Men (dir. 1983-89, sec. 1989-91, v.p. 1991-93, pres. 1993-95, Man of Yr. 1995), Kappa Sigma Alpha Pi chpt. (Hall of Fame 1995). Lodges: Lions, Elks, Eagles. Methodist. Avocations: golf, travel. Home: 1902 E Old Rushville Rd Shelbyville IN 46176-9569

**MCNEELY, PATRICIA GANTT,** communications educator; b. Winnsboro, S.C., Dec. 2, 1939; d. William Adolphus and Alice (Woodson) Gantt; m. Alfred Raymond McNeely, Apr. 8, 1960; children: Allison Patricia, Alan David. BA, Furman U., 1960; MA, U. S.C., 1975. Reporter Greenville (S.C.) News, 1958-60, Columbia (S.C.) Record, 1960-66, 66-72, news editor, 1979-80; reporter The State, Columbia, 1965-66; prof. journalism U. S.C., Columbia, 1972—, Eleanor M. and R. Frank Mundy prof. of journalism, 2000—, dir. print and electronic sequence, 2000—. State mgr. Voter News Svc., N.Y., 1972—; workshop dir. Reader's Digest, Pleasantville, N.Y., 1985—. Author: Fighting Words: A History of the Media of South Carolina, The Palmetto Press: The History of South Carolina's Newspapers and the Press Association. Mem. Assn. for Edn. in Journalism and Mass Comm. (sec. mag. divsn. 1995-96, head newspaper divsn. 1988-89, standing profl. freedom and responsibility com. 1995-98). Office: Univ SC Coll Journalism Mass Comm Blossom At Assembly Sts Columbia SC 29208-0001

**MCNEIL, BARBARA JOYCE,** radiologist, educator; b. Cambridge, Mass., Feb. 11, 1941; d. Archibald Pius and Katherine (Joyce) McNeil. AB, Emmanuel Coll., 1962; MD, Harvard U., 1966, PhD, 1972. Diplomate Am. Bd. Nuc. Medicine. Intern Mass. Gen. Hosp., Boston, 1966—67, resident in nuclear medicine, 1971—73; radiologist nuclear medicine Brigham and Women's Hosp., 1974—, Dana-Farber Cancer Inst., Boston, 1976—; prof. radiology and clin. epidemiology Harvard Med. Sch. and Brigham & Women's Hosp., Boston, 1983—88, dir. ctr. for cost effective care, 1980—93; chmn. Dept. Health Care Policy Harvard Med. Sch., 1988—, Ridley Watts prof. health care policy, 1990—. Chmn. Blue Cross-Mass. Hosp. Assn. Fund for Coop. Innovation, 1981—87; mem. Prospective Payment Assessment Commn., 1983—91; mem. nat. adv. coun. Agy. for Health Care Policy, Rsch. and Evaluation, 1991—96; mem. med. adv. com. Blue Cross Blue Shield, 1993—; mem. coverage adv. com. Medicare, 2001—. Contbr. articles to profl. jours. Recipient Rsch. Career Develop. award, Nat. Inst. Health, 1976—81. Fellow: AAAS, Am. Coll. Nuc. Physicians (Presdl. award 1995); mem.: Soc. Nuc. Medicine, Am. Coll. Radiology. Inst. Medicine (coun. 1999—), Am. Acad. Arts and Scis. Office: Harvard Med Sch Dept Health Care Policy 180 Longwood Ave Rm 202-A Boston MA 02115-5821 Business E-Mail: mcneil@hcp.med.harvard.edu.

**MCNEIL, BARRY,** lawyer; b. Lubbock, Tex., June 29, 1944; BA, Tex. Tech U., 1966; JD, U. Tex., 1969. Bar: Tex. 1969, admitted to practice: US Supreme Ct. 1969, US Dist. Ct. (Ea. Dist.) Tex., US Dist. Ct. (So. Dist.) Tex., US Dist. Ct. (No. Dist.) Tex., US Ct. Appeals (5th Cir.). Trial atty. antitrust divsn. Dept. Justice, 1970-75, chief Dallas office antitrust divsn., 1975-79; ptnr. & head Antitrust & Securities Group Haynes and Boone LLP, Dallas. Co-editor: Internal Corp. Investigations (2nd edit.). Fellow: Am. Coll. Trial Lawyers; mem.: ABA (chmn. Litig. Sect. 1996—97). Office: Haynes and Boone LLP 901 Main St Ste 3100 Dallas TX 75202-3789 Office Phone: 214-651-5580. Office Fax: 214-200-0535. Business E-Mail: barry.mcneil@haynesboone.com.

**MCNEIL, EDWARD WARREN,** real estate company executive; b. Alhambra, Calif., Jan. 5, 1942; s. Murray Charles and Helen Katherine (Curtis) McN.; m. Jutta Bocking, Apr. 1, 1941; children: Anja Britt, Bradley Stuart. Student, U. Calif., Berkeley, 1960-63. Structures engr. Peter Kiewit Sons Co., various cities, Calif., 1961-63; project engr. Huntington Harbour, Sunset Beach, Calif., 1963-64; project supt. Coordinated Realty, Inc., Anaheim, Calif., 1964-65; field ops. mgr. Lear Siegler, Saigon, Vietnam, 1965-67; project engr. Constructora Emkay, Rio Blanco, Chile, 1968-69; ptnr. The Pyramid Cos., Syracuse, NY, 1969-75, The Pioneer Group, Syracuse, 1975-95, ret., 1995. Past chmn., bd. dirs. Crouse Irving Meml. Hosp. Found., Syracuse, 1986—2005; emeritus bd. dirs. Crouse Irving Meml. Hosp. Found., Syracuse, 2005—; trustee, past vice-chmn. Everson Mus. Art, Syracuse, 1981—94; past chmn., vice-chmn., bd. dirs. Syracuse Stage, 1981—93; chmn. Adirondack chpt. Nature Conservancy, 1994—2001, trustee, 2002—, trustee N.Y. state bd., 1998—; trustee Adirondack Land Trust, 1990—2002, chmn., 1994—2001; trustee Manlius Pebble Hill Sch., 1984—86, 1994—99, emeritus, 1999—; vol. pilot Nature Conservancy, No. Wings. Recipient award for svc. to the arts, Cultural Resource Coun., Syracuse, 1987. Mem. Seaplane Pilots Assn., Slocum Soc., Lake Amphibian Flyers Club, Warbirds of Am., No. Lake Flyers Club. Avocations: sailing, canoeing, fly fishing, seaplane flying.

**MCNEIL, HELEN JO CONNOLLY,** nursing educator, public health administrator; b. Olympia, Wash., June 15, 1925; d. James Ambrose and Corinne Marie (Bordeaux) Connolly; m. Robert Phillip McNeil, Aug. 16, 1947; children: Sheryl Ann Andrews, Robert John, Maureen Connolly McNeil, Kevin Charles. BSN, Seattle Coll., 1947; MSN, U. Wash., Seattle, 1961; postgrad., U. Wash., 1974—80. RN Wash., S.C., Tex., Va., cert. pub. health nurse, 1962. Clinic nurse Schutt Clinic, Bremerton, Wash., 1947-49; staff nurse Providence Hosp., Seattle, 1950-60, Overlake Hosp., Bellevue, Wash., 1961-62; pub. health nurse Seattle King County Health Dept. and Vis. Nurse Svc., 1962-64; pub. health nurse supr., 1964-65, assoc. dir. pub. health nursing and vis. nurse svc., 1965-70, health planning and evaluation specialist, 1970-73, adminstr. S.E. dist., 1973-78, adminstr. Ctrl. dist., 1979-81, adminstr. N. dist., 1981-84, dir. nursing rsch., 1984-85; lectr. Sch. Nursing U. Wash., Seattle, 1985-87; mem. faculty S. Puget Sound C.C., Olympia,

1987-88; vis. faculty Sch. Nursing Clemson (S.C.) U., 1988; instr. coll. nursing allied health U. Tex., El Paso, 1988-90; dir. pub. health nursing Commonwealth Va., Richmond, 1990-93; lectr. Sch. Nursing Seattle U., 1995; cons. Seattle, Seaview, Wash., 1995—. Mem. panel in nursing edn. Am. Assn. Colls. of Nursing, 1985—87; adj. assoc. prof. Sch. Pub. Health U. N.C., Chapel Hill, 1980—92; adj. asst. prof. U. Wash. Sch. Nursing, 1965—85; rev. com. nursing census USPHS, 1970—72; health care cons., Kuwait, 1976; lectr. Congress on Nutrition, Rio de Janeiro, 1978. Author: Feasting on a Moveable Island, 1980, Reaching Out, 1998; contbr. articles to profl. jours., chpts. to books. Mem. task force Seattle Health Policy, 1981, Seattle 2000 Commn., 1973; lectr. Internat. Congress Social Psychiatry, Athens, 1973; with Project Hope Internat. Approaches in Health Care of Elderly, Milwood, Va., 1983-84; co-project dir. occupl. health con. edn. for cmty. nurses divsn. nursing U. Wash., 1983-86; mem. ARC Disater Team, Seattle, 1995-97, Parent and Home Health Bd., Richmond, Va., 1990-93; vol. Red Cross, 1994-97. With U.S. cadet nursing corps USPHS, 1943-47. Stress Rsch. grantee Heath Resources Adminstrn., 1974, W. K. Kellog Found. grantee U. Tex., El Paso, 1990, grantee U. Wash., 1983-86; recipient Nursing Adminstrn. Recognition award Jour. Nursing Adminstrn., 1993. Fellow: APHA (nursing sect. pres. 1992—93, Ruth B. Freeman Disting. Career award 1998); mem.: Assn. State and Territorial Dirs. Nursing (emeritus), Seattle Mgmt. Assn. (pres. 1976, Disting Adminstrv. Svc. award City of Seattle 1976), Wash. State Pub. Health Assn. (pres. 1976—77, Adminstrv. Svc. award 1975), Assn. Cmty. Health Nurse Educators (founder, pres. 1985), Seattle U. Alumni (mem. nursing adv. bd. 1993—96, Cmty. Svc. Alumni award 1992), Sigma Theta Tau (internat. rsch. conf. Seoul, South Korea 1984). Avocations: gardening, travel, writing, cooking, paddocks for six hourses. Home and Office: PO Box 173 Seaview WA 98644-0173 Office Phone: 360-642-4958.

**MCNEIL, JAN TORBET,** communications educator; d. James Wesley and Maggie Mae (Eastep) Torbet; children: Torbet, Merica. BS, La. State U., Baton Rouge, 1971; MA, Memphis State U., 1973, U. Memphis, 1996; PhD, Fla. State U., 2000; MEd, U. Hawaii, 2004. Cert. intercultural found. Inst. for Intercultural Comm., Oreg., 2006, internat. practitioner Inst. for Intercultural Comm., Oreg., 2006, tchr. speech and journalism La., tchr. speech Tenn., tchr. ESL added Tenn. Typist La. State Legislature, Baton Rouge, 1967; counselor Camp Merri-Mac for Girls, Black Mountain, NC, 1968; welfare technician La. Dept. Pub. Welfare, Homer, 1972; mgr., prodr. TV program Memphis City Schs., 1974—77; account exec. Memphis Mag., 1978—80; pubs.' rep. Advt. Subscribers Enterprises, Cleve., 1985—86; account mgr. The Image Makers, Memphis, 1987—88; mktg. mgr. Memphis Sash & Door Co., 1988—89; speech instr. State Tech. Inst. at Memphis, 1992—97, N.W. Miss. C.C., Southaven, Miss., 1992—97; instr. English comm. U. Memphis, 1995—97, Fla. State U., Tallahassee, 1997—2001, Ping Tung (Taiwan) Girls' H.S., Ping Tung, 1998, TransPacific Hawaii Coll., Honolulu, 2001, Nat. U. Singapore, 2001—03, TransPacific Hawaii Coll., Honolulu, 2003—06. Corp. trainer Edgesharp GmbH, Wiesbaden, Germany, 2004; vis. prof. English comm. George Simons Internat., Nice, France, 2004; trainer, cons. English comm. U.S. Civilian R & D Corp., Moscow, 2004, Bakuriana, Georgia, 04, TransPacific Hawaii Coll., 2005—06; corp. trainer Japan-Amer. Inst. of Mgmt. Sci., Honolulu, 2006; instr. Taiwanese Summer Prog., Honolulu, 2006; oral examiner U. Cambridge, England, 2006; referee profl. jours. Recipient Am. Legion award, 1967. Mem.: Japan-Am. Inst. Mgmt. Sci., Soc. for Intercultural Edn., Tng., and Rsch., Tchrs. of English as 2d Lang. Internat. (newsletter editor, intercultural comm. interest group 2001—03). Avocations: travel, intercultural events and movies, health and wellness, professional growth activities. Personal E-mail: jantmcneil@yahoo.com.

**MCNEIL, MALCOLM RAY,** speech educator, researcher; b. Cheboygan, Mich., Nov. 2, 1947; s. Richard Lee and Velma May (Collins) McN.; m. Katherine Alice Bonus, Oct. 30, 1971 (div. 1987); children: Sarah Catherine, Matthew Collins; m. Sheila Rose Pratt, Dec. 30, 1989; children: Kealsey Brennan, Meghan Anna. BS, No. Mich. U., 1969, MA, 1971; PhD, U. Denver, 1977. Staff speech pathologist VA Hosp., Denver, 1972-76; predoctoral fellow Dept. Neurology, Mayo Clinic, Rochester, 1976-77; asst. prof. U. Colo., Boulder, 1977-80, U. Wis., Madison, 1980-82, assoc. prof., 1982-87, prof., 1987-92; prof., chair dept. U. Pitts, 1992—. Cons. VA Hosp., Madison, 1980-92, VA Med. Ctr., Pitts. Contbr. over 37 book chpts., 1976—; author: Revised Token test, 1978; contbr. over 100 articles to profl. jours.; assoc. editor Jour. of Speech and Hearing Disorders, 1990-92, Jour. of Speech and Hearing Rsch., 1992-95. Grantee NIH, 1982, 86; named Disting. Alumni award No. Mich. U., 1989. Mem. Am. Speech-Lang.-Hearing Assn.(honors 2004, chancellor's rsch. award 2005, Disting. Svc. prof., 2006), Acad. Aphasia, Acad. Neurol. Communicative Disorders. Democrat. Lutheran. Avocations: golf, theater, music, baseball, basketball. Home: 5445 Aylesboro Ave Pittsburgh PA 15217-1121 Office: U Pitts Comm Sci and Disorder 4033 Forbes Tower Pittsburgh PA 15260

**MCNEIL, MONA MARGARET,** clinical psychologist; b. Bklyn., Sept. 12, 1947; d. William A. and Margaret M. (Kenny) McLoughlin; m. Donald R. Takush, July 7, 1966 (div. 1981); 1 child, Melissa Takush; m. Randall Ring Kleinhesselink, Aug. 5, 1983. Student, Manhattanville Coll., 1965-66; BS in Zoology, U. Wash., 1976; MS in Clin. Psychology, Calif. State, Bakersfield, 1979; PhD in Clin. Psychology, Wash. State U., 1987. Lic. psychologist, Oreg., Wash. Psychology cons. Pioneer Community Hosp., Bakersfield, 1978-79; instr. Wash. State U., Pullman, Wash., 1983; lectr. U. Idaho, Moscow, 1984-85; psychol. asst. Lewiston, Idaho, 1981-85; intern Seattle VA Med. Ctr., 1985-86; lectr., supr. U. Idaho, Moscow, 1986-87; acting dir. alcohol studies Wash. State U., Pullman, 1988; clin. psychologist Affiliated Psychol. Assocs., Inc., Portland, Oreg., 1988—. Adj. faculty Wash. State U., Pullman, 1984—. Vol. therapist Cascade AIDS Project; active NOW, Nat. Abortion Rights Action League, Planned Parenthood. Mem. Oreg. Psychol. Assn., N.W. Woman's Therapy Project, Nat. Register Health Svc. Providers in Psychology. Office: Affiliated Psychol Assocs 5319 SW Westgate Dr Ste 147 Portland OR 97221-2430 Office Phone: 503-297-2019. E-mail: monamcneil@quest.net.

**MCNEIL, PAUL JOSEPH, JR.,** financial analyst; b. Winthrop, Mass., Oct. 11, 1941; s. Paul Joseph Sr. and Helen Margaret (Carr) McN. Cert. in ins., U. R.I., 1965; cert. in travel agts., Travel Sch. of Am., 1968; cert., Labor Sch. of Boston, 1976, Labor Studies Inst., 1989. Field investigator R.I. Food Stamp Unit, Providence, 1965-68; cmty. rels. Coordinator Ecology Action for Rhode Island, 1970-71; sec. and rsch. asst. R.I. Worker Assn., 1973-74; enumerator R.I. Polk & Co., Providence, 1970-83; sr. employment security interviewer R.I. Dept. Employment Tng., Providence, 1984-96; sr. employment & tng. interviewer R.I. Dept. Labor & Tng., Providence, 1996—2003, benefits claims specialist, 2003—. Rec. sec. Local 189 New Eng. chpt., Boston, 1973-76, treas., 1989—; mem. bd. dirs. of R.I. Workers Assn., 1973-74, 75-76, census enumerator U.S. Census Bur., Providence, 1990; mail handler U.S. Post Office, Providence, 1980; claims interviewer R.I. Dept. Employment Security, Providence, 1979-84; rec. sec. R.I. Employment Security Alliance, Providence, 1980-90; v.p. Community Econs. Edn. Ctr., Providence, 1988-91. Exec. com. R.I. State Employees Assn., 1966-68, Community Labor Organizing Com., Providence, 1983-89, Sane Freeze, Washington, 1989-90; shop steward Local 401 SEIU, Providence, 1990-92, 1st v.p., 1992-96; rec. sec. R.I. Sane Freeze, Providence, 1988-94; mem. Nat. Com. Peace Action, 1993—; v.p. Peace Action R.I., 1994-95, pres., 1995—; coord. R.I. Nation Readers Group, 1995—; state committeeman Amvets Dept. R.I., 1994-95, 96—, adj. posts, 1965-68, trustee post 6, 1995-96; v.p. Labor Party R.I., 1994-97, treas., 1997—, pres., 1999, chmn., 1999; exec. bd. R.I. Coalition for Consumer Justice, 1997—; bd. dirs. Injured Workers R.I., 1996—, Warwick Cmty. Action, 1967-69, R.I. Legal Svcs., 1967-69; founder East Greenwich Dem. Youth Club, 1959; co-chmn. Human Rights Action Coun., Warwick, 1968-70; del. R.I. Dem. State Conv., 1976, 78; mem. R.I. Dem. State Com., 1980-86, bd. dirs., 1985-87; mem. Dem. Study Group R.I., 1986-88; organizer United Farm Workers, 1968-71; mem. Fox Point Neighborhood Housing Corp. Dirs., 1980-87, pres., 1981-83, sec., 1983-87; pres. Coalition Consumer Justice, 1990—. With U.S. Army, 1960-63, ETO. Mem. Internat. Assn. Pers. in Employment Security (R.I. chpt. bd. dirs. 1989-93, sec. 1991-93), Greater R.I. Indsl. Rels. Rsch. Assn., R.I. ACLU (bd. dirs. 1974-80,

bd. sec. 1975-77, exec. com. 1979-80), Union of Peace Profls. (exec. bd. 1988-90), Nat. Writers Union, R.I. Cen. Am. Network, Cath. Peace Fellowship, Pax ChristiAncient Order, Order of Hibernians (rec. sec. Providence chpt. 1990-91, 97-98, v.p., 1998-2003, pres. 1991-92, state sec. 1993-96, state pres. 1996-99, sec. Providence County 2003—), K. of C., Sierra Club, Newport Mus. Irish History, Am. Irish Hist. Soc., R.I. Hist. Soc., R.I. Labor History Soc., Gaspee Days Com., Americans for Dem. Action, Debs Found., Edward Bellamy Meml. Assn., R.I. Irish Famine Meml. Com., Am. Legion, Indsl. Rels. Rsch. Assn., Assn. Can.-Am., Am. French Geneal. Soc., Irish Nat. Caucus, Am. Irish Polit. Edn. Com., Friendly Sons of St. Patrick (East Greenwich, R.I.). Democrat. Avocation: writing. Home: PO Box 945 Providence RI 02901-0945

**MCNEIL, RAMSEY ENGLISH,** religious studies educator; b. Franklin County, Va., Sept. 28, 1937; d. George Wilson and Eva Woody English; m. Carl Nixon McNeil, June 2, 1967; 1 child, Carl Nixon. BS in Edn., Radford Coll., Va., 1958; MS in Edn., Radford U., Va., 1968. Sch. tchr. Franklin County Pub. Sch., Rocky Mount, Va., 1958—59, Danville City Pub. Sch., Danville, Va., 1959—63, Roanoke (Va.) City Sch., 1963—67, Mongomery County Sch., Christiansburg, Va., 1967—70; tchr. Bible quiz local chs., Va., 1978—89, tchr. adult Sunday sch. Va., 1996—2006, tchr. Wed. A.M. women's Bible study, 1998—. Den leader Boy Scouts Am., Christiansburg, 1978—80; sch. vol. Montgomery County Va., 1976—91; v.p. Auxiliary Va. Auctioneers, 2005—06; sec. bd. dirs. Montgomery Mus., Christiansburg, Va., 1995—2006; foster parent, 1976—86. Mem.: United Daus. Confederacy (org. new chpts. com. 2005—, pres. 1974—99, 1st dist. chair 1997—99, v.p. 1999—2006, 1st dist. chair 2003—05, org. new chpts. com. 1999—2003), Ea. Star (pianist 1989—96, chaplain 1998—2006). Republican. Baptist. Avocations: reading, antiques, flowers, travel. Home: 5234 Old Pagelyn Rd Radford VA 24141-6518

**MCNEIL, ROBERT L., JR.,** marketing professional; b. Chgo., Oct. 3, 1969; s. Robert L. Sr. and Yvonne McNeil; m. Stacey R. McNeil. Founder, pres. Images USA, Atlanta, 1989—. Mem. Am. Mktg. Assn., Atlanta Ad Club, Ga. Minority Supplier Devel. Coun. Office: IMAGES USA 914 Howell Mill Rd NW #300 Atlanta GA 30316-5546

**MCNEIL, SCOTT,** research scientist; b. Ore., 1964; m. Lisa McNeil, Sept. 1992; children: Nikki, Emma, Sarah, Caleb. BS, Portland State U., Oreg., 1988; PhD, Oreg. Health Scis. U., Portland, 1997. Maj. U.S. Army, 1988—2001; sr. scientist Sci. Applications Internat. Corp., McLean, Va., 2001—04; dir. nanotech. characterization lab. Nat. Cancer Inst., Frederick, Md., 2004—. Author: (book chpt.) Nanotechnology on Cancer Therapy, 2006; contbr. articles to profl. jours. Office: Nat Cancer Inst Rm 246 Bldg 469 1050 Boyles St Frederick MD 21702 Business E-Mail: mcneils@ncicrf.gov.

**MCNEIL, WENDY LAWSON-JOHNSTON,** foundation administrator; d. Peter and Dorothy Stevenson Hammond Lawson-Johnston; m. Thomas K. McNeil; 1 child, Lawson Johnston McNeil Wijesooriya. V.p. Solomon R. Guggenheim Found. Bd. trustees Solomon R. Guggenheim Mus. Office: Solomon R Guggenheim Found 1071 Fifth Ave New York NY 10128

**MCNEILL, CORBIN ASAHEL, JR.,** utilities executive; b. Santa Fe, July 6, 1939; s. Corbin Asahel and Madeline (Thielen) McN.; m. Dorice Schiller, June 16, 1962; children: Michele, Corbin IV, Kevin, Alicia, Timothy. BS in Marine Engring., U.S. Naval Acad., 1962; postgrad., Naval Nuclear Power Sch., Mare Island, Md., 1962-63, U. Calif., Berkeley, 1975-76, Syracuse U., 1983-84. Commd. ensign USN, 1962, advanced through grades to comdr., 1981, ret., 1981; sr. v.p. nuclear generation N.Y. Power Authority, White Plains, 1981-85, Pub. Service Electric & Gas Co., Hancocks Bridge, N.J., 1985-88; exec. v.p. nuclear div. PECO Energy Co., 1988-90; pres., COO Phila. Electric Co., 1990-95, pres., CEO, 1995—, also chmn., 1997—. Pres. Adwin Equipment Co., Phila., 1990—. Trustee The Meml. Hosp. of Salem County (N.J.) Inc., 1986; chmn. TeamWalk March of Dimes, Salem, 1986; bd. dirs. Oswego (N.Y.) C. of C., 1982-83. Mem. Am. Nuclear Soc., Nuclear Utility Mgmt. and Resources Com. Avocations: skiing, reading. Office: PECO Energy Co PO Box 8699 2301 Market St Philadelphia PA 19101

**MCNEILL, DAN K.,** military career officer; b. N.C., July 23, 1946; m. Maureen McNeill; 1 child, Dan. BS in Agr. and Forestry, NC State U., 1968; grad., US Army War Coll., 1989; attended, Inf. Officer Basic and Advanced Cources, US Army Command and Gen. Staff Coll.; degree (hon.), NC State U., 2003. Commd. 2nd lt. US Army, 1968, sr. aide-de-camp to commdg. gen., 1st Inf. Divsn. (mechanized) Fort Riley, Kans., 1971—72, fixed wing avaitor, later asst. ops. officer, later ops. officer, 55th Aviation Co., 52d Aviation Bn., Korea, 1972—73, asst. S-3 (ops.) (air), 2d Bn. (airborne), 505th Inf., 82 Airborne Divsn. Fort Bragg, NC, 1974, commdr., combat support co., 2d Bn. (airborne), 505th Inf., 82 Airborne Divsn., 1974—76, commdr., E Co., 2d Bn. (Airborne), 505th Inf., 82d Airborne Divsn., 1977—78, sec. to gen. staff, US Army So, European Vicenza, Italy, 1984—85, exec. officer, 1st Bn., 509th Inf., later renamed 4th Bn., 325th Inf., 1982—84, commdr.,1st Bn., 325th Inf., 82d Airborne Divsn. Fort Bragg, NC, 1986—88, asst. chief of staff, G-3 (Ops.), 82d Airborne Divsn., Operation Just Cause, Panama and Operation Desert Shield/Storm, Saudi Arabia, 1989—90, commdr., 3d Brigade, 82d Airborne Corps, 1991—93, asst. S-3 (Ops.), later S-3 (Ops.), 3d Brigade, 82d Airborne Divsn., 1976—77, asst. chief of state, G-3 (Ops.), XVIII Airbouore Coprs., 1993—95, asst. divsn. commdr., 2d Inf. Divsn, Korea, 1995—96, chief of staff, XVIII Airborne Corp. Fort Bragg, NC, 1996—97, dep. commdg. gen., I Corps and Fort Lewis Wis., commdg. gen. 82d Airborne Divsn. Fort Bragg, NC, 1998—2000, commdg. gen., combined joint task force-180 Afghanistan, 2000—, commdg. gen., XVIII Airborne Corps and Fort Bragg, NC, 2000—; dep. commdg. gen. chi f of staff US Army Forces Command, Fort McPherson, Ga. Asst. prof. mil. sci., first reserve officer tng. corps region Ga. Mil. Coll., Milledgeville, Ga., 1978—80; doctrine author, dept. tactics US Army Command and Gen. Staff Coll., Fort Leavenworth, Kans., 1981—82. Decorated Defense Superior Svc. medal, Legion of Merit wirh 2 oak clusters, Bronze Star medal with 2 oak leaf clusters, Meritorious Svc. medal with 3 Oak Clusters, Army Commendation medal with 2 Oak Leaf Clusters, Army Achievement medal, Expert Infantryman badge, Army Avaitor badge, Master Parachutist badge with Bronze star, Spl. Forces Tab.

**MCNEILL, DANIEL RICHARD,** writer; b. San Francisco, June 1, 1947; s. Daniel Harry and Maureen Evangeline (Sherriff) McN.; m. Rosalind Deborah Gold, Dec. 20, 1984. AB, U. Calif., Berkeley, 1971; JD, Harvard U., 1982. Author: Fuzzy Logic, 1993 (L.A. Times Book prize in sci. and tech. 1993), The Face, 1998. Mem. Authors Guild. Avocations: photography, bodybuilding. Home and Office: 8110 Redlands St #306 Playa Del Rey CA 90293

**MCNEILL, G. DAVID,** psychologist, educator; b. Santa Rosa, Calif., Dec. 21, 1931; s. Glenn H. and Ethel G. (Little) McN.; m. Nobuko Baba, Dec. 17, 1957; children: Cheryl, Randall L.B. AB, U. Calif. at Berkeley, 1953, PhD, 1962. Research fellow Harvard U., 1962-65; asst. prof. psychology U. Mich., 1965-66, assoc. prof., 1966-68; prof. psychology and linguistics U. Chgo., 1969—2001, chmn. dept. psychology, 1991-97, prof. emeritus, 2001—. Vis. fellow Ctr. for Humanities, Wesleyan U., Middletown, Conn., 1970; mem. Inst. Advanced Study, Princeton, 1973-75; fellow Netherlands Inst. for Advanced Studies, 1983-84; visitor Max Planck Inst. for Psycholinguistics, Nijmegen, Netherlands, 1998-99 Author: The Acquisition of Language, 1970, The Conceptual Basis of Language, 1979, Psycholinguistics: A New Approach, 1987, Gengo Shinrigaku, 1991, Hand and Mind: What Gestures Reveal about Thought, 1992, Gesture and Thought, 2005; editor: Language and Gesture, 2000. Recipient Faculty Achievement award, 1991, Am. Excellence in Pub. award Assn. Am. Pubs., Gordon G. Laing prize U. Chgo. Press, 1995; Guggenheim fellow, 1973-74; grantee NSF, 1983-89, 97—, Spencer Found., 1979-82, 89-92, 95-99, NIDCD, 1992-96, Advanced Rsch. and Devel. Agy., 2003—. Fellow AAAS, Am. Psychol. Soc.; mem. Internat. Soc. Gesture Studies (v.p. 2002-05), Cognitive Sci. Soc., Linguistic Soc. Am.,

Violoncello Soc., Phi Beta Kappa, Sigma Xi Office: U Chgo Dept Psychology 5848 S University Ave Chicago IL 60637-1515 Office Phone: 773-702-8833. Business E-Mail: dmcneill@uchicago.edu.

**MCNEILL, JOHN HUGH,** pharmaceutical sciences educator; b. Chgo., Dec. 5, 1938; s. John and Agnes Margaret (McLean) McN.; m. Sharon Keneffly, July 27, 1963; children: Sandra, Laurie. BS, U. Alta., Can., 1960, MS, 1962; PhD, U. Mich., 1967. Lectr. pharmacy Dalhousie U., 1962-63, U. Alta., 1963; research assoc. U. Mich., Ann Arbor, 1963-65, teaching fellow, 1965-66; asst. instr. Mich. State U., East Lansing, 1966-67, asst. prof., 1967-71; assoc. prof. U. B.C., 1971-72, prof., prof., chmn. div. pharmacology and toxicology, 1972-75, dir. rsch. and grad. studies Faculty Pharm. Scis., 1977-78, prof. Faculty Pharm. Scis., 1975—2004, dean Faculty Pharm. Scis., 1985-96, asst. dean, 1978-81, Med. Rsch. Coun. rsch. prof., 1981-82, prof., assoc. dean rsch. and grad. studies, 1982-84, prof. and dean emeritus, 2004—. Contbr. more than 800 tech. articles to profl. jours. Fellow Royal Soc. Can., Internat. Acad. Cardiovasc. Scis., Can. Acad. Health Scis., Am. Coll. Nutrition; mem. Pharm. Soc. Can. (various coms. 1974-88, coun. 1977-83, v.p. 1979, pres. 1980-81), Am. Soc. for Pharm. and Therapeutics (J.J. Abel award com. 1981, Upjohn award com., 1978-80, chmn. mem. com. 1983-86), Western Pharm. Soc. (coun. 1977-81, pres. 1979-80, past pres. 1980-81), N.Y. Acad. Scis., Internat. Soc. for Heart Rsch. (coun. 1986-95), AAAS, B.C. Coll. Pharms. (coun. 1985-96), Internat. Union Pharmacologists (Can. rep. 1982-88), Am. Pharm. Assn. Office: Univ BC Fac Pharm Scis 2146 East Mall Vancouver BC Canada V6T 1Z3 Office Phone: 604-822-9373. E-mail: jmcneill@interchange.ubc.ca.

**MCNEILL, ROBERT PATRICK,** investment advisor; b. Chgo., Mar. 17, 1941; s. Donald Stephan and Katherine (Bennett) McN.; m. Martha Stephan, Sept. 12, 1964; children— Jennifer, Donald, Victoria, Stephan, Elizabeth BA summa cum laude (valedictorian), U. Notre Dame, 1963; M.Letters, Oxford U., 1967. Chartered investment counselor. Assoc. Stein Roe & Farnham, Chgo., 1967-72, gen. prtnr, 1972-77, sr. prtnr, 1977-86, exec. v.p., 1986-89; pres., mng. dir. Stein Roe Internat., Chgo., 1989—. Underwriting mem. Lloyds of London, 1980—; dir. Comml. Chgo. Corp.; vice chmn. bd. Hill Internat. Prodn. Co., Houston, 1982—; dir., adv. bd. Touche Remnant Investment Counselors, London, 1983—; dir. TR Worldwide Strategy Fund, Luxembourg, Konrad Adenauer Fund for European Policy Studies, Fed. Republic Germany. Voting mem., sec Ill. Rhodes Scholarship Selection Com.; voting mem. Ill. rep. Great Lakes Dist. Rhodes Scholarship Selection Com.; bd. dirs. Kennedy Sch. for Retarded Children, Palos Park, Ill., 1972—; Winnetka United Way, Ill., 1984—; Division St. YMCA, Chgo., 1972—; assoc. Rush-Presbyterian-St. Lukes Med. Ctr., Chgo., 1975—; mem. leadership com. Rush Alzheimer's Disease Ctr. Rhodes scholar, 1963 Fellow Fin. Analysts Fedn.; mem. Chgo. Council on Fgn. Relations (bd. dirs., treas. 1975—), Inst. European Studies (bd. govs., vice-chmn. 1981—), Investment Analysts Soc. Chgo. (chgo. com., com. on fgn. affairs, com. on internat. and domestic issues), Assn. for Investment Mgmt. and Rsch., Chgo. Soc. Clubs, Econ. Club of Chgo, Sunset Ridge Country (bd. dirs. Northfield, Ill., 1983—). Avocations: coin collecting/numismatics, bridge, golf, skiing, art. Office Phone: 312-368-7684. Business E-Mail: rmcneill@sric.net.

**MCNEILL, THOMAS RAY,** lawyer; b. Pitts., June 2, 1952; s. Thomas William McNeill and Mary (Shiveley) Hiss; m. Patsy Lynch, June 25, 1977; children: Elizabeth, Kathleen, Thomas. BSBA, U. Fla., 1974; JD, Emory U., 1977. Bar: Ga. 1977, U.S. Dist. Ct. (no. dist.) Ga. 1977. Assoc. Powell Goldstein LLP, Atlanta, 1977-84, ptnr., 1984—, mgr. corp. dept., 1993-95, bd. ptnrs., 1998—2004, co-leader Bus. Transactions Group, 2003—05, leader, 2005—. Mem. Ga. Bar Assn. (exec. com. bus. law sect., 2001—), Emory U. Alumni Assn. (pres. exec. com. 1988-89, Law Sch. coun. 1990-2000, 2003—, chmn. 2005—), Soc. of Internat. Bus. Fellows, Beta Gamma Sigma. Office: Powell Goldstein LLP 1201 W Peachtree St NW 14th Fl Atlanta GA 30309-3488 Office Phone: 404-572-6681. E-mail: tmcneill@pogolaw.com.

**MCNEILL, WILLIAM HARDY,** retired historian, writer; b. Vancouver, BC, Can., Oct. 31, 1917; s. John Thomas and Netta (Hardy) McN.; m. Elizabeth Darbishire, Sept. 7, 1946; children: Ruth Netta, Deborah Joan, John Robert, Andrew Duncan. BA, U. Chgo., 1938, MA, 1939; PhD, Cornell U., 1947; 20 hon. degrees. Faculty U. Chgo., 1947-87, prof. history, 1957-87, Robert A. Millikan Disting. Svc. prof., 1969-87, prof. emeritus, 1987—, chmn. dept., 1961-67; pres. Demos Fund, 1968-80; chmn. bd. Demos Found., 1980-86. George Eastman vis. prof. Oxford (Eng.) U., 1980-81 Author: Greek Dilemma, War and Aftermath, 1947, Report on the Greeks, 1948, History Handbook of Western Civilization, 1948, rev. and enlarged 6th edit., 1986, America, Britain and Russia, Their Cooperation and Conflict, 1941-46, 1953, Past and Future, 1954, Greece: American Aid in Action, 1947-56, 1957, Rise of the West: A History of the Human Community, 1963, 9th edit., 1991 (Nat. Book award, Gordon J. Laing prize), Europe's Steppe Frontier, 1500-1800, 1964, A World History, 1967, 4th edit., 1998, The Contemporary World, 1967, 2d edit., 1975, The Ecumene: Story of Humanity, 1973, Venice, the Hinge of Europe, 1081-1797, 1974, The Shape of European History, 1974, Plagues and Peoples, 1976, revised edit., 1998, Metamorphosis of Greece since World War II, 1978, The Human Condition, An Ecological and Historical View, 1980, Pursuit of Power, 1982, The Great Frontier, 1983, Mythistory and other Essays, 1986, A History of the Human Community, 1986, 6th edit., 1998, Polyethnicity and National Unity in World History, 1987, Arnold J. Toynbee: A Life, 1989, Population and Politics Since 1750, 1990, Hutchins' University: A Memoir of the University of Chicago 1929-50, 1991, The Global Tradition: Conquerors, Catastrophies and Community, 1992, Keeping Together in Time: Dance & Drill in Human History, 1995, Colebrook: An Historical Sketch, 1996, De excentriciteit van het wiel en andere wereld-historische essays, 1996, The Disruption of Traditional Forms of Nurture, 1998; (with J.R. McNeill) The Human Web: A Birdseye View of World History, 2003, The Pursuit of Truth: A Historian's Memoir, 2005; editor: Ten Autors, Essays in the Liberal Interpretation of History, 1967, (with others) Readings in World History, Vols. I-X, 1968-73, Human Migration, 1978, Jour. Modern History, 1971-79, Jour. Modern Greek Studies, 1983-85, Berkshire Ency. World History, 2005; mem. editl. bd. Ency. Brit., 1981-98; contbr. articles to profl. jours., chpts. to books. Trustee Athens Coll., 1970-88; vice chmn. Christopher Columbus Quincentenary Jubilee Commn., 1985-93; co-chair curriculum task force Nat. Commn. on Social Studies, 1987-89; mem. Bradley Commn. on the Teaching of History, 1986-89; vice chmn. Nat. Coun. for History Edn., 1990-94, Nat. Coun. for History Standards, 1992-94. Fulbright Rsch. scholar Royal Inst. Internat. Affairs, Eng., 1950-51; Rockefeller grantee, 1951-52, 76; Carnegie grantee, 1957-62, 63-64, Josiah H. Macy grantee, 1973-74; Ford Faculty fellow, 1954-55, Guggenheim fellow, 1971-72, 86-87; recipient Erasmus prize, 1996 Fellow Am. Philos. Soc., Am. Acad. Arts and Scis., Brit. Acad. Arts and Scis.; Royal Hist. Soc. (corr.); mem. Am. Hist. Assn. (council, del. Am. Council Learned Socs., pres. 1985) Office: PO Box 45 Colebrook CT 06021-0045

**MCNEILLY, KATHY EDEN,** librarian, library director; b. St. Louis, Mo., Oct. 24, 1948; d. Edwin Winfield Eden and Florence Sybil (Brown) Eden Day; m. Gregory Scott McNeilly, Jan. 13, 1968; 1 child, Meaghan Scott. BS, Fla. State U., Tallahassee, 1966—69; MSc in Libr. Sci., U. Tenn., Knoxville, 1973—74. Libr. asst. Oak Ridge Pub. Libr., Tenn., 1971—76, libr., cataloger, 1976—87, libr., reference, 1987—89, asst. dir., 1989—98, libr. dir., 1998—. Coord. One City, One Book, Oak Ridge, 2005, Oak Ridge, 06. Mem.: ALA, Tenn. Libr. Assn., East Tenn. Libr. Assn. (pres. 2002—03), DAR (historian 2003—06), Oak Ridge Breakfast Rotary (literacy chair 2002—03), Beta Phi Mu. Office: Oak Ridge Pub Libr 1401 Oak Ridge Turnpike Oak Ridge TN 37830 Office Phone: 865-425-3455.

**MC NELLY, FREDERICK WRIGHT, JR.,** psychologist; b. Bangor, Maine, Apr. 14, 1947; s. Frederick Wright and E Frances (Cutter) McNelly; 1 adopted child, Roger McNelly foster children: Joseph, Ronald, Michael, Jeffrey, Jeremy. BA magna cum laude, U. Maine, 1969; MA, U. Mich., 1971; PhD, 1973. Registered clin. psychologist Ill.; cert. profl. qualification, state and provincial bds. of psychology, early intervention program provider Ill. Rsch. coord. NSF project U. Minn., Morris, 1968-69, lab. instr., 1969, trainee

USPHS, 1969-70, 72; teaching fellow psychology U. Mich., Ann Arbor, 1970-72; ednl. examiner Ann Arbor Pub. Schs., 1971; dir. psychol. svcs. Children Devel. Ctr., Rockford, Ill., 1972-82, program dir., 1982-86; cons. psychologist, 1986—. Lectr. Rock Valley Coll., Rockford, 1974—75; part-time pvt. practice psychology, Rockford and Belvidere, Ill., 1980—86, Beloit, Wis., 1985—86; full time, 1986—; mental health cons. Rockford Head Start, 1982—, United Cerebral Palsy, Blackhawk Region, 1986—, Access Svcs., Mendota, Ill., 1992—; mem. health svcs. adv. com. human resources dept. City of Rockford, 1985—; presenter state and regional workshops and confs. Contbr. articles to profl. jours. Active Boy Scouts Am., 1978—83, Big Bros./Big Sisters; chmn. spl. edn. regional adv. com. Bi-County Office Edn., Rockford, 1976—78; mem. Nat. and Ill. Com. Child Abuse, 1975—85; co-chmn. Winnebago County Child Protection Assn., 1980; elder Willow Creek United Presbyn. Ch., Rockford, 1980—83; mem. stronghold renovation session com. Presbytery Blackhawk, Oregon, Ill., 1985. Named U.S. Jaycees Outstanding Young Man of 1977. Mem.: Ill. Assn. Infant Mental Health, No. Ill. Alliance Mentally Ill, Nat. Assn. Mentally Ill, Nat. Assn. Disability Examiners, State Provincial Bds. Psychology, Nat. Register Health Svc. Providers Psychology, Coun. Exception Children, No. Ill. Pvt. Practice Mental Health Assn. (v.p. 1993, pres. 1994—95), No. Ill. Psychol. Assn., Ill. Psychol. Assn. Home: 11591 Beverly Ln Belvidere IL 61008-8708

**MCNELLY, JOHN TAYLOR,** retired journalist, educator; b. Lancaster, Wis., Oct. 2, 1923; s. Stephen Sumner and Caroline Hurd (Taylor) McN.; m. Pamela Edith Thompson, Dec. 20, 1952; children: Barbara, Duncan. BA, U. Wis., 1946, MA, 1957; PhD, Mich. State U., 1961. Reporter AP, Milw., 1948-52, Reuters, London, 1952-53; news editor U. Wis. News Service, Madison, 1957; instr., then assoc. prof. Mich. State U., East Lansing, 1957-66; assoc. prof., then prof. U. Wis., Madison, 1966-82, Evjue-Bascom prof., 1982-88, prof. emeritus, 1988—. Asst. dir. Inter-Am. Mass Communications Program, San Jose, Costa Rica, 1961-62; vis. prof. Berlin Inst. Mass Communication in Developing Nations, W.Ger., 1965, Agrarian U., Lima, Peru, 1968-69; communication cons. UNESCO, Latin Am., 1970-75; lectr. USIA, Latin Am., 1968, 74, 80 Co-author: Communication and Social Change in Latin America, 1968; assoc. editor: Journalism Quar., 1975-77; contbr. monographs and articles to communication publs. Served with USAF, 1942-43. Fulbright-Hays Faculty fellow Lima, Peru, 1968-69 Home: 134 Larkin St Madison WI 53705-5116 Business E-Mail: dtmcnelly@facstaff.wisc.edu.

**MCNERNEY, JAMES, JR., (W. JAMES MCNERNEY),** aerospace transportation executive, former manufacturing executive; b. Providence, R.I., Aug. 22, 1949; m. Haity McNerney, 1987; 3 children. BA in American studies, Yale U., 1971; MBA, Harvard U., 1975. Brand mgr. Proctor & Gamble, 1975—78; sr. mgr. McKinsey & Co., 1978—82; gen. mgr., GE Mobile Communications GE Co., 1982—86; pres. GE Info. Svcs., Rockville, Md., 1988—89; exec. v.p. GE Fin. Services and Capital, Stamford, Conn., 1989—91; pres., CEO GE Elec. Distribution and Control, Plainville, Conn., 1991—92, GE Lighting, Cleveland, Ohio, 1995—97; pres. GE Asia-Pacific, Hong Kong, 1993—95; pres., CEO GE Aircraft Engines, Cin., 1997—2000; chmn., CEO 3M Co, St. Paul, 2001—05; chmn., pres., CEO The Boeing Co., Chgo., 2005—. Bd. dir. The Boeing Co., 2001—, Proter & Gamble Co.; bd. trustee World Bus. Coun. for Sustainable Develop., Bus. Roundtable, Bus. Coun.; mem. spl. programs com. The Boeing Co. Dir. Greater Twin Cities United Way; bd. trustee Northwestern U. Office: The Boeing Co 100 N Riverside Plz Chicago IL 60606-1596*

**MCNEVIN, CHRISTOPHER J.,** lawyer; b. Davenport, Iowa, Sept. 6, 1958; BS summa cum laude, U. Miami, 1979; JD, Stanford U., 1983. Bar: Calif. 1983, Calif. Supreme Ct., US Dist. Ct. (all Calif. dist., we. dist. Pa.), US Ct. Appeals (3d, 9th cir.). Ptnr. Pillsbury Winthrop Shaw Pittman, L.A. Spl. counsel Ohio Atty. Gen., Orange County Water Dist.; co-leader environ. litig. team Pillsbury Winthrop Shaw Pittman, LA. Contbr. articles to profl. jours. Named a So. Calif. Super Lawyer, LA Mag., 2004. Office: Pillsbury Winthrop Shaw Pittman LLP 725 S Figueroa St Ste 2800 Los Angeles CA 90017-5406 Office Phone: 213-488-7507. Office Fax: 213-629-1033. Business E-Mail: chrismcnevin@pillsburylaw.com.

**MCNEW, BENNIE BANKS,** retired finance educator; b. Greenbrier, Ark., Nov. 12, 1931; s. Roland H. and Stella (Avery) McNew; m. Bonnie Lou Stone, Mar. 31, 1956; children: Bonnie Banks, Mary Kathleen. Wilkeman Michael. BS, Ark. State Tchrs. Coll., 1953; MBA, U. Ark., 1954; PhD, U. Tex., 1961. Asst. nat. bank examiner, 1954-56; indsl. specialist Indsl. Rsch. and Ext. Ctr. U. Ark., 1956-59; lectr. finance U. Tex., 1959-61; prof. banking U. Miss., University, 1961-65, dean Sch. Bus. Adminstrn., 1965-79; dean Sch. Bus. Mid. Tenn. State U., Murfreesboro, 1980-88; prof. econs. and fin. U. Ctrl. Ark., Conway, 1988-98; ret. 1998. Asst. dir., v.p. Grad. Sch. Banking La. State U., 1966—97. Author (with Charles L. Prather): (book) Fraud Control for Commercial Banks, 1962; co-author: Money and Banking Casebook, 1966, The Bankers Handbook, 1966, A History of Mississippi, 1973. Pres. Faulkner County Singing Conv., Ark., 2002—04. With U.S. Army, 1950—51. Named Disting. Undergraduate Alumnus, Sch. Bus. Adminstrn., U. Ctrl. Ark., 2002. Mem.: Ward Family Singers and Gospel Music. Soc. (pres. 2002—03), Lions (pres. Oxford, Miss. 1964—65, Edward Dalstrom Disting. Svc. award 2002, Melvin Jones fellow 2003). Home: 12 Bainbridge Dr Conway AR 72034-7217

**MCNICHOLS, GERALD ROBERT,** consulting company executive; b. Cleve., Nov. 21, 1943; s. Charles Wellington and June Beatrice (Kalal) McN.; m. Paula Kay Austin, Dec. 26, 1964; children: G. Robert Jr., Katherine Lynn Loftis, Melissa Sue Cardon. BS with honors, Case-Western Res. U., 1965; MS, U. Pa., 1966; ScD, George Washington U., 1976. Cert. cost estimator/analyst. Sr. ops. analyst Office of Sec., Dept. of Def., Washington, 1970-76; v.p. GenTech, Inc., Bethesda, Md., 1976-77; J. Watson Noah, Inc., Falls Church, Va., 1977-78; pres., chief exec. officer Mgmt. Cons. and Rsch., Inc., McLean, Va., 1978-99; sr. v.p. GRC Internat. (acquired Mgmt. Cons. and Rsch., Inc.), 1999-2000, also bd. dirs.; CEO McNichols & McNichols, Inc., Middleburg, Va., 2000—. Pres. McNichols Family Found., 2000—; chmn. bd. Metier, Ltd.; bd. dirs. Magicsoft Corp., Project Performance Corp., The Wexford Group; bd. adv. Arrowhead Corp., The Baldwin Group; vice chmn. com. arts Kennedy Ctr., Wash., 2005—, bd. dirs. Consortium for Operations Research for Decision Making, 1975; contbg. author: Software Reliability, 1986, Software System Design Methods, 1986, Electronic Systems Effectiveness and Life Cycle Costing, 1983; editor Cost Analysis, 1984; contbr. articles to profl. jours. Pres. Rondelay Civic Assn., Fairfax Sta., Va., 1985-87; bd. dirs. Kennedy Ctr. Cir., 1995-2000. Capt. USAF, 1966-70. Recipient Meritorious Achievement award, Case Western Res U., 1995, Engr. Alumni Achievement award, George Washington U., 1989. Mem. Inst. Cost Analysis (pres. 1985-88), Internat. Soc. Parametric Analysts (bd. dirs. 1982-84, Frieman Lifetime Achievement award 1990), Ops. Rsch. Soc. Am. (chmn. mil. applications sect.), Assn. for Small Rsch., Engring., and Tech. Svcs. Co. (pres.), Mil. Ops. Rsch. Soc. (sec., treas. 1986-87, v.p. administr. 1987-88, bd. dirs. 1985-88, 92-96), Soc. Cost Estimating and Analysis (bd. dirs. 1990-93, Lifetime Achievement award 2000), Century Club George Mason Univ. (bd. dirs. 1997-2000). Home: 23349 Parsons Rd Middleburg VA 20117-2817 Office: McNichols & McNichols Inc PO Box 224 Middleburg VA 20118-2226 Business E-Mail: drmcnichols@mcnichols.org.

**MCNICOL, DAVID LEON,** retired federal official; b. South Gate, Calif., May 18, 1944; s. Charles D. and Mary W. (Heisel) McN.; m. Lore Anne Long, Mar. 25, 1967; children: Katharine Anne, Elizabeth Mary. BA magna cum laude, Harvard U., 1966; MS, MIT, 1968, PhD, 1973. Asst. prof. econs. U. Pa., Phila., 1971-75; sr. staff economist Pres.'s Coun. of Econ. Advisors, Washington, 1976; vis. assoc. prof. econs. Calif. Inst. Tech., Pasadena, 1976-77; sr. economist Office of the Sec., U.S. Dept. of Treasury, Washington, 1977-79; dir. Office of Econ. Analysis U.S. Dept. Energy, Washington, 1980-81, dep. asst. administr. Office of Applied Analysis, 1981-82; dir. Econ. Analysis and Resource Planning Divsn. Office of Sec. of Def., Office of Program Analysis and Evaluation, Washington, 1982-88, dep. asst. sec., dep. dir., 1988—2002, chmn. cost analysis improvement group, 1988—2002; sr.

fellow, mem. rsch. staff, dir., cost analysis and rsch. divsn. Inst. for Def. Analyses, Alexandria, Va., 2002—. Author over 20 publs. on commodity markets, regulatory econs., energy issues and econ. aspects of the U.S. def. program. Recipient Spl. Svc. award Dept. Energy, 1981, Presdl. Rank award U.S. Govt., 1988, 93, 96, 2001, Disting./Meritorious Civilian Svc. medal Dept. Def., 1988, 91, 93, 96, 97, 2001, 2002. Home: 6901 Pineway University Park MD 20782-1163 Office: Inst for Defense Analyses 4850 Mark Center Dr Alexandria VA 22311-1882 Office Phone: 703-845-4369. Business E-Mail: dmcnicol@ida.org.

**MCNIESH, CELESTE ANGELA,** sales executive; b. Vienna, Va., June 28, 1973; d. Barbara Louise Young; m. Michael Lawrence McNiesh, Jan. 17, 2004. BA, James Madison U., 1995; MA, Appalachian State U., 1997. Cert. nationally cert. counselor 1997. Counselor Alamance Burlington Sch. Sys., Graham, NC, 2001—03; coord. sophomore initiative Loyola Coll., Balt. 2003—04; sales mgr. PepsiCo Food Svc. Owings Mills, Md., 2004—; asst. area coord. U. SC, Columbia, SC, 1997—98; asst. dir. residence life Elon U., Elon, NC, 1998—2001. Instr. Dealing with Difficult People, Alamance Burlington Sch. Sys., Graham, NC, 2002—03, Prime for Life Alcohol Prevention Program, Elon U., Elon, NC, 1999—2003; dir. The Thinking CAP, Elon U., 1999—2001; instr. U. 101, U. SC, Columbia, SC, 1997—98, Leadership Devel., Appalachian State U., Boone, NC, 1996—97; crisis team coord. Alamance Burlington Sch. Sys., 2001—03; exec. bd. program chair NC Housing Officers Assn., NC, 1999—2000; conf. chair RA Drive-in Annual Conf., NC, 2000; staff devel. and tng. coord. Elon U., Student Life, 1998—2000. Author: The Space Between, 2003 (10th Nat. Students in Transition Conf. award, 2003). Pres. Five Oaks Homeowners Assn., Owings Mills, Md., 2004—; host com. chair NAMES Project AIDS Meml. Quilt, Elon, NC, 1999—2001. Named Team Player 4th qtr, PepsiCo Food Svc. Mid-Atlantic Zone, 2004; recipient Commitmet to Multiculturalism award, Appalachian State U., 1996, Academic Resource Programming award, South Eastern Housing Officers, 1999—2000. Mem.: Nat. Bd. Cert. Counselors. Independent. Roman Catholic. Avocations: travel, reading. Home and Office: PepsiCo Food Svc and Vending 4664 Mews Dr Owings Mills MD 21117 Office Phone: 410-902-7302. Office Fax: 410-902-7309. E-mail: celeste95@msn.com.

**MCNISH, SUSAN KIRK,** retired lawyer; b. San Jose, Calif., Nov. 4, 1940; d. Wallace Garland and Dorothy (Kirk) Shaw; m. Thomas A. McNish, May 12, 1989; children: Jenifer, Michael. BA, U. Calif., 1962; JD, U. Santa Clara, Calif., 1981; postgrad., Stanford U., 1979, U. Mich., 1981. Bar: Mich. 1981, U.S. Dist. Ct. (ea. dist.) Mich. 1981. Various positions Stanford (Calif.) U., 1968-79; law clk. U.S. Dist. Ct. (no. dist.) Calif., San Francisco, 1979; atty. Consumers Power Co., Jackson, Mich., 1981-88; v.p. gen. counsel, corp. sec. Mich. Consol. Gas Co., Detroit, 1988-98; ret. Mem. clin. svcs. adv. bd. Detroit Med. Ctr., Wayne State U.; dir. Vista Maria Inc., Dearborn Heights, Mich. Mem. Am. Arbitration Assn. (arbitrator, Mich. adv. panel). Home: 1809 Bay Meadow Ct Raleigh NC 27615-5482 E-mail: susankmcnish@yahoo.com.

**MC NITT, WILLARD CHARLES,** food products executive; b. Chgo., June 6, 1920; s. Willard C. and Louise (Richardson) McN.; m. Charlotte D. Boyd, Sept. 14, 1946; children: Willard Charles, James D., Peter B. McNitt. BA, Amherst Coll., 1942; A.M., Harvard Grad. Sch. Bus. Adminstrn., 1942; student, Northwestern Grad. Sch. Bus. Adminstrn., U. Chgo. Sch. Bus. Adminstrn., 1947. Asst. market planning and research Foote, Cone & Belding Co., Chgo., 1946-47; asst. sales promotion and advt. Bell & Gosset Co., Morton Grove, Ill., 1947-48; v.p. sales and mktg. Bowes Industries, Inc., Chgo., 1948-54; gen. mgr. sales and mktg. Clayton Mark & Co., Evanston, Ill., 1954-58; pres., dir. Bowey's, Inc., Chgo., 1958-62; pres., dir., mem. exec. com. H.M. Byllesby Co., Chgo., 1962-63; group v.p., dir. Consol. Foods Corp., Chgo., 1963-67; exec. v.p. consumer products group W.R. Grace & Co., N.Y.C., 1967-72; exec. v.p., dir., mem. exec. com. Ward Foods, Inc., Wilmette, Ill., 1972-73, chief operating officer, pres., dir., mem. exec. com., 1973-76; pres., chief exec. officer, dir. Westgate-Calif. Corp., and Sun Harbor Industries, San Diego, 1977-80; pres., chief exec. officer Nalley's Fine Foods, Tacoma, 1980-83; chmn., dir. Joseph Magnin Inc., 1982-85; chmn. Blue Moon Cheese Co., Thorpe, Wis., 1983—; operating ptnr. Wallner & Co., La Jolla, Calif.; vice chmn., pres., chief exec. officer, dir., mem. exec. com. Foremost Dairies, Inc., San Francisco, 1983-85. Chmn. Epcom; bd. dirs. ATI, NCIC, Blue Moon Cheese, Del. Lightweight. Troop head local Boy Scouts Am., 1957-67. Served to lt. (s.g.) USNR, 1942-46. Mem. Execs. Club (Chgo.), Amherst Club, Harvard Bus. Sch. Club (Chgo., N.Y.C.), Indian Hill Country Club (Winnetka), Dairymen's Club (Boulder Junction, Wis.), Chi Psi. Republican. Congregationalist. Address: 1512 Primrose Ln Glenview IL 60025-7772

**MCNOWN, EDYTHE S.,** music educator; b. Torrington, Wyo., Oct. 18, 1925; d. Charles Mead Sandercock and Ada Mary Guy; m. Myron L. McNown, Dec. 27, 1954; children: Cynthia Ruth Harrington, Douglas Edward, Gregory Bruce. MusB in Piano, U. Wyo., 1948; MA, Kansas City U. Mo., 1951; postgrad., U. Wyo., 1949, U. Mo., 1950—51, Aspen Sch. Music, 1953. Tchr. Laramie Pub. Schs., Wyo., 1948—49, Sunset Hill Girl's Sch., Kansas City, 1952—55, 1965—69; pvt. piano tchr. Fairway, Kans., 1954—. Freelance profl. accompanist, 1950—; organist, choir dir. 3d Presbyn. Ch., Kansas City, Mo., 1951—52; dir. Jr. Boys Choir 2d Presbyn. Ch., Kansas City, Mo., 1966—71; pianist Sigma Alpha Iota Singers, Greater Kansas City, 1976—82, Cmty. Opera Co., Greater Kansas City, 1981—83; music dir. Civic Opera Theater of Kansas City, 1984—90, pianist, 1984—92. Co-founder Civic Opera Theater of Kansas City, 1984, bd. dirs., 1985—2002; vol. performer various area clubs, orgns., schs., chs.; vol. Shawnee Mission Sch. Sys., Kans., 1966—77; mem. Friends of Art Nelson-Atkins Mus. Art, Kansas City, 1988—. Recipient citation, Kans. Fedn. Music Clubs, 1989, Regional Winner, Nat. Fedn. of Music Club Contest, 1947; U. Kansas City fellow, 1949—50. Mem.: Music Tchrs. Nat. Assn., Musical Arts Club, Kansas City Music Club (membership chmn. 1997—99, Annual award 1998, Annual award 1998), Mus. Arts Club of Kansas City (pres. 1980—2000, sec. 1994—96, Jack Henry Pyramid of Arts, Vol. of Yr. award 1994), Phi Kappa Phi, Phi Sigma Iota, Sigma Alpha Iota (pres. 1979—81, 1st v.p. 1987—88, Sword of Honor 1976, Cert. of Merit 1980, Rose of Honor 1981, Rose of Dedication 1992, Nat. Alumni Leadership award, Diamond Sword of Honor 2004). Avocations: needlecrafts, gardening, cooking. Personal E-mail: emmcnown@aol.com.

**MCNULTY, CARRELL STEWART, JR.,** retired manufacturing executive, architect; b. Newark, Dec. 4, 1924; s. Carrell Stewart and Marjorie (Yaegerlehner) McN.; m. Barbara Brokaw, June 21, 1952; children: Peter Carrell, Susan Abigail. Student, Emory U., 1941-43, U. N.C., 1943-44; BArch, Columbia U., 1950, MS in Urban Planning, 1963. Registered architect, Conn. Assoc. SMS Architects, Stamford, Conn., 1950-58, gen. ptnr., 1958-73; pvt. practice architecture Weston, Conn., 1973-76; pres. CMW Co., Weston, 1975-77, HB Products, Inc., Horsham, Pa., 1976-94, HB Instruments, Inc., Horsham, 1979-93, Environ. Svcs. and Products, Inc., Horsham, 1994-96; ret. Mem. Conn. Soc. Architects, 1963-73, sec., 1964-67, pres., 1969-70. Chair S.W. Regional Planning Agy., Norwalk, Conn., 1967-71; mem. Gov.'s Com. on Environment, New Haven, 1970, chair Gov.'s Task Force on Housing, Norwalk, 1972; bd. dirs., sec. Habitat for Humanity of Greater Bucks, Doylestown, Pa., 1990-97; pres. Ctrl. Bucks Crossroads, 1995-96. Lt. (j.g.) USNR, 1943-46; PTO. Recipient citation Am. Assn. Sch. Adminstrs., 1960, 6th Biennial Design award HUD, 1973; grantee HUD, Housing Rsch., 1970. Fellow AIA (mem. urban design com. 1963-73, chmn. 1971); mem. Bucks County Choral Soc., Sigma Nu. Democrat. Mem. United Ch. of Christ (deacon 1965-71, elder 1989-92). Avocations: computers, watercoloring, choral music. Home: 14179 SE 88th Ct Summerfield FL 34491 Personal E-mail: llerracm@earthlink.net.

**MCNULTY, JAMES F.,** construction company executive; m. Judy McNulty; children: Darby, Anne, Brigid. BS in Engring., US Mil. Acad., 1964; MS in Nuc. Physics, Ohio State U., 1970; MS in Mgmt., MIT, 1985. Rsch. assoc. Lawrence Livermore Nat. Lab., 1972—74; asst. dir. Rsch. Off. Mil. Applications

US Dept. Energy, 1978—80; officer nuc. weapon requirements Ops. and Plans Office Dept US Army, 1980—82, sys. mgr. Pershing II Missle Sys., 1982—84, program mgr. ground based laser sys., 1985—88; dir. bus. devel. Parsons Corp., 1988—89, v.p. Washington, 1991—92, sr. v.p. mgr. sys. divsn. Pasadena, 1992—95, pres. infrastructure and tech. group, 1996, pres., CEO, 1996—, chmn., 1998—. Fellow Alfred P. Sloan, MIT. Avocations: hiking, walking, golf, reading. Office: Parsons Corp 100 W Walnut St Pasadena CA 91124-0001 Office Phone: 626-440-2000. Office Fax: 626-440-2630.*

**MCNULTY, JAMES FRANCIS,** engineering executive; b. New Bedford, Mass., July 16, 1929; s. Francis and Mary (Cantwell) McN.; m. Pauline Antoinette Gillotti, Dec. 15, 1962; children: Diana Valencia, Kevin, Irene, James, Theresa. AE in Elec. Engring., Jersey City Tech. Inst.; student, MIT. Supr. Raytheon R&D Lab., Waltham, Mass., 1952-59; elec. engr. Sperry Products, Danbury, Conn., 1959-62; elec. engr. A6A Aircraft Grumman Aircraft, Bethpage, NY, 1963-66; exec. v.p. Adtech Power, Inc., Anaheim, Calif., 1973-80; dir. engring. Datapower, Inc., Santa Ana, Calif., 1980-85; mfg. ops. mgr. Pacific Power Source, Huntington Beach, Calif., 1985-88; v.p., gen. mgr. Powerstar, Inc., Irvine, Calif., 1988-89; dir. engring. and ops. On-Line Power, City of Commerce, Calif., 1989-92; v.p. ops. Tasertron, Corona, Calif., 1992—2001. Cons. On-Line Power, 1993-94, Seimelweis Corp., Bloomington, Calif., 1997, Len Gordon Co., Las Vegas, 1998, Vogt & Resnick Law Corp., Newport Beach, Calif., 1998. Contbr. articles to profl. jours. Sgt. U.S. Army. Mem. VFW. Achievements include patent for ultrasonic testing apparatus and method, patent for control of filament current and voltage, patent for shockley diode pulser, patent for the only non-lethal alternative to the deadly anti-personnel landmine, others. Office: 1731 Medical Ctr Dr Unit #163 Anaheim CA 92801 Office Phone: 714-774-4529. Personal E-mail: jfmcnult@yahoo.com.

**MCNULTY, JAMES FRANCIS, JR.,** lawyer, consultant; s. James Francis, Sr. McNulty and Anna Mae Fiorenza; m. Be Thi Tu, Dec. 19, 1986; 1 child, Thomas Vi. Cert. in Elec. Tech., Santa Ana Coll., 1981, AA, 1982; BA in Sociology, Calif. State U., Fullerton, 1990; JD, Glendale U., 1991; MA in Mgmt., Claremont Grad. U., 2002; AS in Microbiology, Crafton Hills Coll., Calif., 2002. Cert. engring. graphics, Riverside Coll., Calif., 2003; bar: Calif. 1993. Assoc. quality engr. Allen Bradley - West, Fullerton, Calif., 1981—83; plant ops. mgr. Taser Industries, Inc., Monrovia, Calif., 1983—86; CEO E.I.D. Labs, Sierra Madre, Calif., 1986—90; v.p. mktg. and product devel. Tasertron, Newport Beach, Calif., 1990—91; atty. pvt. practice, Calimesa, Calif., 1993—2004; atty., mkt. rsch., product designer Def. Tech. Corp., an Armor Holdings, Inc. Co., 2004—06; atty. Law Enforcement Assoc., Inc., a Sirchie Affiliate, 2004—06; v.p. in ho. counsel Atelier McA'Nulty Designs, Inc., 2006—. Educated for a career in marketing, studied social behavior, social research methods, statistics, law, management and design. At Claremont Colleges, studied under both economist and organizational theorist Peter Ferdinand Drucker and psychologist Mihaly Csikszentmihalyi. An astute product manager recognized for his own novel designs for products responsive to researched markets, James Jr. is named inventor of 17 patents granted for mechanical and electro-mechanical products. Technical expert during trial of U.S. vs. Koon. James Jr. maintains a primarily transactional legal practice. Mem.: Mensa, Phi Theta Kappa, Alpha Gamma Sigma, Alpha Kappa Delta, Delta Theta Phi. Republican. Achievements include patents in field. Avocations: bicycling, forensic science, drafting and designing. Home and Office: 5020 Indian River Dr Unit 421 Las Vegas NV 89103 Personal E-mail: macslaw2000@yahoo.com.

**MCNULTY, JAMES J.,** former mercantile exchange executive; BA, U. Ill., 1973; MA, U. Coll. Dublin, 1974. Ptnr. O'Connor & Assocs., 1989—93; mng. dir., co-head corp. analysis & structuring team Warburg Dillon Read; pres., CEO Chgo. Mercantile Exch., 2000—03, Chgo. Mercantile Exch. Holdings Inc., 2001—03. Bd. dirs. Chgo. Mercantile Exch., 2002—03, Chgo. Mercantile Exch. Holdings Inc., 2002—03; non-exec. dir. ICAP plc., mem. nominating com., mem. risk com., mem. remunerations com.; bd. mem. Archipelago Holdings, Inc., 2004—06, NYSE Group, Inc., 2006—. Office: NYSE Group Inc 11 Wall St New York NY 10005 Office Phone: 212-656-3000.*

**MCNULTY, JOHN KENT,** lawyer, educator; b. Buffalo, Oct. 13, 1934; s. Robert William and Margaret Ellen (Duthie) McN.; m. Linda Conner, Aug. 20, 1955 (div. Feb. 1977); children: Martha Jane, Jennifer, John K. Jr.; m. Babette B. Barton, Mar. 23, 1978 (div. May 1988). AB with high honors, Swarthmore Coll., 1956; LLB, Yale U., 1959. Bar: Ohio 1961, U.S. Supreme Ct. 1964. Law clk. Justice Hugo L. Black, U.S. Supreme Ct., Washington, 0959—1960; vis. prof. Sch. Law U. Tex., 1960; assoc. Jones, Day, Cockley & Reavis, Cleve., 1960—64; prof. law U. Calif., Berkeley, 1964—91, Roger J. Traynor prof. law, 1991—2002, Roger J. Traynor prof. emeritus, 2002—. Of counsel Baker and McKenzie, San Francisco, 1974-75; acad. visitor London Sch. Econs., 1985, Cambridge U., 1994, U. Edinburgh, 1994; vis. fellow Wolfson Coll., Cambridge, 1994, U. Innsbruck, 1996, Trinity Coll., Dublin, 1997; vis. prof. Yale U., U. Tex., U. Leiden, U. Tilburg, U. Tokyo, U. San Diego, Hastings, Vienna Econ. U., Cologne, others; lectr. in field; mem. adv. bd. Tax Mgmt. Author: Federal Income Taxation of Individuals, (with Lathrope) 7th edit., 2004, Federal Estate and Gift Taxation, (with McCouch) 6th edit., 2003, Federal Income Taxation of S Corporations, 1992; (with Westin & Beck) Federal Income Taxation of Business Enterprises, 1995, 2d edit., 1999; mem. bd. overseers Berkeley Jour. Internat. Law. Guggenheim fellow, 1977 Mem. ABA, Am. Law Inst. (life), Internat. Fiscal Assn. (coun. U.S. br.), Order of Coif, Phi Beta Kappa. Home: 1176 Grizzly Peak Blvd Berkeley CA 94708-1741 Office: U Calif Sch Law 422 Boalt Hl Berkeley CA 94720-7200 Office Phone: 510-642-1928. Business E-Mail: mcnultyj@law.berkeley.edu.

**MCNULTY, KATHLEEN ANNE,** social worker, consultant, psychotherapist; b. Hackensack, N.J., Oct. 6, 1958; d. Alfred Edward and Gertrude Natalie (Currie) McN.; m. Henry Stanislaw Kowal, Sept. 16, 1988. BA, Rutgers U., 1980; MSW, Smith Coll., 1984; postgrad., Fielding Grad. Inst., 2001—. Lic. marriage and family therapist; lic. clin. social worker; lic. psychologist. Mental health aide Belleville (N.J.) Mental Health Clinic, 1980-82; clin. social worker Albert Einstein Coll. Medicine, Bronx, N.Y., 1984-86, Family Guidance Bergen, Hackensack, 1986-87, Cliffwood Mental Health Ctr., Englewood, N.J., 1986-87; pvt. practice Rutherford, N.J., 1987-99, Ridgewood, N.J., 1999—. Cons. Meadowlands Weight Control, Rutherford, 1988—, St. Lukes-Roosevelt Hosp. Ctr., N.Y.C., 1988. Contbr. articles to profl. jours. Mem. Am. Orthopsychiat. Assn., Acad. Cert. Social Workers (cert.), Nat. Assn. Social Workers. Avocations: painting, singing, sports, poetry. Office Phone: 201-444-4010. E-mail: kam1058@aol.com, relationsconnect@aol.com.

**MCNULTY, MICHAEL ROBERT,** congressman; b. Troy, NY, Sept. 16, 1947; s. John J. and Madelon McNulty. m. Nancy Ann Lazzaro; children: Michele, Angela, Nancy, Maria. Grad. St. Joseph's Inst., Barrytown, N.Y., 1965, Loyola U. Rome Ctr., 1968, Hill Sch. his., NYC, 1970; BA in Polit. Sci., Coll. Holy Cross, Worcester, Mass., 1969; LHD honoris causa (hon.), Coll. St. Rose, Albany, NY, 1991; LLD honoris causa (hon.), Siena Coll. Loudonville, NY, 1993, Rensselaer Poly. Inst., Troy, NY, 1995, Excelsior Coll., Albany, NY, 2000. Town supr., Green Island, NY, 1969-77; mayor, 1977-81; mem. NY State Assembly from 106th dist., 1982-88, mem. adminstrv. regulations rev. commn., 1983-88; mem. US Congress from 23rd NY dist., 1989-92, US Congress from 21st NY dist., 1993—, at-large whip, mem. ways and means com., ranking minority mem. select revenue measures subcommittee. Chmn. United Way campaign, 1982 Mem. edn. com. on edn. NY State Constl. Conv., 1967; campaign mgr. John J. McNulty Jr. for Sheriff of Albany County, NY, 1973; participant 1974 polit. campaign mgmt. inst. Kent State U., Ohio Recipient Freedom award, Armenian Nat. Com., 1996. Democrat. Roman Catholic. Office: US Ho Reps 2210 Rayburn Ho Office Bldg Washington DC 20515-3221*

**MCNULTY, PAUL J.,** federal agency administrator, former prosecutor; b. Pitts., Jan. 21, 1958; m. Brenda Millican; children: Katy, Annie, Joe, Corrie. BA, Grove City Coll., 1980; JD, Capital U., 1983. Counsel U.S. House Com. on Standards of Official Conduct, Washington, 1983—85; dir. legal svcs. Legal Svcs. Corp., Washington, 1985—87; minority counsel House Judiciary Subcom. Crime, 1987—90; dep. dir. Office Policy Devel., dir. Office Policy and Comms. U.S. Dept. Justice, Washington, 1990—93; counsel Shaw, Pittman, Potts and Trowbridge, 1993—95, U.S. Ho. Reps. Com. on Judiciary, Washington, 1995—99; chief counsel, dir. legis. ops. Office of Majority Leader U.S. Ho. Reps., Washington, 1999—2001; prin. assoc. dep. atty. gen. U.S. Dept. Justice, Washington, 2001, U.S. atty. (ea. dist.) Va. Alexandria, 2001—06, acting dep. atty. gen. Washington, 2005—06, dep. atty. gen., 2006—. Office: US Dept Justice 950 Pennsylvania Ave NW Washington DC 20530*

**MCNUTT, RICHARD HUNT,** manufacturing executive; b. Princeton, N.J., Mar. 11, 1943; s. John and Dorothy Elizabeth (Hunt) McN. Student, Delaware Vly. Coll. Sci./Agr., 1965-68, Temple U., 1978-81; BS in Indsl. Engring., Shelbourn U., 1986. Cert. in vocat. edn.; cert. mfg. engr. Diemaker Custom Tool Co., 1964-67; toolmaker Penn Engring., 1967-69; machine shop mgr., R&D engr. Inertial Motors Corp., 1969-73; machinery design engr. Phila. Rivet Co., Doylestown, Pa., 1973-76; R&D mgr. PHL, Inc., Doylestown, 1976-82; asst. chief engr. PHL Inc./Levr/Air Inc., Prefco Products Inc., 1982-85, chief engr., 1985-86, v.p. ops., 1986-89, dir. engring., 1989—2003; owner Sunrise Solar Heat Co.; cons. Pipersville, Pa.; ptnr. Mediation Assocs., 1990—; R&D engr. fire/smoke divsn. Perfect Air Control, Inc., Pipersville, 2003—04; engring. dir. PHL, Inc., 2004—. Exec. v.p. Del. Water Study Citizens Group for Sound Resource Mgmt.; councillor Probational Vol. Svcs.; founding bd. dirs. Del-Aware Unltd., Inc., Del-Art Inc., Ctr. for Performing Arts, Bucks County, Pa., Del. River Greenway Partnership, Inc.; mem Environ. Polit. Action Com.; founder AWARE, Montgomery County, 1985—, STAND, Bucks County, 1986—, Holicong CSA; mem. exec. bd. Earth Day, 1990, Earth Days Alliance, Bucks County Conservation Dist., 1993—, Del. River Greenway, 1994-96, vice chmn., 1995-96, chmn., 1996-98; v.p. Del. River Greenway Partnership Inc., 1998-99, pres., 1999-2004; mem. econ. devel. com. Del. River Wild and Scenic Study Commn., Dept. Interior Nat. Park Svc., 1994-96; founder Solebury Forum, Bucks County, Environ. Party Com.; mem. Plumstead Twp. Parks and Recreation Commn., sec., 1992-97, vice chmn., 1997-98, chmn., 1998—2004; vice chmn. Plumstead Twp. Shade Tree Commn., NJ, 1992—; planning commn. tech. adv. com. Cape May County, 2001—04; founding ptnr. Rising Nation, Native Am. Cultural Heritage Project, 2000—; Indian Coun. mem. Lenape Nation of Pa., 2003—; founder Tidewaters Gateway Partnership, 2004—, pres. 2005—. Served with USMC, 1960-64. Mem. ASHRAE, NRA (life), VFW, DAV, Soc Mfg. Engrs., Bucks County Assn. Corrections and Rehab., Am. Legion (life), Vietnam Vets. Am. (life), Ctrl. Bucks County C. of C. (environ. and govt. com. 1986—), Internat. Air Movement and Control Assn. (mem. code rev. com., fire-smoke engring. com.), Nat. Fire Protection Assn., Underwriters Lab. (standards com.). Republican. Zen Buddhist. Office: PHL Inc 5556 Stump Rd Pipersville PA 18947-1090 E-mail: phltech@pil.net.

**MCPARLAND, ROBERT PATRICK,** literature educator, writer; b. Mar. 7, 1958; BA, Fordham U.; MA, St. John's U., 1996, Montclair State U., 1997; MPhil, Drew U., 2004, PhD, 2005. Asst. prof. English Felician Coll., Lodi/Rutherford, NJ, 1997—. Author: The Speech of Angels, 2003, In the Nick of Time, 2004, Music and Literary Modernism, 2005, Dickens and Melodrama, 2006. Home: 39 Rosedale Ave Elmwood Park NJ 07407-3033 Office: Dept English 262 S Main St Lodi NJ 07644 Office Phone: 201-559-6105. Business E-Mail: mcparlandr@inet.felician.edu.

**MCPARTLAND, JAMES MICHAEL,** academic administrator; b. NYC, Sept. 26, 1939; s. James J. and Helen M. (Leddy) McP. BS, Cornell U., 1961, MS, 1963; PhD, Johns Hopkins U., 1968. Rschr. U.S. Office Edn., Washington, 1965-67, U.S. Commn. Civil Rights, Washington, 1967-68; asst. dir. Ctr. Social Orgn. Schs., Johns Hopkins U., Balt., 1968-75, co-dir., 1976-94, dir., 1994—. Co-author: Equality of Educational Opportunity, 1966, Encyclopedia of Educational Research, 1992, Review of Research in Education, 1993; co-editor: Violence in Schools, 1977, Comprehensive Urban School Reform, 2002. Mem. Am. Ednl. Rsch. Assn., Am. Sociol. Assn., Am. Statis. Assn. Democrat. Roman Catholic. Avocation: music. Home: 1102 S Streeper St Baltimore MD 21224-4873 Office: Johns Hopkins U CSOS 3003 N Charles St Ste 200 Baltimore MD 21218-3888 Office Phone: 410-516-8803. E-mail: jmcpartland@csos.jhu.edu.

**MCPARTLAND, PATRICIA ANN,** educational association administrator, health educator; b. Passaic, N.J. d. Daniel and Josephine McP. BA, U. Mo., 1971; MCRP, Ohio State U., 1975, MS in Preventive Medicine, 1975; EdD in Higher and Adult Edn., Columbia U., 1988; cert. distance edn., Tex. A&M U., 2000, cert. distance edn. web pub. cert., 2001. Cert. health edn. specialist, distance edn. web pub., grants specialist; workforce devel. profl. Sr. health planner Merrimack Valley HSA, Lawrence, Mass., 1977—79; planning cons., adminstr. Children's Hosp., Boston 1979—80; exec. dir. Mass Workforce Alternatives, Rsch. & Devel., Inc., Marion, Mass., 1980—; evening sch. dir. Upper Cape Cod Regional Tech. Sch., Bourne, Mass., 2005—. V.p., cons. New Bedford (Mass.) Cmty. Health Ctr, 1993—94; chmn. edn. and tng. com. Health and Human Svc. Coalition, 1988—89; mem. project expert panel Office of Minority Health, 1997—2003; mem. New Eng. Regional Minority Health Conf. Com., 1997—99; vis. lectr. Bridgewater State Coll.; lectr. in field; project expert panel Office Minority Health's Culturally and Linguistically Appropriate Svcs.; mem. New Eng. Regional Minority Health Conf. Com., 2001—03; rev. editor Jour. Workforce Devel., Internat. Electronic Jour. Health Edn. Mem. editl. bd. Jour. Healthcare Edn. and Tng., 1989-93, Jour. of Workforce Devel.; author: Promoting Health in the Workplace, 1991; reviewer Qualitative Health Rsch. Jour.; contbr. articles to profl. jours. Vol. spkr. March of Dimes Found., Wareham, Mass., 1992-93; coll.-wide vocat. Cape Cod C.C. Hyannis, Mass., 1989; planning adv. and internat. symposium, Pasco, Wash., 1992; v.p. New Bedford chpt. Am. Cancer Soc., 1985-90. Recipient award Excellence in Continuing Edn. Nat. AHEC Ctr. Dirs. Assn., 1994, 95, 96, 97, Sec.'s awards for Outstanding Progam in Community Health, Nat. Cancer Inst., Washington, 1990. Mem.: APHA, Nat. Assn. Workforce Devel. Profls. (bd. dirs.), Nat. Planning Conf. (mem. com. 1984—87), Southeastern Mass. Health Planning (bd. dirs., sec. 1982—87), Inst. for Disease Prevention (steering com. 1982—). Avocations: writing, acting, dance, theater, travel. Home: PO Box 116 Marion MA 02738-0020 Office: Assn for Workforce Alternatives R&D Inc PO Box 69 2 Spring St Marion MA 02738-1519 Office Phone: 508-759-7711 ext. 258. Personal E-mail: pmcpartland@comcast.net. Business E-Mail: smahec@tiac.net, pmcpartland@uppercapetech.org.

**MCPEAK, MERRILL ANTHONY,** retired military officer; b. Santa Rosa, Calif., Jan. 9, 1936; s. Merrill Addison McPeak and Winifred Alice (Stewart) McPeak Bendall; m. Elynor Fay Moskowitz, Nov. 10, 1956; children—Mark Allen, Brian David AB, San Diego State Coll., 1957; MS, George Washington U., Washington, 1974. Commd. 2d lt. USAF, 1957, advanced through grades to gen., 1988; pilot USAF Thunderbirds, Nellis AFB, Nev., 1966-68; comdr. Misty Forward Air Controllers, Phu Cat, Republic of Vietnam, 1969, 20th Tactical Fighter Wing RAF, Upper Heyford, England, 1980-81, Twelfth Air Force, Bergstrom AFB, Tex., 1987-88; comdr.-in-chief Pacific Air Forces, Hickam AFB, Hawaii, 1988-90; chief of staff USAF, Washington, 1990-94; co. dir., cons., 1994—. Chmn. ECC Internat., 1997-2003, Ethicspoint, 2003-. Decorated DSM, Silver Star, Legion of Merit, DFC. Mem. Air Force Assn., Coun. Fgn. Rels., Daedalians, Sigma Chi. Home: 17360 Grandview Ct Lake Oswego OR 97034-6362 E-mail: mamcpeak@comcast.net.

**MCPETERS, SHARON JENISE,** artist, writer; b. San Bernardino, Calif., Oct. 17, 1951; d. Cecil L. and Mary I. (Tanner) McP.; 1 child, Angela M. Benders. BA in Journalism and English, U. So. Calif., 1981. Proofreader Ventura (Calif.) Coll., 1979. Prin. works include My Professors, 1993, Interpretations, 1994, The Thoughts of Socrates, 1995, Self Portrait, 1995,

Happiness, 1996, My True Self, 1998, Czechoslovakia 1923, 1999, Liszt, 1999, Portrait of Ten Artists, 2000; author: (autobiography) A Human Mind, 1997, (novels) Domestic Symphonies, 1986, The Broken Heart of the World, 1999, An Illuminated Manuscript, 1994, (short stories) The Library of Heaven, 2000, A Girl Without A Name, 2001, A Sanctified Heart, Selected Poems, 1974-2002, 2003, An Intellect's Goodness, 2004, Professor Scapegoat Speaks, 2006. Avocations: classical music, philosophy.

**MCPHEE, GEORGE,** professional sports team executive; BA in Bus., Bowling Green State U., 1982; JD, Rutgers U., 1992. Hockey player Guelph Platers, 1978, Bowling Green State U., 1978—82, NY Rangers, 1982, NJ Devils; v.p. dir. hockey ops. Vancouver Canucks, 1992—97, alt. gov., 1992—; gen. mgr., v.p Washington Capitals, 1997—. Recipient Hobey Baker Meml. award, 1982. Office: Washington Capitals Market Sq N 401 9th St NW Ste 750 Washington DC 20004

**MC PHEE, HENRY ROEMER,** lawyer; b. Ames, Iowa, Jan. 11, 1925; s. Harry Roemer and Mary (Ziegler) McP.; m. Joanne Lambert, May 19, 1956 (div. Dec. 1991); children: Henry Roemer III, Joanne, Larkin, Charles; m. Selby Fleming, Jan. 27, 1999. AB cum laude, Princeton U., 1947; LLB, Harvard U., 1950. Bar: N.J. 1951, Ill. 1961, D.C. 1966. Exec. asst. to gov. State of N.J., Trenton, 1950-52; assoc. R.E. & A.D. Watson, New Brunswick, N.J., 1952-54; asst. to gen. counsel FTC, Washington, 1954; exec. asst. White House, Washington, 1954-57; dep. spl. counsel Pres. U.S., Washington, 1957-58, assoc. spl. counsel, pres., 1958-61; ptnr. Hamel & Park, Washington, 1961-88, mem. mgmt. com., 1975-85, mng. ptnr., 1980-83; ptrnr. Hopkins & Sutter, 1988-93, of counsel, 1994—2002, Foley & Lardner, 2002—. Sec. N.J. Commn. on Interstate Cooperation, 1952-54; gen. counsel Rep. Nat. Fin. Com., 1968-73, Rep. Nat. Com., Washington, 1968. Chmn. bldg. com. Potomac (Md.) Presbyn. Ch., 1965-67; v.p. Rep. Club, Princeton, 1952-54; bd. dirs. Eisenhower Inst., 1983—2006, treas., 1991-93, mem. exec. com., 1991—2006. Mem. ABA, D.C. Bar Assn., N.J. Bar Assn., Lincoln's Inn Soc. Harvard Law Sch. Clubs: Tower (Princeton U.); Princeton (Washington) (pres. 1970-72), Metropolitan (Washington), Capitol Hill (Washington). Republican. Presbyterian. Avocation: tennis. Office: Foley & Lardner 3000 K St NW Ste 500 Washington DC 20007

**MCPHEE, JOAN,** lawyer; b. May 29, 1958; BA, Princeton Univ., 1980; JD magna cum laude, Harvard Univ., 1984. Bar: Mass. 1986, N.Y. 1986, R.I. 1991. Law clk. Judge Abraham D. Sofaer, US Dist. Ct. So. N.Y.; asst. U.S. atty. & dep. chief appeals unit U.S. Dept. Justice, So. Dist. N.Y.; ptnr. litigation dept. Ropes & Gray, Boston, 1990—, chair diversity com. Co-chair Govt. Enforcement Practice Group. Editor (articles): Harvard Law Rev. Mem.: ABA, R.I. Bar Assn., Boston Bar Assn., Phi Beta Kappa. Office: Ropes & Gray 1 International Pl Boston MA 02110-2624 Office Phone: 617-951-7535. Office Fax: 617-951-7050. Business E-Mail: jmcphee@ropesgray.com.

**MCPHEE, JOHN ANGUS,** writer; b. Princeton, NJ, Mar. 8, 1931; s. Harry Roemer and Mary (Ziegler) McP.; m. Pryde Brown, Mar. 16, 1957; children: Laura, Sarah, Jenny, Martha; m. Yolanda Whitman, Mar. 8, 1972; stepchildren: Cole Harrop, Andrew Harrop, Katherine Harrop, Vanessa Speir. AB, Princeton U., 1953; postgrad., Magdalene Coll., Cambridge U., Eng., 1953-54; LittD (hon.), Bates Coll., 1978, Colby Coll., 1978, Williams Coll., 1979, U. Alaska, 1980, Coll. William and Mary, 1988, Rutgers U., 1988; ScD, Maine Maritime Acad., 1992. TV playwright for Robert Montgomery Presents, NYC, 1955-56; contbg. editor, assoc. editor Time mag., 1957-64; staff writer The New Yorker mag., 1965—; Ferris prof. journalism Princeton U., 1975—. Author: A Sense of Where You Are, 1965, The Headmaster, 1966, Oranges, 1967, The Pine Barrens, 1968, A Roomful of Hovings, 1968, Levels of the Game, 1969, The Crofter and the Laird, 1970, Encounters with the Archdruid, 1971, The Deltoid Pumpkin Seed, 1973, The Curve of Binding Energy, 1974, Pieces of the Frame, 1975, The Survival of the Bark Canoe, 1975, The John McPhee Reader, 1976, Coming into the Country, 1977, Giving Good Weight, 1979, Basin and Range, 1981, In Suspect Terrain, 1983, La Place de la Concorde Suisse, 1984, Table of Contents, 1985, Rising from the Plains, 1986, The Control of Nature, 1989, Looking for a Ship, 1990, Assembling California, 1993, The Ransom of Russian Art, 1994, The Second John McPhee Reader, 1996, Irons in the Fire, 1997, Annals of the Former World, 1998, The Founding Fish, 2002, Uncommon Carriers, 2006. Recipient award in lit., Am. Acad. and Inst. Arts and Letters, 1977, Woodrow Wilson award, Princeton U., 1982, Journalism award, Am. Assn. of Petroleum Geologists, 1982, 1987, John Wesley Powell award, US Geol. Survey, 1988, John Burroughs medal, 1990, Walter Sullivan award, Am. Geophys. Union, 1993, James H. Shea award, Nat. Assn. Geology Tchrs., 1995, award for Outstanding Achievement, Am. Inst. Petroleum Geologists, 1997, award of merit, Field Mus. Natural History, 1998, Pulitzer Prize for Gen. Non-Fiction, Annals of the Former World, 1999, Pres.'s award for disting. tchg., Princeton U., 1999, Pub. Svc. award, Geol. Soc. Am., 2002, Gold medal for Distinction in Natural Art. Acad. Natural Scis. Fellow Geol. Soc. Am.; mem. Am. Acad. Arts and Letters.

**MCPHEE, JONATHAN,** music director, conductor, composer, interim artistic coordinator; LRAM, Royal Acad. Music; BM, MM, Juilliard Sch. Music dir., prin. condr. Boston Ballet, 1988—; mus. dir. Symphony by the Sea, Boston, 2004—; prin. condr., artistic advisor Lexington Sinfonietta. Condr.: dance cos. The Joffrey Ballet, The Martha Graham Dance Co., The Dance Theatre of Harlem, Am. Ballet Theatre, N.Y.C. Ballet, The Royal Ballet, Covent Garden, Nat. Ballet of Can., orchs. including Buffalo Philharm., Joffrey Ballet Orch., Rochester Philharm, Opera Orch., BBC Scottish Symphony, Hague Philharm., Boston Pops, Syracuse Symphony, San Diego Symphony, San Francisco Symphony, Orchestre Colonne, The Nat. Philharm, Orch. Danish Radio Symphony Orch, rev. (films) Martha Graham works, Cave of the Heart, Errand Into the Maze, El Penintent, Michael Gandolfi's Caution to the Wind; author: (rev.) version Stravinsky's Rite of Spring; arrangements pub.: by Boosey & Hawkes. Office: Boston Ballet 19 Clarendon St Boston MA 02116-6100 also: P O Box 1425 Marblehead MA 01945

**MCPHEE, KATHERINE HOPE,** singer; b. Sherman Oaks, Calif., Mar. 25, 1984; d. Peisha Burch and Daniel McPhee. Contestant & second-place winner American Idol, 2006; signed to 19 Recordings Ltd./RCA Records, 2006—. Singer: (singles) Somewhere Over the Rainbow/My Destiny, 2006; actor: (plays) Annie Get Your Gun, The Ghost & Mrs. Muir, 2005; (films) Crazy, 2006. Office: 19 Entertainment Ltd 33 Ransomes Dock 35-37 Parkgate Rd London SW11 4NP England Office Phone: 20-7801-1919. Office Fax: 20-7801-1920. E-mail: contact@19.co.uk.

**MCPHEE, MARK STEVEN,** gastroenterologist, educator; b. Kansas City, Mo., Nov. 8, 1951; s. William Robert and Mary Kay (Paige) McP.; m. Christina Marie Luebke, July 14, 1974; children: Molly Amanda, Ian Andrew. BA magna cum laude, Pomona Coll., Claremont, Calif., 1973; MD summa cum laude, U. Kans., Kansas City, 1976. Diplomate Nat. Bd. Med. Examiners; diplomate in internal medicine and gastroenterology Am. Bd. Internal Medicine. Intern, resident, fellow Harvard U. Med. Sch., Boston, 1976-80; dir. gastrointestinal endoscopy unit Kans. U. Med. Ctr., Kansas City, 1980-85; chief sect. gastroenterology St. Luke's Hosp., Kansas City, Mo., 1988-93, chair dept. medicine, 1992-97, assoc. dir. med. edn., 1995-97, dir. med. edn., 1997—; assoc. dean U. Mo.-Kansas City Med. Sch., 1997—. Asst. prof. medicine U. Kans., KansasCity, 1980-85, assoc. prof., 1985; clin. prof. medicine U. Mo.-Kansas City, 1970-97, prof. medicine, 1997—. Author: Annotated Key References in Gastroenterology, 1982; contbr. chpts. to textbook, articles to profl. jours. Bd. dirs. St. Luke's Hosp., Kansas City,Mo., 1993—, Am. Digestive Health Found., Bethesda, Md., 1996—. Fellow ACP, Am. Coll. Gastroenterology; mem. Am. Gastroent. Assn. (mem. governing bd., treas.), St. Lukes Hosp. Physicians Assn. (bd. dirs.), HealthNet Physician Ptnrs. (bd. dirs.), Alpha Omega Alpha. Episcopalian. Avocations: poetry, hiking/camping, golf, tennis, sporting clay target shooting. Office: St Lukes Hosp Dept Med Edn 44th and Wornall Rd Kansas City MO 64111

**MCPHEE, SARAH COLLYER,** art historian, educator; AB, Harvard U., 1982; MA in Art Hist., Columbia U., 1988, PhD in Art Hist., 1997. Editor, writer Met. Mus. Art, 1984—86; asst. prof. Emory U., Art Hist. Dept., 1995—2001, assoc. prof., 2001—. Vis. assoc. prof. Columbia U., Dept. Art Hist. and Archaeology, 2003—04. Co-author: Drawings from the Roman Period 1704-1714, 1999; author: Bernini and the Bell Towers: Architecture and Politics at the Vatican, 2002. Fellow Guggenheim Meml. Found., 2004. Mem.: Inst. for Advanced Study. Office: Art Hist Dept Emory U 128 Carlos Hall Atlanta GA 30322 Office Phone: 404-727-0069. E-mail: smcphee@emory.edu.

**MCPHEETERS, EDWIN KEITH,** architect, educator; b. Stillwater, Okla., Mar. 26, 1924; s. William Henry and Eva Winona (Mitchell) McP.; m. Patricia Ann Foster, Jan. 29, 1950 (div. 1981); children: Marc Foster (dec.), Kevin Mitchell, Michael Hunter; m. Mary Louise Marvin, July 21, 1984. BArch, Okla. State U., 1949; MFA, Princeton U., 1956. Instr. architecture U. Fla., 1949-51; asst. prof. Ala. Poly. Inst., Auburn (Ala.) U., 1951-54; fellow Princeton U., 1955, 81; from asst. prof. to prof. U. Ark., 1956-66; prof. Rensselaer Poly. Inst., 1966-69, dean, 1966-69; prof. Auburn U., 1969-89, dean Sch. Architecture and Fine Arts, 1969-88, dean, prof. emeritus, 1989—. Mem. Ala. Bd. Registration for Archs., 1978-87; profl. adviser South Ctrl. Bell Tel. Co., 1977-79, So. Co., 1979-81, Ala. Power Co., 1979-81, Okla. State U., 1983, Ala. Sch. Fine Arts, 1985-86; cons. Taliesin Archs., 1988-92, adj. prof. Frank Lloyd Wright Sch. of Architecture, 1992-94. Served to 2d lt. USAAC, 1943-45; capt. USAFR 1945-57. Recipient Disting. Arch. award Ala. Archtl. Found., 2001. Fellow AIA (pres. Ala. coun. 1978, Merit award 1976, East Ala. Design awards 1986, 87, 90, 92); mem. Assn. Collegiate Schs. Arch. (bd. dirs. 1970-77, Disting. Prof. 1989), Blue Key, Kappa Sigma, Omicron Delta Kappa, Kappa Kappa Psi, Tau Sigma Delta, Rotary; signature mem. Watercolor Soc. Ala. (pres. 2000—). Episcopalian. Office Phone: 334-887-8779.

**MCPHERSON, ALICE RUTH,** ophthalmologist, educator; b. Regina, Sask., Can., June 30, 1926; came to U.S., 1938, naturalized, 1958; d. Gordon and Viola (Hoover) McP. BS, U. Wis., 1948, MD, 1951, DSc (hon.), 1997. Diplomate Am. Bd. Ophthalmology. Intern Santa Barbara (Calif.) Cottage Hosp., 1951-52; resident anesthesiology Hartford (Conn.) Hosp., 1952; resident ophthalmology Chgo. Eye, Ear, Nose and Throat Hosp., 1953, U. Wis. Hosps., 1953-55; ophthalmologist Davis and Duehr Eye Clinic, Madison, Wis., 1956-57; clin. instr. U. Wis., 1956-57; fellow retina svc. Mass. Eye and Ear Infirmary, 1957-58; ophthalmologist Scott and White Clinic, Temple, Tex., 1958-60; practice medicine specializing in ophthalmology and retinal diseases Houston, 1960—. Staff Meth., St. Luke's, Tex. Children's Hosps., Harris County Hosp. Dist., Houston; clin. asst. prof. Baylor Coll. Medicine, Houston, 1959-61, asst. prof. ophthalmology, 1961-69, clin. assoc. prof., 1969-75, clin. prof., 1975-98, prof., 1998—; cons. retinal diseases VA Hosp., Houston, 1960—, Ben Taub Hosp., Houston, 1960—; mem. adv. com. for active staff appt. sect. ophthalmology Meth. Hosp., 1986-91, mem equipment com., 1993-95, mem. grievance panel, 1997; vol. clin. faculty appts. and promotions com., 1993; bd. dirs. Highlights of Ophthalmology; v.p. N.Am. Highlights of Ophthalmology Internat. Editor: New and Controversial Aspects of Retinal Detachment, 1968, New and Controversial Aspects of Vitreoretinal Surgery, 1977, Retinopathy of Prematurity: Current Concepts and Controversies, 1986. Amb. Houston Ballet, mem. Houston Ballet Found.; mem. pres.'s coun. Houston Grand Opera; condrs. cir. Houston Symphony, mem. Houston Symphony Soc.; mem. campaign for 80s Baylor Coll. Medicine; mem. Assn. for Cmty. TV, BBB, Physicians' Benevolent Fund, South Tex. Diabetes Assn. Inc., Jr. League Houston; bd. dirs. U. Wis. Found., Madison. Recipient Award of appreciation KT Eye Found., 1978, Woodlands Medal for Outstanding Contbn. to the Econ. Devel. of Cmty., 1988, spl. recognition award Assn. for Rsch. in Vision in Ophthalmology, Crystal award Recognizing Generous Support-Ptnrs. with an Eye for Vision Found. Am. Acad. Ophthalmology, 2000, Benjamin Boyd Humanitarian award Pan Am. Assn. Ophthalmology, 2001, Philip Corboy Meml. award Disting. Svc. Ophthalmology, 2002, Women of Vision Houston Delta Gamma Found., 2002; Alice R. Mc Pherson Lab. for Retina Rsch. dedicated Baylor Ctr. for Biotech., 1988; Alice R. Mc Pherson Day proclaimed in her honor Mayor of City of Houston, Mar. 12, 1988. Fellow: ACS (credentials and Tex. credentials com., com. on applications), Am. Acad. Ophthalmology (2nd v.p. 1979, vice chmn. program devel. found. bd. trustees 1993—, nominating com. subspecialty/specialized sect. of coun. 2001, com. for pub. and profl. rels., bd. dirs. ophthalmology ednl. trust fund found., laureate award selection com., mem. coun. representing PAAO, honor award 1956, sr. honor award 1986, guest of honor 1998 meeting, Visionary Soc. Gold Mem.); mem.: AMA, Highlights Ophthal. Internat., Schepens Internat. Soc. (sec. 1986—93, v.p. 1993—95, pres. 1995—97), U. Wis. Ophthal. Alumni Assn. (founding pres. 1990—93, founded Alice R. McPherson lectureship 1994), Assn. Rsch. Surgeons, Pan Am. Assn. Ophthalmology Found., Tex. Ophthal. Assn., So. Med. Soc., Rsch. to Prevent Blindness, Pan Am. Assn. Ophthalmology (v.p. 1991—92, pres. elect 1992—95, AJO lectr. 1993, pres. 1995—97, pres. found. 1997, bd. dirs.; membership com., Benjamin Boyd Humanitarian award 2001), Macula Soc. (credentialing com. 1992), Internat. Soc. Eye Rsch. (credentials com. 1992), Houston Ophthal. Soc. (pres. 1990—91, credentials com.), Harris County Med. Soc., Am. Bd. Laser Surgery, Am. Soc. Contemporary Ophthalmology (Charles Schepens Hon. award), Internat. Coll. Ocular Surgeons (vice regent 1991), Retina Soc. (v.p. 1976—77, pres. 1978—79, credentials com.), Am. Med. Women's Assn., Internat. Coll. Surgeons (vice regent 1991—), Tex. Med. Assn., Vitreous Soc., Jules Gonin Club. Achievements include research in vision and ophthalmology. Office: Tex Med Ctr 6560 Fannin St Ste 2200 Houston TX 77030-2715 E-mail: alicem@bcm.tmc.edu

**MCPHERSON, BRUCE A.,** state official, former state legislator; b. Santa Cruz; m. Mary McPherson; children: Tori, Hunter. Mem. Calif. State Assembly, 1993-96, Calif. State Senate, 1996—2005, vice-chair edn. com., mem. appropriations com., environ. quality com., pub. safety com., revenue and taxation com.; sec. of state State of Calif., Sacramento, 2005—. Mem. joint coms. on arts, headwaters forest and fisheries/aquaculture. Active Santa Cruz City Sch. Dist.; active literacy program Santa Cruz County. Recipient Friend of Higher Edn. award Calif. State U. Alumni Coun., 1995, Simon Wiesenthal Mus. of Tolerance award, 1998; named Legislator of Yr., U. Calif. Alumni Assn., 1997, Pub. Ofcl. of Yr., Monterey Bay Nat. Marine Sanctuary Coun., 1997, 1998 Friend of C.C., Assn. Calif. C.C. Adminstrs., 1998. Mem. Calif. Coastal Conservancy, Santa Cruz Rotary Club (pres.). Republican. Office: Office Secy of State 1500 11th St Sacramento CA 95814 Office Phone: 916-653-7244. Office Fax: 916-653-4620.*

**MCPHERSON, CRAIG A.,** cardiologist, educator; s. Lester F. and Gloria K. Mcpherson; m. Anita K. Kerbesharn, 1948; children: Marianne E., Christina R. AB, Columbia U., N.Y.C., 1972; MD, Tufts U., Boston, 1976. Lic. internal medicine Am. Bd. of Internal Medicine, cardiovasc. diseases Am. Bd. of Internal Medicine, cardiac electrophysiology Am. Bd. of Internal Medicine, Am. Bd. of Internal Medicine. Assoc. prof. of medicine Yale U., New Haven, Conn., 1984—89, assoc. prof. of medicine, 1989—2006, clin. prof. of medicine, 2006—. Dir. cardiac electrophysiology Bridgeport Hosp., Conn., 1992—, dir. cardiology tng., 1995—. Named Tchr. of the Yr., Bridgeport Hosp., 1995, 2005; recipient Hands and Heart award, Dept. of VA, 1989. Fellow: Am. Coll. of Cardiology; mem.: ACP, Am. Heart Assn., Heart Rhythm Soc., Alpha Omega Alpha. Office: Bridgeport Hosp Yale Univ 267 Grant St Bridgeport CT 06610 Office Phone: 203-384-3442. Business E-Mail: pcmcph@bpthosp.org.

**MCPHERSON, DONALD PAXTON, III,** lawyer; b. Balt., Aug. 9, 1941; s. Donald Paxton Jr. and Janet Lewis Russell McPherson; m. Anna Mary Teaff; children: David Russell, Cynthia Quandt. AB, Princeton U., 1963; LLB, Columbia U., 1966. Bar: Md. 1966, U.S. Dist. Ct. Md. 1967, U.S. Ct. Appeals (4th cir.) 1967. Assoc. Piper & Marbury, Balt., 1966-74, ptnr., 1974-98, head real estate dept., 1980-94, of counsel, 1998—. Mem. ABA, Md. Bar Assn. Democrat. Presbyterian. Avocations: swimming, bicycling, hiking. Office: DLA Piper Rudnick Gray Cary LLP 6225 Smith Ave Baltimore MD 21209-3600

**MCPHERSON, DONALD SCOTT,** labor and employment arbitrator/mediator; b. Sharon, Pa., June 11, 1947; s. Donald McMillan and Lily (Smith) McP.; m. Linda Jo Leighty, Aug. 16, 1969; 1 child, Kimra Leigh. BA, Indiana U. of Pa., 1969, MA, 1971; PhD, U. Pitts., 1977. Dir. residence life Indiana U. of Pa., 1969-77, prof. employment rels., 1977-93, chmn. dept., 1977-87, disting. univ. prof., 1993—2004, prof. emeritus, 2005—. Pres. Assn. Pa. State Coll. and Univ. Faculty, Indiana U. Pa. chpt., 1980. Author: Resolving Grievances, 1983; contbr. articles to profl. jours. Elder Calvary Presbyn. Ch., 1983—; sec. St. Andrew's Soc. of Indiana, 1991-94. Recipient disting. faculty award for svc., Commonwealth of Pa., 1983, Outstanding Alumni award, Indiana U. of Pa., 1983. Mem. Nat. Acad. Arbitrators, Assn. for Conflict Resolution, Labor and Employment Rels. Rsch. Assn. (exec. dir. Western Pa. chpt. 1982-89), Found. for Ind. U. of Pa. (bd. dir. 1977-82), Ind. Coun. on the Arts, Ind. U. of Pa. Alumni Assn. (pres. 1975-79), Clan MacPherson Assn. (life), Phi Kappa Phi. Democrat. Presbyterian.

**MCPHERSON, ELIZABETH WRIGHT,** clinical geneticist; b. Battle Creek, Mich., Feb. 27, 1950; d. John Burton and Barbara Cray (Wright) McP.; m. Owen R. Christianson, June 27, 1976; children: Caitlin Ase, Knut Andrew, Olav Iain. BA, Pomona Coll., 1971; MD, U. Wash., 1975; MS, U. Wis., 1975. Diplomate Am. Bd. Pediatrics, Am. Bd. Med. Genetics. Intern and resident U. Wis., Madison, 1975-77, fellow in clin. genetics, 1977-79, clin. geneticist, 1979-81, Children's Hosp. Buffalo, 1981-86, Johns Hopkins U., Balt., 1986-87; pediatrician, geneticist Kaiser Permanent, Washington, 1987-90; pediatric geneticist West Penn Hosp., Pitts., 1990-93; med. geneticist dysmorphologist Magee-Women's Hosp., Pitts., 1993—. Leader Girl Scouts Am., Reston, Va., 1987-90, Boy Scouts Am. McCandless, Pa., 1990—. Fellow Am. Coll. Med. Genetics, Am. Acad. Pediatrics (mem. exec. com. sect. on genetics). Avocations: medieval re-enactment, camping, skiing, Tae Kwon Do. Home: 1462 Bretton Way Pittsburgh PA 15237-6301

**MCPHERSON, GAIL,** publishing and real estate executive; b. Ft. Worth; d. Garland and Daphne McP. Student, U. Tex.-Austin; BA, MS, CUNY. Advt. sales exec. Harper's Bazaar mag., NYC, 1974—76; st. v.p., fashion mktg. dir. L'Officiel/ USA mag., NYC, 1976—80; fashion mgr. Town & Country Mag., NYC, 1980—82; v.p. advt. and mktg. Ultra mag., NYC, 1982—84; fragrance, jewelry and imported automotive mgr. M. Mag., NYC, Tex., 1984—85; st. real estate sales exec. Fredric M. Reed & Co., Inc., NYC, Tex., 1985—88; AT&T security system rep. Home-Watch Inc., Amarillo, Tex., 1989—92; sales rep. Universal Comm., Dallas, 1992—94; acct. exec. Corp. Mktg., Inc., Dallas, 1994—98; sales rep. Pub. Concepts, Dallas, 1998—, NY sponsor Southampton Hosp. Benefit Com.; jr. com. Mannes Sch. Music, NYC, Henry St. Settlement; mem. Dallas Mus. Art League. Mem. Fashion Group NY, Advt. Women NY, Real Estate Bd. NY, U. Tex. Alumni Assn. of NY (v.p.), Corviglia Club (St. Moritz, Switzerland), Doubles, El Morocco Club (jr. com.), Le Club. Republican. Presbyterian. Home: 17850 Sunmeadow Dr #2009 Dallas TX 75252-5382

**MCPHERSON, GUY RANDALL,** ecology educator, researcher; b. Wallace, Idaho, Feb. 29, 1960; s. James Lyle and Edna Carol (Boutinen) McP.; m. Sheila Dianne Merrigan, Aug. 6, 1983. BS, U. Idaho, 1982; MS, Tex. Tech U., 1984, PhD, 1987. Rsch. assoc. Tex. Tech U., Lubbock, 1983-87; postdoctoral rsch. assoc. Inst. of Ecology U. Ga., Athens, 1987-88; vis. asst. prof. Tex. A&M U., College Station, 1988-89; asst. prof. U. Ariz., Tucson, 1989-95, assoc. prof., 1995—2000, prof., 2000—. Vis. assoc. prof. U. Calif., Berkeley, 1995-96, mem. sci. adv. panel, 1993—; dir. David H. Smith postdoctoral fellows program, Arlington, Va., 2000-01; mem. grad. rsch. adv. com. U. Ariz., Tucson, 1989—; moderator in field. Author: Ecology and Management od North American Savannas, 1997, Killing the Natives: Has the American Dream Become a Nightmare, Letters to a Young Academic; author chpts. to books; compiler: (book) Glossary of Fire Management Terms Used in the U.S., 1990; acting assoc. editor Internat. Wildfire Fire, 1990—; contbr. chpt. to book. USDA grantee, 1990, 92, 95, 97, 98, 01, 03, 05, U.S. Dept. Interior grantee, 1999, 02, 04. Mem. AAUP, Soc. for Conservation Biology, Ecol. Soc. Am., Natural Areas Assn. Democrat. Achievements include research in effects of disturbance on community boundary dynamics, direct effects of competition, herbivory effects on plant communities; applied ecology of savannas and grasslands. Office: U Ariz Bse 325srnr Tucson AZ 85721-0001 Home: 1353 N Culpepper Ave Tucson AZ 85745 Office Phone: 520-621-5389. Business E-mail: grm@ag.arizona.edu.

**MC PHERSON, HARRY CUMMINGS, JR.,** lawyer; b. Tyler, Tex., Aug. 22, 1929; s. Harry Cummings and Nan (Hight) McP.; m. Clayton Read, Aug. 30, 1952 (div.); children: Courtenay, Peter B.; m. Mary Patricia DeGroot, Oct. 17, 1981; 1 child, Sam B. BA, U. South, 1949, DCL, 1965; student, Columbia U., 1949-50; LLB, U. Tex., 1956. Bar: Tex. 1955, D.C. 1969. Asst. gen. counsel Democratic policy com. U.S. Senate, 1956-59, assoc. counsel, 1959-61, gen. counsel, 1961-63; dep. under sec. internat. affairs Dept. Army, 1963-64; asst. sec. ednl. and cultural affairs Dept. State, 1964-65; spl. asst. and counsel to Pres. Johnson, 1965-66, spl. counsel, 1966-69; sr. ptnr. Verner Liipfert Bernhard McPherson & Hand, Washington, 1969—2002; ptnr., Fed. Affairs & Legis., Govt. Affairs practices DLA Piper Rudnick Gray Cary, Washington, 2002—. Chmn. task force on domestic policy Dem. Adv. Coun. Elected Ofcls., 1974-76; mem. Pres.'s Commn. on Accident at Three Mile Island, 1979; vice chmn. John F. Kennedy Ctr. for Performing Arts, 1969-76, gen. counsel, 1977-91; bd. dirs. Woodrow Wilson Internat. Ctr. for Scholars, 1969-74; pres. Fed. City Coun., 1983-88; apptd. vice chmn. U.S. Internat. Cultural and Trade Ctr. Commn., 1988-93. Author: A Political Education, 1972, 88, 95. Mem. U.S. Base Closure and Realignment Commn., 1993. 2d lt. USAF, 1950-53. Recipient Disting. Civilian Svc. award Dept. Army, 1964, Arthur S. Flemming award, 1968, Judge Learned Hand Human Rels. award Am. Jewish Com., 1994. Mem. D.C. Bar Assn., N.Y. Council on Fgn. Relations (dir. 1974-77), Econ. Club of Washington (pres. 1992-99). Democrat. Episcopalian. Home: 10213 Montgomery Ave Kensington MD 20895-3325 Office: DLA Piper Rudnick Gray Cary 1200 19th St NW Washington DC 20036-2412 Office Phone: 202-861-6464. Office Fax: 202-689-8570. Business E-mail: harry.mcpherson@dlapiper.com.

**MCPHERSON, JAMES ALAN,** writer, educator; b. Savannah, Ga., Sept. 16, 1943; s. James and Mable (Smalls) McP.; 1 dau., Rachel Alice. BA, Morris Brown Coll., 1965; LLB, Harvard, 1968; MFA, U. Iowa, 1971. Asst. prof. lit. U. Calif., Santa Cruz, 1969-71, Morgan State U., 1975-76; assoc. prof. English U. Va., Charlottesville, 1976-81; prof. English U. Iowa, 1981—. Mem. lit. panel Nat. Endowment for Arts, 1977-80; lectr. Japan, 1989-90; vis. scholar Yale Law Sch., 1978-79. Author: Hue and Cry, 1969, Railroad, 1976, Elbow Room, 1977 (Pulitzer prize 1978), A World Unsuspected, 1987, The Prevailing South, 1988, Confronting Racial Differences, 1990, Lure and Loathing, 1993, Crossings, 1993, Crab Cakes, 1998, Fathering Daughters, 1998, The View From Exile, 2000; editor Double Take Mag., 1995—; contbr. editor Atlantic Monthly, Boston, 1969. Atlantic grantee, 1968; Guggenheim fellow, 1972-73, Ctr. Behavioral Studies fellow, Stanford, Calif., 1997-98, 2002-03; Recipient award in lit. Nat. Inst. Arts and Letters, 1970, MacArthur Found. award, 1981, Excellence in Tchg. award U. Iowa, 1991, Green Eyeshades award Soc. So. Journalists, 1994; stories selected for O'Henry Collection and Best American Short Stories, 1969, 73, Best Am. Short Stories of the 20th Century, Best Am. Essays various Norton Anthologies, 1990, 93, 94, 95, Pushcart prize, 1995, 96, award Cannon Found., 2002. Mem. ACLU, NAACP, P.E.N., Am. Acad. Arts and Scis. (elected mem. 1995), Authors League. Office Phone: 319-335-0416.

**MCPHERSON, JAMES E.,** judge; B in Pub. Adminstrn., San Diego U., 1977, JD, 1981; grad., Naval Justice Sch., 1982; LLM in Mil. Law, Judge Advocate Gen. Sch., 1991. Bar: U.S. Supreme Ct., Calif. Enlisted mil. police USAR; commd. ensign JAGC USNR, 1979, intern Naval Legal Svc. Office San Diego, 1979, asst. force judge advocate comdr. staff U.S. Naval Air

Force, U.S. Atlantic Fleet, 1982—83, with Naval Legal Svc. Office Norfolk, 1983—85, judge advocate Naval Air Sta. Cubi Point, Philippines, 1985—88, command judge advocate USS Theodore Roosevelt, 1988—91, sr. def. counsel Naval Legal Svc. Office, 1991—92, sr. trial counsel, 1992—94, asst. legal and legis. matters to chief naval ops., 1995—97, spl. counsel to chief naval ops., 1997—2000, comdr. Trial Svc. Office East Norfolk, 2000—02, dep. JAG naval legal svc. command, 2002—. Decorated Legion of Merit (two awards), Meritorious Svc. Medal (four awards), Army Commendation Medal, Navy Achievement Medal (two awards). Office: JAGC 1322 Patterson Ave Ste 3000 Washington DC 20374-5066

**MC PHERSON, JAMES MUNRO,** history professor; b. Valley City, N.D., Oct. 11, 1936; s. James Munro and Miriam (Osborn) McPherson; m. Patricia Rasche, Dec. 28, 1957; 1 child, Joanna Erika. BA, Gustavus Adolphus Coll., 1958; PhD, Johns Hopkins U., 1963. From mem. faculty to prof. Princeton U., 1962—91, George Henry Davis '86 prof. Am. history, 1991—2004, prof. emeritus, 2004—. Jefferson lectr., 2000. Author: Struggle for Equality, 1964 (Ainsfield-Wolf award race rels., 1965), The Negro's Civil War, 1965, Marching Toward Freedom: The Negro in the Civil War, 1968, Blacks in America: Bibliographical Essays, 1971, The Abolitionist Legacy: From Reconstruction to the NAACP, 1975, Ordeal by Fire: The Civil War and Reconstruction, 1981, 1992, Battle Cry of Freedom: The Civil War Era, 1988 (Pulitzer prize for history, 1989), Abraham Lincoln and the Second American Revolution, 1991, Images of the Civil War, 1992, What They Fought For 1861-1865, 1994, The Atlas of the Civil War, 1994, Drawn With the Sword: Reflections on the American Civil War, 1996, For Cause and Comrades: Why Men Fought in the Civil War, 1997 (Lincoln prize, 1998), Lamson of the Gettysburg: The Civil War Letters of Lt. Roswell H. Lamson, U.S. Navy, 1997 (Theodore and Franklin D. Roosevelt prize in naval history, 1998), Is Blood Thicker than Water? Crisis of Nationalism in the Modern World, 1998, Writing the Civil War: The Quest to Understand, 1998, To the Best of My Ability, 2000, The American Presidents, 2000, Days of Destiny, 2001, Crossroads of Freedom: Antietam, 2002, Hallowed Ground: A Walk at Gettysburg, 2003, Illustrated Battle Cry of Freedom, 2003. Fellow, Huntington-Nat. Endowment for Humanities, 1977—78, Behavioral Scis. Ctr., Stanford U., 1982—83, Huntington-Seaver Inst., 1987—88; Danforth fellow, 1958—62, Guggenheim fellow, 1967—68. Mem.: Soc. Am. Historians (pres. 1999—2000), Orgn. Am. Historians, So. Hist. Assn., Am. Hist. Assn. (pres. 2003—04), Am. Philos. Soc., Phi Beta Kappa (Jefferson lectr. 2000). Home: 15 Randall Rd Princeton NJ 08540-3609 Office Phone: 609-258-4173. Business E-Mail: jmcphers@princeton.edu.

**MCPHERSON, LARRY EUGENE,** photographer, educator; b. Newark, Ohio, May 1, 1943; s. Eugene Edward and Ethel Grace (Lehman) McP. BA, Columbia Coll., Chgo., 1976; MA, No. Ill. U., 1978. Instr. Columbia Coll. 1971-76; assoc. prof. photography U. Memphis, 1978—. Instr. Sch. of Art Inst. Chgo., spring 1972; workshop instr. Ohio State U., Columbus, summer 1980, VSW Summer Inst., Rochester, N.Y., summer 1988. One-man shows include Art Inst. Chgo., 1969, 78, 81, Dayton Art Inst., 1992; exhibited in group shows at Mus. Modern Art, N.Y.C., 1978, Corcoran Gallery Art, Washington, 1982, George Eastman House, Rochester, N.Y., 1982, New Orleans Mus. Art, 1992, Milw. Art Mus., 1996, Birmingham Mus. Art, 1996, Art Inst. Chgo., 1997; represented in permanent collections Mus. Modern Art, Art Inst. Chgo., George Eastman House, New Orleans Mus. Art, Mus. Fine Arts, Houston, Memphis Brooks Mus. Art, The Dayton Art Inst., Birmingham Mus. Art, Milw. Mus. Art, Ogden Mus. So. Art; author: "Memphis", Santa Fe, NM: Center for American Places, 2002. Faculty Devel. grantee U. Memphis, 1983, 92, 99; grantee-fellow Nat. Endowment for Arts, 1979, 79; Guggenheim fellow, 1980. Mem. Soc. Photog. Edn. Home: 7725 Shadow Bend Ln Arlington TN 38002-8051 Office: U Memphis Dept Art Memphis TN 38152-0001 Business E-mail: lmcphrsn@memphis.edu.

**MCPHERSON, MICHAEL STEVEN,** academic administrator, economist; b. June 6, 1947; married; 2 children. BA Math., U. Chgo., 1967, MA Econs., 1970, PhD Econs., 1974. Instr. econs. dept. U. Ill., Chgo., 1971—74; asst. prof. econs. Williams Coll., 1974—81, assoc. prof. econs., 1981—84, prof. econs., 1984—96, chmn. econs. dept., then dean of faculty, 1986—91; pres. Macalester Coll., St. Paul, 1996—2003, Spencer Found. Chgo., 2003—. Cons. Data Resources, Inc., 1979, Nat. Rsch. Coun. Common. Human Resources, 1979, Modern Lang. Assn., 1980, Nat. Acad. Edn., 1980, Smith Coll., 1982, The Coll. Bd., 1983, Rand Corp., 1985—86, U.S. Dept. Edn. Ctr. Statis., 1986. Co-author (with M.O. Shapiro): Keeping College Affordable: Government and Educational Opportunity, 1991, The Student Aid Game: Meeting Need and Rewarding Talent in American Higher Education, 1998; co-author: (with D. Hausman) Economic Analysis and Moral Philosophy, 1996; editor: The Demand for the New Faculty in Science and Engineering, 1980, Democratic Development and the Art of Trespassing: Essays in Honor of Albert O. Hirschman, 1986; contbr. articles to profl. jours. Trustee Coll. Bd., 1997—. Fellow Study fellow, Am. Coun. Learned Socs., 1977—78, vis. fellow, Princeton U., 1977—78, sr. fellow, Brookings Inst., 1984—86; grantee, Ford Found., 1981—83, Mellon Found., 1984—86. Office: The Spencer Foundation 625 N Michigan Ave Ste 1600 Chicago IL 60611-3109

**MCPHERSON, MILTON MONROE,** retired history professor; b. Beatrice, Ala., Oct. 19, 1928; s. Laurence Milton and Annie Mae (Bell) McP.; m. Carolyn Elizabeth Coley, Dec. 16, 1955; children: Milton Jr., Herbert L., Gretchen M. BA, U. Ala., 1950, MA, 1959, PhD in Am. History, 1970. Asst. prof. history Miss. Coll., Clinton, 1959—60, Mercer U., Macon, Ga., 1960—61, Ala. Coll., Montevallo, 1961—62, Pensacola Jr. Coll., Fla., 1962—68; assoc. prof. history Troy State U., Ala., 1968—87, prof. history, 1987—89; prof. history emeritus 1989—; ret., 1989. Author: The Ninety-Day Wonders: OCS and the Modern American Army, 2001; editor: Memories That Lingered: The Life and Times of Laurence Milton McPherson, 1993, Timeless Moments: Essays in American History, 1995. 1st lt. US Army, 1950-53. Mem. NEA, Ala. Hist. Assn., So. Hist. Assn. Avocations: writing, reading, photography, walking, travel. Home: 206 Sherwood Ave Troy AL 36081-4534

**MCPHERSON, PETER (M. PETER MCPHERSON),** educational association administrator, former academic administrator; b. Grand Rapids, Mich., Oct. 27, 1940; s. Donald and Ellura E. (Frost) McP.; m. Joanne McPherson; 4 children. BA in Polit. Sci., Mich. State U., 1963; MBA, Western Mich. U., 1967; JD, Am. U., 1969; LHD (hon.), Va. State U., 1994, Mt. St. Mary;s Coll. 1996; LLD (hon.), Mich. State U., 1984. Tax law specialist IRS, 1969—75; spl. asst. to Pres. Ford, deputy dir. presdl. personnel The White House, Washington, 1975—77; ptnr. Vorys, Sater, Seymour & Pease, Washington, 1977—80; adminstr. Agy. Internat. Devel., 1981—87; dep. sec. US Dept. Treasury, Washington, 1987—89; group exec. v.p. Bank Am., 1989—93; pres. Mich. State U., East Lansing, 1993—2004, pres. emeritus, 2004—; co-chair, founder Partnership to Cut Hunger and Poverty in Africa, 2005—; pres. Nat. Assn. State Universities and Land-Grant Colleges, 2006—. Chmn. bd. Overseas Pvt. Investment Corp., 1981—87; dir. econ. policy Coalition Provisional Authority, Baghdad, Iraq, 2003. Vol. Peace Corps, Peru, 1964—65; gen. counsel Reagan-Bush Transition, 1980—81. Recipient Humanitarian of Yr. award, Am. Lebanese League, 1983, UNICEF award. Mem. D.C. Bar Assn., Mich. Bar Assn. Republican. Methodist. Office: 499 South Capitol St SW Ste 500B Washington DC 20003 also: NASULGC 1307 New York Ave NW Ste 400 Washington DC 20005-4722 E-mail: McPher20@msu.edu, pmcpherson@nasulgc.org.*

**MCPHERSON, SHERRY LYNN,** social worker; b. Bklyn., Mar. 8, 1969; d. George Cephano and Mary Sue McPherson. BA, Hofstra U., 1992, MSW, Adelphi U., 1996. Cert. sch. social worker. Program coord. Colonial Youth and Family Svcs., Mastic, NY, 1993; sch. social worker Cmty. Counseling Ctr., Franklin Square, NY, 1996—97; cons. Elmont Pre-Kindergarten, NY, 1997, Glen Cove Child Day Care, NY, 1997—98; sch. social worker Patchogue-Medford Schs., NY, 1997—. Bd. dirs. Pronto L.I. Mem. sub com. on youth criminal justice CJCC Suffolk County; mem. site based mgmt. Patchogue-Medford High. Mem.: NASW, NAACP, Sch. Social Work Assn. Am., Nat. Assn. Black Social Workers (treas. 2002—04), Black/Hispanic

Alumni Assn. Hofstra U., Lupus Alliance. Roman Catholic. Avocations: travel, baseball. Office: Patchogue Medford Sch Sys 241 S Ocean Ave Patchogue NY 11772 Personal E-mail: senigma8@aol.com.

**MCPHERSON, STEPHEN,** broadcast executive; b. Pitts., Oct. 28, 1967; BA in polit. sci., Cornell U., 1986. Fgn. exchange trader Commodities Corp., NYC, 1986—91; dir. devel. Witt-Thomas Prodns., LA, 1991—93; dir. current programming Fox Broadcasting Co., LA, 1993—94; sr. v.p. creative affairs ABC Prodns., Burbank, Calif., 1994—95; v.p. Primetime Series NBC, Burbank, 1995—98; exec. v.p. Buena Vista Prodns. Walt Disney Co., 1998—2000, pres. Touchstone TV, 2000—04, pres. ABC Primetime TV, 2004—. Recipient Diversity award, Director's Guild Am., 2005. Office: ABC Entertainment 500 S Buena Vista St Burbank CA 91521*

**MCPHERSON, TED R. (EDWARD RUSSELL MCPHERSON),** federal agency administrator; b. Balt., Sept. 18, 1943; s. Donald Paxton and Janet (Russell) McP.; m. Sally Thompson, May 12, 1969; children: Beth, Edward. BA, Williams Coll., 1967; MS, George Washington U., 1971. Mgmt. cons. Klein & Saks Inc., Washington, 1968, Booz Allen & Hamilton, Washington, 1971-73; v.p. corp. planning & investor relations Republic Bank Dallas, 1973-76; sr. v.p. corp. planning and investor relations RepublicBank Corp., Dallas, 1978-83, sr. v.p., CFO, 1983-84, exec. v.p., CFO, 1984-87, First RepublicBank Corp., Dallas, 1987—2001; pres., CEO InterSolve Group, Dallas, 1989—2001; CFO USDA, Washington, 2001—04; under sec. US Dept. Edn., Washington, 2004—. Mem., Pres. Mngmt. Coun. Trustee Hockaday Sch., Dallas, 1987, Dallas Fiscal Affairs Com., 1983-87. Served to lt. USN, 1968-71. Office: US Dept Edn 400 Maryland Ave SW 7E307 Washington DC 20202

**MCPHERSON, VANZETTA PENN,** magistrate judge; b. Montgomery, Ala., May 26, 1947; d. Luther Lincoln and Sadie Lee (Gardner) P.; m. Winston D. Durant, Aug. 17, 1968 (div. Apr. 1979); 1 child, Raegan Winston; m. Thomas McPherson Jr., Nov. 16, 1985. BS in Speech Pathology, Howard U., Washington, 1969; MA in Speech Pathology, Columbia U., 1971, JD, 1974. Bar: N.Y. 1975, Ala. 1976, U.S. Dist. Ct. (so. dist.) N.Y. 1975, U.S. Dist. Ct. (mid. dist.) Ala. 1980, U.S. Ct. Appeals (2d cir.) 1975, U.S. Ct. Appeals (11th cir.) 1981, U.S. Supreme Ct. Assoc. Hughes, Hubbard & Reed, N.Y.C., 1974-75; asst. atty. gen. Ala. Atty. Gen. Office, Montgomery, 1975-78; pvt. practice Montgomery, 1978-92; magistrate judge U.S. Dist. Ct. (mid. dist.) Ala., Montgomery, 1992—. Former co-owner Roots & Wings, A Cultural Bookplace, Montgomery, 1989—2000. Dir. Ala. Shakespeare Festival, Montgomery, 1987—, Montgomery Symphony Orch., 1995-98; chmn. trustees Dexter Ave. King Meml. Bapt. Ch., Montgomery, 1988; chmn. Leadership Montgomery; bd. mem. Lighthouse Counseling Ctr., Montgomery, 1981-84, Montgomery County Pub. Libr., 1989-90; v.p. Lanier H.S. Parent Tchr. Student Assn., Montgomery, 1990-91, Metro-Montgomery YMCA, 2000-. Mem. ABA Arts Com., 2001-. Recipient cert. Ala. Jud. Coll.; named Woman of Achievement Montgomery Advertiser, 1989, Boss of Yr. Montgomery Assn. Legal Secs., 1992. Mem. ABA (law office design award 1985), FBA (pres. Montgomery chpt.), Nat. Bar Assn., Ala. State Bar Assn. (chmn. family law sect. 1989-90), N.Y. State Bar Assn., Montgomery Inn of Cts. (master bencher 1992—), Ala. Black Lawyers Assn. (pres. 1979-80). Office: US Dist Ct Mid Dist Ala PO Box 1629 One Church St Montgomery AL 36104

**MCPHIE, NEIL ANTHONY GORDON,** federal official; b. Port-of-Spain, Trinidad, June 13, 1945; came to the U.S., 1970; s. Sydney Claudius and Rosarita (Francesca) McP.; m. Judith Butler, June 22, 1972 (div. 1979); m. Regina Chow, June 18, 1982; children: Abigail Clarissa, Sydney Frederick. BA in Econs., Howard U., 1973; JD, Georgetown U., 1976. Bar: Iowa 1977, D.C. 1979, Va. 1982, N.Y. 1982. Journalist Trinidad Guardian, Port of Spain, 1963-65; sales rep. Shell Oil Co., Port of Spain, 1965-70; atty. U.S. EEOC, Washington, 1976-82; asst. atty. gen. State of Va, Richmond, 1982—88, sr. asst. atty. gen., 2002—03; exec. dir. Va. Dept. Employment Dispute Resolution, Richmond, 1998—2002; vice chmn. Merit Systems Protection Bd., Washington, 2003—04, acting chmn., 2003—04, chmn., 2004—. Fellow ABA (vice chair conferm., litigation coms.); mem. Va. State Bar Assn. (chair spl. com. 1988-92), Phi Beta Kappa. Avocations: soccer, horticulture, landscaping. Office: 1615 M St NW Rm 680 Washington DC 20419

**MCQUADE, EUGENE M.,** finance company executive, former bank executive; BBA, St. Bonaventure U. CPA. With Peat Marwick Mitchell & Co., until 1980; dep. contr. Mfrs. Hanover Trust Co., 1980-85, sr. v.p., 1982—, contr., 1985—; sr. v.p. contr. Mfrs. Hanover Corp.; joined Fleet Boston Fin. Group, 1992, CFO, 1993, vice-chmn., 1997, pres.,COO, 2002—04; pres. Bank of Am. Corp., 2004; pres., COO Fed. Home Loan Mortgage Corp. (Freddie Mac), 2004—. Dir. XL Capital Ltd. With USAR. Office: Freddie Mac 1551 Park Run Dr MS D40 Mc Lean VA 22102

**MC QUADE, LAWRENCE CARROLL,** lawyer, investment company executive; b. Yonkers, NY, Aug. 12, 1927; s. Edward A. and Thelma (Keefe) McQuade; m. Morrissey de Rosset Parker, Aug. 3, 1968 (dec. Oct. 1978); 1 child, Andrew Parker McQuade; m. Margaret Osmer, Mar. 15, 1980. BA with distinction, Yale U., 1950; BA, Oxford U., Eng., 1952, MA, 1956; LLB cum laude, Harvard U., 1954; MA (hon.), Colby Coll., 1981. Bar: N.Y. 1955, DC 1968. Assoc. Sullivan & Cromwell, N.Y.C., 1954-60; spl. asst. to asst. sec. internat. security affairs U.S. Dept. Def., Washington, 1961-63; dep. asst. sec. U.S. Dept. Commerce, Washington, 1963-64, asst. to sec., 1965-67, asst. sec., 1967-69; pres. Procon Inc., Des Plaines, Ill., 1969-75, CEO, dir., 1969-75; v.p. Universal Oil Products Co., 1972-75, W.R. Grace & Co., N.Y.C., 1975-78, sr. v.p., 1978-83, exec. v.p., 1983-87, also bd. dirs.; vice chmn. Prudential Mut. Fund Mgmt., N.Y.C., 1988-95; mng. dir. Prudential Securities Inc., 1988-92; chmn. Qualitas Internat., 1994—. Chmn., CEO Universal Money Ctrs., 1987—88; co-chmn. River Capital Internat., 1997—; expert advisor commn. on transnat. corps. UN, 1989—93; bd. dirs. Quixote Corp., Oxford Analytica. Author (with others): The Ghana Report, 1959; contbr. articles to profl. jours. Dir. Paul and Daisy Soros Fellowships New Ams., 1998—, Asian Bus. Cooperation Program, 2006—; bd. dirs. Fgn. Bondholders Protective Coun., N.Y.C., 1978—85, Am. Forum, 1985—96, Am. Coun. on Germany, 1985—94, Asian Programs Found., 2006—; trustee Colby Coll., 1981—89, trustee emeritus, 1989—; Czech and Slovak Am. Enterprise Funds, 1994—96, chmn., 1995—96. Rhodes scholar, Oxford U., 1952. Mem.: Pres.'s Cir. NAS, Overseas Devel. Coun. (bd. dirs. 1974—87), Mgmt. and Devel. Inst. (bd. dirs. 1970—99), Atlantic Coun. U.S. (bd. dirs. 1969—99), Nat. Fgn. Trade Coun. (bd. dirs. 1979—87), Chgo. Coun. Fgn. Rels. (bd. dirs. 1969—75), Coun. Fgn. Rels., N.Y., Met. Club (Washington), Century Club, Harvard Club, Phi Beta Kappa. Office Phone: 212-973-9800. Business E-Mail: lmcquade@rivercapital.com.

**MCQUADE, TYLER,** chemist; BS in chemistry, U. Calif., Irvine, 1993; PhD in chemistry, U. Wis., 1998. Asst. prof. dept. chemistry and chemical biology Cornell U. Contbr. articles to profl. jour. Named one of Top 100 Innovators, MIT Tech. Review, 2004. Office: Cornell U Dept Chemistry and Chemical Biology 360B Spencer T Olin Lab Ithaca NY 14853-1301 Business E-Mail: dtm25@cornell.edu.

**MCQUAID, KIM,** historian, educator, writer; b. Norwalk, Conn., Nov. 2, 1947; s. Francis Walter McQuaid and Margaret Fitzgerald Phelan. BA, Antioch Coll., Yellow Springs, Ohio, 1970; MA, Northwestern U., Evanston, Ill., 1973, PhD, 1975. Asst. prof. dept. history Lake Erie Coll., Painesville, Ohio, 1977—83, assoc. prof., 1989—; prof. emeritus Mary Ball Washington vis. prof. U.S. History U. Coll. Dublin, 1985—86; Fulbright lectr. U. Sci. Malaysia, 1995—96. Co-author: (book) Creating the Welfare State, 1980, 1994; author: Big Business and Presidential Power, 1982, A Response to Industrialism: Liberal Businessmen and The Evolving Spectrum of Capitalist Reform 1886-1960, 2d edit., 2003, The Anxious Years: America in the Vietnam-Watergate Era, 1989, Uneasy Partners: Big Business in American Politics, 1945-1990, 1994; contbr. to profl. jours. Woodrow Wilson fellow,

1970. Green Party. Avocations: wilderness hiking, art. Home: Apt 208 686 E Erie St Painesville OH 44077 Office: Lake Erie Coll 391 W Washington St Painesville OH 44077 Office Phone: 440-375-7177. E-mail: mcquaid@lec.edu.

MCQUARRIE, CLAUDE MONROE, III, lawyer; b. Ft. Benning, Ga., Oct. 15, 1950; s. Claude Monroe Jr. and Rosanne (Sprinkle) McQ.; children: Kevin Andrew, Ryan Christopher, Erin Elizabeth. BS, U.S. Mil. Acad., 1972; JD with distinction, St. Mary's U., San Antonio, 1978. Bar: Tex. 1978, U.S. Dist. Ct. (so. dist.) Tex. 1982, U.S. Ct. Mil. Appeals 1979. Commd. 2d lt. U.S. Army, 1972, advanced through grades to capt., 1976, resigned, 1982; assoc. Fulbright & Jaworski, Houston, 1982-89, ptnr., 1989—. Editor Law Rev., 1977-78. Mem. Houston Bar Assn., John M. Harlan Soc., Phi Delta Phi. Avocations: golf, skiing. Home: 5610 Orchard Valley Ct Kingwood TX 77345-1920 Office: Fulbright & JaworskiLLP 1301 Mckinney St Ste 5100 Houston TX 77010-3031 Office Phone: 713-651-5416. E-mail: cmcquarrie@fulbright.com.

MCQUARRIE, DONALD GRAY, surgeon, educator; b. Richfield, Utah, Apr. 17, 1931; s. John Gray and LoRetta McQ.; m. Dolores Jean Dietrich, July 16, 1956; children: William Gray, Michelle Dolores Colton. BS, U. Utah, 1952, MD, 1956; PhD, U. Minn., 1964. Diplomate Am. Bd. Surgery, Am. Bd. Thoracic and Cardiovascular Surgery. Intern U. Minn. Hosps., 1956—57; resident in surgery U. Minn., Mpls., 1957—59, resident, 1961—65, asst. prof. surgery, 1964—68, assoc. prof. surgery, 1968—72, prof. surgery, 1972—2001, prof. emeritus, 2002—, vice chmn. dept. surgery, 1993—99; mem. surg. staff Mpls. VA Hosp., 1964—99, chief surg. svc., 1993—99, resident in thoracic surgery, 1965—66, dir. surg. rsch. lab., 1964—78. Vis. prof. U. Tex.-San Antonio, 1974, U. Ind. and Indpls. VA, 1977, affiliated program U. Ariz., Phoenix, 1982, Case Western Res. U., 1986. Editor, contbg. author: Head and Neck Cancer, 1986, Reoperations in General Surgery, 1991, 2d edit., 1996; contbr. articles on surg. and basic med. scis. to profl. publs., 1955— Served to lt. M.C., USN, 1959-61 USPHS postdoctoral fellow, 1962-65 Fellow ACS (commn. on cancer 1980-89, exec. council commn. on operating room environ. 1985-91, pres. Minn. chpt. 1983-84, liaison to Assn. Oper. Rm. Nurses 1985-97, gov. 1990-96); mem. Minn. Surg. Soc. (pres. 1980-81), Assn. Acad. Surgery, Mpls. Surg. Soc. (pres. 1978-79), Soc. Head and Neck Surgeons, Central Surg. Assn., Western Surg. Soc., Soc. Univ. Surgeons, Société Internationale de Chirurgie, Am. Surg. Assn., Royal Soc. Medicine, Assn. VA Surgeons (pres. 1987), Soc. Surg. Oncology, Hennepin County Med. Soc., Minn. Med. Assn., Am. Soc. Clin. Oncology, Phi Beta Kappa, Phi Kappa Phi Clubs: Minneapolis, Interlachen Country (Mpls.). Avocations: computer applications to medicine, jewelry design, lapidary work. Home: 6625 Mohawk Trl Minneapolis MN 55439-1029

MCQUARRIE, IRVINE GRAY, neurosurgeon, educator; b. Ogden, Utah, June 27, 1939; s. Irwin Bruce and Ruby Loretta (Epperson) McQuarrie; m. Katharine Gamble Rogers, Mar. 11, 1967 (div.); children: Michael Gray, Mollie; m. Maryann Kaminski, Aug. 14, 1980 (div.); children: Morgan Elizabeth, Gray Luke. BS in Biology, U. Utah, 1961; MD, Cornell U., 1965, PhD, 1977. Diplomate Am. Bd. Neurol. Surgery. Intern, asst. surgeon, surgeon N.Y. Hosp., N.Y.C., 1965—71, 1972—73; rsch. fellow dept. physiology Cornell U. Med. Coll., N.Y.C., 1971—72, 1974—76, asst. prof. depts. physiology and surgery, 1976—81; vis. asst. prof. dept. anatomy Case Western Res. U., Cleve., 1979—81, form asst. prof. neurosurgery, 1981—87, assoc. prof., 1987—, asst. prof. devel. genetics and anatomy, 1981—85, assoc. prof.- 1985—88, assoc. prof. neuroscience, 1988—. Staff neurosurgeon VA Med. Ctr., Cleve., 1981—, clin. investigator, 1981—84, med. investigator neurosurgery, 1984—90; asst. neurosurgeon Univ. Hosps. Cleve., 1981—2003; mem. adv. bd. VA Office Regeneration Rsch. Programs, 1986—88, chmn., 1988—89; Elizabeth Crosby lectr. U. Mich., 1989. Contbr. articles to profl. jours. Comdr. M.C. USNR, 1973—74. Decorated Legion of Merit U.S. Marine Corps; recipient Andrew W. Mellon Tchr.-Scientist award, 1977—79; NIH fellow, 1971—72, 1974—76, VA Individual Rsch. grantee, 1981—2002, Paralyzed Vets. Am. grantee, 1979—82, NIH grantee, 1982—89, Spinal Cord Soc. grantee, 1986—88. Mem.: AAAS, Am. Assn. Neurol. Surgeons, Am. Soc. Cell Biology. Achievements include research in mechanism of axonal regeneration in central nervous system; biochemical investigations on maintenance and replacement of nerve cell processes (called axons and dendrites) by complex intraneuronal transport mechanisms. Home: 12955 Larchmere Blvd Shaker Heights OH 44120 Office: 10701 East Blvd Cleveland OH 44106 Business E-Mail: irvine.mcquarrie@med.va.gov.

MCQUEARY, CHARLES E. (CHUCK MCQUEARY), federal agency administrator; MS in Mech. Engring., U. Tex., PhD in Engring. Mechanics, 1966. Head of dept. Missile OPs. Dept. Bell Labs., AT&T Corp., 1971—73, dir. Undersea Systems Devel. Lab., 1983—87, v.p. Fed. Systems Advanced Technology Divsn., 1987—93; pres., v.p. bus. units AT&T, Lucent Techs., 1994—97; pres. Gen. Dynamics Advanced Tech. Sys., Greensboro, NC, 1997—2002; under sec. for sci. & tech. US Dept. Homeland Security, Washington, 2003—06; dir. operational test & evaluation US Dept. Def., Washington, 2006—. Chair bd. dirs., campaign chair United Way, Greensboro; trustee N.C. Agrl. and Tech. State U.; mem. pres. CEO adv. com. Guilford Tech. C.C.; bd. mem. World Trade Ctr. N.C.; chair Action Greensboro Pub. Edn. Initiative; bd. mem. Guilford County Edn. Network. Named Disting. Engring. Grad., U. Tex., 1997. Office: US Dept Def 1700 Def Pentagon Rm 3A1075 Washington DC 20301*

MCQUEEN, JUSTICE ELLIS (L. Q. JONES), actor, television director; b. Beaumont, Tex., Aug. 19, 1927; s. Justice Ellis and Pat (Stephens) McQ.; m. Sue Helen Lewis, Oct. 10, 1950 (dec.); children: Marlin Randolph, Marilyn Helen, Steven Lewis. Student, Lamar Jr. Coll., 1944, Lon Morris Coll., 1949, U. Tex., 1950-51. Actor, writer, dir.: motion picture films including A Boy and His Dog, 1975 (Hugo award, Sci. Fiction Achievement award for dramatic presentation, Golden Boot award, Internat. Star award, Reel Cowboys Silver Spur award, Western Walk of Fame); actor White Line Fever, 1975, Mother, Jugs & Speed, 1976, Winterhawk, 1976, Fast Charlie, The Moonbeam Rider, 1979; Timerider: The Adventures of Lyle Swann, 1982, The Beast Within, 1982, Sacred Ground, 1983, Lone Wolf McQuade, 1983, Bulletproof, 1988, River of Death, 1989, The Legend of Grizzly Adams, 1990, Lightning Jack, 1994, The Friends of Harry, 1995, Casino, 1995, Ben Johnson: Third Cowboy on the Right, 1996, The Edge, 1997, The Patriot, 1998, The Mask of Zorro, 1998, Route 666, 2001, Prairie Home Companion, 2006, numerous others; tv movies include The Sacketts, 1979, Tornado!, 1996, In Cold Blood, 1996, The Jack Bull, 1999, numerous others; appeared in tv series including Gunsmoke, 1955, Alias Smith and Jones, 1971, Cannon, 1971, Cade's County, 1971, Kung Fu, 1972, Matt Helm, 1975, Charlie's Angels, 1976, Columbo: The Conspirators, 1978, The Dukes of Hazzard, 1979, The Fall Guy, 1981, The Yellow Rose, 1983, The A-Team, 1983, Walker, Texas Ranger, 1993, numerous others; producer The Big Thickett, Come In, Children, The Witchmaker; author, prodr.: The Brotherhood of Satan, 1971; dir., prodr. The Devil's Bedroom, 1964, (tv series) The Incredible Hulk, 1978. Served with USNR, 1945-46. Nominee 4 Emmy awards. Mem. Screen Actors Guild, Dirs. Guild Am. Republican. Methodist. Home and Office: 2144 1/2 N Cahuenga Blvd Los Angeles CA 90068-2708 Office Phone: 323-463-4426. *Contribute to a space that no one can or will fill.*

MCQUEEN, REGENIA, writer; b. Summerville, SC, Oct. 29, 1945; d. William and Mary (Stoutamire) McQueen; m. John Ray Sanders Teasley, Oct. 11, 1961; children: John Ray Sanders Teasley, Tonya Teasley, Ieishia Teasley, Nairobi Teasley, Rhodesia Teasley, Donnish Lindsey Teasley, DeJong Lindsey Teasley, A. Cin. Tech. Coll., 1985; cert., Blackstone Sch. of Law, Dallas, 2000; BA, No. Ky. U., 2005. Clk. Western-So. Life Ins., Cin., 1967-72, IRS, Covington, Ky., 1985-87. Author: Regenia McQueen: Born to Search, 2000, Nairobi Teasley: 1-1/2 Hour Defenseless Lamb, 2001, Witnesses to the Impossible Dreams, 2002, Regenia McQueen: Life Stolen, Name, Land, City Government and History Theft in South Carolina, 2003, Regenia McQueen's Documents, Name, Land, Oil, Government and History Theft of William McQueen in South Carolina vol. 1-4, 2004, John Teasley and Nairobi Teasley: Unlawfully Made Guilty and Lawfully Proven Innocent vol. 1 and 2, 2004,

Regenia McQueen, One of the Richest Women in the World yet, I Have Not a Dime to Spend, 2006, Regenia McQueen A Queen that Lives in the Ghetto, 2006. V.p. 13th St. Tenant Assn., 1979—85; Rosa Parks co-chmn.; trustee Owning the Realty, 1983—85. Recipient Achievement award, Ho. of Reps., Ohio, 2000, Wall of Tolerance award, Nat. Campaign Tolerance, 2002. Avocation: researching. Mailing: PO Box 15311 Covington KY 41015 E-mail: rteasley-3204@fuse.net.

MC QUEEN, ROBERT CHARLES, retired insurance executive; b. Santiago, Chile, Jan. 23, 1921; s. Charles Alfred and Grace Juanita (Abrecht) McQ.; m. Donna Marie Ikeler, Oct. 6, 1945; children: Scott, Jerry, Monte, Donald. AB, Dartmouth Coll., 1942. Mathematician, Equitable Life Assurance Soc., N.Y.C., 1942-49; group actuary Union Central Life Ins. Co., Cin., 1949-57; with Mut. Benefit Life Ins. Co., Newark, 1957-85, exec. v.p., 1969-71, sr. exec. v.p., chief adminstrv. officer, 1971-85, dir., 1978-85. Bd. dirs. St. Barnabas Corp. (formerly Trimark Corp.). Pres. Millburn Twp. (N.J.) Bd. Edn., 1969-71, Naples (Fla.) Bridge Ctr., 1994-96; chmn. BBB Met. N.Y., 1978-80; chmn. bd. trustees St. Barnabas Hosp., Livingston, N.J., 1983-91, trustee, 1991—. With OSS, 1943-45. Fellow Soc. Actuaries; mem. Am. Acad. Actuaries, Canoe Brook Country Club, Quail Creek Club. Republican. Episcopalian. Home: 11408 Oakmont Ct Fort Myers FL 33908 Personal E-mail: coach1921@yahoo.com.

MCQUEEN, SCOTT ROBERT, broadcast executive; b. Peekskill, N.Y., June 30, 1946; s. Robert Charles and Donna Marie (Ikeler) McQ.; children: Geoffrey Scott, Mallory Morgan, Brian Daniel; 1 child, by previous marriage, Tasha Lea. BA, Dartmouth Coll., 1968. Founder Sconnix Radio Ent., Inc., Laconia, NH, 1968, Sconnix Radio Ent., Inc. (became Sconnix Group Broadcasting, Inc.), 1971, pres., 1971; chmn. Bluewater Broadcasting Co., 2003—. Pres. Charisma Ventures, Ltd., 1995—. Chmn. bd. advisors Pine Crest Sch., Boca Raton, Fla., 2000-02, chmn. bd. trustees, 2003—. With N.H. N.G., 1968-69. Mem. Nat. Assn. Broadcasters, Nat. Radio Broadcsters Assn., Lakes Region C. of C. (dir. 1977-81),Royal Palm Yacht and Country Club. Home: 431 E Coconut Palm Rd Boca Raton FL 33432-7915

MCQUEENEY, HENRY MARTIN, SR., publisher; b. NYC, Oct. 29, 1938; s. John Henry and Catherine Mary (Quigg) McQ.; m. Elizabeth Bernino, May 14, 1960; children: Mary E., Henry M. Jr., John P., Matthew S. BBA, St. Johns U., 1961; postgrad., U. Rochester, 1965-67. Advt. sales Curtis Circulation div. Curtis Pub. Co., 1960-62, asst. mgr. N.Y.C., 1962-63, field mgr. Rochester, NY, 1964-67, dept. mgr., account exec. Phila., 1968-74; v.p. sales, exec. v.p. mktg. Manor Books, Inc., N.Y.C., 1974-79; pres. Scott Mag. Dist. Corp., N.Y.C., 1979—93, Kearny Pub., Inc., N.Y.C., 1993-96, Princeton Pub., Inc., N.Y.C., 1996-98; v.p. Irish Connections Mag., N.Y.C., 2000—, Iron Cross, Ltd., N.Y.C., 1998—, Koolhouse Pub. Inc., 2003—, The Irish Examiner USA Newspaper, 2006—. Rep. Western N.Y. Pubs.; cons. Bipad Ednl. Program. Pres. parish bd. Roman Cath. Ch., 1965, editor newspaper, Spencerport, N.Y., 1965, diocesan leader, mem. lay bd., Rochester, 1964-67; certified as tchr. Confraternity Christian Doctrine, Diocese of Rochester, 1964. Served with USAFR, 1956-64. Mem. Am. Legion, Ancient Order of Hibernians. Home: 12 Blenheim Ln Centerport NY 11721-1704 Office: DMI Worldwide PO Box 603 Centerport NY 11721-0603 Fax: 631-261-6532. Office Phone: 631-261-6273. E-mail: dmi33@aol.com.

MCQUERRY, PATRICIA ANN, painter, retired secondary school educator; b. Long Beach, Calif., Dec. 8, 1934; d. Jack Wendell and Estella Woodruff (Atkinson) McQerry; stepmother Hazel Parnell. BA in Art, North Tex. U., 1955; postgrad. in History, U. Ariz., 1961-65; postgrad., Stanford U., 1962-63; diploma in econs., Tex. A&M U., 1974. Tchr. art and social studies Roswell (N.Mex.) Ind. Sch. Dist., 1955-59; grad. asst. history dept. U. Ariz., Tucson, 1959-65; tchr. remedial English, Salpointe Cath. Sch., Tucson, 1961-62; hostess Sequoia-Kings Canyon Nat. Park, 1963; tchr. art Poly. H.S., Ft. Worth, 1966-88; tchr. history Western Hill H.S., Ft. Worth, 1988; tchr. Vision Quest, Elfrida, Ariz., 1991. Counsellor Camp Creators Episc., Tex., 1968. Author: (plays) New World Playhouse, 1981, Larkenportal, 1993; one-woman show Com. for Artist's Ctr., Ft. Worth, 1990 (citation 1990). Eyewitness U.S.-Mex. Border Patrol; mem. Sky Island Alliance; mem. youth criminal justice subcom. Suffolk County Criminal Justice Coord. Com., 2006—. Recipient various art awards; Fredrich Usher scholar U. Ariz., 1964, Senatorial Inner Cir. Commn. award, 2005. Mem.: Phi Alpha Theta, Alpha Rho Tau. Home: 412 Cpmdpi ave Rm 2B Bisbee AZ 85603-5773 Office Phone: 520-432-5733.

MCQUIGG, JOHN DOLPH, retired lawyer; b. Abilene, Tex., Oct. 19, 1931; s. John Lyman and Dorothy Elinor (King) McQ.; m. Sandra Elainea Duke, Oct. 18, 1969 (div. 1989); 1 child, John Revel. BA, Denison U., 1953; LLB, U. Tex., 1962. Bar: Fla. 1962, U.S. Supreme Ct. 1971. Account exec. San Antonio Light, 1957-59; assoc. Shackleford, Farrior, Stallings & Evans, 1962-66, ptnr. Tampa, Fla., 1966-73; pres. John McQuigg, P.A., Tampa, 1973-80; shareholder Fowler, White, Gillen, Boggs, Villareal & Banker, P.A., Tampa, 1980-92; of counsel Stephen Rosen, P.A., Tampa, 1993; pvt. practice Tampa, 1994-2000; ret., 2000. Arbitrator U.S. Dist. Ct., 1990—. Judge Compensation Claims pro hac vice, 1993; bd. dirs. Fla. Gulf Coast R.R. Mus., Inc., Am. Assn. Pvt. Railroad Car Owners; pres. Fla. Coalition R.R. Passengers, 1990-99. 1st lt. USAF, 1953-57. Mem. ABA, Fla. Bar, Tampa Club. Episcopalian.

MCQUIGG, MICHELE BERGER, state legislator; b. Bay Shore, N.Y., Sept. 2, 1947; children: Heather Lukes, Katie Schneider. BS, Mary Washington Coll., 1968; MS, Va. Polytech. Inst. & State U., 1978. Mem. Va. State Legis., 1998—, mem. cts. of justice com., mem. counties cities & towns com., vice chair gen. laws com., mem. sci. and tech. com. Republican. Episcopalian. Office: Gen Assembly Bldg PO Box 406 Richmond VA 23218-0406 E-mail: del_mcquigg@house.state.va.us, michele@mcquigg.com.

MCQUIGGAN, JOHN A., theater producer, writer; b. Detroit, Jan. 12, 1935; s. Paul F. and Elizabeth A. McQuiggan; 1 child, Ruth A. BA, Wash. and Lee U., 1956; degree in Theatre Arts, Neighborhood Playhouse Sch. of Theatre, N.Y., N.Y. 1959. Founder and prodr. Assn. Producing Artists, N.Y., 1959—61; founder, prodr. Milw. (Wis.) Repertory Theatre, 1962—65, Assn. Producing Artists, N.Y., 1967—69; exec. prodr. Unity Theatre*Television*Film Co. Inc., Bklyn., 1979—. Mem. drama bd. Yale U., New Haven, 1985—90. Prodr.: (plays) Quartermaine's Terms (8 Obie awards, 1983), Birds of Paradise (2 Drama Desk awards, 1987), The Baby Dance, The Foreigner (Outer Critics' Cir. award and 2 Obie awards, 1984), prodr.: (plays) The Common Pursuit, (Outer Critics' Cir. award, Lucille Lortel award, 1986), Forbidden Broadway; (films) The Common Pursuit, Project Discovery: The First Film School in Cyberspace; author: (screenplay) Time and Madness, In Your Dreams. Grantee, NEA, 1964—65, 1996—97. Office: Unity TheatreTelevision Film Co Inc 150 Joralemon Street Suite 11B Brooklyn NY 11201 Office Phone: 718-855-6133. Home Fax: 718-855-2228; Office Fax: 718-855-2228. Personal E-mail: mcq@owf.org.

MCQUILKIN, JOHN ROBERTSON, theology studies educator, writer, academic administrator; b. Columbia, SC, Sept. 7, 1927; s. Robert C. and Marguerite (Lambie) McQ.; m. Muriel Elaine Webendorfer, Aug. 24, 1948 (dec. Sept. 2003); children: Helen Marguerite, Robert Paul (dec.), David John, Virginia Anne, Amy Lambie, Douglas Kent; m. Deborah Jones Sink, Jan 1, 2005. BA, Columbia Internat. U., 1947; M.Div., Fuller Theol. Sem., 1950. Prof. Greek, religious edn. and theology Columbia (S.C.) Internat. U., 1950-52; pres. Internat. U., 1968-90. Headmaster Ben Lippen Sch., Asheville, N.C., 1952-55; missionary The Evang. Alliance Mission, Japan, 1956-68; acting pres. Tokyo Christian U., 1963-65. Author: Measuring the Church Growth Movement, 1974, Understanding and Applying the Bible, 1992, The Great Omission, 1984, An Introduction to Biblical Ethics, 1995, Life in the Spirit, 1997, A Promise Kept, 1998, Living the Life, 2000; contbr. articles to profl. jours. Mem. Evangel. Missiological Soc. (gen. dir. 1994-97). Personal E-mail: robertsonmcquilkin@earthlink.net.

MCQUILLAN, LAURENCE JOSEPH, communications consultant, educator; b. Bridgeport, Conn., Aug. 4, 1945; s. John Osborne and Mary Catherine McQuillan; m. Geraldine Marie Kenny, Apr. 8, 1972; 1 child, Sean Patrick. BS in Journalism, St. Bonaventure U., 1969; MA in Polit. Sci., SUNY, Albany, 1975. White House corr. UPI, Washington, 1976—80; asst. Washington bur. chief N.Y. Daily News, Washington, 1980—82; Washington corr. San Francisco Examiner, Washington, 1982—84; news editor Scripps Howard News Svc., Washington, 1984—86; dir. of pub. rels. Am. Fedn. of Tchrs., Washington, 1986—87; sr. White House corr. Reuters News Svc., Washington, 1987—99; White House corr. USA Today, Washington, 1999—2004; spokesman, media cons. U.S. Commn. on the Intelligence Capabilities of the U.S., Washington, 2004—05; dir. of comm. Am. Insts. for Rsch., Washington, 2006—. Adj. prof. Sch. of Comm., Am. U., Washington, 2005—. With U.S. Army, 1969—71, Vietnam. Mem.: White Ho. Corr.'s Assn. (hon.; pres., bd. of dirs. 1993—2004), Gridiron Club of Washington, D.C. (assoc.). Roman Catholic. Office: Am Insts for Rsch 1000 Thomas Jefferson St NW Washington DC 20007 Office Phone: 202-403-5119. E-mail: lmcquillan@air.org.

MCQUILLEN, JEREMIAH JOSEPH, distribution executive; b. Buffalo, Jan. 7, 1941; s. Joseph Bernard and Marca Rita (Ammerman) McQ.; m. Maureen Elaine Brett; children: Michael, Karen, Kathleen. BS, Canisius Coll., 1962. Nat. sales mgr. Birge Wallcoverings, Buffalo, 1973-74, v.p., gen. mgr., 1976-79; v.p. mktg. Reed Decorative Products, Toronto, 1974-76, exec. v.p. Atlanta, 1979-81, Northeastern Wallcoverings, Boston, 1981-88, pres., 1989-91; pres. comml. wallcoverings Forbo Wallcoverings Inc., 1991-92; exec. v.p Hytex Industries, Randolph, Mass., 1992-98, pres., CEO, 1998—. Served to 1st lt., U.S. Army, 1962-64. Mem. Wallcovering Distbrs. Assn. (sec., treas. 1987—, v.p. 1988, pres. 1989-90), Wallcovering Info. Bur. (pres. 1980), Wallcovering Mfg. Assn. (v.p. 1980), Di Gamma (life). Republican. Roman Catholic. Avocations: tennis, racquetball. Home: 3 Nauset St Medfield MA 02052-3006 Office Phone: 781-963-4400. Personal E-mail: jjmhytex@aol.com.

MCQUILLEN, MICHAEL PAUL, neurologist, educator; b. NYC, Sept. 9, 1932; s. Paul and Dorothy Marian (Moore) McQ.; m. Louise Devlin; children: Daniel, Thomas, Patrick, Kathleen. BA cum laude, Georgetown U., 1953, MD, 1957; MA, U. Va., 1994. Diplomate Am. Bd. Psychiatry and Neurology (bd. dirs. 1991-95, exec. com. 1995), added qualification in clin. neurophysiology. Rotating intern Royal Victoria Hosp., Montreal, Que., Canada, 1957—58; resident in neurology Georgetown U. Med. Center, 1958—60; fellow in physiology Johns Hopkins U. Med. Sch. and Hosp., 1960—62, instr. medicine, 1962—65; mem. faculty U. Ky. Med. Center, 1965—74, prof. neurology, 1972—74, prof., chmn. neurology, 1987—93; prof. neurology, chmn. dept. Med. Coll. Wis., Milw., 1974—87; clin. faculty mem. dept. neurology U. Va. Health Sci. Ctr., Charlottesville, 1993—94; prof. neurology U. Rochester, NY, 1995—2005; clin. prof. neurology and neurol. scis. Stanford (Calif.) U., 2006—. Vis. sci. inst. Neurophysiology U. Copenhagen, 1971-72; vis. prof. U. Ky. Med. Ctr., 1978, Royal Coll. Surgeons, Ireland, 1983. Author articles, papers in field. Mem. Cath. Commn. on Intellectual Affairs. Recipient Neurology medal Georgetown U. Med. Sch., 1957; Clin. Teaching award Med. Coll. Wis., 1976; Disting. Service award N.Y. Med. Coll., 1983; named to Johns Hopkins Soc. Scholars, 1981 Fellow Am. Acad. Neurology; mem. AMA, Royal Acad. Medicine Ireland, Nat. Myasthenia Gravis Found. (chmn. 1981-83), Am. Neurol. Assn., Am. Assn. Electromyography and Electrodiagnosis, Wis. Neurol. Assn. (pres. 81-82), Rochester Acad. Medicine, Alpha Omega Alpha. Home: 350 Sharon Pk Dr Apt Q24 Menlo Park CA 94025 Office Phone: 585-240-5479, 650-723-5297. Personal E-mail: michael_mcquillen@comcast.net. Business E-mail: michael_mcquillen@urmc.rochester.edu.

MCQUILLIN, RICHARD ROSS, management consultant; b. Elyria, Ohio, Oct. 15, 1956; s. Wayne Rupp and Frana Rose (Romp) McQuillin; m. Riko Koga; children: Richard K., Sean K. BS, Ohio State U., 1979; MS, U. So. Calif., L.A., 1983; MBA, UCLA, 1990. Sr. staff mem. TRW Inc., Redondo Beach, Calif., 1979-88; sr. cons. Deloitte & Touche, L.A., 1990-91; cons. mgr. NetBase Computing, El Segundo, Calif., 1993-2000; chief tech. officer When2Click.com, El Segundo, Calif., 2000—04, Casting Networks, Inc., Hollywood, 2004—. Treas., contr. Patio Creek Homeowners Assn., Torrance, Calif., 1986—91, pres., 1991—. TRW Investment Club, Redondo Beach, 1984—87. UCLA fellow, 1989. Mem.: IEEE, Beta Gamma Sigma. Home: 1281 Tennyson St Manhattan Beach CA 90266-6956 Office: NetBase Computing Inc 2101 Rosecrans Ave Ste 5250 El Segundo CA 90245-4771 Office Phone: 323-462-8200. E-mail: marquis@mcqcorp.com.

MCQUISTON, ROBERT EARL, lawyer; b. Pitts., Feb. 4, 1936; s. Theodore O. and Bertha L. (Kegley) McQ.; m. Mary Hope Missimer, June 30, 1962; children: Mary Hope, Elizabeth Ann. BA magna cum laude, Yale U., 1958; JD cum laude, Harvard U., 1961. Bar: Pa. 1962. Assoc. Ballard, Spahr, Andrews & Ingersoll, LLP, Phila., Balt., Denver, Washington, Salt Lake City, 1962—69, ptnr., 1969—2001, sr. counsel, 2001—. Mem. nat. adv. group to Commr. IRS, Washington, 1985-87; lectr. in law Temple U., 1968-69, also various tax insts.; bd. dirs. Macromedia Inc., Hackensack, N.J., Gateway Communications, Inc., Binghamton, N.Y. Contbr. articles to profl. jours. Mem. Rep. Fin. Com., Harrisburg, Pa., 1983-86; trustee Am. Soc. Hypertension, 1992-98. Mem. ABA (active numerous coms. sect. taxation 1969—, including coun. mem. 1979-85, vice chmn., sec. 1982-85), Phila. Bar Assn. (bd. govs. 1978-80, mem. coun. 1969-84, sec. treas sect. on taxation 1973-75, vice chmn. 1976-78, chmn. 1978-80), Am. Coll. Tax Counsel (charter, regent 1990-98, vice chmn. 1993-94, chmn. 1994-96), Am. Tax Policy Inst. (trustee 1996-2003, pres. 2001-03), Nat. Conf. Lawyers and CPAs, Exec. Svc. Corps (exec. com. 2005—), Merion Cricket Club, Yale Club N Y C Episcopalian. Home: 1218 Round Hill Rd Bryn Mawr PA 19010-1938 Office: Ballard Spahr Andrews et al 1735 Market St Ste 5100 Philadelphia PA 19103-7599 Office Phone: 215-864-8327.

MCQUOWN, JUDITH HERSHKOWITZ, writer, consultant, financial planner; b. NYC, Apr. 8, 1941; d. Frederick Ephraim and Pearl (Rosenberg) H.; m. Michael L. McQuown, Jan. 13, 1969 (div. 1980); m. Harrison Roth, Dec. 8, 1985 (dec. 1997); m. Harold Allen Lightman, Jan. 2, 2005. AB, Hunter Coll., 1963; postgrad., N.Y. Inst. Fin., N.Y.C., 1965-67. Chief underwriting div. mcpl. securities City of N.Y., 1972-73; CEO Judith H. McQuown & Co., Inc., N.Y.C., 1973—. Author: Tax Shelters That Work for Everyone, 1979, The Fashion Survival Manual, 1981, Playing the Takeover Market, 1982, How to Profit After You Inc. Yourself, 1985, Keep One Suitcase Empty: The Bargain Shopper's Guide to the Finest Factory Outlets in the British Isles, 1987, Keep One Suitcase Empty: The Bargain Shopper's Guide to the Finest Factory Outlets in Europe, 1988, Use Your Own Corporation to Get Rich, 1991, Inc. Yourself: How to Profit by Setting Up Your Own Corporation, 10th edit., 2002, 1,001 Tips for Living Well with Diabetes: Firsthand Advice That Really Works, 2004; contbg. editor Boardroom Reports, Physician's Fin. News, Physician's Guide to Money Mgmt.; contbr. seminars The Learning Annex, seminars The Discovery Ctr., seminars Boston Ctr. for Adult Edn., seminars First Class, seminars Learning Connection, seminars Knowledge Network. Mem. Am. Soc. Journalists and Authors. Home and Office: One Gracie Ter Apt 9C New York NY 10028

MCRAE, CAROL REEVES, secondary school educator, theater director; b. Memphis, Aug. 17, 1948; d. William Rosemary and Rosemary Cedric Reeves; m. Thomas Clark McRae, Sept. 2, 1966; children: Angela Carol Wheat, Thomas Clayton. BS, U. Miss., Oxford, 1980. Tchr. Grenada Sch. Dist., Miss., 1980—94, Davidson Acad., Nashville, 1994—95; tchr., theater dir. Desoto County Schs., Olive Branch, Miss., 1995—. Dir.: (theater director) Northwest Mississippi Drama Festival (various, 2003). Mem. Olive Br. Arts Coun., 2004—06. Home: 475 Woodview Rd Byhalia MS 38611 Office: Olive Branch High School 9366 East Sandidge Rd Olive Branch MS 38654 Office Phone: 662-893-3344. Personal E-mail: carolmcrae@hotmail.com. E-mail: c_mcrae@obhs.info.

**MCRAE, CHARLES R. (CHUCK MCCRAE),** former state supreme court justice; BA, Marietta Coll., 1962; JD cum laude, Miss. Coll. Sch. Law, 1970. Trial atty., Pascagoula, Miss., 1970—90; spl. chancellor, cir. ct. judge Jackson, Forrest and Lincoln Counties, Miss., 1990; justice Miss. Supreme Ct, Jackson, 1991—2003. Mem.: ABA, Magnolia Bar Assn., Fed. Bar Assn., Am. Judicature Soc., ATLA, Miss. Trial Lawyer's Assn. (life).

**MCRAE, HAMILTON EUGENE, III,** lawyer; b. Midland, Tex., Oct. 29, 1937; s. Hamilton Eugene and Adrian (Hagaman) McR.; m. Betty Hawkins, Aug. 27, 1960; children: Elizabeth Ann, Stephanie Adrian, Scott Hawkins BSEE, U. Ariz., 1961; student, USAF Electronics Sch., 1961-62; postgrad., U. Redlands, Calif., 1962-63; JD with honors and distinction, U. Ariz., 1967; LHD (hon.), Sterling Coll., 1992; vis. fellow, Darwin Coll. and Martin Ctr., Cambridge U., Eng., 1996-97. Bar: Ariz. 1967, U.S. Supreme Ct. 1979; cert. real estate specialist, Ariz. Elec. engr. Salt River Project, Phoenix, 1961; assoc. Jennings, Strouss & Salmon, Phoenix, 1967-71, ptnr., 1971-85, chmn. real estate dept., 1980-85, mem. policy com., 1982-85, mem. fin. com., 1981-85, chmn. bus. devel. com., 1982-85; ptnr. and co-founder Stuckey & McRae, Phoenix, 1985—; co-founder, chmn. bd. Republic Cos., Phoenix, 1985—. Magistrate Paradise Valley, Ariz., 1983-85; juvenile referee Superior Ct., 1983-85; pres., dir. Phoenix Realty & Trust Co., 1970—; officer Indsl. Devel. Corp. Maricopa County, 1972-86; instr. and lectr. in real estate; officer, bd. dirs. other corps.; adj. prof. Frank Lloyd Wright Sch. Architecture, Scottsdale, Ariz., 1989—; instr. Ariz. State U. Coll. Architecture and Environ. Design; lead instr. ten-state-bar seminar on Advanced Real Estate Transactions, 1992; evaluation com. for cert. real estate specialist Ariz. Bar, 1994-96; mem. real estate adv. commn. Ariz. Bar, 1996—. Author: Development in Third World Countries, 2002; exec. prodr. film documentary on relief and devel. in Africa, 1990; contbr. articles to profl. jours. Elder Valley Presbyn. Ch., Scottsdale, Ariz., 1973-75, 82-85, 96-98, chair evangelism com. 1973-74, corp. pres., 1974-75, 84-85, trustee, 1973-75, 82-85, chmn. exec. com., 1984, mem. mission com. 1993—, chmn. 1998; trustee Upward Found., Phoenix, 1977-80, trustee, Valley Presbyn. Found., 1982-83, Ariz. Acad., 1971—; trustee, mem. exec. com. Phi Gamma Delta Ednl. Found., Washington, 1974-84; trustee Phi Gamma Delta Internat., 1984-86; bd. dirs. Archon, 1986-87, Hall of Fame Ariz., 1999; founder, trustee, pres. McRae Found., 1980—; bd. dirs. Food for Hungry Inc. (Internat. Relief), 1985-95, exec. com., 1986-95, chmn. bd. dirs., 1987-92; chmn. bd. dirs. Food for Hungry Internat., 1993-95, pres. adv. coun., 1995—, mem. building com., 1999—; trustee, mem. exec. com. Ariz. Mus. Sci. and Tech., 1984—, 1st v.p., 1985-86, pres., 1986-88, chmn. bd. dirs., 1988-90, exec. com. 1984-90, exhibits com. 1990—, strategic planning com., 1999—, svc. recognition 1999; Lambda Alpha Internat. Hon. Land Econs. Soc, 1988-98; sec.-treas. Ariz. State U. Coun. for Design Excellence, 1989-90, bd. dirs. 1988-99, pres. 1990-91, trustee 1999—; mem. Crisis Nursery Office of the Chair, 1988-89, Maricopa C.C. Found., 1988-2002, bd. dirs., 1988-2002, sec. 1990-91, 2d v.p. 1993-94, 1st v.p. and pres. elect 1994-95, pres. 1995-96, mem. Elsner scholarship com., 1999—, web site com., 1999, capital campaign cabinet, 1995-96, 98-99, mem. of chair, 1998-99, mem. nominating com., 1997—, deferred gifts com., 1999—, strategic planning com., 2000—, mem. adv. bd., 2002--; mem. Phoenix Cmty. Alliance, 1998-99, Interchurch Ctr. Corp., 1987-90, Western Art Assocs., bd. dirs., 1989-91, Phoenix Com. on Fgn. Rels., 1988-99, U. Ariz. Pres.'s Club, 1984—, chmn., 1991-92; bd. dirs. Econ. Club of Phoenix, 1987—, sec.-treas., 1991-92, v.p., 1992-93, pres. 1993-94; bd. dirs. Ctrl. Ariz. Shelter Svcs., 1995—, bd. dir., Ariz. Cmty. Found., 1996—, invest. com., 1996—, chair, 2000-- exec. com. 1997—, treas. 1997—, chair nominating com. 1997-98, vice chair bd. dirs., 1999—, chair devel. com., 1999—, advancement com., 1999-2000, chmn. 1999—, fin. and adminstrn. com. 1999—; founding mem. Alliance linking poverty and homelessness, 1996-98, bd. dirs., 1996-98, mem. exec. com., 1996-98, co-chair long range planning com., 1997-98; mem. adv. bd. Help Wanted USA, 1990-92; vol. fund raiser YMCA, Salvation Army, others; bd. dirs. Frank Lloyd Wright Found., 1992—, chair fin. com. 1997-98, chmn. bd. dirs., 1998—; mem. Taliesin Coun., 1985—; bd. dirs. Taliesin Arch., 1992-98, Taliesin Conservation Com. (Wis.), 1992—; founding mem. Frank Lloyd Wright Soc., 1993—; mem. fin. com. Kyl for Congress, 1985-92, bd. dir. campaign bd. Kyl for U.S. Senate, 1993-94, 99—; Senator Kyl Council, 1995-98; campaign com. Symington for Gov. '90, 1989-90, mem. gubernatorial adv. bd., 1990-91; mem. Gov.'s Selection Com. for State Revenue Dir., 1993; mem. bond com. City of Phoenix, 1987-88; mem. Ariz. State U. Coun. of 100, 1985-89, investment com., 1985-89; bd. govs. Twelve Who Care Hon Kachina, 1991; mem. adv. coun. Maricopa County Sports Authority, 1989-93; mem. Ariz. Coalition for Tomorrow, 1990-92; founding mem. bd. dirs. Waste Not Inc., 1990-94, pres., 1990-92, chmn., 1992-94, adv. bd. 1996—; bd. dirs. Garden Homes at Teton Pines Home Owners Assn., 1996—, v.p., 2000-04, pres., 2004—; selected as bearer for the Olympic Torch Relay Team, 1996; adv. bd. KAET TV PBS (Channel 8) 1999-2000. 1st lt. USAF, 1961-64. Recipient various mil. awards; 1st place award Ariz. Bar Assn., 1967; named to Ariz. Hall of Fame, 1999. Mem. ABA, AIEE, AIME, Ariz. Bar Assn., Maricopa County Bar Assn., U. Ariz. Alumni Assn., Nat. Soc. Fund Raising Execs. (Philanthropy award Ariz. chpt. 1991, 97), Clan McRae Soc. N.Am. Phoenix Exec. Club, Internat. Platform Assn., Am. Friends of the U. Cambridge (Eng.), Jackson Hole Racquet Club, Teton Pines Country Club, Tau Beta Pi. Republican. Address: Republic Cos 11811 N Tatum Blvd Ste 1005 Phoenix AZ 85028-1617 Office Phone: 602-494-0202. Personal E-mail: repcos@aol.com, hemcrae3@aol.com.

**MCRAE, JOHN MALCOLM,** dean, educator, architect; b. Vicksburg, Miss., Sept. 4, 1942; s. John L. and Thelma L. (Nabors) McR.; m. Sharon Koscak, July 23, 1971; children: Shane, Kelley, Ryan. BArch, U. Tex., 1966; MArch, Rice U., 1967. Registered architect, Fla. Instr. dept. architecture U. Fla., Gainesville, 1967-70, asst. prof., 1970-75, assoc. prof., 1975-80, prof., 1980-87, asst. dean Coll. Architecture, 1977-79, assoc. dean, 1979-82, dir. instrn., 1979, acting chmn. dept. architecture, 1981-85, chmn., 1983-87, acting chmn. dept. interior design, 1984-86; dean Sch. Architecture Miss. State U., Starkville, 1987—2003; sr. dir. grants and develop. Am. Inst. Architects, 2003—05; dean U. Tenn. Coll. Architecture and Design, Knoxville, 2005—. Pvt. coms., 1971—; advisor Miss. Bd. Licensing Activities, 1987—; assoc. Ctr. Gerontol. Studies U. Fla., 1976—; adv. bd. Pinellas County Fine Arts Coun., Clearwater, Fla., 1979; adv. coun. nat. program Architects-in-School sponsored by Nat. Endowment for Arts, 1978-79; mem. steering com. environments and aging program Gerontol. Soc. Am., 1978-79; chmn. Fla. legis. com. on housing for elderly, 1986-87; awards juror Jacksonville Arts Coun., Fla., 1982; juror archtl. achievements Orlando Mag., 1986; others. Major archtl. projects and consultations include Hist. Am. Bldgs. Survey, Nat. Pk. Svc., Washington, Community Evang. Free Ch., Gainesville, Fla., 1975-76, Bethel Bapt. Ch., Marion Oaks, Fla., 1978-79, Found. for Aging Rsch., Clearwater, 1982, Sunrise Retirement Community, Carrbora, N.C., 1979, 1981, Advent Christian Village, 1986-87, So. Coll. Tech., Atlanta, 1988; employed by John Gifford) Sparks Ave. Shopping Ctr., Comml. Bldg. Federal St., Wannacomet Bldg. Complex, Harbor House Hotel Complex, others, also pvt. residencies, Nantucket, Mass., 1971-73; coms. various archtl. firms including Myrl Hanes and Assocs., Zeisel Rsch. Group; author jour. articles, tchr.'s guides, workbooks, teaching modules, reports. Bd. dirs. Miss. Downtown Devel. Assocs., 1987—. Grantee Nat. Endowment for Arts, 1970-71, 77-79, rsch. grantee U. Fla., 1974, 76-77, Gerontol. Soc. grantee, 1976-77, Fla. Ednl. Rsch. and Devel., 1976-77, State of Fla., 1986, 87, Miss. State U. Rsch. Initiation grant, 1987-88. Fellow AIA (alternate state dir. Fla. chpt. 1979-80, chpt. sec. 1981-82, chm. coms. on design and collegiate rels. 1982-84, corr. mem. com. on health 1986, nat. vice chair designate architects in edn. com. 1992—, nat. archtl. accrediting bd. taks force 1991, juror Sarasota chpt. an. awards program 1985, Mid-Fla. chpt. design awards 1986, chmn. state awards jury S.C. chpt. 1988, mem. landscape archtl. teams various univs. 1981—). Office: U Tenn Coll Architecture and Design 1715 Volunteer Blvd Knoxville TN 37996-2400

**MCRAITH, JOHN JEREMIAH,** bishop; b. Hutchinson, Minn., Dec. 6, 1934; s. Arthur Luke and Marie (Hanley) McR. BA, Loras Coll., Dubuque, Iowa, 1956. Ordained priest Roman Cath. Ch., 1960. Assoc. pastor St. Mary's Ch., Sleepy Eye, Minn., 1960—64, 1968—71; pastor St. Michael's Ch.,

Milroy, Minn., 1964—67, St. Leo's Ch., St. Leo, Minn., 1967—68; dir. Nat. Cath. Rural Life, Des Moines, 1971—78; vicar gen. Diocese of New Ulm, Minn., 1978—82; bishop Owensboro, Ky., 1982—. Roman Catholic. Home: 501 W 5th St Owensboro KY 42301-0765 Office: 600 Locust St Owensboro KY 42301-2130 Office Phone: 270-683-1545 ext 140.

**MCRANEY, GERALD,** actor; b. Collins, Miss., Aug. 19, 1947; m. Beverly Root, 1967, (div. 1971); m. Pat Rae Moran, 1981 (div.); children: Jessica, Angus, Kate; m. Delta Burke, May 28, 1989. Student drama, U. Miss.; studied acting under Jeff Corey, Los Angeles. Repertory experience in New Orleans; 1st TV appearances include Roots II, The Law; co-star TV series Simon & Simon, 1981-88; appeared in films The Never Ending Story, 1984, Jackals, 1986, Murder in the Neighborhood, 1993, Blind Vengeance, 1994, Comanche, 2000, Hansel & Gretel, 2002, Saving Shiloh, 2006; lead role CBS series Major Dad, 1989-93; TV series include Central Park West, 1996, Promised Land, 1996-99, Commando Nanny, 2004, Deadwood, 2005-06, Jericho, 2006-; TV films: Take Me Home: The John Denver Story, 2000, Danger Beneath the Sea, 2001, Untitled Ricky Blitt Project, Tornado Warning, 2002, Untitled Dan Finnerty Project, 2003, Going for Broke, 2003, Ike: Countdown to D-Day, 2004. also: Screen Actors Guild 5757 Wilshire Blvd Los Angeles CA 90036-3635*

**MCRANEY, JOAN KATHERINE,** artist; b. Magee, Miss., Mar. 21, 1936; d. Harold Bryce and Ruth Katherine (Graves) McRaney; m. William Cummings Hollis, Mar. 14, 1966 (div. June 1970); m. Richard Felder, 1997. BFA, Inst. Allende, San Miguel de Allende, Mex., 1975; postgrad., U. So. Miss., Hattiesburg, 1990—; studied with sculptor Dan Askew, 1999—2000. Profl. portrait artist and contemporary sculptor, McComb, Hattiesburg, Miss., 1979—. Lectr. Lauren Rogers Mus. Art, Laurel, Miss., 1996. Exhibitions include Inst. Allende Gallery, 1973, Bellas Artes Gallery, San Miguel de Allende, 1974, Gulf South Gallery, McComb, 1982—84, New Orleans World Fair, 1984, Cottonlandia Mus., Greenwood, Miss., 1985—86, Woods Gallery U. So. Miss., 1990, Saenger Gallery, Hattiesburg, 1990, Woods and Locke Gallery U. So. Miss., 1992—96, Lucille Parker Gallery, William Carey Coll., 1993, Lauren Rogers Mus. Art, Laurel, Miss., 1996, 1999, Meridian (Miss.) Mus. Arts, 1997, USM Mus. Art, 1998, Meridian Mus. Art, 1999, Exit Gallery, Hattiesburg Downtown Gallery Walk, 1999—2000, Impressions Gallery, 2000—01, McComb Pub. Libr., 2000, Southwest C.C., 2002, one-woman shows include Gulf South Gallery, McComb, 2003, Meridian Mus. Art, 2004, Impressions Gallery, 2004, Edgewood Gallery, McComb, 2005—06, Good Karma Gallery, 2005—06, Represented in permanent collections Ole Miss Law Sch. Named winner juried competition, Laurel Arts League, 1999; recipient Louie B. Holmes Meml. award, McComb, 1980, 1981, Hon. Mention, Nat. Portrait Seminar, 1981, 1st pl. Pastel award, S. Miss. Art Assn. Cloverleaf Show, 1992, 1st pl. Drawing award, 1992, Dean's Outstanding Creativity award, 1993, 1994, 1st pl. Painting award, Umpteenth Ann. Student Show, Woods Gallery, 1995, Fred A. Walts Endowment, 1995, 1st Pl. Drawing award, 1995, Best of Show award Mixed Media Sculpture, Miss. Collegiate Art Competition, 1997, Best Sculpture award, Dept. Art Annual Student Exhbn., 1998, Honor, Hattiesburg Arts Coun., 1998, winner juried competition, Meridian Mus. Art, 1999. Mem.: Golden Key Soc., Kappa Delta. Avocations: gardening, photography, yoga, meditation, cooking. Home and Studio: 308 2nd Ave Hattiesburg MS 39401-3879 Office Phone: 601-818-4131. Personal E-mail: mcraneyart@comcast.net.

**MCREE, CELIA,** composer, singer, actress, writer, producer; b. Memphis; d. John Louis and Leta Gwendolyn (Phillips) McR. Student, Phila. Coll. Art (U. of Arts), 1976-77, Herbert Berghof Studio, 1989, Playwrights Horizon Theater, 1989; cert. with distinction, Nat. Acad. Paralegal Studies, Christian Bros. U., 1992. Pres. Mother Records, Memphis, 1984—, You Should Meet My Mother (Publishing), Memphis, 1984—, Wild Thing Music, Memphis, 1987-99, Mother Prodns., Memphis, 1986—; producer, host Indian Talk, WEVL-FM90, Memphis, 1992-95; ptnr. The Cinema Group, N.Y.C., 1997—. Artist, group and solo exhbns. including Eads Gallery, Grover Cleveland Arts Inst., Phila. Mus. Natural History; screenwriter, film scoring; singer, writer (nat. album) including Celia McRee/Back From Under, 1985 (ASCAP Spl. Pop award 1985-86, 86-87), Archives of Modern Music NY., Celia McRee/Passion, 1994; composer, arranger, producer, pub. background and feature music ABC Network, Cable TV and Radio; signature model for KeTukla, 1st Native Am. fashion designer; co-writer Circle of Love, 1999. Entertainer Vets. Bedside Network, N.Y.C., 1981. Recipient cert. of scholarly distinction Nat. Acad. for Paralegal Studies, 1992, cert. of appreciation United Music Heritage, 1990, spl. pop award ASCAP, 1982-84, 87-93, 95-96, 96-97, 97-98, 98-99, 99-2000, 2000-01, Henrietta Hickman Morgan writing award DAR; named Female Pop Songwriter and Female Pop Vocalist of Yr., Entertainer Indi-Assn., 1994, Female Vocalist and Female Entertainer of Yr., 1995; named Most Popular Female Entertainer, Entertainer Indi-Assn., 1996, Female/Artist/Entertainer, 1996, 97, Eia's Female Entertainer/Writer, 1997. Mem. AFTRA, ASCAP, NARAS, Nat. Mus. of the Am. Indian (charter), Animal Legal Def. Fund, N.Y. Acad. Sci., Humane Soc. U.S., Mensa, Memphis Kennel Club. Office: Mother Prodns 5159 Wheelis Dr # 110 Memphis TN 38117-4519

**MCROBBIE, MICHAEL ALEXANDER,** computer scientist, researcher, academic administrator; b. Melbourne, Australia, Oct. 11, 1950; s. Alexander Hewitt and Joyce Victoria (Gair) McRobbie; m. Andrea Shirley Gibson, Dec. 22, 1973; children: Josephine Elizabeth Joyce, Lucien Richard Vernon, Arabella Diana Grace. BA with honors I, U. Queensland, 1974; PhD, Australian Nat. U., 1979. Rsch. fellow La Trobe U., Melbourne, 1979-81, U. Melbourne, 1981-83, Australian Nat. U. Canberra, ACT, 1983-87; head Automated Reasoning Project, 1985-91; reader, assoc. dir. Ctr. for Info. Sci. Rsch., 1987-90; prof., exec. dir. Ctr. for Info. sci. Rsch., 1990-96; CEO CRC for Advanced Computational Systems, 1992-96; v.p. info. tech., chief info. officer Ind. U., Bloomington, 1997—; prof. computer sci., prof. philosophy, prof. computer tech., 1997—. Vis. prof. U. Kaiserlautern, Germany, 1987; Fulbright sr. fellow Argonne Nat. Lab., 1988. Co-author: (book) Automated Theorem Proving in Non-Classical Logics, 1986; author, co-author, editor: over 100 papers, articles, reports and books. Mem.: IEEE, Assn. Computer Machinery, Assn. Automated Reasoning, Columiba Club (Indpls.), Commonwealth Club (Canberra), Univ. Ho. (Australian Nat. U.). Avocations: art, book collecting, weightlifting, cricket. Office: Ind U 601 E Kirkwood Ave Franklin Hall 116 Bloomington IN 47405 E-mail: vpit@indiana.edu.

**MCROBERTS, J. WILLIAMS,** urologist, surgeon, researcher; s. Jerry William McRoberts and Ruth Margeret Parsons; m. Marlie Richards Richards; 1 child, W. Porter; 1 child, Jane Parsons. BA, Princeton, 1955; MD, 1959. Home: 137 Kentucky Ave Lexington KY 40502 Office: UK Medical Ctr Dept Surgery 800 Rose St Lexington KY 40536 Office Phone: 859-225-4785. Personal E-mail: jwilliammcrobertsmd@msn.com.

**MCROBERTS, TERRY ALLAN,** music educator; b. Richmond, Ind., May 11, 1954; s. Roy and Vera McRoberts. BS, Manchester Coll., 1977; MusM, Youngstown State U., 1979; DA, Ball State U., 1984. Assoc. prof. music Blue Mountain (Miss.) Coll., 1983—92; prof. music Union U., Jackson, Tenn., 1992—. Organist/choir dir. First United Meth. Ch., Ripley, Miss., 1985—92, Forest Heights United Meth. Ch., Jackson, Tenn., 1992—2001. Organist First United Meth. Ch., Jackson, Tenn., 2003—. Mem.: Soc. for Am. Music (membership com. mem.), Coll. Music Soc. (bd. mem. so. chpt. 2002), Music Tchrs. Nat. Assn. (nat. cert. tchr. music), Nat. Guild Piano Tchrs. (chair Jackson Ctr.), Am. Matthay Assn. (editor Matthay News 2002), West Tenn. Music Tchrs. Assn. (pres. 1995—97), Tenn. Music Tchrs. Assn. (pres.-elect 2001—03, pres. 2003—, Tchr. of Yr. 2002). Avocations: reading, walking. Home: 319 Parker Dr Jackson TN 38305 Office: Union Univ 1050 Union University Dr Jackson TN 38305 Office Phone: 731-661-5232. Business E-Mail: tmcrober@uu.edu.

**MCRORIE, WILLIAM EDWARD,** retired insurance company executive; b. Rutherfordton, N.C., Apr. 8, 1940; s. Cyrus Brown and Rosalie (Thompson) McR.; m. Hope Evangeline Foster, Sept. 9, 1962; children: Mark Edward, Jennifer Lynn. LLB, U. N.C., 1964. CLU; Bar: N.C., Va. State mgr.

Sturdivant Life Ins. Co., Lynchburg, Va., 1965-68; sr. v.p., gen. counsel First Colony, Lynchburg, 1969-2000. Sec. Jamestown Life Ins. Co., Lynchburg, 1981-2000. Councilman City of Lynchburg. Mem. Va. Bar Assn., Assn. Life Ins. Counsel, John Lynch Soc. (sec. 1970—). Home: 2600 Link Rd Lynchburg VA 24503-3012 E-mail: wem@ntelos.net.

**MC ROSTIE, CLAIR NEIL,** economics professor; b. Owatonna, Minn., Dec. 16, 1930; s. Neil Hale and Myrtle Julia (Peterson) McR.; m. Ursula Anne Schwieger, Aug. 29, 1968. BSBA cum laude, Gustavus Adolphus Coll., 1952; MA in Mktg., Mich. State U., 1953; PhD in Fin., U. Wis., 1963; postgrad., U. Minn., 1971-72, Am. Grad. Sch. Internat. Mgmt., 1980-81; cert., Coll. for Fin. Planning, 1990. Cert. fin. planner. Faculty Gustavus Adolphus Coll., St. Peter, Minn., 1958-96; emeritus prof., 1996—; chmn. dept. econs. and bus. Gustavus Adolphus Coll., 1967-83, chmn., mem. various coms., 1971-96; teaching asst. Sch. Commerce, U. Wis., 1960-62. Lectr. European divsn. U. Md., 1966—67; vis. prof. Am. Grad. Sch. Internat. Mgmt., 1980—81; pres. Minn. World Trade Week, Inc., 1987; bd. dirs. Rite Care Childhood Lang. Clinic. Editor: Global Resources: Perspectives and Alternatives, 1978, The Future of the Market Ecomomy, 1979. Congregation pres. First Luth. Ch., St. Peter, Minn., 1972-73, 93, chmn. pastoral call com., 1968-69, chmn. staffing com., 1975, mem. ch. council, 1968-74, 89-93; chmn. social ministry com. Minn. Synod, Luth. Ch. Am., 1975, mem. long range planning com. Southwestern Minn. Synod; chmn. Rep. council arts professions, scis., Minn., 1968-70, co-chmn. state task force on Vietnam, 1968; mem. adv. commn. Minn. Dept. Manpower Services, 1967-71; mem. North Central Regional Manpower Adv. Com.; bd. dirs. Midwest China Resource Study Center; del. White House Conf. Aging, 1971. Served with U.S. Army, 1954-56. Recipient Leavey Found. award Freedoms Found., Valley Forge, Pa.; rsch. fellow Fed. Res. Bank Chgo., 1962-63. Mem. Fin. Execs. Inst., Fin. Planners Assn., Minn. Econs. Assn. (bd. dirs. 1974-75, 79-80), Masons (master, Royal Arch chpt., Zuhrah Shrine Temple, Scottish Rite), Royal Order Scotland, Alpha Kappa Psi, Iota Delta Gamma, Sigma Epsilon. Lutheran. Avocations: bird watching, backpacking, fitness and health. Home: 1208 Pine Pointe Curv Saint Peter MN 56082-1344

**MCSHAN, CLYDE GRIFFIN, II,** diversified financial services company executive; b. New Orleans, Feb. 8, 1945; s. Clyde G. and Ursula C. (Mumme) McS.; m. Deborah A. Lark, Oct. 16, 1971; children: Madylin, Kristy, Suzanne. BA, Southeastern La. U., 1966. Cert. internal auditor, cert. govt. fin. mgr., cert. office automation profl. Auditor Office of the Inspector Gen., New Orleans, 1965-72; audit br. chief Cen. Voucher Payment Ctr., New Orleans, 1972-73; evaluation staff chief Nat. Fin. Ctr., New Orleans, 1973-74, processing br. chief, 1974, ops. div. chief, 1974-78, acctg. div. chief, 1978-79, ops. div. chief, 1979-80, dep. dir., 1980-81, dir., 1981-93; dep. chief fin. officer, dir. fin. mgmt. U.S. Dept. Commerce, 1993-97; v.p. Affiliated Computer Svcs., Inc., New Orleans, 1997-2001, sr. v.p. affiliated computer svcs., 2001—03; with Lockheed Martin, 2003—04, Savantage Solutions, Inc., 2004—05, Comput. Scis. Corp., 2005—. Contbr. articles to profl. jours. Chmn. CASU Tenant Bd. Dirs., New Orleans, 1989-93, policy com. Fed. Exec. Bd., New Orleans, 1990-93, chmn., 1989-90, 92-93; chmn. unit I United Way of Greater New Orleans, 1989-90, chair mktg. and comm., 1991, vice chmn. cmty. resources divsn. 1991, chair 1992-93, trustee, 1990-94, 98—, chmn. unit VII, 1990, chmn. CFC, 1989, chair cmty.-wide campaign, 2001-02; mem. Tulane U. pub. adv. com. for computer info. sys., 1987—2003; acctg. dept. advt. bd. U. New Orleans, 1991-93; pres. acctg. bd. U. New Orleans, 1992-93, bd. dirs. La. Tech. Coun., vice chair bd., 2004—; bd. dirs. Ctr. for Non-profit Resources, 1997-2002; bd. dirs. YMCA Greater New Orleans, 1990-93, 1997—, chmn. bd., 2002—04. With U.S. Army, 1965-71. Recipient Leadership award United Way, 1989, Communication and Leadership award Toastmasters, 1991, award New Orleans chpt. Federally Employed Women, 1990, 91, Presdl. Meritorious Rank award, 1988, 95, New Orleans Fed. Exec. Bd. award for outstanding leadership, 1989, Spl. award Office of the Comptroller Gen., 1989, Disting. Exec. Svc. award Sr. Exec. Assn. USDA, 1989, Elmer Staats Disting. Leadership award, 1993, Donald L. Scantlebury Meml. award for Disting. Leadership in Fin. Mgmt., 1995, Robert W. King Meml. award for disting. career accomplishments, 1997, Disting. Achievement award Internat. Inst. Bus. Techs.; named one of Outstanding 1990 Campaign Vols. of. Yr., United Way, 1991, Fed. 100 Info. Systems Mgrs., Fed. Computer Wk., 1990, 96, to Info. Tech. Hall of Fame, 1997. Mem. Assn. Govt. Accts. (New Orleans chpt. pres. 1972-73, chm. 1970-71, 73-74, 74-75, 76-77, S.W. region v.p. 1975-76, South Ctrl. region v.p. 1981-82, nat. mem. exec. com. 1983-84, 93-96, chmn. fin. mgmt. enhancement bd. 1988-89, chmn. emerging issues 1990-91, chmn. tech. program com. 1991-93, nat. pres.-elect 1993-94, nat. pres. 1994-95), Inst. Internal Auditors, Sr. Exec. Assn., Fed. Exec. Inst. Alumni Assn. Republican. Roman Catholic. Avocation: gardening. Home: 5500 Toby Ln Kenner LA 70065 Office Phone: 228-813-6034. E-mail: cmcshanii@aol.com, cmcshan@savantage.net, cmcshan@csc.com.

**MCSHANE, IAN,** actor; b. Blackburn, Lancashire, Eng., Sept. 29, 1942; m. Ruth Post (div. 1976); m. Suzan Farmer, 1965 (div. 1968); m. Gwen Humble, 1981; children: Kate, Morgan. Actor: (films) The Pleasure Girls, 1965, Sky West and Crooked, 1966, If It's Tuesday, This Must Be Belgium, 1969, Battle of Britain, 1969, Pussycat, Pussycat, I Love You, 1970, Tam Lin, 1970, Villain, 1971, Freelance, 1971, Sitting Target, 1972, Left Hand of Gemini, 1972, The Last of Sheila, 1973, Ransom, 1975, Journey Into Fear, 1975, The Fifth Musketeer, 1979, Yesterday's Hero, 1979, The Great Riviera Bank Robbery, 1979, Cheaper to Keep Her, 1980, Exposed, 1983, Torchlight, 1984, Ordeal by Innocence, 1984, Too Scared to Scream, 1985, Grand Larceny, 1987, Con Man, 1992, Sexy Beast, 2000, Bollywood Queen, 2002, Agent Cody Banks, 2003, Nemesis Game, 2003, Nine Lives, 2005, Scoop, 2006; (TV series) You Can't Win, 1966, Wuthering Heights, 1967, Bare Essence, 1983, Lovejoy, 1986, Dallas, 1989, Madson, 1996, Deadwood, 2004— (Golden Globe award for best actor TV series - drama, 2005); (TV miniseries) Roots, 1977, Jesus of Nazareth, 1977, Life of Shakespeare, 1978, Disraeli, 1979, Marco Polo, 1982, Evergreen, 1985, A.D., 1985, War and Remembrance, 1988, Trust, 2003; (TV films) The Wild and the Willing, 1962, Funny Noises with Their Mouths, 1963, Funeral Games, 1968, Whose Life Is It Anyway?, 1972, The Lives of Jenny Dolan, 1975, Code Name: Diamond Head, 1977, The Pirate, 1978, High Tide, 1980, The Letter, 1982, Grace Kelly, 1983, Braker, 1985, Rocket to the Moon, 1986, The Murders in the Rue Morgue, 1986, The Great Escape II: The Untold Story, 1988, Young Charlie Chaplin, 1989, Dick Francis: Twice Shy, 1989, Dick Francis: In the Frame, 1989, Dick Francis: Blood Sport, 1989, Perry Mason: The Case of the Desperate Deception, 1990, Columbo: Rest in Peace, Mrs. Columbo, 1990, White Goods, 1994, Soul Survivors, 1995, Babylon 5: The River of Souls, 1998, D.R.E.A.M. Team, 1999, Man and Boy, 2002.*

**MCSHANE, JOSEPH MICHAEL,** academic administrator, priest; b. NYC, June 19, 1949; s. Owen Patrick and Catherine Veronica (Shelley) McS. AB, AM, Boston Coll., 1972; MDiv, STM, Jesuit Sch. Theology, Berkeley, Calif., 1977; PhD, U. Chgo., 1981. Ordained priest Roman Cath. Ch., 1977. English tchr. Canisius H.S., Buffalo, 1972-74; asst. prof. religious studies LeMoyne Coll., Syracuse, NY, 1982-87, assoc. prof. religious studies, 1987-91, prof., 1991-92, chairperson, 1991-92; dean Fordham Coll., Bronx, NY, 1992-98, prof. theology, 1992-98; pres. Fordham U., Bronx, NY, 2003—; pres., prof. theology U. Scranton, 1998—2003. Vis. prof. history Loyola House, Berkley, Mich., 1986—87. Author: Sufficiently Radical: Catholicism, Progressivism and the Bishops' Program of 1919, 1986; author chpt. to book; creator video: The Pilgrimage of the People of God: An Introduction to the Study of Church History, 1991; contbr. articles to profl. jours. Bd. dirs. U. Scranton, Pa., Scranton Prep. Sch., Pa., Fordham U., N.Y.C., Fordham Prep. Sch., Bronx, NY, Regis H.S., N.Y.C., Canisius Coll., Buffalo, St. Joseph's Prep. Sch., Phila. Recipient First prize, Cath. Press Assn., 1992. Mem. Am. Cath. Hist. Assn., Am. Soc. Ch. History, Phi Beta Kappa. Democrat. Roman Catholic. Office: Office of Pres Fordham U Bronx NY 10458 Office Phone: 718-817-3000. Business E-Mail: jmcshane@fordham.edu.

**MCSHEEHY, CORNELIA MARIE,** artist, educator; b. Floral Park, LI, NY, Aug. 10, 1947; d. William Hudson and Mary Teresa (Ball) McS. BFA, Mass. Coll. Art, 1969; MA, SUNY, Albany, 1972. Instr. printmaking Pine Manor Jr. Coll., Chestnut Hill, Mass., 1972-74, Mass. Coll. Art, Boston, 1972-75; asst. prof. printmaking Brown U., Providence, 1976-77; prof, RI Sch. Design, Providence, 1977—, head printmaking program, 1977-89, chief critic European Honors Program Rome, 1986-88. Juror numerous nat. and internat. art exhbn. Grantee Nat. Endowment for Arts, 1974-75, Boston Mus. Fine Arts, Polaroid Corp., 1984, Mellon Found., 1986; visual arts fellow MacDowell Colony, Peterborough, NH, 1983; RI Sch. of Design Frazier Award for Excellence in Tchg. Fellow MacDowell Colony Fellows; mem. Boston Printmakers. Democrat. Roman Catholic. Home: 77 Barney St Rumford RI 02916 Office: RI Sch Design 2 College St Providence RI 02903-2784 Office Phone: 401-454-6221. Business E-Mail: cmcsheeh@risd.edu.

**MCSHEFFERTY, JOHN,** retired research scientist, personal care industry executive, consultant; b. Akron, Ohio, Mar. 14, 1929; s. John and Jean McS.; m. Glenna Gloria Childs, Apr. 18, 1959; children: John III, Amy Childs. BSc, U. Glasgow, 1953, PhD, 1957. Various rsch. positions Sterling Winthrop Rsch. Inst., Rensselaer, NY, 1957-62; dir. pharm. devel. Ortho Pharm. Corp. divsn. Johnson and Johnson, Raritan, NJ, 1962-75; dir. rsch. Janssen R & D, Inc. divsn. Johnson & Johnson, Piscataway, NJ, 1975-77; v.p. R & D family products Internat. Playtex, Paramus, NJ, 1977-79; pres. Gillette Rsch. Inst., Gaithersburg, Md., 1979-97; ret., 1997. Cons. in field. Fellow Royal Pharm. Soc. of Gt. Britain; mem. Indsl. Rsch. Inst. (bd. dirs. 1988-92, emeritt com. 1998—), Am. Acad. Dermatology, Am. Mgmt. Assn. (bd. dirs. 1994-97), Am. Chem. Soc., Am. Pharm. Assn., N.Y. Acad. Scis., Soc. Cosmetic Chemists, Dirs. Indsl. Rsch., Assn. Rsch. Dirs., Rotary, Sigma Xi. Personal E-mail: jmcs2@adelphia.net.

**MCSHERRY, WILLIAM JOHN, JR.,** lawyer, consultant; b. N.Y.C., Oct. 28, 1947; s. William John Sr. and Mary Elizabeth (Dunphy) McS.; m. Elizabeth Ann Crosby, June 8, 1974; children: Brendan, Sean, Rory. AB cum laude, Fordham U., 1969; JD cum laude, Harvard U., 1973. Bar: N.Y. 1974, U.S. Dist. Ct. (so. dist.) N.Y. 1975, U.S. Ct. Appeals (2d cir.) 1977. Assoc. Spengler, Carlson, Gubar, Brodsky & Frischling, N.Y.C., 1973-78, ptnr., 1979-88, Bryan, Cave, McPheeters & McRoberts, N.Y.C., 1989-91, Battle Fowler LLP, N.Y.C., 1991—. Exec. dir. U.S. Football League, N.Y.C., 1985-86; chmn. litigation dept. Battle Fowler, 1992-96; pres., bd. dirs. Playtex Mktg. Corp.; bd. dirs. Questron Tech., Inc. Author: (with others) Tender Offer Regulation: The Federal SEC's Challenge and New York State's Response. Derivatives Risk and Responsibility, 1996, Attorney Client Privilege in tge Second Circuit, 1998. Mem. Zoning Bd. Appeals, Village of Larchmont, N.Y., 1988-91, dep. mayor, 1992-98, bd. trustees, 1991-98. Served with USAR, 1970-75. Mem. ABA (litigation, antitrust, entertainment and sports, corp. banking and bus. law sects., subcom. litigation 1940 Act; vice-chair com. alt. dispute resolution), Assn. of Bar of City of N.Y. (mem. 1979-82 com. state cts. superior jurisdiction, 1987-90, com. arbitration and alternative dispute resolution, mem. sports law com. 1998—), Fed. Bar Council, Council N.Y. Law Assocs. (bd. dirs., treas. 1975), Phi Beta Kappa. Roman Catholic. Avocations: community involvement, sports, writing. Home: 2 Summit Ave Larchmont NY 10538-2930 Address: 75 E 55th St New York NY 10022-3205

**MCSLARROW, KYLE E.,** telecommunications association executive, former federal agency administrator; b. Va. m. Allison McSlarrow. BA, Cornell U., 1982; JD, U. Va., 1985. Asst. to gen. counsel of U.S. Army office sec. U.S. Army, 1985—89; assoc. Hunton & Williams, Washington; dep. chief of staff, chief counsel to majority leaders Bob Dole and Trent Lott US Senate, 1995—97, chief of staff to Senator Paul Coverdell, 1997—2000; nat. chmn. Quayle 2000 Presdl. Campaign, 1998—2000; v.p. polit. and govt. affairs, lead Washington office Grassroots.com, 2000—01; chief of staff to sec. Spencer Abraham US Dept. Energy, Washington, 2001—02, dep. sec., 2002—05; pres., CEO Nat. Cable & Telecom. Assn., Washington, 2005—. Mem. Arlington County, Va. Planning Commn.; co-chmn. US-Russia Energy Working Group, 2002—05. Democrat. Office: Nat Cable & Telecom Assn 1724 Massachusetts Ave NW Washington DC 20036

**MCSORLEY, RITA ELIZABETH,** adult education educator; b. Baraboo, Wis., Feb. 13, 1947; d. Charles Gervase and Bertie Ellen (Baker) Collins; m. William David McSorley III, June 6, 1967; children: William David IV, Kathryn Rita, Stephen Charles, Matthew Thomas. B Liberal Studies, Mary Washington Coll., Fredericksburg, Va., 1988, MEd, U. Va., Charlottesville, 1994. Adult edn. instr. Waipahu (Hawaii) Cmty. Sch. for Adults, 1989-91, literacy coord., 1990-91; dir. religious edn. Marine Meml. Chapel, Quantico, Va., 1992-94; adult edn. instr. Prince William County Schs., Quantico, 1992-93; coord. computer assisted lang. learning project Literacy Coun. No. Va., Falls Church, 1995-96; ednl. cons. Fairfield Lang. Techs., Harrisonburg, Va., 1996-97; adult edn. coord. N.E. Ind. Sch. Sys., San Antonio, 2000—; part-time tng. staff Tex. Ednl. Svc. Ctr. Region XX, 2004—. Presenter Ednl. Svc. Ctr., San Antonio, 2004—; lectr. in field. Mem. sch. bd. Quantico Dependent Schs., 1980-82; vol. Boy Scouts Am., Quantico and Pearl City, Hawaii, 1985-97. Mem. TESOL, U. Va. Alumni Assn. Roman Catholic. Avocations: quilting, genealogy, travel. Office: NEISD 10333 Broadway San Antonio TX 78217 E-mail: rmcsor@neisd.net.

**MCSORLEY, STEPHEN J.,** medical educator; b. Glasgow, Scotland, Apr. 23, 1970; s. David McSorley and Monica Jean Bennett; m. Jean Marion Simpson, Apr. 30, 1994; children: Caitlin Monica, Euan John, Anna Charlotte, Connor David. PhD, U. of Glasgow, Scotland, 1995. Asst. prof. U. Conn. Health Ctr., Farmington, 2001—05, U. of Minn., Mpls., 2005—. Office: U Minn 2001 6th St SE Minneapolis MN 55455-3007 Office Phone: 612-626-9905.

**MCSPADDEN, PETER FORD,** retired advertising agency executive; b. Montclair, N.J., Oct. 2, 1930; s. Chester F. and Janet (Chase) McS.; m. Barbara Dodds, June 30, 1956; children:— Douglas Dodds, David Ford, Peter Chase. AB, Dartmouth, 1952. Account exec. McCann-Erickson, Inc., N.Y.C., 1956-59; with Dancer-Fitzgerald-Sample, Inc., N.Y.C., from 1959, v.p., account supr., 1965-68, sr. v.p., mgmt. supr., 1968-72, exec. v.p., 1972-74, pres., chief operating officer, from 1974; chmn. bd., chief operating officer Saatchi & Saatchi DFS Inc., N.Y.C., 1986-88, also bd. dirs., ret., 1988. Pres., bd. dirs. DFS/Dorland Worldwide; bd. mem. Advt. Fedn., Am. Assn. Advt. Agys., TriState U.; mem. Nat. Advt. Rev. Bd.; bd. trustees Bradford Coll; vice chmn. Broadstreet TV Inc, 1989—. Chmn. bd. visitors Rockefeller Ctr., Dartmouth Coll., 1989-97; pres. Greenwich (Conn.) Young Republican Club, 1966-67; bd. dirs. United Way of Tri-State, 1995 Spl. Olympic Games; campaign mgr. Congressman Lowell P. Weicker, 1968, Senator Weicker, 1970, 76, 82, 88; mem. Rep. Town Com., Greenwich, 1965-68; trustee, mem. exec. com. Greenwich Hosp.; trustee Farnsworth Mus., Rockland, Maine. Served to lt. (j.g.) USNR, 1952-55. Mem. Am. Assn. Advt. Agys. (dir.) Clubs: Riverside (Conn.) Yacht, Greenwich Country, Megunticook Golf. Home: 46 Carriglea Dr Riverside CT 06878-2402

**MC SWAIN, ANGUS STEWART, JR.,** retired law educator; b. Bryan, Tex., Nov. 26, 1923; s. Angus Stewart and Lois (Pipkin) McS.; m. Betty Ann McCartney, June 3, 1956 (dec. May 30, 2002); 1 child, Angus Earl. BS in Civil Engring., Tex. A and M. U., 1947; LLB, Baylor U., 1949; LL.M., U. Mich., 1951. Bar: Tex. 1949. Mem. faculty Baylor U. Sch. Law, 1949—, prof. law, 1956—, dean, 1965-84, ret., 1994. Mem. panel arbitrators Fe. Mediation and Conciliation Service. Author: (with Wendorf) Cases and Materials on Texas Trusts and Probate, 1965, Supplementary Cases and Materials on Property, 1965, 78, (with Norvell and Simpkins) Cases and Materials for Texas Land Practice, 1968. Served to 1st lt., C.E. AUS, 1943-46. Mem. ABA, Tex.Bar Assn. (chmn. family law sect. 1967-69, chmn. com. on standards of admission 1972-73, 77-79), Tau Beta Pi, Phi Alpha Delta Home: 4600 Kenny Ln Waco TX 76710-2059

**MCSWAIN, BYRDIE ENGLE,** laboratory scientist, immunohemotologist; b. Ethel, Ark., Oct. 13, 1939; d. James Marvin and Katherine Engle (Martin) McSwain. BS, U. Ark., 1968; BS in Med. Tech., U. Ark. Sch. Medicine, 1969; MS, U. Ctrl. Ark., 1973; Specialist in Blood Banking, U. Ark. Med. Scis., 1976. Cert. in regulatory affairs (RAPS). Supr. blood bank Univ. Ark. Med. Scis., Little Rock, clin. instr.; dir. tech. svcs., dir. product mgmt. ARC Blood Svcs., dir. transplantation svcs., dir. regulatory affairs, South Ctrl. area dir. tech. and regulatory svcs., acting area dir. quality assurance. Contbr. 13 articles to profl. jours. Grad. scholar Am. Soc. Med. Tech.; recipient Omicron Sigma award, Am. Soc. for Med. Tech., Outstanding Svc. award, Disting. Alumni award U. Ark. for Med. Scis. Mem. Am. Soc. Clin. Lab. Scientists (Med. Technologist of Yr.), Am. Assn. Blood Banks, South Ctrl. Assn. Blood Banks (pres., author, editor), Am. Soc. Clin. Lab. Scientists, Clin. Lab. Mgmt. Assn. (pres. Ark. chpt.), Am. Soc. Clin. Pathologists, Regulatory Affairs Profl. Soc., Am. Soc. Quality Assurance, Phi Beta Kappa. Address: 2619 Fair Park Blvd Little Rock AR 72204-5149

**MCSWAIN, LARRY LEE,** religious studies educator; b. Pond Creek, Okla., Nov. 10, 1940; s. Joseph Kelly McSwain and Glorene May Brown Kirk; m. Rebecca Sue Stidham, Aug. 26, 1963; children: Laura Suzanne, Michael Lee. BA, Okla. State U., 1963; BD, Southwestern Bapt. Theol. Sem., 1966; STD, So. Bapt. Theol. Sem., 1970. Ordained to ministry So. Bapt. Conv., 1962. Pastor Morrison (Okla.) Bapt. Ch., 1961-63, Vernon (Ind.) Bapt. Ch., 1967-69; sr. rsch. asst. urban studies ctr. U. Louisville, 1968-70; asst. to prof. ch. and community So. Bapt. Theol. Sem., Louisville, 1970-88, dean sch. theology, 1988-91, provost, 1991-93; pres. Shorter Coll., Rome, Ga., 1993-2000; prof. ethics/leadership McAfee Sch. Theology, Mercer U., Atlanta, 2002—. Bd. dirs. Acts, Nashville, 1988-91. Co-author: Conflict Ministry in Church, 1981, Church Organization Alive, 1987; contbg. author numerous books; contbr. articles, book reviews to religious jours. Pres. Rome and Floyd County United Way. Curriculum grantee Assn. Theol. Schs., 1976-77; named Cons. of Yr. So. Bapt. Conv., 1987, also Recognition award, 1988. Mem. Rotary Internat. (bd. dirs.), Assn. of So. Bapt. Colls. and Schs., Ga. Found. for Ind. Colls. Democrat. Office Phone: 678-547-6442. E-mail: mcswain_ll@mercer.edu.

**MCSWAIN, NORMAN ELLSWORTH, JR.,** surgeon, educator; b. Albertville, Ala., Feb. 10, 1937; s.Norman Ellsworth Sr. and Mildred (Johnston) McS.; 1 child, Merry Johnston. BS, U. of the South, 1959; MD, U. Ala., 1963; D Emergency Med. Svcs. (hon.), U. Okoboji, 1979. Diplomate Am. Bd. Surgery; cert. diving medicine, hyperbaric medicine. Resident in surgery Bowman Gray Sch. Medicine, Winston-Salem, N.C., 1963-65, Grady Hosp., Atlanta, 1967-70; instr. in surgery Emory U. Affiliated Hosps., Atlanta, 1969-73; pvt. practice Atlanta, 1970-73; assoc. prof. Kans. U. Sch. Medicine, Kansas City, 1973-77; prof. surgery Tulane U. Sch. Medicine, New Orleans, 1977—. Dept. surgeon New Orleans Police Dept., 1979-, vis. prof. Alexandria Hosp., Edmundson, Alta., Can., 1982, Med. Ctr. Cen. Ga., Macon, 1983, Uniformed Svcs. U. of the Health Scis., Bethesda, Md., 1983, 89, Walter Reed Army Hosp., Washington, 1983, Ea. Va. Med. Sch., Norfolk, 1984, Meml. Med. Ctr., Savannah, Ga., 1985, U. Buflao, 1987, Uniformed Svcs. U. of the Health Scis., 1987-88, White House, Washington, 1988, Med. Coll. Wis., 1988, U. Tenn. Med. Ctr., Knoxville, 1988, U. Nijmegen Sch. of Medicine, The Netherlands, 1988, Nederlandsche Vereeniging van Artsen-Automobilisten VVAA, Utrecht, The Netherlands, 1988, Hartford (Conn.) Hosp., 1989, Lothian and Borders Fire Brigaade, Edinburgh, Scotland, 1989; mem. staff Charity Hosp. at New Orleans, sr. vis. surgeon Dept. Surgery, Tulane div., 1988—, also chief Trauma Divsn. Co-author: Retroperitoneal Trauma, 1991, Atlas of Emergency Surgical Procedures, 1991; editorial cons. Emergency Care and Transportation of the Sick and Injured, 3d edit., 1981, 4th edit., 1985; contbr. articles to med. jours., chpts. to textbooks; editor The Emergency Med. Technician Jour., 1978-81, Jour. of Prehosp. Care, 1984-86, Emergency Medicine, Trauma Rounds, 1984—c; sci. editor Am. Assn. Automotive Med. Quar., 1976-82; med. editor Current Concepts in Trauma Care, 1977-85, Current Concepts in Wound Care, 1985-87; edit. cons. Emergency Tng., 1980—, Annals of Emergency Medicine, 1981; mem. editorial bd. Comprehensive Therapy, 1977—, Emergency Med. Care, 1981, Emergency Medicine, 1981—, Emergency Med. Svcs., 1982—, Emergency Medicine Reports, 1983-86, Emergency Medicine Quar., 1984—, Advanced Clin. Updates, 1985—, Jour. Prehosp. Medicine, 1988-89, The Inside Edge, 1988—, Trauma Chronicle, 1990—, Prehosp. and Disaster Medicine, 1990—; editorial cons. Mil. Medicine, 1987—; mem. adv. bd. Rescue-EMS News, 1989—. Capt. M.C., USNR, 1965-90. Recipient New Mem. of Yr. award Atlanta Sports Car Club Am., 1971, Sportmanship award Savannah Internat. Raceway Sports Car Club Am., 1971, Excellence award Kans. Emergency Med. Tng. Assn., 1977, Appreciation award Mid-Am. Regional Coun. Emergency Rescue, 1977, helicopter jump and med. evacuation award Offshore Flight Medic Wings, 1987, Med. Commendation award U.S. Power Boat Assn., 1987. Fellow ACS (sr. mem. com. on trauma 1985—, numerous other coms.), Am. Assn. for Surgery of Trauma, Am. Coll. Surgeons/Com. on Trauma (numerous coms.); mem. ACT Found. (med. adv. bd. 1978-84), Am. Heart Assn. bd. dirs. 1974-76, other offices), Am. Motorcycle Assn. (med. dir. 1975—), Am. Surg. Assn., Am. Trauma Soc. (charter mem., bd. dirs. 1978-83), Assn. for Acad. Surgery (exec. coun. 1974-76), Ea. Assn. for the Surgery of Trauma (publs. com. 1990—), Internat. Soc. Aquatic Medicine (exec. com. 1975, dir. continuing med. edn., 1975—), Internat. Soc. Surgeons, Johnson County Med. Soc. (med. dir. emergency med. svcs 1974-77), La. Med. Soc., Nat. Assn. Emergency Med. Technicians (bd. dirs. 1975-85, chmn. publs. com. 1979-85, bd. govs. 1983-85, med. dir. PHTLS com. 1982—, bd. govs. in Reno 1988—, Pres.'s Leadership award 1980, "Deke" Farrington award 1983, Pres.'s award 1984), Nat. Registry Emergency Med. Technicians (chmn. bd. dirs. 1988—), New Orleans Surg. Soc., Orleans Parish Med. Soc., Shock Soc., Sports Car Club Am. (Southeastern Regional dir. 1972-74, dir. med. safety, 1974-76, Val D. Scroggle award 1977), Surg. Assn. La., J.C. Throughman Surg. Soc., Am. Assn. Emergency Med. Svcs., Am. Assn. Automotive Medicine (A.J. Mirkin Svc. award 1987), Nu Sigma Nu, Sigma Alpha Epsilon. Achievements include first to introduce Pre-Hospital Trauma Life Support (PHLTS), a nationally recognized protocol for the pre-hospital care of trauma patients; one of several health-care workers who helped save numerous lifes in the days following the Hurricane Katrina disaster, recognized for his heroic work by media outlets such as MSNBC and CNN. Office: Tulane U Sch Medicine Dept Surgery 1430 Tulane Ave New Orleans LA 70112*

**MCSWEENEY, FRANCES KAYE,** psychology professor; b. Rochester, NY, Feb. 6, 1948; d. Edward William and Elsie Winifred (Kingston) McSweeney. BA, Smith Coll., 1969; MA, Harvard U., 1972, PhD, 1974. Lectr. McMaster U., Hamilton, Ont., Canada, 1973—74; asst. prof. Wash. State U., Pullman, 1974—79, assoc. prof., 1979—83, prof. psychology, 1983—2004, Regents prof. psychology, 2004—, chmn. dept. psychology, 1986—94, vice provost for faculty affairs, 2003—. Con. in field. Contbr. articles to profl. jours. Woodrow Wilson fellow, Sloan fellow, 1968—69, NIMH fellow, 1973. Fellow: APA, Assn. Behavior Analysis (pres. 2005—06), Assn. for Psychol. Sci.; mem.: Psychonomic Soc., Phi Kappa Phi, Sigma Xi, Phi Beta Kappa. Home: 860 SW Alcora Dr Pullman WA 99163-2053 Office: Wash State U Dept Psychology Pullman WA 99164-4820 Office Phone: 509-335-2738. Business E-Mail: fkmcs@mail.wsu.edu.

**MCSWEENEY, MAURICE J. (MARC MCSWEENEY),** lawyer; b. Chgo., July 3, 1938; s. Thomas J. and Margaret F. (Ahern) McS.; m. Sandra A. Panosh, Sept. 30, 1967; children: Erin, Sean. BS, DePaul U., 1960; JD, U. Chgo., 1963. Bar: Wis. 1963. With Foley and Lardner, Milw., 1963—; mem. mgmt. com., 1984—93, chmn. litig. dept., 1993—2002, chief diversity ptnr., 2003—. Bd. dirs. Harambee Elem. Sch., 1989-00, Internat. Clown Hall of Fame, 1999-02. Bd. dirs. Milw. Pub. Schs., 1973-79, Milw. chpt. ARC, 1979-85, Alverno Coll., Milw., —, chmn., 2005-. Health Edn. Ctr. of Wis., 1987-96. Fellow Am. Coll. Trial Lawyers; mem. ABA, Wis. Bar Assn., Milw. Bar Assn., Am. Judicature Soc. (bd. dirs. 1988-93), Milw. Area Tech.

Coll. Found., Rotary (bd. dirs. Milw. 1986-88). Avocations: skiing, tennis, Karate. Office: Foley & Lardner LLP 777 E Wisconsin Ave Ste 3800 Milwaukee WI 53202-5367 Office Phone: 414-297-5520. Business E-Mail: mmcsweeney@foley.com.

**MCSWEENEY, WILLIAM LINCOLN, JR.,** retired publishing executive; b. Nov. 9, 1930; s. William Lincoln and Ruth Patricia (Desmond) McS.; m. Anne Cornelia Bulman, Aug. 18, 1956; children: Anne C., William L., Siobhan White, Arthur J., Sean B. BS, Boston Coll., 1953; MLA, So. Meth. U., 1980; LHD, Rockhurst Coll., 1997. Tchr. English Killingly (Conn.) H.S., 1956-57; with Hallmark Cards, Inc., Kansas City, Mo., 1957-86, area pers. mgr., 1968, sales tng. mgr., 1969-86, dir. corp. tng. and devel., 1970-86; pub. Nat. Cath. Reporter Co., 1986-96. Bd. dirs. Cath. Social Svcs., Kansas City Archdiocese, 1975-88, pres., 1980-84; bd. dirs. United Cmty. Svcs. Kansas City, 1979-84, mem. exec. com., 1978-84; bd. dirs. Kansas City Amigos De Las Americas, 1977-80, pres., 1979; bd. dirs. Johnson City YMCA, 1978-79, Jesuit Vol. Corps, Midwest, 1989-95, Mex. Am. Cultural Ctr., San Antonio, 1990—, Minority Mus., 1994-2000; bd. dirs. Pan Ednl. Inst., 1979-83, pres., 1980-81; mem. Boston Coll. Alumni Admissions Coun., 1976-96; mem. chancellor's adv. bd. Met. Cmty. Colls., 1979-80; mem. Dem. Com., Johnson County, Kans., 1980-86; bd. advisors Sch. Social Welfare U. Kans., 1983-2000, chair, 1983-91, 93-94, Avila Col., 1991-2000; chair Mayor's UN Day Dinner, Kansas City, Mo., 1990, Mayor's Breakfast, 1994—; trustee NCCJ, 1991-95, co-chmn., 1995—. With U.S. Army, 1953-56. Recipient Kansas City World Citizen of Yr. award, 1995, William V. McKenney award Boston Coll., 2000. Mem. Internat. Rels. Coun. of Kansas City (bd. dirs. 1989-2000), Cath. Press Assn., Assoc. Ch. Press, Internat. Press Inst. (bd. dirs. Am. Com. 1999—), UN Assn., Boston Coll. Alumni Assn. (past bd. dirs.), Boston Coll. Club (Kansas City), Knights of Malta. Roman Catholic. Office: 115 E Armour Blvd PO Box 419281 Kansas City MO 64141-6281

**MCSWEENEY WOODFALL, IRENE FRANCES,** civil engineer, director; b. Olean, N.Y., Jan. 5, 1963; d. James Paul and Bernice Mary McSweeney; children: Joseph, Christopher. AAS in Bldg. Constrn., Wentworth Inst. Tech., Boston, 1983, BEng in Civil Engring., 1985; grad., Worcester Poly. Inst., Mass., 2001—03. Lic. profl. civil engr., Mass. Project mgr. Allen & Major Assoc., Woburn, Mass., 1985—91; dir. constrn. Boston Water and Sewer Commn., Boston, 1991—. Adj. prof. Wentworth Inst. Tech., Boston, 1987—2004, corporator, 2000—. Basketball coach Sacred Heart Sch., Weymouth, Mass., 2000—02, Cath. Youth Orgn., Boston, 2004—05. Recipient Past Pres.' award, New England Water Works, 1995. Mem. Am. Water Works Assn., N.Am. Soc. Trenchless Tech. (bd. dir. 1997—2002, Person of Yr. 2003). Avocations: basketball, skiing, boating, painting. Office: Boston Water and Sewer Commn 980 Harrison Ave Boston MA 02119 Office Phone: 617-989-7447.

**MCSWEENY, WILLIAM FRANCIS,** petroleum company executive, author; b. Haverhill, Mass., Mar. 31, 1929; s. William Francis and Mary Florence (Doyle) McS.; m. Dorothy Pierce, Jan. 20, 1969; children: William Francis III, Cathy Ann, Ethan Madden Maverick, Terrell Pierce. Reporter, columnist, fgn. corr. Hearst Newspapers, 1943—67; dep. chmn., dir. pub. affairs Dem. Nat. Com., 1967—68; spl. asst. to White House Chief Staff, 1968—69; from sr. exec. v.p. to pres. Occidental Internat. Corp., L.A., 1969—91; from exec. v.p. to cons. to chmn. Occidental Petroleum Corp., L.A., 1984—91; bd. dirs. Chevy Chase FSB, 1985—. Mem. Lloyd's of London; pres.'s rep. to USSR, 1979; mem. Pres.'s Inaugural Com., 1980, 84, 92; Presdl. spl. rep. to Oman, 1980, Bolivia, 1982; Pres.'s com. Korean War Meml., 1987; Pres.'s commr. Exec. Exch., 1976-81; Pres.'s trustee The Kennedy Ctr., 1995—, Pres.'s rep. to Korea, 2000; mem. N.E. White Ho. Fellows Bd.; dir. Collaboration Initiatives MIT; mem. U.S. Com. UNESCO; co-chair NATO 50th Summit; spl. counsel spkr. Ho. of Reps., 1971-72; chmn. Maverick-McSweeney Cattle Co Author: Go Up for Glory, 1965, Violence Every Sunday, 1966, The Impossible Dream, 1967; contbr. articles to profl. jours Bd. overseers Fletcher Sch. Law and Diplomacy, Tufts U.; bd. advisors Karl F. Landegger Program Internat. Bus. Diplomacy, Sch. Fgn. Svc., Georgetown U.; trustee, pres. Holton Arms; chmn. Washington Episc. Sch.; chmn. Meridian House Internat., life trustee; mem. World Affairs Coun.; bd. dir. The Atlantic Coun., Overseer Exec. Coun. Fgn. Diplomats, Dept. of State, The Brookings Instn. Coun., 1991-98; vice chmn. Sec. State Fine Arts Commn.; chmn. Ford's Theatre, 1988-95, life trustee; bd. dir. Very Spl. Arts, Arena Stage, Corcoran Gallery Art, Africare, Fed. City Coun., Washington Opera, Folger Shakespeare Theater, Cities in Schs. Nat. Learning Ctr., USO, Arms Control Assn., Nat. Soc. So. Poor, Duke Ellington Sch., Washington Ednl. TV, 1989-95; v.p. Ct. Mary Rose, Portsmouth, Eng.; pres. Commn. to Preserve U.S. Cultural Heritage Abroad; co-chmn. State Dept. diplomatic rooms endowment; chmn. Lombardi Cancer Ctr. Coun., Georgetown U. Med. Ctr.; pres. Ams. Internat. Insts. Advanced Studies; vice-chmn. Kennedy Ctr. Cmty. Bd., 1991-92; trustee V.P. Residence Found., Lyndon Baines Johnson Sch. Pub. Affairs, U. Tex.; trustee Washington Coll.; 1995-05; juror The Heinz Found., 1995-2000; chmn. Chevy Chase Cmty. Com., Coun. Ct. Excellence, 1996-99. Maj. inf. U.S. Army, 1950-53 Decorated Combat Inf. badge; recipient Outstanding Young Man award, Boston Jaycees, 1961, U.S. Disting. Svc. award, 1969, Outstanding Svc. spl. award, 1969, DC Disting. Citizen award, 1981, Paul Hill award, Kennedy Ctr., 1983, DC Cultural award, 1983, Armenian Earthquake Hero medal, 1989, Lincoln medal, 1991, Helen Hayes award, 1991, Washingtonian of Yr. award, 1995, Golden Plate award, Am. Acad. Achievement, 1999, Cultural Alliance award, 2000, Torch of Liberty award, Anti Defamation League, 2001, awards for domestic reports and reporting from Vietnam and Mid. East, including Best U.S. Reporting award, 1964, Angel of Arts award, Cathedral Choral Soc., 2004. Mem. Smithsonian Instn. (nat. adv. com. Kellogg Project), Mus. Native Ams. (dir.), Alfalfa Club, Cosmos Club, 1925 F St. Club (trustee), Internat. Club (trustee)

**MCSWINEY, CHARLES RONALD,** lawyer; b. Nashville, Apr. 23, 1943; s. James W. and Jewell (Bellar) Mc.; m. Jane Detrick McSwiney, Jan. 2, 1970. BA, Kenyon Coll., Gambier, Ohio, 1965; JD, U. Cin., 1968. Assoc. Smith & Schnacke, Dayton, Ohio, 1968-72, ptnr., 1972-89, pres. and mng. ptnr., 1984-89; sr. v.p., gen. counsel The Danis Cos., Dayton, 1992-99, 2000; vice chmn. Carillon Capital, Inc., Dayton, 1992-99; dir. devel. Youth Haven, Inc., 2002—. Chmn., CEO Crysteco, Inc., Wilmington, Ohio, 1995-99; pres. interchange exec. Presdl. Commn. on Pers. Interchange, Washington, 1972-73. Chmn., pres. bd. trustees Dayton Ballet Assn., 1988; trustee Columbus (Ohio) Symphony Orch., 1981-84; chmn. Dayton Performing Arts Fund, 1989-92, Dayton Devel. Coun., 1987-90, Wright State U. Found., Dayton, 1988-94, Miami Valley Sch., Dayton, 1986-2000; mem. bd. advisors Wright State U. Coll. Bus. Adminstrn., 1988-98; bd. vis. U. Cin. Coll. Law, 1987-89; mem. pres.'s coun. Internat. Coll. Recipient Bronze Medal for Performance U.S. EPA, 1973. Mem. Dayton Area C. of C. (trustee 1987-90). Republican. United Ch. of Christ. Home: 1872 Timarron Way Naples FL 34109 E-mail: ronmcswiney@comcast.net.

**MC SWINEY, JAMES WILMER,** retired pulp and paper manufacturing company executive; b. McEwen, Tenn., Nov. 13, 1915; s. James S. and Delia (Conroy) McS.; m. Jewel Bellar, 1940; children: Charles Ronald, Margaret Ann. Grad., Harvard Advanced Mgmt. Program, 1954. Lab. technician, shipping clk. Nashville div. The Mead Corp., 1934-39; asst. office mgr. Harriman div., 1939; plant mgr. Rockport, Ind., 1940; asst. office mgr. Kingsport (Tenn.) div., 1941-44; exec. asst. to pres. Dayton, Ohio, 1957; v.p. devel., 1957-59; adminstrv v.p. Harriman div. (Kingsport (Tenn.) div.), 1959; group v.p. gen. mgr. Mead Bd. div., 1961-63, exec. v.p. corp., 1963-67, pres., chief exec. officer, 1968-71, chmn. bd., chief exec. officer, 1971-78, chmn. bd., 1978-82; ret., 1982. Acct., office mgr., asst. sec.-treas. Brunswick Pulp & Paper Co., Ga., 1944-45; bd. dirs. Ultra-Met, Gosiger, Inc., Sea Island Co. Trustee Com. for Econ. Devel. Aviation cadet USAAF, 1942-44. Home: PO Box 30604 401 Ocean Rd Sea Island GA 31561 Office Phone: 912-638-5262. E-mail: mcswineyj@bellsouth.net.

**MCTAGGART, TIMOTHY ROBERT,** state agency administrator, lawyer; b. Phila., May 6, 1960; s. James Francis and Patricia Ann (Berry) McT. AB cum laude, Harvard U., 1982, JD, 1985. Bar: Mass. 1985, D.C. 1987. Atty.

gen. counsel's office Bd. Govs. FRS, Washington, 1985-87; assoc. Morrison & Foerster, Washington, 1987-89, Fried, Frank, Harris, Shriver & Jacobson, Washington, 1989-91; counsel U.S. Senate Com., 1991-94, Del. Bank Commr., 1994-98; ptnr. Nixon Peabody LLP and predecessor firm, Washington, 1999—2003, Willkie Farr & Gallagher, 2003—. Mem. ABA, Mass. Bar Assn., D.C. Bar Assn. Avocations: reading, basketball, movies. Office Phone: 202-303-1127. E-mail: tmctaggart@willkie.com.

**MCTAGUE, JOHN PAUL,** materials scientist, educator, chemist, researcher; b. Jersey City, Nov. 28, 1938; s. James Aloysius and Teresa Eugenia (Hanley) McT.; m. Carole Frances Reilly, Dec. 30, 1961 (dec. Jan. 1997); children: Kevin W., Catherine E., Margaret A., Maureen E.; m.Margaret Ann Danna, Oct. 15, 2004. BS in Chemistry, Georgetown U., 1960; PhD, Brown U., 1965, DSc (hon.), 1997. Mem. tech. staff N.Am. Rockwell Sci. Ctr., Thousand Oaks, Calif., 1964—70; prof. chemistry, mem. Inst. Geophysics and Planetary Physics UCLA, 1970—82; dep. dir. Office Sci. and Tech. Policy, Exec. Office of Pres., Washington, 1983—86, acting sci. advisor to Pres. Reagan, 1986; v.p. rsch. Ford Motor Co., Dearborn, Mich., 1986—90, v.p. tech. affairs, 1990—99; v.p. lab. mgmt., Office of Pres. U. Calif., Oakland, 2001—, prof. materials Santa Barbara, 2001—. Adj. prof. chemistry Columbia, U., 1982-83. Mem. Pres.'s Coun. Advisors on Sci. and Tech., 1990-93; mem. adv. bd. Sec. Energy, 1990—; chmn. bd. overseers Fermilab, 1994-99. Alfred P. Sloan Research fellow, 1971-73; NATO sr. fellow, 1973; John Simon Guggenheim Meml. fellow, 1975-76. Fellow AAAS, Am. Phys. Soc. (George E. Pake prize 1998), Calif. Coun. Sci. and Tech.; mem. Am. Chem. Soc. (Calif. sect. award 1975), Nat. Acad. Engring., Sigma Xi. Personal E-mail: jmctague1@aol.com.

**MCTAGUE-DOUGHERTY, AMY ELIZABETH,** speech pathology/audiology services professional; d. Edward Patrick and Eileen Frances McTague; m. Patrick C. Dougherty, July 12, 1997; 1 child, Emma Louise Dougherty. BS, Loyola Coll., Balt., 1993, MS, 1995. Cert. clin. competence Am. Speech Lang. Hearing Assn., speech lang. pathologist N.J. Augmentative comm. specialist Cerebral Palsy of Monmouth and Ocean Counties, Inc., Wanamassa, NJ, 1995—; augmentative comm. cons. Prentke Romich Co., Wooster, Ohio, 1997—99; comm. instr. Temple U., Phila., 1999. Adj. prof. Richard Stockton Coll. N.J., Pomona, 1999—2001. Named Employee of the Quarter, Cerebral Palsy of Monmouth and Ocean Counties, 1996. Mem.: Am. Speech Lang. Hearing Assn., Internat. Soc. of Augmentative and Alternative Comm., U.S. Soc. of Augmentative and Alternative Comm., N.J. Speech Lang. Hearing Assn. (co-chair augmentative and alternative comm. com. 1998—99). Roman Catholic. Achievements include development of Vocabulary program for communication devices. Avocations: bicycling, gardening, walking. Office: Ladacin Network 1701 Kneeley Blvd Wanamassa NJ 07712 Office Phone: 732-493-5900. Personal E-mail: pat.doug@verizon.net.

**MCTEE, CINDY,** classical musician, educator; b. 1953; BM, Pacific Luth. U., 1976, studied with David Robbins; MM, Yale U., 1978, studied with Krzysztof Penderecki, Jacob Druckman; and Bruce MacComble; PhD, U. Iowa, 1981, studied with Richard Hervig; studied with Penderecki, Marek Stachowski, and Krystyna Moszumanska-Nazar, Higher Sch. Music, Cracow, Poland. Tchr. Pacific Luth. U., Tacoma, 1981-84; asst. to full prof. music composition U. North Tex., Denton, 1984—. Fulbright-Hayes Sr. Lectr. fellow in computer music Acad. Music, Cracow, 1990. Recipient comms. from Dallas Symphony Orch., Nat. Symphony Orch., Big Eight Band Dirs. Assn., Voices of Change, Barlow Endowment for Music Composition, Am. Guild Organists, Coll. Band Dirs. Nat. Assn., Phi Kappa Lambda Bd. Regents; works performed by Dallas Symphony Orch., Am. Symphony Orch., Detroit Symphony Orch., Chgo. Symphony Orch., Indpls. Symphony Orch., Nat. Repertory Orch., St. Louis Symphony, Memphis Symphony, Honolulu Symphony, Pitts. New Music Ensemble, Nat. Symphony Orch., Nippon Housou Kyoukai (NHK) Symphony Orch., Philharm. Orch., London. Recipient BMI award, Guggenheim Fellowship, 2001; grantee Wash. State Arts Commn.; Composers fellow NEA, Goddard Lieberson fellow AAAL; Acad. award in Music, AAAL, 2002; winner Louisville Orch. Composition Competition, 2001. Home: 1217 Piping Rock St Denton TX 76205-8126

**MCTEER, ROBERT D., JR.,** academic administrator, former bank executive; married; 2 children. BBA in Econ., U. GA, 1963, PhD in Econ., U. 1971. With Fed. Reserve Bank Richmond, 1968—91; sr. v.p. Baltimore branch Fed. Reserve Bank of Richmond, 1980—91; pres., CEO Fed. Res. Bank Dallas, Tex., 1991—2004; chancellor Texas A&M U. System, College Station, Tex., 2004—. Adj. prof. U. Richmond, Va. Commonwealth U., Johns Hopkins U.; bd. dirs. Nat. Coun. on Econ. Edn.; bd. overseers U. Ga. Terry Coll. Bus. Office: Tex A&M U System A&M Bldg 200 Technology Way Ste 2043 College Station TX 77845

**MCTIER, CHARLES HARVEY,** foundation administrator; b. Columbus, Ga., Jan. 28, 1939; s. Roy and Julia (Harvey) McT.; m. Margaret Lucy Ruyl, Aug. 23, 1962; children: Margaret Marie, Charles Harvey Jr. BBA, Emory U., 1961. Administrv. asst. hosp. Emory U., Atlanta, 1961-63, bus. mgr. dept. psychiat. Sch. Med., 1963-66, assoc. dir. personnel, 1966-69, asst. to pres., bd. trustees, 1969-71; sec. Robert W. Woodruff Found., Joseph B. Whitehead Found., Lettie Pate Evans Found., Inc., Lettie Pate Whitehead Found., Inc., Atlanta, 1971-77, sec., treas., 1977-87, v.p., sec., treas., 1987-88, pres., 1988—. Chmn. Atlanta Founds. Forum, 1985-86; trustee Southeastern Coun. Founds., Atlanta, 1985-92, chmn. membership com., 1986-89, chmn. program com., 1989, chmn. bd. trustees, 1989-90; vice chmn. Coun. on Founds., Washington, 1995-97, program com., 1985-87, nominating com., 1987-88, chmn. audit and fin. com., 1996-97, chmn. mgmt. com., 1996-97; chmn. bd. trustees Found. Ctr. N.Y.C., 1994-2000, fin. and audit com., 1991-2000, exec. com., 1992-93, chmn. nominating com.; former pub. mem. Joint Commn. on Accreditation of Health Care Orgns., 1994-2003; dir. SunTrust Bank of Ga., SunTrust Bank Atlanta, 1995—, Coca-Cola FEMSA. Trustee, North Ga. United Meth. Found., 1985—; trustee, treas. Meth. Found. Ret. Mins., 1980; chmn. new ch. devel. com. North Ga. United Meth. Conf., 1980-85; mem. bd. vis. Emory U., 1985-87. Mem. Assn. Emory Alumni (bd. govs. 1987-91), Pres.'s Cir. of NAS/Inst. of Medicine, Commerce Club (bd. dirs.), Peachtree Golf Club, Piedmont Driving Club. Avocations: golf, travel. Office: Robert W Woodruff Found Inc 50 Hurt Plz SE Ste 1200 Atlanta GA 30303-2951 Office Phone: 404-522-6755.

**MCTIQUE, MAURICE P.,** director; Cabinet min., mem. parliament, New Zealand, 1985—97; dir. govt. accountability project Mercatus Ctr., George Mason U., Arlington, Va. Spkr. in field; mem. bd. Performance Mgmt. Adv. Com. Contbr. articles numerous prof. jours. Recipient Queen's Svc. Order, Queen Elizabeth II, 1999; scholar disting. vis. scholar, George Mason U. Office: 3301 N Fairfax Dr Arlington VA 22201-4433 Office Phone: 703-993-4930.

**MCTYEIRE, ROBERT ADAMS,** sound engineer, music company executive, consultant; b. Birmingham, Ala., July 21, 1949; s. William Walter Jr. and Katherine Elizabeth (Meadow) McT.; m. Pamela Ann Huffstutler, Apr. 18, 1978. BS in Commerce and Bus. Adminstrn., U. Ala., 1972. Ind. sound engr., Tuscaloosa, 1972-73; owner, chief engr. Ram Sound, Tuscaloosa, 1973-89, Mary Esther, Fla., 1989—. Charter mem. nominating com. Ala. Music Hall of Fame, Muscle Shoals; cons. Klipsch and Assocs., Inc., Hope, Ark., 1984-; bd. dirs. Iron Art, Inc., The Krewe of Bowlegs, Navarre Land Enterprises, M4 Properties, Ltd., McTyeire Enterprises, Inc. Sound engr. for numerous entertainers including Tony Bennett, Dave Brubeck, Ray Charles, Ry Cooder, Fats Domino, Roy Orbison, Bob Hope, Tom Jones, B.B. King, Wynton Marsalis, Dolly Parton, Bonnie Raitt, Ray Stevens, Ramsey Lewis, George Jones, B.J Thomas, and many others. With U.S. Air N.G., 1969-71. Mem. Muscle Shoals Music Assn. Republican. Avocations: boating, travel, music, motorcycling. Home and Office: Ram Sound 369 W Miracle Strip Pky Mary Esther FL 32569-1833

**MCTYRE, ROBERT EARL,** publishing executive; b. Detroit, Aug. 2, 1955; s. Earl Melvin and Barbara Jean (shorter) McT.; m. Earn Diane Fortune, Mar. 1975 (div. Jan. 1977); m. Dianne Denise Ball, Nov. 1978 (div. Feb. 1982); m. Carmela Ann Baldwin, Sept. 22, 1990; stepchildren: DuJuan Robinson, Tamika Baldwin. Student, Wayne State U., 1988-90. EMT Mich. EMT Detroit Gen. Hosp., 1975-77, Detroit Fire Dept., 1977-85; freelance writer, 1978-86; intern, classified sales Met. Times, Detroit, 1985-86; gen. mgr. Eastside Citizens News, Detroit, 1986-87; reporter Mich. Chronicle, Detroit, 1987-89, assoc. editor, 1989-93, exec. editor, 1993—; pres., CEO BenWil Creative Mgmt. Svcs., Detroit, 1993—. Speaker in field. Author and editor of poems. Assoc. minister New Resurrection Bapt. Ch., Detroit, 1988—. Mem. Soc. Environ. Journalists. Republican. Baptist. Avocations: comic book collecting, martial arts. Office: Mich Chronicle 479 Ledyard St Detroit MI 48201-2641

**MCVAY, MICHEAL RAY,** social sciences educator, department chairman; b. McCook, Nebr., Jan. 19, 1949; s. Harry Ross and Axie Irene McVay; m. Leota Marie McVay, June 1, 1968; children: Scott Alan, Christine Amelia Aschenbrenner. BS, Phillips U., Enid, Okla., 1971; MS, Ft. Hays (Kans.) State U., 1993. Nat. cert. counselor. Philosophy/ethics instr. Colby C.C., Kans., 1993—, chair social scis. divsn., 2000—. Min. Christian Ch. (Disciples of Christ), Oberlin, Kans., 1988—93. Office: Colby CC 1255 S Range Ave Colby KS 67701 Office Phone: 785-462-3984. E-mail: mike@colbycc.edu.

**MCVEIGH, GLENNA FAYE,** minister; b. Holts Summit, Mo., Oct. 3, 1936; d. Frank Edward and Ila Francis Morris; children: Randall, Richard, Kenneth. Student, Southwest Bapt. Coll., 1995, Saint Paul Sch. Theology, 1993—97. Reporter Memphis (Mo.) Dem. Newspaper, 1981—85, editor, 1985—89; receptionist, sec. Fulton (Mo.) Police Dept., 1990—92; minister Bethel United Meth. Ch., Montgomery City, Mo., 1992, Mountain View (Mo.) United Meth. Ch., 1992—2004, Pleasant Grove (Mo.) United Meth. Ch., 1992—2002, Keytesville/Dalton (Mo.) United Meth. Ch., 2004—. V.p. Ministerial Alliance, Mountain View, 2000—04; chaplain Mountain View (Mo.) Healthcare Ctr., 1997—2004. Editor: United Meth. Ch. Jefferson City/Rolla Dist. Newsletter, 1996—99. Bd. dirs. Agape House, Mountain View, 2002—04, FEED Program, Mountain View, 2000—04. Named day in honor, City Mountain View, 2002; recipient Denman Evangelism, Dist. United Meth. Ch., 1995. Mem.: Keytesville (Mo.) C. of C. Avocations: sewing, singing, reading. Home and Office: Keytesville Dalton Immanuel United Methodist 408 West Finnell Dr Keytesville MO 65261

**MCVEIGH, PATRICK (PAT),** software developer company executive; Bachelor's Degree in Psychology, Clark U., Worcester, Mass. Various sales and mktg. positions Apple Computer; with Palm, Inc.; former chmn., CEO Omnisky Corp. (sold to Earthlink); former CEO Aliph Corp.; sr. v.p. worldwide licensing PalmSource, Inc., Sunnyvale, Calif., 2005—, interim CEO, 2005—. Office: Palmsource Inc 1188 E Arques Ave Sunnyvale CA 94085-4602

**MCVEIGH-PETTIGREW, SHARON CHRISTINE,** communications consultant; b. San Francisco, Feb. 6, 1949; d. Martin Allen and Frances (Roddy) McVeigh; m. John Wallace Pettigrew, Mar. 27, 1971; children: Benjamin Thomas Pettigrew, Margaret Mary Pettigrew. BA with honors, U. Calif.-Berkeley, 1971; diploma of edn., Monash U., Australia, 1975; MBA, Golden Gate U., 1985. Tchr., adminstr. Victorian Edn. Dept., Victoria, Australia, 1972—79; supr. Network Control Ctr. GTE Sprint Comms., Burlingame, Calif., 1979—81, mgr. customer assistance, 1981—84, mgr. state legis. ops., 1984—85, dir. revenue programs, 1986—87; comm. cons. Flores, Pettigrew & Co., San Mateo, Calif., 1987—89; telemktg. Apple Computer Inc., Cupertino, Calif., 1989—94; prin. The Call Ctr. Group, San Mateo, Calif., 1995—. Telecomm. cons. PPG Svcs., 1994—; telecomm. spkr. Dept. Consumer Affairs, Sacramento, 1984. Panelist Wash. Gov.'s Citizens Coun., 1984; founding mem. Maroondah Women's Shelter, Victoria, 1978; organizer nat. conf. Bus. Women and the Polit. Process, New Orleans, 1986; mem. sch. bd. Boronia Tech. Sch., Victoria, 1979. Recipient Tchr. Spl. Responsibilities award, Victoria Edn. Dept., 1979. Mem.: Women's Econ. Action League, Am. Telemktg. Assn. (bd. dirs. 1992), Peninsula Profl. Women's Network, Am. Mgmt. Assn., Women in Telecom. (panel moderator San Francisco 1984). Democrat. Roman Catholic. Office Phone: 650-579-1298.

**MCVEY, FRANCIS DANIEL,** mechanical engineer, software developer, educator; b. St. Louis, Jan. 19, 1929; s. Martin Patrick and Marguy Josephine (Boeckler) McV.; m. Anna Elizabeth Moss, Nov. 26, 1958 (dec. Dec. 1990); children: Mark Andrew, Marguy Denise, Michael Sean. BS in Mech. Engring., Washington U., St. Louis, 1952, MS, 1954. Instt. mech. engring. Washington U., St. Louis, 1954-55; group project engr., missiles engring. divsn. McDonnell Aircraft Co., St. Louis, 1955-58, assoc. scientist rsch. divsn., 1961-64, br. mgr. engring. tech. divsn., 1964-74, prin. staff engr., 1974-83; chief aerodynamicist Cleve. Pneumatic Co., Washington, 1959-61; engring. fellow McDonnell Douglas, 1983-86, sr. fellow, 1986-97, dir. CAD/CAM St. Louis, 1986-97; sr. tech. fellow Boeing Co., St. Louis, 1997—, staff engring. dir., 1997-99; retired, 1999. Lectr. St. Louis U., 1964—70, 2000—, U. Mo.-Rolla extension, 1971; adj. prof. aero. and mech. engring. dept. St. Louis U., 2000—; engring. and automotive cons. Mem. exec. adv. com. on engring. St. Louis U., 1998—2006. With AUS, 1946—48. Recipient Lloyd R. Koenig prize in engring. Washington U., 1952. Fellow: AIAA (assoc.; chmn. St. Louis sect. 1963—66, mem. mgmt. com. 1998—2002); mem.: Am. Rocket Soc. (chmn. St. Louis sect.), Sigma Xi. Roman Catholic. Avocation: reading. Home: 7030 Delmar Blvd University City MO 63130-4301 Personal E-mail: fmcveyd@aol.com.

**MCVEY, HENRY HANNA, III,** retired lawyer; b. Richmond, Va., Aug. 12, 1935; s. Henry Hanna Jr. and Eva Lawson (Jennings) McVey; m. Reba Jean Robinson, Dec. 12, 1964; children: Margaret Anne McVey Singleton, Lewis Lawson, Ian Douglas. BS, BA magna cum laude, Hampden-Sydney Coll., Va., 1957; LLB, U. Va., Charlottesville, 1960. Bar: Va. 1960, U.S. Dist. Ct. (ea. dist.) Va. 1960, U.S. Ct. Appeals (4th cir.) 1965, U.S. Supreme Ct. 1970. Assoc. Battle, Neal, Harris, Minor & Williams, Richmond, 1960-66; ptnr. McGuireWoods LLP and predecessor firms, Richmond, 1960—99; ret., 1999. Mem. adv. group under Civil Justice Reform Act of 1990 U.S. Dist. Ct. (ea. dist.) Va. Trustee Hampden-Sydney Coll., 1989—94, 1995—, vice chair, 2001—03, chair bd. trustees, 2003—; mem. Commn. on Archtl. Rev. City of Richmond, 1985—95; mem. Planning Commn. Gloucester County, 2001—, vice chmn., 2006—; bd. dirs. Richmond Symphony, 1977—86, 1987—99, v.p., 1979—81, exec. v.p., 1981—83, pres., 1983—85, chmn. bd. dirs., 1985—87, pres. Symphony Coun., 1999—2001; bd. dirs. Carpenter Ctr. for Performing Arts, 1982—89, Rosewell Found., 1999—2004, pres., 2001—02, v.p., 2002—03. Recipient Algernon Sydney Sullivan medallion for svc. to coll., Hampden Sydney Coll., 2001, Alumni Citation for loyal svc. to the coll., Hampden-Sydney Coll., 2002. Fellow: Am. Bar Found., Am. Coll. Trial Lawyers; mem.: Va. Bar Assn., Va. Assn. Def. Attys. (v.p. 1981—83, treas. 1983—84, pres.-elect 1984—85, pres. 1985—86), Ware River Yacht Club (bd. dirs. 2000—05). Presbyterian. Home: PO Box 8 Ware Neck VA 23178 Personal E-mail: hmcvey@cox.net.

**MC VICKER, CHARLES TAGGART,** artist, educator; b. Canonsburg, Pa., Aug. 31, 1930; s. Carl Walter and Mary Ruth (Washabaugh) McV.; m. Lucy Claire Graves, Mar. 20, 1954; children— Lauri, Bonnie, Heather. BA, Principia Coll., Elsah, Ill., 1952; B.F.A., Art Center Coll. Design, Los Angeles, 1957. Staff artist Alexander Chaite Studios, 1957-58; freelance illustrator and painter, 1958—. Asst. prof. Pratt Phoenix Sch. Art, N.Y.C., 1979-84, Trenton State Coll., 1985—2003. One-man shows include Thompson Gallery, N.Y.C., 1967, Capitol Hill Club, Washington, 1988; represented in permanent collections U.S. Capitol, Am. Hist. Assn., Soc. Illustrators, USAF, Princeton U., DuPont Corp., Zimmerli Art Mus. at Rutgers U., Home Life Ins. Co., Wang Corp. Served with AUS, 1952-54. Recipient Ralph Fabri award Nat. Audubon Artists Ann. Juried Show, 1986, Ralph Fabri medal Nat. Soc. Painters in Casein and Acrylic, 1991, Michael Engel Meml. award Nat.

Audubon Artists, 1992. Mem. Soc. Illustrators (exec. com. 1972-74, pres. 1976-78), Am. Watercolor Soc., Graphic Artists Guild (v.p. nat. exec. com. 1978-79), Audubon Artists, Princeton Artists Alliance (pres. 1989—), Am. Artists Profl. League. Home: 26 Old Orchard Ln Princeton NJ 08540-1939*

**MCVICKER, MICHAEL C.,** dentist; DDS, Ohio State U.; grad., Las Vegas Inst. Advanced Dental Studies. Founder Exceptional Dentistry, Inc, Toledo, 1985—. Mem.: Am. Acad. Cosmetic Dentistry. Office: Exceptional Dentistry, Inc Ste 5 3829 Woodley Rd Toledo OH 43606 Office Phone: 419-474-5955. Fax: 419-473-3533. E-mail: drmike@exceptionalsmiles.com.

**MC VIE, CHRISTINE PERFECT,** musician; b. Eng., July 12, 1943; m. John McVie (div.); m. Eddy Quintela. Student art sch., pvt. student sculpture. Singer, keyboardist, Fleetwood Mac, from 1970; albums with Fleetwood Mac include: Fleetwood Mac, 1968, Fleetwood Mac in Chicago, 1969, Then Play On, 1969, English Rose, 1969, Kiln House, 1970, Future Games, 1971, Bare Trees, 1972, Penguin, Mystery To Me, 1973, Heroes Are Hard to Find, 1974, Fleetwood Mac, 1975, Rumours, 1977, Tusk, 1979, Fleetwood Mac Live, 1980, Mirage, 1982, Jumping at Shadows, 1985, Tango in the Night, 1987, Greatest Hits, 1988, Behind the Mask, 1990, The Dance, 1997; solo albums include Christine Perfect, 1969, Christine McVie, 1984; composer: songs including Spare Me a Little of Your Love, Don't Stop, You Make Loving Fun, Over and Over, Hold Me, Songbird, Got a Hold on Me, Heroes Are Hard to Find, Little Lies, As Long as You Follow, Save Me, Skies the Limit. Office: care Warner Bros Records 3300 Warner Blvd Burbank CA 91505-4632

**MCVIE, JOHN,** musician; b. London, Eng., Nov. 26, 1945; naturalized, U.S., 1986; s. Reg and Dorothy McVie; m. Christine Anne Perfect, Aug. 1968 (div.); m. Julie Anne Rubens, 1978; 1 child, Molly Elizabeth. Band mem. John Mayall & the Bluesbreakers, Fleetwood Mac, 1967—. Musician (bassist): (albums) (solo) John McVie's Gotta Band with Lola Thomas, 1991, (with John Mayall & the Bluesbreakers) John Mayall Plays John Mayall, 1965, Bluesbreakers with Eric Clapton, 1966, Crusade, 1967, Hard Road, 1967, So Many Roads, 1969, As It All Began: The Best of John Mayall & the Bluesbreakers, 1998, Bluesbreakers with Eric Clapton, 2002, (with John Mayall) Looking Back, 1969, Thru the Years, 1971, Banquet in Blues, 1976, John Mayall and the Bluesbreakers (London), 1988, London Blues (1964-1969), 1992, John Mayall and the Bluesbreakers (One Way), 1994, Drivin' On: The ABC Years (1975-1982), 1998, Notice to Appear/A Banquet in Blues, 2000, (with John Mayall & Friends) Along for the Ride, 2001, (with Eric Clapton) History of Eric Clapton, 1972, Crossroads, 1988, Martin Scorcese Presents the Blues: Eric Clapton, 2003, (with Fleetwood Mac) Mr. Wonderful, 1968, Blues Jam in Chicago, Vol. 1 (with Otis Spann), English Rose, 1969, Pious Bird of Good Omen, 1969, Then Play On, 1969, Blues Jam in Chicago (with Otis Span), 1970, Kiln House, 1970, Black Magic Woman, 1971, bassist: (albums) Future Games, 1971, Bare Trees, 1972, Myster to Me, 1973, Penguin, 1973, Heroes Are Hard to Find, 1974, Fleetwood Mac in Chicago, 1975, Fleetwood Mac, 1975, Vintage Years, 1975, Alabatross (Half Christine Perfect), 1977, Original Fleetwood Mac, 1977, Rumours, 1977 (Grammy award for Album of the Yr., 1977), Best of Fleetwood Mac, 1978, Man of the World, 1978, Tusk, 1979, Fleetwood Mac Live, 1980, Mirage, 1982, Rumours/Fleetwood Mac, 1984, Cerulean, 1985, Live in Boston, 1985, London Live '68, 1986, Rattlesnake Shake, 1986, Collection, 1987, Tango in the Night, 1987, Greatest Hits Live, 1988, Live Fleetwood Mac, 1988, Blues Collection, 1989, Interview Disc, 1989, Behind the Mask, 1990, Live at the BBC, 1995, Flletwood Mac/Mr. Wonderful/Pious Bird of Good Omen, 1998, Live at the Boston Tea Party, Pt. 1: 1968 to 1970, 1998; musician: (bassist also vocals) Complete Blue Horizon Sessions: 1967-1969, 1999; musician: (bassist) Shrine '69, 1999, Show-Biz Blues: 1968 to 1970, Vol. 2, 2001, Jumping at Shadows: The Blues Years, 2002, Very Best of Fleetwood Mac, 2002, Say You Will, 2003, (others) Eddie Boyd & His Blues Band, Eddie Boyd, 1967, 7936 South Rhodes, Eddie Boyd, 1968, Long Overdue, Gordon Smith, 1968, Biggest Thing Since Colossus, Otis Spann, Christine Perfect, Christine McVie, 1970, Jeremy Spencer, Jeremy Spencer, 1970, Legendary Christine Perfect, Christine McVie, 1976, Excitable Boy, Warren Zevon, 1978, Night Eyes, Danny Douma, 1979, Perfect Stranger, Robert Fleischman, 1979, Uprooted, Rob Grill, 1979, Quiet Normal Life: The Best of Warren Zevon, 1986, Rock, Rhythm & Blues, Various Artists, 1989, Over, Under, Sideways, Down, The Yardbirds, 1990, Rock of the 70's, Vol. 2, Various Artists, 1992, I'll Sleep When I'm Dead, Warren Zevon, 1996, Under Wheels of Confusion: 1970-1987, Black Sabbath, 1996, Home of the Blues, Various Artists, 1999, Rock: Train Kept a Rollin', 1999, Genius: The Best of Warren Zevon, Warren Zevon, 2002, 20th Century Masters-The Millenium Collection: The Best of Blues Guitar, 2003, Best of British Blues, Vol. 1, 2003, Best of British Blues, Vol. 2, 2003. Named to Rock and Roll Hall of Fame, 1998. Office: Warner Bros Records Inc 3300 Warner Blvd Burbank CA 91505

**MCVISK, WILLIAM KILBURN,** lawyer; b. Chgo., Oct. 8, 1953; s. Felix Kilburn and June (DePear) Visk; m. Marlaine Joyce McDonough, June 20, 1975. BA, U. Ill., 1974; JD, Northwestern U., 1977. Bar: Ill. 1977, Ind. 1999, U.S. Dist. Ct. (no. dist.) Ill. 1977, U.S. Ct. Appeals (7th cir.) 1978, U.S. Dist. Ct. (no. and so. dists.) Ind. 1999, U.S. Ct. Appeals (10th cir.) 2001. Assoc. Jerome H. Torshen, Ltd., Chgo., 1977-80, Silets & Martin, Chgo., 1980-81, Peterson & Ross, Chgo., 1981-85, ptnr., 1985-95, Johnson & Bell Ltd., Chgo., 1995—. Contbr. articles to profl. jours. Mem.: Ill. Assn. Def. Trial Lawyers (chmn. ins. coverage com. 1999—2003), Ill. Assn. Hosp. Attys. (bd. dirs. 1997—2003, pres. 2002), Am. Health Lawyers Assn., Def. Rsch. Inst. Office: Johnson & Bell 33 W Monroe St Ste 2700 Chicago IL 60603-5713 Office Phone: 312-984-0229. Business E-Mail: mcviskw@jbltd.com.

**MCVOY, MICHAEL ARTHUR,** virologist; b. Seoul, Republic of Korea, Mar. 15, 1959; s. James David and Lois Emagene McVoy; m. Julie Rae Secor, Sept. 18, 1982; 1 child, Ian Patrick. BS, Coll. of William and Mary, Williamsburg, Va., 1983; PhD, U. Commonwealth U./Med. Coll. Va., Richmond, 1993. Asst. prof. Va. Commonwealth U., Richmond, 1995—2002, assoc. prof., 2002—, prof., 2006—. Contbr. articles to profl. jours. Recipient Postdoctoral Tng. award dept. microbiology and immunology, Stanford U., 1994—95; grantee, NIH, 1998—99, Jeffress Meml. Trust, 1999—2002, Commonwealth Health Rsch. Bd., 2001—02, NIH, 2001—06, 2003—05, 2003—; Jr. Yr. Exch. scholar, U. St. Andrews, Scotland, 1981—82, Commonwealth fellow, State Coun. of Higher Edn., Va., 1990. Mem.: Am. Soc. Microbiology. Office Phone: 804-828-1739. E-mail: mmcvoy@vcu.edu.

**MCWALTERS, PETER,** school system administrator; b. Oct. 8, 1946; m. Alice Bond McWalters; children: Jennifer, Molly, Katherine. BA in History and Philosophy, Boston Coll., 1968; MS in Pub. Adminstrn., SUNY Brockport, 1979, cert. advanced study ednl. adminstrn., 1981. Permanent N.Y. State Teaching Cert social studies 7-12, Sch. Adminstrn., Sch. Dist. Adminstrn. Tchr.-trainer Eng. for speakers other langs. U.S. Peace Corps., Rep. Philippines; tchr. Eng. for speakers other langs. City Sch. Dist., Rochester, N.Y., 1970-71; tchr. social studies Interim Jr. High Sch., Rochester, 1971-78; Magnet Sch. planning specialist City Sch. Dist., Rochester, 1978-81, coord. Mgmt. 1980-81, supervising dir. planning and budgeting, 1981-85, supt. schs., 1985-91; commr. of edn. State of R.I., 1992—. Bd. dirs. Nat. Ctr. Edn. and Economy, mem. new standards project; bd. dirs. Ctr. Ednl. Devel., Rochester; mem. Edn. Commn. of States, Coun. Chief State Schs. Officers, Coun. Great Cities Schs., 21st Century Edn. Commn. Bd. dirs. Urban League, Rochester; mem. United Way Task Force, Rochester; gov. bd., exec. com. Rochester New Futures Initiative, Inc.; mem. Goals for Greater Rochester, Inc. Mem. Am. Assn. Sch. Adminstrs., Assn. Supervision and Curriculum Devel., Phi Delta Kappa. Office: Elem and Sec Office Shepard Bldg 255 Westminster St Providence RI 02903-3414

**MCWATERS, JEFFREY L.,** healthcare executive; b. Paducah, Ky. m. Cynthia Lamb McWaters; 2 children. B in Acctg., U. Ky., 1978. With Ernst and Young, Nashville, 1978—79. Hosp. Affiliates, 1979—83; founder, pres., CEO Options Mental Health (now Value Options), 1990—94; founder, chmn., CEO Amerigroup Corp., Virginia Beach, Va., 1994—. Bd. dirs. Am. Assn. Health Plans, Man in the Mirror; mem. adv. bd. Monarch Bank, Envest

Entrepreneurial Investments. Chmn. Amerigroup Found., 2000—. Named Entrepreneur of Yr., Ernst and Young, 1999; named to Hall of Fame, Gatton Coll. Bus. and Econs., U. Ky., 2003. Office: Amerigroup Corp 4425 Corporation Ln Virginia Beach VA 23462

**MCWETHY, JOHN FLEETWOOD,** journalist; b. Aurora, Ill., Feb. 28, 1947; s. John Adams and Mary Helen (Bell) McW.; m. Laurie Duncan, June 25, 1971; children: Adam Duncan, James Ian. BA, DePauw U., 1969; MS, Columbia U., 1970; Doctorate in Journalism (hon.), DePauw U., 2002. Def. writer Congl. Quar., Washington, 1970-72; sci. editor U.S. News & World Report, Washington, 1972-77, chief White House corr., 1977-79; chief Pentagon corr. ABC News, Washington, 1979-84; chief corr. ABC News Nat. Security and Sr. State Dept., Washington, 1984—2003; spl. corr. ABC News, 2003—. Sr. media mentor US Army Command Staff Coll., Ft. Leavenworth, Kans., 2005—; moderator program Radio TV Director's Assn. Dept. Homeland Security, 2004—. Contbg. author: Power of the Pentagon, 1972. Recipient DuPont award Columbia U. Sch. Journalism, 1984, 2002; 5 Emmy awards, 1984, 91, 92, 99, 2002, Overseas Press Club award for Inside the Other Side, 1987, Peabody award for coverage of Sept. 11, 2001. Home: 5028 30th St N Arlington VA 22207-2717

**MCWETHY, PATRICIA JOAN,** educational association administrator; b. Chgo., Feb. 27, 1946; d. Frank E. and Emma (Kuehne) McW.; m. H. Frank Eden; children: Kristin Beth, Justin Nicholas. BA, Northwestern U., 1968; MA, U. Minn., 1970; MBA, George Washington U., 1981. Geog. analyst CIA, McLean, Va., 1970-71; rsch. asst. NSF, Washington, 1972-74, spl. asst. to dir., 1975, assoc. program dir. human geography and regional sci. program, 1976-79; exec. dir. Assn. Am. Geographers, Washington, 1979-84, Nat. Assn. Biology Tchrs., Reston, Va., 1984-95, Nat. Sci. Edn. Leadership Assn., Arlington, Va., 1995-97; edn. dir. Nat. Alliance for Mentally Ill, Arlington, 1998-99. Prin. investigator grant on biotech. equipment ednl. resource partnership NSF, 1989-93, NSF funded internat. symposium on Basic Biol. Concepts: What Should the World's Children Know?, 1992-94; co-prin. investigator NSF grant, 1995-97; mem. chmn.'s adv. com. Nat. Com. Sci. Stds. and Assessment, 1992-95; mem. Commn. for Biology Edn. internat. Union Biol. Sci., 1988-97; mem. exec. com. Alliance for Environ. Edn., 1987-90, chmn. program com., 1990; condr. seminars in field; lectr. in field. Author monograph and papers in field; editor handbook. NSF grantee, 1989-93, 95-97; NSF fellow, 1968-69; recipient Outstanding Performance award, NSF, 1973. Mem. Phi Beta Kappa.

**MCWHINNEY, DEBORAH,** finance company executive; BA, U. Mont.; grad., Pacific Coast Banking Sch. With consumer electronic banking divsn. Bank Am. Corp. 17 yrs.; exec. v.p. bus. planning and strategy Visa Internat., 1995—99; group pres. Engage Media Svc., 1999—2001; pres., exec. com. mem. Schwab Instl., Schwab & Co., Inc., 2001—. Exec. advisor to bd. and exec. team Hitachi Data Sys. and Hitachi Ltd., 2003; chair bd. trustees U. Mont. Found.; former bd. chair Electronic Funds Tranfer Assn.; bd. dirs. Novadigm, Inc., PLUS Sys., Touch Am. Holdings, Inc.; past fin. chair Women's Mus.; founding investor, former dir. First Bank Idaho. Named one of 100 Most Influential Women in Bay Area Bus., San Francisco Bus. Times, 2002, 2003, 2004, 25 Most Influential People in Planning Profession, Investment Advisor List, 2004; recipient Movers & Shakers award Fin. Planning, 2004. Achievements include apptd. by Pres. Bush to Securities Investor Protection Corp. (SIPC), 2002.

**MCWHINNEY, EDWARD WATSON,** Canadian government legislator; b. Sydney, Australia, May 19, 1924; s. Walter and Evelyn Annie (Watson) McW.; m. Emily Ingalore Sabatzky, June 27, 1951. LLB, U. Sydney, 1949; LLM, Yale U., 1951, D Juridical Sci., 1953; diploma, Acad. de Droit Internat., The Hague, 1950; LLD, U. Thessaloniki, Greece, 1998. Bar: called to Australian bar 1949, apptd. Queen's counsel, Can 1967. Crown prosecutor, Sydney, 1949-50; lectr., then asst. prof. Law Sch. and Grad. Sch., Yale U., 1951-55; prof. law, mem. Centre Russian Studies, U. Toronto, Ont., Canada, 1955-66; prof. law, dir. Inst. Air and Space Law, McGill U., Montreal, Que., Canada, 1966-71; prof. law, dir. internat. and comparative legal studies U. Ind., Indpls., 1971-74; disting. prof. Simon Fraser U., Burnaby, B.C., 1974-93; mem. Permanent Ct. Arbitration, The Hague, 1985-91; Paul Martin prof. U. Windsor, Canada, 1986; prof. emeritus, 1992; pres., dir. Found. Internat. and Comparative and Fed. Law, 1996—; M.P. Ho. of Commons, Ottawa, Ont., Canada, 1993-2000; co-chmn. joint standing com. Senate and Ho. of Commons, Ottawa, Ont., Canada, 1993-95, parliamentary sec. (fisheries and oceans), 1996-97, parliamentary sec. (fgn. affairs), 1997-2000; fed. govt. rep. nat. unity commn. Govt. of B.C., 1997-98. Vis. prof. Ecole Libre des Hautes Etudes, 1952, Heidelberg and Max-Planck-Inst., 1960-61, 90, NYU, 1954, Faculté Internat. de Droit Comparé, Luxembourg, 1959-60, U. San Antonio, 1963, U. Laval, Que., 1967, U. Paris, 1968, U. Madrid, 1968, U. Aix-Marseille, 1969, U. Nat. Autónoma de México, 1965, Inst. U. Luxembourg, 1972, 74, 76, Acad. Internat. Law, The Hague, 1973, 90, 2002, Aristotelian U., Thessaloniki, Greece, 1974, 78, 85, 96, 2003, U. Nice, 1976-77, Jagellonian U., Cracow, Poland, 1976, U. Paris I (Sorbonne), 1982, 85, Coll. de France, Paris, 1983, Meiji U., Tokyo, 1987, Inst. Internat. Relations, Bejing, 1987, 92, Sch. Internat. Rels., Tehran, 2003; legal cons. UN, 1953-54; cons. Japanese Commn. Constn., mem. prime minister Ont. Adv. Com. Confedn., 1964-71; cons. U.S. Naval War Coll., 1961-68; legal cons. Ministère de la Justice, Que., 1969-70; 74-75; constl. adviser to prime minister of Que., 1974-75; royal commr. Commn. Lang. Rights. Que., 1968-72; cons. U.S. Senate select com. presdl. campaign activities, 1973; spl. commr. inquiry Legislature B.C., 1974-75; chief adv. Fed. Govt.'s Task Force on Nat. Unity, 1978; commr. of enquiry, City of Vancouver, 1979; constl. adv. Fedn. Can. Municipalities, 1978-82; spl. advisor Can. del. UN Gen. Assembly, ann. sessions, 1981-83, 96; constl. adviser Indian Nations (Treaties 6-9), Can., 1980-82; mem. Assoc. de l'Inst. de Droit Internat., 1967, membre titulaire, 1975, pres. 1999-2001; mem. Assoc. de l'Acad. Internat. de Droit Comparé, Paris, 1986, mem. titulaire, 2002-- Author: Judical Review, 4th edit, 1969, Canadian Jurisprudence, 1958, Föderalismus und Bundesverfassungsrecht, 1961, Constitutionalism in Germany, 1962, Comparative Federalism, 2d edit, 1965, Peaceful Coexistence and Soviet-Western International Law, 1964, Law Foreign Policy and the East-West Détente, 1964, Federal Constitution- Making for a Multi-National World, 1966, International Law and World Revolution, 1967, Conflit idéologique et ordre public mondial, 1970, (with M.A. Bradley) The Freedom of the Air, 1968, New Frontiers in Space Law, 1969, The International Law of Communications, 1970, Aerial Piracy and International Law, 1971, (with Pierre Pescatore) Federalism and Supreme Courts and the Integration of Legal Systems, 1973, Parliament and Parliamentary Power Today, 1976, The Executive and Parliamentary Power Today, 1977, (with J-D Gendron and others) La situation de la langue française au Québec (3 vols.), 1973, The Illegal Diversion of Aircraft and International Law, 1974, Parliamentary Privilege and the Broadcasting of Parliamentary Debates, 1976, The International Law of Detente, 1978, The World Court and the Contemporary International Law-making Process, 1979, Quebec and the Constitution, 1979, Municipal Government in a New Canadian Federal System, 1980, Conflict and Compromise: International Law and World Order in a Revolutionary Age, 1981, Constitution-Making: Principles, Process, Practice, 1981, Canada and the Constitution, 1982, United Nations Law Making, 1984, Supreme Courts and Judicial Law-Making, 1986, Les Nations-Unies et la Formation du Droit, 1986, Aerial Piracy and International Terorism, 1987, The International Court of Justice and the Western Tradition of International Law, 1987, (with Nagendra Singh) Nuclear Weapons and Contemporary International Law, 1988, Judicial Settlement of International Disputes, 1990, (with G.I. Tunkin and V.S. Vereshchetin) From Coexistence to Cooperation: International Law and Organisation in the Post-Cold War Era, 1991, (with J. Zaslove and W. Wolf) Federalism-in-the-Making, Contemporary Canadian and German Constitutionalism, National and Trans-national, 1992, Judge Shigeru Oda and the Progressive Development of International Law, 1992, Judge Manfred Lachs and Judicial Law-Making, 1994, The United Nations and a New World Order for a New Millennium, 2000, (with N. Ando and R. Wolfrum) Liber Amicorum Judge Shigeru Oda, 2002, Self-Determination of Peoples and Plural-Ethnic States. Secession and State Succession and the Alternative,

Federal Option, 2003, Chretien and Canadian Federalism, Politics and the Constitution, 1993-2003, 2003, The September 11 Terrorist Attacks and Invasion of Iraq in Contemporary International Law, 2004, The Governor General and the Prime Ministers, 2005, (with Mariko Kawano) Judge Shigeru Oda and the path to judicial wisdom, 2006; bd. editors Australian Quar., 1949-50, Can. Yearbook of Internat. Law, 1963—, Jour. Media Law and Practice, 1980-85, Annuaire International de Justice Constitutionnelle, 1987—; editl. adv. com. Ency. Brit., 1985—; mem. bd. adv. Chinese Jour. Internat. Law, 2002—; contbr. to Ency. Brit. Served as officer Australian Air Force, 1943-45. Recipient Queen's Golden Jubilee medal, 2002; Carnegie Endowment fellow, 1951; Fulbright fellow, 1950-51; Sterling fellow Yale, 1950-51; Rockefeller fellow, 1960-61, 66-68; Can. Coun. fellow, 1960-61; fellow Am. Soc. Internat. Law, 1962-63. Mem. Australian Inst. Polit. Sci. (dir.), Internat. Law Assn. (pres. Toronto br. 1964-66, pres. Montreal br. 1970-71, chmn. exec. com. Canadian br. 1972-75), Canadian Bar Assn. (council Ont. 1956-58), Yale Law Sch. Assn. (pres. Can. 1964-69), Canadian Civil Liberties Assn. (v.p. 1965-67), Am. Soc. Internat. Law (coun. 1965-68, patron 2002—), Am. Fgn. Law Assn., Inst. interamericano de Estudios Juridicos Internacionales (dir. 1965—), Inst. Grand-Ducal de Luxembourg, Internat. Commn. Jurists (mem. coun. Can. br. 1988—), German Soc. for Völkerrecht (hon.), Knights of Mark Twain (U.S., hon., Aristotle Medal 1997, Queen's Golden Jubilee medal 2002). Home: 1949 Beach Ave Ste 402 Vancouver BC Canada V6G 1Z2

**MCWHINNEY, MADELINE H. (MRS. JOHN DENNY DALE),** economist, director; b. Denver, Mar. 11, 1922; d. Leroy and Alice (Houston) McW.; m. John D. Dale, June 23, 1961; 1 child, Thomas Denny. BA, Smith Coll., 1943; MBA, NYU, 1947. Economist Fed. Res. Bank, NYC, 1943-73, chief fin. trade statis. divsn., 1955-59, mgr. market stats. dept., 1960-65, asst. v.p., 1965-73; pres. First Women's Bank, NYC, 1974-76, Dale, Elliott & Co., Inc., Red Bank, NJ, 1977-97. Trustee Retirement System Fed. Res. Bank, 1955-58; vis. lectr. NYU Grad. Sch. Bus., 1976-77; mem. NJ Casino Control Commn., 1980-82, Women's Econ. Round Table, 1978-89, chmn. 1987-88; bd. govs. Am. Stock Exch., 1977-81; trustee Monmouth Mus., 1995—, Vis. Nurse Assn. Ctrl. Jersey, 1995-2004, Planned Parenthood Ctrl. Jersey, 1995-2003, Carnegie Corp. NY, 1974-82, Central Savs. Bank NY, 1980-82, Monmouth Conservatory Music, 2002-; trustee Charles F. Kettering Found., 1975-93, chmn. 1987-91; trustee Inst. Internat. Edn., 1975-, Investor Responsibility Rsch. Ctr., Inc., 1974-81; asst. dir. Whitney Mus. Am. Art, 1983-86; dir. Atlantic Energy Co., 1983-93; trustee Mgrs. Funds, 1983-2004; mem. adv. com. profl. ethics NJ Supreme Ct., 1983-98. Recipient Smith Coll. medal, 1971, Alumni Achievement award NYU Grad. Sch. Bus. Adminstrn. Alumni Assn., 1971, NYU Crystal award, 1982. Mem. Am. Fin. Assn. (past dir.), Money Marketeers (v.p. 1960, pres. 1961-62), Alumni Assn. Grad. Sch. Bus. Adminstrn. NYU (dir. 1951-63, pres. 1957-59), Soc. Meml. Ctr., NJ Com Humanities, Phi Beta Kappa Fellows (v.p. 1979-87). Office: PO Box 458 Red Bank NJ 07701-0458 Home: 192 Heritage Court Little Silver NJ 07739 Personal E-mail: mdale38569@comcast.net.

**MCWHIRTER, BRUCE J.,** retired lawyer; b. Chgo., Sept. 11, 1931; s. Sydney and Martha McWhirter; m. Judith Hallett, Apr. 14, 1960; children: Cameron, Andrew. BS, Northwestern U., 1952; LLB, Harvard U., 1955. Bar: DC 1955, Ill 1955, US Ct Appeals (7th cir) 1963, US Supreme Ct. Assoc. Lord, Bissell & Brook, Chgo., 1958-62; from assoc. to sr. ptnr. Ross & Hardies, Chgo., 1962-95, of counsel, 1996—2003. Editor: Donnelley SEC Handbook, 1972—87; contbr. articles to profl jours. With U.S. Army, 1955—57. Mem.: ABA, Harvard Law Soc Ill., Chgo. Bar Assn., Harvard Club (N.Y.C.), Lawyers Club Chgo., Phi Beta Kappa. Democrat. Home: 111 Sheridan Rd Winnetka IL 60093-4223 Personal E-mail: jbmcw@aol.com.

**MCWHIRTER, GLENNA SUZANNE (NICKIE MCWHIRTER),** retired columnist; b. Peoria, Ill., June 28, 1929; d. Alfred Leon and Garnet Lorene (Short) Sotier; m. Edward Ford McWhirter (div.); children: Suzanne McWhirter Orlicki, Charles Edward, James Richard. BS in English Lang. and Lit., U. Mich., postgrad., 1960-63. Editl. asst. McGraw-Hill Pub. Co., Detroit, 1951-54; staff writer Detroit Free Press, Inc., Detroit, 1963-70, asst. city editor, 1971-77, columnist, 1977-88, Detroit News Inc., Detroit, 1988-97; advt. copy writer Campbell-Ewald Co., Detroit, 1967-68; ret., 1997. Author: Pea Soup, 1984 Winner 1st Place Commentary award UPI, Mich., 1979; 1st Place Columns AP, Mich., 1978, 81; 1st Place Columns Detroit Press Club Found., Mich., 1978; Disting. Service award State of Mich., 1985 Mem. Women in Comm. (Headliner award 1978), Alpha Gamma Delta. Avocations: flower gardening, interior design. Home: 495 Lake Shore Ln Grosse Pointe Woods MI 48236

**MCWHORTER, DIANE,** writer; b. Tupelo, Miss., Nov. 1, 1952; BA in Comparative Lit., Wellesley Coll. Writer, NYC. Author: The NY Times, USA Today (Op-Ed page), The Nation, Slate; author: Carry Me Home: Birmingham, Alabama,The Climactic Battle of the Civil Rights Revolution, 2001 (Pulitzer prize for gen. nonfiction, 2002, named NY Times Notable Book, winner, Southern Book Critics Circle award, 2001, J. Anthony Lukas Book prize, 2002, English Speaking Union Ambassador award, 2002, Sidney Hillman Found. award, 2002), A Dream of Freedom: The Civil Rights Movement from 1954 to 1968, 2004 (NY Times Notable Children's Book, 2004, USA Today Best Children's History, 2004, on ALA Best New Book for Young Adults list, 2004); contbg. author: These United States, 2003, Stories from the Blue Moon Cafe, 2005. Recipient Clarence Cason award, 2003. Personal E-mail: dmcwhorter@earthlink.net.

**MCWHORTER, HOBART AMORY, JR.,** lawyer; b. Birmingham, Ala., Dec. 24, 1931; s. Hobart Amory and Marjorie (Westgate) McW.; remarried Feb. 1, 1997; children: Margaret G., Marjorie W. BA, Yale U., 1953; LLB, U. Va., 1958. Bar: Ala. 1958. Ptnr. Bradley Arant Rose & White, Birmingham, 1958—. 1st lt. U.S. Army, 1953-55. Fellow Am. Coll. Trial Lawyers; mem. Internat. Assn. Ins. Counsel, Nat. Assn. r,R, Counsel Republican, Presbyterian Office: Bradley Arant Rose & White One Federal Pl 1819 Fifth Ave N Birmingham AL 35203-2104 Office Phone: 205-521-8241. Business E-Mail: hmcwhorter@bradleyarant.com.

**MCWHORTER, SHARON LOUISE,** engineering executive, inventor, consultant; b. Feb. 22, 1951; d. Leroy Byron Harris Jr. and Josiebell (Richards) Harris Aaron; m. Abner McWhorter II, Mar. 15, 1969 (div. Aug. 1974); 1 child, Abner III. BA, Wayne State U., 1988; cert., SBA, Detroit, 1978; cert. in sound engring., Detroit Rec. Inst., Warren, Mich., 1982. Directory asst. Mich. Bell Telephone Co., Detroit, 1969; quality control clk. Chevrolet Gear & Axle, Detroit, 1971-74; circulation clk. Wayne County C.C., Detroit, 1977-85, mem. libr. standing com. and open house com., 1983-84; pres. Galactic Concepts & Designs, Detroit, 1977-88, cons., 1983—. Gen. ptnr., mgr. S.M.J. Corridor Devel., Detroit, 1982—, hist. rschr. 1982; del. Small Bus. Conf., 1981; ad hoc mem. Minority Tech. Coun., 1981-82; elected alt. Mich. del. White House Conf. on Small Bus., Washington, 1985-86; lectr., cons. Author, editor: Creative Dilemma newsletter, 1985—; co-patentee cup holding apparatus. Vol. counselor East House/March of Dimes, Detroit, 1977; active Concerned Citizens Cass Corridor, Detroit, 1982-87, Cass Corridor Citizen's Patrol, Detroit, 1983-84, Empowerment Zone Devel. Corp., Detroit, 1996—, bd. dirs., corp. chair, 1997—; pres. Wayne County chpt. MADD, Mich., 1987-88; apptd. citizen rev. com. 1988—; mem. adv. bd. Neighborhood Family Initiative, Southeastern Cmty. Found.; pres. Am. Res. Tng. Sys., Inc., 1990—. Recipient Hist. Landmark award Dept. Interior, 1983, cert. appreciation Tri-County Substance Abuse Awareness Com., 1984. Mem. Inventors Coun. Mich. (bd. dirs. 1985-88), Black Women in Bus. (sec. 1984-85), Greater Detroit C. of C., South Cass Bus. Assn. (v.p. 1987-88, pres. 1988-89), Detroit Econ. Club. Democrat. Methodist. Avocations: photography, filmmaking. Office: SMJ Corridor Devel Co 453 Myrtle St Ste 102 Detroit MI 48201-2311

**MCWHORTER, STANLEY BRUCE,** retired language educator; b. Osco, Ky., June 17, 1930; s. Stanley Vergil and Myrtie Alice (Stearns) M. BA, Transylvania Univ., Lexington, 1954; MA, U. Ky., 1961, PhD, 1963. Life Cert. Edn. Ky., 1950. Instr. English Southwestern Coll., Winfield, Kans.,

1959-60, Morehead State Univ., Ky., 1960-61, Ea. Ky. State Univ., Richmond, 1961-63; asst. prof. English W. Va. Wesleyan Coll., Buckhannon, 1963-67; assoc. prof. English Univ. S. C., Florence, 1967-70; prof. English Xavier Univ., Cincinnati, 1972-75, Univ. Dayton, Ohio, 1975-95; ret., 1995—. Ednl. coord. Natl. Folk Festival Assoc. Am., Wash. D.C., 1963-67. Author: Annotated Bibliography of William Wordsworth's Writings and Ana from 1935-1941, 1961, The Annual Anthology of College English and Literature, 1965, The Idea of Religious Struggle in Four Seventeenth Century English Poets, 1967, The Use of the Folk Ballad in the English Class, 1971, Superstitions of Appalachia, 1975. Dir. civic activities Lions Clubs, Jamestown, Ky., 1953-55. Grantee continued study in chosen field, 1965; recipient Southwestern grant for Tchg. Excellence, 1959-60, Cmty. Leadership award, Lions Club Am., 1961-63, Wesleyan plaque Internat. Rels., 1963-67 Wesleyan grant for study Brit. Am. Balladry, 1963-67. Life mem. MLA Am. (editl. supervisor, 1963-67, scholarship advanced studies, 1963), Nat. Coun. Tchrs. English, Nat. Edn. Assn. Am., Coll. Assn. English Tchrs., Am. Assn. Univ. Profs. D-Conservative. United Methodist. Avocations: running, swimming, travel. Office: Univ Dayton 300 Coll Park Ave Dayton OH 45469 Home: P O Box 3455 Dayton OH 45401 Personal E-mail: mcwhrca@aol.com.

**MCWHORTER, SUSAN CAROL,** English language educator; b. Elkhart, Ind., Apr. 24, 1947; d. Benjamin E. and Anna M. (Pontious) Kirts; m. John R. McWhorter, June 20, 1970 (div. 1984); 1 child, Carole. BA in Speech, Drama and English, Butler U., 1969; MS in English Edn., Troy State U., 1974; EdS in English Edn., Fla. State U., 1985. Tchr. speech and drama Elkhart (Ind.) H.S., 1969-70; tchr. English Ben Davis H.S., Indpls., 1970-72; GED instr. Ala. Tech. Inst., Ft. Rucker, 1972-74; adminstr., coord. Vincennes U., Ft. Benjamin Harrison, Ind., 1974-75; tchr. English Jinks Jr. High, Panama City, Fla., 1975-76; adj. instr. English Gulf Coast C.C., Panama City, 1977—; tchr. Bay High School, Panama City, 1982-98; resource tchr. Bay Dist. Schs. Panama City, 1998—. Mem. Bay Arts Alliance, Panama City, 1985—, Friends of the Libr., Panama City, 1980-90; mem., mentor Orch. of St. Andrew Bay, 1997—. Recipient Golden Apple award News Channel 13, 1989. Mem. Nat. Coun. Tchrs. English, Fla. Coun. Tchrs. of English (cons. 1983—), Bay Lang. Arts Coun. (pres. 1982—), Bay County Reading Coun., Assn. Bay City Educators, Bay Edn. Found. Avocations: playing flute, ballet dancing, swimming. Home: 1880 W 24th Ct Panama City FL 32405-2228 Office: Bay Dist Schs 1311 Balboa Ave Panama City FL 32401-2080 Fax: (850) 873-7128.

**MCWILLIAM, JOANNE ELIZABETH,** retired theology studies educator; b. Toronto, Ont., Can., Dec. 10, 1928; d. Cecil Edward and Edna Viola (Archer) McW.; children, Leslie Mary Giroday, Elizabeth Dewart, Sean Dewart, Colin Dewart; m. C. Peter Slater, June 6, 1987. BA, U. Toronto, 1951, MA, 1953, U. St. Michael's, Toronto, 1966, PhD, 1968; DD honoris causa, Queen's U., Kingston, Ont., 2003. Asst. prof. religious studies U. Toronto, 1968-74, assoc. prof., 1974-87, prof., 1987, chairperson dept. religious studies, 1990-92, 93-94; Mary Crooke Hoffman prof. of Dogmatic Theology Gen. Theol. Sem., N.Y.C. 1994-99; ret., 1999. Author: The Theology of Grace of Theodore of Mopsuestia, 1971, Death and Resurrection in the Fathers, 1986; editor: Augustine: Rhetor to Theologian, 1991, Toronto Jour. Theology. Mem. Can. Soc. for Patristic Studies (pres. 1987-90), Conf. Anglican Theologians (pres. 1990-91), Can. Soc. for the Study of Religion, Can. Theol. Soc., Am. Theol. Soc., Am. Acad. Religion. Anglican. Home: 59 Duggan Ave Toronto ON Canada M4V 1Y1 E-mail: joanne.mcwilliam@utoronto.ca.

**MCWILLIAMS, C. PAUL, JR.,** engineering executive; b. Louisville, June 4, 1931; s. Cleo Paul and Audrey Dora (Hale) McW.; m. Barbara Ann Sparks, Feb. 22, 1950 (div. 1962); children: Bruce Kevin, Craig Tinsley; m. Barbara Ann Heintz, Apr. 25, 1980; 1 stepchild, Kimberly Jean Moorhouse Beaumont. B Chem. Engrng., U. Louisville, 1954, M Engrng., 1972. Lic. profl. engr., N.Y., N.C., Pa. Sr. process devel. engr. Olin Mathieson Chem. Corp., Brandenburg, Ky., 1958-66, Rochester, NY, 1958-66; sr. chem. engr. GTE Sylvania, Seneca Falls, NY, 1966-74, Eastman Kodak Co., Rochester, 1974-81; prin., treas. Flint & Sherburne Assocs., P.C., Rochester, 1981-89; project engr. Roy F. Weston, Inc., Rochester, 1989-92; engring. mgr. ECCO, Inc. (Environ. Cons. Co., Inc.), Buffalo, 1992-94; pres. ECCO Engring., Buffalo, 1993-94; staff engr. Environ. Products & Svcs., Inc., Rochester, NY, 1994-96; pvt. cons. engr. Webster, NY, 1996—. Cons. water tech. Water Tech. Corp., Tonawanda, N.Y., 1973-76; product rsch. panel Chem. Engring. Mag., 1982-83. Author: Waste Disposal Manual, 1976. Life mem. Rep. Presdl. Task Force, Webster, N.Y., 1986—; mem. Rep. Nat. Com., Webster, 1991-92. 1st lt. USAF, 1954-58, ret. lt. col. USAF, 1982. Decorated Meritorious Svc. medal. Mem. NSPE, AIChE, Soc. Am. Mil. Engrs., Res. Officers Assn. (life), Monroe Profl. Engrs. Soc. (environ. com. 1972-75, chmn. 1973-75, bd. dirs. 1982-84, program chmn. 1984), Cons. Engrs. Coun. N.Y. State (program chmn. Rochester chpt. 1986-87, sec. 1987-88, treas. 1989). Episcopalian. Achievements include rsch. in replacing boiler feedwater regulators, related instrumentation and control systems and blowdown; design of dry fabric dust collectors to remove fly ash from coal-fired boilers' flue gas. Home: 1132 Woodbridge Ln Webster NY 14580-8709 Office: C Paul McWilliams PE Cons Engr 1132 Woodbridge Ln Webster NY 14580-8709 Office Phone: 585-872-0505. Business E-Mail: paulmcw@frontiernet.net.

**MCWILLIAMS, CAREY SCOTT,** small business owner, writer; b. Fargo, ND, July 5, 1973; s. Dallas Ora and Jan Marie McWilliams. B of U. Studies, N.D. State U., 1991—97, MA in Mass Commn., 1998—2001. Campus planner Coll. of the Atlantic, Bar Harbor, Maine, 1994; owner C.O.O.P. d' Paw Inc., Fargo, ND, 2002—. Mem. cadet adv. coun. CAP, Fargo, 1987—90. Recipient Comdr.''s Award, CAP, 1988, Lucretia Kuntz Meml. Award, 1989, Billy Mitchell Award, 1989, Braille Flag Award, DAR, 1990. Mem.: NRA, Nat. Honor Soc. (Golden Key Honor Soc, 1996—) Avocations: gun collecting, target shooting, scuba diving, skydiving. Home: 4566 Domingo Rd Fargo ND 58103 Office: COOP d Paw Inc 805 S 15 St Fargo ND 58103 Office Phone: 701-541-5704. Personal E-mail: csmcwilliams73@aol.com. E-mail: books4pets@coopdpaw.com.

**MCWILLIAMS, EDWIN JOSEPH,** banker; b. Spokane, Washington, Aug. 11, 1919; s. Frank S. and Alice (Conlan) McW.; m. Betty J. Galbreath, Aug. 15, 1944; children: Lawrence, Barbara Anne, Marijoan, Peter. Student, U. Notre Dame, Ind., 1937-38, Marquette U., Milw., 1938-40; BS in Bus. Adminstrn, Gonzaga U., Spokane, Wash., 1943. With Fidelity Mutual Savings Bank, Spokane, 1940-82, exec. v.p., 1955-58, pres., 1958-82, Fidelity Service Corp., 1983-87. Mem. adv. council Wash. State Dept. Commerce and Econ. Devel., 1977-80; U.S. del. Internat. Savs. Bank Inst., 1975, 76, 79; vice chair, dir. NW Edn. Loan Assn Pres. United Crusade Spokane County, 1966; pres. mem. exec. bd. Inland Empire coun., region 11 exec. com. Boy Scouts Am.; pres. Spokane Unltd.; mem. adv. coun. Sch. Bus., Gonzaga U.; bd. dirs., mem. exec. com. Expo '74 World's Fair, 1973-74; mem. bd. dirs. Sacred Heart Med. Ctr., 1961-70, Fairmont Meml. Assn.; chmn. bd. mem. Spokane Housing Assn., 1972-87; chmn. Spokane C. of C., 1973-75; bd. regents Wash. State U., 1979-92. Lt. USNR, 1943—45. Mem. Nat. Assn. Mut. Savs. Banks (chmn. 1976-77), Mut. Savs. Banks Assn. State of Wash. (pres. 1980), Am. Savs. and Loan Inst. (past gov. dist. XI), Spokane C. of C. (pres. 1974-75, chmn., 1975-77), Clubs: Rotary of Spokane, K.C. Roman Catholic. Home: 2408 E Deerwood Ct Spokane WA 99223

**MCWILLIAMS, JOHN LAWRENCE, III,** lawyer; b. Phila., Dec. 21, 1943; s. John Lawrence Jr. and Elizabeth Dolores (Chevalier) McW.; m. Paula Ann Root, July 19, 1969 (dec.); children: John Lawrence, IV, Robert Root, Anne Elizabeth, David Stanford, Peter Farrell; m. Kathleen Nolan Pradella, Apr./ 3, 1993. BS, St. Joseph's U., 1965; JD, Seton Hall U., 1969. Bar: N.J. 1969, N.Y. 1975, U.S. Supreme Ct. 1976. Fla. 1977. Trial atty., regional office SEC, N.Y.C., 1969-72; assoc. Mudge Rose Guthrie & Alexanderr, N.Y.C., 1972-77; mem. Freeman, Richardson, Watson & Kelly, P.A., Jacksonville, Fla., 1977-89, chmn., pres., 1984-89; ptnr. Squire, Sanders & Dempsey, Jacksonville, 1989-98, Livermore, Freeman & McWilliams, P.A., Jacksonville, 1998—. Trustee Mcpl. Svc. Dist. Ponte Vedra Beach, 1981-85, chmn. bd. trustees, 1984-85; treas. Ponte Vedra Cmty. Assn., 1980-82; mem. Leadership Jacksonville, 1981, steering com., 1982; dir. Jacksonville Country Day Sch., 1985-87; pres. Jacksonville Beaches Ponte Vedra Unit Am. Cancer Soc., 1988-90; bd. dirs. Sawgrass Property Owners Assn., Inc., 2000-02. Fellow Am. Coll. Bond Counsel; mem. Nat. Assn. Bond Lawyers, The Fla. Bar, Jacksonville C. C., Jacksonville Cmty. Coun. Inc., Univ. Club, Ponte Vedra Club, Sawgrass Club, River Club. Republican. Roman Catholic. Home: 3040 Timberlake Pt Ponte Vedra Beach FL 32082-3726 Office: Livermore Freeman & McWilliams PA 1301 Riverplace Blvd Ste 1825 Jacksonville FL 32207-9029 Office Phone: 904-399-0500. Personal E-mail: jmcwill@comcast.net. Business E-mail: jmcwill@lkfm.com.

**MCWILLIAMS, JOHN MICHAEL,** lawyer; b. Annapolis, Md., Aug. 17, 1939; s. William J. and Helen (Disharon) McW.; m. Frances Edelen McCabe, May 30, 1970; children: M. Edelen, J. Michael Jr., James McC. BS, Georgetown U., 1964; LL.B., U. Md., 1967; LLD (hon.), U. Balt., 1993. Bar: Md. 1967, U.S. Supreme Ct. 1970, U.S. Ct. Internat. Trade 1991, U.S. Ct. Mil. Appeals 1992; cert. mediator NASD. Law clk. Chief Judge Roszel C. Thomsen, U.S. Dist. Ct. Md., 1967-68; assoc. Piper and Marbury, Balt., 1968-69; asst. atty. gen. Md., 1969-76; gen. counsel Md. Dept. Transp., 1971-76; sr. ptnr. Tydings and Rosenberg, Balt., 1977-97; pres. McWilliams Dispute Resolution, Balt., 1997—. Permanent mem. 4th Jud. Conf.; mem. panel of disting. neutrals CPR Inst. for Dispute Resolution, 1994—2001; mem. Md. Alt. Dispute Resolution Commn., 1994—2002. Asst. editor Law Rev., U. Md., 1967; mem. nat. bd. advisors Ohio State Jour. Dispute Resolution. Chmn. Md. adv. coun. to Nat. Legal Svcs. Corp., 1975-78; mem. Gov.'s Commn. to Revise Annotated Code of Md., 1973-78; transition dir. Md. Gov.-Elect Harry Hughes, 1978-79; mem. Md. Indsl. Devel. Financing Authority, 1980; mem. Greater Balt. Commn., 1979-94; mem. exec. com. Econ. Devel. Coun. Greater Balt., 1979-83; vice chmn. bd. Washington/Balt. Regional Assn., 1980-83; mem. Md. Econ. and Cmty. Devel. Adv. Commn., 1983-87; chmn. bd. Md. Econ. Devel. Corp., 1984-89. Served to 1st lt. U.S. Army, 1958-60. Fellow Am. Bar Found. (bd. dirs. 1986-88, 91-93), Internat. Acad. Mediators (pres. 2006—), Coll. Comml. Arbitrators (dir. 2004-05), Md. Bar Found. (dir. 1980-82); mem. ABA (pres. 1992-93, mem. ho. of dels. 1976—, chmn. 1986-88, chmn. Md. del. 1976-86, bd. editors jour. 1986-88, 91-93) Md. Bar Assn. (pres. 1981-82), Nat. Conf. Bar Pres. (exec. coun. 1982-85), Bar Assn. Balt. City, Am. Law Inst., Am. Judicature Soc. (dir. 1974-81, exec. com. 1975-77), Am. Acad. Judicature Edn. (dir. 1977), Md. Law Rev. (trustee 1980-83), Md. Inst. Continuing Edn. Lawyers (trustee 1980-83), Inst. Internat. Bus. Law and Practice (corr.), Md. Club, Rule Day Club. Democrat. Roman Catholic. Home: 3 Merryman Ct Baltimore MD 21210-2815 Office: 1106 N Charles St Ste 300 Baltimore MD 21201 Office Phone: 410-244-8124.

**MCWILLIAMS, MARGARET ANN,** home economist, educator, writer; b. Osage, Iowa, May 26, 1929; d. Alvin Randall and Mildred Irene Edgar; children: Roger, Kathleen. BS, Iowa State U., 1951, MS, 1953; PhD, Oreg. State U., 1968. Registered dietitian. Asst. prof. home econs. Calif. State U., L.A., 1961-66, assoc. prof., 1966-68, prof., 1968-92, prof. emeritus, 1992—, chmn. dept., 1968-76; pres. Plycon Press, 1978—. Author: Food Fundamentals, 1966, 8th edit., 2006, Nutrition for the Growing Years, 1967, 8th edit., 2005, Experimental Foods Laboratory Manual, 1977, 5th edit., 2000, 6th edit., 2005, Lifelong Nutrition, 2001, (with L. Kotschevar) Understanding Food, 1969, Illustrated Guide to Food Preparation, 1970, 8th edit., 1998, 9th edit., 2005, (with L. Davis) Food for You, 1971, 2d edit., 1976, The Meatless Cookbook, 1973, (with F. Stare) Living Nutrition, 1973, 4th edit., 1984, Nutrition for Good Health, 1974, 2d edit., 1982, (with H. Paine) Modern Food Preservation, 1977, Fundamentals of Meal Management, 1978, 4th edit., 2005, (with H. Heller) The World of Nutrition, 1984, Foods: Experimental Perspectives, 1989, 4th edit. 2000, 5th edit., 2005, Food Around the World: A Cultural Perspective, 2003. Chmn. bd. Beach Cities Symphony, 1991-94. Recipient Alumni Centennial award Iowa State U., 1971, Profl. Achievement award, 1977; Phi Upsilon Omicron Nat. Founders fellow, 1964; Home Economist in Bus. Nat. Found. fellow, 1967; Outstanding Prof. award Calif. State U., 1976. Mem. Am. Dietetic Assn., Inst. Food Technologists, Phi Kappa Phi, Phi Upsilon Omicron, Omicron Nu, Iota Sigma Pi, Sigma Delta Epsilon, Sigma Alpha Iota. Home: PO Box 220 Redondo Beach CA 90277-0220 Personal E-mail: mmcwredondo@aol.com.

**MCWILLIAMS, MICHAEL,** writer, publisher; b. Detroit, Aug. 28, 1952; s. Henry and Mary (Toarmina) McW. BA, Wayne State U., 1975; MFA, Columbia U., 1978. Free-lance writer Monthly Detroit mag., 1979-82, Village Voice, Rolling Stone, TV Guide, Adult Age, N.Y. Daily News, LA Herald Examiner, N.Y.C., 1982-87; TV critic, 1988—2001; pub. MaryBooks, 2002—. Author: TV Sirens, 1987, (with others) The Premiere Guide to Movies on Video, 1991. Recipient Assn. of Sunday and Feature Editors award, 1st pl. Arts Criticism, 1992. Mem. Phi Beta Kappa. Avocations: television, movies, theater, music.

**MCWILLIAMS, MIKE C.,** lawyer; b. Dallas, Nov. 10, 1948; s. Earl Dewitt and Mary Louise (Campbell) McWilliams; m. Sally Swatzell, Sept. 1, 1973; children: Michael, Matthew. BBA in Fin., U. Tex., 1969, JD, 1973. Bar: Tex. 1973. Assoc. Elliott, Meer, Vetter, Denton & Bates, Dallas, 1973-78; ptnr. Denton & Generis, Dallas, 1978-80, Moore & Peterson, P.C., Dallas, 1980-89, Winstead, Sechrest & Minick, Dallas, 1989—. Editor: Texas International Law Journal, 1972—73. Mem.: Dallas Bar Assn., Tex. State Bar Assn., Beta Gamma Sigma, Phi Delta Phi. Office: Winstead Sechrest & Minick 5400 Renaissance Tower 1201 Elm St Ste 5400 Dallas TX 75270-2199 Office Phone: 214-745-5631. Business E-mail: mmcwilliams@winstead.com.

**MCWILLIAMS, ROBERT HUGH,** federal judge; b. Salina, Kans., Apr. 27, 1916; s. Robert Hugh and Laura (Nicholson) McW.; m. Catherine Ann Cooper, Nov. 4, 1942 (dec.); 1 son, Edward Cooper; m. Joan Harcourt, Mar. 8, 1986. AB, U. Denver, 1938, LL.B., 1941. Bar: Colo. bar 1941. Dep. dist. atty. Denver, Co, 1941—42; special agent U.S. Office of Naval Intelligence, 1942—45; sgt. U.S. Army, Office of Strategic Services, 1945—46; dist. atty. Denver, Co, 1946—49; private practice Denver, Co, 1949—52; judge municipal ct., Denver, 1949—52, dist., city, and county, Denver, 1952—61, supreme ct. of Co., 1967—70; instructor U. of Denver, 1954—60; judge U.S. ct. of appeals (10th Cir.), Denver, 1970—84; sr. judge, 1984—. Served with AUS, World War II. Mem. Phi Beta Kappa, Omicron Delta Kappa, Phi Delta Phi, Kappa Sigma. Republican. Home: 137 Jersey St Denver CO 80220-5918 Office: Byron White US Courthouse 1823 Stout St Rm 216 Denver CO 80257-1823*

**MCWILLIAMS, SAMUEL ROBERT,** secondary school educator; b. Wilkensburg, Pa., May 4, 1948; s. Paul Wigle and Elizabeth (Witman) McW.; m. Rita Mary Nock, July 31, 1983; 1 child, Karla Marie. BA in Edn./Sci., W.Va. Wesleyan U., 1971; MA in Edn./Curriculum, Pa. State U., 1974; MS in Microcomputers, U. Pitts., 1984. Cert. tchr., Pa.; cert. computer instr., Pa. Tchr. sci. and math. Penn-Trafford Schs., Harrison City, Pa., 1971—. Self-employed master of ceremonies and disc jockey, Level Green, Pa., 1967—. Mem. NEA (life), Alpha Psi Omega Nat. Dramatics Honorary (life), Penn-Trafford Edn. Assn., Pa. Edn. Assn., Pa. Sci. Tchrs. Assn., Bushy Run Lions Club, Psi Omega. Democrat. Presbyterian. Avocations: classic/antique autos, environmental issues, botany/gardening, discography. Home: 348 Meadowbrook Rd Level Green PA 15085-9712 Office: Penn-Trafford Sch Dist Mill St Harrison City PA 15630

**MEACHAM, CHARLES HARDING,** federal agency administrator; b. Newman, Calif., Sept. 21, 1925; s. Vernon A. and Sara (Paulsen) M.; m. June Lorraine Yunker, June 22, 1946; children—Charles Paulsen, Bruce Herbert. BS, Utah State U., 1950. Biologist Calif. Dept. Fish and Game, 1950-56, Alaska Dept. Fisheries, 1956-59; regional supr. regions II and III Alaska Dept. Fish and Game, 1959-68; dir. internat. fisheries Office Gov. Alaska, 1968-69; commr. U.S. Fish and Wildlife Service, Dept. Interior, 1969-70, dep. asst. sec. for fish and wildlife, pks. and marine resources, commr. Internat. North

Pacific Fisheries Commn. and Gt. Lakes Fishery Commn., 1969-70, commr. Internat. Pacific Salmon Fisheries Commn., 1969-70, commr. Great Lakes Fishery Commn., 1969-70, spl. asst. to area dir. Alaska, 1971-74; dir. internat. affairs Office of Gov., Juneau, Alaska, 1975-80; pres. Meacham & Assocs., Anchorage, 1980—. Dep. commr. U.S. North Pacific Fur Seal Commn.; mem. Pacific and North Pacific Fisheries Mgmt. Councils, 1976-81; chmn. nat. park system adv. bd. U.S. Dept. Interior. Bd. dir. Resource Devel. Coun. for Alaska. With USMCR, 1943-46. Mem. Am. Fisheries Soc., Wildlife Soc., Pacific Fisheries Biologists, Internat. Assn. Game, Fish and Conservation Commrs., Ducks Unlimited, Alaska Miners Assn., Am. Legion, U.S.M. Raiders Assn. (pres. 2003—04), Elks. Address: PO Box 428 Sequim WA 98382-0428

**MEACHAM, JON E.,** editor; b. Chattanooga, 1969; m. Keith Meacham; 2 children. BA summa cum laude in English Lit., U. of South, 1991; LHD (hon.), Berkeley Divinity Sch. Yale U., 2005. Writer Newsweek mag., NYC, 1995, nat. affairs editor, 1995—98, mng. editor, 1998—2006, editor, 2006—. Contbg. editor The Washington Monthly; writer NY Times Book Review, Washington Post, LA Times Book Review, Washington Post Book World. Editor: Voices in Our Blood: America's Best on the Civil Rights Movement, 2001; author: Franklin and Winston: An Intimate Portrait of an Epic Friendship, 2003 (NY Times bestseller, LA Times Book of the Year, Emery Reves award; Churchill Centre, 2005), American Gospel: God, the Founding Fathers, and the Making of a Nation, 2006 (NY Times bestseller). Mem. Coun. on Fgn. Relations; bd. regents U. of the South; leadership coun. Harvard Divinity Sch.; nat. advisory group Wash. Nat. Cathedral; communicant, serves on Vestry St. Thomas Ch. Fifth Ave.; Vestry Trinity Ch. Wall St. Office: Newsweek 251 W 57th St New York NY 10019-1894*

**MEACHIN, DAVID JAMES PERCY,** investment banker; b. Teignmouth, Devon, Eng., Jan. 1, 1941; arrived in U.S., 1969; s. James Alfred and Ena Annie Meachin; m. Barbara Marshall Maxwell, Sept. 25, 1971; children: Jonathan J.M., Philip D.M. BS in Phys. Sci., U. Natal, South Africa, 1960; BSChemE, U. Cape Town, South Africa, 1963; MS in Petroleum Engring., French Petroleum Inst., Paris, 1965; diploma in Indsl. Mgmt., Cambridge (Eng.) U., 1966; MBA with distinction, Harvard U., 1971. Project engr. Humphreys and Glasgow Ltd., London, 1966-69; 2nd v.p. investment banking Smith Barney and Co. Inc., N.Y.C. and Tokyo, 1971-75; v.p., gen. mgr. internat. corp. fin. Salomon Bros., N.Y.C. and London, 1975-81; mng. dir. investment banking divsn. Merrill Lynch Capital Markets, N.Y.C., 1981-91; chmn., CEO Cross Border Enterprises L.L.C., 1991—. Bd. dirs. Lyondell Chem. Co.; mem. adv. bd. Gow & Ptnrs., 2003—, South African C. of C. Am. Past chmn. Brit. Am. Ednl. Found.; elder Brick Presbyn. Ch., N.Y.C., 1988—; bd. dirs., vice-chmn. U. Cape Town Fund, N.Y.C., 1985—. Mem.: Kelvin Grove Club (South Africa), Union Club, Harvard Club, United Oxford and Cambridge Club (UK), Misquamicut Club (bd. govs.). Avocations: sailing, golf, tennis, squash. Home: 351 E 84th St New York NY 10028 Office: Cross Border Enterprises LLC 441 Lexington Ave New York NY 10017-3910 Office Phone: 212-682-7400 ext. 230. Business E-mail: dmeachin@crossborderent.com.

**MEAD, CHRISTOPHER,** lawyer; b. Richmond, Va., Mar. 20, 1959; BA magna cum laude, Yale Coll., 1981; JD, Yale Law Sch., 1985. Bar: Md. 1985, DC 1988, Va. 1995, admitted to practice: US Ct. Appeals (4th Cir.) 1986, US Ct. Appeals (2nd Cir.) 1986, US Ct. Appeals (7th Cir.) 1986, US Ct. Appeals (11th Cir.) 1986, US Ct. Appeals (DC Cir.) 1986, US Dist. Ct., Dist. Md. 1986, US Dist. Ct. (DC) 1988, US Dist. Ct. (Ea. and Western Dists. Va.) 1995. Law clk. to Hon. Joseph H. Young US Dist. Ct., Dist. Md., 1985—86; assoc. Williams & Connolly, 1986—89; asst. US atty. Dist. Md., 1989—94, spl. asst. US atty., 1994; ptnr. London & Mead, Washington. Named one of 75 Best Lawyers in Washington, Washingtonian Mag., 2002. Mem.: Va. State Bar, Md. State Bar Assn., DC Bar. Office: London & Mead 1225 Nineteenth St NW Ste 320 Washington DC 20036 Office Phone: 202-331-3334. Office Fax: 202-785-4280. Business E-mail: cmead@londonandmead.com.

**MEAD, FRANK WALDRETH,** taxonomic entomologist; b. Columbus, Ohio, June 11, 1922; s. Arlington Alfred and Edith May (Harrison) M.; widowed; children: David Harrison, Gregory Scott. BS, Ohio State U., 1947, MS, 1949; PhD, N.C. State U., 1968. Rsch. asst. dept. physiology Ohio State U., Woods Hole, Mass., summer 1941; rsch. asst. dept. entomology Columbus, 1948-50; Japanese beetle scout bur. entomology and plant quar. USDA, Columbus, summer 1948, biol. aid bur. entomology and plant quar., 1950-53; entomologist div. plant industry Fla. Dept. Agr., Gainesville, 1953-58, 60, biologist IV, 1983-95, emeritus, 1995—; rsch. asst. N.C. State U., Raleigh, 1958-60; state survey entomologist Fed.-State Coop. Survey, Gainesville, 1969-80. Courtesy assoc. prof. dept. entomology U. Fla., Gainesville, 1973-95, emeritus, 1995—, Fla. A&M U., Tallahassee, 1977-95, emeritus, 1995—. Co-editor Tri-ology Technical Report; contbr. articles to profl. jours. Bd. dirs., treas. Alachua Audubon Soc., Gainesville, 1968-75, 77-82; bd. dirs. Alachua County Hist. Soc. (hon. lifetime mem. 1998), Gainesville, 1980-82; former mem. steering com. Civitan Regional Blood Bank, Gainesville, 1977-79; vol. photographer P.K. Yonge Devel. Rsch. Sch. U. Fla., Gainesville, 1978—; vol. Project Graduation, U. Fla., 1994-2002; mem. Alachua Conservation Trust, 2003—. Nominee Cmty. Svc. award, Gainesville Sun, 2002; named to Registry of Remembrances, Nat. World War II Meml.; recipient award, P.K. Yonge Devel. Rsch. Sch., 2001; fellow, Ohio Acad. Sci. 1966. Mem. VFW, Internat. Order of Merit, Cambridge, Entomol. Soc. Am. (bd. dirs. S.E. br. 1978-79), Ga. Entomol. Soc., Fla. Entomol. Soc. (hon., sec. 1968-82, Cert. of Appreciation 1975, 82, 91, 2004, Cert. of Merit 1986), Fla. Mosquito Control Assn., Entomol. Soc. Washington, Soc. Systematic Biologists, SAR (Benjamin Franklin chpt. Columbus, Ohio), The Am. Legion (life), Sierra Club, Fla. Track Club, Millage Book Club. Avocations: photography, history, birding. Home: 2035 NE 6th Ter Gainesville FL 32609-3758 Office: Fla Dept Agr and Cons Svcs Divsn Plant Industry PO Box 147100 Gainesville FL 32614-7100

**MEAD, JAMES MATTHEW,** insurance company executive; b. Erie, Pa., June 10, 1945; s. James Leonard and Olga (Richter) M.; m. Rhoda Ginsburg, Sept. 2, 1967 (div. 1971); m. Elaine Margaret Lytle, Mar. 8, 1975. BS, Pa. State U., 1967, MA, 1970. Instr. bus. Pa. State U., Middletown, 1968-71; asst. to ins. commr. Commonwealth of Pa., Harrisburg, 1971-74; asst. to pres. Capital Blue Cross, Harrisburg, 1974-78, sr. v.p., 1978-84, pres., CEO, 1984—2004, vice chmn., 2004—; mng. dir. JM Mead, LLC, 2004—. Bd. dirs. BCS Fin., Chgo., Found. Enhancing Cmtys., Harrisburg, Internat. Life Scis. Inst., Wash., Critical Care Sys. Internat., Nashua, NH, Critical Care Sys., Inc.; trustee Lawyers Fund Client Security, Pa. Supreme Ct., Harrisburg, Pa.; trustee Lebanon Valley Coll., Annville, Pa., 2003—; ptnr. Radius Venture LLC, NYC, 2004-2006, venture ptnr., 2006—. Contbr. articles on health care to profl. publs. Mem. bd. advisors Pa. State U., 1985-93; chmn. savs. bond campaign for Ctrl. Pa., U.S. Treasury Dept., Harrisburg, 1986-87; bd. dirs. United Way Capital Region, 1994-98, campaign chair, 1994; bd. dirs. Harrisburg Symphony Assn., 2000-, Found. Enhancing Cmty., 2001-, Pa. Lawyers Fund for Client Security, Pa. Supreme Ct. Paul Harris fellow Rotary Internat., 1988, Alumni fellow Pa. State U., 1986. Mem. Capital Region C. of C. (bd. dirs., treas. 1987-90), West Shore Country Club, Blue Ridge Country Club. Home: 1752 Conway Heath Camp Hill PA 17011 Office Phone: 717-763-1678. Personal E-mail: jamesmmead@aol.com.

**MEAD, KENNETH MINOR,** lawyer, former federal agency administrator; b. May 14, 1947; m. Elizabeth Guerry; children: Jennifer, Hillary. Baccalaurette Degree, So. Conn. U., 1970; JD, U.S.C., 1975; John F. Kennedy Sch. Sr. Mgrs. in Govt., Harvard U., 1991. Sr. atty. Office Gen. Counsel U.S. Gen. Acctg. Office, Washington, 1975-82, asst. dir. Office Quality Assurance, 1982-86, assoc., asst. dir. transp., dir. transp. & telecom. issues, 1986-96, dep. asst. comptr. gen. for policy, 1996-97; inspector gen. U.S. Dept. Transp., Washington, 1997—2006; spl. counsel Baker Botts LLP, Washington, 2006—. Mem. Pres. Coun. on Integrity and Efficiency, 1997-05, Comptr. Gen.'s U.S. Domestic Accountability Bd., 2001-05. With USN, 1970—72. Recipient GAO Disting. Svc. award, Meritorious Svc. award, Mem. Am.

Numismatic Assn., D.C. Bar Assn., Fed. Bar Assn., Assn. Govt. Accountants Office: Baker Botts LLP The Warner 1299 Pennsylvania Ave NW Washington DC 20004 Office Phone: 202-639-7744. Business E-mail: ken.mead@bakerbotts.com.

**MEAD, LAWRENCE MYERS, JR.,** retired manufacturing executive; b. Plainfield, N.J., May 11, 1918; s. Lawrence Myers and Eleanor Whitman (Machado) M.; m. Janet Chase, Feb. 21, 1942; children— Lawrence Myers, Kirtland Chase, Jonathan Taylor, Bradford Machado. BSE., Princeton U., 1940, C.E., 1941; postgrad. mgmt., Harvard Bus. Sch., 1964. With Grumman Corp., Bethpage, NY, 1941-93; v.p. tech. ops. Grumman Aerospace Corp., Bethpage, NY, 1972-75, sr. v.p. dept. ops., 1975-81, sr. v.p. tech. ops., 1981-83; sr. mgmt. cons., 1983-93. Patentee in field. Trustee, police commr., dep. mayor Village of Huntington Bay, N.Y., 1975-80; trustee N.Y.C. Hall of Sci. Fellow Poly. U., 1981. Fellow AIAA; mem. NAE, L.I. Forum on Tech. (bd. dirs., past chmn. bd.), Soc. Logistic Engrs., Soc. Advancement Materials and Process Engring., Princeton U. Alumni Assn. Democrat. Achievements include designing A6A Intruder Navy All Weather Bomber, Gulfstream III Exec. Jet Transport. Home: 88 Notch Hill Rd Apt 253 North Branford CT 06471-1851 E-mail: lmmead@aol.com.

**MEAD, LOREN BENJAMIN,** writer, consultant; b. Florence, S.C., Feb. 17, 1930; s. Walter Russell and Dorothy (Nauss) M.; m. Polly A. Mellette, Aug. 25, 1951; children: Walter Russell, Christopher Allen, Barbara Holladay Mead Wise, Philip Sidney. BA, U. of the South, 1951, DD (hon.), 1982; MA, U. S.C., 1951; MDiv, Va. Sem., Alexandria, 1955, DD (hon.), 1984, Berkeley Div. Sch., New Haven, 1986. Ordained priest Episcopal Ch., 1956. Rector Trinity Episcopal Ch., Pinopolis, S.C., 1955-57, Ch. of the Holy Family, Chapel Hill, N.C., 1957-69; dir. Project Test Pattern, Washington, 1969-74; founder, pres. Alban Inst., Washington, 1974-94. H. Paul Douglas lectr. The Religious Rsch. Assn., 1999. Author: New Hope for Congregations, 1972, Critical Moment, 1988, The Once and Future Church, 1991, More Than Numbers, 1993, Transforming Congregations For The Future, 1994, Five Challenges for the Once and Future Church, 1996, FInancial Meltdown in the Mainline, 1998. Recipient Spl. Achievement award Interim Pastor Network, 1990, Henry Knox Sherill medal, 1999; named DuBose lectr. U. of the South, 1980, Cheney lectr. Berkeley Div. Sch., 1986. Mem. Acad. Parish Clergy (bd. dirs. 1973-75), Soc. for Advancement of Continuing Edn. for Ministry, Religious Rsch. Assn., Soc. for Sci. Study of Religion. Democrat.

**MEAD, MATTHEW HANSEN,** prosecutor; b. 1962; Graduate, Trinity U., U. Wyo. Sch. Law. Deputy Co. Atty. Cambell Co. Atty Office, Wyo., 1987—90; Asst. US atty. and Special Asst. US atty. dist. Wyo. US Dept. Justice, 1991—95; ind. practice, 1995—97; ptnr. Mead and Phillips, 1997—2001; US atty. dist. Wyo. US Dept. Justice, 2001—. Office: US Attys Office PO Box 668 Cheyenne WY 82003-0668*

**MEAD, PHILIP BARTLETT,** healthcare administrator, educator, retired obstetrician; b. Poughkeepsie, N.Y., June 23, 1937; s. Ralph Allen and Altina (Gervin) Mead; m. Ann Elaine Smith, June 27, 1964; children: Ralph Allen II, David Smith. BA, Hamilton Coll., 1959; MD, Cornell U., 1963. Diplomate Nat. Bd. Med. Examiners, Am. Bd. Ob-gyn. Intern in medicine Bellevue Hosp., N.Y.C., 1963-64; resident in ob-gyn. N.Y. Hosp./Cornell Med. Ctr., N.Y.C., 1964-69; asst. prof. U. Vt. Coll. Medicine, Burlington, 1971-76, assoc. prof., 1976-81, prof., 1981—2001, prof. emeritus, 2001—; hosp. epidemiologist Med. Ctr. Hosp. of Vt., Burlington, 1984-93; dir. clin. sys. Vt. Acad. Med. Ctr., Burlington, 1993-95; sr. v.p., med. dir. Fletcher Allen Health Care, Burlington, 1995-97; prof., chmn. ob-gyn. U. Vt. Coll. Medicine, 1997—2001, prof. and chmn. emeritus, 2001—; physician leader women's health care svcs. Fletcher Allen Health Care, Burlington, 1997—2001. Lt. comdr. M.C. USN, 1969—71. Fellow: ACOG, Infectious Disease Soc. Am.; mem.: Soc. Hosp. Epidemiologists, Infectious Disease Soc. Ob-Gyn. (pres. 1987—88), Phi Beta Kappa, Alpha Omega Alpha. Home: 203 Pinehurst Dr Shelburne VT 05482-6882 E-mail: PBMeadMD@aol.com.

**MEAD, SUSANAH M.,** dean; BA, Smith Coll., 1969; JD, Indiana U. Sch. Law, Indianapolis, 1976. Law for Honorable Paul H. Buchanan Jr, chief judge Indiana Court of Appeals, 1976—78; lecturer, legal writing program Indiana U. Sch. Law, Indianapolis, 1978, dir. legal writing, 1980—81, assoc. dean academic affairs, 1997—2004, interim dean, 2005—. Office: Indian U Sch Law Lawrence W Inlow Hall Rm 307 530 W New York St Indianapolis IN 46202-3225 Office Phone: 317-274-2581. Office Fax: 317-374-3955. E-mail: smead@iupui.edu.

**MEAD, WILLIAM CHARLES,** physicist; b. Hazleton, Pa., Dec. 6, 1946; s. Norman Joseph and Ruth Crawford Mead; m. Carol Edna Jerome, May 24, 1969; 1 child, Bennett R. BS, Syracuse U. Syracuse, NY, 1968; MA, Princeton U., Princeton, NJ, 1970, PhD, 1974. Physicist Lawrence Livermore Nat. Lab., 1973—83; physicist, mgr. Los Alamos Nat. Lab., 1983—94; pres., chief scientist Adaptive Network Solutions Rsch. Inc., 1995—. Cons. Lawrence Livermore Nat. Lab., Livermore, Calif., 1995—99. Whistlesoft, Inc., Los Alamos, N.Mex., 1996—98, Ctr. for Adaptive Sys. Applications, Inc., Los Alamos, N.Mex., 1999, Complexica, Inc., Santa Fe, 1999—, Impulse Devices Inc., Grass Valley, Calif., 1999—2003, Los Alamos (N.Mex.) Nat. Lab., 2000—03, Gen. Fusion, Inc., 2003, Environ. Safety Svcs., 2004—. Contbr. articles to profl. jours. Second lt. USAF, 1973—73. Fellow: Am. Phys. Soc. (fellowship 1987); mem.: Internat. Neural Network Soc. Achievements include being head designer for Cairn 50X Intermediate density target, the first laser-driven target to achieve compression of DT to 10 g/cc and a major milestone of the Inertial Confinement Fusion Program; designed and developed C++ engine for Agent-Based Crisis Simulator; development of the Connectionist Hyperprism Classification network to perform task of automated ion mobility spectrum analysis; Adaptive Teaching and Learning Lab. and an Adaptive Tutor for teaching basic arithmetic facts; research in theoretical and computational effort to explore feasibility of Sonic-Cavitation-Driven Fusion; numerical simulations extending knowledge in areas such as the behavior of fluid instabilities in high-gain ICF pellets and the scaling of laser-driven ablation; testing and extending the understanding of ICF physics, providing ideas, simulations and guidance for laser-plasma coupling experiments. Avocations: classical music, photography. Office: Adaptive Network Solutions Research 10 Bonito Pl Los Alamos NM 87544 Office Phone: 505-662-9475. E-mail: wcmead@ansr.com.

**MEADE, ANDREW JOHN,** social studies educator; b. Lincoln, Nebr., Sept. 3, 1960; s. Donald Joseph and Helen Lorraine Meade; m. Nicole Anne Earnhart, July 27, 1996; 1 child, Alexandra Jo. BA, U. Wis., Eau Claire, 1983; MEd, Coll. St. Scholastica, Duluth, Minn., 2002. Cert. tchg. Wis. Social studies instr., coach Colfax (Wis.) HS, 1984—. Head basketball coach Colfax (Wis.) HS, 1984—99, head golf coach, 2001—. Named Dunn County Educator of Yr., 1991; recipient Excellence in Edn., Kiwanis Club, 2005—06. Democrat. Roman Catholic. Avocations: golf, reading, travel. Home: 3138 Tiburon Dr Eau Claire WI 54701 Business E-mail: meade@colfax.k12.wi.us.

**MEADE, DALE MICHAEL,** experimental physicist; b. Lodi, Wis., Aug. 7, 1939; children: Loretta, Carla Fleming. BS with high honors in Elec. Engring., U. Wis., 1961, MS in Physics, 1962, PhD in Physics, 1965. Asst. prof. physics U. Wis., Madison, 1967-69, assoc. prof., 1969-72, prof., 1972-74; from head FM-1 to head Fire Project Princeton (N.J.) Plasma Physics Lab., 1973—98, head Fire Project, 1998—2004. Recipient Disting. Svc. Citation U. Wis. Coll. Engring., Madison, 1990, Disting. Assoc. award U.S. Dept. Energy, Washington, 1994, 2005, Leadership award Fusion Power Assocs., 1999, Disting. Career award Fusion Power Assocs., 2005; Disting. Alumni fellow physics dept. U. Wis., 2002. Fellow AAAS, Am. Phys. Soc. Office: Princeton U Plasma Physics Lab PO Box 451 US Rt 1 N Princeton NJ 08543 E-mail: dmeade@pppl.gov.

**MEADER, JOHN DANIEL,** judge; b. Ballston Spa, NY, Oct. 22, 1931; s. Jerome Clement and Doris Luella (Conner) M.; m. Joyce Margaret Cowin, Mar. 2, 1963; children: John Daniel Jr., Julia Rae, Keith Alan. BA, Yale U.,

1954; JD, Cornell U., 1962. Bar: N.Y. 1963, U.S. Dist. Ct. (no. dist.) N.Y. 1963, U.S. Ct. Appeals (2d cir.) 1966, U.S. Supreme Ct. 1967, U.S. Ct. Mil. Appeals 1973, Ohio 1978, U.S. Dist. Ct. (no. dist.) Ohio 1979, Fla. 1983, U.S. Ct. Appeals (4th cir.) 1992, U.S. Ct. Appeals (fed. cir.) 1993. Sales engr. Albany (N.Y.) Internat. Corp., 1954-59; asst. track coach Cornell U., 1959-62; asst. sec., asst. to mgr. Albany Internat. Corp., 1962-65; asst. atty. gen. State of N.Y., Albany, 1965-68; opns. counsel, attesting sec. GE, Schenectady, 1968-77; gen. counsel, asst. sec. Glidden div. SCM Corp., Cleve., 1977-81; chmn. bd., pres. Applied Power Tech. Co., Fernandina Beach, Fla., 1981-84; pres. Applied Energy, Inc., Ballston Spa, 1984-88; judge N.Y. State Workers Compensation Bd., Albany, 1988—. Dir. Saratoga Mut. Fire Ins. Co. Author: Labor Law Manual, 1972, Contract Law Manual, 1974, Patent Law Manual, 1978. Candidate U.S. Ho. of Reps., 29th Dist. N.Y., 1964, N.Y. Supreme Ct., 1975, 87, 93. Col. JAGC, USAR, 1968-1984, dep. staff judge adv. 3d U.S. Army & Ctrl. Command, 1984, brig. gen. JAGC and Fin. Corps, N.Y. Guard, 1984-2002, state staff judge adv. and state comptr. Nat. AAU High Sch. 1000 Yard Indoor Track Champion, 1949, Nat. AAU Prep. Sch. 440 and 880 Yard Indoor Track Champion, 1950, Nat. AAU Outstanding Performer award, Melrose Games Assn., 1950, Heptagonal Track 880-Yard Champion 1954. Mem. ABA, N.Y. State Bar Assn., Fla. Bar, Amelia Island Plantation Club, Cyprus Temple Club, Yale Club Jacksonville (pres.), Masons. Republican. Presbyterian. Home: 271 Round Lake Rd Ballston Lake NY 12019-1714 Office: NY State Workers Compensation Bd 100 Broadway Albany NY 12241-0001 Office Phone: 518-474-6662. Business E-Mail: john.meader@wcb.state.ny.us.

**MEADER, KEITH ALAN,** social services administrator; s. John Daniel Meader and Joyce Margaret Cowin. BA in Polit. Sci., U.Calif., Berkeley. Pres. Benefit Relief Fund Inc., San Rafael, 1992—95; exec. v.p. InPlace, San Francisco, 1997—. Office: InPlace PO Box 475371 San Francisco CA 94147 Office Phone: 888-467-5223. Personal E-mail: keith@inplace.net.

**MEADOR, CHARLES LAWRENCE,** management and systems consultant, educator; b. Dallas, Oct. 7, 1946; s. Charles Leon and Dorothy Margaret (Brown), m. Diane E. Collins, May 18, 1985. BSME with honors, U. Tex., 1970; MSME, MS in Mgmt., MIT, 1972. Engring. staff Union Carbide Corp., Houston, 1967-68; instr. Alfred P. Sloan Sch. Mgmt. MIT, Cambridge, 1972-75, asst. dir. Ctr. Info. Systems Rsch., 1976-78, lectr. Sch. Engring., co-dir. Macro-Engring. Rsch. Group, 1978-99. Founder, pres. Decision Support Tech., Inc., 1974-92; co-founder, vice-chmn., dir. Software Productivity Rsch., Inc., 1985-87; pres., dir. The Softbridge Group, 1989-92; founder, CEO, Mgmt. Support Tech. Corp., 1992-99; sr. v.p., chief info. officer CIGNA Property and Casualty, 1995-98; vice-chmn., dir. Condor Tech. Solutions, Inc., 1998-2000; co-founder, chmn., dir. MGI Strategic Solutions, 2001—; commr. Nat. Imagery and Mapping Agy., 2000-01; mem. Def. Sci. Bd. Task Force, 2001. Editor: How Big and Still Beautiful? Macro-Engineering Revisited, 1980, Macro-Engineering: The Rich Potential, 1981, Macro-Engineering and the Future: A Management Perspective, 1982, Macro-Engineering: Global Infrastructure Solutions, 1992, Macro-Engineering: MIT Brunel Lectures on Global Infrastructure, 1997; mem. editorial bd. Computer Comm., 1979-91; contbr. articles to profl. jours. NSF trainee, 1970; MIT Wilfred Lewis fellow, 1971, Draper Lab. fellow, 1974. Mem. Computer Soc. IEEE (vice-chmn. Ea. Hemisphere and Latin Am. Area Com. 1977-83), Am. Soc. for Macro-Engring. (bd. dirs. 1992-96), Cosmos Club, Sigma Xi, Tau Beta Pi, Pi Tau Sigma. Office: MGI Strategic Solutions 85 Speen St Framingham MA 01701

**MEADOR, DANIEL JOHN,** law educator; b. Selma, Ala., Dec. 7, 1926; s. Daniel John and Mabel (Kirkpatrick) M.; m. Janet Caroline Heilmann, Nov. 19, 1955; children: Janet Barrie, Anna Kirkpatrick, Daniel John. BS, Auburn U., 1949; JD, Ala., 1951; LLM, Harvard U., 1954; LLD (hon.), U.S.C., 1998. Bar: Ala. 1951, Va. 1961. Law clk. to Justice Hugo L. Black U.S. Supreme Ct., 1954-55; assoc. firm Lange, Simpson, Robinson & Somerville, Birmingham, Ala., 1955-57; faculty U. Va. Law Sch., Charlottesville, 1957-66, prof. law, 1961-66; prof., dean U. Ala. Law Sch., 1966-70; James Monroe prof. law U. Va., Charlottesville, 1970-94, prof. emeritus, 1994—; asst. atty. gen. U.S. Dept. Justice, 1977-79; dir. grad. program for judges, 1979-95. Fulbright lectr., U.K., 1965-66; vis. prof. U.S. Mil. Acad., 1984; chmn. Southeastern Conf. Assn. Am. Law Schs., 1964-65; chmn. Cts. Task Force Nat. Adv. Commn. on Criminal Justice, 1971-72; dir. appellate justice project Nat. Ctr. for State Cts., 1972-74; mem. Adv. Coun. on Appellate Justice, 1971-75, Coun. on Role of Cts., 1978-84; bd. dirs. State Justice Inst., 1986-92; exec. dir. commn. on structural alternatives Fed. Ct. Appeals, 1998-99. Author: Preludes to Gideon, 1967, Criminal Appeals-English Practices and American Reforms, 1973, Mr. Justice Black and His Books, 1974, Appellate Courts: Staff and Process in the Crisis of Volume, 1974, (with Carrington and Rosenberg) Justice on Appeal, 1976, Impressions of Law in East Germany, 1986, American Courts, 1991, 2000 (with J. Bernstein) Appellate Courts in the United States, 1994, His Father's House, 1994, Unforgotten, 1999, (with Rosenberg and Carrington) Appellate Courts: Structures, Functions, Processes, and Personnel, 1994; editor: Hardy Cross Dillard: Writings and Speeches, 1995; editor Va. Bar News, 1962-65; contbr. articles to profl. jours. 1st lt. U.S. Army, 1951-53; col. JAGC, USAR ret. Decorated Bronze Star.; IREX fellow German Dem. Republic, 1983 Mem. ABA (chmn. standing com. on fed. judl. improvements 1987-90), Ala. Bar Assn., Va. Bar Assn. (exec. com. 1983-86), Am. Law Inst., Am. Judicature Soc. (bd. dirs. 1975-77, 80-83), Soc. Pub. Tchrs. Law, Am. Soc. Legal History (bd. dirs. 1968-71), Order of Coif, Raven Soc., Phi Delta Phi, Omicron Delta Kappa, Kappa Kappa Alpha. Presbyterian. Office: U Va Sch Law 580 Massie Rd Charlottesville VA 22903-1738

**MEADOR, JOHN MILWARD, JR.,** dean; b. Louisville, Nov. 4, 1946; s. John Milward and Ruth Inez (Miller) M.; m. Judith Ann Hay, Dec. 22, 1969; children: John Milward III, Elise Kathleen. BA, U. Louisville, 1968; MA, U. Tex., 1972, MLS, 1975; cert. in pub. adminstrn., U. Utah, 1982. Cert. tchr., Ky., Tex. Stacks supr. U. Louisville Librs., 1965-68; English bibliographer M.D. Anderson Libr. U. Houston, 1973-74, head reference dept. social scis. and humanities, 1974-77, head gen. reference dept., 1977-80; asst. dir. pub. svcs. Marriott Libr. U. Utah, Salt Lake City, 1980-84; dean libr. svcs. S.W. Mo. State U., Springfield, 1984-93; dean librs. U. Miss., Univeristy, 1993—2003; dir. librs. SUNY, Binghamton, 2003—. Bd. dirs. S.W. Mo. Libr. Network, Springfield; coun. Dayco Corp., Springfield, 1984-86; chmn. Mo. Northwestern Online Total Integrated Sys. Users Group, 1988-89. Co-author: The Robinson Jeffers Collection at the University of Houston, 1975; contbr. articles to profl. jours. Sponsor Cmty. Alternative Svc. Program, Springfield and St. Louis, 1985-93; governing bd. Mo. Rsch. and Edn. Network, MOREnet, 1991-93; bd. dirs. Broome Libr. Found., Inc., 2005—. With U.S. Army, 1969-71, Vietnam. Recipient Nat. Essay award Propeller Club of U.S., 1964; named to Honorable Order of Ky. Colonels, Gov. Ky., 1978; summer scholar English-Speaking Union, Edinburgh, Scotland, 1968; Apple Computer's Higher Edn. Acad. Devel. Donation Program grantee, 1990. Mem. ALA, Am. Assn. for Higher Edn., Assn. Coll. Rsch. Librs., Bibliog. Soc. Am., Libr. Adminstrn. and Mgmt. Assn., other profl. orgns., English-Speaking Union Club, Rotary (chmn. students guests com. Springfield chpt. 1986-89, chmn. scholarships com. 1989-90, bd. dirs. 1990-91, bd. dirs. Oxford chpt. 1995-96), Phi Kappa Phi. Avocations: raising pure bred airedale terriers, fishing, book collecting. Office: Binghamton Univ SUNY Bartle Library Binghamton NY 13902-6012 Office Phone: 607-777-2346. Business E-Mail: jmeador@binghamton.edu.

**MEADOR, RON,** newspaper editor, writer; b. Buffalo, N.Y., Nov. 24, 1952; s. Meril E. and Evelyn (Lyons) M.; divorced; 1 child, Benjamin Brian. BA, Ind. U., 1975. Copy editor The Courier-Journal, Louisville, 1977-78, The New York Times, 1978-80; reporter, state editor, city editor, asst. mng. editor Star Tribune, Mpls., Minn., 1980-96, mem. editl. bd., editl. writer, 1996—. Mem. Investigative Reporters and Editors, Inc., Nat. Conf. Editl. Writers, Soc. Environ. Journalists, Insts. for Journalism and Natural Resources (mem. adv. bd.). Office: Star Tribune 425 Portland Ave Minneapolis MN 55488-0002

**MEADOR, ROSS DESHONG,** lawyer; b. Mexico City, Aug. 23, 1954; s. Bruce Staffel and Betty Lee M.; m. Michelle Hyunae Chang, Mar. 14, 1997; children: Amy Chang, Leah Chang, Daniel Ross. BA in Comm. and Visual Arts, U. Calif., San Diego, 1980; JD, U. Calif., Berkeley, 1986. Bar: Calif. Co-dir. Overseas Operations Friends of Children of Vietnam, 1974—75; atty. Morrison & Foerster, San Francisco, 1986—89; fgn. legal advisor Kim & Chang, Seoul, 1989—95, Soewito, Suhardiman, Eddymurthy & Kardono, Jakarta, Indonesia, 1996—97; of counsel Morrison & Foerster, 1997—99, Howard, Rice et al, 2000; ptnr. Preston Gates & Ellis, 2001—02, Rogers & Meador, 2003—; internat. legal adv. Vietnam Internat. Law Firm, 2005—. Exec. editor Internat. Tax & Bus. Lawyer, 1985-86. Bd. dirs. Theatre Bay Area, San Francisco, 1988—89. Mem. ABA, Calif. Bar Assn. (exec. com. internat. law sect. 2001-04, sec. 2004-05, adv. emeritus 2006—), Am. C. of C. in Korea (chmn. legal svcs. com. 1993), Korean Am. C. of C. of No. Pacific Coast (v.p. 1998-99, pres. 2000-01), U.S.-Vietnam C. of C. (vice chair 2005), Am. C. of C. Vietnam. Avocation: travel. Home: 1270 Campus Dr Berkeley CA 94708-2045

**MEADORS, ALLEN COATS,** health facility administrator, educator, academic administrator; b. Van Buren, Ark., May 17, 1947; s. Hal Barron and Allene Coats (Means) Meadors. AA, Saddleback Coll., 1981; BBA, U. Ctrl. Arki., 1969; MBA, U. No. Colo., 1974; MPA, U. Kans., 1975; MA in Psychology, Webster U., 1979, MA in Health Svcs. Mgmt., 1980; PhD in Adminstrn., So. Ill. U., 1981. Assoc. adminstr. Forbes Hosp., Topeka, 1971-73; asst. dir. health svcs. devel. Blue Cross Blue Shield of Kans., Topeka, 1973-76; asst. dir. Kansas City Health Dept., Mo., 1976-77; program dir., asst. prof. So. Ill. U., Carbondale, 1977—82, Webster U., St. Louis, 1979—82; mem. faculty Calif. State U., Long Beach, 1977-81; assoc. prof., dir. divsn. health adminstrn. U. Tex., Galveston, 1982-84; exec. dir. N.W. Ark. Radiation Therapy Inst., Springdale, 1984-87; mem. grad. faculty Sch. Bus. Adminstrn. U. Ark., Fayetteville, 1984-87; prof., chmn. dept. health adminstrn. U. Okla., Oklahoma City, 1987-90, dean Coll. Pub. Health, 1989—90; dean Coll. Health, Social and Pub. Svcs. Ea. Wash. U., Cheney, 1990—94; chancellor Pa. State U., Altoona, 1994—99, U.C. Pembroke, 1999—. Cons. Surgeon Gen. Office and Air Force Svc.; bd. dirs. Lumbar Guartoner Bank, Southeastern Regional Med. Ctr. Contbr. articles to profl. jours. Command bd. dirs. Blair County Hall of Fame, Blair County Hist. Soc., Martin Luther King Hosp., Health Care Svcs. Adv. Bd.; bd. dirs., exec. com. Altoona Symphony Orch.; bd. dirs. Home Health Agy., NC Retirement Fund, Southwestern Regional Med. Ctr. With Med. Svc. Corps USAF, 1969—73. Fellow: Am. Coll. Healthcare Execs.; mem.: Am. Hosp. Assn., C. of C. (v.p.). Office: U NC at Pembroke Chancellors Office PO Box 1510 Pembroke NC 28372-1510 Home: PO Box 97 Pembroke NC 28372 Office Phone: 910-521-6201. Business E-Mail: acm@uncp.edu.

**MEADORS, C. BRIAN,** lawyer; b. Lawrence, Kans., Aug. 18, 1969; s. Carey Wayne Meadors and Norma Meadors Senyard; m. Erika Esterbrook, Feb. 12, 2000; children: August Carey, Tabitha Grace. BS in Engring., U. Mich., Ann Arbor, 1991; JD cum laude, Georgetown U., Washington, DC, 1999. Cert. profl. engr., Va., 1998, Ark., 1998; bar: Ark. 2001, DC 2000, Va. 1999. Atty. Morgan, Lewis & Bockius LLP, Washington, 1999—2002, Pryor, Robertson & Barry PLLC, Fort Smith, Ark., 2002—. Elder First Presbyn. Ch., Fort Smith, Ark., 2003—06. Naval nuclear submarine officer USN, 1991—96. Decorated Navy Achievement Medal. US Navy. Mem.: ATLA, Am. Nuc. Soc. Avocations: reading, piano. Home: 10712 Hunters Point Rd Fort Smith AR 72903 Office: Pryor Robertson and Barry PO Drawer 848 315 N 7th St Fort Smith AR 72902-0848 Office Phone: 479-782-8813. Office Fax: 479-785-0254. Personal E-mail: brianmeadors@gmail.com. Business E-Mail: cbmeadors@prblaw.com.

**MEADORS, HOWARD CLARENCE, JR.,** electrical engineer; b. Chgo., July 31, 1938; s. Howard Clarence and Eileen May (Baker) M.; m. Phyllis Anne Rennebaum, July 18, 1964; children: Henry Charles, William Howard, Laura Phyllis, Pamela Susan. SB, MIT, 1960, SM, 1962, Profl. Degree in Elec. Engring., 1964; PhD. Poly. Inst. NY., 1976. Mem. tech. staff Bell Tel. Labs., Inc., Holmdel, NJ, 1966—82; disting. mem. tech. staff AT&T Info. Sys. Labs., Holmdel, 1983—85, supr. product devel., 1985—86; supr. adv. data comm. AT&T Bell Labs., Middletown, NJ, 1986—91; Disting. mem. tech. staff AT&T Bus. Comm. Sys., Holmdel, 1991—91; disting. mem. tech. staff AT&T Network Sys., Holmdel, 1994—96, Lucent Technologies, Holmdel, 1996—2001. Ednl. counselor MIT, 1973-2003, regional vice chmn., 1983-96, ctrl. NJ chmn., 1996-2003. Inventor in field. With Signal Corps, U.S. Army, 1964-66. Mem. IEEE (sr.), Sigma Xi, Eta Kappa Nu. Personal E-mail: hcmeadorsjr@yahoo.com.

**MEADOW, CHARLES,** information scientist, writer; b. Paterson, NJ, Dec. 16, 1929; s. Abraham and Florence (Troub) M.; m. Harriet Reiss, Sept. 9, 1956 (div.); children: Debra Lynne, Sandra Lee; m. Mary Louise Shinskey, June 24, 1972; children: Alison Maria, Benjamin Niland. BA, U. Rochester, 1951; MS, Rutgers U., 1954. Mathematician David Taylor Model Basin USN, Washington, 1954-55; asst. mathematician RAND Corp., Lexington, Mass., 1955-56; unit mgr. GE Co., Bethesda, Md., 1956-60; sr. sys. analyst IBM Corp., Gaithersburg, Md., 1960-68; chief sys. devel. divsn. US Nat. Bur. Stds., Gaithersburg, Md., 1968-71; tech. asst. Office of Sci. and Tech. Exec. Office of the Pres., Washington, 1970-71; asst. dir. divsn. mgmt. info. and telecom. sys. US AEC, Washington, 1971-74; prof. Drexel U., Phila., 1974-82; project mgr. Dialog Info. Svcs., Inc., Palo Alto, Calif., 1982-84; prof. faculty info. studies U. Toronto, 1984—94, assoc. dean, 1990—94, prof. emeritus, 1994—. Vis. prof. U. Sheffield, 1980-81, U. West Indies, 1990-91, U. Wash., 1993, U. NC, 1995; mem. bd. visitors Coll. Communication and Info., U. Tenn., 2002-05. Author or co-author 12 books, including (with Bert R. Boyce and Donald H. Kraft) Text Information Retrieval Systems, 1992, 2nd edit., 1999, (with Bert R. Boyce and Donald H. Kraft) Measurement in Information Science, 1994, Ink Into Bits: A Web of Converging Media, 1998, Making Connections: Communication Through the Ages, 2002, Messages, Meaning and Symbols, 2006; editor Jour. Am. Soc. for Info. Sci., 1976-84, Can. Jour. Info. Sci., 1986-87. 1st Lt. USMC, 1951-53. Mem. Am. Soc. Info. Sci. and Tech. (disting. lectr. award MIT program 1986, ann. rsch. award 1995, info. sci. book of yr. award 2000), Can. Assn. Info. Sci. (pres. 1994), NY Acad. Sci. (honorable mention children's sci. book awards 1975), Ret. Academics and Librs. U. Toronto (exec. com. 2000-02, coms. dir. 2001-02), Sigma Xi. Avocation: photography. Home: 1047 Richardson St Victoria BC Canada V8V 3CG E-mail: ct.meadow@shaw.ca.

**MEADOW, LYNNE (CAROLYN MEADOW),** theater producer; b. New Haven, Nov. 12, 1946; d. Frank and Virginia R. Meadow. BA cum laude, Bryn Mawr Coll., 1968; postgrad., Yale U., 1968-70. Dir. Theatre Communications Group, 1978-80. Adj. prof. SUNY, Stony Brook, 1975-76, Yale U., Circle in the Sq., 1977-78, 89-91, NYU, 1977-80; theatre and music/theatre panelist Nat. Endowment for Arts, 1977-88; artistic advisor Fund for New Am. Plays, 1988-90. Artistic dir. Manhattan Theatre Club, N.Y.C., 1972—; guest dir. Nat. Playwrights Conf., Eugene O'Neill Theatre Ctr., 1975-77, Phoenix Theatre, 1976; dir. Ashes for Manhattan Theatre Club and N.Y. Shakespeare Festival, 1977; prodr. off-Broadway shows Ain't Misbehavin', 1978, Crimes of the Heart, 1981, Miss Firecracker Contest, 1984, Frankie and Johnny, 1987, Eastern Standard, 1988, Lisbon Traviata, 1989, Lips Together, Teeth Apart, 1991, Four Dogs and a Bone, 1993, Love! Valour! Compassion!, 1994; dir. Principia Scritoriae, 1986, Woman in Mind, 1988 (Drama Desk award), Eleemosynary, 1989, Absent Friends, 1991; dir. Broadway prodn. A Small Family Business, 1992, The Loman Family Picnic, 1993, Nine Armenians, 1996 (Drama Desk nominee), Captains Courageous: The Musical, 1999, The Tale of the Allergist's Wife, 2000; (dir. Broadway prodn. and nat. tour), Last Dance, 2003, Rose's Dilemma, 2003, Anna Christie and Magnolias, 2005; co-prodr. Off-Broadway and Broadway show Mass Appeal, 1981. Recipient Citation of Merit Nat. Coun. Women, 1976, Outer Circle Critics award 1977, Drama Desk award 1977, Obie award for Ashes, 1977, Margo Jones award for Continued Encouragement New Playwrights, 1981, Critics Circle award Outstanding Revival on or off Broadway for Loot, 1986, Lucille Lortel award for Outstanding Achievement, 1987, Spl. Drama Desk award, 1989, N.Y. Drama Critics Circle award Best Fgn. Play for Aristocrats, 1989, Torch of

Hope award, 1989, Manhattan Mag. award, 1994, Lee Reynolds award League Profl. Theatre Women, 1994; named Northwood Inst. Disting. Woman of Yr., 1990, Person of Yr., Nat. Theatre Conf., 1992, SDCF "Mr. Abbott" award, 2003. Office: Manhattan Theatre Club 311 W 43rd St Fl 8 New York NY 10036-6413 Office Phone: 212-399-3000 x 114.

**MEADOWS, GWENDOLYN JOANN,** retired behavioral disorders educator; b. Nov. 20, 1944; d. Guss Lee and Bennie Jolene Treadaway; children: Terence Lee Bradley, Melissa Ann Bradley Davis. AA, Norman Coll.; BA, Berry Coll.; M in Behavior Disorders, West Ga. Coll.; ednl. splty. degree in mild learning handicaps, Jacksonville State U., 1988; postgrad. in Adminstrn., U. Ala.; EdD in Human Svcs. and Counseling, U. Sarasota. Cert. tchr. Tchr. Pres. Hillhouse Garden Club, United Daus. of The Confederacy; life mem., bd. dirs. Calhoun Hist. Soc.; life mem. The Deep South Garden Clubs of Ga.; organizer Homebound program for Local Sheriff's Office; mem. Calhoun Red Hats Soc., Calhoun First Bapt. Ch.; bd. dirs. Calhoun Beautification Bd., Garden Club Ga., 2003—04. Named one of Ga. Women of Achievement, 1999. Mem.: Calhoun-Gordon County Ret. Educators Assn., VFW (life), Am. Legion Aux. (pres., 1st v.p., 2d v.p., historian, parliamentarian, chaplain, pres. dept. Ga. 2005—06), Kappa Kappa Iota (1st v.p.). Baptist. Avocations: reading, gardening.

**MEADOWS, JUDITH ADAMS,** law librarian, educator; b. Spartanburg, SC, June 5, 1945; d. Thomas Taylor and Virginia (Dayton) Adams; m. Bruce R. Meadows; children: Beth Ann Blackwood, Ted Adams Meadows. BA, Am. U., 1967; MLS, U. Md., 1979. Law libr. Aspen Sys. Corp., Gaithersburg, Md., 1979-81; dir. Fairfax (Va.) Law Libr., 1981-84, State Law Libr., Helena, Mont., 1984—. Vis. prof. U. Wash., Seattle, 1994; adj. prof. U. Great Falls, Mont., 1989-96; presiding ofcl. Gov's Conf. on Libr. Info. Svc., Helena, Mont., 1991; cons. Nat. Ctr. for State Cts., 2000—. Author: (book chpts.) From Yellow Pads to Computers, 1991, Law Librarianship, 1994; contbr. articles to profl. jours. Bd. dirs. Helena Presents, 1986-92, Holter Mus. Art, 1995-2002, Mont. Supreme Ct. Commn. on Tech., Mont. Equal Justice Task Force, 2001-; bd. dirs. Mont. Supreme Ct. Commn. on Self-Represented Litigants, chair, 2004—; bd. dirs. Helena Edn. Found., v.p., 2003, pres. 2005-06. Recipient Disting. Svc. award State Bar of Mont., 1991, Pro Bono Pub. award, 2002. Mem. Am. Assn. Law Librs. (treas. 1992-95, v.p. 1996—, pres. 1997-98, past pres. 1998—), N.W. Consortium of Law Librs. (pres.), Mont. Libr. Assn. (sec. 1986-88). Office: State Law Libr Mont PO Box 203004 Helena MT 59620-3004

**MEADOWS, VICKERS B.,** federal agency administrator; Grad., Green Mountain Coll. Procuremen, dir. presdl. gifts The White House, Washington, 1985—87, spl. asst. to the v.p. for adminstrn., 1987—89; dep. dir., dir. exec. svc. US Dept. Transp., Washington, 1989—93; dir. adminstrn. to Gov. Bush State of Tex., 1995—2000; spl. asst. to Pres., dir. White House Mgmt. The White House, Washington, 2001, dir. adminstrn. Bush-Cheney Transition; asst. sec. for adminstrn. office, CIO, chief human capital officer US Dept. Housing & Urban Devel., Washington, 2002—04; chief adminstrv. officer, US Patent & Trademark Office US Dept. Commerce, Washington, 2005—. Republican. Office: US Patent & Trademark Office 2121 Crystal Dr Arlington VA 22202

**MEADS, DONALD EDWARD,** management services company executive; b. Salem, Mass., Sept. 23, 1920; s. Laurence G. and Gertrude F. Meads; m. Jane Lightner, June 15, 1943; children: Edward G., Robert C., Laurence G., Judith C. Antrim, Suzanne M. O'Neil, Clifford L., Nancy Chapin. AB in Pre-Law, Dartmouth Coll., 1942; MBA in Fin., Harvard U., 1947. V.p., vice chmn. investment com. N.Y. Life Ins Co., N.Y.C., 1947-61; v.p. dir., chmn. investment com. Investors Diversified Svcs. Inc., Mpls., 1961-65; pres., CEO Internat. Basic Economy Corp., N.Y.C., 1965-67, chmn., CEO, 1967-71; exec. v.p., dir., CFO, chmn. investment com. INA Corp., Phila., 1971-74; chmn. bd., CEO CertainTeed Corp., Valley Forge, Pa., 1974-78, dir., 1973-78; chmn. Mateer-Burt Co., Inc., Plymouth Meeting, Pa., 1984-87, Phila. First Group Inc., 1982-90, Carver Assocs., Inc., West Conshohocken, Pa., 1978—. Hon. life trustee Valley Forge Mil. Acad. and Coll., Wayne, Pa.; hon. dir. Marine Corps Scholarship Found., Princeton, N.J.; adv. bd. World Affairs Coun. Phila. Capt. USMC, 1942-45. Decorated DFC, Air medals (6). Mem. Harvard Club N.Y.C., Union League (Phila.). Personal E-mail: demeads@aol.com.

**MEADS, MINDY,** merchandising and design executive; BS, U. Ill. With Denver Dry Goods, 1974—78; sr. v.p., v.p., merchandising administr., v.p., store mgr., jeans collection buyer R.H. Macy and Company Inc., 1978—89; operating exec. The Limited, 1989—90; v.p., gen. merchandising mgr. Lands End, 1991—94, sr. v.p. merchandising and design, 1994—96; sr. v.p., gen. merchandising mgr., merchandising design planning and allocation Gymboree Corp., 1996—98; exec. v.p. merchandising and design Lands End, 1998—2003; gen. mgr. apparel Sears Roebuck and Co., 2003—04, exec. v.p., 2003—; pres. Lands End, 2003—, CEO, 2004—. Office: Sears Roebuck and Co 3333 Beverly Rd Hoffman Estates IL 60179

**MEADS, WALTER FREDERICK,** communications executive, consultant, writer; b. Ft. Wayne, Ind., Mar. 11, 1923; s. Frederick C. and Minnie E. (Stephenson) M.; m. Mary E. Smith, Mar. 21, 1975; children by previous marriage: Kenneth W., Catherine L. BS, Kent State U., 1948; MA, Fairfield U. With Norman Malone & Assos., Akron, Ohio, 1946-48, Griswold-Eshleman Co., Cleve., 1949-53, Fuller, Smith & Ross, Cleve., 1953-55; sr. v.p., head of creative svc., mem. mgmt. com., vice chmn. plans and rev. bds. J. Walter Thompson Co., N.Y.C., 1955-72; pres. Meads & Assocs., 1972—. With USAAF, 1943-45. Recipient numerous nat. and local advt. industry awards. Home: 6761 Trail Ridge Dr Lakeland FL 33813-1844 Personal E-mail: chipmeads@aol.com. *Creative freedom is probably the core concept in the heart of my life— not only for myself but for others. Life is never static; it either deteriorates or grows. All growth, to me, springs from the creative doers of the world. The rest of humanity goes along for the ride. And creative growth, in any field or endeavor, demands an attitude of freedom to shake off the shackles of habit and find new and better ways of doing things.*

**MEAGHER, ANTHONY L.,** lawyer; b. Balt., Oct. 18, 1963; BA summa cum laude, Tex. Luth. Univ., 1985; JD with honors, Univ. Md., 1988. Bar: Md. 1988. Ptnr., co-chmn. Construction Litigation practice group DLA Piper Rudnick Gray Cary, Balt. Contbr. articles to profl. jours. Mem.: ABA, Md. State Bar Assn., Order of the Coif. Office: DLA Piper Rudnick Gray Cary 6225 Smith Ave Baltimore MD 21209-3600 Office Phone: 410-580-4214. Office Fax: 410-580-3001. Business E-Mail: anthonymeagher@dlapiper.com.

**MEAGHER, GEORGE VINCENT,** mechanical engineer; b. Halifax, N.S., Can., Apr. 23, 1919; s. John Nicholas and Blanche Margaret (Seals) M.; m. Evelyn Margaret Hamm, June 2, 1945; children: Maureen, Lindsey, Lise, Shelagh. BSc, Dalhousie U., Halifax, 1940; B of Engring., McGill U., 1942. Engring. and mgmt. positions in industry, 1942—56; with Dilworth, Secord, Meagher & Assocs. Ltd., Toronto, Canada, 1957—92, chmn., 1985—96; chmn., CEO Champlain Power Products, Ltd., 1970—80; vice chmn. Tata-DSMA, Bombay, 1970—93; pres., CEO DSMA Internat., Inc., 1980—88; dir. State Bank India, Can. Ltd., Toronto, 1984—94; founding dir., past chmn. Can.-India Bus. Coun.; pres. George V. Meagher Ins. Tatacan, Ltd., 1985—. Fellow: Engring. Inst. Can.; mem.: Profl. Engrs. Ont. Home: 500 Avenue Rd Apt 1402 Toronto ON Canada M4V 2J6 Office Phone: 416-929-8286. E-mail: meaghergv@sympatico.ca.

**MEAGHER, JAMES PROCTOR,** editor; b. Rock Island, Ill., June 2, 1935; s. Edmund Joseph and Pauline Marie (Proctor) M.; m. Marie Therese Lyman, Sept. 12, 1959; children: Kathleen Ann Raffa, Christopher James. BA, U. Notre Dame, 1957. Copy editor Chgo. Tribune Co., 1959-61; staff writer Nat. Observer, Washington, 1961-62, news editor Silver Spring, Md., 1962-65, yr. editor, 1965-76, asst. mng. editor, 1976-77; assoc. editor Barron's Bus. and Fin. Weekly, N.Y.C., 1977-78, news editor, 1978-82, asst. mng. editor, 1982-86, dep. editor, 1986-92, mng. editor, 1992-93, editor, 1993-95; exec.

editor Dow Jones Mag. Group, N.Y.C., 1995—2002; ind. editl. cons., 2002—. Served to 1st lt. U.S. Army, 1957—59. Mem. Soc. Profl. Journalists, Sigma Delta Chi. Roman Catholic. Home: 25 Hedges Ave Chatham NJ 07928-2503 Personal E-mail: meagherj@optonline.net.

**MEAGHER, JOSEPH PATRICK,** law educator, consultant; s. Francis and Alma Meagher; m. Rani Parker, June 4, 1989; 1 child, Asha. JD magna cum laude, Harvard Law Sch., 1989. Bar: NY 1990, Washington 1991. Educator Peace Corps, Kisangani, Zaire, 1982—84; atty. Patton, Boggs, Washington, 1989—91, Shearman & Sterling, 1991—92; sr. assoc. Checchi & Co. Cons., Inc., 1992—94; assoc. dir. IRIS Ctr., U. Md., College Park, 1994—. Adj. prof. law Cath. U., Washington, 1991—93. Co-author, editor: Revolution and Development, 2004; contbr. chapters to books, articles to profl. jours. Fellow, Harvard U, Ford Found. 1987—88; grantee, World Bank Netherlands Trust Fund, 1998—2000; Fulbright scholar, Inst. Internat. Edn., 1989. Mem.: Phi Beta Kappa. Office: IRIS Ctr U Md 2105 Morrill Hall College Park MD 20742 Office Phone: 301-405-5468. E-mail: meagher@iris.econ.umd.edu.

**MEAGHER, SANDRA KREBS,** artist; b. N.Y.C., Dec. 18, 1936; d. Oswald Armand and Ella Katherine (Coleman) Krebs; m. John Forsyth Meagher, Oct. 15, 1966. BA, Smith Coll., Northampton, Mass., 1958. Author, artist: (book of drawings and poetry) NORA, 1991. Vice chmn. bd. dirs. Stoneleigh-Burnham Sch., Northampton, 1984-87. Recipient fellowship Va. Ctr. for the Creative Arts, Mt. San Angelo, Va., 1993, Vt. Studio Ctr., Johnson, Vt., 1997. Mem. Art/Place Gallery (pres. 1993, 98, 2005), Silvermine Guild of Artists, Rowayton Arts Ctr., Art Students League (life).

**MEAKEM, CAROLYN SOLIDAY,** investment executive, financial planner, money manager, consultant; b. Columbus, Ohio, Jan. 11, 1936; d. Junius Dean and Mary Elizabeth (Thomas) Soliday: m. Thomas James Meakem, Aug. 26, 1956; children: Thomas James III, Timothy Dean, Traci Lynn. BS, West Liberty Coll., 1959; MEd., U. Md., 1970. cert. fin. planner, cert. trust specialist. Tchr. Westchester Elem. Sch., Ellicott City, Md., 1956-59, Riverdale (Md.) Elem. Sch., 1959-60, Buckingham Elem. Sch., Willingboro, N.J., 1962-64, Beacon Heights Elem Sch., Riverdale, 1964-68; dir. Christian edn. Forest Lake Presbyn. Ch., Columbia, S.C., 1961-62; supr. student tchrs U. Md., College Park, 1968-69; tchr. Norwood Sch., Bethesda, Md., 1975-77; with Ferris and Co. Inc., Bethesda, 1978-88, v.p., 1984-86, sr. v.p., mem. pres.'s coun., chrmn.'s coun., 1986-88, also bd. dirs.; sr. v.p. Legg Mason, Inc., Bethesda, 1988—2005, Smith Barney, Bethesda, 2005—. Guest lectr. George Washington U., 1982-83; trustee, tchr. Wharton Sch. Security Industry Inst., Phila., 1986-95, tchr., speaker Bus. Inst. for Educators, Bethesda, 1987-95. Author: Teachers Activity Guide for Dental Health Education, 1973. Trustee, bd. dirs. Holton-Arms Sch., Bethesda, 1985-94; trustee Nat. Econ. Edn. Found., Security Industry Assn., continuing edn. com., chair ethics edn. sub-com.; founding bd. dirs., treas. Leadership Montgomery, Montgomery County, Md.; hon. bd. dirs. Found. for Boys and Girls Homes Md.; bd. dirs. Child Care Connection; trustee, governing bd. Coun. on Econ. Edn. Md. Mem. LWV (corp. bd. Montgomery County), Nat. Adv. Coun., Security Industry Assn. (regional coord. econ. edn., Best Dist. award 1992), Internat. Assn. Fin. Planners. Presbyterian. Avocations: snow and water skiing, sailing, reading, rose gardening. Home: 10215 Gainsborough Rd Potomac MD 20854-4039 Office: Wachovia Securities 600 Wisconsin Ave Ste 100-Bethesda MD 20814 Office Phone: 301-897-3600. E-mail: carolyn.meakem@wachoviasec.com.

**MEAKIN, FAITH ANNE,** medical library director; b. Phila., Oct. 15, 1943; d. John Blanchard and Dorothy Aileen (Deane) M.; m. Edward J. Frederick, March 23, 2000. Student, Coe Coll., 1961-63; BA, Syracuse U., 1965, MLS, 1966. Intern in med. libr. sci. Biomed. Libr., U. Calif., L.A., 1966-67; head, reference dept. Biomed. Libr., U. Calif. San Diego, La Jolla, 1967-78, head, pub. svcs., 1979-83; mgmt. fellow Biomed. Libr., U. Minn., Mpls., 1978-79; head reference and readers svcs WHO, Geneva, 1983-88; exec. dir. Southeastern/Atlantic regional med. libr. svcs. U. Md. Health Scis Libr., Balt., 1989—94; dir. Health Sci. Ctr. Librs., U. Fla., 1994—. Cons. Netherlands Leprosy Relief Assn., Amsterdam, 1988, Aga Khan U., Karachi, Pakistan, 1987—. Author: (bibliography) Spec Kit 82 Document Delivery, 1982; contbr. articles to profl. jours. USPHS intern, med. libr., L.A., 1966-67; fellow NLM Woods Hole Med. Informatics Course. Fellow Council on Libr. Resources/Nat. Libr. Med. Health Scis. Libr. Mgmt. Intern Program, 1978-79. Fellow: Med. Libr. Assn. (bd. dirs. 2004—, chair med. sch. libr. section); mem.: Acad. of Health Info. Profl. (disting.), Assn. Acad. Health (sci. libr. dir.), Consortium of Biomedical Librs. of the South (chair med. sch. librs. section), Libr. Assn., Beta Phi Mu. Avocations: reading, herbalism. Home: 4015 NW 69th St Gainesville FL 32606-4215 Office: Health Scis Ctr Librs U Fla PO Box 100206 Gainesville FL 32610-0206 E-mail: faith@library.health.ufl.edu, fmeakin@cox.net.

**MEAKIN, MATTHEW,** director; b. Heanor, U.K., Sept. 14, 1971; s. Peter and Christine Sarah Meakin; m. Melanie Louise Bell, June 8, 1996; 1 child, Jacob. Degree in English and Secondary Edn., Mt. St. Mary's U., 1995. Edn. dir. Bowling Brook Prep Sch., Keymar, Md., 2003—. Mem.: ASCD. Office: Bowling Brook Prep Sch 999 Crouse Mill Rd Keymar MD 21757 Office Phone: 410-775-7881.

**MEAL, DOUGLAS H.,** lawyer; b. Feb. 12, 1955; BA summa cum laude, Univ. Pa., 1976; JD cum laude, Harvard Univ., 1980; MALD, Fletcher Sch. Law & Diplomacy, Tufts Univ., 1981. Bar: Mass. 1980, N.Y. 1983, US Dist. Ct. (Mass., So., Ea., We. & No. N.Y.), US Ct. Appeals (1st, 2d, 4th, 7th, 11th & D.C. cir.). Law clk. Judge Robert J. Ward, US Dist. Ct. So. N.Y., 1980—82; assoc. Ropes & Gray, Boston, 1985—89, ptnr. litigation dept., 1989—, chmn. hiring com. Editor (Notes & Comments): Harvard Internat. Law Jour. Office: Ropes & Gray 1 International Pl Boston MA 02110-2624 Office Phone: 617-951-7517. Office Fax: 617-951-7050. Business E-Mail: douglas.meal@ropesgray.com.

**MEAL, LARIE,** chemistry professor, researcher, consultant; b. Cin., June 15, 1939; d. George Lawrence Meal and Dorothy Louise (Heileman) Fitzpatrick. BS in Chemistry, U. Cin., 1961, PhD, 1966. Rsch. chemist U.S. Indsl. Chems., Cin., 1966-67; instr. chemistry U. Cin., 1968-69; asst. prof., 1969-75, assoc. prof., 1975-90, prof., 1990—, rschr., 1980—. Cons. in field. Contbr. articles to profl. jours. Mem. AAAS, N.Y. Acad. Scis., Am. Chem. Soc., NOW, Planned Parenthood, Iota Sigma Pi. Democrat. Avocation: gardening. Home: 2231 Slane Ave Norwood OH 45212-3615 Office: U Cin 2220 Victory Pky Cincinnati OH 45206-2822 Office Phone: 513-556-4364. Business E-Mail: meall@uc.edu.

**MEALEY, GRACE ELEANOR,** music educator; b. Allentown, Pa., Feb. 10, 1927; d. William Jacob Mealey and Ruth May (Knittle) mealey. Attended, Homer Nearing Sch. of Music, 1946—50; studies under, Wilbur Hollman, Cedar Crest Coll., 1950—54, Dr. Ludwig Lenel, Muhlenberg Coll., 1954—58. Pvt. piano, organ tchr., Allentown, Pa., 1948—2005; organist, choir dir. Bethany Evang. Congl. Ch., Allentown, 1948—63; min. of music Emmanuel Evang. Congl. Ch., Bethlehem, Pa., 1963—97; organist, choir dir. Blvd. Evang. Congl. Ch., Allentown, 1997—2002, St. Matthew's Evang. Congl. Ch., Emmaus, Pa., 2002—. Mem.: Am. Guild of Organists, Nat. Guild of Piano Tchrs., Mu Phi Lambda Beta, Pa. Music Tchrs. Assn. Home and Office: 1015 N Arch St Allentown PA 18104

**MEALIE, CARL A.,** emergency physician, educator; b. Astoria, N.Y., Jan. 26, 1948; s. Patrick and Natalie (Previti) M.; m. Maureen Frances Maybury, Apr. 24, 1993; children: David, Ian, Daniel. BA, NYU, 1969; MD, N.Y. Med. Coll., 1974. CCRN. Chmn. Dept. Emergency Medicine St. Mary's Hosp., Roswell, N.Mex., 1975-83; emergency dept. attending physician Guadalupe Med. Ctr., Carlsbad, N.Mex., 1979-83, L.I. Jewish Med. Ctr., New Hyde Park, N.Y., 1993—, chmn. disaster preparation com., 1991—, asst. chief emergency dept., 1989-95, chief clin. ops., 1995; asst. prof. emergency medicine Albert Einstein Coll. Medicine, N.Y.C., 1995. Mem. ambulance adv. bd. Chavez County Med. Soc., Roswell, 1980-83, ambulance bd., 1981-87. Mem. City

Roswell EMS Bd., 1981-93. Fellow Am. Coll. Emergency Physicians (key contact 1987—), N.Y. Acad. Medicine; me., AMA, Am. Acad. Emergency Medicine, N.Y. State Med. Soc., Soc. Acad. Emergency Medicine. Roman Catholic. Avocations: skiing, sailing, hunting, golf. Home: 33 Heights Rd Northport NY 11768-2629 Office: LI Jewish Med Ctr Lakeville New Hyde Park NY 11040 Personal E-mail: carl_mealie@msn.com.

**MEALMAN, GLENN,** corporate marketing executive; b. Prescott, Kans., June 10, 1934; s. Edgar R. and Mary E. (Holstein) M.; m. Gloria Gail Proch, June 12, 1955; children: Michael Edward, Cathy Gail. BS in Bus., Kans. State Coll., Emporia, 1957; postgrad., Harvard U., 1970. With Fleming Cos., Topeka, 1957—, sr. v.p. mktg., 1981-82, exec. v.p. mktg., 1982-86, exec. v.p. Mid-Am. region, 1986-93, exec. v.p. nat. accts., 1994-96; mng. ptnr. Bus. Solutions Assocs. Dir. PBI-Gordon Co., Furrs Supermarkets. Pres. bd. Topeka YMCA, 1981; trustee Ottawa U., Kans., 1980. Served with USNR, 1954-56. Mem. Kans. State C. of C. and Industry (bd. dirs. 1991—), Blue Hills Country Club, Gainey Ranch Country Club, Rotary, Sigma Phi Epsilon (Kans. chpt.). Presbyterian. Office: PO Box 7448 Shawnee Mission KS 66207-0448

**MEALY, J. BURKE,** clinical psychologist; MA in Guidance and Psychology, Assumption Coll., 1966, CAS in Counseling Psychology, 1967; PhD in Clin. Psychology, Duquesne U., 1972. Lic. psychologist, Md; diplomate Profl. Acad. Custody Evaluators, Am. Acad. Forensic Examiners. Clin. psychologist Woodville State Hosp., Carnegie, Pa., 1969-70; dir./psychologist Western State Sch. and Hosp., Canonsburg, Pa., 1970-72; asst. prof. human devel. Calif. State U., Hayward, 1972-73; pvt. practice Md., 1973—; clin. community psychologist Montgomery County Health Dept., Rockville, 1974-78; forensic psychologist Montgomery County Ct., 1978-84. Cons. dist., cir. cts. Montgomery County, 1984-88. Mem.: APA, Am. Orthopsychiat. Assn. Office: JB Mealy and Assocs 15817 Crabbs Branch Way Rockville MD 20855-2635 Office Phone: 301-948-2280.

**MEAMBER, LAURIE ANN,** marketing educator; b. Sacramento, Calif., Aug. 20, 1966; d. Ernest and Holly Meamber. BA, U. Calif., Davis, 1988; MBA, U. Calif., Riverside, 1991; PhD in Mgmt., U. Calif., Irvine, 1997. Mktg. educator George Mason U., Fairfax, Va. Contbr. chapters to books Ethnoconsumerist Methodology for Cultural and Cross-Cultural Research, Art as Life - Life as Art: The Embeddedness of Art in Life and Life in Art in Postmodernity, Cyberspace as the Next Marketing Frontier (?) - Questions and Issues. Fellow Regent's fellow, U. Calif., Irvine, 1991—95, Grad. Sch. Mgmt., U. Calif., Irvine, 1995—96, U. Calif., 1997; Rsch. grant, Sch. Mgmt., George Mason U., 1999—2001, 2003. Mem.: Aesthetics Acad. Network, Assn. Consumer Rsch. (conf. program com. 2000—00), Am. Mktg. Assn. (collegiate chpt. advisor 1999—2004), Beta Gamma Sigma. Avocation: performing arts. Office: George Mason Univ 4400 University Dr Fairfax VA 22030-4444

**MEANS, ANTHONY ROSS,** pharmacology educator; PhD, U. Tex., 1967. Nanaline H. Duke prof., chmn. pharmacology & cancer biology Duke U. Med. Ctr., Durham, NC. Contbr. articles to profl. publs. Fellow AAAS, Am. Acad. Arts and Sci.; mem. Endocrine Soc. (pres. 2004-05, Fred Conrad Koch award 1998), Am. Soc. Pharmacology and Exptl. Therapeutics (Goodman and Gilman award 2006). Office: Duke U Med Ctr PO Box 3813 Durham NC 27710-0001 E-mail: means001@mc.duke.edu.

**MEANS, DAVID HAMMOND,** retired advertising executive; b. Lebanon, Pa., Dec. 15, 1928; s. W. Horace and June (Zimmerman) M.; m. Nancy N. Downes, June 21, 1952; children: Elizabeth N., Susan Z., Emily M., David H. BA, Amherst Coll., 1950. With CIA, 1950-53, N.W. Ayer Inc., 1953-89, exec. v.p., 1976-89; ret., also bd. dirs. Mng. dir. Ayer U.S.A. and Ayer Enterprises, Inc. Bd. dirs. Waveny Care Ctr., New Canaan Nature Ctr., Schoolhouse Apts., Get About Inc. 1st lt. USAF, 1953. Mem. Bus. Profl. Advt. Assn., Merion (Pa.) Golf Club, Amherst Club (N.Y.C.), Country Club New Canaan (Conn.) Gridiron Club (New Canaan), Sr. Men's Club (New Canaan, bd. dirs.), Psi Upsilon. Episcopalian. Home: Wahackme Ln New Canaan CT 06840 Personal E-mail: davenan28@aol.com.

**MEANS, DWIGHT BARDEEN, JR.,** financial consultant, educator; b. Pitts., July 21, 1943; s. Dwight B. Sr. and Betty (Feick) M.; div.; children: Melissa Means Morris, Blake Elizabeth. BSEE, Carnegie-Mellon U., 1965; MBA, U. Pitts., 1969, PhD, 1984. Various positions Bell Telephone Co. Pa., Pitts., 1965-70; asst. prof., dept. chair C.C. Allegheny County, Pitts., 1970-78; from asst. to assoc. prof. Saginaw (Mich.) Valley State U., 1978-86; prof., dept. chair Clarion (Pa.) U. Pa., 1986-88; asst. prof. U. Memphis, 1988-95; adj. prof. numerous univs., 1996—; cons. Pitts., 1995—. Presenter in field. Reviewer Fin. Practice and Edn., Jour. Econs. and Fin., Jour. Real Estate Rsch., Jour. Applied Bus. Rsch; contbr. articles to profl. jours. Mem. Acad. Fin. Svcs. (program com. 1990-95), Am. Econ. Assn., Midsouth Acad. Econs. and Fin. (dir. 1993-95), Fin. Mgmt. Assn. (program com. 1989), Midwest Fin. Assn. (program com. 1995-96), S.W. Fin. Assn. (program com. 1994-95), So. Fin. Assn. (program com. 1992-95). Avocations: hunting, fishing, camping, reading. Home: 138 Owendale Ave Pittsburgh PA 15227-1951 Office Phone: 412-881-0398. Personal E-mail: meansdb@aol.com.

**MEANS, JAMES ANDREW,** engineer; b. Heavener, Okla., Oct. 11, 1937; s. Edward Andrew and Lorena (Nobles) M.; Therese Louise Zimmermann, Feb. 21, 1959; children: James A. Jr., William R., Charles E., Vicky M. BSEE, U. Ariz., 1962, MSEE, 1966; PhD, U. Calif., Santa Barbara, 1972; MS in Computer Sci., Chapman U., Orange, Calif., 1988. Engr. Pacific Missile Test Ctr., Pt Mugu, Calif., 1962-72, engr. mgr., 1972-79; tech. dir. Space and Missile Test Orgn., Vandenberg AFB, Calif., 1979-89; sr. tech. advisor SRI Internat., Menlo Park, Calif., 1990—. Cons. Agri-Craft, Camarillo, Calif., 1968-70, Astro-Geo-Marine, Ventura, Calif., 1972-74; pres. Internat. Found. for Telemetering, 1989-95. Patentee in field. Mem. Internat. Test and Evaluation Assn. (Allen R. Mattews Award, 1991). Democrat. Baptist. Avocations: water-skiing, fishing, hunting, old cars. Home and Office: 284 St Andrews Way Lompoc CA 93436-1355 Business E-Mail: jim.means@sri.com.

**MEANS, JOHN BARKLEY,** director, language educator; b. Cin., Jan. 2, 1939; s. Walker Wilson and Rosetta Miller (Barkley) Means. BA, U. Ill., 1960, MA, 1963, PhD, 1968. U.S. govt. intelligence rsch. analyst on Brazil CIA, Washington, 1962-64; assoc. prof. Spanish and Portugese Temple U., Phila., 1972-82, prof. Portuguese and critical langs., 1982—2003, prof. emeritus, 2003—, co-chmn. dept. Spanish and Portuguese, 1971-75, dir. Center for Critical Langs., 1975—2003, dir. Inst. for Langs. and Internat. Studies, 1987—2003, chmn. dept. Germanic and Slavic Langs. and lit., 1992-94, chair univ. core programs, 1995-97. Cons. on Brazilian-Portuguese and second lang. acquisition and self instrnl. programs for less commonly taught langs., 1968—2003; cons. editor for langs. Norton Pubs., 1979—95; cons. in field. Editor: Essays on Brazilian Literature, 1971; author (with others): Language in Education: Theory and Practice, 1988—; editor: NASILP Manual, 1996; co-dir. CD-ROM Critical Language Series, 1999—; contbr. articles to profl. jours. Trustee Bristol Riverside Theatre, Pa., 1990—2002, 2005—; mng. trustee Means Charitable Trust, 1993—2004. 1st lt. U.S. Army, 1960—62. Fellow, U. Ill., 1967—68; grantee, U.S. Dept. Edn., 1979—83, Japan Found., 1980, 1982, 1989—91, ARCO Chem. Found., 1991, 1993; NDEA fellow, 1962, 1964. Mem.: AAUP, MLA, Joint Nat. Com. for Langs. (bd. dirs.), Nat. Assn. State Univs. and Lang Grant Colls. (commn. on internat. affairs), Nat. Coun. Orgns. Less Commonly Taught Langs. (exec. sec.-treas. 1990—2001), Am. Coun. on Tchg. Fgn. Lang., Nat. Assn. Self-Instrnl. Lang. Programs (exec. dir. 1977—98, editor jour. 1978—94, exec. dir. emeritus 1999—), Nat. Coun. on Langs. and Internat. Studies (bd. dirs.), Sigma Delta Pi, Phi Lambda Beta, Pi Kappa Delta. Home: PO Box 829 Washington Crossing PA 18977-0829 Office: Temple U Ctr for Critical Langs Anderson Hall 1114 W Berks St Philadelphia PA 19122-6090 Business E-Mail: means@temple.edu.

**MEANS, MARIANNE,** columnist; b. Sioux City, Iowa, June 13, 1934; d. Ernest Maynard and Else Marie Johanne (Andersen) Hansen; m. Warren Weaver, Jr. (dec.); m. James J. Kilpatrick. BA, U. Nebr., 1956; JD, George Washington U., 1977. Copy editor Lincoln (Nebr.) Jour., 1955-57; woman's editor No. Va. Sun, Arlington, 1957-59; Washington bur. corr. Hearst Newspapers, 1959-61, White House corr., 1961-65; polit. columnist Hearst Newspapers and King Features Syndicate, 1965—, N.Y. Times News Svc., 1994—; commentator Spectrum CBS radio, Mut. Broadcasting Network, Voice of Am., U.S.I.A. World Network, Post Newsweek Stas., Nat. Pub. Radio. Author: The Woman in the White House, 1963. Recipient Front Page award N.Y. Newspaper Women, 1962; Tex. Headliners award, 1976, Hall of Fame-Sigma Delta Chi, 1988. Mem.: Internat. Women's Media Found. (bd. dirs.), Nat. Press Found. (chmn.), White House Corrs. Assn., Nat. Press Club, Cosmos Club, Gridiron Club (pres.), Sigma Delta Chi (Hall of Fame), Phi Beta Kappa, Delta Delta Delta. Office Phone: 202-263-6415.

**MEANS, MICHAEL DAVID,** hospital administrator; b. Lakeland, Fla., Jan. 19, 1950; married. B. U. Fla., 1971, MHA, 1974. Adminstrv. resident Manatee Meml. Hosp., Bradenton, Fla., 1974, adminstrv. asst., 1974-78; asst. dir. Orlando (Fla.) Regional Med. Ctr., 1978-80, assoc. exec. dir., 1980-81, exec. v.p., chief oper. officer, 1981-88; pres., chief exec. officer Holmes Regional Healthcare System, Melbourne, Fla., 1988—. Health First, Melbourne, Fla. Mem. Fla. Hosp. Assn. Office: Health First 6450 US Highway 1 Rockledge FL 32955-5747

**MEANS, RICHARD NATHANIEL GRIFFITH,** historian; b. Dallas, Jan. 14, 1973; s. Richard Lawrence and Emilia Gay (Griffith) Means. AB, Centenary Coll., 1995; MA, La. State U., 1997; PhD, U. So. Miss., 2001. Exhbn. interpreter Smithsonian Inst. Nat. Mus.of Am. History, Wash., DC, 1994; instr. history U. Southern Miss., Hattiesburg, 1998—99; adj. asst. prof. La. Tech. U., Ruston, 2001—02; lectr. in history Centenary Coll., Shreveport, La., 2002—03; prof. history North Lake Coll., Irving, Tex., 2004—; owner Rosedown Plantation, Caddo Parish, La. Contbr. articles to profl.jours. Mem. bd. dirs. DeSoto Hist. Soc., Mansfield, La., 2003—, Friends of the Mansfield Female Coll., 2004—. Huel Perkins fellow, La. State U., 1995—97, McCain fellow, U. Southern Miss., 2000. Mem.: World Affairs Coun. Greater Dallas, Dallas Hist Soc., Confederate Soc. Am., So. League, So. Hist. Assn., La. Hist. Assn., Shreveport Yacht Club, Plantation Club. Episcopalian. Office: North Lake Coll Divsn Liberal Arts 5001 N MacArthur Blvd Irving TX 75038

**MEANS, ROBERT TAYLOR, JR.,** hematologist, educator; b. Midland, Tex., July 14, 1957; s. Robert Taylor and Anna Therese (Cassidy) M.; m. Stacey W. McKenzie, May 23, 1992; children: Anna, Robert III, Patrick. BA in Biochemistry, Rice U., 1979; MD, Vanderbilt U., 1983. Diplomate Am. Bd. Internal Medicine; cert. in hematology. Resident Baylor Coll. Medicine, Houston, 1983-86; fellow in hematology Vanderbilt U., Nashville, 1986-88, instr. medicine, 1988-90, asst. prof. medicine, 1990-92; assoc. investigator VA Med. Ctr., Nashville, 1988-91, asst. chief hematology/oncology Cin., 1992-98; assoc. prof. med. U. Cin., 1992-98; prof. med., head hematology, assoc. divsn. chief Med. U. S.C., 1998-2000, dir. divsn. hematology-oncology, 2000—04; chief hematology/oncology VA Med. Ctr., Charleston, SC, 1998—2004, prof. internal medicine, 2004—, chief med. svc. Lexington, Ky., 2004—; assoc. chair for rsch., dept. internal medicine U. Ky., 2004—. Contbr. chpts. to books, articles to profl. jours. Recipient Career Devel. award Dept. Veterans Affairs, 1988, Henry Christian award Am. Fedn. Clin. Rsch., 1991. Mem. Am. Soc. Hematology, Internat. Soc. Exptl. Hematology, Phi Beta Kappa. Achievements include being first to report response of anemia of chronic disease to erythropoietin; first description of erythropoietin receptor in polycythemia. Home: 2204 Abbeywood Rd Lexington KY 40515 Office Phone: 859-281-4919. Business E-Mail: robert.means@uky.edu.

**MEANS, TERRY ROBERT,** federal judge; b. Roswell, N.Mex., July 3, 1948; s. Lewis Prude and Doris Emaree (Hightower) M.; m. JoAnn Huffman Harris, June 2, 1973; children: Robert, MaryAnn, Emily. BA, So. Meth. U., 1971, JD, 1974. Bar: Tex. 1974, U.S. Dist. Ct. (no. dist.) Tex. 1976, U.S. Ct. Appeals (5th cir.) 1978, U.S. Dist. Ct. (we. dist., ea. dist.) Tex. 1991. Ptnr. Means & Means, Corsicana, Tex., 1974-88; Presdl. elector, 1980; justice 10th Ct. Appeals, Waco, Tex., 1989-90; judge U.S. Dist. Ct. (no. dist.) Tex., Ft. Worth, 1991— Chmn. Navarro County Rep. Party, Corsicana, 1976-88; pres. YMCA, Corsicana, 1984, Ft. Worth Youth Soccer Assn., 1996-97. Mem. State Bar Tex., Tarrant County Bar Assn., McLennan County Bar Assn. Baptist. Avocations: coaching soccer, racquetball. Office: 201 US Courthouse 501 W 10th St Fort Worth TX 76102-3637

**MEANS, THOMAS CORNELL,** lawyer; b. Charleston, S.C., Oct. 3, 1947; s. Thomas Lucas and Dean (Cornell) M.; m. Judith Faye Perlmutter, Sept. 10, 1977; children: Benjamin, Samuel. AB, Dartmouth Coll., 1969; postgrad., Princeton Theol. Sem., 1970-71; M of Pub. Adminstrn., U. Colo., 1975; JD, George Washington U., 1978. Bar: D.C. 1978, U.S. dist. Ct. (D.C. dist.), U.S. Ct. Appeals (4th and D.C. cirs.) 1979, U.S. Ct. Appeals (10th cir.) 1983, U.S. Ct. Appeals (6th and 11th cirs.) 1989, U.S. Ct. Appeals (9th cir.) 1992, U.S. Ct. Appeals (8th cir.) 1993, U.S. Ct. Appeals (5th cir.) 1996. Social worker Vinyard Childcare, Ann Arbor, Mich., 1969-70; rsch. analyst, registered lobbyist Colo. Counties, Inc., Denver, 1972-75; assoc. Jones, Day, Reavis and Pogue, Washington, 1978-79; assoc. then ptnr. Crowell & Moring LLP, Washington, 1979—. Mem. state adv. coun. on pub. Pers. Mgmt., Colo. State Govt., Denver, 1974-75; lectr. mining law; chmn. coal com. Energy and Mineral Law Found., 1988-89, chmn. spl. insts., ass. sec., 1989-91, sec., 1991-92, v.p., 1992-93, pres., 1993-94, exec. com., 1989-96, trustee, 1989—; mem. bd. editors, 1994—; bd. advisors Nat. Law Ctr., 1993-94, adv. bd. W. Va. Law Review on Nat. Coal Issues, 2001—. Contbr. articles to profl. jours. Named to, Best Lawyers in Am., 2006; recipient Pres.' award, Energy and Mineral Law Found., 2002, Daniel Levy award, Nat. Immigration Project, 2004, John L. McClaugherty award, Energy & Mineral Law Found., 2005. Mem. George Washington Law Alumni Assn. (bd. dirs. 1986-96, exec. com. 1987-96, treas. 1987-88, sec. 1988-90, pres. 1992-94), Order of Coif, Cosmos Club (Washington), Phi Beta Kappa. Home: 6411 Dahlonega Rd Bethesda MD 20816-2101 Office: Crowell & Moring LLP 1001 Pennsylvania Ave NW Fl 10 Washington DC 20004-2595 Office Phone: 202-624-2735.

**MEANY, PHILIP AUGUSTUS,** retired library director; b. Oakland, Calif., Oct. 20, 1938; s. John Philip and Mary Gertrude (Deasy) M. BA, St. Mary's Coll., Moraga, Calif., 1960; M Librarianship, U. Wash., 1963. Asst. libr. Centralia (Wash.) Coll., 1963-68, media svcs. and tech. processes libr., 1969-88, libr. dir., 1988—2002; ret. 2002. Mem. Wash. State Bicycling Adv. Com., Olympia, 1990-99; pres. Destination Centralia Mktg. Assn., 1999-2001. Recipient Platinum Pedal, N.W. Bicycle Fedn., 1997. Mem. Coll. Librs. and Media Specialists Wash. State (pres. 1987-88), N.W. Mgmt. Ednl. Tech. Assn. Avocation: bicycling.

**MEAR, CHARLES EUGENE,** geologist, consultant; b. Dec. 2, 1926; s. Charles Russell Mear and Alice Inez Porche; m. Tonie Margaret Kubesch, Sept. 1, 1951; children: Diane, Charles E. Jr., David R., John P., Mark E., Kathryn, Caroline, Steven. BA in Geology, U. Tex., 1951, MA in Geology, 1953. Cert. petroleum geologist, profl. geoscientist geology Tex., 2003. Petroleum exploration geologist numerous oil cos., Midland, Tex., 1952—67; geologist hard minerals La. Land Exploration Co., Midland, 1967—76, Denver, 1967—76; dist. geologist mgr. Southland Royalty Co., Midland, 1976—82, v.p. geology and geophysics Ft. Worth, 1982—86; v.p. exploration Cross Timbers Oil Co., Ft Worth, 1986—93; rsch. fellow Tex. Archeol. Lab. Austin, Tex., 1993—96; cons. geologist Austin, 1996—2003. Editor: Petroleum Geology of Mississippian Carbonates in North Central Texas, 1989; contbr. articles to profl. jours. Paratrooper 11th airborne divsn. Pacific Theater U.S. Army. Recipient Monroe G. Cheney Sci. award, W. Tex. Geol. Soc., 1991. Mem.: Soc. Sedimentary Geology (hon. life. mem. Permian Basin sect.), Am. Assn. Petroleum Geologists (sec. DPA 1997—99). Home: 7912 Taranto Dr Austin TX 78729-7441

**MEARA, ANNE,** actress, playwright, writer; b. Bklyn., Sept. 20; d. Edward Joseph and Mary (Dempsey) M.; m. Gerald Stiller, Sept. 14, 1954; children: Amy, Benjamin. Student, Herbert Berghoff Studio, 1953-54. Apprentice in summer stock, Southold, L.I. and Woodstock, N.Y., 1950-53; off-Broadway appearances include A Month in the Country, 1954, Maedchen in Uniform, 1955 (Show Bus. off-Broadway award), Ulysses in Nightown, 1958, The House of Blue Leaves, 1970, Bosoms and Neglect, 1986, After-Play, 1996; Shakespeare Co., Two Gentlemen of Verona, Ctrl. Park, N.Y.C., 1957, Romeo and Juliet, 1988; Broadway plays: Spookhouse, 1982, Eastern Standard, 1989, Anna Christie, 1993 (Tony nomination Best Supporting Actress); film appearances include The Out-of-Towners, 1968, Lovers and Other Strangers, 1969, The Boys From Brazil, 1978, Fame, 1979, Nasty Habits (with husband Jerry Stiller), 1976, An Open Window, 1990, Mia, 1990, Awakenings, 1991, Reality Bites, 1994, Daytrippers, 1997, The Fish in the Bathtub, 1998, Southie, 1999, The Independent, 2001, Like Mike, 2002, comedy act, 1963—; appearances Happy Medium and Medium Rare, Chgo., 1960-61, Village Gate, Phase Two and Blue Angel, N.Y.C., 1963, The Establishment, London, 1963, QE II, 1990; syndicated TV series Take Five with Stiller and Meara, 1977-78; numerous appearances on TV game and talk shows, also spls. and variety shows; rec. numerous commls. for TV and radio (co-recipient Voice of Imagery award Advt. Bur. N.Y.); star TV series Kate McShane, 1975, Archie Bunker's Place, 1979, Alf, 1986-88; other TV appearances The Sunset Gang, 1990, Avenue Z Afternoon, 1991, Murphy Brown, 1994, Homicide, 1996 (Emmy nomination), Will and Grace, 2002, Sex in the City, 2002-04, The King of Queens, 2003-05, Good Morning Miami, 2003; (TV movie) Jitters, 1997, All My Children, 1994-99; (TV movie) What Makes a Family, 2001; writer, actress TV movie The Other Woman, 1983 (co-recipient Writer's Guild Outstanding Achievement award 1983), Alf, To Make Up to Break Up, The Stiller and Meara pilot; author, actor (play) After-Play, 1996; author (play) Down the Garden Paths, 2000; video host (with Jerry Stiller) So You Want to Be an Actor? Recipient Outer Critic's Cir. Playwriting award for After-Play, 1995, 4th ann. Alan King award in Jewish Humor, 2003, Productive Aging award Jewish Coun. Aging, 2004, Thalia award (w/ Jerry Stiller) Humbert Coll. Toronto.

**MEARS, CASEY,** race car driver; b. Bakersfield, Calif., Mar. 12, 1978; s. Roger Mears. Profl. race car driver NASCAR, 2002—. Achievements include winner Jim Russell USAC Triple Crown Championship, 2005; finished second Daytona 500, 2006. Office: c/o NASCAR 1801 Internat Speedway Blvd Daytona Beach FL 32115*

**MEARS, PATRICK EDWARD,** lawyer; b. Oct. 3, 1951; s. Edward Patrick and Estelle Veronica (Mislik) M.; m. Geraldine O'Connor, July 18, 1981. BA, U. Mich., 1973, JD, 1976. Bar: N.Y. 1977, Ill. 1996, U.S. Dist Ct. (so. and ea. dists) N.Y. 1977, Mich. 1980, U.S. Dist. Ct. (we. and ea. dists.) Mich. 1980, U.S. Ct. Appeals (6th cir.) 1983, Ill. 1996, U.S. Dist. Ct. (so. dist.) Ill. 1998. Assoc. Milbank, Tweed, Hadley & McCloy, N.Y.C., 1976-79; ptnr. Warner, Norcross & Judd, Grand Rapids, Mich., 1980-91; sr. mem. Dykema Gossett PLLC, Grand Rapids, 1991—2002; equity mem. Dickinson Wright, PLLC, Grand Rapids, 2002—04; equity ptnr. Barnes & Thornburg LLP, 2004—. Adj. prof. Grand Valley State U., Allendale, Mich., 1981-84; dir. Children's Law Ctr., 1994, Grand Rapids Ballet, 1994-99, East Grand Rapids Pub. Sch. Found., 1994-98. Author: Michigan Collection Law, 1981, 2d edit., 1983, Basic Bankruptcy Law, 1986, Bankruptcy Law and Practice in Michigan, 1987, 1995, Revised Article 9 of the UCC in Michigan, 2001; co-author: Strategies for Secured Creditors in workouts and Foreclosures, 2004; contbg. author Collier Bankruptcy Practice Guide; contbr. articles to profl. jours.; editor: Jour. of the Hist. Soc. of the U.S. Dist. Ct. for the Western Dist. of Mich., 2003—. Chmn. legis. com. East Grand Rapids PTA, 1992—94; bd. dirs., sec. Grand Rapids Sister Cities Internat., 2004—. Fellow: Mich. State Bar Found. (sec. coun. real property sect. 1994-97, chair Uniform Comml. Code com. bus. law sect. 2000—), Am. Coll. Bankruptcy; mem.: ABA (chmn. workouts, bankruptcy and foreclosures 2002—04, vice chair real estate financing group 2004—06, chair real estate financing group 2006—), Fed. Bar Assn. (chmn. bankruptcy sect. We. Mich. chpt. 1992—94, newsletter editor 1998—2002, pres. 2001—02), Am. Law Inst., Am. Bankruptcy Inst., Mich. State Bar Assn., East Hills Athletic Club. Office: Barnes & Thornburg LLP 300 Ottawa Ave NW Ste 500 Grand Rapids MI 49503 Office Phone: 616-742-3936. Business E-Mail: pmears@btlaw.com.

**MEARS, WALTER ROBERT,** journalist; b. Lynn, Mass., Jan. 11, 1935; s. Edward Lewis and Edythe Emily (Campbell) M.; m. Sally Danton, Dec. 28, 1956 (dec. Dec. 1962); children: Pamela (dec.), Walter Robert Jr. (dec.); m. Joyce Marie Lund, Aug. 4, 1963 (div. 1983); children: Stephanie Joy, Susan Marie; m. Carroll Ann Rambo, Mar. 1, 1986 (div. 1995); m. Frances R. Richarson, July 5, 1997. BA, Middlebury Coll., 1956, LittD (hon.), 1977. Newsman AP, Boston, 1956, corr. Montpelier, Vt., 1956-60, state house corr. Boston, 1960-61, newsman Washington, 1961-69, chief polit. writer, 1969-72, asst. chief Washington bur., 1973-74, spl. corr., 1975, chief, 1977-83, v.p., 1978-2001, exec. editor, 1984-88, v.p., columnist, 1989-2001. Author: (with John Chancellor) The News Business, 1983, The New News Business, 1995, Deadlines Past, 2003. Trustee Middlebury Coll., 1980-84. Recipient ann. award AP Mng. Editors Assn., 1973; Pulitzer prize for Nat. Reporting, 1977. Mem.: Gvos. Club, Burning Tree Club, Gridiron Club, Delta Kappa Epsilon, Phi Beta Kappa.

**MEATH, JAMES V.,** lawyer; b. Norfolk, Va., May 26, 1948; BA, Old Dominion U., 1971; MUA, Va. Polytechnic Inst. and State U., 1974; JD, U. Richmond, 1979. Bar: Va. 1979, D.C. 1985. Atty. Williams Mullen, Richmond, Va., vice chmn. bd. dirs., regional head Richmond, Charlottesville, chmn. labor and employment sect. Adj. prof. labor law U. Richmond. Mem. bd. assocs., 1998—, mem. dean's advis. coun., 1997—. Co-editor: Virginia Employment Law Letter, 1990—2002; contbr. articles to profl. jours. Bd. dirs. Richmond Soc. Prevention of Cruelty to Animals. Named Number One Employment Defendant Atty in Va., Chambers USA; named one of Legal Elite, Va. Bus. Mag.; fellow, Coll. Labor and Employment Lawyers. Mem.: ABA (mem. developing labor law com., mem. alternate dispute com.), Am. Arbitration Assn. (large complex case panel arbitrator 1985—), comml. panel arbitrator, employment panel arbitrator), D.C. Bar Assn., Va. Bar Assn. (chmn. labor rels. and employment sect. 1995—97, mem. exec. com. 2002—, chmn., bd. govs. 2003, pres.-elect 2004, pres. 2005—). Office: Williams Mullen Two James Ctr 1021 E Cary St PO Box 1320 Richmond VA 23218-1320 Office Phone: 804-783-6507. E-mail: jmeath@williamsmullen.com.

**MEAT LOAF, (MARVIN LEE ADAY),** popular musician, actor; b. Dallas, Sept. 27, 1951; m. Leslie Aday (Edmonds), 1975 (div. 2001); children: Pearl, Amanda. Co-owner prodn. co. Yellow Dog. Albums include featuring Stoney and Meat Loaf, 1970, Free For All, 1976, Bat Out Of Hell, 1977, DeadRinger, 1982, Midnight at The Lost and Found, 1983, Bad Attitude, 1984, Hits Out Of Hell, 1985, Blind Before I Stop, 1986, Meat Loaf Live, 1987, Bat Out Of Hell II: Back Into Hell, 1993, Welcome to the Neighborhood, 1995, Very Best of Meatloaf, 1998, Couldn't Have Said it Better, 2003, Bat Out of Hell III: The Monster is Loose, 2006; (video) Classic Albums-Meat Loaf: Bat Out of Hell, 1999; appeared in (plays) Hair, The RockyHorror Show, National Lampoon Show, More Than You Deserve, Rockabye Hamlet, Billy The Kid & Jean Harlow, As You Like It, Othello; (films) The Rocky Horror Picture Show, 1975, Americathon, 1979, Scavenger Hunt, 1979, Roadie, 1980, Dead Ringer, 1981, The Squeeze, 1986, Out of Bounds, 1986, Motorama, 1990, Gun & Betty Lou's Handbag, 1991, Wayne's World, 1992, Leap of Faith, 1992, Spice World, 1997, Gunshy, 1998, Black Dog, 1998, The Mighty, 1998, Outside Ozona, 1998, Crazy in Alabama, 1999, Fight Club, 1999, The Diary of the Hurdy Gurdy Man, 1999, Blacktop, 2000, Polish Spaghetti, 2000, Rustin, 2001, Focus, 2001, The Salton Sea, 2002, Wishcraft, 2002, Learning Curves, 2003, Extreme Dating, 2004, A Hole in One, 2004, The Pleasure Drivers, 2005, Chasing Ghosts, 2005, Crazylove, 2005, BloodRayne, 2005; (TV films) To Catch a Yeti, 1995, Everything That Rises, 1998, Trapped, 2001, The Ballad of Lucy Whipple, 2001; (TV series) The Equalizer, Tales from the Crypt, The Late Show, Ice TV, The Outer Limits, 2 Newsnight, Nash Bridges, Dead Man's Gun, Behind the Music, (voice) South Park, Never

Mind the Buzzcocks, Have I Got News for You, American Idol, 2006. Received Grammy for Best Rock Vocal Solo Performance, 1993. Office: c/o MCA Records 70 Universal Terrace Pkwy North Hollywood CA 91608-1001*

**MEAUX, ALAN DOUGLAS,** retired computer technician, artist; b. Joliet, Ill., Sept. 10, 1951; s. Berry Lee and Luella Ann (Ferguson) M.; m. Letta Sue Nygaard, Sept. 15, 1984; children: Ashley Nicole, Lacey Marie. Student, Joliet Jr. Coll., 1969-71, Bradley U., 1971-72, U.S. Dept. Agr. Grad. Sch., 1972, Skagit Valley Coll., 1983-85. Cert. specialist water distbn. Wash. state, 2002, Wash. state, 2003. Photographer J.J.C. Blazer, Joliet Herald News, Joliet, 1969-71; auto mechanic Pohanka Olds and Fiat, Hillcrest Heights, Md., 1972-74; Hoffman Olds and Rolls Royce, Hartford, Conn., 1974-75; carpenter Klappenbach Constrn. Co., Moscow, Idaho, 1975-79; property mgr. Olympic Builders, Oak Harbor, Wash., 1979-86; maintenance technician Troubleshooters Inc., Oak Harbor, 1986-87; facilities technician Island County Govt., Coupeville, Wash., 1987—. Chmn. safety com. Island County Govt., 1997, 98, 99, 2000, 03; bronze sculptor Ronin Art Prodns., Oak Harbor, 1979—; appraiser class A Mid-Am. Appraisers Assn., Springfield, Mo., 1986—; bd. dirs. North West Token Kai, U. Wash., Seattle, 1989—; lectr., 1985; contbr. Nanka Token Kai, L.A., 1985-. Author: Japanese Samurai Weapons, 1989; prin. works exhibited at Mini Guild Children's Orthopedic Show, Ballard, Wash., 1986, Worldfest/Ethnic Heritage Coun., Seattle, 1988, 89, 90, Stanwood (Wash.) Invitational Art Show, 1988. Asst. coach Whidbey Islanders Soccer League, 1997-99; safety com. Island County Govt., 1998-2003. Mem. NRA (life), Law Enforcement Alliance Am. (life), Japanese Sword Soc. U.S. (life), N.W. Token Kai (charter, bd. dirs. 1989-91), Western Mus. Conf., Wash. Mus. Assn., Ethnic Heritage Coun., Nanka Token Kai, Japan Soc., Wash. Arms Collectors Assn., North Whidbey Sportmen's Assn. (chmn. range com., trustee), Leisure Acres Water Assn. (pres. 1998-2000), Internat. Defensive Pistol Assn., Ctrl. Whidbey Sportsmen's Club, Whidbey Islanders Futbol Club (asst. coach for girls under 12, 1997-99). Avocations: hunting, fishing, woodworking, reading, collecting Japanese antiques. Office: Ronin Art Prodns 1287 E Hideaway Ln Oak Harbor WA 98277

**MEBANE, JULIE S.,** lawyer; b. San Antonio, Mar. 13, 1957; d. John Cummins and Mildred (Hill) Mebane; m. Kenneth Jerome Stipanov, Jan. 21, 1984; children: Thomas Kenneth Stipanov, Kristen Hill Stipanov. BA in Polit. Sci., UCLA, 1978, JD, 1981. Bar: Calif. 1981, U.S. Dist. Ct. (so. dist.) Calif. 1981. Assoc. Gray, Cary, Ames & Frye, San Diego, 1981-85, Sheppard, Mullin, Richter & Hampton, San Diego, 1986-90; ptnr. Scalone, Stipanov, Yaffa & Mebane, San Diego, 1990-94, Stipanov & Mebane, San Diego, 1994—2004, Duane Morris LLP, San Diego, 2005—. Panelist Calif. Continuing Edn. Bar, 2000—01. Bd. dirs. Episcopal Diocese San Diego, 1992—95, Francis Parker Sch., 2003—. Mem.: San Diego Lawyers Club, San Diego County Bar Assn., ABA, Nat. Assn. Women Bus. Owners (bd. dirs. San Diego chpt. 1996—97), UCLA Alumni Assn. (gen. counsel, bd. dirs. 1992—96), Phi Beta Kappa, Kappa Alpha Theta. Avocations: sports, travel. Office: Duane Morris LLP 101 W Broadway Ste 900 San Diego CA 92101-3544 Office Phone: 619-744-2211. E-mail: jmebane@duanemorris.com.

**MEBANE, WILLIAM BLACK,** controller, financial consultant; b. Vernon, Tex., Dec. 15, 1927; s. David Mitchell and Ida Virginia (Black) M.; m. Joan Hebbard Dumper, Nov. 24, 1956; children— David Alexander, Virginia Ann. BBA, Tex. A&M U., 1952; MBA, Harvard U., 1954. Mem. treas.'s office staff Gen. Motors Corp., N.Y.C., 1954-70; sec.-treas. Alfred P. Sloan Found., N.Y.C., 1971-78; dir. fin. and adminstrn. Am. Diabetes Assn., N.Y.C., 1979-80, dir. planning, 1981; v.p., comptroller NCCJ, Inc., N.Y.C., 1981-86, v.p. for fiscal affairs, 1987-88; fin. cons. Internat. House, N.Y.C., 1989-90; ind. fin. cons., 1990-91; contr. Better Bus. Bur., N.Y.C., 1999. Vol. Essex Council Boy Scouts Am., 1967—. Served with USAAF, 1946-49. Recipient Silver Beaver award Boy Scouts Am., 1982 Mem.: Harvard Bus. Sch. (N.Y.C.); Short Hills (N.J.). Republican. Episcopalian. Home: 36 Haddonfield Rd Short Hills NJ 07078-3402

**MECCIA, FRANCIS (FRANK) ANTHONY,** physician assistant; s. Aniello J. and Marie Celeste Meccia. AA, Kendall Coll., 1976; BS, Columbus Univ., 1998; MS, Trinity So. U., 2000; cert. physician asst., Cook County Hosp., 1989. Cert. advance cardiac life support. Enlisted U.S. Army, 1976, advanced through ranks to staff sgt., 1985, sr. med. aidmen Spangdahlem, Germany, 1976-80, sr. med. advisor Hdqrs. 2d Inf. White House Washington, 1980-83, med. recruiter Ft. Sheridan, Ill., 1983-87, ret., 1987; physician asst. Montefiore Med. Ctr., Bronx, NY, 1989-91; cardiovasc. physician asst. Murphy Otto and Assocs., Evanston, Ill., 1991-98; sr. physician asst. for cardiovasc. svcs. Resurrection Hosp., Chgo., 1998—; staff physician asst. Our Lady of the Resurrection Med. Ctr., Chgo., 2001—; staff physician asst. for cardiovasc. surgery St. Francis Hosp., Evanston, Ill., 2001—. Preceptor U. Health Scis., Chgo. Med. Sch., North Chgo., 1993-94, Cook County Hosp. Physician Asst. Program, Chgo., preceptor 1993—; bd. trustees Alexian Bros. Bonaventure Ho., Chgo., 2005—. Decorated Meritorious Svc. medal USAR Washington, 1992, Army Commendation medal with oak leaf cluster, 1997; recipient The David award Allied Health Pers., Chgo., 1993. Mem. Am. Assn. Physician Assts. (cert., editor/treas. AAPA caucus GLPA 2003—), Am. Assn. Physician Assts. Surgery, Am. Heart Assn. (cert. advance trauma life support), Assn. Physician Assts. Cardiovasc. Surgery, Ill. Acad. Physician Assts. Avocations: scuba diving, sky diving, skiing. Home: 6219 W Cornelia Ave Chicago IL 60634-4120 Office: Resurrection Hosp 7435 W Talcott Ave Ste 1 Chicago IL 60631-3746 Office Phone: 773-792-7942. E-mail: frank1906@aol.com.

**MECH, TERRENCE FRANCIS,** library director; b. Birdorup Park, Wiltshire, Eng., Feb. 24, 1953; s. Emil Paul and Madelyn Mech. BS, U. Wis., Stevens Point, 1975; MS, Ill. State U., 1978; MLS, Clarion U., 1979; EdD, Pa. State U., 1994. Pub. svcs. libr. Tusculum Coll., Greensville, Tenn., 1979-80; libr. dir. Coll. of the Ozarks, Clarksville, Ark., 1980-82, King's Coll., Wilkes-Barre, Pa., 1982—, dir. libr., 1982—, v.p. for info. and instrnl. techs., 1994—2001. Bd. dirs. Northeastern Pa. Bibliographic Ctr., 1982—; mem., officer Coun. Pa. Libr. Networks, 1984-89, chair, 1987-89. Contbr. chpts. to books and articles to profl. jours. Mem. ALA, Pa. Libr. Assn. (bd. dirs. 1986-87, various coms. 1985—). Office: Kings Coll 133 N River St Wilkes Barre PA 18711-0801

**MECHAM, GLENN JEFFERSON,** lawyer, mayor; b. Logan, Utah, Dec. 11, 1935; s. Everett H. and Lillie (Dunford) M.; m. Mae Parson, June 5, 1957; children: Jeff B., Scott R., Marcia, Suzanne. BS, Utah State U., 1957; JD, U. Utah, 1961; grad., Air Command and Staff Coll., 1984, Air War Coll., 1984. Bar: Utah 1961, Supreme Ct. U.S., U.S. Ct. Appeals (10th cir.), U.S. Dist. Ct. Utah, U.S. Ct. Claims. Gen. practice law, 1961-65; atty. Duchesne County, Utah, 1962, City of Duchesne, 1962; city judge Roy City, Utah, 1963-66; judge City of Ogden, Utah, 1966-69, mayor, 1992-2000. Lectr. law and govt. Stevens-Henager Coll., Ogden, 1963-75; asst. U.S. atty., 1969-72; ptnr. Mecham & Richards, Ogden, Utah, 1972-82; pres. Penn Mountain Mining Co., South Pacific Internat. Bank, Ltd.; mem. Bur. Justice Stats. Adv. Bd., U.S. Dept. Justice, U.S. Conf. Mayors; chmn. Marina Capital Inc. Chmn. Ogden City Housing Authority; chmn. bd. trustees Utah State U., Space Dynamics Lab; mem. adv. coun. Fed. Home Loan Bank; pres. Utah League Cities and Towns, 1981—82; vice chmn. Wasatch Front Reg. Coun. Col. USAF, 1957; No. Utah liaison U.S. Sen. Robert F. Bennett. Recipient Disting. Svcs. award, Utah State U., Weber State U. Mem ABA, Weber County Bar Assn. (pres. 1966-68), Utah Bar Assn., Am. Judicature Soc., Weber County Bar Legal Svcs. (chmn. bd. trustees 1966-69), Utah Assn. Mcpl. Judges (sec.), Ogden-Weber C. of C. (Order of the Big Hat), Sigma Chi, Phi Alpha Delta. Home: 1715 Darling St Ogden UT 84403-0556 Office Phone: 801-725-6666.

**MECHAM, STEVEN RAY,** school system administrator; b. Salt Lake City, Oct. 10, 1938; s. Milton Claudius and Marjorie (White) M.; m. Donna Jean Johnson, Jan. 22, 1943; children: Brian Paul, Allan LeRoy. AS, Weber State Coll., 1958; BS, U. Utah, 1963; MA, Tchrs. Coll., Columbia U. 1965; postgrad., McGill U.; PhD, U. Calif., Santa Barbara, 1981. Prin. Montreal Oral Sch., 1966-70; state dir. hearing impaired Conn. Dept. Edn., 1970-71;

dir. guidance Lexington Sch. for Deaf, N.Y.C., 1971-72; supt. Exton Elem., Ana Frank Jr. and sr. H.S., Mexico City, 1972-77; coord. spl. edn. Weber Sch. Dist., Ogden, Utah, 1977-78; prin. Roosevelt Elem. Sch., Ogden, 1978-82; asst. supt. Weber County Schs., Ogden, 1982-87; assoc. supt. Utah Schs., 1990-93; supt. Weber Sch. Dist., 1993-98, dir. Odyssey Sch., 1998—2003. Instr. U. Utah, 1965-66, St. Joseph Coll., Hartford, Conn., 1970-71; pres. Finnish Mission-LDS Russia and Baltic States, 1987-90; adj. prof. McGill U.; instr. Tchrs. Coll., Columbia U., 1968-70; acting chmn. dept. edn. U. Americas, Mexico City, 1976-77; cons. Far West Labs., San Francisco. Contbr. articles to profl. jours. Bd. dirs. Instituto Mexicano Norte Americano de Relaciones Culturales, Mexico City, 1975-76; bishop, stake pres. Ch. Jesus Christ of Latter-day Saints, pres. Finnish Mission; bd. dirs. Am. Cancer Soc. Weber County. Mem. Am. Orgn. Educators Hearing Impaired (pres.), Can. Hearing Soc. (dir.), Utah Assn. Elem. Sch. Prins., Nat. Assn. Elem. Sch. Prins., Internat. Reading Assn., Am. Assn. Sch. Adminstrs., Utah Supt. Assoc., Alexander Graham Bell Assn., PTA, Rotary.

**MECHANIC, DAVID,** social sciences educator; b. NYC, Feb. 21, 1936; s. Louis and Tillie (Penn) Mechanic; m. Kathleen Mars Wiltshire; children: Robert Edmund, Michael Alexander. BA, CCNY, 1956; MA, Stanford U., 1957, PhD, 1959. Faculty U. Wis., Madison, 1960—79, prof. sociology, 1965—73, John Bascom prof., 1973—79; dir. U. Wis. (Center for Med. Sociology and Health Services Research), 1971—79, chmn. dept. sociology, 1968—70; prof. social work and sociology Rutgers U., New Brunswick, NJ, 1979—, acting dean faculty arts and scis., 1980—81, Univ. prof., dean faculty arts and scis., 1981—84, Univ. prof. and Rene Dubos prof. behavioral scis., 1984—, dir. Inst. for Health, Health Care Policy and Aging Research, 1985—. Commn. on med. edn. Robert Wood Johnson Found., 1990—92, nat. dir. investigators awards in health policy rsch. program, 2000—, tech. adv. com. scholars in health policy rsch. program, 2001—, nat. adv. com. scholars in health policy rsch. program, 2002—; panelist on health svcs. rsch. Pres.'s Sci. Adv. Com., 1971—72; treatment com. on reduction of cancer mortality Nat. Cancer Inst., 1984; vice-chmn. com. pain, disability and chronic illness behavior Inst. Medicine-NAS, 1985—86, panel on prevention of disability, 1989—90, panel on new data for an aging world, 1999—2000; com. on capitalizing on social sci. and behavioral rsch. to improve the pubs. health Inst. Medicine, 1999; mem. Nat. Adv. Coun. Aging, NIH, 1982—86, Com. on Prevention of Mental Disorder, 1992—94; coord. panel Pres.'s Commn. Mental Health, 1977—78; expert adv. panel on mental health WHO, 1984—89; health adv. bd. GAO, 1987—95; panel on tech., ins. and health care sys. Office of Tech. U.S. Congress, 1992—95; nat. com. on vital and health stats. HHS, 1988—92; commn. on behavioral and social scis. and edn. NRC, 1992—95; adv. com. Picker/Commonwealth Scholars Program, 1992—99; panel on rethinking disability policy Nat. Acad. Social Ins., 1993—96; vis. scholar Kings Fund Inst., London, 1995; professionalism adv. com. Am. Bd. Internal Med. Found., 2002—05; bd. dirs. Acad. Health. Author: Students Under Stress, 1962, Students Under Stress, 2d edit., 1978, Medical Sociology, 1968, Medical Sociology, rev. edit., 1978, Mental Health and Social Policy, 1969, Mental Health and Social Policy, rev. edit., 1980, 1989, 1999, Public Expectations and Health Care, 1972, Politics, Medicine and Social Science, 1974; author: (with Charles E. Lewis and Rashi Fein) A Right to Health, 1976; author: Growth of Bureaucratic Medicine, 1976, Future Problems in Health Care, 1979, From Advocacy to Allocation: The Evolving American Health Care System, 1986, Painful Choices: Research and Essays on Health Care, 1989, Inescapable Decisions: The Imperatives of Health Reform, 1994, The Truth About Health Care: Why Reform is Not Working in America, 2006; author, editor: Symptoms, Illness Behavior and Help-Seeking, 1982; editor: Handbook of Health, Health Care and the Health Professions, 1983, Improving Mental Health Services: What the Social Sciences Can Tell us, 1987, General Hospital Impatient Psychiatry, 1997, Managed Behavioral Health Care: Current Realities and Future Potential, 1998; co-editor (with Robert Hauser, Archibald Haller and Tess Hauser): Social Structure and Personality, 1982; co-editor: (with Linda Aiken) Applications of Social Science to Clinical Medicine and Social Policy, 1986; co-editor: Paying for Services: Promises and Pitfalls of Capitation, 1989; co-editor: (with Marian Osterweis and Arthur Kleinman) Pain and Disability: Clinical Behavior and Public Policy Perspectives, 1987; co-editor: (with Carl Taube and Ann Hohmann) The Future of Mental Health Services Research, 1989; co-editor: (with Lynn Rogut, David Colby, and James Knickman) Policy Challenges in Modern Health Care, 2005. Recipient Ward medal, CCNY, 1956, Carl Taube award, APHA, 1990, Remc Lapouse award, 2003, Disting. Investigator award, Assn. for Health Svcs. Rsch., 1991, Disting. Contbn. award mental health sect., Soc. for Study of Social Problems, 1991, Emily Mumford medal, Columbia U., 1991, Investigator award in health policy rsch., Robert Wood Johnson Found., 1995—99, Health Svcs. Rsch. prize, Assn. of U. Programs in Health Adminstrn. and the Baxter Allegiance Found., 1997, Senator Frank R. Lautenberg Ann. award, Sch. Pub. Health, U. Medicine and Dentistry NJ, 2003, Benjamin Rush award, Am. Psychiat. Assn., 2004, First Matilde Riley award and lectr., NIH, 2006; fellow Ford Behavioral Sci. fellow, 1956—57, NIMH rsch. fellow, 1965—66, Ctr. for Advanced Study in Behavioral Scis., 1974—75, Guggenheim fellow, 1977—78, Disting. fellow, Assn. Health Svcs. Rsch., 1996. Fellow: AAAS (chmn. sect. social, econ. and polit. scis. 1985), Assn. Health Svcs. Rsch. (disting. 1996); mem.: NAS, Nat. Acad. Sciences, Hogg Found. Mental Health (nat. adv. coun. 1987), Nat. Acad. Social Ins. (founding), Am. Acad. Arts and Scis., Inst. Medicine-NAS (governing coun. 1972—74), Sociol. Rsch. Assn. (pres. 1991—92), Am. Sociol. Assn. (chmn. med. sociol. sect. 1969—70, governing coun. 1977—78, chmn. publs. com. 1989—91, chmn. mental health sect. 1992—93, Disting. Med. Sociologist award 1983, Lifetime Achievement award mental health sect. 1994, Disting. Career award 2001, Disting. Career award for Practice of Sociology 2004), Phi Beta Kappa. Office: Rutgers U Inst Health Policy Aging Rsch 30 College Ave New Brunswick NJ 08901-1283 Home: 5 Overbrook Dr Princeton NJ 08540-3924 Business E-Mail: mechanic@rci.rutgers.edu.

**MECHEM, CHARLES STANLEY, JR.,** retired broadcast executive; b. Nelsonville, Ohio, Sept. 12, 1930; s. Charles Stanley and Helen (Hall) Mechem; m. Marilyn Brown, Aug. 31, 1952; children: Melissa, Daniel, Allison. AB, Miami U., Oxford, Ohio, 1952; LLB, Yale U., 1955. Bar: Ohio 1955. Practice in, Cin., 1955—67; ptnr. Taft, Stettinius & Hollister, 1965—67; chmn. bd. Taft Broadcasting Co., Cin., 1967—90; commr. LPGA, Daytona Beach, Fla., 1990—95, commr. emeritus, 1995—; chmn. U.S. Shoe, 1993—95; chmn. Cin. Bell, Inc., 1996—98, Convergys Corp., 1998—2000; cons. Arnold Palmer Enterprises, Cin., 1996—. Bd. dirs. J.M. Smucker Co., Royal Precision, Inc., Messer Constrn., Inc. Capt. JAGC U.S. Army, 1956—59. Mem.: Cin. C. of C. (pres. 1977), Comml. Club. Office: Taft Stettinius & Hollister LLP 425 Walnut St Ste 1800 Cincinnati OH 45202-4122

**MECHENBIER, CATHERINE,** engineering educator; d. Joe and Lorencita Castillo; m. Mark Mechenbier, May 29, 1982; children: Laura, Priscilla. BS, N.Mex State U., Las Cruces, 1977—82; M of Engring., Tex. Tech U., Lubbock, 1990—95. Engr. Mason & Hanger Silas Mason, Amarillo, Tex., 1982—84; instr. Amarillo Coll., 1984—88. Faculty sponsor Amarillo Coll. Engring. Soc., Amarillo, 2005—. mem.: Tex. CC Tchrs. Assn. Office: Amarillo Coll PO Box 447 Amarillo TX 79178 Office Phone: 806-371-5435.

**MECHLOWICZ, DAVID,** purchasing agent; b. NJ; AS in Culinary Arts, Johnson & Wales U., 2002, BS in Food Svc. Mgmt., 2004. Sous chef Christopher's Cafe, Colts Neck, NJ; server Ten Prime Steak & Sushi; intern cook Food Network Kitchens, 2002, freelancer, Food and Beverage Dept., purchasing mgr.; mgr. Restaurant Assoc., NYC, 2004.*

**MECIMORE, CHARLES DOUGLAS,** retired accounting educator; b. Belmont, N.C., Aug. 20, 1934; s. John Edgar and Hattie (Bolick) M.; m. Barbara Jean Chiddie, June 7, 1959; children: Laura Jean, Charles D. Jr., John Amos. BS, Pfeiffer Coll., 1958; MS, U. N.C., 1962; PhD, U. Ala., 1966. CPA, N.C.; CMA. Asst. prof. U. Ala., Tuscaloosa, 1966-67; assoc. prof. U. Ga. Athens, 1967-71; prof. U. N.C., 1971-79; prof. acctg. Sch. Bus. and Econs., U. N.C., Greensboro, 1980-98; ret., 1998. Head dept. U. N.C. Sch. Bus. and

Econs., 1980-89, 96-98. Served with USAF, 1951-55. Univ. scholar, 1963-66; Haskins and Sells fellow, 1962-64; Beyer bronze medal, 1974. Mem. AICPAs, N.C. Assn. CPAs (Outstanding Educator 1985), Inst. Mgmt. Acctg. Home: 430 Marshall View Ct Winston Salem NC 27101-5285 Personal E-mail: MecimoreC@bellsouth.net.

**MECKE, WILLIAM MOYN,** public information officer; b. Detroit, May 7, 1957; s. Theodore Hart McCalla Jr. and Mary Eleanor (Flaherty) M.; m. Katherine E. Bauer. BA, Georgetown U., 1979; MA, Am. U., 1982; postgrad., Oxford U., 1982, U. N.C., 1982-85. Asst. dir. Found. Study Presdl. and Congrl. Terms, Washington, 1979-82; acct. exec Hill and Knowlton, Inc., Chgo., 1985-86; tchr. The Bolles Sch., Jacksonville, Fla., 1986-88, St. Andrew's Sch., Savannah, 1988-91, Joseph Walker Sch., Marietta, Ga., 1991-92; polit. cons. various Democratic candidates, 1992-95; tech. writer Total Sys. Svcs. Inc., Columbus, Ga., 1995; dir. mktg. Habitat for Humanity Internat., Americus, Ga., 1995-2000, media svcs. mgr., 2000-2001; comm. dir. Ga. Regional Transp. Authority, 2001—. Co-author, editor: Presidential and Congressional Term Limitation: The Issue That Stays Alive, 1981. Asst. dir. Found. Study Presd. and Congl. Terms, Washington, 1979-82; mem. Regional Leadership Forum. Mem. Pub. Rels. Soc. Am., Atlanta Press Club. Office: Ga Regional Transp Authority Ste 900 245 Peachtree Ctr Ave NE Atlanta GA 30303 E-mail: wmecke@grta.org.

**MECKEL, PETER TIMOTHY,** arts administrator, educator; b. Yankton, S.D., Nov. 28, 1941; s. Myron Eugene and Cynthia Ann (Turnblom) Meckel; m. Louise Gloria Mudge, Sept. 8, 1962; children: Christina Louise, Christopher Mark; m. Adrienne Dawn Maravich, Dec. 30, 1972; children: Moya Ann, Jon-Peter. Student, Rockford Coll., Occidental Coll. Founder, gen. dir. Hidden Valley Music Seminars, Carmel Valley, Calif., 1963—; dir. Hidden Valley Opera Ensemble, Masters Festival of Chamber Music, Master Class Series. Cons. in field. Mem. Music Educators Nat. Conf. Congregationalist. Office: Hidden Valley Opera Ensemble PO Box 116 Carmel Valley CA 93924-0116 Office Phone: 831-659-3115. E-mail: hvms@aol.com.

**MECKLENBURG, GARY ALAN,** hospital executive; m. Lynn Kraemer; children: John, Sarah. BA, Northwestern U., 1968; MBA, U. Chgo., 1970. Adminstrv. resident Presbyn.-St. Luke's Hosp., Chgo., 1969-70, adminstrv. asst., 1970-71, asst. supt., 1971-76, assoc. supt., 1976-77, U. Wis. Hosps., Madison, 1977-80; adminstr. Stanford U. Hosp. Clinics, Calif.; pres., CEO St Joseph's Hosp., Milw., 1980-85; pres., dir. Franciscan Health Care Inc., Milw., 1985; pres., CEO Northwestern Meml. Hosp., Chgo., 1985—2001, Northwestern Meml. HealthCare, Chgo., 2001—. Preceptor, guest lectr.; mem. adv. bd. Kellogg Sch. Mgmt., Chgo., 1986—; pres., chief exec. officer, dir. Northwestern Healthcare Network, 1990-92. Recipient Todd Scout award Boy Scouts Am., 1998, Chgo. Bus. Hall of Fame award Jr. Achievement, 2000, GSB Disting. Pub. Svc./Pub. Sector Alumnus award U. Chgo., 2000. Mem. Am. Hosp. Assn. (sect. met. hosps., governing coun. 1984-92, chmn. 1991, 2001, trustee 1996-2002, exec. com. 1997-2002, chmn., 2001, mem. regional policy bd., #5 1984, 87-89, 91-93, 95-99, chmn. 1996-99, 2001, mem. ho. dels. 1984, 87-89, 91—, mem. com. on med. edn. 1976-80), Ill. Hosp. Assn. (bd. dirs. 1988-95, chmn. 1994, mem. adv. panel coun. tchg. hosps. 1997—), U. Chgo. Hosp. Adminstrn. Alumni Assn. (pres. 1985-86), Econ. Club Chgo., Comml. Club Chgo. Office: Northwestern Meml Hosp 251 E Huron St Ste 3-708 Chicago IL 60611-2908

**MECKSEPER, JOSEPHINE,** sculptor; b. Lilienthal, Germany, 1964; MFA, Calif. Inst. Arts, Valencia, 1990—92; attended, Hochschule der Kunste, Berlin, 1986—90. One-woman shows include Shine-oder Jedem das Seine, Galerie Reinhard Hauff, Stuttgart, 2001, IG--Metall und die kunstlichen Paradiese des Politischen, 2004, Lustgarten, Borgmann Nathusius Galerie, Cologne, 2002, Josephine Meckseper, Elizabeth Dee Gallery, 2003, %, 2005, The Bulletin Board, White Columns, NY, 2005, exhibitions include Tattoo Collection, Andrea Rosen Gallery, NY, 1992, This Is Your Home, Stuyvesant Town, NY, 1994, Wheel of Fortune, Lombard-Fried Fine Arts, NY, 1995, Mixing Messages: Graphic Design in Contemporary Culture, Cooper-Hewitt, Nat. Design Mus., NY, 1996, Super Freaks: Post Pop and the New Generation, Part 1: Trash, Green Naftali, NY, 1998, In the Public Domain, 2003, American Idyll, 2004, Overflow, D'Amelio Terras, Marianne Boesky Gallery and Anton Kern Gallery, NY, 1999, Flea Market, Gavin Brown's Enterprise, NY, 2000, Wine, Women and Wheels, White Columns, NY, 2001, Girls on Film, Zwirner & Wirth, NY, 2005, Whitney Biennial: Day for Night, Whitney Mus. Am. Art, 2006, This Ain't No Fooling Around, Rubicon Gallery Contemporary Art, Dublin, 2006. Mailing: c/o Elizabeth Dee Gallery 545 West 20th St New York NY 10011*

**MECKSTROTH, WILMA JEAN,** piano educator, accompanist, music company executive; b. Dayton, Ohio, July 5, 1928; d. Edgar B. and Olive M. Andrew; m. Robert C. Meckstroth, Oct. 7, 1950; children: David, John, Carol. MusB, Northwestern U., Ill., 1950. Nat. cert. tchr. music Music Tchrs. Nat. Assn. Organist The Luth. Ch. of Our Savior, Dayton, 1957—2003; pvt. piano tchr. Dayton, 1957—; accompanist The Music Appreciation Choral Club, 1957—; chmn. Dayton Organ Acad., 1980—; adjudicator Nat. Guild Piano Tchrs., Am. Coll. Musicians, Austin, 1980—2006. Mem.: Am. Guild Organists (dean 1981—83), Ohio Music Tchrs. Assn. (chmn. west dist. 1994—96, Piano Tchr. of Yr. 1999), Dayton Music Club (pres. 1987—89), Dayton Piano Tchrs. Study Club (pres. 1978—79), Mu Phi Epsilon (pres. 1958—60, 2000—02). Lutheran. Avocations: cooking, tennis. Home: 2142 E Rahn Rd Kettering OH 45440

**MECONI, HONEY,** musicologist, writer; d. Patrick and Mary Evelyn Meconi; m. Michel Jean-Marie Godts, Mar. 5, 1988; 1 child, Yannick Corentin Godts. BA, Pa. State U., 1974; AM, Harvard U., 1980, PhD, 1986. From asst. to full prof. Rice U., Houston, 1987—2004, dir. Medieval studies, 1998—2004; prof. music U. Rochester, NY, 2004—; prof. musicology Eastman Sch. Music, Rochester, 2004—. mem. Harvard Grad. Soc. Coun., Cambridge, Mass., 1994—96; mem. adv. bd. Houston Early Music, 2000—02; bd. dir. The Hildegard Project; conf. dir. Constructing Hildegard: Reception and Identity 1089-1998, 1998; music cons. U.S. Cath. Conf., Washington, 1998—99; bd. dirs. Pegasus Early Music. Author: Pierre de la Rue, 2003; editor: Early Musical Borrowing, 2004 (music edit.) Fortuna Desperata, 2001; contbr. articles to profl. jours. Recipient Arts and Architecture Alumna award, Pa. State U., 2006; fellow, Fulbright, Belgium, 1982—84, Villa I Tatti, Florence, Italy, 1986—87, Andrew W. Mellon, U. Pa., 1990—91, Ctr. for the Study of Cultures/Rice U., 2002—03. Mem.: Coll. Music Soc., Internat. Musicol. Soc., Am. Musicol. Soc. (pres. S.W. chpt. 1999—2001, bd. dirs. 2005—06). Avocation: sewing. Office: Univ Rochester 207 Todd Union Rochester NY 14627-0052 Office Phone: 585-275-9399.

**MEDAGLIA, ELIZABETH ELLEN,** small business owner; b. Boston, Jan. 22, 1970; d. Anthony Joseph Medaglia, Jr. and Catherine Louise (Nardelli) Medaglia. BA in Sociology, Coll. of the Holy Cross, 1991; postgrad., Cornell U., 1995—97; cert. in therapeutic massage and hydrotherapy, Finger Lakes Sch. Massage, 1999; M in Acupuncture, Acad. for Five Element Acupuncture, 2003. Lic. massage therapist N.Y., acupuncturist Mass., diplomate acupuncture (NCCAOM), cert. MT educator Finger Lakes Sch. Massage, 2nd degree Reiki, clean needle technique Council Coll. Acupuncture and Oriental, Pan Gu Shengong instr. Litig. legal asst. Ropes & Gray, Boston, 1991—95; founder, pres. DancingPhoenix LLC, Hingham, Mass., 2003—. Fundraiser, cmty. vol. City Year, Mass., 1992—95; intake test vol. Literacy Vol. Am., Mass., 1994—95; rape crisis counselor, adv. Boston Area Rape Crisis Ctr., 1995. Mem.: Am. Acupuncture Coun., Ctr. for Balance, Newton-Needham C. of C., Theosophical Soc. Boston, Acupuncture and Oriental Medicine Alliance, South Shore C. of C., Better Bus. Bur. Office Phone: 617-869-6371.

**MEDAK, SUSAN LEE,** performing company executive; b. Chgo., Dec. 30, 1953; d. Herman and Vivian Hannah (Fried); m. Gregory Scott Murphy, Aug. 1, 1982. BA cum laude, Lawrence U., 1976. Tour asst. The Guthrie Theater, Mpls., 1974; regional svcs. dir. Milw. Repertory Theatre, 1976-80; dir. audience devel., 1980-83; mng. dir. The People's Light and Theatre Co.,

Malvern, Pa., 1983-84, Northlight Theatre, Evanston, Ill., 1984—, Berkeley Repertory Theatre, 1990—. Sec. League of Resident Theatres, 1988; treas. League of Chgo. Theatres, Chgo., 1987-89. Adv. bd. Evanston Jr. League, 1988—, Cameron Kravit Found. of Evanston Hosp., 1989—. Office: Berkeley Repertory Theatre 2025 Addison St Berkeley CA 94704

**MEDALIE, RICHARD JAMES,** lawyer; b. Duluth, Minn., July 21, 1929; s. William Louis and Mona (Kolad) M.; m. Susan Diane Abrams, June 5, 1960; children: Samuel David, Daniel Alexander. BA summa cum laude, U. Minn., 1952; cert., U. London, 1953; A.M., Harvard U., 1955, JD cum laude, 1958. Bar: DC 1958, NY 1963. Law clk. to Hon. George T. Washington U.S. Ct. Appeals, Washington, 1958-59; asst. solicitor gen. U.S., 1960-62; assoc. Kaye, Scholer, Fierman, Hays & Handler, N.Y.C., 1962-65; dep. dir. Ford Found. Inst. Criminal Law and Procedure, Georgetown U. Law Ctr., 1965-68; ptnr. Friedman & Medalie and predecessors, Washington, 1968-98; pres. Pegasus Internat., Washington, 1970—; exec. dir. The Appleseed Found., Washington, 1993-94, chmn. bd., 1993—2002, chmn. emeritus, 2003—, pres., 1995-98; of counsel Brock Ptnrs. LLC, N.Y.C., 1995—; pvt. practice Washington, 1998—2006, Hull, Mass., 2006—. Adj. prof. adminstrv. and criminal law Georgetown U. Law Center, 1967—70; mem. D.C. Law Revision Commn., 1975—87; chmn. Criminal Law Task Force, exec. com., 1978—82; mem. panel commit. arbitrators Nat. Arbitration Forum, 2004—; vice chmn. Harvard Law Sch. Fund, 1981—84, chmn. nat. maj. gifts, 1984—86, dep. chmn., 1986—87, chmn., 1987—89; v.p., bd. dirs. Trial Lawyers for Pub. Justice, Washington, 1998—. Author: From Escobedo to Miranda: The Anatomy of a Supreme Court Decision, 1966; co-author: Federal Consumer Safety Legislation, 1970; co-author, editor: Commercial Arbitration for the 1990s, 1991; co-author, co-editor American Students Organize: Founding the National Student Association after World War II, 2006; co-editor: Crime: A Community Responds, 1967; staff: Harvard Law Rev., 1956-58; case editor, 1957-58; contbr. articles to legal jours. Bd. dir. alumni assn. Experiment in Internat. Living, Brattleboro, Vt., 1961-64, pres., 1962-63. Fulbright scholar, 1952-53; Ford fellow, 1954-55. Fellow Am. Bar Found., Harvard Law Sch. Assn. D.C. (pres. 1976-77, nat. v.p. 1977-78), Harvard Alumni Assn. (law sch. dir. 1991-95); mem. ABA (program chair 1984, 90, chair legis. subcom. 1986-89, ADR/arbitration com., rep. on adv. com. nat. conf. Emerging ADR Issues in State and Fed. Cts. 1991, vice-chmn. 1991-94, arbitration com. litigation sect., co-chair nat. conf. Critical Issues in Arbitration 1993), Am. Arbitration Assn. (panel comml. arbitrators 1964—), D.C. Unified Bar, Assn. Bar City of N.Y., D.C. Estate Planning Coun., Am. Law Inst. (life, consultative group, model penal code sentencing), Cosmos Club, Harvard Club of Washington, Phi Beta Kappa, Phi Alpha Theta. Office Phone: 202-659-0880. Personal E-mail: rmedalie@att.net.

**MEDAROV, BORIS I.,** pulmonologist, researcher, critical care physician; b. Stara Zagora, Bulgaria, Aug. 7, 1971; m. Aniko Holler. MD, Semmelweis U., Budapest, Hungary, 1997. Cert. paramedic Hungarian Nat. Emergency Svc., 1997, lic. physician Conn., 2004, diplomate Am. Bd. Internal Medicine, Am. Bd. Pulmonary Medicine, Am. Bd. Critical Care Medicine. Resident in internal medicine SUNY, Bklyn., 1999—2002; fellow in pulmonary and critical care medicine L.I. Jewish Med. Ctr., L.I. Campus of Albert Einstein Coll. of Medicine, New Hyde Park, NY, 2002—05. Named Dr. of Yr., Kings County Hosp. Ctr., 2002. Mem.: Am. Thoracic Soc., Am. Coll. Chest Physicians. Achievements include research in circadian variation of lung functions. Office: LI Jewish Med Ctr 270-05 76th Ave New Hyde Park NY 11040 Office Phone: 860-496-9669. Business E-Mail: bmedarov@lij.edu.

**MEDAVOY, MIKE,** film company executive, film producer; b. Shanghai, Jan. 21, 1941; arrived in U.S., 1957, naturalized, 1962; s. Michael and Dora Medavoy; m. Irena Medavoy; children: Nicholas, Brian. BA, UCLA, 1963. With Casting dept. Universal Studios, 1963; agt. Bill Robinson Assos., L.A., 1963—64; v.p. motion picture dept. GAC/CMA Co., 1965—71, IFA Co., 1971—74; sr. v.p. United Artists Corp., 1974—78; one of founders, exec. v.p. Orion Pictures Co., Burbank, Calif., 1978—82; exec. v.p. Orion Pictures Corp. (formerly Orion Pictures Co.), Century City, Calif., 1982—90; chmn. Tri-Star Pictures, Inc., Culver City, Calif., 1990—, Phoenix Picture Corp., 1995—. Jury chmn. Tokyo Film Festival 1994; hon. co-chair St. Petersburg (Russia) Film Festival, 1992; adv. bd. Shanghai Film Conf.; co-chmn. Am. Cinematheque, 1997-2004, chmn. emeritus, 2004—. Author: You're Only as Good as Your Next One, 2002. Co-founder Sundance Film Inst.; bd. govs. Sundance Inst., 1980-86; bd. dirs. Calif. Mus. Sci. and Industry, 1984-87, U. Tel-Aviv., UCLA Found.; commr. L.A. Bd. Parks and Recreation, 2001; exec. adv. bd. Calif. Anti-Terrorism Info. Ctr., 2002; bd. advs. Harvard's Kennedy Sch. Gov., co-chair UCLA Burkle Ctr. Internat. Rels., mem. coun. fgn. rels., 2004. Named to Hollywood Walk of Fame, 2005; recipient Acad. award (mem. of team that green lit), One Flew Over the Cuckoo's Nest, Rocky, Annie Hall, Amadeus, Platoon, Dances with Wolves, Silence of the Lambs, Motion Picture Pioneer award, 1992, Career Achievement award, UCLA Alumni, 1997, Prodrs. award, Cannes Film Festival, 1998, Neil H. Jacoby award, 1999, Fred Zinneman award, Anti-Defamation League, 2001, Film Theater and Prodrs. Guild Am. Vision award, UCLA, 2005. Mem. Acad. Motion Picture Arts and Scis. (gov. 1977-81, Hollywood Walk of Fame Star 2005) Business E-Mail: mmedavoy@phoenixpictures.com.

**MEDBURY, SCOT DANIEL,** botanical garden executive; b. Columbus, Ga., Jan. 28, 1959; s. Paul Randall Medbury and Janet Elaine Stewart; m. Brian K. Lym, Oct. 13, 2003. BA in Internat. Studies, U. Wash., Seattle, 1987, MS in Forest Resources, 1990; studied, U. Calif., Berkeley, 1992—97. Nursery mgr. Nat. Tropical Bot. Garden, Kauai, Hawaii, 1982—83; gardener Crown Estate Commn., Windsor, England, 1985, Pukekura Park, New Plymouth, New Zealand, 1986; edn. assoc. Ctr. for Urban Horticulture, Seattle, 1986—90; curator Honolulu Bot. Gardens, 1990—92; dir. San Francisco Bot. Garden and Conservatory of Flowers, 1999—2005; pres., CEO Bklyn. Botanic Garden, 2005—. Hort. cons. Plant Collections Planning and Mgmt., Berkeley, Calif., 1992—99; bd. dirs. Am. Assn. Botanical Gardens & Arboreta, 2001—04. Author: San Francisco Botanical Garden - A World of Plants, 2005; contbr. articles to profl. jours. Mem.: Internat. Dendrology Soc. (coun. mem. 2001—), Garden Club Am. Office: Bklyn Botanical Garden 1000 Washington Ave Brooklyn NY 11225

**MEDDING, WALTER SHERMAN,** retired environmental engineer; b. St. Louis, Mar. 4, 1922; s. Walter Lyman and Elizabeth Steele (Sherman) M.; m. Mary Agnes Patty Johnson, Apr. 22, 1944; children: Jean, Walter, Mauri. BSCE, Va. Poly. Inst., 1947, MS in Sanitary Engring., 1970. Registered profl. engr., Va., N.C., Kans. Various positions U.S. Army, 1942-64; student officer advanced course The Engr. Sch., Ft. Belvoir, Va., 1952—54, head fixed bridges sect., 1954—55; asst. engr. Asmara Eritrea, chief design br. Mediterranean Divsn., Gulf Dist., Tehran, Iran, 1955-57; asst. divsn. engr. 9th Infantry Divsn., Ft. Carson, Colo., 1957-59; resident engr. USACAG, chief constrn. ops. U.S. Army Engring. Command Europe, Frankfurt, Germany, 1959-72; chief contract adminstrn. U.S. Army Engring. Divsn. Europe, Frankfurt, Germany, 1972-75; chief environ. engring. Office, Chief of Engrs., U.S. Army, Washington, 1975-86; sr. army Ctr. for Pub. Works, Ft. Belvoir, Va., 1997-98; music tchr. Co-author: (textbook) Non-standard Military Fixed Bridges, 1954, (with E. Farago) Which Musical Instrument Shall I Play?, 1985; editor, pub. Letter to Lyman, 1978; contbr. articles to profl. jours. Mem. ASCE, Am. Waterworks Assn., Water Environ. Fedn., Conf. of Fed. Environ. Engrs. Republican. Episcopalian. Achievements include development of mil. bridge classification procedures for load carrying and rapid field design. Home: 204 Brooke Dr Fredericksburg VA 22408-2004 Personal E-mail: wsmedding@aol.com.

**MEDEARIS, MARK A.,** lawyer; BS in Civil Engring. with honors, U. Colo., 1975; MS in Structural Engring., Stanford U., 1978; JD, Stanford Law Sch., 1979. Bar: Calif., Colo. Co-founder Venture Law Group (merged with Heller, Ehrman, White, & McAuliffe LLP), 1993—2003; atty., shareholder Heller, Ehrman, White, & McAuliffe LLP, Silicon Valley, Calif., 2003—. Co-author:

Counseling the Boar on Pre-Bid Defensive Planning, 1991. Office: Heller Ehrman 275 Middlefield Rd Menlo Park CA 94025-3592 Office Phone: 650-233-8307. Office Fax: 650-324-0638. E-mail: markm@vlg.com.

**MEDEARIS, MILLER,** lawyer; b. Liberty, Mo., Jan. 19, 1921; s. Thomas Whittier and Mara (Miller) Medearis; children: Christy Crochet, Kellee Reed. LLB, Cumberland U., 1948; JD, Stamford U., 1950. Bar: Okla. 1948, Calif. 1957. Claims adjustor Transit Casualty Co., LA, 1950-56, atty., trial counsel, 1956-58; ptnr. Hagenbaugh, Murphy & Medearis, LA, 1958-69, Medearis and Grimm, LA, 1969—2004; adminstrv. law judge Calif. Employee Ins. Appeals Bd., Sherman Oaks, 2004—. Sec., bd. dirs. Med. Quality Assurance, Sacramento, 1979—84, v.p., 1984—86; commr. LA Bd. Transp., 1986—92; bd. mem. Calif. Unemployment Ins. Appeals Bd., 2000—04; mem. Dem. Bus. Coun., L.A., 1980; adminstrv. law judge Calif. Unemployment Ins. Appeals Bd., 2004—; bd. dirs. Pico Rivera Cmty. Hosp., 1975—85. With USN, 1945—46. Mem.: ABA, Okla. Bar Assn., Calif. Trial Lawyers Assn., State Bar Calif., Lawyers Club LA. Democrat. Baptist. Avocations: boating, water-skiing, downhill skiing. Home: 2175 Ridge Dr Los Angeles CA 90049-1153 Office: 15303 Venture Blvd Ste 1260 Sherman Oaks CA 91403 Office Phone: 818-461-3468.

**MEDEIROS, JENNIFER LYNN,** school psychologist, consultant; b. New Bedford, Mass., Feb. 5, 1974; d. Antone and Joan Elaine Medeiros. BA in Psychology, Bridgewater State Coll., 1995; MEd, U. Mass., Boston, 2004. Tchr. I.H. Schwartz Children's Rehab. Ctr., New Bedford, Mass., 1995—97; children's intensive support services mgr. TILL, Inc., Dedham, Mass., 1997—2001; therapeutic mentor Family Intervention Network, Wakefield, Mass., 1999—2002; cons. Charles River Assn. for Retarded Citizens, Needham, Mass., 2001—; rsch. assist. Ctr. for Social Devel. and Edn., Boston, 2001—04; sch. psychologist Boston Pub. Schools, 2004—. Student rep. Ctr. for Exceptional Children Divsn. of Rsch., Arlington, Va., 2003—04. Mem.: Coun. for Exceptional Children (student rep.divsn. of rsch. 2003—04), Mass. Assn. of Sch. Psychologists, Nat. Assn. Sch. Psychologists. Home: 90A Dexter Ave Watertown MA 02472 Office: Boston Pub Sch 443 Warren St Dorchester MA 02121 Office Phone: 617-635-9676. Personal E-mail: jen_medeiros@yahoo.com.

**MEDEL, REBECCA ROSALIE,** artist; b. Denver, Mar. 26, 1947; d. Natividad and Josefa (Apodaca) Model. BFA, Ariz. State U., 1970; MFA, UCLA, 1982. Asst. prof. fibers dept. head Tenn. Technol. U., Smithville, 1983-88; lectr. Dept. of Design, UCLA, 1989-91; studio artist, 1991—; prof. Tyler Sch. Art Temple U., 1995—. Lectr. N.C. State U., Raleigh, San Diego State U. SUNY, Purchase, 1992, Penland Sch. Asheville, N.C., Textile Study Group, N.Y.C., Calif. Coll. of Arts & Crafts, Oakland, Calif., San Jose State U., Am. Ctr., Kyoto, Japan, City Ctr., Sapporo, Japan, 1986; vis. artist U. N.D., 1985. One-woman shows include Thirteen Moons Gallery, Santa Fe, 2003, 05, Brown Grotta Gallery, Wilton, Conn., 1996, Neuberger Mus. of Art, Purchase, N.Y., 1992-93, Bellas Artes Gallery, N.Y.C., 1991, N.D. Mus. Art, Grand Forks, 1985, Maya Behn Galerie, Zurich, 1984, UCLA, 1982, Thirteen Moons Gallery, Santa Fe, 2003, 05; group shows include Bellas Artes Gallery, Santa Fe, N.Mex., 1992, N.C. State U. Gallery, 1992, Portland Art Mus., 1995, Madison (Wis.) Art Ctr., 1995, Santa Monica (Calif.) Art Gallery, 1995, Maya Behn Gallerie, 1991, Mus. Van Bommel-Van Dam, Venlo, Netherlands, 1990, Palo Alto Cultural Ctr., 1990, Barbican Ctr. Concourse Gallery, London, 1998, Montclair (N.J.) State U. Gallery, 1998, Art Inst. Chgo., 1999, Yokohama (Japan) Mus. Art, 1999, Biennial 2000, Del. Art Mus., Wilmington, L.A. Mus. Art, 2000, Soc. Contemporary Crafts, Pitts., 2001, Westport Arts Ctr., Conn., 2003, many others. Recipient bronze medal Triennial of Tapestry, 1985; visual artist fellow Nat. Endowment for Arts, 1986, 88, fellow for emerging visual artists Soc. Arts Fedn. NEA, 1985; Pew fellow in the arts, 1999, 2003, fellow Pa. Coun. on Arts, 2001, 03; scholar to Arcosanti, Nat. Endowment for Arts, 1986, 88. Home: 2920 Meyer Ave Glenside PA 19038-1920 Office Phone: 215-782-2728. Business E-Mail: rmedel@temple.edu.

**MEDEPALLI, KAMESH,** engineer, researcher, educator; b. Kakinada, Andhra Pradesh, India, Nov. 17, 1975; s. Srirama Rao and Kalyani Alivelu Manga Medepalli; m. Yeshoda Devi Yedevelly; 1 child, Sruthi Kalyanasai. PhD, Stanford U., Calif., 2006. Tech. staff Bell Labs, Holmdel, NJ, 1998—2003; rsch. scientist Telcordia Technologies, Piscataway, NJ, 2003—06; sr. staff engr. Beceem Comm., Santa Clara, Calif., 2006—. Presenter in field. Contbr. articles to profl. jours., chapters to books. Sec. Dept. Electronics & Comm., Visakhapatnam, Andhra Pradesh, India, 1993—94. Analog Devices scholar, Analog Devices, 1996. Mem.: IEEE. Hindu. Achievements include patents for efficient automatic repeat request method using variable length sequence numbers; patents pending for enhancement of framing protocol frame format to support quality of svc; multiplexing IP datagrams inside an MPLS frame; peak-picking enhanced airlink QoS (PEAQ) scheduler for CDMA2000's 1X-EVDO airlink; a channel state dependent method to enforce minimum and maximum throughputs for QoS differentiation in wireless networks; a technique for reliable point to multipoint wireless comm; load equalizing smart antennas for wireless local area networks; channel partitioning for wireless local area networks; collaborative comm. for wireless local area networks. Avocations: running, music, philosophy. Office: Beceem Comm 3960 Freedom Cir Santa Clara CA Office Phone: 408-387-5060.

**MEDEROS, CAROLINA LUISA,** public policy consultant; b. Rochester, Minn., July 1, 1947; d. Luis O. and Carolina (del Valle) Mederos. BA, Vanderbilt U., 1969; MA, U. Chgo., 1971. Adminstrv. asst. Lt. Gov. of Ill., Chgo., 1972; sr. research assoc. U. Chgo., 1972; project mgr., cons. Urban Dynamics, Inner City Fund and Community Programs Inc., Chgo., 1972-73; legis. asst. to Senate pres. Ill. State Senate, Chgo. and Springfield, 1973-76; program analyst Dept. Transp., Washington, 1976-79, chief, trans. assistance programs div., 1979-81, dir. programs and evaluation, 1981-88, chairwoman, sec.'s safety rev. task force, 1985-88, deputy asst. sec. for safety, 1988-89; cons. Patton Boggs LLP, Washington, 1990—. Recipient award for Meritorious Achievement, Sec. Transp. 1980, Superior Achievement award U.S. Dept. Transp., 1981, Sec.'s Gold Medal award for Outstanding Achievement, 1986, Presdl. Rank award, 1987. Home: 2723 O St NW Washington DC 20007-3128 Office: Patton Boggs LLP 2550 M St NW Washington DC 20037-1350 Office Phone: 202-457-5653. E-mail: cmederos@pattonboggs.com.

**MEDH, JHEEM D.,** medical educator, biochemist, researcher; BS in Chemistry and Biochemistry, U. Bombay, India, 1982; MS in Biochemistry, U. Bombay, 1984; PhD in Biochemistry, U. Tex. Med. Br., Galveston, 1990. Jr. rsch. fellow, dept. physiology L.T.M. Med. Coll., Bombay, 1984-86; rsch. asst., dept. human biol. chemistry and genetics U. Tex. Med. Br., 1986-90; postgrad. rsch. biochemist, dept. medicine U. Calif., San Diego, 1991-93; asst. rsch. scientist, adj. asst. prof., dept. medicine U. Iowa Coll. Medicine, Iowa City, 1993—. Presenter in field of role of LDL receptor-related protein, receptor-associated protein and lipoprotein lipase on the regulation of lipoprotein metabolism. Juvenile Diabetes Internat. Found. fellow 1992-93; recipient nat. grand-in-aid award Am. Heart Assn., 1995-98; recipient Gip Hudson award Nat. Student Rsch. Forum, 1989, Stephen C. Silverthorne award Grad. Sch. Biomed. Scis., U. Tex. Med. Br. Mem. Am. Heart Assn. (coun. for basic science), Am. Soc. Cell Biology, Juvenile Diabetes Found. Internat. Office: U Iowa Coll Med 200 CMAB Iowa City IA 52242

**MEDICUS, HEINRICH ADOLF,** physicist, researcher; b. Zurich, Switzerland, Dec. 24, 1918; came to U.S., 1950; naturalized, 1995; s. Friedrich Georg and Clara Anna (Frey) M.; m. Hildegard Julie Schmelz, June 15, 1961. Diploma, Swiss Fed. Inst. Tech., Zurich, 1943, DSc, 1949. Rsch. assoc. Swiss Fed. Inst. Tech., Zurich, 1943-50; visitor Lawrence Berkeley (Calif.) Lab., 1950-51, MIT, Cambridge, Mass., 1951-52, instr., vis. asst. prof., 1952-55; from assoc. prof. to prof. exptl. nuc. physics and history of modern physics Rensselaer Poly. Inst., Troy, NY, 1955-87, prof. emeritus, 1987—. Vis. scientist Atomic Energy Research Establishment Harwell, Eng., 1967-68, Swiss Inst. Nuclear Research, Villigen, 1974-75. Co-author: Fields and

Particles, 1973; contbr. articles to profl. jours. With Swiss Army, 1937-50. Fellow Swiss Found., 1950-52 Mem. Am. Phys. Soc., Swiss Phys. Soc., Hist. of Sci. Soc., Swiss Am. Hist. Soc., Hudson-Mohawk Swiss Soc. (pres. 1974-2006), Delta Tau Delta (pres. house corp. of Upsilon chpt. 1984-91, faculty adv. 1991-95), Swiss Alpine Club Presbyterian. Avocation: wine education. Home: 1 The Knoll East Acres Troy NY 12180 Office: Rensselaer Poly Inst Dept Physics Troy NY 12180 Business E-Mail: medich@rpi.edu.

**MEDICUS, HILDEGARD JULIE,** retired dentist, orthodontist, educator; b. Frankfurt, Germany, July 25, 1928; came to U.S., 1961, naturalized, 1995; d. Gustav and Elizabeth Berta (Neunhoeffer) Schmelz; m. Heinrich Adolf Medicus, June 15, 1961. DMD, U. Marburg, W. Germany, 1953; orthodontics diploma, U. Düsseldorf, W. Germany, 1957. lic. dentist, N.Y. Postdoctoral fellow dental sch. U. Zürich, Switzerland, 1957; postdoctoral fellow U. Liège, Belgium, 1958, Faculté br. Kansas City, 1959, orthodontic rsch. affiliate, 1963—74; sch. dentist Pub. Sch. Sys., Zürich, 1975—76; dental hygiene instr. Hudson Valley C.C., Troy, NY, 1976—77; pvt. practice Troy, NY, 1977—89. Active Hudson Mohawk Swiss Soc. Mem. AAUW, ADA, European Orthodontic Soc., German Orthodontic Soc. Presbyterian. Achievements include study of functional orthodontic appliances and growth and development. Home: 1 The Knoll Troy NY 12180-7284

**MEDIDI, MURALIDHAR,** computer scientist, educator; s. Venkatswamy Naidu and Suryakantham Medidi; m. Sirisha Ramisetti, Mar. 13, 1986; 1 child, Krishna V. B of Tech. in Electronics & Comm. Engring., J. Nehru Technol. U., 1983; M of Tech. in Computer Engring., Indian Inst. Tech., 1985; PhD in Computer Sci., U. Ctrl. Fla., 1994. Lectr. computer sci. J. Nehru Technol. U., Kakinada, Andhra Pradesh, India, 1986—87; proect engr. ADA, Bangalore, Karnataka, 1987—88; asst. prof. computer sci. & engring. No Ariz. U., Flagstaff, 1994—2000, dept. chmn. computer sci. & engring., 2000—02, assoc. prof. Sch. Elec. Engring & Computer Sci. Wash. State U., Pullman, 2002—. Contbr. articles to profl. jours. Fellow, Indian Inst. Tech., 1984. Mem.: IEEE, Sigma Xi. Office: Wash State U PO Box 642752 Pullman WA 99164-2752 Office Phone: 509-335-2126. Business E-Mail: mmedidi@eecs.wsu.edu.

**MEDIN, A. LOUIS,** computer company executive; b. Balt., Oct. 2, 1925; s. Nathan and Bessie (Zell) Medin; m. Julia A. Levin, Dec. 24, 1950; children: Douglas, David, Thomas, Linda. BSChemE, Johns Hopkins U., 1948; PhDChemE, Ohio State U., 1951. Registered profl. engr., Md. Chem. engr. AEC, Wilmington, Del., 1951-53; rsch. engr. Ford Motor Co., Dearborn, Mich., 1953-55; chief chem. nuclear reactor tech. ALCO Products, Schenectady, 1955-58; head nuclear rsch. engr. U.S. Steel, Monroeville, Pa., 1958-63; project mgr. missile design AVCO Corp., Wilmington, Mass., 1963-65; mgr. sci. applications IBM, Manassas, Va., 1965-72, mgr. advanced applications, 1975-87; exec. dir. Inst. for Simulation and Tng., Orlando, Fla., 1987-2000. Chmn. sci. and engring. tech. divsn. Nat. Def. Indsl. Assn.; dir. environment and life scis. Dept. Def., 1972—74; lectr. in field. Contbr. articles to profl. and tech. jours. Mem. Monroeville Parks and Recreation Commn., 1960; chmn. Monroeville Mental Health Assn., 1961; mem. Monroeville Zoning and Planning Commn., 1961; chmn. sci. and engring. tech. divsn. Nat. Def. Indsl. Assn., 1999—; dep. precinct chmn. Montgomery County Rep. Com., 1982. With USN, 1944—46, PTO. Recipient award, Am. Chem. Soc., 1957. Fellow: Am. Inst. Chemists; mem.: Am. Metall. Soc., Am. Def. Preparedness Assn. (chmn. sci. and engring. tech. divsn. 1981—, ednl. advisor Def. Jour., Am. Def. award 1984, Gold medal 1990), Am. Inst. Chem. Engrs., Nat. Security Indsl. Assn. Office: Simulation and Tng., Johns Hopkins U. Alumni Assn. Home: 11401 Ridge Mist Ter Potomac MD 20854-7002 Office Phone: 301-762-1290. Personal E-mail: lmedin@comcast.net.

**MEDIN, ALICE LOUISE,** librarian; b. Eau Claire, Wis., July 17, 1935; d. Ongle Ever and Esther Moholt; m. Myron James Medin, May 14, 1955; children: John, Kären, Anne. BA in Edn., Ea. Wash. U., 1957; MA in Libr. Sci., U. Wis., Madison, 1977. Libr. asst. U. Wis. Fond du Lac Ctr., 1979; reference libr. Plaza br. Kansas City (Mo.) Pub. Libr., 1984-86, describer old and rare books main libr., 1985; dir. Rogers (Ark.) Pub. Libr., 1987—2000. Mem. N.W. Ark. C.C. Found. Bd., Rogers, 1987—95. Bd. dirs. Bella Vista Pub. Libr., 2002—03. Recipient Intellectual Freedom Fighter award, ALA/Freedom to Read Found., 1999. Mem. AAUW (pres. Fond du Lac br. 1973-75), Ark. Libr. Assn. (mem. intellectual freedom com. 1993-2000), N.W. Ark. Libr. Assn. (v.p. 1988-89), Round Table Lectr. Club (v.p. 1979). Lutheran. Avocations: reading, knitting, theater. Home: 1 Audley Cir Bella Vista AR 72714-5645

**MEDIN, JULIA ADELE,** mathematics professor, researcher; b. Dayton, Ohio, Jan. 16, 1929; d. Caroline (Feinberg) Levitt; m. A. Louis Medin, Dec. 24, 1950; children: Douglas, David, Thomas, Linda. BS in Maths. Edn., Ohio State U., 1951; MA in Higher Edn., George Washington U., 1977; PhD in Counseling and Math. Edn., Am. U., 1985. Cert. tchr., Fla., Md. Rsch. engr. Sun Oil Co., Marcus Hook, Pa., 1951-53; tchr. maths. Montgomery County Pub. Schs., Rockville, Md., 1973-88; asst. prof. maths. U. Ctrl. Fla., Orlando, 1988-90, sr. ednl. technologist Inst. for Simulation and Tng., 1990-99; sr. assoc. Mgmt. and Ednl. Tech. Assocs., 1999—. Adv. steering com. U.S. Dept. Edn. Title II, Washington, 1985-89; sr. math. educator, rschr. Inst. for Simulation and Tng., Orlando, 1988-90; judge, co-chair GII Nat. Awards; co-acad. advisor I/ITSEC Conf.; condr. nationwide rsch. project on effective use of technology in the classroom; spkr. in field Author: Loc. of Cont. and Test Anxiety of Mar. Math. Studies, 1985, Single Sex Public Schools, Who Needs Them and Why, 2005; co-author: Single Sex Public Schools, 2005; contbg. author: Math for 14 & 17 Yr. Olds, 1987; editor: Simulation and Computer-Based Technology for Education; contbr. articles to profl. jours. Dem. committeewoman Town of Monroeville, Pa., 1962; religious sch. dir. Beth Tikva Religious Sch., Rockville, 1971; cons. Monroeville Mental Health, 1960 Mem. Nat. Coun. Tchrs. Math., Math. Assn. Am. (task force on minorities in math.). Women in Math. in Edn., Nat. Coalition for Tech. in Edn. and Tng., Phi Delta Kappa, Kappa Delta Pi. Home and Office: 11401 Ridge Mist Ter Potomac MD 20854-7002 Personal E-mail: jmedin@comcast.net.

**MEDIN, LOWELL ANSGARD,** management executive; b. Shafer Twp., Minn., Aug. 28, 1932; s. Ansgaard Phillip Magnus and Adelaide Marie Christine (Grandstrand) M.; m. Frances Irene Knutson, Sept. 13, 1958; children: Kimberly June, James Lowell. AS in Liberal Arts, U. Minn., 1957, BBA, 1959. Dairy farmer Medin Farm, Franconia Twp., 1951-53; silo builder Lindstrom Silo, 1956-58; employment mgr. John Wood Co., St. Paul, 1959; salesperson Diversey Co., LaCrosse, Wis., 1959-60; rebuyer, inventory mgr. Montgomery Ward, St. Paul, 1960-67, rebuyer, rebuyer mgr. Chgo., 1967-85; with sales dept. J.T. Gen. Store, Palatine, Ill., 1986; rebuying mgr. Sportsmen's Guide, Golden Valley, Minn., 1987; inventory mgr. Donald Bruce and Co., Chgo., 1988-91; supr. Pinkerton Security Ops., 1992-96. Pics coord. Hickory Farms, Itasca, Ill., 1995-98. Author: (with others) Shafer Swamp to Village, 1978, The Pioneers of Chisago County 1838-1870, 1992, The Knutson/Stavenau Family Roots, 1994. Candidate for polit. office, Mpls., 1967; del. Minn. State Dem.-Farm Labor Conv., 1956, 58; chmn. cancer drive Village of Palatine, 1968, mem. dist. 6 adv. coun., 1989-97; mem. Homeowners Coun., Palatine, 1976-77; mem. coun. Christ Luth. Ch., Palatine, 1981-86; officer Chicago County DFL Party, 1956-60; del. Chicago County DFL Conv., 1956, 58; pres. Palonis Park Homeowners Assn., Palatine, 1976-82. Cpl. U.S. Army, 1953-55, ETO. Mem. No. Ill. Civil War Roundtable (chartered officer 1983-86, trustee, sec., 2d v.p.), VFW (life, post 981, Arlington Hts.), Am. Legion (life, post 690, Palatine), Alpha Phi Omega. Republican. Lutheran. Avocations: genealogy, gardening, American history, Civil War. Home: 121 S Linden Ave Palatine IL 60074-6342

**MEDIN, MYRON JAMES, JR.,** city manager; b. Ladysmith, Wis., July 8, 1931; s. Myron James and Mildred Clara (Johnson) M.; m. Alice Louise Moholt, May 14, 1955; children: John, Karen. BA, Ea. Wash. Coll., 1954; MPA, U. Mich., 1959. Adminstrv. asst. to city mgr. City of Fond du Lac, Wis., 1959-64, city mgr., 1967-83, City of New Ulm, Minn., 1964-67; city adminstr. City of Kansas City, Kans., 1983-85; pres., gen. mgr. Bella Vista

Village Property Owners Assn., Ark., 1986-92. Mem. com. human devel. Nat. League of Cities, Washington, 1974-80, com. on govtl. relations, 1971-73; chmn. City Plan Commn., Fond du Lac, Wis., 1967-83 Bd. dirs. United Way, Kansas City, Kans., 1984-85, YMCA, 1984-85, Kansas City C.C. Found., 1984-85; mem. Gov.'s Regionalism Task Force Adv. Com., Madison, Wis., 1968-70; trustee Phillips Pro-Celebrity Golf Tennis Charity Classic, 1991-92; mem. transition task force Bella Vista Incorporation, 2005-06; vol. historic house mus. and gardens. Lt. USAF, 1955-57. Recipient Community Service award Fond du Lac Assn. of Commerce, 1978 Mem. Internat. City Mgmt. Assn., Wis. City Mgmt. Assn. (pres. 1975-76), Wis. League of Municipalities (bd. dirs. 1978-80), Wis. Alliance of Cities (v.p. 1972-73), Am. Soc. Pub. Adminstrn. (bd. dirs. 1984-85, Pub. Adminstr. of Yr. award 1985), Bella Vista-Bentonville C. of C. (bd. dirs. 1987-91), Nat. Trust for Hist. Preservation, Benton County Hist. Soc. Lutheran. Avocations: swimming, reading, tennis, gardening, genealogy. Home: 1 Audley Cir Bella Vista AR 72714-5645

**MEDINA, DAVID,** state supreme court justice; b. Galveston Island, Tex., 1958; BS, Southwest Tex. State U., 1980; JD, S. Tex. Coll. of Law, 1989. Joined Cooper Industries Inc., Houston, 1987—89, litigation counsel, 1989; judge 157th State Dist. Ct., Tex., 1990—99; assoc. gen. counsel Cooper Industries Inc., Houston, 2000—04; gen. counsel Gov. Rick Perry, Tex., 2004—05; justice Tex. Supreme Ct., 2005—. Former adjunct prof. S. Tex. Coll. of Law. Former bd. mem. Habitat for Humanity, Houston Metro; bd. mem. Spring Klein Baseball Assn. Mem.: ABA, Mexican Am. Bar Assn., Assn. for Advancement of Mexican Am., Houston Bar Assn. Office: Tex Supreme Ct PO Box 12248 Austin TX 78711*

**MEDINA, JOSE,** philosopher, educator; b. Sevilla, Spain, Nov. 17, 1968; s. Joaquin Medina and Concepcion Garcia. PhD, Northwestern U., Evanston, Ill., 1998. Asst. prof. Vanderbilt U., Nashville, 1999—2005, assoc. prof., 2005—. Author: Speaking from Elsewhere, Language, The Unity of Wittgenstein's Philosophy; editor: Truth: Engagements Across Philosophical Traditions. Recipient Local Coun. award of Academic Excellence to the Best Curriculum, Ministry Edn. and Culture, Spain, 1992; fellow Cognitive Sci. fellow for Interdisciplinary Rsch., Northwestern U., 1995—96, NEH, 2001; Humanities fellow, Penn Warren Ctr. for the Humanities, 2002—03. Mem.: So. Soc. for Philosophy and Psychology, N.Am. Wittgenstein Soc., Soc. for the Advancement Am. Philosophy, Am. Philos. Assn. (com. on hispanics 2001—04). Office: Vanderbilt University Philosophy Dept 111 Furman Hall Nashville TN 37240 Office Phone: 615-343-0322. Business E-Mail: jose.m.medina@vanderbilt.edu.

**MEDINA, KATHRYN BACH,** book editor; b. Plainfield, NJ; d. F. Earl and Elizabeth E. Bach; 1 child. BA, Smith Coll.; MA, NYU. With Doubleday Pub. Co., Inc., NYC, 1965-85; exec. editl. dir., sr. v.p. Random House, NYC, 1985—. Assoc. fellow Jonathan Edwards Coll., Yale U., New Haven, 1982—; fellow Bunting Inst., 1994—95; cons., 1995—96, Coun. Fgn. Rels. Editor: books by James Atlas, Peter Benchley, Elizabeth Berg, Amy Bloom, Bill Bradley, Tom Brokaw, Anita Brookner, Ethan Canin, Michael Chabon, Robert Coles, Agnes deMille, E.L. Doctorow, Jane Fonda, Max Frankel, Charles Frazier, Henry Louis Gates, Jr., Carol Gilligan, Mary Gordon, David Halberstam, Kathryn Harrison, John Irving, Tracy Kidder, Wynton Marsalis, Bobbie Ann Mason, Jon Meacham, James A. Michener, Sandra Day O'Connor, Jane Pauley, Anna Quindlen, Nancy Reagan, James Reston, William Safire, Maggie Scarf, Gloria Steinem, Christopher Tilghman, Alice Walker, Daniel Yergin.

**MEDINA, SANDRA,** social worker, educator; b. Tulsa, Oct. 4, 1947; d. James and Erleen (Austin) Meeks; m. Michael Sellman, 1966 (div. 1979); children: Rhainnie, Morgan; m. Ernest Medina, Aug. 21, 1985; 1 child, Brendyn. Cert., Community Coll. of Denver, 1975; BS summa cum laude, Met. State Coll., Denver, 1981; MSW, U. Denver, 1983, postgrad. Lic. clin. social worker, Colo. Dir. Lafayette (Colo.) Presch./Playtime, 1973-75, Bennett (Colo.) Non-Denominational Presch., 1975-76; intern. in clin. social work Brighton (Colo.) Schs., 1981-82; adminstrv. social work intern Jefferson County (Colo.) Schs., 1982-83; med. social worker Las Animas County Health Dept., Trinidad, Colo., 1985-85; psychiat. social worker Colo. State Hosp., Pueblo, 1985-89; clin. social worker PsychCare, Greeley, 1990-92; counselor high sch. U. Northern Colo. Lab. Sch. Instr. Trinidad State Jr. Coll., 1984-85; field instr. N.Mex. Highlands U., Las Vegas, 1986-87, U. So. Colo., Pueblo, 1988-89; adj. prof. social work U. Denver, 1996-97; asst. prof. social work, practicum coord. Chadron State Coll., 1997-99. Mem. exec. com. Gov.'s Task Force on Child Abuse, Denver, 1985; bd. dirs. Adams County Rep. Advs. for Children Today, Denver, 1978-79; chairperson membership com. Met. Child Protection Coun., Denver, 1982-83. Mem. NASW. Democrat. Presbyterian. E-mail: bestmedfam@netscape.net.

**MEDLAND, WILLIAM JAMES,** university chancellor; b. Logansport, Ind., Jan. 1, 1944; s. Thomas Gallagher and Mary Elizabeth (Hassett) M.; m. Donna Lee Bahnaman, Mar. 12, 1977; children: Bridget Marie, Mark David, Jeanne Nicole. BA, U. Notre Dame, 1966; student, St. Louis U., 1972-74; MA in History, Ball State U., 1967, MA in Edn., 1979, PhD in History, 1980; postgrad., Inst. for Mgmt. Lifelong Edn., Harvard U., 1985, Ctr. Internat. Cooperation and Security Studies, U. Wis., 1988, Ctr. Internat. Studies, MIT, 1989, Freie Universitat, Berlin, 1991; DHL (hon.), Vitelbo U., 2005. Instr. history and philosophy Donnelly coll., Kansas City, Kans., 1967-70; curricular advisor Ball State U., Muncie, Ind., 1970-71, teaching fellow, 1977-80; asst. dean St. Louis (Mo.) U., 1971-75; employee supr. Wilson, Inc., Logansport, 1975-76; ops. mgr. Watson-Jenkins, Inc., Indpls., 1976-77; dean of coll., asst. prof. history Springfield (Ill.) Coll., 1980-81; acad. dean, assoc. prof. history and edn. Marymount Coll., Salina, Kans., 1981-86, exec. v.p., provost, prof. history St. Mary's U., Winona, Minn., 1986-91; pres., prof. history Viterbo U., LaCrosse, Wis., 1991—2006, also bd. dirs., CEO, 1991—2006, univ. chancellor, 2006—. Edn. cons. Am. Inst. Banking, Springfield, 1980-81; advisor Adv. Com. to Sch. Bd., Salina, 1984, Salina Diocesan Bd. Edn., 1981-83; evaluator North Ctrl. Assn., Chgo., 1987-2000. Author: Cuban Missile Crisis of 1962-Needless or Necessary?, 1988, reprint, 1990, A Guide to Writing College Research Papers, 1989, The Catholic School: A Bibliographical Resource Guide, 1990; editor: Int. Acad. Social Scis. jour., 1979, Perspectives: A Liberal Arts Exchange (faculty jour.), 1988. Coll. solicitor United Way, St. Louis, 1973; coord. Coll./Cmty. Artist Series, Salina, 1981—84; mem. Franciscan-Skemp Healthcare Cmty. Bd., 2002—; adv. Hnong Cultural Ctr., 2005; bd. dirs. Immaculate Heart of Mary Sem., Winona, 1987—91, La Crosse Med. Health Sci. Consortium, 1993—. Wis. Found. for Ind. Colls., 1994—98, Assn. Franciscan Colls. and Univs. 1999—2004; chair La Crosse Diocesan Edn. Commn., 1994—2001; bd. dirs. Mathy Ctr., 2003. Named LaCrosse Tribune Person of the Yr./ Iverson-Freking Ecumenical award, 2003; recipient Nat. Man and Youth award, Boys and Girls Clubs, 2004, Collaboration Achievement award, Ladco, 2004, Svc. award, LaCross C.C., 2004, Disting. Svc. award, Pope John XXIII, 2006, Award for Disting. Svc.; Ctr. Internat. Studies fellow, MIT/Harvard U., 1989. Mem.: KC, Wis. Assn. Ind. Colls. and Univs. (bd. dirs. 1991—), Am. Assn. Ind. Coll. Pres., Coun. Coll. Pres., Am. Assn. Higher Edn., La Crosse C. of C. (bd. dirs. 2000—04, exec. com. 2001—04, Cmty. Svc. award 2004), Rotary, KC, Phi Delta Kappa, Phi Alpha Theta (rsch. award Ball State U. 1979). Roman Catholic. Avocations: reading, research. Home: 119 Calla Ct Onalaska WI 54650-8317 Office: Viterbo Univ Office of Chancellor 900 Viterbo Dr La Crosse WI 54601-4777 Office Phone: 608-796-3000. Business E-Mail: wjmedland@viterbo.edu.

**MEDLER, MARY ANN L.,** federal judge; JD, St. Louis U., 1983. Atty. Thompson Coburn, St. Louis, 1983-85; asst. cir. atty. Office of Cir. Atty. City of St. Louis, 1985-92; atty. Union Pacific R.R., St. Louis, 1992-93; magistrate judge U.S. Dist. Ct. (ea. dist.) Mo., St. Louis. Office: 111 S 10th St Rm 13S Saint Louis MO 63102 Office Phone: 314-244-7490. Business E-Mail: Mary_Ann_Medler@moed.uscourts.gov.

**MEDLEY, ALEX ROY,** executive minister; b. Columbus, Ga., Aug. 4, 1948; s. Howard and Clois Mildred (Chumney) M.; m. Patricia Stauffer, May 10, 1975; children: James Ethan, Christopher Jordan. BA magna cum laude, U. Chattanooga, 1970; cert., Grad. Sch. Ecumenical Studies, Celigny, Switzerland, 1973; MDiv, Princeton Sem., 1974. Ordained to ministry Bapt. Ch., 1975. Assoc. pastor First Bapt. Ch. Trenton, N.J., 1974-77; adminstrv. intern Nat. Ministries Am. Bapt. Chs. U.S.A., Valley Forge, Pa., 1977, nat. dir. Christian ctr., 1978-85; min. of world mission support, area min. Am. Bapt. Chs. N.J., East Orange, 1986-92, exec. min., 1992—2001; gen. sec. Am Bap. Chs. in the USA, 2002—. Intern World Coun. Chs., Geneva, Switzerland, 1973; rep. N.Am. Bapt. Fellowship, Washington, 1975-77; mem. domestic hunger/poverty working group Nat. Coun. Chs. of Christ, 1978-85, mem. gen. assembly; conf. speaker Am. Bapt. Chs., 1979; Am. Bapt. Ch. U.S.A. del. to Nat. Coun. Chs. of Christ. Editor (newsletter) Social Edn. for Action Newsletter, 1978-79. Bd. dirs. Ch. World Svc./CROP, N.J., 1975-77, Occupational Tng. Ctr., Burlington, N.J., 1992-99; sec. Key Inmate Edn. Project, Trenton, 1986; participant Nat. Religious Leadership Program, 1997-99, Bapt. World Alliance Commn. on Freedom and Justice, 2000—. Mem. Am. Bapt. Regional Exec. Mins. Coun. Baptist. Avocations: reading, fishing, hiking. Office: American Baptist Churches PO Box 851 Valley Forge PA 19482

**MEDLEY, DONALD MATTHIAS,** retired education educator; b. Faulkton, S.D., Feb. 18, 1917; s. Thomas Arnot and Cecilia Agnes (Kellen) M.; m. Betty Ann Robertsen, Aug. 23, 1948; 1 child, Timothy Laurence. BS, Coll. of St. Thomas, St. Paul, 1938; MA, U. Minn., 1950, PhD, 1954. Tchr. Am. Sch. Guadalajara, Mex., 1941-42, Floodwood (Minn.) Pub. Schs., 1946-48; instr. English, Coll. of St. Thomas, 1948-50; asst. prof. CUNY, 1954-59, assoc. prof., 1959-64, prof., 1964-65; sr. rsch. psychologist Ednl. Testing Svc., Princeton, N.J., 1965-70; disting. prof. U. Va., Charlottesville, 1970-87, prof. emeritus, 1987—2005, ret., 2005. Mem. exec. bd. Consortium for the Improvement of Tchr. Evaluation, Atlanta, 1985-87. Author: (with others) Measurement-Based Evaluation of Teacher Performance, 1984, Handbook of Research on Teaching, 1963, The Teacher's Handbook, 1971, Research on Teaching, Concepts, Findings, and Implications, 1979, Ency. of Educational Research, 5th edit., 1982, 6th edit., 1992, Developing Skills for Instructional Supervision, 1984, Measurement-Based Evaluation of Teacher Performance, 1984, Advances in Teacher Education, 1984, International Ency. of Education: Research and Studies, 1984, 2d edit., 1994, Assessment of Teaching: Purposes, Practices, and Implications for the Profession, 1999; contbr. articles to profl. jours. Staff Sgt. U.S. Army, 1942-46. Fellow APA; mem. Am. Ednl. Rsch. Assn. (divsn. sec. 1962), Nat. Coun. on Measurement in Edn., Assn. Tchr. Educators. Independent. Roman Catholic. Avocation: travel. E-mail: dm4c@aol.com.

**MEDLIN, JOHN GRIMES, JR.,** banker, director; b. Benson, N.C., Nov. 23, 1933; s. John Grimes and Mabel (Stephenson) M. BS in Bus. Adminstrn., U. N.C., 1956; grad., The Exec. Program, U. Va., 1965. With Wachovia Bank & Trust Co., Winston-Salem, NC, 1959—98, pres., 1974; pres., CEO Wachovia Bank and Wachovia Corp., Winston-Salem, NC, 1977-93; chmn. bd. Wachovia Corp., Winston-Salem, NC, 1987-98, chmn. emeritus, 1998—. Trustee Nat. Humanities Ctr., Wake Forest U., The Duke Endowment, The Rsch. Triangle Found., Kenan Inst. for Ethics; mem. State Jud. Coun. N.C., 2000—; active numerous civic and svc. orgns. With USNR, 1956-59. Mem. Phi Delta Theta. Office: Wachovia Corp 100 N Main St Winston Salem NC 27101 Office Phone: 336-732-5000.

**MEDLOCK, DONALD LARSON,** lawyer; b. Port Chester, NY, Mar. 8, 1927; s. Harold and Emma Adelaide (MacLennan) Medlock; m. Katharine Smedes Nicholson, May 21, 1955; children: Katharine Baird, Margaret MacLennan, William Nicholson. BA with honors, Yale U., 1947, LLB, 1950. Bar: N.Y. 1950, U.S. Dist. Ct. (so. dist.) N.Y. 1951, U.S. Ct. Appeals (2d cir.) 1951, U.S. Dist. Ct. (ea. dist.) N.Y. 1952, U.S. Tax Ct. 1952, U.S. Ct. Custom and Patent Appeals. Assoc. Winthrop, Stimson, Putnam & Roberts, N.Y.C., 1950-56, ptnr., 1957-94, sr. counsel, 1995—. Bd. dirs. Bancard Sys. N.Y. Inc. Editor: Yale Law Jour., 1948—50; former dir. Fin. Times Publs., Economist Newspaper Group. Bd. dirs. Yale Alumni Fund, 1955—, chmn., 1984—86, mem. exec. com., 1980—88; bd. dirs. Port Washington Estates Assn., 1958—61; sec., bd. dirs. Port Washington Cmty. Chest, 1959—61; bd. mgrs., mem. exec. com. William Sloane Ho. YMCA Greater N.Y., 1979—84; chmn. Yale Law Sch. Fund, 1974—76; mem. exec. com. Assn. Families U. Denver, 1982—84; mem. ann. fund parents com. Taft Sch., 1979—81; chmn. univ. coun. com. Law Sch. Yale U., 1979—86; mem. devel. bd. Yale U., 1984—88, mem. exec. com., 1984—86, Yale Law Sch., 1975—79, hon., 1979—. Recipient citation, Yale Law Sch., 1977, Yale Alumni Fund Chmn.'s award, 1979, 1987, Yale medal, 1994. Mem.: Assn. Bar City of N.Y. (mem. com. profl. ethics 1958—61), Fed. Power Bar Assn., India House, Corbey Ct. Yale Law Sch., Assn. Yale Alumni (rep.-at-large 1979—82, mem. com. undergraduate admissions 1979—82, mem. com. Yale medal 1981, bd. dirs. 1984—86), Mory's Assn., Yale Club N.Y.C., Manhasset Bay Yacht Club, Tuscarora Club (Margaretville, N.Y.) (bd. dirs. 1963—95, sec. 1970—86, v.p. 1984—86), Country Club Landfall, Scroll and Key Soc., Phi Beta Kappa, Phi Delta Phi. Avocations: trout fishing, tennis, reading, crossword puzzles, golf. Home: Landfall 800 Oyster Landing Wilmington NC 28405-5292

**MEDNICK, ROBERT,** accountant; b. Chgo., Apr. 1, 1940; s. Harry and Nettie (Brenner) Mednick; m. Susan Lee Levinson, Oct. 28, 1962; children: Michael Jon, Julie Eden, Adam Charles. BSBA, Roosevelt U., 1962. CPA Ill. Staff asst. Arthur Andersen, Chgo., 1962-63, sr. acct., 1963-66, mgr., 1966-71, ptnr., 1971-98, mng. dir. SEC policies, 1973-76, mng. dir. auditing procedures, 1976-79. Vice chmn. com. on profl. stds. Andersen Worldwide, 1979-82, chmn., 1982-98, mng. ptnr. profl. and regulatory matters, 1993-98; mem. faculty Northwestern U. Kellogg Grad. Sch. Mgmt., 1999; mem. panel disting. neutrals in banking, acctg. and fin., even. Internat. Inst. for Conflict Prevention and Resolution, 2003—. Contbr. articles to profl. jours. Bd. dirs. Roosevelt U., Chgo., 1977—, vice chmn., 1986-94, sr. vice chmn., 1994—, life trustee, 1999—; bd. dirs. Auditorium Theatre Coun., 1990-96, Lake Shore Drive Synagogue, 1992—; co-chmn. adv. coun. Chgo. Action for Soviet Jewry, Highland Park, Ill., 1983-87; bd. dirs., chmn. House for Soviet Jewry, 1992—; Internat. Fedn. Accts., 1998—; chmn. compliance adv. panel 2003—). Jewish. Avocations: collecting art, travel. Office Phone: 312-642-0571. E-mail: bobmednick@aol.com.

**MEDNICK, SHELDON IRA,** pharmacist; b. Balt., Apr. 8, 1955; s. Sol Abraham and Doris Asbell Mednick. BSc in Pharmacy, Phila. Coll. Pharmacy, 1979. Registered pharmacist Pa., NJ, Md. Pharmacy intern Cooper U. Hosp., Camden, NJ, 1979—80; staff pharmacist Trenton Psychiat. Hosp., NJ, 1981—86, Phila. Geriatric Ctr., 1986—95. Neighborcare Pharmacy, King of Prussia, Pa., 1997—2001, Girard Med. Ctr., Phila., 2001—. Mem.: Masons (sr. deacon Burlington lodge 1984—85). Jewish. Avocations: reading, music, travel. Home: 2801 Wingate Ct Edgewater Park NJ 08010

**MEDOFF, MARK HOWARD,** playwright, scriptwriter; b. Mt. Carmel, Ill., Mar. 18, 1940; s. Lawrence Ray and Thelma Irene (Butt) M.; m. Stephanie Thorne, June 24, 1972; children: Debra, Rachel, Jessica. BA, U. Miami, 1962;

MA, Stanford U., 1966; DHL, Gallaudet Coll. 1981. Instr. English and drama N.Mex. State U., 1966-79, dramatist-in-residence, 1974—, head dept. drama, 1978-87, prof. drama, 1979-93, artistic dir., 1982-87, Am. S.W. Theatre Co., 1984-87. Artistic dir. Creative Media Inst. N.Mex. State U., 2006. Author: (plays) When You Comin' Back, Red Ryder?, 1974, The Wager, 1975, The Kramer, 1975, The Halloween Bandit, 1978, The Conversion of Aaron Weiss, 1978, Firekeeper, 1978, The Last Chance Saloon, 1979, Children of a Lesser God, 1980 (Soc. West Theatres best play award 1982), The Majestic Kid, 1981, The Hands of Its Enemy, 1984, Kringle's Window, 1985, The Heart Outright, 1986, Road to a Revolution, 2001, Prymate, 2004, The Same Live Over, 2004, (novel) Dreams of Long Lasting; (films) When You Comin' Back, Red Ryder?, 1979, Off Beat, 1986, Apology, 1986, Children of a Lesser God, 1986, Good Guys Wear Black, 1978, Clara's Heart, 1988, The Majestic Kid, 1988, City of Joy, 1992, Homage, 1995, Santa Fe, 1997, Who Fly On Angel's Wings, 2000, Children On Their Birthdays, 2002; works appear in Best Plays, 1973-74, 75-75, 79-80, Best Short Plays, 1975, The Homage that Follows, 1987; plays Stumps, 1989, Stefanie Hero, 1990, Showdown On Rio Road, 1995, Gila, 1995, A Christmas Carousel, 1996, Crunch Time, 1996, Gunfighters, A Gulf War Chronicle, 1997, A Christmas Carousel, 1998, Tommy J and Sally, 2000, Prymate, 2004; dir. (film) Children on Their Birthdays. Guggenheim fellow, 1974-75; recipient Obie award, Drama Desk award, Outer Critics Circle award, Media award Pres.'s Com. Employment Handicapped, Tony award, Kennedy Ctr. medal Excellence in Edn. and Artistic Achievement, 2006; Oscar award nominee for Best Screenplay for Children of A Lesser God, 1987; Reynolds Eminent scholar Fla. State U., 2003-06, Artistic Dir. Creative Media Inst N.Mex. State U., 2006-. Mem. SAG, Coll. Fellows Am. Theater, Dramatists Guild, Writers Guild Am., Actors Equity Assn., PEN, Coll. Fellows of the Am. Theatre. Office: PO Box 3072 Las Cruces NM 88003-3072

**MEDVECKY, PATRICIA,** retired elementary school educator; b. N.Y.C., Feb. 2, 1936; d. Patrick and Katherine Conneally; m. Thomas E. Medvecky, Aug. 25, 1967; 1 child, Thomas E. II. BA, Hunter Coll., 1961, MS in Edn., 1965. Cert. notary pub. Conn. Tchr. elem. sch. Bd. Edn., N.Y.C., 1961—67, Ridgefield, Conn., 1967—73, ret., 1973; real property abstractor Law Office of T.E. Medvecky, Bethel, Conn., 1973—96. Mem.: Hunter Coll. Alumni Assn., Sheffield Art League. Republican. Roman Catholic. Avocations: history, watercolor painting and etching. Home: PO Box 23 99 Washinee Heights Rd Taconic CT 06079 Personal E-mail: oldpatsy@yahoo.com.

**MEDVECKY, ROBERT STEPHEN,** lawyer; b. Bridgeport, Conn., Feb. 12, 1931; s. Stephen and Elizabeth (Petro) M.; m. Ellen R. Munt, Nov. 11, 1966; children— Allison L., Beth A., Craig R. AB, Dartmouth, 1952; JD, Harvard, 1955. Bar: Ill. bar 1955, Conn. bar 1958, D.C. bar 1972. Bar 1989. Asso. firm Lord, Bissell & Brook, Chgo., 1955-57; gen. atty. So. New Eng. Telephone Co., New Haven, 1957-71; v.p., gen. counsel, sec. Amtrak, Washington, 1971-75; partner firm Lord, Bissell & Brook, Washington, 1975-78, Reid & Priest, N.Y.C., 1978-87. Clubs: Harvard (N.Y.C.), Fiddlesticks Country (Ft. Meyers, Fla.), Saphire Valley Country (Cashlers, N.C.). Office: 15491 Kilbirnie Dr Fort Myers FL 33912-2424 Personal E-mail: bmedvecky@yahoo.com.

**MEDVED, ROBERT ALLEN,** lawyer; b. Cleve., July 22, 1945; s. Joseph Jack and Mary (Blasko) Medved. BBA, Kent State U., 1968; JD cum laude, Seattle U., 1975. Bar: Wash. 1976, US Ct. Appeals (9th cir.) 1976, US Dist. Ct. (we. dist.) Wash. 1976, US Dist. Ct. (ea. dist.) Wash. 1979, US Supreme Ct. 1981, US Ct. Appeals (DC cir.) 1989. Fin. analyst Ford Motor Co., Sandusky, Ohio, 1972; rsch. asst. Seattle U., 1973—75; law clk Judge U.S. Ct. Appeals (9th cir.), 1974; asst. to labor arbitrator Tacoma, 1975; law clk. to Judge U.S. Dist. Ct. (ctrl. dist.) Calif., 1976; assoc. Graham & Dunn, Seattle, 1976—81, ptnr., 1981—82, Drake and Whiteley, Bellevue, Wash., 1982—86, Foster, Pepper & Shefelman, Seattle, 1986—97; pvt. practice Mercer Island, 1997—. Co-chair intellectual property com. Fed. Bar Assn., Washington; spl. dist. counsel 8th Congl. Dist., Wash., 1983—86. Editor-in-chief: Seattle U. Law Rev. Bd. dirs. Bellevue CC found., 1986—98. Lt. USN, 1968—71. Seattle U. scholar, 1974. Mem.: ABA, Wash. State Bar Assn. Roman Catholic. Office: 7238 SE 32nd St Mercer Island WA 98040-2641 Office Phone: 206-232-5800. Business E-mail: bob@ramedved.com.

**MEDVINSKY, NATHALIA,** library director; b. Kiev, Ukraine, Aug. 1, 1961; arrived in U.S., 2003; d. Vladimir Kroutoy and Ioanna Tabachnikov; m. Boris Dregalo (div.); m. Felix Medvinsky, Jan. 24, 2003. BLS, Kiev Inst. Culture, 1982; MLS, Sch. Libr. Info. and Archives, Jerusalem, Israel, 2001. Chief librarian Conservatory and HS of Jerusalem Acad. Music and Dance, 1992—2002; libr. dir. Fla. Nat. Coll., Hialeah, 2004—. Mem.: ALA, Fla. Libr. Assn. Home: 20336 NE 10th Court Rd N Miami FL 33179-2522 Office: Fla Nat Coll 4425 W 20th Ave Hialeah FL 33012

**MEECE, ROGER A.,** ambassador; b. Indpls., Oct. 1949; BS, Mich. State U., 1971. Former dep. chief of mission Am. Embassy, Brazzaville, Republic of the Congo; consul gen. Halifax, Nova Scotia, Canada; dep. chief of mission Am. Embassy, Kinshasa, Democratic Republic of Congo, 1995—98; dir., Ctrl. African affairs US Dept. State, Washington, 1998—2000, U.S. amb. to Malawi Lilongwe, 2000—03; charge d' affaires Am. Embassy, Abuja, Nigeria, 2003—04; US amb. to Democratic Republic of Congo US Dept. State, Kinsasha, 2004—. Vol. Peace Corps, Sierra Leone, 1971, assoc. dir., Niger, Cameroon, dep. dir., Republic of the Congo, dir., Gabon. Office: 2220 Kinsasha Pl Washington DC 20521-2220*

**MEEHAN, JEAN MARIE ROSS,** human resources, occupational health and safety management consultant; b. Chgo., Mar. 16, 1954; d. A. Ronald Gonzalez and Barbara Marx Shipley; m. John J. Meehan, 1993; 1 child, Jenna A.; 1 child from previous marriage, Justin L. Ross. Diploma in Nursing, St. Mary of Nazareth Hosp., Chgo., 1974; BS in Health Arts with high honors, U. St. Francis, 1988; MPA with honors, Roosevelt U., 2000. Cert. occupl. health nurse specialist, cert. pharmacy technician (CPhT); ordained minister Universal Life Ch., 2003; cert. senior professional in human resources. Staff nurse St. Mary of Nazareth Hosp., Chgo., 1973—75; head nurse ambulatory care Edgebrook Med. Diagnostic Ctr., Chgo., 1975—76; occupl. health nurse Williams Electronics, Inc., Chgo., 1976—84; administr. safety and benefits Reliable Power Products, Franklin Park, Ill., 1984—90; dir. corp. human resources MacLean-Fogg Co., Mundelein, Ill., 1990—2005, Navitus Health Solutions LLC, Madison, Wis., 2005—. Pres. Auriel Mgmt. Group, LLC, Island Lake, Ill., 1992—, Claim Masters, LLC, 1998—99; adv. bd. dir. Gt. Lakes Health Care Alliance, 1996—97; spkr. in workshops. Poetry included in Visions of Beauty, 1999 (Editor's Choice award 1999), Tides of Memory, 2000, America at the Millennium—The Best Poems and Poets of the 20th Century, 2000. Guest spkr. local schs. and environ. groups, also I.E.P.A. and U.S. E.P.A. workshops; mem. Ill. Pollution Prevention Adv. Coun., Springfield, Ill., 1993-98; mem. Lake County Employer Coun. Bus./Govt. Partnership, 1996-99; faculty Am. Occupl. Health Conf., 2003-04. Recipient Leadership Civic intiate United Way Charities of Lake County, 1993, 94. Mem. Am. Assn. Occupl. Health Nurses, Soc. for Human Resources Mgmt., Lake County Violence Intervention and Prevention, Lake County Employer Coun. Avocations: parenting, interior design, reading, art. Office: Auriel Mgmt Group LLC PO Box 86 Wauconda IL 60084 Office Phone: 608-827-7567. Personal E-mail: hrpro@email.com.

**MEEHAN, MARTIN THOMAS,** congressman, lawyer; b. Lowell, Mass., Dec. 30, 1956; s. Martin T. and Alice (Britton) Meehan; m. Ellen T. Murphy; children: Robert Francis, Daniel Martin. BA in Polit. Sci., Edn. cum laude, U. Mass., Lowell, 1978; MPA, Suffolk U., 1981, JD, 1986; student, Harvard U., 1987-88. Administrv. asst. to mayor City of Lowell, Mass., 1978-79; press asst. Congressman James M. Shannon, Mass., 1979-81; del. Dem. Nat. Conv., 1980, 84, 88; head rsch. analyst Joint Com. on Elec. Laws Mass. State Senate, 1981-84; first dep. U. pub. affairs Govt. of Mass., 1985-86, dep. sec. state, 1986-90; 1st asst. dist. atty. Middlesex County, Mass., 1991-92; mem. U.S. Congress from 5th Mass. dist., 1993—. mem. armed svcs. com., judiciary com. Former teacher, adj. instr. U. Lowell, Mass.; lawyer 1986—. Named Student of Yr. Lowell Exchange Club, 1975. Mem. ABA, Mass. Bar Assn., U. Lowell Alumni Assn., The Newspaper Guild, Internat. Fedn. Journalists. Democrat. Roman Catholic. Office: US Ho Reps 2229 Rayburn Ho Office Bldg Washington DC 20515-2105 E-mail: martin.meehan@mail.house.gov.*

**MEEHAN, MICHAEL JOSEPH,** lawyer; b. St. Louis, Aug. 28, 1942; s. Joseph Michael and Frances (Taylor) M.; m. Sharon Kay McHenry (div. 1988); m. Patricia Ann Shive, July 8, 1989 (dec. 1999); m. Shelley Fujiko Lee, 2002. BS in Engring., U.S. Coast Guard Acad., 1964; JD with high distinction, U. Ariz., 1971. Bar: Ariz. 1971, U.S. Ct. Appeals (6th, 8th, 9th and 10th cirs.), U.S. Supreme Ct. 1975. Law clk. Assoc. Justice William H. Rehnquist, U.S. Supreme Ct., 1972; assoc. Molloy, Jones & Donahue, P.C., Tucson, 1971-75; shareholder, 1975-93; chmn. exec. com., head trial dept., 1986-93; founder Meehan & Assocs., Tucson, 1993-2001; ptnr. Quarles & Brady/Striech Long, Tucson, 2001—03; pvt. practice Tucson, 2003—; of counsel Munger Chadwick P.L.C., Tucson, 2004—. Mem. fed. appellate rules adv. com. Jud. Conf. U.S., 1994-99. Author chpt. on appellate advocacy: State Bar of Arizona Appellate Practice Handbook. Fellow Am. Acad. Appellate Lawyers (past pres.); mem. Ariz. Bar Assn. (past chair appellate practice sect. 1999-00), Nat. Conf. Appellate Justice (mem. steering com. 2005). Lutheran. Avocation: golf. Office: Munger Chadwick PLC 333 North Wilmot Rd Ste 300 Tucson AZ 85711 Office Phone: 520-721-1900. Business E-mail: mmeehan@mungerchadwick.com.

**MEEHAN, PATRICK LEO,** prosecutor; b. 1955; BA, Bowdoin Coll., 1978; JD, Temple U., 1986. Assoc. Dilworth, Paxon, Kalish and Kauffman; sr. counsel, exec. dir. U.S. Sen. Arlen Specter; dist. atty. Delaware County, Pa., 1986—2001; US atty. (ea. dist.) Pa. US Dept. Justice, 2001—. Mem. Corp. Fraud Task Force panel, 2002—; mem., adv. subcommittee White Collar Crime, Terrorism, Civil Rights. Office: US Attys Office 615 Chestnut St Philadelphia PA 19106*

**MEEHAN, ROBERT HENRY,** human resources executive, business educator, electronics executive; b. Hackensack, N.J., June 19, 1946; s. Horace Miles and Pauline Jeannette (Pente) M.; m. Ruth Ann Auletta, Sept. 28, 1969; children: Robert Michael, Brian John. BA, Montclair State U., 1968; MA magna cum laude, Fairleigh Dickinson U., 1972; D in Profl. Studies, Pace U., 1997. Cert. secondary sch. tchr. of social studies, N.J., compensation and benefits profl. Job analyst Citicorp, N.Y.C., 1969-70, sr. job analyst, 1970-72, ofcl. asst., 1972, project specialist human resources practices/policy rev., 1973, project specialist attitude surveys, 1973-75, human resources officer nat. banking group, 1975-76; asst. dir. human resources N.Y. Power Authority, White Plains, 1976-84, dir. compensation, 1984-93, dir. compensation and human resources info. sys., 1993-94, dir. compensation and benefits strategy and devel., 1994-95, dir. compensation and benefits, 1995-98; dir. compensation Philips Electronics N.Am., 1998-2000; mng. dir. R.H. Meehan Assocs., Human Capital Cons., Maywood, NJ, 2000—01; dir. compensation, benefits and HRIS, ASML, Tempe, Ariz., 2001—; CEO Chaparral Capital, LLC, Scottsdale, Ariz., 2005—. Instr. World at Work, Scottsdale, Ariz., 1986—, course coord., 1992-94, mem. cert. and currency com., 1988-89, direct compensation com. 1990-91, chmn. 1992-93, bd. dirs. 1993; adj. assoc. prof. Lubin Grad. Sch. Bus., Pace U., 1995-2001; mem. N.Y. Power Pool Salary com., 1990-98, chair, 1998; spkr. at profl. confs. Sr. author: Managing a Direct Pay Program, Cert. Course 4A, 1991, Determining Compensation Costs: An Approach to Estimating and Analyzing Expense, 1991; editor books; mem. exec. adv. panel Acad. Mgmt. Exec., 1993—; contbr. articles to profl. jours. Scoutmaster, Boy Scouts Am., Ridgefield Park, N.J., 1968; also scouting coord., Maywood, N.J., 1982-83; vestryman, sr. warden St. Martin's Episcopal Ch., Maywood, 1977-84. Mem. Soc. for Human Resource Mgmt. (mem. compensation and benefits com. 1998-2001), Metro Phoenix Human Resource Assocs., 2002—, Human Resources Assn. N.Y. (compensation com. 1998-2001), Acad. Mgmt. (exec. adv. panel jour. The Exec.), N.Y. Compensation Assn., 2000—01, Order DeMolay (master councilor 1963, 65, scribe, adv. bd. 1965-68, Meritorious Svcs. award 1965), Psi, Delta Mu Delta, Beta Gamma Sigma. Episcopalian. Avocations: golf, sailing, furniture making. Office: ASML 8555 S River Pkwy Tempe AZ 85284 Office Phone: 480-383-4043. Personal E-mail: rhmeehan@cox.net. Business E-mail: Robert.Meehan@asml.com.

**MEEHAN, SANDRA GOTHAM,** corporate financial executive, consultant, writer; b. Tokyo, June 9, 1948; d. Fred C. and Evelyn (Dirr) Gotham; m. James P. Jenkins, June 15, 1970 (div.); m. Dayton T. Carr, Dec. 27, 1986 (div. 1989). m. Michael J. Meehan, II, Jan. 16, 1992. Student, Stanford-in-France, Tours, 1968-69; BA, Stanford U., 1970, MA, 1971. Acct. exec. Young & Rubicam Inc., N.Y.C., 1972-78, acct. supr., 1978-80; pres. Gotham Prodns., N.Y.C., 1980-82; v.p., mgmt. supr. Ogilvy & Mather, N.Y.C., 1982-85; v.p. Steuben Glass, N.Y.C., 1985-88; sr. v.p. Siegel & Gale, N.Y.C., 1988-92; prin., mng. ptnr. Gotham Meeham Ptnrs., N.Y.C., 1992—. Sr. v.p., dir. corp. comm. Bionutrics, Inc., 1997-98; cons. Congl. coms., FDA, FTC for exec. program Am. Assn. Advt. Agys., Washington, 1978-80; cons. Ctr. Arctic Studies Sorbonne, Paris, in U.S. and Can., 1980-82; seminar dir. N.Y. chpt. Women in Bus., N.Y.C., 1983-84. Author, editor: TV documentary Inuit! The Universal Cry of the Eskimo People, 1981. Trustee, bd. dirs. Rensselaerville (N.Y.) Inst.; exec. com., bd. dirs. Checkerboard Film Found.; NYC Mayor's rep. to bd. dirs. Bot. Gardens; bd. dirs. Paris Rev. Mag., The Overmountained Literary Soc., NYC, Agora Found. Home: 220 E 73rd St New York NY 10021-4319 Office: Gotham Meeham Ptnrs 220 E 73rd St Ste 5G New York NY 10021-4319 Office Phone: 212-628-6810. Office Fax: 212-628-6747. Personal E-mail: gmp7777@aol.com.

**MEEHAN, SHIRLEY,** human services administrator; b. Porterville, Calif., Nov. 2, 1949; d. Melvin Lee Short and Joyce Elaine Brady-Short; m. James Donald Meehan, Feb. 15, 1985; m. Michael Thomas Garin, July 18, 1971 (div.); 1 child, Matthew Thomas Garin. BA, U. Calif., Berkeley, 1970; MBA, George Washington U., Washington, 1976, PhD, 1988. Dep. dir. Health Svcs. R & D, Vets. Health Adminstrn., Washington, 1992—, acting dir., 2004—. Bd. dirs. Knowledge Utilization Soc., Mpls., 1989—95. Contbr. articles to profl. jours. Den leader Chesterbook Cub Scouts, McLean, Va., 1989—90; aux. v.p. Little League, McLean, 1984—90; ch. sch. tchr. United Ch. of Christ, Arlington, Va., 1988—2006; rep. Coun. of Chs. of Greater Wash., Washington, 1992—94; Christian edn. bd. chair United Ch. of Christ, Arlington, 1989—90, assoc. pastor search com., 1989—90. Recipient Elnora M.Rhodes Svc. award, Soc. of Gen. Internal Medicine, 2006, James A. Stockdill award for Excellence in Govt. Svc., Knowledge Utilization Soc., 1991. Mem.: APHA, AcademyHealth, Soc. of Gen. Internal Medicine, Doctoral Assn. (sec./treas. 1987). Christian. Avocations: travel, history. Office: VA Central Office- HSR&D (124) 810 Vermont Ave NW Washington DC 20420 Office Phone: 202-254-0207.

**MEEHAN, TAMIYE MARCIA,** library director; b. Chgo., Oct. 14, 1942; d. Thomas and Virginia Fujibayashi; m. Rudolph J. Trejo, Jr., Sept. 1, 1962 (div. 1980); m. James E. Meehan, Jr., Oct. 4, 1981; children: Terrence, Theodore, Timothy, Rosalind. MALS, Rosary Coll., Fremont, Calif., 1974; MBA, De Paul U., Chgo., 1980. Librarian Chgo. Pub. Libr., 1974-75, br. libr. head, 1975-77, dist. chief, 1977-96, staff devel., 1996-97; dir. Indian Trails Pub. Libr. Dist., Wheeling, Ill., 1997—. Mem. ALA (chmn. ethnic multicultural and info. roundtable 1994-99, chmn. APALA 2001-2002), Ill. Libr. Assn. Bd. dirs. 1999-2002, treas. 2000-02, pres. 2006-), Wheeling Rotary Club (pres. 2004-05). Office: Indian Trails Pub Libr Dist 355 S Schoenbeck Rd Wheeling IL 60090-4467 Office Phone: 847-459-4100. Business E-mail: TMeehan@indiantrailslibrary.org.

**MEEK, FORREST BURNS,** retired trading company executive; b. Tustin, Mich., June 11, 1928; s. Robert B. and Electa I. (Gallup) Meek; m. Jean R. Grimes, June 26, 1953; children: Sally, Thomas, Nancy, Charles. AA, Spring Arbor Coll., 1950; BA, Mich. State U., 1953; postgrad., U. Ga., 1965; MA, Ctrl. Mich. U., 1967. Exec. sec., chmn. bd. Edgewood Press, Clare, 1971—; gen. mgr. Blue Water Imports, 1985; dir. Ctr. for Chinese-Am. Scholarly Exchs., Inc., 1989—97; gen. mgr. Blue-Water Internat. Trading Co., Inc., ret., 1998. Vis. prof. Wuhan U., China, 1986—87; dist. office mgr. Fed. Decennial Census, 1990; instr. phys. geology and astronomy Mid Mich. C.C., 2002,

instr. astronomy, 2001—03; mem., chmn. Red team East Ctrl. Mich. Planning and Devel. Regional Commn.; bd. sec. ITC Shanghai Maglev, Inc., 2003. Author: Michigan Timber Battleground, 1976, Michigan Heartland, 1979, One Year in China, 1988, Michigan Logging Railroad Era, 1850-1963, 1989, Railways and Tramways, 1990, Lumbering in Eastern Canada, 1991, Pearl Harbor Remembered, 1991, Heroes of The Twentieth Century, 2000. Coord. Clare County Bicentennial Com., 1975-76; Rep. fin. chmn., Clare County, 1966-71, asst. treas. 10th dist. Mich, 1967-69; trustee local sch. bd., 1992-96; chmn. local county jury bd., 1991-98; mem. bd. commrs. Clare County Dist. 4 Commn., 1998-2006. Mem. Am. Entrepreneur Assn., Mich. Sci. Tchrs. Assn., Mich. Hist. Soc., Heartland Mich. Geneal. Soc., White Pine Hist. Soc. (exec. sec.), Steam Locomotive History Soc. Republican. Avocations: astronomy, silviculture. Personal E-mail: forrestburns@gmail.com.

**MEEK, KENDRICK B.,** congressman; b. Miami, Sept. 6, 1966; m. Leslie Meek; 2 children. BS, Fla. A&M U., 1989. Devel. rep. Wackenhut Corp.; mem. Fla. Ho. of Reps., Tallahassee, 1994-98, mem. Fla. state 36 Fla. State Senate, Tallahassee, 1998—2002; mem. US Congress from 17th Fla. dist., 2003—; mem. armed svcs. com., homeland security com. Vice chair Com. on Criminal Justice Appropriations Fiscal Responsibility Coun., 1996-97; mem. Com. on Crime and Punishment Justice Coun., 1996-97. Mem. Fla. Young Dems., 1985—, Gtr. Miami Svc. Corp Bd., All Peoples Dem. Club, South Fla. Food Recovery Bd., North Shore Med. Ctr. Bd., IMPACT Miami, Met. Dade County Urban Revitalization Task Force; capt. Fla. Hwy Patrol, 1989-94; founder, mem. Men Against Drugs, Defending Against Drugs and Social Disorder (MAD DADS); founder Positive African-Am. Role Models Lillie C. Evans Elem. Sch., 1990; mem. adv. bd. Dems. 2000 Elected Officials; bd. dirs. Metro-Dade Cmty. Action Agy. Flemming fellow Ctr. for Policy Alternatives, 1996-97; recipient Outstanding Svc. award MADD, 1990, Positive African-Am. Role Models award Lillie C. Evans Elem. Sch., 1991, #1 award Scott-Carver Pack, 1991, award Dade Ptnrs. for Safe Neighborhoods, 1995, Legis. award MADD, 1995, Cmty. Svc. award Fla. Meml. Coll., 1995, award IMPACT Miami, 1996, Stellar Cmty. Svc. award South Fla. Assn. Black Journalists, 1996, Legis. Achievement honor Fla. Divsn. Emergency Mgmt., 1996; named St. Joseph Delaney Hurricane Hero Metro Dade County Commn., 1995, one of 50 Leaders of Tomorrow Ebony Mag., 1995, one of Most Influential Black Americans, 2006, Up and Comers finalist Price Waterhouse, 1996 Quality Floridian Fla. League of Cities, 1996. Mem. NAACP (life, chmn. Miami-Dade br. Oper. Voter Registration 1995-96, v.p., Adams-Powell Civil Rights award 1996, Gwen Sawyer Cherry Meml. award Fla. Conf. NAACP brs. 1997), North Dade Cmty. Assn. (chmn. pub. safety com.), Fla. Agr. and Mech. U. Alumni Assn., Disabled Police Officers Assn. (adv. bd.), Omega Psi Phi. Democrat. Office: US Ho Reps 1039 Longworth Ho Office Bldg Washington DC 20515-0917 Office Phone: 202-225-4506. Office Fax: 202-226-0777.*

**MEEK, LINDA DUKE (LINDA BULLION MEEK),** elementary school educator, writer; b. Charleston, Miss., Oct. 31, 1951; d. Charles Lester and Dell Crosthwait Bullion; m. W. E. Meek, Jr., Dec. 23, 2000; 1 child from previous marriage, Rodney C. Duke. BS in elem. edn., U. Miss., Oxford, 1973. Cert. reading specialist Caohoma Coll., 1976. Tchr. grades 1-3 West Tallahatchie Sch., Webb, Miss., 1973—75; tchr. grade 2 Clarksdale Sch. Dist., 1975—80; tchr. grade 3 Harlingen City Ind. Sch. Dist., Tex., 1980—2000; tchr. grade 6 East Tallahatchie Sch., Charleston, Miss., 2001, tchr. grade 2, 2001—03, reading resource tchr., 2003—. Author: The Long Winding Road, 2004, It's Hard to Say Good-bye, 2006; composer: (recordings) Songs from the Heart, 1999, (songs) A Second Chance, 2003; contbr. articles to mag. Spkr. to groups on breast cancer awareness. Office: 662-647-2679. E-mail: lindameek@bellsouth.net.

**MEEK, VIOLET IMHOF,** retired dean; b. Geneva, Ill., June 12, 1939; d. John and Violet (Krepel) Imhof; m. Devon W. Meek, Aug. 21, 1965 (dec. 1988); children: Brian, Karen; m. Don M. Dell, Jan. 4, 1992. BA summa cum laude, St. Olaf Coll., 1960; MS, U. Ill., 1962, PhD in Chemistry, 1964. Instr. chemistry Mount Holyoke Coll., South Hadley, Mass., 1964-65; asst. prof. to prof. Ohio Wesleyan U., Delaware, Ohio, 1965-84, dean for edml. svcs., 1980-84; dir. annual programs Coun. Ind. Colls., Washington, 1984-86; assoc. dir. sponsored programs devel. Rsch. Found. Ohio State U., Columbus, 1986-91, dean of the Lima, 1992—2003; ret. 2003. Vis. dean U. Calif., Berkeley, 1982, Stanford U., Palo Alto, Calif., 1982, reviewer GTE Sci. and Tech. Program, Princeton, N.J., 1986-92, Goldwater Nat. Fellowships, Princeton, 1990-98. Co-author: Experimental General Chemistry, 1984; contbr. articles to profl. jours. Bd. dirs. Luth. Campus Ministries, Columbus, 1988-91, Luth. Social Svcs., 1988-91, Americom Bank, Lima, 1992-98, Art Space, Lima, 1993—, Allen Lima Leadership, 1993—, Am. House, 1992—, Lima Vets. Meml. Civic Ctr. Found., 1992—; chmn. synodical coms. Evang. Luth. Ch. Am., Columbus, 1982; bd. trustees Trinity Luth. Sem., Columbus, 1996—; chmn. Allen County C. of C., 1995—, chair bd. dirs., 1999; bd. dirs. Lima Syphomy Orch., 1993—, pres. bd. dirs., 1997— Recipient Woodrow Wilson Fellowship, 1960. Mem.: Am. Assn. Higher Edn., Nat. Coun. Rsch. Adminstrs. (named Outstanding New Profl. midwest region 1990), Phi Beta Kappa. Avocations: music, skiing, woodworking, civil war history, travel. Home: 209 W Beechwold Blvd Columbus OH 43214-2012 Office: Ohio State Lima 8521 Libra Rd Dublin OH 43016-9022

**MEEK, WALTER BUCHANAN,** retired lawyer, director; b. Memphis, Jan. 13, 1926; s. Arthur Maurice and Sarah Christine (Buchanan) Meek; m. Patsy Joyce Hayes, June 26, 1949; children: Christine Thrasher, Buchanan, Joyce Yates. BBA, U. Miss., 1948, LLB, 1950. Bar: Miss. 1950, U.S. Ct. Appeals (5th cir.) 1972. Practice, Eupora, Miss., 1950—; mem. Meek and Meek, Eupora, 1975—. With US42, 1943—45. Mem.: ABA, Miss. State Bar. Methodist. Office: PO Box 555 Eupora MS 39744-0555 Office Phone: 662-258-3521.

**MEEKER, GUY BENTLEY,** banker; b. Calcutta, India, Nov. 4, 1945; (parents Am. citizens); s. Lincoln Voght and Fortune Helen (Bentley) M.; m. Lavenia Yale Nelson, Apr. 27, 1967 (div. 1979); children: G. Bentley Jr., Melissa Anne; m. Marcia Lee Zink, Nov. 4, 1984 (div. 1993). BSBA, Georgetown U., 1967; MBA, George Washington U., 1970. Cons. OAS, Washington, 1971-73; v.p. The Deltec Banking Corp., Nassau, Bahamas & N.Y.C., 1973-78, Comml. Credit Internat. Banking Corp., Balt., 1978-82; sr. v.p., gen. mgr. Union Planters Internat. Bank, N.Y.C., 1982-84; exec. v.p., gen. mgr. Worthen Bank Internat., N.Y.C., 1984-86; exec. v.p. and chief exec. officer N.Am. Bank Cen. Asia, N.Y.C., 1984-95; supervisory dir. BCA Bank Europe N.V., Amsterdam, The Netherlands, 1993-95; pres. G.B. Meeker & Co., N.Y.C., 1996—99; writer, mgmt. fin. cons. Miami, 1999—. Author articles and monographs in field. Mem. Bankers Assn. Fgn. Trade (internat. adv. coun. 1992-95, vice chmn. IAC 1994-95), Inst. Internat. Bankers (legis. and regulatory com. 1992-94, bd. trustees 1994-95), Asia Soc. (corp. coun. 1987-95), River Club, Dutch Treat Club, Coffee House Club. Roman Catholic.

**MEEKER, MARY G.,** brokerage house executive; b. Portland, Ind., Sept. 1959; BA in Psychology, DePauw U., 1981; MBA in Fin., Cornell U., 1986. Stockbroker Merrill Lynch, Chgo., 1982; tech. rsch. analyst Salomon Bros., 1989, Cowen & Co., 1991-92; mng. dir. Internet, new media and PC software equity rsch. Morgan Stanley, Dean Witter, Discover & Co. (now Morgan Stanley), N.Y.C., 1991—. Named Queen of the Net, Barron's. Avocations: golf, fishing, skiing. Office: Morgan Stanley 1585 Broadway New York NY 10036-8200 Fax: 212-761-0472. E-mail: mmeeker@ms.com.

**MEEKER, RALPH D.,** computer scientist, information scientist, educator; b. Chgo., Ill., Nov. 15, 1945; s. Ralph A. and Mary J. Meeker; m. Pamela R. Pulver, Sept. 7, 1968; children: Michelle R., Mark D. PhD, Iowa State U., Iowa, 1970. Asst. prof. of physics Benedictine U., Lisle, Ill., 1973—79, assoc. prof. of physics, 1973—79, prof. of physics, 1979—88, prof. of computer sci. and physics, 1988—95, assoc. acad. dean, 1989—98, prof. of computer sci. and info. sys., 1998—. Pres. Exradin, Inc., Lisle, Ill., 1978—2000. Author: (book) CASC Planning and Data Systems: Users' Manual for the Instructional Program Analysis Module; contbr. articles to profl. jours. Vice chair

Lisle Libr. Dist. Found., Lisle, Ill., 2001—04. Recipient Disting. Alumnus award, Benedictine U., 2003. Mem.: Am. Assn. of Physics Tchrs., Computer Soc. of IEEE, Assn. for Computing Machinery, Sigma Xi. Roman Catholic. Avocations: bicycling, reading, travel. Home: 5S518 Arlington Ave Naperville IL 60540-3819 Office: Benedictine Univ 5700 College Rd Lisle IL 60532-0900 Office Phone: 630-829-6561. Office Fax: 630-829-6226.

**MEEKISON, MARYFRAN,** writer; b. Napoleon, Ohio, Apr. 9, 1919; d. Frank J. and Elizabeth (Keyes) Shaff; m. David Meekison, June 17, 1939; children: Maureen Meekison Houppert, David Francis, Beth Ann. Student, St. Mary's Coll., Notre Dame, Ind., 1936-39. Hist. writer, photographer, Napoleon, 1963—, St. Augustine Oh., 1983—; mem. citizen com. Napoleon Area H.S. Award, 2005—. Author: (photographer) Canal Days to Modern Ways Revisited, 1984, History of St. Augustine's 1882-1982, History of St. Augustine Ch., 1983, centennial edit.; (brochure) Canal Days to Modern Ways, 1963; mem. editorial adv. bd. Courier mag., 1989-91; contbr. articles to numerous mags. Steering com. Napoleon Susquicentennial, 1984; trustee Napoleon Pub. Lib., 1976-01. Recipient Spl. citation Courier Alumnae mag., also numerous photography and writing awards, Pres.'s medal, St. Mary's Coll., Notre Dame, Ind., 1991; named Citizen of Yr., Napoleain Area C. of C., 1990; named to St. Mary's Coll. Athletic Hall of Fame Notre Dame, 2001. Mem. Alumnae Assn. St. Mary's Coll. (bd. dirs. 1985-91), Literary Club. Democrat. Roman Catholic. Avocations: tennis, sailing. Home: PO Box 253 Napoleon OH 43545-0253

**MEEKS, GREGORY WELDON,** congressman; b. NYC, Sept. 25, 1953; s. James Weldon and Mary (McNeal) Meeks; m. Simone-Marie Meeks; children: Ebony Renee, Aja J., Nia-Aiyana. BA in Hist., Adelphi U., Garden City, NY, 1975; JD, Howard U. Sch. Law, Washington, 1978. Asst. dist. atty. Queens Dist. Atty.'s Office, 1978-81; asst. narcotics prosecutor Office of Spl. Narcotics Prosecutor, NYC, 1981-83; asst. counsel State Investigations Commn., 1983-84; hearing officer NY Family Ct., 1984-85; judge NY State Workers' Compensation Bd., 1985-87, supervising judge, 1987-93; mem. NY State Assembly, 1993-98, US Congress from 6th NY dist., 1998—, mem. fin. svcs. com., mem. internat. rels. com. Bd. dirs. Rockaway Peninsula Civic Assn., 1983-1991, Peninsula Gen. Hosp., 1989-; chmn. bd. Joseph P. Addabbo Family Health Care Ctr., 1990-92. Recipient NAACP Polit. Leadership award, 1989, Outstanding Vol. Mentor award, NY Mentoring, 1990, Cmty. Leader award Boy Scouts Am., 1992, William Garvin Pub. Svc. award, 2004, Congl. Leadership award, Nat. Urban League, 2006; named one of Most Influential Black Americans, Ebony mag., 2006. Mem. Macon B. Allen Black Bar Assn. (v.p.), Queens County Bar Assn., Far Rockaway NAACP (Polit. Leadership award 1989). Democrat. Baptist. Office: US Ho Reps 1710 Longworth Ho Office Bldg Washington DC 20515-0001 Office Phone: 202-225-3461.*

**MEEKS, JACQUELYNN,** city health department administrator; MPH, Tulane U.; DPH, Harvard U. Corp. dir. quality assurance Mutual of Omaha; dir. quality improvement Group Health Plan, Inc.; rsch. assoc. Washington U. Sch. Medicine; dir. dept. health St. Louis County, 2001—04; health dir. Maricopa County, Ariz., 2005—. Office: Maricopa County Dept Health 4041 N Central Ste 1400 Phoenix AZ 85012 Office Phone: 602-506-6902. Office Fax: 602-506-0272. Business E-Mail: jacquelynnmeeks@mail.maricopa.gov.*

**MEEKS, MARY JANICE,** librarian; b. Newberry, S.C., Sept. 25, 1949; d. Oscar Hugh and Mary Ada (Derrick) Boozer; m. James Thomas Meeks, June 14, 1969; children: Shelley Marie, Stephanie Ann. AA, North Greenville Coll., 1969; BA, Newberry Coll., 1971; MEd in Pers. Svcs., Clemson U., 1979; M in Librarianship, U. S.C., 1982. Cert. secondary social studies and gen. sci. tchr., media specialist. Tchr. Gallman Jr. High Sch., Newberry, 1971-72, Newberry (S.C.) High Sch., 1972-80, 82-84, asst. libr., 1980-82; elem. libr. M.S. Bailey Elem. Sch., Clinton, SC, 1984—. Co-sponsor Literary Club, M.S. Bailey Elem. Sch., Clinton, 1991-1992; child support leader Sistercare, Newberry, 1992-93. Dir. Women's Missionary Union dir., Associational Acteens, 1996—2003, Women's Missionary Union, 2001—. Grantee, Wal-Mart, 2005, 2006. Mem.: NEA, S.C. Edn. Assn. (membership chmn. 1979—80), S.C. Assn. Sch. Librs., Palmetto State Tchrs. Assn. Baptist. Avocations: reading, aerobics, sewing. Home: 1229 Hillcrest Rd Newberry SC 29108-2019 Office: M S Bailey Elem Sch 625 Elizabeth St Clinton SC 29325-1921 Office Phone: 864-833-0836.

**MEEKS, WAYNE A.,** religious studies educator; b. Aliceville, Ala., Jan. 8, 1932; s. Benjamin L. and Winnie (Gavin) M.; m. Martha Evelina Fowler, June 10, 1954 (dec. May 29, 1996); children: Suzanne, Edith, Ellen; m. Judith Colton, Mar. 18, 2000. BS, U. Ala.-Tuscaloosa, 1953; BD, Austin Presbyn. Theol. Sem., 1956; MA, Yale U., 1964, PhD, 1965; Doctor Theologiae honoris causa, U. Uppsala, Sweden, 1990. Instr. religion Dartmouth Coll., Hanover, NH, 1964-65; asst. prof. religious studies Ind. U., Bloomington, 1966-68, assoc. prof., 1968-69; assoc. prof. religious studies Yale U., New Haven, 1969-73, prof. religious studies, 1973-84, Woolsey prof. Bibl. studies, 1984—, emeritus, 1999—, dir. divsn. Humanities, 1988-91. Author: Go From Your Father's House, 1964, The Prophet-King, 1967, Moral World of the First Christians, 1986, First Urban Christians, 1983, 2003, Origins of Christian Morality, 1993, In Search of the Early Christians, 2002, Christ is the Question, 2006; contbr. articles to profl. jours. Fulbright fellow, 1956-57; Kent fellow, 1962-64; NEH fellow, 1975-76; Guggenheim fellow, 1979-80. Fellow Am. Acad. Arts and Sci., Brit. Acad.; mem. Soc. Bibl. Lit. (pres. 1985), Studiorum Novi Testamenti Societas (editl. bd. 1979-82, pres. 2004). Democrat. Presbyterian. Avocations: cabinet-making, hiking. Office: Yale U Dept Religious Studies PO Box 208287 New Haven CT 06520-8287 Business E-Mail: wayne.meeks@yale.edu.

**MEEKS, WILLIAM HERMAN, III,** lawyer; b. Ft. Lauderdale, Fla., Dec. 30, 1939; s. Walter Herman Jr. and Elise Walker (McGuire) M.; m. Patricia Ann Rayburn, July 30, 1965; 1 son, William Herman IV; m. 2d, Miriam Andrea Bedsole, Dec. 28, 1971; 1 child, Julie Marie. AB, Princeton U., 1961; LLB, U. Fla., 1964; LLM in Tax, NYU, 1965. Bar: Fla 1964, U.S. Dist. Ct. (so. dist.) Fla. 1965, U.S. Tax Ct. 1966, U.S. Ct. Appeals (11th cir.) 1981, U.S. Supreme Ct. 1985. Ptnr. McCune, Hiaasen, Crum, Ferris & Gardner, Ft. Lauderdale, 1964-89, Fleming, O'Bryan & Fleming, Ft. Lauderdale, 1990-95, Dobbins, Meeks, Raleigh & Dover, Ft. Lauderdale, 1995—. Dir. Attys. Title Svcs., Inc., 1978-79, Attys. Title Svcs. of Broward County, Inc., 1971—, chmn., 1976-77; mem. Attys. Real Estate Coun. Broward County. Mem. ABA, Fla. Bar Assn., Broward County Bar Assn., Attys. Title Ins. Fund, Ft. Lauderdale Hist. Soc., Ft. Lauderdale Mus., Kiwanis, Lauderdale Yacht Club, Tower Club (Ft. Lauderdale), Phi Delta Phi. Democrat. Presbyterian. Office: Dobbins Meeks Raleigh & Dover Ste 305 2810 E Oakland Park Blvd Fort Lauderdale FL 33306 Office Phone: 954-565-2200. E-mail: whmeeks@ndmrd.com.

**MEENAN, ALAN JOHN,** clergyman, theology studies educator; b. Belfast, No. Ireland, Feb. 7, 1946; came to U.S., 1970; s. John and Elizabeth (Holland) M.; m. Vicky Lee Woodall, May 6, 1974; children: Kelly Elizabeth, Katie Michelle, Kimberly Brooke. BA, Queen's U., Belfast, 1970; MDiv, Asbury Theol. Sem., Wilmore, Ky., 1972, ThM, 1975; PhD, Edinburgh U., 1981. Ordained to ministry Presbyn. Ch., U.S.A., 1973. Pastor Wilmore Presbyn. Ch., 1972-74; asst. pastor St. Giles' Cathedral, Edinburgh, Scotland, 1974-77; sr. pastorf 3d Presbyn. Ch., Richmond, Va., 1984-87; head staff Canoga Park (Calif.) Presbyn. Ch., 1984-89; sr. pastor First Presbyn. Ch., Amarillo, Tex., 1989-97, Hollywood (Calif.) Presbyn. Ch., 1997—2005. Vis. lectr. Nairobi (Kenya) Grad. Sch. Theology, 1983, 89, W. Africa Theol. Sem., Lagos, Nigeria, 2004; founder, Word Is Out, 2005—. Contbr. revs. to religious publs., including Asbury Bible Commentary. Tchr. Chogoria High Sch., Meru, Keyna, 1965-66. Yale U. Tyndale Fellowship for Bibl. Rsch., Theta Phi. Avocations: travel, photography, reading, swimming, squash racquets. Office: 11271 Ventura Blvd Ste 509 Studio City CA 91604 Office Phone: 323-463-7161 x280.

**MEENGS, WILLIAM LLOYD,** cardiologist; b. Zeeland, Mich., Dec. 23, 1942; s. Lloyd Stanley and Gertrude (Wyngarden) M.; m. Helen Delores Van Dyke, June 10, 1964; children: Michelle Rene, William Lloyd, Lisa Ann. AB, Hope Coll., 1964; MD, U. Mich., 1968. Diplomate Am. Bd. Cardiology, Am. Bd. Interventional Cardiology, Am. Bd. Nuc. Cardiology. Intern in internal medicine U. Hosp., Ann Arbor, Mich., 1968-69, resident in internal medicine, 1971-73, fellow in cardiology, 1973-75; practice medicine specializing in cardiology, interventional cardiology and nuc. cardiology Petoskey, Mich., 1975—. Cardiologist Burns Clinic Med. Center, Petoskey, 1975-99, chmn. dept. cardiology and cardiac surgery, 1978-89; med. dir. No. Mich. Heart Center, 1989-95; pres. Petoskey Cardiology, P.C., 1999—; chief sect. cardiology No. Mich. Hosps., 2000—; cardiologist Little Traverse Hosp., Petoskey, 1975—, dir. coronary care unit, 1986-89; dir. cardiac catheterization lab. No. Mich. Hosps., Petoskey, 1985-87, 92—, adult spl. care units, 1986-89; vice chmn. bd. dirs. Burns Clinic Med. Ctr., 1989-92. Contbr. med. articles to profl. jours. Trustee Mich. Heart Assn., 1979-83. Served as surgeon USPHS, 1969-71. Named one of Best Drs. in Am. 2001-02, Best Drs. in Am., 2002, Best Drs. in Am. 2003-04, 2004, Best Drs. in Am. 2005-06. Fellow: Soc. Cardiovasc. Angiography and Interventions, Am. Coll. Cardiology; mem.: Am. Heart Assn. (fellow Coun. on Clin. Cardiology), Alpha Omega Alpha. Home: 1224 Autumn Ln Petoskey MI 49770-9019 Office: Petoskey Cardiology 500 W Mitchell St Ste 400 Petoskey MI 49770-2274 Office Phone: 231-487-2490.

**MEER, JON DOUGLAS,** lawyer; b. Amherst, NY, Dec. 8, 1963; s. Ronald Lewis and Sharon (Fisher) M. BS with honors, Cornell U., 1986; JD, Boston U., 1989. Bar: Calif. 1989, US Dist Ct. (no. & ctrl. dist Calif., Nev., ea. dist Mich.), US Ct. Appeals (6th, 9th cir.). Assoc. Paul, Hastings, Janofsky & Walker, LA; attn. Akin, Gump, Strauss, Hauer & Feld LLP, LA; ptnr., chmn. LA sect. Labor & Employment practice DLA Piper Rudnick Gray Cary, LA, 2002—. Lectr. Lawyer in Classroom prog., Constitutional Rights Found. Named a So. Calif. Super Lawyer, LA Mag., 2004. Mem. ABA, LA County Bar Assn., Beverly Hills Bar Assn., Phi Kappa Phi, Phi Eta Sigma. Office: DLA Piper Rudnick Gray Cary 4th Fl 1999 Ave of the Stars Los Angeles CA 90067-6022 Office Phone: 310-595-3004. Office Fax: 310-595-3304. Business E-Mail: jon.meer@dlapiper.com.

**MEEROW, ALAN WILLIAM,** geneticist, horticulturist, botanist; s. Jack and Lillian Meerow; m. Linda Lee Fisher, May 29, 1982; children: Sara Anne, Andrew Todd, Erica Lynn. BS, U. Calif., Davis, 1978; MS, U. Fla., Gainesville, 1983, PhD, 1986. Prof. U. Fla., Ft. Lauderdale, Fla., 1987—99; rsch. plant geneticist Agrl. Rsch. Svc. USDA, Miami, Fla., 1999—. Rsch. assoc. Fairchild Tropical Bot. Garden, Miami, Fla., 1989—; chmn., bulb specialists group Species Survival Commn. World Conservation Union, Geneva, 1993—2005. Author: Betrock's Guide to Florida Landscape Plants, 1989, Betrock's Guide to Landscape Palms, 1992, Ornamental Palm Horticulture, 2000, Betrock's Cold Hardy Palms, 2005, Betrock's Landscape Palms, 2006; contbr. over 12 chapters to books, over 100 articles to profl. jours. Named Hort. Writer of the Yr., Fla. Nursery and Growers Assn., 1990, Hort. Educator of the Yr., 1991; recipient Presdl. Recognition cert., U. Fla., 1985, Best Ph.D Dissertation of Yr. award, 1986, Superior Accomplishment award, 1996; fellow, World Wildlife Fund/Garden Club Am., 1984, Fla. Fedn. of Garden Clubs, 1985; grantee, NSF, 1984—86, 1996—98, 2002—05, Am. Floral Endowment, 1990—94, Hort. Rsch. Inst., 1992, U. Fla., USDA Coop. Ext. Svc., 1993—99, Floyd L. Wray Found., 1993—96, Growing Technologies, 1993, EZ Soil Co., 1993, Plumeria Soc. Am., 2003, Am. Iris Soc., 2004—06; scholarship, Garden Writers Assn. Am., 1984, H. Harold Hume fellowship, 1985. Mem.: Internat. Soc. Hort. Sci., Internat. Assn. Plant Taxonomy, Am. Soc. Plant Taxonomists (assoc. editor Systematic Botany 2003—, Peter Raven Sci. Outreach award 2005), Am. Soc. Hort. Sci. (assoc. editor Hort Sci. 2001—04), Bot. Soc. Am., Internat. Palm Soc., Internat. Bulb Soc. (life; pres. 2001—06, editor Herbertia 1999—, William Herbert medal 1998). Achievements include research in phylogenetic systematics of Amaryllidaceae and other plant taxa; genetics of coconut varieties; molecular markers in tropical ornamental plants; new tropical plant cultivar development; tropical botany and horticulture; patents in field.

**MEERSCHAERT, JOSEPH RICHARD,** physician; b. Detroit, Mar. 4, 1941; s. Hector Achiel and Marie Terese (Campbell) M.; m. Jeanette Marie Ancerewicz, Sept. 14, 1963; children: Eric, Amy, Adam. BA, Wayne State U., 1965, MD, 1967. Diplomate Am. Bd. Phys. Medicine and Rehab., Am. Bd. Pain Medicine. Intern Harper Hosp., Detroit, 1967-68; resident in phys. medicine and rehab. Wayne State U. Rehab. Inst., Detroit, 1968-71; chief divsn. phys. medicine Naval Hosp., Chelsea, Mass., 1971-73; attending physician William Beaumont Hosp., Royal Oak, Mich., 1973—, med. dir. rehab. unit, 1979-87; pvt. practice medicine specializing in phys. medicine and rehab. Royal Oak, 1973—; pvt. practice specializing in pain medicine 1990—. Mem. med. adv. bd. Nat. Wheelchair Athletic Assn., 1973—, U.S. team physician VII World Wheelchair Games, Stoke Mandeville, Eng.; clin. instr. Wayne State U., 1973-83, clin. asst. prof. phys. medicine and rehab., 1983—; mem. Mich. Dept. Licensing and Regulation State Bd. Phys. Therapy, 1978-81. Contbr. articles to profl. jours. With M.C. USN, 1971-73. Recipient John Hussey award Mich. Wheelchair Athletic Assn., 1981. Fellow Am. Coll. Pain Medicine; mem. Am. Acad. Phys. Medicine and Rehab. (reviewer, presenter) Am. Congress Rehab. Medicine, Mich. Phys. Medicine and Rehab. Soc., Am. Geriatrics Soc., Am. Assn. Electromyography and Electrodiagnosis, Mich. Rheumatism Soc., Mich. Acad. Phys. Medicine and REhab. (pres. 1986-87, chmn. program com. 1977-78, trustee 1980—, pres. bd. dirs. 1994-97), Oakland County Med. Soc. (bd. dirs. 1991, 97), Alpha Omega Alpha. Roman Catholic. Office: 44199 Dequindre Rd Troy MI 48085-1128

**MEESE, CELIA EDWARDS,** pharmaceutical company executive; b. San Diego, May 10; d. Roy Clifford Edwards and Bessie Lucille (Lang) Hill; m. Jud D. Meese; 1 child, Scott Edwards Meese. BA, U. Wis.; BA (hon.), U. Taiwan. Pres. Vitaline Corp., Ashland, Oreg., 1972—; v.p. RenalChem, Inc., San Jose, Calif., 1982-90, Formulations Tech., Inc., Oakdale, Calif., 1982—; dir., trustee Oreg. Shakespeare Festival Endowment, Pacific Retirement Svcs., Medford, Oreg. Mem. Pharm. Mfrs. Assn., Mensa. Home: 88 Granite St Ashland OR 97520-2711

**MEESE, EDWIN, III,** law and public policy educator, former United States attorney general; b. Oakland, Calif., Dec. 2, 1931; s. Edwin and Leone M. Meese; m. Ursula Herrick, 1958; children: Michael James, Dana Lynne. BA, Yale U., 1953; JD, U. Calif., Berkeley, 1958; LLD, Del. Law Sch., Widener U., U. San Diego, Valparaiso U., Calif. Luth. Coll. Dep. dist. atty. Alameda County, Calif., 1959-67; legal affairs sec. staff Gov. Reagan, Sacramento, 1967-69, exec. asst., chief of staff, 1969-75; v.p. Rohr Industries, Chula Vista, Calif., 1975-76; sole pratice law, 1976-80; prof. law U. San Diego, 1977—81, dir. Ctr. for Criminal Justice Policy; counselor to Pres. Reagan Washington, 1981-85; atty. gen. US Dept. Justice, Washington, 1985-88; disting. fellow, Ronald Reagan Chair in Pub. Policy Heritage Found., Washington. Mem. Nat. Security Coun., 1981—85; disting. vis. fellow Hoover Instn. Stanford U.; disting. sr. fellow Inst. for US Studies U. London; bd. regents Nat. Coll. of Dist. Atty.; bd. dirs. Capital Rsch. Ctr., Landmark Legal Found.; co-chmn. bd. governors The Reagan Ranch Program. Author: With Reagan: The Inside Story, 1992. V.p. Lutheran Ch., El Cajon, Calif. Served with US Army. Office: Heritage Found 214 Massachusetts Ave NE Washington DC 20002-4958*

**MEESTER, DONNA JEAN,** costume designer, educator; b. Waterloo, Iowa, July 30, 1963; d. Donald Jacob and Mary Lou Meester. BS, Purdue U., West Lafayette, Ind., 1985; MFA, So. Meth. U., Dallas, 1989. Asst. prof. theatre U. La., Monroe, 1994—98; asst. prof. costume design Ark. State U., Jonesboro, 1998—2002; asst. prof. costume design/prodn. U. Ala., Tuscaloosa, 2002—. Costume designer Okla. Shakespearean Festival, Durant, 2001—05, Ala. Shakespeare Festival, Montgomery, 2006. Mem.: S.E. Theatre Conf., U.S. Inst. for Theatre Design and Tech., Kennedy Ctr. Am. Coll. Theatre Festival (design chair-region iv). Home: 2922 Mayfield Way Northport AL 35476 Office: Univ Alabama Tuscaloosa AL 35401 Office Phone: 205-348-9032. E-mail: dmeester@bama.ua.edu.

**MEESTER, HOLLY,** elementary school educator, music educator, sales executive; b. Grafton, N.D., Sept. 1, 1966; d. Gordon and (Alice) Jane Thompson; m. Brent Meester, Sept. 27, 1991; children: Emily, Daniel. BS in Music Edn., N.D. State U., 1989; MA in Music Edn., U. St. Thomas, 2003. Lic. profl. educator N.D., 1989. Asst. dir. Red River Boy Choir, Fargo, ND, 1988—90; tchr. elem. music Fargo Pub. Schs., 1989—; founder, music dir. Lake Agassiz Girls Choir, Fargo, 1990—97. Ind. cons. Mary Kay Cosmetics, Fargo, 1993—; mentor Fargo Pub. Schs., 1999—2002, dir. elem. hand chimes performing group, 1991—, dir. elem. choir, 1989—; adj. prof. Minn. State U., Moorhead, 2004—. Bldg. liaison Fargo Edn. Assn.; bd. mem. Lake Agassiz Girls Choir, Fargo, 1990—98; steering com. mem. North Ctrl. Accreditation - Lewis & Clark Elem., 1992—2005. Mem.: N.D. Music Educators Assn. (state pres. collegiate chpt. 1988—89, Outstanding Collegiate Music Educator 1989), Music Educators Nat. Conf., Orgn. Am. Kodaly Educators, No. Plains Kodaly Chpt. (pres., v.p., past pres., member-at-large 1997—2005), Kappa Delta (life; corr. sec. 1986—87), Sigma Alpha Iota (life). Achievements include Performance at National Organization of American Kodaly Educators while Director of Lake Agassiz Girls Choir. Avocations: reading, piano, scrapbooks, choir. Office: Fargo Pub Schs 1040 29th St N Fargo ND 58102 Office Phone: 701-446-4854.

**MEEZAN, ELIAS,** pharmacologist, educator; b. N.Y.C., Mar. 5, 1942; s. Maurice and Rachel (Epstein) M.; m. Elisabeth Gascard, May 14, 1967; children: David, Nathan, Joshua. BS in Chemistry, CCNY, 1962; PhD in Biochemistry, Duke U., 1966. Asst. prof. physiology and pharmacology Duke U., Durham, NC, 1969-70; asst. prof. pharmacology U. Ariz., Tucson, 1970-75, assoc. prof., 1975-79; prof., chmn. dept. pharmacology U. Ala., Birmingham, 1979-89, prof., dir. Metabolic Diseases Rsch Lab., 1989-93, prof. dept. pharmacology & toxicology, 1993—. Mem. sci. adv. bd. Aegis Therapeutics, 2004—. Assoc. editor: Life Sci., 1973-79. Helen Hay Whitney postdoctoral fellow, 1966-69; recipient NIH Rsch. Career Devel. award, 1977-79. Mem. Am. Soc. Pharmacology and Exptl. Therapeutics, Am. Soc. Biol. Chemistry, AAUP, AAAS, N.Y. Acad. Sci., Assn. Med. Sch. Pharmacology. Democrat. Jewish. Achievements include isolation of retinal and brain microvasculature; development of method for isolating ultrastructurally and chemically intact basement membranes; co-inventor of method for enhancing nasal absorption of drugs. Home: 1202 Cheval Ln Birmingham AL 35216-2037 Office: U Ala Dept Pharmacology Birmingham AL 35294-0001 Office Phone: 205-934-4577. Business E-Mail: Elias.Meezan@ccc.uab.edu.

**MEEZAN, WILLIAM ALAN,** social work educator, consultant; b. N.Y.C., Mar. 10, 1947; s. Joseph and Beatrice (Rauch) Meezan. BA in Psychology, U. Vt., 1967; MSW, Fla. State U., 1969; cert. in advanced social welfare, Columbia U., N.Y.C., 1973; DSW, Columbia U., 1978. Social worker The Children's Village, Dobbs Ferry, NY, 1969—70; rsch. asst. child welfare rsch. program Sch. of Social Work Columbia U., N.Y.C., 1970-72, part-time rsch. asst. child welfare rsch. program, 1972-73; rsch. assoc. Ctr. for N.Y.C. Affairs New Sch. for Social Rsch., N.Y.C., 1973-75; study dir. Child Welfare League of Am., N.Y.C., 1975-77; cons. Children's Bur., Adminstrn. for Children, Youth and Families, Office Human Devel. Svcs. HEW, Washington, 1978; asst. prof. Jane Addams Coll. of Social Work U. Ill., Chgo., 1978-81, assoc. prof. Jane Addams Coll. of Social Work, 1981-86, chair PhD program, prof. Jane Addams Coll. of Social Work, 1986-88; John Milner prof. child welfare Sch. Social Wk., U. So. Calif., L.A., 1988—99, chair PhD program, 1989—94; Marion Elizabeth Blue prof. children and families U. Mich. Sch. Social Work, 1999—2005; dean Coll. Social Work Ohio State U., Columbus, 2005—. Part-time instr. Ctr. of Social Work and Social Rsch., Fairleigh Dickinson U., Teneck, N.J., 1974-75, Adelphi U. Grad. Sch. of Social Work, Garden City, N.Y., 1978; adj. asst. prof. NYU Sch. of Social Work, N.Y.C., 1975-78; spl. asst. to exec. dir. Jewish Children's Bur., Chgo., 1986-88, steering com., sec. Group for Advancement Doctoral Edn., 1990-94; sec. Soc. For Social Work and Rsch.; bd. dir. Inst. Advancement Social Work Rsch. Author: Adoption Without Agencies: A Study of Independent Adoptions, 1978, Care and Commitment: Foster Parent Adoption Decisions, 1985, Evaluating Family Based Services, 1995, Family Preservation and Family Functioning, 1997, (monographs) The Impact of Welfare on Family Stability, 1975, Foster Care Needs and Alternatives to Placement: A Projection for 1975-85, 1975, Adoptions Services in the States, 1980, Evaluation of the Wayne County Foster Care Pilot Project, 2003; editor: Child Welfare: Current Dilemas-Future Decisions, 1983, Rationing Child Protection, 1995, Research Methods with Gay, Lesbian, Bisexual and Transgender Populations, 2003, The Rewards, Frustrations, Trials and Tribulations of Doing Social Work Research "On the Ground", 2 vols., 2005-2006; mem. editl. bd. Social Work Rsch., Child Welfare, Children and Youth Svcs. Rev., Jour. Pub. Child Welfare, Reflections: Narratives Profl. Helping, others; contbr. chpts. to books, articles to jours. HEW fellow, 1967-68, NIMH fellow, 1972-73, AAAS Congl. Sci. fellow, 1984-85; HEW scholar, 1975-77, U.S. Dept. Health and Human Svcs. scholar, 1989-83, 2000-04; Stuart Found. scholar, 1989-95, Fulbright scholar, 1994-95, State of Calif., 1996-99, Kellogg Found., 2000-04, State of Mich., 2000-02, Aspen Inst., 2000-03, Skillman Found., 2003-04, Mich. Nonprofit Rsch. Program, 2003-05. Mem. NASW, Am. Orthopsychiat. Assn., Acad. Cert. Social Workers, Coun. on Social Work Edn., Soc. Social Work and Rsch. Office: Ohio State U Stillman Hall 1947 College Rd Columbus OH 43210 Home: 2796 Powell Ave Bexley OH 43209 Office Phone: 614-292-5300. E-mail: meezan.1@osu.edu.

**MEFFERT, ROBERT LEE,** music educator; b. Arlington, Minn., Aug. 12, 1937; s. Elmer Henry and Luella Ida Meffert; m. Mary Lundquist, Sept. 24, 1960; children: Mark Robert, James Allen. BA in music edn., Augsburg Coll., 1960; grad. in music edn., U. Minn., 1963. Lic. tchg. Minn., 1960. Music tchr. Edgerton (Minn.) Pub. Sch., 1960—61, Boyceville (Wis.) Pub. Sch., 1961—62, Milroy (Minn.) Pub. Sch., 1963—67, Marshall (Minn.) Pub. Sch., 1967—2000; sr. choir dir. Good Shepherd Luth. Ch., Marshall, Minn., 1967—; dir. Marshall Municipal Band, 1983—; assoc. conductor Southwest Minn. Orch., Marshall, 1989—90. Prin. trombonist Southwest Minn. Orch., Marshall, Minn., 1967—, Marshall Municipal Band, Marshall, 1967—83; tchr. nat. adv. coun. Rep. Nat. Com. Wash., DC, 1984—90. Officer Lyon County GOP Com., Marshall, Minn., 1972—; pres., v.p., sec. Good Shepherd Luth. Ch., Marshall, 1967—. Named Tchr. of Yr., Marshall Jr. HS, 1997. Mem.: NEA, Minn. Music Educators Assn., Music Edn. Nat. Conf. Avocations: woodworking, music, stamp collecting/philately, camping, gardening. Home: 500 Donita Ave Marshall MN 56258

**MEFFERT, ROLAND MATTHEW,** periodontist, educator; b. Cross Plains, Wis., June 30, 1932; s. John Michael and Lorraine Catherine (Garfoot) Meffert; m. Marcella Ann Czarnecki, June 12, 1954; children: Jeffrey, Lisa, Sarah, Gregory, Douglas. DDS, Marquette U., 1955; cert. in periodontics, U. Tex., Houston, 1961; cert. in periodontics, Wilford Hall USAF Med. Ctr., 1962. Commd. 1st lt. USAF, 1954, advanced through grades to col., 1970, ret., 1974; prof. dept. periodontics U. Tex. Health Sci. Ctr., San Antonio, 1974—84, 1992—2003, cons. continuing dental edn. 2003—; assoc. prof. dept. periodontics U. Tex. Med. Ctr., San Antonio, 2003—; prof., chmn. dept. periodontics La. State U. Sch. Dentistry, New Orleans, 1984—92. Editor emeritus Implant Dentistry; editor emeritus: Practical Periodontics and Aesthetic Dentistry; contbr. chapters to books, articles to profl. jours. Recipient Spl. Citation award, Am. Acad. Periodontology, 1993, 1997, Meffert-Mutlu Implant Inst. named in honor, Ankara, Turkey, 1997. Master: Am. Acad. Implant Prosthodontics; fellow: Internat. Colll. Dentists, Am. Coll. Dentists; mem.: Am. Soc. Osseointegration (diplomate, pres. 1992, Oral Implantologist of Yr. 1988), Internat. Congress Oral Implantology (diplomate, pres. 1990, Internat. Edn. award 1992, 1994), Am. Bd. Periodontology (diplomate, dir., chmn. 1990—96). Business E-Mail: meffert@uthscsa.edu.

**MEGAHED, MOHAMED SALAH,** neurologist, educator; b. Aug. 18, 1928; MB, BChir, Cairo U., 1951, MD, 1960. Diplomate Am. Bd. Psychiatry and Neurology. Physician Royal Palace of King Saud, 1954-60; clin. clk. Inst. Nervous Diseases Nat. Hosp. Queen Square, London, 1961-64; resident in neurology SUNY, Buffalo, 1964-67, fellow in neurology, cons. attending neurologist, 1967-69; pvt. practice North Tonawanda, N.Y., 1973; chief EEG and neurology depts. Niagara Falls (N.Y.) Meml. Med. Ctr., Mt. St. Mary's

Hosp., Lewiston, N.Y. Clin. assoc. prof. U. Rochester (N.Y.)-Strong Meml. Hosp., until 1996, clin. prof., 1996—. Fellow ACP, Royal Coll. Physicians (Edinburgh); Am. Acad. Neurology; mem. AMA, N.Y. State Med. Soc. Office: 1089 Kinkead Ave North Tonawanda NY 14120-2840 Office Phone: 716-692-4993.

**MEGALLI, MAGUID RAMZI,** health facility administrator; b. Cairo, Jan. 26, 1942; s. Ramzi and Lydia Megalli; m. Viviane Wassef, Jan. 28, 1968; children: Michael, Mark. MD, MBA, Cairo U., 1965. Lic. Am. Bd. of Urology. Resident in urology Columbia U., N.Y.C., 1970—74; chief of urology St. Joseph Med. Ctr., Yonkers, NY, 1982—88; pres. Benifice Advantage, the Self-Insuring Co. for Archdiocese of N.Y.; chief med. officer Cath. Health Care Sys. Resources, 1999—2002; exec. v.p., chief med. officer Our Lady of Mercy Med. Ctr., Bronx, NY. Founder, chmn. Servitas IPA, N.Y.C., 1994—. Contbr. articles to profl. publs. (Valantine Fellowship award, 1974). Lt. col. USAR, 1972—84. Fellow: ACS (life). Home: 35 Island Dr Rye NY 10580 Office: Our Lady of Mercy Med Ctr 600 E 233d St Bronx NY 10466 Office Phone: 718-920-9590. Home Fax: 914-967-3613. Business E-Mail: mmegalli@chcsnet.org.

**MEGAN, THOMAS IGNATIUS,** retired judge; b. Chgo., Dec. 24, 1913; s. Charles P. and May M. (Magan) M.; m. Lucyanne Flaherty, Apr. 17, 1948; children: Anne, Thomas, Jane, Sarah, William, Molly. AB, U. Ill., 1935; JD, U. Chgo., 1938. Bar: Ill. 1939, N.Y. 1941. Mem. firm Pruitt & Grealis, Chgo., 1939-40, Pruitt, Hale & MacIntyre, N.Y.C., 1941; atty. U.S. Ordnance Dept., Chgo., 1941-42, Chgo., Rock Island and Pacific R.R. Co., Chgo., 1945-70, v.p., gen. counsel, 1970-74, v.p. law, 1974-75; adminstrv. law judge ICC, Washington, 1975-81, HHS, Washington, 1981, FERC, Washington, 1981-96; ret., 1996. Served to maj. AUS, 1942-45. Mem. ABA, Soc. Trial Lawyers Chgo., Chgo. Law Club, Phi Kappa Tau, Phi Delta Phi. Clubs: Union League (Chgo.). Home: 11108 Waycroft Way Rockville MD 20852-3217

**MEGGERS, BETTY JANE,** anthropologist, researcher; b. Washington, Dec. 5, 1921; d. William Frederick and Edith (Raddant) M.; m. Clifford Evans, Sept. 13, 1946. AB, U. Pa., 1943; MA, U. Mich., 1944; PhD, Columbia U., 1952; D (hon.), U. de Guayaquil, Ecuador, 1987, U. Fed. Rio de Janeiro, Brazil, 1994, U. Nat. La Plata, Argentina, 1997, U. Católica de Goiás, Brazil, 1999. Instr. anthropology Am. U., Washington, 1950-51; rsch. assoc. Smithsonian Instn.. 1954—, expert, 1981—; founder, pres. Taraxacum Inc., 1977—. Hon. prof. U. de Azuay, Ecuador, 1991. Author: Environmental Limitation on the Development of Culture, 1954, Ecuador, 1966, Amazonia, 1971, 2d edit., 1996, Prehistoric America, 1972, Evolucion y Dibision Cultural, 1998, Ecologia y Biogeografia de la Amazonia, 1999, (with Clifford Evans) Archeological Investigations at the Mouth of the Amazon, 1957, Archeological Investigations in British Guiana, 1960, (with Clifford Evans and Emilio Estrada) Early Formative Period of Coastal Ecuador, 1965, (with Clifford Evans) Archeological Investigations on the Rio Napo, Eastern Ecuador, 1968; editor: Prehistoria Sudamericana, 1992. Recipient award for sci. achievement Washington Acad. Sci., 1956; gold medal 37th Internat. Congress of Americanists, 1966; Order Al Merito Govt. Ecuador, 1966; Order Bernardo O'Higgins Govt. Chile, 1985; Sec.'s Gold medal for exceptional service Smithsonian Instn., 1986; Order Andres Bello Govt. Venezuela, 1988; Order Al Mérito por Servicios Distinguidos Govt. Peru, 1989. Fellow: AAAS, Assn. Tropical Biology (hon.; councilor 1976—78, pres.-elect 1982, pres. 1983); mem.: Ecol. Soc. Am., New Eng. Antiquities Rsch. Assn., Academia Nacional Historia Ecuador (corr.), Am. Anthrop. Assn. (exec. sec. 1959-61), Museo Antropológico de la Cultura Andina (hon.), Soc. Am. Archaeology (exec. bd. 1962—64), Am. Ethnol. Soc., Anthrop. Soc. Wash. (treas. 1955—60, v.p. 1965—66, pres. 1966—68), Phi Beta Kappa, Sigma Xi. Home: 1227 30th St NW Washington DC 20007-3410 Office: Smithsonian Instn Washington DC 20560-0001

**MEGGINSON, ELIZABETH R.,** legislative staff member, director, lawyer; b. Clarksdale, Miss., Oct. 27, 1947; d. Mitford Ray and Cleo Ruth (Faggard) M.; m. Mark W. Menezes; children: Paige Jennings, Marisa Menezes. BM, La. State U., 1969, MM, 1970, JD, 1977. Pvt. practice, 1977-78; counsel natural resources com. La. Ho. Reps., 1978-81, legis. svc. coord. comml. regulation divsn., 1981-84; asst. atty. gen. environ. enforcement divsn. La. Dept. Justice, 1984-88; asst. sec. for office legal affairs and enforcement La. Dept. Environ. Quality, 1988-89; adminstrv. asst. to Rep. W.J. Billy Tauzin, Washington, 1989-90; staff dir. counsel Subcommittee on Coast Guard and Navigation Com. on Merchant Marine and Fisheries, U.S. Ho. Rep., Washington, 1990—95; counsel to chair Com. on Resources, U.S. Ho. Rep., Washington, 1995—96, chief counsel, 1997—2000, Com. on Transp. & Infrastructure, U.S. Ho. Rep., Washington, 2001—. Mem. Phi Kappa Phi. Office: Committee on Transportation & Infrastructure Room 2165 Rayburn House Office Building Washington DC 20515-6256

**MEGGINSON, LAURA IRENE,** secondary school educator; d. Douglas. BA in History, Auburn U.; MEd, U. Montevallo. Tchr. Lanett (Ala.) H.S., 2003—.

**MEGGS, WILLIAM JOEL,** toxicologist, allergist, emergency physician, educator; b. Newberry, S.C., May 30, 1942; s. Wallace Nat and Elizabeth (Pruitt) M.; m. Susan Nancy Spring, June 11, 1966 (div. June 1998); m. Susan Krause Martin, Apr. 21, 2001; children: Jason Nathaniel, Benjamin Maffey, Thomas Clute. BS, Clemson U., 1964; PhD, Syracuse U., 1969; MD, U. Miami, 1979. Diplomate Am. Bd. Internal Medicine, Am. Bd. Allergy and Immunology, Am. Bd. Emergency Medicine, Am. Bd. Med. Toxicology. Resident in internal medicine Rochester (N.Y.) Gen. Hosp., 1979-82; staff fellow in allergy and clin. immunology Nat. Inst. Allergy and Infectious Diseases, Bethesda, Md., 1982-85; asst. dir. med. edn. emergency Dept. Washington Hosp. Ctr., 1985-88; from asst. prof. allergy, immunology to sr. vice chmn. Sch. Medicine E. Carolina U., Greenville, NC, 1988—2004, sr. vice chmn. Sch. Medicine, 2004—; chmn., dir. emergency dept. Lenoir Meml. Hosp., Kinston, NC, 1990-91. Mem. Emergency Svcs. Com. Lenoir Meml. Hosp., Kinston, 1988-92; mem workshop on immune testing, Agy. for Toxic Substances and Diseases Registry, 1992, workshop on equity in environ. health, U.S. EPA, 1992, workshop on multiple chem. sensitivity syndrome, NRC, 1991; mem. rsch. adv. com. on Gulf War illnesses Dept. VA, 2002-; fellow med. toxicology NYU, 1992-96. Co-author: The Inflammation Cure, 2003; co-editor: Health and Safety in Agriculture, 1997; contbr. numerous articles and abstracts to profl. jours. Vol. physician Indigent Clinic E. Carolina U., Pitt County Med. Soc., 1988—, Pitt County Shelter, 1989—; advanced cardiac life support instr. E. Carolina U. Sch. of Medicine, 1988-2000, advanced trauma life support instr., 1991-2002; mem. Pitt County Traffic Injury Prevention Program, 1989-92; bd. dirs. Rachael Carson Coun., 1988—; mem. adv. bd. Pamplico Tar River Found., 1990—. Named Woodrow Wilson Hon. fellow, 1964, NSF post-doctoral fellow, 1969; grantee N.C. United Way, 1988-89, Greer Labs., 1989-90, Am. Lung Assn. N.C., 1992-93. Fellow Am. Coll. Emergency Physicians, Am. Coll. Med. Toxicology; mem. AMA, Am. Acad. Allergy and Immunology, Am. Acad. Clin. Toxicology, Pitt County Med. Soc., N.C. State Med. Soc., Soc. for Acad. Emergency Medicine, N.C. Thoracic Soc. (physicians' sect.). Achievements include creator of the biological homing theory of the origins of life. Office: E Carolina U Sch Medicine Dept Emergency Medicine Brody Bldg 4-W54 600 Moye Blvd Greenville NC 27858-4300 Office Phone: 252-744-2954. Business E-Mail: meggsw@mail.ecu.edu.

**MEGHANI, SHENI,** geriatrician; b. Rajkot, India, Aug. 16, 1971; d. Nanak and Kusum Meghani. MBBS, Smt. N H L Mcpl. Med. Coll., Ahmedabad, India, 1995; MD, Sheth K M Sch. Postgrad. Medicine and Rsch., Ahmedabad, 1998; postgrad., Des Moines U., 2005—. Diplomate Am. Bd. Internal Medicine, Certificate of Added Qualification in Geriatric Medicine Am. Bd. of Internal Medicine, 2003. Resident dept. medicine Shenth K M Sch. Postgrad. Medicine and Rsch., 1995—98, chief resident dept. medicine, 1998; resident dept. medicine SUNY Health Sci. Ctr. at Bklyn., 1999—2002, chief resident, divsn. of geriat., 2003—04; fellow divsn. geriat. U. Pa., Phila., 2002—03; geriatrician VA Ctrl. Iowa Healthcare Sys., Des Moines, 2004—; Chief divsn. geriat., med. dir. home based primary care, mem. ethics com.,

mem. peer rev. com. VA Ctrl. Iowa Healthcare Sys., 2005—, med. dir. nursing home and palliative care, Knoxville, Iowa, 2005—; adj. clin. faculty internal medicine U. Iowa Carver Coll. of Medicine, Iowa City, 2005—; presenter in field. Mem.: Gerontol. Soc. Iowa, Am. Geriat. Soc. Achievements include research in palliative and end-of-life care; development of comprehensive geriatrics assessment program, innovative program for elder care at VA Des Moines. Office Phone: 515-699-5999. Personal E-mail: shenimeghani@yahoo.com.

**MEGHREBLIAN, ROBERT VARTAN,** manufacturing executive, physicist; b. Cairo, Sept. 6, 1922; arrived in U.S., 1923, naturalized, 1929; s. Vahan V. and Mary (Kurkjian) M.; m. Mary J. Walton, 1955 (div. 1977); Children: David V., Susan M.; m. Margaret M. Gordon, 1987. B in Engring. (Gotshall-Powell scholar), Rensselaer Poly. Inst., 1943; MS (Guggenheim fellow), Calif. Inst. Tech., 1950, PhD magna cum laude (Guggenheim fellow), 1953. Lectr. Oak Ridge Nat. Lab., 1952-55, assoc. project mgr., 1955-58; chief sect. Physics Jet Propulsion Lab., Calif. Inst. Tech., 1958-60, mgr. space scis. divsn., 1960-68, dep. asst. lab. dir., 1968-71, assoc. prof. applied mechanics, 1960-61; v.p. rsch. and engring. Cabot Corp., Boston, 1971-79, v.p., 1971-87; pres. Distrigas Corp., 1979-85; gen. mgr. Cabot Crystals Bus. Unit, 1985-86, dir. corp. planning and devel., 1986-87. Author: Reactor Analysis, 1960. V.p. Art Found. Santa Barbara. Served to lt. (j.g.) USN, 1941-46, PTO, ATO. Fellow AIAA (assoc.), Am. Nuc. Soc.; mem. Tennis Club Santa Barbara, Santa Barbara Club, Montecito Assn. (bd. dirs. 1992-98, v.p. 1994, pres. 1995, 96, chair archtl. rev. com. 1993-95). Montecito Citizen of Yr. 2002, vice chair Montecito planning commn. 2003, chair 2004-06), Sigma Xi. Home: 440 Woodley Rd Montecito CA 93108-2006

**MEGILL, ALLAN D.,** historian; b. Regina, Sask., Can., Apr. 20, 1947; arrived in US, 1980; s. Ralph Peter and Jean Tudhope (Dickson) M.; divorced; children: Jason Robert, Jessica Susan, Jonathan David; m. Rita Felski; 1 child, Maria Megill Felski. BA, U. Sask., 1969; MA, U. Toronto, 1970; PhD, Columbia U., 1975. From instr. to prof. history U. Iowa, Iowa City, 1974—90; prof. history U. Va., Charlottesville, 1990—. Rsch. fellow in history of ideas Australian Nat. U., Canberra, 1977—79, temp. lectr. modern European studies, 1979; dir. d'études invité École des Hautes Études en Scis. Sociales, Paris, 1997—. Author: Prophets of Extremity, 1985, Karl Marx: The Burden of Reason, 2002; editor: Rethinking Objectivity, 1994; co-editor: The Rhetoric of the Human Sciences, 1987; cons. editor Jour. of History of Ideas, 1986—89, mem., editl. bd., 1990—, v.p., 2004—05, pres., 2005—; mem. editl. bd.: U. Press of Va., 1991—94, Rethinking History, 1996—; contbr. articles to profl. jours. Chmn. Page-Barbour and Richard Lectures com. U. Va., 1994-96. Mem.: Am. Hist. Assn. Office: U Va Corcoran Dept of History PO Box 400180 Charlottesville VA 22904 Office Phone: 434-924-6414. Business E-Mail: megill@virginia.edu.

**MEGNA, STEVE ALLAN,** retired secondary school educator; Secondary tchr. Vernon (NJ) H.S., ret., 2006. Recipient Tech. Excellence award Internat. Tech. Edn. Assn. and Tech. Edn. Assn. N.J., 1992, Tech. Program of Yr. award Tech. Edn. Assn. N.J., 1989; named Innovative Tech. Educator, Martinson Family Found., 2002.

**MEHAFFEY, JOHN ALLEN,** marketing executive, publishing executive; b. Brainerd, Minn. m. Mary Jean Mehaffey; children: Mark, Scott, Chris. Student, Minn. Sch. Bus. With Mehaffey Internat., Naples, Fla., 1954—. Bd. govs. Verified Audit Circulations. Ga. Nat. Newspaper Assn., Newspaper Assn. Am., Nat. Press Club (Washington), Ill. Press Assn., Assn. Free Cmty. Papers, Ind. Free Papers Assn., Fla. Free Papers Assn., Am. Mktg. Assn., Inland Press Assn., Fla. Press Assn., Soc. Profl. Journalists, Chgo. Headline Club, Internat. Platform Assn., Am. Telemktg. Assn., Naples Area C. of C., Suburban Newspaper Assn., Ctrl. States Circulating Mgrs. Assn., Inland Press Assn., Southeastern Advt. Pubs. Assn., Brainerd Lakes Area C. of C., St. Joseph's Med. Ctr. Found. (charter), Nat. Alliance for Mentally Ill., Greater Chgo. and AllI. Alliance for Mentally Ill, Motion Picture and TV Assn., Marine Habitat Found. (founding), Naples Aquarium (founding), Founding One Thousand, Naples Philharm. Ctr. for Performing Arts, Naples Conservancy, Northland Arboretum, Paul Bunyan Nature Learning Ctr. (life), Nat. Rails-to-Trails Conservancy, Internat. Press Club (Chgo.), Naples Press Club, Elks, Moose, Sigma Delta Chi. Avocation: boating. Home and Office: Mehaffey Internat PO Box 2956 Naples FL 34106-2956

**MEHALCHIN, JOHN JOSEPH,** entrepreneur, finance company executive; b. Hazleton, Pa., Aug. 8, 1937; s. Charles and Susan (Korba) Mehalchin; 1 child from previous marriage, Martin. BS with honors (1st in class), Temple U., 1964; MBA, U. Calif., Berkeley, 1965; postgrad., U. Chgo., 1964; LHD (hon.), U. Colo., 2002. Supr. costs Winchester-Western, New Haven, 1965-67; mgmt. cons. Booz-Allen & Hamilton, N.Y.C., 1967-68; mgr. planning TWA, N.Y.C., 1968-69; officer Smith Barney, N.Y.C., Paris, 1970-74; pres. Storage Tech. Leasing Corp., Louisville, 1974-79; sr. v.p. Heizer Corp., 1979; pres., founder Highline Fin. Svcs., Inc. and fgn. subs., Boulder, Colo., 1979—, London, Paris, Frankfurt, Germany; chmn. Highline Capital Corp., 1999—; CFO Storage Tech. Corp. Chmn. Highline Capital Corp., Boulder, Colo., 1998—; strategic planning com. Coll. and Grad. Sch. Bus., U. Colo., Denver; bd. advisors U. Colo. Ctr. Entrepreneurship, U. Colo. Bus. Sch., Wolf Ventures. With U.S. Army, 1958—61. Recipient Mack Easton award for Excellence, 1998, Univ. medal, U. Colo., 2002; fellow, U. Calif., Berkeley, 1964, 1965; scholar, U. Chgo., 1964. Mem.: Equipment Leasing Assn., Fin. Execs. Inst., Omicron Delta Epsilon, Beta Gamma Sigma. Home and Office: Highline Fin Svcs Inc 2930 Center Green Ct Ste 200 Boulder CO 80301-5419 Office Phone: 303-443-7267.

**MEHAN, ASHOK,** information technology executive; b. India; arrived in US, 1983; m. Archisha Mehan; 2 children. BA, 1978; MBA, Marymount U., 1987. Founder, CEO SMAC Data Systems, 1990—2001, Adezza Federal Consulting, LLC, 2001—. Adjunct prof. U. Md. Mem. Montgomery County Techn.Develop.Council, Md., County IT Steering Com., Md. Incubator Adv. Bd., County Edu. Workforce Develop. Com.; charter mem. Indian CEO High Tech Council; bd. mem. Indian Am. Leadership Inst. Office: Adezza Fed Consulting LLC 13708 Ginkgo Terrace Rockville MD 20850

**MEHAN, GEORGE TRACEY, III,** former federal agency administrator; b. June 1949; Grad., St. Louis U. Dir. Mo. Dept. Natural Resources, 1989—91; assoc. deputy adminstr. EPA, 1992—93; dir. Office of Great Lakes, Mich. Dept. Environ. Quality; asst. adminstr. water EPA, Washington, 2001—04.

**MEHARG, KAREN,** music educator; b. Ft. Sill, Okla., July 27, 1981; d. Steven W. and Yun Chu Meharg. B of Music Edn., U. Ctrl. Okla., 2003. Cert. tchr. SC. Activities asst. White Oak Estates Nursing Home, Spartanburg, SC, 2003; music tchr. Boiling Springs Mid. Sch., SC, 2004; chorus tchr. Whitlock Jr. H.S., Spartanburg, SC, 2004—. Mem.: Music Educators Nat. Conv., Am. Choral Dirs. Assn., Collegiate Music Educators Nat. Conf. (pres. 2001—02), Spartanburg Music Club, Sigma Alpha Iota (sgt. of arms 2002—03), Alpha Xi.

**MEHIEL, DENNIS,** investment company executive; Co-founder Four M Corp., Balt., 1966, Valhalla, NY, 1970; former owner Box USA, Sweetheart Cup Co.; now chmn., prin. shareholder Four M Capital Inc. Office: Four M Capital Inc 470 Park Ave S New York NY 10016*

**MEHL, ALBERT L.,** pediatrician, poet, composer; s. Clinton Mehl and Alberta Wells; m. Annie Kempe, Aug. 4, 1979; children: Sarah Kempe-Mehl, James Kempe-Mehl. BA, Colo. Coll., Colorado Springs, 1976; MD, U. Colo. Health Scis. Ctr., Denver, 1980. Diplomate Am. Bd. Pediat. Pediatrician Kaiser Permanente, Lafayette, Colo., 1987—. Editl. cons. various publs., Various US states, 1988—; asst. clin. prof. U. Colo. Health Scis. Ctr., Denver, 2001—; chmn. peer rev. com. Exempla Good Samaritan Med. Ctr., Lafayette, Colo., 2005—. Singer, songwriter: albums Asphalt Cowboy, writer, performer: albums Cowboy Pottery; contbr. articles to profl. jours. Mem. expert working group effective interventions infants and young children with hearing

loss U.S. HHS; gubernatorial appointee Colo. Children's Trust Fund Child Abuse Prevention, Denver, 1992—97, vice chmn., 1995—96; chmn. infant hearing adv. com. Colo. State Dept. Health and Environment, Denver, 1997—. Recipient Peak Performance award, Colo. Acad. Audiology, 1998, Communities Helping Young Children award, Frances Owens, First Lady of Colo., 2005; Boettcher Found. scholar, 1973—77. Fellow: Am. Acad. Pediat. (chmn. nat. task force infant hearing 2005—), appointee U.S. joint com. infant hearing 2005—). Avocations: fly fishing, skiing, golf. Office: Kaiser Permanente Med Offices 280 Exempla Cir Lafayette CO 80026

**MEHL, DONALD EDWARD,** retired marketing professional; b. Omaha, Jan. 28, 1923; s. Arthur Julius and Cecilia Mehl; m. Alice Mae Toland, Apr. 15, 1950 (dec. 1997); children: David(dec.), Kathleen Chadwick, Janice Rhodes, Arthur, Therese Sellers. Student, U. Omaha, 1942, U. Minn., 1943—44; BS, Creighton U., 1949. Engring. mgr. Inland Broadcasting Co., 1942—52; telecomm. mktg. mgr. Graybar Electric, Kansas City, Mo., 1952—59; v.p., editor, pub. Tech. Publs., Inc., Kansas City, Mo., 1959—61; advt. and mktg. profl. Collins Radio, Richardson, Tex., 1961—73; mktg. dir. Rockwell Internat., Kansas City, Mo., 1973—87. Author, pub.: Sigsaly - The Green Hornet, 1997, Top Secret Communications of World War II, 2002, founder, editor, pub.: Broadcast Engring. Jour. 1st lt. signal corps U.S. Army, 1943—46. Mem.: Am. Radio Relay League. Avocation: amateur radio. Home: 1327 W Jenkins Blvd Raymore MO 64083

**MEHLENBACHER, DOHN HARLOW,** civil engineer, consultant; b. Huntington Park, Calif., Nov. 18, 1931; s. Virgil Claude and Hayda (Sigfridson) M.; m. Nancy Moss; children: Dohn Scott, Kimberly Ruth, Mark James, Matthew Lincoln. BSCE, U. Ill., 1953; MS in City and Regional Planning, Ill. Inst. Tech., 1961; MBA, U. Chgo., 1972. Registered profl. engr., Ill.; lic. structural engr., Ill. Structural engr., draftsman Swift & Co., Chgo., 1953-54, 56-57, DeLeuw-Cather Co., Chgo., 1957-59; project engr. Quaker Oats Co., Chgo., 1959-61, mgr. constrn., 1964-70, mgr. real property, 1970-71, mgr. engring. and maintenance L.A., 1961-64; chief facilities engr. Bell & Howell Co., Chgo., 1972-73; v.p. design Globe Engring. Co., Chgo., 1973-76; project mgr. I.C. Harbour Constrn. Co., Oak Brook, Ill., 1976-78; dir. estimating George A. Fuller Co., Oak Brook, 1978; pres. Food-Tech. Co., Willowbrook, Ill., 1979-80; dir. phys. resources Ill. Inst. Tech., Chgo., 1980-92; cons. Exec. Svc. Corp., Chgo., 1994—. Arbitrator Am. Arbitration Assn. With USAF, 1954-56. Fellow ASCE. Home and Office: 436 Leitch Ave La Grange IL 60525-6126 Office Phone: 708-354-7131. Personal E-Mail: dohnh@aol.com.

**MEHLER, GORDON,** lawyer; b. Denver, Feb. 27, 1955; s. Irving Martin and Bernice (Steinberg) M.; m. Ariel Zwang; children: Grace, Rachel. BS, U. Colo., 1976; JD, NYU, 1982. Bar: NY 1983, US Dist. Ct. (ea. and so. dists.) NY 1983, US Ct. Appeals (10th cir.) 1984, US Ct. Appeals (2d cir.) 1985, US Supreme Ct. 2000. Assoc. Skadden, Arps, Slate, Meagher & Flom, NYC, 1982-83; law clk. to presiding judge US Ct. Appeals (10th cir.), Denver, 1983-84; fed. prosecutor US Atty.'s Office (ea. dist.), NYC, 1984—99, chief spl. prosecutions (pub. integrity), 1996-98; dep. asst. atty. gen. US Dept. Justice, Washington, 1999-2000; with Law Offices of Gordon Mehler, NYC, 2000—. Adj. assoc. prof. law Fordham U. Law Sch., NYC, 1982-98; US Dept. Justice resident legal advisor to Romania, Bucharest, 1992. Author: (with Gleeson and James) Federal Criminal Practice, Lexis Nexis 7th edit., 2006; editor: (with others) New York Criminal Practice, Lexis Nexis, 2d edit., 2005; contbr. articles in field to profl. jours. and newspapers. Mem. ABA, Assn. Bar City of NY, Fed. Bar Coun., Def. Lawyers Office: 575 Lexington Ave Ste 410 New York NY 10022-6102 Office Phone: 212-527-7503. Business E-Mail: gmehler@mehlerlaw.com.

**MEHLING, CHRISTOPHER JOHN,** lawyer; b. Fremont, Ohio, Dec. 14, 1952; s. Robert E. and Mary (Lehmann) M.; m. Patricia Ann Ebert, June 21, 1975; children: Jennifer, Joshua. BA, Bowling Green (Ohio) State U., 1975; JD, U. Cin., 1978. Bar: Ohio 1978, Ky. 1979, U.S. Dist. Ct. (ea. dist.) Ky. 1980, U.S. Dist. Ct. (so. dist.) Ohio 1978, U. S. Ct. Appeals (6th cir.) 1985. Assoc. Gustin & Lawrence, Cin., 1978-83, Taliaferro, Smith, Mann, Wolnitzek & Schachter, Covington, Ky., 1983-86; ptnr. Taliaferro & Mann, Covington, 1986-93, Taliaferro, Mehling, Shirooni, Carran & Keys, Covington, 1994—. Commr. No. Ky. Area Planning Commn., Kenton, 1984-90; councilman City of Independence, Ky., 1983, bd. adjustments, 1981-83; bd. dirs. Licking Valley coun. Girl Scouts U.S., 1990-93; sec. Ind.-Ky. Synod Evangel. Luth. Ch. in Am., 1991-99; bd. dirs. Covington Bus. coun., 1993-2005, chmn. 1996-97; bd. dirs. Welcome House, 1995-99, CBC Found., pres., 1997-99, bd. dirs. 1997-2005; mem. No. Ky. conv. & Visitors Bur., Champions Club; bd. dirs. No. Ky. C. of C., 2005—, bus advocacy com., 2002—; Dan Beard coun. mem. at large Boy Scouts Am., 2005—. Mem. No. Ky. Bar Assn. (sec. 1990-91, chair conv. 2000.), Ky. Acad. Trial Attys. Democrat. Lutheran. Home: 2528 Nicklaus Lane Crestview Hills KY 41017 Office: 1005 Madison Ave Covington KY 41011-3113 Office Phone: 859-291-9900. Business E-Mail: cmehling@tmsck.com.

**MEHLINGER, HOWARD DEAN,** education educator; b. Hillsboro, Kans., Aug. 22, 1931; s. Alex and Alice Hilda (Skibbe) Mehlinger; m. Carolee Ann Case, Dec. 28, 1952; children: Bradley Case, Barbara Ann, Susan Kay. BA, McPherson Coll., Kans., 1953; MS in Edn, U. Kans., 1959, PhD, 1964. Co-dir. social studies project Pitts. pub. schs., 1963-64; asst. dir. rpt. relations project North Central Assn. Schs. and Colls., Chgo., 1964-65; mem. faculty Ind. U., Bloomington, 1965-97, prof. history and edn., 1974-97, dean Sch. Edn., 1981-90, dir. Ctr. for Excellence in Edn., 1990-99. Social studies adviser Houghton Mifflin Pub. Co.; cons. U.S. Office Edn. Co-author: American Political Behavior, 2d edit., 1977, Count Witte and the Tsarist Government in the 1905 Revolution, 1972, Toward Effective Instruction in the Social Studies, 1974, School Reform in the Information Age, 1995, Technology and Teacher Education: A Guide for Educators and Policymakers, 2002; editl. bd. Education and Society, history tchr.; editor: UNESCO Handbook on the Teaching of Social Studies, 1981; co-editor: Yearbook on the Social Studies, 1981. STAG grantee Dept. State, 1975 Mem. NEA. Nat. Council Social Studies, Phi Beta Kappa, Phi Alpha Theta, Pi Sigma Alpha, Phi Delta Kappa. Home: 3271 N Ramble Rd E Bloomington IN 47408-1094 Business E-Mail: mehlinge@indiana.edu.

**MEHLMAN, BRUCE P.,** former federal agency administrator, trade association administrator; s. Arthur and Judy Mehlman; married; 3 children. Grad., Princeton U., U. Va. Gen. counsel Nat. Rep. Congl. Com., 1996—99; gen. counsel, policy dir. House Rep. Conf.; telecom. policy counsel Cisco Sys., 1999—2001; asst. sec. for tech. policy US Dept. Commerce, Washington, 2001—04; exec. dir. Computer Systems Policy Project, Washington, 2004—. Republican. Office: Computer Systems Policy Project Ste 1100 1341 G St NW Washington DC 20005

**MEHLMAN, EDWIN STEPHEN,** endodontist; b. Hartford, Conn., Nov. 30, 1935; s. Sol Abraham and Rose (Slitt) M.; m. Lesley Judith Lunin, June 13, 1959; children: Jeffrey Cole, Brian Scott, Erik Van. BA, Wesleyan U., 1957; DDS, U. Pa., 1961; cert. endodontics, Boston U., 1965. Diplomate Am. Bd. Endodontists. Instr. clin. instr. endodontics Sch. Dental Medicine Harvard U., Boston, 1965—67; clin. instr. endodontics Sch. Dental Medicine Tufts U., Boston, 1968—70; lectr. endodontics Sch. Dental Medicine, Harvard U., Boston, 1970—72; asst. clin. prof. endodontics, 1972—; staff assoc. Forsyth Dental Ctr., Boston, 1965—; asst. prof. endodontics Boston U. Sch. Dental Medicine, 1995—; pvt. practice Providence, 1965—. Vis. lectr. dental hygiene U. R.I., Kingston, 1965-71, Community Coll. R.I., Lincoln, 1990—; cons. com. on accreditation of Dentists and Dental Aux. Edn. Programs, 1974-78. Contbr. articles to profl. jours. Pres. Temple Habonim, Barrington, R.I., 1968-70, Bur. Jewish Edn. of R.I., 1980-84; area v.p. Jewish Fedn. R.I., 1975-78; mem. R.I. Legis. Commn. to Study Malpractice Crisis, 1985-86; chmn. R.I. Dental Polit. Action Com., 1987-90. Capt. USAF, 1961-63. Recipient Etheringon award Six N.E. Dental Assns. for Outstanding Contbns. to Dentistry, Disting. Fellow Internat. Coll. Dentists, 2004, Dist. Alumni award for svc. to dentistry Boston U. Goldman Sch. Dentistry, 2005 Fellow Am. Coll. Dentists (Vol. Yr. 2004), Internat. Coll. Dentists (dep. regent 1994-98), Pierre Fauchard Acad. (Merit award, Leadership award 2006,

RIOA Kershan award for outstanding contbn. to cmty. 2006); mem. ADA (coun. on govt. affairs and fed. dental svcs. 1988-92, vice-chmn. 1991-92, 1st v.p. 1994-95, 1st dist. trustee 1999-2003); Am. Assn. Endodontists (dir. 1988-91), R.I. Dental Assn. (pres. 1986-87), N.E. Dental Assns. (Outstanding N.E. Dentist 1995, Disting. Practitioner 2000). Jewish. Avocations: reading, civic activities. Home: 3 Hanley Farm Rd Warren RI 02885-4376 also: 130 Waterman St Providence RI 02906-2010

**MEHLMAN, KENNETH B.,** political organization administrator, former federal official; b. Balt., Aug. 1966; s. Arthur and Judy Mehlman. BA, Franklin & Marshall, 1988; JD, Harvard U., 1991. Bar: DC, Md. Assoc. Akin, Gump, Strauss, Hauer and Feld, 1991—94; legis. dir. Rep. Lamar Smith, 1994—96; chief of staff Rep. Kay Granger, 1996—99; mid-west regional polit. dir. Rep. Primaries, 1999; nat. field dir. Bush-Cheney campaign, 2000; dep. asst. & dir. pub. affairs to Pres. George W. Bush The White House, 2001—03; chmn. Bush-Cheney campaign, 2004, Rep. Nat. Com., 2005—. Campaign worker William Weld's campaign for gov. of Mass., 1990, Pres. George H. W. Bush re-election campaign, 1992, Ohio Senator Mike DeWine's campaign, 1994, Senator Bob Dole's campaign, 1996; mem. bd. trustees Franklin & Marshall Coll., 2003—. Mem.: Phi Kappa Tau. Republican. Office: RNC 310 First St SE Washington DC 20003

**MEHLMAN, LON DOUGLAS,** information technology specialist, investment banker, venture capitalist; b. Los Angeles, Apr. 29, 1959; s. Anton and Diane Mehlman. BA, UCLA, 1981; MBA, Pepperdine U., 1983. Cert. project mgmt. profl. Project Mgmt. Inst., 2002. Software developer Ticom Systems Inc., Century City, Calif., 1979—81; systems analyst NCR Corp., Century City, 1981—82; sr. systems analyst Tandem Computers Inc., L.A., 1982—91; sr. computer scientist Computer Scis. Corp., El Segundo, Calif., 1991-97; CIO, dir. info. tech. Globe Cast Corp., Culver City, Calif., 1997-2000; chief tech. officer, v.p. engring. MediaConnex, Inc., Hollywood, Calif., 2000-01; v.p., program mgr. info. tech. Micro Gen. Corp., Santa Ana, Calif., 2001—03; mng. dir. ITF Global Ptnrs., LLC, N.Y.C., 2003—. Author: Establishing an Enterprise Information Systems Infrastructure, 1995, Implementing TQM, 1995, Lessons Learned from the Navstar GPS Engineering Management System Project, 1997. Mem. Am. Mgmt. Assn., Project Mgmt. Inst., Armed Forces Comms. and Electronics Assn., LA Venture Assn., Assn. for Corp. Growth, Sierra Club, Phi Delta Theta. Avocations: golf, tennis, sailing, skiing, world travel. Office: ITF Global Ptnrs 291 7th Ave Penhouse New York NY 10001 E-mail: lonmx@worldnet.att.net.

**MEHLMAN, MARK FRANKLIN,** lawyer; b. LA, Dec. 18, 1947; s. Jack and Elaine Pearl (Lopater) M.; m. Barbara Ann Novak, Aug. 20, 1972; children: David, Jennifer, Ilyse. BA, U. Ill., 1969; LLB, U. Mich., 1973. Bar: Ill. 1973; U.S. Dist. Ct. (no. dist.) Ill. 1973. Assoc. Sonnenschein, Nath & Rosenthal LLP, Chgo., 1973—80, mem. policy and planning com., 1989—. Trustee Groveland Health Svcs., Highland Park (Ill.) Hosp., 1991-97; trustee, treas., exec. com. Spertus Inst. Jewish Studies, Chgo., 1992-97, vice chmn. bd. trustees, 1996—; vice-chmn. regional bd. Anti-Defamation League, 1987-89, hon. life mem. nat. commn., 1993— Fellow Am. Bar Found.; mem. ABA (chmn. mortgages and other debt financing subcom. 1991-95, supervisory coun. 1997—, sec. RPPT sect. 2004-05), Am. Coll. Real Estate Lawyers (exec. com. bd. govs. 2000—, sec. 2003-04, treas. 2004-05, v.p. 2005-06, pres.-elect 2006—, chmn. MDP com. 2000—, chmn. mem. selection com. 2000-01), Anglo-Am. Real Property Inst., Legal Club of Chgo., Lake Shore Country Club, Standard Club, Exec. Club of Chgo. Office: Sonnenschein Nath & Rosenthal LLP Ste 7800 233 S Wacker Dr Chicago IL 60606-6491 Office Phone: 312-876-8023. Business E-Mail: mmehlman@sonnenschein.com.

**MEHLMAN, MAXWELL JONATHAN,** law educator; b. Washington, Nov. 4, 1948; s. Jacob and Betty (Hoffman) M.; m. Cheryl A. Stone, Sept. 15, 1979; children: Aurora, Gabriel. BA, Reed Coll., 1970, Oxford U., England, 1972; JD, Yale U., 1975. Bar: D.C. 1976, Ohio 1988. Assoc. Arnold & Porter, Washington, 1975-84; asst. prof. Case Western Res. U., Cleve., 1984-87, assoc. prof., 1987-90, prof. law, 1990-96, Arthur E. Petersilge prof., 1996—, prof. biomed. ethics, 1998—; dir. Law-Medicine Ctr., Case Western Res. U., 1986—. Spl. counsel N.Y. State Bar, N.Y.C., 1988-94, Nat. Kidney Found., 1991; cons. Am. Assn. Ret. Persons, Washington, 1992. Editor: High Tech Home Care, 1991, (with T. Murray) Encyclopedia of Ethical, Legal and Policy Issues in Biotechnology; author: (with J. Botkin) Access to the Genome: The Challenge to Equality, 1998, (with Andrews and Rothstein) Genetics: Ethics, Law and Policy, 2002, 06, Wondergenes: Genetic Enhancement and the Future of Society, 2003; contbr. articles to profl. jours. Active steering com. AIDS Commn. Greater Cleve., 1986-90. Rhodes scholar, 1970; Rsch. grantee NIH, 1992-94, 97—. Mem. Am. Assn. Law Schs. (chmn. sect. on law, medicine and health care 1990), Phi Beta Kappa. Avocations: skiing, music, kayaking. Office: Case Western Reserve U Sch Law-Law Medicine Ctr Gund Hall 11075 E Blvd Cleveland OH 44106 Office Phone: 216-368-3983.

**MEHLMAN, MYRON A.,** medical educator, toxicologist; m. Constance Mehlman, Sept. 4, 1960 (dec. June 1997); children: Mara Appel, Hope Hurowitz, Alison Fox; m. Karyl Norcross, Apr. 14, 1999. BS, CCNY, 1957; PhD, MIT, 1964. Prof. biochemistry Rutgers U., Newark, 1965-69; prof. biochemistry Coll. of Medicine U. Nebr., Omaha, 1967-71; chief biochem. toxicology FDA, Washington, 1972-73; spl. asst. toxicology dept. HEW, Washington, 1973-75; interagy. liaison officer NIH, Bethesda, Md., 1975-77; dir. toxicology Mobil Oil, Princeton, NJ, 1977-89; prof. U. Medicine and Dentistry of N.J., Piscataway, 1990—, Mt. Sinai Sch. Medicine, NY, 1980, U. Tex. Med. Br., Galveston, 2003—. Editor Jour. Environ. Pathology and Toxicology, 1977-81, Jour. Toxicology and Indsl. Health, 1975-78, Jour. Clean Tech. and Environ. Sci., 1989—; contbr. over 300 articles to profl. jours.; edited over 60 books. 1st It. U.S. Army, 1958-60. Fellow Acad. Toxol. Soc., Am. Coll. Toxicology, Collequim Ramazzin (founding dir., bd. dirs., Ramazzin award 2002). Achievements include research in toxicology, environmental health, and nutritional and biomedical science. Office: 7 Bouvant Dr Princeton NJ 08540-1208

**MEHLTRETTER, KATHLEEN M.,** former prosecutor; b. 1954; BS, Univ. of Dayton; JD, State Univ. of NY at Buffalo. Bar: New York 1979. U.S. atty. (we. dist.) NY U.S. Dept. Justice, Buffalo, 2005—06.*

**MEHNER, ROGER,** lawyer; b. Morristown, N.J., Sept. 29, 1952; s. Kurt Walter and Mae Mehner; m. Joan Helen Kopf, Aug. 14, 1976; children: Caitlin Elizabeth, Allison Leigh. AB in History, Princeton U., N.J., 1974; JD, George Washington U., Washington, D.C., 1977. Bar: N.J. 1977. Jud. clk. N. J. Superior Ct., Somerville, 1977—78; atty. Bourne, Noll & Kenyon, Summit, NJ, 1978—. Trustee Summit Area YMCA, NJ, 1987—95. Recipient Shuart Reed award, Summit Area YMCA, 2000. Mem.: Summit N.J. Bar Assn., N.J. State Bar Assn., Rotary Club (pres. 2002—03). Avocations: antique cars, sports, antiques, music. Office: Bourne Noll & Kenyon 382 Springfield Ave Summit NJ 07901 Business E-Mail: rmehner@bournenoll.com.

**MEHO, LOKMAN I.,** library and information scientist, educator; arrived in US, 1996; s. Ibrahim Y. Meho and Layla S. Hussein. BA in Polit. Sci., Am. U. Beirut, 1991, MA in Polit. Sci., 1996; MS in Libr. Sci., N.C. Ctrl. U., Durham, 1996; PhD in Info. and Libr. Sci., U. N.C., Chapel Hill, 2001. Libr. asst. Am. U. Beirut, 1986—95; freelance bibliographer Lebanon and U.S., 1991—; lectr. Sch. Libr. and Info. Scis. N.C. Ctrl. U., Durham, 1997—98; tchg. fellow Sch. Info. and Libr. Sci. U. N.C., Chapel Hill, 1999—2001; asst. prof. SUNY, Albany, 2001—04, Ind. U., Bloomington, 2004—. Author: Libraries and Information in the Arab World, 1999, Kurdish Culture and Society, 2001, Kurdish Question in U.S. Foreign Policy, 2004, Censorship in the Arab World, 2006. Sec. Lebanese Kurdish Charity Assn., Beirut, 1992—95; youth mem. Lebanese Red Cross, Beirut, 1989—95. Mem.: Assn. Libr. and Info. Sci. Edn., Assn. Coll. and Rsch. Librs., ALA, Am. Soc. Info. Sci. and Tech. Avocations: soccer, reading, painting. Office: Ind Univ 1320 E 10th St LI 011 Bloomington IN 47405 Office Phone: 812-856-2323. Office Fax: 812-855-6166. Business E-Mail: meho@indiana.edu.

**MEHRA, JAGDISH,** economics professor; b. Amritsar, Punjab, India, Nov. 12, 1934; came to U.S., 1962; s. Manmohan and Savitri (Devi) M.; m. Sneh L. Mehra, May 19, 1949; children: Reena, Benu. BA, Birla Inst. Tech., Pilani, Rajasthan, 1955, MA, 1957; PhD, SUNY, Buffalo, 1970. Asst. prof. econs. Banasthali U., Rajasthan, 1959-60; rschr. Nat. Coun. Applied Econ. Rsch., New Delhi, 1960-61; asst. prof. Econs. Birla Inst. Tech., Pilani, 1961-62; grad. asst., econs. instr. SUNY, Buffalo, 1962-65; asst. prof. econs. Youngstown (Ohio) U., 1965-71, assoc. prof. econs., 1971-81, prof. econs., 1981—2003, prof. emeritus, 2003—; sr. rsch. fellow Am. Inst. Econ. Rsch., Great Barrington, Mass., 1982-83. Contbr. articles to profl. jours. Avocations: reading, tennis. Office: Youngstown State U Dept Econs 1 University Plz Youngstown OH 44555 Office Phone: 330-941-1681. Business E-Mail: JCmehra@cc.ysu.edu.

**MEHRA, PUSHKAR,** director, educator; s. Mahendra Kumar and Sheila Mehra; m. Deepika Bhargava, Feb. 17, 2002. DDS, King Georges Med. Coll., India, 1992; DMD, Boston U., 1995; fellowship in Maxillofacial Reconstructive Surgery, Baylor U. Med. Ctr., 2000; postgrad., Tufts U., 1999, Boston U., 1999. Resident Lucknow U., India, 1992—93; clin. dir. Dept of Oral and Maxillofacial Surgery, Boston, 2000—02; asst. prof. Boston U., Boston, 2000—; dir. dept of oral and maxillofacial surgery Boston Med. Ctr., Boston, 2002—. Contbr. articles various profl. jours., chapters to books. Named one of Am.'s Best Dentists Maxillofacial Surgery; recipient Straumann award, Outstanding Rsch., Am. Assn. of Oral and Maxillofacial Surgeons, 2000. Fellow: Am. Coll. of Oral and Maxillofacial Surgeons, Am. Bd. of Oral and Maxillofacial Surgery (life); mem.: ADA (assoc.), Am. Soc. of TMJ surgeons, Mass. Dental Soc. (assoc.), Am. Assn. of Oral and Maxillofacial Surgeons. Achievements include clin. rsrch. in facial reconstructive surgery. Office: Boston U Medl Ctr 100 E Newton St Ste G-407 Boston MA 02118 Office Phone: 617-638-4350. Personal E-mail: pushkar.mehra@bmc.org. E-mail: pmehra@bu.edu.

**MEHRA, RAMAN KUMAR,** aerospace and defense technology executive, automotion and control engineering researcher; b. Lahore, Punjab, India, Feb. 10, 1943; came to U.S., 1964; s. Madan Mohan and Vidya Vati (Khanna) M.; m. Anjoo Talwar; children: Archana, Mandira, Kunal. BEE, Punjab Engring. Coll., 1964; MS in Engring., Harvard U., 1965, PhD, 1968. Assoc. prof. Harvard U., Cambridge, Mass., 1972-76; pres., chief exec. officer Sci. Systems, Co., Inc., Woburn, Mass., 1976—. Author: System Identification, 1976; also tech. papers on model algorithmic control (Best Paper award Internat. Fedn. Automatic Control, 1983). Recipient Eckman award Am. Automatic Control Coun., St. Louis, 1971. Fellow IEEE. Avocations: hiking, golf, tennis. Home: 5 Angier Rd Lexington MA 02420-1608 Office: Sci Systems Co Inc 500 W Cummings Park Woburn MA 01801-6503 Office Phone: 781-933-5355. Business E-Mail: rkm@ssci.com.

**MEHRBERG, RANDALL ERIC,** lawyer; b. Bklyn., Dec. 29, 1955; s. Julius and June (Shapiro) M.; m. Michele Schara, Oct. 20, 1984. BS in economics., U. Pa., 1977; JD, U. Mich., 1980. Bar: Ill. 1980, US Dist. Ct. No. Dist. Ill. 1980, US Ct. Appeals 7th cir. 1981, US Supreme Ct. 1987. With Jenner & Block, Chgo., 1980—93, 1997—2000; gen. counsel, lakefront dir. Chgo. Park Dist., 1993—97; sr. v.p., gen. counsel Exelon Corp., Chgo., 2000—02, exec. v.p., gen. counsel, 2002—. Asst. sec. Chgo. Pacific Corp., 1984-85. V.p. bd. dirs. Gus Giordano Jazzdance Chgo. Recipient Hope for the People award, HOPE Fair Housing, Ill., 1982; commendation for work for the poor, Cath. Charities, 1986, award for def. of civil liberties, ACLU, 1987. Mem. ABA, Chgo. Bar Assn. (exec. com. young lawyers sect. 1988-89, David C. Hilliard award), Chgo. Counsel Lawyers, Law Club Chgo. Avocations: tennis, ice hockey, skiing. Office: Exelon PO Box 805398 Chicago IL 60680-4115

**MEHRENS, CHRISTOPHER EMILE,** musicologist, music librarian; b. Renton, Wash., May 3, 1959; s. George Francis and Gloria Longville Mehrens. MusB in Music History, U. Wash., Seattle, 1982; MA in Music History, U. NC, Chapel Hill 1987; MLS, Ind. U., Bloomington, 2002—02; PhD in Musicology, U. NC, Chapel Hill, 1998. Music libr. Ind. State U., Terre Haute, 2002—. Cons. Shenyang (China) Conservatory of Music, 2006—. Contbr. biog. dictionary, articles to profl. jours. 1st v.p. Vigo County Hist. Soc., Terre Haute, 2005, mem., 2003. Mem.: ALA, Internat. Music Libr. Assn., Music Libr. Assn. (mem. outreach subcom. 2003—, Walter Gerboth award 2005), Am. Musicol. Soc., Am. Assn. of Museums, Beta Phi Mu. Office: Ind State U Cunningham Memorial Library Terre Haute IN 47809 E-mail: libmehr@isugw.indstate.edu.

**MEHRETU, JULIE,** artist; b. Addis Ababa, Ethiopia, 1970; Attended, U. Cheik Anta Diop, Dakar, Senegal, 1990—91; BA, Kalamazoo Coll., 1992; MFA with honors, RI Sch. Design, 1997. Greater New York, P.S.1 Contemporary Arts Ctr., NY, 2000, exhibited in group shows, Ctr. Curatorial Studies, Bard College, Annandale-on-Hudson, 2000, Free Style, Studio Mus. Harlem, 2001, The Americans, Barbican Gallery, London, 2001, Busan Biennale, Korea, 2002, 8th Baltic Triennial Vilnius, Lithuania, 2002, Drawing Now: Eight Propositions, Mus. Modern Art, 2002, Painting at the Edge of the World, Walker Art Ctr., 2003, one-woman shows include, Sol Kofler Gallery, Providence, RI, 1995, Ancestral Reflections, Archive Gallery, NY, 1995, Bombastic Righteous Passively Become Apparent Absurdities, Sol Kofler Gallery, Providence, RI, 1996, Recent Work, Barbara Davis Gallery, Houston, 1998, Module, Project Row Houses, Houston, 1999, The Project, NYC, 2001, Art Pace, San Antonio, Tex., 2001, White Cube, London, 2002, Julie Mehretu: Drawing into Painting, Walker Art Ctr. (travelling), 2003, REDCAT, LA, Calif., 2004, Albright-Knox Art Gallery, Buffalo, NY, 2004, Matrix, U. Calif. Berkeley Art Mus., 2004, earlier 1 gebauer, Berlin, Germany, 2004, Drawing, The Project, NYC, 2005, Current, St Louis Art Mus., 2005, exhibited in group shows at Carnegie Internat., Carnegie Mus. Art, Pitts., Pa., 2004, Sao Paulo Biennial, San Paulo, Brazil, 2004, Whitney Biennial, The Whitney Mus. Am. Art, NYC, 2004, Back to Paint, C&M Arts, NYC, 2004, Firewall, Ausstellungshalle Zeitgenössische Kunst, Munster, Germany, 2004. Recipient Cry of My Birth, Visiting Artist Residency Project, Sch. Art Inst. Chgo., 1999, Excellence Award, RI Sch. Design, 1996, Penny McCall Award, 2001; Core Fellowship, Artist in Residence, Glassell Sch. Art, Mus. Fine Arts, Houston, 1997—99, MacArthur Fellow, John D. and Catherine T. MacArthur Found., 2005. Mailing: c/o Barbara Davis Gallery 5701 Main St 11th Floor Warwick Hotel Houston TX 77005 Address: 37 W 57th St 3rd Fl New York NY 10019

**MEHRINGER, CHARLES MARK,** medical educator; b. Dickinson, N.D., Nov. 21, 1945; m. Ruth Herrman; 1 child, Sydney. BS in Biology, Lamar U., 1966; MD, U. Tex., 1970. Diplomate Am. Bd. Radiology, Am. Bd. Neuroradiology. Intern UCLA Hosp., 1970-71; resident in diagnostic radiology Harbor-UCLA Med. Ctr., Torrance, Calif., 1971-74, fellow in neuroradiology 1976-77; asst. prof. radiology UCLA Sch. Medicine, 1977-80, dir. spl. procedures, 1980-94, assoc. chmn. dept. radiology, 1986-96, prof. dept. radiology, 1996—, acting chmn. radiology, 1996—. Vice-chmn. dept. radiological scis. UCLA Sch. Medicine, Torrance, 1992—, acting chmn. dept. radiology, 1992—; chief diagnostic radiology, 1983-92; chief radiological svcs., cons. U.S. Air Force for Japan and Korea, 1974-76; cons. U. Calif./Irvine (Calif.) Med. Ctr., 1988—, St. Marys Med. Ctr., Long Beach, Calif., 1986—, Long Beach VA Hosp., 1979—, L.A. County Dept. Chief Med. Examiner-Coroner, 1977—; bd. dirs. Rsch. and Ednl. Inst.; presenter in field. Co-author: (with others) Neurological Surgery of the Ear and Skull Base, 1982, Vascular Surgery, 1984, 2d edit., 1994, Youman's Neurological Surgery, 1990, Common Problems in Infertility and Impotence, 1990, Intraluminal Imaging of Vascular and Tubular Organs: Diagnostic and Therapeutic Applications, 1993, Neuroradiology, A Study Guide, 1995; contbr. articles to profl. jours. Bd. dirs., exec. com. Med. Found. Harbor-UCLA Med. Ctr., 1992—. Recipient numerous grants for rsch., 1977—. Mem. Am. Coll. Radiology, Am. Soc. Neuroradiology (sr. mem.), Western Neuroradiologic Soc., L.A. Radiologic Soc. Office: Harbor UCLA Med Ctr Box 27 1000 W Carson St Torrance CA 90502-2004

**MEHRINGER, RICHARD PATRICK,** design educator, artist; s. Joseph A. and Iva D. Mehringer. BFA, Ft. Hays State U., 1981, MA, 1986, cert. in tchg., 1986. Art. lang. arts instr. Fowler Secondary Sch., Colo., 1986—88; art, fine arts chair St. Pauls H.S., NC, 1988—93; art instr., fine arts chair Roosevelt Mid. Sch., Coffeyville, Kans., 1993—99; design instr. Larned H.S., 2000—. Mem., exec. com. Fine Arts League S.E. Colo., LaJunta, 1986—88; mem. Cape Fear Studios Inc., Fayetteville, NC, 1989—93; founding mem. Santa Fe Trail Creative Arts Guild, Larned, 2004—. Artist, photographer (exhibitions) The Dancer, artist, prodr. (one-man shows) Frozen Motion, artist Down Many Roads, Through Many Eons, artist, curator (group shows) Santa Fe Trail Artist and Crafter Guild Invitational; two-person shows, Santa Fe Trail Artist and Crafter Guild Invitational. Named Kans. Secondary Art Educator of Yr., Kans. Art Edn. Assn., 2001-2002, Western Region Secondary Art Educator of Yr., Nat. Art Edn. Assn., 2002-2003, Dist. Tchr. of Yr., Kans. Dept. Edn., 2004-2005; Grad. Assistantship scholar, Ft. Hays State U. Art Dept., 1986. Mem.: Kans. Exemplary Educator's Network (assoc.; team leader 2004—), Santa Fe Creative Arts Guild (assoc.; founding mem. 2004—, pres. 2004), Creative Art Soc. (pres. 1979—81), Phi Delta Kappa (assoc.). Achievements include design of visual arts curriculum. Personal E-mail: arknat@yahoo.com.

**MEHTA, EILEEN ROSE,** lawyer; b. Colver, Pa., Apr. 1, 1953; d. Richard Glenn and Helen (Wahna) Ball; m. Abdul Rashid Mehta, Aug. 31, 1973. Student, Miami U., 1971-73; BA with distinction, Fla. Internat. U., 1974; JD cum laude, U. Miami, 1977. Bar: Fla. 1977, U.S. Dist. Ct. (so. dist.) Fla. 1977, U.S. Ct. Appeals (11th cir.) 1981. Law clk. to presiding judge U.S. Dist. Ct. (so. dist.) Fla., Miami, 1977-79; asst. atty. County of Dade, Miami, 1979-89; shareholder Fine Jacobson Schwartz Nash Block & England, Miami, Fla., 1989-94; ptnr. Eckert Seamans Cherin & Mellott, Miami, 1994-98, Bilzin Sumberg Baena Price & Axelrod, Miami, 1998—. Lectr. in field; v.p. bd. dirs. Shalimar Homes Inc., Anderson, S.C. Miami U. scholar, 1971-73. Mem. Fla. Bar Assn., Dade County Bar Assn. Office: Bilzin Sumberg Baena Price & Axelrod 2500 Wachovia Fin Ctr Miami FL 33131 Office Phone: 305-350-2380. Business E-Mail: emehta@bilzin.com.

**MEHTA, KIRAN H.,** lawyer; AB magna cum laude, Cornell Univ., 1978; JD cum laude, Harvard Univ., 1981. Bar: NC 1983. Law clk. Chief Judge Frank A. Kaufman, US Dist. Ct. (Md. Dist.), 1982—82; ptnr. litigation dept. Kennedy Covington, Charlotte, NC. Contbr. articles to profl. jours., chapters to books. Dean, solid & hazardous waste Charlotte C. of C. Environ. Sch., 1991—94, chmn. hazardous waste/superfund com., 1992—94; dir. Cmty. Sch. Arts, 1997—; mem. supt. council Charlotte-Mecklenburg Sch. Sys., 1999. Mem.: ABA, NC Bar Assn., Mecklenburg County Bar Assn., Phi Beta Kappa. Office: Kennedy Covington Hearst Tower 47th Fl 214 N Tryon St Charlotte NC 28202 Office Phone: 704-331-7437. Office Fax: 704-353-3137. Business E-Mail: khmehta@kennedycovington.com.

**MEHTA, LINN CARY,** literature educator; b. Chgo., Aug. 8, 1955; d. William Lucius and Katherine L.F. (Cooper) Cary; m. Ved Mehta, Dec. 17, 1983; children: Alexandra Sage, Natasha Cary. BA in English and French, Yale U., 1977; MA in English, Oxford U., 1979; MPhil in Comparative Lit., Columbia U., 1989, PhD in Comparative Lit., 2004. Asst. to pres. Ford Found., N.Y.C., 1980—82, asst. program officer, 1982—85; preceptor Columbia U., N.Y.C., 1990—91; instr. Yale U., New Haven, 1993; instr., adj. asst. prof. English dept. Vassar Coll., Poughkeepsie, NY, 1994—97; lectr. English dept. Barnard Coll., N.Y.C., 2000—. Chair bd. Am. Friends St. Hilda's Coll., Boston, 1995-02; sec. bd. alumnae Wrexham Found., New Haven, 1988-94 Actor: (English adaptation of play) Allende, Theater for a New City, 2006. Bd. pres. Ctr. for Traditional Music and Dance, NYC, 1989-94, v.p., 2000—, Lexington 79th Corp., NYC, 1993-97; bd. dirs. Norman Rockwell Mus., Stockbridge, Mass., 1991-96, NY Soc. Libr., 2002—; adv. bd. Appalshop, Whitesburg, Ky., 1990-9; mem. Christ Ch..m Dark Harbor, Maine, 2000-05. Mem. MLA, Am. Comparative Lit. Assn., Thursday Evening Club (pres. 1998-2001) Avocations: music, running, languages. Home: 139 E 79th St New York NY 10021-0324 Office: English Dept Barnard Coll Columbia U 3009 Broadway New York NY 10027 Business E-Mail: lmehta@barnard.edu.

**MEHTA, MINESH P.,** oncologist, educator; s. Praful P. and Sudha P. Mehta; children: Tej, Sanjli. MD, U. Zambia, Lusaka, 1981. Chmn. dept. human oncology U. Wis., Madison, 1997—, prof. 1998—. Chmn. RTOG Brain Tumor Com., Phila., 2000—06. Contbr. articles to profl. jours. Examiner ABR, Tucson, 2004—06. Grantee, NIH, 2001—06. Mem.: ASTRO (ednl. com. mem. 2000—04). Achievements include first to Tomotherapy. Office: U Wis 600 Highland Ave Madison WI 53792 Office Phone: 608-263-5009. Home Fax: 608-263-5009; Office Fax: 608-263-5009. Business E-Mail: mehta@humonc.wisc.edu.

**MEHTA, NARINDER KUMAR,** marketing executive; b. Lahore, Punjab, India, Feb. 18, 1938; came to U.S., 1959; s. Raj Rani Mehta and Puran Chand; m. Narayanaswamy Sampath; children: Kiren, Ravi. B of Commerce, U. Delhi, India, 1958; MA, U. Minn., 1961. Program dir. All India Mgmt. Assn., New Delhi, 1963—67; with Am. Express Co., Chgo., 1968—82, dir. nat. sales N.Y.C., 1975—80, v.p. sales, 1980—82; sr. v.p Shearson Lehman/Am. Express, Boston, 1982—85; sr. v.p. internat. mktg. & sales Capital Credit Corp., Fairfield, NJ, 1985—94; sr. v.p. internat. mktg. Outsourcing Solutions, Inc., 1994—97; pres. Mehta Cons. Group, Dover, Mass., 1997—. Sr. v.p. Temporary Investment Funds, 1982-85, Trust for Short Term Fed. Securities, 1982-85, Mcpl. Fund for Calif. Investors, 1983-85; conducted seminars for profl. assns., colls. and univs. Contbr. articles to profl. jours. Nat. v.p. Muscular Dystrophy Assn., NYC, 1984-86; student body pres. U. Delhi, India, 1958-59. Recipient 1st prize inter-coll. debate, 1958. Mem. Am. Mgmt. Assn., Tau Kappa Epsilon. Avocations: running, swimming, travel, reading. Office: Mehta Cons Group PO Box 547 4 Bryant Ln Dover MA 02030-0547 Personal E-mail: nkmehta@aol.com.

**MEHTA, PARINDA APURVA,** pediatrician, medical educator, hematologist, oncologist; d. J. V. and B. Amlani; m. Apurva C. Mehta, Nov. 26, 1996; children: Parth, Shlok. MBBS, Seth Gordhandas Sunderdas Med. Coll., Mumbai, India, 1993; MD, Upstate Med. U., Syracuse, NY, 2002. Intern King Edward Meml. Hosp., Mumbai, India, 1993—94; resident Lokmanya Tilak Mcpl. Med. Coll., 1994—96; pediatrician pvt. practice, 1996—97; resident Upstate Med. U., SUNY, 1999—2002; fellow Cin. Children's Hosp. Med. Ctr., 2002—05, asst. prof. pediat., blood and marrow transplantation, 2005—. Reviewer: jours. Leukemia, British Jour. Haematology, The Pharmacogenomics Jour., Clin. Cancer Rsch.; contbr. articles to profl. jours. Named Tchr. of Yr., Dept. Pediat., UMU, SUNY, 2000—01, 2001—02; Rsch. grant, FDA, Astellas, Inc., Cancer-Free Kids Pediatric Rsch. Alliance, 2004—05, Translational Rsch. Initiative, Cin. Children's Hosp. Med. Ctr., 2005—06. Mem.: Am. Soc. Pediatric Hematology Oncology, Am. Soc. Blood and Marrow Transplantation, Am. Soc. Clin. Oncology (Young investigator award 2006—, Rsch. grant 2006—), Am. Soc. Hematology (mem. clin. rsch. training inst. 2005—06). Office: Cincinnati Children's Hospital Medical C MLC 7015 3333 Burnet Avenue Cincinnati OH 45229 Office Phone: 513-636-4913. Office Fax: 513-636-3549. E-mail: parinda.mehta@cchmc.org.

**MEHTA, RAJENDRA H.,** cardiologist, researcher; s. Hasmukhrai N and Nila H Mehta. MD, U. Bombay, 1986; MS, U. Mich., 2001. Clin. assoc. Cleve. Clinic Found., 1995—96; clin. asst. prof. U. Mich., Ann Arbor, 1996—, co-investigator, 1996. Recipient Travel award, Bristol Myers Squibb, 1998. Fellow: Am. Heart Assn. (licentiate), Am. Coll. Cardiology (life Proctor Harvey Young Tchr. award 2002). D-Liberal. Hindu. Achievements include research in clinical outcomes. Avocations: jogging, swimming, travel, music. Office: Duke Univ Med Ctr PO Box 17969 2400 Pratt St Durham NC 27715

**MEHTA, RAKESH PETER,** medical educator; b. Princeton, N.J., Mar. 15, 1967; s. Dinesh A. and Susanne Mehta; m. Gloria P. Sachdev, July 5, 1997; children: Cole Sachdev, Sage Promilla, Jade Susanne. MD, Pa. State U., Hershey, 1993. Diplomate Am. Bd. of Internal Medicine, 2000. Staff physician Scott and White Clinic, Temple, Tex., 2000—02; asst. prof. of clin. medicine Ind. Sch. of Medicine, Indpls., 2002—. Recipient Trustee Tchg. award, Ind. U., 2006. Mem.: Am. Soc. of Hematology. Office: Ind Univ Sch of Medicine 535 Barnhill Dr RT-473 Indianapolis IN 46202 Office Phone: 317-278-9776.

**MEHTA, SHAILESH J.,** banker; b. Bombay, Maharashtra, India, Apr. 22, 1949; came to U.S., 1971; s. Jayantilal B. and Manjula J. Mehta; m. Kalpa S. Doshi, Dec. 19, 1973; children: Sameet, Sheetal BS in Mech. Engring., Indian Inst. Tech., 1971; MS in Ops. Research, Case Western Res. U., 1973, PhD in Ops. Research and Computer Sci., 1975. Sr. ops. analyst Cleve. Trust Co., 1973-75, ops. officer, 1975-76, asst. v.p. card ops., 1976-77, v.p. corp. ops. adminstrn., 1979, v.p. advanced systems planning, 1977-78, v.p. info. systems, 1979-82; exec. v.p. banking services AmeriTrust, Cleve., 1974-86; exec. v.p., COO First Deposit Corp., San Francisco, 1986-88, pres., CEO, 1988—; chmn. bd. First Deposit Nat. Bank, Tilton, NH, 1986—; pres., chief exec. officer, chmn. bd. First Deposit Savs. Bank, Redding, Calif., 1986-90; CEO, chmn. bd. First Deposit Nat. Credit Card Bank, Concord, NH, 1990-93; exec. v.p. Providian Corp., San Francisco, 1993-94; pres., COO, 1994-97, chmn., CEO, 1998—. Pres., dir. A.T. Venture Capital Group, Cleve., 1982-86; pres. Granite Hill Capital Ventures LLC. Mem. community adv. coun. U. Calif., Berkeley, 1991—. Mem. Am. Bankers Assn. (telecommunications group 1984—), Ohio Venture Assn., Calif. Commn. for Econ. Devel's. Adv. Coun. on Asia.

**MEHTA, SHREEFAL,** pharmaceutical executive, educator; s. Sudhir Jayantilal and Kokila Mehta; m. Pratibha Gauri Dahanukar; children: Ritam, Anam, Shantala. PhD, U. Tex., Dallas, 2000; MBA, Rensselaer Poly. Inst., Troy, N.Y., 2002. Asst. prof. U. of Tex. Southwestern Med. Ctr., Dallas, 1995—2000; rsch. asst. prof. of biotech mgmt. Lally Sch. of Mgmt. and Tech., Rensselaer Poly. Inst., Troy, NY, 2001—; CEO, Myomatrix Therapeutics, Rensselaer, NY, 2001—04; v.p. bus. and corp. devel. Cytopia, Melbourne, Victoria, Australia, 2004—. Program dir., radical innovation rsch. program Rensselaer Poly. Inst., Troy, NY, 2003—05. Contbr. articles to profl. jours. Bd. dirs. Bioconnex, Albany, NY, 2004—06. Recipient 40 Under 40 Bus. Leaders award, Bus. Rev., 2006. Office: Rensselaer Poly Inst Lally Sch Mgmt 110 8th St Troy NY 12180 Office Phone: 518-276-2852. E-mail: mehtas@rpi.edu.

**MEHTA, SONNY (AJAY SINGH MEHTA),** publishing executive; b. India, 1943; Student, Cambridge U. Worked in paperback pub., England; formerly with Pan and Picador Pubs., England; pub., pres. Alfred A. Knopf divsn. of Random House, NYC, 1987, editor-in-chief; former pres., editor-in-chief Knopf Pub. Group, NYC, chmn., editor-in-chief, 2005—. Office: Knopf Pub 1745 Broadway #B1 New York NY 10019-4305*

**MEHTA, YUSUF A.,** engineering educator; s. Abdulhusain and Tara A. Mehta; m. Munira Y. Shambhoora, Oct. 25, 2002. PhD, Pa. State U., 1999. Tchg. asst. Okla. U., Norman, 1993—94; rsch. asst. Pa. State U., University Park, 1995—99; rsch. assoc. U. Fla., Gainesville, 1999—2001; asst. prof. Rowan U., Glassboro, NJ, 2001—. Adviser Engrs. Without Borders, Glassboro, 2002—06. Recipient award, Lindback Found., 2002. Fellow: ASCE (assoc.); mem.: AAPT, TRB (assoc.). Achievements include research in pavement materials evaluation. Office Phone: 856-256-5327.

**MEHTA, ZARIN,** performing company executive; b. Bombay, Oct. 28, 1938; came to Can., 1962, naturalized, 1969; s. Mehli and Tehmina Mehta; m. Carmen Lasky, July 1, 1966; children: Rohanna, Rustom. Chartered acct., London, 1957. Acct. Frederic B. Smart & Co., London, 1957-62, Coopers & Lybrand, Montreal, Que., Can., 1962-81; mng. dir. Orchestre Symphonique de Montreal, 1981-90; exec. dir., COO Ravinia Festival, 1990-2000; exec. dir. NY Philharm., 2000-. Fellow Inst. Chartered Accts. in Eng. and Wales; mem. Ordre des Comptables Agrees du Que. Office: NY Philharm Avery Fisher Hall 10 Lincoln Center Plaza New York NY 10023-6990 Business E-Mail: mehtaz@nyphil.org.

**MEHURON, WILLIAM OTTO,** retired federal official; b. Hammond, Ind., Nov. 20, 1937; s. Arthur and Margaret Irene (Soroka) M.; m. Charlotte Anne Nyheim, Aug. 26, 1982; children: Kimberly Anne, Kristine Lynn, Susan, Geoffrey. BSEE, Purdue U., 1959; MSEE, U. Pa., 1962, PhD, 1966. Tech. dir. naval intelligence Dept. Navy, Washington, 1974-81; dir. rsch. and engring. Nat. Security Agy., Ft. Meade, Md., 1981-85; v.p., gen. mgr. data systems div. Ampex Corp. subs. Allied-Signal Co., Redwood City, Calif., 1985-86; sr. v.p. product ops. Daisy Systems Corp., Mountain View, Calif., 1986-88; v.p., gen. mgr. Networks and Info. Security div. Security div. Unisys Def. Systems, McLean, Va., 1988-91; pres. Mehuron Assocs. Inc., 1991-95; dir. sys. acquisition office NOAA, USG, Washington, 1995-99; dir. Info. Tech. Lab., Nat. Inst. Stds. and Tech., Gaithersburg, Md., 1999—2002; pres. Mehuron Assocs., Inc., 2002—. Avocations: amateur radio, golf, cooking. Home: 803 S Clay St Hinsdale IL 60521-4541 Office Phone: 630-995-5626. Personal E-mail: mehuron@comcast.net.

**MEI, ANHUA,** mechanical engineer, researcher; b. Chongqing, China, Oct. 5, 1955; arrived in US, 2002; s. Dedong Mei and Jiyu Liu; m. Jinghui Wang, May 28, 1984; 1 child, Da. BS, Chongqing U., 1982; MS, Wuhan Tech. U. Surveying and Mapping, China, 1995; D Engring., Lamar U., Beaumont, Tex., 2006. Asst. prof., lectr. Wuhan Tech. U. Surveying and Mapping, 1982—93, assoc. prof., 1993—98; prin. lectr. Wuhan U., 1998—2002; prin. lectr. Harare Poly. U., Zimbabwe, 1999—2002; sr. mech. engr. Perry Equipment Corp., Mineral Wells, Tex., 2006—. Presenter in field. Contbr. articles to profl. jours. Mem.: ASME, Am. Soc. Optical Engrs. Avocations: swimming, ping pong/table tennis. Home: 1676 Holland Lake Dr # 1206 Weatherford TX 76086 Office: Perry Equipment Corp 118 Washington Ave Mineral Wells TX 76086 Personal E-mail: anhuamei2002@yahoo.com.

**MEI, BETTY MIUCHI,** director; b. Hong Kong, 1960; arrived in U.S., 1979; d. Wai Chung Chan and Yue Mui Wong; m. Joseph Shing Mei, May 25, 1985; children: Joshua, Isaac. BA, SUNY, Plattsburgh, 1982; MA, W.Va. U., Morgantown, 1984, EdD, 1988. Asst. prof. Salem-Teikyo U., W.Va., 1990—93; acad. dir. W.Va. Jr. Coll., Morgantown, 1998—2000; asst. dir. W.Va. U., 2000—. Named one of Top 100 Most Influential People in Morgantown, 2003. Mem.: W.Va. Assn. Ednl. Opportunity Program Personnel, Mid-Ea. Assn. Ednl. Opportunity Programs Personnel, La. Coun. Assn. Avocations: reading, music, photography. Office: WVa U PO Box 6212 Student Svcs Ctr Morgantown WV 26506 Office Phone: 304-293-4316. Business E-Mail: betty.mei@mail.wvu.edu.

**MEI, CHIANG CHUNG,** civil engineer, educator; b. Wuhan, China, Apr. 4, 1935; m. Caroline J. Schmitt, 1965; 1 child. BS, Nat. Taiwan U., 1955; MS, Stanford U., 1958; PhD, Calif. Inst. Tech., 1963. Rsch. fellow engring. sci. Calif. Inst. Tech., 1963-65; mem. tech. staff Nat. Engring. Sci. Co., Calif., 1965; from asst. prof. to prof. MIT, Cambridge, 1965-93, Edmund K. Turner prof. civil engring., 1993—2001, acting head dept., 2001—02, Donald and Martha Harleman prof. civil engring., 2001—. Hon. prof. U. Hong Kong, 1992—; instr. mechanics Chinese Acad. Sci., Beijing, 1994. Recipient J.T. Hsieh award, 1984, Rosenstiel award, 1988, Moffatt & Nichol award, 1992. Fellow Acad. Sinica; mem. ASCE, Nat. Acad. Engring., Am. Phys. Soc., Am. Geophys. Union, Soc. Indsl. and Applied Math. Office: Dept Civil Environ & Engr MIT Cambridge MA 02139 E-mail: ccmei@mit.edu.

**MEI, TOM Y. K.,** lawyer; b. Kuantan, Malaysia, July 24, 1940; came to U.S., 1958. s. Hung Po and Hannah (Chung) M.; m. Margene Suzuki Mei, Sept. 1964; children: Rodney, Todd. BA in econ., Calif. State U., 1963; JD, Western State U. Coll. Law, 1975. Bar: Calif. 1976. Claim rep. CNA Ins., L.A., 1964-66, claim supr. San Diego, 1966-76; assoc. attorney Murchison & Cumming, Santa Ana, 1976-88, ptnr., 1988—. Pres. San Diego Claims Mgr.

Council, 1973. Mem. Am. Bd. Trial Advocates (bd. dirs.), Defense Rsch. Inst., Orange County Bar Assoc. Avocations: skiing, travel. Office: Murchison & Cumming 200 W Santa Ana Blvd Ste 801 Santa Ana CA 92701-4134 Office Phone: 714-972-9977.

**MEIBURG, CHARLES OWEN,** economist, educator; b. Seneca, S.C., Dec. 17, 1931; s. Albert and Gladys Katherine (Burley) M.; m. Elizabeth Rhodes Glenn, June 11, 1955; children: Charles O. Jr., Howard Glenn, Elizabeth Rhodes. BS in Arts and Scis., Clemson U., 1953; MA in Econs., U. Va., 1958, PhD in Econs., 1960. Assoc. prof. U. Va., Charlottesville, 1964-69, prof., 1969-82, J. Harvie Wilkinson, Jr. prof. bus. adminstrn., 1982-99, prof. emeritus, 1999—. Dir. Taylor Murphy Inst. U. Va., 1967-83; assoc. dean Darden Sch. U. Va., 1983-89. Co-author: Cases on Financial Institutions, 1979, Cases in Bank Management, 1986; editor (with others) Loan Officers Handbook, 1986. 1st lt. U.S. Army, 1953-55. Mem. Am. Econ. Assn., Fin. Mgmt. Assn., Assn. for U. Bus. and Econ. Rsch. (pres. 1971). Home: 3345 Kirkwood Ct Keswick VA 22947-9138 Office: U Va Darden Sch PO Box 6550 Charlottesville VA 22906-6550 Office Phone: 434-924-4816. Personal E-mail: com@virginia.edu.

**MEIDES, HOLLY SUE,** music educator; b. Buffalo, Dec. 15, 1968; d. Richard Henry and Margaret Ann Meides. MusB, Potsdam Coll., N.Y., 1991; MusM, Potsdam Coll., 1992. Cert. tchr. music K-12 NY, 1991. Gen. music tchr. Amherst Ctrl. Schs., NY, 1993; orch./band dir., tchr. Lancaster Ctrl. Schs., Lancaster, NY, 1993—. Sec./clarinetist Akron Cmty. Band, Akron, NY, 1984—; solo adjudicator Erie County Music Educator's Assn., East Aurora, NY, 1995—. Recipient Departmental scholar, Crane Sch. of Music, 1991, Presdl. scholar, Potsdam Coll., 1987—91, Presdl. fellow, 1991—92, Gold award, Girl Scouts of Am., 1986. Mem.: NY State Sch. Music Assn., Am. String Tchrs. Assn., Erie County Music Educators Assn., Music Educators Nat. Conf., Maroon Key Soc. (hon.), Pi Kappa Lambda (hon.), Kappa Delta Pi (hon.), Gamma Sigma Sigma (life), Sigma Alpha Iota (life). Roman Catholic. Home: 7061 Maple Rd Akron NY 14001 Office: William Street Sch 5201 William St Lancaster NY 14086 Office Phone: 716-686-3800. Personal E-mail: strings15@aol.com.

**MEIER, BARRY,** reporter; b. May 10, 1949; m. Ellen Joan Pollock; 1 child. BA, Syracuse U. Reporter Wall Street Jour.; spl. reporter NY Newsday; reporter NY Times, 1989—, consumer news reporter. Frequent guest Nat. Pub. Radio. Contbr. chapters to books. Recipient George Polk award for bus. reporting, 2006. Office: NY Times 229 West 43rd St New York NY 10036 Office Phone: 212-556-1917. Office Fax: 212-556-1448. E-mail: meier@nytimes.com.*

**MEIER, CAROLYN K.,** elementary school educator; d. Robert Roy and Vilas Arvilla Meier. BS, Western Ill. U., Macomb, 1978; MS, No. Ill. U., DeKalb, 1991. Cert. phys. edn., health tchr. Ill. Elem. phys. edn. tchr. Sandwich Sch. Dist., Ill., 1979—, Elem. phys. edn. tchr. Sandwich Sch. Dist., 1979—. Mem.: Ill. Assn. Health, Phys. Edn., Recreation and Dance. Presbyterian. Avocations: golf, reading, bicycling. Home: 309 W Knights Rd Sandwich IL 60548 Office: W W Woodbury Sch 322 E 3d St Sandwich IL 60548

**MEIER, CHRISTIAN BEACH,** pastor; b. Kittery, Maine, Sept. 16, 1972; s. Frederick Beach Meier and Carolyn Suzanne Barry; m. Tammy Lynn Swick, Dec. 28, 1996; children: Alexander Christian, Kaitlynn Mae. BS in Biology, U. Nebr., 1994; MDiv, Luther Sem., 1999. Cert. Ordained Pastor Evangelical Luth. Ch. Am. Northeastern Minn. Synod of the ELCA, 1999. Dir. outreach ministries Luth. Student Ctr., U. Nebr., Lincoln, 1993—94; dir. high wilderness ministries Sky Ranch Luth. Camp, Fort Collins, Colo., 1994; pastor Luth. Ch. of the Cross, Nisswa, Minn., 1999—. Adv. bd. mem. Lakes Area Food Shelf, Pequot Lakes, Minn., 1999—2001, Bridges of Hope, Baxter, Minn., 2003—05; cabinet mem. Heartland Conf. Northeastern Minn. Synod, Brainerd, Minn., 2003—; coun. mem. Northeastern Minn. Synod, Duluth, Minn., 2005—. Vol. Brainerd Soup Kitchen, Temple Bapt. Ch., Minn., 1999—2006, Habitat for Humanity, Lakes Area Chpt., Brainerd, 1999—2006. Mem.: NRA (life), Beta Sigma Psi (life; chaplain, steward 1991—94). Luth. Avocations: hunting, fishing, backpacking. Office: Luth Ch of the Cross PO Box 29 Nisswa MN 56468 Office Phone: 218-963-2564. Office Fax: 218-963-0294. Business E-Mail: pastorchris@lccnisswa.org.

**MEIER, GEORGE KARL, III,** minister, lawyer; b. Glen Ridge, NJ, Jan. 13, 1944; s. George Karl and Mary Claire (Myers) M.; children: G.K., Leslie; m. Therese DesCamp, Oct. 10, 1992. BS, Washington and Lee U., 1966; JD, Dickinson Sch. Law, 1969; MDiv, Pacific Sch. of Religion, 1992. Bar: N.J. 1969, Oreg. 1970, U.S. Dist. Ct. N.J. 1969, U.S. Dist. Ct. Oreg. 1970, U.S. Ct. Appeals (9th cir.) 1971, U.S. Ct. Appeals (fed. cir.) 1987, U.S. Supreme Ct. 1973. Law clk. NJ Superior Court Appellate Div., 1969-70; assoc. Stoel, Rives, Boley, Jones & Grey, Portland, Oreg., 1970-75, prtnr., 1976-89; spl. dep. atty. gen. State of Idaho, 1988-89; spl. asst. to pres. Pacific Sch. Religion Berkeley, Calif., 1992; pastor Pioneer Congl. Ch., Sacramento, Calif., 1992-1998, Cmty. Ch. Monterey Peninsula, Carmel, Calif., 1998—. Co-founder Ctrl. City Concern, 1978, SW Youth Svc. Ctr., Portland; chmn. ctrl. adv. bd. Dept. Human Resources; pres. consistory Hillside Cmty. Ch., Portland, 1984-85; acad. com. Pacific Sch. Religion, 1989-91; interim dir. youth programs Epwirth Meth. Ch., 1992; bd. dirs. No. Calif. Nev. Conf. the United Ch. Christ, 1993-97; v.p., 1995-96, pres., 1996-97, Francis House, 1992-98; chmn. 1995-96, Cathedral Pioneer Ch. Homes, Inc., 1992-98; Samaritan Counseling Ctr., 1997-98;co-founder, bd. dirs. InterFaith Pastoral Counseling Ctr. Monterey County, 1999-2005; panel vol. United Way Fund Distbn., 1999-2000; Leadership Monterey Peninsula Class of 2000; bd. dirs. Legal Svcs. for Srs., 2004—. Recipient Outstanding Svc. award Cen. City Concern 1976-89. Mem. Oreg. State Bar Assn; mem. Carmel Valley Rotary Club, 1999—. Mem. United Ch. of Christ. Office Phone: 831-624-8595.

**MEIER, KENNETH JOHN,** political scientist; b. Aberdeen, S.D., Mar. 3, 1950; s. John and Elizabeth (Malsam) M.; m. Diane Jones Meier, Dec. 31, 1972. BA, U. S.D., 1972; PhD, Syracuse U., 1975. Prof. polit. sci. Rice U., Houston, 1975-78, U. Okla., 1978-85, U. Wis., Madison, 1985-89, Milw., 1989-97; Charles Puryear prof. liberal arts Tex. A&M U., College Station, 1998—2005, Sara Lindsey prof. govt., 2001—04, Charles Gregory chair in liberal arts, 2006—. Fellow on hispanic pub. policy issues Inter Univ. Program Social Sci. Rsch. Coun., 1991-92; dir. Ctr. for Presdl. Studies, Policy and Governance, 2001-02. Author: Race, Class and Education, 1989, The Politics of Hispanic Education, 1991, Politics and the Bureaucracy, 1993, The Politics of Sin, 1994, The Case Against School Choice, 1995, Regulation and Consumer Protection, 1995, Applied Statistics for Public Administration, 1997, What Works: A New Approach to Program and Policy Analysis, 2000, The Politics of Fertility Control, 2001, Politics, Policy and Organizations, 2003; editor Am. Jour. Polit. Sci., 1994-98; assoc. editor Jour. Pub. Administrn. Rsch. and Theory. Recipient Clarence A. Kulp award, 1990, Gustavus Myers award, 1991, 93, Herbert Kaufman award, 1992, 2002, Herbert A. Simon award, 1999, award Acad. Mgmt., 2000, distng. rsch. award, Nat. Assn. Schs. Pub. Affairs and Adminstrn./ASPA, 2003; Big XII Faculty fellow, 2003. Fellow: Nat. Acad. Pub. Adminstrn. (Charles Levine award 2005, William Mosher award 2005), Advanced Inst. Mgmt. (Joseph Wholey award 2004); mem.: APHA, MW Polit. Sci. Assn. (pres.-elect 2004—05, pres. 2005—06), Nat. Pub. Mgmt. Rsch. Assn. (pres. 2003—05), SW Polit. Sci. Assn. (pres.-elect 1998—99, pres. 1999—2000), Am. Polit. Sci. Assn. (Latino Mentor award 2005, John Gaus award 2006). Office: Tex A&M U Dept Polit Sci TAMUS 4384 College Station TX 77843-0001 Office Phone: 979-845-4232. Business E-Mail: kmeier@polisci.tamu.edu.

**MEIER, MARK FREDERICK,** research scientist, educator, artist, small business owner; b. Iowa City, Dec. 19, 1925; s. Norman C. and Clea (Grimes) M.; m. Barbara McKinley, Sept. 16, 1955; children: Lauren G., Mark S., Gretchen A. BSEE, U. Iowa, 1949, MS in Geology, 1951; PhD in Geology and Applied Mechanics, Calif. Inst. Tech., 1957. Instr. Occidental Coll., L.A., 1952-55; chief glaciology project office U.S. Geol. Survey, Tacoma, 1956-85;

dir. Inst. Arctic and Alpine Rsch. U. Colo., Boulder, 1985-94; owner MeierArt, 2005—. Vis. prof. Dartmouth Coll., Hanover, N.H., 1964; rsch. prof. U. Wash., Seattle, 1964-86; prof. geol. scis. U. Colo., 1985-96, prof. emeritus, 1997—; pres. Internat. Comn. on Snow and Ice, 1967-71; pres. Internat. Assn. Hydrol. Scis., 1979-83; Mendenhall lectr. U.S. Geol. Survey, 1982, Walter Orr Roberts Disting. lectr. Aspen Global Change Inst., 1992. Contbr. articles to profl. jours. With USN, 1945—46. Named Meier Valley (Antarctica) in his honor; recipient 3 medals, Acad. Scis., Moscow, 1970—85, Disting. Svc. award (Gold medal), U.S. Dept. Interior, 1968, Internat. Hydrology prize, Internat. Assn. Hydrol. Scis./World Meteor. Orgn./UNESCO, 1999, Goldthwait Polar medal, Ohio State U., 2002. Fellow: AAAS (John Wesley Powell Meml. lectr. 1994), Am. Geophys. Union (com. chmn., Robert E. Horton medal 1996); mem.: Arctic Inst. N.Am. (gov. 1987—93), Internat. Glaciol. Soc. (v.p., coun., Seligman Crystal 1985), Geol. Soc. Am. (com. mem.). Office: U Colo Inst Arctic Alpine Rsch 1560 30th St Boulder CO 80309-0450 Business E-Mail: mark.meier@colorado.edu.

**MEIER, RICHARD ALAN,** architect; b. Newark, Oct. 12, 1934; s. Jerome and Carolyn (Kaltenbacher) M.; m. Katherine Gormley, Jan. 21, 1978 (div.); children: Joseph Max, Ana Moss. BArch, Cornell U., 1957; D (hon.), U. Naples, Italy, 1991, The New Sch., N.Y.C., 1995. Registered profl. arch., N.Y., N.J., Conn., Mich., Va., Fla., Ind., Ga., Calif., Ill., Iowa, Tex., Oreg. Architect Frank Grad & Sons, N.J., 1957, Davis, Brody & Wisniewski, N.Y.C., 1958-59, Skidmore, Owings & Merrill, 1959-60, Marcel Breuer & Assocs., 1960-63; architect, prin. Richard Meier & Assocs., N.Y.C., 1963-80, Richard Meier & Ptnrs., 1980—. Resident architect Am. Acad. in Rome, 1973-74; vis. critic Pratt Inst., 1960-62, 65, Princeton, 1963, Syracuse U., 1964; William Henry Bishop vis. prof. architecture Yale U., 1975, 77, vis. critic, 1967, 72, 73, 77; vis. prof. Harvard U., 1977, UCLA, 1988, Eliot Noyes vis. critic in architecture, 1980-81; Harvey S. Perloff vis. prof. architecture UCLA, 1987; adj. prof. architecture Cooper Union, N.Y.C., 1963-73; mem. adv. coun. Cornell U. Coll. Art, Architecture and Planning; mem. Jerusalem Com. Exhbns., XV Triennale, Milan, 1973, Mus. Modern Art, N.Y.C., 1975, 81, Princeton U., Biennale, Venice, Italy, 1976, Cooper-Hewitt Mus., N.Y.C., 1976-77, Leo Castelli Gallery, N.Y.C., 1977, 94, Rosa Esman Gallery, N.Y.C., 1978, 80, N.J. State Mus., 1978, Modernism Gallery, San Francisco, 1978, Wadsworth Atheneum, Hartford, Conn., High Mus. Art, Atlanta Harvard U., Max Protech Gallery, 1980, Syracuse U., Whitney Mus. Art, N.Y.C., 1982, Knoll Internat., Tokyo, Japan, 1988, October Gallery, London, 1990, Royal Palace, Naples, Italy, 1991, Palazzo delle Esposizione, Rome, 1993, Aichi Prefectural Mus. Art, Nagoya, Japan, 1996. Prin. works include Westbeth Artists Housing, N.Y.C., Bronx (N.Y.) Devel. Ctr., Smith House, Darien, Conn., Douglas House, Harbor Springs, Mich., Shamberg House, Mt. Kisco, N.Y., Hoffman and Saltzman Houses, East Hampton, N.Y.; houses in Old Westbury, N.Y., Pound Ridge, N.Y., Palm Beach, Fla., Pitts.; Twin Parks NE Housing, N.Y.C., Atheneum, New Harmony, Ind., N.Y., Hartford (Conn.) Sem., Mus. für Kunsthandwerk, Frankfurt, Germany, Des Moines Art Ctr., High Mus. Art, Atlanta, Bridgeport (Conn.) Ctr., Daimler-Benz Office and Lab. Complex, Ulm, Germany, Weishaupt Forum, Schwendi, Germany, City Hall and Cen. Libr., The Hague, The Netherlands, Corp. Hdqs., Royal Dutch Paper Mills, Hilversum, The Netherlands, Cornell U. Alumni and Admissions Ctr., Ithaca, N.Y., Canal Hdqs., Paris, Espace Pitot, Montpellier, France, Maybury Office Park, Edinburgh, Scotland, Hypolux Bank Bldg., Luxembourg, Mus. Contemporary Art, Barcelona, Spain, Arp Mus., Rolandswerth, Germany, Swiss Volksbank, Basel Office Bldg., Singapore, The Getty Ctr., L.A., SwissAir Hdqs., Melville, N.Y., Fed. Courthouse, Islip, N.Y., Phoenix, Mus. TV & Radio, L.A., Gagosian Gallery, L.A., Rachofsky House, Dallas, Ch. of the Yr. 2000, Rome, Ara Pacis, Rome, 2006, others; author: Richard Meier Architect: Buildings & Projects 1966-1976, 1976, On Architecture, 1982, Richard Meier Collages, 1990, The Getty Ctr. Design Process, J. Paul Getty Trust, 1991, Richard Meier Sculpture, 1994; contbr. articles to profl. jours. Decorated l'Ordre des Arts et des Lettres (France), 1984; recipient Arnold Brunner Meml. prize Am. Acad. Arts and Letters, 1972, Albert S. Bard Civic award City Club N.Y., 1973, 1st honor award for excellence in architecture and urban design, 1977, R.S. Reynolds Meml. award, 1977, Archtl. Record award of excellence for design, 1964, 68, 69, 70, 77, Am. Inst. Steel Constrn. award, 1978, 79, design award 1st prize Kunsthandwerk Competition, Frankfurt am Main, Fed. Republic Germany, 1980, Pritzker Prize for Architecture, 1984, Praemium Imperiale, Japan, 1997, Am. Inst. Architects, LA Chapter Gold Medal, 1998, El Gobierno del Distrito Federal "Huesped Distinguido de la Ciudad de Mexico," 2000, Am. Inst. of Architects 25-Year award for Smith House, 2000, NY Mag. award for Arch., 2003, Frate Sole Internat. award for Sacred Architecture, 2004, Dedalo Minosse Internat. Prize for Commissioning a Building - Quinquennial Hon. award, Associazione Liberi Architetti, 2004, Pratt Legend award, 2004, Sidney L. Strauss award, NY Soc. Architects, 2004. Fellow AIA (medal of honor N.Y. chpt. 1980, nat. design com. 1972-74, 13 AIA nat. awards 1968-97, 40 chpt. awards N.Y. 1965-97, Chgo. Arch. award, 1995, 5 Progressive Architecture awards 1979, 89, 90, 91, 95, Gold medal 1997), Am. Acad. Arts & Sci., 1995; mem. NAD (academician), Internat. Inst. Archs., Royal Inst. Brit. Archs. (Royal Gold medal 1989), Belgian Royal Acad. Art (Lifetime Achievement award Guild Hall 1991, commdr. de l'Ordre des Arts et Lettres, France, 1992). Address: Richard Meier & Ptnrs 475 10th Ave Fl 6 New York NY 10018-1120*

**MEIER, STEVEN W.,** orthopedist, surgeon, consultant; b. Elmhurst, Ill., Jan. 11, 1967; s. William P. and Donna L. Meier. MD, Loyola Med. Sch., Chgo., 1993. Diplomate Am. Bd. Orthop. Surgery, 2003. Orthop. surgeon Ctr. Advanced Sports Medicine, Summit, NJ, 2001—06, Adult and Pediatric Orthop. Specialists, Orange and Mission Viejo, Calif., 2006—. Contbr. articles to profl. jours. Mem.: Am. Acad. Orthop. Surgeons (assoc.). Office: Apos 1310 West Stewart Drive #508 Orange CA 92868-3856 Office Phone: 1.714.633.2111. Office Fax: 1.714.633.5615.

**MEIER, SUE A.,** marriage and family therapist, director; b. Pasadena, Calif., June 21, 1948; d. Don W. and Francys P. Abbott; children: Don Page, Aaron Michael, Thomas James, Jonathan Eric. BA, Calif. State U., Northridge, 1983, MA in Ednl. Psychology, Counseling & Guidance with distinction, 1986, MA in Pub. Admin. with distinction, 2001. Lic. marriage & family therapist Calif. Bd. of Behavioral Sci., 1989. Dir. Child Help USA, Nat. Child Abuse Hotline, Los Angeles, 1992—95; grant rev. U.S. Dept. Health & Human Svcs., Washington, 1996; cons. CSUN Helpline & Calif. Office Child Abuse Prevention, Los Angeles, 1996—; pvt. practice Los Angeles, 1989—; adj. faculty Antioch U., Los Angeles, 1999—, Los Angeles Cmty. Coll., Los Angeles, 1996—; exec. dir., founder Internat. Child Abuse Network, Los Angeles, 1996—. Recipient Nat. Disting. Svc. Registry for Counseling & Devel., Nat. Svc. Registry, 1990, OUtstanding Vol. of Yr. award, San Fernando Valley Child Abuse Coun., 2003. Mem.: LA County Cmty. Coord. Project (treas. 1990—), San Fernando Valley Child Abuse Counsel (pres. 1990—), Alliance of Info. Referral Sys. (bd. dirs. 1993—98). Achievements include development of 1st facilitator training for chatroom support groups; founded Internat. Child Abuse Prevention program. Avocations: crocheting, children & grand children, mystery novels. Office: Internat Child Abuse Network Inc 7657 Winnetka 155 Canoga Park CA 91306-2677 Office Phone: 818-716-8491. E-mail: yesican@yesican.org.

**MEIER, THOMAS KEITH,** academic administrator, language educator; b. Houston, Apr. 12, 1940; s. Herbert H. and Madeleine (Keith) M.; m. Mila Hillard, June 30, 1962; children: John Hillard, Keith Reilly. BA, U. Tex., 1962; AM, Columbia U., 1963, PhD, 1969; MBA, Harvard U., 1967. Fin. mgr., employee rels. mgr. Exxon Co., U.S.A. and Exxon Rsch. Engring. Co., Houston, Florham Park, NJ, 1969-79; pres. Castleton (Vt.) State Coll., 1979-87; pres., Simeon Benjamin prof. English lit. Elmira (N.Y.) Coll., 1987—. Regent Lee Coll., Baytown, Tex., 1972-73; pres. Vt. Higher Edn. Coun., 1981-82; mem. Johnson Found. (Troutbeck) Leadership Seminar, 1991—; mem. adv. coun. The Pres.'s Found. for Support of Higher Edn.; bd. dirs. Chemung Canal Trust Co., Coll. Consortium Finger Lakes, N.Y., Ind. Coll. Fund of N.Y., Coun. Ind. Colls. and Univs., Christopher Isnerwood Found. Author: Defoe and the Defense of Commerce, 1987; contbr. articles to profl. jours. Bd. dirs. Union County Urban League, Elizabeth, N.J., 1973-76,

Rutland Region C. of C., 1982-86, Arnot Art Mus., 1987-99, So. Tier Econ. Growth, 1987—, N.E.-Midwest Congl. Leadership Coun., 1988—; bd. dirs. Chemung County United Way, 1990-93, mem. 1992-93; mem. exec. coun. Five Rivers Coun. Boy Scouts Am., 1998—, mem. exec. bd. N.E. region, 2004—, Boy Scouts Am., 2004—; corp. bd. dirs. Rutland Hosp., 1980-87; bd. dirs. Ind. Coll. Fund, 1995-97. Lt. U.S. Army, 1963-65. Recipient Outstanding Periodical Essay award Tex. Books Rev., 1979, medal of merit Elmira Coll. Alumni Assn., 1991, Medallon Presidencial Univ. InterAm. de Panama, 2002; Weaver fellow, 1968. Mem. Pico Ski Club (Vt.), Elmira Country Club, Elmira City Club, Univ. Club of N.Y.C., Harvard Club of N.Y.C., Phi Beta Kappa, Phi Eta Sigma, Phi Alpha Theta, Omciron Delta Kappa, Theta Xi, Alpha Sigma Lambda, Sigma Beta Delta, Ambda Iota Tau. Episcopalian. Home: The President's Home 855 College Ave Elmira NY 14901-2001 Office: Elmira Coll Office of Pres Elmira NY 14901

**MEIERAN, EUGENE STUART,** materials scientist; b. Dec. 23, 1937; s. Elias and Rae (Linetsky) M.; m. Rosalind Berson, Mar. 25, 1962; children: Sharon Elizabeth, Andrew Marc. BS in Metallurgy, MIT, 1961, ScD in Material Sci., 1963; Doctorate (hon.), Purdue U., 2004. Mem. tech. staff Fairchild R&D, Palo Alto, Calif., 1963-73; engring. mgr. Intel Corp., Santa Clara, Calif., 1973-77, sr. mgr. quality assurance, 1977-84, Intel fellow, 1984—, mgr. applications lab., 1989—, Intel sr. fellow, 2003. Dir. rsch. LFM program MIT, 1993—; vis. lectr. Technion, Haifa, Israel, 1970-71, H.H. Wills Physics Lab., Bristol, Eng., 1970-71; mem. adv. bd. Lawrence Berkeley Lab., 1984— Contbr. articles to profl. jours. AEC fellow, 1960; recipient Internat. Reliability awards, 1970, 79, 85, Carnegie medal, 2004; named Disting. Engring. Alumnus Purdue U., 1988, Purdue Band Alumni, 2000. Mem. AIME (chmn. electronic material symposium 1973—), NAE, Electron Microscope Soc. U.S.A., Tau Beta Pi, Phi Lambda Upsilon. Democrat. Jewish. Home: 5421 E Camello Rd Phoenix AZ 85018-1910 Office. Intel Corp 5000 W Chandler Blvd Chandler AZ 85226-3699 Business E-Mail: gene.s.meieran@intel.com.

**MEIERHENRY, JUDITH KNITTEL,** state supreme court justice; b. Burke, SD, Jan. 20, 1944; m. Mark Vernon Meierhenry, May 14, 1961; children: Todd, Mary. BA in English, U. S.D., 1966, MA, 1968, JD, 1977. Bar: S.D. 1977. H.S. tchr. English Plattsmouth (Nebr.) Pub. Schs., 1966-67; instr. U. SD, 1968-70, Hiram Scott Coll., Scottbluff, Nebr., 1970; tchr. Todd County Pub. Schs., Mission, SD, 1971-74; ptnr. Meierhenry, DeVaney, Krueger & Meierhenry, Vermillion, SD, 1977-79; cabinet sec. SD Dept. Labor, Pierre, 1980-84; sr. mgr., asst. gen. counsel Citibank SD, 1985-88; cabinet sec. edn. and cultural affairs State SD, 1983-84, cir. ct. judge, 1988—2002; justice SD Supreme Ct., 2002—. Mem.: Nat. Assn. Women Judges, SD Bar Assn. Office: SD Supreme Ct 500 E Capital Ave Pierre SD 57501*

**MEIGHER, S. CHRISTOPHER, III,** communications and media executive, publisher; b. NYC, Sept. 23, 1946; s. Stephen Christopher and Denise (Connor) Todd; m. Grace Tebbutt, Aug. 8, 1970; children: Elizabeth, Amanda Powers. BA, Dartmouth Coll., 1968; grad. program mgmt. devel., Harvard U., 1974. Dir. circulation Fortune mag., N.Y.C., 1972-74, Sports Illustrated mag., N.Y.C., 1974-76, Time mag., N.Y.C., 1976-79; v.p. circulation Time, Inc., N.Y.C., 1981-83; pres. Time Distbn. Svc., N.Y.C., 1979-81; pub. People mag., N.Y.C., 1983-85, exec. v.p., group pub., 1985-90; pres. Time Inc. Mags. N.Y., N.Y.C., 1990-92; gen. ptnr., CEO, chmn. Meigher Comm., L.P., N.Y.C., 1993—; CEO Questmedia LLC, 2000—. Bd. dirs. Individual Investor Group, 1998—; bd. vis. Rockefeller Ctr. at Dartmouth Coll., 1997—; delegate U.S. State Dept. USA-USSR, 1988; mem. Bilateral Info. Talks. Moscow. Pub. Saveur mag., Garden Design mag., Quest mag., Smarth Health mag., Friends mag., 1992-2000. Trustee Boys Club N.Y.C., 1979—, Internat. Ho., 1985—92, Am. Ballet Theatre, 1993—, South St. Seaport, 1987—97, St. Paul's Sch., 1997—2002; mem. dream team Meml. Sloan Kettering, 1990—; mem. comm. com. St. James Episcopal Ch., 1989—95. Recipient Disting. Service award Brandeis U., 1983 Mem.: Mag. Publs. Assn. (bd. dirs. 1988—92, 1997—2002), Am. Pubs. Assn. (bd. dirs. 1988—92), Everglades Club (Palm Beach), Saratoga Reading Room, Clove Valley Rod and Gun Club, Lake George Club (trustee 1995—2002), N.Y. Yacht Club (trustee 1987—92), Racquet & Tennis Club (N.Y.), Brook Club, Bath & Tennis Club (Palm Beach), River Club. Office: Meigher Comm LP 920 Third Ave New York NY 10022 Office Phone: 646-840-3402. E-mail: scmiii@aol.com.

**MEIGS, JAMES B.,** editor-in-chief; Editl. dir. Video Review; sr. editor Entertainment Weekly, 1989—93; editor US Mag., 1993—95; editor-in-chief Premiere Mag., 1996—2000, v.p., 1998—2000; dep. editor features Nat. Geographic Adventure, 2001—03, exec. editor, 2003—04; editor-in-chief Popular Mechanics, 2004—. Freelance writer Rolling Stone, Details, Outside, O: The Oprah Mag., Family Life, Popular Mechanics, others. Office: Popular Mechanics 810 7th Ave New York NY 10019

**MEIGS, JOHN FORSYTH,** lawyer; b. Boston, Dec. 4, 1941; s. Charles H. Meigs and Florence S. Truitt; m. Carolyn J. Adams, Aug. 11, 2002; children: Amory, Perry, John. BA, Yale U., 1964; LLB, U. Pa., 1969. Bar: Pa. 1969, U.S. Supreme Ct. 1977. Assoc. Saul, Ewing, Remick & Saul (now Saul Ewing LLP), Phila., 1969-76, ptnr., 1976—. Co-chair estates and trusts Saul Ewing LLP, 1997—2003; chair personal wealth svcs. Group Saul Ewing LLP, 2000—. Contbr. articles to profl. jours. Trustee Independence Seaport Mus., 1978—, Woodmere Art Mus., 1987—. Mem.: ABA, Phila. Bar Assn., Pa. Bar Assn. Episcopalian. Home: 6 Norman Ln Philadelphia PA 19118-3617 Office: Saul Ewing LLP 3800 Centre Sq W Philadelphia PA 19102 Office Phone: 215-972-7812. E-mail: jmeigs@saul.com.

**MEIGS, MONTGOMERY CUNNINGHAM, JR.,** retired military officer, educator; b. Annapolis, Md., Jan. 11, 1945; s. Montgomery Cunningham and Elizabeth Shoemaker (Griggs) M.; m. Mary Ann Mellenbruch, July 6, 1968; children: William Bradford, Matthew Montgomery. BS, U.S. Mil. Acad., West Point, N.Y., 1967; MA in History, U. Wis., 1977, PhD in History, 1982. Commd. 2d lt. U.S. Army, 1967, advanced through grades to gen.; internat. affairs fellow Coun. Fgn. Rels., N.Y.C., 1981-82; exec. officer 2d Armored Cavalry Regiment, Nurnberg, Germany, 1982-84; commdr. 1st Squadron, 1st Cavalry, 1st AD, Schwabach, Germany, 1984-86; rsch. fellow Nat. Def. U., Washington, 1986-87; chief strategic applications br. J-5 Joint Staff, Washington, 1987-90; comdr. 2d Bde 1st Armored Div., Desert Storm, Erlangen, Germany, 1990-91; chief of staff V U.S. Corps, Frankfurt, Germany, 1993-94; dep. chief of staff Ops. HQ USAREUR & 7th Army, Heidelberg, Germany, 1994; comdg. gen. 3d Infantry Divsn., 1995-96, 1st infantry Divsn., Wurzburg, Germany, 1996-97, COMEAGLE, Bosnia-Herzegovina, 1996-97, Combined Arms Ctr., Ft. Leavenworth, Kans., 1997-98; commdg. gen. U.S. Army, COMSFOR, Bosnia-Herzegovina, 1998-99; commdg. gen. U.S. Army Europe and 7th Army, 1998—2002. Tom Slick vis. prof. LBJ Sch., U. Tex., Austin, 2003—04; Louis A. Battle chair Maxwell Sch. Syracuse U., 2004—; dir. OSD's Joint IED Defeat Org., 2005—. Author: Slide Rules and Submarines, 1990; contbr. articles to profl. jours. Decorated Legion of Merit with oak leaf cluster, Bronze Star medal with V device and 2 oak leaf clusters, Purple Heart, officer French Legion of Honor, German Nat. Svc. Order with star, Bavarian Svc. Order, Army Disting. Svc. medal with oak leaf cluster. Avocations: history, hunting. Home: 70 Marvelle Rd Fayetteville NY 13066 Business E-Mail: montgomery.meigs@jieddo.dod.mil.

**MEIJER, AREND,** geochemist, consultant; b. Harm and Trijntje Meijer. PhD, U. Calif., Santa Barbara, 1974. Prof. U. Ariz., Tucson, 1976—83; staff mem. Los Alamos Nat. Lab., 1983—94; geochemist GCX, Inc., Tucson, 1994—2006. Author: (rsch. papers) Geochemical Studies. Mem.: Geochemical Soc., Am. Geophys. Union. Home: 1389 E Stoney Canyon Cir Tucson AZ 85737 Office Phone: 520-229-2036. Personal E-mail: ameijer2@aol.com.

**MEIJER, HANK,** retail company executive; b. 1952; BA, U. Michigan, 1973. Asst. advt. dir. Meijer, Grand Rapids, Mich., mktg. dir., vice chmn. bd. dirs., co-chmn. bd. dirs., 1990—, CEO, 2002—05, co-CEO, 2005—. Office: 2929 Walker Ave NW Grand Rapids MI 49544

**MEIJER, PAUL HERMAN ERNST,** physicist, educator; b. The Hague, Netherlands, Nov. 14, 1921; came to U.S., 1953, naturalized, 1959; s. Herman Willem and Elisabet (Kossmann) M.; m. Marianne Schwarz, Feb. 17, 1949; children: Onko Frans (dec.), Miriam, Daniel, Mark, Corinne. PhD, U. Leiden, Netherlands, 1951. Research assoc. U. Leiden, 1952-53, Duke U., 1954-55; vis. lectr. Case Inst. Tech., 1953-54; asst. prof. U. Del., 1955-56; assoc. prof. Cath. U., Washington, 1956-60, prof. physics, 1960-92, prof. emeritus, 1992—, chmn. dept., 1980-83. Vis. prof. U. Paris, 1964-65, 72, 78, U. Nancy, 1984, 88; part-time appointment Nat. Inst.Stds. and Tech.; short time appointments at Naval Ordnance Lab., Livermore Radiation Lab., Naval Research Lab., Night Vision Lab., Ft. Belvoir. Author:(with P. Papon, J. Leblond) The Physics of Phase Transitions, 2006, (with E. Bauer) Group Theory, 2004; editor: Group Theory and Solid State Physics, 1964. Fulbright grantee, 1953-55, 77-78; Guggenheim grantee, 1964-65; Fulbright sr. fellow, 1978 Fellow Am. Phys. Socs.; mem. European Phys. Soc., Phys. Soc. Netherlands, Inst. Am. Scientists, Fulbright Alumni Assn., Sigma Xi. Research, publs. statis. mechanics solids and liquids, group theory and other fields. Home: 1438 Geranium St NW Washington DC 20012-1518 Office: Cath U Am Dept Physics Hannan Hall Washington DC 20064 Office Phone: 202-319-5324. Business E-Mail: meijer@cua.edu.

**MEIKLE, PHILIP G.,** engineer, retired government agency executive; b. Glendale, W.Va., Dec. 5, 1937; s. Philip and Caroline Elizabeth (Stephens) M.; m. Linda Kay Price, July 14, 1961 (div. Aug. 1976); children: Philip Kevin, Melissa Kay BS in Mining Engring., W.Va. U., 1961, MS in Mining Engring., 1965; M.Engring. Adminstrn., George Washington U., 1980. Registered profl. engr. Mining engr. Duquesne Light Co., Pitts., 1961-63; research engr. W.Va. U., Morgantown, 1963-66; materials engr. Mobay Chem Co., New Martinsville, W.Va., 1966-68; asst. dir. Nat. Ash Assn., Washington, 1968-72; staff mining engr. U.S. Bur. Mines, Washington, 1972-82, divsn. chief, 1982-95; ret., 1995. Mem. U.S. Nat. Com. for Tunneling Tech., Nat. Acad. Scis., Washington, 1985-90, chmn., 1988-89; adj. prof. George Washington U., 1985—; pres. Clan Lamont Soc. N.Am., 1998-2002. Contbr. articles to profl. jours., chpts. to books Recipient Superior Svc. award Dept. Interior, 1980, Meritorious Svc. award, 1986, Disting. Svc. award, 1991, Presdl. Rank award, 1991. Mem. Nat. Assn. Ret. Fed. Employees (life), Sr. Execs. Assn. (life), Coun. Former Fed. Execs. (bd. dirs., 2004-), Sigma Xi, Tau Beta Pi, Sigma Gamma Epsilon, Masons, Shriners. Republican. Baptist. Home: 6819 Brian Michael Ct Springfield VA 22153-1004

**MEIKLEJOHN, ALVIN J., JR.,** state legislator, lawyer, accountant; b. Omaha, June 18, 1923; m. Lorraine J. Meiklejohn; children: Pamela Ann, Shelley Lou, Bruce Ian, Scott Alvin. BS, U. Denver, JD, 1951; LLD (hon.), U. No. Colo., 2000. Mem. Colo. state Senate from 19th Dist., 1976-96, chmn. com. edn.; mem. Edn. Commn. of States, 1981-96; chmn. Colo. Commn. on Ach. in Edn., 1995, mem., 1993-96, Jefferson Sch. Dist. No. R-1 Bd. Edn., 1971-77, pres., 1973-77; commr. Commn. on Uniform State Laws, 1988-96. Dir. Red Rocks C.C. Found., Wings Over the Rockies Air and Space Mus. Capt. U.S. Army, 1944-46, maj. USAF, 1947—51. Mem. Arvada C. of C., Masons, Shriners, Transp. Lawyers Assn. (pres. 1972-73). Republican. Home: 7540 Kline Dr Arvada CO 80005-3732 Office: Jones & Keller PC 1625 Broadway Ste 1600 Denver CO 80202-4727 Office Phone: 303-573-1600. Business E-Mail: ajmeiklejohn@joneskeller.com.

**MEIKSIN, ZVI H.,** electrical engineering educator; b. 1926; BSEE, Israel Inst. Tech., Haifa, 1950, Dipl. Ing., 1951; MSEE, Carnegie Mellon U., 1953; PhDEE, U. Pitts., 1959. Registered profl. engr., Pa. Design engr. McGraw Edison, Cannonsburg, Pa., 1953-54; sr. project engr. Westinghouse Electric Corp., Pitts., 1956-59; prof. elec. engring. U. Pitts., 1959-91, prof. emeritus, 1991—; pres. Transtek, Inc., Pitts., 1995—2004. Cons. entr. 33 orgns. in U.S., Europe, 1959-95; expert witness in field, 1991-95; cons. Transtek, Inc., 2004-. Author: Thin & Thick Films, 1976, Active Filter Design, 1990; co-author: Electronic Design, 1980, 84, Microprocessor Based Design, 1986; jour. referee profl. publs., 1970—; contbr. articles to profl. jours.; inventor, holder 8 patents in field. Fellow IEEE (award coms.); mem. Eta Kappa Nu, Sigma Xi. E-mail: meiksin@pitt.edu.

**MEILI, BARBARA,** lawyer; b. Rhinebeck, NY; BA, Bennington Coll., 1980; JD magna cum laude, NY Law Sch., 1983. Bar: NY 1984. Shareholder, corp. and securities tech., media and telecom. Greenberg Traurig LLP, NYC. Mem.: ABA, Assn. Bar of NYC, Women in Cable and Telecom. Office: Greenberg Traurig MetLife Bldg 200 Park Ave New York NY 10166-1400 Office Phone: 212-801-9200. Office Fax: 212-801-6400. Business E-Mail: meilib@gtlaw.com.

**MEILMAN, EDWARD,** physician; b. Boston, Apr. 6, 1915; s. Harry and Jennie (Sholofsky) M.; m. Rhoeda Berman, Mar. 6, 1946. AB, Harvard U., 1936, MD, 1940. Intern Mt. Sinai Hosp., N.Y.C., 1940-42; resident Beth Israel Hosp., Boston, 1946-48, assoc. in med. and med. research, 1948-53; chmn. dept. medicine L.I. Jewish-Hillside Med. Center, New Hyde Park, NY, 1953-82, chmn. emeritus dept. medicine, 1982—. Prof. medicine SUNY, Stony Brook, 1971— Contbr. articles to profl. jours. Served with USAAF, 1942-46. Fellow N.Y. Acad. Medicine, N.Y. Acad. Scis.; mem. Am. Heart Assn. (fellow council clin. cardiology, council arteriosclerosis), Am. Fedn. Clin. Research, Harvey Soc., Am. Rheumatism Assn., Phi Beta Kappa, Alpha Omega Alpha. Clubs: Harvard (N.Y.C.); Harvard (L.I.). Democrat. Jewish. Office Phone: 516-487-4203. Business E-Mail: emeilman@optonline.net.

**MEILTON, SANDRA L.,** lawyer; b. 1946; BA, Bethany Coll., 1968; attended, U. Pitts.; JD, Dickinson Sch. Law, 1980. Bar: Pa. 1980. Assoc. Hepford, Swartz and Morgan, 1980—87, ptnr., 1987—98; shareholder Tucker Arensberg PC, 1998 ; Bd. dirs. Mechanicsburg Children's Home. Named one of Best Lawyers in Am., 2005. Mem.: ABA, Dauphin County Bar Assn., Am. Acad. Matrimonial Lawyers. Office: Tucker Arensberg PO Box 889 111 N Front St Harrisburg PA 17108-0889 Office Phone: 717-234-4121. Business E-Mail: smeilton@tuckerlaw.com.

**MEIMA, RALPH CHESTER, JR.,** retired diplomat, real estate company executive; b. Chgo., Mar. 29, 1927; s. Ralph Chester and Grace Georgine (Larson) Meima; m. Elizabeth B. Frazier, 1994; children from previous marriage: Ralph Chester III, Stephen H. BA, U. Ams., Mexico City, 1952; MBA, Am. U., 1964. With Carborundum Co., Perth Amboy, 1952-53, Johns-Manville Corp., N.Y.C., 1953-58, Security Storage Co., Washington, 1958-61, Dept. of Commerce, 1961-68; joined U.S. Fgn. Svc., 1968; consul gen. Marseille, France, 1977-80; on loan export devel. cons. State of Md., 1980-82; pres. Atlantic Eastern Corp., 1982-87, Phoenix Internat. Mktg. Corp., 1987-89; pres., chief exec. officer FTI Inc., Annapolis, Md., 1989-95; pres. DERCO, Inc., Balt., 1995—2002. In govt. rels. iJET Travel Risk Mgmt., Inc. With USN, 1945—46. Office: Champion Realty 541-B Baltimore Annapolis Blvd Severna Park MD 21146-3934 Office Phone: 410-975-3358. Personal E-Mail: r.meima@att.net.

**MEINDL, ROBERT JAMES,** language educator, poet; b. Wausau, Wis., Sept. 17, 1936; s. George Martin and Adeline Emilie (Goetsch) M.; m. Victoria Lynn Chavez; children: Karin Rose, George Andrew, Damian Kurt, Erika Wittmer, Christopher Smith, Gabrielle Remelia. BS, U. Wis., 1958; MA, U. Conn., 1960; PhD, Tulane U., 1965; postdoctoral studies, U. Calif., Berkeley, 1967—68, Goethe Inst., Liblar, Germany, 1970, U. Cologne, Germany, 1970. Teaching asst. U. Conn., Storrs, 1958—60; teaching fellow Tulane U., 1960—62; lectr. U. Wis., Green Bay, 1963—65; asst. prof. to full prof. English Calif. State U., Sacramento, 1965—2002, prof. emeritus English, 2002—. Translator: Studies in John Gower, 1981; book rev. editor Studia Mystica Jour., 1984-89; contbr. numerous articles to profl. jours. With USNR, 1953-61, 79-96. Nat. Endowment for the Humanities fellow Stanford U., 1982. Mem. MLA (life), Medieval Acad. Am. (life), John Gower Soc. Office: Calif State U 6000 J St Sacramento CA 95819-2605 Office Phone: 916-278-7704. Business E-Mail: rmeindl@csus.edu.

**MEINE, CURT,** biologist, writer; b. New Castle, Pa., Nov. 29, 1958; s. Kenneth and Evelyn DeVivo Meine. BA in English/History, DePaul U., Chgo., 1980; MS in Land Resources, U. Wis., Madison, 1983, PhD in Land Resources, 1988. Cons., 1998—; staff assoc. US Nat. Rsch. Coun., Washington, 1990—92; rsch. assoc. Internat. Crane Found., Baraboo, Wis., 1993—; sr. fellow Aldo Leopold Found., Baraboo, 2001—. Tchg. asst. Inst. Environ. Studies, 1982—87, project asst., 1987—88; instr. U. Wis., Madison, 1996—; conf. organizer; presenter in field. Author: Aldo Leopold: His Life and Work, 1988 (Book of the Yr. Forest History Soc., 1988), Correction Lines: Essays on Land, Leopold, and Conservation, 2004; editor: Wallace Stegner and the Continental Vision: Critical Essays and Commentary, 1998; editor: (with Marieta Sakalian) Bulgaria's Biological Diversity: Conservation Status and Needs Assessment, 1998; editor: (with Richard L. Knight) The Essential Aldo Leopold, 1999; mem. editl. rev. bd. Wis. Acad. Rev., 1993—99, mem. editl. bd. Environmental Ethics, 1997—; contbr. articles to profl. jours. Founding bd. dirs., pres. Sauk Prairie Conservation Alliance, Priarie du Sac, Wis., 2002—; chair Cmty. Conservation Coalition Sauk Prairie, 1997—98, 2001—02. Recipient Outstanding Achievement award, Wis. Libr. Assn., 1989, award of Merit, State Hist. Soc. Wis., 1989, Biodiversity Leadership award, Bay and Paul Found., 2005—06; Univ. fellow, U. Wis., Madison, 1982—83, Aldo Leopold fellow, Sand County Found., 1985—86, Conservation fellow, Nat. Wildlife Fedn., 1986—87. Mem.: Am. Soc. Environ. History, Soc. Conservation Biology (mem. editl. bd. 1995—, bd. dirs. 1995—2002, White Lady's Slipper award 1998). Office: Internat Crane Found PO Box 447 E11376 Shady Ln Rd Baraboo WI 53913

**MEINEL, ADEN BAKER,** optics scientist; b. Pasadena, Calif., Nov. 25, 1922; s. John G. and Gertrude (Baker) M.; m. Marjorie Steele Pettit, Sept. 5, 1944; children: Carolyn, Walter, Barbara, Elaine, Edward, Mary, David. AB, U. Calif., Berkeley, 1947, PhD, 1949; DSc (hon.), U. Ariz., 1990. Assoc. prof. Yerkes Obs., U. Chgo., Williams Bay, Wis., 1950-58; dir. Kitt Peak Nat. Obs., Tucson, 1958-61; prof. U. Ariz., Tucson, 1961-85; dir. Steward Obs., Tucson, 1962-66, Optical Scis. Ctr., Tucson, 1966-73; Disting. scientist Jet Propulsion Lab., Pasadena, 1985-92; ret., 1993. Regent Calif. Luth. Coll., 1961-71; cons. USAF Spl. Projects Office, 1965-80. Co-author: Applied Solar Energy, 1976, Sunsets, Twilights and Evening Skies, 1983. Recipient Warner prize Am. Astron. Soc., 1954, Van Blesbroeck award Astron. Soc. Pacific, 1990, NASA Exceptional Scientific Achievement medal, 1993; Meinel bldg. U. Ariz. dedicated 1993 Fellow Am. Acad Arts and Scis., Optical Soc. Am. (pres. 1972-73, Adolph Lomb medal 1952, Ives medal 1980), Internat. Optical Engring. Soc. (Goddard award 1984, Kingslake medal, 1993, 2000, Gold medal 1997). Home: 1600 Shoreline Dr Santa Barbara CA 93109-2024 E-mail: ameinel@earthlink.net.

**MEINEL, CAROLYN PETTIT,** industrial engineer, writer; d. Aden Baker and Marjorie Pettit Meinel; m. Michael S. Bertin, Jan. 2, 1997. BA in Gen. Studies, U. Ariz., Tucson, 1981, MS in Indsl. Engring., 1983. COO Analog Precision, Inc., Tucson, 1973—76; pres. L-5 Soc. for Space Devel., 1977—79; sr. scientist Analytic Decisions, Inc., Arlington, Va., 1983—87; pres. M/B Rsch., Cedar Crest, N.Mex., 0187—. Author: (book) Guide to Electromagnetic Launch, two editions, Guide to Electromagnetic Launch, 2nd ed., Emerging Technologies, Vol. 3 and 4, Intermodal Technologies, Emerging Technologies, Vols. 3 and 4, The Happy Hacker, four editions, Intermodal Freight Technologies, Uberhacker, two editions; editor-in-chief (mga.) L-5 News; contbr. chapters to books. Competition ofcl. Ballon Fedn. Am., 1997—2001. Mem.: AAAS, IEEE. Achievements include patents pending for automation of a process-based security modifiction to Linux, filed by Systems Advisory Groupe Enterprises, Inc. Office: M/B Rsch PO Box 1520 Cedar Crest NM 87008 Office Phone: 505-281-9675. E-mail: cmeinel@techbroker.com.

**MEINER, SUE ELLEN THOMPSON,** adult nurse practitioner, consultant, gerontologist; b. Ironton, Mo., Oct. 24, 1943; d. Louis Raymond and Verna Mae Thompson; m. Robert Edward Meiner, Mar. 5, 1971; children: Diane Romeril, Suzanne. AAS, Meramec C.C., 1970; BSN, St. Louis U., 1978, MSN, 1983; EdD, So. Ill. U., Edwardsville, 1991. RN, Nev.; cert. gerontol. nurse practitioner; cert. clin. specialist in gerontol. nursing. Staff RN St. Joseph's Hosp., St. Charles, Mo., 1976-78; nursing supr. Bethesda Gen. Hosp., St. Louis, 1975-76, 71-74; adult med. dir. Family Care Ctr.-Carondelet, St. Louis, 1978-79; program dir., lectr. Webster Coll./Bethesda Hosp., Webster Groves, Mo., 1979-82; diabetes clin. specialist Washington U. Sch. Medicine, St. Louis, 1982; asst. prof. St. Louis C.C., 1983-88; vis. nurse assoc. St. Louis, 1970-71; chmn. dept. nursing, asst. prof. Barnes Hosp. Sch. Nursing, 1988-89; instr. U. Mo., St. Louis, 1989; assoc. prof. St. Charles County C.C., St. Peters, Mo., 1990-92, Deaconess Coll. of Nursing, 1991-93; patient care mgr. Deaconess Hosp., St. Louis, 1993-94; assoc. prof. Jewish Hosp. Coll. of Nursing and Allied Health, 1994-99; gerontol. nurse, rschr. Wash. U. Sch. Med., St. Louis, 1996-2000; prof. nursing U. Nev. Coll. Health Scis., Las Vegas, 2000—05; pvt. practice Nev., 2005—. Nat. dir. edn. Nat. Assn. Practical Nurse Edn. and Svc., St. Louis, 1984-86; mem. task force St. Louis Met. Hosp. Assn., 1987-88; mem. adv. com. Bd. Edn. Sch. Nursing, St. Louis, 1986-90; grant coord. Kellogg Found. Gerontology and Nursing, 1991-92; project dir. NIH, NIA Grant Washington U. Sch. Medicine, St. Louis, 1996-00; mem. editorial bd. Geriatric Nursing Journ., 1999-02; legal nurse cons. Author and editor profl. books; contbr. articles to profl. jours. Chmn. bd. dirs. Creve Coeur Fire Protection Dist. Mo., 1984-89; vice chmn. Bd. Cen. St. Louis County Emergency Dispatch Svc., 1985-87; asst. leader Girl Scouts St. Louis, 1975; treas. Older Women's League, St. Louis, 1992-93. Recipient Woman of Worth award Gateway chpt. Older Women's League, 1993. Mem.: ANA, Am. Soc. of Aging, Nat. League for Nursing, Am. Nurses Found., Am. Coll. Nurse Practitioners, Am. Acad. Nurse Practitioners, Job's Daus. (guardian 1979—80), Order Ea. Star (chaplain 1970), Creve Coeur C. of C., Sigma Theta Tau (fin. chmn. 1984, archivist 1985—87, Zeta Kappa chpt. v.p. 2001—03), Kappa Delta Pi, Sigma Phi Omega (iota chpt. pres. 1990—91). Avocations: travel, reading. Home and Office: 3722 Violet Rose Ct Las Vegas NV 89147-7400 Personal E-mail: agingwell@earthlink.net. *Personal philosophy: From my earliest memories, I have established goals that were obtainable only through very hard work and perseverance. I always sought support and assistance from significant others as each goal was reached before setting another one. My life has been enriched by family and very dear friends. An important belief and practice has been to return the benefits of my education to my community and to be an advocate for those persons needing assistance. I hold a special place for support of all older adults.*

**MEINERT, JOHN RAYMOND,** apparel executive, investment banker; b. White Cloud, Mich., Aug. 11, 1901; m. Joyce Macdonell, Nov. 5, 1955; children: Elizabeth Tinsman, Pamela Martin. Student, U. Mich., 1944-45; BS, Northwestern U., 1949. CPA Ill., 1952. With Hart Schaffner & Marx/Hartmarx Corp., Chgo., 1950-70, exec. v.p., 1975-80, vice chmn., 1981-85, vice chmn., 1985-86, chmn., 1987-90, chmn. emeritus, 1990—; also bd. dirs.; prin. investment banking J.H. Chapman Group, LLC, Rosemont, Ill., 1990—, chmn., 1995-. Bd. dirs. County Seat Stores, Inc., N.Y.C., 1998-99, The John Evans Club, BBB, Chgo. C. of C.; trustee Amalgamated Ins. Fund, 1980-90, Rotary Internat. Retirement Fund, 2000-02; dir. Evanston Hosp., 1988-94, Clothing Mfrs. Assn., pres., 1982-87, chmn. 1987-90. mem. acctg. Northwestern U., 1949; faculty Lake Forest Grad. Sch. Mgmt., 1994-95; arbitrator Am. Arbitration Assn., 1993—. Chmn. bus. adv. coun. U. Ill., 1989-90; mem. Fin. Acctg. Stds. Adv. Coun., 1989-92, Chgo. Coun. Fgn. Rels., Sisters City Com.; mem. adv. coun. Northwestern U. Kellogg Grad. Sch. Recipient Alumni Merit award Northwestern U. Kellogg Grad. Sch., 1989; named Humanitarian of Yr., Five Hosp. Found., 1995. Mem. AICPA (v.p. 1985-86, bd. dirs. 1975-78, coun. 1971-93, trustee benevolent fund 1992-95, gold medal 1987), Ill. CPA Soc. (pub. svc. award 1996, pres. 1982-83, bd. dirs. 1966-68, 81-84, hon. award), Chicagoland C. of C. (bd. dirs.), Rotary (pres. Chgo. 1989-90, trustee found. 1991-95, asst. dist. gov. 1997-2000), Univ. Club, Execs. Club, Rolling Green Country Club. Presbyterian (elder). Home: 634 N Ironwood Dr Arlington Heights IL 60004-5818 Office: J H Chapman Group LLC 9700 W Higgins Rd Rosemont IL 60018-4796 Office Phone: 773-693-4800. Business E-Mail: jmeinert@jhchapman.com.

**MEINHOLD, CHARLES BOYD,** health physicist; b. Boston, Nov. 1, 1934; s. Russell and Jane (Boyd) M.; m. Anne Elizabeth DuVally, Oct. 20, 1956; children: Anne Frances, Patricia Marie, Michael John, Peter Russell, Catherine Louise. BS in Physics, Providence Coll., 1956; postgrad., U. Rochester, 1956-57. Cert. Am. Bd Health Physics 1967. Staff scientist health physics div. Brookhaven Nat. Lab., Upton, NY, 1957-72, head, sr. health physicist safety and environ. div., 1972-88, sr.scientist, div. head, 1988-91, sr. scientist radiol. sci. divsn. Dept. Advanced Tech., 1991-2001; guest scientist Dept. of Non-Proliferation and Nat. Security, 2001—. Mem. Internat. Commn. on Radiol. Protection, 1978-01, vice chmn., 1992-01, emeritus mem., 2002—; mem. Nat. Coun. on Radiol. Protection and Measurement, 1977-01, pres., 1991-02, pres. emeritus, 2002—; Lauren S. Taylor lectr. Pres. South Haven Bd. Edn., Brookhaven, N.Y., 1965-87. Named Hon. Prof., China Inst. Atomic Energy, 1995, China Inst. Radiation Protection, 1997. Fellow Health Physics Soc. (pres. 1980-81); mem. Internat. Radiation Protection Assn. (v.p. 1988-92, pres. 1992-96), Hon. mem. Conf. Radiation Control Program Dirs. Democrat. Roman Catholic. Avocations: woodworking, sailing. Home: 41 Old South Country Rd Brookhaven NY 11719-9526 Office: Brookhaven Nat Lab Bldg 197D Upton NY 11973-5000 Personal E-mail: cbmeinhold@optonline.net.

**MEINIG, DONALD WILLIAM,** geography educator; b. Palouse, Wash., Nov. 1, 1924; s William August and Annie (Malsed) M.; m. Lee McAuliffe, June 29, 1946; children: Laurel, Kristin, Lee. BS, Georgetown U., 1948; MA, U. Wash., 1950, PhD, 1953; DHL (hon.), Syracuse U., 1994. From asst. prof. to assoc. prof. U. Utah, Salt Lake City, 1950-59; assoc. prof. geography Syracuse U., NY, 1959-73, Maxwell prof. geography NY, 1973-89, Maxwell rsch. prof., 1990—2005. Lectr. St. Andrews U., Scotland, 1973, Charles Homer Haskins lectr. ACLS, 1992; vis. prof. Hebrew U., Jerusalem, 1974; adv. editor Wadsworth Pub. Co., 1957-61, Harper & Row, N.Y.C., 1965-83; chief editl. cons. Nat. Geog. Soc., Washington, 1982-88; councilor Am. Geog. Soc., 1993-96. Author: On the Margins of the Good Earth, 1962, The Great Columbia Plain, 1968, Imperial Texas, 1969, Southwest, 1971, The Shaping of America, Vol. 1: Atlantic America 1492-1800, 1986, Vol. 2: Continental America 1800-1867, 1993, Vol. 3: Transcontinental America 1850-1915, 1998, Vol. 4: Global America 1915-2000, 2004; editor: The Interpretation of Ordinary Landscapes, 1979. Mem. N.Y. Council for Humanities, 1979-86. Served to 2d lt. U.S. Army, 1943-46. Recipient Emil and Kathleen Sick award in Western History, 1968, award of Merit Seattle Hist. Soc., 1968, award of Merit Am. Assn. State and Local History, 1969, Summerfield G. Roberts award Sons Republic of Tex., 1969, Faculty Enrichment award Can Embassy, 1980, Master Tchr. award Nat. Coun. for Geog. Edn., 1986, Charles P. Daly medal Am. Geog. Soc., 1986; Fulbright rsch. scholar U. Adelaide, 1958; Guggenheim fellow, 1966-67, NEH fellow, 1987-88. Fellow Brit. Acad. (corr.); mem. Assn. Am. Geographers (councilor 1965-67, Meritorious Contbn. award Presdl. Achievement award 2005, John Brinkerhoff Jackson award 2005), Am. Antiquarian Soc. Office: Syracuse U Dept Geography Syracuse NY 13244-0001

**MEINZER, BEVERLY ANNE,** chemist, educator; d. David Lathrop and Anna Lee (Floyd) Edmiaston; m. Alan Lester Meinzer, Dec. 30, 1989; 1 child, Natalie. BS, Lyon Coll., Batesville, Ark., 1986; MS, U. Ark., Fayetteville, 1989. Chemist IV Tenn. Dept. Health, Jackson, 1990—95; lab. mgr., instr. Lyon Coll., Batesville, 1995—2003; chemistry educator Mid-Ark. CC, Batesville, 2003—. Sci. fair judge various secondary schs. Pianist Faith-Hopewell Cumberland Presbyn. Ch., Batesville, 1996—. Presbyterian. Avocations: piano, sewing. Office: Univ Ark Cmty Coll PO Box 3350 Batesville AR 72503 Business E-Mail: bmeinzer@uacch.edu.

**MEIRELLES, FERNANDO,** film director; b. São Paulo City, Brazil, Nov. 9, 1955; Student in Architecture, Univ. São Paulo. Co-founder Olhar Electronico studio. Dir.: (films) Olhar Electronico, 1986, the Nutty Boy 2, 1998, Golden Gate, 2002, The Constant Gardener, 2005 (ALMA award, Nat. Coun. La Raza for outstanding dir. for motion picture, 2006, Golden Globe nominee for best dir., 2005); co-dir.: City of God, 2002 (Acad. award nomination for direction, 2004); dir., writer: (TV episodes) Brava Gente, 2000, Cidade dos Homens, 2002, 2005; prod: Contra Todos, 2003. Mailing: c/o John Lesher Endeavor Agy 10th fl 9601 Wilshire Blvd Beverly Hills CA 90212*

**MEIRI, KARINA F.,** medical educator; d. Clement Isaac Ormesher and Frida Agnitisch; m. James E. Schwob, Jan. 21, 1988; children: Anneke Schwob, Olivia Schwob. PhD, Liverpool U. Sch. Medicine, Eng., 1978—82. Prof., pharmacology SUNY Upstate Med. U., Syracuse, 1996—2000; prof., anatomy & cellular biology Tufts U. Sch. Medicine, Boston, 2001—. Grantee, NIH, 1987—2004, 1996—, Fogarty Internat. fellowship, 2003—06. Mem. Soc. Neuroscience. Achievements include research in developmental neurobiology. Office: Tufts Univ Sch Medicine 136 Harrison Ave Boston MA 02111 Office Phone: 617-636-2445. Personal E-mail: karina.meiri@tufts.edu.

**MEIROWITZ, CLAIRE CECILE,** publishing executive; b. Frankfurt, Germany, Jan. 14, 1934; came to U.S., 1939; d. Karl and Margot Bier; m. Richard Meirowitz, Sept. 12, 1954 (div., July, 1969); children: Diane, Laura, Linda; m. Joseph, Apr. 20, 1975. AA, Nassau C.C., 1973; BA magna cum laude, Hofstra U., 1976; postgrad., N.Y. Inst. Tech., 1987-90. Pres., owner, editor, writer, pub. rels. and mktg. cons. Profl. Editing Svcs., Babylon, NY, 1972-76, 92—; editl. asst. United Tech. Publs., Garden City, NY, 1976-77; publs. assoc. N.Y. Inst. Tech., Old Westbury, NY, 1977-79; asst. dir. coll. rels., dir. publs. SUNY, Old Westbury, 1979-87, dir. cmty. rels. and publs., 1987-92. Pres. SUNY Coun. for Univ. Affairs and Devel., 1987-89; cons. Guarino Graphics, Greenville, N.Y., 1985-92, editor, copywriter, 1986-92. Manuscript editor Jour. of Collective Negotiations in Pub. Sector, 1972-91, editr., 1991—, Jour. of Individual Employment Rights, 1992—; editor art catalog South Africa/South Bronx, 1981 (art excellence award 1982); author: New Student Prospectus, The College at Old Westbury, 1979, Labor-Management Relations Among Government Workers, 1983; co-editor: Strategies for Impasse Resolution, 1992; editor Alzheimer's Assn. L.I. chpt. newsletter; contbr. articles to profl. jours. v.p., treas., sec., Taxpayers Edn. Assn., Hicksville, N.Y., 1962-68; mem. The Nature Conservancy, Cold Spring Harbor, N.Y., 1980-91; tutor Lit. Vols. Am. Suffolk County Chpt., 1996-99; newsletter editor Babylon Breast Cancer Coalition, 1997—, The Active Retiree, United Univ. Professions, 1999-2002. Recipient Excellence in Profl. Svc. award SUNY, Albany, 1987, Disting. Svc. award SUNY Coun. Univ. Affairs, 1989, award for excellence in communications SUNY Westbury Alumni Assn., 1992, award for disting. leadership L.I. Women's Coun. for Equal Edn., Employment and Tng., 1992, award for newsletter excellence N.Y. State United Tchrs., 2001. Mem. L.I. Communicators Assn., Internat. Assn. of Bus. Communicators (steering com., sec., v.p. L.I. Women's Coun. 1990-99), Babylon Village Womens Club, Babylon Bus. and Profl. Women's Assn. Democrat. Jewish. Avocation: computers. Home: 167 Cadman Ave Babylon NY 11702-1607 Office Phone: 631-422-6804. E-mail: cmeirowitz@yahoo.com.

**MEIS, PAUL JEAN,** obstetrics and gynecology educator; b. Sioux City, Iowa, Oct. 29, 1934; s. Lee Francis and Dorothy (Trexlar) M.; m. Marcia Rose Donsker, June 28, 1958; children: Steven James, Douglas John. BS, U. Iowa, 1956, MD, 1959. Diplomate Am. Bd. Ob-Gyn, Am. Bd. Maternal-Fetal Medicine. Intern Martin Army Hosp., Ft. Benning, Ga., 1959-60; resident ob/gyn. SUNY Upstate Med. Ctr., Syracuse, 1962-65; pvt. practice, La Crosse, Wis., 1965-75; fellow Harbor Gen. Hosp., Torrance, Calif., 1975-77; asst. prof. dept. ob-gyn. Bowman Gray Sch. Medicine Wake Forest U., Winston-Salem, N.C., 1977-80, assoc. prof., 1980-85; prof. Bowman Gray

---

Sch. Medicine Wake Forest U. Sch. Medicine, Winston-Salem, NC, 1985—. Capt. M.C., U.S. Army, 1959-62. Office: Wake Forest U Sch Medicine Dept Ob-Gyn Medical Center Blvd Winston Salem NC 27157-0001 E-mail: pmeis@wfubmc.edu.

**MEISBURG, RONALD EDWARD,** federal agency administrator, lawyer; b. Bowling Green, Ky., July 28, 1947; s. Edward Austin and Jean Lavelle (Knadler) M.; m. Elizabeth Ann Ruark, July 27, 1969 (div. Dec. 1975); m. Roseann Karene Finigan, July 14, 1984 (dec. 1997). BA, Carson-Newman Coll., 1969; JD, U. Louisville, 1974. Bar: Ky., D.C., U.S. Ct. Appeals (2nd, 3rd, 4th, 5th, 6th, 7th, D.C., and 9th cirs.). Atty. U.S. Dept. Labor, Washington, 1974-80; assoc. Smith, Heenan and Althen, Washington, 1980-85, ptnr., 1985-97, Heenan Althen & Roles, Washington, 1997—2002; atty., shareholder Ogletree, Deakins, Nash, Smoak & Stewart LLP, Washington, 2002—06; mem. NLRB, Washington, 2004, spl. asst. to assoc. gen. counsel for enforcement, 2005—06, exec. asst. to dep. gen. counsel, 2005—06, gen. counsel, 2006—. Pres., Energy & Mineral Law Found., 1994-95; mem., exec. com. Ea. Mineral Law Found., W.Va. U., Morgantown, 1990—, asst. v.p., 1991-93, v.p., 1993-94, pres., 1994-95; mem., US Coun. Internat. Bus., 1993-98, Employment Lawyers Advisory Coun., 1996-98, Nat. Assn. Mfrs., 1996-98. Contbr. articles to profl. jours. and proceedings; editl. adv. bd. Jour. Natural Resources and Environ. Law, 1987—. Recipient Disting. Achievement award U.S. Sec. of Labor, Washington, 1978. Mem. ABA, Ky. Bar Assn. Roman Catholic. Office: NLRB Office Gen Counsel 1099 14th St NW Rm 10100 Washington DC 20570*

**MEISEL, ALAN,** law educator; b. Newark, Dec. 24, 1946; s. Stanley and Beatrice (Katz) M.; m. Linda S. Serody, Mar. 6, 1982; 2 children. BA, Yale U., 1968, JD, 1972. Bar: Conn. 1972, Pa. 1973, U.S. Dist. Ct. Conn. 1972, U.S. Dist. Ct. (we. dist.) Pa. 1973, U.S. Ct. Appeals (3d cir.) 1985. Prof. psychiatry U. Pitts., 1973—, prof. law, 1976—, Dickie, McCamey Chilcote prof. bioethics/law and psychiatry, 1995—, dir. Ctr. for Bioethics and Health Law, 1987—. Asst. dir. for legal studies Pres.'s Commn. for Study of Ethical Problems in Medicine and Biomed. and Behaviorial Rsch., Washington, 1982; mem. ethics working group Presdl. Task Force on Healthcare Reform, 1993; mem. adv. coun. NHLBI, 1998—2004. Author: The Right to Die, 1989, 2d edit., 1995, 3d edit. 2004; co-author: Informed Consent: A Study of Decision Making in Psychiatry, 1984, Informed Consent: Legal Theory and Clinical Practice, 1987; contbr. articles to legal and med. jours. Grantee NIMH, grantee Pres.'s Commn. for Study of Ethical Problems in Medicine and Biomed. and Behavioral Rsch., 1981-82, Founds. Fund for Rsch. in Psychiatry grantee, 1979-82, Legal Svcs. Corp. grantee, 1985-87; fellow Hastings Ctr.; award for The Right to Die Am. Assn. Publs., 1989; Pellegrino medal Contbns. Am. Health Care Ethics Law in Selfless Spirit of Edmund D. Pellegrino, Samford U., 2005. Mem.: Am. Soc. Bioethics and Humanities, Am. Soc. Law, Medicine and Ethics, Am. Health Lawyers Assn. Office: U Pitts Sch Law 3900 Forbes Ave Pittsburgh PA 15260 Business E-Mail: meisel@pitt.edu.

**MEISEL, DAN,** chemist; b. Tel Aviv, July 4, 1943; s. Arie and Mariasha Miriam (Ribak) M.; m. Osnat Meisel, Dec. 30, 1965; children: Einat, Omer. BSc, Hebrew U., 1967, MSc, 1969, PhD, 1974. Prof. chemistry U. Notre Dame, Ind., 1998—, dir. Radiation Lab. Ind., 1998—2004. Adv. bd.: Jour. Phys. Chem., 1993—2002; editor: Photochem. Energy Conversion, 1989, Semiconductors Nanoclusters, 1997. Mem. AAAS, Am. Chem. Soc., Am. Phys. Soc. Office: U Notre Dame Radiation Lab Notre Dame IN 46556 Office Phone: 574-631-5457. Business E-Mail: dani@nd.edu.

**MEISEL, GEORGE VINCENT,** lawyer; b. St. Louis, Sept. 24, 1933; s. Leo Otto and Margaret (Duggan) M.; m. Joy C. Cassin, May 18, 1963 BS summa cum laude, St. Louis U., 1956, JD cum laude, 1958. Bar: Mo. 1958. Assoc. Grand Peper & Martin, St. Louis, 1961-64, ptnr., 1965; jr. ptnr. Bryan Cave McPheeters & McRoberts, St. Louis, 1966-69; ptnr. Bryan Cave, LLP, St. Louis, 1970-2000, of counsel, 2000—. Served to 1st lt. USAF, 1958-61 Mem. ABA, Bar Assn. Met. St. Louis, Mo. Bar Assn. Clubs: Saint Louis, Mo. Athletic (St. Louis). Roman Catholic. Home: 2029 S Warson Rd Saint Louis MO 63124-1151 Office Phone: 314-259-2268. Business E-Mail: gvmeisel@bryancavellp.com.

**MEISEL, JOHN,** political scientist; b. Vienna, Oct. 23, 1923; s. Fryda and Ann M. BA, U. Toronto, 1948, MA, 1950; PhD in Polit. Sci., London Sch. Econs., 1959; LLD, Brock U., 1983, U. Guelph, 1985, Carleton U., 1990, U. Toronto, 1993, Queen's U., 1996, U. Regina, 1999, U. Calgary, 2000; DU (hon.), U. Ottawa, 1983; D of Social Scis. (hon.), Laval U., 1988; LittD (hon.), U. Waterloo, 1998. Head dept. polit. studies Queen's U., Kingston, Ont., Canada, 1963-67, Hardy prof. polit. sci., 1963-80, Sir Edward Peacock prof. polit. sci., 1983-93, prof. emeritus. Former chmn. Can. Radio-TV and Telecomms. Commn.; moderator symposia on finding common grounds for polit. issues confronting Yugoslavia, UN, Vienna, 1995. Author: The Canadian General Election of 1957, 1962, Papers on the 1962 Election, 1964, Ethnic Relations in Canadian Voluntary Associations, 1972, Working Papers on Canadian Politics, 1975; editor: Internat. Polit. Sci. Rev., 1979-95, (with Jean Laponce) Debating the Constitution/Débat sur la constitution, 1994. Decorated companion Order of Can.; recipient Killam award Can Coun., 1968-73. Fellow Royal Soc. Can. (pres. 1992-95); mem. Univ. Club (Toronto). Home (Summer): Colimaison Tichborne ON Canada K0H 2V0 Office: Queen's U Kingston ON Canada K7L 3N6 Home (Winter): 70A Johnson St Kingston ON Canada K7L1X7 Business E-Mail: meiselj@post.queensu.ca.

**MEISEL, MARTIN,** English and comparative literature educator; b. NYC, Mar. 22, 1931; s. Joseph and Sally (Rössler) Mörsel; m. Martha Sarah Winkley, Dec. 22, 1957; children: Maude Frances, Andrew Avram, Joseph Stoddard AB, Queens Coll., 1952; MA, Princeton U., 1957, PhD, 1960; postgrad., U. Rome, 1959. Instr. English Rutgers U., New Brunswick, N.J., 1957-58; instr., asst. prof., assoc. prof. Dartmouth Coll., Hanover, N.H., 1959-65; prof. English U. Wis., Madison, 1965-68; prof. English and comparative lit. Columbia U., N.Y.C., 1968—, Brander Matthews prof. dramatic lit., 1987—, chmn. dept., 1980-83, 99-01, acting v.p. arts and scis., 1986-87, v.p. arts and scis., 1989-93, prof. emeritus, 2004—. Trustee Columbia U. Press, 1990-94. Author: Shaw and the 19th Century Theater, 1963, Realizations: Narrative, Pictorial, and Theatrical Arts in 19th Century England (George Freedley Meml. award Theater Libr. Assn. 1984, Barnard Hewitt award Am. Theatre Assn. 1984), 1983; mem. editl. bd. Jour. Victorian Studies, PMLA, Jour. Contemporary Lit., Bull. Rsch. in the Humanities, 19th Century Contexts. Served with U.S. Army, 1954-56 Fellow Guggenheim Found., 1963-64, 1987-88, Am. Council of Learned Socs., 1970-71, Inst. for Advanced Studies in the Humanities, Edinburgh, 1977, Huntington Library and Art Gallery, 1978, 80, 83, Nat. Humanities Ctr., 1983-84, Wilson Ctr., Smithsonian Instn., 1987-88. Mem. MLA, Am. Soc. Theatre Rsch., North Am. Victorian Studies Assn., Assn. of Historians of 19 Century Art, Century Assn., Internat. Shaw Soc. Home: 18 Bacon Hill Rd Pleasantville NY 10570-3502 Business E-Mail: mm28@columbia.edu.

**MEISEL, MICHAEL J.,** lawyer; s. William J. and Patricia A. Meisel; m. Brenda J. Meisel; children: Erin, Nicholas. BA summa cum laude, Siena Coll., 1982; JD, Union U., 1985; MS in Nat. Resource Strategy, Nat. Def. U., 2002. Bar: N.Y. 1985. Judge adv. U.S. Army, Fort Riley, Kans., 1986—89; chief civilian pers. law team U.S Army Legal Svcs., Va.-Agency, Va., 1990—93, chief civilian pers. litig., litig. divsn., 1993—2001, dep. chief litig. divsn., 2002—03, dir. civil law and litig., 2003—. Lectr. Judge Adv. Gen.'s Sch. U. Va., Charlottesville, Va., 1993—2001. Capt. U.S. Army, 1985—90. Decorated Army Commendation medal U.S. Army, Army Achievement medal; recipient Commander's award for Civilian Svc., 1990, Superior Civilian Svc. award, 2001. Mem.: Am. Legion, KC. Avocations: travel, reading. Office: US Army Legal Svcs Agy 901 North Stuart St Ste 716 Arlington VA 22203-1837 Office Phone: 703-696-8112.

---

**MEISELS, GERHARD GEORGE,** academic administrator, chemist, educator; b. Vienna, May 11, 1931; came to U.S., 1951, naturalized, 1961; s. Leo and Adele Josefa Maria (Seehofer) M.; m. Sylvia Claire Knopsnider, June 28, 1958; 1 dau.. Laura Germaine. Student, U. Vienna, 1949-51, 52-53; MS, U. Notre Dame, Ind., 1952, PhD, 1956. Postdoctoral rsch. assoc. U. Notre Dame, 1955-56; chemist Gulf Oil Corp., Pitts., 1956-59; part-time instr. Carnegie Inst. Tech., Pitts., 1956-58; chemist nuclear divsn. Union Carbide Corp., Tuxedo, NY, 1959-63, asst. group leader, 1964-65; assoc. prof. U. Houston, 1965-70, prof., 1970-75, dept. chmn., 1973-75; prof., chmn. dept. chemistry U. Nebr., Lincoln, 1975-81, dean Coll. Arts and Scis., 1981-88; provost, COO U. South Fla., Tampa, 1988-94; dir. Coalition Sci. Literacy, 1994—, Suncoast Area Ctr. for Ednl. Enhancement (SACEE), 1996-99. Cons. Union Carbide Corp., Gearhart-Owen Industries. Editor (spl. issue) Jour. Radiation Physics and Chemistry, 1980; contbr. writings in field to profl. publs. Sec., pres. Ramsey (N.J.) Jr. C. of C., 1959-64; active rsch. bd. All Children's Hosp.; chmn. Fla. Coalition for Improving Math. and Sci. Edn., 1998—, interim exec. dir. Fulbright fellow, Smith-Mundt fellow, 1951-52; sr. fellow Sci. Rsch. Coun., Eng., 1976. Mem. Am. Chem. Soc. (com. chmn.), Am. Soc. for Mass Spectrometry (charter, com. chmn., v.p. 1984-86, pres. 1986-88, bd. dirs. 1988-90), Fla. Acad. Scis., AAAS, Am. Phys. Soc., Coun. Sci. Soc. Pres. (exec. bd. 1989-92, chmn. elect 1990, chmn. 1991, chmn. com. on sci. priorities), Nat. Alliance State Sci. and Math. Coalitions (bd. dirs. 1999—), Coun. for Chem. Rsch. (bd. dirs. 1982-85), Conformation Judges Assn. Fla. (pres. 1996—), Fla. Higher Edn. Consortium Math. and Sci. (ctrl. steering com. 1995—, chmn. 1998-2000), Houston Kennel Club (bd. dirs. 1968-70), Cornhusker Kennel Club (pres., bd. dirs., del. to Am. Kennel Club 1976-88), St. Petersburg Dog Fanciers Club. (sec. 1996-98, 2000-04, del. to Am. Kennel Club 1998—), Lakeland-Winter Haven K.C. (pres. 2006—), Sigma Xi. Home: PO Box 1347 Thonotosassa FL 33592-1347 Office: U South Fla 4202 E Fowler Ave/CHE 205 Tampa FL 33620 Office Phone: 813-974-7183. Business E-Mail: meisels@csl.usf.edu.

**MEISELS, JUDITH A.,** pianist, music educator; b. Budapest, Hungary, July 23, 1938; came to U.S., 1957; d. Stephan and Margaret Benjamin; m. Irving M. Meisels, May 30, 1964; children: Jason D. Meisels, Adrienne C. Meisels. Diploma in piano performance, Buda Acad. Music and Budapest Conservatory of Music, Budapest, Hungary, 1950-54; student, Franz Liszt Acad. Music, Budapest, 1954-56; Matura diploma in Humanities and Natural Scis., Veres Palne Women's Gymnazium & Coll., Budapest, 1956; student, Bklyn. Coll., N.Y.C., 1958-61; Piano pedagogy cert., New Sch. Music Studies, Princeton, NJ, 1977; postgrad., Westminster Choir Coll., Princeton, 1984—90. Cert. profl. tchr. music, N.J. Music Tchrs. Assn., nat. cert. profl. tchr. music Music Tchrs. Nat. Assn. Mem. exec. bd. rsch., planning and selecting internat. artists series, Spectrum Com., Monmouth County Arts Coun., 1980-85; cultural com., exec. bd. internat. concert and lecture series Monmouth County "Y", 1971-93; spkr., lectr. in field; panelist, conductor master classes Piano Tchrs.' Groups, NJ and N.Y.C., 1976-2006; adjudicator high level prestigious piano auditions and competitions. Piano performances: classical solo and ensemble Radio Budapest, Hungary, Ministerium of Fgn. Affairs, 1948-49, Franz Liszt Acad., Budapest, 1948-56, solo performances Hungary, Austria, U.S.A., 1954-56, 73-80. Grantee Franz Liszt Acad., 1956-57. Mem. Music Tchrs. Nat. Assn., N.J. Music Tchrs. Assn., Leschetizky Assn. N.Y., Piano Tchrs. Cong. N.Y., Nat. Guild Piano Tchrs., Shore Music Educators Assn.(exec. bd., publicity chair 1976-80, recording sec. 1987-93), Cecilian Music Club of Freehold, N.J. Avocations: power walking, swimming, reading, music, arts. Office Phone: 732-531-5042. Personal E-mail: jimeisels@aol.com.

**MEISENHEIMER, SHARON LEE,** nurse; b. Princeton, Ill., Apr. 15, 1937; d. Lester Harry and Dorothy Marie Carlson; m. Lester Lee Meisenheimer, June 22, 1958; children: Timothy, Connie, Joel, LuAnn. Nursing diploma, Ft. Wayne Luth. Sch. of Nursing, 1957; studied at, Ft. Wayne Bible Coll., 1957—58, Summer Inst. of Linguistics, 1959. Fl. nurse/newborn nursery Paradise Valley Hosp., Nat. City, Calif., 1958—59; missionary nurse/ch. planting Missionary Ch. World/Peru, in Ecuador, S.A., 1959—96; night supr./staff nurse Colonial Hall Ctr. Nursing Home, Princeton, Ill., 1997—2004. Contbr. articles. Recipient five awards for svc. to children, young people and the cmty., Missionary Ch. of Ecuador. Missionary Ch. Of Ecuador. Avocations: gardening, music, reading, sewing, cooking. Home: 14702 2400 N Ave Walnut IL 61376 Office Phone: 815-379-9034.

**MEISINGER, LOUIS M.,** lawyer; b. NYC, Dec. 12, 1942; BA, UCLA, 1964, JD, 1967. Bar: Calif. 1968. Atty. Hill Wynne Troop & Meisinger, LA; exec. v.p., gen. coun. Walt Disney Co., Burbank, Calif., 1997—2003; sr. advisor Sheppard, Mullin, Richter & Hampton, LLP, Los Angeles, Calif., 2003—. Editor: UCLA Law Rev., 1965-67. Recipient Entertainment Lawyer of the Yr., Beverly Hills Bar Assoc./ Calif., 1999. Mem. State Bar Calif., L.A. County Bar Assn., Century City Bar Assn., Order of Coif, Phi Beta Kappa, Sigma Delta Pi, Phi Delta Phi. Office: Sheppard Mullin Richter & Hampton 333 S Hope St Los Angeles CA 90071

**MEISINGER, SUSAN,** human resources specialist; BA, Mary Washington Coll.; JD, George Washington U. Cert. sr. profl. Human Resources Certification Inst. Spl. legal counsel Associated Builders and Contractors, Washington; dep. under sec. employment standards adminstrn. U.S. Dept. Labor, Washington; v.p. govt. and pub. affairs Soc. Human Resource Mgmt., Alexandria, Va., 1987—97, sr. v.p., 1997—99, exec. v.p., COO, 1999—2002, pres., CEO, 2002—. Mem.: DC Bar Assn. Office: Soc Human Resource Mgmt 1800 Duke St Alexandria VA 22314

**MEISLIN, HARVEY WARREN,** emergency healthcare physician, professional society administrator; b. Rochester, NY, June 19, 1946; s. Milton M. and Celia (Weiner) M.; m. Loretta Marie Bielski, Apr. 30, 1977; children: Justin, Jonathan, Megan. BS in Chemistry, Purdue U., 1968; MD, Ind. U., 1972. Diplomate Am. Bd. Emergency Medicine (chmn.), Am. Bd. Med. Spltys.(del. 1990, fin. com. 1992, exec. com. 1994); cert. cardiac life support, ACLS instr., advanced trauma life support instr. Intern U. Chgo. Hosps. and Clinics, 1973-75, resident, 1975-77, dir. div. emergency medicine, 1975-77; asst. prof. internal and emergency medicine UCLA Emergency Med. Ctr., 1977-80, resident dir. emergency medicine, 1977-80, assoc. dir., 1977-80; assoc. prof. dept. surgery emergency medicine Coll. Medicine, U. Ariz., Tucson, 1980-83, assoc. prof., 1983-85; assoc. head, dept. surgery U. Ariz., Tucson, 1995—; chief. Coll. Medicine, U. Ariz., Tucson, 1985—; chief emergency medicine U. Ariz., Tucson, 1980—; chief sect. emergency medicine dept. surgery Ariz. Health Scis. Ctr., Tucson, 1980—, dir. emergency svcs. Univ. Med. Ctr., 1980—, dir. Ariz. Emergency Med. Rsch. Ctr., 1990—; med. dir. MEDTRAN-Aeromed Ambulance Corp., 1985-88. Mem. emergency med. svc. com. Mid-South Health Planning Orgn., Chgo., 1974; coord. Mid-South Disaster Plan, Chgo., 1974; mem. com. revision of Disaster Plan Billings Hosp., 1974-76; mem. faculty Am. Hosp. Assn. Inst. Disaster Preparedness, 1975; vis. profl. dept. emergency medicine Denver Gen. Hosp., 1977; bd. trustees Emergency Med. Found., 1978-81; mem. med. adv. com. L.A. City Fire Dept., 1979-80; chmn.-elect Tuscon Met. EMS Coun., 1983-84, chmn. 1984-85; chmn. Tuscon Pre-Hosp. Care Coun., 1981; mem. trauma steering com. So. Ariz. Regional Trauma Ctr., 1986-88; mem. ETHICON emergency physicians adv. panel Johnson & Johnson Co., 1987-92; presenter and lectr. in field. Editor: Purdue Rivet, 1971-72, abstract sect. Annals Emergency Medicine, 1982-90, EMS sect., 1989-90; guest editor: Topics in Emergency Medicine, 1979; sci. editor: Drug Therapy, 1984—; mem. editorial bd.: Annals Emergency Medicine, 1977-90, Emergency Dept. News, 1979-87, Emergency Dept. and Ambulatory Care News, 1987-90, Digest of Emergency Medicine Care, 1981-87; contbr. articles and revs. to med. jours. Mem. select med. adv. com. City of Tucson, 1981, med. dir. emergency med. svcs., 1982-83, 84-85; bd. dirs. so. Ariz. divsn. Am. Heart Assn., 1985-90; mem. emergency cardiac care com. so. divsn. Ariz. Heart Assn., 1986-88; mem. med. dirs. commn., dept. health svcs. State of Ariz., 1992—, also mem. Mex. border commn., 1991—; mem. med. direction commn. State of Ariz. (appointed by gov.), 1993—. Recipient Pres. gavel and plaque Am. Bd. Emergency Medicine. Fellow Am. Coll. Emergency Physicians (State of Ill. chpt.); mem. sci. adv. com. 1975, mem. sci. edn. com.

1975-76, mem. grad./undergrad. edn. com. 1976-79, mem. ethics com. 1976-77, mem. surgery/trauma task force bd. cert. exam. 1976-77, bd. dirs. 1976-77, chmn. edn. com. 1976-77; State of Calif. chpt.: mem. hosp. and contract com. 1978-79, mem. EMS and legis. com. 1978-79, mem. spl. task force on emergency dept. distbn. 1979-80, mem. membership com. 1979-80, mem. legis. com. 1979-80, mem. sci. assembly planning com. 1980-81, bd. dirs. 1979-81, mem. rsch. com. 1981; State of Ariz. chpt.: bd. dirs. 1982-92, 92—, chmn. pub. rels. com. 1982-83, v.p. and sec. 1983-84, counselor 1984-87, mem. credentials com. 1986-91, chmn. 1987-90, mem. test com. 1986-87, mem. ad hoc com. for combined tng. 1987-88, chmn. task force on emergency medicine 1987-89, mem. exec. com. 1988—, mem. fin. com. 1988—, sec./treas. 1989-90, mem. EMS com. 1990—, pres.-elect 1990-91, pres. 1991-92, chair stds. com., mem. faculty Nat. Sci. Assembly 1974-76, Cert. Appreciation award 1990); mem. APHA, Am. Coll. Physician Execs., Am. Trauma Soc., Am. Bd. Med. Specialties (mem. fin. com. 1992, mem. exec. com. 1995—, pres., 2004), Ariz. Med. Assn., Pima County Med. Soc. (bd. dirs. 1991—), Phi Rho Sigma. Avocations: racquetball, golf, skiing, automobiles. Office: U Ariz Med Ctr Sect Emergency Med 1501 N Campbell Ave Tucson AZ 85724-0001*

**MEISNER, MARY JO,** foundation administrator, former newspaper editor; b. Chgo., Dec. 24, 1951; d. Robert Joseph and Mary Elizabeth (Casey) M.; 1 child, Thomas Joseph Gradel. BS in Journalism, U. Ill., 1974, MS in Journalism, 1976. Copy editor Wilmington (Del.) News Jour., 1975-76, labor and bus. reporter, 1976-78; labor and gen. assignment reporter Phila. Daily News, 1979, city editor, 1979-83, met. editor, 1983-85; PM city editor San Jose (Calif.) Mercury News, 1985-86, met. editor, 1986-87; city editor The Washington Post, 1987-90; mng. editor The Ft. Worth Star-Telegram, 1991-93; editor and v.p. The Milw. Jour., 1993-95; editor, sr. v p The Milw. Jour. Sentinel, 1995-97; editor, vice chmn. Cmty. Newspaper Co., Needham, Mass., 1997—2001; v.p., comm., external affairs Boston Found., 2001—. Mem. AP Mng. Editors (bd. dirs. 1992-95), Am. Soc. Newspaper Editors, Internat. Press Inst. (bd. dirs. 1994-2000, Pulitzer prize juror 1994, 96). Mass. Newspaper Pubs. Assn. (bd. dirs.); bd. dir., WorldBoston. Office: Boston Foundation 10th Fl 75 Arlington St Boston MA 02116 Business E-Mail: mjm@tbf.org.

**MEISSNER, ANITA COHOON,** retired elementary school educator; b. Lackawanna, N.Y., Mar. 31, 1940; d. Wilbur Thomas and Marie Charlotte (Grube) Cohoon; m. Howard Bernard Meissner, July 22, 1961; children: Jeff, Rick, Amy, Brian. BS in Edn., SUNY, Brockport, 1961; MS in Edn., SUNY, Buffalo, 1965. Tchr. Hamburg (N.Y.) Cen. Schs., 1961—2005, instrml. coach, 1987—2005, staff devel. instr., 1991-92, coord. instrn., 2002—05. Liaison Southtowns Tchrs. Ctr., Hamburg, 1989—2005; facilitator Participative Decision Making Group, Hamburg, 1989-91; clin. field supr. Ctr. Ednl. Studies, Fredonia, 1990—2005. Grace Luth. Ch., Hamburg; mem. Antique Study Group, Hamburg. Democrat. Avocation: travel. Home: 69 Therin Dr Hamburg NY 14075-3838

**MEISSNER, EDWIN BENJAMIN, JR.,** retired real estate broker; b. St. Louis, Dec. 27, 1918; s. Edwin B. and Edna (Rice) Meissner; m. Nina Renard, Dec. 17, 1946; children: Edwin Benjamin III, Wallace, Robert; 1 child, Donald. BS, U. Pa., 1940. Joined St. Louis Car Co., 1934, asst. to pres., v.p., exec. v.p. 1950-56, pres., gen. mgr., 1956-61; pres. St. Louis Car div. Gen. Steel Industries, Inc., 1961-67; sr. v.p. Gen. Steel Industries, Inc., 1968-74; v.p. Bakewell Corp., 1974-85; real estate broker, v.p. Hilliker Corp., St. Louis, 1985-96. Mem. pres.' coun. St. Louis U.; bd. dirs. Washington U. Med. Ctr. Redevel. Corp., Barnard Free Skin and Cancer Hosp.; past bd. dirs. James S. McDonnell USO; overseer St. Louis Symphony Soc.; hon. dir. Humane Soc. Mo.; v.p. Gateway Ctr. Met. St. Louis; chmn. Ladue (Mo.) Police and Fire Commn.; mem. Jefferson Nat. Expansion Meml. Commn.; mil. affairs com. Regional Commerce; dir. Ctrl. Inst. for Deaf. Mem. Am. Ordnance Assn. (life), Internat. Assn. Chiefs of Police (assoc.), Mo. Assn. Chiefs of Police, Mo. Athletics Club, Westwood Country Club, Bridlespur Hunt Club, St. Louis Club, Beta Gamma Sigma. Office: Barton Bldg Ste 302 200 S Bemiston Saint Louis MO 63105-1915 Office Phone: 314-863-2440.

**MEISSNER, KATHERINE GONG,** municipal official; b. Stockton, Calif., 1955; BA, U. Phoenix, Stockton, Calif., 1999. Mem. comty. planning dept. staff City of Stockton, Calif., 1982-85, exec. asst. city clk., 1985-96, city clk., 1996—. Office: City Stockton Office City Clk 425 N El Dorado St Stockton CA 95202-1997 Office Phone: 209-937-8458. Business E-Mail: city.clerk@ci.stockton.ca.us.

**MEISSNER, WALT,** dean; BA, Texas A & M; MFA in theatre mgmt. & directing, Boston U. Assoc. dean-adminstr. affairs Boston U. Coll. Fine Arts, 1993—2001, acting dean, 2001—02, dean ad interim, 2002—. Office: Boston U Coll Fine Arts 855 Commonwealth Ave Room 230 Boston MA 02215 Office Fax: 617-353-3350. E-mail: cfadean@bu.edu.

**MEISTER, BERNARD JOHN,** retired chemical engineer; b. Maynard, Mass., Feb. 27, 1941; s. Benjamin C. and Gertrude M. Meister; m. Janet M. White, Dec. 31, 1971; children: Mark, Martin, Kay Ellen. BSChemE, Worcester Poly. Inst., 1962; PhD in Chem. Engring., Cornell U., 1966. From engring. rschr. to rsch. scientist Dow Chem. Co., Midland, Mich., 1966—92, rsch. scientist, 1992—2005, ret., 2005. Contbr. articles to profl. jours. Mem.: AIChE, Soc. Rheology, Soc. Plastic Engrs., Am. Chem. Soc., Sigma Xi. Methodist. Home: 2925 Chippewa Ln Midland MI 48640-4181 E-mail: bjjml@aol.com. *Free the mind of things you can't change, and let it focus on things you can accomplish.*

**MEISTER, MARK JAY,** museum director, professional society administrator; b. Balt., June 26, 1953; s. Michael Aaron and Yetta (Haransky) M.; m. Carla Rutger, Aug. 7, 1977; children: Rachel, Kaitlin. AB, Washington U., St. Louis, 1974; MA, U. Minn., 1976; cert. mus. mgmt., U. Calif., Berkeley, 1983. Asst. lectr. St. Louis Art Mus., 1974; asst. coord. young people's program Mpls. Inst. Arts, 1975—76, coord. mobile program, 1976, coord. tchrs. resource svcs., 1976—77; dir. Mus. Art and History, Port Huron, Mich., 1978—79, Midwest Mus. Am. Art, Elkhart, Ind., 1979—81; exec. dir. Children's Mus., St. Paul, 1981—86; dir. Mus. Art, Sci. and Industry, Bridgeport, Conn., 1986—89; exec. dir. Archaeol. Inst. of Am., Boston, 1989—99; exec. dir. Am. Inst. Archeological d'Amerique, Boston and Toronto, 1994—99; exec. dir. Dayton Soc. Natural History, 2000—06, pres., 2006—, CEO, 2006—. Adj. lectr. museology Kenyon Coll., Gambier, Ohio, 1977; adj. lectr. art history Ind. U., South Bend, 1980—81; regional reviewer Inst. Mus. Svcs., Washington, 1985—86, Washington, 1989; treas., vice chmn. Minn. Assn. Mus., St. Paul, 1983—86; ex-officio trustee U.S. com. Internat. Coun. on Monuments and Sites, 1995—99. Bd. dirs. Seaway Arts Coun., St. Clair County, Mich., 1978-79; bd. dirs. Dayton Sister Cities Com., 2000-05, chair, 2003-05; bd. dirs. Dayton Peace Accords Project, 2000-05, vice chair 2003; bd. dirs. Glen Helen Ecology Inst., 2003—, Dayton Coun. on World Affairs, 2005—, Greater Dayton Pub. TV, 2005—; mem. Mayor's Arts Adv. Com., Elkhart, 1981; mem. exec. com., Conf. Adminstry. Officers, Am. Coun. Learned Socs., 1994-97; pres. Asian Arts Ctr., Dayton, 2002-05. NEH museology fellow, Mpls. Inst. Arts, 1976-77, Kress fellow U. Minn. 1977-78, Bush leadership summer fellow, Bush Found., St. Paul, 1983; named One of Outstanding Young Men Am., 1981. Mem.: Assn. Children's Mus., Ohio Mus. Assn., Assn. Sci. and Tech. Ctrs., Assn. Zoos and Aquariums, Assn. Sci. Mus. Dirs., Archeol. Inst. Am. Assn. Mus. Office: Dayton Soc Natural History 2600 Deweese Pkwy Dayton OH 45414-5499 Business E-Mail: mmeister@boonshoftmuseum.org.

**MEISTER, PAUL M.,** medical products executive; BA, Univ. Mich., 1974; MBA, Northwestern Univ., 1976. Mng. dir. Henley, 1986—92; sr. v.p. Abex, Inc., 1992—95; v.p., CFO Fisher Sci. Internat., Hampton, NH, 1995—98, exec. v.p., CFO, 1998—2001, vice chmn., 1998—. Bd. dir. M & F Worldwide Corp., Minerals Tech., Inc., Nat. Waterworks, Inc., LKQ Corp. Office: Fisher Sci Internat Liberty Ln Hampton NH 03842*

**MEITZLER, ALLEN HENRY,** electrical engineering educator, automotive scientist; b. Allentown, Pa., Dec. 16, 1928; s. Herbert Henry and Estella Irene (Wagner) M.; m. Joan Catherine Egan, June 13, 1953; children: Thomas Joseph, Peter Michael, David Christopher. BS, Muhlenberg Coll., Allentown, Pa., 1951; MS, Lehigh U., 1953, PhD, 1955. Mem. tech. staff Bell Labs., Whippany and Murray Hill, NJ, 1955-72; prin. research scientist, research staff Ford Motor Co., Dearborn, Mich., 1972-96, elec. engring. educator, 1996—. Adj. prof. U. Mich.-Dearborn. Patentee ultrasonic and ferroelectric devices, automotive electronic devices and systems. Prof. Wackernagel scholar, 1947-51; Hood grad. fellow, 1954-55 Fellow IEEE, Acoustical Soc. Am.; mem. Am. Phys. Soc. Republican. Home: 3055 Foxcroft St Ann Arbor MI 48104-2827 E-mail: allen@meitzler.org.

**MEIXNER, CLIFF DALE,** social studies educator, literature and language professor; b. Abilene, Tex., May 9, 1969; s. Clifford Dale and Cheryl Anne Meixner, Joan Alice Meixner (Stepmother); m. Melanie Mesteller Meixner, Dec. 31, 1994; 1 child, Jacob Harrison. BA in Govt. and English, Angelo State U., San Angelo, Tex., 1995. Cert. gifted and talented edn. Region XI Tex., 1997, advanced placement edn. Coll. Bd. Tex., 2001. Tchr. English and social studies Fossil Ridge H.S., Keller, Tex., 1995—. Veterans advisor Angelo State U., San Angelo, Tex., 1991—94. Mem. Sertoma, Watauga, Tex., 2005—06. With USMC, 1988—96. Decorated Kuwait Liberation medal USMC, Nat. Def. medal, Marine Unit citation - 2nd award, Navy Unit citation; named Tchr. of Yr., Fossil Ridge H.S., 2005—06. Mem.: Am. Legion (assoc.). Roman Catholic. Avocations: coaching, hunting, fishing, travel, antiques. Office: Fossil Ridge HS 4101 Thompson Rd Keller TX 76248 Office Phone: 817-744-1700. E-mail: cmeixner@kellerisd.net.

**MEJIA, BARBARA OVIEDO,** retired chemistry professor; b. San Francisco, Apr. 14, 1946; d. Louis Jerome and Alice May (Beall) O. AA, Sierra Coll., 1967; BS, U. Calif., Davis 1969, PhD, 1973. Cert. community coll. tchr., Calif. Lectr. U. Calif., Davis, summer 1977, Calif. State U., Chico, 1973-76, asst. prof., 1976-80, assoc. prof., 1980-85, prof., 1985—2001, emeritus, 2001—. Contbr. articles to profl. jours. Judge Calif. Cen. Valley Sci.-Engring. Fair, Chico, 1977, 89, 81, 81, 88, bd. dirs., 1978-79; judge Butte County Sci. Fair, Chico, 1985-90. Mem. AAAS, Am. Chem. Soc., Congress of Faculty Assns., Cal Aggie Alumni Assn., Assn. Calif. State Univ. Profs. Sigma Xi. Home: 6 Laguna Ct Chico CA 95928-7431 Office: Calif State U Dept Chemistry Chico CA 95929-0001 Business E-Mail: Bmejia@csuchico.edu.

**MEJIA, JOSE A.,** telecommunications industry executive; b. Venezuela; married; 2 children. BS in Indsl. and Ops. Engring., U. Mich.; MBA in Fin. and Ops. Rsch., Duke U. With IBM, Ford Motor Co.; v.p. supplier mgmt. Bay Networks, Inc., Calif., 1996—98; v.p. external mfg. strategy Nortel Networks (formerly Bay Networks), 1999; joined Lucent Techs., Murray Hill, NJ, 1999, chief procurement officer, 1999—2000, v.p. and chief supply chain officer, 2000—01, pres. supply chain networks, 2001—. Named Engr. of Yr., Hispanic Engr. Nat. Achievement Awards Corp., 2003; named one of Top 25 Execs. That Made A Difference, Electronic Buyer News, 1997, 50 Most Important Hispanics in Tech. & Bus., Hispanic Engr. & Info. Tech. mag., 2005. Office: Lucent Techs 600 Mountain Ave New Providence NJ 07974*

**MEKAS, JONAS,** filmmaker, poet; b. Semeniskiai, Lithuania, 1922; Am.; 1949; Studied philosophy & romance languages, U. Mainz, Germany. Author, Film Culture column Village Voice, 1958—; co-founder Filmmakers' Cooperative, 1962; founder Filmmakers' Cinémathèque (later Anthology Film Archives), 1964, Essential Cinema Collection, 1970. Prodr.: (films) Guns of the Trees, 1961, The Brig, 1963, Walden, 1969, Reminiscences of a Voyage to Lithuania, 1972, Lost Lost Lost, 1975, Zefiro Torna, 1992; Exhibited in group shows at Whitney Biennial, Whitney Mus. Am. Art, 2004; author: (book of poetry) There is No Ithaca, 1996; Exhibited in group shows at Whitney Biennial award, Whitney Mus. Am. Art, 2004. Mailing: c/o Whitney Museum American Art 945 Madison Ave New York NY 10021

**MEKLER, ARLEN B.,** lawyer, chemist; b. NYC, May 4, 1943; s. Lev A. and Ethel (Fox) M.; children from previous marriage: Jeffrey Arlen, Rebecca Ann, Ann-Marie Laura, Victoria Arlene, Lamar Adam, Lars Arlen; m. Molly L. Malone, Feb. 3, 1995. BS in Chemistry, Reed Coll.-San Jose State U., 1953; MS in Organic Chemistry, Iowa State U., 1955; PhD, Ohio State U., 1958-JD, Temple U., 1972. Bar: Del. 1972, Pa. 1972, U.S. Supreme Ct. 1976. Sr. rsch. chemist E.I. du Pont de Nemours & Co., Wilmington, Del., 1958-69; prin. Mekler and Maurer, Wilmington, 1972—. Chief appellate div. Office Pub. Defender, State of Del., 1973-77; pres. Del. Law Ctr., Wilmington, 1973—; instr. constl. law Wilmington Coll., 1976-80; dir. Bar Rev. Del., 1972—; mem. 3d Circuit Ct. Appeal Jud. Nominating Commn., 1977-81, 3d Circuit Ct. Appeals Jud. Conf. Contbr. monographs to legal pubs. Pres. Mental Health Aux. for Gov. Bacon Health Ctr., 1964-66; mem. Citizens Conf. for Modernization of State Legislatures, 1964-68; state chmn., Reform Commn. for Modernization Polit. Party Rules, 1965-68; pres. Del. Citizens for Fair Housing, 1965-69; state commnr. Nat. Conf. on Uniform State Laws, 1972—; pres. Democratic Forum Del., 1966-70; mem. Del. Dem. Platform Com., 1966, 68, 72, 76; research dir. Del. Citizens for Humphrey-Muskie, 1968, Citizens for Biden, 1972, 78, 84, Citizens for McDowell, 1986—, Biden for Pres., 1986, 2005; del. Dem. Nat. Conv., 1980; mem. social action com. Unitarian Ch., Wilmington, 1962-68. Recipient Keyman award, 1964, 65; State Govtl. Affairs award, 1964, 65 Mem. ABA, Del. Bar Assn. (com. on rules of criminal procedure 1973-74, supreme ct. com. on revision of criminal law 1973—, supreme ct. com. on rules of evidence 1976—, com. on revised rules of evidence 1976—, com. on revised rules of Del. Supreme Ct. 1974—, family law com. 1979—, continuing legal edn. com. 1981—), Pa. Bar Assn., Am. Chem. Soc., N.Y. Acad. Socs. (Assn. Chem. Soc. (London), AAAS, Catalyst Club Phila., Wilmington Organic Chemists Club, ACLU (bd. dirs.), Sigma Xi Phi Alpha Delta Home. Brandywine Club, 114 W Matson Run Pky Wilmington DE 19802-1912 Office: PO Box 2285 Wilmington DE 19899-2285 Office Phone: 302-498-5297. Business E-Mail: drlaw@comcast.com.

**MELAMED, ARTHUR DOUGLAS,** lawyer; b. Mpls., Dec. 3, 1945; s. Arthur Charles and Helen Beatrix (Rosenberg) M.; m. Carol Drescher Weisman, May 26, 1983; children: Kathryn Henrie, Elizabeth Allyn. BA, Yale U., 1967; JD, Harvard U., 1970. Bar: D.C. 1970, U.S. Ct. Internat. Trade 1985, U.S. Ct. Appeals (9th cir.) 1971, U.S. Ct. Appeals (2d cir.) 1975, U.S. Ct. Appeals (D.C. cir.) 1978, U.S. Ct. Appeals (8th cir.) 1981, U.S. Ct. Appeals (fed. cir.) 1985, U.S. Ct. Appeals (4th cir.) 1989, U.S. Ct. Appeals (10th cir.) 1993, U.S. Supreme Ct. 1981. Law clk. U.S. Ct. Appeals for 9th Circuit, 1970-71; assoc. Wilmer, Cutler, Pickering, Hale & Dorr, Washington, 1971-77, ptnr., 1978, 96, 2001—, co-chmn. Antitrust & Competition dept.; prin. dep. asst. gen. U.S. Dept. Justice, 1996-2000, acting asst. atty. gen. antitrust divsn., 2000-2001. Vis. prof. Georgetown U. Law Ctr., 1992-93, adj. prof., 1993-94. Editor, Harvard Law Rev.; contbr. articles to profl. jours. Mem. coun. Yale U., 2006—; trustee Nat. Child Rsch. Ctr., 1990-93, Sidwell Friends Sch., 2000—. Mem. ABA, Am. Law Inst., Yale Club (N.Y.C.), Kenwood Country Club. Mailing: Wilmer Cutler Pickering Hale & Dorr 2445 M St NW Washington DC 20037 Office: Wilmer Cutler Pickering Hale & Dorr 1875 Pennsylvania Ave NW Washington DC 20006 Office Phone: 202-663-6090. Office Fax: 202-663-6363. Business E-Mail: doug.melamed@wilmerhale.com.

**MELANCON, CHARLES,** congressman; b. Napoleonville, La., Oct. 3, 1947; s. Joe and Brownie Melancon; m. Alida (Peachy) Clark; children: Charles, Claire. BS, Univ. Southwestern La. Owner Melancon Ins. Agy.; mem. La. Ho. Rep., 1987—93; pres. Am. Sugar Cane League, 1993—2004; mem. US Congress from 3rd La. dist., 2005—. Mem. La. State Dem. Ctrl. Com., 1987—93. Chmn. LSU Agr. Devel. Council; vice chmn. La. Econ. Council. Recipient Outstanding Legislator award, La. Municipal Assn. Disting. Svc. award, La. Restaurant Assn., 1990. Mem.: Ducks Unlimited, UL Lafayette Alumni Assn. Democrat. Roman Catholic. Office: US Ho Reps 404 Cannon Ho Office Bldg Washington DC 20515-1803 Office Phone: 202-225-4031. Office Fax: 202-225-3944.

**MELANDER, ROCHELLE,** writer, life coach; b. Caracas, Venezuela; d. Richard Ira and Diane Elizabeth Melander; m. Harold Webb Eppley; children: Samuel Eppley, Eliana Eppley. BA, Concordia Coll., 1985; MDiv, Luth. Theol. Sem., Phila., 1989, MST, 1990. Pastor Lilly-Portage Lutheran Parish, Lilly, Pa., 1990—94; instr. St. Francis Coll., Laetto, Pa., 1991—93; interim pastor Greater Milw. Synod, Milw., 1995—99; freelance writer, coach, spkr. Milw., 1995—; chaplain Children's Hosp. Wis., Milw. 1998—99. Author: Timeouts With God, 2001, The Spiritual Leader's Guide to Self-Care, 2002, Our Lives Are Not Our Own: Saying Yes to God, 2003, Welcome Forward, 2005; editor: The Word in Season, 1999—; author: Fierce Presence, 2006; contbr. articles to profl. jours. Mem.: SCBWI, Christian Coaches Network, Internat. Coach Fedn. Avocations: reading, walking, baking, crocheting. Home: 3034 N Cramer St Milwaukee WI 53213

**MELANI, KENNETH R.,** insurance company executive; MD, Bowman Gray Sch. of Med., NC, 1979. Pres., CEO West Penn Cares Inc.; pres. Keystone Health Plan West; with Highmark Inc., Pittsburgh, 1989—, exec. v.p. strategic bus. devel. and health services, pres., CEO, 2003—. Mem.: Am. Coll. of Physician Executives, Am. Soc. of Internal Med., Penn. Soc. of Internal Med., Am. Med. Assn., Penn. Med. Soc., Allegheny County Med. Soc. Office: Highmark Inc 120 5th Ave Pittsburgh PA 15222-3099 Office Phone: 412-544-7000.*

**MELANSON, DOROTHY,** political organization administrator; b. Boston, Sept. 21, 1953; AS, Westbrook Coll., Maine, 1980. Com. woman Maine Dem. Nat., Maine, 1996; chairwoman Dem. Com., Cumberland County, Maine, 1996—2002; com. woman Maine Dem. Nat., Maine, 2000; Presdl. Elector Maine, 2000; com. woman Maine Dem. Nat., 2001—03; chairwoman Maine Dem. Party, 2003—; registered nurse Maine Med. Ctr., Maine. A longtime dem. party activist.

**MELAS-KYRIAZI, THEO,** electronics executive; BA in Econs., MBA, Harvard U. Former corp. fin. mgr. Bourgeois Fils & Co., NH; asst. treas. Thermo Electron, Waltham, Mass., 1986—88, treas., 1988—94, pres., CEO ThermoSpectra Corp. subs., 1994—97, chmn. ThermoSpectra, v.p. corp. strategy Thermo Electron, 1997—99, v.p., CFO, 1999—. Bd. dirs. Thoratec. Office: Thermo Electron 81 Wyman St Waltham MA 02454

**MELBINGER, MICHAEL S.,** lawyer; b. Chgo., Sept. 5, 1958; s. Donald G. and Joyce A. (Haynes) M.; m. Karen Mary Melbinger, June 16, 1984; children: Peter Donald, Charlotte Anna, Lucy Grace. BA, U. Notre Dame, 1980; JD, U. Ill., 1983. Bar: Ill., 1983. Assoc. McDermott, Will & Emery, Chgo., 1983-88, ptnr., 1989-93; ptnr., head employee benefits dept. Schiff, Hardin & Waite, Chgo., 1993—97; ptnr., chmn. employee benefits and exec. compensation Winston & Strawn LLP, Chgo., 1997—. William M. Trumbull adj. prof. law Northwestern U.; author, speaker Coll. for Fin. Planning, Denver, 1990—. Mem. editorial bd. Practical Tax Strategies, Taxation for Lawyers, N.Y.C., 1989—; Employee Benefits Counselor, 1993—; Pension Management, 1995—; author Executive Compensation, 2004, author: Employee Benefit Trust Compliance Manual; contbr. articles to profl. jours. Pro bono Adoptive Families Am., Adoption Advocates. Mem. ABA, Nat. Assn. Stock Plan Profls. Home: 2699 Independence Ave Glenview IL 60025-7730 Office: Winston & Strawn LLP 35 W Wacker Dr Chicago IL 60601-9703 Office Phone: 312-558-7588. Office Fax: 312-558-5700. E-mail: mmelbinger@winston.com.

**MELBOURNE, ROBERT ERNEST,** civil engineer; b. Oceanside, Calif., July 17, 1929; s. Thomas Powell and Helen Millicent (Plausse) M.; m. Jeanne Edith Kuhn, Apr. 8, 1961; children: Ann Teresa Farley, Maria Helen Hayes, Steven Thomas, Louise Clare Vance. BSCE, U. So. Calif., 1951; PhD in History, 1996; MSCE, Stanford U., 1955; MA in History, U. San Diego, 1990. Registered civil engr., Calif. Engr. Morrison-Knudsen Co., Boise, Noxon, Mont., 1955-57, J.E. Haddock Ltd., Pasadena, Calif., 1957-58; pres. R.E. Melbourne Co. Inc., San Luis Rey, Calif., 1958-66; engr. constrn. and design, chief engr. San Diego County Water Authority, San Diego, 1966-90; mil. historian in pvt. practice, 1990—. Mem. adv. bd. Colorado River Bd., L.A., 1967-83. Commr. Oceanside Historic Preservation, 1997—. Lt. USN, 1951-54, PTO. Fellow ASCE; mem. U.S. Naval Inst., Soc. Mil. History, Navy League of U.S., Marine Corps Heritage Found. Republican. Roman Catholic. Home: PO Box 9 San Luis Rey CA 92068-0009

**MELBY, DONNA D.,** lawyer; b. 1950; BA, U. Calif., Santa Barbara, 1972; attended, Loyola U. Sch. Law, 1977—78, Calif. Western Sch. Law, 1975—77, JD, 1978. Bar: Calif. 1979. Ptnr. Sonnenschein Nath & Rosenthal LLP, LA, 2002—05. Mem. Calif. Judicial Selection Adv. Coun., 2004. Named one of The Most Influential & Talented Women Trial Lawyers in Calif., LA Daily Jour. & San Francisco Recorder, 2002, 2003, 2004, 16 leading litigators in the US, Minority Corp. Counsel Assn., 2004, The 100 Most Influential Attorneys in State of Calif., LA Daily Jour. & San Francisco Recorder, 2004; named to Top 5% So. Calif. Super Lawyers, LA Mag., 2003—05; recipient Rothchild Pro Bono Award, Sonnenschein Nath & Rosenthall LLP, 2004. Fellow: Internat. Soc. Barristers, Am. Coll. Trial Lawyers; mem.: Fed. Bar Assn., Women Lawyers of LA, Calif. Women Lawyers, Assn. Bus. Trial Lawyers, Assn. So. Calif. Def. Counsel, Def. Rsch. Inst. (labor & employment com.), Fedn. Def. and Corp. Counsel, Internat. Assn. Def. Counsel (faculty mem. trial sch.), Am. Bd. Trial Advocates (faculty mem. trial sch. 1993—, mem. bd. dirs. 1994—, mem. found. bd. trustees 2001—, v.p. 2003, pres.-elect 2004, pres. 2005, pres. LA chpt. 2004), Chancery Club. Office: Sonnenschein Nath & Rosenthal LLP 601 S Figueroa St. Ste 1500 Los Angeles CA 90017 Office Fax: 213 892 5027. Business E-Mail: dmelby@sonnenschein.com.

**MELBY, EDWARD CARLOS, JR.,** veterinarian; b. Burlington, Vt., Aug. 10, 1929; s. Edward C. and Dorothy H. (Folsom) M.; m. Jean Day File, Aug. 15, 1953; children: Scott E., Susan J., Jeffrey T., Richard A. Student, U. Pa., 1948—50; DVM, Cornell U., 1954. Diplomate Am. Coll. Lab. Animal Medicine. Practice vet. medicine, Middlebury, Vt., 1954-62; instr. lab. animal medicine Johns Hopkins U. Sch. Medicine, Balt., 1962-64, asst. prof., 1964-66, assoc. prof., 1966-71, prof. dir. comparative medicine, 1971-74; prof. medicine, dean Coll. Vet. Medicine, Cornell U., Ithaca, NY, 1974-84; v.p R & D SmithKline Beecham Animal Health, 1985-90, v.p. sci. and tech. assessment, 1990-91; ind. cons., 1992—. Cons. VA, NRC, NIH. Author: Handbook of Laboratory Animal Science, Vols. I, II, III, 1974-76. Served with USMC, 1946-48. Mem. Am., N.Y. State, Md., Pa. Vet. Med. Assns., Am. Assn. Lab. Animal Sci., Am. Coll. Lab. Animal Medicine, AAAS, Phi Zeta. Home: PO Box 248 Charlotte VT 05445-0248 Office: 736 Lime Kiln Rd Charlotte VT 05445-9141 Office Phone: 802-985-3368. E-mail: ecmelby@aol.com.

**MELBY, JOHN B.,** composer, educator; b. Whitehall, Wis., Oct. 3, 1941; s. John B. Sr. and Margaret (Edmundson) M.; m. Carol A. Wurtz, July 7, 1961 (div. 1977); 1 child, John; m. Jane H. Thompson, June 15, 1978; children: Kirsten, Charles. MusB, Curtis Inst., 1966; MA, U. Pa., 1967; MFA, Princeton U., 1971, PhD, 1972. Assoc. prof. West Chester (Pa.) U., 1971-73; prof. music U. Ill. Urbana, 1973-97, prof. emeritus, 1997—. Assoc. U. Ill. Ctr. for Advanced Studies, 1989-90. Composer numerous mus. works for live performers, computer-synthesized tape, vocal, chamber, choral and orchestral works including 2 symph., works pub. by Associated Music Pubs., Merion Music, Inc.; recs. on Composers Recs., Inc., New World Records, Advance Records, Centaur Records, Zuma Records. Recipient 1st prize 7th Internat. Electroacoustic Music Awards, Bourges, France, 1979, Am. Acad./Inst. Arts and Letters award, 1984; Guggenheim fellow, 1983. Mem.: ACLU, Am. Composers Alliance (bd. govs.), Am. Music Ctr., Broadcast Music Inc., Herpetologists' League, Am. Atheists. Green Party. Avocations: railroading, cooking, herpetology. Home: 5 Walter St Salem MA 01970-2518 E-mail: jbmelby@johnmelby.com.

**MELCHER, ELIZABETH,** musician; b. Phoenixville, Pa., Oct. 1, 1965; d. William Diehl Lober and Caroline Merroth Melcher; 1 child, Amy Elizabeth Winger. MusB, The Curtis Inst. Music, 1987; MusM, The Juilliard Sch., 1990; DMA, Eastman Sch. Music, 1994. Fellow in ch. music Christ and St. Stephen's Episc. Ch., NYC, 1988—89; asst. organist Brick Presbyn. Ch., NYC, 1989—90; organist/choirmaster Ch. of Ascension, Rochester, NY, 1991—94; min. music Ascension Luth. Ch., Balt., 1994—97; dir. music The Luth. Ch. St. Andrew, Silver Spring, 1997—2001; min. music The Ch. Good Shepherd, Burke, Va., 2001—03; organist/choirmaster Grace and Holy Trinity Episc. Ch., Richmond, Va., 2003—. Asst. organist John Wanamaker Grand Ct. Organ, Phila., 1985—87; pvt. tchr. organ and piano, 1999—. Organist: CD recording Pageant, 2001. Recipient 2d prize, Naples (Fla.) Internat. Organ Festival Competition, 1993, Arthur Poister Nat. Organ Competition, 1995, 1988. Mem.: Am. Guild Organists (recitalist, adjudicator various competitions, 1st prize Nat. Young Artists competition, Region III 1991, Finalist Nat. Young Artists competition 1996). Avocations: tennis, swimming, reading, concerts, travel. Office: Grace and Holy Trinity Episc Church 8 North Laurel St Richmond VA 23220-4797 Office Phone: 804-359-5628 ext. 20. Office Fax: 804-353-2348. Business E-Mail: emelcher@ghtc.org.

**MELCHER, JAMES PATRICK,** political scientist, educator; b. Madison, Wis., Feb. 3, 1963; s. John William and Beatrice Hagensick Melcher; m. Nancy Patricia Finnegan, Jan. 2, 1999. BA, U. Wis., 1985; PhD, U. Minn., 1995. Asst. dept. rsch. Minn. Ho. of Reps., St. Paul, 1989—92; vis. asst. prof. St. John's U., Collegeville, Minn., 1995, Coll. St. Benedict, St. Joseph, Minn., 1995, U. Wis., Eau Claire, 1996; vis. term prof. Cleve. State U., 1996—99; asst. prof. U. Maine, Farmington, 1999—2004, assoc. prof., 2004—. Contbr. articles to profl. jours.; assoc. editor: website Electnet, 1996—2001. Del. Maine Dem. Conv., 2000, 2002; vestry mem. St. Mark's Episc. Ch., Augusta, Maine, 2000—. Named Faculty of Yr., U. Maine, Farmington, 2004; recipient Disting. Faculty award, Cleve. State U. Student Alumni Assn., 1999. Mem.: Am. Polit. Sci. Assn. Episcopalian. Avocations: collecting postcards, fantasy football, fantasy baseball, hiking. Home: 27 Meadow Rd #204 Augusta ME 04330 Office: U Maine Farmington Dept Social Scis and Bus Farmington ME 04938 Business E-Mail: jim.melcher@maine.edu.

**MELCHIOR, IB JORGEN,** scriptwriter, author, film director; b. Copenhagen, Sept. 17, 1917; arrived in U.S., 1938; s. Lauritz Lebrecht Hommel and Inger Thora (Nathansen) M.; m. Harriet Hathaway Kale, Mar. 15, 1942 (div. 1960); 1 child, Leif; m. Cleo Baldon, Jan. 18, 1964; stepchild, Dirk Arin. Degree, Stenhus Kostskole, Denmark, 1936; Cand.Phil., U. Copenhagen, 1937. Actor stage mgr., co-dir. English Players, Paris, 1937—39; stage mgr. Radio City Music Hall, Ctr. Theater, N.Y.C., 1941—42; actor, writer N.Y.C., 1946—49; assoc. dir. CBS-TV, N.Y.C., 1949—50; dir. Perry Como Show, N.Y.C., 1951—54; assoc. prodr. G-L Enterprises, N.Y.C., 1952—53; screen-writer, dir., novelist, 1957—. Author: (novels) Order of Battle, 1973, Sleeper Agent, 1975, The Haigerloch Project, 1977, The Watchdogs of Abaddon, 1979, The Marcus Device, 1980, The Tombstone Cipher, 1983, Eva, 1984, V-3, 1985, Code Name: Grand Guignol, 1987, (biography) Quest, 1990, Order of Battle: Hitler's Werewolves, 1991, (autobiography) Case by Case, 1993; author: (with Cleo Baldon) Steps & Stairways, 1989, Reflections on the Pool, 1997, Lauritz Melchior: The Golden Years of Bayreuth, 2003; screen-writer Live Fast, Die Young, 1957, The Angry Red Planet, 1959, Reptilicus, 1962, Journey to the 7th Planet, 1962, Ambush Bay, 1965, Robinson Crusoe on Mars, 1964, The Time Travelers, 1964, others; dir. Angry Red Planet, The Time Travelers; translator, narrator (tapes) Hans Christian Andersen Fairy Tales, 1986; creator Space Family Robinson (spl. advisor Lost in Space, 1997-98); subject of biography: (by Robert Skotak) Ib Melchior: Man of Imagination, 2000. Adv. bd. Melchior's Narcotics Info. Clinic, LA, 1972-73; adv. coun. Danish Immigrant Mus., Elk Horn, Iowa, 1985—. With U.S. Army Mil. Intelligence, 1942-46. Decorated Bronze Star, Knight Commander Cross, Militant Order of St. Brigitte of Sweden, 1965; recipient King Christian X Erindringsmedalje, 1948, Medal of Merit Old Guard, 1965, Golden Scroll award Best Writing Acad. Sci. Fiction, 1976, Hamlet award Best Legitimate Play Shakespeare Soc. Am., 1982; named Scandinavian of Yr. Am. Scandanavian Found. L.A., 1995, Mem. Writers Guild Am. West, Dirs. Guild Am., Acad. Sci. Fiction (hon.). Manuscript Soc., Authors Guild Inc., Royal Danish Guard Assn., Danish Luncheon Club (L.A.), Adventures Club (L.A.). Home and Office: 8228 Marmont Ln Hollywood CA 90069-1624 Office Phone: 323-654-6679. Personal E-mail: ijmelchior@aol.com.

**MELCHIORRE, DANIELLE MARIE,** psychologist; b. Staten Island, Feb. 6, 1973; d. Donato and Maryann Melchiorre. BA, Bucknell Univ., Lewisburg, Pa., 1995; MSc, St. John's Univ., Jamaica, N.Y., 1998. Cert. Sch. Pschology N.Y. Sch. psychologist Kennedy Pre-sch., Staten Island, NY, 1998, United Cerebral Palsy NYC, 2002—05; psychologist Staten Island Devel. Disabilities Svcs. Office, 2005—. Psychologist ind. contr. Superior Clin. Care, 2005—. Mem.: APA, N.Y. Assn. Sch. Psychologists, Nat. Assn. Sch. Psychologists. Avocations: travel, volleyball, swimming, theater, cooking.

**MELCONIAN, LINDA JEAN,** state senator, lawyer, educator; b. Springfield, Mass. d. George and Virginia Elaine (Noble) Melconian. BA, Mt. Holyoke Coll.; MA, George Washington U.; JD, George Mason U. Asst. counsel to Spkr. Thomas P. O'Neill, Jr. U.S. Ho. of Reps., Washington; pros. atty. Hampden County Dist. Atty., Springfield, Mass.; state senator Mass. Gen. Ct., Boston, 1983—2004, majority leader emeritus Mass. State Senate. Instr. Mt. Holyoke Coll., Am. Internat. Coll.; vis. asst. prof. Suffolk U., Boston. Ex Officio trustee Ella T. Grasso Found., Conn.; active Dem. State Com., Mass. Home: 465 Dwight Rd Springfield MA 01108 Office Phone: 413-374-3671. Business E-Mail: lindamelconian@comcast.net, lindamelconi@suffolk.edu. E-mail: lmelconi@suffolk.edu.

**MELCZEK, DALE J.,** bishop; b. Nov. 9, 1938; AB, St. Mary Coll., Orchard Lake, Mich.; MDiv, St. John Sem., Plymouth, Mich.; MA in Edn., U. Detroit; postgrad., U. Notre Dame. Ordained priest Roman Cath. Ch., 1964, apptd. aux. bishop Roman Cath. Ch., 1982. Assoc pastor St. Sylvester Ch., Warren, Mich., 1964—70, co-pastor, 1970—72; pastor St. Christine Ch., Detroit, 1972—75; vicar West Detroit Vicariate, 1973—75; asst. vicar for parishes Archdiocese of Detroit, 1975—77, sec. to archbishop and vicar gen., 1977—82, archdiocesan consultor, 1972—83, aux. bishop, titular bishop of Trau, 1982—92; regional bishop Detroit N.W. Region, 1983—92; apostolic adminstr. Diocese of Gary, 1992—95, coadjutor Bishop of Gary, 1995—96, bishop of Gary, 1996—. Roman Catholic. Office Phone: 219-769-9292.

**MELDMAN, ROBERT EDWARD,** lawyer; b. Milw., Aug. 5, 1937; s. Louis Leo and Lillian (Gollusch) M.; m. Sandra Jane Setlick, July 24, 1960; children: Saree Beth, Richard Samuel. BS, U. Wis., 1959; LL.B., Marquette U., 1962; LL.M. in Taxation, NYU, 1963. Bar: Wis. 1962, Fla. 1987, Colo. 1990, U.S. Ct. Fed. Claims, U.S. Tax Ct. 1963, U.S. Supreme Ct. 1970. Practice tax law, Milw., 1963—; pres. Meldman, Case & Weine, Ltd., Milw., 1975-85; dir. tax div. Mulcahy & Wherry, S.C., Milw., 1985-90; shareholder Reinhart, Boerner, Van Deuren, S.C., 1991—. Adj. prof. taxation U. Wis., Milw., 1970—2000, mem. tax adv. coun., 1978—2000, dir. Low Income Taxpayer Clinic, 2005—; adj. prof. Marquette U. Sch. Law, Milw., 2001—02, The U. of Queensland T.C. Beirne Sch. Law, 2002; vice chmn. Internat. Revenue Svc. Taxpayer Adv. Panel, 2003—04; sec. Profl. Inst. Tax Study, Inc., 1978—; bd. dirs. Wis. Bar Found., 1988—94; exec. in residence Deloitte & Touche Ctr. for Multistate Taxation, U. Wis., Milw., 1996—2000. Co-author: Federal Taxation Practice and Procedure, 1983, 1986, 1988, 1992, 1998, 2004, Practical Tactics for Dealing with the IRS, 1994, A Practical Guide to U.S. Taxation of International Transactions, 1996, 1997, 2004, Federal Taxation Practice and Procedure Study Guide/Quizzes, 1998; editor: Jour. Property Taxation, 1996—2002; mem. editl. bd.: Tax Litigation Alert, 1995—2000; contbr. articles to legal jours. Recipient Adj. Taxation Faculty award U.W Tax Assn., 1987; named Outstanding Tax Profl. 1992 Top Reports Wis. Mag. and U.W.M Tax Assn. Fellow Am. Coll. Tax Coun.; mem. ABA, Fed. Bar Assn. (pres. Milw. chpt. 1966-67), Milw. Bar Assn. (tax sect. 1970-71), Wis. Bar Assn. (dir. tax sect. 1964-78, chmn. 1973-74), Internat. Bar Assn., The Law Assn. for Asia and the Pacific (chair tax sect.

2000—, dep. chair bus. law sect.), Friends of Gold Meir Libr. (bd. dirs.), Marquette U. Law Alumni Assn. (bd. dirs. 1972-77), Milw. Athletic Club, Wis. Club (bd. dirs. 2003—), B'nai B'rith (trustee, Ralph Harris Meml. award Century Lodge 1969-70), Phi Delta Phi, Tau Epsilon Rho (chancellor Wis. chpt. 1969-71, supreme nat. chancellor 1975-76, v.p. Wis. chpt., tech. 1992-2000). Jewish (trustee congregation 1972-77). Home: 7455 N Skyline Ln Milwaukee WI 53217-3327 Office: 1000 N Water St Ste 2100 Milwaukee WI 53202-3197 E-mail: rmeldman@reinhartlaw.com

**MELDRUM, PETER DURKEE,** venture capitalist, biotechnology company executive; b. Salt Lake City, June 26, 1947; s. Benjamin Nibley and Grace Natalie (Durkee) M.; m. Catherine Roper, June 16, 1970; children: Christopher Shawn. BSChemE, U. Utah, 1970, MBA, 1974. Asst. to pres. Terra Tek, Inc., Salt Lake City, 1974-78; pres., CEO Resource Enterprises, Inc., Salt Lake City, 1978-81, AgriDyne Techs., Salt Lake City, 1981-91, Founder's Fund Inc., 1991—93, Myriad Genetics Inc., Salt Lake City, 1991—. Bd. dirs. Dairy Equipment Co. Utah, Salt Lake City, Amedica, Golden Pine Ventures LLC (sec., chmn.), 2004-. Bd. dirs., vice chmn. ARC Golden Spike, Salt Lake City, 1980-90; mem. State of Utah Coun. Sci. and Tech., 1984-89; mem. adv. bd. Coll. of Sci. U. Utah, Engr. Adv. Bd, U. Utah, adv. bd. High Tech Mktg. Rsch., Austin, Tex., 1986-88; mem. Gov.'s Task Force on Entrepreneurship; Gov.'s Com. on Biomed. Industry, 1988-91; bd. arbitrators NASD, 1991-98; bd. dirs. Ballet West. Salt lt. USAR, 1970-72, bd. trustees, Pioneer Theatre Co. Named Entrepreneur of Yr., 2001; named one of Top 50 Scientific Visionaries in World, Scientific Am. Mag., 2002; recipient Utah Gov. Medal for Sci. and Tech., 1998. Mem. Utah Life Scis. Assn. (bd. dirs. 1995—), Tau Beta Pi, Phi Kappa Phi, Beta Gamma Sigma. Republican. Presbyterian. Avocations: skiing, backpacking, basketball, photography. Office: Myriad Genetics 320 Wakara Way Salt Lake City UT 84108-1214*

**MELE, ALFRED R.,** philosophy educator; b. Detroit, May 22, 1951; s. Alfred Emil and Rosemary (Pardo) M.; children: Al, Nick, Angela. BA, Wayne State U., 1973; PhD, U. Mich., 1979. Asst. prof. philosophy Davidson (N.C.) Coll., 1979-85, assoc. prof., 1985-91, prof., 1991-95, Vail prof., 1995-2000; William H. and Lucyle T. Werkmeister prof. Fla. State U., Tallahassee, 2000—. Author: Irrationality, 1987, Springs of Action, 1992, Autonomous Agents, 1995, Self-Deception Unmasked, 2001, Motivation and Agency, 2003, Free Will and Luck, 2006; contbr. articles to profl. jours. Fellow NEH, 1985-86, 92-93, 99-2000, Nat. Humanities Ctr., Rsch. Triangle Park, NC, 1992-93, Australian Nat. U., 1999. Mem. Am. Philos. Assn., So. Assn. Philosophy and Psychology, Internat. Soc. for Rsch. on Emotion. Avocations: racquetball, tennis. Office: Dept Philosophy Fla State Univ Tallahassee FL 32306-1500

**MELE, JOANNE THERESA,** dentist; b. Chgo., Dec. 5, 1943; d. Andrew and Josephine Jeanette (Calabrese). Diploma, St. Elizabeth's Sch. Nursing, Chgo., 1964; diploma in dental hygiene, Northwestern U., 1977; AS, Triton Coll., 1979; DDS, Loyola U., 1983. RN; registered dental hygienist. Staff nurse medicine/surgery St. Elizabeth's Hosp., Chgo., 1964-66, oper. room nurse, 1966-67; head nurse oper. room Cook County Hosp., Chgo., 1967-76, head nurse ICU, 1976-77; dental hygienist Mele Dental Assocs., Ltd., Oakbrook, Ill., 1977-78; practice dentistry, 1983—. Clin. asst. prof. Loyola U., Chgo., 1988-93. Recipient Northwestern U. Dental Hygiene Clinic award, 1977; Dr. Duxler Humanitarian scholar Loyola U., 1982. Mem. Chgo. Dental Soc., Ill. State Dental Soc., Acad. Gen. Dentistry, Acad. Operative Dentistry, Am. Prosthodontic Soc., Internat. Congress Oral Implantologists, Psi Omega (Kappa chpt.). Roman Catholic. Avocations: reading, music, gardening. Office Phone: 630-573-0420.

**MELEKOTE, SWATHANTHRA KUMAR,** education educator; s. Swathanthra Kumar Melekote and Gayethri Narayanswamy; m. Gayethri Narayanswamy, Dec. 18, 1964; children: Aswini Kumar, Gautami Kumar. MBBS, Jawaharlal Med. Coll., India, 1989; MD in Pediatrics, Bangalore Med. Coll., India, 1993. Lic. Physician, U.S. Chief resident N.Y. Meth. Hosp., Bklyn., 2003—05; asst. prof. U. Conn., Farmington, 2005—. Mng. dir. Aswini Hosp., Bangalore, India, 1993—98. Prodr.: (movie) Graduation, 2004. Recipient Master, Royal Coll. of Pediatrics, London, 1999—2000, Royal Coll. of Physician Child Health, London, 2000. Achievements include patents pending for New type of laryngoscope. Home: 1213 ARbordrive Shrewsbury MA 01545 Office: Uconn Health Ctr 273 Farmington Ave Farmington CT 06032 Office Phone: 860-679-7019. Office Fax: 860-679-1403. Personal E-mail: swathanthra@yahoo.com.

**MELENDY, DAVID RUSSELL,** newscaster, reporter; b. Corpus Christi, Tex., Oct. 19, 1948; s. Harold Orville and Marguerite Doris (Waller) Melendy; m. Lorna Sandra Katz, Mar. 19, 1972; children: Seth Howard, Andrew Scott. Student, George Washington U., 1966-70; BA magna cum laude, U. Hartford, 1972. News dir. Sta. WINY, Putnam, Conn., 1971-77; news anchor, reporter Sta. WPOP, Hartford, Conn., 1977-80; news dir. Sta. WNVR, Waterbury, Conn., 1980-81; news anchor, reporter St. WDRC, Hartford, Conn., 1980—81; news anchor Sta. WCBS-FM, N.Y.C., 1981; prodr., assignment editor, anchor, reporter AP Broadcast Svcs., Washington, 1981—. Instr. journalism Briarwood Coll., Southington, Conn., 1977—81, mem. broadcast adv. com., 1978—81. Prodr., writer, reproter: Star Wars: Strategic Defense Initiative, 1985, Flashback, 1986—2005. Publicity chmn. Woodstock Players Cmty. Theater, Conn., 1972—77, Quinebaug Valley C.C. Found., Danielson, Conn., 1973—75, fundraising chmn., 1976; neighborhood coord. Am. Heart Assn., Washington, 1994, 1999, 2001; troop com. mem. Boy Scouts Am., 1998—99, 2005—, pack com. chmn., 2000—01, asst. scoutmaster, 2001—05, advancement chmn. 2003—, vice chmn. mktg. Horizon dist. news—, Nat. Capital Area coun., 2005—. Mem.: Nat. Press Club, Com. Concerned Journalists, News Media Guild/TNG-CWA (v.p.), Radio and TV News Dirs. Assn., Ho. and Senate Radio-TV Corr. Assn., Elks. Avocations: personal computers, photography, hiking, swimming. Office: AP Broadcast Svcs 1825 K St NW Washington DC 20006-1202 E-mail: david@melendy.us, dmelendy@ap.org.

**MELENHORST, JAN JOSEPH,** immunologist; b. Geldrop, Netherlands, Mar. 6, 1965; s. Jan Marius Melenhorst and Hendrika Josepha Melenhorst-Alsters; m. Ling Zhao, Mar. 30, 1966; children: Anne Xinyi, Matthew Xinwei. PhD, Leiden U., Netherlands, 1997. Postdoctoral fellow Leiden U. Med. Ctr., Netherlands, 1997—98, NIH, Nat. Heart, Lung & Blood Inst., Bethesda, Md., 1998—2002, staff scientist, 2002—. Fogarty Vis. fellowship, NIH, 1998-2002. Mem.: Am. Soc. of Hematology, Am. Assn. of Immunologists. Achievements include the development of a cell culture system for the efficient induction of CD4 and CD8 T cell responses against viral and leukemia antigens for adoptive immunotherapy; Demonstrated that the clonal CD8 population in large granular lymphocyte leukemia consist of memory and effector T cells; Demonstrated that some patients with myelodysplastic syndrome have large expansions of clonal CD8 T cells; isolated and characterized autoreactive Tcells from a patient with aplastic anemia. Office: NIH NHLBI Bldg 10-CRC 10 Center Dr Bethesda MD 20892-1202 Office Phone: 301-435-2622. Office Fax: 301-480-2664. Business E-Mail: melenhoj@nhlbi.nih.gov.

**MELGREN, ERIC FRANKLIN,** prosecutor, lawyer; b. Minneola, Kans., Dec. 16, 1956; s. Carl James and Louise C. (Loechnor) M.; m. Denise Melgren, June 16, 1979; children: David W., Susan C., Peter J., Abigail J. B., Wichita State U., 1979; JD, Washburn U., Topeka, 1985. Bar: Kans. 1985, U.S. Dist. Ct. Kans. 1985, U.S. Ct. Appeals (10th cir.) 1987, U.S. Tax Ct. 1988, U.S. Supreme Ct. 1995. Law clk. US Dist. Ct. Kans., Wichita, 1985-87; assoc. Foulston, Siefkin, Powers & Eberhardt, Wichita, 1987-92; ptnr. Foulston & Siefkin, Wichita, 1992—2001; U.S. atty. dist. Kans. US Dept. Justice, 2002—. Trustee Leadership Wichita, 1994—. Mem. Christian Legal Soc. (state dir. 1994—), Wichita State Alumni Assn. (exec. com. 1993—), West Wichita Rotary Club. Republican. Office: US Attys Office 1200 Epic Ctr 301 N Main Wichita KS 67202 Office Phone: 316-269-6481.*

**MELHUSE, PEDER NYHAGEN,** actor, educator; s. Arthur N. and Isabelle N. Melhuse. MFA in Acting, U. Wis., Madison, 1997. Asst. prof. theatre, dance U. Ala., Tuscaloosa, 2001—05. Guest lectr. theatre, drama U. Wis., Madison, 1999—2000. Mem.: Actors Equity Assn. Avocations: travel, sports. Office Phone: 205-292-8925.

**MELICHER, RONALD WILLIAM,** finance educator; b. St. Louis, July 4, 1941; s. William and Lorraine Norma (Mohart) M.; m. Sharon Ann Schlarmann, Aug. 19, 1967; children: Michelle Joy, Thor William, Sean Richard. BSBA, Washington U., St. Louis, 1963, MBA, 1965, DBA, 1968. Asst. prof. fin. U. Colo., Boulder, 1969-71, assoc. prof., 1971-76, prof. fin., 1976—, chmn. fin. divsn., 1978-86, 90, chmn. fin. and econ. divsn., 1993-2000, MBA/MS programs dir., 1990-93, chmn. fin. divsn., 2003—. Assoc. dir. space law bus. and policy ctr. U. Colo., 1986-87; rsch. cons. FPC, Washington, 1975-76, GAO, Washington, 1981, RCG/Hagler, Bailly, Inc., 1985—, Ariz. Corp. Commn., 1986-87, Comm. Dept. Pub. Utility Control, 1989, US SEC, 1992-95; cons. tech. edn. IBM Corp., 1985-91; dir. ann. Exch. Program for Gas Industry, 1975-94; instr. ann. program Nat. Assn. Regulatory Utility Commrs., Mich. State U., 1981-94. Co-author: Real Estate Finance, 1978, 3d edit., 1989, Financial Management, 5th edit., 1982, Finance: Introduction to Markets, Institutions and Management, 1980, 1984, 1988, 1992, Finance: Introduction to Institutions, Investments and Management, 9th edit., 1997, 12th edit., 2006, Entrepreneurial Finance, 2003, 2d edit., 2006; assoc. editor Fin. Mgmt. Jour., 1975—80, The Fin. Rev., 1988—91. Recipient News Ctr. 4 TV Tchg. award, 1987, MBA/MS Assn. Tchg. award, 1988, Boulder Faculty Assembly Tchg. award, 1988, Grad. Bus. Students Tchg. award, 1995, 98; grantee NSF, 1974, NASA, 1986, 87; scholar W.H. Baughn Disting., 1989-2000, U. Colo. Pres.'s Tchg., 1989—. Mem. Fin. Mgmt. Assn. (mem. prog. com. 1974-76, regional dir. 1975-77, v.p. ann. mtg. 1985, v.p program 1987, pres. 1991-92, exec. com. 1991-93, bd. trustees 1992-99, chmn. 25th Anniversary com. 1994-95, mem. search com. for editor of Fin. Mgmt. Jour., 1995-96, chmn. search com. editor of Fin. Practice and Edn. Jour. 1996, mem. search com. for sec./treas. 1999, 2001), Am. Fin. Assn. Western Fin. Assn. (bd. dirs. 1974-76), Fin. Execs. Inst. (acad. mem. 1975—), Ea. Fin. Assn., Southwestern Fin. Assn., Midwest Fin. Assn. (bd. dirs. 1978-80), Alpha Kappa Psi, Beta Gamma Sigma. Office: U Colo Coll Bus PO Box 419 Boulder CO 80303 Office Phone: 303-492-3182. Business E-Mail: ronald.melicher@colorado.edu.

**MELICK, CLIFFORD FRANCIS,** sociologist, researcher; b. Albany, N.Y., Sept. 6, 1947; s. Francis Joseph Melick, Marion Dorothy Campbell; m. Evelyn Louise Mazo, Feb. 24, 2004, BA, Siena Coll., Loudonville, N.Y., 1971; MA, SUNY, Albany, 1973, PhD, 1979. Rsch. scientist N.Y. State Divsn. for Youth, Albany, 1980—83, dir. revenue and reporting svcs., 1983—86, chief program analysis and rsch., 1986—90; dir. rsch. Greater Balt. Med. Ctr., 1990—2002, dir. clin. info. and rsch., 2002—04; program evaluator Balt. City Pub. Sch. Sys., 2005—. Mem. editol adv. bd. Rsch. in Healthcare Fin. Mgmt., Balt., 2000—; prin. advisor NEMA Rsch., Inc., N.Y.C., 1997—; mem. Greater Balt. Med. Ctr. Instnl. Rev. Bd., Balt., 1990—; bd. dirs. Analytica, Ltd., Albany, NY; adj. Johns Hopkins Sch. Pub. Health, 2005—. Contbr. book Chronic Wound Care, 2d edit., 1997, Chronic Wound Care, 3d edit., 2001, Current Surgical Therapy, 4th edit., 1992, Current Surgical Therapy, 5th edit., 1995, articles to profl. jours. Mem.: APHA, Soc. of Clin. Rsh. Assoc., Am. Urogynecologic Soc., Acad. Health. Soc. for the Art and Sci. Wound Mgmt., Internat. Soc. for Rschs. in Healthcare Fin. Mgmt., Free State Corvette Club. Avocation: sports cars. Home: 8207 Spring Bottom Way Baltimore MD 21208 Office: Balt City Pub Sch Sys Rsch Evaluation Assessment Account 200 E North Ave Baltimore MD 21202 Office Phone: 410-396-8956. Personal E-mail: cmelick@comcast.net. Business E-Mail: cmelick@bcps.k12.md.us.

**MELILLO, JOSEPH VINCENT,** theater producer; b. New Haven, Nov. 15, 1946; s. Vincent and Viola (Fucci) M. BA, Sacred Heart U., 1968; MFA, Cath. U. Am., 1972. Adminstr. City Ctr. Music and Drama, N.Y.C., 1972-75; mktg. dir. The Walnut St. Theatre, Phila., 1975-76; dir. FEDAPT, N.Y.C., 1976-80; gen. mgr. New World Festival of Arts, Miami, Fla., 1982; dir. Next Wave Festival, N.Y.C., 1983-89; artistic dir. N.Y. Internat. Festival, N.Y.C., 1990-91, exec. prodr., 1999—; producing dir. Bklyn. Acad. Music, 1991—, exec. prodr., 1999—. Trustee EnGarde Arts, N.Y.C., 1991-96; v.p., bd. dirs. Assn. Performing Arts Presenters, Washington, 1991-93; cons.-specialist Opera Am. Washington, 1991-93; cons. The Japan Found. "Performing Arts Japan", The Bush Found., St. Paul, Arts Internat., N.Y.C.; adj. prof. Theater Dept. Bklyn. Coll.; co-chair Internat. Presenters Forum; mem. cultural challenge panel N.Y.C. Dept. Cultural Affairs; bd. advisors Etantdonnes, 2000, 2001, 2002; curator Internat. Soc. Performing Arts, 2005 Editor: Market the Arts, 1980. Mem. adv. bd. materials for arts Africa Exch. 651 program com. NJ Performing Arts Ctr., Newark, 1999—; mem. New Haven Festival of the Arts and Ideas; advisor Rolex Mentor and Protege Program, 2002—03; program adv. panel Pew Fellowships in the Arts, 2003, chmn. multidisciplinary panel, 2003, moderator conf., 2005; moderator The Berkshire Conf.; curator panels Internat. Soc. Performing Arts Found., 2005; adv. bd. Rolex Mentor and Protege Program, 2005—. Decorated chevalier Order of Arts and Letters; recipient Documents of Dance award, Dance Library of Israel, 2003, Svc. to Artistic Cmty. award Bang on a Can. Mem.: Century Assn., Order Brit. Empire, L'ordre des Arts et des Lettres (officer 2004). Democrat. Avocations: reading, travel. Office Phone: 718-636-4107. Business E-Mail: programming@bam.org.

**MELIN, ROBERT ARTHUR,** lawyer; b. Milw., Sept. 13, 1940; s. Arthur John and Frances Magdalena (Lanser) M.; m. Mary Magdalen Melin, July 8, 1967; children: Arthur Walden, Robert Dismas, Nicholas O'Brien, Madalyn Mary. BA summa cum laude, Marquette U., 1962, JD, 1967. Bar: Wis. 1966, U.S. Dist. Ct. (ea. dist.) Wis. 1966, U.S. Ct. Appeals (7th cir.) 1966, U.S. Ct. Mil. Appeals 1967, U.S. Supreme Ct. 1975. Law clk. U.S. Dist. Ct. (ea. dist.), Wis., 1966; instr. bus. law U.Ga., Hinesville, 1968; lectr. bus. law U. Md., Asmara, 1970; lectr. law Haile Salassie I. U. Law Faculty, Addis Ababa, Ethiopia, 1971-72; with Walther & Halling, Milw., 1973-74, Schroeder, Gedlen, Riester & Moerke, Milw., 1974-82; ptnr. Schroeder, Gedlen, Riester & Melin, Milw., 1982-84, Schroeder, Riester, Melin & Smith, Milw., 1984—. Author: Evidence in Ethiopia, 1972; contbg. author Ann. Survey African Law, 1974; contbr. numerous articles to legal jours. Rep. Class of 2000, West Point Parent Assn. Wis., 1996—, exec. bd., 1997—; lectr. charitable solicitations and contracts Philanthropy Monthly 9th Ann. Policy Conf., NYC, 1985; chmn. Milw. Young Dems., 1963-64. Capt. JAGC, AUS, 1967-70. Mem.: ABA, Wis. Acad. Trial Lawyers, Wis. Bar Assn., Milw. Bar Assn., Friends Ethiopia, Am. Legion, Delta Theta Phi, Phi Alpha Theta, Pi Gamma Mu. Roman Catholic. Home: 8108 N Whitney Rd Milwaukee WI 53217-2752 Office: 135 W Wells St Milwaukee WI 53203-1807 Office Phone: 414-351-0539.

**MELINSON, GREGG R.,** lawyer; b. Phila., 1954; s. James and Monica Melinson. BA, LaSalle Univ., 1986; JD, Duke Univ., 1989. Bar: Pa. 1989, NJ 1990. Law clerk, Hon. Edward R. Becker US Dist. Ct. Appeals (3d cir.), 1989—90; assoc. Drinker Biddle & Reath LLP, Phila., 1990—94, rejoined, 1997—, now ptnr., chair, govt. affairs practice group; dep. gen. counsel Gov. Tom Ridge, 1994—97. Co-chair Pa. Lawyers for Bush/Cheney. Frequent writer, lectr. in field. Vice chair Am. Heart Assn. Southeastern Pa. affiliate. Mem.: Pa. Economy League (chmn. 2003—). Republican. Office: Drinker Biddle & Reath LLP One Logan Sq 18th & Cherry Sts Philadelphia PA 19103-6996 Office Phone: 215-988-2648. Office Fax: 215-988-2757. Business E-Mail: gregg.melinson@dbr.com.

**MELISSA, HUFF ANN,** secondary school educator; b. Houston, Mo., Nov. 30, 1966; d. Wilburn Eddie and Phyllis Mae Keeney; m. Ronald David Huff; children: Kristin Nicole Huff, Ronald Logan Huff. Ednl. Specialist, William Woods U., Fulton, Mo., 2005. Tchr. Fairview R-XI, West Plains, Mo., 1996—2005; curriculum dir. Fairview R-XI Sch. Dist., West Plains, 2005—. Recipient Tchr. of the Yr., Fairview R-XI Sch. Dist., 2005. Mem.: ASCD. Home: 5101 Couty Road 8940 West Plains MO 65775 Office: Fairview R-XI Sch Dist 4036 State Route K Highway West Plains MO 65775 Office Phone: 417-256-3868.

**MELISSINOS, ADRIAN CONSTANTIN,** physicist, researcher; b. Thessaloniki, Greece, July 28, 1929; came to U.S., 1955, naturalized, 1970; s. Constantin John and Olympia (Abbott) M.; m. Mary Joyce Mitchell, June 7, 1960; children: Constantin John, Andrew William. Student, Royal Naval Acad., Greece, 1945-48; MS, Mass. Inst. Tech., 1956, PhD, 1958. Naval cadet Greek Navy, 1945-48, commd. ensign, 1948, advanced through grades to lt., 1951; ret., 1954; teaching and research asst. Mass. Inst. Tech., 1955-58; instr. U. Rochester, NY, 1958-60, asst. prof. physics, 1960-63, assoc. prof., 1963-67, prof., 1967—, chmn. dept. physics and astronomy, 1974-77. Vis. scientist CERN European Center for Nuclear Research, 1968-69, 77-78, 89-90; cons. Brookhaven Nat. Lab., 1970-72, 75-79; vis. prof. U. Athens, 1996; vis. scientist Deutsches Electronen Synchrotron, 1997; cons. Stanford Linear Accelerator Ctr., 1995-98. Author: Experiments in Modern Physics, 1966, (with J. Napolitano) 2d edit., 2003, (with F. Lobkowicz) Physics for Scientists and Engineers, 1975; (with A. Das) Quantum Mechanics, 1985, Principles of Modern Technology, 1990. Decorated Swedish Order of Sword. Fellow Am. Phys. Soc.; mem. Greek Nat. Acad. (corr.) Achievements include experimentation with elementary particles at most major high energy accelerators in the U.S. and Europe, experimentation with high power lasers, searches for dark matter, search for high frequency gravitational waves. Home: 177 Whitewood Ln Rochester NY 14618-3223 Office: U Rochester Dept Physics Rochester NY 14627 Office Phone: 585-275-2707. Business E-Mail: meliss@pas.rochester.edu.

**MELLBERG, JAMES RICHARD,** retired dental research chemist; b. Manitowoc, Wis., June 3, 1932; s. Millard Filmore Mellberg and Marion Eleanor (Elmer) Zimmerman; m. Gail Maureen Loehning, Sept. 26, 1956; children: Eric, Diane, Laura. BS, Wis. State U., Oshkosh, 1955; MS, Loyola U., Chgo., 1960. Head dental rsch. dept. Kendall Co., Barrington, Ill., 1958-75; assoc. dir. dental rsch. Colgate-Palmolive Co., Piscataway, NJ, 1975-94; ret. Cons. Naval Dental Rsch. Inst., Great Lakes, Ill., 1972-94. Author: Fluoride in Preventive Dentistry, 1983; patentee in field; contbr. over 100 articles in field to sci. publs. Recipient 20 sci. exhibit awards ADA, 1964-87. Mem. Internat. Assn. Dental Rsch. (Disting. Scientist award). Avocations: bicycling, woodworking. Home: 675 Ridge Top Rd Tryon NC 28782 Personal E-mail: mellberg1@alltel.net.

**MELLBERG, LEONARD EVERT,** physicist; b. Springfield, Mass., Dec. 18, 1935; s. Evert and Dorothy (Baker) M.; m. Pamela Narbeth. BS in Physics, U. Mass., Amherst, 1961; MS in Physics, Trinity Coll., Hartford, Conn., 1968. Rsch. physicist Navy Underwater Sound Lab., New London, Conn., 1961—68, SACLANT Undersea Rsch. Ctr., LaSpezia, Italy, 1968—72, Office of Naval Rsch., London, 1968—72, Naval Underwater Sys. Ctr., Newport, RI, 1972—91; sr. scientist Marine Acoustics Inc., Newport, 1991—94; chief scientist Sci. Applications Internat. Corp., San Diego, 1994—2000, Ocean Physics Assocs., South Dartmouth, Mass., 2000—. Govt. and profl. tech. adv. bds. and coms. Contbr. over 70 articles to profl. jours. Pres. Verdandi Swedish Cultural Found., Providence, 1992-97; bd. dirs. Verdandi Chorus Am. Union Swedish Singers, Providence, 1992—. Recipient Naval Underwater Sys. Ctr. Excellence in Sci. award, 1977, 84, Civilian Navy Meritorious Svc. medal Dept. of Navy, 1991. Fellow Acoustical Soc. Am.; mem. IEEE (sr.), AIAA (Svc. award 1977), Am. Geophys. Union, Oceanic Soc. of IEEE. Achievements include research in ocean physics, ocean acoustic propagation, anti-submarine warfare acoustics, Arctic sea-ice ridges and lighter than air vehicles. Home and Office: 109 Wilson St South Dartmouth MA 02748-3021 E-mail: lpmellberg@ieee.org.

**MELLEMA, DONALD EUGENE,** retired radio news reporter and anchor; b. Chgo., Mar. 30, 1937; s. Raymond Cornelius and Dorothy Sofia (Miller) M.; m. Freda Dieterlen Mellema, Sept. 23, 1961; children: Darryl Emerson, Duane Edward. BA in Speech, Beloit (Wis.) Coll., 1959. News dir. WGEZ Radio, Beloit, 1959; evening host, newsman WOSH Radio, Oshkosh, Wis., 1959-63; morning host, newsman WANE Radio, Ft. Wayne, Ind., 1963-65; news dir. WATI Radio, Indpls., 1965-67; news writer WGN Radio, Chgo., 1967-69; news reporter, anchor WBBM Radio, Chgo., 1969-96; ret., 1996. Mem. publs. adv. bd., pres's adv. coun., cons. Beloit Coll., 1996-00, also profl.-in-residence; Lewis and Clark lectr. Taft HS, 2002—; part time faculty Coll. Lake County, Grayslake, Ill., 2002-. Spkr., motivator Chgo. Pub. Sch. Youth Motivation Program, 1993-96; advisor, cons. media rels. to various police and civic orgns.; commr., unit leader Boy Scouts Am., 1971-81; ch. deacon Park Ridge (Ill.) Presbyn. Ch., 1980-83. Recipient regional award Radio TV News Dirs. Assn., 1994, Newsfinder award AP, 1995, career recognition award Chgo. Police Dept., 1997, Mark Twain award Ill. AP, 1997; named to Taft H.S. Hall of Fame, 1995. Mem. Ill. News Broadcasters Assn. (Silver Dome 1st Place award 1994), Soc. Profl. Journalists (Peter Lisagor award 1991, 96, Lewis and Clark lectr. 2002—), Am. Legion. Republican. Avocations: woodworking, reading, photography, birding, travel. Personal E-mail: donmellema@netscape.net.

**MELLEN, FRANCIS JOSEPH, JR.,** lawyer; b. Williamsport, Pa., Dec. 19, 1945; s. Francis Joseph and Mary Emma (Oberst) M.; m. Mary Wilder Davison, Aug. 2, 1975 (div. 1987); m. Beverly Joan Glascock, Sept. 2, 2000; children: Elizabeth, Catherine, Robert, Christine. BA, U. Ky., 1967, MA, 1971; JD, Harvard U., 1973. Bar: NY 1974, Ky. 1975, US Dist. Ct. (so. dist.) NY 1974, US Dist. Ct. (ea. dist.) Ky. 1977, US Dist. Ct. (we. dist.) Ky. 1978, US Ct. Appeals (2d cir.) 1975, US Ct. Appeals (6th cir.) 1982, US Supreme Ct. 2005. Assoc. atty. Rogers & Wells, N.Y.C., 1973-75, Wyatt, Grafton & Sloss, Louisville, 1975-80; ptnr. Wyatt, Tarrant & Combs, Louisville, 1980—. Co-author: Kentucky Mineral Law, 1986, Kentucky Forms and Transactions, 1991; contbr. articles to profl. jours. Spl. study com. Uniform Comml. Code, Ky. Legis. Rsch. Commn., Frankfort, 1984-91; bd. dirs. Leadership Louisville Found., 1995-02, counsel, 1996-98, 2000-02; bd. dirs. Stage One: The Louisville Children's Theatre, 1995-01, v.p., 1997-98, pres., 1998-00; bd. dirs. Louisville-Jefferson County A.W.A.R.E. Coalition, 1994-98, Lt. (j.g.) USNR, 1967-69. Mem. AIJA, Am. Arbitration Assn. (panel), Nat. Arbitration Forum (panel), Ky. Bar Assn. (ho. of dels. 1986-92, ethics com. 2004—, arbitration panel 2005—), Louisville Bar Assn. (chmn. com. profl. responsibility 1992-94), Jefferson Club, Filson Club, Am. Mensa, Hon. Order Ky. Cols. Republican. Home: 2944 Lexington Rd Louisville KY 40206-2934 Office: Wyatt Tarrant & Combs LLP 2800 PNC Plz Louisville KY 40202 Office Phone: 502-562-7290. E-mail: fmellen@wyattfirm.com.

**MELLENCAMP, JOHN (JOHN COUGAR),** singer, lyricist; b. Seymour, Ind., Oct. 7, 1951; m. Vicky C. (div.); children: Michelle, Teddy Joe, Justice; m. Elaine Irwin, Sept. 5, 1992. Student, Vincennes U., Ind. Albums include Chestnut Street Incident, 1977, Biography, 1978, Johnny Cougar, 1979, Nothing Matters and What If It Did, 1980, Night Dancin, 1980, American Fool, 1982, Uh-huh, 1983, Scarecrow, 1985, The Lonesome Jubilee, 1988, Big Daddy, 1989, Whenever We Wanted, 1991, Human Wheels, 1993, Dance Naked, 1994, Mr. Happy Go Lucky, 1996, The Best That I Could Do...1997, John Mellencamp, 1998, Rough Harvest, 1999, Cuttin' Heads, 2001, Trouble No More, 2003, Words & Music: John Mellencamp's Greatest Hits, 2004; performed one song for Folkways: A Vision Shared (A Tribute to Woody Guthrie and Leadbelly), 1988; film actor, dir., soundtrack performer: Falling From Grace, 1992, Seeing in the Dark, 2000; TV appearance Bob Dylan: The 30th Anniversary Concert Celebration, 1993, Farm Aid '96, 1996. Office: Mercury Records 825 8th Ave New York NY 10019-7416

**MELLER, JAROSLAW,** biotechnologist, information scientist, educator; m. Halina Meller; children: Artur, Adam. PhD, Nicholas Copernicus U., Torun, Poland, 1996; D, Polish Acad. Sci., Warsaw, 2004. Lecture. Hebrew U., Jerusalem, 1996—97; fellow Kyoto U., 1997—98; rsch. assoc. Cornell U., Ithaca, NY, 1999—2001; asst. prof. Children's Hosp. Rsch. Found., Cinn. Contbr. articles to profl. jours. Mem.: Internat. Soc. Computational Biology, AAAS. Achievements include discovery of using computational approaches, proposed links between several classes of proteins, including tumor suppressor pVHL and RNA Pol II and a gene regulating the size of the tomato fruit and RAS oncogene. Office: Children's Hosp Rsch Found 3333 Burnet Ave Cincinnati OH 45229 Office Phone: 513-636-0270.

**MELLERT, LUCIE ANNE,** writer, photographer; b. Charleston, W.Va., June 6, 1932; d. Wilbur Conant and Grace Martin (Taylor) Frame; m. William Jennings Mellert, March 15, 1957; 1 child, James Floyd Kelly III. Student, Mason Coll. of Music Fine Arts, Charleston, 1937-49, W.Va. U., Morgantown, 1950-51. Pub. rels. exec., asst. treas., office mgr. J. H. Milam, Inc., Dunbar, W.Va., 1959-71; pub. rels. exec., office mgr. Hallcraft, Inc., Dunbar, 1972-74; office mgr. Kanawha Stone Co. Inc., Nitro, W.Va., 1975-78; freelance writer Dunbar, 1978—; freelance writer, photographer Charleston, W.Va., 1978—. Vol. photographer Charleston Gazette, 1997—. Beautification commr. City of Dunbar, 1969-72; activity coordinator, program dir. Dunbar Bicentennial Com., 1971; founder, coordinator Dunbar City wide Beautification and Improvement Com., 1969-72; coord. Kanawha Valley and Nat. Students Anti-Litter Program, Planting the Seed, 1996-2003; pres. United Meth. Women of St. Marks; active U. Charleston Builders, Friends of Avampato Discovery Mus., W.Va. Humanities Coun., Friends of W. Va. Culture and History; judge various cmty. events, 1995-2004; commr. Kanawha County Pks. and Recreation Commn., 2000—; vol. photographer Charleston Gazette On the Town, 1997-. Named Disting. Mountaineer, W.Va. Gov. Joe Manchin III, 2005; recipient West Virginian award, Gov. Cecil Underwood, 2000, Gov. Bob Wise, 2001, West Va. Vol. Spirit award, W. Va. Women's Commn., 2003, commendation for vol. svc., W.Va. Gov. Bob Wise, 2004. Mem. Nat. Mus. Women in the Arts, Nat. Fedn. Press Women, Pioneer Women's (past pres.), Libr. of Congress Assn., Kanawha Valley and Nat. Trust Hist. and Preservation Soc., East End Assn., Women of Moose, Woman's Club Charleston, W.Va. Soc.Assn. Execs., Mental Health Assn., Mid Atlantic Arts Found. Methodist. Avocations: church activities, piano, music, travel, art. Home: 1604 Virginia St E Charleston WV 25311-2114

**MELLETTE, JULIAN RAMSEY, JR.,** dermatologist, dermatologic surgeon; b. Florence, S.C., June 27, 1939; s. Julian Ramsey and Mary (Brown) Mellette; m. Elizabeth Odom, May 22, 1945; children: Elizabeth Ritland, Julian Ramsey III, Bradford. AB, Wofford Coll., 1961; MD, Med. U. S.C., 1969. Spl. agt. in charge Atlanta field office Mil. Intelligence, 1962—64; chief aerospace medicine Lyster Army Hosp., Fort Rucker, Ariz., 1971—73; chief dermatology Fitzsimmons Army Med. Ctr., Aurora, Colo., 1982—90; prof. dermatology U. Colo. Health Sci. Ctr., 1990—2003, Mohs fellowship dir., 1995—2003. Brig. gen. Joint Svc. Detachment, State of SC, 2003. Contbr. chapters to books, articles to profl. jours. Col. U.S. Army, 1961—90. Mem.: Colo. Dermatology Surg. Soc. (pres. 1989—), Internat. Soc. Dermatology Surgeons (bd. dirs. 1999—2001), Am. Coll. Mohs Surgery and Cutaneous Oncology (bd. dirs. 1993—96). Avocations: skiing, golf, scuba diving, flying. Office: Dept Dermatology PO Box 6510 Campus Stop F703 Aurora CO 80010-0510 Office Phone: 720-848-0510. E-mail: ramsey.mellette@uchsc.edu.

**MELLI, MARYGOLD SHIRE,** law educator; b. Rhinelander, Wis., Feb. 8, 1926; d. Osborne and May (Bonney) Shire; m. Joseph Alexander Melli, Apr. 8, 1950; children: Joseph, Sarah Bonnie, Sylvia Anne, James Alexander. BA, U. Wis., 1947, LLB, 1950. Bar: Wis. 1950. Dir. children's code revision Wis. Legis. Coun., Madison, 1950-53; exec. dir. Wis. Jud. Coun., Madison, 1955-59; asst. prof. law U. Wis., Madison, 1959-66, assoc. prof., 1966-67, prof., 1967-84, Voss-Bascom prof., 1985-93, emerita, 1993—. Assoc. dean U. Wis., 1970-72, rsch. affiliate Inst. for Rsch. on Poverty, 1980—; mem. spl. rev. bd. Dept. Health and Social Svcs., State of Wis., Madison, 1973—2002. Author: (pamphlet) The Legal Status of Women in Wisconsin, 1977, (book) Wisconsin Juvenile Court Practice, 1978, rev. edit., 1983, (with others) Child Support & Alimony, 1988, The Case for Transracial Adoption, 1994; co-editor: Child Support: The Next Frontier, 1999; contbr. articles to profl. jours. Bd. dirs. Am. Humane Assn., 1985-95, Frank Lloyd Wright - Wis., 2004; chair A Fund for Women, Madison, Wis., 2002, 2003. Named one of five Outstanding Young Women in Wis., Jaycees, 1961; rsch. grantee NSF, 1983; recipient Belle Case LaFollette award for outstanding svc. to the profession, 1994, award for Outstanding Contbn. to Advancement of Women in Higher Edn., 1991, award for Lifelong Contbn. to Advancement of Women in the Legal Prof., 1994, Rotary Sr. Svc. award, Madison, Wis., 2002. Fellow Am. Acad. Matrimonial Lawyers (exec. editor jour. 1985-90); mem. Am. Law Inst. (cons. project on law of family dissolution), Internat. Soc. Family Law (v.p. 1994-2000, 2002-05), Wis. State Bar Assn. (reporter family law sect.), Nat. Conf. Bar Examiners (chmn. bd. mgrs. 1989, editl. adv. com.). Democrat. Roman Catholic. Avocations: walking, swimming, collecting art. Home: 2904 Waunona Way Madison WI 53713-2238 Office: U Wis Law Sch Madison WI 53706 Office Phone: 608-262-1610. Business E-Mail: msmelli@wisc.edu.

**MELLINKOFF, SHERMAN MUSSOFF,** medical educator; b. McKeesport, Pa., Mar. 23, 1920; s. Albert and Helen Mussoff Mellinkoff; m. June Bernice O'Connell, Nov. 18, 1944; children: Sherrill, Albert. BA, Stanford U., 1941, MD, 1944; LHD (hon.), Wake Forest U., 1984, Hebrew Union Coll., L.A., 1988. Diplomate Am. Bd. Internal Medicine, Am. Bd. Gastroenterology, Am. Bd. Nutrition. Intern asst. resident Stanford U. Hosp., San Francisco, 1944—45; asst. resident Johns Hopkins Hosp., Balt., 1947—49, chief resident, 1950—51; instr. in medicine, 1951—53; fellow in gastroenterology Hosp. of U. Pa., Phila., 1949—50; from asst. prof. to prof. medicine UCLA Sch. of Medicine, L.A., 1962—86; dean UCLA Sch. Medicine, L.A., 1962—86, emeritus prof. of medicine, 1990—; disting. physician of VA Wadsworth VA Med. Ctr., L.A., 1990-93. Mem. sci. adv. panel Rsch. to Prevent Blindness, Inc., N.Y.C., 1975—93; mem. program devel. com. Nat. Med. Fellowships, Inc., N.Y.C., 1984—. Editl. bd.: The Pharos, 1986; contbr. articles to profl. jours. Apptd. by Gov. of Calif. to McCone Com., 1965. Capt. U.S. Army, 1945—57. Recipient Abraham Flexner award, Assn. Am. Med. Colls., 1981, J.E. Wallace Sterling Disting. Alumnus award, Stanford U. Sch. of Medicine, 1987. Master: ACP; fellow: Royal Coll. of Physicians; mem.: The Johns Hopkins Soc. of Scholars, Am. Acad. of Arts and Scis., Inst. of Medicine of NAS, Assn. Am. Physicians, Am. Gastroenterol. Assn. Assn. Avocations: reading, hiking. Office: UCLA Dept Medicine 44 138 Chs Los Angeles CA 90095 0001

**MELLINS, CLAUDE ANN,** psychologist; BA in Psychology, Brown U., 1982; MS in Clin. Psychology, U. So. Calif., L.A., 1987; PhD in Clin. Psychology, U. So. Calif., 1990. Assoc. prof. clin. psychology HIV Ctr.; co-dir. and dir. rsch. Spl. Needs Clinic Children & Families Columbia Presbyn., N.Y.C., NY, 1992—; assoc. prof. clin. psychology dept. psychiatry and sociomed. scis. N.Y. State Psychiat. Inst. and Columbia U., N.Y.C., 1994—. Neurodevel. supr. Women and Children's Care Ctr., Presbyn. Hosp.; mem. sci. adv. group Pediat. HIV AIDS Cohorts Study. Contbr. chpts. to books and articles to profl. jours. Aaron Diamond Found. fellow. Mem. APA (pediat. psychology subdivsn.).

**MELLINS, HARRY ZACHARY,** radiologist, educator; b. N.Y.C., May 23, 1921; s. David J. and Ray (Hoffman) M.; m. Judith Alice Weiss, Dec. 26, 1950; children: Elizabeth, William, Thomas. AB, Columbia Coll., 1941; MD, L.I. Coll. Medicine, 1944; MS in Radiology, U. Minn., 1951; AM (hon.), Harvard U., 1970. Intern Jewish Hosp., Bklyn., 1944-45, asst. resident in radiology, 1945-46; resident in radiology U. Minn., Mpls., 1948-50, instr. radiology, 1950-52, asst. prof., 1952-53; clin. asst. prof. radiology Wayne State U., Detroit, 1953-56; dir. radiology Sinai Hosp., Detroit, 1953-56; prof., chmn. dept. radiology SUNY, Coll. Medicine, N.Y.C., 1956-69; chief radiology Kings County Hosp. Center, Bklyn., 1956-69; radiologist-in-chief State Univ. Hosp., Bklyn., 1966-69; prof. radiology Harvard Med. Sch., Boston, 1969—87, prof. radiology emeritus, 1991—; dir. diagnostic radiology Peter Bent Brigham Hosp., 1969-79, Brigham and Women's Hosp., 1980-87, dir. edn. and tng., dept. radiology, 1987-94; co-dir. edn. and tng. dept. radiology, 1994-97; chief of radiology Harvard U. Health Svc., 1988-97; radiologist Brigham and Women's Hosp., 1998-99. Nat. cons. in radiology to surgeon gen. U.S. Air Force, 1968-79; mem. radiation study sect. NIH, 1967-71; mem. subcom. for written exam. in diagnostic radiology Am. Bd. Radiology, 1970-75; mem. radiology tng. com. research tng. grants br. Nat. Inst. Gen. Med. Scis.; mem. diagnostic research adv. group div. cancer biology and diagnosis Nat. Cancer Inst., 1975-79; guest examiner Am. Bd. Radiology. Served to capt. M.C. USAAF, 1946-48. Mem. Bklyn. Radiol. Soc. (pres. 1965-66), N.Y. Roentgen Soc. (pres 1966-67), Assn. Univ. Radiologists

**MELLINS, ROBERT B.,** pediatrician, educator; b. NYC, Mar. 6, 1928; s. David J. and Ray H. (Hoffman) M.; m. Sue Mendelsohn, Apr. 19, 1959; children: Claude Ann, David Rustin. AB, Columbia U., 1948; MD, Johns Hopkins U., 1952. Intern Johns Hopkins Hosp.—1952—53; mem. epidemic intelligence svc, founder poison control program Ctr. Disease Control, Chgo., 1953—55; resident in pediat. N.Y. Hosp., 1955—56, Presbyn. Hosp., N.Y., 1956—57, dir. pediat. ICU, 1970—75; assoc. prof. pediat. Columbia U., N.Y.C., 1970—75, prof. pediat., 1975—, dir. Cystic Fibrosis Ctr., 1976—91, dir. pediat. pulmonary divsn., 1972—97. Christmas Seal prof. Can. Lung Assn., 1979-80; 1st Deans Disting. lectr. in clin. scis. Columbia U. Coll. P&S, 1982; mem. Am. Bd. Pediat., founding mem. sub-bd. on pediat. pulmonology; bd. dirs. A.P. Gold Fedn. to promote humanism in medicine. Mem. editl. bd. Am. Rev. Respiratory Diseases, 1974-81, assoc. editor, 1984-90; contbr. articles to profl. jours. V.p. Am. Lung Assn., 1987—89; chmn. steering com. multi-ctr. study heart and lung complications of HIV infection in children NIH, 1989—2003; bd. dir. Am. Lung Assn., 1981—83, LA Jonas Found., 1970—78, 1990—, Symphony of UN, 1990—; bd. dirs. Am. Lung Assn. City of N.Y., 2001—05. Recipient Career Devel. award NIH, 1966-71, Career Scientist award Health Rsch. Coun. NYC Health Rsch. Coun., 1975, Stevens Triennial Rsch. award Columbia U., 1980, Health Edn. Rsch. award Nat. Asthma Edn. Program, 1992, Will Ross medal Am. Lung Assn., 1996, 2001, Life & Breath award Am. Lung Assn. NY, Outstanding Alumnus award Babies Hosp., Columbus, 2006. Mem.: Am. Acad. Allergy and Immunology, Soc. Critical Care Medicine, Am. Thoracic Soc. (bd. dir. 1975, 1981—84, nat. pres. 1982—83, v.p., Disting. Achievement award 1996), Am. Acad. Pediat. (Med. Edn. Lay Edn. award 1995, Kendig award 2003), Am. Soc. Pharmacology and Exptl. Therapeutics, Am. Physiol. Soc., Soc. Pediat. Rsch., Am. Pediat. Soc., Fleischner Soc. (pres. 1995—), Gold Humanism Honor Soc., Alpha Omega Alpha. Office: Childrens Hosp NY-Presbyn 3959 Broadway CHC 746 New York NY 10032 Home: 22 W 66th St Apt 5 New York NY 10023-6207 Office Phone: 212-305-8430. Business E-Mail: rbm3@columbia.edu.

**MELLITS, MARC ANDREW,** composer; b. Balt., Mar. 29, 1966; s. Edwin David and Janet Gloria Mellits; m. Cristina Miruna Buciu, Apr. 25, 1999; children: Nina Ileana children: Mara Rose. MusB, Eastman Sch. Music, 1988; MusM, Yale U., 1991; MusD, Cornell U., 1996. Bd. dirs. Music Journeys, Inc., Fayetteville, NY. Composer: Piano Concerto, 1984, Intervals, 1985, Piano Quartet, 1985, Duo for Alto Flute & Cello, 1986, String Quartet, 1986, 10 Pieces for Piano Solo, 1987, Road Trip, 1987, Whales Save Us, 1988, Insect Heads, 1988, Dark Age Machinery, 1988, Hooley Fooley, 1989, Music for 22 Strings, 1989, Fanfare, 1990, Bucket, 1991, Aggravated Assault, 1991, O, 1991, 11 Pieces for Flute and Piano, 1992, Trio, 1993, Aro, 1993, Polysorbate 60, 1994, Merge Left, 1994, Piccolo Concerto, 1995, Spam, 1995, Blue, 1996, 11 Miniatures for Baroque Ensemble, 1996, Large Man Looms, 1996, Five Chanukah Etudes for the Frascas, 1996, Fruit Loops, 1997, Spank Me, 1997, Jaana, 1997, Fruity Pebbles, 1997, Spin, 1998, Edible Vinyl, 1998, Parking Violation, 1999, 8 Etudes for 2 Guitars, 1999, Phase, Inc., 1999, Zoot Suit Riot, 1999, 5 Machines, 2000, Two Pieces for Flute & Guitar, 2000, Canonada, 2001, Machine V, 2001, Machine III, 2001, Dreadlocked, 2001, Troica, 2001, Opening, 2001, Machine IV, 2001, Lefty's Elegy, 2001, The Misadventures of Soup, 2001, Paranoid Cheese, 2001, Broken Glass, 2001, Zrenden Rodendan, Marija!, 2001, Groove Canon, 2002, M/W, 2002, Haiku, 2003, Season's Songs, 2003, Disciples of Gouda, 2003, Platter of Discontent, 2004, Agu, 2004, String Quartet No. 2, 2004, Tight Sweater, 2005, Gonzalo Speaks, 2005, Brick, 2005, 5 Quiet Machines, 2006, Farfalle Cotte, 2006. Recipient Bernard Rogers Best Composer prize, Eastman Sch. Music, 1987, John Day Jackson prize, Yale U., 1990, award, Found. for Contemporary Performance Arts, 2005; fellow, Cornell U., 1991—95, Tanglewood, 1997; George Eastman scholarship, Eastman Sch. Music, 1984—88. Mem.: Soc. New Music (v.p. 2005—), Common Sense Composers Collective, ASCAP (Young Composers award 1994, 1996).

**MELLMAN, LEONARD,** real estate developer, consultant; b. Mar. 23, 1924; s. Morris and Luba (Levin) Mellman. BA, Temple U., 1949. Prin., owner L. Mellman Co., Phila., 1949-84, Mellman Investments, Phila., 1960—; ptnr. Mellman, Blume Co., Phila., 1979—, Cunniff, Mellman Co., Phila., 1982—. Gen. ptnr. Diamond Acres, Phila., 1981—86, Van Pelt Ct. Ltd., pres., 1985—91, MLC Bd. Settlement Music Sch., Phila., 1985—91, sec. ctrl. bd., 1985—91, v.p. ctrl. bd., 1997—; bd. visitors Temple U. Coll. Liberal Arts, 2004—. Bd. dirs. Art Growth 2000, 1988—; pres. arts and sci. alumni bd. Temple U., Phila., 1976—78, bd. visitors Coll. Liberal Arts, 2004—. With U.S. Army, 1943—46. Mem.: Phila. Bd. Realtors, Credit Mchts. Assn. (pres. 1970—72, Man of the Yr. award 1970), Opera Vols. Internat. (treas. 1999—2003), Union League Phila. (chair, trustee Scholarship Found.), Phila. Vols. Internat., Phila. Opera Guild (bd. dirs. 1995—, pres. 1997—99, chmn. bd. dirs. 1999—2003, hon. chmn. 2003—), Singing City Choir (bd. dirs., pres. 1988—90), Temple U. Gen. Alumni Assn. (pres. 1992—94, Disting. Alumni award 1985). Democrat. Jewish. Home and Office: 220 W Rittenhouse Sq Apt 22C Philadelphia PA 19103 Personal E-mail: mellmanl@aol.com.

**MELLO, CRAIG C.,** molecular medicine educator, researcher; b. 1960; BS in Biochemistry, Brown U., 1982; PhD in Biology, Harvard U., 1990. Postdoctoral rsch. fellow Fred Hutchinson Cancer Rsch. Ctr.; investigator Howard Hughest Med. Inst., 2000—; with U. Mass. Med. Sch., Worcester, Mass., 1994—, Blais U. chair in molecular medicine, 2003—, prof. in the program in molecular medicine. Contbr. articles to profl. journals. Co-recipient Nobel Prize in Physiology or Medicine, Nobel Found., 2006; recipient Lewis S. Rosenstiel award for Disting. Work in Basic Med. Sci., Massry prize, Wiley Prize in Biomedical Sciences, 2003, Gairdner award, Gairdner Found., 2005, Dr. Paul Janssen award for Biomedical Rsch., Johnson & Johnson, 2006, Paul Ehrlich and Ludwig Darmstaedter prize, 2006; Pew scholar, U. Calif., San Francisco, 1995. Mem.: NAS (award in molecular biology 2003). Office: Univ Mass Med Sch Biotech Two Ste 219 373 Plantation St Worcester MA 01605 also: Howard Hughes Inst Medicine 4000 Jones Bridge Rd Chevy Chase MD 20815-6789 Office Phone: 508-856-1602, 301-215-8500. Office Fax: 508-856-2950. Business E-Mail: craig.mello@umassmed.edu.*

**MELLO, DAWN,** retail executive; b. Lynn, Mass. Student, Modern Sch. Fashion and Design, Boston. Model; asst. to fashion dir. B. Altman & Co., N.Y.C., fashion dir., 1971—75; from corp. buying officer to v.p. and gen. merchandise mgr. May Dept. Stores Co.; v.p., fashion dir. to exec. v.p., dir. fashion merchandising Bergdorf Goodman, N.Y.C., 1975—84, pres., 1984—89, 1991—99; creative dir. Gucci, 1989—94; cons. Dawn Mello and Assocs., N.Y.C., 1999—. Office: Dawn Mello and Assocs Inc 12 W 57th St # 802 New York NY 10019

**MELLOAN, GEORGE RICHARD,** editor; b. Greenwood, Ind., Nov. 10, 1927; s. James and Sara Ollie (Merideth) M.; m. Joan Minner, July 1, 1951; children: James, Melissa, Maryanne. BS, Butler U., 1950. Reporter Logansport (Ind.) Press, 1950, Muncie (Ind.) Press, 1951, Wall Street Jour., Chgo. and Detroit, 1951-56, bur. mgr. Cleve. and Atlanta, 1959-61, page one writer N.Y.C., 1961-66, fgn. correspondent London, 1966-70, editl. writer N.Y.C., 1970—, dep. editor, internat., 1973—, op-ed columnist, 1987—. Co-author: The Carter Economy, 1978. Sgt. U.S. Army, 1946-47. Recipient Gerald Loeb award G&R Loeb Found., 1981, Daily Gleaner awards Inter-Am. Press Assn., 1983, 87. Mem. Coun. on Fgn. Rels., Dutch Treat Club, Echo Lake Country Club. Avocations: travel, golf, hiking, photography. Office: Wall Street Jour 200 Liberty St New York NY 10281-1003

**MELLON, MARY REGINA,** librarian; b. Pitts., Sept. 8, 1915; d. Frank and Myrtle (Lewis) Brown; m. Byron Joseph Mellon, Sept. 7, 1936 (dec. July 1970); children: Richard, Terry, Claudia Vidano, James, Byron, Leo, William, Robert. BA with highest distinction, Ind. U. NW., 1976. Libr. St. Bridget Elem. Sch., Hobart, Ind., 1963—70, St. Bridget Parish, Hobart, 1973—85. Libr. aide modern lang. dept. Ind. U., Gary, 1967; VISTA vol. Action, Indpls., 1977—80; dir. Caring Place, Inc., Hobart, 1978—80. Mediator Better Bus. Bur., Merrillville, Ind., 1977—99; allocation vol. Lake Area United Way, Griffith, Ind., 1989—2004, Vision Coun. mem., 2002—04; bd. dirs. Hobart Twp. Lake Ridge Cmty. Svcs., 1980—98. Named Hobart's Most Valuable

Woman, Trade Winds Rehab., Gary, 1980, honoree, Coalition for Internat. Women's Day, East Chicago, Ind., 1983; recipient Angel award, Southlake Ctr. for Mental Health, Merrillville, 1981. Home: 10 N Washington St Hobart IN 46342

**MELLON, SEWARD PROSSER,** brokerage house executive; b. Chgo., July 28, 1942; s. Richard King and Constance Mary (Prosser) Mellon Burrell; m. Karen Leigh Boyd, Sept. 10, 1966 (div. 1974); children— Catharine Leigh, Constance Elizabeth; m. Sandra Springer Stout, 1975. Grad., Choate Sch., 1960; BA, Susquehanna U., 1965, DH, 1993. With Mellon Nat. Corp., Pitts., 1965-69; with T. Mellon & Sons, Pitts., 1969-71; pres. Richard K. Mellon & Sons, Ligonier, 1971—. Bd. dirs. Mellon Bank N.A., Mellon Fin. Corp. Trustee Richard King Mellon Family Found.; trustee, pres. Richard King Mellon Found.; chmn. real estate com., chmn. bd. mem. fin. and exec. com. Valley Sch. Ligonier. Mem. Western Pa. Conservancy (life), Loyal-Hanna Assn. (pres.), Vintage Club (Palm Springs, Calif.), Duquesne Club (Pitts.), Laurel Valley Golf Club (Ligonier), Rolling Rock Club, Rolling Rock Hunt, Phi Mu Delta. Republican. Home: Huntland Downs Box K Ligonier PA 15658 Office: PO Box Rkm Ligonier PA 15658-0780 Office Phone: 724-238-6671.

**MELLON, TIMOTHY,** transportation executive; s. Paul Mellon (dec.). B., Yale Univ, 1964, M., 1966. CEO, chmn. bd. dirs. Guilford Transp. Industries, North Billerica, Mass. Trustee Andrew W. Mellon Found. Office: Guilford Transp Industries High St Iron Horse Pk North Billerica MA 01862 also: Guilford Transp Industries Pease Internatl Tradeport 14 Aviation Ave Portsmouth NH 03801

**MELLOR, CHIP (WILLIAM H. MELLOR),** lawyer; Grad., Ohio State U., 1973; JD, U. Denver, 1977. Public interest lawyer Mountain States Legal Found., 1979—83; pres. Pacific Research Institute for Public Policy, 1986—91; pres., gen. counsel, founder Inst. for Justice, 1991—. Office: Institute For Justice 901 N Glebe Rd Ste 900 Arlington VA 22203-1854 E-mail: wmellor@ij.org.

**MELLOR, J. P.,** education educator; b. Tex., Mar. 15, 1965; s. Richard and Dorothy Mellor; m. Kathryn Mellor, Sept. 3, 1988; children: Phillip, Patrick. BSEE, US Naval Acad., Annapolis, Md., 1987; BS Nuc. Tech., U. State N.Y., Albany, N.Y., 1990; SM, M.I.T., Cambridge, Mass., 1995, PhD, 1999. Cert. chief engr. naval nuc. propulsion plants, Naval Reactors, 1992; registered operator naval nuc. propulsion plants Naval Reactors, 1989. Instr. Naval Nuc. Power Tng. Unit, Ballston Spa, NY, 1989—90; instr. and custom software developer Gt. Ea. Tech., Woburn, Mass., 1996—99; sys. adminstr. Zoesis Studios, Newton, Mass., 1997—99; asst. prof. computer sci. and software engring. Rose-Hulman Inst. Tech., Terre Haute, Ind., 1999—2005, assoc. prof. computer sci. and software engring., 2005—; innovation fellow Rose-Hulman Ventures, Terre Haute, Ind., 2001—. Expert witness Kirkland and Ellis Law Firm, Chicago, Ill., 2000—01; dir. imaging systems lab Rose-Hulman Inst. of Tech., Terre Haute, Ind., 2002—. Trustee Meml. United Meth. Ch., Terre Haute, Ind., 2000—02; pipe sargent Pipes and Drums of the Fountain Trust, Covington, Ind., 2002—; scout leader Cub Scouts of Am., Terre Haute, Ind. Lt. USN, 1983—93, Various. Decorated Navy Achievement Medal Sec. of the Navy, Comdr. in Chief, Pacific Fleet; recipient Morris Joseph Levin Meml. Best Thesis Award, M.I.T. E.E.C.S. Dept., 1995, Excellence in Tng., Naval Nuc. Power Tng. Unit, 1989, Capt Boyd Alexander Award for Elec. Engring., US Naval Acad., 1987, EASCON Student of the Yr., I.E.E.E., 1986; fellow Trident Scholar, US Naval Acad., 1986, 1987; grantee Advanced Biometrics, Dept. of Justic, 2005, Hands-on Computer Vision, Sony, 2002. Mem.: ACM, IEEE, Wabash Valley Scottish Soc., Phi Kappa Phi, Tau Beta Pi, Sigma Xi. Achievements include patents for Sys. and Method for Transforming Graphical Images. Avocations: piping, soccer, music, reading. Office: Rose-Hulman Inst of Tech 5500 Wabash Ave Terre Haute IN 47803 Office Phone: 812-877-8085. Office Fax: 812-872-6060. Business E-Mail: jpmellor@rose-hulman.edu.

**MELLOR, JAMES ROBB,** electronics executive; b. Detroit, May 3, 1930; s. Clifford and Gladys (Robb) Mellor; m. Suzanne Stykos, June 8, 1953; children: James Robb, Diane Elyse, Deborah Lynn. BS in Elec. Engring. and Math., U. Mich., 1952, MS, 1953. Tech. staff Hughes Aircraft Co., Fullerton, Calif., 1955—58; pres. data systems divsn. Litton Industries, Van Nuys, Calif., 1958; exec. v.p. Litton Industries, Inc., Beverly Hills, Calif.; pres., COO AM Internat., Inc., L.A., 1981; exec. v.p. dir. Gen. Dynamics Corp., Falls Church, Va., 1981—90, pres., 1990—, COO, 1990—93, CEO, 1993—97, chmn., 1994—97, USEC, Inc., 1998—, interim pres., CEO, 2004—05; dir. AmerisourceBergen, 2001—06, chmn. bd., 2004—06. Bd. dirs. Bergen Brunswig Corp., Kerr, Computer Scis. Corp., Pinkerton, U.S. Surg. Inc. Contbr. articles to profl. jours. Mem. nat. advisory com. U. Mich.; mem. US-Egypt Pres. Coun. 1st lt. Signal Corps U.S. Army, 1953—55. Recipient Officer of the Order of the Crown, his Majesty King Baudouin of Belgium, 1987. Mem.: IEEE, Computer and Bus. Equipment Mfrs. Assn. (past chmn.), Armed Forces Comm. and Electronics Assn. (bd. dirs.), Am. Mgmt. Assn., Burning Tree Club, Congl. Country Club, Eldorado Club, L.A. Country Club, Calif. Club, Phi Beta Kappa, Eta Kappa Nu, Tau Beta Pi, Sigma Xi. Achievements include patents for storage tubes and display systems. Office: USEC 6903 Rocklegde Dr Bethesda MD 20817 Office Phone: 301-564-3200.*

**MELLOR, JOHN WILLIAMS,** economist, consultant; b. Paris, Dec. 28, 1928; came to U.S., 1929; s. Desmond W. and Katherine (Beardsley) M.; m. Arlene Patton, June 15, 1950 (div. Sept. 1972); children: Michael, Brian, Mark (dec.); m. Uma Lele, Feb. 17, 1973 (div. Apr. 1992); m. Zarmina Said, Oct. 16, 1997. BS, Cornell U., 1950, MS, 1951, PhD, 1954; Diploma, Oxford U., 1952. Prof. Cornell U., Ithaca, NY, 1953—75; chief economist USAID, Washington, 1975—77; dir. Internat. Food Policy Rsch. Inst., Washington, 1977—91; pres. John W. Mellor Assocs., Inc., Washington, 1991—98; v.p. Abt Assocs., Inc., Washington, 1998—. Mem. bd. on agrl. NAS, 1989-92; mem. Agrl. Credit Commn., Res. Bank India, 1986-88. Author: Economics of Agricultural Development, 1966 (Am. Agrl. Econs. award 1968), Accelerating Food Production Growth in Sub-Saharan Africa, 1987, Agricultural Price Policy for Developing Countries, 1988 (hon. mention Am. Agrl. Econs. Assn. 1989); Agriculture on the Road to Industrialization, 1992. Mem. Internat. Common. on Food and Peace, 1988—. Recipient Wihuri Internat. prize Wihuri Found., Helsinki, 1985, Presdl. End Hunger award The White House, 1987, Outstanding Alumni award Cornell U., 1987. Fellow AAAS, Am. Acad. Arts and Scis., Am. Agrl. Econs. Assn. (Best Pub. Rsch. award 1967). Avocations: sailing, walking. Office: John Mellor Assocs Inc Ste PH18 801 Pennsylvania Ave NW Washington DC 20004-2668 Office Phone: 202-347-8802. Personal E-Mail: puanaturally@aol.com. Business E-Mail: john_mellor@abtassoc.com.

**MELLOR, KATHY,** National Teacher of the Year 2004, ESL educator; b. Providence; BS in Elem. Edn., RI Coll., 1970, MEd, 1977; MA in Teaching with ESL and Cross Cultural studies, Brown U., 1989. Substitute tchr. Cranston, RI Sch. Dept., 1970—74; ESL tchr. Internat. Inst. RI, 1980—85; continuing edn. tchr., english dept RI Coll., 1985—86; coros. for ESL North Kingstown Sch. Dept., RI, 1985; ESL tchr. Hamilton Elem. Sch., North Kingstown, RI, Davisville Mid. Sch., North Kingstown, RI, 1985—. Nat. and internat. spokesperson for education, 2004—. Named Nat. Teacher of Yr., Coun. of Chief State Sch. Officers, 2004. Achievements include redesigning her school's ESL program, which provides each student with one to three periods per day in classes for English learners. The amount of instruction given depends on their skill level; providing help to students and their families by forming a local parents group called the "Ladybugs" for speakers of other languages. This improved their ability to help their children; has instructed students from virtually every part of the globe (Laos, Korea, Bolivia, Brazil, Puerto Rico, the Philippines and the Dominican Republic); hosts an International Picnic where her students and their families gather to celebrate their achievements during the school year. Office: Davisville Mid Sch 200 School St North Kingstown RI 02852 Office Phone: 401-541-6300.

**MELLOR, ROBERT E.,** building materials company executive, lawyer; b. 1943; BA, Westminster Coll., 1965; JD, So. Meth. U., 1968. Atty. legal dept. Union Oil Co. of Calif., 1968-73; atty. U.S. Leasing Internat. Inc., 1973-75; v.p. dir. Alexander & Bolton Inc., 1975-76; with Di Giorgio Corp., San Francisco, 1976-79, v.p., 1979-80, v.p., gen. counsel, 1980-81, v.p., sec., gen. counsel, 1981-87, sr. v.p., gen. counsel, sec., 1987, chief adminstrv. officer, exec. v.p., gen. counsel, sec.; counsel Gibson, Dunn & Crutcher, San Francisco, 1990—97; pres., CEO Building Materials Holding Co., 1997—, chmn., 2002—. Bd. dir. Coeur d'Alene Mines Corp., The Ryland Group, Inc., Monroe Muffler Brake, Inc. Office: c/o BMHC 4 Embarcadero Center San Francisco CA 94111*

**MELLOR, RONALD JOHN,** history professor; b. Bklyn., Sept. 30, 1940; s. Ronald Green and Eleanor Teresa (Walsh) M.; m. Anne Tidaback Kostelanetz, June 7, 1969; 1 child, Ronald Blake. AB, Fordham Coll., 1962; cert., U. Louvain, Belgium, 1961; AM, Princeton U., 1964, PhD in Classics, 1968. Asst. prof. Classics Stanford (Calif.) U., 1965-75; assoc. prof. history UCLA, 1976-82, prof. history, 1982—. Vice-chmn. history UCLA, 1985-86, 1991-92, 1998-99, chmn. history, 1992-97; visitor Princeton Inst. Advanced Studies, 1997-98. Author: Thea Rhome, 1975, Tacitus, 1993, Tacitus and the Classical Tradition, 1995, The Roman Historians, 1999, The Ancient Roman World, 2004, The World in Ancient Times: Primary Sources and Reference Volume, 2005; editor: From Augustus to Nero: The First Dynasty of Imperial Rome, 1990, The Historians of Ancient Rome, 2d edit., 2004, Text and Tradition: Studies in Greek History and Historiography in Honor of Mortimer Chambers, 1999, Augustus and the Creation of the Roman Empire, 2005. Fellow NEH, 1969, Am. Coun. Learned Socs., 1972, Humanities Rsch. Ctr. Australian Nat. U., Canberra, Australia, 1990; hon. fellow U. Coll. London, Eng., 1969, 72, 83-85. Mem. Am. Hist. Assn., Am. Philol. Assn., Assn. Ancient Historians, Soc. for the Promotion of Roman Studies. Democrat. Avocations: opera, travel, theater, tennis. Home: 2620 Mandeville Canyon Rd Los Angeles CA 90049-1004 Office: UCLA Dept History 405 Hilgard Ave Los Angeles CA 90095-1473 E-mail: mellor@history.ucla.edu.

**MELLORS, ROBERT CHARLES,** physician, scientist, educator; b. Dayton, Ohio, 1916; s. Bert S. and Clementine (Steinmetz) Mellors; m. Jane K. Winternitz, Mar. 25, 1944; children: Alice J., Robert C., William K., John W. PhD, Western Res. U., 1940; MD, Johns Hopkins, 1944. Diplomate Am. Bd. Pathology. Intern Nat. Naval Med. Ctr., Bethesda, Md., 1944-45; rsch. fellow medicine Meml. Ctr. Cancer and Allied Diseases, NYC, 1946-50, rsch. fellow pathology, 1950-53, asst. attending pathologist, 1953-57, assoc. attending pathologist, 1957-58. Sr. fellow Am. Cancer Soc., 1947-50; sr. clin. rsch. fellow Damon Runyon Meml. Fund, 1950-53; asst. attending pathologist Meml. Hosp., N.Y.C., 1953-57, assoc. attending pathologist, 1957-58; asst. attending pathologist Ewing Hosp., N.Y.C., 1953-57, assoc. attending pathologist, 1957-58; instr. biochemistry Western Res. U., 1940-42; rsch. assoc. Poliomyelitis Rsch. Ctr. and Dept. Epidemiology Johns Hopkins U. Sch. Hygiene, 1942-44; asst. prof. biology Meml. Ctr. Cancer and Allied Diseases, N.Y.C., 1952-53; asst. prof. pathology Sloan Kettering div. Cornell U., 1953-57, assoc. prof., 1957-58; prof. pathology Cornell U. Med. Coll., 1961-90, prof. emeritus, 1990—; adj. prof. pathology N.Y. Med. Coll., 1997—; assoc. attending pathologist N.Y. Hosp., 1961-72, attending pathologist, 1972-86; pathologist-in-chief, dir. labs., 1958-84, emeritus, 1984-85, hon. staff, 1986—; assoc. dir. rsch. Hosp. for Spl. Surgery, N.Y.C., 1958-69, dir. rsch., 1969-84, emeritus, 1984-85, scientist emeritus, 1986—; mem. rsch. adv. com. NIH, 1962-66; adv. com. Nat. Inst. Environ. Health Sci., 1966-69; com. nomenclature and classification of disease Coll. Am. Pathologists, 1960-64. Author: Analytical Cytology, 1955, 2d edit., 1959, Analytical Pathology, 1957, also 5 med. sch. tchg. documents online. Mem. Conservation Bd., Town of North Castle, Westchester, NY. Served as lt. (j.g.), M.C. USNR, 1944-46. Recipient Kappa Delta award Am. Acad. of Orthopedic Surgeons, 1962 Fellow Royal Coll. Pathologists, Molecular Medicine Soc., Am. Soc. Clin. Pathology; mem. Internat. Soc. for Optical Engring., Am. Assn. Pathologists, Am. Assn. Immunologists, Am. Soc. Biochemistry and Molecular Biology, Am. Coll. Rheumatology, Am. Orthopedic Assn. (hon.), Phi Beta Kappa. Home: 3 Hardscrabble Cir Armonk NY 10504-2222 Personal E-mail: rmellors@optonline.net.

**MELLO-THOMS, CLAUDIA,** medical educator, researcher; d. Jose Souto de Mello and Maria Gilvanete Barros de Mello; m. Renny Thoms, Oct. 19, 1996. BSc, U. Fed. de Pernambuco, Recife, 1988; MSEE, U. Fed. do Rio de Janeiro, 1991; PhD, Rutgers U., New Brunswick, 2001. U. Medicine and Dentistry of NJ. Rsch. asst. U. Pa., Phila., 1997—2001; rsch. asst. prof. U. Pitts., 2001—. Cons. Network of Advisors, NYC, 2005—. Author: (short stories) Lavraluz; contbr. articles to profl. jours. Recipient Best Clin. Sci. Paper award, 2003; grantee NIH/Nat. Cancer Inst., 2004—: Med. Image Perception Soc. Buddhist. Achievements include research in determining that radiologists do not make decisions to report or dismiss perceived findings based only on the finding itself, but in comparing the finding with the background; demonstrating that the way a radiologist samples the background offers a good indication about whether they will read the case correctly. Avocations: reading, gardening, cats, hiking, movies. Office: U Pitts 300 Halket St Ste 4200 Pittsburgh PA 15213 Office Phone: 412-641-2570. E-mail: cmellothoms@magee.edu.

**MELLOTT, JOHN,** publishing executive; Grad., Case Western Reserve U. CPA. Controller Atlanta Journal-Constitution, 1987—91, v.p. & gen. mgr., 1992—2000, pub., 2004—; treas. Cox Enterprises, 1991—92, v.p. bus. devel. & planning, 2000—02; pres. Dent Wizard Internat., 2002—04. Office: Atlanta Journal-Constitution 72 Marietta St NW Atlanta GA 30303*

**MELLOY, MICHAEL J.,** federal judge; b. Dubuque, IA, 1948; m. Jane Anne Melloy; children: Jennifer, Katherine, Bridget. BA, Loras Coll., 1970; JD, U. Iowa, 1974. With O'Conner & Thomas P.C. (formerly O'Conner, Thomas, Wright, Hammer, Bertsch & Norby, Dubuque, Iowa, 1974-86; judge U.S. Bankruptcy Ct. (no. dist.) Iowa, 1986-92, U.S. Dist. Ct. (no. dist.) Iowa, Cedar Rapids, 1992—2002; chief judge, 1992—99; judge U.S. Ct. Appeals (8th Cir.), 2002—. With U.S. Army, 1970-72, USAR, 1972-76. Mem. ABA, Comml. Law League Am., Nat. Conf. Bankruptcy Judges, Eighth Cir. Judicial Coun. (bankruptcy judge rep., bankruptcy com.), Iowa State Bar Assn. (coun. mem. bankruptcy and comml. law sect.), Ill. State Bar Assn., Dubuque County Bar Assn., 8th Jud. Dist. Assn., Mason L. Ladd Inn of Ct., Rotary. Address: 625 1st St SE #200 Cedar Rapids IA 52401-2032*

**MELLUM, GALE ROBERT,** lawyer; b. Duluth, Minn., July 5, 1942; s. Lester Andrew and Doris Esther (Smith) M.; m. Julie Murdoch Swanstrom, July 23, 1966; children: Eric Scott, Wendy Jane. BA summa cum laude, U. Minn., 1964, JD magna cum laude, 1968. Bar: Minn. 1968. Assoc. Faegre & Benson, Mpls., 1968-75, ptnr., 1976—, mem. mgmt. com., 1986-98. Mem. planning com. Garret Corp. and Securities Law Inst., Northwestern U. Law Sch., 1984—; bd. dirs.-mem. adv. bd. Quali Tech Inc., Chaska, Minn., 1985-98; corp. sec. Excelsior-Henderson Motorcycle Mfg. Co., Belle Plaine, Minn., 1997-2000. Hockey chmn. LARC Bd., Mpls., 1980—85. Mem. ABA (fed. securities regulation com.), Minn. Bar Assn., Hennepin County Bar Assn. Republican. United Ch. Of Christ. Avocations: tennis, golf, snow and water skiing, handball, boating. Home: 3833 Thomas Ave S Minneapolis MN 55410 Office: Faegre & Benson 2200 Wells Fargo Ctr 90 S 7th St Ste 2200 Minneapolis MN 55402-3901 Office Phone: 612-766-7317. E-mail: gmellum@faegre.com.

**MELMER, RICK,** school system administrator; BA, Dakota Wesleyan U.; MA, SD State U.; EdD, U. Wyo. Supt. schs. Sioux Ctr. Cmty. Sch. Dist., Iowa, 1991—95, Watertown (SD) Sch. Dist., 1995—2003; sec. edn. SD Dept. Edn., Pierre, 2003—. Office: SD Dept Edn 700 Governors Dr Pierre SD 57501*

**MELNICK, ALICE JEAN (AJ MELNICK),** counselor; b. St. Louis, Dec. 25, 1931; d. Nathan and Henrietta (Hausfater) Fisher; m. Harold Melnick, May 24, 1953; children: Susan, Vikki, Patrice. BJ, U. Tex., Austin, 1952;

MEd, U. North Tex., Denton, 1974. Reporter San Antonio Light, 1952-53; instr. journalism project Upward Bound So. Meth. U., Dallas, 1967-71. Instr. writing El Centro Dallas County C.C., Dallas, part time 1972-74; instr. human devel. Richland C.C., Dallas, part-time 1974-79; tchr. English, journalism and psychology Dallas Ind. Sch. Dist., 1969-81; counselor Ursuline Acad., 1981-94; part-time instr. human devel. Sante Fe C.C.; freelance documentary photographer. Author: They Changed the World: People of the Manhattan Project, 2006. Mem. Dallas Sports Car Club, N.Mex. Jewish Hist. Soc., Temple Beth Shalom. Jewish. Home: 101 Monte Alto Rd Santa Fe NM 87508-8865 Personal E-Mail: aj@melnick.net.

**MELNICK, HOWARD A.,** hotel executive; BS in acctg., SUNY, Binghamton; MBA in fin., Fordham U. With Deloitte, Haskell and Sells, The Pepsi Co., 1990—96; now sr. v.p. info. resources application services Marriott Internat. Inc. Named one of Premier 100 IT Leaders, Computerworld, 2005. Office: Marriott Internat Inc One Marriott Dr Washington DC 20058*

**MELNICK, JANE FISHER,** writer, educator, photographer; b. Boston, Sept. 26, 1939; d. Richard T. and Mary (Holcombe) Fisher; m. Burton A. Melnick, Dec. 1962 (div. 1969); 1 child, Benjamin A.; life ptnr. Eileen Willenborg, 1978—. BA cum laude, Radcliffe Coll., 1962; MA, NYU, 1985, PhD in Am. Studies, 1991. News writer, photographer, freelance editor, 1962—75; editor, writer, photographer In These Times, Chgo., 1976-78; grapnics editor, writer Seven Days, N.Y.C., 1978-81; instr. writing, journalism, Am. lit. and history NYU, 1981-86; instr. writing, Am. lit. Loyola U., Chgo., 1988-91; asst. prof. Elmhurst (Ill.) Coll., 1991-96; writer, coll. prep. tutor Chgo., 1997—2004. Recipient Phi Beta Kappa award for best creative work by an undergrad. Radcliffe Coll., 1959; Mademoiselle mag. fiction contest award, 1962, NEA grantee, 1973, dean's dissertation fellow NYU, 1987. Mem. MLA, Mid-Am. Am. Studies Assn. (exec. bd.) Avocations: home renovation, travel. Home: 5000 N Marine Dr Apt 15A Chicago IL 60640-3226

**MELNICK, MICHAEL,** geneticist, educator; b. N.Y.C., Sept. 24, 1944; s. Lester and Evelyn (Rosenberg) M.; m. Anita Goldberger, June 19, 1966; children: Cliff, Lynn. BA in Biology, NYU, 1966, DDS, 1970; PhD in Genetics, Ind. U., 1978. Instr. oral medicine Ind. U., Indpls., 1973-74, fellow in med. genetics, 1974-77, asst. prof. med. genetics, 1977-78; rsch. assoc. prof. U. So. Calif., L.A., 1978-85, assoc. prof., 1985-89, prof. genetics, 1989—. Cons. in human genetics NIH, Bethesda, Md., 1977-88, grant reviewer, 1978—; manuscript referee Am. Jour. Human Genetics, Chgo., 1980—, Am. Jour. Med. Genetics, Helena, Mont., 1980—; MRC vis. prof. McGill U., Montreal, que., 1990. Author, editor 5 books on human genetics; editor-in-chief Jour. Craniofacial Genetics, 1980-2000; contbr. more than 100 articles to profl. jours. Mem. nat. bd. Com. of Concerned Scientists, N.Y.C., 1983—; vice chmn. Youth Towns of Israel, L.A., 1986—. Capt. M.C. U.S. Army, 1970-73. Recipient Ind. U. Disting. Alumnus award, 1984; Warwick James fellow U. London/Guy's Hosp., 1992. Fellow AAAS; mem. Soc. Craniofacial Genetics (pres. 1978-79), Soc. for Developmental Biology, Am. Soc. Human Genetics, Sigma Xi. Achievements include research in delineated major gene causation of cleft lip and palate; delineated insulin-like growth factor, type 2, receptor control of fetal lung, salvary gland and palate development; application of probability neural networks to multi-gene analysis. Avocations: art, philosophy, chess. Office: Univ So California Den 4266 Mc 0641 Los Angeles CA 90089-0641 E-mail: mmelnick@usc.edu.

**MELNYK, EUGENE N.,** pharmaceutical company executive, professional sports team executive; Founder, pres., CEO Trimel, 1983—91; chmn. bd. dirs. BCI, 1991—94; exec. chmn. Biovail Corp., Mississauga, Ont., Canada, 1994—, CEO, 2001—04; owner, gov. & chmn. Ottawa Senators Hockey Club, 2003—. Office: Biovail Corp 7150 Mississauga Rd L5N 8MF Mississauga ON Canada

**MELO, WELTON,** professional soccer player; b. Rio de Janeiro, Apr. 17, 1975; Forward Brazilian Club Am., 1995, New Eng. Revolution, 1996, L.A. Galaxy, 1997—98, Miami Fusion, 1999—2001, Pittsburgh Riverhounds, 2001—02, Fredrikstad FK, Norway, 2003, Seattle Sounders, 2004—. Named Maj. League Soccer All-Star, 1996. Mailing: Seattle Sounders PO Box 80966 Seattle WA 98108

**MELODY, MICHAEL EDWARD,** publishing company executive; b. Streator, Ill., Dec. 22, 1943; s. Giles Lambert and Rose Mary (Moreschi) M.; m. Carol Ann Weir, June 8, 1968 (div.); 1 dau., Alison Anne; m. Bonnie Kaye Binkert, Mar. 26, 1983. BA, Ala. Coll., 1966. Exec. editor, asst. v.p. Prentice-Hall, Inc., Englewood Cliff, NJ, 1974-79; v.p., editor-in-chief coll. divsn. Macmillan Pub. Co., N.Y.C., 1979-80, sr. v.p., pres. coll. divsn., 1980-87, pres. sch. divsn., 1987—88; v.p. higher edn. group Simon & Schuster, N.Y.C., 1988-90; sr. v.p. Houghton Mifflin Co., Boston, 1990-91, exec. v.p., 1991-95; prin. Michael E. Melody Cons., Boston, 1995-96; v.p., gen. mgr. info. prodn. Inso Corp., Boston, 1996-99; pres, CEO, bd. dirs. Sage Pubs., Inc., Thousand Oaks, Calif., 1999—2005. Chmn. bd. dirs. Appleton & Lange, N.Y.C., 1989-90; bd. dirs. Sage Pubs., Ltd., London. Bd. overseers Huntington Theatre Co., Boston, 1993-96; bd. advisors Boston U. Sch. for the Arts, 1997-2000; bd. dirs. Judge Baker Ctr. for Children, Harvard U. Med. Sch., 1997-99, mem. exec. com.; pres. adv. coun. Calif. Luth. U., 2001-05; trustee New West Symphony, 2003-05, So. N.H. U., 2003—; bd. dirs. Santa Fe Symphony Orch., 2006—. Mem. Assn. Am. Pubs. (vice chmn. coll. divsn. 1981-83, chmn. coll. divsn. 1983-86, exec. com. sch. divsn. 1987-88, exec. com. higher edn. divsn. 1990—), Nat. Assn. Coll. Stores (trustee 1986-87, 94-95). E-mail: michael.melody@gmail.com.

**MELONE, JOSEPH JAMES,** retired insurance company executive; b. Pittston, Pa., July 27, 1931; s. Dominick William and Beatrice Marie (Pignone) Melone; m. Marie Jane DeGeorge, Jan. 23, 1960; children: Lisa, Carol. BS, U. Pa., 1953, MBA, 1954, PhD in Econs., 1961. CPCU; ChFC. Assoc. prof. ins. U. Pa., 1959-66, mem. pension rsch. coun., 1961-66; rsch. dir. Am. Coll. Life Underwriters, 1966-68; v.p. Prudential Ins. Co., Boston, 1969-76, sr. v.p. Newark, 1976-81, exec. v.p., 1981-84, pres., 1984-90, Equitable Life Assurance Soc. U.S., 1990-94, COO, bd. dirs.; pres. Equitable Cos., Inc., 1992-96, COO, bd. dirs., pres. NYC, 1996-98, CEO; chmn. Equitable Life Assurance Soc. U.S., NYC, 1994-98. Chmn., CEO Equitable Variable Life Ins. Co.; bd. dirs. Foster Wheeler Corp., BISYS, Inc.; chmn. bd. dirs. Horace-Mann Educators Corp.; chmn. emeritus Equitable Cos. Author: Collectively Bargained Multi-Employer Pension Plans, 1961; co-author: Risk and Insurance, 1963, Pension Planning, 1966. Trustee Newark Mus.; bd. dirs. Greater N.Y. councs. Boy Scouts Am.; chmn. ins. divsn. Cardinal's Commn. Laity N.Y. Archdioceses; bd. overseers Wharton Sch. U. Pa. Mem.: Baltusrol Golf Club, Lost Tree Golf Club, Morris County Country Club, Alpha Tau Omega. Home: Gen Delivery New Vernon NJ 07976-9999 Office: Equitable Cos Inc 1290 Ave of Americas New York NY 10104 Office Phone: 212-314-2060. Business E-Mail: joseph.melone@axa-financial.com.

**MELOY, JUDITH MARIE,** humanities educator; b. Pitts., Oct. 22, 1951; d. John C. and Miriam Meloy. BA, Denison U., 1973; MST, U. Dayton, 1982; PhD, Ind. U., 1986. Admissions counselor Denison U., Granville, Ohio, 1973—74; tchr. Centerville (Ohio) City Schs., 1978—83; program evaluation Conn. State Dept. Edn., Hartford, 1987—89; prof. Vt. State Colls., Castleton, 1989—. Dept. chair, 1994—95; chair tchg. and scholarship com., 2001—03; faculty fellow, 1996—97. Author: (book) Writing the Qualitative Dissertation: Understanding by Doing, 1994, Writing the Qualitative Dissertation: Understanding by Doing, 2d edit., 2002. Comty. Svc., Castleton, 1998—; mem. Hayes Found. Bd., 1992—. Recipient Outstanding Faculty award, Castleton State Coll. Alumni Assn., 2005. Mem.: Am. Ednl. Rsch. Assn. (chmn. qualitative rsch. spl. interest group 2004—06). Office: Castleton State Coll Castleton VT 05735 Business E-Mail: judy.meloy@castleton.edu.

**MELOY, SYBIL PISKUR,** retired lawyer; b. Chgo., Dec. 1, 1939; d. Michael M. and Laura (Stevenson) Piskur; children: William S., Bradley M. BS with honors, U. Ill., 1961; JD, Chgo. Kent Coll. Law, 1965. Bar: Ill. 1965,

Fla. 1985, D.C. 1995, U.S. Dist. Ct. (no. dist.) Ill. 1965, U.S. Supreme Ct. 1972, U.S. Ct. Appeals (fed. cir.) 1983, U.S. Dist. Ct. (so. dist.) Fla. 1985, D.C. 1995. Patent chemist, patent atty., sr. atty., internat. counsel G.D. Searle & Co., Skokie, Ill., 1961-72; regional counsel Abbott Labs., North Chicago, Ill., 1972-78; pvt. practice Arlington Heights, Ill., 1978-79; asst. gen. counsel Alberto Culver Co., Melrose Park, Ill., 1979-83; corp. counsel Key Pharms., Inc., Miami, Fla., 1983-86; assoc. Ruden, Barnett, McCloskey, Smith, Schuster and Russell, Pa., 1987-89, ptnr. Pa., 1990-91, Foley & Lardner, Miami, Washington, 1991—2001. Adj. prof. Univ. of Miami Sch. of Law, 1986-92. Contbr. article on fertility control and abortion laws, book rev. on arbitration to law revs. Recipient Abbott Presdl. award, 1977; Bur. Nat. Affairs prize, 1965; Law Rev. prize for best article. Mem. ABA, Chgo. Bar Assn. (chmn.-elect and vice chmn. internat. and fgn. law com.), Am. Patent Law Assn., Am. Chem. Soc., Licencing Execs. Soc., Phi Beta Kappa, Phi Kappa Phi. Patentee oral contraceptive, 1965. Office: 1676 32d St NW Washington DC 20007-2960

**MELROSE, KENDRICK BASCOM,** manufacturing executive; b. Orlando, Fla., July 31, 1940; s. Henry Bascom and Dorothy (Lumley) M.; children: Robert, Velia, Kendra. BS cum laude, Princeton U., 1962; M.Sc., MIT, 1965; MBA, U. Chgo., 1967. Mktg. mgr. Pillsbury Co., Mpls., 1967-69; dir. corp. planning Bayfield Techs., Inc., Mpls., 1969-70; dir. mktg., consumer products Toro Co. (mfrs. outdoor power equipment), Mpls., 1970—73, pres., Game Time Litchfield, Mich., 1973—76, v.p., outdoor power equipment Mpls., 1976—80, exec. v.p. outdoor power equipment div., 1980-81, pres., 1981-88, chief exec. officer, 1983—2005, chmn., 1987—2005, exec. chmn., 2005. Congregationalist. Office: Toro Co 8111 Lyndale Ave S Minneapolis MN 55420-1196*

**MELROY, PAMELA ANN,** astronaut; b. Palo Alto, Calif., Sept. 17, 1961; d. David and Helen M.; married BS in Physics and Astronomy, Wellesley Coll., 1983; MSc in Earth and Planetary Scis., MIT, 1984. Commd. 2nd lt. USAF, 1983, advanced through grades to lt. col.; co-pilot KC-10, aircraft comdr., instr. pilot Barksdale AFB, Bossier City, La.; test pilot C-17 Combined Test Force; shuttle pilot NASA, Houston, pilot STS-92 (Discovery), 2000, pilot STS-112 (Atlantis), 2002, shuttle comdr. STS-120 to Internat. Space Station, 2006, selected as astronaut, 1994, astronaut, 1995—. Bd. trustee Wellesley Coll. Decorated Air Force Meritorious Svc. medal with oak leaf cluster, Air medal with oak leaf cluster, Aerial Achievement medal with oak leaf cluster, Expeditionary medal with oak leaf cluster. Mem. Soc. Exptl. Test Pilots, Order of Daedalians, 99s. Achievements include being the second female astronaut to command a US orbiter. Avocations: theater, tap and jazz dancing, reading, cooking, flying. Office: Astronaut Office/CB NASA Lyndon B Johnson Space Ctr Houston TX 77058*

**MELSHEIMER, MEL P(OWELL),** venture capitalist; b. L.A., July 9, 1939; s. Oscar Merrill M.; m. Sara Sturdevant, Sept. 1, 1962; children: Heidi, Erich, Douglas. AB, Occidental Coll., 1961; MBA, U. So. Calif., 1965. With United Calif. Bank, Los Angeles, 1962-66; sr. fin. analyst Ford Motor Co., Newport Beach, Calif., 1966-67; v.p., chief fin. officer Pepsi Cola Co. Pepsico, Inc., Purchase, NY, 1968-75; exec. v.p., chief operating officer AZL Resources, Inc., 1975-84; chmn. bd., CEO PHX Pacific, Inc., 1984-89; pres., CEO MPM Capital Corp., 1987-89; exec. v.p. Finevest Foods, Inc., Greenwich, Conn., 1989-92; pres., CEO Land-O-Sun Dairies Inc., 1991-92, Atlanta Dairies, Inc., 1991-92; exec. v.p., sec., COO Dairy Holdings, Inc., Johnson City, Tenn., 1992-94; exec. v.p., COO, CFO Sonex Internat. Corp., Brewster, NY, 1994; pres., CEO M.P. Melsheimer & Co., Ridgefield, Conn., 1994-97; pres. NFX, 1995-96; pres., COO, CFO Harris & Harris Group, Inc., N.Y.C., 1997—2000; pres. Linkhorn Capital Advisors, Inc., 2005—. Served with U.S. Army, 1961-62. Home: 1418 N Woodhouse Rd Virginia Beach VA 23454 E-mail: melmelsheimer@msn.com.

**MELTON, ARTHUR RICHARD,** public health administrator; b. Ysleta, Tex., Apr. 28, 1943; s. Francis Charles and Jean (Graham) M.; m. Frances Bay, Aug. 19, 1965; children: David Bay, Amy Elizabeth. BS, U. Utah, 1969; MPH, U. N.C., 1974, D in Pub. Health, 1976. Dir. labs. S.D. Dept. Health, Pierre, 1976-87; microbiologist Utah Dept. Health, Salt Lake City, 1970-73, dir. divsn. lab. svcs., 1987-92, dep. dir., 1992—. Mem.: Assn. State and Territorial Health Ofcls. (pres. elect 1999—2000, pres. 2000—01), SD Pub. Health Assn. (pres. 1980—81, past pres. 2001—06), Am. Pub. Health Assn. (governing coun. 1980—83). Mem. Lds Ch. Home: 6835 Heather Way West Jordan UT 84084-2304 Office: PO Box 141000 Salt Lake City UT 84114-1000 Office phone: 801-538-6111. Personal E-mail: dickmelton@yahoo.com. Business E-Mail: dmelton@utah.gov.

**MELTON, CAROL A.,** communications executive; b. St. Augustine, Fla., 1954; m. Joseph M. Hassett; children: Matthew, Meredith Hassett. BA with honors, Wake Forest U., 1976; MA in Journalism and Comm., U. Fla., 1977; JD with honors, Am. U., 1981. Assoc. in comm. grp. Hogan and Hartson, Washington, 1981-82; asst. gen. counsel Nat. Cable TV Assn., 1983-86; legal adv. to Chmn. Mark Fowler FCC, Washington, 1986-87; Washington counsel Warner Comm., 1987-91; v.p. law and pub. policy Time Warner Inc., Washington, 1992-97, exec. v.p. v.p. global pub. policy, exec. officer, 2005—; exec. v.p. govt. rels., exec. officer Viacom, Inc., Washington, 1997—2005. Trustee The Media Inst., Washington, 1997—2005, Washington Performing Arts Soc., 1997—99, The Potomac Sch., McLean, Va., 1999—2000, Meridian Internat. Ctr., 2001—03; mem. Fed. City Coun., 1997—, Coun. on Fgn. Rels., 2006—. Office: Time Warner Inc 800 Connecticut Ave NW Washington DC 20006

**MELTON, DAVID REUBEN,** lawyer; b. Milw., Apr. 4, 1952; s. Howard and Evelyn M.; m. Nancy Hillary Segal, May 22, 1981; children: Michelle, Hannah. BA, U. Wis., 1974; JD, U. Chgo., 1977. Bar: Ill. 1977, U.S. Dist. Ct. (no. dist.) Ill. 1977, U.S. Ct. Appeals (7th cir.) 1981, U.S. Supreme Ct. 1982, U.S. Tax Ct. Appeals, 1991. Assoc. Karon, Morrison & Savikas, Ltd., Chgo., 1977-83; ptnr. Karon, Morrison & Savikas, Ltd., Chgo., 1983-87, Karon, Savikas & Horn, Ltd., Chgo., 1987-88, Keck, Mahin & Cate, Chgo., 1988-96; counsel Mayer, Brown & Platt, Chgo., 1996-99, ptnr., 2000—. Office: Mayer Brown Rowe & Maw 71 S Wacker Dr Ste 3200 Chicago IL 60606 Office Phone: 312-701-7358. E-mail: dmelton@mayerbrownrowe.com.

**MELTON, DOUGLAS A.,** molecular and cell biology educator; BS Honors Biology, U. Illinois, Champaign-Urbana, 1971—75; BA History, Phil. of Sci., Cambridge U., 1975—77; PhD Molecular Biology, Trinity Coll. & MRC Lab. Molecular Biology, Cambridge U., Eng., 1980. Asst. prof, dept. bio chem. and molecular biology Harvard U., 1981—84, assoc. prof., 1984—87, J.L. Loeb assoc. prof. nat. sci., 1987, prof. dept. molecular and cellular biology Cambridge, Mass., 1988—; biologist (med.) Mass. Gen. Hosp., Boston; assoc. mem. Children's Hosp., Boston, 1994—; investigator Howard Hughes Med. Inst., 1994—; Thomas Dudley Cabot prof. Natural Sci. Harvard U., Cambridge, Mass., 1999—. Recipient Richard Lounsbery award NAS, 1995; named Policy Leader of Yr. within the Scientific American 50, Scientific American, 2004. Mem.: Inst. Medicine. Office: Harvard Univ Dept Molecular & Cellular Bio 7 Divinity Ave Cambridge MA 02138*

**MELTON, EMMA ALEXANDER,** educational consultant, retired elementary school educator; b. Louisville, Ky., Aug. 26, 1933; d. Jesse Wilson and Reella Odessa Alexander; m. Brady Melton Jr., Apr. 17, 1960; children: Brady Aldred, Tia Meychelle. BA in English and Speech, Ctrl. State Coll., 1954; MA in Elem. Edn., Ohio State U., 1962; cert. in reading, John Carroll U. English tchr. Xenia (Ohio) City Sch., 1955—57; elem. tchr. Cleve. Pub. Sch., 1957—63, reading cons., 1969—90; social skills cons. Soc. Prevention of Violence, Cleve., 1990—92; diversity trainer of educators Anti-Defamation League, Cleve., 1992—97; worksh. Workshop facilitator Inst. Cultural Affairs Internat., various locations, 1970—2000; spkr. at nat. and internat. conf. and workshops, 1984—. Contbg. author: Sister to Sister, 1999. Adv. bd. Nuc. Age Resource Ctr., Cleve., 1994—2004; deacon First Bapt. Ch., Cleve., 1980—; advocacy bd. Interreligious Ptnrs. in Action, Cleve., 2000—; mem. adv. bd.

Cleve. Ecumenical Inst. for Religious Studies, 2006—. Recipient Ecumenical award, Interchurch Coun., Cleve., 1998; grantee, Cleve. Edn. Fund, 1987; Martha Holden Jennings scholar, Jennings Found., 1981. Mem.: Delta Sigma Theta. Democrat. Baptist. Avocations: reading, travel, singing.

**MELTON, GARY BENTLEY,** psychologist, educator; b. Salisbury, N.C., June 4, 1952; s. Harold Sumner Jr. and Marion Adair (Reeves) M.; m. Robin Jo Kimbrough, Aug. 7, 1999; children by previous marriage: Jennifer Lynn, Stephany Beth. BA, U. Va., 1973; MA, Boston U., 1975, PhD, 1978. Asst. prof. psychology Morehead (Ky.) State U., 1978-79, U. Va., Charlottesville, 1979-81; from asst. prof. to full prof. psychology and law U. Nebr., Lincoln, 1981-87, Carl A. Happold prof. psychology and law, 1987-94; prof. neuropsychiatry & behavioral science U. S.C., Columbia, 1994-99, adj. prof. law, pediat. and psychology, 1994-99, dir. Inst. Families in Soc., 1994-99; prof. psychology Clemson U., 1999—. Dir. Inst. Family and Neighborhood Life, Clemson U., 1999—. Author: Child Advocacy: Psychological Issues and Interventions, 1993; co-author: Community Mental Health Centers and the Courts: An Evaluation of Community-Based Forensic Services, 1985, Psychological Evaluations for the Courts: A Handbook for Mental Health Professionals and Lawyers, 1987, 2d edit., 1997, Pediatric and Adolescent AIDS: Research Findings from the Social Sciences, 1992, Ethical and Legal Issues in AIDS Research, 1995, No Place to Go: Civil Commitment of Minors, 1998; editor numerous books. Mem. U.S. Adv. Bd. on Child Abuse and Neglect, 1989-93, vice-chair, 1991-93. Recipient Frederick Howell Lewis award Psi Chi, 1993, Lynn Stuart Weiss award Am. Psychol. Found., 2000. Fellow: APA (chmn. various coms., cert. recognition for psychology in pub. interest 1981, Disting. Contbn. to Psychology in Pub. Interest award 1985, Nicholas Hobbs award 1992, Harold Hildreth award 1992, Disting. Contbn. to Pub. Svc. award 1999, Disting. Contbn. to Internat. Advancement of Psychology award 2005); mem.: Am. Profl. Soc. on Abuse of Children (Career Achievement in Rsch. award 2005), Prevent Child Abuse Am. (Donna Stone award 1992), Am. Orthopsychiat. Assn. (pres. 2004—05), Am. Psychology-Law Soc. (pres. 1990—91). Office: Clemson U Inst Family and Neighborhood Life 158 Poole Agrl Ctr Clemson SC 29634-0132 Office Phone: 864-656-6271. Business E-Mail: gmelton@clemson.edu. E-mail: garybmelton@hotmail.com.

**MELTON, HAROLD D.,** state supreme court justice; b. Wash., DC; BA, Auburn U.; JD, U. Ga., 1991. Former atty. Ga. Dept. of Law, former section leader, consumer interests div.; former exec. counsel Gov. Perdue; justice Ga. Supreme Ct., 2005—. Former volunteer leader Young Life Ministries. Dir. teen ministry Southwest Christian Fellowship Church; bd. mem. Atlanta Youth Academies. Office: Ga Supreme Ct Ste 300 244 Washington St SW Atlanta GA 30334*

**MELTON, HOWELL W., JR.,** lawyer; b. St. Augustine, Fla., Oct. 26, 1951; BA with high honors, U. Fla., 1973; JD, U. Fla. Coll. Law, 1975. Bar: Fla. 1976, DC, Fla. State Cts., US Dist. Ct. (Middle Dist.) Fla.), US Cir. Ct. of Appeals (11th Cir.), US Supreme Ct. With Holland & Knight LLP, NYC, 1975—, practiced in Tampa, Orlando, Chgo. and NYC Offices, mng. ptnr. Orlando, Fla., 2003—. Bd. dir. Enterprise Fla., Inc., chmn. fin. and compensation com.; chmn. Metro Orlando Econ. Develop. Commn. (EDC), 2000—01, mem. policy coun.; past chmn. Ctrl. Fla. Tech. Partnership. Trustee emeritus U. Fla. Coll. Law; officer, mem. exec. com. bd. trustees Orlando Mus. Art, 1991—97; bd. governors Greater Orlando Region, Nat. Conf. for Community and Justice, 1990—; bd. dir. Ctrl. Fla. Fair, Inc., 1993—; trustee Greater Orlando C. of C., U. Fla. Law Ctr. Assn., Inc., 2000—04; mem. Orlando Leadership Class, 1990; founder, bd. dir. and sec. Leadership Orlando Alumni Assn.; mem. Orlando Mus. of Art Acquisition Trust, Savant; pres. Fla. Blue Key. Fellow: Fla. Bar Found., Am. Bar Found.; mem.: DC Bar Assn., Acad. Fla. Trial Lawyers (mem. commercial litig. sect.), Assn. Trial Lawyers Am., Am. Arbitration Assn. (mem. panel arbitrators), Am. Judicature Soc., Fed. Bar Assn., Orange County Bar Assn., Fla. Bar Assn. (mem. litig. sect.), ABA (mem. litig. and law firm mgmt. sects.), Phi Delta Theta (pres. 1976), Omega Delta Kappa, Phi Delta Phi, Phi Eta Sigma. Office: Holland & Knight LLP 195 Broadway New York NY 10007-3189 Office Phone: 212-513-3544, 212-513-3200. Office Fax: 212-513-2339. Business E-Mail: hmelton@hklaw.com, howell.melton@hklaw.com.

**MELTON, HOWELL WEBSTER, SR.,** federal judge; b. Atlanta, Dec. 15, 1923; s. Holmes and Alma (Combee) M.; m. Margaret Catherine Wolfe, Mar. 4, 1950; children—Howell Webster, Carol Anne. JD, U. Fla., 1948. Bar: Fla. 1948. With Upchurch, Melton & Upchurch, St. Augustine, 1948-61; judge 7th Jud. Circuit of Fla., St. Augustine, 1961-77, U.S. Dist. Ct. (mid. dist.) Fla., Jacksonville, 1977-91, sr. judge, 1991—. Past chmn. Fla. Conf. Cir. Judges, 1974; past chmn. coun. bar pres.'s Fla. Bar. Trustee Flagler Coll., St. Augustine. Served with U.S. Army, 1943-46. Recipient Disting. Service award St. Augustine Jaycees, 1953 Mem. ABA, St. Johns County Bar Assn., Jacksonville Bar Assn., Fed. Bar Assn., Fla. Blue Key, Officers Club, Masons, Phi Delta Theta, Phi Kappa Phi, Phi Alpha Theta, Pi Gamma Mu, Methodist. Office: US Dist Ct 300 N Hogan St Ste 11-300 Jacksonville FL 32202 Office Phone: 904-549-1940.

**MELTON, STEPHEN REID,** lawyer; b. Savannah, Ga., Dec. 10, 1949; s. Wallace Reid and Doris Cleone (Bragg) M. BA magna cum laude, Armstrong Coll., 1973; JD, U. Ga., Athens, 1976. Bar: Ga. 1976, D.C. 1979, Tex. 1992, U.S. Supreme Ct. 1980, U.S. Dist. Ct. D.C. 1980, U.S. Ct. Appeals (D.C. cir.) 1980, U.S. Ct. Appeals (7th cir.) 1980, U.S. Ct. Appeals (fed. cir.) 1981, U.S. Ct. Appeals (5th and 11th cirs.) 1985, U.S. Ct. Appeals (4th cir.) 1986, U.S. Ct. Appeals (6th cir.) 1991. Atty., adviser ICC, Washington, 1976-78; staff lawyer FERC, Washington, 1978-81; dep. gen. counsel, 1981-83, acting gen. counsel, 1983-84; assoc. Beveridge & Diamond, Washington, 1984-85; sr. atty. Tex. Oil & Gas Corp., Dallas, 1985-87; asst. gen. counsel United Gas Pipe Line Co., Houston, 1987-89, asst. v.p., asst. gen. counsel, spl. asst. for regulatory affairs, 1989-90, assoc. gen. counsel, 1990-92; of counsel Akin, Gump, Strauss, Hauer & Feld, 1992—97; v.p. gen. counsel and sec. Columbia Gulf Transmission, 1997—2000; asst. sec. Columbia Gas Transmission Corp., 2000—01; assoc. gen. counsel NiSource Corp. Svcs. Co., 2000—02, dep. gen. counsel, 2002—04, dep. gen. counsel FERC compliance officer, 2004—05, v.p., dep. gen. counsel FERC compliance officer, 2005—. Mem. ABA (adminstrv. law sect., utility law sect., bus. law sect.), Energy Bar Assn., Houston Bar Assn., D.C. Bar Assn., Ga. Bar Assn., Tex. Bar Assn., Tex. Gas Assn. (exec. legal com.). Office: NiSource Corp Svcs Co 2603 Augusta Dr Houston TX 77057 E-mail: smelton@nisource.com.

**MELTON, THOMAS RONALD,** history professor; b. Atmore, Ala., Apr. 29, 1948; s. Leroy Eugene and Mary Verona (White) M.; m. Patricia Ann Pickens, Aug. 22, 1970 BA, William Carey Coll., 1970; MA, U. Miss., 1972, PhD, 1985. Prof. history, chmn. dept. social and behavioral sci. Brewton-Parker Coll., Mt. Vernon, Ga., 1977—; v.p. acad. and student affairs, 1997—2001, provost, 2001—. Pres. Ohoopee regional Coun. for the Arts, Vidalia, Ga., 1992-93. Mem. Orgn. Am. Historians, So. Hist. Assn., Ga. Hist. Soc., Ga. Assn. Historians, Phi Kappa Phi, Phi Alpha Theta, Pi Gamma Mu Democrat. Baptist. Home: PO Box 466 Vidalia Ga 30475 Office Phone: 912-583-3238. Personal E-mail: trmelton@bellsouth.net. Business E-Mail: rmelton@bpc.edu.

**MELTON, WAYNE CHARLES,** real estate executive; b. Oak Ridge, Tenn., Aug. 30, 1954; s. Charles Estel and Una Faye (Hull) M.; m. Maria Tobar-Conde; 1 child, Ingrid Tatiana. AB in European Intellectual History, U. Ga., 1975; MS in Real Estate, Shepperton U., 2001, PhD in Real Estate, 2003. Mgr. Household Internat., Athens, Ga., 1975-76; asst. mgr. Athens and Hickory, N.C., Doraville, Ga., 1976-77; pres., ceo Impact Realty-Melton & Assocs. Inc., Athens, 1987—. Cons. Ga. Furniture, Charlotte (N.C.) Realty, 1987—. Trustee Mu, Inc., Page, Ga. Ho. of Reps., 1968; chmn. Madison County Reps., 1973-74; mem. Congl. Bus. Coun., 2002. Recipient Ronald Reagan award, Rep. Congl. Com., 2004. Mem. Pheonix Club, Pres. Club, Zeta Beta Tau. Office: 855 Sunset Dr Ste 11 Athens GA 30606-7718 Business E-Mail: impactrealty@hotmail.com.

**MELTON, WILLIAM EVERETT,** retired music educator; b. Roanoke, Va., June 28, 1940; s. William Everett and Cordelia Mae Melton; m. Carol Ann Drawdy, Aug. 17, 1963; children: John Morris, Marissa Kaye. BS in Music Edn., Carson-Newman Coll., 1962; MS in Music Edn., U. Tenn., 1970, EdD, 1984. Choral music tchr. Carter H.S., Knoxville, Tenn., 1962—93; instr. Carson-Newman Coll., Jefferson City, Tenn., 1993—2006; ret., 2006. Dir. music ministries Fountain City United Meth. Ch., Knoxville, 1993—2003; min. of music Smithwood Bapt. Ch., Knoxville, 2005—. Composer, arranger: choral and handbell works. Asst. dir., music dir. Knoxville Nativity Pageant, 1987—95, mem. adv. bd., 1996—2006; vol. Jubilee Project, Sneedville, Tenn., 2004—06; choral clinician, adjuducator East Tenn. Choral Festivals. Recipient Disting. Alumnus award, Carson-Newman Coll., 2001. Mem.: NEA, Tenn. Ret. Tchrs. Assn., Am. Choral Dirs. Assn. (life). Avocations: travel, gardening.

**MELTZER, ALLAN H.,** economist, educator; b. Boston, Feb. 6, 1928; s. George B. and Minerva I. (Simons) M.; m. Marilyn Ginsburg, Aug. 27, 1950; children: Bruce Michael, Eric Charles, Beth Denise. AB, Duke U., 1948; MA, UCLA, 1955, PhD, 1958. Lectr. econs. U. Pa., Phila., 1956-57; faculty Carnegie Mellon U. Grad. Sch. Indsl. Adminstrn., Pitts., 1957-64, prof. econs., 1964—, Maurice Falk prof. econs. and social sci., 1970-80, John M. Olin univ. prof. polit. economy and pub. policy, 1980-91, Univ. prof. polit. economy and pub. policy, 1991-97, Allan H. Meltzer Univ. prof. polit. economy, 1997—. Vis. prof. U. Chgo., 1964-65, Fundacao Getulio Vargas, Rio de Janeiro, 1976-79, City U., London, 1979-2001; vis. fellow Hoover Instn., 1977-78; vis. scholar Am. Enterprise Inst., Washington, 1989—; co-chmn. Shadow Open Market Com., 1974-89, chmn., 1989-2000; cons. US Treasury, joint econ. com. US Congress, 1960; com. on banking and currency US Ho. of Reps., 1963-64; mem. Pres.'s Econ. Policy Adv. Bd., 1988 90; acting mem. Coun. Econ. Advisors, 1988-89; panel econ. advisors Congl. Budget Office, 1995—; cons., bd. gov. FRS, FDIC; dir. Cooper Tire & Rubber Co., 1983-98, chmn. audit and compensation com., 1996-98; hon. advisor Inst. Monetary and Econ. Studies Bank of Japan, 1987-2003; bd. dir. Sarah Scaife Found., Commonwealth Found.; dir. Stillhalter Vision AG, Zurich, 1994-2002, Advanced Materials Group, 1994-2001; chmn. Internat. Fin. Instn. adv. com. to US Congress, 1999-2000. Author: Monetary Economics, 1989, Keynes's Monetary Theory: A Different Interpretation, 1988; (with Karl Brunner) Money and the Economy: Issues in Monetary Analysis, 1993; (with Alex Cukierman and Scott Richard) Political Economy, 1991, Report of the International Financial Institution Advisory Commission, 2000, A History of the Federal Reserve, vol. 1, 2003 (Book award Econ. History Assn. 2004-05); editor: (with Karl Brunner) Carnegie-Rochester Conf. Series, 1976-89; (with Charles Plosser), 1989-97; contbr. articles to profl. jours. Recipient Outstanding Achievement award UCLA, 1983, Money Marketeers, 1997, Educator of Yr. award Pittsburg Hist. Ctr., 2003, Irving Kristol award Am. Enterprise Inst., 2003, David Horowitz prize Israel Bankers Assn., 2004; Social Sci. Rsch. Coun. fellow, 1955-56, Ford Found. fellow, 1962-63; named Man of Yr. in Fin., Pitts., 1995-96. Fellow: Nat. Assn. Bus. Economists (Adam Smith award 2003); mem.: Am. Fin. Assn., Western Econ. Assn. (pres. 1985—86), Internat. Atlantic Econ. Assn. (pres. 1999—2000), Am. Econ. Assn. (v.p. 1990, Disting. fellow 2002), Phila. Soc. (v.p. 1981—83), Cosmos Club. Achievements include research in macroeconomics. Avocations: political economy, monetary history. Office: Carnegie Mellon U Dept Econs Pittsburgh PA 15213 Office Phone: 412-268-2282. Business E-Mail: am05@andrew.cmu.edu.

**MELTZER, ARTHUR ADAM,** researcher, researcher; s. Mayer and Selma Meltzer; m. Adela Valadez-Plascencia. BA, SUNY, Buffalo, 1979; diploma in human biology, U. Oxford, 1980; MA, U. Mich., Ann Arbor, 1982; MPH, U. Tex., Houston, 1986, PhD, 1991. Rsch. analyst Ctrs. for Medicare and Medicaid Svcs., Balt., 2000—. Contbr. articles to profl. jours. Mem.: Soc. Epidemiol. Rsch. Achievements include research in population-based health. Avocations: yoga, aerobics. Office: Ctrs for Medicare and Medicaid Svcs 7500 Security Blvd Baltimore MD 21224

**MELTZER, BERNARD DAVID,** law educator; b. Phila., Nov. 21, 1914; s. Julius and Rose (Welkov) M.; m. Jean Sulzberger, Jan. 17, 1947; children: Joan, Daniel, Susan. AB, U. Chgo., 1935, JD, 1937; LL.M., Harvard U., 1938. Bar: Ill. 1938. Atty., spl. asst. to chmn. SEC, 1938-40; assoc. firm Mayer, Meyer, Austrian & Platt, Chgo., 1940; spl. asst. to asst. sec. state, also acting chief fgn. funds control div. State, 1941—43; asst. trial counsel U.S. prosecution Internat. Nuremberg War Trials, 1945-46; from professorial lectr. to disting. svc. prof. law emeritus U. Chgo. Law Sch., 1946—; counsel Vedder, Price, Kaufman & Kammholz, Chgo., 1954-55, Sidley and Austin, Chgo., 1987-89. Hearing commr. NPA, 1952-53; labor arbitrator; spl. master U.S. Ct. Appeals for D.C., 1963-64; bd. publs. U. Chgo. Law Sch., 1965-67, chmn., 1967-68; mem. Gov. Ill. Adv. Commn. Labor-Mgmt. Policy for Pub. Employees in Ill., 1966-67, Ill. Civil Service Commn., 1968-69; cons. U.S. Dept. Labor, 1969-70 Author: Supplementary Materials on International Organizations, 1948, (with W.G. Katz) Cases and Materials on Business Corporations, 1949, Labor Law Cases, Materials and Problems, 1970, supplement, 1972, 75, 2d edit., 1977, supplements, 1980, 82 (with S. Henderson), 3d edit. (with S. Henderson), 1985, supplement, 1988; also articles. Bd. dirs. Hyde Park Community Conf., 1954-56, S.E. Chgo. Commn., 1956-57. Served to lt. (j.g.) USNR, 1943-46. Mem. ABA (co-chmn. com. devel. law under NLRA 1959-60, mem. spl. com. transp. strikes), Ill. Bar Assn., Chgo. Bar Assn. (bd. mgrs. 1972-73), Am. Law Inst., Coll. Labor and Employment Lawyers, Am. Acad. Arts and Scis., Order of Coif, Phi Beta Kappa Home: 1219 E 50th St Chicago IL 60615-2908 Office: U Chgo Law Sch 1111 E 60th St Chicago IL 60637-2776 Office Phone: 773-702-9585. Business E-Mail: bernard_meltzer@law.uchicago.edu.

**MELTZER, BRAD,** writer; married. Grad., U. Michigan, Columbia Law Sch. Co-creator (TV series) Jack & Bobby, 2001 05; author The Tenth Justice, 1998, Dead Even, 1999, The First Counsel, 2001, The Millionaires, 2002, Zero Game, 2004, The Book of Fate, 2006, (comic books) Justice League of America, Green Arrow, 2003, Identity Crisis, 2005, (short stories) The Best Seat in the House, Final Farewell, an American Lawyer in London, The Craziest Kid in the World. Address: PO Box 801632 Aventura FL 33180*

**MELTZER, CLIFF,** information technology executive; MS in Computer Sci., Univ. Rochester. With IBM, 1975—91, rschr., T.J. Watson Rsch. Ctr. Rochester Ctr. Yorktown Heights, NY, 1981—91; sr. v.p. IOS Tech. divsn. Cisco Sys., 1992—98, sr. v.p., network mgmt. tech. group San Jose, Calif., 2003—; CEO, pres. Digital Fountain, 1999—2003. Entrepreneur in residence Redpoint Ventures, Menlo Park, Calif., 1999; spkr. in field. Office: Cisco Sys 170 W Tasman Dr San Jose CA 95134 Fax: 408-526-4100.*

**MELTZER, DANIEL J.,** law educator; b. Chgo., Dec. 17, 1951; AB in Economics, Harvard U., 1972, JD, 1975. Bar: Ill. 1975, DC 1978, Mass. 1983. Law clk. to Hon. Carl McGowan, 1975-76; law clk. to Hon. Potter Stewart, 1976-77; spl. asst. to sec. Joseph Califano Jr. Dept. Health, Edn. and Welfare, 1977-78; assoc. Williams & Connolly, 1979-81; asst. prof. law Harvard Law Sch., Cambridge, Mass., 1982-87, prof., 1987—, Story prof. law, 1998—, assoc. dean, 1989-93, vice dean physical planning, 2003—. Co-editor: The Judicial Code and the Rules of Procedure in the Fed. Courts, pub. annually, 1988—2000; co-author: Hart & Wechsler's The Federal Courts and the Federal System, 1973, 1988, 1996, 2003. Fellow: Am. Acad. Arts & Sciences. Office: Harvard Law Sch 1536 Massachusetts Ave Cambridge MA 02138 Office Phone: 617-495-4659. Office Fax: 617-496-4865. Business E-Mail: meltzer@law.harvard.edu.

**MELTZER, DAVID OWEN,** internist, educator, economist; b. N.Y.C., N.Y., Apr. 17, 1964; s. Herbert Yale and Sharon Bittenson Meltzer. BS, Yale U., 1986; PhD in Econs., U. of Chgo., 1992, MD in Econs., 1993. Diplomate Nat. Bd. Med. Examiners, 1994, Am. Bd. Internal Medicine, 1996. Lab. asst. Ill. State Psychiatric Inst., 1982; scientific rsch. asst. U. Chgo., 1983, econs. rsch. asst., dept. econs., 1984, econs. teaching asst., grad. sch. bus., 1988, econs. teaching asst., dept. econs., 1988, econs. rsch. asst., dept. econs., 1988—91, lectr., grad. sch. of pub. policy studies, 1991—93, asst. prof., dept. medicine, dept. econs., and grad. sch. pub. policy studies, 1996—2001, attending physician, Gen. Medicine Svcs., 1997—, physician care physician, Primary Care Group, 1997—, assoc. prof., dept. medicine, dept. econs., grad. sch. pub. policy studies, 2001—; genetics rsch. asst., dept. molecular biophysics and biochemistry Yale U., 1985, econs. rsch. asst., Econs. Growth Ctr., 1985—86; econs. tutor Yale Coll., 1985—86; resident in internal medicine Brigham & Women's Hosp. Harvard Med. Sch., Boston, 1993—96; associated faculty mem. Harris Sch., U. Chgo., 2001—, Dept. Econs., U. Chgo., 2001—. Faculty rsch. fellow Nat. Bur. Econ. Rsch., Cambridge, 1994—; dir. Ctrs. for Disease Control Chgo. Ctr. of Excellence in Health Promotion Econs.; co-dir., MD/PhD Program in the Soc. Sciences U. Chgo., 1997—, bd. dir. Graham Sch. Continuing Edn., 1998—, serves on faculty of graduate program in health adminstrn and policy, Population Rsch. Ctr., and Ctr. on Aging, mem., Com. to Assess Med. Informatics Initiative, 2000—, dir. Academic Hospitalist Iniatiative, dept. medicine, 2000—; co-dir. Robert Wood Johnson Clin. Scholars Program, 2001—; served on panel. "Future for Medicare" Nat. Acad. Social Insurance; served on tech. adv. panel Medicare for the Dept. Health and Human Svcs.; mem. steering com. Health and Retirement Survey, 2000—; invited lectr. and presenter; lectr. in field. Contbr. articles in profl. jours., chapters to books; reviewer Am. Econ. Review, Am. Jour. Medicine, Health Svcs. Rsch., Health Econs., JAMA, Jour. Gen. Internal Medicine, Jour. Health Econs., Jour. Human Resources, Jour. Labor Econs., Jour. Law & Econs., Jour. Polit. Economy, New England Jour. Medicine, Quality and Safety in Health Care, & Rand Jour. Econs., mem. editl. bd. Medical Decision Making, 1992—2002, Quality and Safety in Health Care, 2002—. Recipient Lee Lusted prize, NIH, 1996, Outstanding Paper award, 1998, Garfield award, Rsch. Am., 2002, Health Care Rsch. award, NIH Care Mgmt., Eugene Garfield Economic Impact award, Rsch. Am., Leaders in Gen. Medicine award, Midwest Soc. for Gen. Internal Medicine; John M. Olin Faculty Fellowship, 1999—2000. Mem.: Nat. Acad. Soc. Insurance, Phi Beta Kappa, Alpha Omega Alpha. Office: Univ Chgo 5841 S Maryland MC 2007 Chicago IL 60637 also: Univ Chgo 1155 E 60th St Ste 152 Chicago IL 60637 Office Phone: 773-702-0836. Office Fax: 773-834-2238. Business E-Mail: dmeltzer@medicine.bsd.uchicago.edu, dom2@midway.uchicago.edu.*

**MELTZER, DONALD RICHARD,** retired treasurer; b. Boston, Sept. 1, 1932; s. Leo N. and Betty (Flesher) M.; m. Mary Douglas Seelye, Dec. 7, 1963; children: Kimberly, Christopher. AB, Dartmouth Coll., 1954, MBA, 1955. Mgr. Peat, Marwick, Mitchell & Co., Boston, 1955-67; asst. controller United Fruit Corp., Boston, 1968-69, controller, 1969-70, v.p., controller, 1970-73; v.p., chief acctg. officer United Brands Co., N.Y.C., 1973-74, v.p. fin. and adminstrn., 1974-76; v.p. fin., treas. Instron Corp., Canton, Mass., 1976-88; v.p. fin. and adminstrn., treas., chief fin. officer Dialogue, Inc., Braintree, Mass., 1988-90. Corp. fin. cons., Sudbury, Mass., 1988-96. Overseer Children's Hosp. Med. Ctr., Boston, 1980-94; fin. com. Town of Sudbury, Mass., 1967; chmn. bd. trustees First Parish Ch., Sudbury, 1970-71, treas., 1991-93; pres. Mass. Parents Assn. for Deaf and Hard of Hearing, Boston, 1976-77, bd. dirs., 1973-86. Mem. AICPA, Mass. Soc. CPAs, Fin. Execs. Inst., Am. Assn. Indsl. Mgmt. (bd. dirs. 1980-85), Walk 'N Mass Volkssport Club (co-pres. 1993-95). Avocations: postal history, stamp collecting/philately. Home: 341 Old Lancaster Rd Sudbury MA 01776-2035

**MELTZER, E. ALYNE,** elementary school educator, social worker, volunteer; b. Jersey City, May 16, 1934; d. Abraham Samuel and Fannie Ruth (Nydick) Meltzer. BA, Mich. State U., 1956. Acctg. clk. Louis Marx Co. Inc., N.Y.C., 1957-60; tchr. social studies Haverstraw HS, NY, 1960-61; tchr. Sachem Ctrl. Sch. Dist., Farmingville, NY, 1961-63, East Paterson Sch. Dist., NJ, 1964-65; case worker dept. social svc. Human Resource Adminstrn., N.Y.C., 1966-89. Mem. Yorkville Civic Coun., 1988—93; policy advisor Senator Roy Goodman Adv. Com., Albany, 1987—90; mem. Temple Shaaray Tefila. Recipient Sabra Soc. Plaque award, State of Israel New Leadership Divsn., N.Y.C., 1979, Prime Min. Club Plaque award, State of Israel Bonds, 1986—87, 1996, Pin award, 1986—87, 1990, 1994—96, others. Mem.: AAUW, Jewish Genealogy Soc., Assn. Ref. Zionists Am., Am. Jewish Com., Internat. Coun. Jewish Women (participant Jerusalem seminar 1991, N.Am. region anti semitism seminar 2005), Nat. Coun. Jewish Women (life; rep. evening br. inter br. bd. 1972—74, chmn. program N.Y. sectr. evening br. 1973—74, participant nat. conv. 1987, Albany Inst. 1987, Washington Inst. 1987, N.E. dist. conv. 1988, Albany Inst. 1988, Israel Summit V 1988, Washington Inst. 1989, sec. sect. pub. affairs com. 1990—93, mem. state pub. affairs com. 1990—98, sec. pub. affairs com. 1990—, Albany Inst. 1991, Washington Mission 1991, co-chair Hunger Program Sunday Family Soup Kitchen 1991—93, nat. Israel affairs com. 1991—96, bd. dirs. N.Y. sect. 1991—, Jewish/Israel affairs com. sect. 1991—, Washington Inst. 1992, participant nat. conv. 1993, Albany Inst. 1993, chair Roosevelt Island Svcs. 1993—2003, participant nat. conv. 1996, Israel Roundtable 1996—99, co-chair fundraising 1998—2000, co-chair sec. Yad B'Yad (Hand in Hand with Israel) cmty. svc. project 1999—2005, film festival com. Eleanor Leff Jewish Women's Resource Ctr. 2001—02, co-chair sec. Jewish/Israel Affairs com. 2001—04, advisor sec. Jewish Israeli Affairs com. 2004—, participant nat. conv. 2005, life mem. N.Y. and Rockland County sects. Outstanding Vol. award 1973—74, 1990—91, Donor award 1987—93, 1996), People for the Am. Way, Mich. State U. Alumni Orgn. (life; sec. N.Y. chpt. 1959—60), Women's League for Israel (life), Jewish Hist. Soc. N.Y., Mothers and Others, Hadassah (life), Rockland County Jewish Home for the Aged (life), Sierra Club.

**MELTZER, JAY H.,** lawyer, retail executive; b. Bklyn., Mar. 30, 1944; s. Solomon G. and Ethel L. (Kraft) M.; m. Bonnie R. Rosenberg, June 27, 1965; children: Wendy, Elizabeth, Jonathan. AB, Dartmouth Coll., 1964; JD, Harvard U., 1967. Bar: N.Y. 1968, Mass. 1978, U.S. Dist. Ct. Mass. 1979. Law clk. to U.S. dist. judge, 1967-68; assoc. firm Shearman & Sterling, N.Y.C., 1968-72; with Damon Corp., Needham Heights, Mass., 1972-84, gen. counsel, sec., 1973-84, v.p., 1979-84; v.p., corp. counsel The TJX Cos., Inc., Framingham, Mass., 1984-87, v.p., gen. counsel, sec., 1987-89, sr. v.p., gen. counsel, sec., 1989—2005. Dir. coun. Better Bus. Bur., 1990-93. Mem. ABA, Am. Soc. Corp. Secs., Am. Corp. Counsel Assn. (bd. dirs. N.E. chpt. 1991-2000), Retailers Assn. Mass. (bd. dirs., exec. com., sec.), New Eng. Corp. Counsel Assn. (bd. dirs. 1979-2003). E-mail: jaymeltzer@comcast.net.

**MELTZER, MILTON,** author; b. Worcester, Mass., May 8, 1915; s. Benjamin and Mary (Richter) M.; m. Hilda Balinky, June 22, 1941; children: Jane, Amy. Student, Columbia, 1932-36. Adj. prof. history U. Mass., Amherst, 1977-80. Author: more than 100 books including Mark Twain Himself, 1960; author: (with Walter Harding) A Thoreau Profile, 1962; author: Langston Hughes: A Biography, 1968, Bread and Roses, 1967, Never to Forget: The Jews of the Holocaust, 1976, Dorothea Lange: A Photographer's Life, 1978; editor (with Langston Hughes, C. Eric Lincoln, Jon Michael Spencer): A Pictorial History of African-Americans, 1994; co-editor: Lydia Maria Child: Selected Letters, 1817-1880, 1982, The Black Americans, 1984, Mark Twain: A Writer's Life, 1985, George WAshington and the Birth of Our Nation, 1986, The American Revolutionaries, 1987, Benjamin Franklin: The New American, 1988, Rescue: The Story of How Gentiles Saved Jews in the Holocaust, 1988, Starting From Home: A Writer's Beginnings, 1988, Voices From the Civil War, 1989, Columbus and the World Around Him, 1990, The Bill of Rights: How We Got It and What It Means, 1990, Thomas Jefferson: Revolutionary Aristocrat, 1991, The Amazing Potato, 1992, Slavery: A World History, 1993, Lincoln: In His Own Words, 1993, Andrew Jackson and His America, 1993, Gold, 1993, Cheap Raw Material: How Our Youngest Workers Are Exploited and Abused, 1994, Theodore Roosevelt, 1994, Weapons and Warfare, 1996, Tom Paine, 1996, The Many Lives of Andrew Carnegie, 1997, Ten Queens: Portraits of Women of Power, 1998, Food, 1998, Carl Sandburg, 1999, Witches and Witch Hunts, 1999, Driven from the Land, 2000, They Came in Chains, 2000, Ten Kings, 2001, Ain't Gonna Study War No More, 2002, The Day the Sky Fell, 2002, Great Inventions: The Cotton Gin, 2003, Great Inventions: The Printing Press, 2003, Herman Melville, 2003, Edgar Allan Poe, 2003, Hour of Freedom: American History in Poetry, 2003, Hear That Train Whistle Blow! How the Railroad Changed the World, 2004, Milton Meltzer: Writing Matters, 2005,

Emily Dickinson, 2006. Served with USAAF, 1942-46. Recipient Laura Ingalls Wilder award, Am. Libr. Assn., 2001, Regina medal, Cath. Libr. Assn., 2000. Mem. Orgn. Am. Historians, Authors Guild, P.E.N. Address: 263 West End Ave New York NY 10023-2612

**MELTZER, ROGER,** lawyer; b. NYC, Jan. 31, 1951; s. Irwin Samuel and Beula (Jacobs) Meltzer; m. Robin Hirtz, July 20, 1975; children: Justin, Martin, Elizabeth. BA cum laude, Harvard U., 1973; postgrad., Tulane U., 1974-75; JD cum laude, NYU, 1977. Bar: NY 1978, DC 1979. Assoc. Cahill, Gordon & Reindel LLP, NYC, 1977-84, ptnr., 1984—, mem. exec. com., 2000—, chmn. hiring com. Bd. dir. Hain Celestial Group Inc., 2000—. Mem.: ABA, Order of Coif. Office: Cahill Gordon & Reindel LLP 80 Pine St Fl 17 New York NY 10005-1790 Office Fax: 212-378-2311. Business E-Mail: rmeltzer@cahill.com.

**MELTZER, STEVEN LEE,** lawyer; b. Rochester, N.Y., Sept. 6, 1946; s. Seymour Norman and Ruth (Pekarsky) M.; m. Harriet Vivian Lewis, Aug. 29, 1971; children: Debra, Scott, Jeremy. AB cum laude, Brown U., 1968; MBA with high distinction, Harvard U., 1973, JD, 1973. Bar: Md. 1973, D.C. 1974, Va. 1997. Assoc. Shaw, Pittman, Potts & Trowbridge, Washington, 1973-79, ptnr., 1980—2005, chmn. fin. com., 1985-88, chmn. corp. practice group, 1994—2005; ptnr., Corp. & Securities, Health Care, Emerging Growth & Tech. practices, mem. mng. bd. Pillsbury Winthrop Shaw Pittman, McLean, Va., 2005—. Exec. editor Technology Law Notes, 1986—. Trustee New Eng. Inst. Tech. 1974-, bd. chmn. 1989-; mem. bd, vis. Coll. Life Sci., Univ. Md.; sec., mem. exec. com., legal counsel Tech. Council Md.; founder & legal counsel Md. Angels Council; adv. Stargazer Found. Mem. ABA, Internat. Bar Assn., Info. Tech. Assn. Am., Nat. Venture Capital Assn. Corp. Dir., Mid-Atlantic Venture Assn., No. Va. Tech. Council, Biotechnology Industry Org., D.C. Bar Assn., Md. State Bar Assn., Harvard Bus. Sch. Club. Avocations: golf, tennis. Office: Pillsbury Winthrop Shaw Pittman 1650 Tysons Blvd Mc Lean VA 22102-4859 Office Phone: 703-770-7950. Office Fax: 703-770-7901. Business E-Mail: steven.meltzer@pillsburylaw.com.

**MELVILL, MICHAEL W.,** aircraft company executive, experimental test pilot; b. 1941; arrived in US, 1970; m. Sally Melvill; 1 child. FAA coml. cert., cert. ASEL, AMEL, instrument airplane, Rotorcraft-helicopter and Glider. V.p., gen. mgr., test pilot Scaled Co., Inc., Mojave, Calif., 1985—. Recipient Ivan C. Kincheloe trophy for work on devel. high altitude flight testing of model 281 Proteus, 1999. Mem.: Experimental Aircraft Assn., Aircraft Owners' and Pilots' Assn., Soc. Experimental Test Pilots (assoc. fellow). Achievements include participated in flight testing for Beech Starship prototype (NGBA), Fairchild's Next Generation Trainer for US Air Force (NGT), ARES, Pond Racer; built and flight tested Model 27 Variviggen; built, tested and flew around world in 1997 with Dick Rutan Model 61 Long-EZ; first flight of Model 72 GRIZZLY prototype, Model 77 SOLITAIRE prototype, Model 81 CATBIRD prototype, Model 120 PREDATOR prototype, Model 144 UAV prototype, Model 202 BOOMERANG, Model 226 RAPTOR; first flight of Model 281 PROTEUS, Model 316 SPACESHIPONE; first flight firing of GAU-12/U25mm cannon in Model 151 ARES jet fighter; only person to have flown Voyager Aircraft besides Dick Rutan and Jeana Yeager; holds 4 World and Nat. speed and altitude records in Catbird and Proteus Aircraft; first private manned mission to space, first civilian to fly a spaceship out of the atmosphere, first private pilot to earn astronaut wings, June 21, 2004; Guinness Book of World Records dubbed rocket launch "first ever privately funded manned spaceflight"; manned SpaceShipOne flight on Sept. 29, 2004, which will mark the first of two successful flight that are needed to win the Ansari X Prize. Office: Scaled Composites Inc 1624 Flight Line Mojave CA 93501 Office Phone: 661-824-4541. Office Fax: 661-824-4174.

**MELVIN, BILLY ALFRED,** clergyman; b. Macon, Ga., Nov. 25, 1929; s. Daniel Henry and Leola Dale (Seidell) Melvin; m. Marcia Darlene Eby, Oct. 26, 1952; children: Deborah Ruth, Daniel Henry II. Student, Free Will Baptist Bible Coll., Nashville, 1947—49; BA, Taylor U. Upland, Ind., 1951, LLD (hon.), 1984; postgrad., Asbury Theol. Sem., Wilmore, Ky., 1951—53; BD, Union Theol. Sem., Richmond, Va., 1956; DD, Azusa Coll., Calif., 1968, Huntington Coll., 1995. Ordained to ministry Free Will Baptist Ch., 1951; pastor First Free Will Baptist Chs., Newport, Tenn., 1951—53, Richmond, Va., 1953—57, Bethany Ch., Norfolk, 1957—59. Exec. sec. Nat. Assn. Free Will Baptists, 1959—67; exec. dir. Nat. assn. Evangelicals, 1967—95. Baptist. E-mail: bam1929@verizon.net.

**MELVIN, BOB,** professional baseball player; b. Palo Alto, Calif., Oct. 28, 1961; m. Kelley Melvin; 1 child, Alexi. Attended, Canada Coll.; graduated, Univ. Calif. Bekeley. Catcher Detroit Tigers farm system, 1981—85, Seattle Mariners, 1985, San Francisco Giants, 1985—88, Balt. Orioles, 1989—91, Kans. City Royals, 1992, Boston Red Sox, 1993, White Sox, 1994, NY Yankees, 1994; talent scout Milw. Brewers, 1996, roving instr., 1997, asst. gen. mgr., 1998, asst. mgr., 1999—2000; mgr. Seattle Mariners, 2003—05; bench coach Ariz. Diamondbacks, 2001—02, mgr., 2005—. Juvenile Diabetes Rsch. Found. Office: Chase Field 401 E Jefferson Phoenix AZ 85004*

**MELVIN, CAROLE RAMEY,** educational consultant; d. Roy Earl and Marjorie Smithson Ramey; m. James Preston Melvin, June 4, 1966; children: LindaJean Melvin Eastland, Robert Wesley. Med, Regent U., 1997. Mid. sch. math tchr. Va. Beach City (Va.) Pub. Sch., 1965—72, jr. high math tchr. 1989—94, academic, testing coord., 1994—98, libr., computer, testing coord., 1998—2000, sch. improvement specialist, 2000—; adj. prof. Regent U., Va. Beach, 1997—99. Sch. rep. Va. Beach Edn. Assn., 1997—98; facilitator Sch. Planning Coun., Va. Beach, 1999—; mem. Prins. Adv. Com., Va. Beach. Youth leader Va. Beach Christian Ch., 1989—92. Recipient Disting. Student award, Regent U. Mem.: NEA (assoc.), Assn. Supr., Curriculum Devel. (assoc.), Va. Edn. Assn. (assoc.), Va. Beach Edn. Assn. (assoc. Outstanding Math Tchr. award 1993). Office: Ctr Effective Learning 233 N Witchduck Rd Virginia Beach VA 23462-6507 Office Phone: 757-473-5038. Business E-Mail: crmelvin@vbschool.com.

**MELVIN, CHARLES EDWARD, JR.,** lawyer; b. Greensboro, N.C., July 13, 1929; s. Charles Edward and Mary Ruth (Plunkett) M.; m. Jacklyn McDaniel, Mar. 1, 1958; 1 child, Dana W. BS, U. N.C., 1951, JD with honors, 1956. Bar: N.C. 1956. Of counsel Smith Moore LLP, Greensboro, 1958—. Capt. U.S. Army, 1952-54. Mem. N.C. Bar Assn. (chmn. real property sect. 1981), Am. Coll. Real Estate Lawyers, Greensboro C. of C. (pres. 1978). Office: Smith Moore LLP PO Box 21927 Greensboro NC 27420-1927 Office Phone: 336-378-5204. Business E-Mail: charlie.melvin@smithmoorelaw.com

**MELVIN, PETER JOSEPH,** astrophysicist, educator; b. Seattle, Mar. 12, 1944; s. William Leopold and Virginia (Stevens) M.; m. Bernice Stenman, June 6, 1967 (div. July 1974); m. Alice Sue Pfiester, May 25, 1975 (dec. 1994); children: Robert Dennis, Chloe Anne. BA, Western Wash. State Coll. 1965; MS, U. Ill., 1966, PhD, 1970. NASA trainee U. Ill., Urbana, 1966-68, instr. phys. sci., 1970-72, asst. prof., 1972-77; sr. engr. Martin-Marietta Aerospace Co., Denver, 1977-80, staff engr., 1980-83; sr. specialist engr. engring. tech. applications divsn. Boeing Computer Svcs., Seattle, 1983-86; astrophysicist U.S. Naval Rsch. Lab., Washington, 1986-99, ret., 1999; pres. B-Gravity, Inc., Waldorf, Md., 1999—. Vis. faculty applied math. divsn. Nat. Bur. Stds. Boulder (Colo.) Labs., 1977. Contbr. articles to sci. jours.; patentee in field. Mem. AIAA, Am. Math. Soc., Soc. Indsl. and Applied Math., Am. Geophys. Uion, Am. Astronautical Soc. E-mail: melvin@nrl.navy.mil, pjmelvin@comcast.net.

**MELVIN, RONALD MCKNIGHT,** retired museum director; b. Regina, Sask., Can., Oct. 25, 1927; came to U.S., 1953; s. M. Gordon and Mary Gillespie (McKnight) M.; m. Gwen Ellis, Apr. 30, 1955; children: Mary Fleming, Catharine Melvin. Student, U. B.C., 1945-49. Various positions Powell River Co. Ltd., Vancouver, B.C., Canada, 1947-56; asst. to pres. Trans Union Corp., Chgo., 1956-58; mng. dir. Procor Ltd. subs. Trans Union Corp., Toronto, Ont., Canada, 1958-64; ptnr. Blunt Ellis & Simmons, Chgo.,

1964-71, pres., 1971-78; vice chmn. Blunt Ellis & Loew, Chgo., 1978-80; founding dir. Terra Mus. Am. Art, Evanston, Ill., 1980-84. Dir. Chef Pierre, Traverse City, Mich., 1972-77, Lawter Internat., Chgo., 1977-84. Author, organizer: (art exhbns.) Important Western Art from Chicago Collections, 1980 Five American Masters of Watercolor, 1981, American Naive Paintings From National Gallery of Art, 1982, Solitude--Inner Visions in American Art, 1982, Woman, 1984. Avocation: collecting worcester porcelain. Home: 585 Norfolk Rd PO Box 278 Southfield MA 01259-0278

**MELVIN, RUSSELL JOHNSTON (JAY MELVIN),** magazine publishing consultant; b. New Castle, Pa., Nov. 16, 1925; s. Russell Conwell and Anna Katharine (Johnston) M.; m. Helen Margaret Connery, Aug. 6, 1949; children: Thomas Kirk, Meredith. BA, U. Pa., 1949. Reporter Phila. Inquirer, 1949; copywriter, then asst. to circulation mgr. Time mag., 1949-53; with Newsweek mag., 1953-86, dir. Pacific edits., 1960-64, mng. dir. internat. edits., 1964-68, mng. editor internat. editorial service, 1969-86; cons. internat. affairs and profl. edn. Mag. Pubs. Assn. (formerly Mag. Pubs. Assn.), N.Y.C., 1986—2003. V.p. Newsweek, Inc., 1965-85; founding editor The Journal, Tokyo, 1963; founding dir. Newsweek Feature Service, 1968; mem. UN Communications Adv. Coun. With USNR, 1942—46. Mem. Internat. Advt. Assn. (exec. CEO 1980-85, exec. dir. Chgos. Corp. 1985-86, bd. dirs. 1988-91, mem. world coun. 1990—), Internat. Fedn. Periodical Press (vice chmn. 1990-94, mgmt. bd.), Univ. Club, Chappaqua Tennis Club, The Century Assn. Home: 4214 Kendal Way Sleepy Hollow NY 10591

**MELZACK, RONALD,** psychology professor; b. Montreal, Que., Can., July 19, 1929; s. Joseph and Annie (Mandel) M.; m. Lucy Birch, Aug. 7, 1960; children: Lauren, Joel. BSc, McGill U., Montreal, 1950, MSc, 1951, PhD, 1954; DLitt (hon.), U. Waterloo, 1992, DLaws (hon.), Dalhousie U., 2004. Lectr. Univ. Coll., London, 1957-58; assoc. prof. MIT, 1959-63; lectr. psychology McGill U., 1953-54, prof., 1963—; E.P. Taylor prof., 1986. Author: The Day Tuk Became a Hunter, and Other Eskimo Stories, 1967, Raven, Creator of the World, 1970, The Puzzle of Pain, 1973, Why the Man in the Moon is Happy, and Other Eskimo Creation Stories, 1977; author: (with P.D. Wall) The Challenge of Pain, 1982, 2d edit., 1988; author: Pain Measurement and Assessment, 1983; author: (with P.D. Wall) Textbook of Pain, 1984, 4th edit., 1999; author: (with D.C. Turk) Handbook of Pain Assessment, 1992, 2d edit., 2001; author: (with P.D. Wall) Handbook of Pain Management, 2003. Decorated Officer, Order of Can., 1995, Order of Quebec, 2000; recipient Molson prize Can. Coun., 1985, Gaston Labat award Am. Soc. Regional Anesthesia, 1989, J.J. Bonica award VI World Congress on Pain, 1990, Prix du Que. Marie-Victorin, 1994; recipient Disting. Contbn. award Can. Pain Soc., 1995, Rsch. Recognition award Canadian Anesthesiology Soc., 1997, Janet Travell award Am. Acad. Pain Mgmt., 1997, Killam prize, 2001. Fellow APA, AAAS, Royal Soc. Can., Can. Psychol. Assn. (Disting. Contbns. to Psychol. Sci. award 1986, hon. pres. 1988-89, gold medal award 2002); mem. Internat. Assn. Study of Pain (hon., past pres.). Home: 6111 Du Boisé Apt 5C Montreal PQ Canada H3S 2V8 Office Phone: 514-398-6084. Business E-Mail: rmelzack@mcgill.ca.

**MEMMOTT, SCOTT A.,** lawyer; b. Hartford, Conn., July 15, 1965; BS with high honors, USCG Acad., 1987; JD, U. Va., 1996. Bar: Va. 1996, DC Spl. asst. US atty., Norfolk, Va.; trial atty. civil divsn. US. Dept. Justice, Washington; with Shaw Pittman LLP, Washington; ptnr. Sonnenschein Nath & Rosenthal LLP, Washington, 2004—. Editor-in-chief: Va. Jour. Internat. Law. Founder Sept. 11th Pro Bono Legal Relief Project; mem. standing com. pro bono legal svcs. D.C. Ct. Jud. Conf.; gen. counsel Pentagon Meml. Fund, Inc. Served to lt. comdr. USCG. Mem.: ABA (mem. health law sect. & litig. sect.), Va. Bar Assn., DC Bar Assn. (mem. health law sect.), Am. Health Lawyers Assn. Office: Sonnenschein Nath & Rosenthal LLP Ste 600 E Tower 1301 K St NW Washington DC 20005 Office Phone: 202-408-9169. Office Fax: 202-408-6399. Business E-Mail: smemmott@sonnenschein.com.

**MEMORY, JASPER DURHAM,** academic administrator, physics professor; b. Raleigh, N.C., Dec. 10, 1936; s. Jasper Livingston and Margaret Moore (Durham) M.; m. Carolyn Hofler, June 4, 1961; children — Margaret Carolyn, Jasper William BS summa cum laude, Wake Forest U., 1956; PhD, U. N.C., 1960. Successively asst. prof., assoc. prof. physics U. S.C., Columbia, 1960-64; assoc. prof. N.C. State U., Raleigh, 1964-67, assoc. dean, physics and math. scis., 1973-82, prof. physics 1967—98, vice-provost, grad. dean, 1982—86, dir. corp. and govtl. affairs, 1998-99; v.p. for research U. N.C. System, 1986—98, prof. emeritus 1998—. Bd. govs. Research Triangle Inst., Research Triangle Park, N.C., 1983-84, Triangle Area rsch. dir., 1981-98; cons. NASA Langley, Hampton, Va., 1970-74, Ohio Bd. Regents, 1993-95, Ark. Bd. Regents, 1987, Mass. Bd. Regents, 1998; N.C. State U. rep. Oak Ridge Associated Univs., 1982-85, Grad. Record Exam. Bd., 1985-90, chair, 1989, Policy Coun., Test of English as a Fgn. Lang., 1987-88, chair, 1988. Author: Quantum Theory of Magnetic Resonance Parameters, 1968; (with others) NMR of Aromatic Compounds, 1982, High Resolution NMR in the Solid State: Fundamentals of CP/MAS, 1994. Recipient Outstanding Tchr. award N.C. State U., 1967, Disting. Alumni Service award Wake Forest U., 1981 Fellow Am. Phys. Soc.; mem. Am. Assn. Physics Tchrs., Phi Beta Kappa, Sigma Xi. Democrat. Presbyterian. Home: 4815 Rembert Dr Raleigh NC 27612-6237 E-mail: jmemory@nc.rr.com.

**MEN, HONGSHENG,** biologist, researcher; b. Tongbai, Henan, China, May 18, 1962; s. Jianfeng Men and Shuzhen Li; m. Shunling Tan May, 2, 1989; 1 child, Li. BS, Henan Normal U., Xinxiang, China, 1982—86; MS, Chinese Acad. Scis., Kunming, Yunnan, China, 1986—89; PhD, U. Wis., Madison, 1996—2002. Asst. rschr. Kunming Inst. Zoology, Chinese Acad. Scis. 1986—91, asst. prof., 1992—96; vis. scientist Animal Biotechnology Cambridge Ltd, England, 1991—92; grad. rsch. asst., dept. animal scis. U. Wis., Madison, 1996—2002; rsch. scientist, dept. vet. pathobiology U. Mo., Columbia, 2003—. Rschr. Kunming Inst. Zoology, Chinese Acad. Scis., 1986—96. Contbr. papers to profl. jours. and pubs. Mem.: Soc. Cryobiology, Soc. for Study of Reproduction, Internat. Embryo Transfer Soc. Freedom. Achievements include research in demonstration of cryoinjury to bovine oocytes at DNA level; demonstration of the degeneration mechanism of cryopreserved bovine oocytes to be apototic in nature during culture; improvement in the cryosurvival of porcine embryos produced in vitro through chemical delipation; improved monospermic penetration of porcine oocytes emplying a modified in vitro fertilization system. Home: 1814 E Broadway 2S Columbia MO 65201 Office: Dept Vet Pathobiology Univ Mo 1600 E Rollins St Columbia MO 65211 Office Phone: 573-884-9523. Office Fax: 573-884-7521. Business E-Mail: menho@missouri.edu.

**MENA, DANIEL,** lawyer, arbitrator; s. Oswaldo and Martha Mena; m. Maite Pilar Portuondo, Nov. 21, 1997; children: Eric, Sofia. Cert. in Spanish History, U. Salamanca, 1986. BA, Fla. Internat. U., 1992; JD, U. Fla., 1995. Bar: U.S. Dist. Ct. (so. dist.) Fla. 1996, U.S. Dist. Ct. (mid. dist.) Fla. 1997, U.S. Dist. Ct. (no. dist.) Fla. 1998, U.S. Ct. Appeals (11th cir.) 1995, U.S. Supreme Ct. 1999. Assoc. atty. Baker & McKenzie, Miami, Fla., 1993—94; intern civil litig. U.S. Atty.'s Office, Phila., 1994—95; assoc. atty. Gunster, Yoakley & Stewart, Miami, 1995—98; ptnr. Holland & Knight LLP, Miami, 1998—. Mem. civil procedure rules com. Fla. Bar, Tallahassee, 2004—. Contbr. articles to profl. jours. Mem. legal bd. Amigos Together For Kids, Miami, Fla., 2003. Named Selected Up & Comer, South Fla. Legal Guide, 2002. Mem.: ABA (com. internat. law), Dade County Bar Assn. (com. internat. litig.), Chamber South. Independent. Roman Catholic. Avocations: travel, scuba diving, fishing, boating. Office: Holland & Knight LLP 701 Brickell Ave Suite 3000 Miami FL 33131 Office Phone: 305-789-7528. Office Fax: 305-789-7775. Business E-Mail: daniel.mena@hklaw.com.

**MENAKER, DANIEL,** publishing executive; s. Robert Owen Menaker; m. Katherine Bouton; 2 children. B in English, Swarthmore Coll., 1963; M in English, Johns Hopkins U., 1965. H.S. tchr.; joined as a fact checker The New Yorker, 1969, copy editor, sr. editor; v.p., sr. literary editor Random House, Inc., N.Y.C., 1994—2001; exec. editor Harper Collins, N.Y.C., 2001—03; sr. v.p., editor-in-chief Random House Imprint Random House, Inc., N.Y.C., 2003—04, exec. editor-in-chief, 2004—. Author: (novels) The Treatment,

1998, (collection of short stories) Friends and Relations, 1976, Old Left and other stories, 1987. Office: Random House Inc 1745 Broadway New York NY 10019 Home: 180 Riverside Dr 11E New York NY 10024 E-mail: dmenaker@randomhouse.com.

**MENAKER, FRANK H., JR.,** lawyer; b. Harrisburg, Pa., Aug. 23, 1940; s. Frank H. and Romaine (Sadler) M.; m. Sharon Ann Lynch, Feb. 21, 1981; children: Denise L., Jamie E.; children by previous marriage: David C., Michelle R. BA, Wilkes Coll., 1962; JD, Am. U., 1965. Bar: D.C. 1966, Md. 1975, U.S. Supreme Ct. 1975. Formerly staff counsel Office Gen. Counsel, GAO, Washington; asst. divsn. counsel for aerospace ops. Martin Marietta Corp. Aerospace Divsn., 1970—73, asst. gen. counsel, 1973—77, gen. counsel, 1977—81, Martin Marietta Corp., 1981-95, corp. v.p., 1982—95; v.p., gen. counsel Lockheed Martin Corp., 1995-96, sr. v.p., gen. counsel, 1996—2005; ptnr. DLA Piper Rudnick Gray Cary LLP, 2006—. Spl. counsel U.S. Commn. on Govt. Procurement, 1971. Mem. ABA (mem. sect. pub. contract law, former chair), Md. Bar Assn., Wash. Met. Corp. Counsel Assn. (bd. dirs. 1988-95). Office: DLA Piper Rudnick Gray Cary 1200 Nineteenth St NW Washington DC 20036 Office Phone: 202-861-6302. Business E-Mail: frank.menaker@dlapiper.com.

**MENAKER, MICHAEL,** biology professor; b. Vienna, May 19, 1934; came to U.S., 1934; s. William and Esther (Astin) M.; m. Shirley Ann Lasch, June 4, 1955; children: Ellen Margaret, Nicholas. BA in Biology, Swarthmore Coll., 1955; PhD in Biology, Princeton U., 1960. Asst. instr. Princeton (N.J.) U., 1955-57; postdoctoral fellow Harvard U., Cambridge, Mass., 1960-62; asst. prof. zoology U. Tex.-Austin, 1962-68, assoc. prof., 1968-72, prof., 1972-79; prof. biology U. Oreg., Eugene, 1979-86, dir. interdisciplinary program for neuroscis., 1979-81, dir. Inst. Neurosci., 1981-85; Commonwealth prof. biology U. Va., Charlottesville, 1987—, chmn. dept., 1987-93; dir. Howard Hughes Undergrad. Rsch. Program in Biol. Sci., Charlottesville, 1989-94; core investigator Sci. and Tech. Ctr. in Biol. Timing U. Va., Charlottesville, 1991—. Benjamin Meaker vis. prof. U. Bristol, Eng., 1986. Assoc. editor Behavioral Neurosci., Jour. Biol. Rhythms; contbr. articles to profl. jours. Recipient Lifetime Achievement award Am. Soc. for Photobiology, 2002, Life Achievement in Sci. award Va.'s Outstanding Scientists and Industrialists, 2003; NSF fellow, 1958-59, 60-62; NIH fellow, 1960-62; Guggenheim Found. fellow, 1971-72. Fellow AAAS, Am. Acad. Arts and Scis., Japan Soc. Promotion of Scis. (sr.); mem. Soc. Neuroscis., Am. Physiol. Soc., Soc. Rsch. Biol. Rhythms. Avocations: literature, music, sailing. Office: U Va Dept Biology Gilmer Hall PO Box 400328 Charlottesville VA 22904-4328 Office Phone: 434-982-5767. Business E-Mail: mm7e@virginia.edu.

**MENAKER, RONALD HERBERT,** retired bank executive; b. NYC, Dec. 17, 1944; s. Harold L. Menaker and Gladys (Bleiberg) Ross; m. Kathleen Sager Thomas, Sept. 11, 1966; children: Meredith E., Kyri D. Student, Queen's Coll., 1965—66. Mng. dir. J.P. Morgan & Co., Inc., NYC, 1966—2000; ret., 2000. Bd. dirs. Reckson Assocs. Realty Corp., 2002—. Past trustee NYU Med. Ctr. and Health Sys., NYC, 1991, The Am. Kennel Club Mus. of the Dog, St. Louis, 1989—; bd. dirs., chmn. Am. Kennel Club, NYC, 2002; trustee, vice chmn., past chmn. NYU Downtown Hosp., 1991—; bd. overseers U. Pa. Vet. Sch., 2000—. Mem.: Westminster Kennel Club. Avocations: sporting art, judging dogs. Office Phone: 212-696-8359. Business E-Mail: rhm@akc.org.

**MENAND, LOUIS,** literature educator, writer; m. Emily Menand; 2 children. BA, Pomano Coll., 1973, MA, 1975; PhD in English, Columbia U., 1980. Disting. prof. English Grad. Ctr. CUNY; English Princeton U., Columbia U., U. Va. Sch. Law; Anne T. and Robert M. Bass Prof. of English and Am. Lit. and Language Harvard U., Cambridge, 2003—. Contbg. editor NY Rev. of Books, 1994—; staff writer The New Yorker. Author: Discovering Modernism: T.S. Eliot and His Context, 1986, Metaphysical Club: A Story of Ideas in America, 2001 (Pulitzer Prize for History, 2002, Francis Parkman Prize, 2002, Heartland Prize for Non-Fiction), American Studies, 2002; editor: Pragmatism: A Reader, 1996, The Future of Academic Freedom, 1997, The Best American Essays, 2004; co-editor: The Cambridge History of Literary Criticism, Vol. 7: Modernism and the New Criticism, 2000. Office: Harvard U Barker Ctr Rm 161 12 Quincy St Cambridge MA 02138 Office Phone: 617-495-8780. Office Fax: 617-497-8737. E-mail: menand@fas.harvard.edu.

**MENARD, JOHN R., JR.,** home improvement retail executive; b. Wisc., 1940; Grad., U. of Wis., Eau Claire, 1963. Founder, pres., CEO Menard Inc., Eau Claire, Wis., 1960—; owner, pres. Menard Racing, 1979—. Bd. dirs. Polaris Industries. Named one of Forbes' Richest Americans, 2006. Office: Menard Inc 4777 Menard Dr Eau Claire WI 54703-9625*

**MENCER, GLENN EVERELL,** federal judge; b. Smethport, Pa., May 18, 1925; s. Glenn Hezekiah and Ruth Leona (Rice) M.; m. Hannah Jane Freyer, June 24, 1950; children—Ruth Ann, Cora Jane, Glenn John BBA, U. Mich., 1949, JD, 1952. Bar: Pa. 1953, U.S. Dist. Ct. (we. dist.) Pa. 1953, U.S. Supreme Ct. 1958. Sole practice, Eldred, Pa., 1953-64; dist. atty. McKean County, Pa., 1956-64; judge 48th Jud. Dist. Ct., Smethport, 1964-70, Commonwealth Ct. of Pa., Harrisburg, 1970-82, U.S. Dist. Ct., Erie, Pa., 1982—. Served with U.S. Army, 1943-45, ETO Mem. Fed. Judges Assn., Pa. Bar Assn., McKean County Bar Assn. Lodges: Masons (33 degree). Republican. Methodist. Home: 30 W Willow St Smethport PA 16749-1524 Office: US Dist Ct Fed Courthouse PO Box 1820 Erie PA 16507-0820 Office Phone: 412-644-3576.

**MENCER, JETTA,** lawyer; b. Coshocton, Ohio, Apr. 7, 1959; d. William J. and Virginia M. (Fry) M. BS, Ohio State U., 1980, JD, 1983. Bar: Ohio, U.S. Dist. Ct. (so. dist.) Ohio. Assoc. Berry, Owens & Manning, Coshocton 1983-86; asst. pros. atty. Coshocton County, 1983-86, Licking County, Newark, Ohio, 1986-88, asst. atty. gen., 1988-95; pvt. practice Coshocton, 1995-96; prosecuting atty. Coshocton County (Ohio) Prosecutor's Office, 1997-2001; atty. Lee Smith & Assocs., Columbus, Ohio, 2001—03; pvt. practice Columbus, 2003—. Treas. Coshocton County Dem. Cen. & Exec. Coms., 1984-86; chmn., 1986-88; sec., bd. dirs. Heart Ohio Girl Scout Council, Inc., Zanesville, Ohio, 1985-87; fin. chmn., bd. dirs. YMCA, Coshocton, 1985-87. Mem. Ohio State Bar Assn., Coshocton County Bar Assn., Lions Club. Democrat. Methodist. Office: One S Park Pl Newark OH 43055 Office Phone: 740-345-5171. Personal E-mail: jmencer@columbus.rr.com.

**MENCER, SUE (CONSTANCE SUZANNE MENCER),** former federal agency administrator; b. Nov. 15, 1947; m. John Mencer; children: Jessie, Alex. BA in Spanish, Ohio St. U., 1968; Grad., JFK Sch. Govt., Harvard U., 2003. Tchr. Spanish, 1968—78; spl. agt. FBI, 1978—85, supervisory spl. agt., 1985—90, supr., 1990—98; pvt. cons. Anti-Terrorism Tng., Denver; exec. dir. dept. pub. safety State of Colo., Denver, 2003—05; exec. dir. Office of State & Local Govt. Coordination & Preparedness US Dept. Homeland Security, Washington, 2003—05; sr. policy advisor govt. rels. group Brownstein Hyatt & Farber, PC, Denver, 2005—. Mem.: Commn. on Jud. Discipline, Sec. Former Spl. Agents. Office: Brownstein Hyatt & Farber PC 410 17th St 22nd Fl Denver CO 80202 E-mail: smencer@bhf-law.com.*

**MENCH, JOHN WILLIAM,** retail executive, electrical engineer; b. NYC, Feb. 27, 1943; s. John William and Edna (Ilgen) M.; m. Rose Irene Miller, Aug. 12, 1962 (dec. Jan. 1997); 1 child, William Ilgen; m. Ann Ward Frentress, Mar. 7, 1998. BSEE, U. Sc., 1969; MBA, Ohio U., 1983; PhD, Calif. Coast U., 1994. Registered profl. engr., Ohio; Ga.; cert. in heating, ventilating and air conditioning; accredited profl. Leadership in Energy and Environ. Design. Elec. engr. Uniroyal, Shelbyville, Tenn., 1969-74; facility engr. Kroger, Nashville, 1974-77, asst. mgr. facility engring. Atlanta, 1977-79, Kroger mktg. area mgr. facility engring. Columbus, Ohio, 1979-85; divsn. mgr. facility engring. v.p. Safeway Stores, Inc., Oakland, Calif., 1985-86; v.p. constrn., engring. Big V Supermarkets, Inc., Florida, NY, 1986-95; pres.

Mench & Assocs. Inc., 1994-98. Assoc. prof. Pa. Coll. Tech., 1996-99; lectr. So. Poly. State U., 1999—; prof. Am. Contr. Exch., 1999-2003. Author: (tech. manuals) Comments on Commercial Refrigeration, 1998, Comments on Commercial Air Conditioning, 1998, Plan Review, 1995, others, (textbook) Finance for Construction Management, 2004. Trustee Meth. Ch., 1987—93; bd. dirs. Goshen Day Care Ctr., 1988—95, Elec. Distbn. Systems, 1993—94; past v.p. Tri State V.W. Assn.; exec. adv. bd. Ohio U. Coll. Bus. Adminstrn., 1992—97, life mem.; v.p. Prime Time Group, 2003—05, pres., 2006. Mem. ASHRAE, IEEE (sr.), Assn. Energy Engrs. (sr.). Republican. Methodist. Business E-Mail: jmench@spsu.edu.

**MENCHACA, FRANK,** editorial director; b. Huntington Station, N.Y., Aug. 5, 1961; s. Antonio and Anna (Lopez) M.; m. Deirdre Sullivan, Sept. 16, 1988; children: Gabriel, Aidan, William. BA, NYU, 1983; MA, Yale U., 1986. Jr. editor John Wiley & Sons, N.Y.C., 1983-85; assoc. editor Chelsea Hare Pubs., N.Y.C., 1985-88; lit. editor George Braziller, N.Y.C., 1988-90; assoc. editor Weekly Reader Corp., Middletown, Conn., 1990-92; acquisitions editor Millbrook Press, Brookfield, Conn., 1992-94; editl. dir. Gale Group, Woodbridge, Conn., 1994—. Book reviewer Pubs. Weekly, N.Y.C., 1990-93, participant seminar for acquisition of Latin Am. Libr. materials. Author: (books) Nicolo G and the Days of November, 1991 (VLS award 1991), AL, 1998. Instr. World Prison Poetry Ctr., New Haven, Conn., 1985-88. Mem. MLA, Am. Soc. for 18th Century Studies, Phi Beta Kappa. Democrat. Avocations: writing, publishing. Office: Primary Source Media 12 Lunar Dr Woodbridge CT 06525-2322 Home: 4526 Wagon Wheel Dr Bloomfield MI 48301-1138

**MENCHACA, ROBERT,** elementary school educator; b. Del Rio, Tex., Jan. 24, 1952; s. Antonio and Alicia (Espinoza) M.; m. Fstella Calzada; children. Roberto Jr., Antonio, Rosalva, Mariza, Daniel. BS in Edn., Sul Ross State U., 1973; MEd, East Tex. State U., 1980. Bilingual kindergarten tchr. San Felipe-Del Rio I.S.D., 1974-77, Dallas I.S.D., 1978-84, Seguin I.S.D., 1984-90, North East I.S.D., 1990-92, tchr. 4th grade, 1992-2000, tchr. kindergarten, 2000—. Speaker, presenter in field. Author: Fue David, 1992, Una noche inolvidable, 1992, Daniel y el dia de la pesca, 1992, (with E. Menchaca) Daniel Goes Fishing, 1992. Nominated Tchr. of Yr. Tex. Assn. Bilingual Edn., 1992. Mem. Tex. State Reading Assn. (v.p.-elect Tex. coun. reading and bilingual child group, Tchr. Excellence award 1991), Internat. Reading Assn., Nat. Assn. Bilingual Edn., Tex. Assn. Bilingual Edn. (Bilingual Tchr. of Yr. award 1992), San Antonio Area Assn. Bilingual Edn. (recognized for teaching excellence 1992, Tchr. of Yr. award 1992), Alamo Reading Coun. (bd. dirs., co-chair San Antonio libr. found., treas. 1992-93, Tex. State Tchrs. Assn. Indiv. award for Human and Civil Rights 1995, Excellence in Teaching award 1991). Office: Olmos Elementary School 1103 Allena Dr San Antonio TX 78213-4199

**MENCHER, BRUCE STEPHAN,** judge; b. Washington, May 21, 1935; s. Emanuel and Bertha Miriam (Robbin) M.; m. Janet Patricia Whitfield, Nov. 24, 1974; children by previous marriage: Sean Robbin, Marc Nadzo. BA, George Washington U., 1957, JD with honors, 1960. Bar: D.C. 1960, U.S. Supreme Ct. 1964. Gen. atty. Office Gen. Counsel, Dept. Agr., 1960—61; asst. corp. counsel for D.C., 1961—67; atty.-adviser Office Gen. Counsel, Bur. for Africa, AID, 1967—69; ptnr. Wilkes & Artis, Washington, 1969—75; assoc. judge Superior Ct. D.C., 1975—91, sr. judge, 1991—, presiding judge Family divsn., 1988—90. Professorial lectr. law George Washington U. Nat. Law Ctr., 1982-83; lectr. criminal justice Nat. Cathedral Sch./St. Albans Sch., 1985; faculty advisor Nat. Jud. Coll., 1995. Asst. rsch. editor George Washington Law Rev., 1959-60; contbr. articles to law revs. Mem. gen. alumni gov. bd. George Washington U., 1972-80; bd. dirs. Nat. Child Support Enforcement Assn., 1994-97, The Washington Savoyards Ltd., 1991-96, Trinity Chamber Orch., 2001—. Recipient Alumni Svc. award, 1975, Judge of Yr. award Assn. Plaintiffs Trial Attys., 1983, Samuel Green award for disting. svc. to Washington legal comty. and Phi Delta Phi, 1985, Disting. Alumni Achievement award George Washington U., 1987, also various appreciation and recognition awards local bar assns., D.C. and fed. govts. for work in area of family law and child support enforcement. Mem. ABA, Bar Assn. D.C., D.C. Bar, George Washington Law Assn. (exec. com. 1972-77), The Barristers (exec. com. 1981), George Washington Am. Inn of Ct. (pres. 1999—2000, Phi Delta Phi (pres. Barrister Inn 1974-75) Office: Superior Ct DC 500 Indiana Ave NW Rm 5520 Washington DC 20001-2131 Office Phone: 202-879-1358. *While it may sound old-fashioned, I attribute my appointment to the bench, in large part, to hard work, dedication, a love of the law and respect for my fellow man. One should maintain his sense of balance, always try to understand the other person's position and, at all costs, maintain a sense of humor throughout.*

**MENCHER, MELVIN,** journalist, educator; b. Bklyn., Jan. 25, 1927; s. Peter and Theresa (Sherman) M.; m. Helen Chamberlain, Aug. 27, 1947; children: Thomas, Marianne, Nicholas. Student, U. N.Mex., 1943-44; BA, U. Colo., 1947; postgrad. (Nieman fellow), Harvard, 1952-53. Reporter UP, 1947-50; state polit. corr. Albuquerque Jour., 1951-54; reporter Fresno (Calif.) Bee, 1954-58; asst. prof. journalism U. Kans., Lawrence, 1958-62; asst. prof. Columbia U., N.Y.C., 1962-65, assoc. prof., 1965-75, prof., 1975-90, assoc. dir. summer program for journalism edn. of minorities, 1971, prof. emeritus, 1990—. Contbg. author: Evaluating the Press, 1973; author: News Reporting and Writing, 1977, Basic Media Writing, 1983; editor: The FNMA Guide to Buying, Financing and Selling Your Home, 1973; contbr. articles to profl. jours. Mem. Soc. Profl. Journalists, Nat. Council Coll. Pubs. Advisers, Kappa Tau Alpha. Home: 450 Riverside Dr New York NY 10027-6801 E-mail: mm55@columbia.edu.

**MENCHER, STUART ALAN,** sales and marketing executive; b. NYC, Apr. 25, 1939; s. Meyer H. and Mildred B. Mencher; m. Judith Leslie Schneider; children: Jane Lizabeth, Tracy Ellen. B in Mgmt. Engring., Rensselaer Poly. Inst., 1960; MBA, NYU, 1963. Sales rep. Sperry Rand Univac, Albany, NY, 1960-62; various sales and mktg. mgmt. positions IBM Corp., White Plains, NY, 1965-78, br. mgr. data processing div. Harrison, NY, 1978-81; dir. market ops. planning, bus. mktg. dept. AT&T, Basking Ridge, NJ, 1981-83; dir. market mgmt., sales and mktg. div. AT&T Info. Systems, Morristown, NJ, 1983, dir. data systems mktg., 1983-84, v.p. mktg., large bus. systems div., 1985-87; sr. v.p. sales and mktg. MCI Communications Corp., Washington, 1987-90; sr. v.p., gen. mgr. U.S. distbn. div. Motorola/Codex Corp., Mansfield, Mass., 1990-91; sr. v.p., gen. mgr. Teleport Communications, N.Y.C., 1992-93, v.p. nat. sales and mktg., 1994-98; v.p. strategic planning AT&T Bus. Svcs., Bridgewater, NJ, 1998-99; mng. ptnr. The Mencher Group LLC, East Hampton, NY, 1999—. Bd. dirs. Broadview Networks, N.Y.C., 2000-05. Pres. Westfield Men's Coll. Scholarship Club, NJ, 1977; coach Westfield Young Soccer Assn., 1976—81; mem. budget rev. com. United Fund, Westfield, NJ, 1983—85; mem. adv. bd. N.Y.C. Tech. Coll., 1993; mem. Mayor's Telecomms. Mutual Aid and Restoration Com., N.Y.C., 1992—93; v.p., bd. dirs. Ctr. Children and Families/Safe Space, N.Y.C., 1999—; chmn. mktg. adv. com. YMCA Greater N.Y., N.Y.C., 1999—2004. Lt. USCGR, 1962—65. Avocations: golf, travel, theater, arts. Office: PO Box 5134 East Hampton NY 11937-6165

**MENCHIK, DANIEL ARON,** sociologist, researcher; b. Madison, Wis., Nov. 16, 1976; s. Paul and Bettie Ann (Landauer) Menchik. BA in Polit Sci., U. Wis., Madison, 1995—99; MPhil, U. Cambridge, Eng., 2001—02. Tchr. Yorktown HS, Arlington, Va., 1999—2001; grad. rschr. U. Chgo., 2003—. Recipient Louise Johnson Scholarship, Am. Sociology Assn., 2006. Office: Univ Chgo Sociology Dept 1126 E 59th St Chicago IL 60637

**MENCHIK, PAUL LEONARD,** economist, educator; b. NYC, Sept. 16, 1947; s. Irving and Elinor (Swedlow) M.; m. Bettie Ann Landauer, May 28, 1972; children: Daniel Aron, Jeremy Matthew. BA, SUNY, Binghamton, 1969; AM, U. Pa., 1971, PhD, 1976. Lectr. Rutgers Coll., New Brunswick, NJ, 1974-76; rsch. assoc. Inst. for Rsch. on Poverty, U. Wis., Madison, 1976-79; prof. dept. econs. Mich. State U., East Lansing, Mich., 1979—; chairperson dept. econs., 1992-96, dir. grad. studies, 2005—; sr. economist, econ. policy Office Mgmt. & Budget, Washington, 1990-91. Acad. visitor

Stanford (Calif.) U., 1980, London Sch. Econ., 1987-88; vis. assoc. prof. U. Pa., Phila., 1982-83; vis. scholar Congrl. Budget Office, 1997-98; cons., advisor in field. Mem. editl. bd. Jour. Income Distbn., Amsterdam, 1992—; contbr. articles to profl. jour.; Hon. Rsch. Fellow, Univ. Coll., London, 2003. Grantee NSF, Social Security Adminstrn., U.S. Dept. Health and Human Svcs.; recipient Best Article of Yr. award Econ. Inquiry, 1987. Mem. Am. Econ. Assn., Nat. Tax Assn., Nat. Bur. Econ. Rsch. Conf. on Income & Wealth. Avocations: bowling, racquetball, golf, travel, camping. Office: Mich State U 101 Marshall Hall E Circle Dr East Lansing MI 48824 Office Phone: 517-355-4553. Business E-Mail: menchik@msu.edu.

**MENCHIN, ROBERT STANLEY,** marketing executive; b. Kingston, N.Y., Oct. 31, 1923; s. Abraham H. and Gertrude (Gorline) M.; m. Marylin Barsky, Dec. 26, 1949; children: Jonathan, Scott. BA, NYU, 1948. Acct. exec. DKG Advt., N.Y.C., 1949-51; dir. spl. porjects Am. Visuals Corp., N.Y.C., 1952-59; dir. advt. and pub. rels Arthur Wiesenberger & Co., N.Y.C., 1959-65; pres. Wall Street Mktg. Communs., Inc., N.Y.C., 1967-77; dir. mktg. commn. Chgo. Bd. Trade, 1977-83, v.p. comm. and member rels., 1983-87; pres. Wall Street Mktg., Chgo., 1987—. Author: The Last Caprice, 1964, Where There's a Will, 1977, The Mature Market: A Strategic Marketing Guide to America's Fastest-Growing Population Segment, 1989, New Work Opportunities for Older Americans, 1993, 101 Classic Jewish Jokes: Jewish Humor from Groucho Marx to Jerry Seinfeld, 1997. With AUS, 1942-45. Mem. Am. Mktg. Assn., Pub. Rels. Soc. Am., Fin. Planners Assn. Home: The Breakers 5333 Sheridan Rd Apt 21N Chicago IL 60640 E-mail: robertmenchin@sbcglobal.net.

**MENCIO, GEORGE, JR.,** lawyer; b. Havana, Cuba, Jan. 16, 1951; BS in Polit. sci., Fla. Internat. U., 1978; JD cum laude, U. Miami Sch. Law, 1981. Bar: Fla. 1981, US Dist. Ct. (So. Dist. Fla., US Ct. Appeals (11th Cir.), US Ct. Appeals (DC Cir.), US Supreme Ct. Joined Holland & Knight LLP, 1981—, ptnr. Miami, Fla., 1987—, mem dir. com., bd. dir., head, internat. practice area. Articles and comment editor Miami Sch. Law Law Review; contbr. articles to profl. jours. Mem.: Fla. Bar, Internat. Bar Assn., Inter-Am. Bar Assn., Cuban-Am. Bar Assn., Miami-Dade County Bar Assn. Office: Holland & Knight LLP 701 Brickell Ave Ste 3000 Miami FL 33131 Office Phone: 305-789-7702. Business E-Mail: gmencio@hklaw.com.

**MENDE, HOWARD SHIGEHARU,** mechanical engineer; b. Hilo, Hawaii, Nov. 19, 1947; s. Tsutomu and Harue (Kubomitsu) M. BS in Mech. Engring., U. Hawaii, 1969; MS in Mech. Engring., U. So. Calif., 1975. Registered profl. engr., Calif. Mem. tech. staff I Rockwell Internat., Anaheim, Calif., 1970-71, LA, 1971-73, mem. tech. staff II, 1973-77, mem. tech. staff IV, 1984-86; devel. engr. AiRsch. Mfg. Co., Torrance, Calif., 1977-83; mech. engr. Def. Contracts Mgmt. East, Santa Ana, Calif., 1987-94, electronics engr., 1994—. Lectr. Pacific States U., LA, 1974-75. Mem. ASME. Democrat. Buddhist. Home: 1946 W 180th Pl Torrance CA 90504-4417 Office: Def Contract Mgmt Agy 18901 S Wilmington Ave Bldg DH 2 Carson CA 90746-2856 Personal E-mail: hmende@socal.rr.com. Business E-Mail: howard.mende@dcma.mil.

**MENDE, ROBERT GRAHAM,** retired engineering association executive; b. Newark, Dec. 4, 1926; s. Herman Ernest and Etta (Hillenbrand) M.; m. Joan B. Tamlyn, Apr. 12, 1958; children: Lisa Anne, Robert Graham Jr. Student, Mass. Inst. Tech., 1944-45; degree, N.Y. State Maritime Acad., 1947; BS, Webb Inst. Naval Architecture, 1951. Project engr. Foster Wheeler Corp., N.Y.C., 1953-56; dist. mgr., naval architect Bird-Johnson Co., N.Y.C., 1956-62; sr. naval architect J.J. Henry Co., Inc., N.Y.C., 1962-69; exec. dir. Soc. Naval Architects and Marine Engrs., 1969-91. Mem. marine engring. coun. Underwriters Labs., Inc., 1969-91; ad hoc vis. com. Engrs. Coun. for Profl. Devel., 1970-72. Bd. dirs. Friends of World Maritime U., 1987-91; trustee Webb Inst. Naval Architecture, 1987-91. Lt. USNR, 1951-53. Fellow Royal Inst. Naval Architects, Soc. Naval Architect and Marine Engrs. (hon. life v.p., chmn. N.Y. sect. 1968-69, Vice Admiral E.S. Jerry Land medal 1991, Robert G. Mende Bldg. hdqrs. bldg. named in his honor); mem. ASME, Am. Soc. Naval Engrs., Am. Soc. Assn. Execs., Coun. Engring. and Sci. Soc. Execs. (bd. dirs. 1988-91), Maritime Coll. Assn., N.E. Coast Inst. Engrs. and Shipbuilders, Webb Alumni Assn. (pres. 1970-72). Personal E-mail: robertgmende@aol.com. *Hard work, perseverance, humility and a dash of deprivation almost always insure success. It also doesn't hurt to be in the right place at the right time.*

**MENDEL, JERRY MARC,** electrical engineering educator; b. NYC, May 14, 1938; s. Alfred and Eleanor (Deutch) M.; m. Letty Susan Grossman, June 26, 1960; children: Jonathan, Aileen. BMechE cum laude, Poly. U., 1959, MEE, 1960, PhD in Elec. Engring., 1963. Registered profl. engr., Calif. Instr. elec. engring. Poly. Inst. Bklyn., 1960—63; engring. scientist and sect. chief McDonnell-Douglas Astronautics Co., Huntington Beach, Calif., 1963-74; prof. dept. elec. engring. systems U. So. Calif., L.A., 1974—, chmn. dept., 1984-91, dir. Signal and Image Processing Inst., 1991-94, assoc. dir. edn. Integrated Media Sys. Ctr., 1996—2004. Pres., founder MENTECH, Culver City, Calif., 1983—; pres. United Signals and Systems, Inc., 1989-2001. Author: Discrete Techniques of Parameter Estimation: The Equation Error Formulation, 1973, Optimal Seismic Deconvolution: An Estimation Based Approach, 1983 (Phi Kappa Phi award 1984), Lessons in Digital Estimation Theory, 1987, Maximum-Likelihood Deconvolution, 1990, Lessons in Estimation Theory for Signal Processing, Communications and Control, 1995; editor: Prelude to Neural Networks: Adaptive and Learning Systems, 1994, Uncertain Rule-Based Fuzzy Logic Systems: Introduction and New Directions, 2001; co-editor: Adaptive Learning and Pattern Recognition Systems, 1970. Fellow IEEE (Centennial medal 1984, Third Millennium medal 2000); mem IEEE Control Systems Soc. (Disting. mem. 1986), IEEE Neural Networks Soc. (AdCom 2004—). Office: U So Calif Dept Elec Engring Sys Eeb 400 Los Angeles CA 90089-2564 Office Phone: 213-740-4445. Business E-Mail: mendel@sipi.usc.edu.

**MENDEL, NATE (NATHAN GREGOR MENDEL),** musician; b. Seattle, Dec. 2, 1968; Bassist Sunny Day Real Estate, 1992—95, Foo Fighters, 1995—, The Fire Theft, 2002—. With Sunny Day Real Estate (albums) Diary, 1994, Sunny Day Real Estate, 1995, with Foo Fighters Foo Fighters, 1995, The Colour & the Shape, 1997, There is Nothing Left to Lose, 1999 (Grammy Award, Best Rock Album, 2001), One by One, 2002 (Grammy Award, Best Rock Album, 2004), In Your Honor, 2005, (songs) This is a Call, 1995, Big Me, 1996 (MTV Music Video award, Best Group Video, 1996), Everlong, 1998, My Hero, 1998, Walking After You, 1998, Learn to Fly, 1999 (Grammy Award, Best Short Music Video, 2001, VH1: 100 Greatest Videos, 2001), Breakout, 2000, The One, 2002, All My Life, 2002 (Grammy Award, Best Hard Rock Performance, 2003), Darling Nikki, 2004, Best of You, 2005, DOA, 2005, with The Fire Theft (albums) The Fire Theft, 2003, actor, composer (films) Our Burden is Light, 2005. Achievements include Foo Fighters named one of 100 Greatest Rock Artists, VH1, 2000, 100 Sexiest Artists, VH1, 2002, Top Pop Artists of the Past 25 Yrs., 2004. Office: RCA Records 1133 Ave of the Americas New York NY 10036 Office Phone: 212-930-4000.*

**MENDEL, NATHAN GREGOR See MENDEL, NATE**

**MENDELL, JOSHUA T.,** molecular biologist, geneticist, educator; b. Columbus, Ohio, Nov. 22, 1973; s. Jerry R. and Joyce N. Mendell; m. Kathryn A. O'Donnell, June 18, 2005. BA, Cornell U., Ithaca, NY, 1996; MD, Johns Hopkins U., Balt., PhD, 2003. Asst. prof. Johns Hopkins U., 2004—. Contbr. articles to profl. jours. Recipient Michael A. Shanoff Rsch. award, Johns Hopkins U. Sch. Medicine, 2003, Postdoctoral Basic Sci. award, Am. Soc. Human Genetics, 2003; fellow, Howard Hughes Med. Inst., 1995, Johns Hopkins U., 2003—04; scholar, NSF, 1990; Rita Allen scholar, Rita Allen Found., 2006, Basil O'Connor scholar, Mar. Dimes, 2004—06. Mem.: RNA Soc., Phi Beta Kappa. Achievements include patents for novel therapeutic targets for cancer; novel method to identify mutated genes in human diseases;

research in novel mechanisms through which oncogenes promote tumorigenesis. Office: Johns Hopkins University 733 N Broadway BRB 471 Baltimore MD 21205 Office Phone: 410-502-0428.

**MENDELOW, CLIVE G.,** real estate company executive; b. 1946; V.p. Binswanger Mgmt. Corp., pres.; COO, exec. v.p. Binswanger Co., 1991; vice chmn., COO Chesterton Blumenauer Binswanger, Phila., 1997—. Eminent Profl. fellow, Royal Instn. Chartered Surveyors, London, 2002. Office: Chesterton Blumenauer Binswanger Two Logan Sq Philadelphia PA 19103

**MENDELS, JOSEPH,** psychiatrist, educator; b. Cape Town, South Africa, Oct. 29, 1937; came to U.S., 1964; s. Max and Lily (Turecki) M.; m. Ora Kark, Jan. 22, 1960; children: Gilla Avril, Charles Alan, David Ralph. MB, BChir, U. Cape Town, 1960; MD, U. Witwatersrand, Johannesburg, South Africa, 1965. Asst. prof., assoc. prof. psychiatry and pharmacology U. Pa., Phila., 1967-73; prof. U. Pa. and VA Hosp., Phila., 1973-80; med. dir. Fairmount Inst., Phila., 1980-81; hon. prof. psychiatry and human behavior Thomas Jefferson Med. Ctr., 1986—; med. dir. Med. Inst., Phila., 1981-95, Therapeutics PC, Phila., 1981-98. Cons. NIMH, NIH, numerous pharm. cos., 1968—; lectr. to univs. and hosps. worldwide, 1968—. Author, editor: Concepts of Depression, 1971, Biological Psychiatry, 1973, Psychobiology of Affective Disorders, 1981; contbr. over 200 articles to med. jours. V.p., mem. bd. govs. Am. Jewish Com.; nat. bd. dirs. Project Interchange. Fellow Internat. Coll. Neuropsychopharmacology, Am. Coll. Neuropsychopharmacology. Personal E-mail: jos737@comcast.net.

**MENDELSOHN, BRUCE S.,** lawyer; b. Alexandria, Va. BS with honors, Univ. Md., 1974, JD with honors, 1977. Bar: Md. 1977, DC 1980. Atty., spl. counsel, divsn. corp. fin. US Securities and Exchange Commn., 1977—80, counsel to commr., 1980—82, chief, office regulatory policy, divsn. investment mgmt., 1982—83; joined Akin Gump Strauss Hauer & Feld LLP, 1983—, now. ptnr., co-chair corp. fin. practice group and mem. mgmt com. Washington. Bd. contbr. editors and advisors Securities Regulation Law Journal. Bd. visitors Univ. Md. Sch. of Law. Mem.: ABA, Md. State Bar, DC Bar, Beta Gamma Sigma. Office: Akin Gump Strauss Hauer & Feld LLP Robert S Strauss Bldg 1333 New Hampshire Ave NW Washington DC 20036-1564 Office Phone: 202-887-4446. Office Fax: 202-955-7781. Business E-Mail: bmendelsohn@akingump.com.

**MENDELSOHN, CAROL S.,** television producer; Student, Smith Coll., Cornell U. Writer CSI and CSI: Miami CBS, LA; with Securities and Exchange Commn.; atty. Washington; writer Fame NBC, LA; with Stephen J. Cannell; exec. prodr. Melrose Pl. NBC, 1990—99; exec. prodr. CSI CBS, LA, 2000—. Author: (TV series) Clifford the Big Red Dog, CSI (nominated Emmy Outstanding Drama Series award, 2002, 2003, nominated TV Prodr. of Yr. award, 2003, 2004), CSI: Miami, Gabriel's Fire, Hardcastle & McCormick, J.J. Starbuck, Melrose Place, Providence, Stingray, Teenage Mutant Ninja Turtles, Wiseguy, (films) To Brave Alaska.

**MENDELSOHN, JOHN,** oncologist, hematologist, educator, health facility executive; b. Cin., Aug. 31, 1936; s. Joe and Sarah (Feibel) M.; m. Anne Charles, June 23, 1962; children: John Andrew, Jeffrey Charles, Eric Robert. BA in BioChemical Sciences, Harvard U., 1958, MD, 1963. Diplomate Am. Bd. Internal Medicine, Am. Bd. Hematology, Am. Bd. Med. Oncology. Intern, resident Peter Bent Brigham Hosp., Boston, 1963-65, 67-68; fellow in hematology Washington U. Sch. Medicine, St. Louis, 1968-70; asst. prof. to prof. medicine U. Calif., San Diego, 1970-85, Am. Cancer Soc. prof. clin. oncology La Jolla, 1982-85, dir. Cancer Ctr., 1977-85; prof. medicine, vice-chmn. Cornell U. Med. Coll., NYC, 1985-96; Winthrop Rockefeller chmn. dept. medical oncology, co-head, molecular pharmacology and therapeutics program Meml. Sloan Kettering Cancer Ctr., NYC, 1985-96; pres., prof. medicine U. Tex. M.D. Anderson Cancer Ctr., Houston, 1996—; vice chmn. BioHouston, 2001—. Bd. sci. counselors Nat. Cancer Inst., 1986—90, 1996—2001; cons., mem. sci. adv. bd. Progenics Pharms.; founder, 1st dir. U. Calif. San Diego Cancer Ctr.; mem. Nat. Dialogue on Cancer, 1999, Team on Cancer Rsch., 2001, U. Calif. San Diego External Adv. Com., 2000, Gov.'s Biotech. Panel, Ctr. for Houston's Future; mem. external adv. bd. John Hopkins Oncology Ctr., 1993—; faculty U. Tex. Graduate Sch. Biomedical Sciences. Editor-in-chief (textbook) The Molecular Basis of Cancer; mem. editl. bd. Growth Factors, Jour. Biol. Response Modifiers, Expert Rev. Anticancer Therapy; editor-in-chief Clin. Cancer Rsch.; founding editor Clin. Cancer Rsch.; contbr. articles to profl. jours. Mem. Gov.'s Cancer Coun., Calif., 1981—85; bd. dirs. Am. Cancer Soc., San Diego, 1981—85, Houston Grand Opera, BioHouston, Ctr. for Houston's Future, Houston Forum; bd. dirs., mem. healthcare task force Greater Houston Partnership, 1997; bd. dirs., mem. exec. com. Houston Tech. Ctr., 1998—, nat. cancer policy bd., 1999—; mem. bd. overseers Harvard Med. Sch.; trustee Houston Grand Opera. Named Headliner of Yr. in Medicine, San Diego, 1985; recipient Bourgine award for excellence in cancer rch., Svc. d'Oncologie Med. Pitie-Saltpetriere, 1997, Jill Rose award for oustanding breast cancer rsch., Breast Cancer Rsch. Found., 1999, Gold medal of Paris, 1997, Cancer Rsch. award, Bristol-Myers Squibb, 1997, Joseph H. Burchenal Clin. Rsch. award, Am. Assn. for Cancer Rsch., 1999, Simon Shubitz prize, Univ. Chgo., 2002, David A. Karnofsky award, Am. Soc. of Clin. Oncology, 2002, Freedom to Discover Achievement award in Cancer, Bristol-Myers Squibb, 2004; Fulbright scholar, U. Glasgow, Scotland, 1958—59. Mem.: ACP, AAAS (electorate nominating com. sect. on med. scis. 2001), Am. Clin. and Climatol. Assn., Harvard Overseers' Com., Royal Netherlands Acad. Arts and Scis., Inst. Medicine U.S. NAS, Century Assn., Am. Soc. Hematology, Am. Assn. Cancer Rsch. (4th Joseph H. Burchenal award 1999), Am. Soc. Clin. Oncology (lectr. David A. Karnofsky award 2002), Am. Soc. Clin. Investigation, Assn. Am. Physicians, Phi Beta Kappa. Achievements include rsch. in establishing inhibition of tumor growth by antibodies against growth factor receptors. Office: U Tex MD Anderson Cancer Ctr 1515 Holcombe Blvd # 91 Houston TX 77030-4009 E-mail: jmendelsohn@mdanderson.org.*

**MENDELSOHN, LOUIS BENJAMIN,** financial analyst; b. Providence, R.I., Mar. 26, 1948; s. Alvin Harold and Frances (Leitner) M.; m. Illyce Deborah Greenspan, Aug. 29, 1976; children: Lane Jeffrey, Ean Graham, Forrest Lee. BS, Carnegie Mellon U., 1969; MSW, SUNY, Buffalo, 1973; MBA with hons., Boston U., 1977. Rsch. asst. Mass. Gen. Hosp., Boston, 1969-71; regional health planner Comprehensive Health Planning Coun., Buffalo, 1973-74; adminstv. resident New Eng. Hosp., Boston, 1976; mgmt. specialist Humana Hosp. Bennett, Ft. Lauderdale, Fla., 1977-78; asst. exec. dir. Humana Women's Hosp., Tampa, Fla., 1978-80; pres., CEO Market Technologies Corp., Wesley Chapel, Fla., 1979—; CEO Market Technologies LLC, 2004—, Predictive Techs. Group LLC, 2004—. Author: Trend Forecasting with Techinal Analysis: Unleashing the Hidden Power of Intermarket Analysis to Beat the Market, 2000, Forex Trading Using Intermarket Analysis, 2006; contbg. rschr.: The Encyclopedia of Technical Market Indicators, 1988; contbg. author: High Performance Futures Trading, 1990, Virtual Trading, 1995, Artificial Intelligence in the Capital Markets, 1995, Trade Your Way to Financial Freedom, 1999, Trading Chicago Style, 1999; contbg. writer Tech. Analysis of Stocks and Commodities Mag.; editor newsletter Neural-Financial News, 1991; developer investment software ProfitTaker, 1979—, VantagePoint, 1988—. USPHS fellow, 1975-77. Mem. Market Technicians Assn., Colleague Internat. Fedn. of Tech. Analysts, Beta Gamma Sigma. Achievements include pioneering strategy back-testing and optimization in technical analysis software for microcomputers, 1983; introduction of first commercial strategy testing trading software in financial industry for microcomputers and first intermarket analysis software in fin. industry for microcomputers. Office: Mkt Techs LLC 5807 Old Pasco Rd Wesley Chapel FL 33544-5108 Office Phone: 813-973-0496. E-mail: ww@tradertech.com

**MENDELSOHN, ROY M.,** psychiatrist; b. Chgo., May 24, 1927; s. Abraham Hyman and Bernice Mendelsohn; m. Arlene Joy Pick, Nov. 27, 1949; children: Barie, Gail, Lynn, Mark. BS, U. Ill., 1950; MD, U. Ill. Coll. Medicine, 1952. Cert. adult psychiatry Am. Psychiatry Assn., 1959, child psychiatry Am. Psychiatry Assn., 1961, adult psychoanalysis Am. Psycho-

analysis Assn., 1967, child psychoanalysis Am. Psychoanalysis Assn., 1969. Dir. child clin. Wash. U., St. Louis, 1959—61, dir. tng. child psychiatry, 1961—81; cons. Jewish Family Svcs., St. Louis, 1963—80, Meth. Child Home, St. Louis, 1964—82; dir. Growth Ctr., St. Louis, 1976—84. Author: All Depends on How You Look At It, 1987, I of Consciousness, 1987, Principles of Ideal Therapist, 1987, Believing Is Seeing, 1987, Manifest, 1989, Dream, 1989, Leaps, 1990, How Can Talking Help, 1991, Pearls, 1997, Mister Magoo is My Role Model, 2005; editor: Am. Jour. Psychotherapy. Bd. examiner Am. Bd. Psychiatry and Neurology. With USN, 1945—46, San Diego. Fellow: Am. Ortho. Psychiatric Assn. (life); mem.: Am. Psychiatric Assn. (life). Jewish. Avocations: golf, softball, bridge, music, travel. Office: 404 S Clay Saint Louis MO 63146 E-mail: royboy72@msn.com.

**MENDELSON, ALAN CHARLES,** lawyer; b. San Francisco, Mar. 27, 1948; s. Samuel Mendelson and Rita Rosalie (Spindel) Brown; children: Jonathan Daniel, David Gary; m. Agnès Marie Barbariol. BA with great distinction, U. Calif., Berkeley, 1969; JD cum laude, Harvard U., 1973. Bar: Calif. 1973. Assoc. Cooley Godward LLP, San Francisco, 1973-80, ptnr. Palo Alto, 1980-2000, mng. ptnr. Palo Alto office, 1990-95, 96-97; sec. acting gen. counsel Amgen Inc., Thousand Oaks, Calif., 1990-91; acting gen. counsel Cadence Design Sys., Inc., San Jose, Calif., 1995-96; sr. ptnr. Latham & Watkins LLP, Menlo Park, Calif., 2000—. Bd. dirs. QLT Inc.; co-chair venture & tech. group Latham & Watkins; mem. bd. advisors Santa Clara Computer and High Tech. Law Jour.; mem. emerging cos. sect. governing body Biotech. Industry Orgn., 2004—. Bd. dirs. Bay Bio, Calif. Alumni Assn., 2005-; chmn. Piedmont (Calif.) Civil Svc. Commn., 1978-80; fundraiser Harvard Law Sch. Fund, U. Calif. Berkeley Health Svcs. Initiative, Lucille Packard Children's Hosp.; pres., mem. exec. com. bd. dirs. No. Calif. chpt. Nat. Kidney Found., 1986-98; mem. Overseers' Com. to visit Harvard Law Sch., 2004-. With USAR, 1969-75. Recipient Disting. Svc. award Nat. Kidney Found., 1992; named U. Calif. Berkeley Alumni scholar, 1966, Scaife Found. scholar, 1966, One of 100 Most Influential Attys. in U.S. Nat. Law Jour., 1994, 97, 2000, 06. Mem. Calif. Alumni Assn. (bd. dir.), Bohemian Club, Phi Beta Kappa. Jewish. Home: 76 De Bell Dr Atherton CA 94027-2253 Office: Latham & Watkins LLP 140 Scott Dr Menlo Park CA 94025 Office Phone: 650-463-4693. Business E-Mail: alan.mendelson@lw.com.

**MENDELSON, EDWARD JAMES,** English literature educator; b. NYC, Mar. 15, 1946; s. Ralph and Grace Bernice (Stein) M.; m. Cheryl Neel Noble, 1990; 1 child, James. BA, U. Rochester, 1966; PhD, Johns Hopkins U., 1969. Instr. English Yale U., New Haven, 1969-70, asst. prof., 1970-76, assoc. prof., 1976-79; vis. assoc. prof. Columbia U., N.Y.C., 1979-80, assoc. prof. English, 1981-83, prof., 1983—; vis. assoc. prof. English Harvard U., Cambridge, Mass., 1977-78; lit. executor Estate of W.H. Auden. Author: Early Auden, 1981; editor: Homer to Brecht, 1977, Pynchon: A Collection of Critical Essays, 1978, The English Auden, 1978, Later Auden, 2000, The Things That Matter, 2006; editor: Complete Works of W.H. Auden, 1988—; contbg. editor PC Mag. Fellow Am. Council Learned Socs., 1974-75, NEH, 1980-81, Guggenheim Found., 1986-87 Mem. Acad. Lit. Studies, Societe Européene de Culture Office: Columbia U Dept English 602 Philosophy Hall New York NY 10027

**MENDELSON, ELLIOTT,** mathematician, educator; b. N.Y.C., May 24, 1931; s. Joseph and Helen (Bienstock) M.; m. Arlene Zimmerman, Jan. 25, 1959; children: Julia, Hilary, Peter. AB, Columbia U., 1952; MA, Cornell U., 1954, PhD, 1955. Instr. U. Chgo., 1955-56; jr. fellow Soc. Fellows, Harvard U., 1956-58; Ritt instr. Columbia U., 1958-61; mem. faculty Queens Coll., CUNY, 1961—, prof. math., 1965—. Dir., instr. NSF math. program for high sch. students, 1964-71; researcher axiomatic set theory and math. logic, especially ind. various important propositions of axiomatic set theory, axiom of choice, axiom of restriction; participant NSF Time 2000 Project for future secondary sch. math. tchrs., 1998—. Author: Introduction to Mathematical Logic, 1997, Boolean Algebra and Switching Circuits, 1970, Number Systems, 1973, Beginning Calculus, 1997, 3000 Solved Problems in Calculus, 1988, Differential and Integral Calculus, 1997, Quick Calculus, 1999, Introducing Game Theory and Its Applications, 2004; contbr. articles to profl. jours. Mem. Am. Math. Soc., Math. Assn. Am., Assn. for Symbolic Logic, Phi Beta Kappa. Home: 10 Pinewood Rd Roslyn NY 11576-2420 Office: Queens Coll Dept Math Flushing NY 11367 Office Phone: 516-621-0313. E-mail: emenqc@msn.com.

**MENDELSON, JOAN RINTEL,** lawyer; b. N.Y.C., July 19, 1941; d. Leon and Myra Rintel; m. Neil H. Mendelson, July 30, 1959; children: Debora C., Marie Mendelson Piccarreta. BA with high distinction, with honors in Zoology, Ind. U., 1962, MA, 1963; JD, U. Ariz., 1974. Bar: Ariz. 1975. Co-founder and co-dir. Catonsville Coop. Nursery Sch., Md., 1967—69; assoc. Law Offices of Ann Bowen, Tucson, 1975—76; pvt. practice Tucson, 1977—80; asst. atty. gen. Office of Atty. Gen., Tucson, 1980—2000. Instr. biology U. Md. Balt. County, Catonsville, 1968; spl. magistrate Tucson City Ct., 1984—91; mem. Pima County Child Fatality Rev. Bd., Tucson, 1982—; mem. legal counsel Gov.'s Task Force on Sch. Age Child Care, Phoenix, 1984—86; mem. Pima County Citizen Rev. Bd., Tucson, 2000—; mem. child abuse team Ariz. Health Scis. Ctr., Tucson, 1983—2000; mem. ad hoc com. on child protective svcs. and related child welfare issues Ariz. Legislature, Phoenix, 1994—2000, mem. legal and statutory reform subcom. ad hoc com. on child protective svcs. and related child welfare issues, 1994—2000, chair sys. and policy changes subcom. ad hoc com. on child protective svcs. and related child welfare issues, 1996—2000; mem. model ct. steering com. Pima County Juvenile Ct., Tucson, 1996—2000, mem. model ct. workgroup, 1998—2000; mem. emergency juvenile rules com. Ariz. Supreme Ct., Phoenix, 1998—99, mem. juvenile rules com., 1999—2000, mem. ct. improvement project adv. workgroup, 1998—2003; mem. Pima County Interagency Task Forces on Custodial Interference, Tucson, 1997—2000, Pima County Child Adv. Ctr. Adv. Bd., Tucson, 1997—99; mem. child adv. clinic adv. bd. Coll. Law U. Ariz., Tucson, 1998. Fellow, Ford Found., 1961, NSF, 1962; N.Y. State Regents scholar, 1958. Mem.: Sigma Xi, Phi Beta Kappa. E-mail: njmend@earthlink.net.

**MENDELSON, JOEL STUART,** allergist, immunologist; b. Bklyn., Nov. 2, 1956; BS, Bklyn. Coll., 1978; MD, U. Ctrl. East Dominican Rep., 1982. Diplomate Am. Bd. Allergy/Immunology, Am. Bd. Pediatrics, Am. Bd. Pediatric Infectious Diseases. Pres. pediacatrics St. Lukes Roosevelt Med. Ctr./Columbia U., N.Y.C., 1982-85; fellow allergy, immunology and infectious disease U. Med. and Dentistry N.J., Newark, 1985-87; asst. dir. dept. allergy and immunology Childrens Hosp. N.J., Newark, 1987-88; dir. dept. allergy and immunology Beth Israel Med. Ctr., Newark, 1992—. Cons. in field. Contbr. articles to profl. jours. Fellow Am. Acad. Allergy and Immunology, Am. Coll. Allergy and Immunology, Am. Acad. Pediatrics; mem. Infectious Disease Soc. N.J. Home: 17 Dartmouth Rd Cranford NJ 07016-1651

**MENDELSON, LEE M.,** film company executive, film producer, film director, writer; b. San Francisco, Mar. 24, 1933; s. Palmer C. and Jeanette D. (Wise) M.; children: Glenn, Linda, Jason, Sean. BA, Stanford U., 1954. With Sta. KPIX-TV, 1961-63; chmn. bd., pres. Lee Mendelson Film Prodns. Inc., Los Angeles and Burlingame, Calif., 1963—. Guest instr. in communications Stanford U. Exec. producer, co-writer (miniseries) This Is America, Charlie Brown; producer: Charlie Brown, Cathy, Betty Boop, (TV spls.) John Steinbeck's Travels with Charley, American and Americans, The Fantastic Funnies, You Asked for It, Here Comes Garfield, (animated films) A Boy Named Charlie Brown, Snoopy Come Home, Race for Your Life Charlie Brown, Peanuts, Bon Voyage Charlie Brown (And Don't Come Back), Garfield and Friends, Mother Goose and Grim. Served to 1st lt. USAF, 1954-57. Recipient 7 Emmy awards, 3 Peabody awards. Mem. Writers Guild Am., Dirs. Guild Am. Office: Lee Mendelson Film Prodn Inc 330 Primrose Rd Ste 215 Burlingame CA 94010-4028

**MENDELSON, NINA,** law educator; AB summa cum laude, Harvard U.; JD, Yale U. Law clk. for Judge Pierre Leval So. Dist. NY; for Judge John Walker Jr., Second Cir.; atty. Heller, Ehrman, White & McAuliffe, Seattle, US

Dept. Justice, Environment and Natural Resources Div.; prof. law U. Mich Law Sch., Ann Arbor. Fellow Senate Com. on Environment and Pub. Works. Contbr. articles to law jours. Recipient Thomas Neville Award, Wash. State Bar Assn. Mem.: Phi Beta Kappa. Office: U Mich Law Sch 339 Hutchins Hall 625 S State St Ann Arbor MI 48109-1215 Office Phone: 734-936-5071. Office Fax: 734-763-9375. E-mail: nmendel@umich.edu.

**MENDELSON, RICHARD DONALD,** former communications company executive; b. N.Y.C., Dec. 2, 1933; s. George and Martha (Goodman) M.; m. Marilyn Miller, July 28, 1956; children: Sandra, Kenneth. BS, Wharton Sch. U. Pa., 1955; JD, NYU, 1959. Bar: N.Y. 1960; CPA, N.Y. Asst. atty. gen. N.Y. State Dept. Law, N.Y.C., 1959-70; v.p., treas. Petry TV, N.Y.C., 1971-75; v.p., dir. corp. devel. Katz Communications, Inc., N.Y.C., 1975-77, sr. v.p. ops., 1977-79, sr. v.p., chief fin. officer, 1979-81, exec. v.p., chief operating officer, 1981-82, pres., chief oper. officer, 1982-89; free-lance writer, 1989—. Mem. Employee Stock Ownership Assn. Am. (pres. 1987-88, bd. dirs.), Ballen Isles Country Club (Palm Beach Gardens, Fla.l bd. dirs. 2000-06, pres. 2006). Home and Office: 71 Saint George Pl Palm Beach Gardens FL 33418-4024 Personal E-mail: themeri@aol.com.

**MENDELSON, ROBERT ALLEN,** polymer scientist, rheologist; b. Cleve., 1930; s. Julius and Theodora Anne M.; m. Lura Lauzon, 1971 (dec. 1999); children: John A. Blackstone, Marie L. Taylor. BS in Indsl. Chemistry, Case Inst. Tech., 1952, PhD in Phys. Chemistry, 1956. From sr. rsch. chemist to sci. fellow rsch. dept. Monsanto Co., Texas City, Tex., 1956-72, sci. fellow Springfield, Mass., 1972-89, sr. sci. fellow, 1989-91; rheology focus area leader Baytown (Tex.) Polymers Ctr. Exxon Chem., 1991-94, rheology prin. investigator, 1995-99; ret., 1999. Mem. com. for pub. policy Am. Inst. Physics, 1985-89; collaborator Univ. Rsch. Programs, Cornell U., 1989-91. Mem. editl. bd. Journal of Rheology, 1986-99; contbr. chpts. to books and articles to profl. jours.; patentee in field. Mem. AAAS, Soc. Rheology (pres. 1989-91, v.p. 1987-89, sec. 1974-78), Am. Chem. Soc. (Arthur Doolittle award div. organic coatings and plastics 1982). Home: 5001 Woodway Dr Unit 1803 Houston TX 77056-1701

**MENDELSON, SOL,** physical science educator, consultant; b. Checonovska, Poland, Oct. 10, 1926; came to U.S., 1927; s. David C. and Frieda (Cohen) M. BME, CCNY, 1955; MS, Columbia U., 1957, PhD, 1961. Prof. engring. CCNY, 1955-58; sr. scientist Sprague Electric Co., North Adams, Mass., 1962-64, Airborne Instruments Lab., Melville, NY, 1964-65; phys. metallurgist Bendix Rsch. Lab., Southfield, Mich., 1966-67; cons., rschr., writer, N.Y.C. and Troy, Mich., 1968-72; adj. research phys. sci. CUNY, 1972-87. Contbr. numerous articles to sci. jours. Mem. Am. Phys. Soc., Fedn. Am. Scientists, Sigma Xi, Tau Beta Pi, Pi Tau Sigma. Achievements include research on theory and mechanisms of Martensitic transformations; research on degeneracy in phase transitions and its universal nature which shows that revolutions in science are still possible. *We have to keep reminding each other that data proclaims theory, but theory does not proclaim anything if it is not physical and addresses crucial data. Ambiguous data or unrealistic models have brought prominence to some theories, but those who succeed are based on crucial data and physical models. Such theories give insight into related problems, and to theories of many things and everything.*

**MENDELSON, CORY J.,** music educator, conductor; s. John F. and Lenna Jean Mendelson; m. Aprel Marie Lowder, Apr. 2, 1999; 1 child, Leah Marie. BMus in Choral Edn. and Conducting, Utah State U., Logan, 2003. Choir tchr. Provo H.S., 2003—. Conductor: Mapleton (Utah) Chorale, 2004—. Mem.: Music Educators Nat. Conf., Utah Music Educators Assn., Am. Choral Dir. Assn. Mem. Lds Ch. Avocations: snowboarding, fourwheeling. Office: Provo High Sch 1125 N University Ave Provo UT 84604 Office Phone: 801-373-6550. Office Fax: 801-374-4800. E-mail: corym@provo.edu.

**MENDENHALL, HARRY BARTON,** lawyer; b. Oct. 31, 1946; BA, Colo. Coll., 1968; JD, U. Colo., 1971. Bar: Colo. 1971. Ptnr. Mendenhall & Malouff, R.L.L.P., Rocky Ford, Colo., 1971—. Mem. nominating com. Colo. Supreme Ct., Denver, 1986-91; pres. Colo. Lawyer Trust Account Found., Denver, 1995-97. Mem. Colo. Bar Assn. (pres. 1999-2000). Office: Mendenhall & Malouff 805 Chestnut Ave Rocky Ford CO 81067-1224 Office Phone: 719-254-7606. E-mail: bmendenhall@centurytel.net.

**MENDENHALL, NANCY PRICE,** radiologist, educator; b. Eldorado, Ark., Apr. 18, 1951; d. Delton E. and Betty Jean Price; m. William M. Mendenhall; children: Marisa, Elena. BA in English Lit., U. Fla., 1973, MD, 1980. Diplomate Am. Bd. Radiology. Intern, radiation therapy U. Fla., Gainesville, 1980—81, resident, radiation therapy, 1981—84; asst. prof. dept. radiation oncology U. Fla. Coll. Medicine, Gainesville, 1984-89, assoc. prof., 1989-94, prof., 1994—, chmn. dept. radiation oncology, 1992—; med. dir. Fla. Proton Therapy Inst., also bd. dir.; assoc. chair, radiation oncology U. Fla. Coll. Medicine, Jacksonville. Editor: The Breast; prodr., author video for Am. Coll. Surgeons; contbr. articles to profl. jours. Active Trinity United Meth. Ch.; mem. dean's com., Dept. Veteran Affairs; bd. dir. Am. Cancer Soc., Alachua County; mem. Children's Oncology Group (mem. Hodgkin's com.) Mem. Am. Soc. for Therapeutic Radiology and Oncology (human resources com. 1995, by-laws com. 1995-96), Soc. Chmn. of Academic Radiation Oncology Programs, Am. Radium Soc., Gilbert H. Fletcher Soc., Alachua County Med. Soc., Fla. Soc. Clin. Oncology, Am. Coll. Radiology, Phi Beta Kappa; fellow Am. Coll. Radiology. Methodist. Avocations: horseback riding, sewing, cooking, piano. Office: U Fla Dept Radiation Oncology 2000 SW Archer Rd Dept Gainesville FL 32608-1136 also: UF Coll Medicine Jacksonville 653-1 W Eighth St Jacksonville FL 32209 also: U Fla Proton Therapy Inst 2015 N Jefferson St Jacksonville FL 32206*

**MENDENHALL, ROBERT W.,** information technology executive; b. Pasadena, Calif., Nov. 18, 1954; s. Winton L. and Margaret E. (Kerr) Mendenhall; m. Kathleen A. White, 1978; children: Jamie, Robert, Christina, Virginia, Kathleen, Lori, Emily. BS in Univ. Studies, Brigham Young Univ., 1977, PhD in Instrnl. Psychology and Tech., Brigham Young U., 2003. Gen. mgr. Wicat Inst., Orem, Utah, 1977-80; pres., dir. Wicat Systems Inc., Orem, Utah, 1980—92; exec. v.p., dir. Jostens Learning Corp., San Diego, 1992—94; gen. mgr. IBM K-12 Edn., Atlanta, 1994—96, exec. cons., 1997—98; pres. Western Govs. U., Salt Lake City, 1999—. Mem. bd. bus. and econ. devel. State of Utah, 1997—2001; mem. Commn. Tech. and Adult Learning, 1999—2000; adv. bd. Partnership for 21st Century Skills, 2003—04; mem. Sec. of Edn.'s Commn. on Future of Edn., 2005—. Missionary and bishop LDS Ch.; bd. dir. Oquirrh Inst., 2002—; bd. dir. and chair Gina Bachauer Internat. Piano Found. Office: Western Gov U Ste 700 4001 South 700 East Salt Lake City UT 84107 Office Phone: 801-274-3280. Business E-Mail: rwm@wgu.edu.

**MENDES, EVA,** actress; b. Houston, Mar. 5, 1974; Spokesperson Revlon Cosmetics. Actor: (films) A Night at the Roxbury, 1998, My Brother the Pig, 1999, Urban Legends: Final Cut, 2000, Exit Wounds, 2001, Training Day, 2001, All About the Benjamins, 2002, 2 Fast 2 Furious, 2003, Once Upon a Time in Mexico, 2003, Out of Time, 2003, Stuck on You, 2003, Hitch, 2005; (TV films) The Disciples, 2000; TV appearances include: ER, 1998; Mortal Kombat: Conquest, 1998; VIP, 1999. Office: Creative Artist Agency 9830 Wilshire Blvd Beverly Hills CA 90212-1825

**MENDES, SAM (SAMUEL ALEXANDER MENDES),** film director, theater director; b. Reading, Eng., Aug. 1, 1965; s. James Peter and Valerie Helene Mendes; m. Kate Winslet, May 24, 2003; 1 child. Student, U. Cambridge, Eng. Dir.: (films) American Beauty, 1999 (Outstanding Directorial Achievement in Feature Film Dirs. Guild Am. 1999, Golden Globe for best dir. 1999, Best Dir. award Dallas-Ft. Worth Film Critics Assn. 1999, Best Dir. award Online Film Critics Soc. 1999, Best Dir. award Broadcast Film Critics Assn. 1999, Best Dir. award L.A. Film Critics Assn. 1999, Oscar for best dir. 2000, Dir. of the Yr. London Film Critics Cir. 2000, Hamburg Shakespeare prize 2000), Road to Perdition, 2002, Jarhead, 2005; artistic dir. The Rise and Fall of Little Voice (RNT, Aldwych, Olivier and Evening

Standard awards), 1992, Cabaret (Tony award), 1998, The Blue Room, 1998; dir.: (plays) London Assurance, 1989, Cherry Orchard, 1989, Kean, 1990, Plough & the Stars, 1991, Troilis & Cressida, 1991, The Alchemist, 1991, The Sea, 1991, Richard III, 1992, The Tempest, 1993, The Birthday Party, 1994, Othello, 1997, Assasins, Translations, Glengarry Glen Ross, Glass Managerie, Company, Habelis Corpus, Front Page, To the Green Fields Beyond, The Real Thing (Tony award for Best Revival of Play 2000), Take Me Out (Tony award for Best Revival of Play 2003). Office: Scamp Film & Theatre 26-28 Neal St London WC 2H 9QQ England E-mail: mleigh@scampltd.com.*

**MENDEZ, CELESTINO GALO,** mathematics professor; b. Havana, Cuba, Oct. 16, 1944; came to the U.S., 1962; naturalized, 1970. s. Celestino Andres and Georgina (Fernandez) M.; m. Mary Ann Koplau, Aug. 21, 1971; children: Mark Michael, Matthew Maximilian. BA, Benedictine Coll., 1965; MA, U. Colo., 1968, PhD, 1974, MBA, 1979. Asst. prof. maths. scis. Met. State Coll., Denver, 1971-77, assoc. prof., 1977-82, prof., 1982—2002, chmn. dept. math. scis., 1980—83, asst to the v.p. for acad. affairs/provost, 1989—91; vis. assoc. prof. math. U. Mich., Ann Arbor, 2002—03; asst. dir. math program, lectr. dept. applied math. U. Colo., Boulder, 2003—05. Assoc. editor Denver Met. Jour. Math. and Computer Sci., 1993—2001; contbr. articles to profl. jours. including Am. Math. Monthly, Procs. Am. Math. Soc., Jour. Personalized Instrn., Denver Met. Jour. Math. and Computer Sci. and newspapers. Mem. advt. rev. bd. Met. Denver, 1973-79; parish outreach rep. S.E. deanery, Denver Cath. Cmty. Svcs., 1976-78; mem. social ministries com. St. Thomas More Cath. Ch., Denver, 1976-78, vice-chmn., 1977-78, mem. parish coun., 1977-78; del. Adams County Rep. Conv., 1972, 74, 94, Colo. 4th Congl. Dist. Conv., 1974, Colo. Rep. Conv., 1982, 88, 90, 92, 96, 98, 2000, 02, 04, Douglas County Rep. Conv., 1980, 82, 84, 88, 90, 92, 94, 96, 98, 2000, 02, 04; alt. del. Colo. Rep. Conv., 1974, 76, 84, 2000, 5th Congl. dist. conv., 1976, mem. rules com., 1978, 80, precinct committeeman Douglas County Rep. Com., 1976-78, 89-92, mem. ctrl. com., 1976-78, 89-92; dist. 29 Rep. party candidate Colo. State Senate, 1990; mem. Colo. Rep. Leadership Program, 1989-90, bd. dirs., 1990-98; Douglas County chmn. Rep. Nat. Hispanic Assembly, 1989—95; bd. dirs Rocky Mountain Better Bus. Bur., 1975-79, Rowley Downs Homeowners Assn., 1976-78; trustee Hispanic U. Am., 1975-78; councilman Town of Parker, Colo., 1981-84, chmn. budget and fin. com., 1981-84; chmn. joint budget com. Town of Parker-Parker Water and Sanitation Dist. Bds., 1982-84; commr. Douglas County Planning Commn., 1993-97; dir. Mile High Young Scholars Program, 1995-98. Recipient Excellence in Tchg. award U. Colo. Grad. Sch., 1965-67; grantee Benedictine Coll., 1964-65, Math. Assn. Am. SUMMA grantee Carnegie Found. N.Y., 1994; grantee dir., grantee NSF, 1995-98; nominated candidate for first v.p Math. Assn. Am., 1999, for 2d v.p., 2001. Mem. Math. Assn. Am. (referee rsch. notes sect. Am. Math. Monthly 1981-82, gov. Rocky Mountain sect. 1993-96, investment com. 1996-02, devel. com. 1995-01, task force on reps. 1994-96, sci. policy com. 2000—, bd. govs. 1993-96, 2002-05), Am. Math. Soc., Nat. Coun. Tchrs. Math., Colo. Coun. Tchrs. Math. (bd. dirs. 1994-96), Colo. Internat. Edn. Assn., Assoc. Faculties of State Insts. Higher Edn. in Colo. (v.p. 1971-73). Republican. Roman Catholic. Home: 39 Hummingbird Dr Castle Rock CO 80108-9047 Office: Dept Applied Math Campus Univ Colo PO Box 526 UCB Boulder CO 80309-0256

**MENDEZ, ELSIE NOEMI,** elementary school educator; b. Manhattan, N.Y., May 30, 1970; d. Bolivar and Gaudelia Guim; m. Carlos Alberto Mendez, Feb. 13, 1988; children: Priscilla, Sarah. B in Human Resource Mgmt., cum laude, Trinity Internat. Univ., Miami, 1995; MA in Ednl. Leadership, Stetson Univ., Deland, 2005. Cert. Elem. Edn. Dept. Edn. Kindergarten tchr. Northwest Christian Sch., Miami, 1992—94; 1st grade tchr. Miami Lakes Christian, 1994—2000; tchr. Timbercrest Elem., Deltong, 2002—04, Enterprise Elem., 2004—. Grantee Future Grant, Volusia County Sch., 2005. Mem.: Internat. reading Soc., Volusia Tchr. Orgn. Republican. Baptist. Home: 1100 Glenwood Tr Deland FL 32720

**MENDEZ, FABIO,** economist, researcher; s. Fabio Mendez and Maria de los Angeles Rodriguez; m. Annelyse Lasnier, Oct. 8, 1974; children: Julian Gabino, Anais Belle. PhD, Mich. State U., 2001. Analyst Citigroup, Irving, Tex., 2001—02; asst. prof. U. Ark., Fayetteville, 2002—. Contbr. articles to profl. jours. Mem.: Southern Econ. Assn., Am. Econ. Assn. Home: 5610 Blake Ln Springdale AR 72762 Office: University of Arkansas Business Bldg Rm 402 Fayetteville AR 72701 Office Phone: 479-575-3266. Personal E-mail: fmendez@uark.edu.

**MENDEZ, HERMANN ARMANDO,** pediatrician, educator; b. Guatemala, Apr. 26, 1949; came to U.S., 1980; citizen of El Salvador; s. Hermann and Martha (Abularach) Mendez Fortun; m. Maria Elena Ortiz, Feb. 23, 1971; children: Natalia, Amalia. MD, U. El Salvador, 1977. Diplomate Am. Bd. Pediatrics, Am. Bd. Pediatric Infectious Diseases. Asst. prof. pediats. Health Sci. Ctr. SUNY, Bklyn., 1988-91, assoc. prof. pediat. medicine, 1991—2001, assoc. prof. medicine, 1999—2001; chief dept. pediat. Lincoln Hosp., South Bronx, NY, 2000—; prof. clin. pediat. Weill Coll. Medicine, Cornell U., 2001—. Recipient Asst. Sec. for Health award USPHS, 1990, United U. Professions Excellence award Health Sci. Ctr., Bklyn., 1991, recognition award Bklyn. AIDS Task Force, 1997-98, Humanism in Medicine award Newark Beth Israel Healthcare Found., 1998, Attending of the Yr. award Children's Med. Ctr. of Bklyn., 1998, Gifts for Spl. Children award N.Y.C. Tech. Coll., 1998, N.Y. State Dept. Health Outstanding Svc. award, 1999, cert. of merit State of NY Exec. Chamber, 2002; named Physician of Yr. Salvadorean C. of C., NY, 2002. Fellow Am. Acad. Pediatrics, Infectious Disease Soc. Am. Achievements include clinical research in perinatal transmission of HIV, AIDS in children, adolescents and their families; development of systems of care for these populations and children in general, training of medical students and physicians. Office: Lincoln Med & Mental Health Ctr Dept Pediatrics 234 E 149th Bronx NY 10451-5504 Fax: 718-579-4700. Office Phone: 718-579-5800. E-mail: HAMENDEZ@aol.com.

**MENDEZ, JOHN,** minister; b. N.Y.C., Jan. 7, 1948; m. Sarah Lee Howard; children: Sekou, Jamila. Student, United Theol. Sem., Dayton, Postgrad. Ctr. Mental Health, N.Y.C., Southeastern Theol. Sem., Wake Forest, N.C., Shaw U., Raleigh, N.C., DD (hon.), 1991. Instr. Winston-Salem (N.C.) State U., Shaw U., Raleigh; sr. pastor Emmanuel Bapt. Ch., Winston-Salem, 1983—. Pres. Ministerial Alliance of Winston-Salem, 2003; bd. dirs. Nat. Coun. Chs.; com. mem. World Coun. Chs.; organizer Progressive Nat. Bapt. Conv. and Bapt. Ch. Movement, London and Wolverhampton, England; mentor candidates for D of Ministry degree United Theol. Sem., Dayton. Adv. com. Forsyth Tech. Coll. Sch. Nursing, Winston-Salem; cons. Urban League, Winston-Salem; founder, chairperson Citizens United for Justice, Winston-Salem; bd. dirs. N.C. Psychology Bd. Office: Emmanuel Bapt Ch 1075 Shalimar Dr Winston Salem NC 27107

**MENDEZ, LUIS EDUARDO,** medical educator, researcher; b. Salisbury, Md., Mar. 1, 1968; s. Luis N. and Alicia M. Mendez; m. Nahzaya M. Perez, Nov. 4, 2000. MD, U. Miami, 1993. Diplomate. Fellow Jackson Meml. Hosp., Miami, Fla., 1993—97, Emory U., Atlanta, 1997—98; assoc. prof. divsn. gynecol. oncology U. Miami, 2001—04, South Fla. Gyn. Oncology, 2004—. Office: 3661 S Miami Ave Mercy Profl Bldg #308 Miami FL 33133 Office Phone: 305-663-7001, 305-854-3603. Personal E-mail: lemendez@comcast.net.

**MÉNDEZ, MIGUEL ANGEL,** law educator; b. 1942; AA, Tex. Southmost Coll., 1963; AB in Internat. Affairs & Latin Am. Studies, George Washington U., 1965, JD, 1968. Bar: Tex. 1972. Law clk. US Ct. Claims, Washington, 1968-69; legis. asst. to Sen. Alan Cranston of Calif. Washington, 1969-71; staff atty. Mexican-Am. Legal Def. & Ednl. Fund, San Francisco, 1971-72; dep. dir. Calif. Rural Legal Assistance, San Francisco, 1972-74; dep. pub. defender Office of Monterey County Pub. Defender, Salinas, Calif., 1975-76; assoc. prof. Stanford Law Sch., 1977-84, prof., 1984—, Adelbert H. Sweet prof. law, 1996—. Vis. prof. Santa Clara U. Law Sch., 1977, U. Calif., Berkeley, 1982, U. Vt., 1986, U. San Diego, 1990-91. Author: Evidence: The

California Evidence Code & The Federal Rules, 1995, 1999, 2004. Bd. governors Pub. Advocates, Inc., San Francisco. Recipient Legal Services Award, Mexican-Am. Legal Def. & Ednl. Fund, 1989, Disting. Alumni Award, Tex. Southmost Coll., 1999, Matthew O. Tobriner Pub. Svc. Award, Legal Aid Soc. & Employment Law Ctr. of San Francisco, 2003, Voice of Conscience Award, Pub. Advocates, Inc., 2003, Outstanding Mentor & Padrino Award, Stanford Law Sch. Latino Alumni Assn., 2004. Mem.: Hispanic Nat. Bar Assn. (Pioneer Award 1993), Am. Law Inst. Office: Stanford Law Sch Crown Quadrangle 559 Nathan Abbott Way Stanford CA 94305-8610 Office Phone: 650-723-0613. Office Fax: 650-725-0253. E-mail: mmendez@stanford.edu.

**MENDEZ, RUBEN POLICARPIO,** diplomat, educator, economist; b. Manila, Philippines, June 28, 1933; came to U.S., 1948; s. Mauro and Paz Policarpio M.; m. Matilda Currier McEwen, Apr. 8, 1961; children: Katherine McEwen, Tomas Currier. BA cum laude, Harvard U., 1953; MA, Columbia U., 1959; PhD, NYU, 1984. Economist Merrill Lynch, Pierce, Fenner & Smith, N.Y.C., 1959-63; econ. adviser to chmn. Nat. Econ. Coun., Manila, 1964-66; project officer UN Spl. Fund, N.Y.C., 1963-65; various positions UN Devel. Program, N.Y.C., Africa, Asia, 1966-93; chief econ. advisor UN Environ. Program, Nairobi, Kenya, 1977-81; prin. officer, historian UN Devel. Program, N.Y.C., 1993—. Adj. prof., fellow, vis. lectr. NYU, 1991—; Columbia U., 1992, Yale U., 1994—; cons. Oxford U. Press, N.Y., 1999-2000. Author: International Public Finance: A New Perspective on Global Relations, 1992; contbr. articles to profl. jours., chpts. to books. Yale rep. Acad. Coun. on UN Sys., 1997-98. Grantee Carnegie Corp., N.Y.C., 1995-98, Internat. Devel. Rsch. Ctr., Ottawa, Can., 1994-97. Mem. Am. Econ. Assn., N.Y. Acad. Scis., Soc. Internat. Devel., Harvard Club (N.Y.C.), Harvard Faculty Club, Riverdale Yacht Club, United Kenya Club (Nairobi). Avocations: history, philosophy, classical music, sailing, personal computers. Home: 313 W 263d St Bronx NY 10471 E-mail: rpmendez@post.harvard.edu.

**MENDICINO, ANTHONY J.,** gas company executive; married; 2 children. BS in Civil Engring., Lehigh U.; MBA, U. Pa. Sr. v.p., CFO UTI Energy Corp., 1987—96; CFO, v.p. fin. UGI Corp., King of Prussia, Pa., 1998—2002, sr. v.p., CFO, 2002—. Bd. dir. Superior Well Svcs., 2005—. Office: UGI Corp 460 N Gulph Rd King Of Prussia PA 19406

**MENDINI, DOUGLAS A.,** publishing company executive, writer; b. New Brunswick, N.J., June 13, 1953; s. T.F. Mendini and Helen Victoria Jones Mendini Renninger. BA, Seton Hall U., 1975. Sr. sales mgr. Kensington Pub. Corp., N.Y.C., 1990—. Author: What Was Hot, 1994, others; contbr. articles to numerous mags. Founder Block Assn., Manhattan, NY, 1990; bd. dirs Cmty. Bd., Manhattan, 1990-93, bd. sec., 1993. Recipient Young Writers award Coordinating Coun. Lit. Mags., 1988. Democrat. Roman Catholic. Avocations: presidential history, furniture refinishing, american film history. Home: 403 W 54th St Apt 1D New York NY 10019-4469

**MENDIS, PATRICK,** economist, geographer, educator; b. Polonnaruwa, Sri Lanka, Apr. 7, 1960; came to U.S., 1978; s. B.W. Kamilus and Kusumawati M.; m. Cheryl Lynn Pattison, Oct. 8, 1988; children: Gamini, Samantha. BS in Bus. Adminstrn. and Econs., U. Sri Lanka, 1983; MA in Internat. Devel., Fgn. Affairs, Hubert H. Humphrey Inst. Pub. Affairs, 1986; PhD in Geography/Applied Econs., U. Minn., 1989. Vis. scholar in applied econs. U. Minn., 1990—97, lectr. in internat. rels., 1990—97; grad. prof. econs. and govt. U. Md. U. Coll./U.S. Dept. Def., Heidelburg, Germany, 1997—99, Tokyo, 1999—2000; fgn. affairs officer for sci. and tech. U.S. State Dept., Washington, 2000—01, spl. asst. to Asst. Secy. State and Ednl. and Cult. Affairs, 2001—02, Secretariat Dir., 2001—02; sr. policy advisor World Wildlife Fund / World Bank, 2002—03; vis. prof. econs. & pub. policy U. Pittsburgh's Semester at Sea Program, Spring, 2004. Del. UN, Govt. Sri Lanka, N.Y.C., 1985; cons. World Bank, Washington, 1988, 89 summers, U.S. State Dept., Washington, 1991; Senate Fgn. Rels. Com., Washington; chmn. UN Youth Leadership Summit, N.Y.C., 1995; sr. policy fellow Inst. Agr. and Trade Policy, Mpls., 1996-97; vis. faculty Yale U. Ctr. for Internat. and Area Studies, 1996, 97 summers; spl. asst. former NATO amb. Harlan Cleveland, UN Univ.'s Leadership Acad., 1997, Asian Tour World Acad. Art and Sci., 1995; adj. prof. econs.and mgmt. U. Md., 2000-; vice chmn. Secretary of State's Open Forum, U.S. State Dept, 2001-02; advisor U.S. Del. to the UN Commn. on Sustainable Devel., 2001; cons. Lawrence Livermore Nat. Laboratory's Ctr. for Global Security Rsch., U.S. Dept. of Energy, 2002-03; mem. USDA Grad. Sch Governing Bd., 2003-, The Bureaucrat Inc., 2006-. Author: (book) Human Environment and Spatial Relations, 1992, (e-book) Voyage Around the World: Impact of Globalization, Americanization, and Globalization, Freedom on the March, 2005, Freedom on the March: American Voyage to Explore Globalization, 2006; contbg. editor Asian Am. Press, 1990-94; advisor Internat. Policy Rev. (jour.), 1991—97; editor Global Issues and Economic Perspectives, two electronic journals of the U.S. State Dept., 2002; mem. editl. bd. Energy & Environ., 2001-, The Pub. Mgr., 2005-. Pres. Soc. for Internat. Devel., Minn., 1993-95; v.p. 1995-97; sec. UN Assn., Minn., 1995-96, v.p. 1996-97; founding chmn. Asian-Pacific Endowment for Cmty. Devel. at St. Paul Found., 1993-95, v.p., 1995-97; bd. dirs. Ctr. for Victims of Torture, Minn., 1997-98; trustee Humphrey Inst. Alumni Bd.; endowed two ann. scholarships in Mgmt. Studies and Leadership for Sri Lanka U. students, 1993-, Harlan Cleveland Leadership award for Sri Lanka U. students, 2002; mem. NASA Exec. Leadership Prog., U.S. Fed. Exec. Inst., 2001, Global Environment Change Prog., Harvard Med. Sch. Ctr. Health and Global Environment, 2002, Georgetown U. Prog. for Exec. in Legis. Operations, 2002. Recipient UN medal, 1985, Hubert Humphrey Alumni award for outstanding leadership, 1986, MN Gov.'s Asian-Pacific Heritage award, 1994, Aspen Inst. Global Leadership fellowship, 1995, Salzburg Seminar scholarship, 1995, Kennedy Sch, Leadership scholarship Harvard U., 1996 Sasakawa award Sasakawa Found., 1996, Harold Stassen award for UN Affairs, 1997, UN Univ. scholarship Internat. Leadership Acad., Jordan, 1997, Coolidge fellowship Columbia U., 1997, 21st. Century Trust fellow, Oxford, 2000, Diplomacy fellow AAAS, 2000, Socrates fellow Aspen Inst., 2001, Meritorious Honor award, U.S. State Dept., 2001, Presidential fellow, Salzburg Seminar, 2003, Benjamin Franklin Award, U.S. State Dept., 2003, Uhuru Freedom fellow Internat. Republican Inst., 2005. Fellow World Acad. Arts and Sci.; mem. Am. Com. on Fgn. Rels., U. Minn. Alumni Assn. (bd. dirs.), Internat. Inst. for Strategic Studies, Soc. Internat. Devel. Avocations: running, reading, travel, hiking, swimming. Home: 11628 Newbridge Ct Reston VA 20191 E-mail: pmendis@umuc.edu.

**MENDIUS, PATRICIA DODD WINTER,** editor, educator, writer; b. Davenport, Iowa, July 9, 1924; d. Otho Edward and Helen Rose (Dodd) Winter; m. John Richard Mendius, June 19, 1947; children: Richard, Catherine M. Graber, Louise, Karen M. Chooljian. BA cum laude, UCLA, 1946; MA cum laude, U. N.Mex., 1966. Cert. secondary edn. tchr., Calif., N.Mex. English tchg. asst. UCLA, 1946—47; English tchr. Marlborough Sch. for Girls, LA, 1947—50, Aztec (N.Mex.) HS, 1953—55, Farmington (N.Mex.) HS, 1955—63; chair English dept. Los Alamos (N.Mex.) HS, 1963—86; sr. technical writer, editor Los Alamos Nat. Lab., 1987—2005. Adj. prof. English, U. N.Mex., Los Alamos, 1970-72, Albuquerque, 1982-85; English cons. S.W. Regional Coll. Bd., Austin, Tex., 1975—; writer, editor, cons. advanced placement English test devel. com. Nat. Coll. Bd., 1982-86, reader, 1982-86, proj. equality cons., 1985-88; book selection cons. Scholastic mag., 1980-82. Author: Preparing for the Advanced Placement English Exams, 1975; editor Los Alamos Arts Coun. bull., 1986-91. Chair Los Alamos Art Pub. Places Bd., 1987-92; chair adv. bd. trustees U. N.Mex., Los Alamos, 1987-93; pres. Los Alamos Concert Assn., 1972-73, 95-98, 2000-04, pres. 2003-04; chair Los Alamos Mesa Pub. Libr. Bd., 1990-94, chair endowment com., 1995-99. Named Living Treasure of Los Alamos, 2005. Mem. Soc. Tech. Communicators, AAUW (pres. 1961-63, state bd. dirs. 1959-63, Los Alamos scholarship coun. 1992-93, pres. 1993-94, 2002-04, sec. 2001-04), DAR, Order Ea. Star, Mortar Bd., Phi Beta Kappa (pres. Los Alamos chpt. 1969-72, 99, v.p. 1996-99, pres. 2000-01, dir. 2002—), Phi Kappa Phi, Delta Kappa Gamma, Gamma Phi Beta. Avocations:

swimming, reading, hiking, astronomy, singing. Home: 124 Rover Blvd Los Alamos NM 87544-3634 Office: Los Alamos Nat Lab Diamond Dr Los Alamos NM 87544 E-mail: pmendius@cybermesa.com.

**MENDLIN, RONALD C.,** employment specialist, writer; b. San Francisco, Jan. 8, 1936; s. Joseph and Freda Mendlin; m. Lorraine F. Mendlin, Feb. 15, 1964; children: Andrew Scott, Susan Debra. Student, U. San Francisco, San Francisco State U.; degree, San Francisco City Coll., 1958. Vocat edn. tchg. credential Calif. With City and County of San Francisco, 1962-92; employment specialist No. Calif. Svc. League, San Francisco, 1993—; part-time employment specialist San Mateo, Calif. Job developer San Mateo Employment and Tng. Ctr., Advanced Career Tech., Peninsula Placement Agy.; placement counselor Scofield Employment Agy., San Francisco; lectr. in field. Author (with Marc Polonsky): Putting the Bars Behind You, 5 vols., 2000; author: The Double You, Being Job-Ready, Job Search Tools, Networking and Interviewing for Jobs, Keeping Your Job. Vol. mock job interviewer No. Calif. Svc. League, 1993—. With N.G. USAR, 1954—63. Recipient numerous accolades, Mayor's Office. Mem.: Fiesta Gardens Home Owners Assn. (v.p.), No. Calif. Svc. League (mock interviewer 1993—). Achievements include being credited by California Department of Corrections and California State University's Sacramento Foundation for placing and assisting over 750 ex-felons from state prisons into jobs; obtained jobs for residents in work furlough programs; obtained jobs for residents who had 6 hours to 3 days to obtain a job or be sent back to prison; saved the San Francisco Mcpl. R.R. from fin. embrassement 1974, verbally noted. Office Phone: 415-863-2323.

**MENDON, KAREN JEANETTE,** elementary school educator; b. Oct. 22, 1949; AA, Mt. San Antonio Jr. Coll., 1969; BA, Calif. State U., Long Beach, 1972; std. elem. credential, U. Calif., Irvine, 1976; MA in Curriculum and Devel., Coll. St. Thomas, 1984; Lang Devel. Specialist cert., UCLA, 1993. Phys. edn. tchr. Montebello Intermediate Montebello Unified Sch. Dist., 1972—. Phys. edn. mentor tchr. Montebello Unified Sch. Dist., 1990-93, site adminstrv. internship, 1990, demonstration sch. coord., 1991—; mem. Healthy Kids Healthy Calif. ad hoc com., health cirruculum ad hoc com., mentor tchr., earthquake com., planning com., faculty club, recreation adv. com., coord. personal best program, leadership team, disaster search and rescue team; chair discipline com.; presenter in field. Author: Ideas, Activities and Games to Expend, Enrich and Enhance Your Physical Education Program (grades 3-8). Recipient L.A. County Healthy Fitness Leader award, 1994, Am. Tchr. Honoree award Walt Disney, 1995. Mem. ASCD, NEA, AAHPERD, PTA (Sch. Svc. award 1977), Calif. Assn. Health, Phys. Edn., Recreation & Dance (Unit 413 Outstanding Mid. Sch. Phys. Educator award 1993, Southern Dist. Outstanding Mid. Sch. Phys. Educator award 1993, Calif. Outstanding Mid. Sch. Phys. Educator award 1994).

**MENDONCA, WAYNE D.,** history educator; b. Tularosa, N.M., Nov. 21, 1955; s. Donald R. and Nancy L. Mendonca; m. Paula K. Penner, June 5, 1976; children: Stacy, Adam. BA, Western N.Mex. U., Silver City, 1974—78, MAT, 1979. Cert. N.Mex. Coaches Assn. Tchr. Hot Springs Schs., Truth or Consequences, N.Mex., 1978—84, Silver Schs., Silver City, 1985—. Head track coach, Hot Springs, 1979—84, Silver City, 2000—04; asst. football coach, Silver City, 1985—99. Mem. DWI Task Force, Silver City, 2000—06. Recipient Am. History Tchr. of Yr., NSDAR,Silver City, 1997, Outstanding Am. Tchr., NHR, 2006.

**MENDOZA, GEORGE,** poet, author; b. N.Y.C., June 2, 1934; s. George and Elizabeth Mendoza; m. Ruth Sekora, 1967; children: Ashley, Ryan. BA, State Maritime Coll., 1953; postgrad., Columbia U., 1954-56. Author over 100 books for children and adults published worldwide; many included in Boston U.'s George Mendoza Collection, established 1984; children's books on display at the Centre Nat. d'Art et de Culture Georges Pompidou. Works include: And Amedeo Asked, How Does One Become a Man?, (illustrated by Ati Forberg), 1959, The Puma and the Pearl, 1962, The Hawk Is Humming: A Novel, 1964, A Piece of String, Astor-Honor, 1965, Gwot! Horribly Funny Hairticklers (illustrated by Steven Kellog), 1967, The Crack in the Wall and Other Terribly Weird Tales (illustrated by Mercer Mayer), 1968, Flowers and Grasses and Weeds (illustrated by Joseph Low), 1968, The Practical Man (illustrated by Imero Gobbato), 1968, Hunting Sketches (illustrated by Ronald Stein), 1968, A Beastly Alphabet (illustrated by J. Low), 1969, The Digger Wasp (illustrated by Jean Zallinger), 1969, Herman's Hat (illustrated by Frank Bozzo), 1969, The Starfish Trilogy (illustrated by Ati Forberg), 1969, (compiler) The World From My Window: Poems and Drawings (children's writings), 1969, Are You My Friend? (illustrated by F. Bozzo), 1970, The Marcel Marceau Alphabet Book, 1970, The Thumbtown Toad (illustrated by Monika Beisner), 1970, The Inspector, 1970, The Good Luck Spider & other bad luck stories, 1970, The Fearsome Brat (illustrated by F. Bozzo), 1971, Fish in the Sky (illustrated by Milton Glaser), 1971, Moonfish and owl scratchings, 1971, Moonstring, 1971, The Hunter, the Tick and the Gumberoo, 1971, The Marcel Marceau Counting Book, 1971, The Scarecrow Clock (illustrated by Eric Carle), 1971, Big Frog, Little Pond, 1971, The Scribbler, 1971, The Christmas Tree Alphabet Book, 1971, Shadowplay, 1974, Lord, Suffer me to Catch a Fish, 1974, Fishing the Morning Lonely, 1974, (with Carol Burnett) What I Want to Be When I Grow Up, 1975, (with Zero Mostel) The Sesame Street Book of Opposites, 1975, Norman Rockwell's Americana ABC (illustrated by N. Rockwell), 1975, Doug Henning's Magic Book, 1975, Lost Pony, 1976, Norman Rockwell's Boys and Girls at Play, 1976, Secret Places of a Trout Fisherman, 1977, Norman Rockwell's Diary for a Young Girl (illustrated by N. Rockwell), 1978, Magic Tricks, 1978, Mon livre de magic (French edit. of My Book of Magic), Norman Rockwell's Scrapbook for a Young Boy (illustrated by N. Rockwell), 1979, (with Andres Segovia) Segovia, My Book of the Guitar, 1979, Need a House? Call Ms. Mouse! (illustrated by Doris Susan Smith), 1981, Alphabet Sheep (illustrated by K. Reidy), 1982, The Sheepish Book of Opposites, 1982, Silly Sheep and other sheepish rhymes, 1982, Norman Rockwell's Four Seasons, 1982, Norman Rockwell's Happy Holidays, 1983, Henri Mouse (illustrated by Joelle Boucher), 1985, Henri La Souris, 1987, Norman Rockwell's Patriotic Times, 1986, (with Ivan Lendl) Hitting Hot, 1986, (with Sam Snead) Slammin' Sam, 1986, Norman Rockwell's Love and Remembrance, 1986, Top Tennis, 1987, L'Album des Noeuds, 1988, Norman Rockwell's Old Fashioned American Cookbook, 1988, Hairticklers (illustrated by Gahan Wilson), 1989, The Hunter I Might Have Been, reprint 1989, Were You a Wild Duck, Where Would You Go? (illustrated by Jane Osborn-Smith), 1990, Traffic Jam (illustrated by David Stoltz), 1990; also author screenplays for Petals from a Poem Flower, You Show Me Yours and I'll Show You Mine and scripts for Sesame Street; numerous others; over 15 books of poetry including The Hunter I Might Have Been (Lewis Carroll Shelf award 1968), The Mist Men, Goodbye, River, Goodbye; also dozens of articles in The N.Y. Times, Herald Tribune, Stern, Vogue, Harper's Bazaar, Ms., Esquire, Town & Country, Sports Afield, Men's Journal, Philadelphia Inquirer; special travel corr. Toronto Globe & Mail, 1991-94. Cited by Pres. Reagan for Norman Rockwell's Patriotic Times. Avocation: fishing. *I believe we are living in a world where people no longer see each other as individuals. We have become invisible. It is necessary to save our souls. Go out to a field and pick up a fallen leaf. Look at the veins that river the leaf. Follow them until nothing else matters except for the leaf in your hand. Then you will become visible. You will see others and others will see you.*

**MENDOZA, JESSICA,** Olympic athlete; b. Nov. 11, 1980; BA in Am. studies, Stanford U., MA in Social Sciences Ed. Mem. U.S. Nat. Softball Team, 2002—; U.S. Women's Softball Team, Athens Olympic Games, 2004. Named Stanford Female Conference Athlete of the Yr., 1999, Best Batter, Japan Cup, 2002, MVP, Speedline Invitational, 2002, NFCA First Team All-Am., 1999—2002; named to All-WCWS Tournament Team, 2001. Achievements include mem. Gold medal U.S. Red team, U.S. Cup, 2001; mem. Gold medal U.S. Nat. Team, ISF World Championships, 2003; mem. Gold medal U.S. Nat. Team, Pan-American Games, 2003.

**MENDOZA, JULIE C.,** lawyer; BA summa cum laude, Tufts U., 1977; JD, U. Chgo., 1981. Bar: DC 1981, US Ct. Internat. Trade, US Ct. Appeals, Fed. Cir. Ptnr., co-chair Internat. Trade Group Kaye Scholer LLP, Washington, DC. Office: Kaye Scholer LLP McPherson Bldg 901 Fifteenth St, NW, Ste 1100 Washington DC 20005 Office Phone: 202-682-3640. E-mail: jmendoza@kayescholer.com.

**MENDOZA, KAREN LYNN,** special education educator; b. Artesia, New Mex., Feb. 5, 1970; d. Fred Torrez and Esperanza-Mariscal Alvarez; m. Ramon Mendoza; children: Eris, Jadyn. BSc, Eastern New Mex. U., 1993. Cert. tchr. Tex. Tchr., San Antonio, 1993—97; tchr. Arnett Elem. Sch. Lubbock (Tex.) Ind. Sch. Dist., 1997—. Avocations: scrapbooks, photography, reading. Personal E-mail: kamendoza@cox.net.

**MENDOZA, LOUIS G.,** literature educator, researcher; b. Houston, Aug. 25, 1960; s. Joe and Mary C. Mendoza. PhD, U. Tex., 1994. Asst. prof. English U. Houston, 1994—95; assoc. prof. U. Tex., San Antonio, 1996—. Vis. prof. Brown U., Providence, 1995—96. Author: (critical study) Historia: The Literary Making of Chicana/o History; editor: (anthology) Crossing Into America: The New Literature of Immigration. Chmn. bd. dirs. San Antonio Cultural Arts, 1997—2003. Grantee, NEH, 1999, 2001, 2003. Mem.: Nat. Assn. for Chicana and Chicano Studies (assoc.; gen. coord. 1999—2000). Office: Univ Tex San Antonio 501 W Durango Blvd San Antonio TX 78207 E-mail: lmendoza@utsa.edu.

**MENDOZA, MARTHA,** reporter; b. LA, 1969; BA, U. Calif. Santa Cruz, 1988. Reporter Madera Tribune, Bay City News Svc., Santa Cruz County Sentinel; nat. investigative reporter Associated Press, San Jose, Calif., 1995—. Co-author: The Bridge at No Gun RI: A Hidden Nightmare from the Korean War, 2001. Recipient Pulitzer prize, 2000, Alumni Achievement award, U. Calif. Santa Cruz, 2002; John S. Knight fellow, Stanford U., 2001. Office: Associated Press 675 N 1st St San Jose CA 95112

**MENDOZA, ROBERTO G., JR.,** banker; b. Cuba, 1945; BA, Yale U., 1967; MBA, Harvard U., 1974. Corp. fin. mgmt. positions with J.P. Morgan & Co., NYC, 1967—90, vice chmn., 1990—2000; mng. dir. Goldman Sachs, NYC, 2000—01; founder & chmn. Integrated Finance Ltd., NYC, 2001—. Bd. dir. Prudential plc, Western Union. Office: Integrated Finance Ltd Ste 2750 630 Fifth Ave New York NY 10111*

**MENDOZA, RON,** chef; Grad., Calif. Sch. Culinary Arts. Hot line Nick and Stef's Steakhouse, LA; tng. pastry chef Patina Restaurant; pastry chef Restaurant Jaan, Sona; exec. pastry chef Ortolan, LA, 2006—. Named one of LA's Rising Stars, StarChefs.com, 2006. Office: Ortolan 8338 W Third St Los Angeles CA 90048 Office Phone: 323-653-3300.*

**MENDOZA, RUBEN G.,** anthropologist, educator, archaeologist; b. Frenchcamp, Calif., June 18, 1956; s. Jose and Josephine Mendoza; m. Linda Marie James, June 2, 1990; children: Natalie Dawn Marie, Maya Nicole. BA, Calif. State U., Bakersfield, 1978; MA, U. Ariz., 1980, PhD, 1992. Registered profl. archaeologist 2000. Rsch. asst. SW Mission Rsch. Ctr., Tucson, 1978—79; instr. Bakersfield Coll., Calif., 1982—86; curatorial asst. Photographic Collections, Ariz. State Mus., Tucson, 1988—90; asst. prof. U. Colo., Denver, 1991—95; assoc. prof. Calif. State U., Monterey Bay, Seaside, 1995—2001, prof., 2001—. Instr. Pima Coll., Tucson, 1979—91; prin. investigator Mission San Jaun Bautista, Calif., 1995—; project mgr. mission conservation program, Calif., 2005—; planning faculty Calif. State U. Monterey Bay, Seaside, 1995—97, dir. Inst. Archaeology, 1995—; lit. pl. mentor Scholastic, Inc., N.Y.C., 1996—; contract archaeologist Kaplan McMason, Archaeol. Cons., Salinas, Calif., 2000—; multimedia prodr./content specialist Prentice Hall, Inc., N.Y.C., 2002—03; prin. investigator wireless tech. in archaeology demonstration project, Seaside, 2003—05, Mission San Carlos Borromeo del Rio Carmelo, Calif., 2002—03. Photographer, featured archaeologist: 3d grade science text, video, CD-ROM Time Detectives, 1996, 3d grade science text Science, 2001, editl. cons.: children's book Mission Santa Cruz, Mission San Carlos Borromeo del Rio Carmelo, Mission San Juan Bautista, 2000; contbr. chapters to books; photographer (exhibitions) Loveland Gallery, Colo., Mexican Consulate, Denver, Colo., 1994—95, Mex. Heritage Plaza, 2000; contbr. articles to profl. jours. Curatorial rep., old mission San Juan Bautista Calif. Mission Curators and Dirs. Conf., Santa Barbara, 1997; founding faculty mem. CSU Monterey Bay; mem. grants rev. com. Calif. Missions Found., San Francisco 2000—06, bd. dirs. Riverside. Recipient wireless tech. in tchg. and learning award, Congl. Appropriation, 2002—03; fellow, Ford Found., 1990—91, scholar, Nat. Hispanic Scholarship Fund, 1981, 1982, 1984. Mem.: Register Profl. Archaeologists, Am. Anthrop. Assn. (pres. Assn. Latina and Latino Anthropologists 1997—2000, sect. assembly 1998—2000). Achievements include principal investigator Crescent Rockshelter Archaeological Site, Colorado; principal investigator Old Mission San Juan Bautista, California; principal investigator Mission San Carlos Borromeo del Rio Carmelo, California; discovery of California mission feast day, equinox and solstice alignments. Avocations: photography, golf, writing, videography, gardening. Office: California State Univ Monterey Bay 100 Campus Center Seaside CA 93955-8001 Office Phone: 831-582-3760. Business E-Mail: ruben_mendoza@csumb.edu.

**MENDOZA, SAN JUANA JANE,** school psychologist; b. Elsa, Tex., July 19, 1950; d. Pedro Espinoza Garcia and Maria Mejia Ulloa; children: Oscar Gonzalez, Marcos Gonzalez, Jacinto R., Manuela N. BA, San Jose State U., Calif., 1999; EdS, MA in Sch. Psychology, Chapman U., Concord, Calif., 2002. Interpreter/cmty. liaison Monterey County Office Edn., Salinas, Calif., 1975—82; social worker/case coord. San Andreas Regional Ctr., Gilroy, Calif., 1985—97; sch. psychologist Salinas City Sch. Dist., Calif., 1997—99, Crane Sch. Dist., Yuma, Ariz., 1999—2005. Cons. Monterey County Office Edn., Salinas, Calif., 2004—05. Sch. bd. mem. Chualor Elem. Sch., Calif., 1987—90, Gonzalez Union H.S., Calif., 1990—93; sec. League United Latin Am. Citizens, 1989—92; affirmative action mem. City of Salinas, Calif., 1996; organizer Adelante Mujer Hispana Conf.; Big Sister; sec. Alliance on Aging; bd. dirs. Crisis Ctr. Mem.: NASP, Calif. Assn. Sch. Psychologists, Mex. Am. Polit. Assn. (sec.), Psi Chi, Phi Kappa Phi, Golden Key Soc. Avocations: reading, gardening, travel. Home: 2968 S Broken Arrow Ln Yuma AZ 85364

**MENDOZA, STANLEY ATRAN,** pediatric nephrologist, educator; b. Pitts., May 7, 1940; s. Joseph William and Marian Ruth (Atran) M.; m. Carole Ann Klein, June 23, 1963; children: Daniel, Joseph. Student, Harvard U., 1957—59; BA, Johns Hopkins U., 1961, MD, 1964. Diplomate Am. Bd. Pediat. Intern Johns Hopkins Hosp., Balt., 1964-65; jr. asst. resident dept. medicine Children's Hosp. Med. Ctr., Boston, 1965-66; asst. attending physician, dir. renal rsch. labs. Children's Meml. Hosp., Chgo., 1969-71; asst. prof. pediat. U. Calif. Sch. Medicine, San Diego, 1971—73, assoc. prof., 1973—79, prof. pediat. dept. pediat. divsn. pediatric nephrology, 1979—, vice chmn. dept. pediat., 1986—87, chmn. dept. pediat., 1992—2000. Contbr. article in field to profl. publ. Served With USPHS, 1966-69. Fogarty Sr. Internat. fellow, 1978-79; Alan J. Wurtzburger rsch. scholar, 1964. Recipient Johns Hopkins Med. Soc. award, 1964, hon. mention Borden Undergrad. rsch. award in medicine, 1964; Eleanor Roosevelt internat. fellow Internat. Union Against Cancer, 1984-85. Mem. Am. Fedn. Clin. Rsch., Am. Pediatric Soc., Am. Physiol. Soc., Am. Soc. Nephrology, Am. Soc. Pediatric Nephrology, Internat. Soc. Nephrology. Office: U Calif San Diego Dept Pediat 9500 Gilman Dr # 0696 La Jolla CA 92093-5004 E-mail: samendoza@ucsd.edu.

**MENEELEY, EDWARD STERLING,** artist; b. Wilkes-Barre, Pa., Dec. 18, 1927; s. Edward Sterling and Louina Halter M. Student, Murray Art Sch., Wilkes-Barre, 1947-50, Sch. Visual Arts, N.Y.C., 1952-53. Founder Portable Gallery Press, 1957-67; vis. lectr. Belleville Sch. St. Louis, Art Students League, N.Y.C.; lectr. Lehigh Valley Sch. System, 1987, Rogers College, Istanbul, Turkey, 1991, Lafayette Coll., 1998; pres. ESM Documentations, N.Y.C.; fine arts cons. Arts Initiatives, Inc., N.Y.C.; mem. Penna Artists, 2005. One-man exhbs. include. Donovan Gallery, Phila., 1952, Parma Gallery, N.Y.C., 1962, Teuscher Gallery, N.Y.C., 1966, 68, Inst. Contemporary Arts,

London, 1971, Victoria and Albert Mus., London, 1972, U. Sussex, Eng., 1972, Whitechapel Art Gallery, London, 1973, Demos Gallery, Athens, Greece, 1976, Frank Marino Gallery, N.Y.C., 1978, 79, 80, 81, 82, Sordoni Gallery, Wilkes (Pa.) Coll., 1981, Ericson Gallery, N.Y.C., 1980, Portfolio Gallery, Atlanta, 1983, Angela Flowers Gallery, London, 1985, J.T. Gallery, Jim Thorpe, Pa, 1987, 55 Mercer St., N.Y.C., 1987, Anita Shapolsky Gallery, N.Y.C., 1988, Bucknell U. Gallery Art, Lewisburg, 1988, Recent Painting & Sculpture, Coll. Misericordia, Dallas, Pa., 1989, Mixed Media, Craft Alliance Gallery, St. Louis, 1990, Provincetown (Mass.) Art Mus., 1993, De Arte Magick Gallery, Easton, Pa., 1997, New Works, N.Y.C., 1998, 181 Hudson St. N.Y.C., 1998, 70th St. Gallery Collages, 2001, Soho Creative, N.Y.C., 2002, 03, 04, MCI Gallery, 2003, 2004, Anita Shapulsky Art Found., 2005. Served with USNR, 1945-47, 50-52. Nat. Endowment Arts grantee; Pollock-Krasner Found. grantee, 1986, 90, 2002. Mem. Artist Club N.Y.C., Inst. Contemporary Arts London, Josiah White Soc., Weissport, Pa. Office: Anita Shapcsky Found 20 West Broadway Jim Thorpe PA 18229 Office Phone: 610-379-2176. Personal E-mail: edm7688@yahoo.com.

**MENEFEE, FREDERICK LEWIS,** advertising executive; b. Arkansas City, Kans., Oct. 22, 1932; s. Arthur LeRoy and Vera Mae (Rather) M.; m. Margot Leuze, Sept. 16, 1955; children: Gregory S., Christina Menefee-Anderson. AA, Arkansas City Jr. Coll., 1952; BA, U. Wichita, 1958. Sports editor, bus. mgr. Ark. Light and Tiger Tales, 1949-52; sports reporter Arkansas City Daily Traveler, 1949—52; advt. mgr. Derby Star, Haysville Herald and Sedgwick County News, 1956-57; v.p., account exec. Associated Advt. Agy., 1958-64; with McCormick-Armstrong Adv. Agy. (now Menefee and Ptnrs., Inc.), Wichita, 1964—, agy. mgr., 1964—, account. supr., 1965—, gen. mgr., 1972—, pres., CEO, 1979—, chmn. bd., 1986—2003. Vol. Wichita River Festival, 1974-98; pub. rels. chmn. Wichita Centennial Nat. Art Show and Exhibit, 1969-70. With AUS, 1953-55. Named Henry J. Lawrence Photo award, 1956, Wichita Beacon Advt. award, 1957, KANS Radio award, 1958, Advt. Man of Yr., Advt. Club of Wichita, 1964, Advt. Man of Yr., 9th Dist. Am. Advt. Fedn. Colo., Nebr., Iowa, Mo., Kans., 1965, Adm. Windwagon Smith III Wichita Festivals Inc., 1976. Mem. Am. Advt. Fedn. (nat. bd. dirs. 1969-70, dist. gov. 1968-69, chmn. nat. com. govs. 1969-70, 1st lt. gov. awards chmn. 1967, 68), Wichita Wagonmasters (founding mem. 1973, capt. 1974-75, dir., charter, founder, commodore 1999), Wichita Advt. Club (bd. dirs. 1958-68), v.p. awards 1961-62, v.p membership 1962, v.p. programs 1963, pres. 1964-65), PAWS Inc. (founder, 1st pres. 1978-86), Alpha Delta Sigma (pres. 1957-58, Outstanding Svc. award 1958), Quill & Scroll, 1949-50. Home: 2235 Red Bud Ln Wichita KS 67204-5346

**MENEFEE, JOHN WILLIAM, III,** cinematographer, film producer; b. Washington, Dec. 19, 1944; s. John William Menefee Jr. and Mary Claudia (Tudor) Upchurch. Student, U. Va., 1964-66, Columbia Sch. for Motion Pictures and TV, L.A., 1992. Tour guide Universal Studios, Universal City, Calif., 1970-75, studio transp. driver, 1976; camera asst., trainee Dino d'Laurentiis Orgn., Beverly Hills, Calif., 1976, Panavision (formerly Gen. Camera), N.Y.C., 1978; camera person Paramount Pictures, L.A., 1980, 20th Century Fox Film Corp., L.A., 1987, 96, Sony Pictures Corp., Culver City, Calif., 1992, 97, Paramount Pictures, L.A., 2000. Mem. film and TV action com. Bring Hollywood Home, L.A., 1999—; contbr., supporter World Wildlife Fund, Washington, Lambda Legal Def. Fund, N.Y.C., Cato Inst., Washington. Mem. Internat. Cinematographers Guild (cert.), Jamestown Soc. Episcopalian. Avocations: genealogy, vedic astrology, tennis, acting. Home: 1020 San Rafael Ln Pasadena CA 91105-1531

**MENEFEE, LINNEA-NORMA,** antique dealer; b. Mpls., Mar. 5, 1924; d. Arthur Wesley and Elsie Ida Back. Student, U. Minn., Mpls., U. Minn., Duluth, McPhail Sch. Music, Mpls. Chmn. State Vet. Home, Buffalo. Founder Albert Lea (Minn.) Art Ctr., 1959; county chairwoman Goldwater for Pres., Albert Lea. Recipient Conscientious award, 2001. Mem. AAUW, Am. Med. Assn. Alliance, Nat. Fedn. Rep. Women, Nat. Women of the Arts, Nat. Am. Legion Aux., Nat. VFW Aux., Nat. Assn. Family and Cmty. Edn., Order of Ea. Star, Gillette Blue Blades, Kiwanis Internat., Zeta Phi Eta, Omega Upsilon, Zeta Beta Chi. Episcopalian. Avocations: writing, reading, painting, sculpting, travel.

**MENEFEE, SAMUEL PYEATT,** lawyer, researcher; b. Denver, June 8, 1950; s. George Hardiman and Martha Elizabeth (Pyeatt) M. BA in Anthropology and Scholar of Ho. summa cum laude, Yale U., 1972; diploma in Social Anthropology, Oxford (Eng.) U., 1973, BLitt, 1975; JD, Harvard U., 1981; LLM in Oceans, U. Va., 1982, SJD, 1993; MPhil in Internat. Rels., U. Cambridge, Eng., 1995. Bar: Ga. 1981, U.S. Ct. Appeals (11th cir.) 1982, Va. 1983, La. 1983, U.S. Ct. Mil. Appeals 1983, U.S. Ct. Internat. Trade 1983, U.S. Ct. Claims 1983, U.S. Ct. Appeals (10th cir.) 1983, U.S. Ct. Appeals (fed., 1st, 3d, 4th, 5th, 6th, 7th, 8th and 9th cirs.) 1984, D.C. 1985, Nebr. 1985, Fla. 1985, U.S. Supreme Ct. 1985, U.S. Ct. Appeals (D.C. cir.) 1986, Maine 1986, Pa. 1986. Assoc. Phelps, Dunbar, Marks, Claverie & Sims, New Orleans, 1983-85; of counsel Barham & Churchill PC, New Orleans, 1985-88; sr. assoc. Ctr. for Nat. Security Law U.S. Law, 1985—, fellow Ctr. for Oceans Law and Policy, 1982-83, sr. fellow, 1985-89, Maury fellow 1989—, adv. bd., 1997—. Vis. lectr. U. Cape Town, 1987; vis. asst. prof. U. Mo.-Kansas City, 1990; law clk. Hon. Pasco M. Bowman, U.S. Ct. Appeals (8th cir.), 1994-95; vis. prof. Regent U., 1996-97, scholar-at-large, 1997—, prof., 1998—; adv. The Am. Maritime Forum/The Mariners' Mus., 1997-98; lectr. various nat. and internat. orgns.; mem. ICC Consultative Task Force on Comml. Crime, 1996—. Author: Wives for Sale: An Ethnographic Study of British Popular Divorce, 1981, Contemporary Piracy and International Law, 1995, Trends in Maritime Violence, 1996; co-editor: Materials on Ocean Law, 1982; contbr. numerous articles to profl. jours. Recipient Katharine Briggs prize Folklore Soc., 1992; Bates traveling fellow Yale U., 1971, Rhodes scholar, 1972; Cosmos fellow Sch. Scottish Studies U. Edinburgh, 1991-92, IMB fellow, ICC Internat. Maritime Bur., 1991—, Piracy Reporting Ctr. fellow, Kuala Lampur, 1993—, Huntington fellow The Mariners Mus., 1997. Fellow Royal Anthrop. Inst., Am. Anthrop. Assn., Royal Asiatic Soc., Royal Soc. Antiquaries of Ireland, Soc. Antiquaries (Scotland), Royal Geog. Soc., Soc. Antiquaries; mem. ABA (vice-chmn. marine resources com. 1987-90, chmn. law of the sea subcom. naval warfare, maritime terrorism and piracy 1989—, mem. law of the sea com. steering com. 1996—, mem. working group on terrorism), Southeastern Admiralty Law Inst. (com. mem.), Maritime Law Assn. (proctor, com. mem., chmn. subcom. law of the sea 1988-91, vice chmn. com. internat. law of the sea 1991—, chair working group piracy 1992—, UNESCO study group, 1998—), Marine Tech. Soc. (co-chmn. marine security com. 1991—), Selden Soc., Am. Soc. Internat. Law, Internat. Law Assn. (com. mem., rapporteur Am. br. com. EEZ 1988-90, rapporteur Am. br. com. Maritime Neutrality 1992, observer UN conv. on Law of the Sea meeting of States Parties 1996, chmn. Am. br. com. on Law of the Sea 1996—), rapporteur joint internat. working group on uniformity of the law of piracy 1998—, (Com. Maritime Internat.), Am. Soc. Indsl. Security (com. mem.), U.S. Naval Inst., USN League, Folklore Soc., Royal Celtic Soc., Internat. Studies Assn., Royal Scottish Soc., Royal African Soc., Egypt Exploration Soc., Arctic Inst. N.Am., Internat. Studies Assn., Am. Hist. Soc., Internat. Assn. Rsch. on Peasant Diaries (nat. editor 1996—), Nat. Eagle Scout Assn., Raven Soc., Jefferson Soc., Fence Club, Mory's Assn., Elizabethan Club, Yale Polit. Union, Leander Club, Cambridge Union, United Oxford and Cambridge Univ. Club, Yale Club (N.Y.C.), Paul Morphy Chess Club, Pendennis Club, Round Table Club (New Orleans), Phi Beta Kappa, Omicron Delta Kappa. Republican. Episcopalian. Avocations: anthropology, archaeology, crew, walking. Office: PO Box 5291 Charlottesville VA 22905 also: U Va Ctr Nat Sec Law 580 Massie Rd Charlottesville VA 22903-1738

**MENELL, PETER SETH,** law educator; b. Jersey City, Dec. 2, 1958; s. Allan and Carole M.; m. Clair Marie Sylvia. SB in Econs., MIT, 1980; MA in Econs., Stanford (Calif.) U., 1982; PhD in Econs, 1986; JD, Harvard U., 1986. Law clk. to presiding judge US Ct. Appeals (2d cir.), Hartford, Conn., 1986-87; assoc. prof. law Georgetown U. Law Ctr., Washington, 1987-90; prof. sch. law U. Calif., Berkeley, 1990—; dir. Ctr. Law and Tech., U. Calif., Berkeley, 1995—. Vis. prof. Harvard Law Sch., 1990, Stanford Law Sch., 1992-93. Co-author (with Richard Stewart): Environmental Law and Policy,

1994; co-author: (with R. Merges & M. Lemley) Intellectual Property in the New Technological Age, 2003; co-author: (with M. Lemley, R. Merges & P. Samuelson) Software and Internet Law, 2003; author: Environmental Law, 2002; contbr. articles to profl. jour. Stanford U. fellow, 1980, Olin fellow Harvard U., 1985, Olin Found. fellow, 1989. Mem. Am. Econs. Assn., Calif. Bar Assn. Jewish. Office: University of California School of Law Boalt Hall Berkeley CA 94720-7200

**MENENDEZ, BELINDA,** broadcast executive; Student, St. Andrews U., Scotland. With internat. TV sales Televisa, 1986—95; mgr. TV sales Cisneros; internat. tv distbn. ops. mgr. Michael Solomon's S.I.E.; exec. v.p. sales Studio Canal (formerly Canal Plus DA); co-pres. Universal TV Distbn., Universal City, Calif., 2001—. Office: Universal TV Distbn USA Bldg 1440/3030 100 Universal City Plaza Universal City CA 91608-1002

**MENENDEZ, MARCELINO EULOGIO (MARC MENENDEZ),** marketing professional; b. Mexico City, Mex., June 1974; s. Marcelino and Sharon M. Menendez; m. Susan P. Gildo. BA, Columbia U., N.Y.C., 1996. Analyst Bayerish Vereinsbank, N.Y.C., 1993—95; mng. analyst Forest Labs. N.Y.C., 1996—97, assoc. product mgr., 1997—98; dir. of pharms. SMG Mktg. Group, Inc., N.Y.C., 1998—99; nat. sales dir. health svcs. SMG Mktg. Group, Inc./Quintiles Transnat. Corp, Chgo., 2000—2001; v.p. sales and mktg. Affiliated Network Services, LLC, Chgo., 2001—. Mng. ptnr. Roshamar, Inc., Mex. City, 1999—; prin. Guilmen Cons., Naperville, Ill., 1999—. Treas. Tallgrass Homeowners Assn.; vol. Rep. Party, Chgo., 1997—2003. Recipient Fgn. Langs. award, Bank of Am., 1992. Mem.: Acad. of Managed Care Pharmacy, Nat. Assn. of Dental Plans, Nat. Dental EDI Coun. Orgn. (vice chiar, mktg.), Columbia U. Alumni Assn., Am. Mgmt. Assn., Med. Mktg. Assn. Avocations: exercise, technology/computers, culinary arts. Home: 3703 Mistflower Ln Naperville IL 60564 Office: Affiliated Network Services 20 S Clark St Ste 1810 Chicago IL 60603-1844 Personal E-mail: marquis@elative.com.

**MENENDEZ, ROBERT,** senator, former congressman; b. NYC, Jan. 1, 1954; s. Mario and Evangelina (Lopez) M.; m. Jane Jacobsen, June 5, 1976 (div. 2005); children: Alicia, Robert. BA in Polit. Sci. and Urban Studies, St. Peter's Coll., 1976; JD, Rutgers U., 1979. Bar: NJ 1980. Atty. Diaz and Menendez, Union City, NJ, 1980-92; mayor City of Union City, 1986—92; mem. NJ Gen. Assembly, 1987—91; majority whip NJ State Senate, 1991—92; mem. U.S. Congress from 13th N.J. dist., 1993—2006; Dem. whip at large; US Senator from NJ, 2006—. Com. banking, housing and urban affairs US Senate, com. budget, com. energy and natural resources. CFO Union City Bd. Edn., 1978-82, trustee, 1974-78; mem. Alliance Civic Assn., 1982-92, pres. 1981; mem. Gov.'s Hispanic Adv. Com., Trenton, N.J., 1984—; mem. Gov.'s Ethnic Adv. Com., Washington, 1985. Recipient Cmty. Svc. award Gran Logia del Norte, 1981, Outstanding Svc. award Hispanic Law Enforcement, 1981, Outstanding Cmty. Svc. Revista Actualidades, 1982, US Conf. Mayors award, 1987, 1988, 1991, Disting. Citizen award U. Medicine and Dentistry N.J., 1994, Man of Yr. award Kiwanis, 1994, Lifetime Achievement award Hispanic Bus. Roundtable, 2000, Excellence in Edn. award, Ana G. Mendez U. System, 2003, Capital award Nat. Coun. of La Raza, 2003. Mem. ABA, Fed. Bar Assn. NJ Bar Assn., Hispanic Bar Assn., Hudson County Bar Assn., NJ Employment & Training Commn., NJ Mayors Coalition, NJ Hispanic Leadership Opportunities Program (chmn.), Hispanic Elected and Apptd Ofcls. Orgn. (chmn.); Hoboken Elks Club, North Hudson Lawyers Club (chmn.) Democrat. Roman Catholic. Avocations: chess, racquetball. Office: US Senate 502 Hart Senate Office Bldg Washington DC 20510 also: District Office Ste 1100 One Gateway Ctr Newark NJ 07102 Office Phone: 202-224-4744, 973-645-3030. Office Fax: 202-228-2197, 973-645-0502.*

**MENENDEZ CAMBO, PATRICIA,** lawyer; b. N.Y.C., June 7, 1966; BBA, U. Miami, 1986; JD, U. Pa., 1989. Bar: Fla. 1991, DC 1993. With Greenberg Traurig, PA, Miami, 1994—2000; chief U.S. legal counsel Telefónica S.A., 2000—02; shareholder, chair internat. practice group Greenberg Traurig, PA, Miami, 2002—. Bd. dirs. Coun. of Americas. Contbr. articles to profl. jours. Trustee Nat. Alliance for Autism Rsch. Named one of Top Up and Comers in So. Fla., So. Fla. Legal Guide, 2004, Top 40 Lawyers Under 40, Nat. Law Jour., 2005. Office: Greenberg Traurig 1221 Brickell Ave Miami FL 33131 Office Phone: 305-579-0766. Office Fax: 305-579-0717. Business E-Mail: pmc@gtlaw.com.

**MENEZES, RONALDO P.,** computer scientist, educator; b. Fortaleza, Ceará, Nov. 19, 1969; s. Flávio Augusto O. and Maria do Carmo P. Menezes; m. Sarah O. Oriá, July 19, 1994; children: Kalil O., Adele O. BSc, U. Fortaleza, Fortaleza, Brazil, 1992; MSc, State U. Campinas, São Paulo, Brazil, 1995; PhD, The U. York, England, 2000. Lectr. computer sci. The U. Ulster, Londonderry, Northern Ireland, 1999—2000; asst. prof. computer sci. Fla. Tech, Melbourne, Fla., 2000—06, assoc. prof. computer sci., 2006—. Cons. 8over8 Ltd., Londonderry, Northern Ireland, 1999—2000. Office: Florida Tech Dept of Computer Sciences 150 We University Blvd Melbourne FL 32901 Office Phone: +1 321 6747623.

**MENG, GUNTER RICHARD,** surgeon; b. Brühl, Germany, Mar. 31, 1927; US, 1948; s. Richard and Elise Meng; m. Hilde Maria Farrenkopf, Aug. 14, 1954; children: Karin, Peter. BA, Cornell U., 1951, MD, 1955. Gen. surgeon USAF, 1960—82, chief surgery, chief prof. staff; vice comdr. USAF Wright Patterson Med. Ctr. Surgery cons. for surgeon gen. USAF, Wash., DC, 1978—82. Contbr. articles to profl. jours. Recipient Legion of Merit, USAF, 1982. Mem.: Assn. Mil. Surgeons. Republican. Cath. Home: 12211Lackwood Ct Fort Myers FL 33908

**MENG, HONG,** chemist; s. Xuemin Meng and Shuxia He; m. Yi Wang, Sept. 22, 1995; children: Ziwen Wendy, Cindy Zicong. PhD, UCLA, 1999—2002. Rsch. officer Imre, Singapore, 1997—99; rsch. cons. Lucent Tech., Bell Labs, Murray Hill, NJ, 2000—01; sr. rsch. chemist E.I. DuPont Co. CRD, Wilmington, Del., 2002—. Author: (book) Organic Light Emitting Materials and Dev. Recipient Tan Kan Kee Young Inventors award, Singapore Govt., 1999, John Stauffer Fellowship award, 2001. Mem.: Materials Rsch. Soc. (assoc.). Achievements include patents for high performance and long life time organic light emitting materials; high performance organic semiconductors of anthacene/tetracene/pentacene derivatives; patents pending for high charge mobility organic semiconductors; design of design and synthesis a series F conjugated organic thiol compounds for molecule electronics; highly Stable n-Type Conducting Polymers; first to design rules for high mobility and stable organic semiconductors; first N-Diblock Ccnjugated light emitting polymers; discovery of solid state conducting polymer synthesis PEDOT; invention of high performance and stable organic thin film transistors; organic semiconductor materials design. Office: E I DuPont Co Rt 141 and Henry Clay Bldg E328/R205 Wilmington DE 19880-0328 Office Fax: 302-695-9799. Personal E-mail: hongucla@gmail.com. Business E-Mail: hongdupont@yahoo.com.

**MENG, M. KATHRYN,** lawyer; JD, Fordham U. Former dist. ct. bur. chief criminal divsn. Legal Aid Soc. Nassau County; ptnr. Cianciulli Meng & Panos PC, Garden City, NY. Dean Nassau Acad. Law; adj. prof. Nassau C.C. Columnist Nassau Lawyer. Bd. dirs. Sara's Ctr.; mem. outreach adv. com. St. Brigid's Ch., Westbury, eucharistic ministr. Mem.: ABA (del.), Nassau Legal Aid Soc. (former pres., former bd. dirs.), Attys. to the Bar (com. character and fitnss 2d jud. dept. 1983—), Criminal Cts. Bar Assn. (former pres., former bd. dirs.), N.Y. State Bar Assn. (del.), Nassau County Bar Assn. (pres., chair civil rights com., former chair lawyers assistance com., former mem. judiciary com.). Office: Cianciulli Meng & Panos PC 99 Quentin Roosevelt Blvd Ste 201 Garden City NY 11530 Office Phone: 516-564-6036, 516-683-0901. Business E-Mail: kmeng@cmlawgroup.net.

**MENG, XIAO-LI,** statistician; b. Shanghai, Jan. 24, 1963; PhD, Harvard U., 1990. From asst. to assoc. to prof. stats. U. Chgo., Chicago, 1991—2001; prof. stats. Harvard U., Cambridge, Mass., 2001—, chmn., 2004—. Assoc.

editor: Annals of Stats., 1997—, Jour. Am. Statis. Assn., 1996—2002, Biometrika, 2002—, Statistica Sinica, 1992—97; co-editor, 2005—. Recipient 2001 COPSS award for outstanding statistician under age of 40, Com. of Pres. of Statis. Assn., 2001. Fellow: Royal Statis. Soc. (U.K.), Am. Statis. Assn. (program chair 2004 joint statis. meetings 2002—04), Inst. Math. Stats. (program chair 1999—2000); mem.: Internat. Soc. for Bayesian Analysis, Internat. Chinese Statis. Assn. (life; bd. dirs. 1996—99), Bernoulli Soc. for Math. Stats. and Probability, Biometric Soc. (regional adv. bd. 1995—97). Office: Harvard U Dept Stats Sci Ctr Oxford St Cambridge MA 02138 Business E-Mail: meng@stat.harvard.edu.

**MENGDEN, JOSEPH MICHAEL,** retired investment banker; b. Houston, Sept. 28, 1924; s. Hippolyt Frederick and Amalia (Dittlinger) M.; m. Suzanne Miner, Sept. 30, 1950 (dec. July 1990); children: Anne Elise Mengden Giliberto, Amanda Mary, Michael Joseph, Charles Louis, Melissa Mary Mengden Bunker, Mary Miner Mengden Fitch; m. Dorothy Duggan, July 27, 1991. Ph.B., U. Notre Dame, 1949. V.p. Nat. Bank of Detroit, 1950-67; exec. v.p. First of Mich. Capital Corp., Detroit, 1967-90, sr. cons., 1990-95. Served to 1st lt. USAAF, World War II. Decorated Air medal with 2 oak leaf clusters. Home: 321 Rivard Blvd Grosse Pointe MI 48230-1625 Personal E-mail: men@comcast.net.

**MENGEL, CHARLES EDMUND,** internist, educator; b. Balt., Nov. 29, 1931; s. Charles LeRoy and Anna (Apgar) M.; m. Paula Padgett, June 5, 1978; children: Cheryl Lynn, Charles Edmund, Gregory John, Scott Alan, Carol Ann, Michael Daniel. AB in Chemistry, Lafayette Coll., 1953; MD, Johns Hopkins U., 1957. Intern Johns Hopkins Hosp., 1957-58; resident Duke Hosp., 1958-59, 61-62; clin. assoc. NIH, 1959-61; mem. faculty Duke U. Med. Sch., 1961-65; Doan prof., dir. hematology and oncology Ohio State U., 1965-69; prof. medicine U. Mo., Columbia, 1969-82, chmn. dept., 1969-81; pvt practive gen. medicine Moberly, Mo., 1982-88; prof. medicine Kans. U. Med. Ctr., Kansas City, 1988-98; CEO MEC Enterprises, 1999—. Author textbook; contbr. articles to med. publs. With USPHS, 1959-61. Markle scholar acad. medicine, 1963 Mem. ACP, Am. Fedn. Clin. Rsch., Am. Soc. Hematology, Am. Soc. Clin. Investigation

**MENGELING, WILLIAM LLOYD,** retired veterinarian, virologist; b. Elgin, Ill., Apr. 1, 1933; s. William Paul and Blanche Joyce (Wormwood) M.; m. Barbara Ann Kethcart, Aug. 23, 1958; children: Michelle, Michael. BS, Kans. State U., 1958, DVM, 1960; MS, Iowa State U., 1966, PhD, 1969. Diplomate M. Coll. Vet. Microbiologists (chmn. 1977-78, bd. dirs. 1975-77). Vet. clinician St. Francis Animal Hosp., Albuquerque, 1960-61; vet. med. officer Nat. Animal Disease Ctr., Ames, Iowa, 1961-69, rsch. leader, 1969—2001, U.S. Sr. Exec. Svc., 1991—; ret. 2001. Cons. numerous state, fed., pvt. U.S. and fgn. agys.; collaborative prof., mem. grad. faculty Iowa State U. Co-editor: Diseases of Swine, 5th, 6th, 7th, 8th editions; contbr. articles to jours., chpts. to books. With U.S. Army, 1953-55. Recipient cert. appreciation USDA, 1978, George Fleming award Brit. Vet. Jour., 1978, Disting. Svc. award USDA, 1984, Gov.'s medal sci. State of Iowa, 1985, Vet. Med. Rsch. award Am. Feed Industry Assn., 1989, Leadership Merit awards USDA, 1989, 90, 91, 93, Alumnus award Kans. State U. Coll. Vet. Medicine and Vet. Med. Alumni Assn., 1999, William P. Switzer award Iowa State U. Coll. Met. Medicine, 2000, Howard Dunne Meml. award, Am. Assn. Swine Vets., 2001; elected to Agrl. Rsch. Svc. Hall of Fame, 2001. Mem. AVMA (Vet. Med. Rsch. award 1989), U.S. Animal Health Assn., Conf. Rsch. Workers in Animal Disease (pres. 1987-88, coun. 1981-86), Polish Soc. Vet. Sci. (hon.), Kiwanis (pres. 1975-76). Methodist. Avocations: wilderness survival, canoeing, camping, fishing. Home: 4220 Phoenix St Ames IA 50014-3922 Office Phone: 515-292-7060. Personal E-mail: bbmengeling@aol.com.

**MENGES, JOHN KENNETH, JR.,** lawyer; b. Louisville, Sept. 23, 1957; s. John Kenneth and Barbara Jean (Vick) M. BSBA, Boston U., 1979; JD, Harvard U., 1982. Bar: Tex. 1982. Assoc. Akin, Gump, Strauss, Hauer & Feld, Dallas, 1982-89, ptnr., 1989—, now ptnr.-in-charge Dallas office and mem. mgmt. com. Pres. Dallas County Young Dems., 1985-88, Dallas Dem. Forum, 1990-91, bd. dirs., 1986-89; pres. sch. mgmt. Boston U., 1987—, bd. trustees, 1995—; bd. dirs. Friends of Fair Park; bd. trustees Boston U.; Dallas County chair North Tex. Clean Air Coalition. Mem. ABA, Tex. State Bar Assn., Dallas Bus. League (pres. 1989), Dallas Coun. on World Affairs, Dallas Assn. Young Lawyers, Harvard U. Law Sch. Assn. Tex. (bd. dirs. 1984-87, 90-91, pres. 1993), Boston U. Nat. Alumni Coun. (Young Alumni award 1987), Beta Gamma Sigma. Democrat. Methodist. Avocation: basketball. Office: Akin Gump Strauss Hauer & Feld LLP 1700 Pacific Ave Ste 4100 Dallas TX 75201-4675 Office Phone: 214-969-2783. Business E-Mail: kmenges@akingump.com.

**MENGES, MARTHA,** special education educator; d. John and Mary Blake Duff; children: John A., Katherine. BS in Home Econs., William Woods Coll., Fulton, Mo., 1969; postgrad., Harris Tchrs. Coll., St. Louis, 1970—71, Ea. Ill. U., 1987—88. Cert. elem. edn. Ill., cross categorical spl. edn. Ill. State Bd. of Edn., 1988. Elem. tchr. Granite City Sch. Dist., Ill., 1970—72; substitute tchr. Iroquois County schs., Watseka, Ill., 1982—87; cross categorical spl. edn. tchr. Ford-Iroquois Spl. Edn. Assn., Iroquois County, Ill., 1988—96; spl. edn. tchr. students with behavior disorders Kankakee Dist. #111, Ill., 1996—98; cross categorical spl. edn. tchr. Iroquois Spl. Edn. Assn., Donovan and Watseka, Ill., 1998—. Ednl. diagnostician Nexus Ednl. Ctr., Onarga, Ill., 1995—96; spelling contest coord. King Mid. Sch., Kankakee, 1997—97; instrnl. mentor Iroquois Spl. Edn. Assn., Donovan, 1999—2003; sch. improvement plan com., Donovan, 2000—02; ACT accommodations coord. Watseka Comty. H.S., 2003—04. Iroquois County bd. vol. Am. Cancer Soc., Watseka, 2000—03, Reach to Recovery vol., 2000—03; chairperson wills and memorials com. Watseka United Meth. Ch., 2001—03; steering com. Iroquois Valley Youth for Christ, Watseka, 1995—97. Mem.: NEA, Ill. Coun. for Exeptional Children, Ill. Edn. Assn., Nature Concernvancy, Ill. Corn Growers Assn. Gen. Soc. Mayflower Descendants, Iroquois County Hist. Soc. Avocations: family genealogy, Iroquois county history, prairie plants of Illinois.

**MENGES, SUSAN DEBRA FAVREAU,** management consultant, retired protective services official; b. Cleve., Dec. 15, 1955; d. Donald Francis and Helen Patricia (Rafferty) F.; m. William J. Menges, Nov. 17, 2001. Cert., N.Y. State Police Acad., 1974; student, Cornell U., 1984, SUNY, 1986. Comm. specialist N.Y. State Police, Loudonville, 1974—87, comm. specialist divsn. hdqrs., 1987—98; mgmt. cons., sec.-treas., dir. Don Favreau Assocs., Inc., Clifton Park, NY, 1983—86, v.p., 1986—; comm. specialist divsn. hdqrs. N.Y. State Police, Albany, 1987—98, sys. support specialist divsn. hdqrs. 1998—2005, ret., 2005. Adj. faculty Internat. Assn. Chiefs Police; NYSPIN coord. FBI/Nat. Crime Info. Ctr. cert. program, 1986—; ind. sr. beauty cons. Mary Kay Cosmetics, 2003 Author: Teamwork in the Telecommunication Center, 1986, One More Time: How to be a Mature and Successful Telcommunications Manager, 1987, Law Enforcement Terminal Security, 1991; also NYSPIN cert. manuals. Vol. Suncoast Seabird Sanctuary, Indian Shores, Fla., 2005—06. Recipient Dirs. Commendation N.Y. State Police Acad., 1977, Commendation N.Y. State Police, 1978, Supt.'s Commendation, 1986, Y2K Commendation Gov. George Pataki, 2000 Mem. NAFE, N.Y. State Civil Svc. Assn., Emergency Communicators Profl. Assn. (adv. bd.), Colonie Police Benevolent Assn. (hon.), Am. Soc. Law Enforcement Trainers, Assoc. Pub. Safety Comm. Officers (planning commn. Atlantic chpt. 1991, registration chair ann. N.E. conf. 1991), N.Y. State Troopers Police Benevolent Assn. (hon.), Nat. Bus. Women Assn., Internat. Assn. Chiefs Police, Am. Horse Shows Assn., Am. Soc. Law Enforcement Trainers, Capital Dist. Hunter/Jumper Coun. Republican. Roman Catholic. Avocations: horseback riding, target shooting, reading, sewing. Office: Hdqrs NY State Police State Office Bldg Campus Bldg # 22 Albany NY 12226 Home: 19701 Gulf Blvd Apt 307 Indian Shores FL 33785-2385 E-mail: susan9g6@aol.com.

**MENGLER, THOMAS M.,** dean; b. May 18, 1953; BA in Philosophy magna cum laude, Carleton Coll., 1975; MA in Philosophy, U. Tex., 1977, JD, 1981. Bar: Ill., Tex., D.C., U.S. Ct. Appeals (5th, 7th and 10th cirs.), U.S.

---

Dist. Ct. (we. dist.) Tex. Law clk. to Hon. James K. Logan U.S. Ct. Appeals for 10thCir., Olathe, Kans., 1980-81; assoc. atty. Arnold & Porter, Washington, 1982-83; asst. atty. gen. Office of Atty. Gen. of Tex., Austin, 1983-85; asst. prof. law U. Ill. Coll. Law, Champaign, 1985-89, assoc. prof., 1989-91, prof. law, 1991—2002, assoc. dean for acad. affairs, 1992-93, dean, 1993—2002; dean, prof. law U St Thomas Sch Law, Mpls., 2002—. Contbr. numerous articles to profl. jours. Mem. ABA, Ill. State Bar Assn., Order of Coif, Phi Beta Kappa. Office: U St Thomas Sch Law Mail TMH 440 1000 LaSalle Ave Minneapolis MN 55403-2005*

**MENICHESCHI, EDWARD JOHN,** publishing executive; b. June 20, 1959; Graduate, Fasion Inst. of Tech. Edited the retail trade publ. GQ mag, 1982—86, merchandising editor, 1986—90; v.p. mktg. Bidermann Industries, 1990—92; exec. editor Vogue, 1992—94, assoc. publ., 1994—99; pres. IAM.COM, 1999—2001, WWD Media Worldwide, 2001—06; exec. v.p. Fairchild Publications Inc., 2005—06; v.p., publ. Vanity Fair, 2006—. Named to Digital Coast's Top 100 Internet Exec.; recipient Outstanding Alumni award, Fashion Inst. Tech., 1988. Office: Vanity Fair 4 Time Square 22nd Fl New York NY 10036*

**MENIL, VIOLETA CRUZ,** mathematician, educator, consultant; BSE in Math. magna cum laude, U. San Carlos, Cebu, Philippines, 1965; MS in Applied Math & Stats., SUNY, Stony Brook, 1983; MA in Math. Edn., De la Salle U., Manila, 1976; PhD in Math. and stats., NYU, 1988. Lectr. math. Baruch Coll. CUNY, N.Y.C., 1983—88, instr. stats., 1988—89; assoc. prof. De la Salle U., Manila, 1989—94, rsch. dir., 1990—93; asst. prof. Hostos C.C. CUNY, Bronx, 1994—95, CUNY, Bronx, 2000—; audit statistician N.Y.C. Comptroller's Office, 1995—98. Treas. Corner View Assn., Inc. Bklyn , 2001. Recipient Rotary Outstanding Surigaonon award (ROSA), Rotary Internat., Surigao City Chpt., 1998, Most Outstanding Nicolanian award (MONICA), San Nicolas Colege, Surigao City, 1995; Fulbright Hays scholar, Inst. Internat. Edn., 1981-1984. Mem.: Asian Am. Higher Edn. Coun. (nyc 2001—02), Am. Statis. Assn. (va., alexandria 1999—2002). Home: 4407 4th Avenue Apt B4 Brooklyn NY 11220 Personal E-mail: menilv2@aol.com.

**MENINGALL, EVELYN L.,** retired educational media specialist; b. Dothan, Ala., July 22, 1935; d. Earl and Luella Koonce; m. A. Richard Meningall, Jan. 17, 1958; children: Dawn, Tracy, Richard. BS in Edn., Wayne State U., 1975; MLS, Rutgers U., 1979. Cert. ednl. media specialist Dept. Edn. State N.J., elem. sch. dept. Dept. Edn. State N.J., profl. librs. cert. Dept. Edn. State N.J. Tchr. Detroit Bd. Edn., 1975—76; libr. East Brunswick (N.J.) Pub. Libr., 1978—80; ednl. media specialist Piscataway (N.J.) Bd. Edn., 1980—98; ret., 1998. Author: A Way of Life: An Anthology of Poems, 2004, Reflections: A Collection of Poems, 2005. Active New Detroit, Inc., Delta Sigma Theta Sorority Ctrl. Jersey; vol. tutor/reader pub. schs.; vol. to holisitic score English tests Plainfield (N.J.) H.S.; recording sec. Scholarship Fund of St. Paul AME Ch. Mem.: ALA (life), Ednl. Media Assn., Ill. Edn. Assn. (life), NJ Edn. Assn. (life), Nat. Sorority Phi Delta Kappa, Inc. (life: basileus 1987—89, exec. advisor 1989—91), Delta Sigma Theta (life). St. Paul Ame Church. Avocations: poetry, reading, fishing. Home: 23 Vauxhall Rd East Brunswick NJ 08816-1719

**MENINO, THOMAS M.,** mayor; b. Boston, Dec. 27, 1942; m. Angela Faletra; children: Susan, Thomas Michael, Jr. Degree in Community Planning, U. Mass., 1988; cert. in State and Local Govt. Program, Harvard U. Mem. City Coun., Boston, 1985—, pres., 1993; mayor City of Boston, 1993—. Sr. rsch. asst. Joint Com. Urban Affairs, 1978-83; pres. U.S. Conf. Mayors, 2003. Contbr. articles to historic preservation jours. Regional chmn. Nat. Trust Historic Preservation; bd. dirs. Nat. League Cities, 1985—, mem. various coms. Office: Office of Mayor 1 City Hall Plz Fl 5 Boston MA 02201-1001*

**MENITOFF, PAUL ALAN,** psychiatrist; b. Boston, May 4, 1946; s. Ralph and Ethel (Bickoff) M.; m. Susan Mathilde Hirsch, June 8, 1980. BA cum laude, Harvard U., 1969; MD, Cornell U., 1973. Diplomate Am. Bd. Psychiatry and Neurology, Subspecialty Psychosomatic Medicine. Intern in surgery Univ. Hosp., Boston, 1973-74; psychiat. resident Payne Whitney Clinic N.Y. Hosp./Cornell Med. Ctr., N.Y.C., 1974-77; forensic psychiat. fellow U. So. Calif./L.A. County Med. Ctr., 1977-78; forensic psychiat. fellow Med. Sch. U. Md., Balt., 1978-79; staff psychiatrist Clifton T. Perkins Hosp., Jessup, Md., 1978-80; mem. med. staff St. John's Hosp., Lowell, Mass., 1980-93; Saints Meml. Med. Ctr., 1993—; chief divsn. psychiatry, 1996—; mem. med. staff St. Joseph's Hosp., Lowell, 1980-93, Lowell Gen. Hosp., 1980—, chief dept. psychiatry, 1991-93; pvt. practice, Chelmsford, Mass., 1980—. Clin. inst. psychiatry U. So. Calif. Med. Sch., L.A., 1977-78; clin. asst. prof. psychiatry U. Md. Med. Sch., Balt., 1979-80. Mem. Am. Psychiat. Assn., Mass. Psychiat. Assn., Acad. Psychosomatic Medicine, Am. Acad. Psychiatry and the Law, Mass. Med. Soc. Democrat. Avocations: movies, theater. Office: Greater Lowell Psychiat Assocs 9 Acton Rd Ste 25 Chelmsford MA 01824-3496 Office Phone: 978-256-6579.

**MENIUS, ESPIE FLYNN, JR.,** electrical engineer; b. New Bern, N.C., Mar. 5, 1923; s. Espie Flynn and Sudie Grey (Lyerly) M.; adopted children: James Benfield, Ruben Hughes, James Sechler, Steve Walden. BEE, N.C. State U., 1947; MBA, U. S.C., 1973. Registered profl. engr., N.C., S.C., Tenn., Ga., Fla. With Carolina Power & Light Co., 1947-63, asst. to dist. mgr. Raleigh, Henderson, NC, 1947-50, Sumter, SC, 1947-50, elec. engr. Asheville, Southern Pines and Dunn, NC, 1950-52, dist. engr. Hartsville, SC, 1952-63; sr. elec. engr. Sonoco Products Co., 1963-74, engring. group leader, 1974-89, sr. profl. engr., 1989-91; profl. cons. and elec. engr., 1991—. Instr. Florence-Darlington Tech. Ednl. Ctr. Author: Adoption of Older Children; contbr. articles to profl. jours. Active Hartsville Vol. Fire Dept., 1958-94; Fire dept. and Law Enforcement Chaplain 1985—; Eagle Scout Boy Scouts Am., 1938 scout troop leader New Bern, 1940-41, Raleigh, 1941-47, Henderson, 1948-49, Sumter, 1949-50, Asheville, N.C., 1950, Southern Pines, N.C., 1951-52, Hartsville, 1952-64; bd. mgrs. Nazareth Children's Home, Rockwell, N.C., 1980—; chmn. bd. examiners City of Hartsville, 1980-90; advocate Thornwell Children's Home, Clinton, S.C., 1990—; bd. dir. Darlington (S.C.) County Youth Home, 1992—; active Hartsville Leadership Coun., 1993—; deacon, elder, trustee, tchr. men's Bible class First Presbyn. Ch., Hartsville. Served with US Army, 1943-46. Recipient Citzenship award S.C. State Firemen's Assn., 1993; named Hartsville Citizen of Yr., Rotary, 1960; named to S.C. Fire Fighters Hall of Fame, 1995. Mem. IEEE, AAAS, VFW, Nat. Assn. Engrs., Am. Legion, Knight of St. Patrick, Scabbard and Blade, Eta Kappa Nu, Pine Burr, Phi Eta Sigma, Theta Tau, Beta Gamma Sigma. Presbyterian. Home and office: 423 W Richardson Cir Hartsville SC 29550-5437 Office Phone: 843-332-8502.

**MENKE, ALLEN CARL,** manufacturing executive; b. Huntingburg, Ind., Feb. 16, 1922; s. William Ernest and Clara (Moenkhaus) M.; m. Virginia Lee MacDonald, Apr. 14, 1944; children: Janet, William, Sarah. BS in Mech. Engring, Purdue U., 1943, MS, 1948. Instr. Purdue U., 1946-48; with Trane Co., 1948-63, v.p. sales, 1963-64, exec. v.p. sales, mfg. and engring., 1964-68; v.p. Borg-Warner Corp., Chgo., 1969-76; chmn., pres., CEO Artesian Industries, Northbrook, Ill., 1976-88. Bd. dirs. Trane Co., SPS Techs., Hoover Co., Consolidated Papers Corp., York Corp., Am. Air Filter. Pres. Met. Housing Devel. Corp.; founder, pres. Winnetka Interch. Coun.; bd. dirs., past chmn. Presbyn. Home; past chmn. dean's adv. coun. Krannert Sch. Mgmt. Purdue U.; bd. dirs. McCormick Sem., U. Chgo.; trustee Kenilworth Union Ch. Served to 1st lt. AUS, 1944-46. Named Disting. Alumnus, Purdue U., 1965, Outstanding Engr. Grad., 1991, mem. Purdue Hall of Fame, Ind. Basketball Hall of Fame, 1999. Mem. Sigma Chi (Significant Order Constantine awards). Presbyterian (elder). Lodge: Mason. Home: 2 Arbor Ln #208 Evanston IL 60201

**MENKE, DIANA LYNN,** elementary school educator; d. Thomas E. and Dorothy H. Miller; m. Dave A. Menke, June 19, 1987; 1 child, Kalen Thomas. BS in Edn., Pitts. State U., Kans., 1978. Profl. lic. elem. K-9 Kans. Sate Bd. Edn. Kindergarten tchr. Christ the King Sch., Kansas City, 1978—81, 5th

---

grade tchr., 1981—84; 3rd grade tchr. Queen of the Holy Rosary, Overland Park, Kans., 1984—90; Learning Ctr. tchr. 6th grade lang. arts and 7th and 8th social studies St. Pius X Sch., Mission, Kans., 1995—2005. Preschool art instr. Johnson County Pks. and Recreation, Roeland Park, Kans., 1994—96; dir. religious edn. St. Pius X Parish, Mission, 1995—99. Telephone vol. Muscular Dystrophy, Kansas City, Mo., 1987—92; vol. com. chair Roeland Park PTA, 1995—2002; parent vol. Boy Scouts Am., 2000—05. Nominee Excellence in Tchg. award, C. of C. Kansas City, 1988. Mem.: Nat. Cath. Educators Assn. Roman Catholic. Avocations: travel, crafts, knitting. Home: 13145 Carter St Overland Park KS 66213 Office: Prince of Peace Cath Sch 16000 W 143rd St Olathe KS 66062 Office Phone: 913-764-0650.

**MENKEL-MEADOW, CARRIE JOAN,** law educator; b. N.Y.C., Dec. 14, 1949; d. Gary G. and Margot (Sinn) Menkel; m. Robert Gary Meadow, Aug. 22, 1971. AB magna cum laude, Columbia U., 1971; JD cum laude, U. Pa., 1974; LLD (hon.), Quinnipiac Coll. Law, 1995. Bar: Pa. 1974, U.S. Ct. Appeals (3d cir.) 1975, Calif. 1979, D.C., 1997. Dir. legal writing U. Pa. Law Sch., Phila., 1974-75, clin. supt., lectr., 1976-79; staff atty. Cmty. Legal Svcs., Phila., 1975-77; prof. UCLA, 1979—, prof. law, 1979-99, Georgetown Law Ctr., Washington, 1996—, A.B. Chettle Jr. chair prof. dispute resolution civil procedure, 2005—; holder Phyllis Beck chair Temple U. Law Sch., Phila., 1999. Cons. ABA, Chgo., 1979—84; panel mem. NAS, Washington, 1986—87, NSF, Washington, 1987—90; vis. prof. law Stanford Law Sch., 1990, Harvard Law Sch., 2001, U. Fribourg, Switzerland, 2003; dir. UCLA Ctr. for Conflict Resolution, 1994—99, Georgetown-Hewlett Program on Conflict Resolution and Problem Solving, 2001—; Author: Mediation: Theory, Practice and Policy, 2000, Dispute Processing: Theory, Practice and Policy, 2003, What's Fair: Ethics for Negotiators, 2004, Dispute Resolution: Beyond the Adversarial Model, 2004, Negotiation: Processes for Problem Solving, 2005, Mediation: Practice, Policy and Ethics, 2005; editor-in-chief Jour. Legal Edn., 2003—; editor-in-chief: Internat. Jour. Law in Context, 2004—; contbr. articles to profl. jours. Chairperson Ctr. for Study of Women, UCLA; chair CPR Commn. on Ethics and ADR; bd. dirs. Western Ctr. on Law and Poverty, LA, 1980—86. Recipient William Rutter Found. for Tchg. award UCLA, 1992, 1st prize for Acad. Scholarship on Alternative Dispute Resolution Ctr. for Pub. Resources, 1983, 91, 98, Frank Flegal award for tchg., Georgetown U., 2006. Mem.: Acad. Civil Trial Mediators, Am. Law Inst., Am. Bar Found. (bd. dir., sec., exec. com. 1994—), Law and Soc. Assn. (trustee), Ctr. for Law and Human Values (bd. dir.), Assn. Am. Law Schs. (alt. dispute resolution sect., law and social sci. sect., women in law sect., accreditation com. 1987—90, editor-in-chief Jour. of Legal Edn. 2004—), Soc. Am. Law Tchrs. (trustee), Phi Beta Kappa. Democrat. Office: Georgetown Law Ctr 600 New Jersey Ave NW Washington DC 20001-2075 Office Phone: 202-662-9379. E-mail: meadow@law.georgetown.edu.

**MENKEN, JANE AVA,** demographer, educator; b. Phila., Nov. 29, 1939; d. Isaac Nathan and Rose Ida (Sarvetnick) Golubitsky; m. Matthew Menken, 1960 (div. 1985); children: Kenneth Lloyd, Kathryn Lee; m. Richard Jessor, Nov. 13, 1992. AB, U. Pa., 1960; MS, Harvard U., 1962; PhD, Princeton U., NJ, 1975. Asst. in biostats. Harvard U. Sch. Pub. Health, Boston, 1962-64; math. statistician NIMH, Bethesda, Md., 1964-66; rsch. assoc. dept. biostats. Columbia U., N.Y.C., 1966-69; mem. rsch. staff Office of Population Rsch. Princeton U., 1969-71, 75-87, asst. dir. 1978-86, assoc. dir., 1986-87, prof. sociology, 1980-82, prof. sociology and pub. affairs, 1982-87; prof. sociology and demography U. Pa., Phila., 1987-97, UPS Found. prof. social scis., 1987-97, dir. Population Studies Ctr., 1989-95; prof. sociology U. Colo., Boulder, 1997—, faculty assoc. Population Program, Inst. Behavioral Sci., 1997—; dir. Population Aging Ctr., 2000—, Inst. Behavioral Sci., 2001—; disting. prof., 2002—. Mem. social scis. and population study sect., NIH, Bethesda, 1978-82, chmn., 1980-82, dirs. adv. com., 1995-2000, Nat. Adv. Child Health and Human Devel. Coun., 1988-91, adv. com. Fogarty Internat. Ctr., 2000-02, population adv. com. Rockefeller Found., NYC, 1981-93, com. on population and demography, NAS, Washington, 1978-83, com. on population, 1983-85, 1996-2002, chair 1998-2002, com. nat. stats., 1983-89, com. on AIDS rsch., 1987-93, chair 1990-93; co-chair panel data and rsch. priorities for arresting AIDS in sub-Saharan Africa, 1994-96, Com. on Behavioral and Social Scis. and Edn., 1991-97, chair, steering com., workshop on aging in Africa, 2003-06, chair, sci. adv. com., INDEPTH newtwork, 2002-; coms. Internat. Centre for Diarrhoeal Disease Rsch., Bangladesh, Dhaka, 1984—. Author: (with Mindel C. Sheps) Mathematical Models of Conception and Birth, 1973, (with Ann Blanc and Cynthia Lloyd) Training and Support of Developing Country Population Scientists, 2002; editor: (with Henri Leridon) Natural Fertility, 1979, (with Frank Furstenberg, Jr. and Richard Lincoln) Teenage Sexuality, Pregnancy and Childbearing, 1981, World Population and U.S. Policy: The Choices Ahead, 1986, (with Barney Cohen) Aging in Sub-Saharan Africa: Recommendations for Furthering Research, 2006; contbr. articles to profl. jours. Bd. dirs. Alan Guttmacher Inst., NYC, 1981-90, 93-2000, African Population and Health Rsch. Ctr., Nairobi, Kenya, 2000—. Nat. Merit scholar, 1957; John Simon Guggenheim Found. fellow, 1992-93, Ctr. for Advanced Study in Behavioral Scis. fellow, 1995-96. Fellow AAAS, Am. Statis. Assn.; mem. NAS, Inst. of Medicine, Am. Acad. Arts and Scis., Population Assn. Am. (pres. 1985, Mindel Sheps award 1982), Am. Pub. Health Assn. (Mortimer Spiegelman award 1975), Am. Sociol. Assn., Soc. for Study of Social Biology, Internat. Union for Sci. Study of Population (coun. 1989-97), Sociol. Rsch. Assn. (exec. com. 1991-96, pres. 1996). Office: U Colo IBS#1 483 UCB Boulder CO 80309-0483 Office Phone: 303-492-8148. Business E-Mail: menken@colorado.edu.

**MENKES, JOHN HANS,** pediatric neurologist; b. Vienna, Dec. 20, 1928, came to U.S., 1940; s. Karl and Valerie (Tupler) M.; m. Miriam Trief, Apr. 14, 1957 (div. Feb. 1978); m. Joan Simon Feld, Sept. 28, 1980 (dec. Nov. 2000); children: Simon, Tamara, Rafael C.; m. Myrna Fox (July 1, 2004). AB, U. So. Calif., 1947, MS, 1951; MD, Johns Hopkins U., 1952. Diplomate Am. Bd. Pediat., Am. Bd. Psychiatry and Neurology. Intern, jr. asst. resident Children's Med. Ctr., Boston, 1952-54; asst. resident pediat. Bellevue Hosp., N.Y.C., 1956-57; resident neurology, trainee pediatric neurology Columbia-Presbyn. Med. Ctr., Neurol. Inst. N.Y., N.Y.C., 1957-60; asst. prof. pediat. Johns Hopkins U., Balt., 1960-63, assoc. prof., 1963-66, asst. prof. neurology, 1964-66, chief pediatric neurology divsn., 1964-66; prof. pediat. and neurology UCLA, 1966-74, chief pediatric neurology divsn., 1966-70, prof. psychiatry, 1970-74; chief Neurology-Neurochem. Lab. Brentwood (Calif.) VA Hosp., 1970-74; clin. prof. psychiatry, neurology and pediat. UCLA, 1974-77, clin. prof. pediat. and neurology, 1977-84, prof. pediat. and neurology, 1985-89, prof. emeritus pediat. and neurology, 1989—. Dir. pediatric neurology Cedars-Sinai Med. Ctr., 1997-99, dir. emeritus pediat. neurology, 1999—; mem. metabolism study sect. NIH, 1968-70, project com., 1969-70; mem. adv. com. Nat. Inst. Child Health and Human Devel., 1985-87; mem. Dept. Health Svcs., Calif., 1980-87; mem. vaccine safety commn. Nat. Inst. Medicine, 1995—; mem. Coun. Child Neurology Soc. Dysautonomia Found., med. adv. bd. Nat. Orgn. Rare Diseases, Nat. Wilson's Disease Found.; trustee Dystonia Med. Rsch. Found., Vancouver, Can., 1985—. Author: Textbook of Child Neurology, 6th edit., 2000; (play) The Last Inquisitor, 1985 (Drama-Logue Critics award 1985), The Salvation of Miguel Toruna, 1987; (screen play) Miguel, Open Ward, 1989, The Countess of Sligo, 1992, The White Darkness, 1996, Lady Macbeth Gets a Divorce, 2001, Native Born, 2003; (novels) The Secret Diary of Alice in Wonderland, 1998, The Angry Puppet Syndrome, 1999, After the Tempest, 2003, The Waiting Game, 2000, A View of Fuji, 2000; contbr. numerous articles to profl. jours. Served with USAF, 1954-56. Mem. Am. Acad. Neurology, Am. Acad. Pediatrics, Am. Chem. Soc., Soc. for Pediatric Rsch., Sociedad Peruana de Neuro-Psiquiatria (hon.), Am. Neurochem. Soc., Am. Neurol. Assn., Am. Pediatric Soc., Child Neurology Soc. (Hower award 1980), Dramatist Guild, PEN. Jewish. Home: 10375 Wilshire Blvd Apt 11H Los Angeles CA 90024-4749 Office: 345 N Maple Dr Ste 376 Beverly Hills CA 90210 Office Phone: 310-246-6582. Personal E-mail: jhansmenk@aol.com. Business E-Mail: jmenkes@ucla.edu.

**MENN, JULIUS JOEL,** retired research scientist, consultant; b. Danzig, Free City (now Poland), Feb. 20, 1929; came to the U.S., 1950, naturalized, 1959; s. David Gregory and Regina (Ajzenstadt) M.; m. Alma R. Zito, Aug. 31, 1952 (div. 1981); children: Leslie, David (dec.), Diana (dec.); m. Dianne R. Sagner, Apr. 17, 1992. BS, U. Calif., Berkeley, 1953, MS, 1954, PhD, 1958. Dir. biochem. and insecticide rsch. Stauffer Chem. Co., Mountain View, Calif., 1957-79; dir. agrichem. rsch. Zoecon Corp., Palo Alto, Calif., 1979-85; nat. program leader crop protection Agrl. Rsch. Svc., USDA, Beltsville, Md., 1985-88; assoc. dep. area dir. Beltsville Agrl. Rsch. Ctr., 1988-94; sr. agrl. policy adviser USDA/FAS, 1999—2006. Internat. cons. crop protection and agr. biotechnology, 1994—; chmn. Gordon Rsch. Conf., 1989; adj. prof. environ. toxicology San Jose State U., Calif., 1979-84; adj. prof. entomology U. Md., College Park, 1986-95; vis. prof. Pa. State U., 1999-2002; mem. U.S./USSR Team on Environ. Pollution, 1974-85; tech. expert UNIDO, UNDCP, 1995—, The World Bank, 1998.; tech. cons. Inst. Post Harvest Tech., MARD, Hanoi, Vietnam, 2003-. Editor: Insect Juvenile Hormones, 1972, Insect Neuropeptides, 1991, 12 other tech. books; contbr. over 125 articles to profl. jours. Recipient Bussart Meml. award Ea. Br. Entomol. Soc. Am., 1990, Ciba-Geigy Recognition award Ea. Br. Entomol. Soc. Am., 1991, 92. Mem. Am. Chem. Soc. (fellow pesticide chem. divsn. 1973, chmn. 1976, councilor 1981-89, adv. bd. books dept. 1991-94, Agrochem. Divsn. Internat. award for rsch. in pesticide chem. 1979), Internat. Soc. Study Xenobiotics (councilor 1983-86). Achievements include pioneered pesticide metabolism studies and research on selective insect control agents including juvenile hormones and neuropeptides; patentee in field. Office Phone: 301-854-0145. Personal E-mail: menn03@comcast.net.

**MENNA, GILBERT G.,** lawyer; AB magna cum laude, Syracuse Univ., 1978; JD, Georgetown Univ., 1982, ML in Taxation, 1983. Bar: Calif. 1982, Mass. 1988. Ptnr., bus. law dept. Goodwin Procter LLP, Boston, mem. mgmt. com. Bd. dir. NYU Real Estate Inst.'s REIT Ctr.; bd. assoc. NAREIT. Frequent lectr., writer in field. Mem.: Phi Beta Kappa. Office: Goodwin & Procter Exchange Pl 53 State St Boston MA 02109-2881 Office Phone: 617-570-1433. Office Fax: 617-523-1231. Business E-Mail: gmenna@goodwinprocter.com.

**MENNENOH, BRIAN PHILLIP,** art educator, artist; b. Ill., Jan. 23, 1970; s. William and Sandy Mennenoh; m. Katie Elizabeth Prittie, June 25, 1994; children: Nathan, Abigail. BFA, U. Wis., Eau Claire, 1994. 3d artist The PixelShop, Greenfield, Wis., 1995—98, I V Media, Brookfield, Wis., 1998—2001; instr. Milw. Area Tech. Coll., 2001-. With USAR, 2001. Mem.: IGDA. Office: Milw Area Tech Coll 700 W State St Milwaukee WI 53233 Office Phone: 414-297-6296. E-mail: bmennenoh@wi.rr.com.

**MENNINGA, CLARENCE,** retired geologist; b. Otley, Iowa, Apr. 6, 1928; s. Gysbert and Ethel (Van Engelenhoven) Menninga; m. Irene June Van Prooyen, Oct. 7, 1949; children: Richard Lee children: Douglas Wayne, John Alan, Carol Sue Sunday, Craig Warren, Dianne Joy Shapiro, David Glenn. BA, Calvin Coll., Grand Rapids, 1949; MA in Tchg., Western Mich. U., Kalamazoo, 1959; PhD, Purdue U., West Lafayette, Ind., 1965. Analytical chemist Maytag Co., Newton, Iowa, 1950—56; tchr. Grand Rapids Christian HS, 1956—61; radiochemist Lawrence Radiation Lab., Livermore, Calif., 1966—67; prof. geology Calvin Coll., Grand Rapids, Mich., 1967—90, prof. geology emeritus, 1990—. Author: Science Held Hostage, 1988. Fellow, NSF, 1962—65. Mem.: Nat. Assn. Geology Tchrs., Mich. Basin Geol. Soc., Am. Schools for Oriental Rsch., Am. Sci. Affiliation. Home: 2155 Radcliff Ave SE Grand Rapids MI 49546 Office: Calvin Coll North Hall 1740 Knollcrest Cir SE Grand Rapids MI 49546-4403 Office Phone: 616-526-7093. Office Fax: 616-526-6501. Business E-Mail: menn@calvin.edu.

**MENNINGER, WILLIAM WALTER,** psychiatrist; b. Topeka, Oct. 23, 1931; s. William Claire and Catharine Louisa (Wright) Menninger; m. Constance Arnold Libbey, June 15, 1953; children: Frederick Prince, John Alexander, Eliza Wright, Marian Stuart, William Libbey, David Henry. AB, Stanford U., 1953; MD, Cornell U., 1957; LittD (hon.), Middlebury Coll., 1982; DSc (hon.), Washburn U., 1982; LHD (hon.), Ottawa U., 1986; LLD (hon.), Heidelberg Coll., 1993. Diplomate Am. Bd. Psychiatry and Neurology, Am. Bd. Forensic Psychiatry. Intern Harvard Med. Svc., Boston City Hosp., 1957-58; resident in psychiatry Menninger Sch. Psychiatry, 1958-61; chief med. officer, psychiatrist Fed. Reformatory, El Reno, Okla., 1961-63; assoc. psychiatrist Peace Corps, 1963-64; staff psychiatrist Menninger Found., Topeka, 1965—2001, coordinator for devel., 1967-69; dir. law and psychiatry, 1981-85, dir. dept. edn., dean Karl Menninger Sch. Psychiatry and Mental Health Scis., 1984-90, exec. v.p., chief staff, 1984-93, CEO, 1993—2001, pres., 1993—96, 1999—2001, chmn. bd. trustees, 2001—; clin. supt. Topeka State Hosp., 1969-70, sect. dir., 1970-72, asst. supt., clin., dir. residency tng., 1972-81; pres. Menninger Clinic, Topeka, 1991-96; staff Stormont-Vail Hosp., Topeka, 1984-94, assoc., 1994—2002. Adj. prof. Washburn U.; mem. Fed. Prision Facilities Planning Coun., 1970—73; mem. adv. bd. Nat. Inst. Corrections, 1975—88, chmn., 1980—84; cons. U.S. Bur. Prisons; mem. adv. bd. US Bank, Topeka, 1999—. Syndicated columnist: In-Sights, 1975—83; author: (book) Happiness Without Sex and Other Things Too Good to Miss, 1976, Caution: Living May Be Hazardous, 1978, Behavioral Science and the Secret Service, 1981, Chronic Mental Patient II, 1987; editor: Psychiatry Digest, 1971—74, Bull. of Menninger Clinic, 2001—; contbr. articles to profl. jours., chpts. to books. Mem. health and safety com. Boy Scouts Am., 1970—, chmn., 1980—85, mem. nat. exec. bd., 1980—90, mem. nat. adv. coun., 1990—; bd. dirs. Nat. Com. Prevention Child Abuse, 1975—83; mem. nat. adv. health coun. HEW, 1967—71; mem. Nat. Commn. Causes and Prevention Violence, 1968—69; rsch. adv. com. U.S. Secret Svc., 1990—2005; pres. Jayhawk coun. Boy Scouts Am., 1998—2001; mem. Kans. Gov.'s Adv. Commn. Mental Health, Mental Retardation and Cmty. Mental Health Svcs., 1983—90, Kans. Gov.'s Penal Planning Coun., 1970; chmn. Kans. Gov.'s Criminal Justice Coun., 1970; mem. Kans. Gov.'s Commn. on Crime Reduction and Prevention/Koch Commn., 1994—98; ruling elder 1st Presbyn. Ch., Topeka, 1992—95; trustee Kenworthy-Swift Found., 1980—; bd. dirs. Police Found., Washington, 1996—, Koch Crime Inst., 1998—2000; trustee Midwest Rsch. Inst., Kansas City, Mo., 1996—. With USPHS, 1959—64. Fellow: ACP, Am. Coll. Psychiatrists, Am. Psychiat. Assn. (chmn. com. chronically mentally ill 1984—86, chmn. Guttmacher award bd. 1990—96); mem.: AMA, AAAS, Am. Acad. Psychiatry and Law, Am. Psychoanalytic Assn. (chmn. com. psychoanalysis, cmty. and soc. 1984—93), Inst. Medicine NAS, Group Advancement Psychiatry (chmn. com. mental health svcs. 1974—77, 1991—2002), Stanford Assocs. Office: PO Box 4406 Topeka KS 66604-0406 Office Phone: 785-235-3400. Business E-Mail: wmenninger@menninger.edu.

**MENNIS, EDMUND ADDI,** investment management consultant; b. Allentown, Pa., Aug. 12, 1919; s. William Henry and Grace (Addi) M.; m. Selma Adinoff, Sept. 25, 1945; children: Ardith Grace, Daniel Liam. BA, CCNY, 1941; MA, Columbia U., 1946; PhD, NYU, 1961. Security analyst Eastman, Dillon & Co., NYC, 1945-46; sr. rsch. asst. Am. Inst. Econ. Rsch., Great Barrington, Mass., 1946-50; security analyst Wellington Mgmt. Co., Phila., 1950-61, dir. rsch., 1958-61, v.p., mem. investment com., 1958-66, economist, 1953-66; sr. v.p., chmn. trust investment com. Republic Nat. Bank, Dallas, 1966-72; sr. v.p., chmn. investment policy com. Security Pacific Nat. Bank, LA, 1973-81; pres., dir. Bunker Hill Income Securities, Inc., 1973-81; chmn. bd. Security Pacific Investment Mgrs., Inc., 1977-81; ind. cons. to investment mgmt. orgns., 1982—. Tech. cons. Bus. Coun., Washington, 1962-66, 72-77, 79-81; econ. adviser sec. commerce, 1967-68; mem. investment adv. panel Pension Benefit Guaranty Corp., 1981-83. Author: How the Economy Works, 1991, 2d edit., 1999, Chinese edit., 2000; assoc. editor Fin. Analysts Jour., 1960-88; editor: C.F.A. Digest, 1971-86, Bus. Econs., 1985-99, editor emeritus, 2000—; editor: Banker's Econ. & Investment Alert, 1993—; author or editor books, chpts., numerous articles in field of econs. and investments. Trustee Fin. Analysts Rsch. Found., 1981-86. 1st lt. USAAF, 1942-45; capt. USAF, 1951-53. Fellow Nat. Assn. Bus. Economists (coun. 1967-69, David L. Williams Lifetime Achievement award 1996); mem. Fin. Analysts Fedn. (dir. 1970-72, Graham and Dodd award 1972, Molodovsky award 1972), Am. Econ. Assn., Am. Fin. Assn., LA Soc. Fin. Analysts, Conf.

Bus. Econ. (vice chmn. 1977, chmn. 1978), Inst. CFAs (pres. 1970-72, trustee 1968-74, C. Stewart Sheppard award 1978). Home: 721 Paseo Del Mar Palos Verdes Estates CA 90274-1222 Office: PO Box 1146 Palos Verdes Estates CA 90274-7946 Office Phone: 310-373-3270. Personal E-mail: eamennis@cox.net.

**MENO, JOHN PETER,** chorepiscopus; b. Carlinville, Ill., Aug. 22, 1942; s. John Victor and Margaret Mary (Cena) M.; m. Rolanda A. Abyad, Sept. 14, 1968; 1 child, Peter James. MA, Am. U. Beirut, 1969; STM, Union Theol. Sem., 1972. Ordained priest Syrian Orthodox Ch. of Antioch, 1972, elevated to chorepiscopus, 1983. Gen. sec. Archdiocese of Syrian Orthodox Ch. in the U.S. and Can., Lodi, NJ, 1972—95; cathedral dean St. Mark's Syrian Orthodox Cathedral, Teaneck, NJ, 1975—; gen. sec. Archdiocese of the Syrian Orthodox Ch. for the Ea. U.S., Teaneck, 1996—. Co-sec. Standing Conf. of Oriental Orthodox Chs. in Am., N.Y.C., 1973—; co-chmn. U.S. Roman Cath.-Oriental Orthodox Cons., 1989—. Editor: Hymns of the Syrian Orthodox Church of Antioch, 1976; contbr. The Oriental Orthodox Chs. in the U.S., 1986, Dictionary of Christianity in America, 1990, Oriental Orthodox-Roman Catholic Interchurch Marriages and Other Pastoral Relationships, 1995, Nelson's New Christian Dictionary, 2001, The Encyclopedia of Christianity, 2003. Recipient Golden Cross of the Archdiocese of the Syrian Orthodox Ch in U.S., and Can., 1992. Syrian Orthodox. Home: 263 Elm Ave Teaneck NJ 07666-2323 Office: St Mark's Syrian Orthodox Cathedral 260 Elm Ave Teaneck NJ 07666-2318 Personal E-mail: vrjmeno@aol.com.

**MENO, LIONEL R.,** academic administrator; Commr. edn. Tex. Edn Agy., Austin; dist. supt. Board of Coop. Education Services, Angola, NY, 1995—99; dean Coll. Edn. San Diego State U., 1999—. Office: 5500 Campanile Dr San Diego CA 92182

**MENON, JAI M.,** information technology manager; s. Sreedharan Menon and Radha Sreedharan; m. Sathi Eradi, Aug. 20, 1985; children: Anjali, Vijay V. BS in Tech in Elec. Engring., Indian Inst. Tech., Madras, India, 1977; MS in Computer Sci., Ohio State U., Columbus, Ohio, 1978, PhD in Computer Sci., 1981. From rsch. staff mem. to chief tech. officer IBM, San Jose, Calif., 1982—2003, chief tech. officer, 2003—, dir. storage arch. and strategy, 2003—05, v.p. arch. and strategy, software and storage, 2005—. Session chair CompCon, San Francisco, 1983, 95; mem. of steering com. FAST, File and Storage Sys. Tech., 2003—; mem. program com. conf. Very Large Data Base, 1984, rev. panelist, 1992—96; mem. program com. Internat. Symposium Computer Arch., 1995—95; presenter in field. Author: Relational Database Machine Architecture; co-author: Advanced Database Machine Architecture, Disk Array and parallel I/O - Theory and Practice; contbr. over 47 articles to profl. jours. (Best Paper award HICSS-25, 1992); mem. editl. bd.: Jour. Distributed and Parallel Databases, 1993—94; editor, 1994. Chmn. campaign IBM United Way, San Jose, Calif., 2001. Named Master Inventor, IBM, 1995; recipient Acad. Tech. award, 1994, Corp. award, 2000, Disting. Alumnus award, Ohio State U., 2004, Indian Inst. Tech., Madras, 2006; fellow, IBM, 2001; scholar, Govt. India, 1977. Fellow: IEEE (Wallace McDowell award 2002, Reynold B. Johnson award 2006). Achievements include patents in field. Office Phone: 408-256-1050.

**MENON, MANI,** urological surgeon, educator; b Trichur, Kerala, India, July 9, 1948; came to U.S., 1972, naturalized, 1977; s. Balakrishna and Sumathie Menon; m. Shameem Ara Begum, Oct. 17, 1972; children: Nisha, Roshen. MBBS, Madras U., India, 1971. Diplomate Am. Bd. Urology. Intern Bryn Mawr (Pa.) Hosp., 1973-74; resident Brady Urol. Inst., The Johns Hopkins Hosp., Balt., 1974-80; asst. prof. urology Washington U. Med. Ctr., St. Louis, 1980-83, assoc. prof., 1983; prof. urology, chmn. div. urology and transplant surgery U. Mass. Med. Ctr., Worcester, 1983—; prof. physiology, U. Mass. Med. Ctr., Worcester, 1986—. Mem. AAAS, Am. Assn. Genito Urinary Surgeons, Am. Urol. Assn. (Gold Cytoscope award 1990), Am. Fedn. Clin. Rsch., Am. Soc. Transplantation and Vascular Surgery, Rschrs. on Calculus Kinetics, Johns Hopkins Med. and Surg. Assn., Mass. Med. Soc., Mass. Soc. Med. Rsch. Avocations: tennis, puzzles, mystery fiction. Office: U Mass Med Ctr Div Urology Worcester MA 01655 also: Henry Ford Hosp Vattikuti Urology Inst 2799 W Grand Blvd Detroit MI 48202 Office Phone: 313-916-2066. E-mail: mmenon1@hfhs.org.

**MENOYO, ERIC FELIX,** lawyer; b. NYC, May 9, 1944; s. Enrique and Frances (Villela) M.; m. Deirdre Caitlin Ryan, Aug. 12, 1967; children: Eric Edward, Sarah Micela Holch. AB in English, Georgetown U., 1966, JD, 1969; LLM in Taxation, NYU, 1975. Bar: NY 1969, Mass. 1976, US Dist. Ct. (ea. dist.) Mass. 1976, US Ct. Appeals (1st cir.) 1976. Assoc. Barrett Smith Schapiro & Simon, NYC, 1969-76, Palmer & Dodge, Boston, 1976-77, ptnr., 1978—2005, Edwards Angell Palmer & Dodge LLP, Boston, 2005—. Lectr. law Northeastern U., 1986-87, Mass. Continuing Legal Edn., Boston, 1998—; trustee Cora du Bois Charitable Trust, 1995-. Trustee Nashoba-Brooks Sch. Concord Inc., Mass., 1984-90, 1st Parish Sudbury, 1979-82, Sudbury Valley Trustees, Inc., 1991—, pres., 1994-96. Fellow Am. Coll. Trust and Estate Counsel; mem. ABA, Boston Bar Assn., Am. Law Inst., Larchmont Yacht Club. Unitarian Universalist. Avocations: sailing, hiking. Home: 388 Willis Rd Sudbury MA 01776-1332 Office: Edwards Angell Palmer & Dodge LLP 111 Huntington Ave Boston MA 02199-7613 Office Phone: 617-239-0128. Business E-Mail: emenoyo@eapdlaw.com.

**MENSCHEL, ROBERT BENJAMIN,** investment banker; b. NYC, July 2, 1929; s. Benjamin and Helen (Goldsmith) M.; m. Joyce Virginia Frank, Dec. 5, 1968; children: David F., Lauren E. BS, Syracuse U., 1951, LLD (hon.), 1991; postgrad., NYU, 1951-53. Mem. N.Y. Stock Exchange, N.Y.C., 1950-51; specialist HW Goldsmith and Co., N.Y.C., 1951-54; with Goldman, Sachs & Co., N.Y.C., 1954-66, gen. ptnr. instl. sales, 1966-78, ltd. ptnr., 1979-2000. sr. dir., 2000—. Mem. Pres. Clinton's com. on the arts and humanities; chmn., trustee, exec. and fin. com., mem. investment com., co-chmn. photography com. Mus. Modern Art; trustee Inst. Advanced Study, Princeton, Chess in the Schs., N.Y.C.; trustee, mem. exec. com. Syracuse U.; former trustee, mem. exec. com. Montefiore Hosp., Guild Hall, East Hampton, NY, past chmn. bd.; pres. bd. trustees, mem. exec. com. Dalton Sch., N.Y.C.; past bd. advs. Grad. Sch. Inst. Internat. Bus. Pace U.; mem. exec. bd. N.Y. chpt. Am. Jewish Com., N.Y.C.; bd. dirs., mem. fin. and exec. com. N.Y. Pub. Libr., N.Y.C.; bd. dirs. Parks Coun.; mng. dir. Horace W. Goldsmith Found., Vital Prjects Fund; bd. dirs. associated YM-YWHA; v.p. bd. trustees, mem. fin. and exec. com. Temple Emanu-El, NY; trustee N.Y. Presbyn. Hosp. Recipient George Arents medal Syracuse U., 1984; recipient George Arents medal Syracuse U., City Athletic Club, India Ho. Home: 920 5th Ave New York NY 10021-4160 also: Further Amagansett NY 11930 Office: Goldman Sachs & Co 85 Broad St New York NY 10004-2456 Office Phone: 212-902-6913. Business E-Mail: robert.menschel@gs.com.

**MENSCHER, BARNET GARY,** steel company executive; b. Laurelton, N.Y., Sept. 5, 1940; s. Samuel and Louise (Zaimont) M.; m. Diane Elaine Gachman, June 12, 1966; children: Melissa Denise, Corey Lane, Scott Jay. Student, Centenary Coll., 1958-59; BBA, U. Tex., 1963. Vice pres. mktg. Ella Gant Mfg., Shreveport, La., 1964-66; warehouse mgr. di. material control Gachman Steel Co., Fort Worth, 1966-68, gen. mgr. Houston, 1968-70; v.p. sales Gachman Metal Co., Houston, 1971-76; pres. Menko Steel Service, Inc., Houston, 1979—; CEO NEXTLEVEL, Houston, 1998—. Investment cons. D & L Enterprises, 1966—. Mem. solicitation com. United Fund, 1969-76; mem. Nat. Alliance of Businessmen Jobs Program, 1969—. Served with AUS, 1963-65. Mem. Tex. Assn. Steel Importers, Purchasing Agts. Assn. Houston, Credit Assn. Houston, Am. Mgmt. Assn., Assn. Steel Distbrs., Nat. Assn. Elevator Contractors, Phi Sigma Delta, Alpha Phi Omega. Home: Apt 1002 3388 Sage Rd Houston TX 77056

**MENSE, ALLAN TATE,** research and development engineering executive; b. Kansas City, Mo., Nov. 29, 1945; s. Martin Conrad Mense and Nancy (Tate) Johnson; m. Kim Eisele; children from previous marriage: Melanie Georgia, Eileen Mense Hartzell. BS, U. Ariz., 1968, MS, 1970; PhD, U. Wis., 1977; MS in Indsl. Engring., Ariz. State U., 1999. Registered profl. indsl.

engr., ASQ cert. reliability engring. Scientist Oak Ridge (Tenn.) Nat. Lab, 1976-79; sr. staff sci. and tech. comm. U.S. Ho. Reps., Washington, 1979-81; sr. scientist McDonnell Douglas Astro. Co., St. Louis, 1981-85; from dep. chief scientist to chief scientist Dept. Def. Strategic Def. Initiative Orgn., Washington, 1985-88; v.p. rsch. Fla. Inst. Tech., Melbourne, 1988-92; pres. Advanced Tech. Mgmt., Inc., Tempe, Ariz., 1992-97; lead sys. engr. Motorola Space Sys. Tech. Group, Chandler, Ariz., 1998—2001; chief sci. sr. engring. fellow Raytheon Missile Sys., 2002—. Vis. scholar Sloan Sch., MIT, 1995-96; mem. U.S. Army Sci. Bd., 2005—. Contbr. over 60 articles to profl. jours. Ariz. State U. scholar, 1996-97. Mem. AIAA (sr. mem.), IEEE (chmn. energy com. 1985—, sr. mem.), Nat. Def. Industries Assn., Am. Phys. Soc., Am. Nuclear Soc., Inst. Indsl. Engrs., Fla. Com. Nat. Space Club (charter), Sigma Xi, Theta Tau, Pi Mu Alpha. Episcopalian. Office: 1151 E Hermans Rd B840/MS8 Tucson AZ 85706 Home: 1052 E Baldy Spring Pl Green Valley AZ 85614 Office Phone: 520-794-4720. Business E-Mail: allan_t_mense@raytheon.com.

**MENSES, JAN,** artist, draftsman; b. Rotterdam, Netherlands, Apr. 28, 1933; emigrated to Can., 1960, naturalized, 1965; s. Jan and Elisabeth Wilhelmina (Schwarz) M.; m. Rachel Régine Kadoch, Dec. 7, 1958; children: Salomon, Hnina Sarah, Nechamah Elisabeth Halo. Student, Acad. Fine Arts, Rotterdam, Officers Acad. Royal Dutch Air Force, 1953-55. Cert. Royal Can. Academician, Academician of Nations, Academician of Europe, Academician of Italy. Lectr. in fine arts Concordia U., Montreal, 1973-76, others. One-man shows include Montreal Mus. Fine Arts, 1961, 65, 76, Isaacs Gallery, Toronto, Ont., Can., 1964, Delta Gallery, Rotterdam, 1965, Galerie Godard Lefort, Montreal, 1966, Gallery Moos, Toronto, 1967, Rotterdam Art Found., 1974, Galerie Mira Godard, Toronto, 1977, Montreal, 1978, Seasons Galleries, The Hague, 1980, U. B.C. Fine Arts Gallery, Vancouver, 1981, Galerie Don Stewart, Montreal, 1981, Mead Art Mus., Amherst, Mass., 1983, Agnes Etherington Art Mus., 1984, Blom and Dorn Gallery, N.Y.C., 1985, 86-93, Marywood Coll. Mus., Scranton, Pa., 1985, Saraya-Wolfson Ctr., Safed, Israel, 1987, Mayanot Gallery, Jerusalem, 1987-88, Esperanza Gallery, Montreal, 1988, 89, Gallery Hamaayan Haradum, Safed, Israel, 1989-2000, Blom and Dorn Gallery, Hartford, Conn., 1995, Nora Gallery, Jerusalem, 1995, 96, 97, Artist's Colony, Safed, Israel; over 300 group shows include Montreal World Exhbn., 1967, Salon Internat. Art. Basel, Switzerland, 1972, 74, Can. Nat. Exhbn., 1972, Centennial Exhbn., Royal Can. Acad., Toronto, 1980, Que. Biennale I, II, III, Montreal, 1977, 79, 81, Foire Internat. D'Art Contemporain Paris and Internat. Fair Koln Germany, 1986, Migdal Ha-Emek, Israel, 1988, Group of 8 Israel, Toronto, 1990, Royal Can. Acad. Show, Toronto, 1991, Bezalel Acad., Jerusalem, 2004; represented in permanent exhbn. Gallery Hamaayan Haradum, Safed, Profl. Artists' Assn., Artists Colony, Safed, Menses Mus. Contemporary Art, Safed, Israel; represented in permanent collections Pushkin Mus., Moscow, former Soviet Union, U. Coll. Cape Breton Art Gallery, Sydney, NS, Can. Museo Ciani di Villa Caccia, Lugano, Switzerland, The Art Gallery of Hamilton, Ont.,Can., David Giles Carter Collection, New Haven, Gallery of Nova Scotia-Halifax, Can. Jewish Public Libr. Collection, Montreal, Can., Cadillac Fairview Collection, Toronto, Can, Museum Modern Art, NYC, Phila. Mus. Art, Solomon R. Guggenheim Mus., NYC, Yivo Inst., NYC, Bklyn. Mus., Art Inst. Chgo., Cleve. Mus. Art, Detroit Inst. Arts, Yale U., U. Montreal, Queens U., Kingston, Mead Art Mus., Amherst Coll., Jonathan Edwards Coll., New Haven, Victoria & Albert Mus., London, Vatican Mus., Rome, Quebec Art Bank, Concordia U., Montreal, Haifa Mus. Modern Art, Hebrew U., Jerusalem, Govt. of Que., Yad Vashem Holocaust Meml., Jerusalem, Mus. Boymans-van Beuningen, Rotterdam, Stedelijk Mus., Amsterdam, Rijksmuseum, Amsterdam, Nat. Gallery Can., Ottawa, Gallery Stratford, Montreal Mus. Fine Arts, Musée d'Art Contemporain, Montreal, Que. Provincial Mus., Que. Art Bank, Art Bank of the Can. Coun., Ottawa, Ariz. State Mus., Tucson, Hebrew U., Jerusalem, City of Safed-Israel, Holocaust Mus., Majdeanek, Poland, Holocaust Meml. Ctr., Toronto, Lavalin Mus. Coll, Montreal, Oshawa Mus., Ont.; Dept. External Affairs Govt. Can., Ottawa, Can. Jewish Congress Mus., Montreal, Israel Mus., Jerusalem, Holocaust Mus. Majdanek, Poland, McGill U. Montreal, Olympia & York Collection, Toronto, CBC Collection, Montreal, Kingston (Ont.) U. Mus. Collection, NY Pub. Libr., Worcester (Mass.) Art Mus., Currier Gallery Art, Manchester, NH, Gallery of U. NH, Durham, Mus. Art. RI Sch. Design, Providence, Olympia & York Collection, Toronto, Collection Rishon Le'Zion, Jerusalem, Rose Art Mus., Brandeis U., Waltham, Mass., C.I.L. Collection Montreal, Tel Aviv U., McGill U. Coll., Montreal, Can. Jewish Congress Mus., Montreal, Young Israel of Montreal (Coll.), Can., Confedn. Art Ctr., Charlottetown-Prince Edward Island, Can., Thomas More Inst., Montreal, Menses Mus. Contemporary Art, Safed, Israel, Pushkin Mus., Moscow, The Bronfman Collection Can. Art Montreal Mus. Fine Arts, CEMP Collection Montreal, Mt. Allison U., Sackville, NS, Can., Ont. Heritage Found., Toronto, many others; paintings include Klippoth Series, 1963-78, Kaddish Series, 1964-80, Hechaloth Series, 1973—, Tikkun Series, 1978—, Doomed Children Series, Kings Series, Victor's Series, Metamorphosis Series, Shevirot Hakelim Series, Diabolica Series, Lepers Series, Angels-Series; mural for Montreal Holocaust Meml. Ctr. Mem. Pres.'s Coun. of U. N.H. Served with Royal Dutch Air Force Res., 1953-55. Recipient 5 1st prizes Nat. Art Exhbn., Quebec, Que., 1960-65; Grand prize Concours Artistiques de la Province de Que., 1965; prize X and XI Winnipeg (Man., Can.) Shows, 1966, 68; prize IX Internat. Exhbn. Drawings and Prints, Lugano, 1966; prize Ofcl. Centennial Art Competition, Toronto; 1st prize Hadassah, 1969, 71, 82; Recipient Imago award U. Montreal, 1971; award Reeves of Can., 1969; Tigert award Ont. Soc. Arts, 1970; Loomis and Toles award, 1972; J. I. Segal award J. I. Segal Fund Jewish Culture, 1975; Gold medal Accademia Italia Delle Arte, Italy, 1980; Gold medal Internat. Parliament U.S.A., 1982; Gran Premio delle Nazioni, Italy, 1983, European Banner of Arts with Gold medal, 1984, Oscar d' Italia, 1985, 1st prize III Que. Biennale, 1981, OSA award of merit, Toronto, 1981, 82; World Culture prize Italy, 1984; Golden Flame of World Parliament (U.S.A.) award, 1986; Ish Shalom award Jerusalem, 1993; numerous others; Can. Council sr. arts fellows, 1969-70, 71-72, 81-82; grantee, 1966-67, 67-68; travel grantee, 1968, 73 Mem. Royal Can. Acad. Arts, Acad. Italia Arte e del Lavoro, Acad. Nazioni, Maestro Accademico-Accademia Bedriacense (Italy), Jewish Am. Acad. Arts and Scis., Israeli Art Assn. (Telaviv), Israel Assn. Visual Art (Jerusalem). Jewish. Address: PO Box 43150 HAR NOF Jerusalem 91400 Israel My works have dealt with death, the eclipse of faith, exile, the Galut. They are shaped by my childhood experiences, real and imagined, in Nazi-occupied Europe; influenced by and rooted in my principles and standards of conduct as an Orthodox Jew in the post-holocaust/pre-Messianic era. They are an attempt to translate these experiences into visual contemporary terms (imagery conflicts and reconciliations of conflicts) in order to ascend from the personal/specific to the universal/general. They are a lament, an elegy, a denial and confirmation, an expression of the attitude of the soul in its debasement and dignity towards its Creator; a striving towards serenity in anticipation of the Redemption: a form of prayer.

**MENTHENA, ANURADHA,** research scientist; arrived in US, 2000; d. Bangar Raju and Ammaji Mantena. Student, St. Ann's Coll., Hyderabad, India, 1988—89; MB, BS, U. Health Sci., Hyderabad, 1996. House officer Shanti Nursing Home, Hyderabad, 2000—; rsch. assoc. Albert Einstein Coll. Medicine, Bronx, NY, 2001—05, rsch. assoc. dept. devel. and molecular biology, 2005—. Contbr. articles to profl. jours. Mem.: NY Acad. Scis. Avocations: opera, music, travel, cooking, reading. Office: Albert Einstein Coll Medicine Dept Devel and Molecular Biology 1300 Morris Park Ave Ullman 405 Bronx NY 10461

**MENTZ, HENRY A., III,** plastic surgeon; b. New Orleans, Apr. 9, 1958; s. Henry A. Jr. and Ann (Lamantia) M.; m. Paula Comiskey, May 20, 1989; children: Henry A. IV, James August. BS, La. State U., 1980, MD, 1984. Diplomate Am. Bd. Facial Plastic and Reconstructive Surgery, Am. Bd. Otolaryngology, Am. Bd. Plastic Surgery. Intern otolaryngology Tulane U., New Orleans, 1984-89; resident plastic surgery St. Joseph's Hosp., Houston, 1989-91; founder, ptnr. Aesthetic Ctr. for Plastic Surgeons, Houston, 1991—. Clin. assoc. prof. Baylor U., Houston, 1992—, St. Joseph U., Houston, 1992—; chief surgery Sharpstown Gen. Hosp., Houston, 1994—, chief plastic surgery, 1994—; pres. Houston Soc. of Plastic Surgeons, 2000-01. Fellow

ACS, Internat. Coll. Surgeons, Am. Acad. Otolaryngology; mem. Am. Soc. Plastic and Reconstructive Surgeons, Am. Soc. Plastic Surgeons, Am. Soc. Aesthetic Plastic Surgeons, Internat. Soc Aesthetic Plastic Surgeons, Am. Acad. Otolaryngology Head and Neck Surg, AMA, Tex. Medical Assn., Houston Soc. Plastic Surgeons, Harris County Medical Soc. Republican. Episcopalian. Office: Aesthetic Ctr for Plastic Surgery Ste 300 Kimberly Profl Bldg 12727 Kimberley Houston TX 77024

**MENTZ, HENRY ALVAN, JR.,** retired federal judge; b. New Orleans, Nov. 10, 1920; s. Henry Alvan and Lulla (Bridewell) M.; m. Ann Lamantia, June 23, 1956; children: Ann, Carli, Hal, Frederick, George BA, Tulane U., 1941; JD, La. State U., 1943. Bar: La. 1943, U.S. Dist. Ct. (ea. dist.) La. 1944. With legal dept. Shell Oil, New Orleans, 1947-48; pvt. practice Hammond, 1948-82; judge U.S. Dist. Ct. (ea. dist.) La., New Orleans, 1982—2001, sr. judge, 1992—2001, ret. Editor: Combined Gospels, 1976 Pres. La. Soc. Music and Performing Arts, 1994-97, L.A. Civil Svc. League, 1979-81; bd. dirs. Southea. La. U. Found., Salvation Army; chmn. Tulane U. 50th Anniversary Reunion for 1991. Decorated 2 Battle Stars, Bronze Star; recipient Disting. Svc. award AMVETS, 1950. Mem. SAR, Royal Soc. St. George (pres.), Boston Club New Orleans, Delta Tau Delta. Republican. Episcopalian. Home: 2105 State St New Orleans LA 70118-6255 Office: US Dist Ct C-114 US Courthouse 500 Camp St New Orleans LA 70130-3313

**MENTZ, LAWRENCE,** lawyer; b. N.Y.C., Nov. 5, 1946; s. Joseph Walter and Audrey Cecilia (Armstrong) M.; m. Barbara Antonello, Nov. 10, 1973; children: Kathleen Elizabeth, Lawrence Goodwin. BS in Physics, Rensselaer Poly. Inst., 1968; JD, U. Notre Dame, 1973. Bar: N.Y. 1973, DC 1974. Assoc. Condon & Forsyth, N.Y.C., 1973-80, ptnr., 1981-89, Biedermann, Hoenig, Massamillo & Ruff, N.Y.C., 1990—2005, Kaplan, von Ohlen & Massamillo, LLC, N.Y.C., 2005—; counsellor at law. Worldwide Airlines Customer Rels. Assn. Conf., Singapore, 1983, 2d Cir. Spkrs. Bur., Com. on BiCentennial of U.S. Consts., 1987; arbitrator U.S. Dist. Ct. (ea. dist.) Bklyn., 1986—. With USNR, 1969-70. Mem. ABA, N.Y. State Bar Assn. (exec. com. sect. on comml. and fed. litigation, fed. judiciary com., 1993, com. Supreme Cts.), Assn. of Bar of City of N.Y. (com. on aeronautics law, task force on N.Y. Constl. Conv., com. on state legis.), Wings Club. Roman Catholic. Avocations: swimming, running, stamp collecting/philately. Office: Kaplan von Ohlen & Massamillo LLC 90 Park Ave 18th Fl New York NY 10016 Office Phone: 212-455-9248. E-mail: lwmentz@kvolaw.com.

**MENTZER, JOHN RAYMOND,** electrical engineer, educator; b. Arch Spring, Pa., June 16, 1916; s. Walter Ray and Katheryn Henderson (Barr) M.; m. Bernice Roslyn Simon, Feb. 17, 1945; children— Jacqueline Ferne, Richard Alan. BS, Pa. State U., 1942, MS, 1948; PhD, Ohio State U., 1952. Engr. Westinghouse Electric Corp., Balt., 1942-46, Ordnance Research Lab., 1946-48; research asso. Ohio State U., 1948-52; mem. staff Lincoln Lab., M.I.T., 1952-54; mem. faculty Pa. State U., 1954—, prof. engring. scis., 1956—, head dept. engring. sci. and mechanics, 1974-81, prof. emeritus engring. scis., 1981—. Author: Scattering and Diffraction of Radio Waves, 1955. Recipient Service award Pa. State U., 1979 Sr. mem. IEEE; mem. Am. Soc. Engring. Edn., AAAS, Sigma Xi. Home: 557 Clarence Ave State College PA 16803-3456 Office: 117 Hammond Bldg University Park PA 16802-1401 E-mail: grad1619@adelphia.net.

**MENUTIS, JAMIE,** training services executive, writer; b. Houston, June 4, 1964; d. James P. Menutis and Ruth Ann Pellerin-Menutis; 1 child, Ana Sofia Rosales. BA, Webster U., Vienna, Austria, 1988, cert. refugee studies program, 1988; MA, Georgetown U., 1990. Cert. French lang. proficiency, Spanish lang. proficiency. Campaign asst. Campaign Calif., L.A., 1986—87; rsch. asst. refugee status adv. com. Govt. Can., Ottawa, Ont., Canada, 1986—87; rsch. asst. UN Ctr. for Social Devel. and Humanitarian Affairs, Vienna, 1988, U.S. Cath. Conf.-Migration and Refugee Services, Washington, 1989—90; resettlement program officer Internat. Rescue Com., Freetown, Sierra Leone, 1991—92, liaison officer Nairobi, Kenya, 1992; edn. program mgr.-emergency ops. Trocaire, Gedo, Somalia, 1993; tng. dir. NEU, Inc., New Orleans, 1993—2001; dir. R & M R&D, New Orleans, 1993—. Cons. Ctr. for Effective Non-Profit Mgmt., New Orleans, 1993; fast track trainer U. New Orleans-Small Bus. Devel. Ctr., 1996; staff writer www.Gal.net, 2002—. Author: (book) Where the Natives Feast in New Orleans...A Secret Guide to Local Restaurants, 2002, (government reference) Ten Year Country Profile Reports on Chile, El Salvador and Nicaragua, 1987, (reference) United Nations Center for Social Development and Humanitarian Affairs Bulletin, 1988, (testimonial address for Congress) United States Policy towards Central American and Eastern Europeans Refugees, 1989; contbr. political newsletter Campaign California, 1986; photographic exhbn., portraits of African and Indian Children, 1988; author: (tng. manual) Customer Service Training "Understanding the Customer", 2001, Cultural Orientation Training-International Rescue Committee, Sierra Leone, 1992; contbr. curriculum Somalia-Primary School Materials Development, 1993, articles to profl. jours. Mem. Ladies Philoptochos Soc., New Orleans, 2002; supporter March of Dimes, New Orleans, 1999, Habitat for Humanity, New Orleans, 1998, Amnesty Internat., Washington, 1984. Recipient Medal of Honor for Svc., Internat. Rescue Com., 1992. Mem.: Fgn. Rels. Assn. New Orleans, Georgetown U. Alumni Assn., Pi Sigma. Avocations: photography, travel, yoga, gourmet cooking. Personal E-mail: jmenutis@mindspring.com. Business E-Mail: jamie@nativesfeast.com.

**MENY, ROBERT GEORGE,** former medical research administrator, physician; b. Hackensack, N.J., Jan. 7, 1945; m. Janet McHugh, Apr. 28, 1990; children: Danielle, Ellen, Gus. BS, Tulane U., 1966; MD, Columbia U., 1971. Intern and resident in pediat. N.Y. Hosp., N.Y.C., 1971—73; fellow in neonatology U. Md. Hosp., Balt., 1975—77; mem. staff neonatal ctr. Rutgers Med. Sch., New Brunswick, NJ, 1977—80; dir. Hurley Neonatal Ctr., Flint Mich., 1980—83; dir. Sudden Infant Death Syndrome Inst. U. Md., Balt., 1983—99; pvt. practice Towson, Md., 1999—. Capt. USAF. Mem. Assn. Sudden Infant Death Prevention Physicians (pres.-elect 1995, chmn. bd. 1998). Office: O'Dea Bldg #409 7505 Osler Dr Towson MD 21204

**MENZA, CLAUDIA MARCELLA,** literary agent; b. NYC, June 11, 1947; d. John Gaetano and Antonina (di Lorenzo) M.; m. James R. Forker, May 29, 1971 (div. 1980); m. Charles Anthony Frye, Dec. 16, 1989 (dec. Oct. 1994). BA, Oberlin Coll., 1969. Asst. editor Evergreen Rev., N.Y.C., 1969-73; gen. editor, prodn. mgr. Grove Press, Inc., N.Y.C., 1973-83; sr. editor Art Dir. News, N.Y.C., 1983-85; ptnr. Menza-Barron Agy., N.Y.C., 1983—. Cons. Riverrun Press, N.Y.C., 1983-96; guest lectr. Tex. A&M U., Prairie View, Tex., 1986, NYU, N.Y.C., 1986-87; cons., panelist Nat. Civil Rights Mus. Conf. The Power of the Word, Memphis, 1995; panelist NYU, 1998, The New Sch., N.Y.C., 2000, The Lost State Writers Conf., Greeneville, Tenn., 2000, Harlem Book Fair, 2001; panelist Afrian Am. Lit. Conf., Raleigh, NC, 2003. Author: Cage of Wild Cries, 1990, The Lunatics Ball, 1994, (play), 2006; contbg. author: The Dream Book: An Anthology of Writing by Italian-American Women, 1985 (Am. Book award, 1985); actor: Damned Pub. Riverside Studios, 1999. Working mem. Congress of Racial Equality, Hempstead, N.Y., 1961, Student Nonviolent Coord. Com., Oberlin, Ohio, 1965, Students for Dem. Soc., Oberlin, 1965, The West Village Com., N.Y.C., 1980. Mem. PEN (trustee, chair prison writing com.), Internat. Platform Assn., Acad. Am. Poets, Italian-Am. Writers Assn., Assn. Authors Reps. Avocations: reading, music, theater. Office: Menza-Barron Agy 1170 Broadway Ste 807 New York NY 10001-7507

**MENZA, MATTHEW A.,** psychiatrist; b. Sept. 11, 1950; BA, U. Va., 1973; MD, Temple U., 1980; postgrad., Harvard U., 1985. Intern NYU Med. Sch. Bellvue Hosp., N.Y.C., 1980—81, resident, 1981—84; chief divsn. clin. psychopharmacology Robert Wood Johnson Med. Sch., Piscataway, NJ, 1996—, vice chmn. dept. psychiatry, 2003—. Author. over 65 articles to profl. jours. Bd. govs. Univ. Med. Group, New Brunswick, NJ, 1999—. Office: Robert Wood Johnson Med Sch Dept Psychiatry 675 Hoes Ln Piscataway NJ 08854-5627 Business E-Mail: menza@umdnj.edu.

**MENZEL, IDINA,** actress, singer; b. Syosset, May 30, 1971; d. Stuart and Helene Mentzel; m. Taye Diggs, Jan. 11, 2003. BFA in Drama, NYU. Actor: (Broadway plays) RENT, 1995—97 (Tony award nominee), Aida, 2001, Funny Girl, 2002, Wicked, 2003—05 (Tony award best actress in a musical, 2004); (plays) The Wild Party, 1999, Summer of '42, 2000, Hair, 2001, The Vagina Monologues, 2002, See What I Wanna See, 2005; singer: (albums) Still I Can't Be Still, 1998, Here, 2004; actor: (films) Kissing Jessica Stein, 2001, Just a Kiss, 2002, The Tollbooth, 2004, Rent, 2005; composer: (songs) Follow If You Lead for film "The Other Sister", 1999.*

**MENZEL, MARYBELLE PROCTOR,** volunteer; b. Milledgeville, Ga., Feb. 5, 1940; d. Ennis Hall Proctor and Sara (Evans) McCarthy; m. Robert John Menzel, Sept. 1, 1961; children: Blake, John, Craig. BA cum laude, Wesleyan Coll., Macon, Ga., 1962; MA with highest distinction, U. Ctrl. Fla., 1986. Cert. highest level tchr. Fla. Tchr. Spaulding Jr. HS, Griffin, Ga., 1962, East Syracuse (NY) Minoa HS, 1964—65, Coral Gables (Fla.) HS, 1965—66; dir. Gerber Child Care Ctr., Indialantic, Fla., 1981, Brevard CC Coop Presch., Melbourne, Fla., 1982—85; adj. instr. English and Humanities Brevard CC, Cocoa, Fla., 1985. Host, guide, amb. Denver Art Mus., 2006—. Named Million Dollar Woman, Wesleyan Coll., 2005. Mem.: AAUW (Nat. award Fundraising AAUW Ednl. Found. 2001, Garden of Victories award 1993), Colo. AAUW (dir. ednl. found. 2000—01, pres. elect 2001—02, pres. 2002—04, past pres. 2004—05, pub. policy com. 2004—, women's legis. breakfast com. 2005—, state exec. bd., mem. women's lobby), Wesleyan Coll. Million Dollar Women, Nat. Mus. Women in the Arts (friend), Nat. Mus. Women's History (charter), Nat. Trust for Historic Preservation, Phi Kappa Phi. Democrat. Methodist.

**MENZER, JOHN BRUCE,** retail executive; b. Chgo., Mar 27, 1951; s. John and Lorraine (Glugla) M. m. Kathleen A. Leahy, Oct. 23, 1976; 1 child, Christine. BBA in Pub. Acctg., Loyola U., 1972, MBA in Fin., 1980. CPA, Ill. Supr. acctg. systems Am. Internat., Mount Prospect, Ill., 1973-75; supr. audit Pannell, Kerr, Forster & Co., Chgo., 1975-77; sr. v.p. Bally Mfg. Corp., 1977-85, Ben Franklin Retail Stores, Carol Stream, Ill., 1985—88, exec. v.p., 1988—91, COO, CFO, 1991—93, pres., 1993—95; exec. v.p., CFO Wal-Mart Stores, Inc., 1995—99; pres., CEO Wal-Mart Internat., 1999—2005; vice chmn. Wal-Mart Stores, Inc., 2005—. Bd. dirs. Wal-Mart de Mex., Seiyu Ltd., Japan, Emerson Electric, U.S.-China Bus. Coun., Guangdong Province Gov.'s Econ. Advisors in China. Bd. dirs. Jr. Achievement, Chgo., 1973-75. Mem. Fin. Execs. Inst., Ill. State Soc. CPAs, Nat. Retail Mchts. Assn., Am. Inst. CPAs, Internat. Franchise Assn. (chmn. fin. and tax com., conf. coordinator). Avocations: golf, tennis. Office: Wal-Mart Stores Inc 702 Southwest Eighth St Bentonville AR 72716*

**MENZER, ROBERT EVERETT,** retired toxicologist, educator; b. Washington, Dec. 21, 1938; s. Russell Ernest and Ora Taylor (Oates) M.; m. Sara Lee Gribbon, Dec. 29, 1962; children: R. Eric, Paul D., Joan Coleraine. BS in Chemistry, U. Va., 1960; MS, U. Md., 1962; PhD, U. Wis., 1964. Instr. U. Wis., Madison, 1964; mem. faculty U. Md., 1964-89, asst. prof. entomology, 1964-69, assoc. prof., 1969-73, prof., 1973-89, assoc. dean grad. studies and research, 1974-77, acting dean, 1977-80, chmn. grad. program marine-estuarine-environ. scis., 1978-89, dir. Water Resources Research Ctr., 1981-89; dir. environ. rsch. lab. EPA, Gulf Breeze, Fla., 1989-95, sr. sci. advisor Nat. Ctr. for Environ. Rsch. Washington, 1995—2001; ret., 2001. Prof. emeritus U. Md., 1990—; chmn. hazardous substances data bank rev. panel Nat. Library Medicine, 1973-97; cons. in field, 2001-. Contbr. articles to profl. jours. Recipient U. Md. Alumni award, 1974 Fellow Washington Acad. Scis.; mem. AAAS, Am. Chem. Soc., Soc. Toxicology, Estuarine Rsch. Fedn., Sigma Xi, Phi Kappa Phi. Clubs: Cosmos (Washington). Republican. Episcopalian. Home: 90 Highpoint Dr Gulf Breeze FL 32561-4014 Personal E-mail: remenzer@att.net.

**MENZIES, HENRY HARDINGE,** architect; b. Hickory, N.C., Apr. 20, 1928; s. Henry Hardinge and Hallie (Lloyd) M. AB in Lit., U. N.C., 1948; postgrad., U. So. Calif., 1948-49; Bärch, N.C. State U., 1958. Founder, ptnr. The Architects Group, Boston, 1962-63; individual practice architecture Boston, 1964-78; ptnr. Menzies and LeMieux, N.Y.C., 1978-82; pvt. practice architecture New Rochelle, N.Y., 1983—. Lectr. in field. Works include coll. and seminary, Natick, Mass., 1964, Heights Sch., Washington, 1965, St. Marie's Ch. Lowell, Mass., 1966, Central Cath. H.S., Lawrence, Mass., 1971, Walker Sch., Needham, Mass., 1972, Baird Residence, Sherborn, Mass., 1972, Layton Cultural Ctr., Brookfield, Wis., 1974, Shellbourne Conf. Ctr., Valparaiso, Ind., 1974, Wespine Study Ctr., Pembroke, Mass, 1982, alterations to residences in Greenwich, Conn., 1984, Garwood Bldg. at Arnold Hall, 1986, Midtown Ctr., Chgo., 1986, Student Ctr., Houston, 1986, Windmoor Ctr., South Bend, Ind., 1986, alterations to student residences in Milw. and Providence, 1989-91, renovation of interior St. Aloysius Ch., New Canaan, Conn., 1993-96, chapel at Warwick House, Pitts., 1993, chapel at Westfield Residence, L.A., 1994, chapel at Allview Ctr., Columbia, Md., 1994, chapel at St. John Fisher Residence, Stamford, Conn., 1994, master plan, crypt chapel St. Mary of the Angels Ch., Chgo., 1996—, Shrine at Conf. Ctr., Schulenberg, Tex., chapel Lincoln Green student residence, Urbana, Ill., 1997—, new facade of St. Aloysius Ch., New Canaan, 1997—, Willows Acad., Chgo., 1997—, Cath. Info. Ctr. Washington, 1999-2000, St. Michael's Ch., Gastonia, N.C., 2000—, Cathedral St. Augustine, Bridgeport, Conn., 2003, Paducah, Ky., 2003, H.S. Charlotte, 2003, others; contbr. articles to profl. jours. Served to 1st lt. USNR, 1951-55. Mem. AIA (N.Y. chpt. 1978-84, Westchester/Mid-Hudson chpt. 1985—). Roman Catholic. Office: 99 Overlook Cir New Rochelle NY 10804-4501 Office Phone: 914-637-9597. E-mail: hmenzies@gmail.com.

**MENZIES, IAN STUART,** newspaper editor; b. Glasgow, Scotland, Mar. 11, 1920; came to U.S., 1944, naturalized, 1948; s. John S. and Gertrude (Mephius) M.; m. Barbara Edith Newton, June 16, 1945; children: Marla Ann, Gillian Jean, Alexa Stuart, Deborah Newton. Student, Royal Tech. Coll., 1937-39; Nieman fellow, Harvard U., 1961-62; L.H.D., Salem State Coll., 1978. Reporter Boston Globe, 1948-57, sci. editor, 1957-63, fin. editor, 1963-65, mng. editor, 1965-70, assoc. editor, 1970-85; sr. fellow John McCormack Inst. Pub. Affairs, U. Mass., Boston, 1985—95, sr. fellow emeritus, 1995—. Vis. assoc. Joint Ctr. for Urban Studies, Mass. Inst. Tech.-Harvard, 1970-71. Mem. Hingham (Mass.) Sch. Com., 1962-68. Served to lt. Royal Naval Vol. Res., 1939-46. Decorated D.S.C.; recipient Pub. Service award Nat. Edn. Writers, 1961, Pub. Service award AAAS, 1963, Heywood Broun award, 1961, Sevellon Brown award, 1959, Rudolph Elie award, 1959, A.P. Big City award, 1958, U.P.I. award, 1959. Mem. Harvard Club, Hingham Yacht Club, Brit. Officers Club New Eng. Home and Office: Apt 527 303 Linden Ponds Way Hingham MA 02043-4705

**MEOLA, TONY,** professional soccer player, actor; b. Belleville, N.J., Feb. 21, 1969; s. Vincent and Maria Meola; m. Colleen Meola; 1 child, Jonathan. Student, U. Va., 1986—89. Goalkeeper U.S. Nat. Team, 1988—94, 1999—2002, U.S. World Cup Team, 1990, 1994, 2002, Brighton Football Club, England, 1990, Fort Lauderdale Strikers, 1991, Long Island Roughriders, 1994—95, NY-NJ MetroStars, 1996—98, 2005—, Kansas City (Mo.) Wizards, 1998—2004. Actor: (plays) Tony N' Tina's Wedding, 1995. Named Hermann Trophy winner, MVP, U.S. Cup, 1993; named to MLS All Star Team, 1996—98, 2000, 2002; recipient Mo. Athletic Club Player of Yr., 1989. Achievements include drafted ctr. fielder N.Y. Yankees; tried out as placekicker for N.Y. Jets, 1994; mem. N.J. State HS Soccer Champions, 1986; NCAA Division I Co-Champions, 1989. Office: NY NJ MetroStars 3d Fl 1 Harmon Plz Secaucus NJ 07094

**MÉRAS, PHYLLIS LESLIE,** journalist; b. Bklyn., May 10, 1931; d. Edmond Albert and Leslie Trousdale (Ross) M.; BA, Wellesley Coll., 1955; MS in Journalism, Columbia U., 1954; Swiss Govt. Exchange fellow. Inst. Higher Internat. Studies, Geneva, 1957; m. Thomas H. Cocroft, Nov. 3, 1968. Reporter, copy editor Providence Jour., 1955-57, 59-61; feature writer Ladies Home Jour. mag., 1957-58; editor Weekly Tribune, Geneva, Switzerland, 1961-62; copyeditor, travel sect. N.Y. Times, 1962-68; mng. editor Vineyard Gazette, Edgartown, Mass., 1970-74, contbg. editor, 1974—; assoc. editor

Rhode Islander, Providence, 1970-76; travel editor Providence Jour., 1976-95; editor Wellesley Alumnae mag., 1979-96; assoc. in journalism U. R.I., 1974-75; adj. instr. Columbia U. Sch. Journalism, 1975-76. Author: First Spring: A Martha's Vineyard Journal, 1972, A Yankee Way With Wood, 1975, Miniatures: How to Make Them, Use Them, Sell Them, 1976, Vacation Crafts, 1978, The Mermaids of Chenonceaux and 828 Other Tales: An Anecdotal Guide to Europe, 1982, Exploring Rhode Island, 1984, Castles, Keeps and Leprechauns: Tales, Myths and Legends of Historic Sites in Great Britain and Ireland, 1988, Eastern Europe: A Traveler's Companion, 1991; co-author: Christmas Angels, 1979, Carry-out Cuisine, 1982, New Carry Out Cuisine, 1986, Rhode Island Explorer's Guide, 2004, Country Editor: Henry Beetle Hough and the Vineyard Gazette, 2006. Pulitzer fellow in critical writing, 1967. Mem. Soc. Am. Travel Writers. Home: Music St PO Box 215 West Tisbury MA 02575-0215 Office Phone: 508-693-1439. E-mail: pmcocroft@aol.com.

**MERATI, ALBERT L.,** otolaryngologist; BA with honors, U. Wash., Seattle, 1982, PhD with honors, 1991. Diplomate Am. Bd. Otolaryngology. Chief, divsn. laryngology Med. Coll. Wis., Milw., 2001—. Office: Med Coll Wis 9200 West Wisconsin Milwaukee WI 53226 Office Phone: 414-456-7464.

**MERBLER, CANDACE ANNE,** librarian; b. Bklyn., July 14, 1956; d. Patricia Anne M. Daly and Charles Fuoco; m. Richard Albert Merbler, Feb. 14, 1987 (div. Mar. 5, 2003). BA, U. Albany, 1979, MLS, 1999. Ref. support assoc. U. Albany, 1979—. Pres. United Univ. Profls., Albany, 2001—. Mem. Town of Greenfield UDAG Com., Greenfield Center, NY, 1996—; mem. statewide exec. bd. United Univ. Professions, 2005—; chmn. adv. com. on campus security U. Albany, 2004 . Recipient Excellence award, United U. Professions, N.Y., 1991, Initiatives for Women award, U. Albany, 2002; fellow RASS Dewey fellow, N.Y. Libr. Assn., 1999; scholar Alice-Hastings Murphy scholar, U. Albany Libraries, 1991, Instr. Info. Lit. scholar, Assn. Coll. & Rsch. Libraries, 2002. Mem.: ALA (assoc.), SUNY Librs. Assn. (assoc.), Hudson-Mohawk Libr. Assn. (assoc.), Ea. N.Y. Assn. of Coll. & Rsch. Librs. (assoc.), N.Y. Libr. Assn. (assoc.). Avocations: gardening, crafts, crocheting. Home: 788 Coy Rd Greenfield Center NY 12833 Office: U Albany 1400 Washington Ave Albany NY 12222 Office Phone: 518-442-3564. E-mail: cmerbler@uamail.albany.edu.

**MERCADO, DAVID,** lawyer; b. Houston, Oct. 28, 1958; AB, Columbia Univ., 1981; JD, Yale Univ., 1984. Bar: NY 1985. Assoc. Cravath Swaine & Moore LLP, NYC, 1984—92, ptnr., corp., 1992—. Mem.: ABA, N.Y. State Bar Assn. Office: Cravath Swaine & Moore LLP Worldwide Plz 825 Eighth Ave New York NY 10019-7475 Office Phone: 212-474-1756. Office Fax: 212-474-3700. Business E-Mail: dmercado@cravath.com.

**MERCADO, LILLIAN AMENSINA,** counselor; b. Newark, Dec. 29, 1965; d. Cecil Antonio Davis and Ines Mercedes Serrano; m. Jose Altagricia Mercado, July 30, 1983; children: Celia Mercedes, Matthew Samuel. Data entry installation dept. Sears Roebuck, Wayne, NJ, 1988—93; office mgr. J. Mercado Contracting, Newark, 1992—; cons. asst. Consumers, Montclair, NJ, 1993—94; collector Popular Club Plan, Garfield, NJ, 1994; telemarketer Americana Portraits, West Orange, NJ, 1997—99, customer svc. rep., 1999—2001; bilingual adherence counselor North Jersey Cmty. Rsch. Initiative, Newark, 2001—. Notary pub. Mercado Agy., Newark, 1992—; staff writer Cisco's Artistic Prodn., Jessup, Md., 1995—. Mem. Nat. Black HIV/AIDS Awareness Day, 2003, 2004. Roman Catholic. Avocations: reading, writing, meditation. Home: 474 Summer Ave Newark NJ 07104 Office: North Jersey Cmty Rsch Inst 393 Ctrl Ave Newark NJ 07103 Office Phone: 973-483-3444. Home Fax: 973-482-7142. Personal E-mail: ladyamensina@aol.com.

**MERCADO-RAMOS, FERDINAND,** former Puerto Rican government official; b. Lares, P.R., June 18, 1957; m. Michelle Waters Munoz; children: Ferdinand Giovanni, Andres Fernando. BS in Psychology, U. P.R., 1978; JD, Inter-Am. U. P.R., 1981; postgrad., Universidad Computense Madrid. Sec. of state, San Juan, PR, 2000—03. Author: Grito a la Intimidad, 1976, Un Pensamiento en Viaje, 1990.

**MERCADO-VALDES, FRANK,** broadcast executive; b. 1965; Student, U. Miami. Founder, CEO Heritage Network (formerly African Heritage Network), N.Y., 1993—. Exec. prodr. A Tribute to Alex Haley, 1994. With USMC. Named one of Most Influential People in Art, Culture and Media, City New Pub., 1998.

**MERCANDO, ANTHONY DOMINIC,** cardiologist; b. Yonkers, N.Y., Oct. 6, 1954; s. Dominic and Ida Mercando; m. Lee-Ann Davis, May 3, 1980; children: Michelle, Christina, Andrew, Anne Marie. BSEE, Manhattan Coll., Bronx, 1976; MD, Harvard U., 1980. Lic. physician, N.Y. Med. intern Montefiore Med. Ctr., Bronx, 1980-81, med. resident, 1981-83, cardiology fellow, 1984-86, attending arrhythmia svc., 1986-88; ptnr. Westchester Cardiology Assocs., Tuckahoe, N.Y., 1988—. Founder, pres. Amadeus Multimedia Technologies, Ltd., Irvington, N.Y., 1995—; assoc. dir. ACLS Montefiore Hosp., 1991—. Contbr. articles to profl. jours., chpts. to books; computer editor Jour. Pacing and Clin. Electrophysiology, 1993—. Bd. dirs. Home Nursing Assn. Westchester, Tuckahoe, N.Y., 1994—; tech. com. Irvington Sch. Bd., 1995—. R. Rosen fellow in pacing and electrophysiology N. Am. Soc. Pacing and Electrophysiology, 1986, Sable Meml. Heart fellow United Order Odd Fellows, 1985. Fellow Am. Coll. Cardiology; mem. N.Am. Soc. Pacing and Electrophysiology. Roman Catholic. Avocations: biking, skiing. Office: Westchester Cardiology 688 White Plains Rd # 201 Scarsdale NY 10583-5059

**MERCER, EDWIN WAYNE,** lawyer; b. Kingsport, Tenn., July 19, 1940; s. Ernest LaFayette and Geneva (Frye) M. BBA, Tex. Tech U., 1963; JD, S. Tex. Coll. Law. 1971. Bar: Tex. 1971, U.S. Dist. Ct. (no. dist.) Tex 1975, U.S. Supreme Ct. 1976, U.S. Ct. Appeals (5th Cir.) 1979. Pvt. practice, Houston, 1971-73; gen. counsel, corp. sec. Alcon Labs., Inc., Ft. Worth, 1973-81; ptnr. Gandy Michener Swindle Whitaker Pratt & Mercer, Ft. Worth, 1981-84; v.p., gen. counsel, corp. sec. Pengo Industries, Inc., Ft. Worth, 1984-90, also bd. dirs.; pvt. law practice, 1990—. Bd. dirs. Soc. for Prevention Blindness, 1979—. Mem. ABA, State Bar Tex., Coll. State Bar Tex., South Tex. Coll. Law Alumni assn., Tex. Tech U. Ex-Assn., Ft. Worth Club, Delta Theta Phi, Phi Delta Theta. Methodist. Office: Office: 817-731-1959.

**MERCER, EVELYN LOIS,** retired counseling administrator; b. Ellensboro, N.C., Apr. 25, 1934; d. Milton Bernadine Robinson Sr. and Lois Lenora Robinson; m. Theodore Roosevelt Mercer Sr. (div. June 1978); children: Theodore Roosevelt Jr., Brian Vincent, David Lemuel. BS in Math., Livingstone Coll., 1957; MEd in Guidance and Counseling, U. Cin., 1972; student, U. Akron, 1973, Miami U., Ohio, 1973—75, U. Akron, 1974. Cert. math tchr. Ohio, 1963, guidance counselor Ohio, 1972; lic. profl. counselor Ohio Counselor & Social Worker Bd., 1984. Math tchr. Jackson County Pub. Schs., Gumberry, NC, 1957—60, Cin. Pub. Schs., Cin., 1963—72, guidance counselor, 1972—73, Winton Woods City Sch. Dist., Cin., 1973—94, ret., 1994. Mem. adv. com. conselor edn. U. Cin., 1975—76; admissions adv. bd. Cin. Tech. Coll., Cin., 1975—81, The Ohio State U., Columbus, Ohio, 1982—85; nursing sch. adv. bd. Deaconess Hosp. Sch. Nursing, Cin., 1983—88; dir. Sch. Counseling Cons. Svc., Cin., 1994—, Charlotte, NC, 1994—. Mem. housing commn. City of Forest Park, Cin., 1974—76; Dem. precinct exec. Hamilton County Bd. Elections, Cin., 1974—96. Named Outstanding Counselor of Yr., Inroads of Cin., 1984. Mem.: NEA, AAUW (pres. Charlotte br. 2001—03), Am. Assn. U. Women of NC (v.p. membership 2004—), Am. Assn Coll. Admissions Counselors, Ohio Assn. Coll. Admissions Counselors, Ohio Sch. Counselors Assn., Ohio Edn. Assn., Livingstone Coll. Alumni Assn., U. Cin. Alumni Assn., Nat. Assn. Advancement for Colored People, Les Birdies Golf Club Charlotte (founder 1999, pres. 2000—2001), Order of Eastern Star, Zeta Phi Beta. Democrat. Methodist. Avocations: golf, travel, bridge, volunteering, gardening. Home and Office: 4101 Rye Mill Ct Charlotte NC 28277

**MERCER, FRANCES DECOURCY,** artist, educator; b. Centreville, Miss., June 14, 1944; d. John Homer Jr. and Patricia Powers (Given) Mercer. BA in English Lit., U. Miami, 1969, MA in History of Art, 1971; MFA in Painting, San Francisco Art Inst., 1974. Cert. tchr. Fla. Instr. South Fla. Art Inst., Hollywood, Fla., 1979—81; tchg. asst. San Francisco Art Inst., 1974; instr. Broward C.C., Ft. Lauderdale, Fla., 1979—83; owner 17th St. Galleries, Ft. Lauderdale, 1984—91; tchr. Broward County Sch. Bd., 1980—82; adj. prof. Fla. Atlantic U., 1979—80. Exhibited in group shows at Grove Art Gallery, Coconut Grove, Fla., 1973, Emanuel Walter Gallery, San Francisco, 1975, The Lucian LaBaudt Gallery, 1976, The Both Up Gallery, Berkeley, Calif., 1976, Discover Ctr., Ft. Lauderdale, 1980, Nova U. Artoberfest, Art and Culture Ctr. Hollywood, 1981, Indian Hammock Hunt and Riding Club, Okeechobee, Fla., 1998, A.E. Backus Gallery and Mus., Ft. Pierce, Fla., 2000, pvt. collections. Scholar Tuition scholar, San Francisco Art Inst., 1972, 1973, 1974. Avocations: photography, trail hiking, kayaking, golf, sailing. E-mail: fmercer@floridawatercolors.com.

**MERCER, JAMES LEE,** management consultant; b. Sayre, Okla., Nov. 7, 1936; s. Fred Elmo and Ora Lee (Davidson) M.; m. Karolyn Lois Prince, Nov. 16, 1962; children: Tara Lee, James Lee. BS, U. Nev., 1964, MBA, 1966; postgrad. exec. devel. program, Cornell U., 1979. Cert. in mcpl. adminstrn. U. N.C., 1971, lifetime Jr. coll. tchng. credential Calif., cert. mgmt. cons. Methods and results supr. Pacific Tel. & Tel., Sacramento, 1965-66; prodn. control supr. Gen. Dynamics, Pomona, Calif., 1966-67; nuclear submarine project mgr. Litton Industries, Pascagoula, Miss., 1967-70; asst. city mgr. City of Raleigh, NC, 1970-73; nat. program dir. Pub. Tech., Inc., Washington, 1973-76; gen. mgr. Battelle So. Ops., Atlanta, 1976-79; v.p. Korn/Ferry Internat., Atlanta, 1979-81; pres. James Mercer & Assocs. Inc.; mgmt. cons. Atlanta, 1981-86; chief Indsl. Ext. Divsn. Ga. Inst. of Tech., Atlanta, 1981-83, dir. Ga. Productivity Ctr.; dir. govtl. cons. svc. Coopers & Lybrand, 1983-84; regional v.p. Wolfe & Assocs., Inc., 1984-86; pres., CEO, chmn. Mercer, Slavin & Nevins, Inc., 1986-90; The Mercer Group, Inc., 1990—. Ad hoc prof. N.C. State U., 1972-73; bd. dirs. Taratec Corp., Columbus, Contract Svcs. Assn., Wash., DC., 1990—; lectr., spkr. in field. Author: Public Management Systems, 1978, Public Technology, 1981, Managing Urban Government Services, 1981, Strategic Planning for Public Managers, 1990, Public Management in Lean Years, 1992; contbr. numerous articles to profl. jours. Chmn. Raleigh Mayor's Civic Ctr. Authority Study Commn., 1971; founding bd. dirs. Mordecai Sq. Hist. Soc., Nat. Civic League; founding mem. U. S. C. Master of Pub. Adminstrn. adv. bd., 1987-97; founding mem. Calif. Poly. State U., adv. coun. Coll. Bus. Adminstrn., San Luis Obispo, 1980-95, bd. mem. emeritus, 1995—; founding mem., bd. trustees U. Nev. Found., Reno, 1985-91, trustee emeritus, 1991—. With USN, 1955-59. Mem.: NC League of Municipalities (George C. Franklin award 1971), Instil. Mgmt. Cons. (Atlanta Chpt. (v.p. membership 1991—97, bd. dirs. 1991—97), Contract Svcs. Assn. Am. (bd. dirs. Wash. (D.C.) chpt. 1990—), Ga. Indsl. Devel. Assn., Tech. Transfer Soc. (dir. 1978—87, treas. 1985—86), Internat. Pers. Mgmt. Assn., Govtl. Fin. Officers Assn., Inst. Indsl. Engrs. (chpt. pres. 1969—70, past pres.'s award 1970), Am. Soc. Pub. Adminstrn., Internat. City-County Mgmt. Assn., Raleigh Forward Leadership Orgn., U. Nev. Alumni Assn. (exec. com. 1969—79, Oustanding Alumnus), Shriners, Rotary, Atlanta C. of C., Masons, Beta Gamma Sigma. Home: 28 Sierra del Sol Santa Fe NM 87508-2136 Office: 551 W Cordova Rd Ste 726 Santa Fe NM 87505-1825 Office Phone: 505-466-9500. Personal E-mail: mercer@mindspring.com.

**MERCER, JOHN T.W.,** lawyer; b. Mpls., 1949; AB, Univ. Mich., 1973, JD, 1977. Bar: Ga. 1977. Assoc. Troutman Sanders LLP, Atlanta, 1978—84, ptnr., corp. and securities, 1985—, and practice group leader, project develop. and fin. Mem.: ABA, Nat. Assn. Bond Lawyers, State Bar Ga. Office: Troutman Sanders LLP One Logan Sq Ste 5200 600 Peachtree St NE Atlanta GA 30308-2216 Office Phone: 404-885-3521. Office Fax: 404-962-6632. Business E-Mail: john.mercer@troutmansanders.com

**MERCER, RICHARD JAMES,** lawyer; b. New London, Conn., Oct. 2, 1950; s. James Wilson and Marianne (Wieczorek) M.; m. Ann Holly Gutting, Oct. 9, 1970 (div. 1977); m. Harriet Allston Jopson, May 1, 1982; 1 child, James. BBA, Old Dominion U., 1972; JD, Coll. William and Mary, 1975; LLM in Taxation, Boston U., 1977, LLM in Banking, 1986. Assoc. Epstein & Epstein, Norfolk, Va., 1975, Bernard A. Kaplan, Boston, 1975-76; sole practice, 1976-78, 1979-80; ptnr. Shagory & Shagory, Boston, 1978-79, Alpert, Thurman & Mercer, Boston, 1980-82; assoc. counsel First Nat. Bank Boston, 1983-85, asst. v.p., assoc. counsel, 1985-86, sr. counsel, 1986—. Town coordinator George Bush Presdl. Campaign, Weston, 1980. Mem. ABA, Boston Bar Assn. Am. Arbitration Assn. (arbitrator 1978), Mass. Bar Assn., Va. Bar Assn. Republican. Episcopalian. Office: First Nat Bank Boston 100 Federal St Boston MA 02110-1802

**MERCER, WILLIAM W.,** prosecutor; b. 1964; BA in Polit. Sci., U. Mont., 1986; MPA, Harvard U., 1988; JD, George Mason U., 1993. Counselor to asst. atty. gen., sr. policy analyst Office of Policy Devel. U.S. Dept. Justice, 1989—94; asst. US atty. dist. Mont. US Dept. Justice, 1994—2001, US atty. dist. Mont. Billings, 2001—. Mem. president's adv. coun. U. Mont.; mem. bd. visitors U. Mont. Sch. Law; mem. atty. gen.'s adv. office. Office: US Attys Office PO Box 1478 Billings MT 59103*

**MERCHANT, NATALIE ANNE,** musician, singer; b. Jamestown, N.Y., Oct. 26, 1963; d. Tony and Ann Merchant; 1 child. Lead singer band 10,000 Maniacs, 1981-1993; solo artist, 1993—; founder Myth Amer. Records LLC, 2003—. Albums with 10,000 Maniacs include Human Conflict Number Five, 1982, Secrets of the I Ching, 1983, The Wishing Chair, 1986, In My Tribe, 1987, Blind Man's Zoo, 1989, Hope Chest, 1990, Our Time in Eden, 1992, 10,000 Maniacs MTV Unplugged, 1993; solo album Tigerlily, 1995, Ophelia, 1998, Live In Concert, 1999, Motherland, 2001, Natalie Merchant 2001, Motherland, 2001, The House Carpenter's Daughter, 2003; composer soundtracks: Felicity, 1998, Earthlings, 2003. Office: Myth Amer Records 660 Madison Ave 10th Fl New York NY 10021

**MERCHANT, ROLAND SAMUEL, SR.,** health facility administrator, educator; b. NYC, Apr. 18, 1929; s. Samuel and Eleta (McLymont) M.; m. Audrey Bartley, June 6, 1970; children: Orelia Eleta, Roland Samuel, Huey Bartley. BA, NYU, 1957, MA, 1960; MS, Columbia U., 1963, MSHA, 1974. Asst. statistician NYC Dept. Health, 1957-60, statistician, 1960-63, NY TB and Health Assn., NYC, 1963-65; biostatistician, adminstrv. coord. Inst. Surg. Studies, Montefiore Hosp., Bronx, NY, 1965-72; resident in adminstrn. Roosevelt Hosp., NYC, 1973-74; dir. health and hosp. mgmt. Dept. Health, City of NY, 1974-76; from asst. adminstr. to adminstr. West Adams Cmty. Hosp., LA, 1976; spl. asst. to assoc. v.p. for med. affairs Stanford U. Hosp., Calif., 1977-82, dir. office mgmt. and strategic planning, 1982-85, dir. mgmt. planning Calif., 1986-90; v.p. strategic planning Cedars-Sinai Med. Ctr., LA, 1990-94; cons. Roland Merchant & Assocs., LA, 1994—. Clin. assoc. prof. family, cmty. and preventive medicine Stanford U., 1986—88; dept. health rsch. and policy Stanford U. Med. Sch., 1988—90. Author: Passion-Sustained Commitment to Excellence: Family-Oriented Parenting and Training, 2004. With U.S. Army, 1951—53. Fellow, USPHS. Fellow: APHA, Am. Coll. Healthcare Execs.; mem.: NY Acad. Scis. Home: 27335 Park Vista Rd Agoura Hills CA 91301-3639 Office Phone: 818-879-8732.

**MERCIER, EILEEN ANN,** corporate financial executive; b. Toronto, Ont., Can., July 7, 1947; d. Thomas Sidley and Frances Katherine (Boone) Falconer; m. Ernest Cochrane Mercier, Feb. 8, 1980; children: Jenny, Sheelagh, Peter, Michael, Stuart. BA with hons, Waterloo Luth. U., 1968; MA, U. Alta., Can., 1969; fellow, Instn. Can. Bankers, 1975; MBA, York U., 1977. Mgr. corp. fin. Toronto-Dominion Bank, 1972-78, portfolio mgr. TD capital; dir., U.S. commn. pmt. Canwest Capital Corp., Toronto, 1978-81; mgr. fin. strategy & planning Gulf Can. Ltd., Toronto, 1981-86, mgr. corp. fin.; v.p. The Pagurian Corp., Toronto, 1986-87; v.p., treas. Abitibi-Price, Inc., Toronto, 1987-88, v.p. corp. devel., 1989-90, sr. v.p., CFO, 1990-95. Bd. dirs. Hydro One, Inc., TeeKay Shipping Corp., The CGI Group Inc., ING Bank Can., ING

Can., Inc., Shermag Ltd., Ont. Tchrs. Pension Plan. Past chmn., mem. bd. govs. Wilfrid Laurier U., Waterloo, Ont., York U., U. Health Network. Recipient Outstanding Bus. Leader award Wilfrid Laurier U., 1991, Award for Outstanding Contbn. Schulich Sch. of Bus. York U., 1997. Office: 199 Cranbrooke Ave Toronto ON Canada M5M 1M6

**MERCKER, MARY ALICE,** aviation school administrator; b. Kansas City, Mo., June 29, 1932; d. Kenneth Foster Rhees and Catherine Mary Henel; m. Reid Martin, Nov. 23, 1950 (div. Nov. 1969); children: Reid J., Kenneth C., Mark T., Mary M., Theodore H., Sylvia R., Ben X., Teresa I. Student, Phoenix Coll., 1949-50; AA, Pima Coll., 1990-93; student, U. Ariz., 1994. Fed. aviation adminstr.; comml. pilot; cert. flight instr. Instr. Ariz. Sch. Aviation, Tucson, 1979, Tucson Cmdr., 1990, AVRA Flt. Ctr., Marana, Ariz., 1976-78; pres., founder Alpha Air, Inc., Tucson, 1980—; sec., treas. Manasco Inc., Tucson, 1987—. Aviation cons., Tucson, 1987—; adj. prof. aviation Pima C.C., Tucson, 1988-94, curriculum cons., 1988-93. Author: Northumberland Dreaming, 1998, numerous poems. Recipient 2nd Place Sparrowgrass Poetry Forum, 1996, 1st Place Sparrowgrass Chapbook award, 2001. Mem. Ariz. Pilots Assn., Aircraft Owners and Pilots Assn., 99's (life). Home: 6220 W Belmont Rd Tucson AZ 85743-9212 Office: Alpha Air Inc HC 2 Box 282 Tucson AZ 85735-9709 Personal E-mail: alphair@msn.com.

**MERCURI, JOAN B.,** museum administrator; b. NYC; BA, Va. Commonwealth U., 1984. Mgmt. positions various corps., Ill., 1986-96; exec. dir. Frank Lloyd Wright Home and Studio Found., Oak Park, Ill., 1996—; pres., CEO Frank Lloyd Wright Preservation Trust, Oak Park, 2000—. Dir. Oak Park Area Conv. and Vis. Bur. Mem. Am. Assn. Museums, Nat. Trust for Hist. Preservation, Employment Mgmt. Assn., Soc. Human Resource Mgmt., Frank Lloyd Wright Bldg. Conservancy, Assn. Fundraising Profls., Board Source. Office Phone: 708-848-1976. Business E-Mail: mercuri@wrightplus.org.

**MERCURIO, RENARD MICHAEL,** real estate company executive; b. NYC, June 22, 1947; s. Pasquale J. and Ann F. Mercurio; m. Abbie Gonzalez, June 29, 1968; children— Kristin, Allison. BA, Queens Coll., N.Y.C., 1968; MBA, U. Rochester, 1969. CPA, N.Y.; lic. real estate broker, Calif. Sr. accountant Peat, Marwick & Mitchell, N.Y.C., 1969-73; mgr. Gulf & Western Industries, Inc., N.Y.C., 1973-78; v.p., treas. Famous Players Ltd., Toronto, Ont., Canada, 1978-81; exec. v.p. Famous Players Realty Ltd., Toronto, 1981-84; pres. Design Twenty-Seven Ltd., Toronto, 1984—; v.p. Renric Holdings, Ltd., 1987—; CFO Schickedanz Real Estate, Palm Beach Gardens, Fla., 1999—2003. Mem. AICPA, NY State Soc. CPAs. Personal E-mail: amercu6@aol.com.

**MERDEK, ANDREW AUSTIN,** publishing and media executive, lawyer; b. Portland, Maine, Oct. 11, 1950; s. Philip and Eleanor (Weiss) M.; m. Jeanne Mullen, July 22, 1983; children: David, Jonathan. AB, Middlebury Coll., 1972; JD, U. Va., 1978. Bar: D.C. 1978, U.S. Dist. Ct. D.C. 1979, U.S. Ct. Appeals (D.C. cir.) 1979, U.S. Supreme Ct. 1982. Reporter, editor Portland Press Herald, 1973-75; assoc. Dow, Lohnes & Albertson, Washington, 1978-86, ptnr., 1986-87; v.p., gen. mgr. Atlanta Constitution and Journal, 1987-92; v.p. legal affairs Cox Enterprises, Inc., Atlanta, 1993—, gen. counsel, 1993—, corp. sec., 1993—. Mem. Newspaper Assn. of Am. (chmn. legal affairs com.), Order of Coif, Phi Beta Kappa. Home: 445 Mount Vernon Hwy NW Atlanta GA 30327-4313 Office: Cox Enterprises Inc 6205 Peachtree Dunwoody Rd Atlanta GA 30328- E-mail: andy.merdek@cox.com.

**MERDINGER, CHARLES JOHN,** civil engineer, educator, military officer, academic administrator; b. Chgo., Apr. 20, 1918; s. Walter F. and Catherine (Phelan) M.; m. Mary McKelleget, Oct. 21, 1944; children: Anne, Joan, Susan, Jane. Student, Marquette U., 1935-37; BS, U.S. Naval Acad., 1941; BCE, Rensselaer Poly. Inst., 1945, MCE, 1946; DPhil (Rhodes scholar), Brasenose Coll., Oxford U., Eng., 1949; LHD (hon.), Sierra Nev. Coll., 1987; DLitt (hon.), U. Nev., Reno, 1994. Registered profl. engr., Wis. Commd. ensign USN, 1941, advanced through grades to capt. Civil Engr. Corps, 1959; served aboard USS Nevada, USS Alabama Atlantic and Pacific, 1941-44; design, constrn. pub. works Panama, 1946—47, Washington, Bremerion, Adak, Miramar, 1949—56; comdg. officer, dir. U.S. Naval Civil Engring. Lab., Port Hueneme, Calif., 1956-59; pub. works officer U.S. Fleet activities, Yokosuka, Japan, 1959-62; head English, history and govt. dept. U.S. Naval Acad., Annapolis, Md., 1962-65; asst. comdr. ops. & maintenance Naval Facilities Engring. Command, Navy Dept., 1965-67; pub. works officer Seabees (NSA), DaNang, Vietnam, 1967-68; comdg. officer Western div. Naval Facilities Engring. Command, San Bruno, Calif., 1968-70; pres. Washington Coll., Chestertown, Md., 1970-73; v.p. Aspen Inst. Humanistic Studies, Colo., 1973-74; dep. dir. Scripps Instn. Oceanography, La Jolla, Calif., 1974-80; dir. Avoca, 1978—. Author: Civil Engineering Through the Ages, 1963; contbr.: articles to Ency. Britannica; others. Mem. Md., Calif., Oreg. and Nev. Selection Coms. for Rhodes Scholars, sec. Nev. Com., 1982-89; exec. council. Boy Scouts Am.; sec., mem. exec. com. Md. Ind. Coll. and Univ. Assn., 1971-72; mem. So. Regional Edn. Bd, 1971-73, Nat. Com. History and Heritage of Am. Civil Engring., 1965-72; Alumni trustee U.S. Naval Acad., 1971-74; mem. coun. Rensselaear Poly. Inst., 1972—; trustee Found. for Ocean Rsch., 1976-80, Desert Rsch. Inst. Found., Nev., 1983-92, U. Nev. Reno Found., 1986-93; chmn. bd. trustees Sierra Nev. Coll., 1980-87, chmn. bd. emeritus, 1987; commr. N.W. Assn. Commn. on Colls., 1988-93. Pfc Wis. Nat. Guard, 1935—37. Decorated Legion of Merit with combat V; named All-Am. in lacrosse, 1945, Papal Knight Grand Cross Equestrian Order of Holy Sepulchre of Jerusalem, 1992; inducted into Rensselaer Athletic Hall of Fame, 1983; recipient Disting. Eagle Scout award, 1984. Fellow ASCE (Nat. History and Heritage award 1972), Explorers Club, Soc. Am. Mil. Engrs. (Toulmin medal 1952, 57, 61); mem. NSPE, Soc. History Tech., Am. Soc. Engring. Edn., Brasenose Soc., Pearl Harbor Survivors Assn., Nat. Eagle Scout Assn. (regent), Phalanx, Sigma Xi, Tau Beta Pi, Chi Epsilon. Clubs: Vincent's, Oxford. Roman Catholic. Home: 726 Tyner Way PO Box 7249 Incline Village NV 89452-7249

**MEREDITH, DALE DEAN,** civil engineering educator; b. Centralia, Ill., Mar. 24, 1940; s. Leslie Edward Meredith and Beulah Marie (McClelland) Nattier; m. Linda Jean Hutson, July 3, 1965; children: Sarah Elizabeth, Laura Jane. AA, Centralia Twp. Jr. Coll., 1961; BS, U. Ill., 1963, MS, 1964, PhD, 1968. Registered profl. engr., N.Y., Ill. Asst. prof. U. Ill., Urbana, 1968-73; assoc. prof. civil engring. SUNY, Buffalo, 1973-79, prof., 1979-2000, chmn. dept. civil engring., 1987-96, prof. emeritus, 2000—. Co-author: Design and Planning Engineering Systems, 1973, 2d edit., 1985; also over 50 articles. Vice pres. Baptist Conv. N.Y., Syracuse, 1982-84, 94-95, chmn. 1984-87. Grantee US. Office Water Research and Tech., 1966-73, 75-78, U.S. Dept. Interior, 1968-79, U.S. Dept. Commerce, 1976-79, various pvt. cos., 1979—, N.Y. State Agys., 1980-2000. Fellow ASCE (com. Water Resources Planning and Mgmt. div., 1988, editor jour. Water Resources Planning and Mgmt. 1982-84); mem. Am. Geophys. Union, Am. Soc. Engring. Edn., Am. Water Resources Assn. (editor Water Resources Bull. 1990-91). Office: SUNY Dept Civil Engring Buffalo NY 14260-4300 E-mail: ciedale@eng.buffalo.edu.

**MEREDITH, KEITH EDWARD,** retired academic administrator, educator; b. Clay Ctr., Kans., Oct. 13, 1943; s. Joseph Edward and Eulah Mae Meredith; m. Margaret Rose Meek, May 29, 1964; children: Kurt Edward Merediith, Mark David, Scott Thomas. BS, Kans. State U., Manhattan, Kans., 1965, MS, 1968; PhD, U. Ariz., Tucson, 1973. Mem. faculty Manhattan Pub. Schs., Kans., 1965—66; rsch. assoc. U. Ariz., Tucson, 1972—73, asst. prof. Coll. Edn., 1974—81, assoc. dir. S.W. Arthritis Ctr., 1981—85, assoc. dir. Divsn. Restorative Medicine, 1985—91; adj. assoc. prof. Coll. Edn., 1986—; assoc. dir. Aviz. Ctr. Aging U. Ariz., 1991—98, dir. Gerontol. Studies Interdisciplinary Studies Program, 1993—99, ret., 1999. Chmn. OASIS, Tucson, 2001—02; bd. trustees Ariz. State Ret. Sys., Phoenix, 2003—, chmn. bd. trustees, 2004—. Contbr. articles to profl. jours. Mem. adv. coun. aging Ariz. Gov., Phoenix, 1991—94; chmn. United Way Greater Tucson, 1994—95; chmn. bd. trustees Sonaora Desert Hosp., Tucson; chmn. bd. dirs. United Way Capital Support Corp., Tucson, 1999—2005. Recipient Meritorious Performance in Tchg. award, U. Ariz. Found., 1972, Rsch. award, Assn. Specialists

in Group Work, 1988, Vol. of Yr. award, United Way Greater Tucson, 1989. Democrat. Avocations: reading, golf, music, architectural design. Home: 9711 North Horizon Vista Place Oro Valley AZ 85704-7661

**MEREDITH, LISA ANN MARIE,** social studies educator, consultant; b. Reading, Pa., May 2, 1969; d. Robert Lee and Carol Ann Meredith; life ptnr. Thomas J. Unrath. BA, Alvernia Coll., Reading, Pa., 1990—91. Cert. elem. sch. tchr. Commonwealth of Pa., 1991, mid. sch. tchr. Commonwealth of Pa., 2005. Tchr. Reading Sch. Dist., Pa., 1991—2003, Sch. Dist. Phila., 2001—; edn. coord. Nat. Constn. Ctr., Phila., 2003—04. Asst. coord. Ctr. for Civic Edn., Phila., 2003—04; cons. Pa. Gov.'s Inst. for Social Studies Educators, Harrisburg, 2004—. Mem. Champions for Caring, Phila., 2003—04; activist, rep. Reading Edn. Assn., Pa., 1998—2000; activist Phila., 1992—; Citizens Children and Youth, 2002—03, Phila. Fedn. Tchrs., 2004—05. Grantee, Eisenhower Grants, 1995—96, Tchg. Am. History, 2002—03. Mem.: Nat. Coun. Social Studies Tchrs. (assoc.), Phila. Fedn. Tchrs. (assoc.). Lutheran. Avocations: history, travel, golf, reading. Office: Sch Dist Phila 238 E Wyoming Ave Philadelphia PA 19120 Office Phone: 215-456-3012. Personal E-mail: lamm34@comcast.net. Business E-Mail: lameredith@phila.k12.pa.us.

**MEREDITH, OWEN NICHOLS,** public relations executive; b. Etowah, Tenn., Mar. 27, 1924; s. Owen Habner and Ora (Nichols) M.; m. Mary Virginia Wright, July 19, 1980. BA, U. Va., 1946; MA, Syracuse U., 1952. Editor sub-features Together mag.-Meth. Pub. House, Nashville and Chgo., 1953—57; dir. pub. info. Nashville-Davidson County ARC, 1957—70; exec. dir. Tenn. State Mus., Nashville, 1970—72; owner, mgr. Gazetteer Typesetters, Nashville, 1973—74; dir. pub. rels. Tenn. ARC, Nashville, 1974—89; pvt. practice Nashville, 1989—. Author: The Parish Activities Handbook, 1996, (with R. McBride) The Hedden Family of North Georgia, 1957, The Nichols Family of North Georgia, 1960, (with Lee Seitz) A History of the American Red Cross in Nashville, Tennessee, 1982, (with Mary Virginia Meredith and Susan Wright Lyons) One Cup Love and a Pinch of Catnip, 1998; editor: (with McBride and M. Rothrock) Eastin Morris' 1834 Tennessee Gazetteer, 2d edit., 1971; contbr. articles, photographs and book revs. to hist. jours. Mem. ARC Disaster Rescue, 1989—; vol. archivist Diocese of Nashville, 1992—2005. Mem. Pub. Rels. Soc. Am. (cert.), Tenn. Soc. Health Care Pub. Rels., Internat. Assn. Bus. Communicators, Confederate Meml. Lit. Soc. (Tenn regent 1972-80), Tenn. Exec. Residence Preservation Found., 1971-2005), Coun. for Pastoral Planning and Coun. Devel. Home: 903 Oleson Rd Marengo IL 60152-9261 E-mail: meredithm@k12tn.net.

**MEREDITH, THOMAS C.,** academic administrator; m. Susan Meredith; children: Mark, Matthew. BA, Ky. Wesleyan Coll.; MA, We. Ky. Univ.; EdD, Univ. Miss. Assoc. dir. Bd. Trustees State Inst. of Higher Learning, Miss., 1974—84; vice chancellor exec. affairs U. Miss., 1984—88; pres. Western Ky. U., Bowling Green, 1988-97; chancellor U. Ala. Sys., Tuscaloosa, 1997—2002; chancellor bd. regents Univ. Sys. Ga., Atlanta, 2002—. Pres. Nat. Assn. Sys. Heads; past chmn. Am. Assoc. State Coll. & Univ.; mem. exec. com. So. Regional Edn. Bd., 2002—. Office: Chancellor Univ Sys Ga 270 Washington St SW Atlanta GA 30334-9007 E-mail: chancellor@usg.edu.

**MEREDITH, WENDI SUE,** music educator; d. Dennis Wayne and L Imogene Meredith. BS in Elem. Edn., Bapt. Bible Coll., 1992, BA in Ch. Music, 1997; MusM, SW Mo. State U., 2001. Level 1 Orff Schulwerk Certification Am. Orff Schulwerk Assn., 1999, Improving Strategies in Tchg.AQA GCSE Music Specification Keynote Ednl., 2004, Form Tutors: Role, Skills and Responsibilities Lighthouse Profl. Devel., 2004. English, music tchr. Quint City Bapt. Sch., Davenport, Iowa, 1992—95; prof. voice Bapt. Bible Coll., Springfield, Mo., 1997—2004; head music Egerton Rothesay Sch., Berkhamsted, Hertfordshire, England, 2006—, peripatetic signing tchr., 2005—, coord. musical events, 2006—. Traveling recruiter Bapt. Bible Coll., Springfield, Mo., 1990—92, 1995—2001, coord. traveling recruitment teams, 1999—2001, co-writer, co-producer of drama, 1998—99; soprano Cmty. Choir SW Mo. State U., Springfield, 1998—2003; coord. program for woman's conf. Cherry St. Bapt. Ch., Springfield, 2000—04, dir. woman's conf., 2003—04; children's and musical dir. Bible Bapt. Ch., Wendover, Buckinghamshire, England, 2003—, worship leader, 2004—; mem. chorus Springfield Regional Opera/Messiah Project, 2003—03; soprano Cmty. Choir Bapt. Bible Coll., Springfield, 2003—04; spkr. in field. Composer: (song) For Such a Time as This. Singing team leader for youth camp and youth events Bapt. Bible Fellowship Internat., Springfield, Mo., 1995—2002; children's choir tchr. Cherry St. Bapt. Ch., Springfield, Mo., 1995—2004; christian sch. tchr. Quint City Bapt. Ch., Davenport, Iowa, 1992—95; music coord. youth event, Berkhamsted, 2006; music coord., leader LIFE Camp, Tonbridge, Kent, England, 2006. Civilian day camp worker U.S. Army, 1990—93, Rock Island Illinois. Mem.: Nat. Trust, Nat. Union Tchrs., Gospel Music Assn., Am. Orff Schulwerk Assn.

**MERENDINO, K. ALVIN,** surgeon, educator; b. Clarksburg, W.Va., Dec. 3, 1914; s. Biagio and Cira (Bivona) M.; m. Shirley Emma Jane Hill, July 6, 1943; children: Cira Anne Watts, Nancy Jane Napuunoa, Susan Hill Mitchell, Nina Merendino-Sarich, Maria King Merendino-Stillwell. BA summa cum laude, Ohio U., 1936, LLD (hon.), 1967; MD, Yale U., 1940; PhD, U. Minn., 1946. Diplomate Am. Bd. Surgery, Am. Bd. Thoracic Surgery. Intern Cin. Gen. Hosp., 1940-41; resident U. Minn. Hosp., Mpls., 1941-45; rsch. asst. Dr. Owen H. Wangensteen, 1942-43; trainee Nat. Cancer Inst., 1943-45; dir. program in postgrad. med. edn. in surgery Anchor Hosp., St. Paul, 1946-48; instr. dept. surgery U. Minn., Mpls., 1944-45, asst. prof. dept. surgery, 1945-48; assoc. prof. dept. surgery U. Wash., Seattle, 1949-55, dir. exptl. surgery labs., dept. surgery, 1950-72, prof. dept. surgery, 1955-81, prof. emeritus, 1981—, prof. and adminstrv. officer dept. surgery, 1957-64, prof., chmn., 1964-72; chmn. dept. surgery King Faisal Specialist and Rsch. Ctgr., Riyadh, Saudi Arabia, 1976, dir. med. affairs, 1976-79, dir. Cancer Therapy Inst., spl. cons. to Coun., supr. for exec. mgmt., assoc. dir. med. affairs, 1981-82; dir. ops. King Faisal Med. City, Riyadh, 1981-85. Mem. adv. com. for med. rsch., Boeing Airplane Co., 1959-67, cimmn., 1962l cons. Children's Orthopedic Hosp., Seattle, 1972-82; mem. adv. com. on heart disease and surgery for crippled children's svc., Wash. State Dept. Health and Div. Vocational Rehab., 1961; mem. surgery study sect. NIH, 1958-62, subcom. on prosthetic valves for cardiac surgery, chm. 1st Nat. Conf., 1960, mem. adv. com. 2d Nat. Conf. on Prosthetic Heart Valves, 1969, Surgery A study sect. chmn., 1970-72. Nat. Heart and Lung Inst. Tng. Com., 1965-69; cons. VA, Seattle, 1949-59, 65-81; mem. adv. com. on hosps. and clinics, USPHS, 1963-66; nat. surgery test com. Nat. Bd. Med. Examiners, 1963-67; mem. surgery resident rev. com., 1964-69; mem. adv. com. on Grad. Edn. in Surgery, 1963-73, vice-chmn., 1972-73; chmn. 2d Saudi Arabian Med. Conf., Riyadh, 1978; mem. com. on postgrad. med. edn., Kingdom of Saudi Arabia Ministry of Health, 1978-79; vis. prof. established open heart surgery program Malaysia U. Hosp., Kuala Lumpur, 1971, edn. and tng. jr. faculty (surg. residents) faculty medicine U. Saigon and Mil. M.C. (army surgeons) Binh Dan Hosp. Saigon, Vietnam. Editor in chief: Prosthetic Valves for Cardiac Surgery, 1961; assoc. editor: Prosthetic Heart Valves, 1969; mem. editorial bd. Am. Jour. Surgery.. 1958-83, Jour. Surg. Rsch., 1961-69, Pacific Medicine and Surgery, 1964-68, King Faisal Hosp. Medicine Jour. (renamed Annals of Saudi Medicine), 1981-85; contbr. articles to profl. jours., chpts. to books; producer movies on surgery. Recipient cert. of merit Ohio U. Alumni Assn., 1957, Outstanding W.Va. Italian-Am. award Nat. Italian Heritage Festival Inc., Clarksburg, W.Va., 1984, Spirit of Freedom award A. James Mancin, Sec. State W.Va., 1984, Disting. W. Virginian award Gov. John D. Rockefeller IV., State of W.va., 1984, John Baird Thomas Meml. award Ohio U.; named Surgery Alumnus of Yr., U. Minn., 1981, Disting. Citizen Wash. State, Lt. Gov. John Cherberg, 1981, K. Alvin Merendino Day Seattle, Mayor Charles Royer, 1981; NIH grantee, 1951-76; Verdi scholar Yale U. Fellow ACS (numerous coms., bds.); Soc. of Univ. Surgeons (councilman at large 3 yrs.); Internat. Soc. Surgery; mem. Am. Surg. Assn. (adv. mem. com. 1959-64, v.p. 1972-73), Am. Assn. for Thoracic Surgery, Halsted Soc., Henry N. Harkins Surg. Soc., N. Pacific Coast Surg. Assn., Seattle Surg. Soc. (honored special tribute annual meeting 1997), So. Surg. Soc. (Arthur H. Shipley award 1972), Am. Bd. Surgery 1958-64 (vice chmn. 1962-63, chmn. 1963-64, emeritus

1964—); University Club, Seattle Golf Club, Phi Beta Kappa, Sigma Xi, Beta Theta Pi (sec., pres.), Phi Beta Pi (hon.). Republican. Episcopalian. Avocations: golf, fly fishing, bird hunting, gardening. Home: The Highlands Shoreline WA 98177 Personal E-mail: k.merendinomd@comcast.com.

**MERENLENDER, ADINA MAYA,** biologist; b. Seattle, Oct. 1, 1963; d. Elizabeth Shima and Sylvain Merenlender; m. Kerry Lee Heise, May 30, 1996; children: Noah Douglas Heise, Ariella Rachel Heise. PhD, U. Rochester, N.Y., 1993. Postdoctoral fellow Stanford U., Palo Alto, Calif., 1993—95; assoc. coop. ext. specialists U. Calif., Berkeley, 1995—. Author: (book) Corridor Ecology; contbr. articles to profl. jours. Watershed Sci. And Land Use Change grant, NSF, EPA, 2001-2006. Mem.: Soc. for Conservation Biology (N.Am. bd. mem. 2006). Achievements include research in Effects of land use change on biodiversity; Private land conservation and land use planning; Watershed science and land use. Office: Univ Calif 145 Mulford Hall Berkeley CA 94720-3114 Office Phone: 707-744-1424.

**MERET, ALEXANDRU SASHA,** artist, illustrator; s. Nicolae and Lilia Meret; m. Anca Oana Georgescu, June 24, 1957; m. Cristina Abrihan, Dec. 28, 1956 (div.); children: Colin, Alexandra, Ellis. BA, Fine Arts Sch., Bucharest, Romania, 1974; M in Econs. Sci., Acad. Econ. Scis., Bucharest, 1979; postgrad., Columbia U., 1988—89. Illustrator NY Times, NYC, 1987—. Childrens book, Don Global Suit pe cal (Best Childrens Book, Assn. Romanian Editors, 2003). Office Phone: 917-6490-7342.

**MERGLER, H. KENT,** investment counselor; b. Cin., July 1, 1940; s. Wilton Henry and Mildred Amelia (Pulliam) M.; m. Judith Anne Metzger, Aug. 17, 1963; children: Stephen Kent, Timothy Alan, Kristin Lee. BBA with honors, U. Cin., 1963, MBA, 1964. CFA, C.I.C. Portfolio mgr. Scudder, Stevens & Clark, Cin., 1964 68, exec. v.p. Chgo., 19/0-73; v.p. Gibralter Rsch. & Mgmt., Ft. Lauderdale, Fla., 1968-70; ptnr. Stein Roe & Farnham, Ft. Lauderdale, 1973-84; ptnr., pres., dir., ptnr., mem. exec. com. Stein Roe & Farnham, Inc., Chgo., 1984-91; pres. Stein Roe Investment Trust, 1988—91; mng. ptnr., chief investment officer Loomis, Sayles & Co., L.P., Palm Beach Gardens, Fla., 1992-2000; pres. Northstar Capital Mgmt., Inc., 2002—04, chmn., 2005—. Arbitrator Nat. Assn. Security Dealers, Inc., 1976-82. Chmn. adminstrv. bd. United Meth. Ch., Ft. Lauderdale, 1981—83; mem. fin. com. Kenilworth Union Ch., 1989—92; elder, chmn. fin. com., stewardship com. First Presbyn. Ch., Stuart, 2001—04, 2006; chmn. investment com. Cmty. Found. Broward, 1992—2001, bd. dirs., 1994—2001; mem. Martin County Econ. Coun., 1992—2000; bd. dirs. Pine Crest Prep. Sch., 1982—84, bd. advisors, 1984—87; corp. adv. bd. U. Cin. Coll. Bus. Adminstrn., 1991—94; bd. dirs. Hibiscus House Children's Found., 1993—99, 2001—, chmn. investment com., 1994—99, 2001—; bd. dirs. Coral Ridge Little League, 1976—84, pres., 1980—81. Mem. Fin. Analysts Soc. So. Fla. (bd. dirs. 1974-78, pres. 1975), Bond Club Ft. Lauderdale (bd. dirs. 1978-82), Willoughby Golf Club, Cullasaja Club (Highlands, N.C.), Beta Gamma Sigma, Beta Theta Pi. Republican. Home: 3980 SE Old Saint Lucie Blvd Stuart FL 34996-5119 Office: 3801 PGA Blvd Ste 904 Palm Beach Gardens FL 33410 Office Phone: 561-775-5880.

**MERGLER, NANCY L.,** academic administrator; BA in Psychology, Syracuse U., 1972, MA in Developmental Psychology, 1975, PhD in Developmental Psychology, 1977. Tchg. asst. dept. psychology Syracuse U., 1973—75; asst. prof. dept. psychology Washington Coll., 1976—83, assoc. prof., 1984—94; prof. dept. psychology U. Okla., 1995—, sr. v.p., provost, 1995—. Contbr. articles to profl. jours. Mem.: APA, Okla. Psychol. Assn., Southwestern Psychol. Assn., Ea. Psychol. Assn., Gerontol. Soc. Office: Provosts Office 104 Evans Hall Univ Okla Norman OK 73019-0390

**MERIAM, THOMAS C.,** lawyer; b. Oceanside, NY, Aug. 3, 1951; BA, Coll. Holy Cross, 1973; JD cum laude, Fordham U., 1976. Bar: NY 1977. Ptnr. Chadbourne & Parke LLP, NYC, 1988—, chmn., Bank Fin. Practice Group. Contbr. articles to profl. jour. Mem.: ABA, NY State Bar Assn. Office: Chadbourne & Parke LLP 30 Rockefeller Plz Fl 31 New York NY 10112-0129 Office Phone: 212-408-5355. Office Fax: 212-541-5369. Business E-Mail: tmeriam@chadbourne.com.

**MERIDEN, TERRY,** physician; b. Damascus, Syria, Oct. 12, 1946; arrived in U.S., 1975; s. Izzat and Omayma (Aidi) Meriden; m. Lena Kahal, Nov. 17, 1975; children: Zina, Lana. BS, Sch. Sci., Damascus, 1968; MD, Sch. Medicine, Damascus, 1972, doctorate cum laude, 1973. Diplomate Am. Bd. Internal Medicine. Resident in infectious diseases Rush Green Hosp., Romford, Eng., 1973; house officer in internal medicine and cardiology Ashford Group Univ. Hosps., England, 1973-74; sr. house officer in internal medicine and neurology Grimsby Group Univ. Hosps., England, 1974; registrar in internal medicine and rheumatology St. Annes Hosp., London, 1974-75; jr. resident in internal medicine Shadyside Hosp., Pitts., 1975-76, sr. resident in internal medicine, 1976-77; fellow in endocrinology and metabolism Shadyside Hosp. and Grad. Inst., Pitts., 1976-77; clin. instr. U. Ill., Peoria, 1979; pres. Am. Diabetes Assn., Peoria, 1982-84; dir. Proctor Diabetes Unit, Peoria, 1984—, 1984—. Adviser Gov. of Ill. on diabetes. Mem. editl. bd. Diabetes Forecast mag., Clin. Diabetes, 1990; contbr. articles to profl. jours. Fellow: ACP, Am. Coll. Endocrinology; mem.: ADA (chmn. profl. edn. and rsch. 1980—, mem. editl. bd., mem. Spanish lit. bd., nat. bd. dirs. 1986—, vice chmn. nat. com. on diabetes edn. and affiliate svcs. 1986—), Outstanding Svc. award 1984, Outstanding Diabetes Educator award 1986), AMA (Recognition award 1985), Am. Coll. Endocrinology, Am. Assn. Clin. Endocrinology (founding), Am. Cancer Soc. (Life Line award 1983), Obesity Found. (Century award 1984, Recognition award 1985). Home: 115 E Coventry Ln Peoria IL 61614-2103 Office: 900 Main St Ste 300 Peoria IL 61602-1049 Office Phone: 309-673-1717. Business E-Mail: tmeriden@aol.com.

**MERIDETH, SUSAN CAROL,** business administration educator; b. St. Louis, May 25, 1956; d. George Getzel Brody and Jacquie Jean Lammers; m. John Wolf Merideth, July 28, 1979; children: Laura, Michelle. AAS, St. Louis C.C., 1977; BS, Fontbonne U., 1979; Master of Bus. Adminstrn., Maryville U., 1994. Presch. tchr. various instns., San Diego, 1979—82, Greater San Diego Health Plan, San Diego, 1985—87; supr. Cmty. Care Network, San Diego, 1987—90; mgr. St. John's Mercy Med. Ctr., St. Louis, 1990—95; contracts mgr. Nashua Eye Assocs., Nashua, 1996—98; practice mgr. Found. Med. Ptnrs., Nashua, 1998—99; assoc. prof. bus. adminstrn. Hesser Coll., Manchester, NH, 2000—. Mem.: AAUP, Nat. Bus. Edn. Assn., New England Regional Adv. Bd., Phi Theta Kappa (faculty advisor Alpha Nu Upsilon chpt. 2002—, mem. Pi Kappa chpt.). Office: Hesser Coll 3 Sundial Ave Manchester NH 03103 Office Phone: 603-668-6660. Business E-Mail: susan.merideth@ptk.org.

**MERIN, MITCHELL M,** corporate financial executive; Grad., Trinity Coll., 1975. Pres., dir. Morgan Stanley Investment Advisors, Inc., 1997—98; pres., COO, investment mgmt. Morgan Stanely, 1998—; CEO Morgan Stanley Investment Advisors, Inc., 1998—, pres. for various companies of, 1999—, CEO for various companies of, 2002—. Office: Morgan Stanley 1585 Broadway New York NY 10036

**MERINI, RAFIKA,** humanities educator, writer, language educator; b. Morocco; arrived in U.S., 1972; d. Mohamed M. and Fatima Merini. BA in English cum laude, U. Utah, 1978, MA in Romance Langs. and Lits., 1981; postgrad., U. Wash., 1980-82; cert. in translation, SUNY, Binghamton, 1988, PhD in Comparative Lit., 1992. Tchg. asst. U. Utah, Salt Lake City, 1978-80, U. Wash., Seattle, 1980-82; adminstrv. asst., tchr. French, interpreter The Lang. Sch., Seattle, 1982-83; lectr. Pacific Luth. U., Tacoma, 1983; instr. French and Spanish Ft. Steilacoom C.C. (now Pierce C.C.), 1983—85; tchg. asst. dept. romance langs. SUNY, Binghamton, 1985-87, tchg. asst. women's studies dept., 1988, tchg. asst. comparative lit. dept., 1986-88; vis. instr. humanities and French Union Coll., Schenectady, NY, 1988—89; vis. instr. dept. fgn. langs. and lits. Skidmore Coll., Saratoga Springs, NY, 1989-90; asst. prof. dept. modern and classical langs. State U. Coll., Buffalo, 1990—96,

assoc. prof. dept. modern and classical langs., 1996—. Coord. Buffalo State Coll. women's studies interdisciplinary unit State U. Coll., Buffalo, 1993-99, adviser French Club, 1990-93; founder, dir. Trois-Pistoles French Immersion Program, U. Western Ont.-Buffalo State Coll., London, 1994, 95; presenter, spkr., conf. organizer in field. Author: Two Major Francophone Women Writers, Assia Djébar and Leïla Sebbar: A Thematic Study of Their Works, 1999, 2d printing, paperback edit., 2001; mem. editl. bd. Jour. Middle Eastern and North African Intellectual and Cultural Studies; contbr. articles to profl. jours Grantee Nat. Defense Student award U. Utah, 1974; also numerous other grants and awards. Mem. MLA, Women in French, Pi Delta Phi. Office: State Univ Coll-Buffalo Modern & Classical Langs 1300 Elmwood Ave Buffalo NY 14222-1095 E-mail: merinir@buffalostate.edu.

**MERINO, FERNANDO,** economist, researcher, educator; b. Alicante, Spain, Nov. 7, 1966; s. Cipriano and Esperanza (De Lucas) M. B in Econs., U. de Alicante, 1989; MSc in Econs., Ctr. Monetary and Fin. Study, Madrid, 1991; PhD in Econs., U. de Alcala, 2001. Econs. rschr. Fundacion Empresa Publica, Madrid, 1992—; assoc. prof. U. de Alcala, 1995—. Co-author: Las Empresas Industriales Espanolas, 1992, rev. edit., 1995::; contbr. articles to profl. jours. including Strategic Mgmt. Jour., Barcelona Mgmt. Rev., The Econ. Jour. Office: Fundacion Empresa Publica Quintana 2 3rd E-28008 Madrid Spain Fax: 34 91-5488359.

**MERINO, JUNIOR,** mixologist; Server asst. Boulevard Café, NYC, 1993, bartender, mgr.; wine, bar menu designer Roth's Westside Stakehouse, NYC; sommerlier Terrace 5, NYC, 2005, The Modern, NYC, 2005—. Named Master Mixologist, Cocktail Times; named one of NYC's Rising Stars, StarChefs.com, 2006; recipient Award of Excellence, Wine Spectator. Office: The Modern 11 W 53rd St New York NY 10019 Office Phone: 212-333-1220.*

**MERIWETHER, HEATH J.,** newspaper consultant, retired newspaper publisher; b. Columbia, Mo., Jan. 20, 1944; s. Nelson Heath and Mary Agnes (Immele) Meriwether; m. Patricia Hughes, May 4, 1979; children: Graham, Elizabeth. BA in History, BJ, U. Mo., 1966; MAT, Harvard U., 1967; Advanced Exec. Program, Northwestern U. Journalism fellow Stanford U.; reporter Miami (Fla.) Herald, 1970—72, editor Broward and Palm Beach burs., 1972—77, exec. city editor, 1977—79, asst. mgr. editor news, 1979—80, mng. editor, 1981—83, exec. editor, 1983—87, Detroit Free Press, 1987—95, pub. 1996—2004; newspaper cons., 2004—. Chair Rails to Trails Conservancy. Lt. USNR, 1967—70. Office: 217 River Rd Nyack NY 10960 E-mail: hmeriwether@knightridder.com.

**MERK, FREDERICK BANNISTER,** biomedical educator, researcher; b. Cambridge, Mass., Feb. 21, 1936; s. Frederick and Lois Alberta (Bannister) M.; m. Linda Jean Poole, Oct. 22, 1966 (dec. Dec. 1994); children: John F., R. Daniel; m. Laura Ann Bradford, July 11, 1998; 1 stepchild, Letty A. Bradford. AB, Harvard Coll., 1958; PhD, Boston U., 1971. Asst. prof. pathology Boston U. Sch. Medicine, 1972-73; assoc. prof. dept. pathology Tufts U. Sch. Medicine, Boston, 1973—2002, assoc. prof. dept. anatomy, 1973—2002, emeritus prof. pathology and anatomy, 2002—, part time tchr. anatomy, 2002—; dir. electron microscopy facility, 1975-85. Cons. electron microscopy Mass. Gen. Hosp., Boston, 1964-85; cons. toxicol. testing Transgenic Scis., Worcester, Mass., 1988-91, U.S. Army, 1998-2001. Contbr. more than 60 articles to profl. jours. Trustee Broadway United Meth. Ch., Lynn, Mass., chmn. 1994-2000; lay rep. Grace United Meth. Ch. to ann. New Eng. Conf., 2000—; trustee Frederick and Paula Anna Markus Found., Audubon Soc., Moultonboro, NH, 2005—. Recipient Disting. Career in Tchr. award, 2002; grantee, NIH, 1994—98. Mem. Am. Soc. Cell Biology, Fedn. Am. Soc. Exptl. Biology, Am. Assn. Anatomists, Microscopy Soc. Am., Boston Cancer Rsch. Assn., Sigma Xi. Achievements include research on biology of cells in target organs responding to hormones with emphasis on benign prostatic hypertrophy (enlargement) and prostate cancer. Avocations: gardening, photography, swimming, scuba diving. Home: 28 Warwick Rd Melrose MA 02176 Office: Tufts Univ Sch Medicine Dept Anatomy 136 Harrison Ave Boston MA 02111-1800 Personal E-mail: fmerk@hotmail.com.

**MERK, P. EVELYN,** librarian; b. Macon, Ga., Dec. 8, 1943; d. Charlie B. and Gladys (Perry) M. BA, Mercer U., 1966; MEd, U. Ga., 1973; MLS, Emory U., 1987. Tchr. East Laurens High Sch., Dublin, Ga., 1966-68, Westside Sch., McDonough, Ga., 1968-70, Brantley County High Sch., Nahunta, Ga., 1970-72; sch. media specialist Mary Persons Sch., Forsyth, Ga., 1973-75; tech. services librarian Houston County Pub. Library, Warner Robins, Ga., 1975-76, reference librarian, 1976-77, libr., 1977—96, asst. dir., 1996—2002, libr. cons./trainer, 2002—. Bd. dirs. Warner Robins Day Care Ctr. Inc., chmn. 1984-85, 91. Mem. ALA, AAUW, Southeastern Library Assn., Ga. Library Assn., Warner Robins Pioneers. Avocations: reading, candle making. Home: 293 Peachtree Cir Warner Robins GA 31088-4448 Office: Houston County Pub Libr 721 Watson Blvd Warner Robins GA 31093-3413 E-mail: evelynmerk@aol.com.

**MERKEN, LEO,** lawyer; b. Paris, Feb. 14, 1964; arrived in U.S., 1982; m. Euginia Chen, Nov. 9, 1990; children: Madeleine Chen, Daniel Chen. BA, Occidental Coll., 1985; BS, Calif. Inst. Tech., 1987; MS, U. Calif., Berkeley, 1988; JD, Columbia U., 1995. Bar: U.S. Patent and Trademark Office 1997. Mem. tech. staff, cognizant engr. Jet Propulsion Lab. NASA, Pasadena, Calif., 1989—92; assoc., ptnr. Pennie & Edmonds LLP, N.Y.C., 1995—2003; ptnr. Jones Day, N.Y.C., 2004—. Harlan Fiske Stone scholar, Columbia U. Law Sch., 1995. Mem.: ABA, N.Y. Intellectual Property Law Assn., Am. Intellecutal Property Law Assn., Caltech Alumni Assn. (life), Jones Day N.Y. Ice Hockey Club. Achievements include contributions to the launch and flight operations on the Galileo spacecraft mission. Avocations: travel, ice hockey, soccer. Office: Jones Day 3 Park Plz Irvine CA 92614 Office Phone: 949-851-3939. Business E-mail: leo.merken@jonesday.com.

**MERKER, STEVEN JOSEPH,** lawyer; b. Cleve., Feb. 21, 1947; s. Steven Joseph and Laverne (Zamenik) Merker; m. Janet L. Whyatt; children: Steven, Rena, Ashley, Matthew. BS, Case Inst. Tech., 1968; MS, U. Fla., 1973; JD, George Washington U., 1976. Bar: Ohio 1976, U.S. Dist. Ct. (no. dist.) Ohio 1976, U.S. Dist. Ct. Colo. 1979, U.S. Ct. Appeals (10th cir.) 1979, U.S. Supreme Ct. 1989, U.S. Patent & Trademark Office. Assoc. Jones, Day, Reavis & Pogue, Cleve., 1976-78, Davis, Graham & Stubbs, Denver, 1978-82, ptnr., 1983-96, chmn. labor and employment group, 1989-96; chmn. litig., labor and employment groups Merrick, Calvin & Merker, LLP, 1996-97; ptnr. Dorsey & Whitney LLP, Denver, 1997—, mng. ptnr. Denver office, 2000—. Mem. Tenth Cir. Adv. Com., 1997—2000. Bd. dirs. Very Spl. Arts, Colo., 1994—, Am. Liver Found., 2002—; legal counsel Coloradans for Lamm-Dick campaign, Denver, 1982, Nancy Dick for US Senate Com., Denver, 1984, Cantrell for Dist. Atty., Jefferson County, Colo., 1984. Capt. USAF, 1969—72. Mem.: ABA, Denver Bar Assn., Colo. Bar Assn. Office: Dorsey & Whitney LLP 370 17th St Ste 4700 Denver CO 80202-5644 Office Phone: 303-628-1514. Business E-Mail: merker.steve@dorsey.com.

**MERKERSON, S. EPATHA,** actress; b. Saginaw, Mich., Nov. 28, 1952; BFA, Wayne State U. Broadway and Off-Broadway productions include The Piano Lesson, I'm Not Stupid (Obie award 1992), The Old Settler, Birdie Blue, 2005 (OBIE award Village Voice 2006); appeared in films including Terminator II, Jacob's Ladder, Navy Seals, Loose Cannons, Random Hearts, 1999, The Rising Place, 2001, Radio, 2003, Jersey Girl, 2004; television guest appearances include The Cosby Show, Equal Justice, Elysian Fields, Moe's World; television series roles include Pee Wee's Playhouse, Mann & Machine, Here & Now, Law & Order (Outstanding Supporting Actress in a Drama Series, NAACP Image award, 2006), A Place for Annie, 1994, A Mother's Prayer, 1995, Breaking Through, 1996, An Unexpected Life, 1998, Exiled, 1998, Lackawanna Blues, 2005 (Emmy award for outstanding lead actress in a miniseries or a movie, 2005, best performance by an actress in a mini-series or motion picture made for television, Hollywood Fgn. Press Assn. (Golden Globe award), 2006, outstanding performance by an female actor in a TV movie or miniseries, Screen Actors Guild award, 2006,

Outstanding Actress in a TV Movie, Mini-Series, or Dramatic Spl., NAACP Image awards, 2006). Nominated for Tony award, 1990, Drama Desk award, 1990, Helen Hayes award, 1990, L.A. Theater Critics award, 1990. Office: Law & Order c/o Universal Television 100 Universal City Plz Universal City CA 91608-1002*

**MERKIN, ALBERT CHARLES,** pediatrician, allergist; b. Chgo., Sept. 4, 1924; s. Harry A. and Goldie (Lamasky) M.; m. Eunice Aprill, Aug. 22, 1948; children: Audrey, Ellen, Joseph. Student, U. Ill., 1942-44; MD, U. Ill., Chgo., 1949. Diplomate Am. Bd. Allergy and Immunology, Am. Bd. Pediat. Intern, resident Cook County Hosp., Chgo.; resident Children's Meml. Hosp., Chgo.; with Valley Pediatric and Allergy Clinic, Las Vegas, Nev. Capt. USAF, 1950-53. Fellow Am. Acad. Pediatrics (state chmn. Nev. 1961-64, sect. allergy and immunology), Am. Coll. Allergy; mem. Am. Acad. Allergy, Allergy Subsplty. Group of Acad. Pediatrics (cert. pediatric allergist). Avocations: reading, travel. Office: Valley Pediat & Allergy Clinic 222 S Rainbow Blvd Ste 119 Las Vegas NV 89145-5343

**MERKIN, WILLIAM LESLIE,** retired lawyer; b. NYC, Apr. 30, 1929; s. Jules Leo Merkin and Rae (Levine) Lesser; children: Monica Jo, Lance Jeffrey, Tiffany Dawn. BA, U. Tex., Austin, 1950; JD, St. Mary's U., San Antonio, 1953. Bar: Tex. 1953, U.S. Ct. Mil. Appeals 1954, U.S. Dist. Ct. (we. dist.) Tex. 1957, U.S. Ct. Appeals (5th cir.) 1969, U.S. Supreme Ct. 1970. Pvt. practice, El Paso, Tex., 1956-71; sr. ptnr. Merkin & Gibson, El Paso, Tex., 1972-78, Merkin, Hines & Pasqualone, El Paso, Tex., 1978-90; ret. Lectr. U. Tex.-El Paso, 1978—; cons. in field. Served to capt. JAGC, U.S. Army, 1953-56. Mem. Tex. State Bar Assn., Soc. Profls. in Dispute Resolution, Am. Trial Lawyers Assn., Tex. Trial Lawyers Assn., Common Cause, Internat. Wine and Food Soc. (pres. 1979-80), Am. Arbitration Assn. (part-time arbitrator), Nat. Assn. Securities Dealers (part-time arbitrator), Del Norte Club (El Paso), B'nai B'rith (pres. 1961-62), Phi Delta Phi. Home: 1442 Seacoast Dr Imperial Beach CA 91932-3183 Office Phone: 619-423-1718.

**MERLE, H. ETIENNE,** restaurateur; b. N.Y.C., July 8, 1944; s. Pierre and Josephine Merle. BS, Cornell U., 1969. Mgr. food and beverage DiviDivi Beach Hotel, Aruba, 1969-70; restaurant mgr., chmn. food dept. Tng. Resources for Youth, N.Y.C., 1971; gen. mgr. L'Auberge du Cochon Rouge, Ithaca, N.Y., 1971-92; v.p. Pascale Wine Bar and Restaurant, Syracuse, N.Y., 1982-94; splty. foods broker, pres. Shineola & Assocs., Ithaca, NY, 1999—. Ops. cons. Merle & Roy Assocs., N.Y.C., 1975—; chef, operator Atelier Etienne Corp., Valentine Café, Ithaca, N.Y., 1999-2003. Mem. Cornell Hotel Soc., Chefs de Cuisine Assn. Am., Soc. Culinaire Philanthropique, L'Union Francaise (pres. 1975, 76, 86, 91—). Home: 1146 Danby Rd Ithaca NY 14850-9406 Office: PO Box 6769 Ithaca NY 14851-6769 Office Phone: 607-227-2269.

**MERLIN, LISA RUTH,** neurologist, researcher; d. Walter and Isabel Merlin; m. Bruce Kiel, June 27, 2000; 1 child, Allison Elizabeth Kiel. BA, CUNY Bklyn. Coll., 1983; MD, SUNY Downstate Med. Ctr., Bklyn., 1986. Diplomate Nat. Bd. Med. Examiners, 1987; cert. in neurology Am. Bd. Psychiatry and Neurology, 1991. Intern in internal medicine Brookdale Hosp. Med. Ctr., Bklyn., 1986—87; resident in neurology SUNY Downstate, Bklyn., 1987—90, clin. asst. prof. neurology, 1990—93, asst. prof. neurology and pharmacology, 1993—98, assoc. prof. neurology, physiology and pharmacology, 1998—2004, prof. neurology, physiology and pharmacology, 2004—. Dir. neurology outpatient svcs. Kings County Hosp., Bklyn., 1992—95; dir. adult neurology residency tng. program SUNY Downstate Kings County, 1995—2002; study sect. mem. NIH, Washington, 2001—03; dir. clin. neurosciences pathway med. student programs SUNY Downstate Coll. Medicine, Bklyn., 2004—. Contbr. scientific papers to profl. jours. Recipient Chancellor's Excellence in Tchg. award, SUNY, 2004; grantee Clin. Rsch. Assoc. award, SUNY Downstate, 1992—94, PhRMA Found., 1996—98, Epilepsy Found. Am., 1996—97, Mentored Clin. Scientist Devel. award, NIH, 1996—2002, Ind. Rsch. Grant, 2001—07, Novartis Pharmaceuticals, 2005—06. Fellow: Am. Acad. Neurology (Dreifuss-Penry Epilepsy award 2002); mem.: Am. Neurol. Assn., Soc. Neuroscience, Assn. U. Professors of Neurology, Am. Epilepsy Soc., Alpha Omega Alpha. Achievements include discovery of role of group I metabotropic glutamate receptors in epileptogenesis. Office: SUNY Downstate Med Ctr 450 Clarkson Ave Box 29 Brooklyn NY 11203 Office Fax: 718-270-2241.

**MERLINO, GLENN T.,** medical researcher; BA, Adelphi U., LI, 1975; PhD, U. Mich., Ann Arbor, 1980. Lab. technician NY State Inst. Basic Rsch. in Mental Retardation, 1974—75; grad. fellow Cellular and Molecular Biology Dept. U. Mich., 1975—80; postdoctoral fellow Nat. Cancer Inst., 1980—82, staff fellow Lab. Molecular Biology, 1982—92, sr. investigator Lab. Molecular Biology; now chief Lab. Cell Regulation and Carcinogenesis Ctr. Cancer Rsch., Nat. Cancer Inst., also head Molecular Genetics Group, Lab. Cell Regulation and Carcinogenesis. Past adj. assoc. prof. Dept. Biochemistry George Washington U.; past adj. assoc. prof. Dept. Pathology Georgetown U. Mem.: AAAS, Am. Soc. Investigative Pathology, Am. Assn. Cancer Rsch. Office: Lab Cell Regulation and Carcinogenesis Ctr Cancer Rsch 37 Convent Dr Bldg 37 Rm 5002 Bethesda MD 20892-4264 Office Phone: 301-496-4270. Office Fax: 301-480-7618. E-mail: gmerlino@helix.nih.gov.

**MERLO, LARRY J.,** retail executive; Sr. v.p. stores CVS Pharmacy, Inc., Woonsocket, RI, 1994—98, exec. v.p. stores CVS Corp., Woonsocket, 2000—. Office: CVS Corp Corp Hdqrs 1 CVS Dr Woonsocket RI 02895

**MERMANN, ALAN CAMERON,** retired pediatric educator, chaplain; b. Bklyn., June 23, 1923; s. William Joseph and Ada Fischer (McCrea) M; m Constance Burnou, Sept. 4, 1948 (div. Mar. 1988); children: Edith, Constance, Sarah, Elizabeth; m. Cecily Allen Reynolds, Apr. 15, 1989. BA, Lehigh U., 1943; MD, Johns Hopkins U., 1947; MDiv, Yale U., 1979, MST, 1988, MA, 1999. Diplomate Am. Bd. Pediatrics; med. license, Conn.; ordained to Christian ministry, United Ch. of Christ, 1979. Intern pediatrics Bellevue Hosp., N.Y.C., 1947-48, Johns Hopkins Hosp., Balt., 1948-49; sr. asst. resident pediatrician N.Y. Hosp., N.Y.C., 1949-50; resident pediatrician Meml. Hosp., N.Y.C., 1950-51; rsch. fellow Sloane-Kettering Inst., N.Y.C., 1953-54; pvt. practice pediatrics Guilford, Conn., 1954-82; clin. instr. pediatrics Yale Sch. Medicine, 1954-59, asst. clin. prof. pediatrics, 1959-71, assoc. clin. prof. pediatrics, 1971-79, clin. prof. pediatrics, 1979—2000. Trustee New Eng. Coll., Henniker, N.H., 1969-91; fellow Branford Coll. Yale U., 1979-00; mem. instnl. rev. bd. Union Carbide Corp., Danbury, Conn., 1991—98; lectr. pastoral theology Yale Divinity Sch., 1979-82; asst. pastor First Congregational Ch., Guilford, 1979-82; assoc. pastor Ch. of Christ Congl., United Ch. of Christ, Norfolk, Conn., 1995—2003; chaplain Yale Sch. Medicine, 1982-00, human investigation com., 1983-91, med. ctr. bioethics com., chair pediatrics ethics com., sch. medicine admissions com., com. on well-being of students. Author: Some Chose to Stay: Faith and Ethics in a Time of Plague, 1997, To Do No Harm: Learning to Care for the Seriously Ill, 1999; contbr. articles to profl. jours. Lt. USNR, 1951-53. Fellow Am. Acad. Pediatrics. Democrat. Avocations: dixieland, jazz, gardening. Home: 185 Ashpohtag Rd Norfolk CT 06058

**MEROLLA, CAROL ANN,** writer, consultant; b. Providence, R.I., Aug. 8, 1945; d. Ralph Thomas and Lena Marie Biccicco; m. Anthony Joseph Merolla, May 30, 1964; children: Anthony, Kevin, Kimberly. Diploma, St. Joseph Sch. Nursing, R.I., 1981, U. R.I., 1991, Sch. Children's Lit., 2002. Office mgr. Fabro, Inc., Providence, 1964—80; nurse Cherry Hill Manor, Johnston, RI, 1981—82; pvt. duty nurse self-employed, North Scituate, RI, 1983—86; therapy asst. Providence Phys. Therapy, Warwick, RI, 1987—88; therapy asst., office mgr. Garden City Phys. Therapy, Cranston, RI, 1989—94; office mgr. AFD, Inc., Providence, 1995—; freelance writer self-employed, Johnston, RI, 1994—. Author: (book of poetry) Quiet Reflections, 1999, The Time of Christmas, 2000, The Power of the Pen, 2001, Walk Beside Me, 2002, Scenes of Nature, 2004, (preschool fiction) Two Kittens for Kim, 2002, Sammy and Mouse, 2002, (preteen non-ficiton) Letters to God, 2003, (preschool fiction) Bird in the Bush, 2004. Instr. exercise pool program Muscular Dystophy C.C., RI, 1980—81; capt. Am. Cancer oc., N.Y.C., 1962—64, 1980—83; vol. Salvation Army, North Providence, RI, 1997—; catechist tchr. St. Robert Bellarmine Parish, Johnston, 2004—. Mem.: Soc. Children's Book Writers & Illustrators (assoc. writer 2001—), Internet Soc. Poets (poet laureate 1998—), Poetic award 2002, 2003), Nat. Authors Registry (life Pres. award of lit. excellence for poems 2000, 2002). Republican. Roman Catholic. Avocations: walking, photography, swimming, illustration, recreational programs for seniors. Home and Office: 682 Greenville Ave Johnston RI 02919 Office Phone: 401-231-5083. Office Fax: 401-946-8036. E-mail: afd10@cox.net.

**MERON, THEODOR,** judge, law educator, researcher; b. Kalisz, Poland, Apr. 28, 1930; came to U.S., 1978, naturalized, 1984; s. Yhiel and Bluma (Lipschitz) Znamirowski; m. Monique Jonquet, Mar. 13, 1981; children: Daniel, Amos. M.J., Hebrew U., 1954; LL.M., Harvard U., 1955, S.JD, 1957; diploma in Pub. Internat. Law, Cambridge U., Eng., 1957. Bar: Israel 1971, N.Y. 1984. Legal advisor to Fgn. Ministry of Israel, 1967-71; Israeli ambassador to Can., 1971-75; permanent rep. U.N., Geneva, 1977; prof. law NYU Law Sch., NYC, 1977—94, Charles L. Denison prof., 1994—2005, Charles L. Denison prof. emeritus, 2006—. Carnegie lectr. Hague Acad. Internat. Law, 1980; Sir Hersch Lauterpacht Meml. lectr.; vis. fellow All Souls Coll., Oxford U., England, Max-Planck Inst., Heidelberg, Germany; vis. prof. Grad. Inst. Internat. Studies, Geneva, prof. law, 1991—95; pub. mem. U.S. Del. Conf. on Human Dimension Conf. on Security and Coop. in Europe, Copenhagen, 1998; mem. U.S. del. Rome Diplomatic Conf. on the Establishment of an Internat. Criminal Ct.; vis. prof. law Harvard U., Berkeley Law Sch.; counselor on internat. law U.S. Dept. State, 2000—01; judge appeals chamber Internat. Criminal Tribunal for former Yugoslavia, 2001—, Internat. Criminal Tribunal for Rwanda, 2001—, pres., 2003—05. Author: Investment Insurance in International Law, 1976, The United Nations Secretariat, 1977, Human Rights Law-Making in the United Nations, 1986, Human Rights in Internal Strife: Their International Protection, 1987, Human Rights and Humanitarian Norms as Customary Law, 1989, Henry's Wars and Shakespeare's Laws, 1993, Bloody Constraint: War and Chivalry in Shakespeare, 1998, International Law in the Age of Human Rights, 2004, The Humanization of International Law, 2006; editor: Human Rights in International Law, 1984; editor in chief: Am. Jour. Internat. Law, 1993-88; contbr. articles to profl. jours. Rockefeller Found. fellow, 1975-76; Humanitarian Trust student Cambridge U., 1956-57; recipient Rule of Law award, Internat. Bar Assn., 2004. Mem.: Inst. Internat. Law, Internat. Law Assn., Coun. on Fgn. Rels., Inst. Internat. Humanitarian Law, French Inst. Internat. Law, Am. Soc. Internat. Law (Cert. Merit 1987, Hudson medal 2006), UN Assn. US (hon.). Office: NYU Law Sch 40 Washington Sq S New York NY 10012-1099 also: Churchillplein 2501 EW The Hague Netherlands E-mail: meront@un.org.

**MEROPOL, NEAL J.,** oncologist, researcher; AB, Princeton U., 1981; MD, Vanderbilt U., 1985. Intern, resident in internal medicine Case Western Res. U., Cleve., 1985—88; fellow in med. oncology and hematology U. Pa., Phila., 1988—92; asst. prof. medicine Roswell Park Cancer Inst., 1992—98; dir. Gastrointestinal Cancer Program Fox Chase Cancer Ctr., Phila., 1998—. Prof. medicine Temple U. Sch. Medicine, 2006—. Office: Fox Chase Cancer Ctr 333 Cottman Ave Philadelphia PA 19111

**MEROW, JAMES F.,** federal judge; AB, George Washington U., 1953, JD, 1956. Bar: Va., 1956, DC, 1958. Trial atty., br. dir., civil divsn. US Dept. Justice, Washington, 1959-78; trial judge US Ct. Claims, Washington, 1978-82; judge US Ct. Fed. Claims, Washington, 1982—. With JAGC, U.S. Army, 1956-59. Mem. ABA, Fed. Bar Assn., Va. State Bar, DC Bar. Office: US Ct Fed Claims 717 Madison Pl NW Washington DC 20005

**MEROW, JOHN,** lawyer; b. Little Valley, N.Y., Dec. 20, 1929; s. Luin George and Mildred Elizabeth Merow; m. Mary Alyce Smith, June 19, 1957; 1 child, Alison. Student, UCLA, 1947—48; BS in Engring., U. Mich., 1952; JD, Harvard U., 1958. Bar: N.Y. 1958, U.S. Supreme Ct. 1971. Assoc. Sullivan & Cromwell, N.Y.C., 1958-64, ptnr., 1965-96, vice chmn., 1986-87, chmn., sr. ptnr., 1987-94, sr. counsel, 1997—. Bd. dirs. Seligman Group Investment Cos., Aleris Internat. Inc.; trustee, vice chmn. N.Y. Presbyn. Healthcare Sys., Inc.; trustee N.Y. Presbyn. Hosp.; trustee, sec. Friends of the Archbishop of Canterbury's Anglican Communion Fund. Chmn. bd. dirs. Am.-Australian Assn., 1986—99; bd. dirs. Mcpl. Art Soc. N.Y.; mem. exec. com., sec. U.S Coun. Internat. Bus.; bd. dirs., sec. Met. Opera Club, 1986—94; trustee Anglican Investment Agy. Trust. Lt. USN, 1952—55. Named hon. officer Order of Australia. Mem. Am. Law Inst. (advisor corp. governance project 1978-92), Coun. on Fgn. Rels., Soc. Mayflower Desc., Links Club, Pilgrims, Piping Rock Club, Down Town Assn., Union Club, Griffis Faculty Club, River Club. Home: 435 E 52d St New York NY 10022 also: 51 Fruitledge Rd Glen Head NY 11545-3316 Office: Sullivan & Cromwell LLP 125 Broad St New York NY 10004-2498 Office Phone: 212-558-3616. E-mail: merowj@sullcrom.com.

**MERRELL, JAMES LEE,** writer, minister; b. Indpls., Oct. 24, 1930; s. Mark W. and Pauline F. (Tucker) M.; m. Barbara Jean Burch, Dec. 23, 1951; children: Deborah Lea Merrell Griffin, Cynthia Lynn Archer, Stuart Allen. AB, Ind. U., 1952; MDiv, Christian Theol. Sem., 1956; LittD, Culver-Stockton Coll., 1972. Ordained to ministry Christian Ch., 1955; asso. editor World Call, Indpls., 1956-66, editor, 1971-73; pastor Crestview Christian Ch., Indpls., 1966-71; editor The Disciple, St. Louis, 1974-89; sr. v.p. Christian Bd. Publ., 1976-89; sr. minister Affton Christian Ch., St. Louis, 1989-94; interim chaplain Culver-Stockton Coll., Canton, Mo., 1995; interim sr. pastor Friedens United Ch. of Christ, Warrenton, Mo., 1995-98, St. Johns United Ch. of Christ, Mehlville, Mo., 1998—2002, Hamilton Christian Ch., Creve Coeur, 2002—03, Redeemer Evang. Ch., St. Louis, 2003—05, Trinity United Ch. Christ, 2005—. Bd. dirs Horizons mag., 1995-98. Author: They Live Their Faith, 1965, The Power of One, 1976, Discover the Word in Print, 1979, Finding Faith in the Headlines, 1985, We Claim Our Heritage, 1992, Seeing Life: Finding God, 2006. Chmn. bd. Kennedy Meml. Christian Home, Martinsville, Ind., 1971-73; trustee Christian Theol. Sem., 1978-81. Recipient Faith and Freedom award Religious Heritage of Am., 1983; lifetime achievement award Mo. State Sen., 2000. Mem. Associated Ch. Press (award 1973, 79, 80, 81, 82, dir. 1974-75, 78-81, 1st v.p. 1983-85), Christian Theol. Sem. Alumni Assn. (pres. 1966-68), Religious Pub. Rels. Coun. (awards 1979, 80, 84, 87, 90, pres. St. Louis chpt. 1985-86), Sigma Delta Chi (award 1952), Theta Phi. Home: 248 Greycliff Bluff Dr Saint Louis MO 63129-5081 E-mail: JLeeMer@aol.com. *As a religious communicator and as a pastor, I have always believed in applying the same standards in the sacred realm as in the secular. I have tried to pursue the truth, to keep my constituency informed, to celebrate the noble in life, to fight against those who would lie, distort and hide God's truth in the name of some supposed good.*

**MERRELL, JESSE HOWARD,** writer; b. Shelby, Ala., Dec. 9, 1938; s. James Walton and Emma Thelma (Davis) M.; m. Betsy Lee Davis, Jan. 11, 1964 (div. 1979); children: Sandra, Mark, Brad, Carolyn, Gwen. Grad., Shelby High Sch., Columbiana, Ala., 1957. Pitcher Cin. Redlegs, 1958-62; reporter, news dir. WHAP Radio, Hopewell, Va., 1963; writer/editor Hopewell News, 1963-65; state editor Daily Progress, Charlottesville, Va., 1965-68; assoc. editor Transport Topics, Washington, 1968-75; spl. asst. to pres. Am. Trucking Assn., Washington, 1975-76; editor Transport Topics, Washington, 1976-77; pres. Merrell Ent., Washington, 1977—. Pub. rels. com. Am. Movers Conf., Washington, 1969-72; instr. Dale Carnegie courses, Washington, 1974-81, 1st pres., 1980-81; cons. Mid. Atlantic Conf., Riverdale, Md., 1981-82, Contract Carrier Conf., 1977-82; speechwriter ICC, Washington, 1982. Author: (novel) A Christmas Gift, 1979; syndicated columnist Religion and the Times, Washington Welter, (genealogy) The Merrells of Alabama, 1995, My Name is America! I Was Born at Jamestown!, 2002. Mem. Nat. Trust for Hist. Preservation, Assn. Preservation Va. Antiquities. With U.S. Army, 1960-62. Recipient George Washington Honor award Freedoms Found., 2002, Liberty award Congress of Freedom, Jackson, Miss., 1970, 71, Honor Cert., Freedoms Found., 1972, 1st place editorial

writing Va. Press Assn., 1965, 1st place news writing, 1966. Mem. Nat. Press Club, Assn. Preservation Va. Antiquities, Gen. Washington's Coun. of the 1607 Soc. (charter mem.). Regent's Circle of Mt. Vernon, Jamestown 2007 Spkrs. Bur., Jamestown-Yorktown Found., Colonial Williamsburg Raleigh Tavern Soc. Avocation: photography. Office: Merrell Ent 2610 Garfield St NW Washington DC 20008-4104

**MERRELL, RONALD CLIFTON,** surgeon, educator; b. Birmingham, Ala., June 18, 1946; s. Greene Lawrence and Florence (Jones) M.; m. Marsha Karen Cox, Dec. 24, 1966; children: Alexandria, Alison, R. Clifton. BS in Chemistry, U. Ala., 1967, MD, 1970. Diplomate Am. Bd. Surgery. Resident and fellow in surgery Wash. U., St. Louis, 1970-77; asst. prof. surgery Stanford U., Calif., 1979-84; assoc. prof. surgery U. Tex. Med. Sch., Houston, 1984-88, prof. surgery, 1988-94, M.D. Anderson Cancer Ctr., Houston, 1988-94; assoc. dean clin. affairs U. Tex. Med. Sch., Houston, 1988-92, vice dean, 1992-93; prof. surgery, chmn. dept. surgery Yale U., 1993—99; Stuart McGuire prof. surgery, chmn. dept. surgery Va. Commonwealth U., Richmond, 1999—2003, prof. surgery, 2003—; dir. Med. Informatics Tech. Applications Consortium, 1997—. Author 3 books; contbr. over 200 articles to profl jours., 30 chpts. to books. Maj. U.S. Army, 1977-79. Recipient Basil O'Connor award March of Dimes, 1979, Rsch. Career Devel. award NIH, 1979-84, Henry J. Kaiser award Stanford U., 1982, 83, John P. McGovern Outstanding Tchr. award U. Tex. Med. Sch., 1988, Dean's Teaching Excellence award, 1983-89, Pub. Svc. medal NASA, 1998, 2005, Disting. medal as Friend of Democritus, U. Greece, 1999; grantee NASA, Internat. Coop. medal, Russian Space Agy., 2005. Fellow ACS, Soc. Univ. Surgeons; mem. Am. Assn. Endocrine Surgery, Am. Surg. Assn., Alpha Omega Alpha. Democrat. Episcopalian. Achievements include research in telemedicine and in the transplantation of islets of Langerhans. Office: PO Box 980519 Richmond VA 23298-0519 Office Phone: 804-828-8000. E-mail: ronald.merrell@vcu.edu.

**MERRIAM, DANIEL F(RANCIS),** geologist; b. Omaha, Feb. 9, 1927; s. Faye Mills and Amanda Frances (Wood) M. m. Annie Laura Young, Feb. 12, 1946; children: Beth Ann, John Francis, Anita Pauline, James Daniel, Judith Diane. BS in Geology, U. Kans., 1949, MS, 1953, PhD, 1961; MSc in Geology, Leicester U., England, 1969; DSc, Leicester U., 1975. Geologist Union Oil Co. Calif., 1949-51, 52; asst. instr. U. Kans., 1951-53, instr., 1954, rsch. assoc., 1963-71; geologist Kans. Geol. Survey, 1953-58, head divsn. basic geology, 1958-63, chief geol. rsch., 1963-71; Jessie Page Heroy prof. geology dept. geology Syracuse U., 1971-81, chmn. dept. geology, 1971-80; Endowment Assn. Disting. prof. natural scis. dept. geology Wichita State U., 1981-93, chmn. dept. geology, 1981-87; sr. rsch. scientist Kans. Geol. Survey, U. Kans., 1993-97, emeritus, 1997—. Vis. rsch. scientist Stanford U., 1963; dir. Internat. Field Inst. to Japan, Am. Geol. Inst., 1967; vis. prof. geology Wichita State U., 1968-70; vis. geol. scientist Am. Geol. Inst., 1969; cons. nat. gas survey Fed. Power Commn., 1972-75, 78, chmn. supply tech. adv. com., 1975-77; ad hoc panel earth resources survey NAS/NRC, 1972-73, chmn. U.S. Nat. Com. for Internat. Geol. Correlation program, 1976-79, ex-officio, 1979-80, 81-83, U.S. Nat. Com. on History of Geology, 1989-95; Esso Disting. lectr. U. Sydney, Australia, 1979; mem. U.S. Nat. Commn. for UNESCO, U.S. Dept. State, 1979-85; vis. prof. Centre d'Informatique Geologique, Ecole des Mines de Paris, Fontainebleau, 1980; vis. sr. scientist Kans. Geol. Survey, 1990-91; vis. scientist GeoForschungsZentrum, Potsdam, Germany, 1992; adj. prof. Emporia State U., Kans., 1993—. Author: The Geologic History of Kansas: Kansas Geological Survey, 1963, (with J.W. Harbaugh) Computer Applications in Stratigraphic Analysis, 1968, Computer Fundamentals for Geologists: COMPuTe, 1975, Bibliography of Computer Applications in the Earth Sciences, 1988; founder, editor-in-chief Jour. Math. Geology, 1968-76, 94-97, Computers & Geosciences, 1975-95; founder, editor Kansas Geological Survey, Computer Contributions, 1966-71, Syracuse University Geological Contributions, 1973-81; editor (series) Computer Applications in the Earth Sciences, 1969—, Computers and Geology, 1976-90, Computer Methods in the Geosciences, 1982—, (books and vols.) Mathematical Models of Sedimentary Processes, 1972, The Impact of Quantification on Geology, 1974, Random Processes in Geology, 1976, Geomathematics: Past, Present, and Prospects, 1978, Down-to-Earth Statistics: Solutions Looking for Geological Problems, 1981, Current Trends in Geomathematics, 1988, (colloquium) Geostatistics, 1970; translation editor Statistics for Geoscientists, 1987; co-editor Pacific Geology, 1971-83; editl. cons. Geosystems, 1971-83; mem. editl. rev. bd. Colo. Sch. Mines Quarterly, 1974-90; mem. editl. adv. bd. Geophysical Computer Programs, 1975-76, Applied Geochemistry, 1985-93; mem. editl. bd. History of Earth Science Soc., 1982-2000; reviewer for nat. and internat. jours.; contbr. articles to numerous jours. Bd. dirs Kans Geol. Found., 1989-92. Fullbright-Hayes Sr. Rsch. fellow, U.K., 1964-65. Fellow AAAS (sr., electorate nomination com. 1977-80, chairperson sect. E 1983-84, Sci. software adv. panel 1986-91, SWARM 64th local arrangement com. chmn. 1988), Geol. Soc. Am. (sr., com. on publs. 1973-76, chmn. com. geology dept. 1975-78, history of geology divsn. nominating com. 2006), Geol. Soc. London (William Smith medal 1992), Sigma Xi (sec. Kansas chpt. 1994-96, pres. 1997-98); mem. Am. Assn. Petroleum Geologists (hon., chmn. 1954, 57, ednl. exhibits com., rsch. com., 1964-67, assoc. editor bulletin 1969-75, Geobyte 1985-92, computer applications in geology com. 1971-81, 86-89, N.Y. Dist. rep. 1974-76, Kans. Dist. rep. 1956-57, 1985-91, chmn. 1989-91, Kans. rep. Midcontinent sect. 1988-92, Disting. Svc. award 1987, Cert. of Merit 1987, 93), Soc. Econ. Paleontologists and Mineralogists (hon., chmn. organizer rsch. group in computer tech. 1970-75, 82-82, 89-90, publs. com. 1980-83, chmn. publs. 1981-82, chmn. Pa. Stratigraphy working group Midcontinent sect. 1986-96, ad. hoc. com. databases 1985-88, chmn databases 1986-88, organizer computer applications com. 1988-97, chmn. computer applications 1988-92, procedures com. 1989-2001, chmn 1993-94, spl. advisor headquarters and bus. com. 1988-91, chmn. 1991-98), Nat. Assn. Geology Tchrs. (v.p. Kans.-Okla. sect. 1986, pres. 1987-89, sec. 1994-2003), Geosci. Info. Soc. (program com 1980-81), Internat. Union Geol. Scis., Internat. Geol. Correlations Program (U.S. del. 1969, sec. com. 1975-79, 76-77, chmn. ad hoc com. publs. 1980, adv. bd. publs. 1989-90, chmn. 1980-84), Internat. Geol. Congress (alternate U.S. del. VII ordinary sessions coun. 1984, U.S. del. VIII ordinary sessions coun. 1989), Internat. Assn. Math. Geology (first hon. life mem., mem. coun. 1968—, sec.-gen. 1972-76, pres. 1976-80, interim archivist 1989-92, archivist 1992—, William Christian Krumbein medal 1981, pubs. com. 1997—, organizing com. 8th ann. meeting 2001), Leicester Geol. Soc. (hon. life 1965), Sylvester-Bradley Geol. Soc. (hon. v.p. 1978-79; gold medal 1970), Classification Soc. (chmn. mem. com., bd. dirs. 1968-71), N.Y. State Geol. Assn. (exec. sec. 1972-77, pres. 1977-78, bd. dirs. 1987-83), Kans. Geol. Soc. (hon., bd. dirs., dir. many confs., presdl. citation 1989, chmn future plans com. 1989), Kans. Acad. Sci. (life, mem. coun. at large 1983-86, v.p. 1987, pres.-elect 1988, pres. 1989, chmn. com for 2001, 1989-92, assoc. editor Transactions 1990-92, editor, 1992-2003, strategic planning com. 2000-02, com. chmn. 119th Ann. Meeting 1987, 131st Ann. Meeting 2002; cert. appreciation 2003), History of Earth Sci. Soc. (Earth Science History editl. bd. 1982-2000), Sigma Gamma Epsilon (pres. Alpha chpt. 1952-53, nat. coun. 1983-95, nat. pres. 1990-95, nat. editor The Compass, 1982-93, hon.), Phi Kappa Phi (life), Sigma Xi (Kans. chpt. sec. 1994-96, pres. 1997-98). Office: U Ks Kansas Geol Survey Lawrence KS 66047 Business E-Mail: dmerrian@kgs.ku.edu.

**MERRIAM, DWIGHT HAINES,** lawyer, land use planner; b. Norwood, Mass., Apr. 20, 1946; s. Austin Luther and Lillian Diana (Olsen) M.; m. Cynthia Ann Hayes, May 21, 1966 (div. June 1992); children: Sarah Ann Leilani, Jonathan Hayes; m. Susan Manning Standish, May 6, 1995; children: Alexander Harlan, Lucy Caroline. BA cum laude, U. Mass., 1968; M in Regional Planning, U.N.C., 1974; JD, Yale U., 1978. Bar: Conn. 1978, Mass. 1980, U.S. Dist. Ct. Conn. 1981, U.S. Dist. Ct. Hawaii 1984, U.S. Supreme Ct. 1990, U.S. Ct. Appeals (4th cir.) 1993. Land use planner Charles E. Downe, Newton, Mass., 1968; assoc. Byrne, Buck & Steiner, Farmington, Conn., 1978, Robinson, Robinson & Cole, Hartford, Conn., 1979-83; ptnr. Robinson & Cole LLP, Hartford, Conn., 1984—. Adj. prof. law Western New Eng. Coll., 1978-86, U. Conn., 1982, 84-87, Vt. Law Sch., 1994—; instr. planning U. Bridgeport, 1981-83, U. Conn., 1986-92; mem. faculty Nat. Coll. Dist.

Attys., 1983-87, Nat. Jud. Coll., 1994; mem. faculty Am. Law Inst.-ABA Land Use Inst., 1988—; instr. city and regional planning Memphis State U., 1989, 94; spkr. in field. Author: The Complete Guide to Zoning, 2005; co-author: The Takings Issue, 1999; co-editor: Inclusionary Zoning Moves Downtown, 1985, Eminent Domain Use and Abuse: Kelo in Context, 2006; contbr. more than 200 articles and book revs. to profl. jours. Bd. dirs. Conn. chpt. Appleseed Found., 1997-2000, Am. Boat Builders and Repairers Assn., 1995-1999, Growth Mgmt. Inst., Washington, 1992—, Housing Edn. Resource Ctr., 1984-88, Housing Coalition for Capitol Region, Inc., 1984-86; bd. dirs. Conn. Fund for Environment, 1981-85, legal adv. com., 1985-88, legal adv. bd., 1978-81; mem. Environment 2000 environ. plan adv. bd. Conn. Dept. Environ. Protection, 1987-91; assoc. Environ. Law Inst., 1987—; mem. housing task force Conn. Dept. on Aging, 1981; mem. Gov.'s Housing Task Force, Conn., 1980-81. With USN, 1968—75, Vietnam, capt. USNR, 1975-99. USNR, 1975—99. Fellow: Royal Inst. Chartered Land Surveyors, Am. Inst. Cert. Planners (pres. 1988—90); mem.: ABA (coun. mem. state and local govt. sect. 2000—), Am. Coll. Real Estate Lawyers, Assn. State Floodplain Mgrs., Internat. Mcpl. Law Assn. (chmn. sect. on zoning, planning and land devel. 1988—89, chmn. Conn. 1999—2003), Am. Planning Assn. (chmn. legis. com. Conn. chpt. 1978—80, exec. com. planning and law divsn. 1978—88, chmn. planning and law divsn. 1984—86, editl. adv. bd. 1984—92, bd. dirs. 1988—90), Conn. Bar Assn. (exec. com. zoning and planning sect. 1985—87, 1991—). Democrat. Unitarian Universalist. Avocations: sailing, skiing. Home: 80 Latimer Ln Weatogue CT 06089 Office: Robinson & Cole LLP 280 Trumbull St Hartford CT 06103-3597 Office Phone: 860-275-8228. Business E-Mail: dmerriam@rc.com.

**MERRIAM, ROBERT W.,** engineering executive, educator; b. Providence, July 18, 1923; s. Paul Adams and Marian Lewis M.; m. Nancy Ann Allen, Dec. 21, 1954; children: Susan Allen Jones, Paul Adams, II. BS in Engring. Sci. and Applied Physics, Harvard Coll., 1949; MS in Engring. Sci. and Applied Physics, Harvard Engring. Sch., 1950. Reg. profl. engr., R.I. Instr. elec. engring. Swarthmore (Pa.) Coll., 1950-52; engr. Metals & Controls Corp., Attleboro, Mass., 1953-55; pres. Merriam Instruments, East Greenwich, R.I., 1955-99. Assoc. prof. U. R.I., Kingston, 1969-79. Editor: History of Wireless Communication in the U.S., 1989; patentee in field; contbr. articles to popular publications. Pres., dir. N.E. Wireless and Steam Mus., East Greenwich, 1964—; chmn. Planning Bd., East Greenwich, 1970s; hon. trustee Heritage Trust of R.I. With U.S. Army Signal Corp., 1942-46, ETO. Recipient Antoinette Downing award State of R.I., 1998; named Engr. of Yr., Nat. Assn. Power Engrs., 1998, award Soc. Indsl. Archeology Gen. Tools, 2001, Preserve R.I. Merit award, 2005. Fellow Radio Club Am. (Batcher award 1979); mem. IEEE (life), Am. Radio Relay League (life), Nat. Marine Electronic Assn. (hon., dir. 1957), Nat. Assn. Power Engrs. (hon.), Vet. Wireless Assn. (Marconi Gold medal 1995), 20:00 Club (Meritorious Amateur Seamanship award 1955), Rhode Soc. Profl. Engrs. (Engr. of Yr. 1999), Hope Club, Harvard Club (Boston).

**MERRICK, GEORGE BOESCH,** aerospace transportation executive; b. Burlington, Iowa, Mar. 9, 1928; s. Dale McKeen and Marjorie May (Boesch) M.; m. Eleanor Gamble Moore, Sept. 1, 1951; children: Charles, Ellen, Elizabeth. BS, U. Minn., 1949. With N.Am. Aviation (name changed to Rockwell Internat.), 1949; dir. Apollo Command and Service Module, Space div., 1966-72; v.p.; program mgr. Apollo Program, 1972-74, v.p., program mgr. Space Shuttle Orbiter Program, 1974-76; pres. space div. Rockwell Internat., Downey, Calif., 1976-78, pres. space systems group, 1978-80, corp. v.p., 1980-91, ret., 1991. Recipient Pub. Svc. award, NASA. Fellow Am. Astron. Soc., AIAA.

**MERRICK, RAYMOND F.,** state representative; b. Smith, Alberta, Can., Oct. 18, 1939; m. Phyllis Merrick; children: Michael, Matthew. BBA, Washburn U., 1965. Mgr. sales Folger's Coffee; gen. mgr. Treat Am., sr. v.p.; Myron Green Cafeterias Co., gen. mgr.; owner MSM Mgmt.; mem. Kans. Ho. Reps., Topeka, 2000—. Spkr. pro tem Kans. Ho. Reps., Topeka, 2005—. Pres. booster club Blue Valley H.S., 1995—98; pres. Blue Valley Riding Home Assn. Republican. Lutheran. Office: State Capitol 300 SW 10th Ave Topeka KS 66612 Address: 6874 W 164th Terr Stilwell KS 66085

**MERRIER, HELEN,** actress, writer; b. Chgo., Mar. 10, 1932; d. Miner Thompson and Helen (Hembree) Coburn; m. Tim Meier, Dec. 23, 1954; 1 child, William Frank (dec.). BA, Mills Coll., 1954; BS, Northwestern U., 1955. Radio roles include Ma Perkins, One Man's Family, Standard School House of the Air, 1934-52; stage roles include Finian's Rainbow, 1952, The Happy Time, 1952, The Night of January 16th, 1952, No Exit, 1953, Tiger at the Gates, 1953, Caeser and Cleopatra, 1953, The Cocktail Party, 1953, Streetcar Named Desire, 1953, Misalliance, 1956, Cry the Beloved Country, 1956, Cat in a Tin Roof, 1963, Take Me Along, 1966, Caucasian Chalk Circle, 1967, The Devils, 1968, Electra, 1969, Jean Harlow and Billy the Kid, 1969, Three-Penny Opera, 1969, A Shot in the Dark, 1970, Private Lives, 1970, The Importance of Being Earnest, 1971, Forty Carats, 1972, Paris is Out!, 1972, A Christmas Carol, 1973, The Sea Gull, 1975, Something more than Ordinary, 1976, Three Dollar Bill, 1976, Maid to Marry, 1977, Scrooge, the musical, 1984, Prisoner of Second Avenue, 1985, Tom Sawyer, 1986, Comedy of Errors, 1987, Juno and the Paycock, 1987, Woman of the Year, 1989, Time and the Conways, 1991, Cinderella, 1991, Sweeney Todd, 1991, The Birds, 1993, Dreams of Defiance (rev.), 1994, Lady Lucinda's Scrapbook (solo play), 1996-98, As You Like It hike, 1998-99, A Midsummer Night's Dream hike, 1999, 2001, Vieux Carre, 1999, Woman Talk (cabaret), 1999—, Healthy- Minded Little Old Lady Songs (solo cabaret), 2000—, William Inge Festival, 2000, Robin Hood hike, 2000-01, Rip van Winkle hike, 2001, Stephen Foster in Song and Story (solo cabaret), 2001—, Eleemosynary, 2002, Some Americans Abroad, 2004, Romeo and Juliet, 2004, Ancestral Voices, 2004-2005, All I Really Need to Know I Learned in Kindergarten, 2004. Recipient The Spirit of Theater award, 2000, Disting. Svc. award The Salvation Army, 2000. Mem. Victory Svcs. Club (London), Arts Club Chgo. Home: 915 Linden Ave Wilmette IL 60091-2712 Personal E-mail: hmerrier@worldnet.att.net.

**MERRIFIELD, DONALD PAUL,** ministries coordinator; b. Los Angeles, Nov. 14, 1928; s. Arthur S. and Elizabeth (Baker) M. BS in Physics, Calif. Inst. Tech., 1950; MS, U. Notre Dame, 1951; A.M., Ph.L. in Philosophy, St. Louis U., 1957; PhD, MIT, 1962; S.T.M., U. Santa Clara, Calif., 1966; S.T.D. (hon.), U. So. Calif., 1969; D.H.L. (hon.), U. Judaism, 1984, Hebrew Union Coll.-Jewish Inst. Religion, 1986. Joined Soc. of Jesus, 1951; ordained priest Roman Cath. Ch., 1965; instr. physics Loyola U., Los Angeles, 1961-62; lectr. Engring. Sch., Santa Clara, 1965; cons. theoretical chemistry Jet Propulsion Lab., Calif. Inst. Tech., 1962-69; asst. prof. physics U. San Francisco, 1967-69; pres. Loyola Marymount U., Los Angeles, 1969-84, chancellor, 1984—2002; regent, sr. rsch. fellow Charminade U., Honolulu, 2002—. Mem. Sigma Xi. Office: 2727 Pamoa Rd Honolulu HI 96822-1838 Business E-Mail: dmerrifi@chaminade.edu. E-mail: dmerrifield@calprov.org. *In to-day's world, we all stand in need of that pragmatic hope which allows us to see the possibilities for building a more just society and meeting the challenges before us. Without such hope we are paralyzed before our difficulties. With a less realistic hope, too idealistic, we are continually overwhelmed by failures. But with an openness to possibilities, we can move ahead with determination.*

**MERRIFIELD, DUDLEY BRUCE,** finance educator, federal official; b. Chgo., June 13, 1921; s. Fred and Anna (Marshall) M.; m. Paula Sorensen, June 8, 1949; children: Bruce, Robert, Marshall. AB in Chemistry, Princeton U., 1942; MS in Chemistry, U. Chgo., 1948, PhD in Chemistry, 1950. Disting. vis. prof. Georgetown U. Bus. Sch., Washington. Sr. rsch. chemist Monsanto St. Louis, 1950-56; mgr. polymer tech. Tex.-U.S. Chem. Co., Parsippany, NJ, 1956-63; dir. R & D Petrolite Corp., St. Louis, 1963-68; v.p. tech. and ventures Occidental Petroleum Co., Houston, 1968-77; v.p. tech. and venture mgmt. Continental Group, Stamford, Conn., 1977-82; asst. sec. for productivity, tech. and innovation Dept. Commerce, Washington, 1982-89; undersec. econ. affairs, 1986-87; Walter Bladstrom prof., emeritus Wharton Bus. Sch., U Pa., Phila., 1989-94; pres., CEO Pinnacle Rsch. Inst. Devel. Co., 1991—

Adv. bd. Binat R & D Found., U.S., Israel, France, India, 1979—; disting. vis. prof. mgmt., Georgetown U., Washington. Contbr. articles to profl. jours.; patentee in field. Exec. coun. Episcopal Ch., 1973-79; chmn. Princeton Alumni Coun., 1968-72. With USMC, 1943-46. Fellow AAAS, Inst. for Chemists; mem. Am. Chem. Soc., Indsl. Rsch. Inst. (dir., pres.-elect 1977-82 M. Holland award); Am. Mgmt. Assn. Hall of Fame (trustee, chmn. rsch. coun.), Dirs. Rsch., Sigma Xi Republican. Episcopalian. Office: Pridco Mgmt Corp Ste 604 1316 New Hampshire NW Washington DC 20036 Office Phone: 202-887-0877. Personal E-mail: pridco@verizon.net.

**MERRIFIELD, JEFFREY S.,** commissioner; b. Antrim, NH, 1963; m. Diana M. Merrifield; 3 children. BA magna cum laude, Tufts U., 1985; JD, Georgetown U.Law Ctr., 1992. Bar: NH, DC. Legis. asst. to Senator Gordon Humphrey US Senate, Washington, 1987—90, legis. asst. to Senator Robert Smith, 1990—92; assoc. McKenna & Cuneo LLP, Washington, 1992—95; majority coun. & staff dir. Senate Subcommittee on Superfund, Waste Control and Risk Assessment, Washington, 1995—98; commr. US Nuclear Regulatory Commn., Rockville, 1998—. Mem.: DC Bar Assn., NH State Bar Assn. Achievements include drafting legislation dealing with solid and hazardous waste disposal and cleanup regulation. Office: US Nuclear Regulatory Commn One White Flint N 11555 Rockville Pike Rockville MD 20852-2738 Office Phone: 301-415-1855.

**MERRILL, ARTHUR LEWIS,** retired theologian; b. Tura, Assam, India, Sept. 14, 1930; s. Alfred Francis and Ida (Walker) M.; m. Barbara Jean Mayer, Aug. 18, 1951 (dec. June 1978); children: Margaret Jean, Katherine Merrill Nelson, Robert L.; m. Margaret Z. Morris, Sept. 11, 1985. BA, Coll. of Wooster, 1951; BD with distinction, Berkeley Bapt. Div. Sch., 1954; PhD, U. Chgo., 1962. Ordained to ministry United Ch. of Christ, 1954 Asst. prof. Bapt. Missionary Tng. Sch., Chgo., 1957-58; assoc. prof. Mission House Theol. Sem., Plymouth, Wis., 1958-62, United Theol. Sem. Twin Cities, New Brighton, Minn., 1962-67, prof., 1967-95, prof. emeritus, 1995—. Author: United Theological Seminary of the Twin Cities: An Ecumenical Venture, 1993; co-author: Biblical Witness and the World, 1967; co-editor: Scripture in History and Theology, 1977; contbr. articles to profl. publs. ATS-Lilly postdoctoral fellow, 1966-67. Mem. Soc. Bibl. Lit., Am. Schs. Oriental Rsch., Israel Exploration Soc., Minn. Theol. Libr. Assn. (pres. 1994-95). Home: 36177 Wabana Rd Grand Rapids MN 55744-6446 Personal E-mail: artgaro@northlc.com.

**MERRILL, CHARLES EUGENE,** lawyer; b. San Antonio, Aug. 26, 1952; s. Charles Perry and Florence Elizabeth Merrill; m. Carol Ann Rutter, Apr. 28, 1984; children: Elizabeth C., Charles C. AB, Stanford U., 1974; JD, U. Calif., Berkeley, 1977. Bar: Mo. 1977, Calif. 1983, Ill. 1993. Mem. Husch & Eppenberger, LLC, St. Louis, 1977—. Mem. ABA, Bar Assn. of Met. St. Louis. Office: Husch & Eppenberger LLC 190 Carondelet Plz Ste 600 Saint Louis MO 63105-3441 Business E-Mail: charlie.merrill@husch.com.

**MERRILL, CHRISTOPHER LYALL,** writer; b. Northampton, Mass., Feb. 24, 1957; s. Charles Francis Merrill and Suzanne Sigmund France; m. Lisa Ellen Gowdy, June 4, 1983; children: Hannah Frances, Abigail Rose. BA, Middlebury Coll., 1979; MA, U. Wash., 1982. Dir. Santa Fe Writers Conf., 1987-90, Santa Fe Literary Ctr.; 1988-92; William H. Jenks chair Contemporary Letters Coll. of the Holy Cross, Worcester, Mass., 1995-2000; dir. internat. writing program U. Iowa, Iowa City, 2000—. Author: The Old Bridge: The Third Balkan War and The Age of the Refugee, 1995, Watch Fire, 1994, The Grass of Another Country: A Journey Through The World of Soccer, 1993, From the Faraway Nearby: Georgia O'Keefe As Icon, 1992, Only the Nails Remain: Scenes from the Balkan Wars, 1999, Brilliant Water, 2001, Things of the Hidden God, 2005; poetry editor Orion Mag., 1993-2003; contbg. editor Paris Rev., 1991-95; gen. editor-poetry series Gibbs Smith Pub., Layton, Utah, 1987-2001. Recipient Ingram Merrill Found. award, 1991, Pushcart Prize in Poetry, 1990. Mem. Acad. Am. Poets (Peter Lavan Younger Poets award 1993, Bosnian Stecak award 2001, Kostan Kyriazin Internat. Lit. award 2005). Episcopalian. Avocations: gardening, hiking, reading. Office: U Iowa Internat Writing Program Shambaugh House Iowa City IA 52242-2020 Office Phone: 319-335-2609. Business E-Mail: christopher-merrill@uiowa.edu.

**MERRILL, DANIEL A.,** program manager; Data ctr. shift supr. Volt Info. Scis., 1984—85; image analyst DBA Sys., 1985—87; data ctr. supr. sys. divsn. TRW, 1987—89; info. tech. ops. mgr. advanced client/server devel. group Wollongong/Attachmate, 1989—99; mgr. internat. CPE cert. global product engring. UUNET Tech., 1999—2001; tech. project mgr. IP VPN product devel., comm. svcs. engring. Worldcom, Inc., 2001—02; info. tech. mgr. RDR, Inc., 2003—04; program mgr. Metters Industries, Inc., 2004—06, ManTech IS&T, 2006—. With USN, 1980—84. Mem.: Armed Forces Comm. and Engring. Assn., Internet Engring. Task Force, Am. Mgmt. Assn., US Tennis Assn., Appalachian Mountain Club, Am. Legion. Home: 2015 Chapel Ct Frederick MD 21702-2642 Personal E-mail: dan.merrill@earthlink.net.

**MERRILL, DEANE WHITNEY, JR.,** secondary school educator, consultant; b. Orange, NJ, May 9, 1938; s. Deane Whitney Merrill Sr. and Harriet Mary (Ray); m. Colette Marie Yvonne Bruvry, June 20, 1964 (div. 1971); m. Jane Elizabeth Brockmeyer, Dec. 6, 1975 (div. 1985); m. Anna Christine Morben, July 2, 1995. AB, Williams Coll., 1960; MA in Physics, U. Calif., Berkeley, 1962, PhD in Physics, 1967; DPH, U. Calif., 1998. Scientist Lawrence Berkeley Lab., Berkeley, 1960—98; tchr. Mohawk Trail Regional H.S., Buckland, Mass., 2001—06, Asheville-Buncombe Tech. C.C., Asheville, NC, 2006—. Cons. 22 Mechanic St., Shelburne Falls, Mass., 1998—. Author: numerous publs. in physics, demography, pub. health, biostats. and epidemiology. Achievements include development of density equalizing map projections (cartograms). Home: 96 Beverly Rd Asheville NC 28805

**MERRILL, DONNA,** special education educator; b. Raymond, Nebr., Oct. 30, 1933; d. Donald Frank and Edith Marie (Brightenburg) Spellman; m. Robert Henry Merrill, May 29, 1952; children: Nancy, Catherine, Robert, Barbara. BA, Park Coll., Parkville, Mo., 1955; MA, U. Mo., Kansas City, 1975, PhD, 1983. Editor publs. Park Coll., Parkville, Mo., 1953-57; tchr. Smithville Sch. Dist., Mo., 1965-85, Shawnee Mission Sch. Dist., Mo., 1985—2001, St. Agnes Sch., Kans., 2000—06. Adj. faculty U. Mo., Kansas City, 1985-1995; co-dir. Signet Summer Camp, Kansas City, 1988-98. Mem. Gifted Assn. Mo., Kans. Gifted-Talented Assn., Alpha Delta, Phi Kappa Phi, Pi Lambda Theta, Phi Delta Kappa. Avocation: travel. Home: 19626 Dykes Rd Holt MO 64048-8782 Office: St Agnes Sch 5130 Mission Rd Mission KS 66205 Office Phone: 913-262-1686. Personal E-mail: dmerrill915141@earthlink.net.

**MERRILL, EDWARD WILSON,** chemical engineering professor; b. New Bedford, Mass., Aug. 31, 1923; s. Edward Clifton and Gertrude (Wilson) M.; m. Genevieve de Bidart, Aug. 19, 1948; children: Anne de Bidart, Francis de Bidart. AB, Harvard U., 1945; DSc, MIT, 1947. Research engr. Dewey & Almy div. W.R. Grace & Co., 1947-50; mem. faculty MIT, 1950-98, prof. chem. engring., 1964-98, Carbon P. Dubbs prof., 1973-96, emeritus, 1998—. Cons. in field. Contbr. articles to profl. jours. Pres. bd. trustees Buckingham Sch., Cambridge, 1969-74; trustee Browne and Nichols Sch., Cambridge, 1972-74, hon. trustee, 1974—. Fellow Am. Inst. for Med. and Biol. Engring., Am. Acad. Arts and Scis.; mem. AIChE (Alpha Chi Sigma award 1984, Charles M.A. Stine award 1993, Founders award 2000), Am. Chem. Soc., Soc. for Biomaterials (Clemson U. Award 1990, Founders award 2003). Achievements include patents for chemical and rheological instruments; research in polymers, rheology, medical engineering. Home: 90 Somerset St Belmont MA 02478-2010 Office Phone: 617-253-4593. Office Fax: 617-489-2165. Business E-Mail: emerrill@mit.edu.

**MERRILL, FRANK HARRISON,** data processing executive, consultant; b. Pitts., June 20, 1953; s. Edgar Frank and Harriet Margaret (Gallagher) M.; m. Rita Alice Mae Murray, May 27, 1977; 1 child, Laura Margaret. BSMetE,

Colo. Sch. Mines., 1971-76; M of Computer Info. Systems, U. Denver, 1988. Cert. sys. profl., computer programmer; cert. PICK profl.; cert. computer profl.; A+ cert., MCSE. Metall. engr. Inspiration Copper Co., Miami, Ariz., 1979-80, Cominco Am., Inc., Bixby, Mo., 1980-81; programmer, analyst M.L. Foss, Inc., Denver, 1981-83, Titsch & Assocs., Denver, 1983; data processing mgr. PBI/BAXA, Inc., Denver, 1983-86; owner, sys. cons. Dynamic Solutions, Denver, 1986—2004; dir. software devel. Drycreek Assocs. Corp., 2004—; sr. devel. programmer Trust Co. Am., 2006—. Cons. in field, Denver, 1985—; instr. continuing edn. User's Group, Denver, 1985—2001; instr. computer info. sys. U. Denver, 1990-97; mem. grad. computer info. sys. faculty Colo. campus, U. Phoenix, 1991-94; bd. dirs. Inst. for Cert. of Computer Profls. 1993-96, Drycreek Assocs. Corp., 2004-. Leader Boy Scouts Am., Denver and Globe, Ariz., 1973-86, Denver, 1996—; mem. Marriage Encounter Interfaith Bd., Denver, 1985-89, chair, 1988-89; mem. coun. Rocky Mountain Aldersgate Marriage Encounter, 1986-94, exec. couple, 1990-94; mem. Volksmarch Steering Com. Lakewood on Parade, 1990-95; mem. St. Andrew's Soc. Colo.; nominating com. Free Meth. Ch., 1989-92, ch. bd. property and fin., 1992-94. 2d lt. U.S. Army, 1977-79. Named to PICK Industry Accreditation Coun., 1990; recipient God and Svc. award Free Meth. Ch., 1984. Mem. IEEE, SAR, Assn. Sys. Mgmt. (profl. pres. Mile-Hi chpt. 1992-93, mem. internat. cert. adv. com. 1993-95, chmn. 1994-95, mem. divsn. 17 coun. 1994-96, vice chmn. 1995-96, Distinguished Service award 1996), Colo. Pick Users' Group (edn. chmn. 1984—2001), Info. Sys. Security Assn., Scottish-Am. Mil. Soc. (charter, post contr. Post 100 Colo. 1991-95), Cheyenne High Plains Wanderers Club, A.C. Gilbert Heritage Soc. (Rocky Mtn. Regnl. pres. 1994-2000, mem. nat. exec. bd. 1995—2002), Nat. Soc. Magna Charta Dames & Barons. Republican. Mem. Free Methodist Ch. Avocations: model railroading, model rocketry, hiking, camping, mountain climbing.

**MERRILL, GEORGE VANDERNETH,** lawyer, investment executive; b. NYC, July 2, 1947; s. James Edward and Claire (Leness) M.; m. Janice Anne Humes, May 11, 1985; children: Claire Georgina, Anne Stewart. Student, Phillips Exeter Acad., 1960—64; AB magna cum laude, Harvard U., 1968, JD, 1972; MBA, Columbia U., 1973. Bar: NY 1973, U.S. Dist. Ct. (so. and ea. dists.) NY 1974, U.S. Ct. Appeals (2d cir.) 1974. Assoc. Cleary, Gottlieb, Steen & Hamilton, NYC, 1974-77, Hawkins, Delafield & Wood, NYC, 1977-79; v.p. Irving Trust Co., NYC, 1980-82, Listowel, Inc., NYC, 1982-84, bd. dirs., exec. v.p., 1984-93; v.p. instl. portfolio mgmt. Shawmut Investment Advisors, 1993-95; also co-mgr. Shawmut Growth & Income Equity Mut. Fund; v.p. instl. portfolio mgmt. Fleet Investment Advisors, 1995-96, also co-mgr. Galaxy Growth & Income Equity Mut. Fund.; v.p. trust and instl. portfolio mgmt., mem. Fla. equity com. No. Trust Corp., Chgo., 1996-2000; v.p., sr. personal investment officer, sector head Bank of NY, NYC, 2000—, mem. investment policy com., 2004—. Pres. Northfield Charitable Corp., NYC, 1986-93; v.p., sec. Brougham Prodn. Co., NYC, 1986-89, v.p., sec., 1990-93; v.p., sec. Marinetics Inc., NYC, 1988-90, v.p., sec., 1991-93; v.p. Sci. Design and Engring. Co., Inc., NYC, 1987-88, exec. v.p., 1989-93 Bd. dirs. Pres. Arell Found., NYC, 1985—93. Recipient Detur award, Harvard U., 1968; John Harvard scholar. Mem. ABA, Am. Mgmt. Assn., Nat. Cum Laude Soc., The Brook, Union Club (NYC), Down Town Assn., Racquet and Tennis Club, Somerset Club (Boston), Signet Soc. (Cambridge), Pilgrims of U.S. Home: 2 Pierce Rd Riverside CT 06878 Office: The Bank of NY 5th Fl 1290 Ave of the Americas New York NY 10104 Business E-Mail: gmerrill@bankofny.com.

**MERRILL, HARVIE MARTIN,** manufacturing executive, director; b. Detroit, Apr. 26, 1921; s. Harvie and Helen (Nelson) M.; m. Mardelle Merrill; children— Susan, Linda. BS in Chem. Engring. Purdue U., 1942. Devel. engr. Sinclair Refining Co., 1946-47; research and gen. mgr. 3M Co., St. Paul, 1947-65; v.p. fabricated products Plastics div. Stauffer Chem. Co., N.Y.C., 1965-69; with Hexcel Corp., San Francisco, 1969-86, pres., chief exec. officer, 1969-86, chmn. bd., 1976-88. With USAF, 1942-46. Mem.: Interlachen Country Club. Home: 664 Osceola Ave Winter Park FL 32789

**MERRILL, JEAN FAIRBANKS,** writer; b. Rochester, NY, Jan. 27, 1923; d. Earl Dwight and Elsie (Fairbanks) M. BA, Allegheny Coll., 1944; MA, Wellesley Coll., 1945. Feature editor Scholastic Mags., 1947-50; editor Lit. Cavalcade, 1956-57; publs. div. Bank St. Coll. Edn., 1964-65. Children's books include Henry, the Hand-Painted Mouse, 1951, The Woover, 1952, Boxes, 1953, The Tree House of Jimmy Domino, 1955, The Travels of Marco, 1956, A Song for Gar, 1957, The Very Nice Things, 1959, Blue's Broken Heart, 1960, Shan's Lucky Knife (Jr. Lit. Guild selection), Emily Emerson's Moon, 1960 (Jr. Lit. Guild selection), The Superlative Horse (Jr. Lit. Guild selection), 1961 (Lewis Carroll Shelf award 1963), Tell About the Cowbarn, Daddy, 1963, The Pushcart War (Lewis Carroll Shelf award), 1964 (Boys Club Am. Jr. Book award), High, Wide & Handsome, 1964 (Jr. Lit. Guild selection), The Elephant Who Liked to Smash Small Cars, 1967, Red Riding, 1968, The Black Sheep, 1969, Here I Come-Ready or Not!, 1970, Mary, Come Running, 1970, How Many Kids are Hiding on My Block?, 1970, Please, Don't Eat My Cabin, 1971, The Toothpaste Millionaire (Dorothy Canfield Fisher Meml. award 1975-76), 1972 (Sequoyah award 1977), The Second Greatest Clown in the World, 1972, The Jackpot, 1972, The Bumper Sticker Book, 1973, Maria's House, 1974, The Girl Who Loved Caterpillars, 1992; poetry books edited include A Few Flies and I, 1969; libretto for chamber opera Mary Come Running, 1983. Fulbright fellow, India, 1952—53. Mem. Authors League, Vt. Arts. Coun., Vt. Inst. Natural Sci., Vt. Nat. Resources Coun., Fulbright Assn., Acad. Am. Poets, Women's Internat. League Peace and Justice, Sierra Club, Audobon Soc., Women's Internat. League Peace and Justice, Phi Beta Kappa. Office Phone: 802-728-9549. *My interest in writing children's books may have derived from the impact certain books had on me as a child, and a wish to recreate the quality of that experience. As to my general motivation as a writer, I would say that it is to celebrate those aspects of the human experience that affirm the creative and life-reverencing instinct in man. I always hope that my stories may be essentially liberating, opening the reader to emotional, as well as intellectual experience, and that they may be entertaining, encouraging the capacity for joy by evoking the free play of a reader's curiosity, humor and inventiveness.*

**MERRILL, JOHN,** chef; b. Long Island, NY; Diploma, Culinary Inst. of Am., 1988. Externship JP Morgan Hotel, Hartford, Conn.; line cook Reach Resort, Key West, sous chef, exec. sous chef; mng. chef Boston Harbor Hotel, Marblehead, Mass.; co-founder gourmet catering co., Weston, Mass.; exec. sous chef Aura, Seaport Hotel, Boston, 1998, chef, 1999—. Guest chef (cooking events) Ready, Set, Cook, Food Network, Boston Wine Expo, The Anthony Spinazzola Gala Festival of Wine & Food, Edible, Share Our Strength's Operation Frontline. Named one of Boston's Rising Stars, StarChefs.com, 2006. Office: Aura The Seaport Hotel 1 Seaport Ln Boston MA 02110 Office Phone: 617-385-4000.*

**MERRILL, MARTHA,** library and information scientist; b. Anniston, Ala., Apr. 21, 1946; d. Walter James and Polly (McCarty) M. BA, Birmingham-So. Coll., 1968; MS, Jacksonville (Ala.) State U., 1974; PhD, U. Pitts., 1979. Social worker Tuscaloosa (Ala.) County Dept. Human Resources, 1968-71, Calhoun County Dept. Human Resources, Anniston, 1971-73; social scis./bus. libr. Jacksonville State U., 1974-86, prof. instrnl. media, 1987—. Editor: Reference Services and Media, 1999; co-author: Dictionary for School Library Media Specialists, 2001. Mem. Friends of Libr. bd. Anniston-Calhoun County Pub. Libr., 1984—. Recipient Ala./SIRS Intellectual Freedom award, Intellectual Freedom Coun., Ala. Libr. Assn., 1992, Ala. Beta Phi Mu chpt. Libr. of Yr. award, 1997. Mem. ALA (exec. bd., Intellectual Freedom Round Table 1987-93), Ala. Libr. Assn. (pres. 1990-91, Disting. Svc. award 1995 Outstanding Publ. award, 2004), Ala. Assn. Coll. and Spcl. Librs. (pres. 1989-90), Southeastern Libr. Assn. (chair intellectual freedom com. 1986-88, chair resolutions com. 1990-92). Office: Jacksonville State U Coll Edn Dept Ednl Resources Jacksonville AL 36265 Office Phone: 256-782-5011. E-mail: mmerrill@jsucc.jsu.com.

**MERRILL, MARY H. See BOYD, MARY**

**MERRILL, STEPHEN,** lawyer, consultant, retired governor; Student, U. N.H., Georgetown U. Former personal counsel to Sec. Air Force, Pentagon; atty. gen. State of NH, Concord, 1985—89, gov., 1993—97; of counsel Choate, Hall and Stewart, Boston, 1997—99; pres. Bingham Consulting Group, Boston, 1999—; ptnr. Bingham McCutchen, Boston, 1999—. Mem. NH task force on Child Abuse and Neglect, former pres., legal counsel. Served to capt. USAF. Recipient AG Profl. award. Fellow: ABA; mem.: Nat. Attys. Gen. Emeritus (co-chmn.), Nat. Gov.'s Assn. Emeritus, Ea. Assn. Attys. Gen. (chmn.), Phi Beta Kappa (Ford Found. scholar). Office: Bingham McCutchen 150 Federal St Boston MA 02110-1726

**MERRILL, STEVEN WILLIAM,** research and development company executive; b. Oakland, Calif., Aug. 6, 1944; s. David Howard and Etha Nadine (Wright) M. BA in Chemistry, Calif. State U., Hayward, 2004. Lic. pyrotechnic, Calif. Apprentice Borgman Sales Co., San Leandro, Calif., 1960—64; assembler Calif. Fireworks Display, Rialto, Calif., 1970; pyrotechnician Hand Chem. Industries, Milton, Ont., Canada, 1972—74; dir. R&D Pyrospectaculars, Rialto, 1988—92; pyrotechnic cons., 1993—; owner, dir. Merrill Prodns. Ordnance, Crestline. Experimenter in field, 1958—; chief chemist Baron Blakesly Solvents, Newark, Calif., 1987-88; court expert San Francisco Superior Ct., 1971, Victorville (Calif.) Superior Ct. Counselor Xanthos, Inc., Alameda, Calif., 1970. Mem. AAAS, Am. Chem. Soc., Am. Stats. Assn., Am. Bd. Forensic Examiners, Internat. Platform Assn. Avocations: wood carving, sculpture, photography, electronics, automobile restoration. Home and Office: Merrill Prodns Ordnance PO Box 676 Crestline CA 92325-0676 Office Phone: 909-338-2913. Personal E-mail: birdscare@aol.com.

**MERRILL, SUSAN L.,** lawyer; b. 1957; Grad. cum laude, U. Md., 1979; JD summa cum laude, Bklyn. Law Sch., 1986. Law clk. to Hon. Francis L. Van Dusen US Ct. Appeals (3rd cir.), 1986—87; assoc. Davis Polk & Wardwell, 1987—2004, ptnr., 1994—2004; exec. v.p. enforcement NYSE Group, Inc. (formerly NY Stock Exch.), 2004—. Office: NYSE Group Inc 11 Wall St New York NY 10005 Office Phone: 212-656-3000.*

**MERRILL, THOMAS WENDELL,** lawyer, educator; b. Bartlesville, Okla., May 3, 1949; s. William McGill and Dorothy (Glasener) Merrill; m. Kimberly Ann Evans, Sept. 18, 1973; children: Jessica, Margaret, Elizabeth. BA, Grinnell Coll., 1971, Oxford U., 1973; JD, U. Chgo., 1977. Bar: Ill. 1980, U.S. Dist. Ct. (no. dist.) Ill. 1980, U.S. Ct. Appeals (5th cir.) 1982, U.S. Ct. Appeals (7th cir.) 1983, U.S. Ct. Appeals (9th and DC cirs.) 1984, U.S. Supreme Ct. 1985. Clk. U.S. Ct. Appeals (DC cir.), Washington, 1977-78, U.S. Supreme Ct., Washington, 1978-79; assoc. Sidley & Austin, Chgo., 1979-81, counsel, 1981-87, 90—; dep. solicitor gen. U.S. Dept. Justice, 1987-90; prof. law Northwestern U., Chgo., 1981—2003, John Paul Stevens prof., 1993—2003; Charles Keller Beckman prof. Columbia U., 2003—. Co-author: (book) Property: Takings, 2002; contbr. articles to profl. jours. Rhodes scholar, Oxford U., 1971, Danforth fellow, 1971. Fellow: Am. Acad. Arts & Sci. Office: 435 W 116th St, Rm 727 New York NY 10027 Office Fax: 212-854-7946. E-mail: tmerri@law.columbia.edu.

**MERRILL, WENDY JANE,** financial services company executive; b. Waterbury, Conn., Dec. 4, 1961; d. David Kenneth and Jane Joy (Nevius) Merrill; m. Aidan T. Harrison (div. Nov. 1998); children: Christopher Harrison, Charlotte Harrison, Ryan Harrison; m. Michael G. Kelly, Oct. 2, 1999 (dissolved Nov. 2004). BA in Journalism, George Washington U., 1981; MBA in mgmt., Cornell U., 1992. Intern edn. HEW, Washington, 1978, writer, 1979; rsch. asst. dept. health svcs. adminstrn. George Washington U., Washington, 1979—81; sec. Nat. Assoc. Beverage Importers, Washington, 1981; account exec. Staff Design, Washington, 1982; adminstrv. aide Internat. Food Policy Rsch. Inst., Washington, 1983—86; program assoc. Acad. for Ednl. Devel., Washington, 1986—87; pvt. practice cons. Washington, 1987—88; adminstrv. mgr. food and nutrition policy program Cornell U., Ithaca, NY, 1988—92; cons. mgmt. of med. practices Med. Bus. Mgmt., Ithaca, 1994—95; realtor Century 21 Alpha, 1995—97; compensation mgr. Santa Clara U., Calif., 1996—98; sr. compensation analyst Stanford U., Calif., 1998—99; human resources cons. Siemens Info. and Comm. Networks, 2000; compensation and benefits mgr. Kana Comms., 2000—01; U.S. compensation mgr. KLA-Tencor, 2001—02; pres. Total Solutions Ins. Agy., Inc., Calif., 2003—, Total Solutions Comml. Ventures, Inc., 2003—, Total Solutions Settlement Ptnrs., Inc., 2003—. Cons., editor George Washington U., 1986; cons., rapporteur Internat. Food Policy Restaurant Inst., Washington and Copenhagen, Denmark, 1987; cons., adminstr. Hansell & Post, Washington, 1987-88, Cornell U., Washington and Ithaca, 1988; pvt. practice cons. 2001—. Sponsor Worldvision, Tanzania, 1988-91. George Washington U. scholar, 1979-81. Mem. AMA, Soc. for Human Resources Mgmt., Zonta Club (charter pres. Silicon Valley chpt. 2006—), Sigma Delta Xi (scholar 1980). Democrat. Episcopalian. Avocations: piano, hiking, swimming. Home: 745 S Mary Ave Sunnyvale CA 94087 Office Phone: 408-830-9300. Business E-Mail: wendy@totalsolutionscv.com.

**MERRILL, WILLIAM DEAN,** retired architect, medical facility planning consultant; b. Portland, Oreg., June 1, 1915; s. Charles O. and Grace (Ruhl) M.; m. Bernice E. Wickham, Apr. 19, 1943 (dec. Sept. 1996); 1 child, Sue Ann Merrill Boardman; m. Irene Moe, July 30, 2001. Student in Fine Arts and Forestry, Oreg. State U., Corvallis, 1936-38; student in Architecture, U. Oreg., Eugene, 1939-42. Registered architect, Oreg., Calif., NCARB Prin. W.D. Merrill, Architect, Portland, 1956-64; architect, ptnr. Bissell & Merrill, Architects, Stockton, Calif., 1964-68; architect, ptnr. Kaiser Engrs., Kaiser Found. Hosps. design and constrn., 1968-81; pvt. practice hosp. design and constrn., residential design and constrn., Bay Area, 1981-91; hosp. and sch. constrn. insp. Office of State Health Planning and Devel., State of Calif., 1984-93; ret. 1996. Served as lt (g.g.) USNR, 1942-44. MIU. Mem. AIA (emeritus). Republican. Home: 25411 E Cedar Glen Loop Welches OR 97067

**MERRILL, WILLIAM H., JR.,** lawyer, corporate financial executive; b. Indpls., Apr. 11, 1942; s. William H. and Jane (Robinson) M.; m. Winifred Jane Baur, July 25, 1964; children: Michele Jane, Betsy Diane. BS, Butler U., 1965; JD, Ind. U., 1967. Bar: Ind. 1967. Trust officer Mchts. Nat. Bank, Indpls., 1965—69; gen. counsel Everett I. Brown Co., Indpls., 1969—85; v.p., gen. counsel Landeco, Inc., Indpls., 1970—85; pres. Bash Seed Co., Indpls., 1975—97; gen. ptnr. Meta Ptnrs., 1984—90. Pres. Meta Investment Co., 1988-90, Meta Mgmt. Co., 1988-90, Northwest Devel. Corp., 1975—, Scotts Garden Ctr., Inc., 1977-97; bd. dirs. Custom Molded Products, Inc. Mem. Carmel (Ind.) City Plan Commn., 1975-85, pres. 1982-85. Mem. ABA, Ind. Bar Assn., Indpls. Bar Assn., Crooked Stick Golf Club. Office: 3205 W 71st St Indianapolis IN 46268-2244 Office Phone: 317-291-1441. Personal E-mail: merrillwhmjr@aol.com.

**MERRILL, WILLIAM MELVIN,** electrical engineer; s. H. Kent and Phoebe May Merrill; m. Sarah Ann Levine, July 21, 2005. BS in Elec. and Computer Engring., U. Ariz., Tuscon, Ariz., 1994; MSEE, U. Calif., L.A., Calif., 1996, PhD in Elec. Engring., 1999. Lead wireless arch. Sensoria Corp., San Diego, Calif., 1999—. Contbr. chapters to books. Mem.: IEEE (assoc.). Achievements include patents for method for collecting and processing data using internetworked wireless integrated network sensors; method and apparatus for internetworked wireless integrated network sensor nodes; method and apparatus for distributed signal processing among internetworked wireless integrated network sensors; apparatus for internetworked hybrid wireless integrated network sensors; method for collecting data using compact internetworked wireless integrated network sensors; patents pending for low-latency multi-hop ad hoc wireless network. Office: Sensoria Corporation 15950 Bernardo Center Dr Suite J San Diego CA 92128 Office Phone: 858-673-4460 27.

**MERRIM, LOUISE MEYEROWITZ,** artist, actress; b. N.Y.C. d. Leo and Jeanette (Harris) Meyerowitz; m. Lewis Jay Merrim, June 27, 1948; children: Stephanie, Andrea Merrim Goff (dec.). BFA, Pratt Inst., 1947; MFA, Columbia U., 1951; postgrad., Post Coll., 1971-72, New Sch., 1977-78. Art tchr. pub. schs., N.Y.C., 1947-51, Port Washington, NY, 1970-83. One-woman shows include Plandome Gallery, L.I., Isis Gallery, N.Y., San Diego art Inst., Pan Pacific Hotel, San Diego; exhibited in group shows at Nassau County Fine Arts Mus. (Bronze award), Heckscher Mus. (Nora Mirmont award), Nat. Acad., Nat. Assn. Women Artists (Medal of Honor, Charlotte Whinston award), Audubon Artists. (Stephen Hirsch Meml. award), Cork Gallery, Warner Comm. Gallery, L.I. Art Tchrs. (two awards of excellence), L.I. Art Tchrs. Award Winners Show, Pt. Washington Libr. Invitational, Glen Cove (2nd prize), Manhasset Art Assn. (best in show, five 1st prizes), San Diego Art Inst., San Diego Mus. Art (Gold award), Oceanside Mus. Art, Hank Baum Gallery, San Francisco, Tarbox Gallery, Clark Gallery, Knowles Gallery, San Diego, Golden Pacific Arts Gallery, San Diego, Henry Chastain Gallery, Scottsdale, Boehm Gallery/Palomar Coll., Hyde Gallery/Grossmont Coll., Timmons Gallery, Rancho Santa Fe, Calif.; included in permanent collection of San Diego Mus. Art; appeared in numerous theatrical prodns. including Fiddler on the Roof, Barefoot in the Park, N.Y., Anything Goes, The Musical Comedy Murders of 1940, Anastasia (Drama award), Fiddler on the Roof, The Music Man, What's Wrong With this Picture?, Marvin's Room, San Diego, The Foreigner; dir. Under Milkwood; dir., appeared in Spoon River Anthology. Mem.: Nat. Assn. Women Artists, NY Soc. of Women Artists, Contemporary Artists Guild of NY, Audubon Artist (NY), San Diego Art Inst., Artists Guild of San Diego Art Mus. (pres. 1993), Artists Equity, Actors Alliance. Avocations: tennis, poetry, travel. Home: 3330 Caminito Vasto La Jolla CA 92037-2929 E-mail: louisemer@hotmail.com.

**MERRIMAN, CHRISANN,** marketing professional; d. Daniel Patrick (Stepfather) and Diane Marie Hogan; m. Kelly John Merriman, Nov. 7, 1998; 1 child, Owen Tiernan. BS in mktg., Rivier Coll., 1993—96; MBA, NH. Coll., 1997—99; MS in bus. edn., So. NH. Univeristy, 2000—01. Cert. profl. marketer Am. Mktg. Assn. Mktg. specialist MediaOne Group, Andover, Mass., 1998—2000; industry mktg. mgr. Enterasys Networks, Inc., Andover, Mass., 2000—04; mktg. mgr. VIEO, Inc., Austin, Tex., 2004—. Educator U. of Phoenix Online, 2001—. Mem.: Nat. Assn. of Bus. Educators, Am. Mktg. Assn., Acad. of Mgmt. Office Phone: 512-677-0788.

**MERRIMAN, KEVIN THOMAS,** lawyer; b. Rochester, NY, Sept. 17, 1966; s. William Emmett and Anne Flaherty Merriman; m. Joy Alexandria Mautner, May 23, 1992; children: Samuel, Alexander. BS, Cornell U., 1989; JD, SUNY, Buffalo, 1992. Bar: N.Y. 1993. Assoc. Allen, Lippes & Shonn, Buffalo, 1993-98, Hurwitz & Fine, P.C., Buffalo, 1998—2004; ptnr. Goldberg Segalla LLP, Buffalo, 2004—. Mem. NY Bar Assn., Def. Rsch. Inst., Erie County Bar Assn., Am. Inns of Ct. Democrat. Home: 590 South St E East Aurora NY 14052-2951 Office: Goldberg Segalla LLP 665 Main St Ste 400 Buffalo NY 14203 Office Phone: 716-566-5411. Business E-Mail: kmerriman@goldbergsegalla.com.

**MERRIN, SEYMOUR,** computer company executive; b. Bklyn., Aug. 13, 1931; s. Joseph and Esther Bella (Manelis) M.; m. Elaine Cohen, Sept. 4, 1960 (dec. May 1962); m. Elizabeth Jenifer Slack, Oct. 12, 1963 (dec. Mar. 1995); children: Charles Seymour, Mariamne Jenifer Weights; m. Helene Claire Singer, Sept. 1, 2001 BS, Tufts Coll., 1952; MS, U. Calif., 1954; PhD, Pa. State U., 1962. Geologist Magma Copper Co., Superior, Ariz., 1954, U.S. Geol. Survey, 1956-58; chemist IBM, Poughkeepsie, NY, 1962-64; mgr. package devel., mgr. reliability and failure analysis Sperry Semiconductor divsn. Sperry Rand, Norwalk, Conn., 1965-68; cons. materials tech. Fairfield, Conn., 1967-69; v.p., dir. Innotech Corp., Norwalk, 1969-74; divsn. mgr. Emdex divsn. Exxon Enterprises, Milford, Conn., 1974-78; chmn., dir. Computerworks, Westport, Conn., 1978-85; v.p., dir. personal computing svc. Gartner Group, Inc., Stamford, Conn., 1984-87; pres. Merrin Resources, Southport, Conn., 1987-89, Merrin Info. Svcs., Inc., Santa Fe, 1987—. Bd. dirs. Micrografx Corp., Allen, Tex.; mem. adv. panel Apple Computer Co., Cupertino, Calif., 1982-83; mem. adv. bd. Compaq Computer Corp., Houston, 1984-85, Computer and Software News, N.Y.C., 1984-89; mem. program adv. bd. Comdex, Boston, 1985—; lectr. in field. Contbr. numerous articles to profl. publs.; patentee in field. Bd. dirs. Futures for Children, Albuquerque, 2004—. With U.S. Army, 1954—56. Fellow Geol. Soc. Am., Am. Inst. Chemists; Computing Tech. Industry Assn. (founder, pres. 1981-83, bd. dirs. 1981-84). Home and Office: 840 Camino de las Trampas Santa Fe NM 87501 Personal E-mail: smerrin@aol.com.

**MERRING, ROBERT ALAN,** lawyer, arbitrator, mediator; b. Middletown, N.Y., Oct. 5, 1951; s. Merton George and Mabel Ruth M.; m. Lynn S. Connor, Mar. 16, 1996. Student, Ohio Wesleyan U., 1969—70; AB with distinction and departmental honors, Stanford U., 1973; JD with honors in Internat. and Fgn. Law, Columbia U., 1977; cert. Pepperdine Sch. Law, Inst. for Dispute Resolution, 1996. Bar: Calif. 1977, U.S. Dist. Ct. (cen. dist.) Calif. 1978, U.S. Dist. Ct. (so. and ea. dists.) Calif. 1980, U.S. Ct. Appeals (9th cir.) 1980, U.S. Dist. Ct. (no. dist.) Calif. 1983, U.S. Supreme Ct. 1987, Colo. 1989. Assoc. Pacht, Ross, Warne, Bernhard & Sears, Inc., L.A., 1977-79, Donovan Leisure Newton & Irvine, L.A., 1979-81, Cutler and Cutler, L.A., 1983-88, Friedemann & Hart, Irvine, 1988-89; pvt. practice Orange County, Calif., 1989—. Civil arbitrator, temporary judge, judge pro tem Orange County Superior Ct., 1993—, arbitrator NASD, 2006; mediator U.S. Bankruptcy Ct. (ctrl. dist.) Calif., 1996—; mediator Orange County Superior Ct., 1998-2002; clin. prof. Loyola U. Law Sch., LA, 1981-82. Editor Columbia Jour. Transnat. Law, 1976-77. Columbia U. Internat. fellow, 1975—76. Mem.: ABA, Orange County Patent Law Assn., Am. Arbitration Assn. (panel commcl. arbitrators 1993—, panel mediators 2002—), State Bar Calif. (del. 1998—2003), Assn. Conflict Resolution, Assn. Bus. Trial Lawyers, Orange County Bar Assn. (chair intellectual property and tech. law sect. 2000—01). Office Phone: 714-444-9922. Business E-Mail: rmerring@merringlaw.com.

**MERRINGTON, ADRIAN,** researcher, educator, rheologist; b. Leeds, Yorkshire, Eng., Feb. 17, 1965; came to U.S., 1992; s. George Leslie and Pana Litsa (Georgiou) M.; m. Randi Jean Geiling, Aug. 22, 1997. BSc in Applied Chemistry, U. Greenwich, London, 1988; CChem, U. Bradford, 1990, PhD in Chem. Engring., 1992; CSci, Royal Soc. Chemistry, 2005. Rsch. prodn. asst. Contact Lens Mfrs., Redhill, Eng., 1986-87; vis. scientist Mich. Molecular Inst., Midland, 1992-94, rsch. assoc., 1994-95, assoc. scientist, asst. prof., 1995-2000, sr. assoc. scientist, asst. prof., 2000—. Contbr. articles to profl. jours. Rsch., edn. grantee Sci. and Engring. Rsch. Coun., 1988-92, rsch. grantee NSF Rsch. Ctr. in Coatings, 1992-94, Mich. Materials and Processing Inst., 1995-2000. Mem. Royal Soc. Chemistry, Soc. Plastics Engrs. (bd. dirs. 1998—). Achievements include routes to recycling, multicomponent polymer blends, the effect of and on reprocessed or newly introduced additives; identification and explanation of colloidal phase transitions; identification of colloid stabilizer morphology effects on performance; enhancing mechanical properties of epoxy resins; membrane technology; fuel cell technology. Office: Mich Molecular Inst 1910 W Saint Andrews Rd Midland MI 48640-2657 Office Phone: 989-832-5555 ext. 634. Business E-Mail: merrington@mmi.org.

**MERRION, ARTHUR BENJAMIN,** mathematics professor, tree farmer; b. Williamstown, NJ, Oct. 25, 1938; s. Anthony Robert and Eva May Merrion; m. Martha Jane Banse, Dec. 26, 1965 (div. May 1977); children: Benjamin Thomas, Elizabeth Jane. Attended, Rutgers U., 1957, Drexel Inst. Tech., 1961; fellowship, Appalachian State U., 1965; AB in Math., Pfeiffer Coll. (now Univ.), 1965; MS in Numerical Sci., Johns Hopkins U., 1976. Navigations scientist Oceanographic Office, Suitland, Md., 1966—72, Def. Mapping Agy. Hydrographic Ctr., 1972—78; fellow ops. rsch. analysis Sec. Army Pentagon, Washington, 1978-80; ops. rsch. analyst Asst. Sec. Army, Washington, 1980-86; tree farmer Huntingtown, Md., 1986-98. Instr. math and stats. Embry-Riddle Aeronautical U., 1993-94; math. instr. Charles County C.C., 1990-91; tutor Literacy Coun., navigator Scientist Silas Bent Naval Oceanographic Vessel, 1966. Author: A Short Story By Edgar Allen Pooh. With U.S. Army, 1957-58. Mem. Mod. Soc. SAR, Nat. Soc SAR, Internat. Soc. Poets (Poet of Merit award). Achievements include research in applying math. chaos theory to weather modification; invention of upside-down pear-shaped earth reversal maneuver for correcting earth perturbations. Avocations: chess, violin, Judo, wrestling, ice skating. Home: PO Box 1639

West Jefferson NC 28694-1639 *The Bible says many different things to many different people. To Thomas Alva Edison it was a "Chemist's Handbook". To me it is the source of all man's creativity, directly from the greatest Creator of all. It is a source of inspiration, a solace for periods of depression, and a prescription when I'm in error.*

**MERRISS, PHILIP RAMSAY, JR.,** banker; b. N.Y.C., June 7, 1948; s. Philip Ramsay and Elisabeth (Paine) M.; m. Janet Henry Hylan, Oct. 27, 1973. AB in Econs. magna cum laude, Lafayette Coll., 1970; MBA with high distinction, Dartmouth Coll., 1972. Assoc. corp. fin. dept. A.G. Becker and Co. Inc., N.Y.C., 1972-73; fin. analyst corp. banking dept. Chase Manhattan Bank, 1973, asst. treas. N.Y.C. dist., 1974-75, 2d v.p. mining and metals div., 1976-78, 2d v.p. petroleum div., 1979-86, client exec., v.p. pub. utilities component, 1987-89, credit supv. officer, div. exec., v.p. U.S. Pvt. banking, 1989-94; credit exec. J.P. Morgan Pvt. Bank, N.Y.C., 1994-97, mng. dir. and credit exec., 1997—. Capt. U.S. Army, 1978. Tuck scholar Dartmouth Coll., 1972. Mem. Am. Econ. Assn., Aircraft Owners and Pilots Assn., Weston Gun Club, Yale Club, Fairfield County Hunt Club, Phi Beta Kappa. Republican. Episcopalian. Home: 11 Katydid Ln Weston CT 06883-1808 Office: JP Morgan Chase & Co 345 Park Ave New York NY 10154-1002

**MERRITT, BRUCE GORDON,** lawyer; b. Iowa City, Oct. 4, 1946; s. William Olney and Gretchen Louise (Kuever) M.; m. Valerie Sue Jorgensen, Dec. 28, 1969; children: Benjamin Carlyle, Alicia Marie. AB magna cum laude, Occidental Coll., 1968; JD magna cum laude, Harvard U., 1972. Bar: Calif. 1973, D.C., 1996, N.Y. 1996. Assoc. Markbys, London, 1972—73, Nossman, Krueger & Marsh, L.A., 1973—79, ptnr., 1979—81; asst. U.S. Atty., L.A., 1981—85; ptnr. Hennigan & Mercer, L.A., 1986—88, Debevoise & Plimpton, L.A., 1989—95, N.Y.C., 1996—2001. Adj. prof. law Loyola Law Sch., L.A., 2003—. Fellow Am. Coll. Trial Lawyers; mem. Calif. State Bar Assn. (exec. com. litig. sect. 1992-95), Phi Beta Kappa, Harvard Club (N.Y.C.). Office Phone: 818-521-1812. Personal E-mail: Brucegmerritt@aol.com.

**MERRITT, CAROLYN,** government agency administrator; Diploma, Radford U. Mngr. of solid and hazardous waste and environmental health and safety Champion Intl. Corp., 1989—94; sr. project mngr. RMT/Jones and Neuse, Inc., Houston, 1994; sr. v.p. for Environment, Health and Safety IMC Global Inc., Northbrook, Ill.; chmn, CEO U.S. Chemical Safety and Hazard Investigation Board, 2002—. Office: 2175 K Street NW Ste 400 Washington DC 20037 Office Phone: 202-261-7600.

**MERRITT, EDITH BRADFORD,** elementary school educator; b. Athens, Ga., June 14, 1945; d. Duane Elton and Frances Edith (McCart) Bradford; m. Thomas Wayne Merritt Jr., Jan. 24, 1970; children: Theresa, Jennifer, David, Penny. BS, Auburn U., 1976; MS, Troy State U., 1989. Cert. elem. tchr., Nat. Bd. Edn., 2000. 2d, 4th and 5th grade tchr. Lee-Scott Acad., Auburn, Ala.; tchr. accelerated sci. and social studies 4th gr. Auburn City Schs., tchr. elem. schs. Tuscaloosa, Ala. Workshop presenter ASTA State Conf., U. Ala. In-Svc. Ctr. Finalist Ala. State Tchr. of Yr., 1988-89; recipient commendation for profl. in teaching Ala. Ho. of Reps., 1989, Profl. Best September award Learning Mag.; named Ala. Outstanding Elem. Tchr., 1995. Home: 140 Barnes Lane Eutaw AL 35462-1227

**MERRITT, ELEANOR LYNETTE,** artist, educator; b. N.Y.C., Aug. 17, 1933; d. Wilbert Alexander and Lynette Hyacinth Lipsett; m. Lorenzo Merritt, June 26, 1954 (div. Oct. 1975); m. W.H. Chris Darlington, July 26, 1980; children: Lori Ellen, Lisa Ann. BA, Bklyn. Coll., 1955, MA, 1958. Cert. secondary art tchr. N.Y.C. Art tchr. N.Y.C. Sch. Sys., 1955-59; secondary sch. art tchr. Westbury Schs., L.I., N.Y., 1960-70, dist. chairperson, 1971-82. Lectr. C.W. Post Coll., N.Y., 1978-82, Nassau C.C., N.Y., 1978-82, Art League Manatee County, Bradenton, Fla., 1997—; lectr., docent Ringling Mus. Art, Sarasota, Fla., 1989—. One-woman shows include Nassau County Cultural Mus., Hempstead, N.Y., 1974, Am. Internat. Coll., Springfield, Mass., 1975, 81, The Craftery Gallery, Hartford, Conn., 1976, Women's Resource Ctr., Sarasota, 1987, 92, Shrine of the Black Madonna, Cultural Ctr., Houston, 1988, U. Fla., St. Petersburg, 1988, Manatee C.C., Venice, 1988, Ctrl. Nat. Bank, Sarasota, 1991, Zora Neale Hurston Mus., Eatonville, Fla., 1993, Fine Arts Gallery Ctrl. Libr., Tampa, 1994, Barrier Island Group for the Arts, Sanibel, Fla., 1995, Unit Gallery, Sarasota, 1995, Hillsborough C.C., Tampa, 1997, Palm Harbor, Sarasota, 1998; exhibited in group shows at Salt Creek Art Works, St. Petersburg, Carver Cultural Ctr., San Antonio, Fla. State Capital Gallery, Tallahassee, Hillsborough C.C. Libr., Tampa, Artists Unlimited: The Channel Dist., Tampa, Women's Caucus for Art, Miami, Michael Gold Gallery, N.Y.C., Daytona (Fla.) Beach C.C., City U., Shimonoseki, Japan, 1996, Steinbaum Gallery, N.Y.C., 1997, Self Gallery, Hilton Head, S.C., 1998, Jacksonville Mus. Contemporary Art, 1998, Diverse Origins, Colo., 1998, African Am. Mus., Tampa, 1997, Venice Biennel, 1999, many others; exhibited in corp. exhbns. Atlanta Life Ins. Co., Isphording, Payne, Korp., Inc., Venice, Holiday Inn Crown Plaza, Tampa, Fla., Automatic Data Processing Corp., Roseland, N.J. V.p. Sarasota Arts Coun. Bd., 1996—; chairperson Sarasota County Commn. Art in Pub. Places, 1997—; pres. Venice (Fla.) Art Ctr. Bd., 1998—. Recipient Woman of Impact award County Commn. on the Status of Women, Sarasota, 1997; named Sarasota Artist of the Yr., Sarasota Visual Arts Ctr., 1994. Mem. Women's Mus. Art (charter), Women's Caucus for Art (pres. Sarasota chpt. 1993/94, v.p. nat. prog. 1990-96, Nat. Pres. award 1996), Pen Women Am. (Sarasota chpt.), Fla. Artist Group (area III), Petticoat Painters. Avocations: gardening, travel, lecturing.

**MERRITT, GILBERT STROUD,** federal judge; b. Nashville, Tenn., Jan. 17, 1936; s. Gilbert Stroud and Angie Fields (Cantrell) M.; m. Louise Clark Fort, July 10, 1964 (dec.); children: Stroud, Louise Clark, Eli. BA, Yale U., 1957; LLB, Vanderbilt U., 1960; LLM, Harvard U., 1962. Bar: Tenn. 1960. Asst. dean Vanderbilt U. Law Sch., 1960-61, lectr., 1963-69, 71-75, assoc. prof. law, 1969-70; assoc. Boult Hunt Cummings & Conners, Nashville, 1962-63; asst. metro. atty. City of Nashville, 1963-66; U.S. Dist. atty. for (mid. dist.) Tenn., 1966-69; ptnr. Gullett, Steele, Sanford, Robinson & Merritt, Nashville, 1970-77; judge U.S. Ct. Appeals (6th cir.), Nashville, 1977-2001, chief judge, 1989—96, sr. judge., 2001—. Exec. sec. Tenn. Code Commn., 1977. Mng. editor: Vanderbilt Law Rev, 1959-60; contbr. articles to law jours. Del. Tenn. Constl. Conv., 1965; chmn. bd. trustees Vanderbilt Inst. Pub. Policy Studies. Mem. ABA, Fed. Bar Assn., Tenn. Bar Assn., Nashville Bar Assn., Vanderbilt Law Alumni Assn. (pres. 1979-80), Am. Law Inst., Order of Coif. Episcopalian. Office: US Ct Appeals Customs House 701 Broadway Ste 303 Nashville TN 37203-3967*

**MERRITT, HOWARD SUTERMEISTER,** retired art educator; b. Ithaca, N.Y., June 12, 1915; s. Ernest and Bertha (Sutermeister) M.; m. Florence Sederquest Hill, June 27, 1941; children: Jessica, Stephen, Jonathan, James. BA, Oberlin Coll., Ohio, 1936; M.F.A., Princeton U., N.J., 1942, PhD, 1958. Mem. faculty U. Rochester, N.Y., 1946-80, prof. emeritus, 1980—. Cons. 19th Century Am. Painting, 1960—80. Contbr. exhbn. catalogues and articles to various publs. Served with AUS, 1942-45. Decorated Bronze Star; Nat. Endowment for Humanities summer grantee, 1966-68 Mem. Coll. Art Assn. Home: 85 Bellevue Dr Rochester NY 14620-2703

**MERRITT, JAMES EDWARD,** lawyer; b. Hickory, N.C., June 10, 1938; s. Eddy Schmidt and Dorothy (Hunt) M.; m. Joan L. Hiscock, June 14, 1960 (div. 1983); children: James Edward Jr., Catherine Hunt; m. Kristine McFadden, May 4, 1983. AB, Duke U. 1959; LLB, Harvard U., 1962. Bar: D.C. 1962, Calif. 1968; cert. tax specialist, Calif. Assoc. Pogue & Neal, Washington, 1962-64; trial atty. regional counsel IRS, San Francisco, 1964-68; assoc. Morrison & Foerster, LLP, San Francisco and Washington, 1968-72, ptnr., 1972—98, sr. counsel, 1999—. Lectr. Golden Gate U., San Francisco, 1970-74; cons. chief counsel IRS, Washington, 1982; mem. adv. bd. Tax Mgmt. Inc., N.Y.C., 1987—; Contbr. articles to profl. jours. Mem. Am. Coll. Tax Counsel (regent, chair 1997-2000), ABA (coun., dir., sect. taxation 1990-93, mem. commn. on legal problems of elderly 1993-96), Bar Assn. D.C., Bar Assn. San Francisco (Outstanding Tax Lawyer 1983), J.

Edgar Murdock Inn of Ct. Avocations: travel, gardening, sports. Office: Morrison & Foerster LLP 30 Winster Fax Williamsburg VA 23185-5542 Office Phone: 757-258-3819. E-mail: jimmerritt@aol.com.

**MERRITT, JEAN,** consulting firm executive, psychotherapist; b. N.Y.C., Oct. 29, 1952; d. Harry and Ruth (Happel) Packman; m. Richard L. Kashinsky, Aug. 2, 1976 (div.); m. Richard L. Merritt, May 5, 1985 (div. June 2002); children: Courtney Morgan, Melissa Morgan Grad. high sch., Bayside, N.Y. From contr. to v.p., sec., treas. Kaswol Corp., Richmond Hill, NY, 1973—85; corp. exec. Federated Cons. Svc., Inc., Bayside, NY, CFO Jupiter, Fla., 1985—2002, psychotherapist, 2004—, dir. mktg., 2005—. Coach Queens Spl. Olympics, 1985. Mem. Nat. Trust for Hist. Preservation, Nat. Fedn. Wildlife, Ctr. for Environ. Edn., Defenders of Wildlife, Nat. Resource Def. Coun., Humane Soc. of U.S., Sierra Club, Amnesty Internat. Avocations: flying, art collecting, painting, interior design, gourmet cooking. Home: Apt 2K 520 W 43 St New York NY 10036 Office Phone: 917-319-0184. E-mail: jeanie22m@aol.com.

**MERRITT, NANCY-JO,** lawyer; b. Phoenix, Sept. 24, 1942; d. Robert Nelson Meeker and Violet Adele Gibson; children: Sidney Kathryn, Kurt, Douglas. BA, Ariz. State U., 1964, MA, 1974, JD, 1978. Bar: Ariz. 1978, U.S. Dist. Ct. Ariz. 1978, U.S. Ct. Appeals (9th cir.) 1984. Shareholder Fennemore Craig, P.C., Phoenix. Author: Understanding Immigration Law, 1993; sr. editor: Immigration and National Law Handbook, 1993—; contbr. articles to profl. jours. Chair bd. dirs. TERROS, 1995-97. Fellow Ariz. Bar Found.; mem. ABA, Am. Immigration Lawyers Assn. (chairperson Ariz. chpt. 1985-87, several coms., Pro Bono award), Ariz. Bar Assn. (immigration sect.), Nucleus Club. Democrat. Avocations: modern literature, south american literature, hiking, gardening. Office: Fennemore Craig PC 3003 N Central Ave Ste 2600 Phoenix AZ 85012 Office Phone: 602-916-5411. Business E-Mail: njmerritt@fclaw.com.

**MERRITT, PHYLLIS JUNE,** music educator, director; b. Elizabethton, Tenn., Mar. 28, 1939; d. Earl H. and Willie Greene Merritt. BS in Music Edn., East Tenn. State U., 1960; MusM in Edn., Fla. State U., 1972. Tchr. music Kingsley Elem. Sch., Kingsport, Tenn., 1960—61, Weis Elem. Sch., Pensacola, Fla., 1961—62; dir. choral music Brownsville Jr. H.S., Pensacola, 1962—65, Escambia H.S., Pensacola, 1965—76, Meigs Jr. H.S., Shalimar, Fla., 1976—80, Niceville H.S., Fla., 1980—90; dir. music Trinity United Meth. Ch., Fort Walton Beach, Fla., 1991—98, ret., 1998; founder Phyllis Merritt Singers, Pensacola, 2003—, artistic music dir., 2003—. Singer, conductor Inst. European Studies Concert Tour, 1970, Internat. Assn. Cultural European Concert Tour, 1973, Young Americans Nat. Choral Festival, 1985, Big Apple Choral Festival, 1986. Named Tchr. of Yr., Okaloosa County, Fla., 1986, Escambia County, Fla., 1991; recipient Disting. Alumni in Arts award, East Tenn. State U., 1990. Mem.: Fla. Vocal Assn. (pres. 1988—95, chmn. dist. 1988—95), Am. Choral Dirs. Assn. (sr. pres. 1975—77, pres. divsn. 1979—81, bd. dirs., dir. various convs., musician various concerts, Wayne Hugoboom Disting. Svc. award 1989, So. Divsn. Excellence in Choral Art award 2000). Avocation: travel. Home: 431 Gregory Ave Valparaiso FL 32580

**MERRITT, THOMAS BUTLER,** lawyer; b. Toledo, Apr. 3, 1939; s. George Robert and Bernice (Gerwin) M.; m. Mary Jane Bothfeld, July 23, 1966; children— Thomas Butler, Haidee Soule, Theodore Bothfeld AB magna cum laude, Harvard U., 1961, LLB cum laude, 1966. Bar: Mass. 1966, U.S. Supreme Ct. 1974, N.H. 1994, U.S. Ct. Appeals (1st cir.) 1999. With N.Y. State Dept. Civil Svc., Albany, 1961—63; intern Office of Legal Advisr U.S. Dept. State, Washington, 1965; law clk. to assoc. justice Arthur E. Whittemore Supreme Jud. Ct. Mass., Boston, 1966-67; assoc. Nutter, Mc-Clennen & Fish, Boston, 1967-69, Palmer & Dodge, Boston, 1969-73; asst. counsel to Gov. Mass., 1973; reporter of decisions Supreme Jud. Ct. Mass., Boston, 1974-94; pvt. practice NH, 1994—. Contbr. articles to profl. jours. Mem. Conservation Commn. Town of Sherborn, Mass., 1969-74, chmn. 1972-74; planning bd. Town of Hollis, N.H., 1995-98; mem. N.H. Bd. Natural Scientists, 2005—. 1st lt. U.S. Army, 1962-63, capt. USAR, 1963-69. Mem.: Assn. Reporters of Jud. Decisions (pres. 1983—84), Internat. Law Assn. (Am. br.), Am. Soc. Internat. Law, Fed. Bar Assn., N.H. Bar Assn., Mass. Bar Assn., Am. Law Inst. (life), Harvard Faculty Club (Cambridge), Harvard Club of Boston, Union Club. Episcopalian. Office: PO Box 324 Littleton NH 03561-0324

**MERRITT, WILLIAM ALFRED, JR.,** retired lawyer, real estate company executive; b. NYC, Aug. 7, 1936; s. William Alfred and Florence Anne (O'Connor) M.; m. Christine Marie Cartnick, Sept. 27, 1969; children— William Tyler, Brian Edward, Elizabeth Cody BA in Econs., Holy Cross Coll., Worcester, Mass., 1958; LLB, Harvard U., 1964. Bar: N.Y. 1965. Assoc. Olwine, Connelly, Chase, O'Donnell & Weyher, N.Y.C., 1964-68; v.p. ops. and controls Bunge Corp., N.Y.C., 1968-81; exec. v.p. TIE/Communications Inc., Seymour, Conn., 1981-90; pres. Wiltel Communications Systems Inc, Rolling Meadows, Ill., 1991-92; ptnr. Seaboard Equities Inc., Stamford, Conn., 1992—; gen. counsel Carolina Barnes Capital Inc., Stamford, 1992—99; ptnr. KM Group, Stamford, Conn., 1992—. Served to capt. USNR, 1958-80. Mem. Wee Burn Club, Harvard Club (N.Y.). Avocations: skiing, boating, golf. Home: 83 Brookside Rd Darien CT 06820-3505 Office: Ste 602 One Dock St Stamford CT 06902 Personal E-Mail: w59merr@aol.com.

**MERRIWEATHER, FREDA E.,** education educator; d. Oscar and Eura Merriweather; m. William M. Norvell, III, Apr. 30, 1961 (div.); children: Stacy LePrix Norvell, Tracy Norvell Dukes. BS, So. Ill. U., 1964; MS, U. Wis., Milwaukee, 1971; EdD, U. Louisville, 1992. Cert. tchr. So. Ill. U., 1964, Principal U. Wis., 1972, Superintendent State of Ky., 1991. Tchr. Siefert Elem. Sch., Milw., 1964—73; prin. Md. Ave. Sch., Milw., 1974—76, James Whit Comb Riley, Milw., 1977—80, Pine Elem. Sch. - JCPS, Louisville, 1984—87; vice-principal William McKinley Internat. Sch., Milw., 1976—80; edn. cons. Ingham Internat. Sch. Dist., Holt, Mich., 1982—84; dir. Jefferson County Pub. Sch., Louisville, 1987—91, exec. dir., 1991—93, asst. supt., 1993—2002, 1993—2002; practitioner in residence U. Louisville, Louisville, 2002—. Mem. Gov.'s Literacy Task Force, Frankfort, Ky.; alumni bd. U. Louisville, 1993—95; alumni Supt. Prepared-McKenzie Group, Washington, 1995. Mem. Jr. Achieve., Louisville, Urban League, Louisville. Recipient Adminstrv. Leadership award, Collaborative for Tchg. and Learning, 2001, award, Sarah Scott Leadership, 1978, Valedictorian, H.S. Class, Alumni Fellow, Coll. of Edn., U. Louisville, 1999, Bingham Fellows, 1993, Grad. Sch. Dean's Citation, 1991, Ky. Edn. Leadership Inst., 1990, Outstanding Prin., Nat. Schools of Excellence, 1987; grantee, Leadership Louisville, 1992, Bd. of Alderman, 1992; Doctoral Program scholarship, Scottish Rites Found. Mem.: NAACP, Greater Louisville Alliance of Black Sch. Educators, Nat. Alliance of Black Sch. Educators, Urban League (dir.), Louisville Chpt. of Moles (parliamentation), Delta Sigma Theta Sorority. Avocations: dancing, card games, reading. Office Phone: 502-852-0635. Personal E-mail: femerr01@aol.com.

**MERSEL, MARJORIE KATHRYN PEDERSEN,** lawyer; b. Manila, Utah, June 17, 1923; d. Leo Henry and Kathryn Anna (Reed) Pedersen; m. Jules Mersel, Apr. 12, 1950; 1 child, Jonathan A. BA, U. Calif., 1948; LLB, U. San Francisco, 1948. Bar: D.C. 1952, Calif. 1955. Pvt. practice, Beverly Hills, Calif., 1961—71, L.A., 1997—; staff counsel Dept. Real Estate State of Calif., L.A. 1971—97. Pub. counsel, 2000—02. Active L.A.-Guangzhou Sister City. Mem.: ABA, Current Affairs Forum, World Affairs Coun., So. Calif. Women Lawyers Assn. (treas.-62), Trial Lawyers Assn., L.A. County Bar Assn., Beverly Hills Bar Assn., Beverly Hills C. of C., L.A.-Guanghou Sister City Assn., Sierra Club, L.A. Athletic Club. Home: 13007 Hartsook St Sherman Oaks CA 91423-1616 Office: Dept Real Estate 107 S Broadway Ste 8107 Los Angeles CA 90012-4402

**MERSEREAU, HIRAM STIPE,** wood products company consultant; b. Portland, Oreg., Aug. 4, 1917; s. E.W. and Ruth (Stipe) M.; m. Margaret Daggett, Dec. 25, 1937; children: Hiram Stipe, John Bradford, Timothy Daggett. Student, George Washington U., 1936-37, Harvard U., 1959. With

Weyerhauser Timber Co., Klamath Falls, Oreg., 1937-38, Alexander-Yawkey Lumber Co., Prineville, Oreg., 1938-52; gen. mgr. lumber div. Crossett Co., Ark., 1954-62; corp. sr. v.p., gen. mgr. So. div. Ga.-Pacific Corp., 1963-82, cons., 1982—. Past dir. Citizens & So. Nat. Bank, Augusta, Appalachian Hardwood Mfrs. Inc., Merry Cos., Inc., Augusta. Past bd. dirs. Young Life, Ga. Conservancy, Jr. Achievement Augusta; bd. dirs. Augusta br. Boys Clubs Am., Augusta Cancer Fund; trustee Paine Coll., Augusta. Mem. Nat. Forest Products Assn. (exec. com., dir.) Republican. Presbyterian (elder). Home: 6 Turnberry Ln Sea Pines Plantation Hilton Head Island SC 29928

**MERSEREAU, SUSAN,** information systems company executive, data processing executive; b. Portland, Oreg., Sept. 5, 1946; d. Roland William Mersereau and Barbara Munro; m. Robert Stier, June 19, 1968; 1 child, Arran Elizabeth; m. Philip White, Nov. 17, 1989; children: Richard, Brandon. BA in History, Scripps, 1968; MAT in Edn. History, U. Chgo., 1971; MA in Whole Systems Design, Antioch, 1990. Tchr. South Shore High Sch., Chgo., 1969-70; adminstrv. asst. U. Ill., Chgo., 1970; rsch. analyst U. Wash., Seattle, 1971-72; dir. planning rsch. and evaluation Seattle Sch. Dist., 1972-80; program mgr. Weyerhauser Co., Tacoma, 1980-81, mgr. advanced tech., 1981-83, dir. telecom., 1983-88; gen. mgr., v.p. Weyerhauser Info. Systems, Tacoma, 1988-92, v.p. total quality region adminstrv. svcs. and aviation, 1992—98; v.p. organizational effectiveness Weyerhauser Co., Federal Way, Wash., 1998—2003, sr. v.p. info. tech, chief info. officer, 2003—. Bd. dirs. King County Jr. Achievemen, King County United Way. Avocations: skiing, art, hiking, tennis, fishing. Office: Weyerhaeuser Co 33663 Weyerhaeuser Way S PO Box 9777 Federal Way WA 98063-9777 Office Phone: 253-924-2345.*

**MERSINI - HOUGHTON, LAURA,** physicist, educator; d. Nexhat and Stela Mersini; m. Jeffrey Houghton, Feb. 2, 2003. MSc in Physics, U. Md., 1997; PhD, U. Wis., Milw., 2000. Cert. theoretical physics U. Wis., Milw. Physics Dept., 2000. Rsch. fellow Scuola Normale Superiore, Pisa, Italy, 2000—02; postdoctoral fellow Syracuse U., Physics Dept., NY, 2002—03; vis. prof. Perimeter Inst. Theoretical Physics, Waterloo, Ontario, Canada, 2003—04; asst. prof. physics U. NC, Chapel Hill, 2004—. Contbr. articles to profl. jours. Fellow, Fulbright Found., 1994. Achievements include research in addressing fundamental problems of cosmology and modern physics by means of a new field and direction, string cosmology. Connecting and testing models and the new field to astrophysical observables. Office: U NC Dept Physics and Astronomy Phillips Hall UNC-Chapel Hill Chapel Hill NC 27599 Office Phone: 919-962-4277. Office Fax: 919-962-0480. Business E-Mail: mersini@physics.unc.edu.

**MERSKY, ROY MARTIN,** law educator, legal association administrator; b. N.Y.C., Sept. 1, 1925; s. Irving and Rose (Mendelson) Mirsky; m. Rosemary Bunnage; children: Deborah, Lisa, Ruth. BS, U. Wis., 1948, JD, 1952, MALS, 1953. Bar: Wis. 1952, U.S. Supreme Ct. 1970, Tex. 1972, U.S. Ct. Appeals (5th cir.) 1981, N.Y. 1983. Cataloger U.S. govt. documents U. Wis. Law Libr., 1951—52; reference asst. Madison Free Libr., Wis., 1952; pvt. practice law Wis., 1952—54; readers adv., reference and catalog libr., mcpl. reference libr. at City Hall, Milw. Pub. Libr., 1953—54; chief readers and reference svc. Yale Law Libr., 1954—59; dir. Wash. State Law Libr., 1959—63; exec. sec. Jud. Coun. Commn. Wash. Court Report, State of Wash., 1959—63; prof. law, law libr. U. Colo., Boulder, 1963—65; prof. law, dir. rsch. U. Tex., Austin, 1965—, William Stamps Farish Centennial prof. law, 1996—2001, Harry M. Reasoner Regents chair in law, 2001—, prof. Grad. Sch. Libr. and Info. Sci., 1976—. Vis. prof. law, dir. law libr. N.Y. Law Sch., N.Y.C., 1982-84; M.D. Anderson Found. vis. prof. law Queen Mary and Westfield Coll., U. London, 1994; interim dir. Jewish Nat. and Univ. Libr., Hebrew U., 1972-73; vis. fellow Australian Nat. U. Fac. of Law, Canberra, 1999; cons. to legal pubs. and law schs.; panelist various confs.; lectr. in field. Author: A Treasure in Jerusalem, 1974, (with J. Myron Jacobstein) Fundamentals of Legal Research, 7th edit., 1998, 8th edit., 2002, (with Dunn) Legal Research Illustrated, An Abridgement of Fundamentals of Legal Research, 8th edit., 2002, (with Albert P. Blaustein) The First One Hundred Justices: Statistical Studies on the Supreme Court of the United States, 1978, (with W. Bader) The First One Hundred Eight Justices, 2004, (with Gary R. Hartman, Suzanne F. Young, Jill Duffy and Jake Lisbert) A Documentary History of the Legal Aspects of Abortion in the United States, 1990, 96, 2001 (with Jacobstein Hartman and Bonnie Koneski-White) Reports on Successful and Unsuccessful Nominations, 1992, 95, 96, (with Gary Hartman and Cindy L. Tate) Landmark Supreme Court Cases, 2004 (with Richard Leiter) The Spirit of Lain Librarianship, 2d edit., 2005; contbr. articles to profl. jours., chpts. to books; editor numerous books in field. Bd. dirs. Ctrl. Tex. chpt. ACLU, pres., 1968; bd. dirs. Human Rights Documentation Exch., 1997-2001; mem. bd. advisors Anti-Defamation League, Austin, 1974-78, Tex. Book Festival, 2001-2004; bd. dirs. Hillel Found., 1980-83; bd. dirs. Tex. Com. for Humanities, 1978-80, chair, 1980-82, conf. facilitator, 1982. With U.S. Army, 1944-46, ETO. Decorated Bronze Star. Fellow Am. Bar Found. (life), Tex. Bar Found.; mem. ABA (various coms.), AAUP (chmn. nominating com. 1979-80), Am. Law Inst., Assn. Am. Law Schs. (various coms.), Internat. Assn. Lawyers and Jurists (bd. govs. Am. sect. 1980-95), Nat. Bar Assn., Am. Assn. Law Librs. (chair various coms.), Am. Soc. Info. Sci. (pres. Tex./Okla. chpt. 1992-94), Scribes (bd. dirs. 1974-94, book awards com. 1978-96, pres. 1991-93, chair Scribes Law Review Competition award com. 1993—), Soc. Am. Law Tchrs. (bd. govs. 1979-88, nominations com. 1984), ALA (rsch. librs. group 1987, libr. edn. divsn.), Am. Soc. Indexers, Internat. Assn. Law Librs. (U.S. adv. coun.), Internat. Fedn. Libr. Assns., Nat. Librs. Assn. (pres. 1980-81), Spl. Libr. Assn., State Bar Tex. (mem. editl. bd. jour.), State Bar Wis. (bd. mem. nonresident lawyers divsn. 1992-98, 2003-), Nat. Assn. Coll. and Univ. Attys., Tex. Assn. Coll. Tchrs., Tex. Humanities Alliance (bd. dirs. 1986-88), Tex. Supreme Ct. Hist. Soc. (bd. trustees 1988-94, exec. bd. 2002—, treas. 2003—). Home: 6412 Cascada Dr Austin TX 78750-8157 Office: U Tex Sch Law Tarlton Law Libr 727 E Dean Keeton St Austin TX 78705-3224 Office Phone: 512-471-7735. E-mail: rmersky@law.utexas.edu.

**MERSZEI, GEOFFREY E.,** corporate financial executive; BA, Albion Coll. With Dow Chem. Co., Midland, Mich., 1977—2001, treas. Germany Frankfurt, 1983—85, treas. Ea. Europe, 1985—86, fgn. exch. mgr. Midland, Mich., 1986—88, dir. fin. Asia Pacific Hong Kong, 1988—91, dir. fin. Europe Horgen, Switzerland, 1991—96, v.p., treas. Midland, Mich., 1996—2001; exec. v.p., CFO Alcan, Inc., 2001—05, Dow Chem. Co., Midland, Mich., 2005—, bd. dirs., mem. Office of the Chief Exec., 2005—. Bd. dir. Dow Corning Corpn.; mem. Conf. Bd. Com. Coun. Fin. Execs.; mem. corp. exec. bd. working coun. for CFOs. Office: Dow Chem Co 2030 Dow Ctr Midland MI 48674*

**MERTE, HERMAN, JR.,** mechanical engineering educator; b. Detroit, Apr. 3, 1929; s. Herman and Anna Marie (Mitterer) M.; m. Bernice Marie Brant, Sept. 17, 1952; children: Kenneth Edward, James Dennis, Lawrence Carleton, Richard Brant, Robert Paul. BS in Marine Engring, U. Mich., Ann Arbor, 1950, BS in Mech. Engring, 1951, MS, 1956, PhD, 1960. Faculty U. Mich., 1959—67, prof. mech. engring. Ann Arbor, 1967—2000, prof. emeritus, 2000—. Vis. prof. Tech. U. Munich, Germany, 1974-75 Served to lt. (j.g.) USNR, 1952-55. NSF sr. postdoctoral fellow, 1967-68 Mem. ASME, AIAA, Am. Soc. Engring. Edn., Am. Assn. U. Profs., Sigma Xi. Home: 3480 Cottontail Ln Ann Arbor MI 48103-1706 Office: U Mich Heat Transfer Lab 2026 G G Brown Lab Ann Arbor MI 48109-2125 Office Phone: 734-764-5240. Business E-Mail: merte@engin.umich.edu.

**MERTENS, JOAN R.,** museum curator, art historian; b. NYC, Oct. 10, 1946; d. Otto R. and Helen H. M. BA, Radcliffe Coll., 1967; PhD, Harvard U., 1972. Curatorial asst. Met. Mus. Art, N.Y.C., 1972-73, asst. curator, 1973-76, assoc. curator, 1976-81, curator Greek and Roman dept., 1981—, curator, adminstr., 1983-90, mem. editorial bd. Mus. Jour., 1976—. Lectr. NYU, Inst. Fine Arts, 1992—. Author: Attic White-Ground*Its Development, 1977, Greek Bronzes in the Metropolitan Museum of Art, 1985, (with others) Ancient Art from Cyprus: The Cesnola Collection in the Metropolitan

Museum of Art, 2000, (with others) The Cesnola Collection: Terracottas, 2004. Mem. Archaeol. Inst. Am., German Archael. Inst. (corr. mem.) Home: 124 E 84th St New York NY 10028-0915 Office: Met Mus Art Fifth Ave at 82nd St New York NY 10028

**MERTENS, THOMAS ROBERT,** biology professor; b. Fort Wayne, Ind., May 22, 1930; s. Herbert F. and Hulda (Burg) M.; m. Beatrice Janet Abair, Apr. 1, 1953; children: Julia Ann, David Gerhard BS, Ball State U., 1952; MS, Purdue U., 1954, PhD, 1956. Research assoc. dept. genetics U. Wis.-Madison, 1956-57; asst. prof. biology Ball State U., Muncie, Ind., 1957-62, assoc. prof., 1962-66, prof., 1966-93, dir. doctoral programs in biology, 1974-93, George and Frances Ball disting. prof. biology edn., 1988-93, prof. emeritus, 1993—. Author: (with A. M. Winchester) Human Genetics, 1983 (with R.L. Hammersmith) Genetics Laboratory Investigations, 13th edit., 2006 (co-recipient William Holmes McGuffey Longevity award Text and Acad. Authors Assn. 1998); contbr. numerous articles to profl. jours. Co-recipient Gustav Ohaus award for innovative coll. sci. tchg. NSTA, 1986, recipient Disting. Svc. to Sci. Edn. citation, 1987; fellow NSF, 1963-64, Ind. Acad. Scis., 1969. Fellow AAAS; mem. Nat. Assn. Biology Tchrs. (pres. 1985, hon. mem. 1988), Am. Genetic Assn., Genetics Soc. Am. Episcopalian. Home: 4501 N Wheeling 9B-4 Muncie IN 47304-1277 Office: Ball State U Dept Biology Muncie IN 47306-0001 Personal E-mail: t.mertens@att.net.

**MERTINS, DETLEF,** architect, educator; BArch, U. Toronto, 1980; PhD in Architecture, Princeton U., 1996. Instr. U. Toronto, 1991—2003, Can. Rsch. chair in architecture, 2001—03; prof., chair dept. architecture U. Pa. Sch. Design, 2003—. Vis. prof. Columbia U., Harvard U., Princeton U., Rice U. Author: The Presence of Mies, 1994, The Victory of Building a Style, 2000, others. Recipient Konrad Adenauer Rsch. prize, Alexander von Humboldt Found. and Royal Can. Soc., 2003; vis. scholar fellow, Can. Ctr. for Architecture, 1998. Office: Univ Pa 207 Meyerson Hall Philadelphia PA 19104-6311

**MERTINS, JAMES WALTER,** entomologist; b. Milw., Feb. 18, 1943; s. Walter Edwin and Harriet Ellen (Sockett) M.; m. Marilee Eloise Joeckel, Dec. 8, 1979. BS in Zoology, U. Wis., Milw., 1965; MS in Entomology, U. Wis., 1967, PhD in Entomology, 1971. Project assoc. dept. entomology U. Wis., Madison, 1971-75, rsch. assoc. dept. entomology, 1975-77; asst. prof. dept. entomology Iowa State U., Ames, 1977-84; entomol. cons. Ames, 1984-89; entomologist Nat. Vet. Svcs. Labs. USDA Animal and Plant Health Inspection Svc., Ames, 1989—. Co-author: (textbook) Biological Insect Pest Suppression, 1977, Russian edit., 1980, Chinese edit., 1988; contbr. articles to profl. jours. NSF Grad. fellow, 1970. Mem. Entomol. Soc. Am. (Insect Photography award 1984, 86, 2003), Entomol. Soc. Can., Mich. Entomol. Soc., Wis. Entomol. Soc. (pres., sec., treas., bd. dirs.), Cyclone Corvettes, Inc. (co-founder, pres. 1978, 79; sec., treas., bd. dirs., Mem. of Yr. 1982), Am. Mensa. Avocations: insect photography, Corvette automobile activities, gardening, movies, insect collecting. Office: USDA Animal and Plant Health Inspection Svc PO Box 844 Ames IA 50010-0844 Business E-Mail: James.W.Mertins@aphis.usda.gov.

**MERTON, ROBERT C.,** economist, educator; b. NYC, July 31, 1944; s. Robert K. and Suzanne (Carhart) M., 3 c. BS in Engring. Math., Columbia U., 1966; MS in Applied Math., Calif. Inst. Tech., 1967; PhD in Econs., MIT, 1970; MA (hon.), Harvard U., 1989; LLD (hon.), U. Chgo., 1991; Prof. honoris causa degree, HEC Sch. Mgmt., Paris, 1995; D Econ. Sci. (hon.), U. Lausanne, Switzerland, 1997; Dr honoris causa, U. Paris Dauphine, 1997, Universidad Nacional Mayor de San Marcos, Lima, Peru, 2004; D of Mgmt. Sci. (hon.), Nat. Sun Yat-sen U., Kaoshiung, Taiwan, 1998; DS (hon.), Athens U. Econs. and Bus., 2003; DPhil (hon.), U. Nacional Federico Villarreal, Lima, Peru, 2004. Instr. econs. MIT, Cambridge, 1969-70; asst. prof. fin. Alfred P. Sloan Sch. Mgmt., 1970-73, assoc. prof., 1973-74, prof., 1974-80, J.C. Penney prof. mgmt., 1980-88; vis. prof. fin. Harvard U., Boston, 1987-88, George Fisher Baker prof. bus. adminstrn., 1988-98, John and Natty McArthur University prof., 1998—. Rsch. assoc. Nat. Bur. Econ. Rsch., 1979—; mem. internat. bd. sci. advisors Tinbergen Inst.; co-founder Long-Term Capital Mgmt., L.P., Greenwich, Conn., 1993—99; mem. governing bd. AlphaSimplex Group, 2001—; acad. adv. bd. Real Option Group, 1999—; bd. dirs. Vical Inc., MF Risk, Inc., Dimensional Funds, Cmty. First Fin. Group, Peninsula Banking Group; co-founder, chief sci. officer, mem. bd. dirs. Integrated Fin. Ltd., 2002—; mem. competitive markets adv. coun. Chgo. Merc. Exch., 2004—. Author: Continuous-Time Finance, 1990, rev. edit., 1992; co-author: Casebook in Financial Engineering: Applied Studies of Financial Innovation, 1995, The Global Financial System: A Functional Perspective, 1995, Finance, 2000, Transparency, Risk Management and International Financial Fragility, 2003; editor: The Collected Scientific Papers of Paul A. Samuelson, vol. III, 1972; mem. editl. bd. Internat. Econ. Rev., 1972-77, Jour. Fin., 1973-77, Jour. Money, Credit and Banking, 1974-79, Jour. Fin. Econs., 1974-83, Jour. Banking and Fin., 1977-79, 92-2003, Fin. India, 1988—, Geneva Papers on Risk and Ins., 1989-96, Jour. Fixed Income, 1991—, Fin. Rev., 1992-97, Jour. Fin. Edn., 1995—, European Fin. Rev. (now Rev. Fin.), 1997-2004; mem. adv. bd. The New Palgrave Dictionary of Money and Finance, Math. Fin., Rev. Derivatives Rsch., Nihon Finance Gakkai, The Brookings-Wharton Papers on Financial Policy, Internat. Jour. Theoretical and Applied Finance, Jour. Investment Mgmt., North Holland Series of Handbooks in Finance, Jour. Banking and Fin., 2003—, Annals of Fin., 2004—, Jour. Fin. Lit., 2004—; mem. adv. coun. Fin. Analyst Jour., 2003—; contbr. articles to profl. jours. Mem. hon. bd. Internat. Raoul Wallenberg Found., 2003—, Angelo Roncalli Internat. Com., 2003—. Recipient Leo Melamed prize U. Chgo. Sch. Bus., 1983, Roger Murray prize Inst. for Quantitative Rsch. in Fin., 1985, 86, Disting. Scholar award Ea. Fin. Assn., 1989, Internat. INA-Nat. Acad. Lincei prize Nat. Acad. Lincei, Rome, 1993, FORCE award for fin. innovation Fuqua Sch. Bus., Duke U., 1993, Fin. Engr. of Yr. award Internat. Assn. Fin. Engrs., 1993, Alfred Nobel Meml. Prize in Econ. Scis. 1997, Heroes Among Us award Boston Celtics, 1997, Michael Pupin medal Columbia U., 1998, Disting. Alumni award Calif. Inst. of Tech., 1999, MFD Lifetime Achievement award Boston U., 1999, Lifetime Achievement award Risk Mag., 2003, Nicholas Molodovsky award Assn. Investment Mgmt. Rsch., 2003, Graham and Dodd award Fin. Analysts Jour., 2003; inducted Derivatives Hall of Fame, 1998, named Risk Hall of Fame, Risk Mag., 2002. Fellow Internat. Assn. Fin. Engrs. (sr.), Econometric Soc., Am. Acad. Arts and Scis., Inst. Quantitative Rsch., Fin. Mgmt. Assn., Am. Fin. Assn. (dir. 1982-84, pres. 1986, fellow 2000—); mem. NAS, Bachelier Fin. Soc., Soc. for Fin. Studies (v.p. 1993), Hon. Order Ky. Cols., Tau Beta Pi, Sigma Xi. Office: Harvard U Grad Sch Bus Adminstrn Baker Libr 353 Soldiers Field Rd Boston MA 02163 Business E-Mail: rmerton@hbs.edu.*

**MERTZ, BRYAN PAUL,** science educator; b. Downers Grove, Ill., June 12, 1972; s. William Anton and Clare Karen Mertz. BS, U. Ill., Champaign, 1994; MAT, Colo. Coll., Colorado Springs, 1999. EMT Carle Found. Hosp., Urbana, Ill., 1995—98; intern sci. tchr. Doherty H.S., Colorado Springs, Colo., 1998—99; sci. tchr. Widefield H.S., Colorado Springs, 1999—2000, Air Acad. H.S., Colorado Springs, 2000—; honorarium instr. U. Colo., Colorado Springs, 2002—. Fellow Howard Hughes Sci. Tchrs. Experience in Exptl. Rsch. fellow, Colo. Coll., 2004. Mem.: Human Anatomy and Physiology Soc., Colo. Assn. Biology Tchrs., Nat. Assn. Biology Tchrs. Office: Air Academy High School 6910 Carlton Dr U S A F Academy CO 80840

**MERTZ, FRANCIS JAMES,** university president; b. Newark, Sept. 24, 1937; s. Frank E. and Marian E. (Brady) M.; m. Gail Williams, Apr. 11, 1964; children: Lynn, Christopher, Suzanne, David, Amy, Jonathan. BA, St. Peter's Coll., 1958; JD, NYU, 1961; LLD (hon.), Felician Coll., 1984, Stevens Inst. Tech., Hoboken, N.J., 1988, Fairleigh Dickinson U., 1999, Kunghnam Univ., 1999, Coll. St. Elizabeth, 2002. Bar: N.J. 1967. Exec. v.p. St. Peter's Coll., Jersey City, 1972-78; v.p., CFO N.Y. Med. Coll., Valhalla, 1978-79; dir. adminstrn. Sage Gray Todd and Sims, N.Y.C., 1979-81; pres. Ind. Coll. Fund N.J., Summit, 1981-90, Assn. Ind. Colls. and Univs. N.J., Summit, 1982-90, Fairleigh Dickinson U., Teaneck, NJ, 1990-99, pres. emeritus. Bd. dirs., chmn. St. Joseph's Home for the Blind, 1998—; mem. bd. regents Seton Hall U., 2002-04; chair N.J. Commn. on Higher Edn., 2004-06, N.J. Higher Edn.

Student Assistance Authority, 2004-06, N.J. Ednl. Facilities Authority, 2004-06. Home: 54 Woodcrest Dr Morristown NJ 07960-4541 Office: Fairleigh Dickinson U 285 Madison Ave Madison NJ 07940-1099 Office Phone: 973-267-1506. Business E-Mail: mertz@fdu.edu.

**MERTZ, PAUL ERIC,** history professor, writer; b. Bartlesville, Okla., Feb. 27, 1943; s. Floyd E. and Mary O. Mertz; m. Lyndall Ruth Kauffman, Jan. 28, 1966; children: Mary Kathryn Mertz Carney, Paul Eric Jr. BA, Phillips U., Enid, Okla., 1965; MA, U. Okla., Norman, 1967; PhD, U. Okla., 1971. Instr. history U. Wis., Stevens Point, 1969—72, asst. prof., 1972—77, assoc. prof., 1977—82, prof. history, 1982—. Chair dept. history U. Wis., Steven Point, 1992—98. Author: New Deal Policy and Southern Rural Poverty, 1978. Chair Dem. Party, Portage County, Wis., 1999; elder Frame Meml. Presbyn. Ch., 1972—. Woodrow Wilson Nat. fellow, 1965—66. Mem.: State Hist. Soc., So. Hist. Assn., Orgn. Am. Historians. Democrat. Presbyterian. Avocation: leading bicycle tours in Europe. Office: Dept History U Wis Stevens Point WI 54481

**MERULLO-BOAZ, LISA HELEN,** marketing and fundraising executive; b. N.Y.C., Oct. 25, 1953; d. Irving and Hazel (Jacob) Siegel; m. Edward J. Merullo, Oct. 4, 1975 (div.); children: Aaron E., Jenny L.; m. Jeffrey A. Boaz, July 4, 1993. BA, Northeastern U., 1975. Prodn. and adminstrv. asst. Gennard Andreozzi Inc., N.Y.C., 1978; adminstrv. asst. WNET/13, N.Y.C., 1978-79; prodn. sec. MacNeil/Lehrer Report, N.Y.C., 1979-81, prodn. asst., 1981-82; membership, mktg. and fundraising adminstr. Leventhal-Sidman Jewish Cmty. Ctr., Newton, Mass., 1988-97; devel. assoc. Ben-Gurion U., Newton office, 1997-98; devel. mgr. AIDS Action Com., Boston, 1998—. Exec. prodr. (cable TV show) JCC-TV, 1994-97. Jewish. Avocations: cooking, camping, physical fitness.

**MERWIN, GREGORY KING,** farmer; b. Sacramento, July 16, 1934; s. Samuel Herbert and Daisy Ellen (King) Merwin; m. Patricia Ann Nikula, Aug. 8, 1959; children: Jeffrey Cornell, Elizabeth Juliana Underwood. BS, Stanford U., 1956. Jr. civil engr. Calif. Divsn. Hwys., Bishop, 1956—57; farmer, ptnr. S.H. Merwin & Sons Inc., Clarksburg, Calif., 1959—. Sec.-treas. Calif. Beet Growers Assn. Dist. 3, Delta Region, Calif., 1970—73; pres. Yolo County Farm Bur., Woodland, Calif., 1973—74; steering com. mem. County Agrl. Round Table, Woodland, 1974—2000; bd. mem. Yolo Land Trust, Woodland, 1999—2005. Ch. organist Clarksburg Cmty. C. United Ch. of Christ, 1959—; chmn. Delta Dist. Boy Scouts, Sacramento, 1980—83; com. mem. Clarksburg Plan Com., Calif., 1996—2005. With U.S. Army, 1957—59, Calif. Mem.: Sacramento Chpt. Am. Guild Organists (treas. 1977—80, sub dean 1980—82, dean 1982—84, 1991—92, sec. 2002—05, Colleague cert. 1989). Republican. Mem. United Ch. Of Christ. Achievements include invention of dichondra seed harvester in 1973. Avocations: music, model building, backpacking, history. Home: 39104 Z Line Rd Clarksburg CA 95612

**MERWIN, JOHN DAVID,** lawyer, former governor; b. Frederiksted, St. Croix, VI, Sept. 26, 1921; s. Miles and Marguerite Louise (Fleming) M.; m. Marjorie Davis Spaulding, Feb. 18, 1993. Student, U. Lausanne, Switzerland, 1938-39, U. P.R., 1939-40; BSc, Yale U., 1943; JD, George Washington U., 1948. Bar: Conn., VI 1949, U.S. Supreme Ct. Practice law, St. Croix, VI, 1949-50, 1953-57, 67-85; gen. counsel, v.p. Rob't L. Merwin & Co., Inc., 1953-57; senator-at-large VI Legislature, 1955-57; govt. sec. for VI, 1957-58; gov. VI, 1958-61; rep. Chase Manhattan Bank, Nassau, Bahamas, 1961-65; exec. v.p. Equity Pub. Corp. Orford, NH, 1965-67; ret. Chmn. VI Port Authority, 1972-75; Rep. candidate for Pres. NH Primary Election, 1992; pres. The Nason Found., Cleve., 1981-2002. Capt. F.A. AUS, 1942-46, 50-53. Decorated Bronze Star; Croix de Guerre with silver star. Mem. Conn., NH and VI Bar Assns., US Supreme Ct., Tennis Club St. Croix (VI), Yale Club (NYC), Cosmos Club (Washington), Country Club of Hudson, Phi Delta Phi. Episcopalian. Home and Office: PO Box 1029 Hudson OH 44236 E-mail: jdmerwin@hotmail.com.

**MERWIN, WILLIAM STANLEY,** poet; b. NYC, Sept. 30, 1927; AB, Princeton, 1947. Tutor, France and Portugal, 1949; to Robert Graves' son, Majorca, 1950; translator London, Eng., 1951-54. Playwright Poets' Theatre, Cambridge, Mass., 1956-57; with Roger Planchon's Theatre de la Cite, Lyon, France, 1964-65; author: (poetry) A Mask for Janus, 1952, The Dancing Bears, 1954, Green with Beasts, 1956, The Drunk in the Furnace, 1960, The Moving Target, 1963, Collected Poems, 1966, The Lice, 1969, Animae, 1969, The Carrier of Ladders, 1970 (Pulitzer Prize for poetry 1971), (with A.D. Moore) Signs, 1970, Asian Figures, 1973, Writings to an Unfinished Accompaniment, 1973, The First Four Books of Poems, 1975, The Compass Flower, 1977, Feathers from the Hill, 1978, Finding the Islands, 1982, Unframed Originals, 1982, Opening the Hand, 1983, The Rain in the Trees, 1988, Selected Poems, 1988, Travels, 1993; (prose) The Miner's Pale Children, 1970, Houses and Travellers, 1977, Unframed Originals: Recollections, 1982, Regions of Memory, 1987, The Lost Upland, 1992, Migration, 2005 (Nat. Book award for poetry, 2005); (plays) Darkling Child, 1956, Favor Island, 1957, The Gilded West, 1961; (memoir) Summer Doorways, 2005, editor: West Wind: Supplement of American Poetry, 1961, The Essential Wyatt, 1989; poetry editor: Nation, 1962; translator numerous Spanish, French works; contbr. articles to lit. mags. Kenyon Rev. poetry fellow, 1954; Rockefeller fellow, 1956, grantee, 1969; Nat. Inst. Arts and Letters grantee, 1957; Arts Council Gt. Britain bursary, 1957; Rabinowitz Found. grantee, 1961; Ford Found. grantee, 1964-65; Chapelbrook Found. fellow, 1966; Acad. Am. Poets fellow, 1973; Guggenheim fellow, 1973, 83; recipient Bess Hokin prize Poetry Mag., 1962, Harriet Monroe Meml. prize Poetry Mag., 1967, PEN Translation prize, 1968, Shelley Meml. award, 1974, Bollingen prize for poetry Yale Univ. Libr., 1979, Lannan Literary award for lifetime achievement, 2004. Mem. Nat. Inst. Arts and Letters. Addrerent PO Box 809 Hulku II 96/00-0809 Mailing: care Copper Canyon Press Bldg 313 Ft Worden State Pk PO Box 271 Port Townsend WA 98368*

**MERZ, JAMES LOGAN,** electrical and materials engineering educator, researcher; b. Jersey City, Apr. 14, 1936; s. Albert Joseph and Anne Elizabeth (Farrell) M.; m. Rose-Marie Weibel, June 30, 1962; children: Kathleen, James, Michael, Kimarie. BS in Physics, U. Notre Dame, 1959; postgrad., U. Göttingen, Fed. Republic Germany, 1959-60; MA, Harvard U., 1961, PhD in Applied Physics, 1967; PhD (hon.), Linköping U., Sweden, 1993. Mem. tech. staff Bell Labs., Murray Hill, NJ, 1966-78; prof. elec. engring. U. Calif., Santa Barbara, 1978-94, prof. materials, 1984-94, chmn. dept. elec. and computer engring., 1982-84, assoc. dean for rsch. devel. Coll. Engring., 1984-86, acting assoc. vice chancellor, 1988, dir. semiconductor rsch. corp. core program on GaAs digital ICs, 1984-89, dir. Compound Semiconductor Rsch. Labs., 1986-92, dir. NSF Ctr. for Quantized Electronic Structures, 1989-94; Freimann prof. elec. engring. U. Notre Dame (Ind.), 1994—, v.p. for grad. studies and rsch., dean Grad. Sch., 1996-2001. Mem. exec. com. Calif. Microelectronics Innovation and Computer Rsch. Opportunities Program, 1986-92; mem. NRC com. on Japan, NAS/NAE, 1988-90; mem. internat. adv. com. Internat. Symposium on Physics of Semiconductors and Applications, Seoul, Republic of Korea, 1990, Conf. on Superlattices and Microstructures, Xi'an, China, 1992; participant, mem. coms. other profl. confs. and meetings. Contbr. over 400 articles to profl. jours.; patentee in field. Fulbright fellow, Danforth Found. fellow, Woodrow Wilson Found. fellow; Alexander von Humboldt rsch. awardee, 2002. Fellow IEEE, Am. Phys. Soc.; mem. IEEE Lasers and Electro-Optics Soc. (program com. annual mtg. 1980), IEEE Electron Device Soc. (sec. 1994, 95), Am. Vacuum Soc. (exec. com. electronic materials and processing divsn 1988-89), Materials Rsch. Soc. (editl. bd. jour. 1984-87), Soc. for Values in Higher Edn., Inst. Electronics. Info. and Comm. Engrs. (overseas adv. com.), Sigma Xi, Eta Kappa Nu. Achievements include research in field of optoelectronic materials and devices: semiconductors and ionic materials; optical and electrical properties of implanted ions, rapid annealing; semiconductor lasers, detectors, solar cells, other optoelectronic devices; low-dimensional quantum structures, nanostructures. Home: 1530 Marigold Way South Bend IN 46617-1016 Office: U Notre Dame Dept Elec Engring 203B Cushing Hall Notre Dame IN 46556-5637 Business E-Mail: jmerz@nd.edu.

**MERZBACHER, EUGEN,** retired physics professor; b. Berlin, Apr. 9, 1921; came to U.S., 1947, naturalized, 1953; s. Siegfried and Lilli (Wilmersdoerffer) M.; m. Ann Townsend Reid, July 11, 1952; children: Celia, Charles, Matthew, Mary. Licentiate, U. Istanbul, 1943; AM, Harvard U., 1948, PhD, 1950; DSc (hon.), U. N.C., Chapel Hill, 1993. HS tchr., Ankara, Turkey, 1943–47; mem. Inst. Advanced Study, Princeton, NJ, 1950–51; vis. asst. prof. Duke U., Durham, NC, 1951–52; from mem. faculty to Kenan prof. physics U. N.C., Chapel Hill, 1952–91, Kenan prof. emeritus, 1991—; ret., 1991. Vis. prof. U. Wash., 1967-68, U. Edinburgh, Scotland, 1986; Arnold Bernhard vis. prof. physics Williams Coll., 1993; chair Internat. Conf. on Physics of Electronic and Atomic Collisions, 1987-89; sr. advisor APS, 1998-99. Author: Quantum Mechanics, 3d edit., 1998; also articles. NSF Sci. Faculty fellow U. Copenhagen, Denmark, 1959-60; recipient Thomas Jefferson award U. N.C., 1972; Humboldt sr. scientist award U. Frankfurt, Germany, 1976-77. Fellow AAAS, Am. Phys. Soc. (pres. 1990); mem. Am. Assn. Physics Tchrs. (Oersted medal 1992), Sigma Xi. Achievements include research on applications of quantum mechanics to study atoms and nuclei. Home: 1396 Halifax Rd Chapel Hill NC 27514-2724 Business E-Mail: merzbach@physics.unc.edu, merzie@mindspring.com.

**MESA, JOSE RAMON,** professional baseball player; b. Azua, Dominican Republic, May 22, 1966; Grad., high sch., Dominican Republic. With Balt. Orioles, 1990-92; pitcher Cleve. Indians, 1992—98, Seattle Mariners, 1999—2005, Phila. Phillies, 2001—03, Pitts. Pirates, 2004—. Selected to All-Star Team, 1995-96; named Sporting News Am. League Fireman of the Yr., 1995. Achievements include most saves (46) in American League, 1995, most consecutive saves (38) in American League history, 1995. Office: Pitts Pirates PNC Park 115 Federal St Pittsburgh PA 15212

**MESAK, HANI IBRAHIM,** marketing educator; b. Cairo, Feb. 21, 1944; s. Ibrahim M. Wassif and Mary K. Ghobrial; m. Eugenie Milad Habib, Aug. 23, 1977; 1 child, Irene Ann. BSc, Cairo U., 1965, Grad. Diploma, 1969; PhD, U. Pa., 1974. Engr. Orgn. Small Scale Industries, Cairo; mgmt. rsch. analyst Wharton Sch. U. Pa., Philad., 1970—73; project leader Data Analysis Ctr., NJ, 1974—75; assoc. prof. La. U., Monroe, 1987—89; prof. La. Tech U., Ruston, 1989—. Asst. prof. Kuwait U., 1975—87. Contbr. articles to profl. jours. (Irwin McGraw-Hill Disting. Paper award SW Fedn. Adminstrv. Disciplines, 1996, Best Theoretical/Empirical Paper award Decision Scis. Inst., 02). Mem.: Decision Sciences Inst. (assoc. editor Decision Scis. jour. 1999—2005, named to Hall of Fame). Democrat. Eastern Orthodox. Avocations: travel, ping pong/table tennis. Home: 904 Monterey Dr Ruston LA 71270 Office: La Tech U PO Box 10318 Ruston LA 71272 Office Phone: 318-257-3506. Business E-Mail: mesak@cab.latech.edu.

**MESCHUTT, DAVID RANDOLPH,** historian; b. N.Y.C., May 29, 1955; s. Philip Frederick and Mary Evelyn (Mahanes) M.; m. Sarah Caroline Bevan, July 14, 1990. BA in Journalism, Washington and Lee U., 1977; MA in History Mus. Studies, SUNY, Cooperstown, 1988; postgrad., Attingham Summer Sch., Gt. Britain, 1988, 98, postgrad., 2004, Royal Collection Studies Programme, 2000; PhD in Art History, U. Del., 2005. Rschr. Thomas Jefferson Meml. Found., Charlottesville, Va., 1977-78, Frick Art Reference Libr., N.Y.C., 1980-86; curator art West Point (N.Y.) Mus./U.S. Mil. Acad., 1988-98; consulting curator N.Y. State Office of Pks.; Recreation and Hist. Preservation, Waterford, NY, 1999—. Guest curator N.Y. State Hist. Assn., Cooperstown, 1986-87, Brandywine River Mus., Chadds Ford, Pa., 1992, Va. Hist. Soc., Richmond, 1999; cons. Curatorial Office, U.S. Dept. Treasury, Washington, 1988, Albany (N.Y.) Inst. History and Art, 1988. Author: A Bold Experiment: John Henri Isaac Browere's Life Masks of Prominent Americans, 1988; co-author: The Portraits and History Paintings of Alonzo Chappel, 1992; service. editor Am. Nat. Biography, Oxford U. Press, 1994-99, contbr., 1994—; contbr. articles to profl. jours. Bd. dirs. Friends of Stony Point Battlefield, NJ. Nourse Found. fellow, 1986-87, Nat. Endowment for Arts fellow, 1987, Soc. Colonial Wars fellow, 1988, Andrew W. Mellon fellow Va. Hist. Soc., 1992, Anne S.K. Brown fellow Brown U., 1993, Mayers fellow Huntington Libr. and Art Gallery, 1997. Mem.: Walpole Soc., N.Y. State Hist. Assn., Va. Hist. Soc., Ralph Vaughan Williams Soc., Herbert Howells Soc., Historians Brit. Art, Assn. Historians Am. Art. Methodist. Avocation: music. Office: care Mus of the Shenandoah Valley 901 Amherst St Winchester VA 22601-3802

**MESELSON, MATTHEW STANLEY,** biochemist, educator; b. Denver, May 24, 1930; s. Hymen Avram and Ann (Swedlow) M.; m. Jeanne Guillemin, 1986; children: Zoe, Amy Valor. Ph.B., U. Chgo., 1951, D.Sc. (hon.), 1975; PhD, Calif. Inst. Tech., 1957; Sc.D. (hon.), Oakland Coll., 1964, Columbia, 1971, Yale U., 1987, Princeton U., 1988. Asst. prof. chemistry Calif. Inst. Tech., 1958—59, sr. rsch. fellow chem. biology, 1959—60; assoc. prof. molecular biology Harvard U., 1964—76, Thomas Dudley Cabot prof. natural scis., 1976—. Cons. U.S. Arms Control and Disarmament Agency, 1963; adj. scientist Josephine Bay Paul Ctr. Comparative Molecular Biology and Evolution Marine Biol. Lab., Woods Hole, Mass., 2000—. Recipient Eli Lilly award microbiology and immunology, 1964, Alumni medal U. Chgo., 1971, Lehman award 1975, Presidential award 1983, N.Y. Acad. Scis., 1975; Alumni Disting. Svc. award Calif. Inst. Tech., 1975; Leo Szilard award Am. Phys. Soc., 1978; MacArthur fellow, 1984-89, Lasker award for Special Achievement in Medical Sci., Albert and Mary Lasker Found., 2004. Fellow AAAS (Sci. Freedom and Responsibility award, 1990); mem. NAS (Molecular Biology prize 1963), Inst. Medicine, Am. Acad. Arts and Scis., Fedn. Am. Scientists (chmn. 1986-88, Pub. Svc. award 1972), Coun. Fgn. Rels., Accademia Santa Chiara, Am. Philos. Soc., Royal Society (London), Académie des Sciences (Paris), Genetics Soc. Am. (Thomas Hunt Morgan medal 1995). Office: Harvard U Fairchild Biochem Bldg 7 Divinity Ave Cambridge MA 02138-2019*

**MESEREAU, THOMAS ARTHUR, JR.,** lawyer; b. West Point, NY, 1951; m. Heidi Gold (div.). BA cum laude, Harvard U., 1973; MSc, London Sch. Econ., 1975; JD, U. Calif., 1979. Bar: Calif. 1979. Assoc. Hunton & Williams, Washington, 1979—81; dep. dist. atty. Orange County, Calif., 1981—82; exec. Getty Synthetic Fuels Inc., 1982—85; ptnr. Collins, Mesereau, Reddock & Yu, LLP, LA, 1985—. Vol. legal clinic First African Meth. Episcopal Ch. Named Criminal Def. Lawyer Yr., Century City Bar Assn.; named one of The 10 Most Fascinating People of 2005, Barbara Walters Special; recipient Pro Bono award, State Bar Calif., Commendation, LA Bd. Supr., Sarah Allen Trailblazer award, Cert. Appreciation, LA County Supr., Compton award, Calif. Sch. Bd., Humanitarian award, Nat. Assn. Blacks in Criminal Justice. Mem.: Italian Am. Lawyers Assn. (former mem. bd. gov.), Calif. Atty. Criminal Justice. Achievements include Michael Jackson child molestation trial, 2005. Office: Collins Mesereau Reddock & Yu LLP 1875 Century Pk E 7th Fl Los Angeles CA 90067 Office Phone: 213-384-0982. Office Fax: 213-380-4820. Business E-Mail: mesereau@cmrylaw.com.*

**MESERVE, RICHARD ANDREW,** lawyer; b. Medford, Mass., Nov. 20, 1944; s. Robert William and Gladys Meserve; m. Martha Ann Richards, Sept. 20, 1966; children: Amy, Lauren. BA, Tufts U., 1966; JD, Harvard U., 1975; PhD in Applied Physics, Stanford U., 1976. Bar: Mass. 1975, DC 1980, U.S. Supreme Ct. 1982. Law clk. Mass. Supreme Jud. Ct., Boston, 1975-76; law clk. to presiding justice U.S. Supreme Ct., Washington, 1976-77; legal counsel Pres. Sci. Adviser, Washington, 1977-81; ptnr. Covington & Burling, Washington, 1981-99, sr. of counsel, 2004—; bd. dirs. Carnegie Instn. Washington, 2001—2003, pres., 2003—; chmn. U.S. Nuc. Regulatory Commn., Washington, 1999—2003. Chmn. com. assess safety and tech. issues Dept. Energy reactors NAS, 1987—88, chmn. com. fuel economy automobiles and light trucks, 1991—92, chmn. com. declassification info. Dept. Energy's environ. programs, 1994—95, chmn. nuc. and radiation studies bd. NAS-NAE, 2004—; co-chmn. AAAS-ABA Nat. Conf. Lawyers and Scientists, 1988—94; mem. bd. overseers arts and scis. Tufts U., 1994—2002; mem. adv. bd. Sec. Energy, 1996—99; mem. bd. dirs. Univs. Rsch. Assn., Inc., 2004—; chmn. internat. nuc. safety group IAEA, 2003—. Fellow: AAAS (bd. dirs. 2000—06), Am. Acad. Arts and Scis. (coun. and

exec. com. 2005—), Am. Phys. Soc.; mem.: NAE, Am. Philos. Soc., Sigma Xi, Phi Beta Kappa. Democrat. Home: 708 Berry St Falls Church VA 22042-2402 Office Phone: 202-387-6404. Business E-Mail: rmeserve@ciw.edu.

**MESERVE, WILLIAM GEORGE,** lawyer; b. Medford, Mass., June 14, 1940; s. Robert William and Gladys Evangeline (Swenson) M.; m. Susan Mary Rycroft, Oct. 21, 1967; children: Daniel Scott, Susan Elizabeth, Jonathan Robert. BA, Tufts U., 1962; LLB, Harvard U., 1965; MSc, London Sch. Econs., 1966. Bar: Mass. 1966, U.S. Dist. Ct. Mass. 1970, U.S. Ct. Appeals (1st cir.) 1973. Legal asst. to commr. FTC, Washington, 1966-67; staff counsel com. on commerce U.S. Senate, Washington, 1967-69; assoc. Ropes & Gray, Boston, 1970-76, ptnr., 1976—2002, sr. counsel, 2002—. Geology field asst. McMurdo Sound, Antarctica, 1959-60, Inglefield Land, Greenland, summer 1965. Trustee Tufts U., Medford, 1979—97, AFS Intercultural Programs Inc., N.Y.C., 1979—92, 1993—96, 2006—, New Eng. Med. Ctr., Inc., Boston, 1988—97; Lifespan of Mass., Inc., 1997—2002; bd. visitors Fletcher Sch. Law and Diplomacy Tufts U., Medford, 1971—; bd. dirs. United South End Settlements, Boston, 1979—, Earthwatch Inst., Maynard, 1996—, AFS-USA, N.Y.C., 1999—2006, Conservation Edn. and Rsch. Trust, Oxford, England, 2004—; bd. govs. New Eng. Med. Ctr. Hosps., Boston, 1982—94, 1995—97, 2004—. Fellow Am. Coll. Trial Lawyers; mem. ABA, Boston Bar Assn., Phi Beta Kappa. Clubs: Appalachian Mountain (Boston) (rec. sec. 1977-78). Democrat. Office: Ropes & Gray 1 International Pl Fl 41 Boston MA 02110-2624 Business E-Mail: william.meserve@ropesgray.com.

**MESHACH, JOSEPH ROBERT,** music educator; b. Newton, N.J., Oct. 28, 1962; s. Robert Frankin and Gertrude Meshach; m. Cathy Smith; 1 child, Jennifer Grace. B in Music Edn., Newberry Coll., 1985. Band dir. Barnwell (S.C.) HS, 1985—92, Walterboro (S.C.) HS, 1992—2003, Colleton County (S.C.) High Sch., 2003—. Choir dir. Bethel Presbyn. Ch., Walterboro, 1994—. Named to All-Am. Hall of Fame Band Honors, Purdue U., 1980; recipient Dist. Achievement award, Am. Legion, 1981. Mem.: S.C. Band Dir.'s Assn. (All-State band chmn. 2001—, so. region band chmn. 1994—98, State 4A Marching Band champions 1992, Lower State Marching Band Champions 1992—2001, Outstanding Performance award 1992—2004, State 4A Marching Band champions 1993, 1995, 1997), S.C. Music Educators Assn., Music Educators Nat. Conf., Phi Beta Mu, Phi Mu Alpha Sinfonia (Acad. Achievement award 1984). Home: 301 Canal St Walterboro SC 29488 Office: Colleton County High Sch 1379 Mighty Cougar Dr Walterboro SC 29488 Office Phone: 843-538-2907. Office Fax: 843-538-8151. Personal E-mail: joejoe@lowcountry.com

**MESHACK, GENEVA TUCKER,** retired elementary school educator; b. Marion, Ala., Aug. 31, 1939; d. Lovelace and Louise (Kynard) Tucker; m. Hugh von Meshack, Aug., 1962 (div. 1978). BS, MS, Prairie View A&M. Tchr. Temple ISD, Temple, Tex., 1965—2004; ret., 2004. Mem. PTO, College, music dept. Mt. Zion Bapt. Ch., Temple, Tex., gen. v.p., 2nd v.p. mission. Mem. NEA, Tex. State Tchr. Assn., Nat. Sci. Assn., Ebony Culture Soc., Prairie View A&M Univ. Alumni, Zeta Phi Beta. Democrat. Home: 1016 E Adams Ave Temple TX 76501-4621

**MESHACK, MARQUES D.,** social studies educator; b. San Diego; s. Coleman F. Meshack and Jill Marlene Carroll. AA, San Diego City Coll., 2000; BA in History, Clark Atlanta U., 2004. Team leader San Diego Parks and Recreation Boys and Girls Club, 1996—97; recreation leader I Jackie Robinson YMCA, San Diego, 1997—98; tchr. asst. Euclid Elem. Sch., 1998—99; team leader Hands On Atlanta, 2004—05; social studies tchr. Hapeville Mid. Sch., Atlanta, 2005—. Mentor at-risk students Chollas Elem. Sch., San Diego, 1995; vol. graffitti removal I Love a Clean San Diego, 1996. Mem.: Phi Alpha Phi. Office: Hapeville Charter Mid Sch 3535 S Fulton Ave Hapeville GA 30354-1701 Home: 5796 Old Memory Ln San Diego CA 92114 E-mail: mm3165644@aol.com.

**MESHBESHER, RONALD I.,** lawyer; b. Mpls., May 18, 1933; s. Nathan J. and Esther J. (Balman) M.; m. Sandra F. Siegel, June 17, 1956 (div. 1978); children: Betsy F., Wendy S., Stacy J.; m. Kimberly L. Garnaas, May 23, 1988; 1 child, Jolie M. BS in Law, U. Minn., 1955, JD, 1957. Bar: Minn. 1957, U.S. Supreme Ct. 1966. Prosecuting atty. Hennepin County, Mpls., 1958-61; pres. Meshbesher and Spence Ltd., Mpls., 1961—. Lectr. numerous legal and profl. orgns.; mem. adv. com. on rules of criminal procedure Minn. Supreme Ct., 1971-91; cons. on recodification of criminal procedure code Czech Republic Ministry of Justice, 1994. Author: Trial Handbook for Minnesota Lawyers, 1992; mem. bd. editors Criminal Law Advocacy Reporter; mem. adv. bd. Nat. Affairs Criminal Practice Manual; contbr. numerous articles to profl. jours. Mem.: ABA, ATLA (bd. govs. 1968—71), Attys. for Criminal Justice, Trial Lawyers for Pub. Justice, Minn. Assn. Criminal Def. Lawyers (pres. 1991—92, Disting. Svc. award 2001), Minn. Trial Lawyers Assn. (pres. 1973—74, Lifetime Achievement award 2001), Nat. Assn. Criminal Def. Lawyers (pres. 1984—85), Am. Acad. Forensic Scis., Am. Bd. Criminal Lawyers (v.p. 1983), Am. Bd. Trial Advs., Am. Coll. Trial Lawyers, Internat. Acad. Trial Lawyers, Minn. Bar Assn. Avocations: bicycling, photography, travel, flying, theater. Office: Meshbesher & Spence 1616 Park Ave Minneapolis MN 55404-1695 Office Phone: 612-339-9121. E-mail: rmeshbesher@meshbesher.com.

**MESHEL, HARRY,** former state senator, political party official; b. Youngstown, Ohio, June 13, 1924; s. Angelo and Rubena (Markakis) Michelakis; children: Barry, Melanie. BSBA, Youngstown Coll., 1949; MS, Columbia U., 1950; LLD (hon.), Ohio U., Youngstown State U., Ohio Coll. Podiatric Medicine; LHD (hon.), Youngstown State U. Exec. asst. to mayor City of Youngstown, Ohio, 1964-68, urban renewal dir. Ohio, 1969; mem. 33d district Ohio Senate, Columbus, 1971-93, Dem. minority leader, 1981-82, 85-90, pres. and majority leader, 1983-84, com. mem. econ. develop., sci. & tech., state & local govt., ways & means, commerce & labor, controlling bd., state employment compensation bd., fin. chmn., 1974-81, rules chmn., 1983-84, com. mem. rules, reference & oversight, 1985-90; state chair Ohio Dem. Party, 1993-95. Real estate broker; adj. prof. polit. sci. Ohio U.; faculty mem. (limited svc.) Youngstown State U.; div. mgr. investment firm; Ohio Senate special com. mem. Task Force on Drug Strategies, Ohio Acad. Sci. Centennial Celebration Commn., Motor Vehicle Inspection & Maintenance Program, Legis. Oversight Com., Ohio Boxing Commn., Correctional Inst. Inspection Com., Ohio Small Bus. & Entrepreneurship Coun., Gov.'s Adv. Coun. Travel & Tourism, Legis. Svc. Commn., Capital Sq. Rev. & Adv. Bd., others. Past pres., past lt. gov. Am. Hellenic Ednl. Prog. Assn. (AHEPA); precinct committeeman Mahoning County Dem. Party, ward captain, mem. exec. com.; campaign mgr. local candidates, county campaign mgr. presdl. candidates; del. Dem. Mid-Term Conv., 1981; founder Great Lakes/N.E. Legis. Coalition; chmn., founder Nat. Dem. State Legis. Leaders Assn.; dir. State Legis. Leaders Found.; state/fed. assembly, mem. communications com. Nat. Conf. State Legis., legis. mgmt. com., govt. opers. com.; chair fiscal affairs com. Midwest Conf. Coun. State Govts., task force on econs. & fiscal affairs; del., exec. com. Dem. Nat. Com.; mem. Dem. Leadership Coun., State Dem. Exec. Com.; exec. com. Assn. State Dem. Chairs; bd. trustees Nat. Hall of Fame for Persons with Disabilities; mem. St. Nicholas Greek Orthodox Ch.; mem. Mill Creek Metro Park Bd. Commrs. With USN, 1943-46. Decorated two Bronze Battle Stars; recipient Dist. Svc. award Office of Pres., Top Legislator award Ohio Union Patrolmen Assn., Dist. Citizen award Med. Coll. Ohio, City of Hope Leadership award, 1993, Legis. Leadership award Ohio Coalition for Care of Handicapped Children, Phillips Medal of Pub. Svc., Ohio U., John E. Fogarty award Gov.'s Com. of Employment of Handicapped, Gov.'s award, 1992, U. Cin. Award for Excellence, Lamp of Learning award Ohio Edn. Assn., Black Cultural Soc. award East Liverpool, Mahoning Valley Man of Yr. award, Mahoning Valley Econ. Devel. Corp., Office Holder of Yr. award Truman-Johnson Dem. Women, Best Interest of Children award Fathers of Equal Rights, Founders Day award Circle of Friends Found., Helping Hand award Easter Seal Soc., Honorary Riverboat Captain award Mahoning County Dem. Party, Community Svc. and Special Svcs. awards Eastern Orthodox Men's Soc., Periclean award AHEPA,

Academy of Achievement award Nat. AHEPA Ednl. Found., Nat. Svc. Dem. award AHEPA, 1994, Disting. Citizen award Youngstown State U. Alumni Assn., numerous appreciation and recognition awards; recipient Outstanding Legislator awards Ohio Acad. Trial Lawyers, Ohio Assn. Pub. Sch. Employees, Ohio Rehab. Assn., League Ohio Sportsmen; recipient Dist. Svc. awards Youngstown State U., Ohio Edn. Assn., Ohio Union Patrolmen Assn., Ohio Disabled Vets., AFL-CIO Ohio Barbers Union, AFL-CIO Nat. Assn. of Theatre Owners of Ohio; named Guardian of the Menorah, Youngstown B'nai B'rith, Outstanding Dem., Fairfield Dem. Club, 1993; named to Ohio Vets. Hall of Fame. Mem. (life) NAACP, ACLU, AMVETS (Legislator of Yr. 1993), VFW, Am. Legion, Cath. War Vets (Dist. Legislator award), Vet. Boxers Assn. Mercer County, Pa., Trumbull County Boxers' Legends of Leather (Man of Yr. award Hall of Fame), William Holmes McGuffey Hist. Soc., Buckeye Elks Lodge (hon.); mem. Kiwanis Internat., Urban League, Alliance C. of C., Southern Community Jaycees (hon.), Soc. for Preservation of Greek Heritage, Greek Am. Progressive Assn., Pan Cretan Assn., Arms Hist. Mus. Soc., Eagles, Moose, The Stambaugh Pillars.

**MESHER, JOHN R.,** lawyer; b. Pitts., Nov. 8, 1952; m. Maureen Mesher; children: Dan, Jeffrey, Rachel, Laura. BA, Ind. U. Pa., 1974; JD, Duquesne U., 1977. Bar: Pa. 1977. With Eckert Seamans Cherin & Mellott, Pitts., 1977—80, Alco Standard Corp., Phila., 1980—88; divsn. counsel Certain Teed Corp., 1988—97; v.p., gen. counsel, sec. Saint-Gobain Corp., Valley Forge, 1997—. Mem.: Am. Corp. Counsel Assn. Office: St Gobain Corp 750 E Swedesford Rd PO Box 860 Valley Forge PA 19482 Office Phone: 610-341-7108. Office Fax: 610-341-7087.*

**MESHII, MASAHIRO,** materials science educator; b. Amagasaki, Japan, Oct. 6, 1931; arrived in US, 1956; s. Masataro and Kazuyo M.; m. Eiko Kumagai, May 21, 1959; children: Alisa, Erica. BS, Osaka (Japan) U., 1954, MS, 1956; PhD, Northwestern U., 1959. Lectr., rsch. assoc. dept. materials sci. and engring. Northwestern U., Evanston, Ill., 1959-60, asst. prof., assoc. prof., then prof., 1960-88, chmn. dept. materials sci. and engring., 1978-82, John Evans prof., 1988—2003, John Evans prof. emeritus, 2003—. Vis. scientist Nat. Rsch. Inst. Metals, Tokyo, 1970-71; NSF faculty rsch. participant Argonne (Ill.) Nat. Lab., 1975; guest prof. Osaka U., 1985; Acta/Scripta Metallurgica lectr., 1993-95. Co-editor: Lattice Defects in Quenched Metals, 1965, Martensitic Transformation, 1978, Science of Advanced Materials, 1990; editor: Fatigue and Microstructures, 1979, Mechanical Properties of BCC Metals, 1982; contbr. over 245 articles to tech. publs. and internat. jours. Recipient Founders award Midwest Soc. Electron Microscopists, 1987, Meritorious award for best paper Iron and Steel Soc., 1993; named Best Tchr. of Yr., Engring. Students of Northwestern U., 1978; Fulbright grantee, 1956; Japan fellow, 1957. Fellow ASM (Henry Marion Howe medal 1968, Best Acad. Paper award 1994), Japan Soc. Promotion of Sci.; mem. AIME, Metallurgical Soc., Japan Inst. Metals (hon. Achievement award 1972); clubs: Toastmasters Internat. Office: 22879 NE 127th Way Redmond WA 98053-5657 Office Phone: 425-826-2334. Personal E-mail: mmeshii@hotmail.com.

**MESHKE, GEORGE LEWIS,** drama and humanities educator; b. Yakima, Wash., Oct. 7, 1930; s. George Joseph and Marye Elizabeth (Lopas) Meshke. BA, U. Wash., 1953, MA, 1959, PhD in Drama, 1972. Cert. tchr., Wash. Tchr. English and drama Zillah High Sch., Wash., 1955-58, high sch., Bellevue, Wash., 1958-60, Federal Way, Wash., 1960-70; dir., actor Old Brewery Theatre, Helena, Mont., 1962-66; prof. drama Yakima Valley CC, Yakima, 1970-2000, part-time instr., 1991—05, emeritus, 2005—. Casting dir., dir. summer seminar Laughing Horse Summer Theatre, Ellensburg, Wash., 1989-96, Children's Lit. Inst., 2000; adj. prof. grad. studies Ctrl. Wash. U., Tchr. Exch., London, 1995, People-to People Exch., China, 2000, Mongolia, Manchuria, 2001; lectr. Inquiring Mind series Wash. State Humanities, 1989-91; regional dir. Am. Coll. Theatre Festival, Washington, 1980-86; arts dialogue J.F. Kennedy Ctr., Washington, 1987—; casting dir., actor Hollywood Ind. Prodns.; adv. coun. Kennedy Ctr. Author, producer Towers of Tomorrow, 1985, The Halls of Yesterday-Yakima Hist. drama; appeared in Yakima, Washington, 1998. Regional bd. dirs. Common Cause, Yakima, 1971-73; active Nat. Hist. Soc., Nat. Wilderness Soc., Roosevelt Meml. Found., Wash. State Commn. Humanities, Drama League, People to People Tours, Clinton Libr. With U.S. Army, 1953-55, Austria. Recipient Gold medal Kennedy Ctr., 1985, Wash. State Humanities medal, 1983, NISAD medal, 1989, Wash. State Drama award, 1999. Mem. ACLU, VFW, Wash. Edn. Assn., N.W. Drama Assn., Am. Legion, Am. Edn. Theatre Assn., Am. Fedn. Tchrs., Kennedy Libr., Amnesty Internat. Carter Libr., Libr. Congress (assoc.), Smithsonian Instn., Phi Delta Kappa Democrat. Avocations: travel, mountain climbing, skiing, reading. Home: 5 N 42nd Ave Yakima WA 98908-3214 Office: Yakima Valley CC 16th And Nob Hill Blvd Yakima WA 98907

**MESHKI, HAMED,** lawyer; b. Tehran, Iran, Dec. 28, 1978; s. Cyrus Meshki and Aida S. McNamara. BA, UCLA, 2000; postgrad., Georgetown U., Washington, 2000—01; JD with hons., U. Chgo., 2003. Bar: Calif. 2003. Assoc. Skadden, Arps, Slate, Meagher & Flom LLP, LA, 2003—05, Kirkland & Ellis LLP, LA, 2005—. Presenter in field; founder, chmn. com. Chgo. Transfer Com., 2002—03; mem. Chgo. Investment Law Group, 2002—03; course instr. Law Sch. Admissions Test, 1999—2000; asst. mgr., sales rep. Bernini, Inc., 1997—2000. Contbr. articles to mags. Pro bono atty. Pub. Counsel, LA, 2003; vol. Habitat for Humanity, LA, 2005; pro bono atty. Small Wonders Found, LA, 2004—05, Hope Renews, Inc., LA, 2004—05, Alliance Children's Rights, LA, 2006. John M. Olin scholar in law and econ., U. Chgo. Law Sch., 2001—02. Mem.: Calif. Young Lawyers Assn., LA County Bar Assn., Calif. State Bar Assn., Order of Coif. Avocations: literature, wine, travel. Office: Kirkland & Ellis LLP 777 S Figueroa St Los Angeles CA 90017

**MESHLOVITZ, MARY E.,** educational consultant, special education educator; b. Buffalo, Apr. 6, 1967; d. John and Kathleen C. Kroll; m. Kenneth Peter Meshlovitz, Mar. 15, 1997; 1 child, Kenneth Enn. BS in Elem. and Spl. Edn., SUC, 1989; MS in Reading Edn., SUNY, Buffalo, 1999. Cert. reading, elem. edn., spl. edn. Spl. edn. tchr. Monroe Boces II, Spencerport, NY, 1989—90, Gateway-Longview Sch., Williamsville, NY, 1990—98; spl. edn. resource tchr. Buffalo Pub. Sch., 1998—99, reading tchr., 1999—2003, reading first coach, 2003—. Mem.: Coun. for Exemption Children, Internat. Reading Assn. Democrat. Roman Catholic. Avocations: reading, travel, cross stitch. Home: 37 Mendola St Buffalo NY 14215 Office: Roosevelt ECC #65 249 Skillen St Buffalo NY 14207 Personal E-Mail: new1211997@netzero.net.

**MESHOWSKI, FRANK ROBERT,** business consultant; b. Milw., Sept. 10, 1930; s. Frank Louis and Constance (Mockus) M.; m. Olga Skirka, Jan. 26, 1952; children: David, Laurie, Elaine. B. in Marine Engring., N.Y. State Maritime Acad., 1951; BSME, Newark Coll. Engring., 1954. Project mgr. Curtiss Wright, Woodridge, N.J., 1952-59; v.p. sales/mktg. Gulton Industries, Metuchen, N.J., 1959-68; sr. v.p. Nytronics, Inc., Alpha, N.J., 1968-72; v.p. mktg. Gulf & Western Industries, N.Y.C., 1972-79; pres., chief exec. officer Unicord div. Gulf & Western Industries, Westbury, N.Y., 1979-87; exec. v.p., chief operating officer, dir. OPT Industries, Phillipsburg, N.J., 1987-89. Bus. cons. strategic planning, mktg. and distbn., 1989—. Home and Office: 17 Turnberry Dr Monroe Township NJ 08831 Office Phone: 732-656-3168. Office Fax: 732-656-3169.

**MESHULAM, DEBORAH R.,** lawyer; b. Lancaster, Pa., Nov. 25, 1956; BA magna cum laude, Univ. Va., 1978; JD, Columbia Univ., 1981. Bar: NY 1982, DC 1988, US Dist. Ct. (so. & ea. NY, Md., DC dist.), US Ct. Appeals (2d, 11th, DC cir.), US Supreme Ct. Asst. chief litigation counsel SEC, Washington, 1990—97; ptnr, head of Litigation group DLA Piper Rudnick Gray Cary, Washington. Co-author: Plain English Guidebook to SEC Recordkeeping & Retention, 2003; contbr. articles to profl. jours. Harlan Fiske Stone scholar. Office: DLA Piper Rudnick Gray Cary 1200 19th St NW Washington DC 20036-2412 Office Phone: 202-861-6470. Office Fax: 202-223-2085. Business E-Mail: deborah.meshulam@dlapiper.com.

**MESKILL, THOMAS J.,** federal judge; b. New Britain, Conn., Jan. 30, 1928; s. Thomas J.M. Meskill; m. Mary T. Grady; children: Maureen Meskill Heneghan, John Peter, Eileen Meskill Gallupe, Thomas. BS, Trinity Coll., Hartford, Conn., 1950, LL.D., 1972; JD, U. Conn., 1956; postgrad., Sch. Law, NYU; LL.D., U. Bridgeport, 1971, U. New Haven, 1974. Bar: Conn. 1956, Fla. 1957, D.C. 1957, U.S. Ct. Appeals (2d cir.) 1975, U.S. Supreme Ct. 1971. Former mem. firm Meskill, Dorsey, Sledzik and Walsh, New Britain; mem. 90th-91st Congresses 6th Conn. Dist.; gov. Conn., 1971-75; judge U.S. Ct. Appeals (2d cir.), New Britain, Conn., 1975—, chief judge, 1992-93, sr. judge, 1993—. Pres. New Britain Council Social Agys.; Asst. corp. council City of New Britain, 1960-62, mayor, 1962-64, corp. counsel, 1965-67; mem. Constl. Conv., Hartford, 1965. Served to 1st lt. USAF, 1950-53. Recipient Disting. Svc. award Jr. C. of C., 1964, Jud. Achievement award ATLA, 1983, Learned Hand medal for Excellence in Fed. Jurisprudence, Fed. Bar Coun., 1994. Mem. Conn. Bar Assn. (Henry J. Naruk Jud. award 1994), Hartford County Bar Assn., New Britain Bar Assn., KC. Republican. Office: US Ct Appeals Old Post Office Plz Ste 204 114 W Main St New Britain CT 06051-4223 Office Phone: 860-224-2617.*

**MESKILL, VICTOR P.,** academic administrator, educator; b. Albertson, N.Y., May 9, 1935; s. James Joseph and Ida May (Pfalzer) M.; m. Gail King Heidinger, 1986; children by previous marriage— Susan Ann, Janet Louise, Gary James, Glenn Thomas, Kenneth John, Matthew Adam. BA, Hofstra U., 1961, MA (grad. scholar), 1962; PhD, St. John's U., 1967; postgrad. insts., Ohio State U., 1968; postgrad., Harvard U., 1972, NYU, 1973; DSc (hon.), Samara State Aerospace U., Russia, 1993; LHD (hon.), St. John's U., 1995; DCL (hon.), Moscow Internat. U., Russia, 1996; DCL (hon.), D Ecology/Biosphere (hon.), Coll. Puschino State U., Moscow, 1996; D of Pedagogy (PdD) (hon.), Dowling Coll., 1997; D of Econs. (hon.), U. Istanbul, Turkey, 1997; D of Sci., Yanshan U., Peoples' Republic of China, 1998. Lab. asst., instr. biology Hofstra U., 1960-62; N.Y. State teaching fellow St. John's U., 1962-63; instr. biology Nassau (N.Y.) C.C., 1963-64; tchr. sci. Central H.S. Dist. 2, Floral Park, N.Y., 1963-64; lectr. biology C.W. Post Coll., Greenvale, N.Y., 1963-64, instr. biology, 1964-67, asst. prof., 1967-68, assoc. prof., 1968-74, assoc. dir. Inst. for Student Problems, supr. student tchrs., 1967-68, asst. dean Coll., dean summer sch., coordinator Admissions Office, coordinator adult and continuing edn. programs, 1968-69; dean adminstrn. C.W. Post Ctr. of L.I. U., 1969-70, v.p. adminstrn., 1970-77, prof. biology, 1975-77; pres. Dowling Coll., Oakdale, L.I., 1977-2000, pres. emeritus, 2000—. Cons. in edn. and biology; chem. technician, detective Tech. Rsch. Bur., Nassau County Police Dept., 1958-63; mem. sci. adv. com., 1970; mem. adv. coun. Aerospace Edn. Coun. Inc., 1968; trustee, mem. state legis. com. Commn. Ind. Colls. and Univs.; mem. evaluation teams Mid. States Assn. 1971—; mem. higher edn. adv. com. N.Y. State Senate; mem. Nassau-Suffolk Comprehensive Health Planning Coun.; chmn. Internat. and Mediterranean Studies Group Conf. Contbr. articles to profl. jours. Founding mem., vice-chmn. bd. trustees Nassau Higher Edn. Consortium; bd. dirs. Suffolk County coun. Boy Scouts Am.; mem. N.Y. State Energy Rsch. and Devel. Authority, Town of Islip Devel. Commn.; chmn. bd. trustees L.I. Regional Adv. Coun. Higher Edn.; chmn. L.I. Mid Suffolk Bus. Action; bd. dirs. Southside Hosp., N.Y.; v.p. L.I. Forum for Tech.; former commr. Suffolk County Vanderbilt Mus.; mem. Bus. Coun. N.Y.; hon. mem. U. Pau and Pays de l'Adour, Pau, France, 1994; hon. prof. Minjiang U., Fuzhou, Peoples Republic of China, 1994; active mem. Universal Life Keeping Problems Acad., Dept. Justice Russian Fedn., Moscow. Decorated commendatore dell'Ordine al Merito (Italy); NSF rsch. grantee, 1967-69; Named Tchr. of Year, Aesculapius Med. Arts Soc., C.W. Post Coll. of L.I. U., 1967; Disting. Faculty Mem. of Year, C.W. Post Ctr. L.I. U., 1977, Educator of Yr. WLIW Channel 21, 1996, Officier dans l'ordre des Palmes Académiques, 2001; recipient George M. Estabrook award Hofstra U., 1978, Higher Edn. Leadership award Corning Glass Works, 1987, Disting. Leadership award L.I., 1989, Diploma Merito, Garibaldi Inst., Rome, Diploma of Honor, Rsch. Ctr. for Islamic History, Art and Culture, Istanbul, Turkey, Advancement for Commerce and Industry Disting. Svc. award in field of edn., 1997. Mem. AAAS, Coun. Advancement and Support of Edn., Am. Assn. Collegiate Registrars and Admissions Officers, Am. Assn. Higher Edn., Am. Inst. Biol. Scis., Am. Soc. Zoologists, Am. Assn. U. Adminstrs., Commn. on Ind. Colls. and Univs. (trustee), Nat. Assn. Biology Tchrs., Nat. Sci. Tchrs. Assn., Soc. Protozoologists, N.Y. Acad. Scis., Camilo Josè Cela Found. (hon.), Met. Assn. Coll. and Univ. Biologists (founder, mem. steering com.), Bus. Coun. N.Y., Oakdale C. of C. (founding mem., dir.), Russian Soc. Plant Physiologists (corr.), Universal Life Keeping Problems Acad. Moscow, Tsiolkovski Space Acad. Moscow (fgn.), Univ. Club (N.Y.C.), Wings Club (N.Y.C.), Nat. Arts Club (N.Y.C.), L.I. Coun. Fgn. Rels., L.I. Assn. Commerce and Industry (v.p. edn., dir.), Alpha Chi, Kappa Delta Pi, Phi Delta Kappa, Sigma Xi, Beta Beta Beta, Alpha Eta Rho, Delta Mu Delta, Kappa Delta Rho.

**MESLINSKY, LYNETTE C.,** mathematics professor; b. Buffalo, Dec. 15, 1953; d. Howard A. and Mae M. Hoke; m. Albert E. Meslinsky, Aug. 24, 1973; children: Christopher A., Sheri L., Kelly D., Eric M. M in Secondary Math. Edn., SUNY, Buffalo, 1976. Prof. math. ECC City Campus, Buffalo, 1988—. Recreation dir. North Collins Recreation Dept., NY, 1985—95. Mem.: Amatyc, Nysmatyc. Avocations: reading, skiing, fitness, travel, theater. Office Phone: 716-270-5123. Business E-Mail: meslinskylc@ecc.edu.

**MESNIAEFF, GREGORY,** economist, securities analyst; b. N.Y.C., Jan. 13, 1958; s. Peter G. and Maria A. (Voropajeff) M.; m. Elizabeth Burke, June 18, 1989. BBA Baruch Sch. Bus., CUNY, N.Y.C., 1986; MA in Econs., Trinity Coll., Hartford, 1989. Market rschr. Blair TV, N.Y.C., 1989-90; industry analyst telecomms. Northern Bus. Info./McGraw Hill, N.Y.C., 1990-94; assoc. v.p. equity rsch. Wheat First Butcher & Singer, Richmond, Va., 1994-96; sr. v.p. equity rsch. Robinson-Humphrey Co., Atlanta, 1996—2002; mng. dir. PT Capital LLC, N.Y.C., 2002—. Fellow Trinity Coll. Bd. Fellows, Hartford, 1994-96. Recipient All-Star Analyst Telecom. Equipment Wall St. Jour., 1998. Mem. N.Y. Soc. Security Analysts (investment strategy com.), NY Yacht Club, Russian Nobility Assn. Am. (bd. dir.), Soc. Preservation New England Antiquities, New England Soc. N.Y. Republican. Russian Orthodox. Avocations: skiing, sailing, bicycling, historic preservation. Home: PO Box 1021 Sharon CT 06069 Office Phone: 212-920-4550.

**MESNIKOFF, ALVIN MURRAY,** psychiatrist, educator; b. Asbury Park, N.J., Dec. 25, 1925; s. Nathan and Rachel (Feinberg) M.; m. Wendy Savin, June 15, 1952; children: Nathaniel, Rachel, Joel, Ann. AB, Rutgers U., 1948; postgrad., Yale U., 1948-49, Stanford U., 1949-50; MD, U. Chgo., 1954; cert. Psychoanalytic medicine, Columbia U., 1962. Diplomate: Am. Bd. Psychiatry and Neurology. Pvt. practice, 1958—; collaborating psychoanalyst Columbia U. Psychoanalytic Ctr. for Tng. and Rsch., N.Y.C., 1962—; dir. Washington Heights Cmty., N.Y. State Psychiat. Inst., N.Y.C., 1965—81; assoc. clin. prof. psychiatry Columbia U. Coll. Physicians and Surgeons, 1958—68; prof. psychiatry SUNY, Bklyn., 1968—81; dir. South Beach Psychiat. Ctr., S.I., NY, 1968—75; regional dir. N.Y. State Dept. Mental Health, N.Y.C., 1975—78, dep. commr. rsch., 1978—81; Marion E. Kenworthy prof. Psychiatry Columbia U. Sch. Social Work, 1981—89; lectr. Union Theol. Sem., N.Y.C., 1989—90. Cons. St. Vincent's Hosp., S.I., N.Y.C.; attending psychiatrist S.I. Hosp., 1972-76; sr. attending psychiatrist St. Luke's/Roosevelt Hosp. Ctr., N.Y., 1980-81; cons. Ford Found., N.Y., 1980-81 Contbr. chpts. to books, articles to profl. jours. Bd. dirs. Reality House, 1967-74; mem. task force med. sch. enrollment and physician manpower N.Y. State Bd. Regents, 1973-75; mem. task force on gen. and splty. hosp. care N.Y. State Health Planning Commn., 1973-74. Served with U.S. Army 1943-45. Grantee Ford Found., 1982 Fellow Am. Psychiat. Assn. (life); mem. Am. Psychoanalytic Assn., Assn. Psychoanalytic Medicine Am. Friends Tel Aviv U. (chmn. 1974-75), Phi Beta Kappa. Jewish. Office: 360 Central Park W New York NY 10025-6541 Office Phone: 212-663-5701.

**MESROBIAN, ARPENA SACHAKLIAN,** publishing executive, consultant, editor; b. Boston; d. Aaron H. and Eliza Sachaklian; m. William J. Mesrobian, June 22, 1940 (dec.); children: William S.(dec.), Marian Elizabeth (Mrs. Bruce MacCurdy). Student, Armenian Coll. of Beirut, Lebanon, 1937-38; AA, Univ. Coll., Syracuse U., NY, 1959, BA magna cum laude,

1971; MSsc, Syracuse U., 1993. Editor Syracuse U. Press, 1955-58, exec. editor, 1958-61, asst. dir., 1961-65, acting dir., 1965-66, editor, 1968-85, assoc. dir., 1968-75, dir., 1975-85, 87-88, dir. emeritus, 1985. Dir. workshop on univ. press. pub. U. Malaysia, Kuala Lumpur, 1985; cons. Empire State Coll. Book rev. editor: Armenian Rev., 1967-75; author: Like One Family: The Armenians of Syracuse, 2000; mem. publs. bd. Courier, 1970-94; mem. adv. bd. Armenian Rev., 1981-83; contbr. to Ency. of NY State, 2005; contbr. numerous articles, revs. to profl. jours. Pres. Syracuse chpt. Armenian Relief Soc., 1972-74; sponsor Armenian Assembly, Washington, 1975; mem. mktg. task force Office of Spl. Edn., Dept. Edn., 1979-84, Adminstrn. of Developmental Disabilities, HHS; mem. publs. panel Nat. Endowment for Humanities, Washington; bd. dirs. Syracuse Girls Club, 1982-87; pres. trustees St. John the Bapt. Armenian Apostolic Ch. and Cmty. Ctr., 1991-95. Named Post-Standard Woman of Achievement, 1980; recipient Chancellor's award for disting. service Syracuse U., 1985; Nat. award U.S. sect. World Edn. Fellowship, 1986; N.Y. State Humanities scholar. Mem. Women in Communications, Soc. Armenian Studies (adminstrv. council 1976-78, 85-87, sec. 1978, 85-87), Syracuse U. Library Assocs. (v.p. 1983-88), Am. Univ. Press Services (dir. 1976-77), Armenian Lit. Soc., Armenian Community Center, Assn. Am. Univ. Presses (v.p. 1976-77), UN Assn. (bd. dirs. 1983-88, v.p 1985), Phi Kappa Phi, Alpha Sigma Lambda. Mem. Armenian Apostolic Ch. (past trustee). Club: Zonta of Syracuse (pres. 1979-80, 1st v.p. 1985-86, dist. historian Dist. 2 Zonta Internat. 1993-96).

**MESSA, CHARLES ANGELO, III,** plastic surgeon; b. Phila., Feb. 8, 1963; s. Charles Angelo Jr. and Roberta Elizabeth (Price) M.; m. Linda Mary Schultz, Aug. 13, 1988; children: Charles Angelo IV, William Joseph. BA magna cum laude, LaSalle U., 1985; MD, Pa. State U., 1989. Diplomate Am. Bd. Surgery. Intern U. Mass. Sch. Medicine, 1989-90; resident in surgery II Mass. Sch. Medicine Ctr., Worcester, 1990-94; resident in plastic and reconstructive surgery U. Pa. Med. Ctr., Phila., 1994-96; surgeon Cosmetic Surgery Ctr., Weston, Fla. Presenter in field. Contbr. articles to profl. jours. Fellow ACS (assoc.), Am. Soc. Laser Med. and Surg.; mem. AMA, Pa. Med. Soc., Fla. Med. Assn., Mass. Med. Soc. Republican. Roman Catholic. Office: Weston Cosmetic Surgery Ctr Ste 1 & 2 17180 Arvida Pkwy Weston FL 33326 E-mail: drmessa@westoncosmeticsurgery.com.

**MESSAC, ACHILLE,** mechanical engineer, aerospace engineer; b. Haiti; BS, MS, PhD in Aerospace Engring., MIT, 1986. Assoc. prof. Northeastern U., Boston, 1994—2000; prof. Rensselaer Poly. Inst., Troy, NY, 2000—. Assoc. editor AIAA Jour., Washington, 1999—2002. Recipient CAREER award, NSF, 1997-2002. Fellow: ASME, AIAA (assoc.). Office: Rensselaer Poly Inst JEC 2049 Mech Engring Dept 110 8th St Troy NY 12180

**MESSEMER, GLENN MATTHEW,** lawyer; b. Hartford, Conn., Jan. 7, 1947; s. Joseph M. and Mary S. Messemer. BSBA, Georgetown U., 1968; JD, U. Conn., 1971. Bar: Conn. 1972. Staff atty. Kaman Corp., Bloomfield, Conn., 1972-74; asst. sec., 1974-79; asst. v.p., 1979-81; v.p. gen. counsel, 1981—. Prof. bus. law Sch. Bus. Adminstrn., U. Hartford (Conn., 1974-80 legal counsel Am. Helicopter Soc.; arbitrator Am. Arbitration Assn., 1978-82. Bd. dirs., trustee, regent U. hartford, 1993—. Served with M.I., U.S. Army, 1969-75. Mem. ABA, Conn. Bar Assn. (founding; exec. com., sec.), Hartford County Bar Assn. Clubs: Hartford Golf, Hartford, Masons. Office: Kaman Corp 1332 Blue Hills Ave Bloomfield CT 06002

**MESSENGER, BARBARA BEALL,** artist; d. John Murray and Anne Bryant (Dorsey) Beall; m. Donald White Messenger, Aug. 16, 1960; children: Colleen Beall Messenger-Baldwin, Melanie Dorsey Messenger Davis. BS, Western Md. Coll., 1960; postgrad., Md. Inst. Art, 1978, Howard C.C., Columbia, Md., 1979—80. Art educator, dept. chair Md. Pub. Sch. Sys., New Carrollton, 1960—66; art dir. Bellassai Gallery, Ellicott City, Md., 1980—84; proprietor Art and Frame Shop Ellicott Mills Gallery, Ellicott City, 1984—2000. Set, costume and program designer Calverton Players, Bellsville, Md., 1970—73; art critic, writer Laurel (Md.) Newsleader, 1974—80; substitute tchr. Howard County Pub. Sch. Sys., Ellicott City, 1984, Ellicott City, 85; publicity chmn. Laurel Art Guild. Exhibited in group shows at Laurel Art Guild, 1979, Bellassai Gallery, 1980—84, Villa Julia, Stevenson, Md., 1983, exhibited in group shows, Camden, Maine, 1988, exhibitions include Ellicott Mills Gallery, Md., Represented in permanent collections, Honduras, Turkey, Italy, German, U.S.A., and many islands. Active PTA, Howard County; membership chmn., v.p. Howard County Rep. Women; events coord. Howard County Rep. Party. Recipient Best of Balt. Art Gallery, Balt. Mag., 1980. Mem.: Am. Craft Coun., Howard County Arts Coun., Md. State Arts Coun. (bd. mem. 2003—), Nat. Mus. Women in the Arts (charter). Avocations: painting, crafts, reading, writing, photography. Home and Office: 616 Traveller Lot Lothian MD 20711 Office Phone: 410-741-0959. E-mail: bobbiemessenger@aol.com.

**MESSENGER, GEORGE CLEMENT,** engineering executive, consultant; b. Bellows Falls, Vt., July 20, 1930; s. Clement George and Ethel Mildred (Farrar) M.; m. Priscilla Betty Norris, June 19, 1954; children: Michael Todd, Steven Barry, Bonnie Lynn. BS in Physics, Worcester Poly U., 1951; MSEE, U. Pa., 1957; PhD in Engring., Calif. Coast U., 1986. Rsch. scientist Philco Corp., Phila., 1951-59; engring. mgr. Hughes Semicond., Newport Beach, Calif., 1959-61; divsn. mgr. Transitron Corp., Wakefield, Mass., 1961-63; staff scientist Northrop Corp., Hawthorne, Calif., 1963-68; cons. engr. Las Vegas, Nev., 1968—. Lectr. UCLA, 1969-75; v.p., dir. Am. Inst. Fin., Grafton, Mass., 1970-78; gen. ptnr. Dargon Fund, Anaheim, Calif., 1983—; v.p. tech. dir. Messenger and Assoc., 1987—; registered investment adviser, 1989—. Co-author: The Effects of Radiation on Electronic Systems, 1986, Single Event Phenomena, 1997; contbg. author: Fundamentals of Nuclear Hardening, 1972, Nonvolatile Semiconductor Memory Technology, 1998; contbr. articles to profl. jours.; patentee microwave diode, hardened semicondrs. Recipient Naval Rsch. Lab. Alan Berman award, 1982, Best Paper award HEART Conf., 1992, 3pl. Merit award, 1993, Pete Haas award, 1992, Goddard award for outstanding profl. achievement Worcester Poly. Inst., 1996, Archimedes award for contbns. to semicondr., solid state and nuc. physics rsch., 2006. Fellow IEEE (Merit award 1986); mem. Rsch. Soc. Am., Am. Phys. Soc. Congregationalist. Home and Office: 3111 Bel Air Dr Apt 7F Las Vegas NV 89109-1510 Personal E-mail: gpmessenger@cox.net.

**MESSENKOPF, EUGENE JOHN,** real estate developer, hotel executive; b. N.Y.C., Jan. 26, 1928; s. John Philip and Helen Bessie (Holden) M.; m. Martha Ann Crane, Jan. 29, 1955; children: Diane, Nancy, Eugene John, Susan. BBA, Iona Coll., 1950; MBA, NYU, 1956. CPA, N.Y. Sec.-treas. KLM Process Co., N.Y.C., 1952-54; acct. Am. Tobacco Co., N.Y.C., 1954-56; staff acct. Peat, Marwick & Mitchell, N.Y.C., 1956-60; exec. v.p. Donaldson, Lufkin & Jenrette, Inc., N.Y.C., 1960-84, pres., chief exec. officer real estate div., 1977-84; pres., chief exec. officer Meridian Investing and Devel. Corp., 1977-84; pvt. practice cons., 1984—. Mem. adv. bd. NYU Real Estate Inst., 1981-85; mem. exec. coun. small scale devel. Urban Land Inst., 1983-90; chmn. Wall St. Tax Com., N.Y.C., 1965-68; bd. dirs. SIA Acctg. Div., N.Y.C., 1965-79. Trustee-chmn. fin. com. Mt. Vernon Hosp., 1982-87. Served as sgt. AUS, 1950-52, Korea. Recipient Brother Loftus award Iona Coll., 1976. Mem. AICPA, N.Y. State Soc. CPAs, Fin. Execs. Inst. Republican. Roman Catholic. Achievements include walking 2000 mile Appalachian Trail, 1987.

**MESSER, DONALD EDWARD,** academic administrator, theology studies educator; b. Kimball, SD, Mar. 5, 1941; s. George Marcus and Grace E. (Foltz) M.; m. Bonnie Jeanne Nagel, Aug. 30, 1964; children: Christine Marie, Kent Donald. BA cum laude, Dakota Wesleyan U., 1963, LHD (hon.), 1977, MDiv magna cum laude, Boston U., 1966, PhD, 1969, Asst. to commtr. Mass. Commn. Against Discrimination, Boston, 1968-69; asst. prof. Augustana Coll., Sioux Falls, SD, 1969-71; assoc. pastor 1st United Meth. Ch., Sioux Falls, 1969-71; pres. Dakota Wesleyan U., Mitchell, SD, 1971-81, Iliff Sch. Theology, Denver, 1981-2000, pres. emeritus and prof. practical theology, 2000—. Author: Christian Ethics and Political Action, 1984, Contemporary Images of Christian Ministry, 1989, Send Me? The Intineracy in Crisis, 1991, The Conspiracy of Goodness, 1992, Caught in the Crossfire: Helping Christians Debate Homosexuality, 1994, Calling Church and Seminary Into

the 21st Century, 1995, Unity, Liberty, and Charity: Building Bridges Under Icy Waters, 1996, How Shall We Die? Helping Christians Debate Assisted Suicide, 1997, The Befuddled Stork: Helping Persons of Faith Debate Beginning of life Issues, 2000, Breaking the Conspiracy of Silence: Christian Churches and the Global AIDS Crisis, 2004; co-author: (with George McGovern, Bob Dole) Ending Hunger Now, 2005; contbr. articles to Face to Face, The Christian Century, The Christian Ministry. Active Edn. Commn. of U.S., 1973-79; co-chmn. Citizens Commn. Corrections, 1975-76; vice chmn. SD Commn. on Humanities, 1979-81. Dempster fellow, 1967-68; Rockefeller fellow, 1968-69. Mem. Soc. Christian Ethics, Am. Acad. Religion, Assn. United Meth. Theol. Schs. (v.p. 1986-91, pres. 1991-92). Democrat. Business E-Mail: dmesser@iliff.edu.

**MESSERLE, JUDITH ROSE,** retired medical librarian, retired public relations executive; b. Litchfield, Ill., Jan. 16, 1943; d. Richard Douglas and Nelrose B. Wilcox; m. Darrell Wayne Messerle, Apr. 26, 1968; children: Kurt Norman, Katherine Lynn. BA in Zoology, So. Ill. U., 1966; MLS, U. Ill., 1967. Cert. med. libr. Med. Libr. Assn. Libr. St. Joseph's Hosp. Nursing, Alton, Ill., 1967-71, dir. med. info. ctr., 1971-76, dir. info. svcs., 1976-79; dir. ednl. resources and cmty. rels. St. Joseph's Hosp., 1979-84; dir. Med. Ctr. Libr. St. Louis U., 1985-88; libr. Francis A. Countway Libr. Harvard Med. Sch. and Boston Med. Libr., 1989—2004; ret. Cons., 1973—; instr. Lewis and Clark Coll., 1975, Med. Libr. Assn. bd. dirs. Family Svcs. and Vis. Nurses Assn., Alton, 1976-79. Fellow AAAS, Med. Libr. Assn. (search com. for exec. dir. 1979, dir. 1981-84, pres. 1986-87, legis. task force 1986-90, task force for knowledge and skills 1988-92, nominating com. 1996); mem. OCLC (spl. libr. adv. com. 1994-98), AMA (com. on allied health edn. and accreditation 1991-94), Assn. Acad. Health Sci. Libr. Dirs. (editl. bd. for ann. stats. 1989-94, Region 8 adv. bd. 1992-93, joint legis. task force 1992-97, pres. 1993, charting the future task force 2001-03, scholarly communication task force 2003-05), Am. Med. Informatics Assn. (planning com. 1990, publs. com. 1994-96, ann. mtg. com. 1996-98), Ill. State Libr. Adv. Com., Midwest Health Sci. Libr. Network (divsn. health sci. coun.), St. Louis Med. Librs., Hosp. Pub. Rels. Soc. St. Louis, Nat. Libr. Medicine (biomed. libr. rev. com. 1988-92).

**MESSERLI, DOUGLAS,** writer, publisher; b. Waterloo, Iowa, May 30, 1947; s. John H. and Lorna (Caspers) M.; companion Howard N. Fox. BA in English, U. Md., 1972, MA in English, 1974, PhD in English, 1979. Admissions coord. U. Wis., Madison, 1967-69; asst. head protocol Columbia U., N.Y.C., 1969-70; grad. asst., tchr., coord. interns U. Md., 1973-77; pub. Sun & Moon Press, L.A., 1976—2003; prof. dept. English Temple U., Phila., 1979-84; dir. The Contemporary Arts Ednl. Project, Inc., 1983—; pub. Green Integer, 1998—. Part-time faculty mem. Calif. Inst. Tech., Pasadena, 1987-89, Otis Coll. Art and Sesign, L.A., 1989-2004; pub. Green Integer, 1998—. Author: (poetry) Dinner on the Lawn, 1979, Some Distance, 1982, River to Rivet: A Manifesto, 1985, River to Rivet: A Poetic Trilogy, 1985, Maxims from My Mother's Milk/Hymns to Him: A Dialogue, 1988, An Apple, A Day, 1993, After, 1998, primerias palavras, 1999, (drama) Silence All Round Marked: An Historical Play in Hysteria Writ, 1992, (as Kier Peters) The Confirmation, 1993, also A Dog Tries to Kiss the Sky: Six Short Plays, 2003, (fiction/film/poetry) Along Without: A Fiction in Film for Poetry, 1993, The Walls Come True: An Opera for Spoken Voices, 1996, (fiction as Joshua Haigh) Letters from Hanusse, 2000, (poetry) Primeiras palavras, 1999, (poetry) Bow Down, 2002, (poetry) First Words, 2004; editor: From the Other Side of the Century: A New American Poetry 1960-1990, 1994, The Sun & Moon Guide to Eating Through Literature and Art, 1994, 50: A Celebration of Sun & Moon Classics, 1995, From the Other Side of the Century II: A New American Drama 1960-95, 1998, The PIP Anthology of World Poetry of the 20th Century, Listen to the Mockingbird: American Folksongs and Popular Music Lyrics of the 19th Century. Decorated officier Arts et Lettres (France); recipient Carey-Thomas award Pubs. Weekly, 1987, Harry Ford Editor's award, 1994, Am. Book award, 1998; Found. for Contemporary Performance Arts grantee, 2002. Mem. MLA, Am. Booksellers Assn. Office: Green Integer 6022 Wilshire Blvd Los Angeles CA 90036-3607 Business E-Mail: info@greeninteger.com.

**MESSERSCHMIDT, WILLIAM HARCLERODE,** retired noncommissioned officer, musician; b. Lebanon, Pa., Apr. 30, 1947; s. Harry Edgar and Sylva (Harclerode) M.; m. Janice Andersen, Dec. 28, 1971; children: William F., Ann K., Dorothy R., Edward D. MusB with distinction, Eastman Sch. Music, 1969; postgrad., Cath. U. Am., 1983, Va. Theol. Sem., 1992-96. Enlisted man U.S. Army, 1969, advanced through grades to sgt. maj., 1994; percussionist U.S. Army Field Band, Ft. George G. Meade, Md., 1969-74, U.S. Army Band (Pershing's Own), Ft. Myer, Va., 1974-85, asst. sect. leader, 1985-89, leader percussion sect., 1989-94, leader percussion group, 1994—2002; ret., 2002. Pvt. tchr. percussion No. Va. C.C., Woodbridge, 1983—; adj. instr. percussion No. Va. C.C., Woodbridge 1983—; percussionist Prince William Symphony Orch., Lake Ridge, Va., 1989-93, The Fifes and Drums of Prince William, III, Woodbridge, 2003—, Lynchburg Symphony Orch., Va., 2003—; timpanist, percussionist orchs. with Nt. Christian Choir, Gaithersburg, Md., 1990—, Old Bridge Chamber Orch., Burke, Va., 1999-. Choir dir. Grace Ref. Presbyn. Ch., Woodbridge, 1985-93, Salvation Army Leadership Coun. Mem. Nat. Audubon Soc., Soc. German Am. Studies, Am. Soc. Prevention Cruelty to Animals, Am. Fedn. Musicians, Smithsonian Assocs., SAR, Kappa Delta Pi. Avocations: reading literature, philosophy and art history, tennis, German. Home: 5400 Staples Ln Woodbridge VA 22193-3562 Office Phone: 703-590-9834. E-mail: messpere@verizon.net.

**MESSIA, ROBERT A., III,** social studies educator; b. New Haven, Apr. 7, 1981; s. Robert A. Messia, Jr. and Maureen T. Messia; life ptnr. Julianne Scibetta. B in Polit. Sci. Edn., Siena Coll., Loudonville, NY, 2003; MS in Curriculum Devel. and Instrul. Tech., SUNY, Albany, 2005 Cert. secondary sch. tchr. NY, 2003. Instr. Johns Hopkins U. Ctr. for Talented Youth, Balt., 2002—; social studies tchr. and curriculum leader Averill Pk. (NY) Ctrl. Schs., 2003—. Recipient Outstanding Jr. Male award, Siena Coll., 2002; McCarthy and Presdl. scholar, 1999—2003, Siena Summer Scholars fellow, 2002. Mem.: Capital Regional Coun. for Social Studies, Nat. Coun. for Social Studies, Alpha Kappa Alpha. Office: Algonquian Middle School - Averill Park 333 NYS Route 351 Averill Park NY 12018

**MESSIAH-JILES, SONCERIA,** publishing executive; BA polit. sci., Univ. Houston; MBA, Tex. So. Univ. Talk show host KHOU-TV, KRIV-TV; adv. acct. exec. KMJQ-FM; news reporter KYOK-AM; pub. Houston Defender; pres. Nat. Newspaper Pub. Assn. Office: Nat Newspaper Pub Assn 3200 13th St NW Washington DC 20010 Office Phone: 202-588-8764.

**MESSICK, FREDERIC MORTON,** librarian; b. South Bend, Ind., Apr. 20, 1935; s. Francis Morton Messick and Mary Elizabeth Muessel; m. Carol Louise Reitzel, May 15, 1993; m. Claire Laverne Bowen, Dec. 18, 1965 (div. July 15, 1990); children: Elizabeth Ann Webber, David Morton. AB, Ind. U., 1959, AMT, 1964; MLS, U.Mich., 1965. Social sci. tchr. Elkhart Pub. Schools, Ind., 1963—64; ref. libr. Am. U., Washington, 1965—67; libr. bibliographer Ctrl. Mich. U., Mount Pleasant, Mich., 1967—97, ret., 1997, prof. emeritus, 1997—. Author: (reference book) Primary Sources in European Diplomacy, 1914-1945: A Bibliography of Published Memoirs and Diaries. Bd. dirs. Mt. Pleasant Area Internat. Rels. Com., Mich., 1994—2001. Mem.: Am. Hist. Assn. Unitarian. Avocations: sailing, swimming. Home: 1333 Crestwood Dr Mount Pleasant MI 48858 Personal E-mail: messi1fm@cmich.edu.

**MESSIER, MARK DOUGLAS,** retired professional hockey player; b. Edmonton, Alta., Can., Jan. 18, 1961; Center Indpls. Racers, 1978, Cin. Stingers, 1979, Edmonton Oilers, Canada, 1979—91, NY Rangers, 1991—97, NY, 2000—05, Vancouver Canucks, Vancouver, 1997—2000. Player NHL All-Star Game, 1982—84, 1986, 1988—92, 1994, 1996—98, 2000, 04. Named NHL Player of Yr., 1989, 1990, 1991—92; named to Sporting News All-Star Team, 1981—82, 1982—83, 1989—90, 1991—92; recipient Conn Smythe Trophy, 1984, Lester B. Pearson award, 1989—90,

1991—92, Hart Trophy, 1990, 1992. Achievements include being a member of Stanley Cup Champion Edmonton Oilers, 1984, 1985, 1987, 1988, 1990, NY Rangers, 1994; having his number, 11, retired by NY Rangers, 2006.

**MESSIER, PIERRE,** lawyer, manufacturing executive; b. Montreal, Que., Can., Mar. 3, 1945; s. Lionel and Anita (Caron) M.; m. Ginette Piche, July 11, 1970; 1 child, Mathieu. BA, Coll. St. Viateur, Outremont, Que., 1964; Lic. in Law, U. Montreal, 1968; diploma in adminstrv. scis., Ecole Hautes Etudes Commerciales, Montreal, 1973. Bar: Que. 1969. Assoc. Lemay & Messier, Montreal, 1969-75; v.p.; sec. gen. counsel Can. Cement Lafarge, Ltd., Montreal, 1975-84; v.p., sec. Lafarge Corp., 1983-84; v.p. bus. devel., legal affairs Norsk Hydro Can. Inc., Montreal, 1989-98; lawyer Leduc LeBlanc, Montreal, 1998-2000; pvt. practice, cons., 2000—02, 2003—; sr. legal counsel Bombardier, Inc., Montreal, 2002—03. V.p. Que. Bar Svc. Corp., 1995-2006. Pres. Centre Pedagogique Lucien-Guilbault Inc.; v.p. Coll. Jean de Brebeuf, 1991-97; pres. Greenfield Park Bd. Revision, 1973-74; bd. dirs. Societe Progres Rive Sud, Longueuil, Que., 1974-75, Que. Bar Profl. Liability Ins. Fund, 2006—. Mem. Can. Bar Assn. (pres. young lawyers sect. 1976, nat. exec. 1977-78), Montreal Jr. Bar (treas. 1972), Que. Mfrs. and Exporters Alliance (bd. dirs. 1996-98), St. Denis Club (Montreal), Que. Secs. and Gen. Counsel Assn. (sec. 1998). Office Phone: 450-476-7480. Business E-Mail: pierre.messier@defense.bombardier.com.

**MESSIN, MARLENE ANN,** plastics company executive; b. St. Paul, Oct. 6, 1935; d. Edgar Leander and Luella Johanna (Rahn) Johnson; m. Eugene Carlson (div. 1972); children: Rick, Debora, Ronald, Lori; m. Willard Smith (dec. 1975); m. Frank Messin, Sept. 24, 1982; 5 stepchildren. Bookkeeper Jeans Implement Co., Forest Lake, Minn., 1952-53, 1953—57, Great Plains Supply, St. Paul, 1960-62, Plastic Products Co., Inc., Lindstrom, Minn., 1962-75, pres., 1975—; co-owner, treas. Gustaf's Fine Gifts, Lindstrom, 1985—. Bookkeeper Trinity Luth. Ch., Lindstrom, 1976-81. Recipient award, Diversity 2000/Woman-Owned Bus. in Minn. Mem. Soc. Plastic Engrs., Swedish Inst., Soc. Plastic Industry, Minn. State Hist. Soc., Chgo. County Hist. Soc. Home: 28968 Olinda Trl Lindstrom MN 55045-9429 Office: 30355 Akerson St Lindstrom MN 55045-9456

**MESSINA, PAUL FRANCIS,** finance educator; b. Newport, R.I., Aug. 31, 1962; s. Nunzio Francis and Ilse INgeborg (Maibaum) Messina. BS, SUNY, Albany, 1988; MS, Tex. A&M, Texarkana, 1992; PhD, U. South Africa, 2004; MBA, U. Tex., San Antonio, 2005. Cert. tchr. Tex., La. Instr. math and physics St. Mary's HS, Natcitoches, La., 1989-91, Liberty-Eylau HS, Texarkana, 1991-93, chm. dept. sci., 1992-93; edn. cons. Hewlett-Packard Co., Irving, Tex., 1998—2005; asst. prof. mil. sci. U. Tex., San Antonio, 2001—05, lectr. mgmt. sci. & statis., 2004—. Adj. instr. Northwestern State U., Natchitoches, 1989—91; adj. instr. math Texarkana Coll., 1991—93; adj. instr. physics Ga. Mil. Coll., 1993—95. With U.S. Army, 1988—89. Tandy Tech. scholar, 1992, Eisenhower Mini-grantee, Liberty-Eylau Ind. Sch. Dist., Texarkana, 1992. Mem.: NEA, Internat. Freelance Photographers Orgn., Tex. Acad. Sci., Nat. Coun. Tchrs. Math., Decision Scis. Inst., Inst. Math. Stats., Inst. Ops. Rsch. and Mgmt. Scis., Nat. Tennis Acad., U.S. Profl. Tennis Registry, Ctrl. La. Astronomy Soc., Tex. Acad. Sci., San Tex., Tex. Acad. Sci., Am. Assn. Physics Tchrs., Tex. State Tchrs. Assn. (bldg. rep.), Son's of Italy in Am., Soc. Scabbard and Blade, Omicron Delta Kappa. Roman Catholic. Avocations: photography, tennis, computers, music. Office: U Tex San Antonio 6900 N Loop 1604 W San Antonio TX 78249 Home: 117 1st St Boerne TX 78006-2910 E-mail: pmessina@utsa.edu.

**MESSING, DEBRA,** actress; b. Bklyn., Aug. 15, 1968; m. Daniel Zelman, Sept. 3, 2000; 1 child. Grad., Brandeis U.; M in Drama, NYU. Actor: (films) Walk in the Clouds, 1995, McHale's Navy, 1997, Prey, 1997, Celebrity, 1998, Mothman Prophecies, 2002, Hollywood Ending, 2002, Along Came Polly, 2004, (voice) Garfield, 2004, The Wedding Date, 2005; (TV series) Ned and Stacey, 1995, Prey, 1998, Will & Grace, 1998—2006 (Emmy award best actress in a comedy, 2003); TV appearances include: NYPD Blue, 1994, 1995; Partners, 1995; Seinfeld, 1996, 1997; (voice) King of the Hill, 2002. Office: c/o Gersh Agy 232 N Canon Dr Beverly Hills CA 90210*

**MESSING, ELLEN JEAN,** lawyer; b. Springfield, Mass. AB cum laude, Harvard U., 1973; JD cum laude, Boston U., 1977. Bar: Mass. 1977, U.S. Dist. Ct. (Mass.) 1980, U.S. Ct. Appeals (1st cir.) 1994. Staff atty. Mass. Dept. Pub. Utilities, Boston, 1977-78, Southeastern Mass. Legal Assistance Corp., New Bedford, 1978-79; sole practice Boston, 1979-80; staff atty., clin. instr. U. Mich., Ann Arbor, 1980-82; clin. instr. Boston U. Sch. Law, 1982-83; assoc., of counsel Schreiber & Assocs., Boston, 1983-85; of counsel Westwater & Hernandez, Boston, 1985-86, Stern & Shapiro, Boston, 1986-88; ptnr. Messing & Rudavsky, P.C., Boston, 1988—, Messing, Rudavsky & Weliky PC, Boston. Author: Executive Compensation Packages: An Overview from the Employee's Point of View, The Practical Lawyer, 2002, The Ethical Constraints on Talking to Potential Witnesses, 2003, Representing Plaintiffs in Title VII Actions; contbr. numerous articles to profl. jours. Co-founder, co-chair Alliance for Future of Brookline Schs., Boston, 1991—. Recipient Faculty Award for Exceptional Dedication to Ideals of Community Svc. Boston U. Sch. Law, 1977; named one of Boston's top lawyers Boston Mag. 2004. Mem.: ABA (adv. coun. commn. evaluation rules or profl. conduct ethics commn. 2000), Mass. Bar Assn. (co-chair ethics com. labor & employment law sect. 1988—91, vice chair 1990—91, chair labor and employment law sect. 1991—92), Boston Bar Assn. (co-chair CLE com. labor law sect. 1988—91), Coll. Labor and Employment Lawyers, Boston Inn of Ct. (program dir. 1992—94, co-pres.-elect 1994—95, co-pres. 1995—96), Nat. Employment Lawyers Assn. (chair ethics and sanctions com. 1991—, pres. Mass. chpt. 1992—99, exec. bd. 1992—, co-chair affiliate rels. com. 1993—95, nat. sec. 2002—). Office: Messing Rudavsky & Weliky PC 44 School St Boston MA 02108-4201 Office Phone: 617-742-0004. Business E-Mail: mail@mrwemploymentlaw.com, emessing@mrwemployment.com.

**MESSING, KAREN,** occupational health researcher; b. Springfield, Mass., Feb. 2, 1943; BA, Harvard U., 1963; MSc, McGill U., 1970, PhD in Biology, 1975. Rsch. asst. biochemistry Jewish Gen. Hosp., Montreal, Can., 1970-71; NIH fellow genetics Boyce Thompson Inst. Plant Rsch., 1975-76; prof. ergonomics U. Quebec, Montreal, 1976—, dir. Ctr. Study Biol. Interactions & Environ. Health, 1990—95, 2000—03, dir. grad. ergonomics program, 1999-2000. Disting. fellow Que. Coun. for Social Rsch., 1995-97, Can. Inst. Health Rsch., 2001—; invited rschr. Inst. Cancer Montreal, 1983-95, Sweden Nat. Inst. Working Life, 1997-98; mem. bd. dirs. Quebec Sci. & Tech. Mus., 1984-86, Quebec Coun. Social Affairs, 1984-90. Author: One-Eyed Science: Occupational Health and Working Women, 1998, Integrating Gender in Ergonomic Analysis, 1999; editor: Women and Health, Policy and Practice in Health and Safety, Internat. Jour. Health Svcs., Recherches Feministes Salud y Trabajo, Policy and Practice in Health and Safety; co-editor: Women's Health at Work, 1998. Mem. Am. Pub. Health Assn., Assn. Can. Ergonomists. Office: Univ Que at Montreal CP 8888 succursale Centre-ville Montreal PQ Canada H3C 3P8 Office Phone: 514-987-3000 x 3334. Business E-Mail: messing.karen@uqam.ca.

**MESSINGER, DONALD HATHAWAY,** lawyer; b. Lyons, NY, July 1, 1943; s. Donald H. and Thelma (Hubbard) M.; m. Sara L. Stock, June 3, 1967; children: Michael David, Robert Stephen, Daniel Mark. BA, Colgate U., 1965; JD, Duke U., 1968. Bar: Ohio 1968. Assoc. Thompson Hine LLP, Cleve., 1968-76, ptnr., 1976—, vice chair core practice group 1991-92, ptnr.-in-charge Cleve. office 1991-96, mem. exec. com., 1996-2000. Sec., bd. dirs. Am. Steel and Wire Corp., 1986-93; bd. dirs. Cedar Fair Mgmt. Co., 1993-2002. Trustee Cmty. Info.-Vol. Action Ctr., 1981-88, pres. 1981-84; trustee Free Med. Clinic Greater Cleve., 1970—, sec., 1970-82, v.p. 1982-86, 96-2002, pres. 2002-04; trustee Cleve. Hearing and Speech Ctr., 1980—, v.p. 1984-86, 92-93, pres., 1986-88, 98-2000; trustee U. for Young Ams., 1982-95, sec., 1984-95, pres., 1986-88, chm. 1991-95; mem. exec. bd. Boy Scouts Am., 1983-88; Leadership Cleve., 1984—; trustee, sec. Bus. Vols. Unltd., 1992—; sec. Buckeye Area Devel. Corp., 1970-90; mem. adv. bd. Greater Cleve. New Stadium. Recipient Community Svc. award Fedn. for Community Planning, 1981-82; named one of Outstanding Young Citizens of Greater

---

Cleve., 1971-75. Mem. ABA, Ohio Bar Assn., Cleve. Bar Assn. (trustee 1975-79, chmn. securities law inst. 1983), Nat. Assn. Bond Lawyers Home: 21550 Shelburne Rd Shaker Heights OH 44122 Office: 3900 Key Ctr 127 Public Sq Cleveland OH 44114 Office Phone: 216-566-5571. Business E-Mail: don.messinger@thompsonhine.com.

**MESSITTE, PETER JO,** judge; b. Washington, July 17, 1941; s. Jesse B. and Edith (Wechsler) M.; m. Susan P. Messitte, Sept. 5, 1965; children: Zachariah, Abigail. BA cum laude, Amherst Coll., 1963; JD, U. Chgo., 1966. Bar: Md. 1969, DC 1969, U.S. Ct. Appeals (4th cir.) 1977, U.S. Supreme Ct. 1973, U.S. Ct. Appeals (DC cir.) 1982, U.S. Ct. Appeals (5th cir.) 1983. Assoc. Zuckert, Scoutt & Rasenberger, Washington, 1968-71; solo practice Chevy Chase, Md., 1971-75; mem. Messitte & Rosenberg, P.A., Chevy Chase, 1975-81; prin. Peter J. Messitte, P.A., Chevy Chase, 1981-85; assoc. judge Cir. Ct. for Montgomery County Rockville, Md., 1985-93; judge U.S. Dist. Ct. Md., Greenbelt, 1993—. Mem. Internat. Jud. Rels. Com. Jud. Conf. U.S., 1997-2003. Bd. dirs. Cmty. Psychiat. Clinic, Montgomery County, Md., 1974-85, v.p. 1980-85; Peace Corps vol., Sao Paulo, Brazil, 1966-68; Md. del. Dem. Nat. Conv., N.Y.C., 1980. Recipient tchg. citations Fed. Deposit Ins. Corp. Bank Exam. Sch., 1975, 79, Am. Inst. Banking, 1978, Elizabeth Scull award for Outstanding Svc. to Montgomery County, Md., 1993, Spl. citation Divorce Roundtable Montgomery County, 1993, Gran Cruz da Ordem São José Operário-Brazilian Labor Tribunal, Mato Grosso, 2001, Medalha de Mérito Académico, Academia Paulista de Magistrados, 2002, Contbr. Mental Health Cmty. Psychiat. Clinic, 1986, Leadership in Law award, Md. Daily Record, 2002. Fellow: Md. Bar Found. (H. Vernon Eney award for contbn. to adminstrn. of justice 2001); mem.: ABA, Jud. Inst. Md. (bd. dirs. 1989—93), Charles Fahy Inn of Ct. (master 1987—88), Fed. Judges Assn. (4th jud. cir.), Am. Law Inst., Instituto Paulista de Advogados (hon.), Montgomery County Bar Assn. (Century of Svc. award 1999), Md. Bar Assn., D.C. Bar Assn., Fed. Bar Assn., Montgomery County Inn of Ct. (pres. 1988—90, Leadership in Law award 2002, Md. Daily Record Leadership Law award 2002). Jewish. Office: US Courthouse 6500 Cherrywood Ln Greenbelt MD 20770-1249 Office Phone: 301-344-0632.

**MESSMAN, JACK L.,** network management software company executive; b. Clarksburg, W.Va., Mar. 13, 1940; s. Marvin C. and Betty L. (Jones) M.; m. Maggie Saran, Apr. 18, 1997; children: Valerie Lynne, Kyle Andrew. B in Chem. Engring., U. Del., 1962; MBA with Distinction, Harvard U., 1968. Ptnr. Butcher & Singer, Phila., 1971-73; pres. Norcross, Inc., West Chester, Pa., 1973-80; v.p. corp. devel. UGI Corp., Valley Forge, Pa., 1980-81; exec. v.p. Safeguard Scientifics, Inc., King of Prussia, Pa., 1981-83; pres., CEO Novell Data Sys., Inc., Orem, Utah, 1982—83; exec. v.p., CFO, also bd. dir. Warner Amex Cable Comm. Inc., N.Y.C., 1983-86; mng. dir. Mason Best Co., 1986—88; chmn., CEO Somerset House Corp., Houston, 1986-88; CEO, chmn. bd. dirs. US Pollution Control Inc. (subsidiary of Union Pacific Corp.), Oklahoma City, 1988-91; pres. Union Pacific Resources, Inc., 1991—96, CEO, 1991—99, chmn. Ft. Worth, 1996—99; pres., CEO Cambridge Tech. Ptnrs. (merged with Novell, Inc.), Waltham, Mass., 1999—2001; CEO Novell, Inc., Waltham, Mass., 2001—06, chmn., 2001—06. Bd. dirs. Wawa, Inc. (Pa.), Novell Inc., 1985-, Safeguard Scientifics, Inc., 1994-,Cambridge Technology Ptnrs., 1992-, Tandy Corp., U.S. Data., RadioShack Corp., Timminco, Ltd. Served to 1st lt. U.S. Army, 1963-65. Mem. River Crest Country Club (Ft. Worth), Mira Vista Club (Ft. Worth). Republican. Episcopalian. Office: Novell Inc 404 Wyman St Ste 500 Waltham MA 02451*

**MESSMAN, JAMIE M.,** polymer chemist; b. Two Rivers, Wis., Nov. 17, 1976; s. Michael S. and Michele J. Messman; m. Victoria L. Ulery, Mar. 22, 2003. BS, St. Norbert Coll., DePere, Wis., 1999; PhD, U. of So. Miss., Hattiesburg, 2004. Grad. rsch. asst. U. of So. Miss., Hattiesburg, 1999—2004; early identification intern GEc Global Rsch. Ctr., Niskayuna, NY, 2003; postdoctoral rsch. scholar Ctr. for Nanophase Materials Scis., Oak Ridge (Tenn.) Nat. Lab., 2004—. Mem.: Am. Chem. Soc. (assoc.; POLY divsn.), Pi Mu Epsilon (life). Office: Oak Ridge Nat Lab Bldg 8610 MS 64 One Bethel Valley Rd Oak Ridge TN 37831-6494 Office Phone: 865-576-2394. Office Fax: 865-574-1753. E-mail: messmanjm@ornl.gov.

**MESSMER, DONALD JOSEPH,** business management educator, marketing consultant; b. St. Louis, July 30, 1936; s. Edgar Louis and Lucille Louise (Straub) Messmer; m. Charlotte Jean Fox; 1 child, Angeline Charlotte. BSBA with honors, Washington U., St. Louis, 1969, PhD, 1974. Asst. mgr. M.A. Bell Co., St. Louis, 1956-61; dist. sales exec. U. S. Gypsum Co., St. Louis, 1962-65; br. sales exec. Victor Comptometer Corp., St. Louis, 1965-68; asst. prof. Coll. William and Mary, Williamsburg, Va., 1973-76, assoc. prof., 1976-81, prof., 1981—2006, J.S. Mack prof., 1982—2006; pres. The Wessex Group, Ltd., Williamsburg 1979—. Bd. dirs. Williamsburg Winery, Ltd. chmn. bd. dirs., 2005—; co-founder Coll. William and Mary Exec. Ptnrs. Editor (assoc ed): Decision Scis Jour, 1985—88; contbr. articles to profl jours. Bd dirs, treas Community Action Agency, Williamsburg, 1984—91, United Way Greater Williamsburg, 1985—91, pres, 1989. Recipient Pres.'s cmty. svc. award, Coll. William and Mary, 1999. Mem.: Southeastern Decision Scis Inst (pres 1985—86), Am Mkt Asn (Dissertation Award 1974), Decision Scis Inst (mkt coord 1985—86), Rotary (bd. dirs. 1990—92, program chair 2003, bd. dirs. 2003—, pres. 2004, pres.-elect 2003—04), Beta Gamma Sigma, Alpha Mu Alpha. Republican. Avocations: fishing, golf. Office: The Wessex Group Ltd McLaws Cir Ste 1 Williamsburg VA 23185 Office Phone: 757-253-5606. Business E-Mail: don.messmer@wessexgroup.com.

**MESSMER, HAROLD MAXIMILIAN, JR., (MAX MESSMER),** financial services executive; b. Jackson, Miss., Feb. 20, 1946; s. Harold Maximilian and Margaret (Dee) M.; m. Marcia Elizabeth Nesmith, Apr. 5, 1973; children: Michael Christopher, Matthew Gordon. AB summa cum laude, Loyola U., 1967; JD cum laude, NYU, 1970. Ptnr. corp. law and securities O'Melveny & Myers, Los Angeles, 1970-81; sr. v.p., gen. counsel Pacific Holding Corp., Los Angeles, 1981-82, pres., chief operating officer, 1982-85; pres., dir. chief operating officer Cannon Mills Co. (subs.), Kannapolis, N.C., 1982-85; chmn., dir. Castle & Cook Inc., San Francisco, 1985; chmn., pres., chief exec. officer Robert Half Internat. Inc., Menlo Park, 1985—2004, chmn., CEO, 2004—. Adj. prof. Claremont Grad. Sch. Bus.(exec. mgmt. program), 1979-82; bd. dirs. Health Care Property Investors, Los Angeles, BF Enterprises Inc., N.C. Nat. Bank, Charlotte. Trustee Davidson (N.C.) Coll., 1984—; appointee Pres. Reagan's Adv. Com. on Trade Negotiations, 1985-87. Served with USAR, 1971-75. Mem. ABA, Los Angeles County Bar Assn., Calif. Bar Assn. Served with USAR, 1971-75. Office: Robert Half Internat Inc 2884 Sand Hill Rd Ste 200 Menlo Park CA 94025-7059*

**MESSNER, HOWARD MYRON,** professional association executive; b. Newark, June 10, 1937; s. Elias and Freda (Trachtenberg) M.; m. Aletha Bragg, 1960 (div. 1980); children: Jennifer, Linda, David; m. Melba June Meador, June 22, 1986. BA, Antioch Coll., 1960; MA, U. Mass., 1962. Mgmt. analyst Office Gov., Mass., 1960-61; staff asst. to adminstr. NASA, Washington, 1962-65; mgmt. analyst Bur. Budget, Washington, 1965-71; dir. adminstrn. EPA, Washington, 1971-75, asst. adminstr. for adminstrn., 1983-87; asst. dir. Congl. Budget Office, Washington, 1975-77, Office Mgmt. and Budget, Washington, 1977-83; contr. Dept. Energy, Washington, 1983; exec. v.p. Am. Cons. Engr. Coun., 1987—99; pres. Nat. Acad. Pub. Adminstrn., 2004. Bd. dirs. Kelly, Anderson Inc. Recipient William A. Jump Meml. award, 1971, Presdl. Disting. Exec. award, 1986, Outstanding Pub. Service award Nat. Capital chpt. Am. Soc. Pub. Adminstrn., 1986, Chancellor's medal U. Mass., 1978. Mem. Nat. Acad. Pub. Adminstrn. (trustee), Cosmos Club. Democrat. Jewish. Home: 1683 Justin Dr Gambrills MD 21054-2012 Personal E-mail: messnermeador@msn.com.

**MESSNER, JAMES W.,** advertising executive; b. 1939; Attended, 1959-61. With Sta. WCSM, Celina, Ohio, 1961-63, Sta. WTOD, Toledo, 1961-63, Detroit Advt. Agy., 1965-68, Norman, Navan, Moore & Bard, 1968-77; chmn., CEO J.W. Messner Inc., Grand Rapids, Mich., 1977—. Office: JW Messner Inc 161 Ottawa Ave NW Ste 403 Grand Rapids MI 49503-2760

---

**MESSNER, ROBERT THOMAS,** lawyer, bank executive; b. McKeesport, Pa., Mar. 27, 1938; s. Thomas M. and Cecilia Mary (McElhinny) M.; m. Anne Margaret Lux, Dec. 3, 1966; children: Megan Anne, Michael Thomas. AB, Dartmouth Coll., 1960; LL.B., U. Pa., 1963. Bar: Pa. 1965. With firm Rose, Schmidt & Dixon, Pitts., 1965-68; with G.C. Murphy Co., McKeesport, 1968-86, corp. sec., 1974—; gen. counsel, 1975-86, v.p., 1976-86; v.p., gen. counsel, corp. sec. Dollar Bank, Pitts., 1986—. Dir. G.C. Murphy Found. Mem. Point State Park planning com. City of Pitts.; Rep. candidate Pa. Legis., 1966; mem. Mayor's Com. on Fort Duquesne, Pitts.; bd. dirs. McKeesport YMCA, Downtown Pitts. YMCA, Mon-Yough Heritage Found., 1981—83, Braddock's Field Hist. Soc., Comm., 1968—69; mem. fin. adv. bd. Wilkinsburg, Pa., 1988—. 1st lt. U.S. Army, 1963—65. Decorated Commendation medal. Mem. ABA, Pa. Bar Assn. (chmn. corp. law dept. com.), Allegheny County Bar Assn. (coun. on corp., banking and bus. law), Am. Soc. Corp. Secs. (pres. Pitts. regional group, dir.), Am. Mgmt. Assn., Pa. Assn. Savs. Instns. (chmn. legal com. 1989—), Am. Corp. Counsel Assn., Theta Delta Chi. Clubs: Dartmouth Western Pa., Rivers. Home: 1061 Blackridge Rd Pittsburgh PA 15235-2719 Office: Dollar Bank Three Gateway Ctr Pittsburgh PA 15222

**MESSNER, THOMAS G.,** advertising executive, copywriter; b. NYC, Jan. 26, 1944; s. Malcolm V. Messner and Virginia M. Burkard; m. Terry Carol Bonaccolta, Nov. 28, 1971; 1 child, Zachary. Letter carrier U.S. Post Office, N.Y.C., 1965-67; copywriter Occidental Life Calif., L.A., 1967-68; mail boy D'Arcy Advt., N.Y.C., 1968; copywriter BBDO, N.Y.C., 1968-69, Doyle Dane Bernbach, N.Y.C., 1969-72; creative dir. Ally and Gargano, N.Y.C., 1972-86; founder, ptnr. Messner Vetere Berger Carey Schmetterer, N.Y.C., 1986-92; ptnr. Messner Vetere Berger McNamee Schmetterer Euro RSCG, N.Y.C., 1992-; founder Grand Old Website Co., 1999. Former prof. Sch. Visual Arts, N.Y.C.; copywriter MCI; bd. dirs., US bd., internat. bd. Eurol RSCG; founder, pres. The Grand Old Website Co., Red. Advt. Inc. Copywriter Ronald Reagan 1984 Presdl. campaign Repub. Nat. Com. NY, 1984; copywriter George Bush 1988 presdl. campaign, 1988, Bob Franks Senatorial Campaign, 2000, Andrew O'Rourke for Gov., NY, 1986. Named CLIO Hall of Fame. Mem. Mortons Group, E-Media Investment Group, Fenway Club. Roman Catholic. Office: Messner Vetere Berger McNamee Schmetterer Euro RSCG 350 Hudson St Fl 7 New York NY 10014-4509 E-mail: tom.messner@mvbms.com.

**MESTAS, LUIS HERRERA,** theater educator, dancer; b. L.A., June 21, 1952; s. Ray Mestas and Elvira Herrera. BA, Calif. State U., L.A., 1985, MA in Sch. Adminstrn. and Ednl. Leadership, 1994. Tchg. credential Calif., 1994. Tchr. and dir. after sch. performing arts Twin Lakes Elem. Sch., El Monte, Calif.; tchr. and dir. performing arts Kranz Intermediate Sch., 1999—. Soloist and prin. ballet dancer Christian Groves; founder Christian Dance Acad. Republican. Avocations: violin, the ocean, travel. Office: Charles T Kranz Intermediate Sch 12460 Fineview st El Monte CA 91732-3930 Home: PO Box 4277 El Monte CA 91734 Office Phone: 626-255-6056.

**MESTAYER, MARY FRANCES,** science educator; b. Raceland, La., Sept. 2, 1952; d. Thomas Francis and Del Monte Mary Arabie Mestayer. BA in Edn., U. Southwestern La., Lafayette, 1974; student, Lea Castle Riding Sch., Worcester, Eng., 1977, Moyfield Riding Sch., 1978; student in advanced Bible Study, Layman's Sch. Training Christian Cmty. Ch., Pietersburg, South Africa, 1997—99. Cert. Rhema Bible Training Ctr., Johannesburg, South Africa, 1992; tchr. type B State of La., 1977, tchr. South African Tchr.'s Coun., 1986, South African Coun. Educators, 2000, highly qualified sci. and elem. edn. State of La. Tchr. Raceland (La.) Lower Elem. Sch., 1974—86; sci. tchr. Sunward Park H.S., South Africa, 1986—90; staff Rhema Missions Ctr. Rhema Ministries South Africa, Lanseria, 1991—92; sci. tchr. Southside Elem., Bastrop, La., 1993; sci. tchr., coord. and facilitator Pepps Polokwane Prep. Sch. and Coll., Pietersburg, South Africa, 1994—2001; sci. tchr. Larose-Cut Off Mid. Sch., Cut Off, La., 2001—. Sci. fair coord. Pepps Polokwane Prep. Sch. and Coll., Pietersburg, South Africa, 1994—2000; sci. facilitator Sci. Math. Found., 1996, Power Matric, South Africa, 1996, Africa Growth Network, 1996; sci. dir. after care Pepps Polokwane Prep. Sch. and Coll., 1999; sci. fair coord. Larose- Cut Off Mid. Sch., Cut Off, La., 2002—; sci. fair team mem. Lafourche Parish Schs., Thibodaux, La., 2002—; fellow Ag in the Classroom, La., 2002—; mem. Nat. Energy Ednl. Devel. Project, 2004—. Recipient Mestayer Sci. Trophy, Pepps Polokwane Prep. Sch. and Coll., 2000. Mem.: La. Fedn. Tchrs. Republican. Avocations: missions, horseback riding, gardening, reading, travel. Office: Larose Cut Off Mid Sch 13356 W Main St Cut Off LA 70345-2500 Office Phone: 985-693-3273.

**MESTEL, SHERRY Y.,** social worker, school psychologist, art therapist; b. Bklyn., Dec. 7, 1952; d. Robert and Miriam Mestel; children: Jessica, Iris. MSc in Bilingual Edn., CCNY, 1976; MSW, SUNY, Stonybrook, 1979; MSC in Sch. Psychology, LI U., 1992; PhD, Nat. Inst. Expressive Therapy, 1995; cert. in traumatic brain injury and children, Mt. Sinai Hosp. and Hunter Coll., 1999. Lic. social worker; cert. bilingual Spanish/English elem. tchr. NY, sch. psychologist NY. Puppeteer NYC Dept. Pks., 1972—74; elem. sch. tchr. NYC Bd. Edn., 1974—75, sch. social worker, 1987—92; psychiat. social worker Rockland Children's Psychiat. Ctr., Orangeburg, NY, 1979—81; psychotherapist NY Psychotherapy & Counseling Ctr., Bklyn., 1981—87; sch. psychologist NYC Dept. Edn., Bklyn., 1992—; social worker For the Children, Para los Ninos, PLLC, Bklyn., 2000—. Spkr. NY State Early Childhood Conf., Bklyn., 1999—, YAI, NYC, 1999—; owner Early Intervention, Bklyn., 2000—. Editor: Herbal Remedies, 1978, Women's Rituals, 1979; exhibitions include A.I.R. Gallery, NYC, B.W.A.I.C., Bklyn. Recipient Elem. Sch. Book award, Queens Coll., Flushing, NY, 1974. Mem.: NASP, NASW, Am. Art Therapy Assn. (cert.), Nat. Expressive Therapy Assn., Assn. Humanistic Psychology, Nuyagi Keetowah Soc. Bklyn. Women's Chorus, Bklyn. Working Artist Coalition, Backyard Garden.

**MESTON, CINDY M(AY),** psychologist, educator; b. Abbotsford, B.C., Can., Nov. 6, 1960; arrived in U.S., 1995; d. Joseph Orvil and Mary Elizabeth Meston. BA in Psychology, U. B.C., Vancouver, 1991, MA in Clin. Psychology, 1993; PhD in Clin. Psychology, U. B.C., 1995. Clin. intern. U. Wash. Sch. Medicine, Seattle, 1994—95, sr. post doctoral fellow reproductive and sexual medicine clinic, 1995—96; rsch. fellow Social Sci. Rsch. Coun., Ford Found., 1996—97; acting asst. prof. dept. psychiatry and behavioral scis. U. Wash. Sch. Medicine, Seattle, 1997—98; asst. prof. dept. psychology U. Tex., Austin, 1998—2001, assoc. prof., 2002—. Trainee juvenile svcs. to ct. Willingdon Detention Ctr., Burnaby, B.C., 1990—91; trainee psychology outpatient clinic U. B.C., Vancouver, 1991—94; extern psychiatry outpatient ctr. U. Wash. Med. Ctr., Seattle, 1993, extern Madison Clinic for AIDS, 93, intern Pain Svc., 94, intern dept. rehab. medicine, 95, intern psychiatry outpatient ctr., 95, fellow reproductive and sexual medicine clinic, 1995—96, fellow dept. urology, 95, fellow dept. ob-gyn., 1995—96, psychological reproductive and sexual medicine clinic, 1997—98; intern dept. neuropsychiatry Harborview Med. Ctr., Seattle, 1994—95; spkr. in field. Mem. editl. bd. Archives Sexual Behavior, 2001—, Jour. Sex and Marital Therapy, 2001—, Internat. Jour. Impotence Rsch., 2002—, mem. edit. bd. Jour. Sexual Medicine, 2004—, jour. reviewer numerous jours. in field; contbr. numerous articles to profl. jours., chapters to books; interview subject KXAN-TV, Austin, 1999, NBC Nat. News, 2000, featured in article Wall St. Jour., 1998, NY Times, 1999, Newsweek, 2000. Grantee, Rsch. Coun. Can., 1996—98, Social Sci. Rsch. Coun., Ford Found., 1996—98, Eli Lilly and Co., 1999—2001, Target Health, Inc., 1999—2001, NitroMed, Inc., 1999—2002, Lilly ICOS LLC, 2000—02, Athena Inst. for Women's Wellness, 2000—03, NIH, 2001—; scholar, U.S.B.C., 1989—94. Mem.: APA, Internat. Soc. for Study Women's Sexual Health (sci. program com. ann. meeting 2002, pres. 2003), Soc. Sci. Study Sex, Can. Psychol. Assn., Internat. Acad. Sex Rsch. (sci. program com. ann. meeting 1999, chair poster session 1999, 2000, sci. program com. ann. meeting 2001). Office: U Tex 108 E Dean Keeton Austin TX 78712

**MESTRE, OSCAR LUIS,** financial consultant; b. Havana, Cuba, Nov. 26, 1959; came to U.S., 1960; s. Oscar Luis and Ana Victoria (Arango) M.; m. Margaret M. Bozak, May 17, 1986; children: Melissa Anne, Victoria

Elizabeth, Jessica Margaret. BS and BA, U. Del., 1982; cert. CLU, Am. Coll., Bryn Mawr, Pa., 1988, cert. ChFC, 1988. Account exec. Keystone Fin. Group, Bryn Mawr, 1982-87, New Eng. Fin. Group, Radnor, Pa., 1987—91; ptnr. in charge of mktg. internat. ins., liason for Latin Am., internat. banking and securities AG Transnat., Ltd., Radnor and Huntington, N.Y., 1991—. Founding mem. Tech. Resource Alliance, 1998. Chmn. U. Del. golf fundraising com., Newark, 1986-92; bd. dirs. Haverford (Pa.) Sch. Alumni Assn., 1988-98, chmn. annual giving campaign, 1993-94, planned giving coun. 1998—; mem. profl. adv. coun. Cedars Med. Ctr., Miami, Fla., 1990-93; vol. St. Monica's Ch., Berwyn, Pa., mem. Am. Heart Assn., Pa. chpt.; Am. amateur golf contestant, 1999, British amateur golf contestant, 2000, U.S. Mid-amateur golf contestant, 2000. Named to U. Del. Athletic Hall of Fame, 2001; recipient Hon. Mention All Am. award, NCAA Div. I Golf, 1980—81, Top Club award, Penn Mut. Life Ins. Co., Phila., 1982, Ins. Prodn. Recognition award, Clerical Med. Internat., 1992. Mem. Am. Soc. CLUs and ChFCs (cert.), Tech. Resource Alliance (founding), Leaders Assn. New Eng. Fin., Overbrook Golf Club (bd. dirs. 1999—2003). Avocations: golf, travel, theater, music. Office: Creative Fin Group Ste 200 16 Campus Blvd Newtown Square PA 19073 Office Phone: 610-355-7885. Business E-Mail: omestre@cfg.nef.com.

**MESTRES, JEAN L. See SULC, JEAN LUENA**

**MESTRES, RICARDO A., III,** film company executive; b. NYC, Jan. 23, 1958; s. Ricardo Angelo Jr. and Ann M.; m. Tracy Stewart; children: Alexander Carson, Carrie Ann (dec.). AB, Harvard U., 1980; postgrad. in medicine, U. So. Calif. Creative exec. Paramount Pictures, L.A., 1981-82, exec. dir. prodn., 1982-84, v.p. prodn., 1984-85, Walt Disney Pictures, Burbank, Calif., 1985-86, sr. v.p. prodn., 1986-88; pres. prodn Touchstone Pictures, Burbank, Calif., 1988-89; pres. Hollywood Pictures, Burbank, Calif., 1989-94; co-founder Great Oaks Entertainment, Burbank, Calif., 1995-97; prin. Ricardo Mestres Prodns., Disney Studios, Burbank, Calif., 1997. Prodr: Jack, 101 Dalmations, Flubber, Home Alone 3, The Visitors, The Hunted. Mem. Acad. Motion Picture Arts and Scis. Business E-Mail: ricardo@rmp.com.

**MESTRES, RICARDO ANGELO, JR.,** lawyer; b. NYC, Aug. 12, 1933; s. Ricardo Angelo and Anita (Gwynne) M.; m. Ann Farnsworth, June 18, 1955; children: Laura, Ricardo III, Lynn, Anthony. AB, Princeton U., 1955; LLB, Harvard U., 1961. Bar: N.Y. 1962, U.S. Supreme Ct. 1970. Assoc. Sullivan & Cromwell, N.Y.C., 1961-67, ptnr., 1968-2000, chmn., sr. ptnr., 1995-2000, sr. counsel, 2001—. Trustee Unitarian Ch. All Souls, N.Y.C., 1973-79, 84-87; trustee Phillips Exeter Acad., 1989-99, pres. bd. trustees, 1993-99. Served to lt. USN, 1955-58. Mem.: ABA, Coun. Fgn. Rels., Am. Law Inst., Assn. Bar City N.Y. (corp. law, securities regulation law and state legis. coms.), N.Y. State Bar Assn., Mill Reef Club (Antigua), Links Club, Phi Beta Kappa. Office: Sullivan & Cromwell 125 Broad St Fl 32 New York NY 10004-2498 Office Phone: 212-558-3716.

**MESZNIK, JOEL R.,** investment banker; b. Oct. 3, 1945; m. Lynne Gladstein, Mar. 25, 1979; children: Daniel, Jared, Kara. BS, CCNY, 1967; MBA, Columbia U., 1970. Engr. Ebasco Svcs., N.Y.C., 1967-70; banker Citibank, N.Y.C., 1970-71, Newhouse Capital, N.Y.C., 1971-72, Matthews & Wright, N.Y.C., 1972-76; mng. dir. Drexel Burnham Lambert, N.Y.C., 1976-89; pres. Mesco Ltd., 1990—. Bd. dirs. RAIT, Pharma/wHealth, Greenfield Online. Office: 470 Main St Ste 315 Ridgefield CT 06877-4516

**METALLO, FRANCES ROSEBELL,** mathematics professor; b. Jersey City; d. Vincenzo James and Lucille (Frank) M. BA in Math., Jersey City State Coll., 1985, MA in Math. Edn., 1987. Math. tchr. Emerson HS, Union City, NJ, 1990-92; math tchr. gifted/talented program Jefferson Annex Woodrow Wilson Sch. Dist. Union City, 1992-95; math tchr. Woodrow Wilson Sch., Dist. Union City, 1995—. Adj. tchr. math. Hudson County CC, 1987—, Jersey City State Coll., 1986—, tutor, 1983-86; reviewer for Nat. Coun. Tchrs. Math mag., A Plus for Kids Tchr. Network, 1994, grantee 1993, 96 Contbr. articles to profl. publs.; author, History of the Abacus and Study of Soroban, 1987, The Abacus: It's History and Application Module 17, 1990, A Concise Dictionary of Math and Symbols, 1992, Smile, Basic Algebra is Fun, 1999. Nominee Pres. award for sci. and math tchg., 1996, EWT Com. of NJ, 1996; named Most Admired Woman of Decade; recipient St. Jude's Children's Rsch. Hosp. award, 1995, 1996. Mem. Nat. Coun. Tchrs. Math., Assn. Math. Tchrs. of NJ, Alumni Assn. Jersey City State Coll., Math. Assn. Am., Am. Soc. Prevention of Cruelty to Animals, Assn. of Women in Math., Am. Math. Soc., Dozenal Soc., Kappa Delta Pi (mem. Wall of Tolerance, 2005, 06), Phi Delta Kappa. Avocations: crochet, embroidery, piano. Home: 201 Hancock Ave Jersey City NJ 07307-1916

**METCALF, DONALD,** biomedical researcher; BSc, U Sydney, Sydney, Australia; MB, BS, U Sydney; MD, U. Sydney. Carden fellow, cancer rsch. Walter & Eliza Hall Inst. Med. Rsch., Victoria, Australia, 1954—, head, cancer rsch. unit, asst. dir., 1965—96; emeritus prof. Walter & Eliza Hall Inst. Med. Rsch., Royal Melbourne Hosp., 1996—; rsch. prof., cancer biology U. Melbourne, Australia, 1986—96. Vis. prof., Australia, England, Canada, France, Netherlands, New Zealand, Switzerland, United States. Contbr. articles to profl. jours. Recipient Armand Hammer prize, 1988, Sloan prize, General Motors Cancer Rsch. Foundation, Albert Lasker Clinical Rsch. award, 1993, Louisa Gross Horwitz prize, Columbia U., 1993, Internat. Award, Gairdner Found., 1994, Warren Alpert Found. prize, Harvard Med. Sch., 1996, Ernst Neumann award, Internat. Soc. for Exptl. Hematology, 1995, Amgen Australia prize, 1996, Chiron Internat. award, Nat. Acad. Medicine, Italy, 1999, Victoria prize, Australia, 2000, Prime Minister's prize, 2001, Most Cited Author award, ICI, 2001, Pres. medal, Australia and New Zealand Soc. for Cell and Devel. Biology, 2002, Centenary medal, Australia, 2003, Mentorship award, Days of Molecular Medicine Found, 2004, Mem. NAS (fgn. mem.), Jessie Stevenson Kovalenko medal 1994), Assn. Am. Physicians (hon. fgn. mem.), Royal Soc. (Wellcome prize 1986, Royal medal 1995), Polish Soc. Hematology (hon.), Companion Order of Australia, Alpha Omega Alpha (hon.). Achievements include research in clinical use of molecules called colony-simulating factors (CSFs), which control the growth and development of blood cells. Office: Walter and Eliza Hall Inst Med Rsch 1G Royal Parade Parkville VIC 3050 Australia Office Phone: 61-3-9345-2555. Business E-Mail: metcalf@wehi.edu.au.

**METCALF, JACK,** former congressman, retired state senator; b. Marysville, Wash., Nov. 30, 1927; s. John Read and Eunice (Grannis) M.; m. Norma Jean Grant, Oct. 3, 1948; children: Marta Jean, Gayle Marie, Lea Lynn, Beverlee Ann. Student, U. Wash., 1944-45; BA, BEd, Pacific Luth. U., 1951. Tchr. Elma (Wash.) pub. schs., 1951-52, Everett (Wash.) pub. schs., 1952-81; mem. Wash. Ho. of Reps., 1960-64, Wash. Senate, 1966-75, 80-92, U.S. Ho. of Reps. from 2d Wash. dist., 1995-2001. Chmn. environment and natural resources com., 1988-92; mem. domestic & internat. monetary policy, fin. instns. & consumer credit, aviation, surface transp. coms. Hon. chmn. Innocent Property Owners Protection Initiative. Mem. Coun. State Govts., Wash. Edn. Assn. (bd. dirs.), Wash. Assn. Profl. Educators (state v.p. 1979-81, state pres. 1977-79), Nat. Conf. State Legislatures, Western States Recycling Coalition, South Whidbey Kiwanis. Republican.

**METCALF, JAMES,** manufacturing executive; b. 1959; married; 3 children. BS, Ohio St. Univ., 1980; MBA, Pepperdine Univ., Calif., 1983. Former sr. v.p., L&W Supply Distribution Subs., USG Corp.; with USG Corp., 1981—, dir., retail strategy, 2004, exec. v.p. pres. building sys. divsn., 2005—06, pres., 2006—, also COO, 2006—. Office: USG 125 S Franklin St Chicago IL 60606-4678 Office Fax: 312-606-4093.*

**METCALF, JORDAN PATRICK,** medical educator; b. Bristol, England, Jan. 7, 1961; s. William Kenneth and Norah Frances Metcalf; m. Mary Jane Metcalf; children: Angela Nicole, John Patrick. MD, U. Nebr., Omaha, Nebr., 1984. Lic. physician Nebr., 1984. Asst. prof. Health Scis. Ctr. Okla. U. Okla. City, Okla., 1994-2000, assoc. prof. Health Scis. Ctr., 2000—. Mem. Am.

Lung Assn. Okla., Ctrl. Soc. Clin. Rsch. (sec., treas. 2006), Am. Fedn. Med. Rsch. (chmn. midwest sect. 2004—05), Am. Thoracic Soc. Office: Ouhsc WP1310 920 Stanton Young Blvd Oklahoma City OK 73104 Office Phone: 405-271-6173.

**METCALF, KAREN,** retired foundation executive; b. Reading, Mass., Dec. 12, 1936; d. Albion Edmund and Natalie Viola (Ives) M. AB, Vassar Coll., 1958; MBA, Harvard U., 1968. CFA. Sec. Radio Liberty Com., N.Y.C., 1958-60; rsch. asst. Air Inc., Cambridge, Mass., 1960-64; sys. analyst Keydata Corp., Watertown, Mass., 1964-66; customer edn. cons. Interactive Data Corp., N.Y.C., 1968; portfolio mgr. Scudder, Stevens & Clark, N.Y.C., 1969-81; v.p. fin. and adminstrn. N.Y. Cmty. Trust, N.Y.C., 1981—2002. Episcopalian. Avocations: travel, opera.

**METCALF, LAURIE (LAUREN OPHELIA METCALFE),** actress; b. Edwardsville, Ill., June 15, 1955; m. Jeff Perry (div.); 1 child, Zoe; m. Matt Roth; 2 children Will Theron, Mae BA in Theatre, Ill. State U., 1976. Founding ensemble mem. Steppenwolf Theatre, Chgo. Off-Broadway appearances: Balm in Gilead (debut, Theatre World award), 1984; stage appearances: Who's Afraid of Virginia Woolf?, 1982, Coyote Ugly, 1985, Bodies Rest, and Motion, 1986, Educating Rita, 1987 (Joseph Jefferson award best performance by principal actress in a play), Little Egypt, 1987, Killers, 1988, My Thing of Love, 1995; films: Desperately Seeking Susan, 1985, Making Mr. Right, 1987, Stars and Bars, 1988, The Appointments of Dennis Jennings, 1988, Candy Mountain, 1988, Miles from Home, 1988, Uncle Buck, 1989, Internal Affairs, 1989, Pacific Heights, 1990, Frankie and Johnny, 1991, JFK, 1991, Mistress, 1992, A Dangerous Woman, 1993, Blink, 1994, The Secret Life of Houses, 1994, Leaving Las Vegas, 1995, Dear God, 1996, (voice) Toy Story, 1995, Hellcab, 1997, U-Turn, 1997, Scream 2, 1997, Bulworth, 1998, Toy Story 2, 1999(voice), God, the Devil and Bob, 2000 (voice), Treasure Planet, 2002 (voice), Steel City, 2006, Beer League, 2006; TV movies: Execution of Raymond Graham, 1985, Always Outnumbered, 1998, The Long Island Incident, 1998, Ballon Farm, 1999, Two Families, 2002, Phil at the Gate, 2003; TV series: Saturday Night Live, 1981, Roseanne, 1988-97 (Emmy award, Outstanding Supporting Actress in a Comedy Series, 1993, 94), The Norm Show, 1999, God, The Devil and Bob (voice), 2000; TV appearances: The Equalizer, 1986, The Dharma & Greg, 1997, King of the Hill, 1997, 3rd Rock from the Sun, 1998, The Norm Show, 2001, Malcolm in the Middle, 2004, Frasier, 2004, Without a Trace, 2005, Monk, 2006, Grey's Anatomy, 2006. Address: care ICM 8942 Wilshire Blvd Beverly Hills CA 90211-1934*

**METCALF, PHILIP LESLIE,** mathematics professor, career planning administrator; b. North Webster, Ind., Aug. 28, 1948; s. William Edwin and Edna Lunetta (Lentz) M.; m. Karilyn Sue Fetterhoff, Aug. 9, 1970. BS, Ball State U., 1970; MS, St. Francis Coll., 1975. Tchr. math. Wawasee Cmty. Schs., Syracuse, Ind., 1971-97, career and tech. coord., 1999—. Vis. prof. Ball State U., Muncie, Ind., 1997-99. Mem. study commn. Ind. State Govt., Indpls., 1989-91, mem. profl. stas. bd., 1992-98, chairperson, 1994-98; bd. visitors Butler U.; Tchrs. Coll. alumni bd. Ball State U. Sgt. U.S. Army NG, 1970-76. Awarded Sagamore of the Wabash, Gov. of Ind., 1999. Mem. NEA, Assn. Tchr. Educators, Nat. Coun. Accreditation of Tchrs. Edn. (bd. examiners 1993-98), Ind. State Tchrs. Assn. (bd. dirs. 1991-98), Wawasee Cmty. Educators Assn. (pres. 1981), Am. Assn. Career and Tech. Educators, Ind. ASsn. Area Vocat. Dists., North Ctrl. Assn. (amb. 2002—), Sigma Alpha Epsilon. Democrat. Baptist. Avocations: gardening, body-building, movies, reading, piano. Home: 624 S Dixie Dr North Webster IN 46555-9404 Office: Wawasee High Sch 1 Warrior Path Bldg 1 Syracuse IN 46567-9170 Business E-Mail: pmetcalf@wawasee.k12.in.us.

**METCALF, ROBERT CLARENCE,** architect, educator; b. Nashville, Ohio, Nov. 7, 1923; s. George and Helen May (Drake) M.; m. Bettie Jane Sponseller, Sept. 15, 1943. Student, Johns Hopkins U., 1943; B.Arch., U. Mich., 1950. Draftsman G.B. Brigham, Jr., Architect, Ann Arbor, Mich., 1948-52; pvt. practice architecture Ann Arbor, 1953—; lectr. architecture U. Mich., Ann Arbor, 1955-58, asst. prof., 1958-63, assoc. prof., 1963-68, prof., 1968-91, chmn. dept., 1968-74; dean U. Mich. (Coll. Architecture and Urban Planning), 1974-86; Emil Lorch prof. emeritus U. Mich., 1991—, dean emeritus, 1991—; pvt. practice, 1991—. Sec. Mich. Bd. Registration for Architects, 1975-79, chmn., 1980-82 Designer more than 140 bldgs., Ann Arbor, 1953— Served with U.S. Army, 1943-46, ETO. Decorated Silver Star; recipient Sol King award for excellent teaching in architecture U. Mich., 1974; named Emil Lorch Professor of Architecture, 1989. Fellow AIA (Pres.'s award 1999); mem. AIA Mich., Assn. Collegiate Schs. Architecture, Phi Kappa Phi, Tau Sigma Delta. Home: 1052 Arlington Blvd Ann Arbor MI 48104-2816 Office: U Mich 2150 Art Architecture Bldg Ann Arbor MI 48109 also: Metcalf Architect 2211 Medford Rd Ann Arbor MI 48104-5004

**METCALF, ROBERT JOHN ELMER,** industrial consultant; b. Glen Ellyn, Ill., June 27, 1919; s. Elmer Simpson and Vida Marie Metcalf; B.S.M.E., U. Pitts., 1947; m. Rosemarie Rusch, Sept. 11, 1947; children: Kathleen, Karen, Patti, Pamela. Asst. staff supr. Westinghouse Electric Co., Buffalo, 1949-52, assoc. engr., 1952-54; assoc. Gemar Assocs., Inc., Greenwich, Conn., 1954-66. v.p., 1966-83; cons., 1983-92 Served with U.S. Army, 1943-46. Mem. Inst. Mgmt. Cons. (founding). Roman Catholic. Home and Office: 444 Paula Dr N #331 Dunedin FL 34698-1820

**METCALF, VIRGIL ALONZO,** economics professor; b. Branch, Ark., Jan. 4, 1936; s. Wallace Lance and Luella J. (Yancey) M.; m. Janice Ann Maples, July 2, 1958; children: Deborah Ann, Robert Alan. BS in Gen. Agr., U. Ark., 1958, MS in Agrl. Econs. 1960; Diploma in Econs. U Copenhagen, 1960; PhD in Agrl. Econs., U. Mo., 1964. Asst. prof. U. Mo., Columbia, 1964-65, asst. to chancellor, 1964-69, assoc. prof., 1965-69, prof., exec. asst. to the chancellor, 1969-71; prof. econs., v.p. administrn. Ariz. State U., Tempe, 1971-81, prof. Sch. Agribus. and Natural Resources, 1981-88, prof. internat. bus. Coll. of Bus., 1988—99, prof. emeritus, 2000—. Asst. to the chancellor U. Mo., 1964-69, coord. internat. programs and studies, 1965-69, mem. budget com., 1965-71, chmn., co-chmn. several task forces; cons. Ford Found., Bogota, Colombia, 1966-67; mem. negotiating team U.S. Agy. for Internat. Devel., Mauritania, 1982, cons., Cameroon, 1983, agrl. rsch. specialist, India, 1984, agribus. cons., Guatemala, 1987, 88, asst. dir. Reform Coops. Credit Project, El Salvador, 1987-90; co-dir. USIA univ. linkage grant Cath. U., Bolivia, 1984-89; cons. World Vision Internat., Mozambique, 1989. Contbr. numerous articles to profl. jours. Mem. City of Tempe U. Hayden Butte Project Area Com., 1979; bd. commrs. Columbia Redevel. Authority; mem. workable project com. City of Columbia Housing Authority. Econs. officer USAR, 1963, econ. analyst, 1964-66. Fulbright grantee U. Copenhagen, 1959-60, U. Kiril Metodij, Yugoslavia, 1973. Mem. Am. Assn. Agrl. Economists, Soc. for Internat. Devel., Samaritans (chmn. 1976, bd. dirs. 1976, mem. task force of health svc. bd. trustees 1974, health svc. 1974-78, chmn. program subcom. 1975), Kiwanis, Blue Key, Gamma Sigma Delta, Alpha Zeta, Alpha Tau Alpha. Democrat. Home: 1357 W Crystal Springs Dr Gilbert AZ 85233-6606

**METCALF, WAYNE C., III,** retired insurance company executive; m. Shirley Imada Metcalf. BA in Polit. Sci., U. Hawaii, 1975; JD, 1978; student, Tufts U., 1992-93. Atty. pvt. practice, 1979—; spl. cons. UN, 1994; ins. commr. Dept. Commerce and Consumer Affairs State Hawaii, 1994—97, 2002—. Staff Senate Jud. Com., 1973-75; staff dir. Senate Pres.'s Office, 1975-78; vice-chmn. House Com. on Jud., 1984-86; chmn. House Com. on Jud., 1986-92; mem. house coms. Comsuner Protection and Commerce, 1984-92, Land Use and Hawaiian Affairs Plannong, 1984-86, Labor and Pub. Employment Transp., 1985-88, Housing, Health Human Svcs, 1988-90, Housing, Health, 1990-92. Recipient Disting. Alumni award U. hawaii, 1988, Disting. Legislator award, Nat. Dem. State LEgis. Leaders Assn., 1988; named one of Hawaii's five best legislators by polit. columnist Dan Boylan, 1990, 92.

**METCALF, WILLIAM EDWARDS,** museum curator, educator; b. East Grand Rapids, Mich., Dec. 16, 1947; s. George Ellington and Ruthanne (Schnitzler) M.; m. Margaret Mary Finn, May 21, 1972 (annulled 1984); 1 son, Daniel F.; m. Jane Salinger, Oct. 26, 1991; 1 child, Lydia Qiao Salinger. BA, U. Mich., 1969, MA, 1970, PhD in Classical Studies (Horace H. Rackham prize fellow), 1973. Asst. curator Roman and Byzantine coins Am. Numismatic Soc., N.Y.C., 1973-75, assoc. curator, 1975-78, curator, dep. chief curator, 1978-79, chief curator, 1979-2000, hon. curator, 2000—; prof. classics Yale U., 2002, curator coins and medals Art Gallery, 2002—. Adj. prof. art history and archaeology Columbia U., 1978—97, adj. prof. classics, 1998; adj. prof. history, 1993; adj. prof. classics NYU, 1996, 2000-01, Princeton U., 1999, Bryn Mawr U., 2000; vis. prof. classics NYU, 2001-02. Author: The Cistophori of Hadrian, 1980, The Silver Coinage of Cappadocia, Vespasian-Commodus, 1996; editor: Studies in Early Byzantine Gold Coinage, 1988, America's Gold Coinage, 1990, Mnemata: Papers in Memory of Nancy M. Waggoner, 1991; adv. com. Lexicon Iconographicum Mythologiae Classicae, 1979—; adv. bd. Am. Jour. Archaeology, 1980-97; editor book revs. Am. Jour. Numismatics, 1989-2000; mem. editl. bd. Revue Suisse de Numismatique, 2002—contbr. articles on Roman and Byzantine coinage to profl. jours. NEA fellow for mus. profls., 1978; mem. Inst. for Advanced Study, 1988-89 Fellow Am. Numismatic Soc. (life); mem. Royal Numismatic Soc., Am. Philol. Assn. (subcom. on classical bibliography 1979-89), Archaeol. Inst. Am. (exec. com. NY 1976-80, chmn. numismatics com. 2000--), Columbia U. Seminar on Classical Civilization, Internat. Numismatic Commn. (1st v.p. 1997-2003), Soc. Antiquaries London. E-mail: william.metcalf@yale.edu.

**METCALFE, CHRISTOPHER LEE,** secondary school educator, music educator; b. Rockwood, Tenn., Apr. 30, 1975; s. Danny Lee and Barbara Jean Metcalfe; m. Amy Marie Crabtree, Oct. 24, 1998; 1 child, Olivia Marie. BA of Music Edn., Tenn. Tech. U., 1997. Instr. low brass DeKalb County High Sch., Smithville, Tenn., 1995—98; prin. trombone Cumberland County Playhouse, Crossville, 1997—98; dir. band Lewis County Mid. Sch., Hohenwald, 1998—99, Lewis County High Sch., Hohenwald, 1999—2001, Rockwood High Sch., 2001—. Composer: (choir and band arrangement) Lewis County Alma Mater, 1999. Elder, session mem. 1st Presbyn. Ch., Rockwood, 2002—, pre youth leader, 2003—. Recipient Outstanding Musician award, Phi Mu. Alpha Xi Chi Chpt., 1996, Citation Excellence award, Tenn. Gov. Sch. Arts, 2001; grantee, Roane Choral Soc., Harriman Tenn., 2001. Mem.: NEA, Tenn. Secondary Schs. Band Dirs. Assn., East Tenn. Schs. Band and Orch. Assn., Music Educators Nat. Conf., Tenn. Edn. Assn., Phi Mu Alpha. Avocations: music, fishing, target shooting. Home: 305 Tarwater St Rockwood TN 37854 Office: Rockwood Bands 512 W Rockwood St Rockwood TN 37854

**METCALFE, DEAN DARREL,** medical research physician; b. Medford, Oreg., June 27, 1944; s. Darrell S. and Lucille E. (Moore) Metcalfe; m. Joan I. Peterson, Dec. 21, 1977; children: Justin, Jonathan, Elisabet. BS, No. Ariz. U., 1966; MS in Microbiology, U. Mich., 1968; MD, U. Tenn., 1972. Medicine residency Univ. Mich. Hosps., Ann Arbor, 1972—74; clin. assoc. NIH, Bethesda, Md., 1974—77; Rheum fellow Harvard Med. Sch. and Hosp., Boston, 1977—79; clin. investigator NIH, Bethesda, 1979—85; head mast cell physiology sect. lab. of clin. investigation Nat. Inst. of Allergy and Infectious Diseases, Bethesda, 1985—93, head allergic diseases sect., 1994—95; chief lab. allergic diseases Nat. Inst. of Allergy and Infectious Diseases NIH, Bethesda, 1995—. Co-dir. Allergy-Immunology Tng. Program NIAID/NIH, Bethesda, 1979—; dir. Am. Bd. Allergy-Immunology, Phila., 1990—. Capt. USPHS, 1979—. Recipient Commendation medal, USPHS, 1985, Outstanding Svc. medal, 1991. Fellow: Am. Rheumatism Assn., Am. Acad. Allergy and Immunology (bd. dirs.); mem.: Assn. Am. Physicians, Am. Soc. for Clin. Investigation, Am. Fedn. Clin. Rsch. Office: NIH NI AID Dir 10 Center Dr Msc 1881 Bldg 10 Bethesda MD 20892-0001

**METCALFE, ELIZABETH BROKAW,** art educator; b. St. Louis, Feb. 14, 1941; d. Augustus Van Liew and Elizabeth Cabell Gray Brokaw; m. James Walter Metcalfe, June 7, 1969; children: James Kenneth Brokaw, Elizabeth Cabell. BA, Washington U., St. Louis, 1962, MA, 1965. Instr. Pierce Coll., Athens, Greece, 1966; instr. art history Maryville U., St. Louis, 1968—72, 1981—. Lectr. and book reviewer. Mem. St. Louis Art Mus., 1970—, Chgo. Art Inst., 1970—. Mem.: Archeol. Inst. Am., Nat. Soc. Colonial Dames Am. Republican. Episcopalian. Avocations: reading, walking, running, travel, hiking. Home: 65 Berry Rd Pk Saint Louis MO 63122 Office: Maryville Univ 13550 Conway Rd Saint Louis MO 63141 Personal E-Mail: stlouis65@juno.com.

**METCALFE, LAUREN OPHELIA See METCALF, LAURIE**

**METCALFE, ROBERT DAVIS, III,** lawyer; b. Bridgeport, Conn., July 2, 1956; s. Robert Davis Jr. and Barbara Ann (Peaslee) M. BA summa cum laude, U. Conn., 1978, JD, 1981; MA, Trinity Coll., 1989, Am. Mil. U., 1997. Bar: Conn. 1981, U.S. Supreme Ct. 1986, D.C. 1990, Md. 1991. Judge adv. USN, Norfolk, Va., 1982-85; spl. asst. U.S. atty. U.S. Dept. Justice, Norfolk, 1985, trial atty. Washington, 1985—. Instr. ARC, Hartford, Conn., 1976-80; legis. asst. Conn. Gen. Assembly, Hartford, 1977. Served to lt. USN, 1982-85. Mem. Fed. Bar Assn., Conn. Bar Assn., Judge Adv. Assn., Mensa, Phi Beta Kappa. Republican. Roman Catholic. Avocations: martial arts, reading, sailing, trap and skeet shooting, stamp collecting/philately.

**METCALFE, ROBERT M.,** venture capitalist, former engineer-scientist, former publishing executive, writer; b. Bklyn., 1946; BS in Electrical Engring. and Computer Sci., B in Mgmt., MIT, 1969; MS in Applied Math., Harvard U., 1970, PhD in Computer Sci., 1973; doctorate (hon.). With computer sci. lab. Xerox Palo Alto Rsch. Ctr., 1973-79; founder 3Com Corp., Santa Clara, Calif., 1979-90, v.p. tech. internat. Data Group, Boston, 1990—92; CEO, pub. Info World Pub. Co., San Mateo, Calif., 1992—95, columnist, exec. corr., 1995—2000; venture capitalist, gen. ptnr. Polaris Venture Partners, Waltham, Mass., 2001—. Vis. fellow U. Cambridge, 1991—92; bd. dir. Avistar, EarthLink, Ember, IDC, IDG, Jeknscitt, Media-LabEurope, MIT, Nanosys, Narad, MIT Tech. Review Mag., Paketek; chmn. Paratek; bd. dir. SiCortex; founder (conferences) Pop!Tech, 1997, dir. conferences; produced conferences for Agenda, Vortex. Author: (books) Packet Communication, Internet Collapses and Other InfoWorld Punditry, Beyond Calculation: The Next Fifty Years of Computing. Bd. trustees MIT; bd. dir. St. Mark's Sch. Recipient Grace Murray Hepper award, Assn. for Computing Machinery, 1980, Alexander Graham Bell medal, IEEE 1988, Pub. Understanding of Sci. award, 1995, Medal of Honor IEEE 1996, Nat. Medal Tech., 2005; Marconi Internat. Fellowship 2003; inducted into Bay Shore HS Hall of Fame, 2003. Mem. Am. Acad. Arts and Sciences, NAE, Internat. Engring. Consortium Achievements include helping build the early Internet; invention of Ethernet for which he holds four patents. Office: Polaris Venture Partners Ste 3350 1000 Winter St Waltham MA 02451*

**METCALFE, WALTER LEE, JR.,** lawyer; b. St. Louis, Dec. 19, 1938; s. Walter Lee and Carol Metcalfe; m. Cynthia Williamson, Aug. 26, 1965; children: Carol, Edward. AB, Washington U., St. Louis, 1960; JD, U. Va., 1964. Bar: Mo. 1964. Ptnr. Armstrong, Teasdale, Kramer & Vaughan, St. Louis, 1964—81; sr. ptnr. Bryan Cave LLP, St. Louis, 1982—, former chmn.; chmn. Fed. Res. Bd., St. Louis. BJC Health Care, St. Louis. Bd. dirs. Washington U., St. Louis, Danforth Found., Pulitzer Found. Arts, St. Louis Children's Hosp. Mem.: ABA, St. Louis Bar Assn., Mo. Bar Assn., Noonday Club, Bogey Club. Episcopalian. Home: 26 Upper Ladue Rd Saint Louis MO 63124-1675 Office: Bryan Cave 211 N Broadway 1 Metropolitan Sq Ste 3600 Saint Louis MO 63102-2750 Office Phone: 314-259-2000.

**METHVIN, THOMAS JAMES,** lawyer; b. Eufaula, Ala., Feb. 19, 1963; s. Robert Gordon and Claudia Slade (Lindsey) Methvin; m. Amy Agee, Apr. 13, 1991; children: Thomas Rucker, William Slade. BS, U. Ala. Tuscaloosa, 1985; JD, Samford U., 1988. Bar: Ala. 1988. U.S. Dist. Ct. (mid. and no. dists.) Ala. 1988. Assoc. Beasley Wilson, Montgomery, Ala., 1988—94; ptnr. Beasley Allen Crow Methvin Portis & Miles P.C., Montgomery, Ala.,

1994—98, mng. shareholder, 1998—. Exec. coun. mem. Ala. State Bar, Montgomery, 2001; pres. Montgomery County Bar Assn., Montgomery, Ala., 1996, Montgomery County Trial Lawyers Assn., Montgomery, Ala., 1996; bd. of bar commissions Ala. State Bar, Montgomery, Ala. Bd. mem. Cystic Fibrosis Adv. Panel, Brantwood Children's Home, Let God Arise Ministries. Recipient Top 40 Under 40, Montgomery Advertiser, 2001, Top 40 Litigators Under 40, Nat. Law Jour., 2002. Mem.: Fed. Bar Assn., Ala. Trial Lawyers Assn., Montgomery County Trial Lawyers Assn. (pres. 1996), Ala. State Bar Assn. (exec. coun. 2001, bd. bar commns. 2002—), ABA, Montgomery County Bar Assn. (pres. 1996), Nat. Assn. Consumer Advocates, Trial Lawyers for Pub. Justice, Christian Legal Soc. Avocations: hunting, fishing, travel. Office: Beasley Allen Crow Methvin Portis & Miles 218 Commerce St Montgomery AL 36104 Office Phone: 334-269-2343.

**METOYER, PAMELA PARADIS,** scientific editor, writer; b. Hutchinson, Minn., Sept. 1, 1955; d. Paul Edward, Sr. and Mary LaVerne (Hebert) Paradis; m. Jeffrey Johns Powell, June 17, 1977 (div. July 1982); m. Christopher Allen Tice, Aug. 25, 1997 (div. Sept. 2004).; m. Grady Wilson Metoyer, June 3, 2006. BA, Coll. of St. Scholastica, 1977. Statis./soc. U. Tex. M.D. Anderson Cancer Ctr., Houston, 1978-87; data coord. Baylor Coll. Medicine, Houston, 1987-88, editl. asst., 1988-90, sr. editor, 1992-2000, rsch. assoc. 2000—; dept. editor U. Tex. Med. Sch., Houston, 1990-91; editor, Houston medicine HCA Ctr. for Health Excell., Houston, 1991-92; exec. asst. U. Tex. Sch. Nursing, Houston, 1991-92. Mem. scope and mandate task force, Coun. of Sci. Editors, Chgo., 1996. Editor-in-chief: Am. Med. Writers Assn. Jour., 1992-95 (Apex awards 1995, 96, 97, Matrix award 1996, 2000, 2001, others). Recipient Presdl. Alumni award, Coll. of St. Scholastica, 2003. Mem. Am. Med. Writers Assn. (chpt. sec. 1989-90, chpt. treas. 1990-92, chpt. pres.-elect 1992-93, chpt. pres. 1993-94, chpt. past pres. 1994-95, chpt. dir.-at-large 2001-2003, chair McGovern Award com. 2003—, Chpt. Svc. award 1994, Assn. Pres. award 1993, Assn. Leadership award 1995), Coun. of Sci. Editors, Bd. of Editors in the Life Scis. (diplomate 2002). Office Phone: 713-798-1087. Business E-Mail: pptice@bcm.tmc.edu.

**METREY, GEORGE DAVID,** social work educator, retired academic administrator; b. Milw., July 23, 1939; s. Richard Joseph and Catherine (Evans) M.; m. Cheryl Ann Mosca, June 21, 1969 (dec. May 7, 2000); 1 child, Mary Beth. AB, Marquette U., 1961; MSW, Fordham U., 1963; PhD, NYU, 1970. Lic. ind. clin. social worker RI, NJ. Social worker N.J. Diagnostic Ctr., Edison, 1963-64, asst. social work supr., 1964-66, dir. psychiat. social work, 1966-70; coordinator undergrad. social work program Kean Coll., NJ, 1970-73, assoc. prof. social work NJ 1970-74, prof. NJ, 1974-79, chmn. dept. sociology, anthropology and social work NJ, 1977-73, dir. social work program, acting assoc. dean Sch. Arts and Sci. NJ, 1977-79; dean Sch. Social Work, prof. R.I. Coll., Providence, 1979—, asst. v.p. acad. affairs, 2000—02; ret., 2004. Field instr. Fordham U. Sch. Social Service, 1966-70, adj. prof., 1969-77; adj. assoc. prof. Rutgers U. Grad. Sch. Social Work, 1972-73 Mem. program com. R.I. affiliate Am. Heart Assn., 1980-90, bd. dirs., 1983-89, chmn. program com., 1985-87, exec. com., 1985-87; sec. bd. dirs. Adoption R.I., 1987-89, pres. bd. dirs., 1989-92. Recipient Fordham U. Grad. Sch. Social Svc. Outstanding Alumni, 1984, Spl. Disting. Svc. award R.I. Coll. Alumni Assn., 1996. Mem. NASW (N.J. Social Worker of Yr. 1977, pres. 1978-80, parliamentarian R.I. 1981—, treas. R.I. chpt. 1986-87, nat. competence cert. commn. 1989-91, nat. 2d v.p 1978-80, chair nat. program com. 1981-83), Coun. on Social Work Edn. (bd. dirs. 1979-82, commn. on accreditation 1996-2002, commn. on ednl. policy, 2002—), Acad. Cert. Social Workers, Nat. Assn. Deans and Dirs. Social Work (nominating com. 1993-96, program com. 1993-96), Alpha Phi Omega, Gamma Pi Mu, Alpha Delta Mu (regional v.p.). Roman Catholic. Home: PO Box 206 Wyckoff NJ 07481-0206 Personal E-mail: gmetrey@aol.com.

**METTEE-MCCUTCHON, ILA,** municipal official, retired military officer; b. Mobile, Ala., May 1, 1945; d. John Martin and Anna Ruth (Cleveland) Mettee; m. John Robert McCutchon, Oct. 13, 1974; 1 child, Erin Tempest. BS, Auburn U., Ala., 1967, MS, 1969; grad., various army schs. Rsch. psychologist VA Hosp., Tuskegee, Ala., 1967-69; clin. psychologist U. Ala. Med. Ctr., Birmingham, 1969-71; commd. 1st lt. U.S. Army, 1971, advanced through grades to col., 1992. Officer in charge Alcohol and Drug Abuse Rehab. Ctr., Presidio, San Francisco, 1971-73; strategic intelligence officer 8th Psychol. Bn., 1973-75; tactical intelligence ops. officer, co. comdr. 525th MI Brigade (Airborne), Ft. Bragg, N.C., 1976-79; project officer Command, Control, Commns. and Intelligence Directorate, Combined Arms Combat Devel. Activity, Ft. Leavenworth, Kans., 1979-82; student Command and Gen. Staff Coll., 1982-83; ops. officer Army Spl. Security Group, Washington, 1983-86; Def. Lang. Inst. Presidio of Monterey, 1986-87; chief U.S. So. command Joint Intelligence Ctr., Republic of Panama, 1987-89; comdr. 741st M.I. Bn., Ft. Meade, Md., 1989-91; U.S. Army War Coll., 1991-92; strategic intelligence officer Internat. Mil. Staff NATO, Brussels, 1992-94; comdr. Presidio of Monterey and Ft. Ord, Calif., 1994-96, chief base realignment and closure/environ. mgmt., 1996-97, ret. with honors, 1997. Elected to Marina City Coun., 1998, Rep. ctrl. com. Monterey County, 2000, Mayor City of Marina, 2002—, reelected, 2004; apptd. housing cmty. and econ. devel. policy com. League Calif. Cities,' 1999—; chair bd. dirs. Ftord Reuse Auth., 2004 Decorated Army Commendation medal (3), Meritorious Svc. medal (2), Def. Meritorious Svc. medal, Army Achievement award (2), Legion of Merit (2), Def. Superior Svc. medal; named Woman of Yr. Marina, 2001, Philanthropist of Yr., 2001. Mem. NAFE, Nat. Assn. Univ. Women, Nat. Women's Polit. Caucus, VFW, Assn. U.S. Army, Alumni Assn. U.S. Army War Coll., WAC Found., Women in NATO, Am. Legion (post 694), Ft. Ord Alumni Assn. (adv. bd.), Girl Scouts of Monterey Bay (bd. dirs.), Cmty. Human Svcs. (bd. dirs.), Rotary Internat. (local chpt.), Monterey Rep. Women, Marina C. of C., Marina Bus. Assn., Marina Larger Libr. Com. Home: 3181 DeForest Rd Marina CA 93933 Office: City Hall City of Marina 211 Hillcrest Ave Marina CA 93933-3534 Office Phone: 831-884-1278.

**METTERS, THOMAS WADDELL,** sportswriter; b. Columbus, Ohio, Apr. 17, 1939; s. Thomas Hammond and Charlotte Ann (Waddell) M. BS in Journalism, Ohio U., 1965. Sports editor The Traveller, Ft. Lee, Va., 1960—62; sports writer The Athens Messenger, Ohio, 1965—. Asst. to officials Legion Baseball, Athens, 1962—. Contbr.: Ohio Interscholastic Athletic Media Guide, 1985. Bd. dirs. Athens H.S. Booster Club, 1975—, Athens H.S. Athletic Hall of Fame, 2000; ofcl. scorekeeper Am. Legion World Series, Millington, Tenn., 1989. With U.S. Army, 1959-62. Named to Ohio H.S. Basketball Coaches Assn. Hall of Fame, 1993; recipient Contributor award Ohio H.S. Track & Field Coaches Assn., 1995, Ohio H.S. Athletic Assn. Media Svc. award, 1998. Mem. Soc. Profl. Journalists (Recognition plaque 1973), Ohio Associated Press Sports Writers Assn. (pres. 1984), Green & White Club (sec. 1983-2004, historian 2004—), Jonesy Sams award 1987), Ohio Prep Sports Writers Assn. (Hall of Fame 1990), Ky. Colonels, Am. Legion. Republican. Avocation: bowling. Home: 71 Sunnyside Dr Athens OH 45701-1921 Office: The Athens Messenger 9300 Johnson Rd Athens OH 45701 Office Phone: 740-592-6612 x 221.

**METTINGER, KARL LENNART,** pharmaceutical executive; b. Helsingborg, Sweden, Nov. 1, 1943; came to the U.S., 1989; s. Nils Allan and Anna Katarina (Hallberg) M.; m. Chesne Maree Ryman, 1979; m. Miki Ilaw, 1998. MD, U. Lund, 1973; PhD, Karolinska Inst., 1982. Intern Stockholm Hosps., 1973-74; resident Karolinska Hosp., Stockholm, 1974-77, clin. neurologist 1977-85; med. dir. Kabi Hematology, Stockholm, 1985-87; dep. gen. mgr. Kabi Cardiovascular, Stockholm, 1987-89; med. dir. Ivax/Baker Norton Pharms., Miami, Fla., 1989-93, sr. clin. rsch. dir., 1993-98, exec. dir., clin. rschr., 1998-2000; sr. v.p. chief med. officer SuperGen, San Ramon, 2000—05; chief med. officer Oncolytics Biotech, Calgary/Berkeley, 2005—. Assoc. prof. Karolinska Inst., Stockholm, 1983-91; cons. neurologist Odenplan Med. Ctr., Stockholm, 1984-89. Author: Cerebral Thromboembolism, 1982, Refaat--Myths and Billions in Biotech, 1987; editor: Coronary Thrombolysis: Current Answers to Critical Questions, 1988, Controversies in Coronary Thrombolysis, 1989. Bd. dirs. Boston Bus. Arts, 1999-2001, Oakland East Bay Symphony, 2002—, New Spirit Cmty. Ch., Berteley, 2005—, UNA USA, East Bay, 2006—; v.p. Friends of Music, U. Miami, 2000-2001. Lt.

Swedish Army, 1979 Recipient Silver award Spanish Health Ministry, 1989, Classical Langs. award King Gustav V Found., 1963. Mem. Swedish Stroke Soc. (bd. dirs. 1979-89, pres. 1984-86), Swedish Med. Soc., Swedish Christian Med. Soc. (bd. dirs. 1972-88, pres. 1983-88), Am. Heart Assn., Internat. Assn. Christian Physicians (exec. com. 1975-86). Home and Office: 1367 La Loma Ave Berkeley CA 94708

**METZ, ADAM S.,** real estate company executive; BA, Cornell U.; MMgmt, Northwestern U. Corp. lending officer 1st Nat. Bank Chgo., 1983-87; v.p. Capital Markets Group, JMB Realty, 1987-93; treas., CFO, exec. v.p, dir. acquisitions Urban Shopping Ctrs., Inc., 1993-2000, pres., 2000—01; co-founding ptnr. Polaris Capital LLC, Northbrook, Ill., 2003—. Trustee Amli Residential Properties, 2003—, Ctr. for Urban Land Econs. Rsch., U. Wis., 1997—. Mem. Internat. Coun. Shopping Ctrs. Office: Polaris Capital LLC 1033 Skokie Blvd Ste 660 Northbrook IL 60062 Office Phone: 847-480-9180. E-mail: metza@comcast.net.

**METZ, CARSTEN,** research scientist; b. Goettingen, Niedersachsen, Germany, Feb. 8, 1972; s. Richard and Brigitte Metz; m. Cristina Metz, June 8, 2002; 1 child, Conrad. D with distinction, Tech. U. Braunschweig, Germany, 2001. Mem. rsch. staff Tech. U. Braunschweig, Inst. RF Engring., Niedersachsen, Germany, 1997—2001, Bell Labs., Lucent Techs., Murray Hill, NJ, 2001—. Contbr. scientific papers. Recipient Erwin Marx award, German Engr. Assn., 1997. Mem.: IEEE, German Engr. Assn. Achievements include patents for Phased array metamaterial antenna system; patents pending for Method And Apparatus For Signal Phase Shifting Using Electrowetting; Method And Apparatus For Generating WDM Millimeter-Wave-On-Fiber (MWOF) Signals; Low-Loss Coupler; Reconfigurable Plasma Antenna With Interconnected Gas Enclosures; Planar Power Splitter; research in Nonlinear phased array processing; Anti collision automtive radar; patents for Method and apparatus for intra-layer transitions and connector launch in multilayer circuit boards; Radar sensor and radar antenna for monitoring the environment of a motor vehicle; patents pending for Antenna arrangement; Lightweight signal transmission lines and radio frequency antenna system; Modulation and transmission methods to provide a wireless link and transmitter circuit for providing a wireless link; Low-loss transmission line structure; Media with controllable refractive properties; Improved Antenna Array. Office: 908-582-5301. Office Fax: 908-582-6322. E-mail: cmetz@ieee.org.

**METZ, CATHERINE TAYLOR,** performing arts educator; b. Charlotte, N.C., Feb. 5, 1952; d. Hiera Louis and Norma Roberts Taylor; m. James Milton Metz, Nov. 7, 1987. B of Creative Arts, U. N.C., Charlotte, 1975; MFA, U. N.C., Chapel Hill, 1978, Licentiate of Dramatic Arts, 1979. Cert. tchr. N.C. Substitute tchr. Charlotte-Mecklenburg Schs., NC, 1985—2000; tchr. theatre N.E. Jr. HS, Charlotte, 1986—87, South Mecklenburg HS, Charlotte, 1998—99, East Mecklenburg HS, Charlotte, 2000—06. Actress Playmakers Rep., Chapel Hill, NC, 1976—79, Actor's Theatre, Chapel Hill, NC, 1988—90, Children's Theatre, Chapel Hill, 1988—90. Recipient Joseph Felman scholarship, U. N.C., 1978. Republican. Episcopalian. Avocations: swimming, acting, writing. Home: 10322 Silver Mine Rd Indian Land SC 29715 Office: East Mecklenburg HS 6800 Monroe Rd Charlotte NC 28212 Office Phone: 980-343-6430. E-mail: catherine.metz@cms.k12.nc.

**METZ, CHARLES EDGAR,** radiology educator; b. Bayshore, N.Y., Sept. 11, 1942; s. Clinton Edgar and Grace Muriel (Schienke) M.; m. Maryanne Theresa Bahr, July, 1967 (div. 1988); children: Rebecca, Molly. BA, Bowdoin Coll., 1964; MS, U. Pa., 1966, PhD, 1969. Instr. radiology U. Chgo., 1969-71, asst. prof., 1971-75, assoc. prof., 1976-80, dir. grad. programs in med. physics, 1979-85, prof., 1980—, prof. structural biology, 1984-86, prof. med. physics, 2003—. Mem. diagnostic rsch. adv. group Nat. Cancer Inst., 1980-81; mem. sci. coun. Nat. Coun. on Radiation Protection and Measurements, 1982-85, 2001-, Internat. Commn. on Radiation Units and Measurements, 1988-96, chmn. sci. com., 1992-99; cons. and lectr. in field. Assoc. editor: Radiology Jour., 1986—91, Med. Physics Jour., 1992—95, mem. editl. bd.: Med. Decision Making Jour., 1980—84; contbr. over 200 articles to sci. jours. and chpts. to books. Recipient L.H. Gray medal, Internat. Commn. on Radiation Units and Measurements, 2005. Fellow Am. Assn. Physicists in Medicine; mem. Radiol. Soc. N.Am., Am. Assn. Physicists in Medicine, Soc. Med. Decision Making, Assn. Univ. Radiologists, Phi Beta Kappa, Sigma Xi. Achievements include development of software for ROC analysis used in more than 10,000 labs worldwide. Office: U Chgo Dept Radiology MC2026 5841 S Maryland Ave Chicago IL 60637-1463 E-mail: c-metz@uchicago.edu.

**METZ, CRAIG HUSEMAN,** government relations executive; b. Columbia, SC, Aug. 26, 1955; s. Leonard Huseman and Annette (Worthington) M.; m. Karen Angela McCleary, Aug. 11, 1984; 1 child, Preston Worthington. BA, U. Tenn., 1977; JD, U. Memphis, 1986; cert., U.S. Ho. of Reps. Rep. Leadership Parliamentary Law Sch., 1987. Bar: S.C., D.C., U.S. Ct. Fed. Claims, U.S. Supreme Ct., U.S. Ct. Appeals (4th cir.). Canvass coord., liaison Campaign to Re-elect Congressman Floyd Spence, 1978; del., chmn. Shelby County Del. to 1983 Tenn. Young Rep. Fedn. Conv.; vice chmn. Shelby County Young Reps., 1983-84, chmn., 1984-85; Shelby County adminstr., asst. to Tenn. state exec. dir. Reagan-Bush Campaign, 1984; field rep. Campaign to Re-elect Congressman Floyd Spence, 1986; spl. asst. to Congressman Floyd Spence, 1986-88; counsel com. on labor and human resources U.S. Senate, 1988-90; commr.'s counsel U.S. Occupl. Safety and Health Rev. Commn., Washington, 1990-91; spl. asst. to asst. sec. for legis. and congl. affairs, dep. asst. sec. for congl. liaison US Dept. Edn., 1991—93; asst. dir. Divsn. Congl. Affairs AMA, Washington, 1993; chief of staff Congressman Floyd Spence, Washington, 1993—2001; adminstr. Office of the Second Congl. Dist. of S.C., U.S. Ho. of Reps., Washington, 2001; govt. rels. mgr. EMC Corp., Arlington, Va., 2001—. Judge nat. writing competition U.S. Constn. Bicentennial, SC, 1987—88; mem. U.S. adv. bd. Churchill Archives Ctr., Churchill Coll., U. Cambridge; mem. adv. bd. Salvation Army, Alexandria, Va.; mem. Ch. of the Ascension and Saint Agnes, Washington. Recipient award of merit Rep. Party of Shelby County, 1985, Outstanding Leadership award Shelby County Young Reps., 1985, Meritorious Svc. medal Mil. Dept. S.C., Legis. award Res. Officers Assn. U.S., Order of the Palmetto, Palmetto Patriot award, Pres.'s award of N.G. Assn. S.C.; Hon. Washington fellow U.S. Washington Fellows Program. Mem.: SAR, Soc. Colonial Wars, Rep. Nat. Lawyers Assn. (state chmn. S.C. chpt. 1987—90), U. Tenn. Nat. Alumni Assn., Nat. Cathedral Assn., Friend of Scouting, Nat. Mus. U.S. Army (founding sponsor), German-Am. Heritage Soc. Greater Washington D.C., The Churchill Ctr., Mil. Order Loyal Legion of U.S., Mil. Order Stars and Bars, Sons and Daus. Colonial and Antebellum Bench and Bar 1565-1861, Sons of the Revolution, Soc. King Charles the Martyr, Clan Lockhart, Am. Clan Lockhart Soc., Newcomen Soc. U.S., English Spkg. Union, Palmetto Trust for Historic Preservation, Palmetto Conservation Found., Lowcountry Heritage Soc., Orangeburg County (SC) Hist. Soc., Savannah River Valley Geneal. Soc., The Oyster Bay Hist. Soc., Hist. Soc. of Washington County, Va., Randolph County Geneal. Soc., Fairfax Geneal. Soc., Freedoms Found. Valley Forge, Va. Hist. Soc., Assn. for Preservation Va. Antiquities, Land Trust of Va., Preservation Alliance of Va., Va. Geneal. Soc., U. South Caroliniana Soc., Nat. Trust for Hist. Preservation (assoc. Capital region), Sons of Am. Colonists, St. David's Soc., St. Andrew's Soc. Washington, Royal Soc. St. George/St. George's Soc. Balt., Mil. Soc. War of 1812, Vet Corps Arty. State of N.Y., Gen. Soc. War of 1812, George San Md., Propeller Club Washington, Royal Oak Found., Ky. Col., N.Y. Caledonian Club, Phi Alpha Delta (v.p. McKeller chpt., Outstanding Svc. award 1983), Sigma Alpha Epsilon. Republican. Episcopalian. Home: 8505 Westown Way Vienna VA 22182-2513 Office: Crystal Park One Ste 907 2011 Crystal Dr Arlington VA 22202

**METZ, EMMANUEL MICHAEL,** investment company executive, lawyer; b. Pitts., Sept. 19, 1928; s. Solomon and Gertrude (Krieger) M.; m. Janine Spaner, Apr. 3, 1964. BA, Dartmouth Coll., 1949; LLB, Harvard U., 1952; LLM, NYU, 1958. Bar: N.Y. 1952. Atty. ABC, N.Y.C., 1956-58; security analyst Standard & Poor's, N.Y.C., 1958-68; mng. dir. CIBC Oppenheimer

Corp., N.Y.C., 1968—. Author: Street Fighting at Wall and Broad, 1982. Lt. USN, 1952-56. Home: 150 E 56th St New York NY 10022-3631 Office: 200 Park Ave New York NY 10166 Office Phone: 212-667-5430. Business E-Mail: michael.metz@opco.com.

**METZ, FERDINAND,** chef, educator, academic administrator; b. Munich; BS, U. Pitts., 1973, MBA, 1975; apprenticeship, Sch. for Hotel and Restaurant Adminstrn., Cooking Trade Coll., Munich, Germany. Cert. master chef, Am. Culinary, Fedn., 1982. European apprentice in cooking and baking, 1956—62; commis tounant Hotel Deutscher Kaiser, Munich; saucier, garde manger, decorateur, sous chef Preakness Hills Country Club, Wayne, NJ; poissonier, garde manger, entremetier Le Pavillon, NYC, 1961—64; banquet chef Plaza Hotel, NYC, 1964—65; with Heinz, U.S.A., Pitts., 1965—80, sr. mgr., new product develop., mgr., new product develop., chief, product develop., exptl. chef; pres. Culinary Inst. Am., Hyde Park, NY, 1980—2001, pres. emeritus Beacon, NY, 2001—. Team mem., capt., team mgr., chmn. US Culinary Olympic Team, 1968-1988 (30 gold medals in internat. competition); mgr. Am. Team (Culinary World Cup, Luxemburg, 1986); head, cons., Ferdinand Metz Culinary Innovations, LLC and Master Chefs' Assocs.; lectr. German Hotel and Restaurant Industry; owner Café Cappuccino, Pitts., Gourmet Cooking Sch. for Food Enthusiasts, Pitts.; Internat. Culinary judge representing U.S.A., 1980-. Author: The Culinary Olympics Cookbook, 1976, 1980, 1984, 1988. Trustee St. Francis Hosp., Poughkeepsie, 1981-90. Co-recipient World Championship, hot foods divsn. Internat. Kockkunst Ausstellung, Internat. Culinary Competition, Germany, 1988; recipient Who is Who in Cooking, 1985, Lifetime Achievement award, James Beard Found. 1999, Medal of French Republic, 1967, Gold Plate award Internat. Foodservice Mfrs. Assn., 1983, Hotel Olympia Gold Medal of the British Chef's Soc., Centennial medal, Soc. Culinaire Philanthropique, Grand prize for Culinary Arts, German Govt., Leadership award, Restaurant Bus. Mag., 1985, Team Grand prize, Culinary World Cup Competition, Luxembourg, 1986, Courvoisier "Order of Napoleon", 1986, Caterina de Medici Edu. award, 1987, Corning Higher Edu. award, Commn. Independent Coll. & U., 1990, Silver Spoon award, Food Arts Magazine, 1995, Lifetime Achievement award, Tastemaster, 1992 & 1999, Ty award, NY Restaurant Assn., 1999, Coll. Diplomates, Nat. Restaurant Assn., Diploma and Medal Hon., Maires Cuisiniers de France, 2001, Hon. Gold medal, Masters Chefs of Frame, 2003; inducted into the Am. Acad. of Chefs Hall of Fame, 2003; named Maitre D'Honneur, La Chaine des Rotisseurs, 1997, Man Yr., Innovator Yr. award, MUFSO, 1998, Top 25 Movers and Shakers, Self Magazine, 1998, Escoffier Soc., 2002. Mem. Am. Culinary Fedn. (pres. 1979-83, chmn., mem. honor soc. 1971-, nat. chmn., culinary and master chef cert. com., 1976-85, named Nat. Chef Yr., 1968, Nat. Culinarian Yr., 1985, Educator Yr., 1998), Internat. Foodsvc. Mfrs. Assn., World Assn. of Cooks Societies (hon. mem., v.p. 1981-85, pres. 2004-), Am. Acad. Chefs.; tres. Nat. Restaurant Assn. Edu. Found., 2003-, Societe Culinaire Philanthropique, Vatel Club, Les Amis D'Escoffier Soc., James Beard Found., La Chaine des Rotisseurs; hon. mem. Canadian Chefs de Cuisine, German Chefs' Assn., Am. Dietetic Assn. Internat. Chefs' Assn.; trustee Coun. of Independent Colls. & U. NY, 1983-92, Centre Internat. de Glion, Switzerland, 1987-97, Culinary Inst. Am. 1975-80 (Outstanding Chef Yr., 1975), Nat. Restaurant Assn. Edu. Inst., 1994-. Office: Culinary Inst Am 5 Slocum Rd Beacon NY 12508 Office Phone: 845-838-5448. Office Fax: 845-838-5449. Business E-Mail: F_Metz@msn.com.

**METZ, JEROME JOSEPH, JR.,** lawyer; b. Cin., Dec. 25, 1950; s. Jerome Joseph Sr. and Loretta Ellen (Donnellon) M.; m. Deborah Carolyn Hundemer, July 2, 1976; children: Andrew Thomas, Matthew Jerome, Angela Christina. BS, Xavier U., 1976; JD, U. Cin., 1980. Bar: Ohio 1980, U.S. Dist. Ct. (so. dist.) Ohio 1980, U.S. Ct. Appeals (6th cir.) 1980. Law clk. to judge U.S. Dist. Ct. (so. dist) Ohio, Cin., 1980-82; assoc. Hartsock, Harris & Schneider, Cin., 1982-83, Porter, Wright, Morris & Arthur, Cin., 1983-89, ptnr., 1990—. Trustee Winton Place Devel. Corp., Cin., 1982-91, sec., 1987-91. Vice pres. Mercy Montessori Parents Assn., 1990-91, pres., 1991-92, past pres., 1992-93; sec. Ohio chpt. Scleroderma Found., 2001—; mem. adv. bd. Franciscan Network, 2006-. Mem. ABA, Ohio Bar Assn., Cin. Bar Assn., Social Ministries Immaculate Heart of Mary Parish. Democrat. Roman Catholic. Office: Porter Wright Morris & Arthur 250 E 5th St Ste 2200 Cincinnati OH 45202-4199 Office Phone: 513-369-4200.

**METZ, MARY SEAWELL,** retired foundation administrator, retired academic administrator; b. Rockhill, SC, May 7, 1937; d. Columbus Jackson and Mary (Dunlap) Seawell; m. F. Eugene Metz, Dec. 21, 1957; 1 dau., Mary Eugena. BA summa cum laude in French and English, Furman U., 1958; postgrad., Institut Phonetique, Paris, 1962-63, Sorbonne, 1962-63; PhD magna cum laude in French, La. State U., 1966; HHD (hon.), Furman U., 1984; LLD (hon.), Chapman Coll., 1985; DLT (hon.), Converse Coll., 1988. Instr. French La. State U., 1965-66, asst. prof., 1966-67, 1968-72, assoc. prof., 1972-76, dir. elem. and intermediate French programs, 1966-74, spl. asst. to chancellor, 1974-75, asst. to chancellor, 1975-76; prof. French Hood Coll., Frederick, Md., 1976-81, provost, dean acad. affairs, 1976-81; pres. Mills Coll., Oakland, Calif., 1981-90; dean of extension U. Calif., Berkeley, 1991-98; pres. S.H. Cowell Found., San Fransisco, 1999—. Vis. asst. prof. U. Calif.-Berkeley, 1967-68; mem. commn. on leadership devel. Am. Coun. on Edn., 1981-90, adv. coun. Stanford Rsch. Inst., 1985-90, adv. coun. Grad. Sch. Bus., Stanford U.; bd. dirs. PG&E, AT&T, Inc., Union Bank, Longs Drug Stores. Author: Reflets du monde francais, 1971, 78, Cahier d'exercices: Reflets du monde francais, 1972, 78, (with Helstrom) Le Francais a decouvrir, 1972, 78, Le Francais a vivre, 1972, 78, Cahier d'exercices: Le Francais a vivre, 1972, 78; standardized tests; mem. editorial bd. Liberal Edn., 1982—. Trustee Am. Conservatory Theater. NDEA fellow, 1960-62, 1963-64; Fulbright fellow, 1962-63; Am. Council Edn. fellow, 1974-75 Mem. Western Coll. Assn. (v.p. 1982-84, pres. 1984-86), Assn. Ind. Calif. Colls. and Univs. (exec. com. 1982-90), Nat. Assn. Ind. Colls. and Univs. (govt. rels. adv. coun. 1982-85), So. Conf. Lang. Teaching (chmn. 1976-77), World Affairs Coun. No. Calif. (bd. dirs. 1984-93), Bus.-Higher Edn. Forum, Women's Forum West, Women's Coll. Coalition (exec. com. 1984-88), Phi Kappa Phi, Phi Beta Kappa. Address: PO Box 686 Stinson Beach CA 94970-0686 also: 9 Regulus Ct Alameda CA 94501-1015

**METZ, ROBERT ROY,** publishing executive, media consultant; b. Richmond Hill, N.Y., Mar. 23, 1929; s. Robert Roy, Sr. and Mary (Kissel) M.; m. Susan Lee Blair, 1984; children: Robert Sumner, Christopher Roy. BA, Wesleyan U., Middletown Conn., 1950. Copyboy N.Y. Times, 1951, asst. fgn. news desk, 1952; rewriteman cable desk I.N.S., 1953, overnight cable editor, 1954-56, asst. feature editor, 1956-58; asst. news editor Newspaper Enterprise Assn., 1958, news editor, 1959-63, mng. editor, 1963-66, exec. editor, 1966-68, v.p., 1967-71, editorial dir., 1968-71, pres., editor, dir., 1972-94; dir. Berkeley-Small Inc., 1974-77; chmn. Berkley-Small Inc., 1976-77; v.p., dir. United Feature Syndicate, 1976-77, pres., editor, 1978; pres., editor, dir. United Media, 1978-93, chmn., 1993-94; media cons., 1994—. Pres. Peter Pan Children's Fund, 1997—2005. Mem.: Union League (N.Y.C.). Lutheran. Home: 193 Swamp Rd East Hampton NY 11937

**METZ, ROBIN O.,** writer, educator; b. Pittsburgh, Pa., Jan. 4, 1942; s. Robert Frederick and Isabell Metz; m. Elizabeth Carlin, Dec. 20, 1995; m. Elizabeth Jahnke, Aug. 29, 1992 (dec. Feb. 20, 1993); m. Lynn Hellerstedt Harlan (div.); children: Lisa Metz-Belzer, Ronnah. BA, Princeton U., Princeton, New Jersey, 1964; MFA, U. of Iowa, Iowa City, Iowa, 1967. Phillip sidney post prof. of english Knox Coll., Galesburg, Ill., 1967—, program in creative writing, 1984—; dir, london florence program Associated Colleges of the Midwest, Chicago, Ill., 1993—94, faculty fellow, chgo. urban studies program, 1989—90, faculty fellow, chgo. arts program, 1991—92, 1998—99. Mem. adv. coun Ctr. for Excellence in the Arts and Humanities, Iowa State U.; non-resident fellow Ctr. for Am. Progress, Washington. Author: (book) Unbidden Angel (Rainer Maria Rilke Internat. Poetry Prize, 1999), poetry, fiction, poetry, River Stories (Miss. Valley Internat. Poetry Prize, 1989), poetry/fiction/nonfiction, poetry. Recipient Syndicated Fiction Prize(s), Nat. Endowment for the Arts/PEN USA, Marshall Frankel Am. Fiction Prize, Other Voices, Roll of Honor Citation(s), The Best Am. Short Stories, Phillip Greene Wright Award for Disting. Tchg., Knox Coll.,

Caterpillar Corp. Award for Exceptional Achievement, Environ. Award(s) for Wildlife Habitat and Forestry, State of Wis. (Crawford County); fellow Individual Writer's Fellowship, Ill. Arts Coun. Mem.: Poetry Soc. of Am., Am. Acad. of Poets, Associated Writing Programs, PEN Internat./USA-West. Home: 695 North Broad Street Galesburg IL 61401 Office: Knox College K-50 Galesburg IL 61401 Business E-Mail: rmetz@knox.edu.

**METZ, STEVEN WILLIAM,** small business owner; b. Inglewood, Calif., Nov. 30, 1946; s. Glenn Ludwig and Kathleen Martha (Peterson) M.; m. Michelle Marie McArthur, Aug. 11, 1989; 1 child, Glenn Christian. Student, Fullerton Coll., Calif. Supt. Oahu Interiors, Honolulu, 1969-71, Hackel Bros., Miami, Fla., 1971-73; exec. v.p. Tru-Cut Inc., Brea, Calif., 1974-82; gen. mgr. The Louvre', Grass Valley, Calif., 1983-85; mfg. engring. mgr. Rexnord Aerospace, Torrance, Calif., 1986-87; pres., founder Metz/Calcoa Inc., Torrance, Calif., 1987—. Mfg. rep. consul Orange County Spring, Anaheim, 1987—, TALSCO, 1994—, Precision Resources, 1994—, GEMTECH, 1994—; mfg. rep. consul Alard Machine Products, Gardena, Calif., 1988—, v.p. spl. projects, 1997—. Charter mem. Rep. Presdl. Task Force, 1991—; mem. L.A. Coun. on World Affairs, 1991-92. With U.S. Army, 1966-68. Recipient Appreciation awards DAV, 1968, Soc. Mfg. Engrs., 1991. Fellow Soc. Carbide Engrs.; mem. Soc. Carbide and Tool Engrs. (chpt. pres. 1980-82, Appreciation award 1981), Rep. Presdl. Legion of Merit. Avocations: golf, swimming, riding, boating.

**METZ, T(THEODORE) JOHN,** librarian, educator; b. Erie, Pa., Nov. 5, 1932; s. Theodore John and Dorothy Pearl (Schutte) M.; m. Dorothy Page Neff, June 11, 1955; 1 child, Margaret Elizabeth MusB, Heidelberg Coll., 1954; MA in Music, Miami U., Oxford, Ohio, 1955; MLS, U. Mich., 1959. Libr. II U. Wis., Madison, 1959-61; asst. libr. Lawrence U., Appleton, Wis., 1961-67; dir. librs. U. Wis.-Green Bay, 1967-75; exec. dir. Midwest Region Library Network, Evanston, Ill., 1975-79; coll. libr., assoc. prof. Carleton Coll., Northfield, Minn., 1979-97, coll. libr. emeritus, 1998—. Speaker, participant, coord. numerous confs. and insts., 1969—; chmn. several state libr. groups, 1971-76; mem. several nat. libr. adv. coms., 1974-80; bldg. cons. Carleton Coll., others, 1978—; mem. Citizen Amb. Rsch. Librs. del. to Ea. Europe, 1992. Author: MIDLNET Symposium Report, 1976 Chmn. Green Bay Symphony, 1971-76; mem. various bds. coms., relating to mus. activities; performer Green Bay and other orchs., 1955— Library Service scholar U. Mich., 1957; Library Service fellow U. Mich., 1958 Mem. ALA, Assn. Coll. Rsch. Librs., Internat. Fedn. Libr. Assns. Avocations: music, hunting, fishing, gardening. E-mail: tmetz@carleton.edu.

**METZ, THOMAS FREDERIC,** career military officer; b. Elkin, N.C., Sept. 21, 1948; m. Pamela Redmond; children: Elizabeth, Cade, Patrick. BS, U.S. Mil. Acad., 1971; M in Mech. Engring., N.C. State U., 1980; grad., Command and Gen. Staff Coll., Army War Coll. Registered profl. engr., Va. Enlisted U.S. Army, 1966, commd. 2nd lt. inf., 1971, advanced through grades to lt. gen., 2002, various positions, 1972-76, aide-de-camp for Comdr., Readiness Region VI Ft. Knox, Ky., 1976, comdr. C Co., 4th Bn., 54th Inf., 194th Armor Brigade, 1977-78; asst. prof. mech. engring. dept. U.S. Mil. Acad., West Point, N.Y., 1981-84; S-3/XO 3d Bn., 7th Inf., S-3 197th Separate Inf. Brigade Ft. Benning, Ga.; divsn. chief Inf. Sch. Combat Devel. Directorate, 1984-87; comdr. 4th Bn., 15th Inf., 194th Armor Brigade Ft. Knox, 1987-89; G-3, 2d Inf. Divsn. Republic of Korea, 1990-92; comdr. 2d Brigade, 1st Inf. Divsn., 1992-94; chief of staff Ft. Riley, 1994-95; dir. exptl. force coordination cell, 4th Inf. Divsn. U.S. Army, Fort Hood, 1995-97; asst. divsn. comdr. for support 4th Inf. Divsn., 1997-98; dep. dir. Joint Warfighting Capability Assessment, J8 The Joint Staff, Washington, 1998-2000, vice dir., force structure, resources, & assessment, J-8, 2000—01; comdr., 24th Infantry Divsn. (Mechanized) U.S. Army, Fort Riley, Kans., 2001—03; chief of staff US Centl. Command, Operation Enduring Freedom, 2002—03; comdr., III US Corps U.S. Army, Fort Hood, Tex., 2003—; comdr. Multi-Nat. Corps. Iraq, 2004—05. Decorated Legion of Merit with two oak leaf clusters, Meritorious Svc. medal with three oak leaf clusters, Army Commendation medal with two oak leaf clusters, Good Conduct medal. Office: 6791 Patton Dr Fort Hood TX 76544-1343 E-mail: metztf@js.pentagon.mil.

**METZEN, JAMES P.,** state legislator, bank executive; b. Oct. 1943; m. Sandie Metzen; two children. Student, U. Minn. Banker; mem. Minn. Ho. of Reps., St. Paul, 1975-86, Minn. Senate from 39th dist., St. Paul, 1986—, pres., 2002—. Chmn. govt. op. and vets. com.; mem. jobs, energy and cmty. devel., state govt. fin. divsn. commerce and consumer protection, rules and adminstrn. Minn. State Senate. Home: 412 Deerwood Ct South Saint Paul MN 55075-2102 also: State Senate Rm 322 75 Rev Dr Martin Luther King Jr Blvd Saint Paul MN 55155-1606

**METZER, LAREN WAYNE,** government agency administrator, archivist; b. Bryan, Tex., Mar. 27, 1951; s. Erwin Benjamin Metzer and Mabel Pauline Heid; m. Teena Stern, May 23, 2000; children: Ryan Keith, Sarah Pauline Smith. BA in History, Ctrl. Wash. U., 1973, MA in History, 1974. Archivist Calif. State Archives, 1981—2004, dep. state archivist, 2004—. Coord. Calif. Hist. Records Adv. Bd., Sacramento, 2005—; pres. Soc. of Calif. Archivists, Sacramento, 1998—99; founder We. Archives Inst., 1987. Vol. Peace Corps, Republic of Korea, 1976—77. Recipient Cert. of Recognition, Soc. Calif. Archivists, 1989. Mem.: Coun. of State Archivists, Soc. Calif. Archivists, Soc. Am. Archivists. Avocations: travel, bicycling, aquariums. Office: Calif State Archives 1020 O St Sacramento CA 95814 Office Phone: 916-653-3834.

**METZER, PATRICIA ANN,** lawyer; b. Phila., Mar. 10, 1941; d. Freeman Weeks and Evelyn (Heap) M.; m. Karl Hormann, June 30, 1980. BA with distinction, U. Pa., 1963, LLB cum laude, 1966. Bar: Mass. 1966, D.C. 1972, U.S. Tax Ct. 1988. Assoc., then ptnr. Mintz, Levin, Cohn, Glovsky and Popeo, Boston, 1966—75; assoc. tax legis. counsel U.S. Treasury Dept., Washington, 1975-78; shareholder, dir. Goulston & Storrs, P.C., Boston, 1978-98; stockholder Hutchins, Wheeler & Dittmar, P.C., Boston, 1998—2002; of counsel Vacovec, Mayotte & Singer LLP, Newton, Mass., 2003—. Lectr. program continuing legal edn. Boston Coll. Law Sch., Chestnut Hill, Mass., spring, 1974; lectr. grad. tax program Boston U. Law Sch., 2001—03; adv. com. NYU Inst. Fed. Taxation, NYC, 1981—87; practitioner liaison com. Mass. Dept. Revenue, 1985—90; spkr. in field. Author: Federal Income Taxation of Individuals, 1984; authors' panel Jour. Passthrough Entities, 2003—; mem. editl. bd. Am. Jour. Tax Policy, 1995-98; mem. adv. bd. Corp. Tax and Bus. Planning Rev., 1996—; contbr. articles to profl. jours., chpts. to books. Bd. mgrs. Barrington Ct. Condominium, Cambridge, Mass., 1985-86; bd. dirs. Univ. Rd. Parking Assn., Cambridge, 1988—; trustee Social Law Libr., Boston, 1989-93. Mem. ABA (tax sect., vice-chair publs. 2000-02, mem. coun. 1996-99, chair subcom. allocations and distbns. partnership com. 1978-82, vice-chair legis. 1991-93, chair 1993-95, com. govt. submissions, vice liaison 1993-94, liaison 1994-95, North Atlantic region, co-liaison 1995-96, N.E. region, regional liaison meetings com.), FBA (coun. on taxation, chmn. corp. taxation 1977-81, chair com. partnership taxation 1981-87), Mass. Bar Assn. (coun. tax law sect. 2001-06, chair coun. taxation law sect. 2006—), Boston Bar Assn. (coun. 1987-89, chair tax sect. 1989-91, steering com. solo and small firm sect. 2005—), Am. Coll. Tax Counsel (bd. regents 1999-2004), Boston Estate Planning Coun. (council, pres. 1975, 79-82). Avocation: vocal performances (as soloist and with choral groups). Office: Vacovec Mayotte & Singer LLP Two Newton Pl Ste 340 255 Washington St Newton MA 02458-1634 Office Phone: 617-964-0500. Business E-Mail: pmetzer@vacovec.com.

**METZGAR, DAVID LEE,** biologist; b. Missoula, Mont., Dec. 9, 1968; s. Lee Hollis and Elizabeth Dawley Metzgar; life ptnr. Elizabeth Grace Hunt. PhD, U. of Calif., San Diego, 2001. Rsch. assoc. The Scripps Rsch. Inst., San Diego, 2001—04; lab. dir. Naval Health Rsch. Ctr., San Diego, 2004—; chief sci. officer Evoluqate, LLC, Gainesville, Fla., 2004—. With U.S. Army, 1985—87. Fellowship in exobiology, NASA, 1998 - 2001. Achievements include development of Continuous Culture Devices (Chemostats); Universal Respiratory Pathogen Diagnostics; research in Evolution Of Mutational Dynamics. Avocations: paragliding, scuba diving, rollerblading. Home: Apt 48 4362 Clairemont Mesa Blvd San Diego CA 92117 Office: Naval Health Rsch Ctr PO Box 85122 San Diego CA 92186-5122 Office Phone: 619-553-9106. Business E-Mail: metzgar@nhrc.navy.mil.

**METZGER, BRUCE MANNING,** clergyman, educator; b. Middletown, Pa., Feb. 9, 1914; s. Maurice Rutt and Anna Mary (Manning) M.; m. Isobel E. Mackay, July 7, 1944; children: John Mackay, James Bruce. AB, Lebanon Valley Coll., 1935, DD, 1951; ThB, Princeton Theol. Sem., 1938, ThM, 1939; AM, Princeton U., 1940, PhD, 1942; LHD (hon.), Findlay U., 1962; DD (hon.), St. Andrews U., Scotland, 1964; DTheol (hon.), Münster U., Fed. Republic Germany, 1970; DLitt (hon.), Potchefstroom U., South Africa, 1985. Ordained to ministry Presbyn. Ch. USA, 1939. Teaching fellow N.T. Princeton Theol. Sem., 1938-40, mem. faculty, 1940—, prof. N.T. lang. and lit., 1954-64, George L. Collord prof. N.T. lang. and lit., 1964-84, emeritus, 1984—. Vis. lectr. Presbyn. Theol. Sem. South, Campinas, Brazil, 1952, Presbyn. Theol. Sem. North, Recife, Brazil, 1952; mem. Inst. for Advanced Study, Princeton, 1964-65, 73-74; scholar-in-residence Tyndale House, Cambridge, 1969; vis. fellow Clare Hall, Cambridge, 1974, Wolfson Coll., Oxford U., 1979, Macquarie U., Sydney, Australia, 1982, Caribbean Grad. Sch. of Theology, Jamaica, 1990, Seminario Internacional Teológico Bautista, Buenos Aires, 1991, Griffith Thomas Lectrs., Dallas Theol. Sem., 1992; mem. mng. com. Am. Sch. Classical Studies, Athens, Greece; mem. Standard Bible com. Nat. Coun. Chs., 1952—, chmn., 1975—; mem. seminar N.T. studies Columbia U., 1959-80; mem. Kuratorium of Vetus-Latina Inst., Beuron, Germany, 1959—; adv. com. Inst. N.T. Text Rsch., U. Münster, 1961—; Thesaurus Linguae Graecae, 1972-80; Collected Works of Erasmus, 1977—; chmn. Am. com. versions Internat. Greek N.T., 1950-88; participant internat. congresses scholars, Aarhus, Aberdeen, Bangor, Basel, Bonn, Brussels, Budapest, Cairo, Cambridge, Copenhagen, Dublin, Exeter, Frankfurt, Heidelberg, London, Louvain, Manchester, Milan, Munich, Münster, Newcastle, Nottingham, Oxford, Prague, Rome, St. Andrews, Stockholm, Strasbourg, Toronto, Trondheim, Tübingen; mem. Presbytery, N.B. Author: The Saturday and Sunday Lessons from Luke in the Greek Gospel Lectionary, 1944, Lexical Aids for Students of New Testament Greek, 1946, enlarged edit., 1955, A Guide to the Preparation of a Thesis, 1950, An Introduction to the Apocrypha, 1957, Chapters in the History of New Testament Textual Criticism, 1963, The Text of the New Testament, Its Transmission, Corruption, and Restoration, 1964, (with B.D. Ehrman) 4th enlarged edit., 2005, (with H.G. May) The Oxford Annotated Bible with the Apocrypha, 1965, The New Testament, Its Background, Growth, and Content, 1965, 3d edit., 2003, Index to Periodical Literature on Christ and the Gospels, 1966, Historical and Literary Studies, Pagan, Jewish, and Christian, 1968, Index to Periodical Literature on the Apostle Paul, 1960, 2nd edit., 1970, A Textual Commentary on the Greek New Testament, 1971, 2d edit., 1994, The Early Versions of the New Testament, 1977, New Testament Studies, 1980, Manuscripts of the Greek Bible, 1981, The Canon of the New Testament, 1987, (with Roland Murphy) The New Oxford Annotated Bible with the Apocrypha, 1991, (with M.D. Coogan) The Oxford Companion to the Bible, 1993, Breaking the Code-Understanding the Book of Revelation, 1993, Reminiscences of an Octogenarian, 1997, (with Coogan) The Oxford Guide to People & Places of the Bible, 2001, (with Coogan) The Oxford Guide to Ideas and Issues of the Bible, 2001, The Bible in Translation, Ancient and English Versions, 2001; mem. editl. com. Critical Greek New Testament, 1956-84; chmn. Am. com., Internat. Greek New Testament Project, 1978-88; sec. com. translators: Apocrypha (rev. standard version); editor: New Testament Tools and Studies, 34 vols., 1960-2004, Oxford Annotated Apocrypha, 1965, enlarged edit., 1977; Reader's Digest Condensed Bible, 1982; co-editor: United Bible Societies Greek New Testament, 1966, 4th edit., 1993; compiler: Index of Articles on the New Testament and the Early Church Published in Festschriften, 1951, supplement, 1955, Lists of Words Occurring Frequently in the Coptic New Testament (Sahidic Dialect), 1961, Annotated Bibliography of the Textual Criticism of the New Testament, 1955, (with Isobel M. Metzger) Oxford Concise Concordance to the Holy Bible, 1962, (with R.C. Dentan and W. Harrelson), The Making of the New Revised Standard Version of the Bible, 1991; contbr. articles to jours. Chmn. standard bible com. Nat. Coun. Chs., 1977-2000. Recipient cert. Disting. Svc. Nat. Coun. Chs., 1957, Disting. Alumnus award Lebanon Valley Coll. Alumni Assn., 1961, citation of appreciation Laymen's Nat. Bible Assoc., 1986, Disting. Alumnus award Princeton Theol. Sem., 1989, lit. competition prize Christian Rsch. Found., 1955, 62, 63, E.T. Thompson award, 1991. Mem. Am. Philos. Soc., Soc. Bibl. Lit. (pres. 1970-71, past del. Am. Coun. Learned Socs.), Am. Bible Soc. (bd. mgrs. 1948—, chmn. com. transls. 1964-70), Am. Philol. Assn., Studiorum Novi Testamenti Societas (pres. 1971-72), Cath. Bibl. Assn., N.Am. Patristic Soc. (pres. 1972), Soc. Textual Scholarship (pres. 1995), Am. Soc. Papyrologists; hon. fellow, corr. mem. Higher Inst. Coptic Studies, Cairo; corr. fellow Brit. Acad. (Burkitt medal in Bibl. studies 1994). Republican. Home: 20 Cleveland Ln Princeton NJ 08540-3050 Office: Princeton Theol Sem 64 Mercer St Princeton NJ 08542-0803 Office Phone: 609-921-8300. Business E-Mail: denise.schwalb@ptsem.edu.

**METZGER, ERNEST HUGH,** aerospace engineer, research scientist; b. Nurnberg, Germany, Oct. 22, 1923; came to U.S., 1939, naturalized, 1943; s. Paul Arthur and Charlotte Babette (Kann) M.; m. Sarah Temple Grinnell, Nov. 19, 1956; children: Lisa Metzger Dunning, Charlotte Bennett (dec.), George Grinnell. BS, CCNY, 1949; MS, Harvard U., 1950. Automatic control engr. Bell Aerospace Co. div. Textron, Buffalo, 1950-54, tech. dir. inertial nav. systems, 1954-60, chief engr., inertial instruments, 1960-70, chief engr. gravity gradiometer systems, 1970-83, dir. gravity sensor systems, 1983-86, exec. dir. engring., 1986-89, cons., 1989-95, Bell Geospace Inc., Buffalo, 1995—. Mem. panel future navigation systems Nat. Acad. Sci., com. on geodesy NRC, 1988-89, accelerator criteria com. NASA, tech. com. navigation guidance and control, AIAA, 1989—; vis. lectr. dept. aernautics and astronautics Stanford U., 1990 Contbr. articles to profl. jours.; patentee in field Served with AUS, 1943-46 Recipient Aerospace Pioneer award Niagara Frontier sect AIAA 1977; named to Niagara Frontier Aviation Hall of Fame, 1992. Mem. IEEE, Inst. Navigation (Thurlow award for outstanding contbn. to sci. navigation 1983), AAAS, Air Force Assn., N.Y. Acad. Scis., Explorers Club, Sigma Xi, Tau Beta Pi, Eta Kappa Nu Clubs: Harvard, Buffalo Ski. Home: 663 Downing Ln Williamsville NY 14221 E-mail: semetz@adelphia.net.

**METZGER, EVELYN BORCHARD,** artist; b. N.Y.C., June 8, 1911; d. Samuel and Eva (Rose) Borchard; m. H. A. Metzger, June 28, 1934 (dec. 1974); children: James Borchard, Edward Arthur, Eva Metzger Lanier. AB, Vassar Coll., 1932. One-woman shows include Galeria Muller, Buenos Aires, 1950, S.A.G. Gallery, N.Y.C., 1962, Gallerie Bellechasse, Paris, 1963, Vassar Coll. Art Gallery, Poughkeepsie, N.Y., 1963, Everhart Mus., Scranton, Pa., 1963, Frank Partridge Gallery, N.Y.C., 1964, Norfolk (Va.) Mus. Art, 1965, Van Diemen-Lilienfeld Gallery, N.Y., 1966, Columbus Mus., Ga., 1966, Ga. Mus. Fine Arts, Athens, Ga., 1966, Mex.-Am. Cultural Inst., Mexico City, 1967, Telfair Acad. Arts, Savannah, Ga., 1966, U. Maine, Orono, 1967, Slater Meml. Mus., Norwich, Conn., 1967, Albion (Mich.) Coll., 1969, Graham-Eches Sch., Palm Beach, Fla., 1970, Bartholet Gallery, N.Y.C., 1973, Arsenal Gallery, N.Y.C., 1983, Quogue Libr., N.Y., 1988, Mus. Women in the Arts, Washington 1997, 2002, Joan Whalen Gallery, N.Y.C., 1997, Cornell U., 1998, Washington County Mus. Fine Art, Hagerstown, Md., 1999, Curzen Gallery, Boca Raton, Fla., 2001, AnnNorton Sculpture Garden, Fla., 2001, Am. Norton Sculpture Gardens, West Palm Beach, Fla., 2001, Nat. Mus. Women in Arts, Washington, 2002; represented in permanent collections including Art in Embassies program, U.S. Dept. State. Mem. Artists Equity, Cosmopolitan Club. Avocation: travel. Home: 815 Park Ave New York NY 10021-3276

**METZGER, HENRY,** federal research institution administrator; b. Mainz, Germany, Mar. 23, 1932; came to U.S. 1938; naturalized, 1945; s. Paul Alfred and Anne (Daniel) M.; m. Deborah Stashower, June 16, 1957; children: Eran D., Renée V., Carl E. MD, Columbia U., 1957. Chief chem. immunology sect. Nat. Inst. Arthritis & Musculoskeletal & Skin Disease/NIH, Bethesda, Md., 1973—2002; br. chief USPHS, Bethesda, 1983-94, sci. dir. 1987-98, med. officer grade VI, 1975-98; scientist Sr. Biomed. Rsch. Svc., 1999—2002, scientist emeritus, 2002—. Carl Prausnitz Meml. lectr., 1982; Ecker Meml. lectr. Case Western Res. U., Cleve., 1984; Harvey Soc. lectr., 1984; Eli Nadel Meml. lectr. St. Louis U., 1987; Rodney Porter Meml. lectr., 1993; Burroughs-Wellcome lectr., 1994; R.E. Dyer lectr., 1995; mem. health rsch. coun. BMFT, German Govt., 1994-97. Editor: Fc Receptors & the Action of Antibodies, 1990; assoc. editor Ann. Rev. Immunology, 1982-96; contbr. numerous articles to profl. jours.; mem. editl. bd. numerous sci. jours. Recipient Meritorious Svc. award USPHS, 1978, Disting. Svc. award, 1985, 97, Joseph Mather Smith prize Columbia U., 1984. Fellow AAAS, Am. Acad. Allergy and Immunology; mem. NAS, Am. Assn. Immunologists (pres. 1991-92), Am. Soc. Biol. Chem. Molecular Biology, Am. Soc. Cell Biology, Internat. Union Immunol. Soc. (pres. 1992-95), Found. for Advanced Edn. in the Scis. (pres. 1990-92, 2005-), Alpha Omega Alpha. Home: 3410 Taylor St Chevy Chase MD 20815-4024 Office: NIH Rm 9n228 10 Center Dr 9000 Rockville Pike Bethesda MD 20892-1820 E-Mail: metzgerh@exchange.nih.gov.

**METZGER, JAMES W.,** career military officer; s. Mr. and Mrs. George Metzger; m. Mary Jane Bachmann; children: Jennifer, Amy. Grad. with distinction, U.S. Naval Acad., 1971; MEE, Mich. State U.; student, Nuc. Power Sch., Bainbridge, Md. Commd. ensign USN, advanced through grades to vice adm., 2000; elec. officer, main propulsion asst. USS George Bancroft; engring. officer USS Indpls., 1977-81; nuc. propulsion examining bd. U.S. Pacific Fleet; exec. officer USS Tautog, Pearl Harbor, Hawaii, 1983-86; comdr. USS Mpls.-St. Paul, 1987-90; dir. Submarine Prospective Comdg. Ofiicer Sch., 1991; exec. asst. to comdr. in chief U.S. Atlantic Fleet, Norfolk, Va., 1991-93; comdr. Submarine Devel. Squadron 12, 1993; exec. asst. Vice Chief of Naval Ops. asst., naval aide Sec. of Navy; dep. dir. for strategy and policy USN, Washington, 1997-98, commr. of submarine group 8, 1998—2000, comdr. Seventh Fleet Yokosuka, Japan, 2000—02; asst. to Chmn. of the Joint Chiefs of Staff US Dept. Def., Washington, 2002—04. Decorated Legion of Merit with five gold stars.

**METZGER, JEFFREY PAUL,** lawyer; b. Oct. 13, 1950; s. John E. and Ellen J. M.; m. Stephanie Ann Stahr, Dec. 27, 1977. BA magna cum laude, Amherst Coll., 1973; JD, Georgetown U., 1976. Bar: D.C. 1977. Legis. asst. U.S. Senator Joseph Biden, Jr., Del., 1973; assoc. Collier, Shannon, Rill and Scott, Washington, 1976-79, Cole and Groner PC, Washington, 1979-82; trial atty. commil. litigation br. civil divsn. U.S. Dept. Justice, Washington, 1982-85; mem. prof. staff Pres.'s Blue Ribbon Commn. on Def. Mgmt., Washington, 1985-86; asst. gen. counsel Unisys Corp., 1986—88, v.p., assoc. gen. counsel, 1989—. Mem. ABA. Office Phone: 703-439-5609. Personal E-mail: Jeffrey.Metzger@unisys.com.

**METZGER, PAUL LOUIS,** theologian, director; b. Elgin, Ill., Mar. 9, 1964; s. William Frank and Audrey Louise Metzger; m. Mariko Tomoda, Aug. 11, 1990; children: Christopher Takasumi William, Julianne Misaki. BA, Northwestern Coll., Roseville, Minn., 1987; MDiv. and MA, Trinity Evang. Div. Sch., Deerfield, Ill., 1992; PhD, King's Coll. London, U. London, 1999. Prof. Christian theology and theology of culture Multnomah Bibl. Sem., Portland, Oreg., 1999—. Founder and dir. of the Inst. for the theology of culture: new wine, new wineskins Multnomah Bibl. Sem., Portland, 2000—. Editor: (journal) Cultural Encounters: A Jou. for the Theology of Culture; author: (book) The Word of Christ and the World of Culture, 2003; editor: Trinitarian Soundings in Systematic Theology, 2005; contbr. articles to profl. jours. and newspapers. Mem.: Ctr. Theol. Inquiry. Protestant Christian. Office Phone: 503-251-6741.

**METZGER, ROBERT STREICHER,** lawyer; b. St. Louis, Sept. 27, 1950; s. Robert Stanley and Jean Harriet (Streicher) M.; m. Stephanie Joy Morgan, Nov. 16, 1980; children: Michael, Kristen, Marisa. BA, Middlebury Coll., 1974; JD, Georgetown U., 1977. Bar: Calif. 1978, D.C. 1978. Legis. aide U.S. Rep. Robert F. Drinan, Washington, 1972-73; legis. asst. U.S. Rep. Michael J. Harrington, Washington, 1973-75; rsch. fellow Ctr. for Sci. and Internat. Affairs Harvard U., Cambridge, Mass., 1977-78; assoc. Latham & Watkins, LA, 1978-84, ptnr., 1984-90, Kirkland & Ellis, LA, 1990-93, Troop, Meisinger, Steuber & Pasich and predecessor, LA, 1993-97, Gibson, Dunn & Crutcher LLP, LA, 1997—. Chmn. Aerospace and Govt. Practice Group, 1997—, Telecom. Practice Group, 2000-; cons. Congl. Rsch. Svc., Washington, 1977-78. Contbr. articles to profl. jours. Trustee Sierra Canyon HS Found.; mem. dean's adv. coun. Kennedy Sch. Govt. Harvard U., 2005—. Mem. ABA (litig. pub. contracts sect.), Fed. Comm. Bar Assn., Internat. Inst. for Strategic Studies, Pacific Coun. on Internat. Policy, Dean's Advisory Coun. Kennedy Sch. Govt. Harvard U., Jonathan Club. Office: Gibson Dunn & Crutcher LLP 333 S Grand Ave Los Angeles CA 90071-3197 Office Phone: 213-229-7000. Business E-Mail: rmetzger@gibsondunn.com.

**METZGER, SIDNEY,** retired communications engineer; b. N.Y., Feb. 1, 1917; m. Miriam Lipstein; children: David, Sally, Philip. BSEE, N.Y. Univ., 1937; MEE, Polytech. Inst. Bklyn., 1950. Engr. U.S. Signal Corps. Lab., NJ, 1939—45; head radio relay divsn. Fed. Telecommunications Labs. Internat. Tel. & Tel. Corp., 1945—54; mgr. communications engring. Astro Elect. Prod. Divsn. RCA, 1954—63; engr. engring. divsn. Communications Satellite Corp., 1963-67, asst. v.p. and chief engr., 1968-72, asst. v.p. and chief scientist, 1972-80, v.p. and chief scientist, 1980-82; cons. engr., 1982—93; ret., 1993. Recipient Aerospace award Aerospace & Elec. Systems Soc., 1975, Internat. Communication award IEEE, 1976, Koji Kobayashi Computers & Communication award, 1985, Aerospace Communication award Am. Inst. Aeronaut. & Astronaut., 1984. Fellow IEEE, AIAA; mem. Nat. Acad. Engring, Sigma Xi. Address: 700 John Ringling Blvd Apt N-206 Sarasota FL 34236-1500 Personal E-mail: mimsid7@comcast.net.

**METZGER, VERNON ARTHUR,** management educator, consultant; b. Baldwin Park, Calif., Aug. 13, 1918; s. Vernon and Nellie C. (Ross) Metzger; m. Beth Alrene Metzger, Feb. 19, 1955; children: Susan, Linda, David. BS, U. Calif., Berkeley, 1947, MBA, 1948. Estimating engr. C.F. Braun & Co., 1949; prof. mgmt. Calif. State U., Long Beach, 1949-89, prof. emeritus, 1989—, founder Sch. of Bus. Mgmt. cons. Mem. Fire Commn., Fountain Valley, Calif., 1959—60; mem. mgmt. task force to promote modern mgmt. in Yugoslavia, U.S. State Dept., 1977; mem. State of Calif. Fair Polit. Practices Commn., Orange County Transit Com.; pres. Orange County Dem. League, 1967—68. With USNR, 1942—45. Recipient Outstanding Citizen award, Orange County. Fellow: Soc. Advancement Mgmt. (life; dir.); mem.: Orange County Indsl. Rels. Rsch. Assn. (v.p.), Acad. Mgmt., Tau Kappa Upsilon, Alpha Kappa Psi, Beta gamma Sigma. Home: 1938 Balearic Dr Costa Mesa CA 92626-3513 Office Phone: 714-557-6415.

**METZGER, WYATT K.,** physicist; s. Phillip and Patricia (O' Rorke) Metzger; m. Mercedes Metzger; children: Andre, Sean. BA in Physics, Bowdoin Coll., Brunswick, Maine, 1992; MS in Physics, U. Colo., Boulder, Colo., 1997, PhD in Physics, 2001. Rsch. scientist Battery Automated Tech., 1993—95, Boundless Corp., 1996—97, U. Colo., Boulder, 1997—2001, Nat. Renewable Energy Lab., Golden, 2001—. Author: more than 40 rsch. articles in field. Recipient Dir.'s award, Nat. Renewable Energy Lab., 2003. Mem.: IEEE, Materials Rsch. Soc. Achievements include pioneering contributions in the fields of alternative energy, photovoltaics, and semiconductors. Office: Nat Renewable Energy Lab 1617 Cole Blvd Golden CO 80401 Office Phone: 303-384-6572.

**METZLER, JAMES ROBERT,** musician; b. Worcester, Mass., June 20, 1947; adopted s. Robert Adolph Metzler and Olga Slonin; m. Diane Pearl Fought, Aug. 27, 1988; children: Yurii Wynn Fought, Jeffrey David. MusB, Westminster Choir Coll., 1965—69; MusM, Hartt Coll. of Music, U. of Hartford, 1971—72; Fellowship Diploma, Cambridge Soc. of Musicians; Fellowship Diploma (hon.), Nat. Coll. of Music & Arts; Choir Tng. Diploma, Am. Guild of Organists, 1977. Organist and choirmaster St. James' Episcopal Ch., New London, Conn., 1969—71, First Presbyn. Ch., Hartford, Conn., 1971—72, Trinity Episcopal Ch., Toledo, 1972—96; adj. prof. of organ U. of Toledo, 1984—89; organist and dir. of music Trinity Episcopal Cathedral,

Little Rock, 1996—. Recipient S. Lewis Elmer (First Prize on Guild Exams), Am. Guild of Organists, 1977. Mem.: Royal Sch. of Ch. Music, Am. Guild of English Handbell Ringers, Am. Choral Director's Assn., Am. Guild of Organists. Achievements include organ recital at Notre-Dame Cathedral (Paris), Westminster Abbey (London), St. Paul's Cathedral (London), Norwich Cathedral (England), and Washington National Cathedral (US); director of the Canterbury Singers USA for more than 80 choral services at major British cathedrals and Westminster Abbey. Home: 12411 Cherry Laurel Drive Little Rock AR 72211 Office: Trinity Episcopal Cathedral 310 West 17th St Little Rock AR 72206 Office Phone: 501-372-0294 x 2012. Personal E-mail: jrmetzler@worldnet.att.net.

**METZLER, RUTH HORTON**, genealogical educator; b. Eden, New York, Aug. 4, 1927; d. John Morris and Bernice Louise (Horton); m. Henry George Metzler, Sept. 4, 1948; children: Kathleen, Ronald, Janice, Margaret. Attended, Wheaton Coll., 1945-48; BA (hon.), Wilmington Coll., 1956; MLS, State Univ. of N.Y., Geneseo, 1962. Cert. tchr., libr. media specialist, N.Y. Cataloging typist Peoria Pub. Libr., Ill., 1949-52; cataloging asst. Wilmington Coll. Libr., Ohio, 1953-56; sch. libr. K-12 Nunda Ctrl. Sch., NY, 1956-65; head libr. media ctr. Irondequoit H.S., Rochester, NY, 1965-84; pres. Rochester Geneal. Soc., NY, 1989-93; instr., lectr. Rochester Mus. and Sci. Ctr., NY, 1990—. Author of several family histories. Organizing instr. Genealogy workshops, Rochester Mus. and Sci. Ctr; contbg. lectr. Nat. Geneal. Conf., Rochester, 1990; others. Mem. N.Y. Libr. Assn.;.N.Y. State Tchr. Retirement Sys.; New Eng. Hist. and Geneal. Soc.; Kodak Geneal. Soc., N.Y.; State Coun. of Geneal.; Genealogy Round Table of Monroe County (del. 1996—); Rochester Geneal. Soc.; Geneal. Educators (organizing mem. 1996). Republican. Baptist. Avocations: genealogy, writing.

**METZNER, CHARLES MILLER**, federal judge; b. NYC, Mar. 13, 1912; s. Emanuel and Gertrude (Miller) M.; m. Jeanne Gottlieb, Oct. 6, 1966. AB, Columbia U., 1931, LL.B., 1933. Pvt. practice, 1934; mem. Jud. Council State N.Y., 1935-41; law clk. to N.Y. supreme ct. justice, 1942-52; exec. asst. to U.S. atty. Gen. Herbert Brownell, Jr., 1953-54; mem. firm Chapman, Walsh & O'Connell, 1954-59; judge U.S. Dist Ct. (so. dist.) N.Y., 1959—77; sr. judge, 1977—. Mem. Law Revision Commn. N.Y. State, 1959; chmn. com. administrn. magistrates system U.S. Jud. Conf., 1970-81; chmn. Columbia Coll. Coun., 1965-66. Pres. N.Y. Young Republican Club, 1941; Trustee Columbia U., 1972-84, trustee emeritus, 1984—; bd. dirs. N.Y.C. Ctr. Music and Drama, 1969-74. Recipient Lawyer Div. of Joint Def. Appeal award, 1961, Columbia U. Alumni medal, 1966, Founders award Nat. Coun. U.S. Magistrates, 1989. Mem. ABA, Am. Law Inst., Fed. Bar Coun. (cert. Disting. Jud. Svc. 1989).

**METZNER, RICHARD JOEL**, psychiatrist, psychopharmacologist, educator; b. LA, Feb. 15, 1942; s. Robert Gerson and Esther Rebecca (Groper) M.; children: Jeffrey Anthony, David Jonathan; m. Leila Kirkley, June 26, 1993. BA, Stanford U., 1963; MD, Johns Hopkins U., 1967. Diplomate Am. Bd. Psychiatry and Neurology. Intern Roosevelt Hosp., N.Y.C., 1967-68; resident in psychiatry Stanford U. Med. Ctr., 1968-71; staff psychiatrist divsn. manpower and tng. NIMH-St. Elizabeths Hosp., Washington, 1971-73; chief audiovisual edn. sys. VA Med. Ctr. Brentwood, L.A., 1973-79; from asst. prof. psychiatry to assoc. clin. prof. UCLA Neuropsychiat. Inst., 1980-96, clin. prof., 1996—. Lectr. Sch. Social Welfare, 1975-84; pvt. practice medicine specializing in psychiatry, Bethesda, Md., 1972-73, L.A., 1973—, Sedona, Ariz., 1997—; dir. Western Inst. Psychiatry, L.A., 1977—; pres. Psychiat. Resource Network, Inc., 1984-90. Contbr. articles to profl. jours.; prodr., writer numerous films and videotapes. With USPHS, 1968-71. Recipient 6 awards for film and videotape prodns., 1976-80. Fellow: Am. Psychiat. Assn. (life Disting.); mem.: UCLA Psychiat. Clin. Faculty Assn. (pres. 2001—02), Mental Health Careerists Assn. (chmn. 1972—73), So. Calif. Psychiat. Soc., Phi Beta Kappa. Democrat. Jewish. Office: 25 Cindercone Cir Sedona AZ 86336 Office Phone: 928-204-5850. E-mail: rmetzner@ucla.edu, rmetzner@earthlink.net.

**MEUNIER, MONIQUE**, dancer; b. L.A. Studied with Irena Komoskova, studied with Yvonne Mounsey; student, Sch. Am. Ballet, 1988. Mem. corps de ballet N.Y.C. Ballet, 1990—97, soloist, 1997—98, prin., 1998—2002; soloist Am Ballet Theatre, NYC, 2002—. Dancer (ballets) Agon, Apollo, Harlequinade, The Nutcracker, Swan Lake, Tschaikovsky Piano Concerto No. 2, Vienna Waltzes, The Sleeping Beauty, Ash, Delight of the Muses, A Schubert Sonata, Slavonic Dances. Office: Am Ballet Theatre 890 Broadway New York NY 10003

**MEUNIER, VINCENT**, physicist; BS in Physics, Namur U., Belgium, 1996, MS in Physics, 1998, PhD in Physics, 1999. R&d staff mem. Oak Ridge Nat. Lab., Oak Ridge, Tenn., 2004—; rsch. assoc. Oak Ridge Associated U., Oak Ridge, Tenn., 2002—04, NC State U., Raleigh, NC, 2000—02. Rschr. Oak Ridge Nat. Lab., Oak Ridge, Tenn., 2002—. Contbr. articles to sci. jours. Grantee Rsch. Assoc., Nat. Funds for Sci. Rsch. of Belgium, 2000-2004; scholar Rsch. Asst., Funds for Sci. Rsch. of Belgium, 1996-1999. Mem.: Materials Rsch. Soc., Am. Phys. Soc. E-mail: vm2@ornl.gov.

**MEUSER, FREDRICK WILLIAM**, retired church administrator, historian; b. Payne, Ohio, Sept. 14, 1923; s. Henry William and Alvina Maria (Bouyack) Meuser; m. Jeanne Bond Griffiths, July 29, 1951; children: Jill Martha, Douglas Griffiths. AB, Capital U., 1945, BD, 1948, DD (hon.), 1989; STM, Yale U., 1949, MA, 1953, PhD, 1956; DD (hon.), Tex. Luth. Coll., 1980, Capital U., 1989; LHD (hon.), Augustana Coll., 1985. Ordained to ministry Am. Lutheran Ch., 1948; asst. pastor 1st Luth. Ch., Galveston, Tex., 1948, Christ Luth. Ch., North Miami, Fla., 1949—51; campus minister Yale U. 1951—53; prof. ch. history Luth. Theol. Sem., Columbus, Ohio, 1953—78, dean grad. studies, 1963—69, pres., 1971—78; exec. sec. div. theol. studies Luth. Council in U.S.A., 1969—71; pres. Trinity Luth. Sem., Columbus, 1978—88; del. World Council Chs., 1968, Luth. World Fedn., 1970; v.p. Am. Luth. Ch., 1974—80; mem. Commn. for a New Luth. Ch., 1982—86; asst. pastor St. Paul Luth. Ch., Westerville, Ohio, 1995—97. Author: The Formation of the American Lutheran Church, 1958, Luther the Preacher, 1983; author: (with others) Church in Fellowship, 1963, Lutherans in North America, 1975; translator: (with others) What Did Luther Understand by Religion, 1977, The Reconstruction of Morality, 1979; editor and author: (with others) Interpreting Luther's Legacy, 1967. Recipient Disting. Churchman's award Tex. Luth. Coll., 1972, Joseph Sittler award Trinity Luth. Sem., 1990; named Distinguished Alumnus Capital U., 1977; Am. Assn. Theol. Schs. fellow, 1961-62 Home: 2055 S Floral Ave Lot 240 Bartow FL 33830-7157 E-mail: fredmeuser@aol.com.

**MEVERS, FRANK CLEMENT**, state agency administrator, archivist; b. New Orleans, Oct. 10, 1942; s. Lloyd F. and Mary Ashley (Collins) M.; m. Kathryn Ann Hayes, Dec. 23, 1967; children: John F., Lauren K. BA in History, La. State U., 1965; PhD in Am. History, U. NC, 1972; MA, La. State U., 1967. Editor Papers of James Madison, Charlottesville, Va., 1972-74, Papers of Josiah Bartlett, Concord, NH, 1974-77, Papers of William Plumer, Concord, 1977-79; state archivist State of NH, Concord, 1979—. Editor, author: New Hampshire: State That Made US a Nation, 1989. Mem. Pub. Libr. Bd. Trustees, Concord, 1979-99. With US Army, 1967-69, Korea. Episcopalian. Avocation: stamp collecting/philately. Home: 29 Bradley St Concord NH 03301-6432 Office: NH State Archives 71 S Fruit St Concord NH 03301-2410 Office Phone: 603-271-2236. Personal E-mail: eatright@comcast.net. Business E-mail: fmevers@sos.state.nh.us.

**MEW, CALVIN MARSHALL**, advertising executive; b. Oakland, Calif., Oct. 27, 1947; s. Thomas Bing and May (Jan) m. Mary Farnham Crawford, Oct. 20, 2001. BA, Yale U., 1969; MDiv, Union Theol Sem., 1973; postgrad., Columbia U., 1973-79, Harvard U., 1984. Tutor Union Theol. Sem., 1973-77; adj. lectr. Hunter Coll., 1977-79; market analyst Kenyon & Eckhart Advt. Inc., N.Y.C., 1979-82, v.p. market plans, 1982-83, rev. v.p. strategic plan, 1983-85, v.p. strategic mktg. svcs., 1985-88, sr.v.p. strategic and forward planning, 1988-90; sr. v.p., mng. dir. Bozell, Inc., 1990-93, exec. v.p., mng.

dir., 1993—. Gen. mgr. Bozell Austria, 1994; exec. v.p., regional dir. L.Am. Bozell Worldwide, Inc., 1996; dir. Capritauro Investments, Ltd., 2002. Contbr. articles to profl. jours. Bd. dirs. Union Theol. Sem., 1984—, vice chmn., 1992—. Recipient Cogswell award Yale U., 1969; Columbia U. fellow, Rockefeller Bros. Fund fellow. Mem. Am. Acad. Religion, Soc. Bibl. Lit., Harvard Bus. Sch. Club (mem. adv. bd. N.Y. chpt. 2004). Presbyterian. Home: 895 W End Ave New York NY 10025-3500 Office: Bozell Jacobs Kenyon Eckhart 13801 Fnb Pkwy Omaha NE 68154-5230 Business E-Mail: calvinmew@post.harvard.edu.

**MEW, THOMAS JOSEPH, III, (TOMMY MEW)**, artist, educator; b. Miami, Fla., Aug. 15, 1942; s. Thomas Joseph and Maude Edith (Perry) M.; m. Mary Ann Kelley, June 17, 1966; 1 son, Thomas Joseph IV. BS, Fla. State U., 1962, MA, 1964; PhD, NYU, 1966. Grad. instr. Fla. State U., 1963; asst. prof. art Troy State U., 1966-68, Jacksonville U., 1968-70; prof., chmn. dept. art Berry Coll., 1970—. Dana prof. art. Juror art shows: vis. artist; lectr. in field, cons. art; dir. Fluxus West/Southeast; dir. Moon Gallery. Exhibited in one-man shows Parkway Gallery, Miami, 1962-63, 319 Gallery, N.Y.C., 1968, Meridian (Miss.) Mus., 1976, C.D.O. Gallery, Parma, Italy, 1978, Calif. State U., Sacramento, 1979, Miss. Mus. Art, Jackson, 1979, Art Inst. for Permian Basin, ITex, Arte Studio, Bergamo, Italy, Queen Street Gallery, Belfast, No. Ireland; group shows include High Mus., Atlanta, 1971, 72, 74, New Reform Gallery, Aalst, Belgium, 1975, U. Guelph, Ont., Can., 1975, Neuberger Mus., Purchase, N.Y., 1978, Arte Fiera, Bologna, Italy, 1979; represented in permanent collections, Kansas City Art Inst., Mildura Art Centre, Australia, Wichita Art Mus., Jacksonville (Fla.) Art Mus., Macon Mus. Art, AT&T, Harn Mus., U. Iowa; host; Cable TV show Art: The Mew View, 1978—; Filmmaker, 1966-69; contbr. articles to profl. jours. Bd. dirs. Rome Arts Coun., 1984—, Interface. Recipient Gellhorn award N.Y. U., 1966; Cowperthwaite grantee, 1972; Lilly Found. grantee, 1975; Gulf Life grantee, 1977. Mem. Southeastern Coll. Art Conf., Coll. Art Assn. Am., Am. Fedn. Arts, Nat. Art Edn. Assn., Am. Assn. Art Dealers, Omicron Delta Kappa, Phi Kappa Phi. Home: 28 Virginia Cir Rome GA 30161 Office: Berry Coll Art Dept PO Box 580 Mount Berry GA 30149 Office Phone: 706-236-2219. Business E-Mail: tmew@berry.edu. *I've always moved in the direction of my dreams...always tried to make the great dream a reality.*

**MEWANI, RAJSHREE R.(AMCHAND)**, researcher; b. Bombay, Apr. 3, 1969; d. Narandas and Neena Kotwani; life ptnr. Ramchand Mewani, Dec. 13, 1999. BS, U. Bombay, 1989, diploma in med. lab. tech., 1990, MA, 1994, PhD, 1999. Jr. rsch. fellow Seth G.S. Med. Coll. and K.E.M. Hosp., Bombay, 1990-94, sr. rsch. fellow, 1994-99; parasitologist Inst. of Medicine, Kathmandu, Nepal, 1999-2000; rsch. fellow Georgetown U. Med. Ctr., Washington, 2000—. Contbr. articles to profl. jours. Achievements include patents in field. Office Phone: 202-687-2221. Personal E-mail: dr_rajshreek@yahoo.com. Business E-Mail: rrm6@georgetown.edu.

**MEYBURG, ARNIM HANS**, transportation engineer, educator, consultant; b. Bremerhaven, W. Ger., Aug. 25, 1939; came to U.S., 1965; s. Friedel and Auguste (Kleeberg) M.; m. Ruth Meyburg; 1 child, Jennifer Susan. Student, U. Hamburg, 1960-62, Free U. Berlin, 1962-65; MS (Fulbright travel grantee), Northwestern U., 1968, PhD, 1971. Research assoc. Transp. Center, Northwestern U., 1968-69; asst. prof. transp. engring. Cornell U., 1969-75, assoc. prof., 1975-78, prof., 1978—, acting chmn. dept., 1977-78, chmn. dept., 1980-85, dir. Sch. Civil and Environ. Engring., 1988-98, chmn. bd. Univ. Transp. Rsch. Ctr., 1992-95; dir. Transp. Infrastructure Rsch. Consortium, 1995—. Vis. mem. faculties U. Calif., Irvine, Tech. U. Munich, Germany, (Fulbright lectr.) U. Sao Paulo, Brazil, 1984, Tech. U. Brunswick, W. Ger., 1985-86; Humboldt Found. research fellow, 1978-79; prin. investigator projects Dept. Transp., NSF, Nat. Coop. Hwy. Research Program, N.Y. State Dept. Transp., U.S. Dept. Transp. Author: (with others) Urban Transportation Modeling and Planning, 1975, Transportation Systems Evaluation, 1976, Survey Sampling and Multivariate Analysis for Social Scientists and Engineers, 1979, Survey Methods for Transport Planning, 1995; co-editor: (with others) Behavioral Travel-Demand Models, 1976, New Horizons in Travel-Behavior Research, 1981, Selected Readings in Transport Survey Methodology, 1992; contbr. articles to profl. jours., chpts. to books. NSF Research Initiation grantee, 1973; recipient Humboldt U.S. Sr. Scientist award, 1984, Fulbright sr. lectr. award, 1984. Mem. ASCE, AAUP, Transp. Rsch. Bd., Transp. Rsch. Forum, Sigma Xi, Chi Epsilon. Office: Cornell U 220 Hollister Hall Ithaca NY 14853-3501 Office Phone: 607-255-7519. E-mail: ahm2@cornell.edu.

**MEYER, ALBERT JAMES**, educational researcher; b. Cleve., Sept. 24, 1929; s. Jacob Conrad and Esther Agnes (Steiner) M.; m. Mary Ellen Yoder, Aug. 21, 1954; children: Richard, Anne, Kathryn, Barbara, Elaine. BA, Goshen Coll., 1950; MA, Princeton U., 1952, PhD, 1954. Asst. in teaching and rsch. Princeton (N.J.) U., 1950-53; fellow U. Basel, Switzerland, 1953-54, rsch. assoc., 1956-57; dir. for France, rep. European peace sect. Mennonite Ctrl. Com., 1954-57; asst. prof. physics Goshen (Ind.) Coll., 1958-61, prof., rsch. prof., 1967-89, adj. rsch. prof., 1989—; acad. dean, prof. Bethel Coll., North Newton, Kans., 1961-66, Menno Simons lectr., 1993; exec. sec., pres. Mennonite Bd. Edn., Elkhart, Ind., 1967-95; vis. fellow Princeton (N.J.) U., 1995-96. Exec. for secretariat Puidoux Theol. Confs., 1955-57; former mem. staff Mennonite Student Svcs. Com.; former coord. com. on liberal arts edn. North Ctrl. Mutual Assn. Colls. and Secondary Schs.; vis. rsch. scientist U. Paris, 1974-75; vis. rschr. New Coll. Berkeley, 1986-87; presenter in field; former cons. Conrad Grebel Coll., U. Waterloo, Ont., Can.; mem. peace and social concerns com. Mennonite Ch., 1959-71; former mem. Continuation Com. of Hist. Peace Chs.; mem. interch. rels. staff Mennonite Ch. U.S.A., 1997—; mem secretariat Nat. Assn. Ind. Colls. and Univs. Contbr. articles to profl. jours.; mem. Princeton U. exch. fellow and Charles Foster Kent fellow Nat. Coun. for Religion in Higher Edn., 1953-54. Mem.: Soc. for Values in Higher Edn., Nat. Assn. Ind. Colls. and Univs. (secretariat), Am. Assn. Physics Tchrs., Denominational Execs. for Ch.-Related Higher Edn. (chmn. 1984—86). Avocations: tennis, hiking. Home: 708 Emerson St Goshen IN 46526-3904

**MEYER, ALICE VIRGINIA**, state official; b. N.Y.C., Mar. 15, 1921; d. Martin G. and Marguerite Helene (Houzé) Kliemand; m. Theodore Harry Meyer, June 28, 1947; children: Robert Charles, John Edward. BA, Barnard Coll., 1941; MA, Columbia U., 1942; D of Humanitarian Svcs. (hon.), Briarwood Coll., 2006. Tchr. pub. schs., Elmont, N.J., 1942-43; tchr. Fairlawn (N.J.) High Schs., 1943-47; office mgr., sales rep. N.Y.C., 1948-55; substitute tchr. Pub. Schs., Easton, Conn., 1965-72; state rep., asst. minority leader Conn. State Legislature, Hartford, 1976-93. Mem. Ct. Bd. Govs. for Higher Edn., 1993-2005, vice-chair, chair. bd. govs. for higher edn.; bd. dirs. 3030 Fairfield Health Ctr., 1994-2006. Mem. Edn. Commn. of the States, 1985—87; life trustee Discovery Mus., 1980—; trustee United Way Regional Youth Substance Abuse Project, Bridgeport, 1983—93; mem. strategic planning com. Town of Easton, 1993—; vice chmn. ct. adv. coun. on intergovtl. rels., 1988—; mem. Conn. Commn. on Quality Edn., 1992—93; supporter Conn. Small Towns, 1988; mem. Conn. Humanities Coun., 1974—76, Conn. Film Commn., 1985—88; co-chair Com. on State Plan of Conservation and Devel., 1985—87; mem. Lt. Gov.'s Commn. on Mandate Reduction, 1995; sec. Easton Free Sch. Scholarship Fund, 1980—; pres. Barnard Class of 1941, 1996—; justice of the peace, 2001—; ct. adv. coun. career and vocat. edn., 1980—88; mem. Easton Rep. Town Com., 1965—, vice chmn., 1970—78; bd. dirs. 3030 Park, 1993—2006; Fairfield County Lit. Coalition Bridgeport, 1988—94. Named Legislator of Yr. Conn. Libr. Assn., 1985; Guardian Small Bus. grantee Nat. Fedn. Ind. Bus., 1987; honoree Fairfield YWCA Salute to Women, 1988, Conn. Assn. Small Towns, 1990; named grant to AAUW Fellowship Fund, Bridgeport Br., 1970, Conn. State AAUW, 1974; recipient Conn. Friends of Libr. Hon. award, 1984, Disting. Svc. award Conn. State Coun. on Voc/Tech. Edn., 1986, Sacred Heart U. Ctr. for Policy Issues award, 1988, citation Conn. Bd. for Acad. Affairs, 1992, citation Charter Oak Coll., 1993, Spl. Day Recognition, Town of Weston, 1993, Cert. of Recognition, Town of Westport, 1993, Citation for Fostering Open Access to Higher Edn., AAUW, 1994, Disting. Rep. award Easton Rep. Town Com., 2000, Pub. Svc. award Conn. Sec. of State, 2003, others; named

in her honor Alice U. Meyer Day, Conn., 2005; scholarship named in her honor, 2006. Mem.: LWV, AAUW (local pres. 1976, bd. dirs. 1982), Nat. Order Women Legislators (regional dir. 1987—91, past pres. Conn. chpt.), Conn. Assn. Sch. Adminstrs. (hon.), Bus. and Profl. Women. Congregationalist. Avocations: swimming, sailing, bridge. Home: 18 Lantern Hill Rd Easton CT 06612-2218

**MEYER, ANDREAS S.**, architect, consultant; s. Peter Meyer and Luise Schutzmeister-Meyer; m. Renee LeVerrier, 1999; 1 child, Luis pedro. BS in Elec. Engring., U. Ill., Champaign, 1981; MS, U. Mass., Amherst, 1984—86. Chief tech. officer Zaiq Tech., Inc, Chelmsford, Mass., 2002—04; chief tech. officer Cadence Design Sys., Inc, Chelmsford, Mass., 2002—04; chief tech. officer Assertive Design, Inc., Boston, 2004—. Verification cons. Ind. Cons., Newburyport, Mass., 1994—. Author: (technical book) Principles of Functional Verification, 2004, Newness, 2004. Parent-child mediator Cmty. Diversion Project, Greenland, NH, 2000—06. Achievements include patents pending for automated assertion technology. Office Phone: 603-674-3631. Office Fax: 760-683-2250. Personal E-mail: andreas.meyer@ameyer.org.

**MEYER, ANDREW C. C., JR.**, lawyer; b. N.Y.C., June 28, 1949; s. Andrew and Myra Meyer; m. Kathleen A. Sullivan, May 7, 1982; children— Joshua Andrew, Daniel Gregory, Jessica Kathleen. B.S., C.W. Post Coll., 1971; J.D., Suffolk U., 1974, hon. LLD. Bar: Mass. 1974, U.S. Dist. Ct. Mass. 1974, U.S. Ct. Appeals (1st cir.) 1974. Ptnr. Lubin & Meyer, P.C., Boston, 1974—. Contbr. articles to law jours. Mem. nat. adv. bd., Nat. Ctr. for Patients' Rights. Named one of Boston's Top Lawyers, Boston Mag., one of Top Ten Lawyers, Mass. Lawyers Weekly. Mem. Mass. Bar Assn. (mem. action subcom. Patients' Rights, chmn. trial practice com. 1983-84, award 1984, seminar speaker, 21st Century Club award 1984, Continuing Legal Edn. Faculty award 1984), Mass. Trial Attys. (mem. bd. govs.), Boston Bar Assn. Office: Lubin & Meyer PC 100 City Hall Plz Ste 4 Boston MA 02108 Office Fax: 617-720-1229. Business E-Mail: acmj@lubinandmeyer.com.

**MEYER, ANDREW W.**, retired publishing executive; b. Phila., July 29, 1941; s. John O. and Katherine (Wachter) M.; m. Helen Hope Hogan, Nov. 1963; children: Kelly Ann, Michael, Melissa, Suzanne, Jennifer. BS in Accounting, St. Joseph's U., Phila., 1963; MBA in Finance, U. Conn., 1973. CPA. Sr. accountant Jenkins Fetterolf, Phila., 1963-67; asst. treas. PA & S Small Co., York, 1967-71; v.p. finance Xerox Pub. Group, Greenwich, Conn., 1971-82, R.R. Bowker, N.Y.C., 1982-94; COO Reed Reference Pub., New Providence, N.J., 1995-96; v.p. admin., pub. Bus. Info. Svcs. Grp. Lexis-Nexis, New Providence, 1996-97; v.p. admin. Martindale-Hubbell, New Providence, 1997—2000, CEO and pres., 2000—01.

**MEYER, AUGUST CHRISTOPHER, JR.**, broadcast executive, lawyer; b. Champaign, Ill., Aug. 14, 1937; s. August C. and Clara (Rocke) M.; m. Karen Haugh Hassett, Dec. 28, 1960; children: August Christopher F., Elisabeth Hassett. BA cum laude, Harvard U., 1959, LLB, 1962. Bar: Ill. 1962. Founding ptr. Meyer-Capel, Champaign, Ill., 1962-77, of counsel, 1977—2003; owner, dir., officer Midwest TV, Inc., Sta. KFMB-TV-AM-FM, San Diego, Sta. WCIA-TV, Champaign, Ill., Sta. WMBD-TV-AM, WMXP, Peoria, Ill., 1968—, pres., 1976—. Bd. dirs. BankIll., Main St. Trust Inc.; spl. asst. atty. gen. State of Ill., 1968-76. Chmn. bd. trustees Carle Found. Hosp., Urbana, Ill. Mem. Ill. Bar Assn., Champaign County Bar Assn. Clubs: Champaign Country. Office: Midwest TV Inc PO Box 197 100 W University Ave # 401 Champaign IL 61824-0197 also: Sta KFMB PO Box 85888 7677 Engineer Rd San Diego CA 92111-1515

**MEYER, B. FRED**, small business executive, home designer and builder, product designer; b. LI, NY, Jan. 6, 1918; s. Barthold Fred and Edna May (Clark) M.; m. Mary E. Carman, July 18, 1951; children: Patricia Meyer Sauer, Susan Meyer Sachs. Student, Pratt Inst., 1935-39, Johns Hopkins U., 1946-48, Wayne State U., 1954-55. Registered builder, Fla. Project engr. Lear, Inc., Grand Rapids, Mich., 1948-51; engring. exec. GM Corp., Warren, Mich., 1951-75; pres. BFM Assocs., Inc. (name Fred Meyer, Inc. 1990), Sarasota, Fla., 1975—. Capt. USAAF, 1942-46, ETO. Achievements include 23 patents including pendulum type seat belt retractor, automotive power window switches, automotive power window activator. Avocations: golf, computers, travel. Home and Office: 4753 Antler Trail Sarasota FL 34238 Office Phone: 941-925-1707. Personal E-mail: bfredm@hotmail.com.

**MEYER, BARRY MICHAEL**, motion picture executive; b. NYC, Nov. 28, 1943; s. Perry and Lillian Helen (Katz) M.; m. Barbara Patricia, June 12, 1966; children: Matthew, Elizabeth. BA, U. Rochester, 1964; JD, Case Western Res. U., 1967. Bar: NY, Ohio. Legal counsel ABC, NYC, 1968-70, dir. bus. affairs LA, 1970-71, Warner Bros. TV, LA, 1971—72, v.p. bus. affairs, 1972—78, exec. v.p., 1978—84, Warner Bros. Entertainment, Inc., LA, 1984—94, exec. v.p., COO, 1994—99, chmn., CEO, 1999—. Mem. bd. councilors USC Sch. Cinema-TV; bd. dirs. Motion Picture Assn. Am., Mus. Radio and TV, Am. Film Inst. Contbr. articles to profl. jours. Bd. dirs. Human Rights Watch, San Fernando Valley Child Guidance Clinic, Calif.; bd. trustees U. Rochester. Named one of 50 Most Powerful People in Hollywood, Premiere mag., 2004—06. Mem. Hollywood Radio and TV Soc., Nat. Acad. TV Arts and Scis. (former gov.), Am. Mgmt. Assn., Acad. Motion Pictures Arts & Scis. Office: Warner Bros Entertainment Inc 4000 Warner Blvd Burbank CA 91522-0002 Office Phone: 818-954-1464.*

**MEYER, BETTY JANE**, former librarian; b. Indpls., July 20, 1918; d. Herbert and Gertrude (Sanders) Meyer. BA, Ball State Tchrs. Coll., 1940; BS in Library Sci., Western Res. U., 1945. Student asst. Muncie (Ind.) Pub. Libr., 1936—40; libr. asst. Ohio State U. Libr., Columbus, 1940—44, cataloger 1945—46, asst. circulation librarian, 1946—51, acting circulation librarian, 1951—52, adminstrv. asst. to dir. librs., 1952—57, acting assoc. reference librarian, 1957—58, serials cataloger, 1958—65, head serial divsn. catalog dept., 1965—68, head acquisition dept., 1968—71, asst. dir. librs., tech. svcs., 1971—76, acting dir. librs. 1976—77, asst. dir. librs., tech. svcs., 1977—83; libr. asst. Grandview Heights Pub. Libr., Columbus, 1942—44; student asst. Case Inst. Tech., Cleve., 1944—45. Instr. library adminstrn. Ohio State U. Libr., 1958—63, instr. prof., 1963—67, assoc. prof., 1967—75, prof., 1975—83, prof. emeritus, 1983—; mem. Ohio Coll. Libr. Tech. Adv. Com. on Cataloging, 1971—76; mem. adv. com. on serials, 1971—76; mem. Inter-Univ. Libr. Coun., Tech. Svcs. Group, 1971—83; mem. bd. trustees Columbua Area Libr. and Info. Coun. Ohio, 1980—83. Grantee Ohio State U., 1975—76. Mem.: PEO, AAUP, ALA, Acad. Libr. Assn., Franklin County Libr. Assn., No. Ohio Tech. Svcs. Librarians, Ohio Valley Group Tech. Svcs. Librarians, Ohioana Libr. Assn., Ohio Libr. Assn., Assn. Coll. and Rsch. Librs., Assn. Faculty and Profl. Women Ohio State U., Delta Kappa Gamma, Beta Phi Mu. Home: 6000 Riverside Dr Ofc 52B Dublin OH 43017-1492

**MEYER, BILL**, publishing executive, editor; b. Pratt, Kans., Aug. 6, 1925; s. Otto William and Ruth Clarinda (Jones) Meyer; m. Joan Aileen Wight, Sept. 11, 1949; 1 child, Eric Kent. BS in Journalism, U. Kans., 1948. News editor Marion County Record, Hoch Pub. Co., Inc., Marion, Kans., 1948—67, editor, pub., 1967—2005; owner Cottonwood Valley Agy., Marion, 1990-98, Hoch Pub. Co., Inc., Marion, 1998—. Polit. interviewer Sta. KPTS-TV Wichita, 1983—98; lectr. media law Wichita (Kans.) State U., 1985; mil. cons., travel agt. Battlefield Tours, Slidell, La., 1990—; bd. dirs. Ctrl. Nat. Bank. Past pres. Marion Sch. Dist. Bd. Edn., Marion County Hosp. Dist.; bd. dirs. Marion Manor Nursing Home, Kans. Hist. Soc., 1985—; trustee, past pres. William Allen White Found., Lawrence, Kans. With U.S. Army, 1943—45, ETO. Named Kans. Master Editor, Kans. Leader of the Yr., 2003, Hon. Col., Kans. Cavalry, 1987, Hon. Ky. Col., Kans. Newspaper Hall of Fame, 2004; recipient commendation, Kans. Ho. of Reps., 1982, 99th Inf. Divsn. Assn., 1986, 1989, Clyde Reed Kans. Master Editor award, Kans. Newspaper Found., 1997, Cervi award, Internat. Soc. Weekly Newspaper Editors. Mem.: Soc. Profl. Journalists, Kans. Press Assn. (pres. 1982—83, Boyd Cmty. Svc. award 1979, Outstanding Mentor award 1999), Nat. Newspaper Assn., 99th Inf. Divsn. Assn. (editor 1971—, pres. 1998—99),

Marion C. of C. (past bd. dirs.), Kiwanis (pres. Marion 1957), Shriners, Masons. Republican. Methodist. Avocation: military history. Home: 425 Locust St Marion KS 66861-1429 Personal E-mail: bill@marionkansas.com, meyer@marionkansas.com.

**MEYER, BRECKIN,** actor; b. Mpls., May 7, 1974; m. Dorothy Kaplan, Oct. 14, 2001; 1 child, Caitlin Willow. Actor: (films) Freddy's Dead: The Final Nightmare, 1991, Payback, 1995, Clueless, 1995, The Craft, 1996, Escape from L.A., 1996, Prefontaine, 1997, Touch, 1997, Dancer, Texas Pop. 81, 1998, 54, 1998, Go, 1999, The Insider, 1999, Tail Lights Fade, 1999, Road Trip, 2000, Rat Race, 2001, Kate & Leopold, 2001, (voice) Pinocchio, 2002, Garfield: The Movie, 2004, Blast, 2004, Herbie: Fully Loaded, 2005, Rebound, 2005, Garfield: A Tale of Two Kitties, 2006; (TV films) Camp Cucamonga, 1990, Betrayed: A Story of Three Women, 1995, Rock Times, 2000; (TV series) Child's Play, 1982, Potato Head Kids, 1985, The Jackie Thomas Show, 1992, The Home Court, 1995, (voice) King of the Hill, 2000—, The Near Future, 2000, Inside Schwartz, 2001, Married to the Kellys, 2003, Robert Chicken, 2005—06. Office: c/o the Gersh Agy PO Box 5617 Beverly Hills CA 90210*

**MEYER, BRUCE D.,** lawyer; b. Aug. 31, 1945; BA, Univ. Ill., 1967, JD with high honors, 1970. Bar: Calif. 1971. Assoc. Gibson Dunn & Crutcher, LA, 1970—73, ptnr., 1979—81, Riyadh, Saudi Arabia, 1981—83, ptnr. corp. transactions and securities LA, 1983—; v.p., asst. gen. counsel Whittaker Corp., LA, 1973—79. Mem. exec. com. Gibson Dunn & Crutcher. Mem.: ABA (chmn. Middle East law com., internat. law section 1984—85), LA County Bar Assn., Order of Coif. Office: Gibson Dunn & Crutcher LLP 333 Grand Ave Los Angeles CA 90071-3197 Office Phone: 213-229-7979. Office Fax: 213-229-6979. Business E-Mail: bmeyer@gibsondunn.com.

**MEYER, BRUD RICHARD,** retired pharmaceutical executive; b. Waukegan, Ill., Feb. 22, 1926; s. Charles Lewis and Mamie Olive (Broom) M.; m. Betty Louise Stine (dec. 1970); children: Linda (Mrs. Gary Stillabower), Louise (Mrs. Donald Knochel), Janet (Mrs. Gerald Cockrell), Jeff, Karen, Blake, Amy; m. Barbara Ann Hamilton, Nov. 26, 1970. BS, Purdue U., 1949. With Eli Lilly & Co., Indpls., 1949-87, indsl. engr., 1949-56, supr. indsl. engr., 1956-59, sr. personnel rep., 1960-64, personnel mgr. Lafayette, Ind., 1964-67, asst. dir., 1967-69, dir. adminstrn., 1969-79, dir. personnel and public relations, 1980-87, ret., 1987. Bd. dirs. Lafayette Home Hosp., 1977—, Hanna Community Ctr., 1983—, Tippecanoe Hist. Corp., 1985—; bd. dirs. United Way Tippecanoe County, 1970-76, pres., 1974; bd. dirs. Legal Aid Soc. Tippecanoe County, 1973—, Jr. Achievement, pres., 1979; bd. dirs. Lilly Credit Union, 1969-75, pres., 1973-74; mem. Citizen's Com. on Alcoholism, 1966-72; bd. dirs. Greater Lafayette Cmty. Ctrs., 1975-79, pres., 1977-78; bd. dirs. Tippecanoe County Child Care, 1990—, pres., 1998-99; mem., mng. dir. Battle Tippecanoe Outdoor Drama Bd. With USAAF, 1943-45. Mem. Pi Tau Sigma, Lambda Chi Alpha, C. of C. Greater Lafayette (bd. dirs., v.p. 1969-73), Battleground Hist. Soc. Methodist. Home: 4217 Trees Hill Dr Lafayette IN 47909-3451 Office: Eli Lilly & Co PO Box 7685 Lafayette IN 47903-7685

**MEYER, CATHERINE DIEFFENBACH,** lawyer; b. Seattle, Mar. 27, 1951; d. Patrick Andrew and Hope Dieffenbach; m. Michael E. Meyer, Nov. 21, 1982; children: Catherine. AB, Bryn Mawr Coll., 1973; JD, Northwestern U., 1979. Bar: Calif. 1979, U.S. Dist Ct (cen. dist.) Calif., 1979, U.S. Ct. Appeals (9th cir.) 1982, U.S. Dist. Ct. (ea., no. and so. dists.) Calif. 1987. Assoc. Lillick, McHose & Charles, L.A., 1979-85, ptnr., 1985-88, Lillick & McHose, L.A., 1988-90, Pillsbury Madison & Sutro, L.A., 1990—2001, Pillsbury Winthrop LLP, L.A., 2001—05; past co-chmn. Privacy & Data Protection practice, co-chmn. LA Bus. dept. Pillsbury Winthrop Shaw Pittman LLP, L.A., 2005—; counsel, 2005—. Bd. dirs. House Ear Inst. Mem.: ABA (past co-chmn. Extraterritorial Application of Law subcommittee), LA County Bar Assn. Office: Pillsbury Winthrop Shaw Pittman LLP Suite 2800 725 S Figueroa St Los Angeles CA 90017 Office Phone: 213-488-7362. Office Fax: 213-629-1033. Business E-Mail: catherine.meyer@pillsburylaw.com.

**MEYER, CHRISTOPHER HAWKINS,** lawyer; b. Springfield, Mo., Sept. 29, 1952; s. Richard DeWitt and Nancy (Hawkins) M.; m. Karen Anne Adams, Aug. 8, 1987; 1 child, C. Andrew Meyer. BA in Econs. magna cum laude, U. Mich., 1977, JD cum laude, 1981. Bar: D.C. 1981, U.S. Ct. Appeals (D.C. cir.) 1982, U.S. Ct. Appeals (9th cir.) 1983, Colo. 1985, U.S. Ct. Appeals (10th cir.) 1985, Idaho, U.S. Ct. Appeals (8th cir.) 1985. Counsel water resources program Nat. Wildlife Fedn., Washington, 1981-84, assoc. prof. adjoint, counsel Rocky Mountain Natural Resources Clinic Boulder, Colo., 1984-91; ptnr. Givens Pursley, Boise, 1991—. Contbr. articles to profl. publs. Mem. steering com. Idaho Environ. Forum. Recipient Lawyer of Yr. award Environ. Policy Inst., 1984, Water Conservationist of Yr. Nebr. Wildlife Fedn., 1989. Mem. Phi Beta Kappa. Home: 3443 S Millspur Way Boise ID 83716-8648 Office: Givens Pursley LLP 601 W Bannock St Boise ID 83702-7720 Office Phone: 208-388-1236. Business E-Mail: chrismeyer@givenspursley.com.

**MEYER, SIR CHRISTOPHER J.R.,** former ambassador; b. Beaconsfield, Eng., Feb. 22, 1944; m. Catherine Laylle; 2 sons, 2 stepsons. Student, Lancing Coll., Eng.; Peterhouse, Cambridge, Eng., Paul Nitze Sch., Bologna, Italy; MA in History, Cambridge U., 1965. Joined Diplomatic Svc., London, 1966-68, with Moscow, 1968-70, Madrid, 1970-73; head Soviet sect. East European and Soviet dept. Fgn. and Commonwealth Office, London, 1973-76; speech-writer to fgn. sec. policy planning staff Diplomatic Svc., London, 1976-78; mem. UK rep. to European Comtys., Brussels, 1978-82; polit. counselor British Embassy, Moscow, 1982-84; fgn. office spokesman, press sec. to fgn. sec. Fgn. and Commonwealth Office, London, 1984-88, min. Washington, 1989-92; min., dep. head mission British Embassy, 1992—93, govt. spokesman, press sec. to prime min. London, 1994—96, Brit. amb. to Fed. Rep. Germany, 1997; UK amb. to U.S. Washington, 1997—2003; chmn. U.K. Press Complaints Commn., 2003—. Vis. fellow Harvard U. Ctr. for Internat. Affairs, 1988-89; hon. fellow Peterhouse, Cambridge U., 2001—; chmn. Ambo Consultancy Ltd.; non-exec. dir. GKN plc. Named Knight Comdr. of the Order of St. Michael and St. George, 1998. Avocations: tennis, watching soccer, listening to jazz music. Office: Press Complaints Commn 20/23 High Holborn London EC1N 2JD England Office Phone: 44 207 438 1242. Office Fax: 011 44 207 831 0070.

**MEYER, CHRISTOPHER LEE,** music educator; b. Holland, Mich., May 29, 1980; s. Michael Dean and Karen Ruth Meyer. BA, Hope Coll., Holland, Mich., 2002; MusB, Western Mich. U., Kalamazoo, 2005. Provisional Cert. for Music Edn. (K-12) Mich., 2005. Pvt. cello instr., Holland, Mich., 2005—; cellist Holland Symphony Orch., Holland, Mich., 2002—; gen. mgr. Holland Area Youth Orch., Holland, Mich., 2004—; orch. & band dir. West Ottawa Macatawa Bay Mid. Sch., Holland, Mich., 2005—. Mem.: Am. Symphony Orch. League, Mich. Sch. Band and Orch. Assn., Am. String Tchrs. Assn., Sigma Beta Delta, Pi Kappa Lambda, Phi Beta Kappa.

**MEYER, CHRISTOPHER RICHARD,** lawyer; b. Springfield, Ohio, June 18, 1952; s. Eugene Francis and Marilyn Crawford (Hopping) M.; m. Sharman Elizabeth, Sept. 8, 1973; children: Elizabeth Ann, Emily McClead, Timothy Joseph. BA summa cum laude, Ohio State U., 1974, JD, 1977. Bar: Ohio, U.S. Dist. Ct. (so. and no. dists.) Ohio, U.S. Ct. Appeals (6th cir.), U.S. Supreme Ct. Ptnr. Reese, Pyle, Drake & Meyer, Newark, Ohio, 1977—. Legal counsel Licking Meml. Hosp., Newark Ohio, 1983—, State Farm Ins. Co., Bloomington, Ill., 1977—, St. Paul Ins. Co., Columbus, Ohio, 1977—; spl. coun. Ctrl. Ohio Tech. Coll. Mem. Ohio State Bar Assn. (negligence com., litigation sect.), Ohio Assn. Civil Trial Attys., Soc. Ohio Hosp. Attys., Phi Beta Kappa. Home: 976 Briarhill Dr Newark OH 43055-2249 Office: Reese Pyle Drake & Meyer 36 N 2d St PO Box 919 Newark OH 43058-0919 E-mail: cmeyer@rpdm.com.

**MEYER, DANA LYNN,** music educator; b. Evansville, Ind., Aug. 5, 1965; d. Richard Lowell Meyer and Jacquelyn Claudine Klueg. MusB in Edn., U. Evansville, 1988; MusM in Edn., Ind. State U., 2002. Tchr. music Evansville Day Sch., 1988—91; dir. band Boonville H.S., Ind., 1991—. Clarinetist Rhein Valley Brass German Band, Evansville, 1984—; clarinetist/bass clarinetist Evansville Symphonic Band, 1996—. Scholar Theodore Presser Found., 1986; Col. Ostrum Scholarship Found., 1986. Mem.: Music Educators Nat. Conf. (assoc.), Ind. Bandmasters Assn. (assoc.), Phi Kappa Phi. Lutheran. Avocations: rollerskating, music technology, German language, music, culture, reading, Bible study. Home: 1934 Shepherd Dr Evansville IN 47715 Office: Boonville HS 300 N 1st St Boonville IN 47601 Office Phone: 812-897-4701. Office Fax: 812-897-6061. Personal E-mail: dlmeyer@aol.com. Business E-Mail: dmeyer@warrick.k12.in.us.

**MEYER, DANIEL KRAMER,** real estate executive; b. Denver, July 15, 1957; s. Milton Edward and Mary (Kramer) M. Student, Met. State Coll., Denver, 1977-78, U. Colo., 1978-80. Ptnr., developer RM & M II (Ltd. Partnership), Englewood, Colo., 1981-87; pres. Centennial Mortgage and Investment, Ltd., Englewood, Colo., 1984-87; prin. Capriole Properties, Greenwood Village, Colo., 1983—. Mng. dir. Heritage Capital Group, 2005—06; prin. Courbette Capital, LLC, 2006—. Alumni mem. bd. trustees Kent Denver Country Day Sch., 1981-83; sec. dist. 37 ctrl. and vacancy com. Colo. Ho. of Reps., 1991-92. Recipient Pamela Davis Beardsley devel. award Kent Denver Sch., 1995. Mem.: Chartered Realty Investor Soc., Greenwood Athletic Club. Republican. Avocations: mountain climbing, rollerblading.

**MEYER, DAVID LAVON,** health administration executive; b. Arlington, Va., Dec. 29, 1951; s. Elmer Lavon and Pauline Ellen Meyer; m. Cynthia Karen Collins, May 10, 1980; children: Louisa, Elliot. BA, Randolph-Macon Coll., 1974; MPA, Am. U., 1977. Dir. alumni programs Randolph-Macon Coll., Ashland, Va., 1977—78; chief rules and directives br. U.S. Nuc. Regulatory Commn., Rockville, Md., 1979—2000; sr. exec. Mine Safety and Health Adminstrn., Arlington, Va., 2000—. Author: Pilgrimmages of Faith: History of Churches in Vienna, Virginia, Fairfax, Virginia: A City Traveling Through Time, 1997. Dir. Historic Fairfax City, Inc., 2002—. Avocation: historic preservation. Home: 3508 Cornell Rd Fairfax VA 22030-1814

**MEYER, DEBORA LYNN,** music educator; d. Ronald James and Lorraine Gott; m. Marcus Joseph Meyer, Dec. 20, 1986. BA in K-12 vocal music edn. and vocal performance, Carthage Coll., Kenosha, Wis., 1976; MME in Music Edn., Holy Names Coll., Oakland, Calif., 1990. Cert. Kodaly Orgn. of Am. Kodaly Educators. Pvt. music instr. voice, piano, organ, and guitar, Kenosha and Milwaukee Counties, Wis., 1969—87; profl. vocalist Kenosha, Racine, Milw., Waukesha and Winnebago counties, Wis., 1970—; vocal music specialist K-8, dir. of music St. George Sch. and Ch., Kenosha, Wis., 1976—82; vocal music specialist K-8 St. Stephen Sch., Milw., 1982—87; vocal music specialist K-6, choral dir. Banting Sch. Sch. Dist. Waukesha, Wis., 1987—; clinician music listening, singing sci., children's choral pedagogy Orgn. of Am. Kodaly Educators, Wis. Choral Dirs., Wis. Sci. Tchrs., 1990—. Music mentor acad. decathlon - music mentor Waukesha West H.S., 2001—. Bldg. chairperson campaign United Way of Waukesha County, 2001—05. Recipient Kohl Tchr. Fellowship award, Sen. Herb Kohl, 1998. Mem.: NEA (assoc.), Am. Orff-Schulwerk Assn. (assoc.), Midwest Kodaly Music Educators Assn. (assoc.), Orgn. Am. Kodaly Educators (assoc.; regional rep. mid-west 1 1993—95), Wis. Choral Dirs. Assn. (assoc.; state chair Singing in Wis. and Children's Conv. Choir 1991—94, state chair Conv. Children's Honor Choir 1991—94, rep. Southeastern dist. 1992—94), Am. Choral Dirs. Assn. (assoc.), Nat. Assn. Tchrs. of Singing (assoc.), Wis. Music Educators Assn. (assoc.), Edn. Assn. of Waukesha (assoc.; bldg. union rep. 2000—, NEA del. to nat. assembly in New Orleans 2003), Music Educators Nat. Conf. (assoc.), Sigma Alpha Iota (assoc.). Office: Banting Elem Sch 2019 Butler Dr Waukesha WI 53186-2634 Office Phone: 262-970-1250. Personal E-mail: musicmeyer@wi.rr.com. E-mail: dmeyer@waukesha.k12.wi.us.

**MEYER, DENNIS IRWIN,** lawyer; b. Dayton, Ohio, Oct. 20, 1935; s. Luther Edward and Mary (McGee) M.; m. Rita Murray, June 23, 1962; children: Matthew, Michael, Rita Catherine, Peter, Denise, Abigail. BS, U. Dayton, 1957; LLB, Georgetown U., 1960, LLM, 1962. Bar: Ohio 1960, D.C. 1962. Atty.-advisor U.S. Tax Ct., Washington, 1960—62; sr. counsel Baker & McKenzie, Washington, 1965—. Bd. dirs. United Fin. Banking Cos., Vienna, Va. Mem. ABA, Internat. Fiscal Assn., Met. Club, Belle Haven Country Club, Avenel Golf Club, Robert Trent Jones Golf Club. Roman Catholic. Office: Baker & McKenzie 815 Connecticut Ave NW Washington DC 20006-4004 Office Phone: 202-452-7008. Business E-Mail: dennis.i.meyer@bakernet.com.

**MEYER, DERRICK R.,** information technology executive; BS in Computer Engring., U. Ill.; MBA, Boston U. With Intel Corp., 1983—86, Digital Equipment Corp., 1986—96; dir. engring. Athlon Advanced Micro Devices, Austin, Tex., 1996—99, v.p. engring. computation products group Sunnyvale, Calif., 1999—2001, group v.p. computation products group, 2001—02, exec. v.p. computation products group, 2002—. Office: Advanced Micro Devices One AMD Pl PO Box 3453 Sunnyvale CA 94088-3453

**MEYER, DIANE CHRISTINE,** social worker; b. Meadowbrook, Pa., May 9, 1963; d. Robert Francis and Carole Ann Meyer; children: Stephen Francis, Alexander Gerard, Robert Nathaniel. BA in Psychology, LaSalle U., Phila., 1989. Childcare supr. St. Mary's Villa, Ambler, Pa., 1989—91; caseworker Bucks County Children & Youth, Doylestown, Pa., 1991—2001, casework supr., 2001—. Democrat. Roman Catholic. Avocation: reading. Home: 4218 Miladies Ln Doylestown PA 18901 Office: Bucks County Children and Youth 4259 W Swamp Rd Doylestown PA 18901

**MEYER, DONALD ROBERT,** state agency adminstrator, lawyer; b. Phoenix, June 4, 1942; s. Donald and Eleanor M.; m. Virginia Whitesel, Sept. 3, 1966; 2 children. BA, U. Calif., Berkeley, 1964, JD, 1967; postgrad., Harvard U., 1968. Bar: Calif. 1972, U.S. Peace Corps. Lectr. Seoul Nat. Univ., Korea, 1969-70; assoc. Graham & James, San Francisco, 1971-76; asst. sec. Calif. First Bank (name now Union Bank), San Francisco, 1973-76, v.p., 1976-78, gen. counsel, 1976-96, sr. v.p., 1976-96; corp. sec., exec. v.p. gen. counsel UnionBanCal Corp., 1996—98; commr. Fin. Institutions, Calif., 2000—. Contbr.: Intro to the Law & Legal System of Korea, 1983. Mem. Habitat for Humanity Internat., Sierra Club; co-chmn. San Francisco/Seoul Sister City Com., 1980-90; trustee Asian Art Found. of San Francisco, 1985-92, 97—; commr. Asian Art Mus., San Francisco, 1985-91. Recipient Key to Seoul, Korea, 1984. Mem. ABA, San Francisco Bar Assn., Am. Bankers Assn. (v.p. Calif. State 1982-83), Calif. Bankers Assn. (chmn. legal affairs com. 1982-84, svc. award 1989), Korean-Am. C. of C. (dir. San Francisco sec., bd. dirs. 1974-93, pres. 1996-98, commr. 1998-2002), Soc. Calif. Pioneers, Bohemian Club. Republican. Episcopalian. Personal E-mail: dmeyerberk@cs.com. Business E-Mail: dmeyer@dgi.ca.gov.

**MEYER, EDMOND GERALD,** energy scientist, retired chemistry professor, academic administrator, entrepreneur; b. Albuquerque, Nov. 2, 1919; s. Leopold and Beatrice (Ilfeld) M.; m. Betty F. Knobloch, July 4, 1941; children: Lee Gordon, Terry Gene, David Gary. BS in Chemistry, Carnegie Mellon U., 1940, MS, 1942; PhD, U. N.Mex., 1950. Chemist Harbison Walker Refractories Co., 1940-41; instr. Carnegie Mellon U., 1941-42; asst. phys. chemist Bur. Mines, 1942-44; chemist research div. N.Mex. Inst. Mining and Tech., 1946-48; head dept. sci. U. Albuquerque, 1950-52; head dept. chemistry N.Mex. Highlands U., 1952-59; dir. Inst. Sci. Rsch., dean Grad. Sch. U. Wyo., 1957—63, dean Coll. Arts and Sci., 1963-75, v.p. Rsch., 1974-80, prof. energy and natural resources, 1981-89, prof. and dean emeritus, 1989—. Exec. cons. Diamond Shamrock Corp., 1980; sci. adviser Gov. of Wyo., 1964-90; cons. Coal Tech. Corp., 1981—; cons. Los Alamos Nat. Lab., NFS, HHS, GAO, TVA, Wyo. Bancorp; contractor investigator Rsch. Corp., Dept. Interior, AEC, NIH, NSF, Dept. Energy, Dept. Edn.; Fulbright exch. prof. U. Concepcion, Chile, 1959. Co-author: Chemistry-Survey of Principles, 1963, Legal Rights of Chemists and Engineers, 1977,

Industrial Research & Development Management, 1982; contbr. articles to profl. jours.; patentee in field. Mem. Laramie Regional Airport Bd., 1989-93, treas., 1994-97, chair; active Laramie City Coun., 1997-2001, vice mayor, 1998-2001. Lt. comdr. USNR, 1944-46, ret. Recipient Disting. Svc. award Jaycees; rsch. fellow U. N.Mex., 1948-50. Fellow: AAAS, Am. Inst. Chemists (hon.; pres. 1992—93, chmn. 1994—95); mem.: AIChE (sr.), Coun. Coll. Arts and Scis. (pres. 1971, sec.-treas. 1972—75, dir. Washington office 1993), Biophys. Soc., Am. Chem. Soc. (councilor 1962—90, chmn. Wyo. sect. 1997, 2002, nat. vol. svc. award 2006), Assn. Western Univs. (chmn. 1972—74), Laramie C. of C. (pres. 1984), Sigma Xi. Home: 1058 Colina Dr Laramie WY 82072-5015 Office: U Wyo Coll Arts Scis Laramie WY 82073-0966 Office Phone: 307-766-5445. Business E-Mail: egmeyer@uwyo.edu.

**MEYER, EDWARD HENRY,** advertising agency executive; b. NYC, Jan. 8, 1927; s. I.H. and Mildred (Driesen) M.; m. Sandra Raabin, Apr. 26, 1957; children: Margaret Ann, Anthony Edward. BA with honors in Econ., Cornell U., 1949. With Bloomingdale's div. Federated Dept Stores, 1949-51, Biow Co., 1951-56, Grey Global Group, NYC, 1956—, exec. v.p., 1963-68, pres., 1968—, CEO, chmn., 1970—. Bd. dirs. Ethan Allen Interiors Inc., Harman Internat. Industries, Inc., Jim Pattison Group, Inc. Trustee Solomon R. Guggenheim Mus., NYU Med. Ctr.; bd. mem. Am. Mus. Natural History, Film Soc. of Lincoln Ctr. With USCGR, 1945—47. Mem. Econ. Club (NYC), Univ. Club (NYC), Harmonie Club (NYC), Century Country Club, Atlantic Golf Club. Office: Grey Global Group Inc 777 3rd Ave New York NY 10017-1401*

**MEYER, EDWARD HENRY,** business and economics educator, lawyer; b. Buffalo, June 23, 1949; s. George Louis and Marie Catherine Meyer. BA, Fordham U., 1970, MA, 1972, Columbia U., 1977; JD, NYU, 1980, MBA, 1981. Bar: NY 1981. H.s. tchr. Cardinal Spellman H.S., Bronx, NY, 1972—77; asst. prof. NYU, N.Y.C., 1980—81; assoc. Sullivan and Cromwell, N.Y.C., 1981—82; prof. bus. and econs. Coll. of Mt. St. Vincent, Bronx, 1982—, chmn. dept. bus. and econs., 1982—2005, dean, 2005—. Adj. asst. prof. Fordham U., Bronx, 1972—77, CUNY LaGuardia C.C., N.Y.C., 1973—77; adj. assoc. prof. SUNY Maritime Coll., Bronx, 1986—93. Named Tchr. of Yr., Fordham U. Sch. Gen. Studies, 1975; recipient Tchg. Excellence award, Coll. of Mt. St. Vincent, 1988, 2003. Mem.: Assn. Collegiate Bus. Schs. and Programs (bd. dirs. 1999—2004, commr. baccalaureate and grad. degree bd. commrs. 1996—99, pres., chmn. bd. dirs. 1999—2004), Order of Coif, Delta Mu Delta, Beta Gamma Sigma, Phi Beta Kappa. Office: Coll of Mount St Vincent 6301 Riverdale Ave Bronx NY 10471 Office Phone: 718-405-3373. Office Fax: 718-405-3374. E-mail: edward.meyer@mountsaintvincent.edu.

**MEYER, ELLEN L.,** academic administrator; BA and MS Geo Wash U. Vp for mktg and exten, dean of cont studies and dir of exten prog and summer sch Minneapolis College of Art and Design; dir of cont ed and spec prog RI Sch of Design; pres. Atlanta Coll. Art, 1992—. Mem.: National Black Arts Festival Bd of Dir, Metro Atlanta Arts Fund Adv Bd, vice chair, bd of dir, Atl Reg Consortium for Higher Ed. Achievements include 1992-93 graduate, Midtown Leadership Program, Atlanta; 1994 graduate, Leadership-Atlanta. Office: Atlanta Coll Art 1280 Peachtree St NE Atlanta GA 30309-3502

**MEYER, F. WELLER,** bank executive; b. Washington, Dec. 15, 1942; s. Martin William and Sallie Rita (Weller) M.; m. Brenda Burton, Sept. 27, 1972; children: F. Weller Jr., Brandon Michael. BS, U. Md., 1977. V.p. W.S. Steed Mortgage Co., Wheaton, Md., 1970-73; asst. dir. Mortgage Bankers Assn. Am., Washington, 1973-77; mng. dir. Mortgage Systems Corp., Bethesda, Md., 1977-83; pres., CEO Westmark Mortgage Corp., Rockville, Md., 1983-87, Acacia Fed. Savs. Bank, Falls Church, Va., 1987—. Bd. dirs. Acacia Fed. Svcs. Bank, Calvert Group Ltd.; 1st vice chmn. Am.'s Cmty. Bankers; former pres. Thrift Instns. Adv. Coun. to the Fed. Res.; mem. nat. adv. coun. Fed. Nat. Mortgage Assn.; mem. Nat. Assn. Homebuilders Mortgage Roundtable. Co-author: Residential Mortgage Underwriting, 1981, Construction Lending—Residential, 1981, Construction Lending—Residential Income Property, 1981, Income Property Underwriting, 1981. Dir. Make-A-Wish Found. of the Mid-Atlantic, 1991-97, No. Va. Comty. Found.; Fairfax, Va., 1989; mem. Citizen's Housing Adv. Com., Montgomery County, Md., 1988-90. 1st lt. U.S. Army, 1967-70, Vietnam. Mem. Optimists (pres. Washington 1978-79), Old Guard Assn. Republican. Roman Catholic. Avocations: golf, hunting, jogging. Home: 9809 Kendale Rd Rockville MD 20854-4246

**MEYER, FRANCES MARGARET ANTHONY,** educational consultant; b. Stella, Va., Nov. 15, 1947; d. Arthur Abner Jr. and Emmie Adeline (Murray) Anthony; m. Stephen Leroy Meyer, Aug. 2, 1975. BS, Longwood Coll., 1970; MS, Va. Commonwealth U., 1982; PhD, 1996. Cert. tchr. Va. Tchr. health, phys. edn., and dance Fredericksburg City Pub. Schs., Va., 1970—89; coord. AIDS edn. Va. Dept. Edn., Richmond, 1989—90, specialist health edn., 1990—94, specialist comprehensive sch. health program, 1994—2003; ednl. cons. Fredericksburg, Va., 2003—. Mem. rev. bd. Nat. Commn. for Health Edn. and Credentialing, Inc., conf. and profl. devel. rev., 1996-2000. Author, editor: Dance Education, What is it? Why is it important?, 2002; author (with others): Elementary Physical Education: Growing through Movement-A Curriculum Guide, 1982; contbr. articles to profl. jours. Dir. Va. Children's Dance Festival, 1981—96, 1997—99; vol. ARC, Fredericksburg, 1976—84, 1997—2001, Va. affiliate AHA, 1982—93, 1999—2001; mem. ctrl. steering com. Health, Mental Health and Safety in Schs. Nat. Guidelines Project, Am. Acad. Pediat., 2000—02; Va. Affiliate Am. Cancer Soc. Richmond, Va.; mem. Public Health Edn.Coun., Comprehensive Sch. Health Edn. Team, Va. Alliance Adolescents and Sch. Health, 1990—2004; health com. Va. Healthy Pathways Coalition, 2004—; mem. Am. Heart Assn., 2004—; bd. dirs. Va. HIV/AIDS Network ARC, 1997—2001. Recipient gov.'s medal for substance abuse and prevention edn. fitst of Va., 1997, Alumni Cmty. Svc. award Va. Commonwealth U., 1998, Youth Edn. award for Leadership in the healthy devel. of children Am. Cancer Soc., 2002, Disting. Leadership in Phys. Edn. award Nat. Assn. Sport and Phys. Edn., 2004; Nat. Pub. Health Leadership Inst. fellow, 2000; Va. Coordinated Sch. Health Leadership fellow, 2006. Fellow: Nat. Assn. Sch. Health, Phys. Edn., Recreation, Sport and Dance (hon.); mem.: AAPHERD (chmn. divsn. 1970—, chmn. so. dist. applied strategic planning com. 2002—04, pres. so. dist. 2005—, past v.p., strategic planning com., social justice com., nominating com., pres.'s recognition award 1997, svc. award 1997, nat. honor award 1999), ASCD, AAUW (com. 1989—90, 1995—), NEA, Dance Edn. Orgn. (charter), Va. Assn. for Health, Phys. Edn. Recreation and Dance (various coms. 1970—, health edn. editor Va. Jour. 1994—2003, past pres., Tchr. of Yr. 1983, Va. Honor award 1988, Va. Pioneer award 2003), Va. Alliance for Arts Edn. (adv. bd. 1980—83, 1989—90, 1994—96), Am. Coll. Health Assn. (curriculum and tng. rev. panel 1992—94), Soc. State Dirs. Health, Phys. Edn. and Recreation (legis. affairs com. 1994—98, applied strategic planning com. 1994—2001, pres.-elect 1997, pres. 1998, past pres. 1999, think tank chair 2000—02, Healthis acad. rev. com. 2003, applied policy & legis. com. 2004), Phi Upsilon Omicron award 1996, Presdl. Recognition award 1997, 2000, Simon A. McNeely Honor award 2000, Julian B. Smith award 2004, Va. Health Promotion and Edn. Coun. (bd. dirs. 1996), Internat. Coun. for Health, Phys. Edn., Recreation, Sport and Dance (internat. adv. com. for health edn. and commn. for dance and dance edn., jour. articles rev. com.), Va. Mid. Sch. Assn., Va. Edn. Assn., Nat. Mid. Sch. Assn. Dance Assn. (bd. dirs. 2001—03, Presdl. citation 1998, svc. award 1998, 2000, Pres.'s Merit award 2001), Nat. Network for Youth Svcs. (adv. bd. 1994—98, rev. panel), Longwood Coll. Alumni Coun. (bd. dirs. 1987—90), Delta Kappa Gamma (pres. Beta Eta chpt. 1988—90). Baptist. Avocations: travel, dance, swimming, reading, theatrical performances.

**MEYER, FRED JOSEF,** finance company executive; b. Zurich, Switzerland, Jan. 1, 1931; came to U.S., 1959; s. Josef and Claire (Lehmann) M.; m. Beverly Ruth Carter, Apr. 9, 1961 (div. Feb. 1975); children: Fred Jay, Marcus Clinton, Michael Josef; m. Marie-Nicole Vigneron, Oct. 30, 1975. MS, Fed. Inst. Tech., Zurich, 1956; MBA, Harvard U., 1961; LLD (hon.), Sacred Heart U., 1981. V.p. planning & adminstrn. Sandoz, Inc., Hanover, NJ, 1971-73, exec. v.p., chief fin. officer, 1973-78; pres., CEO Sandoz U.S., Inc., Greenwich, Conn., 1978-81; mng. dir., CEO Wander Ltd., Berne, Switzerland, 1981-82; sr. v.p., chief fin. officer CBS, Inc., N.Y.C., 1982-88; chief fin. officer Omnicom Group, Inc., N.Y.C., 1988-98, vice chmn., 1998-99, spl. advisor exec. office, 2000—03. Bd. dirs. Novartis Corp., N.Y.C., Ptnrs. Group USA Inc., NYC Mem. Fin. Execs. Inst., Econ. Club, Harvard Club (N.Y.C.), Greenwich Country Club. Republican. Congregationalist. Office: Omnicom Group Inc 437 Madison Ave New York NY 10022-7001 E-mail: fjmeyer@aol.com.

**MEYER, G. CHRISTOPHER,** lawyer; b. Fremont, Nebr., Mar. 27, 1948; s. Gerald William and Mildred Ruth (Clausen) M.; children: Kate, Stacy, Jon, Robert. Student, Grinnell Coll., Iowa, 1969; BA, U. Kans., 1970; JD, U. Pa. Law Sch., 1973. Bar: Ohio 1973, U.S. Dist. Ct. (no. dist.) Ohio 1975, U.S. Ct. Appeals (6th cir.) 1982. Assoc. Squire, Sanders & Dempsey, L.L.P., Cleve., 1973-82, ptnr., 1982—. Bd. chairman Cleve. Rape Crisis Ctr. Mem. ABA, Greater Cleve. Bar Assn., Am. Coll. Bankruptcy. Office: Squire Sanders & Dempsey LLP 4900 Key Tower 127 Public Sq Cleveland OH 44114-1304 Home: 5455 N Marginal Rd Cleveland OH 44114-3951 Office Phone: 216-479-8692. Business E-Mail: cmeyer@ssd.com.

**MEYER, GEORGE HERBERT,** lawyer; b. Detroit, Feb. 19, 1928; s. Herbert M. and Agnes F. (Eaton) M.; m. Carol Ann Jones, 1958 (div. 1981) children: Karen Ann, George Herbert Jr.; m. Katherine Palmer White, Nov. 12, 1988. BA, U. Mich., 1949; JD, Harvard U., 1952; cert., Oxford U., Eng., 1955; LLM in Taxation and Labor Law, Wayne U., 1962. Bar: D.C. 1952, Mich. 1953. Assoc. firm Fischer, Franklin & Ford, Detroit, 1956-63, mem. firm, 1963-74; established firm George H. Meyer, 1974-78; sr. mem. firm Meyer and Kirk, 1978-85; sr. mem. Meyer, Kirk, Snyder & Safford PLLC, Bloomfield Hills and Detroit, Mich., 1985-99; mng. mem. Meyer, Kirk, Snyder & Lynch PLLC, Bloomfield Hills, Mich., 2000—. Curator Step Lively exhibit Mus. Am. Folk Art, N.Y.C., 1992; lectr. Am. Folk Art. Author: Equalization in Michigan and Its Effect on Local Assessments, 1963, Folk Artists Biographical Index, 1986, American Folk Art Canes: Personal Sculpture, 1992. Chmn. Birmingham (Mich.) Bd. Housing Appeals, 1964-68; vice chmn. Birmingham Bd. Zoning Appeals, 1966-69; mem. Birmingham Planning Bd., 1968-70; trustee, Bloomfield Village, Mich., 1976-80, pres., 1979-80; trustee Am. Folk Art, N.Y.C., 1987-2004; mem. exec. bd. Detroit Area coun. Boy Scouts Am., 1976—, counsel, 1986-95, v.p., 1996—; mem. nat. adv. bd. Folk Art Soc. Am., 1994—; trustee Detroit Sci. Ctr., 1985-99. 1st lt. JAG, USAF, 1952-55, maj. Res. ret Recipient Silver Beaver award Detroit Area coun. Boy Scouts Am., 1989. Mem. ABA, Detroit Bar Assn., Oakland County Bar Assn., State Bar Mich., Harvard Law Sch. Assn. Mich. (dir. 1959-78, pres. 1970-78), Detroit Sci. Mus. Soc. (pres. 1961-74, chmn. 1974-76), Am. Folk Art Soc. (pres. 2000-04), Cranbrook Writers Guild (pres. 2002-04), Prismatic Club (pres. 2002-03), Scarab Club, Harvard Club, Detroit Athletic Club, Masons, Rotary, Phi Beta Kappa, Alpha Phi Omega, Pi Sigma Alpha Republican. Unitarian. Office: Meyer Kirk Snyder & Lynch PLLC 100 W Long Lake Rd Ste 100 Bloomfield Hills MI 48304-2773 E-mail: gmeyer@meyerkirk.com.

**MEYER, HELEN M.,** state supreme court justice; BSW, U. Minn.; JD, William Mitchell Coll. Law. Ptnr. Pritzker & Meyer, 1987—96, Meyer and Assocs., 1996—2002; assoc. justice Minn. Supreme Ct., St. Paul, 2002—. Office: Minn Jud Ctr 25 Rev Dr Martin Luther King Jr Blv Saint Paul MN 55155

**MEYER, HENRY LEWIS, III,** bank executive; b. Cleve., Dec. 25, 1949; s. Henry Lewis and Anne (Taylor) M.; m. Jane Kreamer, July 15, 1978; children: Patrick Harrison, Andrew Taylor, Christopher Bicknell. BA, Colgate U., 1972, MBA, Harvard U., Boston, 1978. Asst. v.p. Soc. Nat. Bank, Cleve., 1972-76, v.p., 1978-81, sr. v.p., 1981-83; exec. v.p. Soc. Bank, Dayton, Ohio, 1983-85, pres., chief operating officer, 1985-87; sr. exec. v.p. Soc. Nat. Bank, Cleve., 1987-89, vice chmn. bd., 1989-90, pres., COO, 1990-93, pres., CEO, 1993-94, chmn. bd., CEO, 1994-95; exec. v.p. Soc. Corp., 1987-91, vice chmn. bd., 1991-94; exec. v.p. KeyCorp (formerly Soc. Corp.), 1994-95, sr. exec. v.p., COO, 1995-96, vice chmn. bd., COO, 1996-97, pres., COO, 1997—2001; pres., chmn., CEO KeyCorp, 2001. Bd. dirs. Continental Airlines, Inc., Fed. Res. Bank Cleve. Trustee Cleve. Mus. Nat. History, Ideastream (WVIZ/PBS and WCPN); with Law Enforcement Found., Northeast Ohio Coun. Higher Edn., United Way Greater Cleve., Univ. Sch.; bd. dirs. U. Hosps. Health Sys., Inc. Mem.: Club at Key Ctr., Chagrin Valley Hunt Club, Pepper Pike Club, The Union Club, Kirtland Country Club. Republican. Episcopalian.

**MEYER, HORST,** physics professor; b. Berlin, Mar. 1, 1926; BS, U. Geneva, 1949; PhD in physics, U. Zurich, 1953. Fellow Swiss Assn. Rsch. Physics and Math. Studies, Oxford, Eng., 1953-55; Nuffield fellow Clarendon Lab. U. Oxford, 1955-57; lectr., rsch. assoc. dept. engring. and applied physics Harvard U., Cambridge, Mass., 1957-59; from asst. prof. to prof. Duke U., Durham, NC, 1959-84, Fritz London prof. physics, 1984—2004, Fritz London prof. physics emeritus, 2004—. Vis. prof. Technische Hochschule, Federal Republic of Germany, 1965, Tokyo U., 1980, 81, 83; traveling fellow Japanese Soc. for Promotion Sci., 1971, vis. scientist, 1979; guest scientist Inst. Laue-Langevin, France, 1974, 75; Yamada Found. fellow, Japan, 1986; guest scientist USSR Acad. Sci., 1988; guest prof. Toyota Inst. Tech., Nagoya, Japan, Oct. 1998; chmn. Gordon Conf. on Solid H2, 1990; western chmn. conf. quantum crystals, Almaty, Kazakhstan, 1989. Editor Jour. Low Temperature Physics, 1992—, mem. editorial bd., 1988-92; contrb. articles to profl. jours. Alfred P. Sloan fellow, 1961-65. Fellow Am. Phys. Soc. (Jesse Beams prize, 1982, Fritz London prize 1993). Achievements include exptl. rsch. on the properties of liquid and solid helium, critical phenomena in fluids, solid hydrogen and deuterium, magnetic insulators, critical phenomena, convection. Office: Duke U Dept Physics PO Box 90305 Durham NC 27708-0305 Office Phone: 919-660-2520. Business E-Mail: hm@phy.duke.edu.

**MEYER, IRWIN STEPHAN,** lawyer, accountant; b. Monticello, NY, Nov. 14, 1941; s. Ralph and Janice (Cohen) M.; children: Kimberly B., Joshua A. BS, Rider Coll., 1963; JD, Cornell U., 1966. CPA NJ; bar: NY 1966. Tax mgr Lybrand Ross Bros. & Montgomery, NYC, 1966—71; mem. Ehrenkranz, Ehrenkranz & Schultz, NYC, 1971—74; prin. Irwin S. Meyer, 1974—77, 1982—97; mem. Levine, Honig, Eisenberg & Meyer, 1977—78, Eisenberg, Honig & Meyer, 1978—81, Eisenberg, Honig, Meyer & Fogler, 1981—82, Janow & Meyer, LLC., 1997—2004; prin. Irwin S. Meyer, LLC, Pearl River, NY, 2004—. With U.S. Army, 1966—71. Mem.: ABA, NY Bar Assn., Am. Assn. Atty.-CPA, NY Assn. Atty.-CPAs, NJ Assn. CPAs. Office: 1 Blue Hill Plz Ste 1006 Pearl River NY 10965-3100 Office Phone: 845-735-9400. Business E-Mail: irwin@nytaxplanner.com.

**MEYER, JACK ALLEN,** historian, consultant; b. Sugar Camp, Wis., Nov. 13, 1934; s. John Charles Meyer and Loretta Bertha Basch; m. Martha Elise Robinson, Dec. 18, 1970. BA summa cum laude, U. Md., 1973; MA, U. S.C., 1979, PhD, 1984. Enlisted USAF, 1953, advanced through grades to chief master sgt., 1975, ret., 1976; lectr. U. SC, Columbia, 1983—85, vis. asst. prof., 1985—87, sr. lectr., 1993—97; self-employed Tower Armory, Winnsboro, SC, 1993—; commd. SC State Guard, 1993, col., 2001—. Cons. SC State Mus., Columbia, 1979—; presenter in field. Author: South Carolina in the Mexican War, 1996, (monograph) William Glaze & the Palmetto Armory, 1982, 1994; editor: Annotated Bibliography-Napoleonic Era, 1987; contrb. articles to profl. jours. Chmn. Fairfield County Airport Commn., 1976—79, 2006—; bd. mem. Columbia Choral Soc., 1988—90, treas., 1991—92; chmn. Fairfield County Hist. Commn., 1987—89, mem., 1990—94; trustee Greenbrier United Meth. Ch., 1980—87, 1998—2000, 2002—04, chmn., 2005. Decorated Bronze Star, Meritorious Svc. medal, Air Force Commendation medal,; recipient Disting. Faculty award, ROTC, 1992. Fellow: Internat. Napoleonic Soc.; mem.: VFW, SC Soc. Sons of Revolution (pres. 2001—06), State Guard Assn. US, Internat. Chivalric Inst., Am. Inst. for Conservation and Preservation of Historic and Artistic Works, Orders and Medals Rsch. Soc., Orders and Medals Soc. Am. (Lit. medal 1991), Am. Numismatic Assn.,

Arms and Armour Soc., SC Arms Collectors Assn., Univ. South Caroliniana Soc., SC State Mus. Found. (treas. 1981—83, dir. 1983—88), Fairfield County Hist. Soc. (dir. 1978, pres. 1979—80, dir. 1984—87), Co. Mil. Historians, SC Hist. Soc., Soc. for Army Hist. Rsch., US Parachute Assn., Am. Legion, Soc. for Mil. History, Alpha Sigma Lambda, Phi Kappa Phi, Phi Alpha Theta. Methodist. Avocations: private pilot, skydiving, collecting antiques. Home: Aeolia 1029 Greenbrier/Mossydale Rd Winnsboro SC 29180 Personal E-mail: drjameyer@juno.com.

**MEYER, JACK EDWARD,** radiologist, educator; b. Davenport, Iowa, Oct. 21, 1939; s. Russell and Ellen Meyer; m. Mary Jean Meyer, Jan. 9, 1966; children: Heather, Hilary. BA, Grinnell (Iowa) Coll., 1961; MD, Cornell U., 1965; MS (hon.), Harvard U., 1991. Diplomate Am. Bd. Radiology; lic. physician, Mass., Calif. Mich. Intern San Francisco Gen. Hosp., 1965-66; resident in radiology U. Mich., Ann Arbor, 1968-69, Mass. Gen. Hosp., Boston, 1969-71, asst. radiation medicine, 1971-72, head oncologic diagnostic radiology, 1979-83; chief diagnostic radiology Pondville Hosp., Walpole, Mass., 1972-78, chief radiology, chief staff, 1978-79; prof., chmn. dept. radiology U. Louisville, Ky., 1985-87; acting dir. diagnostic radiology Brigham and Women's Hosp., Boston, 1987-88, dir. diagnostic radiology, 1989-99; dir. breast imaging Dana-Farber Cancer Inst., Boston, 2001—. Asst. prof. radiology Boston U., 1972-74, assoc. clin. prof., 1974-79; asst. prof. U. Mass., Boston, 1976-77, assoc. prof. radiology, 1977-79; asst. prof. radiology Harvard Med. Sch., Boston, 1979-82, assoc. prof. radiology, 1982-85, 87-91, prof. radiology, 1991—; dir. diagnostic oncoradiology Dana-Farber Cancer Inst., Boston, 1991-99; dir. breast imaging, Brigham and Womens Hosp, Boston, 1999—2002. Author: (with others) Interventional Radiology, 1981, Cancer: A Manual for Practitioners, 6th edit., 1982, Lymphatic Imaging, 2d edit., 1985; cons. to editorial bd. jours.; contrbr. numerous articles and abstracts to profl. jours. Examiner Am. Bd. Radiology, 1992—. Capt. USAF, 1966-68. Fellow: Soc. Breast Imaging, Am. Coll. Radiology; mem.: Radiol. Soc. N. Am., Mass. Radiol. Soc., Mass. Med. Soc. Office: Brigham and Womens Hosp Dept Diagnostic Radiology 75 Francis St Boston MA 02115-6106 Business E-Mail: jmeyer@partners.org.

**MEYER, JAMES E.,** broadcast executive; b. 1956; Various senior mgmt. positions General Electric, RCA; gen. mgr. high-end color TV div. Thomson-Hughes; senior v.p. product mgmt. Thomson Consumer Electronics, 1992—97, exec. v.p., COO, 1997—99, senior exec. v.p., COO, 1999—2000; senior exec. v.p. digital media solutions Thomson Multimedia, 2000—01; pres. Aegis Ventures, 2001—04; pres. operations & sls. Sirius Satellite Radio, NYC, 2004—. Mem. bd. dirs. Mikohn Gaming Corp., Escient Solutions, Equant. Home: SIRIUS Satellite Radio 1221 Ave of the Americas New York NY 10020 Office Phone: 212-584-5100.

**MEYER, JANE MARY,** elementary school educator; b. Fort Madison, Iowa, Feb. 25, 1947; d. Leo Gehard and Marie Ann Moeller; m. Jerry Allen Meyer (div.); children: Karla, Lance, Brent. AA, Ottumwa Heights Coll., Iowa, 1967; BA in Elem. Edn., Maryerest Coll., 1969; MSc in Edn., We. Ill. U., 1990. Tchr. 1st grade Davenport (Iowa) Cmty. Schs., 1969—74, substitute tchr., 1980—85, tchr. elem. sci., 1985—95, tchr. 1st grade, 1995—. Mem.: Internat. Reading Assn., Iowa Reading Assn. (merit coun. com. 2003—05), Miss. Bend Reading Assn. (bd. dirs. 1999—2003, pres. 2002—03), Davenport Edn. Assn. (sch. rep. 1998—2004). Roman Catholic. Avocations: crafts, travel, gardening. Office: Monroe Elem Sch 1926 W 4th St Davenport IA 52802 Office Phone: 563-322-3559. Personal E-mail: jmm225@msn.com.

**MEYER, JANIS M.,** lawyer; b. NYC, Apr. 29, 1947; BA, SUNY, Stony Brook, 1969; MA, Ohio State Univ., 1971; JD with distinction, Hofstra Univ., 1981. Bar: N.Y. 1982, US Dist. Ct. (ea. & so. dist. N.Y., no. dist. Ill.), US Ct. Appeals (2d, 7th, 9th cir.). Law clerk, Judge George C. Pratt, US Dist. Ct. ea. N.Y. & US Ct. Appeals, 2d cir.; ptnr. litigation & diversity affairs Dewey Ballantine LLP, N.Y.C., 1995—. Contbr. chapters to books. Bd. trustees Hofstra Univ., 1993—, vice chmn., 1996—99, 2002—. Mem.: ABA (vice chmn. Internat. Litigation com. 1993—94), Assn. Bar City of N.Y. Office: Dewey Ballantine LLP 1301 Ave of the Americas New York NY 10019-6092 Office Phone: 212-259-6030. Office Fax: 212-259-6333. Business E-Mail: jmeyer@dbllp.com.

**MEYER, JAROLD ALAN,** oil company research executive; b. Phoenix, July 28, 1938; s. Lester M. and Anita (Walker) M.; m. Diane Louise Wheeler; children: Ronald Alan, Sharon Lynne. BSChemE, Calif. Inst. Tech., 1960, MS, 1961. Mgr. process devel. Chevron Rsch., Richmond, Calif., 1978-82; tech. mgr. Chevron U.S.A., El Segundo, Calif., 1982-84; v.p. process rsch. Chevron Rsch., Richmond, 1984-86, pres., 1986—; sr. v.p. Chevron Rsch. and Tech., Richmond, 1990-93; ret., 1993; prin. J.A. Meyer Assocs., Martinez, Calif., 1993—. Bd. dirs. Gemstar-TV Guide, Solvent Refined Coal Internat., San Francisco; mem. adv. bd. Surface Sci. and Catalysis Program Ctr. for Advanced Materials, Lawrence Berkeley Lab., 1988-91; mem. adv. coun. Lawrence Hall Sci., 1989-94; indsl. advisor Accreditation bd. for Engring. and Tech. Inventor petroleum catalysts; contbr. articles to profl. jours. Bd. visitors U. Calif., Davis, 1986-93, trustee found., 1989—. Mem. Nat. Acad. Engring., Am. Chem. Soc., Nat. Petroleum Refining Assn., Indsl. Rsch. Inst., Conf. Bd. Internat. Rsch. Mgmt. Coun., Accreditation Bd. for Engring. and Tech. Indsl. Advisor, Sigma Xi, Tau Beta Pi. Avocations: electronics design and construction, photography. Home and Office: 849 Corte Briones Martinez CA 94553-5950

**MEYER, JOHN FREDERICK,** engineering educator; b. Grand Rapids, Mich., July 26, 1934; s. Frederick Albert and Harriet (Stibbs) M.; m. Nancy Shaw Briggs, July 4, 1959; children: John, Patricia, James. BS, U. Mich., 1957; MS, Stanford U., 1958; PhD, U. Mich., 1967. Data systems engr. Douglas Aircraft Corp., Santa Monica, Calif., 1957; research engr. Caltech, Jet Propulsion Lab., Pasadena, Calif., 1958-67; asst. prof. U. Mich., Ann Arbor, 1968-71, assoc. prof., 1971-76, prof. elec. engring. and computer sci., 1976—2002, dir. Computing Research Lab., 1984-89, prof. emeritus elec. engring. and computer sci., 2002—. Cons. Calif. Inst. Tech. Jet Propulsion Lab., 1979—91, Indsl. Tech. Inst., Ann Arbor, 1985-92, CIMSA, Paris, 1992, Bendix Advanced Tech. Ctr., Columbia, Md., 1977-85, Thomson CSF, Paris, 1975, Italtel, Milan, 1990—99, Applied Scis. Corp., Reading, Mass., 1993, U. Ill., 2002—. Patentee Time Division Multiplexer, 1963 (NASA Inventions award 1964). Precinct chmn. 3d ward Democratic Party, Ann Arbor, 1971-74. Recipient Disting. Service Award U. Mich., 1964, Silver Core award IFIP, 1995, Golden Core award 1996; IBM fellow, 1957 Fellow IEEE; mem. AAAS, IEEE Computer Soc. (Cert. of Appreciation 1981, 95, Meritorious Svc. award 1985). Home: 1946 Ridge Ave Ann Arbor MI 48104-6306 Office: U Mich 3636 CSE Bldg Ann Arbor MI 48109-2121 Business E-Mail: jfm@eecs.umich.edu.

**MEYER, JOHN ROBERT,** economist, educator; b. Pasco, Wash., Dec. 6, 1927; s. Philip Conrad and Cora (Kempter) M.; m. Lee Stowell, Dec. 17, 1949 (dec.); children: Leslie Karen, Ann Elizabeth, Robert Conrad. Student, Pacific U., 1945-46; BA, U. Wash., 1950; PhD (David A. Wells prize), Harvard U., 1955. Jr. fellow Harvard U., 1953-55, asst. prof., 1955-58, assoc. prof., 1958-59, prof. econs., 1959-68, 1907 Found., prof. transp. and logistics, 1973-83; prof. Yale U., 1968-73; Harpel prof. capital formation and econ. growth Harvard U., 1983-96, prof. emeritus, 1997—. Vice chmn. Union Pacific Corp., 1982-83, dir., 1978-99; trustee Pacific U. Author (with Edwin Kuh): The Investment Decision-An Empirical Inquiry, 1957; author: (with others) Competition in the Transportation Industry, 1959, The Urban Transportation Problem, 1965, Techniques of Transport Planning, 1970, Economics of Competition in the Telecommunications Industry, 1980, Autos, Transit and Cities, 1981, Deregulation and the Future of Intercity Passenger Travel, 1987, Going Private: The International Experience with 'Transport Privatization, 1993, Moving to Market: Restructuring Transport in the Former Soviet Union, 1996, Chile: Political Economy of Urban Development, 2002, other books; contrb. articles. Mem. Presdl. Task Forces on Transp., 1964, 80, Presdl. Comm. on Population Growth and Am. Future, 1970-72; pres. Nat. Bur. Econ. Research, 1967-77. Served with USNR, 1946-48. Recipient Roy W. Crum award, transp. rsch. bd. Nat. Acad. Scis. and Nat. Acad. Engring.,

2002; Guggenheim fellow, 1958. Fellow: Econometric Soc., Am. Acad. Arts and Scis.; mem.: Econ. History Assn., Coun. Fgn. Rels., Am. Econ. Assn. (mem. exec. com. 1971—73). Home: 572 Kinzie Island Ct Sanibel FL 33957-5021 Office: Harvard U Jt Ctr Housing Studies 1033 Massachussetts Ave 5th Fl Cambridge MA 02138-5801 Personal E-mail: jrobtmeyer@aol.com.

**MEYER, JON KEITH,** psychiatrist, psychoanalyst, educator; b. Springfield, Ill., May 6, 1938; m. Eleanor Fumie Yamashita, June 6, 1964; children: David Christopher, Laura Tamiko. AB summa cum laude, Dartmouth Coll., 1960; MD, Johns Hopkins U., 1964; grad., Washington Psychoanalytic Inst, 1980. Intern internal medicine Johns Hopkins Hosp., Balt., 1964-65, resident in psychiatry, 1965-67, 69, St. Elizabeth's Hosp., Washington, 1968; spl. asst. to dir. NIMH, Bethesda, Md., 1969-71; asst. prof. psychiatry Johns Hopkins Med. Sch., Balt., 1971-76, assoc. prof., 1976-83; prof. psychiatry Med. Coll. Wis., Milw., 1983—2003, prof. psychoanalysis, 1996—2003, prof. family medicine, 1990—2003, prof. psychiatry and psychoanalysis emeritus, 2003—; tng. and supervising analyst Chgo. Inst. for Psychoanalysis, 1987—2002; vice chmn. Dept. of Psychiatry, 1993—2003; chief psychiatry Froedtert Meml. Luth. Hosp., Milw., 1994-97; tng. and supervising analyst Wis. Psychoanlytic Inst., Milw., 2001—, Washington Psychoanalytic Inst., 2004—; tchg. analyst Balt.-Washington Psychoanalytic Inst., 2004—; clin. prof. pschiatry Georgetown U. Sch. Medicine, 2006—. Med. dir. Wis. Psychoanalytic Found., Milw., 1987-91, sec. bd. dirs., 1988-91. Author books; editl. bd. Jour. Am. Psychoanalytic Assn., 1991-94; nat. editor: The American Psychoanalyst, 1997-2001; mem. steering com. Psychodynamic Diagnostic Manual; contbr. chpts. to books, numerous articles to profl. jours. Comdr. USPHS, 1967—71. Recipient Dennison Rsch. prize, Johns Hopkins Med. Sch., 1964; Sr. fellow, Dartmouth Coll., 1959—60, Daniel Webster Nat. scholar, 1956—60, Rufus Choate scholar, 1960, Erik Erikson scholar, Austen Riggs Ctr., Stockbridge, Mass., 1991—92, Ctr. Advanced Psychoanalytic Studies, Princeton, NJ, 1998—. Fellow: Am. Coll. Psychoanalysts, Am. Coll. Psychiatrists, Am. Psychiat. Assn.; mem.: Psychodynamic Diagnostic Manual (steering com. 2006—, exec. councilor 2006—), Wash. Psychoanalytic Soc., Balt.-Wash. Psychoanalytic Soc., Can. Psychoanalytic Soc. (hon.), William Alason White Psychoanalytic Soc. (hon.), Wis. Psychoanalytic Soc. (pres. 1989—91), Assn. Child Psychoanalysis (candidate councilor 2001—03), Am. Psychoanalytic Assn. (exec. councilor 1993—97, chmn. com. on exec. coun. structure and function 1995—98, sec. 1997—2001, chmn. com. on cmty. clinics 1997—2002, exec. com. 1997—2002, adminstrv. bd. Jour. Am. Psychoanalytic Assn. 1997—2002, com. on insts 1998—2002, com. on bylaws 2001—02, pres.-elect 2002—04, adminstrv. bd. Jour. Am. Psychoanalytic Assn. 2002—06, exec. com. 2002—06, pres. 2004—06, presiding officer exec. coun. 2004—06, chmn. steering com. 2004—06, exec. councilor 2006—, exploratory subcom. nominating com. 2006—, chmn. exec. com., Edith Sabshin Tchg. award 1999), Internat. Psychoanalytical Assn. (com. on constn. and by-laws 1997—2001, com. on procedural codes 1997—2001, task force on structure and mission 1997—2001, ho. dels. 1998—2001, chair ho. of dels. 1999—2000). Avocations: photography, hiking, kayaking. Office: 2210 Dalewood Rd Lutherville Timonium MD 21093

**MEYER, JOSEPH B.,** state official; b. Casper, Wyo., 1941; m. Mary Orr; children: Vincent, Warren. Student, Colo. Sch. Mines; BA, U. Wyo., 1964, JD, 1967; postgrad., Northwestern U., 1968. Dep. county atty. Fremont County, Wyo., 1967-69; assoc. Smith and Meyer, 1968-71; asst. dir. legis. svc. office State of Wyo., Cheyenne, 1971-87, atty. gen., 1987-95; sec. of state, 1999—; spl. asst. to pres. U. Wyo., Laramie, 1995-98. Condr. numerous govt. studies on state codes including Wyo. probate, criminal, state adminstrn., banking, domestic rels.; negotiator with Office of Surface Mining for Wyo. state preemption; instr. Wyo. Coll. Law, fall, 1986; lectr. Rocky Mountain Mineral Law Found., 1977; chmn. Conf. Western Atty. Gen., 1992—93; mem. exec. com. Nat. Assn. Attys. Gen.; mem. Bush-Cheney Transition Team, 2000—01. Chmn. Cheyenne Bd. of Health, 1999—; bd. dirs. Longs Peak coun. Boy Scouts Am.; dir., chmn. Frontier CDC. Mem. Rotary. Republican. Congregationalist. Avocations: golf, tennis, gardening, wood carving, rock hunting. Office: Office Sec of State State Capital Bldg Cheyenne WY 82002-0001 Office Phone: 307-777-5333. Office Fax: 307-777-6217. Business E-Mail: jmeyer3@state.wy.us.

**MEYER, KARL ERNEST,** journalist; b. Madison, Wis., May 22, 1928; s. Ernest Louis and Dorothy (Narefsky) M.; m. Sarah Nielsen Peck, Aug. 12, 1959 (div. 1972); children: Ernest, Heather, Jonathan; m. Shareen Blair Brysac, Jan. 6, 1989. BA, U. Wis. 1951; MPA, Princeton U., NJ, 1953, PhD, 1956. Reporter N.Y. Times, N.Y.C., 1952, mem. editl. bd., 1979-98; editl. writer Washington Post, 1956-65, chief London Bur., 1965-70, N.Y.C. corr., 1970-71; Washington corr. New Statesman, 1961-65; sr. editor, TV critic Saturday Rev., N.Y.C., 1975-79; corr. in residence Fletcher Sch. Law and Diplomacy, Tufts U., 1979; editor World Policy Jour., N.Y.C., 2000—. Vis. journalist fellow Duke U., Durham, NC, 1988; vis. prof. Yale U., New Haven, 1983, New Haven, 90; McGraw prof. in writing Princeton U., 1993—94; vis. prof. Bard Coll., NY, 2002. Author: The New America, 1961, (with Tad Szulc) The Cuban Invasion, 1962, Fulbright of Arkansas, 1963, The Pleasures of Archaeology, 1971, The Plundered Past, 1973, Teotihuacán, 1975, The Art Museum: Power, Money, Ethics, 1979, Pundits, Poets and Wits: An Omnibus of American Newspaper Columns, 1990, (with Shareen Brysac) Tournament of Shadows: The Great Game and Race for Empire in Central Asia, 1999, The Dust of Empire, 2003. Recipient citation for excellence Overseas Press Club, 1961, Bronze medal for editl. writing Sigma Delta; George Foster Peabody Broadcasting award 1983, Disting. Achievement award Sch. Journalism, U. Wis., 1985; Davenport Coll. of Yale U. fellow; Wisenschaftskolleg Inst. Adv. Studies (Berlin) fellow, 1994-95, Reuter fellow Oxford (Eng.) U., 1996-97. Mem. PEN Club Internat., Coun. on Fgn. Rels., NYU Soc. Fellows, Century Assn., Authors League Am Home: 50 W 96th St New York NY 10025-6526 Office: World Policy Jour 66 5 Th Ave Ste 900 New York NY 10011 Office Phone: 212-229-5808 ext. 4258. Personal E-mail: karlmeyer@att.net. Business E-Mail: meyerk@newschool.edu.

**MEYER, KARL WILLIAM,** retired university president; b. Ft. Wayne, Ind., May 8, 1925; s. K.W. and L. (Hofacker) M.; m. Margery R. Hamman, Apr. 15, 1950; children— Mary, William, Frederick, Ann, Jean. AB, Valparaiso U., 1948; M.F.S., U. Md., 1949; PhD, U. Wis., 1953; postgrad., U. Basel, Switzerland, 1948-49; postdoctoral fellow, U. Mich., 1958-59. Faculty Valparaiso U., 1952-53, Augustana Coll., 1953-55, Wis. State U., 1955-58; dean instrn., dir. grad. studies Wayne State Coll., 1959-63; asst. dir. bd. regents Wis. State Colls., Madison, 1963-64; pres. U. Wis.-Superior, 1964-87. Author: Karl Liebknecht: Man Without a Country, 1957; Contbr. articles to profl. jours. Served with USAAF, 1943-46, ETO. Home: W7861 Homestead Ct Holmen WI 54636-9440 E-mail: meyk25@aol.com

**MEYER, KATHERINE ANNE,** lawyer; BA, Manhattanville Coll., 1973; JD, Columbus Sch. Law, Cath. U. Am., 1976. Bar: DC, Md. With Swankin & Turner, 1976—77, Ctr. for Auto Safety, 1977—79, Pub. Citizen Litigation Group, 1979—89, Harmon, Curran, Gallagher & Spielberg, 1989—93; ptnr. Meyer Glitzenstein & Crystal, Washington, 1993—. Chmn. litigation com. Defenders of Wildlife; adj. prof. law Georgetown U. Law Ctr. (Civil Litigation and Pub. Interest Advocacy), 1986—92; bd. dir. Defenders of Wildlife, Ctr. for Auto Safety, Wildlife Advocacy Project; with DC Cir. Advisory Com. Procedures, 1995—2001; bd. dirs. Ctr. Biol. Diversity. Named one of Best 75 Lawyers in Washington, Washingtonian Mag., 2002. Office: Mayer Glitzenstein & Crystal 1601 Connecticut Ave NW Ste 700 Washington DC 20009-1056 Office Phone: 202-588-5206. Office Fax: 202-588-5049.

**MEYER, LAWRENCE GEORGE,** lawyer; b. East Grand Rapids, Mich., Oct. 2, 1940; s. George and Evangeline (Boerma) M.; children from previous marriage: David Lawrence, Jenifer Lynne; m. Linda Elizabeth Buck, May 31, 1980; children: Elizabeth Tilden, Travis Henley. BA with honors, Mich. State U., 1961; JD with distinction, U. Mich., 1964. Bar: Wis., 1965, Ill. 1965, U.S. Supreme Ct. 1968, D.C. 1972. Assoc. Whyte, Hirschboeck, Minahan, Hardin & Harland, Milw., 1964-66; atty. antitrust div. U.S. Dept. Justice, Washington,

1966-68; legal counsel U.S. Senator Robert P. Griffin, Mich., 1968-70; dir. policy planning FTC, 1970-72; ptnr. Patton, Boggs & Blow, Washington, 1972-85, Arent, Fox, Kintner, Plotkin & Kahn, Washington, 1985-96, Gadsby & Hannah, 1996-2001; pvt. practice Washington, 2001—. Contbr. articles to profl. jours.; asst. editor U. Mich. Law Rev., 1960-61. Bd. dirs. Hockey Hall of Fame, Toronto, 1993-99, Woodrow Wilson House, 1997—. Recipient Disting. Svc. award FTC, 1972. Mem. ABA, D.C. Bar Assn., Wis. Bar Assn. Ill. Bar Assn., US Senate Ex S.O.B.s Club, City Tavern Club, Congl. Country Club Home: 8777 Belmart Rd Potomac MD 20854-1610 Office Phone: 202-661-3910. E-mail: larry@lawlgm.com.

**MEYER, LINDSAY BEARDSWORTH,** lawyer; b. Bridgeport, Conn., Apr. 11, 1961; Student, Universite de Rouen, France, 1982; BS cum laude, Univ. Conn., 1983; JD, George Washington Univ., 1987. Bar: Va. 1987, DC 1988; lic. US Customs Svc. Broker. Assoc. Venable, Baetjer, Howard & Civiletti LLP (now Venable LLP), Washington; ptnr., adv., mktg., new media, homeland security practice areas Venable LLP, Washington, and head, internat. trade practice group. Mem. Md.-Washington Dist. Export Coun. Mem.: ABA (chair, internat. trade and customs com.), DC Bar Assn., Va. Bar Assn., Am. Assn. Exporters and Importers, Beta Gamma Sigma. Office: Venable LLP 575 Seventh St NW Washington DC 20004 Office Phone: 202-344-4829. Office Fax: 202-344-8300. Business E-mail: lbmeyer@venable.com.

**MEYER, MARGARET ELEANOR,** retired microbiologist; b. Westwood, Calif., Feb. 8, 1923; d. Herman Henry and Eleanor (Dobson) M. BS, U. Calif., Berkeley, 1945; PhD, U. Calif., Davis, 1961. Pub. health analyst USPHS, Bethesda, Md., 1945-46; swine Brucellosis control agt. Dept. Agr., Davis, 1946-47; bacteriologist U. Calif., Davis, 1947-61; research microbiologist U. Calif. (Sch Vet Medicine), 1961-77, prof. vet. pub. health and microbiologist exptl. sta., 1977—; rsch. microbiologist U. Calif. Med. Sch., L.A., 1961-77; supr. Brucella identifications lab. WHO, U. Calif., Davis, 1964—87, prof. vet. pub. health, 1973—87, dir. program in preventive vet. medicine, 1987; ret., 1987. Cons. subcom. on Brucella Internat. Com. Bacterial Taxonomy, 1962—, mem., 1966—; mem. 5th Pan Am. Congress Veterinary Medicine, Venezuela, 1966; mem. Internat. Congress Microbiology, Moscow, 1966, Mexico City, 1970, Munich, Ger., 1978, mem., officer, Eng., 1986; mem. Internat. Conf. Culture Collections, Tokyo, 1968; mem. adv. com. to Bergey's Manual Determative Bacteriology, 1967; cons. in resident Pan Am. Health Orgn., Zoonoses Lab., Buenos Aires, 1968; mem. brucellosis tech. adv. com. U.S. Animal Health Assn., 1977; FAO cons. on brucellosis control in dairy animals, Tripoli, Libya, 1981, mem. 3d internat. brucellosis symposium, Algiers, 1981; cons. Alaska Dept. Fish and Game, 1976, FAO, Libya, 1981; Bering Straits Reindeer Herders Assn., Nome, Alaska, 1981; invited speaker Internat. Symposium on Advances in Brucellosis Rsch., Tex. A&M U., 1989, Internat. Bison Conf.; resident cons. on brucellosis control in sheep and goats Am. Near East Refugee Aid, East Jerusalem, 1989; cons. on brucellosis in Yellowstone Nat. Pk., Nat. Pk. Svc., 1991—; invited mem. nat. symposium on brucellosis in the Greater Yellowstone Area, Jackson Hole, Wyo., 1994; cons. on brucellosis control in livestock for Armenia, 1994—. Contbr. articles to profl. jours. Bd. dirs. Carmichael Park and Recreation Dist., Calif., 1975; mem. Sacramento County Grand Jury, 1999-2000. Recipient Research Career Devel. award USPHS-NIH, 1963 Fellow Am. Pub. Health Assn., Am. Acad. Microbiology; mem. Soc. Am. Microbiologists, N.Am. Conf. Animal Disease Research Workers, Am. Coll. Vet. Microbiologists (hon. affiliate), U.S. Animal Health Assn. (chmn. brucellosis tech. advisory com. 1978-79), Internat. Assn. Microbiol. Socs. (mem. 1st intersect. congress 1974), AAUW, No. Calif. Women's Golf Assn., U. Calif. Alumni Assn., Sigma Xi. Clubs: U. Calif. Faculty (Davis); El Dorado Royal Country (Shingle Springs, Calif.); Reno Women's Golf. Home: 5611 Fair Oaks Blvd Carmichael CA 95608-5503 Office: U Calif Sch Vet Medicine Dept Epidemiology & Preventive Medicine Davis CA 95616

**MEYER, MARSHALL WARNER,** sociology educator, finance educator; b. Washington, June 24, 1942; s. Richard Sol and Mildred (Warner) M.; m. Judith Pinsof, Mar. 20, 1966; children: Joshua Micah, Gabriel Sol. BA, Columbia U., 1964; MA, U. Chgo., 1965, PhD, 1967; MA, U. Pa., 1987. Instr., lectr. Harvard U., Cambridge, Mass., 1967-69; asst. prof. Cornell U. Ithaca, N.Y., 1969-73; assoc. prof. U. Calif., Riverside, 1973-75, prof. sociology, 1975-87; vis. prof. UCLA, 1985-86; vis. prof. mgmt. Yale U. Sch. Mgmt., New Haven, 1986-87; prof. mgmt. and sociology Wharton Sch., U. Pa., Phila., 1988—, Richard A. Sapp prof., 2002—. Vis. scholar Russell Sage Found., N.Y.C., 1993-94; vis. prof. mgmt. Hong Kong U. Sci. and Tech., 1996, Tsinghua U., 1999, Chinese U., Hong Kong, 2001. Author: Bureaucracy in Modern Society, 1972, 87, Permanently Failing Organizations, 1989, Rethinking Performance Measurement, 2002; assoc. editor Adminstrv. Sci. Quar., 1987—. Cons. L.A. Police Commn., 1979-80; dir. Chamber Orch. Phila., 2000-; chief exec. Leadership Inst., 1996—. Mem. Acad. of Mgmt., Am. Sociol. Assn. Avocations: computers, music, bicycling, skiing. Office: U Pa Wharton Sch Dept Mgmt Philadelphia PA 19104

**MEYER, MARTIN JAY,** lawyer; b. Wilkes-Barre, Pa., Aug. 1, 1932; s. Max and Rose (Wruble) M.; m. Joan Rosenthal, Aug. 24, 1954; children: Leah, Gary. BA, Wilkes Coll., 1954; postgrad., U. Miami, 1956—57; LLB, Temple U., 1959. Bar: Pa. 1960, U.S. Dist. Ct. (mid. dist.) Pa. 1961, U.S. Ct. Appeals (3d cir.) 1966, U.S. Supreme Ct. 1978. Assoc. Mack, Kasper & Meyer, Wilkes-Barre, 1961-66; ptnr. Mack & Meyer, Wilkes-Barre, 1966—80; sr. ptnr. Meyer & Swatkoski, Kingston, Pa., 1980—. Chmn. disciplinary hearing com. Pa. Supreme Ct.; apptd. spl. trial master State Ct., 1995; apptd. cert. mediator U.S. Dist. Ct. (mid. dist.) Pa., 2000. Legal columnist to local newspapers, creator (TV program) Call The Lawyer, (weekly columns) You Be the Lawyer, You Be the Jury. Chmn. Muscular Dystrophy Assn., 1960; co-chmn. March of Dimes, 1962; trustee Temple Israel Wilkes-Barre; bd. dirs. Jewish Home Scranton, Family Svc. Assn.; arbitrator U.S. Arbitration and Mediation of N.E., Inc., Am. Arbitration Assn. Million Dollar Advocates Forum. With U.S. Army, 1955-56. Fellow Pa. Bar Found.; mem. DAV, ATLA, Am. Arbitration Assn., Am. Bd. Trial Advocates, Pa. Soc., Pa. Bar Assn. (former co-chmn., adoption com. family law sect., alt. dispute resolution com.), Nat. Conf. Bar Pres.'s, Pa. Trial Lawyers Assn. (lectr.), Luzerne County Bar Assn. (pres. 1984-85, chmn. Ct. Rules Com. 1994-2000), N.E. Pa. Trial Lawyers Assn., Elks (trustee), Masons (32 degree), B'nai Brith (pres. 1967), Tau Epsilon Rho. Office: 405 3rd Ave Kingston PA 18704-5802 Office Phone: 570-288-8482. Office Fax: 570-288-1003. E-mail: mmeyer@meyerswatlaw.com.

**MEYER, MAX EARL,** lawyer; b. Hampton, Va., Oct. 31, 1918; s. Earl Luther and Winifred Katherine (Spacht) M.; m. Betty Maxwell Dodds, Sept. 22, 1945; children: Scott Maxwell, Ann Culliford. AB, U. Nebr., 1940, JD, 1942. Bar: Nebr. 1942, Ill. 1946. Assoc. firm Lord, Bissell & Brook, Chgo., 1945-53, ptnr., 1953-85; chmn. Chgo. Fed. Tax Forum, 1965, U. Chgo. Ann. Fed. Tax Conf., 1972; mem. Adv. Group to Commr. of IRS, 1967. Lectr. in field. Bd. dirs. Music Acad. of the West, chmn., 1993—94. Mem.: ABA (coun. tax sect. 1969—72), Am. Coll. Tax Counsel, Chgo. Bar Assn. (chmn. taxation com. 1959—61), Nebr. Bar Assn., Ill. Bar Assn. (coun. tax sect. 1973—76), Birnam Wood Golf Club, Valley Club of Montecito, Law Club (Chgo.), Legal Club, Masons. Republican. Presbyterian.

**MEYER, MICHAEL EDWIN,** lawyer; b. Chgo., Oct. 23, 1942; s. Leon S. and Janet (Gorden) M.; m. Catherine Dieffenbach, Nov. 21, 1982; children: Linda, Mollie, Patrick, Kellie. BS, U. Wis., 1964; JD, U. Chgo., 1967. Bar: Calif. 1968, U.S. Supreme Ct. 1973. Assoc. Lillick & McHose, LA, 1967-73, ptnr., 1974-90, mng. ptnr., 1986-87; ptnr. Pillsbury Madison Sutro, 1990—, mem. mgmt. com. 1990-92; mng. ptnr Pillsbury Winthrop, LA, 1999—2003, Piper Rudnick LLP (now DLA Piper Rudnick Gray Cary), 2004—. Judge pro tem Beverly Hills Mcpl. Ct., Calif., 1976-79, Los Angeles Mcpl. Ct., 1980-86; lectr. in field. Bd. dirs. Bldg. Owners and Mgrs. Assn. Greater L.A., L.A. coun. Boy Scouts Am., L.A. Sports and Entertainment Commn., L.A. Econ. Devel. Corp.; pub. counsel United Way Greater L.A., Los Angeles County Bar Found., trustee, 1997—; Reviving Baseball in Inner Cities; mem. L.A. County Sheriff Youth Found., Jackie Robinson Found. Recipient Good

Scout award L.A. Coun. Boy Scouts Am., 1992, Man of Yr. award United Way, 1996, Real Estate Profl. of Yr. award NACORE. 2002, Reviving Baseball in Inner-Cities CB award Major League Baseball, 2005, Spirit L.A. award L.A. Hdqs. Assn., 2005, Outstanding Cmty. Svc. award Weingart Ctr., 2006; named to Top Ten So. Calif. Super Lawyers LA Mag., 2006, Top Five Calif. Real Estate Lawyers Chambers USA, 2005. Mem. ABA, Am. Arbitration Assn. (arbitrator), Calif. Bar Assn., Los Angeles County Bar Assn. (trustee 1997—), L.A. Bar Assn., Am. Coll. of Real Estate Lawyers, U. Chgo. Alumni Assn. So. Calif. (pres. 1980-82), Calif. Club U. U.A. Club (dir. 1979-85, pres. 1984-85), L.A. Country Club. Jewish. Office: DLA Piper Rudnick Gray Cary Ste 2300 550 S Hope St Los Angeles CA 90071 Office Phone: 213-330-7777. Office Fax: 213-330-7577. Business E-Mail: michael.meyer@dlapiper.com.

**MEYER, MILTON EDWARD, JR.,** retired lawyer, artist; b. St. Louis, Nov. 26, 1922; s. Milton Edward and Jessie Marie (Hurley) M.; m. Mary C. Kramer, Nov. 5, 1949 (dec. Dec. 1999); children: Milton E. III, Melanie M. Meyer Francis, Daniel K., Gregory N.; m. Mildred R. Emrick, Nov. 18, 2003. BS in Bus. Adminstrn, Washington U., 1943; LL.B., St. Louis, U., 1950; LL.M., N.Y. U., 1953. Bar: Mo. 1950, Colo. 1956. Trust adminstr. Mississippi Valley Trust Co., St. Louis, 1946-50; asso. firm Burnett, Stern & Liberman, St. Louis, 1953-56; founding partner firm Hindry & Meyer, Denver, 1956-79, chmn. bd., 1970-79; spl. counsel Schmidt, Elrod & Wills, and predecessors, 1979-83, pres., 1980-82; sec. C.A. Norgren Co., Littleton, Colo., 1960-78, dir., 1971-78; ret. Contbr. articles to profl. jours. Chmn. Denver Rotary's Artists of Am. Exhbn., 1990—92; bd. dirs. Nat. Club Assn., 1971—91, pres., 1976—78; bd. dirs. Denver Cmty. Concert Assn., 1960—64, Sewall Rehab. Ctr., Denver, 1965—68, Carl A. Norgren Found. 1960—70; Denver Lead ership Found., 1983—93, Found. Colo. Women's Coll., 1982—86, chmn., bd. dirs., 1984—86; bd. dirs. Conf. Pvt. Orgns., 1982—89, chmn., bd. dirs., 1984—88. Officer, U.S. Airborne Infantry U.S. Army, 1943—46, World War II, officer, U.S. Airborne Infantry U.S. Army, 1950—52, Korean War. Recipient Wisdom Soc. award of honor. Mem.: ABA, Colo. Bar Assn., Denver Bar Assn., Greater Denver Tax Counsels Assn. (founder, chmn. 1957), Denver Estate Planning Coun. (founder, pres. 1958), Am. Coll. Probate Counsel, Knickerbocker Artists, Pastel Soc. Am., Pastel Soc. West Coast (disting. pastellist award), Internat. Am. Pastel Socs (founder, dir. 1994—2003), Salmagundi Club, Pinehurst Country Clu (pres. 1979—80, dir. 1960—97), Hundred Club Denver, Denver Execs. Club, Cherry Hills Country Club, Rotary (bd. dirs. 1991—93), Phi Eta Sigma, Beta Gamma Sigma, Omicron Delta Kappa, Beta Theta Pi. Republican. Roman Catholic. Home: 7123 W Belmont Dr Littleton CO 80123 E-mail: miltonmeyer@comcast.net.

**MEYER, PAUL,** information technology executive; Studied politics, philosophy and econs., Oxford U.; grad., Pomona Coll.; JD, Yale U. Rschr. & speechwriter for Pres. Clinton The White House, 1993—95; CEO Endeavor Initiative; with Internat. Rescue Com.; sr. fellow Markle Found.; founder, chmn. IPKO, Kosovo, 1999; co-founder, pres. & CEO Voxiva, Washington, DC, 2001—. Named one of the world's 100 Top Young Innovators, MIT Tech. Review, 100 Global Leaders for Tomorrow, World Econ. Forum; recipient Tech. in Service of Humanity Award, MIT Tech. Review. Fellow: Foreign Policy Assn. Office: Voxiva 1725 K St NW Ste 900 Washington DC 20006-1415

**MEYER, PEARL,** compensation executive consultant; b. NYC; d. Allen Charles and Rose Weissman; m. Ira A. Meyer. BA cum laude, NYU, postgrad. Statis. specialist, exec. comp. div. Gen. Foods Corp., White Plains, NY; exec. v.p. and cons. Handy Assocs., Inc., N.Y.C., NY; founder, chair Pearl Meyer & Ptnrs., N.Y.C., NY, 1989—. Lectr. exec. compensation confs. and seminars. Contbr. articles to profl. jours. Recipient Woman of Achievement award, Women Bus. Owners NY, Legal Momentum Aiming High award, 2003. Mem.: Pers. Accreditation Inst., Women's Econ. Roundtable, Soc. Human Resources Mgmt. (cert. accredited pers. diplomate), WorldatWork, Am. Mgmt. Assn., Women's Forum, Sky Club, Sedgewood Club, Phi Beta Kappa, Beta Gamma Sigma, Pi Mu Epsilon. Office: Pearl Meyer & Ptnrs 445 Park Ave New York NY 10022-2606

**MEYER, PHILIP EDWARD,** journalism educator; b. Deshler, Nebr., Oct. 27, 1930; s. Elmer Edward and Hilda Grace (Morrison) M.; m. Sue Quail, Aug. 5, 1956; children: Caroline, Katherine, Melissa, Sarah. BS, Kans. State U., 1952; MA, U.N.C., 1963. Asst. state editor Topeka (Kans.) Daily Capital, 1954-56; reporter Miami (Fla.) Herald, 1958-62; Washington corr. Akron Beacon Jour., 1962-66; nat. corr. Knight-Ridder, Inc., Washington, 1967-78, dir. news research Miami, 1978-81; William Rand Kenan Jr. prof. journalism U. N.C., Chapel Hill, 1981-93; Knight prof., 1993—. Author: Precision Journalism, 1973 (Sigma Delta Chi Disting. Service award 1974), The Newspaper Survival Book, 1985, Ethical Journalism, 1987, The New Precision Journalism, 1991, The Vanishing Newspaper, 2004; co-author: To Keep the Republic, 1975; co-editor: Evaluating Public Journalism, 1998. Project dir. Russell Sage Found., N.Y.C., 1969-70. Served with USNR, 1952-54. Recipient Disting. Contbns. to Journalism award Nat. Press Found., 1994, Disting. Contbns. to Media and Media Studies award Freedom Forum Media Studies Ctr., 1995, award of merit Newspaper Assn. Am. Rsch. Fedn., 1996; Nieman fellow Harvard U., 1966-67, fellow Freedom Forum Ctr. for Media Studies, 1985. Fellow Soc. Prof. Journalists, mem. Am. Assn. for Pub. Opinion Rsch. (pres. 1989-90, award exceptionally disting. achievement 2000), World Assn. for Pub. Opinion Rsch. (pres. 1994-95), Assn. for Edn. in Journalism and Mass Comm. (mem. USA Today bd. contbrs. 1998—), Nat. Press Club (Washington). Democrat. Episcopalian. Avocation: photography. Home: 610 Croom Ct Chapel Hill NC 27514-6706 Office: UNC Sch Journalism & Mass Comm Carroll Hall Cb3365 Chapel Hill NC 27599-3365 Office Phone: 919-962-4085. Business E-Mail: philip_meyer@unc.edu.

**MEYER, PHILIP GILBERT,** lawyer; b. Louisville, June 26, 1945; s. Henry Gilbert and Adele (Gutermuth) M.; m. Jackie Darlene Watson, Jan. 30, 1971 (div. Apr. 1976); m. Sylvia Saunders, Oct. 9, 1976. BBA, U. Mich., Ann Arbor, 1967; JD, U. Tex., Austin, 1970. Bar: Tex. 1970, Mich. 1971, U.S. Tax Ct. 1972, U.S. Dist. Ct. (ea. dist.) Mich. 1971, U.S. Ct. Appeals (6th cir.), 1972, U.S. Dist. Ct. (no. dist.) Ohio 1976, U.S. Dist. Ct. (we. dist.) Mich. 1993, U.S. Dist. Ct. (no. dist.) Ill. 1998. Law clk. Wayne County Cir. Ct., Detroit, 1970-72; atty. Leonard C. Jaques, Detroit, 1972; assoc. Christy & Robbins, Dearborn, Mich., 1972-73; ptnr. Foster, Meadows & Ballard, Detroit, 1973-79; of counsel Christy, Rogers & Gantz, Dearborn, 1979-81, Rogers & Gantz, Dearborn, 1981-86; prin. Philip G. Meyer and Assocs., Farmington Hills, 1986—. Adj. prof. U. Detroit Sch. Law, 1979. Mem. ABA (com. vice chmn. rules and procedure 1982-88), Maritime Law Assn. U.S., Mich. Bar Assn. (vice chmn. admiralty sect. 1978), Tex. Bar Assn., Detroit Bar Assn. (vice chmn. admiralty com. 1991-93, chmn. admiralty sect. 1993-95), Propeller-Port of Detroit (dir. 1984-85). Republican. Home: 5905 Independence Ln West Bloomfield MI 48322-1854 Office: Ste 113 30300 Northwestern Hwy Farmington Hills MI 48334-3212 Office Phone: 248-737-0700. Business E-Mail: pgm@meylaw.com.

**MEYER, PIOTR JAN,** electronics engineer; b. Szczecin, Poland, May 31, 1969; arrived in US, 2000; s. Zygmunt and Maria Meyer. MS in Electronics Engring., Tech. U. Szczecin, 1992. Devel. engr. mechatronic sys. Philips Applied Technologies, Eindhoven, Netherlands, 1994—2000, sr. specialist mechatronic sys. Lynnfield, Mass., 2000—. Guest lectr. series MIT, Cambridge, Mass., 2006. Contbr. scientific papers. Mem.: IEEE, Lynnfield Am. chpt. 2006—), Netherlands-Am. Bus. Group New Eng., Math. Assn. Am., German Scholars Boston (bd. dirs. 2003—06). Achievements include patents for fast and accurate motion of industrial robots; research in mathematical modelling, analysis, simulation and optimization of industrial robot motion for nanometer-level accuracy; development of mathematical modelling, analysis, simulation and optimization of commercial LED-based light sources. Avocations: history, philosophy, fine arts, classical music, mountain climbing. Home and Office: Philips Applied Technologies 20 Lakeview Avenue Lynnfield MA 01940-1920 Office Phone: 617-852-2403. Business E-Mail: p.j.meyer@philips.com.

**MEYER, PRISCILLA ANN,** literature and language professor; b. Aug. 26, 1942; d. Herbert Edward and Marjorie Rose (Wolff) M.; m. William L. Trousdale, Sept. 15, 1974; 1 dau., Rachel V. BA, U. Calif., Berkeley, 1964; MA, Princeton U., 1966; PhD, 1971. Lectr. in Russian lang. and lit. Wesleyan U., Middletown, Conn., 1968-71, asst. prof., 1971-75, assoc. prof., 1975-88, prof., 1988—. Vis. asst. prof. Yale U., 1973, adv. coun. dept Slavic lang. and lit. Princeton U., 1998-2002. Co-editor: Dostoevsky and Gogol, 1979; editor: Life in Windy Weather (by Andrei Bitov), 1986, author: Find What the Sailor Has Hidden: Vladimir Nabokov's Pale Fire, 1988; co-editor: Essays on Gogol: Logos and the Russian Word, 1992, Nabokov's World, 2001, Yuz! Essays on the Occasion of the 75th Birthday of Yuz Aleshkovsky, 2005; translator stories; mem. editl. bd. Slavic and East European Jour., 1999—; contbr. articles to profl. jours. Scholar Internat. Rsch. and Exch. Bd., 1973; grantee Ford Found., 1964-68, 70; hon. vis. fellow Sch. Slavonic and East European Studies London U., 1997, 2001. Mem. Am. Coun. Tchrs. Russian (dir. 1983-86), Am. Assn. Tchrs. Slavic and East European Studies, Internat. Vladimir Nabokov Soc. (v.p. 1983-85, 2002-04, pres. 1985-87, 2004-06), Tolstoi Soc., Dostoevsky Soc., Conn. Acad. Arts and Scis. Office: Russian Dept Wesleyan U Middletown CT 06459-0001 Office Phone: 860-685-3127. E-mail: pmeyer@wesleyan.edu.

**MEYER, PUCCI,** editor; b. NYC, Sept. 1, 1944; d. Charles Albert and Lollo (Offer) M.; m. Michael V. McGill, Oct. 28, 2001. BA, U. Wis., 1966. Asst. editor Look mag., N.Y.C., 1970-71, editorial asst. Paris, 1967-69; reporter Newsday, Garden City, L.I., NY, 1971-73; style editor N.Y. Daily News Sunday Mag., N.Y.C., 1974-76, assoc. editor, 1977-82, editor, 1983-86; sr. editor Prodigy, White Plains, NY, 1987; spl. projects editor N.Y. Post, N.Y.C., 1988-89, style editor, 1990-92, food editor, 1992-93, assoc. features editor, 1993—94, travel editor, 1994—2004. Contbr. articles to various nat. mags. Recipient Pulitzer prize as mem. Newsday investigative team that wrote articles and book The Heroin Trail, 1973.

**MEYER, RACHEL ABIJAH,** foundation administrator, artist, poet; b. Job's Corners, Pa., Aug. 18, 1963; d. Jacob Owen and Velma Ruth (Foreman) M.; children: Andrew Carson, Peter Franklin. Student, Lebanon Valley Coll. Restaurant owner Purcy's Place, Ono, Pa.; restaurant mgr. King's Table Buffet, Citrus Heights, Calif.; product finalizer TransWorld Enterprises, Blaine, Wash.; dir., support svcs. adminstr. Tacticar Found., Sacramento, 1991—; tchr. Tacticar Inst., 1995; chair Conirems, Sacramento, 1996—. Author: Year of the Unicorn, 1994. Avocations: researching, writing, painting. Personal E-mail: ihopinsac@yahoo.com.

**MEYER, RICHARD CHARLES,** microbiologist, educator; b. Cleve., May 2, 1930; s. Frederick Albert and Tekla Charlotte (Schrade) M.; m. Carolyn Yvonne Patton, Apr. 6, 1963; children: Frederick Gustav, Carl Anselm. B.Sc., Baldwin-Wallace Coll., 1952; M.Sc., Ohio State U., 1957, PhD, 1961. Teaching and research asst. Ohio State U., 1956-61, research assoc., 1961-62; microbiologist Nat. Cancer Inst., NIH, Bethesda, Md., 1962-64; asst. prof. vet. pathology and hygiene and microbiology U. Ill., Urbana-Champaign, 1965-68, assoc. prof., 1968-73, prof., 1973-89, prof. emeritus, 1989—. Served with C.E. U.S. Army, 1952-54. Mem. Am. Acad. Microbiology, AAAS, Am. Inst. Biol. Sci., Am. Soc. Microbiology, Sigma Xi, Gamma Sigma Delta, Phi Zeta. Republican. Lutheran. Home: 1504 S Buckthorn Ln Mahomet IL 61853-3632 Office: Dept Vet Pathobiology U Ill at Urbana-Champaign Urbana IL 61801

**MEYER, RICHARD W.,** school librarian; b. St. Louis, Jan. 22, 1943; s. Norman K. Meyer and Melba R. Reisel; m. Clare A. Siesennop, Apr. 12, 1944; children: Sharyn C. Moore, Karyn A. BS in Chemistry, U. Mo., 1967; BA Libr. Sci., U. of Mo., Columbia, MO, 1962—67; MS Libr. Sci., U. of Ill., Champaign, IL, 1969—70; MA Economics, Clemson U., Clemson, SC, 1982—86. Asst. libr. E.I. duPont de Nemours, Aiken, SC, 1967—69; dir. libr. tech services Ind. State U., Terre Haute, Ind., 1976—79; asst. dir. libr. U. Tex. at Dallas, Richardson, 1970—76; assoc. dir. libraries Clemson U., Clemson, 1979—91; dir. libr. Trinity U., San Antonio, 1991—2000; dean and dir. libraries Ga. Inst. Tech., Atlanta, 2000—. Cons. Harris Corp., Melbourne, Fla., 1985—86, Chemists Club N.Y., N.Y.C., 1991—92, Mackenzie U., Sao Paulo, Brazil, 1998—99. Contbr. articles to profl. jours. Field svc. rev. team mem. United Way of San Antonio, 1998—2000. Recipient G.K. Saur Best Article award, Coll. and Rsch. Libraries, 1999; grantee, Andrew W. Mellon Found., 1995—2000; Blackwell scholarship, Coll. and Rsch. Libraries, 2002. Mem.: So. Assn. Colls. and Schs. (mem. reaffirmation rev. team 1999—2002), ALA. Conservative. Home: 2433 Mill Ridge Walk Atlanta GA 30345 Office: Georgia Institute of Technology 704 Cherry St Atlanta GA 30332-0900 Office Phone: 404-894-8914. Business E-Mail: richard.meyer@library.gatech.edu.

**MEYER, ROBERT ALAN,** management consultant; b. N.Y.C., Mar. 20, 1946; s. Leonard and Mildred M.; m. Gail Rein, Oct. 29, 1967; children: Jonathan, Caroline. BA in Econs., Am. Internat. Coll., Springfield, Mass., 1967; MBA, NYU, 1973. 2nd v.p., mgr. mcpl. bond research Smith Barney Harris Upham and Co., Inc., N.Y.C., 1973-76; 1st v.p., dir. mcpl. bond research E.F. Hutton and Co. Inc., N.Y.C., 1976-82; v.p., mgr. mcpl. bond research Merrill Lynch Pierce Fenner and Smith Inc., N.Y.C., 1982-84; pres. Bond Investors Guaranty Ins. Co., N.Y.C., 1984-90; pres., chief exec. officer Greig Fester Fin. Guaranty Brokers, Inc., N.Y.C., 1991-94; prin. Meyer Cons. Group Inc., Holmdel, N.J., 1994-98; chmn., pres., CEO RAM Reinsurance Co. Ltd., Hamilton, Bermuda, 1998-2001; prin. Meyer Cons. Group Inc., Holmdel, N.J., 2001—. Mem. India House. Office: 20 Stoney Brook Rd Holmdel NJ 07733 E-mail: mcgramgm@msn.com.

**MEYER, ROBERT ALLEN,** finance educator; b. Wisconsin Rapids, Wis., May 31, 1943; s. Charles Harold and Viola Bertha (Stockmann) M.; 1 child, Timothy Charles. BA, Valparaiso (Ind.) U., 1966; MA, Mich. State U., 1967, PhD, 1972, postgrad., 1981. Asst. prof. Muskingum Area Tech. Coll., Zanesville, Ohio, 1972-74; adj. prof. U. Fla., Gainesville, 1974-80; dean acad. affairs Santa Fe Community Coll., Gainesville, 1974-80; asst. prof. Purdue U., W. Lafayette, Ind., 1982-84, Ga. State U., Atlanta, 1985-89; assoc. prof., program coord. U. N. Tex., Denton, 1989-91; Fulbright prof. scholar, Bangkok, 1991-92; coord. travel, tourism, hotel, restaurant mgmt. program U. Hawaii Manoa Campus, Honolulu, 1992-97; dir. distance edn., dir. travel, hotel and restaurant mgmt. SPC, St. Petersburg, Fla., 1997—; 21573325. Investor, asst. mgr. LaSiene Restaurant, Ann Arbor, Mich., 1970-72; investor, cons. Cafe Brittany St. Thomas, U.S. V.I., 1974-80, owner, operator, Houston, 1980; pres. RTM Cons., Honolulu, Hawaii, 1989—; educator World Tourism Orgn., 1993—; mem. vis. ind. coun. C. of C., 1993—; club mgr. Assn. Am., 1994—; dir. edn. Am. Assoc. Real Estate License Law Officials. Contbr. articles to profl. jours. Founding mem. Fla. Distance Learning Consortium, 1998—; bd. dirs., founder Fla. Virtual Campus, 1998—, dir. hospitality program, 1998—. Recipient White House Commendation for Partnerships with Industry and Higher Edn.,1984, George Washington Medal of Honor for innovations in higher edn., Freedoms Found., 1985, 86, Achievement award in hospitality edn. Coun. of Hotel, Restaurant & Instl. Edn., 1987. Mem. Assn. Real Estate Lic. Law Ofcls. (distance educ. bd. mem. 1999—), Tarrant County Hotel and Motel Assn., Dallas Hotel Assn., Am. Soc. Tng. and Devel., Travel Ind. Assn. Tex., Hotel Sales & Mktg. Assn. (bd. dirs. 1985-89), Coun. of Hotel, Restaurant and Instl. Edn. (grad. com. 1989-90). Office: St Petersburg Coll PO Box 13489 Saint Petersburg FL 33733-3489 Home: 13108 Angler St Spring Hill FL 34609-5907 Office Phone: 727-394-6165. E-mail: rmeyer1@tampabay.rr.com.

**MEYER, ROBERTA,** mediator, communication consultant; b. San Francisco, July 27, 1936; d. Theodore Robert and Virginia (Organ) Meyer; m. G. William Sheldon; children: Megan McDougall Radeski, Deborah Ann Guerra. Student, U. Utah, 1974. Cert. mediator. Founder, pres., exec. dir. Roberta Meyer Communication Cons., Inc., San Francisco, 1977—. Presenter numerous workshops in alcoholism and communication; nat. spkr. Nat. Found. Alcoholism Comm.; keynote spkr. Calif. Women's Comm. Alcoholism, 1981; mem. adv. bd. Soviet Am. Alliance Alcoholism and Other Addictions; founder Youth Dance Experience, 1999. Author: (book) Facts

About Booze and Other Drugs, 1980, The Parent Connection: How to Communicate with Your Child about Alcohol and Other Drugs, 1984, Listen to the Heart, 1989, (screenplays) Understanding Addition, 1988, Better Relationships Through Effective Communication, 1991; numerous radio and TV appearances; dir.: Meyer Method Dance Program for ballroom dancers, One Meyer Method Dance Training Video, 1998. Mem. adv. bd. Marin Svcs. Women, 1980; vol. Calif. Pacific Med. Ctr., San Francisco Ballet Aux.; mem. N.Y.C. and San Francisco Ballet Cos., 1950—56, San Francisco Ballet Sch., 1956—65; founder, dir. Ballet Arts San Francisco, 1965—78, San Francisco Ballroom Dance Theatre and the accelerated dance programs, 1994—. Named 56th Point of Light, Pres. Bush, 1990; recipient award, Optimists Club. Mem.: Childrens Theatre Assn., Nat. Coun. Alcoholism and Drug Dependence Calif. (pres. 1988—91), San Francisco Womens Rehab. Assn. (pres. 1975—76, dir., founder Youth Dance Project 1999), Nat. Coun. Alcoholism (co-chmn. pub. info. com. 1985—, v.p. Bay area 1988—, bd. dirs. Teen Kick Off 1987—), Alcoholism and Drug Rsch. Comm. Ctr. 1990—, pres. 1988—, creator, cons. youth aware program 1974—), Nat. Collaborative Planning and Cmty. Svc. (cert.), San Francisco C. of C. Address: 2625 Alcatraz Ave #283 Berkeley CA 94705-2702

**MEYER, RON,** film company executive; b. 1944; m. Kelly Chapman; children, Jennifer, Sarah, Carson, Eli. With Paul Kohner Agency, 1964-1970; agent William Morris Agency, Beverly Hills, CA, 1970-1975; co-founder, pres. Creative Artists Agency, Inc., Beverly Hills, CA, 1975-95; pres., COO Universal Studios Inc., Universal City, 1995—. Served with USMC. Named one of 50 Most Powerful People in Hollywood, Premiere mag., 2004—06. Office: Universal Studios Inc 100 Universal City Plz Universal City CA 91608 Office Phone: 818-777-1000.*

**MEYER, RUSSELL WILLIAM, JR.,** air transportation executive; b. Davenport, Iowa, July 19, 1932; s. Russell William and Ellen Marie (Matthews) M.; m. Helen Scott Vaughn, Aug. 20, 1960; children: Russell William, III, Elizabeth Ellen, Jeffrey Vaughn, Christopher Matthews, Carolyn Louise. BA, Yale U., 1954; LLB, Harvard U., 1961. Bar: Ohio 1961. Mem. firm Arter & Hadden, Cleve., 1961-66; pres., chief exec. officer Grumman Am. Aviation Corp., Cleve., 1966-74; exec. v.p. Cessna Aircraft Co., Wichita, Kans., 1974-75, chmn. bd., CEO, 1975-2000, 2002—03, chmn., 2004, chmn. emeritus, 2005. Bd. dirs. Fourth Fin., 1975-1995, Westar Energy, 1978-2000, Gen. Dynamics, 1986-1992, Nations Bank, 1995-2001, Pub. Broadcasting Svc., Welfare to Work Partnership; presdl. appointee Aviation Safety Commn., 1987—; mem. Pres. Airline Commn., 1993, FAA Mgmt. Adv. Counsel, 2004—; dir. Pub. Broadcasting Sys. Chmn. bd. trustees 1st Bapt. Ch., Cleve., 1972-74; bd. dirs. United Way, Wichita and Sedgwick County; trustee Wesley Hosp. Endowment Assn., Wake Forest Univ.; bd. govs. United Way Am., 1993—. With USAF, 1955-58. Recipient Collier trophy Nat. Aeronautic Assn., 1986, George S. Dively award Harvard U., 1992, Wright Bros. Meml. trophy, 1995, Disting. Svc. Citation U. Kans., 2000; named Kansan of Yr., 1998. Mem. ABA, Ohio Bar Assn., Kans. Bar Assn., Cleve. Bar Assn., Gen. Aviation Mfrs. Assn. (chmn. bd. dirs 1973-74, 81-82, 93-94), Wichita C. of C. (chmn. 1988—, bd. dirs.), Wichita Club, Wichita Country Club, Pine Valley Club, Cypress Point Club, Double Eagle Country Club, Flint Hills Nat. Club, Latrobe Country Club, Eldorado Country Club, The Tradition Golf Club. Home: 600 N Tara Ct Wichita KS 67206-1830 Office: Cessna Aircraft PO Box 7704 1 Cessna Blvd Wichita KS 67215-1424 Office Phone: 316-517-8000.

**MEYER, SCOTT,** communications executive; AB, Brown U.; MBA, Harvard U. Cons. Boston Cons. Group; with Merrill Lynch & Co.; v.p., gen. mgr. bus. to bus. consumer divsn. Multex.com; with NY Times Co., 2000—; v.p. NY Times Digital, 2000—03; gen. mgr. NY Times on the Web, 2000—03; v.p. New Eng. Media Group (NEMG), Boston Globe, 2003—05; pres., CEO About, Inc., 2005—. Bd. dirs., former pres. Harvard Bus. Sch. Club, NY; bd. dirs. Online Publishers Assn.; big brother Mass. Bay Big Brothers program; bd. visitors Boston Ctr. Arts. Office: About Inc 29 W 17th St New York NY 10011*

**MEYER, TOBIAS,** auction house executive; Student, Vienna U. Entry-level position contemporary art dept. Christie's, London, 1989—92; head contemporary art Sotheby's, London, 1992, dir. contemporary art worldwide NYC, 1997—. Auctioneer Orange Marilyn (Andy Warhol), 1988, Michael Jackson and Bubbles (Jeff Koons), 2001. Office: Sotheby's 1334 York Ave New York NY 10021 Office Phone: 212-606-7254. Office Fax: 212-606-7011.*

**MEYER, URBAN,** college football coach; b. July 10, 1964; Graduated, Univ. Cin. Tight ends coach Ohio State, 1986—87; asst. coach Ill. State, 1988—89; wide receivers coach Colo. State, 1990—95, Notre Dame, 1996—2000; head football coach Bowling Green, 2001—02, Utah Univ. 2003—04, Univ. Fla., 2005—. Recipient Nat. Coach Yr., The Sporting News, 2003. Office: Ben Hill Griffin Stadium Univ Ave & North South Dr Gainesville FL 32611

**MEYER-BAHLBURG, HEINO F.L.,** psychology professor; b. Hamburg, Germany, Feb. 26, 1940; came to U.S., 1969; s. Wilhelm and Marie Luise Meyer-B. Vordiplom in Psychology, U. Hamburg, 1963, Diplom Psychology, 1966; D in Natural Scis., U. Düsseldorf, Germany, 1970. Sci. asst. U. Düsseldorf, 1970; rsch. asst., then rsch. assoc. prof. psychiatry and pediat. SUNY Med. Sch., Buffalo, 1970-77; rsch. scientist N.Y. State Psychiat. Inst., N.Y.C., 1977—; from assoc. clin. prof. med. psychology to prof. clin. psychology in psychiatry Columbia U. Coll. Physicians and Surgeons, 1978—; pediat. behavioral endocrinologist Presbyn. Hosp., N.Y.C., 1978-90, prof. psychologist in psychiat. svc., 1990—. Contbr. numerous articles to profl. publs. Recipient Disting. Sci. Achievement award Soc. for Sci. Study of Sex, 1993; grantee NIMH, NICHD. Mem. AAAS, APA, Soc. Pediat. Psychology, Internat. Acad. Sex Rsch., German Sexual Rsch. Soc., Internat. Soc. Psychoneuroendocrinology, Soc. Sci. Study Sex, Soc. Rsch. Child Devel., Soc. Sexual Therapy and Rsch., Lawson Wilkins Pediat. Endocrine Soc., Harry Benjamin Internat. Gender Dysphoria Assn. Office: Columbia U Dept Psychiatry 1051 Riverside Dr Unit 15 New York NY 10032-2695 Business E-Mail: meyerb@childpsych.columbia.edu.

**MEYERHOFER, DAVID D.,** physicist, educator; b. Mar. 6, 1959; AB, Cornell U., Ithaca, NY, 1981; PhD, Princeton U., NJ, 1987. Exptl. divsn. dir. and prof. U. of Rochester, Lab. for Laser Energetics, NY, 2000—. Fellow, Am. Phys. Soc., 2002. Office: Lab Laser Energetics 250 East River Rd Rochester NY 14559 Office Phone: 585-275-0255. Business E-Mail: ddm@lle.rochester.edu.

**MEYERHOFF, ERICH,** librarian, director; b. Braunschweig, Germany, Nov. 24, 1919; came to US, 1935; s. Karl and Irma Meyerhoff; m. Inge Zuber; children: Tina, C. Michael BS, CCNY, 1943; MS, NY Sch. Social Work, 1949; MSLS, Columbia U., 1951, cert. advanced librarianship, 1974. Social worker various orgns., to 1951; reference librarian Columbia U. Med. Library, NYC, 1951-57; librarian, asst. prof. Downstate Med. Ctr., SUNY, Bklyn., 1957-61; dir. Med. Library Ctr. NY, 1961-67; librarian Health Scis. Library, SUNY-Buffalo, 1967-70, Cornell U. Med. Coll., NYC, 1970-86, asst. dean, 1977-86; chief library svc. VA Med. Ctr., NYC, 1986-88; archives librarian NYU Med. Ctr., 1980-91; asst. curator Ehrman Med. Libr.-Archives, NYU Sch. Medicine, 1991—. Adj. instr. biomed. comms. Columbia U., 1976-81; cons. U. Mich., Ann Arbor, 1968, NY Met. Reference Rsch. Libr. Agy., 1968-69, Coll. Physicians Phila., 1969-70. Fellow AAAS, Med. Library Assn. (cert., bd. dirs. 1972-76, chmn. various comes. 1968-72, 78-81, Inst. for Sci. Info. awarded 1981-82, Janet Doe lectr. 1977, Marcia C. Noyes award 1997), NY Acad. Medicine; mem. AAUP, Spl. Libraries Assn., Archons Colophon, Am. Assn. History Medicine, Am. Printing History Assn., Met. NY Archivists Roundtable. Avocation: travel. Home: 90 La Salle St New York NY 10027-4719 Office: NYU Med Ctr Archives 550 1st Ave New York NY 10016-6402 Office Phone: 212-263-8280. Business E-Mail: meyere01@library.med.nyu.edu.

**MEYERHOFF, JACK FULTON,** corporate financial executive; b. Joliet, Ill, May 15, 1926; s. Charles F. and Helen (Ferguson) M.; m. Mary Margaret Williams, Jan. 2, 1949; children: Keith F., Greg H., Deborah S., Todd C. Postgrad., Ohio Wesleyan U., 1944-45; BS, Miami U., Ohio, 1947; grad. Advanced Mgmt. Program, Harvard U., 1968. C.P.A., Ohio, Ill. Mgr. Arthur Andersen & Co., Chgo., Cin., Cleve., 1947-59; treas. MacGregor Sports, Cin., 1959-63; v.p. corp. controller Brunswick Corp., Chgo., 1963-77, CFO, 1972-77, v.p. corp. affairs, 1977-80, v.p. human resources, 1980-81; chmn., CEO MarJac Assocs., Nokomis, Fla., 1981—; pres., dir. Charles Oxford Corp., Nokomis, 1984—. Bd. dirs Sherwood Med. Industries, Inc., Old Orchard Bank & Trust Co., Tech: Time Inc., Nokomis; organizer, vice chmn. bd. trustees Caldwell Trust Co. and Trust Cos. Am., Venice, Fla., 1993—. Treas., bd. dirs Cove Sch.; bd. dirs., pres. Skokie Valley Cmty. Hosp., No. Ill. Indsl. Assn.; v.p., bd. dirs. Jr. Achievement; bd. dirs. Chgo. Responsibility Growth, Gulf Area Med. Properties; chmn. bd. Bon Secours-Venice Hosp., HMA Regional Med. Ctr., Venice Hosp. Found.; bd. dirs. J. Clifford MacDonald Handicapped Ctr. of Tampa, Sarasota Com. of 100; bd. dirs., treas. Triangle Econ. Devel. Coun.; bd. dirs., Manatee C.C. Found., Boys and Girls Club of Venice, Pillar Cmty., Venice, Fla.; mem. adv. coun. Miami U., Georgetown U., U. So. Fla. With USNR, 1944-46. Mem. AICPA, Ohio Soc. CPAs, Ill. Soc. CPAs, Fin. Exec. Inst., Nat. Assn. Acct., Harvard Bus. Sch. Alumni Assn., Harvard U. Exec. Alumni Coun. (bd. dirs., treas.), Venice Area C. of C. (bd. dirs., treas.), Sigma Alpha Epsilon, Delta Sigma Pi, Beta Alpha Psi, Beta Gamma Sigma, Venice Yacht Club, Mid Am. Club, Econ. Club, Misty Creek Country Club, Masons, Rotary. Methodist. Home: 3730 Cadbury Cir 819 Venice FL 34293 Personal E-mail: meyerhoffjm@comcast.net.

**MEYERHOFF, KAREN,** museum director; b. Hackensack, NJ, Jan. 15, 1958; d. Hans Peter Meyerhoff and Rose Jakovowicz; m. Roger Gwyn Robert (dec.). BA, U. Minn., Mpls., 1980. Mgr. collections Met. Mus. Art, NYC, 1983—85, sr. restorer, 1985—88; asst. mgr. exhbn. design & prodn. Mus. Modern Art, 1988—97; dir. exhbn. mgmt. & design Guggenheim Mus. 1997—2000; mng. dir. exhbns., collections & design Guggenheim Found., 2000—. Cons., designer Asia Soc., NYC, Mus. Morning Image, Fashion Inst. Tech. Avocations: writing, drawing, skiing. Office: Guggenheim Found 345 Hudson St 12fh fl New York NY 10012

**MEYERHOFF, ROBERT E.,** real estate developer, philanthropist, art collector, horse breeder; b. Jan. 1924; m. Jane M. Bernstein (dec. Mar. 2005); children: Rose Ellen Meyerhoff Greene, Neil, John. Pres. Henderson Webb Inc., Md.; owner Fitzhugh Farm, Phoenix, Md. Mem. of corp. Met. Mus. Art, N.Y.C.; major donor Nat. Gallery Art, DC. Named one of Top 200 Collectors, ARTnews Mag., 2004. Mem.: Jockey Club, Thoroughbred Owners & Breeders Assn. (Outstanding Md. Owner-Breeder 1999). Achievements include establishing Meyerhoff Scholars Program at Univ. Md. Balt. County, 1988. Avocation: collector of modern & contemporary art, especially postwar American abstraction; collection is pledged to National Gallery of Art, Washington. Home: 3615 Blenheim Rd Phoenix MD 21131*

**MEYERINK, VICTORIA PAIGE,** film producer, actress; b. Santa Barbara, Calif., Dec. 27, 1960; d. William Joseph Meyerink and Jeanne Baird; m. Lawrence David Foldes, Apr. 24, 1983. Student, U. So. Calif., 1978-80. Actress, 1962—; v.p. Star Cinema Prodn. Group, Inc., 1981-85; pres. Star Entertainment Group, Inc., L.A., 1985—. Mem. faculty Internat. Film & TV Workshops, 1991—; lectr. colls. & film festivals. Prodr. (motion pictures) The Great Skycopter Rescue, 1982, Young Warriors, 1984, Night Force, 1987, Prima Donnas, 1996, Finding Home, 2004; actress (TV series) The Danny Kaye Show, Green Acres, My Three Sons, Family Affair, The FBI, Adam 12, (motion pictures) Speedway, Night of The Grizzly, Seconds, Brainstorm, The Littlest Hobo, (TV spl.) It Isn't Easy Being a Teenage Millionairess, numerous commls. Recipient Mayoral Proclamation for Outstanding Achievement, City of L.A., Cert. of Recognition for 25 Yrs. Outstanding Contbns. to the Entertainment Industry, City of L.A., Outstanding Achievement award Acad. Family Films & TV. Mem. Acad. Motion Picture Arts & Scis. (exec. com. Student Acad. Awards 1996—), L.A. Film Tchrs. Assn. Avocations: languages, travel, music, scuba diving, gourmet cooking.

**MEYEROWITZ, ELLIOT MARTIN,** biologist, educator; b. Washington, May 22, 1951; s. Irving and Frank (Goldberg) M.; m. Joan Agnes Kobori, June 17, 1984; 2 children. AB, Columbia U., 1973; MPhil, Yale U., 1975, PhD, 1977. Rsch. fellow Stanford U., Calif., 1977-79; asst. prof. biology Calif. Inst. Tech., Pasadena, 1980-85, assoc. prof., 1985-89, prof., 1989—, George W. Beadle prof. biology, 2002—, chair, divsn. biology, 2000—. Mem. editl. bd. Trends in Genetics, Current Biology, Cell, Devel., Genome Biology; contbr. articles to profl. jours. Recipient LVMH Sci. pour l'Art Sci. prize, 1996, Internat. prize for biology, Japan, 1997, Mendel medal, U.K., 1997, Wilbur Cross medal Yale U., 2001; Jane Coffin Childs Meml. fund fellow, 1977-79, Sloan Found. fellow, 1980-82; Ross Harrison prize, Internat. Soc. Devel Biolgist, 2005. Fellow: AAAS; mem.: NAS (councilor 2006—, Lounsbery award 1999), Royal Soc., Soc. for Developmental Biology (pres. 2005—06), Academie des Scis. (fgn. mem./France), Internat. Soc. for Plant Molecular Biology (pres. 1995—97), Genetics Soc. Am. (pres. 1999, medal 1996), Bot. Soc. Am. (Pelton award 1994, Centennial award 2006), Am. Soc. Plant Biologists (Gibbs medal 1995), Am. Acad. Arts and Scis., Am. Philos. Soc. Office: Calif Inst Tech Divsn Biology 156 29 Pasadena CA 91125-0001 Office Phone: 626-395-6889. Business E-Mail: meyerow@caltech.edu.

**MEYERROSE, DALE WILLIAM,** federal official, retired military officer; BS in Econs., USAF Acad., 1975; Grad, Squadron Officer Sch., Maxwell AFB, 1977; MBA, U. Utah, 1978; Grad., Nat. War Coll., Ft Lesley J. McNair, 1992, Sr. Info. Warfare Applications Course, Maxwell AFB, 2000, Program for Nat. & Internat. Security, JFK Sch. Govt., Harvard U., 2001, Joint Flag Officer Warfighting Course, Maxwell AFB, 2003, USN Exec. Bus. Course, U. Calif-Berkeley, 2005. Commnd. 2d lt. USAF, 1975, advanced through grades to major gen., 2002, ret., 2005; maintenance officer 4th Combat Comms. Group, Altus AFB, Okla., 1976-77; aide-de-camp, asst. exec. officer to the comdr. European Comms. Divsn., Kapuan Air Sta., West Germany, 1977-79; aide-de-camp to the comdr. Air Force Comms. Command, Scott AFB, Ill., 1979-80; chief of maintenance 1974th Comms. Group, Scott AFB, 1980-82; mem., air staff tng. program officer Sec. of the Air Pers. Coun., The Pentagon, Washington, 1982-83; various assignments Hdqrs. USAF, The Pentagon, Washington, 1983-85, chief future concepts, dep. chief of staff, 1990-91; comdr. 2048th Comms. Squadron, Carswell AFB, 1985-87; comms. support officer Nat. Mil. Command Ctr. the Joint Staff, The Pentagon, Washington, 1987-90; comdr. 3rd Combat Comms. Group, Tinker AFB, Okla., 1992-94; dir. comms. Operation Southern Watch, Riyadh, Saudi Arabia, 1993; dir. comms. and info. Hdqrs. USAF in Europe, Ramstein AB, Germany, 1994-96; Hdqrs. Air Combat Command, Langley AFB, Va., 1996—2000; dir. command control systems & chief info officer N. Am. Aerospace Def. Command & US Space Command, Peterson AFB, Colo., 2000—02; dir. comm. & info. chief info officer Hdqrs. Space Command, Peterson AFB, Colo., 2002—05; dir. architecture & integration & chief info. officer Hdqrs. US No. Command, Peterson AFB, Colo., 2002—05; assoc. dir. & chief info. officer Office Nat. Intelligence, Washington, 2006—. Decorated Disting. Svc. medal, Def. Superior Svc. medal, Legion of Merit with oak leaf cluster, Def. Meritorious Svc. medal with oak leaf cluster, Meritorious Svc. medal with silver oak leaf cluster, Air Force Commendation medal, Joint Svc. Commendation medal, Air Force Achievement medal, Combat Readiness medal, Nat. Def. Svc. medal with two bronze stars, Southwest Asia Svc. medal with bronze star, Kuwait Liberation medal; Recipient Outstanding Young AFCEAN awars, Armed Forces Comm. & Electronics Assn., 1987, Medal of Merit, 1992; Named Internat. AFCEAN of the Yr., 1999, "Top 100" Info. Tech. Profl., Fed. Computer Weekly, 2005 Office: Office Nat Intelligence NEOB 725 17th St Washington DC 20500*

**MEYER-ROUX, KAREN J.,** archivist, art historian; d. Jean L. and Lois A. Meyer-Roux; m. Allon G. Percus, May 27, 2000; 1 child, Alexander Meyer Percus. PhD, Ecole des Hautes Etudes en Sciences Sociales, Paris, 1999. Archivist Getty Rsch. Inst., LA, 2000—. Author: (publication) La famille, les femmes et le quotidien, textes offerts à C. Klapisch-Zuber; curator (exhibition) Horizons Pluriels. Fellow, European U. Inst., Florence, Italy, 1995, Ecole Francaise de Rome, 1995, 1996. Mem.: Soc. Am. Archivists, Coll. Art Assocation, Am. Assn. Museums.

**MEYERS, ABBEY S.,** foundation administrator; b. Bklyn., Apr. 11, 1944; m. Jerrold B. Meyers, Oct. 23, 1966; children: David, Adam, Laura. AAS, N.Y.C. Community Coll., 1962; LHD (hon.), Alfred U., 1994. Comml. artist various advt. agys., N.Y.C., 1962-65; dir. patient svcs. Tourette Syndrome Assn., Bayside, NY, 1980-85; exec. dir., founder Nat. Org. for Rare Disorders, Danbury, Conn., 1985—, pres. U.S. commr. Nat. Commn. on Orphan Diseases, Washington, 1986-89; subcom. human gene therapy NIH, Bethesda, Md., 1989-92, recombinant DNA adv. com., 1992-96; mem. Health Care Payor Adv. Commn. on Conn. Commn. on Hosps. and Health Care, 1992-94; mem. FDA Biol. Response Modifiers Com., 1995-99; DHHS Nat. Human Rsch. Protection Adv. Com., 2000-2002; Partnership for Human Rsch. Protection Pub. Adv. Coun., 2005—. Author: (with others) Orphan Drugs and Orphan Diseases: Clinical Reality and Public Policy, 1983, (with others) Cooperative Approaches to Research and Development of Orphan Drugs, 1985, (with others) Tourette Syndrome: Clinical Understanding and Treatment, 1988, (with others) Physicians Guide to Rare Diseases, 1992. Bd. dirs. Nat. Orphan Drug and Device Found., N.Y.C., 1982-85; leader Coalition to Pass Orphan Drug Act of 1983, 1979-82. Recipient Pub. Health Svc. award HHS, 1985, Commr.'s Spl. citation FDA, 1988. Mem. Nat. Health Coun. (bd. dirs. 1989-94), Alliance of Genetic Support Groups (bd. dirs. 1987-89), European Orgn. for Rare Disorders (hon. pres. 1997—). Avocations: reading, horseback riding. Office: Nat Orgn for Rare Disorders PO Box 1968 Danbury CT 06813-1968 E-mail: orphan@rarediseases.org.

**MEYERS, ALBERT IRVING,** chemistry professor; b. NYC, Nov. 22, 1932; s. Hyman and Sylvia (Greenberg) M.; m. Joan Shepard, Aug. 10, 1957; children: Harold, Jill, Lisa BS, NYU, 1954, PhD, 1957. Rsch. chemist Cities Svc. Oil Co., Cranbury, NJ, 1957-58; asst., assoc. prof., prof. La. State U., New Orleans, 1958-70, Boyd prof., 1969; prof. Wayne State U., Detroit, 1970-72, Colo. State U., Fort Collins, 1972—2003, disting. prof., 1986—2003, John K. Stille prof. chemistry, 1993—2003, prof. emeritus chemistry, 2003—. Spl. postdoctoral fellow Harvard U., Cambridge, 1965-66; cons. G.D. Searle Co., Skokie, Ill., 1972-84, Mid-West Rsch. Inst., Kansas City, Mo., 1974-77, NIH, Bethesda, Md., 1977-79, 85-89, Bristol-Myers Squibb Co., 1983-95, Roche Colo., 1989—, GlaxoSmithKline Co., 1994-2001; mem. sci. adv. bd. La Jolla, Calif., Avanir Bioscis., La Jolla. Assoc. editor Jour. Am. Chem. Soc., 1979-85; mem. editl. adv. bd. Jour. Organic Chemistry, 1990-95, Tetrahedron, 1990-2003, Jour. Chem. Soc. Perkin, 1993, Jour. Chem. Soc. Chem. Commun., 1996, Heterocycles, 1974—; contbr. over 500 articles to profl. jours. Recipient Alexander von Humboldt award Fed. Republic of Germany, 1984, Disting. Alumni award NYU, 1990, award in synthetic chemistry Am. Chem. Soc., 1985, A.C. Cope Scholar award, 1987, Yamada prize, Japan, 1996, award Internat. Soc. Heterocyclic Chemistry, 1997; named Man of Yr., New Orleans Jaycees, 1968, Boyd Prof. La. State U., 1969; recipient pioneer award Am. Insts. Chemists, 1998. Fellow AAAS, Nat. Acad. Sci.; mem. Royal Soc. Chemistry (silver medalist 1982), Phila. Organic Chemistry Soc. (Allan Day award 1987). Home: 1500 Hepplewhite Ct Fort Collins CO 80526-3822 Office: Colo State Univ Dept Chemistry Fort Collins CO 80523-0001 Office Phone: 970-491-7060. E-mail: aimeyers@colostate.edu.

**MEYERS, AMY,** museum director; m. Jack Meyers; 1 child, Rachel. BA, U. Chgo.; PhD in Am. Studies, Yale U. Rschr. Dumbarton Oaks; rschr. Ctr. for Advanced Study in Visual Arts, Nat. Gallery; curator Am. Art, Henry E. Huntington Libr., Art Collections and Bot. Gardens, San Marino, Calif.; dir. Yale Ctr. for Brit. Art; prof. art Yale U. Adj. faculty Calif. Inst. Tech.; vice chair, Huntington rep. Assn. Rsch. Insts. in History of Art, 1995—2000. Editor (with Margaret Pritchard): Empire's Nature: Mark Catesby's New World Vision; editor: (with Alan Trachtenberg) Classic Essays on Photography. Office: Yale Ctr for Brit Art PO Box 208280 1080 Chapel St New Haven CT 06520-8280

**MEYERS, ARLEN,** physician; b. Philadelphia, Pa. Prof. U. Colo. Sch. of Medicine, Denver, 1976—2006. Office: U Colo 4200 E 9th Ave B-205 Denver CO 80262 Office Phone: 303-315-8642. Business E-Mail: arlen.meyers@uchsc.edu.

**MEYERS, CAROLYN WINSTEAD,** academic administrator, mechanical engineer, educator; b. Hampton, Va., May 11, 1946; d. John Selner and Eva Carroll (Tonsler) Winstead; divorced; m. James E. Cofield, Jr.; children: Timothy C. III, Leslie C., Lisa A.; m. James E. Cofield, Jr. BSME, Howard U., 1968; MSME, Ga. Inst. Tech., 1979, PhD in Metallurgy, 1984. Steam generator analyst Machinery Apparatus Operation div. Machinery Apparatus Ops. div. GE, Schenectady, 1968; systems analyst Info. Svcs. div. Info. Svcs. div. GE, Bethesda, Md., 1969; instr. Atlanta U. Ctr. Corp., 1972-77; instr. mech. engring. Ga. Inst. Tech., Atlanta, 1979-84, asst. prof., 1984-90, assoc. prof., 1990-96; dir. SUCCEED Coalition Ctr. for Profl. Success, 1992-93; assoc. dean rsch. Coll. Engring. Ga. Inst. Tech., Atlanta, 1993-96; dean Coll. Engring. NC A&T State U., Greensboro, 1996, prof. mech. engring., 1996—2006, vice chancellor acad. affairs, 2000—06, provost, 2001—06; pres. Norfolk State U., Va., 2006—. Summer faculty fellow USAF Materials Lab., Wright-Patterson AFB, Ohio, 1988; program officer NSF, 1996-99. Contbr. articles to profl. jours. Chmn. waste volume reduction subcom. Atlanta Mayor's Commn. on Solid Waste Disposal, 1989-92; trustee Westminster Schs., Atlanta, 1989-93; program dir. divsn. undergrad edn. NSF, 1997-99, divsn. human resources devel. Arlington, V., 1999—; bd. dirs. Piedmont Triad Coun. Internat. Visitors, N.C. Sch. Sci. and Math, 2000-, Moses Cone Health Sys., 2003-, United Way Greater Greensboro, 2002-03, Rsch. Triangle Inst., MentorNet; chair, bd. dirs. Nat. Inst. Aerospace, 2003—. Recipient Faculty award for women NSF, 1991, Disting. Alumni award Atlanta-Howard U. Alumni Assn., 1992; named Black Engr. of Yr. in Higher Edn. U.S. Black Engr. Mag. and Coun. Engring Deans, 1990; Pres. Young Investigator grantee NSF, 1988; inducted to Acad. of Disting. Engring. Alumni Ga. Tech. U., 1996; honored alumna in edn. on Charter Day Howard U., 1997. Fellow ASME (Engr. of Yr. 1990); mem. AIME, SAE (Ralph Teetor Ednl. award 1986), Am. Soc. Engr. Edn. (v.p. pub. affairs 2001-2003), Foundry Ednl. Found. (key prof. 1985-95), Soc. Women Engrs. (state pres. Atlanta sect. 1987-90), Am. Foundrymen's Soc. (sponsor student sect. 1987-95, aluminum divsn. sci. merit award 1994), Soc. Black Engrs. (Golden Torch award 2002, Emerald honors Women in Sci and Tech. 2003), Links (pres. Atlanta chpt. 1987-88); Jack and Jill Am., The Girl Friends, Golden Key, Sigma Xi, Tau Beta Pi, Phi Kappa Phi, Alpha Kappa Alpha, Beta Gamma Sigma. Roman Catholic. Office: Office of Pres Norfolk State U 700 Park Ave Norfolk VA 23504 E-mail: president@nsu.edu.

**MEYERS, CHRISTINE LAINE,** marketing and media executive, consultant; b. Detroit, Mar. 7, 1946; d. Ernest Robert and Eva Elizabeth (Laine) M.; 1 child, Kathryn Laine; m. Oliver S. Moore III, May 12, 1990. BA, U. Mich. 1968. Editor indsl. rels. diesel divsn. Gen. Motors Corp., Detroit, 1968; nat. advt. mgr. J.L. Hudson Co., Detroit, 1969-72, mgr. internal sales promotion, 1972-73, dir. pub., 1973-76; nat. advt. mgr. Pontiac Motor divsn., Mich., 1976-78; pres., owner Laine Meyers Mktg. Cos., Inc., Troy, Mich., 1978—; founder, owner CORP! Mag., 1998—. Dir. Internat. Met. Detroit. Inc. Contbr. articles to profl. publs. Bus. adv. coun. Ctrl. Mich., 1977-79; pub. adv. com. on jud. candidates Oakland County Bar Assn.; adv. bd. Birmingham Cmty. Hosp., Bank of Am., 1999-2001; bd. dirs. YMCA, Mich., 1992-98, Haven, 1997—; Automation Alley, Oakland County, 1999—. Named Mich. Ad Woman of Yr., 1976, one of Top 10 Working Women, Glamour mag., 1978, one of 100 Best and Brightest Advt. Age, 1987, one of Mich.'s top 25 female bus. owners Nat. Assn. Women Bus. Owners, One of Top 10 Women Owned Bus., Mich., 1994; recipient Vanguard award Women in Comm. 1986, Lifetime Achievement award Northwood U., 2002. Mem. Internat. Assn. Bus. Communicators, Adcraft Club, Women's Advt. Club (1st v.p. 1975), Women's Econ. Club (pres. 1976-77), Internat. Women's Forum Mich. (founding pres. 1986-97), Internat. Inst. Detroit (bd. dirs. 1986-89), Detroit C.

of C., Troy C. of C., Mortar Bd., Quill and Scroll, Pub. Rels. Com. Women for United Found., Founders Soc. Detroit Inst. Arts, Fashion Group, Pub. Rels. Soc. Am., First Soc. Detroit (exec. com. 1970-71), Kappa Tau Alpha. Home: 5165 Longmeadow Rd Bloomfield Hills MI 48304-3657 Office: Laine Meyers Mktg Cos Inc 3645 Crooks Rd Troy MI 48084-1642 Office Phone: 248-458-2677 ext.301. Business E-Mail: cmyers@corpmagazine.com.

**MEYERS, CHRISTOPHER,** humanities educator, consultant; s. Diana Meyers and Ehrhard Bahr (Stepfather); m. Donna Elsdon, Apr. 6, 1997; 1 child, Natasha Leigh Meyers-Cherry stepchildren: Renee Elsdon, Jonathon Elsdon. BA, U. Calif., Santa Cruz, 1980; cert. in clin. ethics, U. Tenn., 1984, D, 1986. Prof. philosophy Calif. State U., Bakersfield, 1986—, exec. dir. Kegley Inst. Ethics, 1987—; clin. ethicist Kern Med. Ctr., Bakersfield, 1997—. Ethics cons.; instr. Mercy Healthcare, Bakersfield, 1991—, San Joaquin Cmty. Hosp., Bakersfield, 1995—. Contbr. articles to profl. jours. Ethics cons.; instr. Multiple Bus. and Philanthropic Groups, Bakersfield, 1987—2006. Mem.: Am. Soc. Bioethics and Humanities, Assn. Practical and Profl. Ethics, Am. Philos. Assn. Avocations: fly fishing, hiking, bicycling. Office: Calif State U Bakersfield 9001 Stockdale Hwy Bakersfield CA 93311

**MEYERS, DALE (MRS. MARIO COOPER),** artist; b. Chgo. d. Walter Herman and Gertude (Pettee) Wetterer; m. Mario Cooper, Oct. 11, 1964; children: Dale, Steven R. Student, Glendale Coll., Corcoran Gallery Sch. Art, Washington, 1962-63, Art Student's League, N.Y.C., 1964-78. Instr. Art Students League, 1979—; ofcl. artist NASA, USCG.; lectr. Parson's Sch. Design, Nat. Acad. Sch. Author The Sketchbook, 1983; contbr.: Watercolor Bold and Free, Am. Artist mag. Diversion mag.; solo exhbns. include, West Wing Gallery, Ringwood (N.J.) State Park, 1970, Manor Club, Pelham Manor, N.Y., 1970, Apollo Art Gallery, Oklahoma City, 1972, Quadrangle Gallery, Dallas, 1972, Galveston Ctr. for Arts, 1974, Fla. Gulf Coast Art Ctr., 1977, 86, Okura Hotel, Tokyo, Japan, 1977, Owensboro Mus. Art, 1983, Salmagundi Club, 1986, 88, Stehle-Reed Gallery, Midland, Tex., 1987, others; artist-in-residence, Galveston Arts Ctr., 1974, Owensboro Mus. Art, 1983, Asilomar, Calif., 1983, 84; group exhbns. include Two Hundred Years of Watercolor Painting in Am, Met. Mus. Art, 1966, Eyewitness to Space, Nat. Gallery Art, Washington, 1969, Smithsonian Instn., 1961-63, Corcoran Gallery, 1963, Museo de la Acuarela, Mexico City, 1968, 89, London (Ont., Can.) Mus. Art, 1971-72, Art Gallery Hamilton (Can., 1971-72, Ont. Inst. Edn., 1971-72, Butler Inst. Art, 1962—, Frye Mus., 1962—; represented in permanent collections, Calif. Palace of Legion of Honor, San Francisco, Nat. Acad. N.Y.C., Avon Fine Arts Collection, NASA, EPA, Museo de la Acuarela, Schumacher Gallery, Columbus, Ohio, Slater Mus., Conn., Portland (Maine) Mus., U. Utah Fine Arts Collection, Frye Mus., Seattle, Owensboro Mus. Art, Coll. Misericordia, Dallas, Pa, Canton Art Inst., Ohio, Arnot Mus., Elmira, N.Y., internat. watercolor exhbn. Can., U.S., Gt. Britain, 1991-94, Chung Cheng Gallery, Taipei, 1994. Recipient Henry W. Ranger award Nat. Acad. Design, 1968, Samuel F.B. Morse medal, 1973, Anna Hyatt Huntington Bronze medal, 1971, Knickerbocker Artists Gold medal, 1981, 88, Allied Artists Am. award, 1969, Gold medal honor Nat. Arts Club, 1972, Anna Hyatt Huntington Gold medal, 1974, Adolf and Cara Obrig award Nat. Acad., 1974, 81, Walter Biggs award, 1976, Allied Arts Gold medal, 1978, Audubon ARtists Silver medal, 1984. Fellow Royal Soc. Arts (Grumbocher Gold medals 1988, 90); mem. Am. Watercolor Soc. (pres. 1973-03, pres. emeritus 2003-, editor jours. 1962-79, Bronze medal honor award 1968, awards 1970, 72, 78, 79, 81, 82, 83, 85, 87, 89, 93, 98, High Winds medal 2001, 05, Dolphin medal 2000), Nat. Acad. (academician), Allied Artists Am. (pres. 1975-78), Art Students League N.Y., La. Watercolor Soc. (hon.), Ky. Watercolor Soc., Ohio Watercolor Soc. (hon.), Watercolor Soc. Mex., Fla. Watercolor Soc. (hon.), Audubon Artists, Salimagundi Club (medal of honor 1994). Office: Art Students League 215 W 57th St New York NY 10019

**MEYERS, ERIC MARK,** religion educator; b. Norwich, Conn., June 5, 1940; s. Karl D. and Shirlee M. (Meyer) M.; m. Carol Lyons, June 25, 1964; children: Julie Kaete, Dina Elisa. AB, Dartmouth Coll., 1962; MA, Brandeis U., 1964; PhD, Harvard U., 1969. Lerner prof. religion, archeol., bibl. study, ancient hist. Duke U., Durham, NC, 1969—, dir. grad. program in religion, 1979-86, 2001—; dir. Annenberg Inst., Phila., 1991-92. Pres. Am. Schs. Oriental Rsch., Balt., 1990—96, Balt., 2006—; commentator on biblical archaeology; dir. 8 digs Israel, Italy, 1970—2000; co-dir. NEH seminar Duke U., 2004; dir. Jewish St. Program, 1972—90, 2002—. Author: 10 books; co-author: The Cambridge Companiion to the Bible, 1997; editor (in chief): The Oxford Encyclopedia of Archaeology in the Near East, 5 vols., 1997; contbr. articles more than 400 to profl. jours.; frequent guest (TV series) A&E channel, Discovery channel; frequent guest: History Channel. Jewish. Avocations: singing (baritone), golf, the arts, travel. Home: 3202 Waterbury Dr Durham NC 27707-2416 Office: Duke U 118 Gray Bldg PO Box 90964 Bldg Durham NC 27708-0964 Office Phone: 919-660-3517. Business E-Mail: emc@duke.edu.

**MEYERS, HOWARD L.,** lawyer; b. Dec. 22, 1948; BS, U. Del., 1970; JD, U. Va., 1973. Bar: Pa. 1973. Sr. ptnr. in bus. and fin. sect., mng. ptnr. Phila. office Morgan, Lewis & Bockius LLP, chmn. firm fin. com. Mem. ABA, Phila. Bar Assn., Greater Phila. C. of C. (mem. exec. com., bd. dirs., gen. counsel), Phila. Flower Show (exec. com.), Coun. Pa. Horticultural Soc. Office: Morgan Lewis & Bockius LLP 1701 Market St Philadelphia PA 19103-2903 Office Phone: 215-963-5000. Office Fax: 215-963-5001. Business E-Mail: hmeyers@morganlewis.com.

**MEYERS, JAN,** retired congresswoman; b. Lincoln, Nebr., July 20, 1928; m. Louis Meyers; children: Valerie, Philip AA in Fine Arts cum laude, William Woods Coll., 1948; BA in Communications (hon.), U. Nebr.-Lincoln, 1951; LittD, William Woods Coll., 1986; LLD, Baker U., 1993. Mem. Overland Park (Kans.) City Coun., 1967-72; pres. Overland (Kans.) Park City Council; mem. Kans. Senate, 1972-84, comm. pub. health and welfare com., local govt. com.; mem. 99th-103rd Congresses from 3rd Kans. Dist., 1985-97, mem. com. internat. rels., mem. small bus. com., mem. com. on econ. and ednl. opportunities. Chmn. pub. health and welfare com., chmn. local govt. com., vice chmn. transp. com., vice chmn. utilities com. Kans. Senate. 3rd Dist. co-chmn. Bob Dole for U.S. Senate, 1968; chmn. Johnson County Bob Bennett For Gov., 1974; mem. Johnson County Cmty. Coll. Found.; bd. dirs. Johnson County Mental Health Assn.; mem. fundraising com. Johnson County Am. Cancer Soc.; mem. com. for Ctr. for Aging, Kans. U. Med. Ctr.; bd. dirs. Johnson County Libr. Assn. Recipient Outstanding Elected Ofcl. of Yr. award Assn. Cmty. Mental Health Ctrs. Kans., Woman of Achievement Matrix award Women in Communications, Disting. Service award Bus. and Profl. Women Kansas City, William Woods Alumna award of distinction, Cmty. Svc. award Jr. League Kansas City, 1st Disting. Legislator award Kans. Assn. C.C.s, Outstanding Svc. award Kans. Library Assn., United Community Services, Kans. Pub. Health Assn., award Gov.'s Conf. Child Abuse and Neglect, Outstanding Legislator award Kans. Action for Children, Friend award Nat. Assn. County Park and Recreation Ofcls., 1987, Disting. Alumna award, 1991, Spirit of Enterprise award U.S. C. of C., Guardian of Small Bus. award Nat. Fedn. Ind. Bus. Mem. LWV (past pres. Shawnee Mission) Methodist.

**MEYERS, JOHN ALLEN,** magazine publisher; b. Winnetka, Ill., Feb. 21, 1929; s. Fred W. and Ruth B. (Burras) M.; m. Jane Bowers, Sept. 18, 1954; children: Jennifer, Katherine, John. BA, Mich. State U., 1951, Litt.D. (hon.), 1978; postgrad., Columbia U., 1965. Mgr. Cleve. Time mag., 1960-63, mgr. Chgo., 1963-65, mgr. N.Y.C., 1965-68, worldwide advt. sales dir., 1968-72; v.p. Time, Inc., publisher Sports Illustrated mag., 1972-78; pub. Time mag., 1978-85; chmn. Time Inc. Mag. Co., 1985-88; chmn. emeritus Time Inc., 1988—. Appointed presdl. bd. adv. on Pvt. Sector Initiatives; chmn. J.A.M. Enterprises. Editor-in-chief Constitution mag. Bd. dirs., pres., Found. for the U.S. Constn., 1986-2004; Served with USMC, 1951-53. Decorated Purple Heart.

**MEYERS, JONATHAN EVAN,** lawyer; b. NYC, Oct. 7, 1974; s. Fred Barry and Caren Nora Meyers. BA, Columbia U., 1996; JD, Fordham U., 2002. Bar: NY 2003. Regional promotion mgr. Crave Records, San Francisco,

1996—98; local promotion mgr. Columbia Records, L.A., 1998—2000; assoc. Hogan & Hartson, NYC, 2002—05; assoc. counsel Forbes.com Inc., 2005—. Mem.: NY State Bar Assn. Office: Forbescom Inc 90 Fifth Ave New York NY 10011 Office Phone: 212-366-8974. E-mail: jmeyers@forbes.net.

**MEYERS, KAREN DIANE,** lawyer, educator; b. Cin., July 8, 1950; d. Willard Paul and Camille Jeannette (Schutte) M.; m. William J. Jones, Mar. 27, 1978. BA summa cum laude, Thomas More Coll., 1971; MBA, MEd, Xavier U., 1978; JD, U. Ky., Covington, 1978. Bar: Ohio 1978, Ky. 1978; CLU; CPCU; cert. structured settlement cons. Clk. to mgr. Baldwin Co., Cin., 1970-78; adj. prof. bus. Thomas More Coll., Crestview Hill, Ky., 1978—, CSSC-U. Notre Dame, 1994, CSSC, 1994; asst. sec., asst. v.p., sr. counsel The Ohio Life Ins. Co., Hamilton, 1978-91; prin. KD Meyers & Assocs., 1991; v.p. Benefit Designs, Inc., 1991-96, Little, Meyers & Assocs., Ltd., Cin., 1996—; adj. prof. Miami U., 1998—. Adj. lectr. U. Notre Dame, South Bend, Ind., 2005—. Bd. dirs. ARC, Hamilton, 1978-83, vol., 1978—; bd. dirs. YWCA, Hamilton, 1985-91. Gardner Found. fellow, 1968-71; recipient Ind. Progress award Bus. & Profl. Women, 1990. Fellow Life Mgmt. Inst. Atlanta; mem. ABA, Soc. Chartered Property Casualty Underwriters (instr. 1987—), Cin. Bar Assn., Butler County Bar Assn., Ohio Bar Assn., Ky. Bar Assn. Roman Catholic. Avocations: aerobics, jogging, crafts. Home: 7903 Hickory Hill Ln Cincinnati OH 45241-1363

**MEYERS, LAUREN ANCEL,** biologist; BA, Harvard U., 1996; PhD in biol. scis., Stanford U., 2000. Asst. prof. section integrative biology U. Tex., Austin. Contbr. articles to profl. jour. Named one of Top 100 Young Innovators, MIT Tech. Review, 2004. Office: U Tex Section Integrative Biology PAT 638 1 University Station C0930 Austin TX 78712 Business E-Mail: laurenmeyers@mail.utexas.edu.

**MEYERS, LAWRENCE EDWARD,** state judge; m. Barbara Meyers; children: Kelli Kelli, Clay. BA in History and Chemistry, So. Meth. U., 1970; JD, U. Kans., 1973; postgrad., U. Tex., Arlington, Tex. Wesleyan U. Asst. dist. atty. Montgomery County, Kans., 1973—75; pvt. practice Ft. Worth, 1975—88; assoc. justice U.S. Ct. Appeals (2nd cir.), Ft. Worth, 1988—92; judge Ct. Criminal Appeals, Ft. Worth, 1992—. Instr. Tex. Christian U., Ft. Worth. Mem. parish coun. St. Mary's of Assumption, Ft. Worth. Mem.: Tarrant County Bar Assn., State Bar Kans., State Bar Tex. Republican. Office: Court of Criminal Appeals Supreme Ct Bldg 201 W 14th St Austin TX 78701-1614 also: PO Box 12308 Austin TX 78711-2308

**MEYERS, LINDA DEE,** non-profit administrator, researcher; b. Chgo., Dec. 31, 1945; m. L. Richard Meyers; 2 children. BA in Phys. Edn. & Health with honors, Goshen Coll., 1968; MS in Nutrition, Colo. State U., 1974; PhD in Human Nutrition, Cornell U., 1978. Tchr. Swaneng Hill Secondary Sch., 1968-71; staff Bioteko Rural Coop., Serowe, Botswana, 1972; rsch. asst. dept. food sci. and nutrition Colo. State U., 1973-74; scientist Nat. Ctr. Health Statistics HHS, Washington, 1976-78, sr. nutrition advisor, 1986—, dep. dir. and team leader nutrn., environ. hlth. & sci. coord., 1996—2001; dep. dir. food and nutrition Inst. of Med. of Nat. Acads., Washington, 2001—03, exec. dir., food and nutrition bd., 2003—. Contbr. articles to profl. jours. Mem. APHA, IFT, Am. Soc. Nutrition, Omicron Nu, Phi Kappa Phi. Office: Inst of Med 500 Fifth St NW Washington DC 20001

**MEYERS, MARLENE O.,** retired hospital administrator; m. Eugene Meyers; children: Lori, Lisa, Dean. BSN, U. Sask., 1962; postgrad., U. Oslo, Norway, 1973; MSc, U. Calgary, Alta., Can., 1976; continuing edn., Harvard U., 1980, Banff Sch. Mgmt., 1985, U. Western Ont., Can., 1993; EMT-B, Scottsdale C.C., 2000. RN, Ariz. Various nursing positions, Alta. and B.C., Can., 1962-69; instr., chair Mount Royal Coll. Allied Health, Calgary, 1969-82; asst. exec. dir. Rockyview Hosp., Calgary, 1982-85; v.p. patient svcs. Calgary Gen. Hosp., 1985-91, pres., CEO, 1991-95, Meyers and Assocs. Health Care Mgmt. Cons., Calgary, 1995—98; clin. nurse Scottsdale Behavioral Health Ctr., 1999—. Surveyor Can. Coun. on Health Facilities Accreditation, 1986-97; mem. adv. com. for South Caucasus Health info. project, Can. Adv. Coun. Named Calgary Woman of Yr. in field of Health, 1982; recipient Heritage of Svc. award, 1992. Mem. Alta. Assn. RNs (hon.), Can. Coll. Health Svcs. Executives, Can. Exec. Svcs. Orgn., Can. Soc. for Internat. Health (bd. dirs. 1997-2001, South Caucasus adv. com. 2001—), Rotary Internat. also: 10464 E Cannon Dr Scottsdale AZ 85258-4929

**MEYERS, MARY ANN,** foundation administrator, consultant, writer; b. Sodus, NY, Sept. 30, 1937; d. Harold Galpin and Clarice Mildred (Daniel) Dye; m. John Matthew Meyers, Aug. 22, 1959; children: Andrew Christopher, Anne Kathryn. BA magna cum laude, Syracuse U., 1959; MA, U. Pa., 1965, PhD, 1976. Editorial asst. Ladies' Home Jour., Phila., 1959-62; editor, asst. dir. news bur. U. Pa., Phila., 1962-65, asst. to pres., 1973-75, univ. sec., lectr. Am. civilization, 1980-90; contbg. writer The Pennsylvania Gazette, Phila., 1965—97; dir. coll. rels., editor Haverford Horizons, lectr. in religion Haverford (Pa.) Coll., 1977-80; pres. The Annenberg Found., St. Davids, Pa., 1990-92; v.p. for external affairs Moore Coll. Art and Design, Phila., 1995-97; sr. fellow The John Templeton Found., Radnor, Pa., 1997—. Vis. com. dept. biology U. Pa., 1996—2002; mem. bd. advisors The Peter Gruber Found., St. Thomas, U.S. V.I., 2001—. Author: A New World Jerusalem, 1983, Art, Education and African American Culture: Albert Barnes and the Science of Philanthropy, 2004, 06; contbg. author: Death in America, 1975, Gladly Learn, Gladly Teach, 1978, Coping with Serious Illness, 1980, Religion in American Life, 1987; contbr. articles to profl. jours. Judge recognition program Coun. for Advancement and Support Edn., Washington, 1977—78, chair creative editing and writing workshop, 1978; mem. Picker Found. Program on Human Qualities in Medicine, N.Y.C., Phila., 1980—83; del. Phila.-Leningrad Sister Cities Project, 1986; trustee U. Pa. Press., 1985—2003; vice chmn. U. Pa. 250th Anniversary Commn., 1987—90; mem. steering com. of bd. trustees U. Pa. Annenberg Sch. for Comm., 1990—92, mem. adv. bd. U. Pa., Annenberg Ctr. for the Performing Arts, 1990—98; mem. bd. overseers U. Pa., Sch. Arts and Scis., 1990—97; mem. steering com. of bd. trustees Annenberg Ctr. for Comm., U. So. Calif. L.A., 1990—92, The Annenberg Washington Program in Comm. Policy Studies of Northwestern U., Washington, 1990—92; dir., sec. Am. Acad. Polit. and Social Sci., 1992—, World Affairs Coun. Phila., 1990—95; dir. Diagnostic and Rehab. Ctr., Phila., 1993—2002. Recipient Excellence award Women in Communications, Inc., 1973-74, award for pub. affairs reporting Newsweek/Coun. for Advancement and Support Edn., 1977, Silver medal Coun. for Advancement and Support Edn., 1986. Mem. Am. Acad. Polit. and Social Sci. (sec. and dir. 1992-), Cosmopolitan Club, Sunday Breakfast Club, Phi Beta Kappa (mem. steering com. Delaware Valley chpt. 1995-97). Roman Catholic. Home: 217 Gypsy Ln Wynnewood PA 19096-1112

**MEYERS, MIRIAM WATKINS,** retired language educator; b. Atlanta, Jan. 22, 1941; d. William Craton Watkins and Carolyn Grey (Franklin) Burtz; m. Chester Albert Meyers, July 29, 1967. AB with honors, Peabody Coll., 1962; MS, Georgetown U., 1968; postgrad., Yale U., U. Minn., Hamline U., Met. State U. Tchr. English, French Fairfax (Va.) County Pub. Schs., 1962-66; jr. editor, writer NASA Hdqrs., Washington, 1966-67; supr. practice teaching, instr. Yale U., New Haven, 1967-68; asst. to dir. and research coordinator Inst. for Interdisciplinary Studies, Mpls., 1969-71; exec. asst. to pres. Met. State U., St. Paul, 1971-72, asst. prof., 1971-76, assoc. prof., 1976-83, prof., 1983—2001, prof. emerita, 2001—. Author: A Bite off Mama's Place, 2001; mem. editl. bd. Women and Lang.; contbr. articles to profl. jours., chpts. to books. Vol. Minn. Civil Liberties Union, 1970-80. Recipient Algernon Sidney Sullivan award Peabody Coll., 1962, Teaching Excellence citation Met. State U., 1980, 86; named Outstanding Faculty Advisor Met. State U., 1986. Mem. Am. Dialect Soc., Minn. Assn. for Continuing Adult Edn. (sec. 1983-84, bd. dirs. 1983-84, 86-87), Orgn. for Study of Comm., Lang. and Gender (bd. dirs. 1990-91). Democrat. Home: 2200 W 21st St Minneapolis MN 55405-2414

**MEYERS, MORTON ALLEN,** radiologist, educator; b. Troy, N.Y., Oct. 1, 1933; s. David and Jeanne Sarah (Dunn) M.; m. Beatrice Applebaum, June 1, 1963; children:— Richard, Amy. MD, SUNY, Upstate Med. Coll., 1959.

Diplomate Am. Bd. Radiology, 1965. Intern Bellevue Hosp., N.Y.C., 1959-60; resident in radiology Columbia-Presbyn. Med. Ctr., N.Y.C., 1960-63; fellow Am. Cancer Soc., 1961-63; prof. dept. radiology Cornell U. Med. Ctr., N.Y.C., 1973-78; radiologist in chief Stony Brook U. Hosp., 1978—91; prof. chmn. dept. radiology SUNY Sch. Medicine, Stony Brook, 1978-91, prof. dept. radiology, 1991-98, disting. univ. prof., 1998—. Cons. Northport VA Hosp.; vis. investigator St. Mark's Hosp., London, 1976; ann. orator Radiol. Soc. N.Am., 1986. Author: Diseases of the Adrenal Glands: Radiologic Diagnosis, 1963, Dynamic Radiology of the Abdomen: Normal and Pathologic Anatomy, 1976, 5th edit., 2000, trans. in Spanish, 1980, Japanese, 1985, 91, Italian, 1992, Portuguese, 1999; Iatrogenic Gastrointestinal Complications, 1981; series editor: Radiology of Iatrogenic Disorders, 1981-86; editor: Computed Tomography of the Gastrointestinal Tract: Including the Peritoneal Cavity and Mesentery, 1986, Neoplasms of the Digestive Tract: Imaging, Staging, and Management, 1998; founding editor in chief Abdominal Imaging, 1976—; mem. editl. bd. Radiology, Surg. and Radiol. Anatomy; contbr. chpts. to books, articles to profl. jours.; spkr. in field. Served to capt. M.C. U.S. Army, 1963-65. Recipient Gold medal, U. Leeds, 1980, Radiol. Soc. Republic of China, 1986, Asian-Oceanian Congress Radiology, 1987, European Congress of Radiology, 1995, Indian Radiol. and Imaging Assn., 1999. Fellow: European Soc. Gastrointestinal and Abdominal Radiology, Am. Coll. Gastroenterology, Am. Coll. Radiology; mem.: European Soc. Urogenital Radiology, NY Acad. Gastroenterology, NY Roentgen Ray Soc., Assn. Univ. Radiologists, Israel Radiol. Soc. (hon.), Italian Radiol. Soc. (hon. Medal of Honor 1983), Royal Belgian Soc. Gastroenterology (hon.), Spanish Radiol. Soc. (hon.), European Assn. Radiology (hon.), Soc. Gastrointestinal Radiologists (Cannon medal 1993, Hartman medal 1995), Soc. Uroradiology, Am. Gastroenterol. Assn., Am. Roentgen Ray Soc. (Gold medal 1975, 1980), Radiol. Soc. N.Am., Alpha Omega Alpha. Home: 14 Wainscott Ln East Setauket NY 11733-3816 Office: SUNY Health Scis Ctr Sch Medicine Dept Radiology Stony Brook NY 11794-8460

**MEYERS, NICHOLAUS,** music educator; s. Walden Augustus and Cheryl Renee Meyers; m. Erica Kupinski, July 6, 2001. MusB, Augusta State U., 1997—2002; MusM, U. of Tenn., 2002—04. Grad. libr. asst. U. Tenn., 2003—04; instr. of music Augusta State U., 2004—. Percussion instr. Lakeside H.S., Evans, Ga., 2001—; percussionist Augusta Opera, Augusta, Ga., 2002—; timpanist Augusta Choral Soc., Augusta, Ga., 2004—; percussionist Oakridge Symphony, Oakridge, Tenn., 2004. Composer: (composition) A Glimpse Ahead, Reflections, Three Shorts, Altered Stages, Contrasting Opinions, Two Holy Songs. Maxwell Meml. Music scholarship, Augusta State U., 1998—2002, Mauldin Music scholarship, 1999—2002. Mem.: ASCAP, Percussive Arts Soc., Soc. of Composers, Coll. Music Soc. Achievements include research in Guide to Timpani Concertos. Home: 151 Stonemill Dr Martinez GA 30907 Personal E-mail: nmeyers@aug.edu.

**MEYERS, PAMELA SUE,** lawyer; b. Lakewood, N.J., June 13, 1951; d. Morris Leon and Isabel (Leibowitz) M.; m. Gerald Stephen Greenberg, Aug. 24, 1975; children: David Stuart Greenberg, Allison Brooke Greenberg. AB with distinction, Cornell U., 1973; JD cum laude, Harvard U., 1976. Bar: N.Y. 1977, Ohio 1990. Assoc. Stroock & Stroock & Lavan, N.Y.C., 1976-80; staff v.p., asst. gen. counsel Am. Premier Underwriters, Inc., 1980-96; legal counsel Citizens Fed. Bank, Dayton, Ohio, 1997-98; gen. counsel, sec. Mosler Inc., Hamilton, Ohio, 1998—2001. Bd. dirs. Hamilton County Alcohol and Drug Addiction Svc. Bd., 1996-2000, Adath Israel Congregation, 1999-2005; dir. Gorman Heritage Farm Found., 2006—; trustee Carpenters Creek Civic Assn., 2004-06; mem. Village Evendale Recreation Commn., 2006—. Mem. Cin. Bar Assn., Harvard Club of Cin. (pres. 1998-99, bd. dirs. 1993-2000), Phi Beta Kappa. Jewish. Avocations: piano, reading, tennis. Home: 3633 Carpenters Creek Dr Cincinnati OH 45241-3824 Personal E-mail: psmeyers@fuse.net.

**MEYERS, REBECKA LOUISE,** pediatric general surgeon; b. Salt Lake City, May 11, 1958; MD, Oreg. Health Sciences U. Sch. Medicine, 1985. Cert. Gen. Surgery, Pediatric Gen. Surgery. Intern, gen. surgery U. Calif. Med. Ctr., San Francisco, 1985—88, fellow, cardiovascular diseases, 1988—90, resident, gen. surgery, 1990—92; fellow St. Christopher's Hosp. for Children in Pediatric Surgery, Phila., 1992—94; pediatric surgeon Primary Children's Med. Ctr., Salt Lake City, 1994—; chief, divsn. pediatric surgery Univ. Utah Hosp. (now called U. Utah Health Sciences Ctr.), Salt Lake City, 2001—; asst. prof. U. Utah, Salt Lake City, 1994—99, assoc. prof., 1999. Mem.: Utah Med. Assn., Pacific Assn. of Pediatric Surgeons, Internat. Pediatric Endosurgery Group, Assn. Women Surgeons, Am. Pediatric Surgical Assn., Am. Coll. Surgeons, Am. Acad. Pediatrics. Office: Primary Childrens Med Ctr 100 N Medical Dr Ste 2600 Salt Lake City UT 84113 also: U Utah Health Services Ctr 50 N Medical Dr Salt Lake City UT 84132 Office Phone: 801-588-3350.*

**MEYERS, STUART IRWIN,** real estate developer; b. N.Y.C., Aug. 7, 1941; s. Herman and Helen Noah Meyeroff; m. Carol Ann Goldstein, Sept. 26, 1964 (div. Apr. 1970); m. Arlene Merryl Meyers, June 20, 1976 (div. Sept. 1998); children: Wendy Jill Meyers-Crabb, Jeffrey Brian. BS in Econ., U. Pa., 1963; MBA in Acctg., Columbia U., 1964. CPA N.Y., Fla. Sr. auditor Price Waterhouse & Co., NYC, 1964-68; dir. corp. devel. mergers and acquisitions ITT Corp., NYC, 1969-73; staff v.p. mergers and acquisitions RCA Corp., NYC, 1973—75; v.p. contr./CFO trucks equipment div. Hertz Corp., 1975—76; v.p. mergers and acquisitions Kraft Inc., Glenview, Ill., 1976-81; sr. v.p. mergers and acquisitions United Brands Corp., 1981-84; sr. v.p. devel. The Related Co., Miami, Fla., 1985-93; chmn., founder, prin. The Cornerstone Group, Coral Gables, Fla., 1993—; chmn. Cornerstone Strats., LLC, St. Thomas. Bd. dirs. Affordable Housing Tax Credit Coalition, Washington; bd. dirs., founder Affordable Housing Providers, Tallahassee; bd. dirs., trustee Nat. Assn. Home Builders Multifamily Coun., Chgo., 1997. Named Pillars of the Industry Freddie Mac "Builder of the Yr.", 2003; recipient Builder of the Yr. Award, Multifamily Exec. Mag., 2003. Mem.: AICPA, N.Y. State CPA Soc., Fla. CPA Soc., St. Thomas Yacht Club, LaGorce Country Club (founder), Penn Club, Dade Alumni Club U. Pa. (bd. dirs.), Wharton Sch. Club S. Fla. (bd. dirs.). Jewish. Avocations: piano, golf, ranching, skiing, yachting. Home: Elysian Beach Resort Unit # 349 St Thomas VI 00802 Office Phone: 340-715-6099.

**MEYERS, WAYNE MARVIN,** microbiologist, physician; b. Huntingdon County, Pa., Aug. 28, 1924; s. John William and Carrie Venca (Weaver) Meyers; m. Esther Louise Kleinschmidt, Aug. 26, 1953; children: Amy, George, Daniel, Sara. BS in Chemistry, Juniata Coll., 1947, DSc (hon.), 1986; diploma, Moody Bible Inst., 1950; MS in Med. Microbiology, U. Wis., 1953, PhD in Med. Microbiology, 1955; MD, Baylor Coll. Medicine, 1959. Instr. Baylor Coll. Medicine, 1955-59; intern Conemaugh Valley Meml. Hosp., Johnstown, Pa., 1959-60; staff physician Berrien Gen. Hosp., Berrien Center, Mich., 1960-61; missionary physician Am. Leprosy Missions, Congo/Zaire, Burundi, 1961-73; prof. pathology Sch. Medicine U. Hawaii, Honolulu, 1973-75; chief microbiology divsn. Armed Forces Inst. Pathology, Washington, 1975-89, chief mycobacteriology, 1989—2005, registrar leprosy registry, 1975—2005, asst. to registrar leprosy registry, 2005—, vis. scientist, 2005—; mem. leprosy panel U.S.-Japan Coop. Med. Sci. Program, 1976-83; mem. sci. adv. bd. Leonard Wood Meml., 1981-85, sci. cons. dir., 1985-87, sci. dir. 1987-90, cons., 1990—2004; rsch. affiliate Tulane U. 1981—. Bd. dirs. Gorgas Meml. Inst. Tropical and Preventive Medicine, Inc., Leonard Wood Meml. Bd. dirs. Jour. Leprosy, 1978—93; contbr. chapters to books, articles to profl. jours. Adv. bd. Damien-Dutton Soc. Leprosy Aid, Inc., 1983—96, corp. bd. dirs., 1996—; adv. bd. Am. Leprosy Missions, Inc., 1979—88, chmn. bd. dirs., 1985—88, program cons. to bd. dirs., 1988—2003, mem. bd. references, 1988—; mem. Hansen's Disease rsch. adv. com. Gillis W. Long Hansen's Disease Ctr., Carville, La., 1985—92, chmn., 1985—92; mem. Buruli Ulcer task force WHO, 1998—2004; bd. dirs. Leonard Wood Meml., 2006—. With U.S. Army, 1944—46. Allergy Found. Am. fellow, 1957, 1958, WHO Rsch. grantee, 1978—87. Mem.: Internat. Soc. Travel Medicine, Binford-Dammin Soc. Infectious Disease Pathologists (sec.-treas. 1988—91, pres. 1995—96), Am. Soc. Microbiology, Am. Soc. Tropical Medicine and Hygiene, Internat. Soc. Tropical Dermatology, Internat. Acad. Pathology,

Internat. Leprosy Assn. (councillor 1978—88, pres. 1988—93), Sigma Xi. Achievements include research in human and experimental leprosy, and other mycobacterial diseases. Office: Armed Forces Inst Pathology Washington DC 20306-6000 Office Phone: 202-782-1873. E-mail: wmekmeyers@comcast.net.

**MEYERSON, ADAM,** foundation administrator; b. Phila., Aug. 2, 1953; s. Martin and Margy Ellin (Lazarus) M.; m. Nina Hope Shea, Sept. 13, 1986; children: Thomas Abraham, William Ulysses, Henry Elijah. BA, Summa Cum Laude, Yale U., 1974; student, Harvard U., 1977-79. Mng. editor The Am. Spectator, Bloomington, Ind., 1977-87; editorial writer Wall St. Jour., NYC, 1979-83; editor Policy Rev. The Heritage Found., Washington, 1983-98, v.p. ednl. affairs, 1993—2001; pres. Philanthropy Roundtable, Washington, 2001—. Co-editor: The Wall Street Journal on Management, 1985. Home: 3714 Ingomar St NW Washington DC 20015-1820 Office: Philanthropy Roundtable 1150 17th St NW # 503 Washington DC 20036 Office Phone: 202-822-8333. E-mail: ameyerson@philanthropyroundtable.org.*

**MEYERSON, HAROLD,** journalist; b. LA, 1950; Grad. Columbia Univ. Exec editor L.A. Weekly mag, 1989—2001, polit editor & columnist, 2001—; editor at large The American Prospect. Contbr. columns in newspapers, articles in polit jours. Office: The American Prospect Suite 717 2000 L St NW Washington DC 20036

**MEYERSON, IVAN D.,** lawyer, corporate financial executive; AB, U. Calif., Berkeley, 1966; JD, Stanford U., 1969. Bar: Calif. 1970. Assoc. Herzstein & Maier, San Francisco, 1970-75, ptnr., 1976-78; atty. SEC, 1975-76; assoc. gen. counsel McKesson Corp., San Francisco, 1984-87, v.p., gen. counsel, 1987-98; exec. v.p., gen. counsel McKesson - HBOC Inc., San Francisco, 1998—. Office: McKesson Corp 1 Post St Ste 3275 San Francisco CA 94104-5292

**MEYERSON, LEE A.,** lawyer; b. NYC, May 11, 1956; AB magna cum laude, Duke U., 1977; JD, NYU, 1981. With Simpson, Thacher & Bartlett, LLP, NYC, 1981—, ptnr., 1989—. Editor: NYU Law Review, 1981. Mem.: Assn. Bar City of NY. Office: Simpson Thacheer & Bartlett LLP 425 Lexington Ave New York NY 10017-3954 Office Phone: 212-455-3675. Office Fax: 212-455-2502. E-mail: lmeyerson@stblaw.com.

**MEYERSON, MARGY ELLIN,** urbanist, civic volunteer; b. Washington, Feb. 25, 1923; d. Arthur and Frieda (Langer) Lazarus; m. Martin Meyerson, Dec. 31, 1945; children: Adam, Laura (dec.), Matthew. BA, U. Chgo., 1943; postgrad., Harvard U., 1947-48, U. Pa., 1953-56; MA, Bryn Mawr Coll., 1953, U. Pa., 1993. Asst. to gen. counsel Pa. Postwar Planning Commn., 1944-45; assoc. Phila. Housing Assn. and Citizens Council on City Planning, 1945; mgmt. staff Chgo. Housing Authority, 1946. Cons. Ill. Postwar Planning Commn., 1948; assoc. Com. on Nat. Policy, Yale U., 1948-49; lectr. social scis. Drexel U., 1956-57, city and regional planning U. Calif., Berkeley, 1965-66; bd. dirs., exec. com Phila. Housing Assn., 1952-57; v.p., treas. Community Devel Co., Inc., 1957-63; bd. dirs., exec. com. Niagara Frontier Housing Devel., 1967-70; co-chmn. Cathedral Pk. Devel., Buffalo, 1968-70; commr. Phila. City Planning Commn., 1971-81; bd. dirs. Tensiodyne, Inc., Girard Bank Co-editor: Urban Housing, 1966, Japanese translation 1975; co-editor abstracts sect. Jour. Am. Inst. Planners, 1952-60. Trustee Oakland (Calif.) Mus., 1965-66; trustee Rosenbach Found., Rosenbach Mus. and Library, 1975—, chmn. 1979-92; trustee Presby.-U. Pa. Med. Ctr., 1983-95, exec. com. 1985-95; trustee Lewis Stevens Community Trust, 197785, v.p. 197985; mem. Pa. Humanities Council, 1981-86; adv. council Hampshire Coll., 1981—; bd. dirs. World Affairs Council, Am. Coll. in Paris Found., 1982-87; trustee Presbyn. Hosp. Phila., 1995-, New Courtland Elder Svcs., 1985-; overseer U. Pa. Libr., 1990-, co-chmn. Friends of the Libr., 1990-. Recipient Susan B. Anthony prize Bryn Mawr Coll., 1953, ann. award for best paper Nat. Hwy Rsch. Bd., 1953; named Disting. Dau. of Pa., 1982; Martin and Margy Meyerson Professorship named in their honor U. Pa., 1995, Martin and Margy Meyerson chair fgn. affairs named in their honor Philippine Women's U., Manila. Mem. Prytanean Soc., Martin Margy Meyerson Conf. Ctr., Cosmopolitan Club (Phila.). Address: 2016 Spruce St Philadelphia PA 19103-6524

**MEYERSON, MARTIN,** academic administrator, urban planner; b. NYC, Nov. 14, 1922; s. Samuel and Etta (Berger) M.; m. Margy Ellin Lazarus, Dec. 31, 1945; children: Adam, Laura (dec.), Matthew. BA, Columbia U., 1942; MCP, Harvard U., 1949; LLD, U. Pa., 1970, Queen's U., Can., 1968, Shiraz U., Iran, 1973, U. Edinburgh, 1976; PhD honoris causa, Hebrew U., 1987; also 18 other hon. doctorates including ScD, LHD, LittD, DFA, DHum, 1967-98. Mem. staff Michael Reese Hosp., Chgo., 1945-47; asst. prof. coll. and grad. social scis. U. Chgo., 1948-52; assoc. prof., dept. chair city and regional planning U. Pa., 1952-56, prof., 1956-57, pres., 1970-81, pres. emeritus, 1981—, chmn. U. Pa. Press, chmn. adv. bd. Inst. Rsch. Higher Edn., Fels Ctr. Govt., 1981—; bd dirs. Lauder Inst. Mgmt. and Internat. Studies, co-chmn. Commn. for U. Pa. 250th Anniversary, 1987-90, Univ. prof., 1977—; exec. dir. action Am. Coun. to Improve Our Neighborhoods, 1955-56, trustee, 1956-66; Frank Backus Williams prof. city planning and urban rsch. Harvard U., 1957-63, acting dean Grad. Sch. Design, 1963; founding dir. Joint Ctr. for Urban Studies, MIT and Harvard U., 1958-63; dean, prof. urban devel. Coll. Environ. Design, U. Calif., Berkeley, 1963-66; interim chancellor U. Calif., Berkeley, 1965; pres., prof. public policy SUNY, Buffalo, 1966-70; prof. Inst. Urban Rsch. U. Pa.; dir. visitor Inst. for Advanced Study, Princeton, N.J., 1983-84; pres. U. Pa., 1986-99. Dir. Real Estate Rsch. Corp., 1961-67, Marine Midland Bank, 1966-70, 1st Fidelity Bancorp. (now First Union), Scott Paper Co., Penn Mut. Life, Saint Gobain Corp., Certain Teed, Norton, Avatar, Universal Health Svcs.; cons. to govts., pvt. firms U.S. and abroad, UN missions, urban/econ. devel. to Japan, Indonesia and South Asia, Yugoslavia, 1958-65; sr. advisor urban and regional pub. and pvt. devel. Arthur D. Little, Inc., 1958-66; cons. Sears Roebuck Found., 1958-69; chmn. bd. Western N.Y. Nuclear Rsch. Ctr., 1966-70; adv. coun. NASA, 1965-70; White House presdl. task forces, urban policy, 1960-69; mem. coun. Electric Power Rsch. Inst., 1973-77; mem. U.S. del. UN Conf. on Sci. and Tech. for Less Developed Areas, 1963. Author: (with E. C. Banfield) Politics, Planning and the Public Interest, 1955, Housing, People and Cities, 1962, Face of the Metropolis, 1963, Boston, 1966, Gladly Learn and Gladly Teach, 1978; editor: Conscience of the City, 1970, McGraw-Hill Series on Cmty. Devel.; mem. editorial bd. Ency. Britannica, 1980-98, Daedalus, 1972-90. Mem. Air Conservation Commn., 1962-66; mem. Bay Area Conservation and Devel. Commn., 1965-66; chmn. Assembly Univ. Goals and Governance, 1969-74; commr. N.Y. State Commn. on Post-Secondary Sch. Edn., 1976-77; hon. prof. Nat. U. Asuncion, 1969—, Beijing U., 1996—; bd. dirs. Phila. Bicentennial Corp., 1970-76, Greater Phila. Partnership, 1973-81, Afro-Am. Film Festival, 1966-70, Niagara U., 1968-70, Center for Community Change, 1968-72, Acad. Religion and Mental Health, 1970-78, Center for Ednl. Devel., 1967-70, Phila. Mus. Art, 1974—, Nat. Urban Coalition, 1969-78; trustee, Niagara U., 1968-70, Am. Coll., 1982-92, Curtis Inst. Music, 1987-94, United World Coll.N. Mex., 1984—, Am. Schs. Oriental Rsch., 1985—, Tel Aviv U., Coll. Bd., 1986-92, Hebrew U., Internat. House Ctr., Monell Chem. Senses Ctr., chmn., 1993—, Fgn. Policy Rsch. Inst., 1981—, Panasonic Found., 1982—, Ctr. for Visual History, U.S. Com. on the Constl. System; founding dir. Internat. Centre for Study East Asian Devel. Japan; Inst. for Internat. Edn., 1971—, chmn., 1981-85; bd. dirs. Internat. Council Ednl. Devel., 1971-94, Am. Council Financial Aid to Edn., 1975-81, Open Univ. Found., U.K., 1979-82; chmn. council pres. Nat. Accelerator Lab., 1972-73; co-chmn. Images (French TV), 1976-79, Salzburg Seminar Bd., 1978—, sr. fellow, 1997—; co-chmn. Marconi Internat. Fellowship Found., chair exec. com., 1978-96, chmn. bd. dirs., 1996—; Internat. gov. Center Environ. Studies, London, 1966-84; mem. sr. exec. council Conf. Bd., 1970-77; trustee Aspen Inst., 1976-96; chair coun. UN Centre for Regional Devel., Nagoya, Japan, 1983-93; chair internat. selection commn. Phila. Liberty Medal, 1988—; bd. overseers Koc Univ., Bosphorus, Turkey, 1994—; bd. dirs. Internat. Literacy Inst., 1996—. Decorated commendature Knight-Commdr. (Italy); chevalier de l'Ordre Nat. de Mérite (France); Order of the Rising Sun Emperor of Japan; recipient Einstein medal Am. Technion

---

Soc., 1976, Disting. Achievement award U. Calif. Berkeley, 1984, John Jay award Columbia U., 1982, Disting. Educator award Assn. Collegiate Schs. of Planning, 1996; overseas fellow Churchill Coll. Urban Planning, Cambridge U., 1983; hon. fellow Soc. for Tech. Communication, 1988; Wheelwright fellow Harvard U.; Meyerson Hall named in his honor U. Pa. Grad. Sch. Fine Arts; Martin and Margy Meyerson Professorship named in honor U. Pa., 1995, Philippine Women's U., Manila. Fellow Am. Acad. Arts and Scis., Royal Soc. Arts (Franklin fellow), Buckminster Fuller Inst. of Design Scis. (founder), Am. Philos. Soc. (exec. com.), Nat. Acad. Edn.; mem. Am. Soc. Planning Ofcls. (past dir., aide to exec. dir.), Am. Inst. Planners (past gov., spl. award winner), Internat. Assn. Univs. Paris (Am. dir. 1975—, head 1982-85, hon. pres. 1985—), Coun. Fgn. Rels., European Acad. Arts, Scis. and Letters (academician), Phi Beta Kappa. Clubs: Philadelphia, Century (N.Y.C.), Cosmos (Washington), U. Pa. (N.Y.C.). Office: Univ Pa Library 225 Van Pelt Philadelphia PA 19104

**MEYERSON, SEYMOUR,** retired chemist; b. Chgo., Dec. 4, 1916; s. Joseph and Rena (Margulies) M.; m. Lotte Strauss, May 22, 1943; children: Sheella, Elana. SB, U. Chgo., 1938, postgrad., 1938-39, 47-48, George Williams Coll., 1939-40; DSc (hon.), Valparaiso U., 1995. Inspector powder & explosives Kankakee Ordnance Works, Joliet, Ill., 1942; chemist Deavitt Labs., Chgo., 1941-42; from chemist to rsch. cons. Standard Oil Co. (Ind.) Rsch. Dept. (now BP Corp. N.Am. Inc.), Whiting, Ind. and Naperville, Ill., 1946—84. Mem. indsl. adv. coun. chemistry dept. U. Okla., Norman, 1967-69; Frontiers in Chemistry lectr. Wayne State U., 1965; invited spkr. James L. Waters Symposium, Pitts. Conf., Chgo., 1995. Charter mem. editl. adv. bd. Organic Mass Spectrometry, 1968-87, Mass Spectromony Revs., 1980-87; author, co-author 190 sci. publs. 2d. lt. AUS, 1943—46, ETO. Mem. Am. Chem. Soc. (Frank H. Field and Joe L. Franklin award for outstanding achievement in mass spectrometry 1993), Am. Soc. for Mass Spectrometry., Phi Beta Kappa. Secular Humanist. Achievements include research in chemistry of gas-phase organic ions; patents in field. Home: 43 Vermont Ct Unit A1 Asheville NC 28806-3058 Personal E-mail: meyerson43@hotmail.com.

**MEYERSON, STANLEY PHILLIP,** lawyer; b. Apr. 13, 1916; s. Louis A. and Ella Meyerson; m. Sherry Maxwell, Nov. 30, 1996; children: Marianne Martin, Camilla, Margot Ellis, Stanley P. AB, Duke U., 1937, JD, 1939. Bar: SC 1939, NY 1940, Ga. 1945, US Supreme Ct. Ptnr. Johnson Hatcher & Meyerson, Atlanta, 1945-55, Hatcher, Meyerson, Oxford & Irvin, Atlanta, 1955-78, Westmoreland, Hall, McGee, Oxford & Meyerson, Atlanta, 1978-88, McGee & Oxford, Atlanta, 1988—. Former adj. prof. Ga. State U.; dir., officer various corps. Contbr. Co-founder West Paces Ferry Hosp., Atlanta, Annandale at Suwanee for the Handicapped; trustee Hudson Libr., Inc., Highlands, NC, MetroGroup, Atlanta; del. Moscow Conf., Law and Bilateral Econ. Rels., 1990. Lt. comdr. USNR, 1943—45. Mem.: ABA (former professionalism com.), Atlanta Bar Assn. (former sec.), Ga. Bar Assn. (former chmn. tax com.), Georgians for Nixon (chmn. 1960), Duke U. Alumni Assn. (former pres. Atlanta chpt., former sec. N.Y.C. chpt.), Cherokee Town and Country Club (Atlanta), Highlands Country Club, Rotary Club Highlands N.C.

**MEYER WEISGERBER, MARTHA LINDSEY,** medical products executive; b. Summit, N.J., May 28, 1955; d. William Harold and Hattie Griffin (Ward) Meyer; m. James Curtis Weisgerber, June 22, 1991; 1 child, Emily Griffin. BA, Wake Forest U., 1977. Sales-mfrs. rep. Philip Morris Tobacco Co., Winston-Salem, 1977-82; pharm. sales rep. USV Pharm. Divsn.-Revlon Corp., Winston-Salem, 1982-84, Upjohn Pharms., N.J., 1984-89; hosp. sales rep., med. sys. mgr., area account mgr. Lederle Labs. divsn. Am. Cyanamid, 1989—. Deacon, elder First Presbyn. Ch., Cranford, N.J., 1995—. Mem. Jr. League Elizabeth Plainfield (bd. mem. 1991-92). Republican. Avocations: swimming, gardening. Home: 313 N Union Ave Cranford NJ 07016-2414 Office: Wyeth Ayerst Pharm PO Box 7447 Philadelphia PA 19101-7447

**MEYINSSE, JOSEPH APPOLINAIRE,** mathematics professor, researcher; s. Appolinaire Paul and Theresa Meyinsse; m. Patricia Elizabeth McClean; 1 child, Jerome. BS, Xavier Coll., Tenn., 1980; MS, So. U., Baton Rouge, 1985, MS, 1983; PhD, La. State U., 1995. From asst. to assoc. prof. So. U., Baton Rouge, 1992—2003, prof., chmn., 2003—. Named Tchr. of Yr., So. U., 2002; grantee. La. Bd. Regents, 2004—. Mem.: Nat. Coun. Tchrs. Math., Math. Assn. Am. Office: Southern Univ 156 Elton C Harrison Dr Baton Rouge LA 70813 Office Phone: 225-771-5180. Business E-mail: joseph_meyinsse@subr.edu.

**MEYROWITZ, CAROL,** retail executive; With The TJX Cos., Inc., Framingham, Mass., 1983—, exec. v.p. merchandising, Marmaxx group, exec. v.p., pres. Marmaxx group, 2001—04, sr. exec. v.p., 2004—05, adv. cons., 2005, pres., 2005—. Office: TJX Companies 770 Cochituate Rd Framingham MA 01701*

**MEYSTEL, MICHAEL A.,** Internet company executive; b. Moscow, Feb. 12, 1973; arrived in U.S., 1978; s. Alexander M. and Marina M. (Selitsky) M.; m. Robin L. Weiss, May 25, 1997 (div.); 1 child, Jacob. Student, Drexel U., 1989—94; BBA in Computer Sci. magna cum laude, Ursinus Coll. Sys. and network adminstr. Drexel U., Phila., 1991—94; sr. sys. analyst Bell Atlantic, Malvern, Pa., 1994—95; pres., CEO Cognisphere, Inc., West Chester, Pa., 1995—; sr. sys. analyst Decision One Corp., Malvern, 1995—96; cons., application developer Shared Med. Sys., Malvern, 1996—97, Conectiv Energy, Newark, Del., 1997—98, Anderson BDG, Inc., Allentown, Pa., 1998; project mgr. The Vanguard Group, Valley Forge, Pa., 1998—; dir. info. tech. MRDS, Inc., 1999—2003, COO, 2003—05. Sys. cons. ADREM, Inc., Bala, Pa., 1991-94; rsch. asst. Siemens Corp. Rsch., Princeton, N.J., 1992; pres., CEO ICSC Corp., West Chester, 1995-2000. Chmn. Citizens for Youth Devel. Through Sports, 2005—06. Achievements include inventor/patentee apparatus for text structuring. Office: Cognisphere Inc PO Box 2591 West Chester PA 19380

**MEZA, LUIS ALBERTO,** internist, researcher; s. Luis Alberto and Susana Cartes Meza; m. Teresa I. Ibarra, Sept. 3, 1966; children: Luis A. Jr., Monica Meza Hernandez, Leticia Ann Canizaro, Lisa Cristina Harrell. MD, U. Nat. Asuncion, Paraguay, 1966. Diplomate Am. Bd. Internal Medicine, Am. Bd. Oncology, Am. Bd. Hematology. Intern Mercy Hosp., Des Moines, 1970—71; resident in internal medicine La. State U., New Orleans, 1971—74; fellow Ochsner Found. Hosp., New Orleans, 1974—76; assoc. prof. medicine La. State U., Lafayette, 1976—; physician SW Oncology, Lafayette, 1979—. Chief med. staff Southpark Hosp., Youngsville, La., 2005—06. Capt. Paraguay Nat. Army, 1964—69. Fellow: ACP, Internat. Soc. Hematology; mem.: Am. Soc. Hematology, So. Assn. for Oncology, La. State Med. Soc., So. Med. Assn., Am. Soc. of Clin. Oncology, Lafayette Parish Med. Soc. Roman Catholic. Achievements include research in growth factor support in treating side effects related to chemotherapy. Avocations: travel, golf, photography. Office: Southwest Oncology 443 Heymann Blvd Ste A Lafayette LA 70503 Office Phone: 337-234-4535. Office Fax: 337-235-4272. Personal E-mail: lamezamd@aol.com.

**MEZACAPA, EDNA S.,** music educator, elementary school educator; b. Flint, Mich., Jan. 23, 1948; d. Jack E. and Vlasta A. Tremayne; m. Nicklas A. Mezacapa, July 25, 1970; children: Amy Anne, Sara Marie. MusB, Heidelberg Coll., Tiffin, Ohio, 1970. Gen. music tchr. Bellevue (Ohio) City Schs., 1969—73; youth choir dir. Findlay Episc. Ch., Findlay, Ohio, 1975—78; subs. tchr. Rochester (N.Y.) Schs., 1979—81; youth choir dir. Ch. of the Epiphany, Rochester, 1979—81; music tchr., K-8 St. Mary's Cath. Sch., Kalamazoo, 1981—82, St. Ludmila Cath. Sch., Cedar Rapids, Iowa, 1984—86; tchr. Christian edn. Calvary Episc. Ch., Rochester, Minn., 1986—87; subs. music tchr., 1-6 Rochester City Schs., Rochester, Minn., 1988—90, music tchr., 1-6, 1990—. Dir. Calvary Episc. Youth Choir, 1995—96, Suzuki Orch., 2001—03. Dir. youth choir Calvary Episcopal Ch., 1996—97; dir. Suzuki Orch. 2001—03.

---

**MEZEI, GEOFFREY D.,** physiologist; b. Madison, Wis., Dec. 11, 1974; s. Donald Harry and Kathryn Ann Mezei; m. Lisa Ann Houpas, June 22, 2002; 1 child, Joseph Louis. BS in Kinesiology, U. Wis., Madison, 1997. Clin. exercise physiologist Beaver Dam (Wis.) Cmty. Hosp., 2001—. Recipient Harold F. Ames award, Western Golf Assn., 1996; Evans scholar, 1993—97. Mem.: Wis. State Soc. Cardiotherapy and Pulmonary Rehab., Am. Coll. Sports Medicine (cert. exercise specialist). Avocations: hunting, fishing, cooking, sports. Office: Beaver Dam Cmty Hosp 707 S University Ave Beaver Dam WI 53916

**MEZEY, ROBERT,** poet; b. Phila., Feb. 28, 1935; s. Ralph and Clara M.; m. Olivia Simpson (div.); children: Naomi, Judah, Eve. Student, Kenyon Coll., 1951-53; BA, U. Iowa, 1959; postgrad., Stanford U., 1960-61. Lectr. Western Res. U., Cleve., 1963-64, Franklin & Marshall Coll., Lancaster, Pa., 1965-66; asst. prof. Fresno (Calif.) State U., 1967-68, U. Utah, Salt Lake City, 1973-76; prof., poet-in-residence Pomona Coll., Claremont, Calif., 1976-99; ret., 1999. Author: (poems) The Lovemaker, 1960 (Lamont award), White Blossoms, 1965, The Door Standing Open, 1970, Selected Translations, 1981, Evening Wind, 1987 (Bassine citation, PEN prize 1989), Collected Poems 1952-1999, 2000 (Poets prize 2002); editor Naked Poetry, 1968, Poems from the Hebrew, 1973, Collected Poems of Henri Coulette, 1990, Selected Poems of Thomas Hardy, 1998, The Poetry of E.A. Robinson, 1999, Poems of the American West, 2002, A Word Like Fire: Selected Poems of Dick Barnes, 2005; translator: Tungsten (César Vallejo), 1988. With U.S. Army, 1953—55. Fellow Ingram Merrill, 1973, 89, Guggenheim Found., 1977, Stanford U., 1960, NEA, 1987; recipient Poetry prize Am. Acad. Arts and Letters, 1982. Avocations: tennis, chess. Home: 960 E Bonita Ave # 28 Pomona CA 91767 Personal E-mail: mezteadancer@aol.com.

**MEZO, RICHARD EUGENE,** literature and language professor, writer; b. Carterville, Ill., Aug. 17, 1938; s. William Leonard Mezo and Madeline Helen Wilkerson; m. Sun Hee Choe Mezo; children: Harmony Suzanne, Julie Ann. AA, San Diego City Coll., 1969; MA, Calif. State U., 1972; PhD, U. ND, 1978. Cert. Teacher 6-12 Western Wash. U., 1988. English instr. Several Overseas U. (Saudi Arabia, Taiwan, Korea), 1979—85, Pierce Coll., Tacoma, 1985—86, Olympic Coll., Bremerton, Wash., 1986—87; asst. prof. Meyille State U., ND, 1988—89; assoc. prof. U. Guam, 1989—99; lectr. U. Md., Asian Divsn., 1992—2001; tchr. Dept. Def. Edn. Activity, Arlington, Va., 2001—. Reader ETS Coll. Bd., Daytona, Fla., 1997—; chmn., divsn. English and applied linguistics U. Guam, 1990—92. Author: (reference book) Am. Nat. Bio., 1999, World Edn. E.ncy, 2001. Mem.: MLA (field bibliographer 2002—), Assn. Lit. Scholars and Critics, Acad. Am. Poets. Democrat. Protestant. Avocation: reading. Home: 109 Waters Landing Stafford VA 22554 Office: Dept Def Edn Activity 4040 N Fairfax Dr Arlington VA 22203 Personal E-mail: remezo@yahoo.com.

**MEZVINSKY, EDWARD M.,** lawyer; b. Ames, Iowa, Jan. 17, 1937; m. Marjorie Margolies; 11 children. BA, U. Iowa, 1960; MA in Polit. Sci., U. Calif., Berkeley, 1963, JD, 1965. Bar: Iowa. Iowa State Legislature, 1969-70; U.S. congressman 1st Dist., Iowa, 1973-77; U.S. rep. UN Commn. on Human Rights, 1977-79; chmn. Pa. Dem. State Com., 1981-86. Author: A Term to Remember; contbr. articles to law jours. Mem. Pa. Bar Assn., Bar of the Supreme Ct. of U.S., Omicron Delta Kappa. Office: 9 Elliott Ave Bryn Mawr PA 19010-3407

**MEZZULLO, LOUIS ALBERT,** lawyer; b. Balt., Sept. 20, 1944; m. Judith Scales, Jan. 2, 1970. BA, U. Md., 1967, MA, 1976; JD, T.C. Williams Law Sch., 1976. Bar: Va. 1976. Sales rep. Humble Oil (name now Exxon), Richmond, Va., 1970-72; acctg. Marcoin, Inc., Richmond, 1972-73; pvt. practice bookkeeping, tax preparation, Richmond, 1973-76; assoc. McGuire, Woods, Battle and Boothe, Richmond, 1976-79; dir. Mezzullo & McCandlish, Richmond, 1979-2000; mem. Mezzullo & Guare, PLC, Richmond, 2000—03. Contbr. articles to profl. jours. Former bd. dirs. Richmond Symphony; bd. dirs. Va. Mus. Fine Arts Found.; former pres. Southampton Citizens Assn., Richmond, 1986. Served with USAR, 1969-75. Mem. ABA (tax sect.), Internat. Acad. Estate and Trust Law, Am. Coll. Trust and Estate Counsel, Am. Coll. Tax Counsel (chair), Va. State Bar (tax sect.), Am. Coll. Employee Benefit Counsel, Va. Bar Assn., Am. Bar Found., Va. Law Found., Estate Planning Coun. Richmond, Trust Adminstrs. Coun., Am. Coll. Employee Benefits Counsel, Willow Oaks Country Club. Home: 2961 Westchester Rd Richmond VA 23225-1842 Office: Luce Forward Hamilton & Scripps 6050 El Toro Ranch Rancho Santa Fe CA 92067 Office Phone: 804-775-4312. Business E-Mail: Lmezzullo@mcguirewoods.com, lmezzullo@luce.com.

**MFORMBELE, AKONGNWI CLEMENT,** mathematician, educator; b. Bamenda, Cameroon, Dec. 16, 1976; BSc in Math. & Computer Sci. (hon.), Buea U., Cameroon, 1997, MSc (hon.) in Math., 1999; MSc in Applied Math. (hon.), Lehigh U., Bethlehem, Pa., 2005. Tchr. math., computer sci., applied math., physics Presbyn. Ch., Buea, Cameroon, 1997—2003; lectr. U. Buea, 1999—2003; summer excel prof. Lehigh U., Bethlehem, 2003, tchg. asst., 2003—. Author: (textbooks) Effective Mathematics Book1 with Workbook 1, Effective Mathematics Book 2 with Workbook 2, Effective Mathematics Book 3 with Workbook 3, Advance Level Mathematics for Cameroon Schools, (book) Ordinary Level Mathematics for Cameroon Schools. Recipient award, Presbyn. Ch., Cameroon, 1987—93, Cameroon Govt. Academic Excellence, 1987—94, Cameroo GCE Bd., 1992, Cameroon GCE Bd., 1994; fellow, Coll. Arts & Sci., Lehigh U., 2003—; scholar, Cameroon Govt., 1997; grant, 1999. Avocations: swimming, Scrabble, soccer, travel. Home: 519 E Morton St Bethlehem PA PA180 Office: Lehigh U 14 E Packer Ave Bethlehem PA PA180 Office Phone: 610-758-4463. Personal E-mail: akongwi@yahoo.com. Business E-Mail: cma5@lehigh.edu.

**MFUME, KWEISI,** civil rights association executive, former congressman; b. Balt., Oct. 24, 1948; divorced; children: Donald, Kevin, Keith, Ronald, Michael, Christopher. BS, Morgan State U., 1976, MA, Johns Hopkins U., 1984. Mem. Balt. City Council, 1979-87, 100th-104th Congresses from 7th Md. dist., 1987-96, chmn. congl. black caucus, ranking minority mem., mem. banking and fin. svcs. subcom. on gen. oversight and investigations; mem. small bus. com., mem. telecom. subcom. pres. NAACP, Balt., 1996—2005. Former adj. prof. polit. sci. Morgan State U., Balt. Author (with Ronald Stodghill II): (autobiography) No Free Rule: From the Mean Street to the Mainstream, 1997. Recipient Drum Major for Justice award, SCLC, 1997. Baptist. Home: PO Box 1557 Baltimore MD 21203-1557

**MGMEME, FESTUS N.,** biology professor, pharmacist; b. Akatta, Nigeria, Aug. 22, 1955; arrived in U.S., 1977; s. Jacob O. and Juliana E. Mgbeme; m. Lyne Mgbeme, Sept. 15, 1984; children: Crystal, Ceasar, Cherylisa, Zepherus. BS with hons. in Pharmacy, L.I. U., Bklyn., 1952; MSc, Okla. State U., Stillwater, Okla., 1981, PhD, 1989. Rsch. asst. Okla. State U. 1982—89; rev. instr. med. chemistry L.I. U., 1989—95; dir. pharmacy MGB Pharm. Inc., Newark, 1996—99; prof. biology Houston C.C., 2001—. Pharmacist Lazaroff Pharmacy, Newark, 1992—95; prin., owner Fest Holdings Nigeria Ltd., Lagos, Nigeria, 1998—; prof. biology Colleman Coll., Houston, 2001—; CEO MGB Pharm. Inc., Newark, 1996—. Mem.: Pharm. Assn., Am. Chem. Soc., Lords Clubs Internat. (asst. pro lords 2005—), KC (dir. 1986—87). Avocation: basketball. Office: HCCS Southeast Coleman 1900 Pressler St Houston TX 77030-3117

**MHANNA, MAROUN JEAN,** pediatrician; s. Jean and Amira Mhanna; m. Cynthia O Farajian, Nov. 5, 1966; children: Christiane, Stephanie, John Louis. MD, St. Joseph U. Sch. Of Medicine, Beirut, Lebanon, 1989. Lic. physician Beirut, 1989, diplomate pediats. Am. Bd. of Pediat., 1995, in neonatal perinatal medicine Am. Bd. of Pediat., 1999, in pediat. critical care Am. Bd. of Pediat., 2000. Pediatric intensivist and neonatologist MetroHealth Med. Ctr., Cleve., 1999—. Asst. prof. pediat. Case Western Res. U., Cleve., 1999—. Fellow: Am. Acad. of Pediat.; mem.: Soc. of Pediat. Rsch., Am.

Thoracic Soc., Soc. of Critical Care Medicine. Office: MetroHealth Medical Center 2500 MetroHealth Dr Cleveland OH 44109 Office Phone: 216-778-1346. Office Fax: 216-778-4223. Business E-Mail: mmhanna@metrohealth.org.

**MI, CHUNTING CHRIS,** engineering educator; s. Zhanyou Mi and Shunei Liu; m. Yuhong Fu, Nov. 15, 1990; children: Juliana, Jonathan. BSc, N.W. Poly. U., Xi'an, China, 1985, MSc, 1988; PhD, U. Toronto, 2000. Assoc. prof. Northwestern Poly. U., Xi'an, 1992—94, Xi'an Petroleum Inst., 1994—96; elec. engr. GE, Peterborough, Ontario, 2000—01; asst. prof. elec. engring. U. Mich., Dearborn, 2001—. Contbr. articles to profl. jours. Recipient Nat. Innovation award, China State Coun., 1990, Govt. Spl. Allowance award, 1995, Dist. Tchg. award, U. Mich., Dearborn, 2005. Mem.: IEEE (sect. vice chiar 2005—06). Office: Univf Mich Dearborn 4901 Evergreen Rd Dearborn MI 48128-1491 Office Phone: 313-583-6434.

**MIAH, MOHAMMAD SOLAIMAN,** economics professor, researcher; b. Tangail, Bangladesh, Jan. 1, 1955; arrived in US, 1975; s. Mohammad Serajuddin and Sufia (Khatoon) Miah; m. Syeda Salma Khatoon, Aug. 5, 1988; children: Abdul Rahman, Abid. BA, Eastern Ill. U., Charleston, 1979; MS, U. Ky., Lexington, 1985; PhD, No. Ill. U., Dekalb, 2001. Asst. prof. Bethany Coll., Lindsburg, Kans., 2001—02, W.Va. State U., Institute, 2002—. Faculty Rsch. grantee, W.Va. State U., 2003—05. Mem.: Pa. Econ. Assn., Midwest Econ. Assn., Am. Econ. Assn. Office: WVa State U Econs Dept Institute WV 25112

**MIALON, HUGO,** economics professor; b. Apr. 25, 1977; s. Yves and Elly Mialon; m. Sue Mialon. BA in Econ., McGill U., Montreal, 1999; MS in Econ., U. Tex., Austin, 2001, PhD in Econ., 2004. Asst. prof. Emory U., Atlanta, 2004—. Contbr. articles to profl. jours. Recipient Tchg. Consultation Pairs award, Emory U., 2005; Tchg. Rsch. grant, 2005. Mem.: Can. Econ. Assn., Am. Econ. Assn., Golden Key Nat. Honors Soc. Achievements include research in the economic theory of the Second Amendment's right to bear arms; the economic theory of the Fifth Amendment's right to silence; the economic theory of the Fourth Amendment's search and seizure law; the economic theory of private and public enforcement of the antitrust laws; the economic theory of sexual and domestic violence. Home: 732 Ladson Ct Decatur GA 30033 Office: Emory U Econs Dept 1602 Fishburne Dr Atlanta GA 30322-2240 Office Phone: 404-727-0355. Office Fax: 404-727-4639. E-mail: hmialon@emory.edu.

**MIAN, AHSAN,** engineering educator, mechanical engineer; b. Rajbari, Bangladesh; PhD, Auburn U., Ala., 1999. Asst. prof. Mont. State U., Bozeman, 2005—. Contbr. articles to profl. jours. Grantee, NASA-EPSCoR, 2006—. Mem.: MRS. Office: Montana State Univ 220 Roberts Hall Bozeman MT 59717 Office Phone: 406-994-6296. E-mail: amian@me.montana.edu.

**MIANO, LOUIS STEPHEN,** arts advisor; b. N.Y.C., July 28, 1934; s. Louis Clyde and Zefira (Palombo) M. BA, Dartmouth Coll., 1955; MA, Columbia U., 1958. Writer Look Mag., N.Y.C., 1960-61; editor Show Mag., N.Y.C. and L.A., 1961-63; assoc. producer ABC-TV, N.Y.C. and L.A., 1963-66; vice-chmn., dir. creative services AC&R Advt., N.Y.C., 1966-90. Sec. EEE Theatrical Ventures, N.Y.C., 1974—; bd. trustees Met. Opera Guild; cons. in field. Co-producer plays: Design for Living, Corpse, The Seagull, Legends, Inner Voices, 1974-86 Trustee Marymount Manhattan Coll., N.Y.C., 1989-2002; cons. Home Box Office, 1991-92; bd. dirs. Nat. Bd. of Rev. of Motion Pictures, 1995—, Gotham Chamber Opera, 2000—, Met. Opera Guild, 2005—, Circle-in-the Square, sec.; gen. dirs. coun. N.Y.C. Opera, 1998—; bd. dirs. Metro. Opera Guild, 2005— Mem. Century Assn. Home and Office: 430 E 57th St New York NY 10022-3061 Office Phone: 212-753-2860.

**MIAO, WUJIAN,** chemistry professor; b. Rudong, Jiangsu, China, Dec. 26, 1962; s. Siyou Miao and Bafeng Yang; m. Zhilan Ge, Nov. 25, 1986; children: Jingfan, Kevin Liu. BS, Nantong U., Nantong, China, 1979—82; MSc Courses Diploma, Jinan U., Guangzhou, China, 1985—86; MSc, Zhongshan U., Guangzhou, China, 1988—91; PhD, Monash U., Melbourne, Australia, 1996—99. U. tchr. qualification credential Edn. Commn., Jiangsu Province, China, 1996. Chemistry technician, dir. chemistry dept. labs, lectr., vice-head, dept. chemistry Nantong U., 1982—95; vis. scholar Monash U., Melbourne, Australia, 1995—96; rsch. scientist Commonwealth Sci. and Industrian Orgn., Melbourne, 2000; post-doctoral fellow U. Tex., Austin, 2001—04; asst. prof. U. So. Miss., Hattiesburg, 2004—. Adv. Overseas Exch. Assn. of Nantong City, Jingsu, China, 1998—2002; sec. gen. Chinese Student Club, Monash U., 1996—98. Named Top Young Tchr. in Gen. Univs. and Colls., Edn. Commn, Jiangsu Province, China, 1994; recipient Top Postgrad. award, Zhongshan U., 1991, Dean's Rsch. Initiative Program award, U. So. Miss., 2004; Guanghua Edn. scholar, Zhongshan U., 1990, Yao Wannian scholar, 1990, Study Abroad scholar, State Edn. Commn., China, 1995, Grad. scholar, Monash U., 1996—99, Study Abroad scholar, State Edn. Commn., China, 1997, Internat. Planning Visit grantee, NSF, 2006. Fellow: China's Tchrs. Coll. Assn. Analytical Chemistry, Universities & Colleges Laboratorial Mgmt. Soc., Jiangsu Province; mem.: Miss. Acad. Scis., Soc. Electroanalytical Chemistry, Electrochem. Soc., Am. Chem. Soc. Achievements include patents for methods and compositions for the detection of biological molecules using a two particle complex. Office: Univ So Miss 118 College Dr Box 5043 Hattiesburg MS 39406 Office Phone: 601-266-4716. Office Fax: 601-266-6075. Business E-Mail: wujian.miao@usm.edu.

**MICA, JOHN L.,** congressman; b. Binghamton, N.Y., Jan. 27, 1943; s. John and Adeline Resciniti M.; m. Patricia Szymanek, 1972; children: D'anne, Clark. AA, Miami-Dade C.C., 1965; BA, U. Fla., 1967. Pres. MK Devel. Inc., 1975—92; mem. Fla. Ho. of Reps., 1977—81, mem. appropriations com., mem. ethics com., mem. elections com., mem. cmty. affairs com.; chief of staff US Senate, Washington, 1981—85; mng. gen. ptnr MD Cellular Comm., 1986—92; mem. US Congress from 7th Fla. Dist, Washington, 1992— Mem. transp. and infrastructure com., govt. reform and oversight com., chmn. subcom. on aviation, 1993— Author: Factor affecting local government reorganization efforts in Florida, Urban and Environmental Issues. Formerly with Beth Johnson Mental Health Bd., PTA Bd., Zora Neale Hurston Meml. Com. Recipient Outstanding Svc. award Fla. Conservative Union, Outstanding Svc. award Fla. Cancer Soc., Outstanding Svc. award Sertoma, Outstanding Young Men of Am. award; named one of five outstanding Young Men in Fla. Mem.: Fla. Jaycees Statewide (Good Govt. award 1973), Winter Park Jaycees (Good Govt. award 1972), Tiger Bay Club, Kiwanis. Republican. Episcopalian. Office: US HoReps 2313 Rayburn HO Office Bldg Washington DC 20515-0907 Office Phone: 202-225-4035.

**MICCICHE, DANIEL JOHN,** lawyer; BA, SUNY, Stony Brook, 1978; JD, U. Chgo., 2982. Profl. corp. ptnr. Akin Gump Strauss Hauer and Feld LLP, Dallas, 1988—. Mem. comptroller's tax adv. group Tex. Comptroller Pub. Accounts. Mem. sch. fin. task force Greater Dallas Chamber; bd. dirs. Tex. C-BAR (Cmty. Bldg. through Atty. Resources), Am. Found. Blind S.W. Region; bd. adv. entrepreneurship program U. Dallas Grad. Sch. Mgmt. Mem. ABA, State Bar Tex.(chair state taxation com., 2002-04, chair corp. taxation com., 1998-99), Dallas Bar Assn. (chair tax section, 2001), State Bar N.Y. Office: Akin Gump Strauss Hauer & Feld LLP 1700 Pacific Ave Ste 4100 Dallas TX 75201-4675 Business E-Mail: dmicciche@akingump.com.

**MICCIO, ELIZABETH PETRICK,** artist; b. Mt. Vernon, N.Y., Sept. 27, 1922; d. Alfred and Ruth Petrick; m. Edward Miccio Jr, May 8, 1943; children: Edward Louis, Kathleen Elizabeth. AD, Rocky Mountain Coll. Art, 1967. Designer, illustrator Gibson Greeting Cards, Inc., 1971-75; instr. Colo. Inst. Art, Denver, 1977-90; freelance artist, 1990—. Home: 468 26th Ave Greeley CO 80634-2621

**MICHA, DAVID ALLAN,** chemistry professor, physics professor; b. Argentina, Sept. 12, 1939; came to U.S., 1966, naturalized, 1974; s. Simon David and Catalina (Cohen) M.; m. Rebecca Stefan, 1991; children: Michael F., Anna K. MS, U. Cuyo, Bariloche, Argentina, 1962; DSc, U. Uppsala,

---

Sweden, 1966. Rsch. assoc. Theoretical Chemistry Inst. U. Wis., Madison, 1966-67; asst. rsch. physicist Inst. Pure and Applied Sci. U. Calif., La Jolla, 1967-69; assoc. prof. chemistry and physics U. Fla., Gainesville, 1969-74, prof., 1974—, dir. Ctr. Chem. Physics, 1982-91, head phys. chem. divsn., 1999—2004. Vis. prof. U. Gothenburg, Sweden, 1970, Harvard U., 1972, 90, 98, 2000, 01, Max-Planck Inst., Göttingen, Germany, 1976, 96, Imperial Coll., London, 1977, U. Calif., Santa Barbara, 1982, U. Colo. and Weizmann Inst., Israel, 1983, U. Buenos Aires, 1988, 95, Supercomputer Inst., Fla. State U., 1991, Ecole Normale Superieure, Paris 2004, 05; mem. adv. panel div. advanced sci. computing NSF, 1990-92, Max-Planck Inst. Astrophysik, Munich, Germany, 1996, 97. Mem. editl. bd. Internat. Jour. Quantum Chemistry, 1979-88, Few-Body Systems, 1985—; editor Finite Systems and Multiparticle Dynamics, 1990-2005, symposium procs.; contbr. several book chpts., numerous articles to sci. jours. Recipient U.S. Sr. Scientist award A. Von Humboldt Found., 1976, Sr. Faculty Rsch. award Sigma Xi, 1985; Alfred P. Sloan Found. fellow, 1971-74; Nat. Bur. Standards JILA fellow, 1983. Fellow Am. Phys. Soc. (vice chmn. topical group on few body sys. and multi-particle dynamics 1986-88, chmn. 1988-89); mem. Am. Chem. Soc. Office: U Fla 2318 New Physics Bldg Gainesville FL 32611-8435

**MICHAEL, ALFRED FREDERICK, JR.,** physician, medical educator; b. Phila. s. Alfred Frederick and Emma Maude (Peters) M.; m. Jeanne Jones; children: Mary, Susan, Carol. MD, Temple U., 1953. Diplomate Am. Bd. Pediatrics (founding mem. sub-bd. pediatric nephrology, pres. 1977-79). Pediat. diagnostic lab. immunology and pediatric nephrology intern Phila. Gen. Hosp., 1953-54; resident Children's Hosp. and U. Cin. Coll. Medicine, 1957-60; postdoctoral fellow dept. pediatrics and biochemistry Med. Sch., U. Minn., Mpls., 1960-63, prof., 1965-68, prof. pediatrics, lab. medicine and pathology, 1968-88, co-dir. pediatric nephrology, 1968—86, Regents' prof., 1986—, head dept. pediatrics, 1986-97, dean, 1996—2002. Established investigator Am. Heart Assn., 1963-68. Past mem. editl. bd. Internat. Yr. Book of Nephrology, Am. Jour. Nephrology, Kidney Internat., Clin. Nephrology, Am. Jour. Pathology; contbr. articles to profl. jours. Physician founder, Vikings Children's Fund, Univ. Pediats. Found.; served with USAF, 1955-57. Recipient Alumni Achievement award Temple U. Sch. Medicine, 1988, John Peters award, 1992, Diehl award, 2003; NIH fellow, 1960-63, Guggenheim fellow, 1966-67, NIH Merit awardee, 1992-2002, Bolles Rogers award, Shotwell award. Fellow AAAS; mem. AMA, Am. Soc. Clin. Investigation, Assn. Am. Physicians, Am. Pediat. Soc., Soc. for Pediat. Rsch., Am. Assn. Investigative Pathology, Am. Soc. Cell Biology, Am. Soc. Nephrology (coun., pres.-elect 1992—, pres. 1993, John Peters award), Internat. Soc. Nephrology, Soc. for Exptl. Biology and Medicine, Minn. Med. Assn. Home: 1986 Lower Saint Dennis Rd Saint Paul MN 55116-2820 Office Phone: 612-626-4949. Business E-Mail: micha003@umn.edu.

**MICHAEL, ANDREW JAY,** geophysicist; s. Paul Andrew and Norma Michael; m. Stephanie Louise Ross. BS, MIT, Cambridge, Mass., 1981; MS, Stanford U., Calif., 1983, PhD, 1985. Postdoctoral scholar and tchr. dept. geophysics Stanford U., 1985—86; postdoctoral scholar br. seismology US Geol. Survey, Menlo Park, Calif., 1986—88, geophysicist Earthquake Hazards Team, 1988—. Editor: (jour.) Bulletin Seismol. Soc. Am., 2004—; composer: (music) Earthquake Quartet #1; lectr., musician (performance) The Music of Earthquakes. Mem., pres. Coastside Cmty. Orch., Half Moon Bay, Calif., 1995—2003; founding dir. Coastside Jewish Cmty., Half Moon Bay; bd. mem. Patients Against Lymphoma, Rieglesville, Pa., 2005—. Mem.: Seismol. Soc. Am., Am. Geophys. Union (life). Achievements include research in Stress and Structure Around Active Faults, Earthquake Prediction, Hazards Assessment, Rapid Dissemination of Earthquake Information. Avocations: jazz, classical music, squash, canoe camping, winemaking. Office: USGS - Ms 977 345 Middlefield Rd Menlo Park CA 94025 Office Phone: 650-329-4777. Business E-Mail: michael@usgs.gov.

**MICHAEL, ANN DOZIER MARINO,** real estate broker; b. Durham, N.C., Apr. 22, 1944; d. Walter Joseph and Ellen G. (Cheek) Dozier; m. John Harrison Marino, Oct. 15, 1966 (div. Jan. 1981); children: John Harrison Jr., Ann Southerlyn; m. G. Revell Michael, July 4, 1998. BA, Salem Coll., 1966. Sales assoc. Rector Assocs. Realtors, Alexandria, Va., 1984-96, Pardoe and Graham, Alexandria, 1997—2002; assoc. broker McEnearney Assocs. Realtors, Alexandria, 2002—. Vol. Jr. League, Chgo., 1970-74; bd. dirs. Jr. League, Washington, 1979-95, Vol. Clearing House, Washington, Project Open Rd., Chgo., Fire and Burn Inst., Washington; mem. parents coun. Burgundy Farm Sch., 1983; mem. parish coun. St. Mary's, Alexandria, 1977-80. Recipient Rookie of Yr. award No. Va. Bd. Realtors, 1985, Lifetime Top Prodr. Club, Lifetime Million Dollar Club, No. Va. Bd. Realtors, 1985-2002. Mem.: Fairfax Hunt Club, Salem Coll. Alumnae Club (pres. Chgo. chpt. 1970—73). Republican. Roman Catholic. Office: McEnearney Assocs 109 S Pitt St Alexandria VA 22314

**MICHAEL, ERNEST ARTHUR,** mathematics professor; b. Zurich, Switzerland, Aug. 26, 1925; came to U.S., 1939; s. Jakob and Erna (Sondheimer) M.; m. Colette Verger Davis, 1956 (div. 1966); children: Alan, David, Gerard; m. Erika Goodman Joseph, Dec. 4, 1966; children: Hillary, Joshua. BA, Cornell U., 1947; MA, Harvard U., 1948; PhD, U. Chgo., 1951. Mem. faculty dept. math. U. Wash., Seattle, 1953—, asst. prof., 1953-56, assoc. prof., 1956-60, prof., 1960-93, prof. emeritus, 1993—. Mem. Inst. for Advanced Study, Princeton, 1951-52, 56-57, 60-61, 68, Math. Research Inst., E.T.H. Zürich, 1973-74; vis. prof. U. Stuttgart, Ger., 1978-79, U. Munich, Fed. Republic Germany, 1987, 88, 92-93. Editor: Procs. Am. Math. Soc., 1968-71, Topology and Its Applications, 1972-94, Set-Valued Analysis, 1993—; contbr. articles to profl. jours. With USNR, 1944—46. Grantee, AEC, Office Nav. Rsch., NSF, Guggenheim Found., Humboldt Found. Mem. Am. Math. Soc., Math. Assn. Am., ACLU, Amnesty Internat. Jewish. Home: 22200 Chinook Rd Woodway WA 98020-7200 Office: U Washington Dept Math Box 354350 Seattle WA 98195-4350 Personal E-mail: ernie@eemichael.net

**MICHAEL, GEORGE JOSEPH,** political science professor; BS, Widener U., Chester, Pa., 1990; MS, Temple U., Phila., 1992; PhD, George Mason U., Fairfax, Va., 2002. Asst. prof. adminstrn. of justice and polit. sci. U. Va., Wise, Va., 2003—. Author: Confronting Right-Wing Extremism and Terrorism in the USA, 2003, The Enemy of My Enemy: The Alarming Convergence of Militant Islam and the Extreme Right, 2006; contbr. articles to profl. jours. Staff sgt. nat. guard USAF, 1985—90. Recipient Faculty Outstanding Rsch. award, U. Va. Coll. at Wise. Mem.: European Consortium Polit. Rsch. Office: University of Virginia College One College Avenue Wise VA 24293-4412 Office Phone: 276-376-4581. Office Fax: 276-328-0247. Business E-Mail: gjm3a@uvawise.edu.

**MICHAEL, GEORGE T.,** real estate manager, real estate developer; s. Lorriane Cooper; m. Terrelyn Michael, Sept. 9, 1989. AA, Bronx C.C., 1978; diploma, NYU Grad. Sch. of Bus., 1980. Mgr., owner various real estate properties, N.Y.C., 1980—. Author: (sch. newspaper) The Communicator, 1975. V.p. Adults & Youth for a Better Baisley Inc., Jamaica, 1984. Avocations: book collecting, stamp collecting/philately, track. Office Phone: 718-468-4481. Office Fax: 718-468-1512. E-mail: gtmdred@aol.com.

**MICHAEL, HART E.,** pharmaceutical executive; Degree in Bus. Econ. & Geography, U. Calif., Santa Barbara; MBA, Calif. State U., Fresno. Various fin. positions with high technology cos.; treas., dir. fin. Avantek, Inc., 1982—90; exec. v.p., CFO Vestar, Inc., 1990—95, chmn., pres., 1994—95; v.p., CFO NeXstar Pharma., Inc., 1995—99, chmn. mgmt. com., 1998—99; CFO, sr. v.p., pres. Allos Therapeutics, Inc., Westminster, Colo., 1999—, pres., CEO 2001—. Office: Allos Therapeutics Inc 11080 Circle Point Rd Ste 200 Westminster CO 80020

**MICHAEL, JERROLD MARK,** public health service officer, educator, retired dean; b. Richmond, Va., Aug. 3, 1927; s. Joseph Leon and Esther Leah M.; m. Lynn Y. Simon, Mar. 17, 1951; children: Scott J., Nelson L BCE, George Washington U., 1949; MSE, Johns Hopkins U., 1950; MPH, U. Calif., Berkeley, 1957; DrPH (hon.), Mahidol U., 1983; ScD (hon.), Tulane U., 1984.

---

Commd. ensign USPHS, 1950, advanced through grades to rear adm., asst. surgeon gen., 1966; ret., 1970; dean Sch. Pub. Health, U. Hawaii, Honolulu, 1971-92, prof. pub. health, 1971-95; emeritus prof. pub. health U. Hawaii, Honolulu, 1995—; adj. prof. global health George Washington U., 1997—. Bd. dirs. Nat. Health Coun., 1967-78, Nat. Ctr. for Health Edn., 1977-90; mem. nat. adv. coun. on health professions edn., 1978-81; chmn. bd. dirs. Kuakini Med. Ctr., Honolulu; sec., treas. Asia-Pacific Acad. Consortium Pub. Health; vis. prof. U. Adelaide, 1993, George Washington, 1994; hon. prof. Beijing Med. U., 1994; adj. prof. internat. pub. health Goerge Washington U., 1997- Contbr. articles to profl. jours.; assoc. editor Jour. Environ. Health, 1958-80, Asia-Pacific Jour. of Pub. Health, 1986-95 Pres. Commd. Officers Found., 2000—. Served with USNR, 1944-47 Decorated Meritorious Svc. medal, comdr. Royal Order of Elephant (Thailand); recipient Walter Mangold award, 1961, J.S. Billings award for mil. medicine, 1964, Gold medal Hebrew U., Jerusalem, 1982, San Karcil Gold medal, Malaysia, 1989, Disting. Svc. award Pacific Island Health Officers Assn., 1992, USPHS awards, Commd. Officers Assn. Brutsche award, 1999, Founders award Asia-Pacific Acad. Consortium Pub. Health, 2003, U.S. Surgeon Gen.'s medallion, 2005, others Fellow Am. Public Health Assn.; mem. Am. Acad. Health Adminstrn., Am. Soc. Cert. Sanitarians, Nat. Environ. Health Assn., Am. Acad. Environ. Engrs. Clubs: Masons

**MICHAEL, M. BLANE,** federal judge; b. Charleston, SC, Feb. 17, 1943; AB, W.Va. U., 1965; JD, NYU, 1968. Bar: NY 1968, US Dist. Ct. (so. and ea. dists.) NY 1968, W.Va. 1973, US Ct. Appeals (4th cir.) 1974, US Dist. Ct. (so. dist.) W.Va. 1981. Counsel to Gov. W.Va. John D. Rockefeller IV, 1977—80; atty. Jackson & Kelly, Charleston, W.Va., 1981—93; fed. judge US Ct. Appeals (4th cir.), Charleston, W.Va., 1993—. Mem.: ABA, Kanawha County Bar Assn., W.Va. Bar Assn., Phi Beta Kappa. Office: US Circuit Judge Robert C Byrd US Courthouse 300 Virginia St E Rm 7404 Charleston WV 25301-2504*

**MICHAEL, MARK DIXWELL,** lawyer; b. Palo Alto, Calif., Feb. 27, 1951; s. J.L. and Elizabeth (Ketcham) M.; m. Eileen Susan Landauer; children: Sarah Kristen Michael, Emily Christine Landauer. BA, Stanford U., 1972; JD, UCLA, 1977. Bar: Hawaii 1977, Calif. 1979. Assoc. Carlsmith, Carlsmith, Wichman & Case, Honolulu, 1977-78, Char, Hamilton, Taylor & Thom, Honolulu, 1979-81, Law Offices of Jerry E. Berg, San Francisco, 1981-84; sr. v.p., gen. counsel, sec. 3Com Corp., Santa Clara, Calif., 1984—2003. Dir. Nollenberger Capital Ptnrs., Inc., Natus Med., Inc. Mem. ABA, Am. Soc. Corp. Secs., Silicon Valley Assn. Gen. Counsel, Calif. State Bar Assn., Hawaii State Bar Assn. E-mail: mark_michael@myway.com.

**MICHAEL, NOREEN,** school system administrator; PhD in Ednl. Psychology, U. Ill. Commr. of edn. Virgin Islands Dept. Edn., Charlotte, Amalie, Virgin Islands, 2002—. Office: Commr of Education 44-46 Kongena Gade St Thomas VI 00802

**MICHAEL, ROBERT,** history educator; s. Gilbert and Jeanne Friedberg; m. Susan Michael; children: Stephanie, Andrew, Carolyn. BA, Boston U., 1958; MA, U. Conn., 1968, PhD, 1972. Book editor Thomas Yoseloff Univ. of Pa. Press, N.Y.C., 1962—63, Hawthorn Books / Prentice Hall, N.Y.C., 1963—64, Bobbs-Merrill, N.Y.C., 1964—65; prof. Inter Am. U., Aguadilla, PR, 1970—71; emeritus prof. European history U. Mass., Dartmouth, 1971—. Vis. prof. Cen. European U., Budapest, Hungary, 1996, U. Vienna, 1996, Ringling Sch. Art and Design, Sarasota, Fla., 2005—, Fla. Gulf Coast U., Ft. Myers, 2005—, U. South Fla., Sarasota, 2005—; vis. lectr. U. Venice, Italy, 2000. Editor: (scholarly email lists) Humanities Network (James Harvey Robinson prize Am. Hist. Assn., 1997); author: (scholarly book) Nazi-Deutsch/Nazi-German: An English Lexicon of the Language of the Third Reich; editor: (memoir) Branded on My Arm and in My Soul: The Holocaust Memoirs of Abraham Landau; author: (reference book) Dictionary of Antisemitism, (scholarly book) A Concise History Of American Antisemitism, Holy Hatred: A History Of Christian Antisemitism, History of Catholic Antisemitism, (novel) Odysseus The Jew; editor: (essays) Menorah Review; author: (scholarly book) The Radicals and Nazi Germany, Fatal Vision, Fatal Image, (reference book) The Houghton-Mifflin Guide to the Internet for History, (scholarly book) The Holocaust: A Chronology and Documentary, The Holocaust Chronicle: A History in Words and Pictures, (poetry) Whispers of Inspiration; contbr. articles to scholarly jours. With U.S. Army. Mem.: Phi Beta Kappa. Democrat. Jewish. Avocations: writing, reading. Office Phone: 508-999-8301. Personal E-mail: leahcimrobert@yahoo.com. E-mail: robertomichael@verizon.net.

**MICHAELIDES, CONSTANTINE EVANGELOS,** architect, educator; b. Athens, Greece, Jan. 26, 1930; came to U.S., 1955, naturalized, 1964; s. Evangelos George and Kalliopi Constantine (Kefallonidis) M.; m. Maria S. Canellakis, Sept. 3, 1955; children: Evangelos Constantine, Dimitri Canellakis. Diploma in Architecture, Nat. Tech. U., Athens, 1952; M.Arch., Harvard U., 1957. Practice architecture, Athens, 1954-55, St. Louis, 1963—; asso. architect Carl Koch, Jose Luis Sert, Hideo Sasaki, Cambridge, Mass., 1957-59, Doxiadis Assos., Athens and Washington, 1959-60, Hellmuth, Obata & Kassabaum, St. Louis, 1962; instr. Grad. Sch. Design Harvard U., 1957-59, Athens Inst. Tech., 1959-60; asst. prof. architecture Washington U., St. Louis, 1960-64, assoc. prof., 1964-69, prof., 1969-94, assoc. dean Sch. Architecture, 1969-73; dean Washington U., Sch. Architecture, 1973-93, dean emeritus, 1993—; Ruth and Norman Moore vis. prof. Washington U., St. Louis, 1995. Vis. prof. (Sch. Architecture), Ahmedabad, India, 1970; counselor Landmarks Assn. St. Louis, 1975-79 Author: Hydra: A Greek Island Town: Its Growth and Form, 1967, The Aegean Crucible: Tracing Vernacular Architecture in Post-Byzantine Centuries, 2003; contbr. articles to profl. jours. Mem. Mcpl. Commn. on Arts, Letters, University City, Mo., 1975-81. With Greek Army Res., 1952-54. Fellow AIA (Rsch. award 1963-64, Presdl. Citation 1992); mem. Tech. Chamber of Greece, Soc. Archtl. Historians, Modern Greek Studies Assn., Hellenic Soc. St. Louis (pres. 1991, 95, 96). Home and Office: 735 Radcliffe Ave Saint Louis MO 63130-3139 E-mail: info@delospress.com.

**MICHAELIDES, DOROS NIKITA,** internist, medical educator; b. Nicosia, Cyprus, Jan. 7, 1936; came to U.S., 1969; s. Nikita P. and Elpinike (Taliadorou) M.; m. Eutychia J. Loizides, Feb. 27, 1965; children: Nike-Elsie, Joanna-Doris. MD magna cum laude (Royal Greek Govt., Scholar) U. Athens, 1962; DTM and H (Greek State Scholarship, Found. Scholar) U. Liverpool, Eng., 1967; MSc in Clin. Biochemistry (Greek State, Scholarship Found. Scholar), Newcastle-upon-Tyne (Eng.) 1969. Diplomate Am. Bd. Family Practice, Am. Bd. Allergy and Immunology; qualified Am. Bd. Internal Medicine; cert. in infectious diseases and immunochemistry, Eng. Clk., intern U. Uppsala, Sweden, 1962; resident Nicosia Gen. Hosp., 1963—66; fellow U. Liverpool Hosps., 1967; fellow internal and clin. medicine Royal Infirmary U. Edinburgh, 1967—68; rsch. fellow Royal Victoria Infirmary U. Newcastle-upon-Tyne, 1968—69; resident internal medicine Bapt. Meml. Hosp., Memphis, 1969—72; fellow in chest diseases We. Okla. Chest Disease Hosp., 1970—71; chief clin. immunology/respiratory care ctr. Erie, Pa.; chief respiratory care ctr. VA Med. Ctr., Erie, 1972—84, acting chief dept. medicine, 1980—81; asst. clin. prof. medicine Hahnemann U. Sch. Medicine, Phila., 1977—, Gannon U., Erie, 1977—. Mem. staff internal medicine Hamot Med. Ctr., immunology and chest diseases Metro Health Ctr., Erie; preceptor medicine St. Vincent's Health Ctr.; affiliate staff Cleveland Clinic Found.; vol. physician Greek Nat. Guard, Cyprus, 1964. Author: The Occurrence of Proteolytic Inhibitors in Heart and Skeletal Muscle, 1969; Blood Gases, Acid-Base and Electrolytes Disturbances, 1980; Immediate Hypersensitivity: The Immunochemistry and Therapeutics of Reversible Airway Obstruction, 1980; The Equivalent Potency of Corticosteroid Preparations used in Reversible Airway Obstruction, 1981; contbr. articles to med. jours. Recipient citation for outstanding svcs. to vets. DAV, 1975, citation Adminstr. U.S. Vets. Affairs, 1978. Fellow ACP (life), Am. Immune. Cert. Allergists, Am. Coll. Allergy and Immunology (com. autoimmune diseases), Am. Assn. Immunology and Allergy (pulmonary com.), Am. Coll. Chest Physicians (life; critical care com.), Royal Soc. Medicine, Am. Coll. Angiology, N.Y. Acad. Scis., Am. Coll. Clin. Pharmacology, Am. Assn. Cert.

Allergists. Greek Orthodox. Home: 4107 State St Erie PA 16508-3129 Office: Doros N Michaelides Md 4107 State St Erie PA 16508-3129 E-mail: dnm777@pol.net, dorosmichaelides@yahoo.com.

**MICHAELIS, BETTY JANE,** sculptor, retired small business owner; b. Champaign County, Ohio, Feb. 6, 1928; d. Charles Edward and Mable Augusta (Stevens) Hendricks; m. Philip Alvin Russell, July 25, 1947 (div. Feb. 1965); children: Barbara Ann Russell Clifford, Karen Sue Russell Geist, Philip Edward; m. Larry Edward Michaelis, Nov. 29, 1986. Student, Sinclair C.C., 1987-88. 2d v.p. Credit Life Ins., Springfield, Ohio, 1984-86; sculptor of public art Miamisburg, Ohio, 1987—. Avocation: reading. Home: 9616 Yorkridge Ct Miamisburg OH 45342-5208

**MICHAELIS, MICHAEL,** management and technical consultant; b. Berlin, June 8, 1919; s. George and Martha (Bluth) M.; m. Diana Ordway Tead, Sept. 11, 1954; children: Ordway Peter, David Tead; m. Cintra McIlwain Williams, Mar. 19, 1966 (div. Nov. 1975); m. Caroline Crutcher Bishop, Mar. 17, 1984. BSc in Engring., U. London, 1941. Rsch. asst., group leader Rsch. Labs. Gen. Electric Co., Ltd., U.K., 1935-45, staff physicist and cons., 1945-49; dir. physics divsn. Radiochem. Centre, U.K. Atomic Energy Authority, 1949-51; cons. Arthur D. Little, Inc., Cambridge, Mass., 1951-52, staff cons., 1952-61, sr. asso., 1957-61, head nuclear mgmt. cons. services, 1956-61, internat. bus. devel. services, 1959-61, policy adviser to several large corps, 1954-61, mgr. Washington ops., 1963-72, sr. cons., 1972-81; pres., CEO Partners In Enterprise, Inc., 1981—2000. Cons. to Pres.'s Spl. Asst. Sci. and Tech., The White House, 1961-63; exec. sec. The White House Panel on Civilian Tech., 1961-63; exec. dir. rsch. mgmt. adv. panel, com. on sci. and tech. U.S. Ho. of Reps., 1963-67; dep. coord. then Pres.-elect Carter's Task Force on Sci. and Tech. Policy, 1976; mem. tech. adv. bd. to U.S. Sec. Commerce, 1978-81; mem. citizens adv. coun. Congl. Caucus for Sci. and Tech., 1983-86; mem. nat. com. Am. Goals and Resources, Nat. Planning Assn., 1964-67, mem. adv. com. sci., tech. and economy, 1966-68; vice chmn. com. internat. affairs Atomic Indsl. Forum, 1958-60; assoc. with Anglo-Am. Radar Rsch. Project, World War II. Editor, project dir.: Federal Funding of Civilian Research and Development, 1976; Contbr. articles to profl. jours. Fellow AAAS (chmn. engring. sect. 1980-82, exec. dir. sr. scientists and engrs. program 1989-90); mem. IEEE (sr.), Sci. Film Assn. (founder 1943, sec. 1943-48, v.p. 1948-51), Am. Nuclear Soc., Boston Com. Fgn. Rels., Royal Inst. Physics and Phys. Soc., Soc. Internat. Devel., Royal Instn. Elec. Engrs., Assn. Hosp. Physicists, Nat. Planning Assn., World Future Soc. (dir.), U.S. C. of C. (chmn. com. on govt.-industry rels. in sci. and tech. 1963-64), Interdisciplinary Comm. Assocs. Inc. (dir. 1969-79), Am. Econ. Assn., Am. Soc. Cybernetics, Am. Soc. for Pub. Adminstrn., Atlantic Coun. U.S., Cosmos Club (Washington, sec. 1994-97, v.p. 1997-98, pres. 1998-99), Harvard Faculty Club. Home and Office: 6812 Meadow Ln Chevy Chase MD 20815-5018 Office Phone: 301-986-1950. Personal E-mail: zmichael@verizon.net. *The Constitution of the U.S. diffuses power so as to better secure liberty. But it also intends that practice will integrate the dispersed powers into a workable government. It confers upon its branches autonomy but also reciprocity, separateness but also interdependence. It is incumbent on each of us to help make this system work, and to make it responsive to the human needs of our country and the world.*

**MICHAELIS, PAUL CHARLES,** engineering physicist executive; b. Bronx, June 18, 1935; s. Paul Fredrick and Rose (Landsbury) M.; m. Geraldine A. DeCuollo, June 29, 1958; 1 son, Paul Charles. BS in Elec. Engring, Newark Coll. Engring., 1964, MS in Physics, 1967. With AT&T Bell Labs., Murray Hill and Whippany, NJ, 1953-96; assoc. mem. tech. staff Bell Telephone Labs., 1963-67, mem. tech. staff, 1967-82, tech. mgr., 1982-96, ret., 1996; founder P.C. Michaelis Tech. Cons. Inc., Watchung, NJ, 1996—. Lectr. USSR Acad. Scis., 1972 Contbr. articles to profl. jours.; patentee in optics, magnetics, mechanics and electronics. Mem: IEEE (life; Morris N. Liebmann award 1975), AAAS, Am. Phys. Soc., U.S. Naval Inst., Am. Soc. Naval Engrs., Lions (past pres. Watchung club, Melvin Jones fellow), Raritan Yacht Club (sec.). Home: 103 High Tor Dr Watchung NJ 07069-5424 also: 151 Amherst Dr Bayville NJ 08721 Office: P C Michaelis Tech Cons Inc 103 High Tor Dr Watchung NJ 07069-5424 E-mail: pmichaelis@optonline.net.

**MICHAELS, AL (ALAN RICHARD MICHAELS),** sports commentator; b. Bklyn., Nov. 12, 1944; s. Jay Leonard and Lila Ruth (Ross) Michaels; m. Linda Anne Stamaton, Aug. 27, 1966; children: Steven, Jennifer. BA, Ariz. State U., 1966. TV/radio play-by-play announcer Cin. Reds, 1971—73, San Francisco Giants, 1974—76; sports commentator ABC TV Network, NYC, 1976—, lead announcer, Monday Night Football, 1986—2006, lead announcer, NBA, 2003—06, NBC Sunday Night Football, 2006—. Recipient Nat. Sportscaster of Yr. award, Nat. Sportscasters and Sportswriters Assn., 1980, 1983, 1986, Emmy award, 1987. Avocations: reading, tennis. Office: c/o NBC Sports 30 Rockefeller Plaza New York NY 10112

**MICHAELS, DEBORAH DOWNEY,** lawyer; b. Princeton, Ill., Feb. 14, 1959; m. Jeremy D. Michaels, June 2, 1984. BA, U. Wyo., 1982, JD, 1984. Bar: Wyo. 1985, U.S. Ct. Appeals (10th cir.) 1985. Assoc. Banks, Johnson, Wolfe & Hallock, Gillette, Wyo., 1985-86; ptnr. Banks, Johnson, Wolfe, Hallock and Michaels, Gillette, 1986-87, Banks, Johnson, Wolfe and Michaels, Gillette, 1987-88, Michaels & Michaels, Gillette, 1988—. Instr. Northeast Wyo. Community Coll., Gillette, 1985-87; pres. Youth Emergency Svcs. Dir. Youth Emergency Services, Gillette; vol. Soup Kitchen, Gillette. Mem. ABA, ATLA, Wyo. Trial Lawyers Assn., Delta Theta Phi. Avocations: tennis, horseback riding, fly fishing, figure skating. Home: 1202 Hilltop Ct Gillette WY 82718-5625 Office: Michaels & Michaels 1st Interstate Bank Bu Ste 7 Gillette WY 82716 Office Phone: 307-682-2037. E-mail: dmichaels@vcn.com.

**MICHAELS, EDWARD G.,** music educator, musician; b. McKeesport, Pa., July 16, 1948; s. George Francis and Martha (Zolyak) Buddick; m. Mary Kay Sneller, Dec. 6, 1975; children: George, Matthew. BSc in Music Edn., Duquesne U., Pitts., Pa., 1970; MusM, Northwestern U., Evanston, Ill., 1971. Lic. tchr. Ohio. Dir. band Gilmour Acad., Gates Mills, Ohio, 1974—84; instr. saxophone Sch. Fine Arts, Willbughby, Ohio, 1984—96; instr. instrumental music Willoughby-Eastlake (Ohio) Sch. Dist., 1985—. Dir. River Run Jazz Camp Cuyahoga Valley Nat. Pks., Penisula, Ohio, 2006—. Dir.: Lakeland C.C. Jazz Festival, 1997—, Lakeland C.C. Jazz Impact, 1990, Lakeland C.C. Summer Jazz Festival, 1990—; prodr.: (CD) Going Beyond, 1996. Mem. Ohio Music Educators Assn., Internat. Assn. Jazz Educators. Home: 6595 Ivana Ct Mentor OH 44060

**MICHAELS, JACK D.,** manufacturing executive; BSME, U. Cin. Various postions Internat. Harvester Co., sr. v.p., gen. mgr. Paris, mng. dir. Germany, worldwide pres. agrl. and constrn. equipment ops., J. I. Case Co.; pres.-internat. Hussmann Corp., pres., CEO; pres. Hon Industries, Inc., Muscatine, Iowa, 1991—96, CEO, 1991—96, chmn., 1996—2004; chmn., pres., CEO Snap-on Inc., Pleasant Prarie, Wis., 2004—. Office: Snap-on Inc 10801 Corporate Dr Pleasant Prairie WI 53158*

**MICHAELS, JENNIFER TONKS,** foreign language educator; b. Sedgley, England, May 19, 1945; d. Frank Gordon and Dorothy (Compston) Tonks; m. Eric Michaels, 1973; children: Joseph, David, Ellen. MA, U. Edinburgh, 1967, McGill U., 1971, PhD, 1974. Teaching asst. German dept. Wesleyan U., 1967-68; instr. German dept. Bucknell (Pa.) U., 1968-69; teaching asst. German dept. McGill U., Canada, 1969-72; prodn. asst. Pub. TV News and Polit. program, Schenectady, NY, 1974-75; from asst. prof. to assoc. prof. Grinnell (Iowa) Coll., 1975-87, prof., 1987—. Vis. cons. German dept. Hamilton Coll., 1981; cons. Modern Lang. dept. Colby Coll.; panelist NEH, 1985; spkr. in field. Author: D.H. Lawrence, The Polarity of North and South, 1976, Anarchy and Eros: Otto Gross' Impact on German Expressionist Writers, 1983, Franz Jung: Expressionist, Dadaist, Revolutionary and Out-sider, 1989, Franz Werfel and the Critics, 1994; contbr. numerous articles, revs. to profl. jours. Mem. MLA, Rocky Mt. MLA (v.p. 2005), Am. Assn. Tchrs. of German, Soc. Exile Studies, German Studies Assn. (sec. treas.

1991-92, v.p. 1992-94, pres. 1995-96, numerous coms.). Democrat. Avocations: music, travel, reading. Office: Grinnell Coll German Dept PO Box 805 Grinnell IA 50112-0805 Business E-Mail: michaels@grinnell.edu.

**MICHAELS, JOHN PATRICK, JR.,** investment banker, media broker; b. Orlando, Fla., May 28, 1944; s. John Patrick and Mary Elizabeth (Slemons) M.; 1 child, Kimberly Lynn. Grad., Jamaica Coll., Kingston, 1961; BA magna cum laude, Tulane U., 1966; MA in Comm. (ABC fellow), U. Pa., 1968; MA (hon.), St. Leo Coll., 1981. With Times Mirror Co., 1968-72; v.p. mktg. and devel. TM Comms. Co., 1968-72; v.p. Cable Funding, NYC, 1973; founder, chmn. Comm. Equity Assoc., 1973—; chmn. Atlantic Am. Corp. Group, 2000—. Dir. Enterprise Fla. Tulane scholar, 1962-66; Tulane fellow, 1963-66. Fellow Inst. Dir. (London), Royal Overseas Club (UK), RNC Regents (co-chmn.); mem. Master of Fox Hounds, Nat. Cable TV Assn., Cable TV Pioneers, Broadcast Pioneers, Phi Beta Kappa, Phi Eta Sigma, Sigma Chi (Significant SIG). Home: 5117 S Nichol St Tampa FL 33611-4132 Office: 101 E Kennedy Blvd Ste 3300 Tampa FL 33602-5151 Office Phone: 813-226-8844. Business E-Mail: rmichaels@ceaworldwide.com.

**MICHAELS, LORNE,** television writer, producer; b. Toronto, Ont., Can., Nov. 17, 1944; m. Rosie Schuster, 1973 (div. 1980); m. Susan Forristal, 1984 (div. 1987); m. Alice Barry, 1991; 3 children. Grad., U. Toronto, 1966; doctorate (hon.), Ryerson U. Former prodr. CBC, Toronto; writer Rowan and Martin's Laugh-In, NBC, also other TV series, L.A., 1968-75; chmn. bd., founder Broadway Video, 1997—. Writer, prodr. (TV series) The Hart & Lorne Terrific Hour, 1970, writer, exec. prodr. Saturday Night Live, 1975—80, 1985—; prodr.: (TV series) The New Show, 1984; exec. prodr.: Sunday Night, 1988, The Kids in the Hall, 1989—94, Late Night with Conan O'Brien, 1993—, The Vacant Lot, 1994; writer, prodr. (TV special) Lily Tomlin, 1975, The Paul Simon Special, 1977, Steve Martin's Best Show Ever, 1981, The Best of John Belushi, 1985; prodr.: (TV special) Saturday Night Live - Robbin Williams, 1986, The Best of Gilda Radner, 1989, Saturday Night Live: The Best of Eddie Murphy, 1998, Saturday Night Live: The Best of Steve Martin, 1999, Saturday Night Live: The Best of Dana Carvey, 1999, Saturday Night Live: The Best of Chris Rock, 1999, Saturday Night Live: The Best of Will Ferrell, 2002; writer, exec. prodr. (TV special) The Best of Dan Aykroyd, 1986; exec. prodr.: (TV special) Saturday Night Live: The Best of Chris Farley, 1998, Saturday Night Live: The Best of Phil Hartman, 1998, Saturday Night Live: The Best of Mike Myers, 1998, Saturday Night Live: The Best of Adam Sandler, 1999, Late Night with Conan O'Brian: 10 Anniversary Special, 2003, Night of Too Many Stars, 2003, Saturday Night Live: The Best of Cheri Oteri, 2004; co-exec. prodr. (TV special) Rolling Stone Presents Twenty Years of Rock & Roll, 1987; prodr.: (TV films) Things We Did Last Summer, 1977; exec. prodr.: The Rutles: All You Need Is Cash, 1978, Mr. Mike's Mondo Video, 1979, Simon and Garfunkel: The Concert in Central Park, 1982, The Rutles 2: Can't Buy Me Lunch, 2002, America's Most Terrible Things, 2002; (TV series) The Colin Quinn Show, 2002, The Tracy Morgan Show, 2003—04, Sons & Daughters, 2006—; writer, prodr. (TV films) Gilda Live, 1980, (films) Three Amigos, 1986; prodr.: (films) Coneheads, 1983, Nothing Lasts Forever, 1984, Wayne's World, 1992, Coneheads, 1993, Wayne's World II, 1993, Tommy Boy, 1995, Stuart Saves His Family, 1995, Black Sheep, 1996, Kids in the Hall: Brain Candy, 1996, A Night at the Roxbury, 1998, Superstar, 1999, The Ladies Man, 2000, Enigma, 2001, Mean Girls, 2004. Recipient 4 awards Writers Guild Am., 9 Emmy awards NATAS; named Broadcaster of Yr. Internat. Radio and TV Soc., 1992; recipient George Foster Peabody award for Saturday Night Live, 1990, Order of Canada, 2002, Mark Twain Prize, John F. Kennedy Ctr. for Performing Arts, 2004; named to TV Acad. Hall of Fame, 1999; received star on Hollywood Walk of fame. Office: Broadway Video 1619 Broadway Fl 9 New York NY 10019-7463*

**MICHAELS, MARION CECELIA,** newswriter, editor, news syndicate executive; b. Black River Falls, Wis. d. Leonard N. and Estelle O. (Payne) Doud; m. Charles Webb (div.); children: Charles, David, Robert; m. Mark J. Michaels (div.); 1 child, Merry A. BS in Bus. Edn., U. Wis., 1978, MS in Sys. Edn., 1981. Mgr., instr. bus. program Blackwell Job Corps Ctr., 1987-89; mgr. Michaels Secretarial Svc., Black River Falls, Wis., 1979-83; columnist, editor Michaels News, Black River Falls, 1983—, pres. 1989—. Hon. appt. rsch. bd. advisors Am. Biog. Inst., 1996-2001. Author: The Little Cowboy: Pursuing Dana's Dream, 1998, September's Song, 2003—, Dana's Dream, 2004, Loving Lisa, 2005; columnist Single Parenting, 1983—94, Parenting Plus, 1990—2004, editor, contbr. (column) Surviving Single, 1990—95, To Read or Not (Fiction), 1985—, To Read or Not (Non-Fiction), 1985—2004, Report From Planet Earth, 1985—, Travel Tidbits, 1995—, Surviving Sane, 1995—98. Chmn. Brockway Cmty. Orgn., 1969-71; chair, counselor Brockway Youth Group, 1970-72; chmn. labor com. Dem. Platform Com., Wis., 1975-76; candidate State Assembly, 1978, 82; co-founder Franklin Delano Roosevelt Meml., 1997; mem. LWV. Named to Internat. Poetry Hall of Fame, 1997. Mem.: Assn. Rsch. and Enlightenment, Physicians for Social Responsibility, Union Concerned Scientists, Internat. Soc. Poets (founding laureate mem. 2006, Internat. Poet of Merit award 1999, Outstanding achievement in poetry award 2005, 2006), Humane Soc. of U.S., Nat. Com. to Protect Soc. Security and Medicare, Peale Ctr. for Positive Living, Friends of the Earth, Nat. Trust for Pub. Edn., Smithsonian (assoc.), Pub. Citizen, Am. United, Nat. Parks, Clean Wis., So. Poverty Law Ctr., Natural Resources Def. Coun., Co-op Am., Amnesty Internat., Inst. for Noetic Scs., League of Conservation Voters, Wilson Ctr., Common Cause, Internat. Fund for Animals, Women's History Mus. (charter mem.), Phi Delta Kappa, Pi Omega Pi. Avocations: singing, dance, walking, swimming.

**MICHAELS, RICHARD EDWARD,** lawyer; b. Chgo., June 10, 1952; s. Benjamin and Lillian (Borawski) Mikolajczewski; m. Karen Lynn Belau Michaels, May 17, 1980; children: Jonathan R., Timothy R., Matthew R. BS in Commerce summa cum laude, DePaul U., 1973; JD, Northwestern U., 1977. Bar: Ill. 1977, U.S. Dist. Ct. (no. dist.) Ill. 1977, U.S. Ct. Appeals (7th cir.) 1977; CPA, Ill. Acct. Touche Ross & Co., Chgo., 1973-74; assoc. Schuyler, Roche & Zwirner and predecessor firm Hubachek & Kelly Ltd., Chgo., 1977-83; ptnr. Schuyler, Roche & Zwirner, Chgo., 1983—, pres., 1994—. Mem. adv. bd. Thrivent Fin., 2002—. Mem. Northwestern U. Law Rev., 1976-77. Mem. adv. bd. Greater Chgo. agy. Luth. Brotherhood, 1999—2002; chmn. Hawkswimming Maine South H.S., 2001—02; vice chmn. congregation St. Andrew's Luth. Ch., Park Ridge, Ill., 1990—92, chmn. congregation, 1992—94. Mem. ABA, Internat. Bar Assn., Ill. Bar Assn., Chgo. Bar Assn., DePaul U. Alumni Assn., DePaul U. Boosters, Chgo. Athletic Assn., Northwestern Club, C.A.A. Club, Beta Gamma Sigma, Pi Gamma Mu, Beta Alpha Psi. Lutheran. Avocations: photography, golf. Home: 808 Elm St Park Ridge IL 60068-3312 Office: Schuyler Roche & Zwirner 130 E Randolph St Ste 3800 Chicago IL 60601-6342 Office Phone: 312-565-8438. Business E-Mail: rmichaels@srzlaw.com.

**MICHAELS, ROBERT A.,** real estate development company executive; BSBA, JD, U. S.D. With Gen. Growth, 1972—, gen. counsel, exec. v.p., dir. corp. leasing; pres., CEO Gen. Growth Mgmt., Inc.; pres., COO Gen. Growth Properties, Inc. Bd. dirs. Gen. Growth Properties, Inc., Gen. Growth Mgmt., Inc.; bd. dirs. Ctr. for Urban Land Econs. Rsch., Sch. of Bus. U. Wis.-Madison; spkr. in field. Editor Law Rev., U. S.D.; contbr. articles to profl. jours. Mem. ABA, S.D. Bar Assn., Iowa Bar Assn., Minn. Bar Assn., Internat. Coun. of Shopping Ctrs. (exec. com., bd. trustees, govt. affairs chmn. states Iowa, Nebr., S.D., state dir. Minn., S.D., N.D.). Office: 110 N Wacker Dr Chicago IL 60606-1511

**MICHAELS, WALTER BENN,** English professor, writer; b. 1948; BA, U. Calif., Santa Barbara, 1970, PhD, 1975. Asst. prof. English Johns Hopkins U., 1974—77, prof. English and humanities, 1988—2001; asst. prof. English U. Calif., Berkeley, 1980—86, prof., 1987—88; prof., head Dept. English U. Ill., Chgo., 2001—. Sunderland fellow U. Mich. Law Sch., 1987; Joseph Warren Beach lectr. U. Minn., 1987; Whitney J. Oates fellow humanities Princeton U., 1989; Leventritt lectr. arts Harvard U. Mus., 1994; disting. prof. Am. lit. Tel Aviv U., 1996, Vardi lectr., 99; prof. Sch. Criticism and Theory Cornell U., 1997; Ian Watt lectr. History and Theory of Novel Stanford U., 2001. Editor:

The American Renaissance Reconsidered, 1984; author: The Gold Standard and the Logic of Naturalism: American Literature at the Turn of the Century, 1987, Our America: Nativism, Modernism and Pluralism, 1995, The Shape of the Signifier: 1967 to the End of History, 2004, The Trouble With Diversity, 2006; contbr. Promises of American Life: 1880-1920, 2005, editl. bd. mem. Nineteenth Century Studies, 1995—, Cambridge U. Press Am. Lit., 1999—; contbr. articles to profl. jours. Office: U Chgo Dept English 601 S Morgan St Chicago IL 60607-7120 Office Phone: 312-413-2200. E-mail: wbm@uic.edu.*

**MICHAELS, WILLARD A. (BILL MICHAELS),** retired broadcasting executive; b. Omaha, May 13, 1917; s. Gus M. and Bessie (Kerstine) M.; m. Helen Louise Mintel, Nov. 20, 1938 (dec. Sept. 2000); children: Marcella, Lawrence Richard, Betty Michaels Westbrook BA, Trinity U., 1940. Asst. sports editor San Antonio Express, 1937-40; sports announcer, sales mgr., gen. mgr. KABC, San Antonio, 1940-53; gen. mgr. KGBS-TV, 1954; v.p. WJBK-TV, Detroit, 1955-61; dir. Storer Broadcasting Co., Miami Beach, Fla., 1960-85, TV v.p., 1961-66, exec. v.p., 1966-67, pres., 1967-74, chmn., 1974-82, ret., 1982. Chmn. New Boston Garden Corp. (Boston Bruins), 1972-75; dir., mem. exec. com. Northeast Airlines, 1965-72, pres., 1970-72; dir. Delta Airlines, 1972-90, adv. dir., 1990—. Trustee Storer Found. Home: 154 Manchester Way Shavano Pk San Antonio TX 78249

**MICHAELSEN, O.V. See OFTENESS, OVE**

**MICHAELS HOLLANDER, ERICA,** law educator; d. Harold Mogin; life ptnr. Thomas James Crowley, Sept. 9, 2006; children: David Benjamin, Joel Benjamin, Daniel Benjamin, Michael Thomas. JD, Union U., Albany, N.Y., 1976; PhD, U. of Denver, 2003. Bar: Colo. 1998, N.Y. 1977, Calif. 1984, Nev. 1983. Lectr. Met. State Coll. of Denver, 2000—. Contbr. articles to law jours. V.p. Roxborough Pk. Found., Littleton, Colo., 1998—2001. Recipient Pres.'s fellowship, U. of Denver, 1999. Home: 6910 Fairway Vista Littleton CO 80125 Office: Erica Michaels Hollander Inc 10561 Sandstone Run Littleton CO 80125 Personal E-mail: ericahollander@comcast.net.

**MICHAELSON, ARTHUR M.,** lawyer; b. NYC, May 16, 1927; s. Samuel H. and Augusta L. M.; m. Arline L. Kahn, June 30, 1957; children: Barbara L., Sarah E., David N. AB, Columbia U., 1947; LLB, Yale U., 1950. Bar: N.Y. 1950, U.S. Supreme Ct 1964. Partner Wachtel & Michaelson, N.Y.C., 1957-66; v.p. McCrory Corp., N.Y.C., 1966-68, Glen Alden Corp., N.Y.C., 1968-73; partner Miller, Singer, Michaelson & Raives, N.Y.C., 1973-84; counsel Hofheimer Gartlir & Gross, 1984—. Author: (with J. Blattmacdr) Income Taxation of Estates and Trusts, 1980, 85, 89, 95, 96, 98. Bd. dirs., mem. exec. com. Amnesty Internat. of U.S.A., Inc., 1972-81, vice chmn., 1975-76. Served with USN, 1945-46. Mem. ABA, Assn. Bar City N.Y. Office: 530 5th Ave New York NY 10036-5101

**MICHAELSON, JON,** lawyer; b. Jersey City, Apr. 2, 1948; BA, Pomona Coll., 1969; MA, Univ. Tex., Austin, 1973; JD, Boalt Sch. Law, Univ. Calif., Berkeley, 1978. Bar: Calif. 1978, US Dist. Ct. (Calif. districts), US Ct. Appeals (9th & Fed. cir.), US Supreme Ct. Ptnr., Global Intellectual Property practice Coudert Bros. LLP, San Francisco. Editor: Indsl. Rels. Law Jour., 1976—77; editor: (articles), 1977—78. Mem.: ABA, Internat. Trademark Assn., State Bar Calif., Santa Clara County Bar Assn. Office: Coudert Brothers Llp 555 S Flower St Los Angeles CA 90071-2300 Office Phone: 415-267-6200. Office Fax: 415-977-6110. Business E-Mail: michaelsonj@coudert.com.

**MICHAELSON, MARTIN,** lawyer; b. Boston, Apr. 12, 1943; s. Eliot D. and Charlotte (Selib) M.; m. Anne Taylor, Aug. 30, 1987; children: Andrew M., Daniel M.; stepchildren: Rachel T., Hannah T. BA, U. Chgo., 1965; JD, Boston Coll., 1968. Bar: N.Y. 1968, D.C. 1973, U.S. Supreme Ct. 1973, Mass. 1983, U.S. Dist. Ct. N.Y. 1969, D.C. 1973, U.S. Ct. Appeals (1st, 2d, 3d, 4th, 6th and 9th cirs.). Atty. Cravath, Swaine & Moore, N.Y.C., 1968-71; legis. asst. Congressman Robert F. Drinan, Washington, 1971-73; atty. Hogan & Hartson, Washington, 1973-76, ptnr., 1976-83, 89—. Dep. gen. counsel Harvard U., Cambridge, Mass., 1983-88, univ. counsel, 1989, lectr. Harvard Grad. Sch. of Education, 1999. Consulting editor Trusteeship mag. Fellow: Nat. Assn. Coll. and Univ. Attys. Office: Hogan & Hartson Columbia Square 555 13th St NW Ste 800E Washington DC 20044-1161 Office Phone: 202-637-5748. Business E-Mail: mmichaelson@hhlaw.com.

**MICHAELSON, PETER LEE,** lawyer; b. NYC, Aug. 29, 1952; BS in Elec. Engring. and Econs., Carnegie-Mellon U., 1974, MSEE, 1975; JD, Duquesne U., 1979; LLM in Trade Regulation, NYU, 1985; postgrad., Harvard U., 1993, 96, 97, postgrad., 96, 97, 99. Bar: Pa. 1979, NJ 1980, (US Patent and Trademark Office) 1980, (US Dist. Ct. NJ) 1980, (US Ct. Claims) 1980, (US Ct. Mil. Appeals) 1980, (US Tax Ct.) 1980, (US Supreme Ct (3rd cir.)) 1981, (US Ct. Appeals (fed. cir.)) 1983, NY 1986, (US Supreme Ct.) 1986, Alaska 2000, cert.: Ctr. Effective Dispute Resolution (mediator), lic.: Chartered Inst. Arbitrators, Eng. (arbitrator). Electronics project engr. Control Systems Research, Inc., Pitts., 1975-76; electronics devel. engr. Aluminum Co. Am., Alcoa Tech. Ctr., Prodn. Equip. Lab., Pitts., 1976-77, Rockwell Internat. Corp., Pitts., 1977-79; corp. patent atty. mem. patent and legal staff Bell Telephone Labs., Holmdel, NJ, 1979-82; atty. Pennie & Edmonds, N.Y., 1982-84; prin. Michaelson & Assocs., Counsellors at Law, Red Bank, NJ, 1984—. Mem. disting. panel neutrals tech. ICANN domain names and Y2K panels CPR Inst. Dispute Resolution, NYC; accredited mediator Centre for Effective Dispute Resolution, London; approved mediator/arbitrator in intellectual property and ICANN domain name and keyword disputes World Intellectual Property Orgn., Geneva; arbitrator ICANN domain name disputes, mem. adv. coun. IP panel, bd. dirs., mem. dispute resolution policy panel Nat. Arbitration Forum, Mpls.; arbitrator, mediator U.S. Dist. Ct. (ea. dist.) N.Y.; arbitrator London Ct. Internat. Arbitration, N.Am. Coun., Internat. C.of C., Paris, Internat. Ct. Arbitration, U.S. Coun. for Internat. Bus., NYC, Nat. Assn. of Securities Dealers; mediator NJ Superior Ct.; mem. CPR Inst. Dispute Resolution; master Justice Marie Garibaldi Am. Inn of Ct. for Alternative Dispute Resolution; mem. CEDR, London, CPR Arbitration Com. and Patent Commn.; presenter in field US and abroad; chartered arbitrator Chartered Inst. Arbitrators, London; arbitrator comml. and tech. panels Am. Arbitration Assn. Contbr. articles to profl. jours. Mem. Sch. Budget Adv. Com., Rumson, NJ, 1981—85, Zoning Bd. Adjustment, Rumson, 1988—93. Fellow: Australian Ctr. Internat. Comml. Arbitration (arbitrator), Chartered Inst. Arbitrators; mem.: AIPPI, Internat. Bar Assn., Am. Arbitration Assn. (nat. patent adv. coun., arbitrator, commercial and tech. panels), Assn. Fed. Bar N.J., Monmouth County Bar Assn., Fed. Bar Assn., Monmouth County Bar Assn., Assn. Conflict Resolution, N.J. Intellectual Property Law Assn., Am. Intellectual Property Law Assn. Home: 15 Holly Tree Ln Rumson NJ 07760-1950 Office: Michaelson & Assocs 1161 Broad St Ste 118 Shrewsbury NJ 07702 Office Phone: 732-542-7800. Office Fax: 732-542-7858. Business E-Mail: pete@mandw.com.

**MICHAILOFF, IAN ROBERT,** real estate broker, land use planner; b. Santa Clara, Calif., Sept. 13, 1973; s. Michael Gregory and Victoria Jean Michailoff; m. Robyn Michelle Clark, Mar. 10, 2001; children: Raiden Anthony, Jennika Simone. Diploma in bus. mgmt. info. sys. and acctg., Calif. State U., Sacramento, 1998; Microsoft Cert. Sys. Engr., HEALD, Calif., 1999. Cert. Real Estate Broker Calif., 2004. Broker, founder HouseLynk Realty & Loan, Stockton, Calif., 2003—, RentLynk Property Mgmt., Stockton, Calif., 2003—. Land developer DYB, LLC, Stockton, Calif., 2004—. Sgt. U.S. Army, 1991—95. Decorated Airborne Jump Wings U.S. Army, Ranger Tab, Can. Jump Wings, Jordanian Jump Wings. Mem.: Santa Clara Assn. Realtors (licentiate), Lodi Assn. Realtors (licentiate), Calif. Assn. Realtors (licentiate), Nat. Assn. Realtors (licentiate), Stockton C. of C. (assoc.), Stockton Golf & Country Club (licentiate), Gracie Jiu Jitsu (assoc.), Sigma Phi Epsilon Frat. (assoc.; social chmn. 1997—98). Conservative. Roman Catholic. Avocations: golf, Ju Jitsu, kickboxing, renovating properties. Office: HouseLynk Realty & Loan 1904 Country Club Blvd Stockton CA 95204 Office Phone: 209-462-8300. Business E-Mail: robm@houselynk.com.

**MICHAJLOW, EUSTACHY IOM,** artist; b. Jeziory, Poland, Apr. 23, 1930; arrived in U.S., 1951; s. Victor Michajlow and Lidia Naumezyk; m. Dorina Boisjole Michajlow, Mar. 10, 1973; children: Vadim, Kora. Home: 2319 Travelers Palm Dr Edgewater FL 32141-4403

**MICHALAK, EDWARD FRANCIS,** lawyer; b. Evanston, Ill., Sept. 6, 1937; s. Leo Francis Michalak and Helen Sophie (Wolinski) Krakowski. BSBA, Northwestern U., 1959; LLB, Harvard U., 1962. Bar: Ill. 1962. Assoc. McDermott, Will & Emery, Chgo., 1963-69, ptnr., 1969—. Served to sgt. USAR, 1962-68. Mem. Ill. Bar Assn., Chgo. Bar Assn., Beta Gamma Sigma, Beta Alpha Psi. Roman Catholic. Avocations: golf, opera. Home: 3455 Harrison St Evanston IL 60201-4953 Office: McDermott Will & Emery 227 W Monroe St 47th Fl Chicago IL 60606-5096 Office Phone: 312-984-7506. Business E-Mail: emichalak@mwe.com.

**MICHALAK, JANET CAROL,** childhood education educator, coordinator; b. Buffalo, Mar. 22, 1949; d. Theodore and Thelma Ruth (Roesch) Vukovic; m. Gerald Paul Michalak, June 19, 1971; children: Nathan, Justin. BS in Edn., SUNY Coll. at Buffalo, Buffalo, 1970; MS in Edn., SUNY, Buffalo, 1971, EdD, 1981. Cert. tchr. nursery, kindergarten, grades 1-6, reading tchr., English tchr. grades 7-12, N.Y. Reading tchr. Tonawanda (N.Y.) Sch. System, 1971-80; instr. Niagara County C.C., Sanborn, N.Y., 1980-82, asst. prof., 1982-85, assoc. prof., 1985-91, prof., 1991—2004, prof. emeritus, 2004, coord., prof. childhood edn. Adj. lectr. SUNY, Buffalo, 1990—91. Recipient Pres.'s award for Excellence in Teaching, Niagara County C.C., 1990, Nat. Inst. for Staff & Orgnl. Devel. Excellence award, 1991, SUNY Chancellor's award for Excellence in Teaching, 1991. Mem. Coll. Reading Assn., Internat. Reading Assn., N.Y. Coll. Learning Skills Assn., Niagara Frontier Reading Coun. (bd. dirs. 1986-88, 97—). Republican. Avocation: reading. Home: 184 Montbleu Dr Getzville NY 14068-1329 Office: Niagara County CC 3111 Saunders Settlement Rd Sanborn NY 14132-9487

**MICHALAK, JO-ANN,** library director; Grad., Syracuse U., U. Ill., Columbia U. Libr. U. Ill., Ind. U., Columbia U., U. Pitts.; now dir. Tisch Libr. Tufts. U., Medford, Mass. Pres. Boston Libr. Consortium, 2006—; mem. adv. bd. for univ. libbrs. Carnegie Mellon U., 2006—; bd. dirs. NELINET. Mem.: Soc. For Scholarly Pub. Office: Tisch Libr Tufts U 35 Professors Row Medford MA 02155 Office Phone: 617-627-3345. Office Fax: 617-627-3002. E-mail: jo-ann.michalak@tufts.edu.*

**MICHALAK, SARAH C.,** university librarian; BA in English, Univ. Calif. Riverside, 1969; MLS, UCLA, 1970. Previous head Bio-Agrl. Dept. Univ. Calif. Riverside; previous libr. Univ. Wash., Seattle; dir. J. Willard Marriot Libr. Univ. UT, Salt Lake City, 1995—2004; univ. libr. and assoc. provost for univ. libraries U. NC, Chapel Hill, 2004—. Mem.: Scholarly Pub. and Academic Resources Coalition (steering com.), Libr. Adminstrn. and Mgmt. Assn., Assn. Rsch. Libr. Office: CB 3900 Davis Libr Univ NC Chapel Hill NC 27514 Office Phone: 919-962-1301. E-mail: smichala@email.unc.edu.*

**MICHALEK, JOHN JAMES,** legal association administrator; b. Bemidji, Minn., Aug. 1, 1945; m. Diane Marie Olson, Dec. 21, 1968; children: Matthew John, Nicole, Shane. BA, U. Minn., 1967, JD, 1970. Legal editor Lawyers Coop. Pub. Co., Rochester, NY, 1970—75; dir. continuing legal edn. Wash. State Bar Assn., Seattle, 1975—81, exec. dir., 1981—91; asst. dean devel. and cmty. rels. Sch. Law U. Wash., 1991—95; dir., CEO Assn. Legal Adminstrs., Lincolnshire, Ill., 1995—. Fellow: Coll. Law Practice Mgmt.; mem.: Nat. Trust Hist. Preservation, Am. Mgmt. Assn., Am. Soc. Assn. Execs. Lutheran. Office: Assn Legal Adminstrs 75 Tri-State Internat Ctr # 222 Lincolnshire IL 60069-4435 Office Phone: 847-267-1360. Business E-Mail: jmichalik@alanet.org.

**MICHALSKI, PAUL PETER,** lawyer; b. Amsterdam, NY, Aug. 11, 1961; s. Steven Robert (stepfather) and Marilyn Lee (Januszewski) Cevera; m. Elizabeth L. Butterworth, 1990; children: James, Anne. AB, Harvard U., 1983, JD, 1986. Bar: Mass. 1986, N.Y. 1987. Assoc. Cravath, Swaine & Moore LLP, N.Y.C., 1986-94, ptnr., corp., 1994—. Adv. bd. Capital Markets Law Jour., James Beard Found. Fellow. Mem. ABA, Internat. Bar Assn., N.Y. State Bar Assn., City of N.Y. Bar Assn., The Blue Hill Troupe Ltd., Mosimann's Club, Harvard Club, New Canaan Soc., Roton Point Assn., Royal Soc. for Encouragement of Arts (Mfg. and Commerce fellow), NY Law Inst. (exec. com.). Republican. Office: Cravath, Swaine & Moore LLP Worldwide Plz 825 Eighth Ave New York NY 10019-7475 Office Phone: 212-474-1868. Office Fax: 212-474-3700.

**MICHALSKI, STANLEY FRANKLIN,** music educator, conductor; b. Nanticoke, Pa., Aug. 15, 1934; s. Stanley and Lottie Michalski; m. Joan Marilyn Michalski, Nov. 16, 1957; children: Stanley III, Lisa Joan. BS in Music Edn., cum laude, Pa. State U., 1956, MEd in Music Edn., 1959, EdD in Music Edn., 1966; postgrad., U. Pitts., Wyo. Sem., Clarion U.; diploma (hon.), El Centro Estudios Comm. Social, 1990, La Casa Cultra Acapulco. Supr. instrumental music Cen. Dauphin Sch., Harrisburg, Pa., 1956—58; grad. asst., asst. condr. univ. bands Pa. State U., 1958—59; music supr. Juniata Joint Schs., Mifflintown, Pa., 1959—60; prof. music and music edn. Clarion U., 1961—92; condr. instrumental music Charlotte Diocese Mecklenburg Area Cath. Schs., 1993—. Adj. prof. U. N.C., 1999—, Winthrop U., 1999—; vis. artist prof., condr. in residence Catawba Coll., 2003—; mem. editl. bd. Brass and Percussion Jour.; guest condr., adjudicator, soloist numerous worldwide appearances. Contbr. articles to profl. publs. Bd. dirs. Clarion Area Schs., Clarion County Area Vocat. Tech. Sch., Clarion Hosp., Clarion Borough Employee Pension Com.; chmn. United Way Faculty Fund Dr., 1984—87. Recipient Cert. Commendation, Am. Fedn. Musicians, 1971, Citation of Excellence, Nat. Band Assn., 1977, Cert. Exceptional Acad. Svc., Clarion State Coll., 1978, 1981, Disting. Faculty award, Clarion Alumni Assn., 1986, A. Frank Martin award, Kappa Kappa Psi, 1986, Clarion Borough Mayor's award, 1983, 1991, Disting. Svc. to Music award, Kappa Kappa Psi, 1991. Mem.: NEA (life), N.C. Music Educators Assn., Internat. Mil. Music Soc., Nat. Bandmasters Assn., Am. Fedn. Musicians, Am. Bandmasters Assn. (pres. 1998—99, chmn. bd. 1992—97), Coll. Band Dirs. Nat. Assn. (pres. ea. divsn. 1975—77, Pa. state chmn. 1969—71), Pa. Music Educators Assn. (pres. 1976—78, cont. chmn. 1975, 1976), Pa. State Alumni Assn. (life), Pa. Coll. Bandmasters Assn. (life; treas. 1965—71), Tau Beta Sigma, Kappa Kappa Psi, Omicron Delta Kappa, Phi Beta Mu (pres. 1977). Avocations: travel, golf. Home: 9013 Raintree Ln Charlotte NC 28277 Office Phone: 704-541-8016, 704-516-7902.

**MICHAUD, GEORGES JOSEPH,** physics professor; b. Quebec, Can., Apr. 30, 1940; s. Marie-Louis and Isabelle (St. Laurent) M.; m. Denise Lemieux, June 25, 1966. BA, U. Laval, Que., 1961, BSc, 1965; PhD, Calif. Tech. Inst., Pasadena, 1970. Prof. U. Montreal, Canada, 1969—2005, prof. emeritus, 2005—; dir. Ctr. Rsch. en Calcul Appliqué, 1992-96, assoc. dean of grad. studies, 1997—2000. Recipient Steacie prize NRC, 1980, Medaille Janssen, Acad. Scis., Paris, 1982, Prix Vincent, ACFAS, 1979; Killam fellow Conseil des Arts, 1987-89. Mem.: Royal Soc. Can., Internat. Astron. Union, Can. Astron. Soc. (Beals award 2006), Am. Astron. Soc. Office: Univ Montreal Dept de Physique Montreal PQ Canada H3C 3J7 Office Phone: 514-343-6672. Business E-Mail: michaudg@astro.umontreal.ca.

**MICHAUD, MICHAEL HERMAN,** congressman; b. Millinocket, Maine, Jan. 18, 1955; s. James Leroy and Jean (Morrow) M. Grad., Schenck H.S., 1973; student, U. Maine, 1979. Papermaker Gt. No. Paper Co., 1973-80, mem. staff finishing dept., 1981—; mem. dist. 134 Maine Ho. Reps., Augusta, 1980—94, mem. regional conf. task force on environment, chmn. energy and natural resources com., spkr. pro tem, chmn. appropriations and fin. affairs com., mem. legis. svc. com.; mem. Dist. 3 Maine Senate, Augusta, 1994—2002, pres. pro tem.; mem. US Congress from 2nd Maine dist., 2003—. Mem. com. Eastmill Fed. Credit Union, 1979—; area coord. Merril for Gov. campaign, 1978; v.p. Maine Young Dems., 1978-80, del. state conv., 1980, 82, 84, del. nat. conv., 1979. Mem. Nat. Conf. State Legislators, Katahdin Friend of Retarded Children Assn., East Br. Snow Rovers, KC.

Democrat. Office: US Ho Reps 437 Cannon Ho Office Bldg Washington DC 20515-1902 also: Great Northern Paper Co Bowater Main St East Millinocket ME 04430 Home: 3 Birch St East Millinocket ME 04430-1001

**MICHEAS, ATHANASIOS CHRISTOU,** finance educator; b. Volos, Greece, Jan. 4, 1974; s. Christos and Vasiliki Micheas; m. Lada Kotlov, Nov. 7, 2001; children: Vasiliki, Eudokia. PhD in Statistics, U. Conn., Storrs, 2001. Asst. prof. stats. U. Mo., Columbia, 2001—. Contbr. articles to profl. jours. Grantee Nowcasting Precipitation grant, NSF, 2005—. Office: U Mo 146 Middlebush Hall Columbia MO 65211 Office Phone: 573-884-8828. Office Fax: 573-884-5524. Business E-Mail: amicheas@stat.missouri.edu.

**MICHEL, ANTHONY NIKOLAUS,** electrical engineering educator, researcher; b. Rekasch, Romania, Nov. 17, 1935; came to U.S., 1952; s. Anton Michel and Katharina (Metz) Malsam; m. Leone Lucille Flasch, Aug. 17, 1957; children: Mary Leone, Katherine Jean, John Peter, Anthony Joseph, Patrick Thomas. BSE.E., Marquette U., 1958, MS in Math., 1964, PhD in Elec. Engring., 1968; D.Sc. in Math., Tech. U. Graz, Austria, 1973. Registered profl. engr., Wis. Engr. in tng. U.S. Army C.E., Milw., 1958-59; project engr. AC Electronics div. Gen. Motors Corp., Milw., 1959-62, sr. research engr., 1962-65; asst. prof. elec. engring. Iowa State U., Ames, 1968-69, assoc. prof., 1969-74, prof., 1974-84; prof. elec. engring. U. Notre Dame, Ind., 1984-87, chmn. dept. elec. and computer engring. Ind., 1984-88, Frank M. Freimann prof. engring. Ind., 1988—2002, dean coll. engring. Ind., 1988—98, dean emeritus, 1998—, prof. emeritus, 2002—. Cons. Houghton Mifflin Co., 1975, Acad. Press, 1983; cons. editor William C. Brown Co. Pubs., Dubuque, Iowa, 1982-83; vis. prof. Tech. U. Vienna, 1992, Ruhr U., Bochum, Germany, 1999, Johannes Kepler U., Linz, Austria, 2004. Author: (with others) Qualitative Analysis of Large Scale Dynamical Systems, 1977, Mathematical Foundations in Engineering and Science, 1981, Ordinary Differential Equations, 1982, Applied Linear Algebra and Functional Analysis, 1993, (with Derong Liu) Dynamical Systems with Saturation Nonlinearities, 1993, (with Kaining Wang) Qualitative Theory of Dynamical Systems, 1994, (with Kaining Wang) Qualitative Theory of Dynamical Systems, 2d edit., revised and expanded, 2001, (with Panos J. Antsaklis) Linear Systems, 1997, (with Derong Liu) Qualitative Analysis and Synthesis of Recurrent Neural Networks, 2002; contbr. articles to profl. jours., chpts. to books. Grantee NSF, 1972—, Dept. Def., 1968-72; fellow Fulbright Found., 1992; recipient Alexander von Humboldt Rsch. award U.S. Sr. Scientists, 1998, Disting. Alumnus award Coll. Engring. Marquette U., 2005 Fellow IEEE (mng. editor Trans. on Cirs. and Sys. 1981-83, Best Trans. Paper award 1978, 83, 93, Centennial medal 1984, Millenium medal 2000); mem. IEEE Cirs. and Sys. Soc. (pres.s 1989, Myril B. Reed Outstanding Paper award 1993, Tech. Achievement award 1995, Golden Jubilee medal 1999), IEEE Control Sys. Soc. (Disting. Mem. award 1998), Russian Acad. Engring. (hon.), Sigma Xi, Eta Kappa Nu, Pi Mu Epsilon, Phi Kappa Phi. Home: 17001 Stonegate Ct Granger IN 46530-6948 Office: U Notre Dame Dept Elec Engring Coll Engring Notre Dame IN 46556 Office Phone: 574-631-4395. Business E-Mail: amichel@nd.edu, anthony.n.michel1@nd.edu.

**MICHEL, DONALD CHARLES,** editor; b. Ventura, Calif., Nov. 17, 1935; s. Charles J. and Esther Caroline (Heilert) M.; m. Loretta Perron, May 4, 1963; children: Edwin, Robert. Photographer. BA, UCLA, 1958, MS, 1959. Editor San Fernando (Calif.) Sun, 1958-60; successively reporter, weekend editor, mng. editor Valley Times Today, North Hollywood, Calif., 1960-63; feature editor Houston Chronicle, 1963-68; asst. mng. editor features Chgo. Daily News, 1968-77; exec. v.p., editor Chgo. Tribune-N.Y. News Syndicate, 1984; v.p. adminstrn. and editl. devel. L.A. Times Syndicate, 1984-93, dir. book devel., 1993-97; cons. L.A. Times Syndicate, 1998-99; ret. Photo exhbn., Sedona, 2001; founder DLM Images, 2003. Home: 3000 Adornos Way Burbank CA 91504-1609 Personal E-mail: donmichel@charter.net.

**MICHEL, ELIZABETH CHENEY,** social reform consultant; b. Pitts., Feb. 11, 1951; d. George Philip and Charlotte Elizabeth (Cowser) Cheney; m. Raymond Joseph Michel, Oct. 21, 1973 (div. June 1997); children: Keith Raymond, Grant Petersen. BA, Rollins Coll., 1973; M in Comm., U. Ctrl. Fla., 1988, PhD, 1992. Vis. prof. Univ. Ctrl. Fla., Orlando, Fla., 1989-92; assoc. prof., chair comm. program Mars Hill (N.C.) Coll., 1993-99; comms. cons., v.p. Comms. Strategies-Healthcare.com, Corp., 1999-2000; dir. change mgmt. Ga. Tech. Authority, 2001—. Pres. Kairos Commn. Strategies, Atlanta, 1998—; bd. dirs. Biltmore Inst., 1997—, cons., 1996—; bd. dirs. Commn. on Industries of the Mind, Atlanta; vice-chair 21st Century Comm., 1996—; project coord. for joint comm. with Chinese Acad. Social Scis., China; del. to Consortium for Global Edn., China, 1998; vis. comm. Kennesaw State U.; mem. internat. del. to Conf. on Environ. Sustainability, Shanghai, 2000, Implementation Strategies for SMEs, Networking 2000, Paris, 2000; v.p. Systems and Strategies; mem. bd. advisor Atlantic U. Chinese Medicine, 2000—, chair bd. dirs., 2001—. Author: 4 Simple Steps to Communications that Connect! and Kairos Community Strategies Interactive CD-ROM, 2000; chief editor: An Orchestra of Voices: Making the Argument for Press and Speech Freedom in the People's Republic of China, 2000; contbr. articles to mag. Bd. dirs. Atlanta Women's Network, 2000—01. Internat. Rsch. grant Appalachian Coll. Assn., 1994, 96, 97, Mellon Found., 1994, 95, 96, 97; Vis. Rsch. fellow Chinese Acad. Social Scis., 1996, 97. Mem.: Women's Network, Brit. Am. Bus. Group, Am. Educators Journalism and Mass Comm., Nat. Comm. Assn., Atlanta Coun. on Internat. Rels., Dem. Women's forum, Metro Atlanta C. of C., Women's Commerce Club, Ga. Exec. Women's Network, Atlanta Women's Network-Strategic Planning, Kappa Delta Phi, Phi Kappa Phi. Presbyterian. Avocations: acting, music, drawing.

**MICHEL, H. JOHN, JR.,** lawyer; b. Lewistown, Pa., 1947; AB, Wesleyan, 1970; MA, Univ. Chgo., 1977; JD, Univ. Pa., 1985. Bar: Pa. 1985. Joined Drinker Biddle & Reath LLP, Phila., 1985, ptnr., chair bus., fin. dept. Office: Drinker Biddle & Reath LLP One Logan Sq 18th & Cherry Sts Philadelphia PA 19103-6996 Office Phone: 215-988-2515. Office Fax: 215-988-2757. Business E-Mail: john.michel@dbr.com.

**MICHEL, HARTMUT,** biochemist; b. Ludwigsburg, Germany, July 18, 1948; s. Karl and Frieda Michel; m. Ilona S. Leger, 1979; children: Andrea, Robert Joachim. Doctorate, U. Wurzburg, 1969—74. With Max Planck Inst. Biochemistry, Martinsried, Germany, 1979-87. Co-recipient Nobel prize for chemistry, 1988; recipient Biophysics Prize, Am. Phys. Soc., Otto Klung Prize, Leibniz Prize, Otto-Bayer Prize. Office: Max Planck Inst Biophysics Max-von-Laue-Str 3 60438 Frankfurt Germany E-mail: hartmut.michel@mpibp-frankfurt.mpg.de.*

**MICHEL, JACQUELINE,** geochemist; BS, U. SC, Columbia, 1974, MS, 1976, PhD in Geochemistry, 1980. Registered geologist SC. Prin. investigator NOAA Hazardous Materials Response and Assessment Divsn., Seattle, 1978—; project mgr. Office of Pipeline Safety, 1996—; pres. Rsch. Planning Inc., 2000—. Mem. com. spills on nonfloating oil NRC, 1998—99; mem. com. oil in the sea, 1999—2002; chmn. com. spills of emulsified fuels: risks and responses, 2001; mem. Oceans Study Bd. NAS; mem. sci. adv. panel US Commn. Ocean Policy; adj. prof. U. SC School of Environment. Contbr. articles to profl. jours., chapters to books. Mem.: Carolina Geol. Soc., Sigma Xi. Office: RPI Louisiana Inc Twin Heights Office Pk Ste E 27999 Old S Walker Rd Walker LA 70785*

**MICHEL, MARY ANN KEDZUF,** nursing educator; b. Evergreen Park, Ill., June 1, 1939; d. John Roman and Mary Kedzuf; m. Jean Paul Michel, 1974. Diploma in nursing, Little Company of Mary Hosp., Evergreen Park, 1960; BSN, Loyola U., Chgo., 1964; MS, No. Ill. U., 1968, EdD, 1971. Staff nurse Little Co. of Mary Hosp., 1960-64; instr. Little Co. of Mary Hosp. Sch. Nursing, 1964-67, No. Ill. U., DeKalb, 1968-69, asst. prof., 1969-71; chmn. dept. nursing U. Nev., Las Vegas, 1971-73; prof. nursing, 1975—, dean Coll. Health Scis., 1973-90; pres. PERC. Inc.; mgmt. cons., 1993—95. Mgmt. cons. Nev. Donor Network, 1993; mem. So. Nev. Health Manpower Task Force, 1975; mem. manpower com. Plan Devel. Commn., Clark County Health Sys. Agy., 1977-79, mem. governing body, 1981-86; mem. Nev.

Health Coordinating Coun., Western Inst. Nursing, 1971-85; mem. coordinating com. assembly instnl. adminstrs. dept. allied health edn. and accreditation AMA, 1985-88; mem. bd. advisors So. Nev. Vocat. Tech. Ctr., 1976-80; sec.-treas. Nev. Donor Network, 1988-89, chmn. bd., 1988-90. Contbr. articles to profl. jours. Trustee Desert Spring Hosp., Las Vegas, 1976-85; bd. dirs. Nathan Adelson Hospice, 1982-88, Bridge Counseling Assocs., 1982, Everywoman's Ctr., 1984-86; chair Nev. Commn. on Nursing Edn., 1972-73, Nursing Articulation Com., 1972-73, Yr. of Nurse Com., 1978; moderator Invitational Conf. Continuing Edn., Am. Soc. Allied Health Professions, 1978; mgmt. cons. Nev. Donor Network, 1994-95, Donor Organ Recovery Svc., Transplant Recipient Internat. Orgn., S.W. Eye Bank, S.W. Tissue Bank. Named Outstanding Alumnus, Loyola U., 1983; NIMH fellow, 1967-68. Fellow Am. Soc. Allied Health Professions, 1991, (chair nat. resolutions com. 1981-84, treas. 1988-90, sec.'s award com. 1982-83, 92-93, nat. by-laws com. 1985, conv. chair 1987); mem. AAUP, Am. Nurses Assn., Nev. Nurses Assn. (dir. 1975-77, treas. 1977-79, conv. chair 1978), So. Nev. Area Health Edn. Coun., Western Health Deans (co-organizer 1985, chair, 1988-90), Nat. League Nursing, Nev. Heart Assn., So. Nev. Mem. Hosps. (nursing recruitment com. 1981-83, mem. nursing practice com. 1983-85), Las Vegas C. of C. (named Woman of Yr. Edn.) 1988, Slovak Catholic Sokols, Phi Kappa Phi (chpt. sec. 1981-83, pres.-elect 1983, pres. 1984, v.p. Western region 1989-95, editl. bd. jour. Nat. Forum 1989-93), Alpha Beta Gamma (hon.), Sigma Theta Tau, Zeta Kappa. Office: U Nev Las Vegas 4505 S Maryland Pky Las Vegas NV 89154-9900 Office Phone: 702-895-3719. Personal E-mail: m.a.michel@worldnet.att.com.

**MICHEL, NICOLAS,** international organization administrator; b. Nov 7, 1949; married with children. PhD in Law, U. Fribourg, Switzerland; MA in Internat. Rels., Georgetown U. Washington, DC. Lic.: (attorney at law). Sec.-gen. Dept. of Edn. and Culture of the canton, Fribourg, Switzerland, 1980—85; acted as the head of the Swiss del. for the presentation of nat. reports before internat. com.; dir., Internat. Law Directorate Swiss Fed. Dept. of Foreign Affairs, 1998—2003, legal advisor, 1998—2004; under-sec.-gen. Legal Affairs and UN Legal Counsel, 2004—. Chmn., consultation and preparatory mtg. on a third protocol to the Geneva Convs. (Emblems), 2000; chmn. Com. of the Legal Advisors on Pub. Internat. Law of the Coun. of Europe, 2003—04; prof., Internat. Law and European Law U. Fribourg, Switzerland, 1987—2004, vice dean of the law faculty, 2003—04; bd. dir. European Law Faculties Assn., 2003—04. Author of numerous books and articles on Internat. and European law. Office: UN Hdqs First Avenue at 46th St New York NY 10017 Office Phone: 212-963-5339. Office Fax: 212-963-6430.*

**MICHEL, PAUL REDMOND,** federal judge; b. Phila., Feb. 3, 1941; s. Lincoln M. and Dorothy (Kelley) Michel; m. Brooke England, 2004; children: Sarah Elizabeth, Margaret Kelley. BA, Williams Coll., 1963; JD, U. Va., 1966. Bar: Pa. 1967, U.S. Supreme Ct. 1970. Asst. dist. atty. Phila. Atty.'s Office, Phila., 1967—71, dep. dist. atty. investigations, 1972—74; asst. spl. prosecutor Watergate investigation US Dept. Justice, Washington, 1974—75, dep. chief pub. integrity sect., Criminal div. and prosecutor "Koreagate" investigation, 1976—78, assoc. dep. atty. gen., 1978—81; asst. counsel intelligence com. US Senate, 1975—76, counsel and adminstrv. asst. to Sen. Arlen Specter, 1981—88; judge US Ct. Appeals (Fed. cir.), Washington, 1988—, chief judge, 2004—. Instr. appellate practice and procedure George Washington U. Nat. Law Ctr., 1991—2002. 2d lt. USAR, 1966—72. Office: US Ct Appeals Fed Cir 717 Madison Pl NW Washington DC 20439 Office Phone: 202-633-6297. E-mail: michelp@cafc.uscourts.gov.*

**MICHELI, FRANK JAMES,** lawyer; b. Zanesville, Ohio, Mar. 23, 1930; s. John and Theresa (Carlini) Micheli; m. Doris Joan Clum, Jan. 9, 1954; children: Michael John, James Carl, Lisa Ann, Matthew Charles. Student, John Carroll U., Cleve., 1947-48, Xavier U., Cin., 1949-50; LL.D., Ohio No. U., Ada., 1953. Bar: Ohio 1953. Pvt. practice, Zanesville; ptnr. Leasure & Micheli, 1953-65, Kincaid, Micheli, Geyer & Ormond, 1965-75, Kincaid, Cultice, Micheli & Geyer (and predecessor), 1982-92, Micheli, Baldwin, Bopeley & Northrup, 1992—. Instr. bus. law Meredith Bus. Coll., Zanesville, 1956; lectr. med. malpractice, hosp. and nurse liability. Dir. pub. svc. City of Zanesville, 1954. Mem.: ABA, Am. Bd. Trial Advs. (bd. dirs. Ohio chpt. 1991—95, pres. 1997), Am. Arbitration Assn. (mem. nat. panel), Am. Judicature Soc., Ohio Bar Assn., Ohio Def. Assn., Def. Rsch. Inst., Internat. Assn. Ins. Counsel, Elk. Home: 160 E Willow Dr Zanesville OH 43701-1249 Office: PO Box 788 3808 James Ct Ste 2 Zanesville OH 43702-0788 Office Phone: 740-454-2545. E-mail: micheli@cyberzane.net.

**MICHELINI, SYLVIA HAMILTON,** auditor; b. Decatur, Ala., May 16, 1946; d. George Borum and Dorothy Rose (Swatzell) Hamilton; m. H. Stewart Michelini, June 4, 1964; children: Stewart Anthony, Cynthia Leigh. BSBA summa cum laude, U. Ala., Huntsville, 1987. CPA, Ala.; cert. govt. fin. mgr., fraud examiner. Acct. Ray McCay, CPA, Huntsville, 1987-88; auditor Def. Contract Audit Agy., Huntsville, 1989-92; auditor-office of inspector general George C. Marshall Space Flight, Center, Ala., 1992-97; contr. Hamilton Hotels, Inc., 1997-2001; ret. Exec. bd. Decatur City PTA, 1976-78; pres., v.p. Elem. Sch. PTA, Decatur, 1977-79; leader Girl Scouts U.S. and Cub Scouts, Decatur, 1972-77; active local ARC, 1973-77. Mem.: AAUW (chpt. treas. 1988—90), AICPA, Inst. Mgmt. Accts. (v.p. comm., dir. program book 1991—94, Dixie coun. dir. newsletters 1992—93, dir. ednl. programs 1992—93, 1993—94, nat. coun. ethics 1990—97, nat. fin. com. 1997—98, nat. bd. dirs. 1994—97), Inst. Internal Auditors (dir. awards and recognition 1996—97, sec. 1999—2001, 2003—04), Ala. Soc. CPAs (profl. ethics com. 1993—94, govtl. acctg. and auditing com. 1994—95), Assn. Govt. Accts. (sec. 1992—93, chmn. pub. rels. 1993—94), Am. Soc. Women Accts (chpt. treas. 1989—90, dir. chpt. devel. 1989—90), Nat. Notary Assn., Nat. Assn. Accts. (dir. cmty. svc. 1987—88, v.p. adminstrn. and fin. 1988—89, pres. 1989—90, nat. coun. on ethics 1990—91), Phi Kappa Phi. Baptist. Avocations: reading, walking, sewing, research, music. Home and Office: 2801 Sylvia Dr SE Decatur AL 35603-5643 E-mail: nimi@hiway.net.

**MICHELIS, MICHAEL FRANK,** nephrologist; b. Bklyn., Dec. 11, 1938; s. Michael and Gisella (Gammer) M.; m. Mary Ann Wolak, July 28, 1973; children: Elizabeth Ann, Katherine Clare. BA, Columbia U., 1959; MD, George Washington U., 1963. Intern, resident Lenox Hill Hosp., N.Y.C., 1963-65; resident Mosp. Med. Coll. Pa., Phila., 1965-67; fellow in renal disease, dept. medicine U. Pitts. Sch. Medicine, 1969-70, asst. prof. medicine, 1971-75; chief renal diagnostic unit VA Hosp., Pitts., 1971-75; asst. prof. clin. medicine NYU Med. Sch., 1975-93; assoc. prof. clin. medicine N.Y. Med. Coll., 1980-87, prof.; asst. prof. clin. medicine Cornell U. Med. Coll., 1992-93; prof. clin. medicine NYU Med. Coll., 1993—; dir. nephrology sect. Lenox Hill Hosp., N.Y.C., 1975—. Spl. lectr. Georgetown U. Med. Sch., 1973-85; lectr. Western Pa. Continuing Edn. for Physicians, 1972-75, vis. prof., 1976; merit rev. bd. VA, 1973-76; cons. clin. fellowship rev. com. NIH, 1981-85; mem. exec. com. End Stage Renal Disease Network, N.Y.C., 1981-85; mem. med. Kidney Found. of N.Y./N.J., 1987-2001; vice-chair med. adv. bd., trustee Kidney and Urology Found. Am., 2001—, v.p., 2005—. Mem. editl. bd. Clin. Nephrology, 1979-89, Geriat. Nephrology, 1986, Jour. Geriatric Nephrology and Urology, 1989—, mem. editor, 1989-98; contbr. articles to profl. jours. Served to maj. M.C., AUS, 1967-69. Decorated Army Commendation medal; Health, Rsch. and Svcs. Found. grantee, 1970, 72, 74. Mem. AMA (invited lectr. 1973-75), ACP, Am. Fedn. Clin. Rsch., Am. Soc. Nephrology, Internat. Soc. Nephrology, Internat. Soc. for Geriatric Nephrology and Urology (pres. 1999-2003), Ctrl. Soc. Clin. Rsch. Greek Orthodox. Home: 16 Woodland Park Dr Tenafly NJ 07670-3027 Office: Lenox Hill Hosp 100 E 77th St New York NY 10021-1850 Office Phone: 212-988-3506. E-mail: mfmich@ix.netcom.com.

**MICHEL-KERJAN, ERWANN O.,** finance educator; b. Paris; PhD, Ecole Poly., Paris, 2002. Mng. dir. Ctr. for Catastrophic Risk Mgmt., Wharton Sch. Fin., Phila., 2002—. Author: Treatise on New Risks; author, editor: Seeds of Disaster. Roots of Response. How Can Private Action Reduce Public

Vulnerability, 2006. Mem.: Econometric Soc., Am. Risk and Ins. Assn., Am. Econ. Assn. Office: The Wharton School 3730 Walnut St Philadelphia PA 19104 Office Phone: 215-503-0515. Business E-Mail: erwannmk@wharton.upenn.edu.

**MICHELL, AURIEL IBN,** lawyer, writer; b. Miami, Fla., Apr. 8, 1948; s. Sylva Rivkah Mazoulay and Arie Stepthen Michell. DD, Hamilton State U., 1975; LLD, Southland Coll. Law, 1976; LLM, Clearwater Coll. of Law, 1979; ThD, Slidell Bapt. Sem., 1989; JD, Kensington U., 1993. Bar: Calif. Bar 1979. Tax lawyer City of Refuge, El Paso, Tex., 1994—; gen. counsel Intl Inst. for Health & Wellness, Orem, Utah, 1999—. Author: (book) Let's Talk Jewish, 1998 (religious best seller, 2000), Visions, 2000 (New Poet of the Yr. award, 2001), (poetry) From Deep Inside My Soul, 2001 (Internat.Poet of Merit award, 2002). Bd. of dirs. Tampa (Fla.) Food Bank, 1982—85. Maj. U.S. Army, 1967—73. Mem.: ABA, Fed. Bar Assn. Democrat. Jewish. Avocation: travel, writing, speaking. Office: City of Refuge c/o Rio Verde University POBox 971166 Orem UT 85097 E-mail: ctyrfugedu3@hotmail.com.

**MICHELMAN, FRANK I.,** law educator; b. New Rochelle, NY, May 26, 1936; BA in History, Yale U., 1957; LLB, Harvard U., 1960. Bar: NY 1961, Mass. 1967. Pvt. practice, NY, 1960—61; law clk. to Assoc. Justice William J. Brennan, Jr. US Supreme Ct., Washington, 1961-62; asst. to asst. atty. gen. tax divsn. US Dept. Justice, 1962-63; asst. prof. law Harvard Law Sch., Cambridge, Mass., 1963-66, prof., 1966—, Robert Walmsley Univ. prof., 1992—, assoc. dean, 1981—85. Cons. HUD, 1966 Co-author: (with Sandalow) Government in Urban Areas, 1970; author: Brennan and Democracy, 1999. Cons. Boston Model City Program, 1968-69; mem. Boston Home Rule Commn., 1969-71; mem. Gov.'s Task Force on Met. Devel., 1974-75. Mem. Am. Soc. for Polit. and Legal Philosophy (pres. 1998-2000), Am. Acad. Arts and Sciences. Office: Harvard Law Sch 1563 Massachusetts Ave Cambridge MA 02138 Office Phone: 617-495-4628. Office Fax: 617-496-5156. Business E-Mail: fmichel@law.harvard.edu.

**MICHELMAN, KATE,** advocate; married; 3 daughters. Dir. Planned Parenthood, Harrisburg, Pa., 1980-85; pres. Nat. Abortion and Reproductive Rights Action League, Washington, 1985—2004. Spkr. in field. Named one of 100 Most Powerful Elites in the Nation's Capitol Washingtonian Mag., named a fellow of John F. Kennedy Sch. Govt.'s Inst. of Politics Harvard U., 1994. Office: Nat Abortion Rights Action League 1156 15th St NW Ste 700 Washington DC 20005-1744

**MICHELS, DALE E.,** physician; b. Wayne, Nebr., Mar. 24, 1948; s. R.B. and Florence A. (Peterson) M.; m. Roylene C. Gustafson, Jan. 25, 1969; children: Gretchen, Sheila, Joel. BA in Medicine, U. Nebr., Omaha, 1969, MD, 1973. Diplomate Am. Bd. Family Practice with added qualifications in geriatrics. Practicing family physician Lincoln (Nebr.) Family Med. Group, 1974—. Med. cons. Comm. Blood Bank of LCMS, Lincoln, 1992—; med. dir. Nebr. Found. for Med. Care, 2001—; pres. EMS, Inc., 2002—; v.p. Wellmark Health Plan of Nebr., Lincoln, 1996-2000; vice-chair bd. trustees Back to the Bible, Lincoln, 1986-2004 chair bd. trustees, 2004—; sec.-treas. Family Care, P.C., Lincoln, 1986-97. Pres. Lancaster County Med. Soc., Lincoln, 1991-92, Nebr. Acad. of Family Physicians, Omaha, 1987, Nebr. Heart Assn., 1983, Lincoln Christian Sch. Bd., Lincoln, 1990-97. Recipient J.J. Hanigan award Lincoln Lancaster Comm. Health Dept., 1994, Pub. Health Leadership awrd, 2000; named Family Physician of Yr., Nebr. Acad. Family Physicians, 1999. Mem. Am. Med. Dirs. Assn. (pres.-elect N.E.), Lancaster County Med. Soc., Nebr. Acad. Family Physicians (Family Physician of Yr. 1999), Christian Med. Dental Soc., Am. Acad. Family Physicians, Nebr. Med. Assn. (pres. 1999-00). Republican. Avocations: flying, photography, gardening. Office: Lincoln Family Med Group PC 7441 O St Ste 400 Lincoln NE 68510-2466 Office Phone: 402-488-7400. E-mail: daromichels@cs.com.

**MICHELS, DIRK,** lawyer; b. Wupperful, Germany, Mar. 10, 1962; s. Wolfgang and Ingrid Michels; m. Claudia I. Olson, Aug. 2, 1995. BWL Vordiplom, Univ. Hamburg, Germany, 1986, doctorate Erstes Staatsexamen, 1988; LLM, U. San Diego, 1996. Bar: Hamburg 1992, Calif. 1996. Law clk. Hamburg Ct. Appeals, 1989-92; assoc. Hutth Dietrich Hahn, Hamburg, 1992-95, Hillyer & Irwin, San Diego, 1996-2000; assoc. to ptnr. & pro bono coord. Kirkpatrick & Lockhart Nicholson Graham LLP, San Francisco, 2000—. Bd. dirs. UN Trade Point, San Diego. Contbr. articles tp profl. jours. Mem. ABA (internat. sect.), Council of Bars & Law Soc. of European Cmty., German-Am. Commerce Club Silicon Valley (bd. dir.), Internat. Angel Investor Inst. (bd. adv.), German-Am. Lawyers Assn., German-Am. Cultural Soc., Am. Coun. on Germany. Office: Kirkpatrick & Lockhart Nicholson Graham LLP 10th Fl 4 Embarcadero Ctr San Francisco CA 94111-4121 Office Phone: 415-249-1022. Office Fax: 415-249-1001. Business E-Mail: dmichels@klng.com.

**MICHELS, JOSEPH B.,** military officer, dean; b. Spokane, Wash., Dec. 6, 1952; BS in Elec. Engring., Weber State U., Ogden, Utah, 1976; MS in Systems Mgmt., U.S.C., 1978; PhD Indsl. Engring., Tex. A&M, Coll. Sta., 1982. Registered profl. engr., Tex., 2000. Commd. 2d lt. USAF, 1976, advanced through grades to col., 1999; Chief electronics and workload control divsns. Comm. and Installation Group USAF, Norton AFB, Calif., 1977—80; test engr. USAF, Scott AFB, Ill., 1980—81, test dir. Wright AFB, Dayton, Ohio, 1981—82; chief logistics mgmt. systems modernization USAF Pentagon,.Washington, 1986—88, chief logistics spares analysis, 1988—89; maintenance supr. USAF Equipment Maintenance Squadron, Aircraft Generation Squadron, Moody AFB, Ga., 1989—90; commdr. USAF Equipment Maintenance Squadron, Moody AFB, Ga., 1990—92; mem. chief of staff ops. group Hdqtrs. USAF Pentagon, Washington, 1992; mgr. joint program elec. commerce, elec. data interchange Hdqtrs, Defense Logistics Agy., Cameron Sta., Va., 1992—95; dir. logistics 12th Space Warning Squadron, Thule AFB, Greenland, 1995—96; chief support svcs. br. Albuquerque (N. Mex.) Field Ops. Def. Threat Reduction Agy., Kirkland (N.Mex.) AFB, 1997—99; cmmdr. logistics group USAF 11th Wing, Bolling AFB, Washington, DC, 1999—2001; dean Sch. of Systems and Lighting Air Force Inst. Tech., Wright- Patterson AFB, Dayton, Ohio, 2001—. Recipient Legion of Merit, James D. Forrestal award, U.S. Naval War Coll. 1996. Mem.: Soc. Logistics Engrs. (cert. profl. logistician 1985), Inst. Cost Analysts (cert. 1984). Office: Air Force Inst Tech Office Pub Affairs Wright Patterson AFB Dayton OH 45433-7765

**MICHELS, ROBERT,** psychiatrist, educator; b. Chgo., Jan. 21, 1936; s. Samuel and Ann (Cooper) M.; m. Verena Sterba, Dec. 23, 1962; children—Katherine, James. BA, U. Chgo., 1953; MD, Northwestern U., 1958. Intern Mt. Sinai Hosp., N.Y.C., 1958-59; resident in psychiatry Columbia Presbyn.-N.Y. State Psychiat. Inst., N.Y.C., 1959-62; mem. faculty Coll. Physicians and Surgeons, Columbia U., N.Y.C., 1964-74, assoc. prof., 1971-74; psychiatrist student health service Columbia U., 1966-74; supervising and tng. analyst Columbia U. Center for Psychoanalytic Tng. and Research, 1972—; attending psychiatrist Vanderbilt Clinic, Presbyn. Hosp., N.Y.C., 1964-74; Barklie McKee Henry prof. psychiatry Cornell U. Med. Coll., N.Y.C., 1974-93, chmn. dept. psychiatry, 1974-91, Stephen and Suzanne Weiss dean, 1991-96; provost for med. affairs Cornell U., 1991-96, Walsh McDermott U. prof. of medicine, 1996—; univ. prof. psychiatry, 1996—; psychiatrist-in-chief N.Y. Hosp., 1974-91, attending psychiatrist, 1991—. Attending psychiatrist St. Luke's Hosp. Ctr., N.Y.C., 1966—. Co-author: The Psychiatric Interview in Clinical Practice, 1971, 2d edit., 2006; contbr. articles to profl. jours. Served with USPHS, 1962-64. Mem. Am. Psychiat. Assn., Am. Coll. Psychiatrists, N.Y. Psychiat. Soc., Royal Medico-Psychol. Assn., Psychiat. Rsch. Soc., Assn. Rsch. in Nervous and Mental Diseases, Acad. Psychiatry, Am. Psychoanalytic Assn., Internat. Psychoanalytic Assn., Ctr. Advanced Psychoanalytic Studies, N.Y. Acad. Scis., Alpha Omega Alpha. Office: Cornell U Med Coll 418 E 71st St New York NY 10021-4894 Office Phone: 212-746-6001. E-mail: rmichels@med.cornell.edu.

**MICHELS, RUTH YVONNE,** retired cytologist; b. Denver, Aug. 23, 1942; d. James John Crumb and Ruth Marie Hoglund; m. Robert Allen Michels, June 5, 1960; children: Danna Lynn Michels Hardy, Anita Kay Michels Bornschein. AS, Mesa State Coll., Grand Junction, Colo., 1973. Registered cytotechnologist Am. Soc. of Clin. Pathologist, 1974. Rsch. cytotechnologist St. Mary's Hosp. & Med. Ctr., Grand Junction, Colo., 1973—83, clin. cytotechnologist, 1983—85, cytology/histology supr., 1985—93; edn. coord. -cytology program Grand Junction campus U. Utah, Salt Lake City, 1987—88, clin. instr., 1988—93; cons. Shandon, Inc., Pitts., 1988—99; dir. of ops. Saccomanno Rsch. Inst., Grand Junction, Colo., 1993—99; cons. Bayer Diagnostic, Emeryville, Calif., 1999—2001; cytotechnologist - call in position Cmty. Hosp., Grand Junction, Colo., 2000—; cons. Inspire Pharms., Inc., Durham, NC, 2000—01; rsch. cons. Opacity, Inc. (Bio-Imaging Tech.), Grand Junction, Colo., 2001—03; contract employee Mesa County Dept. Pub. Health, 2005—. Mem. nat. adv. com. Am. Soc. of Cytology, Phila., 1990—92; chmn. quality assurance com. on pap smears Colo. State Dept. of Health Women's Health Initiative, Denver, 1991—94; mem. adv. com. on papanicolaou technique: approved guidelines Nat. Com. for Clin. Lab. Stds., Wayne, Pa., 1993—94; human subjects adv. com. mem. U.S. Dept. of Energy, Washington, 1993—99; exec. com. ASSIST - Colo. Dept. of Pub. Health, Denver, 1994—99; developer mass fatalities plan Mesa County Coroner's Office, 2005. Author: (sci. paper) Cancer in Children, Pulmonary Cytologic Specimens using the Shandon Megafunnel (Nat. Soc. of Histology Sci. Paper of the yr., 1998), Geno Saccomanno, MD, Ph.D. Pioneer Pathologist 1915 -1999, Examination of p53 Alterations and Cytokeratin Expression in Sputa Collected from Patients Prior to Histologic Diagnosis of Squamous Cell Carcinoma, Concurrent Flourescence In Situ Hybridization and Immunocytochemistry for the Detection of Chromosome Abberations in Exfoliated Bronchial Epithelial Cells, Cytologic Evaluations of Pulmonary Infiltrates: Tumor vs. Inflammation, (tech. video) The Saccomanno Brush Wash Collection Tube; contbr. documentary film - universal studios Early Warning Lung Cancer; author (presenter): (presentation) Early Detection of Lung Cancer, (human subjects meeting) Educating the Nations IRBS, (lung cancer seminar) Where Do We Go From Here?; author: (sci. paper) The Cytologic Diagnosis of Small Cell Carcinoma of the Lung., A comparison of Saccomanno Smear Slides and the New Large Format Cytospin, Megafunnel Slides of sputum Specimens. Co-chmn. Drug Free Mesa County, Grand Junction, Colo., 1999—2003; mem. Rocky Mountain Divsn., Am. Cancer Soc., Denver, 1995—2003, Colo. Divsn. Am. Cancer Soc., Denver, 1974—95; chmn. bd. dirs. Colo. Divsn., Am. Cancer Soc., Denver, 1991—92; stakeholder on peer rev. grant application com. - cell cycle and growth Nat. Home Office - Am. Cancer Soc., Atlanta, 2000—04. Named Vol. of Yr., Colo. divsn. Am. Cancer Soc., 1982; recipient St. Geroge medal, Nat. Home Office, Am. Cancer Soc., 1995, Bonnie Forquer award for substance abuse prevention, Drug Free Mesa County and the Mesa County Dept. of Pub. Health, 2002, Disting. Alumni award, Mesa State Coll., 2003. Mem.: Internat. Acad. of Cytology (assoc.), Am. Soc. of Cytology (assoc.), Sigma Xi Sci. Rsch. Soc. (assoc.). Independent-Republican. Lutheran. Achievements include patents for Cell Block Collection Method and Apparatus for Cytology Specimens; Cytological Sampling Method and Device using a liquid Based Fixative for Pap smears; Cytological Sampling Method and Device for non gynecological cytology specimens. Avocations: creative writing, reading, bike riding, outdoors activities. Home: 2151 Hawthorne Ave Grand Junction CO 81506- 4164 Personal E-mail: rmichels@acsol.net.

**MICHELSEN, CHRISTOPHER BRUCE HERMANN,** surgeon; b. Boston, Aug. 18, 1940; s. Jost Joseph and Ingeborg Elizabeth (Dilthey) M.; children: Heidi Elizabeth, Matthew Christopher, Joshua Jost. BA, Bowdoin Coll., 1961; MD, Columbia U., 1969. Diplomate Am. Bd. Orthop. Surgery, Am. Bd. Forensic Medicine. Intern Columbia Presbyn. Med. Ctr., N.Y.C., 1969—70, resident, 1970—71; orthop. resident N.Y. Orthop. Hosp., N.Y.C., 1971—73, jr. Anne C. Kane fellow, 1973—74, sr. Anne C. Kane fellow and hip fellow, 1974—75, traveling fellow, 1975—76; internat. A-O fellow, postgrad. fellow in biomechanics Case Western Res. U., N.Y.C., 1975—76, instr. biomed. engring., 1975—76; prof. clin. orthop. surgery, orthop. surgeon Columbia Coll. Physicians and Surgeons, 1976, vice chmn. dept. orthop. surgery, 2002—; chief orthop. svc. Allen Pavillion, Columbia Presbyn. Med. Ctr., 1993—, chief orthop. spine surgery svc., 1998—. Col. USAR, ret. Fellow ACS, Am. Assn. for Surgery of Trauma, Am. Orthop. Assn., N.Am. Spine Soc., Am. Acad. Orthop. Surgeons, Internat. Coll. Surgeons, N.Y. Acad. Medicine; mem. AMA, Am. Coll. Physicians Execs., Orthop. Rsch. Soc., Am. Soc. Bone and Mineral Rsch., Royal Soc. Medicine (affiliate). Office: 5141 Broadway New York NY 10034-1159 Home: 10 Rossa Ln Ossining NY 10562-2568

**MICHELSON, GARY KARLIN,** orthopedic surgeon, inventor; b. Jan. 14, 1949; MD, Hahnemann U., Phila. Cert. Orthopaedic Surgery. Intern, spinal surgery Hahnemann U., Phila., resident, 1971—75; fellow St. Lukes Episcopal Hosp., Houston, 1979; former hosp. appointment Centinela Hosp., Calif.; hosp. appointment Daniel Freeman Hosp., Calif.; founder Karlin Tech. Named one of Forbes' Richest Americans, 2006. Patents and applications covering inventions and techniques related to spinal fusion, surgical implants and surgical techniques. Inventions have revolutionized spinal surgery by introducing minimally invasive devices an durgical techniques, including widely used threaded and alternative non-threaded spinal interbody implants. The technology has significantly reduced the risks and improved the success of spinal surgery by reducing incision size, shortening the operation, reducing blood loss and improving recovery time. In 2005, Medtronic Inc. paid several billion dollars to settle a patent lawsuit and also to acquire the spine surgery-related patents.*

**MICHELSON, GERTRUDE GERALDINE,** retired retail executive; b. Jamestown, NY, June 3, 1925; d. Thomas and Celia Rosen; m. Horace Michelson, Mar. 28, 1947 (dec. Apr. 2002); children: Martha Ann (dec.), Barbara Jane. BA, Pa. State U., 1945; LLB, Columbia U., 1947; LLD with honors, Adelphi U., 1981; DHL with honors, New Rochelle Coll., 1983; LLD with honors, Marymount Manhattan Coll., 1988; PhD in Policy Analysis, Rand Grad. Sch., 2002. Mgmt. trainee Macy's NY, 1947-48, various mgmt. positions, v.p. employee personnel, 1963-70, sr. v.p. labor consumer rels., 1970—72; sr. v.p. pers. labor consumer rels. Macy & Co., Inc., 1972-79, sr. v.p. external affairs, 1979-80, R.H. Macy & Co., Inc., 1980-92, sr. advisor, 1992-94; ret., 1995. Chmn. Helena Rubinstein Found.; bd. dirs. Markle Found.; chmn. emeritus bd. trustees Columbia U.; life trustee Spelman Coll.; past pres. bd. overseers Tchrs. Ins. Annuity Assn. Am. Coll. Retirement Equities Fund. Recipient Disting. Svc. medal Pa. State U., 1984. Mem. NYC Ptnrship. (vice chmn.), Women's Forum, Econ. Club NY Home: 70 E 10th St New York NY 10003-5102 Office: Federated Dept Stores Inc 151 W 34th St New York NY 10001-2101

**MICHELSON, LILLIAN,** librarian, researcher; b. NYC, June 21, 1928; d. Louis and Dora (Keller) Farber; m. Harold Michelson, Dec. 14, 1947; children: Alan Bruce, Eric Neil, Dennis Paul. Vol. Goldwyn Libr., Hollywood, Calif., 1961-69; owner Former Goldwyn Rsch. Libr., Hollywood, 1969—; ind. location scout, 1973—. Mem. Motion Picture Libr. Found., 2002—; Friends L.A. Pub. Libr. Mem.: Acad. Motion Picture Arts and Scis. Office: c/o Dreamworks SKG Rsch Librb 1000 Flower St Glendale CA 91201-3007 Office Phone: 818-695-6445. E-mail: hmichelson@dreamworks.com.

**MICHELSTETTER, STANLEY HUBERT,** lawyer; b. Milw., July 8, 1946; s. Donald Lee and Gloria (Menke) M.; m. Joyce Bladow, Apr. 29, 1972 (div. Jan. 2006); children: Chad S., Chris E. BA in Math., U. Wis., 1968, JD, 1972. Bar: Wis. 1972, U.S. Dist. Ct. (we. dist). Wis. 1972. Staff atty. Wis. Employment Rels. Commn., Milw., 1972-80; pvt. practice, Milw., 1980—; adminstrv. law judge, equal rights div. adminstrn. Wis. Dept Industry, Labor and Human Rels., Milw., 1992-93. Chmn. North Shore Rep. Club, Milw., 1984-86; bd. dirs. Jewish Family Svcs., 2002-06; with Wis. EMployment Rel. Commn., 2005—. Served to 2d lt. Wis. N.G., 1968-74. Mem. Wis. Bar Assn. (chmn. 1993), Milw. Bar Assn., Nat. Acad. Arbitrators, Indsl. Rels. Rsch.

Assn. (bd. dirs. 1987—), Nat. Assn. R.R. Rels. Republican. Jewish. also: PMB 37 5185 Broadway Gary IN 46409-2708 Home: 3032 Providence St Sun Prairie WI 53590 Office Phone: 608-266-1180. Business E-Mail: stan@stanm.com.

**MICHENER, JAMES LLOYD,** medical educator; b. Dec. 19, 1952; m. Gwendolyn Curtis Murphy; children: Rebecca Liane, Joshua Kieran. BA, Oberlin (Ohio) Coll., 1974; MD, Harvard Med. Sch., 1978. Diplomate Am. Bd. Family Practice. Resident in family medicine Duke U. Med. Ctr., Durham, NC, 1978-81, Kellogg fellow, 1981-82, clin. prof. dept. cmty. and family medicine, 1994—, chmn. dept. cmty. and family medicine, 1994—. V.p. Durham Health Care, Inc., 1985-86; project reviewer Ctrs. Disease Control and Prevention, 2002-; vis. prof. work group pub. health and med. edn. Ctrs. Disease Control, Atlanta, 2005. Co-author: Nutrition in Practice, 1990, 2d edit., 1992; contbr. numerous articles to med. pubs. including Academic Medicine, The Jour. of Family Practice, Medical Care, others; mem. editl. bd. Rx Nutrition, 1989-91; presenter in field. Bd. dirs. N.C. Med. Soc. Found., 1995—2004; STFM rep. resource com. on nutrition edn. Am. Acad. Family Practice Found., 1987-91. Grantee The Fullerton Found., Inc., The Josiah Macy, Jr. Found., U.S. Dept. Health and Human Svcs., Kate B. Reynolds Charitable Trust, N.C. Health and Wellness Trust. Mem. AMA, NIH (Fogarty/Ellison fellowship selection com. 2005-06), Assn. Am. Med. Colls. (exec. com., exec. coun. 2001—), Assn. Tchrs. Preventive Medicine (chmn. coun. acad. units 2002—), Am. Acad. Family Physicians Found., N.C. Acad. Family Physicians, Assn. Dept. Family Medicine (bd. dir. 1997—, sec. 1998—2005), Coun. Acad. Socs. (adminstrm. bd. 2000—, chair 2005), World Orgn. Nat. Colls., Acads. and Academic Assn. Gen. Practitioners and Family Physicians, Am. Austrian Founds. Internat. Health Forum (mem. steering com.). Home: 4011 Duck Pond Trail Chapel Hill NC 27514-9758 Office: Duke U Med Ctr PO Box 2914 Durham NC 27710-0001 Business E-Mail: miche001@mc.duke.edu.

**MICHENFELDER, ALBERT A.,** lawyer; b. St. Louis, July 21, 1926; s. Albert A. and Ruth Josephine (Donahue) M.; m. Lois Barbara Sullivan, Sept. 03, 1949 (div. May 2, 1967); children: Michael J., Ann C. Michenfelder Yancey, Elizabeth D. Michenfelder Brown; m. Ramona Jo Dysart, July 12, 1968 (dec. Jan. 2, 1998); 1 child, Julie D. Michenfelder Wolfe. B of Naval Sci., Marquette U., 1946; LLB, St. Louis U., 1950. Bar: Mo. 1950, U.S. Dist. Ct. (ea. dist.) Mo. 1950, U.S. Supreme Ct. 1975. Assoc. Flynn & Challis, St. Louis, 1950-54; pvt. practice St. Louis, 1954-55; of counsel Husch & Eppenberger LLC, St. Louis. Mem. 21st Cir. Jud. Commn., St. Louis, 1981-87. Contbr. articles to profl. jours. City atty. City of Webster Groves, Mo., 1966-79; mem. John Marshall Club, St. Louis. Lt. (j.g.) USNR, 1944-47. Mem. Mo. Bar Assn., Bar. Assn. Met. St. Louis, St. Louis County Bar Assn. (pres. 1966), Westborough Country Club. Republican. Avocations: golf, tennis. Office: Husch & Eppenberger LLC 190 Carondelet Plz Ste 600 Saint Louis MO 63105-3441 Office Phone: 314-480-1730. Business E-Mail: al.michenfelder@husch.com.

**MICHERO, WILLIAM HENDERSON,** retired retail executive; b. Fort Worth, June 19, 1925; s. William Alvin and Lela Belle (Henderson) M.; m. Nan Elaine Henderson, July 9, 1948; children— Jane Elaine Michero Christie, William Sherman, Thomas Edward. BS in Commerce, Tex. Christian U., 1948. Sec. Tandy Corp., Fort Worth, 1960-75, v.p., 1970-75; with Tandycrafts, Inc., Fort Worth, 1975-90, sr. v.p., sec., dir., 1979-83, chmn. bd., 1983-90, ret., 1990. Sec. B.F. Johnston Found., Fort Worth, 1962-90. Bd. dirs. David L. Tandy Found., Fort Worth, 1968-99, Oakwood Cemetery Assn., 1979-89, Panther Boys Club, 1974-78, Fort Worth Mus. Sci. and History, 1973-75, pres. 1975, United Way; chmn. Distributive Edn. Council, 1970. Served with U.S. Navy, 1943-46. Mem.: Colonial Country Club, Fort Worth Club. Home: 1600 Texas St #1617 Fort Worth TX 76102-3434

**MICHIE, SARA H.,** pathologist, educator; b. Tulsa, Okla., Jan. 3, 1955; BS in Biology, Stephen F. Austin U., 1977; MD, U. Tex., Houston, 1981. Diplomate Am. Bd. Pathology. Resident anatomic pathology Stanford (Calif.) U. Med. Ctr., 1981—83, postdoctoral fellow immunology dept. pathology, 1983—84, 1986—87, postdoctoral fellow diagnostic immunopathology, 1984—85; resident dept. pathology U. Iowa, Iowa City, 1985—86, postdoctoral fellow, 1986; assoc. investigator lab. svc. VA Hosp., Palo Alto, Calif., 1988—89, staff physician 1989—, assoc. investigator, 1990—91; clin. instr. pathology dept. Stanford U., 1989—92, asst. prof. pathology, 1992—. Contbr. articles to profl. jours. Recipient Rsch. award, Am. Diabetes Assn., 1996. Mem.: Bay Area Flow Cytometry Group, Soc. Investigative Pathology, Am. Soc. Investigative Pathology, Alpha Omega Alpha, Sigma Xi. Office: VA Hosp Palo Alto 3801 Miranda Ave Stop 154F Palo Alto CA 94304-1207

**MICHNEY, TODD MICHAEL,** history professor; b. Cleve., Ohio, Oct. 1, 1971; s. Michael A. and Patricia A. Michney; m. Laura M. D'Alessandro, July 20, 1996. BA, Case We. Res. U., 1993; MA, U. Minn., 1997, PhD, 2004. Lectr. U. Minn., Mpls., 1999—2000; adj. prof. Cleve. State U., 2005—06; vis. asst. prof. Tulane U., 2006—. Contbr. articles to profl. jours.; actor: Barebores Prodns., 1998, In the Heart of the Beast Mask and Puppet, 2005. Organizer, canvasser Green Party Ohio, Cleve., 2000. Mem.: Orgn. Am. Historians, Am. Hist. Assn., Phi Beta Kappa. Avocations: birdwatching, tai chi. Office: Tulane Univ 125A Hebert Hall Annex New Orleans LA 70118 Office Phone: 504-862-8607. Business E-Mail: tmichney@tulane.edu.

**MICHNICH, MARIE E.,** health policy analyst, consultant, educator; M Health Svs. Adminstrn., UCLA, DrPH Health Svs. Rsch. Asst. prof. health svs. U. Washington; sr. exec. v.p. Health Policy, Am. Coll. Cardiology Clin. Practice and Sci. Svs. Divsn.; dir. Health Policy Programs and Fellowships Nat. Acad. Scis. Inst. Medicine, 2002—. Cons, spkr. in field; legis. asst. health policy Medicare, Medicaid, maternal and child health; legis. asst. U.S. Senate Majority Leader Robert Dole; mem. several nat. health policy groups. Robert Wood Johnson Health Policy fellow. Mem.: Am. Pharm. Assn. Found. (1st pub. mem. bd. dirs. 2002—), Robert Wood Johnson Health Policy Fellows Program (mem. adv. bd., dir.), Health Care Quality Alliance (former chmn.). Office: Office Health Policy Programs Fellowship 500 5th St NW Washington DC 20001

**MICHOD, SUSAN ALEXANDER,** artist, painter; b. Toledo, Ohio, Jan. 3, 1945; d. Harold Milne and Caroline (Simonds) Alexander; m. Charles Louis Michod Jr., Aug. 16, 1969; children: Alexander Charles, Richard Simonds, Michael Wise. Student, Smith Coll., 1963-66; BS, Univ. Mich., 1967; MFA, Pratt Inst., 1969. Exhibiting mem. Artemisia Gallery, Chgo., 1973-78; exhibitor Jan Cicero Gallery, Chgo., 1978-88, Andre Zarre Gallery, N.Y.C., 1978-80, Susan Caldwell Gallery, N.Y.C., 1980-83, Gwenda Jay Gallery, Chgo., 1988-89, State of Ill. Gallery, Chgo., 1991, Jan Cicero Gallery, Chgo., 1991, Andre Zarre Gallery, N.Y.C., 2003, Biennale Internat. Dell' Arte Contemporanea, Florence, Italy, 2003, That 70's Show- The Age of Pluralism in Chgo., Munster, Ind., 2004, Hinsdale (Ill.) Ctr. Arts, 2004, Whitney Mus. Am. Art, N.Y.C., 2006. Faculty Chgo. Acad. Fine Arts, Chgo., 1969-74; mentor Columbia Coll., Chgo., 1980-90; collaborator and set designer Fluid Measure Organic Theatre, Chgo., 1989, Kast & Co., Links Hall., Chgo., 1992. Author: Some Thoughts on Pattern Painting, 1977; contbr. articles to books. Visual arts panel Ill. Arts Coun., 1977-79. Recipient Artist's grant Ill. Arts Coun., 1984, Collaboration grant Paper Press Gallery, 1987. Mem. Artimisia Gallery (pres. 1973—, founding mem.). Home: 2242 N Dayton St Chicago IL 60614-3612 Office: 1523 N Kingsbury St Chicago IL 60622-2533 E-mail: cmichod@cs.com.*

**MICHOPOULOS, ARISTOTLE V.,** humanities educator, researcher; b. Kotylion, Arcadia, Peloponnesos, Greece, Apr. 22, 1944; s. Vassilios A. Michopoulos and Anastasia D. Papazafeiropoulos; m. Despina Dimitropoulos (div. Jan. 30, 1996). BA, U. of Athens, Athens, Greece, 1967; MA, Grad. Ctr. of C.U.N.Y., New York, NY, 1976; PhD, Fla. State U., Tallahassee, FL, 1980. Translator Greek Orthodox Archdiocese of N. & S. Am., New York, NY, 1970—71; translator and adminstr. Hellenic indsl. Devel. Corp., New York, NY, 1972—74; h.s. tchr. Bd. of Edn. of NYC, New York, NY, 1975—76; adj.

instr. Fla. State U., Tallahassee, 1977—78, asst. project dir. and curriculum writer, 1978—80; asst. prof. U. of Fla., Gainesville, Fla., 1980—87; prof. of greek studies dir. at Hellenic Coll., Brookline, Mass., 1987—2005. Dean Hellenic Coll., Brookline, Mass., 1995—2002, Greek studies dept. dir., 1987—; translator, cons. Various Organizations, Many, 1980—. Rep. to u.s. dept. of edn. Greek Orthodox Archdiocese, New York, NY, 1992—98; del., com. mem. Coun. on Hellenes Abroad, Chicago, Ill., 1995—2002; nat. coord. Paideia project, Greece, 1999—2004. Recipient Fulbright award, Fulbright Program, 1977, Socratic award, U. Fla., 1999; fellow, US Dept. of H.E.W., 1976—79. Mem.: Kotylion Syllogos (cons. 1980—2005, Merit Award 2000), Am. Hellenic Edn. Assn. (AHEPA), Modern Greek Studies Assn. Avocations: tennis, swimming, backgammon, travel. Office: Hellenic College 50 Goddard Avenue Brookline MA 02445 Office Phone: 617-850-1271.

**MICK, HOWARD HAROLD,** lawyer; b. Newton, Kans., Oct. 21, 1934; s. Marvin Woodrow and Edith (Bergen) M.; m. Susan Siple, Sept. 5, 1957 (dec. July 1997); children: Martha, Julie, Elizabeth; m. Patricia Willson, Apr. 4, 1998. Student, U. Okla., 1952-54; BS, LLB, U. Colo., 1958. Bar: Colo. 1958, Mo. 1959. Assoc. Stinson, Mag & Fizzell, Kansas City, Mo., 1959—62, shareholder, 1962—2002; of counsel Stinson Morrison Hecker LLP, 2002—. Bd. dirs. Ctr. Mgmt. Assistance, Kansas City, Mo., 1984-88; mem. adv. coun. Kansas City Salvation Army, 1987—; Milbank Mfg. Co., Kansas City, Mo., 1996—; mem. adv. coun. Gordon Parks Elem. Sch., Kansas City, Mo., 2000—. Mem. ABA, Lawyers Assn. Kansas City, Kansas City Bar Assn., Rotary, Kansas City Club, Indian Hills Country. Democrat. Presbyterian. Avocations: golf, tennis, bridge. Office: Stinson Morrison Hecker LLP PO Box 419251 Kansas City MO 64141-6251 Office Phone: 816-691-3175. E-mail: howardmick@kc.rr.com.

**MICK, JAMES PAUL,** music educator; b. Salina, Kans., Aug. 27, 1979; s. Theodore and Katherine Mick. B in Music Edn., Tex. Christian U., 2002; MusM, Ithaca Coll., 2005. Cert. tchr. Tex., 2002. Resident asst. Tex. Christian U., Ft. Worth, 1999—2002; long-term orch. substitue tchr. Arlington (Tex.) Ind. Sch. Dist., 2003; grad. asst. Ithaca (N.Y.) Coll., 2003—05; head orch. dir. Plano (Tex.) Ind. Sch. Dist., 2005—. Mem. Newton Mid-Kansas Symphony Orch., 1996—; intern summer orch. dir. Newton Unified Sch. Dist., 2000; pres. Music Educator's Orgn. Tex. Christian U., Ft. Worth, 2001—02; all-graduate coun. music rep. Ithaca Coll., 2004—05. Musician (prin. double bassist): Pergine Spettacolo Aperto. Pres. Beta Upsilon Chi Frat., Ft. Worth, 2001—02. Dean's scholar, Tex. Christian U., 1998—2002, Undergrad. scholar, Southwestern Bell, 2000—02. Mem.: Nat. Assn. Music Edn., Internation Soc. Bassists, Am. String Tchrs. Assn., Music Educators Nat. Conf., Tex. Music Educators Assn., Pi Kappa Lambda. Independent. Achievements include Completion of three 26.2 mile marathons. Avocations: running, travel, volunteering, bicycling. Home: 3304 Wentworth St Plano TX 75075 Personal E-mail: jpmick@hotmail.com.

**MICKEL, EMANUEL JOHN,** foreign language educator; b. Lemont, Ill., Oct. 11, 1937; s. Emanuel John and Mildred (Newton) M.; m. Kathleen Russell, May 31, 1959; children: Jennifer, Chiara, Heather. BA, La. State U., 1959; MA, U.N.C., 1961, PhD, 1965. Asst. prof. U. Nebr., Lincoln, 1965-67, assoc. prof., 1967-68, Ind. U., Bloomington, 1968-73, prof., 1973—, dir. Medieval Studies Inst., 1976-91, chmn. French and Italian, 1984-95. Cons. NEH; French advisor Soc. Rencevals, 1995-98; adv. bd. mem. Nineteenth Century French Studies, 1995—. Author: Marie de France, 1974, Eugene Fromentin, 1982, Ganelon Treason and the Chanson de Roland, 1989, Jules Vernes Complete Twenty Thousand Leagues Under the Sea, 1992, Enfances Godefroi and Retour de Cornumarant, 1999. Capt. U.S. Army, 1963-65. Grantee NEH, Washington, 1978-84; Lilly Open fellow Lilly Found., Indpls., 1981-82; Chevalier dans l'Ordre des Palmes Academiques, 1997. Avocations: music, theater, sports, travel, ancient literature. Office: French & Italian Dept Indiana Univ 642 Ballantine Hall Bloomington IN 47401-5020 Office Phone: 812-855-8253. Business E-mail: mickel@indiana.edu.

**MICKEL, RUTH PHELPS,** commentator, librarian; b. Gonzales, Fla., Mar. 8, 1922; d. James Cochran and Ella Yount Phelps; m. Toufick Mickel (dec.); children: Diana Austin, Joseph T., Timothy J., Martha, Sarah. BA, U. La., 1973. Writer, announcer, operator, reporter WDSU Radio, New Orleans, 1943—46; continuity editor, reporter WKRG Radio, Mobile, Ala., 1946—47, KNOE Radio, Monroe, La., 1948—49; med. libr. Glenwood Med. Ctr., West Monroe, La., 1974—79; reference libr. Ouachita Parish Libr., Monroe, 1979—92; sr. reporter Daily Med., Health News KNOE TV, Monroe, 1995—. Author poetry. News releases, interviews LWV, Monroe, 1949—70; pres. Georgia Tucker PTA, Monroe, 1969, Beauceant, Monroe, 1970—72. Named Poet Laureate, Order Ea. Star, State La., 1975, Mother of Yr., Am. Mothers, Inc., State La., 1995; recipient life membership, Presbyn. Women, 1995. Mem.: N.E. La. Poetry Soc. (pres. 1997—99, treas. 1999—2003), DeNova Book Club (pres. 1994—96), Ea. Star (worthy matron 1953, dist. dep. 1956). Democrat. Presbyterian. Avocations: Bible study, walking, poetry, flower arranging. Home: 1500 McKeen Pl Apt 313 Monroe LA 71201 Office Phone: 318-323-5309.

**MICKELSON, PHIL (PHILIP ALFRED MICKELSON JR.),** professional golfer; b. San Diego, June 16, 1970; s. Philip and Mary Mickelson; m. Amy McBride, Nov. 19, 1996; children: Amanda Brynn, Sophia Isabel, Evan. BS in Psychology, Ariz. State U., 1992. Profl. golfer PGA, 1992—. Co-author (with Donald T. Phillips): One Magical Sunday (But Winning Isn't Everything), 2005. Founder The Phil and Amy Mickelson Charitable Fund. Recipient Fred Haskins award, 1990, 91, 92, Jack Nicklaus award, 1990, 91, 92; won NCAA Championships, 1989, 90, 92; 1st team All-Am. with Sun Devils; Espy Award for Best Male Golfer, Best Championship Performance, ESPN, 2004. Achievements include 1st left-hander to win U.S. Amateur, 1990, 1st player in PGA history to win same tournament as amateur and profl. (No. Telecom Open); winning The Masters Tournament, 2004, 2006; PGA Championship, 2005; Presidents Cup, 1994, 1996, 1998, 2000, 2003; Ryder Cup, 1995, 1997, 1999, 2001, 2004; 25 career PGA Tour Victories; runner-up US open, 2006; shot a career-low 60 in the second round of the 2005 FBR Open. Avocation: flying. Office: care PGA Box 109601 100 Avenue Of Champions Palm Beach Gardens FL 33418*

**MICKELSON, STACEY,** state legislator; BA, Minot State U., 1994. Govt. rels. dir. Artspace Projects, Inc.; rep. Dist. 38 N.D. Ho. of Reps., 1994-2000, mem. fin. and taxation com., vice-chmn. transp. com. Mem. interim taxation, adminstrv. rules coms. Bowhay Inst. for Legis. Leadership and Devel. fellow. Mem. Am. Coun. Young Polit. Leaders, Darden Program Emerging Polit. Leaders, Flemming Fellows. Home: 3120 Roosevelt St Ne Minneapolis MN 55418-2360

**MICKENBERG, DAVID,** museum director, art director, historian; b. Bklyn., Apr. 24, 1954; s. Morton and Florence Geri (Merenstein) M.; m. Judith Hope, Apr. 25, 1980; children: Danielle, Julia, Mia. BA with honors, Colgate U., 1976; M in Art History, U. Wis., Milw., 1979. Asst. to dir. Bklyn. Mus., 1975-76; asst. curator Picker Art Gallery, Hamilton, N.Y., 1977-79; program coordinator, asst. dir. adult edn. Indpls. Mus. of Art, 1979-81; exec. dir. Okla. Mus. Art, Oklahoma City, 1981-86; dir. Mary & Leigh Block Gallery Northwestern U., Evanston, Ill., 1986—2001; Ruth Gordon Shapiro dir. Davis Mus. and Cultural Ctr., Wellesley Coll., Mass., 2001—. Editor: (exhbn. catalogue) Maurice Prendergast Large Boston Public Garden Sketchbook, 1981; editor, author: (exhbn. catalogue) Songs of Glory: Medieval Art from 900 to 1500, 1985. Trustee Chamber Orch. of Oklahoma City, 1984-86, Oklahoma City Pub. Sch. Found., 1984-86, Infant Crisis Services, Oklahoma City, 1985-86; advisor mktg. and pub. rels. Okla. Symphony Orch., Oklahoma City, 1984-86, masters of mus. studies program, U. Okla., Norman, 1985; bd. govs. Ill. Art Alliance, 1988-90. Ind. U. fellow, 1979-80, scholar, 1980-81 Mem. Coll. Art Assn., Am. Assn. Museums, Internat. Ctr. of Medieval Art Office: Davis Mus and Cultural Ctr Wellesley Coll 106 Central St Wellesley MA 02481-8203

**MICKEY, PAUL F(OGLE), JR.,** lawyer; b. Washington, Sept. 25, 1949; s. Paul Fogle and Margaret Snowden (Stanley) M.; m. Carol Lynne Forsyth, Mar. 19, 1977; children: Alison Langlands, Suzanne Snowden, Scott Forsyth. AB summa cum laude, Princeton U., 1971; JD, U. Va., 1974. Bar: D.C. 1974, US Ct. Appeals (DC, 7th, 10th cir.), U.S. Supreme Ct. 1981. Law clk. to George E. MacKinnon, U.S. Ct. Appeals, D.C. Circuit, 1974-75; with office of legal adv. U.S. Dept. State, Washington, 1975-77; assoc. Covington & Burling, Washington, 1977-79; v.p., gen. counsel Nat. R.R. Passenger Corp. (Amtrak), Washington, 1979-83, exec. v.p. law and pub. affairs, 1983-85; ptnr. Shaw, Pittman, Potts & Trowbridge, Washington, 1985—2005, mng. ptnr., chmn., 1995—2003; ptnr. Employment & Labor, Litigation practices Pillsbury Winthrop Shaw Pittman, Washington, 2005—. Articles editor, Va. Law Rev.; contbr. articles to legal revs. Mem., bd. govs. Nat. Cathedral Sch.; mem. corp. bd. dirs. Children's Hosp., Nat. Med. Ctr.; bd. dirs. St. Francis Ctr. Mem. ABA, D.C. Bar Assn. (chmn. Individual Employee Rights & Responsibilities subcom.), Am. Arbitration Assn. (arbitrator), Met. Club, Chevy Chase Club. Episcopalian. Office: Pillsbury Winthrop Shaw Pittman 2300 N St NW Washington DC 20037-1128 Office Phone: 202-663-8233. Office Fax: 202-663-8007. Business E-Mail: paul.mickey@pillsburylaw.com.

**MICKLE, MARLIN HOMER,** electrical engineer, educator; b. Windber, Pa., July 5, 1936; s. Howard T. and Ruth Elma (Corle) Mickle. BS, U. Pitts., 1961, MS, 1963, PhD, 1967. Jr. engr. IBM, 1962; engr. Westinghouse Co., 1964; mem. faculty U. Pitts., 1962—, assoc. prof. elec. engring., 1968-75, prof., 1975—, dir. computer engring. program, 1982-84, Nickolas A. De-Cecco prof., 2001—. Program dir. sys. theory & applications NSF, 1974—75, cons., Batelle, Contraves-Goerz, TASC, Westinghouse, AMSCO, Tex. Instruments, Inc., Compunetics, others; pres. Mickle Computer Techs., Inc., Pitts., 1979—85; v.p., dir. Power Resources, Inc., Pitts., 1980—84; dir. Univ. R & D Assocs., Inc., 1985—2004; exec. dir. Swanson Ctr. Product Innovation, 2004—06, Radio Frequency Indentification Ctr. Excellence, 2005—; dir. Radio Frequency Identification Ctr. Excellence. Author (with T. W. Sze): Optimization in Systems Engineering, 1972; mem. editl. bd. Jour. Interdisciplinary Modeling and Stimulation, 1978—80; editor-in-chief: Internat. Jour. Paralle and Distributed Systems and Networks, 1997—2002; editor: Internat. Jour. Radio Frequency Tech. Applications, 2004—; contbr. articles to profl. jours. Bd. dirs. Asbury Heights, Pitts., 1982—, Wesley Hills Mt. Lebanon, Pitts., 1985—86; chmn. bd. dirs. Emory Sr. Housing, Pitts., 2000—; dist. lay leader Pitts. dist. United Meth. Ch., 1971—73; elder Shadyside Presbyn. Ch., 2004—. Radar tech. Airborne USAF, 1954—58. Recipient excellence in corp. innovation award, Carnegie Sci. Ctr., 2005, sys. rsch. and cybernetics award, Internat. Inst. Advanced Studies in Sys. Rsch. and Cybernetics, 1988. Fellow: IEEE (life). Republican. Home: 4601 5th Ave Apt 723 Pittsburgh PA 15213-3657 Office: U Pitts Dept Elec and Computer Enring Pittsburgh PA 15261-0001 Office Phone: 412-600-3606. Business E-Mail: mickle@pitt.edu.

**MICKO, ALEXANDER S.,** corporate financial executive, educator, treasurer; b. Munich, May 8, 1947; came to U.S., 1952, naturalized, 1957; s. Zygmunt and Maria (Huber) M.; m. Sharon E. Judge, June 7, 1969; 1 child, Brian A. BS, LaSalle U., 1969. CPA, N.J., Pa. Audit mgr. Price Waterhouse, Phila., 1970-77; asst. chief fin. investigations div. of Casino Gaming Enforcement, State of N.J., Trenton, 1977-79; v.p. fin. TeleScis., Inc., Mt. Laurel, NJ, 1979-87; v.p. fin., chief fin. officer, asst. sec. Dechert, Price & Rhoads, Phila., 1987-89; v.p. fin., treas., sec. NET Atlantic, Inc., Thorofare, NJ, 1989-92; v.p., contr. AAA Mid-Atlantic, Inc., Phila., 1999—2006; pres. Alexander & Assocs., 2006—. Owner AM Fin. Services, Medford, N.J., 1986—; cons. United Computer Services, Berlin, N.J., 1982—; lectr. in field. Bd. dirs. Forest Hills Civic Assn., Williamstown, N.J., 1976. With USMC, 1969-75. Recipient Michael A. DeAngelis Outstanding Profl. Achievement award, LaSalle U., Phila., 1985. Mem. AICPA, N.J. Soc. CPAs, Pa. Inst. CPAs, Fin. Execs. Inst., Nat. Assn. Accts. Roman Catholic. Avocations: skiing, golf. Home: 5 Huntington Cir Medford NJ 08055-3315 Personal E-mail: amicko@aol.com.

**MICOZZI, MARC STEPHEN,** health executive, physician, educator; b. Norfolk, Va., Oct. 27, 1953; s. Edio Dominic and Huguette (Picon) M.; m. Carole Ann O'Leary, Oct. 8, 1982; 1 child, Alicia Madeleine. Cadet, USAF Acad., 1971-72; BA, Pomona Coll., 1974; MD, U. Pa., 1979, PhD, 1986. Diplomate Am. Bd. Pathology. Rsch. fellow City of Hope Nat. Med. Ctr., Duarte, Calif., 1973; chem. engr. Gould Corp., El Monte, Calif., 1974; Luce Found. scholar Mindanao State The Philippines, 1976-77; clin. applications chemist McDonnell-Douglas Corp., Pasadena, Calif., 1978; postdoctoral fellow Allied Inst. Environ. Health, Princeton, N.J., 1979; resident in pathology Pa. Hosp., Phila., 1980-83; med. examiner Dade County Med. Examiner's Office, Miami, Fla., 1983-84; sr. investigator Nat. Cancer Inst., Bethesda, Md., 1984-86; dir. Nat. Mus. Health and Medicine, Washington, 1986-95; exec. dir. Coll. Physicians' of Phila., 1995—2002; exec. dir. Integrative Medicine Thomas Jefferson U. Hosp., Phila., 2002—. Adj. prof. Uniformed Svcs. U. Health Scis., Bethesda, 1986-95, U. Pa. Sch. Medicine, 1996—; vis. lectr. Georgetown U. Sch. Medicine, Washington, 1986—, Johns Hopkins U. Sch. Medicine, Balt., 1988—; adj. prof. dept. phys. medicine U. Pa., 1996—. Editor: Nutrition and Cancer, 1989; assoc. editor Health Care, Jour. Human Orgn., 1983-89; contbr. chpts. to books and numerous articles to profl. jours. Del. White House Conf. on Youth, Estes Park, Colo., 1971, UN Conf. on Human Environ., Stockholm, 1972, NATO Advanced Study Inst., Brussels, 1982; mem. Calif. Gov.'s Adv. Com., 1972-74. Fellow Human Biology coun., Soc. for Applied Anthropology, Am. Anthrop. Assn.; Am. Acad. Forensic Scis., Am. Pub. Health Assn., N.Y. Acad. Scis. Roman Catholic.

**MICZEK, KLAUS ALEXANDER,** psychology professor; came to U.S., 1967; s. Erich and Irene (Werthl) M.; m. Christiane Baerwaldt, Aug. 8, 1970; 1 child, Nikolai A. Tchrs. cert., Paedagogische Hochschule, Berlin, 1966; PhD, U. Chgo., 1972. Asst. prof. Carnegie-Mellon U., Pitts., 1972-74, assoc. prof., 1974-79, Tufts U., Medford, Mass., 1979-83, prof., 1983-93, Moses Hunt prof. psychiatry, psychology, pharmacology and neuroscience, 1993—. Cons. Solvay-Pharma v.b., Weesp, The Netherlands, 1984-99, NIH, Rockville, Md., 1984—, Forest Labs., N.Y.C., 2003—; Boehringer Ingelheim, Germany, 2003—; Boerhaave prof. U. Leiden, The Netherlands, 1987; mem. panel on violence, NAS, 1989-92. Editor: Ethopharmacology, 1983, Ethopharmacological Aggression Research, 1984; field editor, coord. editor Behavioral Pharmacology, Jour. Psychopharmacology; contbr. articles on psychopharmacology, 1973—. Rsch. grantee Nat. Inst. Drug Abuse, 1973—, Nat. Inst. Alcoholism and Alcohol Abuse, 1981—; recipient Solvay-Duphar award APA, 1993, Bundesverdienstkreuz Cross of Merit, Fed. Republic of Germany, 1996, Gold medal Charles U., Prague, 2004; named disting. scholar Tufts U., 2006. Fellow AAAS (Tufts U. Disting. scholar 2006), APA (program chmn. 1981, pres. div. psychopharmacology 1990-91, master lectr. 1999), Behavioral Pharmacol. Soc. (pres. 1992-94), Internat. Soc. for Rsch. on Aggression (councilor 1987); mem. Soc. Neurosci., N.Y. Acad. Scis., Internat. Primatol. Soc. Office: Tufts U Dept Psychology 530 Boston Ave Medford MA 02155-5532 Business E-Mail: klaus.miczek@tufts.edu.

**MIDCALF, RANDALL,** language educator, director; b. Saginaw, Mich., Feb. 10, 1959; MA in English, Oakland U., Rochester, Mich., 1989. Assoc. prof. English Maranatha Bapt. Bible Coll., Watertown, Wis., coord. English program, 1997—. Contbg. editor (mag.) In Focus. Instr. Sunday sch. Calvary Bapt. Ch., Watertown, 1994—2006. Mem.: NCTE. Office: Maranatha Bapt Bible Coll 745 W Main St Watertown WI 53094 Office Phone: 920-206-2361. E-mail: rmidcalf@mbbc.edu.

**MIDDAUGH, ROBERT BURTON,** artist; b. Chgo., May 12, 1935; s. John Burton and Mae Knight (Cronk) M. Student, U. Chgo., 1960-62; BFA, Art Inst. Chgo., 1964. Curator art collection 1st Nat. Bank Chgo., 1971-83. Designed, executed ednl. display, Prehistoric Project at Oriental Inst. of U. Chgo., 1968; one-man shows include, Kovler Gallery, Chgo., 1965, 67, 69, Martin Schweig Gallery, St. Louis, 1970, 72, 79, 83, U. Wis., 1976, 81, 82, Fairweather Hardin Gallery, Chgo., 1977, 80, 83, 85, Rockford Art Mus., 1987, Zaks Gallery, Chgo., 1992, 93, 97, Printworks Gallery, Chgo., 2006; group shows, including, Art Inst. Chgo., 1964, 66, 78, 79, Evanston (Ill.) Art

Ctr., 1966, Joslyn Art Mus., Omaha, 1968, U. Notre Dame, 1969, Va. Mus. Fine Arts, Richmond, 1966; represented in permanent collections, Art Inst. Chgo., Boston Mus. Fine Arts, Fine Art Mus. of South, Mobile, Ala., Los Angeles County Mus., Phoenix Art Mus., Worcester (Mass.) Art Mus., Ill. State Mus., Springfield. Served with U.S. Army, 1958-60. Archivist, Chgo. Park Dist., 1998-2005. Mem. Arts Club Chgo.

**MIDDELJANS, APRIL LYNN,** literature educator; b. Oaklawn, Ill., Sept. 25, 1971; d. Daniel Jon Diephouse and Dora Mae Wyngarden; m. John William Middeljans, June 19, 1993. BA, Calvin Coll., 1993; PhD, U. Ill., 2005. English instr. U. Ill., 1993—. Recipient Outstanding Tchr. award, U. Ill., 2005. Mem.: Modern Lang. Assn. Avocations: singing, creative writing. Office: U Ill 608 S Wright St Urbana IL 61801

**MIDDELKAMP, JOHN NEAL,** pediatrician, educator; b. Kansas City, Mo., Sept. 29, 1925; s. George H. and Clara M. (Ordelheide) M.; m. Roberta Gill, Oct. 3, 1949 (div. 1970); children— Sharon Ann, Steven Neal, Susan Jean, Scott Alan; m. Lois Harper, Mar. 1, 1974 BS, U. Mo., 1946; MD, Washington U., St. Louis, 1948. Diplomate Am. Bd. Pediatrics. Intern D.C. Gen. Hosp., Washington, 1948-49; resident St. Louis Children's Hosp., 1949-50, 52-53; instr. pediatrics Washington U., 1953-57, asst. prof. pediatrics, 1957-64, assoc. prof., 1964-70, prof., 1970-98, prof. emeritus, 1998—; dir. ambulatory pediatrics St. Louis Children's Hosp., 1974-91. Author: Camp Health Manual, 1984; contbr. articles, chpts. to profl. publs. Served to comdr. M.C., USNR, 1943-66. NIH postdoctoral fellow, 1961-62 Mem. Am. Acad. Pediatrics, Am. Soc. Microbiology, Infectious Diseases Soc. Am., Am. Pediatric Soc., Ambulatory Pediatric Assn., Sigma Xi, Alpha Omega Alpha Home: 8845 Paragon Cir Saint Louis MO 63123-1114 Office: Office Assoc Dean for Grad Med Edn Washington Univ Sch Medicine 660 S Euclid Box 8033 Saint Louis MO 63110 Office Phone: 314-747-4479.

**MIDDEN, WILLIAM ROBERT,** chemist, educator; b. Wood River, Ill., May 19, 1952; BS, St. Johns U., 1974; PhD in Biochemistry, The Ohio State U., 1978. Postdoctoral fellow The Ohio State U., 1978-79, The Johns Hopkins U., Balt., 1980-81, rsch. assoc. dept. environ. health scis., 1981-83, asst. prof. dept. environ. health scis., 1983-87; adj. assoc. prof. dept. pathology Med. Coll. of Ohio, Toledo, 1988-97; asst. prof. dept. chemistry Ctr. for Photochemical Scis., Bowling Green (Ohio) State U., 1988-95, assoc. prof., 1995—. Vis. scientist Laboratoire Acide Nucleique, Departement de Recherche Fondamentale sur La Matiére Condensée, Service D'études des Systémes et Archit ctures Moléculaires, Centre D'Etudes Nucléaires, Grenoble, France, 1989; lectr. and seminar presenter in field; cons. Synergistic Lab., Libby, Mont., 1988, Fresh Products, Inc., Toledo, 1989, Calderon Automation, Inc., Bowling Green, 1989, Ricerca, Inc., Painesville, Ohio, 1988-91. Contbr. numerous articles to profl. jours. and monographs/ Dir. Ptnrs. in Contest and Cmty., 2000—, Chapman Cmty., 2004—. Recipient Master Tchr. award Bowling Green State U., 1993, Grad. Rsch. Asst. award, 1992-93; grantee NIH, 1986, 87, Bowling Green State U., 1988, 1992-93, NSF, 1989, 2003-05, U.S. Dept. Edn., 2001-06. Mem. AAAS, Am. Chem. Soc., Omicron Delta Kappa. Office: Bowling Green State U Dept Chemistry Bowling Green OH 43402

**MIDDENDORF, ALICE CARTER,** volunteer; b. Balt., Dec. 7, 1940; d. John William and Alice Temple (Carter) M. BA, Wellesley Coll., 1963, Oxford U., Eng., 1972. Libr. Boston Athenaeum Libr., 1963—68; editor Houghton Mifflin Co., Boston, 1966—68; bd. dirs. Balt. Zool. Soc., 1976; cons. Nat. Zoo, Washington, 1976—77, G. Ward & Assocs., Ridgefield, Conn., 1976—79; from bd. dirs. to bd. govs. Nat. Aquarium Balt., 1975—88, sec. bd. govs., 1987—88, animal policy com., 1982—88; bd. dirs. Total Health Care (merger Constant Care and West Balt. Cmty. Health Ctrs.), Balt.; sec. bd. dirs. Total Health Care, Balt., 1990—93, 1997—98, treas., 1998. Adv. bd. Nat. Aquarium in Balt., 1989-94, 99-2005, bd. govs., 1994-99, sec. bd. govs., 1995-99; bd. dirs. Constant Care Med. Ctr., Balt., Park Heights Street Acad., Balt., 1985—88; 1985-980; pres. Fulmar Corp., Cayman Islands, Brit. West Indies, 1991-99; pres., chmn. bd. dirs. Lystra Hill Farms, Inc., Goleta, Calif., 1996-97 Bd. dirs. Scenic Md. Recipient Pres.'s Citation, Pres. City Coun. Balt., 1974, 76, Award of Appreciation, Mayor of Balt., 1981 Avocations: scuba, underwater photography, marine biology, malacology, travel, reading. Home and Office: 1301 Hillside Rd Stevenson MD 21153-2019

**MIDDENDORF, J. WILLIAM, II,** investment banker; b. Balt., Sept. 22, 1924; m. Isabelle Paine, Mar. 7, 1953; children: Frances, Amy, John W. IV, Ralph Henry. B in Naval Sci., Holy Cross Coll., 1945; AB, Harvard U., 1947; MBA, NYU, 1954; LLD (hon.), Troy State U.; LittD (hon.), Sch. of Ozarks, Am. Christian Coll.; D. Social Scis. (hon.), Netherlands-Am. Inst. Commd. ensign USN, 1945, advanced through grades to lt. (j.g.), ret., 1946; with credit dept. Chase Manhattan Bank, 1947-52; ptnr. Wood Struthers and Co., 1958-61; sr. ptnr. Middendorf, Colgate and Co., 1962-69; ambassador to The Netherlands, 1969-73; sec. USN, 1974-77; pres., CEO Fin. Gen. Bankshares, Inc., 1977-81; ambassador to Orgn. Am. States, 1981-85, European Communities, 1985-87; chmn. Middendorf & Assocs., Inc., 1989—. Chmn. presdl. task force Project Econ. and Social Justice, 1986-90; mem. U.S. Del. to supervise elections in Suriname, 1988; treas. Internat. Rep. Inst. Composer 8 symphonies, 100 marches, (opera) King Richard, nat. independence march for Belize, other compositions for Latin Am. countries; guest condr. Boston Pops, St. Louis Symphony, Ind. U., others; contbr. articles to profl. jours. Mem. U.S. Olympic com., 1979-89, U.S. Olympic Selection com. for field hockey; judge field hockey Olympics, Rome, 1960; former mem. vis. com. dept. Am. paintings Met. Mus. Art, N.Y.C., vis. com. dept. Am. Art, Mus. Fine Arts, Boston; hon. v.p. Naval Hist. Found.; treas. Goldwater for Pres. com., 1962-64, Presdl. Transition com. 1968, Rep. Nat. Com., 1964-69; alt. del. for Gov. Reagan, 1980; del. State of Conn. 1964, 68, State of Va., 1996, co chmn. Virginians for Reagan, 1980, hon. com. Va. GOP, 1980-81; coord. internat. econ. and naval adv. com. Reagan for Pres. campaign, 1980; chmn. Congl. Boosters com., 1978-81; chmn. CIA Transition Team, 1980-81; chmn. fin. com. Pres. Reagan's 1981 Inaugural com.; trustee Naval War Coll. Found., Heritage Found., Washington; past trustee Hoover Instn. for War Revolution and Peace, Corcoran Gallery, N.Y. Hist. Soc., Balt. Mus. Art, Greenwich Hist. Soc., Boston Symphony, Middlesex Sch., Concord, Mass., Nat. Symphony Orch., Mass. Gen. Hosp., Boys Club N.Y.; bd. electors Ins. Hall of Fame; bd. dirs. Georgetown U., John Philip Sousa Meml. Found., Newport Art Mus. and Mariners' Mus., Norfolk, Va.; chmn. bd. dirs. council statesmen Ludwig von Mises Inst.; chmn. Com. for Monetary Rsch. and Edn. Inc., Netherlands-Am. Amity Trust, Def. Forum Found., Navy League Awards com., 1977—; former mem. com. Dept. State Fine Arts Com.; founding chmn. U.S. Navy Meml. Found.; past chmn. Netherlands-Am. Inst., Wolf Trap Farm Park, John Carter Brown Library Assocs., Providence, Asian Composers Expo., European Council of Boy Scouts. Decorated Grand Master Order of Orange Nassau (Netherlands), Order of Arab (Republic Egypt), Grand Master of Order of Naval Merit (Republic Brazil); recipient Superior Honor award Dept. State, 1974, Disting. Pub. Svc. award Dept. Def., 1975, 76, Navy Disting. Pub. Svc. award, 1976, Naval Disting. Svc. medal Republic Brazil, 1976, Ludwig von Mises Free Market award, 1985, Inter-Am. Music Coun. award, 1985, Edwin Franko Goldman award Am. Bandmasters Assn., 1987, Assn. Harvard Clubs Am. award, Disting. Svc. medal Purdue Univ. Bands, Netherlands Soc. Phila. Gold medal, Good Citizenship medal Nat. Soc. SAR, Medal of Honor, Midwest Nat. Band Assn., Invest in Am. Am. Eagle award, 1988, Eugene J. Keogh Disting. Pub. Svc. award NYU, 1989, Nat. Commendation award Pres.' Coun. Phys. Fitness and Sports, 1989, Leadership award. Am. Friends of Turkey, 1989, Adm. Arleigh Burke Leadership award, 1998, Arleigh Burke award 1998; named Alumnus of Yr. NYU, 1978; Nat. Masters Sculling champion, 1979, Gold medal The Holland Soc. Mem. Am. Antiquarian Soc., Harvard Alumni Assn. (permanent class mem. 1947), Soc. Cin. (hon.), ASCAP, Walpole Soc., Co. Mil. Historians, Mil. Order Loyal Legion, SAR, Soc. of SAR, Field Hockey Assn. Am. (past pres., player/mgr. nat. team 1963), U.S. Naval Inst., Navy League. Clubs: Angler's, Downtown Assn., Union (N.Y.); Army-Navy, Capitol Hill, Met., Potomac Boat (Washington); Sakonnet Golf (Little Compton, R.I.); Somerset (Boston). Mailing: PO Box 1037 Little Compton RI 02837

**MIDDENDORF, JOHN HARLAN,** English literature educator; b. N.Y.C., Mar. 31, 1922; s. George Arlington and Margaret (Hofmann) M.; m. Beverly Bruner, July 14, 1943 (dec. 1983); children: Cathie Jean Middendorf Hamilton, Peggy Ruth Middendorf Brindisi; m. Maureen L. MacGrogan, Jan. 31, 1986. AB, Dartmouth Coll., 1943; AM, Columbia U., 1947, PhD, 1953. Lectr. English CCNY, 1946, Hunter Coll., 1946–49; faculty Columbia, 1947—, prof. English, 1965-89, prof. emeritus, 1990—, dir. grad. studies, 1971-74, vice-chmn., 1976-80. Chmn. English test com. Coll. Entrance Exam. Bd., 1967—69. Contbr. articles, revs. to profl. jours.; Editor: English Writers of the Eighteenth Century, 1971; asst. editor: Johnsonian News Letter, 1950-58; co-editor, 1958-78; editor, 1978-90; assoc. editor: Yale edit. Works Samuel Johnson, 1962-66; gen. editor, 1966—. Lt. (j.g.) Japanese translator USNR, 1943–43. Faculty fellow Fund Advancement Edn., 1951-52; grantee Coun. Rsch. Humanities, 1958-59, Am. Philos. Soc., 1962. Mem. Am. Coun. Learned Socs., 1962, NEH, 1976-88. Mem. Johnsonians (sec.-treas. 1958-68, chmn. 1969, 79), Univ. Seminar on 18th Century European Culture (chmn. 1973-75, 85-87), Oxford Bibliog. Soc., Grolier Club, English Inst. (mem. supervisory com. 1963-66), Modern Lang. Assn., Soc. Sr. Scholars, Am. Soc. 18th Century Studies, Phi Beta Kappa. Home: 404 Riverside Dr New York NY 10025-1861 Office: Columbia U Dept English New York NY 10027

**MIDDLEBROOK, DIANE WOOD,** English language educator, writer; b. Pocatello, Idaho, Apr. 16, 1939; d. Thomas Isaac and Helen Loretta (Downey) Wood; m. Jonathan Middlebrook, June 15, 1963 (annulled 1976); 1 child, Leah Wood; m. Carl Djerassi, June 21, 1985. BA, U. Wash., 1961; MA, Yale U., 1962, PhD, 1968; LittD (hon.), Kenyon Coll., 1999. Asst. prof. Stanford (Calif.) U., 1966—73, assoc. prof., 1978—83, prof., 1983—2001, prof. emerita, 2002—, dir. Ctr. for Rsch. on Women, 1977—79. Author: Walt Whitman and Wallace Stevens, 1974, Worlds into Words: Understanding Modern Poems, 1980, Anne Sexton, A Biography, 1991, Suits Me: The Double Life of Billy Tipton, 1998, Her Husband: Hughes and Plath, a Marriage, 2003; editor: Coming to Light: American Women Poets in the Twentieth Century, 1985; author: (poetry) Gin Considered as a Demon, 1983. Founding trustee Djerassi Resident Artists Program, Woodside, Calif., 1980—83, chair, 1994; trustee San Francisco Art Inst, 1993. Finalist Nat. Book award, 1991; recipient Yale Prize for Poetry; fellow Ind. Study, NEH, 1982—83, Bunting Inst., Radcliffe Coll., 1982—83, Guggenheim Found., 1988—89, Rockefeller Study Ctr., 1990. Fellow: Royal Soc. Lit.; mem.: MLA, Authors Guild, Christs Coll. Cambridge (hon.), The Athenaeum Club, Biographers Club. Avocations: collecting art, theater. Home: 1101 Green St Apt 1501 San Francisco CA 94109-2012 Office: Agent Georges Borchardt 136 E 57th St New York NY 10022 Office Phone: 415-474-1866. E-mail: dwm@stanford.edu.

**MIDDLEBROOK, GEOFFREY COLE,** environmental educator; s. John E. and Phyllis C. Middlebrook; m. Sachiko Matsunaga, Dec. 23, 1990. PhD, U. Hawaii, 1995. Lectr. Calif. State U., L.A., 1995—2001, U. So. Calif., 2001—. Mem. various environ. and animal rights organizations, 1995—2005. Mem.: Nat. Coun. Tchrs. English. Personal E-mail: middlebr@usc.edu.

**MIDDLEBROOK, JOHN G.,** marketing executive, advertising executive; BS in Engring., GM Inst.; M in Mktg., Mich. State U. With GM Oldsmobile Div., 1959—67, GM Pontiac Div., 1967, asst. sales mgr., 1969—70, sales analysis mgr., 1970, dir. mktg. svcs., 1977; zone mgr. GM Corp., Washington, 1977, dir. mktg. ops., 1978, mgr. product planning, devel., 1979—81; dir. passenger car planning GM Worldwide, 1981—83; dir. car distbn., sales analysis, strategic planning GM Pontiac Div., 1983, asst. gen. sales mgr., merchandising, ops., 1984—85; v.p. sales, svc, mktg. Saturn Corp., 1985—87; v.p. mktg product planning staff GM Corp., 1987—89; gen. mgr. GM Pontiac Motor Div., 1989, GM Chevrolet Div., 1996, GM Corp., 1999—2000, v.p. mktg, advt., 2000—. Pres. Boy Scouts, Detroit. Office: GM Corp 300 Renaissance Ctr PO Box 300 Detroit MI 48265-3000

**MIDDLEBROOKS, DELORIS JEANETTE,** retired nursing educator; b. Cedar Rapids, Iowa, Apr. 9, 1931; d. Harland R. and Rosa V. (Anderson) Hickey; m. Johnnie L. Middlebrooks, Apr. 25, 1962 (dec.); children: James, Kathleen. Diploma, Evang. Hosp. Sch. Nursing, 1956; BSN, State U. Iowa, 1958; MS in Nursing, U. Calif., San Francisco, 1960; EdD, U. Nev., Las Vegas, 1985. Instr., coord. Nev. State Hosp. Sch. Practical Nursing, Sparks, 1963-66; staff nurse St. Mary's Hosp., Reno, 1968; instr., coord. Reno VA Sch. Practical Nursing, 1968-72; instr,. coord. health occupations Wooster High Sch., 1972-73; nursing faculty Truckee Meadows C.C., 1973-94, ret., 1994; intermittent staff nurse VA Hosp., 1984-86; instr., review course Stanley Kaplan Ednl. Ctr., 1987-89; clin. nursing faculty Western Nev. C.C., Carson City, 1987, Northern Nev. C.C., Elko, 1979-93; guest assoc. prof. nursing Lewis-Clark State Coll., Lewiston, Idaho, 1989. Cons. Irish Bd. Nursing, Dublin, Ireland, 1985. Nominated Nev. Voc. Tchr. of Yr., 1975, 79, 88, 89; Recipient March of Dimes Community Leadership award, 1990. Mem.: ANA, Am. Assn. for the History of Nursing, Nev. Nurses Assn., Phi Kappa Phi, Sigma Theta Tau. Home: 1385 Ebbetts Dr Reno NV 89503-1918

**MIDDLEBROOKS, EDDIE JOE,** environmental engineer; b. Crawford County, Ga., Oct. 16, 1932; s. Robert Harold and Jewell LaVerne (Dixon) M.; m. Charlotte Linda Hardy, Dec. 6, 1958; 1 child, Linda Tracey. BCE, U. Fla., 1956, MS, 1960; PhD, Miss. State U., 1966. Registered profl. engr., Ariz., Miss., Utah, Wash., Colo.; registered land surveyor, Fla. Asst. san. engr. USPHS, Cin., 1956-58; field engr. T.T. Jones Constrn. Co., Atlanta, 1958-59; grad. teaching asst. U. Fla., 1959-60; research asst. U. Ariz., 1960-61; asst. prof., then assoc. prof. Miss. State U., 1962-67; research engr., asst. dir. San. Engring. Research Lab., U. Calif.-Berkeley, 1968-70; prof. Utah State U., Logan, 1970-82, dean Coll. Engring., 1974-82; Newman chair natural resources engring. Clemson U., 1982-83; provost, v.p. acad. affairs Tenn. Tech. U., 1983-88, U. Tulsa, 1988-90, prof. chem. engring., 1988-92, Trustees prof. chem. engring., 1990-92, acting pres., 1990; prof. civil engring. U. Nevada, Reno, 1992-97. Mem. nat. drinking water adv. council EPA, 1981-83; cons. EPA, UN Indsl. Devel. Orgn., Calif. Water Resources Control Bd., City and County of San Francisco, State of Colo., South Fla. Water Mgmt. Dist. (Everglades), also numerous indsl. and engring. firms. Author: Modeling the Eutrophication Process, 1974, Statistical Calculations-How to Solve Statistical Problems, 1976, Biostimulation and Nutrient Assessment, 1976, Water Supply Engineering Design, 1977, Lagoon Information Source Book, 1978, Industrial Pollution Control, Vol. 1: Agro-Industries, 1979, Wastewater Collection and Treatment: Principles and Practices, 1979, Water Reuse, 1982, Wastewater Stabiliation Lagoon Design, Performance and Upgrading, 1982, Reverse Osmosis Treatment of Drinking Water, 1986, Pollution Control in the Petrochemicals Industry, 1987, Natural Systems for Waste Management and Treatment, 1988, 2d edit., 1995, Japanese transl., Natural Wastewater Treatment Systems, 2006; contbr. tech. articles to profl. jours. Fellow ASCE; mem. Water Environment Fedn. (dir. 1979-81, 91-92), Eddy medal 1969), Assn. Environ. Engring. Profs. (pres. 1974), Utah Water Pollution Control Assn. (pres. 1976), Internat. Assn. on Water Quality, Am. Soc. Engring. Edn., Am. Acad. Environ. Engrs. (diplomate, trustee 1992-95, v.p. 1995, pres. 1997-98), Sigma Xi, Omicron Delta Kappa, Phi Kappa Phi (Disting. mem.), Tau Beta Pi, Sigma Tau. Home and Office: 2128 Imperial Ln Superior CO 80027 Office Phone: 303-664-5292. Personal E-mail: Joemiddle@aol.com.

**MIDDLEDITCH, LEIGH BENJAMIN, JR.,** lawyer, educator; b. Detroit, Sept. 30, 1929; s. Leigh Benjamin and Hope Tiffin (Noble) M.; m. Betty Lou Givens, June 27, 1953; children: Leigh III, Katherine Middleditch McDonald, Andrew B. BA, U. Va., 1951, LLB, 1957. Bar: Va. 1957. Assoc. James H. Michael, Jr., Charlottesville, 1957-59; ptnr. Battle, Neal, Harris, Minor & Williams, Charlottesville, 1959-68; legal adviser U. Va., Charlottesville, 1968-72; ptnr. McGuire, Woods, Battle & Boothe (now McGuire Woods LLP), Charlottesville, 1972-99, of counsel, 2000—; v.p. McGuire Woods Cons. LLC, Charlottesville, 2001—. Lectr. Grad. Bus. Sch., U. Va., Charlottesville, 1958-94, lectr. Law Sch. 1970-90. Co-author: Virginia Civil Procedure, 1978, 2d edition, 1992; contbr. articles to profl. jours. Chmn. U. Va. Health Svcs. Found., 1988-97; bd. mgrs. U. Va. Alumni, 1994-2001, pres., 2000-01; bd. dirs., chmn. Va. Health Care Found., 1997-98; trustee Claude Moore Found., 1991—; bd. visitors U. Va., 1990-94; trustee Thomas Jefferson Meml. Found., Monticello, 1994-2002; chair U. Va. Miller Found. for Study of Presidency, 2000—. Fellow Am. Bar Found., Va. Bar Found.; mem. ABA (bd. govs. 1999-2002), Va. State Bar (coun., chmn. bd. govs. various sects.), Charlottesville-Albemarle Bar Assn. (pres. 1979-80), U. Va. Law Sch. Alumni Assn. (pres. 1979-81), U.S. C. of C. (bd. dirs. 1998—2004), Va. C. of C. (pres. 1988-90), Omicron Delta Kappa. Episcopalian. Office: McGuire Woods LLP PO Box 1288 Charlottesville VA 22902-1288 Office Phone: 434-977-2543. E-mail: lmiddleditch@mcguirewoods.com.

**MIDDLEKAUFF, ROBERT LAWRENCE,** historian, educator, academic administrator; b. Yakima, Wash., July 5, 1929; s. Harold and Katherine Ruth (Horne) M.; m. Beverly Jo Martin, July 11, 1952; children: Samuel John, Holly Ruth. BA, U. Wash., 1952; PhD, Yale U., 1961. Instr. history Yale U., New Haven, 1959-62; asst. prof. history U. Calif., Berkeley, 1962-66, assoc. prof., 1966-70, prof., 1970-80, Margaret Byrne prof. history, 1980-83, prof. history, 1988-92, emeritus prof., 2000—, Preston Hotchkis prof., 1992—; dir. Huntington Libr., Art Gallery and Bot. Gardens, San Marino, Calif., 1983-88; Harmsworth prof. history Oxford (Eng.) U., 1996-97. Mem. coun. Inst. Early Am. History and Culture, Williamsburg, Va., 1974-76, 85-88, chair exec. bd., 1992-96. Author: Ancients and Axioms, 1963, The Mathers, 1971, The Glorious Cause: The American Revolution, 1763-1789, 1982, 2nd edit., rev., 2005, Benjamin Franklin and His Enemies, 1996. Served to 1st lt. USMC, 1952-54, Korea. Recipient Bancroft prize, 1972, Commonwealth Club Gold medal, 1983; fellow Am. Coun. Learned Socs., 1965, NEH, 1973, Huntington Libr., 1977. Fellow Am. Acad. Arts and Scis.; mem. Am. Hist. Assn., Orgn. Am. Historians, Am. Philos. Soc., Soc. Am. Historians, Am. Antiquarian Soc., Assocs. Early Am. History and Culture (mem. exec. com.), Colonial Soc. Mass. (corr.), Mass. Hist. Soc. Home: 5868 Ocean View Dr Oakland CA 94618-1535 Office: Univ Calif Dept History Berkeley CA 94720-2550 Office Phone: 510-642-1971.

**MIDDLEMAN, RAOUL FINK,** artist; b. Balt., Apr. 3, 1935; s. Paul B. and Elizabeth (Fink) M.; m. Pat Bird (div.); m. Ruth Katherine Channing, Dec. 2, 1971; children: Raphael Bachrach, Benjamin Jacob, Nathaniel John. BA, Johns Hopkins U., 1955; postgrad., Penn. Acad. Fine Arts, 1957—61, Bklyn. Mus., 1961. Faculty Md. Inst. Coll. of Art, Balt., 1961-85. Vis. critic Vt. Studio Sch. Summer Program,1 985; resident dir. Summer Landscape Painting Program, Md. Inst. Coll. of Art, 1981-83; vis. artist Artists for Environment Found., Walpack Ctr., 1977-81; artist-in-residence Hoffberger Sch. of Painting, 1973-74; lectr. for Figurative Alliance, Studio Sch., N.Y.C., Nat. Gallery in Edinborough, Yale Norfolk, 1980, Md. Inst. Coll. of Art, 1985. One-man shows include Swanston Fine Arts, 1988, Allan Stone Gallery, 1985, 1981,1975, 1972, 1969, 1968, Grimaldis Gallery, 1984, 1981, 1979, 1978, 1999, 2003, William Capro Gallery, 1983, The Water Gap Art Gallery, 1982, The Md. Inst., Coll. of Art, 1974, Krasner Gallery, 1966, Ice Gallery, NYC, 1996, 1997, 1998, Univ. Md., 1999, Troika Gallery, Easton, Md., 1999, MB Modern Gallery, NYC, 2000, Rodger LaPelle Galleries, Phila., 2001, Bavarian Paintings, Murnau, Germany, 2001, Md. Art Place, Balt., 2002; exhibited in groups shows at Nat. Acad. Design, 1990, Md. Inst., 1989-90, Gaumann Cicchino Gallery, 1989, Ingber Gallery, 1989, Bendann Gallery, 1989, Swanston Fine Arts, 1988, Haus der Kunst, 1986, Kornbluth Gallery, 1985, Steven Scott Gallery, and others; represented in permanent collections at ABC Network, Balt. Mus. Art, Corcoran Gallery, Frye Mus. Art, Johns Hopkins Hosp. NAD, Met. Mus. Art, NY Public Libr., Syracuse Univ., Towson Univ., Univ. Md. Recipient Robert and Rochelle Phillipp prize Nat. Acad. Design, 1990. Mem. Nat. Acad. Design (pres. 1998-2001). Avocation: violin. E-mail: rmiddleman@earthlink.net.

**MIDDLETON, ANTHONY WAYNE, JR.,** urologist, educator; b. May 6, 1939; s. Anthony Wayne and Dolores Caravena (Lowry) M.; m. Carol Samuelson, Oct. 23, 1970; children: Anthony Wayne, Suzanne, Kathryn, Jane, Michelle. BS, U. Utah, 1963; MD, Cornell U., 1966. Intern U. Utah Hosps., Salt Lake City, 1966-67; resident in urology Mass. Gen. Hosp., Boston, 1970-74; practice urology Middleton Urol. Assocs., Salt Lake City, 1974—2005. Mem staff LDS Hosp., chmn. divsn. urology, 1995—2004, Salt Lake Regional Med. Ctr., 1977—79, 1984—86; assoc. clin. prof. surgery U. Utah Med. Coll., 1977—2005; vice-chmn. bd. govs. Utah Med. Self-Ins. Assn., 1980—81, 1996—2005, chmn., 1985—87; chmn. med. adv. bd. Uroquest Co., 1996—99; med. dir. Uromed, prostate microwave co., 1999—2000, Utah divsn. Rocky Mountain Prostate, 2001—04, Utah-Idaho Lithotripsy, 2001—03. Editor: AACU-FAX, 1992-2005; assoc. editor Millenial Star Brit. LDS mag., 1960-61; contbr. articles to profl. jours. Mem. U. Utah Coll. Medicine Dean's Search Com., 1983—84; bd. dirs. Utah Symphony, 1985—2002, Primary Children's Found., 1989—96; mem. Utah Crime Reparations Bd., 2000—05, chmn., 2002—05; staff pres. Primary Children's Med. Ctr., 1982; vice chmn. Utah Med. Polit. Action Com., 1978—81, chmn., 1981—83, Utah Physicians for Reagan, 1983—84; del. Utah State Rep. Conv., 2000—01; bishop, later stake presidency Ch. Jesus Christ Latter-day Saints; mission pres. Canada Vancouver Mission, 2005—; bd. dirs. Utah chpt. Am. Cancer Soc., 1978—86, Utah Symphony and Opera, 2002—05, Timpanogos Club, 1978—, 2d asst. to pres., 2002—03, 1st asst. to pres., 2003—04, pres., 2004—05. Capt. USAF, 1968—70. Mem.: AMA (del. to Ho. of Dels. 1998—2005, chmn. ref. com. I 2001, mem. governing coun. SSS 2002—05, alt. del. to Ho. of Dels., 1987-88, 89-92, 94, 96-98), ACS, Am. Assn. Clin. Urologists (bd. dirs. 1989—90, nat. pres.-elect 1990—91, pres. 1991—92, nat. bd. chmn. urologic polit. action com. UROPAC 1992—98, Disting. Svc. award 2000), Salt Lake Surg. Soc. (treas. 1977—78), Utah Urol. Assn. (treas. 1977—78, pres. 1978—79), Salt Lake County Med. Assn. (sec. 1965—76, treas. 1980—81, pres. liaison com. 1988—81, pres.-elect 1981—83, pres. 1984), Am. Urologic Assn. (socioecons. com. 1987—90, chmn. western sect. socioecons. com. 1988—90, chmn. western sect. health policy com. 1990—2002, pres.-elect western sect. 1999—2000, pres. 2000—01, Outstanding Svc. award 2005), Utah Med. Assn. (pres. 1987—88, bd. dirs. 1998—2005, Disting. Svc. award 1993), Beta Theta Pi (chpt. pres. Gamma Beta 1962), Alpha Omega Alpha, Phi Beta Kappa. Republican. Home: 2798 Chancellor Pl Salt Lake City UT 84108-2835 Office: 1060 East 1st South Salt Lake City UT 84102-1520 Office Phone: 604-271-3587. Personal E-mail: awmiddleton@msn.com.

**MIDDLETON, CHRISTOPHER,** Germanic languages and literature educator; b. Truro, Cornwall, Eng., June 10, 1926; arrived in US, 1966; s. Hubert Stanley and Dorothy May (Miller) M. BA, U. Oxford, Eng., 1951, DPhil, 1954. Lectr. King's Coll., London, 1955-65; prof. Germanic langs. and lit. U. Tex., Austin, 1966-98. Author: Selected Writings, 1989, Andalusian Poems, 1993, The Balcony Tree, 1992, Intimate Chronicles, 1996, Twenty Tropes for Doctor Dark, 2000, The Word Pavilion and Selected Poems, 2001, Of the Mortal Fire, 2003, Jackdaw Jiving: Essays on Poetry and Translation, 1998, In the Mirror of the Eighth King, 1999, Faint Harps and Silver Voices-Selected Translations, 2000, Crypto-Topographia: Stories of Secret Places, 2002, Palavers and A Nocturnal Journal, 2004, The Anti-Basilisk, 2005. Recipient trans. prize Schlegel-Tieck/Govt. Fed. Republic Germany, 1985, Anglo-Swiss Cultural Rels. prize Max Geilinger Stiftung, Zurich, Switzerland, 1987; Guggenheim Found. poetry fellow, 1974-75, NEH poetry fellow, 1980. Mem. Akademie der Künste Berlin. Office: U Tex Dept Of Germanic Langs Austin TX 78712

**MIDDLETON, DAVID,** physicist, applied mathematician, educator; b. NYC, Apr. 19, 1920; s. Charles Davies Scudder and Lucile (Davidson) M.; m. Nadea Butler, May 26, 1945 (div. 1971); children: Susan Terry, Leslie Butler, David Scudder Blakeslee, George Davidson Powell; m. Joan Bartlett Reed, 1971; children: Christopher Hope, Andrew Bartlett, Henry H. Reed. Grad. Deerfield Acad., 1938; AB summa cum laude, Harvard U., 1942, AM, 1945, PhD in Physics, 1947. Tchg. fellow electronics Harvard U., Cambridge, Mass., 1942, spl. rsch. assoc. radio rsch. lab., 1942-45, NSF predoctoral fellow physics, 1945-47, rsch. fellow electronics, 1947-49, asst. prof. applied physics, 1949-54; cons. physicist Cambridge, 1954—2004, Concord, Mass., 1957-71, N.Y.C., 2005—; adj. prof. elec. engring. Columbia U., 1960-61; adj. prof. applied physics and comm. theory Rensselaer Poly. Inst., Hartford Grad. Ctr., 1961-70; adj. prof. communication theory U. R.I., 1966—; adj. prof. math. scis. Rice U., 1979-89. U.S. del. internat. conf. Internat. Radio Union, Lima, Peru, 1975; lectr. NATO Advanced Study Inst., Grenoble, France, 1964, Copenhagen, 1980, Luneburg, Germany, 1984; invited lectr. Russia Acad. Sci. Acoustic Inst., 1973, 76, 79, 84; mem. Naval Rsch. Adv. Com., 1970-77; mem., cons. Inst. Def. Analyses; mem. sci. adv. bd. Supercomputing Rsch. Ctr., 1987-91; cons. physicist since 1946, orgns. including Johns Hopkins U., SRI Internat., Rand Corp., USAF, Cambridge Rsch. Ctr., Comm. Satellite Corp., Lincoln Lab., NASA, Raytheon, Sylvania, Sperry-Rand, Office Naval Rsch., Applied Rsch. Labs., U. Tex., GE, Honeywell Transp. Sys. Ctr. of Dept. Transp., Dept. Commerce Office of Telecom., NOAA, Office Telecom. Policy of Exec. Office Pres., Nat. Telecom. and Info. Adminstrn., Sci. Applications Inc. (SAIC), Naval Undersea Warfare Ctr., Lawrence Livermore Nat. Labs., Planning Rsch. Corp., Applied Physics Labs. U. Wash., 1992—, Kildare Corp., 1995—, Karmanos Cancer Inst., 1997-01, others. Author: Introduction to Statistical Communication Theory, 1960, 3d edit., 1996, Russian edit. Soviet Radio Moscow, 2 vols., 1961, 62, Topics in Communication Theory, 1965, 87, Russian edit, 1966; sci. editor English edit. Statistical Methods in Sonar (V.V. Ol'shevskii), 1978; mem. editl. bd. Info. and Control, Advanced Serials in Electronics and Cybernetics, 1972-82; contbr. articles to tech. jours. Recipient Prize paper award (with W.H. Huggins), Nat. Electronics Conf., 1956, Wisdom award of honor, 1970, First prize, 3d Internat. Symposium on Electromagnetic Compatibility Rotterdam, Holland, 1979, Prize paper awards, U.S. Dept. Commerce, 1978. Fellow: AAAS, IEEE (life Prize paper award 1977, 1979), Electromagnetics Acad. MIT, N.Y. Acad. Scis., Acoustical Soc. Am., Am. Phys. Soc.; mem.: NAE, Am. Math. Soc., Author's Guild Am., Dutch Treat (N.Y.C.), Explorers Club, Cosmos Club (Washington), Harvard Club (N.Y.C.), Sigma Xi, Phi Beta Kappa. Achievements include research in radar, telecommunications, underwater acoustics, oceanography, seismology, systems analysis, electromagnetic compatibility, communication theory; pioneering research in statistical communication theory. Home and Office: 127 E 91st St New York NY 10128-1601 Office: David And Joan Middleton 127 E 91st St New York NY 10128-1601 Office Phone: 212-831-8565.

**MIDDLETON, ELIZABETH MCPHEE,** research scientist; d. George Edward McPhee, Jr. and Elizabeth LaFond McPhee; children: Edward Lloyd III, Christine Elizabeth. BS in Zoology, U. Md., 1967, MS in Ecology, 1976, PhD in Botany, 1993. Rsch. asst. dept. zoology U. Md., College Park, 1965—67; instr. phys. scis. Md. Pub. Sch. Sys., Prince George's County, Mount Ranier, 1967—72, Greenbelt, 1967—72; grad. tchg. asst. dept. zoology U. Md., 1974—75; analyst, programmer, project coord. Computer Sciences Corp., Silver Spring, 1975—78; project mgr., remote sensing specialist Ea. Regional Remote Sensing Applications Ctr., NASA/Goddard Space Flight Ctr., Greenbelt, 1978—83; rsch. scientist Biospheric Sciences Br., NASA/Goddard Space Flight Ctr., 1984—. Project mgr., plant fluorescence project, joint nat. aeronautics and space agy., U.S. dept. of agr. Nat. Aeronautics and Space Agy., Goddard Space Flight Ctr., Greenbelt, 2000—, dep. project mgr., the ecology component of the large scale atmosphere-biosphere study in amazonia, lba-ecology, 1996—98. Choir mem. Christ Episcopal Ch., Columbia, Md., 1988—2003; chorus mem. Columbia Pro Contare, 1984—2003. Named to Mortar Bd., Sr. Women's Hon., U. Md., 1966. Mem.: IEEE, Ecol. Soc. Am. (assoc.). R-Liberal. Christian. Achievements include research in The effect of UV-B irradiation on plants and amphibians; The spectral and bidirectional reflectance properties of vegetation canopies; The interaction of carbon and nitrogen cycles on plant physiology, spectral reflectance properties, and spectral fluorescence properties. Avocations: singing, swimming, tennis, skiing, knitting, reading, travel. Office: National Aeronautics and Space Agency Goddard Space Flight Ctr Greenbelt MD 20771 E-mail: elizabeth.m.middleton@nasa.gov.

**MIDDLETON, GEORGE, JR.,** clinical child psychologist; b. Houston, Feb. 26, 1923; s. George and Bettie (McCrary) M.; m. Margaret MacLean, Nov. 17, 1953. BA in Psychology, Birmingham-Southern Coll., 1948; MA in Psychology, U. Ala., Tuscaloosa, 1951; PhD in Clin. Psychology, Pa. State U., 1958. Lic. psychologist, La.; diplomate Am. Coll. Forensic Examiners, Am. Bd. Psychol. Specialities. Asst. clin. psychology Med. Coll. Ala., Birmingham, 1950-52; dir. dept. psychology Bryce Hosp., Tuscaloosa, 1952-54; instr. counseling Coll. Bus. Adminstrn. Pa. State U., 1956-58; asst. prof. edn. McNeese State U., 1962-65, assoc. prof. spl. edn., 1962-65; dir. La. Gov.'s Program for Gifted Children, 1962—; prof. spl. edn. McNeese State U., 1965-73, prof. psychology, 1973-74; pvt. practice clin. psychology and neuropsychology, 1974—; cons. psychologist Calcasieu Parish Sch. Bd., 1975—. Vis. scholar U. Victoria, BC, Can., 1970-71. Mem. Am. Psychol. Assn., Nat. Acad. Neuropsychology, Internat. Neuropsychol. Soc., La. Psychol. Assn. (pres. 1973-74), La. S. Psychol. Assn., S.W. La. Psychol. Assn. (pres. 1965, 73, 84), La. State Bd. Examiners Psychologists (chmn. 1977-78), Coun. for Exceptional Children, Am. Coll. Forensic Examiners, 1996. Assn. for the Gifted. Episcopalian. Home and Office: 2001 Southwood Dr Ste A Lake Charles LA 70605-4139

**MIDDLETON, HARRY JOSEPH,** foundation administrator; b. Centerville, Iowa, Oct. 24, 1921; s. Harry J. and Florence (Beauvais) M.; m. Miriam Miller, Oct. 29, 1949; children— Susan, Deborah, James Miller, Jennifer. Student, Washburn U., 1941-43; BA, La. State U., 1947. Reporter AP, N.Y.C., 1947-49; news editor Archtl. Forum mag., N.Y.C., 1949-52; writer March of Time, N.Y.C., 1952-54; free lance writer, author, film dir., 1954-66; staff asst. to Pres. Lyndon B. Johnson, Washington, 1966-69, spl. asst. Austin, Tex., 1969-70; dir. Lyndon Baines Johnson Libr., U. Tex., Austin, 1970—2002; exec. dir. Lyndon Baines Johnson Found., 2002—05. Author: Compact History of the Korean War, 1965, LBJ: The White House Years, 1990, Lady Bird Johnson: A Life Well-Lived, 1992. With AUS, 1943-46, With AUS, 1950—52. Mem. Sigma Delta Chi. Home: Apt 8C 1801 Lavaca St Austin TX 78701-1306

**MIDDLETON, HERMAN DAVID, SR.,** retired theater educator; b. Sanford, Fla., Mar. 24, 1925; s. Arthur Herman and Ruby Elmerry (Hart) Middleton; m. Amelia Mary Eggart, Dec. 1, 1945; children: Herman David, Kathleen Hart. BS, Columbia U., 1948, MA, 1949; PhD, U. Fla., 1964; postgrad., N.Y. U., 1950, Northwestern U., 1951. Instr. dir. drama and speech Maryville (Tenn.) Coll., 1949-50; instr., designer, tech. dir. theatre U. Del., 1951-55; asst. prof., head dept. drama U. N.C., Greensboro, 1956-59, assoc. prof., head dept. drama and speech, 1959-64, prof., head dept., 1965-74, prof., 1974-79, Excellence Fund prof. dept. communication and theatre, 1979-90, prof. emeritus, 1990. Stage mgr. Unto thee Hills Cherokee Hist. Assn., 1953—56; designer Chucky Jack Gt. Smokey Mountains Hist. Assn., Gatlinburg, Tenn., 1956, designer, dir., 57; comm. cons. NC Nat. Bank, 1968, Jefferson Std. Life Ins. Co., Greensboro, NC, 1969, Gilbarco, Inc., Greensboro, 1969—70, Greensboro, 1973. Drama critic, columnist: Sunday Star, 1952, theater editor: Players Mag., 1959—61, theater columnist: Sunday edits. Greensboro Daily News, 1959—62; contbr. articles to profl. jours. Mem. NC Arts Coun. Commn., 1964—66, Guilford County Bi-Centennial Celebration Commn., 1969—70; pres. Shanks Village Players, Orangeburg, NYC, 1947—48, Univ. Drama Group, Newark, Del., 1954—55; bd. dirs. Broadway Theatre League Greensboro, 1958—60, Greensboro Cmty. Arts Coun., 1964—67, 1969—72, Greensboro Cmty. Theatre, 1983—86, Carolina Theatre commn., 1990—93; organizer-cons. Market Players, W. Market St. United Meth. Ch., 1979—82. With USN, 1943—46. Recipient O. Henry award, Greensboro C. of C., 1966, Gold medallion, Amoco Oil Co., 1973, Suzanne M. Davis award, Southeastern Theatre Conf., 1975, Marian A. smith Disting. Career award, NC Theatre Conf., 1990. Mem.: Assn. Theater Higher Edn., NC Theater Conf. (co-organizer 1971, bd. dirs. 1984—92, pres. 1987—88), NC Drama and Speech Assn. (pres. 1966—67), Carolina Dramatic Assn. (bd. dirs. 1958—59), Southeastern Theatre Conf. (bd. dirs. 1963—68, 1987—92, pres. 1965, pres. pro tem 1966), Nat. Collegiate Players, Speech Communication Assn. Am., Assn. Theatre Higher Edn. (founding mem. 1986—87), Am. Coll. Theatre Festival (regional festival dir. 1973, 1980, regional dir., mem. nat. com. 1978—80), Am. Theatre Assn. (chmn. bd. nominations 1971—72), Am. Nat. Theatre and Acad. (organizer exec. v.p. Piedmont chpt. 1957—60), Alpha Psi Omega, Theta Alpha Phi, Phi Kappa Phi, Phi Delta Kappa. Democrat. Methodist. Home: 203 Village Ln Unit A Greensboro NC 27409-2517 Personal E-mail: hmiddleton@triad.rr.com.

**MIDDLETON, J. RICHARD,** religious studies educator; b. Kingston, Jamaica, Jan. 14, 1955; s. Jack Reginald and Phyllis Merle Middleton; m. Marcia Ann Berry, Aug. 27, 1977; children: Andrew Derek, Kevin Timothy. BTh, Jamaica Theol. Sem., Kingston; MA, U. Guelph, Ont., Canada; PhD, Vrije Universiteit, Amsterdam, Netherlands. Inter-varsity campus min. U Guelph, 1981—83; assoc. Protestant chaplain U. Rochester, 1986—88; christian ref. chaplain Brock U., St. Catharines, Ontario, Canada, 1988—90; adj. prof. of philosophy Redeemer U. Coll., Ancaster, Ontario, Canada, 1989—91; adj. prof., worldview studies Inst. Christian Studies, Toronto, 1990—95; asst. prof. O.T. interpretation Colgate Rochester Div. Sch., NY, 1996—2001; assoc. prof. Bibl. studies Roberts Wesleyan Coll., Rochester, 2002—. Mem. adv. bd. Brazos Press, Grand Rapids, Mich. Author: The Liberating Image: The Imago Dei in Genesis 1; co-author: Truth Is Stranger Than It Used to Be: Biblical Faith in a Postmodern Age, The Transforming Vision: Shaping a Christian World View; contbr. articles to profl. publs. Recipient Faculty award for Profl. Devel., Roberts Wesleyan Coll., 2004; Grad. scholar, Provincal Govt., Ont., Can., 1983—84, Doctoral fellow, Social Scies. and Humanities Rsch. Coun. Can., 1992—94. Mem.: Am. Acad. Religion, Can. Evang. Theol. Assn., Can. Theol. Soc., Can. Soc. Bibl. Studies, Soc. Bibl. Lit. Office: Roberts Wesleyan Coll 2301 Westside Dr Rochester NY 14624 Office Phone: 585-594-6981. Business E-Mail: middleton_richard@roberts.edu.

**MIDDLETON, JACK BAER,** lawyer; b. Phila., Jan. 13, 1929; s. Harry C. and Mildred Cornell (Baer) M.; m. Ann (Dodge), Aug. 22, 1953; children: Susan D., Jack B. Jr., Peter C. BA, Lafayette Coll., 1950; JD (hon.), Boston U., 1956. Bar: NH 1956, US Dist. Ct. Vt. 1988, US Ct. Appeals (1st cir.) 1957, US Supreme Ct. 1972. Assoc. McLane, Graf, Raulerson and Middleton, Manchester, NH, 1956—62; ptnr., dir. McLane, Graf, Raulerson and Middleton, Manchester, NH, 1962—. Spl. justice Merrimack, NH Dist. Ct., 1964-87; commr. Uniform State Laws, 1971-74. Author: (with others) Summary of New Hampshire Law, 1964, Compendium of New Hampshire Law, 1969, Trial of a Wrongful Death Action in New Hampshire, 1977; editor Boston U. Law Rev., 1954-56; contbr. articles to profl. jours. Active Mt. Washington Commn., 1969—; Bedford, NH Sch. Bd., 1960-66; adv. bd. Merrimack Valley Coll.; trustee, sec. Mt. Washington Obs., 1957—; chmn. bd. trustees White Mountain Sch., 1976-79; campaign chmn. United Way Greater Manchester, 1987, bd. dirs., 1986-92, chmn., 1990-91; bd. dirs. NH Pub. Radio, 1988-91; bd. gov. NH Pub. TV, 1994-2003, chmn., 1997-99; trustee New Eng. Law Inst., 1977-80, Franklin Pierce Law Ctr., 2003—. Sgt. USMCR, 1950-52. Fellow Am. Coll. Trial Lawyers (chmn. NH sect. 1988-90), Am. Bar Found. (life); mem. ABA (ho. dels. 1984-2005, bd. gov. 1996-2002, sec. elect 1998-99, sec. 1999-2002), New Eng. Bar Assn. (bd. dir. 1977-88, pres. 1982-83), NH Bar Assn. (pres. 1979-80), NH Bar Found. (bd. dir. 1979-92, chair 1983-90), Nat. Ctr. State Ct. (dir. 1999-2005), Nat. Conf. Bar Found. (trustee 1985-92, pres. 1989-90), Nat. Conf. Bar Pres. (exec. coun. 1987-95, pres. 1993-94), NH Bus. and Industry Assn. (bd. dir. 1988-2005, sec. 2000-2005), Manchester C. of C. (bd. dir. 1967-89, chmn. 1984-85), New Eng. Coun. (bd. dirs. 1991-2004), New Eng. Legal Found. (bd. dirs. 2001-04). Office: McLane Graf Raulerson and Middleton 900 Elm St Ste 1001 Manchester NH 03101-2029

**MIDDLETON, JAMES ARTHUR,** oil and gas company executive; b. Tulsa, Mar. 15, 1936; s. James Arthur and Inez (Matthews) M.; m. Victoria Middleton; children: Robert Arthur, James Daniel, Angela Lynn; stepson: Andrew Davis Fitzhugh. BA, Rice U., 1958, BS in Mech. Engring., 1959. With Atlantic Richfield Co., 1959-96; design engr. Dallas, 1962-67; tech. planner, 1967-69; mgr. shale devel. Grand Junction, Colo., 1969-72; mgr. engring. dept. Los Angeles, 1972-74; mgr. Prudhoe Bay project Pasadena, Calif., 1974-80; v.p. mgr. corp. planning Los Angeles, 1980-81; pres. ARCO Coal Co., Denver, 1981-82; sr. v.p. ARCO Oil and Gas Co., Dallas, 1982-85, pres., 1985-90, sr. v.p. parent co., 1981-87, exec. v.p. parent co., 1987-94, also bd. dirs.; chmn., CEO Crown Energy Corp., Salt Lake City, 1996-2000; pres. Jam Energy Co., 2000—. Bd. dirs. Tex. Utilities Co., Dallas., ARCO Chem. Co., Berry Petroleum Co. Corp. rep. Circle Ten coun. Boy Scouts Am.; bd. dirs. L.A. coun. Boy Scouts Am., United Way Met. Dallas, Dallas Coun. on World Affairs, Jr. Achievement So. Calif. 2d lt. C.E., AUS, 1959-60 Reicpient ASME Petroleum dir. Oil Drop award. Mem. Soc. Petroleum Engrs. of AIME, Tex. Mid-Continent Oil and Gas Assn., Am. Petroleum Inst., Rocky Mountain Oil and Gas Assn., We. States Petroleum Assn. (chmn. bd. dirs.), Nat. Gas Suppliers Assn. (chmn.), L.A. C. of C. (bd. dirs.), L.A. Music Ctr. Founders, Ctr. for Strategic and Internat. Studies (CSIS)-Dallas Round Table, Am. Enterprise Forum Chief Execs. Round Table, Dallas Petroelum Club, Tower, Northwood, Calif. Club, Bel-Air Country Club, L.A. Country Club, Preston Trail Golf Club. Office: 3609 Euclid Ave Dallas TX 75205 Office Phone: 214-599-2824.

**MIDDLETON, MARC STEPHEN,** corporate insurance risk manager; b. Louisville, Dec. 7, 1950; s. Joseph Scott and Virginia Marie (Schuler) M.; m. Carmen Teresa Fauscette, Feb. 22, 1969; 1 child, Marc Christopher. AA, Dalton Jr. Coll., 1970; BBA, U. Ga., 1972. Sr. risk analyst Deere and Co., Moline, Ill., 1973-78, mgr. corp. claims, 1978-79, mgr. corp. ins. dept., 1980-86; v.p. risk mgmt. svcs. John Deere Ins. Group, Moline, Ill., 1987-91; dir. risk mgmt. Deere and Co., Moline, Ill., 1992—. V.p. bd. dirs. Tahoe Ins. Co., Reno, 1981-83, Sierra Gen. Life Ins. Co., Reno, 1981-83, Continental Guaranty, Ltd., Hamilton, Bermuda, 1981-83; v.p. John Deere Ins. Co., Rock River Ins. Co., Tahoe Ins. Co., 1990-91, John Deere Life Ins. Co., Sierra Gen. Life Ins. Co., 1991; mem. M200 Risk Mgmt. Forum; mem. FM Global Risk Mgmt. Exec. Coun. Mem. Citizen's Adv. Council to East Moline (Ill.) Sch. Bd., 1978-80; coach YMCA Youth Basketball, Moline, 1978. Mem. Risk and Ins. Mgmt. Soc., Risk Mgmt. Council of Mfrs. Alliance (formerly Machinery and Allied Products Inst.), Captive Ins. Cos. Assn., ESIS (Delphi panel 1985—), Internat. Platform Assn. Roman Catholic. Avocations: tennis, hunting, fishing, woodworking. Home: PO Box 369 6 Eagle Pointe Pass Rapids City IL 61278 Office: Deere & Co 1 John Deere Pl Moline IL 61265-8098 Office Phone: 309-765-5865. Business E-Mail: middletonmarcs@johndeere.com.

**MIDDLETON, NORMAN GRAHAM,** social worker, psychotherapist; b. Jacksonville, Fla., Jan. 21, 1935; s. Norman Graham and Betty (Quina) M.; m. Judy Stephens, Aug. 1, 1968; stepchildren: Monty Stokes, Toni Stokes. BA, U. Miami, Fla., 1960; MSW, Fla. State U., 1962. Casework counselor Family Svc., Miami, 1962-64; psychiat. social worker assoc. firm Drs. Warson, Steele, Wiener, Sarasota, Fla., 1964-66; psychotherapist Sarasota, 1966—. Instr. Manatee Jr. Coll., Bradenton, Fla., 1973-76. Author: The Caverns of My Mind, 1988, Imaginative Healing, 1993, Spirited Imagination, 2002. Pres. Coun. on Epilepsy, Sarasota, 1969-70. Served with USAF, 1954-58. Fellow Fla. Soc. Clin. Social Work (pres. 1978-80); mem. Am. Group Psychotherapy Assn., Am. Assn. Sex Educators and Counselors (cert. sex educator). Democrat. Episcopalian. Home: 16626 Winburn Dr Sarasota FL 34240-9221 Office: 1257 S Tamiami Trail Sarasota FL 34239-2219 Office Phone: 941-366-3334. E-mail: imageside@aol.com.

**MIDDLETON, TERESA MUIR,** Internet company executive, researcher; b. London; d. Francis Robert and Marjorie Banwell Muir; children: Christopher, Andrew, Claire. BSc, Syracuse U., 1978; MBA, Pepperdine U., 1982. Rschr. SRI Internat., Menlo Park, Calif., 1970—90, program mgr., 1990—94, assoc. dir., 1994—98, assoc. dir. emeritus, 1998—; CEO PatchWorx, Inc., Menlo Park, 1998—. Founding dir. Nat. Cristina Found., Greenwich, 1989—; mem. com. Nat. Conf. Tech. and Disabilities, Northridge, 1989; chmn. Virtual Reality Conf., Menlo Park, 1991; rschr. in field. Editor: Virtual Worlds: Real Challenges, 1991. Dir. telecom. for the deaf Deafnet Dissemination Project,

1984. Recipient Mimi award, SRI Internat., 1997. Avocations: swimming, music, travel. Office: Patchworx Inc 333 Ravenswood Ave BS372 Menlo Park CA 94025 Personal E-mail: tmiddleton@aol.com. Business E-Mail: tmiddleton@patchworx.org.

**MIDDLETON-DOWNING, LAURA,** psychiatric social worker, artist, small business owner; b. Edinburg, Ind., Apr. 20, 1935; d. John Thomas Jr. and Rowene Elizabeth (Baker) Middleton; m. George Charles Downing, 1974 (div. 1986). BA in English Lit., U. Colo., 1966, MFA, 1969, BA in Psychology, 1988; MSW, U. Denver, 1992; Doctor of Clin. Hypnotherapy, Am. Inst. Hypnotherapy, 1995. Cert. clin. hypnotherapist, Calif., Colo.; cert. past life therapist, Colo., In ternat. Bd. for Regression Therapy-Level II cert. Profl. artist, Silver Plume and Boulder, Colo., 1965—; profl. photographer Silver Plume, Boulder, 1975—; art tchr. U. Colo., Boulder and Longmont, 1971-73; mem. survey crew Bur. of Land Mgmt., Empire, Colo., 1984-85; cons. social work and psychotherapy Boulder, 1992—; psychiat. and med. social worker Good Samaritan Health Agy., Boulder, 1993-97; pvt. practice clin. hypnotherapy Boulder, 1995—; pvt. practice past-life therapist, 1995—. Pres. Phoenix LG, Inc., 1998-2004 Author, photographer Frontiers, Vol. IV, No. 1, 1979; works exhibited in 15 one-woman shows, 1969—; numerous group exhbns. including group exhbn., Colo. History Mus., Denver, 1997-98. Trustee Town of Silver Plume, Colo., 1975-84; co-founder, pres. Alma Holm Rogers Nat. Orgn. Women, Clear Creek County, 1975-82; mem. Ctrl. Mountain Coun., Clear Creek County, 1980; chairperson Mary Ellen Barnes Cmty. Ctr. Project, Silver Plume, Colo., 1983; vol. Rape Crisis Team, Boulder, 1989-90, Child & Family Advocacy Program, Boulder, 1992-97; adv. bd. mem. Good Samaritan Agy., Boulder, 1993-97; caring minister vol. First Congl. Ch., Boulder, 1995-98; founding mem. Front Range Women in the Visual Arts, Boulder, Colo., 1974. Recipient Juried Exhbn. Merit award Colo. Women in the Arts, 1979; Women's Incentive scholar U. Colo., Boulder, 1999; Grad. Sch. Social Work scholar U. Denver, 1991; Colo. Grad. grantee U. Denver, 1992. Mem. AAUW, NASW, DAR, Colo. Advs. for Responsible Mental Health Svcs., Eye Movement Desensitization Reprocessing Network, Internat. Assn. for Regression Rsch. and Therapies, Inc. (Ecocycle, Colo. block leader), Natural Resources Def. Coun., The Nature Conservancy, World Wildlife Fedn., Bus. Women's Leadership Group, Sierra Club, Defender of Wildlife, Psi Chi. Avocations: skipping, photography, travel, volunteerism, bicycling. Office: PO Box 2312 Boulder CO 80306-2312

**MIDELFORT, HANS CHRISTIAN ERIK,** history professor; b. Eau Claire, Wis., Apr. 17, 1942; s. Peter Albert and Gerd (Gjems) M.; m. Corelyn Forsyth Senn, June 16, 1965 (div. Dec. 1981); children: Katarina, Kristian; m. Cassandra Clemons Hughes, May 25, 1985 (div. April 1996); 1 child, Lucy; m. Anne L. McKeithen, June 22, 1996. BA, Yale U., 1964, MPhil, 1967, PhD, 1970. Instr. Stanford U., Calif., 1968-70; asst. prof. U. Va., Charlottesville, 1970-72, assoc. prof., 1972-87, prof., 1987—, Charles Julian Bishko prof. history, 1996—. Vis. prof. Harvard U., Cambridge, Mass., 1985, U. Stuttgart, Germany, 1988, U. Bern, Switzerland, 1988, Wolfson Coll., Oxford U., 2002, Yale U., 2003; prin. Brown Coll., U. Va., 1996-2001; Dwight Terry lectr. Yale U., 2003; vis. fellow All Souls Coll., Oxford U., 2005. Author: Witch Hunting in Southwestern Germany, 1972 (Gustave Arlt prize 1972), Mad Princes of Renaissance Germany, 1994 (Roland H. Bainton prize 16th Century Studies Conf. 1995), A History of Madness in 16th Century Germany, 1999 (Ralph Waldo Emerson prize, Phi Beta Kappa, 1999, Roland H. Bainton prize 16th Century Studies Conf. 2000), Exorcism and Enlightenment, 2005; editor: Johann Weyer, On Witchcraft, 1998; co-editor: Europe, 1450-1789. Encyclopedia of the Early Modern World, 2003; translator: Imperial Cities and the Reformation (Bernd Moeller), 1972, Revolution of 1525 (Peter Bickle), 1981, Shaman of Oberstdorf (Wolfgang Behringer), 1998. Mem. Soc. Reformation Rsch. (pres. 1992-93). Office: U Va Dept History Charlottesville VA 22903 Office Phone: 434-924-7949. Business E-Mail: hem7e@virginia.edu.

**MIDKIFF, DINAH LEE,** retired elementary and middle school educator; b. Ashland, Ky., Dec. 23, 1954; d. Marie Ramey Midkiff. AA, Ashland Cmty. Coll., 1974; BA, Morehead State U. 1976, MA, 1978, cert. in adminstrn. and supervision, 1980. Tchr. Boyd County Bd. Edn., Ashland, 1976—85, Boone County Bd. Edn., Hebron, Ky., 1989—90, Franklin County Bd. Edn., Frankfort, Ky., 1990—2003, Jessamine County Bd. Edn., Nicholasville, Ky., 2003—04; ret., 2004—. Cons. Ky. Dept. Edn., Frankfort, Ky., 1986—89. Co-author: Jazz Up Reading: A Conference Overview, Informal Selection Process for Grade One Placement. Named Ky. Col., 2001, Maker's Mark Amb., 2005; recipient Drug Abuse Resistance Edn. award, 2002. Mem.: NOW, AAUW, Am. Assn. Ret. Persons, Ky. Ret. Tchr. Assn., Sierra Club (mem. mission trips to Ky., SD, Tex., Mexico, Jamaica). Democrat. Avocations: travel, reading. Home: 1338 Shun Pike Nicholasville KY 40356

**MIDKIFF, ROBERT RICHARDS,** trust company executive, finance company executive, consultant; b. Honolulu, Sept. 24, 1920; s. Frank Elbert and Ruth (Richards) M.; m. Evanita Sumner, July 24, 1948; children: Mary Lloyd, Robin Starr, Shelley Sumner, Robert Richards Jr., David Wilson. BA, Yale U., 1942; grad. Advanced Mgmt. Program, Harvard U., 1962; LHD, U. Hawaii, 2002. Asst. sec. Hawaiian Trust Co., 1951—56, asst. v.p., 1956—57, v.p., 1957—65; dir. Am. Factors, Ltd., 1954—65; v.p. Amfac, Inc., 1965—68; exec. v.p., dir. Am. Security Bank, Honolulu, 1968—69, pres., dir., 1969—71; pres., CEO, dir. Am. Trust Co. Hawaii, Honolulu, 1971—93; chmn. bd. dirs. Bishop Trust Co. Ltd., Honolulu, 1984—93; pres., CEO Am. Fin. Svcs. of Hawaii, 1984—93. Co-chmn. Gov.'s Archtl. Adv. Com. on State Capitol, 1960-65; co-chmn. Gov.'s Adv. Com. on Fine Arts for State Capitol, 1965-69; past chmn., bd. dirs. Hawaii Visitors Bur.; past pres., bd. dirs. Downtown Improvement Assn., Lahaina Restoration Found., Hawaii Cmty. Found.; bd. dirs., pres. Atherton Family Found.; past chmn. Profit Sharing Rsch. Found.; chmn., bd. dirs. Hawaii Theatre Ctr.; past chmn. bd. dirs. Good Beginnings Alliance; chmn. bd. dirs. Honolulu Cultural and Arts Dist. Mem. Coun. on Founds. (past bd dirs.), Profit Sharing Coun Am (past bd. dirs.) Small Bus. Coun. Am. (past bd. dirs.), ESOP Assn. Am. (past bd. dirs.), Pacific Club, Waialae Golf Club, Phi Beta Kappa. Episcopalian. Office: 4477 Kahala Ave Honolulu HI 96816-4924 Office Phone: 808-734-8132. Office Fax: 808-737-9007. Personal E-mail: rrmhi@aol.com.

**MIDLARSKY, ELIZABETH RUTH,** psychology professor; b. NYC; d. Abraham Allan and Frances Lucille (Wiener) Steckel; m. Manus Issachar Midlarsky, June 25, 1961; children: Susan Rachel, Miriam Joyce, Michael George. BA, CUNY, 1961; MA, Northwestern U., 1966, PhD, 1968. Lic. psychologist, N.J., Mich., Colo. Asst. prof. U. Denver, 1968-73; dir. rsch. and evaluation Malcolm X Mental Health Ctr. (now Park East), Denver, 1973-75; assoc. prof., dir. psychol. tng. program Met. State Coll., Denver, 1975-77; assoc. prof. psychology U. Detroit, 1982—90. prof. psychology, 1983-90, chair dept. psychology, 1978-81, dir. Ctr. Study Devel. and Aging, 1977-83; prof. clin. psychology Tchrs. Coll. Columbia U., N.Y.C., 1990—, dir. Ctr. for Lifespan and Aging Studies, 1992—; rsch. scholar Phila. Geriatric Ctr., 1997—2000. Mem. initial rev. group NIMH, Bethesda, Md., 1976-82; mem. ad hoc rev. groups NHLBI, Bethesda, 1985-95; mem. study sect. NIH, Bethesda, 1986-91; mem. task force on prevention, 1991-94. Author: Altruism in Late Life, 1994; co-editor Humboldt Jour. Social Rels., 1985-86, Violence in Schools, 2005; editor Acad. Psychol. Bull., 1982-86, mem. editl bd. Jour. Traumatic Stress, 2000—; contbr. chpts. to books and articles to profl. jours. Mem. exec. coun. Mich. Psychol. Assn. Grantee Nat. Inst. Aging, 1982-85, 87-90, AARP, 1982-83, 88-89, 92-95; postdoctoral rsch. fellow AAUW, 1974-75. Fellow APA (divsn. 12, 20, publs. com. 1990-92, election com. 2005—, student award com. 1990), Am. Psychol. Soc., Am. Orthopsychiat. Assn., Gerontol. Soc. Am. (exec. com. on program com. 1983-84); mem. Soc. Psychol. Study Social Issues, Internat. Assn. Genocide Scholars. Home: 3 Falcon Rd East Brunswick NJ 08816-2716 Office: Columbia U Tchrs Coll Dept Couns & Clin Psych PO Box 148 New York NY 10027-0148 Office Phone: 212-678-3124. Business E-Mail: em142@columbia.edu.

**MIDLER, BETTE,** singer, entertainer, actress; b. Honolulu, Dec. 1, 1945; m. Martin von Haselberg, 1984; 1 child, Sophie. Student, U. Hawaii. Debut as actress (films) Hawaii, 1965, then cast Fiddler on the Roof, N.Y.C.,

1966—69, Salvation, 1970, Tommy, Seattle Opera Co., 1971, nightclub concert performer on tour U.S., from 1972; appearance Palace Theatre, N.Y.C., 1973, Radio City Music Hall, 1993, TV appearances include The Tonight Show, Bette Midler: Old Red Hair is Back, 1978, Gypsy, 1993 (Golden Globe award best actress in a mini-series or movie made for television, 1994, Emmy nomination, Lead Actress - Special, 1994), Seinfeld, 1996, Diva Las Vegas, 1997, Murphy Brown, 1998, appeared Clams on The Half-Shell Revue, N.Y.C., 1975, recs. include The Divine Miss M, 1972, Bette Midler, 1973, Broken Blossom, 1977, Live at Last, 1977, The Rose, Thighs and Whispers, 1979, Songs for the New Depression, 1979, Divine Madness, 1980, No Frills, 1984, Mud Will Be Flung Tonight, 1985, Beaches (soundtrack), 1989, Some People's Lives, 1990, Bette of Roses, 1995, Bathhouse Betty, 1998, Bette, 2000, Bette Midler Sings The Rosemary Clooney Songbook, 2003; actor: (films) Hawaii, 1966, The Rose, 1979 (Academy award nomination best actress, 1979), Divine Madness, 1980, Jinxed, 1982, Down and Out in Beverly Hills, 1986, Ruthless People, 1986, Outrageous Fortune, 1987, Oliver and Company (voice), 1988, Big Business, 1988, Beaches, 1988, Stella, 1990, Scenes From a Mall, 1991, For the Boys, 1991 (Academy award nomination best actress, 1991), Hocus Pocus, 1993, Get Shorty, 1995, The First Wives Club, 1996, That Old Feeling, 1997, Get Bruce, 1999, Isn't She Great, 1999, Drowning Mona, 2000, Isn't She Great, 2000, The Stepford Wives, 2004; appeared in cable TV (HBO) prodn. Bette Midler's Mondo Beyondo, 1988; author: A View From A Broad, 1980, The Saga of Baby Divine, 1983; exec. prodr., composer (TV show) Bette, 2000, exec. prodr. Some of My Best Friends, 2001, (films) Divine Secret of the Ya-Ya Sisterhood, 2002. Recipient After Dark Ruby award, 1973, Grammy awards, 1973, 1990, spl. Tony award, 1973, Emmy award for NBC Spl., Ol' Red Hair is Back, 1978, 2 Golden Globe awards for The Rose, 1979, Golden Globe award for The Boys, 1991, Emmy award The Tonight Show appearance, 1992.

**MIEKKA, JEANETTE ANN,** retired science educator; b. Kenmore, NY, Aug. 25, 1931; d. Harry Whittier and Beulah Laura Lambe; m. Richard George Miekka, June 22, 1958; children: James Richard, Frederick Noah, Cynthia Marie Bordas-Miekka. BSc, Boston U., 1949—53, MEd, 1954—57. Teacher of All Sciences Mass., 1954. Tchr. of chemistry, physics, biology, gen. sci. Meridith H.S., Meridity, NH, 1953—54; sci. tchr. and dept. chmn. Hicksville Jr. H.S., 1954—56; biology and physiology tchr. Newton H.S., Mass., 1956—60; instr. of comparative physiology Allied Health Jr. Coll., Holliston, Mass., 1978—79; ret., 1979. Sophomore class advisor Meridith H.S., NH, 1953—54; supr. of student teachers Newton H.S., Mass., 1957—60, advisor, future teachers of am., 1956—60. Contbr. articles to profl. jours. Pres. Am. Field Svc., Natick, Mass., 1964—65; dir. F.I.S.H., Natick, Mass., 1964—65; chmn., publicity Sudbury Women's Club, Mass., 1971—74; mem. Sun Coast Opera Guild; cons. St. Francis Sch., Loiseau, Haiti, 2002—05; assoc. St. Margaret's Convent, Boston; lay eucharistic min. St. Matthews Ch., St. Petersburg, Fla., 2004—05. Mem.: Internat. Women's Writing Guild (assoc.). Episcopal. Avocations: travel, bridge, book club, cooking, writing.

**MIELCARZ, SHARON MARIE,** assistant principal; b. Waterbury, Conn., Sept. 19, 1950; d. Richard J. and Antoinette C. Hannon; m. Robert T. Mielcarz, Aug. 18, 1973; 1 child, Jeffrey A. AS, Mattatuck C.C., Waterbury, 1971; BS, Ctrl. Conn. State U., 1972, MS, 1978. Lic. tchr. Conn. Bus. tchr. St. Paul Cath. HS, Bristol, Conn., 1974—2003, asst. prin., 2003—. Faculty advisor United Way Youth Bd., Bristol, Conn., 1980—. Named to St. Paul Cath. HS Hall of Fame, 2004. Home: 60 Dorset Horn Ln Bristol CT 06010 Office: St Paul Cath HS 1001 Stafford Ave Bristol CT 06010 Office Phone: 860-584-0911. E-mail: smmielcarz@comcast.net.

**MIELE, ANGELO,** engineering educator, researcher, consultant, author; b. Formia, Italy, Aug. 21, 1922; arrived in U.S., 1952, naturalized, 1985; s. Salvatore and Elena (Marino) Miele. DCivil Engring., U. Rome, Italy, 1944, DAero. Engring., 1946; DSc (hon.), Inst. Tech., Technion, Israel, 1992. Asst. prof. Poly. Inst. Bklyn., 1952- 55; prof. Purdue U., 1955-59; dir. astrodynamics Boeing Sci. Rsch. Labs., 1959-64; prof. aerospace scis., math. scis. Rice U., Houston, 1964-88, Foyt Family prof. engring., 1988-93, Foyt prof. emeritus engring., aerospace scis., math. scis., 1993—, rsch. prof., 2001—. Cons. Douglas Aircraft Co., 1956—58, U.S. Aviation Underwriters, 1987, Boeing Comml. Airplane Co., 1989, European Space Tech. Engring. Ctr., 2002; cons. Allison divsn. GM Corp., 1956—58; Breakwell Meml. lectureship Internat. Astron. Fedn., 1994; Gaspare Santangelo Meml. lectureship Italian Assn. of Aeronautics and Astronautics, 2001. Author: Flight Mechanics, 1962; editor: Theory of Optimum Aerodynamic Shapes, 1965, Applied Mathematics in Aerospace Science and Engineering, 1994, Advanced Design Problems in Aerospace Engineering, 2003; editor-in-chief Jour. Optimization Theory and Applications, 1966—, assoc. editor Jour. Astronautical Scis., 1964—93, Applied Math. and Computation, 1975—, series editor Math. Concepts and Methods in Sci. and Engring., 1975—, Optimal Control Applications and Methods, 1979—, mem. editl. bd. RAIRO-Ops. Rsch., 1990—, mem. adv. bd. AIAA Edn. Series, 1991—98; contbr. articles to profl. jours. Pres. Italy in Am. Assn., 1966—93. Decorated knight comdr. Order Merit Italy; recipient Levy medal, Franklin Inst. of Phila., 1974, Brouwer award, AAS, 1980, Schuck award, Am. Automatic Control Coun., 1988, Latina prize, 2002, Flight Mechanics award, AIAA, 1982, Pendray Aerospace Lit. award, 1982. Fellow: Am. Astronautical Soc., AIAA (hon. Pendray Aerospace Lit. award 1982, Mechs. and Control of Flight award 1982), Franklin Inst.; mem.: Tex. Acad. Engring., Scis. and Medicine, Nat. Acad. Engring. of Argentina (corr.), Internat. Acad. Astronautics, Acad. Scis. Turin (corr.), Russian Acad. Scis. (corr.), NAE. Achievements include research in aerospace engring., windshear problems, hypervelocity flight, interplanetary flight, math. programming, optimal control theory and computing methods. Home: 3106 Kettering Dr Houston TX 77027-5504 Office: Rice Univ MS-322 Aero-Astronaution Group 6100 Main St Houston TX 77005-1827 Office Phone: 713-348-4907. Business E-Mail: miele@rice.edu.

**MIELE, JOEL ARTHUR, SR.,** civil engineer; b. Jersey City, May 28, 1934; s. Jene Gerald Sr., and Eleanor Natalie (Bergida) M.; m. Faith Roseann Trombetta, July 21, 1952 (div. 1954); m. 2d Josephine Ann Cottone, Feb. 14, 1959; children: Joel Arthur, Jr., Vita Marie, Janet Ann. BCE, Poly. Inst. Bklyn., 1955. Lic. profl. engr. NY, NJ, Fla.; profl. planner NJ; chartered engr., U.K. Civil engr. Yudell & Miele, Queens, NY, 1955-57; chief engr. Jene G. Miele Assocs., 1960—68; prin. and CEO Miele Assocs., 1968—94; commr. N.Y.C. Planning Commn., 1990—94; commr. dept. bldgs. City of N.Y., 1994—96; commr. Dept. Environ. Protection, 1996—2002, N.Y.C. Bd. Stds. and Appeals, 2002—05; pvt. practice cons. engr., 2005—. Mem. NY State Bd. for Engring. and Land Surveying, 1997—, chmn. 2005-. Patentee masonry wall constrn. Mem. Cmty. Bd. 10, Queens, 1971-90, chmn., 1978-90; mem. bd. visitors Creedmoor State Hosp., 1978—, pres., 1979—; trustee Queens Borough Pub. Libr., 1979—, pres., 1995-96; bd. dirs. Peninsula Hosp. Ctr., 1984—, chair, 1990—; bd. mem. Peninsula Gen. Nursing Home, 1985—, chair, 1990—; bd. mem. Queens County Overall Econ. Devel. Corp., 1989-94, pres., 1991-94; trustee Queens Pub. Comm. Corp., 1983—; exec. v.p. Queens County and mem. Nat. Coun. Boy Scouts Am., 1991—; bd. mem. Am. Parkinson Disease Assn., 1985—, mem. exec. com., 1987—, v.p., pres. Internat. Parkinsons Fond, Netherlands, 1997—; dir. Queens Libr. Found., 1997—; dir. Assn. Met Water Agys., 1997-02, Assn. Met. Sewerage Agys., 1997-02; mem. Nat. Coun. Examiners Engring. & Surveying, 1997—, founder, co-pres., Internat. Parkinsons Fond gGmbH, Germany, 2006-. Lt. (j.g.) USN, 1957-60; capt. USNR, 1960-88, ret., 1988; RADM LH NY Naval Militia, 1998. Named Italian-Am. of Yr. Ferrini Welfare League, Queens, 1980, Hon. Mem. of Queens Chpt. AIA, 1994, Hon. Profl. Affiliated Mem. NY Soc. Archs., 1994; recipient Outstanding Engring. Mgr. award Boy Scouts Am., 1987, Pride of Queens award, 1990, Pub. Servant Extraordinaire award United Cerebral Palsy of Queens, 1994, Good Scout award Greater NY Coun. Boy Scouts Am. 1994, Nat. Silver Beaver Court of Honor award, Boy Scouts of America, 1997, United Hosp. Funds Disting. Trustee award for Extraordinary Svc., 1997, NYSSPE Outstanding PE Mgr. of Yr. award, 1997, Disting. Alumni award, Poly. U., 1998, Humanitarian of Yr. award Guide Dog Found., 2000, Spl. Recognition for Pub. Svc. award NY Bldg. Congress, 2002, Golden Eagle award Boy Scouts Am., 2002. Fellow ASCE (life), NSPE (trustee polit. action com. 1990-96); mem. N.Y. State Soc. Profl. Engrs. (v.p. 1984-86, pres. 1988-89, nat. dir. 1987-90, Engr. of Yr. 1983), Soc. Am. Mil. Engrs., N.Y. State Assn. of Professions (founding). Democrat. Congregationalist. Office Phone: 718-848-8013. Personal E-mail: jmiele2@nyc.rr.com.

**MIELE, LUCIO,** physician, medical researcher, pharmacologist; b. Naples, Italy, Mar. 13, 1957; s. Armando and Agata Liana (Vassallo-Paleologo) Miele; m. Carolyn Margaret Duncan, Oct. 16, 2005; stepchildren: Charles Joseph Duncan, Margaret Ann Duncan, Caroline Elizabeth Duncan. MD, U. Naples, Italy, 1981—81, PhD, 1987. Vis. fellow NIH, Bethesda, Md., 1986—89, vis. assoc., 1989—93; tenure-track prin. investigator Ctr. for Biologics Evaluation and Rsch., FDA, Bethesda, 1994—96, acting chief lab. cell biology, 1996—98; asst. prof. pathology Loyola U. Med. Ctr., Maywood, Ill., 1998—2001; assoc. prof. pharmacology U. Ill., Chgo., 2001—05; prof. pathology, pharmacolgy and exptl. therapeutics Loyola U. Med. Ctr., Maywood, Ill., 2005—. Vis. prof. Temple U., Phila., 2005—06; dir. breast cancer pre-clinical rsch. program Cardinal Bernardin Cancer Ctr., Loyola U. Chgo., Maywood, Ill., 2005—; organizer EMBO Conf. on Notch Signaling, 2002; spkr., cons. in field. Editor: Jour. Expt. Clin. Oncology, 2004—06; mem. editl. bd.: Jour. Cell Biochem., 2003—06, Women's Oncology Reviews, 2002—06; contbr. articles to profl. jours. Drug discovery and molecular pharmacology study sect. Nat. Cancer Inst./NIH, Bethesda, 2002—06; breast cancer rsch. study sections Dept. of Def., Washington, 2002—06; dept. pub. health penny severns women's oncology rsch. awards study sect. State of Ill., Springfield. Recipient Outstanding Young Scientist award, Italian Acad. Medicine and Surgery, 1983, FDA award, 1997, Excellence in Women's Oncology Rsch. award, Ill. Dept. Pub. Health, 2000—01; grantee, NCI, 1999—2004, Ill. Dept. Pub. Health, 1999—2002, 2006—, Nat. Inst. Child Health and Human Devel., 2002—06; Idea grant, DOD, 2004—, Program Project grant, NCI/NIH, 2006—. Mem.: Am. Assn. for Cancer Rsch. Democrat-Npl. Roman Catholic. Achievements include development of recombinant human CC10/Uteroglobin; research in role of notch signaling in various cancers, notch inhibition has anti-neoplastic activity in vivo. Avocations: horsemanship, scuba diving, photography, poetry, philosophy. Office: Loyola Univ Med Ctr 2160 S First Ave Maywood IL 60153 Office Phone: 708-327-3298. Office Fax: 708-327-2245. Business E-Mail: lmiele@lumc.edu.

**MIELE, STEFANO M.,** lawyer; b. 1966; BS, Georgetown U.; JD, Emory U. Atty. Jones, Day, Reavis, & Pogue; with Mariner Health Care, Inc., Atlanta, 1995—, sr. v.p., assoc. gen. counsel, asst. sec., sr. v.p., gen. counsel, sec., 2002—. Office: Mariner Health Care Inc One Ravinia Dr Ste 1500 Atlanta GA 30346 Office Phone: 678-443-6786. Office Fax: 770-393-8054. E-mail: smiele@marinerhealthcare.com.

**MIELKE, CLARENCE HAROLD, JR.,** hematologist; b. Spokane, Wash., June 18, 1936; s. Clarence Harold and Marie Katherine (Gillespie) M.; m. Marcia Rae, July 5, 1964; children: Elisa, John, Kristina. BS, Wash. State U., 1959; MD, U. Louisville, 1963. Intern San Francisco Gen. Hosp., 1963-64; resident in medicine Portland VA Hosp., 1964-65, San Francisco Gen. Hosp., 1965-67; fellow in hematology U. So. Calif., 1967-68; tchg. fellow, asst. physician, instr. Tufts-New Eng. Med. Ctr. Hosps., Boston, 1968-71; sr. scientist Med. Rsch. Inst., San Francisco, 1971-90; chief hematology Presbyn. Hosp., San Francisco, 1971-82; asst. prof. clin. medicine U. Calif. Sch. Medicine, San Francisco, 1971-80, assoc. clin. prof., 1979-90, bd. dirs. Inst. Cancer Rsch., 1992—, Trustee, bd. dirs. Med. Rsch. Inst. San Francisco, Sacred Heart Hosp. Found., 1997-2000, Rockwood Clinic Found., 1994—; dir. emeritus Inst. Cancer Rsch.; trustee emeritus, bd. dirs. Med. Rsch. Inst., 1988—; dir. Health Rsch. and Edn. Ctr., Wash. State U., 1989—, prof. pharmacology, 1989—, prof. vet. medicine, 1989—, assoc. dean rsch., 1992-2004; dir. Spokane (Wash.) Heart Study, 1994—. Editor emeritus Jour. Clin. Aphesis, 1981; contbr. chpts. to books, articles to med. jours. Named Nat. Disting. Eagle Scout, 1998; NIH grantee, 1973-88. Fellow ACP, Am. Heart Assn.; mem. AAAS, AMA, Am. Heart Assn., Internat. Acad. Clin. and Applied Thrombosis and Hemostasis, Internat. Soc. Hematology, Am. Coll. Angiology; mem. Am. Soc. Internal. Medicine, Internat. Soc. Thrombosis and Hemostasis, N.Y. Acad. Scis., Spokane Med. Soc., Internat. Soc. Angiology. Office: PO Box 1495 Spokane WA 99210-1495 Office Phone: 509-358-7630. Business E-Mail: mielkeh@wsu.edu.

**MIELKE, JAMES EDWARD,** geochemist; b. Toledo, Oct. 6, 1940; s. Herbert Edward and Naomi Hilletje (Raabe) M.; m. Laurie Beth Retter, Dec. 19, 1966; children: Erin Christine, Emily Jane. BS, MIT, 1962; MS, U. Ariz., 1965; PhD, George Washington U., 1974. Mine geologist potash exploration N.S. Rsch. Found., 1962; geologist S.W. field party Universal Engring. Corp., Boston, 1963-64; geochemist C-14 dating lab. Smithsonian Instn., Washington, 1964-73; specialist in marine and earth scis. Congl. Rsch. Svc./Libr. of Congress, Washington, 1973-2000, retired, 2000. Liaison to Nat. Materials Adv. Bd., Nat. Rsch. Coun., Washington, 1981-86. Author more than 170 publs. including articles in profl. jours., com. prints, Congl. Rsch. Svc. reports; co-author: Strategic and Critical Materials, 1985, Review of Research in Modern Problems in Geochemistry, 1979. Pres. Home Buyers, Inc., Washington, 1976-83. Smithsonian Instn. Rsch. grantee, 1966-69. Mem. AAAS, Am. Geophys. Union, Marine Tech. Soc. Republican. Lutheran. Avocation: folk dancing. Home: 2803 Washington Ave Chevy Chase MD 20815-3009

**MIELKE, PAUL WILLIAM, JR.,** statistician, consultant; b. St. Paul, Feb. 18, 1931; s. Paul William and Elsa (Yungbauer) M.; m. Roberta Roehl Robison, June 25, 1960; children: William, Emily Spear, Lynn Basila. BA, U. Minn., 1953, PhD, 1960; MA, U. Ariz., 1958. Tchg. asst. U. Ariz., Tucson, 1957—58, U. Minn., Mpls., 1958—60, statis. cons., 1960—62, lectr., 1962—63; from asst. to assoc. prof. dept. stats. Colo. State U., Fort Collins, 1963—72, prof. dept. stats., 1972—. Co-author: Permutation Methods: a Distance Function Approach; contbr. articles Am. Jour. Pub. Health, Jour. of Statis. Planning and Inference, Ednl. and Psychol. Measurement, Biometrika, Earth-Sci. Revs., Weather and Forecasting, Jour. Behavioral and Ednl. Stats. Capt. USAF, 1953-57. Fellow Am. Statis. Assn.; mem. Am. Meteorol. Soc. (Banner I. Miller award 1973, 94). Biometric Soc. Achievements include rsch. in common statistical methods (t test and analysis of variance) related to counter intuitive geometric foundations and provided alternative statistical methods which are based on appropriate foundations. Home: 736 Cherokee Dr Fort Collins CO 80525-1517 Office: Colo State U Dept Stats Fort Collins CO 80523-1877 Office Phone: 970-491-6465. Business E-Mail: paul.mielke@colostate.edu.

**MIERA, LUCILLE CATHERINE MIERA,** artist, retired art educator; b. Socorro, N.Mex., Nov. 25, 1931; d. Stephen Maurice and Carmen Rosela (Baca) Miera; m. Vito Modesto Miera Jr., Aug. 22, 1953; children: Stephanie Lucille Miera Mansfield, Jennifer Ann Miera Eberhart. BA, U. N.Mex., 1973, MA, 1976, Ednl. Specialist Sch. Adminstrn., 1984. Cert. tchr., adminstr., N.Mex. Apprentice land surveying and draftsmen Stephen M. Miera, Regional Land Surveyor, Albuquerque, 1946-49; typist Albuquerque Abstract & Title, 1950; typist, engring. draftsman U.S. Army Corps Engrs., Albuquerque, 1950-57; engring. draftsman U.S. Dept. Interior, Albuquerque, 1957-59; art tchr., art dept. chair Albuquerque Pub. Sch. Sys., 1973-93, reviewer curriculum devel. plan jr. high schs.; reviewer mid. schs.; ret. Prof. asst. U. N.Mex., Albuquerque, 1974; mid. sch. articulation rep. Taylor Middle Sch., Albuquerque, 1974-83; art rep. North Ctrl. Evaluation Middle Sch., Albuquerque, 1978; pres., art tchr. N.Mex Art League, Albuquerque, 1996, 97, 99; founder art program Emeritus Acad., Tech. Vocat. Inst., 1997, art tchr., bd. dirs. 1997—. Exhibitions include Mus. Art, Toledo, Ohio, 1966, Kirtland AFB Officers Club, Albuquerque, 1967—68, U. N.Mex., 1969—76, 1999—2000, Albuquerque Pub. Schs. Adminstrn. Bldg., 1973—93, United Bank N.Mex., 1982, Albuquerque U. of C., 1999, exhibited in group shows at N.Mex. State Fair Fine Arts Gallery, N.Mex. State Fair Hispanic Art Gallery, Scottsdale Village Ctr. Art Gallery, Old Town Albuquerque De Colores Soaring Eagle and La Hacienda Galleries, Coronado Airport Gallery. Mem., flyer distbr. Rep. Party, Albuquerque, 1954; poll clk. Bernalillo County, Albuquerque,

1960; leader Campfire USA, Albuquerque, 1966, 80; treas. Manzano Band, Albuquerque, 1977; pres. Glenwood Neighborhood Assn., Albuquerque, 1984-87; pres., nat. area dir. Res. Officers Assn. Ladies, Washington, 1989-91. Mem. Nat. Mus. Women's Art (charter), Nat. Hist. Soc., N.Mex. Assn. Educators Ret., N.Mex. Watercolor Soc., N.Mex. Res. Officer Ladies (pres.), N.Mex. Archdiocesan Coun. Cath. Women (pres. 1974), Epsilon Sigma Alpha. Avocations: travel, instructing and displaying art to promote art in the community. Home: 4405 Glenwood Hills Dr NE Albuquerque NM 87111-4260 E-mail: lmierart@aol.com.

**MIERS, HARRIET ELLAN,** federal official, lawyer; b. Dallas, Aug. 10, 1945; BS in Mathematics, So. Meth. U., 1967, JD, 1970. Bar: Tex. 1970. Law clk. to Hon. Joe E. Estes US Dist. Ct. (no. dist.) Tex., 1970—72; assoc. Locke Purnell Rain Harrell (formerly Locke, Purnell, Boren, Laney & Neely PC), Dallas, 1972—78, ptnr, 1978—99, pres., 1996—99; mng. ptnr. Locke Liddell & Sapp L.L.P., 1999—2001; asst. to Pres. & staff sec The White House, Washington, 2001—03, asst. to Pres. & dep. chief of staff for policy, 2003—05, gen. counsel to Pres., 2005—; nominee for assoc. justice US Supreme Ct., 2005, withdrew nomination, 2005. Chairwoman, Tex. Lottery Commn., 1995-2000; mem. bd. dirs. Capstead Mortgage Corp., Coamerica Bank, Tex. Comments editor Southwestern Law Jour., 1969-70. Mem.-at-large Dallas City Coun., 1989-91; trustee Southwestern Legal Found. Named 1 of Top 50 Most Influential Lawyers Nat. Law Jour., 1998; named Outstanding Young Lawyer of Dallas, Dallas Assn. of Young Lawyers, 1978, Woman of the Year, Today's Dallas Woman, 1997; Woman of Excellence award, Women's Enterprise Mag., Louise B. Raggio award, Dallas Women Lawyers Assn., Jurisprudence award, Anti-Defamation League, 1996, Hon. Merrill Hartman award, Legal Svcs. of No. Tex., Sarah T. Hughes award, Women in Law Section State Bat of Tex., Am. Jewish Comm. Human Relations award, DBA's Justinian award for Community Svc. Fellow Am. Bar Found., Tex. Bar Found. (life); mem. ABA (jour. bd. editors, ho. dels., chair credentials and admissions com., election law com., bus. and cmty. activities), Dallas Bar Found., Dallas Bar Assn. (chmn. bd. dirs. 1981, pres., 1985-90), State Bar Tex. (pres. 1992-93, dir. 1986-89), Attys. Liability Assurance Soc. (bd. dirs.). Office: The White House 1600 Pennsylvania Ave NW 2nd Fl Washington DC 20502

**MIERSWA, RUTH MILDRED,** counselor, writer; b. Rice Lake, Wis., Apr. 4, 1917; d. John Peter Stoik and Julia Margaret Hessel; m. Richard Darrel Mierswa, June 12, 1941; children: Daniel, Richard, Peter. BA, U. Wis., Whitwater, 1939. Tchr. H.S., Sheboygan Falls, Wis., 1939—41; metaphys./astrolgical counselor, 1973—. Author: Ray Centered Astrology, 1986, Who You Are and Why You Are Here, 1998. Mem.: Am. Fedn. Astrology, Nat. Coun. Geomic Rsch. Achievements include development of a phase of astrology for finding one's life purpose and personality type. Avocations: gardening, hiking, reading. Home: 1092 Turk Hill Rd Fairport NY 14450 Personal E-mail: ruthmiersiva@aol.com.

**MIES, JOHN CHARLES,** Internet company executive; b. Peoria, Ill., Aug. 24, 1946; s. Ernest Gregory and Clara Emma (Reese) M. BS, Ea. Ill. U., 1968. Tchr. Centennial High Sch., Champaign, Ill., 1969-74; ptnr. The Leather Shop, Champaign, 1974-78, The Waterbed Shop, Champaign, 1978-82; pres. CEO Mies Corp., Champaign, 1982—. Mem. adv. bd. Bedroom mag., 1991-93; v.p. gen. mgr. AdvanceNet, 1996; pres. Online Svcs.; v.p. gen. mgr. Cambert Ltd., 1997, COO, 1999; ptnr. Ravecomm, LLC. Editor-in-chief The Sleep Connection newsletter; columnist Bedroom Industry Newsletter. Faculty rector Flotation Healthcare Found., chmn. bd., 1996. Mem. Nat. Waterbed Retailers Assn. (exec. com. 1987-92, sec.-treas. 1988-89, pres. 1991, chmn. long-range planning com., co-chmn. liaison com., joint pub. rels. com., named to Waterbed Hall of Fame 1992), Ctrl. State Mktg. Group (pres. 1986-89, 93, sec.-treas. 1992, sec. 1994-98, editor New Bedding Vision newsletter), Urbana C of C. (chmn. leadership planning com.), Monticello C of C. (bd. dirs. 1998-2003, treas. 2001-02), Champaign C. of C., Waterbed Advt. Coun. (com. mem., bd. dirs. 1990-91), Waterbed Coun. (com. mem., bd. dirs. 1990-91), Waterbed Coun. (bd. dirs. 1994, sec. 1994, dir. pubs. 1995, pres. 1996). Avocations: computers, motorcycle. Office: Mies Corp 201 W Springfield Ave Champaign IL 61820-4834

**MIESSE, JAMES EVERETT,** librarian; b. Columbus, Ohio, Oct. 14, 1952; s. Everett Warner and Dorothy Ann (Adams) M. BA in Classical Studies, U. Mo., Columbia, 1975, MA in Library Sci., 1984. Head automation/circulation svcs. S.W. Mo. State U., Springfield, Mo., 1985—87; user svcs. librarian Notis Systems, Inc., Evanston, Ill., 1987—88, account mgr. conversion svcs., 1988—90; sr. account mgr. conversion svcs., 1991—97; mgr. release integration and distbn., 1991—95; dir. customer svc. Endeavor Info. Systems, Inc., Des Plaines, Ill., 1995—2001; dir. product delivery and quality, 2001—. Mem. ALA, Assn. Coll. and Rsch. Librs., Libr. Adminstrn. and Mgmt. Assn. (com. chmn. 1988-90), Libr. Info. and Tech. Assn. Home: 835 Chilton Ln Wilmette IL 60091-2152 Office: Endeavor Info System 1350 E Touhy Ave Des Plaines IL 60018-3303

**MIFFLIN, JEFFREY ALLEN,** archivist, consultant, historian, researcher; s. Lewis Allen and Helen Louise Mifflin; m. Wendy Sue Kalish, 1988. AB cum laude, Harvard U., Cambridge, Mass., 1980; JD, Northeastern U., Boston, 1983; MA in History, U. Mass., Boston, 1992; MS in Libr. and Info. Sci., Simmons Libr. Sch., Boston, 1998. Asst. archivist McLean Hosp., Belmont, Mass., 1986—90, Harvard Collection Hist. Scientific Instruments, 1990—92; archives and manuscript specialist Mass. Inst. Tech., 1992—; archivist and curator Mass. Gen. Hosp., 1998—. Cons. Pioneer Group, Boston, 1998—2002. Contbr. articles to profl. jour., chapters to books. Recipient Infinite Mile award, Mass. Inst. Tech., 2001. Mem.: Archivists and Libr. in the History Health Scis., Am. Assn. for the History Medicine, Soc. Am. Archivists. Achievements include research in relationship of historical objects to the documentary record. Home: 18 Douglas Rd Medford MA 02155 Office: Mass Gen Hosp RSL 110 55 Fruit St Boston MA 02114 Office Phone: 617-726-3180.

**MIFTAHOF, ROUSTEM NARIMANOVICH,** science educator, researcher; b. Kazan, Russia, Apr. 5, 1957; s. Nariman A. and Sofie K. Miftahof; m. Grace Sh. Sawan, May 20, 1997; 1 child, Jasmine Sofie. MD (hon.), Kazan Med. Inst., Russia, 1980; MS in Applied Math., Kazan State U., Russia, 1981, PhD in Math. and Physics, 1983; DS in Technical Scis., Moscow, 1989. Prof. Korea Advanced Inst. Sci. and Tech., Daejeon, Republic of Korea, 2006. Prin. scientist Acad. Scis., Kazan, 1984—87. Author: Biomechanics of the Small Intestine. Recipient Bronze medal, Acad. Scis., USSR, 1984. Achievements include design of software to simulate the neurogastrobiology of the gastrointestinal tract. Office Phone: 82-042-869-4878. Personal E-mail: rmif@amath.kaist.ac.kr.

**MIGALA, LUCYNA J.,** journalist, broadcast executive, artistic director; b. Krakow, Poland, May 22, 1944; came to U.S., 1947, naturalized, 1955; d. Joseph and Estelle (Suwala) M.; m. Frank A. Cizon, Oct. 9, 1998. Student, Loyola U., Chgo., 1962-63, Chgo. Conservatory of Music, 1963-70; BS in Journalism, Northwestern U., 1966. Radio announcer, prodr. Sta. WOPA, Oak Park, Ill., 1963—66; writer, reporter, prodr. NBC News, Chgo., 1966—69, 1969—71; prodr. NBC local news, Washington, 1969; prodr., coord. NBC network news, Cleve., 1971—78, field prodr. Chgo., 1978—79; v.p. Migala Comm. Corp., 1979—. Program and news dir., on-air personality Sta. WCEV, Cicero, Ill., 1979—; lectr. City Colls., Chgo., 1981, Morton Coll., 1988. Columnist Free Press, Chgo., 1984-87. Founder, artistic dir., gen. mgr. Lira Ensemble (formerly The Lira Singers), Chgo., 1965—, Artist-in-residence, Loyola U., Chgo.; mem., chmn. various cultural coms. Polish Am. Congress, 1970-80; bd. dir. Nationalities Svcs. Ctr., Cleve., 1973-78; bd. dir. v.p. Cicero-Berwyn Fine Arts Coun., Cicero, Ill., 1980-87; mem. City Arts I and II panels Chgo. Office Fine Arts, 1986-89, 94; v.p. Chgo. chpt. Kosciuszko Found., 1983-86; bd. dir. Polish Women's Alliance Am., 1983-87, Ill. Humanities Coun., 1983-89, mem. exec. com., 1986-87; bd. dir. Ill. Arts Alliance, 1989-92; founder, gen. chmn. Midwest Chopin Piano Competition (later Chgo. Chopin Competition), 1984-86; founding mem. ethnic and folk arts panel Ill. Arts Coun., 1984-87, 92-94; mem. Polonia Census 2000 Com.;

bd. dir.Polish-Am. Leadership Initiative, Chgo., 2001—; trustee Lincoln Acad. Ill., 2005—. Fellow Washington Journalism Ctr., 1969; decorated Cavalier's Cross of Merit Govt. Poland; recipient AP Broadcasters award, 1973, Emmy award NATAS, 1974, Cultural Achievement award Am. Coun. Polish Culture, 1990, award of merit Advocates Soc. Polish Am. Attys., 1991, Human Rels. Media award City of Chgo., 1992, Outstanding Achievement award Minister Fgn. Affairs Rep. of Poland, 1994, Civic Achievement award Polish Am. Hist. Assn., 2000, Nat. Creative Arts award Polish Am. Hist. Soc., 2003, Beautiful Spirit award Keep Chgo. Beautiful, Inc., 2005. Mem. Soc. Profl. Journalists. Office: Sta WCEV 5356 W Belmont Ave Chicago IL 60641-4103 also: The Lira Ensemble 6525 N Sheridan Rd # Sky905 Chicago IL 60626-5344 Business E-Mail: limgala@liraensemble.com.

**MIGDAL, NELSON,** lawyer; b. Bronx, May 4, 1953; BA cum laude, Hofstra U., 1975; JD cum laude, Union U. (Albany Law Sch.), 1978. Bar: NY 1979, US Dist. Ct. (No. Dist. NY) 1978, DC 1988. Exec. ptnr. Holland & Knight LLP, Washington, 1998—2001, ptnr., mem. dir. com., chmn., real estate dept., Nat. Practice Development Task Force. Adj. prof. Broome Community Coll., 1985—88; instr. Real Estate Tng. Inst., 1986, Graduate Realtor Inst., 1991—95, Real Estate Edn. Found., 1992—94, Nat. Edn. Network, 1992—95, Comml. Property News, 1998—2002, featured spkr., 1999—, BOMA Broadband Confs., 2000—02, IRR Bldg. Access Confs., 2000—04, Lodging Conf., 1999—2004, RealShare, 2000—04, RealCom, 2001—02; co-chair Global Hospitality Industry Practice Group; mem. Directors Com.; co-chmn. Nat. Client Development Policy Com. Mem. Albany Law Review, 1977—78; author: "The Model Agreement" for Telecommunications Building Access, "Building Access Made Easy"; Contbg. author Real Estate Forum, Real Estate Investor, Legal Times, Washington Bus. Jour., founding editor and regular contbr. Property Writes (Holland & Knight LLP), 1997—2004; contbr. articles to profl. jours. Mem.: ABA, DC Bar, Justinian Soc., Phi Sigma Alpha. Office: Holland & Knight LLP 2099 Pennsylvania Ave NW Ste 100 Washington DC 20006 Office Phone: 202-457-5925. Business E-Mail: nmigdal@hklaw.com.

**MIGDOL, MARVIN JACOB,** public relations and marketing executive, consultant; b. Rochester, N.Y., Jan. 11, 1937; s. Frank and Dorothy (Krieger) M.; m. Frances Scheiner, June 13, 1959 (div. June 1970); children: Helene Ellen, Steven Gary, Larry Jay; m. Grace Miron, Dec. 26 1970 (div. Aug. 1986); children: Michael Alan, Susan Renee, Honi Faith; m. Roni Habel, June 30, 1991 (div. Dec. 1992); m. Fay Herschberg, Dec. 27, 2003. BA in Sociology, U. Buffalo, 1959; postgrad., U. Miami, 1959-60; MS in Communications, Boston U., 1961. Dir. pub. rels. United Fund, Reading, Pa., 1961-63, Rensselaer Poly. Inst., Troy, NY, 1963-64, Touro Infirmary, New Orleans, 1964, Hamot Hosp., Erie, Pa., 1964-65, United Jewish Fedn., Buffalo, 1965-68; pres. Marvin J. Migdol Inc., Dallas, 1968—. Instr. Boston U., 1962—, Pa. State U., U. Tex., 1962—; Collin County C.C., Plano, 1990-91. Author: Public Relations Handbook, 1963, Comics as a Public Relations Tool in Communications, 1971, The Migdol Manual, 1972, Success in the 1990's, 1987, Greater Virility: Overcoming Impotence, 1993; contbr. numerous articles to profl. jours. Reporter Rep. Nat. Conv., Dallas, 1964; asst. dist. commr. Boy Scouts Am., Dallas, 1980-85; exec. bd. dirs. EPCOT Resorts, Lake Buena Vista, Fla., 1992—; v.p. Am. Jewish Congress, S.W. Region, 2001-05; v.p. Am. Friends of Magen David Adoin, 2004—; commencement U. Phoenix, Dallas, 2005. Recipient Pub. Rels. award Coun. Jewish Welfare Funds & Fedn., N.Y.C., 1967, Nat. Bus. League, West Palm Beach, Fla., 1968, Merit award Big Brothers & Sisters, Dallas, Tex., 1987, Major League Volleyball award San Jose, Calif., 1987.; named Entrepreneur of the Yr. Venture Mag., Dallas, Tex., 1987 Mem. U.S. Profl. Mktg. Assn. (pres. 1990—), Am. Assn. Indsl. Editors (bd. dirs. 1967-70), Am. Coll. Pub. Rels. Assn. (bd. dirs. 1964-66), Inst. for Info. and Comm. (bd. dirs. 1971—), Dallas Belles (dir. mktg. and pub. rels. 1987—), Jewish Nat. Fund (area dir.), Dallas Bridge Assn. (chmn. publicity), Dallas C. of C. (mem. econ. and internat. coun.), U. Buffalo Alumni Assn. We. Pa. and Tex., 1964-65, Temple Shalom (vice chmn. bldg. fund 1971-72, mem. Brotherhood bd. 1985-86), Jewish Cmty. Ctr., Am. Contract Bridge League (chmn. pub. rels. 1989—; award Memphis chpt. 1983-87), Alpha Epsilon Pi (gov., 1970-79), Phi Delta Phi, (v.p. 1959-60, treas. 1960—). Jewish. Avocations: writer, lecturer, baseball and softball umpire, Boy Scout leader. Office: CAREington Internat Corp 7400 Gaylord Pkwy Frisco TX 75034 Home: 18715 Gibbons Dr Dallas TX 75287 Office Phone: 469-252-5816. Personal E-mail: fmmigdol@comcast.net.

**MIGHELL, KENNETH JOHN,** lawyer; b. Schenectady, N.Y., Mar. 17, 1931; s. Richard Henry and Ruth Alice (Simon) M.; m. Julia Anne Carstarphen, Aug. 24, 1961; children: Thomas Lowry, Elizabeth Anne. BBA, U. Tex., 1952, JD, 1957. Bar: Tex. 1957. Assoc. Scurry, Scurry, Pace & Wood, Dallas, 1957-61; asst. U.S. Atty. Justice Dept., Dallas, 1961-77; 1st asst. No. Dist. Tex., 1972-77; U.S. Atty. No. Dist., Tex., 1977-81; ptnr. Cowles & Thompson, Dallas, 1981-96, of counsel, 1996—. Chmn. bd. mgmt. Downtown Dallas YMCA, 1974-76; pres. Dallas Area Am. Lung Assn., 1985-87; bd. dirs. YMCA Met. Dallas, 1987—; imm. adv. bd. Southwestern Law Enforcement Inst., 1994-98; mem. SW Legal Found., CLE adv. com. 1999-2003. With USN, 1952-54; capt. USNR, 1954-78. Mem.: FBA, Nat. Assn. Former U.S. Attys. (pres. 1995), State Bar Tex. (bd. dirs. 1994—95), Dallas Bar Found. (trustee 1994—, chmn. 1999—2000, chmn. 2001—02), Dallas Bar Assn. (bd. dirs. 1984—89, chmn. 1989, v.p. 1990—91, pres. 1993). Democrat. Methodist. Office: Cowles & Thompson 901 Main St Ste 4000 Dallas TX 75202-3793 E-mail: kmighell@cowlesthompson.com.

**MIGID, ADEL A.,** theater educator, set designer, consultant; arrived in U.S., 1970; s. A. Migid Hamzza and Fatma Ibraheem; m. Somaya A. Migid, June 20, 1969; children: Jeffrey Adel, Amy Adel. MFA in Theatre and Prodn. Design and Tech., Ohio U., Athens, 1972. Grad. tchg. fellow Ohio U., Athens, 1969—72; asst. prof. W.Va. U., Morgantown, 1972—75; assoc. prof. and guest artist U. Mont., Missoula, 1975—76; assoc. prof. and designer Wright State U., Dayton, Ohio, 1976—79; assoc. prof. and guest artist U. S.D., Vermillion, 1979—80; prof. Sch. Dance, Theatre and Arts Adminstrn. Coll. Fine Arts U. Akron, Ohio, 1980—. Asst. prof. and guest artist U. Tex., Austin, 1974; acting dept. head Sch. Dance, Theatre and Arts Adminstrn. Coll. Fine Arts U. Akron, Ohio, 1980—82, coord. undergrad. theatre program, 1983—86, dir. design and tech. program, 1983—85; U.S. del. Prague Internat. Conf. Design and Arch., 1983, 87, 91, 95, 99; vice commr. scenic design commn. U.S. Inst. Theatre Tech., 1983—86, ednl. commn. condr. survey grad. and undergraduate theatre programs, 1986—88, vice commr. and chair programming ednl. commn., 1988—92; mem. U.S. cultural exch., England, Austria, Czechoslovakia, Poland and Russia, 1987; guest artist and master class condr. Nat. Inst. Arts, Beijing, 1985; vis. prof. and guest artist Ohio U., 1986; lectr. and presenter Ohio Ednl. Theatre Assn. Ann. Confs., 1995—2003; cons. theatre arch. Performing Arts Facility, Brunswick, Ohio, 1997—99, Guzzetta Hall U. Akron, 2000; invited mem. People to People Theatre Prodn. Delegation, Australia, 1999; mem. bd. trustees Fulbright Commn., 2005; mem. rev. and evaluation com. Internat. Fulbright Sr. Scholars Program, 2005—05; internat. prodn. and design cons.; lectr. and presenter profl. seminars and confs. Designer: (work published in) Design and Stage Lighting, by Parker, Smith and Wolf, 1985—88; contbr. designs to profl. publs., articles to profl. jours.; one-man shows include Cairo Opera House Art Gallery, 2004, prin. works include prodn. design Dionne Warwick and Burt Bacharach "Las Vegas" tour, Kool and the Gang "Funky" tour, Anne Murray "Tastefully Glitzy" tour, ARACEMCO Indsl. Exhibit Wing, Cairo Internat. Trade Fair, 1992, Our Town, Cairo Opera House, 2004, exhibitions include Ann. Theatre Design Exhbn. Contest, Ohio U., Athens, 1971 (First prize), Nat. Intercollegiate Scene Design Exhbn. and Competition, Carbondale, Ill., 1972 (First prize), Nat. Intercollegiate Costume Designs Exhbn. and Competition, 1972 (First prize), Internat. Prague Quadrennial Theatre Design and Arch., 1987 (First prize, Internat. Gold medal), Art Gallery Lincoln Ctr. Performing Arts, N.Y.C., 1989, Internat. Opera Am. and Opera Guild Internat. Conf., Vancouver, B.C., 1999, Art Gallery Myers Sch. Art, Akron, Ohio, 1999, Profl. Design Expo 2000 U.S. Inst. Theatre Tech., Denver, 2000. Mem. bd. trustees Friends of Egypt, 2005. Recipient Outstanding Tchr. of Yr., W.Va. U., 1972, U. Tex., 1975, Dept. Theatre Arts U. Akron, 1984, 1985; fellow,

Carnegie Tchg. Acad., 2003; grantee, Ednl. Rsch. Ctr. U.Akron, 1983, 1986, 1987, Ednl. Commn. U.S. Inst. Theatre Tech., 1992—95, Carnegie Tchg. Acad. SOTAL, 2003—04, Fulbright Sr. scholar award, 2004, U. Akron, 2005. Mem.: United Scenic Artists N.Y. Avocations: sports, tennis, swimming, gardening. Office: Coll Fine Arts U Akron Akron OH 44325-1005 Home: 481 N Portage Path Akron OH 44303 Office Phone: 330-972-6082.

**MIGIELICZ, GERALYN,** photojournalist; b. St. Louis, Feb. 15, 1958; d. Edward J. and Mary Ann (McCarthy) M. BJ, U. Mo., 1979. Photographer Emporia (Kans.) Gazette, 1979-80; chief photographer St. Joseph (Mo.) News-Press & Gazette, 1980-83; photo editor, photographer Seattle Times, 1984; picture editor Rocky Mountain News, Denver, 1985-86; graphics editor San Jose (Calif.) Mercury News, 1986-92, dir. photography, 1992—. Mem. faculty Poynter Inst., U. Mo. Workshop, Latin Am. Photojournalism Conf., Stan Kalish Picture Editing Workshop. Knight fellow Stanford U., 2005; recipient Individual Editing awards Soc. Newspaper Designers, 1988-04, Editing awards, 91-01; named for Overall Excellence in Editing, Picture of Yr. Contest, U. Mo., 1993. Office: San Jose Mercury News 750 Ridder Park Dr San Jose CA 95131-2432

**MIGIMOTO, FUMIYO KODANI,** retired secondary school educator; b. Oxnard, Calif, Jan. 2, 1918; d. Katsutaro and Yoshio Kodani; m. Tadao Migimoto, June 1956. BA, UCLA, 1939, cert. teaching, 1940; MA, Oberlin Coll., 1953; cert. in teaching, U. Hawaii, 1956. Cert. secondary tchr., Calif., Hawaii. Asst. to dean of coll. Oberlin Coll., Ohio; English tchr. Jackson Coll., Honolulu, Hawaii State Dept. Edn.; Honolulu; retired. Mem. textbook evaluation com., Hawaii. Author many poems, editor, military newsletters 1993-1999. Grantee, Hawaii State Dept. Edn. Mem ASCD, Internat. Soc. Poets, Pan-Pacific S.E. Asia Women's Assn. Hawaii (past exec. v.p.), Hawaii Edn. Assn., Hawaii State Retired Tchr. Assn., Oahu Retired Tchr. Assn., Alliance for Drama Edn., UCLA Alumni Assn., Oberlin Alumni Assn., Poetry Acad., Alpha Delta Kappa (past chpt. exec. pres., chmn. frat. edn.). Home: 999 Wilder Ave Apt 303 Honolulu HI 96822-2628

**MIGITA, RUSSELL,** pediatrician, emergency physician; b. Honolulu, Hawaii, Dec. 23, 1967; s. Roy and Janice Migita; m. Jenni Zanatta. AB, Stanford U., Palo Alto, Calif., 1991; MD, U. Calif., San Diego, Calif., 1995. Staff physician Emergency Svcs. Children's Hosp. and Regional Med. Ctr., Seattle, 1998—; clin. asst. prof. pediat. Sch. Medicine U. Wash., Seattle, 2005—. Fellow: Am. Acad. Pediat. Office: Seattle Children's Hospital 4800 Sand Point Way NE Seattle WA 98105 Office Phone: 206-987-2599.

**MIGLIARO, MARCO WILLIAM,** electrical engineer; b. N.Y.C., Mar. 29, 1948; s. Marco Salvatore and Anna (Dalton) M.; children: Kristen Marie, Meredith Anne, Marie Angela, Marco Thomas; m. Jasoda Badlu, Nov. 19, 1988. BEE, Pratt Inst., 1969; postgrad., N.J. Inst. Tech., 1970-72. Registered profl. engr., N.Y., N.J., Pa., Mass., Fla. Engr. Am. Electric Power, N.Y., 1969-78; staff engr. Gibbs & Hill, Inc., N.Y.C., 1978-81; sr. cons. engr. Ebasco Svcs., Inc., N.Y.C., 1981-88; tech. mgr. ABB Impell Corp., Melville, NY, 1988-90; sr. staff specialist for nuc. engring. Fla. Power & Light, Juno Beach, 1990-96, chief elec./I&C engr., 1996—2003; pres. ESA Cons. Engrs., PA, Jupiter, Fla., 2003—; pres., CEO IEEE Industry Stds. and Tech. Orgn., 2003—. Developer seminar on stationary batteries, 1987. Contbg. author: Handbook of Power Calculations, 1984, 99, Standard Handbook for Electrical Engineers, 1999, 2006; also articles. Recipient Meritorious Svc. award Am. Nat. Standards Inst., 1994. Fellow IEEE (pres. 2001—, stds. assn. bd. govs. 1998—, bd. dirs. 1990-92, 2001, fin. com. 1990-92, dir. stds. 1990-91, mem. exec. com. 1992, v.p. stds. activities, 1992, 2001, Stds. medal 1984, Stds. Bd. Disting. Svc. award 1993, Charles Proteus Steinmetz award 1996, Third Millennium medal 2000); mem. IEEE Power Engring. Soc. (Disting. Svc. award 1988, 92), Industry Standards and Tech. Orgn. (bd. dirs. 2000—, chmn. 2000-03). Avocations: fishing, travel. Home: PO Box 9253 Jupiter FL 33468-9253 Office: ESA Cons Engrs PA PO Box 9251 Jupiter FL 33468-9251 Office Phone: 561-691-1946. Business E-Mail: marco@esaconsulting.com.

**MIGLIO, SHERYL ANN,** computer scientist; d. Henry Roger and Eileen Miglio; m. George Grant Miglio; m. Dean Boudway Miglio, Nov. 8, 1979; children: Eric Brian Hiltpold, Kevin Andrew Hiltpold. MA in Curriculum Devel., George Mason U., 2002. Specialist employee devel. Manpower and Resources Affairs U.S. Army, Alexandria, Va., 1989—96; specialist employee devel. Dept. of Army, Fort Belvoir, Va., 1996—2001; program and mgmt. analyst Def. Energy Support Ctr., Fort Belvoir, Va., 2001—. Trainer americans with disabilities act Disability Law, Richmond, Va., 1990—93. Recipient Cold War cert., Dept. Def., 1945—91. Mem.: ASCD (assoc.), Soc. Applied Learning Tech. Conservative. Achievements include design of FEMA emergency response online training. Avocations: rock gardening, music, dog training. Office: Defense 8725 John J Kingman Road Fort Belvoir VA 22060

**MIGLIORATO, LYNNE GYURISIN,** elementary school educator; b. Homestead, Pa., Feb. 27, 1940; d. Frank and Margaret (Turoczy) Gyurisin; m. Andrew Migliorato, Feb. 14, 1967. BS in Edn., Duquesne U., 1962. Elem. tchr. West Mifflin (Pa.) Area Sch. Dist., tchr. kindergarten, 1962-97; retired, 1997. Mem. Pa. Assn. Sch. Retirees, Allegheny County Tchrs. Ret. Assn., Am. Fedn. Tchrs., Delta Kappa Gamma (v.p. membership, chmn.) Office: Clara Barton Elem Sch 764 Beverly Dr West Mifflin PA 15122-3235

**MIGLIS, THOMAS G.,** financial services company executive; BBA, Baruch Coll. Mem. audit staff Coopers & Lybrand; various positions including chief info. officer Salomon Smith Barney; mng. dir. to exec. mng. dir. global systems group Bankers Trust NY Corp., also prnr.; chief info. officer Citadel Investment Group LLC, Chgo., 2001—, also mem. mgmt. com. Named one of Premier 100 IT Leaders, Computerworld, 2005. Office: Citadel Investment Group LLC 131 S Dearborn St Chicago IL 60603*

**MIGNONE, MARIO B.,** language educator; came to U.S., 1960; m. Lois Mignone, June 29, 1968; children: Pamela Anne, Cristina Maria, Elizabeth Maria. BA, CCNY, 1967; MA, Rutgers U., 1969, PhD, 1972. Disting. prof. Italian lang. SUNY, Stony Brook, 1970—, dir. undergrad. studies, 1976-83, dir. grad. studies, 1983-87; founder, exec. dir. Ctr. for Italian Studies, chmn. French and Italian dept., Stony Brook, 1988—98. Author: The Theater of Eduardo De Filippo, 1974, Abnormality and Anguish in the Narrative of Dino Buzzati, 1981, Eduardo De Filippo, 1984, Pirandello in America, 1988, Columbus: Meeting of Cultures, 1993, Italy Today: A Country in Transition, 1995, Italy Today: At the Crossroads of the New Millennium, 1998; assoc. mng. editor Forum Italicum, 1986-94, editor, 1994—; contbr. articles to profl. jours. Mem. coll. coun. SUNY, Old Westbury. Mem. Am. Assn. Tchrs. Italian (pres. 1982-84), Am. Italian Am. Educators (pres. 1997—), Am. Italian Hist. Assn. (mem. coll. coun. SUNY, Old Westbury). Office: SUNY Dept European Langs Lits Stony Brook NY 11794-3359 Office Phone: 631-632-6223. Business E-Mail: mmignone@notes.cc.sunysb.edu.

**MIGNOT, EMMANUEL,** medical researcher; Student, Ecole Normale Supérieure, Paris; MD, René Descartes Sch. Medicine, Paris V Univ., 1984; PhD, Paris VI Univ., 1984. Cert. Sleep Disorders Am. Bd. Sleep Medicine. Resident Necker Enfants Malades Hosp., Paris, 1985, intern, 1984; dir. Stanford Ctr. for Narcolepsy Stanford U. Sch. Med., 1993—, acting asst. prof. psychiatry & behavioral sciences, 2001—2001, prof. psychiatry & behavioral sciences, 2001—, assoc. prof. medicine; founder Hypnion Inc., 2000—; investigator Howard Hughes Med. Inst., 2002—. Editorial bd. Sleep, Sleep Medicine, Sleep Rsch. Online; bd. dirs. Nat. Sleep Found., chair Narcolepsy Coun.; Nat. Ctr. for Sleep Disorders adv. panel NIH. Recipient Health Rsch. award, Nat. Sleep Found., Rsch. award, NIH, Profl. Svc. award, Narcolepsy Network, Drs. C. & F. Demuth 11th award for Young Ingestigators in the Neurosciences, WC Dement Academic Achievement award, McKnight Achievement award, W. Alden Spencer award, Jacobaeus Prize. Mem.: Inst. Medicine. Achievements include discovery of cause of narcolepsy. Office: Stanford Hosp Sleep Disorders Clinic #3301 MC 5730 401 Quarry Rd Stanford CA 94305*

**MIGNOUNA, HODEBA-JACOB DOUWEHAN,** geneticist, researcher; arrived in U.S., 2000; s. Issoga Douwehan Mignouna and Homnaka Memina Ganda; m. Enyonam-Philomene Adjoua Messanvi; children: Dila Dahlia, Harry Salim Jonathan. Baccalaureat, Coll. Chaminade, Kara, Togo, 1971—78; Chem. engring., Faculty of Agronomic Sci., Louvain-La-Neuve, Belgium, 1978—83; D of Agrl. Sci., Faculty of Agronomic Sci., Louvain-La-Neuve- Belgium, 1984—90. Sr. scientist internat. Inst. of Tropical Agr., Ibadan, Nigeria, 1992—2000; vis. rsch. fellow Cornell U., Ithaca, NY, 2000—02; chem. engr. Dept. of Agrl. Products and Control Services, Lome, Togo; assoc. rsch. prof. Va. State U., Petersburg, Va., 2002—. Cons. World Bank, Washington, 2002. Mem. polit. party Union for Justice and devel., Lome, Togo, 1990—97. Grantee Tech. Vol. assistance for Devel., USAID, 2002-2008. Mem.: AAAS, Crop Sci. Soc. of Am. (assoc.). Achievements include research in many markers for developing improved rice cltivars. Office: African Agricultural Tech Foundation c/o ILRI PO Box 30709 Nairobi Kenya Office Phone: 1-650 833 6660. Office Fax: 1-650 833 6661. Business E-Mail: h.mignouna@aatf-africa.org.

**MIGOYA, CARLOS,** bank executive; b. Cuba; Grad., Fla. Internat. U., 1976. With Southeast Bank, 1974—91; pres. Consolidated Bank, 1991; with First Union Nat. Bank; pres. Miami-Dade County region Wachovia Corp., CEO Atlantic region, 2006—. Bd. dirs. Take Stock in Children, Miami-Dade County Cultural Affairs Coun., chmn., 2006; bd. dirs. Miami Bus. Forum. Office: Wachovia Corp 1 Wachovia Ctr Charlotte NC 28288-0013*

**MIGUE, JEAN LUC,** economics professor; b. Montreal, Que., Can., Apr. 13, 1933; s. Joseph Alfred and Marie Laurence (Venne) M.; m. Renee Caron, Sept. 13, 1958; children: Paule, Pascal, Nicolas. BA in Econs, U. Montreal, 1953, MA, 1956; PhD in Econs, Am. U., 1968. Researcher Bank of Can., 1957-58; prof. Laval U., 1962-70; prof. econs. Nat. Sch. Public Adminstrn., Quebec, 1970-99. Mem. staff Econ. Coun. Can., 1973-74 Author: The Price of Health, 1974, Le Prix du Transport, 1978, Nationalistic Policies of Canada, 1979, L'Economiste et La chose Publique, 1979, The Public Monopoly of Education, 1989, Federalism and Free Trade, 1993, Etatisme et Declin du quebec, 1999, Le Monopole de La Santé, 2001, Statism and Health in France, 2005, On N'a Pas Les Gouvernements Qu'on Merite, 2006. Fellow Massey Found., 1956, sr. fellow, The Fraser Inst. Fellow Royal Soc. Can.; mem, Mont Pelerin Soc. Roman Catholic. Office Phone: 418-655-5733. E-mail: jlmigue@videotron.ca.

**MIHAILA, GEORGE ANDREI,** computer scientist, researcher; b. Bucharest, Romania, June 18, 1967; arrived in U.S., 2000; s. Gheorghe and Violeta Marcela Mihaila; m. Haritina Gratiela Dobrescu, Nov. 28, 2000; children: Maria, Irina Violeta. BS, U. Bucharest, 1990; MS, U. Toronto, 1996, PhD, 2000. Jr. rschr. Informatics Rsch. Inst., Bucharest, 1990—91; asst. prof. U. Bucharest, 1990—93; software engr. Omnis Group Inc., Bucharest, 1991—92, Ciel Romania, Bucharest, Romania, 1992—93, Ahearn & Soper Inc., Toronto, Canada, 1993—94; rsch. staff mem. T. J. Watson Rsch. Ctr. IBM, Hawthorne, NY, 2000—. Adj. asst. prof. Columbia U., N.Y., 2002—. Author: Publishing, Locating, and Querying Networked Information Sources (award Romanian Acad., 2002). Mem.: Assn. Computing Machinery. Home: 1724 Central St Yorktown Heights NY 10598 Office: IBM TJ Watson Research Center 19 Skyline Drive Hawthorne NY 10532 Office Phone: +1-914-784-7803. Personal E-mail: george.mihaila@gmail.com. Business E-Mail: mihaila@us.ibm.com.

**MIHAL, SANDRA POWELL,** research scientist; b. Balt., Dec. 15, 1941; d. Sanford William and Mary Louise (Barry) Powell; m. James George Anderson, June 15, 1963; children: Robin Marie, James Brian, Melissa Lee, Derek Clair; m. Charles Turner Barber, Apr. 18, 1978; stepchildren: Gretchen Jayco, Katrina Hope; m. Ladislaw Paul Mihal, May 25, 1991; stepchildren: Alexander Paul, Suzie May, Natasha Elizabeth, Rudy Darius. BA, Mt. St. Agnes Coll., 1963; MA, N.Mex. State U., 1970, PhD, 1975; EdD, Vanderbilt U., 1990. Cert. tchr., Md. Tchr. Ridgely-Dulaney Jr. H.S., Towson, Md., 1964; grad. asst. N.Mex. State U., Las Cruces, 1967—69; acad. advisor, instr. polit. sci. Purdue U., West Lafayette, Ind., 1974—78; prof., acad. sys. analyst U. So. Ind., Evansville, 1978—82; assoc. prof., chair dept. computer info. sys. Henderson Ky. C.C., 1982—88; prof. computer tech., divsn. chair Anne Arundel C.C., Arnold, Md., 1988—91; sys. analyst immigration and naturalization svc. Dept. of Justice, Washington, 1991—92, sr. rsch. sys. analyst immigration and naturalization svc. Glynco, Ga., 1995—; dep. program mgr. distributed learning Fed. Law Enforcement Training Ctr., Homeland Security, Glynco, Ga., 2002—. Bd. dirs. Ind. Polit. Sci. Assn. Muncie, 1984-88, Internat. Studies Assn.-Midwest, Chgo., 86-88; pres. Ky. Acad. Computer Users' Group, Lexington, 1985-86; telecom. adv. bd. C.C. Sys., Annapolis, Md., 1990-91; computer sys. network analyst CLARC Svcs., Pt. Charlotte, Fla., 92-95; adj. prof. history and polit. sci. Edison C.C., Punta Gorda, Fla., 1993-95; spkr. in fied Author: Learning By Doing BASIC, 1983, Computers Learning By Doing, 1984; contbr. articles to profl. jours Block coord. several neighborhood assns.; computer adv. bd. Henderson County Sch., 1982-88; chmn. Newburgh (Ind.) Youth Orgn., 78-86; judge Sci. Fair, Annapolis, 1989-90; nomination bd. Ky. Higher Edn. Assn., 1989-91; mem Charlotte Chorale, Port Charlotte, 1992-94, Peace River Power Squadron, Port Charlotte, 1994-96. Coast Guard Aux., 1995-97. Fellow, Sloan Found., 1973—75, U. Ky. Award, Ky. C.C., 2003; scholar, Md. State Tchr. Bd. Edn., 1960—63. Mem, Soc. Applied Learning Tech., Assn. Computing Machinery (v.p. 85—), Am. Legion, Pi Gamma Mu. Democrat. Mem. Ch. Of Christ. Avocations: sailing, singing, swimming, cooking, music. Home: 112 Oak Ridge Rd Brunswick GA 31523-9741 Business E-Mail: sandy.mihal@dhs.gov.

**MIHALAS, DIMITRI MANUEL,** astrophysicist, educator; b. LA, Mar. 20, 1939; s. Emmanuel Demetrious and Jean (Christo) M.; children: Michael Demetrious, Alexandra Genevieve. BA with highest honors, UCLA, 1959; MS, Calif. Inst. Tech., 1960, PhD, 1963. Asst. prof. astrophys. scis. Princeton U., 1964-67; asst. prof. U. Colo., 1967-68; assoc. prof. astronomy and astrophysics U. Chgo., 1968-70, prof., 1970-71; adj. prof. astrogeophysics, also physics and astrophysics U. Colo., 1972-80; sr. scientist High Altitude Obs., Nat. Center Atmospheric Research, Boulder, Colo., 1971-79, 82-85; G.C. McVittie prof. astronomy U. Ill., 1985-98; astronomer Sacramento Peak Obs., Sunspot, N.Mex., 1979-82; mem. staff Los Alamos (N.Mex.) Nat. Lab., 1998—2004, fellow, 2004—. Cons. Los Alamos Nat. Lab. 1981-98; vis. prof. dept. astrophysics Oxford (Eng.) U., 1977-78; sr. vis. fellow dept. physics and astronomy Univ. Coll., London, 1978; mem. astronomy adv. panel NSF, 1972-75 Author: Galactic Astronomy, 1969, 2d edit, 1981, Stellar Atmospheres, 1970, 2d edit., 1978, Theorie des Atmospheres Stellaires, 1971, Foundations of Radiation Hydrodynamics, 1984; assoc. editor Astrophys. Jour, 1970-79, Jour. Computational Physics, 1981-87, Jour. Quantitative Spectroscopy, 1984-94; mem. editorial bd. Solar Physics, 1981-89. NSF fellow, 1959-62; Van Maanen fellow, 1962-63; Eugene Higgins vis. fellow, 1963-64; Alfred P. Sloan Found. Research fellow, 1969-71; Alexander von Humboldt Stiftung sr. U.S. scientist awardee, 1984. Mem. U.S. Nat. Acad. Sci., Internat. Astron. Union (pres. commn. 36 1976-79), Am. Astron. Soc. (pub. bd. 1995-99, mem. coun. 2000—03, Helen B. Warner prize 1974). Astron. Soc. Pacific (dir. 1975-77) Home: PO Box 806 Los Alamos NM 87544-0806 Office: Los Alamos Nat Lab X-3 MS-F644 Los Alamos NM 87545-0001 Office Phone: 505-665-4529. Business E-Mail: dmihalas@lanl.gov.

**MIHALY, EUGENE BRAMER,** diversified financial services company executive, consultant; b. The Hague, The Netherlands, Nov. 11, 1934; arrived in US, 1940; s. Eddy and Cecile (Bramer) Kahn; stepson of Eugene Mihaly; m. Stacey Beth Pulner, Apr. 21, 1996; children: Lisa Klee, Jessica; stepchildren: Stephanie Pulner, Andrew Pulner. AB magna cum laude, Harvard U., 1956; PhD, London Sch. Econs. and Polit. Sci., 1964. Aviation/space editor Hartford (Conn.) Courant, 1960-61; internat. economist AID, Washington, 1964-65; dep. dir. Peace Corps, Tanzania, 1966, dir., 1967-68, dep. dir. East Asia/Pacific bur. Washington, 1969, dir. office program devel., evaluation and rsch., 1969-70; assoc. dir. Inst. Internat. Studies, U. Calif., Berkeley, 1970-72; pres. Mihaly Internat. Corp., 1972—; chmn. bd. Mihaly Internat. Can., Ltd.,

1992—; sr. lectr. Haas Sch. Bus. U. Calif., Berkeley, 1991-95. Adj. prof. Amos Tuck Sch. Dartmouth Coll., 1997-2002; chmn. adv. bd. Northwood Fund Mgmt. Inc. Author: Foreign Aid and Politics in Nepal: A Case Study, 1965; contbr.: Political Development in Micronesia, 1974, Management of the Multinationals, 1974; also articles to various publs. Chmn. emeritus Calif.-S.E. Asia Bus. Coun.; chmn. Global R.I.; pres. Found. for Ocean State Pub. Radio; dir. Common Cause R.I.; trustee CC of RI Found. Mem. Coun. on Fgn. Rels., Appalachian Mountain Club (vice chmn.), Narragansett Hdqs. Club. Home: 4 Half Mile Rd Barrington RI 02806 Office Phone: 401-247-1418.

**MIHAN, RICHARD,** retired dermatologist; b. Dec. 20, 1925; s. Arnold and Virginia Catherine (O'Reilly) M. MD, St. Louis U., 1949. Diplomate Am. Bd. Dermatology. Intern L.A. County Gen. Hosp., 1949-51, resident in dermatology, 1954-57; pvt. practice in dermatology L.A., 1957-95; prof. emeritus U. So. Calif., 1989—. Lt. Comdr. USNR, 1951-53. Fellow ACP; mem. AMA, Pacific Dermatol. Assn. (exec. bd. 1971-74), Am. Acad. Dermatol., Calif. Med. Assn. (chmn. dermatol. sect. 1973-74), L.A. Met. Dermatology Soc. (pres. 1975-76), L.A. Acad. Medicine (pres. 1988-89), Order of St. John of Jerusalem, of Rhodes, and of Malta, Order of St. Lazarus (comdr.), Calif. Club. Roman Cath. Home: 3278 Wilshire Blvd Apt 503 Los Angeles CA 90010-1431

**MIHELIC, TRACEY L.,** lawyer; b. Lake Forest, Ill., Sept. 12, 1965; BA, Ill., 1990. With Gardner, Carton & Douglas, Chgo., 1990—2000, ptnr., 1998—2000, Baker & McKenzie, Chgo., 2000—. Mem.: ABA, Internat. Emissions Trading Assn., Emissions Mktg. Assn., Ill. State Bar Assn. Office: Baker and McKenzie One Prudential Plz 130 E Randolph Dr Chicago IL 60601

**MIHM, JOHN CLIFFORD,** chemical engineer; b. Austin, Tex., July 28, 1942; s. Clifford Henry and Adeline (Cleary) M.; m. Janet Eleanor Skales, May 29, 1964; 1 child, Mary Lynn AA, Frank Phillips Coll., 1962; BSChemE, Tex. Tech. U., 1964. Registered profl. engr., Tex., Okla. With Phillips Petroleum Co., 1964—2003, v.p. corp. engring. Bartlesville, Okla., 1987-92, v.p. R & D, 1992-93, sr. v.p. corp. tech., 1993-99, sr. v.p. tech. and project devel., 1999—2002; engr. mgr. E & P Phillips Petroleum Co., Stavanger, Norway, 1977-82; chmn. bd. Far East Energy Corp., 2005—. Mem. adv. bd. Tex. Tech U., Lubbock, 1985—, tres. deans coun., 1996-98. Bd. dirs. Boy Scouts Am., Bartlesville, 1986—; area III pres. 1998-2002, So. region bd. dirs., 1998—. Named Disting. Engr., Tex. Tech. U., 1984; named to Okla. State U. Coll. of Engring. Arch. and Tech. Hall of Fame, 1999. Fellow ASME (ind. adv. bd. 1989-2002, found. bd. dirs. 2000-03); mem. NSPE (mem. adv. bd. 1994-2002), AIChE (ECC divsn., bd. dirs. 1989-93, chmn. 1992-93), Okla. Soc. Profl. Engrs. (Outstanding Engr. in Mgmt. award 1991), Soc. Petroleum Engrs. (bd. dir. 2004-, Disting. Mem. 2000), Okla. Engring. Found. (bd. dirs., pres. 1993-97), Nat. Acad. Constrn. Republican. Roman Catholic. Home: 5413 Braemar Dr Frisco TX 75034 Office Phone: 972-658-8583. E-mail: jcmihmr66@aol.com.

**MIHM, MARTIN CHARLES, JR.,** pathologist, educator; s. Martin Charles and Cecilia Matilda (Hepp) M. AB, Duquesne U., 1955; MD, U. Pitts., 1961; MA (hon.), Harvard U., Cambridge, Mass., 1990. Diplomate Am. Bd. Dermatology, Am. Bd. Pathology. Intern Mt. Sinai Hosp., N.Y.C., 1961-62, resident in medicine, 1963-64; resident in dermatology Mass. Gen. Hosp., Boston, 1964-67, resident in Pathology, 1968-72, chief dermatopathology, 1973-94; asst. prof. pathology Harvard U. Med. Sch., Boston, 1972-75, assoc. prof., 1975-79, chief dermatopathology, 1982-93; prof. pathology Mass. Gen. Hosp.-Harvard U., Boston, 1980-93; prof., chief dermatopathology, dermatology Albany (N.Y.) Med. Coll., 1993—. Pathologist Malignant Melanoma Coop. Group, 1972—77; chmn. pathology com. Intergroup Melanoma Study, 1983—88; chief sr. adminstr. Wellman Labs., Mass. Gen. Hosp., 1985—93; cons. WHO, 1985—; adj. prof. pathology Vanderbilt U., 1989—; chmn. pathology standing com., 1991—; clin. prof. pathology Harvard Med. Sch., 1996—; sr. dermatopathologist and pathologist Mass. Gen. Hosp., 1996—; adj. prof. Thomas Jefferson Med. Sch., 2000—; prof. otolaryngology U. of Ark. Sch. of Med. Scis., 2002—. Author: Primer of Dermatopathology, 1984, 2d edit., 1992, Problematic Pigmented Lesions, 1990; co-author: Melanoma and Nevi, 1997, The Melanocytic Proliferations, 1991; editor: Lymphoproliferative Disorders of the Skin, 1986, Pathbiology and Recognition Malignant Melanoma, 1988, Dermatologia Practica, 2005; contbr. articles to med. jours.; overseer Boston Symphonic Orch., 2001—. Bd. overseers Boston (Mass.) Symphony Orch., 2001—. Served to comdr. USPHS, 1967-69. Recipient Gold Humanism award, Harvard Med. Sch., 2004. Fellow: ACP, Am. Soc. Dermatopathology, Am. Acad. Dermatology; mem.: AMA (Harvard Med. Sch. rep. to med. sch. sect. 1991), Annenberg Cir. of Dermatologic Found., Italian Assn. Ambulatory Dermatologists (hon.), Soc. of Dermatology, Mexico (hon.), Italian Soc. of Anatomic Pathology (hon.), Austrian Dermatology Soc. (hon.), Harvard Dermatology House Officer's Assn. (pres. 1982), Fort Orange Club, Albany, Harvard Club (Boston, N.Y.C.), Pi Gamma Mu, Alpha Omega Alpha. Independent. Roman Catholic. Home: 27 Chilton St Brookline MA 02446 Office: Mass Gen Hosp Warren Bldg 827 55 Fruit St Boston MA 02114 Office Phone: 617-724-1350. Business E-Mail: mmihm@partners.org.

**MIHM, MICHAEL MARTIN,** federal judge; b. Amboy, Ill., May 18, 1943; s. Martin Clarence and Frances Johannah (Morrissey) M.; m. Judith Ann Zosky, May 6, 1967; children— Molly Elizabeth, Sarah Ann, Jacob Michael, Jennifer Leah BA, Loras Coll., 1964; JD, St. Louis U., 1967. Asst. prosecuting atty. St. Louis County, Clayton, Mo., 1967-68; asst. state's atty. Peoria County, Peoria, Ill., 1968-69; asst. city atty. City of Peoria, Ill., 1969-72; state's atty. Peoria County, Peoria, Ill., 1972-80; sole practice Peoria, Ill., 1980-82; U.S. dist. judge U.S. Govt., Peoria, Ill. 1982—; chief U.S. dist. judge U.S. Dist. Ct. (ctrl. dist.) Ill., 1991—98. Chmn. com. internat. jud. rels. U.S. Jud. Conf., 1994—96. mem. exec. com. 1995—97, mem. com. jud. br., 1987—93, mem. com. internat. jud. rels., 1998—2002; mem. Supreme Ct. Fellows Commn., 2000—; adj. prof. law John Marshall Law Sch., 1990—. Past mem. adv. bd. Big Brothers-Big Sisters, Crisis Nursery, Peoria; past bd. dirs. Salvation Army, Peoria, W.D. Boyce council Boy Scouts Am., State of Ill. Treatment Alternatives to Street Crime, Gov.'s Criminal Justice Info. Council; past vice-chmn. Ill. Dangerous Drugs Adv. Council; trustee Proctor Health Care Found., 1991-2002. Recipient Good Govt. award Peoria Jaycees, 1978, Vincent C. Immel Alumni Merit award St. Louis U. Sch. Law, 1997, Disting. Alumnus in Pub. Svc. award Loras Coll., 2000, U.S. AID award for Outstanding Vol. Svc. in Russia, 2004. Mem. Peoria County Bar Assn. Roman Catholic. Office: US Dist Ct 204 Federal Bldg 100 NE Monroe St Peoria IL 61602-1003 Office Phone: 309-671-7113. Business E-Mail: michael_mihm@ilcd.uscourts.gov.

**MIHUC, TIMOTHY BRIAN,** science foundation director; b. Sierra Vista, Ariz., Dec. 14, 1963; s. Willard and Norma Mihuc; m. Janet Duncan, May 12, 1989; children: Sarah, Joshua. BS in Biology, Oral Roberts U., Tulsa, Okla. 1986; MS in Zoology, Okla. State U. Stillwater, 1989; PhD, Idaho State U., Pocatello, 1994. Rsch. asst. prof. coop fish and wildlife rsch. unit La. State U., Baton Rouge, 1994—96; field sta. dir. Ill. Natural History Survey, Alton, 1996—98; from asst. to assoc. prof. SUNY, Plattsburgh, 1999—. Contbr. over 25 articles to profl. jours. Bd. dirs. Lake Champlain Com., Burlington, Vt., 2004—06. Named Outstanding undergrad. student, Okla. Acad. Sci., 1986; fellow, USDA, 1996; grantee, NSF, 2001—05. Mem.: Internat. Soc. Theoretical and Applied Limnology, Ecol. Soc. Am., N.Am. Benthological Soc. (Best Poster Presentation- Hydrolab award 1994), Phi Kappa Phi. Office: LCRI SUNY Plattsburgh 101 Broad St Plattsburgh NY 12901 Home: 264 Clocqk Hill Rd Saranac NY 12981 Office Phone: 518-564-3038.

**MIKA, JOSEPH JOHN,** library director, educator; b. McKees Rocks, Pa., Mar. 1, 1948; s. George Joseph and Sophia Ann (Stec) Mika; m. Marianne Hartzell; children: Jason-Paul Joseph, Matthew Douglas, Meghan Leigh. BA in English, U. Pitts., 1969, MLS, 1971, PhD in Libr. Sci., 1980. Asst. libr., instr. Ohio State U., Mansfield, 1971-73; asst. libr., asst. prof. Johnson State Coll., Vt., 1973-75; grad. asst., tchg. fellow Sch. Libr. and Info. Sci., U. Pitts.,

1975-77; asst. dean, assoc. prof. libr. svc. U. So. Miss., Hattiesburg, 1977-86; dir. libr. and info. sci. program Wayne State U., 1986—95, 2002—, prof., 1986—. Cons. to librs.; co-owner Libr. Jobs Network, Libr. Tng. Network. Editor: Jour. Edn. Libr. and Info. Sci., 1995—2005. Col. USAR. Decorated DSM. Mem.: ALA (councilor 1983—86, chmn. constn. and bylaws com. 1985—86, councilor 1998—2001), Mich. Ctr. for Book (chair 1994—2001), Soc. Miss. Archivists (treas., exec. bd. 1981—83), Assn. Coll. and Rsch. Librs. (chmn., chmn. budget com. 1982—83), Leadership Acad., Mich. Libr. Assn., Miss. Libr. Assn. (pres.-elect 1985, chair libr. edn. com. 1989), Assn. Libr. and Info. Sci. and Edn. (chmn. nominating com. 1982, chmn. membership com. 1982—83, exec. bd. 1986), Kiwanis (Hattiesburg), Phi Delta Kappa, Beta Phi Mu (pres.-elect. 1987—89, pres. 1989—91). Home: 222 Abbott Woods Dr East Lansing MI 48823-1995 Office: Wayne State U Libr and Info Sci Program 106 Kresge Library Detroit MI 48202 Office Phone: 313-577-6196. Business E-mail: aa2500@wayne.edu.

**MIKAELIAN, TSOLINE,** aerospace engineer; b. Beirut, Feb. 15, 1980; d. Hratch Kaspar Mikaelian and Alice Karapet Koucherian. BS in Space and Comm. Scis., York U., Toronto, Ont., Can., 2002; MS in Aeronautics and Astronautics, MIT, Cambridge, Mass., 2005. Tchg. asst., rschr. Atomic Physics Lab., York U., 2000—02; rschr. Spectral Applied Rsch., Inc., Concord, Ont., 2002, MIT Computer Sci. and Artificial Intelligence Lab., Cambridge, 2003—. Rsch. cons. Toyota Tech. Ctr., Inc., Cambridge, 2004—. Contbr. articles to profl. jours. Gen. advisor Armenian Generic Benevolent Union, Young Profls. Group, Boston, 2005. Recipient Herschel prize dept. physics and astronomy, York U., 2000, Ruth Hill Meml. award, 2001, Gold medal of the Faculty of Pure and Applied Sci., 2002, Normal Bethune Coll. Master's prize for academic excellence, 2002, Academic medal, Gov. Gen. of Can., 2002; scholar, Canada Gulbenkian Found., Portugal, 1999, 2000, 2001; Presdl. fellow, MIT, 2003, Amelia Earhart fellow, Zonta Internat. Found., 2004—05. Mem.: Can. Assn. Physicists, Am. Assn. Artificial Intelligence, MIT Enterprise Forum. Armenian Orthodox. Avocations: painting, photography, travel. Home: 70 Pacific St Apt 407 Cambridge MA 02139 Office: MIT 32 Vassar St Cambridge MA 02139 Personal E-mail: tsoline@alum.mit.edu.

**MIKALOW, ALFRED ALEXANDER, II,** deep sea diver, marine surveyor, marine diving consultant; b. N.Y.C., Jan. 19, 1921; m. Janice Brenner, Aug. 1, 1960; children: Alfred Alexander, Jon Alfred. Student, Rutgers U., 1940; MS, U. Calif., Berkeley, 1948; MA, Rochdale U., Can., 1950. Owner Coastal Diving Co., Oakland, Calif., 1950—; Divers Supply, Oakland, 1952—; dir. Coastal Sch. Deep Sea Diving, Oakland, 1950—. Capt. and master rsch. vessel Coastal Researcher I; mem. Marine Inspection Bd., Oakland. marine diving contractor, cons. Mem. adv. bd. Medic Alert Found., Turlock, Calif., 1960—. Author: Fell's Guide to Sunken Treasure Ships of the World, 1972; (with H. Rieseberg) The Knight from Maine, 1974. Lt. comdr. USN, 1941-47, PTO, 1949-50, Korea. Decorated Purple Heart, Silver Star. Mem. Divers Assn. Am. (pres. 1970-74), Treasury Recovery, Inc. (pres. 1972-75), Internat. Assn. Profl. Divers, Assn. Diving Contractors, Calif. Assn. Pvt. Edn. (no. v.p. 1971-72), Authors Guild, Internat. Game Fish Assn., U.S. Navy League, U.S. Res. Officers Assn., Tailhook Assn., U.S. Submarine Vets. WWII, Explorer Club (San Francisco), Calif. Assn. Marine Surveyors (pres. 1988—), Soc. Naval Archs. and Marine Engrs. (assoc.), Masons, Leions, Am. Legion, VFW. Home and Office: 4943 South Pt Discovery Bay CA 94514-9490

**MIKALSON, JON DENNIS,** classics educator; b. Milw., Aug. 1, 1943; s. John Martin and Evelyn Kathryn (Heuser) M.; m. Mary Helen Villemonte, Aug. 28, 1966; children: Melissa, Jacquelyn. BA, U. Wis., 1965; postgrad., Am. Sch. Classical Studies, Athens, Greece, 1968-69; PhD, Harvard U., 1970. Asst. prof. classics U. Va., Charlottesville, 1970-75, assoc. prof., 1975-84, prof., 1984—, William R. Kenan Jr. prof. classics, 1999—, chmn. dept. classics, 1978-90. Dir. Echols Scholar Program, 1997-2000; vis. scholar Corpus Christi Coll., Cambridge, Eng., 1977-78; mem. Inst. for Advanced Study, Princeton, N.J., 1984-85; Whitehead prof. Am. Sch. Classical Studies, 1995-96. Author: The Sacred and Civil Calendar of the Athenian Year, 1975, Athenian Popular Religion, 1983, Honor Thy Gods: Popular Religion in Greek Tragedy, 1991, Religion in Hellenistic Athens, 1998, Herodotus and Religion in the Persian Wars, 2003, Ancient Greek Religion, 2004; contbr. articles to profl. and scholarly jours. James Rignall Wheeler fellow Am. Sch. Classical Studies, 1968-69, NEH fellow, 1977-78, Herodotus fellow Inst. for Advanced Study, 1984-85. Mem. Am. Philol. Assn., Am. Sch. Classical Studies, Archeol. Inst. of Am., Classical Assn. of Middle West and South (pres. so. sect. 1988-90), Classical Assn. of Va., Phi Beta Kappa, Phi Eta Sigma, Phi Kappa Phi, Omicron Delta Kappa. Clubs: Lions. Home: PO Box 664 Crozet VA 22932-0664 Office: U Va Dept Classics PO Box 400788 B002 Cocke Hall Charlottesville VA 22904-4788 Office Phone: 434-823-2163. Business E-mail: jdm9x@virginia.edu.

**MIKATA, YOZO,** mechanical engineer, application developer; b. Nichinan, Miyazaki, Japan, Jan. 29, 1956; arrived in U.S., 1981; s. Chotaro and Fumiko (Kato) Mikata. BSCE, U. Tokyo, 1979, MSCE, 1981; PhD in Mech. Engring., U. Del., Newark, 1984. Postdoctoral fellow Northwestern U., Evanston, Ill., 1984-87; postgrad. rsch. engr. U. Calif., San Diego, 1987-89; rsch. assoc. U. Ill., Urbana-Champaign, 1989-90; asst. prof. Old Dominion U., Norfolk, Va., 1990-96; sr. rsch. scientist ICAM, NASA Langley Rsch. Ctr., Hampton, Va., 1996-99; software engr. Bell Atlantic Network Svcs., Silver Spring, Md., 1999-2000; structural mechanics engr. Lockheed Martin Co., Schenectady, N.Y., 2000—. Contbr. articles to profl. jours. Rsch. grantee, Engring. Found., 1992, NASA Langley Rsch. Ctr., 1993, 1994. Mem.: ASME, Am. Acad. Mechanics, Soc. Indsl. and Applied Math. Achievements include research in on micromechanics of coated fiber composite materials providing analytical solutions, and thereby contributed to the understanding of local mechanical behavior of coatings; on wave propagation, fracture mechanics, dynamic phase transformation. Avocations: swimming, dance, jazz, astronomy, number theory. Office: Lockheed Martin Co PO Box 1072 Schenectady NY 12301

**MIKELL, FRANK LEONARD,** cardiologist; b. Augusta, Ga., Apr. 26, 1947; s. Frank Leonard and Mary (Herndon) M.; three children. BA, Emory U., 1969; B in Med. Scis., Dartmouth Med. Sch., 1972; MD, Emory U. Med. Sch., 1974. Asst. prof. medicine U. Minn., Mpls., 1979-82; interventional cardiologist Prairie Cardiovasc. Cons., Springfield, Ill., 1982—. Clin. assoc. prof. medicine So. Ill. U. Med. Sch., Springfield, 1987—. Fellow Am. Coll. Cardiology, Am. Coll. Chest Physicians, Am. Coll. Physicians, Soc. Cardiac Angiography & Intervention, Coun. Clin. Cardiology Am. Heart Assn. Avocations: golf, hunting. Office: Prairie Cardiovasc Cons PO Box 19420 Springfield IL 62794-9420

**MIKELS, RICHARD ELIOT,** lawyer; b. Cambridge, Mass., July 14, 1947; s. Albert Louis and Charlotte Betty (Shapiro) M.; m. Deborah Gwen Katz, Aug. 29, 1970; children: Allison Brooke, Robert Jarrett. BA in Govt. Adminstrn., Boston U., 1969, JD cum laude, 1972. Bar: Mass. 1972, US Dist. Ct. Mass. 1974, US Ct. Appeals (1st Cir.) 1978. Legal examiner ICC, Washington, 1972-74; prtnr. Riemer & Braunstein, Boston, 1974-80; ptnr., chmn. Comml. Law Sect. Peabody & Brown, Boston, 1980-88; mem., chmn. Comml. Law Sect. Mintz, Levin, Cohn, Ferris, Glovsky and Popeo, PC, Boston, 1988—; ptnr. Contbr. articles to profl. jour.; editor: Boston U. Law Rev., 1971—72. Tng. adv. com. Jewish Vocat. Svc., Boston, 1991, 1995, 1996, bd. dir. 1995—99, vice chair microenterprise adv. com., 1997; vice chair lawyers com. Combined Jewish Philanthropies, 1994, 1995; mem. bd. visitors Boston U. Fellow Am. Coll. Bankruptcy (1st cir. regent 2005-06); mem. ABA, Am. Bankruptcy Inst. (bd. dirs. 2000-06), Assn. Comml. Fin. Attys., Comml. Law League Am., Mass. Bar Assn., Boston Bar Assn., Boston U. Law Alumni Assn. (mem. exec. com., pres. exec. com. 2000-01). Office: Mintz Levin Cohn Ferris Glovsky & Popeo PC 1 Financial Ctr Fl 39 Boston MA 02111-2657 Office Phone: 617-348-1691. Office Fax: 617-542-2241. Business E-mail: rmikels@mintz.com.

**MIKELSONS, J. GEORGE,** air transportation executive; Founder, chmn., CEO Am. Trans Air, Inc., Indpls., 1973—2005. Office: Am Trans Inc Indpls Internat Airport PO Box 51609 Indianapolis IN 46251-0609

**MIKESELL, MARVIN WRAY,** geography educator; b. Kansas City, Mo., June 16, 1929; s. Loy George and Clara (Wade) M.; m. Reine-Marie de France, Apr. 1, 1957. BA, UCLA, 1952, MA, 1953; PhD, U. Calif.-Berkeley, 1959. Instr. to prof. geography U. Chgo., 1958—, chmn. dept. geography, 1969-74, 83-86. Del. U.S. Nat. Commn. for UNESCO Author: Northern Morocco, 1961; editor: Readings in Cultural Geography, 1962, Geographers Abroad, 1973, Perspectives on Environment, 1974. Fellow Am. Geog. Soc. (hon.); mem. Assn. Am. Geographers (pres. 1975-76, Disting. Career award 1995). Clubs: Quadrangle. Home: 1155 E 56th St Chicago IL 60637-1530 Office: Com Geog Studies 5828 S University Ave Chicago IL 60637-1583 Office Phone: 773-702-8313. Business E-Mail: mmikesel@uchicago.edu.

**MIKESELL, RICHARD LYON,** lawyer, financial counselor; b. Corning, N.Y., Jan. 29, 1941; s. Walter Ray and Clara Ellen (Lyon) M.; m. Anna May Creese, Mar. 16, 1973; 1 child, Joel. BSChemE, U. Calif., Berkeley, 1962; LLB, Duke U., 1965; BA in Liberal Studies, UCLA, 1977. Bar: U.S. Supreme Ct. 1971, Ohio 1965, Calif. 1967, U.S. Ct. Appeals (9th cir.) 1982, U.S. Ct. Appeals (2d cir.) 1993, U.S. Patent Office 1967. Patent atty. Procter & Gamble, Cin., 1965-66, Rocketdyne divsn. N.Am. Aviation, L.A., 1966-69; pvt. practice law L.A., 1969-81; prin. Law Offices of R.L. Mikesell, L.A., 1981—. Fin. counselor L.A. Police Dept., 1986—; arbitrator Am. Arbitration Assn., L.A., 1980—. Pres. San Fernando Valley Fair Housing Coun., L.A., 1969-72, Valley Women's Ctr., L.A., 1990; line res. officer L.A. Police Dept., 1969-72. Named Res. Officer of Yr. L.A. Police Dept., 1990, 98; recipient 1st Place award Nat. SPAM Recipe Contest, 1998. Avocation: target rifle shooting. Office Phone: 818-376-0376. Personal E-mail: richlyon6713@sbcglobal.net.

**MIKESELL, WALTER R., JR.,** mechanical engineer, engineering executive; BSChemE, MSChemE, Purdue U., 1957. Registerd profl. engr., Ill., Tenn. Engr. Chgo. Bridge and Iron Co., Oakbrook, Ill., 1957-59, project engr. Operation Cryogenics, 1959-60, devel. engr., cons., 1960-66, mgr. stress analysis, 1968-72, from mgr. design engring. to asst. chief engr., 1976-83, from asst. chief engr. to chief mech. engr., 1983-86; mgr. engring. CBI Nuclear Co., Memphis, 1972-76; sr, cons. Robert L. Cloud & Assocs., Berkeley, Calif., 1986—. Former mem. com. engring. Am. Bur. Shipping. Fellow ASME (boiler code coms., chmn. bd. accreditation, chair coun. codes and stds., J. Hall Taylor medal 1989, Codes and Stds. medal 1992), Materials and Properties Coun.

**MIKESKA, NOEL RHEA,** entrepreneur, health advocate; b. Garland, Tex., Nov. 28, 1975; s. Gary and Kimberlee Mikeska; m. Erinn Teresa Blake, Sept. 22, 2001. BA, Abilene Christian U., Tex., 2000. Cert. Nat. Assn. Health and Fitness Am.,Tex., 2000. CEO Your Body Fitness Inc, Dallas, 1997—, America's Fitness Corp., 2001—, Abb-Solute Fitness, Dallas, 2003—; exec. dir. Noel Mikeska Enterprises Inc., Irving, 2004—. Founder America's Fitness Inst., 2006; pres. Fitnex Comml.; health expert ABC-TV; talk show host local Dallas TV. Contbr. articles to periodicals. Mem.: CEO Club, Sigma Nu. Achievements include being featured in the Dallas Morning News. Office Phone: 214-352-4001.

**MIKHAILICHENKO, ALEXANDER A.,** physicist, researcher; b. Chita, Russia, Aug. 3, 1948; arrived in U.S., 1995; s. Alexy Georgy and Luba A. Mikhailichenko; m. Irina V. Makhort; children: Alexy, Andrew. PhD in Physics, Novosibirsk BINP, 1986. Sr. rsch. assoc. BINP Novosibirsk, Russia, 1972—95, Cornell U., Ithaca, NY, 1995—2005. Achievements include invention of radio frequency generator; method of acceleration; research in optical stochastic cooling method; polarized positron production method. Home: 909 Triphammer Rd Ithaca NY 14853-2508 Office: Cornell Univ Ithaca NY 14853 Office Phone: 607-255-3785. Business E-Mail: mikhail@lepp.cornell.edu.

**MIKHAILOV, STEPAN FEDOROVICH,** physicist, researcher; b. Norilsk, Krasnoyarsk region, Russia, Nov. 29, 1960; arrived in U.S., 2000; s. Feodor K. and Valentina M. Mikhailov; m. Natalia A. Makhanova, June 8, 2000; 1 child, Andrei M. Makhanov. MS, Novosibirsk Physics, Novosibirsk, 1982—2000; sr. rsch. scientist FEL Lab. Duke U., Durham, NC, 2000—. Office: Duke U DFEL Lab PO Box 90319 LaSalle St Extension Durham NC 27708-0319 Home: 103 Misty Woods Cir Apt K Chapel Hill NC 27514 Office Phone: 919-660-2647. Office Fax: 919-660-2671. Business E-mail: smikhail@fel.duke.edu.

**MIKHAILOVSKY, ALEXANDER,** research and development company executive; MS in Elec. Engring., Perm State U., Russia, 1994; PhD in Physics, Moscow State U., 1998. Postdoctoral rschr. Los Alamos (N.Mex.) Nat. Lab., 1998—2002; staff rschr., rsch. facility coord. U. of CA Santa Barbara, 2002—. Office: Univ of Calif Santa Barbara Dept Chemistry and Biochemistry Santa Barbara CA 93106-9510 Office Phone: 805-893-2327. Business E-mail: mikhailovsky@chem.ucsb.edu.

**MIKHELSON, SERGEI,** mathematician, educator; b. Saint Petersburg, Russia, May 17, 1970; s. Stanislav and Eleonora (Guretskaya) Mikhelson. BA, Russian State Pedagogical U., St. Petersburg, Russia, 1993; MA, Russian State Pedagogical U., 1993, Columbia U., N.Y.C., 1994. Math. and logic tchr. Gymnasia 56, St. Petersburg, Russia, 1991—97; program dir., dept. head Ctr. of Alternative Edn., St. Petersburg, 1994—98; vice-prin. Gymnasia 56, St. Petersburg, 1995; math. adj. instr. NYU, N.Y.C., 1999—2005, Borough of Manhattan C.C., N.Y.C., 1998—2001; math. tchr. Bklyn Friends Sch., 2002—. Internat. debate trainer Internat. Debate Edn. Assn., N.Y.C., 1998—2002. Co-author (publication) Mathematics Education in Russia. Mem.: Nat. Coun. of Tchrs. of Math. Business E-Mail: ssm21@columbia.edu.

**MIKIEWICZ, ANNA DANIELLA,** marketing and international business export manager; b. Chgo., Dec. 22, 1960; d. Zdislaw and Lucy (Magnuswska) M. BS in Mktg., Elmhurst Coll., 1982; postgrad., Triton Coll. Asst. to midwestern regional mgr. Melster Pub. Co., Chgo., 1983; sales rep. First Impressions, Elk Grove, Ill., 1984; asst. to Midwestern dist. mgr. Airco Ind. Gases, Broadview, Carol Stream, Ill., 1985; customer svc. & ops. mgr. Yamazen USA, Inc., Schaumburg, Ill., 1985-88; nat. sales & mktg. coord. Kitamura Machinery U.S.A. Inc., 1988-95; mktg. mgr. Beth Lee Boutique, 1995-97; internat. bus. export control sales coord. MHI Machine Tool USA, Inc. subs. Mitsubishi Heavy Industries, 1997-99; internat. bus. asst. to exec. v.p. sales America Excel, Inc., Elk Grove Village, Ill., 1999—; internat. bus. Brazil Market IST Sales Am., Inc., Waukegan, Ill., 2000—04; internat. export bus. mgr. global worldwide market Anixter, Inc., 2005—. Named Chgo. Polish Queen Polish Am. Culture Club, 1983-84. Mem.: NAFE. Republican. Roman Catholic.

**MIKITA, JOSEPH KARL,** broadcast executive; b. Va., Oct. 3, 1918; s. John and Catherine (Wargofcak) M.; m. Mary Therese Benya, Nov. 26, 1942; children: Patty-Jane Mikita McGlynn, Michael, M. Noël Mikita Garagiola. BS, Fordham U., 1939; MS, Columbia U., 1940. Treas., controller Capital Cities Broadcasting Co., Albany, NY, 1955-58; controller Westinghouse Broadcasting Co., Inc., N.Y.C., 1958-60, v.p. fin., 1960-64, v.p. fin. and adminstrn., 1964-65, sr. v.p., 1965-69, 1975—; also dir., exec. v.p. Westinghouse Electric Corp. for Broadcasting, Learning and Leisure Activities, N.Y.C., 1969-75. Dir. Sutro Tower, Inc.; ptnr. Emerald Bay Resort Co. Exuma, Bahamas Author: (with others) The Business of Broadcasting, 1964. Bd. dirs. Fordham U. Council, Albany County Workshop, Albany County Heart Assn., Citizens For Reasonable Growth, Boca Raton; chmn. bd. Instructional TV. Served to maj. AUS, 1940-45, ETO. Recipient Order of Merit (Silver), Westinghouse Electric Corp., Disting. Service Alumni award Fordham U., 1969. Mem. AICPA, Internat. Radio and TV Soc., N.Y. Soc. CPAs, Fin. Execs. Inst. (dir., past pres. Manhattan chpt.), Inst. Broadcasting Fin. Mgmt. (past dir.), Town Club, Westchester Country Club, Boca Raton Club, M.G.A.; JDM Country Club, Royal Palm Yacht and Country Club,

Palm Beach County Golf Assn., Golden Harbour Yacht Club (commodore), Rotary (1st v.p. N.Y.). Home: 3125 NE 7th Dr Boca Raton FL 33431-6906 Office: 90 Park Ave New York NY 10016-1301 Personal E-mail: jkmikita1@bellsouth.net.

**MIKITKA, GERALD PETER,** brokerage house executive, consultant; s. Michael and Nancy Lee, 1977; children: Richard, Jeffrey, Jennifer. BSBA in Fin., Roosevelt U., 1966, postgrad., 1967. Diplomate: registered investment advisor. Sr. investment exec. Shearson Hammill & Co., Chgo., 1967-73; chmn., pres. Capital Directions, Inc., Chgo., 1973—. Pres. CDI Fin. Advisors, Chgo., 1974—, CDI Properties, Chgo., 1974—, CDI Communications, Inc., Chgo., 1978—, A.B. Properties Inc., Chgo., 1986—, Am. Eagle Realty Inc., Chgo., 1988—, Grand Caribbean Properties Inc., Chgo., 1988, Cain Estates Inc., Chgo., 1988—, Caribbean Sea Properties Inc., Chgo., 1989—. Served with U.S. Army, 1967-69. Mem. Nat. Assn. Securities Dealers, Securities Investment Protection Assn., Broadcast Film. Mgmt. Assn., Nat. Radio Broadcast Assn., Internat. Assn. Fin. Planning. Lodges: Rotary.

**MIKKELSEN, BARBARA BERRY,** retired retail executive, rancher; b. Wichita Falls, Tex., June 16, 1942; d. Marshall Keith Berry and Louie Arlene Williams; m. John Hardie Mikkelsen, Nov. 24, 1967. B.A., New Orleans, 1965. Pres. White Rabbit, Inc, Vernon, Tex., 1980—96, Plum Creek Farms, Inc, Vernon, Tex., 1985—. Adv. bd. Vernon Humane Soc., Tex., 1983—2003; mem. Adv. Bd. for Vernon State Hosp., Vernon, Tex., 1974; mem. of bd. Vernon Boys and Girls Club, Vernon, Tex., 1969—2003; chmn. spl. events Santa Fe Opera, 2003—05, mem. of bd., 2003—, Anson County Hist. Soc., Wadesboro, NC, 1988—89, Red River Valley Mus., Vernon, Tex., 1983—2000, Wilbarger Country Hist. Soc., Vernon, Tex., 1988—99; pres. Vernon Jr. League, Vernon, Tex., 1969—71, mem. of bd., 1971—76, Broadway Theatre League, Wichita Falls, Tex., 1970—72. Recipient 25 Yr. Award, Vernon Boys and Girls Club, 1994, Donor, Vernon Humane Soc., 1984. Avocations: raising and training horses, art, travel, opera, theater. Office: 2429 Texas St Vernon TX 76384 Home: 8 Altazano Dr Santa Fe NM 87505 Personal E-mail: eagle505@earthlink.net.

**MIKOLAJCZYK, MARK S.,** publishing executive; b. 1961; Grad., Rochester U., 1982. Prodn. coord. to night ops. mgr. USA Today, 1982—84; spl. projects mgr. Cin. Enquirer, 1984—87; prodn. dir. Times Herald, Port Huron, Mich., 1987—89; v.p. prodn. Cin. Enquirer, 1989—96; dir. prodn. Gannett Co. Newspaper Div., 1996, v.p. prodn., 1997—2003, sr. v.p. ops., 2003—05; pres., CEO Detroit Newspaper Partnership, Mich., 2005—06; pres., publisher Fla. Today, Melbourne, 2006—. Named Corp. Staffer of Yr., Gannett Co., Inc., 2002. Office: Florida Today PO Box 419000 Melbourne FL 32941-9000 Office Phone: 321-242-3500.*

**MIKULAS, DANA CAMERON,** voice educator, music educator; b. Birmingham, Ala., Nov. 13, 1977; d. Terry Ray and Patricia Ann Wade; m. Jonathan Michael Mikulas. MusB, Dallas Bapt. U., 1998—2000. Kodaly cert. Plano ISD, Tex., 2003. Voiceteacher RMTA, Richardson, Tex., 1999—; music tchr. Plano ISD, Plano, Tex., 2000—. Performer: (opera) Hansel & Gretel; musician: (albums) The Love I Found in You. Praise & worship leader, soloist, choir mem. First Bapt. Ch., Plano, Tex., 2000—03. Recipient All-Level Music award, Dallas Bapt. U., 2000; Music scholarship, 1998—2000, grant, Plano Futures Found., 2003. Mem.: Tex. Music Educators Assn., Music Teachers Nat. Assn., Tex. Music Teachers Assn., Richardson Music Teachers Assn. (co-chairman of sacred festival, monitor chmn. for festivals 2001—03), Nat. Honors Soc., Zeta Tau Alpha (music & svc. committees 1996—98).

**MIKULAY, MARK P.,** music educator; b. New Orleans, Dec. 23, 1962; s. Stephen and Margaret Mikulay; m. Tammy Mikulay; children: Adam children: Andrew. MusM, Southeastern La. U., 1987; MS in Bus. Mgmt., No. Ill. U., 2002. Cert. chief sch. bus. ofcl., prin., instrumental music educator Ill. Band dir. Civic Meml. HS, Bethalto, Ill., 1987—90; tchr. Murphyboro (Ill.) Schools, 1990—2002; educator Sesser (Ill.)-Valier Cmty. Unit Sch. Dist., 2002—. Craig Schilling IASBO Conf. scholar, IASBO, 2002. Mem.: Ill. Grade Sch. Music Assn. (chmn. Sesser 2004—), Ill. Music Educators Assn. (assoc.).

**MIKULSKI, BARBARA ANN,** senator; b. Balt., July 20, 1936; d. William and Christine (Kutz) M. BA in Sociology, Mt. St. Agnes Coll., 1958; MSW, U. Md., 1965; LLD (hon.), Goucher Coll., 1973, Hood Coll., 1978, Bowie State U., 1989, Morgan State U., 1990, U. Mass., 1991; DHL (hon.), Pratt Inst. 1974. Tchr. Vista Tng. Ctr. Mount St. Mary's Sem., Balt.; social worker Balt. Dept. Social Services, 1961-63, 66-70; mem. Balt. City Council, 1971-76, 95th-99th Congresses from 3d Md. Dist., 1977-87; US Senator from Md., 1987—; sec. Dem. Conf. 104th-106th Congress. Adj. prof. Loyola Coll., 1972-76; mem. U.S. Senate labor and human resources com., 1987—, ranking mem. subcom. on aging, 1993—; mem. appropriations com., 1987, ranking mem. subcom. on vets., housing, and ind. agys., 1987—. Bd. visitors U.S. Naval Acad.; bd. adv. Space Awareness Alliance. Recipient Nat. Citizen of Yr. award Buffalo Am.-Polit. Eagle, 1973, Woman of Yr. Bus. & Profl. Women's Club Assn., 1973, Outstanding Alumnus U. Md. Sch. Social Work, 1973, Govt. Social Responsibility award, 1991, Disting. Svc. award Ctrl. and East European Coalition, 1996, Louis D. Brandeis award Baltimore, Md. Zionist Dist., 1996, Public Svc. award Am. Inst. Aeronautics and Astronautics, 1998, Order of Merit Commanders Cross with Star Govt. Poland, 2001, Good Housekeeping/Wyeth award women's health, 2002, Connie Mack Lifetime Avhievement award Susan G. Komen Breast Cancer Found., 2003, Elmer P. Martin Public Svc. award Great Blacks in Wax Mus., 2003, Public Svc. award Emergency Nurses Assn., 2004, Nat. Leadership award Big Brothers and Big Sisters of Ctrl. Md., 2005. Mem. LWV. Democrat. Roman Catholic. Office: US Senate 503 Hart Sen Office Bldg Washington DC 20510-0001 also: Brown's Wharf Ste 400 1629 Thames St Baltimore MD 21231 Office Phone: 202-224-4654, 410-962-4510. Office Fax: 202-224-8858, 410-962-4760.*

**MIKUMO, AKIKO,** lawyer; b. Kyoto, June 18, 1953; BA, U. Calif., Berkeley, 1978; JD, NYU, 1982. Assoc. Weil, Gotshal & Manges LLP, N.Y.C., 1983—90; ptnr. Weil U.S. practice London, 1998—2000. Mem.: ABA (mem. com. on corp. law 1993—), Assn. of the Bar of the City of N.Y. Office: Weil Gotshal & Manges LLP 767 Fifth Ave New York NY 10153 Office Phone: 212-310-8000.

**MIKUS, ELEANORE ANN,** artist; b. Detroit, July 25, 1927; d. Joseph and Bertha (Englot) M.; m. Richard Burns, July 6, 1949 (div. 1963); children: Richard, Hillary, Gabrielle. Student, Mich. State U., 1946-49, U. Mex., summer 1948; B.F.A., U. Denver, 1957, MA, 1967; postgrad., Art Students League, 1958, NYU, 1959-60. Asst. prof. Cornell U., Ithaca, NY, 1979-80, assoc. prof., 1980-92, prof. art, 1992-94, prof. emerita, 1994—. Asst. prof. art Monmouth Coll., West Long Branch, N.J., 1966-70, prof. Cornell, Rome, 1989; vis. lectr. painting Cooper Union, N.Y.C., 1970-72, Central Sch. Art and Design, London, 1973-77, Kensington Inst., London, 1974-77, Harrow (Eng.) Coll. Tech. and Art, 1975-76. One-woman shows at Pace Gallery, N.Y.C. (1963, 64, 65) and O.K. Harris Gallery (1971, 72, 73, 74), N.Y.C., Baskett Gallery, Cin., 1982, 84-85, Claudia Carr Gallery, 1998—, Mitchell Algus Gallery, N.Y.C., 1998, 2003, 04; represented in permanent collections including Met. Mus. Art, N.Y.C., Mus. Modern Art, N.Y.C., Whitney Mus., N.Y.C., Los Angeles County Mus., Cin. Mus., Birmingham (Ala.) Mus. Art, Norton Simon Mus., Pasadena, Bklyn. Mus., Honolulu Acad. Arts, Indpls. Mus. Art, Nat. Gallery Art, Washington, Victoria and Albert Mus., London, Libr. of Congress, Washington, Tucson Mus. of Art, Blanton Mus. U. Tex., U. Ariz. Mus. Art, Tucson, Univ. Ariz., Tucson, De Cordova Mus., Lincoln, Mass.; subject of book Eleanore Mikus, Shadows of the Real (by Robert Hobbs and Judith Bernstock), 1991. Fellow, Guggenheim, 1966—67, Tamarind, 1968, McDowell, 1969, Yaddo drawing and painting, 2004. Home: PO Box 4775 Ithaca NY 14852-4775 Office: Cornell U Dept Art Tjaden Hall Ithaca NY 14853 also: 270 Luce Rd Groton NY 13073-9747 Office Phone: 607-533-7766. Personal E-mail: mikusart44@hotmail.com.

**MIKVA, ABNER JOSEPH,** lawyer, retired judge; b. Milw., Jan. 21, 1926; s. Henry Abraham and Ida (Fishman) M.; m. Zoe Wise, Sept. 19, 1948; children: Mary, Laurie, Rachel. JD cum laude, U. Chgo., 1951; DL (hon.), U. Ill., 1980, Am. U., 1991, Northwestern U., 1991, Tulane U., 1993, Ill. Inst. Tech., 1997, Santa Clara U., 2000, Wm. Mitchell Coll. Law, 2001; DHL (hon.), Hebrew U., 1989, U. Wis., 1995, De Paul U. Law Sch., 2002, So. Ill. U., 2006. Bar: Ill. 1951, D.C. 1978. Law clk. to Hon. Sherman Minton U.S. Supreme Ct., 1951; prtnr. Devoe, Shadur, Mikva & Plotkin, Chgo., 1952-68, D'Ancona, Pflaum, Wyatt & Riskind, 1973-74; lectr. Northwestern U. Law Sch., Chgo., 1973-75, U. Pa. Law Sch. 1983-85, Georgetown Law Sch., 1986-88, Duke U. Law Sch., Durham, NC, 1990-91, U. Chgo. Law Sch., 1992-93; mem. Ill. Gen. Assembly from 23d Dist., 1956-66, 91st-92d Congresses from 2d Dist. Ill., 94th-96th Congresses from 10th Dist. Ill.. mem. ways and means com., judiciary com.; chmn. Dem. Study Group, 1979; judge U.S. Ct. Appeals (D.C. cir.), 1979-94; chief judge U.S. Ct. Appeals (D.C. cir), 1991-94; counsel to the Pres. The White House, Washington, 1994-96; arbitrator JAMS, Inc., 1997—. Vis. prof., Walter Schaefer chair in pub. policy U. Chgo., 1996-98; vis. prof. U. Ill. Coll. Law, 1998-2000, U. Chgo., 2000—. Author: The American Congress: The First Branch, 1983, The Legislative Process, 1995, An Introduction to Statutory Interpretation, 1997. With USAAF, WWII. Sr. fellow Inst. Govt. & Pub. Affairs U. Ill., 1998-2000; recipient Page One award Chgo. Newspaper Guild, 1964, Best Legislator award Ind. Voters Ill., 1956-66, Alumni medal U. Chgo., 1996, Paul Douglas Ethics in Govt. award, 1998, Thurgood Marshall award, ABA, 2005; named one of Ten Outstanding Young Men in Chgo., Jr. Assn. Commerce and Industry, 1961. Fellow Am. Acad. Arts and Scis.; mem. ABA, Chgo. Bar Assn. (bd. mgrs. 1962-64), D.C. Bar Assn., Am. Law Inst., U.S. Assn. Former Mems. Congress, Order of Coif, Phi Beta Kappa. Home: Ph 6 5020 S Lake Shore Dr Chicago IL 60615-3253 Office Phone: 773-834-5852. Business E-Mail: amikva@law.uchicago.edu.

**MILAČ, METOD M.,** retired school librarian; b. Prevalje, Slovenia, Oct. 2, 1924; arrived in U.S., 1950; s. Ivan Milač and Jerica Ivač; m. Herta M. Schiffer; children: Andrew(dec.), Thomas I., Michael J. MusM in Musicology, Cleve. Inst. Music, 1960; MLS, We. Res. U., Cleve., 1962; MPH, Syracuse U., NY, 1987, PhD in Humanities, 1991. Libr. Cleve. Twist Drill Co., 1952—62; from music libr. to assoc. libr. Syracuse U., NY, 1962—84, assoc. libr., 1984—92; ret., 1992. Mem. Ctrl. N.Y. Libr. Resources Coun., 1973—90; founder, condr. Singing Soc. Korotan, Cleve., 1951—62; spkr. in field. Author: Resistance, Imprisonment, & Forced Labor: A Slovene Student in World War II, 2002; translator (in Slovene): Kdo solze nae posui: Doivetja slovenskega diaka med drugo svetovno vojno, 2003; contbr. articles to profl. jours.; composer: String Quartet, 1958, Duma, 1960, Pozdravljena zemljia, 1961; trancscriber and editor: songs Missa super undique flammatis, 1962. Recipient Libr. Svc. award, Post Standard Newspaper, 1982, Disting. Svc. award, Syracuse (N.Y.) U. Libr., 1989; grantee, Syracuse (N.Y.) U., 1967, 1984—85. Mem.: Am. Musicol. Soc., American Slovene Congress, Am. Assn. Advancement Slavic Studies, Soc. Slovene Studies (pres. 2000—06, sec. 1996—2000, coord. program 1979—84), Adirondack Mountain Club, Theta Chi Beta (hon.). Avocations: tennis, hiking. Home: 259 Kensington Pl Syracuse NY 13210 E-mail: mmilac@syr.edu.

**MILAM, BEN WILLIAM,** music educator; b. Marietta, Ga., Feb. 7, 1980; s. George Russell Milam and Deborah Sue Davies; m. Darenda Leigh Young, May 11, 2002; 1 child, Benson William. BA summa cum laude, Jacksonville State U., Ala., 2003. Cert. tchr. music P-12 Ga. Band dir. Westside Middle Sch., Rocky Face, Ga., 2003—. Mem.: Music Educators Nat. Conf., Ga. Music Educators Assn., Profl. Assn. of Ga. Educators. Home: 100 Woodberry Ct Calhoun GA 30701

**MILAM, JOHN DANIEL,** pathologist, educator; b. Kilgore, Tex., May 22, 1933; s. Ott G. and Effie (White) Milam; m. Carol Jones, Aug. 1, 1959; children: Kay, Beth, John Daniel, Julie. BS, La. State U., 1955, MS, 1957, MD, 1960. Attending pathologist St. Luke's Episcopal Hosp., Houston, 1967—89, chief of staff, 1981—83; emeritus Tex. Children's Hosp., Houston, 2000—; adj. prof. lab. medicine M.D. Anderson Cancer Ctr., U. Tex., Houston, 1990—2001; prof. pathology and lab. medicine U. Tex. Med. Sch., Houston, 1989—2001, prof. emeritus, 2001—; active med. staff Hermann Hosp., Houston, 1988—, med. dir. lab. svcs., 1990—95; chief pathology Lyndon B. Johnson Gen. Hosp., Houston, 1995—2001. Trustee Am. Bd. Pathology, 1985—96, pres., 1995, life trustee, 1996—; cons. in field. Contbr. articles and abstracts to profl. jours., chapters to books. Bd. dirs. Greater Houston area chpt. ARC, 1978—. Recipient Disting. Physician award, Harlan J. Spjut award 2003, Am. Soc. Clin. Pathologists (Commn. on Continuing Edn. Disting. Svc. award 1993, Israel Davidsohn Disting. Svc. award 2001), Tex. Soc. Pathologists (pres. 1978, George T. Caldwell award 1981), Am. Assn. Blood Banks (pres. 1984, Disting. Svc. award 1988). Republican. Baptist. Home: 11927 Arbordale Ln Houston TX 77024-5001 Office: U Tex Houston Med Sch Rm 2-022 Dept Pathology 6431 Fannin St Houston TX 77030-1501 Office Phone: 713-500-5336. Business E-Mail: john.d.milam@uth.tmc.edu.

**MILAM, LYNNE MORGAN,** special education educator; b. Harlan, Ky., Oct. 19, 1943; d. James T. and Dorothy O. Morgan; m. Jon Milam, June 20, 1970; 1 child, Morgan M. Cressman. BA with distinction in Edn., U. Ky., Lexington, 1967; MA in Spl. Edn., West Ga. Coll., Carrollton, 1990. Cert. tchr. speech grades 7-12 Ky., 1967, Ga., 1989, tchr. learning disabilities grades K-12 Ga., 1991. Tchr. English/speech Loyall Jr. H.S., Ky., 1966—73; tchr. speech/drama James A. Cawood H.S., Harlan, 1969—73; tchr. learning disabilities The Bedford Sch., Fairburn, Ga., 1985—. Named one of Outstanding Young Women in Am, 1967, 1970; recipient Outstanding Young Ky. Speech Tchr., Ky. Assn. Comm. Arts, Lexington, 1969, Outstanding Harlan County Educator, Harlan County Jaycees, 1970. Mem.: Orton Dyslexia Assn., Ga. Coun. Tchrs. of English, Phi Kappa Phi. Republican. Christian. Avocations: reading, writing, singing. Office: The Bedford Sch 5665 Milam Rd Fairburn GA 30213 Business E-Mail: lmilam@thebedfordschool.org.

**MILAM, WILLIAM BRYANT,** former ambassador, senior policy scholar; b. Bisbee, Ariz., July 24, 1936; s. Burl Vivian and Alice Vera (Pierce) M.; step-children: Erika, Fred. AB, Stanford U., 1959; MA, U. Mich., 1970; postgrad., Am. U., 1973. Polit. officer Dept. State, Washington, 1967-69; fin. economist Dept. State and Am. Embassy, Washington and London, 1970-75; energy economist Dept. State, Washington, 1975-77, dep. office dir., 1977-80, office dir., 1980-83; dep. chief of mission Am. Embassy, Yaounde, Cameroon, 1983-85; dep. asst. sec. Dept. State, Washington, 1985-90; U.S. amb. to Bangladesh, 1990-93; spl. negotiator oceans environ. sci. Dept. State, Washington, 1993-95; chief of mission Am. Embassy, Monrovia, Liberia, 1995-98, U.S. amb. to Pakistan, Islamabad, 1998-2001; with Woodrow Wilson Internat. Ctr. for Scholars, 2002—. Calif. State scholar, 1956-59; recipient James Clement Dunn award Dept. of State, 1981, Superior Honor award, 1983, Pres.'s Meritorious Svc. award U.S. Govt., 1990, Pres. Outstanding Svc. award, 1991. Avocations: reading, golf, writing. Office: One Woodrow Wilson Plz 1300 Pennsylvania Ave NW Washington DC 20004 Business E-Mail: william.milam@wilsoncenter.org.

**MILANA PANOPOULOS, MARIA,** artist; b. Oceanside, NY, Nov. 13, 1965; d. Thomas F. and Angelina M. Milana; m. Michael S. Panopoulos, May 1988; children: Thomas, Nicholas Student, Kingsborough C.C., Manhattan Beach, N.Y., 1983-84, Nassau C.C., Garden City, N.Y., 1984-85. Freelance model, N.Y., Fla., 1981—; model Home Shopping Network, N.Y., Fla., 1992-93; owner Artistic Creations, Custom Faux You, Maria Panopoulos Artist, 2006—. Poet. Mem. adv. bd. Trinity Oaks Homeowners Assn., New Port Richey, Fla., 1992-93. Mem. Tarpon Springs Art Assn. (bd. dirs 1998—), Herbal Healer Acad. Republican. Catholic. Achievements include patent for knee brace. Business E-Mail: cre8tive@tampabay.rr.com.

**MILANDER, HENRY MARTIN,** educational consultant; b. Northampton, Pa., Apr. 17, 1939; s. Martin Edward and Margaret Catherine (Makovetz) M.; children: Martin Henry, Beth Ann. BS summa cum laude, Lock Haven U., Pa.,

1961; MA, Bowling Green State U., Ohio, 1962; EdS (Future Faculty fellow 1964), U. No. Iowa, 1965; EdD, Ill. State U., Normal, 1967. Instr. Wartburg Coll., Waverly, Iowa, 1962-64; asst. prof. Ill. State U., 1966-67; dean instrn. Belleville (Ill.) Area Coll., 1967-69; v.p. acad. affairs Lorain County Community Coll., Elyria, Ohio, 1969-72; pres. Olympic Coll., Bremerton, Wash., 1972-87, Northeastern Jr. Coll., Sterling, Colo., 1988-95; ednl. cons., 1995—. Pres. Bremers, Inc., 1986-87. Contbr. articles to profl. jours. Pres. Kitsap County Comprehensive Health Planning Council, 1975-76; pres. Logan County Colo. United Way, 1992-93. Recipient Faculty Growth award Wartburg Coll., 1963, Community Service award, 1975, Chief Thunderbird award, 1985. Mem. Am. Assn. C.C., Am. Assn. Sch. Adminstrs., N.W. Assn. Cmty. and Jr. Colls., Wash. Assn. C.C. (pres. 1984-85), Wash. C.C. Computing Consortium (chmn. bd. dirs. 1985-87), Puget Sound Naval Bases Assn. (pres. 1982-86), Wash. Assn. C.C. Pres. (pres. 1984-85), Bremerton Area C. of C. (pres. 1977-78), Colo. Assn. C.C. Pres. (pres. 1993-94), Rotary (pres. Sterling Club 1992-93), Kappa Delta Pi, Phi Delta Kappa. Lutheran. Home: 709 E Pointes Dr West Shelton WA 98584-6305

**MILANICH, JERALD THOMAS,** archaeologist, curator; b. Painesville, Ohio, Oct. 13, 1945; s. John Joseph and Jean Marie (Bales) M.; m. Maxine L. Margolis, Dec. 20, 1970; 1 child, Nara Bales. BA, U. Fla., 1967, MA, 1968, PhD, 1971. Fellow Smithsonian Inst., Washington, 1971-72; asst. prof. anthropology U. Fla., Gainesville, 1972-75; asst. curator Fla. Mus. Natural History, 1975-77, assoc. curator, 1977-81, chmn. dept. anthropology, 1981-83, 91-94, curator, 1981—. Author: (with Samuel Proctor) Tacachale -- Essays on the Indians of Florida and Southeastern Georgia During the Historic Period, 1978; (with Charles Fairbanks) Florida Archaeology, 1980; McKeithen Weeden Island, 1984; Early Prehistoric Southeast, 1985; (with Susan Milbrath) First Encounters, Spanish Explorations in the Caribbean and the United States, 1492-1570, 1989; The Hernando de Soto Expedition, 1990; Earliest Hispanic-Native America Interactions in the Greater American Southwest, 1991; (with Charles Hudson) Hernando de Soto and the Indians of Florida, 1993, Archaeology of Precolumbian Florida, 1994, Florida Indians and the Invasion of Europe, 1995, The Timucua, 1996, Archaeology of Northern Florida, 1997, Florida Indians From Ancient Times to the Present, 1998, Laboring in the Fields of the Lord: Spanish Missions and Southeastern Indians, 1999, 2006, Famous Florida Sites: Mount Royal and Crystal River, 1999, (with Theodore Morris) Florida's Lost Tribes: Through the Eyes of an Artist, 2004, Frolicking Bears Wet Vultures and Other Oddities: A New York City Journalist in Nineteenth Century Florida, 2005; mem. editl. bd.: Archaeology Mag., 1992-2002, contbg. editor, 2002—. Trustee Archeol. Inst. Am., 2004—. Recipient Ripley P. Bullen award, 1980, Rembert Patrick Book award, 1994-95, James Mooney Book award, 1995, medal Fla. Acad. Sci., 2004, Lifetime Achievement award Fla. Archeol. Coun., 2006; grantee NSF, 1970-71, 73-75, 77-82, Wentworth Found., 1976-77, 81-84, 91, NEH, 1985, 87-89, Fla. Divsn. Hist. Resources, 1981, 83-89, 91, 96-97, 00-02, 03-04. Mem. Soc. Am. Archaeology (exec. bd. 1990-93), Soc. Profl. Archeologists (cert., pres. 1981-82), So. Anthrop. Soc., S.E. Archeol. Conf. (pres. 1986-88). Office: Fla Mus Natural History Gainesville FL 32611-7800

**MILANO, ALYSSA,** actress; b. N.Y.C., Dec. 19, 1972; d. Thomas M. and Lin Milano.; m. Cinjun August Tate, Jan. 1, 1999 (div. Nov. 20, 1999). Student, Bel Air Prep. Sch., L.A. Appeared on TV series Who's the Boss?, 1984-92, Melrose Place, 1997-98, Charmed, 1998-2006 (also prodr.); appeared in TV movies The Canterville Ghost, 1986, Dance'Til Dawn, 1988, Conflict of Interest, 1992, Candles in the Dark, 1993, Casualties of Love: The Long Island Lolita Story, 1993, Confessions of a Sorority Girl, 1994; appeared in various TV spls.; on TV shows Body by Jake, 1988, The Arsenio Hall Show, 1989, various shows for American Treasury, 1989, To Brave Alaska, 1996; film actress Old Enough, 1982, Commando, 1985, Speed Zone, 1989, Where the Day Takes You, 1992, Little Sister, 1992, Double Dragon, 1993, Embrace of the Vampire, 1995, At Home with the Webbers, 1993, The Surrogate, 1995, Public Enemy # 1, 1995, No Fear, 1996, Glory Daze, 1996, Jimmy Zip, 1996, Below Utopia, 1997, Hugo Pool, 1997, Buying the Cow, 2002, Kiss the Bride, 2002, Dickie Roberts: Former Child Star, 2003, (voice) Dinotopia: Quest for the Ruby Sunstone, 2005; stage debut in Annie, various cities, 1980-81; stage appearances include All Night Long, Second Stage Theatre Co., N.Y.C., 1984, Jane Eyre, Theatre Opera Music Inst., N.Y.C., others; TV guest appearances include The Outer Limits, 1995, Spin City, 1996, Fantasy Island, 1998; prodr. Below Utopia, 1997. Recipient Best Supporting Actress award Youth Films Awards; Silver prize Tokyo Music Festival, 1989. Mem. SAG, AFTRA, Actors' Equity Assn.*

**MILASKI, JOHN JOSEPH,** management consultant; b. Johnson City, N.Y., Sept. 16, 1959; s. John Walter and Nellie Joan (Panaro) Milaski; m. Ann Mildred Caldwell, Jan. 22, 1994; children: Ian Alexander, Isaac Nicholas, Natalie Ann. AAS, Broome C.C., 1979; BSEE, Rochester Inst. Tech., 1984; MBA, Syracuse U., 1991. Registered engr., N.Y.; cert. bus. transformation cons. Design engr. IBM, Endicott, NY, 1979-84, systems engr., 1984-85, mktg. cons., 1985-91, cons. Cons. & Sys. Integration Svcs. upstate N.Y., 1992-94, cons. Worldwide Document Mgmt. Solutions Group, 1995-96, con. Worldwide Cons. Svcs., 1996-99; prin. IBM WW BT Cons. Svcs., 2000— Ga. state advisor to Nat. Rep. Senatorial Com., 1997. Inventor. Vol. IBM Olympic Force Team 1996 Summer Olympics; trust mgr. Nat. Trust for Hist. Preservation; charter mem., life mem. Statue of Liberty-Ellis Island Found., Inc.; charter mem. Nat. WWII Meml.; founding mem. Nat. Wall of Tolerance; charter mem. Nat. D-Day Mus.; active IBM Corp. Tech. Leadership Coun.; life mem. Republican Nat. Com.; mem. presdl. victory team Rep. Nat. Com. Recipient Utilities Industry Mktg. Excellence award IBM Systems Engring. Symposium, 1989, 91. Mem. IEEE (sr.), ASME (sr.), Am. Mgmt. Assn., Am. Prodn. and Inventory Control Soc. (sr.), Internat. Platform Assn., Computer and Automated Sys. Assn., NY State Sheriff's Assn., Ga. State Sheriff's Assn., Ga. State Troopers Assn., U.S. Holocaust Meml. Mus. (charter), IBM 100 Percent Club, U.S.C. of C., Internat. Directory of Disting. Leadership, Nat. Mus. of the Am. Indian (charter), Nat. WWII Meml. Fnd. (charter), Am. Battle Monuments Commn. (charter), Libr. Congress (charter), Nat. Trust for Historic Preservation, Centennial Olympic Pk. Atlanta (constructing donor). Republican. Roman Catholic. Avocations: skiing, travel, boating. Home: 2315 Sagramore Pl Cape Coral FL 33914-2571

**MILAVETZ, BARRY,** academic administrator, molecular biologist; b. Virginia, Minn., Sept. 22, 1948; s. David and Frances Milavetz; m. Judith Podell, June 25, 1972; 1 child, Adam. PhD, U. Ill., Champaign-Urbana, 1974. Assoc. prof. U. ND, Grand Forks, 1992—, assoc. v.p. for rsch., 2004—. Grantee NIH, 2006—. Mem.: Can. Soc. Biochemistry, Molecular and Cellular Biology, NY Acad. Scis., Am. Soc. Biochemistry and Molecular Biology, Am. Soc. Virology, Am. Chem. Soc., Am. Soc. Microbiology, Sigma Xi. Democrat. Achievements include patents for Assay for Identifying Anti-Viral Agents Specific Protein-Coated Double-Stranded DNA Viruses; research in characterization of chromatin structure in the papovavirus simian virus 40. Home: 916 Shakespeare Rd Grand Forks ND 58203 Office: U ND 264 Centennial Dr Grand Forks ND 58202 Office Phone: 701-777-4280. Business E-Mail: barrymilavetz@mail.und.nodak.edu.

**MILAZZO, DAVID ANTHONY,** mathematics educator; b. Buffalo, N.Y., Aug. 29, 1982; s. Sam and MaryEllen Milazzo. BS in Math., Buffalo State Coll., 2003, MS in Math. Edn., 2006. Cert. secondary math. edn. N.Y. State. Tchr. Lake Shore H.S., Angola, NY, 2005—. Adj. prof. SUNY, 2004—. Recipient Legacy scholarship, Buffalo State Alumni Assn., 2003, Buffalo State Coll. Honors Program scholarship, Buffalo State Honors Program, 2000—03; scholar Balanced Man award and scholarship, Sigma Phi Epsilon, 2000. Mem.: Nat. Coun. Tchrs. of Math., Am. Math. Assn., Math. Assn. of Am., Omicron Delta Kappa (treas. 2002—03), Kappa Delta Pi. Home: 59 Gary Ln Buffalo NY 14227 Personal E-mail: milada89@mail.buffalostate.edu.

**MILAZZO, RICHARD T.,** writer; b. N.Y.C. s. Thomas and Linda Milazzo; BA, Franklin and Marshall Coll., 1968—72; MA, City Coll. of NY, 1973—75. Editor, co-pub. Edgewise Press, Inc., NY, 1995—; sr. critic Yale U., 1988—89; coord. New Observations, NY, 1987; am. co-editor Kunst

Forum, 1986—88; co-editor, pub. Effects Mag., NYC, 1982—84; co-editor Feltrinelli, Italy, 1981; editor, co-pub. Out of London Press, 1975—82. Curator Emilio Mazzoli Gallery, Modena, Italy, 1999—, Alain Noirhomme Gallery, Brussels, 1998—; curator1997 Sidney Janis Gallery, NYC, 1995—97. Author: Hyperframes vol. I, 1989, vol. II, 1990, Streets of Gold, 2000, Malcolm Morley, 2000, Caravaggio on the Beach, 2001, Hotel of the Heart, 2002, Le Violon d'Ingres, 2004, Saint Clair Cemin, 2005, Jonathan Lasker, 2005, Ross Bleckner, 2006, Alogon, 2006, Small China Moon, 2006, According to What, 2006. Supporter Greenwich Village Soc. for Hist. Preservation, NYC, 2001—. Nat. Trust for Hist. Preservation, 1998—. Scholarship, Franklin and Marshall Coll., 1968—72. Mem.: Archives of Am. Art, St. Louis Mus. of Art, Mus. Modern Art, Met. Mus. of Art. Avocations: travel, art collecting, reading. Home and Office: 24 Fifth Ave No223-224 New York NY 10011 Personal E-mail: rtamilazzo@mindspring.com.

**MILBANK, JEREMIAH,** foundation executive; b. NYC, Mar. 24, 1920; s. Jeremiah and Katharine (Schulze) M.; m. Andrea Hunter, July 19, 1947 (dec. Oct. 1982); children: Jeremiah III, Victoria Milbank Whitney, Elizabeth Milbank Archer, Joseph H.; m. Rose Jackson Sheppard, May 4, 1991 (dec. Feb. 1998); m. Margy B. Rockefeller, Jan. 25, 1999. BA, Yale U., 1942; MBA, Harvard U., 1948; L.H.D. (hon.), Ithaca Coll., NY, 1976, Sacred Heart U., Conn.; LL.D. Manhattan Coll. With J.M. Found., N.Y.C., pres., 1971—. Pres. Turkey Hill Corp., 1972—. Author: First Century of Flight in America, 1942. Chmn. emeritus Boys and Girls Clubs Am.; hon. pres. Internat. Ctr. for the Disabled, 1991—; fin. chmn. Rep. Nat. Com., 1969-72, 75-77. Lt. USNR, 1943-46. Mem. River Club (N.Y.C.), Round Hill Club (Greenwich), Yale Club. Republican. Office: 60 E 42nd St New York NY 10165-0006

**MILBERG, JOACHIM,** retired automotive executive; b. 1943; Doctorate in prodn. engring., Tech. U. Berlin, 1971. Head automatic lathe divsn. Werkzeugmaschinenfabrik Gildemeister AG, 1978; prof. machine tools and ops. rsch. Munich Tech. U., 1981; mem. bd. mgmt. in charge of prodn. BMW, 1993, ret. chmn. bd. mgmt., 1999—2002, dir.; ret. CEO BMW A.G., 1999—2002. Mem. audit review com. Deere and Co., mem. corp. governance com.; dir. Allianza A.G., Festo A.G., MAN A.G. Achievements include raced in the 24hrs of LeMans and won with the BMW LMR. Office: Deere & Co World HQ One John Deere Pl Moline IL 61265

**MILBOURNE, WALTER ROBERTSON,** lawyer; b. Phila., Aug. 27, 1933; s. Charles Gordon and Florie Henderson (Robertson) M.; m. Georgena Sue Dyer, June 19, 1965; children: Gregory Broughton, Karen Elizabeth, Walter Robertson, Margaret Henderson AB, Princeton U., 1955; LL.B., Harvard U., 1958. Bar: Pa. 1959. Assoc. firm Pepper, Hamilton & Sheetz, Phila., 1959-65, Obermayer, Rebmann, Maxwell & Hippel, Phila., 1965-67, prtnr, 1968-84, Saul, Ewing, Remick & Saul, 1984-2000, of counsel, 2001—. Bd. dirs. Pa. Lumbermen's Mut. Ins. Co., Phila. Reins. Corp.; co-chmn. Nat. Conf. Lawyers and Collection Agys., 1979-90; chmn. bus. litigation com. Def. Rsch. Inst., 1986-89, mem. law instsn. com., 1989-95; mem. panel of disting. neutrals CPA Inst. Dispute Resolution, 2000- Chmn. mental health budget sect. Phila. United Fund, 1967—70; pres. Found. Internat. Assn. Def. Counsel, 1997—2001. Fellow: Am. Coll. Trial Lawyers. mem. internat. com. 1992—96); mem.: ABA, Phila. Bar Assn., Pa. Bar Assn., Phila. Lawn Tennis Assn. (pres. 1969—70), Merion Cricket Club. Republican. Home: 689 Fernfield Cir Wayne PA 19087-2002 Office: Saul Ewing Remick & Saul 3800 Centre Sq W Philadelphia PA 19102 Office Phone: 215-972-1975. Personal E-mail: Waltermilb@aol.com.

**MILBRATH, ROBERT HENRY,** retired petroleum industry executive; b. Apr. 17, 1912; s. Paul and Mabel (Volkman) M.; m. Margaret Ripperger, Jan. 19, 1940; children: Robert S., Constance, Susan. BS, U.S. Naval Acad., 1934. With Standard Oil Co. N.J., 1934-74; v.p., gen. mgr. Esso Sociedad Anonima Petrolera Argentina, 1938-42, 45-50; area contact East Coast South Am., mktg. coordination, 1950-52; dir. Internat. Petroleum Co., 1954—, v.p., 1956; v.p., dir. Esso Export Corp. N.Y., 1957-59, exec. v.p., dir., 1959-61; pres., dir. chmn. exec. com. Esso Internat., Inc. (formerly Esso Export Corp.), 1961-66; exec. v.p. Esso Europe, 1966-68; logistics coordinator Standard Oil Co. (N.J.) (now Exxon Corp.), 1968-69, dir., v.p., 1969-70, dir., sr. v.p., 1970-73, ret., 1974. Cons. Boys Clubs Am., 1978-84. Served to lt. comdr. USNR; asst. naval attache 1942, Buenos Aires; chief Latin Am. sect. Army-Navy Petroleum Bd. 1943-45, Washington. Mem. U.S. Naval Acad. Alumni Assn. Clubs: U. (N.Y.C.). Republican. Home: Apt 3221 5200 SW 25th Blvd Gainesville FL 32608 Personal E-mail: rmil@gator.net.

**MILBRETT, TIFFENY CARLEEN,** professional soccer player; b. Portland, Oreg., Oct. 23, 1972; Degree in comms. mgmt., U. Portland. Mem. U.S. Women's Nat. Soccer Team; profl. soccer player N.Y. Power, 2001—03. Mem. championship team, Montricoux, France, 1993. Named World Cup Champion, 1999; recipient Gold medal, Centennial Olympic Games, 1996, 3d place medal, 1995, Silver medal, World Univ. Games, 1993, Sydney Olympic Games, 2000. Office: c/o US Soccer Fedn 1801 S Prairie Ave # 1811 Chicago IL 60616-1319

**MILBURN, RICHARD HENRY,** physics professor; b. Newark, June 3, 1928; s. Richard Percy and Lucy Elizabeth (Karr) M.; m. Nancy Jeannette Stafford, Aug. 25, 1951; children— Sarah Stafford, Anne Douglas. AB, Harvard U., 1948, A.M., 1951, PhD, 1954. Instr. Harvard U., Cambridge, Mass., 1954, 56-57, asst. prof., 1957—61; assoc. prof. physics Tufts U., Medford, Mass.. 1961-65, prof., 1965-98, John Wade prof., 1990-98, rsch. prof., 1998—2003, prof. emeritus, 2003. Fulbright lectr., India, 1984 Trustee Cambridge Friends Sch., 1989-95. With U.S. Army, 1954-56. Sheldon travelling fellow, 1948-49; NSF fellow, 1952-53; Guggenheim fellow, 1960 Fellow Am. Phys. Soc. (past chmn. New Eng. sect.); mem. Am. Assn. Physics Tchrs., AAAS, AAUP. Achievements include research on high energy and elementary particles physics. Home: 1 Plymouth Rd Winchester MA 01890-3620 E-mail: rmilburn@tufts.edu.

**MILBURY, MIKE,** professional sports team executive, former professional hockey coach; b. Brighton, Mass., June 17, 1952; m. Ginger Milbury; children: Owen, Luke, Jake, Jake Patrick, Caitlin, Alison. Grad., Colgate U. Player Boston Bruins, 1976-87, asst. coach, 1985—86, head coach, asst. gen. mgr., 1989-91, asst. gen. mgr., 1991—95; head coach Maine Mariners (Am. Hockey League), 1987—89, NY Islanders, 1995—97, 1998, gen. mgr., 1996—98, 1999—2006; sr. v.p. NY Islanders, Bridgeport Sound Tigers, NY Dragons, 2006—. In-studio analyst ESPN, 1994—95; gen. mgr. US Nat. Hockey Team, 1995—96, 1996—97. Named Coach of Yr., The Hockey News and The Sporting News, 1990. Office: NY Islanders Nassau Veterans Meml Coliseum 1255 Hempstead Turnpike Uniondale NY 11553*

**MILCH, THOMAS H.,** lawyer; b. Dec. 27, 1950; BA summa cum laude, Yale Univ., 1973, JD, 1976. Bar: Ind. 1976, D.C. 1977. Ptnr., Environ. Practice Group Arnold & Porter, Washington. Adj. prof. Georgetown Univ. Law Sch., 1989—97. Dir. Migrant Legal Action Project, 1991—93, Environ. Law Inst., 1993—99; bd. dir. RESOLVE, Inc., 1993—, Wildlife Trust Internat. Mem.: ABA (vice chmn., Com. on Environ. Litigation 1994—; chmn. Spec. Com. on Environ. Litigation Techniques 1992—94, mem. Standing Com. on Environ. Law 1996—98), Lawyers Com. on Human Rights (past co-chmn., D.C. Adv. Council). Office: Arnold & Porter 555 Twelfth St NW Washington DC 20004-1206 Office Phone: 202-942-5030. Office Fax: 202-942-5999. Business E-Mail: thomas.milch@aporter.com.

**MILCHAN, ARNON,** film producer; b. Britis Palestine (now Israel), Dec. 6, 1944; Prodr. (plays) Tomb, It's So Nice To Be Civilized, Amadeus (Paris prodn.), (TV) MASADA, 1981, (TV series) The Client, 1995, (films) Black Joy, 1977, The Medusa Touch, 1978, Dizengoff 99, 1979, The King of Comedy, 1983, Once Upon a Time in America (also actor), 1984, Brazil, 1985, Stripper, 1986, Legend, 1986, Man on Fire, 1987, The Adventures of Baron Munchausen, 1989, Who's Harry Crumb, 1989, The War of the Roses, 1989, Big Man on Campus, 1990, Pretty Woman, 1990, Q&A, 1990, Guilty by Suspicion, 1991, JFK, 1991, Switch, 1991, The Mambo Kings, 1992,

Memoirs of an Invisible Man, 1992, The Power of One, 1992, Under Siege, 1992, Sommersby, 1993, Falling Down, 1993, Made in America, 1993, Free Willy, 1993 (exec. prodr.), The Nutcracker, 1993, That Night, 1993, Heaven and Earth, 1993, The New Age, 1993, Striking Distance, 1993, Six Degrees of Separation, 1993, Second Best, 1994, Boys on the Side, 1994, Natural Born Killers, 1994, The Client, 1994, Cobb, 1994, Bogus, 1995, Under Siege 2: Dark Territory, 1995, Free Willy 2: The Adventure Home, 1995, Empire Records, 1995, Copycat, 1995, Heat, 1995, The Sunchaser, 1996, Carpool, 1996, Bogus, 1996, A Time to Kill, 1996, The Mirror Has Two Faces, 1996, Tin Cup, 1996, L.A. Confidential, 1997, Murder at 1600, 1997, Free Willy 3: The Rescue, 1997, The Devil's Advocate, 1997, Breaking Up, 1997, The Man Who Knew Too Little, 1997, Dangerous Beauty, 1998, City of Angels, 1998, The Negotiator, 1998, A Midsummer Night's Dream, 1999, Simply Irresistable, 1999, Goodbye Lover, 1999, Fight Club (exec. prodr.), 1999, Entrapment, 1999, The Hunt for the Unicorn Killer, 1999, Big Momma's House, 2000, Tigerland, 2000, Joe Somebody (exec. prodr.), 2001, Don't Say A Word, 2001, Black Knight, 2001, Freddy Got Fingered (exec. prodr.), 2001, Joy Ride (exec. prodr.), 2001, High Crimes, 2002, Life or Something Like It, 2002, Unfaithful (exec. prodr.), 2002, Daredevil, 2003, Runaway Jury, 2003, Down with Love (exec. prodr.), 2003, The Girl Next Door (exec. prodr.), 2004, Man on Fire, 2004, First Daughter (exec. prodr.), 2004, Elektra, 2005, Mr. and Mrs. Smith, 2005, Bee Season (exec. prodr.), 2005, Stay, 2005, Date Movie, 2006; (TV); exec. prodr.: Squach, 2000, Noriega: God's Favorite, 2000 (TV), Up at the Villa, 2000 Office: New Regency Enterprises 10201 W Pico Blvd Bldg 12 Los Angeles CA 90064-2606*

**MILDER, JAY,** artist; b. Omaha, May 12, 1934; s. Leo and Jeanette M.; children: Rachael, Rifka, Joshua, Isobella. Student, U. Nebr., Omaha, 1953-54, Sorbonne, Paris, 1954-56, Art Inst. of Chgo., 1956-57, Hans Hofmann Sch., Provincetown, Mass., 1958-62. Dfsdfsdfsd. Tchr. art Dayton Art Inst., 1963-65, N.Y. Inst. Tech., N.Y.C., 1965, Pratt Inst., Bklyn., 1966, Brandeis Inst., Santa Susana, Calif., 1967-68, Md. Art Inst., Balt., 1969, Chrysler Mus. Sch., Norfolk, Va., 1970, CUNY, 1971-89, U. Studio Sch., Johnson, 1989. Numerous one man shows at various mus. and galleries including City Gallery, NYC, 1958, Sun Gallery, Provincetown, Mass., 1958, Allan Stone Gallery, NYC, 1960, 61, 62, Fulton Gallery, NYC, 1960, Zabriskle Gallery, NYC, 1960, Museo Bellas Artes, San Juan, 1961, Dayton Art Inst., 1963, Ohio Wesleyan U., Del., 1964, Antioch Coll., Ohio, 1965, Gallery Fore, LA, 1965, Bienville Gallery, New Orleans, 1968-72, 73, 74, 77, Rosen Gallery, Laguna Beach, 1968, Temple Israel, Long Beach, 1969, The Chrysler Mus., Norfolk, Va., 1972, Mint Mus. Art, Charlotte, NC, 1973, Ryder Gallery, LA, 1973, Thompson Gallery, Aspen, Colo., 1974, Lerner-Heller Gallery, NYC, 1975, Gallery One, 1976, Art Latitude Gallery, NYC, 1978, Mint Mus. Art, Charlotte, NC, 1978, Ingber Gallery, NYC, 1979, Ad Summun Arts Gallery, NYC, 1980, Ronald Hunning Gallery, NYC, 1981, Oscarsson Hood Gallery, NYC, 1982, Shahin Requicha Gallery, Rochester, NYC, 1984, Sid Deutsch Gallery, 1986, Richard Green Gallery, NYC, 1986, Gallery Four, Charlotte, Va., 1986, Harcourts Contemporary, San Francisco, 1987, Richard Green Gallery, NYC, 1987-89, Gallery Jupiter, Little Silver, NJ, 1987-89, Anton Gallery, Washington, 1987-89, Yares Gallery, Scottsdale, 1987-89, Eleonore Austerer Fine Art, San Mateo, Calif., 1988, Girgis & Klym Gallery, Fitzroy, Australia, 1988, Yares Gallery, Scottsdale, Ariz., 1989, Schick Art Gallery, Skidmore Coll., Saratoga Springs, NYC, 1991-92, Va. Beach Ctr. Arts, 1991-92, Elizabeth Harris Gallery, NYC, 1994, Alitash Kebede Gallery, LA, 1994, Horace Richter Gallery, Tel Aviv, 1996, Hugo Pagano Gallery, NYC, 1997, Nat. Mus. Fine Arts, Rio de Janeiro, 1999, Andre Zarre Gallery, NYC, 2001, Mus. Modern Art, Salvador, Bahia, Brazil, 2003; numerous group shows including City Gallery, NYC, 1958, 10th St. Gallery, NYC, 1958, Phoenix Gallery, 1958, 77, Sun Gallery, Provincetown, 1959, Ellison Gallery, Ft. Worth, 1959, Stuttman Gallery, NYC, 1960, Zabriskie Gallery, 1960, Dayton Art Inst., Ohio, 1961, Mus. Modern Art, NYC, 1962, 67, Yale U. Art Gallery, New Haven, 1962, Nat. Graphics Show, 1963, Yale U. Art Gallery, New Haven, 1964, Martha Jackson Gallery, NYC, 1965, Am. Fedn. Art U. Mich. Mus. Art, Ann Arbor, 1965, Mus. Modern Art, Mex. City, Mex., 1968, Karen Horney Clinic, NYC, 1969, Sonraed Gallery, NYC, 1970-71, New Sch. Social Rsch., NYC, 1970-71, Mus. NY, 1970-71, North Shore Cmty. Art Ctr., Gt. Neck, NY, 197-71, Dayton Art Inst., 1970-71, Living Arts Ctr. Gallery, 1970-71, Joseloff Gallery, U. Hartford, Conn., 1970-71, East Ctrl. State Coll., Ada, Okla., 1970-71, Gardiner Art Gallery, Okla. State U., Stillwater, 1970-71, Contemporary Arts Found., Okla. City, 1970-71, Bienville Gallery, New Orleans, 1970-71, 74, The Chrysler Mus., Norfolk, Va., 1970-71, Westbeth Artists Gallery, NYC, 1971, City Coll. NYC, 1973, Santa Barbara Mus. Calif., 1974, Mass. U., 1974, San Francisco Art Inst., 1974, Ankrum Gallery, LA, 1974, Aida Hernandez Gallery, NYC, 1974, Pace Coll., NYC, 1974, The Chrysler Mus., Norfolk, 1974, Humanist Ctr., NYC, 1974, La. State U. Gallery, Baton Rouge, 1975, Landmark Gallery, NYC, 1977, Aaron Berman Gallery, NYC, 1977, Skidmore Coll., Saratoga Springs, NYC, 1977, Noyes, Van Cline and Davenport Gallery, NYC, 1977, 10th St. Mexican Mus., Guadalajara, Mex., 1978, Bienville Gallery, New Orleans, 1978, Landmark Gallery, NYC, 1978, Myers Arts Gallery, SUNY, Plattsburgh, 1978, U. Art Gallery, SUNY, Albany, 1978, Union Coll., Cranford, NJ, 1978, St. John's Coll., Annapolis, Md., 1979-80, Castellani Gallery, Niagara Falls, NY, 1979-80, Dowd Art Gallery, SUNY, Cortland, NY, 1979-80, Root Art Ctr., Hamilton Coll., Clinton, NY, 1979-80, Brainerd Art Gallery, SUNY, Potsdam, 1979-80, Del. Art Mus., Wilmington, 1979-80, Bruce Mus., Greenwich, Conn., 1979-80, Tyler Art Gallery, SUNY, Oswego, 1979-80, Firehouse Gallery, Nassau CC, Garden City, NY, 1979-80, Warehouse Gallery, Orlando, Fla., 1984, Provincetown Assn. and Mus., Mass., 1985, Equitable Life AssuranceSoc. and Mendik Co., NYC, 1985, Kenkeleba Gallery, NYC, 1986, Shanghai, China and City U. NY, 1986, Newton Art Ctr., Newtonville, Mass., 1986, Anita Shapolsky Gallery, NYC, 1987, 55 Mercer St. Gallery, 1987, Galerie Helen Grubair, Miami, Fla., 1988, Arthur Robbins Studio, NYC, 1988, Manattan Borough Pres. Gallery, NYC, 1988, Newport Art Mus., RI, 1988, Unipas Gallery, NYC, 1988, RFM Studio, NYC, 1988, Limelight, NYC, 1988, Galerie Helene Grubair, Miami, Fla., 1988, Barbara Ingber Gallery, NYC, 1989, Horace Richter Gallery, Jaffa, Israel, 1990, Anita Shapolsky Gallery, NYC, 1990, Alitash Kebede Fine Art, LA, 1991, Anderson Gallery, Va. Commonwealth U., Richmond, Va., 1991, Greenville Mus., SC, 1993, Kathleen Ross Gallery, Soho, NYC, 1995, Elizabeth Harris Gallery, NYC, 1998, Hugo Pagano Gallery, NYC, 1999, Reina Sofia Mus., Madrid, 2000, many others; represented in permanent collections including New Orleans Mus. Art, Grey Mus., NYU, Mus. Tucson, Pinacoteca Mus., Sao Paulo, RI Sch. Design Mus., Providence, Va. Beach Art Mus., Wichita Art Mus., Kans., Anderson Gallery, Va. Commonwealth U., Richmond, AT&T Corp., NYC, Bayonne Jewish CC, NJ, Brandeis Inst., LA, Best Products, Richmond, Beth El Synagogue, Long Beach, The Chrysler Mus., Dayton Art Inst., Ein Hod Mus., Jerusalem, Flossie Martin Gallery, Radford U., Va., Herbert F. Johnson Mus., Cornell U., Ithaca, Lakeland Cultural Arts Ctr., Littleton, NC, Maler Mus. Art, Randolph-Macon Women's Coll., Lynchburg, Va., Mint Mus. Art, Charlotte, NC, Muscarelle Mus. Art, Williamsburg, Va., Mus. Art, San Juan, Mus. Solidarity, Titograd, Yugoslavia, Neuberger Mus., Purchase, Newark Mus., New Mus., NY, Oakleigh Collection, Boston, Palm Springs Desert Mus., Provincetown Mus., Simon and Shuster Co., NYC, Sinai Temple, LA, Skidmore Coll., Saratoga Springs, Skirball Mus., Hebrew Union Coll., LA, State U. NY, Binghamton, Tel Aviv Mus., Weatherspoon Art Gallery, Greensboro, NC, Yale U., New Haven; contbr. various catalogues and publs. Home and Office: 108 Wooster St New York NY 10012-5207

**MILDREN, JACK,** bank executive, retired state official; b. Kingsville, Tex., Oct. 10, 1949; s. Larry J. and Mary Glynne (Lamont) M.; m. Janis Susan Butler, Jan. 14, 1972; children: Leigh, Lauren, Drew. BBA, U. Okla., 1972. Cert. petroleum landman. Mem. Balt. Colts Football Team, 1972-73, New England Patriots Football Team, 1974; v.p. Saxon Oil Co., 1972-79; co-founder, pres. Regency Exploration Inc., 1977-88; ind. oil oper., 1988-90; lt. gov. State of Okla., Oklahoma City, 1990-95; pres., CEO Pre-Paid Legal Svcs. Inc., Ada, Okla., 1995; owner LJM Fin., 1997—; vice chmn. Arvest Banks, 2003—. Bd. dirs. Children's Med. Rsch. Found., Arts Coun. Oklahoma City, Nat. Football League Players Found. and Hall of Fame, State Ctr. Com., Jim Thorpe Club; mem. Leadership Okla., Leadership Oklahoma City; mem. Com. to Devel. Biotech. Industry in Okla. Named All-Am. Football Player, 1971, Acad. All-Am., 1971, Nat. Football Found. Hall Fame, 1971,

Most Valuable Player Sugar Bowl, 1972, Best QB in U. Oklahoma history, numerous other athletic awards; inducted into Okla. Sports Hall of Fame, 1998, GTE Acad. Hall of Fame, 1998. Mem. Beta Gamma Sigma, Phi Delta Theta (past pres., bd. dirs.) Meth. Home: 1701 Guilford Ln Oklahoma City OK 73120-1013 Office: PO Box 55500 Oklahoma City OK 73155 Office Phone: 405-419-3721. Business E-Mail: jmildren@arvest.com.

**MILDVAN, DONNA,** infectious diseases physician; b. Phila., June 20, 1942; d. Carl David and Gertrude M.; m. Rolf Dirk Hamann; 1 child, Gabriella Kay. AB magna cum laude, Bryn Mawr Coll., 1963; MD, Johns Hopkins U., 1967. Diplomate Am. Bd. Internal Medicine and Infectious Diseases. Intern, resident Mt. Sinai Hosp., N.Y.C., 1967-70, fellow, infectious diseases 1970-72; asst., assoc. prof. clin. medicine Mt. Sinai Sch. Medicine, N.Y.C., 1972-87; prof. clinical medicine Dept. Medicine, Mt. Sinai Sch. Medicine, N.Y.C., 1987-88, prof. medicine, 1988-94; physician-in-charge infectious diseases Beth Israel Med. Ctr., N.Y.C., 1972-79, chief, div. infectious diseases, 1980—; prof. medicine Albert Einstein Coll. of Medicine, N.Y.C., 1994—. Mem. AIDS charter rev. com., NIH/Nat. Inst. Allergy and Infectious Diseases, Bethesda, 1987—; cons. FDA, Rockville, 1987—, Ctrs. for Disease Control, Atlanta, 1985-86; among first to describe AIDS, "Pre-AIDS", AIDS Dementia, 1982, among first to study AZT, 1986; Keynote speaker, II Internat. Conf. on AIDS, Paris, 1986 and other achievements in field; Sophie Jones Meml. lectr. in infectious diseases U. Mich. Hosps., 1984. Contbr. numerous articles to profl. jours; co-editor two books, many book chpts. and abstracts on infectious diseases and AIDS; editor: Atlas of AIDS, edits. 1-3. Grantee N.Y. State AIDS Inst., 1986-87; Henry Strong Denison scholar Johns Hopkins U. Sch. Medicine, 1967; recipient Woman of Achievement award AAUW, 1987, Hero in Medicine award Internat. Assn. Physicians in AIDS Care, 2000; contract for antiviral therapy in AIDS, Nat. Cancer Inst./Nat. Inst. Allergy and Infectious Diseases, 1985-86, subcontract Nat. Inst. Allergy and Infectious Diseases, ACTU, 1987-99, prin. investigator, 2000—. Fellow Infectious Diseases Soc. Am.; mem. Am. Soc. Microbiology, AAAS, Harvey Soc., Internat. AIDS Soc. Democrat. Jewish. Avocation: old movies. Office: Beth Israel Med Ctr 1st Ave New York NY 10003-7903

**MILEDI, RICARDO,** neurobiologist; b. Mexico City, N.Mex., Sept. 15, 1927; m. Ana Mela Garces, Dec. 17, 1955; 1 child, Rico. BSc, Instituto Cientifico y Literario, Chihuahua, Mex., 1945; MD, U. Nacional Autonoma de Mex., 1955; DSc (hon.), Universidad del Pais Vasco, 1992, U. Trieste, Italy, 2000, U. Chihuahua, Mex., 2000, U. Queretaro, 2001. Researcher Instituto Nacional de Cardiologia, Mexico, 1954-56; fellow John Curtin Sch. Med. Res., Canberra, Australia, 1956-58; mem. faculty U. Coll., London, 1959-85, Foulerton research prof. of Royal Soc., 1975-85, head dept. biophysics, 1978-85; disting. prof. dept. neurobiology and behavior U. Calif., Irvine, 1984—. Recipient Principe de Asturias prize, Spain, 1999. Fellow Royal Soc. London (Royal medal 1999), Am. Acad. Arts and Scis.; mem. AAAS, NAS, 3d World Acad. Scis., (titular) European Acad. Arts, Scis., Humanities, N.Y. Acad. Scis., Hungarian Acad. Scis. (hon.), Mex. Acad. Scis., Mex. Acad. Medicine. Home: 9 Gibbs Ct Irvine CA 92612-4032 Office: U Calif Dept Neurobiology Behavior 2205 Bio Sci Ii Irvine CA 92697-4550 Office Phone: 949-824-4730. Business E-Mail: rmiledi@uci.edu.

**MILES, AMY E.,** recreational facility executive; With PricewaterhouseCoopers, LLC, 1989—98; sr. mgr. Deloitte & Touche, 1998—99; from sr. v.p. fin. to exec. v.p., CFO, treas. Regal Entertainment Group, Englewood, Colo., 1999—2000, exec. v.p., 2000—, CFO, 2000—, treas., 2000—. Office: Regal Entertainment Group 9110 East Nichols Ave Ste 200 Englewood CO 80112

**MILES, ARTHUR J.,** financial planner, consultant; b. N.Y.C., Sept. 2, 1920; s. Levi and Rachel Goldsworthy (Hiscock) M.; m. Pearl Cooper, Nov. 27, 1947; children: Beverly Miles Kerns, Douglas Robert. BBA, Pace U., 1958; MBA, NYU, 1963; postgrad., Dartmouth Coll., 1966, Brown U., 1970-71. Instr. Brown U., Providence, 1970-71; with Dime Savs. Bank, N.Y.C., 1938-81, exec. v.p., treas., 1975-78, sr. exec. v.p., treas., 1978-81; pres. AJM Assocs., Floral Park, N.Y., then Sarasota, Fla., 1981—. Newscaster Sta. WUSF-FM, Tampa, Fla.; bd. dirs. Cultural Instns. Retirement System, N.Y.C., 1968—89; fin. cons. Bklyn. Inst. Arts and Scis., 1972—89. Trustee, nat. treas. Alcoholics Anonymous, N.Y.C., 1970-79; tech. adviser N.Y.C. Fin. Liason Com., 1975-76. Served to sgt., inf. U.S. Army, 1942-45, Philippines. Fellow Fedn. Fin. Analysts; mem. Nat. Assn. Bus. Economists, Internat. Assn. Fin. Planners, Broadcast Pioneers, NYU Club, Marco Polo Club (N.Y.C.), Tournament Players Club. Republican. Office: AJM Assocs 8325 Shadow Pine Way Sarasota FL 34238-5624

**MILES, CHRISTINE MARIE,** museum director; b. Madison, Ind., Mar. 2, 1951; d. Leland Weber and Mary Virginia (Geyer) M. BA, Boston U., 1973; MA, George Washington U., 1982; postgrad., Mus. Mgmt. Inst., 1985. Curatorial asst. Mus. City of N.Y., 1973-75; art gallery dir. South Street Seaport Mus., N.Y.C., 1975-77; rschr. The Octagon, AIA Found., Washington, 1978-80; dir. Fraunces Tavern Mus., Washington, 1980-86, Albany (N.Y.) Inst. History and Art, 1986—. Bd. dirs. SUNY-Albany Found. Author, writer/coordinator, compiler of catalogs in field. Mem. Arts Commn. City of Albany; pres. Gallery Assn. N.Y. State, 1991-93, N.Y. State. Mem. Am. Assn. Mus. Office: Albany Inst History and Art 125 Washington Ave Albany NY 12210-2296

**MILES, DAVID LOREN,** museum director; b. Charlevoix, Mich., Feb. 14, 1940; s. Robert Clarence and Esther Miles. BA, MA, U. Mich., 1963. Asst. cashier U. Mich., Ann Arbor, 1966—68, dir. statistical svcs., 1968—70; night mgr. Lodge Motel, Charlevoix, 1972—2000; co-dir. Charlevoix Hist. Soc. Harsha House Mus., 2000—. Writer, prodr., rschr. (town heritage book) Bob Miles' Charlevoix II, 2002. Mem. C. of C. Home: 109 Pk Ave Charlevoix MI 49720 Office: Charlevoix Hist Soc 103 State St Charlevoix MI 49720 Office Phone: 231-547-0373. Business E-Mail: chxhistory@core.com.

**MILES, DAVID MICHAEL,** lawyer; b. Jackson, Mich., Aug. 5, 1954; s. Richard George and Joann Marie (Stefanoff) M.; m. Noelle Suzanne McHugh, Sept. 6, 1986; children: Amy Elizabeth, Margaret Noelle, Lane McHugh. Student, U. Mich., 1972-74; BA cum laude, Clark U., 1976; JD magna cum laude, George Washington U., 1979. Bar: D.C. 1979, U.S. Ct. Appeals (4th cir.) 1980, U.S. Dist. Ct. Md. 1980, U.S. Dist. Ct. D.C. 1983, U.S. Supreme Ct. 1983, U.S. Ct. Appeals (D.C. cir.) 1981, U.S Ct. Appeals (9th cir.) 1984, U.S. Ct. Appeals (2d cir.) 1984. Law clk. to Chief Judge Edward Northrop, U.S Dist. Ct. Md., 1979-80; law clk. to Cir. Judge George MacKinnon U.S. Ct. Appeals, Washington, 1980-81; assoc. Fried, Frank, Harris, Shriver & Jacoboson, Washington, 1981-86, ptnr., 1986-92; Sidley Austin LLP, Washington, 1992—. Co-author: The Law of Financial Services, 1988; contbr. articles to profl. jours. Home: 5229 Westpath Way Bethesda MD 20816 Office: Sidley Austin LLP 1501 K St NW Washington DC 20005 Office Phone: 202-736-8556. Personal E-mail: DavidM9876@aol.com. Business E-Mail: dmiles@sidley.com.

**MILES, DON CLIFFORD,** architect; b. Ft. Knox, Ky., Sept. 17, 1942; s. Don and Kathrine Eva (Gray) M.; m. Pamela Wait, Aug. 6, 1972; children: Katherine Wait, Lesley Gray, Nicole Conel. BArch with honors, U. Wash., 1966; MArch, M of City Planning in Urban Design, Harvard U., 1971. Registered architect, Wash. Assoc. ptnr. Zimmer, Gunsul, Frasca Partnership, Seattle. Cons., lectr. numerous orgns., cities, corps. Prin. projects include Pedestrian Corridor, Major Pub. Open Spaces, CBD Transit Ctr., Bellevue, Wash., Banfield Light Rail Project, Portland, Boise (Idaho) Downtown Major Pub. Open Space, Street Improvements and Transit Malls, Honolulu Rapid Transit Project, Revitalization of State St., Chgo., Midway Corridor Project, Mpls., High Capacity Transit Project, Seattle, Ctrl. Orange County Aerial Fixed Guideway, Mission Valley West Extension Light Rail Project, San Diego, Master Plan for Capitol of State of Wash., Seattle Union Sta. Redevel. Plan, Weyerhauser Corp. Campus, Quadrant Corp. site, Lake Union, Seattle, Whitman Coll. Bd. dirs., founder Project for Pub. Spaces, 1975—; bd. dirs. Seattle Children's Mus., 1978-82; trustee Queen Ann Community Coun.,

1978-80. Fellow AIA, Inst. Urban Design. Avocations: skiing, jogging. Home: 611 W Comstock St Seattle WA 98119-3422 Office: Zimmer Gunsul Frasca 925 4th Ave 2400 Seattle WA 98104-1146

**MILES, DONALD F.,** lawyer; b. Marysville, Calif., Apr. 11, 1949; AB with honors, Stanford U., 1971; JD, U. Calif., San Francisco, 1974. Bar: Calif. 1974, U.S. Dist. Ct. (no. dist.) Calif. 1974, U.S. Dist. Ct. (ea. dist.) Calif. 1977, U.S. Dist. Ct. (so. dist.) Calif. 1986, U.S. Supreme Ct. 1987, U.S. Dist. Ct. (ctrl. dist.) Calif. 1991. Law clk. to Hon. William P. Clark Jr. Supreme Ct. Calif., 1974-75; mem. Howard, Rice, Nemerovski, Canady, Falk & Rabkin, P.C., San Francisco. Spl. master U.S. Dist. Ct. (no. dist.) Calif.; instr., adj. faculty mem. Hastings Coll. Law U. Calif.; faculty mem., bd. dirs. Hastings Nat. Coll. Advocacy; mem. adv. com. Calif. Legis. Joint Com. Tort Liability. Author: (with others) Civil Procedure During Trial, vol. II, 1984, 95, California Liability Insurance Practice, 1991, Continuing Education of the Bar Action Guide, 1991; author, narrator: (videotape) Laying a Foundation to Introduce Evidence, 1989; contbr. articles to profl. jours. Bd. chmn. The Glenwood Sch. Found. Mem. ABA (sect. torts and ins. practice), State Bar Calif., Assn. Def. Counsel No. Calif., Bar Assn. of San Francisco, Internat. Assn. Def. Counsel, Def. Rsch. Inst., Thurston Soc., Order of Coif. Office: Howard Rice Nemerovski Canady Falk & Rabkin PC 3 Embarcadero Ctr Ste 700 San Francisco CA 94111-4074 Office Phone: 415-434-1600. Business E-Mail: dmiles@howardrice.com.

**MILES, DORIS COOPER,** bank executive; b. Camp Le June, N.C., Jan. 16, 1963; d. Thomas Wayne and Linda Gene (DuVall) Cooper; 1 child, J. Brian. Sales and mktg. sec. Hawthorne at Leesburg, Fla., 1989—91; contr. to Delta Techop and Credit Union Norrell Svcs., Atlanta, 1991—93; workers compensation administr. Riscorp, Maitland, Fla., 1995—96; sales and leasing adminstr. Jaymark Bldrs., Clermont, Fla., 1996—98; EAS contr. to IBM Norrell Spherion, Atlanta, 1998—2000, Orlando, Fla., 2000—01; dealer fin. sec. Independent Bank, Cleveland, Tenn., 2001—. Author: (booklet) To the Policy Holder, 1994, (book) Mommy and the Masher, 1996, The Storm's Heart, 1998, Between Love and Duty, 2001. Avocations: motivational speaking, travel, photography. Home: 102 Janes Way Ne Cleveland TN 37323-4521

**MILES, FRANK CHARLES,** retired newspaper executive; b. Detroit, Jan. 1, 1926; s. Nelson and Ethel Jane (Mennill) M.; m. Catharine Estelle Coleman, Sept. 4, 1948 (dec. Aug. 2000); children: Barbara Ann, Diana Estelle; m. Joan Ashkin, Feb. 1, 2003. Student, Westervelt Bus. Coll., 1947-48. With Thomson Newspapers Ltd.: Cambridge, Ont., Canada, 1950-52, 54-55; bus. mgr. Sarnia (Ont.) Obs., 1952-54; gen. mgr. Pembroke (Ont.) Obs., 1956-58. Moose Jaw (Sask.) Times-Herald, Canada, 1958-62; pub. Austin (Minn.) Daily Herald, 1962-66; sr. v.p., gen. mgr. Thomson Newspapers Inc., Des Plaines, Ill., 1966-89, exec. v.p. acquisitions 1990-91, ret., 1991, also bd. dirs. Vol. assignments Internat. Media Fund, Baltics, Albania, 1992-93; Knight fellowship Moscow, 1994, Ctrl. for Ind. Journalism, Bucharest, Romania, 1995, Kocise Slovakia, 1996, Internat. Rsch. & Exch. Corps., Zagreb, Croatia, Belarus, 1997, Brest, Minsk, Belarus, 1997-98. Mem. Assn. Integration of Whole Person, Sigma Delta Chi. Republican. Mem. United Ch. of Christ. Home: 3892 Bordeaux Dr Punta Gorda FL 33950

**MILES, HARRY LEHMAN,** lawyer, educator; b. May 4, 1944; s. Sidney and Beatrice (Lehman) M. AB, Dartmouth Coll., 1965; JD, Bklyn. Law Sch., 1969; MA in Comms., U. Mass., Amherst, 1972. Tchr. James Madison H.S., Bklyn., 1966-70; instr. U. Mass., Amherst, 1970-72; practice law Amherst, 1971-75; asst. dist. atty. Northwestern Dist., Mass., 1975-79, 1st asst. dist. atty. Mass., 1979-80; ptnr. Growhoski, Callahan & Miles, Northampton, Mass., 1980-94, Green, Miles, Lipton, & Fitz-Gibbon, Northampton, Mass., 1994—. Past adj. prof. law Western New Eng. Coll. Sch. Law, Greenfield Cmty. Coll.; v.p., dir. Western Mass. Legal Services Corp. Mem. Shutesbury (Mass.) Bd. Health, 1972-74, Shutesbury Fin. Com., 1973-74. Fellow Am. Acad. Forensic Scis. (jurisprudence sect.), Am. Coll. Trial Lawyers, Mass. Bar Found.; mem. ABA, Mass. Bar Assn., Hampshire County Bar Assn. Mass. Assn. Criminal Defense Lawyers, Dartmouth Lawyers Assn. Democrat. Office: Green Miles Lipton Fitz-Gibbon 77 Pleasant St PO Box 210 Northampton MA 01061-0210 Office Phone: 413-586-8218 3012. E-mail: Hmiles@greenmiles.com

**MILES, JACK (JOHN RUSSIANO),** journalist, educator; b. Chgo., July 30, 1942; s. John Alvin and Mary Jean (Murphy) Miles; m. Jacqueline Russiano, Aug. 23, 1980; 1 child, Kathleen. LittB, Xavier U., Cin., 1964; PhB, Pontifical Gregorian U., Rome, 1966; student, Hebrew U., Jerusalem, 1966—67; PhD, Harvard U., 1971. Asst. prof. Loyola U., Chgo., 1970—74; asst. dir. Scholars Press, Missoula, Mont., 1974—75; postdoctoral fellow U. Chgo., 1975—76; editor Doubleday & Co., N.Y.C., 1976—78; exec. editor U. Calif. Press, Berkeley, 1978—85; book editor L.A. Times, 1985—91, mem. editl. bd., 1991—95; dir. Humanities Ctr. Claremont (Calif.) Grad. U., 1995—97; Mellon vis. prof. Calif. Inst. Tech., 1997—98; sr. advisor to pres. J. Paul Getty Trust, L.A., 1999—. Contbg. editor: Atlantic Monthly, 1995—; author: Retroversion and Text Criticism, 1984, God: A Biography, 1995, Christ: A Crisis in the Life of God, 2001; contbr. learned and popular articles to various periodicals; book reviewer. Recipient Pulitzer Prize for biography, 1996; Guggenheim fellow, 1990—91, 2002—, MacArthur fellow, 2003—. Mem.: PEN, Amnesty Internat., Am. Acad. Religion, Nat. Book Critics Cir. (pres. 1990—92). Episcopalian. Office: J Paul Getty Trust 1200 Getty Center Dr Ste 1100 Los Angeles CA 90049-1688

**MILES, JESSE MC LANE,** retired accounting company executive; b. De Funiak Springs, Fla., June 17, 1932; s. Percy Webb and Dora (Pippin) M.; m. Catherine Rita Eugenio, July 18, 1959; children: Jesse Jr., Catherine, Teresa, John, Thomas, Robert BSBA, U. Fla., 1954. CPA NY. Mem. staff, mgr., prin. Arthur Young & Co., N.Y.C., 1954-63, ptnr., 1963-89, dep. chmn.-internat., 1985-89; chmn. Arthur Young Internat., 1985-89; ptnr. Ernst & Young, 1989-92; co-chmn. Ernst & Young Internat., 1989-92; ret., 1992. Mem. AICPA, N.Y. Inst. CPAs, Boca Pointe Country Club. Home: 7077 Via Mediterrania Boca Raton FL 33433

**MILES, JOANNA,** actress, playwright, director; b. Nice, France, Mar. 6, 1940; came to U.S., 1941, naturalized, 1941; d. Johannes Schiefer and Jeanne Miles; m. William Burns, May 23, 1970 (div. 1977); m. Michael Brandman, Apr. 29, 1977; 1 child, Miles. Grad. H.S., Putney, Vt., 1958. Mem. Actors Studio, Playwrites and Dirs. Workshop, NYC, 1966; co-founder, mem. LA Classic Theatre, 1986; playwright, dir. Unit Actor's Studio, LA, 2002—05. Founder, mem. Playwrights Group/LAWW, 1991-98, L.A. Writer's Workshop, 1996-98. Starred in: (motion pictures) The Way We Live Now, 1969, Bug, 1975, The Ultimate Warrior, 1975, Golden Girl, 1978, Cross Creek, 1983, As Is, 1986, Blackout, 1988, Rosencrants and Guildenstern are Dead, 1991, The Rhinghart Theory, 1994, Judge Dredd, 1994, Alone, 1996, Sex & Breakfast, 2006; numerous television films including In What America, 1963, My Mothers House, 1963, Glass Managerie, 1974, Born Innocent, 1974, Aloha Means Goodbye, 1974, The Trial of Chaplain Jensen, 1975, Harvest Home, 1977, Fire in the Sky, 1978, Sophisticated Gents, 1979, Promise of Love, 1982, Sound of Murder, 1983, All My Sons, 1987, The Right to Die, 1987, The Habitation of Dragons, 1991, Heart of Justice, 1991, Water Engine, 1991, Cooperstown, 1992, Legionnaires, 1992, Life Lessons, 1992, Willing to Kill, 1992, The American Clock, 1993, Dark Reflections, 1993, Outcry, 1994, Everything to Gain, 1995, Small Vices, 1998, Crossfire Trail, 1999, Thin Aire, 1999, Monty Walsh, 2002, Jane Doe: Shaken & Stirred, 2006; episodes in numerous TV series including: Barney Miller, Dallas, St. Elsewhere, The Hulk, Trapper John, Kaz, Cagney and Lacey, Studio 5B, 1989, Star Trek: The Next Generation, 1990, 91, Life Stories, 1991, HBO Life Stories, 1993, Total Security, 1997, Nothing Sacred, 1998, Chicago Hope, 1998-99, ER, 2000, 01, Family Law, 2000, Judging Amy, 2003; stage plays include Once in a Life Time, 1963, Cave Dwellers, 1964, Drums in the Night, 1968, Dracula, 1968, Home Free, 1964, One Night Stands of a Noisy Passenger, 1972, Dylan, 1974, Dancing for the Kaiser, 1976, Debutante Ball, 1985, Kramer, 1977, One Flew Over the Cuckoo's Nest, 1989, Growing Gracefully, 1990, Cut Flowers, 1994; performed in radio shows Sta. KCRW Once in a Lifetime, 1987,

Babbit, 1987, Sta. KPFK, Grapes of Wrath, 1989, The White Plague, Sta. KCRW, 1991, Chekhov Short Stories, Sta. KCRW, 1992; playwright, v.p. Brandman Productions; author: (plays) Ethanasia, A Woman in Reconstruction, Hostages, Feathers, On the Shelf, (films) An Offereing of Oranges, Breaking the Rules. Pres. Children Giving to Children. Recipient 2 Emmy awards, 1974, Women in Radio and TV award, 1974, Actors Studio Achievement award, 1980, Dramalogue award, 1996, Vision award 2003; nominated Golden Globe, 1974. Mem. Acad. Motion Picture Arts and Scis. Office: Brandman Prodns 2062 Vine St Apt 5 Hollywood CA 90068-3928 Office Phone: 323-463-3224. Personal E-mail: jmilesb@aol.com.

**MILES, JOHN BILL,** retired accountant, retired tax specialist; b. Knox County, Ky., Sept. 18, 1931; s. John Ishmael and Allie Arizona (Engle) M.; m. Mary Patricia Wilson, May 25, 1963; children: Melanie, Jennifer, Dennis. BS in Commerce, Salmon P. Chase Coll., 1962; BS in Acctg., U. Cin., 1972; MBA, Lincoln Grad. Sch. Mgmt., Des Moines, 2001. CPA; accredited tax advisor; enrolled agt. Cost acct. Avco Corp., Cin., 1956—58; chief auditor Pepsi-Cola Bottling Co., Cin., 1958—64; property acct. Monsanto Co., Addyston, Ohio, 1964—66; sec.-treas. Shur-Good Biscuit Co., Inc., Cin. 1966—79; acct. Fabritec Internat. Corp., Cold Spring, Ky., 1980—98; ind. practice acctg. Cheviot, Ohio, 1999—. Lt. Col. ret. Ohio Mil. Res. Mem.: NRA, AICPA, Nat. Assn. Legal Assts., Ohio Assn. Ind. Accts., Nat. Soc. Accts., Ohio Soc. CPAs, State Guard Assn. U.S., Am. Legion, Assn. U.S. Army, Honorable Order Ky. Cols., Fur Takers of Am., Ohio Mil. Res. Assn., Accts. for Pub. Interest, Cheviot Rep. Club. Home: 3816 Roswell Ave Cincinnati OH 45211-3329

**MILES, JOHN JEFFRIES,** lawyer; b. Roanoke, Va., Mar. 29, 1946; s. Hugh Smith Jr. and Helen Mary (Jeffries) M.; m. Carolyn Ward, Aug. 30, 1969. BS, Va. Tech., 1968, MA, 1971; JD, Washington & Lee U., 1973. Bar: Va 1973, U.S. Tax Ct. 1973, U.S. Claims Ct. 1973, U.S. Dist. (we. dist.) Va. 1974, U.S. Ct. Appeals (4th cir.) 1974, U.S. Supreme Ct. 1980, D.C. 1982, U.S. Ct. Appeals (D.C. cir.) 1982, U.S. Ct. Appeals (3d cir.) 1983, U.S. Ct. Appeals (fed. cir.) 1990, U.S. Ct. Appeals (8th cir.) 1997. Assoc. Martin Hopkins & Lemon, Roanoke, 1973-75; asst. atty. gen. Office of Atty. Gen., Richmond, Va., 1976-78; trial atty. antitrust divsn. U.S. Dept. Justice, Washington, 1979-92; ptnr. O'Connor & Hannan, Washington, 1982-84, Powers Pyles Sutter & Miles, Washington, 1984-87, Baker & Hostetler, Washington, 1987-88; sr. atty. Jones Day Reavis & Pogue, Washington, 1988-92; ptnr. Ober Kaler, Washington, 1993—. Author: Antitrust Guide for Health Care Coalitions, 1983, Health Care and Antitrust Law, 1992, Antitrust Bull., 1984, Antitrust Law Jour., 1979, 1998. Episcopalian. Home: 6254 Kingfisher Ln Alexandria VA 22312-3913 Office: Ober Kaler 1401 H St NW Fl 5 Washington DC 20005-2175 Office Phone: 202-326-5008.

**MILES, JOHN R.,** real estate development company executive; b. York, Pa. married; 2 children. Grad., US Naval Acad. V.p., global head client systems and services Lend Lease Corp Ltd. Named one of Premier 100 IT Leaders, Computerworld, 2005. Office: Lend Lease Corp Ltd 200 Park Ave New York NY 10166*

**MILES, KENNETH ONTARIO,** academic program director; b. Washington; s. Lessie Olivia Walker. BA, U. Va., 1992, MEd, 1998. Tchr., coach Gonzaga Coll. High Sch., Washington, 1993-95; acad. lifeskills coord. U. Va., Charlottesville, 1995-97; coord. acad. support football Syracuse (N.Y.) U. Athletic Dept., 1997—2002; dir. student svcs. Sch. Info. Studies Syracuse (N.Y.) U., 2002—. Mem. Nat. Assn. of Student Personnel Adminstrs., Nat. Assn. of Grad. Admissions Profls., Black Coaches Assn., Nat. Assn. Advisors Athletics (chmn. ethnic concerns com. 1999-2000). Democrat. Baptist. Avocation: weight training. Office: Syracuse U Sch Info Studies 4-206 Ctr for Sci and Tech Syracuse NY 13244-4100 E-mail: komiles@syr.edu.

**MILES, LAVEDA ANN,** advertising executive; b. Greenville, S.C., Nov. 21, 1945; d. Grady Lewis and Edna Sylvia (Mahaffey) Bruce; m. Charles Thomas Miles, Nov. 10, 1974; 1 child, Joshua Bruce. A in Bus. Adminstrn., North Greenville Jr. Coll. Traffic mgr. WFBV-TV, Greenville, 1968-74; pub. svc. dir., traffic mgr. WTCG-TV, Atlanta, 1974-75; traffic mgr. Henderson Advt. Co., Greenville, 1975-77, broadcast coord., 1977-79, dir. broadcast bus., 1979-82, v.p., dir. broadcast bus., 1982-89, bus. mgr. creative dept., 1989-91, dir. creative svcs., 1991-93, sr. v.p., dir. creative svcs., 2000—; owner Altamont Mktg., 1996-99. Mem. Leadership S.C., 1994-95; bd. dirs. Boys Home of the South, 2003—. Named one of 100 Best and Brightest Women, Ad Age and Advt. Women of N.Y., 1988. Mem. Advt. Fedn. Greenville (sec. 1979-81), Greenville Ad Club (sec. 1999-2000, pres. 2000—; Silver medal award 2003). Republican. Baptist.

**MILES, LELAND WEBER,** retired academic administrator; b. Balt., Jan. 18, 1924; s. Leland Weber and Marie (Fitzpatrick) M.; m. Mary Virginia Geyer, July 9, 1947; children: Christine Marie, Gregory Lynn. AB cum laude, Juniata Coll., 1946; MA, U. N.C., 1947, PhD, 1949; postgrad., Duke U., 1949; DLitt (hon.), Juniata Coll., 1969; LLD (hon.), Rosary Hill Coll., 1970; LLD (hon.), Far East U., 1979; DHC (hon.), U. Guadalajara, Mex., 1984; Order of Merit, Alfred U., 1986. Assoc. prof. English Hanover Coll., 1949-50, prof., chmn. English dept., 1950-60; assoc. prof., asst. to head English dept. U. Cin., 1960-63, prof., 1963-64, founder humanities reading program for engrs., 1961; dean Coll. Arts and Scis., U. Bridgeport, Conn., 1964-67; pres. U. Bridgeport, 1974-87; founder U. Bridgeport Sch. Law, 1977; pres. emeritus U. Bridgeport, 1987—; pres. Alfred U., 1967-74. Bd. dirs. United Illuminating, 1978-94, chmn. audit com., 1992-94, Grolier, 1984-88, Wright Managed Investment Funds, 1988-04, Internat. Peace Acad., 1982-90; Danforth scholar Union Theol. Sem., 1956; Lilly fellow Sch. Letters Ind. U. 1959; Am. Council Learned Socs. fellow Harvard, 1963-64; Sr. Fulbright Research scholar Kings Coll. U. London, 1964, vis. scholar, 1972; seminar leader, deans and presidents insts. Am. Council on Edn., 1973-79; chmn. bd. Acad. Collective Bargaining Info. Service, Washington, 1977-79; producer, moderator Caring the Challen CBS Sta. WHAS-TV, Louisville, 1958-61; moderator Aspen (Colo.) Inst. for Humanistic Studies, 1969-70; lectr. Keedick Lecture Bur., N.Y.C., 1956-83; vis. prof. New Coll., Sarasota, Fla., 1989. Author: John Colet and the Platonic Tradition, 1961; editor: Thomas More's Dialogue of Comfort Against Tribulation, 1965, Where Do You Stand On Linquistics?, 1964, revised, 1968; sr. editor: (with Stephen Graubard and later Stephen B. Baxter) Studies in British History and Culture, 1965-79, Provoking Thought: What Colleges Should Do For Students, 2001; contbg. editor Nat. Forum, 1983-91; contbr. articles to learned jours., chpts. in books. Trustee Western NY Nuc. Rsch. Ctr., 1967-73; chmn. bd. Coll. Ctr. Finger Lakes, 1968-71; vice-chmn. bd. Empire State Found., 1969-71, chmn., 1971-73; mem. New Eng. Bd. Higher Edn., 1985-87, Ambs. Roundtable World Affairs Forum, 1986-92, Fuld Found./Nat. League Nursing Adv. Coun. on Accreditation, 1986-88; chmn. Ettinger scholarship com. Ednl. Found. Am., 1987-93; bd. dirs. Conn. Grand Opera, 1978-89, Bridgeport Bus. Coun., 1982-88; bd. dirs. Save the Children, 1988-95, chmn. adv. coun., 1990-95; adviser Asolo Theater-Fla. State U. Conservatory Actors Tng., 2004-. 1st lt. USAAF, 1944-45; capt. USAFR. Decorated DFC with oak leaf cluster, Crown Decoration of Honor 3rd Order Iran, 1978; chevalier l'Ordre des Palmes Académique (France), 1984; recipient Rosa and Samuel Sachs prize Cin. Inst. Fine Arts, 1961, Cultural medal Republic of China, 1983, Disting. Svc. award Greater Bridgeport Bar Assn., 1986, Outstanding Civilian Svc. medal Dept. Army, 1988; Miles scholars Alfred U., 1995—. Fellow Royal Soc. Arts, Manufactures and Commerce (life); mem. Renaissance Soc. Am., English Speaking Union (bd. dirs. Greenwich, Conn. chpt. 1998-04), UN Assn. (bd. dirs. Sarasota Manatee chpt., young profl. for internat. coop. 2005-), Internat. Assn. Univ. Pres. (pres. 1981-84, pres. emeritus 1984—, chief UN mission 1988-97, World Peace award 1987, chmn. UN commn. on oranges control edn. 1991-96, mem. coun. sr. advisers 1992—), Knights of Malta (order of the Orthodox Knights Hospitaller of St. John of Jerusalem, Russian Orthodox br.), Mil. Officers Assn. Sarasota, West Coast Symphony Assn., Sarasota Opera Guild, Univ. Club (NYC), Phi Delta Kappa. Episcopalian. Home (Summer): 87 Field Point Dr Fairfield CT 06824-6329 Home (Winter): 2110 Ben Franklin Dr Sarasota FL 34236 Office Phone: 941-525-3095. Personal E-mail: lelandwmiles@yahoo.com.

**MILES, LES,** college football coach; b. Nov. 10, 1953; m. Kathy Miles; children: Kathryn, Leslie, Benjamin, Gracie. BS in Econ., Mich. Univ., 1976. Asst. NFL coach. Dallas Cowboys, 1998—2000; grad. asst. Univ. Mich., 1980—81, asst. coach., 1987—94, Univ. Colo., 1982—86, Okla. State, 1995—97, head football coach, 2001—04, LSU, 2005—. Office: Tiger Stadium Staadium Rd Baton Rouge LA 70803 E-mail: football@lsu.edu.*

**MILES, MICHAEL A., JR.,** retail executive; BA, Yale Univ., 1983; MBA, Harvard Univ., 1987. Sr. v.p. concept develop. & franchise Pizza Hut Yum! Brands, Inc., 1996—99, COO Pizza Hut, 2000—03; COO Staples, Inc., Framingham, Mass., 2003—06, pres., COO, 2006—. Bd. dir. Western Union. Office: Staples Inc 500 Staples Dr Framingham MA 01702*

**MILES, MICHAEL ARNOLD,** consumer products executive; b. Chgo., June 22, 1939; s. Arnold and Alice (Morrissey) Miles; m. Pamela L. Miles; children: Michael Arnold Jr., Christopher. BS, Northwestern U., 1961. Various mgmt. positions to v.p., account supr. Leo Burnett Co., Chgo. 1961—71; with Heublein, Inc., 1971—82; sr. v.p. mktg. Ky. Fried Chicken, 1971—72; v.p. gen. mgr. grocery products Heublein, Inc., 1972—75, group v.p. internat. ops., 1976—77, v.p. group exec. Internat. group, chmn. food svc. and franchise group Ky. Fried Chicken, 1977—81, sr. v.p. foods Louisville, 1981—82; pres., COO Kraft Gen. Foods, Glenview, Ill., 1982—89; CEO, vice chmn. Philip Morris Cos., Inc., 1989—91, dep. chmn., 1991, CEO, 1991—94; special ltd. ptnr. Forstmann Little & Co., 1995—. Bd. dirs. Sears Holding Corp., Time Warner, 1995—, AMR Corp., Citadel Broadcasting Corp., Dell Inc. Bd. dirs. Jr. Achievement Chgo., Coun. Fgn. Rels., Nat. Multiple Sclerosis Soc., Lyric Opera Chgo.; mem. adv. coun. J.L. Kellogg Grad. Sch. Mgmt. Northwestern U., Evanston, Ill.*

**MILES, RAYMOND EDWARD,** retired dean, organizational behavior and industrial relations educator; b. Cleburne, Tex., Nov. 2, 1932; s. Willard Francis and Wilma Nell (Owen) M.; m. Lucile Dustin, Dec. 27, 1952; children: Laura, Grant, Kenneth. BA with highest honors, U. North Tex., 1954, MBA, 1958; PhD, Stanford U., 1963. CLR, Santa Fe R.R., Gainesville, Tex., 1950-55; instr. mgmt. Sch. Bus. U. North Tex., Denton, 1958-60; asst. prof. organizational behavior and indsl. relations Sch. Bus. Adminstrn. U. Calif.-Berkeley, 1963-68, assoc. prof., 1968-71, prof., 1971—, assoc. dean Haas Sch. of Bus., 1978-81, dean, 1983-90; dir. Inst. Indsl. Relations, 1982-83; cons. various pvt., pub. orgns. Author: Theories of Management, 1975; (with Charles C. Snow) Organization Strategy, Structure and Process, 1978, Fit, Failure, and the Hall of Fame, 1994; co-author: Organizational Behavior: Research and Issues, 1976; co-editor, contbg. author: Organization by Design: Theory and Practice, 1981. Served to 1t. USAF, 1955-58. Mem.: Acad. Mgmt. Democrat. Unitarian Universalist. Home: 8640 Don Carol Dr El Cerrito CA 94530-2733 Office: U Calif Walter A Haas Sch Bus Berkeley CA 94720-0001 Business E-mail: miles@haas.berkeley.edu.

**MILES, RICHARD,** former ambassador; b. Little Rock, Ark., 1937; m. Sharon O'Brien, June 18, 1960; children: Richard, Elizabeth. AA, Bakersfield Coll., 1960; AB, U. Calif., Berkeley, 1962; MA, Ind. U., 1964; grad., U.S. Army Russian Inst., Garmisch-Partenkirchen, Germany. With voter registration, political leadership tng. S.C. Voter Edn. Project, 1964-67; with Fgn. Svc., Oslo, Moscow, Belgrade, 1967-88; consul gen. Leningrad, 1988-91; prin. officer U.S. Embassy Office, Berlin, 1991-92; with Soviet, East European, Yugoslav Affairs, Politico-Military Bureau US Dept. State, amb. to Azerbaijan, 1992-93; dep. chief mission Am. Embassy, Moscow, 1993-96, chief of mission Belgrade, 1996—99; polit. advisor U.S. Dept. State, Washington. With USMC, 1954-57. Am. Polit. Sci. fellow for Sen. Ernest F. Hollings, 1983-84; fellow Harvard U. Ctr. Internat. Affairs, 1987-88.

**MILES, RICHARD BRYANT,** mechanical and aerospace engineering educator; b. Washington, July 10, 1943; s. Thomas Kirk and Elizabeth (Bryant) M.; m. Susan McCoy, May 14, 1983; children: Thomas, Julia. BSEE, Stanford U., 1966, MSEE, 1967, PhD in Elec. Engring., 1972. Rsch. assoc. elec. engring. dept. Stanford (Calif.) U., summer 1972; asst. prof. mech. and aerospace engring. dept. Princeton (N.J.) U., 1972-78, assoc. prof., 1978-82, prof., 1982—, chmn. engring. physics program, 1980-96, acting chmn. dept. mech. and aero. engring., 2002. Lectr. Northwestern Poly. U., Xian, China, 1987; rsch. scientist CNRS; vis. prof. U. Marseilles, France, 1995. Contbr. articles to profls. publs.; chpt. to book and conf. procs.; patentee in field. Bd. dirs. Fannie and John Hertz Found., Livermore, Calif., 1989—. Fannie and John Hertz Found. fellow, 1969-72. Fellow AIAA (Aerodynamic Measurement Tech. TC award 2000) Optical Soc. Am.; mem. IEEE (sr.), Am. Phys. Soc. Office: Princeton U Mech & Aerospace Engring D-414 Eng Quad Olden St Princeton NJ 08544-0001 Office Phone: 609-258-5131. Business E-mail: miles@princeton.edu.

**MILES, SHARON KATHLEEN,** microbiologist, educator; b. Tupelo, Miss., Dec. 26, 1958; d. Harry Willis and Cora Jane York; m. Timothy Ira Miles, Apr. 29, 1978; children: Stephen Dewayne, Timothy Ira Jr. MAT in Microbiology, Miss. State U., Starkville, 1989. Cert. Am. Soc. Clin. Pathologist, North Miss. Med. Ctr. Sch. Med., 1980. Med. technologist North Miss. Med. Ctr., Tupelo, 1980—87, Itawamba C.C., Fulton, Miss., 1992—. Biol. sci. coord. for distance learning Itawamba C.C., Tupelo, 2006—. Mem. funds distbn. com. United Way, Miss., 2004—06; mem. friends of scouting Boy Scouts Am. Yocona Area Coun., Miss., 2000—06. Recipient Meritorous Achievement award, Itawamba C.C., 2004. Mem.: Am. Soc. Clin. Pathologist (assoc.). Republican. Baptist. Avocations: equitation, scuba diving. Office: Itawamba Community College 2176 S Eason Blvd Tupelo MS 38804 Office Phone: 662-620-6219.

**MILES, STEVEN HAVERSTOCK,** geriatric medicine educator; b. Mpls., Jan. 26, 1950; s. James Gillespie and Laura Haverstock Miles; m. Susan Jane Moore, Dec. 23, 1972 (div. Mar. 1976); m. Julie Olds, Aug. 21, 1982; children: Erica, Esme. BA in Biology, Psychology, St. Olaf Coll., 1972; MD, U. Minn., 1976; postgrad., United Theol. Sem., 1977. Diplomate geriatric medicine Am. Bd. Internal Medicine. Chief med. resident, internal medicine resident Hennepin County Med. Ctr., Mpls., 1976-81; med. program dir. Am. Refugee Com., Thailand, 1981-82; asst. prof. medicine dept. internal medicine U. Minn., 1982-86; asst. prof. medicine, assoc. dir. ctr. for clin. med. ethics U. Chgo. Pritzker Sch. Medicine, 1986-89; assoc. faculty ctr. for biomed. ethics U. Minn., Mpls., 1990—; affiliate faculty ctr. for advanced feminist studies, 1990—; assoc. prof. medicine Hennepin County Med. Ctr., U. Minn., Mpls., 1990—. Cons. CPR policy in nursing homes Atty. Gen. State of Minn., 1990—, health facility policy design for limiting life-prolonging therapies Office Tech. Assessment, U.S. Congress, 1987-88, health facility policy for limiting treatment Minn. Hosp. Assn., 1986; mem. med. staff Meridian Hospice, Chgo., 1986-87; mem. ethics com. Hennepin County Med. Ctr., 1990—. Mem. editorial bd. Jour. of Am. Geriatrics Soc., 1990—, Second Opinion, 1990—; Gerontologist; author: (with C.K. Cassel, M. Siegler, C.F. Gomez, B.J. Marsh) Institutional Protocols for Decisions about Life-Sustaining Treatments, 1988; co-author: (with C.F. Gomez) Protocols for Elective Use of Life-Sustaining Treatments: A Design Guide, 1989; author articles. Bd. dirs. Hennepin Faculty Assocs., 1991—, Minn. Internat. Health Vols., 1989—, Minn. Planned Parenthood, 1985-86; mem. delivery mechanisms com. and benefit design, 1990—; foster parent Hennepin County and Cook County Social Svcs., 1985-87; chair med. ethics resource com. VA Med. Ctr., 1985-86; chmn. ethics com. Emergency Med. Svcs. Coun., Hennepin County, Minn., 1984-85; health profl. network coord. Amnesty Internat. Torture Network, 1986-87. Kaiser Found. Faculty scholar Henry J. Kaiser Faculty Found., 1988-92. Fellow ACP, Hastings Ctr.; mem. Am. Geriatric Soc., Gerontol. Soc. Am., Am. Sco. Law, Medicine and Health Care, Soc. for Gen. Internal Medicine, Minn. Med. Soc., Hennepin County Med. Soc. Home: 1517 E River Pky Minneapolis MN 55414-3626 Office: Hennepin County Med Ctr 701 Park Ave Minneapolis MN 55415-1623

**MILES, THOMAS CASWELL,** aerospace engineer; b. Atlanta, Mar. 21, 1952; s. Franklin Caswell and Eugenia Frances (Newsom) M.; m. Linda Susan Duggleby, Aug. 10, 1980. BMET, So. Poly. State U., 1977; postgrad.,

Troy State U., 1978-80. Assoc. engr. aircraft design Lockheed Martin Aero. Co., Marietta, Ga., 1980-82, engr., aircraft design, 1982-85, sr. engr., aircraft design, 1985-89, group engr., 1989-90, specialist engr., 1990-98, sr. specialist engr., 1998-2001, staff engr., 2001—. Mem. SAE-A-6 Mil. Aircraft & Helicopter Panel, 1987-91, SAE-A-10 Aircraft Oxygen Equipment Com., 1996—. Mem. AIAA, (assoc. fellow), ASME, ASTM, Nat. Mgmt. Assn. (bd. dirs. 1996-2000), Soc. Automotive Engrs. (SAE co. rep., SAE Atlanta sect. vice chmn. aircraft), Oxygen Standardization Coord. Group, Assn. Fraternity Advisors (affiliate), Wick's Lake Homeowners Assn. (pres. 1995, v.p. 1996, 97), Tau Kappa Epsilon (Providence advisor 1999-2002, dist. pres. 1987-88, dist. v.p. 1984-99, chpt. advisor 1980-87, key leader 1985, 90, So. Order of Honor 1989, Edn. Found. medal of excellence 2002). Avocations: sailing, screen printing. Home: 1926 Wicks Ridge Ln Marietta GA 30062-6777 Personal E-mail: tekezeke@aol.com.

**MILES, WENDELL A.,** federal judge; b. Holland, Mich., Apr. 17, 1916; s. Fred T. and Dena Del (Alverson) M.; m. Mariette Bruckert, June 8, 1946; children: Lorraine Miles, Michelle Miles Kopinski, Thomas Paul. AB, Hope Coll., 1938, LLD (hon.), 1980; MA, U. Wyo., 1939; JD, U. Mich., 1942; LLD (hon.), Detroit Coll. Law, 1979. Bar: Mich. Ptnr. Miles & Miles, Holland, 1948-53, Miles, Mika, Meyers, Beckett & Jones, Grand Rapids, Mich., 1961-70; pros. atty. County of Ottawa, Mich., 1949-53; US dist. atty. Western Dist. Mich., Grand Rapids 1953-60, U.S. dist. judge, 1974—, chief judge, 1979-86, sr. judge, 1986—. Cir. judge 20th Jud. Cir. Ct. Mich., 1970-74; instr. Hope Coll., 1948-53, Am. Inst. Banking, 1953-60; adj. prof. Am. constl. history Hope Coll., Holland, Mich., 1979—; mem. Mich. Higher Edn. Commn.; apptd. Fgn. Intelligence Surveillance Count, Washington, 1989—. Pres. Holland Bd. Edn., 1952-63. Served to capt. U.S. Army, 1942-47. Recipient Liberty Bell award, 1986. Fellow Am. Bar Found.; mem. ABA, Mich. Bar Assn., Fed. Bar Assn., Ottawa County Bar Assn., Grand Rapids Bar (Inns of Ct. 1995—), Am. Judicature Soc., Torch Club, Rotary Club, Masons. Office: US Dist Ct 236 Fed Bldg 110 Michigan St NW Ste 452 Grand Rapids MI 49503-2363 Home (Winter): 16380 Kelly Cove Dr #305 Fort Myers FL 33908 Office Phone: 616-456-2314. Business E-mail: miles@miwd.uscourts.gov.

**MILETICH, IVO,** library and information scientist, bibliographer, educator, linguist, literature research specialist; b. Pucisca, Yugoslavia, Apr. 18, 1936; came to U.S., 1966, naturalized, 1972; s. Josip and Mandina (Bagich) M.; m. Mira Pilja, Mar. 11, 1967; children: George Edward, Marina Julie. AB, Acad. Edn., Split, Yugoslavia, 1960; AM in History. U. Skopje, Macedonia, Yugoslavia, 1966; cert. advanced study, Berlitz Inst., Chgo., 1969; MA in Libr. Sci., Rosary Coll., River Forest, Ill., 1971. Cert. libr., Va. Tchr. various schs., Yugoslavia, 1959-65; asst. bibliographer Slavic langs. and lit. Joseph Regenstein and Sam Harper Librs., U. Chgo., 1967-71; tchr. Croatian lang. co-edn. YMCA Community Coll., Chgo., 1969-71, 74-; bibliographer Old Dominion U., Norfolk, Va., 1971-74; assoc. prof. libr. sci., bibliographer Chgo. State U., 1974—. Translator, interpreter English, Latin, Croatian, Serbian, Macedonian, Bulgarian, Old Ch. Slavic, Slovene, 1969—; interpreter Berlitz Trans. Ctr. Sch. Langs.; lectr. South Slavonic langs., lit., history and culture, Balkan states culture, heritage and folk lit., transl. techniques; lectr. in field. Contbr. various confs., seminars, workshops, jours., transl. of articles, studies, work on dictionary, Berlitz Transl. Svc. transl. and interpretation. Recipient cert. of appreciation YMCA Transl. Ctr., Chgo., 1976, cert. Beta Phi Mu, U. Pitts., 1972, Am. Translators Assn., 1980, Assn. Coll. and Rsch. Librs., 1986. Mem. ALA, Am. Fedn. Tchrs., Assn. Coll. and Rsch. Librs., Chgo. Acad. Libr. Coun. Libr. of Congress (assoc.), Soc. Scholarly Publishing, Beta Phi Mu. Home: 618 Exchange Ave Calumet City IL 60409-3903 Office: Chgo State U Rm Lib 203 95th St at King Dr Chicago IL 60628

**MILEWSKI, BARBARA ANNE,** pediatrics nurse, neonatal/perinatal nurse practitioner, critical care nurse; b. Chgo., Sept. 11, 1934; d. Anthony and LaVerne (Sepp) Witt; m. Leonard A. Milewski, Feb. 23, 1952; children: Pamela, Robert, Diane, Timothy. ADN, Harper Coll., Palatine, Ill., 1982; BS, Northern Ill. U., 1992; postgrad., North Park Coll. RN Ill., cert. CPR instr. Staff nurse N.W. Cmty. Hosp., Arlington Heights, Ill., Resurrection Hosp., Chgo.; nurse neonatal ICU Children's Meml. Hosp., Chgo.; day care cons. Cook County Dept. Pub. Health; owner, CEO Child Care Health Cons. CPR instr. Stewart Oxygen Svcs., Chgo., Harper Coll., Children's Meml. Hosp.; instr., organizer parenting and well baby classes and clinics; health coord. CEDA Head Start; mem. adv. bd. Cook County Child Care Resource and Referral; dir. Albany Park Head Start. Vol. Children's Meml. Hosp., Boy Scouts Am. Mem.: Am. Mortar Bd., Sigma Theta Tau. Personal E-mail: barbmilewski@aol.com.

**MILEY, GEORGE H.,** nuclear and electrical engineering educator, plasma engineer, energy conversion scientist; b. Shreveport, La., Aug. 6, 1933; s. George Hunter and Norma Angeline (Dowling) M.; m. Elizabeth Burroughs, Nov. 22, 1958; children: Susan Miley Hibbs, Hunter Robert. BS in Chem. Engring., Carnegie-Mellon U., 1955; MS, U. Mich., 1956, PhD in Chem.-Nuclear Engring., 1959. Nuclear engr. Knolls Atomic Power Lab., Gen. Electric Co., Schenectady, 1959-61; mem. faculty U. Ill., Urbana, 1961—, prof., 1967—, chmn. nuclear engring. program, 1975-86, dir. Fusion Studies Lab., 1976—, fellow Ctr. for Advanced Study, 1985-86; dir. rsch. Rockford Tech. Assocs. Inc., 1990-94; pres., dir. rsch. NPL Assocs. Inc., 1994—; chief scientist Lattice Energy, LLC, 2001—03. Vis. prof. U. Colo., 1967, Cornell U., 1969-70, U. New South Wales, 1986, Imperial Coll. of London, 1987; mem. Ill. Radiation Protection Bd., 1988—; mem. Air Force Studies Bd., 1990-94; chmn. tech. adv. com. Ill. Low Level Radioactive Waste Site, 1990-96; chmn. com. on indsl. uses of radiation Ill. Dept. Nuclear Safety, 1989-2000. Author: Direct Conversion of Nuclear Radiation Energy, 1971, Fusion Energy Conversion, 1976; editor Jour. Fusion Tech., 1980-2001; U.S. regional editor Laser and Particle Beams, 1982-86, mng. editor, 1987-91, editor-in-chief, 1991-2002; U.S. editor Jour. Plasma Physics, 1995-2003. Served with C.E. AUS, 1960. Recipient Western Electric Tchg.-Rsch. award, 1977, Halliburton Engring. Edn. Leadership award, 1990, Edward Teller medal, 1995, Scientist of Yr. award Inst. New Energy, 1996, Cert. Recognition award NASA, 2003; NATO sr. sci. fellow, 1975-76, Guggenheim fellow, 1985-86, Japanese Soc. Promotion of Sci. fellow, 1994. Fellow IEEE (Fusion Engring. and Sci. award, 2004), Am. Nuclear Soc. (dir. 1980-83, Disting. Svc. award 1980, Outstanding Achievement award Fusion Energy divsn. 1992, Radiation Sci. and Tech. award 2004), Am. Phys. Soc., AIAA (assoc.); mem. Am. Soc. Engring. Edn. (chmn. energy conversion com. 1967-70, pres. U. Ill. chpt. 1973-74, chmn. nuclear divsn. 1975-76, Outstanding Tchr. award 1973), Sigma Xi, Tau Beta Pi. Presbyterian. Achievements include research in fusion, energy conversion, reactor kinetics, and fuel cells. Avocations: tennis, hiking. Office: U Ill 214 Nuc Engring Lab 103 S Goodwin Ave Urbana IL 61801-2901 Office Phone: 217-333-3772. E-mail: georgehm@aol.com. *My professional goal has been to insure that future generations have a plentiful supply of economical, readily available energy such as offered by fusion. Not only should this insure a continued improvement in the standard of living for persons in all nations, but it should help maintain peace which is threatened by the struggle to obtain and control limited natural sources of energy.*

**MILEY, JENNA YVONNE,** education educator, consultant; b. S. Charleston, W.Va., Nov. 23, 1951; d. Edgar M. and Retha M. (Barnes) Gillespie; m. Stanley Leon Miley, Apr. 19, 1985; 1 child, James E. Caruthers. AS, Mohegan C.C., Norwich, Conn., 1990; BS, So. Ill. U., 1993; MA, Webster U., St. Louis, 1994; postgrad., Capella U., 2006—. Instr. Owensboro C.C., Ky., 1995—96; summer intern GRADD, Owensboro, Ky., 1996; instr. Jefferson C.C., Louisville, 1997, Carolina C.C., Sanford, NC, 1998—99, Al Ain Women's Coll., United Arab Emirates, 1999—2002; asst. prof. Bainbridge (Ga.) Coll., 2002—. Dir. mini-grant Svc. Learning. Author: (newsletter) College Success. Mem. steering com. Leadership Decatur County, 2004—05. Decorated Outstanding Unit Ribbon USAF; Gov.'s Tchg. fellow, 2005—06. Mem.: AAUW (pres. Bainbridge chpt. 2005—06), AAUP, Lions. Republican. Pentecostal. Avocation: travel, reading. Office: Bainbridge Coll 2500 E Shotwell St Bainbridge GA 39819 Office Phone: 229-248-2567. Personal E-mail: jmiley@bainbridge.edu.

**MILFORD, FREDERICK JOHN,** retired research and development company executive; b. Cleve., July 1, 1926; s. Frederick Charles and Florence M.; m. Jean Irene Olson, Sept. 8, 1951; 1 child, Cheryl Lynn. BS in Physics, Case Inst. Tech., 1949; PhD in Physics, M.I.T., 1952. Instr. Case Inst. Tech., Cleve., 1952-56, asst. prof., 1956-59; div. cons. Battelle Columbus Labs., 1959-62, div. chief, 1962-64, sr. fellow, 1964-66, dir. research in phys. scis., 1966-73, scientist, 1973, dept. mgr., 1973-76, assoc. dir., 1976-85, chief scientist, 1985-87, v.p. spl. programs, 1987-89, ret., 1989. Vis. prof. physics U. Wash., 1969 Author: (with J.R. Reitz) Foundations of Electromagnetic Theory, 1960, 4th edit., 1993. Emeritus mem. adv. bd. Central Ohio Salvation Army. Served with USNR, 1945-46. George Eastman fellow, 1951-52; Focke scholar, 1948-49 Fellow Am. Phys. Soc.; mem. Masons, Kit Kat Club, Ctrl. Ohio Lions Eye Bank (oper. bd., 1983-). Home: 1411 London Dr Columbus OH 43221-1543

**MILFORD, MURRAY HUDSON,** retired soil science educator; b. Honey Grove, Tex., Sept. 29, 1934; s. Murray Lane and Vivian Ione (Hudson) M.; m. Marsha Ann Rasmussen, July 21, 1961; children: Rebecca Ione, Murray Daniel. BS in Agronomy, Tex. A&M, 1955, MS in Agronomy, 1959; PhD in Soil Science, U. Wis., 1962. Cert. profl. soil scientist. Rsch. assoc. Cornell U., Ithaca, NY, 1962-63, asst. prof., 1963-68, assoc. prof., 1968, Tex. A&M U., College Station, 1968-74, prof., 1974-2001; ret., 2001. Author: (lab. manual) Soils and Soil Science-Lab. Exercises, 1970. 1st lt. USAR, 1955-57. Recipient so. region award for excellence in coll. and univ. tchg. in food and agrl. scis. Nat. Assn. State Univs. and Land Grant Colls., Higher Edn. Program, USDA, 1995. Fellow AAAS, Am. Soc. Agronomy (pres. Tex. chpt. 1982-83, Resident Edn. award 1978), Soil Sci. Soc. Am. (Edn. award 1988); mem. Soil and Water Conservation Soc. (pres. Tex. coun. of chpts. 1987). Democrat. Presbyterian. Home: 3606 Tanglewood Dr Bryan TX 77802-3320 E-mail: mmilford@tca.net.

**MILGRAM, JEROME H.,** marine and ocean engineer, educator; b. Phila., Sept. 23, 1938; s. Samuel J. and Fannie M. BSEE, MIT, 1961, MS, 1962, PhD in Hydrodynamics, 1965. Registered profl. engr., Mass. With Scripps Inst. Oceanography, San Diego, summer 1961; project engr. Block Assocs., Cambridge, Mass., 1961-67; asst. prof. MIT, Cambridge, 1967-70, assoc. prof., 1970-77, prof. ocean engring., 1977-89, William I. Koch prof. marine tech., 1989—, prof. mech. engring., 2005—. Rsch. assoc. in biophysics Harvard U. Med. Sch., 1974-76; vis. prof. in naval architecture and marine engring. U. Mich., 1988-89; design dir. Am. 3 Found., 1991-95; guest investigator Woods Hole Oceanog. Instn., 1996—; vis. prof. Johns Hopkins U., 1996-97; investigator and expert witness for marine casualties. Contbr. articles to profl. jours.; patentee in field. Recipient Am. Bur. Shipping award, 1961, Alan Berman Outstanding Rsch. Publ. award U.S. Naval Rsch. Lab., 1990, AT&T Design Innovation award, 1992. Fellow Soc. Naval Archs. and Marine Engrs. (life); mem. NAE (life), Nat. Rsch. Coun. (marine bd. 1998-2001). Home: 20 Blossom Hill Rd Winchester MA 01890-3455 Office: MIT 77 Massachusetts Ave Rm 5-318 Cambridge MA 02139-4307 Business E-Mail: jmilgram@mit.edu.

**MILGRIM, DARROW A.,** insurance company executive; b. Chgo., Apr. 30, 1945; BA, Calif. State U., San Bernardino, 1968; postgrad., U. So. Calif., 1972. Accredited ins. advisor, cert. ins. counselor; sch. adminstr. Tchr. Rialto Unified Sch. Dist., Calif., 1969-70, Las Virgenes Unified Sch. Dist., Westlake Village, Calif., 1970-78; instr. Calif. State U., Northridge, 1980-84; pres. Darrow Milgrim Ins. Svcs., Inc.; ins. broker, dir. Speare Ins. Brokers, Blade Ins. Svcs., Sherman Oaks, Calif., 1884—2004; sr. v.p. Acordia Calif., Inc., a Wells Fargo Co., Sherman Oaks, 2004—. Cons. Ronald McDonald House Charities, SC, L.A., 1986—95, ACA Legis. Task Force and Nat. Pub. Policy com.; bd. dirs. Calamigos Star C Ranch Summer Camp, Malibu, Calif., Calamigos Environ. Edn. Ctr., Malibu. Editor: Legislation and Regulations for Organized Camps, 1987. Pres. Calif. Camping Adv. Coun., Long Beach, 1985—87, 1999—2000; bd. dirs. Calif. Collaboration Youth, Sacramento, 1985—, Camp Ronald McDonald Good Times, 1989—95; commr. dept. pks. and recreation City of Agoura Hills, Calif., 1987—93. Mem.: Agts. and Brokers State Legis. Coun., Ins. Brokers and Agts. L.A. Coun., Am. Camping Assn. (bd. dirs. So. Calif. sect., mem. nat. pub. policy com. Martinsville, Ind. 1980—98, nat. bd. dirs. 1990—95, legis. liaison, regional honor 1986). Office: Acordia Calif Inc 15303 Ventura Blvd 7th Fl Sherman Oaks CA 91403 Office Phone: 818-464-9308. Business E-Mail: darrow_milgrim@acordia.com.

**MILGRIM, ROGER MICHAEL,** lawyer; b. NYC, Mar. 22, 1937; s. Israel and Iola (Lash) Milgrim; 1 child, Justin. BA, U. Pa., 1958; LLB, NYU, 1961, LLM, 1962. Bar: N.Y., U.S. Supreme Ct. Assoc. Baker & McKenzie, Paris, 1963-65, Nixon Mudge et al, N.Y.C., 1965-68; mem. Milgrim Thomajan & Lee P.C., N.Y.C., 1968-92; ptnr., chmn. intellectual property group Paul, Hastings, Janofsky & Walker LLP, N.Y.C., 1992—2003, chmn. litig. dept., 1999—2000. Adj. prof. sch. law NYU, N.Y., 1974—95. Author: Milgrim on Trade Secrets, 1967, supplement, 2005, Milgrim on Licensing, 1990, supplement, 2005. Trustee Coll. Wooster, 1994-97, Bklyn. Hosp., 1982-91; bd. dirs. Fulbright Assn., 1998—2004, chmn. Fulbright Prize com., 1999-01; bd. dirs. Technip, 1998—; bd. advs. UniStates LLC, 2000—. Mem. Knickerbocker Club. Republican. Home: 431 Paxinosa Rd E Easton PA 18040-1337 Office: Paul Hastings Janofsky & Walker LLP 75 E 55th New York NY 10022-3205 Office Phone: 212-318-6010. Business E-Mail: rogermilgrim@paulhastings.com.

**MILGROM, FELIX,** immunologist, educator; b. Rohatyn, Poland, Oct. 12, 1919; came to U.S., 1958; naturalized, 1963; s. Henryk and Ernestina (Cyryl) M.; m. Halina Miszel, Oct. 15, 1941; children: Henry, Martin Louis. Student, U. Lwow, Poland, 1937-41, U. Lublin, 1945; MD, U. Wroclaw, Poland, 1947; MD (hon.), U. Vienna, Austria, 1976, U. Lund, Sweden, 1979, U. Heidelberg, Fed. Republic Germany, 1979, U. Bergen, Norway, 1980; DSc (hon.), U. Med. Dent., N.J., 1991. Rsch. assoc., prof. dept. microbiology Sch. Medicine U. Wroclaw, 1946-54, chmn. dept., 1954; prof., head dept. microbiology Sch. Medicine, Silesian U., Zabrze, Poland, 1954-57; rsch. assoc. Svc. de Chime Microbienne, Pasteur Inst., Paris, 1957; rsch. assoc. dept. bacteriology and immunology U. Buffalo Sch. Medicine, 1958-62; assoc. prof., then prof. and disting. prof. microbiology Sch. Medicine, SUNY, Buffalo, 1962—, chmn. dept., 1967-85. Author: Studies on the Structure of Antibodies, 1950; co-editor: International Convocations on Immunology, 1969, 75, 79, 85, Principles of Immunology, 1973, 2d edit., 1979, Principles of Immunological Diagnosis in Medicine, 1981, Medical Microbiology, 1982; editor in chief Internat. Archives of Allergy and Applied Immunology, 1965-91; contbg. editor Vox Sanguinis, 1965-76, Transfusion, 1966-73, Cellular Immunology, 1970-83, Transplantation, 1975-78; contbr. numerous articles to profl. jours. Recipient Alfred Jurzykowski Found. prize, 1986, Paul Ehrlich and Ludwig Darmstaedter prize, 1987. Mem. Am. Assn. Immunologists, Transplantation Soc. (v.p. 1976-78), Am. Acad. Microbiology, Coll. Internat. Allergologicum (v.p. 1970-82, pres. 1978-82, hon. mem. 1990—), Polish Acad. Arts and Scis., Sigma Xi. Achievements include research in the serology of syphilis, Tb, rheumatoid arthritis, organ and tissue specificity including blood groups, transplantation and autoimmunity. Home: 474 Getzville Rd Buffalo NY 14226-2555 Office Phone: 716-829-3316. Business E-Mail: milgrom@buffalo.edu.

**MILHAUPT, CURTIS J.,** law educator; BA, Notre Dame U., 1984; JD, Columbia U., 1989. Attv. Shearman & Sterling, NYC, Tokyo, 1989—94; assoc. prof. law Washington U. Sch. Law, 1994-98, prof., 1998—99; faculty mem. Columbia U. Law Sch., NYC, 1999—, Fuyo prof. law. Ctr. for Japanese Legal Studies, chair Transactional Studies Prog. Vis. prof. UCLA, 1997. Author: Japanese Law in Context: Readings in Society, the Economy, and Politics, 2001, Global Markets, Domestic Institutions: Corporate Law and Governance in a New Era of Cross-Border Deals, 2003, Economic Organizations and Corporate Governance in Japan: The Impact of Formal and Informal Rules, 2004. Fellow Japan Found.; U. of Tokyo Faculty of Law, 1992—93; vis. scholar Bank of Japan Inst. for Monetary and Econ. Studies,

1998; vis. fellow, Rsch. Inst. of Econ., Trade and Industry, 2002. Office: Columbia Law Sch 435 W 116th St New York NY 10027 Office Phone: 212-854-4926. E-mail: milhaupt@law.columbia.edu.

**MILHORAT, THOMAS HERRICK,** neurosurgeon; b. NYC, Apr. 5, 1936; s. Ade Thomas and Edith Caulkins (Herrick) M.; m. Edith Mostile, 1961; children: John Thomas, Robert Herrick. BA, Cornell U., 1957, MD, 1961. Intern, asst. resident in gen. surgery N.Y. Hosp.-Cornell Med. Ctr., 1961—63, asst. resident, chief resident in neurosurgery, 1965—68, asst. neurosurgeon NIH, 1968—71; clin. assoc., dept. surg. neurology Nat. Inst. Neurol. Diseases and Blindness, Bethesda, 1963—65; assoc. prof. neurol. surgery, assoc. prof. child health and devel. George Washington U. Sch. Medicine, Washington, 1971—74, prof. neurol. surgery, prof. child health and devel., 1974—81; chmn. dept. neurosurgery Children's Hosp. Nat. Med. Ctr., Washington, 1971—81; prof. neurol. surgery, dept. chmn. SUNY Health Sci. Ctr., Bklyn., 1982—2001; chmn. dept. neurosurgery North Shore/L.I. Jewish Health System, 2002—; founder dir. Chiari Inst. North Shore Univ. Hosp., 2002—; dir. Harvey Cushing Insts. Neurosci., Northshore-LI Jewish Health System, 2006—; prof. neurol. surgery NYU Sch. Medicine, 2002—. Neurosurgeon-in-chief Kings County Hosp. Ctr., 1982—2001; regional chmn. neurol. surgery L.I. Coll. Hosp., 1986—2001; program dir. Neurosurgery Rsch. Tng. Program, 1982—2001; mem. Nat. Coun. Scientists NIH, 1969—82; dir. Harvey Cushing Inst. Neurosci. North Shore L.I. Jewish Health Sys., NY, 2006—. Author: Hydrocephalus and Cerebrospinal Fluid, 1972, Pediatric Neurosurgery, 1978, Cerebrospinal Fluid and the Brain Edemas, 1987; (with M.K. Hammock) Cranial Computed Tomography in Infancy and Childhood, 1981; mem. editl. bd. Neurosurgery, 1997—, Neurosug Focus: Syringomyelia, 2000—; contbr. more than 325 articles to profl. jours. Lt. comdr. USPHS, 1963—65. Recipient 1st prize in pathology, Cornell U. Med. Sch. Dept. Ob-Gyn., 1960, Charles L. Horn prize Cornell Med. Sch., 1961, Best Paper award ann. combined meeting N.Y. Acad. Medicine/N.Y. Neurosurg. Soc., 1965, Pudenz award for Excellence in CSF Physiology, 1994, E. Jefferson Browder award for excellence in Neurosurgery, 1996, Arthur A. Kaplan award for excellence in neurosurgery, 1999. Mem. AAAS, Internat. Soc. Pediat. Neurosurgery, Am. Assn. Neurol. Surgery, Am. Syringomyelia Alliance Project (chmn. med. adv. bd. 1996—), Am. Acad. Pediat. (surg. sect.), Soc. Pediat. Rsch., N.Y. Acad. Medicine, N.Y. Soc. Neurosurgery (pres. 1988-90), Bklyn. Neurologic Soc. (pres. 1988-95), Soc. Neurosci., Internat. Soc. Neurosci., Soc. Neurol. Surgeons, Sigma Xi. Avocations: golf, billiards, gardening. Office: North Shore Univ Hosp Dept Neurosurgery Manhasset NY 11030 Office Phone: 516-562-3020. Business E-Mail: milhorat@nshs.edu.

**MILIC-EMILI, JOSEPH,** physiologist, educator; b. Sezana, Slovenia, May 27, 1931; arrived in Can., 1963; s. Joseph Milic-Emili and Giovanna Milic-Emili Perhavec; m. Ann Harding, Nov. 2, 1957; children: Claire, Anne-Marie, Alice, Andrew. MD, U. Milan, 1955; Dr. honoris causa, U. Louvain, Belgium, 1987, Kunming Med. Coll. China, 1987, U. Montpellier, France, 1994, U. Ferrara, Italy, 1996, U. Athens, Greece, 1998, U. Ljubljana, Slovenia. Asst. prof. physiology and exptl. medicine McGill U., Montreal, Que., Canada, 1963-65, assoc. prof., 1965-69, prof., 1969-77, prof. emeritus, 1998—; dir. Meakins-Christie Labs., 1979-94. Vis. prof. Lab. de Physiologie Faculte de Medecine Saint-Antoine, Paris, Svc. de Pneumologie Hosp. Beaujon, Paris, 1978-79, 94-95, chmn. dept. physiology, 1973-78; vis. cons. medicine Royal Postgrad. Med. Sch., London, 1958-60; cons. Aeronautics Imperial Coll. Tech., London, 1969-70; asst. prof. physiology U. Liege, Belgium, 1958-60; asst. prof. U. Milan, 1956-58. Mem. editl. bd. Jour. Applied Physiology, 1970-76, Rev. Française des Maladies Respiratoires, 1979-96, Rivista de Biologia, 1979-86, Am. Rev. Respiratory Disease, 1982-89, Reanimation, Soins Intensifs, Medicine d'Urgence, 1984-95. Mem. applied physiology and bioengring. study sect. NIH, 1975-78. Decorated Order of Can.; recipient Gold medal C. Forlanini U. Pavia, Italy, 1982, Am. Coll. Chest Physicians medal, 1984, 98, Harry Wunderly medal Thoracic Soc. Australia, 1988, medal Italian Sch. Mil. Medicine, 1990, medal Med. Sch. Brest, 1997, medal Med. Sch. Ferrara, 1997, medal Med. Sch. Bologna, 2006, Trudeau medal Am. Thoracic Soc., 2006; author of one of 100-most cited articles in clin. rsch. of 1960s; named one of 1,000 most-cited contemporary scientists, 1965-78, 1998 Presdl. award European Respiratory Soc., 1998 Disting. Lectr. in Physiology Am. Coll. Chest Physicians. Fellow Royal Soc. Can., Slovenian Acad. Sci. (fgn. corr.), Soc. Med. Clin. Bononiensis Sci.; mem. Am. Physiol. Soc., Can. Physiol. Soc., Can. Thoracic Soc., Med. Rsch. Coun. (mem. grants com. 1980), Soc. Pneumologie Belge (hon.), Brazilian Physiol. Soc. (hon.), Hellenic Thoracic Soc. (hon.), Polish Pneumological Soc. (hon.), Chilean Resp. Soc. (hon.). Home: 4394 Circle Rd Montreal PQ Canada H3W 1Y5 Office: McGill U Meakins-Christie Labs 3626 St Urbain St Montreal PQ Canada H2X 2P2 Office Phone: 514-398-3864 ext. 80144. Business E-Mail: joseph.milic-emili@mcgill.ca.

**MILIOTIS, DEMITRIOS,** physics professor; b. Korinth, Greece, Jan. 1, 1930; s. Menelaos and Angellika Miliotis; m. Louly Grifsa, June 10, 1960; 1 child, Menelaos. Diploma in Physics, Nat. U., Athens, Greece, 1957, PhD in Physics, 1964. Rsch. asst. Nat. Found. Rsch., Athens, 1958-65, rsch. assoc., 1969-71; rsch. asst. physics dept. U. Ill., Urbana, 1965-66, rsch. assoc., 1966-68; asst. prof. physics dept. U. Athens, 1971-72; assoc. prof. U. Ioannina, Greece, 1972-75, prof., chmn. applied physics 1975-77, head physics and math. depts., 1978-80, prof. dept. physics, 1981-85, prof. emeritus, 1985—. Invited prof. U. Crete, Heraklion, Greece, 1977-78; vis. prof. physics dept. U. Ill., 1980-81. Author books on circuit analysis and semiconductor physics; contbr. articles to profl. jours. Lt. Greek Army, 1954-56. Home: 27A Kifissias Ave 11523 Athens Greece

**MILITA, MARTIN JOSEPH,** lawyer; b. Vineland, N.J., May 14, 1953; s.Martin Joseph and Mary Elizabeth (Gavigan) M.; m. Janet D. Milita, Oct. 3, 1981; 1 child, Samantha Anne. BA, Kings Coll., 1976; JD, Temple U., 1979. Bar: Pa. 1979, N.J. 1979, U.S. Dist. Ct. N.J. 1979. Tchg. fellow Temple U., Phila., 1978; asst. dist. atty. Bucks County Dist. Atty.'s Office, Doylestown, Pa., 1979-81; asst. prosecutor Hunterdon County Prosecutor's Office, Flemington, NJ, 1981-84; dep. atty. gen. State of N.J., Trenton, 1984-90; assoc. Sills Cummis et al, Newark, 1990-94; counsel Riker, Danzig, Scherer, Hyland & Perretti, LLP, Morristown, NJ, 1994—. Contbr. articles to law jours. Mem. adv. bd. Rep. Nat. Com., Washington, 1994—. Mem. N.J. Bar Assn. Roman Catholic. Avocations: Civil War history, collecting civil war art and artifacts. Office: A Fiore & Sons 1230 McCarter Hwy Newark NJ 07104-3710

**MILITO, CONNIE MARIE,** education administrator, government relations administrator; b. Tampa, Fla., Nov. 12, 1958; d. Frederick Anthony and Costantina Milito. BA, U. South Fla., 1981; MA, Nova U., 1990. Cert. adminstrn. and supervision early childhood edn. Elem. tchr. Sch. Dist. Hillsborough County, Tampa, Fla., 1982—90, acting supr. early childhood edn., 1990—92, dir. govt. rels., 1993—. Mem. exec. com. Cmty. Advocates for Resources for Edn. and Social Svcs., Tampa 1993—2002; mem. Horace Mann League, 1994—, Tiger Bay Club Tampa; mem. exec. bd. Bipartisan Polit. Club, 2000—02. Mem.: Fla. Edn. Legis. Liaisons (pres. 1998—99, exec. bd. 1996—2002), Phi Delta Kappa, Kappa Delta Phi. Office: Sch Dist Hillsborough County 901 E Kennedy Blvd Tampa FL 33602 Office Phone: 813-272-4519. Business E-Mail: milito_c@firn.edu.

**MILIUS, JOHN FREDERICK,** film writer, director; b. St. Louis, Apr. 11, 1944; s. William Styx and Elizabeth (Roe) M.; 3 children. Grad., U. So. Calif., 1967. Instr. motion pictures script analysis U. So. Calif., fall 1973, advanced motion picture script analysis, spring 1974 Films include: (screenwriter) Devil's 8, 1969, Evel Knievel, 1971, Dirty Harry (uncredited), 1971, Jeremiah Johnson, 1972 (Heritage Wrangler Award), The Life and Times of Judge Roy Bean, 1972, Magnum Force, 1973, Apocalypse Now, 1979 (with Francis Ford Coppola, Academy Award nominee Best screenplay), Extreme Prejudice, 1987, Geronimo: An American Legend, 1993, Clear and Present Danger, 1994, Mexico, 1999, (TV) Melvin Purvis: G-Man, 1974; dir., screenwriter: Dillinger, 1973, The Wind and the Lion, 1975 (National Bell Ringers ednl. award, Writers Guild nom. for Best Orig. Screenplay), Big Wednesday, 1978, Conan the Barbarian, 1982, Red Dawn, 1984, Farewell to

the King, 1989, Flight of the Intruder, 1990, The Northmen, 1999, (TV) Rough Riders, 1997; (prodr., screen writer) (TV series) Rome; exec. prodr.: Hardcore, 1979, Used Cars, 1980, Uncommon Valor, 1983; exec. prodr., co-screenwriter: 1941, 1979; dir.: (TV) The Twilight Zone, 1985, Motorcycle Gang, 1994; actor: Deadhead Miles, 1974, Hearts of Darkness: A Filmmaker's Apocalypse, 1991, Ben Johnson: Third Cowboy on the Right, 1996, (TV) American Cinema, 1994, Frank Capra'a American Dream, 1997; writer (video game): Medal of Honor: European Assault, 2005; spiritual advisor: Lone Wolf McQuade, 1983. Recipient Nat. Student Film Festival award U. So. Calif., 1968; numerous gun shooting awards; honored by Winchester for The Wind and the Lion. Office: care Jeff Berg International Creative Mgmt 8942 Wilshire Blvd Beverly Hills CA 90211-1934

**MILIZIANO, JOHN C.,** social studies educator; b. York, Pa., July 8, 1958; s. George and Anna Miliziano; m. Kelly R. Miliziano, Aug. 6, 1996; children: Sophia, Joseph. BA, York Coll. Pa., 1980; MEd Leadership, U. South Fla., Tampa, 1997. Tchr. social studies Fairfax Mid. Sch., Va., 1980—81, Tampa H.S., Fla., 1981—. Sponsor Model UN Orgn., 2001—. Finalist Econ. Edn. award, Nat. Coun. Econ. Edn., 2005; recipient Fla. Gov.'s Econ. Edn. award, Fla. Coun. Econ. Edn., 2005. Democrat. Roman Catholic. Home: 5309 Redfield Ln Tampa FL 33624

**MILKEN, MICHAEL R.,** think-tank executive, philanthropist; b. 1946; m. Lori Milken, Aug. 11, 1968; 3 children. Grad. summa cum laude, U. Calif., Berkeley; MBA, U. Pa. Securities trader Drexel Burnham Lambert, until 1990; chmn. The Milken Inst., 1991—; founder Prostate Cancer Found. (formerly CaPCure), 1993—; chair Knowledge Universe, 1996—; chmn. FasterCures/Ctr. for Accelerating Med. Solutions, 2003—. Author: Taste for Living Series cookbooks. Chair Assn. Cure of Cancer of the Prostate; co-founder Milken Family Found., 1982. Named one of 400 Richest Ams., Forbes mag., 2006. Office: Milken Inst 1250 Fourth St Ste 200 Santa Monica CA 90401*

**MILKMAN, MARIANNE FRIEDENTHAL,** retired city planner; b. Berlin, May 13, 1931; arrived in US, 1957; d. Ernst Leopold and Margarethe (Goldschmidt) Friedenthal; m. Roger Dawson Milkman, Oct. 18, 1958; children: Ruth, Louise, Janet, Paul. BA, Cambridge (Eng.) U., 1952, MA, 1956; teaching diploma, London U., 1953. Tchr. biology Milham Ford High Sch., Oxford, Eng., 1953-57; teaching fellow, rsch. asst. U. Mich., Ann Arbor, 1957-59; sci. dir. Children's Sch. Sci., Woods Hole, Mass., 1971-72; planning technician dept. planning and program devel. City of Iowa City, 1975-76, planner I, 1976-79, assoc. planner, 1979-85, coord. comty. devel., 1986-96; ret., 1996. Bikeways chmn Project Green, Iowa City, 1968—75; chmn. comprehensive plan com. Town of Falmouth, 2002—. Fellow, English Speaking Union, 1957—58; scholar State, Cambridge Univ and London Univ, 1949—53, Fulbright Traveling, Univ Mich, 1957. Mem.: Nat Community Develop Asn, Nat Asn Housing and Redevelopment Offs, Am Planning Asn (secy-treas Iowa chpt 1982—84, vpres 1984—86, pres 1986—88, chmn univ relations comt 1987—91, Pres's Award 1988). Jewish. Avocations: mountain hiking, wild flowers, music. Home: 12 Fells Rd Falmouth MA 02540-1626

**MILKMAN, ROGER DAWSON,** genetics educator, molecular biologist, researcher; b. NYC, Oct. 15, 1930; s. Louis Arthur and Margaret (Weinstein) M.; m. Marianne Friedenthal, Oct. 18, 1958; children: Ruth Margaret Milkman Atkinson, Louise Friedenthal, Janet Dawson Milkman Lussenhop, Paul David. AB, Harvard U., 1951, A.M., 1954, PhD, 1956. Student, asst. instr., researcher, investigator Marine Biol. Lab., Woods Hole, Mass., 1952-72, 88-96; instr., assoc. prof. U. Mich., Ann Arbor, 1957-60; assoc. prof. Syracuse U., NY, 1960-68; prof. biol. scis. U. Iowa, Iowa City, 1968-2001, prof. emeritus, 2001—, chmn. univ. genetics PhD program, 1992-93. Vis. prof. biology Grinnell (Iowa) Coll., 1990; mem. genetics study sect. NIH, 1986-87; NSF panelist, 1996-99; adj. scientist Marine Biol. Lab., Woods Hole, 2002—, Josephine Bay Paul Ctr. Translator: (from German) Developmental Physiology, 2d edit., 1971; editor: Perspectives on Evolution, 1982, Experimental Population Genetics, 1983, Evolution jour., 1984-86; mem. editl. bd. Jour. Bacteriology, 1998-2000; contbr. articles to profl. jours. Sec. Soc. Gen. Physiologists, 1963-65, Am. Soc. Naturalists, 1980-82; alumni rep. Phillips Acad., Andover, Mass., 1980-94. NSF grantee, 1959—; USPHS grantee, 1984-87. Fellow AAAS; mem. Am. Soc. for Microbiology, Genetics Soc. Am., Corp. Marine Biol. Lab., Soc. for Gen. Microbiology (U.K.), Soc. study Evolution. Jewish. Avocation: mountain hiking. Home and Office: 12 Fells Rd Falmouth MA 02540-1626 Office Phone: 508-289-7390. Business E-Mail: rmilkman@mbl.edu, roger-milkman@uiowa.edu, rogmilkman@adelphia.net.

**MILL, THEODORE,** chemist, researcher; b. Apr. 17, 1931; came to U.S., 1932; BS, Wayne State U., 1953; PhD, U. Wash., 1956. Fellow Hickrill Rsch. Found., Katonah, NY, 1956-57; chemist DuPont Expt. Sta., DuPont Co., Wilmington, Del., 1957-60, Stanford Rsch. Inst., Menlo Park, Calif., 1960-64, dir. phys. organic chemistry dept., 1964-85, sr. scientist, 1985—. Cons. in field. Contbr. articles to profl. jours. Patentee in field. Grantee NSF, 1975-80, NIH, 1976-82, EPA, 1976-99; SRI fellow, 1996, Dept. Energy, 2002-04. Mem. ACS (chmn. local sect. 1976), AAAS, Am. Geophys. Union, Soc. Environ. Toxicol. and Chem., Sierra Club, Audubon Soc. Democrat. Office: SRI 333 Ravenswood Ave PS 239 Menlo Park CA 94025-3493 Office Phone: 650-859-3605. Personal E-mail: ted.mill@srl.com.

**MILLAN, ALVIN,** speech pathology/audiology services professional, educator; b. San Juan, P.R., Mar. 28, 1968; s. William Millan and Aura Fuentes; m. Norma Rodriguez, Dec. 19, 1992; children: Liz C., Kenneth X. B in Speech Therapy, U.P.R., 1990, M in Speech Lang. Pathology, 1992, cert. in early intervention devel. deficiencies, 1996. Cert. speech lang. pathologist P.R., assistive tech. cert. Prof. speech lang. and comm. disorders U. P.R. Med. Scis. Campus, San Juan, 1991—; program coord. speech therapy program Caribbean U., Bayamon, 2002—. Contbr. articles to profl. jours. Recipient Outstanding Profl. in Speech Lang. Pathology, 2002. Fellow: Assn. Reading Devel., Assn. Curriculum Devel.; mem.: Am. Speech and Lang. Assn. (advocacy spkrs. bur. 1999—2001), P.R. Orgn. Speech-Lang. Pathology and Audiology (pres. adv. bd. 1996—99, v.p. 1999—2000, sec. 2000—, v.p. 2001—02). Avocations: reading, writing, meditation, spirituality, travel. Home: Calle San Patricio aa-15 Alturas de San Pedro Fajardo PR 00738 Office: Ctr Rehab del Habla Lenguaje Ave Gen Valero 313-B Fajardo PR 00738 Office Phone: 787-863-0673. Business E-Mail: malf35@icepr.net.

**MILLAN, BRETT JORGE,** education educator; BA Anthropology, U. Tex.-Pan Am., Edinburg, 1992, MA in English, 1999, MA in Interdisciplinary Studies Anthropology, 2005. Specials mgr. Jones & Cook Stationers, McAllen, Tex., 1996—2000; lead instr. English dept. South Tex. Coll., McAllen, 2000—. Active Zoning Bd. of Adjustments and Appeals, McAllen, Tex., 2003—06; steering bd. Leadership McAllen, Tex., 1998—2001; exec. bd. ARC Hidalgo County, McAllen, 1988—92. Recipient Jaguar award, South Tex. Coll., 2003, Award of Excellence, NISOD, 2005; Promotion of Excellence grant, Phi Kappa Phi, 2003, Ednl. Leadership Doctoral scholar, Tex. A & M Kingsville U., 2005—06. Mem.: Soc. Applied Anthropology (assoc.), Am. Anthrop. Assn. (assoc.), Am. Mensa (assoc.), Lambda Alpha (life), Phi Kappa Phi (life). Office: South Texas Coll 3201 W Pecan Blvd Mcallen TX 78501 Office Phone: 956-872-7263.

**MILLANE, LYNN,** retired municipal official; b. Buffalo, Oct. 14, 1928; d. Robert P. and Justine A. Schermerhorn; m. J. Vaughan Millane Jr., Aug. 16, 1952; children: Maureen, Michele, John, Mark, Kathleen. EdB, U. Buffalo, 1949, EdM in Health Edn. 1951. Coun. mem. Amherst Town Bd., NY, 1982—96, dep. town supr. 1990-96, supr., 1996. Founder, liaison 1st adult day svcs. adv. bd. Town of Amherst, 1988, liaison to ad hoc cable TV com., 1992—96, liaison to Amherst C. of C., 1993—96, 1st records mgmt. adv. bd., liaison ethics bd., 1994—96; legis. liaison SUNY Family Violence Clin. Sch. Law, Buffalo, 1997—98; pres. E.J. Meyer Hosp. Jr. Bd., 1962—64; commr. (apptd. by Gov. George Pataki) NY State Ethics Commn., 1999—2004, 2004—; adv. bd. NY State Office Aging, 1996—2005, chair adv. bd.,

1997—2005; spkr. in field. Pres. Aux. to Erie County Bar Assn., 1966-68, Womens Com. Buffalo Philharm. Orch., 1976-78, v.p. adminstrn., 1975-76, v.p. pub. affairs, 1974-75, chair. adv. bd., 1979-82; v.p. Buffalo Philharm. Orch. Soc., Inc., 1976-78, coun. mem., trustee, 1979-87, bd. overseers, 1987-92; dir. 8th jud. dist. NY State Assn. Large Towns, 1989-91; bd. dirs. oper. bd. Millard Fillmore Suburban Hosp., 1992-98; 1st v.p. Fams for 17, 1980-82, Friends of Baird Hall SUNY, Buffalo, 1980-82; exec. bd. Womens Exec. Coun. Erie County Rep. Com., 1969-71, Longview Protestant Home for Children, 1979-85, 2d v.p., 1982-85; bd. dirs. Amherst br. ARC, 1982-91, by-laws com., 1981, 84, chair sr. concerns com., 1982-91, liaison code of ethics com., 1987-89; nat. music com. Womens Assn. for Symphony Orch. in Am. and Can., 1977-79; coun. mem. Am. Symphony Orch. League; sec. Amherst Sr. Citizens Adv. Bd., 1980-81, liaison from Amherst Town Bd., 1982-96; liaison to the Alternate Fuel and Clean Cities Com., 1994-96; dir.-at-large cmty. adv. coun. SUNY, Buffalo, 1981-91; co-assoc. chair maj. gift divsn. capital campaign Daeman Coll., 1998-; chair mem. com. Daeman Coll Trustees, 2003—; co-chair Women United Against Drugs Campaign, 1970-72; founding mem. Lunch and Issues, Amherst, 1981—; edn. com.; bd. dirs. Network in Aging of Western N.Y., Inc., 1982-89, housing com., 1987-89; bd. dirs. Amherst Elderly Transp. Corp., 1982-99; committeeman dist. Town of Amherst Rep. Com.; treas. Town and Country Rep. Club, 1980-81; nominating com. Fedn. Rep. Womens Clubs Erie County, 1980; del. N.Y. State Govs. Conf. on Aging, 1995, White House Conf. on Aging, 1995, named mem. aging svcs.; mem. Erie County Indsl. Devel. Agy. Erie County Regional Devel. Corp., 1996-97; mem. adv. bd. Amherst Symphony Orch., 2003-; vol. life project Greater Buffalo chpt. ARC, 2002-05, mem. svc. to older adults com., 2002-05. Named Homemaker of Yr., Family Circle mag., 1969, Woman of Substance, 20th Century Rep. Women, 1983, Woman of Yr., Buffalo Philharm. Orch. Soc., Inc., 1982, Outstanding Woman in Cmty. Svc., SUNY, Buffalo, 1985; recipient Good Neighbor award, Courier Express, 1978, Merit award, Buffalo Philharm. Orch., 1978, edn. Rep. Womens Clubs Erie County award, 1982, Disting. Svc. award, Town of Amherst Sr. Citr., 1985, Amherst Adult Day Care and Vis. Nurses Assn., 1994, Susan B. Anthony award, nterclub Coun. Western N.Y., 1991, Cmty. Svc. award, Amherst Rep. Com., 1991, D.A.R.E. award, Town of Amherst Police Dept., 1994, Amherst South Rotary Club, 1997, Outstanding Cmty. Svc. award, Amherst Sr. Citizen Found., 1997, Lynn Millane Cmty. Svc. award named in her honor, Rep. honoree, award for svc., Town of Amherst Youth Bd., 1996, award for care and assistance to sr. citizens of N.Y. State, Batavia Nursing Home, 2000, Woman of Distinction award, NY State Senate, 2003; hon. Paul Harris fellow. Mem. Amherst C. of C. (VIP dinner com. 1984), LWV, SUNY Buffalo Alumni Assn. (life, presdl. advisor 1977-79), Amherst Symphony Orch. Assn. (bd. dirs. 1981-87, roster chair. 1982-84, nominating chair 1985-86, vice-chair 50th ann. com. 1994-96, adv. com. 2003-), Niagara Connect, Amherst Rep. Womens Club (bd. dirs. 1963-65, 99), Zonta (pres. Amherst chpt. 1986-88, Zontian of Yr. 1992), Pi Lambda Theta (hon.).

**MILLAR, GORDON HALSTEAD,** mechanical engineer, agricultural products executive; b. Newark, Nov. 28, 1923; s. George Halstead and Dill E. (McMullen) M.; m. Virginia M. Jedryczka, Aug. 24, 1957; children: George B., Kathryn M., Juliet S., John G., James H. B.M.E., U. Detroit, 1949, D.Sc. (hon.), 1977; PhD, U. Wis., 1952; L.H.D., West Coast U., 1984; D.Sc. (hon.), Western Mich. U., 1986. Registered profl. engr., Fla., Ill., Iowa, Mich., Minn., Ohio. Supr. new powerplants Ford Motor Co., 1952-57; engring. mgr. Meriam Instrument Co., Cleve., 1957-59; dir. new products McCulloch Corp., Los Angeles, 1959-63; with Deere & Co., 1963-84, v.p. engring. Moline, Ill., 1972-84; exec. assoc. Southwest Research Inst., 1987. Mem. Fed. Adv. Com. Indsl. Innovation, 1979; chmn. West Ctrl. Ill. Ednl. Telecom. Corp.; pres. Accreditation Bd. for Engring. and Tech., 1983-85; pres., fellow Accreditation Bd. for Engring. and Tech. Editor: The Sheerline, Antique and Classic Boat Soc. (Sunnyland chpt.), 1995-; contbr. articles to profl. jours.; patentee in field. Chmn. Quad Cities chpt. United Way, 1976-77; bd. dirs.; adv. council Bradley U. Coll. Engring. and Tech.; mem. exec. com. Illowa council Boy Scouts Am., 1977-79. Served with U.S. Army, World War II. Decorated Purple Heart; recipient Alumnus of Year award U. Detroit, 1976, Comdrs. medal for pub. svc. Dept. Army, 1989 Fellow ASME (hon. life mem.), Soc. Automotive Engrs. (pres. 1984, bd. dirs. 1984-86, mem. nat. nominating com.); mem. NAE, NSPE, Engrs. Joint Coun., Indsl. Rsch. Inst., Engring. Soc. Detroit, Am. Soc. Agrl. Engrs., Ill. Soc. Profl. Engrs., Moline C. of C., Aviation Coun. Home: 1840 Wiley Post Trl Port Orange FL 32128-6756 Office Phone: 386-788-0213.

**MILLAR, JAMES ROBERT,** economist, educator, university official; b. San Antonio, Tex., July 7, 1936; s. James G. and Virginia M. (Harrison) M.; m. Gera Ascher, July 4, 1965; children: Leo Schaeg (dec.), Mira Gail. BA, U. Tex., 1958; PhD in Econs., Cornell U., 1965. Asst. prof. dept. econs. U. Ill., Urbana, 1965-70, assoc. prof., 1970-72, prof., 1973-89, assoc. vice chancellor for acad. affairs, 1984-89, dir. internat. programs and studies, 1984-89; prof. econs. and internat. affairs George Washington U., Washington, 1989—2004, prof. emeritus, 2004—, dir. Inst. for European, Russian and Eurasian Studies, 1989-01, assoc. dean Elliott Sch. Internat. Affairs, 1989-95, acting dean, 1994. Mem. acad. coun. Kennan Inst. Advanced Russian Studies, 1975-84; young faculty exchange Moscow State U., 1966; cons. to congressmen and various U.S. govt. depts., 1972—; dir. Soviet Interview Project, 1981-88; sec., bd. dirs. Midwest Univs. Consortium for Internat. Activities, 1984-88, chmn. bd., 1988-89; bd. dirs., chair fin. com. Internat. Rsch. and Exchs. Bd., 2002—. Author: The ABCs of Soviet Socialism, 1981 (non-fiction award Soc. Midland Authors, 1981), The Soviet Economic Experiment, 1990; editor, contbr. The Soviet Rural Community, 1971; editor: Slavic Rev., Am. Quar. Soviet and East European Studies, 1975-80, Problems of Post-Communism, 1996-2003; editor, contbr. Politics, Work and Daily Life, A Survey of Former Soviet Citizens, 1987; editor, contbr. Cracks in the Monolith: Party Power in the Brezhnev Era, 1992, The Social Legacy of Communism, 1994; editor-in-chief: Encyclopedia of Russian History, 4 vols., 2004; contbr. articles on studies on Soviet/Russian economy and econ. history to scholarly jours. Served with ___ ___ ___ ___, ___ ___, 1960 ___ ___, ___ ___ fellow, 1961-64, sr. scholar rsch. travel grantee to USSR, 1972; Internat. Rsch. and Exchs. Bd./USSR Acad. Scis. travel exchangee, 1979; fellow Woodrow Wilson Internat. Ctr. for Scholars, 1988-89, Guggenheim fellow, 1995-96; Internat. Rsch. and Exchs. Bd. advanced rsch. grantee, 1996. Mem. AAAS, Internat. Com. Ctrl. and East European Studies (bd. dirs., v.p.; 2001—), Econ. History Assn., Am. Assn. Advancement Slavic Studies (del. Am. Coun. Learned Soc. 1992-98, bd. dirs. 1995-2001, v.p. 1998-99, pres. 1999-2000, chair coun. of member insts. 1995-99, treas. 2004—), Am. Coun. Learned Soc. (treas., bd. dirs. 1996-2002, sec. 1994-96, mem. exec. com. and nominating com.); mem. joint com. with Social Sci. Rsch. Coun. 1990-95), Nat. Coun. for Ea. Europe and Eurasia (bd. dirs. 2004—), N.Y. Acad. Sci., Phi Beta Kappa (pres. Alpha chpt. 1998-01). Home: 2801 New Mexico Ave NW Apt 1215 Washington DC 20007-3942 Office: George Washington U Inst Eur Russ Eurasian Studies 1957 E St NW Ste 412 N Washington DC 20052-0001 Office Phone: 202-994-1645. Business E-Mail: millar@gwu.edu.

**MILLAR, JOCELYN G.,** entomologist, educator; PhD in Organic Chemistry, Simon Fraser U., Burnaby, B.C. Canada, 1983. From asst. to prof. dept. entomology U. Calif., Riverside, 1988—. Assoc. editor: Jour. Chem. Ecology, 2003—; contbr. articles to profl. jours., chapters to books. Mem.: AAAS, Internat. Soc. Chem. Ecology (pres. 2005—), Entomol. Soc. Am. (Syngenta Recognition award Crop Protection 2001, IPM award 2005, C.W. Woodworth award 2006, Recognition award 2001), Am. Chem. Soc. Office: University of California Department of Entomology Riverside CA 92521 Office Phone: 1 951 827 5821. Office Fax: 1 951 827 3086.

**MILLAR, JOHN DONALD,** physician, environmental services administrator, essayist, consultant, musician; b. Newport News, Va., Feb. 27, 1934; s. John and Dorothea Virginia (Smith) M.; m. Joan M. Phillips, Aug. 17, 1957; children: John Stuart, Alison Gordon, Virginia Taylor. BS, U. Richmond, 1956; MD, Med. Coll. Va., 1959; D.T.P.H., London Sch. Hygiene and Tropical Medicine, 1966; D of Pub. Svc. (hon.), Greenville Coll., Ill., 1994. Cert. specialist in Gen. Preventive Medicine 1969. Intern U. Utah Affiliated Hosps., Salt Lake City, 1959-60, asst. resident in medicine, 1960-61; chief

Epidemic Intelligence Svc., Ctr. for Disease Control, USPHS, HEW, Atlanta, 1961-63, dep. chief surveillance sect. epidemiology br., 1962-63, chief smallpox unit, 1963-65, dir. smallpox eradication program, 1966-70, dir. Bur. State Svcs., 1970-78, asst. dir. Ctr. for Disease Control for Pub. Health Practice, 1979-80; dir. Nat. Ctr. Environ. Health, Atlanta, 1980-81, Nat. Inst. for Occupation Safety and Health, Atlanta, 1981-93, chmn. exec. com. Nat. Toxicology Program, 1989-93; pres. Don Millar & Assocs., Inc., Atlanta, 1993—. Adj. prof. occupational and environ. health Sch. Pub. Health Emory U., Atlanta, 1988-98; cons. on smallpox, smallpox eradication, immunization programs and occupational and environ. health WHO; mem. WHO expert adv. panel on occupational health. Co-chmn. Task Force 4 Just Kids, 1993-98; tech. adv. bd. Ctr. Protect Workers' Rights, 1993; disting. fellow. vice chmn. Pub. Health Policy Adv. Bd., Inc., Washington, 1998—; mem. string bass sect. DeKalb Symphony Orch., 1982-06, Gainesville (Ga.) Symphony Orch., 2000-04, N.E. Ga. Mountain Chamber Orch., 2001-05, Truett-Macconnell Coll. Wind Symphony, 2002—, Toccoa Falls Coll. Orch., 2005—, Toccoa Symphony Orch., 2005—. Mem. editl. bd. Am. Jour. Indsl. Medicine, 1985-05, Am. Jour. Occupl. Psychology, 1993-00, Am. Jour. Preventive Medicine, 1993-00; contbr. articles to profl. jours. Recipient Surgeon Gen's. Commendation medal, 1965, Okeke prize London Sch. Hygiene and Tropical Medicine, 1966, Presdl. award for mgmt. improvement, 1972, W.C. Gorgas medal Assn. Mil. Surgeons U.S., 1987, Lucas lectr. Faculty Occupational Medicine Royal Coll. Physicians, London, 1987, Outstanding Med. Alumnus award Med. Coll. Va., 1988; also recipient Equal Employment Opportunity award, 1975, Medal of Excellence, 1977, Joseph W. Mountin lectr. award, 1986, Alexander D. Langmuir MD Meml. lectr. award, 2001, all from Ctrs. for Disease Control, Disting. Svc. medal USPHS, 1983, 88, Exemplary Svc. medal Surgeon Gen. U.S., 1988, Giants in Occupational Medicine lectr. U. Utah, 1989, William S. Knudsen award Am. Coll. Occupational Medicine, 1991, presdl. citation APA, 1991, William Steiger Meml. award Am. Conf. Govtl. Indsl. Hygienists, 1993, Health Watch award for outstanding contbns. toward improving health of minority populations, 1992, Award of Merit Minerva Edn. Inst., 1993, Alumni Disting. Svc. award U. Richmond, 1993, Jeff Lee Mem. Lectr. Am. Indusl. Hygiene Assoc. San Diego, Calif., 2002; named to Order Bifurcated Needle, World Health Orgn., 1978, Faculty Occupational Medicine, Royal Coll. Physicians, London, 1990; elected Safety and Health Hall of Fame Internat., Nat. Safety Coun., 1997. Mem. Am. Indsl. Hygiene Assn. (hon.), Am. Coll. Occupl. and Environ. Medicine, Am. Epidemiol. Soc., Collegium Ramazzini, Am. Assn. Pub. Health Physicians., Assn. Mil. Surgeons U.S., Pub. Health Svc. Commissioned Officers Assn., Alpha Omega Alpha.

**MILLAR, MICHAEL WILLIAM,** musician; b. N.Y.C., June 22, 1953; s. W. Llewellyn and Janet Josephine (Dean) M.; m. Lisa Rochelle Branch, July 30, 1983 (dec. Aug. 1987); m. Dana Grace Smart, June 25, 1989; children: Emily Ellyn, Matthew Ian. MusB in Performance, U. Colo., Boulder, 1976; MA in Music Performance, Calif. State U., L.A., 1980; D in Musical Arts, Claremont Grad. U., 1999; studied with George Roberts, Jeffrey Reynolds, Roy Main, Peter F. Drucker, Jean Lipman-Blumen, Nancy van Deusen. Trombonist Harry James Orch., 1980-85; exec. dir. Santa Clarita Symphony, 2005—. Mem. faculty U. Colo., Denver, 1987, Calif. State Poly. U., Pomona, 2004-, Internat. Trombone Festival, 2001; dir. Entrepreneurship Ctr. for Music, U. Colo., Boulder, 2002-03; has appeared with various brass ensembles, big bands, symphony orchs. and other mus. groups; performed in TV and radio jingles for Budweiser, Toyota, IBM, Texaco, Am. Express, Honda, Delta Airlines, Qantas, Sunny Delight, Disney World, AT&T, numerous others. Appeared in films Patch Adams, Hot to Trot, Sing, For the Boys, The Doors, on TV in Hull High, Jerry Lewis MDA Telethon Orch., 1995-2005; performed with L.A. Philharm., Steve Allen, Ray Anthony, Tex. Beneke Orch., Tony Bennett, George Burns, Ray Charles Orch., Rosemary Clooney, Ray Conniff, Merv Griffin, Jerry Lewis, Shari Lewis, Mills Bros., Liza Minnelli, Helen O'Connell, Patti Page, Debbie Reynolds, Kenny Rogers, Artie Shaw, The Smothers Brothers, numerous others; rec. with Southwest Chamber Music, Ray Anthony, Poco, Les Hooper, Joey DeFrancesco, Bruce Lofgren Jazz Orch., others. Co-recipient Grammy award, with S.W. Chamber Music, 2004. Mem. NARAS, Rec. Musicians Assn., Am. Fedn. Musicians, Ams. for the Arts. Home: 25430 Via Impreso Valencia CA 91355-2709 Office Phone: 818-901-6843. E-mail: millar@music.org.

**MILLAR, RICHARD WILLIAM, JR.,** lawyer; b. LA, May 11, 1938; LLB, U. San Francisco, 1966. Bar: Calif. 1967, U.S. Dist. Ct. (cen. dist.) Calif. 1967, U.S. Dist. Ct. (no. dist.) Calif. 1969, U.S. Dist. Ct. (so. dist.) Calif. 1973, U.S. Supreme Ct. Assoc. Iverson & Hogoboom, Los Angeles, 1967-72; ptnr. Eilers, Stewart, Pangman & Millar, Newport Beach, Calif., 1973-75, Millar & Heckman, Newport Beach, 1975-77, Millar, Hodges & Bemis, Newport Beach, 1979—. Trustee Western State U. Coll. Law, 2004—. Fellow: Am. Bar Found. (life); mem.: ABA (litigation sect. trial practice com., ho. of dels. 1990—), Orange County Bar Assn. (chmn. bus. litig. sect. 1981, chmn. judiciary com. 1988—90, sec. 1999, treas., pres. charitable fund 2000, pres.-elect 2001, pres. 2002, treas., dir. charitable fund 2003), Calif. Bar Assn. (lectr. CLE), Pacific Club, Bohemian Club (San Francisco). Home: 71 Hillsdale Newport Beach CA 92660 Office: Millar Hodges & Bemis One Newport Pl Ste # 900 Newport Beach CA 92660 Office Phone: 714-752-7722. Personal E-mail: millar@mhblaw.net.

**MILLARD, CHARLES WARREN, III,** museum director, writer; b. Elizabeth, N.J., Dec. 20, 1932; s. Charles Warren and Constance Emily (Keppler) M. AB magna cum laude, Princeton U., 1954; MA, Harvard U., 1963, PhD, 1971. Asst. to dir. Fogg Art Mus. Harvard U., Cambridge, Mass., 1963-64; asst. to dir. Dumbarton Oaks, Washington, 1965-66; dir. Washington Gallery Modern Art, 1966-67; teaching fellow Harvard U., 1968-69; curator 19th Century European art L.A. County Mus. Art, 1971-74; chief curator Hirshhorn Mus. and Sculpture Garden Smithsonian Instn., Washington, 1974-86; adj. prof. Johns Hopkins U., Balt., 1983-86; dir. Ackland Art Mus., 2000-04. Author: The Sculpture of Edgar Degas, 1977, La Vie d'Auguste Preault, Auguste Preault Sculpteur Romantique, 1809-1879, 1997; art editor Hudson Rev., 1972-87; contbr. articles to profl. jours. With USN, 1956-59.

**MILLARD, DONALD REX,** financial executive; b. Atlanta, Ga., June 24, 1947; s. Rex and Martha Nell (Gilstrap_M.; m. Fay Simmons, Mar. 15, 1968; children: Lisa, Bradley. BBA, U. Ga., 1968. CPA Ga. Audit mgr. Peat, Marwick, Main & Co., Atlanta, 1968-78; v.p. fin. Chick-fil-A Inc., Atlanta, 1978-82; pres. Dental One Inc., Atlanta, 1982-87; v.p. fin, CFO HEalthdyne Inc., Marietta, Ga., 1987—. Pub. chmn., Fin. Execs. Inst., Atlanta, 1987—. Mem. AICPA, Ga. Assn. CPA, Assn. Corp. Growth, Fin. Execs. Inst. (publicity chmn. 1987—). Avocations: racquetball, skiing.

**MILLARD, JAMES KEMPER,** marketing executive; b. Lexington, Kentucky, Oct. 28, 1948; s. Lyman Clifford and Cora (Carrick) M.; m. Madelyn (Hooper), Nov. 26, 1983; children: Lyman Clifford III, Sean Duffy, James Kemper Jr., Caroline Carrick. BA, Transylvania Univ., Lexington, Ky., 1971. Writer AP, Lexington, Ky., 1970—71; asst. news. dir. Sta. WLEX-TV, FM, Lexington, Ky., 1971—76; prod. Ky. Dept. Pub. Info., Frankfort, 1973; dir. Univ. rels. Transylvania Univ., Lexington, Ky., 1973—79; acct. supr. Abbott Advt., Inc., Lexington, Ky., 1979—85; mktg. dir. Steak N' Shake, Inc. Indpls., 1985; field mktg. mgr. Blue Bell, Pa., 1985—86; field mktg. dir. Nutri Sys. Inc., Blue Bell, Pa., 1986—88, v.p. comm., 1988—90, sr. v.p. mktg., 1990—91; pres. Mktg. Comm. Overview, Inc., Exton, Pa., 1991—93, Waterwild Mktg., Lexington, Ky., 1993—94; dir. promotion and devel. Sta. WKYT-TV, Lexington, Ky., 1994—99; exec. cons. E Corp., Lexington, Ky., 1999—2000; pres. ConnectedCampus.com., 1999—2000; sr. v.p. devel. strategy Equity Technologies and Resources, Inc., Lexington, Ky., 2000—02; pres. ETCR Mergers and Acquisitions, Inc., Lexington, Ky., 2001—; pres., CEO Equity Technologies and Resources, Inc., Lexington, Ky., 2002—; Verified Prescription Safeguards, Inc., Lexington, Ky., 2002—; ptnr. Waterwild Farm, LLC, Lexington, Ky., 2003—; pres., CEO Found Affordable Housing, Inc., 2006—. Mem. acad. adv. com. Ea. Ky. U., Richmond, 1983-87; treas. Bluegrass Integrated Pest Mgmt., Lexington, 1983-85; case

study spkr. Radio Advertisers Bur., 1989-90. Author: C and O Streamliners, 1994. Mem. Comdr. in Chief Leadership Cir., 1990—; pres. Swan Kitchen Car Co., 1990—; mem. Hon. Order Ky. Colonels, 1976—; cons. Jr. Achievement; mem. campaign cabinet United Way Bluegrass, 1995, mem. dream team, 1998—99; mem. devel. coun. Midway Coll., 1995—99; deacon Ctrl. Christian Ch., Lexington, Ky., 1984—86; bd. dir. Chesapeake and Ohio Hist. Soc., Clifton Forge, Va., 1983—98; v.p. Chesapeake and Ohio Hist. Soc., Clifton Forge, Va., 1994—97; bd. dir. Found. for Affordable Housing, 1995—, Friends of McConnell Springs, 1998—; chmn. Friends of Mc Connell Springs, 2001—; bd. dir. Bluegrass Trust for Hist. Preservation, 1998—2003, v.p., 1999, pres., 2000—02; trustee Lexington History Mus., Ky., 2000—; mem. bd. Lexington, Fayette Rural Land Mgmt., Ky., 2001—; mem. Am. Assn. Pvt. R.R. Car Owners, 1990—, R.R. Passenger Car Alliance, 1990—. Recipient Great Menu Award Nat. Restaurant Assn., 1982; Key Man Award Jerrico Inc., 1981; Silver and Bronze ADDY Awards Lexington Advt. Club, 1982; Gold Award Fla. Restaurant Assn., 1984; Innovative Idea Award Ky. Broadcasters Assn., 1995. Mem. Rotary Internat., Delta Sigma Phi (pres. U. Ky. corp. bd. 1994-97). Democrat. Address: Waterwild Farm PO Box 12012 Lexington KY 40579-2012 Personal E-mail: jmillard@usa.com. Business E-Mail: jmillard@foundhousing.org.

**MILLARD, NEAL STEVEN,** lawyer, educator; b. Dallas, June 6, 1947; s. Bernard and Adele (Marks) Millard; m. Janet Keast, Mar. 12, 1994; 1 child, Kendall Layne. BA cum laude, UCLA, 1969; JD, U. Chgo., 1972. Bar: Calif. 1972, U.S. Dist. Ct. (ctrl. dist.) Calif. 1973, U.S. Tax Ct. 1973, U.S. Ct. Appeals (9th cir.) 1987, N.Y. 1990. Assoc. Willis, Butler & Schiefly, L.A., 1972-75; ptnr. Morrison & Foerster, L.A., 1975-84, Jones, Day, Reavis & Pogue, L.A., 1984-93, White & Case, L.A., 1993—. Instn. Calif. State Coll., San Bernardino, 1975—76; lectr. Practising Law Inst., N.Y.C., NY, 1983—90, Calif. Edn. Bar, 1987—90; adj. prof. U. So. Calif Law Ctr., L.A., 1994—. Mem. citizens adv. com. L.A. Olympics, 1982—84; trustee Altadena (Calif.) Libr. Dist., 1985—86; bd. dirs. Woodcraft Rangers, L.A., 1982—90, pres., 1986—88; bd. dirs. Los Angeles County Bar Found., 1990—2000, pres., 1997—98; mem. Energy Commn. county and cities of L.A., 1995—99; mem. jud. procedures commn. Los Angeles County, 1999—, chair, 2000—02; mem. pub. safety com. City of LaCanada-Flintridge, 2006—; mem. Pub. Safety Commn. LaCanada-Flintridge, 2006—; bd. dirs. Inner City Law Ctr., 1996—99; bd. dirs. sec. LaCanada-Flintridge Ednl. Found., 2002—06; bd. dirs. Alliance Coll.-Ready Pub. Schs., 2004. Mem.: ABA, Am. Law Inst., Pub. Counsel (bd. dirs. 1984—87, 1990—93), Los Angeles County Bar Assn. (trustee 1985—87), N.Y. State Bar Assn., Calif. Bar Assn., U. So. Calif. Inst. Corp. Counsel (mem. adv. bd. 1998—2006), U. Chgo. Law Alumni Assn. (pres. 1998—2001), Flintridge Riding Club, Calif. Club, Chancery Club, Beach Club, Phi Beta Kappa, Phi Delta Phi, Pi Gamma Mu. Office: White & Case 633 W 5th St Ste 1900 Los Angeles CA 90071-2087 Office Phone: 213-620-7773. Business E-Mail: nmillard@whitecase.com.

**MILLARD, RICHARD STEVEN,** lawyer; b. Pasadena, Calif., Feb. 6, 1952; s. Kenneth A. and Kathryn Mary (Paden) M.; m. Jessica Ann Edwards, May 15, 1977; children: Victoria, Elizabeth, Andrew. AB, Stanford U., 1974; JD magna cum laude, U. Mich., 1977. Bar: Calif. 1977, Ill. 1985. Assoc. Heller, Ehrman, White & McAuliff, San Francisco, 1977-81, Mayer, Brown & Platt, Chgo., 1982-83, ptnr., 1984-99, Weil, Gotshal & Manges, Redwood Shores, Calif., 1999—. Mem. ABA, Order of Coif. Office: Weil Gotshal & Manges 201 Redwood Shores Pkwy Redwood City CA 94065 Office Phone: 650-802-3015. Business E-Mail: richard.millard@weil.com.

**MILLARD, ROBERT B.,** investment company executive; b. 1950; m. Bethany Millard; 4 children. BS, MIT, 1973; MBA, Harvard U., 1976. Joined Kuhn Loeb & Co., 1976; mng. dir. Lehman Brothers Inc., 1983—. Bd. dirs. Weatherford Internat., Inc., 1989—, GulfMark Offshore, Inc., 1996—, L-3 Comm. Corp., 1997—, non-exec. chmn., 2006—; chair vis. physics com. MIT, vis. linguistics & philosophy com., vis. architecture com. Bd. trustees, oper. & adminstrn. com. Assoc. Universities Inc.; bd. trustees, exec. com. Population Coun., 1993—, MIT Corp., 2003—; bd. trustees, exec. com., treas. New Sch. Univ.; bd. govs. Parsons Sch. Design; bd. dirs. Remarque Inst., NYU. Mem.: Coun. Fgn. Rels., The Brook, Edgarton Golf Club, NY Yacht Club. Office: Lehman Brothers 9th Fl 399 Park Ave New York NY 10022 Office Phone: 212-526-9370. Office Fax: 212-526-3597.*

**MILLAUER, LISELOTTE,** journalist; b. Danzig, Prussia, Germany, July 4, 1945; came to U.S., 1991; d. Ernst and Eva Millauer; 1 child, Alex. Grad., U. Hamburg. Chief reporter Bild am Sonntag, Hamburg; chief corr. Welt am Sonntag, Hamburg. Interviewer TV show exclusiv ZDF; freelance journalist for mags. including Harper's Bazaar, Playboy, Vogue, Madame; one-on-one interviews (Liselotte Millauer Face to Face with the World's Prominence), Pres. Ford, Pres. Reagan, Gov. Nelson Rockefeller, Pres. Sadat, Shah of Iran, Indira Ghandi, Archbishop Makarios, Chancellor Kohl, Chancellor Schmidt, Leonard Bernstein, Federico Fellini, Gianni Bulgari, Karl Lagerfeld, King Hussein, Prince Ranier of Monaco, Alfred Hitchcock, Cary Grant, Mae West, others; moderator NDR Talkshow. Pub. (biography) Christian Anders, German Popstar, 2005. Home and Office: 1530 N Detroit St Los Angeles CA 90046-3286 Office Phone: 323-876-3979. E-mail: lmillauer@aol.com.

**MILLBERG, JOHN C.,** lawyer; b. New London, Conn., Jan. 4, 1956; s. Melvin Roy and Dorothy (Van Zandt) M.; m. Lori Bruce, Oct. 18, 1981; children: Kathryn Faye, Rebecca Ann, Melvin Roy III. BA, Bowling Green State U., 1977; JD, Wake Forest U., 1980. Bar: Tex. 1980, N.C. 1986, S.C. 2000, U.S. Dist. Ct. (so. dist.) Tex. 1981, U.S. Ct. Appeals (5th and 11th cirs.) 1981, U.S. Dist. Ct. (ea., mid. and we. dists.) N.C. 1986, U.S. Ct. Appeals (4th cir.) 1986, U.S. Dist. Ct. S.C. 2002. Assoc. Crain Caton James & Womble, Houston, 1981-85; assoc. dir. Maupin, Taylor, Ellin & Adams, Raleigh, NC, 1985—94; mng. ptnr. Millberg, Gordon & Stewart, PLLC, Raleigh, NC, 1994—. Mem. bar candidate com. N.C. Bd. Law Examiners, 1988-90. Scholar Wake Forest U. Sch. Law, 1977-80. Mem. N.C. Assn. Def. Attys. (exec. com., v.p. southeastern region), Nat. Assn. R.R. Trial Counsel. Office: Millberg Gordon & Stewart PLLC S 104 1101 Haynes St Raleigh NC 27604-1455

**MILLEN, MATT,** professional sports team executive; b. Hokendauqua, Pa., Mar. 12, 1958; m. Patricia Millen; children: Marianne, Michalyn, Marcus; 1 child, Matthew Jr. Student Pa. State U. Linebacker Oakland/L.A. Raiders, 1980—88, San Francisco 49ers, 1990, Washington Redskins, 1991; game analyst CBS, Fox TV; pres., CEO Detroit Lions, 2001—. Named to NFL Pro Bowl Team, 1988. Office: Detroit Lions Inc 222 Republic Dr Allen Park MI 48101-3650

**MILLENDER-MCDONALD, JUANITA,** congresswoman; b. Birmingham, Ala., Sept. 7, 1938; d. Shelly and Everlina (Dortch) M.; m. James McDonald III, July 26, 1955; children: Valeria, Angela, Sherryll, Michael, Roderick. BS, U. Redlands, Calif., 1980; MS in Edn., Calif. State U., L.A., 1986; postgrad., U. So. Calif. Manuscript editor Calif. State Dept. Edn., Sacramento; dir. gender equity programs L.A. Unified Sch. Dist.; mem. U.S. Congress from 37th Calif dist., Washington, 1996—; mem. small bus. com., transp. and infrastructure com.; mem. Ho. Com. on Ho. Adminstrn.; tchr.; sch. adminstr., 1981—90; Carson mayor pro-tempore; mem. Calif. Assembly, 1992—96, Jt Com. Libr., Dem. Homeland Security Task Force, New Democrat Coalition, Regional Whip. City councilwoman, Carson; bd. dirs. S.C.L.C. Pvt. Industry Coun. Policy Bd.; West Basin Mcpl. Water Dist., Cities Legis. League (vice chmn.; mem. Nat. Women's Polit. Caucus; mem. adv. bd. Comparative Ethnic Tng. U. So. Calif.; founder, exec. dir. Young Advocates So. Calif. Recipient Most Influential Black Americans, Ebony mag., 2006. Mem. NAACP, NEA, Nat. Assn. Minority Polit. Women, NAFE, Nat. Fedn. Bus. and Profl. Women, Assn. Calif. Sch. Adminstrs., Am. Mgmt. Assn., League African Women, L.A. World Affairs Coun., Nat. Female Execs., Nat. Coun. Jewish Women, Carson C. of C., Phi Delta Kappa. Democrat. Office: 2445 Rayburn HOB Washington DC 20515-0537 also: 970 W 190 St Ste 900 Torrance CA 90502 Office Phone: 202-225-7924. Office Fax: 202-225-7926.*

**MILLER, ALAN B.**, hospital management executive; b. NYC, Aug. 17, 1937; s. Daniel and Mary (Blumenthal) M.; m. Jill K. Stein, Oct. 5, 1968; children: Marc Daniel, Marni Elizabeth, Abby Danielle. BA, Coll. William and Mary, 1958; MBA, U. Pa., 1960. V.p. Young & Rubicam, Inc., N.Y.C., 1964-69; sr. v.p. Am. Medicorp., Inc., L.A., 1970, pres., chief exec. officer Phila., 1973-77, chmn. bd., 1977, Hosp. Underwriting Group, 1977-78; founder, pres., chmn. bd. Universal Health Svcs., King of Prussia, Pa., 1978—; chmn., founder UHT-Real Estate Trust, King of Prussia, 1986—. Formerly health care adviser Fed. Mediation and Conciliation Svc.; chmn., pres. Universal Health Svcs. Real Estate Investment Trust, N.Y. Stock Exch., 1986—; bd. dirs. CDI Corp., N.Y. Stock Exch., Broadlane, Penn Mut. Life Ins.; mem. exec. bd. Wharton Sch., U. Pa., 1996-2004, mem. bd. overseers, 2005-. Chmn. Opera Co. of Phila.; dir. Regional Performing Arts Ctr. Capt. 77th Inf. Divsn. U.S. Army. Recipient Ellis Island Medal of Honor, 1998. Mem.: Phila. C. of C. (bd. dirs.). Home: 57 Crosby Brown Rd Gladwyne PA 19035-1512 Office: Universal Health Svcs Inc PO Box 61558 367 S Gulph Rd King Of Prussia PA 19406*

**MILLER, ALAN JAY**, rare book dealer, author; b. Bklyn., July 11, 1936; s. Louis and Claire (Maltz) M.; m. Susan Ruth Morris, Oct. 29, 1961; children— Laurie Ann, Adam Louis. BA, Cornell U., 1957. Chartered fin. analyst. Pres. Analysis-in-Depth Inc., N.Y.C., 1965-67; mng. editor Value Line Investment Survey, N.Y.C., 1967-68; rsch. dir. Emanuel Deetjen & Co., N.Y.C., 1968-69; exec. v.p., dir. Intersci. Capital Mgmt. Corp., N.Y.C., 1969-71; pres., dir. ICM Equity Fund Inc., N.Y.C., 1970-71, ICM Fin. Fund Inc., N.Y.C., 1970-71; v.p., assoc. rsch. dir. Bache & Co., Inc., N.Y.C., 1972, G.H. Walker & Co., Inc., N.Y.C., 1972-73; 1st v.p., assoc. rsch. dir. Blyth Eastman Dillon & Co. Inc., N.Y.C., 1974-76; dir. rsch. E.F. Hutton & Co., Inc., N.Y.C., 1976-81, sr. v.p. 1976-80, exec. v.p. Hutton Investment Mgmt., 1976-88; mng. dir. SLH Asset Mgmt. Shearson Lehman Hutton, Inc., N.Y.C., 1988-90; sr. v.p. Martin E. Segal Co., N.Y.C., 1990-92. Adj. assoc. prof. Columbia U. Grad. Sch. Bus., 1978-79; mem. faculty N.Y. Inst. Fin., 1977-98; adj. prof. Adelphi U. Coll., 1993-98; rare book dealer, 1998—. Author: Socially Responsible Investing: How to Invest with Your Conscience, 1991, Standard and Poor's 401(k) Planning Guide, 1995. Personal E-mail: alan@alansbooks.com

**MILLER, ALAN M.**, editor, writer, educator, television host; b. NYC, July 24, 1934; s. Philip and Sylvia (Lubash) M.; children: Neil, Peter, Stephanie Cook, Douglas; m. Sharon A. Tanenbaum, Aug. 29, 1996; step-children: Holly Harouche, Becky Theodoratos. AB, Syracuse U., 1955, LLB, 1958, JD, 1968. Asst. counsel 3 joint legis. coms. N.Y. State Legislature, 1968-70; counsel to minority Nassau County Bd. Suprs., 1974-75; prin. atty. editor Thomson/West, Eagan, Minn., 1985—2004. Faculty film and screenwriting Mpls. Coll., 1999—, Hofstra U., 1990-97, Discovery Ctr., 1990-94, NY Inst. Tech., Old Westbury, 1987-89; humanities faculty, Inver Hills CC, 2004—; bd. mem. Inver Hills Found., 2005—. Columnist South Shore Record, Woodmere, NY, Another Viewpoint, 1985-99 (awards NY Press Assn. 1988, 89, 94, Best column award 1992), Single-Minded, 1991-92, NY Bowler, 1991-93 (Bowling Mag. awards 1990-93, Best column award 1992), Nostalgia Mag., 1990-91; writer-editor USCAdvantage, 1995-99 (Immy awards 1996, 97); editor: Beyond the Bar, Thomson West Group, 2000-02, 05; contbr. articles to publs., including NY Times, Newsday, Newsday Mag., Mpls. Star-Tribune, Humanistic Judaism. Assembly dist. leader NY State Dem. Com., 1965-76; Commr. Village of Woodsburgh, NY, 1980, telecom. com. City of Eagan, Minn., 1999-2005, chmn., 2002, vice-chmn., 2003; citizens adv. com. Minn. Twins, 2000-02; vice-chmn. Minn. Assn. Cable TV Administrs., 2002-03; host and prodr. cable TV Access to Democracy, 2001—, TwinsTalk, 2003-04; guest host Air Am. Radio, Minn., 2005—. Recipient multiple awards for coverage of Persian Gulf War from Israel, 1991, Citizens Impact award Burnsville/Eagan Telecomm., 2003-04, Millenium Club award, 2004, Century Club award, 2005. Mem. Screenwriters Workshop, Ind. Film Pub., Assn. Holocaust Orgns. Jewish. Home: 4316 Aries Ct Eagan MN 55123 Office: 1501 Hennepin Ave T-3068 Minneapolis MN 55403 Personal E-mail: alanmillermn@comcast.net.

**MILLER, ALBERT JAY**, retired library director; b. Beaver Falls, Pa., Dec. 7, 1927; s. Joseph Jefferson and Alberta Fae (Shaffer) Miller. BS, Geneva Coll., 1952; MLS, Rutgers U., 1958; postgrad. U. Chgo., 1960-61, U. Pitts., 1963-68, U. Mich., 1969. Libr. West Allegheny Jr. H.S., Imperial, Pa., 1959-60, Butler (Pa.) Area Sr. H.S., 1962-67, Pa. State U., New Kensington, 1969-89, rsch.-libr. continuing edn. dept., 1970-89, ret. libr. and info. svcs. dir. emeritus, 1989, prof. emeritus. Author: A Selective Bibliography of Existentialism in Education and Related Topics, 1969, Confrontation, Conflict and Dissent, 1972, Death: A Bibliographical Guide, 1977; book and media rev. editor: Learning Today, 1978—; mem. editl. bd. Learning Today, 1979—. Tchr., judge Nat. Baton Twirling Assn., 1998; instr. water safety ARC, New Kensington, 1969—, Citizens Gen. Hosp., 1971—72; active Boy Scouts Am., 1970—; bd. dirs. Westmoreland County, Butler County mental health issues; mem. Allegheny-Kiski Human Rels. Coun., 1976—77; bd. dirs. Allegheny-Kiski Sr. Citizens Ctr., 1976—77, fund raising chmn., 1989—90, 2d v.p., 1997—98, pres., 1998—; mem., pub. rels. dir. Twirling Unlimited, Akron, Ohio; baton twirler Kensington Firemens Band; entrepreneur Al's Terrific Twirling Tricks-Catch It; book reader People's Libr., New Kensington; Sunday sch. tchr. Manchester Reformed Presbyn. Ch., 1970—, elder, clk. session, 1984—, Sabbath sch. supt., 1990; elder emeritus Eastvale Reformed Presbyn. Ch., mem. Christian edn. com., tchr. adult Sabbath sch., 2003; bd. corporators Geneva Coll., Beaver Falls, Pa., 1987—. Named Twirling champion, N.Y. State Hall of Fame, 1999. Mem.: ALA, NEA (life), U.S. Twirling Assn., Pa. Libr. Assn., Pa. Edn. Assn. (life). Democrat. Home: 160 Crosswynds Dr Beaver Falls PA 15010-1182 Office Phone: 724-891-2369. Personal E-mail: millercrosswynds@comcast.net.

**MILLER, ALFRED MONTAGUE**, lawyer; b. Augusta, Ga., Jan. 5, 1940; s. Dessie Ford and May Belle (Power) M.; m. Lynthia Wofford, Aug. 25, 1962 (div. 1979); children— William Montague, Stephen Mathews; m. Peggy Elaine Mays, July 26, 1980. B.B.A., U. Ga., 1961, J.D., 1963. Bar: Ga. 1962, Superior Ct. Ga. 1962, U.S. Dist. Ct. (so. dist.) Ga. 1963, U.S. Ct. Appeal (11th cir.) 1981, U.S. Supreme Ct. 1978. Ptnr. Fulcher, Fulcher, Hagler, Harper and Reed, Augusta, 1963-71, Dye, Miller, Tucker and Everitt, P.A., Augusta, 1971—90, of counsel 1990-; pres. Club Car, Inc., 1990-2001; dir. First Bank of Ga., 2001-. Fellow Ga. Bar Found., Am. Coll. Trial Lawyers; mem. Am. Judicature Soc., ABA, State Bar Ga. (bd. govs. 1977-85), Augusta Bar Assn. (pres. 1985), Internat. Assn. Def. Counsel, Beta Gamma Sigma, Chi Phi (pres. 1960-61), Phi Delta Phi. Presbyterian. Home: 4384 Deer Run Haven GA 30809-4440 Office: Tucker Everitt Long Brewton & Lanier PO Box 2426 Augusta GA 30903-2426 Office Phone: 404-722-0771. E-mail: mill4384@aol.com.

**MILLER, ALLAN JOHN**, lawyer; b. Beachwood, Ohio, Oct. 17, 1921; s. Carl Frederick and Rhoda (Warren) M.; m. Marjorie Hewitt Pirtle, Aug. 10, 1946; children: James W., Patricia Anne. BBA, Fenn Coll., 1946; LL.B., Western Res. U., 1948; D. (hon.), Dyke Coll., Cleve., 1986. Bar: Ohio 1948. With Standard Oil Co., Ohio, 1948-77, treas., 1967-77; mem. firm Kiefer, Knecht, Rees, Meyer & Miller, Cleve., 1977-81. Dir. United Screw & Bolt Corp., 1977—97. Home: Apt 531 900 Tamiami Trl S Venice FL 34285-3627 bd. trustees Dyke Coll., Cleve., 1971-86. With AUS, 1943-46, PTO; vol. tax aide AARP, 2005—. Mem. Cleve. Treas.'s Club. Clubs: Capri Isles Golf Club (Venice, Fla.). Presbyterian. Home: Apt 531 900 Tamiami Trl S Venice FL 34285-3627

**MILLER, ALWIN VERMAR**, educational association administrator, consultant; b. Dardanelle, Ark., Oct. 12, 1922; s. William Marshall and Ollie Vernice (Green) M.; m. Patricia Jane Knox, Dec. 31, 1945; children: Carol, Alwin, William, Nitiya, Thomas. AA, Ark. Poly. Inst., 1939; BS, UCLA, 1947, BA with honors, 1947, MEd, 1948, EdD, 1956; cert., Internat. Inst. Ednl. Planning, (UNESCO), 1967—68. Instr. Chico (Calif.) State Coll., 1948-49; assoc. prof. So. Oreg. Coll., Ashland, 1949-57; edn. advisor AID, Washington, 1957-75; pvt. practice Upper Marlboro, Md., 1975—. Cons. in

**MILLER, ANDRE**, professional basketball player; b. Mar. 19, 1976; BS in Soc., Univ. Utah, 1998. Basketball player Cleveland Cavaliers, 1999—2002, LA Clippers, 2002—03, Denver Nuggets, 2003—. Named to NBA All-Rookie Team, 1999—2000. Office: Denver Nuggets 1000 Chopper Cir Denver CO 80204*

**MILLER, ANDREW PICKENS**, lawyer; b. Fairfax, Va., Dec. 21, 1932; s. Francis Pickens and Helen (Hill) M.; m. Penelope Farthing, Nov. 18, 1990; children: Julia Lane, Andrew Pickens, Elise Givhan, Winfield Scott, Lucia Holcombe. AB magna cum laude, Princeton U., 1954; postgrad., New Coll., Oxford U., Eng., 1954-55; LLB, U. Va., 1960. Bar: Va. 1960, U.S. Supreme Ct. 1967, D.C. 1979. Asso. Penn, Stuart & Stuart, 1960-62; ptnr. Penn, Stuart & Miller, Abingdon, Va., 1963-69; atty. gen. State of Va., 1970-77; ptnr. Mays, Valentine, Davenport & Moore, Richmond, Va., 1977-78, Dickstein, Shapiro, Morin & Oshinsky, LLP, Washington, 1979—2002, Powell Goldstein LLP, Washington, 2002—. Pres., Young Democratic Clubs Va., 1966-67; chmn. Washington County Dem. Com., 1967-69; Dem. nominee for U.S. Senate from Va., 1978; bd. dirs. Barter Found., 1962-69, Nat. Heritage Found., 2005—; trustee King Coll., 1966-74; mem. adv. bd. Ams. for Effective Law Enforcement, 1973-77, Ctr. for Oceans Law and Policy, 1975-79; vice-chmn. Va. Bd. Corrections, 1983-86. Served to 1st lt. AUS, 1955-57. Fellow Am. Bar Found., ABA (ho. dels. 1971-76, action commn. to reduce ct. costs and delay 1979-84, commn. on pub. understanding about the law 1992-95); mem. So. Conf. Attys. Gen. (vice chmn. 1972-73, chmn. 1973-74), Nat. Assn. Attys. Gen. (exec. com. 1973-74, chmn. antitrust com. 1971-76, Wyman Meml. award 1976), Va. Bar Assn. (chmn. young lawyers sect. 1967-68, exec. com. 1985-88), Am. Judicature Soc. (bd. dirs. 1973-76, exec. com. 1974-76), Soc. of Cin. (Va. standing com. 1988-89, 93-96, asst. sec., 1992-95, sec. gen. 1995-98), The John Marshall Found. (pres. 1987-89), Phi Beta Kappa, Omicron Delta Kappa. Presbyterian. Home: 1503 35th St NW Washington DC 20007-2729 Office: Powell Goldstein LLP 3rd Fl 901 New York Ave NW Washington DC 20001-4413 Office Phone: 202-624-7386. Business E-Mail: amiller@pogolaw.com.

**MILLER, ANITA DIANE**, psychologist; b. Lewistown, Pa., Oct. 31, 1968; d. Fred A. and Sarah A. Miller; life ptnr. James McMartin Long; 1 child, Hannah Nicole Keener. BA, Bucknell U.; PhD, Vanderbilt U., 1998. Lic. clin. psychologist NY, 2002. Rsch. cons. James Long Co., Caroga Lake, NY, 2002—05; asst. prof. Skidmore Coll., Saratoga Springs, 2005—. Contbr. articles to profl. jours. Mem. Resident's Com. Protect Adirondacks, Blue Mountain Lake, NY, 2004—05, Adirondack Nature Conservancy, Keene Valley, 2004—05. Recipient Still prize, Bucknell U., 1989, Nat. Rsch. Svc. award, NIMH, 1994—97, 1999—2002, Rsch. award, 1999, Young Investigator award, Nat. Alliance for Rsch. on Schizophrenia and Depression, 2000—03; fellow, Pew Sci. Found., 1989, U. Pitts., 1998—2002; scholar, U. Wis., 1999. Mem.: APA (assoc.), Am. Psychol. Soc., NY Psychol. Assn. (assoc.), Soc. Rsch. Child Devel. (assoc.), Soc. Neurosci. (assoc.), Soc. Rsch. Psychopathology (assoc.), Internat. Neuropsychological Soc. (assoc.), Soc. Psychophysiological Rsch. (assoc.), Sigma Xi, Phi Beta Kappa, Psi Chi, Alpha Lambda Delta, Phi Eta Sigma. Achievements include research in Psychophysiology Device Development, with James Long. Home: PO Box 685 Caroga Lake NY 12032-0685 Office: Skidmore Coll 815 North Broadway Saratoga Springs NY 12866-1632 Personal E-mail: anita_miller_phd@yahoo.com.

**MILLER, ANN G.**, lawyer; b. San Francisco, Nov. 1, 1944; BA, U. San Diego, 1966; JD, U. San Francisco, 1970. Bar: Calif. 1971. Law clk. U.S. Dist. Ct. (no. dist.) Calif., 1970-71; ptnr. Lillick & Charles, San Francisco, Nixon Peabody LLP, San Francisco, 2001—. Mem. Ninth Cir. Judicial Nominating Com. Mem.: ABA, Computer Law Assn., Bar Assn. San Francisco, Maritime Law Assn. (chair Passenger Vessel and Cruise Com.). Office: Nixon Peabody LLP Two Embarcadero Ctr San Francisco CA 94111-3996 Office Phone: 415-984-8236. Office Fax: 415-984-8300. E-mail: amiller@nixonpeabody.com.

**MILLER, ANNETTE K. See MATEMA, ZSUN-NEE**

**MILLER, ANTHONY BERNARD**, physician, researcher; b. Woodford, Eng., Apr. 17, 1931; married, 1952; 5 children. BA, U. Cambridge, 1952, MB, BChir, 1955; MA, 2004, MD, 2006. House officer Oldchurch Hosp., Romford, Eng., 1955-57; med. registrar Luton and Dunstable Hosp., Eng. 1959-62; mem. sci. staff Med. Research Council Tb and Chest Disease Unit, London, 1962-71; assoc. prof. preventive medicine and biostats. U. Toronto, 1972-76, prof., 1976-96, chmn. dept., 1992-96, dir. grad. program in epidemiology, 1986-91; dir. epidemiology unit Nat. Cancer Inst. Can., Toronto, 1971-86; dir. Nat. Breast Screening Study, 1980—, WHO Collaborating Ctr. on Evaluation of Screening for Cancer, 1991-2000; prof. emeritus pub. health scis., 1997—; head divsn. of clin. Epidemology German Cancer Rsch. Ctr., Heidelberg, 1999—2003. Nat. Health scientist, 1988-93; mem. working cadre Bladder Cancer Project, U.S., 1973-75; mem. epidemiology com. Breast Cancer Task Force, U.S., 1973-77, chmn., 1975-77; mem. Fed. Task Force Cervical Cytol. Screening, Can., 1974-76, 80-81, Union Internat. Contre le Cancer com., controlled therapeutic trials, 1978-82, Multidisciplinary project breast cancer, 1978-82, chmn. project on screening, 1982-93; mem. sci. council Internat. Agy. Research Cancer, Lyon, 1981-85, chmn., 1985; mem. com. on diet, nutrition and cancer NRC of U.S., 1980-83, mem. oversight com. radioepidemiologic tables, 1983-84, com. on diet and health, 1986-89, com. on dietary guidelines implementation, 1988-91, chmn. com. on environmental epidemiology, 1990-94; chmn. Ont. Task Force on Primary Prevention of Cancer, 1994-95. Served with RAF, 1957-59. Mem. Can. Oncology Soc. (sec.-treas. 1975-79, pres. 1980-81), Soc. Epidemiology Research, Internat. Epidemiology Assn., Am. Soc. Preventive Oncology (pres. 1983-85), Am. Coll. Epidemiology (bd. dirs. 1987-89), Coun. Can. Strategy for Cancer Control. Personal E-mail: ab.miller@sympatico.ca.

**MILLER, ARJAY**, retired university dean; b. Shelby, Nebr., Mar. 4, 1916; s. Rawley John and Mary Gertrude (Schade) M.; m. Frances Marion Fearing, Aug. 18, 1940; children: Kenneth Fearing, Ann Elizabeth (Mrs. James Olstad). BS with highest honors, UCLA, 1937. LL.D. (hon.), 1964; postgrad., U. Calif.-Berkeley, 1938-40; LL.D. (hon.), Washington U., St. Louis; LL.D., Whitman Coll., 1965, U. Nebr., 1965, Ripon Coll., 1980. Teaching asst. U. Calif. at Berkeley, 1938-40; research technician Calif. State Planning Bd., 1941; economist Fed. Res. Bank San Francisco, 1941-43; asst. treas. Ford Motor Co., 1954-63, controller, 1953-57, v.p., controller, 1957-61, v.p. finance, 1961-62, v.p. of staff group, 1962-63, pres., 1963-68, vice chmn., 1968-69; dean Grad. Sch. Bus., Stanford U., 1969-79, emeritus, 1979—. Former chmn. Automobile Mfrs. Assn., Econ. Devel. Corp. Greater Detroit; councillor The Conf. Bd.; past chmn., life trustee Urban Inst.; mem. Public Adv. Commn. on U.S. Trade Policy, 1968-69, Pres.'s Nat. Commn. on Productivity, 1970-74. Trustee Internat. Exec. Svc. Coirps.; hon. trustee The Brookings Instn.; dir. emeritus S.R.I. Internat.; former chmn. Pub. Policy Inst. Calif.; former chmn. Detroit Press Club Found.; former chmn. Boy Area Coun. Capt. USAAF, 1943—46. Recipient Alumnus of Year Achievement award UCLA, 1964; Distinguished Nebraskan award, 1968; Nat. Industry Leader award B'nai B'rith, 1968 Fellow Am. Acad. Arts and Scis. Clubs: Pacific Union, Bohemian. Presbyterian.

**MILLER, ARNOLD**, electronics executive; b. NYC, May 8, 1928; s. Sam and Mina (Krutalow) M.; m. Beverly Shayne, Feb. 5, 1950; children: Debra Lynn, Marla Jo, Linda Sue BS in Chemistry, UCLA, 1948, PhD in Phys. Chemistry, 1951. Registered profl. engr., Calif. Rsch. phys. chemist Wrigley Rsch. Co., Chgo., 1951; supr. phys. chemistry Armour Rsch. Found., Chgo., 1951-54, mgr. chemistry and metals, 1954-56; chief materials sci. dept. Borg-Warner Rsch. Ctr., Des Plaines, Ill., 1956-59; dir. rsch. Rockwell Corp., Anaheim, Calif., 1959-66, dir. microelec. ops., 1967-68; group exec. materials ops. Whittaker Corp., L.A., 1968-70; pres. Theta Sensors, Orange, Calif., 1970-72; mgr. xeroradiography Xerox Corp., Pasadena, Calif., 1972-75, corp. dir. rsch. and adv. devel. Stamford, Conn., 1975-78, El Segundo, Calif., 1978-81, v.p. electronics div., 1981-84, pres. electronics div., 1984-87, corp. officer Stamford 1984-87; pres. Tech. Strategy Group, Fullerton, Calif., 1987—; prodr. Remembrance Films, 2004—. Bd. dirs. Spectro Diode Labs, San Jose, Calif., Semicondr. Rsch. Corp., Colorep Inc., Carlsbad, Calif.; bd. dirs., chair audit com. Merisel Computer Products, El Segundo, Calif., lead dir. 1989—; mem. vis. com. on materials sci. U. So. Calif., L.A., 1966-68; mem. State of Calif. Micro Bd., 1984-2000. Editorial adv. bd. Advances in Solid State Chemistry; co-editor Electronics Industry Development; contbr. numerous articles to profl. jours. and monographs; patentee in field. Mem. civilian adv. group Dept. Commerce, 1959-60; mem. 5th decade com., also adv. com. on engring. and mgmt. program UCLA, 1984-; mem. com. on scholarly commn. with People's Republic of China, Tech. Transfer Task Force, Nat. Acad. Sci., Washington, 1985; bd. dirs. Orange County Pacific Symphony, Fullerton, Calif., 1982-; mem. univ.'s adv. bd. Calif. State U.-Fullerton, 1986-2006, chair, 1991-2006; v.p., bd. dirs. Heritage Pointe Home for the Aging, 1987-97; chmn. Indsl. Assocs. sch. engring. and computer sci. Calif. State U., 1987-97, trustee continuing learning ctr., 1993-; mem. Overseas Devel. Coun., 1988-; mem. Nat. Com. U.S.-China Rels., 1990-; trustee So. Calif. Coll. of Optometry, 1996-, sec.-treas. 1997-2003; bd. mem. Cmty. Found., 1995-, v.p., 1997-. Recipient Sci. Merit award Navy Bur. Ordnance/Armour Rsch. Found., 1952, IR-100 award, 1964, 69; named hon. alumnus Calif. State U., Fullerton, 1996, Univ. medal. Inst. Gerontology Calif. State U., Fullerton, 2002. Fellow AAAS; mem. IEEE, AIME, Am. Chem. Soc., So. Calif. Coalition Edn. Mfg. Engring. (bd. dirs. 1994-98), Elec. Industry Assn. (past chmn. microelectronics), Phi Beta Kappa, Sigma Xi, Phi Lamda Upsilon Home: 505 Westchester Pl Fullerton CA 92835-2706 Office: Tech Strategy Group PO Box 5769 Fullerton CA 92838-0769 Office Phone: 714-447-8887. Business E-Mail: amiller@fullerton.edu.

**MILLER, ARTHUR HAWKS, JR.**, librarian, archivist; b. Kalamazoo, Mich., Mar. 15, 1943; s. Arthur Hawks and Eleanor (Johnson) M.; m. Janet Carol Schroeder, June 11, 1967; children: Janelle Miller Moravek, Andrew Hawks. Student, U. Caen, Calvados, France, 1963-64; AB, Kalamazoo Coll., 1965; AM in English, U. Chgo., 1966, AM in Librarianship, 1968; PhD, Northwestern U., 1973. Reference libr. Newberry Libr., Chgo., 1966-69, asst. libr. pub. svcs., 1969-72; coll. libr. Lake Forest (Ill.) Coll., 1972-94, archivist and libr. for spl. collections, 1994—. Co-author: 30 Miles North: A History of Lake Forest College, Its Town, and Its City of Chicago, 2000, Lake Forest Estates, People, and Culture, 2000, Classic Country Estates Lake Forest, 2003, One Hundred Rare and Notable Books, 2004. Pres. Lake Forest/Lake Bluff Hist. Soc., 1982-85, bd. dirs., 2003—; pres. Ill. Ctr. for Book Bd., 1992-93; pres. Ragdale Found., 1992-96; dir. Lake Forest Found. for Hist. Preservation, 1997—, v.p., 2000-02; dir. Ctr. For Railroad Photography and Art, 1999—, sec., 2005. Mem. Caxton Club. Presbyterian. Home: 169 Wildwood Rd Lake Forest IL 60045-2462 Office: Lake Forest Coll Donnelley and Lee Libr/LIT 555 N Sheridan Rd Lake Forest IL 60045-2399 Office Phone: 847-735-5064. E-mail: amiller@lakeforest.edu.

**MILLER, ARTHUR MADDEN**, lawyer, investment banker, brokerage house executive; b. Greenville, SC, Apr. 10, 1953; s. Charles Frederick and Kathryn Irene (Madden) M.; m. Roberta Beck Connolly, Apr. 17, 1993; children: Isabella McIntyre Madden, Roberta Beck Connolly. AB in History, Princeton U., 1973; MA in History, U. NC, 1976; JD with distinction, Duke U., 1978; LLM in Taxation, NYU, 1982. Bar: N.Y. 1979, U.S. Dist. Ct. (so. dist.) N.Y. 1979. Assoc. Mudge Rose Guthrie Alexander & Ferdon, N.Y.C., 1978—85; v.p. pub. fin. Goldman, Sachs & Co., N.Y.C., 1985—. Trustee Convent of the Sacred Heart, NY, 2003—, St. Andrew's Sch., Del., 2003—; adv. bd. Mary Baldwin Coll., Staunton, Va., 1982—86; trustee Princeton U. Rowing Assn., NJ, 1980—, pres., 1986—95; trustee Rebecca Kelly Dance Co., NYC, 1984—86; steward Power Ten, 1992—95. Mem. ABA (tax sect. com. on tax exempt financing 1985—), Nat. Assn. Bond Lawyers (lectr. 1985—), Pub. Securities Assn. (cons. 1985—), Practising Law Inst. (lectr. 1980, editor/author course materials 1980—), Bond Attys. Workshop (editor/author course material 1983—, lectr. 1983—), Princeton Club. Office: Goldman Sachs & Co 85 Broad St New York NY 10004-2456

**MILLER, ARTHUR RAPHAEL**, law educator; b. NYC, June 22, 1934; s. Murray and Mary (Schapin) Miller; m. Ellen Monica Joachim, June 8, 1958 (div. 1978); 1 child, Matthew Richard; m. Marilyn Tarmy, 1982 (div. 1988); m. Sandra L. Young, 1992 (div. 2001). Student, Bklyn. Coll., 1952, 55, CCNY, 1955; AB in History, U. Rochester, 1955; LLB, Harvard U., 1958. Bar: NY 1959, US Supreme Ct. 1959, Mass. 1979. Assoc. Cleary, Gottlieb, Steen & Hamilton, NYC, 1958-61; assoc. dir. Columbia Law Sch. Project Internat. Procedure, NYC, 1961-62; lectr. Columbia Law Sch., NYC, 1961-62; assoc. prof. U. Minn. Law Sch., 1962-65; prof. U. Mich. Law Sch., 1965-72; vis. prof. Harvard Law Sch., Cambridge, Mass., 1971-72, prof., 1972-86, Bruce Bromley prof. law, 1986—. Rsch. assoc. Mental Health Rsch. Inst. 1966-68; dir. project computer assisted instn. Am. Assn. Law Schools, 1968-75; spl. rapporteur State Dept. concerning chpt. II of Hague Conv., 1967; del. US-Italian Conf. Internat. Jud. Assistance, 1961, 62; chmn. task force external affairs Interuniv. Communications Coun., 1966-70; mem. law panel, com. sci. and tech. info. Fed. Coun. Sci. and Tech., Pres.'s Office Sci. and Tech., 1969-72; mem. adv. group to chief justice Supreme Ct. on Data Banks, 1970-78; mem. spl. adv. group to chief justice Supreme Ct. on Fed. Civil Litig.; mem. com. on automated personal data systems HEW, 1972-73; chmn. Mass. Security and Privacy Coun., Mass. Commn. on Privacy; mem. US Commn. New Technol. Uses Copyrighted Works, 1975-79; reporter US Supreme Ct.'s Adv. Com. on Civil Rules, 1978-86, mem. 1986-91; faculty Fed. Jud. Ctr.; reporter study on complex litig. Am. Law Inst.; bd. dirs. Rsch. Found. on Complex Litigations, 1975-80; bd. overseers Rand Inst. on Civil Justice, 1998-2002. Author: The Assault on Privacy: Computers, Data Banks, and Dossiers, 1971, Miller's Court, 1982; (with others) New York Civil Practice, 8 vols., Civil Procedure Cases and Materials, 7th edit., 1997, Federal Practice and Procedure: Civil, 34 vols., 1969—; CPLR Manual, 1967; host syndicated TV shows in Context, Miller's Law, Miller's Court, Headlines on Trial; legal expert Good Morning America. Served with AUS, 1958-59. Recipient Nat. Emmy award for The Constitution, That Delicate Balance. Mem. Am. Law Inst. Office: Harvard Law Sch 1563 Massachusetts Ave Cambridge MA 02138 Office Phone: 617-495-4111. Office Fax: 617-495-9191.

**MILLER, AUDREY THORNTON**, retired vice principal; b. Glassboro, N.J., June 22, 1937; d. Aubrey and Rebecca Thornton; m. Kenneth C. Miller, Sr., Nov. 20, 1967; children: Yvette A. Rudd, Kenneth C. Jr. BS, Cheyney U., 1963; MEd, Rutgers U., 1973; EdD, Nova Southeastern U., 1998. Cert. prin., supr. N.J. Tchr. Camden (N.J.) Bd. Edn., 1963-74, asst. to prin., 1974-97, vice prin. H.C. Sharp Sch., 1997-2000; ret., 2000. Advisor Theta Chi City Wide chpt. Rowan U., 1980-85, Sharp Sch. Safety Patrol, Camden, 1991-95, Network III Drug Program, Camden, 1993-96; adv. bd. Carter's Psychol. Svc., Camden County, 1995—. Author: Using the Writing Process to Enchance Elementary Students Writing Proficiency and Teachers' Instructional Strategies, 1998. Vice-pres. Garden City Alumnae of Delta Sigma Theta Sorority, Inc., Sicklerville, N.J., 1989-91; chair Career Women's Ministry, St. Matthews Bapt. Ch. Williamstown, N.J., 1993-96, chief ednl. svcs. comty. devel. ctr. programs SMCDC, 2003-05; mem. Camden County LWV. Recipient Set a Good Example award Gov. Christie Whitman, Trenton, 1994, Disting. Achievement award, Camden Bd. Edn., 1994, 96, Proclamation, Bd. Chosen Freeholders, Camden County, 2000, Cheyney U. Alumni Outstanding Service Award, 2003. Mem. NAACP, AFL-CIO, Black Women's

Edn. Alliance (Educator's award 1992), Camden City Fedn. Sch. Adminstrs., N.J. Fedn. Colored Women's Club (Outstanding Svc. in Edn. award 2000, African-Am. Women Achievers award 2006), Cheyney U. Alumni Assn. (life, area rep. S. Jersey chpt., 2000-02), Nova Southeastern U. Alumni Assn., Rutgers U. Alumni, Delta Sigma Theta (life, mem. ea. region leadership team 2005), Kappa Delta Pi, Kappa Alpha Psi (Africna-Am. Women Archives award 2006). Democrat. Avocations: interior decorating, travel, tennis. Home: 4 Pierson Pl Sicklerville NJ 08081-2006 Personal E-mail: milerau@aol.com.

**MILLER, BARBARA KENTON,** retired librarian; b. N.Y.C., Sept. 21, 1934; d. Robert Alfred and Kathleen Hope (Levy) Kenton; m. John Arnold Miller, June 15, 1955; children: Valerie Ann Miller, Jennifer Karen Kraft. BA distinction, Finch Coll., 1960; MLS, C.W. Post, 1976. Cert. libr. N.Y. Libr., cons. archivist Coun. Fgn. Rels., N.Y.C., 1977—2000; ret., 2000. Cons. archivist Coun. on Fgn. Rels. Mem. Spl. Librs. Assn., Beta Phi Mu. Avocations: dogs, golf. Office: Coun Fgn Rels 58 E 68 St New York NY 10021-5953 Personal E-mail: bkmiller55@aol.com.

**MILLER, BARRY,** researcher, psychologist; b. NYC, Dec. 25, 1942; s. Jack and Ida (Kaplan) M.; m. Susan Hallermeier; children: Eric, Arianne, Kristina, Barrie. BS in Psychology, Bklyn. Coll., 1965; MS in Psychology, Villanova U., 1967; PhD in Psychiatry, Med. Coll. Pa., 1971. Instr. psychology Villanova (Pa.) U., 1971-73; asst. dir. dept. behavioral sci., med. rsch. scientist Ea. Pa. Psychiatric Inst., Phila., 1971-73, sr. med. rsch. scientist 1973-80; dir. Pa. Bur. Rsch. and Tng., Harrisburg, 1973-81; asst. prof. psychology U. Pa. Med. Sch., Phila., 1975-78, asst. clin. prof. psychology 1978—; assoc. prof. psychiatry Med. Coll. Pa., Phila., 1981-90, rsch. assoc. prof. medicine, 1983-90, assoc. dean for rsch., 1981-90; dir. for rsch. devel. Albert Einstein Healthcare Network, Phila., 1990-95; dir. The Permanente Med. Group Rsch. Inst., Oakland, Calif., 1995-99; adj. assoc. prof. psychiatry Med. Coll. Pa., Phila., 1990—; rsch. assoc. prof. psychiatry Temple U. Sch. Med., Phila., 1990—; adminstrv. dir. rsch. ops. Divsn. Rsch., Oakland, Calif., 1999—. Mem. sci. and tech. task force Pa. Econ. Devel. Partnership, Harrisburg, 1987-88, mem. Sage Woman Mag., 1980's; contbg. editor: Idaho Women in History, 1990. Mem. cancer control prgram Pa. Dept. Health, 1994; vis. rsch. assoc. prof. Med. Coll. Pa., Phila., 1991—. Contbr. articles to profl. jours.; mem. editorial bd. Jour. Mental Health Adminstrn., 1988—, assoc. editor, 1989—. Bd. dirs. Community Mental Health Ctr. 6A, Phila., 1969-73, Northwest Jewish Youth Ctrs., Phila., 1974-75; mem. Lafayette Hill Civic Assn., 1973-86, Citizens Coun. Whitemarsh (Pa.) Twp., 1975-86; pres., bd. dirs. Golden Eagle Luxury Homeowners Assn., Pleasanton, Calif., 1995-97. Grantee HHS, NIH. Mem. AAAS, Am. Psychol. Assn., Assn. Mental Health Adminstrs., Assn. Univ. Tech. Mgrs., Soc. Rsch. Adminstrs., Calif. Psychol. Assn. Avocation: hiking. Office: Divsn Rsch 2000 Broadway Oakland CA 94612-3429 Office Phone: 510-891-3408. Business E-mail: barry.x.miller@kp.org.

**MILLER, BARRY RIXMANN,** lawyer; b. Tempe, Ariz., Feb. 8, 1945; s. Ray E. and Dorothy (Rixmann) M.; m. Patricia A. Cunningham, Aug. 10, 1968; children: Christy, Brandy Ann. BS with honors, U. Ill., 1967; JD with honors, 1970. Bars: Ill. 1970, Tex. 1972, US Tax Ct. 1972. Mem. firm Andrews & Kurth, Houston, 1972-79, ptnr., 1979, emprt. com., 1990-92, ptnr., co-head Tax Law Sect., Vinson & Elkins, LLP, 2003-05. Treas Askew PTO, 1980. Served to 1st lt. US Army, 1970-72. Decorated Army Commendation medal. James scholar, 1963; recipient Bronze Tablet, U. Ill., 1967. Mem. Tex. Bar Assn., ABA (sect. on taxation), Order of the Coif, Beta Alpha Psi, Phi Alpha Mu, Sigma Chi. Republican. Contbr. articles to profl. jours. Office: Vinson & Elkins LLP First City Tower 1001 Fannin St, Ste 2300 Houston TX 77002 Office Phone: 713-758-4438. Business E-mail: brmiller@velaw.com.

**MILLER, BENJAMIN K.,** retired state supreme court justice; b. Springfield, Ill., Nov. 5, 1936; s. Clifford and Mary (Luthyens) M. BA, So. Ill. U., 1958; JD, Vanderbilt U., 1961. Bar: Ill. 1961. Ptnr. Olsen, Cantrill & Miller, Springfield, 1964-70; prin. Ben Miller-Law Office, Springfield, 1970-76; judge 7th jud. cir. Ill. Cir. Ct., Springfield, 1976-82, presiding judge Criminal div., 1977-81, chief judge, 1981-82; justice Ill. Appellate Ct., 4th Jud. Dist., 1982-84, Ill. Supreme Ct., Springfield, 1984-2001, chief justice, 1991-93, ret. 2001. Adj. prof. So. Ill. U., Springfield, 1974—; mem. Ill. Cts. Commn., 1988-90; mem. Ill. Gov.'s Adv. Coun. on Criminal Justice Legis., 1977-84, Ad Hoc Com. on Tech. in Cts., 1985—. Mem. editorial rev. bd. Illinois Civil Practice Before Trial, Illinois Civil Trial Practice Pres. Cen. Ill. Mental Health Assn., 1969-71; bd. govs. Aid to Retarded Citizens, 1977-80; mem. Lincoln Legals Adv. Bd., 1988—. Lt. USNR, 1964-67. Mem. ABA (bar admissions com. sect. of legal edn. and admissions to bar 1992—), Ill. State Bar Assn. (bd. govs. 1970-76, treas. 1975-76), Sangamon County Bar Assn., Ctrl. Ill. Women's Bar Assn., Am. Judicature Soc. (bd. dirs. 1994—), Abraham Lincoln Assn. (bd. dirs. 1988-98). Address: 100 E Bellevue PL Apt 29F Chicago IL 60611-5194 Office Phone: 312-840-7216.

**MILLER, BENNETT,** film director; b. 1967; Student, NYU. Dir.: over 200 commercials, (Documentary) The Cruise, 1998, New York Minute Video: A Film from 9/09/1999 at 9:09 A.M., 1999; (films) Capote, 2005 (Best First Film, NY Film Critics Circle, 2005). Avocations: chess, drawing, yoga. Office: c/o Endeavor Agency 9601 Wilshire Blvd 10th Fl Beverly Hills CA 90212*

**MILLER, BERNARD JOSEPH, JR.,** advertising executive; b. Louisville, July 31, 1925; s. Bernard J. Sr. and Myrtle (Herrington) M.; m. Jayne Hughes, Aug. 7, 1948 (div. Oct. 1970); children: Bernard J. III, Jeffrey, Janet Marie.; m. Brita Naujok, Nov. 24, 1970; 1 child, Brian. BS, Ind. U., 1949. Merchandising mgr. Brown-Forman Distillers, Inc., Louisville, 1949-54; v.p. Phelps Mfg. Co., Terre Haute, Ind., 1954-60; pres. Columbian Advt. Inc., Chgo., 1960-87, chmn., 1987—. 2d lt. USAF, 1943-46 PTO Mem. Point of Purchase Advt. Inst. (dir. 1970-73), Saddle and Cycle Club (bd. dirs. 1987-90, 99—). Avocations: tennis, downhill skiing, collecting first edition autographed books.

**MILLER, BETH MCCARTHY,** television director; Dir.: (TV series) Saturday Night Live, 1995, The Jon Stewart Show, 1993—, The Colin Quinn Show, 2002, (TV spl.) Eagles: Hell Freezes Over, 1994—, Nirvana Unplugged, 1994—, James Taylor Live, 1998—, Saturday Night Live: The Best of Adam Sandler, 1999—, Saturday Night Live Christmas, 1999—, Saturday Night Live: 25th Anniversary, 1999, America: A Tribute to Heroes, 2001, NBC 75th Anniversary Spl., 2002, Saturday Night Live: The Best of Will Ferrell, 2002, GQ Men of the Yr. Awards, 2003; dir., prodr.: MTV Video Music Awards, 2003. Nominee Outstanding Directorial Achievement in Musical/Variety award, DGA, 2000, 2004, Emmy award, 1999, 2000, 2003; recipient Outstanding Directorial Achievement in Musical/Variety award, DGA, 2001, 2002. Office: Saturday Night Live 30 Rockefeller Plaza 50th St and 6th Ave New York NY 10112

**MILLER, BETTY BROWN,** freelance writer; b. Altus, Ark., Dec. 21, 1926; d. Carlos William and Arlie Gertrude (Sublett) Brown; m. Robert Wiley Miller, Nov. 15, 1953; children: Janet Ruth, Stephen Wiley. BS, Okla. State U., 1949; MS, U. Tulsa, 1953; postgrad., Am. U., 1966—68. Tchr. LeFlore (Okla.) H.S., 1947-48, Osage Indian Reservation H.S., Hominy, Okla. 1948-50, Jenks (Okla.) HS, 1950—51; instr. Sch. Bus. U. Tulsa, 1950-51; tchr. Tulsa pub. schs., 1951-54; instr. Burdette Coll., Boston, 1954-55; reporter Bethesda-Chevy Chase Tribune, Montgomery County, Md., 1973-75; freelance writer, contbr. newspapers and mags., 1973—. V.p. Kenwood Park (Md.) Citizens Assn., 1960; mem. Ft. Sumner Citizens Assn., editor newsletter, 1969; mem. Md. State PTA, editl. coord. leadership conf., 1973-74; founder, chair Montgomery County Forum edn., 1970-75; trustee Friends Valley Forge Nat. Hist. Park; bd. dirs Friends Curtis Inst. Music; active Nat. Mus. Women in the Arts, Musical Fund Soc. Phila.; trustee adv. Help the Aged Internat. Mem.: DAR, PEO, Union League Phila. (past mem. ladies com., mem. ladies adv. com.), The Nat. Gravel Soc., Internat. Platform Assn., Montgomery County Press Assn., Nat. Soc. Arts & Letters (past editor mag.).

bd. dirs. pub rels., past nat. corr. sec.), Huguenot Soc. Pa. (v.p. 1989—92, pres. 1993—95, past bd. dirs., hon. pres. 1997—), Nat. League Am. Pen Women (former budget chmn., past nat. treas.), Soc. Descandants of Washington's Army at Valley Forge (past nat. comdr. in chief, past inspector gen. Nat. Huguenot Soc., past. mem. gen. coun.), Acorn Club Phila., Sedgeley Club (pres. Phila. 1985—88), Washington Club, U.D.C., Adventures Unltd. (chmn. Washington chpt.), Capital Spkrs. Club Washington (past pres.), Melba T. Croft Music Club, Order Ea. Star (life). Republican. Address: PO Box 573 Valley Forge PA 19481-0573

**MILLER, BEVERLY A(NN),** reference librarian; b. Tulsa, Dec. 22, 1941; d. Buford Maxwell and Wilda (Durfee) M. BA, Thiel Coll., Greenville, Pa., 1964; MA in Libr. Sci., U. Denver, 1965; MA in History, Boise (Idaho) State U., 2003. Periodicals libr. Minot (N.D.) State Coll., 1966-67; asst. libr. Rocky Mountain Coll., Billings, Mont., 1967-68; circulation libr. Boise (Idaho) State Coll., 1968-71; reference and interlibr. libr. Boise (Idaho) State U., 1971—, bd. dirs., faculty advisor Women's Ctr., 1992-93. Bd. dirs. Higher Edn. Resource Svcs./West, Boise, 1991—. Book reviewer Libr. Jour., 1975-95; author, adv. bd. mem. Sage Woman Mag., 1980's; contbg. editor: Idaho Women in History, 1990. Mem. AAUP (bd. dirs. Boise State U. chpt. 1994-2003, treas.), NOW (bd. dirs. Boise 1978-79, Idaho 1979-80), Am. Fedn. Tchrs. (v.p. 1979-81 Boise State U.), Pacific N.W. Libr. Assn., Pacific N.W. Women's Studies Assn., Idaho Libr. Assn., Idaho Womens Network (bd. dirs 1987-92), Snake River Alliance (bd. dirs. 1986). Avocations: women's history, dog sports. Office Phone: 208-426-1626. Business E-mail: bmiller@boisestate.edu.

**MILLER, BEVERLY WHITE,** former college president, educational consultant, b. Willoughby, Ohio, 1923; d. Joseph Martin and Marguerite Sarah (Storer) White; m. Lynn Martin Miller, Oct. 11, 1945 (dec. 1986); children: Michaela Ann, Craig Martin, Todd Daniel, Cass Timothy, Simone Agnes. AB, Western Res., 1945; MA, Mich. State U., 1957; PhD, U. Toledo, 1967; LHD (hon.), Coll. St. Benedict, St. Joseph, Minn., 1979; LLD (hon.), U. Toledo, 1988. Chem. and biol. researcher, 1945-57; tchr. schs. in Mich., also Mercy Sch. Nursing, St. Lawrence Hosp., Lansing, Mich., 1957-58; mem. chemistry and biology faculty Mary Manse Coll., Toledo, 1958-71, dean grad. div., 1968-71, exec. v.p., 1968-71; acad. dean Salve Regina Coll., Newport, RI, 1971-74; pres. Coll. St. Benedict, St. Joseph, Minn., 1974-79, Western New Eng. Coll., Springfield, Mass., 1980-96, pres. emerita, 1996—. Higher edn. cons., 1996—; cons. U.S. Office Edn., 1980; mem. Springfield Pvt. Industry Coun./Regional Employment Bd., exec. com., 1982-94; mem. Minn. Pvt. Coll. Coun., 1974-79, sec., 1974-75, vice chmn., 1975-76, chmn., 1976-77; cons. in field. Author papers and books in field. Corporator Mercy Hosp., Springfield, Mass. Recipient President's citation St. John's U., Minn., 1979; also various service awards; named disting. alumna of yr. U. Toledo, 1998. Mem. AAAS, Am. Assn. Higher Edn., Assn. Cath. Colls. and Univs. (exec. bd.), Internat. Assn. Sci. Edn., Nat. Assn. Ind. Colls. and Univs. (govt. rels. adv. com., bd. dirs. 1990-93, exec. com. 1991-93, treas. 1992-93), Nat. Assn. Biology Tchrs., Assn. Ind. Colls. and Univs. of Mass. (exec. com. 1981-96, vice chmn. 1985-86, chmn. 1986-87), Nat. Assn. Rsch. Sci. Tchg., Springfield C. of C. (bd. dirs.), Am. Assn. Univ. Adminstrs. (bd. dirs. 1989-92), Delta Kappa Gamma, Sigma Delta Epsilon. Office: 6713 County Road M Delta OH 43515-9778

**MILLER, BILL (WILLIAM H. MILLER III),** diversified financial services company executive; BA, Washington and Lee U., 1972; attended, John Hopkins U. CFA 1986. Treas. J.E. Baker Co.: dir. rsch. Legg Mason, Inc., Balt., 1981—85, co-mgr. value trust fund, 1982—90, portfolio mgr., 1990—, CEO Legg Mason Capital Mgmt. Vice chmn. Santa Fe Inst., 2001—05, chmn., 2005—. Former military intelligence officer. Office: Legg Mason Cds Inv Serv PO Box 55214 Boston MA 02205-5214*

**MILLER, BIRTHALENE,** writer; b. Chester, Miss., Jan. 3, 1931; d. Charlie Sylvester and Maggie Miller. Tutor high sch. and jr. coll. students, Ackerman, Miss. Contbr. short stories, poetry to anthologies and mags.; newspaper columnist. Chmn. Friends for Mabos for Gov., Choctaw County, Miss., 1987, Friends to Re-elect Mabos campaign, 1991; vol. writer Adult Literacy of Choctaw County; chairperson Friends for Musgrove for Gov., Choctaw County, Miss., 1999, Friends to Re-elect Gov. Musgrove. Democrat. Methodist. Avocations: reading, sketching, word puzzles. Home: 235 N Commerce St Ackerman MS 39735-9114

**MILLER, BLONDELL STEPHENSON,** social worker, minister; b. Hartsville, S.C. d. Johnnie and Marie Belvin Stephenson; m. James Lee Miller, Apr. 6, 1974; children: Taris Lydell, James Richard, Brandon Jerel. BA in History, Morris Coll., 1973; degree in Social Work, Winthrop U., 1980; student in Religious Edn., Duke U., 2004—05. Lic. pastor S.C. Conf. United Meth. Ch. 2003; LCSW S.C. Bd. Social Work, 1989. Tchr. Lee County Bd. Edn. Bishipville, SC, 1973—74; social worker Lee County Dept. Social Svc., Bishipville, 1974—2005; pastor Hartsville (S.C.) Dist. United Meth., 2000—. Chmn. bd. FEMA, Bishopville; bd. dir. Lee First Step, Bishopville, Waterse Head Start Program Health, Sumter, SC. Mem.: NAACP, Morris Coll. Alumni (sec.), Ea. Star (treas.), Delta Sigma Theta (chaplin 1986—). Meth. Avocations: cooking, reading, singing, travel, basketball. Home: 503 Pleasantview Dr Hartsville SC 29550 Office: Lee County Dept Social Svc 820 Brown St Bishopville SC 29010 Office Phone: 803-484-5376. Personal E-mail: blon1949@aol.com.

**MILLER, BODE,** skier; b. Easton, NH, Oct. 12, 1977; s. Woody and Jo Miller. Attended, Carrabassett Valley Acad. Co-author (with Jack McEnany): Bode: Go Fast, Be Good, Have Fun, 2005. Named Champion, FIS World Cup, 2005; recipient Six US Nat. Championship Medals, Two Silver-Medals, Winter Olympic Games, 2002, One Silver-Medal, Two Gold-Medals, World Championship, 2003, World Cup Super G Title, 2005. Achievements include first US skier in 22 yrs. to win World Cup overall championship, 2005. Office: US Ski and Snowboard Assoc Box 100 1500 Kearns Blvd Park City UT 84060 E-mail: bode@bodemillerusa.com.*

**MILLER, BONNIE SEWELL,** marketing professional, writer; b. Junction City, Ky., July 24, 1932; d. William Andrew and Lillian Irene (McCowan) Sewell; m. William Gustave Tournade Jr., Nov. 5, 1950 (div. 1974); children: Bonnie Sue Tournade Zaner, William Gustave III, Sharon Irene Tournade Leach; m. Bruce George Miller, Nov. 15, 1981. BA, U. South Fla., 1968, MA, 1973. Cert. tchr., Fla. Dept. English Tampa Cath. H.S., Fla., 1972—78; tchr. Clearwater H.S., Fla., 1978—80; mgr. prodn. svcs. Paradyne Corp., Largo, Fla., 1980—83; freelance writer, cons. Tampa, 1983—84; mgr. product documentation PPS, Inc., Largo, 1984—86, mgr. mktg. comm., 1986—87; writer Nixdorf Computer Corp., Tampa, 1988—89; mktg. dir. Suncoast Schs. Fed. Credit Union, Tampa, 1989—98; co-owner, v.p., writer, cons. Need-A-Writer, Inc., Tampa, 1998—; instr. profl. and tech. writing U. South Fla., 2004—. Instr. English, Hillsborough C.C., Tampa, Fla., 1975—87; cons. bus. writing Coronet Instrnl. Media Writing Project, 1976, Nat. Mgmt. Assn., 1981—87; adj. instr. profl. writing U. South Fla., 1993; adj. instr. tech. writing U. Tampa, 2002, English instr., 2002—; adj. instr. profl. and tech. writing U. South Fla., 2004—. Author: Youth Financial Literacy, 1999, Effective Business Writing for Credit Unions, 2000, Meeting for a Lifetime, 2006; contbr. articles to profl. jours. Bd. dir. SERVE, Tampa, Credit Union Mktg. Assn. Coun., Sing Parent Displaced Homemakers Group; legis. chair Tampa PTA, 1985; judge speech contest Am. Legion, Tampa, 1976; vol. North Tampa Vol. Libr., 1988. NEH fellow, 1975. Mem. NAFE, Soc. Tech. Communicators, Am. Assn. Bus. Women, Kappa Delta Pi. Democrat. Methodist. Avocations: writing, sewing, gardening, travel, decorating. Home and Office: 516 2d Ave SE Lutz FL 33549 E-mail: bsmiller@suntarcom.net.

**MILLER, BRAD (RALPH BRADLEY MILLER),** congressman; b. Fayetteville, NC, May 19, 1953; s. Nathan David and Margaret Virginia (Hale) Miller; m. Esther Susan Hall, Dec. 19, 1981. BS in Polit. Sci., U. NC, Chapel Hill, 1975; MSc in Polit. Sci., London Sch. Econs., 1978; JD, Columbia U., 1979. Bar: NC 1979, US Dist. Ct. (ea. dist.) NC 1980, US Ct. Appeals (4th

cir. 1980), US Dist. Ct. (mid. dist.) NC 1983. Law clk. to Hon. J. Dickson Phillips, Jr. US 4th Cir. Ct. Appeals, 1979-80; assoc. Allen, Steed & Allen, Raleigh, NC, 1980-82, Barringer, Allen & Pinnix, Raleigh, NC, 1982-84, LeBoeuf, Lamb, Leiby & MacRae, Raleigh, NC, 1985-88; prin. Nichols, Miller & Sigmon, Raleigh, NC, 1988-90; pvt. practice Raleigh, NC, 1991—; mem. NC State Ho. Reps., 1992—96, NC State Senate, 1997—2002, chmn. sen. jud. II com.; mem. US Congress from 13th NC dist., 2003—. Mem. fin. svcs. com. US Congress, mem. sci. com. Chmn. Wake County Dem. Com., 1985-87; mem. state exec. com. NC Dem. Com., 1985-89, 91-97; mem. NC Environ. Rev. Commn., 1994-95, mem. sentencing and policy adv. com. Mem. ATLA, NC Bar Assn., Wake County Bar Assn., NC Acad. Trial Lawyers, Am. Judicature Soc. Democrat. Episcopalian. Office: US Ho Reps 1722 Longworth Ho Office Bldg Washington DC 20515 Office Phone: 202-225-3032.*

**MILLER, BRIAN DANIEL,** music educator, organist; b. Charlotte, NC, Nov. 3, 1971; s. Vincent LaFollette and Jettie Rea Miller. BA in History, U. NC, 1994, B in Music Edn., 1995. Band tchr. Louisburg HS, NC, 1995—. Mem. NC Music Educators Conf., 1995—; fine arts dept. chair Louisburg HS, 1996—, mem. sch. planning team; mem. supt. dropout adv. team Franklin County Schs., 2004—05. Composer: The Louisburg March, 2001. Pianist Lions Club, Louisburg, NC, 2000—. Named Young Educator of Yr., Louisburg Jaycees, 2000, Tchr. of Yr., Franklin County Schs., 2000, Artist of Yr., Franklin County Arts Coun., 2001, Tchr. of Yr., Wal-Mart, 2002, 2003, 2004; recipient Never Stop Learning Educator award, WTVD-11. Mem.: Am. Theatre Organ Soc., Am. Guild Organists, Ctrl. Dist. Bandmasters Assn., James A. Johnson Masonic Lodge, Phi Mu Alpha Sinfonia, Phi Eta Sigma, Phi Beta Kappa. Republican. So. Baptist. Avocations: reading, collecting books and music, antique lamp repair, restoring typewriters and reed organs. Home: 102 Person St Louisburg NC 27549 Office Phone: 919-496-4722 ext. 225. Personal E-mail: bdmiller1935@aol.com.

**MILLER, BRIAN DOUGLAS,** science educator; b. Indpls., May 21, 1958; s. Edna C. Miller; m. Tamara Sue McKinley, Sept. 4, 1976; children: Aaron David, Allison Paige. BA, Berea Coll., Ky., 1980; MEd, Xavier U., Cin., Ohio, 1989. Tchr. sci. Reading Mid. Sch., Cin., 1982—84, Deer Park H.S., Cin., 1984—. Chairperson sci. dept. Deer Park H.S., 1992—, mentor specialist, 1997—99, nat. honor soc. advisor, 2001—05. Co-author: (paper on wolf spiders) Jour. Behavioral & Ecol. Sociobiology, 1996, (paper on atrial fibrillation) Jour. Thoracic & Cardiovascular Surgery, 2005. Recipient Meritorious award for Academic Excellence, Deer Park Schs., 1994, Cin. Outstanding Sci. Tchr. award, U. Cin., Xavier U., NKU, 2005; Martha Helen Jennings scholar, U. Dayton, 1992. Mem.: Greater Cin. Herpatol. Soc., Nat. Assn. Biology Tchrs. Avocations: reading, fitness, travel. Home: 12172 Village Woods Dr Cincinnati OH 45241 Office: Deer Park HS 8351 Plainfield Rd Cincinnati OH 45236 Personal E-mail: dougmiller521@yahoo.com.

**MILLER, BRYAN MICHAEL,** music educator; b. Berwyn, Ill., Sept. 8, 1966; s. Donald Harold and Jean Ann Miller. BS in Music Edn., No. Ill. U., 1989; MusM, U. Notre Dame, 1991; diploma, Acad. Mil. Sci., 2000. Asst. dir. bands U. Notre Dame, Ind., 1989—91; band dir. Reavis H.S., Buizbank, Ill., 1991—94; music dept. chair Leyden H.S., Franklin Park, Ill., 1994—. Adj. faculty Vander Cook Coll., Chgo., 1999—2004; music dir. Elmhurst (Ill.) Coll., 2005—; comdr. 566th Air Force Band, Peoria, Ill., 2000—; music dir. Ill. Ambassadors of Music, 2005—. Bd. dirs. Chgo. Youth Symphony Orch., 2002—; mem. leadership team Opus Chamber Music Camp, 2004—. Capt. USAF, 1998—. Decorated Achievement medal USAF, Ill. N.G., Commendation medal; recipient Citizen Soldier award, Acad. Mil. Sci., 2000. Mem.: Am. Fedn. Tchrs., Ill. Music Educators Assn., N.G. Assn., Moose, Am. Legion. Home: 5 S 738 Hummingbird Ln Naperville IL 60540 Office: Leyden High Sch 3400 N Rose St Franklin Park IL 60131

**MILLER, BUFFY,** dancer; b. Atlanta; Studies with, Patricia Bromley; student, New Ballet Sch. Mem. Feld Ballet Tech. Soc., 1986—97; with Ballet Tech., 1997—. Office: 108 High St 2 Portland ME 04101-3815

**MILLER, C. ARDEN,** physician, educator; b. Shelby, Ohio, Sept. 19, 1924; s. Harley H. and Mary (Thuma) Miller; m. Helen Meihack, June 26, 1948; children: John Lewis, Thomas Meihack, Helen Lewis, Benjamin Lewis. Student, Oberlin Coll., Ohio, 1942—44; MD cum laude, Yale U., New Haven, Conn., 1948. Intern, then asst. resident pediatrics Grace-New Haven Community Hosp., 1948—51; faculty U. Kans. Med. Center, 1951—66, dir. childrens rehab. unit, 1957—60, dean Med. Sch., 1960—66; prof. pediatrics and maternal and child health U. N.C., Chapel Hill, 1966—98, emeritus, 1998—, vice chancellor health scis., 1966—71, chmn. dept. maternal and child health, 1977—87. Chmn. exec. com. Citizens Bd. Inquiry into Health Svcs. for Am., 1968—71. Mem. editl. bd.: Jour. Med. Edn. 1960—66; contbr. articles to profl. jours. Trustee Appalachian Regional Hosps., 1974—84, Planned Parenthood Fedn.; chmn. Alan Guttmacher Inst., 1978—84, 1986—. Recipient Robert H. Felix Disting. Svc. award, St. Louis U., 1977, Martha Mae Eliot award in pub. health, 1984, O. Max Gardner award, U. N.C., 1987; scholar Am. Markle scholar in med. scis., 1955—60. Fellow: Royal Soc. Health (hon.), Clare Hall Cambridge (Eng.) U. (life); mem.: APHA (chmn. action bd. 1972—75, pres. 1974—75, Sedgewick Meml. medal 1986), Inst. of Medicine NAS, Assn. Am. Med. Colls. (v.p. 1965—66), Soc. Pediat. Rsch., Delta Omega, Alpha Omega Alpha, Sigma Xi. Home: 350 Carolina Meadows Villa Chapel Hill NC 27517-7549

**MILLER, CANDICE S.,** congresswoman; b. Clair Shores, Mich., May 7, 1954; m. Donald G. Miller; 1 child, Wendy Nicole. Student, Macomb County C.C., 1973—74, Northwood U., 1974. Sec., treas. D.B. Snider, Inc., 1972-79; trustee Harrison Twp., 1979-80, supr., 1980-92; treas. Macomb County, 1992-95; sec. of state State of Mich., Lansing, 1995—2003; mem. US Congress from 10th Mich. dist., 2003—. Mem. Lake St. Clair Blue Ribbon Commn. Chair John Engler for Gov. campaign, Macomb County; del. Rep. Nat. Conv., 1996; co-chair Rep. Platform Com., 1996, Dole/Kemp Presdl. Campaign, Mich., 1996, Bush/Cheney Presdl. Campaign, Mich., 2000; mem. Carehouse-Macomb County Child Adv. Ctr., Selfridge Air Nat. Guard Base Cmty. Coun., Detroit Econ. Club. mem. adminstrv. bd. Mich. State. mem. safety commn. Recipient Macomb Citizen of Yr. award, March of Dimes, 1997, Woman of Distinction award, Macomb County Girl Scouts, Adjutant General's Patriot award, Mich. Nat. Guard, 2002, GH award women in govt., Good Housekeeping mag., 2003, Econ. Excellence award, Macomb C. of C.; Paul Harris Internat. fellow. Mem.: Nat. Assn. Secretaries of State, Boat Town Assn. Republican. Presbyterian. Avocations: boating, yacht racing. Office: US Congress 228 Cannon HOB Washington DC 20515 also: District Office 48653 Van Dyke Ave Shelby Township MI 48317-2560 Office Phone: 202-225-2106, 586-997-5010. Office Fax: 202-226-1169, 586-997-5013.*

**MILLER, CAROLYN LYONS,** microbiologist, military officer; b. Birmingham, Ala., June 28, 1955; d. John Henry and Annie Lois Lyons; m. Brian Lenny Miller, July 28, 1984; 1 child, Brian Lenny Miller, Jr. BS, U. Ala., 1977; MS, Ala. A&M U., 1979; PhD, Rutgers U., 1984; degree, Air U., 2000. Lic. medical technologist Am. Soc. Clin. Pathologists, 1984, cert. clin. lab. scientist Nat. Certification Agy. Lenexa, KS, 1984. Student asst. Dept. Biology and Microbiology U. Ala., Birmingham, Ala., 1973—77; rsch. asst. Dept of Biology and Food Sci. and Tech. Ala. A&M U., Normal, Ala., 1977—79; rsch. asst. Dept Pedodontics Sch. of Dentistry U. Ala., 1980; tchg. asst. biology and microbiology Cook Coll. Rutgers U., New Brunswick, NJ, 1980—83, asst. area coord. student life Douglass Coll., 1983—84; med. tech. intern Wilford Hall Med. Ctr., Lackland Air Force Base, Tex., 1985—86; chief quality control/epidemiology divsn. Air Force Sch. Aerospace Medicine, Brooks Air Force Base, Tex., 1986—89; comdr. 421st med. svc. squadron Wilford Hall Med. Ctr., Lackland Air Force Base, 1997—98; assoc. prof. Dept. Biology USAF Acad., Colorado Springs, Colo., 1989—93, exec. officer to the dean of the faculty, 1993—95; exec. officer to the comdr. Human Sys. Ctr., Brooks Air Force Base, Tex., 1995—97; ops. staff officer/dir., quality assurance & regulatory affairs 59th Med. Diagnostics and Therapeutics Group, Lackland Air Force Base, Tex., 1998—2000; v.p. recruitment & diversity affairs Uniformed Svcs. U. Health Scis., Bethesda, Md.,

1999—2002; pathology flight comdr. 375th Med. Group, Scott AFB, Ill., 2002—05; dep. med. support squadron comdr. 375th Med. Support Squadron, Scott Air Force Base, Ill., 2002—05; biomed. sci. corps exec. 375th Airlift Wing, Scott AFB, Ill., 2002—05; dir. chem., biol., nuc. and clin. surveilance Air Force Inst. for Operational Health, Brooks City AFB, Tex., 2005—. Faculty advisor for vol. cmty. med. clinic Med. Sch. Uniformed Svcs. U., Bethesda, 1999—2002; coach odyssey of the mind White Oaks Elem. Sch., Burke, Va., 2000—02; vol. instr. Incarnate Word Coll., San Antonio, 1995—97; chmn. parent adv. com. Child Devel. Ctr., Colorado Springs, Colo., 1991—95; mem., leadership coun. for cmty. svc. Alamo Fed. Exec. Bd., San Antonio, 1995—99; cons. in field. Contbr. articles to profl. jours. Cmty. mem. Alamo Fed. Exec. Bd., San Antonio, Tex., 1995—99; ch. med. vol. Emmanuel Ch., San Antonio, Tex., 1985—89; advisor to the bd. Uniformed Svcs Med. Sch., Bethesda, Md., 1999—2002; mil. deployment Mil., Overseas, Non-U.S., Classified, 2003—03. Col. USAF, 1985, Scott and various other Air Force Bases, over 20 years of service. Decorated Expeditionary Svc. Ribbon with Gold Border USAF, Air Force Outstanding Unit Award with Valor US; fellow, 81Rutgers U., 1984; Pell grant, U. of Ala., 1974—77. Master: Biomedical Scis. Corps (licentiate; licensure 1985, Chief Mastery badge 1995); mem.: Soc. Armed Forces Mil. Lab. Scientists (sr. mem. 1986, Best Rsch. Poster Presentation 1999), Am. Soc. Microbiologists (corr.; mem. 1978, Grad. Student award 1983), Assn.Mil. Surgeons of U.S. (corr.; mem. 1996), Am. Soc. Clin. Pathologists (assoc.; assoc. mem. 1990), Officers Club (assoc.; mem. 1986), Beta Beta Beta (hon.; honor mem. 1979), Zeta Phi Beta (corr.; pres. 1975—77, Cmty. Charity Supporter 1976). Achievements include research in converting urine to potable water to prevent discharge in space; development of medical laboratory in deployed location; first to tri-service military and federal medical school recruitment to help meet nation's need for physicians, women and minorities. Avocations: reading, horseback riding, running, walking, interior decorating. Home: 23003 Whisper Canyon San Antonio TX 78258-3211 Office: 2350 Gillingham Dr Brooks City-Base TX 78235 Office Phone: 210-536-8305. Personal E-mail: bbcmiller@earthlink.net. Business E-Mail: carolyn.miller@brooks.af.mil.

**MILLER, CHARLES,** investor, retired investment company executive; b. Galveston, Tex., Feb. 13, 1934; s. Samuel and Rose M.; m. Beth Birdwell. BA in Math., U. Tex., 1959. Investment officer Tchr. Retirement System, Austin, Tex., 1961-66; v.p., portfolio mgr. Funds, Inc., Houston, 1966-71; pres., chief exec. officer Funds Adv. Co., Houston, 1971-76; pres., chief exec. officer Criterion Mgmt. Co., Houston, 1971-98; pres., chief exec. officer Transamerica Mgmt. Group, 1976-92; chmn. State Pension Rev. Bd. of Tex., 1979-83; bd. dirs. Tex. Commerce Bank, Houston, Cen. Houston, Inc.; mem. Tex. Govs. select com. on Edn., Tex. govs. Task Force on State Trust and Asset Mgmt; former chmn. Tex. Ednl. Econ. Policy Ctr.; mem. Bd. Regents, U. Tex. Sys., 1999-2004, chmn. 2001-04; chair. Sec. of Edn.'s Commn. on Future of Edn., 2005. Trustee Houston Ballet Found., Houston Mus. Natural Sci. and Planetarium, Am. Leadership Forum; mem. council overseers Jesse H. Jones Grad. Sch. Adminstrn. Rice U., Houston; chair. bd. trustees U. Houston Found.; bd. trustees Tomas Rivera Ctr., Tex. Rsch. League, Santa Fe Inst.; mem. bd. visitors and govs. St. John's Coll.; pres. Sol y Sombra Found., Ctr. for the Study of Community Found.; past chair and mem. Greater Houston Partnership; founder, chmn. Charter Sch. Resource Ctr. of Tex. Served with USN, 1957-58. Mem. Fin. Analysts Fedn., Am. Statis. Assn., Nat. Assn. Bus. Economists, Houston C. of C. (bd. dirs.), U. Tex. Cancer Ctr. ((bd. visitors), Downtown Houston Assn. (bd. dirs.). Episcopalian. Clubs: Petroleum (Houston); Headliners (Austin); Ponte Vedra (Jacksonville, Fla.); Coronado, Century. *

**MILLER, CHARLES E. (CHUCK MILLER),** judge; b. Washington, Sept. 26, 1944; s. Charles Edward Miller and Mary (Cox) M.; divorced; 1 child, Samantha Mcgill Cox. BA, So. Meth. U., 1971, JD, 1972. Bar: Tex. 1972. Assoc. Roseborough & Curlee, Dallas, 1972-77; judge County Criminal Ct. #7, Dallas, 1977-82, Ct. Criminal Appeals, Austin, Tex., 1983-94; state judge at large State of Tex., 1995—. Adj. prof. criminal law So. Meth. U. Law Sch., Dallas, 1980—82; arbitrator comml., employment and labor panels Am. Arbitration Assn., 1995—; labor abitrator Fed. Mediation and Conciliation Svc., 2002—, arbitrator, labor roster, 2003—; arbitrator comml. and employment Nat. Arbitration Forum, 2004. Author and lectr. in field. Mem. nat. adv. coun. Nat. victim Ctr., NYC and Washington; mem. nat. steeringcom. Victims Constitutional Amendment Network; mem. adv. bd. victims Organized to Ensure Rights and Safety; mem. victim assistancecom. Tex. Young Lawyers Assn.; parliamentarian state exec. bd. People Against Violent Crime. With US Army, 1966-70. Named Disting. Mil. Grad., Officer Candidate Sch., Ft. Sill, Okla., 1968, Best Dallas Misdemeanor Ct. Judge, Dallas Bar Assn., 1982, Best Dallas Criminal Ct. Judge, Dallas County Criminal Bar Assn., 1982; decorated Army Commendational medal, 1970; recipient Sunny von Bulow Nat. Victim Advocacy Ctr. Appreciation cert., 1987, US Dept. Justice Victims of Crime Appreciation cert., 1992, Victims Organized to Ensure Rights and Safety Advocate for Justice award, 1993, People Against Violent Crime Appreciation cert., 1993. Mem. SAR, State Bar Tex. (chmn. criminal law sect. 1981-82, course dir. advanced criminal law course 1990, chmn. crime victim com. 1992-94, crime victim & witness, 1994, cert. specialist in criminal law), Coll. State Bar Tex., Tex. Bar Found. Republican. Home and Office: 1701 Foggy Glen Cv Ste 100 Dallas TX 75233-1541 Office Phone: 512-496-6666. Personal E-mail: judgechuckmiller@att.net.

**MILLER, CHARLES E.,** gynecologist; b. Iron Mountain, Mich., Aug. 18, 1953; s. Alfred and Muriel Miller; m. Laura Miller; children: Benjamin, Abagayle, Alec. BS in Medicine, Northwestern U., Chgo., 1975, MD, 1977. Diplomate Am. Bd. Ob-gyn., 1984. Dir. reproductive endocrinology and infertility Luth. Gen. Hosp., Park Ridge, Ill., 1983—85, dir. Ctr. for Advanced Reproduction for In-vitro Fertilization and Gamete Intrafallopian Transfer, 1989—95, dir. minimally invasive gynecol. surgery, 2005—; med. dir., med. dir. divsn. endoscopic surgery Ctr. for Human Reproduction, Schaumburg, Ill., 1995—99; dir. Ctr. for Minimally Invasive Gynecologic Surgery Glenbrook Hosp., Ill., 1997—2001; pvt. practice Arlington Heights, Ill., 1999—2001, Charles E. Miller, MD & Assocs., Arlington Heights and Naperville, Ill., 2001—. Cons. Ethicon Endo-Surgery, Cin., 2004—, Ethicon Women's Health and Urology, Somerville, NJ, 2004—, Galil Med., Ltd., Yokneam, Israel, 2006—, Serono, Rockland, Mass.; cons.. mem. spkrs. bur. Smith & Nephew, Andover, Mass., 2005—; mem. spkrs. bur. Boston Sci., Natick, Mass., 2005—; clin. assoc. prof. dept. ob-gyn. U. Ill., Chgo., clin. assoc. dept. ob-gyn. Mem. adv. bd.: Jour. Minimally Invasive Gynecology, mem. editl. bd.: OB/GYN News; contbr. chapters to books, articles to profl. jours. Fellow: ACOG (cert. accreditation coun. for gynecologic endoscopy); mem.: Chgo. Assn. Gynecologic Endoscopists, Chgo. Assn. Reproductive Endocrinology, Soc. Reproductive Surgeons, Endometriosis Assn. (clin. adv. bd., bd. dirs. 2006), Am. Assn. Gynecologic Laparoscopists (pres. elect, sec. - treas. 2006), RESOLVE - The Nat. Fertility Assn. (clin. adv. bd. mem., Lifetime Achievement award 2005), Am. Soc. Reproductive Medicine (bd. mem.). Office: Charles E Miller MD & Associates 120 Osler Dr Naperville IL 60540 Office Phone: 630-364-1119. Office Fax: 630-428-0083. Business E-Mail: lmaki@charlesemillermd.org.

**MILLER, CHARLES HAMPTON,** lawyer; b. Southampton, NY, Jan. 25, 1928; s. Abraham E. and Ethel (Simon) M.; m. Mary Fried, Aug. 26, 1956; children: Cathy Lynn Castaneda, Steven Scott, Jennifer Lee Miller-Grady. BA, Syracuse U., 1949; LLB, Columbia U., 1952. Bar: N.Y. 1952, Republic of Korea 1954, U.S. Ct. Appeals (2d cir.) 1958, U.S. Supreme Ct. 1969, U.S. Ct. Appeals (3d cir.) 1972, U.S. Ct. Appeals (7th cir.) 1973, U.S. Ct. Appeals (9th cir.) 1995; cert. mediator (so. and ea. dists.) N.Y., mediator Supreme Ct. N.Y. County; arbitrator Ea. Inst. N.Y. Asst. counsel Waterfront Commn., N.Y. Harbor, 1954-56; asst. atty. U.S. Atty. for So. Dist. N.Y., 1956-58; assoc. Cole & Deitz, NYC, 1958-61; Marshall Bratter Greene Allison & Tucker, NYC, 1961-64, ptnr., 1964-82; Hess Segall Guterman Pelz Steiner & Barovick, NYC, 1982-86, Loeb & Loeb LLP NYC, 1986-2000, counsel, 2000—. Mem. faculty Continuing Legal Edn., Columbia U. Law Sch., 1976-82. With U.S. Army, 1952-54. Fellow: Am. Bar Found.; mem.: ABA, Assn. of Bar of City

of NY. Home: 171 Ralph Ave White Plains NY 10606-3813 Office: Loeb & Loeb LLP 345 Park Ave Fl 18 New York NY 10154-1895 Office Phone: 212-407-4910. Personal E-mail: marbuzz@msn.com.

**MILLER, CHARLES MAURICE,** lawyer; b. L.A., Sept. 7, 1948; BA cum laude, UCLA, 1970; postgrad., U. So. Calif., L.A., 1970-71; JD, U. Akron, 1975. Bar: Calif. 1978, U.S. Dist. Ct. (cen. dist.) Calif. 1978, U.S. Ct. Appeals (9th cir.) 1978, U.S. Supreme Ct. 1981. Gen. atty. U.S. Immigration & Naturalization Svc., U.S. Dept. Justice, L.A., 1976-79; ptnr. Miller Law Offices, L.A., 1979—. Adj. prof. law U. West L.A., 1989-90 Co-editor: The Visa Processing Guide: Process and Procedures at U.S. Consulates and Embassies, 12th edit., 2005-06; articles editor U. Akron Law Rev., 1974-75 Mem. Calif. Bd. Legal Specialization, San Francisco, 1988-89 Mem. Bar of Calif. (chmn. immigration splty. 1988-89, commr. immigration splty. 1987-90), Am. Immigration Law Found. (bd. trustees 1995-98), Am. Immigration Lawyers Assn. (bd. dirs. 1998-2001, mem. bd. govs., chair So. Calif. chpt. 1993-94, INS headquarters liaison com. 1997-98, co-chair mentor program 1990-91, co-chair visa office liaison 1991-92, vice chair 1994-95, co-chair consular rev. task force 1993-95, Jack Wasserman Meml. award for excellence in immigration litigation 1995) Office: Miller Law Offices 12441 Ventura Blvd Studio City CA 91604-2407

**MILLER, CHARLES P.,** lawyer; b. Charlestown, W.Va., May 14, 1961; BA cum laude, W. Va. Univ., 1983, JD, 1986. Bar: W. Va. 1986, Tex. 1987. Ptnr., Banking, Bus. Transactions, Securities practices, head Bus. Dept., mem. mgmt. com. Patton Boggs LLP, Dallas. Founder Dallas Private Equity Forum; mem. selection com. Tex. Investment Forum, 1997—2003. Named a Tex. Super Lawyer, Tex. Monthly Mag., 2003—04. Mem.: ABA, Dallas Bas Assn., Tex. Bankers Assn., Order of the Coif. Office: Patton Boggs LLP Suite 3000 2001 Ross Ave Dallas TX 75201-8001 Office Phone: 202-457-6000. Office Fax: 214-758-1550. Business E-Mail: cmiller@pattonboggs.com.

**MILLER, CHARLES RICKIE,** systems analyst, engineering executive; b. New Albany, Ind., Oct. 4, 1946; s. Marshall Christian and Thelma Virginia (Martin) M.; m. Janel Howell, Nov. 24, 1968; children: Kimberly, Brian, Audrey, Rachel. BA in Physics, DePauw U., 1969; postgrad., Rice U., 1969-70, U. Houston, 1972-76. Tech. editor ITT/Fed. Electric Corp., Houston, 1970-71, LTV/Svc. Tech. Corp., Houston, 1971; sys. safety engr. Boeing Aerospace Corp., Houston, 1971-76; thermal analyst space sys. divsn. Rockwell Internat. Corp., Houston, 1976-89; mgr. thermal and fluid sys. for space shuttle payloads Space Shuttle Program Office, NASA/L.B. Johnson Space Ctr., Houston, 1989—. Mem. editl. team Apollo 14, 15 preliminary sci. reports, 1971-72; mem. sys. integration negotiating team for Space Shuttle to Mir Space Sta. rendezvous and docking missions, 1993-98, chmn. negotiating team for Space Shuttle to Mir Space Sta. water preparation and transfer, 1994-98, space shuttle program co-chmn. for shuttle/internat. space sta. program joint tech. working groups for thermal control, environ. control and life support sys., 1996—. Bd. dirs. Space City Aquatic Team, Houston, 1990-91. Rector scholar DePauw U., 1964-68; Rice fellow Rice U., 1969-70. Mem. AIAA, ASME, Nat. Space Soc., Air Force Assn., Am. Inst. Physics, Planetary Soc., Sigma Pi Sigma. Avocations: children's sports, jogging, science fiction, military history. Home: 806 Walbrook Dr Houston TX 77062-4030 Office: NASA Mail Code MO2 LB Johnson Space Ctr Houston TX 77058 Office Phone: 281-483-1229. E-mail: cmiller@ems.jsc.nasa.gov.

**MILLER, CHARLES T.,** prosecutor; b. Winslow, Wash., June 27, 1948; s. Charles Wilbur and Pharoeba M. (Good) M.; m. Rebecca Louise Campbell, Aug. 17, 1974; chidren: Angela Dawn, Emily Grace, Kathryn Louise. BS in Criminal Justice, W.Va. State Coll., 1973; JD, W.Va. U., 1977. Bar: W.Va. 1977, U.S. Ct. Appeals (4th cir.) 1977. Asst. prosecuting atty., Kanawha County, W.Va., 1977-82; assoc. and ptnr. E. F. Thaxton Attys., Charleston, 1982-84; 1st asst. US atty. (so. dist.) US Dept. Justice, Charleston, 1984—93, 1994—, interim US atty., 1991—92, 1993, 2001, 2005—. With USN, 1966-69, Vietnam; maj. W.Va. Army Nat. Guard; lt. col. W.Va. Air Nat. Guard. Decorated Navy Achievement medal, Rep. of Vietnam Svc. medal, Rep. of Vietnam Campaign ribbon, Rep. of Vietnam Cross of Gallantry, Combat Action ribbon, Presdl. Unit citation. Presbyterian. Avocation: carpentry. Office: US Atty's Office PO Box 1713 Charleston WV 25326*

**MILLER, CHARLES WALLACE,** historian, environmental geologist, educator; b. Phoenix, July 7, 1946; s. Charles W. and Emabel O. Miller; m. Connie Raschke, June 3, 1972; 1 child, Geoffrey Wallace. BA, U. Md., 1969; MA, U. Tex., 1970; BS, SUNY, Albany, 1978; PhD, Union Inst., 1990. Tchr. pub. schs., San Antonio, 1971-76; instr. San Antonio Coll., 1972-78, St. Mary's Univ., San Antonio, 1976-78, Cochise Coll., Sierra Vista, Az., 1989-90, Pima C.C., Tucson, 1998—; environ. geologist U.S. Geol. Survey, Metairie, La., 1978-80; field geologist U.S. Bur. Land Mgmt., Moab, Utah, 1980-84; historian U.S. Bur. Reclamation, Salt Lake City, 1990-94; environ. scientist USAF, Tucson, 1994—. Mineral cons., Tucson, 1984-89. Author: Stake Your Claim! The Tale of America's Enduring Mining Law, 1991, The Spirit of the Pioneers Still Rules, 1997, The Automobile Gold Rushes, 1998. Vol. East Tucson Bapt. Ch., Tucson, also various youth orgns. including Boy Scouts and one-on-one mentoring program for troubled youth; group coord. Combined Fed. Campaign. Recipient Outstanding Alumni award, SUNY Albany (now Excelsior Coll.), 2005. Mem. SAR (sec. Tucson chpt.), Nat. Eagle Scout Assn., Mining History Assn., James Madison Brigade for Preservation of the U.S. Constn., Mensa, Hist. Soc., Golden Key, Phi Alpha Theta, Pi Sigma Alpha. Achievements include climbed two tallest peaks in the lower 48; rim-to-rim trek across Grand Canyon. Avocations: backpacking, scuba diving, photography, lifeguarding. Home: 136 S Shadow Creek Pl Tucson AZ 85748-3278 Office: USAF 355 CES CEVA Davis Monthan Afb AZ 85707

**MILLER, CHARLOTTE FAYE,** speech pathology/audiology services professional; b. Weir, Miss., Feb. 19, 1959; d. John Samuel and Gertha Lee (Warren) Miller; m. Phillip William Miller, July 14, 1978. BS, Jackson State U., 1981; MS, Miss. State U., 1996. Cert. sch. clinician, sch. adminstr. Miss. Speech lang. pathologist Choctaw County Schs., Ackerman, Miss., 1981-90, Attala County Schs., Kosciusko, Miss., 1990—. Ins. salesperson Pre Paid Legal Svcs., Inc., Jackson, Miss., 1996—. Chairperson spl. edn. svcs. Greenlee Elem. Sch., McCool, Miss., 1996—98, Image Award Martin Luther King Celebration, Kosciusko, 1997—98; lay spkr. United Meth. Ch.; dir. Miss Black Choctaw County Pageant, Weir, 1983—93; coord. Buttons and Beaus Pageant, Ehtel, Miss., 1996—98; property mgr. Millers - Colemans - Satterfields Found., Inc. Named Woman of the Yr., Star Herald Newspaper, 1992; recipient Gratitude award, Attala County Assn. Educators, 1995. Mem.: Miss. Educators (Ist Yr. Tchr. award 1993—95, Outstanding Achievement award 1993), Miss. Speech Hearing Assn., Nat. Coun. Negro Women (membership chair mem. 1996—, pres. 1998—, award 1996), Heroines of Jericho (jr. matron 1988—, dist. sec. 1994—95), Zeta Phi Beta (local, state, regional officer 1990—98, Appreciation award 1990, 1993, 1997, 1998). Democrat. Methodist. Avocations: travel, quilting, houseplants. Home: 2472 Allala Rd 2126 Mc Cool MS 39108 Office: Greenlee Elem Sch RR 3 Box 66 Mc Cool MS 39108-9110

**MILLER, CHERYL DEANN,** former professional basketball coach, broadcaster; b. Riverside, Calif., Jan. 3, 1964; BA in Broadcast Journalism, U. So. Calif., 1985. Basketball player Jr. Nat. Team, 1981, U.S. Nat. Team, 1982, U.S. Olympics, 1984; commentator ABC Sports; head coach women's basketball U. So. Calif., 1993-94; commentator TNT Sports, Atlanta, 1996; gen. mgr., head coach Phoenix Mercury, 1997—2000. Player JC Penney All-Am. Team Five, U. So. Calif. Women's Basketball Team, World Championship Team, 1983. Recipient Sports Illustrated Player of Yr., 1986, Naismith Player of Yr. award, Kodak All-Am. award, more than 1,140 trophies and 125 plaques including Nat. Sports Festival, 1981, Pan Am. Games, 1983, FIBA World Championship, Goodwill Games, gold medal 1984 Olympic Games; elected to Naismith Basketball Hall of Fame, 1995.

**MILLER, CHERYL LYNN,** former paralegal, artist, art educator; b. Chgo., Nov. 6, 1946; d. Joseph Julius and Sue (Baker) Ronto (Budnovich) Roberts; m. William Albert Miller, Dec. 31, 1965; children: Karin Wells, Brent. BA, So. Ill. U., 1997; postgrad., Coll. Santa Fe, 2003, U. No. Colo., 2004, Adams State Coll., 2005. Tchr. Douglas County Sch. Dist., Castle Rock, Colo., 2000—03; art tchr. Shepherd of the Hills, Centennial, Colo., 2004—. Tchr. participant Diversity Club, Douglas County H.S., Castlerock, Colo., 2002—03. Mem.: Colo. Art Edn. Assn., Nat. Art Edn. Assn., Alumni Assn. So. Ill. U., Phi Kappa Phi. Methodist. Office: Shephard of the Hills Christian Sch 7691 S University Centennial CO 80122 Office Phone: 303-798-0711. E-mail: wmillertime1@aol.com.

**MILLER, CHRISTINE ODELL COOK,** federal judge; b. Oakland, Calif., Aug. 26, 1944; m. Dennis F. Miller; 2 children. BA in Polit. Sci., Stanford U., 1966; JD, U. Utah, 1969. Bar: D.C., Calif. Law clk. to Hon. David T. Lewis U.S. Ct. Appeals (10th cir.), Salt Lake City; trial atty. U.S. Dept. Justice, U.S. Ct. Claims; team leader atty. FTC; atty. Hogan & Hartson, Washington; spl. counsel Pension Benefit Guaranty Corp.; dep. gen. counsel U.S. Ry. Assn.; ptnr. Shack & Kimball, Washington; judge U.S. Ct. Fed. Claims, Washington, 1982—. Comment editor Utah law Rev. Scholar U. Utah Coll. Law. Mem. D.C. Bar Assn., Calif. State Bar, Order of Coif, Univ. Club, Cosmos Club. Avocation: genealogy. Office: US Ct Fed Claims 717 Madison Pl NW Ste 716 Washington DC 20005-1011

**MILLER, CLAIRE ELLEN,** editor, educator, writer; b. Milw., July 17, 1936; d. Emil George Benjamin and Phyllis Dorothy (Rahn) Holtzen; m. Gerald Ray Miller, June 21, 1958; children: Karin, Russell. BS in Edn., Concordia U., 1961. Tchr. Grace Episcopal Day Sch., Silver Spring, Md., 1971-77, The Norwood Sch., Bethesda, Md., 1977-79; writer Media Materials, Balt., 1980; project editor Ednl. Challenges, Alexandria, Va., 1981; asst. mng. editor Ranger Rick Mag., Nat. Wildlife Fedn., Vienna, Va., 1981-87, mng. editor, 1988-2001, contbg. editor, 2002—; propr. Claire Ellen Miller, Writer and Editor, Rockville, Md., 2001—. Author numerous activity books for presch. thru mid. sch., 1979-80; project editor 6 vocabulary books, 1981; author numerous children's mag. and newspaper stories and books, 1981—. Mem. Assn. Ednl. Pubs., Md. Ornithol. Soc. Democrat. Lutheran. Avocation: birding. Home and Office: 17501 Kirk Ln Rockville MD 20853-1033 Personal E-mail: clairemiller@erols.com.

**MILLER, CORBIN RUSSELL,** investment company executive; b. Huntington, W.Va., Apr. 6, 1948; s. Corbin Russell and Ernestine (Thorne) M.; m. Kathryn Ann Anderson, Sept. 16, 1978. AB cum laude, Princeton (N.J.) U., 1971. Trainee Morgan Guaranty Trust Co., NYC, 1972-74, asst. treas., 1974-77; assoc. Wm. Sword & Co. Inc., Princeton, 1977-79; v.p. J. Henry Schroder Corp., NYC, 1979-83, J. Henry Schroder Bank & Trust Co., NYC, 1983-87; v.p. IBJ Schroder Bank & Trust Co., NYC, 1987-90; chmn. Koala Techs. Corp., Pleasanton, Calif., 1990-91; mng. dir. Regent Ptnr. Inc., NYC and Denver, 1991-92; exec. v.p. S.N. Phelps & Co., Greenwich, Conn., 1992-95; exec. v.p., CFO, dir. Carey Internat., Inc., Washington, 1995-96; pres. Lombard North Am. Inc., San Francisco, 1997-99; sr. ptnr. Continuum Ventures LLC, NYC, 2000—. Bd. dirs. Met. Opera Guild, N.Y.C., 1994—. Mem. Am. Soc. Order St. John of Jerusalem (chancellor 1999-2002), Met. Opera Club (pres. 1992-94), Knickerbocker Club, Rockaway Hunting Club, Racquet and Tennis Club, The Brook. Republican. Episcopalian. Avocation: golf. Home: 1165 5th Ave New York NY 10029-6931 Office: Continuum Ventures LLC 300 Park Ave Fl 17 New York NY 10022-7402 E-mail: cm@corbinmiller.us.

**MILLER, DANIEL HARLAN,** lawyer; b. Huntington, W.Va., Mar. 20, 1960; s. Kenneth Harlan and Charlotte Jane (Anderson) M.; m. Lisa Carole Jacobs, June 15, 1991. BBA, U. Ky., 1982; JD, U. Louisville, 1988. Bar: Ky. 1989, U.S. Dist. Ct. (ea. dist.) Ky. 1990, U.S. Supreme Ct. 1999. Assoc. Summers, Fox & McGinty, Lexington, Ky., 1989—90; pvt. practice Lexington, 2000, 2006—; ptnr. Elam & Miller, PSC, Lexington, 1990—2004; sr. title counsel Metropolitan Title Co., Lexington, 2004—05. Legal counsel Lexington Jaycees, 1991-93. Legal counsel bar. First Presbyn. Ch. Learning Ctr., Lexington, 1991-97, deacon, 1997-2000; profl. affiliates com. Lexington Bd. Realtors, 1992-96; exec. com. 1990-91, 94—, legal counsel 1990-91, Fayette County Rep. Party, Lexington; bd. dirs. Lincoln Club of Fayette County, 1991-96; vice-chmn. Fayette County Young Reps., Lexington, 1990-91; unit commr. Boy Scouts Am., Lexington, 1987-88, assoc. den. leader, com., 1994-96, coun. exec. bd., 1996—, v.p., 1996-2004, Cub Scout den leader, 2004—, chmn. Henry Clay Dist., 2006—. James West fellow. Fellow Ky. Bar Found.; mem. Ky. Bar Assn. (vice chair real property sect. 2004-05), Fayette County Bar Assn. (pro bono project mem. 1989—, chmn. real property sect. 1999-2001), Lexington Home Builders Assn. (assoc.), Lexington Mortgage Bankers Assn., Nat. Eagle Scout Assn., Sons Confederate Vets. Civil War, Sons Union Vets. Civil War, Soc. Colonial Wars, Lexington Rotary Club (chmn. Boy Scout com. 1996-2003, Paul Harris fellow Rotary Internat.), Internat. Fellowship Scouting Rotarians (historian 2006—). Home: 2109 Lakeside Dr Lexington KY 40502-3018 Office: PO Box 22606 Lexington KY 40522-2606 Office Phone: 859-402-8006. Business E-Mail: dan@danmilleratty.com.

**MILLER, DANIEL RAYMOND,** prosecutor; b. Evansville, Ind., Sept. 20, 1963; s. Daniel Edgar and Virginia Sue (Baumgart) M. BA magna cum laude, DePauw U., 1985; JD cum laude, Ind. U., 1989. Bar: Ind. 1989. Clk. to Hon. William I. Garrard, Ind. Ct. of Appeals, Indpls., 1989-90; dep. pros. atty. Vanderburgh County Pros.'s Office, Evansville, 1990—, dir. gun violence program, 2003—04, dir. drug law enforcement program, 2004—. Pres. Substance Abuse Coun. Vanderburgh County, 1997-98; chmn. pastoral coun. St. John Cath. Ch., Evansville, 1995-98; mem. Diocese of Evansville Pastoral Coun., 1997-2000; pres. 4-H Coun., 1999, 2003-2004, Nat. 4-H Leadership Trust, 2004-06. Mem.: Nat. Dist. Attys. Assn., Ind. Bar Assn., Vanderburgh County Coop. Ext. Svc. (bd. dirs. 2000—05), St. Vincent DePaul Soc. (pres. 1994, sec. conf. 1995—2003, pres. 2003—), 4-H Club Assn. (leader Energetics club 1991—, bd. dirs. 1995—2001, treas. 2000—01, pres. Vanderburgh County 4-H Leaders 2001—02). Republican. Roman Catholic. Avocations: gardening, church choir. Home: 13521 N Green River Rd Evansville IN 47725-9769 Office: Vanderburgh Co Pros Office Rm 108 City County Adm Bldg Evansville IN 47708 Office Phone: 812-435-5118. E-mail: drmprosec@aol.com.

**MILLER, DANIEL WEISS,** psychologist; b. Sept. 14, 1924; s. Paul and Helen (Weiss) M.; children: Sarah, David, Larissa. BA, New Sch. Social Rsch., 1952; MA in Psychology, CUNY, 1955; postgrad., NYU, 1956-57, Yeshiva U., 1957-58, Humanistic Psychology Inst., 1978-81; PhD in Psychology, Internat. Inst. Advanced Study, 1989. Lic. psychologist, N.Y. Psychology intern N.J. State Psychologists Tng. Program Trenton State Hosp., 1953-55; probation officer N.Y.C. Surrogate Ct., 1955-57; sr. psychologist Ctrl. Islip State Hosp., N.Y., 1957-58; chief psychologist Kings Park (N.Y.) State Hosp., 1958-62; rsch. psychologist Elmhurst Gen. Hosp., Queens, N.Y., 1962-63, Rockland State Hosp., N.J., 1964; pvt. practice N.Y.C., 1972—. Dir. organic process therapy Primal-Gestalt; lectr.; tng. therapist ctrs., Paris, Greece, Frankfurt, Germany, Brazil, Montreal, Can.; mem. media com. for mental health UN. Author: The Unseen Universe of Mind and Matter, 1993, The Web and the Cloth Science, Consciousness and Chemodynamics, 2003. Mem. Assn. Past Life Rsch. and Therapy, Assn. Spirituality and Psychotherapy (past v.p.), N.Y. Acad. Sci., Internat. Primal Assn. (bd. dirs.), Soc. Chaos Theory in Psychology and Life Scis., Lyceum Club. Home and Office: 106 Saint Marks Ave Brooklyn NY 11217-2412 E-mail: danielwmiller@earthlink.net.

**MILLER, DARCY M.,** publishing executive; b. Glen Ridge, N.J., June 17, 1953; d. Paul Richardson and Susan (Alling) Miller; m. James R. Donaldson III, Feb. 6, 1988 (div.); 1 child, Zoe Alling Donaldson; m. Richard G. Powers, Aug. 23, 2003. Co-founder, assoc. pub. Mus. Mag., N.Y.C., 1979-83; pub. Crop Protection Chems. Ref., N.Y.C., 1983-85; assoc. pub. Chief Exec. Mag., N.Y.C., 1986-87, pub., 1987-89, exec. v.p., 1989-96; pub. Stagebill, N.Y.C.,

1996-97; group pub. Am. Baby Group, 1997-2000, pres., 2000—01; pres. corp. sales Primedia Inc., N.Y.C., 2001—03; sabbatical, 2003—. Mem.: ASCAP, Advt. Women of N.Y. Democrat. Episcopalian.

**MILLER, DAVID ALLEN,** air force officer; b. Galion, Ohio, Sept. 3, 1963; s. Richard Allen and Dorothy S. (Stoyanovich) M.; m. Regina Denise Fulkerson, Mar. 16, 1987; children: Christopher David, Alexandra Lauren. BS, Bowling Green (Ohio) U., 1985, Tex. A&M U., 1987; MS, U. Md., 1994. Commd. 2d lt. USAF, 1986, advanced through grades to lt. col., 1998, ret., 1996; comdr., dir., CFO Palehua Solar Obs., Honolulu, 1996—99; chief of weather staff officer 14th Air Force, 1999—2001; dep. dir. internat. fellows program Internat. Student Mgmt. Office, 2001—. Team chief Air Force Space Forecast Ctr., Falcon, Colo., 1994-96 Contbg. author, editor: Maryland Pilot Earth Science and Technology Education Network, 1994; author, editor: Financial Services Report, 2004. Vol. St. Andrew's Epis. Cathedral, Honolulu, 1996-99, Camp Timberline, Hawaii, 1999; earth sci. instr. Md. High Sch. Tchrs., 1993-94; clean air forecaster U. Md., College Park, 1993-94, trooper, stable mgr. cavalry, 1993; sailor Pacific Yacht Club, Hickam AFB, 1997. Decorated Commendation medal, first oak leaf, Meritorious Svc. first oak leaf medal. Mem. AAAS, Air Force Space Command Officers Club, Am. Phys. Soc. Achievements include development of technique to forecast spacecraft internal changing conditions. Home: 6528 Osprey Point Ln Alexandria VA 22315-5908 Office: Internat Fellows Program Eisenhower Hall Rm 124 408 4th Ave Fort Mcnair DC 20319

**MILLER, DAVID EDMOND,** physician; b. Biscoe, N.C., June 6, 1930; s. James Herbert and Elsie Dale (McGlaughon) M.; m. Marjorie Willard Penton, June 4, 1960; children: Marjorie Dale, David Edmond. AB, Duke U., 1952, MD, 1956. Diplomate Am. Bd. Internal Medicine (subspecialty bd. cardiovasular disease). Interned. ctr. Duke U. Durham, N.C., 1956-57, resident in internal medicine, 1957-58, 59, 60, research fellow cardiovascular desease, 1958-59, 61, assoc. internal medicine and cardiology, 1963-79, clin. asst., prof. medicine cardiology, 1979-91; practice medicine specialising in internal medicine and cardiology Durham, 1964-2000; attending physician internal medicine div. cardiology Watts Hosp., Durham, 1964-76, chief medicine, 1975-76; attending physician cardiology divsn. internal medicine Durham Regional Hosp. (formerly Durham County Gen. Hosp.), 1976-2000, chmn dept. internal medicine, 1976-82, pres. med. staff, 1980-81, ret., 2000. Adv. com. Duke Med. Ctr. Contbr. articles to profl. jours. Council clin. cardiology N.C. chpt. Am. Heart Assn., 1963—. Served to lt. comdr. USNR, 1961-63. Fellow ACP, Am. Coll. Cardiology, Royal Soc. Medicine, Royal Soc. Health; mem. AMA, So. Med. Assn., N.C. Med. Soc. (del. ho. of dels. 1981, 82, 83), N.C. Durham-Orange County Med. Soc., Am. Soc. Internal Medicine, N.C. Soc. Internal medicine (exec. coun. 1984-92), Am. Fedn. Clin. Rsch. Clubs: Hope Valley Country, Carolina Yacht. Methodist. Home: 1544 Hermitage Ct Durham NC 27707-1680

**MILLER, DAVID GROFF,** insurance agent; b. Kansas City, Kans., Aug. 17, 1949; s. Vincent G. and Ruth (Whitton) M.; m. Marjorie Zwiers, 1979. BA, U. Kans., 1972. CLU. Press aide to U.S. Senator James B. Pearson, 1974-75; fed. grant adminstr. Kans. Gov. Robert Bennett, 1975-78; brokerage rep. Paul Revere Co., Overland Park, Kans., 1979-85; prin. Miller Agy. Inc., Eudora, 1985—. Rep. dist. 4 Kans. State Reps., 1981-91; chmn. Kans. State Rep. Party, 1995-98. Mem.: Ind. Ins. Agts., Omicron Delta Kappa. Methodist. Office: Miller Agy Inc PO Box 460 Eudora KS 66025-0460

**MILLER, DAVID L.,** lawyer; b. Bklyn., Nov. 4, 1954; BA with distinction, George Washington Univ., 1976; JD magna cum laude, Univ. Mich., 1979. Bar: DC 1979, Va. 1986. Ptnr. Real Estate practice, mem. bd. dir., chmn. Legal Opinion com. Pillsbury Winthrop Shaw Pittman, McLean, Va. Bd. mem. Appleseed Found., Langley Sch., McLean, Va. Mem.: ABA (chmn. Com. on Legal Opinions in Real Estate Transactions), Am. Coll. Real Estate Lawyers, Urban Land Inst., Nat. Assn. Industrial & Office Properties, Va. State Bar Assn., DC Bar Assn. (vice chmn. steering com., Real Estate Housing & Land Use sect.), Phi Beta Kappa, Order of the Coif. Office: Pillsbury Winthrop Shaw Pittman 1650 Tysons Blvd Mc Lean VA 22102-4859 Office Phone: 703-770-7925. Office Fax: 702-770-7901. Business E-Mail: david.miller@pillsburylaw.com.

**MILLER, DAVID R.,** academic administrator; BS, U. Calif., Berkeley; PhD, Princeton U. Acting dean engring. U. Calif. San Diego, La Jolla, assoc. dean engring., assoc. vice chancellor, acting sr. vice chancellor, assoc. vice chancellor. Office: UCSD Office Sr Vice Chancellor Acad Affairs 9500 Gilman Dr Dept 0001 La Jolla CA 92093-0001 Business E-Mail: milleravc@ucsd.edu.

**MILLER, DAVID W.,** lawyer; b. Indpls., July 1, 1950; s. Charles Warren Miller and Katherine Louise (Beckner) Dearing; m. Mindy Miller, May 20, 1972; children: Adam David, Ashley Kay, Amanda Katherine Kupfer. BA, Ind. U., Bloomington, 1971; JD summa cum laude, Ind. U., Indpls., 1976. Bar: Ind. 1976. Investigator NLRB, Indpls., 1971-76; assoc. Roberts & Ryder, Indpls., 1977-80, ptnr., 1981-86, Baker & Daniels, Indpls., 1986—. Bd. dirs. Everybody's Oil Corp., Anderson, Ind. Bd. dirs. S. Madison Cmty. Found., Pendleton, Ind. Mem. Ind. Bar Assn. (chmn. labor law sect. 1981-82). Republican. Office: 300 N Meridian St Ste 2700 Indianapolis IN 46204-1750 Office Phone: 317-237-1316. E-mail: dwmiller@bakerd.com.

**MILLER, DAVID WILLIAM,** historian, educator; b. Coudersport, Pa., July 9, 1940; s. Arthur Charles and Kathryn Marie (Long) M.; m. Margaret Vick Richardson, Aug. 22, 1964; 1 child, Roberta Neal. BA, Rice U., 1962; MA, U. Wis., 1963; PhD, U. Chgo., 1968. Instr. history Carnegie Mellon U., Pitts., 1967-68, assoc. prof., 1968-73, assoc. prof., 1973-80, prof., 1980—. Adj. prof. religious studies U. Pitts., 1998—. Author: Church, State and Nation in Ireland, 1898-1921, 1973, Queen's English Ulster Loyalism in Historical Perspective, 1978; editor: Peep o'Day Boys and Defenders: Selected Documents on the Disturbances in County Armagh, 1784-1796, 1990; co-editor: Piety and Power in Ireland, 1760-1960, 2000; assoc. editor: Oxford Dictionary of National Biography, 2004, Encyclopedia of Irish History and Culture, 2004; prin. developer: (interactive atlas) Great American History Machine, 1994. Sr. research fellow Inst. Irish Studies Queen's U., Belfast, Northern Ireland, 1975-76. Mem. Am. Conf. for Irish Studies. Democrat. Presbyterian. Avocations: walking, singing. Office: Carnegie Mellon Univ Dept of History Schenley Park Pittsburgh PA 15213 Office Phone: 412-268-2953. Business E-Mail: dwmiller@cmu.edu.

**MILLER, DAWN L.,** composition literature educator; d. John Merritt and Cora Armenda (LaRue) Hyndman; m. Louis J. Miller, June 11, 1966; 1 child, Daniel Louis. BS, St. Mary-of-the-Woods, 1963; MS in Edn., St. Francis U., 1971; MA, Ind. U., Ft. Wayne, 1994; cert. in organ, Notre Dame U., 2000. Profl. life tchg. lic. Ind. Tchr. St. Vincent Sch., Ft. Wayne, 1964—67, St. Joseph Sch., Garrett, Ind., 1974—90; tchr. Hebrew scriptures Bishop Luers H.S., Ft. Wayne, 1990—91; adj. faculty Ivy Tech. State Coll., Ft. Wayne, 1991—96; adj. faculty composition lit. Ind. U.-Purdue U., Ft. Wayne, 1992—. Nominee Ind. Tchr. of Yr., Diocese of Ft. Wayne-South Bend, 1990. Mem. AAUP. Democrat. Roman Catholic. Avocations: piano, organ. Office: Ind Univ Purdue Univ 2101 Coliseum Blvd Fort Wayne IN 46805 Business E-Mail: millerd@ipfw.edu.

**MILLER, DAWN MARIE,** retired meteorologist; b. Hartford, Conn., Sept. 17, 1963; d. Eugene E. Miller and Audrey E. (Flagg) Laurel; m. Dennis James Miller, Sept. 9, 1989; children: Zackarey, Amanda. BS in Meteorology, SUNY, Oneonta, 1985. Customer support specialist WSI Corp., Bedford, Mass., 1985-87, from media TV mktg. to product mktg. specialist-data svcs. Billerica, Mass., 1987-97, sr. meteorologist, product mktg. specialist, 1997-99, sr. meteorologist, assoc. product mgr., 1999—2001, sr. meteorologist, media mktg. and promotion, 2001—03, etc., 2004; salon coord. Shear Class, LLC, Hudson, NH, 2005—. Mem.: Nat. Weather Assn., Am. Meteorol. Soc., Am. Hort. Soc., Nature Conservancy, Nat. Audubon Soc., Nat. Arbor Day Found., Oneonta Alumni Assn. Republican. Episcopalian. Avocations: meteorology, astronomy, photography, gardening, bird watching. Home: 37 Wren Dr Litchfield NH 03052-2540 E-mail: dawn.miller@gmail.com.

**MILLER, DEANE GUYNES,** salon and cosmetic studio owner; b. El Paso, Tex., Jan. 12, 1927; d. James Tillman and Margaret (Brady) Guynes; m. Richard George Miller, Apr. 12, 1947; children: J. Michael, Marcia Deane. Degree in bus. adminstrn., U. Tex., El Paso, 1949. Owner four Merle Norman Cosmetic Studios, El Paso, 1967-96; pres. The Velvet Door, Inc., El Paso, 1967-96. Pres., bd. dirs. YWCA, 1967; v.p. Sun Bowl Assn., 1970; bd. dirs. El Paso Symphony Assn.; bd. dirs., treas. El Paso Mus. Art, trustee, 1990, pres., 1990—93; chmn. bd. El Paso Internat. Airport; bd. dirs., sec. Armed Svc. YMCA, 1987, 1st v.p., 1990; trustee Internat. Mus. Art, 1999, pres., 2003, 2004—05. Named Outstanding Woman field of civic endeavor El Paso Herald Post. Mem. Women's C. of C. (pres. 1969), Pan Am. Round Table (dir., pres. 1987), Internat. Assn. for Visual Arts (v.p. 1998, 2000), Internat. Mus. Art (pres. 2004-05) Home: 1 Silent Crest Dr El Paso TX 79902-2160 Office: 1211 Montana Ave El Paso TX 79902

**MILLER, DECATUR HOWARD,** lawyer; b. Balt., June 29, 1932; s. Lawrence Vernon and Katherine Louise (Baum) M.; m. Sally Burnam Smith, Nov. 23, 1963; 1 dau., Clemence Mary Katherine. BA, Yale U., 1954; LL.B., Harvard U., 1959. Bar: Md. 1959. Assoc. Piper & Marbury, Balt., 1959-62, 1963-66, ptnr., 1967-94, ptnr. emeritus, 1995—, mng. ptnr., 1974-87, chmn., 1987-94; Md. Securities commr., 1962-63. Bd. dirs. Mercantile Funds. Trustee Enoch Pratt Free Libr., 1975—2003, v.p., 1977—85, pres., 1985—89; trustee Calvert Sch., Balt., 1976—89, pres., 1982—87; trustee Walters Art Gallery, Balt., 1987—91; bd. sponsors Sellinger Sch. Bus. and Mgmt. Loyola Coll., 1990—98; active Mayor's Bus. Adv. Coun., 1993—99; hd. vis. U. Md. Balt. County, 1994—2000; bus. sch. adv. coun. Morgan State U., 1994—96; chmn. Equal Justice Coun., 1999—2003; bd. dirs. Balt. Symphony Orch., 1970—, v.p., 1978—86, 1988—90, pres., 1990—92, life dir., 2002—; bd. dirs. United Way Ctrl. Md., 1988—91, The Leadership, 1990—93, Empower Balt. Mgmt. Corp., 1995—, Coll. Bound Found., 1990—2001, chmn., 1994—96; bd.dirs. Greater Balt. Com., 1988—96, chmn., 1992—94; bd. dirs. U. Md. Found., 2000—03. With U.S. Army, 1954—56. Mem. Md. Bar Assn., Am. Law Inst., Am. Bar Found., Md. Bar Found., Elkridge Club, Ctr. Club, Elizabethan Club, Lawyers Round Table. Home: 3704 N Charles St Apt 1305 Baltimore MD 21218 Personal E-mail: dhm26@mindspring.com.

**MILLER, DENNIS,** comedian; b. Pitts., Nov. 3, 1953; m. Ali Espley, April 10, 1988; 2 children, Holden, Marlon. BA, Point Park Coll. Stand-up comic, cast mem. Saturday Night Live, 1985-91; prodr., writer, host Dennis Miller Show, 1992; exec. prodr., writer, host Dennis Miller Live, 1994—2002; announcer Monday Night Football, 2000—02; exec. prodr., host Dennis Miller, 2004—05; contbr., Hannity & Colmes Fox News, 2006—. HBO spls. include: Mr. Miller Goes to Washington (also exec. prodr.), 1988, host 13th Annual Young Comedians Show (also prodr., writer), 1989, Black & White, 1990, They Shoot HBO Specials, Don't They? (also exec. prodr.), 1993, Dennis Miller: Citizen Arcane (also exec. prodr.), 1996, Dennis Miller: The Millenium Special-1,000 Years, 100 Laughs, 10 Really Good Ones (also exec. prodr., writer), 1999, Raw Feed (also writer), 2003; host Freedomfest: Nelson Mandela's 70th Birthday Celebration, The America's Choice Awards, 1990, 43d Annual Primetime Emmy Awards Presentation, 1991; albums include The Off-White Album, 1989; actor (films) Disclosure, 1994, The Net, 1995, Tales From the Crypt Presents: Bordello of Blood, 1996, Murder at 1600 Pennsylvania Avenue, 1997, Joe Dirt, 2001; TV appearances include Sam Kinison: NewsRadio, 1995, Why Did We Laugh?, 1998, Saturday Night Live: The Best of Phil Hartman, 1998, The Best of Chris Farley, 1998, Bad Boys of Saturday Night Live, 1998; (video) The Best of Mike Myers, 1998, 25th Anniversary, 1999, SportsCenter, 2000, Primetime Glick, 2001, Boston Public, 2003, The View, 2004; author: The Rants, 1996, Ranting Again, 1998, I Rant Therefore I Am, 2000, The Rant Zone: An All-Out Blitz Against Bush League Politics, Twisted Child Stars, Soul-Sucking Jobs and People Who Eat Their Jobs, 2001. Recipient Best Writing Emmy award for a Variety/Music Program for Dennis Miller Live, 1994, 1995, 1996, 1998. Office: Fox New Network LLC 1211 Ave Americas New York NY 10036*

**MILLER, DENNIS EDWARD,** health medical executive; b. Detroit, Dec. 21, 1951; m. Deborah Ann Keith, Feb. 12, 1977. BS, Austin Peay State U., 1973; MBA, U. South Fla., 1981. CPA. Chief exec. officer Hosp. Corp. of Am., Bennettsville, SC, 1976-84; div. v.p. Westworld Community Healthcare, Waco, Tex., 1984-86; group v.p. Nat. Healthcare, Inc., Dothan, Ala., 1986-87; COO Healthcare Connections, Brentwood, Tenn., 1988; cons. VHA Physician Svcs., Inc., Dallas, 1988-90; asst. adminstr., CFO Clarksville (Tenn.) Meml. Hosp., 1990; Franklin, Tenn., 1990; sr. v.p., COO Eastside Ventures, Inc., Birmingham, Ala., 1990-93; sr. v.p. Ea. Health System, Inc., Birmingham, Ala., 1990-93; CEO Williamson Med. Ctr., Franklin, 2002—. Chmn. Minority Leadership Task Force, Ea. Health System, Inc., 1994-95. Sec. Ala. Health Svcs. Bd.; mem. Literacy Coun. Ala., Ala. Hosp. Assn. State Legis. Com., future directions com.; chmn. Birmingham Regional Healthcare Exec. Forum; chmn. friends of scouting campaign Boy Scouts Am., 1996; mem. Franklin Land Use Steering Com. subcom., Leadership Franklin, 2002, Franklin Tomorrow, Williamson 25, 2004, 05, Franklin Bus. Leadership Coun., 2006, Hosp. Alliance Tenn., 2006, Tenn. Hosp. Ass., 2006; chmn. Healthcare Exec. Forum Mid. Tenn., 2006; mem. coun. Boy Scouts Mid. Tenn., 2006; mem. archives and mus. com. Williamson County, 2006. Fellow Am. Coll. Healthcare Execs. (chmn diplomate credentials com., pres. mid. Tenn. chpt. 2006, Ala. Regent's award for exec. excellence 1995), Hosp. Fin. Mgmt. Assn. (Follmer Bronze Merit award for outstanding svc.); mem. AICPA, Tenn. Soc. CPAs, Ala. Soc. CPAs (chmn. state legis. com.), Ala. Hosp. Assn. (future directions com.), Birmingham C. of C. (chmn. membership com.), Birmingham East Rotary Club (pres., chmn. membership com.), Leadership Franklin Class 2003, Franklin Noon Rotary Club, Mensa, Shriners, Masons, Birmingham Touchdown Club, Sigma Chi Assn. alumni. hunting, fishing, gardening, antiques. Office: Williamson Med Ctr 2021 Carothers Rd Franklin TN 37067 Office Phone: 615-435-5151.

**MILLER, DENYCE KARLINA,** tax specialist; b. Chgo., July 2, 1963; d. Sidney Miller, Vera Miller. BS in Commerce, DePaul U., 2001, M in Acctg., 2002. CPA Ill. Tax cons. Denyce Miller Tax Svc., Bellwood, Ill., 2001—; postal employee devel. tng. technician USPS, Chgo., 1985—2005, auditor office inspector gen., 2005—. Mem. fin. com. Am. Postal Workers Union, Chgo., 2001—03. Author: Blind Love, 1996. Coord. hearing impaired Am. Postal Workers Union, Chgo., 1992—94, dir. ctk. craft, 2001—03, coord. hearing impaired, 2001—03; combined fed. campaign key worker USPS, Chgo., 1989. Recipient Taekwondo First Dan award, Kukkiwon World Taekwondo Hdqs., 1996. Mem.: AICPA (Scholarship award 2001), Inst. Mgmt. Accts. (Scholarship award 2001), Ill. Cert. Pub. Accts. Soc. Democrat. Mem. Apostolic Ch. Avocation: Tae Kwon Do. Home: 1012 Marshall Bellwood IL 60104-2322 Office Phone: 708-268-1554. Home Fax: 708-544-8419. Personal E-mail: karlina2@yahoo.com, dmtaxes@hotmail.com.

**MILLER, DIANE ILLIAN,** cultural organization administrator; b. Englewood, N.J., Apr. 19, 1952; d. Norman and Grace Estelle (Clark) Illian; m. Walter Frederick Miller, Jan. 31, 1976; children: Jeremy S., Brian K. BA in Comm. cum laude, Glassboro State Coll., NJ, 1974. Staff writer The Gloucester County Times, Woodbury, NJ, 1974—77; presch. tchr. Atco Children's Program, 1984—90; svcs. coord. Atlantic Heritage Ctr., Somers Point, NJ, 2002—06. Freelance writer The Bulletin, Phila., 1978, The Mainland Jour., Pleasantville, NJ, 1992, Hammonton, NJ, 2002. Author: A Century of History, 1986; editor: The Atlantic County Hist. Soc. Yearbook, 2002, 2003, 2004. Mem. choir United Meth. Ch., Absecon, NJ, 1998—, comm. liaison, 2002—. Recipient Hon. mention, NJ Press Assn., 1976. Avocations: reading, camping, travel, genealogy.

**MILLER, DIANE WILMARTH,** retired human resources director; b. Clarinda, Iowa, Mar. 12, 1940; d. Donald and Floy Pauline (Madden) W.; m. Robert Nolen Miller, Aug. 21, 1965; children: Robert Wilmarth, Anne Elizabeth. *Husband Robert N. Miller, BA 1962 Cornell College, JD 1965*

*University of Colorado Law School, Boulder, is currently a partner in the law firm Perkins Coie in Denver. He is a past U.S. Attorney for the District of Colorado. Son Robert Wilmarth Miller, BA 1996 Hastings College, JD 1999 University of Wyoming College of Law, Laramie, is currently employed as a deputy district attorney in the DA's office in Greeley, Colorado. Daughter, Anne Elizabeth Miller, BA 1999 University of Denver, was awarded Denver University's prestigious Pioneer Award and is currently a State Farm agent in Westminster, Colorado.* AA, Colo. Women's Coll., 1960; BBA, U. Iowa, 1962; MA, U. No. Colo., 1994. Cert. tchr., Colo.: vocat. credential, Colo.; cert. sr. profl. in human resources; lic. Colo. Ins. Prodr. Sec.-counselor U. S.C. Rep., Myrtle Beach AFB, 1968-69; instr. Coastal Carolina Campus U. S.C., Conway, 1967-69; tchr. bus. Poudre Sch. Dist. R-1, Ft. Collins, Colo., 1970-71; travel cons. United Bank Travel Svc., Greeley, Colo., 1972-74; dir. human resources Aims C.C., Greeley, 1984—2001, ret., 2001. Instr. Aims CC, 1972—89; bd. dirs. U. No. Colo. Found., Greeley, 2003—. Bd. trustees 1st Congl. Ch., Greeley, 2005—. Mem.: Philanthropic Ednl. Orgn. (pres. 1988—89), Women's Panhellenic Assn. (pres. 1983—84), Questers (pres. 2002—04), WTK Club (pres. 2006—), Scroll and Fan Club (pres. 1985—86). Home: 3530 Wagon Trail Pl Greeley CO 80634-3405

**MILLER, DON ROBERT,** surgeon, educator; b. Highland, Kans., July 6, 1925; s. Pleasant V. and Lucy Anna (Hammond) M.; m. Geraldine Ellen Nelson, Sept. 6, 1947; children: Don R., Laurie, Todd, Marcia, Kristen, Felicia. AB, Southwestern Coll., 1944; MD, U. Kans., 1948. Mem. faculty U. Kans., Kansas City, 1957-73, prof. surgery, 1970-73, U. Calif. Irvine, 1973-92, prof. emeritus, 1992—, vice chmn., chief dept. surgery, pres. med. staff, 1989-91. Dir. surgery Orange County (Calif.) Med. Center, 1973-77. Contbr. articles to profl. jours. Gov. 1988-92. Served with USNR, 1943-45, 50-52. Spl. research fellow Zurich, Switzerland, 1965-66 Fellow A.C.S., Am. Coll. Cardiology; mem. Am. Soc. Univ. Surgeons, Am. Surg. Assn., Soc. Vascular Surgery, Am. Assn. Thoracic Surgery, Am., Central, Western surg. assns., Internat. Cardiovascular Soc., Sigma Xi, Alpha Omega Alpha. Achievements include research on extracorporeal circulation, myocardial function. Home: 743 Louisiana St Lawrence KS 66044-2339

**MILLER, DON WILSON,** nuclear engineering educator; b. Westerville, Ohio, Mar. 16, 1942; s. Don Paul and Rachel (Jones) M.; m. Mary Catherine Thompson, June 25, 1966; children: Amy Beth, Stacy Catherine, Paul Wilson Thompson. BS in Physics, Miami U., Oxford, Ohio, 1964, MS in Physics, 1966; MS in Nuc. Engring., Ohio State U., 1970, PhD in Nuc. Engring., 1971. Rsch. assoc. Ohio State U., Columbus, 1966-68, univ. fellow, 1968-69, tchg. assoc., 1969-71, asst. prof. nuc. engring., 1971—74, assoc. prof., 1974-80, chmn. nuc. engring. program, 1977-97, prof., 1980—2004, dir. nuc. reactor lab., 1977—2002, prof. emeritus, 2004—, dir. Advanced Sys. and Safety, 2005—. Sec., treas. Cellar Lumber Co., Westerville, Ohio, 1972-84, 85—; cons. Monsanto Rsch. Corp., Miamisburg, Ohio, 1979, NRC, Washington, 1982-84, 99—, Scantech Corp., Santa Fe, 1984-95, Neoprobe Corp., Columbus, 1990, Electric Power Rsch. Inst., Palo Alto, Calif., 1992-94; mem. adv. com. on reactor safeguards Nuc. Regulatory Commn., 1995-99. Patentee in field; contbr. articles to profl. jours. Mem. Westerville Bd. Edn., 1976-91, pres., 1977-78, 86-88; mem. Ohio Sch. Bd.'s Assn., Columbus, 1976-91; mem. fed. rels. com. Nat. Sch. Bd.'s Assn., Washington, 1984-86. With USAR, 1960-68. Named Tech. Person of Yr. Columbus Tech. Coun., 1979; named to All Region Bd. Ohio Sch. Bd's Assn., 1981, 86, Westerville South H.S. Hall of Fame, 1996; recipient Achievement award Mid Ohio Chpt. Multiple Sclerosis Soc., 1988. Fellow Am. Nuc. Soc. (chmn edn. divsn. 1986-87, bd. dirs. 1989-91, chair human factors divsn. 1993-94, v.p./pres. elect 1995-96, pres. 1996-97, Cert. Appreciation 1991); mem. IEEE (sr. mem.), Am. Soc. Engring. Edn. (chmn. nuc. engring. divsn. 1978-79, Glenn Murphy award 1989), Nuc. Dept. Heads Orgn. (chmn. 1985-86), Westerville Edn. Assn. (Friend of Edn. award 1992), Rotary (Courtright Cmty. Svc. award 1989), Kiwanis, Hoover Sailing Club, Alpha Nu Sigma (chmn. 1991-93). Avocations: American history, travel, amateur radio. Home: Friendship Village 5675 Ponderosa Dr Columbus OH 43231 Office: Ohio State U Dept Mech Engring Nuc Engring Program EA30 Scott Lab 201 W 19th Ave Columbus OH 43210-1142 Office Phone: 614-292-7979. Business E-Mail: miller.68@osu.edu.

**MILLER, DONALD EUGENE,** lawyer; b. Providence, Mar. 20, 1947; s. Meyer Samuel and Beatrice (Wattman) M.; m. Deborah Neary Miller, Mar. 14, 1987. BA, Boston U., 1968; JD, U. Pa., 1972. Law clk. Assoc. Justice Alfred H. Joslin Supreme Ct., Providence, 1972-73; prin. lawyer Temkin, Merolla & Zurier, Providence, 1973-81, Temkin & Miller, Ltd., Providence, 1981-91; exec. v.p., gen. counsel, corp. sec. The Fairchild Corp., McLean, Va., 1991—. Author: (treatise) Buying and Selling a Small Business, 1987. Mem. RI Bar, Mass. Bar, DC Bar. Avocation: dog breeding and exhibiting. Home: 10704 Riverwood Dr Potomac MD 20854-1332 Office: The Fairchild Corp 1750 Tysons Blvd Mc Lean VA 22102

**MILLER, DONALD EUGENE,** retired air traffic controller; b. Twin Falls, Idaho, Aug. 17, 1931; s. James Alonzo and Goldia Belle Miller; m. Betsy Jean Doty; children: Michelle Anne, Mihak Lynne. Studied, Aeronautical Acad., Okla. City, 1954—56. Lic. pilot FAA, 1977. Air traffic controller FAA, Des Moines, 1956—68, St. Louis, 1968—70; instr., air traffic control FAA Acad., Oklahoma City, 1970—74; automation specialist, air traffic control FAA Tower, Portland, Oreg., 1974—75, mgr., air traffic control Hillsboro, Oreg., 1975—77; liasion officer, air traffic control Marine Corps. Air Station, Yuma, Ariz., 1977—80; air traffic quality assurance FAA Regional Hdqs., L.A., 1980—81, air traffic internat. br., 1985—90; air traffic mgr. FAA Radar Facility, Bakersfield, Calif., 1981—85; ret., 1990. Cons. Hughes Aircraft Fullerton, Calif., 1991 Author, (manual) Automated Radar Terminal System, 1971. County treas. Union County, Creston, Iowa, 1953—55. Staff sgt. USAF, 1949—52, Korea. Mem.: Air Traffic Control Assn. (bd. mem. 1980—82). Avocations: writing, golf, dance, travel. Home: 4963 Poseidon Way Oceanside CA 92056

**MILLER, DONALD LANE,** publishing executive; b. Pitts., May 14, 1918; s. Donald Edwin and Arvilla (Lane) M.; A.B., Kenyon Coll., 1940; Russian interpreter cert. U. Colo., 1946; postgrad. U. Pitts., 1947-48; m. Norma Reno, Feb. 2, 1951. Reporter, Pitts. Sun-Telegraph, 1940-42, Washington Post, 1946; with pub. rels. dept. Westinghouse Electric Corp., Pitts., 1947-51; reporter Billboard and Tide, 1953; pub. rels. dir. Nat. Agrl. Chem. Assn., Washington, 1954-58; sec. Donald Lerch & Co., Washington, 1958-61; pres. Asso. Pub. Rels. Counselors, Washington, 1961-77; chmn. Braddock Comm., Inc.; chmn. emeritus Children's Aid Internat.; exec. dir. All Am. Conf., Washington, 1962-75. Editor GOP Nationalities News, Rep. Nat. Com., 1960; pub. rels. nationalities div. Rep. Nat. Com., 1964; coord. life underwriters sect. Citizens for Nixon-Agnew, 1968; co-pub. Cmty. Forum, 1996-2002. Served from ensign to lt., USNR, 1942-46; from lt. to lt. comdr., 1951-53. Decorated Knight of Europe. Mem. English Speaking Union, SAR, Phi Beta Kappa, Delta Tau Delta. Clubs: Nat. Press. Author: Strategy for Conquest, 1966, George to George: 200 Years of Presidential Quotations, 1989, Call of the Northern Neck, 1992. Office: PO Box 710720 Herndon VA 20171-0720

**MILLER, DONALD LESESSNE,** publishing executive; b. N.Y.C., Jan. 10, 1932; s. John H. and Mamie (Johnson) M.; m. Ann Davie, Aug. 12, 1951 (div. 1981); children: Lynn, Mark; m. Gail Aileen Wallace, June 27, 1981. BA, U. Md., 1967; cert., Harvard Grad. Sch. Bus. Adminstrn., 1969. Enlisted U.S. Army, 1948, advanced through grades to maj., 1966, ret., 1968; spl. asst. to pres., mgr. corp. recruitment Inmont Corp., N.Y.C., 1970-71; dep. asst. sec. def. U.S. Dept. Def., Washington, 1971-73; v.p. personnel mgmt. Columbia U., N.Y.C., 1973-78; dir. personnel devel. and adminstrn. Internat. Paper, N.Y.C., 1978-79; v.p. employee relations Consol. Edison N.Y., N.Y.C., 1979-86, Dow Jones & Co., Inc., N.Y.C., 1986-95; CEO, pub. Our World News. Author: An Album of Black Americans in the Armed Forces, 1969. Chmn. bd. emeritus Associated Black Charities, N.Y.C., 1982-94. Decorated Legion of Merit;

decorated Army Commendation Medal; recipient Disting. Civilian Service medal Dept. Def., 1973, Disting. Alumnus award U. Md., 1977. Mem. Alpha Sigma Lambda, Pi Sigma Alpha, Phi Kappa Phi, Alpha Phi Alpha, Sigma Pi Phi.

**MILLER, DONALD MUXLOW,** accountant; b. Luverne, Minn., Feb. 21, 1924; s. Henry Clay and Mildred Eva (Muxlow) M.; m. Eunice Jean Gibson, Feb. 19, 1944 (dec. Feb. 17, 2004); children: SueRilla M., Donna Jean Eichten, Patsy Ann Pushee. Student, Metro State, St. Paul, 1973-84. CPA. Mgr. Hines & Paulus, CPA, Worthington, Minn., 1952-65; commandant Minn. Vets. Home, Mpls., 1965-68; prin. D.M. Miller, Acct., 1968-70, 76-78; asst. sec. Minn. State Senate, St. Paul, 1970-72; comptr. Western Oil Co., Mpls., 1972-76; commr. Dept. VA, State of Minn., St. Paul, 1978-81; pres. D.M. Miller & Assoc., Ltd., Mpls., 1981-97; chief exec. officer MARD, Inc., Mpls., 1985-95; v.p. Miller, Micketts & Assocs Ltd., Mpls., 1993-96; pres. D.M. Miller Ltd., Worthington, 1997—2004. Trustee Heart Professorship Found., 1987-91; pres. Legionnaire Sch. Patrol Camp, Brainerd, Minn., 1963-64; pres. Big Island Vets. Camp, Mpls., 1986-88. 2d lt. USAAC, 1942—46, 1st lt. USAF, 1951—52. Recipient Volunteer of the Year award Kidney Found., 1975. Mem. VFW, Minn. Assn. Pub. Accts. (dist. 2002—04), Nat. Assn. State Vets. Homes (hon. life mem., reg. v.p. 1967-68), Nat. Assn. State Dirs. Vets Affairs (reg. v.p. 1978-79), Minn. Gaming Assn. (exec. sec. 1987-92), Am. Legion (hon life mem., comdr. Minn. 1962-63, nat. com. chmn. 1980-84, pres. Minn. Found. Bd. 1990-91). Presbyterian.

**MILLER, DONALD ROSS,** management consultant; b. Huntington, N.Y., Aug. 5, 1927; s. George Everett and Ethel May (Ross) M.; m. Constance Higgins, 1948 (div. 1955); children: Donald Ross Jr., Cynthia Lynn, Candace Lee; m. Janet Heyman Behr, Apr. 15, 1965; children: Jeffrey Lawrence, Wendy Lorraine. BS/BEA, MIT, 1950. Cert. mgmt. cons. Inst. of Mgmt. Cons. Staff engr. Stop & Shop, Inc., Boston, 1950-56; v.p., dir. Cresap, McCormick and Paget, Inc., N.Y.C., 1956-76; mng. dir. Donald R. Miller Mgmt. Cons., Palm Desert, Calif., 1977—2005. Pres., CEO Carl Fischer Inc., N.Y.C., 1996; chmn. bd. dirs. Nash Finch Co., Mpls., 1995-2000; bd. dirs. Michael Anthony Jewelers, Inc., Mt. Vernon, N.Y., Western Horizon Resorts, Inc., Gunnison, Colo. Author: Management Practices Manual, 3 vols., 1963, (booklet) Management of Managerial Resources, 1969. Bd. dirs. Queens Mus. Art, Flushing, N.Y., 1982-93; pres. Lexington House, Forest Hills, 1984-2001; mem. MIT Alumni Adv. Coun., Cambridge, Mass., 1955-75; bd. govs. Alumni Ctr. N.Y.C., 1965-75, chmn. 1968-72; bd. dirs. Vol. Cons. Group, N.Y., 1969-79; trustee Queens Theatre in the Park, Flushing Meadow, N.Y., 1976-82; mem. vestry St. Margaret's Episcopal Ch., Palm Desert, Calif., 2003—05, sr. warden, 2004—05. With U.S. Maritime Svc., 1945-46, ETO, U.S. Army, 1946-48. Mem. Nat. Assn. Corp. Dirs., Inst. Mgmt. Cons., Sky Club. Episcopal. Avocations: tennis, reading. Home and Office: 73850 Fairway Dr #10 Palm Desert CA 92260 E-mail: donmilleo@aol.com.

**MILLER, DOROTHY ANNE SMITH,** retired cytogenetics educator; b. N.Y.C., Oct. 20, 1931; d. John Philip and Anna Elizabeth (Hellberg) Smith; m. Orlando Jack Miller, July 10, 1954; children: Richard L., Cynthia K., Karen A. BA in Chemistry magna cum laude, Wilson Coll., Chambersburg, Pa., 1952; PhD in Biochemistry, Yale U., 1957. Rsch. assoc. dept. ob-gyn Columbia U., N.Y.C., 1964-72; from rsch. assoc. to asst. prof. dept. human genetics-devel., 1973-85; prof. dept. molecular biology and genetics Wayne State U., Detroit, 1985-94, prof. dept. pathology, 1985-96, prof. Ctr. for Molecular Medicine and Genetics, 1994-96. Vis. scientist clin. and population cytogenetics unit Med. Rsch. Coun., Edinburgh, Scotland, 1983-84; vis. prof. dept. genetics and molecular biology U. la Sapienza, Rome, 1988; vis. disting. fellow La Trobe U., Melbourne, Australia, 1992. Contbr. numerous articles to sci. jours. Grantee March of Dimes Birth Defects Found., 1974-93, NSF, 1983-84. Mem. Am. Soc. Human Genetics, Genetics Soc. Am., Genetics Soc. Australia, Phi Beta Kappa. Presbyterian. Home: 19365 Cypress Ridge Terr #817 Lansdowne VA 20176 Personal E-mail: damiller@smartneighborhood.net.

**MILLER, DOUGLAS LINN,** lawyer; b. Reading, Pa., Nov. 17, 1950; BA, MA, Yale U., 1972; JD, Harvard U., 1975. Bar: Ga. 1975. Lawyer Troutman Sanders, Atlanta, 1975—99, mng. ptnr. having oversight of the Project Develop. and Fin. Practice Group Hong Kong, China, 1997—99; sr. v.p., gen. counsel, chief compliance officer Mirant Corp., Atlanta, 1999—. Miller acted as lead counsel in state regulatory rate case proceedings, as well as fuel cost recovery and demandside cost recovery riders, prudence reviews of nuclear power plant construction, nuclear power plant ops., fossil plant construction, and coal procurement practices. Mem. ABA, State Bar Ga. Office: Mirant Corp 1155 Perimeter Ctr W Atlanta GA 30338 Office Phone: 678-579-7924. Business E-Mail: douglas.miller@mirant.com.

**MILLER, DUANE KING,** health and beauty care company executive; b. NYC, Mar. 1, 1931; s. Henry Charles and Helen Marion (King) M.; m. Nancy L. Longley, June 6, 1954; children: Cheryl L., Duane L. AB in Econs. and Fin., NYU, 1953. V.p. mktg. Warner-Chilcott divsn. Warner Lambert Co., Morris Plains, NJ, 1970-72, pres. divsn., 1973-77; exec. v.p. Am. Optical div., pres. Am. Optical Internat div. Warner Lambert Co., Southbridge, Mass., 1978; pres. biol. and proprietary products divsn., v.p. Revlon Health Care Group, Revlon Corp., Tuckahoe, NY, 1978-80, pres. ethical, proprietary and vision care divsns., 1981-82, corp. v.p. parent co., 1982, pres. Revlon Health Care Group, 1983-92, corp. exec. v.p. parent co., 1984-92, pres. Revlon Health Beauty Care and Internat. Group, 1988-92, ret., 1992; pres. DKL Properties, health care cons., Promedex Techs., 1992—. Author: (with others) Marketing Planning for Chief Executives and Planners, 1966. Mem. Rep. Nat. Com. Mem. Princeton Club N.Y., Masons, Shriners. Office: 483 Rte 520 Marlboro NJ 07746 Home: 9 Winding Way Greenville DE 19807

**MILLER, DWIGHT MERRICK,** archivist, historian; b. Keosauqua, Iowa, July 25, 1932; s. Leo Albert and Beryl Irene Miller; m. Frances Florine Olney, Nov. 19, 1961 (dec. Sept. 1977); 1 child, Dianne; m. Judith Spencer, 1979 (div. 1988); m. Pauline K. Leaverton, 1999. BA, U. Iowa, Iowa City, 1959; MA, Truman State U., Kirksville, 1961; attended, The American U., Washington, 1963-64. Asst. archivist Manuscript Divsn., Library of Congress, Washington, 1961-64; sr. archivist Herbert Hoover Presdl. Libr., West Branch, 1964-99. Compiler, state editor: The Public Papers of the Presidents: Herbert Hoover; 1929-1933 (6 vols.), 1974-77; co-editor: Herbert Hoover and Harry S. Truman: A Documentary History, 1992, Historical Materials in the Herbert Hoover Presidential Library, 1996, Herbert Hoover and Franklin D. Roosevelt: A Documentary History, 1998; editor: Laura Ingalls Wilder and the American Frontier: Five Perspectives, 2002. Co-chmn. Iowa Sesquicentennial Commn. Cedar Cty., Tipton, 1995-97. Mem. Herbert Hoover Presdl. Libr. Assn., Friends of the Univ. of Iowa Libraries (adv. bd. 1976-81), Ft. Ticonderoga Assn. (adv. bd. 1991—). Presbyterian. Avocations: book collecting, historical Iowa pottery. Home: 10 Rita Lyn Ct Iowa City IA 52245-3504

**MILLER, DWIGHT RICHARD,** professional hair care industry executive, cosmetologist, consultant; b. Johnstown, Pa., Jan. 24, 1943; Grad., Comer & Doran Sch., San Diego; DSci. (hon.), London Inst. for Applied Rsch., 1973. Cert. aromatherapist; lic. cosmetologist.; instr.; Brit. Mastercraftsman. Styles dir. Marinello-Comer, Hollywood, Calif., 1965-67; expert Pivot Point Internat., Chgo., 1967-68; styles dir. Lapins, L.A., 1969; dir. Redken, L.A., 1970, Vidal Sassoon, London, 1971-74; world amb. Pivot Point, New Zealand and Australia, 1974-75, internat. artistic dir. Chgo., 1975-78; internat. dir., co-founder Hair Artists Inst. & Registry, 1968-81; internat. artistic dir. Zotos Internat., Darien, Conn., 1981-87, Matrix Essentials, Inc., Solon, Ohio, 1987-92; bd. dirs., founder, v.p. creative Anasazi Exclusive Salon Products, Inc., Dubuque, Iowa, 1992-96; pres. Anasazi Salon Sys., Santa Fe, 1996-98; cons., 1998—; pres. Sahag Products, 2004—; owner Salon Sante Fe, 2004—. Judge hairdressing competitions Norwegian Masters, Australian Nat. Champions, N.Am. Hairstyling Awards; pres. Intercrimpers, London, 1974-75; celebrity stylist Doris Day, Juliet Prowse, Cindy Crawford, Monica Setes; cons. in field. Author: Sculptic Cutting Pivot Point 75, Prismatics, 1983, Milady's Standard System of Salon Skills, 1998, Amos Master Cutting

System, 2000; prodr.(and dir.): (documentaries, 15), (numerous tech. and industry videos); contbr. articles and photographs to popular mags.; mem. editl. bd.: Shades mag., Launchpad mag. With USMC, 1960—64. Named Artistic Dir. Yr. Am. Salon mag., Intercoiffure Educator of the Century; presented with Order of White Elephant, 1976; recipient London Gold Cup for Best Presentation London Beauty Festival, 1982, Dr. Everett G. McDonough award for Excellence in Permanent Waving, World Master award Art and Fashion Group, 1992, N.Am. Hairstylist of the Yr. award, 2000. Mem. Cercle des Arts et Techniques de la Coiffure, Intercoiffure, Haute Coiffure Franchaise, Soc. Cosmetic Chemists, Hair Artists Great Britain, Internat. Assn. Trichogists, Nat. Cosmetologists Assn. (HairAmerica, cert. instr.), Am. Soc. Phytotherapy and Aromatherapy, HairChicago (hon.), Art and Fashion Group (pres. 1993), 'Dressers MC (pres. 1990—), London's Alternative Hair Club (patron), Salon Assn., Am. Beauty Assn., Profl. Beauty Assn., Alternative Hair Club North Am. (hon. pres. 2003—). Achievements include development of several profl. product lines including Vidal Sassoon-London, Design Freedom, Bain de Terre, Ultra Bond, Vavoom!, Systeme Biolage, Anasazi, Sheer Blonde. Home and Office: 707 Don Gaspar Ave Santa Fe NM 87505-2629 Business E-Mail: dwight@dwightmiller.com.

**MILLER, EDWARD DORING,** anesthesiologist, hospital administrator, dean; b. Rochester, NY, Feb. 1, 1943; s. Edward D. and Natalie (Sidam) Miller; m. Leslie Coombs, June 15, 1968 (dec. Apr. 1987); children: Sara Davenport, Katherine Coombs; m. Lynne Root, Apr. 30, 1988; children: Lawrence Root, Elizabeth Root Fusco. AB, Ohio Wesleyan U., 1964; MD, U. Rochester, 1968. Diplomate Am. Bd. Anesthesiology, Am. Coll. Anesthesiology; cert. critical care medicine. Surg. intern Univ. Hosp., Boston, 1968-69; anesthesia resident Peter Bent Brigham Hosp., Boston, 1969-71; fellow in physiology Harvard Med. Sch., Boston, 1971-73; dir. anesthesia research Brooke Army Med. Ctr., Ft. Sam Houston, Tex., 1973-75; asst. prof. anesthesiology U. Va. Med. Ctr., Charlottesville, 1975-79, assoc. prof. anesthesiology, 1979-82, prof. anesthesiology, 1982-83, prof. anesthesiology, surgery, 1983-86; E.M. Papper prof. anesthesiology, chmn. dept. Columbia U. Coll. Physicians and Surgeons, N.Y.C., 1986-94; Mark C. Rogers prof., chmn. dept. anesthesiology Johns Hopkins U., Balt., 1994—, interim dean med. faculty, vp. medicine Sch. of Medicine, 1996-97, dean Sch. of Medicine, 1997—, CEO Sch. of Medicine, 1997—. Sr. scientist physiology, pharmacology Hosp. Necker, Paris, 1981-82; examiner Am. Bd. Anesthesiology; v.p. clin. faculty U. Va., 1983-85, pres. 1985-86. Editor Anesthesia and Analgesia, 1982-92; contbr. numerous articles to profl. jours. Pres. Barracks-Rugby-Preston Neighborhoods, Va., 1977-79; vestry Christ Episc. Ch., Va., 1985-86. Served to maj. M.C., U.S. Army, 1973-75. Recipient Rsch. Career Devel. award Nat. Inst. Gen. Med. Scis., 1978-83; NIH grantee, 1977-87, Inst. Nat. de la Sante et de la Recherche Medicale grantee, 1981-82. Mem. Assn. U. Anesthetists (sec. 1984-87), Am. Soc. Anesthesiologists, Am. Physiol. Soc., Internat. Anesthesia Research Soc. (trustee 1988—), Soc. Critical Care Medicine, Soc. Cardiovascular Anesthesiologists, Assn. Univ. Anesthesiologists (pres. 1990-92), Found. for Anesthesia Edn. and Rsch. (bd. dirs. 1986—), Up Med. Bd. Presbyn. Hosp. Office: Johns Hopkins U Sch Med Adminstrn 733 N Broadway Ste 100 Baltimore MD 21205-2196 Office Phone: 410-955-3180. Business E-Mail: emiller@jhmi.edu.

**MILLER, ELEANOR,** English language and literature educator; b. Mill Valley, Calif. BA with honors, U. Nev., 1966, PhD in English with honors, 1970. Instr. English Valley Coll., San Bernardino, Calif., 1983-84, Crafton Hills Coll., Redlands, Calif., 1984-86, Coll. of the Desert, Palm Springs, Calif., 1986-90; prof. English Composition & Literature So. Nev. C.C., Las Vegas, 1990—. Chair teaching-learning excellence com. So. Nev. C.C., Las Vegas, 1991-94, new faculty mentor, 1995—. Author: English Placement Grading, 1991, CCSN Writing Across the Curriculum, 1994, New Faculty Mentoring, 1997, Teaching Excellence, 1998. Advisor/participant Women's Re-entry Ctr., Palm Springs/Las Vegas, 1989-94; vol. Womyn's Festival Com., U. Nev., Las Vegas, 1994—; mem. adv. bd. Collegiate Press, 1998—. Mem. AAUW, Nat. Coun. Tchrs. English, Nev. State Tchrs. English, Nev. Adult Edn. Assn., Nev. Humanities Com., Mountain Plains Adult Edn. Assn., U. Nev. Alumni Assn., Women in Comm., Phi Kappa Phi. Avocations: reading, travel. Office: So Nev CC 3200 E Cheyenne Ave North Las Vegas NV 89030-4228

**MILLER, ELEANORA GENEVIEVE,** freelance/self-employed poet; b. Gowrie, Iowa, Nov. 17, 1916; d. Alfred Theodore and Jennie Wilhelmina (Carlon) Liljegren; m. Chester Forest Miller, June 1, 1941; children: Carolin Miller Gibson, Loring. BA, Augustana Coll., Rock Island, Ill., 1938; MA, Drake U., 1983. Tchr. English and speech Keota (Iowa) High Sch., 1938-39, Moulton (Iowa) High Sch., 1940-41; reporter Des Moines Register, 1956—; bookkeeper Miller Ins. Ltd., Leon, Iowa, 1980—98; writer pvt. practice, Leon, 1938—. Author: (books of poetry) Poems in Iowa Annual of Lyrical Poetry, 1955, Interviewing the Ghosts, 2001, numerous poems published; winner of over 18 awards for poetry, (book) Interviewing the Ghosts, 2001; editor (newsletter) For Front, 1971-75. Vol. ARC, 1962-73; sec. South Ctrl. Iowa Theatre, Leon, 1978—; mem. Iowa Gov.'s Civil Rights Commn., 1961-65; state chmn. Iowa Citizens for Human Rights, 1965; mem. bd. ch. and society Iowa Conf. United Meth. Ch., 1985-90; lay speaker United Meth. Ch., Creston Dist., 1980—. Mem. VFW Aux. (Iowa state pres 1955-56), Nat. League of Am. Penwomen (br. pres. 1964-66, state pres. 1966-68, 1st pl. lyric poetry 1972), Iowa Poetry Assn. (state pres. 1972-74). Republican. Avocations: vocal music, book collecting. Home: 1405 NW Church St Leon IA 50144-1267

**MILLER, ELLEN S.,** marketing executive; b. Indpls., June 28, 1954; d. Harold Edward and Lilian (Gantner) M. BA, DePauw U., 1976; postgrad., Sch. Visual Arts, N.Y.C., 1981-82. Editorial asst. Daisy mag., N.Y.C., 1976-77; asst. dept. mgr., Christmas hiring mgr. Bloomingdale's, N.Y.C., 1978; sales rep. Rosenthal USA Ltd., N.Y.C., 1979, mktg. asst., 1980-81, dir. mktg. comms., 1982-90; mgr. consumer mktg. Creamer Dickson Basford, Providence, 1990, v.p., 1991-94; prin. E.S. Miller Comm., Providence, 1994—. Instr. Learning Connection. Editor Community Prep. Sch. newsletter, 1993. Trustee Cmty. Prep Sch., Providence, 1993—, mem. exec. com., 1997—. Recipient Bell Ringer award New Eng. Pub. Club, 1992, 93, Iris award N.J. chpt. Internat. Assn. Bus. Communicators, 1993, Silver Quill award Dist. I, 1993, Holland award Ctrl. Mass. Advt. Club, 1997. Mem. Pub. Rels. Soc. Am., Nat. Tabletop Assn. (com. chair 1989), Internat. Tabletop Awards (bd. dirs. 1989), Rotary Club. Republican. Presbyterian. Office Phone: 401-724-3773. E-mail: ellensmiller@att.net.

**MILLER, ELLIOTT CAIRNS,** retired bank executive, lawyer; b. Cambridge, Mass., May 4, 1934; s. James Wilkinson and Mary Elliott (Cairns) M.; m. Mary Killion, July 2, 1960; children: Jonathan Vaill, Stephen Killion. AB, Harvard Coll., 1956; JD, U. Mich., 1961; LLM, Boston U., 1970. Bar: Conn. 1962. Assoc. Robinson & Cole, Hartford, Conn., 1961-66, ptnr., 1967-72; v.p., counsel Svc. for Savs., Hartford, Conn., 1972-73; v.p., 1973-78, exec. v.p., 1978, pres., CEO, dir., 1979-90; pres., CEO Soc. for Savs. Bancorp Inc., 1987-90. Bd. dirs. nat. council Savs. Inst., Washington, 1984-88. Trustee, chmn. Kingswood-Oxford Sch. West Hartford, 1977-87; trustee Coordinating Coun. on Founds., 1987-90; bd. dirs. Downtown Coun., Hartford, 1975-90; trustee Greater Hartford Arts Coun., 1980-88; trustee Wadsworth Atheneum, 1990-99; trustee Hartford Stage Co., 1973-85, 1985—; corporator Hartford Hosp., Inst. of Living; mem. transition com. Conn. State Treas. Denise Napier, 1998-99. With U.S. Army, 1956-58. Mem. Conn. Bar Assn., 21st Century Club (Hartford), Monday Evening Club (Hartford), Dauntless Club (Essex, Conn.), Ferrari Club Am., Bernese Mountain Dog Club. Methodist. Home: 9 Champlain Sq Essex CT 06426-1101 E-mail: soleoak@aol.com.

**MILLER, EMILIE F.,** former state senator, consultant; b. Chgo., Aug. 11, 1936; d. Bruno C. and Etta M. (Senese) Feiza; m. Dean E. Miller; children: Desireé M., Edward C. BSBA, Drake U., 1958. Asst. buyer Jordan Marsh Co., Boston, 1958-60, Carson, Pirie, Scott & Co., 1960-62; dept. mgr., asst. buyer Woodward & Lothrop, Washington, 1962-64; state labor coord. Robb Davis Daliles Joint Campaign; legis. aide Senator Adelard Brandt, Va.,

1980-83; fin. dir. Saslaw for Congress, 1984; legis. cons. Va. Fedn. Bus. Profl. Women, 1986-87, 98-00; senator Va. Gen. Assembly, Richmond, 1988-92; cons. apptd. by Gov. Wilder to bd. dirs. Innovative Tech. Authority, 1992-94, Ctr. for Innovative Tech., 1992-94; cons., 1992—; sr. mgr. Thompson, Cobb, Bazilio & Assocs., 1999—. Bus. tng. seminars, Moscow, Nizhny Novgorod, Russia, 1993, Novgorod, St. Petersburg, 95; cons. in field. Guest editl. writer No. Va. Sun, 1981; host, prodr. weekly TV program, Channel 61. Active State Ctrl. Com. Dem. Party Va., Richmond, 1974—, steering com., 2000—, chair 11th congrl. dist., 2001—; mem. Fairfax County Dem. Com., 1968—, chair, 1976-80, 98-2000, Presdl. Inaugural Com., 1977, 1992 Dem. Nat. Platform Com., Va., Dem. Adv. Com. Robb-Spong Commn., 1978-79; chair 11th Congrl. Dist. Dem. Com., 2001—; founder, chair Va. Assoc. Dem. County and City Chmn., 1976-80; chmn. Fairfax County Dem. Com., 1976-80, 1998-00; security supr. 1980 Dem. Nat. Conv.; v.p. Va. Fedn. Dem. Women, 1992-94; bd. dirs. Stop Child Abuse Now, 1988, Ctr. Innovative Tech., 1992-94, Ct. Apptd. Spl. Advs., 1993-96; nat. alumni bd. J.A. Achievement, BRAVO adv. com. for the first Gov.'s Awards for Arts in Va., 1979-80; lay tchr. St. Ambrose Cath. Ch., 1963-80; del. to White House Conf. on Children, 1970; chair Va. Coalition for Mentally Disabled, 1992-94; com. of 100, Va. Opera Bd., 1994-99; bd. dirs. Social Action Linking Together. Recipient Disting. Grad. award Jr. Achievement, 1973, Woman of Achievement award Fairfax (Va.) Bd. Suprs. and Fairfax County Commn. for Women, 1982, Cmty. Svc. award Friends of Victims Assistance Network, 1988, Founders award Fairfax County Coun. of Arts, 1989, Mental Health Assn. of Northern Va. Warren Stambaugh award, 1991, Ann. Svc. award Va. Assn. for Marriage and Family Therapy, 1991, Psychology Soc. of Washington Cmty. Svc. award, 1993, pacesetter award So. Women in Pub. Leadership Conf., 1996. Mem. NOW, Nat. Mus. Women in the Arts, Va. Assn. Female Execs. (mem. adv. bd., bd. dirs., v.p. 1992-99), Va. Assn. Cmty. Svc. Bds. (chmn. 1980-82), North Va. Assn. Cmty. Bds. (chmn. 1978-79, 95-98), Fairfax County Coun. Arts (v.p. 1980—, mem. exec. com. internat. children's festival, Founders award 1989), Fairfax County C. of C. (mem. legis. com.), Greater Merrifield Bus. and Profl. Assn., Mental Health Assn. No.Va. (bd. dirs.), Ctrl. Fairfax C. of C., Falls Church C. of C., Bus. and Profl. Women's Fedn. Va., Mantua Citizens Assn. (exec. bd.), Bus. and Profl. Women's Club (pres. Falls Church chpt. 1994-96, Woman of Yr. award 1990), Women's Nat. Dem. Club (past v.p., mem. bd. govs.), Downtown Club (Richmond), Va. Assn. Female Execs. (bd. dirs. 1992-99), Phi Gamma Nu. Democrat. Roman Catholic. Avocations: tennis, art, baseball. Home: 8701 Duvall St Fairfax VA 22031-2711 Office Phone: 703-560-0291. Personal E-mail: emiliemiller@cs.com.

**MILLER, ERNEST CHARLES,** management consultant; b. Bronx, N.Y., July 14, 1925; s. Ernest Philip and Elizabeth (Hellwig) M.; m. Edith Grosvenor Porterfield, Nov. 11, 1947 (div. Oct. 3, 1963); children: Laura Lee, Marcy Rogers, Ernest Charles; m. Tung-fen Lin, Jan. 8, 1985. AB, Yale U., New Haven, Conn., 1945; MA, U. Pa., 1949. Lic. psychologist, N.Y. Instr. U. Pa., 1947-51, cons., 1950-53; br. mgr., bd. dirs. Richardson, Bellows, Henry & Co., Inc., 1953-55; mgr. personnel tech. Am. Standard, Inc., 1955-59; mng. prin. Hellwig, Miller & Assos., Westport, Conn., 1959-61; sr. assoc. Cresap, McCormick & Paget, Inc., N.Y.C., 1961-63; with Am. Mgmt. Assns., N.Y.C., 1964-83, pres. AMACOM div., 1978-81, group v.p. AMA Publs. Group, 1981-83; pres. Miller, Hellwig Assocs., 1984—. Author works in strategic planning, orgn. devel., human resources, exec. compensation and mgmt. Bd. dirs. La Jolla Inst. for Allergy and Immunology, chair compensation com., audit com.; mem. Columbia U. All-Univ. Seminar, China Internat. Bus. Orgn. and Mgmt. NEH fellow, 1980 Mem. APA, Soc. Indsl. and Orgnl. Psychology. Episcopalian. Office: Miller Hellwig Assocs 150 W End Ave New York NY 10023-5713

**MILLER, EUGENE,** academic administrator, finance educator; b. Chgo., Oct. 6, 1925; s. Harry and Fannie (Prosterman) M.; m. Edith Sutker, Sept. 23, 1951 (div. Sept. 1965); children: Ross, Scott, June; m. Thelma Gottlieb, Dec. 22, 1965; stepchildren: Paul Gottlieb, Alan Gottlieb. BS, Ga. Inst. Tech., 1945; AB magna cum laude, Bethany Coll., 1947, LLD, 1969; diploma, Oxford U., Eng., 1947; MS in Journalism, Columbia U., 1948; MBA, NYU, 1959; postgrad., Pace U., 1973—. Reporter, then city editor Greensboro (N.C.) Daily News, 1948-52; S.W. bur. chief Bus. Week mag., Houston, 1952-54, assoc. mng. editor N.Y.C., 1954-60; dir. pub. affairs and communications McGraw-Hill, Inc., 1960-63, v.p., 1963-68; sr. v.p. CNA Fin. Corp., Chgo., 1973-75; chmn. Eugene Miller & Assos., Glencoe, Ill., 1975-77; v.p. USG Corp., Chgo., 1977-82, sr. v.p., 1982-85, mem. mgmt. com., 1982-91, exec. v.p.; CFO, 1985-87, elected vice chmn., CFO, 1987-91, mem. exec. com., also bd. dirs.; prof., exec.-in-residence Coll. Bus. Fla. Atlantic U., 1991—; chmn., CEO Ideon Group, Inc., Jacksonville, Fla., 1996. Speechwriter for Pres. Dwight Eisenhower during 1956 campaign; adj. prof. mgmt. NYU, 1963-65; prof. bus. adminstrn. Fordham U., 1969-75; prof. fin., chmn. dept. Northeastern Ill. U., 1975-78; lectr. to bus. and ednl. groups; bd. dirs. MRFI, Inc., Chgo., bd. dirs., mem. adv. bd. dirs. Nationwide Acceptance Corp., Chgo.; cons. to sec. Dept. Commerce, 1961-66; editor-in-residence U. Oreg., 1992; exec.-in-residence U. Ill., 1991, U. Wis., 1991, U. Toronto, 1992; exec.-in-residence, POHL fellow U. Wyo., 1992; mem. adv. bd. CFO mag., 1991-99; bd. dirs. the Strive Group, Chgo.; cons. Arthur Andersen & Co., Chgo., 1992-97; arbitrator NYSE, 2002—, NASD, 2005-; speech writer Pres. Eisenhower 1956 campaign. Author: Your Future in Securities, 1974, Barron's Guide to Graduate Business Schools, 1977, 14th edit., 2005; contbg. editor: Public Relations Handbook, 1988, Boardroom Reports, 1986—; writer syndicated bus. column, 1964-86; mem. editl. bd. IRQ mag., 1997—. Trustee Bethany Coll., 1970—; mem. alumni bd. Columbia U. Sch. Journalism. Comdr. USNR, World War II, ret. Recipient outstanding achievement award Bethany Coll., 1963, 50th anniversary award Sch. Journalism Columbia U., also honors award, 1963, Sch. Journalism Ohio U., 1964, disting. svc. award in investment edn. Nat. Assn. Investment Clubs, 1980, Roalman award Nat. Investor Rels. Inst., 1987; honored with Eugene Miller Bd. Rm. Bethany Coll., 1999, Eugene Miller Bd. Rm. Coll. Bus. Fla. Atlantic U., 2006. Fellow Pub. Rels. Soc. Am.; mem. Soc. Am. Bus. Editors and Writers (founder, Pres.'s award 2003), Fin. Execs. Inst., St. Andrew's Country Club, Sigma Delta Chi, Alpha Sigma Phi. Home: 7351 Ballantrae Ct Boca Raton FL 33496-1423 Office: Fla Atlantic U Coll Business 777 Glades Rd Boca Raton FL 33431-6424 Office Phone: 561-297-3630. Personal E-mail: Gene160@aol.com.

**MILLER, EUNICE A.,** marriage and family therapist, sex therapist, foundation administrator; b. Phila., Mar. 29, 1940; d. Henry and Elizabeth Eisenberg; m. Melvin Norman Miller, May 12, 1963; children: Emily, Rachel, Deborah. BA, Adelphi U., 1961; MSW, U. Pa., 1965. Dir. Crossroads Counseling Ctr., Malvern, Pa., 1979—. Book reviewer Dan's Papers, 2005—, talk show host Plain Wrapper, Voiceamerica Health and Wellness Channel, 2005—. Mem. Lower Merion Twp. (Pa.) Cable Adv. Com., 1985—97; pres. Melvin and Eunice A. Miller Found., Malvern, 1996—. Mem.: Counselors and Therapists (book reviewer, cert. sex therapist), Am. Assn. Sex Educators. Personal E-mail: eunicemiller@hotmail.com.

**MILLER, EWING HARRY,** retired architect; b. Toledo, Ohio, Oct. 5, 1923; s. Ewing Harry and Esther Alice (Graves) M.; children: Victoria Alice, Paul Ewing; m. Donna Barnard Ari. BA, U. Pa., 1947, MA, 1948. Draftsman Harbeson, Hough, Livingston & Larson, Phila., 1948; designer Nolen & Swinburne, Phila., 1950-52; project architect Gilboy & O'Malley, London, 1953-55; partner Miller, Vrydagh & Miller, Terre Haute, Ind., 1955-65; pres. Ewing Miller Partnership, Terre Haute, 1965-70, Archonics Corp., 1970-76, chmn. bd., 1976-79; sr. ptnr. for design Archonics Design Partnership, Indpls., 1979-84; assoc. ptnr. architecture eastern region U.S. Howard Needles, Tammen & Bergendoff, 1984-92; archtl. cons. Design & Bldg. Industry, 1992—; gen. ptnr. Lockerbie Devel. Co. 1978-86, Lockerbie Glove Devel. Co. 1983-86, East St. Devel. Co., 1979-86. Contbr. articles to profl. jours.; archtl. critic Indpls. Monthly Mag.; major archtl. works include: various bldgs. Ind. U., including grad. biology lab., Ind. State U., master plan and edn. bldgs., residence halls and sci. bldg., Ind. and various classroom bldgs., Southwestern Ind. U., master plan and edn. bldgs., Ind. and Ohio Laborers Tng. Ctrs., master plan U. San Diego. Westin Conv. Hotel; various office parks, Indpls. Pub. Transp. Corp. facility, addition to Duesenberg Factory; master plan Ind. State Govt. Complex, State of Ind. and design of new state office bldg.; prin. in charge printing facility Ho. of Rep. Architect of the Capitol, prin. in charge of Mastser Plan for design and restoration of Old Exec. Office Bldg., Washington; master plan for remodeling The Pentagon, Washington; prin. in charge design for remodeling Dept. of State, Washington; client rep. for remodeling Midwest Direct Mktg. Ctr., B.M.G., Inc., N.Y. Mem. Ind. Gov.'s Commn. on Aging, 1959-62; pres. Gov.'s Commn. on Comprehensive Health Planning, Ind., 1970-75, Behavioral Research Found., 1965-85; bd. mgrs. Sheldon Swope Art Gallery, 1965-80, pres., 1965-73; bd. dirs. Center for Exploration of Values and Meaning, 1978-85, Herron Art Gallery, 1980-88; chmn. Indpls. Arts and Cultural Alliance, 1983; v.p. Am. Chestnut Land Trust, Port Republic, Md.; chmn. bd. Cove Point Natural Heritage Trust, Losby, Md., 1995—, bd. mem. The Environmnental Fund of Maryland. Recipient design citation, biennial awards program Ind. Soc. Architects; Honor awards, triennial design awards East Central Region AIA; Nat. Archtl. award of excellence Am. Inst. Steel Constrn.; 1st Honor award and winner Internat. Competition for Housing, Indpls.; nat. award of excellence for univ. bldgs. Am. Sch. and Univ. Mag.; Ind. Soc. Architects Honor award restoration of Circle Theater, various office bldgs. Fellow AIA (mem. com. on design, chmn. com. on architecture for edn., mem. Vision 2000 study, architecture in coming decade), Lambda Alpha Hon. Soc. also: The Pennsylvania Apts #1202 601 Pennsylvania Ave NW Washington DC 20004-2601 Home: 601 Pennsylvania Ave NW Apt 1202 Washington DC 20004-2644

**MILLER, FLEMON MARSHALL,** public works manager; b. L.A., Sept. 15, 1942; s. Flemon Harris Miller and Claudia Cameron; m. Peggy Ann Torres, Mar. 14, 1992; 1 child, Diane Barboza; m. Lowida Jarmon Penland (div.); 1 child, Marguet Marshall. Cert. course instr. in supplier diversity 2000, hazardous waste and materials handling Dept. Transp. Warehouse man City of L.A., 1969—75, auto parts storekeeper, 1975—77, storekeeper dept. water and power, 1977—89, sr. storekeeper dept. power and water supply supr., 1989—92, sr. storekeeper dept. power and water, 1992—99, sr. storekeeper dept. power and water and supr. investment recovery, 1999—. Chmn. advisory coun. Normandie Ave. Elem. Sch., L.A., 1972—77. Recipient Recycler of Yr., City of L.A., 2006, Law Enforcement Hero award, Nat. Assn. Police Orgns., 2006. Office: Investment Recovery 11797 Truesdale St Sun Valley CA 91352

**MILLER, FORREST E.,** telecommunications industry executive; BS in acctg., Univ. So. Calif.; MBA, Stanford Univ. CPA. Acct. Coopers & Lybrand; sr. assoc. Marakon Assoc.; mgmt. positions through pres. Pacific Bell directory Pacific Telesis, 1984—97; pres., CEO SBC directory ops. SBC Comm., 1997—99, pres., CEO SNET, 1999, pres., CEO Southwestern Bell, group pres. corp. planning, group pres. external affairs & planning, 2004; group pres. AT&T Comm. Corp. AT&T Inc. (merger of SBC Comm. with AT&T Corp.), San Antonio, 2005—. Office: AT&T Inc 175 E Houston San Antonio TX 78205 Mailing: AT&T Inc PO Box 2933 San Antonio TX 78299-2933*

**MILLER, FREDERICK EDWIN, JR.,** history professor, government agency administrator; b. Stamford, Conn., Jan. 27, 1939; s. Frederick Edwin and Florence Baker Miller; m. Louise Ellen Wood, July 20, 1985. B of Social Sci. in Edn. cum laude, Fairfield U., 1960; MA in History, Boston U., 1961; postgrad., NYU, 1965—67; JD, Fordham U., 1976. Tchr. dept. spl. pupil svcs. Stamford Pub. Schs., Conn., 1961—62; tchr. social studies Stamford Cath. High Sch., 1965—67; lectr. history and gov. N.Y.C. C.C., 1966—73; lectr. CUNY, Queens, 1968—69; state rep. Conn. Ho. Reps., Hartford, 1971—73; asst. clk. Superior Ct. Jud. Dist. Stamford-Norwalk, 1976—95; justice of peace Fairfield. Ajd. prof. Norwalk C.C., Concordia Coll., Bronxville, NY, Coll. New Rochelle, St. Basils Coll., Stamford, Fairfield U., Sacred Heart U.; incorporator Stamford Hosp., Stamford, Conn.; mem. bd. Drug Liberation Inc, Stamford, Conn., Stamford Forum for World Affairs, Stamford, Conn., South Edn Cmty. Ctr., Stamford, Conn., Spanish Internat. Ctr., Stamford, Conn.; mem. bd. trustees Catholic Charities, Diocese Bridgeport, Conn. Mem. adv. task force desegregation Stamford Pub. Schs., 1971—72; mem. Bd. Assessment Appeals, Fairfield, 1995—99, chmn., 1997—99; mem. Stamford Bd. Reps., 1967—77, pres., 1973—77. Mem.: AAUP, Am. Polit. Sci. Assn., Am. Cath. Hist. Assn., Am. Hist. Assn., Ancient Order Hibernians, KC 4th Degree, Phi Alpha Theta. Democrat. Roman Catholic. Home: 167 Rock Major Rd Fairfield CT 06824

**MILLER, GALE TIMOTHY,** lawyer; b. Kalamazoo, Sept. 15, 1946; s. Arthur H. and Eleanor (Johnson) M.; m. Janice Lindvall, June 1, 1968; children: Jeremy L., Amanda E., Timothy W. AB, Augustana Coll., 1968; JD, U. Mich., 1971. Bar: Mich. 1971, Colo. 1973, U.S. Dist. Ct. Colo. 1973, U.S. Ct. Appeals (10th cir.) 1979, U.S. Supreme Ct. 1997. Trial atty. FTC, Washington, 1971-73; assoc Davis Graham & Stubbs LLP, Denver, 1973-77, ptnr., 1978—, chmn. exec. com., 1998—2001. Bd. dirs. Colo. Jud. Inst., 1999—, v.p., 2005—, chair, 2006—, Colo. Lawyers Com., 1989—91, bd. dirs., 1987—2006, mem. exec. com., 2004—06; chair Colo. Jud. Inst., 2006—. Recipient Cmty. Svc. award Colo. Hispanic Bar Assn., 1996, Sustained Contbn. award Colo. Lawyers Com., 2005; named Individual Lawyer of Yr. Colo. Lawyers Com., 1994. Mem. ABA (antitrust sect. task force on model civil antitrust jury instrns. 1985-87), Colo. Bar Assn. (chair antitrust sect. 1996-98), Denver Bar Assn. Democrat. Lutheran. Office: Davis Graham & Stubbs LLP 1550 17th St Ste 500 Denver CO 80202 Office Phone: 303-892-7368.

**MILLER, GARFIELD LANKARD, III,** investment banker; b. Buffalo, Apr. 8, 1950; s. Garfield Lankard and Johanne (Cunningham) M.; m. Martha Ellen McGarry, Aug. 24, 1974; 1 child, Cornelia Lawton. BBA, Middlebury (Vt.) Coll., 1972; MBA, U. Pa., 1975. Account mgr. Citibank, N.A., N.Y.C., 1975-79; ltd. ptnr. Bear, Stearns & Co., N.Y.C., 1979-85; mng. dir. CS First Boston, Inc. N.Y.C., 1985-91, Salomon Bros Inc., N.Y.C., 1991-94, pres. Aegis Energy Advisors Corp., N.Y.C., 1994—. Office: Aegis Energy Advisors Corp 6th Fl 708 3rd Ave New York NY 10017-4119 Office Phone: 212-245-2552. E-mail: glmiller@aegisenergy.com.

**MILLER, GARY C.,** lawyer; b. Little Rock, Ark., May 23, 1955; s. William Scott, Jr. and Margaret Imogene (Puckett) M.; m. Mary Catherine Miller, Oct. 23, 2000; children: Daniel, Sarah. BA in Econs. and Managerial Studies, Rice U., 1977; JD, U. Tex., 1980. Bar: Tex. 1980, U.S. Dist. Ct. (so. dist.) Tex. 1981, U.S. Dist. Ct. (no. and we. dists.) Tex. 1991, U.S. Dist. Ct. (ea. dist.) Tex. 1993, U.S. Ct. Appeals (5th cir) 1980, U.S. Supreme Ct. 1995. Atty. Wood, Campbell, Moody & Gibbs, Houston, 1980-83, Gibbs & Ratliff, Houston, 1983-85, Andrews & Kurth LLP and prececeessor, Houston, 1985—. Contbr. articles to profl. jours. Chmn. Westminster Weekday Sch., Houston, 1993—96; chmn., bd. trustees Westminster United Meth. Ch., Houston, 1996—98; bd. dirs. Houston Vol. Lawyers Program, 2000—04, Houston Lawyer Referral Svc., 2004—05; co-chair HBA Legalines, 2002—03. Fellow Tex. Bar Found.; mem. ABA (bus. in bankruptcy com., bus. and corp. litigation com.), Houston Bar Assn., Order of Coif, Phi Beta Kappa. Office: Andrews & Kurth LLP 600 Travis Ste 4200 Houston TX 77002 Office Phone: 713-220-3829. Business E-mail: garymiller@andrewskurth.com.

**MILLER, GARY EVAN,** psychiatrist, mental health services professional; b. Cleve., Aug. 19, 1935; s. Henry M. and Mollie (Price) M.; m. Karen Ann Marie Barrett, Sept. 16, 1972; children: Anna Charis, Rebecca Elizabeth. MD, U. Tex., Galveston, 1960. Diplomate in psychiatry, addiction psychiatry, and geriatric psychiatry Am. Bd. Psychiatry and Neurology. Intern Montefiore Hosp., NYC, 1960-61; resident in psychiatry U. Hosp. Cleve., 1961-62, Austin State Hosp., Tex., 1963-65; dep. commr. mental health services Dept. Mental Health and Mental Retardation, Tex., 1967-70; dir. Rio Grande State Ctr. for Mental Health and Mental Retardation, Dept. Mental Health, Harlingen, Tex., 1966-67; asst. commr., dir. Rochester regional office State Dept. Mental Hygiene, NY, 1970-72; clin. asst. prof. psychiatry U. Rochester Sch. Medicine and Dentistry, 1970-72; asst. clin. prof. psychiatry SUNY, Buffalo, 1970-72; cons. mental health Ga. Dept. Human Resources, Atlanta,

1972, dir. div. mental health, 1972-74; clin. prof. psychiatry Emory U. Sch. Medicine, Atlanta, 1972-74; vice chmn. Ga. State Planning and Adv. Coun. for Devel. Disabilities Services and Constrn., 1972-73; cons. mental health services orgn. and adminstrn., 1974-76; dir. mental health and devel. services State of NH Concord, 1976-82; commr. Tex. Dept. Mental Health and Mental Retardation Austin, 1982-88; clin. prof. psychiatry U. Tex. Health Sci. Ctr., Houston, adj. assoc. prof. psychiatry San Antonio, 1984-95; dir. med. dir. HCA Gulf Pines Hosp., Houston, 1988-94, chief of staff, 1993; clin. dir. adult psychiatry Cypress Creek Hosp., Houston, 1994-2000, med. dir., 2000—03, pres. med. staff, 1996; assoc. clin. psychiatry Post Oak Psychiatry Assoc., Houston, 1988-90; pres. Alternative Svc. Network, Houston, 1990—; chief of staff Kingwood (Tex.) Pines Hosp., 2003—04, dir. Psychiatric Svcs., 2004—. Dir. state alcoholism program in South Tex. region, 1966-67; dir. state alcoholism program in Ga., 1972—74; mem. faculty U. SC Sch. Alcohol and Drug Studies, 1975; mem. quality assurance com. Aetna US Healthcare Pharmacy, 1999—2001. Contbr. articles to profl. jours. Served as capt. M.C., US Army, 1962-63. Recipient Cert. of Recognition, Ga. Psychol. Assn., 1973. Fellow Am. Psychiat. Assn. (disting. life; cert. in adminstrv. psychiatry, com. on psychiat. adminstrn. and mgmt. 1999-2002); mem. AMA, Am. Soc. Clin. Psychopharmacology (cert.), Am. Soc. Addiction Medicine (cert. alcoholism and other drug dependencies), Am. Acad. Addiction Psychiatry, NH Psychiat. Soc. (pres. 1981-82), Nat. Assn. State Mental Health Program Dir. (bd. dir. 1984-88, sec. 1986-88), NH Med. Soc., Am. Acad. Psychiatry and the Law, Am. Assn. Psychiat. Adminstr. (pres. Tex. chpt. 1986), Tex. Med. Assn., Tex. Soc. Psychiat. Physicians, Mental Health Assn. Greater Houston (bd. dir. 1989-95, v.p. advocacy 1990-95, adv. coun. 1999—), Alpha Omega Alpha. Home: 5314 Westminister Ct Houston TX 77069-3338 Office: 530 Wells Fargo Dr Ste 110 Houston TX 77090-4026 Office Phone: 281-440-6899. Personal E-mail: gemhou@yahoo.com.

**MILLER, GARY G.,** congressman; b. Huntsville, Ark., 1948; m. Cathy, 1972; 4 children. Student, Mt. San Antonio C.C. Founder G. Miller Devel. Co.; mem. U.S. Congress from 42nd Calif. dist., Washington, 1999—; mem. budget com., fin. svcs. com., sci. com. Bd. dirs. Sonrise Christian Sch., 1982; appointed to Diamond Bar (Calif.) Mcpl. Adv. Coun., 1988; elected to 1st Diamond Bar City Coun., 1989; mayor, 1992; elected to Calif. State Assembly, 1995 (chmn. budget com. and banking and fin. com., vice chmn. transp. com.). With U.S. Army. Republican. Achievements include proposing 24 bills signed into law, successfully negotiated funding of 1st class size reduction program, and produced balanced budget that reduced the bus. tax. to 1973 levels while maintaing a $310 million reserve. Office: US Ho Reps 1037 Longworth Ho Office Bldg Washington DC 20515-0542

**MILLER, GARY J.,** political economist; b. Urbana, Ill., Jan. 2, 1949; s. Gerald J. and Doris Elaine (Miner) M.; m. Anne Colberg, Jan. 29, 1971; children: Neil, Ethan. BA, U. Ill., 1971; PhD, U. Tex., 1976. Asst. prof. Calif. Inst. Tech., Pasadena, 1976-79; assoc. prof. Mich. State U., East Lansing, 1979-86; Taylor prof. polit. economy Washington U., St. Louis, 1986-97; assoc. dean for acad. affairs Olin Sch. Bus., St. Louis, 1995-96, prof. polit. sci. Author: Cities by Contract, 1981, Reforming Bureaucracy, 1987, Managerial Dilemmas, 1992. NSF grantee, 1981, 83, 92, 03. Mem. Phi Beta Kappa, Phi Kappa Phi (Disting. Faculty award 1994). Democrat. Office: Washington U Dept Polit Sci 1 Brookings Dr Dept Polit Saint Louis MO 63130-4899 Office Phone: 314-935-5874. Business E-mail: gjmiller@artsci.wustl.edu.

**MILLER, GARY LEE,** secondary school educator; b. Taft, Calif., Jan. 4, 1957; s. John Darvel Miller and Dorothy Donnetta Bennett; m. Kathlyn Ruth Kuhre, Sept. 8, 1957; children: Michael John, Karolina Ruth, Gary David, Kristal Dorothy Moberly, Martin Calvin. Degree in zoology, Brigham Young U., Provo, Utah, 1981; degree in petroleum engring., Tex. A&M U., College Station, 1984. Oil field tool repair i Brady Well Svc., Bakersfield, Calif., 1984—87; tchr. h.s. sci. Porterville Unified Sch. Dist. Home: 2056 Chris Court Porterville CA 93257 Office: Monache High School 960 N Newcomb Porterville CA 93257 Office Phone: 559-782-7150. Office Fax: 559-781-3377.

**MILLER, GENEVIEVE,** retired medical historian; b. Butler, Pa., Oct. 15, 1914; d. Charles Russell and Genevieve (Wolford) Miller. AB, Goucher Coll., Balt., 1935; MA, Johns Hopkins U., Balt., 1939; PhD, Cornell U., Ithaca, N.Y., 1955. Asst. in history medicine Johns Hopkins Inst. History of Medicine, Balt., 1943—44, instr., 1945—48, rsch. associate, 1979—94; asst. prof. history of sci. Case Western Res. U. Sch. Medicine, Cleve., 1953-67, assoc. prof., 1967-79, assoc. prof. emeritus, 1979—; rsch. assoc. med. history Clevel. Med. Libr. Assn., 1953-62; curator Howard Dittrick Mus. Hist. Medicine, 1962-67, dir., 1967-79. Author: William Beaumont's Formative Years: Two Early Notebooks 1811-1821, 1946; The Adoption of Inoculation for Smallpox in England and France, 1957 (William H. Welch medal Am. Assn. History Medicine 1962), Bibliography of the History of Medicine of the U.S. and Canada, 1939-1960, 1964, Bibliography of the Writings of Henry E. Sigerist, 1966, Letters of Edward Jenner and Other Documents Concerning the Early History of Vaccination, 1983; assoc. editor Bull. of History of Medicine, 1944-48, acting editor, 1948, mem. adv. editl. bd., 1960-92; mem. bd. editors Jour. History of Medicine & Allied Scis., 1948-65; editor Newsletter Am. Assn. History of Medicine, 1986-96; contbr. articles to profl. jours. Alumna trustee Goucher Coll., Balt., 1966-69; trustee Judson Retirement Cmty., Clevel., 1993-99, Am. Coun. Learned Socs. fellow, 1948-50, Dean Van Meter fellow, Goucher Coll., 1953-54. Fellow Clevel. Med. Libr. Assn. (hon.); mem. Am. Assn. History Medicine (pres. 1978-80, mem. coun. 1960-63, Lifetime Achievement award 1999), Am. Hist. Assn., Internat. Soc. History of Medicine, Soc. Archtl. Historians, Phi Beta Kappa. Democrat. Home and Office: Judson Manor Apt 616 1890 E 107th St Cleveland OH 44106-2251

**MILLER, GEOFFREY,** child neurologist; b. Manchester, Eng., Feb. 1, 1947; came to U.S., 1990. s. Erwin and Cynthia Sarah Miller; m. Patricia Sarah Craigie, June 21, 1985; children: Joanne, Sally, Alethea. BA, MB, ChB, BAO, Trinity Coll., Dublin, Ireland, 1972, MA, 1982; MD, U. Western Australia, 1985; MPhil, U. Glasgow, Scotland, 2002. Diplomate Am. Bd. Psychiatry and Neurology, Am. Bd. Child Neurology, Am. Bd. Neurodevelopmental Disabilities. Fellow Royal Postgrad. Med. Sch., London, 1982-83; devel. pediatrician Princess Margaret Hosp. for Children, Perth, Australia, 1983-85; med. dir. Sir David Brand Ctr. for Cerebral Palsy, Perth, Australia, 1983-84; assoc. prof. pediat. Pa. State U., Hershey, 1988-92; co-dir. Muscular Dystrophy Assn. Clinic, Hershey, 1988-92, clinic physician Houston, 1998—; prof. pediat. & neurology Baylor Coll. Medicine, Houston, 1992—2004, chief devel. pediat. sect., 2000—02; dir. Meyer Ctr. Devel. Pediat., Tex. Childrens Hosp., 2000—02; prof. pediat. & neurology Yale U., 2004—. Vis. specialist West Australian Soc. for Crippled Children, Perth, 1983; investigator Neuromuscular Rsch. Inst., Perth, 1984-87; clin. dir. Child Neurology Svc. Yale U. Sch. Medicine, 2004—; mem. Yale Bioethics Ctr., 2004. Editor: Static Encephalopathies, 1992, Cerebral Palsies, 1998, Extreme Prematurity; contbr. articles to jours. in field. Capt. Royal Army Med. Corps, 1970-78. Elected and inducted into Am. Neurol. Assn., 1996. Fellow Royal Coll. Physicians, Royal Coll. Australasian Physicians; mem. Royal Coll. Physicians (London), Child Neurology Soc. (membership com. 1996-97, internat. affairs com. 1997—, chmn. 2002-), Internat. Child Neurology Soc., Soc. for Devel. Pediat., Am. Acad. Cerebral Palsy and Devel. Medicine (outcomes com. 2001—). Avocations: rugby, soccer. Business E-mail: geoffrey.miller@yale.edu.

**MILLER, GEORGE,** congressman; b. Richmond, Calif., May 17, 1945; s. George and Dorothy (Rumsey) M.; m. Cynthia Caccavo, 1964; children: George, Stephen. BA, San Francisco State Coll., 1968; JD, U. Calif., Davis, 1972. Legis. counsel Calif. senate majority leader, 1969-73; mem. U.S. Congress from 7th Calif. dist., 1975—; mem. edn. and workforce resources com., chmn. dem. policy com. Chmn. subcom. on oversight and investigations, 1985—, chmn. subcom. on labor stds., 1981-84, chmn. select com. on children, youth and families, 1983-91, chmn. com. on natural resources, 1991-94; mem. com. on edn. and lab., dep. majority whip, 1989-94; vice chair Dem. Policy Com., 1995—. Mem. Calif. Bar Assn. Democrat. Office: US Ho Reps 2205 Rayburn Ho Office Bldg Washington DC 20515-0507

**MILLER, GEORGE ARMITAGE,** psychologist, educator; b. Charleston, W.Va., Feb. 3, 1920; s. George E. and Florence (Armitage) M.; m. Katherine James, Nov. 29, 1939 (dec. Jan. 1996); children: Nancy, Donnally James. BA, U. Ala., 1940, MA, 1941; AM, Harvard U., 1944, PhD, 1946; PhD (hon.), U. Louvain, 1976; D Social Sci. (hon.), Yale U., 1979; DSc (hon.), Columbia U., 1980, U. Sussex, 1984, New Sch. Social Rsch., 1993; LittD (hon.), Charleston U., 1992; DSc (hon.), DSc (hon.), New Sch. Social Rsch., 1993, Princeton U., 1996, Williams Coll., 2000; DSc (hon.), Carnegie Mellon U., 2003. Instr. psychology U. Ala., 1941-43; rsch. fellow Harvard Psycho-Acoustic Lab., 1944-48; asst. prof. psychology Harvard U., 1948-51, assoc. prof., 1955-58, prof., 1958-68, chmn. dept psychology, 1964-67, co-dir. Ctr. for Cognitive Studies, 1960-67; prof. Rockefeller U., N.Y.C., 1968-79, adj. prof., 1979-82; prof. psychology Princeton U., 1979-90, James S. McDonnell Disting. prof. psychology, 1982-90, James S. McDonnell Disting. prof. psychology emeritus, 1990—, program dir. McDonnell-Pew Program in Cognitive Neurosci., 1989-94; assoc. prof. MIT, 1951-55. Vis. Inst. for Advanced Study, Princeton, 1972-76, 82-83, mem., 1950, 70-72; vis. prof. Rockefeller U., 1967-68, MIT, 1976-79, group leader Lincoln Lab., 1953-55; fellow Ctr. Advanced Study in Behavioral Scis., Stanford U., 1958-59; Fulbright research prof. Oxford (Eng.) U., 1963-64; Sesquicentennial prof. U. Ala., 1981. Author: Language and Communication, 1951, (with Galanter and Pribram) Plans and the Structure of Behavior, 1960, Psychology, 1962, (with Johnson-Laird) Language and Perception, 1976, Spontaneous Apprentices, 1977, Language and Speech, 1981, The Science of Words, 1991; editor Psychol. Bulletin, 1981-82. Recipient Disting. Service award Am. Speech and Hearing Assn., 1976, award in behavioral scis. N.Y. Acad. Scis., 1982, Hermann von Helmholtz award Cognitive Neurosci. Inst., 1989, Nat. Medal Sci. NSF, 1991, Gold Medal Am. Psychological Found. 1990, Nat. Medal of Sci. 1991, Louis E. Levy medal Franklin Inst., 1991, John P. Govern award, Am. Assn. for Advancement of Sci., 2000; Guggenheim fellow, 1986, William James fellow Am. Psychological Soc., 1989; Fondation Fyssen Priz Internat. for cognitive sci., 1992. Fellow Brit. Psychol. Assn. (hon.); mem. NAS, AAAS (chmn. sect. J 1981, John P. McGovern award 2000), APA (pres. 1968-69, Disting. Sci. Contbn. award 1963, William James Book award divsn. gen. psychology 1993, Outstanding Lifetime Contbn. to Psychology award 2003), Eastern Psychol. Assn. (pres. 1961-62), Acoustical Soc. Am., Linguistic Soc. Am., Am. Statis. Assn., Am. Philos. Soc., Am. Physiol. Soc., Psychometric Soc., Soc. Exptl. Psychologists (Warren medal 1972), Am. Acad. Arts and Scis., Psychonomic Soc., Royal Netherlands Acad. Arts and Scis. (fgn.), Sigma Xi. Home: 16 Willow St Princeton NJ 08542-6923 Office: Princeton Univ Dept Psychology Green Hall Princeton NJ 08544

**MILLER, GEORGE DAVID,** retired military officer, not-for-profit executive; b. McKeesport, Pa., Apr. 5, 1930; s. George G. and Nellie G. (Cullen) M.; m. Barbara Aex; 1 child from previous marriage: George David Jr.; stepchildren: Jason Dunn, Elizabeth Dunn. BS, U.S. Naval Acad., 1953; MS in Aerospace Engring. Air Force Inst. Tech., 1966; postgrad., Nat. War Coll., 1970-71. Commd. 2d lt. U.S. Air Force, 1953, advanced through grades to lt. gen., 1981; ops. officer, comdr. 22d Spl. Ops. Squadron, Nakhon Phanom Royal Thai AFB, Thailand, 1969—70; dep. comdr. for ops., vice comdr., comdr. 55th Strategic Reconnaissance Wing, Offutt AFB, Nebr., 1971-74; comdr. 17th Air div., 307th Strategic wing, U-Tapao Airfield, Thailand, 1974-75; comdr. 57th Air Div. Minot AFB, ND, 1975-76; asst. dep. chief staff ops. hdqrs. SAC, Offutt AFB, Nebr., 1976-77; dir. single integrated operational plan Joint Strategic Target Planning Staff, Joint Chiefs of Staff, 1977-79; dir. plans USAF, Washington, 1979-80, asst. dep. chief staff ops., plans and readiness, 1980-81; vice comdr.-in-chief SAC, Offutt AFB, Nebr., 1981-84; exec. dir., sec.-gen. U.S. Olympic Com., 1984-87; pres. exec. dir. Morris Animal Found., 1987—92; pres., CEO The Nat. Fire Protection Assoc., 1992—2002; pres. Miller Assocs. Consulting. Chmn. bd. dirs. RJA Group Inc.; bd. dirs. Target Safety Inc. Decorated Def. D.S.M., Air Force DSM, Legion of Merit, D.F.C. with 3 oak leaf clusters Air medal with 18 oak leaf clusters, others. Mem.: VFW, World Orgn. of Bldg. Ofcls. (pres. 2003—), Confedn. of Fire Protection Assns. Internat. (chmn. 1992—2005), Metro Fire Chiefs Assn., Nat. Fire Protection Assn. (pres. emeritus), Mil. Officers Assn., Air Force Assn., Daedalians, Shriners, Scottish Rite, Masons, Am. Legion. Lutheran. Home: 20 Phillips Pond Natick MA 01760-5643 Office Phone: 508-380-9218. Business E-mail: george.d.miller@comcast.net.

**MILLER, GEORGE DEWITT, JR.,** lawyer; b. Detroit, Aug. 20, 1928; s. George DeWitt and Eleanor Mary Miller; m. Prudence Brewster Saunders, Dec. 28, 1951; children: Margaret DeWitt, Joy Saunders. BA magna cum laude, Amherst Coll., 1950; JD with distinction, U. Mich., 1953. Bar: Mich. 1953, U.S. Dist. Ct. (so. dist.) Mich. 1953, U.S. Ct. Appeals (6th cir.) 1960, U.S. Tax Ct. 1960. Assoc. Bodman, Longley & Dahling, Detroit, 1957-61, ptnr., 1962—. Trustee, mem. Matilda R. Wilson Fund, 1993—, pres., 1998—; trustee Maplegrove Ctr./Kingswood Hosp., Henry Ford Health Sys., 1995—, Music Hall Ctr. Performing Arts, 2002—; dir. Detroit Symphony/Orch. Hall, 2001—. Capt. USAF, 1953-56. Recipient Commendation medal. Fellow Mich. State Bar Found.; mem. ABA, State Bar Mich., Detroit Bar Assn., Orchard Lake Country Club, Order of Coif, Phi Beta Kappa. Episcopalian. Avocations: yacht racing, shooting, gardening. Home: 320 Dunston Rd Bloomfield Hills MI 48304-3415 Office: Bodman LLP 100 Renaissance Ctr Ste 34 Detroit MI 48243-1001 Business E-mail: gmiller@bodmanllc.com.

**MILLER, GEORGE H.,** architectural firm executive; b. Berlin, June 7, 1949; naturalized; BArch, Pa. State U., 1973. Registered Iowa, N.Y., Mass., Pa., Ohio, Okla., Tex., Fla., Ind., D.C. With Liu Urban Design Assocs., 1974—75, I.M. Pei & Ptnrs., 1975—89; ptnr. Pei Cobb Freed & Ptnrs., N.Y.C., 1989—. Studio critic Columbia U. Sch. Arch., 1978; tchr., lectr., guest critic Columbia U., Yale U., Pa. State U., N.Y. Inst. Tech. Contbr. articles to profl. jours. Fellow: AIA (participant N.Y.C. justice com. symposium, mem. large firm roundtable); mem.: Mcpl. Arts Soc., Soc. Archtl. Historians, Ordre des Archs. Archtl. League N.Y., Nat. Coun. Archtl. Registration Bds. Office: Pei Freed & Ptnrs LLP 88 Pine St New York NY 10005

**MILLER, GEORGE W.,** federal judge, lawyer; b. Schenectady, N.Y., July 12, 1941; m. Mary Katherine, three children. BA magna cum laude, Princeton Univ., 1963; JD, Harvard Univ., 1966; LLM, George Washington Univ., 1968. Bar: N.Y. 1966, D.C. 1968, Va. 1978. Law clk. to Hon. Bruce M. Forrester U.S. Tax Ct., 1966—67; assoc. Hogan & Hartson, 1970—77, spec. ptnr., 1977—79, ptnr., 1979—2004; judge US Ct. Fed. Claims, Washington, 2004—. Mem. U.S. Ct. Fed. Claims Adv. Council, 1994—2004; mem. Litigation Practice task force US. Ct. Fed. Claims, 1995; mem. U.S. Ct. Appeals D.C. cir. adv. com., 2002—04; mem. task force Racial Ethnic Bias & Adv. Com. D.C. Courts, 1990—92; mem. D.C. Ct. Appeals Bd. Prof. Responsibility, 1985—91, vice-chmn., 1988—89, chmn., 1989—91. Judge Adv. Gen Corps USN, 1967—70 USNR, 1970—77. Mem.: U.S. Ct. Fed. Claims Bar Assn. (bd. gov.). Office: US Ct Fed Claims 717 Madison Pl Washington DC 20005

**MILLER, G(ERSON) H(ARRY),** science administrator, mathematician, computer scientist, chemist; b. Phila., Mar. 2, 1924; m. Mary Alexa Heath, Jan. 28, 1961; children: Byron, Alexandra. BA, Pomona Coll., 1949; MEd in Counseling and Pers., Temple U., 1951; PhD. in Edn. Psychology, U. So. Calif., 1957; MS in Math., U. Ill., 1982, postgrad., 1963-65. Jr. high sch. and jr. coll. math teacher L.A. Sch. Dist., 1953-57; assoc. prof. Western Ill. U. Macomb, 1957-60; prof. Towson State U., Balt., 1960-61; prof. math. and edn. Parsons Coll., Fairfield, Iowa, 1961-65; prof. Tenn. Technol. U., Cookeville, 1966—68; prof. math. and computer sci. Edinboro (Pa.) U., 1968-71, 81-89, asst. dir. Institutional Rsch., 1972-80, emeritus prof., 1989—; dir. Studies On Smoking, Inc. and SOS Stop Smoking Clinic, Edinboro, 1972—. Dir. Nat. Study Math. Requirements for Scientists and Engrs., 1966-73; condr. Nat. Symposium for Am. Inst. Biol. Scis., Am. Chem. Soc. and Am. Soc. Engring. Educators, 1970-75; dir. Math. for Industry Confs.; spkr., presenter in field Contbr. numerous articles to profl. jours. Pres. Edinboro YMCA, 1972-83; bd. dirs. Common Cause, Harrisburg, Pa., 1975-80; Sgt. USAAF, 1943-46, PTO. Grantee U.S. Office Edn., 1968, 70, No Other World, 1973, NAS, 1980, ITT Life Ins. Corp., 1983, Erie County Found., 1987. Fellow Am. Inst. Chemists (cert. profl. chemist), AAAS; mem.

APHA, Am. Assn. World Health, Am. Chem. Soc., Am. Soc. Engring. Edn., Internat. Assn. Pure and Applied Chemists, Internat. Soc. for Preventive Oncology, Math. Assn. Am., Am. Diabetes Assn., Sch. Sci. and Math. Assn., N.Y. Acad. Scis. (hon.), Acad. Sr. Profls. (hon.). Home and Office: Studies on Smoking 125 High St Edinboro PA 16412-2552 Home (Summer): 25 Crescent Pl S Saint Petersburg FL 33711-5118 Personal E-mail: drghmiller@aol.com.

**MILLER, GRAY HAMPTON,** federal judge, lawyer; b. Houston, Dec. 9, 1948; Student, US Merchant Marine Acad.; BA, U. Houston, 1974, JD, 1978. Bar: Tex. 1978. Assoc. Fulbright & Jaworski LLP, Houston, 1978—86, head admiralty dept, 1996—2004, ptnr., 1986—2004, sr. ptnr., 2004—06; judge US Dist. Ct. (so. dist.) Tex., Houston 2006—. Mem. ABA, Maritime Law Assn. U.S., State Bar Tex., Houston Bar Assn., Southeastern Admiralty Law Inst. (bd. dirs. 1989-91), Order of Barons. Office: US Dist Ct 515 Rusk Ave Houston TX 77002

**MILLER, GREEN RUSSELL,** economist, educator; b. Kenvir, Ky., Mar. 10, 1939; s. Clifford Wesley and Lorene (Farmer) M.; m. Carolyn Sue Blackburn, Oct. 7, 1966; children: Laura Marie, Russell Wesley. BA, U. Tex., El Paso, 1969; MA, U. Oreg., 1971; PhD, U. Ky., 1985. Instr. Transylvania U., Lexington, 1973—79; asst. prof. Sch. Pub. Affairs Ky. State U., Frankfort, 1977; prof. econs. Morehead State U., Ky., 1979—, dir. Ctr. for Econ. Edn. 1979—96. Bd. dirs. Ky. Coun. Econ. Edn., Louisville, 1979-96; cons. to various law firms, Ky., 1973—; supr. Cash-Fiscal Agy, El Paso Br. Fed. Reserve Bank of Dallas, 1959-1969. Contbr. numerous articles to profl. jours. Coach Little League Baseball, Morehead, 1982-85, Youth Soccer League, 1985-86; bd. dirs. St. Albans Ch., Morehead, 1979-82, Gethsemane Luth. Ch., 1989-97; vol. One-on-One program Dept. of Corrections, Lexington, 1973-82, Morehead Cmty.Fed. Credit Union (treas. 1999-). With inf. U.S Army, 1957-59. Mem. Midwest Econ. Assn., Ky. Econs. Assn., Internat. Bus. and Econ. Rsch. Assn. (Best Paper award, 2003), Mo. Valley Econ. Assn. (Jerome F. Schwier meritorious svc. award 1997), So. Econ. Assn., Ky. Assn. Econl. Opportunity Program Pers., Joint Coun. on Econ. Edn., Nat. Assn. Econ. Educators, Ky. Coun. on Econ. Edn. (bd. dirs. 1979-96, Outstanding Ctr. Dir. 1981-82), Assn. Ky. Econ. Educators (charter, original bylaws com., nominating com. 1985-93), Nat. Assn. Forensic Econs. (charter, bd. dirs. 1986-87, bus. editor Jour. Econs. 1990-97, chair acctg.-econs.-fin. 1988-2002), Southeastern Ky. Econ. Assn. (charter, chair 2004-06), Internat. Acad. Bus. and Pub. Rels. Adminstrn. Disciplines. Democrat. Lutheran-Episcopal. Avocations: hiking, reading. Home: 1240 Rodburn Hollow Rd Morehead KY 40351-9092 Office: Morehead State U UPO 1280 150 University Blvd Morehead KY 40351 Business E-Mail: g.miller@moreheadstate.edu.

**MILLER, GREGORY JAMES,** lawyer; b. New Bedford, Mass., Aug. 5, 1959; s. Martin. E. and Marjorie D. (Cohen) M. BA in History, Kalamazoo Coll., 1981; JD, N.Y. Law Sch., N.Y.C., 1984. Bar: Conn. 1985, N.Y. 1985, U.S. Dist. Ct. Conn. (2d dist.) 1987. Assoc. Benenson & Kates, N.Y.C., 1984-88, of counsel, 1988—2004; gen. counsel Gold Line Connector, Inc., West Redding, Conn., 1992—2004; of counsel Bainton McCarthy, LLC, Redding, Conn., 2004—. Bd. dirs. Command Security Corp., chmn. warrant com., mem. compensation and audit com., chmn. ind. dirs. com. Editor N.Y. Law Sch. Jour. of Human Rights, 1983-84. With U.S. Coast Guard, 2004—. Named Outstanding Young Man in Am. Jr. C. of C., 1984. Mem. N.Y. State Bar Assn., Conn. Bar Assn. Avocations: astronomy, Arabian horses, sailing. Home: 40 Great Pasture Rd West Redding CT 06896-2303 Office: Three Stamford Ave Stamford CT 06902-0500 Office Phone: 203-323-8080. E-mail: gmiller@gold-line.com.

**MILLER, GREGORY KENT,** structural engineer; b. Anaconda, Mont., July 6, 1951; s. Robert Bruce and Lois Patricia (Arvish) Miller. BS in Civil Engring./Engring. Mechanics, Mont. State U., 1973, MS in Engring. Mechanics, 1974. Project engr. U.S. Energy R&D Adminstrn., Idaho Falls, Idaho, 1974-77; structural engr. EG&G Idaho, Inc., Idaho Falls, 1977-93; supr. Lockheed Martin Idaho Technologies Co., Idaho Falls, 1994-99, BBWI, Idaho Falls, 1999—2005, Idaho Nat. Lab., Idaho Falls, 2005—. Contbr. articles to profl jours. Mem.: ASME (comt mem boiler and pressure vessel code sect III 1995—), Phi Kappa Phi (Sr of Yr 1973), Tau Beta Pi. Achievements include research in advanced modeling and analysis methods for evaluating failure of fuel particles in high-temperature gas-cooled reactors; contributed to technology for analyzing complex material behavior in pressure vessels; advanced methods for evaluating containers bearing nuclear materials for impact loads associated with accidental drop events. Office: Idaho Nat Lab Technologies Co PO Box 1625 Idaho Falls ID 83415-3855 Office Phone: 208-526-0360. Business E-Mail: gregoryk.miller@inl.gov.

**MILLER, GREGORY R.,** prosecutor; BA, Drew U.; JD, Ohio N. U. Chief asst. U.S. atty. (no. dist.) Fla. US Dept. Justice, Tallahassee, U.S. atty. (no. dist.) Fla., 1993-98, asst. U.S. atty. (no. dist.) Fla., 2000—02; US atty (no. dist.) Fla. US Dept Justice, Tallahassee, 2002—; assoc. Fowler, White, Gillen, Boggs, Villareal and Banker, PA, Tallahassee, 1998-2000. Office: US Attys Office 111 N Adams St Tallahassee FL 32301 Office Phone: 850-942-8430. Business E-Mail: gregory.miller@usdoj.gov.*

**MILLER, H. TODD,** lawyer; b. Buffalo, N.Y., Sept. 19, 1947; s. Henry Opel and Irene Teresa (Hauck) M.; m. June Diehl Lancaster, Aug. 1, 1970; children: Catharine Maclay, Todd Lancaster, Peter Hanes. BA, SUNY, Buffalo, 1969; JD, Duke U., 1971. Bar: N.C. 1971, D.C. 1973. Jud. clerk to Hon. Charles R. Simpson U.S. Tax Ct., Washington, 1971-73; assoc. atty. Hogan & Hartson LLP, Washington, 1973-78, ptnr, 1979—. Mem. Phi Beta Kappa, Order of the Coif. Episcopalian. Office: Hogan & Hartson Columbia Sq 555 13th St NW Ste 9W-312 Washington DC 20004-1161 Office Phone: 202-637-5667.

**MILLER, HAROLD ARTHUR,** lawyer; b. St. Marie, Ill., Aug. 18, 1922; s. Arthur E. and Luletta (Noé) M.; m. Michele H. Rogivue, Nov. 21, 1947; children: Maurice H., Jan Leland, Marc Richard. BS in Acctg., U. Ill., 1942, JD, 1950. Bar: Ill. 1950, U.S. Dist. Ct. 1950, U.S. Tax Ct. 1950. Fgn. svc. officer U.S. State Dept., Paris, France, 1945-48; ptnr. Filson, Williamson & Miller, Champaign, Ill., 1950-60, Williamson & Miller, Champaign, 1960-72, Miller & Hendren, Champaign, 1972—. Atty. Christie Clinic Found., Champaign, 1960—; atty. pub. schs. dists., Champaign & Vermilion Counties, Ill., 1960—; atty. for municipalities in Champaign County, Ill., 1970—. Author: Estate Planning for Doctors, 1961, Intervivos Trusts Alternative to Probate 1996. Bd. dirs., officer Urbana Ill. Sch. Dist., 1957-69; chmn., trustee Parkland Coll., Champaign, 1971-91; founding bd. mem. CCDC Found., Champaign-Urbana Ednl. Found., Moore Heart Found., Christie Found.; life mem. PTA. With Spl. Svcs., U.S. Army, 1942-45, ETO. Mem. ABA, Am. Judicature Soc., Ill. and Local Bar Assns., Ill. Trial Lawyers Assn., Alpha Kappa Psi, Presbyterian. Office: Miller & Hendren Attys 30 E Main St #200 Champaign IL 61824-0980 Office Phone: 217-352-2171. Business E-Mail: ham@mhlawoffice.com.

**MILLER, HAROLD EDWARD,** retired manufacturing conglomerate executive, consultant; b. St. Louis, Nov. 23, 1926; s. George Edward and Georgenia Elizabeth (Franklin) M.; m. Lilian Ruth Gantner, Dec. 23, 1949; children— Ellen Susan, Jeffrey Arthur. BSBA, Washington U., St. Louis, 1949. Vice pres. Fulton Iron Works Co., St. Louis, 1968-71, pres., 1971-79, chmn. bd., 1979-90; v.p. Katy Industries Inc., Elgin, Ill., 1976-77, exec. v.p., 1978-90, also dir., to 1990; pres. HM Consulting, Palatine, Ill., 1990—. Internat. cons. Vigel Spa, Italy; v.p. Vigel U.S.A. Inc., 1996—. Served with U.S. Army, 1945-46. Mem. Barrington Tennis Club, Inverness Golf Club. Presbyterian. Office Phone: 847-991-7852. Personal E-mail: hmillercons84@sbcglobal.net.

**MILLER, HARVEY S. SHIPLEY,** foundation trustee, philanthropist; b. Phila., Sept. 28, 1948; s. Frank Leroy and Betty Charlotte (Elfont) M. BA, Swarthmore Coll., 1970; JD, Harvard U., 1973. Bar: N.Y. 1973. Assoc.

Debevoise & Plimpton, N.Y.C., 1973-75; curator and dir. dept. collections and spl. exhbns. Franklin Inst., Phila., 1975-81; v.p. Energy Solutions, Inc., N.Y.C., 1982-84; pres., chief exec. officer, dir. Daltex Med. Scis., Inc., N.Y.C. 1983-86, dir. exec. com., 1983-94, chief operating officer, vice chmn., 1986-91, pres., chief operating officer, 1991-93; trustee The Judith Rothschild Found., N.Y.C., 1993—. Author: Milton Avery: Drawings and Paintings, 1976, It's About Time, 1979; author, editor: New Spaces: Exploring the Aesthetic Dimensions of Holography, 1979; co-author: Rapid Inactivation of Infectious Pathogens by Chlorhexidine-coated Gloves, 1992; contbr. articles to profl. jours. Mem. vis. com. on photography George Eastman House, Rochester, N.Y., 1976-78; trustee Milton and Sally Avery Arts Found., N.Y.C., 1983—, sec., 1996—; trustee The Franklin Inst., Phila., 1993-95, Phila. Mus. Art, 1985—, exec. com., 1993-96; assoc. trustee U. Pa., 1981-95; trustee Arcadia U., 2002-2005; bd. govs. Print Club, Phila., 1976-87; bd. overseers U. Pa. Sch. Nursing, 1981—, Edith C. Blum Art Inst. Bard Coll., 1984-87; bd. dirs. Fabric Workshop, Phila., 1976-86, hon. trustee, Miami Mu. Modern Art, 2004—; mem. prints and drawings and photographs trustees adv. com. Phila. Mus. Art, 1974—, trustee, 1985—, vice chmn., 2004—, investment com., 1989-95, exec., devel. and exhbn. coms., 1993-96, chair 125th ann. campaign, 1999-2002; mem. vis. com. modern art Met. Mus. Art, 1998—; bd. assocs. Swarthmore Coll. Librs., Phila., 1978-86; treas., dir. Arcadia Found., Norristown, Pa., 1981—; chmn. adv. bd. Inst. Contemporary Art U. Pa., 1982-84; trustee, vice chmn. coms. on instrn. Pa. Acad. Fine Arts, 1982-91; trustee emeritus, 1991—, chmn. collections and exhbns. coms., 1985-87; trustee N.Y. Studio Sch., 1974-80, U. of the Arts, 1979-86; mem. exec. bd. Citizens for Arts in Pa., 1980; adv. bd. The Highlands Hist. Soc., 1999—; bd. dirs. Once Gallery, Inc., 1974-75, Wildlife Preservation Trust Internat., Inc., 1990-95; mem. Mayor's Cultural Adv. Coun., Phila., 1987-91; chair Mayor's Art-in-City Hall Program, Phila., 1992-94; trustees coun. Nat. Gallery Art, Washington, 1995-2000, 2001—; mem. collections com. Hist. Soc. Pa., 1991-93; councilor trustee, 1992-93; mem. vis. com. photographs Met. Mus. Art, 1996—, vis. com. modern art, 1998—; mem. trustees' com. on drawings Mus. Modern Art, 1996—, trustee, 2003—, Prints and Illustrated Books, Museum of Modern Art, 2001—; mem. photography accessions com. San Francisco Mus. of Modern Art, 1997-2002; arts adv. com. Fund for the Waterworks, 1999-2001; founding mem. bd. trustees Maltz Jupiter (Fla.)Theatre, 2001—; bd. dirs. Am. Patrons of the Tate Gallery, 2003—; charter mem. The Drawings Group, L.A. County Mus. Art, 2003—; mem. drawings com. L.A. Mus. Contemporary Art, 2003—; bd. trustees Whitney Mus. Am. Art, 2004—; mem. Commn. on Drawing, 2005—, chmn. com. on drawings, 2004; bd. overseers Hammer Mus., L.A., 2004—; trustee Ursinus Coll., 2004—, Point Found., 2004—; collections com. Harvard U. Art Mus; bd. dirs. Salzburg Festival Soc., 2006—. Named 1st non-Russian recipient of Diploma of Merit, Russian Ministry of Culture, 2002; recipient Disting. Civic Svc. award, City Phila., 1997, Hon. Alumni award, U. Pa. Sch. Nursing, 2005. Fellow The Pierpont Morgan Libr., Coll. Physicians Phila.; mem. ABA, Assn. of Bar of City of N.Y., Athenaeum, Libr. Co. Phila., Am. Philos. Soc., Hist. Soc. Pa., Phila. Art Alliance, Union League of Phila., Harvard Club of N.Y.C., Swarthmore Club Phila., Palm Beach Yacht Club, Sunnybrook Golf Club, Phi Sigma Kappa. Republican. Home: Plumlyn 7036 Sheaff Ln Fort Washington PA 19034-2017 Office: 1110 Park Ave New York NY 10128-1201

**MILLER, HARVEY WILLIAM,** retired military officer; b. LaCrosse, Wis., Nov. 20, 1919; s. Carl William and Charlotte (Lumley) Miller; m. Marylin Buck Grindle, May 16, 1995; m. Daphne Olive Roddy, Dec. 29, 1942 (dec. Jan. 1995); children: Charlene, David, Peggy. BS with honors, U. Wis., Madison, 1941; MS, Mont. State Coll., Bozeman, 1942. Cert. tchr. history and bus. econs. grades 9-12 Va. Officer and pilot to lt. comdr. US Navy, 1943—65, prof. naval scis., 1955—58; mideast navy intelligence officer Morocco, 1959—61; intelligence officer USS Enterprise CVA(N) 65, 1961—63, Def. Intelligence Agy., Arlington, Va., 1963—65; indusl. intelligence CIA, Langley, Va., 1965—76. Mgr. officers club, Honolulu, 1947. Pres. Country Club Hills Civic Assn., Fairfax City, Va., 1968—74; mgr. Little League, Port Lyautey, Morocco, 1960—61; chmn. Hawaiian Island Luth. Evang. Inst.; mem. sch. bd. Lutheran Sch., Richfield, Minn., 1956—58; tchr. adult Bible sch. base chapel Port Lyautey, Morocco, 1959—61. Mem.: Mil. Officer Assn. Am., Nat. Active and Ret. Fed. Employees Assn. (pres. Va. Chpt. 1885 1985—, pres. Fla. Chpt. 583 2005—06). Democrat. Lutheran. Avocations: genealogy, square dancing, bowling, golf, softball. Home: 6332 Lomand Ave New Port Richey FL 34653 Personal E-mail: harlinmill@juno.com.

**MILLER, HEIDI G.,** diversified financial company executive; b. 1951; married; 2 children. BA in History, Princeton U., 1974; PhD in History, Yale U., 1979. Various positions to mng. dir. emerging markets structured finance group Chemical Bank, 1979—92; joined as v.p. and asst. to the pres. Travelers Group, 1992, CFO, 1995—98, Citigroup (merger of Citibank and Travelers Group), NYC, 1998—2000; CFO, sr. exec. v.p. strategic planning and adminstrn. Priceline.com, Norwalk, Conn., 2000; vice chmn. Marsh & McLennan Co., Inc., NYC, 2001—02; exec. v.p. strategy and devel., CFO Bank One Corp., 2002—04; exec. v.p., CEO, treasury & securities div. J.P. Morgan Chase & Co. (merger of Bank One Corp. and J.P. Morgan Chase & Co.), NYC, 2004—. Bd. dirs. General Mills Inc., 1999—, Merck & Co., Inc., 2000—04, Bank One Corp., 2000—02, Local Initiatives Support Corp., 2004—. Trustee Princeton U., NYU Med. Sch. Office: JP Morgan Chase & Co 270 Park Ave New York NY 10017*

**MILLER, HELEN,** history educator; b. Bronx, N.Y., Jan. 15, 1955; d. Jack and Frieda (Ringelheim) Greenberg; m. Mark Steven Miller, Sept. 17, 1978; children: Matthew, Adam. BA in History summa cum laude, Lehman Coll., 1976; AM in History, Harvard U., 1978. With Jewish Chautauqua Soc., N.Y.C., 1977-80, Conceptual Planning, Inc., N.Y.C., 1980-81; with dept. pers. mgmt. Dept. Employment City of New York, 1981-83; with dept. material scis. & engring. MIT, Cambridge, Mass., 1984-86; adj. instr. history Frederick (Md.) CC, 1988-90; adj. instr. history arts & scis. divsn. Pellissippi State Tech. CC, Knoxville, Tenn., 1992-95, instr. history dept. humanities, 1995-97; adj instr. Davidson County CC, Lexington, NC, 1997—99; social studies tchr. S.E. Mid. Sch. Winston-Salem/Forsyth County Schs., 2000—. Mem.: Nat. Coun. Social Studies, N.C. Assn. Educators. Office: SW Mid Sch 1200 Old Salem Rd Kernersville NC 27285

**MILLER, HELEN ELIZABETH,** art educator, adult education educator, artist; b. Granit City, Ill., Feb. 18, 1969; d. David Allen Busch and Christine Delores Mistarz; m. Todd Charles Miller, Apr. 25, 1967; 1 child, Samantha Alexandria. BA magna cum laude, Calumet Coll., 1995; MA, Ind. U., 1999. Tchr. art Waukegan (Ill.) Sch. Sys., 2002—03, 2004—, Round Lake (Ill.) H.S., 2003—04. Organizer clothing drive Carman Buckner Sch., Waukegan, Ill., 2004. Prin. works include mural, Waukegan (Ill.) Sch. Sys. Grantee, Walmart, 2004. Avocations: painting, drawing, scuba diving, bicycling, ceramics. Home: 330 Greenview Ln Lake Villa IL 60046 Office: Waukegan School Dist Sheridan Rd Waukegan IL 60046 Office Phone: 847-336-3100. Personal E-mail: helenemiller@yahoo.com.

**MILLER, HENRY FORSTER,** architect; b. Sept. 16, 1916; s. Rutger Bleecker and Dorothy (Forster) M.; m. Maria Stockton Bullitt, May 6, 1942; children: Maria, Andrew, Dorothy, Steven, Henry Jr. BA, Yale U., 1938, MArch, 1948. Registered architect, Conn., R.I., Mass. Instr. archtl. design Yale Sch. Architecture, New Haven, 1948-49; dir. facilities planning office Yale U., New Haven, 1974-90; assoc. Harold H. Davis Architect, New Haven, 1949-56; ptnr. Davis, Cochran & Miller, New Haven, 1956-69, Davis, Cochran, Miller, Baerman, Noyes, New Haven, 1969-74; pvt. practice Orange, Conn., 1990—. Pres. Conn. Bldg. Congress, 1957-58. Prin. works include Booth Meml. Boys Club Bldg. (Archtl. Design award 1971), Columbus Sch. New Haven (HUD Design Excellence award 1970), Orange Conn. residence (listed on Nat. Register of Historic Places 2001). Mem. bd. govs. New Haven Boys and Girls Club, 1956-93; v.p. Comty. Coun. Greater New Haven, 1964-66; apptd. mem. State Housing Commn., Conn., 1970-72; mem. Conn. Rev. Bd. for Nat. Register of Hist. Places, 1974-81; founding dir. Conn. Trust for Hist. Preservation, 1975-86, pres., 1975-77; bd. dirs. New Haven Preservation Trust. Maj. F.A. AUS, 1941-46, ETO. Decorated Bronze

Star medal (2). Fellow AIA (Conn. state preservation coord. 1965-90, exec. com. 1967-69), Mory's Assn. Democrat. Roman Catholic. Avocations: drawing, painting. Home and Office: 30 Derby Ave Orange CT 06477-1403 Office Phone: 203-387-5917. E-mail: henry.miller@yale.edu.

**MILLER, HENRY FRANKLIN,** lawyer; b. Phila., May 19, 1938; s. Lester and Bessie (Posner) M.; m. Barbara Ann Gendel, June 20, 1964; children: Andrew, Alexa. AB, Lafayette Coll., 1959; JD, U. Pa., 1964. Bar: Pa. 1965. Law clk. U.S. Dist. Ct. Del., Wilmington, 1964-65; assoc. Wolf, Block, Schorr & Solis-Cohen LLP, Phila., 1965—71, ptnr., 1971—. Pres. Soc. Hill Synagogue, Phila., 1978-79, Big Brothers/Big Sisters Assn. of Phila., 1980-81, Jewish Family & Children's Agy., Phila., 1986-88. 1st lt. U.S. Army, 1959-60. Mem. Am. Coll. Real Estate Lawyers. Avocations: swimming, hiking, bicycling, reading. Office: Wolf Block Schorr & Solis-Cohen LLP 1650 Arch St Fl 21 Philadelphia PA 19103-2029 Office Phone: 215-977-2182. Business E-Mail: hmiller@wolfblock.com.

**MILLER, HERBERT DELL,** petroleum engineer; b. Oklahoma City, Sept. 29, 1919; s. Merrill Dell and Susan (Green) M.; m. Rosalind Rebecca Moore, Nov. 23, 1947; children: Rebecca Miller Wheeler, Robert Rexford. BS in Petroleum Engring., Okla. U., Norman, 1941. Registered profl. engr., Okla., Tex. Field engr. Amerada Petroleum Corp., Hobbs, N.Mex., 1947—48, Houston, 1948—49, dist. engr. Longview, Tex., 1949—57, sr. engr. Tulsa, 1957—62; petroleum engr. Moore & Miller Oil Co., Oklahoma City, 1962—78; owner Herbert D. Miller Co., Oklahoma City, 1978—. Maj., F.A. AUS, 1941—47, ETO. Decorated Bronze Star with oak leaf cluster, Purple Heart (U.S.); Croix de Guerre (France). Mem. AIME, Oklahoma City Golf. Republican. Episcopalian. (pres. Men's Club 1973). Home and Office: 1819 W Wilshire Blvd Oklahoma City OK 73116-4115

**MILLER, HERBERT ELMER,** accountant; b. DeWitt, Iowa, Aug. 11, 1914; s. Elmer Joseph and Marian (Briggs) M.; m. Lenore Snitkey, July 1, 1938; 1 dau., Barbara Ruth. AB, State U. Iowa, 1936, MA, 1937; PhD, U. Minn., 1944; Dr. h.c., Free U. Brussels, 1982; D.H.L. (h.c.), De Paul U., 1983. C.P.A., Iowa. Acctg. prof. U. Minn., U. Mich., Mich. State U., 1938-70; ptnr. Arthur Andersen & Co., Chgo., 1970-78; dir. Sch. Acctg., U. Ga., Athens, 1978-83. Co-author: Finney-Miller accounting series, 1950-70; editor, contbr.: C.P.A. Rev. Manual, 1951-79. Mem. AICPA (bd. dirs. 1968-70), Am. Acctg. Assn. (pres. 1965-66), Federated Schs. Acctg. (pres. 1982), Beta Gamma Sigma, Beta Alpha Psi (nat. pres. 1961-62) Home: 145 S Stratford Dr Athens GA 30605-3025

**MILLER, HOLLY DARA,** physician, director, healthcare educator, researcher; d. Algernon Maxwell and Constance Arlene (Becker) Miller; m. Allan Eric Siperstein, Nov. 12, 1995; children: Alden David Siperstein, Marion Alice Siperstein; m. Eric Albert Leon Meary, June 8, 1988 (div. 1995); 1 child, Aldea Marine Meary. MD, Albert Einstein Coll. of Medicine, N.Y.C. 1987; Internship, St. Vincent's Hosp., N.Y.C., 1989; MBA, ISA, Groupe HEC, Paris, 1994; Residency, Gen. Internal Medicine, U. Calif., San Francisco, 1996. Rsch. project mgr. Ciba-Geigy, Paris, 1990—92; staff physician On Lok Sr. Health Svcs., U. Calif., San Francisco, 1996—98; product mgr., mktg. dept. Oacis Healthcare Sys., San Rafael, Calif., 1998—99; mng. dir. The Cleve. Clinic, 1999—. Mem. editl. bd. MD Net Guide, Plainsboro, NJ, 2004—; mem. bd. dirs. Alpha - 1 Found., Fla., 2005—. Author: (articles) JAMIA. Grantee French-American Exch. Program, The French Govt., 1987, Rsch. in Healthcare Informatics, Robert Wood Johnson Found., 2004, Healthcare Informatics Rsch., Agy. for Healthcare and Rsch., 2004; scholar Josiah Macy Scholarship for Basic Sci. Rsch., Columbia U., 1982, Internat. Exch. Program, ISA, Groupe Hautes Etudes Commercials, 1993. Mem.: AMA. Achievements include research in ongoing funded research in Heathcare Informatics. Office: The Cleveland Clinic 9500 Euclid Ave CL30 Cleveland OH 44195 Office Phone: 216-444-2200.

**MILLER, I. GEORGE,** physician, educator, researcher; b. Chgo., Apr. 18, 1937; s. Irving George and Florence (Levy) M.; m. Arlette Goldmuntz, Mar. 25, 1962; children: Lisa, John, David. AB, Harvard U., 1958, MD, 1962. Intern Univ. Hosp., Western Res., U., Cleve., 1962-63; resident Univ. Hosp., Western Res., U., Cleve., 1962-65; epidemiology intelligence oficer Communicable Disease Ctr. USPHS, Atlanta, 1964-66; research fellow in medicine Harvard U. Med. Sch., Boston, 1966-69; asst. prof. pediatrics, epidemiology, biophysics and biochemistry Yale Sch. Medicine, New Haven, 1969-72, J.F. Enders prof., 1979—. Mem. exptl. virology study sect. NIH, 1974-77; mem. sci. adv. com. Damon Runyon Fund, 1979-85, dir., 1985-94; Leukemia Soc. Am., 1976-81. Contbr. numerous articles, chpts. to profl. publs.; editl. bd. Jour. Virology, 1981-87, Virology, 1982-86. Recipient epidemic Intelligence Service Alumni Assn. prize, 1967; Macy faculty scholar, 1977, Am. Cancer Soc. scholar, 1990; Howard Hughes Med. Inst. investigatorship, 1972-80 Fellow Infectious Diseases Soc. (Squibb award 1982, Enders award 1989); mem. Am. soc. Clin. Investigation, Am. Pediatric Soc., Am. Soc. Virology, Assn. Am. Physicians. Inst. Medicine. Jewish. Office: Yale U Sch Medicine Pediatrics Infectious Diseases PO Box 208064 New Haven CT 06520-8064 Office Phone: 203-785-4758. Business E-Mail: george.miller@yale.edu.

**MILLER, IRVING FRANKLIN,** chemical engineer, educator, biomedical engineer, academic administrator; b. N.Y.C., Sept. 27, 1934; s. Sol and Gertrude (Rochkind) M.; m. Baila Hannah Milner, Jan. 28, 1962; children: Eugenia Lynne, Jonathan Mark. BS in Chem. Engring., NYU, 1955; MS, Purdue U., 1956; PhD, U. Mich., 1960. Rsch. scientist United Aircraft Corp., Hartford, 1959-61; from asst. prof. to profl., head chem. engring. Poly. Inst. Bklyn., 1961-72; prof. bioengring., head bioengring. program U. Ill., Chgo., 1973-79, acting head sys. engring. dept., 1978-79, assoc. vice chancellor rsch., dean Grad. Coll., 1979-85, prof. chem. engring., head chem. engring. 1986-95, dir. Ctr. for Advanced Edn. and Rsch., 1989-90, dir. Office of Spl. Projects, 1990-92, dir. bioengring. program, 1992-95; dean Coll. Engring. U. Akron, Ohio, 1995-98, prof. biomed. engring., 1998-2000; dir. corp. ops. BioTechPlex Corp., 2002—. Cons. to industry; cons. NAS, NIH; dir. distance learning programs Ohio Aerospace Inst., 1998—2000. Editor: Electrochemical Bioscience and Bioengineering, 1973; contbr. articles profl. jours. Mem. AIChE, AAAS, Am. Chem. Soc., Biomed. Engring. Soc., N.Y. Acad Scis. Home: 1746 N Larrabee St Chicago IL 60614-5634 Office Phone: 312-266-1728. Personal E-mail: ifmiller@sbcglobal.net. Business E-Mail: ifmiller@uic.edu.

**MILLER, J. ALLEN,** lawyer; b. July 21, 1951; BA cum laude, U. NH, 1972; JD, Cornell U., 1979. Bar: NY 1980. Ptnr., co-coord. & chmn. Corp. Dept. Chadbourne & Parke LLP, NYC, co-coord., Latin Am. Practice Group. Spkr. in field; contbr. articles to profl. jour.; note & comment editor Cornell Internat. Law Jour., 1978—79. Mem.: ABA, NY State Bar Assn. Office: Chadbourne & Parke LLP 30 Rockefeller Plz New York NY 10112 Office Phone: 212-408-5454. Office Fax: 212-541-5369. Business E-Mail: amiller@chadbourne.com.

**MILLER, JACK DAVID R.,** radiologist, physician, educator; b. Johannesburg, Apr. 15, 1930; s. Harold Lewis and Inez (Behrman) M.; m. Miriam Sheckter, Dec., 1988. B.Sc., M.B., Ch.B., U. Witwatersrand, Johannesburg, 1956. Diplomate: Am. Bd. Radiology. Intern Coronation Hosp., Johannesburg, 1957-58; resident in radiology Passavant Meml. Hosp., Chgo., 1959-62, Wesley Meml. Hosp., Chgo., 1959-62; fellow in radiology Northwestern U. Med. Sch., 1962-63; chmn. dept. radiology U. Hosp., Edmonton, Alta., Canada, 1971-83; radiologist, dept. radiology U. Alta Hosp., 1963—2004, head, dir. neuroradiology, 1984—92; prof. emeritus radiology U. Alta., 1997—. Clin. prof. radiology U.Alta., 1971—Fellow Royal Coll. Physicians Can., Am. Coll. Radiology. Personal E-mail: miribud@shaw.ca.

**MILLER, JACQUELINE WINSLOW,** library director; b. N.Y.C., Apr. 15, 1935; d. Lynward Roosevelt and Sarah Ellen (Grevious) W.; 1 child, Percy Scott. BA, Morgan State Coll., 1957; MLS, Pratt Inst., 1960; grad. Profl. seminar, U. Md., 1973. Cert. profl. libr. With Bklyn. Pub. Libr., 1957-68; head ext. svcs. New Rochelle (N.Y.) Pub. Libr., 1969-70; br. adminstr. Grinton Will

Yonkers (N.Y.) Pub. Libr., 1970-75; dir. Yonkers Pub. Libr., 1975-96. Mem. adj. faculty grad. libr. studies Queens Coll., CUNY, 1989, 90. Mem. commr.'s com. Statewide Libr. Devel., Albany, N.Y., 1980; mem. N.Y. Gov.'s Commn. on Librs., 1990, 91; bd. dirs. Cmty. Planning Coun., Yonkers, N.Y., 1987; mem. Yonkers Black Women's Polit. Caucus, 1987; pres. bd. Literacy Vols. of Westchester County, 1991-92; mem. fair campaign practices com. LWV, 1996—. Recipient Yonkers Citizen award Ch. of Our Saviour, 1980, 2d Ann. Mae Morgan Robinson award Yonkers chpt. Westchester Black Women's Polit. Caucus, 1992, 3d Ann. Equality Day award City of Yonkers, 1992, African-Am. Heritage 1st award YWCA, 1994; named Outstanding Profl. Woman Nat. Assn. Negro Bus. and Profl. Women's Clubs Inc., 1981. Mem. ALA (councilor 1987-91), N.Y. State Libr. Assn., Pub. Libr. Dirs. Assn. (exec. bd.), N.Y. State Pub. Libr. Dirs. Assn., Westchester Libr. Assn., Yonkers C. of C. (bd. dirs. 1992-95), Educate the Girls, Inc. (bd. dirs., 2003—) Rotary (Yonkers chpt.). Personal E-mail: jacki@sprynet.com.

**MILLER, JAMES CLIFFORD, III,** economist; b. Atlanta, June 25, 1942; s. James Clifford and Annie (Moseley) M.; m. Demaris Humphries, Dec. 22, 1961; children: Katrina Demaris, John Felix, Sabrina Louise. BBA, U. Ga., 1964; PhD in Econs., U. Va., 1969; LLD (hon.), U. of Pacific, 1987; PhD (hon.), Kennesaw Coll., 1988. Asst. prof. Ga. State U., Atlanta, 1968-69; economist U.S. Dept. Transp., Washington, 1969-72; assoc. prof. econs. Tex. A&M U., College Station, 1972-74; economist U.S. Coun. Econ. Advs., Washington, 1974-75; asst. dir. U.S. Council Wage and Price Stability, Washington, 1975-77; resident scholar Am. Enterprise Inst., 1977-81; adminstr. Office Info. and Regulatory Affairs, Office Mgmt. and Budget and exec. dir. Presdl. Task Force on Regulatory Relief, Washington, 1981; chmn. FTC, Washington, 1981-85; dir. Office Mgmt. and Budget, Washington, 1985-88; disting. fellow, chmn., counsellor Citizens for a Sound Economy, 1988—2002; disting. fellow Ctr. for Study of Pub. Choice George Mason U., 1988—2002; sr. fellow Hoover Instn., 1988—. Pres., chmn. bd. Econ. Impact Analysts, Inc., 1978-02; chmn. and owner emeritus CapAnalysis Group of Howrey, 2002-06; bd. govs. US Postal Svc., 2003-, chmn., 2005-; sr. advisor Blackwell Sanders Peper Martin. Author: Why the Draft?: The Case for a Volunteer Army, 1968, Economic Regulation of Domestic Air Transport: Theory and Policy, 1974, Perspectives on Federal Transportation Policy, 1975, Benefit-Cost Analyses of Social Regulation: Case Studies from the Council on Wage and Price Stability, 1979, Reforming Regulation, 1980, The Federal Trade Commission: The Political Economy of Regulation, 1987, The Economist as Reformer, 1989, Fix the US Budget: Urgings of an "Abominable No-Man", 1994, Monopoly Politics, 1999. Candidate for Rep. nomination for U.S. Senate for Va., 1994, 96. Thomas Jefferson fellow, 1965-66, DuPont fellow, 1966-67, Ford Found. fellow, 1967-68. Mem. Am. Econ. Assn., Pub. Choice Soc., So. Econ. Assn. (exec. com. 1980-81, v.p. 1990-91), Adminstrv. Conf. U.S. (vice chmn. 1987-88). Republican. Baptist. Office: 750 17th St NW #1000 Washington DC 20006 Office Phone: 202-378-2302. Business E-Mail: jim@jimmiller.org.

**MILLER, JAMES FORREST,** lawyer; b. Sioux City, Ia., Jan. 28, 1952; AB magna cum laude, Dartmouth Coll., 1974; JD, Columbia Univ., 1977. Bar: DC 1978. Litigator, tax divsn. US Dept. Justice; sp. counsel US Dept. Treasury, 1989—93; ptnr., regulated industries, govtl. rels. Hunton & Williams LLP, Washington. Recipient Stone Scholar. Office: Hunton & Williams LLP 1900 K St NW Washington DC 20006-1109 Office Phone: 202-955-1934. Office Fax: 202-778-2201. Business E-Mail: jfmiller@hunton.com.

**MILLER, JAMES GEGAN,** research scientist; b. St. Louis, Nov. 11, 1942; s. Francis John and Elizabeth Ann (Caul) M.; m. Judith Anne Kelvin, Apr. 23, 1966; 1 child, Douglas Ryan. AB, St. Louis U., 1964; MA, Washington U., 1966, PhD, 1969. Asst. prof. physics Washington U., St. Louis, 1970-72, assoc. prof., 1972-77, prof. physics, 1977—, dir. lab for ultrasonics, 1987—; rsch. asst. prof. medicine, 1976-81, rsch. assoc. prof. medicine, 1981-88, rsch. prof. medicine, 1988-2000, prof. biomed. engring., 1998—, Albert Gordon Hill prof. physics, 1999—, prof. medicine, 2000—. Contbr. articles to profl. jours.; patentee in field. Recipient I-R 100 award, Indsl. Research Devel. Mag., 1974, 1978, Merit award, NIH, 1998, Tchg. award, Emerson U., 2004; grantee, NIH, NASA. Fellow IEEE (sr., gov. com. Ultrasonics, Ferroelectrics and Frequency Control Soc. 1978-80,86-88, 92-94, Achievement award 2006), Am. Inst. Ultrasound in Medicine, Acoustical Soc. Am. (Silver medal 2004), Am. Inst. Med. and Biol. Engring.; mem. Am. Phys. Soc., Sigma Xi (nat. lectr. 1981-82). Office: Washington Univ St Louis Physics Dept CB 1105 One Brookings Dr Saint Louis MO 63130 Office Phone: 314-935-6229. E-mail: james.g.miller@wustl.edu.

**MILLER, JAMES H.,** electric power industry executive; BSEE, U. Del. Plant engr. Pub. Svc. Electric & Gas, Salem, NJ; various Delmarva Power & Light Co.; v.p. ops., constrn. and engring. ABB Resource Recovery Sys., pres., 1990-93, U.C. Oper. Svcs., 1993-94, ABB Envrion. Sys. Inc., Birmingham, Ala., 1994-95; exec. v.p. prodn., nuc. regulatory and environ. affairs USEC Inc., Bethesda, Md., 1995—99, exec. v.p., COO, 1999—2001; pres. PPL Generation PPL Corp., Allentown, Pa., 2001—04, exec. v.p., COO, 2004—05, pres., COO, 2005—. With USN. Office: PPL Corp 2 N 9th St Allentown PA 18101-1179*

**MILLER, JAMES M.,** lawyer; b. Berwyn, Ill., Apr. 25, 1950; m. Luz Angela Aristizabal, July 13, 1991; children: Hillary Daniela, Maxwell James. BA magna cum laude, U. Miami, 1972; JD, U. Chgo., 1975. Bar: Fla. 1975. Shareholder Akerman & Senterfitt, Miami, Fla. Bd. dirs. Miami Mus. Sci., pres. 1989-91. Mem. ABA (litigation sect., corp., banking and bus. law sect.), Fla. Bar (vice-chmn. 11th jud. cir. grievance com. B 1982-84), Dade County Bar Assn. Office: Akerman Senterfitt SunTrust International Center One SE 3d Ave 28th Fl Miami FL 33131 Office Phone: 305-982-5624. Business E-Mail: james.millen@akeeman.com.

**MILLER, JAMES MCCALMONT,** pediatrician; b. Springfield, Mass., Sept. 25, 1938; s. John Haynes and Josephine (Darrah) M.; m. Jane Rose, July 7, 1975; children: John, Charlotte, Willard. AB, Hamilton Coll., 1960; MD, Cornell U., 1964. Resident U. Colo. Med. Ctr., Denver, 1964-67; staff pediatrician Kaiser Permanente Med. Ctr., Walnut Creek, Calif., 1969-87, chief pediatrician, 1971-82, Pleasanton, Calif., 1982-87; staff pediatrician Appalachian Regional Health, Hazard, Ky., 1987-92, N.W. Pediat. Ctr., Centralia, Wash., 1992—. Clin. assoc. U. N.Mex., Albuquerque, 1967-69; instr. U. Calif., San Francisco, 1969-87, U. Ky., Lexington, 1988-92. With U.S. Army, 1967-69. Fellow Am. Acad. Pediat.; mem. Wash. State Med. Assn. Office: Northwest Pediatric Ctr 1911 Cooks Hill Rd Centralia WA 98531-9027 Office Phone: 360-736-6778. E-mail: jmiller@localaccess.com.

**MILLER, JAMES ROBERT,** lawyer; b. McKeesport, Pa., Aug. 2, 1947; s. Robert Charles and Ethel Margaret (Yahn) M.; m. Kathleen Ann Galka, June 6, 1975; children: Jesse J., Cassidy A. BA, NYU, 1969; JD, Duquesne U., 1972. Bar: Pa. 1972, U.S. Dist. Ct. (we. dist.) Pa. 1974, U.S.Ct. Appeals (3d cir.) 1978, U.S. Ct. Appeals (11th cir.) 1989, U.S. Supreme Ct. 1990. Law clerk to Hon. James C. Crumlish, Jr. Commonwealth Ct. of Pa., Phila., 1972-74; shareholder Dickie, McCamey & Chilcote, Pitts., 1974—. Mem. ABA, Am. Coll. Trial Lawyers, Pa. Bar Assn., Acad. Trial Lawyers. Avocation: sports. Office: Dickie McCamey & Chilcote Two PPG Pl Ste 400 Pittsburgh PA 15222

**MILLER, JAMES RUMRILL, III,** finance educator; b. Phila., Dec. 21, 1937; s. James Rumrill and Elizabeth Pleasants (King) M.; m. Bettie M. Studer, May 1, 1969; children from previous marriage: Elizabeth, Katharine, Kerry. AB, Princeton U., 1959; MBA (Woodrow Wilson fellow), Harvard U., 1962; PhD, MIT, 1966. Sys. analyst MITRE Corp., Bedford, Mass., 1962—67; asst. prof. bus. adminstrn. Stanford U., 1967—69, assoc. prof., 1970—73, prof., 1973—, Walter and Elise Haas prof. bus. adminstrn., 1977—97, assoc. dean Bus. Sch., 1974—76, Walter and Elise Haas prof. bus. adminstrn. emeritus, 1997—. Cons. in field. Author: Professional Decision

Making, 1970; contbr. numerous articles to profl. jours. Mem. Phi Beta Kappa. Republican. Episcopalian. Office: 16641 W Loma Verde Trail Surprise AZ 85387 E-mail: mdmsinc@aol.com.

**MILLER, JAMES VINCE,** university president; b. Waynetown, Ind., July 16, 1920; s. J. Vince and Hazel B. (Spore) M.; m. Mildred Mae Hockersmith, June 13, 1943; children: Maryllyn Jean, Rachel Katherine. BA in Philosophy and English, U. Indpls., 1942; M.Div. in History and Lit., United Sem., Dayton, Ohio, 1945; postgrad., Earlham Coll., 1945-46; PhD in Philosophy, Boston U., 1955; LL.D. (hon.), Otterbein Coll., 1971, U. Indpls., 1979. Ordained to ministry Evang. United Brethren Ch., 1945; pastor Greensfork, Ind., 1944-46, Stow, Mass., 1946-48; faculty dept. philosophy and religion Bates Coll., Lewiston, Maine, 1950-64, prof., 1960-64, chmn. dept., 1958-64; acad. dean Otterbein Coll., Westerville, Ohio, 1964-68, v.p. for acad. affairs, acad. dean, 1968-71; pres. Pacific U., Forest Grove, Oreg., 1971-83, pres. emeritus, 1983—; pres. Nat. Coll. of Naturopathic Medicine, Portland, Oreg., 1989-93, pres. emeritus, 1993—. Adj. prof. Union Grad. Sch., 1970-78, San Francisco Theol. Sem., 1979-86; chmn. N.W. Assn. Pvt. Colls. and Univs., 1974-76; treas. Oreg. Ind. Coll. Assn., 1974-76, 76-78, chmn., 1978-79; adv. com. Oreg. Ednl. Coordinating Commn., 1976-79; chmn. council for higher edn. United Ch. Bd. Homeland Missions, 1975-76; former mem. adv. com. Gov.'s Listening Post; former mem. spl. com. on future of edn. in Oreg., Oreg. Ednl. Coordinating Commn.; mem. Oreg. Bd. Optometry, 1988-92. Mem.: Rotary. Methodist. Address: 1633 Mowry Sq Richland WA 99354-2612

**MILLER, JAN DEAN,** metallurgy educator; b. Dubois, Pa., Apr. 7, 1942; s. Harry Moyer and Mary Virginia (McQuown) M.; m. Patricia Ann Rossman, Sept. 14, 1963; children: Pamela Ann, Jeanette Marie, Virginia Christine. BS, Pa. State U., 1964; MS, Colo. Sch. of Mines, 1966, PhD, 1969. Rsch. engr. Anaconda Co., Mont., 1966; asst. prof. metallurgy U. Utah, Salt Lake City, 1968-72, assoc. prof., 1972-78, prof., 1978-2000, Ivor D. Thomas prof., 2000—, dept. chmn., 2002—; rsch. engr. Lawrence Livermore Lab., Calif. 1972. Cons. on processing of mineral resources to various cos. and govt. agys. Editor: Hydrometallurgy, Research, Development, and Plant Practice, 1983, others; contbr. over 425 articles to profl. jours.; 25 patents in field. Recipient Marcus A. Grossman award Am. Soc. Metals, 1974, Van Diest gold medal Colo. Sch. of Mines, 1977, Student award excellence in tchg. metall. engring. U. Utah, 1978, 82, 94, Extractive and Processing Lectr. award The Minerals, Metals and Materials Soc., 1992, Disting. Achievement medal Colo. Sch. of Mines, 1994, Best Paper award for fundamental rsch. 2000 TAPPI Recycling Symposium, 2000, Oustanding Tchg. award Coll. Mines and Earth Scis. U. Utah, 2000, J.D. Miller Symposium honor for innovations in resource processing, SME Annual meeting, Salt Lake City, 2005, Spl. Meritorious Recognition medal Gdansk U. Tech., Poland, 2005; Centennial fellow Coll. of Earth and Mineral Scis., Pa. State U., 1996. Mem. NAE, AIME (Henry Krumb lectr. 1987, Richards award 1991, Mineral Industry Edn. award 1997, Aplan award 2003), Soc. Mining, Metallurgy and Exploration (chmn. mineral processing divsn. 1980-81, Disting. Mem. award 1992, Antoine M. Gaudin award 1992), Fine Particle Soc., Am. Chem. Soc., Soc. Mining Engrs. (bd. dirs. 1980-83, program chmn. 1982-83, Taggart award 1986, 05, Stefanko award 1988, 02, symposium honoring J.D. Miller, 2005), Metall. Soc. (Extractive Metallurgy Tech. award 1988), Salt Lake Water and Tennis Club, U. Utah Faculty Club. Baptist. Office: U Utah Metall Engring 135 S 1460 E Rm 412 Salt Lake City UT 84112-0114 Office Phone: 801-581-5160. Business E-Mail: jdmiller@mines.utah.edu.

**MILLER, JAN PAUL,** lawyer, former prosecutor; b. Md. married; 2 children. BA in polit. sci., U. N.C., 1982; JD cum laude, Harvard U., 1985. Assoc. Christy & Viener LLP, 1985—86, Casner, Edwards & Roseman LLP, 1986—88, Gordon, Feinblatt, Rothman, Hoffberger & Hollander LLP, 1988—89; asst. U.S. atty. dist. Md US Dept. Justice, 1989—2002, U.S. atty. Ctrl. dist. Ill. Springfield, 2002—05; ptnr. Thompson Coburn LLP, Belleville, Ill., 2005—. Adj. prof. George Washington U. Recipient numerous commendations from law enforcement agencies, including FBI, U.S. Customs Svc., Drug Enforcement Adminstrn., U.S. Secret Svc., U.S. Postal Ins. Office: Thompson Coburn LLP 525 W Main St Belleville IL 62220*

**MILLER, JANEL HOWELL,** psychologist; b. Boone, N.C., May 18, 1947; d. John Estle and Grace Louise (Hemberger) Howell; m. C. Rick Miller, Nov. 24, 1968; children: Kimberly, Brian, Audrey, Rachel. BA, DePauw U., 1969; postgrad., Rice U., 1969; MA, U. Houston, 1972; PhD, Tex. A&M U., 1979. Lic. clin. psychologist, sch. psychologist Tex. Assoc. sch. psychologist Houston Ind. Sch. Dist., 1971-74; rsch. psychologist VA Hosp., Houston, 1972; assoc. sch. psychologist Clear Creek (Tex.) Ind. Sch. Dist., 1974-76; instr. psychology, counseling psychology intern Tex. A&M U., 1976-77; clin. psychology intern VA Hosp., Houston, 1977-78; coord. psychol. svcs. Clear Creek Ind. Sch. Dist., 1978-81, assoc. dir. psychol. svcs., 1981-82; pvt. practice Houston, 1982—. Faculty U. Houston-Clear Lake, 1984—; adolescent suicide cons., 1984—. DePauw U. Alumni scholar, 1965-69; NIMH fellow U. Houston, 1970-71. Mem. APA, Am. Assn. Marriage and Family Therapists, Soc. for Personality Assessment, Am. Coll. Forensic Examiners, Internat. Rorschach Soc., Tex. Psychol. Assn., Tex. Assn. Marriage and Family Therapists, Houston Psychol. Assn. (media rep. 1984-85), Houston Assn. Marriage and Family Therapists. Home: 806 Walbrook Dr Houston TX 77062-4030 Office: 16854 Royal Crest Dr Houston TX 77058-2529 Office Phone: 281-461-4098. Business E-Mail: shrinkskate@sbcglobal.net.

**MILLER, JEANNE-MARIE ANDERSON (MRS. NATHAN J. MILLER),** language educator, academic administrator; b. Washington, Feb. 18, 1937; d. William and Agnes Catherine (Johns) Anderson; m. Nathan John Miller, Oct. 2, 1960. BA, Howard U., 1959, MA, 1963, PhD, 1976. Instr. dept. English Howard U., Washington, 1965-76, asst. prof., 1976-79, assoc. prof., 1979-92, prof., 1992-97, prof. emeritus, 1997—, asst. dir. Inst. Arts and Humanities, 1973-75, asst. acad. planning office v.p. for acad. affairs, 1976-90. Cons. Am. Studies Assn., 1972—75, Silver Burdett Pub. Co., NEH, 1978—; mem. adv. bd. D.C. Libr. for Arts, 1973—. Editor, Black Theatre Bull., 1977-86; Realism to Ritual: Form and Style in Black Theatre, 1983; assoc. editor Theatre Jour., 1980-81; contbr. articles to profl. jours., chpts. to books. Mem. Washington Performing Arts Soc., 1971—, Friends of Sta. WETA-TV, 1971—, Mus. African Art, 1971—, Arena Stage Assocs., 1972—, Washington Opera Guild, 1982—, Wolf Trap Assocs., 1982—, Drama League N.Y., 1995, Shakespeare Theatre, 2001—, Met. Opera Guild, 2002—, Ford Found. fellow, 1970-72. So. Fellowships Fund fellow, 1973-74; Howard U. rsch. grant, 1975-76, 94-97, ACLS grant, 1978-79, NEH grant, 1981-84. Mem.: LWV, MLA, ACLU, AAUP, Nat. Archives Found., Folger Shakespeare Libr., Acad. Am. Poets, Am. Theatre and Drama Soc., Studio Mus. Harlem, Nat. Mus. Women in Arts, Nat. Bldg. Mus., Winterthur Guild, Hist. Soc. Washington, D.C. Preservation League, Nat. Trust Historic Preservation, Zora Neale Hurston Soc., Langston Hughes Soc., Ibsen Soc., Friends of Kennedy Ctr. for Performing Arts, Am. Higher Edn., Coll. Lang. Assn., Common Cause, Am. Assn. Higher Edn., Am. Studies Assn., Coll. English Assn., Nat. Coun. Tchrs. English, Sierra Club, Pi Lambda Theta. Democrat. Episcopalian. Home: 504 24th St NE Washington DC 20002-4818 E-mail: jmamiller@verizon.net.

**MILLER, JEFF,** congressman; b. St. Petersburg, Fla., June 27, 1959; m. Griswold Vicki Miller; 2 children. BA, U. Fla., 1984. Mem. Fla. Ho. of Reps., 1998—2002, U.S. Congress from 1st Fla. Dist., 2002—. Past chmn. Escambia County Legislative Del., 1999—2000. Mem. Fla. Hist. Soc., various areas of C. of C., Elizabeth Chapel United Meth. Ch., Chumuckla; mem. bd. dirs. Santa Rosa County United Way; Pregnancy Resource Ctr. Milton Milton; Gulf Coast Coun. Boy Scouts Am.; Fla. FFA Found. Mem.; Coun. Ready Infrastructure, Com. on Rules, Ethics and Elections, Com. on Gen. Govt. Appropriations, Congl. Redistricting Com., Utilities and Telecommunications Com. (chmn.), Com. on Vet. Affairs, Ho. Armed Svcs. Com. Republican. Office: Congress 324 Cannon HOB Washington DC 20515-0901

**MILLER, JEFFREY CLARK,** lawyer; b. Boston, Aug. 17, 1943; s. Andrew Otterson and Jeanne (White) M.; m. Susanne Jackson, Oct. 23, 1970; children: Gordon, Andrew, Katharine, Eric. BA, Yale U., 1965; JD, Cornell U., 1968. Bar: N.Y. 1970. Assoc. Miller, Montgomery, Spalding & Sogi, N.Y.C., 1968-69; sec. Jamaica Water & Utilities Inc., Greenwich, Conn., 1969-72; assoc. Reid & Priest, N.Y.C., 1972-86, ptnr., 1986-93; asst. gen. coun. Northeast Utiles Svc. Co., Berlin, Conn., 1993—. Bd. dirs. Wilson Point Property Owners Assn., Norwalk, Conn., 1972-74, pres., 1988-92; trustee St. Luke's Sch., New Canaan, Conn., 1991—, chmn., 1995-97; sec. Yale U. Class 1965, 1990-2000. Mem. ABA, N.Y. State Bar Assn. (sec. pub. utility com. 1983-87). Home: 1 Valley Rd Norwalk CT 06854-5010 Office: Northeast Utilities Svc Co PO Box 270 Hartford CT 06141-0270 E-mail: millejc@nu.com.

**MILLER, JENNIFER JEAN,** lawyer, law educator; b. Sault Sainte Marie, Mich., Dec. 26, 1976; d. Glenys Joy Miller. BSc in Polit. Sci., Pre-Law, Lake Superior State U., 1998; JD, Thomas M. Cooley Law Sch., 2001. Bar: Mich. 2003, Chippewa County Bar Assn. 2003, Sault Tribe Chippewa Indians 2003, Bay Mills Tribal Ct. 2004. Law clerk Mahjoory, Mahjoory & Berry PC, Lansing, 1999—2001, Law Office WM. Dyke Justin, PC, 2001—02, Law Office of Mark Dobias PC, 2001—02; law clerk, atty. Chippewa County Pub. Defender, 2002—04; atty., pvt. practice Jennifer J. Miller Atty. At Law, 2003—. Adj. prof. Lake Superior State U., 2002—. Office: Jennifer J Miller Attorney At Law 613 Eureka St Sault Sainte Marie MI 49783 Office Phone: 906-632-4157.

**MILLER, JENNIFER L.,** elementary school educator, small business owner; d. Frank L. and Patricia M. Warfel; m. Ryan G. Miller, July 2, 1994; children: Calleigh L., Garrett R., Trevor R. BA in Elem. Edn. (hon.), U. Portland, 1992. Cert. tchr. A-regular classroom Alaska, spl. edn. endorsement. Dir. summer recreation City of Wrangell, 1990—91; summer acad. tchr. geology; pvt. tutor Wrangell, 1991—92; 1st grade tchr. Wrangell City Schs., 1992—95, asst. coach h.s. girls basketball, 1993—94, multiage tchr. 1-2, 1995—96, multiage tchr. 2-3, 1996—2002; substitute tchr. 1998—92; multiage tchr. 1-2-3 Wrangell City Schs., 2002—03, multiage tchr. 2-3, 2003—04; tchr. 3rd grade Wrangell (Alaska) City Schs., 2004—; co-owner Clearwater Packing. Benchmark cut score com. dept. edn. State of Alaska, benchmark test bias com. edn. and early devel., stds. based assessment validation com., 2004—, content rev. com., 2005—, mem. dept. edn. data review com., 2006; adv. bd. Evergreen Elem., 2002—. Co-founder Evergreen Agtrl. Testing Site; leader Girl Scouts, Wrangell, 2002; active Friends of the Libr., Wrangell, Master Gardener's, Alaska; cmty. fair vendor Alaska, 1997; vol. Wrangell Little League, 2002, Alaskans for Drug Free Youth, Alaska, 1991, Hershey Track and Field, Alaska, 1990—91, Stikine River Rats Swim Team, Alaska, 1992; judge Wrangell H.S. Cheerleaders, Alaska, 1990—92. Recipient Youth Garden grant, Nat. Gardening Assn., 1999, Clay Muralist grant, Alaska Arts in Edn. Mem.: ASCD, NEA, NSTA, Alaska State Literacy Assn., Alaska Coun. Tchrs. Math., Internat. Reading Assn., Wrangell Tchr.'s Assn. (sec. 2000—, negotiations com., bldg. rep., tchr. of Yr. 1997, 2001, 2006), Nat. Coun. Tchrs. English, Assn. for Childhood Edn. Internat., Juneau-Haines Reading Coun., Nat. Coun. Tchrs. Math., Elk. Home: PO Box 1899 25 Mile Zimovia Hwy Wrangell AK 99929 Home Fax: 907-874-3182. Personal E-Mail: rjcgmill@aptalaska.net.

**MILLER, JERRY HUBER,** retired university chancellor; b. Salem, Ohio, June 15, 1931; s. Duber Daniel and Ida Claire (Holdereith) M.; m. Margaret A. Setter, 1958; children: Gregory, Joy, Carol, Beth, David. BA, Harvard U., 1953; MDiv., Hamma Sch. Theology, 1957; DD (hon.), Trinity Luth. Sem., 1981. Ordained to ministry Luth. Ch., 1957. Research assoc., intern Cornell U., Ithaca, NY, 1955-56; instr. Wittenberg U., Springfield, Ohio, 1956-57; parish pastor Ch. of Good Shepherd, Cin., 1957-62; asst. to pres. Ohio Synod Luth. Ch. Am., 1962-66; sr. campus pastor, dir. campus ministry U. Wis., Madison, 1966-69; regional dir. Nat. Luth. Campus Ministry, Madison, 1969-76, exec. dir. Chgo., 1977-81; pres. Calif. Luth. U., Thousand Oaks, 1981-92, chancellor, 1992-94, pres. emeritus, 1994—; ret. Ventura County Maritime Mus., Channel Islands Harbor, Calif., 1993-95. Chmn. Los Robles Bank, Thousand Oaks, 1987-2000; mem. exec. com. Coun. Nat. Colls., Washington, Assn. Ind. Calif. Colls. and Univs., 1981-92, Coun. Luth. Colls., Luth. Ednl. Conf. N.Am., 1977-94; vice chair bd. behavioral sci. State Calif.; bd. dirs. Santa Barbara Bank and Trust. Editor: The Higher Disciplines, 1956; contbr. articles to profl. jours. Bd. dirs. Wittenberg U., Augustana Coll., Rock Island, Ill., United Way, Thousand oaks, Ventura County chpt. ARC, Thousand Oaks, YMCA; chmn. bd. dirs. Los Robles Hosp.; vice chair Stagecoach Inn Mus. Found., 1998—; bd. govs. Thousand Oaks Civic Arts Plaza, 2005—. Recipient Patrick Henry medal, Mil. Order of World Wars, 1992; named Man of Yr., Salem, 1975, Man of Yr. Conejo Valley, 1999; Siebert Found. fellow, 1975. Mem. Am. Assn. Higher Edn., Council Advancement and Support Edn., Harvard Alumni Assn., Western Coll. Assn. (bd. dirs.), Conejo Valley C. of C. (bd. dirs.), Conejo Symphony Orch. (bd. dirs.), Conejo Valley Hist. Soc. (bd. dirs. 1995—), Sr. Concerns Conejo Valley. Clubs: Harvard (Ill., Ohio, Wis., Calif.), YMCA (regional bd. dirs., vice chair 1996-99), Rotary. Avocations: skiing, golf, hiking, travel. Personal E-Mail: msmjhm@aol.com.

**MILLER, JO CAROLYN DENDY,** family and marriage counselor, educator; b. Gorman, Tex., Sept. 16, 1942; d. Leonard Lee and Vera Vertie (Robison) Dendy; m. Douglas Terry Barnes, June 1, 1963 (div. June 1975); children: Douglas Alan, Bradley Jason; m. Walton Sansom Miller, Sept. 19, 1982. BA, Tarleton State U., Stephenville, Tex., 1964; MEd, U. North State, 1977; PhD, Tex. Woman's U., 1993. Tchr. Mineral Wells (Tex.) H.S., 1964-65, Weatherford (Tex.) Mid. Sch., 1969-74; counselor, instr. psychology Tarrant County Jr. Coll., Hurst, Tex., 1977-82; pvt. practice Dallas, 1982—. Author: (with Velma Baker, Jeannene Ward) Becoming: A Human Relations Workbook, 1981. Mem. ACA, Tex. State Bd. Examiners Profl. Counselors, Tex. State Bd. Marriage and Family Therapists, Tex. Counseling Assn., North Ctrl. Tex. Counseling Assn., Dallas Symphony Orch. League, Nat. Coun. Family Rels., Tex. Mental Health Counselors Assn., Internat. Assn. for Marriage and Family Counselors. Methodist. Office: 8222 Douglas Ave Ste 777 Dallas TX 75225-5938 Office Phone: 214-691-0400. Personal E-Mail: jcdmphd@sbcglobal.net.

**MILLER, JOEL STEVEN,** inorganic and organic materials chemist; b. Detroit, Oct. 14, 1944; s. John and Rose M.; m. Elaine J., Sept. 20, 1970; children: Stephen D., Mark A., Alan D. BS in Chemistry, Wayne State U., 1967; PhD, UCLA, 1971. Mgr. rsch. Occidental Rsch. Corp., Irvine, Calif., 1979-83; supr. rsch. Cen. R & D Lab. E. I. Du Pont Nemours & Co., Wilmington, Del., 1983-93; prof. chemistry U. Utah, 1993—, adj. prof. materials sci., 1994—2000. Disting. prof., assoc. Inorganic Synthesis Corp., Chgo.; vis. prof. U. Calif., Irvine, 1980, Weizmann Inst., Rehovot, Israel, 1985, U. Pa., Phila., 1988, U. Paris-Sud, 1991; Schmidt lectr. Weizmann Inst. Sci. Editor 16 books; mem. adv. bd. Jour. Materials Chemistry, 1991—2003, Advanced Materials, 1994—; mem. editl. bd. CrystEngComm, 1999—; mem. editl. adv. bd. Inorganic Chemistry, 2001-03, Chemistry-A European Journal; contbr. over 450 articles to sci. jours. Indsl. fellow in material sci. northwestern U., 1991-93; Wilhelm Manchot rsch. fellow 1996; fellow Japan Soc. Promotion Sci., 2000; recipient Disting. Rsch./Creative award, U. Utah, 2001, Gov. of Vt.'s medal for sci. and tech., 2004. Mem. Am. Chem. Soc. (chmn. solid state subdiv. 1989, Utah award, 2003, Award Chemistry of Materials, 2000). Achievements include discovery and development of organic magnets and conductors. Office: U Utah Dept Chemistry Salt Lake City UT 84112 Office Phone: 801-585-5455. Business E-Mail: jsmiller@chem.utah.edu.

**MILLER, JOHN,** federal agency administrator, former news correspondent; married. Grad., FBI Nat. Exec. Inst. Correspondent WNEW-TV, 1973, WNBC-TV, 1988—94, ABCNEWS Law & Justice Unit, 1997—2002; co-anchor 20/20 ABC, 2002—03; dep. police commr., chief spokesman for commr. NYC Police Dept., 1994—95; bur. chief, counter-terrorism 7 criminal intelligence bur. LA Police Dept., 2003—05; asst. dir. pub. affairs FBI, Washington, 2005—. Co-author (with Michael Stone & Chris Mitchell): The Cell: Inside the 9/11 Plot, and Why the FBI and CIA Failed to Stop It, 2003.

Recipient Emmy awards for broadcast journalist (9), Peabody awards (2), Dupont-Columbia award. Mem.: Internat. Assn. Police Chiefs, Internat. Assn. Bomb Technicians. Office: FBI 950 Pennsylvania Ave NW Washington DC 20535*

**MILLER, JOHN EDDIE,** lawyer; b. Wayne, Mich., Nov. 14, 1945; s. George Hayden and Georgia Irene (Stevenson) M.; m. Nancy Carol Sanders, Jan. 7, 1968; children: Andrea Christine, Matthew Kit. BA, Baylor U., 1967; JD, U. Memphis, 1973; LLM, U. Mo., 1980. Bar: Mo. 1974, U.S. Dist. Ct. (we. dist.) Mo. 1974, Tex. 1982. Asst. prof. Central Mo. State U., Warrensburg, 1973-74; sole practice Sedalia, Mo., 1974-79; sr. contract administr. Midwest Research Inst., Kansas City, Mo., 1979-81, Tracor Inc.. Austin, Tex., 1981-84; contract negotiator Tex. Instruments, Austin, 1984-86; sr. contract administr. Tracor Aerospace Inc., Austin, 1986-87, Radian Corp., Austin, 1987-96; counsel., asst. co. sec. Radian Internat. LLC, Austin, 1996—. Corp. sec. Radian Southeast Asia Ltd., Bangkok, 1995—, dir. Radian Southeast Asia Ltd., Bangkok, 1996—; corp. sec. Radian Internat. Overseas Mgmt. Co., 1996—; instr. bus. law State Fair CC, Sedalia, 1974-79, Austin CC, 1983-84. Bd. dirs. Legal Aid Western Mo., 1977—79, Boy's Club, Sedalia, 1974—79. With U.S. Army, 1968—71. Mem.: U.S. Tennis Assn., Tex. Bar Assn. (intellectual property law sect., internat. law sect., computer law sect.), Mo. Bar Assn. (internat. law com., patent, trademark and copyright law com., tech. law com.), Phi Alpha Delta. Office Phone: 512-231-6062. E-mail: johnemiller@excite.com, ttjohnemiller@hotmail.com.

**MILLER, JOHN EDWARD,** military officer, educational association administrator, information technology executive; b. Paragould, Ark., May 8, 1941; s. Wardlow Knox and Anna Mae (Danford) M.; m. Joan Carolyn Capano, Oct. 5, 1968; children: C. Claire, J. Andrew, JoAnna M., Mary Ellen. BS in Math., S.W. Mo. State U., 1963; MS in Ops. Tech., Ga. Inst. Tech., 1971; postgrad., Yale U., 1991. Commd. 2d lt. U.S. Army, 1963, advanced through grades to lt. gen., 1993; student, then author, instr., grad. studies faculty mem. U.S. Army Command and Gen. Staff Coll., Ft. Leavenworth, Kans., 1974—77; bn. comdr. 4th Brigade, 4th Inf. Divsn., Wiesbaden, Germany, 1977—79; ops. and tng. officer 8th Inf. Div., Badkreuznach, Germany, 1979—81; student U.S. Army War Coll., Carlisle, Pa., 1982; divsn. chief Office Dep. Chief of Staff for Rsch. Devel. and Acquisition, Dept. Army, Washington, 1982—84; brigade comdr., chief of staff 9th Inf. Divsn., Ft. Lewis, Wash., 1984—87; asst. for combat devels. U.S. Army Tng. and Doctrine Command, Ft. Monroe, Va., 1987—88; asst. divsn. comdr. for ops. and tng. 8th Inf. Divsn., Baumholder, Germany, 1988—89; dep. comdt. U.S. Army Command and Gen. Staff Coll., Ft. Leavenworth, 1989—91; comdt. 101st Airborne Divsn., Ft. Campbell, Ky., 1991—93; comdt. U.S. army command, gen. staff coll. U.S. Army, Ft. Leavenworth, 1993—95; dep. comdg. gen. U.S. Army Tng. and Doctrine Command, Ft. Monroe, Va., 1995—97; exec. dir. learning solutions Oracle Corp., Reston, Va., 1997—2000, v.p. bus. develop. 2000—02, exec. dir. def. bus. ops., 2000—03, v.p. govt. ops., 2003—05, 2005—; pres., gen. mgr. Titan linguist ops. and tech. support L-3 Comms., Inc., 2005—. Apptd. mem. Am. U. MBA adv. bd., 1999; apptd. chair exec. bd. Nat. Academies, Army Sci. and Tech., 2001, Army Sci. Bd., 1999, Mem. Def. Sci. Bd., 2003; selected guest lectr. Def. Experts Exch., JFK Sch. Govt., Harvard U. and Peoples Liberation Army, China. Chair Army Distaff Found., 2003—. Decorated Disting. Svc. medal U.S. Army; recipient Outstanding Alumni award, S.W. Mo. State U., 1993. Mem. Assn. U.S. Army, Disabled Am. Vets Assn., 101st Airborne Divsn.Assn. Republican. Avocations: tennis, skiing, sailing. Office: 1900 Campus Commons Reston VA 20191 Office Phone: 703-390-7300. Personal E-mail: john.e.miller@l-3com.com.

**MILLER, JOHN GRIDER,** writer; b. Annapolis, Md., Aug. 23, 1935; s. John Stanley and Ruby Corinne (Young) M.; m. Susan Bradner Bailey, Oct. 26, 1974; children: Kerry, John, Alison. BA, Yale U., 1957. Commd. 2d lt. USMC, 1957, advanced through grades to col., inf./ops. advisor Vietnamese Marine Corps., 1970-71, prin. speechwriter for Commandant Washington, 1971-76, commd. officer Battalion Landing Team, 1977-78, asst. chief of staff ops. and plans III Amphibious Force Okinawa, 1982-83, dep. dir. Marine Corps History Washington, 1983-85, ret., 1985; mng. editor Procs. and Naval History U.S. Naval Inst., Annapolis, Md., 1985-2000. Author: The Battle to Save the Houston, 1985. (Pocket Books edit., 1992, Bluejacket edit., 2000), The Bridge at Dong Ha, 1989, (Dell edit. 1990, Bluejacket edit., 1996, Audiobook edit., 1997), Punching Out: A Guide to Post-Military Transition, 1994, The Co-Vans: U.S. Marine Advisors in Vietnam, 2000; contbr. author: The Marines, 1998, Commandants of the Marine Corps, 2004. Decorated Legion of Merit with gold star, Bronze Star with combat V, Cross of Gallantry, Vietnamese Marine Corps.; recipient Author of Yr. award Naval Inst., 1990, Alfred Thayer Mahan award Navy League of U.S., 2002. Mem. Marine Corps. Hist. Found. (bd. dirs., Gen. Wallace M. Greene Jr. Book award 1989, Disting. Svc. award 1998), Mil. Order of World Wars (past chpt. comdr., chmn. nat. mag. com.), Civitan Internat. (past chpt. pres.), Washington Naval and Maritime Corrs.' Cir., New Providence Club, Annapolis Chorale. Avocations: music, piano, choral singing, boating. Home: 21 Sands Ave Annapolis MD 21403-4426 E-mail: millerjohng@comcast.net.

**MILLER, JOHN PETER (JACK MILLER),** journalist; b. Aug. 3, 1928; s. Wesley and Margaret (Baker) M.; m. Helen DeMars, July 30, 1949 (dec.); children: Candice(dec.), Gregory(dec.). Student, Welland and Toronto. From sports page editor to front page editor Welland Evening Tribune, 1949—53; with Hamilton (Ont.) Spectator, 1953—71, radio and TV columnist, 1955—71; with Toronto Daily Star, 1971—91, radio and TV columnist, 1971—78, comm. editor, 1979—85, sci. columnist, 1982—85, sci. writer, 1985—89, sci. editor, 1989—91, sci. corr., 1991—95; prof. journalism Niagara Coll., 1996—99. Frequent TV and radio appearances. Contbr. stories to mags. Mem.: Can. Sci. Writers Assn. (2 writing awards 1985, writing award 1987, 2 writing awards 1988, writing award 1989). Office: 162 Martindale Rd Apt 101 Saint Catharines ON Canada L2S 3S4 E-mail: jackasinmiller@yahoo.com.

**MILLER, JOHN ROBERT,** oil industry executive; b. Lima, Ohio, Dec. 28, 1937; s. John O. and Mary L. (Zickafoose) M.; m. Karen A. Eier, Dec. 30, 1961; children: Robert A., Lisa A., James E. BSChE with honors, U. Cin., 1960, D.Comml. Sc. hon., 1983. With Standard Oil Co., Cleve., 1960-86, dir. fin., 1974-75, v.p. fin., 1975-78, v.p. transp., 1978-79, sr. v.p. tech. and chems., 1979-80, pres., COO, bd. dirs., 1980—86; chmn., CEO TBN Holdings, Cleve., 1986—2000, Petroleum Ptnrs., Cleve., 2000—03; chmn. SIRVA, Inc., 2006—. Bd. dirs. Cambrex Corp., Eaton Corp., Graphic Packaging Corp.; former chmn. Fed. Res. Bank, Cleve. Mem. Pepper Pike Club, The Country Club, Chagrin Valley Hunt Club, Tau Beta Pi. Office: SIRVA Inc 7511 Creek View Trl Chagrin Falls OH 44023 Office Phone: 440-543-2128. Business E-Mail: office@johnrmiller.com.

**MILLER, JOHN RONALD,** minister; b. LA, Jan. 4, 1938; s. Clarence Raymond and Yolanda Sarah (Capenaro) M.; m. Madelon Louise Tetaz, Mar. 26, 1966; children: Sarah Louise, John Ronald. BA, Southwestern Coll., 1960; MDiv, Drew U., 1963; MA, Rutgers U., 1968. Ordained to ministry United Meth. Ch., 1965, United Ch. Christ, 1966. Pastor Burden (Kans.) Meth. Ch., 1958-60; min. Wilson Meml. Union Ch., Watchung, NJ, 1961—. Mem. Consultation on Ch. Union, Princeton, N.J., 1982—, com. on disabled United Ch. of Christ, Montclair, N.J., 1982—. Chmn. Dorthea Dix Chapel Bldg. Program; pres. Trenton Psychiat. Hosp.-State of N.J., 1985; mem. N.J. State Bd. Human Svcs., 1996—. Southwestern Coll. scholar, 1960, Tipple scholar, 1960. Mem. Nat. Coun. Chs. of Jesus Christ (governing bd. 1985—), Internat. Coun. Community Chs. (moderator ecumenical commn. 1984—, regional trustee, exec. bd. 1987, v.p. exec. bd. 1991), pres. communion 1995-97), Optimists. Mem. United Ch. Of Christ. Office: Mary E Wilson Meml Union Ch 7 Valley Rd Watchung NJ 07069-6034 Office Phone: 908-755-5020.

**MILLER, JOHN T., JR.,** lawyer, educator; b. Waterbury, Conn., Aug. 10, 1922; s. John T. and Anna (Purdy) M.; children: Kent, Lauren, Clare, Miriam, Michael, Sheila, Lisa, Colin, Margaret. AB with high honors, Clark U., 1944;

JD, Georgetown U., 1948; Docteur en Droit, U. Geneva, 1951; postgrad., U. Paris, 1951. Bar: Conn. 1949 (inactive), D.C. 1950, U.S. Ct. Appeals (2d, 3d, 5th, 10th, 11th and D.C. cirs.), U.S. Supreme Ct. 1952. With Econ. Cooperation Adminstn. Am. Embassy, London, 1950-51; assoc. Covington & Burling, 1952-53, Gallagher, Connor & Boland, 1953-62; pvt. practice Washington, 1962—. Adj. prof. law Georgetown U. Law Ctr., Washington, 1959—; mem. Panel on Future of Internat. Ct. Justice. Co-author: Regulation of Trade, 1953, Modern American Antitrust Law, 1958, Major American Antitrust Laws, 1965; author: Foreign Trade in Gas and Electricity in North America: A Legal and Historical Study, 1970, Energy Problems and the Federal Government: Cases and Material, 8th edit., 1996, Deregulated Natural Gas and Electric Power Industries Seminar: Case Material, 5th edit., 2006; contbr. articles to profl. jours. Trustee Clark U., 1970-76, De Sales Sch. of Theology, 1993-97; mem. bd. advisors Georgetown Visitation Prep. Sch., 1978-94, trustee, 1994-96, emeritus trustee, 1996—; former fin. chmn. troop 46 Nat. Capital Area coun. Boy Scouts Am.; pres. Thomas More Soc. Am., 1996-97. 1st lt. U.S. Army, 1943-46, 48-49. Decorated Bronze Star; recipient 10 yr. teaching award, Nat. Jud. Coll., 1983. Mem. ABA (coun., former administrv. law sect. 1972-73, ho. dels. 1991-93), AAUP, D.C. Bar Assn., Energy Bar Assn. (pres. 1990-91), Congl. Country Club, Army and Navy Club (bd. govs. 2000—), DACOR, Prettyman-Leventhal Am. Inn of Ct. (master 1988-99, pres. 1995-96), Sovereign Mil. Order of Malta (knight). Republican. Roman Catholic. Home: 4721 Rodman St NW Washington DC 20016-3234 Office: 1001 Connecticut Ave NW Washington DC 20036-5504 Office Phone: 202-331-1630. E-mail: jtmillerjr@erols.com.

**MILLER, JOHN WINSTON,** academic administrator; m. Barbara Miller; children: Lauren, Elizabeth, Raymond. BS in Guidance, Ohio U., 1969; MS in Edn., No. Ill. U., 1972; PhD in Edn., Purdue U., 1975. Pub. sch. tchr., Chgo. and Ind.; from asst. prof. to prof., assoc dean edn. Wichita State U., 1974—86; prof., dean Coll. Edn. Ga. So. U., 1986—93, Fla. State U., 1993—99; chancellor U. Wis., Whitewater, Wis., 1999—2005; pres. Ctrl. Conn. State U., New Britain, 2005—. Office: Ctrl Conn State U 1615 Stanley St New Britain CT 06050*

**MILLER, JON PHILIP,** marketing professional, pharmaceutical executive; b. Moline, Ill., Mar. 30, 1944; s. Clyde Sheldon and Alice Lenora (Taes) M.; m. Shirley Ann Hymes, Aug. 21, 1965; children: Melissa, Elizabeth. AB, Augustana Coll., 1966; PhD, St. Louis U., 1970; MBA, Pepperdine U., 1983. Rsch. assoc. to sr. biochemist ICN Pharm., Inc., Irvine, Calif., 1970—72, leader molecular pharmacology group, 1972—73, head molecular pharmacology/drug metabolism dept., 1973—76, dir. biology divsn., 1975—76; dir. SRI-NCI liaison group SRI Internat. (formally Stanford Rsch. Inst.), Menlo Park, Calif., 1976—78; sr. bioorganic chemist SRI Internat., Menlo Park, 1978—80, head medicinal biochemistry program, 1980—84, dir. biotech. rsch. dept., 1982—85, dir. biotech. and biomed. rsch. lab., 1985—92, assoc. dir. life scis. divsn., 1989—92; dir. bus. devel., strategic mktg. MDS Panlabs, Inc., Bothell, Wash., 1992—98; dir. pharm. mktg. Applied Biosys., Foster City, Calif., 1998—2001; dir. bus. devel ACLARA Bioscis., Mountain View, Calif., 2001—03; pres. Miller & Co., Foster City, 2003—. Office: Miller & Co 1147 Blythe St Foster City CA 94404 Personal E-mail: jm330@sbcgobal.net.

**MILLER, JONATHAN F.,** Internet company executive; b. 1957; V.p., programming and NBA entertainment NBA, NYC; launched Paramount Comedy Channel, London; joined Nickelodeon, 1993; CEO, mng. dir Nickelodeon UK, 1993; mng. dir. Nickelodeon Internat.; pres., CEO USA Broadcasting, 1997—99, USA Electronic Commerce Solutions, 1999—2000, USA Info. and Services (USAIS), 2000—02; chmn., CEO American Online, Inc., Dulles, Va., 2002—. Recipient Vanguard award, Producers Guild Am., 2006. Office: American Online Inc 22000 AOL Way Dulles VA 20166 Office Phone: 703-265-1000.*

**MILLER, JONATHAN WOLFE,** theater and film director, physician; b. London, July 21, 1934; s. Emanuel Miller; m. Helen Rachel Collet, 1956; 3 children. Ed., St. John's Coll., Cambridge U.; MB Ch, Univ. Coll. Hosp. Med. Sch., London, 1959; DLitt (hon.), U. Leicester, 1981, Cambridge U., 1996; Dr. (hon.), Open U., 1983. Dir. Nottingham Playhouse, 1963-69; assoc. dir. nat. Theatre, 1973-75; mem. Arts Coun., 1975-76; artistic dir. Old Vic, 1988-90; lectr. Nat. Gallery, 1995, Met. Mus., N.Y.C., 1995; curator major exhbn. Nat. Gallery, London, 1998. Vis. prof. drama Westfield Coll., U. London, 1977-78; lectr. wide variety of subjects. Co-author, actor in Beyond the Fringe, 1961-64; dir. Under Plain Cover Royal Ct. Theatre, 1962, The Old Glory, N.Y.C., 1964, Prometheus Bound, Yale Drama Sch., 1967, Oxford and Cambridge Shakespeare Co. prod. of Twelfth Night, on tour in U.s., 1969; dir. for Nat. Theatre, London: The Merchant of Venice, 1970, Danton's Death, 1971, The School for Scandal, 1972, The Marriage of Figaro, 1974; other prodns. include: The Tempest, London, 1970, Prometheus Bound, London, 1971, The Taming of the Shrew, Chichester, Eng., 1972, The Seagull, Chichester, 1973, The Malcontent, Nottingham, Eng., 1973, The Family in Love, 1974, The Importance of Being Earnest, 1975, All's Well That Ends Well, Measure For Measure, Greenwich Season, 1975, Three Sisters, 1977; dir. operas Arden Must Die, 1973, Sadler's Well Theatre, 1974, The Cunning Little Vixen, Glyndebourne, 1975, 77, Marriage of Figaro, Vienna State Opera, 1991, Robert Devereux, Monte Carlo, 1992, Die Gezeichnete, Zurich, 1992, Maria Stuarda, Monte Carlo, 1993, the Secret Marriage, Opera North, 1993; dir. for English Nat. Opera: The Marriage of Figaro, 1978, The Turn of the Screw, 1979, 91, Arabella, 1980, Othello, 1981, Rigoletto, 1982, 85 (alwo at Met. Opera, N.Y.C.), Fidelio, 1982, 83, Don Giovanni, 1985, The Magic Flute, 1986, Tosca, 1986, The Mikado, 1986, 88, The Barber of Seville, 1987, Cosi fan Tutte, 1995, Carmen, 1995; dir. for Kent Opera: Cosi Fan Tutte, 1975, Rigoletto, 1975, Orfeo, 1976, Eugene Onegin, 1977, La Traviata, 1979, 96, Falstaff, 1980, 81, Fiedlio, 1982, 83, 88; dir. for La Scala Milan: La Fanciulla del West, 1991, Manon Lescaut, 1998; dir. for Maggio Musicale, Florence: Don Giovanni, 1990, Cosí fan Tutte, 1991, 94, Marriage of Figaro, 1992, La Bohéme, 1994, La Bohéme, which transfered to La Bastille, 1995, dir., Strass Ariadne auf Naxos, 1997; dir. Met. Opera, N.Y.: Katya Kabanova, 1991, Pelléas et Mélisande, 1995; dir in co-prodn. with L.A. Music Ctr. and Houston Grand Opera House Der Rosenkavalier, 1994, King Lear at Lincoln Centre, N.Y., 2004; dir. Broadway play Long Day's Journey Into Night, 1986, The Taming of the Shrew at Royal Shakespeare Co.. Stratford, 1987, Andromache, One Way Pendulum, Bussy D'Ambois, all at Vic, 1988, The Tempest, 1988, Turn of the Screw, 1989, King Lear, 1989, The Liar, 1989, Cosi Fan Tutte at Lincoln Centre, N.Y., 2004; films include: Take a Girl Like You, 1969; TV films include: Whistle and I'll Come to You, 1967, Alice in Wonderland, 1967, The Body in Question Series, 1978, Henry the Sixth, part I, 1983, States of Mind Series, 1983, A Braief History of Disbelief Series, 2005; exec. prodr. Shakespeare TV series, 1979-81; author (TV) McLuhan, 1971, The Body in Question, 1978, States of Mind, The Facts of Life, Subsequent Performances, 1986, Who Cares, Born Talking, Museums of Madness, Anthropology, Opera Works; editor: Freud: The Man, His World, His Influence, 1972, The Don Giovanni Book, 1990; actor (TV) Jonathan Miller on Reflection, 1998, (TV mini-series) The Talk Show Story, 2000. Decorated Order of Brit. Empire; named Dir. of Yr., Soc. West End Theatre Awards, 1976; recipient Silver medal Royal TV Soc., 1981; fellow Univ. Coll. London; hon. fellow St. John's Coll., Cambridge U.; rsch. fellow in history of medicine Univ. Coll., London U., 1970-73. Fellow Royal Coll. Physicians (London and Edinburgh); mem. AAAS (fgn. mem.). Office: care IMG Artists 616 Chiswick High St London W45RX England Office Phone: 44 207957 5832. E-mail: cdyer@imgartists.com.

**MILLER, JORDAN D.,** physiologist; b. St. Paul, Minn. BS, Winona State U., Minn., 1998; MS, U. Wis., La Crosse, 2000; PhD, U. Wis., Madison, 2005. NHLBI pre-doctoral fellow U. Wis., Madison, 2000—05; NHLBI post-doctoral fellow U. Iowa, Iowa City, 2005—. Contbr. articles to profl. jours. Internat. young scientist mentor Am. Heart Assn., Dallas, 2006. Mem.: Am. Physiol. Soc. (Mil. Physiology Pre-doctoral award 2003, Proctor and Gamble Predoctoral award 2004, Mil. Physiology Pre-doctoral award 2005,

Cardiovascular sect. rsc h. recognition award 2006), AAAS, Am. Heart Assn. Office: University of Iowa 340B Eckstein Medical Research Building Iowa City IA 52242 Office Phone: 319-335-6778. E-mail: jordan-miller@uiowa.edu.

**MILLER, JOSEF M.,** otolaryngologist, educator; b. Phila., Nov. 29, 1937; married, 1960; 3 children. BA in Psychology, U. Calif., Berkeley, 1961; PhD in Physiology and Psychology, U. Wash., 1965; MD (hon.), U. Göteborg, Sweden, 1987; MD (h.c.), U. Turku, Finland, 1995. USPHS fellow U. Mich., 1965-67, rsch. assoc., asst. prof. dept. Psychology Ann Arbor, 1967-68, prof., dir. rsch. dept. Otolaryngology, dir. Kresge Hearing Rsch. Inst., 1984—; asst. prof. depts. Otolaryngology, Physiology and Biophysics U. Wash., Seattle, 1968-72, rsch. affiliate Regional Primate Rsch. Ctr, 1968-84, assoc. prof., 1972-76, acting chmn. dept. Otolaryngology, 1975-76, prof., 1976-84; Lunn and Ruth Townsend prof. comm., 1996—. Mem. study sect. Nat. Inst. Neurol. and Communicative Disorders and Stroke, NIH, 1978-84, ad hoc bd. dirs. sci. counselors, 1988; sci. rev. com. Deafness Rsch. Found., 1978-83, chair, 1983—; mem. faculty Nat. Conf. Rsch. Goals and Methods in Otolaryngology, 1982; adv. com. hearing, bio-acoustics and biomechanics Commn. Behavioral and Social Scis. and Edn., Nat. Rsch. Coun., 1983—; hon. com. Orgn. Nobel Symposium 63, Cellular Mechanisms in Hearing, Karlskoga, Sweden, 1985; cons. Otitis Media Rsch. Ctr., 1985-89, Pfizer Corp., 1988; faculty opponent U. Göteborg, Sweden, 1987; rsch. adv. com. Galludet Coll., 1987; chair external sci. adv. com. House Ear Inst., 1988-91; author authorizing legis. Nat. Inst. Deafness and Other Comm. Disorders, NIH, 1988, co-chair adv. bd. rsch. priorities com., bd. dirs. Friends adv. coun., 1989—, chair rsch. subcom., 1990-93, treas., bd. dirs., 1996—; grant reviewer Mich. State Rsch. Fund, NSF, VA; reviewer numerous jours. including Acta Otolaryngologica, Jour. Otology, Physiology and Behavior, Science. Mem. editorial bd. Am. Jour. Otolaryngology, 1981—, AMA, Am. Physiology Soc., Annals of Otology, Rhinology and Laryngology, 1980—, Archives of Oto-Rhino-Laryngology, 1985-93, Hearing Rsch., Jour. Am. Acad. Otolaryngology-Head and Neck Surgery, 1990—. Bd. dirs. Internat. Hearing Found., 1985—. Fellow U. Wash., 1962-65, Kresge Hearing Rsch. Inst., U. Mich., 1965-67; recipient award Am. Acad. Otolaryngology; grantee Deafness Rsch. Found., U. Wash., 1969-71; rsch. grantee NIH, 1969-73. Mem. AAAS, Am. Acad. Otolaryngology and Head and Neck Surgery (com. rsch. in otolaryngology 1971-82, continuing edn. com. 1975-79, NIH liaison com. 1988—, program steering com. jour. 1990, Pres. Citation 1997), Am. Auditory Soc., Am. Otological Soc., Am. Neurotological Soc., Am. Otologic Honor Soc., Acoustical Soc. Am. (com. rsch. psychol., physiol. acoustics 1969-78), Fedn. Am. Physiol. Soc., Fedn. Am. Socs. Exptl. Biology, Soc. Neurosci., Assn. Rsch. Otolaryngology (sec.-treas. 1979-80, Pres. elect 1981, pres. 1982. program dir. mtg. 1983, award of merit com. 1985, 95-96, chair 1988, program dir., pres. symposium homeostatic mech. of inner ear 1993), Finnish Acad. Otolaryngology (hon.), Sigma Xi. Office: U Mich Kresge Hearing Rsch Inst 1301 E Ann St Rm R5032 Ann Arbor MI 48109-0506

**MILLER, JOSEPH A.,** chemicals executive; b. West Pittston, Pa., Jan. 1942; BS, Va. Mil. Inst., 1963; PhD in Chemistry, Pa. State U., 1966. Various positions in R&D, mfg., bus., and mktg. E.I. DuPont de Nemours & Co., 1966—2001, sr. v.p., 1994-96, chief tech. officer, 1996, sr. v.p. R&D Wilmington, Del., 1994—2001, sr. v.p., chief tech. officer, 2001—02; exec. v.p., chief tech. officer Corning (N.Y.) Inc., 2002—. Mem. Nat. Sci. Math. and Engring. Edn., NRC. Mem. U. Del. Rsch. Found.; bd. trustees U. Del.; mem. adv. bd. dept. chem. engring. U. Del., Ga. Tech.; co-chair symposium to reform sci. edn. in Del. pub. schs. Capt. U.S. Army, 1967-69. Pa. State U. Alumni fellow. Fellow AAAS; mem. NAE, AIChE, Am. Chem. Soc. (Barnes award for rsch. leadership 1998, mem. adv. steering com. for chemistry in a biol. context), Indsl. Rsch. Inst., Nat. Sci. Bd., Chem. Heritage Found., Coun. for Competitiveness, Nat. Sci. and Tech. Bd. Internat. Adv. Panel of Singapore, Nat. Sci. Resources Ctr. (chmn. of bd.), Del. Sci., Math. and Tech. Edn. Found., Del. Pub. Policy Inst. Office: Corning One Riverfront Plaza Corning NY 14831

**MILLER, JOSEPH ARTHUR,** manufacturing engineer, consultant, educator; b. Brattleboro, Vt., Aug. 28, 1933; s. Joseph Maynard and Marjorie Antoinette (Hammerberg) Miller; m. Ardene Hedwig Barker, Aug. 19, 1956; children: Stephanie L., Jocelyn A., Shana L., Gregory J. BS in Agrl., Andrews U., Berrien Springs, Mich., 1955; MS in Agrl. Mechs., Mich. State U., 1959; EdD in Vocat. Edn., UCLA, 1973. Constrn. engr. Thornton Bldg. & Supply, Inc., Williamston, Mich., 1959-63, C & B Silo Co., Charlotte, Mich., 1963-64; instr. and dir. retraining Lansing C.C., Mich., 1964-68; asst. prof./prog. coord./coop coord. San Jose State U., 1968-79; mfg. specialist Lockheed Martin Missiles and Space (and predecessor cos.), Sunnyvale, Calif., 1979-81, rsch. specialist, 1981-88, NASA project mgr., 1982-83, staff engr., 1988-96, rsch. staff engr., 1996-98, coord. flexible mfg. system simulation project, 1994-96, team mem. machining outsource initative project, AIMS agile mfg. project, 1995—97, coord. productivity improvement program, 1996—98; engring. and constrn. cons. Berry Creek, Calif., 1998—. Agrl. engring. cons. USDA Poultry Expt. Sta., 1960—62; computer numerical control cons. Dynamechtronics, Inc., Sunnyvale, 1987—90; machining cons. Space Sys. divsn. Lockheed, 1986—96; instr. computer numerical control DeAnza Coll., Cupertino, Calif., 1985—88, Labor Employment Tng. Corp., San Jose, Calif., 1988—93; career counselor Pacific Union Coll., Angwin, Calif., 1985—92; instr. computer-aided mfg. and non traditional machining San Jose State U., 1994—97; team leader pursuit of excellence machine tool project Lockheed Martin Missiles and Space, Sunnyvale, 1990—95, coord. safety award program, 1997—98, quality awareness program screening com., 1998. Author: Student Manual for CNC Lathe, 1990; contbr. articles to profl. jours. UCLA fellow, 1969—73. Mem.: Am. Soc. Indsl. Tech. (pres. 1980—81), Calif. Assn. Indsl. Tech. (pres. 1974—75, 1984—85), Nat. Assn. Indsl. Tech. (pres. industry divsn. 1987—88, mem., chmn. accreditation visitation teams 1984—, bd. cert. 1991—92), Soc. Mfg. Engr. (sr.; chmn. edn. com. local chpt. 1984—85, career guidance counselor 1986—88). Adventist. Avocations: violin, cabinet making, gardening, feeding hummingbirds. Home: PO Box 190 Berry Creek CA 95916-0190 Personal E-mail: jodenie@cncnet.com.

**MILLER, JOYCE CATHERINE,** chemistry professor, research scientist; d. Richard Norman and Gretna Mae Jones; m. John E. Miller, June 30, 1973. BA, Olivet Nazarene U., Kankakee, Ill., 1969—73; MA, Ball State U., Muncie, Ind., 1973—75; PhD, Ohio State U., Columbus, 1995—99. Cert. medical technologist Am. Soc. Clin. Pathologists, 1976. Rsch. technician in organic chemistry Ball Corp., Muncie, 1973—74; med. technologist Ball Meml. Hosp., Muncie, 1975—76; chemistry supr. Knox Cmty. Hosp., Mount Vernon, Ohio, 1976—78; evening supr. clin. lab. Bethesda Hosp., Zanesville, Ohio; clin. lab. dir. Joel Pomerene Meml. Hosp., Millersburg, Ohio, 1982—95; medical technologist Wooster Cmty. Hosp., Ohio, 1995—; tchg. asst. Ohio State U., 1996—98; assoc. prof. chemistry Mt. Vernon Nazarene U., Ohio, 1998—. Ch. pianist, Sunday sch. tchr. Loudonville Ch. Nazarene, Ohio, 1981—2006. Mem.: AAAS. Protestant. Avocations: golf, bicycling. Home: 874 Fairway Dr Howard OH 43028 Office: Mt Vernon Nazarene Univ 800 Martinsburg Rd Mount Vernon OH 43050 Business E-Mail: joyce.miller@mvnu.edu.

**MILLER, JUDITH A. (JUDY MILLER),** retired journalist; b. NYC, 1948; m. Jason Epstein, 1993. BA in Economics, Barnard Coll., 1969; MA, Princeton U., 1971. Corr. The Progressive, Nat. Pub. Radio; reporter, Washington Bur. NY Times, Washington, 1977, chief Cairo Bur. Egypt, 1983, Paris correspondent of France, 1986—87, news editor and dep. bur. chief, Washington Bur., 1987—88, spl. correspondent to Persian Gulf crisis, 1990, spl. correspondent, Sunday Mag., 1990, sr. writer, ret. 2005. Lectr. in field. Author: One, By One, By One, 1990, God Has Ninety-Nine Names, 1996; co-author (with Laurie Mylroie): Saddam Hussein and the Crisis in the Gulf, 1990; co-author: (with William Broad and Stephen Engelberg) Biological Weapons & America's Secret War, 2002. Co-recipient Pulitzer Prize, explanatory journalism, 2002; recipient Emmy award, 2002, DuPont award, 2002. Achievements include first woman to be named chief of NY Times Cairo Bur. E-mail: miller@nytimes.com.*

**MILLER, JUDITH ANN,** historian, educator; b. Ohio, Mar. 15, 1956; d. Rolland and Carol Miller. BA, Coll. of Wooster, 1978; PhD, Duke U., 1987. Asst. prof. U. Tenn., Knoxville, 1987—88, Emory U., Atlanta, 1988—97, assoc. prof., 1997—. Author: Mastering the Market, 1998; co-editor: Taking Liberties, 2003. Recipient Gerschenkron prize, Econ. Hist. Assn., 1987. Mem.: Am. Hist. Assn., Soc. French Hist. Studies (Korn prize 1993). Office: Emory U Dept History 561 S Kilgo Cir Atlanta GA 30322

**MILLER, JUDITH BRAFFMAN,** writer; b. St. Louis, Feb. 21, 1947; d. William and Lorraine Shirley Braffman; m. Mark Ellis Miller, June 9, 1968. BA, U. Calif., Berkeley, 1969. Freelance writer, 1978—. Active Amnesty Internat., NYC, 2002—, Am. Friends Svc. Com., 2005. Fellow: Royal Astron. Soc. Gt. Britain; mem.: AIAA, ACLU, AAAS, Internat. Dark Sky Assn., Astron. Soc. of the Pacific, Nat. Space Soc., Planetary Soc., Am. Inst. Physics, Brit. Astron. Assn., Am. Astron. Soc., Am. Chem. Soc., NY Acad. Scis., Am. Soc. Journalists and Authors, Union Concerned Scientists. Avocations: naturalist, poetry, politics. Home and Office: 1149 Partridge Ave Saint Louis MO 63130 Office Phone: 314-725-7096.

**MILLER, JUDSON FREDERICK,** lawyer, retired military officer; b. Tulsa, Dec. 5, 1924; s. Herbert Frederick and Martha (Davidson) M.; m. June Hirakis, Aug. 4, 1967; children by previous marriage: Kathleen, Shelley, Douglas, Judson Frederick. BS, U. Md., 1961; postgrad., Army War Coll., 1961-62; MA, George Washington U., 1962; JD, U. Puget Sound, 1980. Bar: Wash. 1981. Commd. 2d lt. U.S. Army, 1943, advanced through grades to maj. gen., 1975; platoon leader, co. comdr. 4th Cav. Group, Europe, 1944-46, 82d Airborne Div., 1947-50; with 187th Airborne RCT and Hdqrs. 8th Army, 1950-52; instr. Armored Sch., 1953-56; bn. comdr. 14th Armored Cav. 1958-60; with Hdqrs. U.S. Strike Command, 1963-65; brigade comdr., chief of staff 4th Inf. Div., Vietnam, 1966-67; mem. gen. staff Dept. Army, 1967-68; dep. comdg. gen. Ft. Ord, Cal., 1968-69; asst. chief of staff Hdqrs. Allied Forces Central Europe, 1969-71; asst. comdr. 3d Inf. Div., Germany, 1971-73; chief of staff I Corps Group, Korea, 1973-75; dep. comdg. gen. VII Corps, Germany, 1975-77; ret., 1977; assoc. F.G. Enslow and Assocs., Tacoma, 1981—. Decorated Silver Star, Legion of Merit, Bronze Star with V device and oak leaf cluster, Joint Service Commendation medal, Air medal with 8 oak leaf clusters, Purple Heart, Vietnamese Gallantry Cross with palm; named to Okla. Mil. Acad. Hall of Fame, 1988. Mem. ABA, Assn. U.S. Army. Clubs: Tacoma Country, Lakewood Racquet. Home: 8009 75th St SW Tacoma WA 98498-4817 Office: Tacoma Mall Office Bldg 4301 S Pine St Ste 205 Tacoma WA 98409-7205 Personal E-mail: jud7@comcast.net.

**MILLER, JUSTIN ALLEN,** artist, art educator; b. Fredricksburg, Va., Oct. 14, 1978; s. Keith Allen and Joyce Miller. BFA, Va. Commonwealth U., 2001; MFA, N.Y. Acad. of Art, 2004. Freelance illustrator Little, Brown and Co., N.Y.C., 2003—; adj. prof. Va. Commonwealth U., Richmond, Va., 2004. Instr. All Arts and Sci. Camp, Greensboro, NC, 2002; sub. tchr. Stafford County (Va.) Pub. Schs., 2002; developed curriculum All Arts and Sci. Camp, Greensboro, NC, 2003. Illustrator (children's book) Brassy the Fire Engine Saves the City, 2005. Dean Scholarship, Va. Commonwealth U., 1999—2000, Fulbright Full Grant, Mar. of Ag., 2005. Mem.: Golden Key Nat. Hon. Soc., Phi Eta Sigma. Avocation: photography. Home: 1130 Bristol Mine Rd Colonial Beach VA 22443 Office Phone: 540-903-0689. E-mail: jamill71@hotmail.com.

**MILLER, KAREN L.,** dean, nursing educator; BSN, Case Western Res. U.; MSN, U. Colo.; PhD in Nursing. V.p. The Children's Hosp., Denver; assoc. prof. Coll. Nursing U. Colo. Health Scis. Ctr.; dean, prof. Sch. Nursing U. Kans., 1996—, dean Sch. Allied Health, 1998—. Mem. editl. bd. IMAGE: Jour. Nursing Scholarship. Grantee NIH, 1992. Fellow Am. Acad. Nursing; mem. ANA, ANA Coun. Nurse Rschrs., Am. Orgn. Nurse Execs., Coun. on Grad. Edn. for Nursing Adminstrn., Midwest Alliance in Nursing, Midwest Nursing Rsch. Soc., Sigma Theta Tau (collateral reviewer rsch. com.). Office: U Kans Sch Nursing 390 Rainbow Blvd Kansas City KS 66160-0001

**MILLER, KARLA PATRICIA,** elementary school educator; b. Takoma Park, Md., Apr. 6, 1968; d. James Roland and Patricia Melvin Miller. BS, U. Md., 1990, MEd, 1994, postgrad., 1997—2005. Advanced profl. cert. elem. grades and reading Md. State Dept. Edn., 2001. Tchr. 1st and 2d grade Montgomery County Pub. Schs., Olney, Md., 1991—95, reading specialist Silver Spring, 1995—98, tchr. 1st grade, 1998—2005. Mem. travel group observe best practices schs. Australia and New Zealand Montgomery County Pub. Schs., Rockville, 1993, first grade team leader, 1999—2000; mem. travel group observe schs. Australia and New Zealand, IRA's world congress Jr. Class Learning, Auckland, 2000; lect. Am. U., Washington, 2003; clin. supr. reading U. Md., College Park, 1997; cons. Md. State Dept. Edn., Balt., 1996—97 Participant Out of the Darkness Pallotta Teamworks, Washington, 2002. Mem.: IRA's Publ. Com., Internat. Reading Assn. (young author's chair Montgomery County coun. 1994—95, v.p Montgomery County coun. 1995—96, pres.-elect Montgomery County coun. 1996—97, pres. Montgomery County coun. 1997—98, mem. internat. reading assn. pub. coun. 1998—2000), Am. Edn. Rsch. Assn., Golden Key Nat. Honor Soc., Kappa Delta Pi, Phi Delta Kappa. Avocations: French, reading, writing. Office: Montgomery County Pub Schs 2111 Porter Rd Silver Spring MD 20910 Personal E-mail: kmiller4@umd.edu.

**MILLER, KENDRA DANETTE,** art services business owner, consultant; b. Jackson, Miss., Jan. 24, 1970; d. William Jerome Miller and Linda B. Walker. BA, Northwestern U., 1992; MA in Arts Adminstrn., Sch. of Art Inst. Chgo., 1997. Cert. fine and decorative art appraisal studies George Wash. U. Ctr for Profl. Devel., D.C., 2004. External affairs dir. Phoenix Inst. for Conservation, Wash., 2000—04; prin. Strata Fine Art Svcs., Silver Spring, Md., 2004—. Docent Nat. Mus. Women in the Arts, Wash., 2000—05; vol. Nativity Youth Ctr., Wash., 2004—05; adv. bd. McClinton Musical Theatre Arts Found., Bucharest, Romania, 2003—05. 1st mum. Woman Made Gallery, Chgo., 1997—99, treas., 1999; bd. mem. Imani Found. & Art Gallery, Kent, Ohio, Better Existence with HIV, Evanston, Ill., 1992—94. Scholar, Assn. Fundraising Profls., Greater N.Y. chpt., 2000, Nat. Capital Gift Planning Coun., 2002. Mem.: Am. Soc. Appraisers (assoc.). Conservative. Avocations: scuba diving, tennis, reading, art, travel. Office: Strata Fine Art Svcs LLC 8201 Schrider St Ste 4 Silver Spring MD 20910-4637 Office Phone: 202-491-6084. Business E-mail: info@stratafineartservices.com.

**MILLER, KENNETH EDWARD,** sociologist, educator; b. N.Y.C., June 17, 1929; s. Joseph F. and Irene (Edersheim) M.; m. Andrée Nora Barthelemy, Feb. 14, 1959 (div. Nov. 1984); children: Jennifer Andrée, Christopher Kenneth; m. Janet Sue Daniels, May 21, 1990. BA, U. Ala., 1953, MA, 1956; PhD, Duke, 1965; MS, Drake U., 1986. Asst. to pres., dir. devel. Jacksonville (Fla.) U., 1957-60; dir. Health Council, assoc. dir. Community Planning Council, Birmingham, Ala., 1960-62; asst. prof. sociology Emory U., Atlanta, 1966-70, acting chmn. dept., 1969-70; prof. sociology Drake U., Des Moines, 1970-96, chmn. dept., 1970-79, 82-88, asst. to dean for grad. studies, 1991-92, prof. emeritus, 1996—. Research sociologist U. Ala., 1956-57; research asso. U.S. Civil Service Commn., summer 1968. Served with USN, 1946-48. Postdoctoral research fellow Duke, 1965-66. Mem. Midwest Sociol. Soc. Home: 2129 NW 140th St Clive IA 50325-8730

**MILLER, KENNETH GREGORY,** retired air force officer; b. Bryan, Tex., July 28, 1944; s. Max Richard and Catherine Mae (Sultzman) M.; m. Ann Marguerite Perpich, Nov. 25, 1966; children: Keith G., Deborah J., Craig S. BS in Aero. Engring., Purdue U., 1966; MS in Systems Mgmt., U. So. Calif., 1970; grad., Nat. War Coll., Washington 1986; postgrad., U. Va., 1988. Commd. 2d lt. USAF, 1966, advanced through grades to brig. gen., 1995; with Office Sec. Def., Washington, 1980-81; various positions to dir. field ops. F-16 System Program Office, Wright-Patterson AFB, Ohio, 1981-86; chief engring. div. Sacramento Air Logistics Ctr., McClellan AFB, Calif., 1986-87; dir. materiel mgmt. Ogden Air Logistics Ctr., Hill AFB, Utah, 1987-89; vice comdr. Acquisition Logistics Div., Wright-Patterson AFB, 1990-91; comdr. Air Force Contract Mgmt. Divsn., Kirtland AFB, N.Mex., 1990; comdr.

western dist. Def. Contract Mgmt. Command, L.A., 1990-91; dir. C-17 Program Office, Wright-Patterson AFB, 1991-93; dep. asst. sec. for acquistion USAF, Washington, 1993-94, dir. supply hdqrs., 1994-95; v.p. for gulf ops. BDM Fed., 1995-96; group v.p. for advanced tech. svcs. group RJO Enterprises, Inc., 1997; sr. v.p. Dayton ops. CACI, Inc., 1997-99; group v.p. Air Force programs Anteon Corp., 1999—. Mem. engring. bd. visitors Purdue U. Decorated Disting. Svc. medal, Legion of Merit (2), Def. Superior Svc. medal; recipient award of merit Freedom Found.; named Outstanding Aerospace Engr., Purdue U., Disting. Engring. Alumnus, Purdue U., 2001; named to ROTC Hall of Fame, 2001. Mem. Nat. Contract Mgmt. Assn. (bd. advisors 1990-92), Soc. Logistics Engrs., Nat. Def. Indsl. Assn. Office: 1560 Wilson Blvd Ste 800 Arlington VA 22209 Home: 9061 Daybreaker Drive Park City UT 84098 E-mail: kmiller@anteon.com.

**MILLER, KENNETH LEE,** counselor, educator; s. Arthur Jerome and Geraldine Marie Miller; m. Suellyn Mary Hetrick, May 28, 1983. BA in Sociology, Purdue U., 1979, MEd in Counseling, 1985, PhD, 1990. Diplomate Am. Bd. Med. Psychotherapists, 1988; profl. clin. counselor Ohio Counselor, Social Worker, and Marriage and Family Therapist Bd., 2002, nat. cert. counselor Nat. Bd. for Cert. Counselors, Inc./Va., 1988, approved clin. supr. Ctr. for Credentialing and Edn., Inc./N.C., 1998, life skills educator Teachers Coll., Columbia U., 1982. Co-dir. gender equity grant Purdue U., West Lafayette, Ind., 1987—89; asst. prof. Calif. State U., San Bernardino, 1990—92; asst. prof., capt. The Citadel, Charleston, SC, 1992—93; asst. prof. U. Hawaii at Manoa, Honolulu, 1993—95; assoc. prof. Youngstown (Ohio) State U., 2000—. Dir. U. Counseling Ctr./Cmty. Counseling Clinic Youngstown State U., 2000—04, dept. chair counseling, 2003—05; cons. Hunt County Dept. Mental Health, Greenville, Tex., 1995—95. Co-author: Gender-fair Counseling Strategies, 1988, Working for Change: Planning a Gender Equity Workshop, 1988; contbr. chapters to books, articles to profl. jours.; co-developer (videotape) A Model for Gender-fair Counseling, Freedom, Fairy Tale, Assembly Line, Your Choice/Your Future, Comedian, Obsolete, Inequality: A Subtle Disaster. Mem. San Bernardino County Mental Health Assn., 1990—92; adv. com. Tri-County Child Advocacy Ctr., Youngstown, 2000—02; mem. bd. mgrs. John Will Anderson Boy's Club, Gary, Ind., 1983—83; sec. Hawaii Multicultural Counseling and Devel. Assn., Honolulu, 1994—95; com. mem. Multicultural Ethics Rev. Com., ACA, Honolulu, 1994—94; western divsn. rep. Nat. Orgn. for Human Svc. Edn., Seattle, 1991—92; judge Calif. Academic Decathlons, San Bernardino, Calif., 1990—91. Recipient Disting. Professorship award, Youngstown State U., 2001—02. Mem.: APA, ACA, Ohio Assn. for Counselor Edn. and Supervision, East Ohio Counseling Assn., Ohio Counseling Assn., Soc. for the Psychol. Study of Social Issues, Am. Coll. Counseling Assn., Assn. for Counselor Edn. and Supervision (Robert Frank Outstanding Counseling Program award 2002—03), Am. Edni. Rsch. Assn., Kappa Delta Pi, Pi Lambda Theta, Chi Sigma Iota. Avocations: swimming, tennis, scuba diving. Office: Youngstown State Univ One University Plaza Youngstown OH 44555

**MILLER, KENNETH MICHAEL,** electronics executive, director; b. Chgo., Nov. 20, 1921; s. Matthew and Tillie (Otto) M.; m. Dolores June Miller, Jan. 16, 1943 (dec. Dec. 1968); children: Barbara Anne Reed, Nancy Jeanne Hathaway, Kenneth Michael, Roger Allan; m. Sally J. Ballingham, June 20, 1970 (dec. Apr. 2002). Student, Ill. Inst. Tech., 1940-41, UCLA, 1961. Electronics engr. Raytheon Corp., Chgo., 1941-48; gen. mgr. Lear, Inc., Santa Monica, Calif., 1948-59; v.p., gen. mgr. Motorola Aviation Electronics, Inc., Culver City, Calif., 1959-60; v.p., gen. mgr. instrument divsn. Daystrom, Inc., L.A., 1961; gen. mgr. metrics divsn. Singer Co., L.A. and Bridgeport, Conn., 1961-65; v.p., gen. mgr. Lear Jet Corp., 1965-66; pres., dir. Infonics, Inc., 1967-68; v.p., gen. mgr. Computer Industries, Inc., 1968-69; dir. ops., tech. products group Am. Std. Corp., McLean, Va.; also v.p., gen. mgr. Wilcox Elec. divsn. Kansas City, Mo., 1969-71; pres. Wilcox Elec., Inc. subs. Northrop Corp., Kansas City, 1971-72; v.p., dir. World Wide Wilcox, Inc. subs., McLean, 1971-72; pres., CEO, dir. Penril Corp., Rockville, Md., 1973-86; pres. K-M Miller and Assocs., Rockville, 1986—. Dir. George Mason Bank, NA, Washington, Palmer Nat. Bank, Washington. Mem. adv. bd. Washington Bus. Jour.; contbr. articles to profl. jours. Mem. regional planning coun. Cmty. Mental Health Svcs., Bridgeport, 1964; mem. Bridgeport Capital Fund Com.; trustee Park City Hosp.; vice dir. Montgomery County Arts Coun.; bd. dirs. U. Bridgeport; mem. Md. State Com. High Tech. Recipient Job Makers award Mfrs. Assn. Bridgeport, 1963. Fellow Radio Club Am. (dir., chmn grants-in-aid com.); mem. AIAA, IEEE, Aircraft Owners and Pilots Assn., Am. Mgmt. Assn., Armed Forces Comm. and Electronics Assn. (life), Electronic Industries Assn., Instrument Soc. Am. (life), Nat. Aero. Assn., Soc. Non-Destructive Testing, Soc. Automotive Engrs., Air Force Assn., Am. Radio Relay League (life), Amateur Satellite Corp. (life), Am. Def. Preparedness Assn. (life), Aero. Elec. Soc. (life), Nat. Capital DX Assn. (pres. 1987-88), Assn. Old Crows (life), Mfrs. Assn. Bridgeport (dir.), Bridgeport Engring. Inst., Bridgeport C. of C. (pres. 1964), Quarter Century Wireless Assn. (life, Disting. Svc. award 1994), Soc. Wireless Pioneers, Rolling Hills Country Club (Wichita), Algonquin Club (Bridgeport). Home and Office: 16904 George Washington Dr Rockville MD 20853-1128 Office Phone: 301-774-7709. E-mail: kmm@prodigy.net.

**MILLER, KENNETH W.,** lawyer; b. Chgo., Oct. 25, 1960; BS, U. Ill., 1982; JD magna cum laude, Northwestern U., 1985. Bar: Ill. 1985. Ptnr., co-chmn. pvt. equity practice Katten Muchin Zavis Rosenman, Chgo. Mem.: ABA, Am. Inst. of CPAs. Office: Katten Muchin Zavis Rosenman 525 W Monroe St Chicago IL 60661 Office Phone: 312-902-5261. Office Fax: 312-577-8747. E-mail: ken.miller@kmzr.com.

**MILLER, KHADIJAH OLIVIA,** education educator; d. Joseph Richard and Eunice Verdell Turner; m. L. Eric Miller, Oct. 27, 1997; 1 child, Ericka Olivia. BA in Print Journalism, NYU, 1993; MA in African Am. Studies, Temple U., 1995, PhD in African Am. Studies, 2001. Dir. women's studies program and women's ctr. Norfolk (Va.) Coll., 2000—02, asst. prof. interdisciplinary studies Norfolk (Va.) State U., 2002—. Recipient award for innovative excellence in tchg., learning and tech., 17th Internat. Conf. Coll. Tchg. and Learning, 2006; grantee, NEH, 2005. Mem.: AAUW, Am. Democracy Project (v.p. Norfolk State U. chpt. 2005—06). Office: Norfolk State U 700 Park Avenue Norfolk VA 23504 Office Phone: 757-823-2864. Office Fax: 757-823-8602. Business E-Mail: komiller@nsu.edu.

**MILLER, KLEBER C.,** lawyer; b. Austin, Tex., Aug. 11, 1924; LLB, Univ. Tex., 1951. Bar: Tex. 1951. Asst. dist. atty. Travis County, Tex., 1951; ptnr., litigation, energy practices Shannon Gracey Ratliff & Miller LLP, Fort Worth, Tex. Fellow: Am. Bar Found., Am. Coll. Trial Lawyers (past state chmn.), Tex. Bar Found. (life; chmn. of fellows); mem.: ABA, Am. Bd. Trial Advocates, Def. Rsch. Inst. (past state chmn.), Fedn. Def. & Corp. Counsel (v.p. 1966—68), Trial Lawyers Am., State Bar Tex. (bd. dir. 1976—79, chmn. 1978), Tex. Assn. Def. Counsel (bd. dir. 1973—76, pres. 1977), Fort Worth Tarrant County Bar Assn. (pres. 1967—68, Blackstone award 1992, Professionalism award 2000), Delta Sigma Rho. Office: Shannon Gracey Ratliff & Miller LLP Ste 3800 777 Main St Fort Worth TX 76102 Office Phone: 817-336-9333. Office Fax: 817-336-3735. Business E-Mail: kmiller@shannongracey.com.

**MILLER, L. MARTIN,** accountant, financial planner; b. N.Y.C., Sept. 17, 1939; s. Harvey and Julia (Louis) M.; m. Judith Sklar, Jan. 21, 1962; children: Philip, Marjorie. BS, Wharton Sch., U. Pa., 1960; M Taxation, Villanova Law Sch., 2001. CPA; CFP; accredited fin. planning specialist. Jr. acct. Deloitte, Haskins & Sells, N.Y.C., 1960-62, sr. acct. Phila., 1962-64; mng. ptnr. Morison Cogen LLP, Phila., 1964—2005. Treas. Coronet Container Co., Inc., Phila., Val Mar Realty Corp., NYC; dir. Penn Internat. Trading Co., Phila.; mng. dir. CPA Tax Forum, 1986-69; underwriting mem. Lloyds of London, 1978-95, chmn. Mid-Atlantic region, 1991-92; faculty Wharton Sch. U. Pa., 1992-2004, Villanova U., 2003—; MBA program faculty LaSalle U., 2003—; continuing edn. faculty AICPAs, 2006; lectr. in field. Author: Accountants Guide to S.E.C. Filings, 1968, Salaries, Penn. Non-Profit Report, 1997, Worker Compensation, Practical Tax Strategies, 2000; contbr. articles to profl. jours. Mem. Phila. Rep. Com., 1963-67, treas. Daerr-Bannon for state rep.

com., 1997; chmn. Lower Merion Twp. scholarship fund, 1975-78; bd. dirs. Main Line Br. ARC, 1997-2000; bd. dirs. Penn Valley Civic Assn., 1973-79, Gladwyne Civic Assn., 1992-95; mem. Lower Merion Planning Commn., 1978-82, Gov.'s Tax Study Commn.; pres. Mensa Edn. and Rsch. Found., 1984-86; mem. SEC Forum on Small Bus. Capital Formation, 1983, Pa. Impact, 1995; apptd. to Pa. State Bd. Accountancy, 1985-94, chmn., 1990-91; elected sch. bd. dir. Lower Merion Twp., 1993-97, also chmn. fin. com. Served with U.S. Army, 1961-62. Recipient Outstanding Achievement award Germantown Civic Assn., 1965. Mem. NASD (industry arbitrator 2005—)Pa. Inst. CPAs (com. chmn. 1975-78, bd. dirs. 1979-81, by-laws chmn. 1980-83, mem. non-profit orgns. com. 1995-99, fin. planning com. 2002-2003), Nat. Assn. State Bds. Accountancy (edn. com. 1987, nominating com. 1989, experience com. 1990, continuing edn. com. 1995—), Am. Arbitration Assn. (mem. comml. panel, 2002—), Cert. Fin. Planner (bd. ethics 1995-97), AICPAs (nat. tax com. 1979-82, exec. com. self regulation divsn. for CPA firms 1984-87, acctg. and rev. svcs. com., long range planning com., ethics divsn. 1985-88, specialization bd. 1989-90, ethics exec. com. 1990-93, mem. curriculum and acctg. edn. 1993-96, chmn. fin. assistance task force 1995, bd. dirs. Estate Planning Coun. 1998-2004, nomination com. 1999, discussion leader continuing edn. 2005), Little 10 Acctg. Assn. (edn. chmn. 1980-84), Main Line C. of C. (govt. affairs com. 1991-99), Mensa (internat. fin. officer 1970-74), Masons (past master), Plays and Players Club (treas. 1978-79), Beta Alpha Psi. Home: 204 Dove Ln Haverford PA 19041-1902 Office: Morison Cogen LLP 150 Monument Rd Bala Cynwyd PA 19004-1702

**MILLER, LARRY H.,** professional sports team executive, auto dealer, broadcast executive; b. Salt Lake City; m. Gail Miller; 5 children. LLD (hon.), Univ. Utah, 1991; degree (hon.), Utah Valley State Coll., Salt Lake Cmty. Coll. Formerly with auto parts bus., Denver and Salt Lake City; now owner auto dealerships, Salt Lake City, Albuquerque, Denver and Phoenix; part-owner Utah Jazz, NBA, Salt Lake City, 1985—86, owner, 1996—, Larry H. Miller Group, Salt Lake City, KJZZ-TV, Salt Lake City, 1993—. Office: c/o Utah Jazz 301 W South Temple Salt Lake City UT 84101-1216 also: Larry H Miller Group 5650 S State St Murray UT 84107-6131

**MILLER, LAURA,** mayor, journalist; b. Balt., Nov. 18, 1958; m. Steven Wolens; children: Alex, Lily, Maxwell. Grad. U. Wis., Madison. Mem. Dallas City Coun., 1998—2002; mayor City of Dallas, 2002—. Columnist, investigative reporter Dallas Observer, metro columnist Dallas Times Herald, New York Daily News, The Dallas Morning News, The Miami Herald; freelance writer: The Miami Herald. Recipient H.L. Mencken Writing award, Balt. Sun, 1995, 6 Katie awards, Dallas Press Club, 2 Tex. Headliner awards, 2 Philbin awards, Dallas Bar Assn., cert. of merit, ABA. Office: Dallas City Hall 1500 Marilla St Rm 5EN Dallas TX 75201-6390

**MILLER, LEE I.,** lawyer; b. Nov. 16, 1947; BSBA, Georgetown U., 1969, JD, 1973. Bar: Md. 1973, Ill. 1976. Ptnr., Real Estate practice Rudnick & Wolfe, Chgo., mng. ptnr., 1992—99; ptnr, co-chmn. Piper Marbury Rudnick & Wolfe, Chgo., 1999—2004; ptnr., joint CEO DLA Piper Rudnick Gray Cary, Chgo., 2005—. Bd. dir. Griffindor Capital Ptnrs. LLC. Editorial asst. Tax Lawyer, 1972-73. Bd. visitors Georgetown Univ. Law Ctr.; mem. adv. bd. Georgetown Univ. Corp. Counsel Inst. Recipient Judge Learned Hand Human Rels. award, Am. Jewish Com., 2001. Mem.: Ill. State Bar Assn., Chgo. Bar Assn., Am. Coll. Real Estate Lawyers, Real Estate Roundtable (pres. club mem.), Phi Alpha Delta. Office: DLA Piper Rudnick Gray Cary Suite 1900 203 N La Salle St Chicago IL 60601-1293 Office Phone: 312-368-4029. Office Fax: 312-236-7516. Business E-Mail: lee.miller@dlapiper.com.

**MILLER, LEROY PAUL, JR.,** language educator; b. Holyoke, Mass., Feb. 21, 1949; s. Leroy Paul Sr. and Rose Marie (Danehey) Miller. AA, Northampton (Mass.) Jr. Coll., 1972; BA, U. New Eng., Biddeford, Maine, 1974; MEd, Springfield (Mass.) Coll., 1977; postgrad., Am. Internat. Coll., Springfield. Cert. elem. tchr., English tchr., history tchr., guidance counselor Mass. Sch. adjustment counselor Holyoke Pub. Schs., 1978-79; edni. programmer, 1979-80, tutor Chpt. I, 1980-81; tutor Amherst (Mass.) Pub. Schs., 1982-84; tchr. West Springfield (Mass.) Pub. Schs., 1985-86; tchr. English Springfield Pub. Schs., 1986—. Fundraiser M. Marcus Kiley Mid. Sch.; alumni counselor U. New Eng., 1977—. Mem. NEA, ASCD, Nat. Coun. Tchrs. English, Mass. Tchrs. Assn., Springfield Edn. Assn. (faculty rep. 1986—), U. New Eng. Alumni Assn. (v.p. 1990—), Elks, Psi Chi. Democrat. Roman Catholic. Avocations: reading, bowling. Home: 2 Gerard Way Holyoke MA 01040-1204 Office: M Marcus Kiley Mid Sch 180 Cooley St Springfield MA 01128-1108 Office Phone: 413-787-7240. Personal E-Mail: lmill55169@aol.com.

**MILLER, LESLIE ANNE,** lawyer; b. Franklin, Ind., Nov. 4, 1951; d. G. Thomas and Anne (Gaines) Miller; m. Richard B. Worley, Feb. 14, 1987. AB cum laude, Mt. Holyoke Coll., 1973; MA in Polit. Sci., Rutgers U., 1974; JD, Dickinson Sch. Law, 1977; LLM with honors, Temple U., 1994; LLD (hon.), Thomas Jefferson U. Coll. Health Profls., 2002; HHD (hon.), Wilson Coll., 2001. Bar: Pa. 1977, U.S. Dist. Ct. (ea. dist.) Pa. 1977, U.S. Ct. Appeals (3d cir.) 1980, U.S. Dist. Ct. (ea. dist.) Pa. 1987. Assoc. LaBrum & Doak, Phila., 1977—81, ptnr., 1982—86, Goldfein & Joseph, Phila., 1986—95, McKissock & Hoffman, P.C., Phila., 1995—2003; gen. counsel Gov. Pa., 2002—. Bd. dirs. WHYY-TV, 1996—; del. Third Circuit Jud. Conf., 1981, 82, 85; mem. Jud. Inquiry and Rev. Bd., 1990-94, chair, 1993-94; mem. faculty trial advocacy program Dickinson Sch. Law, 1992, 94; mem. hearing com., disciplinary bd. Supreme Ct. Pa., 1996—; mem. faculty Acad. Advocacy Temple U., 1994—; judge pro tem Ct. of Common Pleas; interm pres. Kimmel Ctr. for the Performing Arts, 2001-02 Mem. acad. ball com. Phila. Orch., 1986-87, 89-91, 95-96, mem. acad. music com. 1998—; mem. Open Space Task Force Com., Lower Merion Twp., Pa., 1990, bd. dirs., 1990-94, mem. counsel, 1990, Lower Merion Conservancy 1995-97, 2000 , others 1st divn. Med. Coll. Pa., 1985-96, sec. 1987-92, chair presdl. search com., 1993, chair presdl. inauguration, 1987, chair com. on acad. affairs, 1989-95, chair dean's search com., 1994-95, chair nomenclature com., 1996; bd. dirs. Med. Coll. Hosps., 1991-96, Allegheny Health Edn. and Rsch. Found., 1993-96, Hahnemann U. Med. Sch., 1994-96, Pa. Ballet, 1994—, St. Christopher's Hosp. for Children, 1991-94, vice chair, 1990-94; bd. dirs. Phila. Free Libr., 1997—, bd. dirs. Kimmel Ctr. for the Performing Arts, 1999—, interim pres., 2001-02, vice chair bd. dirs., 2002—; hon. chair Pa. Breast Cancer Coalition, 2003, exec. v.p. Pa. chpt., 2005; bd. trustees Mt. Holyoke Coll., 2000—, chair, 2005—; bd. govs. Dickinson Sch. Law, Pa. State U., 2001—. Recipient Mary Lyon award Mt. Holyoke Alumni Assn., 1985, Alumnae Medal of Honor, 1988, Hon. Alumnae award, 1989, Pres.'s award Med. Coll. Pa., 1993, Sylvia Rambo award Dickinson Sch. of Law, 1997, Star award Forum of Exec. Women, 1998, Ann Alpern award PBA Women in the Profession, 1999, Sandra Day O'Connor award Phila. Bar Assn., 1999, Outstanding Leadership in Support of Legal Svcs. award Pa. Legal Svcs., 1999, Women Making History Nat. Assn. of Women Bus. Owners, 2002, Women of Distinction award, Phila. Bus. Jour., 2001, Internat. Women's Forum "Women Who Make a Difference" award, 2003, Pink Ribbon award Pa. Breast Cancer Coalition, 2003, Woman One award Drexel U. Inst. for Women's Health and Leadership, 2004, Pa. Meritorious Svc. medal, 2005; named to Pa. Honor Roll of Women, 1996; named Disting. Dau. of Pa., Gov. of Pa., 1999. Fellow Am. Bar Found., Pa. Bar Found.; mem. ABA, Pa. Bar Assn. (exec. com. divsn. young lawyers 1983-85, bicentennial com. 1986-87, bd. govs. 1990-93, gender bias task force 1992-97, chair com. on jud. selection and retention 1987-89, vice chair 1985-87, investigative divsn. 1982-85, chair Andrew Hamilton Ball 1989, trustee Phila. Bar Found. 1990-97, co-chair century three commn. 1993-97, others), Pa. Bar Assn. (found. ho. dels. life fellow, bd. govs. 1980-83, 84-87, 91-93, chair young lawyers divsn. 1982, long range planning com. 1985-87, com. on professionalism, 1987-91, vice chmn. jud. inquiry and rev. bd. study com. 1989-91, sec. 1984-87, chair ho. dels. 1991-93, chair commn. on women in the profession 1993-95, v.p. 1996-97, pres. 1998-99, immediate past pres. 1999—, apptd. mem. ct. jud. discipline 1999), Pa. Bar Inst. (faculty, course planner), Pa. Assn. Def. Counsel (exec. com. 1987-90, 94, chair trial demonstration with Phila. Trial Lawyers Assn. 1993), Def. Rsch. Inst. (spkr. toxic torts seminar 1983), Phila. Bar Edn. Advocacy Women Litigators (course planner, faculty 1995), Women's Assn. Women's Alternatives (bd. dirs. 1983-94, vice chair 1985-94), Phila. Forum Exec. Women, Pa. Women's Forum (pres. 2002-04), Com. of Seventy, Mt. Holyoke Alumnae Assn. (bd. dirs. 1986-89, 1999—). Democrat. Lutheran. Avocations: collecting American antiques, gardening, running. Office: Governors Office of Gen Counsel 225 Main Capitol Bldg Harrisburg PA 17120 Office Phone: 610-940-5325. Personal E-mail: millesq@aol.com.

**MILLER, LINDA B.,** political scientist; b. Manchester, NH, Aug. 7, 1937; d. Louis and Helene (Chase) M. AB cum laude, Radcliffe Coll., 1959; MA, Columbia U., 1961, PhD, 1965. Asst. prof. Barnard Coll., 1964-67; rsch. assoc. Princeton U., 1966-67, Harvard U., 1967-71, 76-81, lectr. polit. sci., 1968-69; assoc. prof. Wellesley (Mass.) Coll., 1969-75, prof. polit. sci., 1975—2004, chmn. dept., 1985-89. Vis. prof. rsch. Watson Inst., Brown U., 1997, adj. prof. internat. rels., 1998—2000, 2003—, sr. fellow, 2000—03; vis. prof. polit. sci. Brown U., 1997. Author: World Order and Local Disorder: The United Nations and Internal Conflicts, 1967, Dynamics of World Politics: Studies in the Resolution of Conflicts, 1968, Cyprus: The Law and Politics of Civil Strife, 1968; co-author, co-editor: Ideas and Ideals: Essays on Politics in Honor of Stanley Hoffmann, 1993; editor Internat. Studies Rev., 1999-2002; contbr. articles to profl. jours. Internat. Affairs fellow Coun. Fng. Rels., 1973-74, Rockefeller Found. fellow, 1976-77, Oceanographic Instn. sr. fellow, 1979-80, 82-83, NATO social sci. rsch. fellow, 1982-83. Mem. Inst. Strategic Studies, Internat. Studies Assn., Coun. Fgn. Rels., Phi Beta Kappa. Home: PO Box 415 South Wellfleet MA 02663-0415 Office: Wellesley Coll Dept Polit Sci Wellesley MA 02482 also: Watson Inst Brown U PO Box 1970 Providence RI 02912-1970 Office Phone: 401-863-1598. Business E-mail: Linda_Miller@brown.edu.

**MILLER, LINDA KAREN,** retired secondary school educator, social studies educator, law educator; b. Kansas City, Jan. 22, 1948; d. Bennie Chris and Thelma Jane (Richey) M. B of Secondary Edn., U. Kans., 1970; M of Secondary Edn., U. Va., 1978, EdD, 1991. Tchr. social studies Fairview Jr. H.S., Kansas City, 1970—72; substitute tchr. Fairfax Pub. Schs., Va., 1972—73; reading aide Lake Braddock Secondary Sch., Burke, Va., 1973—74; tchr. social studies Mark Twain Intermediate Sch., Alexandria, Va., 1974—75, Herndon Intermediate Sch., Va., 1975—78, Fairfax H.S., 1978—86, 1987—2002; ret., 2002. Cons. in field; instr. Sch. Law Cmty. Coll. So. Nev., Las Vegas, 2003; del. People to People, China, 2005. Ambassador to China People to People, 2003; Nev. coord. Nat. Coun. for History Edn., 2005. Named Pre-Collegiate Tchr. of Yr., Orgn. Am. Historians, 1996, Secondary Tchr. of Yr., Nat. Coun. for Social Studies, 1996, U. Va., 1997, Outstanding Secondary Tchr. of Yr., Nat. Peace Corps Assn., 1999, Nat. Peace Educator, 2002; recipient George Washington medal, Valley Forge Freedom Found., 1988, Excellence in Tchg. award, U. Kans. Sch. Edn., 1999, Celebrating Tchg. Excellence award, Am. Coun. Tchrs. Russian, 1998, World History Tchg. prize, World History Assn., 2002, Humanities Leadership award, NEH, 2003; fellow, Korean Soc., 2000, 2004, Am. Revolution fellow, NY Hist. Soc., 2001. Mem. Nat. Coun. Social Studies (curriculum com. 1991-94), Am. Legal History Soc., Orgn. Am. Historians, Nat. Coun. for History Edn., Nev. Coun. Social Studies, U. Va. Alumni Assn. Republican. Episcopalian. Avocation: doll collecting.

**MILLER, LORING ERIK,** insurance agent, broker; b. N.Y.C., Apr. 6, 1951; s. Martin and Frances (Kaufman) M.; m. Ilene Jane Cook, Dec. 18, 1983; children: Justin, Jennifer, Mallory. Student, L.I. U., 1968—72; diploma, GM Sch. Dealership Mdse./Mgmt., 1977. Treas. Dial Chevrolet Inc., Westbury, NY, 1970—77, v.p., owner, 1977—88; pres. Mid. Country Brokerage Inc., Westbury, 1984—87, Loring E. Miller Agy. Inc., Mineola, NY, 1978—. Bd. dirs., pres. Nassau County Police Res. Assn., 1985—; chmn. bd. dirs., founder Suffolk County Police Res., 1997—; assoc. dir. N.Y.C. Police Res. Assn., 1986—, N.Y. Finest Found.; state trustee, lodge pres. N.Y. State Fraternal Order of Police.; bd. dirs., Suffolk County Crime Stoppers; scoutmaster Boy Scouts Am., 1994-97; hon. mem. Nassau County Police Dept.; dir. N.Y. Law Enforcement Found.; main bd. dirs., peace officer, dir. spl. ops. divsn. law enforcement Nassau County Soc. Prevention Cruelty to Animals. Mem.: Chiefs of Police Assn. Suffolk County, Profl. Ins. Agts. N.Y. Office: 398 Willis Ave Mineola NY 11501-1819

**MILLER, LOUIS H.,** lawyer; b. Lampeter, U.K., Apr. 22, 1945; m. Diane Matuszewski, Dec. 31, 1973; children: Margaret, Anthony. BA in History, Rutgers U., 1967; JD, Temple U., 1970. Bar: N.J. 1970, U.S. Dist. Ct. N.J. 1970, U.S. Supreme Ct. 1996. Law clk. to Judge Thomas Beetel Hunterdon County Ct., Flemington, NJ, 1970-71; law clk. to Judge Baruch Seidman Superior Ct. N.J. Chancery, Trenton, NJ, 1971-72; assoc. Jefferson, Jefferson & Vaida, Flemington, 1972-75; ptnr. Vaida & Miller, Flemington, 1975-78; pvt. practice Flemington, 1978-81, 88—; judge Superior Ct. N.J., Flemington, 1981-88; of counsel Levinson Axelrod Wheaton & Grayzel, Flemington, 1990-97. Spl. dep. atty. gen. N.J. Hunterdon County Prosecutor Office, Flemington, 1972-73; condemnation commr. Appt. Superior Ct. N.J., Flemington, 1988—, N.J. Assembly spkrs. commr.; commr. N.J. State Commn. Investigation, Trenton, 1993-97; arbitrator U.S. Fed. Dist. Ct. N.J., 1989—. Twp. committeeman Alexandria Twp. Com., R.D. Milford, N.J., 1978-81. Mem. Am. Judges Assn., Am. Judicature Soc., N.J. State Bar Assn. (mem. dist. ethics com. 1980-81, mem. mcpl. ct. practice com. 1996—), Hunterdon County Bar Assn., Consular Law Soc., Welsh Am. Geneal. Soc., Welsh North Am. C. of C. (bd. dirs.), USF Constellation Mus. (mem. bd. trustees 2003-). Republican. Avocations: paleontology, travel, hiking. Office: PO Box 850 40 Main St Flemington NJ 08822-1411 Office Phone: 908-782-1818. Personal E-mail: millerlh@earthlink.net.

**MILLER, LOUIS HOWARD,** biologist, researcher; b. Balt., Feb. 4, 1935; s. David and Daisy (Arenson) Miller; m. Susan K. Pierce; 1 child, Jennifer. BS, Haverford Coll., 1956; MD, Washington U., St. Louis, 1960; MS in Parasitology, Columbia U., 1964. Asst. prof. then assoc. prof. Coll. of P & S, Columbia U., N.Y.C., 1967—71; head malaria sect. NIAID, NIH, Bethesda, Md., 1971—92, chief lab. parasitic diseases, 1992—. Contbr. articles to profl. jours. Capt. U.S. Army, 1965—67. Recipient Paul Ehrlich/Ludwig Darmstaedter prize, 1989, Award for Disting. Achievement in Infectious Disease Rsch., Bristol-Myers Squibb, 1996, Commonwealth award in sci. and invention, 1999. Fellow: ACP, Queensland Inst. Med. Rsch., Royal Soc. Tropical Medicine and Hygiene; mem.: Assn. Am. Physicians, Inst. of Medicine, NAS, Am. Soc. Tropical Medicine and Hygiene (pres. 1988). Office Phone: 301-435-2177.

**MILLER, LYNN FIELDMAN,** lawyer; b. Newark, Oct. 9, 1938; d. George Martin and Helene G. (Friedman) Fieldman; m. Arthur Harold Miller, Aug. 24, 1958; children: Jennifer Lyn, Jonathan Daniel. BA in English, Barnard Coll., 1959; MLS, Rutgers U., 1971, MA in Theater Arts, 1977, JD, 1990. Bar: N.J. 1990, U.S. Dist. Ct. N.J. 1990, U.S. Ct. Appeals (3d cir.) 1992. Head libr. Alma White Coll., Zarapheth, N.J., 1971; reference libr. Douglas Coll., New Brunswick, 1971-79; media libr. Rutgers U. New Brunswick, 1979-87; intern Hon. Anne E. Thompson Fed. Dist. Ct., Trenton, NJ, 1988; assoc. Wilentz, Goldman & Spitzer, Woodbridge, NJ, 1989, Greenbaum, Rowe, Smith, Woodbridge, 1990-91, Miller & Littman, New Brunswick, 1991-93; ptnr. Miller & Miller, New Brunswick, 1993-2001, Miller, Miller & Tucker, P.A., 2001—. Editor in chief: (jour.) Women's Rights Law Reporter, 1989-90. Active Highland Park (NJ) Environ. Commn., 1991-97, Supreme Ct. Com. on Women in the Cts.; trustee Middlesex County Bar Found., 2002—. Mem. NJ State Bar Assn. (trustee 2000-06, individual rights com. 1989-95, chair individual rights com. 1995-97, div. entertainment and arts law sect. 1992-96, bd. trustees Women in the Profession sect. 1997-98, sec. 1998-99, chmn. 2000-01, chair spl. com. consumer protection law 2002-2004), Middlesex County Bar Assn. (chair women lawyers sect. 1995-96, bd. trustees 1996-2002, treas. 2003-04, 2d v.p. 2004-05, 1st v.p. 2005-06, pres.-elect 2006—). Avocations: walking, bicycling. Office: 96 Paterson St New Brunswick NJ 08901-2109 Office Phone: 732-828-2234. Business E-mail: lmiller@millerandmiller.com.

**MILLER, LYNNE MARIE,** environmental services administrator; b. NYC, Aug. 4, 1951; d. David Jr. and Evelyn (Gulbransen) M. AB, Wellesley Coll., 1973; MS, Rutgers U., 1976. Analyst Franklin Inst., Phila., 1976-78; dir. hazardous waste div. Clement Assocs., Washington, 1978-81; pres. Risk Sci. Internat., Washington, 1981-86; CEO, Environ. Strategies Consulting, LLC, Reston, Va., 1986—. Bd. dirs. Scana Corp., Adams Nat. Bank. Editor: Insurance Claims for Environmental Damages, 1989, editor-in-chief Environ. Claims Jour.; contbr. chpts. to books. Named Ins. Woman of Yr. Assn. Profl. Ins. Women, 1983. Mem.: Wellesley Bus. Leadership Coun. Office: Environ Strategies Consulting LLC 11911 Freedom Dr Ste 900 Reston VA 20190-5631 E-mail: lmiller@escva.com.

**MILLER, MALCOLM HENRY,** manufacturing sales executive, real estate developer; b. Elgin, Ill., Feb. 6, 1934; s. Carl Theodore and Alice Lucy (Garbisch) M. BA, U. Wis., 1957; postgrad., Am. Inst. Fgn. Trade, 1961, U. N.Mex., Albuquerque, 1963. Sales engr. Fairbanks Morse Corp., Beloit, Wis., 1962; pvt. practice real estate Albuquerque, 1964-75; supt., v.p. Walworth Foundries, Inc., Darien, Wis., 1959-61, exec. v.p. sales, co-owner, 1975—; v.p. sales, co-owner Waukesha Specialty Co., Inc., Darien, 1975—. Treas. Fastcast, Inc., Albuquerque, 1993—. Loan advisor, developer Community Assn. for Sr. Housing, Albuquerque, 1967-70; Rep. candidate for state senator N.Mex., 1970; active fin. com. Bernalillo County Reps., N.Mex., 1970-80, Walworth County Reps., Wis., 1976-77; mem. Congressman Ryan's 1st Dist. Small Bus. Adv. Com. Served to 1st lt. US Army, 1957-59. Mem. Am. Foundrymen's Assn., Dairy Food Industries Supply Assn., Dairy Food Industries Supply Assn. (bd. dir. 1992-95), Santa Fe Opera Guild, Big Foot Country Club, Nat. "W" Club, Masons, The Madison Club, Sigma Alpha Epsilon. Republican. Episcopalian. Avocations: exercise, films, opera, fly fishing. Home: 223 Fremont St PO Box 37 Walworth WI 53184-0037 Office: Walworth Foundries Inc PO Box 160 Hwy 14 and I-43 Interchange Darien WI 53114

**MILLER, MARGERY,** psychologist, educator, speech pathology/audiology services professional, mental health services professional; m. Donald F. Moores; children: Kip Lee, Tige Justice. BA, Elmira Coll., 1971; MA, NYU, 1972; EdS, MS, SUNY, Albany, 1975; MA, Towson State U., 1987; PhD, Georgetown U., 1991. Lic. speech pathologist Md., psychologist Md.; cert. tchr. nursery-6th grades, spl. edn. N.Y., nationally cert. sch. psychologist. Speech and lang. pathologist Mental Retardation Inst. Flower and Fifth Ave. Hosp., NYC, 1971—72; cmty. speech/lang. pathologist, dir. speech and hearing svc. NY State Dept. Mental Hygiene, Troy, 1972—74; instr. comm. disorders dept. Coll. St. Rose, Albany, NY, 1975—77; clin. supr. U. Md., College Park, 1978; speech/lang. pathologist Md. Sch. for Deaf, Frederick, 1978—84; auditory devel. specialist Montgomery County Pub. Schs., Rockville, Md., 1984—87; coord. Family Life program Nat. Acad. Gallaudet U., Washington, 1987—89; interim dir., 1988—89; dir. Counseling and Devel. Ctr. N.W. Campus, Washington, 1989—93; prof. psychology, coord. psychology internship program, dir. undergrad. psychology program Gallaudet U., Washington, 1993—; lic. practicing psychologist Bethesda, Md., 1998—. Instr. sign-lang. program Frederick CC; pause instr. for deaf adolescents; diagnostic cons. psychology and speech pathology; presenter at confs.; profl. coaching, Md., Fla., 2002—. Author: It's O.K. to Be Angry, 1976; co-author: Cognition, Education and Deafness: Directions for Research and Instruction, 1985; mem. editl. rev. com. Gov.'s Devel. Disabilities Coun., Md.; contbr. articles to profl. jours. Vol., choreographer Miss Deaf Am. Pageant, 1984. Office Edn. Children's Bur. fellow, 1971. Mem.: APA, Montgomery County Md. Mental Health Assn., Am. Assn. Higher Edn., Nat. Assn. Sch. Psychologists, Am. Assn. Deaf, Am. Speech, Lang. and Hearing Assn. (cert. clin. competence in speech/lang. pathology). Office: Gallaudet U 800 Florida Ave NE Washington DC 20002-3660 Office Phone: 202-651-5540. Business E-Mail: margery.miller@gallaudet.edu.

**MILLER, MARILYN LEA,** library and information scientist, educator; AA, Graceland Coll., 1950; BS in English, U. Kans., 1952; AMLS, U. Mich., 1959, PhD of Librarianship and Higher Edn., 1976. Bldg.-level sch. libr. Wellsville HS, Kans., 1952-54; tchr.-libr. Arthur Capper Jr. HS, Topeka, 1954-56; head libr. Topeka HS, Topeka, 1956-62; sch. libr. cons. State of Kans. Dept. of Pub. Instrn., 1962-67; from asst. to assoc. prof. Sch. Librarianship Western Mich. U., Kalamazoo, 1967-77; assoc. prof. libr. sci. U. NC, Chapel Hill, 1977-87, prof., chair dept. libr. and info. studies Greensboro, 1987-95, prof. emeritus, 1996—. Vis. faculty Kans. State Tchrs., Emporia, 1969, 63, 64, 66, U. Minn., Mpls., 1971, U. Manitoba, Winnipeg, Can., 1971; vis. prof. Appalachian State U., Boone, NC, 1987; adv. bd. sch. libr. media program Nat. Ctr. for Ednl. Stats., 1989 user rev. panel, 1990; chair assoc. dean search com. Sch. Edn., 1988, coord. Piedmont young writers conf., 1989-94, 97-99, chair race and gender com., 1990-93, SACS planning and evaluation com., 1990-91, learning resources ctr. adv. com., 1991-93; hearing panel for honor code U. NC Greensboro, 1988-91, assn. women faculty and administrv. staff, 1987-95, faculty coun., 1987-95, chair, 1994-95, univ. libr. com., 1987-88, com. faculty devel. in race and gender scholarship, 1990-92; lectr. and cons. in field. Editor: Pioneers and Leaders in Library Service to Youth, 2003; mem. editl. bd. The Emergency Librarian, 1981-97, Collection Building: Studies in the Development and Effective Use of Library Resources, 1978-96; contbr. chpt. to books, articles to profl. jour. Children's libr. specialists to visit Russian sch. and pub. libr., book publs., Moscow, Leningrad, Tashkent, 1979; hon. del. White House Conf. on Libr. and Info. Svcs., Washington, 1991; head del. Romanian Summer Inst. on Librarianship in U.S., 1991; citizen ambr. People to People Internat. Program, People's Republic of China, 1992, Russian and Poland, 1992, Russia, 1994, Barcelona, 1995; exec. bd. dirs. Friends of Greensboro Pub. Libr., 1996-99, chair gift shop and coffee shop adv. com., 1996-02, v.p., 2003-05, pres. 2005—; chair Citizens Materials Adv. com., 1999-; chair Citizens Strategic Long Range Planning com., 1994-95, 01-03, chair, 2003, Sch. Pub. Libr. com., 2002—, chair, 2003—; pub. libr. trustee, 2005- NC State Libr. Commn., 2006-. Recipient Freedom Found. medal, 1962, Disting. Svc. to Sch. Librs. award Kans. Assn. Sch. Librs., 1982, Disting. Svc. award Graceland Coll., 1992, Disting. Alumnus award Sch. Libr. and Info. Studies, U. Mich., 1988, Contribution to Libr. Info. Sci. award Am. Libr. Info. Sci., 1999; Delta Kappa Gamma scholar, 1972. Mem.: ALA (awards com. 1971—72, chair Chgo. conf. resolutions 1972, chair 1973—75, resolutions com. 1976—78, adv. com. Nat. Ctr. Ednl. Stats. 1984, standing com. libr. edn. 1987—91, yearbook adv. com. 1988—90, chair 1989—90, pres. 1992—93, exec. dir. 1994, chair rsch. com., chair search com., Disting. Svc. award Am. Assn. Sch. Librs. 1993), Friends of N.C. Pub. Librs. (bd. dirs. 2000—), So. Assn. Colls. and Schs. (accreditation team 1988), Southeastern Libr. Assn. (chair libr. educators sect. 1990—92), N.C. Assn. Sch. Librs. (Disting. Svc. award 2004), Assn. Libr Svc. to Children (bd. dirs. 1976—81, pres. 1979—80, rsch. com. 1982—85, chair 1984—85, Disting. Svc. award 2005), Assn. Ednl. Comms. and Tech., Am. Assn. Sch. Librs. (nominating com. 1980, pub. com. 1981—82, chair search com. exec. dir. 1985, v.p., pres.-elect 1985—86, pres. 1986—87, coord. coms. nat. stds. vision and implementation 1995—98), N.C. Libr. Assn. (life; edn. libr. com. 1978—80, 1982—86, bd. dirs. 1987—99, exec. bd. status women roundtable 1989—2003, chmn.-elect 1995—97, chmn. 1997—99, common. on status of sch. librs. 1999—2000). Personal E-mail: marilynl@bellsouth.net.

**MILLER, MARK A.,** information technology training executive; B in Bus. Adminstrn., U. Mich. V.p. Nutri/System, Inc., sr. v.p., pres.; founder, pres. Foxboro Group; chmn., CEO Signature Plastic Surgery, Inc., 1997—2000; group exec. v.p. Ea. U.S. Right Mgmt. Cons., Inc.; CEO New Horizons Worldwide, Inc., 2006—. Office: New Horizons Worldwide Inc 1900 South State Coll Blvd Ste 200 Anaheim CA 92806-6135 Office Phone: 714-940-8000. Office Fax: 714-938-6002.*

**MILLER, MARK C.,** waste management administrator; BS in Computer Sci., Purdue U. From mgr. to v.p. Internat. Divsn. Abbott Labs., 1976—89, v.p. Internat. Divsn., 1989—92; pres. Stericycle Inc., Lake Forest, Ill., 1992—, CEO, 1992—. Bd. dir. Ventana Med. Sys., Inc., Lake Forest Hosp. Mem.: Phi Beta Kappa. Office: Stericycle Inc 28161 North Keith Drive Lake Forest IL 60045

**MILLER, MARK KARL,** journalist, editor; b. Meadville, Pa., Aug. 5, 1953; s. Richard Karl and Ellener Louise (Zimber) M. BA in Comms. and Journalism, Shippensburg U. of Pa., 1975. Editl. asst. Broadcasting mag., Washington, 1975, staff writer, 1976—77, asst. editor, 1977—80, sr. news editor, 1980—87, asst. mng. editor, 1987—91; mng. editor Broadcasting & Cable mag., Washington, 1991—98, Digital TV mag., Washington, 1999; freelance editor, writer, photographer, rsch., 2000—; dep. editor TVNewsday.com, 2006—. Mem. editl. adv. bd. Shippensburg U. of Pa., 1989-94, mem. profl. adv. bd. comm./journalism dept., 1994-96. Recipient Outstanding Alumnus award Shippensburg U., 1992. Mem. Soc. Profl. Journalists, Art Deco Soc. of Washington (bd. dirs., publs. chair 1986-97), Nat. Press Club. Home and Office: 2425 Valley Way Cheverly MD 20785-2956 Office Phone: 301-773-0058. E-mail: mkmiller@comcast.net.

**MILLER, MARSHALL LEE,** lawyer; b. Chattanooga, Tenn., Oct. 18, 1942; BA, Harvard U., 1964; student, Oxford U., Eng., Heidelberg U., Germany; JD, Yale U., 1970. Bar: D.C. 1971, U.S. Supreme Ct. 1979. Spl. asst. to adminstr. U.S. EPA, 1971-73; assoc. dep. atty. gen. U.S. Dept. Justice, 1973-74; asst. sec. labor (acctg.), dep. adminstr. OSHA, 1975-76; ptnr. Baise & Miller, Washington. Bd. editors: Yale Law Jour.; Soviet Mil. editor: Armed Forces Jour., 1983-87; author books internat. and environ. topics. Bd. dirs. Bulgarian-Am. Enterprise Fund, Electronic Warfare Assocs., Am. Coun. of Internat. Living, Am. Assn. Advancement Sci. Home: PO Box 1311 Bethany Beach DE 19930-1311 Office: Baise Miller Pc PO Box 14368 Washington DC 20044-4368

**MILLER, MARTIN EUGENE,** management labor negotiator, lobbyist; b. Decatur, Ill., May 14, 1945; s. Floyd Homer and Vivian LaVerne (Gould) M.; m. Sherry Kay Bandy, May 25, 1968; children: Liane, Laura. BS, U. Ill., Champaign-Urbana, 1968; MEd, U. North Fla., Jacksonville, 1974. Cert. math. tchr.; cert. ednl. adminstrn. and supervision. Tchr. Decatur Pub. Schs., Ill., 1968, Clay County Sch. Bd., Green Cove Springs, Fla., 1970—74, coord. cert. pers., 1974—77, dir. instrnl. pers., 1977—78, dir. pers. svcs., 1978—81, asst. supt. for human resources and labor rels., 1981—93, dir. cmty. and govtl. rels., 1993—97; gen. dir. govtl. rels. Duval County Pub. Schs., Jacksonville, Fla., 1997—2001; pres. Miller Consulting Group, Inc., 2001—. Past mem. Edn. Stds. Commn., Tallahassee, 1985-93, vice chmn. 1988-92; past mem. Blue Cross-Blue Shield Adv. Coun., Jacksonville, Fla.; past mem. Fla. Ednl. Leaders Forum. Served as staff sgt. USAF, 1968-70. Mem.: Fla. Ednl. Legis. Liaisons (past pres.), Fla. Edn. Negotiators (past pres.), Fla. Assn. Sch. Adminstrs., Am. Assn. Sch. Adminstrs., Phi Delta Kappa. Republican. Presbyterian. Avocations: home computers, music, swimming, photography. Home: 1612 Bay Cir W Orange Park FL 32073-4746 Office: 1612 Bay Circle West Orange Park FL 32073 E-mail: martinmiller@MillerConsultingGroup.com.

**MILLER, MARY HELEN,** retired state government administrator; b. Smiths Grove, Ky., June 30, 1936; d. Walter Frank and Lottie Belle (Russell) Huddleston; m. George Ward Wilson, Sept. 12, 1958 (div. Sept. 1973); children: Ward Glenn, Amy Elizabeth Huddleston; m. Francis Guion Miller Jr., June 6, 1981. BA, Western Ky. U., 1958. Tchr. Fayette County Schs., Lexington, Ky., 1958-60, Seneca High Sch., Louisville, 1960-63, Shelby County High Sch., Shelbyville, Ky., 1963-69; rsch. analyst Legis. Rsch. Com., Frankfort, Ky., 1973-79, asst. dir., 1973-89, 90-91; chief exec. asst. Office Gov., Frankfort, 1983-87, 93-95, legis. liaison, 1991-93; cabinet sec. Natural Resources and Environ. Protection Cabinet, Frankfort, 1987-88; sales assoc. W. Wagner, Jr. Comml. Real Estate, Louisville, 1989-91; ret., 1996. Author: (constl. revision) Citizens Guide To/Perspective, 1978, (booklet) A Look at Kentucky General Assembly, 1979, A Guide to Education Reform, 1990, (handbook) Gubernatorial Transition in Kentucky, 1991. Mem. Leadershi Ky. Alumni, Frankfort, 1986, Waterfront Devel. Corp. Bd., Louisville, 1986—87, Greater Louis Partnership Econ. Devel., 1988—92, Shelbyville 2000 Found. Bd., 1991—92; mem. ass. Regional Airport Authority Bd., Louisville, 1986—89; mem. Shelby County Cmty. Theatre Bd., Shelbyville, 1978—83, 1988—91, treas., 1979—83, pres., 1989—91; chair Shelby County Cmty. Found., 1995—2000; mem. Ky. Long Term Policy Bd., 1992—99, chair, 1995; mem. Ky. Hist. Properties Commn., 1995—99; exec. com. Ky. Hist. Soc., 2002—, v.p., 2004—; mem. Shelby Devel. Found., 2003—05. Recipient Vic Hellard Jr. Pub. Svc. in Ky. award, 1999; named Shelbyville Citizen of Yr., 1998. Mem. Caryatid Book Club (pres. 1999), Women's Initiative Networking Groups (pres. 1998), Western Ky. U. Alumni Assn. (bd. dirs. 1992-95). Democrat. Episcopalian. Avocations: reading, theater, gardening, antiques. Home: 1116 Main St Shelbyville KY 40065-1420 E-mail: mhm1116@aol.com.

**MILLER, MARY JEANNETTE,** retired management consultant; b. Washington, Sept. 24, 1912; d. John William and David Evengline (Hill) Sims; children: Sylvenia Delores Doby, Ferdi A., Cecil Jr.(dec.). Student, Howard U., 1929—30, U. Ill., 1940—42, U. Md., 1975; cert. in Vocat. Photography, Prince George C.C., 1986. Chief mail processing unit Bur. Reclamation, Washington, 1940—57; records supr. AID, 1957—71, records mgmt. cons., 1980—84; office engr. Bechtel Assocs., Washington, 1976—79; docent Mus. African Art Smithsonian Instn., Washington, 1986—89; circulation asst. Prince George County Libr. System, Hyattsville, Md., 1987—91; ret., 1991. Real estate assoc., tchr. English as Second lang. Ministry Edn., Seoul, Korea, Saint Helena, 1960—61; cons. Ministry Fin., Laos, 1968—70, Ministry Fin. Royal Lao Govt., 1971—74, AID Missions, Yemen, Sudan, Somalia, 1982; mem. Friends of Internat. Edn. Com., 1985—92; sec., treas., bd. dirs. Miller Transitional, Inc. Author Handbooks on Office Mgmt.; contbr. articles to travel books. Mem.: AARP, NAFE, Montgomery County Bd. Realtors, Am. Mgmt. Assn., Soc. Am. Archivists, Nat. Trust Hist. Preservation, Am. Fgn. Svc. Assn., Zeta Phi Beta. Roman Catholic. Home: 700 7th St SW Apt 27 Washington DC 20024-2453 Office Phone: 703-575-8013.

**MILLER, MARY KATHLEEN,** secondary school educator; b. Mishawaka, Ind., Nov. 24, 1943; d. John Edward and Carolyn M.; m. Robert Alan Miller, Jan. 1, 1971; children: Brendan Alexander, Stacey Ann. BA, U. Ill., 1965, MA, 1968. Cert. secondary educator, tchr., N.J. Tchr. French, English, Beaumont H.S., St. Louis, 1965-66; tchr. English as a Fgn. Lang., Raghunath H.S., Meerut, India, 1968-69; tchr. English as a 2d Lang., Milw. Area Tech. Coll., 1969-71, Coll. William and Mary, Williamsburg, Va., 1971-73; tchr. English, French, religion St. Pius H.S., Piscataway, N.J., 1973-74; tchr. English as a 2d Lang. grades 7-12 East Windsor Bd. Edn., Hightstown, 1982—. State secondary rep. N.J. TESOL/BE, 1992-96; mem. bilingual adv. bd. N.J. Office Bilingual Edn., 1996-98; mem. Mercer County Profl. Devel. Bd., 1998-2002. Gov.'s tchr.'s grant Commr. of Edn., N.J., 1986, India tchr.'s grant Fulbright Edn. Found., 1968-69. Mem. TESOL, N.J. Edn. Assn. (bldg. rep. 1992-98), East Windsor Edn. Assn., Cranbury Hist. Soc., Kappa Delta Pi. Avocations: tennis, biking, travel, swimming, writing. Office: Hightstown HS 25 Leshin Ln Hightstown NJ 08520-4001 Office Phone: 609-443-7738. E-mail: mkmiller@ewrsd.k12.nj.us.

**MILLER, MARY LYNN,** nurse; b. Miflinburg, Pa., Dec. 15, 1935; d. Harold William and Ruth (Wohlheiter) Miller. Diploma, Pa. Hosp. Sch. Nursing, Phila., 1956; BSN, U. Pa., Phila., 1964, MSN, 1968. RN Pa. Hosp. Staff/ward nurse, supr. Pa. Hosp., 1956-68; dir. ednl., instr. U. Pa., 1968—70; dir. patient care svcs. Inst. Pa. Hosp., Phila., 1970—94. Bd. dirs. Center City Christian Coun., Phila., 1956—60; mem. met. bd. ARC, Phila., 1970—76, 1994—. Recipient Disting. Alumnae award, U. Pa. Sch. Nursing, 1970. Democrat. Mem. United Ch. Of Christ. Home: 421 Market St Mifflinburg PA 17844

**MILLER, MAURICE LIM,** cultural organization administrator; BS in Mech. Engring., U. Calif., Berkeley, 1968, M in Design, 1977; Cert. in Housing and Bus. Develop., Develop. Training Inst., 1985. Exec. dir. Asian Neighborhood Design, San Francisco, 1981—2003; founder Family Independence Initiative, 2001—. Bd. dirs. Corp. for Enterprise Develop., Public Private Ventures, Calif. Endowment, 2005—. Named Gerbode Found. Fellow,

1993, Eureka Leadership Fellow, 1997; recipient Asian Pacific Heritage Month's Local Hero of Yr. award. Office: Family Independence Initiative 1204 Preservation Pkwy Oakland CA 94612*

**MILLER, MAYNARD MALCOLM,** geologist, educator, science administrator, former state legislator; b. Seattle, Jan. 23, 1921; s. Joseph Anthony and Juanita Queena (Davison) M.; m. Joan Walsh, Sept. 15, 1951; children: Ross McCord, Lance Davison. BS magna cum laude, Harvard U., 1943; MA, Columbia U., 1948; PhD, St. John's Coll., Cambridge U., 1957; student, Naval War Coll., Air War Coll., Nat. Def. U., Oak Ridge Inst. Nuc. Sci.; DSc (hon.), U. Alaska, 1990. Registered profl. geologist, Idaho. Asst. prof. naval sci. Princeton U., NJ, 1946; organizer, dir. Office Naval Rsch., Juneau Icefield Rsch. project Am. Geog. Soc., NYC, 1946—55, rsch. assoc., 1948—55; geologist Gulf Oil Co., Cuba, 1947; staff scientist Swiss Fed. Inst. for Snow and Avalanche Rsch., Davos, 1952—53; instr. dept. geography Cambridge U., 1953—54, 1956; assoc. prodr., field unit dir. film Seven Wonders of the World Cinerama Corp., Europe, Asia, Africa, Mid. East, 1954—55; rsch. assoc. Lamont Geol. Obs., N.Y.C., 1955—59; sr. scientist dept. geology Columbia U., N.Y.C., 1957—59; asst. prof. geology Mich. State U., East Lansing, 1959—61, assoc. prof., 1961—63, prof., 1963—75; dean Coll. Mines and Earth Resources U. Idaho, Moscow, 1975—88, dean emeritus, prof. geology, dir. Glaciological and Arctic Scis. Inst., 1975—; dir., state geologist Idaho Geol. Survey, 1975—88, dir. emeritus; rep. Legislature of State of Idaho, Boise, 1992—2000. Geophys. cons. Nat. Park Svc., NASA, USAF, NAS; mem. mapping expdn. Brady Icefield and Glacier Bay, Alaska, 1940, 41; co-initiator, organizer, leader USAF-Harvard Mountaineering Club Mt. St. Elias Expdn., 1946; chief geologist Am. Mt. Everest Expdn., Nepal, 1963; dir. Nat. Geog. Soc. Alaskan Glacier Commemorative Project, 1964—; co-initiator, organizer, field leader Nat. Geog. Soc. Joint U.S.-Can. Mt. Kennedy Yukon Meml Mapping Expdn., 1965; leader Muséo Argentino de Ciencias Naturales, Patagonian expdn. and glacier study for Inst. Geologico del Peru and Am. Geog. Soc., 1949-50; with adv. missions People's Republic of China, 1981, 86, 88, 98; with geol. expdns. Himalaya, Nepal, 1963, 84, 87; with USAF ice survey mission to Ellesmere Land, North Pole and Polar Sea, 1951; organizer, ops. officer pioneering USN-LTA blimp geophysics flight to Ice Island T-3 and North Pole area Office Naval Rsch., 58; ONR-LTA coord. SS Nautilus First Transit North Pole; prin. investigator U.S. Naval Oceanog. Office sea and pack ice rsch. Ice Island T-3 Polar Sea, 1967-68, 70-73; dir. lunar field sta. Mt. Rainier summit simulation USAF-Boeing Co., 1959-60; prin. investigator Nat. Geog. Soc. 30 Yr. Remap of Lemon, Taku and Cathedral Massif Glaciers, Juneau Icefield, 1989-2005; exec. dir. Found. for Glacier and Environ. Rsch., Pacific Sci. Ctr., Seattle, 1955-95, 97—, chmn., 1992—, pres., 1955-85, trustee, 1960—, cons. Dept. Hwys. State of Alaska, 1965; chmn., exec. dir. World Ctr. for Exploration Found., N.Y.C., 1967; dir., adv. bd. Idaho Geol. Survey, 1975-88; chmn. nat. coun. JSHS program U.S. Army Rsch. Office and Acad. Applied Sci., 1982-90; sci. dir. U.S. Army Rsch. Office and DOD Nat. Sci. and Humanities Symposia programs, 1991—; disting. guest prof. China U. Geoscis., Wuhan, 1981. Changchun U. Earth Scis., People's Republic of China, 1988—; adj. prof. U. Alaska, 1986—; lectr. in field Author: Field Manual of Glaciological and Arctic Sciences; co-author books on Alaskan glaciers and Nepal geology; contbr. articles to profl. jours., chpts. to books. Past mem. nat. exploring com., nat. sea exploring com. Boy Scouts Am.; past mem. nat. adv. bd. Embry Riddle Aero. U.; bd. dirs. Idaho Rsch. Found.; pres. state divsn. Mich. UN Assn., 1970-73; mem. Centennial and Health Environ. Commns., Moscow, Idaho, 1987—. With USN, 1943-46, PTO. Decorated 11 campaign and battle stars; Fulbright scholar Cambridge U., 1951-53; named Leader of Tomorrow Seattle C. of C. and Time mag., 1953, one of Ten Outstanding Young Men U.S. Jaycees, 1954; recipient commendation for lunar environ. study USAF, 1960, Hubbard medal (co-recipient with Mt. Everest expdn. team) Nat. Geog. Soc., 1963, Elisha Kent Kane Gold medal Geog. Soc. Phila., 1964, Kavo award Soc. Mil. Engrs., 1966, Franklin L. Burr award Nat. Geog. Soc., 1967, Nat. Commendation Boy Scouts Am., 1970, Disting. Svc. commendation plaque UN Assn. U.S., Disting. Svc. commendation State of Mich. Legis., 1975, Outstanding Civilian Svc. medal U.S. Army Rsch. Office, 1977, Outstanding Leadership in Minerals Edn. commendations Idaho Mining Assn., 1985, 87, Nat. Disting. Tchg. award Assn. Am. Geographers, 1996; recipient numerous grants NSF, Nat. Geog. Soc., NASA, ARO, M.J. Murdock Trust, Dept. of Interior, others, 1948—. Fellow Geol. Soc. Am., Arctic Inst. N.Am., Explorers Club; mem. AAAS (councillor, Pacific divsn. 1978-88), AIME, ASME (hon. nat. lectr.), Am. Geophys. Union, Internat. Glaciological Soc. (past councilor), Assn. Am. State Geologists (hon.), Am. Legis. Exch. Coun., Am. Assn. Amateur Oarsmen (life), Am. Alpine Club (hon., past councilor, life), Fulbright Assn., Alpine Club (London), Appalachian Club (hon. corr.), Brit. Mountaineering Assn. (hon., past v.p.), The Mountaineers (hon.), Cambridge U. Mountaineering Club (hon.), Himalyan Club (Calcutta), English Speaking Union (nat. lectr.), Naval Res. Assn. (life), Dutch Treat Club, Circumnavigators Club (life), Adventurers Club N.Y. (medalist), Am. Legion, VFW, Harvard Club (N.Y.C. and Seattle), Sigma Xi, Phi Beta Kappa (past pres. Epsilon chpt.), Phi Kappa Phi. Republican. Methodist. Avocations: skiing, mountain climbing, photography. Home: 514 E 1st St Moscow ID 83843-2814 Office: Univ Idaho Coll Sci Moscow ID 83844-3022 also: Found Glacier & Environ Rsch 4470 N Douglas Hwy Juneau AK 99801-9403 Office Phone: 208-885-6192, 208-882-1237. Office Fax: 208-882-6207. Business E-Mail: jirp@uidaho.edu.

**MILLER, MERRILL ANTHONY, JR.,** oil industry executive; b. Burlington, Iowa, July 4, 1950; s. Merrill Anthony Sr. and Florence Mae (Douglas) M.; m. Diana Sue Wagner, June 17, 1972; 1 child, Diana B. in Engring., U.S. Mil. Acad., 1972; MBA, Harvard U., 1980. Team mgr. Procter & Gamble, Mehoopany, Pa., 1977-78; asst. to pres. Helmerick & Payne, Tulsa, 1980-82, v.p. and gen. mgr. no. div. Okla. City, 1982; with Nat. Oilwell Varco, Houston, 1996—, pres., 2000—, COO, 2000—05, CEO, 2001—, chmn., 2002—. Bd. dirs. Internat. Computer Exchange, Inc., Boulder, Colo. Mem. Internat. Assn. Drilling Contractors (bd. dirs. 1985—, chmn. midcontinent chpt. 1986-87). Roman Catholic. Avocations: sports, reading. Office: National Oilwell Varco 10000 Richmond Ave Houston TX 77042-4200

**MILLER, MICHAEL,** physician, educator; b. Queens, N.Y., June 19, 1957; s. Irving Maltz and Lenore (Goldstein) Miller; m. Lisa L. Miller; children: Avery Lauren, Ilana Frieda, Myles Solomon. BA, Rutgers U., 1979; MD, Robert Wood Johnson Med. Sch., 1983. Diplomate Am. Bd. Internal Medicine, Am. Bd. Cardiovascular Disease, Nat. Bd. Med. Examiners. Intern dept. medicine Med. Ctr. U. Cin., 1983-84, resident internal medicine 1984-86; lipoprotein metabolism fellow Sch. Medicine Johns Hopkins U., Balt., 1986-89, cardiovascular disease fellow, 1988-91; dir. ctr. preventive cardiology U. Md. Med. Sys., Balt., 1991—; assoc. prof. medicine divsn. cardiology Sch. Medicine U. Md., Balt., 1991—; asst. prof. medicine divsn. cardiology Sch. Medicine Johns Hopkins U., Balt., 1991—; adj. asst. prof. dept. medicine Baylor Coll. Medicine, Houston, 1992—. Tchr. Sch. Medicine U. Md., 1994—; Johns Hopkins U., 1993—, Balt. Pub. Sch. Sys., 1991—; lectr. in field. Author: The Practice of Coronary Disease Prevention, 1996, The Cholesterol Planner, 3d edit., 2004, 5th edit., 2006; contbr. chpts. to books and articles to profl. jours.; reviewer numerous jours.; featured in ednl. recordings, 1990—. Mem. Gov.'s Task Force Cardiovasc. Disease Prevention. Grantee NIH/Am. Heart Assn., 1989—, Bristol-Myers Squibb, 1991-93, Sandoz, 1992-93, Pfizer, 1992—, Merck, 1997—; recipient Robert Galbraith award, 1979, William F. Grupe award, 1983, Samuel Kaslev award, 1994. Fellow Am. Coll. Cardiology (co-author Preventive Cardiology, 1998—), Am. Heart Assn. Coun. Arteriosclerosis; mem. AAAS, Am. Soc. Preventive Cardiology (past pres.), Am. Heart Assn. Coun. Epidemiology, Phi Beta Kappa. Jewish. Avocations: skiing, tennis, hiking. Home: 5 Green Heather Ct Baltimore MD 21208 Office: U Md Divsn Cardiology 22 S Greene St Baltimore MD 21201-1544 Office Phone: 410-328-6299. E-mail: mmiller@medicine.maryland.edu.

**MILLER, MICHAEL DOUGLAS,** lawyer; b. Tucson, Dec. 25, 1948; s. Robert Friend and Mary (Fawcett) M.; m. Jennifer Louise Hunter, Dec. 23, 1960; 1 child, Hunter Douglas. BS, U. Ariz., 1973, JD, 1976. Bar: Ariz. 1977. Pvt. practice, Tucson, 1977—. Mem. Ariz. Bar Assn., Ariz. Trial Lawyers

Assn., Pima County Bar Assn. Avocations: fishing, camping, outdoor activities. Office: 2830 N Swan Rd Ste 140 Tucson AZ 85712-6301 Office Phone: 520-327-3801. E-mail: mdm@mdmlaw.com.

**MILLER, MICHAEL JEFFREY,** editor, columnist; b. Chgo., Dec. 10, 1958; s. Kenneth Maynard and Joan (Callner) Miller; m. Joan A. Slobin, Oct. 18, 1987. BS in Computer Sci., Rensselaer Poly., Troy, N.Y., 1979; MS in Journalism, Northwestern U., Evanston, Ill., 1980. Sr. editor Bldg. Design and Constrn., Chgo., 1980—83; west coast bur. chief Popular Computing, San Francisco, 1983—85; exec. editor InfoWorld, Menlo Park, Calif., 1985—89, editor, 1989—90, editor-in-chief, 1991, PC Mag., NYC, 1991—2005; exec. v.p., editl. dir. Ziff-Davis Pub., 1997—2005; chief content officer Ziff-Davis Media, 2005—. Mem.: Soc. Profl. Journalists, Am. Soc. Technion. Office: Ziff Davis Media Inc 28 E 28th St New York NY 10016-7930

**MILLER, MICHAEL PATIKY,** lawyer; b. Huntington, N.Y., Apr. 16, 1944; s. George J. and Alida (Patiky) Miller; m. Dorothy Denn, Dec. 25, 1966; children: Lauren M. Golubtchik, Jonathan M., Rachel Miller Lazarus. AB, Rutgers U., 1965; JD, NYU, 1968. Bar: N.J. 1968, U.S. Dist. Ct. N.J. 1968, Calif. 1975, U.S. Dist. Ct. (no. dist.) Calif. 1975, U.S. Tax Ct. 1977, U.S. Ct. Appeals (9th cir.) 1977, U.S. Ct. Appeals (fed. cir.) 1984, U.S. Dist. Ct. (cen. dist.) Calif. 1982, U.S. Supreme Ct. 1983, U.S. Claims Ct. 1986. Chief of procurement and admin. law U.S. Army, 1973—74; atty. Electric Power Rsch. Inst., Palo Alto, Calif., 1974—77; assoc. Weinberg, Ziff & Kaye, Palo Alto, 1977—78; ptnr. Weinberg, Ziff & Miller, Palo Alto, 1978—, mng. ptnr., 1990—98; lectr. on tax and estate planning U. Calif. Extension, 1980—. Author: Creditor Rights in Proceedings Outside Estate Adminstrn., 1995, rev., 1999, Estate Planning for Foreign Nationals in Silicon Valley, 2000, Death, Debts and Taxes 2000, rev. 2006, Building A Better Boiler, Doing the Math in Estate Planning, 2006, Don't Make Mistakes with Judicial Council Forms, 2006; co-author: Decedents Estate Practice, 2001, rev. annually, Trust Administration, 2d edit., 2001—; contbg. author: California Wills and Trusts, 1991, Estate Planning for Unmarried Couples, 1998, Doing the Math of Estate Planning, 1999, Trust and Estate Litigation, 2004; contbr. chpts. in books and articles to profl. jours. Treas. No. Calif. region United Synagogue Am., 1985-89, pres., 1992-95. Capt. U.S. Army, 1969-74, Vietnam, Ethiopia. Recipient Lion of Judah award, 1984, Cert. Merit U. Judaism, 1992. Mem. ABA (chmn. region VI pub. contract law sect. 1975-78, commn. tax practice in small law firms, com. on taxation of trusts, estates, taxation sect. 1986—), N.J. State Bar, State Bar of Calif. (commr. tax law adv. commn. 1989-92, 93-95, chair 1994-95, mem. bd. legal specialization 1994-95, chair probate sect. 1982), Silicon Valley Bar Assn. (pres. 2000-02, trustee 2002—, treas. 2006—). Office: Weinberg Ziff & Miller 400 Cambridge Ave Palo Alto CA 94306-1507 Office Phone: 650-329-0851. Business E-Mail: mpmiller@taxattorney.com.

**MILLER, MICHAEL THURMAN,** architect; b. Chgo., Nov. 26, 1956; s. Wallace Howard and Joanne (Thurman) M.; m. Deborah Walton, July 21, 1984; children: Jessica Nicole, Elissa Danielle, Jordan Alexander. BArch, U. Ill., 1978, MArch, MBA, 1982. Lic. architect, Ill. Architect Enviro-Technics Ltd., Skokie, Ill., 1978, A.M. Kinney Assocs., Evanston, Ill., 1978—79; architect, project planner Murphy/Jahn Inc., Chgo., 1982—84; sr. project mgr. Litton Industries, Schiller Park, Ill., 1984—89; sr. assoc. Grunsfeld and Assocs., Architects, Chgo., 1989—2000; CFO, COO Lucien Lagrange Archs., Chgo., 2000—04; prin. Zweig White Info. Svcs., Chgo., 2005—06; asst. v.p. Hyatt Hotels Corp., Chgo., 2006—. Home: 1655 Marcie Ct Deerfield IL 60015-3979

**MILLER, MICHELLE D.,** lawyer; b. 1952; BA cum laude, Boston Univ., 1974; JD magna cum laude, Boston Coll., 1979. Bar: Mass. 1979. Law clk. Judge Paul J. Liacos, Supreme Judicial Ct. Mass., 1979—80; assoc. to ptnr. Wilmer Cutler Pickering Hale & Dorr, Boston, 1980—, vice chmn. Litigation dept., vice chmn. Antitrust & Competition dept.; mem. exec. com. Contbr. articles to profl. jours. Named one of Top 50 Female Mass. Lawyers, Boston Mag., 2004. Mem.: ABA, Boston Bar Assn. (former co-chmn. Antitrust com.), Order of the Coif. Office: Wilmer Cutler Pickering Hale & Dorr 60 State St Boston MA 02109 Office Phone: 617-526-6116. Office Fax: 617-526-5000. Business E-Mail: michelle.miller@wilmerhale.com.

**MILLER, MILTON ALLEN,** lawyer; b. L.A., Jan. 15, 1954; s. Samuel C. and Sylvia Mary Jane (Silver) Miller; m. Mary Ann Toman, Sept. 10, 1988; 1 child, Mary Ann. AB with distinction and honors in Econs., Stanford U., 1976; JD with honors, Harvard U., 1979. Bar: Calif. 1979, U.S. Ct. Appeals 9th cir.) 1979, U.S. Supreme Ct. 1989, Calif. (U.S. Dist. Ct. (cen., no. and so. dists.)) 1981. Law clk. U.S. Ct. Appeals (9th cir.), Sacramento, 1979—80; assoc. Latham & Watkins, L.A., 1979—87, ptnr., 1987—. Chmn. ethics com. Latham & Watkins, L.A., 1986—. Author: (non profit) Attorney Ethics, 1993; editor: (articles) Harvard Law Rev., 1978—79; contbr. articles to profl. jours. Mem.: ATLA, ABA, L.A. County Bar Assn. (chmn. profl. responsibility and ethics com.), Calif. State Bar Assn. (mem. com. on profl. responsibility), Harvard Club (Boston and NY), Phi Beta Kappa. Office: Latham & Watkins Ste 4000 633 W 5th St Los Angeles CA 90071-2005 Office Phone: 213-485-1234. Business E-Mail: milt.miller@lw.com. *Notable cases include Medavoy vs. Klein and Raquel Welch vs. MGM Corp.; served as trial and insurance counsel in San Juan Dupont Plaza Hotel Fire litigation.*

**MILLER, MONTE BALDWIN,** retired internist; b. Independence, Mo., Sept. 4, 1930; s. Marshall Baldwin and Frances Lee Miller; m. Christine Faye Vielguth, Sept. 6, 1953; children: Mitchell, Mark, Michelle. BA, U. Kans., 1951; MD, U. Kans., Kansas City, 1955. Bd. cert. internal medicine. Intern Tacoma (Wash.) Gen. Hosp., 1955—56; flight surgeon USAF, Williams AFB, Ariz., 1956—58; pvt. practice Garnett, Kans., 1958—62; resident internal medicine Wilford Hall USAF Med. Ctr., Lackland AFB, Tex., 1962—65; asst for ing dept. medicine David Grant USAF Med. Ctr., Travis AFB, Calif., 1965—67, chmn. dept. medicine, 1968—73, dir. hosp. svcs. and dep. comdr., 1973—75, comdr., 1975—77; chief of medicine 12th USAF Hosp., Cam Rahn Bay, 1967; asst. clin. prof. Dept. Medicine Calif., Davis, 1968—78; med. directorate br. chief Hdqrs. Air Force Inspection and Safety Ctr., Norton AFB, Calif., 1978—79; chief med. inspection divsn., 1979—80; comdr. Malcolm Grow USAF Med. Ctr., Andrews AFB, DC, 1980—81; command surgeon Mil. Airlift Command, Scott AFB, Ill., 1981—85; comdr. Wilford Hall USAF Med. Ctr., Lackland AFB, Tex., 1985—86; command surgeon Hdqrs. U.S. European Command, Stuttgart, Germany, 1986—88; surg. gen. USAF, 1988—91; med. dir. Birch and Davis Internat. Project King Abdulaziz U., Saudi Arabia. Cons. internal medicine USAF Surgeon Gen., Washington, 1970—88. Contbr. articles to profl. jours. Bd. mem. Meth. Ch., Winchester, Tenn., 1994—98, Franklin County Adult Activity, Winchester, 2000—; bd. mem., past pres. Timsford Coun., Winchester, 2000—. Lt. gen. USAF, 1988—91. Fellow: ACP (Air Force gov. 1985, Laureate award); mem.: U. Kans. Med. Alumni (Disting. Alumni 1990), AMA (bd. govs. 1988—91), hosp. dels. 1988, mem. reference com. on med. edn. 1991), Phi Beta Kappa. Republican. Avocation: bass fishing. Home: 306 Cooper Ln Winchester TN 37398-4316

**MILLER, MORRIS HENRY,** lawyer; b. Thomasville, Ga., June 14, 1954; s. Gibbes Ulmer and Marianne (Morris) M.; m. Anita Carol Payne, Mar. 23, 1985; children: Morris Payne, Rose Elizabeth, David Gibbes, Paul Louis Henry, John Henry. BS in Acctg. summa cum laude, Fla. State U., 1976; JD, U. Va., 1979. Bar: Fla. 1979. Assoc. Holland & Knight, Tampa, Fla., 1979-84, ptnr. Tallahassee, 1984—, chmn. health law practice, 1989—2001, knowledge mgmt. ptnr., 2001—04. Dist. chm. comm. Gulf Ridge coun. Boy Scouts Am., 1988-89, mem. pack com., cubmaster Pack 23, Suwannee River Area coun., 1995-98, scoutmaster Troop 182, 1997-99, scoutmaster Troop 10, 2000-01, asst. scoutmaster 2002—, dist. nominating com., exec. bd., 2005-; mem. Leadership Tampa, 1986, Leadership Tampa Bay, 1989; bd. dirs. John G. Riley House Mus. Ctr. for African-Am. History and Culture, 1998-99, Tallahassee YMCA, 1994-2002, chmn. long range planning com., 1997; founder, chmn. Tampa Bus. Com. for Arts, Inc., 1988-89; elder Presbyn. Ch. Mem. ABA (health and bus. law sects.), Fla. Bar (chmn., vice chmn. computer

law com. 1983-89, Fla. corp. law revision com. 1986-89, health and bus. sects.), Tallahassee Bar Assn. Office: Holland & Knight 315 S Calhoun St Ste 600 Tallahassee FL 32301-1897 Office Phone: 850-425-5655. Business E-Mail: morris.miller@hklaw.com.

**MILLER, NANCY CELESTA,** music educator, director; b. Cleve., Sept. 10, 1941; d. Paul Milton and Margaret Marie (Hinkle) Meares; m. Glenn David Miller, Aug. 17, 1963; children: Suzanne Marie (Miller) Geis, Paula Jean (Miller) Mohr. B in Music Edn., Baldwin-Wallace Coll., Berea, Ohio, 1963. Lic. music teacher K-12 Ohio. Music tchr. k-12 gen./vocal/instrumental Fla. Twp. (Ohio) Schs., 1964—65; gen. music tchr. Defiance (Ohio) City Schs., 1967—68, Bryan City Schs., Ohio, 1972—2006. Children's and youth choir dir. St. Paul's Meth. Ch., Defiance, 1965—69; childrens choir camp dir. Wesley United Meth.-West Ohio Conf., Texas, 1993—96; children's choir dir. Wesley United Meth., Bryan, Ohio, 1972—2005, dir. music and worship, 1996—2005. Editor: (carillon newsletter) Randscrifden, 1971—72; composer: Delta Kappa Gamma Song- VI songbook (Cert., 1990), (musical) American Leaders, 2003—04, 2006; musician: Markey Meml. Carillon, Classy Clarinets Quartet, U. Mich. Clarinet player Bryan City Band, 1968—; keyboard, clarinet performer sch. and cmty. musicals, Williams County, Ohio, 1990—. Mem.: NEA, Cmty. Concerts Assn. Williams County (pres. 1995—97), Buick Club Am., Delta Kappa Gamma (pres. 1992—94). Methodist. Avocations: gardening, sewing, playing, cards and board games. Home: 17190 US 20a West Unity OH 43590

**MILLER, NANCY ELLEN,** computer scientist, consultant; b. Detroit, Aug. 30, 1956; d. George Jacob and Charlotte M. Miller. BS in Computer and Comm. Scis. U. Mich., 1978; MS in Computer Scis., U. Wis., 1981. Product engr. Ford Motor Co., Dearborn, Mich., 1977; computer programmer Unique Bus. Sys., Inc., Southfield, Mich., 1978; tchg. asst. U. Wis., Computer Scis. Dept., Madison, 1978—82; computer scientist Lister Hill Nat. Ctr. Biomed. Commns., Nat. Libr. Medicine, NIH, Bethesda, Md., 1984—88; pvt. practice West Bloomfield, Mich., 1993—. *Nancy E. Miller's professional interests in the field of artificial intelligence include: knowledge representation, expert systems, default logic, planning, knowledge-based systems, case-based reasoning, logic programming, agents, fuzzy logic, neural networks, and genetic programming. She is also interested in object-oriented programming and design. Ms. Miller is highly skilled in the following computer languages, systems, and tools: Lisp, Prolog, C++, C, Pascal, UNIX, Windows, Framekit, HTML, etc. She has used rapid prototyping and structured programming methodologies. Ms. Miller has worked in many facets of computer science, from research and development to end-user applications, in academia, government and industry, and on all sizes of computers.* Recipient Jour. of Am. Soc. for Info. Sci. Best Paper award, 1988. Mem. Assn. for Computing Machinery (sec. S.E. Mich. spl. interest group on artificial intelligence 1993-94), Am. Assn. for Artificial Intelligence, Assn. for Logic Programming, U. Wis. Alumni Assn. (life), U. Mich. Alumni Assn. (life), Am. Contract Bridge League, Nat. Women's Polit. Caucus, NARAL Pro-Choice Am., Jewish Fedn. Met. Detroit, Planned Parenthood Fed. Am., Hadassah: The Women's Zionist Orgn. Am. (life). Democrat. Jewish. Address: PO Box 4224 Southfield MI 48037-4224

**MILLER, NANCY K.,** literature educator; PhD, Columbia U. Disting prof of Eng and comparative lit at Grad Ctr City U. N.Y., N.Y.C. Contbr. articles to profl. jours.; author: (books) Bequest and Betrayal: Memoirs of a Parent's Death, and, But Enough about Me: Why We Read Other People's Lives. Office: CUNY Grad Ctr PhD Program in Eng 365 5th Ave New York NY 10016-4309 E-mail: nmiller@gc.cuny.edu.

**MILLER, NANCY LOIS,** senior pastor; b. Lancaster, Pa., July 20, 1954; d. William Martin and Dorothy DeBoer Miller. BA, Lebanon Valley Coll., 1976; MDiv, Garrett-Evangelical Theol. Sem., 1980. Cert. deacon Ea. Pa. Ann. Conf. United Meth. Ch., 1977, elder Ea. Pa. Ann. Conf. United Meth. Ch., 1981, basic quarter clin. pastoral edn. Rush Presbyn. St. Luke's Med. Ctr., Ill., 1979. Student assoc. pastor Cmty. Ch. Wilmette, Ill., 1977—78; vesper intern Vesper Soc., San Leandro, Calif., 1978—79; sr. pastor Milton Grove United Meth. Ch., Mount Joy, Pa., 1980—82, Bellegrove United Meth. Ch., Annville, Pa., 1992—94, Water Works United Meth. Ch., Cleona, Pa., 1992—94, Radnor United Meth. Ch., Rosemont, Pa., 1994—98, Coventryville United Meth. Ch., Pottstown, Pa., 1998—2003, Messiah United Meth. Ch., Lafayette Hill, Pa., 2003—; assoc. in resident svs., assoc. chaplain Cornwall Manor Retirement Cmty., Pa., 1983—84; founding pastor Faith United Meth. Ch., Lititz, Pa., 1984—92. Mem. dist. com. min. Lancaster Dist. United Meth. Ch., Pa., 1981—83; chairperson Evaluation Com. Conf. Coun. on Mins. of The Ethnic Minority Local Ch. Task Force, Valley Forge, Pa., 1982—82; chairperson, mem. commn. Comission on Status & Role Women Ea. Pa. Ann. Conf. The United Meth. Ch., Valley Forge, Pa., 2000—; mem. United Meth. Ch. Camp Pocono Plateau Site Com., Cresco, Pa., 1981—85; co-chair Harry Hosier Dist. Ministerium of The United Meth. Ch., Phila., 1994—96; chair worship com. & retreat com., mem. of steering com. Women of Faith (sub-com. The Met. Christian Coun. of Phila.), 1994—98. Actor: (plays) Musical Carnival. Founding pastor Faith United Methodist Ch. Mem.: Conshohocken Bus. and Profl. Women, Whitemarsh Twp. Bus. Assn. Democrat. Avocations: travel, camping, needlework, singing, piano. Office: Messiah United Meth Ch 527 Ridge Pike Lafayette Hill PA 19444 Office Phone: 610-828-0118. Office Fax: 610-828-2463. Personal E-mail: nancymiller@verizon.net.

**MILLER, NATHANIEL GREGORY,** mathematics professor; b. Berkeley, Calif., Sept. 5, 1972; s. Douglas Edward and Eleanor Goudsmit Miller. AB, Princeton U., NJ, 1994; PhD, Cornell U., Ithaca, NY, 2001. Instr. Cornell U., Ithaca, 1994—2001; asst. prof. math. scies. U. No. Colo., Greeley, 2001—. Contbr. articles to profl. jours. Mem.: Math. Assn. Am. Avocations: cello, hiking. Home: 464 Morrison Alley Boulder CO 80302 Office: University of Northern Colorado Ross Hall Greeley CO 80631 Office Phone: 970-351-2297. Business E-Mail: nat@alumni.princeton.edu.

**MILLER, NEIL STUART,** advertising executive; b. NYC, July 30, 1958; s. Irving Israel Maltz and Lenore (Goldstein) M.; m. Karen Joyce Salomon, Nov. 22, 1987; children: Lindsay Alexandra, Jacqueline Olivia, Sara Allison. BS, SUNY, Buffalo, 1980; MBA, SUNY, Binghamton, 1982. CPA, N.Y. Staff auditor Peat Marwick Mitchell & Co., N.Y.C., 1982-83; ops. auditor Gulf & Western Industries, N.Y.C., 1983-84; spl. projects acct. Mickelberry Comms., N.Y.C., 1984-86; v.p. fin. Ptnrs. & Shevack Inc. (subs. Mickelberry Comms. Inc.), N.Y.C., 1986-87, sr. v.p. fin., 1987-89, exec. v.p., CFO, 1989-96, exec. v.p., COO, 1996-98; sr. v.p., fin. dir. McCann Erickson New York (subs. Interpublic Group of Cos.), N.Y.C., 1998-2000; CFO N.Am. MindShare (subs. WPP Group PLC), N.Y.C., 2000; COO TN Media (subs. True North Comm./Interpublic Group of Cos.), NYC, 2000—01; CFO N.Am. Foote, Cone & Belding (subs. Interpub. Group of Cos.), N.Y.C., 2001—04; exec. v.p., CFO N.Am. McCann Erickson, N.Y.C., 2004—. Mem. AICPA, N.Y. State Soc. CPAs (past mem. com. CFOs and advt.). Avocations: skiing, motorcycling, golf. Home: 594 W Saddle River Rd Upper Saddle River NJ 07458-1115 Office: McCann Erickson 622 Third Ave New York NY 10017 Office Phone: 646-865-2255. Business E-Mail: Neil.Miller@mccann.com.

**MILLER, NICOLE,** art columnist; "Arts Beat" columnist Washington Post, visual arts columnist for Sunday Source. Office: Washington Post 1150 15th St NW Washington DC 20071 Business E-Mail: nmiller@washpost.com.

**MILLER, NICOLE JACQUELINE,** fashion designer; b. Ft. Worth, Mar. 20, 1951; d. Grier Bovey and Jacqueline (Mahieu) M. BFA, RISD, 1973; cert. de coursspeciale, École de la Chambre Syndicale de la Couture Parisienne, Paris, 1971. Opened boutique Gamine, Stockbridge, Mass., 1973—74; asst. designer Clovis Ruffin, NYC, 1974; designer Raincheetahs, NYC, 1974—75, P.J. Walsh, NYC, 1975-82, Nicole Miller, NYC, 1982—; Nicole by Nicole Miller, J.C. Penney, 2005—. Mem. Sports Commn. of N.Y., Commn. on Status of Women; bd. trustees R.I. Sch. of Design. Bd. dirs. Smith's Food and Drug. Recipient Dallas Fashion award, 1991, Earnie award for children's wear, Michael award for fashion. Mem. Fashion Group, Fashion Roundtable, Coun. of Fashion Designers of Am., N.Y. Athletic Club. Avocations: skiing, ice skating, waterskiing, wind surfing. Office: 525 7th Ave Fl 20 New York NY 10018-4901

**MILLER, NIDI R.,** artist, sculptor, educator; b. Camaguey, Cuba, Feb. 6, 1958; d. Robert A. and Nydian R. Ynda; m. William R. Miller, July 4, 1991; children: Alexis C., Albert R., Patrick R. BA in Fgn. Langs., BA in Art and Sculpture, George Mason U., 2004. Artist, sculptor, educator Fairfax County, Centreville, Va., 2000—. Exhibits include Group House/Earl House Exhibit, mural, September 11 Commemoration. Vol. Fairfax Area Christian Emergency and Transitional Svcs., 2000—01, Centreville United Meth. Ch., 1999—2002. Recipient Vision awards for acad. excellence, Office of Diversity Programs and Svcs., 2004. Mem.: Alpha Chi (hon.), Golden Key (hon.)

**MILLER, NORMAN CALVIN,** economist; b. Greensburg, Pa., May 28, 1939; s. Harold C. and Helen (Kovaleski) M.; m. Patricia Luan, Dec. 27, 1977; children: Doug, Scott, Craig, Pamela, Joshua. BS, St. Vincent Coll., 1961; MA, U. Pitts., 1964, PhD, 1966. Asst. prof. econs. Bowling Green (Ohio) U., 1966-67, Carnegie-Mellon U., Pitts., 1967-71; cons. U.S. Treasury Dept., Washington, 1971-72; prof. econs. U. Pitts., 1972-85; Lange prof. econs. and Am. enterprise Miami U., Oxford, Ohio, 1985—. Author: Macroeconomics, Open Economy Macroeconomics; editor: International Reserves in Developing Countries, Balance of Payments and Exchange Rate Theories; contbr. more than 30 scholarly articles to profl. jours. Grad. fellowship NSF, 1963-66, grantee NSF, 1967-69, U.S. State Dept., 1972. Mem. Am. Econ. Assn. Office: Miami U Laws Hall Oxford OH 45056-3628 Office Phone: 513-529-2836. E-mail: millernc@muohio.edu.

**MILLER, NORMAN CHARLES, JR.,** editor, reporter; b. Pitts., Oct. 2, 1934; s. Norman Charles and Elizabeth (Burns) M.; m. Mollie Rudy, June 15, 1957; children—Norman III, Mary Ellen, Teri, Scott. BA, Pa. State U., 1956. Reporter Wall Street Jour., San Francisco, 1960-63, reporter N.Y.C., 1963-64, bur. chief Detroit, 1964-66, Washington corr., 1966-71; Washington Bur. chief, 1973-83; nat. editor Los Angeles Times, 1983-97; lectr. journalism U. So. Calif., 1997—2001; ret., 2001. Author: The Great Salad Oil Swindle, 1965 Served to lt. (j.g.) USN, 1956-60. Recipient Disting. Alumnus award Pa. State U., 1978; George Polk Meml. award L.I. U., 1963; Pulitzer Prize, 1964 Mem.: Gridiron (Washington). Roman Catholic. Avocation: tennis.

**MILLER, NORMAN LESLIE,** meteorologist, hydrologist, researcher; s. William and Elizabeth Topp Miller. BS in Engring. Sci., U. Md., 1978; MS in Atmospheric Sci., U. Wis., 1981, PhD Atmospheric Sci., 1987. Atmospheric and oceanic sci. group leader U. Calif. - Berkeley Nat. Lab., 1998—; adj. full prof. hydrology and w Hydrology and Water Resources Dept., Univ. Ariz. - Tucson, Tucson, 2000—05. Contbg. author Intergovernmental Panel on Climate Change, 1995—; mem. Calif. climate change panel Calif. Energy Commn., Sacramento, 2000—; sci. rev. bd. mem. Port of L.A., 2003—; ad. prof. hydrology and water resources dept. U. Ariz., Tucson, 2000—05; presenter in field. Avocation: prof. emeritus, 1996—. Office: U Calif Berkeley Nat Lab One Cyclotron Rd Berkeley CA 94720 Office Phone: 510-495-2374.

**MILLER, ORLANDO JACK,** obstetrician, gynecologist, educator, geneticist; b. Okla. City, May 11, 1927; s. Arthur Leroy and Iduma Dorris (Berry) M.; m. Dorothy Anne Smith, July 10, 1954; children: Richard Lawrence, Cynthia Kathleen, Karen Ann. BS, Yale U., 1946, MD, 1950. Intern St. Anthony Hosp., Okla. City, 1950-51; asst. resident in obstetrics and gynecology Yale-New Haven Med. Center, 1954-57, resident, instr., 1957-58; vis. fellow dept. obstetrics and gynecology Tulane U. Service, Charity Hosp., New Orleans, 1958; hon. research asst. Galton Lab., Univ. Coll., London, 1958-60; instr. Coll. Physicians and Surgeons Columbia U., N.Y.C., 1960, asso. dept. obstetrics and gynecology, 1960-61, asst. prof., 1961-65, asso. prof., 1965-69, prof. dept. human genetics and devel., dept. obstetrics and gynecology, 1969-85; asst. attending obstetrician, gynecologist Presbyn. Hosp., N.Y.C., 1964-65, assoc., 1965-70, attending obstetrician and gynecologist, 1970-85; prof. molecular biology, genetics and ob-gyn. Wayne State U. Sch. Medicine, Detroit, 1985-94, prof. Ctr. for Molecular Medicine and Genetics, 1994-96, prof. emeritus, 1996—, chmn. dept. molecular biology and genetics, 1985-93, dir. Ctr. for Molecular Biology, 1987-90. Bd. dirs. Am. Bd. Med. Genetics, 1983-85, v.p., 1983, pres., 1984, 85. Author: (with E. Therman) Human Chromosomes, 2000; editor Cytogenetics, 1970-72; assoc. editor: Birth Defects Compendium, 1971-74, Cytogenetics and Cell Genetics, 1972-97; mem. editl. bd. Cytogenetics, 1969-69, Am. Jour. Human Genetics, 1969-74, 79-83, Gynecologic Investigation, 1970-77, Teratology, 1972-74, Cancer Genetics and Cytogenetics, 1979-84, Jour. Exptl. Zoology, 1989-92, Chromosome Rsch., 1994-99; mem. editl. bd. com. Genomics, 1987-93, assoc. editor, 1993-96; mem. adv. bd. Human Genetics, 1978-98; cons. Jour. Med. Primatology, 1977-94; consulting editor McGraw-Hill Yearbook of Sci. and Tech., 1995—, Encyclopedia of Science and Technology, 1997—; contbr. chpts. to textbooks and articles to med. and sci. jours. Mem. sci. adv. com. on rsch. Nat. Found. March of Dimes, 1967-96, mem. sci. com., 1996—; mem. sci. rec. com. Basil O'Connor starter grants, 1973-77, 86-94; mem. human embryology and devel. study sect. NIH, 1970-74, chmn., 1972-74; mem. com. for study of inborn errors of metabolism NRC, 1972-74; mem. sci. adv. com. virology and cell biology Am. Cancer Soc., 1974-78, mem. sci. adv. com. cell and devel. biology, 1986-90; mem. human genome study sect. NIH, 1991-94; U.S. rep. permanent com. Internat. Congress of Human Genetics, 1986-91. With AUS, 1951-53. James Hudson Brown Jr. fellow Yale U., 1947-48; NRC fellow, 1953-54; Population Council fellow, 1958-59; Josiah Macy Jr. fellow, 1960-61; NSF sr. postdoctoral fellow U. Oxford, 1968-69; vis. scientist U. Edinburgh, 1983-84; Disting. vis. fellow, Fogarty Internat. fellow LaTrobe U., Melbourne, Australia, 1992; recipient Pres. Disting. Scientist award Soc. for Gynecol. Investigation, 1999. Fellow AAAS; mem. AAAS, Am. Soc. Human Genetics (bd. dirs. 1970-73, 86-90), Genetics Soc. Am., Acad. Scholars. Wayne State U. (life, pres. 1996-97), Sigma Xi. Home: 19365 Cypress Ridge Terr # 817 Lansdowne VA 20176 Office: 540 E Canfield St Detroit MI 48201-1928 E-mail: ojmiller@smartneighborhood.net.

**MILLER, PAMELA GUNDERSEN,** mayor; b. Cambridge, Mass., Sept. 7, 1938; d. Sven M. and Harriet Adams Gundersen; m. Ralph E. Miller, July 7, 1962; children: Alexander, Erik, Karen. AB magna cum laude. Smith Coll., 1960. Feature writer Congl. Quar., Washington, 1962-65; dir. cable TV franchising Storer Broadcasting Co., Louisville, Lexington, Ky., 1978—80; mem. 4th dist. Lexington Fayette County Urban Coun., 1973-77; councilwoman-at-large, 1982-93; vice mayor, 1984-86, 89-93; mayor, 1993—2003. Dep. comm. Ky. Dept. Local Govt., Frankfort, 1980-81; pres. Pam Miller, Inc., 1984-94, Cmty. Ventures Corp., 1985-95. Mem. Fayette County Bd. Health, 1975—77, Downtown Devel. Commn., 1975—77; bd. dirs. YMCA, Lexington, 1975—77, 1985—90, Fund for the Arts, 1984—93, Coun. of Arts, 1978—80, Sister Cities, 1978—80; chmn. Prichard Com. for Acad. Excellence, 2004—; treas. Planned Parenthood, 2003—, Fayette Edn. Found., 2005—; alt. del. Dem. Nat. Com., 1976; bd. dirs. Lexington Opera Soc., 2003—; chair Fund for Arts Campaign, 2003—04. Named woman of achievement YWCA, 1984, outstanding Woman of Blue Grass AAUW, 1984. Mem. LWV (dir. 1970-73), Profl. Women's Forum. Home: 140 Cherokee Park Lexington KY 40503-1304

**MILLER, PAMELA SUE,** elementary school educator; b. Jefferson City, Mo., Feb. 3, 1952; d. Raymond Adolph and Nina Mae Loesch; m. Leslie Jay Miller, July 27, 1974; children: Joy, Aaron, Paul. AA, St. Paul's Coll., 1972; BS, Concordia U., 1974. Tchr. St. James Luth. Sch., Lafayette, Ind., 1975—76, St. Paul/Cmty. Luth. Sch., Readlyn, Iowa, 1976—79, St. John's Luth. Sch., Arnold, Mo., 1990—, chapel coord., 2000—. Mem. hand bell choir St. John's Ch., 1992—98, mem. adult choir, 2000—; organist St. Paul's Ch., Readlyn, Iowa 1976—80, tchr. Sunday sch., 1981—90; sec. Aid. Assn. Luth., Appleton, 1988—2001; congregational coord. Thrivent Fin. Luth., Appleton, Wis., 2001—; team capt. walk Luth. Children and Family Svcs., St. Louis, 2002—05. Lewis and Clark grant, Mo. Conservation, 2004. Mem.: Luth. Educators Assn. Lutheran. Office: St John's Luth Sch 3511 Jeffco Blvd Arnold MO 63101

**MILLER, PATRICIA A.,** music educator, opera and concert artist; b. Washington, June 16; d. Robert Lee and Bernice (Echols) Miller. MusB, Boston U.; MusM, New Eng. Conservatory; artist's diploma, Accademia di Santa. Cecilia, Rome; postdoctoral diploma, Mozarteum, Salzburg. Artist Thea Dispeker Artist's Mgmt., Inc., N.Y.C., 1981—95; assoc. prof. music, artist-in-residence U. Mo., Columbia 1983—85; prof. music, dir. vocal studies, artist-in-residence George Mason U., Fairfax, Va., 1991—; prof. voice Oberlin Coll. Conservatory, Oberlin, Ohio, 2000—01. Dir. vocal studies George Mason U., 1995—, prodr. opera theater, 2000—, dir. Inst. Vocal Arts, 2004—; lectr. Smithsonian, Wash., DC, 2000—02. Performer: (Operas) ERCOLE Amante, 1986, Carmen, 1985, Porgy & Bess, 1996,; concert/recital artist Kennedy Ctr., Washington, 2000, Kiev, 2002, Ambassador Embassy, 2003, Salzburg, Austria, 2004, Kaynon Concert Hall, Seoul, Korea, 2005; performer (soloist): Schloss Leopolskron Great Hall, 2004, Kiev Philharmonic Orch., 2004, New Strathmore Music Ctr., 2005, Nat. Philharmonic Orch. and Chorus, 2005. Mem. opera panel Nat. Endowment for the Arts, 2003—04; mem. panel Va. Commn. for the Arts, 2004—05. Recipient Shining Star Cmty Svc. award, Nat. Urban League, Sojourner Truth Leadership award, George Mason U., 2004; grantee, Am. Embassy, 2002; Fulbright scholar, Rome. Mem.: Fulbright Assn. (bd. dirs. Nat. Capitol area), Nat. Assn. Tchrs. Singing (state bd. dirs.), Sigma Alpha Iota (Alumni Artistry Leadership award 2004, Outstanding Artist award 2004). Methodist. Avocations: travel, walking, swimming, cooking. Office: George Mason Univ Dept Music MSN-3E3 4400 University Dr Fairfax VA 22030-4444 Office Phone: 703-993-1382. Personal E-mail: labellavoce1@aol.com. Business E-mail: pmiller@gmu.edu.

**MILLER, PATRICIA ANN,** secondary school educator; b. Charleston, W.Va., Oct. 26, 1938; d. William Jennings and Frankie Marguerite (Bragg) Nutter; m. Maurice E. Miller, July 20, 1963; children: Elizabeth, Jeffrey, Joel. BS Mus Edn., Charleston U., 1961; postgrad., Cin. Conservatory Music, 1962, 63, Miami U., Oxford, Ohio, 1965. Tchr. Ross (Ohio) High Sch., 1961-65, Hamilton (Ohio) Pub. Schs., 1973-95; retired, 1995. Choir dir. Immanuel Bapt. Ch., Hamilton, 1968-84, 1986-94, Grace United Meth. Ch., Hamilton, 1994-1998; featured soloist Hamilton Symphony Chorale. Mem. Music Educators Nat. Conf., Ohio Music Edn. Assn., Great Miami Choral Soc. (featured soloist), Am. Choral Dir's. Assn. Home: (Winter): 1590 E Firestone Dr Chandler AZ 85249-4382

**MILLER, PATRICIA LOUISE,** state legislator, nurse; b. Bellefontaine, Ohio, July 4, 1936; d. Richard William and Rachel Orpha (Williams) M.; m. Kenneth Orlan Miller, July 3, 1960; children: Tamara Sue, Matthew Ivan. RN, Meth. Hosp. Sch. Nursing, Indpls., 1957; BS, Ind. U., 1960. Staff nurse Cmty. Hosp., Indpls., 1958, Meth. Hosp., Indpls., 1959; office nurse A.D. Dennison, MD, 1960-61; rep. State of Ind. Dist. 50, Indpls., 1982-83; senator State of Ind. Dist. 32, Indpls., 1983—, chair senate health and provider svcs. com., 1999—; mem. labor and pension com., 1985—94; mem. edn. com., 1989—92; legis. appt. and elections com., chmn. interim study com. pub. health and mental health Ind. Gen. Assembly, 1986; chair Senate Environl. Affairs, 1990—91; health and environ affairs, 1992—; mem. election com., 1992—; mem. budget subcom. Senate Fin. Com., 1995—. Mem. Bd. Edn. Met. Sch. Dist., Warren Twop., 1974-82, pres., 1979-80, 80-81; mem. Warren Twp. Citizens Screening Com. for Sch. Bd. Candidates, 1972-84, Met. Zoning Bd. Appeals, Divsn. I, apptd. mem. City-County Coun. on Aging, Indpls. 1977-80; mem. State Bd. Vocat. and Tech. Edn., 1978-82, sec., 1980-82; mem. gov.'s Select Adv. Commn. for Primary and Secondary Edn., 1983; precinct committeeman Rep. Party, 1967-74, ward vice-chmn., 1974-78, ward chmn., 1978-85, twp. chmn., 1985-87; vice chmn. Marion County Rep., 1986-2000; sgt. at arms, 1982, mem. platform com., 1988, 90, 92, co-chmn. Ind. Rep. Platform Com., 1992; rep. Presdl. Elector Alternate, 1992; active various polit. campaigns; bd. dirs. PTA, 1967-81; pres. Grassy Creek PTA, 1971-72; state del. Ind. PTA, 1978; mem. child car adv. com. Walker Career Ctr., 1976-80, others; bd. dirs. Ch. Fedn. Greater Indpls., 1979-82, Christian Justice Ctr., Inc., 1983-85, Gideon Internat. Aux., 1977, Ctrl. Ind. Coun. Aging; mem. United Meth. Bd. Missions Aux. Indpls., 1974-80, v.p., 1974-76, mem. nominating com., 1977; bd. dirs. Lucille Raines Residence, Inc., 1977-80; exec. com. S. Ind. Conf. United Meth. Women, 1977-80, lay del. s. Ind. Conf. United Meth. Ch., 1977—, fin. and adminstrn. com., 1979-88, planning and rsch. com., 1980-88, co-chmn. law adv. com., chmn. health and welfare, conf. coun. ministries, also mem. task force, bd. ordained ministry, also panel, chmn. com. on dist. superintendency, dist. coun. on ministries; sec. Indpls. S.E. Dist. Council on Minstries, 1977-78, pres. 1982; chmn. council on ministries Cumberland United Meth. Ch., 1969-76; chmn. stewardship com. Old Bethal United Meth. Ch., 1982-85, fin. com., 1982-85, adminstrv. bd., mem. council on ministries, 1981-85; co-chair Evangelism Com., 1994—; jurisdictional del. United Meth. Ch., 1988, 92, 96-2000; alternate del. United Methodist Ch. Gen. Conf., 1988, del. 1992; mem. adv. com. Warren Fine Arts Found., 1991—; mem. adv. bd. St. Francis Hosp., 1992-2005; mem. health and human svcs. com. Midwest Legis. Conf., 1995; del rep. various confs. and convs. Recipient Lambda Theta Honor for Outstanding contbr. in fiedl of end., 1976; named Woman of Yr. Cumberland Bus. and Profl. Women, 1979; Ind. Vocat. Assn. citation award, 1984, others. Mem. Indpls. dist. Dental Soc. Women's Aux., Ind. Dental Assn. Women's Aux., Am. Dental Assn. Women's Aux., Coun. State Govt. (intergovtl. affairs com.), Nat. Conf. State Legis. (vice chmn. health com. 1994—), Warren Twp. Rep., Franklin Rep., Lawrence Rep., Center Twp. Rep., Fall Creek Valley Rep, Marion County Coun. Rep. Women (3rd v.p. 1986-89), Ind. Women's Rep. (legis. chair 1988-89), Nat. Fedn. rep. Women, Beech Grove Rep., Perry Twp. Rep., Indpls. Women's Rep. Club (3rd v.p. 1989—), Indpls. Press Club. Office Phone: 317-232-9400. Business E-Mail: s32@in.gov.

**MILLER, PATRICK DWIGHT, JR.,** religious studies educator, minister; b. Atlanta, Oct. 24, 1935; s. Patrick Dwight and Lila Morse (Bonner) M.; m. Mary Ann Sudduth, Dec. 27, 1958; children: Jonathan Sudduth, Patrick James. AB, Davidson Coll., 1956; BD, Union Theol. Sem., Va., 1959; PhD, Harvard U., 1964. Ordained to ministry Presbyn. Ch., 1963. Pastor, minister Trinity Presbyn. Ch., Traveler's Rest, S.C., 1963-65; asst. prof. Bibl. studies Union Theol. Sem., Richmond, Va., 1966-68, assoc. prof., 1968-73, prof., 1973-84, dean of faculty, 1979-83; Charles T. Haley prof. of Old Testament Theology Princeton (N.J.) Theol. Sem., 1984—. Author: The Divine Warrior in Early Israel, 1973, The Hand of the Lord, 1977, Sin and Judgment in the Prophets, 1982, Interpreting the Psalms, 1986, Deuteronomy, 1990, They Cried to the Lord, 1994, The Religion of Ancient Israel, 2000, Israelite Religion and Biblical Theology, 2000; editor: Theology Today, 1990-2005 Mem. Soc. of Bibl. Lit. (sec.-treas. 1987-88, pres. 1998), Rev. Std. Version Translation Com. Democrat. Presbyterian. Office: Princeton Theol Sem PO Box 821 Princeton NJ 08542-0803

**MILLER, PATRICK M.,** social studies educator; b. Butler, Pa. s. Edward Leyland and Erma Mae Miller; m. Bridget Miller, Sept. 15, 1984; children: Gretchen, Melinda, Alexis. BA, U. South Fla., Tampa. Social studies tchr. Butler Area Schs., Pa. Office: Butler Area Interm HS 551 Fairground Hill Rd Butler PA 16001-2633

**MILLER, PATRICK WILLIAM,** research scientist, educator; b. Toledo, Sept. 1, 1947; s. Richard William and Mary Olivia (Rinna) M.; m. Jean Ellen Thomas, Apr. 5, 1974; children: Joy, Tatum, Alex. BS in Indstrl. Edn., Bowling Green State U., 1971, MEd in Career Edn. and Tech., 1973; PhD in Indstrl. Tech. Edn., Ohio State U., 1977; Master's cert. Govt. Contract Adminstrn., George Washington U., 1995. Tchr. Montgomery Hills Jr. High Sch., Silver Spring, Md., 1971-72, Rockville (Md.) High Sch., 1973-74; asst. prof. Wayne State U., Detroit, 1977-79; assoc. prof., grad. coordr. indstrl. edn. and tech. Western Carolina U., Cullowhee, NC, 1979-81; assoc prof. U. No. Iowa, Cedar Falls, 1981-86; dir. grad. studies practical arts and vocat.-tech. edn. U. Mo., Columbia, 1986-89; devel. editor Am. Tech. Pubs., Homewood, Ill., 1989-90; proposal mgr. Nat. Opinion Rsch. Ctr. U. Chgo., 1990-96; dir. grants & contracts City Colls. Chgo., 1996-99; assoc. v.p. acad. affairs Prairie State Coll., 1999—2001, also dean workforce devel. and career edn., 1999—2001; prof. Govs. State U., University Park, Ill., 2001—. Pres. Patrick W. Miller and Assocs., Munster, Ind., 1981—; presenter, cons. in field Author: Nonverbal Communication: Its Impact on Teaching and Learning, 1983,

Teacher Written Tests: A Guide for Planning, Creating, Administering and Assessing, 1985, Nonverbal Communication: What Resarch Says to the Teacher, 1988, How To Write Tests for Students, 1990, Nonverbal Communication in the Classroom, 2000, Nonverbal Communication in the Workplace, 2000, Grant Writing: Strategies for Developing Winning Proposals, 2d edit., 2002, Test Development: Guidelines, Practical Suggestions and Examples, 2001, Body Language: An Illustrated Introduction for Teachers, 2005, Body Language on the Job, 2006; mem. editl. bd. Jour. Indsl. Tchr. Edn., 1981-88, Am. Vocat. Edn. Rsch. Jour., 1981-85, 94—, Tech. Tchr., 1982-84, Jour. Indsl. Tech., 1984—, Jour. Vocat. and Tech. Edn., 1987-90, Human Resource Devel. Quar., 1989—; contbr. articles to profl. jours. Sec. U. No. Iowa United Faculty, Cedar Falls, 1983-84, pres. 1984-86. Lance cpl. USMC, 1966-68, Vietnam. Named one of Accomplished Grads. of Coll. Tech., Bowling Green State U., 1995; recipient editl. recognition award, Jour. Indsl. Tchr. Edn., 1984, 1986, 1988. Mem. ASTD, Am. Ednl. Rsch. Assn., Assn. for Career and Tech. Edn., Am. Vocat. Edn. Rsch. Assn., Nat. Assn. Indsl. Tech. (chmn. rsch. grants 1982-87, pres. industry divsn. 1991-92, chmn. exec. bd. 1992-93, past pres. 1993-94, Leadership award 1992, 93), Nat. Assn. Indsl. and Tech. Tchr. Educators (pres. 1988-89, past pres. 1989-90, trustee 1990-93, Outstanding Svc. award 1988, 90), Internat. Tech. Edn. Assn., Coun. Tech. Tchr. Edn., Epsilon Pi Tau, Phi Delta Kappa. Personal E-mail: patrickwmiller@sbcglobal.net.

**MILLER, PAUL AUSBORN,** adult education educator; b. East Liverpool, Ohio, Mar. 22, 1917; s. Harry A. and Elizabeth (Stewart) M.; m. Catherine Spiker, Dec. 9, 1939 (dec. Dec. 1964); children— Paula Kay, Thomas Ausborn; m. Francena Lounsbery Nolan, Jan. 15, 1966. BS, U. W.Va., 1939; MA, Mich. State U., 1947, PhD, 1953. County agrl. agt. in, W.Va., 1939-42; extension specialist sociology and anthropology Mich. State U., East Lansing, 1947-55, asst. prof., 1947-52, assoc. prof., 1953, prof., 1953-61, dir. coop. ext. svc., 1954-58, provost Morgantown, 1959-61; pres. W.Va. U., Morgantown, 1962-66; asst. sec. for edn. HEW, Charlotte, 1966-68; disting. prof. edn., dir. univ. planning studies U. N.C., Charlotte, 1966-68; prof. adult edn. N.C. Sate U. at Raleigh, 1668-69; pres. Rochester (N.Y.) Inst. of Tech., 1969-79, pres. emeritus, 1979—, prof., 1979-83. Sr. program cons. W.K. Kellogg Found., 1979-83; adj. prof. rural sociology U. Mo.-Columbia, 1994—. Author: Community Health Action, 1953; co-author: Patterns for Lifelong Learning, 1973; contbr. to publs. in field. Mem. Colombian Commn. Higher Edn., 1960-61. Served as 1st lt. USAAF, 1942-46. Named to the Internat. Adult and Continuing Edn. Hall of Fame. Fellow Am. Sociol. Assn.; mem. Rural Sociol. Soc., Phi Kappa Phi, Epsilon Sigma Phi. Home: 1909 Walden Ct Columbia MO 65203-5407 Personal E-mail: millerpaul@missouri.edu.

**MILLER, PAUL DAVID,** aerospace transportation executive. retired admiral; BA, Fla. State U.; MBA, U. Ga. Commd. USN, advanced through grades to four star adm.; comdr.-in-chief U.S. Atlantic Command; supreme allied comdr.-Atlantic NATO; with Litton Marine Sys., 1995-99; pres. Sperry Marine Inc.; CEO Alliant Techsystems, Inc., Hopkins, Minn., 1999—2004, chmn., 1999—2005.

**MILLER, PAUL DEAN,** breeding consultant, geneticist, educator; b. Cedar Falls, Iowa, Apr. 4, 1941; s. Donald Hugh and Mary (Hansen) M.; m. Nancy Pearl Huser, Aug. 23, 1965; children: Michael, Steven. BS, Iowa State U., 1963; MS, Cornell U., 1965, PhD, 1967. Asst. prof. animal breeding cornell U., Ithaca, N.Y., 1967-72; v.p. Am. Breeders Svc., De Forest, Wis., 1972-95; exec. dir. Nat. Dairy Herd Improvement Assn., 1996—2003; pres. Windsor (Wis.) Park Inc., 1985—. Adj. prof. U. Wis., Madison, 1980—, sr. scientist, 2003—; dir. Internat. Com. on Animal Recording, 1998-2003. Contbr. articles to profl. jours. Mem. Beef Improvement Fedn. (disting. svc. award 2005), Am. Soc. Animal Sci., Am. Dairy Sci. Assn., Nat. Assn. Animal Breeders (dir. 1983-92, v.p. 1986). Republican. Office: Univ Wis 446 Animal Sci Bldg 1675 Observatory Dr Madison WI 53706-1284 Home: 6301 Fox Run Sun Prairie WI 53590-9357 E-mail: pdmil@aol.com, pdmiller2@wisc.edu

**MILLER, PAUL J.,** lawyer; b. Boston, Mar. 27, 1929; s. Edward and Esther M.; children— Robin, Jonathan; m. Michal Davis, Sept. 1, 1965; children— Anthony, Douglas BA, Yale U., 1950; LL.B., Harvard U., 1953. Bar: Mass. 1953, Ill. 1953. Assoc. Miller & Miller, Boston, 1953-54; assoc. Sonnenschein Nath & Rosenthal, Chgo., 1957-63, ptnr., 1963—; bd. dirs. Oil-DriCorp. Am., 1975—2004. Trustee Latin Sch. of Chgo., 1985-91. 1st lt. JAGC, U.S. Army, 1954-57. Fellow Am. Bar Found.; mem. Tavern Club, Saddle and Cycle Club, Law Club, Phi Beta Kappa. Avocation: gardening. Office: Sonnenschein Nath & Rosenthal 233 S Wacker Dr Ste 8000 Chicago IL 60606-6491 E-mail: pjm@sonnenschein.com

**MILLER, PAUL J.,** orthopedist, surgeon; b. NYC, July 19, 1927; s. Murray and Kitty Miller; m. Nanci Franco; children: Jimmy, Andrew, Michael. BA, Columbia U.; MD, NYU. Orthop. surgeon, pvt. practice, Queens, NY, 1958—. Attending orthopedist LI Jewish Hosp., New Hyde Park, NY, 1962—. Capt. USAF, 1953—55, Germany. Fellow, AADS, 1961—, AMA, 1961—, FICS, 1961—, FACS, 1961—. Avocations: golf, travel. Home: 101 Brook St Garden City NY 11530 Office: Mishkin Miller Fueman PC Bellerose NY 11426

**MILLER, PAUL SAMUEL,** lawyer; b. Paterson, N.J., Apr. 8, 1939; s. Louis and Etta (Wolff) M.; m. Carol Plesser, Mar. 26, 1961; children: Nicole F., Margo H., Jason E. BA, Rutgers U., 1960. JD magna cum laude. 1962. Bar: N.Y. 1963. Assoc. Kaye, Scholer, Fierman, Hayes & Handler, N.Y.C., 1962-63, Rubin, Baum & Levin, N.Y.C., 1964; ptnr. Fishman, Miller & Zimet, N.Y.C., 1964-70; counsel Leasing Cons., Inc., Rosyln, N.Y., 1970-71; with Pfizer Inc., N.Y.C., 1971—2002, assoc. gen. counsel, v.p., gen. counsel, 1986-92, sr. v.p., gen. counsel, 1992-99, exec. v.p., gen. counsel, 1999—2002; spl. counsel Kaye Scholer LLP, N.Y.C., 2002—. Ofcl. corr. Pharm. Mfrs. Assn., mem., chmn. exec. com. law sect., 1989-90. Mem. United Jewish Appeal Com., Essex County, 1981-83, co-chmn. Livingston sect., 1982; former chmn. bd. dirs. Citizens Crime Commn. of N.Y.C., inc.; bd. dirs. Am. Israel Pub. Affairs Com., Am. Jewish Congress, Jewish Theol. Sem., U.S. C. of C., chmn. Nat. Chamber Litigation Coun.; mem. bus. adv. coun. Touro Law Sch.; mem. bd. overseers Inst. Civil Justice, RAND. Albert Einstein Coll. Medicine, Jaffee Inst. Strategic Studies at Tel Aviv U. Recipient Jerusalem Humanitarian award, Shaare Zedek Medical Ctr. 1999, Louis Marshall Award, Jewish Theological Seminar, 2001. Mem. ABA (antitrust law sect., corp. banking and bus. law sect., natural resources law sect. sci. and tech. sect., mem. health law forum com.), N.Y. State Bar Assn. (antitrust law sect., food and drug law sect.). Office: Kaye Scholer LLP 425 Park Ave New York NY 10022 Business E-mail: pmiller@kayescholer.com.*

**MILLER, PEGGY GORDON ELLIOTT,** academic administrator; b. Matewan, W.Va., May 27, 1937; d. Herbert Hunt and Mary Ann (Renfro) Gordon; m. Robert Lawrence Miller, Nov. 23, 2001; stepchildren: Rohn J., Robert K.;children from previous marriage: Scott Vandling Elliott III, Anne Gordon Elliott. BA, Transylvania Coll., 1959; MA, Northwestern U., 1964; EdD, Ind. U., 1975; degree (hon.), Transylvania U., 1993, Chungnam Nat. U., Korea, 2000. Tchr. Horace Mann H.S., Gary, Ind., 1959-64; instr. English Am. Inst. Banking, Gary, 1969-70, Ind. U. N.W., Gary, 1965-69, lectr. Edn., 1973-74, asst. prof. edn., 1975-78, assoc. prof., 1978-80, supr. secondary student tchg., 1973-74, dir. student tchg., 1975-77, dir. Office Field Experiences, 1977-78, dir. profl. devel., 1978-80, spl. asst. to chancellor, 1981-83, asst. to chancellor, 1983-84, acting chancellor, 1983-84, chancellor, 1984-92; pres. U. Akron, Ohio, 1992-96, SD State U., 1998—. Sr. fellow Nat. Ctr. for Higher Edn., 1996-97; vis. prof. U. Ark., 1979-80, U. Alaska, 1982; bd. dirs. Lubrizol Corp., A. Schulman Corp., Commn. on Women in Higher Edn., SD Mus. Art, Akron Tomorrow, Ohio Aerospace Consortium, Ohio Super Computer Com., Brookings O. of C.; holder VA Harrington disting. chair in edn., 1994-96, Charles G. Herbrich chair in leadership mgmt., 1996—; chmn. Growth partnership Rsch. Pk. Author: (with C. Smith) Reading Activities for Middle and Secondary Schools: A Handbook for Teachers, 1979, Reading Instruction for Secondary Schools, 1986, How to Improve Your Scores on Reading Competency Tests, 1981, (with C. Smith and G. Ingersoll) Trends in

Educational Materials: Traditionals and the New Technologies, 1983, The Urban Campus: Educating a New Majority for a New Century, 1994, also numerous articles. Bd. dirs. Am. Humanics Meth. Hosp., N.W. Ind. Forum, N.W. Ind. Symphony, S.D. Art Mus., Boys Club N.W. Ind., Akron Symphony, NBD Bank, John S. Knight Conv. Ctr., Inventure Pl., Akron Roundtable. Cleve. Com. Higher Edn., 4-H Found., S.D. Art Mus., S.D. Value. Recipient Disting. Alumni award Northwestern U., UA Disting. Alumni award, 1994, Dist. Alumni award, Ind. U., 2004, numerous grants; Am. Council on Edn. fellow in acad. administrn. fund. U., Bloomington, 1980-81. Mem. Assn. Tchr. Educators (nat. pres. 1984-85, Disting. Mem. 1990), Ind. Assn. Tchr. Educators (past pres.), North Ctrl. Assn. (mem. commn. at large), Am. Assn. State Colls. and Univs. (acting v.p. divsn. acad. and internat. programs 1997, bd. dirs., treas., chmn. global priorities commn.), Am. Coun. Edn. (bd. dirs., exec. com.), Leadership Devel. Coun. ACE, Office Women Higher Edn. (mem. emerita of exec. bd), Am. Humanics (bd. dirs.), Ohio Inter Univ. Coun. (chairperson), Internat. Reading Assn., Akron Urban League (bd. dirs.), P.E.O., Cosmos Club, Phi Delta Kappa (Outstanding Young Educator award), Delta Kappa Gamma (Leadership/Mgmt. fellow 1980), Pi Lambda Theta, Pi Kappa Phi, Chi Omega. Episcopalian. Avocation: music. Home: 929 Harvey Dunn St Brookings SD 57006-1347 Office: Office of the Pres South Dakota State Univ Adminstrn Bldg 201 Brookings SD 57007-0001 Office Phone: 605-688-4111, 605-688-4112. Business E-Mail: Peggy_Miller@sdstate.edu.

**MILLER, PETER A.,** lawyer; b. May 2, 1958; m. Amy Elizabeth Faust, 1985. BS, U. Pa., 1980; JD, NYU, 1984. Assoc. Stroock & Stroock & Lavan LLP, N.Y.C., ptnr., 1993—2004, Akin, Gump, Strauss, Hauer & Feld LLP, N.Y.C., 2004—. Mem. exec. com. lawyers divsn. UJA Fedn. NY. Mem. bd. overseers Jewish Theological Seminary Rabbinical Sch.; bd. dirs. Madeleine Borg Cmty. Svcs. Jewish Bd. Family Children Svcs., Inc.; bd. dirs. Vacamas Programs for Youth. Mem.: NY Bar Assn. Office: Akin Gump Strauss Hauer & Feld LLP 590 Madison Ave New York NY 10022-2524 Office Phone: 212-872-1004. Office Fax: 212-872-1002. E-mail: pamiller@akingump.com.

**MILLER, PETER C.,** lawyer; b. 1965; BA, Marquette U., 1987; JD, DePaul U., 1990. Bar: Ill. 1990. Ptnr. Seyfarth Shaw LLP, Chgo., chmn. Employee Benefits Practice Group. Mem.: Employee Stock Ownership Plans (ESOP) Assn., Ill. State Bar Assn., ABA. Office: Seyfarth Shaw LLP 55 East Monroe St Ste 4200 Chicago IL 60603 Office Phone: 312-269-8513. Office Fax: 312-269-8869. Business E-Mail: pmiller@seyfarth.com.

**MILLER, PETER KARL,** music educator; b. York, Pa., Sept. 11, 1959; s. Paul Wilson and Gertrud Dorothea Miller; m. Mary Elizabeth Feldmann, Oct. 16, 1982; children: Emily Elizabeth, Christina Anna, Marissa Allison. BS in music edn., U. Pa., 1981; MusM in vocal performance, Cleve. Inst. Music, 1983, MusM in organ performance, 1994. State Tchr. Cert. Bd. State of Ill., 2002, State of Ohio, 1994. Dir. of music St. Ignatius of Antioch Ch., Cleveland, Ohio, 1983—91; organist, choir dir. Temple Emanu-El, University Heights, Ohio, 1983—96; dir. of music ministries St. Dominic Ch., Shaker Heights, Ohio, 1991—96; min. of music Grace United Meth. Ch., Decatur, Ill., 1996—2001; asst. adj. prof. of music Millikin U., Decatur, 1999—2002; elem. string tchr. Decatur Pub. Sch. Dist. 61, Decatur, Ill., 2001—02; asst. prof. of music Ind. Wesleyan U., Marion, Ind., 2002—. Music faculty Cuyahoga C.C., Cleve., 1983—87; artistic dir. Sacred Madrigal Singers, Decatur, Ill., 1996—. Dir.: Spring Choral Concert; musician: Karl Stamitz Bassoon Concerto, Senior recital accompanist; dir.: Feast of Christmas Past and Present; musician: (songs) various Faculty Recitals, 2004—. Mem.: Music Tchrs. Nat. Assn., Nat. Acad. Advising Assn. (assoc.), Am. Guild of Organists (assoc.), Music Educators Nat. Conf. (assoc.), Nat. Assn. of Tchrs. of Singing (assoc.), Decatur Running Club, Phi Mu Alpha. Conservative Luth. Avocations: running, bicycling, numismatics, philatelics, travel. Home: 413 W Decatur St Decatur IL 62522 Office: Ind Wesleyan U 4201 S Washington St Marion IN 46953 Office Phone: 765-677-2162. Office Fax: 765-677-2120. Personal E-mail: pmmiller@insightbb.com. E-mail: peter.miller@indwes.edu.

**MILLER, PETER M.,** lawyer; b. 1959; BA magna cum laude, Miami U., 1982; JD cum laude, Georgetown U., 1985. Bar: Ill. 1985, Mass. 1988. Ptnr., Trusts & Estates Sect. & Tax Sect. Mintz Levin Cohn Ferris Glovsky & Popeo PC, Boston. Office: Mintz Levin Cohn Ferris Glovsky & Popeo PC One Financial Ctr Boston MA 02111 Office Phone: 617-348-1726. Office Fax: 617-542-2241. Business E-Mail: pmiller@mintz.com.

**MILLER, PETER N.,** historian, educator; b. NYC, Dec. 13, 1964; BA, Harvard Coll.; MA, Harvard U.; PhD, U. Cambridge. Rsch. fellow U. Cambridge, 1990—93; Mellon instr. in social scis. U. Chgo., 1993—96; asst. prof. U. Md., 1998—2001; prof. cultural history Bard Grad. Ctr., NY, 2001—, chair academic programs. Author: Defining the Common Good: Empire, Religion and Philosophy in Eighteenth-Century Britain, 1994, Peiresc's Europe: Learning and Virtue in the Seventeenth-Century, 2000; contbr. The Song of the Soul: Understanding Poppea, 1992; contbr. articles to profl. jours. Fellow, NEH, John D. and Catherine T. MacArthur Found., Wissenschaftskolleg zu Berlin, Warburg Inst., John Simon Guggenheim Meml. Found., 2003. Office: Bard Grad Ctr 18 W 86th St New York NY 10024*

**MILLER, PHILIP EFREM,** librarian; b. Providence, Feb. 18, 1945; s. Jacob and Natalie (Rouslin) M.; m. Zenia Weiner, Dec. 20, 1969; 1 son, Paul Jeremy. BSL., Georgetown U., 1967; MS, U. Mich., 1968, A.M.L.S., 1973; PhD, NYU, 1984. Asst. libr. Hebrew Union Coll., N.Y.C., 1973-76, acting libr., 1976-78, librarian, 1978—. Author: Karaite Separatism in 19th Century Russia, 1993. Mem.: Assn. Jewish Librs. (pres. 1982—84). Home: 56 Truman Dr Marlboro NJ 07746-1122 Office: Hebrew Union Coll-Jewish Inst of Religion Klau Libr 1 W 4th St New York NY 10012-1186 E-mail: pmiller@huc.edu.

**MILLER, PHILIP GRAY,** artist; b. Seattle, Aug. 18, 1947; s. Robert Chester and Agnes Minto (Weston) M. Student, Whitman Coll., Walla Walla, Wash., 1965-69. Artist, musician Gallery Functional Art, Santa Monica, L.A., 1970—. Furniture maker Sonrisa Bernice Steinbaum Gallery, N.Y.C.; cons. Inner Cities Murals Project, L.A., 1992—, Met. Transp. Agy., L.A., 1993-94. Author (novella) Death Valley Girls, 1989, (screenplay) Hurt By Love, 1993, (book) Cynic's Guide to Spiritual Awakening, 1993; curator Punch Gallery, L.A., 1993; permanent exhibihbn., a Colony for AVT Nespelem, Washington, 1997—, writer, actor, film maker; works represented in permanent collections Conrado Terasas City Coun., L.A., Laguna Beach (Calif.) Mus., Venice (Calif.) Family Clinic, AIDS Project L.A.; represented in group shows Punch Gallery, 1996, Gallery Function al Art, 1997; Plates of the Vain pictorial book, 1999. Min. Universal Life Ch., Seattle, L.A., 1969—. Recipient Design 100 award Met. Home, 1989. Avocations: yoga, cats, gardening, basketball. Home: 10845 Vanowen St Ste A North Hollywood CA 91605-6418

**MILLER, PHILIP JOHN,** insurance agent, consultant; b. Yonkers, N.Y., Apr. 28, 1945; s. Arnold Norris and Shirley Miller; m. Violet Ann Miller, Oct. 6, 1968; 1 child, Andrea Marie. BA, L.I. U., 1966; M, CCNY, 1967. Lic. property/casualty/health ins. broker. V.p. Montgomery and Montgomery, N.Y.C., 1970—77; sr. v.p. Kornreich Orgns., N.Y.C., 1977—95; pres. Creative Resources Group, Hauppauge, NY, 1995—2000, Prosulting Inc., Northport, NY, 2000—. Cons. ins. fraud FBI, 1995—; cons. U.S. Govt., Washington, 2000—; established and managed specialized insurance programs for food industry, hazardous material trucking, non-profit organizations, and geriatric cmty. Author: Serious on Safety, 2002; co-author: Food Equipment Facts, 1988; author: Onwards and Upwards, 2003, Onwards and Upwards, Book II, 2006; guest appearances for various topics on insurance for Fox Five and CNBC, guest spkr. Dr. Bernard Meltzer show, 1990; author: Arbitration Insurance - the Need to Know, 2006. Presdl. Roundtable, Washington, 2000—; Senatorial Inner Cir., Washington, 2001—, Senatorial Inner Cir. Commn., Washington, 2005, Senatorial Trust, Washington, 2001—; Presdl. Task Force Commn. of Accomplishment, 2005. Capt. spl. ops. U.S. Army, 1962—67. Nominee medal of Freedom; named Businessman of Yr.,

NRCC, Washington, 2005. Mem.: Associated Risk Mgrs. Avocations: martial arts, architecture, writing. Office: Prosulting Inc 111 Soundview Ter Northport NY 11768 Office Phone: 631-757-9458. Fax: 631-757-9458.

**MILLER, PHILLIP EDWARD,** environmental scientist; b. Waterloo, Iowa, May 29, 1935; s. Joe Monroe and Katherine Elva (Groom) Miller; m. Cathy Ann Love, Sept. 15, 1962; children: Eric Anthony, Bryan Edward, Sean Patrick, Gregory Joseph. BA Sci. Edn., U. No. Iowa, 1961; MA Sci. Edn., U. Iowa, 1964; postgrad., U. Wis., 1966—68. Tchr. physics and chemistry Millersburg Cmty. H.S., Iowa, 1961—62; supervising tchr. NSF Insvc. Inst. U. Iowa, Iowa City, 1962—64; instr. biology, area coord. OEO We. Ky. U., Bowling Green, 1964—66; sci. editor, journalism instr.-sci. and tech. writing Mich. State U., East Lansing, 1968—74; asst. prof. agr., forestry and home econs. U. Minn., St. Paul, 1974—77; sr. editor atomic energy divsn. E.I. du Pont de Nemours and Co., Aiken, SC, 1977—89; sr. scientist environ. protection dept. Westinghouse Savannah River Co., Aiken, 1989—99; pres. Agy. Book Authors, Collectors and Understanding Sci., Aiken, 1994—2004. Radiol. air and drinking water program owner environ./govt. group Morrison Knudsen Corp., Aiken, 1999—2000; prin. scientist Washington Group Internat., Inc., Aiken, 2000—03; panelist 26th Internat. Tech. Comm. Conf., LA, 1979; participant Dept. Energy/Westinghouse Sch. Environ. Excellence, Cin., 1991; invited contbr. to procs. 1st Tatarstan Symposium Energy, Environment and Econs., Kazan, Russia, 1992; cert. pilot U.S. Power Squadrons, 2004—. Mem. publs. com. Ctrl. Assn. Sci. and Math. Tchrs., Iowa City, 1969—72; editor: Nat. Task Force Agrl. Energy R & D, 1976; editor, contbr.: Minn. Sci. Mag., 1974—77; contbr. articles to profl. jours. Judge speech Optimist and 4-H Club Contests, Aiken, 1985—86. Sgt. U.S. Army, 1955—58. Recipient Disting. Marksman Badge Gold medal, 1st pl. Sci. Writing, Argonne Labs. Assn., 1973, Profl. Achievement Permanent Profl. cert., Iowa State Bd. Pub. Instrn., 1974, Blue ribbon, Am. Assn. Agrl. Coll. Editors, 1ex. A&M, 1976. Achievements include the discovery that low-zinc root environment causes delay of development and acceleration of senescence in tobacco plants; research in the causes and timing of pre-adolescent initial interest in science.

**MILLER, PIERRE VALCOUR, II,** lawyer; b. New Orleans, Aug. 9, 1961; s. Pierre Valcour and Adrienne (Dainko) M.; m. Kelly Marie Harper, Dec. 4, 1993; children: P. Valcour III, Andrew Payne, Harper James, Elise Marie. BBA, U. Notre Dame, 1983; JD cum laude, Tulane U., 1986. Assoc. Jones, Walker, Waechter, Poitevent, Carrere & Denegre, New Orleans, 1987-92; jud. law clk. Judge Earl E. Veron, Lake Charles, La., 1986-87; ptnr. Kiefer & Rudman, New Orleans, 1992-95, Trinchard & Trinchard, New Orleans, 1995-97, Patrick, Miller, Burnside & Belleau LLC, New Orleans, 1997—. Vol. New Orleans Pro Bono Project, 1987—. Republican. Roman Catholic. Office: Patrick Miller Et Al 400 Poydras St Ste 1680 New Orleans LA 70130-7215 Office Phone: 504-527-5400.

**MILLER, R. CHARLES,** lawyer; BA cum laude, Harvard Univ., 1980; JD cum laude, Univ. Pa., 1985. Bar: D.C. 1989, US Supreme Ct. Law clk. Judge Spottswood W. Robinson III, US Ct. Appeals (D.C. cir.), Chief Justice William H. Rehnquist, US Supreme Ct.; spec. counsel Office of the Gen. Counsel, SEC, Washington, 1992—95; regional atty. Dole presidential campaign, 1996; adminstrv. ptnr. & mem. mgmt. com. Kirkpatrick & Lockhart Nicholson Graham LLP, Washington. Editor (in chief): Univ. Pa. Law Rev.; co-author: Mutual Fund Regulation - An A to Z Workshop; contbr. articles to profl. jours. Mem.: Am. Law Inst., Order of the Coif. Office: Kirkpatrick & Lockhart Nicholson Graham LLP 2nd Fl 1800 Massachusetts Ave NW Washington DC 20036-1221 Office Phone: 202-778-9372. Office Fax: 202-778-9100. Business E-Mail: cmiller@klng.com.

**MILLER, R. TERRY,** lawyer; b. San Jose, Calif., Feb. 28, 1947; BA, U. Calif., Berkeley, 1968; JD, So. Meth U., 1971. Bar: Tex. 1971. Sr. ptnr. Fulbright & Jaworski LLP, Dallas; now ptnr., co-chair real estate and fin. practice group and mem. mgmt. com. Akin Gump Strauss Hauer & Feld LLP, Dallas. Mem. ABA, State Bar Tex., Dallas Bar Assn., Phi Alpha Delta. Office: Akin Gump Strauss Hauer & Feld LLP ste 4100 1700 Pacific Ave Dallas TX 75201-4675 Office Phone: 214-969-4237. Office Fax: 214-969-4343. Business E-Mail: tmiller@akingump.com.

**MILLER, R. WARBURTON,** psychologist, farmer; b. Bellefonte, Pa., Nov. 23, 1921; s. Joseph Frederick and Mary (Warburton) Miller; m. Joyce Larayne Miller; children: Pamela Joyce, Page Layne. AB, Pa. State U., 1942; MA, U. Redlands, 1951; PhD, U. So. Calif., 1957; postgrad., San Bernardino Valley Coll., Columbia U., U. Mich., U. Minn., L.A. State Coll., U. Internat., Saltillo, Coah, Mex., Inst. Mex. Cultura Internat.; JD, Loma Linda Coll. Law, 1985. Lic. clin. psychologist, marriage, family and child counselor, clin. speech pathologist. Capt. USN, 1942—44, 1951—53; officer USNR, 1942—74; staff psychologist San Bernardino County Med. Ctr., 1968—74; forensic psychologist/clin. psychologist; pvt. practice with Dr. Joyce Miller. Mem. psychology examining com. State Bd. Med. Examiners, 1970—74; dir. Mojave Valley Coordinating Coun. Family Mental Health, 1971—72; lectr. U. So. Calif., U. Redlands, Loma Linda U.; bd. dirs., v.p. E. Pioneer Mut. Water Co.; expert witness in forensic psychology; chmn. bd. dirs. AVORA Corp. Author (with Joyce Miller): Dealing with the Behavioral Problems in the Elementary School, 1968, A Layman's Handbook for Aphasic Rehabilitation, 1973; contbr. articles to profl. jours. Mem. State of Calif. Psychologists Polit Action Com.; past pres. Carriage Club, Civic Light Opera Assn., San Bernardino chpt. City of Hope Hosp. # 434, San Bernardino County Navy League; bd. dirs., past pres. Goodwill Industries Inland Counties; pres. San Bernardino Libr. Found., 1995—. Recipient George Washington medal, Freedoms Found. Valley Forge, 1970, 1972, 1973, honor cert., 1974, Disting. citizens Lifetime Achievement award, Calif. Inland Empire Coun., Boy Scouts Am., 2000. Fellow: Am. Assn. Marriage Counselors; mem.: SAR (nat. trustee 1970—74, chmn. nat. soc. Ind. Day com. 1971—73, v.p. gen. nat. soc. we, dist. 1977—74, nat. exec. com 1977—74, vev. gen. nat. soc. 1974—76, past pres. So. Calif. chpt. Riverside, past pres. State of Calif.), Inland So. Calif. Soc. Clin. Psychologists, Calif. Sate Psychol. Assn., San Bernardino Area C. of C. (bd. dirs., pres. 1999), Naval Res. Assn., Rotary (Paul Harris award), Hon. Order Ky. Cols., Masons, Kappa Sigma, Pi Delta Sigma, Tau Kappa Alpha. Avocation: travel. Home and Office: 6836 Palm Ave Highland CA 92346-2513 Office Phone: 909-881-2786.

**MILLER, RAY,** state senator; BA in Polit. Sci., MA in Polit. Sci., Ohio State U., CEO Prof. Employment Svcs. Am.; state rep. Ohio Ho. of Reps., Columbus, 1981—93, 1998—2002; state sen., dist. 15 Ohio State Senate, Columbus, 2003—, ranking minority mem., fin. instns. and human svcs. and aging subcoms., and commerce and labor com., mem. fin. and fin. instns., health, and ins. coms. Founder, chmn. Ohio Commn. on Minority Health, Ohio Commn. on African-Am. Males; mem. exec. com. Ohio Dem. Party; chmn. Nat. Progressive Leadership Caucus. Recipient Dist. Legis. award, Am. Assn. Counseling and Devel., Trailblazer award, Ohio Legis. Black Caucus, C.J. Mclin, Jr. award, Urban Minority Alcoholism Drug Abuse Outreach Programs Ohio, Internat. Pathfinder award, World Congress on the Family, Dr. Martin Luther King Jr. Humanitarian award, Columbus Edn. Assn., 300 other cmty. and civic awards. Mem.: Coalition of 100 Black Men, Children's Hunger Alliance, NAACP, Alpha Phi Alpha. Democrat. Office: Senate Bldg Rm # 52 Ground fl Columbus OH 43215 E-mail: rmiller@maild.sen.state.oh.us.

**MILLER, RAYMOND EDWARD,** computer science educator; b. Bay City, Mich., Oct. 9, 1928; s. Martin Theophil and Elizabeth Charlotte (Zierath) M.; m. Marilyn Lueck, June 18, 1955; children: Patricia Ann, Laura Jean, Donna Lyn, Martha Eileen. BS in Mech. Engring., U. Wis., 1950; BEE, U. Ill., 1954, MS in Math., 1955, PhD in Elec. Engring., 1957. Design engr. IBM, Endicott, Poughkeepsie, NY, 1950—51, mem. rsch. staff Yorktown Heights, NY, 1957—81; dir., prof. Ga. Inst. Tech., Atlanta, 1980—89, prof. emeritus, 1989—; dir. Ctr. Excellence in Space Data and Info. Scis. NASA, Greenbelt, Md., 1988—93; prof. U. Md., College Park, 1989—2001, prof. emeritus, 2002—. Pres. Computing Scis. Accreditation Bd., N.Y.C., 1985-87. Author:

Switching Theory, Vols. I and II, 1965; editor: (with J.W. Thatcher) Complexity of Computer Computation, 1972; patentee in field. Lt. USAF, 1951-53. Fellow AAAS, IEEE, Assn. for Computing Machinery, IEEE Computer Soc. (v.p. edn. acts 1991-92). Lutheran. Avocations: tennis, fishing. Office: U Md Dept of Computer Sci A V Williams Bldg College Park MD 20742-0001 Office Phone: 301-405-2675.

**MILLER, RAYMOND JARVIS,** agronomy educator; b. Claresholm, Alta., Can., Mar. 19, 1934; came to U.S., 1957, naturalized, 1975; s. Charles Jarvis and Wilma Macy (Anderson) M.; m. Frances Anne Davidson, Apr. 28, 1956; children: Cheryl Rae, Jeffrey John, Jay Robert. BS, U. Alta., Edmonton, 1957; MS, Wash. State U., 1960; PhD, Purdue U., 1962; Doctorate (hon.), Moscow State Agro Engring. U., 2000. Mem. faculty N.C. State U., 1962-65, U. Ill., 1965-69; asst. dir., then assoc. dir. Ill. Agrl. Expt. Sta., 1969-73; dir. Idaho Agrl. Expt. Sta., 1973-79; dean U. Idaho Coll. Agr., 1979-85, v.p. for agr.; dean Coll. Agr. and Coll. Life Sci. U. Md., College Park, 1986-89, vice chancellor agr. and natural resources, 1989-91; pres. Md. Inst. for Agrl. and Natural Resources, 1991-93, prof. agronomy, 1986—, dir. internat. program agrl. natural resources, 1998—. Internat. expert in areas of agrl. sci. and edn. with spl. emphasis on Russia, former Soviet Union, East Europe, China, L.Am. and the Pacific Rim. Author numerous papers in field. Pres. Idaho Rsch. Found., 1980-85; bd. govs. Agrl. Rsch. Inst., 1979-80; chmn. legis. subcom. Expt. Sta. Com. on Policy, 1981-82; chmn. bd. divsn. agr. Land Grant Assn., 1985-86; co-chmn. Nat. Com. Internat. Sci. Edn. Joint Coun., USDA, 1991-94; bd. dirs. C.V. Riley Found., 1985-93; chmn. budget com. Bd. Agr., Nat. Assn. State Univs. and Land Grant Colls., 1993; mem. U.S./Russian Subcom. on Agrl. Rsch., Edn. and Ext., 1996—. Fed. Provincial grantee U. Alta., 1954-56, Dan Baker scholar U. Alta., 1954-56; grantee Internat. Congress Soil Sci., 1960, Purdue U. Rsch. Found., summers 1960, 61 Fellow AAAS, Am. Soc. Agronomy, Soil Sci. Soc. Am.; mem. Internat. Soc. Soil Sci., Clay and Clay Minerals Soc., Am. Chem. Soc., Am. Soc. Plant Physiolotists, Elks, Lions, Sigma Xi, Phi Kappa Phi, Gamma Sigma Delta, Alpha Zeta. Office: Symons Hall Univ Md College Park MD 20742 Office Phone: 301-405-1316. E-mail: millerrj@umd.edu.

**MILLER, REBECCA LYNN,** software engineer; b. Jasper, Tex., Feb. 9, 1948; d. Estelleen Odom Miller. BA, Lamar U., Beaumont, Tex., 1992. Lead software engr. GE Healthcare (formerly IDX Sys.), Dallas, 1994—. Singer: Sweet Adelines Internat. (2d pl. Internat. medal, 1989). Ct. apptd. child adv. CASA, Sherman, Tex., 2003—05. Mem.: Mensa (life). R-Consevative. Methodist. Avocation: travel. Home: 201 S College Dr Keene TX 76059 Personal E-mail: bebbaboo@hotmail.com.

**MILLER, REUBEN GEORGE,** retired economics professor; b. Phila., Mar. 28, 1930; s. George and Edna (Fuchs) M.; m. Sylvia Raigla, June 9, 1955. BA, LaSalle Coll., 1952; diploma, U. Stockholm, 1954; MA, U. Mont., 1956; PhD, Ohio State U., 1966. Asst. instr. Ohio State U., 1954-57; acting asst. prof. Oberlin (Ohio) Coll., 1957-58; asst. prof. U. Mass., Amherst, 1959-67; assoc. prof. econs. Smith Coll., Northampton, 1967-70; Charles A. Dana prof. econ., chmn. dept. Sweet Briar Coll., Va., 1970—2004, chmn. div. social scis., prof. emeritus, 2004—. Mem. adv. staff Computer Sci. Corp., Washington; cons. Dept. Def.; Fulbright-Hayes lectr. econs. Coll. Law, Nat. Taiwan U., Republic China, 1965-66 Contbr. articles to profl. jours. Am.-Scandinavian Found. fellow, 1952-53; Research Trng. fellow Social Sci. Research Council, 1958-59 Mem. Am. Econ. Assn., Am. Fin. Assn., Royal Econ. Soc. Office: Sweet Briar Coll Dept Econs Sweet Briar VA 24595 Business E-Mail: miller@sbc.edu. E-mail: rsmiller@uscyber.net.

**MILLER, RICHARD ALAN,** economist, educator; b. Springfield, Ohio, Feb. 25, 1931; s. Ross and Beatrice Miller; m. Joan Taylor Walton, July 7, 1956; children: Carol Elizabeth, Jean Anne, Eric Ross. BA, Oberlin Coll., 1952; MA, Yale U., 1957; MA (hon.), Wesleyan U., 1972; PhD, Yale U., 1962. Mem. faculty Wesleyan U., Middletown, Conn., 1960—2006, chmn. dept. econs., 1968-69, 71-73, 75-76, 92-94, Andrews prof., 1995-98, Woodhouse/Sysco prof., 2002—06, Woodhouse/Sysco prof. emeritus, 2006—. Vis. lectr. Yale U., New Haven, 1961-62, vis. assoc. prof., 1967-68, vis. prof., 1973, 83, 85, 95; vis. assoc. prof. U. Calif., Berkeley, 1969-70; vis. prof. U. Adelaide, Australia, 1981; vis. lectr econs. U. Conn., Storrs, 1983; economist Econ. Policy Office, Antitrust Div., U.S. Dept. Justice, Washington, 1973-74, cons., 1974-75; cons. antitrust sect. State Conn., 1980, 82; dir. Kawanhee, Inc., Maine, 1975-81, 82-86 Contbr. articles to indsl. orgn. and antitrust econs. to profl. jours. Mem. cert. adv. coun. Dept. Edn., State Conn., 1982-86; mem. coms. Bd. for State Acad. Awards. State Conn., 1978-97; dean faculty of Cons. Examiners., 1985-87; trustee Conn. Joint Coun. Econ. Edn., 1982-85. Served to lt. (j.g.) USNR, 1952-55. Ford Found. fellow Yale U., 1958-59; NSF fellow MIT, 1964-65, Wesleyan U., 1965-69; Shelby Cullom Davis Found. grantee Wesleyan U., 1979-82; Fulbright fellow N.Z. Inst. Econ. Research, 1986, 88. Mem. Am. Econs. Assn., Indsl. Orgn. Soc. Congregationalist. Home: 83 Paterson Dr Middletown CT 06457-5138 Office: Wesleyan U Dept Econs Middletown CT 06459-0001 Office Phone: 860-685-2354. Business E-Mail: ramiller@wesleyan.edu.

**MILLER, RICHARD ALLEN,** lawyer; b. East Chicago, Ind., Nov. 22, 1945; s. Ernest R. and Sophie D. (Kurmis) M.; m. Patricia Annette Bratton, July 26, 1969 (div. May 1974); 1 child, Jason Todd; m. Kathleen Patrice Sills, Jan. 3, 1976; children: Andrew Christian, Caroline Grace. BS, Ind. U., 1967; JD, Valparaiso U., 1973. Bar: Ind. 1974, U.S. Dist. Ct. (no. dist.) Ind. 1974, U.S. Supreme Ct. 1985, U.S. Ct. Appeals (7th cir.) 1987, U.S. Claims Ct. 1990. Assoc. Owen W. Crumpacker & Assocs., Hammond, Ind., 1974-76; Benjamin, Greco & Gouveia, Gary, Ind., 1976-77; ptnr. Greco, Gouveia, Miller & Pera, Gary, 1978-79, Greco, Gouveia, Miller, Pera & Bishop, Merrillville, Ind., 1979-85, Gouveia & Miller, Merrillville, 1985—2004, Richard A. Miller & Assocs., Merrillville, Ind., 2004—. Spl. counsel City of Hammond, 1974; fiscal counsel Ind Toll Rd. Comn., South Bend, 1981-83, Ind. Dept. Highways Toll Rd. Div., Granger, 1982-87; spl. asst. U.S. Rep. Peter J. Visclosky, Gary and Washington, 1985-86. Author: Indiana Rules of Evidence Applying to Expert Testimony, 1991. Campaign mgr. Visclosky for U.S. Congress, 1st Congl. Dist., Ind., 1983-88; dist. coordinator Nat. Bicentennial Competition on U.S. Constitution and Bill of Rights, 1st Congl. Dist., Ind., 1987-88. Mem. Ind. Bar Assn., Assn. Trial Lawyers Am., Ind. Trial Lawyers Assn. Democrat. Lutheran. Avocations: fly fishing, walking dog. Office: Law Offices Richard A Miller & Assocs 370 W 80th Pl Merrillville IN 46410-6173 Home: 1018 Sterling Ct Crown Point IN 46307-2686 Office Phone: 219-756-9390. Business E-Mail: ram@ramalaw.com.

**MILLER, RICHARD JACKSON (RICK MILLER),** lawyer; b. Milw., July 17, 1946; s. Wayne D. and Margarite M. (Von Sitany) Miller; m. Irene Nikki Tsacoyeanes, May 28, 1972; children: Nicole Elizabeth, Andrew James, Katherine M., Penelope Constance. BA, U. N.C., 1968; JD, U. Va., 1971. Bar: NY 1973, US Dist. Ct. (so. dist.) NY 1975, US Ct. Appeals (2nd cir.) 1975, Fla. 1988. Assoc. Brown and Wood, NYC, 1971-78, Wood and Dawson, NYC, 1978-82; ptnr. Alexander and Green, NYC, 1982-86, Mudge, Rose, Guthrie, Alexander & Ferdon, West Palm Beach, Fla., 1986-95, Edwards, Angell, Palmer and Dodge, LLP, West Palm Beach, Fla., 1995—. Contbr. articles to jours., chpts. to books; co-author: State and Local Govt. Debt Financing, Capt. USAR, 1972-79. Mem. Fla. Bar Assn., NY State Bar Assn., Univ. Club, NYC. Episcopalian. Avocations: golf, tennis. Office: Edwards Angell Palmer and Dodge 1 N Clematis St Ste 400 West Palm Beach FL 33401 E-mail: rmiller@eapdlaw.com.

**MILLER, RICHARD KEITH,** academic administrator, engineering educator; b. Fresno, Calif., June 12, 1949; s. Albert Keith and Gloria Mae (Pittman) M.; m. Elizabeth Ann Parrish, July 10, 1971; children: Katherine Elizabeth, Julia Anne. BS in Aerospace Engring., U. Calif., Davis, 1971; MS in Mech. Engring., MIT, 1972; PhD in Applied Mechanics, Calif. Inst. Tech., Pasadena, 1976. Asst. prof. mech. engring. U. Calif., Santa Barbara, 1975-79; assoc. prof. civil engring. U. So. Calif., LA, 1979-85, prof., 1985-92, assoc. dean engring., 1989-92; prof., dean Coll. Engring. U. Iowa, 1992-99; founding pres., prof. mech. engring. Franklin W. Olin Coll. Engring., Needham, Mass., 1999—. Cons. Astro Aerospace Corp., The Aerospace Corp., Jet Propulsion

Lab. Contbr. numerous articles to sci. and profl. jours. Mem. AIAA, ASME, ASCE, Am. Soc. Engring. Edn. Office: Franklin W Olin Coll Engring Office of Pres Olin Way Needham MA 02492-1200 Office Phone: 781-292-2301. Office Fax: 781-292-2314. E-mail: richard.miller@olin.edu.*

**MILLER, RICHARD KIDWELL,** artist, actor, educator; b. Fairmont, W.Va., Mar. 15, 1930; s. Maurice Entler and Lillian (Reed) M.; m. Teresa Marie Robinson, Apr. 27, 1957. Student, Pa. Acad. Fine Arts, 1948-49; BA, Am. U., 1953; MFA, Columbia U., 1956. Asst. prof. Kansas City Art Inst., 1968-69; instr. painting Scarsdale (N.Y.) Community Sch., 1970-75. Participated extensively in profl. theater as actor and singer including roles in Broadway Prodn. Baker Street, Oliver, Funny Girl, Wonderful Town, Illya, Darling, Indians, Rise and Fall of the City of Mahogonny; actor stock cos. including Fiddler on the Roof; one-man art shows include Trans-Lux Gallery, Washington, 1951, Bader Gallery, Washington, 1954, Balt. Mus. Art, 1955, Graham Gallery Ltd., N.Y.C., 1960, 62, 65, Argas Gallery, Madison, N.J., 1966, Jefferson Place Gallery, Washington, 1966, Albrecht Kemper Mus. Art, St. Joseph, Mo., 1969, L.I. U., 1973, Aaron Berman Gallery N.Y.C., 1983, Westbeth Gallery, N.Y.C., 1982, John Jay Gallery, N.Y.C., 1998, 2000, JCC of Mid-Westchester, 2001, Retrospective Exhbn., U. W.Va., 2004; group shows include Corcoran Gallery Art., 1950-51, 53, Pa. Acad. Fine Arts, 1951, 64, Carnegie Internat., 1961, Salon de National, Paris, 1954, Whitney Mus., 1958, U. Nebr., 1963, Martha Jackson Gallery, N.Y.C., 1973, Nat. Acad. Design, N.Y.C., 1996, 2002, 04, Art of the Northeast, New Caanan, Conn., 1996, others; represented in permanent collections Albrecht Kemper Mus. of Art, St. Joseph, Mo., Hirshorn Mus. and Sculpture Garden, Washington, Phillips Collection, Washington, Rochester Mus. Art, U. Ariz. Mus. of Art, Tucson, Watkins Gallery Collection, Washington, U. W.Va., Morgantown, NAD Mus., also numerous private collections; featured in Jan. edit. Am. Artist Mag., 1988, Christian Sci. Monitor, 1990, World Artists (Claude Marks), 1991. Washington Times Herald scholar, 1944, 45, 46; Gertrude Whitney scholar, 1948-53, 55-56; Fulbright fellow, 1953-54 Mem.: Nat. Acad. Design Mus. Address: 222 W 83d St Apt 8C New York NY 10024-4913 *I have an insatiable need to express myself— I suppose I was born with it. I was given more than one talent to satisfy this need, and for that I thank God. I have endeavored to use these talents to the absolute best of my ability. I can do no more than that. Some times I have succeeded, and many times I have failed, but the real joy and meaning is in the doing. All the pain has been worth it.*

**MILLER, RICHARD N.,** former medical association administrator; b. Jan. 27, 1938; m. Janet Olin, 1966; children: Margaret, Julia. Grad., Loras Coll.; MD, U. Iowa, 1963; MPH, Harvard U., 1967. Diplomate Am. Bd. Preventive Medicine. Intern Washington Hosp. Ctr., 1963-64; resident Walter Reed Army Inst. Rsch., Washington, 1967-69; pub. health officer Third Civil Affairs Detachment U.S. Army, Canal Zone, 1964-66, chief preventive medicine activity USARSUPTHAL Bangkok, 1970-72, chief preventive medicine activity USAMEDDAC Frankfurt, Germany, 1972-75, regional preventive medicine cons. Ft. McPherson, Ga., 1975-79; dir. divsn. preventive medicine Walter Reed Inst. Rsch., Washington, 1979-93, dir. residency program in gen. preventive medicine, 1979-88, 91-93, dir. WRAIR ann. tropical medicine course, 1979-93; asst. prof. preventive medicine and biometrics USUHS, Washington, 1981-93; dir. Med. Follow-up Agy. Inst. of Medicine, Washington, 1993—2001. Contbr. articles to profl. jours. Mem. Am. Coll. Epidemiology, Am. Soc. for Tropical Medicine and Hygiene, Soc. for Epidemiology Rsch., Infectious Disease Soc. Am. Office: Inst Med Med Follow-up Agy 2101 Constitution Ave NW Washington DC 20418-0007

**MILLER, RICHARD SHERWIN,** law educator; b. Boston, Dec. 11, 1930; s. Max and Mollie Miller; m. Doris Sheila Lunchick, May 24, 1956 (dec. April 23, 2005); children: Andrea Jayne Armitage, Matthew Harlan. BSBA, Boston U., 1951, JD magna cum laude, 1956; LLM, Yale U., 1959. Bar: Mass. 1956, Mich. 1961, Hawaii 1977. Pvt. practice law, Boston, 1956—58; assoc. prof. law Wayne State U., Detroit, 1959—62, prof.; 1962—65; prof. law Ohio State U., Columbus, 1965—73, dir. clin. and interdisciplinary programs, 1972—73; prof. U. Hawaii, Honolulu, 1973-95, prof. emeritus, 1995—, dean, 1981-84, dir. summer externship program, 2006. Vis. prof. law USIA/U. Hawaii, Hiroshima U. Affiliation Program, Japan, 1986, Victoria U., Wellington, New Zealand, 1987; del. Hawaii State Jud. Conf., 1989-92 Author: Courts and the Law: An Introduction to our Legal System, 1980; editor: (with Roland Stanger) Essays on Expropriations, 1967; editor-in-chief: Boston U. Law Rev., 1955-56; contbr. articles to profl. jours. Mem. Hawaii Substance Abuse Task Force, 1994-95; mem. Hawaii Patients Rights Task Force, 2005-06; arbitrator Hawaii Ct. Annexed Arbitration Program, 1995-99; bd. dirs. Drug Policy Forum Hawaii, 1996—; mem. Save our Star-Bulletin Com., 1999-2001, Citizens for Competitive Air Travel, 2002, Citizens Against Gasoline Price Gouging, 2003-; cons. Hawaii Coalition for Health, 1997-. 1st Lt. USAAF, 1951—53. Sterling-Ford fellow Yale U., 1958-59; named Lawyer of Yr. Japan-Hawaii Lawyers Assn., 1990; recipient Cmty. Svc. award Hawaii Med. Assn. Alliance, 1999. Mem. ABA, Hawaii State Bar Assn., Hawaii ACLU, Am. Inn of Ct. IV (emeritus founding mem., master of the bench), Am. Law Inst., Honolulu Cmty.-Media Coun. (chair 1994-89, treas. 2000-02, vice chair 1998-2000), Yale Club of Hawaii. Democrat. Office: U Hawaii Richardson Sch Law 2515 Dole St Honolulu HI 96822-2328 Business E-Mail: rmiller@aya.yale.edu.

**MILLER, RICHARD STEVEN,** lawyer; b. Mt. Vernon, NY, Dec. 5, 1951; s. Norman and Mildred (Curtis) M. BA, U. Pa., 1974; JD, NYU, 1977. Bar: N.Y. 1978, U.S. Dist. Ct. (so. and ea. dists.) N.Y. 1978, U.S. Ct. Appeals (2d cir.) 1978. Asst. dist. atty. Kings County, NY, 1977-79; with Hahn & Hessen, NYC, 1979-82, Levin & Weintraub & Crames, NYC, 1982-87; counsel, then ptnr. Rogers & Wells, NYC, 1987-91; ptnr. Dewey Ballantine LLP, NYC, 1991-2001; prin. shareholder Greenburg Traurig LLP, NYC, 2001—, and co-chmn. nat. reorgn., bankruptcy and restructuring practice, 2001—. Mem. ABA, Internat. Bar Assn., Am. Bankruptcy Inst. Office: Greenberg Traurig LLP MetLife Bldg 200 Park Ave New York NY 10166 Office Phone: 212-801-6767. Office Fax: 212-805-5567. Business E-Mail: millerr@gtlaw.com.

**MILLER, RICHARDS THORN,** naval architect, engineer; b. Jan. 31, 1918; s. Herman Geistweit and Helen Buckman (Thorn) M.; m. Jean Corbat Spear, Sept. 13, 1941 (dec.); children: Patricia (Mrs. Charles G. Fishburn), Linda (Mrs. John X. Carrier); m. Alice Johnson Houghton, May 19, 1984. BS in Naval Arch. and Marine Engring., Webb Inst. Naval Arch., Glen Cove, N.Y., 1940; Naval Engr., MIT, Boston, 1951. Registered profl. engr. Commd. ensign USN, 1940, advanced through grades to capt., 1960; head preliminary design br. Bur. Ships, 1960-63; dir. Mine Def. Lab., Panama City, Fla., 1963-66; dir. ship design Naval Ship Engring. Ctr., 1966-68; specialized work design oceanographic rsch. ships, mine sweepers, torpedo boats, destroyers; ret., 1968. Mgr. ocean engring. Oceanic divsn. Westinghouse Electric Corp., 1969-75, adv. engr., 1975-79; cons. naval arch. and engr., 1968—; arbitrator admiralty and ship bldg. contract cases, 1978—; mem. com. naval arch. Am. Bur. Shipping, 1960-63, mem. tech. com., 1978-92; mem. ship structure com., 1966-68. Author: (with R.G. Henry) Sailing Yacht Design, 1963, (with K.L. Kirkman) Sailing Yacht Design—A New Appreciation, 1990; also sects. in books, articles. Decorated Navy Legion of Merit; recipient William Selkirk Owen award Webb Alumni Assn., 1983. Fellow Soc. Naval Archs. and Marine Engrs. (chmn. S.E. sect. 1965-66, chmn. marine sys. com. 1970-77, chmn. tech. and rsch. steering com. 1977-78, chmn. small craft com. 1983-87, v.p. tech. and rsch. 1979-81, hon. life v.p. 1981—, mem. coun. 1976—, mem. exec. com. 1977-81, Capt. Joseph H. Linnard prize 1964, Disting. Svc. award 1988); mem. Am. Soc. Naval Engrs. (mem. coun. 1976-78), U.S. Naval Inst., Christie Soc., Mil. Bd. for Profl. Engrs., N.Y. Yacht Club, Annapolis Yacht Club, Sailing Club of the Chesapeake, Sigma Xi. Home and Office: BayWoods of Annapolis 7101 Bay Front Drive Apt 316 Annapolis MD 21403-3701

**MILLER, RITA,** personnel consultant, diecasting company executive; b. Bklyn., Jan. 15, 1925; d. Joseph and Etta M.; BA, Bklyn. Coll., 1947; MA, Boston U., 1949; children: Erika Greenwald, Roy Barnet Glickman. Person-

nel officer, sec. to pres. Marine Elec. Corp., Bklyn., 1943-47; script writer Song Debut, Boston, 1949-50; dir. Writers' Workshops, interviewer pub. opinion surveys, New Rochelle, N.Y., 1962-64; dir. pers. and indsl. rels. Dynacast divsn. Coats & Clark, Inc., Yorktown Heights, 1966-89. Mem. Am. Soc. Personnel Adminstrn., Westchester Personnel Mgmt. Assn. (dir.), Personnel Council New Rochelle, Bus. and Profl. Women U.S.A., Nat. Sociology Hon. Soc. Editor: The Management Consultant (George Kenning), 1965; contbr. articles to profl. jours. Home: 29-I Windsor Ct Keene NH 03431

**MILLER, ROBERT,** advertising executive; b. NYC, June 2, 1923; s. Samuel and Adele (Elswit) M.; m. Frances Fitzgerald, June 10, 1944 (dec. 1978); children: Marc Robert, William Fitzgerald, Daniel Bates, Ellen Minette (Mrs. John Meyer); m. Sandra Gold, 1980; 1 child, Richard Scott. Student, NYU, 1940-42, Syracuse U., 1943. Newsroom employee N.Y. Daily Mirror, 1942; with Miller Advt. Agy., Inc., N.Y.C., 1946—, v.p., 1948-54, chmn. bd., 1954-57, pres., 1958—, Miller Advt. Service Corp., 1956-62, Miller Advt. Agy. Ill., Inc., 1965-73, also bd. dirs. Bd. dirs. Hereford Ins. Co., Inc., 1988-94. Author: Clash of Cultures, 2003; Contbg. editor Madison Avenue mag., 1975-78. Bd. govs. Roslyn Democratic Club, 1957-61, 68-73; mem. Nassau County Dem. Com., 1958-61, 68-73; Bd. dirs. Shalom Peace Found., 1970-89. Served to 1st lt. USAAF, 1942-46. Mem.: VFW, Jewish War Vets., Am. Legion. Home: 301 E 52nd St New York NY 10022-6319 also: 17 Shelly Dr Ellenville NY 12428-1809 Office: Miller Advt Agy Inc 71 Fifth Ave New York NY 10003-3004

**MILLER, ROBERT CARL,** retired library director; b. May 9, 1936; m. Jeanne M. Larson. BS in History and Philosophy, Marquette U., 1958; MS in Am. History, U. Wis., 1962; MA in Libr. Sci., U. Chgo., 1966. Head telephone reference Library of Congress, Wash., 1959-60; reference librarian Marquette U., Milw., 1960-62, acquisition librarian, 1962-66; head tech. services/librarian Parsons Coll., Fairfield, Iowa, 1966-68; head acquisitions dept. U. Chgo. Library, 1968-71, assoc. dir (reader services), 1971-73; assoc dir (gen. service) U. Chgo., 1973-75; dir. of libraries U. Mo., St. Louis, 1975-78; dir of libraries U. of Notre Dame, Ind., 1978-97, ret. Ind., 1997. Vis. prof. IBIN-U. Warsaw, Poland, 1992, 93, 97, 2000, 02. Contbr. articles to profl. jours. Fellow Woodrow Wilson Found. (sr.), Coun. on Libr. Resources; mem. ALA, Polish Inst. of Arts and Letters of Am. Roman Catholic. Home: 27752 Woodland Dr Chisago City MN 55013 Personal E-mail: miller.l@nd.edu.

**MILLER, ROBERT CHARLES,** retired physicist; b. State College, Pa., Feb. 2, 1925; s. Lawrence P. Miller and Eva Mae (Gross) Wiedemann; m. Virginia Callaghan, Aug. 30, 1952; children: Robin Miller Storey, Jeffrey Lawrence Miller, Lauren Miller Lynch. AB, Columbia U., 1948, MA, 1952, PhD, 1956. Staff mem. Johns-Manville Research Ctr., Finderne, NJ, 1948-49; teaching asst. in physics Columbia U., N.Y.C., 1949-51, lectr. in physics, 1951-53; mem. tech. staff Bell Telephone Labs., Murray Hill, NJ, 1954-63, head solid state spectroscopy research dept., 1963-67; staff mem. Inst. Defense Analyses, Arlington, Va., 1967-68; head optical elec. research dept. Bell Telephone Labs., Murray Hill, 1968-77; mem. tech. staff AT&T Bell Labs., Murray Hill, 1977-84, disting. mem. tech. staff, 1984-88, ret., 1988. Cons. Office of Sec. Def., Arlington, Va., 1968-75. Inventor (with Dr. J.A. Giordmaine) Optical Parametric Oscillator, 1965 (co-recipient R.W. Wood prize, 1986); contbr. articles to profl. jours. Served with U.S. Army, 1943-46, ETO. RCA predoctoral fellow Columbia U., 1953-54. Fellow Am. Phys. Soc.; mem. AAAS, N.Y. Acad. Scis., Sigma Xi. Avocations: sailing, sports cars, tennis. Home: 65 Eaton Ct Cotuit MA 02635-2908 E-mail: rvcmiller@prodigy.net.

**MILLER, ROBERT FRANK,** retired electronics engineering educator; b. Milw., Mar. 30, 1925; s. Frank Joseph and Evangeline Elizabeth (Hamann) M.; m. La Verne Boyle, Jan. 10, 1948 (dec. 1978); children: Patricia Ann, Susan Barbara, Nancy Lynn; m. Ruth Winifred Drobnic, July 26, 1980. BSEE, U. Wis., 1947, MSEE, 1954, PhD in Elec. Engring., 1957. Profl. engr.; Wis. Instr. physics Milw. Sch. Engring., 1949-53; sr. engr. semicondr. Delco Electronics/GMC, Kokomo, Ind., 1957-67, asst. chief engr., 1967-70, mgr. product assurance, 1970-73, dir. quality control, 1973-85; asst. prof. elec. engring. tech. Purdue U., Kokomo, Ind., 1986—2005, ret., 2005. Ind. cons., Kokomo, 1990—; mem. Ind. Microelectronics Commn., Indpls., 1987—. Author tech. papers; co-author lab. manuals. Bd. dirs. Howard Community Hosp. Found., Kokomo, 1974—, participating in med. end. support; trustee YMCA, Kokomo, 1990—, bd. dirs., 1967-90. Named Disting. Alumnus U. Wis., Madison, 1980, 90. Mem. IEEE (life), Am. Soc. Quality Control (bd. dirs. sect. 0918, advisor Cen. Ind. sect. bd. 1988—), Sigma Xi, Tau Beta Pi, Phi Kappa Phi, Eta Kappa Nu. Presbyterian. Achievements include active in local medical and scientific education. Home: 3201 Susan Dr Kokomo IN 46902-7506

**MILLER, ROBERT G.,** drug store chain company executive; b. 1944; With Albertson's Inc., 1961-89, exec. v.p. retail ops., 1989-91; chmn. bd., pres., CEO Fred Meyer Inc., Portland, Oreg., 1991-99; COO Kroger Co., Cin., 1999; CEO Rite Aid Corp., Camp Hill, Pa., 1999—2003, chmn., 1999—. Dir. Harrah's Entertainment Inc., Wild Oats Markets Inc. Office: Rite Aid Corp 30 Hunter Ln Camp Hill PA 17011-2410*

**MILLER, ROBERT HAROLD,** otolaryngologist, educator; b. Columbia, Mo., July 2, 1947; s. Harold Oswald and Ruth Nadine (Ballew) M.; m. Martha Guillory, Apr. 18, 1981 (div.); children: Morgan Guillory, Reed Thurston. BS in Biology, Tulane U., 1969, MD, 1973, MBA, 1996. Diplomate Am. Bd. Otolaryngology. Resident otolaryngology, head/neck surgery UCLA, 1978; from asst. prof. to assoc. prof. otolaryngology-head and neck surgery Baylor Coll. Medicine, Houston, 1978—87; prof., chmn. otolaryngology-head and neck surgery Tulane Sch. Medicine, New Orleans, 1987—98, vice-chancellor for clin. affairs, 1997—99; dean U. Nev. Sch. Medicine, 1999—2001, prof., 1999—2002; prof. otolaryngology-head and neck surgery Tulane Sch. Medicine, New Orleans, 2002—03; exec. dir. Am. Bd. Otolaryngology, Houston, 2004—. Bd. dirs. Am. Bd. Otolaryngology; chief of staff Tulane Hosp., 1995-96; vis. prof. otolaryngology Baylor Coll. Medicine, Houston, Tex., 2004—. Mem. editl. bd. Archives of Otolaryngology, 1986-05, Head & Neck Surgery, 1987-03, Laryngoscope, 1996-, ENToday, chmn., 2006-. Named Outstanding Young Man, Houston C. of C., 1980; Robert Wood Johnson Health Policy fellow, 1996-97. Fellow ACS, Am. Soc. Head & Neck Surgery, Am. Acad. Oto-Head & Neck Surgery (Disting. Svc. award 1994, Honor award 1991), Triological Soc. (exec. sec. 1992-97, treas. 1997-2004). Avocations: tennis, computers. Home: 2616 Wroxton Rd Houston TX 77005 Office: Am Bd Otolaryngology 5615 Kirby Dr 600 Houston TX 77005 Office Phone: 713-850-0399. Business E-Mail: rmiller@aboto.org.

**MILLER, ROBERT J.,** lawyer; BS, Ctrl. Mich. U., 1982; MBA, U. Okla., 1986, JD, 1990. Bar: Ariz., US Dist. Ct., Dist. of Ariz. Ptnr., group dep. Bankruptcy, Restructuring and Creditors' Rights Bryan Cave LLP, Phoenix. Office: Bryan Cave LLP 1 Renaissance Square Two N Ctrl Ave, Ste 2200 Phoenix AZ 85004 Office Phone: 602-364-7043. E-mail: rjmiller@bryancave.com.

**MILLER, ROBERT J.,** lawyer; b. 1949; married; 2 children. BA, Bklyn. Coll., CUNY, 1971; JD, Georgetown U., 1974. Bar: NY 1975, US Supreme Ct. 1978. Ptnr. Blutrick, Falcone & Miller LLP, NYC, Blutrick, Herman & Miller LLP, NYC, Parker Duryee Rosoff & Haft (combined with Reed Smith in 2002), NYC, 1996—2002, mng. ptnr.; ptnr. Reed Smith LLP, NYC, 2002—, NY/NJ practice group leader litig. group. Pro-bono counsel Fedn. of Italian-Am. Organizations of NY. Mem.: Assn. of the Bar of the City of NY (mem. litig. com., mem., arbitration com.). Office: Reed Smith LLP 599 Lexington Ave 29th Fl New York NY 10022 Office Phone: 212-549-0249. Office Fax: 212-521-5452. Business E-Mail: rmiller@reedsmith.com.

**MILLER, ROBERT JAMES,** educational association administrator; b. Mansfield, Ohio, Jan. 27, 1926; s. Dennis Cornelius and Mabel (Snyder) M.; m. Jerri Ann Burran, June 5, 1952; children: Robert James Jr., Dennis Burran.

Student, Heidelberg Coll., 1946-47; BS, U. N.Mex., 1950, MA, 1952; postgrad., Miami U., Oxford, Ohio, 1951-55; MBA, Fla. Atlantic U., 1978. Asst. exec. sec. Phi Delta Theta Hdqrs., Oxford, 1951-54, adminstrv. sec., 1954-55, exec. v.p., 1955-91; pres. Phi Delta Theta Found., Oxford, 1984-96; bus. mgr. The Scroll, Oxford, 1955-91; cons., 1997—. Editor: Phikeia—The Manual of Phi Delta Theta, 1951, 19 edits., 1989, Phis Sing, 1958, Constitution and General Statutes of Phi Delta Theta, Fraternity Education Foundations, 1962, Directory of Phi Delta Theta, 1973. Chmn. United Appeal, Oxford, 1960; bd. dirs. Interfrat. Found., 1995—, Oxford Cmty. Arts Ctr., 2005—; pres. Miami U. Art Mus., 1993-94, McCullough-Hyde Hosp., Oxford, 1966, comm. endowment adv. com., 1988-89; vol. leader Boy Scouts Am., Oxford, 1966-79. Named Citizen of Yr., City of Oxford, 1968; recipient citation Theta Chi, 1967, Order of Interfrat. Svc. Lambda Chi Alpha, 1994, Interfrat. Leadership award Sigma Nu, 1994, accolate for intrafraternity svc. Kappa Alpha, Meritorious Svc. award Boy. Scouts Am., 1977, others; Interfrat. Inst. fellow Ind. U., 1988. Mem. Nat. Intrafraternity Conf. (com. mem. 1954-96, Gold medal 1992), Am. Soc. Assn. Execs. (cert.), Cin. Soc. Assn. Execs., Fraternity Execs. Assn. (pres. 1962-63, Disting. Svc. award 1991), Edgewater Conf. (pres. 1978-79), Summit Soc., Country Club Oxford (bd. dirs.), Work Devel. Assn. (pres. 1999—), Order of Symposiarchs, Order of Omega, Rotary (founder Oxford club 1965, pres. 1966, Merit award 1974, dist. gov. S.W. Ohio 1978-79, study group exch. leader South Africa 1992), Blue Key, Phi Delta Kappa, Omicron Delta Kappa Home: 15 Woodcrest Way Oxford OH 45056-9485 Office: Phi Delta Theta Ednl Found 2 S Campus Ave Oxford OH 45056-1801 Office Phone: 513-523-6966.

**MILLER, ROBERT JOSEPH,** lawyer, former governor; b. Evanston, Ill., Mar. 30, 1945; s. Ross Wendell and Coletta Jane (Doyle) Miller; m. Sandra Ann Searles, Oct. 17, 1949; children: Ross, Corrine, Megan. BA in Polit. Sci., U. Santa Clara, 1967; JD, Loyola U., 1971. First legal advisor Las Vegas (Nev.) Met. Police Dept., 1973—75; justice of the peace Las Vegas Twp., 1975—78; dep. dist. atty. Clark County, Las Vegas, 1971—73, dist. atty., 1979—86; lt. gov. State of Nev., 1987—89, gov., 1989—98; sr. ptnr. Jones Vargas, Las Vegas, 1999—2005; prin. Dutko Worldwide, Las Vegas, Nev., 2005—. Bd. dir. Newmont Mining Corp., Zenith Nat. Ins. Corp., Wynn Resorts Ltd. Chmn. Nev. Commn. on Econ. Devel., Carson City, 1987—91, Nev. Commn. on Tourism, Carson City, 1987—91; mem. Pres. Reagan's Task Force on Victims of Crime, 1982; chmn. Nev. divsn. Am. Cancer Soc., 1988—90. Mem.: Nev. Dist. Attys. Assn. (pres. 1979, 1983), Nat. Govs. Assn. (vice chmn. exec. com. 1995—96, chmn. 1996—97, past chmn. com. on justice and pub. safety, chmn. legal affairs com. 1992—94, lead gov. on transp. 1992—), Western Govs. Assn. (chmn. 1993—94), Nat. Dist. Attys. Assn. (pres. 1984—85). Democrat. Roman Catholic. Office Phone: 702-240-0831.

**MILLER, ROBERT LOUIS,** dean, chemistry professor; b. Chgo., Jan. 26, 1926; s. Sam P. and Ida (Reich) M.; m. Virginia Southard, Oct. 26, 1947 (dec. Sept. 1973); children: Ruth, Stephen, Martin, Andrew; m. Bonnie Seay Berard, Nov. 28, 1975; children: Edouard, Derek. PhB, U. Chgo., 1947, BS, 1949, MS, 1951; PhD, Ill. Inst. Tech.; PhD (NSF Sci. faculty fellow), 1963. Mem. faculty U. Ill. Chgo. Circle Campus, 1953-67, asst. dean Coll. Liberal Arts and Scis., 1963-65, assoc. dean Coll. Liberal Arts and Scis., 1965-67; prof. chemistry U. N.C.-Greensboro, 1968-98, dean arts and scis., 1968-85, acting dean Grad. Sch., 1989-91, spl. asst. to the provost, 1993-94, acting assoc. provost, 1994-96, spl. asst. to provost, 1996-97, interim head dept. math. scis., 2001—03. Am. Coun. Edn. adminstrv. intern SUNY-Binghamton, 1967-68. Mem. exec. com. of com. environ. affairs Piedmont Council Govts., 1971-76; mem. Greensboro Task Force on Energy; chmn. residential and transp. subcom Greensboro Energy Commn.; mem. Bd. Edn., Oak Park, Ill., 1965-66; bd. dirs. Hospice at Greensboro, 1981-87, pres., 1982-84, vol. 1988-89; vol., mem. bd. dirs. Cities in Schs., 1988-92; bd. dirs. Gilbert Pearson Audubon Soc., Greensboro Civil Liberties Union, Weatherspoon Gallery, 1981-85. Served with AUS, 1944-46, ETO. Mem. AAAS, Sigma Xi (treas. chpt.). Home: 4020 Watauga Dr Greensboro NC 27410-4502 Office: Dept Computer Sci Univ NC Greensboro NC 27412 Personal E-Mail: rmill07@bellsouth.net. Business E-Mail: rlmiller@uncg.edu.

**MILLER, ROBERT NOLEN,** lawyer; b. Monmouth, Ill., May 30, 1940; s. Robert Clinton and Doris Margaret (Nolen) M.; m. Diane Wilmarth, Aug. 21, 1965; children: Robert Wilmarth, Anne Elizabeth. BA, Cornell Coll., Mt. Vernon, Iowa, 1962; JD, U. Colo., 1965. Bar: Colo. 1965. Assoc. firm M. Quiat, Denver, 1965-66, Fischer & Beaty, Ft. Collins, Colo., 1969-70; dist. atty. Weld County Dist. Atty's. Office, Greeley, Colo., 1971-81; U.S. atty. U.S. Dept. Justice, Denver, 1981-88; chief counsel litigation and security US West Inc., Englewood, Colo., 1988-93; of counsel Patton, Boggs & Blow, Denver, 1993-94; ptnr., head litig. LeBoeuf, Lamb, Greene & Mac Crae, Denver, 1994—2003; ptnr. Perkins Coie, Denver, 2003—. Instr. bus. law Am. U., U. S.C., Myrtle Beach, 1966-69; mem. Gov.'s Commn. for Columbine and Civil Justice Reform, 1999—; mem. Supreme Ct. Nominating Commn., 1999—. Co-author: Deathroads, 1978 Bd. dirs. Boys Club, Greeley, 1974-78, 1st Congl. Ch., Greeley, 1975-78; Rep. candidate for atty. gen. Colo., 1977-78. Capt. USAF, 1966-69. Recipient Citizen of Yr. award Elks Club, Greeley. Mem. Fed. Bar Assn. (pres. Colo. chpt. 1983-84), Colo. Dist. Atty's Coun. (pres. 1976-77), Colo. Bar Assn., Weld County Bar Assn., Rotary (pres. local chpt. 1980-81). Republican. Avocations: fishing, hunting, reading. Office: Perkins Coie 1899 Wynkoop Ste 700 Denver CO 80202-1043 Office Phone: 303-291-2300. Business E-Mail: rmiller@perkinscioe.com.

**MILLER, ROBERT SCOTT,** social worker, hospital administrator; b. Seattle, Dec. 12, 1947; s. Bert Lester and Carol Theresa (Gustafson) M.; m. Karen Ann Staake, Nov. 12, 1977; children: Sarah, Megan, Emily. BA in Sociology cum laude, Seattle Pacific U., 1970; AM in Social Work, U. Chgo., 1972; MA in Human Resources Mgmt., Pepperdine U., 1977; diploma in life skills coaching, Stonebridge Associated Colls., U.K., 2002; postgrad., Calif. Pacific U., 2006—. LCSW. Br. supr. Wash. State Dept. Social and Health Svcs., Oak Harbor and Anacortes, 1975—78, supr. casework Everett, 1973—75; lectr., coord. rural cmty. mental health project U. Wash., Seattle, 1978—83; exec. dir. Armed Svcs. YMCA, Oak Harbor, 1984—86; area dir. United Way of Island County, Oak Harbor, 1986—88, exec. dir., 1988—92, Saratoga Cmty. Mental Health, Coupeville, Wash., 1992—99; outpatient therapist, attention-deficit/hyperactivity disorder mental health specialist Cath. Cmty. Svcs. Northwest, Oak Harbor, Wash., 1993—96; dir. Cath. Cmty. Svcs. N.W., Oak Harbor, Wash., 1996—2001, Mount Vernon, Wash., 1996—99, clin. dir. Everett, Wash. 1998—2004; privacy officer Health Ins. Portability and Accountability Act (HIPAA), 2001—04; pvt. practice counselor. 2001—; cons., psychiat. hosp. surveyor, quality control reviewer Ascellon Corp., Balt., 2004—. Internship supr. counseling program, Seattle U., 1998-99, Bastyr U., 2000-01; instr. sociology and psychol. Chapman U. Naval Air Sta. Whidbey Island, Orange, Calif., 1988-95, 2004; practicum instr. sch. social work Ea. Wash. U., 2003. Contbr. articles to profl. jours. Bd. dir. Puget Sound chpt. Huntington's Disease Soc. Am., 1989-93, pres., 1991, fundraising chmn., 1989-91, v.p., 1990; adv. bd. United Ways Wash., 1991-92; chmn. Island County bd. emergency food and shelter program Fed. Emergency Mgmt. Agy.; vice chmn. Cmty. Resource Network, Oak Harbor, 1991; steering com. Greater Oak Harbor Econ. Summit, 1991; strategic planning com. Whidbey Gen. Hosp., Coupeville, 1992-93; exec. com. Mt. Baker coun. Boy Scouts Am., 1993; bd. dir. Opportunity Coun., Bellingham, 1993-94, Concerts on the Cove, Coupeville, 1993-94, v.p., 1994-95; active Oak Harbor Citizen's Comprehensive Plan Task Force, 1994, Readiness to Learn Coupeville Cmty. Team, 1996; risk mgmt. subcom. chair Assoc. Provider Network, 1997-98; child study team Island County, 1996-99, child protective team, 1997-99; health adv. bd. Head Start, Mt. Vernon, Wash., 1999-2002. Recipient outstanding svc. award Armed Svcs. YMCA of the U.S. Dallas, 1985, two program merit awards McDonald's Corp., Oak Harbor, 1986; named Alumni of a Growing Vision, Seattle Pacific U., 1991, Diplomat of Yr. Greater Oak Harbor C. of C., 1991, Celebrating Excellence award, Ascellon Corp., 2005, Celebrating Excellence award, Ascellon Corp., 2005. Mem. NASW. bd. dirs. Wash. chpt. 1982-85), Wash. Assn. Social Welfare (pres. 1975-76), Acad. Cert. Social Workers, Sunrise Rotary Club (sec. Oak Harbor chpt. 1998-99), Greater Oak Harbor C. of C. Democrat. Roman

Catholic. Avocations: reading, genealogy, fishing, computers, 3rd degree mason. Home: 2450 Rocky Way Coupeville WA 98239-9610 Office: Ste B206 275 SE Cabot Dr Oak Harbor WA 98277 E-mail: robertmiller@onebox.com

**MILLER, ROBERT STEVENS, JR.,** automotive executive; b. Portland, Oreg., Nov. 4, 1941; s. Robert Stevens and Barbara (Weston) Miller; m. Margaret Rose Kyger, Nov. 9, 1966 (dec. Aug. 11, 2006); children: Christopher John, Robert Stevens, Alexander Lamont. AB with distinction, Stanford U., 1963; LLB, Harvard U., 1966; MBA, Stanford U., 1968. Bar: Calif. 1966. Fin. analyst Ford Motor Co., Dearborn, Mich., 1968-71, spl. studies mgr. Mexico City, 1971-73; dir. fin. Ford Asia-Pacific, Inc., Melbourne, Australia, 1974-77, Ford Motor Co., Caracas, Venezuela, 1977-79; v.p., treas. Chrysler Corp., Detroit, 1980-81, exec. v.p. fin., 1981-90, vice chmn., 1990-92; sr. ptnr. James D. Wolfensohn, Inc., NYC, 1992-93; chmn. Morrison Knudsen, 1995—96; chmn., CEO Waste Management, 1997—99; dir. Fed. Mogul Corp., Smithfield, Mich., 1993—, chmn., CEO, 1999-2000, 2004—05, non exec. chmn., 2001; chmn., CEO Bethlehem Steel Corp., 2001—03, Delphi Corp., Troy, Mich., 2005—. Office: Delphi Corp 5725 Delphi Dr Troy MI 48098*

**MILLER, ROBERT W.,** music educator, musician; b. Iron Mountain, Mich., Dec. 25, 1950; s. Walter Harry and Caroline Louise Miller. BMus, U. Mich., 1973; MMus, Peabody Conservatory of Music, Balt., 1974; Dr.Musical Arts, Peabody Inst. of Johns Hopkins U., Balt., 1979. Disting. prof. of music, artist-in-residence East Stroudsburg U. of Pa., 1977—. Adj. prof. music Essex C.C., Balt., 1975—77; piano faculty Interlochen Ctr. of Arts, Mich., 1978—80; summer faculty Mansfield Coll./Oxford U., England, 1986—89, IFK U. of Salzburg and Cultural Studies Acad., Austria, 1991—; guest artist N.Y. Philharm. Ensembles, N.Y.C., 1998, N.Y.C., 2002, N.Y.C., 05; solo and chamber music recitals Weill Recital Hall at Carnegie Hall, N.Y.C., 1998—; rehearsal pianist Van Cliburn at Interlochen Ctr. for the Arts, 1975—80. Musician: (solo piano recital) Salle Cortot, 1992, 2000, Weill Recital Hall at Carnegie Hall, 1992, 2000, (piano concerto soloist) World Youth Symphony, Peabody Symphony, Montclair Chamber Ensemble, Pine Mountain Music Festival; recording artist Media Rite Prodns., Educo Records. Founder, artistic dir. Carter Chamber Music Series, East Stroudsburg, 1993—; competition judge Pa. Gov.'s Sch. of Arts, Tatamy, 1978—. Named to Outstanding Young Men of Am., 1980; recipient Disting. Prof. award, East Stroudsburg U., 2002; scholar F. Lammot Belin Arts scholar, Waverly, Pa., 1991. Mem.: Assn. of Pa. State Coll. and Univ. Faculty, Music Tchrs. Nat. Assn., Am. Liszt Soc. Avocations: swimming, scuba diving, water-skiing, hiking. Mailing: East Stroudsburg Univ Dept Music Fine Arts Bldg East Stroudsburg PA 18301 Office Phone: 570-422-3759. E-mail: Robert.Miller@po-box.esu.edu.

**MILLER, ROBERT WARD,** music educator; b. Auburn, Ala., June 19, 1978; s. Robert Ward and Kathy Gibson Miller; m. Carrie Sims, July 7, 2001. MusB in Edn., Auburn U., Ala., 2001; MusM in Trombone Performance, Ariz. State U., Tempe, Ariz., 2003. Cert. music tchr. Ala., 2001. Dir. bands Andalusia (Ala.) H.S., 2003—04, Pleasant Grove (Ala.) H.S., 2004—. Musical arranger Marching Band Auburn (Ala.) U., 1998, webmaster Marching Band, 98. Composer: Three Etchings in Brass, 2006. Scholar, U. Iowa Sch. Music, 2006—. Mem.: Nat. Band Assn., Internat. Trombone Assn., Coll. Band Dirs. Nat. Assn. (assoc.), Auburn (Ala.) U. Alumni Assn. (life), Pi Kappa Lambda (life), Golden Key (life). Office: Pleasant Grove High School Band 805 7th Avenue Pleasant Grove AL 35127 Office Phone: 334-804-5172.

**MILLER, ROBERT WARREN,** entrepreneur; b. Apr. 17, 1939; m. Chantel Miller, 1965; children: Mrs. Christopher R. Getty, Princess Pia Marie-Chantel of Greece, Princess Alexandra von Fürsterberg. BS in Hotel Adminstr., Cornell U. Co-founder Duty-Free Shoppers (DFS), 1960—97; founder, chmn. Search Group, Hong Kong, 1974—. Trustee Asian Soc.; co-chmn. Ann. Internat. Asian Fair, 1997—; goodwill amb. Hong Kong Tourist Assn.; co-founder Mari-Cha Collection. Named one of Top 200 Collectors, ARTnews Mag., 2004; recipient Millennium Cup, Am. Cup races, Super Yachts Regatta, New Zealand, 2000. Mem.: Royal Yacht Squadron, Hong Kong Mus. Art, Conservatory of Music Bd., Hong Kong Arts Ctr. Achievements include holding west to east transatlantic speed record, monohull sailboat, 1998-2001; crossed Atlantic Ocean from NY to Cornwall, Eng. in 8 days 23 hours 59 minutes 41 seconds, Oct. 1998. Avocations: wing-shooting, sailing, skiing, yachting, collecting art, especially old masters, 19th century painting; Am. abstraction.

**MILLER, ROBERTA DORIS,** elementary school educator; b. Lynn, Mass., May 14, 1940; d. Morris and Lorraine Miller. BS in Edn. cum laude, Lesley Coll., Cambridge, Mass., 1961; M in Edn., Salem (Mass.) State Coll., 1964; postgrad., Boston U. Tchr. Brookline (Mass.) Pub. Schs., 1968—. Pilot math. programs Edni. Devel. Corp., Newton, Mass., 1988-89; pilot sci. programs TV series 3! 2! 1! Contact!, 1991; developer curriculum materials in math. and lang. arts Brookline Pub. Schs., 1969—; faculty Suffolk U., Boston, 2000—; presenter in field. Coord. presentation of programs to nursing homes and vets. hosps.; coord. fundraising victims and schs. of Hurricane Andrew, 1992; chair, coord. fundraising for victims of the Midwest floods, 1993. Mem.: MATSOL (Mass. Assn. Tchrs. of Speakers Other Langs., Inc.), NEA, Mass. Tchrs. Assn. Avocations: travel, reading, music. Personal E-mail: bobdorrob@yahoo.com.

**MILLER, ROBIN,** chef, nutritionist, editor; M in Food and Nutrition, NYU, 1998. Contbg. nutritionist Am. Heart Assn., Am. Inst. for Cancer Rsch., Weight Watchers, Inc.; health cons. www.HealthAtoZ.com. Contbg. editor: Health mag., Cooking Light mag.; author: The Newlywed Cookbook, 1991, Jane Fonda, Cooking for Healthy Living, 1996, The Daily Soup, 1999, The Newlywed Cookbook, 1999, Verduro, 2001 Picnics, 2003; host (TV series) Quick Fix Meals with Robin Miller, Food Network.*

**MILLER, RODNEY D.,** health facility administrator, consultant; b. Granite City, Ill., Jan. 21, 1951; s. Ralph Delmar and Hanna Frances (Poe) Miller; m. Kelly Ann Abernathy, Sept. 23, 1982; children: Timothy Aaron, Stephen Andrew. MBA, Wayland Bapt. U., 1994. Cert. Med. Practice Exec. Am. Coll. Med. Practice Execs., 1997. Adminstr. Med. Arts Clinic, Spring Creek Clinic, Elko, Nev., 1998—99; exec. dir. Valley Diagnostic Clinic, PA, Harlingen, Tex., 1999—. Exec. dir. Border Palms Ltd., Harlingen, Tex., 2000—. Actor: Disciple of Jesus, Beyond Calvary Ch. Bd. mem. Am. Heart Assn., Harlingen, 1999—2001. Sgt. USAF, 1970—74, Sheppard AFB. Decorated Nat. Def. ribbon USAF, Good Conduct medal. Mem.: Med. Group Mgmt. Assn. (CMPE 1997). Conservative-R. Avocations: swimming, bicycling, motorcycling, weightlifting, fishing. Home: 917 Lantana Harlingen TX 78550 Office: Valley Diagnostic Clinic PA 2200 Haine Dr Harlingen TX 78550 Home Fax: 956-421-5220; Office Fax: 956-421-5220. Business E-Mail: rmiller@vdcpa.com.

**MILLER, ROGER ALLEN,** physicist; b. Chillicothe, Ohio, June 27, 1934; s. Joseph Perrin and Mary Josephine (Somers) M.; m. Barbara Pauline Rice, Aug. 31, 1957; children: Erich Rice, Gretchen Rice, Carl Rice. BS, Ohio U., 1956; PhD, Case Inst., 1963. Rsch. assoc. Case Inst., Cleve., 1963-64; rsch. physicist Corning (N.Y.) Inc., 1964-71, sr. rsch. physicist, 1971-79, devel. assoc., 1979-87, sr. rsch. assoc., 1987—. Spl. lectr. physics Elmira Coll., N.Y., 1966-69; mem. edit. bd. Fiber and Integrated Optics, Pasadena, Calif., 1976-86, mem. adv. bd. 1986-88. Contbr. articles to profl. jours. AART award Assn. for the Advancement Radiation Tech., 1990. Mem. Am. Phys. Soc., Optical Soc. Am., Am. Assn. Physics Tchrs., Sigma Xi, Phi Beta Kappa, Phi Kappa Phi. Achievements include contributions to the development of lead free Steuben crystal; development of optical waveguide coatings and coating applicators; design and development of the first, all dielectric, low-loss optical waveguide cable; patentee in field. Office: Corning Inc Sullivan Pk Sp Fr 03 # 1 Corning NY 14831-0001 Personal E-mail: ramiller@localnet.com.

**MILLER, ROGER L.,** architectural firm executive; b. Brooklandville, Md. BS, MArch, Ga. Inst. Tech. Registered Ga., Tenn., S.C., N.C., cert. NCARB. Joined Cooper Carry Inc., Atlanta, 1979, prin., 1990, v.p., 1994—. Recipient Kenneth M. Murchison award, Ga. Inst. Tech. Mem.: Nat. Assn. Office and Indsl. Pks. Office: Cooper Carry Inc Ste 200 3520 Piedmont Rd NE Atlanta GA 30305-1595

**MILLER, RONALD,** journalist, critic; b. Santa Cruz, Calif., Feb. 28, 1939; s. Fred Robert and Evelyn Lenora Miller; m. Darla-Jean Irene Rode, Nov. 2, 1963. AA, Monterey Peninsula Coll., 1958; BA, San Jose State U., 1961. Reporter Santa Cruz (Calif.) Sentinel, 1959-62; reporter, chief news bur. San Jose (Calif.) Mercury News, 1962-77, editor T.V., 1977-99; syndicated TV columnist Knight Ridder Syndicate, 1978-99. Commentator, critic Sta. KLOK, San Jose, 1981-83; nat. judge Cableace awards, 1987; adj. instr. Whatcom C.C., Bellingham, Wash., 2001-04, Western Wash. U., 2003—. Author: (foreword) Les Brown's Encyclopedia of Television, 1992; coauthor: Masterpiece Theatre, 1995, Author: Mystery! A Celebration, 1996 (Agatha, Anthony, and Macavity award nominee 1996-97); columnist, mng. editor The Columnists.com website, 1999—; mystery columnist Alibris.com. website, 2000, PBS mystery.com website, 2001-2002; program host Am. Mus. Radio and Electricity, 2003; TV columnist Mystery Scene Mag., 2004-. Recipient Nat. Spot News Photo award Sigma Delta Chi, 1961, Outstanding Alumnus award San Jose State U. Dept. Journalism and Mass Comm., 1985, Nat. Headline award Press Club Atlantic City, 1994. Democrat. Home and Office: 5437 Canvasback Rd Blaine WA 98230

**MILLER, RONALD ALFRED,** family physician; b. Orange, Calif., Sept. 27, 1943; s. Alfred Casper and Inez Geraldine (Gunderson) M.; m. Jean Ilene Andrews, June 18, 1966; children: Jon, Lauri, Bryan. BA, Pacific Luth. U., 1965; MD, U. Wash., 1969. Diplomate Am. Bd. Family Practice (bd. dirs. 1985-90, pres. bd. 1989-90). Intern in medicine Parkland Meml. Hosp., Dallas, 1969-70; gen. practice residency USPHS Gallup Indian Med. Ctr., Gallup, N.Mex., 1970-72; prin. Medical Doctor Glacier Med Assocs., Whitefish, Mont., 1972—. Clin. prof. U. Wash., Seattle, 1975—; coord. community clin. unit in family medicine, U. Wash., Whitefish, 1975—; bd. dirs. Utah Med. Ins. Assn., Salt Lake City, 1987—. Bd. dirs. Whitefish Housing Authority, 1977-82; mem. alumni bd. Pacific Luth. U., Tacoma, 1976-81, pres., 1979-80; mem. Glacier Community Chorale, Whitefish, 1984—, bd. dirs., 1990-92. Lt. comdr. USPHS, 1970-72. Mem. Am. Acad. Family Physicians (com. on continuing med. edn. 1977-81, com. on edn. 1984-89, Mead Johnson award Grad. Edn. in Family Practice 1972), Mont. Acad. Family Physicians (bd. dirs., sec./treas, v.p., pres. 1982-83, del. nat. congress 1978-84), Rotary, Alpha Omega Alpha. Republican. Lutheran. Avocations: hunting, fishing, skiing, backpacking, singing. Home: 1046 7th St W Whitefish MT 59937-3227 Office: 1111 Baker Ave Whitefish MT 59937-2905

**MILLER, RONALD BAXTER,** language educator, writer; b. Rocky Mount, NC, Oct. 11, 1948; s. Marcellus Cornelius and Elsie (Bryant) M.; m. Jessica Garris, June 5, 1971 (div. Dec. 1998); 1 child, Akin Dasan; m. Diana L. Ranson, Sept. 3, 2000. BA magna cum laude, N.C. Ctrl. U., 1970; AM, Brown U., 1972, PhD, 1974. Asst. prof. English Haverford Coll., Haverford, Pa., 1974-76; assoc. prof. English, dir. Black lit. program U. Tenn., Knoxville, Tenn., 1977-81, prof. English, dir. Black lit. program, 1982-92, Lindsay Young prof. liberal arts and English, 1986-87; prof. English, dir. Inst. for African Am. Studies U. Ga., Athens, 1992—2006, prof. English, African Am. studies, 2006—. Instr. summer sch. Roger Williams Coll., Bristol, R.I., 1973; lectr. SUNY, 1974; Mellon prof. Xavier Univ., New Orleans, 1988; Irvine Found. visiting scholar Univ. San Francisco, 1991. Author: (reference guide) Langston Hughes and Gwendolyn Brooks, 1978, The Art and Imagination of Langston Hughes, 1989 (Am. Book award, 1991); editor, contbr.: Black American Literature and Humanism, 1981, Black American Poets Between Worlds, 1940-60, 1986; co-author, co-editor: Call and Response The Riverside Anthology of African American Literary Tradition, 1998, ed., "The Short Stories", Collected Works of Langston Hughes 15, 2002; mem. editl. bd. Tenn. Studies in Lit., 1991-93, Black Fiction Project (Yale-Cornell-Duke-Harvard), 1985—, U. Ga. Press, 1994-97; contbr. articles to profl. jour. Recipient award Am. Council on Learned Soc., 1978, Golden Key Faculty award Nat. Golden Key, 1990, 95, Alpha award for disting. svc. U. Ga. Athens, 1993, Am. Book award, 1991; Sr. Tchg. fellow U. Ga. Athens, 1994, Lanston Hughes prize, 2001, Outstanding Tchg. award Student Govt. Assn., 2005-06; Nat. Rsch. Coun. sr. fellow, 1986-87, NDEA fellow, 1970-72, Ford Found. fellow, 1972-73, NEH fellow, 1975; Nat. Fellowships Fund dissertation grant, 1973-74, ACLS Conf. grantee, 1978. Mem. MLA (exec. com. Afro-Am. Lit. Discussion Group 1980-83, chair 1982-83, mem. del. assembly 1984-86, 97-99, com. on langs. and lits. of Am. 1993-97, chair 1996), Langston Hughes Soc. (pres. 1984-90, exec. editor Langston Hughes Review 1993—). Office: U Ga Inst African Am Studies Athens GA 30602 Personal E-mail: rbmiller6@charter.net. Business E-Mail: rbmiller@uga.edu.

**MILLER, RONALD D.,** medical educator, researcher; Prof. cellular & molecular pharmacology Univ. Calif., San Francisco, chmn. Dept Anesthesia and Perioperative Care. Office: Univ Calif Dept Anesthesia C-450 Box 0648 521 Parnassus St San Francisco CA 94143-0648 E-mail: millerr@anesthesia.ucsf.edu.

**MILLER, RONALD K.,** real estate broker, educator; b. Penn Yan, Ny, Apr. 8, 1948; s. Harold and Helen Miller; m. Marguerite Miller, July 16, 2001; children: Jennifer McKay, Kristoffer; m. Jane Miller, Jan. 2, 1970 (div. May 1, 2001). BA, MacMurray Coll., Jacksonville, Illinois, 1970; MA, Elmira Coll., Elmira, NY, 1975. Educator Canandaigua Schools, Canandaigua, NY, 1970—71, Dundee Schools, Dundee, NY, 1972—. broker Finger Lakes Properties, Penn Yan, NY, 1992—. Choir dir. First Presbyn. Ch., Penn Yan, NY, 1970—2002. Avocations: gardening, woodworking. Office: Dundee Central School 55 Water Street Dundee NY 14837

**MILLER, RONALD LYNN,** director; b. Pitts., Sept. 1, 1950; s. Calvin John and Virginia (Ricca) Miller; children: Veronica Lynn, Maria Eileen. B Westminster Coll., 1972; M in religion, Pitts. Theol. Sem., 1975; vis. scholar, U. Oxford, 1990—92; PhD in sociology and internat. studies, U. Pitts., 1994. Prof., sociology U. Pitts., 1980—88, prof., religion, 1988—92, prof., global studies, 1996—; founder to dir. Ctr. Global Studies Internat. Interdisciplinary, Pitts., 1995—. Lectr. various Universities. Author: Introduction to Global Studies, 2003, Revolution in Japan and England, 1996, Individual Identity Formation, 1984. Mem.: Somatics Soc., Somatics Soc., World Hist. Assn., Am. Sociol. Assn., Am. Acad. of Religion, Assn. for Psychol. Sci., Am. Polit. Sci. Assn., Am. Phys. Soc., Am. Philos. Assn., Internat. Neural Network Soc., Assn. for the Study of Ethnicity and Nationalism, Am. Musicolog. Soc., Am. Math. Soc., Linguistics Soc. Am., Law and Soc. Assn., Modern Lang. Assn., Internat. Studies Assn., Am. Hist. Assn., Geol. Soc. Am., Internat. Geog. Union, Assn. Am. Geographers, Coun. for European Studies, Am. Econ. Assn., Econ. Soc. Am., Communal Studies Assn., Internat. Soc. for Comparative Study of Civilizations, Internat. Union of Pure and Applied Chemistry, Am. Chem. Soc., Genetics Soc. of Am., Am. Soc. for Micro., Am. Astron. Soc., Assn. for Asian Studies, Am. Assn. for Artificial Intelligence, Am. Anthrop. Assn., Am. Studies Assn., African Studies Assn. Achievements include patents pending for a module for doing global studies at the university level. Office: Ctr Global Studies Internat Interdisciplinary 40 Beltzhoover Ave Pittsburgh PA 15210 Office Phone: 412-381-3753. Business E-Mail: ronaldlynnmiller@centerforglobalstudies.com.

**MILLER, RONALD MELLADO,** education educator; b. El Paso, Texas, Nov. 3, 1970; s. Donald Hale and Corina Mellado Miller; m. Patricia Marie Addicks, Feb. 4, 1995; children: Hannah Aurora, Gideon McKay, Shiloh Marie, Eve Asenath. MS, Purdue Univ., 1997—99, PhD, 2000—03. Sci. rschr. Purdue Univ., West Lafayette, Ind., 1997—2003; prof. Brigham Young Univ., Laie, Hawaii, 2003—. Statis., human factors engring. cons. Miller Consulting, West Lafayette, Ind., 1995; human factors engrng. cons. Purdue Univ. Human Factors in Aviation Rsch. Group, West Lafayette, Ind., 1998—; statis., human factors engrng. cons. Miller Consulting, Laie, Hawaii, 2003—.

Internat. cmty. activist Purdue Univ., West Lafayette, Ind., 1998—2003, Brigham Young U., Hawaii, Laie, Hawaii, 2003. Grantee Rsch. Grant, Purdue U., 2002; scholar Mosell-Watt Bell Scholarship, Brigham Young U., 1995—97; Grad. Fellowship, Purdue Univ., 1997—2003. Mem.: APA, Psychonomic Soc., Am. Statis. Assn., Human Factors and Ergonomic Soc. Mem. Church Of Jesus Christ Latter Day Saint. Achievements include research in refuting the fundamental theoretical difference between pavlovian and instrumental conditioning; co-author of the only current theory how mental chunking operates. Avocations: travel, swimming, surfing. Office: Brigham Young Univ Hawaii 55-220 Kulanui St BYUH Box #1970 Laie HI 96762 Home: 55-457 Moana St Laie HI 96762 Office Phone: 808-293-3831. Business E-Mail: millerr@byuh.edu.

**MILLER, ROSS HAYS,** retired neurosurgeon; b. Ada, Okla., Jan. 30, 1923; s. Harry and Helen (Rice) M.; m. Catherine Railey, May 2, 1943; children: Terry Hays, Helen Stacy. BS, East Central State Coll., Ada, 1943; MD, U. Okla., 1946; MS in Neurosurgery, U. Minn., 1952. Diplomate: Am. Bd. Neurol. Surgery (chmn. exam. com. 1978-84). Intern St. Luke's Hosp., Cleve., 1946-47; fellow in neurosurgery Mayo Clinic, Rochester, Minn., 1950-54; instr. in neurosurgery Mayo Med. Sch., 1954-63, asst. prof. neurosurgery, 1963-73, asso. prof., 1973-75, prof., chmn. dept. neurosurgery, from 1975, now ret. Vis. prof. neurol. surgery Med. Coll. Ga., Augusta Contbr. articles to profl. jours. Trustee East Central State U. Found. Served as capt., M.C. U.S. Army, 1947-49, Korea. Named to Okla. Hall of Fame, 1977, Athletic Hall of Fame, East Central U. Okla., 1977; recipient Disting. Alumnus award East Central U. Okla., 1974, Mayo Found. Disting. Alumnus award, 1992. Mem. AMA, ACS, Am. Assn. Neurol. Surgeons (chmn. com. profl. practice 1976-79, dir. 1976-79, v.p. 1979, rep. to Council Med. Splty. Socs. 1980-84), Congress Neurol. Surgeons (exec. com. 1963-65), Minn. Soc. Neurol. Scis., Neurosurg. Soc. Am. (v.p. 1975), Soc. Neurol. Surgeons (v.p. 1983), Sigma Xi.

**MILLER, ROWLAND SPENCE,** psychologist, writer; s. Donald W. and Charlotte Miller; m. Carolyn Cobb, Sept. 23, 2006; children: Erin Elizabeth Cobb, Christopher Rowland, Jonathon Spence. BA, Cornell U., Ithaca, NY, 1973; MA, U. Fla., Gainesville, PhD, 1978. Assoc. editor Jour. Social Clin. Psychology, 1996—2002. Author: Poise and Peril in Everyday Life (Psi Chi Newman award Excellence Rsch., 1980), Intimate Relationships. Mem.: APA, Internat. Assn. Relationship Rsch., Soc. Exptl. Social Psychology, Soc. Personality and Social Psychology, Assn. Psychol. Sci. Office: Psychology Dept Sam Houston State U Huntsville TX 77341

**MILLER, RUANE,** artist, educator; d. Edward F. and Helen B. Miller; children: Rian Bogle, Adrea Bogle. BFA, Tyler Sch. Art, Phila., 1962—65; MFA, Tyler Sch. Art, Rome, 1966—68, Rochester Inst. Tech., NY, 1984—86. Asst. prof. art history & fine arts Lycoming Coll., Williamsport, Pa., 1977—78; instr. silkscreen SUNY, Albany, 1981—81; instr. drawing & painting Rochester Inst. Tech., NY, 1985—86; vis. artist & lectr. digital art UCLA, 1986—87; prof. digital & fine arts Coll. NJ, Ewing, 1986—. Computer graphics chairman Coll. NJ, 1986—94; juried paper presenter, panel discussant natl. conf. on liberal arts & edn., Sch. Visual Arts, NYC, 1988; juried workshop participant Siggraph's Internat. Conf., 1990; chmn. Coll. NJ, Ewing, NJ, 1994—97, fine arts chmn., 1998—2002, digital arts chmn., 2002—04. Exhibitions include William Penn Mem. Mus., Harrisburg, PA, 1980, Middlesex County Mus., Piscataway, NJ, 1990, Lycoming Coll., Williamsport, Pa., 1990, Condesco-Lawler gallery, NYC, 1995, Silvermine Guild, New Canaan, Conn., 1996, Art Inst. Phila., 1997, Lycoming Coll., 2000, Newark Mus. Art, Newark, NJ, 2002, Hunterdon Mus. Art, Clinton, NJ, 2003, Bristol-Myers Squibb gallery, 2005, State Mus., Trenton, NJ, 2006, Princeton U., NJ, 2006, Represented in permanent collections Phila Mus. Art, Mus. Art San Francisco, US Embassy, Rome, Mercer County Cultural & Heritage Com. Recipient Dodge Fellowship award & partial residency grant, Vt. Studio Ctr., 1996, Artist Residency fellowship, Ucross Found., 1998, Sustained Rsch. awards, Coll. NJ, 1998—; scholar NCGEF Ednl. Scholarship award, Natl. Computer Graphics Assn., 1989; Ednl. Resource grant, Siggraph's Internat. Conf., 1987, Computers in Curriculam grant, Dept. Higher Edn., NJ, 1988. Mem.: Nat. Assn. Schs. Art & Design, Am. Print Alliance, So. Graphics Coun., Princeton Artist's Alliance (co-pres. 2003—05). Office: Coll NJ Dept Sch Art Media & Music PO Box 7718 Trenton NJ 08628-0718 Personal E-mail: ruane@ruanemiller.com.

**MILLER, RUBY SILLS,** retired gerontologist; b. Montpelier, Ind., July 7, 1919; d. Elijah Bert and Alma (Beasley) Sills; m. Glenn Kenneth Miller, Mar. 26, 1966. BS in Edn., Ball State Tchrs. Coll., 1957; MBA, U. Wis., 1958; MPS, New Sch. Social Rsch., 1983; post-masters cert., Hunter Brookdale Ctr. on Aging, 1988. Reporter Montpelier Herald, 1937-41; soc. editor, reporter Hartford City News-Times, Ind., 1941-44, bus. office supr., 1945-57; asst. to dean, instr. U. Wis. Sch. Bus., 1958-60; exec. dir. Nat. Fedn. Bus. and Profl. Women's Clubs, 1960-64; asst. to nat. exec. dir. Girl Scouts U.S.A., NYC, 1964-66, spl. asst. to nat. exec. dir., 1972-74; dir. exptl. project for adminstrv. trainees Camp Fire Girls, Inc. and Girl Scouts U.S.A., 1966-68; dir. regional confs. Nat. Assembly for Social Policy and Devel., Inc., 1968-71; project dir. Nat. Ctr. for Vol. Action, 1971-72; cons. Nat. Coun. for Homemaker-Home Health Aide Svc., Inc., 1972, 76; asst. dir. Gustavus Adolphus Cmty. Lounge Sr. Ctr., 1977-78; cmty. program officer Queens County NYC Dept. Aging, 1978-89; gerontologist cons., 1989—. Sec. Hartford City Retailers Assn., 1951-54 Mem. bd. life mem. Bellevue Day Care Ctr., 1979—, pres., 1980—82; bd. mem. Bellevue Hosp. Adv. Coun., 1978—82, 1991—97; region 1 field rep. NY State Wide Sr. Action Coun., 1989—91, bd. trustees, 1992—2002, region 1 pres., 1996—98, state pres., 1996—98; coord. vol. nat. study guardianship system NY Older Women's League and Ctr. Social Gerontology, Ann Arbor, Mich., 1990—91; pres. Ind. Bapt. Youth Fellowship, 1944—46; supt. Sunday sch. 1st Bapt. Ch. in Montpelier Bapt. Ch., 1949—51; bd. trustees Cmty. Ch. Unitarian Universalist, 1987—92, 1998—2003, vice chair, 1999—2002. Mem.: State Soc. Aging NY. Home: 165 E 32nd St Apt 5G New York NY 10016-6009 Personal E-mail: RMille7030@aol.com.

**MILLER, RUSH GLENN, JR.,** dean; b. Atlanta, Mar. 13, 1947; s. Rush Glenn and Gene (Ramsey) M.; m. Johnnye Mize, July 21, 1967; children: Lisa, Glenn, John, Edward. BA in History, Delta State Coll., Cleveland, Miss., 1969; MA in History, Miss. State U., 1971, PhD in medieval History, 1973; MLS, Fla. State U., 1974. Asst. prof. U. Miss., Oxford, 1974-75; dir. libr. svcs. Delta State U., 1975-82; dir. libr. Sam Houston State U., Huntsville, Tex., 1982-86; dean librs. Bowling Green State U., 1986-94; dir. univ. libr. sys. U. Pitts., 1994—. Del. White House Conf. on Librs., Washington, 1979; del. to users coun. Online Computer Libr. Ctr., Inc., Dublin, Ohio, 1992-94. Contbg. author: Diversity and Multiculturalism in Libraries, 1994, also others; editor Miss. Librs., 1982-84; contbr. articles to profl. jours. Recipient Past President's award Miss. Libr. Assn., 1976. Mem. ALA (various coms. 1976—), Southeastern Libr. Assn. (exec. bd. 1976-82), Acad. Libr. Assn. Ohio. Democrat. Methodist. Avocations: golf, reading. Office: U Pitts Hillman Libr 3960 Forbes Ave Pittsburgh PA 15260 Office Phone: 412-648-7710. Office Fax: 412-648-7887. E-mail: rgmiller@pitt.edu.*

**MILLER, RUTH ANN,** artist; b. Columbia, Mo., Dec. 7, 1930; d. Carl Elmer and Marjorie May (Harris) Miller; m. Rowland Procter Elzea, June 1958 (div.); children: Jessica Mary, Cathlin Suzanne, Lucas James; m. Andrew Murray Forge, Dec. 24, 1974. BA, U. Mo., 1954; student, Art Students League, N.Y.C., 1954-56. Tchr., adj. prof. Queens Coll., N.Y.C., 1974-75, U. Hartford, Conn., 1975-78, N.Y. Studio Sch., N.Y.C., 1973—, Parsons Sch. Design, N.Y.C., 1991-93. One-person exhbns. include Lincoln Gallery, Westchester, Pa., 1964, Del. Art Mus., Wilmington, 1967, Washington Art Assn., N.Y. Studio Gallery, 1979, 88, Washington Depot, Conn., 1982, 92, Bowery Gallery, N.Y.C., 1993, others; group shows include Am. Acad. and Ist. Arts and Letters, N.Y.C., 1990, N.Y. Studio Sch. Gallery, N.Y.C. 1990, Waterbury (Conn.) Arts, 1991, NAD, N.Y.C., 1992, 93, 94, 95, Bryn Mawr Coll., 1993, NAD Mus. Art, 1993; works in collections at Del. Art Mus., U. Del., Corcoran Gallery, pvt. collections. Ingram Merril Found. grantee, 1981, 95. Mem. NAD (academician), Washington Art Assn.

**MILLER, SABRINA WARES,** librarian; d. Margaret Ann Bonds and Edson Brigham Wares; children: Adrian Matthew, Brandon Thomas. BA, Sul Ross State U., Alpine, Tex., 1992; MLS, NC Ctrl. U., Durham, 2000. Cert. health info. profl. Med. Libr. Assn., 2005. Med. libr. intern Laupus Libr., East Carolina U. Sch. of Medicine, Greenville, NC, 2000—00; edn. ctr. libr. Mid-Am. Cancer Ctr., Springfield, Mo., 2000—01; pub. svcs. med. libr. John B. Coleman, M.D., Health Scis. Libr., Houston CC, 2001—06; tech. libr. Champion Techs., Fresno, Tex., 2006—. Accreditation cons. Acad. of HealthCare Professions, Houston, 2004—. Vol. Poe Elem. Sch., Houston, 2003; vol. charity work Salvation Army. Bedichek Faculty Devel. grant, Houston C.C. Sys., 2001. Mem.: Spl. Libr. Assn., Mensa Internat., Acad. Health Info. Profls., Tex. Med. Ctr. Health Scis. Libr. Consortium, Med. Libr. Assn. Democrat. Office: PO Box 450499 Houston TX 77245

**MILLER, SAM SCOTT,** lawyer; b. Ft. Worth, July 26, 1938; s. Percy Vernon and Mildred Lois (MacDowell) M.; m. Mary Harrison FitzHugh, May 10, 1969. BA, Mich. State U., 1960; JD, Tulane U., 1964; LLM, Yale U., 1965. Bar: La. 1965, N.Y. 1966, Minn. 1969. Assoc. Simpson Thacher & Bartlett, N.Y.C., 1965-68; sr. counsel Investors Diversified Services, Mpls., 1968-73; ptnr. Ireland Gibson Reams & Miller, Memphis, 1973-74; gen. counsel Paine Webber Group, Inc., N.Y.C., 1974-87, sr. v.p., 1976-87; ptnr. Orrick, Herrington & Sutcliffe, N.Y.C., 1987—. Adj. prof. NYU Law Sch., 1986-90; vis. lectr. Yale Law Sch., 1980-85, Inst. for Internat. Econs. and Trade, Wuhan, China, 1983, U. Calif., 1986; trustee Omni Mut., Inc., 1988-; ombudsman Kidder Peabody Group, 1988-, Charles Schwab & Co., 1991-, Gruntal & Co., 1995-. Contbr. articles to profl. jours.; editor-in-chief Tulane Law Rev., 1964-65; bd. editors Securities Regulation Law Jour., 1982—. Bd. dirs. Guthrie Theatre Found., Mpls., 1971-74; bd. dirs. Minn. Opera Co., 1971-74, Yale U. Law Sch. Fund., 1981—; bd. govs. Investment Co. Inst., 1980-87. Fellow Fgn. Policy Assn.; mem. ABA (chmn. subcom. market regulation 1985-93, vice chmn. com. fed. regulation of securities 1995-98, chmn. subcom. electronic comm. 1999—), Assn. Bar City N.Y. (treas. and mem. exec. com. 1994-96, chmn. broker-dealer investment co. and regulations subcom. 1982-83), Internat. Bar Assn., Securities Industry Assn. (chmn. fed. regulation com. 1976-78), Down Town Assn., Knickerbocker Club, Order of Coif, Omicron Delta Kappa. Democrat. Baptist. Office: Orrick Herrington & Sutcliffe 666 5th Ave Rm 203 New York NY 10103-1798

**MILLER, SANFORD,** car rental company executive; b. 1954; Grad., SUNY-Oswego, 1975. Licensee ops, mgr. Budget Group, Inc., Daytona Beach, Fla., from 1980, ptnr. franchises N.Y.C., owner franchises through no. Fla., from 1984; dir. mktg. and spl. accounts Budget Corp., 1989-91; v.p. Tranex Rental N.Y., Inc. operators Albany and Rochester brs., 1991-94, Capital City Leasing, Inc., operators Richond, Va. franchise, 1991-94, chmn. bd. dirs., CEO Budget Group Inc., 1994—. Mem. Travel Bus. Roundtable; chmn. licensee local market adv. bd. Budget Sys., 1989-90. Mem. Fla. Commn. Tourism, 1999—. Named Fla.'s Ernst & Young Master Entrepreneur of Yr., 1998. Mem. Travel Industry Assn. Am. (exec. com. 1999—), Am. Car Rental Assn. (pres. 1993), World Travel and Tourism Coun.

**MILLER, SCOTT D.,** lawyer; b. Redondo Beach, Calif., 1961; BSE, Ariz. State U., 1982; JD, Columbia U., 1985. Bar: Calif. 1987. Law clk. William A. Norris, US Ct. of Appeals (9th cir.), 1985—86; assoc. Sullivan & Cromwell, Palo Alto, ptnr., and co-head, tech. practice specialty group. Named one of 12 "Dealmakers of the Yr.", The American Lawyer, 2003—04. Office: Sullivan & Cromwell 1870 Embarcadero Rd Palo Alto CA 94303-3308 Office Phone: 650-461-5620. Office Fax: 650-461-5700. Business E-Mail: millersc@sullcrom.com.

**MILLER, SHANNON,** Olympic athlete; b. Rolla, Mo., Mar. 10, 1977; Student, Boston Coll. Gymnast U.S. National Gymnastic Team, 1990—97. Named Female Athlete of Yr., Nat. March of Dimes Found., 1993; named to U.S. Olympic Hall of Fame, 2005, Internat. Gymnastics Hall of Fame, 2006. Achievements include most decorated gymnast in US history; won a total of 58 International and 49 National Competition medals; won 9 World Championship medals including 2 back to back All-Around Gold medals; won a Silver All-Around and Silver medal for the balance beam at the Barcelona Olympic Gymnastics in 1992; was a member of the Bronze Team for winning the Bronze medal for floor exercise and uneven bars at the Barcelona Olympic Gymnastics in 1992; was a member of the Gold Team for winning the Gold medal for the balance beam at the Olympics in 1996.

**MILLER, SHEILA,** state legislator; d. Vernon and Mildred M.; m. Michael Miller; 1 child, Emilie C. BS cum laude, Pa. State U., 1974. Rep. dist. 129 State of Pa., 1993—. Bd. dirs. Berks County Farmland Preservation. Mem. Nat. Cattlemens Assn., Berks Farm Bur., Berks Cattlemens Assn., Pa. Cattlemens Assn., Heidelberg Heritage Soc., Berks County Rep. Women, Phi Kappa Phi, Gamma Sigma Delta Agrl. Alumni Soc. Republican. Office: Pa Ho of Reps PO Box 202020 Harrisburg PA 17120-2020

**MILLER, SIENNA,** actress; b. NYC, Dec. 28, 1981; d. Ed and Jo Miller. Attended, Lee Strasberg Inst. Actor: (films) South Kensington, 2001, High Speed, 2002, Layer Cake, 2004, Alfie, 2004, Casanova, 2005; (TV series) Bedtime, 2002, Keen Eddie, 2003; guest appearance Late Night with Conan O'Brien, 2003. Office: c/o Endeavor Talent Agency 9701 Wilshire Blvd, 3rd Fl Beverly Hills CA 90212*

**MILLER, STANLEY LLOYD,** chemistry and biochemistry professor; b. Oakland, Calif., Mar. 7, 1930; s. Nathan Harry and Edith (Levy) M. BS, U. Calif., Berkeley, 1951; PhD, U. Chgo., 1954. F.B. Jewett fellow Cal-Tech., Pasadena, Calif., 1954; asst. prof. Coll. Physicians and Surgeons, N.Y.C., 1955-60; from asst. to full prof. U. Calif., San Diego, 1960—. Mem. Am. Chem. Soc., Am. Soc. Biol. Chemists, Nat. Acad. Sci., Internat. Soc. Study of the Origin of Life (pres. 1986-89). Office: Univ Calif San Diego Dept Chemistry & Biochem 9500 Gilman Dr Dept & La Jolla CA 92093-0506 E-mail: smiller@ucsd.edu.

**MILLER, STEPHEN BLAINE,** plastic surgeon; b. Huntington, W.Va., Dec. 10, 1962; s. Albert Blaine and Chestene Miller; m. Kim Constantino, Apr. 21, 2001; 1 child, Evan Blaine. MD, Marshall U., 1994. Diplomate Am. Bd. Plastic Surgeons. Plastic surgeon Cosmetic & Reconstructive Plastic Surgery, Huntington, W.Va., 2001—. Mem.: Am Soc. Plastic Surgeons. Baptist. Avocation: shooting sports. Office: Cosmetic & Reconstructive Plastic Surg 2828 First Avenue Suite 203 Huntington WV 25702 Office Phone: 304-529-4450. Personal E-mail: dr25702@netzero.net.

**MILLER, STEPHEN HERSCHEL,** surgeon, educator; b. N.Y.C., Jan. 12, 1941; s. Morris Louis and Mildred Lily (Beller) M.; children: Mark, David. MD, UCLA, 1966; MPH, San Diego State, 1996. Diplomate Am. Bd. Surgery, Am. Bd. Plastic Surgery (mem. exec. com. 1985—, chmn. written examination sect. 1985—, bd. dirs. 1984—, chmn. 1989-90). Asst. prof. surgery U. Calif., San Francisco, 1973-74; from asst. prof. to prof. surgery Milton S. Hershey Med. Ctr., Hershey, Pa., 1974-78; chief div. plastic surgery Oreg. Health Scis. U., Portland, 1979-88, Staff Scripps Clinic, La Jolla, Calif., 1988—98; clin. prof. surgery U. Calif., San Diego, 1989—98; adj. prof. surgery Northwestern U., Evanston, Ill., 1998—; pres., CEO Am. Bd. Med. Specialities, Evanston, Ill., 2004—. Bd. dirs. Nat. Resident Matching Program, 1998—, Edn. Commn. for Foreign Med. Grads., 1998—. Editor-in-chief Yearbook of Plastic, Reconstructive and Aesthetic Surgery, 1988-95. Physician advisor Boy Scouts Am.. dist. chmn. scoutmaster exec. coun., 1983-84; bd. dirs. Temple Beth Israel, Portland, 1984-86. Recipient Physician Recognition award, 1976; grantee Med. Rsch. Found. of Oreg., 1980, Oreg. Health Scis. U., 1980. Mem. ACS (chmn. program com. 1983-87), Am. Soc. Plastic and Reconstructive Surgery (bd. dirs. 1980-89, v.p. 1985-86, pres.-elect 1986-87, pres. 1987-88, grantee 1976), Am. Assn. Plastic Surgeons (chmn. rsch. com. 1983-84, trustee 1988-91, sec. 1990-93, pres. 1994-95), Assn. Acad. Chmn. Plastic Surgery (sec./treas. 1985—); Am. Bd. Med.

Specialites (sect., exec. v.p., 1998). Avocations: reading, golf. Home: 808 Judson Ave Apt 4D Evanston IL 60202-2456 Address: Am Bd Med Specialities 1007 Church St Ste 404 Evanston IL 60201-5913 Office Phone: 847-491-9091. Fax: 847-328-3596.

**MILLER, STEPHEN RALPH,** lawyer; b. Chgo., Nov. 28, 1950; s. Ralph and Karin Ann (Olson) Miller; m. Sheila L. Krysiak, Feb. 2, 1998; children from previous marriage: David Williams, Lindsay Christine. BA cum laude, Yale U., 1972; JD, Cornell U., 1975. Bar: Ill. Assoc. McDermott, Will & Emery, Chgo., 1975-80, income ptnr., 1981-85, equity ptnr., 1986—, mgmt. com. mem., 1992-95. Mem. spl. task force on post-employment benefits Fin. Acctg. Stds. Bd., Norwalk, Conn., 1987—91. Contbr. articles to profl. jours. Trustee Police Pension Bd., Wilmette, Ill., 1992—98; mem. Seabury Coun., 2004—, Chgo. Coun. Fgn. Rels., 1978—, mem. devel. com., 1997—2002, chair devel. subcom., 1999—2002, mem. external rels. com., 2002—03, mem. pres.'s cir. steering com., 2005—; trustee Seabury Western Theol. Sem., Evanston, Ill., 1994—2002, chancellor, 1996—97, 2004—05, chair trusteeship com., 2000—02. Mem.: ABA, Hundred Club Cook County, Cornell Club Chgo., Lawyers' Club Chgo., Yale Club Chgo. Avocations: sailing, water-skiing, cross country skiing. Office: McDermott Will & Emery 227 W Monroe St Ste 4700 Chicago IL 60606-5096 Office Phone: 312-984-7634. Business E-Mail: smiller@mwe.com.

**MILLER, STEVEN,** medical administrator; Grad., U. Mo., Kansas City. Hosp. staff, faculty Wash. U., 1990—, nephrology fellow, 1988, asst. prof., 1991—97, assoc. prof., 1997—, dir. hypertension clinic divsn. nephrology; med. dir. systemwide renal network Barnes-Jewish Hosp.; chief med. officer Wash. U. Sch. Medicine-Barnes Jewish Hosp., 1999—2005; now v.p. of rsch. Express Scripts Inc., St. Louis. Mem.: Internat. Soc. Nephrology, ACP. Office: Express Scripts Inc 13900 Riverport Dr Maryland Heights MO 63043

**MILLER, STEVEN E.,** professor of international affairs; b. North Hollywood, Calif. m. Deborah K. Louis; children: Jonathan, Nicholas. B, Occidental Coll., LA; MA in Law and Diplomacy, Fletcher Sch. Law and Diplomacy, PhD in Internat. Relations. Sr. rsch. fellow Stockholm Internat. Peace Rsch. Inst.; tchr. defense and arms control studies Dept Polit. Sci. MIT; dir. Internat. Security Program Belfer Ctr. Sci. and Internat. Affairs Harvard U., Mass., co-prin. investigator Mass. Editor-in-chief Internat. Security jour.; co-chmn. US Pugwash Com.; mem. Coun. Internat. Pugwash; mem. adv. com. Stockholm Internat. Peace Rsch. Inst.; mem. scientific com. Landau Network Centro Volta, Italy; coun. mem. Internat. Inst. Strategic Studies; steering com. Kokkalis Program on Southeastern and East-Central Europe John F. Kennedy Sch. Govt. Harvard U., steering com. Ukrainian Project. Editor: The Rise of China, 2000, Nationalism and Ethnic Conflict, 2001, The Russian Military: Power and Policy, 2004, Offense, Defense, and War, 2004; co-author: (monograph) War with Iraq: Costs, Consequences, and Alternatives, 2002; contbr. to Nezavisimaya Gazeta. Mem.: Am. Acad. Arts and Sciences (com. internat. security studies, fellow 2006). Office: Belfte Ctr Sci and Internat Affairs Littauer 378 79 John f Kennedy St Cambridge MA 02138 Office Phone: 617-495-1411. Office Fax: 617-495-8963. E-mail: steven_miller@harvard.edu.*

**MILLER, STEVEN H.,** museum director; b. Phila., 1947; m. Jane McClure Pelson; children: Andrew Steven, Katherine Ann. BA, Bard Coll., 1970; cert. in conservation sci., Internat. Ctr. for Study of Preservation and Restoration of Cultural Property, Rome, 1978. Asst. to sr. curator Mus. of City of N.Y., N.Y.C., 1971-72, asst. curator paintings, prints and photographs, 1973-77, curator prints and photographs, 1977-79, curator, dept. head fine art collections, history and spl. collections, 1979-85, sr. curator, 1985-87; asst. dir. Maine State Mus., 1987-91; dir. of mus. Western Res. Hist. Soc., Cleve., 1991-95; exec. dir. The Bennington (Vt.) Mus., 1995—2001, Morris Mus., Morristown, NJ, 2001—; exec. v.p Morris Mus. Found., Morristown, NJ, 2001—. Adj. prof. mus. studies Case Western Res. U., 1991—94, Seton Hall U.; lectr. NYU, 1978—87, Columbia U., N.Y.C., 1981, 82, New Sch. for Social Rsch., N.Y.C., 1978, 83, Maine State Mus., 1987—91. Author catalogs; contbr. articles to profl. jours. Charter and former mem. hist. preservation com. City of Gardiner, Maine; mem. Williamstown Art Conservation com.; bd. trustees ArtPride, NJ; bd. govs. Bard-St. Stephen's Alumni Assn.; bd. trustees Hist. Deerfield, Mass.; past bd. dirs. Vt. Mus. and Gallery Alliance; former mem. landmarks preservation com. Shaker Heights, Ohio; former mem. adv. com. Blaine House Restoration, Maine; former mem., art adv. com. Gracie Mansion Conservancy, N.Y.C.; former mem. adv. coun. Mus. Moving Image, Astoria, NY. Mem.: NARAS (assoc.), Century Assn., Maine Assn. Mus. (co-founder, charter coun. mem.), Am. Assn. Mus. (mem. mus. advocacy team, mem. mus. accreditation vis. com.), Park Ave. Club (Morristown). Home: 45 Washington Ave Morristown NJ 07960-5622 Office Phone: 973-971-3702.

**MILLER, STEVEN MAX,** humanities educator; b. Portland, Me., Feb. 9, 1950; s. J. Max and Belva Kathryn (Kitty Booher) M.; m. Fran Felice Koski, May 30, 1985 (div. 1992). BA in English with high honors, Coll. of William and Mary, 1972; MA in English Lang. and Lit., Ind. U., 1975. PhD in English Lang. and Lit., 1985. Sr. libr. asst. cataloger rare books and spl. collections Lilly Libr., Bloomington, Ind., 1972-76; prof. English Millersville U., Pa., 1985—, dir. univ. honors program, 1999-2001, dir. Honors Coll., 2001—06. Cons. women writers project Brown U., Providence, 1990-95. Contbr. articles to profl. jours. Grantee NEH, 1991, 92. Mem. MLA, John Donne Soc. Am., Spenser Soc. Episcopalian. Avocation: gardening. Office: Millersville U Honors Coll PO Box 1002 Millersville PA 17551-0302

**MILLER, STUART A.,** real estate executive, lawyer; s. Leonard and Sue Miller. Grad., Harvard U.; JD, U. Miami, 1982. Various positions homebuilding divsn. Lennar Corp., Miami, Fla., v.p., 1988—97, pres. homebuilding divsn. and former investment divsn., 1991—97, bd. dirs., 1990—, pres., CEO, 1997—; chmn. bd. LNR Property Corp., 1997—2005. Bd. dirs. Union Bank Fla.; mem. Joint Ctr. for Housing Studies Policy Adv. Bd., Harvard U. Named one of 50 Most Generous Philanthropists, BusinessWeek, 2005. Office: Lennar Corp 700 NW 107th Ave Ste 400 Miami FL 33172-3154*

**MILLER, STUART A.,** lawyer; b. Suffern, NY; BA, Hamilton Coll., 1994; JD, Bklyn. Law Sch., 1997. Bar: NY 1997, NJ 1998, Fla. 1998, US Dist. Ct. Ea. Dist. NY, US Dist. Ct. So. Dist. NY, US Dist. Ct. Dist. NJ. Ptnr. Wilson, Elser, Moskowitz, Edelman & Dicker LLP, NYC. Mem.: NY State Bar Assn., Def. Rsch. Inst., Assn. of the Bar of the City of NY. Office: Wilson Elser Moskowtiz Edelman & Dicker LLP 23rd Fl 150 E 42nd St New York NY 10017-5639 Office Phone: 212-490-3000 ext. 2403. Office Fax: 212-490-3038. Business E-Mail: millers@wemed.com.

**MILLER, SUE,** writer; b. NY, 1943; Student, Harvard Univ. Author: (novels) The Good Mother, 1986, Family Pictures, 1990 (Nat. Book Awards Critics Cir. award nominee), For Love, 1993, The Distinguished Guest, 1995, While I Was Gone, 1999 (Oprah Book Club pick), The World Below, 2001, Lost in the Forest, 2005, (short stories) Inventing the Abbots, 1987, (non-fiction) The Story of My Father, 2003. Bunting Fellow, Radcliffe. Mailing: c/o Knopf Pub Author Mail 1745 Broadway New York NY 10019

**MILLER, SUE,** information technology executive; Owner Sue Miller & Assoc., Atlanta. Leadership roles Tech. Assn. Ga., Digital Ball Exec. Com. Mem.: Women in Tech. Found. (pres.), Women in Tech. (pres. 2000, interim pres. 2006—, v.p., dir. fin.). Office: Women in Tech Ste A Box 473 4780 Ashford Dunwoody Rd Atlanta GA 30338-5504 Office Phone: 678-234-7329.*

**MILLER, SUSAN ANN,** retired school system administrator; b. Cleve., Nov. 24, 1947; d. Earl Wilbur and Marie Coletta (Hendershot) M. BS in Edn., Kent State U., 1969; MEd, Cleve. State U., 1975; PhD, Kent State U., 1993. Cert. supt.; cert. elem. prin., cert. elem. supervisor; cert. Learning Disabled/Behavior Disabled tchr.; cert. tchr. grades 1-8; cert. sch. counselor; lic. counselor. Tchr., guidance counselor, interim prin. North Royalton City

Schs., Ohio, 1969-84; dir. elem. and spl. edn., acting supt., asst. supt. Ednl. Svc. Ctr. of Cuyahoga County, Valley View, Ohio, 1984—. Contbr. articles to profl. jours. Grantee Latchkey Program, State Dept. Edn., North Coast Leadership Program, Peer Assistance and Rev., Cuyu Yr. Program, Alt. H.S. Mem. ASCD, Coun. Exceptional Children, Phi Delta Kappa. Office: ESC Cuyahoga County 5700 W Canal Rd Valley View OH 44125-3326 Home: 7236 Morning Star Trail Sagamore Hills OH 44067 Personal E-mail: sumrtoi47@yahoo.com.

**MILLER, SUSAN L.,** social services administrator; Student, Santa Monica Coll., 1980—85; cert. in mktg. and advt., Loyola Mount U., 1994; BA in Sociology and Mgmt., Eckerd Coll., 2006. Comptr., dir. fin. and adminstrn. Westside Ctr. for Ind. Living, Inc., LA, 1979—85; exec. dir. Placer Ind. Resource Svcs., Inc., Auburn, Calif., 1995—. Bd. dirs. Auburn Area Access, Inc. dba Auburn Cmty. TV, treas., 2000—. Bd. dirs. Capital Unity Coun., 2001—04, program adv. coun., 2004—; bd. dirs. Golden Sierra Workforce Investment, 2001—, v.p., 2004—; treas. CA Found. for Ind. Living Ctrs., 2004—, sec., 1999—2004; adv. coun. Placer County Social Svcs. Transp., 1997—, chair, 1998—99, Tahoe regional planning agy. com., 2001—, adv. coun. Alpine County, 2001—; chair adv. coun. Alpine County IHSS, 2004; client, family rels. com., cultural competency com. Placer County Health & Human Svcs., 2001—; bldg., fire and other codes adv. com. Calif. State Bldg. Commn., 1999—2002; active Tahoe Area Coord. Coun. on Disability, 1999—; bd. dirs. CA Found. for Ind. Living Ctrs., 1995—, treas., 1996—99; steering com. Best Step Trans. Collaborative, 1996—; bd. dirs. Foothill Employers Adv. Coun., 2003—; steering com. Vision 2020 for Greater Auburn, 1998—2003. Avocations: genealogy, painting, reading. Office: Placer Ind Resource Svcs Inc 11768 Atwood Rd Ste 29 Auburn CA 95603

**MILLER, SUSAN LAURA,** real estate company executive, retired special education educator; d. Martin and Bertha (Bottenstein) Fried; m. Carl William Miller, Apr. 5, 1970; children: Ryan Scott, Brent Todd. BA, Western Ky. U., 1970, MA in Spl. Edn., 1973. Cert. Tchr. in English, Spl. Edn., Psychology NY, Fla., Ga. Spl. edn. tchr. Morgantown Schs., Ky., 1970—73, Clayton County Schs., Jonesboro, Ga., 1973—80, Mid. Island Longwood HS, LI, NY, 1980—2001; v.p. Carl Miller Am. Yearbook Inc., 1992—2005; mktg. dir. Classic Experience; pres., owner Island Coastal Properties Mgmt. LLC, 2002—. Asst. developer spl. edn. curriculum. Mem. planning com. Ga. Spl. Olympics. Mem.: N.Y. State Retired tchrs. Assn., Flagler Point Condo Assn., Silver Sands Condominium Assn. (v.p. 2000—05), Ga. Jaycettes (Woman of Yr. 1976), Eau Gallie Yacht Club, Women's Club of Brevard, Sigma Kappa. Avocations: world travel, yachting, home designing. Home: 795 Loggerhead Island Way Satellite Beach FL 32937

**MILLER, SUZANNE MARIE,** library director, educator; b. Feb. 25, 1954; d. John Gordon and Dorothy Margaret (Sabatka) M.; 1 child, Altinay Marie. BA in English, U. S.D., 1975; MA in Library Sci., U. Denver, 1976, postgrad. in law, 1984. Librarian II U. S.D. Sch. of Law, Vermillion, 1977-78; law libr. U. LaVerne, Calif., 1978-85, instr. in law Calif., 1980-85; asst. libr. tech. svcs. McGeorge Sch. Law, Calif., 1985-99, prof. advanced legal rsch. Calif., 1994-99; state librarian S.D. State Library, Pierre, 1999—2004; state libr. Minn. State Libr. Svcs. and Sch. Tech, Roseville, 2004—. Co-author (with Elizabeth J. Pokorny) U.S. Government Documents: A Practical Guide for Library Assistants in Academic and Public Libraries, 1988; contbr. chpt. to book, articles to profl. jours. Pres. Short Grass Arts Coun., 2001—03; bd. dirs. Black Hills Playhouse Bd., 1999—2004, S.D. Ctr. for the Book Bd., 2002—04. Recipient A. Jurisprudence award Bancroft Whitney Pub. Co., 1983. Mem.: ALA, Minn. Ednl. Media Orgn., Minn. Libr. Assn., Western Coun. State Librs. (sec. 2001—02), Chief Officers of State Libr. Agys. (sec. 2002—04), Western Pacific Assn. Law Librs. (sec. 1990—94, pres. elect 1994—95, pres. 1995—96, local arrangements chair 1997), No. Calif. Assn. Law Librs. (mem. program com., inst. 1988), Mt. Plains Libr. Assn. (S.D. rep. to exec. bd. 2001—04), So. Calif. Assn. Law Librs. (arrangements com. 1981—82), Am. Assn. Law Librs., S.D. Libr. Assn. Roman Catholic. Home: 448 Marcotts Blvd So Roseville MN 55113 Office: Minn Dept Edn 1500 Hwy 36 West Roseville MN 55113-4266 Office Phone: 651-582-8251. Business E-Mail: suzanne.miller@state.mn.us.

**MILLER, TED ROBERT,** management consultant; b. Sept. 17, 1947; s. Marvin Lester and Carolyn Ruth Miller; m. Valerie Sue Nelkin. BS in Engring., Case Western Res. U., 1968; MS in Ops. Rsch., U. Pa., 1971, M in City Planning, 1970, PhD in Regional Sci., 1975. Ops. rsch. analyst U.S. Dept. Commerce, Nat. Bur. Stds. and HEW, Washington, 1971-75; staff dir. task force on Nat. Blood Data Ctr. Am. Blood Commn., Rosslyn, Va., 1975-77; asst. dir. urban and econ. devel. Nat. Inst. Advanced Studies, Washington, 1977-78; v.p. Granville Corp., Washington, 1978-84; sr. rsch. assoc. Urban Inst., Washington, 1984-93; dir. Children's Safety Network Econ. and Ins. Rsch. Ctr., 1992—. V.p. Nat. Pub. Svcs. Rsch. Inst., Calverton, Md., 1993-96, pres., 1997-2002; prin. rsch. scientist Pacific Inst. Rsch. and Evaluation, Calverton, 1997—. Mem. editl. bd. Jour. Safety Rsch., 1991—, Jour. Forensic Econs., 1991-2004, Acc. Analysis and Prevention, 1993—, Inj. Prev., 2002-; contbr. articles to profl. jours. Mem. Bd. Proprs. Ea. N.J., 1974-98; pres. Adelphi Ter. Condo. Assn., 1979-81. Recipient Nationwide on Your Side Hwy. Safety award, 1996, State and Territorial Injury Prevention Dirs. Assn. Vision award, 2005. Fellow Assn. Advt. Automotive Medicine, Am. Inst. Cert. Planners; mem. AAAS, APHA (Excellence in Sci. award injury control sect. 1999), So. Regional Sci. Assn. (exec. coun. 1990-92), Am. Econ. Assn., Pi Delta Epsilon. Democrat. Office: 11701 Beltsville Dr Ste 300 Beltsville MD 20705

**MILLER, TERRY ALAN,** chemistry professor; b. Girard, Kans., Dec. 18, 1943; s. Dwight D. Miller and Rachel E. (Detjen) Beltram; m. Barbara Hoffmann, July 16, 1966; children: Brian, Stuart. BA, U. Kans., 1965; PhD, Cambridge (Eng.) U., 1968. Disting. tech. staff Bell Telephone Labs, 1968-84; vis. asst. prof. Princeton U., 1968-71; vis. lectr. Stanford U., 1972; vis. fgn. scholar Inst. Molecular Sci., Okazaki, Japan, summer 1983; Ohio eminent scholar, prof. chemistry Ohio State U., Columbus, 1984—. Chair Molecular Spectroscopy Symposium, Columbus, 1992—. Mem. editl. bd. Jour. Chem. Physics, 1978-81, Laser Chemistry, 1986—, Rev. of Sci. Instruments, 1986-89, Jour. Phys. Chemistry, 1989-95, Jour. Optical Soc. Am., 1989-95, Chemtracts, 1989-90, Ann. Revs. Phys. Chemistry, 1989-94, Jour. Molecular Structure, 1996—; mem. editl. bd. Jour. Molecular Spectroscopy, 1982-87, editor 2005; contbr. articles to profl. jours. Recipient Bourke medal Royal Soc. Chemistry, 1998; Marshall fellow Brit. Govt., 1965-67, NSF fellow, 1967-68. Fellow Optical Soc. Am. (Meggars award 1993), Am. Phys. Soc. (H.P. Broida award 1999), AAAS; mem. Am. Chem. Soc. (councilor), Coblentz Soc. (Bomen-Michaelson award 1995). Office: Ohio State U 120 W 18th Ave Columbus OH 43210-1106

**MILLER, TERRY MORROW,** lawyer; b. Columbus, Ohio, Mar. 11, 1947; s. Robert E. and Elizabeth Jane (Morrow) M.; m. Martha Estella Johnson, Mar. 20, 1976; 1 child, Timothy. BS, Ohio State U., 1969, JD, 1975. Bar: Ohio 1975, U.S. Ct. Appeals (6th cir.) 1979, U.S. Supreme Ct. 1980. Asst. atty. gen. State of Ohio, Columbus, 1975—77; ptnr. Miller & Noga, Columbus, 1977—81; assoc. Vorys, Sater, Seymour and Pease, Columbus, 1981—85, ptnr., 1986—. Trustee Columbus Lit. Coun., 1997—2004. Sgt. U.S. Army, 1969-71, Okinawa. Mem. Ohio State Bar Assn., Columbus Bar Assn., Lakes Golf and Country Club, Rattlesnake Ridge Golf Club. Avocations: golf, Ohio history. Home: 288 E North Broadway Columbus OH 43214-4114 Office: Vorys Sater Seymour et al PO Box 1008 52 E Gay St Columbus OH 43216-1008 Office Phone: 614-464-5645. Business E-Mail: tmmiller@vssp.com.

**MILLER, THEODORE NORMAN,** lawyer; b. Chgo., Oct. 9, 1942; s. Alexander Hyman and Bertha Helen (Swidler) M.; m. Marylyn Sue Zaye, June 21, 1964; children — Henry, Amy. B.A., U. Mich., 1964; LL.B., Yale U., 1967. Bar: Ill. 1967, Calif. 1991, U.S. Dist. Ct. (no. dist.) Ill. 1967, U.S. Ct. Appeals (7th cir.) 1968, U.S. Supreme Ct. 1972. Law clk. U.S. Ct. Appeals (7th cir.), 1967-68; assoc. Sidley & Austin, Chgo., 1968-73, ptnr., 1973—, now mng. ptnr. NYC office, and vice chmn., mgmt. com. and mem. exec.

com. Mem. ABA, Chgo. Bar Assn., Chgo. Council Lawyers, Phi Beta Kappa, Order of Coif. Office: Sidley Austin Brown & Wood LLP 787 Seventh Ave New York NY 10019-6018 Office Phone: 212-839-5886. Office Fax: 212-839-5599. Business E-mail: tmiller@sidley.com.

**MILLER, THEODORE T.,** radiologist; b. N.Y.C., Mar. 1, 1961; BA, U. Pa., 1983; MD, Vanderbilt U., 1987. Diplomate Am. Bd. Radiology, 1993. Intern N.Y. Hosp., N.Y.C., 1987—88; resident Mt. Sinai Hosp., N.Y.C., 1988—92; fellow Hosp. Spl. Surgery, 1992—93; attending radiologist Columbia Presbyn. Med. Ctr., 1993—96, North Shore U. Hosp., Manhasset, 1996—2006; staff radiologist Hosp. Spl. Surgery, N.Y.C., 2006—. Dir. North Shore Imaging Assocs., Great Neck, NY, 1996—; chief musculoskeletal imaging North Shore U. Hosp., Manhasset, 2000—; assoc. prof. radiology N.Y. U. Sch. Medicine, N.Y.C., 2001—; v.p. N.Y. Roentgen Soc., 2006. Mem. editl. bd.: Radiology, Skeletal Radiology, Seminars Musculoskeletal Radiology, Radiographics, 2005; author: (textbook) Diagnostic Musculoskeletal Imaging, 2005. Recipient Pres.'s medal, Internat. Skeletal Soc., 2006. Mem.: Radiol. Soc. N.Am. (editl. bd. mem. 2003, Edidl. fellow 2001). Achievements include patent for Temporary vena cava filter. Office: Hosp Spl Surgery 535 E 70th St New York NY 10021 Office Phone: 516-465-8686, 212-606-1810.

**MILLER, THOMAS EUGENE,** lawyer, writer; b. Bryan, Tex., Jan. 4, 1929; s. Eugene Adam and Ella Lucille (Schroeder) M. BA, BS, Tex. A&M U., 1950; MA, U. Tex., 1956, JD, 1966; postgrad., U. Houston, 1956-58. U. Calif., 1983. Bar: Tex. 1966. Rsch. technician M.D. Anderson Hosp., Houston, 1956-58; claims examiner trainee Social Security Adminstrn., New Orleans, 1964; trademark examiner U.S. Patent and Trademark Office, Washington, 1966; editor Bancroft-Whitney Co., San Francisco, 1966-72; ret., 1992. Author: (under pseudonym Millard Thomas) Home From 7-North, 1984; contbr. to numerous legal publs. Mem. Dem. Nat. Com., 1981—; mem. Celebrate Bryan Com., chmn. Bryan Med. Heritage Com. Mem. ABA, World Lit. Assn., World Inst. Achievement, United Writers Assn. India, Nat. Trust for Hist. Preservation, Tex. Bar Assn., U. Tex. Sch. of Law, Non-practicing Alumni Adv. Coun., African Wildlife Found., World Wildlife Fund, Internat. Platform Assn., Nat. Writers Assn., Scribes, Acad. Polit. Sci., Press Club, Commonwealth Club, Westerners Internat., Rotary Club (Paul Harris fellow, Found. fellow), Menninger Soc., Tex. A&M U. Faculty Club, Phi Kappa Phi, Psi Chi, Phi Eta Sigma. Methodist. Home: 101 N Haswell Dr Bryan TX 77803-4848 Office Phone: 979-822-1907. *Personal philosophy: Use your experience and abilities not only to understand life and to succeed, but also to help others' journeys through life.*

**MILLER, THOMAS J.,** state attorney general; b. Dubuque, Iowa, Aug. 11, 1944; s. Elmer John and Betty Maude (Kross) Miller; m. Linda Cottington, Jan. 10, 1981; 1 child, Matthew. BA, Loras Coll., Dubuque, 1966; JD, Harvard U., 1969. Bar: Iowa 1969. With VISTA, Balt., 1969—70; legis. asst. to U.S. rep. John C. Culver, 1970—71; legal edn. dir. Balt. Legal Aid Bur., part-time faculty U. Md. Sch. Law, 1971—73; pvt. practice McGregor, Iowa, 1973—78; city atty., 1973—79, Marquette, Iowa; atty. gen. State of Iowa, 1978—90, 1994—; ptnr. Faegre & Benson, Des Moines, 1991—95. Chmn. Microsoft case settlement com.; co-chmn. Airline Competition Working Group; pres. 2d Dist. New Dem. Club, Balt., 1972. Mem.: NAAG (pres. 1989—90, chmn. consumer protection, ins., budget, and antitrust coms., Wyman award 1990), ABA, Iowa Bar Assn., Common Cause. Democrat. Roman Catholic. Office: Office of Atty General Hoover State Office Bldg 1305 E Walnut St Des Moines IA 50319-0112*

**MILLER, THOMAS J.,** former ambassador; b. Chgo., 1948; m. Bonnie Miller; 2 children. BA in Polit. Sci., U. Mich., 1969, MA in Asian Studies and Polit. Sci., 1973, PhD in Polit. Sci., 1975. Various to sr. fgn. svc./min. counselor U.S. Dept. State, 1976—, analyst for Vietnam, Laos, & Cambodia, 1976—77, spl. asst. to under sec. polit. affairs, 1977—79; dep. prin. officer U.S. Consulate, Chiang Mai, Thailand, 1979—81; dep. chief of mission U.S. Embassy, Athens, 1994-97; spl. coord. for Cyprus (amb.) U.S. Dept. State, 1997-99, U.S. amb. to Bosnia and Herzegovina, 1999—2001, U.S. amb. to Greece Athens, 2001—04. Lectr. in field; initiator Model UN programs at three Washington high schs. Recipient numerous awards in field. Avocations: speaks greek, spanish, thai, indonesian, japanese.

**MILLER, THORMUND AUBREY,** lawyer; b. Pocatello, Idaho, July 14, 1919; s. Roy Edmund and Lillian (Thordarson) Miller; m. Hannah A. Flansburgh, Feb. 10, 1946 (dec. Jan. 2003); children: Karen Lynette Van Gerpen, Christine Alison Westall; m. Barbara Singelyn, May 8, 2004. BA, Reed Coll., 1941; LLB, Columbia U., 1948; grad., Advanced Mgmt. Program, Harvard Bus. Sch., 1961. Bar: Calif. 1949, D.C. 1951, U.S. Supreme Ct. 1960. Assoc. McCutchen, Thomas, Matthews, Griffiths & Greene, San Francisco, 1948-50; atty. So. Pacific Transp. Co., Washington, 1950-56, asst. gen. atty., 1956-59, gen. atty., 1959—66, sr. gen. atty. San Francisco, 1966—75, gen. solicitor, 1975—79, gen. commerce counsel, 1979—83, dir., mem. exec. com., 1983—87, v.p., gen. counsel, 1983—89; gen. counsel So. Pacific Comms. Co., San Francisco, 1970—79, dir., 1970—81. Pres. Wood Acres Citizens Assn., Bethesda, Md., 1955-56; exec. com. Holbrook Palmer Recreation Park Found., 1979—, pres., 1982-84; bd. dirs. Atherton Civic Interest League, 1981—, pres., 1992-94; mem. Atherton Park and Recreation Commn., 1991-95, Atherton Waste Reduction Commn., 1999-2005, San Mateo Civil Grand Jury, 1997; alumni bd. Reed Coll., 1971-72, trustee, 1987-2002, campaign com., 1995-2000, Atherton Westa Reduction Com. 1999-2005; joint donor Thormund A. Miller/Walter Mintz chair in econ. history; bd. dirs. Assocs. U. Calif. Press, 1994—2006. Lt. USNR, 1942-46. Mem.: ABA, Calif. Bar Assn. Presbyterian.

**MILLER, TIMOTHY ALDEN,** plastic and reconstructive surgeon; b. Inglewood, Calif., Dec. 11, 1938; s. Henry Bernard and Florence Algena (Maddock) M.; 1 child Matthew Christopher Student, U. Calif., Berkeley, MD, UCLA, 1963. Diplomate Am. Bd. Surgery, Am. Bd. Plastic Surgery (dir. 1991-97). Intern Vanderbilt U. Hosp., Nashville, 1963-64; resident in surgery, dept. surg. pathology UCLA, 1966-67, resident, then chief resident gen. and thoracic surgery, 1967-69, acting asst. prof., 1969-70, prof. surgery, 1981—; asst. surg. resident John Hopkins Hosp., 1967; fellow plastic and reconstructive surgery U. Pitts., 1970-72; chief plastic surgery West L.A. VA Med. Ctr., 1973—; prof., chief plastic and reconstructive surgery UCLA Sch. Medicine, 2002—. Author: (novel) Practice to Deceive, 1991; assoc. editor Jour. Plastic & Reconstructive Surgery, 1987-93, co-editor, 1994—. Trustee Children's Inst. Internat., 1995-2000. Capt. U.S. Army, 1964-66, Vietnam. Decorated Bronze Star; recipient Thomas Symington award Pitts. Acad. Medicine, 1971. Mem. Am. Soc. for Plastic Surgery (co-editor Jour. Plastic and Reconstructive Surgery), Am. Soc. for Aesthetic Plastic Surgery (bd. dirs. 1990-95), Plastic Surgery Ednl. Found. (bd. dirs. 1991-95), Phi Beta Kappa. Office: UCLA Med Ctr 200 Ucla Medical Plz Ste 465 Los Angeles CA 90095-8344 Office Phone: 310-825-5644.

**MILLER, TONYA ALICIA,** training and development specialist; b. Newark, Sept. 16, 1970; d. Mike Joe and Janette Miller. BA, Hampton U., 1992; MS, Old Dominion U., 1994, PhD, 1999. Assoc. mgr. AT&T, Morristown, NJ, 1996—97; prof./instr. Old Dominion U., Norfolk, Va., 1997—2000; human resources and developement specialist Gen. Electric, Atlanta, 2000—02; S.E. regional tng. and devel. specialist ADT/Tyco Fire & Security, Norcross, Ga., 2002—04; human resources mgr. Tyco Fire & Security, 2004—. Orgnl. devel. specialist Sentara Health Systems, Norfolk, 1995—96; bus. devel. specialist Gen. Electric, Richmond, Va., 1997—98; orgnl. devel. specialist City of Norfolk, 1998—2000; spkr./presenter in field. Chairperson United Way, Morristown, 1996—97; mentor Delta Sigma Theta, Norfolk, 1997—2000; big sister Big Sister Program, Norfolk, 1998—2000; campaign fellow City of Norfolk, 1999—2000. Named one of 30 leaders of the Future, Ebony Mag., 2001; Am. Doctoral Rsch. Assistantship, Old Dominion U., 1992—95, 1999, Commonwealth of Va. fellow, State of Va., 1995—97, One Yr. Dissertation fellow, So. Regional Ednl. Bd., 1998—99. Mem.: Soc. for Indsl. and Orgnl. Psychology (assoc.), Alpa Kappa Mu, Psi Chi (sec. 1991—92), Beta Kappa

Chi, Delta Sigma Theta. Achievements include research in work-life role integration. Office: Tyco Fire & Security One Town Ctr Rd Boca Raton FL 33468 Personal E-mail: tam1929@aol.com.

**MILLER, TRACY LYNN,** medical office administrator; d. David Gene and Nancy Louise Miller. Cert. in Med. Assisting, Jefferson Cmty. Coll., Steubenville, Ohio, 1995; AS, Franciscan U. of Steubenville, Ohio, 2004, BS in Bus. Mgmt., 2005. CMA Am. Assn. Med. Assts. Ohio, 1996. Med. asst. Med. Group Assoc., Steubenville, Ohio, 1995—2001, Riverside Med. Ohio, Steubenville, 2001, office mgr., 2001—. Adj. instr. Jefferson Cmty. Coll., Steubenville, Ohio, 2005—, adv. bd. med. asst. program, 2005—. Mem. bd. dir. Charity Hospice, Steubenville, Ohio, 2005—. Recipient Nat. Leadership award, US Congress, 2004. Mem.: Am. Assn. Med. Assts., Ohio State Soc. Med. Assts. (dist. councilor, bd. trustees 2000—), Ohio Valley Chpt. Med. Assts.

**MILLER, VALERIE CAROL,** journalist; b. Chgo. d. V. Heinz and Arlene Elizabeth Miller. A in Gen. Studies, C.C. So. Nev.; BA Comms., U. Nev., 1998. Travel coord. Great Escape Travel, Las Vegas, 1996—97; staff writer, reporter U. Nev. Las Vegas Rebel Yell Students Newspaper, 1997—98; travel coord. World Travel and Accessories, Las Vegas, 1998—2000; reporter, freelance writer, intern Las Vegas Sun Newspaper, 1998—2000; broadcaster, disk jockey Sta. KLAV AM 1230, Las Vegas, 1997—; reporter, staff writer Las Vegas Bus. Press Newspaper, 2000—; staff writer Las Vegas Sr. Press. Host radio show Valerie's Music Magic. Vol. Shade Tree Shelter, Las Vegas, 2002; vol. writer Nev. Times Newspaper, Las Vegas, 1995, 1997. Nominee Journalist of Merit award, Nev. Press Assn., 2002, 2003, Small Bus. Journalist of Yr., Nev. Small Bus. Adminstrn., 2003; recipient Best Feature Story award third prize, Nev. Press Assn., 2001, Small Bus. Journalist of Yr. award for Nev., U.S. Small Bus. Assn., 2002, Merit award for news writing, Internat. Assn. Bus. Comm., 2003, Merit award for series writing, 2003, 2005, Best Bus. Story award, Nev. Press. Assn., 2002, 2004. Fellow: Soc. for the Advanced Placement of Materials, Working in Comms., Soc. Profl. Journalists, 3rd Wave Nev., Tortois Group; mem.: Phi Lambda Eta. Avocations: travel, writing poems and song lyrics, movies. Office: Las Vegas Bus Press 1385 Pama Ln Ste 111 Las Vegas NV 89119 Office Phone: 702-871-6780 ext. 331. Personal E-mail: millerv52@hotmail.com. Business E-mail: vmiller@lvpress.com.

**MILLER, VELVET G.,** health science association administrator; b. Reading, Pa., Aug. 16, 1945; d. Louis L. and Pattee J. Miller; m. Calvin E. Davis, Sept. 14, 1991; 1 child, Toby L. C. BSN, Wagner Coll., 1967; MEd, Temple U., 1976; MPA, Harvard U., 1984; PhD, Boston U., 1997. RN. Assoc. commr. Mass. Dept. Pub. Welfare, Boston, 1988-89, Mass. Dept. Health, Boston, 1989-91; v.p. Wagner Coll., S.I., 1991-92; Medicaid dir. N.J. Dept. Human Svcs., Trenton, 1994-96, dep. commr., 1996-98; exec. dir. Children's Futures N.J., Princeton, 1998-99; ptnr. Davis Miller Group, Trenton, 1991—; pres., CEO Horizon/Mercy, Trenton, 2001—02, My Parent's Concierge, 1999—. Mem. adv. bd. Urban Inst., Washington, 1996—2004, Finding Common Ground, Columbia U., N.Y.C., 1997—2003. Co-author: (book) Renegotiating Healthcare, 1995 (ANA CPR inst. award, 1995, 1996); contbr. articles and reports to profl. jours. Bd. dirs. Families USA, Washington, 1993—99. Recipient Pub. Svc. award, N.J. Pub. Policy Rsch. Inst., 1998, Carballo award for excellence in pub. svc., Commonwealth of Mass., 1988. Fellow: Am. Acad. Nursing; mem.: ANA, APHA. Democrat. Presbyterian. Home and Office: 219 Cornwall Ave Trenton NJ 08618-3321 E-mail: vmiller8529@comcast.net.

**MILLER, VERNE WILLIAM,** computer engineer, consultant; b. Chgo., Mar. 22, 1953; s. Fritz Henry and Dorothy Ruth Miller. BS Computer Engring. cum laude, DeVry U., 2005. Registered: State of Ill. (Police Officer) 1983, lic.: Glock, Inc. (Glock Armorer & Instr.) 1996; cert. CPR instr. ARC, 1995, emergency first aid instr. ARC, 1995, lic. emergency rescue technician State of Ill., 1987, controlled Substance Class I and II State of Ill., 1989. Mech. engr. Sheldons Mfg. Corp., Elgin, Ill., 1973—76; law enforcement officer Chgo. Union Sta. R.R. Police, 1982—87, Amtrak Police Dept., Chgo., 1987—2001; cons., rschr. LETCON, Harwood Heights, Ill., 1990—. Cons. U.S. Dept. Justice, Office Justice Stats., Washington, 1990—94; adv. bd. mem. Nat. Tactical Officers Assn., 1992—94; cons., trainer Midwest Tactical Tng. Inst., Freeport, Ill., 1989—91. Author: (book) Police Identification Guide to Street Gangs: Volumes I & II; contbr. articles to profl. jours. Spkr. - anti-drug edn. Bartlett Sr. Citizens Groups, Ill., 1989—91. Mem.: IEEE, NRA (life), Clan Kincaid Scottish Heritage Soc., Ill. State Rifle Assn., Law Enforcement Alliance Am., North Am. Hunting Club (life), Alpha Chi, Tau Alpha Pi (Nu Beta chpt. v.p. 2003—04, Nu Delta chpt. pres. 2004—05). Republican. Lutheran, Mo. Synod. Avocations: photography, writing. Home: 5654 W Gunnison St Chicago IL 6060-3216 E-mail: vernemiller@sbcglobal.net.

**MILLER, W. KIEVIT,** writer; b. Bklyn., Mar. 5, 1950; d. Walter Benedict Miller and Gladys Christina Marie Swadba; children: Cove Kievit, Brook Kievit. BA in Environ. studies, Fla. Internat. U., Tamiami, 1984; D candidate in natural health, Clayton Coll. Dist. coord. Broward Soil and Water Conservation Dist., Davie, Fla., 1985; tchr. Mus. of Discovery and Sci., Fort Lauderdale, Fla., 1984, 1993; head guide Seminole Tribe of Fla., Big Cypress Reservation, 1999; founder, CEO BIOKIND Tours, LLC, Venus, Fla., 2000—. Author: (book) BIOKIND Rhetoric for a New Paradigm, A Field Guide to the Future, 2000, BIOKIND Tracks, Traces of & Whispers for (and from) the Soul, 2003, The BIOKIND Body, A Naturapathic Approach to Health and Fitness, 2005. Capt. USCG. Scholar, Audubon Soc., 1984, Art of Living Found., 1996. Office Phone: 863-531-0093. Business E-Mail: biokindtours@biokind.

**MILLER, WALKER DAVID,** judge; m. Susanne Hauk, 3 children. LLB, U. Colo., 1963; M in Comparative Law, U. Chgo., 1965. Bar: Colo. 1963, U.S. Dist. Ct. 1965, U.S. Ct. Appeals 1971, U.S. Supreme Ct. 1970. Asst. prof. Sch. Law, U. Kans., Lawrence, 1966-69; ptnr. Miller & Ruyle, Greeley, Colo., 1969, Miller, Ruyle, Steinmark & Shade, Greeley, 1970-74; solo practice, Greeley, Colo., 1974-92; ptnr. Karowsky, Witwer, Miller and Oldenburg, Greeley, 1992-96; judge U.S. Dist. Ct. Colo., Denver, 1996—. Office: US Dist Ct Colo 901 19th St Rm A938 Denver CO 80294-1929 Office Phone: 303-844-2468. E-mail: walker_d_miller@cod.uscourts.gov.

**MILLER, WALTER JAMES,** retired literature educator, writer; b. McKee City, NJ, Jan. 16, 1918; s. Walter Theodore and Celestia Anna (Simmons) Miller; m. Mary T. Hume; children: Naomi, Jason, Robin, Jared, Elizabeth. BA, CUNY, 1941; MA, Columbia U., 1952. Instr. English Poly. Inst. Bklyn., 1946—53, asst. prof., 1953—55; asst. prof. English and modern langs. Colo. State U., Ft. Collins, 1955—56; assoc. prof. English NYU, 1956—66, prof. English, 1966—84, prof. emeritus, 1984—. Dir. Summer Writers Conf. Hofstra U., Hempstead, NY, 1972—79, NYU, NYC, 1983—85. Author: Engineers as Writers, 1953, Making an Angel; Poems, 1977, 1001 Ideas for English Papers, 1994, Love's Handmaid: New and Selected Poems, 2001, Joseph in the Pit: A Verse Drama, 2002; author, translator: Annotated Jules Verne, 1995; editor, translator: Verne's 20,000 Leagues Under the Sea, 1993, The Meteor Hunt, 2006; contbg. editor Simon and Schuster, 1969-97. Recipient Spl. award, Engrs. Coun. Profl. Devel., 1966, Charles Angoff award, The Lit. Rev., 1983, Gt. Tchr. award, NYU Alumni Assn., 1980, Fisher Second Harvest award, CUNY Alumni Assn., 1997; fellow, Ruttenberg Found., 1999—2006. Business E-Mail: wjm2@nyu.edu.

**MILLER, WALTER LUTHER,** pediatrician, educator; b. Alexandria, Va., Feb. 21, 1944; s. Luther Samuel and Beryl (Rinderle) M. SB, MIT, 1965; MD, Duke U., 1970. Diplomate Am. Bd. Pediatrics. Intern, then resident Mass. Gen. Hosp., Boston, 1970-72; staff assoc. NIH, Bethesda, Md., 1972-74; sr. resident U. Calif., San Francisco, 1974-75, rsch. fellow, 1975-78, asst. prof. pediatrics, 1978-83, assoc. prof., 1983-87, prof., 1987—, dir. Child Health Rsch. Ctr., 1992—2003, faculty biomed. scis. grad. program, 1982—, faculty genetics grad. program, 1998—, dir. pediat. endocrinology tng. program,

1994—, chief divsn. endocrinology, 2000—, assoc. prof. metabolic rsch. unit, 1983-87, prof., 1987—. Bd. scientific counselors Nat. Inst. of Child Health & Human Devel., 2004—. Editor DNA and Cell Biology Jour., 1983—; mem. editl. bds. numerous sci. jours.; contbr. articles to profl. jours., chpts. to books. Del. Dem. Nat. Conv., N.Y.C., 1976. Served with USPHS, 1972-74. Recipient Nat. Rsch. Svc. award NIH, 1975, Clin. Investigator award, 1978, Albion O Bernstein award NY Med. Soc., 1993, Clin. Endocrinology Trust medal Brit. Endocrine Soc., 1993, Henning Andersen prize European Soc. Pediatric Endocrinology, 1993, Samuel Rosenthal Found. prize for excellence in acad. pediatrics, 1999. Fellow: AAAS, Molecular Medicine Soc.; mem.: Androgen Excess Soc. (founding mem., bd. dirs. 2002—05), Am. Soc. Biochem. Molecular Biology, Lawson Wilkins Pediat. Endocrine Soc. (edn. com. 1992—96, coun. 1995—96, corp. adv. bd. 1998—2002, program dirs. com. 2004—), Am. Soc. Clin. Investigation, Am. Soc. Human Genetics, Endocrine Soc. (fin. com. 1999—2002, annual meeting steering com. 2005—, Edwin B. Astwood lecture award 1988, Clin. Investigator Lectr. award 2006), European Soc. for Paediatric Endocrinology (hon.), Japanese Soc. for Pediat. Endocrinology (hon.), We. Soc. Pediat. Rsch. (Ross Rsch. award 1982), Soc. Pediat. Rsch., Am. Pediat. Soc., Am. Acad. Pediats., Assn. Am. Physicians, Am. Soc. for Microbiology, Theta Delta Chi. Achievements include patents in field; published in over 300 publs. Office: U Calif Med Ctr Dept Pediat Rm 672 S San Francisco CA 94143-0978

**MILLER, WALTER NEAL,** insurance company consultant; b. N.Y.C., Nov. 26, 1929; s. Morton and Kathryn (Gersten) M.; m. Nancy Louise Clapp, Sept. 11, 1954; children— Scott, Timothy, David, Kathryn Wallace, Amy Tully. BA, Swarthmore Coll., 1951. With N.Y. Life Ins. Co., N.Y.C., 1951-86; sr. v.p., actuary Prudential Ins. Co., Newark, 1986-93; sr. v.p., chief actuary Prudential Preferred Fin. Svcs., Liberty Corner, NJ, 1993-94; pvt. practice cons., 1994—. Author: (with others) Analysis of Actuarial Theory for Variable Life Insurance, 1969; contbr. articles to profl. jours. Mem. Soc. Actuaries (bd. dirs.), Am. Acad. Actuaries (bd. dirs., v.p.), Actuarial Stds. Bd. (chmn.), Estuary Coun. Srs. (pres. bd. dirs.). Home: 48 Eagle Ridge Dr Essex CT 06426-1370 Personal E-mail: walterm746@aol.com.

**MILLER, WARREN LLOYD,** lawyer; b. Bklyn., July 18, 1944; m. Jana Morris, May 1978. BA with high honor, Am. U., 1966; JD with honors, George Washington U., 1969. Bar: Va., 1969, DC, 1969, various US Dist. Cts., US Ct. Appeals (various US cirs.), US Supreme Ct., 1981. Law clk. to Hon. Edward A. Beard Superior Ct. D.C., 1968-69; asst. U.S. atty. for D.C., 1969-74; ptnr. Stein, Miller & Brodsky, 1974-85; pres. Warren L. Miller, P.C., 1986—; of counsel Smith, Shaw & McClay, 1986-93. Lectr. Am. U., 1972-73, mem. adv. coun. Sch. Pub. Affairs, 2004—; mem. Jud. Conf. DC Cir., 1984—; pres. Asst. US Attys. Assn. DC, 1983-84; spkr. in field. Contbr. articles to profl. jours. Parliamentarian credentials and rules coms. Rep. Nat. Conv., 1984; mem. D.C. Law Revision Commn., 1987-91 (apptd. by Pres. Reagan), mem. U.S. Common Preservation Am.'s Heritage Abroad, 1992— (apptd. by Pres. Bush, reapptd. by Pres. Clinton 1996, 99), now chmn. (apptd. by Pres. Bush), 2001—; bd. dirs. Found. for Buchenwald and Mittelbau-Dora Memls., 1994—; spkr. ceremonies commemorating 50th anniversary of liberation of Buchenwald Concentration Camp, Buchenwald, Germany, 1995, Ceremony Dedicating Little Camp Meml., Buchenwald, Germany, 2002; spkr. U.S. Holocaust Meml. Mus., 1995, 02; fundraiser for Rep. Nat. Com. and Pres. Bush, 1988 92; co-chmn. dinner for V.P. Bush, 1988; vice-chmn. Pres.'s Dinner, 1989; co-chmn. Pres.'s Club, Washington, 1990-92; chmn. fundraiser for U.S. Senator Christopher Bond, 1992, 97, 03; chmn. fundraiser U.S. Senator John Warner, 1996; vice-chmn., fundraiser Senator Bob Dole, 1996; co-chmn., fundraiser Gov. George W. Bush Presdl. Exploratory Com., 1999, honoring Pres. George W. Bush, 2003; mem. host com., fundraiser for Gov. George W. Bush, 2000, U.S. Sen. John Warner, 2001, Gov. Jeb Bush, 2002, v.p. Dick Cheney, 2003; co-leader U.S. Del. to Internat. Conf., Warsaw, Poland, 2002 (apptd. by. Sec. State Colin Powell); mem. adv. bd. Am. U. Sch. Pub. Affairs, 2004—. Decorated Order of Three Stars Pres. of Latvia, comdr.'s cross Order of Merit Poland, Order of Morning Star Pres. Croatia. Mem. Congl. Country Club (Bethesda, Md.), Phi Delta Phi, Omicron Delta Kappa, Pi Gamma Mu. Achievements include negotiating and concluding bi-lateral agreements with the following governments: Bosnia and Herzegovina, Latvia, Lithuania, Bulgaria, Macedonia, Estonia, Czech Republic, Germany, Austria, Hungary, Poland, Armenia, Albania, Serbia and Croatia. Office Fax: 703-848-1841.

**MILLER, WENTWORTH,** actor; b. Chipping Norton, Eng., June 2, 1972; BA, Princeton U. Actor: (films) Romeo and Juliet, 2000, Room 302, 2001, The Human Stain, 2003, Underworld, 2003, (voice) Stealth, 2005.; (TV miniseries) Dinotopia, 2002; (TV series) Prison Break, 2005—.*

**MILLER, WILBUR HOBART,** retired management consultant; b. Boston, Feb. 15, 1915; s. Silas Reuben and Muriel Mae (Greene) Miller; m. Harriett I. Harmon, June 20, 1941; children: Nancy Iber Miller Harray, Warren Harmon, Donna Sewall Miller Davidge. BS, U. N.H., 1936, MS, 1938; PhD, Columbia U., 1941. Rsch. chemist Am. Cyanamid Co., Stamford, Conn. 1941—49, Washington tech. rep., 1949—53, dir. food industry devel., 1953—57, tech. dir. products for agr. Cyanamid Internat. N.Y.C., 1957—60; sr. scientist Dunlap & Assocs., Darien, Conn., 1960—63; sr. assoc. Dunlap & AssoCs., Darien, 1963—66; coord. new product devel. Celanese Corp., N.Y.C., 1966—67, mgr. comml. rsch., 1967—68, dir. corp. devel., 1969—84; ret., 1984. Lectr. bus. and soc. Western Conn. State Coll., 1977—79; pres.'s coun. U. NH, 1982—; internat. fellow U. Bridgeport, 1985—88; cons. in field. Contbr. scientific papers to profl. jours.; patentee in field. Chmn. Stamford Forum World Affairs, 1954—87, hon. chmn., 1987—; adv. bd Ctr Study Presidency 1980 90, 1st dir. Stamford Symphony, 1974—80, v.p., 1978—80; bd. dirs. Stamford Hist. Soc., 1988, v.p., 1991—92, pres., 1993—95; bd. dirs. Coun. Continuing Edn., Stamford, 1960—70, pres., 1963; bd. dirs. Stamford Sr. Ctr., 1991—, vice chmn., 2002—03, chmn., 2003—04, trustee, 2005—; elder United Presbyn. Ch., nominating com., 1960—63; pres. Interfaith Coun. Stamford, 1973. Recipient Am. Design award, 1948, Outstanding Achievement award, Coll. Tech., U. N.H., 1971, Golden Rule award, J.C. Penney & Co., 1986; Univ. Fellow, Columbia U., 1940—41. Fellow: AAAS, Am. Inst. Chemists (councillor N.Y. chpt. 1984—85); mem.: Am. Acad. Polit. and Social Scis., Soc. Internat. Devel., Inst. Food Tech., Société de Chimie Industrielle (v.p. fin. Am. sect. 1980—84, bd. dirs. 1984—, chmn. com. 1997—), N.Y. Acad. Scis., Am. Chem. Soc. (news svc. adv. bd. 1948—53), Chemists Club (treas. 1982—84), Sigma Xi, Phi Kappa Phi, Alpha Chi Sigma. Home: 122 Palmers Hill Rd #1111 Stamford CT 06902-2134

**MILLER, WILBUR RANDOLPH,** academic administrator; b. Elsberry, Mo., Nov. 12, 1932; s. Charles Clifton and Pauline Jean (Dryden) M. Student, SE Mo. U., 1951-53; BEd, U. Mo., 1954, MEd, 1955, EdD, 1960. Cert. secondary tchr., Mo. Tchr. indsl. arts Hazelwood Sch. Dist., St. Louis, 1955-56, U. Lab. Sch., Columbia, Mo., 1956-60; indsl. tchr. educator Purdue U., West Lafayette, Ind., 1960-63; asst. prof. U. Mo., Columbia, 1963-67, assoc. prof. and chmn. dept. coll. edn., 1967-76, prof. and assoc. dean coll. edn., 1976-86, dean coll. edn., 1986-91, prof., dean emeritus, 1992; cons. Rep. of Turkey, 1993, 94; assoc. v.p. for devel. Auburn U., 1996—. Chmn. adv. coun. Fed. Rsch. Ctr. in Vocat. Edn., Ohio State U., Columbus, 1981-84; internat. edn. cons. 1992—; edn. adv. bd. DeVry Inc., Oakwood Terrace, Ill., 1986—; mem. pvt. post-sec. tech. sch. accreditation commn. Accrediting Commn. Career Schs. and Colls. Tech., 1994-98. Author: Teaching Children Through Construction Activities, 1985, Instructors and Their Jobs, 1998, 2d edit., 2002, The Golf Primer, 1991, Handbook for College Teaching, 1997, 2d edit., 2003; editor: (series) Basic Industrial Arts, 1978; contbr. more than 94 articles to profl. jours. Pres., bd. dirs. Lenoir Inc., Columbia, 1977-84; mem. Woodhaven Sch. Bd., Columbia, 1982-83. With USNR, 1955-63. Recipient U. Mo. Faculty/Alumni award 1985. Mem. Nat. Assn. Indsl. Tchr. Educators (pres., officer 1965-74), Am. Indsl. Arts Assn. (v.p. 1980), Mo. Vocat. Assn. (pres. 1974-75), Mo. Assn. Colls. for Tchr. Edn. (pres. 1987-90), Am. Vocat.

Assn. (Outstanding Svc. award 1979), U. Mo. Faculty Club (officer 1977-82), Kiwanis. Mem. Christian Ch. (Disciples Of Christ). Avocations: golf, travel, home maintenance. Office: PO Box 2683 Auburn AL 36831-2683 Office Phone: 334-844-1139.

**MILLER, WILLIAM ALVIN,** clergyman, author, lecturer; b. Pitts., Jan. 1, 1931; s. Christ William and Anna Ernestine (Wilhelm) M.; m. Marilyn Mae Miller, Aug. 8, 1953; children: Mark William, Eric Michael. BA, Capital U., 1953; MDiv, Luth. Theol. Sem., Columbus, Ohio, 1957; MST, Andover Newton Theol. Sch., Newton Centre, Mass., 1958, D of Ministry, 1974. Ordained to ministry Luth. Ch.; lic. marriage & family therapist, Minn.; cert. chaplain Assn. of Profl. Chaplains. Pastor St. James Luth. Ch., Balt., 1958—66; chaplain Fairview Hosp., Mpls., 1966—73, dir. dept. religion & health, 1973—87; instr. Fairview Sch. Nursing, Mpls., 1967—75, Luther Northwestern Theol. Sem., St. Paul, 1973—85; pres. Woodland Pub. Co., Wayzata, Minn., 1979—2000; dir. Woodland Pastoral Assocs., Mpls., 1987—96; assoc. pastor Ctrl. Luth. Ch., Mpls., 1989—94. Chair bd. dirs. Luth. Social Svcs. Md., Balt., 1963-65; administr. Dialogue 88, Mpls., 1987-88; marriaage & family therapist emeritus, Minn. Author: Why Do Christians Break Down?, 1973, Big Kids' Mother Goose, 1976, When Going to Pieces Holds You Together, 1976, You Count, You Really Do!, 1976, Mid Life, New Life, 1978, Conversations, 1980, Make Friends With Your Shadow, 1981, Prayers at Mid Point, 1983, The Joy of Feeling Good, 1986, Your Golden Shadow, 1989, 91, Meeting the Shadow, 1991; assoc. editor Jour. Pastoral Care, Decatur, Ga., 1984-88, editl. cons., 1988—; contbr. articles to profl. jours. Chaplain, Jr. C. of C., Randallstown, Md., 1962-64; bd. dirs. Am. Protestant Health Assn., Schaumburg, Ill., 1983-89; clin. mem. Am. Assn. Marriage & Family Therapy, 1989-96, Minn. Assn. Marriage & Family Therapy, 1989-96. Fellow Coll. Chaplains (pres. 1985-87), Assn. Mental Health Clergy (Anton T. Boisen award 1989); mem. Assn. Clin. Pastoral Edn. (supr. emeritus 2000—), Am. Assn. Marriage and Family Therapy, Minn. Assn. Marriage and Family Therapy. Avocations: woodworking, publishing, construction. Home and Office: 2005 Xanthus Ln N Minneapolis MN 55447-2053

**MILLER, WILLIAM CHARLES,** theological educator; b. Mpls., Oct. 26, 1947; s. Robert Charles and Cleithra Mae (Johnson) M.; m. Brenda Kathleen Barnes, July 24, 1969; children: Amy Renee, Jared Charles. BA, Ind. Wesleyan U., 1968; MLS, Kent State U., 1974, PhD, 1983; postgrad., U. Kans., 1984; MA in Religious Studies, Ctrl. Bapt. Theol. Sem., 1988; MBA, MidAm. Nazarene U., 1997; STM, Nashotah House, 2001. Ordained to ministry Ch. of Nazarene, 1986. Libr. technician Kent State U., 1972—74; catalog libr. Mt. Vernon Nazarene Coll., Ohio, 1974—76, libr. catalog and acquisitions, 1976—78; dir. libr. svcs., prof. theol. bibliography Nazarene Theol. Sem., Kansas City, Mo., 1978—2005, dean adminstrn., 1996—98, 1999—2005; dir. accreditation Assn. Theol. Schs., Pitts., 2005—. Adj. rsch. assoc. U. Kans., 1984-85; adj. prof. MidAm. Nazarene U., Olathe, Kans., 1994-2000, Ind. Wesleyan U., 2005, Nazarene Theol. Sem., 2005—; bd. dirs. Small Libr. Computing Inc.; pres. Mo. Libr. Network Corp., St. Louis, Mo., 1998-2001. Author: Holiness Works: A Bibliography, 1986; editor TUG Newsletter, 1984-87, bd. dirs., 1985-88; editor Jour. Religious and Theol. Info., 1990-98. With U.S. Army, 1968-72. Mem. Assn. Study Higher Edn., Bibliog. Soc. Am., Am. Theol. Libr. Assn. (bd. dirs 1985-88), Wesleyan Theol. Soc., Eng. Record Soc., Beta Phi Mu. Home: 18290 W 155th Ter Olathe KS 66062-6718 Office: Assn Theol Schs 10 Summit Park Dr Pittsburgh PA 15275-1103 Office Phone: 412-788-6505. Business E-mail: miller@ats.edu.

**MILLER, WILLIAM CHARLES,** lawyer; b. Jacksonville, Fla., Aug. 6, 1937; s. Charles and Mary Elizabeth (Kiger) M.; m. Hadmut Gisela Larsen, June 10, 1961; children: Monica Lee, Charles Andreas. BA, Washington and Lee U., 1958, LLB, 1961; LLM, NYU, 1963; postgrad., Harvard U., 1978. Bar: Fla. 1961, Calif. 1984, Ind. 1987, U.S. Supreme Ct. 1968. Counsel to electrochem., elastomers and internat. depts. E.I. duPont de Nemours & Co., Wilmington, Del., 1963-66; counsel S. Am. ops. Bristol-Myers Co., N.Y.C., 1967-69; internat. counsel Xerox Corp., Stamford, Conn., 1969-79, assoc. gen. counsel, 1979-80; v.p., gen. counsel, sec. Max Factor & Co., Hollywood, Calif., 1981-85, Boehringer Mannheim Corp. (now Roche Diagnostics), Indpls., 1985-92; v.p., gen. counsel Collagen Corp., Palo Alto, Calif., 1992-95, GenProbe Inc., San Diego, 1995-96, Safeskin Corp., San Diego, 1996-98; exec. v.p. Lipomatrix Inc., Neuchatel, Switzerland, 1998-99; gen. counsel Turbostar Comm. Corp., 2000—02, exec. v.p., gen counsel, 2002—03; exec. v.p., dir. gen. counsel Aesthetic and Reconstructive Techs., Inc., 2002—. Bd. dirs. Southwestern Legal Found., 1975-85. Fulbright scholar, 1959-60; Ford Found. fellow, 1961-62; Hague Acad. fellow, 1963; German Govt. grantee, 1962-63; Kappa Sigma scholar, 1959. Mem. Internat. Bar Assn., ABA, Calif. Bar Assn., Fla. Bar Assn., Ind. Bar Assn., Masons, Elks, Phi Beta Kappa, Phi Eta Sigma, Delta Theta Phi. Republican. Mem. Christian Ch. Home: 4521 Randag Dr North Fort Myers FL 33903-4731 Personal E-mail: wcmesq@comcast.net.

**MILLER, WILLIAM CHARLES,** academic administrator, retired naval officer; b. LA, Dec. 1, 1940; s. John Benjamine and Marianne Georgette (Lyons) M.; m. Barbara Jean Leach, June 8, 1962; children: Linda, William, Julie, James, Marianne. BS, U.S. Naval Acad., 1962; MSEE, Stanford U., 1965, PhDEE, 1967. Commd. ensign USN, 1962, advanced through grades to rear adm.; instr. elec. engring. U.S. Naval Acad., Annapolis, Md., 1975-76, exec. asst. to supt., 1976-79; comdg. officer USS Cushing (DD-985), 1979-81; exec. asst. Office Asst. Sec. Navy, Washington, 1981-83; program mgr. Office Naval Tech., Washington, 1983-86; comdg. officer Naval Rsch. Lab., Washington, 1986-87; dir. ofc. Office Chief Naval Ops., Washington, 1987-90; chief naval rsch. Dept. Navy, Washington, 1990—93; assoc. provost W.Va. Univ., 1993—97; exec. dir., vice chmn. W.Va. Univ. Rsch. Corp., 1993—97; associate dean U.S. Naval Acad., Annapolis, 1997—. Dir. Joint Counter Low Observables Office, Washington, 1989-90; keynote speaker 18ty Internat. Symposium on Naval Hydrodynamics, 1990. Decorated Legion of Merit with 3 oak leaf clusters. Mem. IEEE (keynote speaker Ocean Engring. Systems symposium OCEANS 1990, Internat. Conf. on Naval Networks 1991). Roman Catholic. Avocations: fishing, boating. Office: US Naval Academy Office of Academic Dean 121 Blake Rd Annapolis MD 21402-5000

**MILLER, WILLIAM CHARLES,** architect, educator; b. San Francisco, May 11, 1945; s. Francis Leland and Ethel Lorene (Britt) M.; m. Beverly Jean McConnell, Dec. 22, 1968; children: Britt A., David A. BArch, U. Oreg., 1968; MArch, U. Ill., 1970. Cert. arch. Nat. Coun. Archtl. Registration Bds., Ariz., Kans., Utah. Asst. prof. Coll. Architecture U. Ariz., Tucson, 1970—77; asst. prof. architecture Kans. State U., Manhattan, 1977-86, prof., 1986-92, head dept., 1990-92; prof. Coll. of Architecture and Planning U. Utah, Salt Lake City, 1992—, dean, 1992—2002; architect various firms. Guest lectr. in field; presenter numerous profl. socs. and orgns.; dir. west ctrl. region Assn. Collegiate Schs. Architecture, 1988-91, chair theme paper sessions ann. meeting, San Francisco, 1990, chair regional paper sessions ann. meeting, Washington, 1991, co-chair adminstrv. conf., Milw., 1995; bd. dirs. Nat. Archtl. Accrediting Bd., 1996-99; mem. Utah Architects Lic. Bd., 2000—; chair edn. com. NCARB, 2005—; vis. disting. prof. U. Ill., Urbana Champaign, 2003. Author: Alvar Aalto: An Annotated Bibliography, 1984; co-editor: The Architecture of the In-Between, 1990, Architecture: Back to Life, 1991; contbr. over 60 articles to profl. jours., chpts. to books. Bd. Assist. Inc., 1992-2002, Artspace, Inc., 1997-2002, Contemporary Arts Group, 1992-96, Salt Lake City Art Design Bd., 1995-2003. Recipient Disting. Prof. award Collegiate Schs. Architecture, 2004, Svc. awards Nat. Coun. Archtl. Registration Bds., Nat. Archtl. Accrediting Bd. Fellow AIA (pres-elect Flint Hills, treas. Utah, exec. com., treas., exec. com. Western Mountain region, elected coll. of fellows 1997); mem. Am.-Scandinavian Found., Soc. for Advancement Scandinavian Studies, Tau Sigma Delta. Office: U Utah Coll Architecture & Planning Salt Lake City UT 84112 Office Phone: 801-581-8254. Business E-Mail: miller@arch.utah.edu.

**MILLER, WILLIAM FREDERICK,** research and development company executive, educator, financial consultant; b. Vincennes, Ind., Nov. 19, 1925; s. William and Elsie M. (Everts) M.; m. Patty J. Smith, June 19, 1949; 1 son, Rodney Wayne. Student, Vincennes U., 1946-47; BS, Purdue U., 1949, MS, 1951, PhD, 1956; DSc (hon.), 1972. Mem. staff Argonne Nat. Lab., 1955-64, assoc. physicist, 1956-59, dir. applied math. div., 1959-64; prof. computer sci. Stanford U., Palo Alto, Calif., 1965-97, Herbert Hoover prof. pub. and pvt. mgmt. emeritus, 1997—, assoc. provost for computing, 1968-70, v.p. for rsch., 1970-71, v.p., provost, 1971-78; mem. Stanford Assocs., 1972—; pres emeritus., CEO SRI Internat., Menlo Park, Calif., 1979-90; chmn. bd., CEO SRI Devel. Co., Menlo Park, David Sarnoff Rsch. Ctr., Inc., Princeton, NJ, 1987—90. Chmn. emeritus bd. dirs. Borland Software, Sentius Corp.; founder, chmn. Nanostellar, Inc.; professorial lectr. applied math. U. Chgo., 1962-64; vis. prof. math. Purdue U., 1962-63; vis. scholar Ctr. for Advanced Study in Behavioral Scis., 1976; mem. adv. coun. BHP Internat., 1990-97; computer sci. and engring bd. NAS, 1968-71; mem. Nat. Sci. Bd., 1982-88; corp. com. computers in edn. Brown UU., 1971-79; mem. policy bd. EDUCOM Planning Coun. on Computing in Edn., 1974-79, chmn., 1974-76; mem. ednl. adv. bd. Guggenheim Meml. Found., 1976-80; com. postdoctoral and doctoral rsch. staff NRC, 1977-80, computer sci. and telecom.; dir. Fund Am., 1977-91, Fireman's Fund Ins., 1977-91, Wells Fargo Bank and Co., 1996-97, Varian Assocs. Inc., 1973-96. Mem. editl. bd. Pattern Recognition Jour, 1968-72, Jour. Computational Physics, 1970-74. Served to 2d lt. F.A. AUS, 1943-46. Recipient Frederic B. Whitman award United Way Bay Area, 1982, Sarnoff Founders medal, 1997, David Packard Civic Entrepreneurship Team award, 1998, Robert K. Jaedicke Silver Apple award Stanford U. Bus. Sch. Alumni, 1998, The Dongbaeg medal Order of Civil Merit, The Rep. of Korea, 2000, The Okawa prize, The Okawa Found. for Info. and Telecoms., 2000, Most Mentor award Internat. Angel Investors, 2002; named to Silicon Valley Engring. Hall of Fame, 2001, Jr. Achievement Bus. Hall of Fame, 2002. Fellow IEEE (life), Am. Acad. Arts and Scis., AAAS; mem. Soc. Indsl. and Applied Math., Assn. Computing Machinery, Nat. Acad. Engring., Sigma Xi, Tau Beta Pi (Eminent Engr. 1989). Office: Stanford U Grad Sch Bus Stanford CA 94305

**MILLER, WILLIAM GREEN,** former ambassador; b. NYC, Aug. 15, 1931; m. Suzanne Lisle; 2 children. BA, MA, Oxford U., U.K.; postgrad., Harvard U. Tutor Winthrop House Harvard U., 1956-59; with Fgn. Svc., 1959; vice consul, polit. officer Isfahan, Iran, 1959-62; polit. officer Tehran, Iran, 1962-64; line officer, exec. secretariat Dept. of State, 1965-66; mem. Sr. Interdepartmental Group, 1966-67; spl. asst. fgn. affairs and def. Senator John Sherman Cooper, 1967-73; staff dir. Senate Select Com. Emergency Powers, 1973-75, Senate Select Com. to Study Govtl. Ops. with Respect to Intelligence Communities, 1975-76, Senate Select Com. Intelligence, 1976-81; assoc. dean, adj. prof. internat. politics Fletcher Sch. Law and Diplomacy, 1981-83, rsch. assoc., 1983-85; faculty assoc. Harvard Ctr. Middle Eastern Studies, 1983-86; pres. Am. Com. U.S.- Soviet Rels., 1986-92; U.S. amb. to Ukraine, 1993-98. Cons. D.H. Sawyer and Assocs., Ltd., N.Y.C., 1985; bd. dirs. Internat. Found., pres. 1986-92; pres. Com. Am.- Russian Rels., cons. Catherine T. MacArthur Found., 1992-93. Contbr. articles to profl. jours. Bd. mem. UN Assn., 2002—; co-chmn. bd. Myiv-Mohyla U. Found., 2002—; bd. dirs. The Andrei Sakharov Found., 1998—, Inst. Soc. Action and Renewal in Eurasia, 1998—; bd. mem. US - Ukraine Found., 2002—. Rsch. fellow Harvard Ctr. Sci. and Internat. Affairs, 1984-86, John F. Kennedy Sch. of Govt. fellow Harvard U., 1986. Fellow Rsch. Inst. of Politics; mem. Nat. Acad. Pub. Diplomacy, Nat. Acad. Pub. Adminstrn., Internat. Inst. Strategic Studies, Coun. Fgn. Rels., Children of the 21st Century, Middle East Inst., Soc. Iranian Studies, Search for Common Ground. Office: Woodrow Wilson Internat Ctr Scholars 1 Woodrow Wilson Plaza 1300 Pennsylvania Ave NW Washington DC 20004-3002 Office Phone: 202-691-4000. Business E-Mail: wmiller@igc.org.

**MILLER, WILLIAM HUGHES,** theoretical chemist, educator; b. Kosciusko, Miss., Mar. 16, 1941; s. Weldon Howard and Jewel Irene (Hughes) M.; m. Margaret Ann Westbrook, June 4, 1966; children: Alison Leslie, Emily Sinclaire. BS, Ga. Inst. Tech., 1963; AM, Harvard U., 1964, PhD, 1967. Jr. fellow Harvard U., 1967-69; NATO postdoctoral fellow Freiburg (Germany) U., 1967-68; asst. prof. chemistry U. Calif., Berkeley, 1969-72, assoc. prof., 1972-74, prof., 1974—, dept. chmn. 1989-93, chancellor's prof., 1998—, Kenneth S. Pitzer disting. prof., 1999—. Fellow Churchill Coll., Cambridge (Eng.) U., 1975-76; hon. prof. Shandong U., People's Republic of China, 1994. Alfred P. Sloan fellow, 1970-72; Camille and Henry Dreyfus fellow, 1973-78; Guggenheim fellow, 1975-76, Christensen fellow St. Catherine's Coll., Oxford, 1993; recipient Alexander von Humboldt-Stiftung U.S. Sr. Scientist award, 1981-82, Ernest Orlando Lawrence Meml. award, 1985, Hirschfelder prize in theoretical chemistry, U. Wis., 1996, Alumni Achievement award Ga. Inst. Tech., 1997, Spiers medal Faraday divsn. Royal Soc. Chemistry, London, 1998. Fellow AAAS, Am. Acad. Arts and Scis., Am. Phys. Soc. (Irving Langmuir award 1990); mem. NAS, Am. Chem. Soc. (Theoretical Chemistry award 1994, Ira Remsen award 1997, Peter Debye award 2003), Internat. Acad. Quantum Molecular Sci. (Ann. prize 1974). Office: U Calif Dept Chemistry Berkeley CA 94720-0001

**MILLER, WILLIAM IAN,** legal educator; b. 1946; BA, U. Wis., 1969, M of Philosophy, 1973, PhD, 1975; JD, Yale U., 1980. Assoc. prof. U. Houston, 1981-85; prof. U. Mich. Law Sch., Ann Arbor, 1984—, Thomas G. Long Prof. Law. Vis. assoc. prof. U. Mich., Ann Arbor, 1984-85; vis. prof. Yale U., fall 1988. Author: Bloodtaking and Peacemaking: Feud, Law, and Society in Saga Iceland, 1990, Humiliation, 1993, The Anatomy of Disgust, 1997, The Mystery of Courage, 2000, Faking It, 2003, An Eye for an Eye, 2006. Mem. Law and Soc. Assn., Am. Soc. Legal History, Am. Hist. Assn. Office: U Mich Law Sch 411 Hutchins Hall 625 S State St Ann Arbor MI 48109-1215 Office Phone: 734-763-9014. Office Fax: 734-763-9375. E-mail: wimiller@umich.edu.*

**MILLER, WILLIAM IRWIN,** finance company executive; b. Columbus, Ind., Apr. 30, 1956; s. Joseph Irwin and Xenia Ruth (Simons) M.; m. Lynne Marie Maguire, Oct. 29, 1983; children: Katherine Maguire, Laura Marie, Emily Elizabeth. BA, Yale U., 1978; MBA, Stanford U., 1981. Sect. mgr. Cummins Engine Co., Inc., Charleston, SC, 1978-79; assoc. Warburg Pincus Capital Corp., N.Y.C., 1981-83; pres. Irwin Mgmt. Co., Inc., Columbus, 1984-90, also bd. dirs.; chmn. Irwin Fin. Corp., Columbus, 1990—. Chmn. Irwin Mgmt. Co. and Tipton Lakes Co., Columbus, 1984—; bd. dirs. Cummins Inc., Irwin-Sweeney-Miller Found., Columbus, New Perspective Fund, L.A., New World Fund, LA. Trustee The Taft Sch., Watertown, Conn., 1979-2006, Christian Theol. Sem., Indpls., 1988-94, Europacific Growth Fund, L.A., 1992—, Yale U., New Haven, 2005—; bd. dirs. Cummins Found., Columbus, Ind., 1989—, Irwin Fin. Found., Columbus, 1991—, Tennant Co., 1993-2005, The Heritage Fund of Bartholomew County, Columbus, 1998—, John D. and Catherine T. MacArthur Found., 2005—; mem. overseers com. Yale U., New Haven, 1995-99, 2000—; mem. Ctrl. Ind. Corp. Partnership, Indpls., 1999—, Nat. Bldg. Mus., 2001—. Office: Irwin Fin Corp 500 Washington St PO Box 929 Columbus IN 47202-0929

**MILLER, WILLIAM LEE, JR.,** minister; b. Mammoth Spring, Ark., Dec. 27, 1926; s. William L. and Janie Katherine (Murrell) M.; m. Marion Evelyn O'Neal, Mar. 23, 1947 (div. 1976); children: Georgia Katherine Miller Beach, William Lee III; m. Judith Ann Bell, Nov. 28, 1977 (dec. July 1997); m. Delores Bryan, Dec. 27, 1998. AB, Phillips U., 1950, LittD, 1968; postgrad., U. Ark., 1951-52, Tex. Christian U., 1958, U. Ky., 1961; BD, Lexington Theol. Sem., 1961, MDiv, 1997. Ordained to ministry Christian Ch. (Disciples of Christ), 1950. Pastor 1st Christian Ch., Rogers, Ark., 1952-59, Rogers Heights Christian Ch., Tulsa, 1961-62; v.p. Bd. Higher Edn., Indpls., 1962-68; pres. Bd. Higher Edn. Christian Ch. (Disciples Of Christ), 1968-77; v.p. devel. Nat. City Christian Ch. Corp., Washington, 1977-82; upper Midwest regional min., pres. Christian Ch. (Disciples Of Christ), Des Moines, 1982-93; pres. Miller Devel. Assoc. Dir. Christian Ch. Found., Indpls., 1968-77, 84-93; trustee Bethany Coll., W.Va., 1972-85, Culver Stockton Coll., 1970-77, 82-94, Tougaloo Coll., Jackson, Miss., 1970-76, Christian Theol. Sem., Indpls., 1987-94. Author: Vision with Passion, A Church history

of the Christian Church (Disciples of Christ), 2004. Precinct committeeman Dem. Party, Indpls., 1968-72; mem. Reagan First Inaugural Religious Com.; bd. dris. St. Louis Christian Home, 1956-59; chmn. Coop. Coll. Registry, Washington, 1963-70; mem. Disciples of Christ Ch., Disciples Soc. for Faith & Reason; bd. dirs., exec. com. Christian Ch. D.C., N.C., 1995-98; pres. Friends of Dare County (N.C.) Librs., 1997-99; v.p. North Dare County Ministerial Assn., 1998-99. Mem. Disciples of Christ Hist. Soc., Coun. Christian Unity (exec. com. 1968-77), Nat. Evangelitic Assn. (bd. dirs. 1983-86), Am. Assn. Higher Edn., Masons, KT, NAACP, Sigma Chi, Am. Legion, Interfaith Alliance, Amnesty Internat., Sierra Club. Mem. Christian Ch. (Disciples Of Christ). Home and Office: Miller Devel Assocs 1710 W Long Blvd Raymore MO 64083-9116 Office Phone: 816-331-5790.

**MILLER, WILLIAM NAPIER CRIPPS,** lawyer; b. Long Branch, NJ, June 7, 1930; adopted s. Julia (Erwin) M.; m. Carolyn Anderson, Jan. 19, 1951 (div. 1963); children: Bruce Douglass, Jennifer Erwin; m. Hannelore Steinbeck, Dec. 4, 1970 AA. Coll. Marin, 1949; student, U. Calif.-Berkeley, 1949-51, JD, 1955. Bar: N.Y., Calif. 1956, U.S. Supreme Ct. 1983. Assoc. Mudge, Stern, Baldwin & Todd, N.Y.C., 1955-58, Pillsbury, Madison & Sutro, San Francisco, 1959-65; ptnr. Pillsbury, Winthrop Shaw Pittman LLP, San Francisco, 1966—; staff NYU Law Sch., 1957-58; ct. adv. com. Calif. State Assembly Judiciary Com., 1979-80. Author: Long Pig, 2002. Bd. dirs. Laguna Honda Hosp., San Francisco, 1966—; bd. visitors U. Calif.-Hastings Law Sch. Served with USAF, 1951-52. Recipient Bur. Nat. Affairs award U. Calif.-Hastings, 1955; recipient Thurston Soc. award, 1953. Fellow Am. Coll. Trial Lawyers; mem. ABA, San Francisco Bar Assn., Order of Coif, St. Francis Yacht Club. Home: 16 George Ln Sausalito CA 94965-1890 Office: Pillsbury Winthrop Shaw Pittman LLP PO Box 7880 San Francisco CA 94120-7880 Office Phone: 415-983-1464. Business E-Mail: william.miller@pillsburylaw.com.

**MILLER, WILLIAM NAPIER CRIPPS,** lawyer; b. Red Bank, NJ, June 7, 1930; LLB, Univ. Calif., Hastings, 1955. Bar: Calif. 1956, NY 1956, US Supreme Ct. Sr. ptnr. Litigation practice Pillsbury Winthrop Shaw Pittman, San Francisco. Co-author (& co-editor): Trial of a Criminal Antitrust Case; author: Long Pig: A Fantasy Concerning Cannibals, Courts and Other Consumers, 2003 (Best Fiction/Humor award, Bay Area Independent Publishers, 2003). Served USAF, 1950—52. Fellow: Am. Coll. Trial Lawyers; mem.: ABA, Calif. Bar Assn., San Francisco Bar Assn. Office: Pillsbury Winthrop Shaw Pittman 50 Fremont St San Francisco CA 94105 Office Phone: 415-983-1464. Office Fax: 415-983-1200. Business E-Mail: william.miller@pillsburylaw.com.

**MILLER, WILLIAM RICHEY, JR.,** lawyer; b. Oklahoma City, Apr. 4, 1947; s. William Richey and Edna Rosalind (Nielsen) M.; m. Susan Hammond, Aug. 2, 1970; children: Brooke, Karen. BA, Pomona Coll., Claremont, Calif., 1969; MA, Claremont Grad. Sch., 1972; JD, Lewis and Clark Coll., 1975. Bar: Oreg. 1975, U.S. Dist. Ct. Oreg. 1976, U.S. Ct. Appeals (9th cir.) 1976. Staff atty. Oreg. Ct. Appeals, Salem, 1975-76; with firm Griffith, Bittner, Abbott & Roberts, Portland, Oreg., 1976-83; ptnr. Davis Wright Termaine, Portland, 1983—. Adj. prof. Lewis and Clark Law Sch., 1975-78. Bd. dirs. Portland Civic Theatre, 1988-91, Am. Lung Assn. Oreg., Portland, 1985-88, Oreg. Bus. Com. for the Arts, Portland, 1991-93. Mem. Oreg. State Bar (sect. chair 1990-91), Comml. Fin. Assn., Oreg. Bankers Assn., Lewis and Clark Alumni Assn. (bd. dirs. 1989-92). Presbyterian. Home: 843 Lakeshore Rd Lake Oswego OR 97034-3704 Office: Davis Wright Tremaine 1300 SW 5th Ave Ste 2300 Portland OR 97201-5682 Office Phone: 503-778-5304.

**MILLER, WILMA HILDRUTH,** education educator; b. Dixon, Ill., Mar. 8, 1936; d. William Alexander and Ruth Karin (Hanson) M. BS in Edn., No. Ill. U., DeKalb, 1958, MS in Edn., 1961; DEd, U Ariz., 1967. Cert. reading specialist. Elem. tchr. Dist. 170, Dixon, Ill., 1958-63, Dist. 1, Tucson, Ariz., 1963-64; asst. prof. edn. Wis. State U., Whitewater, 1965-68; assoc. prof. edn. Ill. State U., Normal, 1968-72, prof., 1972-98, prof. emeritus, 1998—. Author: Diagnosing and Correcting Reading Difficulties in Children, 1988, Reading Comprehension, 1990, Complete Reading Disabilities Handbook, 1993, Alternative Assessment Techniques in Reading and Writing, 1995, Reading and Writing Remediation Kit, 1997, The Reading Teacher's Survival Kit, 2001, Reading Skills Problem Solver, 2002, Survival Reading Skills for Secondary School Students, 2003, 101 Ways for Developing Emergent Literacy, 2004, others; contbr. over 225 articles to profl. jours. Altar Guild, usher, greeter, communion asst. Our Saviour Luth. Ch., Normal, 1990—. Recipient Outstanding Contbn. to Edn. award No. Ill. U., 1998. Mem. Internat. Reading Assn. (parent and reading com. 1972-74, editl. adv. bd. 1995-98, Outstanding Dissertation award 1968), Mid-State Reading Coun. (editl. adv. bd. 1991-98), Alpha Upsilon Alpha (advisor Reading chpt. 1993-98), Pi Lambda Theta, Kappa Delta Pi, Phi Delta Kappa. Avocations: travel, writing, reading, antiques. Home: 302 N Coolidge St Normal IL 61761-2435 Personal E-mail: whmille@ilstu.edu.

**MILLER, YOLANDA,** publisher, writer; b. Chicago Heights, Ill., Aug. 5, 1957; m. Andrew Miller, Apr. 2, 1983. BS cum laude, U. Wis., Stout, 1978; MS in Rehab. Counseling, U. Wis., Milw., 1984. Pub. Victory Publs., Racine, Wis., 1996—. Author: (poetry) Ode to Precious, Priceless and Irreplaceable African-American Men, 1996. Avocation: reading. Home: 2526 Delaware Ave Racine WI 53403-3432

**MILLER, ZELL BRYAN,** former senator, former governor; b. Young Harris, Ga., Feb. 24, 1932; s. Stephen Grady and Birdie (Bryan) M.; m. Shirley Carver, Jan. 14, 1954; children: Murphy Carver, Matthew Stephen. Student, Young Harris Coll., 1951; AB in History, U. Ga., 1957, MA in History, 1958. Dir. Ga. Bd. Probation, 1965-66; dep. dir. Ga. Dept. Corrections, 1967-68; exec. sec. to Gov., 1968-71; mem. State Bd. Pardons and Paroles, Atlanta, 1973-75; lt. gov. State of Ga., 1975-90, gov., 1990-98; prof. polit. sci. and history U. Ga., 1999; U.S. senator from Ga., 2000—05; sr. advisor McKenna Long & Aldridge LLP, Atlanta, 2005—. Prof. Young Harris Coll., 1959-64, Emory U., Young Harris Coll., U. Ga.; bd. dirs. various corps., including Overseas Pvt. Investment Corp. (OPIC), Ga. Power, Gray Comms., Ezgov.com, Post Properties, Kollmann USA; keynote speaker Democratic Nat. Convention, NYC, 1992, Republican Nat. Convention, NYC, 2004; retired Jan. 2005; commr., Am. Battle Monuments Commn., 2005-, part-time commentator, Fox News Channel, 2005-. Author: The Mountains Within Me, 1985, Great Georgians, 1983, They Heard Georgia Singing, 1996, Corps Values: Everything You Need to Know I Learned in the Marines, 1996, Listen to this Voice: Selected Speeches of Governor Zell Miller, 1998, A National Party No More: The Conscience of a Conservative Democrat, 2003, Deficit of Decency, 2005. Mem. Ga. Senate, 1960-64; mayor Young Harris, 1959; exec. dir. Democratic Com. Ga., 1971-72; pres. Coun. State Govts., 1991; vice chmn. So. Gov.'s Assn., 1991; So. States County Dem. Authority. Served with USMC, 1953-56. Mem. Ga. Sch. Food Services Assn. (life), Ga. Peace Officers Assn. (life), Gridiron Soc. U. Ga., Blue Key, Lions Club. Democrat. Meth. Office: McKenna Long & Aldridge LLP 303 Peachtree St NE Ste 5300 Atlanta GA 30308 also: Am Battle Monuments Commn 2300 Clarendon Blvd Ste 500 Arlington VA 22201

**MILLER, ZOYA DICKINS,** civic worker, consultant; b. Washington, July 15, 1923; d. Randolph and Zoya Pavlovna (Klementinovska) Dickins; m. Hilliard Eve Miller, Jr., Dec. 6, 1943; children: Jeffrey Arnot, Hilliard Eve III. Grad., Stuart Sch. Costume Design, Washington, 1942; student, Cochran Galleries of Fine Arts, 1942, Sophie Newcomb Coll., 1944, New Eng. Conservatory Music, 1946, Colo. Coll., 1965; grad., Internat. Sch. Reading, 1969; student, Cochran Galleries of Fine Arts, 1942. Lic. pvt. pilot. Instr. Stuart Summer Sch. Costume Design, Washington, 1942; fashion coord. Julius Garfinckel, Washington, 1942-43; fashion coord., cons. Mademoiselle mag., 1942-44; star TV show Cowbelle Kitchen, 1957-58, Flair for Living, 1958-59; model mags. and comml. films, also nat. comml. recs., 1956-80; dir. rsch. devel. Webb-Waring Inst. Cancer, Aging and Antioxidant Rsch., Denver, 1973—2006, devel. cons., 2006—. Contbr. articles, lectrs. on health care sys. and fund raising. Mem. exec. com., bd. dirs. El Paso County chpt. Am. Lung

Assn. Colo., 1965—84, bd. dirs., 1965—87, chmn. radio and TV coun., 1963—70, mem. med. affairs com., 1965—70, pres., 1965—66, procurer found. funds, 1965—70; developer nat. radio ednl. prodns. for internat. use Am. Lung Assn., 1963—70, coord. statewide pulmonary screening programs Colo., other states, 1965—72; chmn. benefit fund raising El Paso County Cancer Soc., 1963; co-founder, coord. Colorado Springs Debutante Ball, 1967—; coord. Nat. Gov.'s Comprehensive Health Planning Coun., 1967—74, chmn., 1971—72, Colo. Chronic Care Com., 1969—73, chmn. fund raising, 1970—72, chmn. spl. com. conl. studies on nat. health bills, 1971—73; mem. Colo.-Wyo. Regional Med. Program Adv. Coun., 1969—73, Colo. Med. Found. Consumers Adv. Coun., 1972—78; mem. decorative arts com. Colorado Springs Fine Arts Ctr., 1972—75; founder, state coord. Nov. Noel Pediat. Benefit Am. Lung Assn., 1973—87; founder, chmn. bd. dirs. Newborn Hope, Inc., 1987—; mem. adv. bd. Wagon Wheel Girl Scouts, 1991—94; mem. cmty. adv. coun. Beth-El Nursing Sch., 1998—; chmn. Colo. Festival World Theatre Gala, 2005; gala chmn. Colorado Festival World Theatre, 2005; maj. donor devel. dir. Meml. Health Sys., Colorado Springs, 2006—; bd. dirs. Episcopal Columbarium Assn., 2001, The Family Attachment Ctr., Inc., Meml. Hosp. Found., Colo. Springs, Colo., 2004; hon. bd. mem. KCME 88.7 FM, Colorado Springs, Colo., 2004; gala chmn. Colo. Festival of World Theatre, 2005; maj. donor devel. dir. Meml. Health Sys., Colo. Springs, 2006—. Zoya Dickins Miller Vol. of Yr. award established Am. Lung Assn. of Colo., 1979; recipient James J. Waring award Colo. Conf. on Respiratory Disease Workers, 1963, Nat. Pub. Rels. award Am. Lung Assn., 1979, Gold Double Bar Cross award, 1980, 83, Jefferson award Am. Inst. Pub. Svc., 1991, Thousand Points of Light award The White House, 1992, Recognition award So. Colo. Women's C. of C., 1994, Silver Spur Cmty. award Pikes Peak Range Riders, 1994, Silver Bell award Assistance League Colorado Springs, 1996, Svc. to Mankind award Centennial Sertoma Club, 1997, Help Can't Wait award Pikes Peak chpt. ARC, 1997, Cmty. Weaver award The Independent News, 1997, Apgar award Colo. March of Dimes, 1998; named Humanitarian of Yr., Am. Lung Assn. of Colo., 1987, El Pomar Found. award for Excellence, Russell Tutt Leadership award, 2004. Mem.: Nat. Soc. Fund Raising Execs., Denver Round Table for Planned Giving, Colo. Assn. Fund Raisers, Nat. Soc. Colonial Dames, The Family Attachment Ctr., Nat. Cowbell Assn. (El Paso county pres. 1954, TV chmn., chmn. nat. Father of Yr. contest Colo. 1956—57), Broadmoor Garden Club, Garden of the Gods Club, Cheyenne Mountain Country Club. Home: 74 W Cheyenne Mountain Blvd Colorado Springs CO 80906-4336 E-mail: hope4455@adelphia.net.

**MILLER-ENGEL, MARJORIE,** foundation administrator, commissioner, small business owner; d. David Harry Siegel and Ruth Joan Gord; m. Robert Alan Engel, May 4, 1984; 1 child, Liana Laura Engel. BA, Syracuse U.; cert. in interior design, N.Y. Sch. Interior Design. Assoc. dir. devel. Planned Parenthood Fedn., N.Y.C.; account exec. Harold Oram Consulting, N.Y.C.; pres., owner Marjorie Miller Pub. Rels., N.Y.C.; founder, chmn. Life Ctr. Youth, Inc., Santa Fe, 1982—; pres., owner M. M. Designs, Inc., Santa Fe, 1989—. Co-owner Greenkey Property Investments, Santa Fe, 1989—. Commr. N.Mex Commn. Status Women, 2003—. Mem.: Intl. Women's Forum. Office: Life Ctr Youth Inc PO Box 8718 2725 Agua Fria St Santa Fe NM 87504

**MILLER-LANE, BARBARA See LANE, BARBARA**

**MILLER-LERMAN, LINDSEY,** state supreme court justice; b. L.A., July 30, 1947; BA, Wellesley Coll., 1968; JD, Columbia U., 1973; LHD (hon.), Coll. of St. Mary, Omaha, 1993. Bar: N.Y. 1974, U.S. Dist. Ct. (so. dist.) N.Y. 1974, U.S. Appeals (2d cir.) 1974, Nebr. 1976, U.S. Dist. Ct. (ea. dist.) N.Y. 1975, U.S. Dist. Ct. Nebr. 1976, U.S. Appeals (8th cir.) 1979, U.S. Supreme Ct. 1982, U.S. Ct. Appeals (6th cir.) 1984, U.S. Ct. Appeals (10th cir.) 1987. Law clk. U.S. Dist. Ct., N.Y.C., 1973-75; from assoc. to ptnr. Kutak Rock, Omaha, 1975-92; judge Nebr. Ct. Appeals, Lincoln, 1992-98, chief judge, 1996-98; justice Nebr. Supreme Ct., 1998—. Contbr. articles to profl. jours. Bd. dirs. Tuesday Musical, Omaha, 1985—. Office: Nebr Supreme Ct State Capitol Rm 2222 Lincoln NE 68509 Office Phone: 402-471-3734.

**MILLER UDELL, BRONWYN,** judge; b. Danbury, Conn., Aug. 7, 1972; BA, Barnard Coll., Columbia U., 1994; JD, U. Miami, 1997. Bar: (Fla.) 1997. Asst. state atty. State of Fla., Miami, 1997—2005; judge Dade County, 2005—. Adj. faculty Fla. Internat. U., 2001—02; mem. Witness Justice Adv. Bd. Mem. Cmtys. in Schs. Miami Mentoring Program, Coral Gables Sr. H.S. Parent Tchr. Assn.; co-chair Expert Corps. Vol. Mem.: League of Prosecutors (bd. dir.), Fla. Assn. Women Lawyers, Fla. Pros. Attys. Assn., Federalist Soc. Lawyer's Divsn., Elephant Forum, Fla. Dist. Phi. Office: South Dade Justice Ctr 10710 SW 211th St Miami FL 33189 Office Phone: 305-252-5840.

**MILLETT, STEPHEN MALCOLM,** futurist, consultant, historian; b. N.Y.C., Feb. 22, 1947; s. John David and Catherine (Letsinger) M.; m. Sherry Richards, Sept. 2, 1989; children: Jennifer Ann, Ann E. AB, Miami U., Oxford, Ohio, 1969; MA, Ohio State U., 1970, PhD, 1972. Rschr. Battelle, Columbus, Ohio, 1979—2006, Futurist Sound Technologies, 2006—. Mgr. tech. forecasts incl. Strategic Technologies 2005 and 2020 and Energy Innovations 2010. Author: Manager's Guide to Technology Forecasting, 1991, Scottish Settlers of America, 1996; pub. and editor U.S. Scots, 1992-97. Mem. at large State Bd. Edn. Ohio, 2003—. Capt. USAF, 1973—79. Mem. World Futures Soc., Assn. of Profl. Futurists (founding mem.), Phi Delta Theta. Avocations: scottish history and culture, antiques. Home: 3673 Tillbury Ave Columbus OH 43220-5068 Office: Battelle 505 King Ave Columbus OH 43201-2693 E-mail: milletts@battelle.org.

**MILLGATE, MICHAEL (MICHAEL HENRY MILLGATE),** retired literature educator; b. Southampton, Eng., July 19, 1929; arrived in Can., 1964; s. Stanley and Marjorie Louisa Millgate; m. Jane Barr, Feb. 27, 1960. BA, Cambridge U., 1952, MA, 1956; postgrad., U. Mich., Ann Arbor, 1956-57; PhD, U. Leeds, 1960. Tutor Workers' Ednl. Assn., Eng., 1953-56; lectr. English lit. U. Leeds, 1958-64; prof., chmn. dept. English York U., Ont., Can., 1964-67; prof. English U. Toronto, 67-94, univ. prof., 87-94, univ. prof. emeritus, 1994—. Carpenter lectr. Ohio Wesleyan U., 1978; vis. scholar Meiji U., 1985. Author: William Faulkner, 1961, American Social Fiction, 1964, The Achievement of William Faulkner, 1966, Thomas Hardy: His Career as a Novelist, 1971, Thomas Hardy: A Biography, 1982, Testamentary Acts: Browning, Tennyson, James, Hardy, 1992, Faulkner's Place, 1997, Thomas Hardy: A Biography Revisited, 2004; editor: Tennyson: Selected Poems, 1963, Thomas Hardy: The Life and Work of Thomas Hardy, 1985, William Faulkner Manuscripts, 20 (4 vols.), 21 (2 vols.), 22 (4 vols.), 23 (2 vols.), 1986, New Essays on Light in August, 1987, Thomas Hardy: Selected Letters, 1990, Letters of Emma and Florence Hardy, 1996, Thomas Hardy's Public Voice, 2001; co-editor: Transatlantic Dialogue, 1966, Lion in the Garden, 1968, The Collected Letters of Thomas Hardy, Vol. I, 1978, Vol. II, 1980, Vol. III, 1982, Vol. IV, 1984, Vol. V, 1985, Vol. VI, 1987, Vol. VII, 1988, Thomas Hardy's Studies, Specimens, Etc. Notebook, 1994. Mem. ednl. adv. bd. John Guggenheim Meml. Found., 1994—2005. Can. Coun. leave fellow, 1968-69, S.W. Brooks fellow U. Queensland, 1971; Killam sr. rsch. scholar, 1974-75; John Simon Guggenheim Meml. fellow, 1977-78, Connaught sr. fellow, 1979-80; Social Sci. and Humanities Rsch. Coun. Can. leave fellow, 1981-82, grantee, 1977—; Can. Coun. grantee, 1973-77; Killam rsch. fellow, 1986-88. Fellow Royal Soc. Lit., Royal Soc. Can. (Pierre Chauveau medal 1999); mem. MLA (adv. com. Ctr. for Edit. Am. Authors 1971-74, com. on scholarly edits. 1985-89), Victorian Studies Assn. Ont. (pres. 1972), Thomas Hardy Soc. (v.p. 1973—), Tennyson Soc. Home: 1 Balmoral Ave Apt 809 Toronto ON Canada M4V 3B9 E-mail: michael.millgate@utoronto.ca.

**MILLHAUSER, STEVEN,** writer; b. N.Y.C., Aug. 3, 1943; BA, Columbia Coll., 1965; postgrad., Brown U., 1968-71. Vis. assoc. prof. English Williams Coll., 1986—88; assoc. prof. Skidmore Coll., Saratoga Springs, NY, 1988—92, prof. English, 1992—. Author: Edwin Mullhouse: The Life and Death of an American Writer, 1972, Portrait of a Romatic, 1977, In the Penny Arcade, 1985, From the Realm of Morpheus, 1986, The Barnum Museum,

1991, Little Kingdoms, 1993, Martin Dressler: The Tale of an American Dreamer, 1996, The Knife Thrower and Other Short Stories, 1998, Enchanted Night, 1999; contbr. short stories to periodicals. Recipient Pulitzer Prize for fiction, 1997. Office: Skidmore Coll Dept English 307 Palamountain Bldg Saratoga Springs NY 12866

**MILLIAN, JOHN C.,** lawyer; b. Jan. 30, 1958; BA in Econ., Univ. Calif., Berkeley, 1980; JD, Yale Univ., 1983. Bar: Wash. 1984, Calif. 1987, DC 1988. Law clk. Judge Gerhard A Gesell US Dist. Ct., Washington, 1983—84; ptnr. litig. dept. Gibson Dunn & Crutcher LLP, Washington, 1991—, former ptnr.-in-charge DC office. Pro bono atty. Wesley Theol. Sem.; bd. dir Wesley Sem. Found.; mem. exec. com. Gibson Dunn & Crutcher. Mem.: ABA, Coun. for Ct. Excellence (bd. dir.). Office: Gibson Dunn & Crutcher LLP 1050 Connecticut Ave NW Washington DC 20036 Office Phone: 202-955-8213. Business E-Mail: jmillian@gibsondunn.com

**MILLICHAP, JOSEPH GORDON,** neurologist, educator; b. Wellington, Eng., Dec. 18, 1918; came to U.S., 1956, naturalized, 1965; s. Joseph P. and Alice (Flello) M.; m. Mary Irene Fortey, Feb. 25, 1946 (dec. Oct. 1969); children: Martin Gordon, Paul Anthony; m. Nancy Melanie Kluczynski, Nov. 7, 1970 (dec. Apr. 1995); children: Gordon Thomas, John Joseph. MB Surgery honors, St. Bartholomew's Med. Coll., U. London, 1946, MD Internal Medicine, 1951, diploma child health, 1948. Diplomate Am. Bd. Pediat., Am. Bd. Neurology and Child Neurology, Am. Bd. Electroencephalography. Intern. resident St. Bartholomew's Hosp., 1946—49, Hosp. Sick Children, London, 1951—53, Mass. Gen. Hosp., Boston, 1958—60; pediat. neurologist NIH, 1955—56; USPHS fellow neurology Mass. Gen. Hosp., Boston, 1958—60; cons. pediat. neurology Mayo Clinic, 1960—63; pediat. neurologist Children's Meml. Hosp., Northwestern Med. Ctr., Chgo., 1963—; prof. neurology and pediat. Northwestern U. Med. Sch., 1963—. Cons. surgeon gen. USPHS; mem. med. adv. bds. Ill. Epilepsy League, Muscular Dystrophy Found., Cerebral Palsy Found., 1963—; vis. prof. Gt. Ormond St. Hosp., U. London, 1986-87 Author: Febrile Convulsions, 1967, Pediatric Neurology, 1967, Learning Disabilities, 1974, The Hyperactive Child with MBD, 1975, Nutrition, Diet and Behavior, 1985, Dyslexia, 1986, Progress in Pediatric Neurology, 1991, Vol. II, 1994, Vol. III, 1997, Environmental Poisons in Our Food, 1993, A Guide to Drinking Water, Hazards and Health Risks, 1995, Attention Deficit Hyperactivity and Learning Disorders, 1998, (with G.T. Millichap) The School in a Garden, 2000; editor Jour. Pediatric Neurology Briefs; contbr. articles to profl. jours., chpts. to books Chmn. rsch. com. med. adv. bd. Epilepsy Found., 1965—. Served with RAF, 1949-51 Named New Citizen of Year in Met. Chgo., 1965; recipient Americanism Medal DAR, 1972, Brennemann award Chgo. Pediat. Soc., 1998; USPHS rsch. grantee, 1957 Fellow Royal Coll. Physicians; mem. AMA, Am. Neurol. Assn., Am. Pediat. Soc., Am. Soc. Pediat. Rsch., Am. Acad. Neurology, Am. Soc. Pharmacology and Exptl. Therapeautics, Soc. Exptl. Biology and Medicine, Am. Bd. Psychiatry and Neurology (asst. examiner 1961—) Episcopalian. Office: Children's Meml Hosp Box 51 2300 N Childrens Plz Chicago IL 60614-3394

**MILLIEN, RAYMOND,** lawyer; b. Bklyn. m. Tiffani Millien; children: Spencer, Katherine. BS, Columbia U., 1972; JD, George Washington U. Bar: Va. 1997, NY, DC, registered: U.S. Patent and Trademark Office, bar: Ill. Software design engr. Gen. Electric; with Sterne, Kessler, Goldstein, & Fox PLLC, 1997—2001, DLA Piper Rudnick Gray Cary, 2001—04; v.p, group IP counsel Am. Express Co., 2004—06; gen. counsel Ocean Tomo LLC, 2006—. Nat. lectr. BAR/BRI Patent Bar Rev. course; lectr. IP law George Washington U. Co-author: (books) From Finals to the Firm: Top Ten Things New Law Firm Associates Should Know, 2003, Little Blues: How to Build a Culture of Intellectual Property within a Small Technology Company, 2006. Office: Ocean Tomo, LLC 200 W Madison 37th Fl Chicago IL 60606-3414 Office Phone: 312-327-4407. Office Fax: 312-327-4401. E-mail: rmillien@oceantomo.com.

**MILLIGAN, CYNTHIA HARDIN,** dean, lawyer; BA, U. Kans., 1967; JD, George Washington U., 1970. Bar: D.C. 1970, Nebr. 1977. Assoc. Arent, Fox, Kintnor, Plotkin & Kahn, Washington, 1970-77; ptnr. Rembolt, Ludtke, Milligan & Berger, Lincoln, Nebr., 1977-87; div. Nebr. Dept. Banking and Fin., Lincoln, 1987-91; pres. CMA, Lincoln, 1991-98; dean U. Nebr. Coll. Bus. Adminstrn., Lincoln, 1998—. Bd. dirs. Wells Fargo & Co., San Francisco, Gallup Orgn., Princeton, N.J., Calvert Funds, Bethesda, Md. Trustee, bd. chmn. W.K. Kellogg Found., Battle Creek, Mich. Fellow Nebr. Bar Found.; mem. Nebr. Bar Assn. Office: U Nebr Coll Bus Adminstrn PO Box 880405 Lincoln NE 68588-0405*

**MILLIGAN, JOHN DRANE,** historian, educator; b. N.Y.C., Oct. 11, 1924; s. Carl Glover and Hazel Gray (Drane) M.; m. Joyce Mary Jervis, Nov. 16, 1946; children: Jacqueline M., Paula J., Mary M., Elizabeth Y. BA, U. Mich., 1952, MA, 1953, PhD, 1961. Tchg. asst. U. Mich., 1951-52, tchg. fellow, 1954-56; from asst. prof. to prof. history SUNY, Buffalo, 1962-2000, dir. grad. programs in history, 1963-68, 94-95, dir. undergrad. programs in history, 1979-86, acting dept. chmn., summers, 1977, 78-80, 88, prof. emeritus, 2000. Vis. prof. McMaster U., Hamilton, Ont., Can., summer 1964, 69-70 Author: Gunboats Down the Mississippi, 1965, From the Fresh-Water Navy, 1861-1864, 1970; also chpts. in books, articles in jours., encys. Mem. Ann Arbor chpt. NAACP, exec. bd., 1956-61; mem. ACLU, exec. bd., 1959-61; mem. campaign coms. for various candidates for local and nat. office, 1960-76; mem. Buffalo NAACP, Buffalo Housing Opportunities Made Equal, Citizens Council on Human Relations, Physicians for Social Responsibility, Common Cause, Amnesty Internat.; faculty chmn. United Fund dr., 1977; active Foster Parents Plan, 1955-70; adoptive parent Internat. Social Services; founder charitable trust for minority coll. scholarships. Served with USAAF, 1943-46, USAFR, 1946-56. James B. Angell scholar U. Mich.; grantee Research Found. SUNY; grantee U.S. Naval Inst.; Citation of Civil War Round Table, Moncado Award of Am. Mil. Inst. Mem.: Soc. Civil War Historians, Afro-Am. Hist. Soc., Buffalo and Erie County Hist. Soc., So. Hist. Assn., Assn. Am. Historians, Am. Hist. Assn., SUNY Buffalo Founders' Soc., Buffalo Coun. for Responsibility in Fgn. Policy, SUNY Buffalo Pres.'s Assocs., Civil War Round Table, Silver Wings Assn., Cambria Flying Soc., Niagara Soaring Club, Aircraft Owners and Pilots Assn., Soaring Soc. Am., Exptl. Aircraft Assn., Phi Alpha Theta, Phi Kappa Phi, Tau Sigma Delta. Home: 21 Allenhurst Rd Buffalo NY 14214-1201 *If an individual cannot influence for the better the course of humankind, one can sometimes influence for the better the life of another individual.*

**MILLIGAN, LAURA ANN KASSING,** director; d. Nemo Walter and Jacqueline Sue (Harper) Kassing; 1 child, Jaime Lynn Milligan Miller. AAS honors, Three Rivers C.C., Poplar Bluff, Mo., 1999; B in Applied Sci. cum laude, Mo. State U., 2001. Asst. dir. fin. aid Three Rivers CC, Poplar Bluff, 2002—04, dir. student housing, 2004—, dir. fin. aid, 2006. V.p. student govt. Three Rivers C.C., 1998—99. Named Outstanding Senator of Yr., Three Rivers CC, 1998—99; recipient Proclaimation, Mo. Ho. Reps., 2002, Nat. TRIO Day honors, TRIO, 2002; scholar, Claudia Found., Linda Bloodworth-Thomason, 1997—99, Mo. State U., 1999. Mem.: Mo. Coll. PA (assoc.), Mo. Assn. Student Fin. Aid Pers. (assoc.), Three Rivers C.C. Alumni Assn. (assoc.; treas. 2002—03), Mo. Pacific Women's Club (hon.), Nat. Residence Hall Hon. (life; exec. coun., chmn. edn. com. 2001), Epsilon Pi Tau (assoc.). Democrat. Avocations: travel, reading, photography, geocaching. Office: Three Rivers CC Rivers Ridge Apts 1998 Herschel Bess Blvd Poplar Bluff MO 63901 Office Phone: 573-840-9106. Office Fax: 573-840-9115. Business E-Mail: housing@trcc.edu.

**MILLIGAN, SISTER MARY,** theology studies educator, consultant; b. LA, Jan. 23, 1935; d. Bernard Joseph and Carolyn (Krebs) M. BA, Marymount Coll., 1956; Dr. de l'Univ., U. Paris, 1959; MA in Theology, St. Mary's Coll., Notre Dame, Ind., 1966; STD, Gregorian U., 1975; D. honoris causa, Marymount U., 1988. Tchr. Cours Marymount, Neuilly, France, 1956-59; asst. prof. Marymount Coll., Los Angeles, 1959-67; gen. councillor Religious of Sacred Heart of Mary, Rome, 1969-75, gen. superior, 1980-85; asst. prof. Loyola Marymount U., Los Angeles, 1977-78, provost, 1986-90, prof.,

1990—96, dean liberal arts, 1992-97, provincial superior, 1997—2003; prof. St. John's Sem., 2003—. Pres. bd. dirs. St. John's Sem., Camarillo, Calif., 1986-89; mem. exec. com. Internat. Union Superiors Gen., Rome, 1983-85; mem. planning bd. spiritual renewal program Loyola Marymount U., Los Angeles, 1976-78. Author: That They May Have Life, 1975; compiler analytical index Ways of Peace, 1986; contbr. articles to profl. jours. Vis. scholar Grad. Theol. Union, Berkeley, 1986. Mem. Coll. Theology Soc., Cath. Biblical Assn. Democrat. Roman Catholic. Business E-Mail: mmilligan@stjohnssem.edu.

**MILLIGAN, STEVE,** retail executive; BA in Acctg., The Ohio State U. CPA AICPA. Sr. mgr. Price Waterhouse; corp. asst. controller Dell Inc.; sr. v.p. Western Digital Corp., Lake Forest, Calif., 2002—, CFO, 2002—. Recipient Elijah Watt Sells award, 1985. Office: Western Digital Corp 20511 Lake Forest Dr Lake Forest CA 92630-7741

**MILLIGAN, VICTOR,** consulting engineer; b. Belfast, No. Ireland, Nov. 11, 1929; arrived in Can., 1956; s. Albert and Margaret (Walker) M.; m. Mary Ann Pelikan, July 20, 1955 (dec. 1988); children: Jeffrey, Michael; m. Audrey Morrow, Oct. 9, 1990 (dec. Oct 2003). BS, Queen's U., No. Ireland, 1951, MS, 1952, DSc (hon.), 1993; D Engring. (hon.), Waterloo U., Ont., Can., 1990. Registered profl. engr. Ont., Alta., Nfld. Asst. engr. James Williamson & Ptnrs., Glasgow, Scotland, 1952-54; rsch. fellow Purdue U., Lafayette, Ind., 1954-55; tech. officer Imperial Chem. Industries Ltd., Cheshire, England, 1955-56; from dist. to asst. chief engr. Geocon, Ltd., Toronto, Ont., Canada, 1956-60; prin. Golder Assocs., Toronto, 1960-74, pres., CEO, chmn., 1974-84, sr. prin., chmn., cons., 1984-94. Mem. faculty engring. sci. adv. com. U. Western Ont., 1973-76; adj. prof. dept. geol. engring. U. Toronto, 1980-83; pres. Consulting Engrs. Ont., 1982-83; chmn. assoc. com. on geotechnical rsch. NRC, 1984-89. Co-author: Stability in Open Pit Mining, 1971, Geotechnical Practice in Open Pit Mining, 1972; founding editor Can. Geotechnical Jour., 1963-68; contbr. over 50 sci. papers. King George VI Meml. Rsch. fellow 1954-55; recipient Engring. Excellence medal Assn. Profl. Engrs. Ont., 1988, Beaubien award Assn. Consulting Engrs. Canada Outstanding Excellence, 1997; fellow Can. Acad. Engring., 1994. Fellow ASCE, Instn. Civil Engrs. (hon.), Geol. Soc. Can., Engring. Inst. Can. (Julian C. Smith medal 1991, Sir John Kennedy medal, 2005), Royal Acad. Engring.; mem. Can. Geotech. Soc. (R.F. Legget award 1973), Internat. Soc. Soil Mechanics and Geotech. Engring.

**MILLIKAN, CLARK HAROLD,** physician; b. Freeport, Ill., Mar. 2, 1915; s. William Clarance and Louise (Chamberlain) M.; m. Gayle Margaret Gross, May 2, 1942 (div. Apr. 1966); children: Terri, Clark William, Jeffry Brent; m. Janet T. Holmes, July 21, 1966 (div. Dec. 1987); m. Nancy Futrell, Dec. 28, 1987. Student, Parsons Jr. Coll., Kans., 1935; MD, U. Kans., 1939. Diplomate Am. Bd. Psychiatry and Neurology. Intern St. Luke's Hosp., Clev., 1939-40, asst. resident medicine, 1940-41; from resident neurology to asst. prof. neurology State U. Iowa, Iowa City, 1941-49; staff Mayo Clinic, Rochester, Minn., 1949—, cons. neurology, 1958—; dir. Mayo Center for Clin. Rsch. in Cerebrovascular Disease; prof. neurology Mayo Sch. Medicine; physician-in-chief pro tem Cleve. Clinic, 1970; prof. neurology U. Utah Sch. Medicine, Salt Lake City, 1976-87, U. Miami (Fla.) Sch. Medicine, 1987-88; scholar in residence, dept. neurology Henry Ford Hosp., Detroit, 1988-92; prof. neurology Sch. of Medicine Creighton U., Omaha, 1992-94; clin. prof. neurology Med. Coll. Ohio, Toledo, 1994-97; dir. acad. affairs Intermountain Stroke Rsch. Found., Salt Lake City, 1997—. Asst. chmn., editor trans. 2d Princeton Conf. Cerebrovascular Disease, 1957, chmn. confs., 1961, 64; chmn. com. classification and nomenclature cerebrovascular disease USPHS, 1955-69; mem. council Nat. Inst. Neurologic Diseases and Blindness, NIH, USPHS, 1961-65, div. regional med. program, 1965-68; A.O.A. lectr. Baylor U., Waco, Tex., 1952; James Mawer Pearson Meml. lectr., Vancouver, B.C., Can., 1958; Conner Meml. lectr. Am. Heart Assn., 1961; Peter T. Bohan lectr. U. Kans., 1965, 73 Editor: Jour. Stroke, 1970-76, assoc. editor, 1976—. Recipient Outstanding Alumnus award, U. Kans., 1973. Fellow ACP, Am. Acad. Neurology (founding chmn. sect. on stroke and vascular neurology 1994), Royal Soc. Medicine; mem. AMA, AAUP, AAAS, Assn. Rsch. Nervous and Mental Disease (pres. 1961), Am. Neurol. Assn. (1st v.p. 1969-70, pres. 1973-74), Minn. Med. Assn., Four County Med. Soc. South Minn., Cen. Neuropsychiat. Assn., N.Y. Acad. Sci., Am. Heart Assn. (chmn. coun. cerebrovascular disease 1967-68, Gold Heart award 1976, Spl. Merit award 1981), Nat. Stroke Assn. (pres. 1986, editor Jour. Stroke and Cerebrovascular Disease 1990—), Sigma Xi. Office Phone: 801-263-0611. Office Fax: 801-263-9141. Personal E-mail: clarkmillikan@yahoo.com.

**MILLIKAN, JAMES ROLENS,** cleaning service executive, fitness consultant; b. Beaumont, Tex., Jan. 15, 1950; s. George Lee and Gertrude Louise (Mann) M.; m. Dorothy Jane Albright, Apr. 22, 1989. BFA, U. Houston, 1968; MFA, Juilliard Sch., 1971. Mgr. ptnr. Edward, Bankers & Co., Houston, 1971-73; prop. gen. Max M. Kaplan Properties, San Antonio, 1973-75; gen. bldg. mgr. Property Mgmt. Systems, Atlanta, 1975-79; dir. real estate Sun Life Group Am., Atlanta, 1979-81; prin. The Millikan Cos., Atlanta, 1981-85, J.R. & Co., Atlanta, 1985-87; sr. v.p., gen. mgr. east coast Nat. Cleaning Contractors, Inc., Atlanta, 1987-93; prin., pres. Master Bldg. Cleaners Inc., Atlanta, 1993—; owner Atlanta Kicksport. Owner ATlanta Kicksport; cons. Sun Life Group Am., 1982-84, McFaddin Ventures, Houston, 1983-84. Composer: Crystal Blue Persuasion (gold record 1969), Crimson & Clover (gold record 1969), Mony Mony (gold record 1969), I Love You More Today than Yesterday (gold record 1970), 1000 Yesterday (gold record 1971), others; instrumentalist for orchs. of Duke Ellington, Count Basie, Buddy Rich, Woody Herman and Glenn Miller, 1965-68; drummer, arranger, conductor for recording artist Petula Clark, 1968-71, leader J.R. and Co., Jazz Ensemble. Founder, pres. St. Luke's Econ. Devel. Corp., Atlanta, 1979, bd. dirs.; bd. dirs. St. Jude's Hosp. Atlanta, 1984, Am. Suicide Found., chmn. Goodwill. Am Diven. Nat. Bd. Am. Found. for Suicide Prevention; mem. Home Bldg. with Habitat for Humanity. With U.S. Army, 1970-76. Mem. Bldg. Owners and Mgrs. Atlanta, Am. Mktg. Assn., Am. Suicide Found. (bd. dirs.), Bldg. Svc. Contractors Assn. Internat. Democrat. Episcopalian. Avocations: music, golf, skiing, white water rafting, running, kick boxing. Home and Office: Master Bldg Cleaners Inc 2722 Vinings Oak Dr SE Atlanta GA 30080

**MILLIKAN, LARRY EDWARD,** dermatologist; b. Sterling, Ill., May 12, 1936; s. Daniel Franklin and Harriet Adeline (Parmenter) M.; m. Jeanine Dorothy Johnson, Aug. 27, 1960; children: Marshall, Rebecca. BA, Monmouth Coll., 1958; MD, U. Mo., 1962. Intern Great Lakes Naval Hosp., Ill., 1962-63; housestaff in tng. U. Mich., Ann Arbor, 1967-69, chief resident, 1969-70; asst. prof. dermatology U. Mo., Columbia, 1970-74, assoc. prof., 1974-81; chmn. dept. dermatology Tulane U., New Orleans, 1981—, chair/prof. emeritus, 2006—. Cons. physician Charity Hosp., New Orleans, Tulane U. Hosp., New Orleans, Riley Hosp., Anderson Hosp., Rush Hosp., all Meridian, Miss.; mem. bd. trustees Sulzberger Inst. for Dermatological Edn., 1995-99; chmn. com. med. edn. com. La. State Med. Soc., 1994-97. Assoc. editor Internat. Jour. Dermatology, 1980-99, Clinics in Dermatology, 1999—; mem. editl. bd. Current Concepts in Skin Disorders, Am. Jour. Med. Scis.; mem. editl. bd. Clinics in Dermatology, 1985—, assoc. editor, 1999—; contbr. articles to med. jours. Bd. dirs. Women's Dermatol. Assn., 1990—. With USN, 1960-67. Recipient Andres Bello awrd Govt. of Venezuela, 1989, citation of merit Sch. Medicine, U. Mo., 1993, Faculty Alumnus award U. Mo., 1997; named Disting. Alumnus, Monmouth Coll., 1990; Nat. Cancer Inst. grantee, 1976-84. Fellow ACP; mem. AAAS, AMA, Am. Acad. Dermatology (bd. dirs. 1986-90), Am. Dermatol. Assn., Am. Dermatol. Soc. for Allergy and Immunology (pres., bd. dirs.), Soc. for Investigative Dermatology (past pres. South sect.), So. Med. Assn. (vice chmn. dermatology sect. 1984, chmn. 1994), Coll. Physicians Phila. Assn. Profs. Dermatology (bd. dirs. 1984-86), Orleans Parish Med. Soc., La. Med. Soc., Pan Am. Med. Assn., Internat. Soc. Dermatol. (dep. sec. gen. 1989-99), Mo. Allergy Assn. (past pres.), Am. Coll. Cryosurgery, Assn. Acad. Dermatol. Surgeons, Internat. Soc. Dermatol. Surgery, Internat. Acad. Cosmetic Dermatology (sec. gen. 1996-), Dermatol. Found. Leaders Soc. (state chmn. 1993-97). Office: Tulane Univ Sch Medicine Dept of Dermatology 1430 Tulane Ave TB36 New Orleans LA 70112-2699

**MILLIKEN, DOUGLAS GORDON,** financial consultant, municipal official; b. Denver, June 13, 1957; s. J. Gordon and Marie (Machell) M. M in Acctg. and Fin. Mgmt., U. Denver, 1980; M in Taxation, U. Denver Law Sch., 2005. CPA, 1980. Ind. fin. cons., Centennial, Colo. 1990—. Mem. fin., acctg., intergovtl. rels. com. Nat. League Cities, 2002—; elected. treas. City of Centennial, 2001. Bd. mem., Colo. Legal Initiatives Project, Denver, 1993-96. Mem. Colo. Soc. CPAs, Rocky Mountain Wrestling Club (founding mem. 1994). Avocation: amateur wrestling. Home: 5315 S Nepal Way Centennial CO 80015-2143 Office: City of Centennial Ste 200 12503 E Euclid Dr Centennial CO 80111-6400 E-mail: doug@dougmilliken.com

**MILLIKEN, JOHN GORDON,** research economist; b. Denver, May 12, 1927; s. William Boyd and Margaret Irene (Marsh) M.; m. Marie Violet Machell, June 13, 1953 (dec. 2004); children: Karen Marie, Douglas Gordon, David Tait, Anne Alain. BS, Yale U., 1949, BEng, 1950; MS, U. Colo., 1966, PhD, 1969. Registered profl. engr., Colo. Engr. U.S. Bur. Reclamation, Denver, 1950-55; asst. to plant mgr. Stanley Aviation Corp., Denver, 1955-56; prin. mgmt. engr., dept. mgr. Martin-Marietta Aerospace Divsn., Denver, 1956-64; mgmt. engr. Safeway Stores, Inc., Denver, 1964-66; sr. rsch. economist, prog. analyst. div. head U. Denver Rsch. Inst., 1966-86; pres. Univ. Senate, 1980-81; prin. Milliken Chapman Rsch. Group, Inc., Littleton, Colo., 1986-88, Milliken Rsch. Group, Inc., Littleton, 1988—. Vis. fellow sci. policy rsch. unit U. Sussex, Eng., 1975-76; cons. mgmt. engr. Author: Aerospace Management Techniques, 1971, Federal Incentives for Innovation, 1974, Recycling Municipal Wastewater, 1977, Water and Energy in Colorado's Future, 1981, Metropolitan Water Management, 1981, Technological Innovation and Economic Vitality, 1983, Water Management in the Denver, Colorado Urban Area, 1988, Benefits and Costs of Oxygenated Fuels in Colorado, 1990, Water Transfer Alternatives Study, 1994, Colorado Springs Water Resources Plan Alternative Assessment Study, 1995, Colorado Springs Utilities Wastewater Infrastructure Alternatives Study, 1998; contbr. articles to profl. jours. Bd. dirs. S.E. Englewood Water Dist., 1963—, South Englewood San. Dist., 1965—; bd. dirs. South Suburban Pk. and Recreation Dist., 1971-96, chmn., 1990-92; v.p. South Suburban Land and Facilities Corp., 2001—; chmn. Dem. Com. of Arapahoe County, 1969-71, 5th Congl. Dist. Colo., 1972-73, 74-75; mem. exec. com. Colo. Faculty Adv. Coun., 1981-85; mem. Garrison Diversion Unit Commn., 1984; trustee Colo. Local Govt. Liquid Asset Trust, 1986-2005, chmn., 1991-93; bd. dirs. Colo. Spl. Dist. Assn. Property and Liability Pool, 1989—, pres. 1997-98. With M.C., U.S. Army, 1945-46. Recipient Adlai E. Stevenson Meml. award, 1981, cert. of Appreciation for svc. to Nation, U.S. Sec. Interior, 1984, hon. title "Amicus Universitatis," U. Denver, 1994, Disting. Svc. award Spl. Dist. Assn. Colo., 1995; Milliken Park named in his honor for svcs. to Littleton/Centennial Cmty., 1996. Mem. Acad. Mgmt., Nat. Assn. Bus. Economists, Yale Sci. and Engring. Assn. Water Works Assn., Sigma Xi, Tau Beta Pi, Beta Gamma Sigma, Sigma Iota Epsilon. Congregationalist. Home and Office: 6502 S Ogden St Centennial CO 80121-2561 Personal E-mail: jgordonmil@aol.com.

**MILLIKEN, KEVIN DAVID,** music educator; s. Marlin D. and Carol A. Milliken. MusB, Lycoming Coll., Williamsport, Pa., 1995. Music tchr. East Juniata HS, McAlisterville, Pa., 1995—. Mem.: Music Educators Nat. Conf., Pa. Music Edn. Assn. (county rep. 1995—), Loyal Order Moose, Zembo Shriners, Ancient Accepted Scottish Rite, Union Lodge. R-Consevative. Lutheran. Avocations: music, auto racing. Home: RR 4 Box 656 Mifflintown PA 17059 Office: East Juniata HS RR 2 Box 2411 Mc Alisterville PA 17049 Office Phone: 717-463-2111 ext. 40.

**MILLIKEN, KITTY LOU,** research scientist; b. Nashville, Tenn., Mar. 15, 1954; d. Edna Myers and Charles Duncan Milliken; m. Steven John Seni, Feb. 14, 1981; 1 child, Katherine Lynne. BA, Vanderbilt U., Nashville, Tenn., 1975; MA, U. Tex., Austin, 1977, PhD, 1985. Rsch. assoc. Bur. of Econ. Geology, Austin, Tex., 1979—80; rsch. geologist Exxon Prodn. Rsch., Houston, 1985—86; vis. rschr. Inst. Francais du Petrole, Rueil-Malmaison, France, 1996—97; rsch. assoc. U. Tex., Austin, 1997—99, rsch. scientist, 1999—2004, sr. rsch. scientist, 2004—. Co-editor Jour. of Sedimentary Rsch. 2004—, assoc. editor 1993—2000; j. ben carsey disting. lectr. Am. Assn. of Petroleum Geologists, 2005—06. Mem.: Am. Assn. of Petroleum Geologists, Geol. Soc. of Am. (sepm coun. 2006—), Soc. for Sedimentary Geology (sepm coucil 2004—). Achievements include research in diagenesis of siliciclastic rocks; applications of electron microbeam techniques to the study of sandstones and shales; reservoir quality assessment. Avocations: spinning, knitting, quilting, hiking. Office: Dept of Geological Sci U of Tex at Austin Austin TX 78712 Office Phone: 512-471-6082. Business E-Mail: kittym@mail.utexas.edu.

**MILLIKEN, MARY SUE,** chef, television personality, writer; Former mem. staff Le Perroquet, Chgo., Restaurant d'Olympe, Paris; formerly chef, co-owner City Cafe, L.A.; chef, co-owner CITY, L.A., 1985—94, Border Grill, L.A., 1985—91, Santa Monica, 1990—. Co-host (TV series) Too Hot Tamales, 1995—, Tamales' World Tour, (radio show) Good Food; co-author: City Cuisine, 1989, Mesa Mexicana, 1994, Cantina, 1996, Cooking with Too Hot Tamales, 1997; guest appearances (TV series) Oprah Winfrey Show, Maury Povich, Today Show, Sabrina the Teenage Witch, featured in USA Today, People Mag., Entertainment Weekly. Active Scleroderma Rsch. Found. Named Chef of Yr., Calif. Restaurant Writers, 1993. Mem.: Chef's Collaborative 2000, Women Chefs and Restaurateurs. Office: Border Grill 1445 4th St Santa Monica CA 90401*

**MILLIKEN, ROGER,** textile/chemical company executive; b. NYC, Oct. 24, 1915; s. Gerrish and Agnes (Gayley); m. Justine V. R. Hooper, June 5, 1948 (dec.); children: Justine, Nancy, Roger, David, Weston. Student, Groton Sch., 1929-33; AB, Yale U., 1937; LLD (hon.), Wofford Coll., Rose-Hulman Inst. Tech., Phila. Coll. Textiles and Sci., Brenau Coll., The Citadel; D. Textile Industry (hon.), Clemson U.; DHL (hon.), Converse Coll.; D. Bus. admin. (hon.), U. S.C., Spartanburg; LLD (hon.), LaGrange Coll., Furman U.; HHD (hon.), Presbyterian Coll. Bd. dirs. Milliken & Co. (formerly Deering Milliken), Spartanburg, SC, 1941—, pres. 1947-83, chmn., CEO, 1983—2005, chmn. 2006—. Chmn. bd. Inst. Textile Tech., 1948—97, chmn. emeritus, 1997—; bd. dirs. S.C. Textile Mfrs. Assn. Chmn. Greenville-Spartanburg Airport Commn.; trustee Wofford Coll., SC. Named Businessman of the Yr., SC C. of C., 1981, Citizen of the Carolinas, NC C. of C., 1991, Leader of the Century, Textile World Mag., 1999; named to SC Bus. Hall of Fame, 1985, SC Hall of Fame, 1998, Nat. Bus. Hall of Fame, 2000; recipient Neville Holcombe Disting. Citizenship Award, Spartanburg Area C. of C., 1985, Lifetime Achievement Award, No. Textile Assn., 1999. Mem.: AIA (hon.), Garden Club Am. (mem.-at-large), Yeamans Hall, Augusta Nat. Golf Club, Links, Union League. Office: Milliken & Co PO Box 3167 Spartanburg SC 29304

**MILLIMET, ERWIN,** lawyer; b. N.Y.C., Oct. 7, 1925; s. Maurice and Henrietta (Cohen) Millimet; children: Robert, James, Rachel, Sarah. BA magna cum laude, Amherst Coll., 1948; LLB cum laude, Harvard U., 1951. Bar: N.Y. 1952. Formerly sr. ptnr., chmn. exec. com. Stroock & Stroock & Lavan, N.Y.C.; ret., 1991. Mem. faculty Grad. Sch. Mgmt., U. Mass. Mem. bd. visitors U. San Diego Law Sch.; mem. Five Coll. LIR (learning in retirement), Northhampton, Mass.; active Nat. Support Group for Africa; founder Citizens for Am., Washington, 1984; mem. Rep. Presdl. Task Force. Mem. N.Y. State Bar Assn., Assn. of Bar of City of N.Y., Fed. Bar Assn., Rep. Club (N.Y.C. and Washington), Phi Beta Kappa. E-mail: emill@gis.net.

**MILLIN, LAURA JEANNE,** museum director; b. Elgin, Ill., June 11, 1954; d. Douglas Joseph and Patricia Ruth (Feragen) M. BA in Interdisciplinary Studies, The Evergreen State Coll., 1978. Dir. On The Boards, Seattle, 1979; art dir. City Fair Metrocenter YMCA, Seattle, 1980; dir. Ctr. on Contemporary Art, Seattle, 1981; co-owner Art in Form Bookstore, Seattle, 1981-89; co-dir. 3d internat festival of films by women dirs. Seattle Art Mus. & 911 Contemporary Arts, 1988; auction coord. Allied Arts of Seattle, 1989; dir. Missoula (Mont.) Mus. of the Arts, 1990—. Dir. Visual AIDS Missoula Mus. of the Arts, 1998; curator Radio COCA, Ctr. on Contemporary Art, Seattle, 1986, co-curator, 1981, 83; lectr. in field. Co-editor: Another (ind. feminist

newspaper), Seattle, 1989; editor: (exhibition catalog) James Turrell: Four Light Installations, 1981. Bd. dirs. Internat. Festival of Films by Women Dirs., Seattle, 1987, 89, Nine One One Comtemporary Arts Ctr., Seattle, 1981-87, bd. chmn. 1981-85; bd. advisors REFLEX (art mag.), Seattle, 1988-89, Ctr. on Contemporary Art, Seattle, 1983-86; state vis. Mont. Arts Coun., Missoula, 1991, NEA, Mpls., 1988, Chgo., 1987;; panelist Mont. Arts Coun., Helena, 1990; cons. Seattle Arts Commn., 1989, juror, 1985. Home: 1721 S 9th St W Missoula MT 59801-3432

**MILLING, BERT WILLIAM, JR.,** judge; b. Mobile, Ala., Mar. 5, 1946; s. Bert William and Marjorie Ann (Smith) M.; m. Priscilla Pitman, Apr. 15, 1966; children: Brooks Pitman, Jeremy Bacon, Maran Celeste. AB in Philosophy, The Coll. of William and Mary, 1968; JD, U. Ala., 1971. Bar: Ala. 1971. Legal officer 212th Arty. Group, Fort Lewis, Wash., 1971-72; legal asst. officer Judge Advocate Gen.'s Office, Ft. Sill, Okla., 1972-74; spl. asst. atty. gen. Dist. Atty.'s Office, Mobile, 1974-75, asst. dist. atty., 1977-78; assoc. Sintz, Pike, Campbell & Duke, Mobile, 1975-77; ct. referee Juvenile Div. of Cir. Ct., Mobile, 1978-81; counsel U.S. Senate Com. on Jud., Subcom. on Security & Terrorism, Washington, 1981-83; asst. U.S. atty. Justice Dept., Mobile, 1983-86; U.S. magistrate judge U. S. Dist. Ct. So. Dist. Ala., Mobile, 1986—. Mem. Administrv. Office U.S. Cts.; mem. adv. group Magistrate Judges and Tech. Facilities Adv. Coun., 2005—06. Capt. U.S. Army, 1971-74; maj. N.G., USAR, 1975-87. Mem. Ala. Bar Assn., Mobile Bar Assn., Fed. Magistrate Judges Assn. (budget and fin. com. 2005-06), Christian Legal Soc. Anglican. Avocations: photography, music, reading, exercising. Office: US Courthouse 113 Saint Joseph St Mobile AL 36602-3606

**MILLING, MARCUS EUGENE, SR.,** geologist; b. Galveston, Tex., Oct. 8, 1938; s. Robert Richardson and Leonora Mildred (Currey) M.; m. Sandra Ann Dunlay, Sept. 11, 1959; 1 child, Marcus Eugene Jr. BS in Geology, Lamar U., 1961; MS in Geology, U. Iowa, 1964, PhD in Geology, 1968. Cert. petroleum geologist. Rsch. geologist Exxon Prodn. Rsch. Co., Houston, 1968-76; prodn. geologist Exxon Co. U.S.A., Kingsville, Tex., 1976-78, dist. exptl. geologist New Orleans, 1978-80; mgr. geol. rsch. Arco Oil and Gas Co., Plano, Tex., 1980-86, chief geologist Dallas, 1986-87; assoc. dir. Bur. Econ. Geology U. Tex., Austin, 1987-92; exec. dir. Am. Geol. Inst., Alexandria, Va., 1992—. Vice-chmn. Offshore Tech. Conf., Dallas, 1984-87; dir. Geosci. Inst. for Oil and Gas Recovery Rsch., Austin, 1988-91. NSF fellow, 1966. Fellow Geol. Soc. Am. (councilor 1986-89); mem. Am. Assn. Petroleum Geologists, Soc. Petroleum Engrs., Am. Inst. Profl. Geologists (Ben H. Parker Meml. medal 1997), Blue Key, Sigma Xi. Home: 11457 Hollow Timber Ct Reston VA 20194-1980 Office: Am Geol Inst 4220 King St Alexandria VA 22302-1507 E-mail: mmilling@dgiweb.org.*

**MILLIS, ROBERT LOWELL,** astronomer, science observatory director; b. Martinsville, Ill., Sept. 12, 1941; m. Julia Drean, 1965; children: David, Daniel. BA, Ea. Ill. U., 1963; PhD in Astronomy, U. Wis., 1968. Staff astronomer Lowell Obs., Flagstaff, Ariz., 1967—86, assoc. dir., 1986—90, acting dir., 1989—90, dir., 1990—. Bd. dir. Mus. of No. Ariz., United Way of No. Ariz. Mem. Am. Astron. Soc., Internat. Astronomy Union, Divsn. Planetary Sci. (sec.-treas. 1985-88, chmn. 1994-95). Achievements include discovery of the Rings of Uranus (with J.L. Elliot); research in planetary satellites and ring systems; the occultation studies of solar system objects; comet and Kuiper belt objects. Office: Lowell Observatory 1400 W Mars Hill Rd Flagstaff AZ 86001-4499 Business E-Mail: rlm@lowell.edu.

**MILLISOR, KENNETH RAY,** lawyer; b. Belle Center, Ohio, Jan. 31, 1937; s. Darrel R. and Clara Sue (Miller) M.; m. Annette M. Seifert Ross, June 7, 1985. BA, Ohio Wesleyan U., 1959; JD, Ohio State U., 1960. Bar: Ohio 1960, U.S. Dist. Ct. (no. dist.) Ohio, 1965, U.S. Ct. Appeals (6th cir.) 1965, U.S. Ct. Appeals (D.C. cir.) 1975, U.S. Supreme Ct. 1970. Ptnr. Poetzel & Andress, Akron, Ohio, 1960-74, Millisor & Nobil, Akron and Cleve., 1975—. Past v.p. Akron Area coun. Boy Scouts Am.; active United Way. Mem. ABA, Ohio Bar Assn., Cleve. Bar Assn., Order of Coif, Shoreby Club (pres. 2000-03). Democrat. Home: 864 Beach Rd Lakewood OH 44107 Office: Millisor & Nobil Co 9150 S Hills Blvd Ste 300 Cleveland OH 44147-3599 Office Phone: 440-838-8800. E-mail: KMillisor@millisor.com.

**MILLMAN, AMY J.,** government official; b. Bklyn., June 12, 1954; m. Aug. 3, 1984; 2 children. BA in History, Carnegie Mellon U., 1976; MPA, George Washington U., 1978. Rschr. Congl. Quar., Inc., Washington, 1976-79; analyst OSHA, Dept. Labor, Washington, 1979-81; Washington rep. The Philip Morris Cos., Inc., 1981-91; dir. legis. affairs The Am. Trucking Assn., Inc., Washington, 1991-93; exec. dir. Nat. Women's Bus. Coun., Washington, 1993—2001; pres. Springboard Enterprises, 2001—. Adj. prof. George Washington U., Sch. Bus. and Public Mgmt., 2001—; bd. advisors Enterprising Woman Magazine, 2001—. Mem. Phi Kappa Phi.

**MILLMAN, BRUCE RUSSELL,** lawyer; b. Bronx, NY, June 4, 1948; s. Meyer and Garie (Solomon) M.; m. Lurrie Jan Liss, Aug. 12, 1973; children: Noemi, Avi. AB, Princeton U., 1970; JD, Columbia U., 1973. Bar: N.Y. 1974, U.S. Dist. Ct. (ea. and so. dists.) N.Y. 1975, U.S. Ct. Appeals (2d dir.) 1978, U.S. Supreme Ct. 1978. Assoc. Rains & Pogrebin and predecessors, Mineola, NY, 1973-79, ptnr., 1980—2004; prin. Grotta, Glassman & Hoffman, P.A., N.Y.C., 2004—. Arbitrator Nassau County Dist. Ct., Mineola, 1981-83. Contbr. New York Employment Law, 1995, Labor and Employment Law for the Corporate Counselor and General Practitioner, 1994, Updating Issues in Employment Law, 1986, Public Sector Labor and Employment Law, 1988. Bd. dirs. West Side Montessori Sch., N.Y.C., 1984-90, sec., 1985-87, pres., 1987-90. Harlan Fiske Stone scholar Columbia U. Law Sch., N.Y.C., 1971, 73. Mem. ABA, N.Y. State Bar Assn. (chair labor and employment law sect. 1997-98), Nassau County Bar Assn., Indsl. Rels. Rsch. Assn. (bd. dirs. L.I. chpt. 1984—, pres. 1995-96). Home: 60 Riverside Dr New York NY 10024-6108 Office: Grotta Glassman & Hoffman PC 650 Fifth Ave New York NY 10019 also: 532 Broadhollow Rd Melville NY 11747 Office Phone: 212-261-2175. Business E-Mail: millmanb@gghlaw.com.

**MILLMAN, RICHARD GEORGE,** architect, educator; b. St. Johns, Mich., Feb. 12, 1925; s. Harold Fildew and Elizabeth Hill (Van Deusen) M.; m. Mary Louise Manley, June 17, 1950; children: John Richard, Ruth Barbara. BArch, U. Mich., 1951, MArch, 1962. Registered arch., Mich., Ohio, Ala. Job capt. Smith Hinchman & Grylls, Detroit, 1951-52; designer assoc. Eliot Robinson, AIA, Birmingham, Mich., 1952-55; designer Eero Saarinen Assocs., Bloomfield Hills, Mich., 1955-56; assoc. Chas. W. Lane Assocs. Inc., Ann Arbor, Mich., 1956-59; prin. Kainlauri, MacMullan, Millman, Ann Arbor, 1959-62; assoc. prof. Ohio U., Athens, 1962-68; prof. Auburn (Ala.) U., 1968—, head architecture dept., 1968-73, 84-85, head indsl. design dept., 1988-89. Prof. Mid. East Tech. U., Ankara, Turkey, 1966-67, King Faisal U., Dammam, Saudi Arabia, 1979-81. One man shows include Dhahran Art Group, Saudi Arabia, 1981, Peet Gallery, Auburn U., 1983, 91, Heritage Hall Mus., Talladega, Ala., 1998; author: Washtenaw Community College, 1962, Auburn U. Tour Guide, 1990. With U.S. Army, 1943-46, ETO, PTO. Decorated Bronze Star; recipient Cert. of Honor Ala. Hist. Comm., 1977; Alumni scholar U. Mich., 1961; Fulbright lectr. Exch. Comm., Mid. East Tech. U., 1966. Mem. AIA (treas. Ala. coun. 1969, v.p. 1970, pres. 1972, emeritus 1990, Auburn chpt. pres. 1970, emeritus), Nat. Coun. Archtl. Registration Bd. (cert.), Auburn Arts Assn., Ga. Watercolor Soc. (signature mem.), Watercolor Soc. Ala. (signature mem.; pres. 2003), So. Watercolor Soc. (signature mem.). Avocations: painting, photography. Home: 736 Brenda Ave Auburn AL 36830-6038 Office Phone: 334-887-6428. E-mail: millmmm@charter.net.

**MILLNER, THOMAS,** manufacturing and holding company executive; Pres. The Pilliod Cabinet Co., High Point, N.C., Pilliod Holding Co., Swanton, Ohio, Remington Arms Co., Madison, WI. Office: Remington Arms Co 870 Remington Dr PO Box 700 Madison NC 27025-0700

**MILLOY, FRANK JOSEPH, JR.,** surgeon; b. Phoenix, June 26, 1924; s. Frank Joseph and Ola (McCabe) M. BS, Notre Dame U., 1946; MS, Northwestern U., 1949, MD, 1948. Diplomate Am. Bd. Surgery and Thoracic

Surgery. Intern Cook County Hosp., Chgo., 1947-49, resident, 1953-57; practice medicine, specializing in surgery Lake Forest, Ill., 1958—. Hon. attending staff Presbyn.-St. Lukes Hosp.; former mem. attending staff Cook County Hosp.; assr. staff U. Ill. Rsch. Hosp.; clin. assoc. prof. surgery, U. Ill. Med. Sch.; assoc. prof. surgery Rush Med. Sch. Contbr. articles to profl. jours., chapters to books. Cons. West Side Vet. Hosp. Served as apprentice seaman USNR, 1943-45; lt. M.C., USNR, 1950-52; PTO. Mem.: ACS, Soc. Med. History Chgo. (pres.), Cook County Hosp. Surg. Alumni Assn., Karl Meyer Surg. Soc. (sec.), Warren Cole Surg. Soc. (past sec.), Ill. Thoracic Surg. Soc. (past pres.), Soc. Thoracic Surgeons, Am. Coll. Chest Physicians, Internat. Soc. Surgery, Chgo. Surg. Soc., Univ. Club (Chgo.), Met. Club, Knights of Malta, Phi Beta Pi. Home: 574 Jackson Ave Glencoe IL 60022-2036 Office Phone: 847-835-5578.

**MILLS, AGNES EUNICE KARLIN,** artist; b. N.Y.C., Apr. 2, 1915; d. Herman Karlin and Celia (Ducoffe) Karlin; m. Saul Mills, May 10, 1938 (dec. Nov. 1993); children: Karen, Marghe. Grad., Cooper Union Art Sch., N.Y.C., 1938; BFA, Pratt Inst., 1975; student, NYU. One-woman shows include Carus Gallery, N.Y.C., Unitarian Soc. Manhasset, N.Y., Harbor Gallery, Cold Spring Harbor, N.Y., Harbor Gallery, Cape Cod, Mass., Alfredo Valente Gallery, N.Y.C., Robbins Gallery, East Orange, N.J., Nuance Galleries, Tampa, Friends of Tampa Ballet, Graphic Eye Coop Gallery, Pt. Washington, N.Y., City Ctr. Gallery, N.Y.C., Lincoln Ctr. Art Gallery, N.Y.C., North Shore Cmty. Arts Ctr., Great Neck, N.Y., Delray Beach Works in Progress Gallery, Boca Raton Cmty. Ctr., Palm Beach Pub. Libr., Gramercy Park Armory, N.Y.C.; exhibited in group shows at Alfredo Valente Gallery, N.Y.C., Audubon Soc., N.Y.C., Bowdoin Coll. Mus. Art, Brunswick, Maine, Brandeis U., Waltham, Mass., Bklyn. Mus. Art, Brown U., Providence, Butler Inst. Am. Art, Youngstown, Ohio, Colgate U. Libr., Hamilton, N.Y., Cornell U., Ithaca, N.Y., East Hampton (N.Y.) Guild Artists, Gallery K, Woodstock, N.Y., Graphic Eye Coop Gallery, Port Washington, N.Y., Heckscher Mus., Huntington, N.Y., Hunterdon County Mus., Clinton, N.J., Joan Avnet Gallery, Great Neck, N.Y., Lincoln Ctr. Libr. Performing Arts, N.Y.C., Madison Gallery, N.Y.C., Boca Raton City Hall, Boca Raton Cmty. Ctr., Boca Raton Libr.; represented in permanent collections at Boca Raton Mus. Art, Nat. Women in the Arts Mus. Home: 1070 SW 22nd Ave Villa 13#3 Delray Beach FL 33445-6030

**MILLS, BARRY,** academic administrator, lawyer; b. Providence, Sept. 8, 1950; m. Karen Gordon Mills. BA in Biochemistry and Govt. cum laude, Bowdoin, 1972; PhD, Syracuse U., 1976; JD, Columbia U., 1979. Bar: N.Y. 1980. Mem. Debevoise & Plimpton, NYC, 1979—86, ptnr., 1986—2001; pres. Bowdoin Coll., Brunswick, Maine, 2001—. Bd. trustees Bowdoin Coll., Brunswick, Maine, 1994—2000. Harlan Fiske Stone scholar, Columbia Law Sch., 1979. Mem. Assn. of Bar of City of N.Y. Office: Bowdoin Coll Hawthorne-Longfellow Hall 5700 College Station Brunswick ME 04011-8448 Office Phone: 207-725-3221.

**MILLS, BELEN COLLANTES,** early childhood education educator; b. Philippines; d. Ricardo and Epifania (Tomines) C.; children: Belinda Mills Keiser, Roger A. BSE, Leyte Normal Coll., Tacloban, Leyte, Philippines, 1954; MS in Edn., Ind. U., 1955, EdD, 1967. Asst. prof. Fla. State U., Tallahassee, 1968—74, assoc. prof., 1974—89, prof., 1989—98, prof. emeritus early childhood edn., 1998—. Author books on early childhood edn., phonics-based children's books and acad. readiness computer programs; contbr. articles to profl.jours. Smith-Mundt Fulbright scholar. Mem. Nat. Assn. for Edn. of Young Children, Nat. Assn. Early Childhood Tchr. Edn., World Coun. for Curriculum and Instrn., Assn. Childhood Edn. Internat. Home: PO Box 20023 Tallahassee FL 32316-0023 Office Phone: 850-576-2251.

**MILLS, BOB,** member of Canadian parliament; b. Young, Sask., Can. m. Nicole Mills; children: Ken, Kari Anne, Melinda, Rosanno, Ric, Amanda. BA in Sci. and Edn., U. Sask. Tchr. biology Lindsay Thurber Comprehensive H.S., 1965-79; founder Mills Travel, Ltd., 1979—; elected to House of Commons, Red Deer, Alta., Canada, 1993—. Parliamentary activities include mem. steering com. on fgn. affairs and internat. trade, Ofcl. Opposition Fgn. Affairs Critic, Opposition Health Critic, 2000—, mem. standing com. on health, chief environ. critic. gen., 2001-06. Mem. Am. Express Network (recipient Travel Hall of Fame award 1992). Avocations: farming, gardening, photography, travel. Office: 534-N Centre Ottawa ON Canada K1A 0A6 Office Phone: 613-995-0590. Business E-Mail: millsb@parl.gc.ca.

**MILLS, BRADFORD,** merchant banker; b. NYC, Dec. 16, 1926; s. Dudley Holbrook and Louise (Morris) M.; m. Cheryl Ann Di Paolo; children: Elizabeth Lee, Bradford Alan, Barbara Louise, Ross Dudley. BA cum laude in Econs., Princeton U., 1948; postgrad., Oxford U., Eng., 1950-51. Asst. to dir. overseas pers. divsn. ECA, Paris, 1948-50; assoc. corp. fin. dept. F. Eberstadt & Co., N.Y.C., 1954-62, ptnr., 1960-62; mng. ptnr. N.Y. Securities Co., 1962-70; chmn., dir. Specialized Svcs., Inc., Atlanta, 1968-85; pres., CEO Overseas Pvt. Investment Corp., Washington, 1971-73, dir., 1971-75; chmn. bd., dir. F. Eberstadt & Co. Internat., 1973-74; mng. ptnr. Bradford Assocs., 1974-92; ltd. ptnr. Bradford Investment Ptnrs. Ltd., 1992-96. Past chmn. Diamond Glass, MMX Corp., HWC Corp., Chgo. Stock Tab Corp., O.S. Kelly Co., Filtration Scis., Overseas Pvt. Investors Ltd., Overseas Pvt. Equities, Overseas Equity Investors, Inc., Specialized Svcs., Inc. U.S. Precision Glass, Inc., Amwell Valley Conservancy, Bradford Ventures, Stonecare Internat.; chmn. Bradford Investment Group, HDMR Discovery Inc.; bd. dirs. The Princeton Packet, Pulsed Instruments; former dir. over 50 pub. and pvt. cos. Pres. Mills Found.; trustee, vice chmn. Millbrook Sch., NY, 1978-05; sec., trustee, mem. exec. fin., investment and strategic planning coms., 1995, Princeton Healthcare Sys.; trustee SAVE/Friends of Homeless Animals. Mem. Coun. Fgn. Rels., Blooming Grove Club (Pa.), Links Club, Leash Club, Anglers Club N.Y., Nassau Club (trustee 1998-04), Bedens Brook Club, Amwell Valley Conservancy, Inc., Amwell Conservancy Found. (chmn.), TPC at Jasna Polona. Office: 2ND FL 92 Nassau St Princeton NJ 08542-4519 Office Phone: 609-921-3880. Personal E-mail: patchesteddy@msn.com.

**MILLS, CAROL MARGARET,** public relations executive, consultant; b. Salt Lake City, Aug. 31, 1943; d. Samuel Lawrence and Beth (Mansell) M. BS magna cum laude, U. Utah, 1965. With S. Hatch Co., Woods Cross, Utah, 1965-87, corp. sec.; 1970-87, traffic mgr., 1969-87, dir. publicity, 1974-87, cons. various orgns., 1988—. Dir. bus. Intermountain Tariff Bur. Inc., 1978-88, chmn., 1981-82, 1986-87; bd. dirs. Mountainwest Venture Group. Fund raiser March of Dimes, Am. Cancer Soc., Am. Heart Assn.; active senatorial campaign, 1976, gubernatorial campaign, 1984, 88, congl. campaign, 1990, 92, 94, vice chair voting dist., 1988-90, congl. campaign, 1994, chmn. 1990-92, chmn. party caucus legis. dist.; witness transp. com. Utah State Legislature, 1984, 85; apptd. by gov. to bd. trustees Utah Tech. Fin. Corp., 1986—; corp. sec., mem. exec. com., 1988—; mem. expdn. to Antaractica, 1996, Titanic '96 expdn.; mem. Iceland and Greenland expdn., 2001; mem. Pioneer Theatre Guld, 1985--. Recipient Svc. awards S. Hatch Co., 1971, 80; VIP chpt. Easter Seal Telethon, 1989, 90, Outstanding Vol. Svc. award Easter Seal Soc. Utah, 1989, 90. Mem. Nat. Tank Truck Carriers, Transp. Club Salt Lake City, Am. Trucking Assn. (mem. pub. rels. coun.), Utah Motor Transport Assn. (bd. dirs. 1982-88), Internat. Platform Assn., Traveler's Century Club, Titanic Internat., Beta Gamma Sigma, Phi Kappa Phi, Phi Chi Theta. Home: HC 11 Box 329 Kamiah ID 83536-9410

**MILLS, CHARLES GARDNER,** lawyer; b. Griffin, Ga., Feb. 29, 1940; s. Charles G. and Marguerite (Powell) M. AB, Yale U., 1962; JD, Boston Coll., 1967; LLM, Touro Coll., 2002. Bar: N.Y. 67, U.S. Dist. Ct. (so. and ea. dists.) 72, U.S. Ct. Appeals (2d cir.) 75, U.S. Supreme Ct. 77, U.S. Ct. Fed. Claims 91, U.S. Ct. Appeals for Vets. Claims 96, U.S. Dist. Ct. (no. dist.) N.Y. 99. Assoc. Smart & McKay, N.Y.C., 1967-68, Smart & Mills, N.Y.C., 1969-71, Eaton & VanWinkle, N.Y.C., 1971-82, Payne, Wood & Littlejohn, Glen Cove and Melville, N.Y., 1982-91; pvt. practice, Glen Cove, 1991—. With U.S. Army, 1962-64, ETO. Mem. Assn. Bar City N.Y., Nassau County Bar Assn., Rotary (pres. Glen Cove Club 1989-90), Am. Legion (comdr. Locust Valley,

N.Y. post 1988-90, comdr. Nassau County com. 1995-96, N.Y. Judge Advocate, 1998—), Soc. Colonial Wars, SCV, Order of the Arrow. Republican. Roman Catholic. Office: 56 School St Glen Cove NY 11542-2512

**MILLS, CHARLES N.,** healthcare supplies and products company executive; b. Sept. 30, 1961; BS, MBA, Cornell U. With IBM; then joined Medline Industries, Mundelein, Ill., 1986, pres. textile divsn., 1991—97, CEO, 1997—.*

**MILLS, CORINNE C.,** music educator; d. William P. and Cynthia L. Channon; children: Kristen Danielle, Pamela Dawn. MusB, Hartt Sch., West Hartford, Conn., 1977. Cert. Conn. Dept. Edn. Traffic coord. Fafair Bearing Co., New Britain, Conn., 1980—82; cello tchr. U. Conn. Cmty. Sch. Arts, Storrs, 1990—93; music tchr. Hartford (Conn.) Pub. Sch., 1995—2001, dist. music coach, 2001—; cello tchr., ensemble coach Hartford Conservatory, 1992—2000. Tchr., coach, dir. summer program Hartford Conservatory, Conn., 1992—2000. Musician (asst. prin. cellist): Ea. Conn. Symphony Orch., 1982—; musician (cellist) Oakdale Music Theater, 1991—, Andrea Bocelli Am. Tour, 2001—; co-author: Teaching Music in the Urban Classroom: A Guide to Survival, Success and Reform, 2006. Mem.: Am. Orff Schulwerk Assn., Am. Fedn. Tchrs., Am. Fedn. Musicians, Alpha Chi. Democrat. Avocation: gardening. Office: Hartford Pub Sch 960 Main St Hartford CT 06103 Office Phone: 860-695-8724. Business E-mail: millcool@hartfordschools.org.

**MILLS, DALE DOUGLAS,** journalist; b. Seattle, Oct. 4, 1930; d. Donald Emery and Antoinette (Kinleyside) Douglas; m. William Russell Mills, Aug. 13, 1955; children: Lida Susan, William Tad Jr., Peter Donald, Jane Douglas. BA, U. Wash., Seattle, 1952. Reporter Seattle Times, 1954-55, 74-83; asst. libr. Harvard U., 1955-56; editor Puget Soundings mag., 1968-71. Author: Deliver Us From Squid Roe, 1995, Mem com. sign control Seattle City Coun., 1970-72; rsch. dir. City Coun. campaign; bd. mgrs. King County Juvenile Ct.; trustee Allied Arts Seattle; bd. dirs. King County Coun. for Prevention of Child Abuse and Neglect. Recipient awards for excellence in journalism Wash. Press Assn., Nat. Fedn. Press Women, Allied Daily Newspapers, C.B. Blethen Meml. award for disting. investigative reporting, Excellence award Soc. Profl. Journalists/Sigma Delta Chi; named Disting. Alumnus Lakeside-St. Nicholas Sch., 1984. Mem.: Jr. League Seattle, Helen T. Bush Children's Hosp Guild, Earthjustice, Sunset Club, Seattle Yacht Club, Kappa Kappa Gamma. E-mail: ddmills@comcast.net.

**MILLS, DANIEL QUINN,** business educator, consultant, author; b. Houston, Nov. 24, 1941; s. Daniel Monroe and Louise (Quinn) M.; children: Lisa Ann, Leandra, Shirley Elizabeth, Eliza Day, Sargent; m. Elizabeth Moore. BA, Ohio Wesleyan U., 1963; MA, Harvard U., 1965, PhD, 1968. Prof. MIT, Cambridge, 1968-75, Harvard Bus. Sch., Boston, 1976—. Impartial umpire Plan to Settle Disputes in Constrn., 1973-79, Trans-Alaska Pipeline, 1975-78, AFL-CIO Internal Disputes Plan, 1975-82; commr. Nat. Commn. on Employment Policy, Washington, 1982-86. Author: Industrial Relations in Construction, 1971, Labor, Government and Inflation, 1975, Labor-Management Relations, 1978, 5th edit., 1993, The New Competitors, 1985, Not Like Our Parents: The Baby-Boom Generation, 1987, The IBM Lesson, 1988, The Rebirth of the Corporation, 1990, The GEM Principle, 1994, Broken Promises: What Went Wrong at IBM, 1996, e-Leadership, 2000, Buy, Lie and Sell High: How Investors Lost Out on Enron and The Internet Bubble, 2002, Wheel, Deal and Steal: Deceptive Accounting, Deceitful CEO's and Ineffective Reforms, 2003, Having It All, 2004, How to Lead-How to Live, 2005, Principles of Management, 2005, Masters of Illusion, 2006. Mem. Am. Econ. Assn., Indsl. Rels. Rsch. Assn., Phi Beta Kappa Office: Harvard U Harvard Bus Sch Soldiers Field Rd Allston MA 02163 Office Phone: 617-495-6206. Business E-Mail: dmills@hbs.edu.

**MILLS, DAVID HARLOW,** psychologist, professional society administrator; b. Marshalltown, Iowa, Dec. 26, 1932; s. Harlow Burgess and Esther Winifred (Brewer) M.; m. Janet Louise Anderson, June 15, 1957 (div. 1984); children: Ross Harlow, Anne Louise; m. Susan S. Greene, Aug. 3, 1984. BS, Iowa State U., 1955, MS, 1957; PhD, Mich. State U., 1964. Postdoctoral fellow USPHS U. Ill., Champaign, 1964-65; from asst. prof. psychology to assoc. prof. Iowa State U., Ames, 1965-69, asst. dir. counseling ctr., 1967-69; faculty U. Md., College Park, 1969-81, prof. psychology 1972-81, asst. dir. counseling center, 1969-81; adminstrv. officer Am. Psychol. Assn., Washington, 1981-86; pvt. practice Bangor, Maine, 1989—, Blue Hill, Maine, 1990—. Cons. Iowa Women's Reformatory, 1966-69, VA, Rockwell City, Iowa, 1966-69; rsch. assoc. Nat. Register Health Svcs. Providers in Psychology; mgmt. cons. Ctr. Creative Leadership U. Md., 1980—; mem. Maine Bd. Psychologists; mem. exam com. Assn. State and Provincial State Psychology Bds., 1995-98; mem. Maine State Bd. Examiners Psychologists, 1994-2003, cons., 20030172,, chair, 1996-99. Contbr. articles to profl. jours. Pres. Woodman-Pinecrest Citizens Assn., Silver Spring, Md., 1973-74; mem. com. higher edn. Allied Civic Group Montgomery County, 1974, sr. fellow Consortium of Univs. of the Washington D.C. Met. Area., 1987—; mem. diocesan rev. bd. Portland (Maine) Roman Cath. Diocese, 1997-2002. Served with U.S. Army, 1957-61. Fellow APA (chair ct. on profl. stds., 1988-1989, ethics 1981-1989, ethics cons. 1990—); mem. Internat. Assn. Counseling Svcs. (accrediting bd. 1972-74, v.p 1975-77, pres. 1977-79). Democrat. Unitarian Universalist. Office: PO Box 108 Little Deer Isle ME 04650-0108 E-mail: bigskye@acadia.net.

**MILLS, DON HARPER,** pathology and psychiatry educator, lawyer; b. Peking, China, July 29, 1927; came to U.S., 1928; s. Clarence Alonzo and Edith Clarissa (Parrett) M.; m. Lillian Frances Snyder, June 11, 1949; children: Frances Jo, Jon Snyder. BS, U. Cin., 1950, MD, 1953; JD, U. So. Calif., 1958. Diplomate Am. Bd. Legal Medicine. Intern L.A. County Gen. Hosp., 1953-54, admitting physician, 1954-57, attending staff in pathology, 1959—; pathology fellow U. So. Calif., L.A., 1954-55, instr. pathology, 1958-62, asst. clin. prof., 1962-65, assoc. clin. prof., 1965-69, clin. prof. 1969 , clin. prof psychiatry and behavioral sci., 1986—. Asst. in pathology Hosp. Good Samaritan, L.A., 1956-65, cons. staff, 1962-72, affiliate staff, 1972-91; dep. med. examiner Office of Los Angeles County Med. Examiner, 1957-61; instr. legal medicine Loma Linda (Calif.) U. Sch. Medicine, 1960-66, assoc. clin. prof. humanities, 1966-95; cons. HEW, 1972-73, 75-76, Dept. Def., 1975-80; trustee Am. Bd. Legal Medicine, Inc., Chgo., 2004—; med. dir. Profl. Risk Mgmt. Group, 1989-2001, Octagon Risk Svcs., Inc., 2001—. Column editor Newsletter of the Long Beach Med. Assn., 1960-75, Jour. Am. Osteo. Assn., 1965-77, Ortho Panel, 1970-78; exec. editor Trauma, 1964-88, mem. editl. bd., 1988-2006; mem. editl. bd. Legal Aspects of Med. Practice, 1972-90, Med. Alert Comms., 1973-75, Am. Jour. Forensic Medicine and Pathology, 1979-87, Hosp. Risk Control, 1981-96; contbr. numerous articles to profl. jours. Bd. dirs. Inst. for Med. Risk Studies, 1988—; mem. adv. bd. Pacific Ctr. for Health Policy and Ethics, 1997—, chmn., 1999—. With USN, 1946—47. Recipient Ritz Heerman award Calif. Hosp. Assn. 1986, Disting. fellow Am. Acad. Forensic Scis., 1993, Genesis award Pacific Ctr. for Health Policy and Ethics, 1993, Founder's award Am. Coll. Med. Quality, 1994. Fellow Am. Coll. Legal Medicine (pres. 1974-76, bd. govs. 1970-78, v.p 1972-74, chmn. malpractice com. 1973-74, jour. editl. bd. 1984—, gold medal 1999), Am. Acad. Forensic Sci. (gen. program chmn. 1966-67, chmn. jurisprudence sect. 1966-67, 73-74, exec. com. 1971-74, 84-88, v.p 1984-85, pres. 1986-87, ethics com. 1976-86, 91-2001, chmn. ethics com. 1994-2001, long-term planning com. 1990—2004, jour. editl. bd. 1965-79); mem. AMA (jour. editl. bd. 1973-77), AAAS, ABA, Am. Coll. Med. Quality (hon. life), Calif. Med. Assn., Los Angeles County Med. Assn., Los Angeles County Bar Assn., Am. Health Lawyers Assn. Clubs: SC Hosp. Attys. Home: 700 E Ocean Blvd Unit 2606 Long Beach CA 90802-5039 Office: 5000 Airport Plaza Dr Ste 250 Long Beach CA 90815-4959 Office Phone: 562-420-5987.

**MILLS, DOROTHY ALLEN,** investor; b. New Brunswick, N.J., Dec. 14, 1920; d. James R. and Bertha Lovilla (Porter) Allen; m. George M. Mills, Apr. 21, 1945; children: Dianne Adele McKay, Dorothy Louise Sphatt. BA, Douglass Coll., New Brunswick, N.J., 1943. Investment reviewer Ctrl.

Hanover Bank, N.Y.C., 1943-44; asst. to dir. of admissions and sec. undergrad. yrs. Douglass Coll., New Brunswick, 1944-45; sec., regional dir. O.P.A., Ventura, Calif., 1945-46; corp. sec. George M. Mills Inc., Highland Park, NJ, 1946-75; pvt. investor N. Brunswick, 1975—. Sr. v.p. Children Am. Revolution, N.J., 1965; active alumni com. Douglass Coll., 1990—. Recipient Douglass Alumni award, 1992. Mem. AAUW, New Brunswick Hist. Soc., DAR, English Speaking Union, Rutgers Alumni Faculty Club, Woman's League of Rutgers U., Princeton-Douglass Alumni Club, N. Brunswick Women's Club, Auxiliary Robert Wood Johnson Hosp. and Med. Sch. Republican. Mem. Dutch Reformed Ch. Avocations: travel, gardening, bridge. Home: 1054 Hoover Dr New Brunswick NJ 08902-3244

**MILLS, DOROTHY JANE (DOROTHY Z. SEYMOUR),** editor, consultant; b. Cleve., July 5, 1928; d. Henry Zander and Katherine Helen Reinert; m. Harold Seymour, May 21, 1949 (dec. Sept. 25, 1992); m. Roy Elburt Mills, Feb. 15, 1995. Student, Cleve. State U., 1946—49; BS, Case-Western Res. U., 1950, MA, 1952. Cert. elem. and H.S. tchr. Ohio, N.Y. Tchr. Cleve. Pub. Schs., 1950—54, Parma Heights (Ohio) Pub. Schs., 1955—57, Pelham (N.Y.) Pub. Schs., 1957—63, Warwick (N.Y.) Pub. Schs., 1963—66; sr. editor Ginn & Co., Pubs., Boston, Lexington, Mass., 1967—73, Lexington, 1979—81; freelance writer, editor, cons., 1981—; owner Patrician Publs., Naples, Fla., 1998—. Cons. Stillpoint Pub., Walpole, NY, 1987—; freelance editor, 1987—95; lectr. in field. Author: (children's textbooks) Bill and the Fish, 1965, Brad and Nell, 1965, Stop Pretending, 1965, Ballerina Bess, 1965, Ann Likes Red, 1965, The Rabbit, 1965, The Tent, 1965, The Sandwich, 1965, Big Beds and Little Beds, 1965, (edn. text) Toad Charts, 1987, (novels) The Sceptre, 1998, 1999, The Labyrinth, 2003, The Treskel, 2005, (cookbook) Meatless Meat: A Book of Recipes for Meat Substitutes, 2001; co-author, editor: Fear Not to Sow Because of the Birds, 1988;; co-author (with Harold Seymour): Baseball: The Early Years, 1960, Baseball: The Golden Age, 1971, Baseball: The People's Game, 1990; author: (autobiography) A Woman's Work: Writing Baseball History with Harold Seymour, 2004; co-author: (edn. text) Word Recognition, 1987. Author short stories; contbr. articles to pubs. Mem.: NASSH, SABR, AAUW. Avocations: piano, singing, travel. Home and Office: Patrician Publs 770 Goodlette Rd N # 311 Naples FL 34102 Office Phone: 239-775-2840. E-mail: dorothyjanemills@comcast.net.

**MILLS, DOUGLAS L.,** physics professor; b. Berkeley, Calif., Apr. 2, 1940; s. Eli J. and Bruna G. Mills; m. Sandra Ann Thrall, June 18, 1961; children: Scott Alan, Sherylle Mills Englander. PhD, U. Calif., Berkeley, 1965. Postdoctoral fellow U. Paris, Orsay, France, 1965—66; asst. prof. physics U. Calif., Irvine, 1966—69, assoc. prof. physics, 1969—83, prof. physics, 1983—2005, rsch. prof. physics, 2005—. Co-author with H. Ibach (textbook) Electron Energy Loss Spectroscopy and Surface Vibrations; author: (textbook) Non Linear Optics; Basic Concepts; contbr. scientific papers. Staff commodore Bahia Corinthian Yacht Club, Newport Beach, Calif., 1995—96. Fellow: Am. Phys. Soc. Office Phone: 949-824-5148. Business E-Mail: dlmills@uci.edu.

**MILLS, EDWARD WARREN,** corporation executive, lawyer; b. N.Y.C., Apr. 7, 1941; m. Maria Parascandolo, Sept. 19, 1971; children: Edward Warren, Foy Fitzhugh, Joseph V.O. BS, Washington and Lee U., 1962; MBA, Hofstra U., 1974; JD, N.Y. Law Sch. 1977. Bar: N.Y., D.C. 1978. Acct. Wasserman & Taten, N.Y.C., 1962-69; exec. v.p. L.H. Keller, Inc. and Hugo P. Keller, Inc., N.Y.C., 1969-74; pres. Gen. Ruby & Sapphire Co., 1974-94, Qualistar Corp., 1974-94, EWM Gen. Corp., 1993—; sole practice, N.Y., 1978—. Mem. ABA, N.Y. State Bar Assn., D.C. Bar Assn. Office: 7700 Massachusetts Ave New Port Richey FL 34653-3024 Home: PO Box 610 New Port Richey FL 34656-0610 Business E-Mail: genrus73@aol.com.

**MILLS, EDWIN SMITH,** economics professor; b. Collingswood, N.J., June 25, 1928; s. Edwin Smith and Roberta (Haywood) M.; m. Barbara Jean Dressner, Sept. 2, 1950; children: Alan Stuart, Susan Dorinda; m. Margaret M. Hutchinson, Jan. 22, 1977. BA, Brown U., 1951; PhD, U. Birmingham, Eng., 1956. Asst. lectr. Univ. Coll. North Staffordshire, Eng., 1953-55; instr. MIT, 1955-57; mem. faculty Johns Hopkins, Balt., 1957-70, prof. econs., 1963-70, chmn. dept. econs., 1966-69; prof. econs. and pub. affairs, Gerald L. Phillippe prof. urban studies Princeton U., 1970-75, prof. econs., 1975-87, chmn. dept., 1977; Gary Rosenberg prof. real estate and fin. Kellog Sch. Mgmt. Northwestern U., Evanston, Ill., 1987—96, emeritus prof., 1996—. Vis. rsch. fellow Cowles Found., Yale, 1961; sr. profl. staff Coun. Econ. Advisers, 1964—65. Author: Urban Economics, 1972, The Burden of Government, 1986; editor: Jour. Urban Econs., 1973—90; contbr. articles to profl. jours. 2d lt. U.S. Army, 1946—48. Recipient numerous rsch. grants and contracts, 1960—95. Mem.: Am. Econ. Assn., Phi Beta Kappa. Home: 1 Calvin Cir Apt A413 Evanston IL 60201-1953 Office: Northwestern U Ctr Real Estate Rsch Kellogg Graduate School 2001 Sheridan Rd Evanston IL 60208-2001 Office Phone: 847-491-8340. Business E-Mail: e_mills@kellogg.northwestern.edu.

**MILLS, ELIZABETH JENNINGS,** art educator; b. Baton Rouge, La., Feb. 19, 1947; d. Robert Bernard Jennings and Virginia Adelia (Lobdell) Jennings; m. Wilmer Riddle Millsm Dec. 28, 1967; children: Wilmer Hastings, Evelyn Kate, Virginia Young, John Jennings. BA in Art and English, La. State Univ., 1969. Agrl. missionary to Brazil S.Am. Presbyn. Ch. in U.S., La., 1972-80. Weaving demonstrator ch. and civic groups, St. Francisville, La., 1983—; guest lectr. James Madison U., Harrisonburg, Va., 1995. Dramatic monologue Fanny Mendelsolhm, 2004; exhbns. include Zeigler Mus., Jennings, La., 1993, La. State U., 1995, Cabaret Theater, 1995, La. Arts and Science Ctr. Mus., 1996; weaving exhibit Magnolia Mound Plantation, 2000; portrait show Eight First Ladies and Lecture, 2000; juried art show Grand Isle, La., 2003, 2004. Mem., officer, tchr. The Plains Presbyn. Ch., Zachary, La., 1980—; mem., officer Study Clubs/Book Clubs, Baton Rouge and Zachary, 1982—; vol. Baton Rouge Symphony, 1987-90; tour guide Plantation Homes St. Francisville Pilgrimage, West Feliciana, La. 1985-90, c. 1790 home on Melugh House tour, 2004, film location of Dukes of Hazard movie, 2004-05; mem. award grants panel, E.B.R. Parish, 2003, art com. Zachary Sch. Sys., 2004. Mem. Assoc. Women in the Arts (sec. 1991-93), Artist Guild of West Feliciana (bd. dirs. 1992—), The Weaving Group. Avocations: writing, poetry, weaving, book making, travelling to museums. Home: 22552 Old Scenic Hwy # 964 Zachary LA 70791-6222

**MILLS, ELIZABETH SHOWN,** historical writer, genealogist; b. Cleve., Miss., Dec. 29, 1944; d. Floyd Finley Shown and Elizabeth Thulmar (Jeffcoat) Carver; m. Gary B. Mills, 1963; children: Clayton Bernard, Donna Rachal, Daniel Garland. BA, U. Ala., 1980. Cert. Genealogist, geneal. lectr. Hist. writer, educator, 1972—; editor Nat. Geneal. Soc. Quar., Arlington, Va., 1987—2002. Faculty Samford U. Inst. of Genealogy and Hist. Rsch., Birmingham, Ala., 1980—; trustee Assn. for Promotion of Scholarship in Genealogy, N.Y., 1984-90; contract dir., cons. U. Ala., 1985-92; faculty Nat. Inst. of Geneal. Rsch., 1985-97. Author, editor, translator Cane River Creole Series, 6 vols.; author: Evidence: Citation and Analysis for the Family Historian, 1997, Professional Genealogy: A Manual for Researchers, Writers, Editors, Lecturers, and Librarians, 2001, Isle of Canes: A Historical Novel, 2004; contbr. articles to profl. jours. Trustee Nat. Bd. Certification Genealogists, 1984—, v.p., 1989-94, pres., 1994-96; trustee Assn. Profl. Genealogists, 1984-90, 92-94, presidng v.p., 1988-89. Named Outstanding Young Women of Am. Jaycees, Gadsden, 1976, Outstanding Alumna award U. Ala. New Coll., Tuscaloosa, 1990. Fellow Am. Soc. Geneal. (sec. 1992-95, v.p. 1995-98, pres. 1998-2001), Nat. Geneal. Soc. (councilor 1987-92), Utah Geneal. Assn., Grady McWhiney Rsch. Found. (sr.); mem. Assn. Profl. Genealogists (Smallwood Svc. award, 1989). Republican. Roman Catholic.

**MILLS, EUGENE SUMNER,** academic administrator; b. West Newton, Ind., Sept. 13, 1924; s. Sumner Amos and Lela (Weatherly) M.; m. Dorothy Frances Wildman, Oct. 22, 1945; children: David Walden, Sara Anne. AB, Earlham Coll., 1948; MA, Claremont Grad. U., 1949, PhD, 1952; Spl. Postdoctoral Auditor, Harvard, 1958-59; LLD (hon.), N.H. Coll., 1979, U. N.H., 1988; LHD (hon.), Earlham Coll., 1987. From instr. to prof. psychology Whittier (Calif.) Coll., 1950—60, prof., 1960—62, chmn. dept. psychology,

1952—62; pres. Whittier (Calif.) Coll. and Whittier Coll. Sch. of Law, 1979-89; prof. psychology Whittier (Calif.) Coll., 1979-89, emeritus prof. psychology, pres. emeritus 1989—; faculty U. NH, Durham, 1962—79, dean Grad. Sch., 1963—67, dean Coll. Liberal Arts, 1967—70, acad. v.p., 1970—71, provost, 1971—74, pres., 1974—79. Vis. prof. U. Victoria, B.C., 1958, 60; bd. dirs. Elderhostel, Inc., 1977-97, chmn., 1984-90, vice chmn., 1996-97; vice chmn. Fedco Inc., 1996-98; interim pres. Earlham Coll., 1996-97; mem. NH Psychol. Assn., 1962-79, pres., 1969-70, bd. dirs., 1967-70; trustee Earlham Coll., 1966-69, 96-97, hon. lifetime trustee, 1997—. Author: George Trumbull Ladd: Pioneer American Psychologist, 1969, The Story of Elderhostel, 1993; contbr. articles to profl. jours. Bd. dirs. LA County coun. Boy Scouts Am., 1981—89; bd. dirs. Fedco Charitable Found., 2001—. Danforth Found. grantee; NSF grantee. Fellow Am. Psychol. Assn.; mem. Western Psychol. Assn., Sigma Xi, Phi Kappa Phi., Omicron Delta Kappa Mem. Soc. Of Friends.

**MILLS, FREDERICK VANFLEET,** art educator, watercolorist; b. Bremen, Ohio, June 5, 1925; s. Frederick William and Juanita Ellen (VanFleet) M.; m. Lois Jean Rademacher; children: Mark Steven (dec.), Michael Sherwood, Mollie Sue, Merre Shannon, Randal Dean, Susan Lynn, Todd Patrick, Shondra Marie. BS, Ohio State U., 1949; MS, Ind. U., 1951, EdD, 1956; postgrad., U.S. Army Staff and Command Coll., 1973-76. Tchr. art, supr. Celina (Ohio) Pub. Schs., 1949-51; instr. univ. h.s. Ind. U., 1951-55, prof. art, art edn., chmn. dept. art edn. Bloomington, 1959-65; vis. prof. U. Tex.-Austin, 1965; chmn. dept. related arts, crafts and interior design U. Tenn., Konxville, 1966-68; prof. art, chmn. dept. art Ill. State U., 1968-85, prof. emeritus, 1985—; dist. prof. art Lincoln Coll., Normal, 1986—. Rsch. reader humanities HEW, 1968-69; resource person arts, edn. and Arts. panel Rocketeler Report Am Coun. Arts in Edn., 1977-78; cons. Latin Am. Fulbright Scholarship Program Harvard U., 1981-82; mem. com. III. Fine Arts Rev. for Capital Devel. Bd., 1987—, planning com. Nat. Inst. Advanced Studies in Art and Design and Archives of Am. Art Sch., 1988—, rsch. com. Nat. Sch. Art and Design. One-man shows include McLean County Arts Ctr., Bloomington, Ill., Lincoln (Ill.) Coll., Ill. Agriculture Assn. Credit Union Art Exhbn. Series, Bloomington, Suzette Schochet Gallery, Newport, R.I.; represented in permanent collections Ill. State U. Credit Union, Normal, Ill. State U. Computer Lab., Normal, Mid-Ill. Credit Union, Bloomington, I Wonderlin Gallery, Normal, Ill., State Farm Ins. Co., Kemper Fin. Securities/Kemper Fin. Fund, First of Am. Bank, Ill., Diamond Star Motors Corp., Easter Seal Assn., City of Vladimir, Russia, City of Asahikawa, Hokkaido, Japan, County of McLean, City of Bloomington, Town of Normal; author, editor: The Status of the Visual Arts in Higher Education, 1976, New Perspectives in Visual Arts Administration, 1977, Issues in the Administration of Visual Arts, 1978, Politics and the Visual Arts, 1979, The Visual Arts in the Ninth Decade, 1980; editor Western Arts Bull., 1958-62; featured in 12 part ser. As An Artist Sees local pub. access; contbr. to profl. jours. Pres. Ill. Alliance Art Edn., 1975-77, Ill. Task Force for Arts Edn. in Gen. Edn., 1976-77; mem. Tenn. Arts Commn., 1967-68, Nat. Alliance Arts Edn./Kennedy Ctr., 1975-77; charter trustee Ill. Summer Sch. for Arts, v.p., v.p. Found. Bd., 1988-94; bd. dirs., co-founder Sugar Creek Arts Festival, Normal, 1985—; chair major gifts com. Normal Theater Restoration Project, 1992—; bd. dirs., v.p. McLean County Arts Ctr., Bloomington, 1980-90, sponsor Skilled Crafts award, 1968—. Served to maj. USAR; Col. Ill. Militia. Recipient Recognition award Alliance for Arts Edn., 1984, Outstanding Svc. award Ill. Alliance Arts Edn. 1984, 1994 Ornament of Yr./Alliance of Yr. award, Ill. State U. Alumni Assn. Svc. Awd.; subject articles, TV interviews Mem. Nat. Council Art Adminstrs. (charter, sr. rsch. editor bd. dirs. 1973-81), Nat. Assn. Schs. Art (instnl. del. 1974-84, nominating com. 1977-78, rsch. com. 1976-77), Western Arts Assn. (pres. 1962-64), Coll. Art Assn., Nat. Art Edn. Assn. (bd. dirs. 1980-84), Scabbard and Blade, Phi Delta Kappa, Delta Tau Delta, Delta Phi Delta. Clubs: Rotary Internat. Home: 25306 Arrowhead Lne Hudson IL 61748-9414 *As I reflect on my life and career up to this point, I feel that consistency and humaneness are two words that come to mind. It seems extremely important to be consistent when a person relates to others, and if that is coupled with humaneness and consideration of the value of others, being aware of their strengths and weaknesses, their likes and dislikes, it becomes easier to relate to them in this most complex world of ours.*

**MILLS, GARTH ALLEN, SR.,** not-for-profit fundraiser, consultant; s. Harry Earl Mills, Jr. and Ruth May (Stowe) Mills; m. Ann W. Budd, Dec. 1, 1979; children: Garth Allen Mills, Jr., Daniel Winston, Molly Payne. BA in Internat. Rels., Whittier Coll., Calif., 1978; MEd, James Madison U., Harrisonburg, Va.; advanced grad. studies in philanthropy & leadership, U. Va., Charlottesville, 1986—88. LUTCF Am. Coll., 1991; cert. fund raising exec. Nat. Soc. Fund Raising Execs., 1985, lic. series 7 Nat. Assn. Securities Dealers, 1988. Founding dir. Bridgewater Healthcare Found., Va., 1983—86; chief advancement officer Mary Baldwin Coll., Staunton, Va., 1986—88; council Massanutten Mil. Acad. Found., Woodstock, Va., 1999—2001; exec. dir./counsel Va. War Meml. Ednl. Found., Richmond, Va., 2001—03. Author: (screenplay) To Touch A Memory. Pres. Kiwanis, Harrisonburg, Va., 1990—91. 2nd lt U.S. Army, 1972—73, Korea. Decorated DMG Claremont ROTC. Mem.: Assn. Fund Raising Profls. R-Conservative. Catholic. Avocations: Tae Kwon Do, golf, motorcycling, skeet shooting.

**MILLS, GEORGE MARSHALL,** financial consultant; b. Newton, NJ, May 20, 1923; s. J. Marshall and Emma (Scott) M.; m. Dorothy Lovilla Allen, Apr. 21, 1945; children: Dianne (Mrs. Thomas McKay III), Dorothy L.A. (Mrs. Edward Sphatt). BA, Rutgers U., 1943; MA, Columbia U., 1951. CLU, CPCU; chartered fin. cons.; cert. govt. fund mgr. Pres. George M. Mills Inc., North Brunswick, NJ, 1946—75; pres. CORECO, Inc. Newark, 1960-78; risk mgr. N.J. Hwy. Authority, Woodbridge, 1976-95; pres. Assoc. Risk Mgmt., North Brunswick, NJ, 1995—. Cons. Govs.'s Com. on Bus. Efficiency in Pub. Schs. 1979-90; coun. Risk Mgmt. Ins. Real Estate. Bd. dirs. Alpha Chi Rho Ednl. Found., vice-chmn. 1991-95; workshop Easter Seal Soc.; mem. Gov.'s Task Force on Sound Mcgl. Govt., 1981-82; pres. Nat. Interfrat. Conf., 1979-80. With USNR, 1943-46. Mem. Congl. Bus. Adv. Coun. (chmn. 2003-, co-chair Presdl. Inauguration Com.), Am. Coll. Life Underwriters, Am. Coll. Property Liability Underwriters, Internat. Bridge Tunnel and Turnpike Assn. (chmn. risk mgmt. com. 1980-95, bus. ins. risk mgmt. bd. 1988-95, chair Congress Bus. Adv. Coun. 2003-04, co-chair presdl. inauguration com. 2005, Matthew J. Lenz Jr. medal 1989, Paul K. Addams award 1992, Businessman of Yr. 2003-06, Ronald Reagan Gold medal 2005-06, Presdl. Ronald Reagan Gold medal 2006, Congl. Order of Merit 2006), New Brunswick Hist. Soc., English Congl. Speaking Union, Rutgers Club (trustee), Alpha Chi Rho (nat. councillor 1964-70, nat. pres. 1970-73, nat. treas. 1975-78), Kappa Kappa Psi, Tau Kappa Alpha, Phi Delta Phi. Mem. Reformed Ch. Am. Home: 1054 Hoover Dr New Brunswick NJ 08902-3244 Office Phone: 732-828-2700.

**MILLS, HELENE AUDREY,** retired education educator; b. Oct. 6, 1933; d. Paul Albert and Mabel Meister; m. Ray Mills, Apr. 17, 1954; children: Keith, Katherine(dec.), Kevin. BS in Family Life Edn., Wayne State U., 1954, MEd in Human Resources, 1965, EdD in Gen. Administrn., 1980. Supr., instr. Wayne State Coll. Edn., 1958-67; tchr. life studies, health edn. Seaholm HS, Birmingham, Mich., 1967-72, 74-77, asst. to prin., 1974-77, asst. prin., 1978-79, prin., 1990-97, Derby Mid. Sch., Birmingham, 1980-90; asst. prof. Oakland U., Rochester Hills, Mich., 1997—2002; ret., 2002. Adj. prof. Oakland U., Rochester, 1985—89, Wayne State U., Detroit, 1989—91; consulting editor Clearing Ho., 1985—97. Contbr. articles to profl. jours. Mem. steering com. Meadowbrook Leadership Acad., 1984—87; mem. Detroit Strategic Planning Task Force, 1986—88; mem. exec. bd. Oakland County Youth Assistance, 1987—90; v.p. Cmty. Ho. Sr. Women's Club, Birmingham, Mich., 2004—; program chairperson women's group Northbrooke Ch., 1997—99; mem. adult ministries purpose com., 1998—99. Recipient PTSA Coun. Pres. award, 1982, Celebration of Women award, Greater Detroit Coun. NA'AMAT U.S. 1986, Exemplary Secondary Sch. award, State of Mich., 1991. Mem.: NASCD, Oakland County Secondary Prins. Assn. (pres. 1983—85, Prin. of the Yr. 1991), Mich. Secondary Prins. Assn., Mich. Coun. Family Rels., Mich. Assn. Supervision and Curriculum

Devel., Nat. Secondary Prins. Assn., Nat. Staff Devel. Assn., Birmingham Area Sr. Citizens Assn. (bd. mem., program chair 2003—), Phi Delta Kappa (chmn. mem. Oakland br. 1998—2002).

**MILLS, JAMES,** language educator; s. James and Christina Noble Rutherford (Crawford) Mills; m. Jo Anne Homer, 1968; children: Michael, Shauna, Robert, Joseph. BA in French, Brigham Young U., 1969, MA in French, 1972; PhD, U. Utah, 1980. Cert. tchr. Utah. Instr. French So. Utah State Coll., Cedar City, 1972—76, asst. prof. French, 1976—81, assoc. prof. French, 1981—91, prof. French, 1991—2005; asst. prof. French U. Pa., Clarion, 1987—89. Lectr., presenter in field. Contbr. articles to profl. jours. Vol. Boy Scouts Am., Enoch, Utah, 1982—87; panelist Camp Shakespeare, Cedar City, 1993. Sgt. U.S. Army, 1969—71 USAR, 1971—72. Recipient numerous Rsch. grants. Mem.: Utah Acad. Scis., Arts and Letters, Rocky Mountain MLA, So. Utah Univ. Faculty Senate. Avocations: reading, piano, walking, writing, travel. Office: So Utah Univ Dept Fgn Lang Humanities & Philosophy 531 W Center Cedar City UT 84720 Business E-Mail: mills@suu.edu.

**MILLS, JEFFREY D.,** prosecutor; b. Bedford, Ind., Oct. 3, 1973; s. Christina L. and Jan D. Mills; m. Jessica L. Kopp, June 27, 1998; children: Savanna M., Syney L., Cannon J. BS in Bus. Mgmt., Ind. U., 1997; JD, Ind. U. Sch. of Law, 2000. Assoc. atty. Foley & Lardner LLP, Milw., 2000—01, Baker & Daniels LLP, Indpls., 2001—02, Barnes & Thornburg LLP, Indpls., 2002—04; v.p., assoc. counsel Old Nat. Bank, Indpls., 2004—. Merit scholarship, Ind. U., 1996, 1999, 2000. R-Consevative. Office: Old National Bank 101 W Ohio St Ste 2200 Indianapolis IN 46204 Office Phone: 317-693-2544. Office Fax: 317-693-2541. Business E-Mail: jeff_mills@oldnational.com.

**MILLS, JERRY WOODROW,** lawyer; b. Springfield, Mo., July 17, 1940; s. Woodrow Wilson and Billie Louise M.; m. Marion Cargile, Mar. 27, 1964; children: Eric E., Brendon W. BSEE, Tex. A&M U., 1963; JD, Georgetown U., 1967. Bar: Tex. 1967, U.S. Patent & Trademark Office 1967, US Ct. Fed. Claims, US Dist. Ct. No. Tex., US Ct. Appeals 5th 10th 11th & Fed. Cir. Ptnr. Richards, Harris & Hubbard, Dallas, 1970-82, Baker, Mills & Glast, Dallas, 1982-90; sr. ptnr., chmn. intellectual property dept. & mem. exec. com. Baker Botts LLP, Dallas, 1990—. Adj. prof. So. Meth. U. Law Sch., 1994-97. Bd. dirs. Dallas Legal Svcs. Project, 1972-75, Entrepreneurs Found. No. Tex., trustee & sec. Dallas Theater Ctr., mem. national adv. & develop. council Tex. A&M Univ. Named a Texas Super Lawyer, Texas Monthly mag. & Law & Politics mag., 2003—04. Fellow Tex. Bar Found., Dallas Bar Found.; mem. ABA, Tex. State Jr. Bar Assn. (treas. 1975. dir.), Dallas Jr. Bar Assn. (pres. 1971, Outstanding Young Lawyer award 1975), Dallas Bar Assn. (bd. dirs. 1983-85), Eta Kappa Nu, Phi Eta Sigma, Phi Kappa Phi, Tau Beta Pi. Methodist. Office: Baker Botts LLP 800 Trammell Crow Ctr 2001 Ross Ave Ste 900 Dallas TX 75201-2980 Office Fax: 214-661-4665. Business E-Mail: jerry.mills@bakerbotts.com.

**MILLS, JOHN W.,** academic administrator; BS, U. RI; PhD in Biology, Brown U., 1973. Provost, v.p. academic affairs Paul Smith's College, NY, pres. NY, 2004—. Prof. anatomical scis. Dartmouth U., Harvard U., Temple U., Clarkson U., U. Copenhagen. Office: Paul Smith's Coll Route 86 & 30 PO Box 265 Paul Smiths NY 12970-0265 Office Phone: 518-327-6223. E-mail: millsj@paulsmiths.edu.

**MILLS, JON,** dean, law educator; b. Miami, Fla., July 24, 1947; s. Herb J. and Marguerite (Sweat) M.; m. Beth Bechard; children: Marguerite, Elizabeth. BA, Stetson U., 1969, LLD, 1986; JD, U. Fla., 1972. Mem. Fla. Ho. of Reps., 1978-88, majority leader, 1986-87, speaker, 1987-88; ptnr. McGalliard, Mills, DeMontomollin, Smith, Monaco & Sieg; mem. faculty U. Fla., Gainesville, 1973—80, prof. law, 1996—, interim dean, 1999—2001, dean, 2001—03. Bar Ct Appeals (11th Cir.); mem. Fla. Constitution Revision Commn., 1997—98. Co-author: Voting Rights and Democracy, 1996; contbr. articles to profl. jours. 1st lt. USAR. Decorated Order of Coif; recipient Allen Morris award, 1979-80, 1985-86, Outstanding Legis. award Fla. Health Care Assn., 1982, Most Valuable Member award Fla. Constn. Revision Commn., 1998; named Rep. of Yr. Assn. Retarded Citizens Fla., 1981. Fellow Am. Bar Found.; mem. ABA, Fla. Bar Assn., Pi Kappa Alpha, Fla. Blue Key. Methodist. Home: 2727 NW 58th Blvd Gainesville FL 32606-8516 Office: U Fla Coll Law 230 Bruton-Geer Hall Gainesville FL 32611 also: PO Box 117625 Gainesville FL 32611

**MILLS, KEVIN LEE,** computer scientist, researcher; b. Frederick, Md., Oct. 21, 1951; s. John Lee and Doris Jean (Comer) M.; m. Karen June Davis, Dec. 30, 1972; children: Colin Walter, Elizabeth Anne. BS in Polit. Sci. and Econs., Frostburg (Md.) State U., 1973; MS in Tech. Mgmt., Am. U., 1979; PhD in Info. Tech., George Mason U., 1996. Sr. computer analyst System Devel. Corp., McLean, Va., 1976-81; project mgr. Tesdata Systems Corp., McLean, 1981-82; computer scientist Nat. Bur. of Stds., Gaithersburg, Md., 1982-84, group leader, 1984-87; divsn. chief Nat. Stds. and Tech., Gaithersburg, 1987-95; program mgr. Def. Advanced Rsch. Projects Agy., Arlington, Va., 1996-98; adj. prof. George Mason U., 1996—2006; divsn. chief Nat. Inst. Standards & Technology, Gaithersburg, Md., 1999-2001, sr. rsch. scientist, 2001—. Cons. in field, 1980-82. Contbr. articles to jours. Capt. USMC, 1972-78. Mem. IEEE (sr.), Assn. for Computing Machinery. Avocations: hiking, writing, reading, photography. E-mail: kmills@nist.gov.

**MILLS, LAWRENCE,** lawyer, business and transportation consultant; b. Salt Lake City, Aug. 15, 1932; s. Samuel L. and Beth (Neilson) M. BS, U. Utah, 1955, JD, 1956. Bar: Utah 1956, ICC 1961, U.S. Supreme Ct. 1963. With W.S. Hatch Co. Inc., Woods Cross, Utah, 1947-89, gen. mgr., 1963-89, v.p., 1970-89, also dir. Bd. dirs. Nat. Tank Truck Carriers, Inc., Washington, 1963—, pres., 1974-75, chmn. bd., 1975-76; mem. motor carrier adv. com. Utah State Dept. Transp., 1979—; keynote speaker Rocky Mountain Safety Suprs. Conf., 1976; mem. expedition to Antartica, 1996, Titanic Expedition, 1996. Contbr. articles to legal and profl. jours. and transp. publs. Del. to County and State Convs., Utah, 1970-72; v.p. Utah Safety Coun., 1979-82, bd. dirs., 1979—, pres., 1983-84; mem. Utah Gov's Adv. Com. on Small Bus.; capt. Easter Seal Telethon, 1989, 90; state vice chmn. High Frontier, 1987—; mem. adv. com. Utah State Indsl. Commn., 1988—, chmn. com. studying health care cost containment and reporting requirements 1990—; mem. expdn. to Antarctica, 1996, Titanic '96 expedition, Iceland expedition, 2001, Greenland expedition, 2001. Recipient Safety Dir. award Nat. Tank Carriers Co., 1967, Outstanding Svc. and Contbn. award, 1995, Trophy award W.S. Hatch Co., 1975, Disting. Svc. award Utah State Indsl. Commn., 1992, Outstanding Svc. award Utah Safety Coun., 1994. Mem. Salt Lake County Bar Assn., Utah Motor Transport Assn. (dir. 1967—, pres. 1974-76, Outstanding Achievement Award 1989), Utah Hwy. Users Assn. (dir. 1981—), Indsl. Rels. Coun. (dir. 1974—), Salt Lake City C. of C., U.S. Jaycees (life Senator 1969—, ambassador 1977—, pres. Utah Senate 1979-80, Henry Giessenbier fellow 1989), Nat. Petroleum Coun., Utah Associated Gen. Contractors (assoc. 1975-77, 88—), Silver Tank Club, Hillsdale Coll. President's Club, Traveler's Century Club. Home: HC 11 Box 329 Kamiah ID 83536-9410 *Personal philosophy: Excessive government regulation stifles individual initiative. We should learn from the downfall of communism.*

**MILLS, MARGARET H.,** linguist; b. Davenport, Iowa, Jan. 8, 1954; d. Oliver Wendell and Elizabeth Barrett Hill; m. Marcus M. Mills, May 22, 1976; children: Olivia Lauren, Hillary Barrett, Caroline Manning. BA; MA, U. Iowa; PhD in Slavic Linguistics, U. Mich., 1985; MPH, U. Iowa, 2005. Instr., asst. prof. Russian Ill. State U., Normal, 1984—86; asst. prof. Russian Georgetown U., Washington, 1986—89, U. Iowa, Iowa City, 1989—93, assoc. prof. Russian, 1993—2000, prof. Russian, 2000—. Author: Topics in Colloquial Russian, 1990, UI Neonatology Handbook, 1997, Slavic Gender Linguistics, 1999, Medical Issues and Health Care Reform in Russia, 1999; contbr. articles to profl. jours. Grantee, Nat. Rsch. Coun., 1997, Social Sci. Rsch. Coun., 1996—98, NIH, 2000, Eurasia Found., Washington and Moscow, 2000, Am. Coun. Internat. Edn., Moscow, 2001. Office: U Iowa Dept Russian Iowa City IA 52242

**MILLS, MARK S.,** biology professor; BS in Biology, U. Nebr., Omaha, 1986, MA in Biology, 1991; PhD, U. Ga., 1990—98. Contbr. chapters to books, articles to profl. jours. and pubs. Merit badge counselor Boy Scouts Am., Marshall; ch. bd. and worship team Marshall Ch. of the Nazarene, Marshall. Recipient John McCallum Tchg. award, Mo. Valley Coll., 2006. Mem.: Soc. for Study of Amphibians and Reptiles, Herpetologists League, Am. Soc. Ichthyologists and Herpetologists, Sigma Xi. Mem. Christian Ch. Office: Missouri Valley Coll 500 E College St Marshall MO 65340 Office Phone: 660-831-4203.

**MILLS, MICHAEL PAUL,** judge; b. Charleston, South Carolina, Aug. 25, 1956; s. Paul H. and Shirley (Dulaney) M.; m. Mona (Robinson), Aug. 2, 1976; children: Alysson, Chip, Rebekah, Penn. AA, Itawamba Cmty. Coll., Fulton, Miss., 1976; BA, U. Miss., 1978, JD, 1980; LLM, U. Va., 2001. Bar: Miss., 1980; U.S. Ct. Appeals (Fed. Cir.), 1986; U.S. Ct. Appeals (5th cir.), 1980; U.S. Supreme Ct., 1990. Pvt. practice, Miss., 1980-95; legis. Miss. Ho. of Reps., Jackson, Miss., 1983-95; mem. Nat. Conf. Commr. on Uniform State Laws, 1993—; justice Miss. Supreme Ct., Jackson, Miss., 1995—2001; judge US Dist. Ct. (no. dist.), Miss., Oxford, 2001—. Adj. prof. law U. Miss. Office: Fed Bldg Rm 335 911 Jackson Ave Oxford MS 38655 Office Phone: 662-234-1538. Office Fax: 662-234-1447.

**MILLS, OLAN, II,** photography company executive; b. 1930; married. Grad., Princeton U., 1952. With Olan Mills, Inc., Chattanooga, 1955—, now chmn. Office: Olan Mills Inc Gen Offices 4325 Amnicola Hwy Chattanooga TN 37406-1014

**MILLS, RICHARD HENRY,** federal judge; b. Beardstown, Ill., July 19, 1929; s. Myron Epler and Helen Christine (Greve) M.; m. Rachel Ann Keagle, June 16, 1962; children: Jonathan K., Daniel Cass. BA, Ill. Coll., 1951; JD, Mercer U., 1957; LLM, U. Va., 1982. Bar: Ill. 1957, U.S. Dist. Ct. Ill. 1958, U.S. Ct. Appeals 1959, U.S. Ct. Mil. Appeals 1963, U.S. Supreme Ct. 1963. Legal advisor Ill. Youth Commn., 1958-60; state's atty. Cass County, Virginia, Ill., 1960-64; judge Ill. 8th Jud. Cir., Virginia, 1966-76, Ill. 4th Dist. Appellate Ct., Springfield, Ill., 1976-85, U.S. Dist. Ct. (cen. dist.) Ill., Springfield, 1985—. Adj. prof. So. Ill. U. Sch. Medicine, 1985-06; mem. adv. bd. Nat. Inst. Corrections, Washington, 1984-88, Ill. Supreme Ct. Rules Com., Chgo., 1963-85. Contbr. articles to profl. jours. Pres. Abraham Lincoln coun. Boy Scouts Am., 1978-80. With U.S. Army, 1952-54, Korea, col. res.; maj. gen. Ill. Militia. Recipient George Washington Honor medal Freedoms Found., 1969, 73, 75, 82, Disting. Eagle Scout Boy Scouts Am., 1985. Fellow Am. Bar Found.; mem. ABA, Nat. Conf. Fed. Trial Judges (chmn. 1999-00), Ill. Bar Assn., Chgo. Bar Assn., Cass County Bar Assn. (pres. 1962-64, 75-76), Sangamon County Bar Assn., 7th Cir. Bar Assn., Am. Law Inst., Fed. Judges Assn., Army and Navy Club (Washington), Sangamo Club, Masons (33 degree), Lincoln-Douglas Am. Inn of Ct. 150 (founding, pres. 1991-93). Republican. Episcopalian. Home: US Dist Ct 600 E Monroe St Ste 117 Springfield IL 62701-1659 Office Phone: 217-492-4340.

**MILLS, RICHARD PAUL,** school system administrator; b. Paris, Nov. 28, 1944; m. Judith Mills. BA with honors, Middlebury Coll., 1966; MA in Am. History, Columbia U., 1967, MBA, 1975, EdD, 1977. Tchr. history Dalton Sch., NYC, 1967—71; creator with others Elizabeth Seeger Sch., NYC, 1971—73; planning assoc. N.J. Dept. of Edn., 1975-78, dir. policy analysis, 1978-80, dep. asst. commr., 1980-82, spl. asst. to the commr., 1982-84; spl. asst. to Gov. Thomas H. Kean of N.J., 1984-88; commr. of edn. State of Vt., 1988-95, State of N.Y., 1995—; pres. Univ. of the State of N.Y., 1995—. Adj. asst. prof. Columbia Univ. Tchrs. Coll., 1977; adj. assoc. prof. Rider Coll., N.J., 1979; cons. task force to oversee fiscal reform in Newark, 1975; tchr. The Dalton Sch., N.Y.C., 1967-71, Elizabeth Seeger Sch., N.Y.C., 1971-73; mem. Carnegie Task Force on Learning in the Primary Grades; chair mgmt. group Nat. Alliance for Restructuring Edn.; bd. New Stds. Project; mem. bd. Nat. Ctr. on Edn. and the Economy. Contbr. articles to profl. jours. U.S. rep. to standing com. European Ministers of Edn., 1987. Office: NY State Edn Dept 111 Edn Bldg 89 Washington Ave Albany NY 12234-4909

**MILLS, ROBERT BRUCE (BOB MILLS),** retired deputy county clerk; b. LA, Calif., Aug. 2, 1930; s. John Gordon and Mabelle Agnes (Kent) Mills; m. Diane Parcel (div.); 1 child, Susan Lynne; m. Charlotte Ann Schmutz, June 8, 1963. BA, U. So. Calif., LA, 1953; MEd, Whitworth Coll., Spokane, Wash., 1982. Secondary tchr. Glendale Unified Sch. Dist., Calif.; supr. tng. Calif. Water & Tel. Co., Monrovia; exec. dir. Lockheed Mgmt. Assn., Burbank, Calif.; dir., pub. rels. S.F. Valley Child Guidance Clinic, Van Nuys, Calif.; dep. county clk.-superior ct. Office of County Clk., Spokane County, Wash.; ret., 2001. Regional v.p. Nat. Mgmt. Assn., Dayton, Ohio, 1969—72; shop steward AFSCME Union AFL/CIO, Spokane, Wash., 1978—84. Author: (book chpt.) Human Resources in Aerospace, 1972. Co-founder, treas., pres. Daybreak Youth Svcs., spokane, Wash., 1972—86; bd. mem. Habitat for Humanity, Spokane, Wash., 1996—2002. With U.S. Army, 1954—56. Democrat. Presbyn. Home: 410 Hare Ln Deer Park WA 99006 Personal E-mail: sirbob830@earthlink.net.

**MILLS, ROBERT LEE,** retired academic administrator; b. Erlanger, Ky., Nov. 13, 1916; s. John Clifford and Dixie Lee (Morris) M.; m. Mildred Sizer, June 24, 1942 (div.); children: Robert Lee, Dixie Louise, Barbara Jean. AB in Math. and Physics, U. Ky., 1938, MA in Ednl. Adminstrn, 1941, Ed.D., 1951; LLD, William Jewell Coll., 1971. Tchr. Covington (Ky.) pub. schs., 1938-41; head hydraulics br. Air Force Tech. Sch., Lincoln, Nebr., 1942-44; mem. supervisory staff electromagnetic plant Oak Ridge, Tenn., 1944-48; rsch. asst. U. Ky., Lexington, 1948-51, dean admissions, registrar, 1954-57; dir. rsch., head bur. adminstrn. and fin. Ky. Dept. Edn., 1951-54; chmn. dept. ednl. adminstrn. U. Tex., Austin, 1957-59; pres. Georgetown (Ky.) Coll., 1959-78, chancellor, 1978-86, ret., 1986, pres. emeritus, 1987—. Exec. sec. Ky. Adv. Commn. Ednl. Policy, 1952-54; v.p. Ky. Assn. Colls. and Secondary Schs., 1962-63, exec. com., 1959-64, pres., 1963-64; chmn. exec. com. Ky. Ind. Coll. Found.; mem. Commn. on Higher Edn., 1970-77, Ky. Govt. Council, 1968-72; adviser Texas Assn. Sch. Bds., 1957-59 Contbr. articles to profl. jours. Cons. Pres.' Com., White House Conf. Edn., 1955; mem. Ky. Devel. Council, 1961-65, Ky. Constn. Revision Commission, 1964-66. Recipient Distinguished Alumni award U. Ky., 1963, Centennial award, 1964 Mem. Nat., Ky. edn. assns.; Newcomen Soc., So. Assn. Bapt. Colls. (pres. 1965-66), Bapt. World Alliance (mem. exec. com. 1965-70, chmn. men's dept. 1965-67), So. Assn. Colls. and Schs. (commn. on colls. 1971-77), Kappa Delta Pi, Phi Delta Kappa, Phi Kappa Tau. Lodges: Kiwanis. Democrat. Baptist.

**MILLS, STACEY WEBSTER,** music educator, musician; b. New Orleans, Aug. 1, 1959; d. Charles Peyton Webster and Bobbye Cole Wilson; m. David James Mills, Dec. 22, 1984; children: John Dav9d, Robert Tucker. B Music Edn., U. NC, Chapel Hill, 1981. Cert. tchr. NC. Band dir. Charlotte Mecklenburg Schs., 1981—86, Charlotte County Day Schs., 1996—; trumpet player Charlotte Symphony Orch., 1989—94, Brass Charlotte Quintet, 1992—. Instrumental music coord. Montreat (NC) Music and Worship Conf., 2002, 03, 05. Mem. music com. Covenant Presbyn. Ch., Charlotte, 2003—04, mem. coll. coun., 2006—. Recipient O'Herron award, Charlotte Country Day Sch., 2004. Mem.: NC Music Educators Assn., Music Educators Nat. Conf. Democrat. Presbyterian. Avocations: pets, exercise, reading, brass quinette. Office: Charlotte Country Day Sch 1440 Carmel Rd Charlotte NC 28226

**MILLS, STEPHEN,** artistic director; Prin. dancer Ballet Austin, 1987, choreographer, 1988, resident choreographer, 1992, assoc. artistic dir., 1999—, artistic dir., 2002—. Instr. Internat Theatrical Inst., Cyprus; master tchr. Booker T. Washington H.S. for the Performing Arts, Dallas, U. Va. Sch. of the Arts, New Orleans Ctr. for Creative Arts, Stephens Coll., Mo., Point Park Coll., Pitts., Ballet Austin. Choreographed works have been shown at Ballet Builders at Lincoln Ctr., 1998, Rencontres Chorégraphiques Internat. des Seine-Saint-Denis, Paris, Cuballet, Havana, The Dayton Ballet, The Sarasota (Fla.) Ballet, Ballet Pacifica, Dallas Black Dance Theatre, Dance Kaleidoscope, Ontario Ballet Theatre, Toronto, Icelandic Ballet Co., Reykjavik;

performing mem. Harkness Ballet, Am. Dance Machine, Cin. Ballet, Indpls. Ballet Theatre, Balanchine Repertoire. Bd. trustees Dance USA. Office: Ballet Austin 3002 Guadalupe St Austin TX 78705-2818*

**MILLS, STEVEN A.,** information technology executive; Sales trainee, mktg. rep. IBM, N.Y.C., 1974—80, mem. bus. planning staff divsn. data processing, 1981—82, mgr. bus. planning staff, 1982—84, adminstrv. asst. to v.p. and asst. group exec. plans and controls, 1984—85, dir. planning info. sys. and comm. group, 1985—88, dir. fin. planning, 1988—89, dir. ops. programming sys., 1989—90, asst. gen. mgr. fin. and planning, 1990—92, gen. mgr. Santa Teresa lab., 1992—95; gen. mgr. global software strategy and solutions IBM Software Group, 1995—2000, sr. v.p., group exec., 2000—. Mem. ops. com. IBM, mem. worldwide mgmt. coun., mem. corp. tech. com. Office: IBM 1133 Westchester Ave White Plains NY 10604

**MILLS, THOMAS L.,** lawyer; b. Elmira, NY, Jan. 4, 1948; BS, U.S. Coast Guard Acad., 1970; JD, George Washington U., 1975. Bar: DC 1975. Mng. ptnr., chmn. health law practice Winston & Strawn LLP, Washington, 1995—. Dir. bd. control U.S. Coast Guard Acad. Alumni Assn. Lt. U.S. Coast Guard, 1970—75. Mem.: DC Bar Assn., Order of Coif. Office: Winston & Strawn LLP 1400 L St NW Washington DC 20005-3502 Office Phone: 202-371-5714. Office Fax: 202-371-5950. E-mail: tmills@winston.com.

**MILLS, WILLIAM HAROLD, JR.,** construction executive; b. St. Petersburg, Fla., July 24, 1939; s. William Harold and Caroline (Bonfoey) M.; m. Sylvia Ludwig, Jan. 4, 1962 (div. 1975); children— William Harold III, Robert Michael, Leslie Anne; m. Kimberly Keyes, May 4, 1985 (div. 1988); m. Gigi Alice Schmidt, Aug. 1, 1990. Grad., Woodberry Forest Sch., 1954-57; BS in Civil Engring., U. Fla., 1961. Cert. Class A gen. contractor, Fla. V.p. bus. devel. Mills & Jones Constrn., St. Petersburg, Fla., 1964-68; v.p. Wellington Corp., Atlanta, 1968-71; exec. v.p. Mills & Jones Constrn., St. Petersburg, Fla., 1971-79; pres., chmn. Federal Constrn. Co., St. Petersburg, 1979-88, vice chmn., 1988—; pres., chair Univ. Housing Svcs., Inc., St. Petersburg. Mem. adv. com. St Petersburg Port, 1993—. Pres. St. Petersburg Progress, inc., 1986-87; active mem. Suncoasters, St. Petersburg, 1974—, St. Anthony's Devel. Found., St. Petersburg, 1983-86; past chmn. Pinellas Marine Inst., St. Petersburg, Blue Ribbon Zoning Com., City of St. Petersburg; mem. Tony Janus Award Com.; former mem. Pinellas County Constrn. Licensing Bd., Tampa Bay Aviation Adv. Com., United Fund Pinellas County; former mem. U. South Fla. Campus Adv. Bd. Served with USPHS, 1962-64. Named Hon. Royal Navy Liaison officer Her Majesty's Royal Navy, 1984. Mem. ASCE, NSPE, Am. Mgmt. Assn., Mensa, St. Petersburg Area C. of C. (bd. govs. 1983-85), Fla. Sports Adv. Coun., Order of Salvador/Salvador Dali Mus., St. Petersburg Yacht Club, Dragon Club, Les Ambassadurs Club (London), Annabel's Club (London), Useppa Island Club (past bd. govs.), Sigma Alpha Epsilon, U.S. Croquet Assn., Univ. Fla. Pres.'s Coun. (life). Republican. Episcopalian. Home: 1260 Brightwaters Blvd NE Saint Petersburg FL 33704-3728 E-mail: wmillsjr@uhsi.com.

**MILLS, WILLIAM HAYES,** lawyer; b. Gordo, Ala., Mar. 30, 1931; s. Early S. and Bama (Cameron) M. LLB, U. Ala., 1956. Bar: Ala. 1956. Pvt. practice, Birmingham, Ala.; ptnr. Rogers, Howard, Redden & Mills, 1961—79, Redden, Mills & Clark, 1979—. Arbitrator Fed. Mediation and Conciliation Svc., Am. Arbitration Assn. Served with AUS, 1948-50, 50-51. Mem. ABA, Ala. Bar Assn., Birmingham Bar Assn. Baptist. Home: 2105 Williamsburg Way Birmingham AL 35223-1740 Office: Redden Mills & Clark 940 Financial Ctr Birmingham AL 35203 Office Phone: 205-322-0457. Business E-Mail: whm@rmclaw.com.

**MILLS, WILLIAM JAMES, JR.,** orthopedist, surgeon, researcher; b. San Francisco, Calif., July 7, 1918; s. William James Mills and Rose Lena Conrad; m. Elaine Mary Nagelvoort, Aug. 23, 1952; children: Sarah, Janet, William, Martha, Mary, John, Matthew. BA, U. Calif., 1942; MD, Stanford U., 1950; LittD (hon.), U. Alaska, 2003; DSc (hon.), U. Man., 2006. Cert. Am. Coll. Surgery, Am. Acad. Orthopedic Surgery, Am. Orthopedic Assn., Arctic Inst. N. Am. Intern U. Mich. Hosp., Ann Arbor, Mich., 1949—51, resident, 1951—54; pvt. practice orthopaedist Anchorage, 1955—66; pvt. practice orthop. surgeon, 1968—; surgeon U.S. Naval Hosp., DaNang, Vietnam, 1966—67; asst. prof. Vanderbilt U. Hosp., Nashville, 1967—68. Founder, dir. Alaska Arctic Med. Rsch. Found., Anchorage, 1978—; adj. prof. U. Alaska, Anchorage, 1980—; clin. prof. dept. orthop. surgery U. Wash. Editor-in-chief: Alaska Medicine Jour., 1959; contbr. scientific articles, photographs to jours. Rear admiral USNR, 1942—78, WWII, Vietnam, ret. USNR, 1978. Recipient Dr. Helen Whaley award, Alaska Treatment Ctr., Alpine Team medal, City of Lecco, Italy, 1961, Disting. Achievement award, U. Mich., 2002, Jack Hildes medal, Circumpolar Health Soc., 2003, Disting. Achievement, U. Mich., 2001. Fellow: ACS, Am. Orthop. Assn., Am. Acad. Orthop. Surgeons. Avocations: camping, fly fishing, reading, stamp collecting/philately, gardening. Home and Office: 1544 Hidden Lane Anchorage AK 99501

**MILLS, WILLIAM R.,** food products executive; V.p. fin., sec. Weis Markets, Sundbury, Pa., 1992—2002, sr. v.p., 2002—, CFO, 2002—, treas., 2002—. Bd. dirs. Weis Markets. Office: Weis Markets 1000 S Second St Sunbury PA 17801

**MILLSAPS, FRED RAY,** investor; b. Blue Ridge, Ga., Apr. 30, 1929; s. Samuel Hunter and Ora Lee (Bradshaw) M.; m. Audrey Margaret Hopkins, June 22, 1957; children: Judith Gail, Stephen Hunter, Walter Scott. AB, Emory U., 1951; postgrad., U. Wis. Sch. Banking, 1955-57, Harvard Bus. Sch., 1962; LLD, Fla. So. Coll., 1991. V.p. Fed. Res. Bank, Atlanta, 1958-64: fin. v.p. Fla. Power & Light Co., 1965-69; chmn., pres. Landmark Banking Corp. of Fla., Ft. Lauderdale, 1969-78. Bd. dirs. Franklin Templeton Mut. Funds, Mut. Shares Funds. Chmn. South Fla. Coordinating Coun., 1976-78, WPBT Cmty. TV Found. of South Fla., 1973-75, Fla. So. Coll., Lakeland, 1976-95, Broward Performing Arts Authority, Honda Classic, Broward Workshop, Holy Cross Health Corp.; mem. Fla. Coun. of 100. Mem. Coral Ridge Country Club. Methodist.

**MILLSAPS, WILLIAM HOBART, JR.,** retired editor; b. Chattanooga, July 1, 1942; s. William Hobart and Myra Sue (Bryant) M.; m. Nancy Dickenson Hurt; children: Katherine Gail Millsaps Renick, Camerian Sue. Student, U. Tenn., 1960-66. Sports writer The Knoxville (Tenn.) Jour., 1963-66, Richmond (Va.) Times-Dispatch, 1966-71, assoc. sports editor, 1972, exec. sports editor, 1973-76, sports editor, 1977-91, mng. editor, 1992-93, exec. editor, 1994—2005; ret., 2005. Pres. U.S. Basketball Writers Assn., 1986, AP Sports Editors, 1980; pres. Leadership Metro Richmond Alumni Assn., 1995. Named to, U.S. Basketball Writers Assn. Hall of Fame, media wing Va. Sports Hall of Fame, Va. Comm. Hall of Fame; recipient 11 Va. Sports Writer of Yr. awards, Nat. Sportscasters and Sportswriters Assn. Mem. Willow Oaks Country Club (Richmond) Presbyterian. Avocations: reading, golf.

**MILLSON, RORY OLIVER,** lawyer; b. Capetown, Republic of South Africa, Nov. 26, 1950; s. Harry E. and Fay Leonard (Liesching) M.; m. Linda Ellen Rodd, June 15, 1985; children: Helen Fay, John Rodd, Henry Francis. BA, Yale U., 1973, JD, 1977; MA, Oxford U., Eng., 1975. Bar: N.Y. 1978, U.S. Dist. Ct. (so. and ea. dists.) N.Y. 1978, U.S. Ct. Appeals (D.C. cir.) 1990, U.S. Ct. Appeals (2d cir.) 1991, U.S. Supreme Ct. 1991. With Cravath, Swaine & Moore, N.Y.C., 1976—, ptnr., litig., 1984—. Office: Cravath Swaine & Moore 825 8th Ave Fl 38 New York NY 10019-7475 Office Phone: 212-474-1672. Office Fax: 212-474-3700. Business E-Mail: rmillson@cravath.com.

**MILLSPAUGH, MARTIN LAURENCE,** real estate developer, consultant; b. Columbus, Ohio, Dec. 16, 1925; s. Martin Laurence and Elisabeth (Park) M.; m. Meredith Plant, May 10, 1952; children: Elisabeth, M. Laurence, Meredith, Thomas. AB summa cum laude, Princeton U., 1949. Reporter, columnist Richmond News Leader, Va., 1949-53; urban affairs writer Balt. Evening Sun, 1953-57; asst. commr. Urban Renewal Adminstrn., Washington, 1957-60; dep. gen. mgr. Charles Ctr., Balt., 1960-65; pres., chmn., CEO

Charles Ctr.-Inner Harbor Mgmt., Inc., 1965-85; exec. v.p., pres., vice chmn. Enterprise Devel. Co., Columbia, Md., 1985—2005; pres. Enterprise Internat. Devel. Co., Columbia, 1988-91, vice chmn., 1991—2005, Enterprise Real Estate Svcs., Inc., 1996—2005; pvt. practice Balt., 2005—. Conducted seminars in Nagasaki and Kagoshima, Japan, 1991-92; lectr. Columbia U., Princeton U., Johns Hopkins U., U. Md., U. New Orleans, NYU, Acad. Polit. Sci., AAAS, Lambda Alpha Internat. Urban Land Inst., 1985-95, U.K. Inst. Travel and Tourism, 1993, Can. Water Resources Assn., 1991, Nat. Bldg. Mus., 1995, Internat. Property Market, Cannes, 1996, others; appeared on USIA Worldnet TV Dialogue, Montevideo, Uruguay, 1990, Recife and Rio de Janeiro, 1995; cons. in field. Author: (with others) The Human Side of Urban Renewal, 1958; author (newspaper series) Design for Living (hon. mention Heywood Broun award 1957); profl. appearances include VOA, 1994, CBS Sunday News, 1994; contbr. articles to profl. jours. Trustee Enoch Pratt Free Libr., Balt., 1965-85, Gilman Sch., 1975-80, Bryn Mawr Sch. for Girls, 1978-81; bd. dirs. Planned Parenthood Assn. Md., 1962-65, Roland Park Civic League, 1962-64, sec., 1963-64, Blue Cross of Md., Inc., 1970-80, Balt. Symphony Orch. Assn., 1974-78, YMCA Greater Balt. area, 1977-81; Md. Internat. Coun., Balt., 1992-96, mem. long range planning com., 1994-96, sec., 1995-96; chair nominating com. World Trade Ctr. Inst., 1996-01; task force Twentieth Century Fund, NYC, 1984-85; adv. coun. real estate devel. program Columbia U. Grad. Sch. Architecture and Planning, 1985-94; bd. advisors Fight-Blight Fund, Balt., 1961-62, Waterfront Ctr., Washington, 1987-90; adv. bd. Nat. Aquarium, Balt., 1988-2001, Sch. Bus. Mgmt. Morgan State U., 1993-94, Real Estate Inst., Sch. Profl. and Bus. Studies Johns Hopkins U., 1994-2006, chair, 2000-2002; pres.'s adv. bd. U. Md. Balt. County, 1989-94; adv. bd. Ctr. for Balt. Studies/U. Balt., 2001-02; adv. panel Ctr. Strategic and Internat. Studies, Washington, 1993-94; mem. Md. Transp. Real Estate Adv. Group, 1996; mem. U.S. Senate Productivity Award Selection Com. for Md., 1987. Sgt. USAF, 1944-46, PTO. Recipient Disting. Svc. award U.S. Housing and Home Fin. Agy., Washington, 1960, Urban Planning award The Waterfront Ctr., 1995, Awd. for Civic Accomplishment Greater Balt. Comm., 1981, Prix d'Excellence Awd. Internat. Real Estate Fedn., 1997. Mem. Urban Land Inst. (hon., exec. group internat. coun., 1989-97, vice chmn. internat. coun. 1995-96, chair adv. panel for city of Harrisburg, Pa., 1984, internat. com. 1987-88, Balt. dist. coord. 1987-91, vice-chmn. dist. coun. 1991-94, Balt. dist. coun. exec. com. 1992-, adv. panel for Oklahoma City, 1995, chair Project Analysis Chattanooga, 1999, awards com. 1995-97, Award of Excellence, 1980), Internat. Real Estate Fedn. (greater Balt. com. 2005—), urban affairs coun. 1982-87), Coun. on Urban Econ. Devel., Internat. Downtown Assn., Internat. New Town Assn. (adv. panel for waterfront devel. for City of Malmo, Sweden 1987), Phi Beta Kappa, Lambda Alpha. Clubs: Center, Balt., 14 W Hamilton St (Balt.); Ivy (Princeton, NJ). Democrat. Episcopalian. Home: 203 Ridgewood Rd Baltimore MD 21210-2538 E-mail: mmillsii@aol.com.

**MILLSTEIN, IRA M.,** lawyer, educator; b. NYC, Nov. 8, 1926; s. Harry M. and Birdie E. (Rosenbaum) M.; m. Diane G. Greenberg, July 3, 1949; children: James Eliot, Elizabeth Jane. BS, Columbia U., 1947, LL.B., 1949. Bar: N.Y. 1949, U.S. Supreme Ct. 1973. Atty. antitrust div. Dept. Justice, Washington, 1949-51; assoc. firm Weil Gotshal & Manges LLP, N.Y.C., 1951-57, ptnr., 1957—. Fellow faculty govt. John F. Kennedy Sch. Govt., Harvard U., 1983-87; Eugene F. Williams Jr. vis. prof. in competetive enterprise and strategy Yale Sch. Mgmt., 1996—; chmn. emeritus pvt. sector adv. group on corp. Global Corp. Governance Forum sponsored by World Bank/OECD-Paris, Washington, 1999—; counsel, bd. dirs. Lower Manhattan Devel. Corp., 2002-; bd. mem. World Trade Ctr. Meml. Found.; chmn. NY State Commn. Pub. Authority Reform. Author: (with Katsh) The Limits of Corporate Power, 1981, (with McAvoy) The Recurrent Crisis in Corporate Governance, 2003; contbr. articles to profl. jours. Mem. Nat. Commn. on Consumer Fin., 1969-72, chmn., 1971-72; chmn. exec. com. bd. overseers Albert Einstein Coll. Medicine, Yeshiva U., Bronx, N.Y., 1981—, chmn., 2004—; chmn. bd. trustees Cen. Pk. Conservancy, 1990-99; co-chair NYSE, NASD Blue Ribbon com. on improving audit coms., 1999. Decorated chevalier Nat. Order of Merit, France. Mem. Am. Acad. Arts and Scis. (elected), ABA (chmn. antitrust law sect. 1977-78), N.Y. State Bar Assn. (chmn. antitrust law sect. 1967-68), Nat. Assn. Corp. Dirs. (bd. dirs. 1994—2004, governance coun. 2004—), Met. Club, Quaker Ridge Golf Club. Home: 1240 Flagler Dr Mamaroneck NY 10543-4601 Office: Weil Gotshal & Manges LLP 767 5th Ave Ste 3201 New York NY 10153-0023 Business E-Mail: ira.millstein@weil.com.

**MILLSTEIN, JULIAN STUART,** lawyer; b. NYC, Sept. 14, 1944; s. David and Elizabeth Millstein. BA, Brandeis U., 1965; JD, Fordham U., 1978. Bar: NY 1979, NJ 1994, US Dist. Ct. (so. dist.) NY 1979, US Dist. Ct. (ea. dist.) N.Y. 1980, US Ct. Appeals (2d and 9th cirs.) 1982. Computer programmer Met. Life Ins. Co., NYC, 1965-66; cons. Programming Methods Corp., NYC, 1966-73; systems officer Mfrs. Hanover Trust Co., NYC, 1973-77; assoc. Hughes Hubbard & Reed, NYC, 1978-82; ptnr. Brown Raysman Millstein Felder & Steiner LLP, NYC, 1982—2005. Adj. prof. Fordham Law Sch., NYC, 1991—. Author: Doing Business on the Internet: Forms and Analysis, 1997; editor-in-chief Computer Law Strategist, 1984—, Multimedia and Web Strategist, 1994—, e-Commerce Law and Strategy, 1984-2002. Mem. Computer Law Assn., NY State Bar Assn. (chair com. on internet and tech. law 1995-98), Assn. Bar City NY (computer law com. 1997-99). Office: Brown Raysman Millstein Felder & Steiner LLP 900 Third Ave New York NY 10022 Office Phone: 212-895-2420. E-mail: JMillstein@brownraysman.com.

**MILLSTEIN, LINCOLN,** media company executive; BA in Polit. Sci., U. Conn.; postgrad., Stanford U., 1980—81. Reporter, editor The Hartford Courant, 1973—83; bus. editor, 1981—83; varous editor positions The Globe, 1983—85; v.p. new media The Boston Globe, 1995—99; CEO Boston.com, 1998—99; group v.p., pub. N.Y. Times Digital, N.Y. Times Co., NY, 1999—2000, exec. v.p. NY, 2000—04; sr. v.p., dir. digital media Hearst Newspapers, 2005—. Profl. Journalism fellow, NEH, 1980—81 Achievements include development and introduction of The Globe 100 list of the top companies in Massachusetts in 1989. Office: Hearst 250 W 55th St New York NY 10019-5201

**MILLSTEIN, RICHARD ALLEN,** federal agency administrator; b. N.Y.C., Jan. 21, 1945; s. Abraham and Minnie (Zahn) M.; m. Nancy Louise Karelitz, Aug. 10, 1968; children: Danna Karen, Eric Jon, Todd David. BA, NYU, 1964; JD cum laude, Boston U., 1968. Bar: N.Y. 1968. Spl. asst. to dir. NIMH, Chevy Chase, Md., 1968-70, from legal asst. to acting chief legis. svcs. br. Rockville, Md., 1970-73; chief legis. svcs. unit Alcohol, Drug Abuse and Mental Health Adminstrn., Rockville, 1973-77, 78-79, assoc. adminstr. planning, policy analysis and legis., 1979-85, assoc. adminstr. for policy coordination, 1986-87; profl. staff liaison Pres.'s Commn. on Mental Health The White House, Washington, 1977-78, sr. staff mem. Drug Abuse Policy Office, 1987-88; exec. asst. to asst. sec. for health HHS, Washington, 1985-86; dep. dir. Nat. Inst. on Drug Abuse, Rockville, 1988—92, 1994—2003, acting dir., 1992—94; acting dep. dir. John G. Fogarty Internat. Ctr. for Advanced Study in Health Scis., NIH, Bethesda, Md., 2004—. Editor Periodic Summaries of Proposed and Enacted Fed. Legis., 1971-77; columnist On the Federal Scene Adminstrn. in Mental Health, 1973-76; contbr. articles to profl. jours. Bd. dirs., chmn. youth commn., sec., v.p. Congregation Har Shalom, Potomac, Md., 1984-85, 87-89. Recipient cert. appreciation Spanish Heritage Pub. Health Svc. Workers, 1981, Equal Employment Opportunity award Parklawn Asian/Pacific Am. Community, 1985, Superior Svc. award USPHS, 1986; Meritorious Exec. Rank award Pres. of U.S., 1988, Disting. Exec. Rank award, 1991. Mem. Md. Congress Parents and Tchrs. (hon. life). Office: Fogarty Internat Ctr NIH 31 Center Dr Rm B2C02 Bethesda MD 20892-2220

**MILLSTONE, DAVID JEFFREY,** lawyer; b. Morgantown, W.Va., 1946; AB, Johns Hopkins U., 1968; JD, W.Va. U., 1971. Bar: Ohio 1971. Ptnr. Squire, Sanders & Dempsey LLP, Cleve. Co-author: Wage Hour Law--How to Comply, 2001; editor: Ohio and Fed. Employment Law Manual, 2001; contbr. chapters to books. Past chair regional bd., nat commr., nat. exec. com. mem. Anti-Defamation League, 2002—05. Mem.: ABA, Ohio Mgmt. Law-

yers Assn., Cleve. Bar Assn. Office: Squire Sanders & Dempsey 4900 Key Tower 127 Public Sq Ste 4900 Cleveland OH 44114-1304 Office Phone: 216-479-8574. E-mail: dmillstone@ssd.com.

**MILLWOOD, KEVIN,** professional baseball player; b. Gastonia, NC, Dec. 24, 1974; Pitcher Atlanta Braves, 1997—2003, Phila. Phillies, 2003—04, Cleveland Indians, 2005, Tex. Rangers, 2006—. Named to NL All-Star Team, 1999. Achievements include pitching no-hitter vs. San Francisco Giants, 2003. Office: Tex Rangers Ameriquest Field 1000 Ballpark Way Arlington TX 76011*

**MILMAN, DORIS HOPE,** retired pediatrician, psychiatrist, educator; b. NYC, Nov. 17, 1917; d. Barnet S. and Rose (Smoleroff) Milman; m. Nathan Kreeger, June 15, 1941; 1 child, Elizabeth Kreeger Goldman. BA, Barnard Coll., 1938; MD, NYU, 1942. Diplomate Am. Bd. Pediat.; lic. physician, N.Y. Intern Jewish Hosp., Bklyn., 1942-43, resident, 1944-46, fellow in pediat., 1946-47; postgrad. extern in psychiatry Bellevue Hosp., N.Y.C., 1947-49; attending pediat. psychiatrist Jewish Hosp., Bklyn., 1950-56; asst. prof. pediat. Health Sci. Ctr. at Bklyn. SUNY, 1956-67, assoc. prof., 1967-73, prof., 1973-93, prof. emeritus 1993—, acting chmn. dept. pediat., 1973-75, 82. Pvt. practice child and adolescent psychiatry, Bklyn., 1950-90; vis. prof. Ben Gurion U. of the Negev, Beersheva, Israel, 1977. Co-editor: AAP Adolescent Newsletter, 1993—; copyeditor: Bellevue Lit. Rev., 2001—. Mem. adv. bd. N.Y. Assn. for the Learning Disabled, N.Y.C., 1975-80. Recipient Disting. Alumna award Barnard Coll., 1986, Solomon R. Berson Achievement award NYU Sch. Medicine, 1991; Grace Potter Rice fellow Barnard Coll., 1938-39. Fellow Am. Acad. Pediat. (emeritus), Am. Psychiat. Assn. (disting. life fellow); mem. AAAS, Am. Orthopsychiat. Assn. (life), Am. Pediat. Soc. (emeritus), N.Y. Pediat. Soc. (emeritus), Phi Beta Kappa, Alpha Omega Alpha. Home: 2373 Broadway Apt 2028 New York NY 10024-2842

**MILMAN, NATALIE,** education educator; BA in English and Spanish, Tulane U., 1991; PhD, U. Va., 2000. Tchr. Long Beach (Calif.) Unified Sch. Dist., 1991—96; asst. prof. George Washington U., Washington, 2001—. Author: The Digital Teaching Portfolio: A How-To Guide for Teachers, 2003. Named Luminary, Gelman Libr., George Wash. U., 2005; recipient Outstanding Grad. Tchg. Asst. award, U. Va., 1999; Curry Ctr. for Tech. and Tchr. Edn. fellow, 1997—2000. Mem.: Am. Ednl. Rsch. Assn. (chmn. spl. interest group 2005—). Office: George Washington U 2134 G St NW Washington DC 20052 Office Phone: 202-994-1884.

**MILMOE, J. GREGORY,** lawyer; b. White Plains, NY, 1947; AB, Cornell U., 1970; JD, Fordham U., 1975. Bar: NY 1976. Joined Skadden, Arps, Slate, Meagher & Flom, NYC, 1971—; mailroom asst., 1971, ptnr., co-leader corp. restructuring. Lectr. on fiduciary and restructuring issues for legal and business audiences. Articles editor: Fordham Law Review, 1974-75. Office: Skadden Arps Slate Meagher & Flom 4 Times Sq New York NY 10036 Office Phone: 212-735-3770. Office Fax: 917-777-3770. Business E-Mail: jmilmoe@skadden.com.

**MILNE, CHRISTOPHER MCQUISTON WILMOTH,** photographer, journalist, educator; b. N.Y.C., June 6, 1934; s. C. Lee Wilmoth and Helen Milne; m. Vesta Seymour, Jan. 6, 1999; children: Bruce, Milne, Geoffrey, David, James, Kevin. BA, Geneva Coll., 1956; studied color photography, Roman Vishniak, Montreal, 1973; MA, U. Fla. Writer U.S. Steel, Pitts., 1957-61; owner Interprel Corp., Pitts., 1961—; photographer Robert F. Kennedy Funeral Train, 1968; writer, corr. U.S.A. Washington, 1968—94; pub., editor Ea. Shore Echo, Halifax, 1976-77; founder Marine Gallery and Mus., Canada, 1978; instr. various colls., 1988—; publ. Safe Harbour Press, Crescent, Pa., 1989—; CEO, Milne Inst., Crescent, 1999—. Spl. investigator Scranton commn. investigating killings Kent State U., 1971; mem. speaker's bureau Ethics in Journalism. Editor: RR Stations of Pennsylvania, 1967; author: Ethics for Journalists, 2000; contbr. articles & photographs to Official Railway Guide, 1978-79; photographer traveling exhibit A Brutal Season, Northern Ireland, 1988-, When Trains Were King, 1992—; asst. editor Can. Nat. Rlwys., 1978; official photographer CPR, 1974. Mem. primetimers policy com. Christ Ch. at Grove Farm; counselor House Trailer Com. on Aging, 1970; spl. investigator Agy. for Social Concerns of United Meth. Ch., 1970 Mem. SAR, VFW, Nat. Geog. Soc. (life), Soc. Profl. Journalists, Train Collectors Assn., Profl. Photographers Am., Nat. Multiple Sclerosis Soc., N.H. Art Assn., Newburyport (Mass.) Art Assn., Pitts. History and Landmarks Found. (docent), Scottish Rite Masonic Orders Achievements include one of three official news photographers on Robert F. Kennedy funeral train. Office: Milne Inst PO Box 331 Glenwillard PA 15046 Office Phone: 724-457-7753.

**MILNE, GORDON A.,** construction executive, mortgage company executive; BA in Econs., Brigham Young U., 1975; MBA, U. Chgo., 1977. CPA. Various positions Kaufman and Broad Mortgage Co., 1986—91; sr. v.p., dir. CFO Bow Valley Energy Inc., Calgary, Canada, 1991—94; v.p. Fin. Divsn. Can. Occidental Petroleum Ltd., Calgary, 1994—96; sr. v.p. fin., CFO Agrium Inc., Calgary, 1996—2000; exec. v.p. Ryland Group, Inc., Calabasas, Calif., 2000—, CFO, 2000—. Office: The Ryland Group Inc 24025 Park Sorrento Ste 400 Calabasas CA 91302

**MILNER, CAROLYN ROSE,** artist, educator; b. Atlanta, Ga., Aug. 1, 1955; d. Wesley J. and Frances M. Rose; m. Bradford Milner; 1 child, James. BFA in Drawing and Painting, Atlanta Coll. Art, 2001; postgrad., Ga. State U. Prof. Ga. State U., Atlanta, 2003—. Mem.: exhibitor: Fordham Law Review, 1974-75. Mem.: DAR (Cherokee chpt.), Jr. League Atlanta (sustaining mem.), Coll. Artists Assn. Home: 900 Edgewater Dr Atlanta GA 30328

**MILNER, CHARLES FREMONT, JR.,** manufacturing executive; b. Durham, NC, July 21, 1942; s. Charles Fremont and Eloyse Sargent Milner; m. Molly Frane Wakefield, Aug. 28, 1965; children: Bernadette Ann Milner Gardner, Eloyse Lee Milner Ellerman. BA, Guilford Coll., 1963; MBA, Harvard U., 1965. Asst. to comptroller Harvard U., 1965-66; instr. Northeastern U., Boston, 1965-66; with Burlington Hosiery Co. divsn. Burlington (N.C.) Industries, 1966-71, asst. v.p., 1971-74; pres. v.p. Parklane Hosiery Co., Inc., New Hyde Park, N.Y., 1971-74; pres. Rudin & Roth, Inc. divsn. NCC Industries, N.Y.C., 1974-75; v.p. apparel group M. Lowenstein and Sons, N.Y.C., 1975-76; pres., CEO BBC, Inc. and Camp Industry divsns. Genesco, Inc., 1978-80; gen. mgr. Johnston and Murphy Shoe Co. divsn., 1979—82; gen. mgr. footwear mktg. and mfg. Genesco, Inc., 1980-81, v.p., 1981-82; pres., CEO Hope Hosiery Mills and C.M. Industries, Inc., Denver, Pa., 1983—. Trustee Friends Acad., Locust Valley, N.Y., 1974-79, Guilford Coll., 1982-97, vice chmn., 1989, chmn., 1990-97; mem. class chief fund agt. Harvard Bus. Sch., 1986-91, 40th reunion co-chmn. 2005, alumni bd., 1992-2001, v.p., 1995-97, pres., 1997-99, past pres., 1999-2001. Mem. Nat. Assn. Hosiery Mfrs. (dir. 1978-82, 87—, exec. com 1989-93, 99—, 2d vice-chmn. 1991-92, vice-chmn. 1992, chmn. 1993), Lancaster Country Club (bd. govs. 2004—), Hamilton Club, Moselem Springs Golf Club. Home: 158 Hamilton Rd Lancaster PA 17603-4734 Office: 205 Washington St Denver PA 17517 E-mail: mmilner@socksmyway.com.

**MILNER, CLYDE A., II,** historian; b. Durham, N.C., Oct. 19, 1948; s. Charles Fremont and Eloyse (Sargent) M.; m. Carol Ann O'Connor, Aug. 14, 1977; children: Catherine Carol, Charles Clyde. AB, U. N.C. 1971; MA, Yale U., 1973, MPhil, 1974, PhD, 1979. Admissions counselor Guilford Coll., Greensboro, NC, 1968-70; acting instr. Yale U., New Haven, 1974-75; research fellow McNickle Ctr., Chgo., 1975-76; instr. Utah State U., Logan, 1976-79, asst. prof., 1979-82, assoc. prof., 1982-88, prof., 1988—2002; dir. Mountain West Ctr. for Regional Studies, 1997-2000; dir. PhD program in heritage studies Ark. State U., 2002—, prof., 2002—. Reader of manuscripts History Book Club, Inc., 1986—; exec. dir. Am. Studies program Utah State U., 1997-2000, vis. prof., Yale U., 2006-. Author: With Good Intentions, 1982; editor: Major Problems in the History of the American West, 1989, co-editor 2d edit., 1997; editor: A New Significance: Re-envisioning the History of the American West, 1996; assoc. editor The Western Hist. Quar., 1984-87, co-editor, 1987-89, editor, 1990-97, exec. editor, 1998-2002; co-

editor: Churchmen and the Western Indians, 1985, Trails: Toward a New Western History, 1991, Oxford History of the American West, 1994 (Western Heritage award for non-fiction Nat. Cowboy Hall of Fame 1994, Caughey Western History Assn. award for best book on history of Am. West 1995). Recipient Paladen Writing award The Montana Mag. Western History, 1987, Faculty Svc. award Associated Students Utah State U., 1987, Outstanding Social Science Researcher award Utah State U., 1983, (with Carol A. O'Connor) Charles Redd prize Utah Acad. Scis., Arts and Letters, 1996; fellowship fund established in his honor Western Hist. Quar. Utah State U., 2002, Grad. Editl. Assistantship in his honor with Anne M. Butler, 2004. Mem. Western History Assn., Orgn. Am. Historians (Disting. lectr. 2004—, adv. bd. newsletter 2005—), Phi Alpha Theta, Phi Beta Kappa. Mem. Soc. Of Friends. Home: 1306 E Country Club Terr Jonesboro AR 72401-4325 Office: Ark State U Heritage Studies PhD Program PO Box 69 State University AR 72467 Office Phone: 870-972-3509. Business E-Mail: cmilner@astate.edu.

**MILNER, HAROLD WILLIAM,** hotel executive; b. Salt Lake City, Nov. 11, 1934; s. Kenneth W. and Olive (Schoettlin) Milner; m. Susan Emmett, June 19, 1959 (div. 1976); children: John Kenneth, Mary Sue; m. Lois Friemuth, Aug. 14, 1977; 1 child, Jennifer Rebecca. BS, U. Utah, 1960; MBA, Harvard, 1962. Instr. Brigham Young U., Provo, Utah, 1962-64; v.p. Gen. Paper Corp., Mpls., 1964-65; dir. finance Amalgamated Sugar Co., Ogden, Utah, 1965-67; corp. treas. Marriott Corp., Washington, 1967-70; pres., chief exec. officer, trustee Hotel Investors, Kensington, Md., 1970-75; pres., CEO Americana Hotels Corp., Chgo., 1975-85, Kahler Corp., Rochester, Minn., 1985-97, Kensington Co., Salt Lake City, 1997—. Trustee Baron Asset Funds, 1987—. Author: A Special Report on Contract Maintenance, 1963. Lt. U.S. Army, 1960. Mem.: Minn. Bus. Partnership (bd. dirs. 1991—). Mem. Lds Ch. Office: The Kensington Co 2293 Morning Star Dr Park City UT 84060-6725 Office Phone: 435-640-1129. Personal E-mail: hmilner@aol.com.

**MILNER, IRVIN MYRON,** retired lawyer; b. Cleve., Feb. 5, 1916; s. Nathan and Rose (Spector) M.; m. Zelda Winograd., Aug. 15, 1943 AB cum laude, Western Res. U. (now Case Western Res. U.), 1937, JD, 1940, LL.M., 1970. Bar: Ohio 1940, U.S. Dist. Ct. (no. dist.) Ohio 1946. Pvt. practice, Cleve., 1946—2005; ret. Exec. sec., counsel Men's Apparel Club Ohio, Cleve., 1947-48; adj. instr. Sch. Law, Case Western Res. U., 1965-66; spl. counsel Ohio Office Atty. Gen., 1960-70; legal counsel Korean Am. Assn. Greater Cleve., 1973-95. Mem. Cleve. Fgn. Consular Corps., 1970-96, hon. consul Rep. of Korea for Cleve., 1970-96; bd. dirs. Internat. Human Assistance Programs, Inc., 1973-79, voting corp. mem., 1980-88; mem. Republican Nat. Com. Served with U.S. Army, 1941-45, ETO. Decorated Order Diplomatic Svc. Merit-Heung-in medal (Republic of Korea), 1975; named to Disting. Alumni Hall of Fame, Cleveland Heights (Ohio) High Sch., 1983. Fellow Internat. Consular Coll., Ohio Bar Found.; mem. ABA (small bus. com., corp. bus. law sect. 1971-74), Greater Cleve. Bar Assn., Cuyahoga County Bar Assn. (pres. 1975-76, co-chmn. jud. standards com. 1987-88, life trustee, award of Special Merit 1976, Pres.' award 1988), Ohio State Bar Assn. (coun. dels., 1976-86, com. on legal ethics and profl. conduct 1984-97), Cuyahoga County Bar Found. (sec.-treas. 1980-84, bd. dirs. 1984—), Cuyahoga County Coun. Ohio VFW (comdr. 1958, Merit award 1958), Am. Security Coun. (nat. adv. bd.), Cleve. Coun. on World Affairs, Greater Cleve. Vets. Coun. (pres. 1957), Western Res. Coll. Alumni Assn. (bd. dirs. 1982-88), Cleve. City Club, Masons (32 deg.), Tau Epsilon Rho (chancellor Cleve. Grad. chpt. 1987-88), Delta Phi Alpha. Jewish.

**MILNER, RICHARD GERARD,** physicist; b. Cork, Ireland, Dec. 2, 1956; s. William and Maura (McGrath) M.; m. Eileen Troy, June 21, 1980; children: William, Samuel, David. BS with honors, Univ. Coll. Cork, 1978, MS, 1979; PhD, Calif. Inst. Tech., 1985. Rsch. assoc. Calif. Inst. Tech., 1985-88, rsch. scientist, 1988; asst. prof. MIT, Cambridge, 1988-93, assoc. prof., 1993-98, prof., 1998—, dir. Bates Linear Accelerator Ctr., 1998—. Mem. medium energy physics group MIT Lab. Nuc. Sci. Contbr. articles to profl. jours. Recipient Presdl. Young Investigator award NSF, 1989. Office: MIT Dept Physics Rm 26-447 77 Massachusetts Ave Cambridge MA 02139-4301 E-mail: milner@mitlns.mit.edu.*

**MILNES, ARTHUR GEORGE,** electrical engineer, educator; b. Heswall, Eng., July 30, 1922; came to U.S., 1957, naturalized, 1964; s. George and Marion (Teasdale) M.; m. Mary Laverne Wertz, Dec. 4, 1955; children: Sheila Rae, Brian George, John Teasdale. BSc, U. Bristol, Eng., 1943, MSc, 1947, DSc, 1956. With Royal Aircraft Establishment, 1943-57, prin. sci. officer, 1952-57; mem. faculty Carnegie-Mellon U., Pitts., 1957-87, prof. elec. engring., 1960-87, assoc. head dept., 1966-69, Buhl prof., 1973-87, prof. emeritus Pitts., 1987—. Cons. to industry on semiconductor devices, 1957 Author: Transductors and Magnetic Amplifiers, 1957, (with D.L. Feucht) Heterojunctions and Metal-Semiconductor Junctions, 1972, Deep Impurities in Semiconductors, 1973, Semiconductor Devices and Integrated Electronics, 1979; contbr. articles to profl. jours. FOA rsch. fellow NAS-Royal Soc. London, 1954. Fellow IEEE (J.J. Ebers award 1982, van der Ziel award 1993), Am. Phys. Soc., Instn. Elec. Engrs. (London). Home: 1417 Inverness St Pittsburgh PA 15217-1157

**MILNOR, HAZEL,** nurse; b. Marble, Ark., Apr. 2, 1921; d. Andrew Jackson and Laura Jane (Davis) Spencer; m. John Champion Milnor, June 21, 1951 (dec. Aug. 1989); children: Mary Christine, Jean Ann Laura. RN, Calif. Hawaii. Nurse pvt. duty, Calif., 1942—; surg. nurse Queen's Hosp., Hawaii, 1944-46; flight attendant United Airlines, San Francisco, 1946-51. Author: Entertaining in Hawaii, 1977, (poetry) As Angels Watch, 1997, Founding pres. Spl. Angels Ministry, Hawaii; chair develop. com. Spl. Angels; vol. various orgns., 1951—. Recipient Disting. Svc. award Assn. for Retarded Citizens in Hawaii, 2005; inducted Internat. Poetry Hall of Fame. Mem. Assn. Retarded Citizens, Clipped Wings (mem.-at-large, mem. coms.), Internat. Soc. Poets (disting.), Oahu Country Club. Republican. Episcopalian. Avocations: collecting angels, travel.

**MILNOR, JOHN WILLARD,** mathematician; b. Orange, N.J., Feb. 20, 1931; AB, Princeton, 1951, PhD, 1954; DSc (hon.), Syracuse U., 1965, U. Chgo., 1967. Mem. faculty Princeton U., 1953—62, prof., 1960—62, Henry Putman chair, 1962; prof. math., dir. Inst. Math. Scis. SUNY, Stony Brook NY, 1988—. Editor: Annals of Mathematics, 1962—, Morse Theory, Characteristic Classes, —, Dynamics in One Complex Variable, —, Singular Points of Complex Hypersurfaces, —, Topology from the Differentiable Viewpoint, —. Recipient Fields medal, Internat. Congress Math. in Stockholm, 1962, Nat. medal of Sci., 1967, Leroy P. Steele prize, 1982, Wolf prize in math., Wolf Found., Israel, 1989; Henry Putman fellow, 1949, 1950, Alfred P. Sloan fellow, 1955—59. Mem.: NAS, Russian Acad. Scis. (fgn. mem.), Am. Math. Soc. (Steele prize 2004), Am. Philos. Soc., Am. Acad. Arts and Sci. Achievements include proof that a 7-dimensional sphere can have several differential structures; research in holomorphic dynamics. Office: SUNY Inst Math Sci Math Bldg 5D 148 Stony Brook NY 11794-3660*

**MILNOR, WILLIAM ROBERT,** physician; b. Wilmington, Del., May 4, 1920; s. William Robert and Virginia (Sterling) Milnor. m. Gabriella Mahaffy, Aug. 19, 1944; children: Katherine Alexander, William Henry. AB, Princeton U., 1941; MD, Johns Hopkins U., 1944. Diplomate Am. Bd. Internal Medicine. Intern, resident Johns Hopkins Hosp., 1944-46; rsch. fellow Nat. Heart Inst., 1949-51; physician-in-charge heart sta. Johns Hopkins Hosp., 1951-60, physician, 1952—; mem. faculty Johns Hopkins Med. Sch., 1951—, prof. physiology, 1959—. Vis. Stu. Catherine's Coll. Oxford U., England, 1968; mem. med. adv. panel Am. Inst. Biol. Scis., 1971—; assessor Nat. Med. Rsch. Coun. Australia, 1976—. Author: Hemodynamics, 1989, Cardio-vascular Physiology, 1990; contbr. articles to med. textbooks and med. jours. Capt. med. corps USAAF, 1946—48. Fellow: ACP; mem.: Heart Assn. Md., Am. Heart Assn. (nat. rsch. com. 1966), Biomed. Engring. Soc., Am. Fedn. Clin. Rsch., Am. Physiol. Soc.

**MILONAS, E. LEO,** lawyer, former state judge; b. Oct. 23, 1936; BA, CCNY, 1957; LLB, Bklyn. Law Sch., 1960. Bar: NY 1960. Judge, Criminal Ct. City of NY, 1973—76, supervising judge, Bronx County Criminal Ct., 1973—74, supervising judge, NY County Criminal Ct., 1974—77; justice, Supreme Ct. State of NY, 1978—82, dep. chief adminstrv. judge, 1979—81, assoc. justice, appellate div., 1982—98, chief adminstrv. judge, 1993—95; ptnr., Litigation practice Pillsbury Winthrop Shaw Pittman, NYC, 1998—. Mem. NY State Commn. on Judicial Nomination, 2000—, Governor's Departmental Judicial Screening Com., 2000—, Commn. on Fiduciary Appointments; chmn. First Dept. Pre-Argument Conf. Appellate div. NY State Supreme Ct.; co-chmn. Comml. Courts Task Force NY State. Bd. dir. Legal Aid Soc., 2001—, Fund for Modern Courts, 2000—, Nat. Ctr. for State Courts, 1974, 1980, 2002—; bd. dir. & mem. exec. com. Nat. Urban League, 1990—; bd. dir. Judges & Lawyers Breast Cancer Alert, co-pres., 1997—99; bd. dir. Fund for the City of NY. Fellow: ABA (mem. Ho. Del. 2000—); mem.: Assn. Bar City of NY (v.p. 2000—01, pres. 2002—04), NY State Bar Assn. (mem. Council on Judicial Assns. 1978—). Office: Pillsbury Winthrop Shaw Pittman 1540 Broadway New York NY 10036 Office Phone: 212-858-1615. Office Fax: 212-858-1500. Business E-Mail: eleo.milonas@pillsburylaw.com.

**MILONAS, MINOS,** artist; b. Heraklion, Crete, Greece, Apr. 28, 1936; came to U.S., 1964, naturalized, 1968; s. Stavros and Maria (Kaplantzis) M.; m. Arlene Watson, Dec. 23, 1963 (div. 1970); m. Sarah Brown, Dec. 1973 (div. 1974); m. Elaine Maucelli, May 26, 1988. BA, Calif. State U., Northridge, 1970; MFA, U. Wash., Seattle, 1972. Freelance writer and poet, Athens, 1960-64; freelance artist L.A., 1964-66; instr. U. Wash., 1971-72, Studio Milonas, Seattle, 1972-76, artist N.Y.C., 1977—, textile designer, 1984-94. One man shows include Second Story Gallery, Seattle, 1971, Henry Art Gallery, Seattle, 1972, Polly Friedlander Gallery, Seattle, 1973, Stavrakakis Gallery, Crete, Greece, 1977, West Broadway Gallery, N.Y.C., 1979, 81, 82, Heraklion Art Gallery, Crete, 1983, Kreonides Gallery, Athens, 1983, 84, Doma Gallery, N.Y.C., 1988, Hellenic Cultural Ctr., N.Y., 1990, 93, Cypriot Consulate, N.Y.C., 1990; exhibitions in group shows at Calif. State U., Northridge, 1968-69, Mcpl. Art Gallery, L.A., 1969, U. Wash. Libr., Seattle, 1971, 72, Panaca Gallery, Bellevue, Wash., 1973, Mercer Island Art Gallery, Seattle, 1973, Henry Art Gallery, Seattle, 1973, Tacoma Art Mus., 1973, 75, N.W. Watercolor Soc., 1974, Gordon Woodside Gallery, Seattle, 1974, Coll. of the Cisciyous, Calif., 1975, Laguna Gloria Art Mus., Austin, Tex., 1975, Redmonds (Wash.) Arts Festival, 1975, Univ. Dist. Arts Festival, Seattle, 1976, Bellevue Art Mus., 1976, Sunne Savage Gallery, Boston, 1976, Cretan Artists, Stavrakakis Gallery, Heraklion, Crete, 1978, Internat. Drawing Biennale, Cleveland, Eng., 1981-82, Bowes Mus., Barnard Castle, Eng., 1982, Shipley Art Gallery, Gateshead, Eng., 1982, House of Commons, London, 1982, Haggin Mus., Stockton, Calif., 1985-86, U. N.D., Grand Forks, 1987, Greek Cultural Ctr., Springfield, Mass., 1987, 89, Del Bello Gallery, Toronto, Ont., Can., 1987, Ball State U., Muncie, Ind., 1989, Morin-Miller Galleries, N.Y.C., 1989-90, Columbia (Md.) Coll., 1989, Grand Prospect Hall, Bklyn., 1990, Kenneth Raymond Gallery, Boca Raton, Fla., 1993-96, Pan Cretan Art Exhbn. Rethymnon Mcpl. Art Gallery, Crete, Greece, 2003—, Melina Merkouri Cultural Ctr., Athens, 2003; author: The Small Caravan, 1962, short stories; author 12 books of poetry in Greek, From A to Z, Poems in English, 2003, Look At Manhattan, Poems in English, 2004, Autobiography, in Greek, 2005, Poems from April, Bilingual Poems in English and Greek, 2005, For Her, Bilingual Poems in English and Greek, 2005; videos include Multimedia Artist, 1988, 500 Definitions--Art Is, 1991; donated paintings to various orgns. Recipient 4 Sculpture awards Summer Art Festivals, 1970-76, 2 Merit awards Greek Cultural Ctr., 1987; U. Wash. grantee, 1970; U. Wash. scholar, 1971. Mem. Nat. Artists Equity Assn., Inc., N.Y. Artists Equity Assn., Inc., Poetry Soc. Am., Greek-Am. Writers Assn., Acad. Am. Poets, Poets House. Democrat. Home and Office: 790 11th Ave Apt 39A New York NY 10019-3521

**MILONE, FRANCIS MICHAEL,** lawyer; b. Phila., Pa., June 18, 1947; s. Michael Nicholas and Frances Theresa (Fair) Milone; m. Maida R. Crane, Nov. 25, 1991; children: Michael, Matthew. BA, LaSalle Coll., 1969; MS, Pa. State U., 1971; JD, Pa., 1974. Bar: Pa. 1974, U.S. Dist. Ct. (ea. dist.) Pa. 1974, U.S. Dist. Ct. (mid. dist.) Pa. 1979, U.S. Dist. Ct. (ea. dist.) Mich. 1983, U.S. Ct. Appeals (3d cir.) 1978, U.S. Ct. Appeals (4th and 5th cirs.) 1979, U.S. Supreme Ct. 1979. Assoc. Montgomery, McCracken, Walker & Rhoads, Phila., 1974—77; ptnr.,firm chmn., chmn. firm mgmt. com. Morgan, Lewis & Bockius, Phila., 1981—. Mem.: ABA (labor and litig. sects.), Phila. Bar Assn., Pa. Bar Assn. Office: Morgan Lewis & Bockius 1701 Market St Philadelphia PA 19103-2903 Office Phone: 215-963-5670. Office Fax: 215-963-5001. E-mail: fmilone@morganlewis.com.

**MILORO, PROTOPRESBYTER FRANK,** religious organization administrator, theology studies educator; b. Wilmington, Del., Jan. 26, 1947; m. Constance Ann Evanisko, Apr. 20, 1969; children: Alexandra, Stephanie, Christopher. Grad. summa cum laude, Saviour Sem., 1969; grad. with high honors, St. Vincent Coll., 1972; attended, U. Pitts. Ordained to Diaconate and Priesthood, 1969. Assigned St. John's Ch., Ligonier, Pa., 1969-72, St. Stephen's Ch., Latrobe, Pa., 1969-72, St. John's Ch., Rahway, NJ, 1972-76; dir. Camp Nazareth, diocesan dir. youth, 1976-86; dean Christ the Saviour Sem.; elevated to dignity of Very Rev., 1985; sec. to bishop; instr. homiletics and parish administrn.; diocesan chancellor Am. Carpatho-Russian Orthodox Diocese, 1990—; dean Christ the Savior Cathedral, 1997—. Chaplain Ea. Orthodox residents Polk Ctr., Commonwealth Pa., established chapel. Assoc. editor The Ch. Messenger. Russian Orthodox. Office: 312 Garfield St Johnstown PA 15906-2122

**MILSOM, ROBERT CORTLANDT,** banker, director; b. Butler, Pa., Dec. 15, 1924; s. Robert C. and M. Ethel (Leyland) M. BS, John Carroll U., 1948. With PNC Bank (formerly Pitts. Nat. Bank), 1948-90; asst. sec., asst. cashier customer relations div. PNC Bank, 1953-56, asst. v.p. loan div., 1956-60, v.p. charge comml. loan group, 1960-65, sr. v.p. charge comml. banking div., 1965-68, exec. v.p., 1968-72, pres., 1972-85, chmn., CEO, 1985-90, also bd. dirs., 1972—; vice chmn., dir. PNC Bank Corp, 1972-90. Bd. dirs. PNC Bank N.A., PNC Equity Mgmt. Corp., Exec. Svc. Corps., Foxwall Med. Svc.; chmn. bd. trustees Mercy Hosp. Pitts., 1994—. Bd. dirs. Pitts. Mercy Health System, Inc., Pitts. Ballet Theatre, Regional Indsl. Devel. Corp.; hon. trustee John Carroll U., Cleve.; mem. adv. bd. Mon Valley Renaissance program California U. Pa. Mem. Duquesne Club of Pitts., Fox Chapel Golf Club of Pitts., Laurel Valley Golf Club, Rolling Rock Club. Office: PNC Bank NA Two PNC Plz 2-PTPP-20-2 620 Liberty Ave Pittsburgh PA 15222-2719

**MILSON, BERTRAM IRVING,** surgeon; b. Green Bay, Wis. s. Louis and Marion Milson; m. Patti Salscheider, Jan. 30, 1991; children: Michael, Debra, James. BS, Northwestern U.; MD, Marquette Med. Coll. Diplomate Am. Bd. Surgery. Surgeon Dousman Clinic, Green Bay, 1961—2005. Med. advisor N.W. Tech. Sch., Green Bay, Wis. Col. USAR, 1957—94. Fellow: Am. Coll. Emergency Physicians, Am. Coll. Surgeons. Republican. Jewish. Office: Dousman Clinic 1745 Dousmaw Green Bay WI 54303

**MILSTED, AMY,** biomedical educator; BSEd, Ohio State U., 1967; PhD, CUNY, 1977. Lectr. Hunter Coll./CUNY, 1970-76; instr. Carnegie-Mellon U., Pitts., 1976-77; postdoctoral fellow Muscular Dystrophy Assn./Carnegie-Mellon U., Pitts., 1978-79; rsch. assoc. Case Western Res. U., Cleve., 1979-82; rsch. chemist VA Med. Ctr., Cleve., 1982-87; project staff The Cleve. Clin. Found., 1987-89; asst. staff dept. brain and vascular mol. Cleve. Clinic Found., 1989-93; grad. faculty Sch. Biomed. Scis. Kent (Ohio) State U., 1995—; assoc. prof. dept. biology U. Akron, Ohio, 1993-2000, prof. biology, 2000—. Contbr. articles to profl. jours. Fellow Am. Heart Assn.; mem. AAAS, Inter-Am. Soc. Hypertension, Am. Chem. Soc., Endocrine Soc., Assn. Women in Sci. Office: Univ Akron Dept Biology Asec 279 Akron OH 44325-3908 E-mail: milsted@uakron.edu.

**MILSTEIN, ELLIOTT STEVEN,** lawyer, educator, academic administrator; b. Oct. 19, 1944; s. Samuel M. and Mildred K. Milstein; m. Bonnie Myrun, Oct. 1, 1967 (div. Oct. 1992); 1 child, Jacob. BA, U. Hartford, 1966,

LLD (hon.), 1997; JD, U. Conn., 1969; LLM, Yale U., 1971; LLD (hon.), Nova Southeastern U., 2001. Bar: conn. 1969, D.C. 1972, U.S. Dist. Ct. Conn. 1969, U.S. Ct. Appeals (D.C.) 1972. Lectr. law U. Conn. Clin. Program, 1969-70; staff counsel New Haven Legal Assistance Assn., 1971-72; asst. prof. law, dir. clin. programs Washington Coll. Law Am. U., 1972-74, assoc. prof., dir. clin. programs, 1974-77, prof., dir. clin. programs, 1977-88, interim dean, 1988-90, dean, 1990—. Prof. law, Washington Coll. Law Am. U., 1995—; co-dir. Nat. Vets. law Ctr., 1978-84; cons. Calif. Bar Bd. of Bar Admissions, Nat. Conf. Bar Examiners, law tng. Practising Law Inst., N.Y.C.; chmn. D.C. Law Students in Ct. Program, 1982-83; mem. Law Tchrs. for Legal Svcs. Bd. dirs. Alliance for Justice, 1996-97. Ford Urban Law fellow, 1971-72. Mem. ABA (skills tng. com. 1983-85, govt. rels. com. 1992—), ACLU, Soc. Am. Law Tchrs., Assn. Am. Law Schs. (chmn. sect clin. edn. 1982, accreditation com. 1984-86, chmn. standing com. clin. edn. 1993—, exec. com. 1996-2001, pres.-elect 1999, parliamentarian, 2004—, pres. 2000, William Pincus award for outstanding contbns. to clin. legal edn. 1992). Democrat. Home: 3216 Brooklawn Ct Bethesda MD 20815-3941 Office: Am U Washington Coll Law 4801 Massachusetts Ave NW Washington DC 20016-8196

**MILSTEIN, HOWARD P.,** bank executive; b. May 15, 1951; BA, Cornell U., 1973; MBA, JD, Harvard U., 1977. Co-chmn., pres., CEO Emigrant Savings Bank, NY Pvt. Bank & Trust; mng. ptnr. Milstein Properties; founding chmn. FriedbergMilstein; chmn. MB Real Estate. Mem. Nat. Bd. Smithsonian Inst.; trustee Cornell U.; mem. bd. overseers Weill Cornell Med. Coll., 1989—; mem. bd. trustees Thomas Jefferson Found., Inc., 2006—. Named one of Forbes' Richest Americans, 2006. Home: NY Pvt Bank & Trust 5 E 42nd St #7 New York NY 10017*

**MILSTEIN, LAURENCE BENNETT,** electrical engineering educator, researcher; b. Bklyn., Oct. 28, 1942; s. Harry and Sadie (Kaplan) M.; m. Suzanne Barbara Hirschman, Oct. 3, 1969; children: Coreen Roxanne, Renair Marissa. BEE, CUNY, 1964; MSEE, Poly. Inst. Bklyn., 1966, PhD in Elec. Engring., 1968. Mem. tech. staff Hughes Aircraft Co., El Segundo, Calif., 1968-69, staff engr., 1970-72, sr. staff engr., 1972-74; asst. prof. Rensselaer Poly. Inst., Troy, NY, 1974-76, U. Calif.-San Diego, La Jolla, 1976-79, assoc. prof., 1979-82, prof. elec. engring., 1982—, chmn. dept., 1984-88, Ericsson endowed chair, 2005. Cons. Hughes Aircraft Co., Culver City, Calif., 1976—78, Lockheed Missiles and Space Co., Sunnyvale, Calif., 1978—93, Motorola Satellite Comm., 1992—96, InterDigital Comm. Corp., 1992—96, Golden Bridge Tech., 1995—99; cons. various govt. agys., pvt. cos., 1975—. Contbr. articles to profl. jours.; co-editor: Tutorials in Modern Communications, 1983, Spread Spectrum Communications, 1983. Recipient Outstanding Tchr. award Warren Coll., U. Calif.-San Diego, La Jolla, 1982, Disting. Tchg. award, 1999; grantee Army Rsch. Office, 1977-84, 86-89, 91-2001, Office of Naval Rsch., Arlington, Va., 1982-05, TRW, San Diego, 1983-89, 92-97, NSF, 1993-04. Fellow IEEE (Millennium medal 2000, Edwin Armstrong Achievement award 2000, MILCOM long term tech. achievement award 1998, F.W. Ellersick MILCOM prize paper award 2002), IEEE Coms. Soc. (bd. govs. 1983, 85-87, 93-95, v.p. for tech. activities 1990-91), IEEE Info. Theory Soc. (bd. govs. 1989-94). Jewish. Office: U Calif San Diego Dept Elec Computer Engring La Jolla CA 92093 Office Phone: 858-534-3096. Business E-Mail: milstein@ece.ucsd.edu.

**MILSTEIN, MONROE GARY,** retail executive; b. NYC, Jan. 14, 1927; s. Abe Herman and Ann Ethel (Isaacs) M.; m. Henrietta Haas, Dec. 22, 1949; children— Lazer, Andrew, Stephen Bs, NYU, 1946. Pres. Monroe G. Milstein Inc., N.Y.C., 1947—; chmn. bd., pres., chief exec. officer Burlington Coat Factory Warehouse Corp., N.J., 1972—; dir. Fidelity Bank & Trust Co. of N.J., 1972—. Trustee, pres. bd. Long Beach Pub. Library, N.Y., 1967-76; pres. bd. trustees Nassau Library System, Roosevelt Field, N.Y., 1971-73 Recipient Man of Yr. awards Coat and Suit Buyers Assn., 1964, Long Beach C. of C., Youth Service award B'nai B'rith Mem. Am. Gen. Mdse. Assn., U.S. C. of C. Clubs: Dads (Long Beach) (pres. 1966). Lodges: B'nai B'rith (v.p. 1960-62). Jewish. Avocations: fishing, reading, music.

**MILSTEIN, PAUL,** real estate developer; b. NYC, 1923; s. Morris Milstein; m. Irma Milstein; 3 children. Student, NYU Sch. Architecture. Pres. Circle Floor Co. Inc., NYC, 1961; founder & pres. Milstein Properties, NYC. Former chmn. bd. Starrett Corp.; co-chmn. Emigrant Savings Bank. Life trustee NY Presbyn. Hosp., NYC; trustee Am. Mus. Natural Hist., NYC. Named one of 400 Richest Americans, Forbes, 2006. Office: Emigrant Bank 5 E 42nd St New York NY 10017-6994*

**MILSTEIN, RICHARD CRAIG,** lawyer; b. NYC, July 16, 1946; s. Max and Hattie (Jacobson) Milstein; children: Brian Matthew, Rachel Helanie. AA with hons., Miami-Dade Jr. Coll., 1966; AB cum laude, U. Miami, Fla., 1968; JD, U. Miami, 1973. Bar: Fla. 1974, US Dist. Ct. (so. dist.) Fla. 1974, US Ct. Appeals (5th cir.) 1974, US Ct. Appeals (11th cir.) 1982, U.S. Supreme Ct. 1977. Assoc. August, Nimkoff & Pohlig., Miami, Fla., 1974—76; mng. ptnr. Jepeway, August, Gassen & Pohling. Miami, 1976—78, August, Pohlig & Milstein, P.A., Coral Gables, Fla., 1980—83; sr. ptnr. Milstein & Wayne, Coral Gables, 1983—85; ptnr. Tescher & Milstein, PA, Coral Gables, 1986—90, Akerman, Senterfitt & Eidson, P.A., 1990—. Named to U. Miami Iron Arrow Hon. Soc., U. Miami, 1998—; recipient Extraordinary Service Award, Mothers' Voices S. Fla., 2000, Establishment of the Richard C. Milstein Excellence Award, Dade County Bar Assoc., 1999, Outstanding Alumnus Award, U. Miami Sch. of Law, 1999, Tobias Simon Pro Bono Service Award, FL Supreme Ct., 1996, John Minor Wisdom Professional and Public Service Award, American Bar Association Section of Litigation, 1996, Pro Bono Service Award for the Eleventh Judicial Circuit, FL Bar Pres., 1996, Pro Bono awards, 1986, Pro Bono Service Award for the Eleventh Judicial Circuit, FL Bar Pres., 1986. Mem.: U. Miami Law Alumni, Fla. Bar Assn., Coral Gables Bar Assn., Dade County Bar Assn., Am. trial Lawyers Assn., ABA, Nat. Coun. Aging, Nat. Acad. Elder Law, Am. Coll. Trust and Estate Counsel, Dade County Cultural Alliance, U. Miami, South Fla. Inter-Profl. Council Inc., South Fla. Mediation Ctr., Ops. SafeDrive. Met. Dade County Ind. Rev. Panel, Acad. Fla. Trial Lawyers, Miami Coalition Inc., Ptnr. for Youth, Metro Dade County Cultural Affairs Coun., Dade County Vol. Lawyers for Arts, Bet Shira Congregation, Dance Umbrella Inc., Zeta Epsilon Nu, Alpha Kappa, Phi Kappa Phi, Delta Pi, Phi Alpha Theta, Omicron Delta Kappa, Delta Theta. Maj. Phi Theta Kappa. Democrat. Office: Akerman Senterfitt & Eidson One SE 3rd Ave Fl 28 Miami FL 33131

**MILSTEIN, RICHARD SHERMAN,** lawyer; b. Westfield, Mass., May 9, 1926; s. Abraham and Sarah (Yudman) M. BA, Harvard, 1948; JD, Boston U., 1952. Bar: Mass. 1952, U.S. Supreme Ct. 1959. Ptnr. Ely & King, Springfield, Mass., 1954-95, Chaplin & Milstein, Boston, 1984-91; sr. counsel Robinson, Donovan, Madden & Barry P.C., Springfield, 1995-98. Dir. Mass. Continuing Legal Edn., 1969-80; cons. dir., 1980—. Commr. Springfield Parking Authority, 1984—90; trustee Cmty. Music Sch., Springfield, 1994—96, Springfield Symphony Orch., 1995—99, Springfield Libr. Mus. Assn., 1990—2000, Baystate Hosp. Found., 2001—03; overseer Mass. Supreme Jud. Ct. Hist. Soc., 1995—, Boston Lyric Opera, 1999—; trustee Baystate Hosp. v.p., 1995—97; vice chmn. Westfield Acad., 1980—99; chmn. Horace Smith Fund, 1977—93; bd. dirs. Boston Ctr. for Adult Edn., 1998—, v.p., 1998—2003; bd. overseers Huntington Theater, Boston, 1999—; mem. vis. com. Mus. Fine Arts, Boston, 2000—; bd. dirs. Friends of Boston U. Libraries, 2005—; life trustee Sta. WGBY Pub. TV, Springfield, former chmn. bd. trustees. Lt. commdr. USCGR, 1952—64. Recipient Am. Law Inst.-ABA Harrison Tweed Spl. Merit award for contbn. to CLE, 1997, Mass. Bar Cmty. Svc. award, 1998, William Pynchon award for Cmty. Svc. City of Springfield, 1999. Fellow Am. Coll. Trust and Estate Counsel, Mass. Bar Found. (life); mem. Am. Law Inst. (life), Am. Bar Found. (life), Soc. Four Arts Palm Beach. Home: 300 Boylston St Boston MA 02116-3923 also: Mass Continuing Legal Edn 10 Winter Pl Boston MA 02108-4751 Home (Winter): 330 S Ocean Blvd Apt 2E Palm Beach FL 33480 Office Phone: 617-350-7006 ext. 1241. Personal E-mail: rsmilstein@aol.com. E-mail: rsmilstein_ab@post.harvard.edu.

**MILSTEN, ROBERT B.,** lawyer; b. Tulsa, Nov. 6, 1932; s. Travis I. and Regina (Jankowsky) M.; m. Jane Herskowitz, June 24, 1956; children: Stuart Paul, Leslie Jane. BS, Ind. U., 1954; LL.B., U. Okla., 1956; postgrad., So. Meth. U., 1959. Bar: Okla. 1956, U.S. Ct. of Appeals 1956, U.S. Tax Ct 1956. Practiced in, Oklahoma City, 1962—; govt. atty. Office Chief Counsel, IRS, 1958-62; atty. Fuller, Smith, Mosburg & Davis, 1962-63; sr. counsel Andrews, Davis, Legg, Bixler, Milsten & Price, Inc., 1964—, mem. firm, 1966—, dir., 1977-82, 96-98. Mem. S.W. region IRS/Bar Liaison Com., 1994-97; docent, Nat. Cowboy Western Heritage Mus. Past pres., trustee Temple B'nai Israel. Served as lt., JAGC USAF, 1956-58. Mem. ABA (com. civil and criminal tax penalties sect. taxation 1962—98), Okla. Bar Assn., Fed. Bar Assn. (2d v.p. local chpt. 1976), Econ. Club Okla., Gaillardia Country Club, Men's Dinner Club, Phi Delta Phi (treas. 1955-56)

**MILTON, CATHERINE HIGGS,** entrepreneur; b. NYC, Jan. 6, 1943; d. Edgar Homer and Josephine (Doughty) Higgs; m. A. Fenner Milton (div.); m. Thomas F. McBride, Aug. 25, 1974 (dec. Oct. 31, 2003); children: Raphael McBride, Luke McBride. BA, Mt. Holyoke Coll., 1964, PhD (hon.), 1992. Reporter, travel writer Boston Globe, 1964-68; with Internat. Assn. Chiefs Police, Washington, 1968-70; asst. dir. Police Found., Washington, 1970-75; spl. asst. US Treasury Dept., Washington, 1977-80; project staff Spl. Com. Aging/Senate, Washington, 1980-81; spl. asst. to pres., founder/exec. dir. Stanford U. Haas Ctr. for Public, Calif., 1981-91; exec. dir. Commn. for Nat. and Cmty. Svc., Washington, 1991-93; v.p. Corp. for Nat. Svc., Washington, 1993-95; exec. dir. Presidio Leadership Ctr., 1995-96; exec. dir. US Programs Save the Children, Westport, Conn., 1996—2002; pres. Friends of the Children, Portland, Oreg., 2002—05. Mem. US Atty. General's Task Force on Family Violence, 1981-82; chair nat. forum Kellogg Found., 1990; bd. dirs. Inst. Higher Edn. Policy, Generation United. Author: Women in Policing, 1972, Police Use of Deadly Force, 1976; co-author: History of Black Americans, 1965, Team Policing, Little Sisters and the Law, 1970. Bd. dirs. Youth Svc. Calif., L.A., 1986-91, Trauma Found., San Francisco, 1982-90, Generation United, 1985-, Inst. Higher Edn. Policy, 1985-; spl. advisor Campus Compact, 1986-91. Nat. Kellogg Found. fellow, Battle Creek, Mich., 1985-88; recipient Dedication and Outstanding Efforts award Bd. Suprs., Santa Clara, Calif., 1989, Outstanding Vol. Contbn. award Strive for Five, San Francisco, 1991, Dinkelspiel award Stanford U., 1991; named Outstanding Campus Adminstr. COOL, 1987. Avocations: backpacking, skiing, hiking, travel. Home: 3652 SE Oak St Portland OR 97214

**MILTON, CHAD EARL,** lawyer; b. Brevard County, Fla., Jan. 29, 1947; s. Rex Dale and Mary Margaret (Peacock) M.; m. Ann Mitchell Bunting, Mar. 30, 1972; children: Samuel, Kathleen, Kelsey. BA, Colo. Coll., 1969; JD, U. Colo., 1974; postgrad., U. Mo., 1976-77. Bar: Colo. 1974, Mo. 1977, U.S. Dist. Ct. Colo. 1974, U.S. Dist. Ct. (we. dist) Mo. 1977. Counsel Office of Colo. State Pub. Defender, Colo. Springs, 1974-76; pub. info. officer, counsel Mid-Am. Arts Alliance, Kansas City, Mo., 1977-78; claims counsel Employers Reinsurance Corp., Kansas City, Mo., 1978-80; sr. v.p. Media/Profl. Ins., Kansas City, Mo., 1981-2000; sr. v.p. nat. practice leader, intellectual property & media Marsh, Kansas City, Mo., 2000—. Reporter, photographer, editor Golden (Colo.) Daily Transcript, 1970; investigator, law clk. Office of Colo. State Pub. Defender, Denver, Golden, 1970-74; participant Annenberg Project on the Reform of Libel Laws, Washington, 1987-88; adj. prof., comm. and advt. law Webster U., 1989-93; lectr. in field. Pres. bd. dirs. Folly Theater, 1992-94, Kans. City Chamber Orch., 1995—. Mem. ABA (chair intellectual property law com. of the torts and ins. practice sect., forum com. on comm. law, ctrl. and Ea. European law initiative), Mo. Bar Assn., Kansas City Met. Bar Assn., Libel Def. Resource Ctr. (editorial bd., exec. com.). Avocations: tennis, golf, skiing, sailing, antique maps. Home: 8821 Alhambra St Shawnee Mission KS 66207-2357 Office: Marsh 2405 Grand Blvd Kansas City MO 64108-2510 Office Phone: 816-556-4365. E-mail: chad.e.milton@marsh.com.

**MILTON, JOHN CHARLES DOUGLAS,** nuclear physicist, researcher; b. Regina, Sask., Can., 1924; s. William and Frances Craigie; m. Gwendolyn Margaret Shaw. Oct. 10, 1953; children: Bruce F., Leslie J.F., Neil W.D., Theresa M. A.M. in Music, U. Man., 1943, B.Sc. with honors, 1947; MA, Princeton U., 1949, PhD in Physics, 1951. Asst. rsch. officer Atomic Energy Can., Ltd., Chalk River, Ont., 1951-57, assoc. rsch. officer, 1957-62, sr. rsch. officer, 1962-70, prin. rsch. officer, 1970-91, head nuclear physics br., 1967-83, dir. physics div., 1983-85, v.p. physics and health scis., 1986-90, researcher emeritus, 1990-97. Vis. scientist Lawrence Berkeley Lab., 1960-62, Centre de Recherches, Strasbourg & Bruyeres-le-Chatel, 1975-76; chmn. nuclear physics grants Natural Sci. and Engring. Research Council, 1977-82; adv. bd. TRIUMF 1984-92; bd. dirs. Can. Fusion Fuels Tech., 1986-90, Tokamak de Varennes, 1986-90. Pres. Deep River Hort. Assn., 1997-98; mem., bd. gov. Deep River and Dist. Hosp., 2004-. Fellow: Royal Soc. Can., Am. Phys. Soc.; mem.: Can. Assn. Physicists (pres. 1992). Home: 3 Alexander Pl Deep River ON Canada K0J 1P0 E-mail: dmilton@magma.ca.

**MILTON, JOSE,** real estate development company executive; b. Cuba; arrived in US, 1962; Architect, Cuba, Miami; founder J. Milton & Associates, Coral Gables, Fla., 1962—. Office: J Milton & Associates Ste 301 3211 Ponce De Leon Blvd Coral Gables FL 33134 Office Phone: 305-460-6300. Office Fax: 305-442-0778.*

**MILTON, JOSEPH,** real estate development company executive; b. Miami; s. Joseph Milton. Degree in engring., U. Miami. Pres., CEO J. Milton & Associates, Coral Gables, Fla. Office: J Milton & Associates Ste 301 3211 Ponce De Leon Blvd Coral Gables FL 33134 Office Phone: 305-460-6300. Office Fax: 305-461-0531.

**MILTON, JOSEPH PAYNE,** lawyer; b. Richmond, Va., Oct. 24, 1943; s. Hubert E. and Grace C. Milton; children: Michael Payne, Amy Barrett, David King; m. Cela Cabler Milton, Apr. 8, 1989. BS in Bus. Adminstrn., U. Fla., 1967, JD, 1969. Bar: Fla. 1969, U.S. Ct. Appeals (5th cir.) 1971, U.S. Supreme Ct. 1972, U.S. Ct. Appeals (11th cir.) 1981. Assoc. Toole, Taylor, Moseley & Gabel, Jacksonville, 1969-70; ptnr. Toole, Taylor, Moseley, Gabel & Milton, Jacksonville, 1971-78, Howell, Liles, Braddock & Milton, Jacksonville, 1978-89; sr. ptnr. Milton, Leach, Whitman, D'Andrea, Cherek & Milton, P.A., Jacksonville, 1990—. Mem. jud. nominating commn. Fla. Supreme Ct., 2002, chmn., 2005—06. Mem. Mayor's Blue Ribbon Task Force; mem. Law Ctr. Coun., U. Fla. Coll. Law, 1972-78, mem. alumni coun., 1995—; campaign chmn. N.E. Fla. chpt. March of Dimes, 1973-74, v.p., 1974-75; pres. Willing Hands, 1974-75; chmn. attys.' divsn. United Way, 1977; pres. Civic Round Table of Jacksonville, 1980-81; mem. exec. com. Jacksonville Area Legal Aid, Inc., 1982-83; chmn. pvt. bar involvement com. Legal Aid Bd. Dirs., 1982-83; mem. Hist. Soc. Fla. Supreme Ct., membership chmn. N. Fla. US Supreme Ct. Hist. Soc. Recipient Outstanding Svc. award for individual contbns. in support of legal svcs. for the poor, 1981; named Superlawyer of Fla., 2006. Fellow: Soc. Lawyers for Pub. Svc., Southeastern Admiralty Law (dir. Port, Jacksonville 1996—99), Am. Bar Found., Internat. Soc. Barristers; mem.: ATLA, Nat. ABOTA Found. (treas. 2004—05, pres. 2006—), Am. Judicature Soc., Acad. Fla. Trial Lawyers, Maritime Law Assn. U.S. (mem. com. professionalism 1996—), Nat. Assn. R.R. Trial Counsel (exec. com. 1979—2004, v.p. southeastern region 1984—86, pres. 1990—91), Jacksonville Assn. Def. Counsel (pres. 1981—82, lectr. CLE programs, guest lectr. U. Fla. Nat. Assn. R.R. Trial Counsel), Fla. Coun. Bar Assn. Pres. (exec. com. 1982—88, v.p. 1984, pres. 1985—86, Outstanding Past Bar Pres. award 2001), Fla. Bar (grievance com. 1975—77, chmn. grievance com. 1976, 4th jud. cir. nominating commn. 1980—82, voluntary bar liaison com. 1982—83, mem. exec. coun. for trial sect. 1982—89, chmn. 1987, 1988, bd. passim 1982—89, charter mem. admiralty and maritime law bd. cert. 1996—2000, chmn. 1998, chmn. 4th jud. cir. professionalism com. 1998—, bd. cert civil trial lawyer, bd. cert. admiralty and maritime law, mem. Hist. Soc. for 11th cir.; recipient Outstanding Professionalism Program 1999, 2001), Jacksonville Bar Assn. (young lawyers sect. 1974—75, pres. 1980—81, Lawyer of Yr. award 1999), Am. Bd. Trial Advs. (pres. Jacksonville chpt. 1997, FLABOTA bd. mem. 1997—, treas. 1999, nat. bd. mem. 1999—, pres.-elect 2000, treas. 2004, charter, chpt. selected as Best in Nation

1997, Jacksonville chpt. Trial Lawyer of Yr. 2000, selected as Fla. Trial Lawyer of Yr. 2000, named Master In Trial Master of Yr. 2003), Country Club Sapphire Valley (NC), Gulf Life Tower Club, Univ. Club, San Jose Country Club. Republican. Home: 4655 Corrientes Cir N Jacksonville FL 32217-4329 Office: Milton Leach Whitman D'Andrea Charek & Milton PA 815 S Main St Ste 200 Jacksonville FL 32207-8181 Office Phone: 904-346-3800. Personal E-mail: jmilton@miltonleach.com.

**MILTON, PETER WINSLOW,** artist; b. Lower Merion, Pa., Apr. 2, 1930; s. William Hammond and Lois (Preston) M.; m. Edith Hanna Cohn, June 3, 1961; children: Jeremy Lawrence, Naomi Helen. BFA, Yale U., 1954, MFA, 1962. Tchr. art Md. Inst., Balt., 1961-68, Yale Summer Sch. of Music and Art, 1970; artist-in-residence Dartmouth Coll., winter 1983, Rockefeller Found., Bellagio, Italy, 1990, Pasadena (Calif.) City Coll., 1999, Weber State U., Ogden, Utah, 2004. Guest lectr. J. Paul Getty Mus., 1999. Exhibited in over 80 one-man shows including, Balt. Mus., 1965, De Cordova Mus., Lincoln, Mass., 1970, Phillips Exeter Acad., 1971, 83, The Franz Bader Gallery, Washington, 1967, 71, 80, 82, 86, 87, 88, 89, 91, Museo La Tertulia, Cali, Colombia, 1972, Corcoran Gallery Art, Washington, 1972, Asso. Am. Artists, N.Y.C., 1975, Galerie Georges Bernier, Paris, 1975, Biblioteca Luis Angel Arango, Bogota, Colombia, 1975, Galerie Petites Formes, Osaka, Japan, 1979, Francis Kyle Gallery, London, 1980, 88, 91, 94, 06, Bklyn. Mus., 1980, 88, Hood Mus., Dartmouth Coll., 1983, Louis Newman Galleries, Beverly Hills, Calif., 1984, 87, 94, Graystone Gallery, San Francisco, 1985, Edith Caldwell Gallery, San Francisco, 1992, 94, Mary Ryan Gallery, N.Y.C., 1993, Currier Mus. Art, Manchester, N.H., 1997, De Young Mus., San Francisco, 1998, Jack Rutberg Fine Arts, Los Angeles, 2001, Ayle Gallery, 2006; 2 traveling exhbns. to 40 Am. cities, 1977-81; exhibited in numerous group shows; represented in numerous permanent collections. Yale traveling fellow, 1954; Louis Comfort Tiffany Found. grantee, 1964; recipient numerous nat. and internat. awards and prizes including Medal of Honor Interprint Exhbn., Lvov, USSR, 1990, awards exequo Internat. Triennial Graphics Arts, Crocow, Poland, 1991, 94, 03, 04, Commendary award Miniprint Exhbn., Finland, 1998, Hon. award Internat. Biennial, Varna, Bulgaria, 1997, Internat. Triennial Graphic Arts, Poland, 2003, Miniprint Exhbn., Finland, 2004, Spl. Jury award Internat. Biennial, Varna, 2005. Subject of: Peter Milton: Complete Etchings 1960-1976, 1977, The Jolly Corner, 21 etchings (Henry James) 1980, The Primacy of Touch: The Drawings of Peter Milton, 1993, The Aspern Papers, 18 drawings, 1 etching (Henry James) 1992, Peter Milton: Complete Prints, 1960-96, Chronicle Books, 1996. Home: PO Box 237 Francestown NH 03043-0237 Personal E-mail: emilton@earthlink.net.

**MILTON-JONES, DELISHA,** professional basketball player; b. Riceboro, Ga., Sept. 11, 1974; d. Beverly Milton; m. Roland Jones, June 30, 2003. BA in Sports Mgmt., U. Fla. Forward Portland Power, 1997—99, L.A. Sparks, 1999—. Forward Ekaterinburg team/EuroLeague, Russia, 2002—; mem. USA Basketball Women's Sr. Nat. Team, 2004. Recipient gold medal, Olympic Games, 2000, World Championships, 1998, 2002, U.S. Olympic Cub, 1999, World Univ. Games, 1997, U.S. Olympic Festival, 1994. Office: Los Angeles Sparks 555 N Nash St El Segundo CA 90245

**MILUNAS, J. ROBERT,** health care organization executive; b. Aug. 7, 1947; s. Joseph John M.; m. Glenetta Graham; children: Amy, Joseph, Anna Kate. BS, Tulane U., 1969; postgrad., Samford U., 1973; MBA, Ga. State U., 1977. Mgr. internal and govt. reporting, corp. contr.'s staff Arvin Industries Inc., Columbus, Ind., 1977-80; mgr. consol. acctg., corp. contr.'s staff Mattel Inc., Hawthorne, Calif., 1980-82; asst. contr. Times Mirror Cable TV Inc., Irvine, Calif., 1982-83; Western Divsn. contr. SCA, Santa Ana, Calif., 1983-84; v.p., corp. contr. Tchrs. Mgmt. Investment Corp., Newport Beach, Calif., 1984-86; v.p., CFO Beech St. Inc., Irvine, 1987-89; v.p. fin. and adminstrn. ConsumerHealth Inc., Newport Beach, Calif., 1989-93; pres. Aegis Consulting Svcs., Dana Point, Calif., 1994—. 1st lt. U.S. Army Transp. Corps., 1969-71. Decorated Bronze Star. Roman Catholic. Office Phone: 404-321-4232. Personal E-mail: bob@milunas.com. *Life is a precious gift to be nurtured daily through interaction with friends and family and helping others achieve their potential.*

**MILUNSKY, AUBREY,** geneticist, pediatrician, educator; b. Johannesburg, Nov. 3, 1936; came to U.S., 1969; 1 child. Jeffrey M. MB, BCh, U. Witwatersand, Johannesburg, 1960, DSc, 1982; postgrad., Gt. Ormond St. Hosp., London, 1965. Diplomate Am. Bd. Pediatrics, Am. Bd. Med. Genetics. Intern Johannesburg Gen. Hosp./Baragwanath Hosp., Johannesburg, 1961; resident in internal medicine and pediat. Baragwanath Hosp., 1961-64; pediat. registrar Queen Mary's Hosp. for Children, Surrey, Eng., 1965-66; asst. pediatrician New England Med. Ctr. Tufts U., Boston, 1966-70, from instr. to asst. prof. pediat. Sch. Medicine, 1966-70; rsch. fellow and assoc. in neurology Mass. Gen. Hosp./Harvard Med. Sch., Boston, 1969-70; dir. Birth Defects and Genetics Clinic Mass. Gen. Hosp., Boston, 1971-73, asst. pediatrician, 1971-82, assoc. dir. Cystic Fibrosis Clinic, 1975-79; asst. prof. pediatrics Harvard Med. Sch., Boston, 1971-81; prof. pediatrics and ob-gyn. Sch. Medicine, dir. Ctr. for Human Genetics, assoc. physician Univ. Hosp. Boston U., 1981—; prof. pathology, 1985—, Endowed chair human genetics, 1991—; pediatrician Boston City Hosp., 1981—. Mem. Mass. State Genetics Adv. Bd., 1983-84; profl. adv. bd. Nat. Tuberous Sclerosis Assn., 1990-93; quality assurance com. New England Regional Genetics Group, 1990-96. Author: The Prenatal Diagnosis of Hereditary Disorders, 1973, Know Your Genes, 1977, How to Have the Healthiest Baby You Can, 1987, Choices, Not Chances: An Essential Guide to your Heredity and Health, 1989, Heredity and Your Family's Health, 1992, Your Genetic Destiny: Know Your Genes, Secure Your Health, Save Your Life, 2001; editor: Clinics in Perinatology, Vol. II, 1974, The Prevention of Genetic Disease and Mental Retardation, 1975, Genetic Disorders and the Fetus: Diagnosis, Prevention and Treatment, 1979, 5th edit., 2004, Coping with Crisis and Handicap, 1981, (with G.J. Annas) Genetics and the Law 1, 1976, Genetics and the Law II, 1980, Genetics and the Law III, 1986, (with E.A. Friedman and L. Gluck) Advances in Perinatal Medicine, Vol. II, 1982, Vol. III, 1983, Vol. IV, 1985, Vol. V, 1986, mem. editl. bd. Am. Jour. Law and Medicine, 1974-93, Am. Jour. Med. Genetics, 1977-94, Bioethics Digest, 1977-78, Prenatal Diagnosis, 1980-90, 92—, Intelligence Reports in Ob-Gyn., 1982-88, Fetal Therapy, 1986—; peer reviewer New England Jour. Medicine, Pediatrics, Am. Jour. Med. Genetics, Am. Jour. Ob-Gyn., Am. Jour. Law and Medicine, Am. Jour. Pub. Health, Prenatal Diagnosis, Fetal Therapy, Ob-Gyn., Epidemiology, Jour. Pediatrics; contbr. over 300 articles to profl. jours. Recipient First Place Film award Nat. Coun. Family Rels. Media Awards Co., 1990, Tinsley Harrison award Soc. for Clin. Investigation, 1991; Aubrey Milunsky Endowed Chair in Human Genetics named in his honor Boston U., 1991. Fellow Am. Coll. Med. Genetics (founding), Royal Coll. Physicians (diploma in child health 1965); mem. Am. Pediat. Soc., Am. Soc. Human Genetics (social issues com. 1983-87), Am. Soc. Law and Medicine, (v.p. 1982-83, pres.-elect 1983-85, pres. 1985-86, bd. dirs. 1986-88, 90-93), Soc. for Pediat. Rsch., Mass. Med. Soc. Office: Boston U Sch Medicine Ctr for Human Genetics 715 Albany St Boston MA 02118-2307

**MIMS, JOYCE ELAINE,** lawyer; b. Chgo., Mar. 6, 1942; d. Thomas Samuel Mims and Hortense Bernice Miller; m. John Young. BA, U. Wis., 1964; MA, Northwestern U., 1965; JD, NYU, 1975. Bar: Ill. 1976. Tchr. Lane Tech. High Sch., Chgo. Bd. Edn., 1965—67; edn. specialist IBM World Trade Corp., NYC, 1968—69; adminstr. tech. CUNY-Brooklyn, 1969—75; assoc. firm Bell, Boyd & Lloyd, Chgo., 1975—78; atty. Am. Hosp. Supply Corp., Evanston, Ill., 1978—82, div. counsel, 1982—83, asst. gen. counsel, 1983—89; gen. counsel Ancilla Systems Inc., 1989—95, sr. v.p., gen. counsel, 1999—98; v.p., gen. counsel, sec. Ryerson Tull, Inc., Chgo., 1999—2001, v.p., gen. counsel, 2001—. Mem. Evanston Zoning Bd. Appeals, 1977—82; mem. bd. dirs. Evanston Community Devel. Corp., Evanston Hosp. Corp. Mem.: ABA, Chgo. Bar Assn. Office: Ryerson Tull Inc 2621 W 15th Pl Chicago IL 60608

**MIMS, MERRILL TED,** computer scientist, department chairman; PhD, U. N.Tex. Chair computer sci. U. Ill., Springfield, 1990—. Office: Univ Illinois One University Plaza Springfield IL 62703 Office Phone: 217-206-7326.

**MIMS, WILLIAM CLEVELAND,** state legislator, lawyer; b. Harrisonburg, Va., June 20, 1957; s. David Lathan and Lurleen Shirley (Stovall) M.; m. Jane Ellen Rehme, Dec. 20, 1980; children: Katherine Grace, Emily Anne, Sarah Joy. AB, Coll. of William & Mary, 1979; JD, George Washington U., 1984; LLM, Georgetown U., 1986. Bar: Va. Legis. asst. Congressman Paul Trible, Washington, 1981-82; dep. legis. dir. Senator Paul Trible, Washington, 1983-85; chief of staff Congressman Frank Wolf, Washington, 1986-87; atty. Hazel & Thomas, P.C., Leesburg, Va., 1987-91, Worcester, Mims & Atwill, P.C., 1993—2002, Mims, Atwill & Leigh, P.C., Leesburg, 2002—; mem. Va. Gen. Assembly, Richmond, 1991—, del., 1992-98, senator, 1998—. Adj. prof. law George Mason U., 2002—; mem. Va. Housing Commn., 1994—, chmn. 2000—2003; mem. Va. Code Commn., 2000, chmn., 2003—. Bd. dirs. Dulles Area Transp. Assn., Herndon, Va., 1994—, Marshall Home Preservation Fund, Leesburg, 1992—, Youth for Tomorrow, 1995-97; treas., bd. dirs. Loudoun Bar Assn., Leesburg, 1988-89; active Nat. Eagle Scout Assn., 1992--. Flemming fellow, 1995-96. Mem. Va. Bar Assn. (Boyd-Graves Conf. 1996—, bd. govs. 2002—), Va. Trial Lawyers Assn., Christian Legal Soc., No. Va. Transp. Assn. Republican. Episcopalian. Office: Mims Atwill & Leigh PC PO Box 741 Leesburg VA 20178-0741

**MIN, BALSHIK,** pathologist; b. Seoul, Republic of Korea, Jan. 15, 1942; s. Young-Ock and Yang-Hee (Kim) M.; m. Jungsoon Ahn, Apr. 25, 1970; children: James, Susan. MD, Seoul Nat. U., 1966. Pathologist Faxton-St. Luke's Healthcare, Utica, NY, 1978—2005, dir. labs., 1984—2005; pathologist Centrex Clin. Labs., New Hartford, NY, 1978—, dir. labs., 1990—96; pathologist, dir. labs Rome (NY) Meml. Hosp., 2005—. Capt. Korean Army, 1966-70. Fellow Coll. Am. Pathologists; mem. AMA, Am. Soc. Clin. Pathology, Nat. Soc. Histotechnology, Ctrl. N.Y. Acad. Medicine. Avocations: reading, classical music, gardening, golf. Office: Rome Meml Hosp 1500 N James St Rome NY 13440 Office Phone: 315-338-7045.

**MIN, DAVID BYONG,** chemist, educator, research scientist; b. Seoul, Republic of Korea, Sept. 12, 1942; arrived in U.S.A., 1965; s. Yun S. Min and Sun D. Yoon; m. Hyung Ok Lee, Aug. 1, 1953; children: Peter K., Stephen K. BS, Seoul Nat. U., Republic of Korea, 1965; MS, U. Minn., Mpls., 1968; PhD, Rutgers U., New Brunswick, NJ, 1973. Mgr. CP, Best Foods Rsch. Ctr., Union, NJ, 1976—79; prof. Ohio State, Columbus, 1979—. Hon. prof. Rutgers U., 1976—79; cons. Ministry of Agr., Seoul, 2001—; sci. editor Jour. of Food Sci., Chgo., 2001—. Author: Flavor Chemistry of Foods, 1998, Chemistry of Food Lipids, 2002. Pres. Korean Cath. Ch., Columbus, Ohio, 2000—02. Recipient Rsch. Achievement award, Inst. of Food Technologists, 1995, Disting. Sr. Faculty Rsch. award, Ohio State, 1999, Rsch. award, Korean Soc. of Food Sci. and Tech., 2002; fellow, Am. Oil Chemicals Co., 2001, Inst. of Food Technologists, 2002. Roman Catholic. Achievements include development of singlet oxygen oxidation of foods; research in oxygen quenching to improve flavor stability of foods; mechanism of light sensitivity of riboflavin. Avocations: golf, travel. Home: 1306 Lakeside Pl Worthington OH 43085 Office: Ohio State Univ 2015 Fyffe Rd Columbus OH 43210 Office Phone: 614-292-7801. Personal E-mail: min.2@osu.edu.

**MIN, JANICE BYUNG,** editor-in-chief; b. Atlanta, 1969; m. Peter Sheehy, 1997; 1 child. BA in Journalism, Columbia U., NYC, 1990. Reporter, Westchester County, NY, 1990—92; writer to sr. editor People mag., NYC, 1992—97; with Life mag., NYC, 1997—98; mng. editor In Style mag., NYC, 1998—2001; exec. editor Us Weekly mag., NYC, 2002—03, editor-in-chief, 2003—. Recipient Editor of Yr., AdWeek mag., 2005. Office: Us Weekly 1290 Ave of Americas New York NY 10104-0298 Office Phone: 800-283-3956. Office Fax: 212-651-7890.

**MIN, TAEGEE,** aerospace engineer, researcher, mechanical engineer; b. Jinju, Gyeongnam, Republic of Korea, July 7, 1971; s. Byungchul Min and Jeolja Park; m. Noo Mi Moon, Dec. 10, 1975. PhD, Seoul Nat. U., 2001. Rschr. Ctr. for Turbulence and Flow Control Rsch., Seoul Nat. U., Republic of Korea, 2001—03; rschr. dept. mech./aerospace engring. UCLA, 2003—. Mem.: Am. Phys. Soc. Achievements include patents pending for shaft assembly using cavities for skin-friction torque reduction. Office: UCLA Dept Mech/Aerospace Engring 420 Westwood Plz Los Angeles CA 90095 Office Phone: 310-825-0875. Personal E-mail: ilyitch@freechal.com.

**MINA, RICHARD T.,** apparel executive; Pres. Footlocker Europe Footlocker Inc., 1996—99, pres., CEO Champ Sports, 1999—2003, pres., CEO, 2003—. Office: Footlocker Inc 112 W 34th St New York NY 10120

**MINAHAN, DANIEL FRANCIS,** lawyer, retired manufacturing executive; b. Orange, N.J., Dec. 3, 1929; s. Alfred A. and Katherine (Kelly) M.; m. Mary Jean Gaffney, May 2, 1953; children: Daniel F. Jr., John A. AB magna cum laude, U. Notre Dame, 1951; JD magna cum laude, U. Conn., 1964; grad., Advanced Mgmt. Program, Harvard, 1975. Bar: Conn. 1964, U.S. Supreme Ct 1969, U.S. Ct. of Appeals (2d cir.), U.S. Dist. Ct. Conn. 1971. Mgr. indsl. engring. Uniroyal, Inc., Naugatuck, Conn., 1952-59, mgr. indsl. relations, 1959-64, dir. labor relations N.Y.C., 1964-66; v.p. indsl. relations and labor counsel Phillips Van Heusen Corp., N.Y.C., 1966-69; v.p. personnel-adminstrn. Broadway-Hale Stores, Inc., L.A., 1969-70; v.p. employee relations, sec. Magnavox-N.Am., Philips Corp., 1970-73, v.p. ops., group exec., 1973-83, sr. v.p. adminstrn., 1984-89, exec., v.p., 1989-93, vice-chmn., 1991-93; vice-chmn. nat. found. bd. Robert Anderson Sch. Mgmt., U. N.Mex., 1993-98; pvt. practice, 1998—. Trustees adv. coun., Fairfield U. mem. dean's coun. Grad. Sch. Bus. Co-author: The Developing Labor Law, 1971. Chmn. bd. Internat. Fedn. Keystone Youth Orgns., London and Chgo., 1984-88; vice-chmn. nat. found. bd. Anderson Sch. Mgmt., U. N.Mex., 1993-98. With USMC. Mem. The Forum for World Affairs, Conn. Bar Assn., Harvard Club, Club Internat. (Chgo.). Office Phone: 203-255-0746.

**MINAHAN, JESSICA ANGELA,** special education service professional; b. Boston, Mar. 6, 1975; d. Neal and Rita Minahan. BS in Intensive Spl. Edn., Boston U., 1997; MS in Tchg. Spl. Needs and Elem. Edn., Wheelock Coll., Boston, 2001; CGS in Tchg. Children with Autism, U. Albany, NY, 2005. Cert. intensive spl. needs all levels Mass., 1997, early childhood edn. Mass., 1997, tchr. students with spl. needs Mass., 2001, elem. edn. Mass., 2001, Wilson reading Mass., 2005, Behavior Analyst Certification Bd., 2007. Head spl. needs tchr. The League Sch. Boston, Walpole, Mass., 1998—99; educator Good Start Early Intervention Mass. Soc. Prevention Cruelty to Children, Lynn, Mass., 1999—2000; inclusion specialist Cambridge Pub. Schs., Cambridge, Mass., 2001—06; inclusion facilitator Newton Pub. Schs., Mass., 2006—. Adj. prof. Lesley U., Cambridge, 2006—; spkr. in field. Mem.: Asperger's Assn. New Eng., Boston Pub. Libr. Young Profls. Avocations: cooking, travel.

**MINAI, OMAR AHMAD,** physician; b. Lahore, Pakistan; s. Idris Ahmad and Riaz Fatima Minai; m. Beena Ahmad, Dec. 7, 1998. MB BS, Aga Khan U., Karachi, Pakistan, 1990. Diplomate Am. Bd. Internal Medicine, Am. Bd. Pulmonary Medicine, Am. Bd. Critical Care Medicine, Am. Bd. Sleep Medicine. Intern in internal medicine U. Conn., Farmington, 1992-93, resident in internal medicine, 1992-96; fellow in pulmonary and critical care medicine Cleve. Clin. Found., 1996-99, staff physician in pulmonary and critical care medicine, 1999—. Contbr. Mem.: ACP, Am. Thoracic Soc., Am. Coll. Chest Physicians. Office: Cleve Clinic Found 9500 Euclid Ave Ste A-90 Cleveland OH 44195-0001 Office Phone: 216-445-2610. E-mail: minaio@ccf.org.

**MINAR, PAUL G.,** interior designer, consultant; b. Phoenix, July 12, 1932; s. Aaron Crowther and Ione Anna (Schmid) Mortensen. Student, Ariz. State U., 1950-54, John F. Kennedy U., 1978-80, Antioch West U., 1980. Sound effects technician, TV stage mgr. Sta. KHJ-AM-TV, L.A., 1955-63; displayer W.&J. Sloane Furniture Co., Beverly Hills, Calif., 1963-66, Bullock's Dept. Store, L.A., 1966-68, Macy's Dept. Store, San Francisco, 1968-70; interior designer Lloyd's Furniture Co., San Diego, 1970-71, Bonynge's Furniture Co., Oakland, Calif., 1971-72, Breuner's Furniture Co., Oakland, 1972-74; design cons. The Other Artist, San Francisco, 1974—. Archival rschr. and

conservation Petaluma Hist. Mus., 1994—; cons. Human Svcs. Dept., Oakland, Calif., 2003—; profl. numerologist; lectr. in onomatology. Author: Numbers: The Energy Force in Your Name, 2003; writer, producer (documentary) The Modern Nursing Home, 1959. Vol. talent agt. San Francisco Symphony Black and White Ball, 1983; mem. Fine Arts Mus. of San Francisco. Mem. Inst. Noetic Scis., Petaluma Mus. Assn., Interant. Assn. Numerologists, Calif. Soc. Psychical Study. Democrat. Roman Catholic. Avocations: wilderness exploration, tennis, classical music, parapsychology, world history. Office: The Other Artist 3200 Buchanan St San Francisco CA 94123-3517 E-mail: pminar@shasta.com.

**MINARD, MARYANN JOHNSON,** elementary school educator, secondary school educator, director; b. Springfield, Mass. d. William Richard and Geraldine Grady Johnson; m. Michael P Minard, June 30, 1973; 1 child, Megan Elizabeth. BS in elem. edn., Westfield State Coll., 1971; MPA, Troy State U., 1988; PhD in Ednl. Leadership and Policy, U. N.H., 2002. Tchr. West Springfield Pub. Schools, Mass., 1971—74, Rutland Pub. Schools, 1974—75, Adelento Sch. Dist., Calif., 1976—78, Dept. Def. Dependents School, Germany, 1978—81, 1984—89, Maine Sch. Adminstrv. Dist. #35, South Berwick, Maine, 1989—97; faculty in residence U. N.H., Durham, 1997—2000; dir. K-12 curriculum York Sch. Dept., 2000—. Mem.: ASCD, Am. Ednl. Rsch. Assn. (Disting. Paper award 2005), New England Assn. Schs. and Colls. (commr. elem. and mid. schs. 1995—2001, commr. Am. and internat. schs. abroad 2004—), New England Ednl. Rsch. Assn. (bd. dirs. 2005—), Rubovits Best Paper award 2004). Avocations: skiing, travel, boating. Home: 14 Beech Rd South Berwick ME 03908 Office: York Sch Dept 469 US Route One York ME 03909 Business E-mail: mminard@yorkschools.org.

**MINARDI, ANN SEGURA,** lawyer, musician; d. William A. and Mary Louise Segura; m. John Christopher Minardi, June 10, 1983; children: Christine Ann, Angela Rose. BA, U. Mich., 1980; JD, Boston U., 1984. Bar: Md. 1988, U.S. Ct. Internat. Trade 1988, U.S. Ct. Appeals (fed. cir.) 1988, U.S. Supreme Ct. 1989. Atty. Office of Regulations and Rulings, Washington, 1988—. Musician: (professional flutist) Friday Morning Music Club, 1998—. Recipient Academic award, U. Mich., 1980. Mem.: Customs Lawyers Assn. (chair, program com. 2004—05). Avocation: equestrian sports. Office: Customs and Border Protection 1300 Pennsylvania Ave NW Washington DC 20229

**MINARDI, RICHARD A. (RICK), JR.,** lawyer; b. Mobile, Ala., Aug. 15, 1943; s. Richard A. and Martha F. (Beck) Minardi; m. Frances Archer Guy, Oct. 21, 1989. BA, Yale U., 1965, LLB, 1968. Bar: Va. 1969. Assoc. McGuire Woods & Battle, Richmond, Va., 1968-71; ptnr. Staples, Greenberg Minardi & Kessler, Richmond, 1971-86, Mays & Valentine, Richmond, 1986-2000; ptnr., mem. exec. com. Troutman Sanders LLP, Richmond, 2001—. Mem.: ABA, Richmond Bar Assn., Va. Bar Assn. Office: Troutman Sanders LLP Troutman Sanders Bldg 1001 Haxall Point Richmond VA 23219 Office Phone: 804-697-1252. Office Fax: 804-698-5128. Business E-Mail: rick.minardi@troutmansanders.com.

**MINARIK, JOSEPH JOHN,** economist, researcher; b. Lancaster, Pa., July 27, 1949; s. Joseph John and Helen Elizabeth M.; m. Eileen Marie Dowds; children: Mara Christina, Sara Elizabeth. BA, Georgetown U., 1971; MA, Yale U., 1972, M.Phil., 1973, PhD, 1974. Rsch. assoc. Brookings Instn., Washington, 1974-81; dept. asst. dir. Congl. Budget Office, Washington, 1981-84; sr. rsch. assoc. Urban Inst., Washington, 1984-88; exec. dir. Joint Econ. Com. U.S. Congress, Washington, 1988-90; exec. dir. for policy, chief economist House Budget Com., 1991-93; assoc. dir. econ. policy Office Mgmt. and Budget, 1993-2001; policy dir., chief economist House Budget Com. Dem. Staff, 2001—05; sr. v.p., dir. rsch. Com. Econ. Devel., 2005—. Author: Making Tax Choices, 1985, Making America's Budget Policy, 1989; contbr. articles to profl. jours. Fellow NSF, 1971-74, Yale U., 1971 Mem. Am. Econ. Assn., Nat. Tax Assn. Democrat. Home: 11656 Mediterranean Ct Reston VA 20190-3401 Office: Com Econ Devel 200 L St NW Washington DC 20036 Business E-Mail: joseph.minarik@ced.org.

**MINAYA, OMAR,** professional sports team executive; b. Valverde Mao, Dominican Republic; Scout Tex. Rangers, 1985—97; dir. pers. and internat. scouting, 1995—97; sr. asst. gen. mgr. N.Y. Mets, 1997—2002; v.p. Montreal (Can.) Expos, 2002—04; gen. mgr., 2002—04; exec. v.p. baseball operations, gen. mgr. New York Mets, 2004—. Office: c/o New York Mets Shea Stadium 123-01 Roosevelt Ave Flushing NY 11368*

**MINC, HENRYK,** mathematics professor; b. Lodz, Poland, Nov. 12, 1919; s. Izrael and Haja (Zyngler) M.; m. Catherine Taylor Duncan, Apr. 16, 1943; children: Robert Henry, Ralph Edward, Raymond. MA with honors, Edinburgh U., Scotland, 1955, PhD, 1959. Tchr. Morgan Acad., Dundee, Scotland, 1956-58; lectr. Dundee Tech. Coll., 1957-58, U. B.C., Vancouver, Canada, 1958-59, asst. prof., 1959-60; assoc. prof. U. Fla., Gainesville, 1960-63; prof. U. Calif., Santa Barbara, 1963-90, prof. emeritus, 1990—. Vis. prof. Technion Israel Inst. Tech., Haifa, 1969-80. Author: A Survey of Matrix Theory and Matrix Inequalities, 1964, Russian translation, 1972, Chinese translation, 1990, Introduction to Linear Algebra, 1968, Spanish translation, 1968, Modern University Algebra, 1966, Elementary Linear Algebra, Spanish translation, 1971, New College Algebra, 1968, Elementary Functions and Coordinate Geometry, 1969, Algebra and Trigonometry, 1970, College Algebra, 1970, College Trigonometry, 1971, Integrated Analytic Geometry and Algebra with Circular Functions, 1973, Permanents, 1978, Russian translation, 1980, Chinese translation, 1991, Nonnegative Matrices, 1988, Chinese translation, 1991; contbr. over 80 rsch. articles to math. jours., 9 rsch. papers to archaeol. and ancient numismatic jours.; articles to Burns Chronicle; referee and reviewer math jours. 2nd lt. Polish Army 1940-48, France, U.K. Recipient Lester Ford award Math. Assn. Am., 1966, rsch. contract Office Naval Rsch., 1985-88, Air Force Office Sci. Rsch. grantee, 1960-83, Lady Davis fellow, 1975-78. Fellow: Soc. Antiquaries of Scotland; mem.: Friends of Ellisland, Robert Burns Assn. N.Am., Saltire Soc., Scots. Lang. Soc., Scottish Soc. Santa Barbara (past chieftain), Robert Burns World Fedn. (hon. pres.), Am. Math. Soc. Democrat. Home: 4076 Naranjo Dr Santa Barbara CA 93110-1213 Office: U Calif Dept Math Santa Barbara CA 93106 Personal E-mail: hmincburns@cox.net.

**MINDELL, DAVID A.,** engineering educator; BA in Elec. Engring., Yale U., 1988, BA in Lit., 1988; PhD, Mass. Inst. Tech., 1996. Ocean engr. deep submergence lab. Woods Hole Oceanographic Instn., 1990—95; grad. fellow NSF, 1993—95, Dibner Inst. History Sci. and Tech., 1995—96; asst. prof. Mass. Inst. Tech., 1996—2000, Frances and David Dibner prof. history engring. and mfg., 2000—, prof. engring systems. Tech. cons. Hermetic Scis. Co., 1986—; vis. investigator deep submergence lab. Woods Hole Oceanographic Instn., 1996—; vis. rsch. fellow Smithsonian Instn., 1999; adj. rschr. Inst. Exploration, Mystic, Conn. Editor: Technology, Archaeology, and the Deep Sea; author: (book) War, Technology and the Experience Aboard the USSS Monitor, 2000, Between Human and Machine: Feedback, Control, and Computing before Cybernetics, 2002; contbr. articles to profl. jours., chapters to books. Recipient Sally Hacker Prize, Soc. History Tech. for War, 2001, Abbott Payson Usher Prize, 1998; MacVicar faculty fellow, Mass. Inst. Tech., 2001—. Fellow: Explorer's Club; mem.: IEEE, History Sci. Soc., Soc. History Tech. Office: Mass Inst Tech 77 Massachusetts Ave Bldg E51-185 Cambridge MA 02139 Office Phone: 617-253-0221. Office Fax: 617-258-8118. Business E-Mail: mindell@mit.edu.

**MINDELL, EUGENE ROBERT,** surgeon, educator; b. Chgo. Feb. 24, 1922; s. Leon and Tillie (Rosenthal) M.; m. June A. Abrams, Sept. 19, 1945; children: Barbara, Ruth, David, Douglas. BS, U. Chgo., 1943, MD, 1945. Diplomate Am. Bd. Orthopaedic Surgery. Intern orthopaedic surgery U. Chgo. Clinics, 1948-52; instr. U. Chgo., 1952; mem. faculty dept. orthopaedic surgery Sch. Medicine SUNY, Buffalo, 1953—, prof. Sch. Medicine, 1964—; chmn. dept. SUNY Sch. Medicine, Buffalo, 1964-88, dir. orthopaedic oncology Sch. Medicine, 1988—. Mem.

bd. mgrs. Erie County Med. Ctr., 1990-96. Assoc. editor Jour. Bone and Joint Surgery, 1984-88, trustee, 1991—; dep. editor Clin. Orthopaedics and Related Rsch. representing Musculoskeletal Tumor Soc., 1997—; contbr. articles to profl. jours. Lt. (j.g.) M.C. USNR, 1946-48. Eugene R. Mindell Endowed Chair of Orthopaedic Surgery established in his honor SUNY, Buffalo, 1996; recipient Disting. Svc. award Alumni U. Chgo. Sch. Medicine, 1990, award for achievement in health care D'Youville Coll., 2002, Lifetime Achievement Excellence in Tchg. award, SUNY Buffalo Dept. Orthop. Surgery, 2002; NRC fellow, 1949-50. Fellow ACS; mem. Am. Acad. Orthopaedic Surgeons (bd. dirs. 1991-92), Am. Orthopaedic Assn. (v.p. 1990-91), Assn. Orthopaedic Chmn., Am. Assn. Surgery of Trauma, Am. Orthopaedic Rsch. Soc. (pres. 1972-73, residency rev. com. 1985-91), Musculoskeletal Tumor Soc. (pres. 1989-90), Coun. Musculoskeletal Specialty Socs. (chmn. elect 1991, chmn. 1992). Jewish. Home: 85 Depew Ave Buffalo NY 14214-1509 Office: 100 High St Buffalo NY 14203-1126 Office Phone: 716-859-1531. Business E-Mail: emindell@kaleidehealth.org.

**MINDES, GAYLE DEAN,** education educator; b. Kansas City, Mo., Feb. 11, 1942; d. Elton Burnett and Juanita Maxine (Mangold) Taylor; m. Marvin William Mindes, Aug. 15, 1969 (dec.); 1 child, Jonathan Seth; m. Matilde Delich-Funes Mindes Jun. 27, 2002. BS, U. Kans., Lawrence, 1964; MS, U. Wis., Madison, 1965; EdD, Loyola U., Chgo., 1979. Tchr. pub. schs., Newburgh, N.Y., 1965-67; spl. educator Ill. Dept. Mental Health, Chgo., 1967-69; spl. edn. supr. Evanston (Ill.) Dist. 65 Schs., 1969-74; lectr. Loyola U., Chgo., 1974-76, Coll. St. Francis, Joliet, Ill., 1976-79; asst. prof. edn. Oklahoma City U., 1979-80; prof. edn. DePaul U., 1993-99, acting dean, 1998-99, prof. edn., 1999—, dir. EdD program, 2000—02, chair tchr. edn., 2003. Lectr. Northeastern Ill., U. Chgo., 1974, North Park Coll., Chgo., 1978; vis. asst. prof., rsch. assoc. Roosevelt U. Coll. Edn., Chgo, 1983-87, Albert A. Robin campus prof., dir. R&D dir. tchr. edn., dir. early childhood, dir. grad. edn. ctr., 1993; senate chair Roosevelt U., 1986-89, trustee Roosevelt U., 1987-93; search com. multicultural affairs v.p. advancement, DePaul U., co-chair tchg., learning, tech. com, 2000—; strategic planning univ. com, 2004, search com., 2004, sr. v.p. advancement, 2004, faculty coun. budget com., 2004—, univ. tenure and promotion bd., 2005—, pers. com. tech., 2005—, sch. edn. NCA com., 2005-06; co-chair ILAEYC Bldg. Bridges; faculty adv. com. to univ. plan. and info. tech. DePaul U. Sch. Edn., panel on grievances, 1995-99, comprehensive pers. devel. com., 1995-99; tng. sub-com. adv. Ill. Dept. Children & Family Svcs., 1993-95; panel of advisers comprehensive pers. devel. sys. Ill. State Bd. Edn., 1995-99; mentor, cons. to partnerships project tng. early intervention svcs. U. Ill., Champaign; panelist Ill. Initiative for Articulation between Ill. Bd. Higher Edn. and Ill. CC Bd., Early Childhood Assessment Sys.; co-chair, panelist Bansenville Pub. Schs.; cons. in field; project evaluator Chgo. Tchr. Collaborative, Dept. Edn., 1999-2004; chair U. Tchg. Learning Tech. com., 2001—; mem. partnership com. Ill. State Bd. Edn., 2002, content expert panel, 2003; faculty coun. De Paul Budget Com., 2004—; active Sch. Edn. North Ctrl. Commn., 2005—; cons. Heinemann Libraries. Author: Assessing Young Children, 1996, 2d edit., 2003, Teaching Young Children Social Studies, 2006; co-author: (with Marie Donovan) Building Character: Five Enduring Themes for a Stronger Early Childhood Curriculum PK-3, 2000; (with Allan C. Ornstein and Thomas Lesley II) Secondary and Middle School Methods, 2005; editor: DePaul U. Sch. Edn. Newsletter; co-author: Planning a Theme Based Curriculum for 4's or 5's, 1993, Assessing Young Children: 1996, Encyclopedia of Children's Play, 1997, 2d edit., 2006; mem. editl. bd. Ill. Sch. R&D, Ill. Divsn. Early Childhood Edn. Adv. Com. to Ill. Bd. Edn.; cons. editor: NAEYC, 2003; contbr. articles to profl. jours. Bd. dir. North Side Family Day Care, 1981; northside affiliate Mus. Contemporary Art, 1991-96; active Gov's Task Force on Alternative Rts. to Cert., 1999; edn. adv. com. Okla. Dept. Edn., 1979-80; adv. bd. bilingual early childhood program Oakton C.C.; adv. bd. early childood tech. assistance project Chgo. Pub. Schs., Lake View Mental Health, 1986-90; planning com. Lake View Citizens Coun. Day Care Ctr., 1978-79; local planning coun. Ill. Dept. Child and Family Svcs.; childcare block grant tng. sub. com.; chair teen com. Florence G. Heller JCC, membership com.; adv. bd. Harold Washington Coll. Child Devel., regional tech. assistance grant LICA; parents. com. Francis W. Parker Sch.; assessment task force Dept. Human Svcs., City of Chgo., 2001-02; trustee Congregation Kol Ami., 2000-03; vol. gardener Lincoln Park Zoo, 2002—; resale shop vol. Mt. Sinai Hosp., 2004—. U. Kans. scholar, 1960, Cerebral Palsy Assn. scholar, 1965; U. Wis. fellow, 1964-65. Fellow: Am. Orthopsychiat. Assn.; mem.: ASCD, North Ctrl. Assn. (mem. sch. bd. com. 2005—), Found. for Excellence in Tchg. (selection com. Golden Apple 1989—94), Ill. Assn. for Edn. Young Children (co-chair bldg. bridges project), Ill. Coun. for Exceptional Children, Coun. for Exceptional Children, Am. Ednl. Rsch. Assn., Nat. Assn. for Edn. Young Children (tchr. edn. bd. 1990—94, editl. panel 2003—, editl. rev. bd.), Pi Lambda Theta, Phi Delta Kappa, Alpha Sigma Nu. Office: DePaul Univ Sch Of Edn Chicago IL 60614 Office Phone: 773-325-7769. Business E-Mail: gmindes@depaul.edu.

**MINDICH, ERIC,** investment company executive; Sr. exec., ptnr. Goldman Sachs Group Inc.; founder Eton Pk. Capital Mgmt., 2005—. Leadership coun. New Am. Found.; trustee Whitney Mus. Am. Art. Office: Eton Park Captial Mgmt 825 Third Ave New York NY 10022 Office Phone: 212-593-0766, 212-756-5300.

**MINDLIN, PAULA ROSALIE,** retired reading educator; b. N.Y.C., Nov. 27, 1944; d. Simon S. and Sylvia (Naroff) Bernstein; m. Alfred Carl Mindlin, Aug. 14, 1965; 1 child, Spencer Douglas. BA in Edn., Bklyn. Coll., 1965; MS in Edn., Queens Coll., 1970, Specialist Sch. Adminstrn, 1973. Tchr. Dist. 16 Pub. Sch., Bklyn., 1965—68; reading tchr. Dist. 29 Pub. Sch. and Dist. 16, Bklyn., 1968—85; instr. insvc. courses Cmty. Sch. Dist. 29, Queens Village, NY, 1984—93, reading coord. Reading/Comm. Arts Program, 1985—90. dir. reading, 1990—94. Adj. lectr. York Coll., 1989; dir. Chpt. 1 Program (Nat. Recognition 1994, U.S. Sec. of Edn.); curriculum cons., 1997—98. Recipient svc. award N.Y. State Reading Assn. Coun., 1996. Mem. Queensboro Reading Coun. (pres. 1994-96, Educator of Yr. award 1994). Avocations: reading, gardening, travel.

**MINDLIN, STEVEN TODD,** lawyer; b. Phila., Feb. 4, 1958; s. Wilford Gilbert and Florence (Fisher) M. BA, Haverford Coll., 1980; JD, U. Miami, Fla., 1983. Bar: Fla., 1983, U.S. Dist. Ct. (so. dist.) Fla. 1984, D.C. 1984. Assoc. Wood, Lucksinger et al., Miami, 1983-85, Haben, Parker et al, Tallahassee, 1986-87; ptnr. Haben & Culpepper, P.A., Tallahassee, 1987-93; of counsel Ruden, Barnett et al, Tallahassee, 1993-95; ptnr. Rose, Sundstrom & Bentley, Tallahassee, 1995—. Mem. ABA, Nat. Health Lawyers Assn., Healthcare Fin. Mgmt. Assn. (chmn. task force com. Fla. chpt. 1989), Fla. Assn Hosp. Attys. Democrat. Avocations: music, sports. Office: Rose Sundstrom & Bentley LLP 2548 Blairstone Pines Dr Tallahassee FL 32301-5915

**MINEAR, RICHARD HOFFMAN,** history professor; b. Evanston, Ill., Dec. 31, 1938; s. Paul S. and Gladys (Hoffman) M.; m. Edith C.; children: Robert C., Edward L. AB, Yale U., 1960; MA, Harvard U., 1962, PhD, 1968. Asst. prof. history Ohio State U., 1967-70; from assoc. prof. history to prof. history U. Mass., Amherst, 1970—. Author: Japanese Tradition and Western Law, 1970, Victors' Justice, 1971, Dr. Seuss Goes To War, 1999; translator: Requiem for Battleship Yamato, 1985, Hiroshima: Three Witnesses, 1990, Black Eggs, 1994, When We Say Hiroshima, 1999, One Historian's Progress, 2000. Mem. Amherst Town Mtg., 1976-91, Amherst Select Bd., 1981-90. Fulbright fellow, Kyoto, Japan, 1964-66, 70-71, Japan Found. fellow, Tokyo, Sapporo, 1992-93. Office: Dept History U Mass Amherst MA 01003

**MINEHAN, CATHY ELIZABETH,** bank executive; b. Jersey City, Feb. 15, 1947; d. Harry Manford Jones and Rita Jane (Decora) Jones Leary; m. Gerald Paul Minehan, July 18, 1970; children: Melissa Jane, Brian Patrick. BA, U. Rochester, 1968; MBA, NYU, 1977. Various positions to sr. v.p. Fed. Reserve Bank N.Y., N.Y.C., 1968—75, ops. analysis officer, 1975, mgr. mgmt. info. dept., 1976—78, asst. v.p., 1979—82, v.p., 1982—87, sr. v.p., 1987—91; chief operating officer Fed. Reserve Bank Boston, 1991-94, pres., 1994—. Cons. IMF, Washington, 1990-91; bd. dirs. Boston Mcpl. Rsch. Bur., Park St. Corp., The New Eng. Coun.; mem. Gov's Coun. Econ. Growth and Tech. Bd.

---

dirs. Boston Pvt. Industry Council, Boston Mcpl. Rsch. Bur., Jobs for Mass., New Eng. Council, Boston Pub. Libr. Found.; mem. Mass. Women's Forum, Boston, 1991—; bd. advisors Caroll Sch. Mgmt. Boston Coll.; trustee Bentley Coll., 1992—; trustee coun. U. Rochester, 1993—. Mem. Pub. Securities Assn. (ex officio, govt. ops. com. 1986-91), Beta Gamma Sigma. Democrat. Roman Catholic. Avocations: golf, skiing, jogging. Office: Fed Res Bank Boston PO Box 2076 600 Atlantic Ave Ste 100 Boston MA 02210-2204*

**MINEHART, JEAN BESSE,** tax accountant; b. Cleve., Nov. 8, 1937; d. Ralph and Augusta Besse; m. Ralph Conrad Minehart, Aug. 28, 1959; children: Patricia Minehart Miron, Deborah Minehart Rust, Elizabeth Minehart Biedermann, Stephen. BA, Mass. Wellesley Coll., 1959; MEd, U. Va., 1971. Rsch. assoc. Age Ctr. of New Eng., Boston, 1959-61; substitute tchr. Charlottesville Sch. Sys., Va., 1976-81; tax acct. H&R Block, Charlottesville, 1982-94, Huey & Bjorn, Charlottesville, 1997—. Past pres. Ephphatha Village Housing for the Deaf, Charlottesville, 1984-87; bd. dirs. Tues. Evening Concert Series, Charlottesville, 1990-94; sec., bd. dirs. Family Svc., Inc., Charlottesville, 1987-91; bd. dirs. Westminster Organ Concert Series; elder Westminster Presbyn. Ch., 1979-81, 94-96, trustee, 2005—. Scholar, Wellesley Coll. scholar. Mem. LWV (v.p., treas. 1991-95) Blue Ridge Wellesley Club (pres. Charlottesvillechpt. 1989-91, dorm rep. 1996-2004). Avocations: reading, music. Home: 1714 Yorktown Dr Charlottesville VA 22901 Office Phone: 434-971-7642.

**MINEKA, SUSAN,** psychology professor; b. Ithaca, N.Y., June 2, 1948; d. Francis Edward and Muriel Leota (McGregor) M. BA in Psychology magna cum laude, Cornell U., 1970; PhD, U. Pa., 1974. Lic. psychologist Ill. Prof. psychology U. Wis., Madison, 1974-85, U. Tex., Austin, 1986-87; prof. Northwestern U., Evanston, Ill., 1987—. Co-dir. Panic Treatment Ctr., Evanston Hosp., 1988—99; co-dir. Anxiety and Panic Treatment Clinic Northwestern U., 2001—; mem. NIH Panic Consensus Panel, 1991. Editor: Jour. Abnormal Psychology, 1990—94; assoc. editor Emotion, 2003—; contbr. articles to profl. jours. Fellow, Ctr. for Advanced Study in the Behavioral Scis., Stanford, Calif., 1997—98; grantee, NSF and NIMH, 1978—. Fellow APA (bd. sci. affairs 1992-94, chair 1994, pres. divsn. 12, sect. 3 1995), Am. Psychol. Soc. (bd. dirs. 2001-04); mem. Assn. for Advancement Behavior Therapy, Midwestern Psychol. Assn. (pres. 1996-97), Soc. for Rsch. in Psychopathology (mem. exec. bd. 1992-94, 2000-03), Phi Beta Kappa, Sigma Xi. Democrat. Office: Northwestern U Psychology Dept Evanston IL 60208-0001

**MINER, JACQUELINE,** political consultant; b. Dec. 10, 1936; d. Ralph E. and Agnes (McGee) Mariani; m. Roger J. Miner, Aug. 11, 1975; children: Laurence, Ronald Carmichael, Ralph Carmichael, Mark. Ind. polit. cons., Hudson, NY; instr. history and polit. sci. SUNY, Hudson, 1974—79. Mem. nat. steering com. Fund for Am.'s Future, 2d cir. Hist. Com.; mem. White House Outreach Working Group on Central Am.; candidate for Rep. nomination U.S. Senate, 1982; co-chair N.Y. state steering com. George Bush for Pres. campaign, 1986—88; del. Rep. Conv., 1992, GOP Conv., 1992; Rep. county committeewoman, 1958—76; vice chmn. N.Y. State Ronald Reagan campaign, 1980, N.Y. State Rep. Com., 1991—93; co-chmn. N.Y. State Reagan Roundup Campaign, 1984—86; chmn. Coll. Consortium for Internat. Studies. Mem.: PEO, U.S. Supreme Ct. Hist. Soc. Address: 1 Merlins Way Hudson NY 12534-4157

**MINER, JAMES ROSS,** emergency physician, educator; b. Minneola, N.Y., Jan. 11, 1970; MD, Mayo Med. Sch., Rochester, Minn., 1996. Lic. physician MN, 1997. Assoc. prof. of emergency medicine U. of Minn. Med. Sch., Mpls., 1999—. Assoc. editor Acad. Emergency Medicine, 2003—06. Fellow: Am. Coll. of Emergency Physicians. Achievements include research in pain management. Office: Hennepin County Medical Center 701 Park Ave S Minneapolis MN 55415 Office Phone: 612-873-8791. E-mail: jimminer@hotmail.com.

**MINER, JOHN BURNHAM,** industrial relations educator, writer; b. NYC, July 20, 1926; s. John Lynn and Bess (Burnham) M.; children by previous marriage: Barbara, John, Cynthia, Frances; m. Barbara Allen Williams, June 1, 1979; children: Jennifer, Heather. AB, Princeton U., 1950, PhD, 1955; MA, Clark U., 1952. Lic. psychologist, N.Y. Rsch. assoc. Columbia U., 1956-57; mgr. psychol. svcs. Atlantic Refining Co., Phila., 1957-60; mem. faculty U. Oreg., Eugene, 1960-68; prof., chmn. dept. orgnl. sci. U. Md., College Park, 1968-73; rsch. prof. Ga. State U., Atlanta, 1973-87, Disting. prof., 1974; pres. Orgnl. Measurement Systems Press, Eugene, Oreg., 1976—; prof. human resources SUNY, Buffalo, 1987-94, chmn. dept. orgn. and human resources, 1989-92; profl. practice Eugene, Oreg., 1995—. Cons. McKinsey & Co., N.Y.C., 1966-69; vis. lectr. U. Pa., Phila., 1959-60; vis. prof. U. Calif., Berkeley, 1966-67, U. South Fla., Tampa, 1972; researcher on orgnl. motivation, theories of orgn., human resource utilization, bus. policy and strategy, entrepreneurship. Author: Personnel Psychology, 1969, Personnel and Industrial Relations, 1969, 1973, 1977, 1985, The Challenge of Managing, 1975; author: (with Mary Green Miner) Policy Issues Personnel and Industrial Relations, 1977; author: (with George A. Steiner) Management Policy and Strategy, 1977; author: (with M.G. Miner) Employee Selection Within the Law, 1978; author: Theories of Organizational Behavior, 1980, Theories of Organizational Structure and Process, 1982, People Problems: The Executive Answer Book, 1985, The Practice of Management, 1985, Organizational Behavior: Performance and Productivity, 1988, Industrial-Organizational Psychology, 1992, Role Motivation Theories, 1993; with Donald P. Crane Human Resource Management: The Strategic Perspective, 1995; author: The 4 Routes to Entrepreneurial Success, 1996; author: (with Michael H. Capps) How Honesty Testing Works, 1997; author: A Psychological Typology of Successful Entrepreneurs, 1997, Organizational Behavior: Foundations, Theories and Analyses, 2002, Organizational Behavior: Essential Theories of Motivation and Leadership, 2005, Organizational Behavior: Essential Theories of Process and Structure, 2006, Organizational Behavior: Historical Origins, Theoretical Foundations, and the Future, many other books and monographs; contbr. numerous articles, papers to profl. jours. With U.S. Army, 1944—46, ETO. Decorated Bronze Star, Combat Infantryman's badge. Fellow APA, Acad. of Mgmt. (editor Jour. 1973-75, pres. 1977-78), Soc. for Personality Assessment, Am. Psychol. Soc.; mem. Soc. for Human Resource Mgmt., Inst. Operations Rsch. Mgmt. Sci., Am. Sociolog. Assn., Indsl. Rels. Rsch. Assn., Internat. Coun. for Small Bus., Strategic Mgmt. Soc., Internat. Pers. Mgmt. Assn., Human Resource Planning Soc. Republican. Home and Office: 34199 Country View Dr Eugene OR 97408-9440 Office Phone: 541-484-2715.

**MINER, ROGER JEFFREY,** federal judge; b. Apr. 14, 1934; s. Abram and Anne M. Miner; m. Jacqueline Mariani; 4 children. BS, SUNY; LLB cum laude, N.Y. Law Sch., 1956; postgrad., Bklyn. Law Sch., Judge Advocate Gen.'s Sch., U. Va.; LLD (hon.), N.Y. Law Sch., 1989, Syracuse U., 1990, Albany Law Sch./Union U., 1996; attended, Emory U. Bar: N.Y. 1956, U.S. Ct. Mil. Appeals 1956, Republic of Korea 1958, U.S. Dist. Ct. (so. and ea. dists.) N.Y. 1959. Ptnr. Miner & Miner, Hudson, NY, 1959—75; corp. counsel City of Hudson, 1961—64; asst. dist. atty. Columbia County, 1964, dist. atty., 1968—75; justice N.Y. State Supreme Ct., 1976—81; judge U.S. Dist. Ct. (no. dist.) N.Y., 1981—85; sr. judge U.S. Ct. Appeals (2d cir.), Albany, NY, 1997—. Adj. assoc. prof. criminal law State U. Sys., NY, 1974—79; adj. prof. law N.Y. Law Sch., 1986—96, Albany Law Sch. Union U., 1997—2002; faculty assoc. Ariz. State U. Coll. Law, 2004; lectr. state and local bar assns.; lectr. SUNY, Albany, 1985; with N.Y. Law Sch. Bd. Trustees, 1991—96; hon. trustee N.Y. Law Sch. bd. trustees, 1996—; chmn. 2d Cir. Com. on Hist. and Commemorative Events, 1989—94; mem. jud. coun. 2d Cir., 1992—96; with No. Dist. Hist. Com., 1981—85, State, Fed. Jud. Coun. of N.Y., 1986—91, Cameras in the Courtroom com., 1993—96; chmn. Jud. Conf. on U.S. com. on fed.-state jurisdiction, 1987—; skiing, State, Fed. Jud. Coun. of N.Y., 1990—91; trustee Practicing Law Inst., 1995—2002. Mng. editor: N.Y. Law Sch. Law Rev.; contbr. articles to law jours. 1st lt. JAGC U.S. Army, 1956—59, capt. USAR, ret. Named Columbia County Man of Yr., 1984; recipient Dean's medal for disting. profl. svc., N.Y. Law Sch., Disting. Alumnus award, Charles W. Froessel award for Valuable Contbn. to Law,

---

Albany Jewish Fedn. award, Abraham Lincoln award, Cmty. Svc. award, Kiwanis, others, Ellis Island medal of honor. Mem.: ATLA, ABA, Columbia County Magistrates Assn., Am. Soc. Writers on Legal Subjects, Fed. Bar Coun., Fed. Judges Assn., Am. Judicature Soc., Am. Law Inst., Columbia County Bar Assn., Assn. of Bar of City of N.Y., N.Y. State Bar Assn., B'nai Brith, N.Y. Law Sch. Alumni Assn. (hon.; bd. dirs.), Supreme Ct. Hist. Soc., Columbia County Hist. Soc., Elks (past exalted ruler). Jewish. Office: US Ct Appeals 445 Broadway Ste 414 Albany NY 12207-2926*

**MINER, THOMAS HAWLEY,** entrepreneur; b. Shelbyville, Ill., June 19, 1927; s. Lester Ward and Thirza (Hawley) M.; m. Lucyna T. Minciel, July 22, 1983; children: Robert Thomas, William John. Student, U.S. Mil. Acad., 1946—47; BA, Knox Coll., 1950; JD, U. Ill., 1953. Bar: Ill. 1954. Counsel Continental Ill. Nat. Bank & Trust Co., Chgo., 1953—55; pres. Harper-Wyman Internat. S.A., Venezuela and Mex., 1955—58, Hudson Internat. S.A., Can. and Switzerland, 1958—60, Thomas H. Miner & Assoc., Inc., Chgo., 1960—; chmn. Miner, Fraser & Gabriel Pub. Affairs, Inc., Washington, 1982—88, Miner Sys., Inc., 1981—; internat. dir. Urban Retail Properties Inc., 2005—; chmn., CEO Ill. Global Partnership, Inc., 2005—. Bd. dirs. Lakeside Bank, Worldschool, Bright Oceans Internat. Corp.; chmn. Ill. dist. export coun. U.S. Dept. Commerce, 1971—; sec. Consular Corps. Chgo., 1986—88; chmn. Mid-Am. China Mgmt. Tng. Ctr., Global Software Source, Geo Vision, Inc., U.S.-Iraq Bus. Alliance. Chmn. bd. dirs. Sch. Art Inst. Chgo., 1977-81; bd. govs., life mem., sustaining fellow Art Inst. Chgo.; former chmn. UN Assn., Chgo.; founder, chmn. Mid-Am. Com., 1968—; former mem. bd. dirs. UNICEF, NAM, Internat. Trade Policy Com. and Working Group on Commonwealth of Ind. States and Ea. Europe; trustee 4th Presbyn. Ch., Chgo., Roosevelt U., Chgo., 1996; bd. advisors Mercy Hosp.; vice chmn. Chgo. Sister Cities; mem. adv. bd. Internat. Inst. Edn.; bd. dirs. Internat. Sister Cities. With USNR, 1945-46; mem. Pres. Coun. U. Ill. Found.; dir. Internat. Urgan Retail Properties Co.; chmn. Ill. Global Partnership, Inc. Capt. U.S. Army, 1946-47. Decorated comdr. Crown of the Kingdom of Belgium, 2003, commendatore Ordine al Merito della Repubblica Italiana; recipient Alumni Achievement award Knox Coll., 1974, Gold Medallion award Internat. Visitors Ctr. Chgo., 1989; named One of Chgo.'s 10 Outstanding Young Men, 1962, Chicagoan of Year Chgo. Assn. Commerce and Industry, 1968, Alumni of Month Coll. Law U. Ill., Nov. 1970, Aug. 1984; hon. consul Republic of Senegal, 1970-88. Mem. Am. Mgmt. Assn., Chicagoland C. of C., Mid-Am. Arab C. of C. (founder, former pres.), Chgo. Bar Assn., Chgo. Coun., Chgo. Coun. Fgn. Rels. (past dir.), Coun. of the Ams., Internat. Trade Club (past dir., pres.), Japan-Am. Soc., Nat. Coun. U.S.-China Trade, Nat. Acad. Scis. (pres. coun.), English Speaking Union (dir., past chmn.) Trade and Econs. Coun. USA-CIS (dir.), U.S.-Russia Bus. Coun., Mus. Contemporary Art, Newcomen Soc. N.Am., U.S.-China Bus. Coun., U.S.-Arab C of C. (bd. dirs.), U.S.-Mex. C. of C. (bd. dirs.), Thomas Minor Soc., Chgo. Club, Econ. Club, Grant Park Concerts Soc., Chgo. Farmers Club, Mid-Am. Club, Univ. Club (Washington), Univ. Club (Milw.), Hillsboro Club (Fla.), Tryall Golf and Beach Club (Jamaica), Rotary, Phi Delta Phi, Phi Gamma Delta. Office: Ste 2500 150 N Michigan Ave Chicago IL 60601-7553 also: 900 N Michigan Ave STe 1300 Chicago IL 60611 Office Phone: 312-236-8745. Personal E-mail: ltminer@aol.com. Business E-Mail: tminer@mid-americacenter.com.

**MINETA, NORMAN YOSHIO,** former secretary of transportation, management consultant; b. San Jose, Calif., Nov. 12, 1931; s. Kay Kunisaku and Kane (Watanabe) M.; m. Danealia; children: David, K., Stuart S.; stepchildren: Robert M. Brantner, Mark Brantner. BS, U. Calif.-Berkeley, 1953; D of Pub. Svc., Santa Clara U., 1989; HHD (hon.), Rust Coll., 1993. Agt./broker Mineta Ins. Agy., San Jose, 1956-89; mem. adv. bd. Bank of Tokyo, Calif., 1961-75; mem. city coun. City of San Jose, 1967-71, vice mayor, 1969-71, mayor, 1971-75; mem. US Congresses from 13th (now 15th) Calif. dist., 1975-95; subcom. surface transp., 1989-92; former dep. Dem. whip; ranking minority mem. transp. and infrastructure com.; sr. v.p., mng. dir. transp. sys. & srvs. Lockheed Martin, Washington, 1995-2000; sec. US Dept. Commerce, Washington, 2000-2001, US Dept. Transp., Washington, 2001—06; vice chmn. global comm. consultancy Hill & Knowlton Inc., Washington, 2006—. Chmn. fin. com. Santa Clara County (Calif.) Council Chs., 1960-62; commr. San Jose Human Relations Commn., 1962-64, San Jose Housing Authority, 1966-67; bd. dirs. Nat. RR Passenger Corp.(AMTRAK), 2001-; mem. adv. bd. Carolinks 2006- Precinct chmn. Community Theater Bond Issue, 1964; mem. spl. gifts com. Santa Clara County council Boy Scouts Am., 1967; sec. Santa Clara County Grand Jury, 1964; bd. dirs. Wesley Found., San Jose State Coll., 1956-58, Pacific Neighbors, Community Council Cen. Santa Clara County, Japan Soc., San Francisco, Santa Clara County chpt. NCCJ, Mexican-Am. Community Services Agy.; mem. exec. bd. No. Calif.-Western Nev. dist. council Japanese Am. Citizens League, 1960-62, pres. San Jose chpt., 1957-59; bd. regents Smithsonian Instn., 1979-95; chmn. Smithsonian vis. com. for Freer Gallery, 1981-95; mem. bd. regents Santa Clara U.; chmn. Nat. Civil Aviation Rev. Commn., 1997; mem. Smithsonian Nat. Bd., 1996—. Served to lt. AUS, 1954-56. Mem. Greater San Jose C. of C., Nat. Assn. Indsl. Ins. Agts., Calif. Assn. Indsl. Ins. Agts., San Jose Assn. Ind. Ins. Agts. (dir. 1960-62), North San Jose Optimists Club (pres. 1956-58), Jackson-Taylor Bus. and Profl. Assn. (dir. 1963). Democrat. Methodist. Office: Hill & Knowlton Inc Ste 601 600 New Hampshire Ave NW Washington DC 20037 *Personal philosophy: My two greatest responsibilities are accountability and accessibility to everyone I represent, and to anyone who comes to me for help.*

**MINETREE, JAMES LAWRENCE, III,** retired military officer, educator; b. Balt., Feb. 21, 1937; s. James Lawrence and Rhoda (Blossom) M.; m. Martha Milling, Apr. 9, 1983; children: James Lawrence IV, Peter Milling, Jennifer Grace, Margaret Warner; stepchildren: Rachael, Aubrilyn. B, U. Nebr., Omaha. 1971; MA, U. So. Calif., L.A., 1973. Commd. 2d lt. U.S. Army, 1964, advanced through grades to lt. col., 1979; mem. Nat. Intelligence Coun. CIA, Langley, Va., 1979-82; ret. U.S. Army, 1982; with GE Aerospace Sys., Reston, Va., 1982-85; sr. cons. Fed. Emergency Mgmt. Agency, 1985; dir. Crisis Mgmt. Info. Sys. BDM, Tysons Corner, Va., 1985-86; pres. Analytical Scis. Inc., Vienna, Va., 1986-90; founder Nat. Inst. for Urban Search and Rescue, Santa Barbara, Calif., 1982—; adj. prof. U. Md. U. Coll., College Park, 1992—; founder, pres. Wilson Inst. for Humanitarian Assistance, Springfield, Va., 1998—. Trustee Nat. Assn. Search and Rescue, Fairfax, Va., 1984—88; mem. nat. adv. bd. Congl. Fire Svcs. Inst., Washington, 1990—96; designated army strategist. Author. U.S. Govt. rep. European Coun., Athens, Greece, 1990; conceived U.S. Nat. and Internat. Urban Search and Rescue Teams, 1987; disaster mgmt. officer Fed. Emergency Mgmt. Agy., Washington, 1993—2000. With USCG Res., 1954—58. Decorated Legion of Merit (2), Bronze Star (2), Air medal, Meritorious Svc. medal, Army Commendation medal (3), Vietnam Cross of Gallantry, Civic Action medal, others, Dominican Republic and Republic of Vietnam; recipient Presdl. citation Pub. Svc. The White House, Washington, 1995. Mem. VFW, Nat. Def. Exec. Res., Assn. U.S. Army, Am. Legion. Republican. Episcopalian. Home: Grace Hill Farm 5425 Mill Creek Rd Millboro VA 24460 E-mail: peteminetree@mgwnet.com.

**MING, JENNY J.,** retail apparel company executive; married; 3 children. BA in clothing merchandising, San Jose State U. Mdse. mgr. brand activewear Gap Inc., 1986, v.p., divsn. mdse. mgr., sr. v.p. merchandising, Old Navy, 1994—96, exec. v.p. merchandising, Old Navy, 1996—99, pres., Old Navy, 1999—, mem., sr. v.p. com., 1999—. Bd. dirs. Epiphany, Inc., 2001—. Bd. dirs. Big Brothers Big Sisters, San Francisco; mem. Com. of 100. Named one of 50 Most Powerful Women in Am. Bus., Fortune mag., 2003. Office: Gap Inc 1 Harrison St San Francisco CA 94105-1602

**MING, SI-CHUN,** pathologist, educator; b. Shanghai, Nov. 10, 1922; arrived in US, 1949, naturalized, 1964; s. Sian-Fan and Jan-Teh (Kuo) M.; m. Pen-Ming Lee, Aug. 17, 1957; children: Carol, Ruby, Stephanie, Michael, Jeffrey, Eileen. MD, Nat. Central U. Coll. Medicine, China, 1947. Resident in pathology Mass. Gen. Hosp., Boston, 1952-56; assoc. pathologist Beth Israel Hosp., Boston, 1956-67; asst. prof. pathology Harvard U. Med. Sch., 1965-67; assoc. prof. U. Md., 1967-71; prof. Temple U., Phila., 1971-93, prof. emeritus, 1993—, acting chmn. dept. pathology, 1978-80, dep. chmn. dept.

path., 1980-86. U.S. rep. WHO Collaborating Ctr. for Primary Prevention, Diagnosis and Treatment of Gastric Cancer, 1984-98; hon. prof. Tianjin Med. Coll., Shanghai Second Med. U., Fourth Mil. Med. U., China, 1988—. Author: Tumors of the Esophagus and Stomach, 1973, supplement, 1985, Precursors of Gastric Cancer, 1984, Pathology of the Gastrointestinal Tract, 1992, 2d edit., 1998; mem. editl. bd. World Jour. Gastroenterology, 1998-05, Gastric Cancer, 1998-05. Nat. Cancer Inst. sr. fellow Karolinska Inst. Stockholm, 1964-65. Mem. AAAS, U.S. Canadian Acad. Pathology, Am. Soc. Investigative Pathology, Am. Gastroenterol. Assn., N.Y. Acad. Scis. Achievements include development of classification method for stomach carcinoma based on the growth pattern of the cancer; establishment of pathological criteria for the diagnosis of premalignant lesions of the digestive tract. Office: 3401 N Broad St Philadelphia PA 19140-5104 Business E-Mail: ming@temple.edu.

**MING, YAO,** professional basketball player; b. Shanghai, Sept. 12, 1980; s. Yao Zhie Yuan and Fang Feng Di. Studied, Shanghai Physical & Sport Technic Edn. Inst., Shanghai Foreign Lang. Inst. Player Shanghai Sharks, Chinese Basketball Assn., 1997—2002, Houston Rockets, Nat. Basketball Assn., 2002—. Mem. Chinese Olympic Basketball Team, Athens, 2004; ctr. Western Conf. NBA All-Star Game, 2003, 04, 05, 06. Author: Yao: A Life in Two Worlds, 2004; film appearances The Year of the Yao, 2004, guest appearances (voice TV series) The Simpsons, 2005. Named NBA All-Rookie First Team, 2002; named to People Mag. 100 most influential people, 2004; recipient Laureus World Newcomer of Yr. award, 2003. Achievements include 1st player to be #1 overall pick to come from an internat. basketball league; appeared on covers of Sports Illustrated, The Sporting News, ESPN the Mag. SLAM, Inside Stuff and Basketball Digest; featured in Visa, Apple Computer and Gatorade TV commercials. Avocation: computer games. Office: Houston Rockets 1510 Polk St Houston TX 77002-1099*

**MINGE, DAVID,** former congressman, lawyer, law educator; b. Clarkfield, Minn., 1942; m. Karen Aaker; children: Erik, Olaf. BA in History, St. Olaf Coll., 1964; JD, U. Chgo., 1967. Atty. Faegre & Benson, Mpls., 1967-70; prof. Law U. Wyo., 1970-77; atty. Nelson, Oyen, Torvik, Minge & Gilbertson, 1977-93; mem. 103d-106th Congresses from 2nd Minn. Dist., 1993-2001; judge Minn. Ct. Appeals, Minn., 2002—. Cons. Ho. Jud. Com., Subcom. Adminstrv. Law U.S. Congress, 1975; chair Agrl. Law Sect., Minn. State Bar Assn. 1990-92, adv. bd. Western Minn. Legal Svcs., 1978-84; bd. dirs. Legal Advice Clinics, Ltd., Hennepin County, Western Minn. Vol. Atty. Program; lectr. U. Minn., Morris, 2001-02 Coord. Montevideo area CROP Walk for the Hungry; clk. Montevideo Sch. Bd., 1989—92; dir. Montevideo Cmty. Devel. Corp.; steering com. Clean Up the River Environ., 1992. Fellow Kellogg Found. Food and Soc. fellow, 2002; scholar, Woodrow Wilson Ctr. for Internat. Studies, 2002. Mem.: Minn. Bar Assn. Office: 25 Dr Martin Luther King Jr Blvd Saint Paul MN 55155 Office Phone: 651-297-1003.

**MINGHELLA, ANTHONY,** film director, screenwriter; b. Ryde Isle of Wight, Eng., Jan. 6, 1954; Dir. (films) Mr. Wonderful, 1993, Play, 2000; dir., screenwriter (films) Truly, Madly, Deeply, 1991 (BAFTA award for Best Original Screenplay, 1992), The English Patient, 1996 (Acad. award for Best Dir. 1997, Dir.'s Guild Am. award for feature directing 1997), The Talented Mr. Ripley, 1999 (National Board of Review award for Best Dir., 1999) Cold Mountain, 2003 (National Board of Review award for Best Adapted Screenplay, 2003), exec. prodr. (films) Iris, 2001, Heaven, 2002, The Quiet American, 2002, screenwriter (TV series) Grange Hill, 1978, Boon, 1986, Inspector Morse, 1987, The Storyteller, 1987. Office: MacCortendale & Holton 1640 5th St Ste 205 Santa Monica CA 90401-3325

**MINGLE, JAMES JOHN,** lawyer; m. Barbara O'Neil; children: Christina, Jonathan. AB in English, St. Joseph's Coll., Phila., 1968; JD, U. Va., 1973. Bar: Md. 1974, Va. 1990, N.Y. 1996. Asst. to pres. Frostburg State Coll., 1973-77, adj. prof. bus. law, 1975-77; asst. atty. gen. State of Md., 1977-89; chief counsel Md. State Univ. and Coll. Sys., U. Md. Pub. TV, 1981-89; gen. counsel U. Va., Charlottesville, 1989-95, lectr. law, 1994-95; gen. counsel, sec. corp., adj. prof. law Cornell U., Ithaca, NY, 1995—. Adj. prof. law U. Md., 1984-88; asst. to bus. mgr. Phila. 76ers NBA Club, 1968-69; city atty. City of Frostburg, Md., 1974-76; joint adv. bds., Cornell Med. Coll. Qatar, 2001 Mem.: Cornell-Nanyang Inst. Hospitality Mgmt., Nat. Assn. Coll. and U. Attys. Office Phone: 607-255-3903. Business E-Mail: jjm19@cornell.edu.

**MINGLE, JOHN ORVILLE,** engineer, educator, lawyer, consultant; b. Oakley, Kans., May 6, 1931; s. John Russell and Beulah Amelia (Johnson) M.; m. Patricia Ruth Schmitt, Aug. 17, 1957; children: Elizabeth Lorene, Stephen Roy. BS, Kans. State U. Manhattan, 1953, MS, 1958; PhD, Northwestern U., 1960; JD, Washburn U., 1980. Bar: Kans., Wyo., U.S. Patent Office; registered profl. engr., Kans. Tng. engr. Gen. Electric Co., Schenectady, 1953-54; mem. faculty Kans. State U., 1956-90, prof. nuclear engring., 1965-90, prof. emeritus, 1990—, Black & Veatch Disting. prof., 1973-78; dir. Inst. Computational Research Engring., 1969-88; exec. v.p., patent counsel Kans. State U. Research Found., 1983-88. Instr. Northwestern U., 1958-59; vis. prof. U. So. Calif., 1967-68; cons. govt. and industry; engring. legal cons. 1990—. Author: The Invarient Imbedding Theory of Nuclear Transport, 1973; also articles. Bd. dirs. Laramie Regional Airport, 1994-97. Officer AUS, 1954—56, lt. U.S. Army, 1954—56. Mem. ABA (chairperson sci. and tech. phys. scis. com. 1982-92), NSPE (sect. exec. com. 1985-87, chmn. 1985-86), Am. Nuclear Soc. (sect. pres. 1976-77), Am. Inst. Chem. Engrs. (profl. devel. com. 1982-95), Am. Soc. Engring. Edn. (chmn. Midwest sect. 1985-86, exec. com. 1984-87), Profl. Engrs. in Edn. (vice chmn. 1978-80, workshop chairperson 1983), Kans. Engring. Soc. (past chpt. pres.), Kans. Bar Assn., Licensing Execs. Soc., Sigma Xi (past chpt. pres., lectr.), Soc. Univ. Patent Adminstrs. (exec. com. 1985-87, v.p. com. region 1985-87). Home: 1409 Downey St Laramie WY 82072-1867 Office Phone: 307-742-0171. In times past workaholic behavior produced prudent contributions. Now in our world of paradox, the philosophy has been turned on its head, and an iota of "wisdom work" often overshadows everything else.

**MINGO, JOE LOUIS,** elementary school educator; b. Kershaw, S.C., Nov. 14; s. John L. and Ella (Wilson) M. BA in Elem. Edn., U. S.C., 1980, MEd, 1982, postgrad., 1994—. Cert. tchr. elem. edn., early childhood edn. Singer operator Springs Industries, Lancaster, SC, 1972-79; with BJH Realty, Columbia, SC, 1980-81, Carabo Inc., Columbia, 1980-85; tchr. 3d grade Sumter County (S.C.) Sch. Dist. #2, 1982-86, tchr. 4th grade, 1986-94, tchr. math, 1994—; lead tchr. math Shaw Heights Elem. Sch., Shaw AFB, SC, 1993—; asst. principal Sumter Co. Sch. Dist. #2, 2000-01. Author poetry in New Voices in Am. Poetry, 1986, 88. With USAF, 1984—. Desert Storm. Avocation: writing. Office: 345 Eastern School Rd Sumter SC 29153 E-mail: jmingo@scsd2.k12.sc.us, joemingo@aol.com.

**MINGWEI, LEE,** artist; b. Taichung, Taiwan, 1964; MFA, Yale U., Isabella Steward Gardner Mus., Boston, Cleve. Museum Art, Mus. Modern Art, NY, Whitney Biennial, Whitney Mus. Am. Art, 2004. Mailing: c/o Lombard-Freid Fine Arts 531 West 26th St New York NY 10001

**MINICHELLO, DENNIS,** lawyer; b. Cleve., June 9, 1952; s. Ernest Anthony and Mary Theresa (Rocci) M.; m. Janine Stevens, Feb. 14, 1987. BA in Econs., MA in Econs., Ohio U., 1974; JD, Northwestern U., 1978. Bar: U.S. Dist. Ct. Ill., U.S. Ct. Appeals (7th cir.), Supreme Ct. Ill., U.S. Supreme Ct. Assoc. Haskell & Perrin, Chgo., 1978-84; ptnr. Tribler & Marwedel, Chgo., 1984-89, Keck, Mahin & Cate, Chgo., 1989—97; shareholder Marwedel, Minichellot & Reeb, P.C., 1997—. Contbr. articles to profl. jours. Bd. dirs. Great Lakes Naval and Maritime Mus. Fulbright scholar, 1974-75. Mem. ABA, Ill. State Bar Assn., Chgo. Bar Assn. (mem. transp. com.), Maritime Law Assn. (proctor), Ohio U. Alumni Assn. (bd. dirs.), The Propeller Club US (pres. 1983-84), Port Chgo., Transp. Lawyers Assn., Conf. Freight Counsel, Midwest High Speed Rail Coalition (pres. 2000—), Def.

Rsch. Inst., Leading Lawyers Network. Roman Catholic. Avocations: reading, exercise. Office: Marwedel Minichello & Reeb PC 10 S Riverside Plz Ste 720 Chicago IL 60606-3709 Office Phone: 312-902-1600 ext. 5065. Business E-Mail: dminichello@mmr-law.com.

**MINICK, MICHAEL,** publishing executive; b. Albany, NY, Mar. 26, 1945; s. Jason and Ruth Isabelle (Solomon) M. Student, U. Va., 1963-66; BA in History, L.I. U., 1968. Editorial dir. Mag. Mgmt., N.Y.C., 1969-73; mng. editor Gentlemen's Quarterly, N.Y.C., 1975-76; pub., ptnr. Beauty Digest, N.Y.C., 1978-90; pub. Pa. Ofcl. Wine and Liquor Quar., N.Y.C., 1985—, Ohio Liquor Quar., 1990—. Adj. prof. NYU Sch. Journalism. Author: The Kung Fu Exercise Book-Health Secrets of Ancient China, 1974, The Wisdom of Kung Fu, 1974; contbr. numerous articles to popular mags. Mem.: Pa. Wine and Spirit Assn., Sir Harold Actors Soc., 25 Yr. Club of Ind. Distbrs. Democrat. Home: 440 W 22nd St New York NY 10011-2526

**MINICOZZI, ROB,** electronics executive; B in computer sci., NY Inst. Tech.; MBA, Adelphi U. Joined Arrow Electronics, Inc., 1988, now v.p. applications devel. Named one of Premier 100 IT Leaders, Computerworld, 2005. Office: Arrow Electronics Inc 50 Marcus Dr Melville NY 11747*

**MINICUCCI, RICHARD FRANCIS,** lawyer, former hospital administrator; b. NYC, Jan. 16, 1947; s. Daniel Michael and Marie Felice (Trotta) M.; m. Nancy Jean Moran, Aug. 16, 1969; children: Jonathan, Elizabeth, Richard. BA, Rutgers U., 1969; MHA, Duke U., 1971; JD, Memphis State U., 1976. Bar: Tenn. 1977, N.Y. 1978. Adminstrv. asst. Duke Hosp., Durham, NC, 1971; health planner Mid-South Med. Ctr. Coun., Memphis, 1971-73; dir. adminstrn. Memphis & Shelby County Hosp. Authority, 1973-77; assoc. Hayt Hayt & Landau, Great Neck, NY, 1977-81, ptnr., 1981-89, Nixon Peabody LLP (Nixon Hargrave Devans & Doyle, LLP), Garden City, NY, 1989—. Lectr. various health law assns. Editor: New York Environmental Law Handbook, 2d edit.; author: Residency Training Program Accreditation, 1st-5th edits., Mastering the Accreditation Process, 1999; editor-in-chief Accreditation Alert, Trouble in Academia: Ten Years of Litigation in Medical Education, 2003; contbr articles to profl. jours. Co-chmn. fund raising Luth. High Sch., Brookville, N.Y., 1991. Capt. U.S. Army, 1971-79. Mem. Am., Nassau Bar Assn., Am. Health Lawyers Assn. Republican. Roman Catholic. Avocations: tennis, skiing, hockey, travel. Office: Nixon Peabody LLP 990 Stewart Ave Ste 350 Garden City NY 11530-4838

**MINICUCCI, ROBERT A.,** investment company executive; b. Waterbury, Conn., May 7, 1952; s. Arnold A. and Mary (Garafola) M.; children: Robert A. Jr., Alexandra H. BA, Amherst (Mass.) Coll., 1975; MBA, Harvard U., 1979. CPA. Staff acct. Price Waterhouse, Boston, 1975-77; assoc. Lehman Bros., N.Y.C., 1977-82, v.p., 1982-85, sr. v.p., 1985-88, mng. dir., 1988-91; sr. v.p., treas. Am. Express Co., 1991-92; CFO First Data Corp., N.Y.C., 1992-93; gen. ptnr. Welsh, Carson, Anderson & Stowe, N.Y.C., 1993—. Bd. dirs. Amdocs Ltd. Inc., Attachmate Corp., Global Knowledge Network Inc., BancTec, Inc., Alliance Data Systems, Inc., Ruesch Internat., Inc., Electronic Evidence Discovery, Inc Home: 159 Long Neck Point Rd Darien CT 06820 Office: Welsh Carson Anderson Stowe 320 Park Ave Ste 2500 New York NY 10022-6815

**MINIER, JEAN-FRANCOIS RAYMOND,** investment banker; b. Bagneux, France, Nov. 20, 1970; arrived in Japan, 1992; s. Christian and Claudine (Sauvant) M.; m. Satomi Yamashita, Sept. 3, 1993; children: Jiro, Maya, Lili. Engr., Ecole Polytechnique, Palaiseau, France, 1992. Lic. pvt. pilot. Trader Banque Indosuez/W.I. Carr, Tokyo, 1992—93, Bankers Trust Asia, Tokyo, 1993—95; v.p. Morgan Stanley, Tokyo, 1995—97; assoc. dir. Natwest Securities, Tokyo, 1997—98; head equity derivatives trading Dresdner Kleinwort Wasserstein, London, 1998—2001, head capital markets Japan/Asia, Tokyo br. mgr. Tokyo, 2001—. Treas. X-Projects, Palaiseau, 1990-92, X-Entreprises, Palaiseau, 1991-92; chmn. banking and securities com. European Bus. Cmty., Tokyo, 2002—. Lt. French Gendarmerie, 1989-92. Decorated Nat. Def. medal French Def. Ministry, Paris, 1990. Avocations: tennis, golf, skiing, piloting, classical music. Office: Dresdner Kleinwort Wasserstein 1-6-1 Roppongi Minato-ku Tokyo 106-6014 Japan E-mail: jfminier@r0l.itscom.net.

**MINIER, LEE N.,** funeral director; b. Utica, N.Y., Feb. 17, 1950; s. Hugh B. and Ann D. Minier; m. Meredith L. Leigh, July 7, 1974; 1 child, Marissa. AB, Ill. Coll., Jacksonville, 1972; MS, SUNY, Brockport, N.Y., 1974; PhD, U. Colo., Denver, 1979. Lic. funeral dir. N.Y. Postdoctoral fellow Nat. Multiple Sclerosis Soc., Richmond, Va., 1979—81; rsch. assoc. U. Colo. Health Sci. Ctr., Denver, 1981—83; v.p., funeral dir. Christopher-Mitchell Funeral Homes, Inc., Albion, NY, 1990—. Contbr. articles to profl. jours. Pres., bd. dirs. Oak Orchard Comty. Health Ctr., Albioon and Brockport, NY, 1990—92; bd. dirs. Ea. Orleans Red Cross, Albion, 1993; campaign chairperson United Way, Orleans County, NY, 2000, 2002. Mem.: Nat. Ctr. for Sci. Edn. Avocations: weightlifting, canoeing, bicycling. Office: Christopher-Mitchell Funeral Homes Inc 21 West Ave Albion NY 14411

**MINIERE, MICHAEL ANTHONY,** mathematician, educator; b. Plainfield, N.J., Apr. 3, 1945; s. Matthew Salvatore Miniere and Josephine Mineire; m. Lynn Marie Gauker, Aug. 18, 1996; children: Nicole, Samantha, Michael Jr. AA, Hagerstown C.C., Md., 1969; BSc, Montclair State U., NJ, 1985; MSc, Stevens Inst. Tech., 1987, PhD, 1997. Freelance musician, 1969—87; tchg. asst. Stevens Inst. Tech., Hoboken, NJ, 1987—92; prof. Dept. Math. Middlesex County Coll., Edison, NJ, 1992—. Adj. prof. math. Rutgers U., New Brunswick, NJ, 1999—; bus. dir. Coll. Gifted Programs, Parsippany, NJ 1992—. Mem.: Am. Math Soc., The Math. Assn. Am., Phi Kappa Phi. Republican. Roman Catholic. Avocations: fishing, swimming, boating, kayaking. Home: 5 Campbell Rd Kendall Park NJ 08824-1302 Office: Middlesex County College 2600 Woodbridge Ave Edison NJ 08818 Office Phone: 732-548-6000 x3741.

**MINIKES, STEPHAN MICHAEL,** ambassador, lawyer, banker; b. Berlin, Aug. 29, 1938; came to U.S., 1949; naturalized, 1957; married; 1 child. BS, Cornell U., 1961; JD, Yale U., 1964. Bar: N.Y. State 1965, U.S. Ct. Appeals 2nd Circuit, 1967, U.S. Supreme Ct. 1972, U.S. Ct. Mil. Appeals, 1973, DC, 1977. Assoc. firm Milbank, Tweed, Hadley & McCloy, N.Y.C., 1964-68, Borden & Ball, N.Y.C., 1968-72; counsel to spl. cons. for energy Pres. U.S., 1973; counsel to chief Naval Ops., Washington, 1972-74; sr. v.p. Export-Import Bank of U.S., Washington, 1974-77; resident mng. partner firm Butler & Binion, Houston and Washington, 1977-84; Thelen Reid & Priest, N.Y., L.A., San Francisco, and Wash., 1984—2001; amb. Org. Security and Coop. in Europe, Vienna, 2001—. Contbr. articles to profl. jours. Mem. exec. com. Yale U. Law Sch., 1979-82, 86-89, 93-97; trustee, chmn. fin. com. Washington Opera, 1979-84. Mem. ABA, Fed. Bar Assn., D.C. Bar Assn., Assn. of Bar of City of N.Y., Am. Soc. Internat. Law, Am. Coun. Germany (bd. dirs.), Cornell U. Alumni Assn., Yale U. Alumni Assn. (law sch. rep. 1981-83, 86-90). Clubs: Yale (Washington), Metropolitan (Washington). Office Phone: 43-31339-3901.

**MINK, JONATHAN W.,** medical educator, researcher; b. Mpls., Nov. 11, 1958; s. Walter David and Shirley Holt Mink; m. Janet L. Cranshaw, July 7, 1962; children: Laura C., David C. BA, Wesleyan U., Middletown, Conn., 1980, MA, 1981; MD, PhD, Washington U., St. Louis, 1989. Diplomate neurology with spl. qualifications in child neurology Am. Bd. Psychiatry and Neurology, 1997, inc. State of NY, 2001. Asst. prof. Washington U., St. Louis, 1996—2001; assoc. prof. U. Rochester (NY) Sch. Medicine, 2001—. Fellow: Am. Acad. Pediat., Am. Acad. Neurology; mem.: Am. Neurol. Assn. (Derek Denny-Brown Neurol. Scholar award 2002), Soc. for Neuroscience, Movement Disorders Soc., Child Neurology Soc. Office: University of Rochester Box 631 601 Elmwood Ave Rochester NY 14642 Home Phone: 1-585-275-3669. Business E-Mail: jonathan_mink@urmc.rochester.edu.

**MINKEL, CLARENCE WILBERT,** university official; b. Austin, Minn., Feb. 9, 1928; s. Rudolph Herman and Lenora (Buhr) M.; m. Jeanette Edith Borgstrom, Nov. 29, 1947 (div. 1973); children: Thomas, Sandra, Theresa, Lorraine, Joanna; m. F. Phyllis Macari, Apr. 27, 1974. BA, Colo. State Coll., 1953, MA, 1955; PhD, Syracuse U., 1960. Instr. Colo. High Sch., Greeley, Colo., 1953-55; grad. asst. Syracuse (N.Y.) U., 1955-56; asst. prof. SUNY, Buffalo, 1960; from asst. to assoc. prof. Colo. State Coll., 1960-65; assoc. dir. asst. dean then assoc. dean Mich. State U., East Lansing, 1967-79; dean Grad Sch., vice provost, assoc. vice chancellor U. Tenn., Knoxville, 1979—. Advisor USAID, Guatemala, 1963-65; adj. prof. Lanzhou U., China, 1987—; pres. Conf. So. Grad. Schs., 1988-89, Pan Am. Inst. Geography and History, OAS, 1990-93; trustee S.E. Consortium Internat. Devel., Washington, 1989-2005. Co-author: Latin America, 1986; contbr. articles to profl. jours. With U.S. Army, 1945-47, Japan. Mem. Nat. Coun. Geographic Edn., Assn. Am. Geographers, Am. Geographical Soc., Am. Name Soc., Conf. Latin Americanist Geographers, Phi Kappa Phi. Office: U Tenn 316 Burchfiel Bldg Knoxville TN 37996-0925 Office Phone: 865-974-0407. E-mail: cminkel@utk.edu.

**MINKEL, HERBERT PHILIP, JR.,** lawyer; b. Boston, Feb. 11, 1947; s. Herbert Philip and Helen (Sullivan) M. BA, Holy Cross Coll., 1969; JD, NYU, 1972. Bar: Mass. 1973, US Dist. Ct. Mass., 1973, NY 1976, US Dist. Ct. (so. dist.) NY 1978. Law clk. U.S. Dist. Ct. Mass., Boston, 1972-73; assoc. Milbank, Tweed, Hadley & McCloy, N.Y.C., 1973-79; ptnr. Fried, Frank, Harris, Shriver & Jacobson, N.Y.C., 1979-94; mem. adv. com. on bankruptcy rules Jud. Conf. U.S., 1987-93; sr. ptnr. Minkel and Assoc., N.Y.C. and Boston, 1994—. Adj. assoc. prof. NYU Law Sch., 1987-94. Contbg. author: American Bankers Assn. Bankruptcy Manual, 1979; contbg. editor: 5 Collier on Bankruptcy, 15th edit., 1979-96; contbr. articles to profl. jours. Bd. advisors Internat. Yacht Restoration Sch., Newport, R.I., Spl. Olympics, Spl. Smiles. Root-Tilden scholar NYU, 1969-72. Mem. ABA, Nat. Bankruptcy Conf., Assn. Bar City of N.Y. Home: 68 Bumps River Rd Osterville MA 02655-1525 Office: Minkel and Assocs 131 E 62d St New York NY 10021 also: 112 Revere St Boston MA 02114 Office Phone: 212-319-2797. Personal E-mail: hminkel@nyc.rr.com.

**MINKER, JACK,** computer scientist, educator; b. Bkyln., July 4, 1927; s. Harry and Rose (Lapuck) M.; m. Rita Goldberg, June 24, 1951 (dec. Oct. 11, 1988); children: Michael Saul, Sally Anne; m. Johanna Cartee Weinstein, Jan. 19, 1997. BA cum laude with honors in Math., Bkyln. Coll., 1949; MS in Math., U. Wis., 1950; PhD in Math., U. Pa., 1959. Grad. teaching asst. U. Wis., 1949-50; tchr. math. Erasmus Hall High Sch., Bkyln., 1950-51; engr. Bell Aircraft Corp., Buffalo, 1951-52; mgr. info. tech. sect. RCA, Bethesda, Md., 1952-63; dir. tech. staff Auerbach Corp., Washington, 1963-67, tech. cons., 1967-72; mem. Faculty NIH Grad. Sch., 1965-66; vis. mem. faculty U. Md., 1967-68, assoc. prof. computer sci., 1968-71, prof., 1971-98, prof. emeritus, 1998—, 1st chmn. dept. computer sci., 1974-79; cons., speaker, lectr. in field; cons. NSF, 1979-82, chmn. adv. bd. on computer sci., 1980-82. Prof. Inst. Advanced Computer Studies, 1986—; vice-chmn. Com. Concerned Scientists, 1973—; past mem. U.S. Acad. for Rech. Info. Documentalists. Author: (with H. Gallaire and J.M. Nicolas) Logic and Data Bases a Deductive Approach, 1984; editor: (with H. Gallaire and J.M. Nicolas) Advances in Data Base Theory, vol. 1, 1980, vol. 2, 1984, (with H. Gallaire) Logic and Data Bases, 1978, Foundations of Deductive Databases and Logic Programming, 1988, (with J. Lobo and A. Rajasekar) Foundations of Disjunctive Logic Programming, 1992; editor: Logic-Based Artificial Intelligence, 2000; founding editor-in-chief Theory and Practice of Logic Programming, 2000-2001; contbr. articles to profl. jours.; publs. reviewer; mem. editl. bd. numerous jours. Vice chmn. Com. Concerned Scientists, 1972—. With U.S. Army, 1945-46. Recipient U. Md. Presdl. medal, 1996, Allen Newell award ACM/AAAS, 2005; named Disting. Scholar-Tchr. U. Md., 1997-98, fellow Acad. Excellence in Tchg. and Learning, 2002—. Fellow: IEEE (editl. bd. Expert Info.Sys. jour.), ACM, AAAS, Am. Assn. Artificial Intelligence; mem.: Assn. Computing Machinery (chmn. nat. program com. 1968—69, vice chmn. com. on sci. freedom and human rights 1979—89, founding, Outstanding Contbn. award 1985). Jewish. Office: U Md Dept Computer Sci Dept and Inst Advanced Computer College Park MD 20742-0001 Business E-Mail: minker@cs.umd.edu.

**MINKOFF, ALICE SYDNEY,** interior designer stylist; b. Washington, Jan. 29, 1948; d. Lawrence and Ellen (Altman) Glassman; children: Adam Pollin, Shane Pollin, Jacob Minkoff, Sam Minkoff. Student, U. Md. Owner Fredrick, Miley & Assocs., Inc., 1983—2003, Showroom at Washington Design Ctr., 1983—2003. Interior designer for homebuilders, 1975-82; interior designer high end residential homes and hotel interiors, 1980—. Vol. Food and Friends, Washington, 1991—; chair Heartstrings, Washington, 1990; active AIDS Awareness. Mem. NOW, ACLU, Nat. Trust Hist. Preservation, Nature Conservancy, Human Rights Campaign, Dem. Nat. Com., HillPac. Avocations: gourmet cooking, travel, antiques. Home and Office: 3018 New Mexico Ave NW Washington DC 20016-3519 E-mail: moonalice@aol.com.

**MINKOFF, HILDA BRESSLER,** secondary and adult education educator; b. Havana, Cuba, Oct. 10, 1933; d. Isaac and Augustina (Draiman) Bressler; m. Paul Norman Minkoff, Nov. 24, 1957; children: David Jay, Debra Carol. BS Indsl. Labor Rels., Cornell U., 1955; MEd Counseling and Guidance, Temple U., 1969, EdD Vocat./Edn. Adminstrn., 1983. Counselor various schs., Phila., 1967—74, King H.S., Phila., 1975—83, Washington H.S., Phila., 1984—85; supr. student support svcs. Sch. Dist. Phila., 1984—91; counselor Ctrl. H.S., Phila., 1994—97; ret., 1997. Adj. prof. Arcadia U., Glenside, Pa., 1990—2003; pres. Pa. Sch. Counselor Assn., 1979—80, Counseling Assn. Greater Phila., 1990—91. Pres. Hanna Senesch Hadassah, 2003—05, hon. pres., 2005—; chmn. com. Hadassah of Greater Phila., 2005—06; pres. Am. Sch. Counselor Assn., 1983—84; mem. exec. bd women's divsn. State of Israel Bonds, 1997; assoc. chair Ann. Fashion Show, 2002—. Mem.: Retired Educators and Profls. Personal E-mail: hminkoff@verizon.net.

**MINKOFF, JACK,** retired economics professor; b. NYC, Jan. 29, 1925; s. Isidore and Yetta (Fine) M.; m. Anne B. Johnson, June 19, 1948; children—Ellen, Paul. AB, Cornell U., 1948; A.M., Columbia U., 1950, PhD (Ford Found. fellow), 1960. Instr. econs. Western Res. U., 1952-53; instr. econs. Sarah Lawrence Coll., 1959-60; prof. econs., chmn. dept. social sci. Pratt Inst., Bkyln., 1960—, acting dean Sch. Liberal Arts and Scis., 1985-86, dean, 1986-93, acting provost, 1993-95, prof. emeritus, 1996—2002, ret., 2002. Served with USAAF, 1943-45. Social Sci. Rsch. Coun. fellow, 1950-51. Mem. Phi Beta Kappa. Home: 57 Ruxton Rd Great Neck NY 11023-1528

**MINKOFF, JOHN,** mathematician, educator; b. Bklyn. s. Alvin Minkoff and Mollie Schwartz; m. Susan Alder, Nov. 19, 1966; 1 child, John. BSEE, Columbia U., 1962, MSEE, 1963, PhD, 1967. Rsch. engr. Columbia U., NYC, 1964-67, rsch. associate, 1967-73; mgr. analysis activities Riverside Rsch. Inst., NYC, 1973-77; mem. tech. staff Bell Tel. Labs., Whippany, NJ, 1977-86; disting mem. tech. staff ATT/Lucent Techs. Bell Labs., Whippany, 1986—2001; staff scientist space sys. divsn. ITT, 2001—. Adj. prof. elec. engring. Polytech. U. NY, 1989-90; adj. prof. applied math. NYU, NYC, 1990-95. Author: Signals Noise and Active Sensors, 1992, Signal Processing Fundamentals and Applications for Communications and Sensing Systems, 2002; contbr. articles to profl. jours. Music dir. Hawthorne (NJ) Symphony Orch. NSF grantee, 1991. Mem. Am. Phys. Soc. Jewish. Avocation: music. Home: 578 Jones Rd Englewood NJ 07631 Office: ITT Space Sys Divsn 100 Kingsland Rd Clifton NJ 07014 Office Phone: 973-284-2011. Office Fax: 973-284-2849. Business E-Mail: john.minkoff@itt.com.

**MINKOVA, DONKA,** language educator; b. Sofia, Bulgaria; d. Lubomir Zhekov and Kalina Zavoeva-Zhekova; m. Robert P. Stockwell; children: Dimo Diakov, Lubomir Diakov. PhD, U. Sofia; lectr. in English lang. U. Sofia, 1969—83; prof. English lang. UCLA. Author: History of Final Vowels in English, 1991; author: (with Robert Stockwell) English Words: History and Structure, 2001; author: Alliteration and Sound Change in Early English, 2003; co-editor: Studies in the History of the English Language: A

Millennial Perspective, 2002, Chaucer and the Challenges of Medievalism, 2003. Fellow Pres.'s Rsch. fellow in the humanities, U. Calif., 1994—95, John Simon Guggenheim Found., 2000—01; hon. fellow, Inst. Advanced Studies in Humanities, U. Edinburgh, Scotland, 1980—81. Office: English Dept UCLA 149 Humanities Bldg Los Angeles CA 90095 Office Phone: 310-825-4978. E-mail: minkova@humnet.ucla.edu.

MINKOWITZ, MARTIN, lawyer; former state government official; b. Bklyn., 1939; s. Jacob and Marion Minkowitz; m. Carol L. Ziegler; 1 son from previous marriage, Stuart Allan. AA, Bklyn. Coll., 1959, BA, 1961; JD, Bklyn. Law Sch., 1963, LLM, 1965. Bar: N.Y. 1963, U.S. Supreme Ct. 1967, U.S. Tax Ct. 1974, all four U.S. Dist. Cts. N.Y. Ptnr. Minkowitz, Hagen & Rosenbluth, N.Y.C., 1964—76; gen. counsel State of N.Y. Workers' Compensation Bd., 1976—81; dep. supt. and gen. counsel State of N.Y. Ins. Dept, 1981—88; instr. CUNY, 1975; ptnr. Stroock & Stroock & Lavan, NY, 1988—. Adv. bd. Coll. Ins., 1987-90; adj. prof. law N.Y. Law Sch., N.Y.C., 1982—; lectr. ABA, N.Y. C. of C., Practicing Law Inst., N.Y. State Bar Assn. Nat. Assn. Ins. Commrs., Nat. Conf. Ins. Legis.; hearing officer N.Y.C. Transp. Dept., 1970-75; cons. City Coun. N.Y.C. 1969. Author: West's New York Workers' Compensation, 2003-; (with others) Rent Stabilization and Control, 1973, Handling the Basic Workers' Compensation Law Case, 1996, West's New York General Practice, 2003; co-author: Workers Compensation, Insurance and Law Practice-The Next Generation, 1989; commentaries to McKinney's Consol. Laws, 1982—; mem. editl. bd. Jour. Occupl. Rehab. U. Rochester, 1991—; contbr. articles to profl. jours. Bd. dir., sec. Kingsbay YM-YWHA, Bklyn., 1978-99, elected dir. emeritus, 1999—; pres. bd. dir. Shore Terrace Co-op., Bklyn., 1982-83; co-chmn. exec. bd., met. coun., nat. v.p. Am. Jewish Congress, N.Y.C., 1983-91; bd. dir. Met. Coord. Coun. on Jewish poverty, 1993—, Nat. Conf. Cmty. and Justice (bd. dir. N.Y. divsn. 1994-2001, nat. bd. trustees 1995-2001, chair N.Y. divsn. 1998-2001); bd. Am. Soc. Workers Compensation, 2003—. Recipient cert. meritorious svc. Bklyn. Law Sch., Outstanding Pub. Svc. award Ind. Ins. Agt. Assn., citation outstanding performance State of N.Y. Workers' Compensation Bd., Disting. Leadership award N.Y. Claims Assn., City of Peace award State of Israel Bonds, Brotherhood award NCCJ, 2003, Man of Yr. awards Congregation B'Nai Avraham, Bklyn., 2003, Kingsbay YM-YWHA, 2005. Fellow N.Y. State Bar Found. (mem. fed. bar coun., com. on 2d cir.); mem. N.Y. County Lawyers Assn. (chmn. unlawful practice of law com. 1982-86, mem. profl. ethics com. 1985-91, chair worker's compensation com. 1988-91, bd. dir. 1997-2002, 2006-, chair profl. ethics com. 2001-2006, bd. dir., exec. bd. 2003-05), N.Y. State Bar Assn. (mem. ho. of dels. 1999-2003, 2004—, chmn. unlawful practice of law com. 1981-83, mem. com. on profl. ethics 1981-84, chmn. com. profl. discipline, mem. com. on jud. nominations, editor One on One publ. 2001—, Sustaining Mem. of Yr. award 1995), Soc. Ins. Receivers, Bklyn. Law Sch. Alumni Assn. (pres. 1984-92, pres. elect 1993-94, pres. 1995-96). Office: Stroock Stroock & Lavan 180 Maiden Ln Fl 17 New York NY 10038-4937 Office Phone: 212-806-6256. Business E-Mail: mminkowitz@stroock.com.

MINKOWYCZ, W. J., mechanical engineering educator; b. Libokhora, Ukraine, Oct. 21, 1937; came to U.S., 1949; s. Alexander and Anna (Tokan) M.; m. Diana Eva Szandra, May 12, 1973; 1 child, Liliana Christine Anne BS in Mech. Engring., U. Minn., 1958, MS in Mech. Engring., 1961, PhD in Mech. Engring., 1965. From asst. prof. to James P. Hartnett prof. U. Ill., Chgo., 1966—2006, James P. Hartnett prof., 2006—. Cons. Argonne Nat. Lab, Ill., 1970-82, U. Hawaii, Honolulu, 1974-94. Founding editor-in-chief (jour.) Jour. Numerical Heat Transfer, 1978—; editor-in-chief: Internat. Jour. Heat and Mass Transfer, 1968-, Rheologically Complex Fluids, 1972, Internat. Comms. in Heat and Mass Transfer Jour., 1974-, Handbook of Numerical Heat Transfer, 1988; editor: (book series) Computational and Physical Processes in Mechanics and Thermal Sciences, 1979—, Advances in Numerical Heat Transfer, 1996—, Vol. 1, 1997—, Vol. 2, 2000—; contbr. articles to profl. jours. Recipient Silver Circle for Excellence in Teaching, U. Ill.-Chgo., 1975, 76, 81, 86, 90, 94, Harold A. Simon award Excellence in Teaching, 1986, Ralph Coats Roe Outstanding Tchr. award Am. Soc. Engring. Edn., 1988, U. Ill. Disting. Tchr. award, 1989. Fellow ASME (Heat Transfer Meml. award 1993); mem. Sigma Xi, Pi Tau Sigma. Republican. Ukrainian Catholic. Office: U Ill Dept Mech Engring Mail Code 251 842 W Taylor St Chicago IL 60607-7021 Office Phone: 312-996-3467. Business E-Mail: wjm@uic.edu.

MINNA, MARIA, member of Canadian Parliament; b. Pofi, Frosinone, Italy, Mar. 14, 1948; arrived in Can., 1957. Grad. in Sociology with honors, U. Toronto. Policy advisor to former Ont. Premier David Peterson; pres. COSTI-IIAS Immigrant Svcs.; v.p. pub. affairs cons. co., Toronto; M.P. from Beaches-Woodbine dist. Ho. of Commons, Toronto, 1993-97, MP from Beaches-East York dist. Ottawa, Ont., Can., 1997—; parliamentary sec. Min. Citizenship and Immigration, 1996—98; chmn. to social policy com. Nat. Liberal Caucus, 1998—99, min. for internat. cooperation, 1999—2002. Life-long liberal, mem. Nat. Platform Com., 1988; apptd. vice chair standing com. Human Resources Devel., 1994. Contbr. reports on cmty. devel. and provision of svcs. to immigrants and minority groups. Former mem. campaign cabinet United Way Gtr. Toronto; former dir. Nat. Coun. Welfare Recipient Premio Italia nel Mondo award, 2001, President's Award, Indo-Canada Chamber of Commerce, 2001, Outstanding Leadership Award, RESULTS Canada, 2002. Mem. Nat. Congress Italian-Canadians (former exec. dir. Toronto dist., former pres.). Liberal. Office: House of Commons 406 West Block Ottawa ON Canada K1A 0A6 also: 1912 Danforth Ave M4C1J4 Toronto ON Canada E-mail: Minna.M@parl.gc.ca.

MINNELLI, LIZA, singer, actress; b. Los Angeles, Mar. 12, 1946; d. Vincente and Judy (Garland) M.; m. Peter Allen, Mar. 3, 1967 (div. June 24, 1972); m. Jack Haley Jr., Sept. 15, 1974 (div. 1979); m. Mark Gero, Dec. 4, 1979 (div. 1992); m. David Gest, Mar. 16, 2002 (div. 2003). Appeared in Off-Broadway revival of Best Foot Forward, 1963; appeared with mother at London Palladium, 1964; nightclub debut at Shoreham Hotel, Washington, 1965; appeared in Flora, the Red Menace, 1965 (Tony award), The Act, 1977 (Tony award), The Rink, 1984, Victor Victoria; films include Charlie Bubbles, 1967, The Sterile Cuckoo, 1969, Tell Me That You Love Me, Junie Moon, 1970, Cabaret, 1972 (Oscar award), That's Entertainment, 1974, Lucky Lady, 1975, A Matter of Time, 1976, Silent Movie, 1976, New York, New York, 1977, Arthur, 1981, Rent A Cop, Arthur on the Rocks, 1988, Stepping Out, 1991, The OH in Ohio, 2006; recorded You Are For Loving, 1963, Tropical Nights, 1977, Liza Minnelli at Carnegie Hall, 1987, Results, 1989, Maybe This Time, 1996, Gently, 1996, Minnelli on Minnelli, 2000, (with Herbie Hancock, Johnny Mathis, Donna Summer), Liza's Back!, 2003; (TV films) Parallel Lives, 1994, The West Side Waltz, 1995, Jackie's Back!, 1999; appeared on TV in own spl. Liza With a Z, 1972 (Recipient Emmy award); other TV appearances include Goldie and Liza Together, 1980, Baryshnikov on Broadway, 1980, The Princess and the Pea, Showtime, 1983, A Time to Live, 1985, Sam Found Out, 1988, Liza Minnelli Live from Radio City Music Hall, PBS (Emmy nomination, Music Program Performance, 1993), The Wonderful World of Oz: 50 Years of Magic, 1990, A Century of Cinema, 1994, My Favorite Broadway: The Leading Ladies, 1999, (TV series) Arrested Development, 2003-05; internat. tour with Frank Sinatra, Sammy Davis Jr., 1988. Awarded the Brit. equivalent of the Oscar for Best Actress, 1972, Italy's David di Donatello award (twice), the Valentino award. Address: Capitol Records Inc 1750 Vine St Hollywood CA 90028-5209 also: Angel EMI Guardian Records 304 Park Ave S New York NY 10010-5339*

MINNEMAN, KENNETH PAUL, pharmacology educator; b. Sacramento, Calif., Sept. 1, 1952; s. John Jesse and Esther Annette Minneman; children: Jennifer, Rebecca, Jeffrey. BS, MIT, 1974; PhD, U. Cambridge, England, 1977. Asst. prof. pharm. Emory U., Atlanta, 1980-85, assoc. prof. pharm., 1985-90, prof. pharm, 1990-2000, Charles Howard Candler prof. pharm., 2000—. Editor: Brody's Human Pharmacology: Molecular to Clinical, 2005 Undergraduate Fellowship, Nat. Sci. Found., 1970-74; biomed. rsch. grantee NIH, 1981-2005; postdoctoral fellow U. Colo. Med. Ctr., Denver, 1977-80; John Jacob Abel award, 1986, Award for Excellence in Basic Pharmacology, PhRMA Found., 2000. Mem. AAAS, Am. Soc. Pharm. & Exptl. Therapeutics

(exec. coun. 1999-02, pres.-elect 2006-07), Soc. Neurosci., Internat. Soc. Neurochem. Home: 206 Eleventh St Atlanta GA 30309 Office: Emory U 1510 Clifton Rd Atlanta GA 30322 Fax: 404-727-0365. Office Phone: 404-727-5985. Business E-Mail: kminneman@pharm.emory.edu.

MINNER, RUTH ANN, governor; b. Melford, Del., Jan. 17, 1935; m. Frank Ingram (dec. 1967); 3 children; m. Roger Minner (dec. 1991). Student, Del. Tech. and Community Coll. Office receptionist to Gov. State of Del., Dover, 1972—74; mem. Del. Ho. of Reps., Dover, 1974—82, Del. State Senate, Dover, 1982—92; lt. gov. State of Del., Dover, 1993—2001, gov., 2001—. Mem.: Dem. Nat. Com. Democrat. Office: Office Gov William Penn St Tatnall Bldg 3d Fl Dover DE 19901 Office Phone: 302-744-4101. Office Fax: 302-739-2775.*

MINNERLY, ROBERT WARD, retired headmaster; b. Yonkers, N.Y., Mar. 21, 1935; s. Richard Warren and Margaret Marion (DeBrocky) M.; m. Sandra Overmire, June 12, 1957; children: Scott Ward, John Robert, Sydney Sue. AB, Brown U., 1957; MAT, U. Tex., Arlington, 1980. Tchr., coach Rumsey Hall Sch., Washington, Conn., 1962—64, Berkshire Sch., Sheffield, Mass., 1964—70, asst. head, 1969—70, headmaster, 1970—76; dir. Salisbury Summer Sch. Reading and English, Conn., 1970; prin. upper sch. Ft. Worth Country Day Sch., 1976—86; headmaster Charles Wright Acad., Tacoma, 1986—96; ednl. cons. The Edn. Group, 1996—2000; interim dir. Harold E. LeMay Mus., 2001—02; exec. dir. R. Merle Palmer Minority Students Scholarship Fund., 2004—. Cons. Tarrant County Coalition on Substance Abuse, 1982-84; mayor's task force Tacoma Edn. Summit, 1991-92; bd. dirs. World Cultural Interaction, Gig Harbor, Wash. Contbr. articles to profl. jours. Bd. dirs. Tacoma/Pierce County Good Will Games Art Coun., 1989, Multicare Found., Tacoma, 2002, Tacoma Baseball Found., 2003—; mem. exec. com. Am. Leadership Forum, 1991-95; bd. dirs. Broadway Ctr. for Performing Arts, Tacoma, 1988-94, 96-98, mem. exec. com., 1990-93; elected Wash. State Bd. Edn., 1996-2001; bd. dirs. Tacoma Youth Choir, 2000-03. Named Adminstr. of Yr. Wash. Journalism Edn. Assn., 1991; recipient Columbia award, Wash. Fedn. Ind. Schs., 2000. Mem. Pacific N.W. Assn. Ind. Schs. (chmn. long-range planning com. 1989-92, exec. com. 1990-92, 91, v.p. 1994). Presbyterian. Home: 4214 39th Avenue Ct NW Gig Harbor WA 98335-8029 Office Phone: 253-752-9008. Personal E-mail: rwmin@centurytel.net. E-mail: bob@palmerscholars.org.

MINNERS, HOWARD ALYN, federal agency administrator, researcher, preventive medicine physician; b. Rockville Center, N.Y., Sept. 1, 1931; s. Howard A. and Marie Henriette (Soberski) M.; m. Gretchen Paffenbarger, Oct. 25, 1958; children: Todd, Bradford. AB, Princeton U., 1953; MD, Yale U., 1957; MPH, Harvard U., 1960. Diplomate Am. Bd. Preventive Medicine, Nat. Bd. Med. Examiners. 2d. lt. USAF, 1956; intern Wilford Hall USAF Hosp., San Antonio, 1957-58; resident Sch. of Aerospace Medicine, USAF, Brooks AFB, Tex., 1960-62; advanced through grades to maj. USAF, 1966; advanced through grades to rear adm. USPHS, ret., 1987; dir. office rsch. promotion and devel. WHO, Geneva, Switzerland, 1977-80; dir. Office of Sci. Advisor Agy. Internat. Devel., Washington, 1981-91; dep. dir. Office Internat. Health USPHS and Asst. Surgeon Gen., 1980-81. Assoc. dir. NIH NIAID, 1966-77; astronaut flight surgeon NASA, Houston, 1962-66. Pres. Model A Ford Found., 1994-2000. Fellow World Acad. Art and Sci., Am. Coll. Preventive Medicine; mem. AAAS, Internat. Found. Sci. Stockholm (pres., chmn. bd. trustees 1991-97), Yale Med. Alumni Fund (chmn. bd. trustees 2003-06). Avocations: Model A Ford restoration, history.

MINNICH, DIANE KAY, legal association administrator; b. Iowa City, Feb. 17, 1956; d. Ralph Maynard Minnich and Kathryn Jane (Obye) Tompkins. BA in Behavioral Sci., San Jose State U., 1978. Tutorial program coord./instr. Operation SHARE/La Valley Coll., Van Nuys, Calif., 1979-81; field exec. Silver Sage Girl Scout Coun., Boise, Idaho, 1981-85; continuing legal edn. dir. Idaho State Bar/Idaho Law Found. Inc., Boise, 1985-88, dep. dir., 1988-90, exec. dir., 1990—. Sec.-treas. Western States Bar Conf., 2001-2005; bd. dirs. Atty. Liability Protection Soc.--A Fmily of Profl. Svc. Cos.; mem. adv. bd. legal asst. program Boise State U. Mem. Assn. CLE Adminstrs., Chgo., 1985-90; bd. dirs. Silver Sage coun. Girl Scouts, Boise, 1990-93, 99-2001, mem. nominating com., 1990-94, 97-2001, chair nominating com. 1991-92; mem. legal asst. program adv. bd. Boise State U.; bd. dirs. Boise Schs. Found., 2004—. Named one of Outstanding Young Women in Am., 1991. Mem. ABA (standing com. on pub. edn. adv. com. 2004—), Nat. Orgn. Bar Execs. (membership com. 1992-97, chair 1996-97), Zonta Club Boise (pres. 1991-92, bd. dirs. 1989-93), Rotary Club Boise (chair mem. com. 1994-97, bd. dirs. 1994-97, 99—, pres. 2003-04). Avocations: jogging, golf. Office: Idaho State Bar Idaho Law Found PO Box 895 525 W Jefferson St Boise ID 83702-5931 Home: 1118 Harrison Blvd Boise ID 83702-3448 Office Phone: 208-334-4500. E-mail: dminnich@isb.idaho.gov.

MINNICH, THOMAS GAYLE, director; s. Virgil and Mamie F Minnich; m. Penny L. Hamilton; children: Gayle R. Zeller, Anne M. Frampton, Susan M. Haines, Jennifer L., John T., Michael J. BSEE, U. Okla., Norman, 1970; MSEE, Air Force Inst. Tech., Wright-Patterson AFB, Ohio, 1972. Comm. engr. SAIC, Papillion, Nebr., 1989—93; chair elec. engring. dept. CTC W.Va. U. Tech., Montgomery, 1993—. Comm. engr. Ultra Sys., Colorado Springs, 1987—89, Tracor, Inc., 1986—87; assoc. prof. elec. engring. Western Ky. U., Bowling Green, 1984—86. Zoning enforcement officer City of Montgomery, W.Va., 2001—06. Maj. USAF, 1962—84. Mem.: IEEE (assoc.), Am. Soc. Elec. Engrs. (assoc.). Achievements include development of numerous works for government in the area of satellite communication systems needs identification, implementation planning, and system anaysis. Office: CTC at WVU Tech 405 Fayette Pike Montgomery WV 25136 Office Phone: 304-442-3351. E-mail: thomas.minnich@mail.wvu.edu.

MINNICK, BRUCE ALEXANDER, lawyer; b. New London, Conn., Apr. 16, 1943; s. Robert Wood Minnick and Nedra Louise (Alexander) Wiesman; m. Judith Anita Saxon, Sept. 23, 1967 (div. 1981); children: Audra Anne, Lisa Michelle; m. Charlotte Ann Springfield, Apr. 10, 1983 (div. 1991); 1 child, Matthew Alexander; m. Debra C. Williams, July 3, 1997; 1 stepchild, Brandy Michelle Williams. AA, Broward Community Coll., 1970; BS with honors, Fla. State U., 1971, JD, 1977. Bar: Fla. 1978, U.S. Dist. Ct. (no. dist.) Fla. 1979, U.S. Dist. Ct. (mid. and so. dists.) Fla. 1982, U.S. Supreme Ct. 1981, U.S. Ct. Appeals (11th cir.) 1982, U.S. Tax Ct. 1983, U.S. Ct. Claims 1983, U.S. Dist. Ct. (ea. dist.) Mich. 1990; cert. Expert in Labor and Employment Law, The Fla. Bar, 2003. Asst. v.p., asst. comptroller Pan Am. Bank Miami, 1971—74; staff dir., counsel rules com. Fla. Ho. Reps., Tallahassee, 1976-78; v.p., gen. counsel Fla. Credit Union League, Tallahassee, 1978-80; asst. atty. gen. dept. legal affairs State of Fla., Tallahassee, 1981-86, chief advocate, 1985—86; ptnr. Mang, Rett & Collette, P.A., Tallahassee, 1986-93, Mang, Rett & Minnick PA, Tallahassee, 1994-95; pvt. practice Bruce A. Minnick PA, Tallahassee, 1996—; resident ptnr. Kahn & Assocs., LLC, Cleve., 2005—. Chief advisor Fla. Commn. on Ethics, 1985—86; lectr. state agys., 1982—, Fla. Bar. 1986—; pres. Civil Rights Dispute Resolution Ctr. Mem. Leon County Dist. Adv. Com., 1980—82, 1992—94; mem. exec. com. Leon County Dems., 1984—2000, 2001—05. Mem.: ABA (labor sect., local govt. and law sect.), Fed. Bar Assn. (pres.-elect Tallahassee chpt. 1995, pres. 1996), Fla. Women Lawyers Assn. (hon. Fla. Govt. Bar Assn., Tallahassee Bar Assn., Fla. Bar Assn. (chmn. com. labor sect. 1987—91, exec. coun. labor sect. 1989—93, founding chmn. Fed. Ct. practice com. 1990—92, del. to 11th Cir. Jud. Conf. 1990—92, rep. mem. pub. rels. com. 1991—93, com. chmn. govt. lawyer sect. 1991—2000, cert. expert labor and employment law 2003, ann. meeting com. 2004—2006), Golden Eagle Country Club, Univ. Ctr. Club, Phi Alpha Delta. Christian Scientist. Avocations: golf, astronomy, writing. Home: 9017 Eagles Ridge Dr Tallahassee FL 32312-4046 Office: 2815 Remington Cir Ste 200 PO Box 15588 Tallahassee FL 32317 Fax: 850-385-8414. Office Phone: 850-386-9444. Personal E-mail: baminnick@earthlink.net. Business E-Mail: bruce@minnicklaw.com.

MINNICK, MALCOLM DAVID, lawyer; b. Indpls., July 5, 1946; s. Malcolm Dick and Frances Louise (Porter) M.; m. Heidi Rosemarie Klein, May 24, 1972. BA, U. Mich., 1968, JD, 1972. Bar: Calif. 1972, U.S. Dist. Ct.

(ctrl. dist.) Calif. 1972, U.S. Ct. Appeals (9th cir.) 1984, U.S. Dist. Ct. (no. dist.) Calif. 1986, U.S. Supreme Ct. 1986. Assoc. Lillick McHose & Charles, LA, 1972-78; ptnr. Lillick & McHose, LA, 1978-91, Pillsbury Winthrop Shaw Pittman LLP, San Francisco, 1991—. Group mgr. Creditors Rights and Bankruptcy Group, 1993-98; panelist Calif. Continuing Edn. of Bar, LA, 1982-86, 88, Practicing Law Inst., 1992, 93, 94, Banking Law Inst., 1999, 00; bd. govs. Fin. Lawyers Conf., LA, 1981-84; mem. exec. com. Lillick & McHose, 1982-85. Co-author: Checklist for Secured Commercial Loans, 1983. Pres. Ross Sch. Found., 1997-98. Mem. ABA (corp., banking and bus. law sect.), Am. Bankruptcy Inst., Calif. Bar Assn. (Uniform Comml. Code com. 1983-86), LA County Bar Assn. (exec. com. comml. law and bankruptcy sect. 1987-90), Bar Assn. San Francisco (comml. law and bankruptcy sect., panelist 2004), LA Country Club, Univ. Club (bd. dirs. 1983-86, pres. 1985-86). Avocation: golf. Office: Pillsbury Winthrop Shaw Pittman LLP 50 Fremont St San Francisco CA 94105-2230 Office Phone: 415-983-1351. Business E-Mail: dminnick@pillsburylaw.com.

MINNICK, MARY E., beverage company executive; b. Evanston, Ill., Nov. 27, 1959; BS in Bus., Bowling Green St. U., 1981; MBA, Duke U., 1983. With fountain sales, bottle/can divsn. Coca-Cola USA; asst. v.p., dir non-carbonated beverages The Coca-Cola Co., 1993—95, v.p., Middle & Far East mktg., 1996—97, pres. South Pacific divsn., 1997—2000, pres., Coca-Cola Japan, 2000—01, pres., COO, Asia Group, 2001—05, exec. v.p., 2002—, pres. mktg., strategy & innovation, 2005—. Mem. Dean's Coun. John F. Kennedy Sch. Bus., Harvard U.; bd. visitors Fuqua Sch. Bus. Named one of Most Powerful Women in Bus., Fortune mag., 2005, 100 Most Powerful Women in World, Forbes mag., 2005, 25 Masters of Innovation, Business-Week, 2006. Office: The Coca-Cola Co PO Box 1734 Atlanta GA 30301*

MINNIGH, JOEL DOUGLAS, library director; b. Greenville, Pa., Apr. 9, 1949; s. Wendell Ellsworth and Frances Alene (Hyde) M.; m. Margaret Beth Crowther, Dec. 26, 1972; children: Bradley Dean, Douglas Knox. BA, Allegheny Coll., 1971; MLS, U. Pitts., 1975. Cert. libr., Pa. Asst. libr. Wilkinsburg (Pa.) Pub. Libr., 1976-77, head libr., 1977—. Bd. dirs. Goodwill Industries Pitts., 1980-90, Mulberry Sr. Citizens Ctr., Wilkinsburg, Pa., 2001—; vice chmn. bd. dirs. Bach Choir Pitts., 1984-87; sec., bd. dirs. United Meth. Ch. Union, Pitts., 1987-88; elder, deacon Fox Chapel Presbyn. Ch., 1987—, soloist, 1998—. Recipient honor Goodwill Industries Pitts., 1990, citation Pa. Senate, 1991. Mem. Pa. Libr. Assn. (treas. S.W. chpt. 1988-89, 2004-05), Allegheny County Libr. Assn. (pres. librs. adv. coun. 2001-02, bd. dirs. 2002-05), Wilkinsburg C. of C. (dir. 1998-03, sec. 1999-2003). Republican. Avocations: travel, cooking, gardening, music, reading. Home: 1009 Blackridge Rd Pittsburgh PA 15235-2719 Office: Wilkinsburg Pub Libr 605 Ross Ave Pittsburgh PA 15221-2145

MINNIS, KAREN, state representative; b. Portland, Oreg., July 20, 1954; m. John Minnis, 1972; 3 children. Legis. aide State Rep. John Minnis. 1987—98; mem. Oreg. Ho. of Reps., 1998—; majority leader, 2001—03. Spkr. of the Ho., 2003—. Republican. Office: 900 Court St NE Rm 269 Salem OR 97301 Office Phone: 503-986-1200.

MINNIX, BRUCE MILTON, television and theatre director; b. Henderson-ville, N.C., Apr. 26, 1923; s. Bruce Milton and Jane Irene (Leverett) M.; m. Corinne McClure, Aug. 5, 1950; 1 child, Tracy Logue. BA, U. N.C., 1948. Mem. faculty New Sch., N.Y.C., 1977-80; adj. prof., Bklyn., 1985; AT&T sales tng. program, 1987. Dir. numerous TV shows including: U.S. Steel Hour, 1961-63; Shakespeare in Central Park- Merchant of Venice, 1962—, Anthony and Cleopatra, 1963—, Hamlet, 1964; Essay on Doors, 1963, Never Too Young, 1965-66, Galileo Oratorio, 1967 (Emmy nomination) On Being Black, 1969, The Haggadah Oratorio, 1981, Search for Tomorrow, 1968-74, All My Children, 1978-79, Another World, 1981, Texas, 1981-82, Body Talk, 1983, As the World Turns, 1985-86; The Cradle Will Rock, 1986 (Emmy nomination), Minolta Tng. series Minolta Info. Network, 1980-81; dir. Citibank, 1984, N.J. Bell (AT&T), 1985; writer, dir. Victorian Cape May A Video Visit to a Town out of Time, 1988 (medal Houston Film Festival), dir. Ricardo Muti and the Future of the Philadelphia Orchestra, 1988, Pitney Bowes Copier Intro 1992, Time Warner Cable 1991, Rain, 2005; producer, writer: Mt. Washington Valley, A Video Visit in Four Seasons, 1990; Actor: Music Video by Little Texas What Might Have Been, 1993, The New York Idea, 2002-03 Mayor, City of Cape May, N.J., 1972-76; founding mem. 3-term pres. Mid-Atlantic Center for Arts. Served with USN, 1943-45. Mem. Dirs. Guild Am. Achievements include earning the designation of National Historic Landmark. Office Phone: 609-884-7365.

MINOCHA, ANIL, physician, educator, researcher; b. India, Feb. 4, 1957; Came to U.S., 1982; s. Ram Saroop and Kamla Devi M. Pre-med. diploma, Punjab U., India, 1974; MD, Med. Coll., Rohtak, India, 1980; postgrad. studies in pharmacology, Baylor Coll. Medicine, 1982-84. Diplomate Am. Bd. Internal Medicine, Am. Bd. Gastroenterology, Am. Bd. Forensic Medicine, Am. Bd. Geriatric Medicine. House officer depts. ophthalmology and dermatology Med. Coll. Hosp., Rohtak, India, 1980-81; med. officer State Health Svcs. Govts. of Punjab and Haryana, India, 1981-82; rsch. asst. Baylor Coll. Med., Houston, 1982-84; fellow clin. pharmacology U. Tex., Charlottes-ville, 1984-86; resident physician Franklin Square Hosp., Balt., 1986-89; fellow gastroenterology Mich. State U., East Lansing, 1989-91; asst. prof. U. Louisville, 1991-95; assoc. prof. medicine U. Okla., Oklahoma City, 1995-99, mem. faculty ctr. of toxicology, 1997-99, assoc. prof. geriatric medicine. 1998-99; chief gastroenterology So. Ill. U. Sch. Medicine, Springfield, 1999—2002; dir. divsn. digestive diseases U. Miss. Med. Ctr., Jackson, 2002—. Instr. dept. medicine Mich. State U., 1989-91; staff physician dept. medicine VA Med. Ctr., Louisville, 1991-95; mem. credentials com. Humana Hosp., U. Louisville, 1992, other coms., 1992-94; mem. R&D com. VA Hosp., 1992-95; presenter in field; mem. pharmacy and therapeutics com. Heartland Health Plan, Oklahoma City, 1996-98: mem. R&D com. VA Med. Ctr., Oklahoma City, 1996-99, chmn. med. record com., 1996-99; mem. world lit. rev. panel Am. Jour. Gastroenterology, 1996; mem. Formulary Adv. Coun. of the Okla. State Bd. of Nursing, 1997-99. Author: The Gastroenterology Resident Pocket Survival Guide, 1999. Minocha's Guide to Digestive Diseases, 2000, How to Stop Heartburn. 2001, Natural Stomach Care, 2003, Handbook of Digestive Diseases, 2004, Encyclopedia of the Digestive System and Digestive Disorders, 2004; contbr. articles to profl. jours. Prin. investigator Gulf Biosystems, Charlottesville, 1985; biomed. rsch. grantee Mich. State U., 1990; sch. medicine rsch. grantee U. Louisville, 1993. Fellow ACP, Am. Coll. Gastroenterology, Am. Coll. Forensic Examiners; mem. Am. Gastroenterol. Assn., Am. Assn. for Study of Liver Disease. Office: U Miss Med Ctr Divsn Digestive Diseases 2500 N State St Jackson MS 39216 Office Phone: 601-984-4549. Business E-Mail: aminocha@medicine.umsmed.edu. E-mail: docwrite@aol.com.

MINOGUE, JOHN P., academic administrator, educator, priest; b. Chgo., Jan. 1946; B in Philosophy, St. Mary of the Barrens; MDiv, Deandreis Inst. Theology, 1972; M in Theology, DePaul U., 1975; PhD in Ministry, St. Mary of the Lake Sem., 1987. Ordained Vincentian priest, 1972. Vincentian priest Congregation of the Mission; instr. theology, dir. clin. pastoral placement programs St. Thomas Sem., Denver, 1972-76; instr. grad. theology, asst. then acad. dean DeAndreis Inst., 1976-83; pres. DePaul U., Chgo., 1993—. Trustee DePaul U., 1991—; bd. dirs. DePaul U. Corp., 1991-91; adj. prof. Sch. New Learning DePaul U., 1984—, instr. law and med. ethics Coll. Law DePaul U., 1989—; asst. prof. clin. ob.-gyn. Northwestern U.; instr. health care ethics St. Joseph Coll. Nursing, Joliet, Ill., Northwestern Sch. Nursing, Chgo.; cons. nat. health care ethics, patient decision-making, mem. Congregation of the Missions Bd. mem. Children's Meml. Hosp. Mem.: NASA (bd. mem.). Office: De Paul U Office of the Pres 55 E Jackson Blvd 22nd Fl Chicago IL 60604-2287

MINOGUE, ROBERT BROPHY, retired nuclear engineer; b. Covington, Ky., Jan. 31, 1928; s. Joseph and Catherine Ann (Brophy) M.; m. Marie Joan Clarke, June 12, 1954; children: Patrick, Margaret, Marie, Francis. BS, Thomas More Coll., 1949; MS, U. Cin., 1951; grad., Oak Ridge Sch. Reactor Tech., 1952. Nuclear engr., then head nuclear tech. sect. naval reactors br.

AEC, Washington, 1952-56; head research reactor design and enngring., then head nuclear power plant engring. sect. Gen. Atomic div. Gen. Dynamics Corp., 1957-67; chief spl. projects br. div. reactor standards AEC, Washington, 1967-72, asst. dir., then dep. dir. regulatory standards, 1972-74; dir. office standards devel. Nuclear Regulatory Commn., Washington, 1975-80, dir. office research, 1980-86; pvt. practice Temecula, Calif., 1986—. U.S. mem. sr. adv. group Safety Standards IAEA, 1974-86; mem. Com. on Interagy. Radiation Research and Policy Coordination, 1982-86. Author: Reactor Shielding Design Manual, 1956; patentee: Triga Research Reactor. Served with AUS, 1946-48. Recipient Bernard F. Langer award, ASME, 1982. Roman Catholic. Home and Office: 29743 Marhill Cir Temecula CA 92591-1809

**MINOR, EDWARD COLQUITT,** paper company executive, lawyer; b. Balt., Dec. 1, 1942; s. Edward Essau and Mary Newell (Schultz) Minor; m. Joan Slade, Aug. 29, 1964; 1 child, Elizabeth Colquitt. AB in Econ., Western Md. Coll., 1964; LLB cum laude, Boston U., 1967. Bar: Md. 1967, Ga. 1972, Va. 1974, U.S. Supreme Ct. Assoc. Semmes Bowen & Semmes, Balt., 1967-68; judge adv. U.S. Army, Savannah and Vietnam, 1968-72; assoc. Connerat Dunn & Hunter, Savannah, 1972-73; sr. atty. Kraft Paper Union Camp Corp., Savannah, 1973, asst. gen. counsel, asst. sec Fine Paper Franklin, Va., 1974-85, assoc. gen. counsel, asst. sec. Fine Paper, 1985-99, mgr. Fine Paper, 1988-95, divsn. procurement mgr. purchasing Fine Paper, 1995-99; pvt. practice, 2003—; m2 consulting Fed. Contracting. Mem. citizens adv. bd. Va. Dept. Environ. Qualtiy; energy cons., 2001—02. Mem. Gov.'s Commn. Efficiency, 1988; chmn. Franklin Constl. Bicentennial Commn.; chmn. bd. dirs. Southampton Acad., Courtland, Va., 1985—88; dep. mem. Va. Bus. Coun., 1985—88; chmn. citizens adv. bd. Va. Dept. Air Pollution Control, 1992, mem., 1993—99, Roundtable Environ. Standing, 1991; mem. exec. bd. Diocese S.E. Va., Episcopal Ch., 1985—89; vestryman Emmanual Episcopal Ch., Franklin, 1985, 1987, 1991; bd. dirs. Tidewater Heart Assn., Norfolk, Va., 1980—86, Future of Hampton Rds., Inc., Rawles Mus. Arts, 1992—93. Decorated Bronze Star. Fellow: Royal Soc. Encouragement Arts Am.; mem.: Ga. Bar Assn., Md. Bar Assn., Va. Bar Assn. (co-chmn. corp. counsel sect. 1990—92, bd. govs. adminstrv. law sect., jud. com. 1997—, bd. govs. corp. counsel sect. 1998—2000), Va. State Bar (chmn. environ. sect. 1990—91), Courtland Ruritan Club (pres. 2003), Town Point Club, Norfolk Yacht Club, Rotary (pres. Franklin 1992—93). Home: 23456 Thomas Cir Courtland VA 23837-1336 Personal E-mail: ecminor@verizon.net.

**MINOR, GEORGE GILMER, III,** drug and hospital supply company executive; b. 1940; married. BA, Va. Mil. Inst., 1963; MBA, U. Va., 1966. With Owens & Minor, Inc., Richmond, Va., 1963—; mgr. sales Acme Candy Co. div., 1966-68, mgr. retail mktg., 1968-73, div. wholesale drug br., 1973-77, v.p., 1977-80, exec. v.p., 1980-81, pres., 1981—99, CEO, 1984—2005, chmn., 1994—. Bd. dir. SunTrust Banks Inc. Bd. dir. Va. Biotechnology Rsch. Park Authority, Richmond Renaissance; v.p. bd. vis. Va. Mil. Inst.; chmn. bd. trustees Va. Health Care Found.; mem. adv. bd. Univ. Va. Sch. Nursing. Named Va. Industrialist of the Year, 2001; named to Greater Richmond Bus. Hall of Fame, 2003. Office: Owens & Minor Inc 4800 Cox Rd Glen Allen VA 23060-6292*

**MINOR, HALSEY,** multimedia company executive; married; 3 children. BA in Anthropology, U. Va., 1987. Investment banker Merrill Lynch Capital Markets, San Francisco, 1987—89; founder, CEO Global Publishing Corp., 1989—90; cons. Russell Reynolds Associates, 1991—92; founder, chmn., CEO CNET: The Computer Network, San Francisco, 1992—2000; chmn. emeritus CNET Networks, Inc., 2000—; founder, chmn., CEO Grand Central Communications, 2000—. Founding investor Listen.com (acquired by Real Media and Salesforce.com); bd. dirs. salesforce.com, Inc. Office: Grand Central Communications 50 Fremont St 16th Fl San Francisco CA 94105 Office Phone: 415-344-3200. Office Fax: 415-344-3250.

**MINOR, JOSEPH EDWARD,** civil engineer, educator; b. Corpus Christi, Tex., June 2, 1938; s. William Smoot Jr. and Irene (Schiller) M.; m. Treva Ann Edmiston, Sept. 3, 1960; children: Joseph Edward Jr., Sharon Diane. BSCE, Tex. A&M U., 1959, M of Engring., 1960; PhD, Tex. Tech U., 1974. Registered profl. engr., Tex., Mo., Fla. Sr. rsch. engr. Southwest Research Inst., San Antonio, 1962-69; P. Whitfield Horn prof. Tex. Tech U., Lubbock, 1969-88; Thomas Reese prof., chmn. dept. civil engring. U. Mo., Rolla, 1988-93, rsch. prof., 1993—. Pres. Insulating Glass Cert. Council, N.Y., 1986-89; vis. prof. Tex. A&M U., Kingsville, 2003-. Contbr. articles to profl. jours. Served with USAR. Recipient Disting. Engr. award Tex. Tech U., 1989, Disting. Svc. award Nat. Hurricane Conf., 1999; Nat. Def. fellow, 1959-60; Fulbright scholar, 1978. Fellow ASCE (pres. Tex. sect. 1984-85, award of honor 2003); mem. NSPE, Tex. Soc. Profl. Engrs. (Engr. of Yr. Nueces chpt. 2006). Presbyterian. Avocation: fishing. Office: Joseph E Minor PE Consulting Engineer PO Box 603 Rockport TX 78381-0603 E-mail: josephminor@sbcglobal.net.

**MINOR, ROBERT ALLEN,** lawyer; b. Washington, Oct. 20, 1948; s. Robert Walter and Joan (Allen) M.; m. Sue Ellyn Blose, June 13, 1981; children: Robert Barratt, Sarah Allen. AB in English, Duke U., 1970; JD, Ohio State U., 1975. Bar: Ohio 1975, U.S. Dist. Ct. (so. dist.) Ohio 1976, D.C. 1979. Assoc Vorys, Sater, Seymour & Pease, LLP, Columbus, Ohio, 1975-82, ptnr., 1982—. Author seminar articles. With U.S. Army, 1970-72. Mem. Ohio Bar Assn., Columbus Bar Assn., Athletic Club Columbus, Scioto Country Club. Republican. Presbyterian. Office: Vorys Sater Seymour & Pease LLP PO Box 1008 52 E Gay St Columbus OH 43215-3161 Office Phone: 614-464-6410. Business E-Mail: raminor@vssp.com.

**MINOR, RONALD RAY,** minister; b. Aliceville, Ala., Nov. 3, 1944; s. Hershel Ray and Minnie Orell (Goodson) M.; m. Gwendolyn Otelia Newsome, July 25, 1970; 1 child, Rhonda Rene. BA in Ministerial, Southeastern Bible Coll., 1971, BA in Secondary Edn., 1973; DDiv, Southern Bible Coll., 1984. Ordained to ministry Pentecostal Ch. of God, 1968. Gen. sec. Pentecostal Ch. of God, Joplin, Mo., 1979—2005, dist. supt. Philadelphia, Miss., 1975-79, pastor LaBelle, Fla.; now pastor Orient Park Tabernacle, Tampa, Fla.; pastor Lafayette (Ind.) Pentecostal Ch. of God. Pres. Pentecostal Young People's Assn., Fla. and Miss.; sec. Gen. Bd. Pentecostal Ch. of God, Joplin, 1979; bd. dirs. Nat. Assn. Evangs., Wheaton, Ill., 1981-96; adv. coun. Am. Bible Soc., N.Y.C., 1979-2003; sec. Commn. Chaplains, Washington, 1991-95. Office: Pentecostal Ch of God 3511 S 9th St Lafayette IN 47909 E-mail: ronald.minor@insight66.com.

**MINOR, STERLING ARTHUR,** lawyer; b. Sioux City, Iowa, July 1, 1952; s. Harold DeForrest and Mary Ruth (Thompson) M.; children: Elizabeth Anne, Lauren Camille; m. Ellen L. Luby, June 28, 1998. BS, Duke U., 1974; JD, So. Meth. U., 1977. Bar: Tenn. 1977, Tex. 1982, U.S. Ct. Appeals (6th cir.) 1978, U.S. Ct. Appeals (D.C. cir.) 1978, U.S. Ct. Appeals (5th cir.) 1982; bd. cert. bus. bankruptcy law Tex. Bd. Legal Specialization. Ptnr. Martin & Cochran, Nashville, 1977-81; participating assoc. Sheinfeld, Maley & Kay, Houston, 1981-86; ptnr. Bracewell & Zeluff, 1986—88; mem. Baker, Brown, Sharman & Parker, Houston, 1989-91; pvt. practice Houston, 1991—. Spkr. in field. Reviewing editor: Guide to Asset Protection Planning, 1998, 99; columnist Legal Minutes, West U Mag., The Mag. River Oaks, Meml./Villages Mag., Tanglewood Mag., Bellaire Mag., Downtown Voice, 1993-95; contbr. numerous articles on bus. entities, asset protection and bankruptcy to profl. jours. Chmn. Zoning Bd. Adjustment, City West University Place, Tex., 1987-97; adminstrv. bd. mem. West University United Meth. Ch., 1988-90, 96-98; bd. mem. West University Elem. Sch. PTA, 1989-92, Rotary Club West University, 1995-96, The Sentinel Club, Inc., 1996-97; pres. Art League Houston, 1998-2000. Fellow Houston Bar Found.; mem. Coll. State Bar Tex., Tunraround Mgmt. Assn. Home: 2031 Dunstan Rd Houston TX 77005-1621 Office: 808 Travis St Ste 1418 Houston TX 77002-5734 Office Phone: 713-223-8585. Office Fax: 713-223-4324. Business E-Mail: sminor@sterlingminor.com.

**MINOW, JOSEPHINE BASKIN,** civic volunteer; b. Chgo., Nov. 3, 1926; d. Salem N. and Bessie (Sampson) Baskin; m. Newton N. Minow, May 29, 1949; children: Nell, Martha, Mary. BS, Northwestern U., Evanston, Ill., 1948. Asst. to advt. dir. Mandel Brothers Store, Chgo., 1948-49; tchr. Francis W. Parker Sch., Chgo., 1949-50; vol. in civil and charitable activities, 1950—; bd. dirs. Juvenile Protective Assn., Chgo., 1958—, pres., 1973-75. Bd. dirs. Parnham Trust, Beaminster, Dorset, England. Author: Marty the Broken Hearted Artichoke, 1997. Founder, coord. Children's divsn. Hospitality and Info. Svc., Washington, 1961-63; mem. Caucus Com., Glencoe, Ill., 1965-69; co-chmn. spl. study on juvenile justice Chgo. Cmty. Trust, 1978-80; chmn. Know Your Chgo., 1980-83; bd. dirs. Chgo. Coun. Fgn. Rels., 1977-2003, hon. life mem., 2003; trustee Chgo. Hist. Soc., Ravinia Festival Assn.; mem. women's bd. Field Mus., U. Chgo.; founding mem., v.p. women's bd. Northwestern U., 1978; bd. govs. Chgo. Symphony, 1966-73, 76-; mem. Citizens Com. Juvenile Ct. of Cook County, 1985-96; exec. com. Northwestern U. Libr. Coun., 1974-96; co-chair grandparents' adv. com. Chgo. Children's Mus., 1999; bd. dirs. Jane Addams Juvenile Ct. Found.; dir. Abraham Lincoln Presdl. Libr. and Mus., 2005—. Recipient spl. award Chgo. Sch. and Workshop for Retarded, 1975, Children's Guardian award Juvenile Protective Assn., 1993. Mem. Hebrew Immigrant Aid Soc. (bd. dirs. 1977-98, award 1988), Friday Club, The Arts Club. Democrat. Jewish. Office: Chgo Hist Museum Clark St at North Ave Chicago IL 60614

**MINOW, MARTHA LOUISE,** law educator; b. Highland Pk., Ill., Dec. 6, 1954; AB in History, U. Mich., 1975; EdM, Harvard U., 1976; JD, Yale U., 1979; EdD (hon.), Wheelock Coll., 1998. Bar: Mass. 1981. Law clk. to Judge David L. Bazelon US Ct. Appeals DC Cir., 1979-80; law clk. to Assoc. Justice Thurgood Marshall US Supreme Ct., 1980-81; asst. prof. law Harvard Law Sch., Cambridge, Mass., 1981-86, prof., 1986—; William Henry Bloomberg prof. law, 2003—; acting dir. program on ethics and the professions Harvard U., Cambridge, Mass., 1993—94, acting dir. ctr. on ethics and the professions, 2000—01; co-dir. Children's Studies at Harvard, 1996—99. Sr. fellow Harvard Soc. Fellows, 1997-. Author: Making All the Difference: Inclusion, Exclusion, and American Law, 1990, Not Only For Myself: Identity, Politics, and Law, 1997, Between Vengeance and Forgiveness: Facing History After Genocide and Mass Violence, 1998, Partners, Not Rivals: Privatization and the Public Good, 2002; co-author: Teacher's Manual, Civil Procedure: Doctrine, Practice, and Context, 2004; editor: Family Matters: Readings on Family Lives and the Law, 1993; co-editor: Narrative, Violence, and the Law, 1992, Law Stories, 1996, The Free Exercise of Culture, 2001, Engaging in Cultural Differences, 2002, Imagine Coexistence: Restoring Humanity After Violent Ethnic Conflict, 2003, Mary Joe Frug's Women and the Law, 2004. Trustee emeritus Judge Baker Children's Ctr.; trustee William T. Grant Found.; bd. dirs. Judge David L. Bazelon Ctr. for Mental Health Law, The Covenant Found, Am. Bar Found., 1985-94. Mem. Law and Soc. Assn. Office: Harvard Law Sch 1563 Massachusetts Ave Cambridge MA 02138 Office Phone: 617-495-4276. Office Fax: 617-496-5156. Business E-Mail: minow@law.harvard.edu.

**MINOW, NEWTON NORMAN,** lawyer, educator; b. Milw., Wis., Jan. 17, 1926; s. Jay A. and Doris (Stein) Minow; m. Josephine Baskin, May 29, 1949; children: Nell, Martha, Mary. BS, Northwestern U., 1949, JD, 1950, LLD (hon.), 1965, U. Wis., Brandeis U., 1963, Columbia Coll., 1972, Govs. State U., 1984, De Paul U., 1989, RAND Grad. Sch., 1993, U. Notre Dame, 1994, Roosevelt U., 1996, Barat Coll., 1996, Santa Clara U. Sch. Law, 1998, Cath. Theol. Union, 2001. With firm Mayer, Brown & Platt, Chgo., 1950-51, 53-55; law clk. to chief justice U.S. Supreme Ct., 1951-52; adminstrv. asst. to Ill. Gov. Stevenson, 1952-53; spl. asst. to Adlai E. Stevenson in presdl. campaign, 1952, 56; ptnr. firm Stevenson, Rifkind & Wirtz, Chgo., N.Y.C. and Washington, 1955-61; chmn. FCC, Washington, 1961-63; exec. v.p., gen. counsel, dir. Ency. Brit., Chgo., 1963-65; ptnr. Sidley Austin LLP, Chgo., 1965—91, sr. counsel, 1991—. Former trustee, past chmn. bd. dirs., adv. trustee Rand Corp.; past chmn. Chgo. Ednl. TV; chmn. pub. rev. bd. Arthur Andersen & Co., 1974—83; trustee Carnegie Corp. N.Y., 1987—97, chmn. bd. trustees, 1993—97; Annenberg prof. comm. law and policy Northwestern U., 1987—2003, prof. emeritus, 2003—; dir. Annenberg Washington Program, 1987—96; chmn. tech. and privacy adv. com. Soc. Def., 2003—04. Author: (book) Equal Time: The Private Broadcasters and the Public Interest, 1964; co-author: Presidential Television, 1973, Electronics and the Future, 1977, For Great Debates, 1987, Abandoned in the Wasteland: Children, Television, and the First Amendment, 1995, As We Knew Adlai. Bd. govs. Pub. Broadcasting Svc., 1973—80, chmn. bd. dirs., 1978—80; vice chmn. presdl. debates LWV, 1976, 1980, 1993—; chmn. bd. overseers Jewish Theol. Sem., 1974—77; trustee Notre Dame U., 1964—77, 1983—96, life trustee, 1996; trustee Mayo Found., 1973—81, Northwestern U., 1975—87, life trustee, 1987—. With U.S. Army, 1944—46. Named one of Am.'s 10 Outstanding Young Men, 1961; recipient George Foster Peabody Broadcasting award, 1961, Ralph Lowell award, 1982, Lifetime Achievement award, Am. Lawyer, 2004, Woodrow Wilson award for pub. svc., 2006. Fellow: Am. Acad. Arts and Scis., Am. Bar Found.; mem.: Northwestern U. Alumni Assn. (medal 1978), Century Club (N.Y.C.), Chgo. Club, Comml. Club (pres. 1987—88). Democrat. Office: Sidley Austin LLP One S Dearborn St Chicago IL 60603 Office Phone: 312-853-7555. Business E-Mail: nminow@sidley.com.

**MINSHALL, GREG,** computer programmer; b. Carmel, Calif., Apr. 21, 1952; s. Glenn Almon and Martha Jane (Hardesty) M.; m. Maria Concepción Gonzalez, Dec. 30, 1976 (div. Mar. 1984); children: Matthew, Cecilia; m. Carol Ann Mendel, Oct. 4, 1987 (div. Feb. 1992); children: Oriana, Jacob. BA in Math., U. Calif., Berkeley, 1985. Computer programmer Stanford Linear Accelerator Ctr., Menlo Park, Calif., 1969-70, 72-73; computer programmer/engr. Inst. for Advanced Computation, Sunnyvale, Calif., 1978-80; computer programmer U. Calif. Berkeley, 1980-83; cons., 1984-88; computer programmer Novell, Inc., Walnut Creek, Calif., 1988-95, Ipsilon Networks, Inc., Mountain View, Calif., 1995—97; founder Siara Sys., 1998—2002; mem. tech. adv. bd. Netillion, 2004—05. Bd. dirs Kronos Quartet. Mem. Assn. for Computing Machinery, Usenix

**MINSKOFF, EDWARD,** architectural firm executive; s. Leo Minskoff and Isabelle; m. Julie Minskoff. Grad., Mich. State U.; MBA, U. Calif., LA. CEO Olympia & York; founder, chmn. Edward J. Minskoff Equities Inc. Chair endowment, pediatric oncology NYU Med. Ctr. Trustee NYU Med. Ctr.; bd. dirs. NYU Med. Ctr. Cancer Inst.; vice chmn. bd. trustee NYU Sch. Medicine Found. Named one of Top 200 Collectors, ARTnews Mag., 2006. Mem.: Assn. for a Better NY (exec. com.), Real Estate Bd. NY (gov.). Avocations: squash, golf, exercise. Office: 1325 Ave of Americas 53rd St New York NY 10019*

**MINTER, DAVID LEE,** English literature educator; b. Midland, Tex., Mar. 20, 1935; s. Kenneth Cruse and Frances (Hennessy) M.; m. Cynthia Caroline Sewell, Dec. 22, 1957; children: Christopher Sewell, Frances Elizabeth. BA, N. Tex. State U., 1957, MA, 1959; BD, Yale U., 1961, PhD, 1965. Univ. lectr. Hamburg (W. Ger.) U., 1965-66; lectr. Yale U., 1966-67; asst. prof. Rice U., Houston, 1967-69, assoc. prof., 1974-80; prof. English Emory U., Atlanta, 1981-89, Asa G. Candler prof. Am. lit., 1989-90, dean Coll. Arts and Scis., 1981-90, v.p. arts and scis., 1984-90; Libbie Shearn Moody prof. English Rice U., Houston, 1990-99, interim vice provost, univ. libr., 1995-96, interim provost, 1999-2000, Bruce and Elizabeth Dunlevie prof. English, 1999—2002. Author: The Interpreted Design as a Structural Principle in American Prose, 1969, William Faulkner: His Life and Work, 1980, 82, 91, 97, French edit., 1984, Korean edito., 1999, A Cultural History of the American Novel: Henry James to William Faulkner, 1994, 96, Faulkner's Questioning Narratives: Fiction of the Major Phase, 2001, 04; editor: Twentieth-Century Interpretations of Light in August, 1969, The Norton Critical Edit. of The Sound and the Fury, 1987, 93; co-editor: The Harper American Literature, 1986, 93, 96, 97, The Columbia Literary History of the United States, 1987 (Italian edit. 1990, Chinese edit. 1994, Japanese edit. 1997); also articles and revs. Fulbright Travel fellow, 1966; Nat. Endowment

for Humanities fellow, 1969-70; Am. Council Learned Socs. grantee, 1975; Fred Harris Daniels fellow, 1980 Mem. MLA, Am. Lit. Group, Am. Studies Assn., Phi Beta Kappa. Methodist. Home: 2145 Swift Houston TX 77030-1215 E-mail: dcmint@rice.edu.

**MINTER, JERRY BURNETT,** electronics executive; b. Ft. Worth, Oct. 31, 1913; s. Claude Joe and Roxie (Ayers) M.; m. Monica Rose Hanlon, Mar. 2, 1940; children: Claude, Mark (dec.), Byron, Claire, Maureen. BSEE, MIT, 1934. Engr. Boonton (N.J.) Radio Corp., 1935-36, Ferris Instruments Co., Boonton, 1936-39; v.p., chief engr. Measurements Corp., Boonton, 1939-53; pres. Components Corp., Denville, NJ, 1946—. Contbr. articles to tech. jours. Pilot CAP, Morristown, N.J., 1947-50. Fellow IEEE (life, past chmn. No. N.J. sect.), Audio Engring. Soc. (past pres.), Radio Club Am. (life, pres. emeritus, past pres., Armstrong medal 1968); mem. AIAA, Am. Soc. for Metals (life), N.Y. Acad. Scis., Soc. Motion Picture and TV Engrs. (life), Internat. Soc. Photo-Optical Instrumentation Engrs., Quiet Birdmen. Achievements include 26 patents in field. Home: 48 Normandy Heights Rd Morristown NJ 07960-4613 Office: Components Corp 6 Kinsley Pl Denville NJ 07834 Office Phone: 973-627-0290.

**MINTER, PHILIP CLAYTON,** retired communications company executive; b. Sydney, Australia, Aug. 9, 1928; came to U.S., 1957; s. Roy Dixon and Adeline Claire (Bradly) M.; m. Mary Bashford Schettler, Jan. 24, 1959 (dec. July 1999); children: Elizabeth C., Margaret S. BSc with honours, U. Sydney, 1951; MS, U. Wyo., 1958; PhD, U. Wis., 1960. Tchr. King's Sch., Parramatta, Australia, 1951-57; mng. dir. Motivational Rsch. Assocs., Sydney, 1960-62; dir. rsch. Nat. Fund Raising Coun., Sydney, 1962-65; project dir. USDA, Ft. Collins, Colo, 1965-67; chief info. pesticides program USPHS, Atlanta, 1967-68; mgr. data bases div. Pa. Rsch. Assocs., Phila., 1968-70; pres. Ednl. Communications Inc., King of Prussia, Pa., 1970-94; v.p. Medication Mgmt. Systems Internat., LLC, 2001—; dir. Unmaned Ocean Vehicles, 2005—. Pres. Svc. Tng. Ltd., Kenilworth, Eng., 1976-88; cons. Westinghouse Learning Corp., 1972. Author: Handbook for Pesticide-Chemicals Program Coordinators, 1967. Recipient Terry Magill award Australia Soc., N.Y., 1994. Mem. Soc. Automotive Engrs., Sci. Rsch. Soc. Am., Royal Heritage Soc. (bd. dirs.), U. Wis. Alumni Assn. (bd. dirs. Delaware Valley br.), Australian/Am. C. of C. Phila. (pres.), Union League, Brit. Officers Club Phila. (pres. 1992-93), The Order of Autralia, Sigma Xi. Republican. Episcopalian. Home: 1576 Stapler Dr Yardley PA 19067-4214 Personal E-mail: aacc@comcast.net.

**MINTER, REBECCA MANGET,** surgeon; b. Rapid City, S.D., Aug. 12, 1970; d. John Anderson Minter and Janet MacEachin Wagstaff; m. John Edward Rectenwald, June 12, 1999. BA, U. Denver, 1992; MD, U. Tex. Southwestern, Dallas, 1996. Diplomate gen. surgery Am. Bd. Surgery, 2004. Intern U. Fla., 1996—97, resident, 1997—98, rsch. fellow sepsis and inflammation, 1998—2000, resident, 2000—03; asst. prof. U. Mich., Ann Arbor, 2003—. Contbr. articles to profl. jours. Mem. Coun. on Grad. Med. Edn., Washington, 2003—06. Recipient Achievement award for exceptional leadership abilities in medicine, AMA/Glaxo, 1995, Upjohn Med. Student Achievement award for Cmty. Svc., Upjohn Pharmaceuticals and UTSW Med. Ctr., 1996, Med. Student Tchg. award, U. Fla. Dept. Surgery, 2003, Edward R. Woodward Surg. Resident's award, 2003, Tchg. award, U. Mich. Dept. Surgery, 2005; grantee, NSF, 1991, Assn. for Surg. Edn. Ctr. for Excellence in Surg. Edn., Rsch., and Tng., 2004—05, Soc. U. Surgeons Found., 2005, NIH-NIGMS, 2005—, U. Mich., 2006—; scholar, Student Interact/Rotary, San Antonio, 1988, U. Denver, 1988—92; Hornbeck scholar, 1988—92. Fellow: ACS (assoc.); mem.: Soc. U. Surgeons (social and legislative issues com.), Am. Hepato-Pancreato-Biliary Assn., Soc. for Surgery of the Alimentary Tract, Assn. for Surg. Edn., Assn. for Academic Surgery (councilor, edn. com. mem., instl. rep. 2006—), Assn. Women Surgeons. Achievements include patents pending for Gene Therapy for Pulmonary Disease; research in computer aided laparoscopic simulators for training surgical residents; immunomodulation of sepsis in biliary obstruction; systematic development of a comprehensive competency-based curriculum and assessment framework for surgical training. Office: University of Michigan 1500 E Medical Center Drive TC 2920 Ann Arbor MI 48109-0331 Office Phone: 734-936-5823. Office Fax: 734-769-7056.

**MINTON, JERRY DAVIS,** lawyer, consultant, retired banker; b. Ft. Worth, Aug. 13, 1928; s. Robert Bruch and Anna Elizabeth (Davis) M.; m. Martha Drew Fields, Nov. 28, 1975; children: Marianne, Martha, John Morgan. BBA, U. Tex., Austin, 1949, JD, 1960; grad. cert., Nat. Trust Sch., Northwestern U., 1960. Of counsel Michener, Larimore, Swindle, Whitaker, Flowers et al., 1991—96; adv. dir. Kanaly Trust Co., Houston, 1992-2000. Vice chmn. 1st Nat. Bank Ft. Worth, 1982-84; chmn., CEO 1st City Nat. Bank Ft. Worth, 1986-91. Pilot USAF, 1951-55, pilot Tex. Air N.G., 1955-57; capt. USAFR Ret. Decorated D.F.C., Air medal with 3 oak leaf clusters. Mem. Air Force Assn., State Bar Tex., Tarrant County Bar Assn., Soc. Descs. of Washington's Army at Valley Forge, SAR, SCV, Mil. Order Stars and Bars, Mil. Order World Wars, D.F.C. Soc., Ft. Worth Air Power Coun., Order Quiet Birdmen, Order of Daedalians, River Crest Country Club, Breakfast Club, Wildcatters Club, Sigma Iota Epsilon, Phi Delta Phi. Episcopalian. Home: 5404 El Dorado Dr Fort Worth TX 76107-3236

**MINTON, JOHN D., JR.,** state supreme court justice; m. Susan Lenell Page. BA in English & History, Western Ky. U., 1974; JD, U. Ky. Coll. of Law, 1977. Atty., priv. practice Bowling Green, Ky., 1981—95; chief administrative judge Green River Region, Ky., 1996—2003; circuit judge Warren County, Ky., 1992—2003; judge Second Appellate Dist. Ky. Ct. of Appeals, 2003—06; justice Ky. Supreme Ct., 2006—. Leader Ky. Conf. of United Methodist Church; bd. mem. Student Life Found. Western Ky. U. Office: Ky Supreme Ct Warren Cty Justice Ctr 1001 Ctr St 2nd Fl Rm 204 Bowling Green KY 42101*

**MINTON, JOHN DEAN,** historian, educator; b. Cadiz, Ky., July 29, 1921; s. John Ernest and Daisy Dean (Wilson) M.; m. Betty Jo Redick, June 8, 1947; children—John Dean, James Ernest. AB in Edn, U. Ky., 1943, MA in History, 1947; PhD, Vanderbilt U., 1959. Instr. history U. Miami, Fla., 1951; tchr. Broward County Pub. Sch. Sys., U. Miami evening divsn., 1951-53; prin. Trigg County (Ky.) H.S., 1953-58; prof. history We. Ky. U., Bowling Green, 1958-86, ret., dean Grad. Coll., 1964-71, v.p. for adminstrv. affairs, 1970-79, interim pres., 1979, v.p. for student affairs, 1981-86, part-time prof. 1986-96. Author: The New Deal in Tennessee, 1932-1938, 1979; contbr. articles to profl. jours. Former mem. Gen. Bd. Discipleship, United Meth. Ch.; with Louisville Bd. Discipleship; lay spkr. Louisville Conf. Meth. Ch.; bd. dirs. Higher Edn. Found., Meth. Ch., Jesse Stuart Found. Served with USNR, 1943-46. Mem. NEA, Ky. Edn. Assn., So. Hist. Assn., Ky. Hist. Soc., Bowling Green C. of C. (bd. dirs.), Civitan Club (pres. 1966), Phi Alpha Theta, Phi Eta Sigma, Kappa Delta Pi Home: 645 Ridgecrest Way Bowling Green KY 42104-3818

**MINTON, JOSEPH PAUL,** retired safety organization executive; b. Houston, Oct. 20, 1924; s. Joseph Marion and Stella (Fite) M.; m. Nancy Fettig, June 19, 1948; children: Joan M., Michael J., Jane A., Mary B., John E., Diane C. BS in Air Transp., Purdue U., 1949; Grad., U.S. Air Force Air Command and Staff Coll., 1958. Commd. 2d lt. USAF, 1944, advanced through grades to col., 1966, combat Burma, World War II, assignments in crew, staff and command, ret., 1967; v.p. Purdue Airlines Inc., Lafayette, Ind., 1967-68, pres., CEO, 1969-71, mng. dir., chief exec. officer Saber Air Ltd., Singapore, 1971-73; sr. v.p. Brit. Caledonian Airways, N.Y.C., 1974-76; mng. dir. Nat. Transp. Safety Bd., Washington, 1977-78; exec. dir. Nat. Safety Coun., Washington, 1978-88. Decorated D.F.C. with oak leaf cluster, Air medal with 3 oak leaf clusters, 3 battle stars, Air Force Commendation medal with oak leaf cluster. Roman Catholic. Address: 1720 Lake Shore Crest Dr Apt 15 Reston VA 20190-3243

**MINTON, YVONNE FAY,** mezzo-soprano; b. Sydney, Australia; d. Robert Thomas and Alice Violet M.; m. William Barclay, Aug. 24, 1965; children— Malcolm Alexander, Alison Elizabeth. Student, Sydney Conservatorium

Music, 1960-61. Mezzo-soprano with all maj. orchs. in, Australia, 1958-61; moved to London, 1961, joined, Royal Opera House, Covent Garden, 1965-70, guest artist, Cologne (Germany) Opera, 1969—, U.S. debut as Octavian in Der Rosenkavalier, 1970; appeared, with Lyric Opera, Chgo., 1970, Met. Opera, N.Y.C., 1973, San Francisco Opera, 1974, Paris Opera, 1974, Bayreuth, 1974, Salzburg, 1978; sang regularly with maj. symphony orchs. throughout world, 1968—; recs. include The Knot Garden, 1970, Cosi Fan Tutte, 1971, Lulu, 1979; maj. vocal works include Mahler songs with, Chgo. Symphony; condr. master classes across Europe and vocal coach in London. Comdr. Order Brit. Empire, 1980 Hon. mem. Royal Acad. Music. Office: care Ingpen & Williams 7 St Georges Ct 131 Putney Bridge Rd London SW15 2PA England

**MINTZ, ALBERT**, lawyer; b. New Orleans, Oct. 19, 1929; s. Morris and Goldie (Goldblum) M.; m. Linda Barnett, Dec. 19, 1954; children— John Morris, Margaret Anne Easthope. BBA, Tulane U., 1948, JD, 1951. Bar: La. 1951; cert. tax specialist, estate and adminstrn. specialist. Since practiced in, New Orleans; ptnr. Montgomery, Barnett, Brown, Read, Hammond & Mintz, Hurwitz-Mintz Realty Cos., New Orleans. Bd. dirs Strauss Distbrs., Avrico, Inc. Mem. editl. bd. Tulane Law Rev. Adv. bd. Law Sch. Tulane U.; chmn., dir. adv. bd Tulane Summer Lyric Theater; bd. dirs. Tulane Ctr. Stage Talent and Shakespearean Theatre; bd. dirs. Jewish Cmty. Ctr., New Orleans, 1965-72, Jewish Fedn., 1968-, Home for Jewish Aged, 1968-71, Jewish Family Svc., New Orleans, 1968-72; trustee, bd. mgrs. Touro Infirmary Hosp. and Found.; trustee Jewish Endowment Found.; charter mem. La. Hist. Assn. bd. trustees, mem. Temple Sinai. Recipient Judah Touro Society Award, 1999, Tulane Outstanding Alumnus award, Class of 1951, 2001, Outstanding Vol. award Tulane U., 2003, Role Model award Young Leadership Coun., 2004, Young award for professionalism and comty. svc., 2005. Mem. ABA, La. Bar Assn. (lectr., publ. on corp., tax, real estate law), New Orleans Bar Assn. (exec. com. 1971-74), Am. Law Inst., U.S. Hist. Assn., New Orleans C. of C. (chmn. com. civic affairs and state legis. 1968-69), Tulane Emeritus Club (chmn. exec. com., pres. 2004), Phi Delta Phi, Omicron Delta Kappa, Zeta Beta Tau. Jewish. Home: 1915 State St New Orleans LA 70118-6251 Office: 3200 Energy Ctr 1100 Poydras St New Orleans LA 70163-1101 Office Phone: 504-585-7635. Business E-Mail: amintz@monbar.com.

**MINTZ, DANIEL HARVEY**, endocrinologist, educator, academic administrator; b. N.Y.C., Sept. 16, 1930; s. Jacob A. and Fanny Mintz; m. Dawn E. Hynes, Jan. 15, 1961 (dec.); children: David, Denise, Debra; m. Marge Kleiman, Nov. 30, 1996. BS cum laude, St. Bonaventure Coll., 1951; MD, N.Y. Med. Coll., 1956. Diplomate Am. Bd. Internal Medicine. Intern Henry Ford Hosp., Detroit, 1956-57; resident Georgetown med. div. D.C. Gen. Hosp., Washington, 1957-59, Georgetown U. Hosp., Washington, 1958-59; fellow medicine Nat. Inst. Arthritis and Metabolic Diseases, 1959-60, Am. Diabetes Assn., 1960-61; practice medicine, specializing in diabetes and endocrinology U. Miami. (Fla.) Sch. Medicine, prof. medicine, 1969—, Mary Lou Held prof. medicine, 1981-96, chief div. endocrinology and metabolism, dept. medicine, 1969-80, sci. dir. Diabetes Research Inst., 1980-96, sci. dir. emeritus, 1996—; asst. prof. medicine Georgetown U. Sch. Medicine, 1963-64; assoc. prof. medicine U. Pitts. Sch. Medicine, 1964-69; chief svc. Georgetown U. Med. div. D.C. Gen. Hosp., Washington, 1963-64; chief medicine Magee-Women's Hosp., Pitts., 1964-69. Guest prof. U. Geneva, 1976—77. Contbr. articles to profl. jours. Fellow: ACP; mem.: Am. Assn. Physicians. Soc. Soc. Clin. Investigation, Ctrl. Soc. Clin. Investigation, Am. Soc. Clin. Investigation, Am. Fedn. Clin. Rsch., Am. Diabetes Assn., Endocrine Soc. Office: U Miami Diabetes Rsch Inst PO Box 016960 R-77 Miami FL 33101-6960

**MINTZ, DONNA PIERCE**, elementary school educator; d. George Franklin and Eva Lawrence Pierce; m. Ronald Lee Mintz, Aug. 3, 1980; children: Holly Melissa, Joshua Kyle, Rebecca Leigh, Ronald Lee Jr.(dec.). BS, Appalachian State U., Boone, N.C., 1979. Cert. reading instrm. K-12 N.C., 1979. Reading tchr. Kings Mountain Schs., NC, 1980—82, elem. tchr., 1982—87; preschool educator First Bapt. Ch., Jamestown, NC, 1989—90; elem. tchr. Guilford County Schs., Greensboro, NC, 1993—94; reading specialist Davidson County Schs., Lexington, NC, 1994—. Staff devel. leader Davidson County Schs., Thomasville, NC, 1996—. Vol. United Way, Thomasville, NC, 2005—06. Named Tchr. of Yr., Brier Creek Elem. Sch., 2006. Mem.: N.C. Reading Assn., Internat. Reading Assn., Appalachian State U. Alumni ASsn., Phi Delta Kappa (assoc.). Home: 916 New Hampshire Dr Jamestown NC 27282 Office: Davidson County Schools 175 Watford Rd Thomasville NC 27360 Business E-Mail: dmintz@davidson.k12.nc.us.

**MINTZ, JACK MAURICE**, think tank executive, economics educator; b. Edmonton, Alta., Can., Mar. 6, 1951; s. David Benjamin and Clara (Abramovich) M.; m. Eleanor Janice Schwartz, Aug. 31, 1975; children: Avi Ilan, Gaela Lana. B.A. with honors, U. Alta., Edmonton, 1973; M.A., Queen's U., Kingston, Ont., Can., 1974; Ph.D., U. Essex, Colchester, Eng., 1980. Cons. Econ. Council Can., Ottawa, Ont., 1974-75; assoc. prof. econs. Queen's U., Kingston, 1978-89; prof. J.L. Rotman Sch. Mgmt., U. Toronto, 1989-; pres., CEO, C.D. Howe Inst.; bd. dirs. Brascan, Ont. Financing Authority, CHC Ltd. Author: Most Favored Nation, 2001 (Donner prize, Davis prize); contbr. articles to profl. jours. Royal Ont. Mus. Found. Commonwealth fellow, Eng., 1975-78; postdoctoral fellow Social Sci. and Humanities Rsch. Coun. Can., 1981-82, Inst. Mgmt., 1984. Mem. Can. Econs. Assn., Am. Econs. Assn., Am. Fin. Assn., Nat. Stats. Coun. Lodge: B'nai B'rith Youth Orgn. (internat. pres. 1969-70, exec. mem. 1983-84). Avocations: running, squash. Office: CD Howe Inst 67 Yonge St Toronto ON M5E 1J8 Canada Office Phone: 416-865-1904.

**MINTZ, M. J.**, lawyer; b. Phila., Oct. 29, 1940; s. Arthur and Lillian (Altenberg) Mintz; m. Judith E. Held; children: Robert A., Christine L. BS, Temple U., 1961, JD, 1968. CPA Pa., D.C.; bar: D.C. Atty. adv. to judge U.S. Tax Ct., Washington, 1968-70; asst. gen. counsel Cost of Living Coun. Exec. Office of Pres., Washington, 1971-73; ptnr. Dickstein, Shapiro & Morin, Washington, 1973—2005, M.J. Mintz, P.C., Washington, 2006—. Adj. prof. George Mason U. Law Sch., Va., 1974—78; advisor U.S. Sec. Labor, Employee Ret. Income Security Act, 1974, Adv. Coun., Washington, 1982—85. Contbr. articles to profl. jours. Apptd. by Pres. Ronald Reagan to adv. com. Pension Benefit Guaranty Corp., 1987, reapptd. and designated chmn. by Pres. George Bush; apptd. by Gov. George Allen of Va. Bd. Va. Pub. Bldg. Authority, 1996—2001, reapptd. by Gov. James Gilmore, 2001—; Rep. candidate Fairfax County Bd. Suprs., 1971. Fellow: Nat. Assn. Watch & Cook Collectors (star), Freeman of the Worshipful Co. of Clockmakers (London); mem.: AICPA, ABA, Antiquarian Horological Soc. (London), Naval Club (London), Chappaquiddick Beach Club, Met. Club (Washington), Belle Haven Country Club, Cosmos Club. Avocation: antiquarian horologist.

**MINTZ, MARSHALL GARY**, lawyer; b. Detroit, May 28, 1947; BA, UCLA, 1968, JD, 1971. Bar: Calif. 1972. Law clk. appellate dept L.A. County Superior Ct., 1971-72; ptnr. Kelly Lytton Mintz & Vann, LLP, L.A., Calif., 1995-2001; of counsel Sidley & Bell LLP, L.A., 2001—03; mem. Mintz & Werner, L.A., 2003—. Moderator, panelist Calif. Continuing Edn. of Bar, 1980—; mem. arbitration adminstrv. com. L.A. County Superior Ct., 1979, mem. 1984 Olympics spl. settlement panel; mem. arbitration panel L.A. Superior Ct., 1999—; lectr. Lorman Ednl. Seminars, 2002-. Mem. ABA State Bar Calif., L.A. County Bar Assn. (arbitrator arbitration and client rels. com. 1978-99), Assn. Bus. Trial Lawyers (bd. govs. 1976-77, program chmn. 1976). Office: 1801 Century Park E Ste 2400 Los Angeles CA 90067-2326 Office Phone: 310-556-9692. E-Mail: mgmintz@earthlink.net.

**MINTZ, MORTON ABNER**, writer, reporter; b. Ann Arbor, Mich., Jan. 26, 1922; s. William and Sarah (Solomon) M.; m. Anita Inez Franz, Aug. 30, 1946; children— Margaret Ruth, Elizabeth Diane (dec.), Roberta Joan, Daniel Robert. AB in Econs, U. Mich., 1943. Reporter St. Louis Star-Times, 1946-50; reporter, asst. city editor St. Louis Globe-Democrat, 1951-58; reporter Washington Post, 1958-88. Former chair Fund for Investigative Journalism; sr. advisor niemanwatchdog.org. Author: The Therapeutic Nightmare, 1965, By Prescription Only, 1967, The Pill: An Alarming Report, 1969,

At Any Cost: Corporate Greed, Women, and the Dalkon Shield, 1985, (with Jerry S. Cohen) America, Inc.: Who Owns and Operates the United States, 1971, Power, Inc.; Public and Private Rulers and How to Make Them Accountable, 1976, (with others) In the Name of Profit: Profiles in Corporate Irresponsiblity, 1972, More Bucks, Less Bang: How the Pentagon Buys Ineffective Weapons, 1983. Recipient Heywood Broun, Raymond Clapper, George Polk awards for journalism, 1962, A.J. Liebling award, 1974, Worth Bingham Meml. award, 1976, Columbia Journalism award, 1983, Hugh M. Hefner First Amendment award for lifetime achievement, 1996. Mem.: Com. Concerned Journalists. E-mail: mintzm@earthlink.net.

**MINTZ, NORMAN NELSON**, investment banker, educator, retired academic administrator; b. N.Y.C., Sept. 18, 1934; s. Alexander and Rebecca (Nelson) M.; m. Marcia Lynn Belford, Aug. 27, 1960; children: Geoffrey Belford, Douglas Nelson. AB, Bucknell U., 1955; PhD, NYU, 1966. Asst. gen. mgr. Ross Products Inc., N.Y.C., 1957-59; media analyst Benton & Bowles Inc., N.Y.C., 1960; asst. prof. fin. Syracuse (N.Y.) U., 1965-69; asst. prof. econs. Columbia U., N.Y.C., 1968-72, assoc. dean Grad. Sch. Arts and Scis., 1972-77, dep. provost, 1977-80, acting provost, 1978-79, sr. v.p., 1980-82, exec. v.p. for acad. affairs, 1982-89, exec. v.p., ret., 1990—; mng. dir. Loeb Ptnrs. Corp., 1990—. Economist U.S.-P.R. Commn. on Status of P.R., 1965-66; bd. dirs. Loeb Holding Corp., Loeb Ptnrs. Corp., Sr. Network, Inc., KmX Corp., AdChek, Inc., Evare, L.L.C., Intersections, Inc., Loeb Arbitrage Fund., Ultramercial, LLC. Author: Monetary Union and Economic Integration, 1970; contbr. articles to profl. jours. Dir. Citizens Budget Commn., Conf. on Jewish Social Studies, 1975—94, N.Y.C. Coun. on Econ. Edn., 1993—. 1st lt. Signal Corps. U.S. Army, 1955—57. Earhart Found. fellow, 1963-65. Mem. Am. Econ. Assn., Am. Fin. Assn., Royal Econ. Soc., India House Club, Phi Beta Kappa, Omicron Delta Epsilon. Office: care Loeb Ptnrs 61 Broadway New York NY 10006-2701 Office Phone: 212-483-7041. E-mail: nmintz@loebpartners.com.

**MINTZ, SAMUEL ISAIAH**, language educator, writer; b. N.Y.C., Nov. 20, 1923; Nathan and Anna (Sheinkman) M.; m. Eleanor Streichler, Mar. 2, 1947; children: Joel Alan, Jonathan. BA, Bklyn. Coll., 1948; MA, Columbia U., 1949, PhD, 1958. Prof. City Coll. N.Y., N.Y.C., 1948-86, prof. doctoral faculty, 1965-86, prof. emeritus, 1986—, CUNY Grad. Ctr., N.Y.C., 1986—. English faculty Cambridge U., Eng., 1964-65, vis. prof. Columbia U., N.Y.C., 1969-70, Barnard Coll., N.Y.C., 1987-89; vis. fellow Wolfson Coll. Oxford U., 1973. Author: The Hunting of Leviathan, 1962, 2d edit., 1996; editor: From Smollett to Henry James, 1980; founder, editor History Ideas Newsletter, N.Y.C., 1954-60; contbr. articles to profl. jours. With Army Air Force, 1943—46. Fulbright fellow Cambridge U., 1956-57, rsch. scholar, 1964-65, Guggenheim fellow, 1964. Office: City U NY Grad Sch 365 5th Ave New York NY 10016-4309

**MINTZ, SHLOMO**, conductor, violist; b. Moscow, Oct. 30, 1957; came to U.S., 1974; s. Abraham and Eve (Labko) M.; m. Corina Ciacci; children: Eliav David, Alexander. Studied with Ilona Feher; Diploma, Juilliard Sch. Music, 1979. Judge internat Tchaikovsky Competition, Moscow, 1990; juror queen Elisabeth Internat. Music Competition, Brussels, 1993. Concerto debut with Israel Philharm.; violin solo recordings include Violin Concertos by Mendelssohn and Bruch (Grand prix du Disque Diapason d'or), 1981, Complete Sonatas and Partitas for Solo Violin by J.S. Bach, The Miraculous Mandarin-Two Portraits (with Abbado/Chicago Symphony Orchestra) by Bartok, Compositions and Arrangements (with Clifford Benson, piano) by Kreisler, Violin Concerto; also Bruch: Violin Concerto Number 1 (with Abbado/Chgo. Symphony Orchestra) by Mendelssohn, Twenty-Four Caprices by Paganini, Two Violin Concertos (with Abbado/London Symphony Orchestra) by Prokofiev, The Four Seasons (with Stern, Perlman, Mehta) by Vivaldi, Vivaldi violin concertos, Vols. I & II (with Israel Chamber Orch.), 1992, Collection String Symphonies, Vol. III to X, (with Israel Chamber Orch.), 1992, Violin and Viola Sonatas by Chostakovich (with V. Postnikova); apptd. music advisor, chief condr., soloist Israel Chamber Orch., 1989-93; artistic advisor, prin. guest condr. Limburg Symphony Orch., Maastricht, The Netherlands, 1994; condr. London Symphony Orch., Berlin Radio Symphony, Balt. Symphony, Detroit Symphony, Rotterdam Philharm.; soloist with Montreal Symphony, Nat. Symphony, Washington, Carnegie Hall, Tonhalle Orch. of Zurich, Spanish Nat. Orch., Israel Philharm., others. Recipient Premio Accademia Musicale, Chigiana Siena, Italy, 1984. Uses Zahn violin made by Stradivarius, and a Carlo-Guiseppe Testrove viola. Office: ICM Artists Inc 40 W 57th St Fl 16 New York NY 10019-4098

**MINTZ, STEVEN H.**, history professor; b. Detroit, Feb. 16, 1953; s. Marvin F. and Esther (Sklar) M.; m. Susan Kellogg, July 18, 1983; children: Seth, Sean. BA, Oberlin (Ohio) Coll., 1973; MA, Yale U., 1975, PhD, 1979. Asst. prof. history Oberlin Col., 1978-80; assoc. prof. history U. Houston, 1981—, and John and Rebecca Moores Scholar. Guest prof. Universitat Siegen, Fed. Republic of Germany, 1985-86; vis. scholar Ctr. for European Studies, Harvard U., Cambridge, Mass., 1989-90; cons. Nat. Mus. Am. History, Smithsonian Inst., Washington, 1988—. Author: A Prison of Expectations, 1983, America and Its People, 1988, African American Voices: The Life Cycle of Slavery, 1999, Moralists and Modernizers: America's Pre-Civil War Reformers, 1995, Native American Voices: A History & Anthology, 2000, Huck's Raft, 2004 (Carr P. Collins Award for Best Book of Nonfiction, Tex.Inst. Letters, 2005), (with others) Domestic Revolutions, 1988. Mem. Phi Beta Kappa. Jewish. Office: Dept History Bldg AH Univ Houston 4800 Calhoun Rd Houston TX 77204-0001*

**MINTZ, SUZANNE**, association executive; b. Feb. 1946; m. Steven Mintz. BA, Queens Coll., City U. NY; MS, U. Md. Architect; pres., co-founder Nat. Family Caregivers Assn., Wash., DC, 1993—. Bd. dirs. Nat. Patient Safety Found.; adv. bd. Easter Seals, Nat. Assn. Hosp. Hospitality Houses. Author: Love, Honor and Value: A Family Caregiver Speaks Out About the Choices and Challenges of Caregiving, 2002; writer about caregiver issues. Recipient Lilly Welcome Back award for lifetime achievement, 2004. Achievements include has testified before Congress about caregiver issues. Office: Nat Family Caregivers Assn 10400 Conn Ave #500 Kensington MD 20895-3944 Office Phone: 800-896-3650. Office Fax: 301-942-2302.

**MINTZES, JOEL J.**, biology professor, researcher; b. LA, Dec. 13, 1947; s. Herbert and Shirley Mintzes; m. Susan S. Solomon, June 22, 1969; 1 child, Aaron Lewis. BS, U. Ill., 1970, MS, 1971; PhD, Northwestern U., Evanston, Ill., 1974. Asst. prof. U. Ill., Chgo., 1974, U. Windsor, Ontario, Canada, 1974—79; assoc. to full prof. biology U. NC, Wilmington, 1979—. Vis. prof. sci. edn. Tata Inst. Fundamental Rsch., Bombay, 2003; vis. ecology scholar Providence U., Taichung, Taiwan, 2004. Editor: Handbook of College Science Teaching; contbr. scientific papers. Mem. B'nai Israel Congregation, Wilmington, NC, 1990—95. Recipient Sci. Edn. Award Merit, Editl. Bd., Sci. Edn., 1984; Fulbright-Technion fellow, Israel Inst. Tech., Haifa, 2004. Mem.: NSTA, Nat. Assn. Rsch. in Sci. Tchg. Achievements include research in conceptual development and cognitive processes in biology; environmental education. Home: 2305 N Lumina Av Wrightsville Beach NC 28480 Office: U NC 601 S College Road Wilmington NC 28403 Office Phone: 910-962-3437. Home Fax: 910-962-4066; Office Fax: 910-962-4066. Business E-Mail: mintzes@uncw.edu.

**MINTZ-HITTNER, HELEN ANN**, physician, researcher; b. Houston, Aug. 12, 1944; d. Bert and Jeanette (Haydis) Mintz; m. David Hittner, Sept. 8, 1968 (div. May 11, 1989); children: Miriam Annette Hittner Tondera, Susan Michelle Hittner, George Jacob Hittner. BA, Rice U., 1965; MD, Baylor Coll. Medicine, 1969. Lic. Tex. Bd. of Med. Examiners, 1969. Intern pediat. Baylor Affiliated Hosps., Houston, 1969—70, resident ophthalmology, 1970—73; fellow pediat. ophthalmology Tex. Children's Hosp., Houston 1973—74; pediat. ophthalmologist Houston, 1974—95; Alfred W. Lasher III prof. pediat. ophthalmology U. Tex. Houston Med. Sch., 1995—. Author: several rsch. reports and jour. articles. Fellow: Am. Acad. Ophthalmology (Honor award 1986, Sr. Honor award 2005); mem.: N.Y. Acad. Medicine, N.Y. Acad. Sci., Ciba Found., Soc. Heed Fellows (life), Assn. Rsch. in Vision and Ophthalmology, Am. Assn. Pediat. Ophthalmology and Strabismus, Phi Beta

Kappa (life), Alpha Omega Alpha (life). Liberal. Jewish. Achievements include discovery of Primary etiology of retinopathy of prematurity; research in Genetic linkage of aniridia to chromosome 11p13 (PAX6); Genetic identification of anterior segment dysgenesis on chromosome 10q25 (PITX3); Genetic identification of anterior segment dysgenesis on chromosome 1p32 (FOXE3); Genetic identification of anterior segment dysgenesis on chromosome 20p11.2 (VSX1). Home: 2400 N Braeswood Blvd #125 Houston TX 77030-4357 Office: U of Tex-Houston Med Sch 6410 Fannin St #920 Houston TX 77030-5204 Personal E-mail: mintzhittner@aol.com. Business E-Mail: Helen.A.Mintz-Hittner@uth.tmc.edu.

**MINUDRI, REGINA URSULA**, librarian, consultant; b. San Francisco, May 9, 1937; d. John C. and Molly (Halter) M. BA, San Francisco Coll. for Women, 1958; MLS, U. Calif., Berkeley, 1959. Reference libr. Menlo Park (Calif.) Pub. Libr., 1959-62; regional libr. Santa Clara County (Calif.) Libr., 1962-68; project coord. Fed. Young Adult Libr. Svcs. Project, Mountain View, Calif., 1968-71; dir. profl. svcs. Alameda County (Calif.) Libr., 1971, asst. county libr., 1972-77; libr. dir. Berkeley Pub. Libr., 1977-94; city libr. San Francisco Pub. Libr., 1997-2000. Lectr. U. San Francisco, 1970-72, U. Calif., Berkeley, 1977-81, 91-93, San Jose State U., 1994-97; cons., 1975-90; mem. adv. bd. Miles Cutter Ednl., 1992-98. Author: Getting It Together, A Young Adult Bibliography, 1970; contbr. articles to publs. including Sch. Libr. Jour., Wilson Libr. Bull. Bd. dirs. No. Calif. ACLU, 1994-96, Cmty. Memory, 1989-91, Berkeley Pub. Libr. Found., 1996-99; bd. dirs. Berkeley Cmty. Fund, 1995-99, chair youth com., 1994-96; mem. bd. mgrs. ctrl. br. Berkeley YMCA, 1988-93. Recipient proclamation Mayor of Berkeley, 1985, 86, 94, Citation of Merit, Calif. State Assembly, 1994; named Woman of Yr., Alameda County North chpt. Nat. Women's Polit. Caucus, 1985, Outstanding Alumna, U. Calif. Sch. Libr. and Info. Scis., Berkeley, 1987, Lifetime Achievement award Berkeley Cmty. Fund, 2001. Mem. ALA (pres. 1986-87, exec. bd. 1980-89, coun. 1979-88, 90-94, Grolier award 1974), Calif. Libr. Assn. (pres. 1981, coun. 1965-69, 79-82), LWV (dir. Berkeley chpt. 1980-81, v.p. comm. svcs. 1995-97). Office: Reality Mgmt 836 The Alameda Berkeley CA 94707-1916

**MINZNER, PAMELA BURGY**, state supreme court justice; b. Meridian, Miss., Nov. 19, 1943; BA cum laude, Miami U., 1965; LLB, Harvard U., 1968. Bar: Mass. 1968, N.Mex. 1972. Pvt. practice, Mass., 1968—71, Albuquerque, 1971—73; adj. prof. law U. N.Mex., Albuquerque, 1972—73, asst. prof., 1973—77, assoc. prof., 1977—80, prof. law, 1980—84; judge N.Mex. Ct. Appeals, Albuquerque, 1984—94, chief judge, 1993—94; justice N.Mex. Supreme Ct., Santa Fe, 1994—, chief justice, 1999—2001. Mem. faculty Inst. Preparatoi Legal U., N.Mex. Sch. Law, 1975, 79; participant NEH Summer Seminars for Law Tchrs. Stanford Law Sch., 1982, U. Chgo. Law Sch., 1978. Author (with Robert T. Laurence): A Student's Guide to Estates in Land and Future Interests: Text, Examples, Problems & Answers, 1981, 2d edit., 1993. Mem.: ABA, State Bar N.Mex. (co-editor newsletter 1979—83, bd. dirs. 1978—79, 1983—84, sect. on women's legal rights and obligations), Gamma Phi Beta. Democrat. Avocations: reading, bridge, movies. Office: Supreme Ct NMex PO Box 848 Santa Fe NM 87501-0848*

**MIOTKE, DAVID ROY**, music educator; b. Appleton, Wis., Nov. 30, 1956; s. George Charles and Mary Mae Miotke; m. Sherril Grace Miotke, Oct. 23, 1982. BS, Carroll Coll., 1979. Band dir., music tchr. Reedsburg (Wis.) Sch. Dist., 1979—. Instrumental dir. Choraliers Show Choir, Reedsburg, 1981—2004; tech. coord. Cal Ctr., Reedsburg, 1999—; pres. Reedsburg (Wis.) Players, 2005—. Composer: (full band commn.) Shiva Dance, 1989, March for Bosiphus, 1989. Hand bell choir dir. St. John Luth. Ch., Reedsburg, 1992—. Recipient Woodson Outstanding Tchr. award, Reedsburg Edn. Found., 2002. Mem.: Wis. Youth Band Dirs. Assn. (pres.), Music Educators Nat. Conf. Avocation: working puzzles, writing music, painting. Office: Webb Mid Sch 707 N Webb Ave Reedsburg WI 53959 Office Phone: 608-524-2328. E-mail: david.miotke@verizon.net.

**MIQUELON, MIRIAM F.**, former prosecutor, lawyer; b. Elmhurst, Ill. children: Aaron, Rachel. Grad., U. Ariz., 1975, DePaul U., 1978; LLM in Taxation, Chgo.-Kent Coll. Law; postgrad. in Taxation, DePaul U.; postgrad. in History, Northwestern U. Lawyer, Houston, Stone, McGuire, Benjamin & Kocoras, Miquelon and Assocs., 1981—88, Keck, Mahin & Cate, Chgo., 1988—91; asst. U.S. atty. Ea. Dist. N.Y., Bklyn., 1991—93, So. Dist. Ill., 1993—99; asst. spl. counsel to Spl. Counsel John C. Danforth, 1999—2000; asst. U.S. atty. So. Dist. Ill., 2000—02, U.S. atty., 2002—03. Adj. prof. law Washington U. Sch. Law, St. Louis; adj. faculty Northwestern U. Coll. Law, Chgo. Recipient Chief Postal Inspector's award, U.S. Postal Inspection Svc., 2001, Spl. commendations, FBI, Drug Enforcement Adminstrn., U.S. Customs Svc., IRS. Avocations: volunteering, sports activities.

**MIR, ALEKSANDRA**, artist; b. Lubin, Poland, 1967; Communication & Media studies, Schillerska/Gothenburg U., Gothenburg, 1986—87; BFA in Media Arts, Sch. Visual Arts, NY, 1992; Grad. Faculty Cultural Anthropology, New Sch. Social Rsch., NY, 1994—96. One-man shows include Life is Sweet in Sweden, Trixter, Gothenburg, 1995, Pick UP (oh baby), Lyd/Galerie, Copenhagen, 1997, City Forest (prototype), Tompkins Sq. Pk., NY, 1998, Conspiracy Night, Swiss Inst., NY, 1999, Gavin Brown's enterprise, NY, 2001, Corp. Mentality, Lukas & Sternberg, NY, 2002, Naming Tokyo (part II), Swiss Inst., NY, 2003, Happy Holidays, The Wrong Gallery, NY, 2003, The Big Umbrella (NY), PS1 Contemporary Art Ctr., NY, 2004, New Commission, Fundacion NMAC, Montenmedio, 2005, exhibited in group shows at Empires without States, Swiss Inst., NY, 1999, Democracy!, Royal Coll. Art, London, 2000, COPY, Roth Horowitz Gallery, NY, 2002, The Twentieth Anniversary Show, Gavin Brown's enterprise, NY, 2003, Sandwiched, Jacob Fabricius, NY, 2003, Power, Corruption & Lies, Roth Horowitz, NY, 2004, Calif. Earthquakes, Daniel Reich Gallery, NY, 2004, Whitney Biennial, Whitney Mus. Am. Art, 2004. Mailing: c/o Andrew Roth 160 A East 70th St New York NY 10021 E-mail: aleksandra_mir@hotmail.com.

**MIRABELLO, FRANCIS JOSEPH**, lawyer; b. Ft. Lauderdale, Fla., Mar. 2, 1954; s. Frank Guy and Mary (Sorce) M.; m. Marianna Hay O'Neal, Aug. 5, 1978; childen: Diana H., A. Paul. BS in Civil Engring., Princeton U., 1975; JD, Harvard U., 1978. Bar: Calif. 1978, Pa. 1981, Fla. 1983. Assoc. Irell & Manella, Los Angeles, 1978-81; ptnr. Morgan, Lewis & Bockius, Phila., 1981—, mng. personal law practice group. Lectr. law Villanova (Pa.) U. Law Sch., adj. prof. law U. Pa., Phila. Mem. ABA, ACTEC. Clubs: Merion Cricket, Phila. Skating, Commonwealth Nat. Golf. Avocations: tennis, golf. Office: Morgan Lewis & Bockius 1701 Market St Philadelphia PA 19103-2903 Office Phone: 215-963-5248. Office Fax: 215-963-5001. Business E-Mail: fmirabello@morganlewis.com.

**MIRABILE, RUSSELL MICHAEL**, lawyer; b. Bklyn., Sept. 29, 1947; s. Nicholas Robert and Ann (Cardello) M.; children: Melissa, Danielle, Jordan. BA, Bklyn. Coll., 1969; JD, St. John's U., 1971; LLM, NYU, 1980. Bar: N.Y. 1975, U.S. Dist. ct. (ea. dist) N.Y. 1975, U.S. Ct. Appeals (2d cir.) 1975, U.S. Supreme Ct. 1978. Asst. dist. atty. County of N.Y., N.Y.C., 1974-78; claims atty. U.S. Aviation Underwriters, Inc., N.Y.C., 1978-83, v.p. claims, v.p. subrogation dept., 1983-85, v.p., products liability counsel, 1985-87, v.p. products liability counsel 1987-90, sr. v.p., dir. claims, 1990—. Mem. ABA (co-chair aviation litigation sect. 1987-97, chmn. aviation and space law com. 2000-02), N.Y. State Bar Assn., Internat. Assn. Def. Counsel, Assn. Bar City N.Y. (aeronautics com.), Fedn. Ins. Counsel. Avocations: golf, skiing, tennis. Office: US Aviation Underwriters 199 Water St 15th Fl New York NY 10038-3580 Office Phone: 212-859-3810. E-mail: rmirabil@usau.com.

**MIRABITO, ANTHONY JASON**, law educator, lawyer; b. NYC, Jan. 29, 1948; s. Anthony Joseph Mirabito and Jean Theresa (Cultrone) Mirobito; m. Marjorie Rose Berger, July 7, 1974; children: Katherine Rose, Andrew. BS in Engring. Physics, NYU, 1965—69; JD, Am. U., 1973; LLM in Taxation, Georgetown U., 1975. Bar: Pa. 1974, DC 1975, Mass. 1981, registered: US Patent & Trademark Office 1977. Patent examiner, atty. US Patent & Trademark Office, Arlington, Va., 1969—75; atty. US Dept.

Commerce, Washington, 1975—77, US Internat. Trade Commn., Washington; in-house counsel Westinghouse Electric Co., Pitts., 1979—80; legal cons. Mass. computer & software cos., Boston area, 1980—; of counsel Gaston Snow & Ely Bartlett, Boston, 1984, head, patent dept.; ptnr., Intellectual Property Law Wolf, Greenfield & Sacks; founding ptnr., co-chmn., Intellectual Property Law Sect. Mintz Levin Cohn Ferris Glovsky & Popeo PC, Boston. Assoc. prof. law Suffolk U. Law Sch., Boston, 1980—; lectr. in field. Contbr. articles to law reviews; editor: Foreign Investment in US, 1977. Mem.: Pa. Bar Assn., Mass. Bar Assn., ABA, DC Bar Assn. (Internat. Law Sect.), Boston Bar Assn., Small Bus. Assn. of New Eng., Boston Patent Law Assn. (former pres.), Winchester Boat Club (Mass.). Achievements include being named inventor on two US Patents. Office: Mintz Levin Cohn Ferris Glovsky & Popeo PC One Financial Ctr Boston MA 02111 also: Suffolk U Law Sch 41 Temple St Boston MA 02114-4241 Office Phone: 617-348-1805. Office Fax: 617-542-2241. Business E-Mail: jmirabito@mintz.com.

**MIRACLE, DORIS JEAN,** retired medical/surgical nurse; b. Louisville, July 23, 1931; d. Bernard Louis and Catherine Federle; m. Earl Miracle, Aug. 31, 1951; 1 child, David. Surg. nurse Norton Hosp., Louisville, 1951, Norton-Children's Hosp., Louisville, 1969—86; ret., 1986. Poetry (albums) Sounds of Poetry, 2003; contbr. poems to mags., poetry to anthologies, articles to profl. jours. Recipient Editors Choice award, 2003, 2006. Mem.: Wilderness Rd. Writers, Gaslight Writers, Ky. Writer's Coalition, Internat. Soc. of Poets, Soc. Children's Book Writers and Illustrators, Louisville Astronomical Soc. Avocations: reading, poetry, astronomy, art, music. Personal E-mail: doriskitm@aol.com.

**MIRACLE, GORDON ELDON,** advertising educator; b. Olympia, Wash., May 28, 1930; s. Gordon Tipler and Corine Adriana (Orlebeke) M.; m. Christa Stoeter, June 29, 1957; children. Gary, Gregory, Glenn. BBA, U. Wis., 1952, MBA, 1958, PhD, 1962. Case officer, civilian intelligence analyst U.S. Army, Fed. Republic Germany, 1955-57; instr. commerce U. Wis. Grad. Sch. Bus., Madison, 1958-60; instr., then asst. prof. mktg. U. Mich., Ann Arbor, 1960-66; assoc. prof. advt. Mich. State U., East Lansing, 1966-70, chmn. PhD program in mass media, 1973-74, chmn. dept., 1974-80, prof. advt., 1970-99, prof. emeritus, 1999—. Vis. prof. mktg. mgmt. N. European Mgmt. Inst., Oslo, 1972-73; cons., lectr. in field. Author: Management of International Advertising, 1966; co-author: International Marketing Management, 1970, Advertising and Government Regulation, 1979, Instructor's Manual for International Marketing Management, 1971, European Regulation of Advertising: Supranational Regulation of Advertising in the European Economic Community, 1986, Voluntary Regulation of Advertising: A Comparative Analysis of the United Kingdom and the United States, 1987, (in Korean) Cultures in Advertising: Advertising in Cultures, 1990; contbr. articles to scholarly and profl. jours.; editor: Marketing Decision Making: Strategy and Payoff, 1965, Sharing for Understanding, Proc. Ann. Conf. Am. Acad. Advt., 1977. Served with AUS, 1952-55. Recipient first Biennial Excellence in Advt. award, U. Ill., 1995; Ford Found. fellow, 1961-62, 64, Am. Assn. Advt. Agys. fellow Marsteller, Inc., 1967, Advt. Ednl. Found. fellow McCann-Erickson Hakuhodo, 1985, Fulbright rsch. fellow Waseda U., Tokyo, 1985; recipient numerous grants; recipient Viktor-Mataja medal Austrian Advt. Rsch. Assn., Vienna, 1999. Fellow: Am. Acad. Advt. (treas., exec. com. 1978—79); mem.: Internat. Advt. Assn., Internat. Advt. Assn. ((ednl. accreditation com. 1993—95, internat. advt. edn. group 1996—2001), Am. Mktg. Assn., Acad. Internat. Bus. (sec., exec. com. 1973—75), Adcraft Club Detroit. Home: 10025 Oak Island Dr Laingsburg MI 48848-8718 Office: Mich State U Dept Advt East Lansing MI 48824 Business E-Mail: miracle@msu.edu.

**MIRACLE, NANCY,** foundation administrator, writer; b. NYC, Sept. 14, 1946; Acting student with Lee Strasberg, Carnegie Hall Studios, N.Y.C., 1955—62; tutored in classical lit. and writing, N.Y.C., 1963—66; student, Manhattan C.C., N.Y.C., 1965—69; student, creative writing, New Sch. for Social Rsch., N.Y.C., 1971—76; MFA in Creative Writing, Goddard Coll., 1979; tutored, Ibiza, Spain, 1979—80. Lectr. Marymount Coll., N.Y.C., 1979; tutor CUNY, N.Y.C., 1983; condr. workshops Women's Internat. Writing Group, N.Y.C., 1976—82; tchr. YMCA Writing Workshops, Honolulu, 1988—89, St. Louis Sch., Honolulu, 1993—94; tutor U. Hawaii, Honolulu, 1990—2000; pres. and founder Marilyn Monroe Found., Honolulu, N.Y.C., 1985—. Actor(lead): 2 plays, 1955—58; author: (novels) Lesser Sins, 1979, Venus Oh So Bright, 1994, Here I Am Mother, 1985; contbr. chapters to books; author: (play) Here I Am Mother, 2004 (Am. Book award, 1985). Mem.: Dramatists Guild. Avocations: dance, theater, gym, swimming, yoga. Office Phone: 212-560-7505. Business E-Mail: marilynmonroefoundation@yahoo.com.

**MIRAGLIA, PETER F.,** artist, photographer; b. Glen Cove, N.Y., July 11, 1953; s. Anthony and Frances (Pitrone) M. Group and solo exhbns. include Painted Bride Art Ctr., Phila., 1982, Calif. Mus. Photography, Riverside, 1983, Marcuse Pfeifer Gallery, N.Y.C., 1987, Haupert Art Gallery, Bethlehem, Pa., 1988, Viridian Gallery, N.Y.C., 1988, Helio Galleries, N.Y.C., 1988, Del. Ctr. for Contemporary Arts, Wilmington, 1989, Creative Photography Gallery, Dayton, Ohio, 1989, Phila. Mus. Art, 1990, Hartnett Art Gallery, Rochester, N.Y., 1991, Alternative Mus., N.Y.C., 1991, C.C. Phila., 1992, Ctr. Photography at Woodstock, N.Y., 1993, Allentown (Pa.) Art Mus., 1993, Phila. Art Alliance, 1994, Ctr. Photog. Art, Carmel, Calif., 1994, Photog. Resource Ctr., Boston, 1996, Levering Gallery, Phila., 1996, Bucks County C.C., Pa., 1997, Pitts. Filmmakers Gallery, 1997, Tyler Sch. of Art, Temple U., Phila., 1997, Del. Art Mus., Wilmington, 1998, Samuel S. Fleisher Art Meml. of Phila. Mus. Art, 1998, The Print Ctr., Phila., 2000, Del. Ctr. for the Contemporary Arts, Wilmington, 2000, Lancaster Mus. Art, Pa. 2001, Phoenix Gallery, N.Y.C., 2001, Krasdale Gallery, N.Y.C., 2001, The Print Ctr., Phila, 2002, 06, Univ. Arts, Phila., 2002, Del Ctr. Contemporary Arts, Wilmington, 2002, JMS Gallery, Phila, 2004, Allentown Art Mus., 2005, Villanova U. Gallery, 2006; represented in permanent collections Villanova U., Rowan U. N.J., PNC Bank, The Print Ctr, Moravian Coll, Lehigh U. Art Gallerion, Erie Art Cu., Dayton Art Inst., The Ctr. Photography, Woodstock, N.Y., Calif. Mus. Photography, Balt. Mus. Art, Phila. Mus. Art; featured in: Contemporary Philadelphia Artists - The Phila. Mus. Art, 1990, Beyond Aesthetics: Artworks of Conscience, 1991, The Photo Rev., 2000, Photographer's Forum, 2000, About Face, 2000. Recipient Excellence award Perkins Ctr. for Arts, 1984, Pa. Coun. Arts Spl. Opportunity Stipend award, 2002, 1st prize Photo Rev. Nat. Competition, 1994; named one of Outstanding Young Men of Am., 1987; Visual Arts fellow Pa. Coun. on Arts, 1987, 97, 99, 2005, Visual Arts fellow NEA, 1988; grantee, Artists Space, 1988. Home: 208 Catharine St Philadelphia PA 19147-3303 Personal E-mail: petermiraglia@mac.com.

**MIRAN, PATRICIA MARIE,** art educator; b. Seattle, Apr. 6, 1951; d. Robert Glenroy Hancock and Bernice Iris Brisky; m. Maynard Alvin Miran, May 1, 1983; children: Maxwell, Jacob, Emma. Diploma in fine arts illustration, Art Students League, N.Y.C., 1974; BS cum laude, Excelsior Coll., 2001. Childrens story hr. dir. Sayre Libr., 1989—95; exec. dir. Lincoln Acad., Waverly, NY, 1998—2004; tchr. Jewish Cmty. Sch., Elmira, NY, 1999—. Libr. dir. Cady Libr., Nichols, NY, 1996; tutor, remedial reading M-G Edn., Elmira, 2001—; instr. Elmira Bus. Inst., 2005—06, pvt. painting lessons, 2006—. Rep. 4-H Cornell Coop. Ext., Owego, NY, 1999—2001. Grantee, N.Y. State Coun. on Arts, 1994—96; scholar, Calif. Coll. Arts and Crafts, 1969—70, Art Student League, 1974. Avocations: gardening, birdwatching, hiking, canoeing, painting. Home and Office: 21 Lincoln St Waverly NY 14892 Office: Jewish Cmty Sch PO Box 3087 1008 W Water St Elmira NY 14905 Personal E-Mail: mmiran@stny.rr.com.

**MIRANDA, CARLOS SA,** food products company executive; b. Fall River, Mass., Nov. 16, 1929; s. Carlos Sa and Annette (Pratt) M.; m. Natalie Cardoso, Sept. 5, 1949; children: Carla, Lucy, John. BS in Mech. Engring., Marquette U., 1956. With internat. divsn. Kellogg Co., Battle Creek, Mich., 1964—65; gen. mgr. Kellogg Co. Brazil, 1965—80; v.p. Kellogg Internat., Battle Creek, 1980—89; gen. mgr. Kellogg's Spain, 1983—84; country dir. internat. exec. svc. corps. Costa Rica, 1990—91; mediator Fla. County Cts.

1994—. Recipient Pero Vaz Caminha award, Brazil, 1976; conferred title Comdr. of Legion of Honor of Marshal Rondon, Brazil, 1971. Mem. ASME. Independent. Roman Catholic. Home: 8949 Wildlife Loop Sarasota FL 34238

**MIRANDA, M. JEANNE,** psychiatrist; BS, Idaho State U., 1976; MA, U. Kansas, 1983, PhD, 1986. Asst. clin. prof. psychology U. Calif. San Francisco (UCSF), 1988—95, asst. prof. in residence in psychology, 1992—95; assoc. prof. psychology Georgetown U., Washington, 1995—2001; assoc. prof. biobehavioral sciences & psychiatry UCLA Neuropsychiatric Inst., 2001—, assoc. dir. Health Svcs. Rsch. Ctr. Sr. scientific editor Mental Health: Culture, Race, & Ethnicity, 2001. Recipient Interdisciplinary Achievement award, LPPI-UCSF Alumni-Faculty Assn., 1986, R.E. Harris award, UCSF, 1986; fellow, Rehabilitation Svc. Adminstrn., 1980—84; NIMH Clin. Svcs. Rsch. Fellowship, 1986—88. Mem.: Inst. Medicine. Office: Health Svcs Rsch Ctr UCLA Wilshire Ctr Ste 300 10920 Wilshire Blvd Los Angeles CA 90024-6505 Office Phone: 310-794-3710. E-mail: mirandaj@ucla.edu.*

**MIRANDA, ROBERT NICHOLAS,** publishing executive, director; b. Bklyn., July 9, 1934; m. Marilyn H. Pils, May 25, 1958; children: Marilyn, Robert, Susan, Lori, Jennifer. AA in Acctg. and Bus. Adminstrn., SUNY, Farmingdale, 1967. Pres. Pergamon Press, Inc., Elmsford, NY, 1965—92; chmn., CEO Cognizant Communication Corp., Elmsford, 1992—; owner Miranda Press, 2002. Bd. dirs., exec. v.p., vice chmn. Soc. and Assoc. Svc. Corp., McLean, Va., 1979-82; bd. dirs., chmn. electronics com. Copyright Clearance Ctr., 1984-93. Pub. Acupuncture and Electro Therapeutics Rsch., Analgesia, Bird Behavior, Cancer Prevention Internat., Cell Transplantation, Festival Mgmt. and Event Tourism, Gene Expression, Info. Tech. and Tourism, Life Support and Biosphere Sci., Oncology Rsch., Tourism Analysis, Technology: Jour. of Regulatory Sci., Failure and Lessons Learned in Info. Tech., Pacific Tourism Rev., Tourism, Culture and Comm., Tourism Dynamic Book Series, Tourism in Marine Environments, Habitation: An Internat. Jour., Revs. in Analgesia, Event Mgmt., Tourism Rev. Internat., Info. Tech. in Hospitality. Served with USNR, 1954-59. Mem. Internat. Soc. Intelligent Sys. (founder, bd. dirs., fin. dir 1992—). Avocations: hunting, fishing, horseback riding. Office: Cognizant Comm Corp 3 Hartsdale Rd Elmsford NY 10523-3701 Office Phone: 914-592-7720. Personal E-mail: cogcomm@aol.com.

**MIRANDA-LEVI, JASON,** film producer, writer; s. Jose Antonio Miranda and Mercedes Bertolin-Levi; m. Maria L Maria Luisa Echaurren, Nov. 24, 1962; 1 child, Mychele Lina-Marie. BS, Fordham U., 1954—58; JD, St. Johns U., 1958—61. Lic.: NY (Attorney) 1963. Pvt. law practice, NYC, 1964—74. Prodr.: (film and television) Han Matado a Un Cadaver; (TV series) Cara a Cara; author: (novels) The Spanish Enigma, Dancer in the Dark; exhibitions include Photographic Surrealism. Lance cpl. USMC, 1951—53, Korea. Recipient Dama del Paraguas, City of Barcelona, Spain, 1973, La Font de Canaletas, City Coun. of the City of Barcelona, Spain, 1973, Medal of San Jordi, Province of Barcelona, Barcelona, Spain, 1976, Font de Canalinska, City Coun. of Barcelona, Spain, 1975. Mem.: SAG, NY Bar. R-Consevative. Jewish. Avocations: antique watch collector, travel, reading, haute cuisine. Personal E-mail: jmlevi@sbcglobal.net.

**MIRE, WELDON J.,** oil industry executive, human resources specialist; B of Fgn. Lang., U. La., 1971; postgrad., U. Costa Rica. Joined Halliburton, Houston, 1978, sr. shared svcs. mgr., 1998—99, dir. bus. devel., global dir. strategic bus. devel., 1999, sales mgr. Asia Pacific sales, 1999—2001, divsn. v.p., country v.p. for Indonesia, 2001—02, v.p. human resources, 2002—. Office: Halliburton 10200 Bellaire Blvd Houston TX 77020-5299 Office Phone: 281-575-3000. E-mail: weldon.mire@halliburton.com.

**MIRELES, JESSE,** architecture educator, department chairman, academic administrator; b. Houston, Dec. 10, 1947; s. Louis Gomez and Ruth Duron Mireles; m. Mary Louis Phillips, Mar. 25, 1966. AAS in Engring. Draft Tech., San Jacinto CC, Pasadena, Tex., 1971; EdB in Instrn. Indsl. Tech. Edn., U. Houston, 1972, MEd in Curriculum and Instrn., 1973, EdD in Curriculum and Instrn. & Edn. Adminstrn., 1977. Instr. San Jacinto CC, Pasadena; exec. v.p., prin. ptnr. Dickens, Mireles, Patel & Assocs., Inc., 1978—85; asst. prof. Bowling Green State U., Ohio, 1986—87; prof., program dir. Phoenix Coll., 1987—89, exec. asst. to pres., 1990—92, 2002—04, assoc. dean instrn., 1996—97, sr. assoc. dean instrn., 1997—98, dept. chair, 1998—2002, 2004—, caucus chair, 2001—02. Mem. doctoral dissertation com. No. Ariz. U., Flagstaff, 1994—95; mem. strategic planning coun. Phoenix Coll., 2001—; presenter in field. Pres. Pinnacle Peak Crossing Homeowners Assn., 1993—94; mem. planning com. Ariz. Regional Transit Authority, 1996—98. With U.S. Army, 1968—69, Vietnam. Decorated Nat. Def. Svc. medal, Vietnam Svc. medal, Vietnam Campaign medal, Bronze Star; named Maricopa Employee Recognition Tchg. Excellence and Leadership named in his honor, 2001; recipient Brown & Root Tchg. Excellence award, San Jacinto CC, 1977, Assn. Women's Active Return to Edn. award, Phoenix Coll., 1988; grantee Fred. C. Stone Endowment grantee, Bowling Green State U., 1988. Mem.: Phi Theta Kappa. Democrat. Avocation: golf. Home: 4409 W Cielo Grande Glendale AZ 85310 Office: Phoenix Coll 1202 W Thomas Rd Phoenix AZ 85013

**MIRELS, HAROLD,** aerospace engineer; b. N.Y.C., July 29, 1924; s. Hyman and Lily (Efron) M.; m. Nell Segal, Oct. 4, 1953; children: Lily, Laurence Franklin, Jeremy Mark. BSME, Cooper U., 1944; MSME, Case Inst. Tech., 1949; PhD in Aero. Engring., Cornell U., 1953. Sect. head NACA, Cleve., 1944-57; br. chief NASA, Cleve., 1957-61; dept. head Aerospace Corp., El Segundo, Calif., 1961-78, assoc. dir., 1978-84, prin. scientist, 1984-93; cons., 1993—. Co-inventor continuous wave chem. laser. Recipient Tech. Achievement award Cleve. Tech. Socs., 1960. Fellow AIAA (Fluid and Plasmadynamics award 1988), Am. Phys. Soc.; mem. Nat. Acad. Engring. Home: 3 Seahurst Rd Palos Verdes Peninsula CA 90274-1700

**MIRENGOFF, PAUL E.,** lawyer, political blogger; married; 2 children. AB summa cum laude, Dartmouth Coll., 1971; JD, Stanford Law Sch., 1974. Lawyer with Office of Gen. Counsel Equal Opportunity Commn., 1976—81; with Hunton & Williams, Washington, 1981—99; ptnr. Akin Gump Strauss Hauer & Feld LLP, Washington, 1999—. Contbr. (book) Employment Discrimination Law, (book) Sexual Harassment in Employment Law, articles to profl. jours.; published a column about affirmative action Washington Post; author: (blog website) powerlineblog.com, 2002—. Mem.: DC Bar. Office: Akin Gump Strauss Hauer & Feld LLP Robert S Strauss Bldg 1333 New Hampshire Ave NW Washington DC 20036-1564 Office Phone: 202-887-4354. Office Fax: 202-887-4288. Business E-Mail: pmirengoff@akingump.com. E-mail: powerlinefeedback@gmail.com.*

**MIRICK, JOHN O.,** lawyer; b. Worcester, Mass., Nov. 27, 1946; s. Richard W. and Margaret (Whittemore) M.; m. Diane Kay LaHman, Aug. 2, 1969; children: Christopher R., Seth H. BA magna cum laude, Amherst (Mass.) Coll., 1968; MA, University Coll., London, 1969; JD cum laude, Harvard U., 1972. Bar: Mass. 1973, U.S. Dist. Ct. Mass. 1973, U.S. Ct. Appeals (1st cir.) 1974, U.S. Ct. Appeals (2nd cir.) 1979, U.S. Supreme Ct. 1980, U.S. Ct. Appeals (fed. cir.) 2006. Assoc. Hale & Dorr, Boston, 1972-76; ptnr. Mirick, O'Connell, DeMallie & Lougee, Worcester, Mass., 1976—. Trustee Mass. Continuing Legal Edn., 1988-92. Trustee Dynamy, Inc., Worcester, 1979—89, Mass. Bd. Bar Overseers, 1999—2002, chair, 2001—02; mem. Mass. Jud. Nominating Commn., 2003—06. Fulbright scholar, 1969. Mem. ABA, Mass. Bar Assn, Mass. Acad. Trial Attys., Assn. Trial Lawyers Am., Am. Antiquarion Soc., Phi Beta Kappa. Office: Mirick O'Connell DeMallie & Lougee 100 Front St Worcester MA 01608 Office Phone: 508-791-8500. E-mail: jomirick@modl.com.

**MIRIPOL, JERILYN ELISE,** poet, writer, writing therapist; b. Chgo., Jan. 22; d. Albert and Janice (Tuchin) M.; m. Richard Palmer Van Duyne, Dec. 30, 1986. BA in English Lit., Northeastern U., 1974. Writing therapist Northshore Retirement Hotel, Evanston, Ill., 1983; creative writing tchr. Oakton Community Coll., Evanston, 1985—; writing therapist St. Francis

Hosp., Evanston, 1989—. Artist-writer-in-residence Dawes Sch., Evanston, 1985; artist-in-residence Evanston Twp. High Sch., 1988; writing facilitator for individual students, Chgo., 1987—; tchr. writing therapy to mental health profls. and caregivers U. Wis., Milw., 1989; presenter writing therapy workshop, 1990, Nat. Assn. Poetry-Therapy, Chgo., 1991. Author: Discovering Self-Awareness Through Poetry, 1987, (poetry) The Sounds Were Distilled, 1977; author numerous poems; contbr. articles to profl. jours. Vol. Ridgeview Nursing Home, Evanston, 1982-83; advocate of children of abuse, human and civil rights. Talent scholar in creative writing Northeastern Ill. U., Squaw Valley Community Writers scholar, 1980, Radgale Found. scholar, 1985, Aspen Writer's Workshop Breadloaf Writer's Conf. scholar; Danforth fellow nominee; Dawes Sch. grantee, 1987. Mem. NOW, PEN, UNICEF, ACLU, Nat. Assn. Poetry Therapy, Women's Internat. League for Peace, Humanitas Internat. (human rights com.), Amnesty Internat., Am. Acad. Poets, Ill. Alliance of Arts, Pan Pacific Southeast Asia Women's Assn. (v.p.), 11th Ann. Poetry Therapy Conf. (keynote speaker), Greenpeace, Death Penalty Foes. Avocations: music, dance, art, reading, drama, films. Home: 1520 Washington Ave W Wilmette IL 60091-2417 Office Phone: 847-251-6721. Personal E-mail: jmiripol@webtv.net.

**MIRK, JUDY ANN,** retired elementary school educator; b. Victorville, Calif., June 10, 1944; d. Richard Nesbit and Corrine (Berghoefer). BA in Social Sci., San Jose (Calif.) State U., 1966, cert. in teaching, 1967; MA in Edn., Calif. State U., Chico, 1980. Cert. elem. edn. tchr. Calif. Profl. psychology trainee John F. Kennedy U., Orinda, Calif., 1977—99; tchr. Cupertino (Calif.) Union Sch. Dist., 1967-95; lead tchr. lang. arts Dilworth Sch., San Jose, 1988-90, mem. supt.'s adv. team, 1986-90, mem. student study team, 1987-95; ret. Mem. student study team, 1987-95; mem. Dilworth Sch. Site Coun., 1981-95. Mem.: The Commonwealth Club of Calif., Phi Mu. Independent. Avocations: photography, natural history, watercolors.

**MIRKIN, BERNARD LEO,** pharmacologist, pediatrician; b. Bronx, N.Y., Mar. 31, 1928; s. Max and Esther M.; m. Phyllis Korduner, Aug. 1954 (dec. 1982); children: Lisa Mia, Mara Rebecca; m. Sarah Solotaroff, 1986; stepchildren: Jennifer, Rachel, Jacob. AB, NYU, 1949; PhD, Yale U., 1953; MD, U. Minn., 1964. Asst. prof. pharmacology SUNY, Downstate Med. Center, 1954-60; Ford Found. postdoctoral fellow Karolinska Inst., Stockholm, 1960-61; USPHS post-doctoral fellow Yale U., 1961-62; resident in pediatrics U. Minn. Hosp., Mpls., 1964-66; asst. prof. U. Minn. Med. Sch., Mpls., 1966-67, asso. prof., 1967-72; prof. pediatrics, pharmacology and biol. chemistry, dir. div. clin. pharmacology U. Minn. Health Sci. Ctr., 1972-89; prof. pediatrics and molecular pharmacology Northwestern U. Med. Sch., Chgo., 1989—; head, dir. rsch. Inst. for Edn. and Rsch. Children's Meml. Hosp., Chgo., 1989—99; assoc. dean rsch. Northwestern U. Med. Sch., 1994—96; dir. rsch. emeritus Inst. for Edn. and Rsch. Children's Meml. Hosp., Chgo., 2000—. Cons. Office of Technology Assessment, U.S. Congress, WHO, U.S. Pharmacopeia, PhARMA Found., Nat. Inst. Health; fellow Jesus Coll., Oxford U., 1974; Ford Found. postdoctoral fellow Karolinska Inst. Stockholm 1960-61. Author: Perinatal Pharmacology and Therapeutics, 1976, Clinical Pharmacology: A Pediatric Perspective, 1978. Served with M.C. U.S. Army, 1954-56. Mem. AAAS, Soc. Pediat. Rsch., Am. Assn. Cancer Rsch., Am. Pediat. Soc., Am. Soc. Pharm. Exptl. Therapeutics, Am. Soc. Clin. Pharm. and Therapeutics. Home: 427 Greenleaf St Evanston IL 60202-1328 Office: Childrens Meml Inst Edn and Rsch Mailcode # 117 2300 N Childrens Plz Chicago IL 60614-3363 E-mail: b-mirkin@northwestern.edu.

**MIRKIN, GABE BARON,** physician, medical educator, writer, radio personality; b. Brookline, Mass., June 18, 1935; s. Mitchell and Vera (Baron) M.; children: Gene, Jan, Jill, Geoffrey, Kenny; m. Diana Purdie Rich, 1998. BA, Harvard U., 1957; MD, Baylor U., 1961. Diplomate Am. Bd. Pediatrics, Sub Bd. Allergy, Am. Bd. Allergy and Immunology, Am. Bd. Sports Medicine. Resident in pediatrics Mass. Gen. Hosp., Boston, 1961-63; fellow allergy, immunology, dermatology Johns Hopkins Hosp., Balt., 1963-65; allergy, immunology, dermatology, sports medicine pvt. practice, Silver Spring, Md., 1966—. Tchg. fellow pediat. Harvard Med. Sch., 1962-63; tchg. fellow allergy and immunology Johns Hopkins Med. Sch., 1963-65; asst. prof. dept. phys. edn. U. Md., College Park, 1976-83; assoc. clin. prof. pediat. Georgetown U. Sch. of Medicine, 1984—. Author: The Sportsmedicine Book, 1978, Getting Thin, 1983, Dr. Gabe Mirkin's Fitness Clinic, 1986, The Complete Sportsmedicine Book for Women, 1985, 2d rev. edit. 1991; (with Shangold) Women and Exercise, 1988, Dr. Gabe Mirkin's Fatfree, Flavorful Book, 1995; (with Diana Mirkin) The 20 Gram Diet, 1995, The 20/30 Fat and Fiber Diet Plan, Dr. Gabe Mirkins Pocket Guide to Fitness & Sports; (with Rich) The Whole Grains Cookbook, 1997, The Good Food Book, 2001, Healthy Heart Miracle, 2004; author (newsletter) The Mirkin Report, 1990—; columnist: N.Y. Times, 1976-89, United Features, 1989-94, Washington Post, 1976, Singer Media Corp., 1994-99; appearances on P.M. Mag. WDVM-TV, Washington, 1979, House Party, NBC TV, 1990, The Learning Channel; host internationally syndicated radio talk show, 1996-2003; daily radio spots on fitness and nutrition, CBS Radio Stations News Svc., 1979—; host talk show on health fitness and nutrition, KMOX Radio, St. Louis, 1982-98; nightly talk show host NBC Washington, WRC, 1982-84, 87—, WNTR, 1984-86; weekly spots for Physicians Radio Network, 1984-85; daily talk show syndicated by Sun Radio Network, 1992; weekly talk show WEEI, Boston, 1993-94, others; columnist and contbg. editor to health and fitness mags.; contbr. articles to profl. jours., chpts. to books. Major USAF, 1968-70. Fellow Am. Coll. Allergists, Am. Assn. Cert. Allergists, Am. Assn. for Clin. Immunology and Allergy, Am. Acad. Pediatrics, Am. Acad. Allergy and Immunology. Avocation: bicycle tandem racing. Office: 10901 Connecticut Ave Kensington MD 20895-1645 Office Phone: 301-942-7900. Business E-Mail: gabe@drmirkin.net.

**MIRKIN, MICHAEL V.,** chemistry professor, b. Alma-Ata, Kazakhstan, USSR, May 18, 1961; s. Vulf and Ninel Mirkin; m. Marina Gert, May 5, 1960; 1 child, Alexander. BS, MS in Chemistry, Kazakh State U., Alma-Ata, Kazakhstan, 1982, PhD, 1987. Postdoctoral assoc. chemistry U. Tex., Austin, 1990—93; asst. prof. chemistry Queens Coll., CUNY, Flushing, 1993—98, assoc. prof. chemistry, 1998—2004, prof. chemistry, 2004—. Co-editor (co-editor): (monograph) Scanning Electrochemical Microscopy, 2001. Mem.: Soc. Electroanalytical Chemistry, Electrochem. Soc., Am. Chem. Soc. Office: Dept Chemistry Queens Coll 65-30 Kissena Blvd Flushing NY 11367 Office Phone: 718-997-4111. Office Fax: 718-997-5531. Business E-Mail: mmirkin@qc.cuny.edu.

**MIRKOW, FRANK J.,** lawyer; b. Bogota, Colombia, Feb. 4, 1965; s. Italo and Cristina Mirkow; m. Andrea C. Frank, May 26, 2001; children: Hamilton Kennan, Harrington Frank. Ba, U. Md., 1987; MPA, Harvard U., 1990; JD, Cornell U., 2000. Cons. Price Waterhouse, LLP, Washington and Riyadh, Saudi Arabia, 1990—93; sr. cons. Arthur Andersen, LLP, Washington and Moscow, 1993—97; assoc. Shaw Pittman, LLP, Washington, 2000—02, Hale and Dorr, LLP, Washington, 2002—04, Haynes and Boone, LLP, Washington, 2004—. Bd. dirs. Fgn. Policy Discussion Group, Washington, 2000—; corp. sec. Internat. Ctr. for Religion and Diplomacy, Washington, 2000—. Fgn. policy intern Sen. Edward M. Kennedy, Washington, 1987—88; term mem. Coun. of Fgn. Rels., Washington, 2000—05; adj. fellow Ctr. for Strategic and Internat. Studies, Washington, 2004. Mem. DC Bar Assn., ABA. Internat. Law, Phi Kappa Phi, Phi Alpha Theta, Phi Beta Kappa. Home: 4831 Alton Pl NW Washington DC 20016 Office Phone: 202-654-4502. E-mail: fjm5@yahoo.com.

**MIRMAN, JOEL HARVEY,** lawyer; b. Toledo, Dec. 3, 1941; s. Benjamin and Minnie Mirman; children: Lisa, Julie, Benjamin. BBA, Ohio U., 1963; JD, Ohio State U., 1966. Bar: Ohio 1966, U.S. Dist. Ct. (so. dist.) Ohio 1966, U.S. Supreme Ct. 1972. Ptnr. Topper, Alloway, Goodman, DeLeone & Duffey, Columbus, Ohio, 1966-85, Benesch, Friedlander, Coplan & Aronoff, 1986-93; shareholder Buckingham, Doolittle & Burroughs, Columbus, 1994—2003; ptnr. Gamble Hartshorn & Johnson, LLC, Columbus, 2004—. Lectr. Ohio CLE Inst., Columbus, 1972—; mem. Supreme Ct. of Ohio Commn. on Certification of Specialists. Author direct examination CLE materials; contbr. articles to profl. jours. Mem. Ohio Elections Commn., 1976-80, vice-chmn. 1980. Named one of Ohio's Top 100 Super Lawyers, 2004—06, Best Lawyers in Am., 2003—04, 2004—05; recipient, 2005—06. Mem. Ohio State Bar Assn. (coun. of dels.), Worthington Hills Country Club, Worthington Hills Civic Assn. (pres. 1992-93). Office: Gamble Hartshorn & Johnson LLC 1 E Livingston Ave Columbus OH 43215 Office Phone: 614-324-5985. Business E-mail: mirman@ghjlaw.com.

MIRMAN, MERRILL JAY, physician, surgeon; b. Darby, Pa., Jan. 24, 1941; s. Nathan and Rosalie (Applebaum/Yablotchnick) M. BS in Pharmacy, Phila. Coll. Pharmacy and Sci., 1962; D of Osteopathy, Phila. Coll. Osteo. Medicine, 1966; diploma, Ethical Hypnosis Tng. Ctr. Diplomate Am. Acad. Pain Mgmt.; Am. Bd. Gen./Family Practice; cert. flight instr., residential sales, sclerotherapy; lic. real estate broker, Pa., Del.; lic. pharmacist, Pa.; lic. airline transport pilot; lic. ins. provider life accident, health, health, property, casualty, rabbi; lic. physician, Calif., D.C., Fla., Ga., N.J., Md., Pa., Tex., Nev., Del.; lic. acupuncturist, Pa.; radio amateur extra class; FCC lic. gen. radio telephone with radar endorsement; pvt. detective; ordained rabbi, Am. Bd. Rabbis. Mem. faculty dept. osteo. principles and practice Pa. Coll. Osteo. Medicine, 1970-75; acting med. dir. S.E. Pa. Transp. Authority, Phila., 1970; mem. psychopharmacology rsch. unit Phila. Gen. Hosp., 1972-77; vice chmn. dept. gen. practice Tri-County Hosp., 1975, chmn. dept. gen. practice, 1976; mem., preceptor dept. family and cmty. medicine Milton S. Hershey Med. Ctr. Pa. State U., 1978; founder, dir. Mirman Sch. Hypnosis, 1978-79; physician, surgeon Mirman Med. Ctr., Pa. Clinic for Pain, Springfield, Pa., 1979—; clin. asst. prof. medicine Temple U., Phila., 2005—06. Osteo. med. cons. West Phila. Mental Health Consortium, 1971; mem. pvt. practice rsch. group U. Pa., 1972-77; chmn. osteo. principles and practice com. Tri-County Hosp., 1976, chmn. pharmacy and therapeutics com., 1977, med. exec. com. of osteo. prin. and methods com., 1977, libr. com., 1977, Coll. Osteo. Medicine, Kansas City, 1985, Riverside Hosp. Wilmington, Del.; physician reviewer region V Pa. Peer Review Orgn., 1985; reviewer Keystone Peer Review Orgn., 1986; pvt. investigator. Editor Sclerotherapy, 1986, 88, 89, 94; originator, prodr., dir. (cable TV series) To Your Health, 1982-86; author: Foundation Course in Hypnosis and Self Hypnosis, 1979, Advanced Course in Hypnosis, 1979, Foundation Course in Hypnosis, Examination, 1979, Advanced Course in Forensic Hypnosis, 1980; editor: Sclerotherapy of Aches, Pains and Varicose Veins, 1982. Pres. planning commn., Glenolden, Pa., 1970-72; pres. Boro of Glenolden Fourth of July assn., 1969-2002; vol. radio and TV sta. operator Franklin Inst. Sci. Mus., Phila.; vol. examiner Am. Radio Relay League. Capt. M.C., U.S. Army, 1968-69, Vietnam. Recipient Four Chaplains Legion Honor award Chapel Four Chaplains, 1982, Air medal with oak leaf clusters; World Aviation recordholder. Fellow Am. Coll. Pain and Sclerotherapy Mgmt. (sec.-treas. 1981-83, v.p. 1983-85, pres. elect 1985-87, pres. 1987-89, bd. dirs. 1991-95), Acad. Psychosomatic Medicine, Am. Back Soc., Internat. Acad. Behavioral Medicine, Counseling and Psychotherapy, Coll. Physicians Phila. Oculoplastic Fellowship Soc. N.Y.; mem.AAAS, Am. Bd. Sclerotherapy (cert., v.p. 1989-91, pres. 1991-95, sec. 1995—), Am. Coll. Gen. Practice (cert.), Am. Osteo. Assn., Am. Acad. Osteopathy (mem. hosp. com. 1973), Assn. to Advance Ethical Hypnosis (cert. pres. Pa. chpt. #2 1972-73, 79-80), Acad. Psychosomatic Medicine, Internat. Assn. for Forensic Hypnosis (cert., exec. bd. 1982—; advisor 1979—), Can. Orthopedic Med. Assn., Nat. Aero. Assn., Am. Radio Relay League (vol. examiner), Pa. Osteo. Med. Assn. (chpt. #2 alt. del. 1971-77), Del. County Pharm. Assn., Peer Review Orgn. Commonwealth Pa., Exptl. Aircraft Assn., Del. County Amateur Radio Assn., Airplane Owners and Pilots Assn., Chaverim Del. Valley, Holmesberg Amateur Radio Club, Haraboním Am., Rho Pi Phi. Office: Mirman Med Ctr 652 E Springfield Rd Springfield PA 19064-3644 Office Phone: 610-626-8588.

MIRMIRA, RAGHAVENDRA G., endocrinologist, researcher, educator; b. 1964; BA in chemistry with honors, U. Chgo., 1986, PhD in biochemistry and molecular biology, 1991, MD in medicine with honors, 1993; postdoctoral in beta transcription, U. Calif., San Francisco, 1996—2000. Cert. in internal medicine Am. Bd. Internal Medicine, 1996, in endocrinology, diabetes, and metabolism Am. Bd. Internal Medicine, 1998. Medical resident in medicine Sch. Medicine, U. Calif., San Francisco, 1993—95; clinical and rsch. fellow Endocrinology and Hormone Rsch. Inst., Sch. Medicine, U. Calif., San Francisco, 1995—2000; asst. prof. clinical internal medicine Dept. Medicine, Sch. Medicine, U. Va., Charlottesville, 2000—. Contbr. articles to numerous profl. jour. Recipient Career Devel. award, Juvenile Diabetes Found., 1999, Rsch. Career award, NIH, 1999—, Discovery Health Channel Med. Honors, 2004; Physician Postdoctoral fellowship, Howard Hughes Med. Inst., 1996—99. Mem.: Alpha Omega Alpha. Achievements include first to develop transplant for treatment of diabetes that can be performed without the aid of immunosuppressant drugs; widely considered to be at the forefront of diabetes rsch. for his efforts in understanding islet cells, the cells that produce insulin. Office: Univ Va Health Sys Charlottesville VA 22908*

MIROLA, WILLIAM ANDREW, sociologist, educator; b. Middletown, NY, Dec. 4, 1963; s. John B. and Doris M. (Muszynski) Mirola; m. James Elvis Le Grand, Oct. 21, 1991. BA in Biology, Houghton Coll., 1985; MA in Sociology, Ind. U., 1990, PhD in Sociology, 1995. Assoc. prof. sociology Marian Coll., Indpls.; 1995—, chmn. dept. history and social sci., 2002—. Rschr. religion and urban culture project Polis Ctr., Indpls., 1999—2002; rschr., cons. St. Richard's Sch., Indpls., 1999—2000. Editor: Sociology of Religion: A Reader, 2001; assoc. editor: Sociology of Religion; contbr. articles to profl. jours. Active Trinity Episcopal Ch., Indpls., 2004—; bd. trustees St. Richard's Sch., Indpls., 2004—. Fellow Young Scholars in Am. Religion, Pew Charitable Trusts, 1997—99. Mem.: Soc. for Sci. Study Religion, Assn. for Sociology Religion, Am. Sociol. Assn. Democrat. Episcopalian. Avocations: travel, cooking, antiques, gardening, art. Office: Marian College 3200 Cold Spring Rd Indianapolis IN 46222-1997 Office Phone: 317-955-6033. Business E-Mail: mirola@marian.edu.

MIRONER, MERRIL A., lawyer; b. Gloversville, NY, Dec. 28, 1940; BS with honors, Union Coll., 1962; JD cum laude, Columbia U., 1965. Bar: NY 1966, US Dist. Ct., No. Dist. NY, US Dist. Ct., So. and Ea. Dists. NY, US Ct. Appeals, 2nd Cir. Confidential legal asst. Appellate Div. of Supreme Ct., Third Dept., 1965—67; ptnr. Katten Muchin Rosenman, NYC. Mem.: NY State Bar Assn. Office: Katten Muchin Rosenman 575 Madison Ave New York NY 10022 Office Phone: 212-940-8910. Office Fax: 212-940-8776. E-mail: merril.mironer@kattenlaw.com.

MIROWSKI, PHILIP EDWARD, economics professor; b. Jackson, Mich., Aug. 21, 1951; s. Edward and Elizabeth Mirowski. BA, Mich. State U., 1973; MA in Econs., U. Mich. 1976, PhD in Econs., 1979. Asst. prof. U. Santa Clara, Calif., 1978-81, Tufts U., Medford, Mass., 1981-84, assoc. prof. econs., 1984-90; Carl Koch prof. econs. and history and philosophy of sci. U. Notre Dame, Ind., 1990—. Vis. assoc. prof. Yale U., New Haven, 1987-88; vis. prof. Tinbergen Inst., Erasmus U., Rotterdam, Holland, 1991, U. Paris, 1997, U. Modena, Italy, 1998, Santa Fe Inst., 2001; Fulbright sr. fellow, 2003, Internat. Ctr. for Advanced Studies, NYU, 2004. Author: Reconstruction of Economic Theory, 1986, Against Mechanism, 1988, More Heat Than Light, 1989, Machine Dreams, 2002, Science Bought and Sold, 2002, Effortless Economy of Science, 2004; editor: Natural Images in Economics, 1994, Edgeworth on Chance, 1994, Collected Works of William Thomas Thornton, 1999, Agreement on Demand, 2006; mem. editl. bd. History Polit. Econ., Duke U., 1986—, Social Concept, 1988-94, Jour. Instnl. Econs., 2004—, Jour. History of Econ., 2001—; contbr. articles to profl. jours. Mem. AAAS, Am. Econs. Assn., History Sci. Soc., History Econs. Soc. Soc. for Social Studies of Sci. (Fleck prize 2006), Philosophy of Sci. Assn. Office: U Notre Dame 400 Decio Hall Notre Dame IN 46556 E-mail: mirowski.1@nd.edu.

MIRRA, SUZANNE SAMUELS, pathologist; BA, Hunter Coll., 1962; MD, SUNY, Bklyn., 1967. Instr. pathology Yale U. Sch. Medicine, New Haven, 1971-73; staff pathologist Atlanta VA Med. Ctr., Decatur, Ga., 1973-97; asst. prof. pathology Emory U. Sch. Medicine, Atlanta, 1973-80, assoc. prof. pathology, 1981-93, prof. pathology, 1993-97; prof., chair dept. pathology SUNY Health Sci. Ctr., Bklyn., 1997—. Dir. prin. investor Emory Alzhe-

imer's Disease Ctr., Atlanta, 1991—97. Mem. editl. bd. Arch Pathol. Lab. Med., 1988-2000, Jour. Neuropathology Exptl. Neurology, 1991-95, Brain Pathology, 1995-99, Alzheimer's Disease Reviews, 1995-2000. Recipient Albert E. Levy Sci. Faculty Rsch. award Emory U., 1987, Disting. Alumnus Achievement award SUNY, 1992; named to Hunter Coll. Hall of Fame, 1996. Fellow Coll. Am. Pathologists (Presdl. award 1987,89, Herbert Lansky award 1990, chair neuropathology commn. 1992-95); mem. Am. Assn. Neuropathologists (v.p. profl. affairs 1992-97, pres. 1999-2000, Meritorious Contributions to Neuropathology award, 2005), Alzheimer's Assn. (bd. dir. Atlanta chpt. 1987-97, nat. bd. dir. 1997-05), Alpha Omega Alpha. Office: SUNY Health Sci Ctr 450 Clarkson Ave Brooklyn NY 11203-2056 Business E-Mail: suzanne.mirra@downstate.edu.

MIRRLEES, SIR JAMES ALEXANDER, economics professor; b. Minnigaff, Scotland, July 5, 1936; s. George Barlas MacNab and Nan Lindsay (Purdie) M.; m. Gillian Marjorie Hughes, July 29, 1961 (dec. 1993); children: Catriona, Fiona; m. Patricia Wilson, May 12, 2001. MA, Edinburgh U., Scotland, 1957; BA, Cambridge U., Eng., 1959, PhD, 1963; DLitt (hon.), Warwick U., Eng., 1982, Portsmouth U., 1997, Brunel U., 1997, Edinburgh U., Scotland, 1997, Oxford U., 1998. Lectr. in econ. U. Cambridge, England, 1963-68; Edgeworth prof. econs. U. Oxford, England, 1968-95; prof. polit. economy U. Cambridge, 1995—2003, emeritus prof. polit. economy, 2003—, fellow Trinity Coll., 1995—; disting. prof.-at-large Chinese U. of Hong Kong, 2002—; hon. prof. Peking U.; vis. eminent scholar faculty economics and commerce U. Melbourne, Australia, 2005—. Vis. prof. MIT, 1968, 70, 71, 76, U. Calif., Berkeley, 1986, Yale U., 1989. Co-author: (with Little) Project Appraisal and Planning for Developing Countries, 1974; contbr. articles to profl. publications. Recipient Nobel Prize in Econ. Sciences, 1996; Knighted for contributions to econ. sci., Eng., 1997. Fellow Brit. Acad., Roy. Soc. of Edinburgh, Econometric Soc. (pres. 1983-84); mem. NAS (fgn. mem.), Royal Econ. Soc. (pres. 1989-92), Am. Econ. Assn. (hon.), Am. Acad. Arts and Sci., Assn. Univ. Tchr. Econ. (chmn. 1983-87). Office: Trinity Coll CB2 1TQ Cambridge England Office Phone: +44 1223 339 516, +852 2609 7831.

MIRSKY, ARTHUR, retired geologist, educator; b. Phila., Feb. 8, 1927; s. Victor and Dorothy M.; m. Patricia Shorey, Dec. 22, 1961; 1 dau., Alexis Catherine. Student, Bklyn. Coll., 1944, student, 1946—48; BA, U. Calif., 1950; MS, U. Ariz., 1955; PhD, Ohio State U., 1960. Cert. geologist, Ind. Field uranium geologist AEC, S.W. U.S., 1951-53; cons. uranium geologist Albuquerque, 1955-56; asst. dir. Inst. Polar Studies, Ohio State U., 1960-67; adj. asst. prof. geology Ohio State U., 1964-67; from asst. prof. geology to prof. Ind. U.-Purdue U., Indpls., 1967-94, prof. emeritus, 1994—, coord. geology, 1967-69, chmn. dept. geology, 1969-93. Contbr. articles to profl. jours. Served with USN, 1944-46. Mem. AAAS, AAUP, Am. Inst. Profl. Geologists, Geol. Soc. Am., Nat. Assn. Geosci. Tchrs., Am. Geol. Inst., Soc. Sedimentary Geology, Ind. Acad. Sci., Sigma Xi. Office: Indiana U-Purdue U Dept Earth Scis 723 W Michigan St Indianapolis IN 46202-5132 Office Phone: 317-278-0229, E-mail: amirsky@iupui.edu.

MIRVAHABI, FARIN, lawyer; b. Tehran, Iran; d. Ali and Azar Mirvahabi; m. Richard C. Powell; children: Bobby Naemi, Jimmy Naemi. Degree in Law, Tehran U., Iran, 1968; M of Comparative Law, Georgetown U., 1972; LLM, George Washington U., 1976; JSD, NYU, 1978; diploma, The Hague Acad. Internat. Law, 1983. Bar: Va. 1989, U.S. Dist. Ct. (ea. and we. dists.) Va. 1990, D.C. 1990, U.S. Dist. Ct. D.C. 1990, U.S. Supreme Ct. 1997. With Gold & Cutner, N.Y.C., 1979-80; in-house counsel IRA Engring. and Constrn., Tehran, London, 1981-82; legal advisor Bank Markazi, Tehran, 1981-82; practiced law The Hague, The Netherlands, 1982-87; arbitrator Iran Air-Pan Am Arbitration Tribunal, Paris, 1984-87; legal cons. Rooney, Barry & Fogerty, Washington, 1987-88; atty. sole practice, Washington, 1989—. Law prof. No. Va. Law Sch., Alexandria, 1989-90; instr. Paralegal Inst., Arlington, Va., 1988-89; prof. Tehran U., 1982; panelist Am. Arbitration Assn.; guest speaker in field; life dep. gov. Am. Biog. Inst. Rsch. Assn., 19995—. Contbr. numerous articles to profl. jours. Named Maxplank fellow Maxplank Inst. of Internat. Law, 1986; recipient Clyde Eagleton award NYU, 1977, Woman of Yr. medallion honoring Cmty. Svc. and Profl. Achievement, 1995, Spl. Merit award DC Bar, 2005. Mem. ABA, Internat. Bar Assn., Arbitration Forum Inc., D.C. Bar Assn. (panelist client-atty. arbitration bd. 1990—), D.C. Bar & Lawyers Assn., Trial Lawyers Assn., Va. Bar Found., Am. Soc. Internat. Law, Am. Film Inst. The Kennedy Ctr. Avocations: reading, writing, Broadway shows, picnic, swimming. Office: Ste 613-6 1000 Connecticut Ave NW Washington DC 20036 Office Phone: 703-534-6677.

MIRZA, AZAM A., insurance company executive; BS in computer sci., Wash. U., St. Louis; MS in engring. mgmt., U. Mo., Rolla. Various positions most recently dir. tech. G.A. Sullivan, 1992—98; with Oracle Corp.; head advanced tech. group Arthur Andersen LLP, St. Louis; joined Reinsurance Group of Am. Inc., Chesterfield, Mo., 2002, now v.p. global software. Named one of Premier 100 IT Leaders, Computerworld, 2005. Office: Reinsurance Group of Am Inc 1370 Timberlake Manor Pkwy Chesterfield MO 63017 Office Phone: 636-736-7000.*

MIRZA, HUMAIR, cardiologist, educator; b. Karachi, Pakistan, Feb. 18, 1966; arrived in U.S., 1993; s. Hasan and Qamar Jehan Mirza; m. Mahwash Khan, Dec. 20, 2001. MBBS, Dow Med. Coll., Karachi, 1991. Diplomate Am. Bd. Internal Medicine, Am. Bd. Cardiology, Am. Bd. of Interventional Cardiology. Rsch. fellow nephrology and hypertension SUNY, Stony Brook, 1993—96, resident interanl medicine, 1994—97, chief med. resident, 1997—98, asst. clin. instr., 1994—2001, cardiology fellow, 1998—2001, interventional cardiology fellow, 2001—02, asst. prof. medicine and cardiology, 2002—, asst. program dir., cardiology fellowship program; mem. med. bd. Univ. Hosp., SUNY, Stony Brook, 1999—2002, mem. grad. sch. med. edn. com., 1997—2002. Contbr. articles to profl. jours. (Pfizer Abstract award, 2001). Grantee Nat. Kidney Found., 1994—96. Mem.: ACP, Am. Soc. Internal Medicine. Avocations: classical music, tennis, jogging, theater. Office: SUNY Health Sci Ctr Bldg T 17 Stony Brook NY 11794 E-mail: humirza@excite.com.

MIRZA, LEONA LOUSIN, elementary school educator, director; b. Chgo., July 1, 1944; d. Max B. and Opal Lousin; m. David B. Mirza; children: Sara Anush, Elizabeth Ann. BA in Math., North Park Coll., Chgo., 1965; MA in Edn., Western Mich. U., Kalamazoo, 1967, EdD in Edn., 1972; cert. in computer studies, North Park Coll., 1983. Specialist in elem. curriculum and adminstrn. Tchr. Kalamazoo Pub. Schs., 1965-69; prof. math. edn. North Park U., Chgo., 1969-2001, asst. acad. dean, 1999—2001, chair dept. stats., 2004—; dir. Inst. for Internat. and Cultural Studies, 2001—06. Editor The Ill. Math. Tchr., 1992-95; contbr. articles to profl. jours. Chmn. adv. com. on edn. in Ill., 1975-77. Mem. Nat. Coun. Tchrs. Math., Ill. Coun. Tchrs. Math., Ill. Assn. Colls. of Tchr. Edn., Ill. Assn. Tchrs. Edn. in Pvt. Colls. (officer 1974-86). Home: 5241 N Sawyer Ave Chicago IL 60625-4715 Office: 3225 W Foster Ave Chicago IL 60625-4823 Office Phone: 773-244-5731. Business E-Mail: lmirza@northpark.edu.

MIRZAIE, IDA A., economics professor; b. Tehran, Iran; PhD, U. Wis., Milw., 1999. Faculty Ohio State U., Columbus, 2000—, John Caroll U., Cleve., 2002—06. Office: Ohio State U 410 Arps Hall 1945 N High St Columbus OH 43210 Business E-Mail: mirzaie.1@osu.edu.

MISA, KENNETH FRANKLIN, management consultant; b. Jamaica, NY, Sept. 24, 1939; s. Frank J. and Mary M. (Soszka) M. BS in Psychology cum laude, Purdue U., 1963; PhD in Psychology, St. John's U., 1966. Cert. mgmt. cons.; lic. psychologist, Calif. Staff psychologist Rohrer, Hibler & Replogle, L.A., 1966-67; assoc. A.T. Kearney, Inc., L.A., 1968-71, sr. assoc., 1972-74, prin., 1975-78, v.p., ptnr., 1979-86; pres. HR Cons. Group, 1987—. Mem. APA, Am. Psychol. Soc., Calif. State Psychol. Assn., Soc. for Human Resources Mgmt., Human Resources Planning Soc., Indsl. Rels. Rsch. Assn., Soc. for Indsl. and Orgnl. Psychology, World Affairs Coun. L.A., Town Hall So. Calif., Glendale C. of C., Jonathan Club. Republican. Roman Catholic.

Home: One Bristol Ct Rancho Mirage CA 92270 Office: HR Cons Group 100 N Brand Blvd Ste 200 Glendale CA 91203-2642 Office Phone: 818-241-0060. Home Fax: 323-254-8553. Personal E-mail: kfmhrcg@aol.com.

MISAGE, MARK ALAN, physics educator; Physics tchr. Westlake H.S., Austin, Tex., 1990—.

MISAKIAN, JO ELLEN PRIEST, school librarian, dean; d. Frederick and Velma Priest; m. John L. Misakian, Nov. 3, 1956; children: Johnny Lee, Jeffrey Dale, James Kevin. BS, N.Y. Inst. Tech., N.Y.C., 1992; MLS, San Jose State U., 1993; cert. in tchg., Nat. U., Fresno, Calif., 1994; cert. in libr. media svc., San Jose State U., 1994. Libr. technician Sanger (Calif.) Unified Sch. Dist., 1970—94; libr. media coord. Fresno County Office of Edn., 1994—99; libr. media program dir. Fresno Pacific U., 9999—, interim dean Sch. Edn., 2005—. Mem. adv. bd. Infopeople, Calif., 2002—, Ame Nixon Ctr. for Study of Children's Lit., Fresno, 2002—. Mem. adv. bd. Tchr. Libr. Mag., 2002—; author: The Essential School Library Glossary, 2004; contbr. articles to profl. jours. Chair Ctrl. Valley Libr. Com., 2000—, Fresno Reads Roundtable, 2001—04; ex-dir. Heartland Regional Libr. Network, 2002—. Mem.: ALA, Calif. Sch. Libr. Assn. (pres. 2000—01, chair libr. standards task force 2002—04, Profl. Svc. award 2005). Republican. Protestant. Home: 253 N DeWolf Fresno CA 93727 Office: Fresno Pacific Univ Sch Edn 1717 S Chestnut Fresno CA 93702 Office Phone: 559-453-2291. Office Fax: 559-453-7168. Business E-Mail: jmisakian@fresno.edu.

MISBIN, ROBERT, medical executive; b. Bklyn., N.Y., Mar. 20, 1947; m. Eloise Harman, Oct. 20, 1974. MD (hon.), Johns Hopkins U., Balt., 1971. Med. officer FDA, Rockville, Md., 1995—. Home: 8505 NW 4th Pl Gainesville FL 32607 Office: FDA 10903 New Hampshire Ave Silver Spring MD 20903-1058 Office Phone: 301-796-1259. Personal E-mail: misbinr@surfglobal.net. E-mail: robert.misbin@fda.hhs.gov.

MISCAVIGE, DAVID, head of religious order; b. Phila., 1960; s. Ron and Loretta Miscavige; m. Shelly Barnett, 1981. Mem. Sea Orgn. and Commodore's Messenger Orgn. Ch. of Scientology, 1976, asst. to L. Ron Hubbard; chmn. bd. Religious Tech. Ctr., 1987—. Scientologist. Avocations: photography, snorkeling, motorcycling. Office: Religious Tech Ctr Internat 1710 Ivar Ave, Ste 1100 Los Angeles CA 90028 Office Phone: 323-663-3258. Office Fax: 323-667-0960.*

MISCELLA, MARIA DIANA, humanities educator; b. NYC, July 11, 1929; d. Nicola and Giovanna (Tangorra) Torelli; m. Emilio Miscella, Feb. 27, 1954 (dec. Sept. 30, 1996); children: Delia, Marisa, Giuliana. Tchr. Degree, Istituto Magistrale, Lecce, Italy, 1946; postgrad., U. Naples, 1946-48; BA, Hunter Coll., 1954, MA, 1972. Cert. secondary educator NY. English corr. GE Co., Rome, 1950-51; corr. Spanish & French Pettinos Import & Export Co., N.Y.C., 1952-53; tchr. Italian Harrison (N.Y.) H.S., 1967-87, St. John's U., Queens, NY, 1987-89; lectr. Italian various orgsn., N.Y. State, 1987—; lectr. Italian lit. and history various colls. and univs., NY, 1987—. Moderator of club Harrison (N.Y.) H.S., 1967-87. Mem. Little Neck (N.Y.) Civic Assn., 1970-95, Am. Assn. Ret. People, Douglaston, N.Y., 1994—; founder, treas. Italian Am. Women's Ctr., 1997—. Recipient scholarship Columbia U., 1954, Letter of Commendation, Bd. Regents, Albany, N.Y., 1980, Cert. Recognition and Gratitude for Contbn. to the Arts and Dedication to Cmty., N.Y.C. Coun., 2004, Spl. Lit. Contest prize The Salt Queen Found., 2005; named Woman of Yr., Consortium of L.I. Italian Am. Orgns., 1992. Mem. AAUW (hostess, v.p 1990-93, cert. of commendation 1996), Am. Assn. Tchrs. of Italian (sec. Societa Onoraria Italica 1979-91), Ams. Italian Heritage (bd. mem. 1982—, Women of the Yr. 2004), Sons of Italy (John Marino Lodge cultural com. mem 1994—, Merit award 1995), Assn. Italian Am. Educators (dir./historian by-laws com. 2000), N.Y. State United Tchrs., Am. Fedn. Tchrs., Nat. Italian Am. Found., Douglaston Women Club, Retirees Club. Roman Catholic. Avocations: reading, writing, travel, going to theatre, playing bridge.

MISCHEL, WALTER, psychology professor; b. Vienna, 1930; BA in psychology, NYU, 1951; MA in psychology, City Coll. NY, 1953; PhD in psychology, Ohio State U., 1956, DSc (hon.), 1997. Asst. prof., dept. psychology Harvard U., 1958—62, Stanford U., 1962—83; Niven prof. psychology, dept. psychology Columbia U., 1983—. Author: Introduction to Personality, 2004, Personality and Assessment, 1996, numerous other works. Recipient Merit award, Nat. Inst. Mental Health, 1989. Fellow: Am. Psychological Assn. (Disting. Sci. Contribution award 1982), Am. Acad. Arts and Scis.; mem.: NAS. Office: Columbia U 401A Schermerhorn Hall New York NY 10027 Business E-Mail: wm@paradox.psych.columbia.edu.*

MISCHKA, JAMES, fashion designer; b. Burlington, Wis., Dec. 23, 1960; BA in Mgmt. and Art Hist., Rice Univ., Houston, 1982; BFA in Fashion Design, Parsons Sch. Design, NYC, 1985. Apprenticeship with Yves St. Laurent, Paris; apprenticeship with Willi Smith NYC, 1985—88; co-founder, ptnr. Badgley Mischka, NYC, 1985—; ptnr. Badgley Mischka Dress, NYC. Named one of Top 10 American Designers, Vogue; recipient Mouton Cadet Young Designers award, 1989, Dallas Internat. Apparel Rising Star award, 1992. Office: 525 7th Ave Fl 18 New York NY 10001-4901

MISCHKE, CARL HERBERT, retired religious association executive; b. Hazel, S.D., Oct. 27, 1922; s. Emil Gustav and Pauline Alvina (Polzin) M.; m. Gladys Lindloff, July 6, 1947; children: Joel, Susan Mischke Blahnik, Philip, Steven. BA, Northwestern Coll., Watertown, Wis., 1944; M.Div., Wis. Luth. Sem., Mequon, 1947. Ordained to ministry Evang. Lutheran Ch. Parish pastor Wis. Synod, 1947-79; pres. Western Wis. Dist. Evang. Luth. Ch., Juneau, 1964-79; v.p. Wis. Luth. Synod, Milw., 1966-79, pres., 1979-93; retired, 1993. Lutheran.

MISCHKE, FREDERICK CHARLES, retired manufacturing executive; b. Benton Harbor, Mich., Sept. 21, 1930; s. Fred William and Clara Adeline (Ruhno) M.; m. Kathleen Ann Schultz, Nov. 19, 1955 (dec. Aug. 1980); children: Stephanie Ann, Michael Frederick (dec. Oct. 12, 1996), Eric William; m. Lori Ann Leonard, Dec. 23, 1983. AA, Lake Mich. Coll., 1956; BBA, Western Mich. U., 1958. CPA, Ind., Mich. Staff acct. Lybrand, Ross Bros. & Montgomery, Chgo., 1958-63; supr. acctg. Niles, Mich., 1963-65; v.p., treas. Skyline Corp., Elkhart, Ind., 1965-91, ret., 1991. Vol. Svc. Corps. Ret. Execs., 1992—, local v.p., 1993-99, treas. 2000—; chmn. Meml. Endowment Fund Luth. Ch., 1995-2006. Mem. AICPA, Ind. Assn. CPAs (Civic Achievement award, 1976), Mich. Assn. CPAs, Fin. Execs. Inst. (Michiana chpt. pres. 1974-75), Elcona Country Club (pres. 1975), Rotary (local pres. 1976-77). Republican. Lutheran. Avocations: photography, boating, golf. Home: 23322 Greenleaf Blvd Elkhart IN 46514-4508 Personal E-mail: freddycm@aol.com.

MISDOM, AMANDA MICHELLE, elementary school educator, music educator; b. Chicago Heights, Ill., July 19, 1980; d. John Hobbs and Linda Dian Kommers; m. Theodore Henry Misdom, July 24, 2004; 1 child, Christian Theodore. BS in Elem. Edn., So. Ill. U., Charleston, 2002; MA in Elem. Edn., Olivet Nazarene U., Bourbonnais, Ill., 2004. Tchr. grade 5 Sch. Dist. 163, Park Forest, Ill., 2002—03; tchr. music grades k-6 and choir grades 4-6 Sch. Dist. 194, Steger, Ill., 2003—. Office: Saukview Elem Sch 3341 Miller Ave South Chicago Heights IL 60411 Office Phone: 708-755-9600. E-mail: amisdom@sd194.org.

MISE, JESSE SHERDEN, structural engineer, consultant; b. Jonesville, Va., July 13, 1933; s. Clabe Moss and Gladys Elizabeth (Orr) M.; m. Betty Joy Curtiss, July 8, 1984; children: Nancy Miller, Linda Andrews, Doug Hinshaw. BS in Math., Tenn. Tech., 1957. Registered profl. engr., Tenn., Mo. Road designer Va. Dept. Hwys., Petersburg, 1958-64; structural designer various archtl., engring. firms, 1964-67; structural engr. Combustion Engring., Windsor, Conn., 1967-72, Tenn. Eastman, Kingsport, 1973-76, TVA, Knoxville, 1976-87, ABB Environ., Knoxville, 1988-91; cons. Jesse S. Mise, P.E., Knoxville, 1992—; chief engr. James Thomas Engring., Knoxville, 1992—. Author: Engineers Guide to Unusual Opportunities, 1972. Mem. Patriots of

East Tenn., Knoxville, 1996—. Mem. ASCE, Nat. Coun. of Examiners for Engring. and Surveying, 1993—. Home and Office: 5704 Melstone Rd Knoxville TN 37912-4629 Personal E-mail: alt2000tec@aol.com, jessemise@aol.com.

**MISELSON, ALEX J. (JACOB MISELSON)**, portfolio manager, securities analyst, investment theorist; b. NYC, Feb. 23, 1926; s. Aaron and Bertha (Guskin) M. BS in Social Sci. with honors in History, CCNY, 1947; MA in History, Columbia U., 1950; MA in Econs., Queens Coll., 1975. Instr. dept. history CCNY, 1949—55; tchr. Kearny (N.J.) HS, 1955—57, Uniondale HS, L.I., NY, 1957—76; reg. rep. Herzfeld and Stern, N.Y.C., 1977—81, Haas Securities Corp., N.Y.C., 1981—83, Fahnestock and Co., N.Y.C., 1983—85, Dominick and Dominick, N.Y.C., 1985; dir. rsch. A.T. Brod and Co., Inc., N.Y.C., 1986—94, Investors Assocs., N.Y.C., 1994—96, Paragon Capital Markets, N.Y.C., 1996—2003, dir. investment strategy, 2000—03; sr. v.p., investment strategist View Trade Securities, Jersey City, 2003—. Instr. econs. Nassau CC, 1969-75; head coach basketball Kearny HS, NJ, 1955-57; asst. coach basketball C.W. Post Coll., Greenvale, L.I., 1958-59; spl. guest TV talk shows; commentator in fin. field, 1988—. Contbr. Dick Davis Digest; contbr. articles to profl. jours., interviewed by talk shows with appearances on host Joe Franklins radio show in NYC, 2000-04. Active L.I. Coun. for Econ. Edn., Hofstra U., Hempstead, N.Y., 1968-75. With U.S. Army, 1944-45. Mem. Phi Delta Kappa, Phi Alpha Theta, Phi Beta Kappa. Avocations: reading, writing, theater. Office Phone: 800-839-9706 ext. 208.

**MISHAAN, EMILIO**, transplant surgeon, educator; b. Guatemala, Guatemala, Aug. 20, 1960; s. Ezra Mishaan and Ivonne Smeke; 1 child, Isabella. BS, U. del Valle, Guatemala, 1981; MD, U. Francisco Manoquin, Guatemala, 1985. Chief resident surgery Hosp. San Juan de Dios, Guatemala, 1989—90, emergency surgeon, 1992—94; gen. surgeon Hosp. Militar, Guatemala, 1990—99, prof. surgery U. Francisco Marroquin, Guatemala, 1992-; transplant surgeon Hosp. San Juan de Dios, 1994—. CEO Venoclinic, Guatemala, 2001—06, Guatemala Laser Inst. Fellow: ACS, SAGES. Jewish. Avocations: running, hunting, fishing. Home: Km 19 9 Carretera El Salvador Guatemala City Guatemala Office: Gae 3-22 Z10 of 403 CMII Guatemala City Guatemala Personal E-mail: emishaans@yahoo.com.

**MISHEL, LAWRENCE**, economics research director; BA, Pa. State U., 1974; MA, Am. U., 1977; PhD in Econs., U. Wis., 1982. Prof. of Econs. Cornell U., Ithaca, N.Y., 1982-83; economist UAW, Detroit, 1983-85, IUD, AFL-CIO, Washington, 1986-87; rsch. dir. through pres. Econ. Policy Inst., Washington, 1987—. Co-author: (book) The State of Working America, 1991. Office: Econ Policy Inst 1660 L St NW Washington DC 20036

**MISHELEVICH, DAVID JACOB**, medical products executive; b. Pitts., Jan. 26, 1942; s. Benjamin and Sarah (Bachrach) M.; m. Bonnie Gray McKim, Dec. 6, 1981; 1 child, Cory Jane. BS in Physics, U. Pitts., 1962; MD, Johns Hopkins U., 1966, PhD in Biomed. Engring., 1970. Lic., Md., Tex. Intern in medicine Balt. City Hosps. (now The John Hopkins Bayview Med. Ctr.), 1966-67; active duty USPHS, 1967—69, inactive reserve, 1969—; staff assoc. Nat. Inst. Neurol. Diseases and Stroke, NIH, Bethesda, Md., 1967-69; exec. v.p. Nat. Ednl. Consultants, Balt., 1971-72; prof., dept. chairperson, dir. med. computing resources ctr. U. Tex. Health Sci. Ctr., Dallas, 1972-82; attending physician/sr. attending physician internal med. Dallas County Hosp., Dist. Parkland Meml. Hosp., 1973-82; v.p. computer and software tech. EAN-TECH, Mountain View, Calif., 1983-84; CEO Garden Gate Software, Cupertino, Calif., 1984-86; dir., then v.p. and gen. mgr. applications and rsch. divsn. IntelliCorp, Inc., Mountain View, 1986-89; v.p. mktg. and sales Viewpoint Engring., Mountain View, Calif., 1989-90; v.p. engring. AirWays Med. Techs., Inc., Palo Alto, Calif., 1991-93; dir., then v.p. R&D, chief tech. officer Circadian, Inc., San Jose, Calif., 1993-95, v.p., gen. mgr. AirWays Asthma Ctrs. divsn., 1995-96; CEO Sterling Healthcare Outcomes, Inc., Cupertino, 1996—2002, Playa del Rey, Calif., 2002—; founder, exec. v.p., chief tech. officer QENM.com, 1999-2001; chief tech. officer HealthShore, Inc., 2001—04; lead technologist Outbreak! Music Sys., 2002—; chief tech. officer TeleCath, 2003—. Pres. Mishelevich Assocs., Dallas, 1982-83; Cupertino, 1990-91, cons. prof. of neurosurgery Stanford U. Sch. Medicine, 2003-; dir. biomed. engring. and med. affairs Aubrey Group, Inc., Irvine, Calif., 2005—; mem. biomed. libr. rev. com. NIH-Nat. Libr. Medicine, 1978-82; cons. in field. Former tech. reviewer IBM Sys. Jour., Jour. of AMA; rev. IEEE computer Soc. Internet, 2001-03; contbr. numerous articles to profl. jours.; patentee in field. V.p. Dallas chpt. Am. Jewish Congress, 1980-84, Am. Jewish Fund, 1980-81; pres. Westport Bch. Club Villas, Homeowners Assn., 2003-06. Fellow Am. Coll. Med. Informatics; mem. AAAS, IEEE, IEEE Computer Soc. (exec. bd. tech. com. on computational medicine 1981-83), Am. Assn. for Artificial Intelligence, Assn. for Computing Machinery (chair Dallas chpt. 1974-75), Am. Med. Informatics Assn., Internat. Tandem Users Group (past pres.), Model T Ford Club of Am., Am. Radio Relay League (life), Phi Beta Kappa, Omicron Kappa. Democrat. Jewish. Home and Office: 7301 Vista del Mar #B111 Playa Del Rey CA 90293 Office Phone: 310-305-2791. E-mail: david@mishelevich.com. *Working with computers for some forty-five years has made me particularly sensitive to human needs and productivity. Two principles in which I believe are the human resources principle (maximize people's strengths and minimize or neutralize their weaknesses so they perform personally and professionally better than they would otherwise expect of themselves), and the optimality principle (I would rather do a 92% job in two weeks than a 97% job in 2 years).*

**MISHKIN, BARBARA FRIEDMAN**, lawyer; b. Phila., Feb. 19, 1936; d. Maurice Harold and Gertrude (Sanders) F.; m. Martin S. Thaler, Mar. 22, 1958 (div. 1970); children: Diane Sanders, Paul Sanders, David Emile, Amy Suzanne; m. Mortimer Mishkin, May 27, 1971. AB, Mount Holyoke Coll., 1957; MA, Yale U., 1958; JD, Am. U., 1981. Bar: D.C. 1982, U.S. Supreme Ct. 1989, U.S. Ct. Appeals (4th cir.) 1995. Rsch. psychologist NIMH, Bethesda, Md., 1968-69; spl. asst. to chief judge U.S. Ct. Appeals (D.C. cir.) Washington, 1970 71; spl. asst. to scientific dir. Nat. Inst. Child Health, Bethesda, 1971-74; asst. staff dir. Nat. Commn. for the Protection of Human Subjects, Washington, 1974-78; staff dir. Ethics Adv. Bd. HEW, Washington, 1978-80; dep. dir. Pres.' Commn. on Ethics in Medicine and Rsch., Washington, 1980-83; assoc. Hogan and Hartson, Washington, 1983-89, counsel, 1990-93, ptnr., 1994—2006, of counsel, 2006—. Cons. Ctr. for Law and Health Scis., Boston, 1970-73; cons., lectr. Johns Hopkins U. Sch. of Medicine, Balt., 1971-73; bd. dirs. Bon Secours Health Systems, Inc., Columbia, Md., 1984-90. Contbr. numerous articles on health law, med. ethics and biomed. research to jours. in field. Mem. policy bd. Legal Counsel for the Elderly, Washington, 1984-88, vice chair, 1988-90; trustee Mt. Holyoke Coll., 1985-90; mem. Mayor's Adv. Task Force on Hospice Licensure, Washington, 1985-87; bd. dirs. Hebrew Home Greater Washington, 1987-91. Recipient Lifetime Achievement award, Health Improvement Inst., 2004. Mem. ABA (chair sect. on health and environment 1988-92, chair com. on regulating rsch. 1996-98), D.C. Bar Assn. (subcom. rights of the elderly and the handicapped 1985-92, Pro Bono Atty. Yr. 1988), AAAS (com. on sci. freedom and responsibility 1986-92, AAAS/ABA Nat. Conf. Lawyers and Scientists 1992, ABA co-chair 1993-94). Am. Soc. Law, Medicine and Ethics (bd. dirs. 1995-98). Home: 5610 Wisconsin Ave Apt 402 Chevy Chase MD 20815-4429 Office: Hogan & Hartson Columbia Sq 555 13th St Washington DC 20004-1109 Office Phone: 202-637-5680. Business E-Mail: bfmishkin@hhlaw.com.

**MISHKIN, FREDERIC STANLEY**, bank executive, economics educator; b. NYC, Jan. 11, 1951; s. Sidney and Jeanne (Silverstein) M.; m. Sally A. Hammond; children: Matthew, Laura. Student, Oxford (Eng.) U., 1971-72; BS in Economics, MIT, 1973, PhD in Economics, 1976. Tchg. asst. MIT, 1974—76; asst. prof. U. Chgo., 1976-81, assoc. prof., 1981-83; vis. assoc. prof., dept. economics and dept. fin., Kellogg Grad. Sch., Northwestern U., Evanston, Ill., 1982-83; faculty rsch. fellow Nat. Bur. Econ. Rsch. Cambridge, Mass., 1979—80, rsch. assoc., 1980—; prof. econs. Columbia U. Grad. Sch. Bus., NYC, 1983-91, A. Barton Hepburn prof. econs., 1991—99, Alfred Lerner prof. Banking and Fin. Institutions, 1999—; exec. v.p. and dir. rsch. Fed. Res. Bank NY, NYC, 1994—97; mem. bd. govs. Fed. Res. Sys.,

Washington, 2006—. Economist, bd. govs., Fed. Res. System, Washington, 1977, acad. cons. bd. govs., 1993, vis. scholar, Divsn. Internat. Fin., bd. govs., 1993; mem. Conf. on Income and Wealth, 1984-; vis. scholar, Inst. for Fiscal and Monetary Policy, Ministry of Fin., Japan, Tokyo, 1986, Res. Bank of Australia, 1994, Bank of Eng., 2001; mem. Brookings Panel on Econ. Activity, Washington, 1977-78; mem. acad. adv. panel Fed. Res. Bank of N.Y., NYC, 1990-94, 1997- academic cons., 1997-; vis. prof. Princeton U., 1990-91; mem., Ctr. for Latin Am. Economics, Fed. Res. Bank Dallas, 1996-; Harry Johnson Lecture, Money Macroeconomics and Finance Rsch. Group Annual Conf., 1993; hon. prof. Renmin (Peoples) U. China, 1999; Homer Jones Lecture, 2000; Henry George Lecture, Univ. Scranton, 2004; John Kuszczak Meml. Lecture: Bank of Can., 2005; JMCB-FDIC invited lecture, 2005; chmn., External Evalution Com. for Rsch. Activities, Internat. Monetary Fund, 1999; advisor, Inst. Contemporary Fin., Shanghai Jiao Tong U., 2000-, Bank of Korea, Inst. for Monetary and Econ. Rsch., 2005-06; mem. Financial Economists Roundtable, 2001-04; mem. internat. adv. bd. financial supervisory svc., S. Korea, 2000-01; vis. rsch. fellow, The World Bank, 2000-01; sr. fellow, FDIC Ctr. for Banking Rsch., 2003-. Author: A Rational Expectations Approach to Macroeconometrics, 1983, The Economics of Money, Banking and Financial Markets, 1986, 4th edit. 1995, Money, Interest Rates and Inflation, 1993, Financial Markets, Institutions and Money, 1995, also articles; mem. editl. bd. American Economic Review, 1982-85, journal of International Money and Finance, 1992-, Fianance India, 1999-, Ctrl. Bank of Chile Series, Central Banking Analysis, and Economic Policy, 2001-; assoc. editor Journal of Business and Economic Statistics, 1986-93, Journal Applied Econometrics, 1985-2000, Journal Money, Credit and Banking, 1992-, Journal Economic Perspectives, 1994-2004; mem. adv. bd. International Finance, 1997-, Macroeconomics and Monetary Economics Abstracts, 1996-; editor Fed. Res. Bank NY, Economic Policy Review, 1994-97, mem. editl. bd., 1997- NSF Grad. Fellowship, 1973—76, Alfred P. Sloan Found. Fellowship, 1982—86. Mem. Am. Econ. Assn., Am. Fin. Assn., Ea. Econ. Assn. (v.p., 2002-03, pres.-elect, 2003-04, pres. 2004-05), Phi Beta Kappa, Sigma Xi. Avocations: sailing, cross country skiing, long distance cycling, reading. Office: Fed Res Sys 20th St & Constitution Ave NW Rm 2010 Washington DC 20551 Business E-Mail: fsm3@columbia.edu.*

**MISHKIN, MORTIMER**, neuropsychologist; b. Fitchburg, Mass., Dec. 13, 1926; AB, Dartmouth Coll., 1946; MA, McGill U., Montreal, Can., 1949, PhD, 1951; DSc (hon.), McGill U., 2004. Asst. in research and physiology and psychiatry Yale U. Med. Sch., New Haven, 1949-51; research asst. Inst. of Living, Hartford-Conn. and NYU Bellevue Med. Ctr., N.Y.C., 1951-55; research physiologist, sect. on neuropsychology NIMH, Bethesda, Md., 1955-75, research physiologist, Lab. of Neuropsychology, 1976-78, chief sect. cerebral mechanisms Lab. of Neuropsychology, 1979-80, chief Lab. of Neuropsychology, 1980-97, assoc. dir. basic rsch. DIRP, 1994-97, chief sect. cognitive neuroscience, 1997—, acting chief, lab neuropsychology, 2005—. Part-time instr. psychology Howard U., 1956-58; vis. scientist Nencki Inst. Exptl. Biology, Warsaw, Poland, winter 1958, 68, Tokyo Met. Inst. Neuroscis., summer 1978, Oxford U. Dept. Exptl. Psychology, summer 1979, Inst. Child Health U. Coll. London, 1993, vis. prof., 2000-; mem. psychol. scis. panel NIH, 1959-61, exptl. psychology study sect., 1965-69; mem. NIMH Assembly of Scientists Council, 1962-64, 72-74; mem. NIMH Scientist Promotion Rev. Com., 1984-86; mem. adv. com. Cognitive Neurosci. Inst., 1982-86; mem. NIH Fogart Internat. Scholars-in-Residence Adv. Panel, 1985-89, McDonnell Found. Study panel, 1987-89; adv. bd. McDonnell-Pew Program Cognitive Neurosci., 1989-94; cons. Developmental Cognitive Neurosci. Unit, Inst. Child Health, U. Coll. London, 1990—, vis. prof., 2000—; active Human Frontier Sci. Program, 1992-94, chmn. 1993; adv. bd. Ctr. for the Neural Basis of Cognition, U. Pitts. and Carnegie Mellon U., 1994-96, chair, 1999, 2004; adv. bd. La. State U. Neurosci. Ctr., 1994-96, Frontier Rsch. Program, RIKEN, Japan, 1994-96, Zanvyl Krieger Mind-Brain Inst., Johns Hopkins U., 1994-2000, Cognitive and Behavioral Neurosci. Panel, SUNY, Stony Brook, 1996, Mental Health and Neurosci. Clin. Rsch. Ctr., U. N.C., Chapel Hill, 1996-98, Krasnow Inst., George Mason U., Fellow Mentor Program, 1997-2002. Cons. editor Jour. Comparative and Physiol. Psychology, 1963-73, Exptl. Brain Rsch., 1965—, Brain Rsch., 1974-78, Neuropsychologia, 1963-92, Human Neurobiology, 1981-87, Jour. Cognitive Neurosci., 1989—, Jour. NIH Rsch., 1989-97, Cerebral Cortex, 1990-95, Advances in Neurobiology, 1990—, Handbook Behavioral Neurology, 1991—, Current Opinion in Neurobiology, 1991—, Neurobiology of Learning and Memory, 1992—, Learning and Memory, 1993—, Jour. Internat. Neuropsychol. Soc., 1995-99, Internat. Encyclopedia of the Social and Behavioral Scis., 1998-2002; reviewing editors sci., 1985-93; assoc. editor Neuroreport, 1990-2000; contbr. numerous articles to profl. jours., also abstracts and book revs. Served to lt. (j.g.) USNR. Recipient U.S. Presdl. Disting. Rank award, 1992, Karl Spencer Lashley prize Am. Philos. Soc., 1996, Found. Ipsen Neuronal Plasticity prize, 1995, Med. Rsch. award Met. Life Found., 2000. Fellow AAAS (chair-elect 1990-91, chair 1991-92, past chair 1992-93), APA Assn. (officer, divsn. 6 mem. at large 1964-66, coun. rep. 1967-69, pres. 1968-69, Disting. Scientific Contribution award, 1985); mem. NAS (officer, sect. 52 chmn. 1998-92), Ea. Psychol. Assn., Internat. Brain Research Orgn. (officer, rep.-at-large governing coun. 1993-98), Internat. Neuropsychol. Soc., Internat. Neuropsychol. Symposium, Internat. Primatological Soc., Internat. Soc. Neuroethology, Cognitive Neuroscience Soc. (Hermann von Helmholtz award, 1989) Soc. Exptl. Psychologists (Howard Crosby Warren medal 1998), Soc. Neurosci. (officer, pres.-elect 1985-86, pres. 1986-87, past pres. 1987-88), Inst. Medicine, Brazilian Acad. Sci., Sigma Xi, Phi Beta Kappa. Achievements include research in behavioral and cognitive neuroscience in primates. Office: NIMH Lab Neuropsychology 49 Convent Dr Msc 4415 Bldg 49 Bethesda MD 20892-0001 Business E-Mail: mishkinm@mail.nih.gov.

**MISHKIN, PAUL J.**, lawyer, educator; b. Trenton, NJ, Jan. 1, 1927; s. Mark Mordecai and Bella (Dworetsky) M.; m. Mildred Brofman Westover; 1 child, Jonathan Mills Westover. AB, Columbia U., 1947, JD, 1950; MA (hon.), U. Pa., 1971. Bar: N.Y. State bar 1950, U.S. Supreme Ct. bar 1958. Mem. faculty Law Sch. U. Pa., Phila., 1950-72; prof. law U. Calif., Berkeley, 1972-75, Emanuel S. Heller prof., 1975—2000, Emanuel S. Heller prof. emeritus, 2000—. Cons. City of Phila., 1953; reporter study div. jurisdiction between state and fed. cts. Am. Law Inst., 1960-65; mem. faculty Salzburg Seminar in Am. Studies, 1974; Charles Inglis Thompson guest prof. U. Colo., 1975; John Randolph Tucker lectr., 1978, Owen J. Roberts Meml. lectr., 1982; vis. fellow Wolfson Coll., Cambridge U., 1984; vis. prof. Duke U. Law Sch., 1989. Author: (with Morris) On Law in Courts, 1965, (with others) Federal Courts and the Federal System, 2d edit, 1973, 3d edit, 1988; contbr. articles to profl. jours. Trustee Jewish Publ. Soc. Am., 1966-75, Ctr. for Law in the Pub. Interest, 2001-04; mem. permanent com. Oliver Wendell Holmes Devise, 1979-87. With USNR 1945-46. Rockefeller Found. rsch. grantee, 1956; Center for Advanced Study in Behavioral Scis. fellow, 1964-65; recipient Russell Prize for Excellence in Teaching, 1996. Fellow Am. Acad. Arts Scis., Am. Bar Found.; mem. Am. Law Inst., Order of Coif, Phi Beta Kappa. Home: 91 Stonewall Rd Berkeley CA 94705-1414 Office: U Calif Sch Law Boalt Hall Berkeley CA 94720 Business E-Mail: pjm@law.berkeley.edu.

**MISHLER, CLIFFORD LESLIE**, publisher; b. Vandalia, Mich., Aug. 11, 1939; s. Nelson Howard and Lily Mae (Young) M.; m. Sandra Rae Knutson, Dec. 21, 1963 (dec. July 8, 1972); m. Sylvia M. Leer, Feb. 27, 1976; children: Sheila, Sharon, Susan. Student, Northwestern U., 1957-58. Author, pub. ann. edits. Ann. Studies U.S. and Can. Commemorative Medals and Tokens, 1958-63; assoc. editor Numismatic News, Krause Publs., Iola, Wis., 1963-64, editor, 1964-66, numismatic editor all publs., 1966-75, exec. v.p., pub. all numismatic publs., 1975-78, exec. v.p., pub. all products, 1978-88, sr. v.p., pub. all Numismatic products, 1988-89, sr. v.p. ops., 1989-90; pres Krause Publs., Iola, Wis., 1991-99; dir. numismatic devel. Whitman Pub., 2005—. Bd. dirs. First State Bank Iola, 1972-83, Scandinavia Telephone Co., 1981-97, TDS Telecom cmty. bd., 1997-2000; mem. coins and medals adv. panel Am. Revolution Bicentennial Commn., 1970-75; mem. an assay commn. U.S. Mint, 1973. Co-author: Standard Catalog of World Coins, ann. 1972-2005; contbr. articles New Book Knowledge, ann. 1969-81. Co-founder Iola Old Car Show, Inc., 1972, ex-officio dir., 1985—2003; mem. Wis. Commemora-

tive Quarter Coun., 2001—03; bd. dirs. William R. Higgins, Jr. Found., 1991—; chmn. fund drive Iola-Scandinavia Cmty. Fitness and Aquatic Ctr., 1999—2001. Recipient The Internat. Vreneli Preistrager: The "Friendly Prize" for lifetime numismatic achievements, Munzen-Revue, Basel, Switzerland, 2001, Numis. Amb. award, Numis. News/Balt., Md., 2003. Fellow Am. Numismatic Soc. (life, coun. mem. 1997-2003, trustee 2003—); mem. Am. Numismatic Assn. (life, medal of merit 1983, Farran Zerbe Meml. Disting Svc. award 1984, Glen Smedley meml. dedicated svcs. award 1991, Lifetime Achievement award 1997, Numismatist of Yr. 2002, hall of fame 2004, Burnett Anderson Meml. award for Excellence in Numismatic writing, 2005), Token and Medal Soc. (life, pres. 1976-78, editor jour. 1964-68, Disting. Svc. award 1966, 80), Numismatists of Wis. (life, pres. 1974-76, Meritorious Svc. award 1972), Soc. Internat. Numismatics (award of excellence 1981), Blue Ridge Numismatic Assn. (life, hall of fame 1994), Tex. Numismatic Assn. (life, hall of fame 1993), Ind. State Numismatic Assn. (life, founders award 1993), Ctrl. States Numismatic Soc. (life, medal of merit 1984), Iola Lions (Melvin Jones fellow 1996). Home: 100 Island Dr Iola WI 54945-9485 Office: 105 N Main St Iola WI 54945-0001 Office Phone: 715-445-5050. Personal E-mail: mish@athenet.net.

**MISHLER, JOHN JOSEPH**, sculptor, art educator; b. Nazareth, Ethiopia, May 28, 1948; came to U.S.; 1949; s. Dorsa J. and Mary K. (Diller) M.; m. Phyllis M. Emerson, June 27, 1970; 1 child, Nathan M. BA, Goshen (Ind.) Coll., 1972; MFA, U. Tenn., 1977. Assoc. prof. art Goshen Coll., 1985—. Executed sculptors for Recreation Ctr., Goshen Coll., 1995, Chandler Grade Sch., Goshen, 1995, U. Notre Dame, 1996, also pvt. comms; exhbns. include Midwest Mus., Elkhart, Ind., 1992, Western Mich. U., Kalamazoo, 1992, U. Notre Dame, Ind., 1995-96, Midwest Mus. Am. Art, Elkhart, 1995 (Purchase award), Michiana Regional Airport, South Bend, Ind., 2002, Krasl Art Ctr., St. Joseph, Mich., 2002, Art & Cultural Ctr., Fall Brook, Calif., 2002, Field Mus., Chgo., 2002, Sculpture in the Park 2002, Loveland, Chgo., 2002, Pier Walk 2002, Navy Pier, Chgo., 2002. Genesis grantee, 1995; recipient 2 purchase awards Elkhart (Ind.) Regional Midwest Mus. Art, 1997. E-mail: johnjm@goshen.edu.

**MISHLER, JOHN MILTON (YOCHANAN MENASHSHEH BEN SHAUL)**, science educator, artist; b. Cairo, Ill., Sept. 25, 1946; s. John Milton and Mary Jane (Woodbury) Mishler; m. Mary Therese Stember, Apr. 15, 1972 (div. Nov. 1981); m. Sigrid Ruth Elizabeth Fischer, Dec. 15, 1981; 1 child, Joshua Evan. AA with honors, Orange Coast Coll., Costa Mesa, Calif., 1966; AB in Molecular Biology, U. Calif., San Diego, 1969, ScM in Engring. Scis., 1971; DPhil in Immunohematology, St. John's Coll., Oxford U., 1978. Cert. cmty. coll. instr. Calif. Clin. coord. McGaw Labs., Costa Mesa, 1972-78; rsch. fellow Royal Postgrad. Med. Sch., Eng., 1977-78, Med. U., Cologne, Fed. Republic Germany, 1978-80; br. chief Nat. Heart, Lung and Blood Inst. NIH, Bethesda, Md., 1980-82; prof. med., basic life scis. and pharmacol. U. Mo., Kansas City, 1983-89, asst. vice chancellor, 1983-85, dir. div. basic med. scis., 1985-86, assoc. vice chancellor, 1985-89; prof. nat. scis. U. Md. Ea. Shore, Princess Anne, 1989-94, dean grad. studies and research, 1989-91; prof. biology Delaware Valley Coll. Sci. and Agrl., Doylestown, Pa., 1994—, dean of Coll., 1994-95. Frequent nat. and internat. lectr.; chmn. 13 nat. and internat. meeting sects. Author: Pharmacology of Hydroxyethyl Starch. Use in Therapy and Blood Banking, 1982; mem. editl. bd. Jour. Soc. Rsch. Adminstrs., 1987-91; book rev. editor Grants Mag., 1987-89; contbr. over 100 articles to profl. jours. Bd. dirs. Ctr. for Bus. Innovation, Inc., 1987, Bucks Assn. for Retarded Citizens, 1995-96; v.p. Artsbridge, 1999-2000. Sr. rsch. fellow Alexander von Humboldt Foun. (Germany), 1978-80; recipient Outstanding Adminstrn. Svc. award U. Mo., Kansas City, 1987, Excellence award Soc. Rsch. Adminstrn., 1989, Cert. Appreciation, 1991, Silver and Bronze awards Artist Guild of Delaware Valley, 1998, Second prize Chester County Art Assn., 1998, Bd. Dirs. award Gtr. Norristown Art League, 1998, Award of Merit Westmoreland Art Nats., 1998, Perkins Ctr. for Arts, 2000, Robert Ransley Outstanding Talent award, 1999, 2d prize drawing Ctr. for the Creative Arts, 1999, 1st prize graphics Perkiomen Valley Art Ctr., 1999, 2d prize, 2002, Wayne Art Supply award Wayne Art Ctr., 2002, Pres.'s award Salmagundi Club, 2002, Best of Show/1st Pl. award Louisville Art Assn., 2003, Jerry's Artarama award Montana Watercolor Soc., 2003, honorable mention Associated Artists Southport, 2004, Franklin Square Gallery, 2004, hon. mention Taos Nat. Watercolor Soc., 2004, Winston Churchill award Mo. Watercolor Soc., 2005, Ursus Abstract award Tubac Ctr. of Arts, 2006, 3rd prize Conneaut Cmty. Ctr. for Arts, 2006. Fellow Internat. Soc. Haematology, Royal Coll. Pathologists; mem. Am. Soc. Hematology, German Soc. Hematology, Nat. Coun. Univ. Rsch. Adminstrn., Nat. Assn. State Univs. and Land-Grant Colls. (mem. exec. com. coun. on rsch. policy and grad. edn. 1990-91), Coun. Grad. Schs. N.Y. Acad. Scis., Sigma Xi. Jewish. Avocations: reading, abstract art painting, writing, music. Home: 475 North St Apt 6F Doylestown PA 18901-3863 Office: Delaware Valley Coll 700 E Butler Ave Doylestown PA 18901-2607 Office Phone: 215-489-2351. Business E-Mail: mishlerj@devalcol.edu.

**MISHRA, AMITABH**, computer engineer, educator; s. Brij Mohan and Devmani Mishra; m. Tanuja Tiwari, Feb. 21, 1992; children: Meghana Noni, Anant Shubham. BE, Jabalpur U., India, 1973; MTech, Indian Inst. Tech., Kharagpur, India, 1975; PhD, McGill U., Montreal, Can., 1985; MS, U. Ill., Urbana Champaign, 1996. Mem. tech. staff Bell Labs, Naperville, Ill., 1987—2000; assoc. prof. Va. Tech., Blacksburg, Va., 2000—. Contbr. articles to profl. jours. Grantee, NSF, 2000—06. Mem.: IEEE (sr.). Achievements include patents in field. Office: Virginia Tech 2040 Torgersen Hall Blacksburg VA 24061 Office Phone: 540-231-9689.

**MISHRA, PIYUSH**, computer engineer, researcher, educator; b. Allahabad, Uttar Pradesh, India, Apr. 17, 1975; m. Anusha Gopal, Dec. 13, 2004. BS in Engring., Birla Inst. Tech., India, 1993—97; PhD in Elec. Engring., Poly. U., Bklyn., 1999—2004. Mem. engr. Infosys. Tech. Ltd., Bangalore, Karnataka India, 1998 98; rsch fellow Poly. U., Bklyn., 1999—2004; internship Symbol Techs. Inc., Holtsville, NY, 2001; asst. prof. Mich. Technol. U., Houghton, Mich., 2004—. Reviewer IEEE ACM Transactions, Jours., Confs.; tech. referee John Wiley & Sons, 2004—, Handbook Computer Networks; co-chair, tech. program com. mem. Internat. Conf. Info. & Comm.; tech. program com. mem. IEEE Internat. Conf. on Communication, 2006—. Contbr. scientific papers, chapters to books. Grantee Info. Assurance Group scholarship, Cisco Sys., 2003, IEEE Design Automation Conf. Graduate scholarship, Rsch. fellowship, Polytechnic U. Mem.: IEEE (tech. program com. mem. 1996—, tech. referee 2000—), Sigma Xi (assoc.). Hindu. Office: Mich Technol Univ 121 EERC 1400 Townsend Dr Houghton MI 49931 Office Phone: 906-487-2869. Office Fax: 906-487-2949. Personal E-mail: mishrapiyush@gmail.com. Business E-Mail: mishra@mtu.edu.

**MISIC, MARK M.**, exercise physiologist, researcher; s. Donald and Mildred Misic. BS in Mktg., No. Ill. U., DeKalb, 1984, MS in Info. Sys., 1987, EdD, 1994, MSEd in Exercise Physiology, 2000. Cert. strength & conditioning specialist Nat. Strength & Conditioning Assn., 2001, personal trainer Nat. Strength & Conditioning Assn., 2001. Analyst Unisys, Elk Grove, Ill., 1984—86; mgr. JP Faivre, DeKalb, Ill., 1987—90; instr. No. Ill. U., 1990—2004, dir. tech. coll. bus., 1991—2004; instr. U. Ill., Urbana, 2004—, rsch. coord., 2005—. Contbr. articles to profl. jours. Chmn. bd. elders Immanuel Luth. Ch., DeKalb, 2001—03. Mem.: Nat. Strength & Conditioning Assn., Am. Coll. Sports Medicine. Lutheran. Avocations: resistance training, running, swimming, bicycling, horseback riding. Office: U Ill 906 S Goodwin Urbana IL 61820 Office Phone: 217-244-7299. Business E-Mail: mmisic2@uiuc.edu.

**MISIOROWSKI, ELISE BESSON**, museum director; b. N.Y.C., Jan. 17, 1947; d. John Case Besson and Louise Katrina Foot; m. Robert Alan Misiorowski, June 10, 1966; 1 child, Rebecca Alexis. Student, Knox Coll., 1966; diploma in gemology, Gemol. Inst. Am., 1981. Diamond grader Gemol. Inst. Am. Gem Trade Lab., Santa Monica, Calif., 1979—82; rsch libr. Gemol. Inst. Am. Libr., Santa Monica, 1984—97; mus. dir. Gemol. Inst. Am. Mus., Carlsbad, Calif., 2000—. Faculty Antique, Period Jewelry and Gem Conf., Maine, 1994, Maine, 98, RI, 97, RI, 99; lectr. Gemol. Inst. Am. Alumni Assn., Basel, Switzerland, 1998, Hong Kong, 99. Contbr. articles to profl. jours., column to Profl. Jeweler's Mag. Vol. Peace Corps, Honduras, 1966—69. Mem.: Am. Soc. Jewelry Historians, Soc. Jewellery Historians, Women's Jewelry Assn. Democrat. Episcopalian. Avocations: jewelry fabrication, pearl stringing, crocheting, book collecting. Office: Gemological Inst Am Robert Mollawad Campus 5345 Armada Dr Carlsbad CA 92008 Office Phone: 760-603-4073.

MISKUS, MICHAEL ANTHONY, electrical engineer; b. East Chicago, Ind., Dec. 10, 1950; s. Paul and Josephine Miskus; m. Daphne Christine Headley, Nov. 19, 1998. BS, Purdue U., 1972, AAS in Elec. Engring. Tech., 1972; cert. mgmt., Ind. U., 1972, Ind. Ctrl. Coll., 1974; MA in Orgnl. Mgmt., U. Phoenix, 1996, postgrad., 1997; PhD in Orgnl. Behavior, Columbia U., 1998. Cert. plant engr. IIPFE; registered environ. assessor REA, Calif. Svc. engr. Reliance Electric & Engring. Co., Hammond, Ind., 1972-73; maintenance supr., maintenance mgr. Diamond Chain Co./AMSTED Industries, Indpls., 1973-76; primary and facilities elec. engr. Johnson & Johnson Baby Products Co., Park Forest South, Ill., 1976-81; prin. Miskus Cons., indsl./comml. elec. cons., 1979—; plant and facilities engring. mgr. Sherwin Williams Co., Chgo. Emulsion Plant, 1981-85; with Miscon Assocs., Riverside, Calif., 1985—; acting dir. plant and facilities engring. Bourns Inc., 1982-90; facility mgr. Cardiovascular Devices Inc., 3M Healthcare, 1990—; mgr. Metrology and Corp. Metrology Lab. & ISO 9000, 3M, St. Paul; facilities ops. mgr. Press Enterprise, Riverside, 1997-2001; dir. facilities and plant engring. Shell Solar Industries LP, Camarillo, Calif., 2001—; project mgr. Devel. mktg. svcs. tng. sales tools Siemens, Power Conversion Divsn., NYC, 2002—. Instr., lectr. EET program Moraine Valley C.C., Palos Hills, Ill., 1979; instr. cert. program plant engring. U. Calif.; lectr. energy engring., bldg. automation sys. Prairie State Coll., Chicago Heights, Ill., 1980—; mem. adj. faculty, faculty adv. bd. Orange Coast Coll., Costa Mesa, Calif.; bd. dirs., v.p. adminstrn. Internat. Inst. Plant & Facilities Engring.; commr., chmn. Riverside Energy Commn., 1988—; mem. Elec. Industry Evaluation Panel; siemens project mgr. Siemens Energy and Automation LD Motors, 2002—; chief cons. Miscon Cons. Productivity, Improvement Sys. Self Elec. Use Sys. Author: (text) The New Business Society. Mem. faculty adv. bd. Moraine Valley C.C., 1980—. Mem. IEEE, Am. Inst. Plant Engrs. (pres. Pomona chpt. 1989—, chmn. western region VI membership, chmn. nat. coun. stds. labs. region II Twin Cities sect. 1995—), Assn. Facility Engrs. (pres. Inland Empire chpt. III 1997—), Assn. Energy Engrs. (sr., So. Calif. chpt.), Assn. Profl. Energy Mgrs. (bd. dirs. Orange County chpt. 1992), Internat. Inst. Plant and Facilities Engring. (dir. tech. 1999—), Illuminating Engring. Soc. N.Am., Internat. Platform Assn., Riverside C. of C., Purdue Alumni Orgn. L.A. (v.p. Inland chpt.), Purdue Club L.A. (v.p. Inland Empire sect.). Personal E-mail: columbia503@yahoo.com, jackeyboy@ezz.net.

MISLOW, KURT MARTIN, chemist, educator; b. Berlin, June 5, 1923; came to U.S., 1940, naturalized, 1946; s. Max and Ida (Bingen) M.; m. Jacqueline Ford, 1966; children: Christopher, John. BS, Tulane U., 1944, DSc (hon.), 1975; PhD, Calif. Inst. Tech., 1947; Doctorate (hon.), Free U., Brussels, 1974, Uppsala U., 1977, Düsseldorf U. 1994, Zurich U., 2004. Instr. NYU, 1947-51, asst. prof., 1951-56, asso. prof., 1956-60, prof., 1960-64; Hugh Stott Taylor prof. chemistry Princeton, 1964-88, chmn. dept. chemistry, 1968-74, prof. emeritus, 1988—. Vis. prof. Stanford U., 1960, Calif. Inst. Tech., 1994; M.S. Kharasch vis. prof. U. Chgo., 1989; Univ. lectr. U. London, 1965; J.A. McRae Meml. lectr. Queen's U., 1967; H.A. Iddles lectr. U. N.H., 1972; Solvay lectr. and medalist Free U. Brussels, 1972; E.C. Lee lectr. U. Chgo.; A.A. Vernon lectr. Northeastern U., 1976; PPG lectr. Ohio U., 1977; J. Musher Meml. lectr. Hebrew U. Jerusalem, 1978; North Country lectr., 1978; Honor lectr. Ariz. State U., 1981; E. Ritchie meml. lectr. Sydney U., 1983; Fuson lectr. U. Nev., 1983; Research Scholar lectr. Drew U., 1983; McGregory lectr. Colgate U., 1984; Sandia lectr. U. Alta., 1984; Purves lectr. McGill U., 1985; Arnold lectr. So. Ill. U., 1985; Bergmann lectr. Yale U., 1986; H.C. Brown lectr. Purdue U., 1988; Irvine lectr. U. St. Andrews, 1988; Eyring lectr. Ariz. State U., 1989; Disting. Scientist lectr. Bard Coll., 1991; Syntex Disting. lectr. Colo. State U., 1991; Disting. scientist lectr. Bard Coll., 1991; J.W.T. Spinks lectr. U. Saskatchewan, 1992; Bristol-Myers-Squibb disting. lectr. Syracuse U., 1992; Churchill fellow Cambridge U., 1974-75; mem. adv. panel chemistry NSF, 1963-66; mem. panel medical and organic chemistry NIH, 1963-66. Author: Introduction to Stereochemistry, 1965; also numerous articles; bd. editors: Jour. Organic Chemistry, 1965-70; mem. editl. adv. bd. Monatshefte für Chemie, Topics in Stereochemistry, Accounts of Chem. Rsch., Chem. and Engring. News, Bull des Sociétés Chimiques Belges, Symmetry, Jour. Math. Chemistry. Recipient Solvay medal Free U. Brussels, 1972, Prelog medal, ETH Zurich, 1986, W.H. Nichols medal, 1987, Sci. Achievement award medal CCNY, 1988, Disting. Alumni award Calif. Inst. Tech., 1990, Chirality medal, 1993, Sesquicentennial medal Tulane U., 1997, Arthur C. Cope Scholar award Am. Chem. Soc. 1995; Guggenheim fellow, 1957-58, 74-75, Alfred P. Sloan fellow, 1959-63, Sherman Fairchild disting. scholar Calif. Inst. Tech., 1990, 91, 94. Fellow AAAS, Am. Acad. Arts and Scis.; mem. NAS, AAUP, Am. Chem. Soc. (James Flack Norris award 1975), Academia Nazionale dei Lincei (fgn. mem.), Phi Beta Kappa, Sigma Xi. Personal E-mail: kmislow@princeton.edu.

MISNER, CHARLES WILLIAM, physics professor; b. Jackson, Mich., June 13, 1932; s. Francis deSales and Madge B. (Mee) M.; m. Susanne Elisabeth Kemp, June 13, 1959; children: Benedicte Elisabeth, Francis Frithjof, Timothy Charles, Christopher Kemp. BS, U. Notre Dame, 1952; MA, Princeton U., 1954, PhD, 1957. Instr. Princeton U., NJ, 1956-59, asst. prof. NJ, 1959-63; assoc. prof. physics U. Md., College Park, 1963-66, prof., 1966-2000, assoc. chair physics dept., 1995-99, prof. emeritus, sr. rsch. scientist, 2000—. Vis. fellow Inst. for Theoretical Physics, U. Calif., Santa Barbara, 1980-81, All Souls Coll., Oxford, Eng., 1973, Max Planck-Albert Einstein Inst., Potsdam, Germany, 2000, 02, 05; vis. faculty Calif. Inst. Tech., 1972, Princeton U., 1969 Author: (with Wheeler and Thorne) Gravitation, 1973, (with Patrick J.Cooney) Spreadsheet Physics, 1991; contbr. articles to profl. jours. Recipient Sci. Centennial award U. Notre Dame, 1965, Dannie Heineman prize (with R. Arnowitt and S. Deser) for math. physics Am. Phys. Soc., 1994; NSF sr. postdoctoral fellow, 1966-67; Guggenheim fellow, 1972-73; Einstein Centennial lectr., 1979. Fellow Am. Phys. Soc., Royal Astron. Soc., Am. Acad. Arts and Scis., Am. Assn. Advancement Sci. mem. Philosophy of Sci. Assn., Am. Math. Soc. Fedn. Am. Scientists. Democrat. Roman Catholic. Office: U Md Dept Physics College Park MD 20742-4111 E-mail: misner@physics.umd.edu.

MISNER, CHARLOTTE BLANCHE RUCKMAN, retired community organization administrator; b. Gifford, Idaho, Aug. 30, 1937; d. Richard Steele and Arizona (Hill) Ruckman; m. G. Arthur Misner, Jr., Aug. 29, 1959; children: Michelle, Mary, Jennifer. BS in Psychology, U. Idaho, 1959. Vol. numerous orgns., India, Mexico, The Philippines, 1962-70; sec., v.p. pres., trustee St. Luke's Hosp., Manila, 1970-84; founding mem., 3d v.p., pres. Am. Women's Club of Philippines, 1977-84; exec. dir. Friends of Oakland (Calif.) Parks and Recreation, 1986-2000, ret., 2000. Active Lincoln Child Ctr., Oakland, 1984—. Recipient Vol. Svc. award Women's Bd. St. Luke's Hosp., 1977, Mid. Sch. Vol. award Internat. Sch.-Manila, 1980. Me. Alpha Gamma Delta (alumnae treas., pres. East Bay 1985-89, province dir. alumnae 1989-98, bd. dirs. alumni devel. 1998-2005, mem. steering com. centennial capital campaign 1999—), Cum Laude Soc. (hon.).

MISNER, JEFFREY J., air transportation executive; b. 1954; married; 3 children. BA, San Deigo State Univ. With Kenneth Leventhal and Co., Newport, Calif., 1979—81; tax & bus. cons. Ernst & Young, Orange County, Calif., 1981—91; v.p. treas. ops. Continental Airlines Inc., 1995—2000, sr. v.p., CFO, 2001—. With USMC, 1971—73. Office: Continental Airlines Inc PO Box 4607 Houston TX 77210-4607

MISNER, LORRAINE, lab administrator; b. Fitchburg, Mass., June 24, 1948; d. Cedric Winfield and Pearl Erma (Hallisey) M. BA in Biology, Fitchburg State Coll., 1971; MS in Biology, Anna Maria Coll., 1983. Cert. Novell engr. Lab. technologist Leominster (Mass.) Hosp., 1971-87; rsch. asst. U. Lowell Rsch. Found. (now U. Mass. Lowell Rsch. Found.), 1987-99; sys. engr. TeleSpectrum Worldwide Inc., 1999—. Piccolo Townsend (Mass.) Mil.

Band, 1964-93; mem. choir United Ch. of Christ, 1961—. Mem. Am. Soc. Clin. Pathologists (assoc., registrant). Avocations: bowling, music, travel, dance. E-mail: lorrainemisner@earthlink.net.

MISNER-ELIAS, MICHAEL BRYAN, bank executive, consultant; s. Norman F. and H. Karen Misner; m. Gayle Andrea Elias, Nov. 1, 1992; children: Benjamin Samuel, Simon Christopher, Sarah Grace. BS, Franciscan U. Steubenville, 1988. Naval flight officer USN, Brunswick, Maine, 1989—94; dir. mktg. Mmedia.com, Manhattan, Kans., 1995—96; dir. competitive intelligence Little Diversified Archtl. Consultants, Charlotte, NC, 1997—2001; portfolio mgr. Bank of Am., Charlotte, 2002—. Lt. USN, 1989—94, Brunswick, Maine. Mem.: Soc. Competitive Intelligence Professionals (life). Conservative. Roman Catholic. Avocations: running, theology, apologetics, early church history. Office Phone: 704-387-7523. Business E-Mail: michael.misner-elias@bankofamerica.com.

MISRA, RAGHUNATH PRASAD, physician, educator; b. Calcutta, West. Bengal, India, Feb. 1, 1928; came to U.S., 1964; s. Guru Prasad and Anandi M.; m. Therese Rettenmund, Sept. 13, 1963; children: Sima, Joya, Maya, Tara. BSc honors, Calcutta U., 1948; MBBS, Med. Coll., Calcutta, 1953; PhD, McGill U., Montreal, Que., 1965. Diplomate Am. Bd. Anat. and Clin. Pathology. Asst. prof., dir. kidney lab. U. Louisville Sch. Medicine, 1964—68; assoc. investigator and dir. kidney lab Mt. Sinai Hosp., Cleve., 1968—73; asst. prof. Case We. Res. Med. Sch., Cleve., 1973—76; asst. prof., dir. kidney lab. Sch. Medicine La. State U., Shreveport, 1976—80, assoc. prof. Sch. Medicine, 1990—96, prof. Sch. Medicine, 1986—98, emeritus prof. Sch. Medicine, 1998—. Cons. VA Med. Ctr., Shreveport, 1977-98, EA Conway Meml. Hosp., Monroe, La., 1980-98; dir. Ocular Pathology Lab. Sch. Medicine La. State U., Shreveport, 1988— Author: Atlas of Skin Biopsy, 1983 Pres. India Assn. of Shreveport, 1979, 81 Tallisman fellow Mt. Sinai Hosp., 1970-73. Fellow Am. Coll. Pathologists, Am. Soc. Clin. Pathologists, Am. Coll. Internat. Physicians, U. Calcutta Med. Alumni Assn. Am. (pres. 1992-93), Sigma Xi (pres. 1987-89) Democrat. Hindu. Avocations: photography, travel. Office: La State U Sch Medicine 1501 Kings Hwy Shreveport LA 71103-4228 Office Phone: 318-675-5012. Business E-Mail: rmisra@lsuhsc.edu.

MISRACH, RICHARD LAURENCE, photographer; b. LA, July 11, 1949; s. Robert Laskin and Lucille (Gardner) M.; m. Debra Bloomfield, Jan. 18, 1981 (div. 1987); 1 son, Jacob Luke; m. Myriam Weisang, Apr. 17, 1989. AB in Psychology, U. Calif., Berkeley, 1971. Instr. Assoc. Students Studio, U. Calif.-Santa Barbara, 1984. Juror Nat. Endowment Arts, 1986; lectr. Calif. Inst. for Arts, 1990. Exhbns. include Whitney Biennial, 1981, 91, Musèe d'Art Moderne, Paris, 1979, Mus. Modern Art, N.Y.C., 1978, Grapestake Gallery, San Francisco, 1979, 81, Young-Hoffman Gallery, Chgo., 1980, Oakland Mus., 1982, 87, San Francisco Mus. Modern Art, 1983, Centre Georges Pompidou, Paris, 1983, L.A. County Mus. Art, 1984, Fraenkel Gallery, San Francisco, 1985, 89, 91, 95, 97, 99, Min Gallery, Tokyo, 1975-87, Univ. Art Mus., Berkeley, Curt Marcus Gallery, 1995, 96, 97, 2000, James Danziger Gallery, 1995, Robert Mann Gallery, N.Y., 1999, Melbourne Internat. Festival, Australia, 1995, G. Gibson Gallery, 2000, High Mus. Art, Atlanta, 2000, Froenhel Gallery, 2002, 04, 06, Grant/Selwyn Fine art, 2003, Pace MacGill Chelsea, 2004, 06, Marc Selwyn Fine Art, 2005, others; one person exhbns. at Art Inst. Chgo., 1988, Milw. Art Mus., 1988, Carpenter Ctr., Harvard U., 1988, Fotomann, Inc., N.Y., 1989, 91, Photographers Gallery, 1990, Parco Gallery, Tokyo, 1990, Arles Festival, France, 1990, Jan Kesner Gallery, 1990, 91, 94, 2000, Houston Mus. Fine Arts, 1996, Ctr. Creative Photography, Tucson, 1996, Mus. Contemporary Art, Chgo., 1997, Contemporary Mus. of Art Art, Hawaii, 1997, San Jose Mus. of Art, 1998, Diputacion de Granada, Spain, 1997, art commn. cover Time mag., July 4, 1988; books include Telegraph 3 A.M., 1974, Grapestake Gallery, 1979, (A Photographic Book), 1979, Hawaii portfolio, 1980, Graecism dye-transfer portfolio, 1982, Desert Cantos, 1987, (Internat. Ctr. of Photography award 1988), Bravo 20: The Bombing of the American West, 1990 (Pen Ctr. U.S.A. West award for nonfiction 1991), Richard Misrach, Minn. Gallery, 1988, Violent Legacies, Aperture, 1992, Crimes and Splendors, 1996, Cantos del Desierto, Di putacion de Granada, 1999, The Sky Book, 2000, Richard Misrach: Golden Gate, 2001, Pictures of Paintings, 2002, Chronologies, 2005. Guggenheim fellow, 1978; Ferguson grantee, 1976; NEA grantee, 1973, 77, 84, 92; AT&T commn., 1979; Eureka fellow, 1991; recipient Koret Israel prize, 1992. *Photographs are the shadows of reality much like dreams. On the one hand, they appear to literally transcribe the real world, while on the other, they defy our linear concept of time and meaning. Because the primary illusion of photography is fact, it is the most powerful art medium of our time.*

MISSAR, CHARLES DONALD, retired librarian; b. Cleve., July 16, 1925; s. Charles Frank and Genevieve Catherine (Buechele) M.; m. Margaret Mary du Fief, Feb. 17, 1962 (dec.); children: Charles David, Stephen du Fief. Student, Sacred Heart Sem., Detroit, 1943-45, St. Mary's Sem., Cleve., 1945-49; BA, John Carroll U., 1951; MLS, Cath. U. Am., 1960. Referral specialist Libr. of Congress, Washington, 1963-66; ERIC info. specialist U.S. Office Edn., Washington, 1966-72; head Ednl. Reference Ctr. Nat. Inst. Edn., Washington, 1973-78, supervisory libr., 1978-85; sr. libr. U.S. Dept. Edn., 1985-86; sr. editor Computer Scis. Corp. Profl. Svcs. Group, 1986-94, Missar Assocs., Washington, 1994—2001. Agy. rep. Fed. Libr. Com., Washington, 1978-86; ann. lectr. Fed. Libr. Resources Workshop, Catholic U. Am., Washington, 1981-96. Editor: Management of Federally Sponsored Libraries: Case Studies and Analysis, 1995; compiler, author: A Checklist of Ohio Imprints From 1821 to 1825, 1960; editor monthly jour. Tech. Abstract Bull., 1958-60; mem. editl. bd. Online Mag., 1977-80 Bd. dirs. Shrine of the Most Blessed Sacrament St. Pius X Libr., 1995—. Recipient Superior Svc. Group award U.S. Office Edn., 1968, Superior Performance award Nat. Inst. Edn., 1974, 84; inductee Spl. Libraries Assn. Hall of Fame, 1991. Mem. ALA, D.C. Libr. Assn. (treas. 1972-74), Spl. Librs. Assn. (chmn. edn. divsn. 1980-81, chmn. 1989-90), Am. Soc. Info. Sci. (chmn. info. svcs. for edn. group 1984-86), John Carroll Soc., Cleve. Club, Serra Club (pres. 1992-93, 94-96), Arimathean Club, Ohio Soc., Cosmos Club. Roman Catholic. Home: 5617 32nd St NW Washington DC 20015-1622 E-mail: cdmissar@aol.com.

MISSEL, ESTHER BARBARA, artist; b. Hartford, Conn., Apr. 4, 1926; d. Gasper and Lucy Melandrillo Lissandrello; m. Frederick F. Missel, June 16, 1949; children: Deborah, Gillian, Frederick Allen. AA, Bay Path Coll., 1949. One-woman shows include Framer's Gallery, Moorestown, N.J., 1973, Perkins Ctr. for Arts, 1979, Newman Galleries, Phila., Kalyn's Fine Arts, Princeton, N.J., Cannon House Office Bldg., Washington, 1985, Moorestown Sch. Music, N.J., 2006, exhibited in group shows at Burlington County Art Guild, 1974, South Jersey All Profl. Art Show, Cape May, 1973, Rider Coll., 1973, Nat. League Am. Pen Women Club House, Washington, 1977, N.J. Ctr. Performing Arts, 1974, Haddon Fortnightly, Haddonfield, N.J., 1970, Am. Artists Profl. League, Princeton, N.J., 1981, Perkins Ctr. Arts, Moorestown, N.J., 1982, Phila. Mus. Art, 2004, 2005, Arnold Art Gallery, Newport, R.I., Represented in permanent collections 1st Presbyn. Ch., Moorestown, Squibb Co., Princeton, Farmers & Mechanics Bank, Moorestown, N.J., also pvt. collections, U.S., abroad, pub. in. Yacht Portraits, Sheridan House, N.Y.C. Contr. design and artwork to local hosps., non-profit groups. Recipient 1st Pl. in oils, Burlington County Art Guild, 1970, 2d Pl., 1972, 1st in oils, Haddonfield Fortnightly, 1973, Popular Vote award, Cape May Art League Nat. Summer Art Show, 1969. Mem.: United So. of Marine Painters, Am. Artists Profl. League, Am. Soc. Marine Artists, at. League Am. Pen Women, Inc., Internat. Soc. Marine Painters. Presbyterian. Home and Office: 264 E Main St Moorestown NJ 08057-2906 E-mail: finmtown@aol.com.

MISSETT, JUDI SHEPPARD, dancer, jazzercise company executive; b. Iowa; BA in Theater, Radio/TV, Northwestern U., Chgo., 1966. Profl. dancer, Chgo., 1966-77; jazzercise instr., choreographer, tchr. Jazzercise, Inc., Calif., 1977—; pres. worldwide dance-fitness franchise orgn. Jazzercise, Inc., Carlsbad, Calif.; prin. JM TV Prodns.; prin. mail-order catalog bus. Jazzertogs. Instr. convs., children's fitness progs. Author: (comprehensive nutrition prog.) The Jazzercise Know More Diet; author weekly fitness column for Los Angeles Times

Syndicate; performer, prodr. home exercise videos. Mem. Calif. Gov.'s Coun. on Phys. Fitness & Sports; bd. dirs. San Diego Inner-City Games; contbr. millions of dollars for charities by leading spl., large-scale workout classes. Recognized for contbns. to growth and advancement of fitness industry by Pres. Reagan in his White House Conf. on Women in Bus., 1986, Aerobics and Fitness Assn. Am., Am. Coun. on Exercise, Pres.' Coun. on Phys. Fitness & Sports; named Entrepreneur of Year, Working Woman Mag., 1988; recipient Lifetime Achievement award Internat. Assn. Fitness Profls., 1991, Women Who Mean Bus. award San Diego Bus. Jour., 1995, A Woman of Accomplishment award Soroptimist Internat. of San Diego, 1996; inducted into Internat. Assn. Fitness Profls. Hall of Fame, 1992. Mem. Nat. Fitness Leaders Assn. (exec. dir., Charles Bucher Meml. award 1996). Office: Jazzercise Inc 2460 Impala Dr Carlsbad CA 92008-7226

MISSIMER, THOMAS MICHAEL, geologist; b. Lancaster, Pa., Mar. 10, 1950; s. Jacob M. and Lorraine L. (Bilodeau) M. AB in Geology, Franklin and Marshall Coll., 1972; MS in Geology, Fla. State U., 1973; PhD in Marine Geology and Geophysics, U. Miami, Fla., 1995. Registered profl. geologist, Fla., Ga., Ind., Va., Tex. Hydrologist U.S. Geol. Survey, Ft. Myers, Fla., 1973-75; rsch. assoc. sedimentology U. Miami, Coral Gables, 1975-76; pres. Missimer & Assocs., Inc., Cape Coral, Fla., 1976-92; vice chmn. ViroGroup, Inc., Cape Coral, 1991-93; pres. CDM Missimer, Ft. Myers, 1993-99; v.p. Camp, Dresser & McKee, Inc., Ft. Myers, 1994—2004, CDM Missimer, Ft. Myers, 1999—2004; pres. Missimer Groundwater Sci., Inc., Ft. Myers, 2004—. Mem. Bd. Fla. Profl. Geologists, 1991-97, avice chmn., 1993, chmn., 1994; apptd. by Gov. J. Bush to the Fla. Forever Adv. Coun., 1999—2003; mem. tech. adv. com. Gov.'s Com. for a Substantial South Fla., 1995-98, chmn., 1996-98. Author Water supply development for membrane water treatment facilities, 1994, Lender's Guide to environmental liability management, 1996; contbr. hydrogeol. and geol. studies of Southeastern U.S. to sci. jours.; contbr. more than 200 articles to profl. jours. Mem. citizens planning adv. com. Be Lee County (Fla.), 1981-82, chmn., 1982-83. Recipient Best Paper award, Internat. Desalination Assn., D.C. World Conf. on Desalination, 1991, Acad. Merit award U. Miami, 1997. Mem. Geol. Soc. Am., Am. Inst. Profl. Geologists (cert. profl. geol. scientist), Am. Water Resources Assn., Am. Water Works Assn., AAAS, Am. Inst. Hydrology (cert. profl. hydrogeologist), Am. Groundwater Assn. (Hydrogeologist), Fla. Acad. Scis. (chmn. earth and planetary sci. sect. 1973-74, 95), Internat. Desalination Assn., Southeastern Geol. Soc., Phi Beta Kappa (bd. dirs. 1996-98). Republican. Home: 3214 Mcgregor Blvd Fort Myers FL 33901-6723 Office: Missimer Groundwater Sci Inc 3214 McGregor Blvd Fort Myers FL 33901 Office Phone: 239-810-3009. Personal E-mail: missimertm@aol.com.

MISTACCO, VICKI E., foreign language educator; b. Bklyn., Nov. 18, 1942; d. Anthony Sebastian and Lucia (Lalli) M. BA, NYU, 1963; MA, Middlebury Coll., 1964; M of Philosophy, Yale U., 1968, PhD, 1972. Instr. French Wellesley Coll., Mass., 1968-72; asst. prof. French, 1972-78, assoc. prof. French, 1978-84, prof. French, 1984—, chmn., 1978-81. Nat. adv. bd. Sweet Briar Jr. Yr. in France, Va., 1978—. Author: Women and Literary Tradition: Anthology from the Middle Ages to the Present, 2006—; contbr. articles to profl. jours. Fulbright fellow, 1963-64, Woodrow Wilson fellow, 1964-67; NEH fellow, 1983-84, 94-95. Mem.: N.E. MLA, MLA, Soc. Internat. pour l'Etude des Femmes de l'Ancien Regime, Women in French, Am. Assn. Tchrs. French, Phi Beta Kappa. Democrat. Roman Catholic. Avocations: photography, travel. Office: Wellesley Coll Dept French 106 Central St Wellesley MA 02481-8268 Office Phone: 781-283-2406. Business E-Mail: vmistacco@wellesley.edu.

MISTRAL, JACQUES, economist; b. Toulouse, France, Sept. 22, 1947; s. Léon and Lucienne (Bataillard) M.; m. Bernadette Tricou, July 1, 1970; 3 children. D Econ. Sci., U Paris, 1976; diploma, Ecole Polytechnique, Paris, 1969. Economist French Ministry of Fin., Paris, 1970—76; prof. econs. U. Paris, 1977—81; rsch. officer Centre D'Etudes Prospectives et D'Economie Mathematique, 1980—84; dep. dir. Nat. Sch. Stats. and Econ. Adminstrn., Paris, 1984—88; econ. adviser Prime Minister of France, Paris, 1988—91; exec. v.p. Axa Group, Paris, London, Beijing, Melbourne, 1992—2000; spl. advisor to Minister of Economy, Fin. and Industry Paris, 2000—01; minister, counselor for econ. and fin. affairs Embassy of France, Washington, 2001—. Bd. dirs. Ctr. d'Etudes Prospectives et d'Economie Internationale. Notre Etat, 2000, Etat t'urgence, 2004, La raison du plies tort, 2004. Lt. arty., French armed forces, 1969. Fellow, Harvard U., Kennedy Sch. Govt., 2005—06. Mem.: Le Cercle des Economistes, Le Siècle. Office: Embassy of France 4101 Reservoir Rd Washington DC 20007 Office Phone: 202-944-6380. E-mail: jacques_mistral@ksg.harvard.edu.

MISTRETTA, THERESA MARY, retired elementary school educator; b. Mt. Morris, NY, June 11, 1940; d. Michael Carmelo and Therese Mary Mistretta. BS, SUNY, Geneseo, 1963, MS, 1968. Tchr. 2d grade Cayuga Dr. Elem. Sch. Bd. Edn., Niagara Falls, NY 1963—66; tchr. 1st grade Fyle Elem. Sch., Henrietta, NY, 1966—79, Monica Leary Elem. Sch., Henrietta, 1979—97; ret., 1997. Co-founder, v.p. Mt. Morris Hist. Soc., 1973—83, 1999—2006, site mgr. archaeology field sch. Mills Mansion, 2003—06; founder, chair Mt. Morris Italian Festival Com., 1996—2004. Recipient Golden Apple award, Rush-Henrietta Tchrs. Assn., 1980. Mem.: Livingston County C. of C. (tourism com. 2001—06, Tourism Advocate of Yr. 2004), Bonsai Soc., Mt. Morris C. of C. (sec. 2005—06, Tourism Advocate of Yr. 2004, Sr. Citizen of Yr. 2006), Ikebana Internat. (pres. chpt. 53 2000—02). Roman Catholic. Avocations: bonsai, travel, archaeology, Ikebana. Home: 22 State St Mount Morris NY 14510

MISTRY, PERCY SHIAVAK, investment banker; b. Bombay, July 22, 1947; arrived in U.K., 1987; s. Shiavak P. and Banoo S. (Engineer) M.; m. Pauline Earnshaw, Oct. 15, 1969. B of Tech. with honors, Loughborough (U.K.) U., 1969; MBA, U. Toronto, 1970, MPhil, 1971. Sr. advisor to exec. v.p. Internat. Fin. Corp., Washington, 1977-78; mng. dir. SGV-SUN Hung Kai Corp. Fin., Hong Kong, 1978-81; dir., sr. fin. advisor The World Bank, Washington, 1981-87; sr. fellow Oxford (Eng.) U., 1987-92; chmn. Oxford Internat. Assoc., 1988—, Oxford Internat. Fin., 1992-97; CEO Synergy Power Corp., 1998-2000, Acad. Coun. Willon Park, 1999—2004. Chmn. Ukraine Fin. Corp., 1995-98, D.C. Gardner & Co., London, 1992-93; bd. dirs. Indsl. Credit & Investment Corp. India, Bombay, 1993-97, Forum on Debt & Devel., The Hague, Holland, 1988-98, Synergy Power Corp., Hong-Kong, 1987-2003, Small Enterprises Assistance Funds; columnist The Banker, 1987-91; advisor DBSA, UN-ECA, 1999—, Commonwealth Secretariat on Internat. Fin. Svcs., 2005, Govt. of Mauritius, 2005-06; chmn. high-level expert com. on making Mumbai an IF Ctr., 2006. Author: Multilateral Development Banks, 1995, African Debt: The Case for Relief, 1988, African Debt Revisited: Procrastination or Progress?, 1991, Inflation in Ethiopia, 1992, Economic Integration in Southern Africa, 1993, The Financial Condition of the African Development Bank, 1993, Multilateral Debt: An Emerging Crisis, 1994, Multilateral Development Bank, 1995, Resolving Africa's Multilateral Debt Problem, 1996, Regional Integration and Economic Development, 1996, Adjustment, Investment and Development Finance in Southern Africa, 2000, Role of the Commonwealth in International Negotiations, 2001, Mobilizing Support and Resources for the UN, 2001, Financing for Development, 2001, Regulation of International Financial Service in Mauritices; Cost/Benefit Study, 2006, Mitigating Risks for Foreign Investments in Least Developed Countries, 2003, Cost-Benefit Study of AML-CFT Regulations in Commonwealth Countries, 2006; co-author: Development Finance in Southern Africa, 1998, Zambia: Exchange Rate Policy, 1989, Financing the Multilateral System, 1991, The Conversion of Official Bilateral Debt, 1992, Adjusting Privatization, 1992 (Acad. Book of Yr. 1993). Dir. US-Caresbac, Atlanta, 1988-92; trustee The P.C. Mistry Found., Bombay, 1987—, F.S. MisCry Found. Mem. The Reform Club, The Willingdon Club, Cricket Club of India, The Royal Western India Turf Club. Avocations: dog breeding, swimming, squash, tennis, reading. Office Phone: 4419 9383 1567. Personal E-Mail: OxfordIntluk@aol.com, percysmistryuk@aol.com

**MITAKIDES, LOUELLA JANE,** entrepreneur; b. Dayton, Ohio, Mar. 24, 1949; d. Lester Calvin Helsley and Nettie May Gann; m. John Mitakides, June 5, 1982; children: Katherine Wynn VanderKaay, Andrew John. Copywriter Calderhead Advt., NYC, 1970; promotion dir. Cox Broadcasting, Dayton, Ohio, 1971—76; owner, CEO Helsley Advt., Cin., 1977—84; investor, entrepenuer DRNA, Inc., NYC, 1999—2006; owner Mitakides, Inc., Dayton, Ohio, 1985—. Candidate US Congress, 2004; fundraising strategist Clinton/Gore Lieberman, 1992, 1996, 2000; founding mem. Dem. Nat. Com. Small Bus. Coun., 2000, Dem. Senatorial Campaign Com. Women's Coun., 1992. Mem.: DAR, Am. Hellenic Inst. Avocations: genealogy, national history. Home: 5323 Split Rail Rd Dayton OH 45429

**MITAL, DINESH PRAKASH,** healthcare educator, consultant; b. Kosi Kalan, Uttar Pradesh, India, July 28, 1947; s. Manohar Lal and Chander Vati Mital; m. Sushma Garg, Jan. 27, 1973; children: Rashmi, Rahul. BS, Indian Inst. Tech., Kanpur, India, 1968; MS, SUNY, Stony Brook, 1970—70, PhD, 1974. Elect. engring., IEE, 1983. Project engr. NCR corp., Dayton, Ohio, 1973—76; prof. U. Roorkee, Uttar Pradesh, India, 1976—83; assoc. prof. Nanyang Technol. U., Singapore, 1983—99, UMDNJ- SHRP, Dept. Health Informatics, Newark, 1999—. Head instr. and control divsn. info. engring. Nanyang Technol. U., Singapore, 1990—98; supr. in field; gen. chmn., organizer rsch. sessions internat. confs. Editor: (edited book) Collection of Papers- Roboticsand Computer Vision; contbr. scientific papers, 60 papers internat. jours., 200 papers internat. conf., revs. rsch. papers internat. jours. Chmn. SINDA, 1994—99. Grantee microprocessor based solar contr., Applied Rsch. Corp., 1984-1986, automation small and medium size industries, 1986-1994, vision sys. automatic aircraft repairs, ARC, 1988-1994, automated signature identification, AcRF, 1988-1994, automated human face recognition sys., 1994-1998. Fellow: IEE; mem.: IFEE (sr.). Office: UMDNJ-SHRP Health Informatics 65 Bergen St Newark NJ 07107 Home Fax: 973-972-8540; Office Fax: 973-972-8540. Personal E-mail: mitaldp@umdnj.edu.

**MITAU, LEE R.,** lawyer, bank executive; b. Oct. 17, 1948; AB cum laude, Dartmouth Coll., 1969; JD magna cum laude, U. Minn., 1972. Bar: Minn. 1972, NY 1973. Law clk. to Hon. George E. MacKinnon US Ct. Appeals DC cir., 1972-73; assoc. Cleary, Gottlieb, Steen & Hamilton, 1973—79; ptnr. Oppenheimer, Wolff & Donnelly, 1979—83, Dorsey & Whitney, Mpls., 1983—95, mem. policy com., 1988—99, chmn. corp. dept., 1989—95; exec. v.p., gen. counsel US Bancorp, Mpls., 1995—. Adj. prof. law William Mitchell Coll. Law, 1982—83; bd. dirs. H.B. Fuller Co., St. Paul, 1996—, Graco Inc., Mpls., 1990—, chmn., 2002—. Trustee Mpls. Inst. Arts, Minn. Pvt. Coll. Coun.; bd. governors Mpls. Club.

**MITCH, WILLIAM EVANS,** nephrologist; b. Birmingham, Ala., July 22, 1941; s. William Evans and Mary Elizabeth (Ackerman) Mitch; m. Frances Alexandra Fisher, Aug. 21, 1965; children: Eleanor Baylor, William Armistead. BA, Harvard Coll., 1963; MD, Harvard Med. Sch., 1967. Intern Brigham & Women's Hosp., Boston, 1967-68, resident, 1968-69, 1973—78, Johns Hopkins Hosp., Balt., 1972-73; clin. assoc. NIH, Bethesda, Md., 1969-72; from asst. prof. to assoc. prof. dept. pharmacology Johns Hopkins U., Balt., 1974-78; assoc. prof. medicine Harvard Med. Sch., Boston, 1978-87; prof. Emory U. Sch. Medicine, Atlanta, 1987—2002; disting. prof. U. Tex., Galveston, 2002—04; prof. Baylor Coll. Medicine, Houston, 2004—. Mem. study sect. NIH, 1988—92. Editor: The Progressive Nature of Renal Disease, 1986, 2d edit., 1992, Nutrition and the Kidney, 1988, 5th edit., 2005. Pres. region II Nat. Kidney Found., 1990—92, chmn. sci. adv. bd., 1996—98; chmn. exec. coun. kidney Am. Heart Assn. Grantee, NIH, 1979—. Mem.: Internat. Soc. Nephrology (treas. 1997—2003), Am. Soc. Nephrology (pres. 2004), Am. Clin. and Climatol. Assn., Assn. Am. Physicians, Am. Soc. Clin. Investigation. Office Phone: 713-798-8350. Business E-Mail: mitch@bcm.edu.

**MITCHAM, JULIUS JEROME,** accountant; b. Pine Bluff, Ark., Jan. 2, 1941; s. James Vernon and Bertha Lee (Robertson) M.; m. Janet Claire Berry, Mar. 31, 1970 (div. Sept. 1981); m. Marsha Lee Henderson, Oct. 22, 1983; 1 child, Timothy John. BBA, U. Cen. Ark., 1971. CPA Ark., Okla.; cert. healthcare fin. mgr. Br. mgr. Comml. Nat. Bank, Little Rock, 1961-66; auditor, acctg. supr. Ark. Blue Cross and Blue Shield, Little Rock, 1971-77; contr. Riverview Hosp., Little Rock, 1977-81; pvt. practice acctg. Little Rock, 1981-82; contr. Henryetta (Okla.) Med. Ctr., 1982-83; fin. report supr. Am. Med. Internat., Inc., Houston, 1983; dir. corp. acctg. Ft. Myers (Fla.) Cmty. Hosp., 1984-86; contr. Med. Ctr. of Southeast Okla., Durant, 1986-87; CFO Gulf Coast Cmty. Hosp./Qualicare of Miss., Inc., 1987-88; asst. adminstr. fin. S.W. Gen. Hosp., San Antonio, 1988-89; pvt. practice San Antonio, 1989-90; CFO Bapt. Meml. Hosps. of Mississippi County, Blytheville, Ark., 1991-94; Med. Arts Hosp., Texarkana, Tex., 1994-96, Healthsouth Rehab. Hosp., Texarkana, Tex., 1997-98; pres. Mitcham & Assocs., 1998—2001; CFO Muscogee (Creek) Nation Divsn. Health Adminstrn., Okmulgee, Okla., 2002—04, Booneville (Ark.) Meml. Hosp., Ark., 2004—05, Okmulgee Meml. Hosp., 2005—. With USN, 1959—61. Mem. AICPA, Ark. Soc. CPAs, Healthcare Fin. Mgmt. Assn. (cert. fellow), Lions (sec. 1985-86, 2d v.p. 1995-96), Masons. Republican. Baptist. Home: PO Box 277 Okmulgee OK 74447 Office: PO Box 1038 Okmulgee OK 74447 Office Phone: 918-758-3102. E-mail: jmitch41@aol.com.

**MITCHARD, JACQUELYN,** writer; b. 1953; H.S. English tchr., 1974—76; mng. editor, reporter Pioneer Press, Chgo., 1976—79; reporter The Capital Times, Madison, Wis., 1979—84; metro reporter, columnist Milw. Jour., 1984—88; speechwriter for Donna Shalala, 1989—93. Author: Mother Less Child, 1985, Jane Addams: Pioneer in Social Reform and Activist for World Peace, 1991, Jane Addams: Peace Activist, 1992, The Deep End of the Ocean, 1996, The Rest of Us: Dispatches from the Mothership 1997, The Most Wanted, 1998, A Theory of Relativity, 2001, Twelve Times Blessed, 2003, Christmas Present, 2003, Starring Prima!, 2004, Baby Bat's Lullaby, 2004, The Breakdown Lane, 2005, Cage of Stars, 2006.

**MITCHELHILL, JAMES MOFFAT,** retired civil engineer; b. St. Joseph, Mo., Aug. 11, 1912; s. William and Jeannette (Ambrose) Mitchelhill; m. Maurine Hutchason, Jan. 9, 1937 (div. 1962); children: Janis Maurine Mitchelhill Leas, Jeri Ann Mitchelhill Riney; m. Alicia Beuchat, 1982. BS, Northwestern U., 1934, MSCE, 1935. Registered profl. engr., Mont., P.R., Tex. Engring. dept. C., M., St. P. & P.R.R. Co., Chgo., Miles City, Mont., 1935-45; asst. engr. Ponce & Guayama R.R. Co., Aguirre, PR, 1945-51, v.p., gen. mgr., 1969-70; engr. Ctr. Cortada, Santa Isabel, PR, 1951-54; r.r. supt. Braden Copper Co., Rancagua, Chile, 1954-63; staff engr. Coverdale - Colpitts, N.Y.C., 1963-64; asst. to exec. v.p. Central Aguirre Sugar Co., 1964-67; v.p., gen. mgr. Coddea, Inc., Dominican Republic, 1967-68; asst. to gen. mgr. Land Adminstrn. P.R., La Nueva, 1970-71; with Centrals Aguirre Lafayette and Mercedita, 1971-72; asst. to gen. mgr. Corporacion Azucarera de P.R., 1973-76, asst. to exec. dir., 1977-79, asst. exec. dir. for environ., 1979-82, engring. cons., 1982-92; Kendall County engr., 1985-97; ret., 1997. Fellow: ASCE; mem.: Colegio de Ingenieros y Agrimensores de P.R., Am. Ry. Engring. Assn., Travellers Century Club, Circumnavigators Club, Explorers Club, Sigma Xi, Tau Beta Pi. Home: 11505 Altantic City NE Albuquerque NM 87111

**MITCHELL, ALISON N.,** newspaper reporter, editor; b. Bay Shore, N.Y., May 2, 1961; d. Sidney L. and Audrey (Auerhahn) M. BA, Radcliffe Coll., 1976. Reporter The Record, Bergen County, NJ, 1976-77; reporter Newsday, Melville, NY, 1977-81, Capital bur. chief, 1981-84; Congl. corr., Capital Bureau chief, fgn. correspondent Washington & Moscow, 1985—91; reporter, White House correspondent, Washington bureau chief New York Times, Washington & NYC, 1991—2003; dep. nat. editor, 2003—. Recipient Walter Brown award for coverage of state govt., Legis. Corr. Assn., 1983, Everett McKinley Dirksen award, Nat. Press Found., 1999. Mem. N.Y. Legis. Corr. Assn. Office: New York Times 229 W 43d St New York NY 10036 Office Phone: 212-556-7356. Office Fax: 212-556-7614.*

**MITCHELL, ANDREA,** journalist; b. NYC, Oct. 30, 1946; d. Sydney and Cecile Mitchell; m. Alan Greenspan, Apr. 6, 1997. BA in English Literature, U. Pa., 1967. Polit. reporter KYW Newsradio, Phila., 1967-76; polit. corr. Sta. KYW-TV, Phila., 1972-76; corr. Sta. WTOP-TV, Washington, 1977-78; gen. assignment and energy corr. NBC News, Washington, 1978-81, White House corr., 1981-88, chief congl. corr., 1989-92, chief White House corr., 1993-94, chief fgn. affairs corr. Washington, 1995—. Substitute host Meet the Press, 1988-; host MSNBC The Mitchell Report, Decision 2000. Author: (book) Talking Back: ...to Presidents, Dictators, and Assorted Scoundrels, 2005. Trustee U. Pa., 1995—. Recipient award for pub. affairs reporting Am. Polit. Sci. Assn., 1969, Pub. Affairs Reporting award AP, 1976, AP Broadcast award, 1977; named Communicator of the Yr., Phila. chpt. Women in Comms., 1976, Woman of the Yr., Phila. chpt. Am. Women in Radio and TV, 1989, Lucretia Mott award Woman's Way, 1991, Welles Hangen award superior achievement journalism, Brown U., 2003, Lifetime Achievement award RTNDA, 2004, Harvard U. Goldsmith Career Achievement prize, 2005. Office: NBC News 4001 Nebraska Ave NW Washington DC 20016-2733

**MITCHELL, ANGELA CAROL,** elementary school educator; b. Carbondale, Ill., June 26, 1980; d. Samuel Everett Childers and Carol Ann (Jacobs) Mitchell; 1 child, Justyn Tyler Maschhoff. BS, Vanderbilt U., Nashville, 2002, M in Edn., 2004. Cert. tchg. Tenn. Tchg. aide U. Sch. Nashville, 2003—04; tchr. Jones Paideia Magnet Sch., Met. Nashville Pub. Sch., 2004—05, Oak Hill Sch., Nashville, 2005—. Mem.: NEA, Student Tenn. Edn. Assn. (v.p. 1999—2002), Kappa Delta Pi, Kappa Delta Epsilon, Gamma Beta Phi, Phi Eta Sigma, Alpha Lambda Delta, Pi Lambda Theta, Psi Chi (life). Independent. Avocations: writing, reading, travel. Office: Oak Hill Sch 4815 Franklin Rd Nashville TN 37220 Office Phone: 1-615-297-6544.

**MITCHELL, ARTHUR,** dancer, choreographer, performing company executive, educator; b. NYC, Mar. 27, 1934; s. Arthur and Willie Mae Mitchell. Student, Sch. Am. Ballet.; D. Arts (hon.), Columbia Coll., Chgo., 1975; cert. of competence, Peter U., 1978; DFA (hon.), City Coll., CUNY, 1979, N.C. Sch. Arts, 1981, L.I. U. Sch. Bus. Pub. Adminstrn., 1982, Fordham U., 1983, Princeton U., 1986, Williams Coll., 1986, Juilliard Sch., 1990; DHS (hon.), Urbana Coll., 1979; DA (hon.), Harvard U., 1987. With William Dollar's Ballet Theatre Workshop, 1954, John Butler Co., 1955; prin. dancer NYC Ballet, 1955-72; artistic dir., founder Am. Negro Dance Co., NYC, 1966—; founder, dir., choreographer Dance Theatre of Harlem, NYC, 1969—; former resident choreographer, artistic dir. Nat. Ballet Co., Brazil. Tchr. dance Karel Shook Studio, Melissa Hayden Sch., Cedarhurst, L.I., Jones-Haywood Sch. Ballet, Washington. Dancer Kiss Me Kate, Orpheus, Carmen Jones, Allegro, Creation of the World, Episodes, House of Flowers, choreographer with Rod Alexander Newport Jazz Festival, Rhythmetron, 1971, Ode to Otis, 1969, Lil' Gal, 1969, Tones, 1970, Biosfera, 1970, Fun and Games, 1970, Holberg Suite, 1970, Manifestations, 1975, Concerto for Jazz Band and Orch., 1971, Fête Noire, 1971, Spiritual Suite: Dance In Praise of His Name, 1976, Breezin', 1977, The Greatest, 1977, El Mar, 1977, Doin' It, 1978, Porgy and Bess, 1985, Phoenix Rising, 1987, John Henry, 1988, Ribbon in the Sky, 1990, Bach Passacaglia, 1993; co-choreographer Broadway prodn. Shinebone Alley, dancer, choreographer, actor Spoleto Festival of Two Worlds, 1960; dancer tv prodns. A Streetcar Named Desire, PBS dance prodn. Songs of Mahler, Dance in America: Dance Theatre of Harlem, Stravinsky's Firebird, NBC prodn. Creole Giselle, A&E prodn. Fall River Legend. Active Nat. Conf. on Social Welfare, 1973, U.S. Dept. State Dance Adv. Panel; pres. Task Force on Arts and Humanities, 1981; mem. Commn. for Cultural Affairs, NYC, 1982; mem. adv. bd. Arts and Entertainment, NYC; mem. Partnership, Inc., 1983, Nat. Coun. Arts, 1987, Pres. Commn. on White House Fellowships, 1991. Named to Hall of Fame, NAACP Image Awards, 1986; recipient Changers award, Mademoiselle Mag., 1970, award, North Shore Commn. Arts Ctr., 1980, Capezio Dance award, 1971, Ann. Excellence award, John F. Kennedy Ctr. for Performing Arts, 1980, award, Am. Dance Guild, 1982, Am. Black Achievement award, Ebony Mag., 1983, Pres.'s Cabinet award, U. Detroit, 1982, Paul Robeson award, Actors Equity Assn., 1986, Lion of the Performing Arts award, NY Pub. Libr., 1986, Arnold Gingrich Meml. award, 1987, Banquet of Golden Plate, 1989, Harkness Disting. Artist award, Adelphi U., 1990, Disting. Svc. to Arts award, Am. Acad. Arts and Letters, 1994, Zenith award for Fine Arts, 1994, Handel Medallion, NYC, 1993, Barnard Medal of Distinction, Barnard Coll., 1994, Lifetime Achievement award, Sch. Am. Ballet, 1995, Nat. Medal of Arts, Nat. Endowment Arts, 1995, Living Landmarks award, NY Landmarks of Conservancy, 1995; grantee Fletcher Fellowship, Fletcher Found.; Conroy fellow, St. Paul's Sch., Concord, N.H., 1982, MacArthur fellow, 1994. Office: Dance Theatre Harlem 466 W 152nd St New York NY 10031-1896*

**MITCHELL, BETTY JO,** publishing executive, writer; b. May 2, 1931; d. Edith Darrah McWilliams. BA, S.W. Mo. State U.; MSLS, U. So. Calif.; MBA, PhD, Calif. Coast U., 2002. Asst. acquisitions libr. Calif. State U., Northridge, 1967—69, libr. for pers. and fin., 1969-71, acting assoc. libr. dir., 1971-72, assoc. dir. univ. librs., 1972-81; mgr. info. sys. City Santa Monica Rent Control, Calif., 1984-93; owner Viewpoint Press, Tehachapi, Calif. Cons. We. Interstate Commn. for Higher Edn. USOE Inst. for Tng. in Staff Devel. Problem Solving; participant workshops in field; spkr. at profl. confs. in field; bd. dirs. Tehachapi Cmty. Orch. Author: ALMS: A Budget Based Library Management System, 1982, The Secret of Hilhouse: An Adult Book for Teens, 1993, The Huckenpuck Papers: The Tale of a Family's Secret and a Young Girl's Search for Self-Esteem, 2001, Seeds of Violence, 2005; co-author: Cost Analysis of Library Functions: A Total System Approach, 1978, How to See the U.S. on $12 a Day; contbr. writings to profl. publs.; editor Staff Development column in Spl. Librs., 1975-76. Bd. dirs. San Fernando Valley coun. Girl Scouts U.S., 1974-77, employed pers. com., 1979-81; bd. dirs. Bear Valley Springs Condominium Owners Assn., 1978, Empyrean Found., 1978-81, Tehachapi Cmty. Orch. Found., 1998. Tehachapi Performing Arts Ctr. Found., 2003—, Tehachapi Heritage League, 2005— Mem. AAUP, AAUW, ALA (chmn. various coms.), Assn. Women in Computing (bd. dirs. 1989), Nat. Libr. Assn., Author's Guild, Calif. Libr. Assn., Assn. Calif. State U. Profs. (sec., exec. com. 1971-72), Phi Beta Chi, Alpha Mu Gamma. Office: PMB 400 785 Tucker Rd Ste G Tehachapi CA 93561-2523 Personal E-mail: joie99@aol.com.

**MITCHELL, BEVERLY SHRIVER,** hematologist, oncologist, educator; b. Balt., May 14, 1944; m. John Robert Pringle; children: Robert Mitchell, Elizabeth Greene. AB summa cum laude in Biochemistry, Smith Coll., 1965; MD, Harvard U., 1969. Hematology fellow U. Mich., Ann Arbor, 1975-77, from instr. to asst. prof. internal medicine, 1977-81, assoc. prof., 1981-87, prof. internal medicine and pharmacology, 1987-91, U. N.C., Chapel Hill, 1991—, divsn. chief hematology/oncology, 1994—2003; assoc. dir. Lineberger Cancer Ctr., Chapel Hill, 1994—2005; deputy dir. Stanford Cancer Ctr., Stanford U., 2005—. Mem. bd. sci. counselors Cancer Treatment divsn. Nat. Cancer Inst. Vice chair med. and sci. affairs Leukemia and Lymphoma Soc., 2003—05. Recipient Stohlman award Leukemia Soc., 1988. Mem. Am. Soc. Hematology (treas. 1991-96, v.p. 1998, pres. 2000), Phi Beta, Inst. Medicine. Achievements include research in nucleotide metabolism and the development of novel therapies for hematologic malignancies. Office: Stanford Cancer Ctr 800 Welch Rd Stanford CA 94305-5796 Office Phone: 650-725-9621. Business E-Mail: bmitchell@stanford.edu.

**MITCHELL, BRENDA KING,** training services executive; b. NYC, Jan. 9, 1943; d. William Franklin and Ola Mae (Ross) K.; divorced; 1 child, Corrie Nelson. BA, Fordham U., 1973; MA, Hunter Coll., 1977; PhD in Pub. Adminstrn., Nova U., 1981. Dir. manpower planning Addictive Disease Agy., N.Y.C., 1973-77; project and contract mgr. Pub./Pvt. Ventures Corp., Phila., 1978-80; exec. dir. Devel. Corp., Phila., 1980-84; bus. mgr. Control Data Corp., Mpls., 1984-87; dep. sec. Pa. Dept. Comml., 1987—91; spl. asst. to Gov. of Pa. in community econ. devel. initiatives, 1989—91; sec. Commonwealth of Pa., Harrisburg, 1991-94; pres. CEO African Am. Delaware Valley Devel. Corp., Phila., 1993—94, Mgmt. & Environ. Tech. Inc., Phila., 1995—; co-founder, mng. ptnr. Cmty Leadership Devel. Inst., Allegheny County, Pa., 1999—. Sole propr. bus. in real estate devel. & property

mgmt., Phila., Harrisburg, adv. coun. US Dept. Commerce Industry sector, 1994-, bd. dir. Penns Landing Corp, 2001-, adv. bd. Benjamin Franklin Tech. Ptnrs., 2002-. Author: They Crossed Together, 1975. Recipient citation for Outstanding Leadership in Econ. Devel., City of Phila. Mayor's Office, 1987; named for Outstanding Leadership, People United to Serve Humanity, Inc., 1991, Disting. Alumni, Nova U., 1992, Policy Advocate of Yr., Nat. Assn. Bus. Women Owners, 1992. Mem. NAACP (life), Nat. Congress of Black Women, Nat. Forum Black Pub. Adminstrs. (pres. 1987), Forum Exec. Women, Black Women's Leadership Conf. Home: 5204 Overbrook Ave Philadelphia PA 19131-2409 Office: Mgmt & Environ Tech Inc Ste 1108 1315 Walnut St Philadelphia PA 19107 Office Phone: 215-546-7991. Office Fax: 215-546-7995.

**MITCHELL, BRIAN CHRISTOPHER,** academic administrator; b. Lowell, Mass., Feb. 23, 1953; s. Christopher Joseph and Doris Katherine (McEvoy) M.; m. Maryjane Murphy, June 28, 1975; children: Jeffrey Ryan, Patrick Joseph. BA, Merrimack Coll., 1974; MA, U. Rochester, 1976, PhD, 1981. Chair history dept. Anna Maria Coll., Paxton, Mass., 1982-85; program officer Nat. Endowment Humanities, Washington, 1985-91; pres. Commn. Ind. Colls. and Univs Pa., Harrisburg, 1991-98, Washington and Jefferson Coll., Washington, Pa., 1998—2004, Bucknell U., Lewisburg, Pa., 2004—. Instr. U. Mass., Lowell, 1977-85; adj. prof. George Mason U., Fairfax, Va., 1988-91; cons. Lowell Nat. Hist. Park, 1977-81, Lowell Heritage State Park, 1977-78. Author: The Paddy Camps: The Irish of Lowell, 1821-1861, 1988, On The North Bank, 1984; editor: Building the American Catholic City, 1986; contbg. author: From Paddy to Stud, 1986. Mem. Pa. Humanities Coun.; mem. Pa. Hist. and Mus. Commn.; chair Pa. selection com. Rhodes Scholarship Trust. Grantee Am. Coun. Learned Socs., 1985, NEH. Mem. Am. Hist. Assn. (Albert J. Beveridge award), Orgn. Am. Historians, Nat. Assn. Ind. Colls. and Univs. Roman Catholic. Office: Off of President Bucknell U Box A0527 Lewisburg PA 17837 Office Phone: 570-577-1511. E-mail: bmitchel@bucknell.edu.*

**MITCHELL, BRIAN STOKES,** actor; b. Seattle, Oct. 31, 1958; s. George Thomas and Lillian (Stokes) M. Prin. actor 12th Night Repertory Co., San Diego, 1977-80; co-star Roots: The Next Generations, L.A., 1980, Trapper John, M.D., L.A., 1980-86, The Good War, L.A., 1987, The Fresh Prince of Bel Air, 1993, In the House, 1996, Crossing Jordan, 2002, Frasier, 2002—03; co-star Mail Kennedy Ctr., Washington, The Music Box Theatre, Broadway, N.Y.C., and Pasadena, Calif., 1987-88; star David Merrick's Broadway play Oh Kay Richard Rodgers Theatre, 1990. Guest tchr., speaker San Diego Jr. Theater, 1984; guest star The White Shadow, 227, Houston Knights, Alf, Night Court, L.A., 1987; voice-over actor, series reg. California Raisins, New Kids on the Block, Kid 'n Play, 1988—; trustee Actor's Fund, 1999—; mem. honors artists com. Kennedy Ctr., 2001, 02, 04; pres. Actors Fund Am., 2004; mem. artist's com. Ams. for the Arts, 2004. Appeared in Broadway prodn. Jelly's Last Jam, 1992, Kiss of the Spider Woman, 1994-95, Ragtime, Ford Theater for Performing Arts, 1996 (Drama League Disting. Performance award, Can.'s Dora award, Drama League award); Shubert Theatre, L.A., 1997 (L.A. Critics award), Kiss Me Kate, 1999-2001 (Tony Award, 2000, Drama Desk award, Outer Critics Circle award), Do Re Mi, 2000, Carnival, 2001, King Hedley II, 2001, Sweeney Todd, 2002, South Pacific, 2005; appeared in National Theater prodn. Man of La Mancha, 2002 (Helen Hayes award), National Symphony Orchestra Pops: An Evening with Brian Stokes Mitchell, 2005; composer: (symphonic suite) 3 Scenes for Clipper Ships, 1983; (Trapper John, M.D. TV scores) The Wunderkind, Friends and Lovers, I Only Have Ice For You, 1984; film work includes Ghost Dad, 1990, (voice) The Prince of Egypt, 1998, Ruby's Bucket of Blood, 2000, Call me Clause, 2001. Ambassador March of Dimes, U.S. Tour, 1984-85; performer USO, European Tour, 1984, Far East/Middle East Tour, 1985, Calif. Orgn. of Police and Sheriffs, L.A., 1986. Recipient Best Pop Song and Composer of Yr. awards Los Angeles Songwriters Showcase, 1986, Drama League Distinguished Performance Award, 1998, Nightlife award, outstanding cabaret male vocalist in a major engagement, 2006. Mem. Acad. of TV Arts and Scis. (blue ribbon panelist 1987), ASCAP, Screen Actors' Guild, AFTRA, Actors Equity Assn. Avocations: flying, skiing, composing.*

**MITCHELL, BRIANE NELSON,** lawyer; b. Seattle, July 4, 1953; s. Robert Max and Frances Marie (Nelson) M.; m. Suzanne Harmatz; children: Brianne Nelson, Brittany Suzanne. AB, Columbia U., 1975; JD, U. Idaho, 1978. Law clk. U.S. Ct. Appeals (9th cir.), 1978-80; assoc. Debevoise & Plimpton, N.Y.C., 1980-84, Paul, Hastings, Janofsky & Walker, L.A., 1984-86, ptnr., 1986-93, McCambridge, Deixler & Marmaro, L.A., 1994-95, Shapiro, Mitchell & Dupont LLP, Santa Monica, 1996-2000, Manatt, Phelps & Phillips LLP, L.A., 2000—03. Assoc. dir. Pacific regional office SEC, 2004—. Mem.: ABA, Calif. Bar Assn., N.Y. State Bar Assn., Idaho Bar Assn. Business E-Mail: MitchellBN@sec.gov.

**MITCHELL, BRUCE TYSON,** lawyer; b. San Francisco, Nov. 6, 1928; s. John Robert and Lorraine C. (Tyson) M.; m. Adrienne Means Hiscox, Oct. 14, 1951; 1 son, Mark Means. AB with great distinction, Stanford U., 1949, JD, 1951. Bar: Calif. 1952, U.S. Dist. Ct. (no. dist.) Calif 1952, U.S. Ct. Appeals (9th cir.) 1952, U.S. Supreme Ct. 1971. Estate adminstr. Crocker Nat. Bank, San Francisco, 1955-57; atty. Utah Internat. Inc., San Francisco, 1957-87, sec., 1974-87, sr. counsel, 1961—87, ret., 1987; pvt. practice securities arbitrator. Mem. non-securities panel arbitrators N.Y. Stock Exch., Pacific Exch., NASD Bd. Arbitrators; mem. adv. bd. archaeology, Stanford U. Chmn. San Mateo County Rep. Ctrl. Com., 1964-70; mem. Calif. Rep. Ctrl. Com., 1964-74, 77-83; alt. del. Rep. Nat. Conv., 1968; co-chmn. San Mateo (Calif.) County Pres. Ford Com., 1976; mem. bd. visitors sch. law Stanford U., 1980-83; exec. v.p., bd. dirs. San Francisco Jr. C. of C., 1961; bd. dirs. No. Calif. chpt. Arthritis Found., 1972-85, 1987-92, St. Francis Hosp. Found., San Francisco, 1992-98, 99—, hon. dir. 1998-99— Lt. (j.g.) USNR, 1952-55, Japan. Mem. ABA, Calif. Bar Assn., San Francisco Bar Assn., Am. Judicature Soc., Am. Soc. Corp. Secs. (v.p. 1976-77, dir. 1976-79), Assn. Former Intelligence Officers, Commonwealth Club of Calif. (pres. San Francisco 1973), Stanford Assocs., Pacific Union Club, Olympic Club, Capitol Hill Club, Travelers Century Club, Masons. Congregationalist. Home: 165 Redwood Dr Hillsborough CA 94010-6971 Office: 225 Bush St Fl 16 San Francisco CA 94104-4213 Office Phone: 415-439-8801.

**MITCHELL, BURLEY BAYARD, JR.,** lawyer; b. Oxford, N.C., Dec. 15, 1940; s. Burley Bayard and Dorothy Ford (Champion) M.; m. Mary Lou Willett, Aug. 3, 1962; children: David Bayard (dec.), Catherine Morris. BA with honors, N.C. State U., 1966, DHL (hon.), 1995; JD, U. N.C., 1969; LLD (hon.), Campbell U., 1998. Bar: N.C. 1969, U.S. Ct. Appeals (4th cir.) 1970, U.S. Ct. Appeals (3d cir.) 2002, U.S. Supreme Ct. 1972. Asst. atty. gen. State of N.C., Raleigh, 1969-72, dist. atty. 1973-77, judge Ct. Appeals, 1979, sec. crime control, 1979-82; justice Supreme Ct. N.C., Raleigh, 1982-94; chief justice Supreme Ct. of N.C., Raleigh, 1995-99; ptnr. Womble Carlyle Sandridge and Rice, Raleigh, 1999—. Served with USN, 1958-62, Asia. Recipient N.C. Nat. Guard Citizen Commendation award, 1982. Mem. ABA, VFW, Am. Bar Assn., Mensa, Am. Legion, Phi Beta Kappa. Democrat. Methodist. Home: 4301 City of Oaks Wynd Raleigh NC 27612-5316 Office: Wacovia Capital Ctr 150 Fayetteville St Mall Ste 2100 PO Box 831 Raleigh NC 27602-0831 Office Phone: 919-755-8166.

**MITCHELL, CAROL L.,** lawyer; b. 1955; BA, Boston Coll., 1978; JD, U. Maine, 1987. Bar: Maine 1988. Sr. v.p. legal affairs Peoples Heritage Fin. Group, 1991—99; exec. v.p., chief adminstrn. officer, gen. counsel, corp. clerk Banknorth Group, Inc., Portland, Maine, 2000—. Dir. New Eng. Legal Found.; mem. Gov.'s Bus. Adv. Coun.; mem. bd. visitors U. Maine Sch. Law; spkr. in field. Mem.: Am. Soc. Corp. Secs., Internat. Women's Forum (treas.). Office: Banknorth Group Inc Two Portland Sq Portland ME 04101 Office Phone: 207-761-8500. E-mail: cmitchell@banknorth.com.

**MITCHELL, CATHY (C.C.) CHRISTINE,** art educator; b. Phoenixville, Pa., 1954; d. William Douglas and Christine (Donshietz) Mitchell. AA, Cuyahoga C.C., Parma Heights, Ohio, 1975; BFA, Sch. of the Art Inst. Chgo., 1987, MA in Art Edn., 1994. Cert. art tchr. grades K-12 Ill., 1987, Ohio, 1998.

Dir./arts coord. Howland Sch. Arts, Chgo. Pub. Schs., 1987—98; interim coord. dept. edn. Wexner Ctr. for the Arts, Columbus, Ohio, 1998—2000; arts educator - visual art Columbus (Ohio) Pub. Schs., 2000—. Mem. adv. bd. Art Inst. Chgo., 1991—98; mem. edn. bd. Mus. Contemporary Art, Chgo., 1997—99; adj. faculty dept. art edn. Elmhurst (Ill.) Coll., 1997. Co-prodr. writer (video) School Improvement Planning, Chicago Public Schools. Mem. Cliff Dwellers, Chgo., 1997; com. chair Columbus Arts Festival, 1998—; trustee Parkview NE Condominium Assn., Lewis Center, Ohio, 2001—; active Joel Hall Dance Co., Chgo., 1997—2001. Recipient Nat. Grand prize, Tchr.-Student Photography, Canon Photography with USA Today, 1997, Outstanding Svc. in Arts Edn. for the State of Ill. award, Ill. Alliance for the Arts, 1997, Art Tchr. of Yr., Ill. Alliance for Arts, 1997. Mem.: NEA (assoc.), Ohio Edn. Assn. (assoc.), Nat. Art Edn. Assn. (assoc.). Office: CC Mitchell PO Box 1674 Powell OH 43065-1674 Personal E-mail: box1674@ameritech.net.

**MITCHELL, CONNIE,** director; m. George Mitchell, Sr.; children: Carlata, George Jr. Tchr. adv. Office Adminstrv./Instrnl. Pers. Detroit Pub. Schs. Dir. Ednll. Enrichment Acad.; mem. bd. dir. Nat. Bd. Profl. Tchg. Standards, 1995—2003. Active Meth. Children's Home Soc. Named Middle Sch. Tchr. of Yr., Newsweek Mag./WDIV-TV, 1994, Tchr. of Yr., Detroit Pub. Schs., 1994; recipient Golden Apple Tchr. award, Wayne County Regional Edn. Svc. Agy. Mem.: Nat. Bd. for Profl. Tchg. Stds. (bd. mem.), Alpha Kappa Alpha. Office: Detroit Pub Schs Schs Ctr Bldg 3031 W Grand Blvd Detroit MI 48202*

**MITCHELL, DAVID BENJAMIN,** lawyer, arbitrator, mediator; b. Miami Beach, Fla., Nov. 3, 1950; s. Quintus Eugene and Gertrude (Ziegler) M.; m. Lynn Stewart, Dec. 11, 1993. BA, U. Miami, Coral Gables, Fla., 1973; JD, Stetson U., 1978. Bar: Fla. 1979, U.S. Dist. Ct. (so. dist.) Fla. 1979, U.S. Tax Ct. 1987, U.S. Supreme Ct. 2004; cert. family mediator; cert. arbitrator; cert. ins. mediator. Assoc., sr. assoc. Semet, Lickstein, Morgenstern & Berger, P.A., Coral Gables, 1987. Pvt. practice, 1987—; pres. David B. Mitchell, P.A., Coral Gables, 1990—. Pres. South Fla. Mediation Assocs., Inc., Coral Gables, 1990-92. Author: Magna Carta: It's American Legacy, 2005. Active Coral Gables Cmty. Found., 1996—; grad. Leadership Miami, 1987; bd. dirs. Ponce de Leon Devel. Assn., pres., 1992-93; bd. dirs. Internat. Zen Found. of Fla., 1997—, Coral Gables Citizens Crime Watch, 1998—, pres., 2001-03; vice chmn. Coral Gables City-Wide Anti-Crime Com., 2002-05, chmn., 2005-06; active Coral Gables Emergency Ops. Dept., 2005—; chmn. Coral Gables Pub. Safety Com., 2006—. Recipient Key to the City of Coral Gables, 1993, 2006. Mem. The Fla. Bar (family law sect.), Dade County Bar Assn. (family law com., county cts. com., vice chair, 2004, Cert. of Appreciation 1994-95), Coral Gables Bar Assn. (law day com. 1996, scholarship com. 1996, bd. dirs. 1997-2005, pres. 2003-04), Cuban-Am. Bar Asssn., Fed. Bar Assn., Fla. Acad. Profl. Mediators, U. Miami Alumni Club of Greater Miami (sec., dir. 1996-98), Republican Nat. Lawyers Assn., Federalist Soc., SAR (chpt. pres., 2005-06), Jamestown Soc., Soc. Descs. of Knights of the Garter, Order of Crown of Charlemagne, Baronial Order of Magna Carta, Rotary Club Coral Gables (dir. 2001-03, pres.-elect 2006—), Royal Soc. St. George, Mil. Order Crusades, ORder Mergovinian Dynasty, Order Founders and Patriots Am., Son Confederate Vets. Republican. Buddhist. Office Phone: 305-461-5015. Personal E-mail: mitchellesq@aol.com.

**MITCHELL, DAVID LANCASTER,** research educator; b. LA, Dec. 13, 1954; s. Eugene M. and Elizabeth B. Mitchell. BS in Chemistry, Calif. Polytechnical U., San Luis Obispo, Calif. PhD, U. Nev., 1995. Rsch. scientist Desert Rsch. Inst., Reno, 1989—95, asst. rsch. prof., 1995—2000, assoc. rsch. prof., 2000—. Cons. Atmospheric and Environ. Rsch., Inc., Lexington, Mass., 2000—01. Contbr. articles to profl. jours. Pres. Divine Mission USA, Reno, 2002—. Recipient Peter B. Wagner medal of excellence, Desert Rsch. Inst., 2000; grantee, Dept. Energy, NOAA, NSF. Mem.: Am. Meteorol. Assn. (chmn. com. on cloud physics 2000—). Achievements include research in accurate analytical treatment of ice particle-radiation interactions; dependence of North American monsoon on sea surface temperatures; satellite remote sensing of atmospheric ice mass. Avocation: teaching meditation and yoga. Office: Desert Rsch Inst 2215 Raggio Pky Reno NV 89512-1095 Office Phone: 775-674-7039. Office Fax: 775-674-7007. E-mail: mitch@dri.edu.

**MITCHELL, DAVID WALKER,** lawyer; b. Oakland, Calif., Nov. 11, 1935; s. Theodore Boyd and Helen Louise (Walker) M.; m. Carolyn Hilliard Graves, July 29, 1961; children: Sarah, Betsy. AB in History, Stanford U., 1957; JD, Harvard U., 1960. Bar: Calif. 1961. Assoc. Kindel & Anderson, L.A., 1961-65, Weir, Hopkins, Donovan, San Jose, Calif., 1965-68; ptnr. Hopkins, Mitchell & Carley, San Jose, 1968-87, McCutchen, Doyle, Brown & Enersen, San Jose, 1987-93, Hoge, Fenton, Jones & Appel, San Jose, 1993-2000, of counsel, 2001—. Bd. dirs. Peninsula Open Space Trust, Menlo Park, Calif., 1982—2005, pres., 1984-92; bd. dirs. Cmty. Found. Silicon Valley., San Jose, 1977-94, 99-2003; chair bd. trustees United Way Santa Clara County, 1983-85. Fellow Am. Bar Found.; Am. Leadership Forum (sr.); mem. Santa Clara County Bar Assn. (trustee 1972-75), San Jose C. of C. (bd. dirs. 1975-80). Mem. United Ch. of Christ. Avocations: music, hiking. Office: Hoge Fenton Jones Appel 60 S Market St Ste 1400 San Jose CA 95113-2396 Office Phone: 408-287-9501. Business E-Mail: dwm@hogefenton.com.

**MITCHELL, DENNIS ANTHONY,** dentist, educator; b. Port of Spain, Trinidad and Tobago, May 1, 1962; s. Victor O'Reilly Mitchell and Ulyth Lamour Lewis, Cyril Theodore Lewis (Stepfather) and Maria Mitchell (Stepmother); m. Bridgette Vanera Joyner, July 8, 2001; children: Angelique Victoria children: Danielle Lindsey. BA, Cornell U., 1984; DDS, Howard U., 1989; MPH, Columbia U., 1996. Gen. practice dental resident Harlem Hosp. Ctr., N.Y.C., 1989—90, chief resident, 1990—91; clin. instr. Columbia U. Sch. Dental and Oral Surgery, N.Y.C., 1991—94, dental pub. health resident, 1994—96, dir. cmty. dentcare network Harlem, 1996—2002, asst. dean diversity and multicultural affairs, 2004—; cmty. health services fellow Columbia U. Ctr. Cmty. Health Partnerships, N.Y.C., 2002—04. Cons. HIV dental standards of care com. NY State Dept. Health AIDS Inst., N.Y.C., 1995—2002; cons. NY State oral cancer control partnership workgroup com. NY State Dept. Health, Bur. Dental Health, N.Y.C., 2001—04, cons. NY State oral health planning com., Albany, 2004—; cons. Ctr. Health and Health Care in Schs. Robert Wood Johnson Found., Lawrenceville, NJ, 2001—04, cons. pipelines, profession and practice, community-based dental edn., 2002—. Named to Disting. African Americans in Dentistry Calendar, Aetna Inc., 2004; recipient Cmty. Svc. award, Harlem Cmty. Dental Soc., 1991, Chief Resident award, Harlem Hosp. Ctr. Dept. of Dentistry, 1991, Nat. Rsch. Svc. award, Nat. Inst. Allergy and Infectious Diseases, 1994, Outstanding Achievement award, Nat. Dental Assn., 1997, Cmty. Leadership award, 2002, Disting. Alumni award, Howard U. Coll. Dentistry, 2002, Leadership award, West Harlem Group Assistance, 2004; grantee Minority Clin. Assoc. Physician's award, Nat. Inst. Craniofacial Rsch., 1998, Nat. Inst. Dental and Craniofacial Rsch., 2001. Mem.: APHA, Am. Dental Edn. Assn., Greater Met. NY Dental Soc. (pres. 1998—2000), Internat. Assn. of Dental Rsch., Am. Assn. Pub. Health Dentistry, Nat. Dental Assn. (trustee 1993—99, Cmty. Leadership award and Outstanding Achievement Award 1997, 2002), Omicron Kappa Upsilon, Alpha Phi Alpha. Democrat. Achievements include first to dental service network for children and adults in Harlem, New York; research in oral manifestations of HIV disease in injecting drug users; dental caries experience in Northern Manhattan adolescents; effects of periodontal therapy intervention on preterm birth. Avocations: reading, travel, golf. Home: 190 Cherry Ln Teaneck NJ 07666 Office: Columbia U Coll Dental Medicine P& S Bldg Box 20 630 West 168th St New York NY 10032 Office Phone: 212-342-3714. Home Fax: 212-305-1034; Office Fax: 212-305-1034. Personal E-mail: dml48@columbia.edu.

**MITCHELL, DONALD G.,** physicist; s. H. Rees and Elizabeth B. Mitchell. PhD, U. NH, 1975. Rsch. assoc. JHU/APL, Laurel, Md., 1979—84, sr. staff physicist, 1985—91, prin. profl. physicist, 1991—. Grantee, NASA, 1978—, NSF, 1978—. Mem.: Am. Geophys. Union. Independent. Achievements

include invention of Energetic Neutral Atom imagers. Avocations: sailing, hiking, photography. Office: Johns Hopkins Applied Physics Lab 11100 Johns Hopkins Rd MP3-E183 Laurel MD 20723 Office Phone: 240-228-5981.

**MITCHELL, EARL NELSON,** physicist, researcher; b. Centerville, Iowa, Aug. 30, 1926; s. Earl Nelson and Nina (Swank) M.; m. Marlys Marie Panning, July 23, 1955. AB magna cum laude, U. Iowa, 1949, MS, 1951; PhD, U. Minn., 1955. Research scientist Sperry Rand Corp., St. Paul, 1955-58; asst. prof., then assoc. prof. physics U. N.D., Grand Forks, 1958-62; vis. assoc. prof., then assoc. prof. and prof. physics U. N.C., Chapel Hill, 1962-91, prof. emeritus, 1991—, asst. chmn. dept., 1968-76. Lectr. Hamline U., 1956, 57; cons. Sperry Rand Corp., 1958-62 Contbr. articles to profl. jours.; author textbooks. Mem. Chapel Hill Planning Bd., 1970-71; pres. Chapel Hill Concert Series, 1967-70; mem. bd. for missions to deaf Luth. Ch. Mo. Synod, 1958-64. Served in USNR, 1945-46. Mem.: Am. Soc. Enologists (bd. dirs. ea. sect. 1984—91, pres.-elect 1988, pres. 1989, past pres. 1990), Am. Phys. Soc., N.C. Wine Growers Assn. (pres. 1994—98, past pres. 1998—2003), Phi Eta Sigma, Sigma Xi, Phi Beta Kappa. Democrat. Office: U NC Dept Physics Chapel Hill NC 27599-0001

**MITCHELL, EARL WESLEY,** clergyman; b. Excelsior Springs, Mo., Mar. 16, 1931; s. Earl Van and Ora Leah (Butterfield) M.; m. Mary Lou Bell, June 8, 1956; children: Susan Yvonne, Randall Bruce. Ordained to ministry Christian Union Ch., 1971. Min. Vibbard (Mo.) Christian Union Ch., 1962-69, Liberty (Mo.) Christian Ch., 1969—77, Barwick Christian Union Ch., Cameron, Mo., 1977-80, Independence (Mo.) Christian Union Ch., 1980—95; assoc. pastor Flack Meml. Christian Union Ch., Excelsior Springs, Mo., 1995—. Former mem. state exec. bd. Christian Union Ho., 1995-98; area rep. Mo. Christian Union USA; former mem. gen. exec. bd., former editor C.U. Witness. Sgt. USAF, 1951-55. Avocations: music, woodworking, painting, photography. Home and Office: 618 Henrie St Excelsior Springs MO 64024-2022

**MITCHELL, EDWARD JOHN,** economist, retired educator; b. Newark, Aug. 15, 1937; s. Edward Charles and Gladys (Werner) M.; m. Mary Josephine Osborne, June 14, 1958; children: Susan, Edward. BA summa cum laude, Bowling Green State U., 1960; postgrad. (Social Sci. Research Council fellow), Nuffield Coll., Oxford U., Eng., 1963-64, PhD in Econs. (NDEA fellow 1960-63, NSF fellow 1964-65), 1966. Lectr. in econs. Wharton Sch., U. Pa., 1964-65; economist Rand Corp., 1965-68; mem. Inst. Advanced Study, Princeton, 1968-69; sr. economist Pres.'s Council Econ. Advs., Washington, 1969-72; vis. assoc. prof. econs. Cornell U., 1972-73; assoc. prof. bus. econs. U. Mich., 1973-75, prof., 1975-88, prof. emeritus bus. econs. and pub. policy, 1988—; pres. Edward J. Mitchell Inc., Ann Arbor, 1977—94. Dir. nat. energy project Am. Enterprise Inst., 1974-76; pres. Fountainhead Investment Co., 1984—94. Author: U.S. Energy Policy: A Primer, 1974, Dialogue on World Oil, 1974, Financing the Energy Industry, 1975, Vertical Integration of the Oil Industry, 1976, The Deregulation of Natural Gas, 1983; contbr. articles to profl. jours. Home: 310 Penny Ln Santa Barbara CA 93108-2601 Office: Grad Sch Bus U Mich Ann Arbor MI 48109 E-mail: mitchell296@cox.net.

**MITCHELL, ELIZABETH MARELLE,** family practice nurse practitioner, medical/surgical nurse, nursing educator; b. Bemis, Tenn., Dec. 2, 1937; d. William Columbus and Ruth Marelle (Wadley) Latham; m. Thomas Alton McNatt, June 20, 1953 (dec. Mar. 1984); children: Glenn McNatt, Craig McNatt, Chris McNatt; m. Charles Leon Mitchell, Sept. 7, 1985; stepchildren: Melanie Campbell, Mike, Allyson Webb. AA in Nursing, Union U., 1965; BSN, U. Tenn., Martin, 1994; MSN, FNP, U. Tenn., Memphis, 1996. RN Tenn., cert. CNOR, BCLS, BCLS instr., BCLS instr. trainer, ACLS, ACLS instr., family nurse practitioner, ANCC. Staff nurse med.-surg. units Jackson-Madison County Gen. Hosp., Tenn., 1965-66; physician 1st asst. Jackson Clinic Surgeons, 1966-74; nursing instr. Jackson Area Vo-Tech Sch., 1974-78, nursing instr. supr., 1978-81; supr. oper. rm. Jackson Splty. Hosp. (acquired by Jackson-Madison County Gen. Hosp. 1983), 1981-85; instr. nurse edn. Jackson-Madison County Gen. Hosp., 1985-96; family nurse practitioner Perry County Med. Ctr., 1996—. Nursing adv. bd. mem. Jackson Area Vo-Tech Sch., 1987—96; task force nursing sch. curriculum devel. mem. State of Tenn., Nashville, 1992; clin. skills judge Health Occupations Student Assn. Tenn. State Competition, Nashville, 1992. Tchr. Sun. sch. Malesus Bapt. Ch., Malesus, Tenn., 1975—86. Mem.: ANAA, West Tenn. Healthcare Edn. and Tng. Conf. Group (pres. 1987, regional rep. 1988, sec. 1994), Tenn. Nursing Assn., Am. Soc. Healthcare Edn. and Tng. (svc. rep. West Tenn. 1988, Outstanding Regional Rep. Tenn. chpt. 1988), Assn. Oper. Rm. Nurses (program com. 1993, 1994), Am. Acad. Nurse Practitioners, U. Tenn. Martin Nursing Honor Soc., Sigma Theta Tau, Phi Theta Kappa. Avocations: reading, swimming, crafts. Home: 4963 Hwy 412 w Linden TN 37096-5611 Office: Perry County Med Ctr 115 E Brooklyn St Linden TN 37096

**MITCHELL, ELLEN CLABAUGH,** investment executive; b. Omaha, Mar. 2, 1942; d. Joseph Franklin and Dorothy (Newton) Carpenter; m. Dixon L. Mitchell, Aug. 25, 1962; 1 child, Lara Ellen. BS in Fin. & Econs., U. Nebr., Omaha, 1965; MBA, Va. Poly. Inst., 1983. Chartered Fin. Analyst. Asst. v.p. Firstier Fin., Omaha, 1965-69, 1971-75, Bridges Investments, Omaha, 1970-71; analyst U.S. Securities and Exchange Commn., Washington, 1983-85; v.p. Nat. Bank of Washington, 1985-87, Foxhall Investment Mgmt., Washington, 1987-93; pres. Mitchell Advisors Inc., Reston, Va., 1993—. Mem. Washington Soc. Investment Analysts, Inst. Chartered Fin. Analysts, Garden Club (v.p., treas. 1980). Episcopalian. Home: 2017 Turtle Pond Dr Reston VA 20191-4045 Office: Mitchell Advisors Inc 2017 Turtle Pond Dr Reston VA 20191-4045

**MITCHELL, ERIC EHRMAN,** photographer, stock broker; b. Phila., Nov. 24, 1954; s. Ehrman Burkman and Hermine (Strickler) M.; m. Leslie Ann March, Aug. 18, 1984; children: Meredith Hermine, Lauren Calder. BS in Photography and Bus., Skidmore Coll., 1977. Accredited asset mgmt. specialist. Head photographer Phila. Mus. Art, 1978-86; freelance photographer St. Peters, Pa., 1986-94; stockbroker Montanto Securities, Bluebell, Pa., 1994-95, Boenning & Scattergood, Inc., Pottstown, Pa., 1996—, v.p., 1996—. Photographs have appeared in various books, catalogues and mags. worldwide. Planning commr. South Coventry Twp., Chester County, Pa., 1990-96, 2001—, supr., 1992-98; mem. Fedn. No. Chester County Cmtys., Pa., 1992-2003; bd. dirs. Pottstown Meml. Med. Ctr., 2003—, Kimberton Waldorf Sch. 2006-; bd. dirs., pres. Pottstown Rotary Cmty. Endowment Fund, 2006—. Fellow Paul Harris, 2002. Mem.: Am. Soc. Media Photographers, St. Andrews Soc., Pottstown Club (pres. 2005—06), Rotary. Avocations: skiing, hiking, woodland management, technical analysis of the stock market. Office: Boenning & Scattergood 601 High St Pottstown PA 19464 Office Phone: 610-327-0600.

**MITCHELL, GARY EARL,** physicist, researcher; b. July 5, 1935; s. Earl Raymond and Delma Kathlene (Lockard) Mitchell; m. Carolyn Fey Stutz, Aug. 4, 1957; children: Scott Frederick, Karen Lee(dec.). BS, U. Louisville, 1956; MA, Duke U., 1958; PhD, Fla. State U., 1962. Rsch. assoc. Columbia U., N.Y.C., 1962—64, asst. prof., 1964—68; assoc. prof. NC State U., Raleigh, 1968—74, prof. physics, 1974—, assoc. head physics dept., 1982—97; assoc. dir. Triangle Univs. Nuclear Lab., 1992—. Sr. scientist Alexander von Humboldt Found., Bonn, Germany, 1975, Bonn, 97. Contbr. numerous articles to sci. publs. Recipient Alumni Disting. Prof. award, NC State U. Fellow: Am. Phys. Soc. (Jesse Beams award 1997); mem.: numerous sci. assns. Avocation: history. Home: 2913 Harriman Rd Durham NC 27705-5423 Office: NC State U Dept Physics PO Box 8202 Raleigh NC 27695-0001 Office Phone: 919-660-2638. Business E-Mail: mitchell@tunl.duke.edu, gary_mitchell@ncsu.edu.

**MITCHELL, GEORGE CHARLES,** diplomat, international consultant, mediator, educator, writer; b. Aug. 6, 1920; s. Charles Peter and Athena N. (Kapotas) Mitchell; m. Nina Catherine Chaconas, Oct. 22, 1955; children: Martina, Melinda, Marlena. BS, U. Nebr., Kearney, 1941; postgrad., U. Nebr.,

Lincoln, 1941-42; cert., Oxford U., 1947; MA, Georgetown U., 1947; cert., Acad. Internat. Law, The Hague, The Netherlands, 1948; PhD summa cum laude, Sorbonne U., Paris, 1949; postgrad., Inst. d'Etudes Politiques, Paris, 1947-49, George Washington U. Law Sch., 1959-61, Fgn. Svc. Inst., 1962, 69, U. Pitts., 1974, U.S. Army War Coll., 1980, U.S. Naval War Coll., 1981. News corr., Washington and Western Europe, 1946-49; polit. analyst U.S. Dept. State, Washington, 1951-54, specialist, 1954-55; dep. prin. officer, econ. com. officer, consul Am. Consulate Gen., Belfast, No. Ireland, 1955-58; fgn. rels. officer, UNESCO rels. staff U.S. Dept. State, Washington, 1958-62; prin. officer, polit. officer, consul Am. Consulate, Arequipa, Peru, 1962-67; dean Consular Corps, 1965-66; polit.-mil. officer, lst sec. Am. Embassy, Santo Domingo, Dominican Republic, 1967-68; prin. officer, polit.-econ. officer, consul Am. Consulate, San Luis Potosi, Mex., 1968-71; chief Speakers Bur. U.S. Dept. State, Washington, 1971-72, plans officer Bur. Pub. Affairs, 1971-72; exec. dir. World Affairs Coun. Pitts., 1973-91; internat. con., mediator Pitts., 1989—; exec. dir. internat. tng. Lang. Ctr., Pitts., 1990-91. Adj. prof. grad. internat. bus. mgmt. Point Pk. U., 1991—2003; internat. mgr. U.S. Arbitration and Mediation, Pa., 1992—93; bd. dirs. Stas. KGFW and KQKY, Kearney, Stas. KKAR and KQKQ, Omaha, Stas. KXNP-KODY, North Platte, 1954—96; leader del. to China World Affairs Coun., 1978; leader del. to Taiwan and Philippines Nat. Coun. World Affairs, 1988. Author: (book) Matthew B. Ridgway: Soldier, Statesman, Scholar, Citizen, 1999; editor: World Affairs Coun. newsletter, Nat. Coun. World Affairs Orgns. newsletter; co-editor: (book) Asian/Pacific Dynamics-Economic, Political, Security, 1984; radio interviewer on internat. affairs, judge (TV series) Battle of Wits; contbr. articles to U.S. govt. publs., profl. jours., newspapers. Founder Prescott Sch., Arequipa; mem. Western Pa. Dist. Export Coun., Pitts., 1979—92; founder, pres. Atheneum Soc., Washington, 1952; founder Am. Soc. Arequipa, 1963. Lt. (j.g.) USNR, 1942—45, ETO. Recipient Meritorious Honor award, U.S. Dept. State, 1966, Disting. Svc. award, U. Nebr., 1972, 1988; scholar AHEPA, 1939; Paul Harris fellow, Rotary Found., 2004, scholar, U. Nebr., 1941. Mem.: Am. Arbitration Assn., Midwest Conf. World Affairs (adv. coun. 1988—90), Assn. Conflict Resolution, Internat. Exec. Svc. Corps, Fgn. Affairs Rels. Corps, Nat. Coun. World Affairs Orgns. (v.p. 1985—87, pres. 1987—89, bd. dirs., exec. com. 1974—91), Com. Present Danger (founding, bd. dirs.), Am. Fgn. Svc. Assn., Rotary, Mortar Bd. Avocations: reading, writing, public speaking, antiques, travel. Home and Office: 3416 Brookdale Dr Upper Saint Clair Pittsburgh PA 15241-1558

**MITCHELL, GEORGE ERNEST, JR.,** zoology educator; b. Duoro, N.Mex., June 7, 1930; s. George Ernest and Alma Thyrza (Hatley) M.; m. Billie Carolyn McMahan, Mar. 14, 1952; children: Leslie Dianne, Karen Leigh, Cynthia Faye. BS, U. Mo., 1951, MS, 1954; PhD, U. Ill., 1956. Asst. prof. animal sci. U. Ill., 1956-60; assoc. prof. U. Ky., Lexington, 1960-67, prof., 1967-98, prof. emeritus, 1998—, dir. grad. studies in animal scis., 1964-96, coord. beef cattle and sheep, 1974-90. Contbr. articles to profl. jours. Served with USAF, 1951-53. Fulbright research scholar New Zealand, 1973-74; Rsch. scholar Japan Soc. for Promotion of Sci., Japan, 1989 Mem. Am. Soc. Animal Sci. (sec. 1969-70, v.p. 1970-71, pres. So. sect. 1971-72, rsch. fellow 1989, Disting. Svc. award 1994), Am. Dairy Sci. Assn., Am. Inst. Nutrition, AAAS, Council for Agrl. Sci. and Tech., Sigma Xi, Alpha Zeta, Gamma Sigma Delta, Omicron Delta Kappa. Democrat. Methodist. Home: 690 Hill N Dale Rd Lexington KY 40503-2164 Office: U Ky 809 W P Garrigus Bldg Lexington KY 40546-0001 Personal E-mail: gmitchel@earthlink.net.

**MITCHELL, GEORGE JOHN,** entertainment company executive, lawyer, former senator; b. Waterville, Maine, Aug. 20, 1933; s. George J. and Mary (Saad) M.; m. Heather MacLachlan; children: Andrea, Andrew, Claire. BA, Bowdoin Coll., 1954; LL.B., Georgetown U., 1960. Bar: Maine 1960, D.C. 1960. Trial atty. anti-trust divsn. US Dept. Justice, Washington, 1960-62; exec. asst. to Senator Edmund Muskie US Senate, 1962-65; ptnr. Jensen, Baird, Gardner & Henry, Portland, Maine, 1965-77; US atty. Dist. Maine US Dept. Justice, 1977-79; judge US Dist. Ct. Maine, 1979-80; US Senator from Maine, 1980-95; majority leader, 1988-95; mem. environ. and pub. works com., 1980-95; mem. vet. affairs com., fin. com., 1981-95; mem. nat. ocean policy study group, arms control observer group; ex officio mem. intelligence com.; chmn. Dem. Senatorial Campaign Com., 1984-86; spl. counsel Verner, Liipfert, Bernhard, McPherson and Hand, Washington, 1996—2002, Preti, Flaherty, Beliveau, Pachios & Haley, Portland, Maine, 1997—2005; ptnr. Piper Rudnick, Washington, 2002—04; ptnr., chmn. global bd.; co-chmn. Govt. Controversies practice group DLA Piper Rudnick Gray Cary, 2005—; chmn. The Walt Disney Co., Burbank, Calif., 2004—. Chmn. Maine Democratic Com., 1966-68; nat. committeeman, Maine, 1969-77; dep. dir. Edmund S. Muskie presdl. campaign, 1968, 1972; asst. county atty. Cumberland County, 1971; spl. adv. to Pres.& Sec. of State for Econ. Initiatives in Ireland, 1995-2000; chmn., Sharm el-Sheikh Internat. Fact-Finding Com. to Examine Crisis in Middle East, 2000-01; head, Investigation of Steroid Abuse in Major League Baseball, 2006-; bd. dirs. Staples, Inc., FedEx Corp., Starwood Hotels & Resorts, The Walt Disney Co., 1995- Author: World on Fire: Saving an Endangered Earth, 1990, Not For America Alone: The Triumph of Democracy and The Fall of Communism, 1997, Making Peace, 1999; co-author (with William S. Cohen): Men of Zeal: A Candid Inside Story of the Iran-Contra Hearings, 1988. Served with U.S. Army, 1954-56; overseer Red Cross 9-11 Disaster Fund. Recipient Phila. Liberty medal, 1998, Presdl. Medal of Freedom, 1999, Truman Inst. Peace Prize, German Peace Prize, UNESCO Peace Prize, Harry Hopkins medal. Chaired Northern Ireland peace talks which led to the Good Friday Agreement, 1998. Office: DLA Piper Rudnick Gray Cary 1251 Ave of the Americas New York NY 10020-1104 Business E-Mail: george.mitchell@dlapiper.com.

**MITCHELL, GEORGE PHYDIAS,** gas and petroleum company executive; b. Galveston, Tex., 1919; m. Cynthia BS, Tex. A&M U., 1940. Exploration engr., geologist Amoco Prodn. Co., 1940-41, cons. geologist, engr., 1940-41; pres. Mitchell Energy & Devel. Corp., 1947-72, chmn. bd. dirs., CEO, 1972—. With Mitchell Energy & Devel. Corp., The Woodlands, Tex., 1947—, chmn., pres., 1972—, chief exec. officer, from 1972, also bd. dirs.; pres. George Mitchell & Assocs. Served to maj. U.S. Army, 1942-46. Recipient Michel T. Halbouty Human Needs award, Am. Assn. Petroleum Geologists 1994; named one of Forbes' Richest Americans, 2006. Office: Mitchell Energy & Devel PO Box 4000 The Woodlands TX 77387-4000*

**MITCHELL, GREGORY ALAN,** management consultant; s. Norman Lee and Bonnie Lou Mitchell; children: Desiree Lynnette, Annette Renee. BA in Bus., St. Leo U., 1999. Ceo, pres. Greg Mitchell Svcs., Inc., Virginia Beach, Va., 2000—. Tech. dir., mdcip U.S. No. Command, Colorado Springs, 2002—05; chief se&i Dhs-Uscg-Deepwater, Washington, 2005—. Author (tech. dir.): Maritime Critical Infrastructure Protection Technical & Operational Architecture, With USN, 1979—2000. Recipient Commendation, Standing Joint Forces Homeland Security, 2004. Avocations: music, guitar, travel.

**MITCHELL, J. BARRY,** corporate financial executive; m. Beth Mitchell; 3 children. BBA, Lehigh Univ., 1970, MBA, 1971. With PECO Energy Co., 1971—2000, v.p., treas., 1994—2000, Exelon Corp. (formed by merger of PECO Energy & Unicom Corp.), Chgo., 2000—02; sr. v.p., treas. Exelon Corp., Chgo., 2002—03, sr. v.p., treas., bus. unit CFO, 2003—05, sr. v.p., treas., CFO, 2005—. Bd. dir. Energy Ins. Mutual; mem. adv. bd. Factory Mutual Ins. Co. Mem. exec. com. Juvenile Diabetes Rsch. Found.; trustee Merit Sch. Music. Office: Exelon Corp 10 S Dearborn St Chicago IL 60603 also: Exelon Thermal Technologies 200 W Jackson Blvd Ste 1310 Chicago IL 60606-6941*

**MITCHELL, JAMES ANDREW,** education educator; b. Fort Campbell, Ky., Feb. 16, 1953; s. James Andrew and Joyce Anne (Smith) M.; m. Oana Geodoiu, Aug. 13, 1999; 1 child, Magdalena Amelie. AB, Vassar Coll., 1975; MA, Princeton U., 1979, PhD, 1985. Instr. Princeton U., Princeton, NJ, 1981—82; asst. prof. Haverford Coll., Pa., 1981—82, U. Redlands, Calif., 1982—85; escort/interpreter U.S. Dept. State, Washington, 1983—86; project mgr. Delphi Internat. Group, Washington, 1986—89; asst. prof. Mt. Vernon Coll., Washington, 1990—94; assoc. prof. Calif. State U., Northridge, 1994—2003, prof., 2003—. Vis. faculty fellow Am. U. in Kygyzstan, 2001, U. Bucharest, 2001; bd. dirs. South East European Inst. of Internat. Affairs; Am. fgn. policy adv. bd. Dushkin Publ., 2006—. Contbr. articles to profl. jours. Mem. African policy issues group George Bush for Pres. Campaign, Washington, 1988. J. William Fulbright fellow CIES and USIA, U. Bucharest, 1977, NEH fellow, Washington, 1989, John Parker Compton pre-doctoral fellow Ctr. for Internat. Studies, Princeton U., 1981; Rsch. grantee Woodrow Wilson Sch., Princeton U., 1989 Mem.: Princeton Club of N.Y. Avocations: exercise, aerobics. Office: Dept Polit Sci/Calif State 18111 Nordhoff St Northridge CA 91330-0001 Office Phone: 818-677-3488. Business E-Mail: james.mitchell@csun.edu.

**MITCHELL, JAMES B.,** medical researcher; PhD in cellular radiation biology, Colo. State U., 1978. Joined Radiation Br. Nat. Cancer Inst., 1979, independent investigator, 1984, past chief Radiobiology Sect., past dep. chief Radiation Oncology Br.; chief Radiation Biology Br. Ctr. Cancer Rsch., Nat. Cancer Inst., 1993—, head Tumor Biology Sect., acting chief Radiation Oncology Br: Radiation Oncology Br Ctr Cancer Rsch 10 Center Dr Bldg 10 Rm B3B69 Bethesda MD 20892 Office Phone: 301-496-7511. Office Fax: 301-480-2238. E-mail: jbm@helix.nih.gov.

**MITCHELL, JAMES EDWARD,** physician, educator; b. Chgo., June 19, 1947; s. James Edward and Elizabeth Latimer M.; m. Karen Antrim, June 14, 1969; children: James, Katherine. BA, Ind. U., 1968; MD, Northwestern U., 1972. Diplomate Am. Bd. Psychiatry Neurology. Intern Indpls. U., Mpls., 1972—73; resident U. Minn., Mpls., 1973—76, from asst. prof. to prof., 1979-90, prof., 1990-96; prof., chmn. dept. neuroscience sch. medicine & health sci. U. N.D., Fargo, 1996—. Pres., scientific dir. Neuropsychiat. Rsch. Inst., Fargo, 1996—. Named Tchr. of Yr., N.D. Psychiat. Residents Assn., 1997-98, 98-99. Fellow Am. Psychiat. Assn., Am. Assn. Social Psychiatry; mem. Acad. Eating Disorders (pres. 1999-2000), Eating Disorders Rsch. Soc. (sec.-treas. 1995—). Avocations: canoeing, art, travel. Office: Neuropsychiat Rsch Inst PO Box 1415 700 1st Ave S Fargo ND 58107 Fax: 701-293-3226. Office Phone: 701-293-1335. E-mail: mitchell@medicine.nodak.edu.

**MITCHELL, JAMES KENNETH,** civil engineer, educator; b. Manchester, NH, Apr. 19, 1930; s. Richard N. and Henrietta (Moench) M.; m. Virginia D. Williams, Nov. 24, 1951; children: Richard A., Laura K., James W., Donald M., David L. BBCE, Rensselaer Poly. Inst., 1951; MS, MIT, 1953, DSc, 1956. Mem. faculty U. Calif., Berkeley, 1958-93, prof. civil engring., 1968-89, chmn. dept., 1979-84, Edward G. and John R. Cahill prof. civil engring., 1989-92, Edward G. and John R Cahill prof. civil engring. emeritus, 1993—; Via prof. civil engring. Va. Poly. Inst. and State U., Blacksburg, 1994-99, Univ. Disting. prof., 1996-99, Univ. Disting. prof. emeritus, 1999—. Geotech. cons., 1960—. Author: Fundamentals of Soil Behavior, 1976, 3d edit., 2005; contbr. articles to profl. jours. Asst. scoutmaster Boy Scouts Am., 1975-82; mem. Moraga (Calif.) Environ. Rev. Com., 1978-80. Served to 1st lt. AUS, 1956-58. Recipient Exceptional Sci. Achievement award NASA, 1973, Berkeley citation, 1993, Chief of Engrs. Outstanding Svc. award U.S. Army Corps Engrs., 1999. Mem. ASCE (hon., Huber prize 1965, Middlebrooks award 1962, 70, 73, 01, Norman medal 1972, 95, Terzaghi lectr. 1984, Terzaghi award 1985. H. Bolton Seed medal 2004, Outstanding Projects and Leaders award in edn., 2006, pres. San Francisco sect. 1986-87), NAS, Nat. Acad. Engring. (vice chair civil engring. sect. 2001-03, chair 2003-05), Am. Soc. Engring. Edn, (W. Electric Fund award 1979), NRC (geotech. bd. chmn. 1990-94, bd. on infrastructure and constrn. environ. 1994-96, transp. rsch. bd. exec. com. 1983-87), Internat. Soc. Soil Mechanics and Geotech. Engring. (v.p. N.Am. 1989-94, Kevin Nash Gold medal 2001), Earthquake Engring. Rsch. Inst., Japanese Geotech. Soc. (internat. hon. mem.), Brit. Geotech. Soc. (Rankine lectr. 1991), Sigma Xi, Tau Beta Pi. Office: Va Tech Dept Civil Engring Blacksburg VA 24061-0105 Office Phone: 540-231-7351. Business E-Mail: jkm@vt.edu.

**MITCHELL, JAMES MARSHALL, JR.,** artist, educator; b. Cordele, Ga., Feb. 26, 1948; s. James Marshall and Sidney Price Mitchell; m. Shirley Phillips Mitchell, Aug. 16, 1970; children: Krista, Jay. BA in Art Edn., Valdosta State Coll., Ga., 1970; MS in Art, Ga. So. Coll., 1977. Tchr. art Griffin-Spaulding (Ga.) H.S., 1970—71, Crisp County H.S., Cordele, Ga., 1976—. Recipient Pottery award, Mus. Art, Albany, Ga., Purchase award, Cone Box Show; scholar, Fulbright Found., 1999. Mem.: Ga. Art Edn. Assn. Baptist. Avocations: fishing, reading. Office: Crisp Co Sr High Sch 2402 Cougar Aly Cordele GA 31015-2044

**MITCHELL, JERRY,** choreographer, actor; Choreographer (Broadway plays) Jerome Robbins' Broadway, 1989, Three Men on a Horse, 1993, Grease, 1994, You're a Good Man, Charlie Brown, 1999, The Full Monty, 2000, The Rocky Horror Picture Show, 2000, Hairspray, 2002, Imaginary Friends, 2002, Gypsy, 2003, Never Gonna Dance, 2003, La Cage aux Folles, 2004 (Tony award, best choreography, 2005, Drama Desk award, outstanding choreography, 2005, Outer Critics Circle award, outstanding choreography, 2005), Dirty Rotten Scoundrels, 2005, Catch Me If You Can, 2005, conceiver and dir. Broadway Bares (annual charity event), choreographer (films) Scent of a Woman, 1992, Jeffrey, 1995, In & Out, 1997, Drop Dead Gorgeous, 1999, Hedwig and the Angry Itch, 2001, Camp, 2003, Marci X, 2003, dance consultant Meet Joe Black, 1998, choreographer (TV series) The Drew Carey Show, 1995, (TV films) Geppetto, 2000, art dir. The New Gladiators, 1983; actor: The Secret of the Purple Reef, 1960.*

**MITCHELL, JERRY,** reporter; b. Texarkana, Tex., 1962; BA, Harding U., Ark. Spl. projects reporter Clarion-Ledger, Jackson, Miss., 1986—. Author: The Preacher & the Klansman, 1998; cons. (documentaries) Killed by the Klan, 1999. Finalist Pulitzer Prize, 2006; recipient NAACP Comty. Svc. award, Kennedy Ctr. honors ADI , 1998, Heywood Broun award for burning journalism, 1999, Outstanding Alumnus award, Harding U., 1999. Nat. Assn. Black Journalists award, 1999, newspaper award, Sidney Hillman Found., 1999, Sigma Delta Chi award for pub. svc. in journalism, Soc. Professional Journalists, 1999, 2 Best of Gannett awards, 1999, Silver Em award, U. Miss. Dept. Journalism, 2000, Outstanding Achievement Award of Excellence, Gannett Co., 2002, John Chancellor award for Excellence in Journalism, Columbia U., 2005, Pres.'s medal, CUNY Queen's Coll., 2005, Vernon Jarrett award, NC Agricultural & Technical State U. Inst. Advanced Journalism Studies, 2006, Tom Renner medal for outstanding crime reporting, Investigative Reporters & Editors, 2006, George Polk award for justice reporting, 2006. Achievements include investigative reporting leading to the prosecution and conviction of white supremacists who had committed murders in the 1960s; including the murders of three civil rights activists in Mississippi and the 1963 bombing of a church in Birmingham that killed four girls. Office: Clarion-Ledger PO Box 40 Jackson MS 39205 Office Phone: 601-961-7000. Office Fax: 601-961-7224.*

**MITCHELL, JOAN LAVERNE,** research scientist; b. Palo Alto, Calif., May 24, 1947; d. William Richardson and Doris LaVerne (Roddan) M. BS in Physics, Stanford U., 1969; MS in Physics, U. Ill., 1971, PhD in Physics, 1974. Rsch. staff mem. T.J. Watson Rsch. Ctr. IBM, Yorktown Heights, NY, 1974-88, 96-98, mgr. T.J. Watson Rsch. Ctr., 1979-88, image tech. cons. mktg. White Plains, NY, 1989-91, rsch. staff mem. T.J. Watson Rsch. Ctr. Hawthorne, NY, 1991-94, mgr. T.J. Watson Rsch. Ctr., 1992-94, supplemental employee Burlington, NY, 1994-96; vis. prof. U. Ill., Urbana, 1996; with IBM Printing Systems Divsn., Boulder, Colo., 1999—, IBM fellow, 2001—. Del. CCITT Study Group XIV, 1978-79, ISO JPEG Com. 1987-94, ITU-T Study Group 16 Working Party 3, 2005—. Co-author: JPEG Still Image Data Compression Standard, 1993, MPEG Video Compression Standard, 1997; contbr. articles to profl. jours. Recipient U. Ill. Coll. Engring. Disting. Alumni Svc. award, 2006, Leadership award Internat. Multimedia Telecoms. Consortium, 2006; Xerox Indsl. fellow, 1970-71. Fellow IEEE; mem. NAE, Am. Phys. Soc., Soc. for Imaging Sci. and Tech., Sigma Xi (chpt. sec. 1976, v.p. 1977, pres. 1978). Democrat. Achievements include co-inventor on numerous

patents. Home: 1172 Fall River Cir Longmont CO 80501 Office: IBM Printing Systems Divsn 6300 Diagonal Hwy MS004N Boulder CO 80301-9270 Office Phone: 303-924-4271. Business E-Mail: joanm@us.ibm.com.

**MITCHELL, JOHN CHARLES,** marketing professional; b. Bedford, Ind., May 25, 1947; s. John Lewis and Mary Ellen (Rowe) M.; m. Marie Elizabeth Bruland, Aug. 21, 1971; 1 child, Allison Anne. BA in Econs., Va. Mil. Inst., 1969; MBA, JD, Ind. U., 1975. Bar: Ind., 1975, Fed. Cts., 1975. Brand mgr. Procter and Gamble Co., Cin., 1975-82; group product mgr. RJR/Del Monte, San Francisco, 1982-84; dir. mktg. RJR/Nabisco, Parsippany, NJ, 1984-87, v.p. mktg., 1987-88, v.p., gen. mgr., 1988-90, pres. sales and logistics co., 1991-94, pres. Planters, Lifesavers co. Winston-Salem, NC, 1994-96; pres. bus. printer divsn. Lexmark Internat., Lexington, Ky., 1997-99; founder Collaborative Leaders, Inc., Chapel Hill, NC, 2001—. 1st lt. US Army, 1969-71. Inductee Va. Mil. Inst. Sports Hall of Fame, 1981. Republican. Methodist. Avocations: golf, skiing. E-mail: jandmmitchell@nc.rr.com.

**MITCHELL, JOHN LAURIN AMOS,** biological science educator; b. Lincoln, Nebr., July 18, 1944; s. William A. and Ruth Chilla (Cobbey) M.; m. Gail Ann Kurtz, July 13, 1968; children: Jill, Todd. BA, Oberlin Coll., 1966; PhD, Princeton U., 1970. Postdoctoral fellow McArdle Inst. Cancer Rsch., Madison, Wis., 1970-73; asst. prof. No. Ill. U., DeKalb, 1973-78, assoc. prof., prof., 1983—; dir. Biochem. Biophys. Rsch., 1997—. Inventor in field; contbr. articles to profl. jours.

**MITCHELL, JOHN W.,** pharmaceutical executive; B of Engring., Yale U. Various positions Pfizer, Inc., Bklyn., 1964—68, dir. prodn. planning and inventory control N.Y.C., 1968—72, product dir. constrn and startup new plants, 1972—75, v.p., gen. mfg. ops. PR, 1975—78, pres. profn. pharms. N.Y.C., 1978—97, pres. mfg., 1997—99, sr. v.p. global mfg., 1999—2000, pres., team leader global mfg., 2000—, v.p., 2001—

**MITCHELL, JON CEANDER,** music educator, conductor; b. Chgo., June 18, 1949; s. James William and Violet Linnea Mitchell; m. Ester Morales, Dec. 22, 1973; children: Monica Mitchell Finn, Lydia, David. MusB, Millikin U., 1971; MS in Music Edn., U. Ill., 1972, EdD in Music Edn., 1980. Asst. prof. music Hanover (Ind.) Coll., 1982—87; condr. wind ensemble Carnegie Mellon U., Pitts., 1987—91; asst. prof. music U Ga., Athens, 1991—92; prof. music U. Mass., Boston, 1992—96, chair dept., 1996—. Music dir. North Pitts. Civic Symphony, Pitts., 1988—92; guest conducting various bands and orchs. Author: From Kneller Hall to Hammersmith, 1990, A Comprehensive Biography of Gustav Holst, 2001, The Braunschweig Scores: Felix Weingartner and Erich Leinsdorf on Beethoven's First Four Symphonies, 2005; contbr. articles to profl. jours.; condr.: CD Beethoven: Piano Concerto in D, Op. 61, Concerto in D, 2004, The Youthful Beethoven, 2005, Beethoven: Piano Concerto in E Flat, Wio.0.4, 2005. Mem.: Coll. Band Dirs. Nat. Assn., Music Educators Nat. Conf., World Assn. Symphonic Bands and Ensembles (asst. editor newsletter 2000, editor WASBE jour. 1994), Condrs. Guild, Phi Kappa Phi. Avocations: travel, model railroading, coaster collecting. Office: Dept Performing Arts U Mass 100 Morrissey Blvd Boston MA 02125-3393

**MITCHELL, JONI (ROBERTA JOAN ANDERSON),** singer, songwriter; b. Ft. Macleod, Alta., Can., Nov. 7, 1943; d. William A. and Myrtle M. (McKee) Anderson; m. Chuck Mitchell (div.); m. Larry Klein, Nov. 21, 1982. Student, Alta. Coll. Albums Song to a Seagull, Clouds, Ladies of the Canyon, Blue, For the Roses, Court and Spark, 1974, Miles of Aisles, The Hissing of Summer Lawns, 1975, Hejira, 1976, Don Juan's Reckless Daughter, 1979, Mingus, 1979 (Jazz Album of Year and Rock-Blues Album of Year, Downbeat mag., 1979), Shadows and Light, 1980, Wild Things Run Fast, 1982, Dog Eat Dog, 1985, Chalk Mark in a Rainstorm, 1988, Night Ride Home, 1991, Turbulent Indigo, 1994, Hits, 1996, Taming the Tiger, 1998, Both Sides Now, 2000, Travelogue, 2002, screenwriter/actor (films) Love, 1982; contbr. album dog Eat Dog/Wild Things Run Fast, 1996. Named to Rock and Roll Hall of Fame, 1997; recipient Grammy award for Best Folk Performance, 1969, Grammy award for Best Arrangement Accompanying Vocalists (with Tom Scott), 1974. Address: care Reprise Records 3300 Warner Blvd Burbank CA 91505-4632

**MITCHELL, JOSEPH PATRICK,** architect; b. Bellingham, Wash., Sept. 29, 1939; s. Joseph Henry and Jessie Delila (Smith) Mitchell; m. Marilyn Ruth Jorgenson, June 23, 1962; children: Amy Evangeline, Kirk Patrick, Scott Henry. Student, Western Wash. State Coll., 1957-59; BA, U. Wash., 1963, BArch, 1965. Assoc. designer, draftsman, project architect Beckwith Spangler Davis, Bellevue, Wash., 1965-70; prin. J. Patrick Mitchell, AIA & Assocs./Architects/Planners/Cons., Kirkland, Wash., 1970—. Del. various internat. confs.; charter mem. Northshore Bapt. Ch., 1969, elder, 1984—90; bd. ext. and cert. com. Columbia Bapt. Conf., 1977—83, vice-moderator, 1995—96, moderator, 1996—97, overseer ch. ministries bd., pres., 1997—99; charter mem. Cascade Cmty. Ch., 1997—; trustee Bakke Libr./Cultural Ctr., 1994—96; chmn. long range planning com. Lake Retreat Camp, 1965—93; active Deming Hist. Cemetery Assn., 1997—. Recipient Internat. Archtl. Design award, St. John Vianney Parish, 1989. Mem.: AIA, Christian Camp and Conf. Assn., Wash. Farm Forestry Assn., Internat. Conf. Bldg. Ofcls., Nat. Coun. Archtl. Registration Bds., Nat. Fedn. Bus., Interfaith Forum Religion, Art, and Architecture (arch. edn. tour. Finland and St. Petersburg, Russia 1998), Construm. Specification Inst., Woodinville C. of C. Office: 12620 120th Ave NE Ste 208 Kirkland WA 98034-7511

**MITCHELL, KAREN FRANCES,** artist, jewelry designer; b. Denver, Aug. 24, 1953; d. Harry Francis and Mary Jane Magrete (Jensen-Borg) Mitchell. BFA, U. Colo., 1975; postgrad., Gemological Inst. Am., 1986, Kulicke Jewelry Arts Inst., 1988, Cecilia Bauer Studio, 1992, Fashion Inst. of Tech., 1993, Nat. Acad. Design, 1994. Cert. tchr. art specialist. Jewelry designer, pres. Karen Mitchell Design, Aspen, Colo., 1978 ; cultural rschr., cons. various Italian newspapers and mags., NY, Colo., 1992-94, Italian Consulate Cultural Inst., NY, 1992—94. Instr. workshops design and goldsmithing technique; apprentice Van der Schoot Disegno e Fabricazione, Milan, 1989—91. Co-designer, co-author (book) World Gold Coun. Jewelry Trend Book, 1991—95; exhibitions include World Gold Coun., Aaron Faber Gallery, N.Y.C., Yaw Gallery, Mich., SOFA, Chgo., NY, J. Cotter Gallery, Cindy Griem Fine Jewels, Somerhill Gallery, N.C., Facere Gallery, Wash., Concepts Gallery, Calif., Greene & Greene Gallery, NY, Yann Gallery, Chgo., Master's Showcase Park Ave., N.Y.C., Fall Crafts Park Ave., The Artful Hand Gallery, Boston, Works Gallery, N.Y.C., Am. Craft Coun. Shows, Balt., Am. Craft Coun. San Francisco, Positive Images Gallery, Austin, Tex., Telluride Gallery, Colo. Vol. chmn. benefit com. Aspen Art Mus.; co-chmn. benefit com Aspen Music Festival; mem. Les Dames d'Aspen; vol. Profl. Women's Orgn., Milan, Am. Craft Mus., NY, 1993, Coun. Fashion Designers Am., NY, Internat. Design Conf. of Aspen, Screening Com. Aspen Film Fest, Soprano, Aspen Choral Soc.; vol. benefit Aspen Ski Club/U.S. Olympic Equestrian Team, 1995; trustee Aspen Snowmass Coun. Arts. Named Vol. of the Yr. Aspen Art Mus., 2001. Mem.: Jewelry Design Profl.'s Network, Am. Craft Coun., Soc. N.Am. Goldsmiths. Address: PO Box 4885 Aspen CO 81612-4885 E-mail: kmdaspen@hotmail.com.

**MITCHELL, KENNETH DAVID,** physiologist, educator; b. Musselburgh, Scotland, Mar. 5, 1959; children: Elaine J., Fraser K., Keith J. BSc with upper 2d class honors, U. Edinburgh, Scotland, 1981, PhD in Physiology, 1986. Physiology tutor Univ. Med. Sch., Edinburgh, 1981-84; rsch. assoc. dept. physiology and biophysics Nephrology Rsch. and Tng. Ctr. U.A., Birmingham, 1984-86, postdoctoral rsch. fellow, 1986-87, rsch. instr., 1987-88, scientist I, 1987-88; asst. prof. dept. physiology Tulane U. Sch. Medicine, New Orleans, 1988-95, assoc. prof., 1995—. Contbr. articles to profl. jours. Fellow Am. Heart Assn. (fellow Coun. High Blood Pressure Rsch. 1993—; Established Investigator award 1995-2000), Am. Soc. Nephrology; mem. Am. Physiol. Soc., Am. Soc. Nephrology, Internat. Soc. Nephrology. Office: Tulane U Sch Medicine Dept Physiology SL39 1430 Tulane Ave New Orleans LA 70112-2699 Office Phone: 504-988-2593. Business E-Mail: kdmitch@tulane.edu.

**MITCHELL, LEE MARK,** communications executive, investment banker, lawyer; b. Albany, NY, Apr. 16, 1943; s. Maurice B. and Mildred (Roth) M.; m. Barbara Lee Anderson, Aug. 27, 1966; children: Mark, Matthew. AB, Wesleyan U., 1965; JD, U. Chgo., 1968. Bar: Ill. 1968, D.C. 1969, U.S. Supreme Ct. 1972. Assoc. Leibman, Williams, Bennett, Baird & Minow, Chgo. and Washington, 1968-72, Sidley & Austin, Washington, 1972-74, ptnr., 1974-84, 92-94; exec. v.p. and gen. counsel Field Enterprises, Inc., Chgo., 1981-83, pres., CEO, 1983-84, Field Corp., 1984-92; prin. Golder, Thoma, Cressey, Rauner, Inc., Chgo., 1994-98; ptnr. Thoma Cressey Equity Ptnrs., Inc., Chgo., 1998—. Chmn. Chgo. Stock Exch., Inc. Author: Openly Arrived At, 1974, With the Nation Watching, 1979; co-author: Presidential Television, 1973. Bd. visitors U. Chgo. Law Sch., 1984—86, Medill Sch. Journalism, Northwestern U., 1984—91; pres. bd. govs. Chgo. Met. Planning Coun., 1988—; mem. midwest regional adv. bd. Inst. Internat. Edn., 1987—99; trustee Ravinia Festival Assn., 1989—97, Northwestern U., Northwestern Meml. Hosp.; U.S. del. Brit. Legis. Conf. on Govt. and Media, Ditchley Park, England, 1974; adv. com. LWV Presdl. Debates, Washington, 1979—80, 1982; vice chair Chgo. Met. Planning Coun., 1999—. Mem.: Econ. Mid-Am. Club, ABA, Comml. Club Chgo. Home: 135 Maple Hill Rd Glencoe IL 60022-1252 Office: Thoma Cressey Equity Ptnrs Sears Tower Ste 9200 233 S Wacker Dr Chicago IL 60606-6331 Business E-Mail: lmitchell@thomacressey.com.

**MITCHELL, LOUISE TYNDALL,** special education educator; b. St. Louis, Oct. 25; d. Walter Eugene and Nellie May (Otey) Tyndall; m. Felix Mitchell Sr., Sept. 30, 1958; children: Felix Jr., Jeane Mitchell-Carr. AA, Stowe Tchrs. Coll., St. Louis, 1947; BA, Harris Tchrs. Coll., St. Louis, 1958; MA, St. Louis U., 1965. Cert. elem. tchr., secondary English and math., reading clinician. Tchr. math. Hadley High Sch., St. Louis, 1958-59; tchr. Emerson Elem. Sch., St. Louis, 1969-67; head dept. spl. edn. Laclede Elem. Sch., St. Louis, 1967-68, coord. curriculum, 1968-70; adminstrv. asst. Delmar High Sch., St. Louis, 1970-72; assoc. prof., reading clinician, mgr. apprentice tchrs. Harris Tchrs. Coll., 1972-78; chair dept. spl. edn. Cleveland High Sch., St. Louis, 1978-84, chmn. faculty, 1982-84; head dept. spl. edn. S.W. High Sch., St. Louis, 1984-87, tchr., mentor, 1987—. Mentor St. Louis Pub. Schs., 1988-89. Author: (handbook) Teachers Aide, 1987, curriculum guides, 1974, 78; co-author (curriculum guide) Fundamental Curriculum, 1990. Chair Rsch. and Status Black Women, St. Louis, 1974; charter mem. Triagle Club YWCA, 1970. Recipient Community Svc. award Top Ladies Distinction, St. Louis, 1981, 50 Yrs. Outstanding Svc. award A.M.E. Ch., St. Louis, 1987, Salute to Excellence in Edn. recognition St. Louis Am. Newspaper, 1991. Mem. NAACP, Am. Fedn. Tchrs., Nat. Coun. Negro Women, Colored Womens' Fed. Clubs, Women Achievement (coord. youth 1989), St. Louis U. Alumni Assn., (Svc. award 1986), Ch. Women United, Order Ea. Star (past Worthy Matron 1978), Sigma Gamma Rho (chaplain 1988-90), Phi Delta Kappa. Avocations: reading, writing, drama, singing, public speaking. Home: 4537 Fair Ave # A Saint Louis MO 63115-3054

**MITCHELL, LUCILLE ANNE,** retired elementary school educator; b. Dayton Corners, Ill., Oct. 19, 1928; d. Roy Rollin and Edna May (Whitehouse) Sheppard; m. Donald L. Mitchell; children: David, Diane, Barbara Rock, Patricia Reaves. BS in Edn., Augustana Coll., 1966; MS in Edn., Western Ill. U., 1972, Edn. Specialist, 1974. Tchr. Carbon Cliff (Ill.) Elem. Sch., 1962-65, Moline (Ill.) Bd. Edn., 1967-92. Mem. textbook selection com. Moline Bd. Edn., 1967-84, rep. Moline Bd. Edn., Ill. Network Sch. Devel., 1973. Author: numerous poems. Counselor to pastor Cmty. of Christ, 2001—02, elder in priesthood. Named Ill. Master Tchr., State of Ill., 1984; recipient Internat. Peace prize United Cultural Convention, 2005 Mem. Ill. Edn. Assn. (com. mem.), Moline Edn. Assn. (com. mem.), Delta Kappa Gamma (program chmn. 1978-79, recording sec. 1980-81) Avocations: organ, piano, oil and water color painting, poetry, teaching Bible study classes. Home: 3214 55th Street Ct Moline IL 61265-5740 Personal E-mail: donnlucy@mchsi.com.

**MITCHELL, LYNN HATFIELD,** music educator, director, musician; d. Gus Davis and Bobbie Coffelt Hatfield, Jr.; m. Stephen Park Mitchell, June 18, 1983; children: Davis Park, Melissa Lee, Hannah Jane. MusB in Edn., Fla. State U., 1976; MusM in Edn., U. Ga., 1981. Cert. Level I Orff-Schulwerk, 1995, Level II Orff-Schulwerk, 1997, Level III Orff-Schulwerk, 1999, Master Orff-Schulwerk, 2001, Level I Doreen Rao Choral Music Experience, 2005. Choir dir. Jonesboro Jr. HS, Clayton County Schs., Ga., 1977—80; music tchr., asst. band dir. Martins Ferry Schs., Ohio, 1982—88; elem. music tchr. Jefferson County, Birmingham, Ala., 1995—97, Shelby County Schs., Columbiana, Ala., 1997—2001; choir dir., tchr. Riverchase Mid. Sch., Birmingham, 2001—; music tchr. Wilsonville Elem. Sch. Children's choir dir. Lafayette Presbyn. Ch., Tallahassee, 1989—93; handbell and children's choir dir. Riverchase Presbyn. Ch., Hoover, Ala., 1995—2001; choir dir. Shades Valley Presbyn. Ch., Birmingham, 2001—04; music dir. Centerstage Prodns., Birmingham, 2002—03, South City Theatre, Alabaster, Ala., 2005. Actor: (cmty. musical theater) Cinderella, 42nd Street. Bd. mem. Magic City Children's Opera, Birmingham, 1998—2002; treas. Ala. Orff Assn., Birmingham, 1998—2002; dist. chmn. Ala. Vocal Assn., Birmingham, 2005—06. Named Tchr. of Yr., Wilsonville Elem. Sch., 2001. Mem.: Nat. Educator's Assn., Am. Choral Dir.'s Assn., Music Educator's Nat. Conf. Democrat-Npl. Presbyterian. Avocations: singing, reading, theater. Office: Riverchase Middle Sch 853 Willow Oak Dr Birmingham AL 35244 Office Fax: 205-682-5515. Business E-Mail: lmitchell@shelbyed.k12.al.us.

**MITCHELL, MARCIA JEANNE,** writer; b. San Jose, Calif., Feb. 20, 1932; d. Eugene Lewis Wilcox and Gladys Delphine Shoemaker; m. John Alexander Donnan (div. June 1, 1975); children: Alan James Donnan, Kristen Elizabeth Donnan; m. Thomas Francis Mitchell, June 29, 1985. Student, Colo. State U., 1965—67; BA, Norwich U., Vt. Coll., 1989. Writer, editor Rapid City (S.D.) Jour. 1968 73; cabinet officer, Leo, junior S.D. State Govt., Pierre, SD, 1973—75; sr. exec. Corp. for Pub. Broadcasting, Washington, 1975—80; assoc. dir. Am. Film Inst., Washington & L.A., 1980—87; freelance writer, prodr., 1988—. Lectr., seminar leader mgmt. strategies for women, 1980—82; lectr. Crystal Cruise Lines, 1999, Cunard QE2, 2001; motivational sem. spkr. Prodr.: world premieres of maj. motion pictures, 1980—86, A Daughter's Tribute to Fred Astaire, 2001; author: Cosmetics from the Kitchen, 1972, Raindance to Research, 1977, Management Strategies for Women, 1980, 1981, The Spy Who Seduced America: Lies and Betrayal in the Heat of the Cold War, 2002. Past sec. Nat. Assns. Commns. on Women; vice chair Montserrat Found. for Charitable Giving, West Indies, 1995—2001; chair spl. events Hill City (S.D.) Arts Coun., 2001; mem. Montserrat Nat. Trust, Montserrat, 2001; past chair grants com. State Fine Arts Coun., SD; past mem. State Commn. on Status of Women, SD; mem. S.D. Humanities Found. Bd., 2005—06; mem., organizer S.D. Dem. Women, 2001—02; past bd. dirs. Women's Equity Action League, N.Y.C., NY; past chair TV broadcasting com. PBS Sta. WETA-TV, Washington. Recipient 1st pl. feature writing, S.D. Press Women, 1995, Counter-Intelligence Book of Yr., Assn. Former Intelligence Officers, 2002, 1st pl., Non-fiction Books, 2003. Mem.: S. D. Humanities Found., Nat. Fedn. Press Women (Top Press Woman of Yr. 1972—73). Roman Catholic.

**MITCHELL, MELVIN CLIFFORD,** music educator; b. Talihina, Okla., Dec. 1, 1942; s. Lem Granville Mitchell and Evelyn Irene Gale, J. E. Gale (Stepfather); m. Joyce Elaine Anglin, June 23, 1962; children: Matthew Clark, Daniel Dale. MusB in Edn., Okla. State U., 1964; MEd, Southwestern Okla. State U., 1975. Cert. vocal music dir. K-12 Okla. State U. Vocal music dir. Shelbyville (Mo) Pub. Sys., 1964—65, Littleton (Colo.) Sch. Dist., 1965—66, Lone Wolf (Okla.) Pub. Sch. Sys., 1967—70, Woodward (Okla.) Pub. Sch. Sys., 1970—75; chmn. and vocal music dir. Ea. Okla. State Coll., Wilburton, 1975—83; vocal music dir. Lewisville (Tex.) Ind. Sch. Dist. 1986—. Musical cast mem. and soloist Okla. State U., Stillwater, 1961—64; contest dir. N.W. Okla Vocal Music Dist., Woodward 1970—75; vocal music adjudicator/clinician, Okla. 1970—83; mem. all-state music com. Okla. Music Educators Assn., Oklahoma City, 1972—75; dir. sweepstakes choirs Woodward choral orgns., Enid, Okla., 1973—75; dir. musicals Woodward Pub. Schs., 1973—75; vocal music dir. Okla. State 4-H Round-Up,

Stillwater, 1975—79; dir. musicals Ea. Okla State coll., 1975—83; vocal choral arranger Griffin Mid. Sch. A cappella Choir, The Colony, Tex., 1998—. Fellow: Phi Delta Kappa (assoc.; found. rep. 1998—2004); mem.: Tex. Choral Dirs. Assn. (assoc.), Tex. Music Educators Assn. (assoc.), Am. Choral Dirs. Assn. (life). Republican. Baptist. Avocation: golf. Home: 2216 Swallow Ln Lewisville TX 75077 Office: Griffin Mid Sch 5105 N Colony Blvd The Colony TX 75056 Office Phone: 469-713-5973 x 2960. Home Fax: 972-317-9863. Business E-mail: mitchellmc@lisd.net.

**MITCHELL, MEMORY FARMER,** retired communications executive; b. Raleigh, N.C., Jan. 21, 1924; d. James S. and Foy Johnson Farmer; m. Thornton W. Mitchell, Sept. 7, 1963 (dec.); children: James Thornton, David Wingate. BA, Meredith Coll., 1944; LLB, JD, U. N.C., 1946, MA in History, 1949. Bar: N.C. 1947. Staff mem. Inst. Govt., Chapel Hill, NC, 1946—47; instr. in history Meredith Coll., Raleigh, NC, 1949—50; asst. state archivist N.C. Divsn. Archives and History, NC, 1956—61; adminstrv. asst. N.C. State Bd. Pub. Welfare, Raleigh, 1950—54; judge Cabarrus County Domestic Rels. Ct., Concord, NC, 1954—56; hist. pubs. adminstr. N.C. Divsn. Archives and History, 1961—82, ret., 1982. Pres. Hist. Soc. N.C., 1973—74. Author: Legal Aspects of Conscription and Exemption in North Carolina, 1861-1865, 1965; editor: Messages and Address of Governors Terry Sanford, Daniel K. Moore, Robert W. Scott, James Holshouse, Jr., James B. Hunt, 5 vols., 1966—82; mem. editl. bd.: Am. Archivist, 1972—74. Pres. Meredith Coll. Alumnae Assn., 1982—84; dir. Carolina Charter Corp., 1970—, Wake County Resources for Srs., NC, 1992—98; active Pullen Meml. Bapt. Ch., Raleigh, NC, 1st Bapt. Ch., Raleigh. Named Tar Heel of Wk., News and Observer, Raleigh, N.C., Oct. 1, 1961; recipient Outstanding Alumna award, Meredith Coll. Alumnae, 1978. Mem.: So. Hist. Assn. (coun. 1977—79), N.C. Soc., N.C. Lit. and Hist. Assn. (sec.-treas. 1976—77, Christopher Crittenden award 1981), Friends of the Archives (dir.). Democrat. Baptist. Avocations: reading, travel, cooking, embroidery, crocheting. Home: 2431 Medway Dr Raleigh NC 27608

**MITCHELL, MOZELLA GORDON,** language educator, minister; b. Starkville, Miss., Aug. 14, 1936; d. John Thomas and Odena Mae (Graham) Gordon; m. Edrick R. Woodson, Mar. 20, 1951 (div. 1974); children: Cynthia LaVern, Marcia Delores Woodson Miller. AB, LeMoyne Coll., 1959; MA in English, U. Mich., 1963; MA in Religious Studies, Colgate-Rochester Divinity Sch., 1973; PhD, Emory U., 1980. Instr. in English and Speech Alcorn A&M Coll., Lorman, Miss., 1960-61; instr. English, chmn. dept. Owen Jr. Coll., Memphis, 1961-65; asst. prof. English and religion Norfolk State Coll. U. Norfolk, Va., 1965—81; assoc. prof. U. South Fla., Tampa, 1981—93, prof., 1993—, chmn.-elect religious studies dept., 2005—, chair religious studies dept., 2006—; pastor Mount Sinai AME Zion Ch., 1882—89; presiding elder Tampa dist. AME Zion Ch., 1988—; pastor, founder Love of Christ AME Zion Tabernacle, Branden, 1993—; candidate for bishop AME Zion Ch., 2003—04, presiding Elder, 1998—2004. Vis. assoc. prof. Hood Theol. Sem., Salisbury, N.C., 1979-80, St. Louis U., 1992-93; vis. asst. lectr. U. Rochester, N.Y., 1972-73; co-dir. Ghent VISTA Project, Norfolk, 1969-71; cons. Black Women and Ministry Interdenominational Theol. Ctr; lectr. Fla. Humanities Coun., 1994-95; Meml. lectr. Mordecai Johnson Inst., Colgate Rochester Div. Sch., 1997. Author: Spiritual Dynamics of Howard Thurman's Theology, 1985, Howard Thurman and the Quest for Freedom, Proc. 2d Ann. Howard Thurman Convocation (Peter Lang), 1992, African American Religious History in Tampa Bay, 1992;, New Africa in America: The Blending of African and American Religious and Social Traditions Among Black People in Meridian, Mississippi and Surrounding Counties (Peter Lang), 1994, Crucial Issues in Caribbean Religions (Peter Lang), 2006, Crucial Issues in Caribbean Religion, 2006; editor: Martin Luther King Meml. Series in Religion, Culture and Social Devel.; editorial bd. Cornucopia Reprint Series; contr. articles and essays in field. Mem. Tampa-Hillsborough County Human Rels. Coun., 1987—; founder Women at the Well, Inc.; del. 7th assembly World Coun. Chs., Canberra, Australia, 1991, 17th World Meth. Coun., Rio de Janiero, 1996; del. 18th World Meth. Coun., Brighton, England, 2001; mem. connectional coun. A.M.E. Zion Ch., Charlotte, 1984—; staff writer Sunday sch. lit., 1981—, mem. jud. coun., candidate for bishop, 2002—04; pres. Fla. Coun. Chs., Orlando, Fla., 1988—90, pres.-elect, 1998—, pres. exec. bd., 2000. Recipient ecumenical leadership citation Fla. Coun. Chs., 1990, Inaugural lectr. award Geddes Hanson Black Cultural Ctr. Princeton Theol. Sem., 1993; fellow Nat. Doctoral Fund, 1978-80; grantee NEH, 1981, Fla. Endowment for Humanities, 1990—, U. South Fla. Rsch. Coun., 1990—. Mem. Coll. Theology Soc., Am. Acad. Religion, Soc. for the Study of Black Religion (pres. 1992-96), Joint Ctr. for Polit. Studies, Black Women in Ch. and Soc., Alpha Kappa Alpha. Phi Kappa Phi. Democrat. Methodist. Avocations: piano, poetry, tennis, bicycling, Scrabble. Office: Univ South Florida Religious Studies Dept CPR 107 Tampa FL 33620 Office Phone: 813-974-1852. Business E-Mail: mozellam@aol.com. *In my estimation, people are people, whatever the race, class or status. Between the front yard and the back porch of each individual dwells the real person, to whom I like to direct my approach.*

**MITCHELL, NICOLE MARGARET,** flutist, composer; b. Syracuse, NY, Feb. 17, 1967; d. Michael Eugene and Joan Beard Mitchell; life ptnr. David Corey Boykin; 1 child, Aayonealya Samadhi Joan McDaniel. BA in Music Performance, Chgo. State U., 1998; Masters in Jazz and Classical Performance, No. Ill. U., 2000. Founder, dir., composer, flutist Black Earth Ensemble, Chgo., 1997—, Black Earth Strings, 2002—. Adj. prof. of music Northeastern Ill. U. at Ctr. for Inner City Studies, Chgo., 2000—; adj. prof. of flute Chgo. State U., 2000—; co-pres. Dreamtime Records Inc., Chgo., 2003—; edn. coord. Jazz Inst. of Chgo., 2004—; adj. prof. of music No. Ill. U., Dekalb, Ill., 2006—. Composer (playwright, conceptualist, producer) (multi-arts community play) Vision Quest: Hope, Future and Destiny; composer: (arranger) (string quartets) Love has no Boundaries, Wondrous Birth, Sweet Tooth; composer: (trio for flute, cello and frame drum) Waterdance; composer: (arranger) (large ensemble pieces) Afrika Rising Trilogy, Umoja, Bluerise, Peaceful Village, Wheatgrass, Wondrous Birth, Curbside Fantasee, Skating, Future's Meditation, Wanna Make You Smile, Time For Change, The Creator has Other Plans for Me, Navigator, Off the Clock, Cause and Effect, Sun Cycles, For New Orleans, (chamber ensemble pieces) Episodes of an Obscure Life, Sanctuary, Waris Dirie, Ice, On the Nile, Sweet Tooth, Journey for 3 Blue Stones, In the Garden, Message from Mothergoddess, For Daughters of Young Love, Healing Ritual; composer: (creative flutist) (music cd) Vision Quest, Afrika Rising, Hope, Future and Destiny. Recipient Critic's Poll Top Ten Rising Star Flutist, Downbeat Mag., 2001—05, Critic's Poll Winner Rising Star Flutist, 2006; fellow Music Composition, Ill. Arts Coun., 2003, 2005; grantee Music, CAAP, Cultural Arts Program-Chicago, 2001, 2003, 2005; scholar, Am. Symphony Orch. League, 1997, 1998, 1999. Mem.: ASCAP, Assn. for the Advancement of Creative Musicians (vice chairperson 2004—). Humanist. Achievements include Performed original music in Paris, Verona, Vancouver, Montreal, New York, Guelph, Kerava and Moscow. Avocations: poetry, tap dancing, meditation, rollerskating, art. Personal E-mail: www.nicolemitchell.com.

**MITCHELL, ORLAN E.,** clergyman, academic administrator; b. Eldora, Iowa, Mar. 13, 1933; s. Frank E. and Alice G. (Brown) M.; m. Verlene J. Huehn, June 10, 1952; children: Jolene R., Stephen M., Nadene A., Timothy M., Mark E. BA, Grinnell Coll., 1955; B.D., Yale U., 1959, M.Div., 1965; D.Min., San Francisco Theol. Sem., 1976. Ordained to ministry United Ch. of Christ, 1959; pastor chs. Sheridan Twp., Iowa, 1954-55, New Preston, Conn., 1956-59, Clarion, Iowa, 1959-69, Yankton SD, 1969-77; pres. Yankton (S.D.) Coll., 1977-96; conf. minister Iowa Conf. United Ch. Christ; ret., 1996. Cons. in field. Mem. Sch. Bd., Clarion, Iowa, 1965-69, mem., Yankton, S.D., 1973-77, pres., 1976; bd. dirs. Lewis and Clark Mental Health Center. Mem. S.D. Found. Pvt. Colls., S.D. Assn. Pvt. Colls., Colls. of Mid-Am. Lodges: Kiwanis; Masons. Democrat. Mem. United Ch. Of Christ. Office: 725 Park St Grinnell IA 50112-2235 Personal E-mail: orlanm@pcpartner.net.

**MITCHELL, PAMELA LEE,** elementary school educator; b. Lafayette, Ind., Feb. 28, 1950; d. Edward John and Olive Maude Brenner; m. Kenneth David Mitchell; 1 child, David Edward. BA, Purdue U., 1968—72, MS in Edn., 1977. Tchr. North Newton Sch. Corp., Roselawn, Ind., 1973—78,

Lafayette Sch. Corp., 1978—. Head 4th and 5th grade sci. dept. Vinton Elem. Sch., Lafayettte, Ind., 1991—95, head 1st grade tchr., 1996—. Four R's grant for computers, Vinton Elem. Sch., 1996. Mem.: AARP, Am. Edn. Assn., Nat. Edn. Assn. Office: Vinton Elem Sch 3101 Elmwood Ave Lafayette IN 47904

**MITCHELL, PATRICIA EDENFIELD,** broadcast museum administrator; b. Swainsboro, Ga., Jan. 20, 1943; d. James Otis and Bernice Tucker Edenfield; m. Jay Addison Mitchell, Aug. 20, 1964 (div. June 1970); 1 child, Mark Addison. BA magna cum laude, U. Ga., 1964, MA, 1965. English instr. U. Ga., Athens, 1965—69; English, drama instr. Va. Commonwealth U., Richmond, 1969—70; researcher, writer LOOK Mag., NYC, 1970; cons., speech writer Garth Assocs., NYC, 1970—71; TV prodr., reporter WB2-TV, Boston, 1971—77; anchor, talk show host WTTG-TV, Washington, 1977—79; corr. NBC-TV Today, NYC, 1984—89, CBS-TV Sunday Morning, NYC, 1989—90; exec. prodr., writer documentaries VU Prodns., LA, 1990; pres. CNN Prodns. and Time Inc. TV TBS, 1992—2000; pres., CEO PBS, 2000—06; pres. Mus. TV & Radio, 2006—. Creator, prodr., host, owner Woman to Woman (nationally syndicated program), L.A., 1983—; spkr., conf. leader on women's issues, 1973—; bd. trustees Sundance Inst.; former mem. exec. com. TBS, Inc., CNN Exec. Com.; bd. mem. Internews, 2002—. Mem. adv. com. Nat. Coun. on Rsch. on Women, N.Y.C., 1990—92; mem. adv. bd. Schlesinger Libr. on History of Women, Radcliffe Coll., Cambridge, Mass., 1985—92; media com. Hollywood Women's Polit. Com., L.A., 1989—92; former trustee Metro Atlanta YMCA, High Mus. Art, Atlanta; mem. adv. bd. Santa Barbara Sch. Comm. U. Calif.; pres. Global Green USA (Am. affiliate Mikhail Gorbachev's worldwide conservation orgn.); nat. bd. mem. Girls Inc. Named One of the 100 Most Powerful Women in Television, The Hollywood Reporter; recipient Emmy for Best Daytime Program, TV Acad., 1984, Emmy for Best Host-Daytime, 1971, numerous film festival awards, 1989—92, Women in Cable & Broadcasting Woman of the Year, CINE Golden Eagle for Lifetime Achievement, Sandra Day O'Connor award for Leadership. Avocations: hiking, bicycling, horseback riding, reading. Office: Mus TV & Radio 25 W 52nd St New York NY 10019 Office Phone: 212-621-6800.*

**MITCHELL, PATRICK E.,** lawyer; b. Oconomowoc, Wis., June 6, 1957; BS, Christian Bros. Coll., 1979; JD, U. Va., 1982. Bar: Tex. 1982. Shareholder, tax practice group Jenkens & Gilchrist, P.C., Dallas, v.p. bd. dirs. Mem.: ABA, Dallas Bar Assn. Office: Jenkens & Gilchrist PC 1445 Ross Ave Ste 3200 Dallas TX 75202-2799 Office Phone: 214-855-4363. Office Fax: 214-855-4300. Business E-Mail: pmitchell@jenkens.com.

**MITCHELL, PATSY MALIER,** religious school founder, administrator; b. Greenwood, Miss., Aug. 28, 1948; d. William Lonai and Lillian (Walker) Malier; m. Charles E. Mitchell, Apr. 20, 1970; children: Christopher, Kara, Angela. BS in Edn., Delta State U., 1970, MEd, 1974, Edn. Specialist, 1979; MA in Ch. Ministries, Ch. of God Sch. Theology, 1990; PhD in Psychology and Counseling, La. Bapt. U., 1994; D in Edn. Christian Sch. Adminstrn., Baptist Christian U., 1992. Cert. sch. adminstr. Youth, Christian edn. dir. Ch. of God, Minter City, Miss., 1975—, teen talent dir., 1983—, missions rep., 1975—; dist. Christian edn. dir. Cleveland, Miss., 1983-85, sch. adminstr., 1985—. Del. Ch. of God Edn. Leadership, Cleveland, Tenn., 1990; del., spkr. Christian Sch. Internat., Chattanooga, 1991. Contbr. Dir. St. Jude Children's Hosp., Memphis, 1991; vol. 4-H Club, Greenwood, Miss., 1985—91. Named Outstanding Young Women of Am., 1983, Top 10 of 50 Leading Bus. Women in Miss., 2001; recipient Cmty. Pride award, Chevron, 1988, Internat. Woman of Yr. award, 1993, One of One Thousand Greatest Ams., 2004, Top 100 Educators in the World, 2005—06, Internat. Educator of the Yr., 2004. Mem.: NAFE, Ch. of God Edn. Assn., Christian Schs. Internat., Christian Sch. Adminstrs., Gospel Music Assn., Ch. of God Sch. of Theology Alumni assn., Delta State Alumni Assn. Republican. Home: 5642 County Rd 544 Minter City MS 38944 Office Phone: 662-299-4592. *The greatest gift that God has given mankind is the capacity to love and encourage others. It is God's gift to us and our gift to others.*

**MITCHELL, PAUL,** computer graphics designer, educator; MFA in Paintin, No. Ill. U., DeKalb, 1975. Prof. computer graphic design Lewis U., Romeoville, Ill., chairperson dept. art and design, 1977—2005. Dir., website creator giveforart.org, Lockport, Ill., 2005—06. Recipient Joie De Vivre award, 2006. Home: 19330 W Airport Rd Lockport IL 60441 Office: Lewis University One University Pkwy Romeoville IL 60446 Office Phone: 815-838-0500. Personal E-mail: mitchepa@lewisu.edu.

**MITCHELL, PAULA LEVIN,** biology professor, editor; b. NYC, Nov. 2, 1951; d. Louis X. and Jane (Schanfeld) Levin; m. Forrest Lee Mitchell, July 28, 1979 (div. 1993); children: Robert, Evelyn; m. Edward S. Haynes, June 6, 1994. BA in Biology, U. Pa., 1973; PhD in Zoology, U. Tex., 1980. Rsch. assoc. dept. entomology La. State U., Baton Rouge, 1981-84; vis. prof. dept. biol. scis Tarleton State U., Stephenville, Tex., 1984-93; asst. prof. dept biology Winthrop U., Rock Hill, SC, 1993—99, assoc. prof., 1999—2005, prof., 2005—. Adj. asst. prof. Tex. Christian U., Fort Worth, 1988-89, Clemson U., SC, 1996—; editor Entomol. Soc. Am., Lanham, Md., 1986-93; vis. fellow U. Delhi, 2005. Subject editor Jour. Agrl. Entomology, 1994-98; contbr. articles to profl. jours. Branch sec. AAUW, Stephenville, 1986-87. U. fellow U. Tex., Austin, 1973—76, Fulbright Sr. Rsch. Scholar, New Delhi, India, 2001—02. Mem.: Internat. Heteropterists' Soc. (sec. 2002—), Southwestern Entomol. Soc., SC Entomol. Soc. (pres. 2001), Ga. Entomol. Soc. (editor 1986—93), Entomol. Soc. Am. Office: Winthrop U 202 Life Sci Bldg Rock Hill SC 29733-0001 Office Phone: 803-323-2111. Business E-Mail: mitchellp@winthrop.edu.

**MITCHELL, PETER KENNETH,** educational consultant; b. Bklyn., June 12, 1949; s. Peter Kenneth and Joan Marie (Hayes) Mitchell; 1 child, Elyse Alexandra. Cert. in French lang. proficiency, U. de Neuchatel, Switzerland, 1969; BA, SUNY, Geneseo, 1970; MS in French, L.I. U., 1975. French, Spanish and English Mid. Country Sch. Dist., Selden, NY, 1972-81; tech. asst. to dir. internat. affairs dept. Am. Fedn. Tchrs., Washington, 1981—90; asst. to gen. sec. Internat. Fedn. Free Tchrs. Unions, Amsterdam, Netherlands, 1986—91; exec. dir. Internat. Reading Assn., Newark, Del., 1990-91; owner Insights Out Assocs., Newark, Del., 1992—97. Dir. mktg. Jr. Achievement Del., 1994—99. Contbr. articles to profl. jours. Recipient Father of the Yr. award, Nat. Multiple Sclerosis Soc., 1998. Mem.: Amnesty Internat., Washington U. Club, Blue and Gold Club. Avocations: reading, music. Home and Office: Insights Out Assocs 5702 Vicky Dr Newark DE 19702

**MITCHELL, REGINALD EUGENE,** mechanical engineering educator; b. Houston, May 16, 1947; s. Clifford Eugene and Juanita Beatrice (Thomas) M.; 1 child, Erika Gene; m. Shirley Ann Myers, Nov. 9, 1990. BS in Chem. Engring., U. Denver, 1968; MS in Chem. Engring., N.J. Inst. Tech., Newark, 1970; ScD in Chem. Engring., MIT, 1975. Mem. tech. staff Sandia Nat. Labs., Livermore, Calif., 1975-89, disting. mem. tech. staff, 1989-91; assoc. prof. mech. engring. dept. Stanford (Calif.) U., 1991—. Recipient Outstanding Tchr. award Tau Beta Pi, 1994. Mem.: Nat. Orgn. Black Chemists and Chem. Engrs. (Percy Julian award 1987), Combustion Inst., Sigma Xi. Avocations: board games, card games, tennis. Home: 6143 Viewcrest Dr Oakland CA 94619-3728 Office: Stanford U Mech Engring Dept Bldg 520 Rm 520C Stanford CA 94305-3032 Business E-Mail: remitche@stanford.edu.

**MITCHELL, RICHARD BOYLE,** security firm executive; b. St. Louis, June 20, 1947; s. Samuel West and Blair R. (Boyle) M.; m. Sallie Jean Gear, Dec. 4, 1999; children: Rebecca, Jessica. BS in Mktg., NYU, 1969. Account exec. D.L. Blair Corp., N.Y.C., 1967—70, NW Ayer Advt. Agy., N.Y.C., 1970-74; sr. account exec. Ted Bates Agy., N.Y.C., 1974-75; sr. v.p. DKG Advt., N.Y.C., 1975-81, McCaffrey/McCall, N.Y.C., 1981-86; pres., CEO Marshall Jaccoma Mitchell, N.Y.C., 1986-96; sr. ptnr. Modem Media, N.Y.C., 1996-97; mng. dir., mgmt. cons. MJM Cons., N.Y.C., 1997—2001; pres. 911 Consulting, Wilton, Conn., 2001—. Commr. Wilton (Conn.) Police Dept., 1984-01.

Served with USAR, 1969-74. Mem.: Wilton Riding. Democrat. Roman Catholic. Avocations: military history, running, weightlifting. Home: 20 Indian Hill Rd Wilton CT 06897-1319 Office Phone: 203-563-9999. E-mail: bomitchell@911consulting.net.

**MITCHELL, RICHARD R.,** principal; b. Lubbock, Tex., Oct. 9, 1951; s. William T. and Margarite Mitchell; children: Tandy, Michael, Christopher. BA in Phys. Edn., Wayland Bapt. Coll., 1975; MA in Adminstrn., U. Phoenix, 2000. Tchr. Church on The Rock, Rockwall, Tex., 1986—95, The Christian Ctr. Sch., West Columbia, Tex., 1995—2000, Evangel Temple Christian Sch., Grand Prairie, Tex., 2000—02; prin. Family Christian Acad., Dallas, 2002—. Care pastor COTR, Rockwall, 1992—95; asst. football coach RCA, Rockwall, basketball coach, 1994—95; asst. football coach CCS, West Columbia, Tex., 1998—2000. Participant Sheriff's Posse, Rockwall, 2004. Recipient Scripture Promise award, 2004. Mem.: IACSA, Assn. Christian Schs. Internat. Republican. Non-Denominational. Avocations: golf, travel, weightlifting, exercise. Office: 10715 Garland Rd Dallas TX 75218 Home: 11055 Wallbrook Dr Dallas TX 75238-3038 Office Phone: 214-324-4399.

**MITCHELL, RICK,** journalist, writer; b. San Jose, Calif., Nov. 27, 1952; s. Maurice Dale Mitchell and Mary Margaret (Woody) Gron; m. Lori Sumako, May 3, 1987; 1 child, Chelsea Pearl. BA in Am. Studies, Calif. State U., Fullerton, 1974. Music critic Oreg. Jour., Portland, 1978-82, Willamette Week, Portland, 1983, The Oregonian, Portland, 1984-85; music critic, sports columnist Willamette Week, 1986; freelance writer L.A., 1987; arts and entertainment reporter The Bakersfield Californian, 1988; music critic Houston Chronicle, 1989-99. Author: Garth Brooks: One of A Kind, Workin' on A Full House, 1993. Mem. Houston Zen Cmty.; artistic dir. Houston Internat. Festival, 2000—. Mem. Amnesty Internat. Avocations: athletics, reading, music. E-mail: mitchako@aol.com.

**MITCHELL, RIE ROGERS,** psychologist, counselor, educator; b. Tucson, Feb. 1, 1940; d. Martin Smith and Lavaun (Peterson) Rogers; m. Rex C. Mitchell, Mar. 16, 1961; 1 child, Scott Rogers. Student, Mills Coll., 1958-59; BS, U. Utah, 1962, MS, 1963; postgrad., San Diego State U., 1965-66; MA, PhD, UCLA, 1969. Diplomate Am. Bd. Psychology; registered play therapist, supr.; cert. sandplay therapist. Tchr. Coronado (Calif.) Unified Sch. Dist., 1964-65; sch. psychologist Glendale (Calif.) Unified Sch. Dist., 1968-70; psychologist Glendale Guidance Clinic, 1970-77; asst. prof. ednl. psychology Calif. State U., Northridge, 1970-74, assoc. prof., 1974-78, prof., 1978—. Chmn. dept. ednl. psychology, 1976-80, 2000—06, acting exec. asst. to pres. Calif. State U., Dominguez Hills, 1978-79; cons. to various Calif. sch. dists.; pvt. practice psychology, Calabasas, Calif. Author: Sandplay: Past Present & Future, 1994; contbr. numerous articles to profl. jours. Recipient Outstanding Educator award Maharishi Soc., 1978, Woman of Yr. award U. Utah, 1962, Profl. Leadership award Western Assn. Counselor Edn., 1990, Disting. Tchg. award Calif. U. Northridge, 1994. Mem. APA, Calif. Assn. Counselor Edn., Supervision and Adminstrn. (dir. 1976-77), Western Assn. Counselor Edn. and Supervision (officer 1978-82, pres. 1980-81), Assn. Counselor Edn. and Supervision (dir. 1980-81, program chmn. 1981-82, treas. 1983-86, Presdl. award 1986, Leadership award 1987), UCLA Doctoral Alumni Assn. (pres. 1974-76), Am. Ednl. Rsch. Assn., Calif. Women in Higher Edn. (pres. chpt. 1977-78), Calif. Concerns (treas. 1984-86), Sandplay Therpists of Am. (fin. officer 1996-2000, bd. mem. 1993—, media chair, 1995, bylaws chair, 1994-96, exceptions com. chair, 1995-96), Pi Lambda Theta (pres. chpt. 1970-71, chairwoman nat. resolutions 1971-73). Home: 4503 Alta Tupelo Dr Calabasas CA 91302-2516 Office: Calif State U Counselor Edn Dept Northridge CA 91330-0001 Office Phone: 818-677-4976. Business E-Mail: rie.mitchell@csun.edu.

**MITCHELL, ROBERT DALE,** engineer, consultant; b. Worthington, Minn., Aug. 2, 1910; s. Karl V. and Margaret Dumont (Steigleder) M.; m. Carol Sherman Northrop, June 17, 1939; children: Constance Remington, Robert Brown. BS, S.D. State U., 1932; S.M. (grad. fellow), Harvard U., 1939. Engr. J. Emberg, Madison, SD, 1932-35; instr. S.D. State U., 1935-37; engr. Malcolm Pirnie Engrs., N.Y.C., 1939-42, project engr., 1945-70; sr. v.p., sec., chief engr. Malcolm Pirnie, Inc., 1970-75; cons. Malcolm Pirnie Engrs., 1975—. Served to maj. San. Corps AUS, 1942-45. Recipient Distinguished Engr. award S.D. State U., 1977 Fellow Am. Coun. Engring. Cons.; mem. ASCE (life), Am. Water Works Assn., New Eng. Water Works Assn. (commemorative award 1963) Office: 104 Corporate Park Dr White Plains NY 10604-3804 Home: 795 Wash Rd Rye NH 03870-2204

**MITCHELL, ROBERT JOSEPH,** insurance executive; b. Chgo., Mar. 2, 1947; s. Charles Robert and Rita (Cagney) M.; m. Nancy Telfer, Dec. 24, 1970; children: Laura Mage, Claire Clagett. BS, Loyola U., Chgo., 1970. CLU, ChFC. Asst. cashier Mich. Ave. Nat. Bank, Chgo., 1970-74; asst. v.p. First Nat. Bank of Lake Forest, Ill., 1974-78, United Bank of Skyline, Denver, 1978-79, v.p. comml. loan adminstrn., 1979-82; pres., chief exec. officer United Bank of Cherry Creek, Denver, 1982-83; exec. v.p. Capital Nat. Bank, Ft. Worth, 1983-87; ins. agt./broker, CEO Mitchell & Moroneso Ins. Svcs. Inc., Ft. Worth, 1987—; pres. The More Fin. Group, Ft. Worth. Bd. dirs., pres. Easter Seals, Ft. Worth, 1988-95, Internat. Sister Cities of Ft. Worth, 1989—; chmn. bd. dirs. Big Bros./Big Sisters of Tarrant County, 1987; priorities com. United Way, 1985—; exec. bd. mem. Mus. Sci. and History, Ft. Worth, 1990, Boys and Girls Club Ft. Worth, 1997-2000, bd. govs., 2005; bd. dirs. Ptnrs. in Health Found. Recipient Pres. Hon. award Comm. Mut. Life Ins. Co., 1990-91. Mem. Nat. Assn. Life Underwriters (Nat. Quality award 1990-93), Am. Soc. CLUs, Ft. Worth Bus. and Estate Coun., Ft. Worth Million Dollar Roundtable (life, Ct. of Table 1999-2000, 02-03, Top of Table 2004, 2005), Ft. Worth Rotary (exec. bd., Paul Harris fellow). Roman Catholic. Avocations: racquetball, squash. Office: Mitchell & Moroneso Ins Svcs Inc 306 W 7th St Ste 888 Fort Worth TX 76102-4912 Office Phone: 817-338-0888.

**MITCHELL, ROGER LOWRY,** retired agronomy educator; b. Grinnell, Iowa, Sept. 13, 1932; s. Robert T. and Cecile (Lowry) M.; m. Joyce Elaine Lindgren, June 26, 1955; children: Laura, Susan, Sarah, Martha. BS in Agronomy, Iowa State Coll., 1954; MS, Cornell U., 1958; PhD in Crop Physiology, Iowa State U., 1961. Mem. faculty Iowa State U., 1959-69, prof. agronomy, 1966-69, prof. charge farm operation curriculum, 1962-66; prof. agronomy, chmn. dept. U. Mo., Columbia, 1969-72, 81-83, emeritus prof. 1998—, dean agr., dir. expt. sta., 1983-98, dean extension, 1972-75, emeritus dean, 1998—; v.p. agr. Kans. State U., Manhattan, 1975-80; exec. dir. Mid-Am. Internat. Agrl. Consortium, 1981; ret. 1998. Exec. bd. divsn. agr. Nat. Assn. State Univs. and Land Grant Colls., 1978-80, 85-90, chmn., 1988-89; mem. bd. agr. NRC/NAS, 1983-86. Author: Crop Growth and Culture, 1970; co-author: Physiology of Crop Plants, 1985 Served to 2d lt. USAAF, 1954-56. Danforth fellow, 1956-61; Acad. Adminstrn. fellow Am. Council Edn., 1966-67; recipient Henry A. Wallace award Iowa State U., 1993, Sec's Honor award USDA, 1998. Fellow AAAS (chmn. sect. O 1980-81), Am. Soc. Agronomy (pres. 1979-80), Crop Sci. Soc. (pres. 1975-76); mem. Soil Sci. Soc. Am., Coun. Agrl. Sci. and Tech., Sigma Xi, Gamma Sigma Delta, Alpha Zeta, Phi Kappa Phi. Home: 502 W Lathrop Rd Columbia MO 65203-2804 Business E-Mail: mitchellrj@missouri.edu.

**MITCHELL, ROY SHAW,** lawyer; b. Sherwood, N.Y., Jan. 16, 1934; s. Malcolm Douglas and Ruth Landon (Holland) M.; m. Nancy Elizabeth Bishop, Aug. 27, 1955; children: Mark E., Jeffrey B., Jennifer R. BS, Cornell U., 1957; JD with honors, George Washington U., Washington, D.C., 1959. Bar: D.C. 1959, Ohio 1960, Va. 1967, U.S. Ct. Fed. Claims 1963, U.S. Supreme Ct. 1965. Atty. Squire, Sanders & Dempsey, Cleve., 1960-61; Hudson & Creyke, Washington, 1961-67, Lewis, Mitchell & Moore, Vienna, Va., 1967-87, Morgan, Lewis & Bockius LLP, Washington, 1987-99; pres., CEO constrn. claims group Hill Internat., Inc., Washington, 1999—2004. Vice-chmn. Ameribanc Savs. Bank, Annandale, Va., 1980-95; trustee Ameribanc Investors Group, Annandale, 1980-95; chmn. The Ctr. Mgmt. Devel. and Tng., Inc., 2004—. Co-author: (with others) Handbook of Construction Law and Claims, 1982, 89; contbr. numerous articles to profl. jours. Fellow ABA (pub. contract law sect.), Am. Coll. Construction Lawyers, Va. Bar Assn. D.C. Bar Assn. Presbyterian. Avocation: boating. Home: 5 Jefferson Run Rd Great Falls VA 22066-3200 Office Phone: 571-435-7191. E-mail: roysmitchell@aol.com.

**MITCHELL, RUSSELL HARRY,** dermatologist; b. Erie, N.D., Oct. 19, 1925; s. William John and Anna Lillian (Sögge) M.; m. Judith Lawes Douvarjo, May 24, 1968 (dec. Mar. 2000); children: Kathy Ellen, Gregory Alan, Jill Elaine, Crystal Anne. BS, BA, U. Minn., Mpls., 1947, BM, 1949, MD, 1951; postgrad., U. Pa., 1968-69. Diplomate Am. Bd. Dermatology. Intern Gorgas Hosp., C.Z., 1951-52; commd. lt. (j.g.) M.C. USN, 1953, advanced through grades to capt., 1968, commdg. officer 1st Med. Bn., 1st Marine divsn. Vietnam, ret., 1981; resident in dermatology U.S. Naval Hosp., Phila., 1967-70; asst. chief out-patient dept. Gorgas Hosp., 1955-64; chief med. and surg. wards Army. State Hosp., Phoenix, 1965; pvt. practice Leesburg, Va., 1978—. Staff Loudoun Health Ctr., 1973—; dermatologist Nat. Naval Med. Ctr., Bethesda, Md., 1973-81; asst. prof. Georgetown U. Med. Sch., 1975-85. Contbr. articles to proff. jours. Pres. Archaeol. Soc. Panama, 1962-64. Decorated bronze star with combat V; Vietnam Gallantry Cross with Palm and clasp; Condecoration Vasco Nuñez de Balboa in orden de Caballero (Panamá). Fellow: Am. Acad. Physicians (life), Am. Acad. Dermatology (life), Explorers' Club; mem.: Loudoun County Med. Soc., Am. Soc. Contemporary Medicine and Surgery, Assn. Mil. Surgeons, Assn.Mil. Dermatologists (life), Marine Corps League, Ctr. for Study of First Americans, Am. Archeology Soc., Marines' Meml. Club (assoc.), Phi Chi. Office: 823 S King St Ste J Leesburg VA 20175-3916 Office Phone: 703-777-6009.

**MITCHELL, RUTHIE YVETTE,** human services administrator, director; b. Harrisburg, Pa., Nov. 14, 1960; d. Jerry Mitchell and Nina Walters; children: Edmond Vincent, Sharrow, Tyrone, DeAndre Diggs. B in Human Svcs., M in Human Svcs., Lincoln U., 2004; student, Capella U., Mpls., Minn., 2004—. Armed correctional officer supr. DC Dept. Corrections, Lorton, Va., 1985—90; campus police officer Howard U., Washington, 1998—2002; preventive case mgmt. counselor Us Helping Us, Washington, case mgr., 2000—, transitional discharge planner, project mgr., 2002—; exec. dir. Jewel In the Night, Washington. Facilitator Dept. Corrections Tng. Acad., 1985, Fed. Protective Svc. Divsn. Acad., 1998, Ct. Svcs. Offender Supervision Agy., Washington, 2004. Editor: (book) So This Is Nina, 2004. Vol. substance abuse counselor Pilgrim Rest Bapt. Therapeutic Svcs., Washington, 1998—. Recipient Outstanding Performance Duty, HUH Security Divsn., 2000. Mem.: Pi Gamma Mu. Avocations: writing, ballet. Home: 5802 Southern Ave Washington DC 20019 Office: Jewel in Night 5802 Southern Ave Washington DC 20019 Office Phone: 202-446-1105. Office Fax: 202-204-0808. Personal E-mail: ruthiemitchell2002@yahoo.com.

**MITCHELL, SHAWNE MAUREEN,** author; b. Tacoma, Wash., Jan. 09; d. F. King and Nona Margaret Burnside (Hayes) M.; m. J.D. Cook, Spt. 4, 1982; children: Travis, Austin. BA, U. Wash.; postgrad., U. Santa Monica, 1997—. CEO Adventures of the Spirit, Santa Barbara, Calif., 1994—; author, spkr. Soul Style, 1995—; columnist Feng Shui-Soul Style, Calif., 1996—. Cons. real estate, Wash., Calif., 1980—; dir. Small Luxury Hotels, L.A., 1986-87; internat. spkr., author on subject of higher consciousness; internat. spkr. on Feng Shui. Author: Soul Style, 1997, Exploring Feng Shui, Ancient Secrets and Modern Insights, 2001, Creating Home Sanctuaries with Feng Shui, 2002, Simple Feng Shui, 2004; editor: Home Sanctuaries mag.; contbr. articles to proff. jours. Bd. dirs. Montecito (Calif.) Ednl. Found., 1997-99, Los Positas Park Found., Santa Barbara, 1995. Mem.: Womens Exec. Network, Seattle Tennis Club, Santa Barbara Polo Club, Wash. Athletic Club. Avocations: boating, hiking, travel, music, art. Office: Adventures of the Spirit Inc PO Box 5765 Santa Barbara CA 93150-5765 Office Phone: 805-565-8885. E-mail: shawne@shawnemitchell.com.

**MITCHELL, STEPHEN MILTON,** investment company executive; b. Atlanta, Oct. 23, 1943; s. Judge Stephenson and Elizabeth Ruth (Morgan) M.; m. Carolyn Docia Goss, June 29, 1968; children: William Stephenson, Scott Milton, Gregory Stephen. B of Indsl. Engring. with honors, Ga. Inst. Tech., 1965, MS in Indsl. Engring., 1966. Registered proff. engr., Ga. Sr. engr. Lockheed-Ga. Corp., Marietta, 1966-70; mgr. material control Snapper Power Equipment, McDonough, Ga., 1970-73; pres. Atlanta Processing Co., Conley, Ga., 1973-86; sr. v.p., gen. mgr. Norcom, Inc., Norcross, Ga., 1986-93; chmn., CEO Atlanta Processing B, Inc., Tucker, Ga., 1993-94; CEO Internat. Processing Corp., Atlanta, 1994, Sertec Corp., Atlanta, 1995—, also bd. dirs. Bd. dirs. Atlanta Processing Co., Conley, Ga., Norcom, Inc., Norcross, APB Inc., Tucker, Ga., IPC, Atlanta; mem. exec. com., chmn., bd. dirs. Clairmont Oaks, Inc., 1988—. Bd. dirs., treas. Common Cause, Ga., 1989—; active First Bapt. Ch. of Decatur, Ga., 1968—, chmn. bd. deacons, 1993, 95. Mem. Young Presidents Orgn., World Presidents Orgn., Ga. Tech. Alumni Assn. (trustee 1981-87). Republican. Home: 5268 Browning Way SW Lilburn GA 30047-7029 Office: Sertec Corp 2100 Powers Ferry Rd NW Ste 200 Atlanta GA 30339-5014

**MITCHELL, STUART,** medical entomologist, consulting physician; m. Martha Mitchell. BS in Physics, Iowa State U., Ames, 1981; MS in Pest Mgmt., Purdue U., 1999; PhD in Entomology, Trinity Coll., Metairie, La., 2000, PhD in Zoology, 2002, PhD in Biology, 2003, PhD in Naturopathy, 2005, D of Naturopathy; DSc (hon.), Breyer State U., 2005; DSc in Osteo. Medicine, Belford U., 2005. Bd. cert. entomologist, cert. in homeland security, wildlife control proff., trainer in food safety Nat. Environ. Health Assn., med. investigator, in traditional naturopathy. Cons. physician, med. entomologist Springer Svcs., Des Moines, 1996—. Tchr., food mgr. NSF Internat., Des Moines, 2002—; tchr. HACCP, 2002—. Author: (pest mgmt. tng. manual) Guidelines On Training; contbr. articles to proff. jours. Developer The Springer Inst.; mem. Des Moines Parks Bd., 2002—03; bd. dirs. Blank Pk. Zoo, Des Moines, 2002—03, Des Moines Bot. Ctr., 2002—03., Whitmire Micro-Gen Labs. grantee, 2003. Mem. AAAS, Entomol. Soc. Am., Am. Inst. Biolog, Phi Chi Omega. Democrat. Lutheran. Avocations: science, walking. Office: Springer Svcs 5360 NE 14th Str Ste A Des Moines IA 50313-2002 Office Phone: 515-360-7981, 800-793-1833. Office Fax: 515-262-9149. Personal E-mail: docmitchell@hotmail.com.

**MITCHELL, TEDDY LEE,** physician; b. Columbia, La., Feb. 24, 1962; s. Oliver Clayton nad Mary Elizabeth (Johnston) M.; m. Janet Luisa Tornelli, Apr. 9, 1988; children: Mary Katherine, Oliver Charles, Christopher Tornelli. BS in Biology, Stephen F. Austin State U., 1983; MD, U. Tex. Med. Br., 1987. Diplomate Am. Bd. Internal Medicine, Cert. of Added Qualification-Sports Medicine. Intern U. Tex. Med. Br., Galveston, 1987-88, resident, 1988-91, 90-91; staff physician Cooper Aerobics Ctr., Dallas, 1991—, med. dir. wellness program, 1991—. Mem. Rep. Sen. Inner Cir., Washington, 1993, Heritage Found., Washington, 1993. Capt. U.S. Army Res. Med. Corps, 1988-96. Fellow ACP (cert. Merit 1990), Am. Coll. Sports Medicine; mem. AMA, Tex. Med. Assn., Dallas County Med. Soc. Methodist. Avocations: exercise, travel, music. Home: 3224 Lovers Ln Dallas TX 75225-7626 Office Phone: 972-560-2667.

**MITCHELL, TERENCE EDWARD,** materials scientist; b. Haywards Heath, Sussex, Eng., May 18, 1937; came to U.S., 1963, naturalized, 1978; s. Thomas Frank and Dorothy Elizabeth (Perrin) M.; m. Marion Wyatt, Dec. 5, 1959; children: Robin Norman, Jeremy Neil. BA, St. Catharine's Coll., Cambridge, U., Eng., 1958, MA, 1962, PhD in Physics, 1962; ScD, U. Cambridge, 1994. Research fellow Cavendish Lab., Cambridge, 1962-63; asst. prof. metallurgy Case Inst. Tech., 1963-66; assoc. prof. Case Western Res. U., 1966-75, prof., 1975-87, adj. prof., 1987—, chmn. dept., 1983-86, dir. high voltage electron microscopy facility, 1970-82, co-dir. materials research lab., 1982-83; vis. scientist NASA at Ames Lab., Stanford U. and Electric Power Research Inst., Palo Alto, Calif., 1975-76; scientist Ctr. Materials Sci. Los Alamos (N.Mex.) Nat. Lab., 1987—, lab fellow, 1991—; lab fellows chair Los Alamos (N.Mex.) Nat. Lab., 1993-95. Chmn. steering com. Electron Microscopy Ctr. Argonne (Ill.) Nat. Lab., 1979-83; cons. in field; mem. vis. metals and ceramics div. Oak Ridge Lab., 1987-91; vis. com. solid state scis. div. Ames Lab., 1987-89; sci. adv. com. Sci. and Tech.

Ctr. for Superconductivity, 1989-93. Materials sci. editor Microscopy Rsch. and Technique, 1986—; sr. editor North Am., 1994—; contbr. 400 articles to proff. jours. Pres. Cleve. Ethical Soc., 1970-72; bd. dirs Am. Ethical Union, 1972-74; steward Los Alamos Unitarian Ch., 1992-94; mem. policy com. Univ. Materials Coun., 1986-89; mem. policy com. Argonne Electron Microscopy Steering Com., chmn. 1978-82. Electric Power Research Inst. fellow, 1975-76; NSF grantee, 1966-88; Dept. Energy grantee, 1970-86, 87—; NIH grantee, 1969-72; NASA grantee, 1974-77, 81-87; USAF Office Sci. Research grantee, 1974-85; U.S. Army Research Office grantee, 1970-75, 79-83, EPRI grantee, 1986-89; spl. issue in his honor Philos. Mag. A, Sept. 1998; spl. symposium in his honor TMS Ann. Meeting, San Diego, 2003; named Van Horn Disting. Lectr., Case Western Res. U., 2004. Fellow Am. Soc. Metals, Am. Phys. Soc., Am. Ceramics Soc. (assoc. editor jour. 1989-v.p. 1999-2000), Minerals, Metals & Materials Soc., Los Alamos Nat. Lab., Japan Inst. Metals; mem. Japan Soc. Promotion of Sci., Electron Microscopy Soc. Am. (program chmn. 1981-82, dir. 1984-86, pres.-elect 1994, pres. 1995, past pres. 1996), Materials Rsch. Soc., Soc. Francaise de Microscopie Electronique (sci. com. 1982-90). Office: Los Alamos Nat Lab Ctr Materials Sci Ms # G755 Los Alamos NM 87545-0001 Office Phone: 505-667-0938. E-mail: temitchell@lanl.gov.

**MITCHELL, THEODORE REED,** educational association administrator, former academic administrator; b. San Rafael, Calif., Jan. 29, 1956; s. Theodore Robert and Genevieve Dolores (Doose) Mitchell; m. Christine M. Beckman, July 8, 1995; children: Caroline Mitchell Beckman, Theo Beckman. BA, Stanford U., 1978, MA, 1980, PhD, 1983. Asst. prof. Dartmouth Coll., Hanover, NH, 1981—86, assoc. prof., 1986—87, chair dept. edn., 1987—91; dep. to pres. and provost Stanford U., Calif., 1991—92; dean Sch. Edn. and Info. Studies UCLA, 1992; vice chancellor, 1996—98; v.p. for edn. and strategic initiatives The J. Paul Getty Trust, 1998—99; pres. Occidental Coll., 1999—2005; CEO NewSchools Venture Fund, San Francisco, 2005—. Trustee Stanford U., 1985—90, Thetford Acad., Vt., 1989—91; bd. dirs. L.A. Edn. Partnership, L.E.A.R.N. Author: Political Education, 1985, Sociology of Education, 1998. Bd. dirs. Children Now, Oakland, Calif., 1994—, Gateway Learning Corp., 1996—. Office: NewSchools Venture Fund 49 Stevenson St, Ste 575 San Francisco CA 94105 Office Phone: 415-615-6860. Fax: 415-615-6861.*

**MITCHELL, THOMAS EDWARD, JR.,** communications cabling executive; b. Sacramento, Apr. 12, 1946; s. Thomas Edward and Violet Mae (Southall) M.; m. Terri Kathleen Vance, Apr. 20, 1969; children: Anthony E., Brian C. BA, Nat. U., 1987, MBA, 1988. Enlisted USMC, 1966, advanced through grades to maj., 1980, retired, 1989; sr. exec. Nat. Decision Sys., Encinitas, Calif., 1989-90, Equifax Mktg. Decision Sys., San Diego, 1990—94; exec. v.p Holocom Networks, Carlsbad, Calif., 1994—2002; pres. Holocomm Sys. Inc., San Diego, 1994—2002. Bd. dirs. Cal-Pacific Steel Structure Inc., Hawaii, Calif., Holocomm. sys. Inc., San Diego, Calif., Holocom Networks, Carlsbad, Calif.; instr. bus. mgmt. San Diego (Calif.) Golf Acad., 2003—. Contbr. articles to proff. jours.; patentee in field. Dir. Toys for Tots, L.A./ORange Counties, Calif., 1974-77. Recipient Silver Star medal U.S. Pres., 1968, Meritorious Svc. medal, Joint Chiefs of Staff Commendation medal, others. Mem. World Trade Assn. (assoc. 1989—), Am. Legion, Internat. Platform Assn. Avocations: restoring old cars, racquetball, golf, history. Home: 3264 Chase Ct Oceanside CA 92056-3809 Office: San Diego Golf Acad 1910 Shaowridge Dr Ste 111 Vista CA 92083

**MITCHELL, TIMMY J.,** principal; b. Hammond, Ind., Nov. 2, 1954; s. Thomas E. and Diane E. Mitchell; m. Rhonda J. Matthews, Apr. 18, 1984; 1 child, Terry E.; 1 child from previous marriage, Crystal Marie. BA, Purdue Calumet U., 1995, MS, 2000. Police officer Schererville (Ind.) Police Dept., 1977—97; tchr. Grimmer Mid. Sch., Schererville, 1997—2002; prin. Lincoln Elem. Sch., Roselawn, Ind., 2002—. Mem. Lincoln PTA; D.A.R.E. Officer Friendly Schererville Police Dept., 1990—92. Sgt. USAF, 1972—76. Mem.: Fraternal Order Police. Avocations: motorcycling, motorcross. Office: Lincoln Elem Sch 10280 N 450 E Demotte IN 46310 Office Phone: 219-345-3458. Fax: 219-345-3488. Business E-Mail: tmitchell@nn.k12.in.us.

**MITCHELL, TIMOTHY LYNN,** music educator; b. Maysville, Ky., Sept. 4, 1959; s. Charles Harrison and Gwendell Mae Mitchell. BA in Music, No. Ky. U., Highland Heights, 1982, MusB Edn., 1982; MA in Edn., Georgetown Coll., Ky, 1993. Min. of music Main St. Bapt. Ch., Alexandria, Ky., 1985—92; gen. music tchr. Kelly Elem. Sch., Burlington, Ky., 1990—. Tchr. rep. Kelly Sch. Site-Based Coun., Burlington, 1994—96; sch. tech. coord. Kelly Elem. Sch., Burlington, 2005—. Mem.: NEA, Ky. Edn. Assn., Ky. Music Educators Assn., Nat. Assn. for Music Edn. Avocations: writing plays and musicals, travel. Home: 2265 West Horizon Dr Hebron KY 41048-9577 Office: Kelly Elem Sch 6775 McVille Rd Burlington KY 41005-8659 Office Phone: 859-334-4450.

**MITCHELL, WAYNE ANTOINE,** retired music educator; b. Tracy, Minn., Mar. 19, 1936; s. Lloyd Benton and Marie Susan Mitchell; m. Miriam Alene Tollefson (dec.); children: Phillip Paul, David Kirk; m. Doris Lorraine Bjordahl, Feb. 21, 2004. BA, Augustana Coll., 1958; MusM, U. Colo., 1965; D in Musical Arts, U. Iowa, 1978. Jr.-sr. HS vocal tchr. pub. schs., Tracy, Minn., 1958—66; music prof. Westmar Coll., Le Mars, Iowa, 1966—83, music prof., admissions, 1985—87; music prof. Dordt Coll., Sioux Center, Iowa, 1983—84, Bethany Coll., Lindsborg, Kans., 1984—85, Mt. Mercy Coll., Cedar Rapids, Iowa, 1988—89, Luther Coll., Decorah, Iowa, 1989—98; ret., 1998. Singer: various operas and concerts. Mem., pres. Le Mars Arts Coun., 1970—84; musical dir. Pub. Opera N.W. Iowa, 1975—77; recitalist Iowa Arts Coun., 1979—80. Mem.: Nat. Tchrs. Singing (state pres., sec. 1966—98), Am. Choral Dirs. Assn., Pi Kappa Lambda. Republican. Lutheran. Avocations: refinishing antique furniture, gardening, carpentry. Home: 102 E 7th St Dell Rapids SD 57022-1640

**MITCHELL, WAYNE LEE,** retired health facility administrator; b. Mar. 25, 1937; s. Albert C. and Elizabeth Isabelle (Nagel) M.; m. Marie Galletti. BA, U. Redlands, Calif., 1959; MSW, Ariz. State U., 1970, EdD, 1979. Social worker various county, state, and fed. agys., 1962-70; social worker Bur. Indian Affairs, Phoenix, 1970-77, USPHS, 1977-79; asst. prof. Ariz. State U., 1979-84; with USPHS, Phoenix, 1984—2003, ret., 2003; pvt. practice cons. Phoenix, 2003—. Lectr. in field. Contbr. articles to proff. jours. Bd. dirs. Phoenix Indian Comty. Sch., 1973-75, ATLATL, 1994-98, Partnership for Comty. Devel. Ariz. State U.-West, 1996-99, Cen. Ariz. Health Sys. Agy., 1982-85; mem. Phoenix Area Health Adv. Bd., 1975, Comty. Behavioral Mental Health Bd., 1976-80, Fgn. Rels. Com., Phoenix; trustee Heard Mus. Anthropology, Phoenix, 1996; apptd. Ariz. State Bd. Behavioral Health Examiners, 2000-2002. With USCG, 1960-62. Named in Voices and Faces, 2003; recipient Comty. Svc. award, Ariz. Temple of Islam, 1980, Ariz. State U., 1996, Dir. Excellence award, Phoenix Area IHS Dir., 1992, 1993, Nat. IHS Dir.'s award for outstanding svc., 2001, NARD Lifetime Achievement award, 2005. Mem. NASW (Lifetime Achievement award 2003), Fgn. Rels. Coun., U.S.-China Assn., Kappa Delta Pi, Phi Delta Kappa, Tau Sigma Chi. Democrat. Congregationalist. Home: PO Box 9592 Phoenix AZ 85068-9592 Personal E-mail: drwlmitch@cox.net.

**MITCHELL, WILLIAM EDMUND,** electronics executive; b. LA, Mar. 13, 1944; s. John Stewart and Helen (Fine) M.; m. Jan Marie Scheyer, Feb. 16, 1969; children: Alden, Amanda, Alyssa. BS in Engring., Princeton U., 1966; MS in Engring., U. Mich., 1967. Analyst Exxon Corp., N.Y.C., 1969-72; dept. mgr. Baton Rouge, 1972-73; ops. mgr. Raychem Corp., Menlo Park, Calif., 1973-76; regional mgr. Raychem Internat., Menlo Park, Calif., 1977-83, v.p., 1985-88; sr. v.p. Raychem Corp., Menlo Park, 1988-93; pres., CEO Nashua (N.H.) Corp., 1993—95; chmn., pres., CEO Sequel Inc., 1995—99; pres. Solectron Global Sys., 1999—2002; v.p. Solectron Corp., 1999—2002; pres., CEO Arrow Electronics Inc., Melville, NY, 2003—, chmn., 2006—. Bd. dirs. Rogers Corp., Conn. Mem. Orgn. for Corp. Growth, Am. Electronics Assn. (bd. dirs. 1993—), Ladera Oaks Club. Republican. Avocations: swimming, tennis, literature. Office: Arrow Electronics Inc 50 Marcus Dr Melville NY 11747*

**MITCHELL, WILLIAM GRAHAM CHAMPION,** lawyer, corporate officer; b. Raleigh, N.C., Dec. 24, 1946; s. Burley Bayard and Dorothy Ford (Champion) Mitchell; children: William Graham, Margaret Scripture. AB, U. N.C., 1969, JD with highest hons., 1975. Bar: N.C. 1975, U.S. Dist. Ct. (ea., mid., and we. dists.) N.C. 1976, U.S. Ct. Appeals (4th cir.) 1978. Ptnr. Womble, Carlyle, Sandridge & Rice, Winston-Salem, 1975-87; sr. v.p. for external affairs RJR Nabisco, Atlanta, 1987-89; exec. v.p. R.J. Reynolds Tobacco Co., Winston-Salem, 1988-89; ptnr. Howrey & Simon, Washington, 1990-94; spl. counselor to chmn. bd. True North Comm., Inc., Chgo., 1996; chmn. bd., CEO Global Exch. Carrier Co., Leesburg, Va., 1997-00; pres., CEO Global Comms. Techs. Inc., Reston, Va., 1999-2000; chmn. bd., CEO Convergence Equipment Co., Manassas, Va., 1999-2000; chmn. bd. Qfactor Inc., Bethesda, Md., 2000-01; exec. v.p., gen. mgr. Verisign Inc., Mountainview, Calif., 2001—03; chmn. bd., CEO Network Solutions, Inc., Dulles, Va., 2003—. Bd. dirs. Fed. Agrl. Mortgage Corp., Washington. Mem. Pres.'s Adv. Com. Trade Policy and Negotiations, Indsl. Policy Adv. Com., Washington, 1991—; bd. dirs. Washington Performing Arts Soc., 1988—92; founding trustee Prog. Policy Inst., 1988—; bd. advisors Dem. Leadership Coun., 1988—; vice chmn. fin. Bush Campaign; mem. exec. com. Nat. Assn. Mfrs., Washington, 1988—89, Nat. Fgn. Trade Coun., 1988—89; chmn. Tobacco Inst., Washington, 1988—89. Mem.: ABA (vice chmn. antitrust sect., pvt. litigation com. 1987—89, chmn. FTC com. 1986), Forsyth Country Club, City Club Washington, Georgetown Club, Order of Coif. Personal E-mail: champ@champmitchell.com. Business E-Mail: cmitchell@networksolutions.com.

**MITCHELL, WILLIAM J.,** academic administrator, architecture educator; BArch, U. Melbourne, Victoria, Australia, 1967; M of Environ. Design, Yale U., 1969; MA, U. Cambridge, Eng., 1977. Arch. Yuncken-Freeman Architects, Melbourne, Australia, 1967—68; asst. prof. architecture, urban design UCLA, 1970—74, head architecture, urban design program, 1973—77, assoc. prof. architecture, urban design, 1974—80, prof. architecture, urban design, program head', 1980—86; pres. The Urban Innovations Group, LA, 1973—74; founding ptnr. The Computer-Aided Design Group, Marina Del Rey, Calif., 1978—91; prof. architecture Harvard U., Cambridge, Mass., 1986—89, dir. Master in Design Studies Program, 1986—92, G. Ware and Edythe M. Travelstead prof. architecture, 1989—92; prof. architecture and media arts & sci. MIT, Cambridge, 1992—, dean Sch. of Architecture and Planning, 1992—2003, head media arts and scis. program, 2003—. Vis. critic Yale U., New Haven, 1970—75, Tulane U., New Orleans, 1981; lectr. dept. architecture U. Cambridge, England, 1978—80; vis. prof. U. Calif., Berkeley, 1982, Carnegie-Mellon U., Pitts., 1979—83, U. Sydney, NSW, Australia, 1985; disting. vis. scholar U. Adelaide, SA, Australia. Author: Computer-Aided Architecture Design, 1983, The Logic of Architecture: Design, Computation and Cognition, 1990, The Reconfigured Eye: Visual Truth in the Post-Photographic Era, 1992, City of Bits: Space, Pl., and the Infobahn, 1995, Me++: The Cyborg Self and the Networked City, 2003, e-topia: Urban Life Jim But Not as We Know It, 1999, Info. Tech. and Low-Income Communities, 1999; author: (with others) The Art of Computer Graphics Programming, 1987, The Poetics of Gardens, 1988, The Electronic Design Studio: Architectural Knowledge and Media in the Computer Era, 1990, Digital Design Media, 2d edit., 1991; contbr. numerous articles to proff. jour. Fellow: Royal Australian Inst. Architecture. Office: MIT Media Lab E15-401 77 Massachusetts Ave Cambridge MA 02139-4307

**MITCHELLL, PAULA RAE,** nursing educator, dean; b. Independence, Mo., Jan. 10, 1951; d. Millard Henry and E. Lorene (Denton) Gates; m. Ralph William Mitchell, May 24, 1975. BS in Nursing, Graceland U., 1973; MS in Nursing, U. Tex., 1976; EdD in Ednl. Adminstrn., N.Mex. State U., 1996. RN, Tex., Mo.; cert. childbirth educator. Instr. nursing El Paso (Tex.) C.C., 1979-85, dir. nursing, 1985—2003, acting divsn. chmn. health occupations, 1985-86, divsn. dean, 1998-99, dean health occupations, 1999-2000, curriculum facilitator, 1984—85, dean health occupations, math and sci., campus dean Rio Grande, 2000—. Ob-gyn. nurse practitioner Planned Parenthood, El Paso, 1981-86, med. com., 1986-98; cons. in field, army med. dept. officer Acad. Health Scis.Ft. Author: (with Grippando) Nursing Perspectives and Issues, 1989, 93; contbr. articles to proff. jours. Founder, bd. dirs. Health-CREST, El Paso, 1981—85; mem. pub. edn. com. Am. Cancer Soc., El Paso, 1983—84, mem. proff. activities com., 1992—93; mem. El-Paso City-County Bd. Health, 1989—91; mem. Govt. Applications Rev. Com. Rio Grande Coun. Govts., 1989—91; mem. collaborative coun. El Paso Magnet H.S. for Health Care Professions, 1992—94; co-chair health and human svcs. task force Unite El Paso Health, 1996—98, mem. steering com., 1999—2000; co-chair health taskforce El Paso Cmty. Legis. Agenda, 1997—99; mem. adv. com. Ctr. for Border Health Rsch., Paso del Norte Health Found., 1998—2004; mem. Leadership El Paso, 1999; mem. health proff. shortage task force Greater El Paso C. of C., 2001—; mem. health care coun., 2002—; mem. star adv. com. Canutillo Tex. Ind. Sch. Dist., Canutillo, Tex., 2003—; bd. dirs. Border Health Inst., El Paso, 2001—, sec.-treas., 2003—. Capt. U.S. Army, 1972—78. Decorated Army Commendation medal, Meritorious Svc. medal. Named to Women's Hall of Fame, El Paso Commn., 1999, named Outstanding Alumni, N.Mex. State U. Dept. Edn. Mgmt. and Devel., 2002-03. Mem. Nat. League Nursing (resolutions com. Assocs. Degree coun. 1987-89, accreditation site visitor, AD coun. 1990—). Tex. edn. com. 1991-92, Tex. 3d v.p. 1992-93, Tex. 1st v.p. 1997-99, nominating com. 1999-2000), Am. Soc. Psychoprophylaxis Obstetrics, Nurses Assn. Am. Coll. Ob-Gyn. (cert. in ambulatory women's healthcare, chpt. coord. 1979-83, nat. program rev. com. 1984-86, cert. 1987-89), Advanced Nurse Practitioner Group El Paso (coord. 1980-83, legis. com. 1984), Am. Phys. Therapist Assn. (commn. on accreditation, site visitor for phys. therapist asst. programs 1991-), Orgn. Assoc. Degree Nursing (Tex. membership chmn. 1985-89, chmn. goals com. 1989-2004, nat. bylaws com. 1989-93), Am. Vocat. Assn., Am. Assn. Women Cmty. and Jr. Colls., Tex. Orgn. Nurse Execs., Nat. Coun. Workforce Edn. (articulation task force 1986-89, program standards task force 1991-93), Nat. Coun. Instrnl. Adminstrs., Tex. Soc. Allied Health Profls. (sec., 2004-2005), Tex. Nurses Assn. (pres.-elect dist. one 2002-03, pres. 2003-05), Nat. Soc. Allied Health Profls. coun. El Paso C. of C. (healthcare program focus coun. 2001-05), Sigma Theta Tau, Phi Kappa Phi. Mem. Christian Ch. (Disciples Of Christ). Home: 4616 Cupid Dr El Paso TX 79924-1726 Office: El Paso C C PO Box 20500 El Paso TX 79998-0500 Office Phone: 915-831-4030. Business E-Mail: paulam@epcc.edu.

**MITCHELTREE, DENNIS,** musician, educator; b. Milw., Sept. 25, 1964; 1 child, Antoinette Mitcheltree-Briguglio. Diploma in jazz performanne, Berklee Coll. of Music, Boston, 1987. Jazz musician Am. Music Group, Bklyn., 1976—. Music tchr., N.Y.C., 1987—2005. Jazz musician, composer: music recs. Home: #209 285 Fifth Ave Brooklyn NY 11215 Office: Am Music Group # 209 285 Fifth Ave Brooklyn NY 11215 Office Phone: 917-498-9100. Personal E-mail: dengor@pipeline.com. E-mail: amgorg@pipeline.com.

**MITCHEM, ALLEN P.,** lawyer; b. Burley, Idaho, Oct. 30, 1918; s. James Edgar and Adah Elizabeth (Allen) Mitchem; m. Katherine I. Webber, Aug. 21, 1993; children: Allen P., James E., Lowell E. AB, Ft. Hays State U., 1940; JD magna cum laude, Washburn U., 1947; LLM, Columbia U., 1948. Bar: Kans. 1947, Colo. 1949, US Supreme Ct. 2004. Assoc. prof. Coll. Law U. Denver, 1948—53; pvt. practice law Denver, 1953—60, 1963—; minority counsel interior and insular affairs com. U.S. Senate, Washington, 1961—62. Vis. lectr. Sch. Law, U. Colo., 1954, 57, 59; lectr. Sch. Law, U. Denver, 1953—63; arbitrator, Denver, 1965—. Contbr. articles to legal rev. Dist. gov. Colo. Civitan Internat., 1957—58, judge adcv., 1958—59; pres. Denver Execs. Club, 1986—88; chmn. gen. bd. Civil. Christian Ch., 1963—65, 1975—76; trustee Endowment Assn. Ft. Hays State U., 1968—78; dir. Colo. Christian Home, Denver, 1974—80; pres. Denver Civitan Club, 1955—56; dir. Denver Area Coun. Civitans, 1955, 1957. Capt. USMC, 1942—45. Recipient Alumni Achievement award, Ft. Hays State U., 1970. Mem.: ABA, Denver Bar Assn., Colo. Bar Assn. Home: 420 S Marion Pkwy Apt 2002 Denver CO 80209-5526 Personal E-mail: apmitchem@msn.com.

**MITCHENER, JOHN EDWARD,** music educator, musician; b. Laurinburg, N.C., June 30, 1964; s. James Samuel and Sara (Carton) M. BM, N.C. Sch. Arts, Winston-Salem, 1986; MM organ, Eastman Sch. Music, Rochester, N.Y., 1989, MM harpsichord, 1994, D.Mus. Arts, 1995. Organist The Am. Cathedral in Paris, Paris, Ile-de-France, 1989; dir. music, organist Zion Episcopal Ch., Palmyra, NY, 1991—95; grad. asst. harpsichord Eastman Sch. Music, 1991—92, assoc. instr. organ cmty. edn. divsn., 1992—95; instr. organ Colgate Rochester Divinity Sch., Rochester, 1992—95; grad. tchg. asst. in organ Eastman Sch. Music, 1992—95, grad. tchg. asst. in baroque ensembles, 1994—95; assoc. prof. organ and coll. organist Salem College, Winston-Salem, NC, 1995—; Kenan prof. organ N.C. Sch. of the Arts, Winston-Salem, NC, 1995—. Organist St. Paul's Episc. Ch., Winston-Salem, NC, 2001—, Wesley Meml. United Meth. Ch., High Point, NC, 1996—2001. Musician: (classical organ recitals and concerts) Complete organ works of Johann Sebastian Bach, 2000—03 (Faculty Development Grant from North Carolina School of the Arts, 2001), concerts of Am. music performed througout Europe (Austria, France, Germany, Poland, and Switzerland), 2001, (organ concerts) organ music of Bach performed throughout Europe, 2000, concerts and master classes in USA and Europe, performances heard on Nat. Pub. Radio and Austrian Nat. Radio, —, collaborative artist for 5 CD recordings, —. Mem. exec. com. bd. trustees and chmn. music com. Moravian Music Found., Winston-Salem. Recipient organ competition winner, Music Tchrs. Assn., 1986, Nat. Winner nat. organ competition, Music Tchrs. Nat. Assn., 1986, Winner music competition, N.C. Music Tchrs. Assn. (so. divsn.), 1986, Winner 3rd prize, Dublin Internat. Organ Competition, 1990, Winner Gold Medal in harpsichord, Nat. Conservatory Rueil-Malmaison, France, 1990, Winner Prix d'Excellence in organ, 1990, Winner Prix de Virtuosité, 1991. Mem.: Moravian Music Found. (pres., bd. trustees), Am. Guild of Organists (Winner AGO competition, Phila. 1987, dean Winston-Salem chpt. 1997—99, Winner organ competition Winston-Salem chpt. 1983). Avocations: golf, reading, running, walking, hiking. Office: NC Sch Arts 1533 S Main St Winston Salem NC 27117-2189 Office Phone: 336-631-1543, etx. 143. Business E-mail: mitchenerj@ncarts.edu.

**MITCHUM, CASSANDRA,** poet, writer; b. Greensboro, N.C., June 11, 1950; m. Preston Mitchum Sr., Dec. 17, 1973; children: Preston Jr., Cynthia, Vanessa. Bus. cert., Monroe Bus. Inst., 1970. Receptionist, typist Royal Nat. Bank, N.Y.C., 1970-72, Metcalf & Eddie Engrs., N.Y.C., 1972-74; sec. Bendix Internat., N.Y.C., 1975-80; receptionist Chrysler Corp., N.Y.C., 1980-81; sec. Nat. Assn. Securities, Washington, 1981-83; word processor, sec. Lewis, Kominers & James, Counselors-at-Law, 1983-84, 86. Author numerous poems. Recipient Merit certificate World of Poetry, Sacramento, 1990, Editor's Choice award Nat. Libr. Poetry, 1996-97; named Golden Poet, World of Poetry, Sacramento, 1991; named to Internat. Poetry Hall of Fame, 1997; named one of Best Poets of 1997, 98, Outstanding Poet of 1998. Mem. Internat. Soc. Poets. Democrat. Penecostal. Home: 9507 Garwood St Silver Spring MD 20901

**MITELMAN, BONNIE COSSMAN,** editor, writer; b. Flint, Mich., Feb. 15, 1941; d. Maurice B. (dec.) and Frieda H. (Ragir) Cossman; m. Stanley D. Lelewer, Mar. 12, 1961 (div. 1969); children: Joanne, Stephen(dec.); m. Alan N. Mitelman, July 23, 1972; 1 child, Geoffrey. BA, Northwestern U., 1969; MA, Manhattanville Coll., 1977. Copywriter trainee Dancer-Fitzgerald-Sample, Inc., Chgo., 1956—60; advt. copywriter Spiegel, Inc., Chgo., 1961—63; freelance advt. and pub. rels. writer Chgo., NYC, 1963—72; co-founder Mitelman & Assocs., Briarcliff Manor, NY, 1972—92, pub. rels. assoc., 1992—94, asst. dir. publ. rels., 1994—97; dir. publs. and mktg. Anti-Defamation League, NYC, 2005—. Adj. lectr. dept. history Mercy Coll., Dobbs Ferry, NY, 1979—85. Author: Mothers Who Work: Strategies for Coping; mem. editl. bd.: Reform Judaism, 1977—; contrbr. articles to profl. jours. and newspapers. Mem.: Am. Hist. Assn., Authors Guild, Women in Comm. E-mail: bmitelman@adl.org.

**MITGANG, HERBERT,** writer, journalist; b. NYC, Jan. 20, 1920; s. Benjamin and Florence (Altman) M.; m. Shirley Kravchick, May 13, 1945; children: Esther, Lee, Laura. LLB, St. John's Law Sch., Bar: N.Y. 1942. Sports stringer Bklyn. Eagle, 1938-39; screen writer Universal-Internat. Pictures, 1945; copy editor, reviewer N.Y. Times, N.Y.C., 1945-54; supervising editor Sunday Times drama sect., 1955-62; editorial writer, mem. editorial bd. N.Y. Times, 1963-64, 67-76, deputy editor Op-Ed page, 1970-76, publishing, cultural corr., book critic, 1976-94; asst. to pres., exec. editor CBS News, 1964-67. Instr. English evening divsn. CCNY, 1948-49; vis. lectr. English, guest fellow Silliman Coll., Yale U., 1975-76; lit. advisor White House Libr., 1977-81. Writer, prodr.: (film documentaries) Henry Moore: Man of Form (award Ohio U. 1966), D-Day Plus 20 Years, Sandburg's Prairie Years, Degas' Racing World (Duke Ellington score), Ben-Gurion on the Bible, Anthony Eden on Vietnam; author: Lincoln As They Saw Him, 1956, (novel) The Return, 1959, The Man Who Rode the Tiger: The Life and Times of Judge Samuel Seabury, 1963 (Pulitzer Prize finalist in biography, Silver Gavel award ABA), Working for the Reader, 1970, (novel) Get These Men Out of the Hot Sun, 1972, The Fiery Trial: A Life of Lincoln, 1974, (novel) The Montauk Fault, 1981, (novel) Kings in the Counting House, 1983, Dangerous Dossiers: The Secret War Against America's Authors, 1988, Words Still Count With Me: A Chronicle of Literary Conversations, 1995, Once Upon a Time in New York: Jimmy Walker, Franklin Roosevelt, and the Last Great Battle of the Jazz Age, 2000, Newsmen in Khaki: Tales of a World War II Soldier Correspondent, 2004; editor: Washington, D.C., in Lincoln's Time, 1958, Civilians Under Arms: Stars and Stripes, Civil War to Korea, 1996, The Letters of Carl Sandburg, 1968, America at Random, 1969, Spectator of America, 1971, Selected Writings of Abraham Lincoln, 1992; (plays) Mister Lincoln, 1980, Adlai, Alone, 2005; contrbr. to the New Yorker, Art News, Am. Heritage, The Progressive, The Nation, Chicago Tribune, Newsday, New York Times, Washington Post. Mem. exec. bd. Newspaper Guild of N.Y., CIO, 1948-49; bd. dirs. Theatre for a New Audience, N.Y., 1998—. Served with counter-intelligence sect. 5th wing USAAF, 1942-43, MTO; Army corr., mng. editor Stars and Stripes, Oran-Casablanca and Sicily edits. 1943-45. Decorated six battle stars, Knight Order of Merit (Italy); recipient Human Rights award Newspaper Guild of N.Y., 1958, Broadcast Preceptor award San Francisco State Coll., 1970, N.Y. State Bar Assn. Media award, 1976, Lincoln award Civil War Roundtable of N.Y., 1981, George Polk Career award L.I. U., 1993, 25 Yr. News Achievement award Soc. of Silurians, 1993, Lit. Lions award N.Y. Pub. Libr. Fellow Soc. Am. Historians; mem. Authors League (council 1962—, pres. fund 1976-97, pres. emeritus 1998—), Dramatists Guild (bd. dirs. 1999—), Authors Guild (pres. 1971-75, trustee, corrs. fund 1975—), Internat. P.E.N. (U.S. del. London) Clubs: Century Assn. (N.Y.C.). Jewish. Office: 203 E 72nd St Apt 18A New York NY 10021-4551

**MITRA, ASOKE NATH,** retired physicist, educator; b. Rajshahi, India, Apr. 15, 1929; s. Jatindra Nath and Rama Rani (Bose) M.; m. Anjali Ghosh, Nov. 27, 1956; children: Bani, Gargi. BA with honors in Math., Ramjas Coll., Delhi, 1947, MA in Math., 1949; PhD in Physics, Delhi U., 1952, Cornel U. 1955. Lectr. physics U. Delhi, 1949-52; ctrl. states scholar Govt. India, Cornell U., Ithaca, N.Y., 1952-55; reader in physics Aligarh Muslim U., India, 1955-60, Delhi U., 1960-62; vis. prof. physics Ind. U., Bloomington, 1962-63; prof. physics Delhi U., 1963-69, sr. prof., 1969-89; Einstein rsch. prof. U. Delhi, 1989—94; freelance writer-rschr., 1996—. Proff. cons. Rutherford Lab., 1968; vis. scientist UCLA, 1967, CERN, 1968, 83, 85, U. Tex.-Austin, 1971, Bonn, 1974, U. Paris, 1977, Deutsche Elektronen Synchrotron, 1979, Internat. Ctr. for Theoretical Physics, Trieste, 1962, 65, 67, 68, 69, 70, 71, 74, 77, 83, Tubingen, 1985, Ind U., Bloomington, 1986; nat. lectr. Univ. Grants Commn., India, 1973; vis. prof. U. Ill., Chgo., 1986-87, Nat. Inst. Adv. Studies, Bangalore, 1995; vis. lectr. Nuffield Found., Australia, 1973; mem. internat. adv. coun. for successive internat. conf. series on few body problems in nuc. and particle physics and other internat. confs.; convenor, organizer 7th Internat. Conf. on Few Body Problems, Delhi U., 1975-76; sr. exch. visitor U.S. univs., Indo-U.S. Joint Program, 1976; sr. exch. visitor Brit. univs., Indian Nat. Sci. Acad. Royal Soc. Exch. Programme, 1979. Editor: Few Body Dynamics, 1976, Niels Bohr-A Profile, 1985, Quantum Field Theory, 2000, India's Role in Global Physics: Then & Now,

2006, Indian Contributions to Post-War Global Physics: A Profile, 2006; bd. editors: Few Body Systems, 1985-2000; contrbr. over 200 articles to revs. to profl. jours. Mem. physics panel Univ. Grants Commn., India, New Delhi, 1974-76, 80-82; mem. coun. Raman Rsch. Inst., Bangalore, India, 1978-88; mem. Nat. Bd. for Higher Maths., Bombay, 1982-88; mem. phys. adv. com. dept. sci. and tech. Govt. India, 1982-87; mem. physics coms. Coun. for Sci. and Indsl. Rsch., New Delhi, 1974-78, 81—; mem. nat. accelerator com. Dept. Atomic Energy, India, 1979-83. Recipient S.S. Bhatnagar award Coun. for Sci. and Indsl. Rsch. India, New Delhi, 1969, Megh Nad Saha award Univ. Grants Commn., New Delhi, 1975, S.K. Mitra Birth Centenary medal Indian Sci. Congl. Assn., 1999; nat. fellow Univ. Grants Commn., 1977-78; assoc. Internat. Ctr. for Theoretical Physics, Trieste, 1967-70, sr. assoc., 1972-77, hon. assoc., 1978-83. Fellow Third World Acad. Scis., Indian Nat. Sci. Acad. (sec. 1975-79, editor publ. 1983-86, Albert Einstein rsch. prof. 1989-94, S.N. Bose medal 1986), Indian Acad. Sci. (coun. 1975-78), Am. Phys. Soc. Avocations: stamp collecting/philately, philosophy of science. Home: 244 Tagore Park Delhi 110009 India Office Phone: +911127444731. Personal E-mail: ganmitra@nde.vsnl.net.in.

**MITRA, SANJIT KUMAR,** electrical and computer engineering educator; b. Calcutta, West Bengal, India, Nov. 26, 1935; came to U.S., 1958; MS in Tech., U. Calcutta, 1956; MS, U. Calif., Berkeley, 1960, PhD, 1962; D of Tech. (hon.), Tampere (Finland) U., 1987; Academician, Acad. Finland, 2000; D in Tech. (hon.), Bucharest (Romania) U., 2004. Asst. engr. Indian Statis. Inst., Calcutta, 1956-58; from teaching asst. to assoc. Univ. Calif., Berkeley, 1958-62; asst. prof. Cornell U., Ithaca, NY, 1962-65; mem. tech. staff Bell Telephone Labs., Holmdel, NJ, 1965-67; prof. U. Calif., Davis, 1967-77, prof. elec. and computer engring. Santa Barbara, 1977—, chmn. dept. elec. and computer engring., 1979-82; dir. Ctr. for Info. Processing Rsch., 1993-96. Cons. Lawrence Livermore (Calif.) Nat. Lab., 1974-95; cons. editor Van Nostrand Reinhold Co., N.Y.C., 1977-88; mem. adv. bd. Coll. Engring. Rice U., Houston, 1986-89; mem. adv. coun. Rsch. Inst. for Math. and Computing Sci., U. Groningen, The Netherlands, 1995—; mem. adv. bd. Internat. Signal Processing Ctr., Tampere U. of Tech., Finland, 1997—; external assessor Faculty of Engring., U. Putra Malaysia, Serdang, 1997—2000; hon. prof. No. Jiatong U., Beijing, China, 1985, Tech. U. Cluj-Napoca, 2005. Author: Analysis and Synthesis of Linear Active Networks, 1969, Digital and Analog Integrated Circuits, 1980; co-editor: Modern Filter Theory and Design, 1973, Two-Dimensional Digital Signal Processing, 1978, Miniaturized and Integrated Filters, 1989, Multidimensional Processing of Video Signals, 1992, Handbook for Digital Signal Processing, 1993, Digital Signal Processing: A Computer-Based Approach, 1997, 3d edit., 2005, Nonuniform Discrete Fourier Transform and Its Signal Processing Applications, 1998, Digital Signal Processing Laboratory Using MATLAB, 1999, Nonlinear Image Processing, 2000. Named Disting. Fulbright Prof., Coun. for Internat. Exch. of Scholars, 1984, 1986, 1988, Disting. Sr. Scientist, Humboldt Found., 1989; recipient F.E. Terman award, 1973, award, AT&T Found., 1985, Edn. award, Am. Soc. Eng. Edn., 1988, U. medal, Tech. U. Slovakia, 2005. Fellow: IEEE (Tech. Achievement award 1996, Mac Van Valkenburg award 1999, Millennium medal 2000, McGraw-Hill/Jacob Millman award 2001, Best Paper award 2002, John H. Mulligan Jr. Edn. medal 2006, Soc. award 2006, Edn. award 2006), AAAS, Internat. Soc. Optical Engring. (Tech. Achievement award 2005); mem.: IEE U.K. (Blumlein-Browne-Wilans premium 2000), Acad. Engring. Mex., U.S. Nat. Acad. Engring., Norwegian Acad. Technol. Scis., Croatian Acad. Arts and Scis., Acad. of Finland, European Assn. for Signal Processing (Tech. Achievement award 2001). Achievements include patents for two-port networks for realizing transfer functions; non-reciprocal wave translating device; discrete cosine transform-based image coding and decoding method; method and apparatus for multipath channel shaping; method for embedding and extracting digital data in images and videos. Office: Univ Calif Dept Elec Computer Eng Santa Barbara CA 93106

**MITROPHANOV, ALEXANDER YURYEVICH,** mathematician, researcher; b. Novosibirsk, Russia, Apr. 24, 1976; s. Yuri Ivanovich Mitrophanov and Lydia Dmitriyevna Mitrophanova. MS with highest distinction, Saratov State U., Russia, 1998, MS with highest distinction, 2001, PhD, 2002. Cert. profl. translator Gymnasium 3, Saratov, Russia, 1993. Jr. rsch. scientist Saratov State U., Russia, 2001—02, mathematician, 2002—04, sr. rsch. scientist, 2003—04; postdoctoral fellow Ga. Inst. Tech., Atlanta, 2004—. Jour. reviewer Zentralblatt MATH, 2003—06; jour. referee Briefings in Bioinformatics, 2005—06, BMC Bioinformatics, 2004—06, Bioinformatics, 2006. Contbr. articles to profl. jours. Participant, Freedom Support Act Future Leaders Exch. Program U.S. Govt., 1993—94, A. M. Bogomolov scholar, Saratov State U., 1995—98. Mem.: Internat. Soc. Computational Biology. Achievements include development of modern sensitivity theory for Markov chains; novel approach to the quantitative analysis of signal transduction/transcriptional regulatory systems in bacteria; first to develop inequality-based sensitivity theory for hidden Markov models. Office: Georgia Inst Tech 310 Ferst Dr Atlanta GA 30332-0230 Office Fax: 404-894-0519. Business E-mail: amit@amber.biology.gatech.edu.

**MITSAKOS, CHARLES LEONIDAS,** education educator, consultant; b. Lowell, Mass., Oct. 17, 1939; s. Leonidas A. and Vasiliki (Sampatakakis) M.; m. Stella Martakos, June 23, 1963; children: Charles L. Jr., Andria Estelle. BS in Edn., Lowell State Coll., 1961; EdM, Boston U., 1963, EdD, 1977. Tchr., team leader, social studies curriculum specialist Lexington (Mass.) Pub. Schs., 1961-67; social studies coord., cons. Chelmsford (Mass.) Pub. Schs., 1967-78; asst. supt. of schs. Andover (Mass.) Pub. Schs., 1978-83; supt. of schs. Winchester (Mass.) Pub. Schs., 1984-92; clin. faculty supr. Nashua, Boston Coll., Chestnut Hill, Mass., 1992-93; prof. edn., chair divsn. edn. Rivier Coll., Nashua, NH, 1993—. Ednl. cons. to schs. and sch. dists. in 15 states, U.S. V.I., U.S. Dept. Def. Dep. Schs. and Ministries of Edn., 1970—; facilitator Sch. Administrs. Leading with Tech. (SALT), Bill and Melinda Gates Found. funded project, 2002-05; dir. Mid. Sch. Staff Devel. Inst. for Social Desegregation Program, Fairfield County, S.C., 1972; mem. staff, lectr. in team tchg. and social studies edn. NSF Insts., Stanford U., Ind. U., SUNY, Geneseo, Xavier U., U. NC, Boston U., 1968-75; sr. lectr. sch. adminstrn. and curriculum devel. Sch. Grad. Studies, Rivier Coll., 1977-93, numerous others. Author, gen. editor: (multimedia program for elem. sch.) The Family of Man Social Studies Program, 1971-77; co-author: (textbooks) America! America!, 1977, revised 2d edit., 1987, Ginn Social Studies, 1987; author: (workbook) America! America! Workbook, 1982, (textbook) Earth's Geography and Environment, 1991, others. Mem. Coun. Tchr. Ed NH Dept. Edn.; mem. bd. dirs., treas., past pres. Social Sci. Edn. Consortium, Fin. Com. and Steering Com. So. NH Sch. to Careers Partnership; past chmn. task force on teenagers and religious edn. Greek Orthodox Archdiocese of North and South Am.; former trustee U. Lowell; chairperson affirmative action com., chairperson com. to oversee U. Lowell Rsch. Found.; former mem. ad hoc budget com. Town of Winchester; former mem. bd. dirs., chairperson nominating com. and search com. for resident dirs. Andover Com. for A Better Chance; fund-raising chairperson, mem. edn. com.; former trustee, newsletter editor local ch. Recipient Disting. Alumni award U. Lowell, Coll. of Edn., 1987. Democrat. Greek Orthodox. Avocations: writing, mosaic iconography, travel, reading. Office: Rivier Coll 420 Main St Nashua NH 03060-5086 Office Phone: 603-897-8582. E-mail: cmitsakos@rivier.edu.

**MITSCHER, LESTER ALLEN,** chemist, educator; b. Detroit, Aug. 20, 1931; s. Lester and Mary Athelda (Pounder) M.; m. Betty Jane McRoberts, May 29, 1953; children: Katrina, Kurt, Mark. BS, Wayne U., 1953, PhD, 1958. Rsch. scientist, group leader Lederle Labs., Pearl River, NY, 1958-67; prof. Ohio State U., Columbus, 1967-75, U. Kans., Lawrence, 1975—, chmn. dept. medicinal chemistry, 1975-92; intersearch prof. Victorian Coll. of Pharmacy, Monash U., Melbourne, Australia, 1975—. Cons. NIH, Abbott Labs. Author: (with D. Lednicer) The Organic Chemistry of Drug Synthesis, Vol. 1, 1976, Vol. 2, 1980, Vol. 3, 1984, Vol. 4, 1990, The Chemistry of the Tetracycline Antibiotics, 1978; co-author: The Green Tea Book, 1997; editor-in-chief Medicinal Research Reviews, 1995-99; contbr. over 250 articles to profl. jours. Recipient Disting. Alumnus award Sch. Pharmacy, Wayne State U., 1980, 97, Rsch. Achievement award Acad. Pharm. Scis., 1980, 97, Volweiler Rsch. award Am. Assn. Colls. Pharmacy, 1985, Higuchi-

Simmons award U. Kans., 1986. Fellow AAAS; mem. Am. Soc. Pharmacognosy (pres. 1992-93), Am. Chem. Soc. (former chmn. councilor medicinal chemistry divsn., Bristol-Myers Smissman rsch. award 1989, Med. Chemistry award 2000), Japanese Antibiotics Assn., Soc. Heterocyclic Chemistry, Internat. Orgn. for Chemistry in Developing Countries (steering com.). Presbyterian. Office: Dept Medicinal Chemistry U Kans Lawrence KS 66045 Office Phone: 785-864-4562. Business E-Mail: lmitscher@ku.edu.

**MITSEFF, CARL,** lawyer; b. Detroit, Nov. 16, 1928; s. Frank H. and Katherine (Schaffer) M.; m. Phyllis Schlitters, June 28, 1952; children: C. Randall, Bradley Scott, Julie, Emily, Faye. BS, Wayne State U., 1952, LL.B., 1955. Bar: Mich. 1956. Practiced in Detroit, 1956—; staff atty. Burroughs Corp., 1955-60; mem. firm LeVasseur, Mitseff, Egan & Capp, 1960-80, Mitseff & Baril, 1980-85, Fitzgerald, Hodgman, Cox, Cawthorn & McMahon, 1986-90, Cox & Hodgman, 1990—. Spl. asst. atty. gen. State of Mich.; lectr. in field. Named to Mich. Workers Compensation Hall of Fame, 2000. Mem. ABA, State Bar Mich., Internat. Assn. Ins. Counsel, Internat. Assn. Indsl. Accident Bds. and Commns., Detroit Athletic Club (bd. dirs.), Beavers (pres.). Exec. Club (pres.). Bus. Round Table (chmn.), Lochmoor Club, Grosse Pointe Yacht Club, Pi Kappa Alpha, Delta Theta Phi. Home: 612 N Brys Dr Grosse Pointe Woods MI 48236-1247 Office: 1001 Woodward Ave Ste 1000 Detroit MI 48226-1904 Office Phone: 313-963-3210. Personal E-mail: c.mitseff@aol.com.

**MITSELMAKHER, GUENAKH,** physics professor, researcher; b. Vilnius, Lithuania, Dec. 5, 1945; arrived in U.S., 1991; s. Viktoras and Anna (Bannikova) M.; m. Antonina Lavrova, Aug. 22, 1970; children: Irina, Victor. M Physics, Moscow State U., 1968; PhD in Physics, Joint Inst. Nuclear Rsch., Dubna, Russia, 1974; DS, USSR State Com. Higher Edn., Moscow, 1987. Staff scientist Joint Inst. for Nuc. Rsch., Dubna, Russia, 1968-91, dept. head, 1983-91, dep. dir. lab., 1987-89; staff scientist Superconducting Supercollider Lab., Dallas, 1991-94; Fermi Nat. Accelerator Lab., Batavia, Ill., 1994-98; prof. physics U. Fla., Gainesville, 1995—2004, dir. Inst. for High Energy Physics and Astrophysics, 2000—, disting. prof. physics, 2004—. Mem. adv. com. Program Fundamental Nuc. Physics, Ministry of Sci. of Russian Fedn., Moscow, 1993-2000; mem. steering com. compact muon solenoid CMS, experiemet European Ctr. for Nuc. Rsch., CERN, Geneva, 1997—; cons. to dir. Joint Inst. Nuc. Rsch., Dubna, 2000—. Contbr. articles over 200 articles to profl. publs. Recipient Commemorative medal, Faculty of Math. and Physics, Charles U., Prague, 2003. Fellow: Am. Phys. Soc.; mem.: AAAS. Achievements include contributions to physics of pions and muons, study of electroweak interactions, particle detectors development. Home: 4929 SW 95th Ter Gainesville FL 32608-4189 Office: U Fla Dept Physics Gainesville FL 32611 Business E-Mail: mitselmakher@phys.ufl.edu.

**MITTEL, JOHN J.,** diversified financial services company executive, economist; b. L.I., N.Y. s. John and Mary (Leidolf) M.; 1 child, James C. BBA, CUNY. Rschr. econs. dept. McGraw Hill & Co., N.Y.C.; mgr., asst. to pres., Indsl. Commodity Corp., J. Carvel Lange Inc., and J. Carvel Lange Internat., Inc., N.Y.C., 1956-64; corp. sec., 1958-86, v.p., 1964-80, exec. v.p., 1980-86; pres. I.C. Investors Corp., N.Y.C., 1972—, I.C. Pension Adv., Inc., N.Y.C., 1977—. Bd. dir. several corps.; plan adminstr., trustee Combined Indsl. Commodity Corp. and J. Carvel Lange Inc. Pension Plan, 1962-86, J. Carvel Lange Internat. Inc. Profit Sharing Trust, 1969-86, Combined Indsl. Commodity Corp. and J. Carvel Lange Inc. Employees Profit Sharing Plan, 1977-86. Co-author: How Good a Sales Profit Are You, 1961, The Role of the Economic Consulting Firm. Mem. grad. adv. bd. Bernard M. Baruch Coll., CUNY, 1971-72. Mem. Conf. Bd., Am. Statis. Assn., Newcomen Soc. N.Am., Union League (N.Y.C.). Office: 10633 Saint Andrews Rd Boynton Beach FL 33436-4714

**MITTELSTADT, BEVERLY ANNE,** elementary school educator; b. White Plains, N.Y., Mar. 22, 1954; d. William Miller and Peggy Anne Voltz; m. Robert Edward Mittelstadt, June 23, 1978; children: Robert William, Brittany Anne. BS in Edn., Springfield Coll., Mass., 1976; MS in Early Childhood Edn., Coll. New Rochelle, 1982. Head tchr. Village Nursery Sch., Chappaqua, NY, 1976—88; kindergarten tchr. North Salem (N.Y.) Cen. Sch. Dist., 1988—. Camp counselor, assn. dir. North Castle Recreation, Armonk, NY, 1971—82. Scholar, Coll. New Rochelle, 1981. Mem.: Westchester Assn. Edn. Young Children, Nat. Assn. Edn. Young Children, Kappa Delta Pi. Independent. Episcopalian. Avocations: reading, sewing, skiing, walking, cooking. Home: 32 Meads Ln Stormville NY 12582 Office: North Salem Cen Sch Dist 230 June Rd North Salem NY 10560

**MITTELSTAEDT, JANET RUGEN,** music educator, composer; b. Port Washington, NY, Mar. 30, 1941; d. Chester Davis and Harriet Helen (Goodman) Rugen; m. Ronald Edward Mittelstaedt, Aug. 24, 1963; children: Edward D., Amy C. Leimbach, Thomas A. BS in Edn., Bucknell U., 1963; BA in Music, Marylhurst U., 1984; MM in Composition, U. Portland, 1993. Nat. cert. in piano and composition Music Tchrs. Nat. Assn. Tchr. 6th grade Spring Branch Sch. Dist., Houston, 1964-66; piano tchr. Houston, 1964-66, Pitts., 1967-74, Portland, Oreg., 1978—; composition tchr., 1988—. Composer: Solo Snips, 1991, Splashes of Color, 1992, Sonatina for Youth, 1993, Fabric and Frills, 1994, Beehive, 2002, Animal Antics, 2004; contbr. articles to profl. jours. Pianist, music coord. Evergreen Presbyn. Ch., Portland, 1994—2000, dir. children's mus., 1996, 1997; youth choir accompanist First Presbyn. Ch., Portland, 2003—05. Recipient award, Ernest Bloch Composers Symposium, 1993, spl. awards, ASCAP, 1994—95, 1997—2004. Mem.: Oreg. Music Tchrs. Assn. (music composition clinician 1990—, composition adjudicator 1990—, chmn. Portland ensemble 1992—94, state composition clinician 1992—95, Portland composition 1998—99, chair Portland program 1999—2001, syllabus adjudicator 2002—, co-chmn. syllabus far west area 2004—, chmn. Pt. syllabus 1980, music theory clinician 1980, Composer of Yr. 1994), Oreg. Fedn. Music Clubs (chair composition 1980). Republican. Presbyterian. Avocations: reading, travel, poetry. Home: 4485 NW 187th Ave Portland OR 97229-2911 Personal E-mail: janrm@att.net.

**MITTELSTEDT, SARAH ANNA,** elementary school educator; b. Huron, S.D., Dec. 28, 1940; d. John and Alice Harriett (Stillman) Ellingsen; m. Richard Rudolph Mittelstedt, Aug. 29, 1964; children: Richard Lee, Rodney Lynn. BA, Huron (S.D.) Coll., 1962. Sec., receptionist H.R. Lee & Co., Huron, 1958-62; tchr. 5th grade Huron Pub. Schs., 1962-64; tchr. grades 5 - 8 Ohio Sch. in Hand County, 1964-67; substitute tchr., Title I aide Huron Pub. Schs., 1974-77, elem. tchr., 1977-99, substitute tchr., Title I aide, 2001—. Mem. tchr. assistance team McKinley Sch., Huron, 1987—90; mem. textbook adoption com. Huron Pub. Schs., 1989; sec. bd. dirs. Huron Area Edn. Fed. Credit Union, 1987—93; North Ctrl. evaluation team Huron Pub. Schs., 1991; participant Nat. Tchrs. Forum, Washington, 1997. Pub.: Huether Family Tree, 2004; contbr. genealogy, pictures and recipes to recipe book. Mem. sch. com. 4-H, Huron, SD, 1975—86, asst. leader to leader, music leader, activities leader; mem. Huron Coll. Cmty. Orch., 1956—61; den mother Cub Scouts, 1974—75; solicitor Huron Coll. Share Campaign, 1974—76; vol. tchr. beginning crochet Cornerstone Learning Ctr., 2004—05; sec. fellowship com. Congl. United Ch. Christ, 1981—83, cradle roll chmn., 1986—89, mem. bell choir, 1978—81, mem. Christian edn. com., 1983—89, mem. stewardship com., 1989—95, stewardship mem., sec., 2000—06, trustee, 1995—2000, mem. pastor search com., 1991—92, 1999—2001. Named Tchr. of Yr., S.D. Soc. Studies Coun., 1993, Huron S.D. Tchr. of Yr., 1997. Mem. NEA, S.D. Edn. Assn., Huron Edn. Assn. (sec., bldg. rep., Sunshine person 1987-89), PTA, Huron Rovers Camping Club (pres., v.p., sec.-treas.), Heartland Garden Club (sec. 2001-02, pres. 2002—04), Huron Area Ret. Tchrs., Delta Kappa Gamma (pres. 1990-92). Republican. Avocations: camping, genealogy, crafts, travel, gardening. Home: 726 Frank Ave SE Huron SD 57350-2947 Personal E-mail: richardsarah64@hotmail.com.

**MITTEN, DAVID GORDON,** classical archaeologist; b. Youngstown, Ohio, Oct. 26, 1935; s. Joe Atlee and Helen Louise (Boyd) M.; children: Claudia Antonia Sabina, Eleanor Elizabeth. BA, Oberlin Coll., 1957; MA in Classical Archaeology, Harvard U., 1958, PhD in Classical Archaeology, 1962. From instr. dept. fine arts to assoc. prof. Harvard U., Cambridge, Mass., 1962-69,

James Loeb prof. classical art and archaeology, 1969—; curator ancient art Harvard U. Art Mus., Cambridge, 1976-96, George M.A. Hanfmann curator ancient art, 1996—2005, curator emeritus, 2006—. Assoc. dir. Harvard-Cornell Sardis Expdn., 1976—; Whitehead vis. prof. archaeology Am. Study of Classical Studies, Athens, Greece, 1990-91. Author: (with S.F. Doeringer) Master Bronzes from the Classical World, 1967; Classical Bronzes: Mus. Art, RISD, 1975, (with Arielle P. Kozloff) The Gods Delight: The Human Figure in Classical Bronze, Cleve. Mus. Art, 1988. Woodrow Wilson fellow Harvard U., 1958; Fulbright fellow Am. Sch. Classical Studies at Athens, 1959-60; Archaeol. Inst. Am. Olivia James fellow, 1969-70; John Simon Guggenheim Found. fellow, 1976-77. Mem. Archaeol. Inst. Am., Assn. Field Archaeology (co-founder), Am. Schs. Oriental Rsch., Brit. Sch. Archaeology (Athens, Greece), Am. Numismatic Soc. Office: Sackler Mus 316 Harvard Univ 485 Broadway Cambridge MA 02138-3845 Office Phone: 617-495-3355. E-mail: mitten@fas.harvard.edu.

**MITTEN, MATTHEW J.,** law educator, lawyer; b. Tiffin, Ohio, Apr. 26, 1959; BA in Econs., Ohio State Univ., 1981; JD magna cum laude, Univ. Toledo, 1984. Bar: Ga. 1984. Atty. antitrust and intellectual property law Kilpatrick Stockton LLP, Atlanta, 1984—89; prof. law So. Tex. Coll. Law, Houston, 1990—99; prof. law, dir. Nat. Sports Law Inst. Marquette Univ. Law Sch., 1999—, assoc. dean for academic affairs, 2002—04; dir. Sports Law Inst., Marquette Univ., 1999—. Sr. fellow U. Melbourne Law Sch., 2005—06; faculty, comparative sports law TC Beirne Sch. Law, Univ. Queensland, Brisbane, Australia; vis. prof. Univ. Toledo Coll. Law; vis. lectr., sports medicine Univ. Tenn. Grad. Sch. Medicine; spkr. in field; cons. in field. Note and comment editor U. Toledo Law Review; contbr. articles i profl. jours. and chapters in books; co-author: Sports Law and Regulation-Cases, Materials and Problems, 2005. Chair NCAA Com. Competitive Safeguards and Med. Aspects Sports, 2002—05. Mem.: Am. Assn. Law Sch. (past chmn., sect. Law & Sports), Sports Lawyers Assn. (bd. dir.), ABA (entertainment and sports law), Order of the Coif. Office: Marquette University Law School Sensenbrenner Hall PO Box 1881 Milwaukee WI 53201-1881 Office Phone: 414-288-7494. Business E-Mail: matt.mitten@marquette.edu.

**MITTEN, RUSS,** lawyer, telecommunications industry executive; BA in History, Political sci. & Philosophy, Southeast Missouri State U.; JD, Wash. U. Sch. of Law. Bar: Conn., Mo., Tex., Wash., Hawaii, US Supreme Ct., US Ct. of Appeals, U.S. Dist. Ct. Gen. counsel Missouri Public Service Commn., Gen. Telephone Co. of Southwest, Gen. Telephone Co. of Northwest, GTE Service Corp.; v.p., gen. counsel, sec. GTE Hawaiian Telephone; gen. counsel Citizens Communications, 1990—91, v.p., gen. counsel, asst. sec., 1991—2000, v.p., gen. counsel, sec., 2000—02, sr. v.p., gen. counsel, sec., 2002—. Office: Citizens Communications 3 High Ridge Park Stamford CT 06905

**MITTERAND, HENRI C.,** literature educator, writer; b. Vault-De-Lugny, Yonne, France, Aug. 7, 1928; arrived in U.S., 1989; s. Joseph and Helene (Dangauthier) Mitterand; m. Helene T. D'Afflitto, Dec. 24, 1955; children: Marie-Helene, Jacques-Olivier. Lic., U. Paris, 1969, Maitrise, 1950, Agregation, 1951, PhD, 1969; degree (hon.), U. Athens, 1997. From asst. to assoc. prof. U. Besancon, France, 1957-65; assoc. prof. U. Reims, France, 1965-68; prof. in French lit. U. Paris 8, 1968-78; prof. U. Paris 3, 1978-90, Columbia U., N.Y.C., 1990—2004, prof. emeritus, 2004—. Vis. prof. Stanford U, 1966, U. Toronto, Canada, 1970—93, U. Pa., 1999; editl. cons., Paris, 1971—; mem. numerous adv. bds. in field; lectr. in field. Editor: (book) Zola, 5 Vols., 1959—67 (award, 1968), Zola, 15 Vols., 1970; author: Le Discours du roman, 1980, L'Illusion réaliste, 1994, Zola et le Naturalisme, 1986, Le Regard et le Signe, 1987, Le Roman à l'oeuvre, 1998, Zola I, 1999, Zola II, 2001, Zola III, 2004. Decorated officer Palmes Academiques France, chevalier Legion d'Honneur, comdr. Order Arts and Letters; recipient Prix de l'Academie Française, Grand Prix de la Ville de Paris, 2000. Mem.: Soc. Fellows/Columbia U., Acad. du Morvan, Inst. Pierre Larousse, Soc. des Amis de Zola (pres. 1990—), Royal Soc. Can. Avocations: sailing, music, films, reading. Office: Columbia U Broadway/116th St W New York NY 10027 E-mail: hm12@columbia.edu.

**MITTERMILLER, JAMES JOSEPH,** lawyer; b. Washington, Apr. 13, 1953; s. Jack and Alice Marie (Froeba) M.; m. Elizabeth Gaillard Simons, June 23, 1979; children: Samuel Stoney, Paul Andrew, Laurie Alice, Claire Mary. Student, U. Heidelberg, 1973-74; BA, Claremont McKenna Coll., 1975; JD, U. Calif. Berkeley, 1978. Bar: Calif., U.S. Dist. Ct. (so., ctrl. and ea. dists.) Calif., U.S. Ct. Appeals (9th cir.), U.S. Supreme Ct. Assoc. Sheppard, Mullin, Richter & Hampton, L.A., 1978-86, ptnr., 1986—. Panelist Calif. Continuing Edn. of Bar, L.A. and San Diego, 1984—. Dir. Legal Aid Soc. of San Diego, 1990—, pres., 1998-2000; bd.dirs., LaJolla YMCA, 2001-04. Recipient Wiley Manuel Pro Bono award Calif. State Bar, 1992, 2001. Mem. Assn. Bus. Trial Lawyers (bd. dirs 1998-2001), Am. Inns of Ct., Claremont McKenna Coll. Alumni Assn. San Diego (bd. dirs.). Avocations: swimming, surfing. Office: Sheppard Mullin Richter & Hampton 501 W Broadway Fl 19 San Diego CA 92101-3536

**MITTLEBERG, ERIC MICHAEL,** pharmaceutical executive; b. NYC, Nov. 7, 1951; s. Irving Ralph and Rose (Schnieder) M.; m. Jane Susan Baumoehl, Dec. 25, 1977; children: Scott, Alyson, Lauren. BS in Pharmacy, St. Johns U., Jamaica, N.Y., 1974, MS in Ind. Pharmaceutics, 1978, PhD in Pharmaceutics, 1982. Registered pharmacist, N.Y. Assoc. scientist Hoffmann-LaRoche Inc., Nutley, NJ, 1974-78; dept. head process improvement Lederle Labs, Pearl River, NY, 1978-83; mgr. mfg. devel. Key Pharm., Miami, Fla., 1983-86; dir. prodn. and tech. svcs. Schering Labs, Miami, 1986-89; sr. dir. pharm. devel. and tech. svcs worldwide R.W. Johnson Pharm. Rsch. Inst., Raritan, NJ, 1989-97; v.p. sci., med. affairs Ivax Corp., 1997—2006; sr. v.p. devel. Par Pharm., Inc., 2006—. Mem. Internat. Soc. Pharm. Engrs., Acad. Pharm. Sci., Am. Pharm. Assn. Office: Par Pharm Inc 120 Belmont Dr Somerset NJ 00073 Business E-Mail: eric.mittleberg@parpharm.com. emittleberg@parpharm.com.

**MITTLEMAN, RICHARD SAMUEL,** lawyer; b. Boston, Feb. 26, 1941; s. Irving I. and Marcia (Rosenzweig) M.; m. Linda Ann Weiner, June 24, 1962; children: Michael, David. AB, Colby Coll., Waterville, Maine, 1962; JD, Boston U., 1965. Bar: RI 1965, US Dist. Ct. RI 1965. Ptnr. Zietz, Sonkin, Radin & Mittleman, 1967-85, Cameron & Mittleman LLP, Providence, 1986—. Office: Cameron & Mittleman LLP 56 Exchange Ter Providence RI 02903-1772 Office Phone: 401-331-5700. Business E-Mail: rmittleman@cm-law.com.

**MITTLEMAN, STEVEN DAVID,** physicist, researcher; b. Boston, Oct. 20, 1942; m. Sarah Egerton, June 6, 1976; children: Carrie, Adam. BSEE, Worcester Poly. Inst., 1964; ScM, Brown U., 1966, PhD, 1974. Physicist NASA, Cambridge, Mass., 1966-70, Sperry Rsch. Ctr., Sudbury, Mass., 1979-83; prof. U. Maine, Orono, 1974-79; prin. engr. Alpha Industries, Woburn, Mass., 1983-85; mgr. radiation facility Dept. Air Force Rome Lab, Hanscom AFB, Mass., 1985-92, chief component tech., 1993-97; dep. divsn. chief Air Force Rsch. Lab., Hanscom AFB, 1997—. Cons. in solar energy, 1972-79; actual. coord. Northeastern U., Dedham, Mass., 1982-2005. Contbr. numerous articles to profl. jours., chpt. to book. Office: Air Force Rsch Lab Electromagnetics Tech Divsn 80 Scott Dr Hanscom Afb MA 01731-2909 Office Phone: 781-377-4038. Business E-Mail: steven.mittleman@hanscom.af.mil.

**MITTLER, DIANA (DIANA MITTLER-BATTIPAGLIA),** music educator, pianist; b. NYC, Oct. 19, 1941; d. Franz and Regina (Schilling) Mittler; m. Victor Battipaglia, Sept. 5, 1965 (div. 1982). BS, Juilliard Sch., 1962, MS, 1963; DMA, Eastman Sch. Music, 1974. Choral dir. William Cowper Jr. H.S. and Springfield Gardens Jr. H.S., Queens, NY, 1963-68; coord. music Flushing H.S., Queens, 1968-79; asst. prin. music Bayside H.S., Queens, 1979-86; assoc. prof. music Lehman Coll., CUNY, 1986-87, prof., 1987—; choral dir., 1986—. Cons. ednl. projects New World Records, 1987—; ednl. cons. Flushing Coun. on Culture and the Arts; cons. Sta. WNET; assoc. condr.

Queens Borough-Wide Chorus, 1964-70; pianist, founder Con Brio Chamber Ensemble, 1978; faculty So. Vt. Music Festival, 1979-83; soloist with N.Y. Philharm., 1956; examiner NYC Bd. Edn. Bd. Exams., 1985—. Author: 57 Lessons for the H.S. Music Class, 1983, Franz Mittler: Austro-American Composer, Musician and Humorous Poet, 1993; contbr. articles to profl. jours.; performance Internat. Summer acad. Mozarteum, Salzburg, Austria, 1995, Weill Recital Hall, 1996, Merkin Hall, 1997, Herbert von Karajan Centrum, Vienna, Austria, 1998; rec. Franz Mittler, Preiser Records, Trio and Piano Pieces, 2003; featured on Study with the Best Series, CUNY TV, 2005. Choral dir., accompanist various charitable, religious, mil., civic holiday functions. N.Y. State Regents scholar, 1958-62; scholarships Juilliard Sch. and Eastman Sch. Music; recipient Excellence in Tchg. award, 1993, Prism award, 1996. Mem. Am. Choral Dirs. Assn., Music Edn. Nat. Conf., Golden Key Soc. Democrat. Home: 10857 66th Ave Forest Hills NY 11375-2247 Office: Lehman Coll Music Dept Bedford Pk Blvd W Bronx NY 10468 Office Phone: 718-960-7795. Personal E-Mail: dianamittler@aol.com.

**MITTMAN, LAWRENCE,** lawyer; b. NYC, Mar. 17, 1951; s. Joseph and Esther (Yarmark) Mittman; m. Ellyn Roth, Aug. 27, 1978; children: Wesley, Jordan. BA magna cum laude, Yeshiva Coll., 1972; JD, Columbia U. Law Sch., 1975. Bar: N.Y. 1976, cert.: U.S. Dist. Ct. So. & Ea. Dist. N.Y. 1976, U.S. Ct. Appeals, second cir. 1978. Ptnr. Paul, Hastings, Janofsky & Walker LLP, N.Y.C., co-chmn. fin. svc. & creditors' rights practice group. Spl. prof. Hofstra U. Sch. Law, 1981. Co-author (with Rees W. Morrison): Bankruptcies: Assets Often Can Be Picked Up At Bargain Prices, 1981; author: Bargain Leases From Bankrupt Tenants, 1982; co-author (with Rees W. Morrison & Burton R. Lifland): Bankruptcy Commentary-Second Cir. Rev. 1981-1982 Term, 1983. Office: Paul Hastings Janofsky & Walker LLP 75 E 55th St First Floor New York NY 10022-3205 Office Phone: 212-318-6300. Office Fax: 212-230-7721. Business E-Mail: lawrencemittman@paulhastings.com.

**MITTON, MICHAEL ANTHONY,** environmental technology company executive; b. Bremen, Germany, Mar. 13, 1947; came to U.S., 1948 (parents Am. citizens); s. Ralph Walter and Aniela (Pilarz) M.; m. Lisa Van der Veer, Mar. 7, 1986 (div. 1991); m. Marilyn Kay Bowen, Sept. 18, 1993. BS, U. Wyo., 1970. Asst. mgr. ops. Moller Steamship Co., N.Y.C., 1970-72; investment analyst Moller Industries, N.Y.C., 1972-73; internal auditor Corning (N.Y.) Glass Works, 1973-75, supr. acctg., 1975-76; dir. acctg. Autotrain Corp., Washington, 1977-78; pres. RMA Ltd., Ft. Collins, Colo., 1978-81; contr. Purecycle Corp., Boulder, Colo., 1981-83; pres., chief exec. officer, treas. Synthetech Inc., Albany, Oreg., 1983-90, bd. dirs., chmn., 1990-95; ret., 1995; pres., CEO Chemical Biosensors, Inc., Beaverton, Oreg., 1992-95; technology entrepreneur, founder environ. tech. co., 1995—. Co-chmn. Oreg. Biotech. Industry Coun., 1989-90. Mem. Gov.'s Task Force Tech. Transfer, 1992-94. Fellow Am. Leadership Forum; mem. Soaring Soc. Am., Oreg. Biotech. Assn. (bd. dirs., chmn. 1990-91, pres. 1991-92), Multnomah Athletic Club. Avocations: flying, squash, skiing, sailing. Home: PO Box 4275 Incline Village NV 89450-4275

**MITZNER, KENNETH MARTIN,** electrical engineer, consultant; b. Bklyn., May 7, 1938; s. Louis Bernard and Dora (Sandler) Mitzner; m. Ruth Maria Osorio, Dec. 26, 1968; children: Camille Lorena Mitzner Zeiter, Esther Jeannette Mitzner Lin, Sharon Michelle Mitzner Mentkowski. BS, MIT, 1958; MS, Calif. Inst. Tech., 1959, PhD, 1964. Mem. tech. staff Hughes Aircraft, Malibu, Calif., 1959-64; prin. engr. B-2 divsn. Northrop Corp., Pico Rivera, Calif., 1964-94; owner Mitzner Sci. and Tech., Oceanside, Calif., 1995—. Instr. U. Calif., Santa Barbara, 1964—65; lectr. in field. Author: (handbook) Demonstrations Against Abortion & Death Selection, 1970; contbr. chapters to books, articles to profl. jours. Bd. dirs. Nat. Right to Life Com., 1980—81; pres. Mobilization for Unnamed, Oceanside, 1970—; bd. dirs. Ams. United for Life, 1991—sec. Calif. Pro Life Coun., Sacramento, 1972; mem. Los Angeles County Select Citizens Com. Life Support Policies, LA, 1983—85; bd. dirs. Jewish Life Issues Com., Solana Beach, 1983—. Named Patron of Life, Calif. Pro Life Coun., 1976; recipient Pres.'s award, 1979; Howard Hughes fellow, 1959—64, Fulbright Found. grantee, Govt. of Italy, 1961—62. Fellow: IEEE (life); mem.: Electromagnetics Acad., U.S. Nat. Commn. Internat. Union Radio Sci. (del. 20th gen. assembly). Avocations: history, stamp collecting/philately, birdwatching. Personal E-Mail: kmitzner@aol.com.

**MIURA, ROBERT MITSURU,** mathematician, researcher, educator; b. Selma, Calif., Sept. 12, 1938; s. Richard Katsuki and Frances Yoneko Miura; m. Kathryn Bannai; children: Derek Katsuki, Brian Robert, Jared Bannai Nagae, Sean Takeo. BS, U. Calif.-Berkeley, 1960, MS, 1962; MA, Princeton U., 1964, PhD, 1966. Rsch. assoc. Princeton U. Plasma Physics Lab., 1965-67; assoc. rsch. scientist Courant Inst. Math. Sci., N.Y.C., 1967-68; asst. prof. math. N.Y.U., N.Y.C., 1961—71; assoc. prof. math. Vanderbilt U., Nashville, 1971—75, U. B.C., Vancouver, Canada, 1975—78, prof., 1978—2001; prof. math. sci. and biomed. engring. N.J. Inst. Tech., Newark, 2005—. Assoc. chmn. math. sci. N.J. Inst. Tech., 2003—05, dir. divsn. biol. scis., 2004—05, acting chmn. math. sci., 2005—06. Editor: Backlund Transformations, 1976, Nonlinear Phenomena in Physics and Biology, 1981, Some Mathematical Questions in Biology-Neurobiology, 1982, Muscle Physiology, 1986, DNA Sequence Analysis, 1986, Plant Biology, 1986; mem. editl. bd. Can. Applied Math. Quar., 1991—; co-editor-in-chief: Analysis and Applications, 2000—, mem. editl. bd.: Integrative Neurosci., 2001—06; contbr. articles to profl. jours. Mem. steering com. Ctr. Math. Rsch., U. Montreal, 1990-94; mem. sci. adv. panel Fields Inst.; Toronto, 2002-06, mem. sci. nominating com., 2003—. Recipient Leroy P. Steele prize, 2006; John Simon Guggenheim fellow, 1980-81; U. B.C. hon. Killam fellow, 1980-81. Fellow Royal Soc. Can., AAAS (nominating com., math. sect.); mem. Am. Math. Soc. (Leroy P. Steele prize 2006), Soc. Indsl. and Applied Math. (chmn. joint com. on math. in life scis. 1981-84, vice chair activity group on the life scis. 2005-), Can. Applied Indsl. Math. Soc., Can. Math. Soc. (internat. affairs com.), Soc. Math. Biology (bd. dirs. 1995-98, nominating com. 1998), Pacific Inst. Math. Sci. (interim exec. bd. 1996), Sigma Xi. Office: NJ Inst Tech Dept Math Sci Univ Hgts Newark NJ 07102 Business E-Mail: miura@njit.edu.

**MIVILLE, MARIE LUCIA,** psychologist, educator; b. Miami, Fla. d. Roland Wilfred and Beatriz Miville; life ptnr. J. M. Rohrbacker. PhD, U. of Md., College Park. Lic. health svc. psychologist Okla. Assoc. prof. Okla. State U., Stillwater, 1995—2003, Tchrs. Coll., Columbia U., N.Y.C., 2003—. Author: (book chpt.) From Prejudice and Discrimination to Awareness and Acceptance; contbr. articles to profl. jours. Mem.: Coun. of Counseling Psychology Tng. Programs (chair 2006—). Achievements include development of Miville-Guzman Universality-Diversity Scale. Office Phone: 212-678-3342.

**MIXON, AARON MALACHI, III,** medical products executive; b. May 22, 1940; m. Barbara Weber; 2 children. BA, Harvard U., 1962, MBA, 1968. CEO, chmn. Invacare Corp., Elyria, Ohio, 1979—. Chmn. bd. trustees Cleve. Clinic Found. Office: Invacare Corp 1 Invacare Way PO Box 4028 Elyria OH 44036-2125 Office Phone: 440-329-6000. Office Fax: 440-366-9008.*

**MIXON, KENNETH WAYNE,** history professor, department chairman; b. Winnsboro, SC, Aug. 19, 1945; s. Cornelius Burch and Lucille Daughtry Mixon; m. Frances Frazier Mixon, Feb. 10, 1967; children: Phillip Eldridge, Eleanor Mixon Attwood. BA, U. SC, 1967, MA, 1970. PhD, U. NC, 1974. Asst. prof. history U. So. Miss., Natchez 1975—77; from asst. to full prof. dept. history Mercer U., Macon, Ga., 1977—96; prof., chair dept. history Augusta (Ga.) State U., 1996—. Author: Southern Writers and the New South Movement, 1980, The People's Writer, 1995; editor: My Young Master, 1987; contbr. more than 25 articles to profl. jours. Neighborhood fundraiser Am. Cancer Soc., Augusta, 2001—, Am. Heart Assn., Augusta, 2001—. Served with U.S. Army, 1967—69, Korea. Mem.: MLA (South Atlantic divsn.), So. Hist. Assn., Am. Hist. Assn. Democrat. Presbyterian. Avocation: running. Office: Augusta State U Dept History Augusta GA 30904

**MIXSON, ARCHIBALD JAMES,** research scientist, internist, endocrinologist; b. Louisville, Oct. 25, 1952; s. James Goodwin and Loraine Lyle Mixson; m. Nancy Ruth Gavin, Oct. 3, 1981; children: Claire Loraine, James Gavin. BA in Math., Vanderbilt U., Nashville, 1974; MD, Emory Sch. Medicine, Atlanta, 1979. Lic. internal medicine ACP, 1983. Post-doctoral fellow NIH, Bethesda, Md., 1986—89; sr. staff fellow, 1989—95; rsch. asst. prof. U. Md., Balt., 1995—98, asst. prof., 1998—2006, assoc. prof., 2006—. Grantee, NIH, Nat. Cancer Inst., 1997—2002, 2004—, Md. Indsl. Partnerships, 2002—04. Achievements include patents for carrier: DNA complexes containing DNA ecoding anti-angiogenic peptides and their use in gene therapy; branched histidine copolymers and methods for using same. Avocations: tennis, travel. Office: U Md 10 South Pine St Bldg MSTF Rm 759 Baltimore MD 21201 Office Phone: 410-706-3223.

**MIYAGAWA, CHIORI,** theater educator, playwright; life ptnr. Hap Tivey. MFA, CUNY, 1989. Asst. lit. mgr. Actors Theatre of Louisville, 1991—91; lit. mgr. Arena Stage, Washington, 1991—92; assoc. artist Pub. Theater, N.Y.C., 1992—93; artistic assoc. N.Y. Theatre Workshop, N.Y.C., 1993—2000; assoc. prof. theater Bard Coll., Annandale-on-Hudson, NY, 2001—. Playwritht-in-residence Yale Sch. Drama, New Haven, 1996—2000; bd. dir. Alliance of Resident Theatre, N.Y.C., 2003—. Author (plays) America Dreaming, 1995 (Rockefeller Mulit-Artist Prodn. award, 1994), Nothing Forever (Rockefeller Mulit-Artist Prodn. award, 1995), Yesterday's Window, FireDance, 1997, Jamaica Avenue, 1998, Broken Morning, 1998 (TCG Extended Collaboration grant, 1998), Awakening, 1999 (Japan Found. award, 2000), Woman Killer, 2001, Antigone's Red, 2002, Antigone Project/Red Again, 2004; author: (plays) Leaving Eden, 2005. Recipient, Ensemble Studio Theatre/Alfred P. Sloan Found., 2002; fellow, N.Y. Found. for Arts, 1994, Van Lier Playwriting fellow, N.Y. Theatre Workshop, 1997, Asian Cultural Coun., 1999, MacDowell Colony, 2002—03; McKnight Playwriting fellow, Playwrights Ctr., 1998. Democrat. Buddhist. Office: Bard Coll Theater Dept Annandale On Hudson NY 12504 Office Phone: 845-758-7938. E-mail: miyagawa@bard.edu.

**MIYAGAWA, HIROAKI,** materials scientist, researcher; b. Sendai, Japan, Aug. 13, 1972; s. Kazuhiko and Emiko Miyagawa. BS, Nagoya U., Japan, 1996; MS, Tokyo Inst. Tech., 1998, PhD, 2000. Postdoctoral rsch. assoc. Ctr. Intelligent Processing Composites Northwestern U., Evanston, Ill., 2000—01; vis. rsch. assoc. Composite Materials and Structures Ctr. Mich. State U., East Lansing, Mich., 2002—04, vis. rsch. assoc. Dept. of Packaging, 2004—05; sci. rschr. Nitto Denko Tech. Corp., Oceanside, Calif., 2006—. Contbr. articles to profl. jours. Vol. train operator Fox River Trolley Mus., South Elgin, Ill., 2001—05, Orange Empire Rlwy. Mus., Perris, Calif., 2006. Mem.: ASME, Soc. Advancement Material and Process Engring. (1st Pl. Outstanding Tech. Paper award 2001), The Japan Soc.Mech. Engrs. Achievements include patents pending for biobased epoxy, their nanocomposites and methods for making those. Home: 3760 North Way Oceanside CA 92056 Office: Nitto Denko Technical Corporation 501 Via Del Monte Oceanside CA 92054 Office Phone: 760-435-2717. Personal E-Mail: hiroaki.miyagawa@gmail.com.

**MIYAGAWA, ICHIRO,** physicist; b. Hiratsuka, Kanagawa, Japan, Mar. 5, 1922; s. Shigejiro and Tsuma (Itoh) M.; m. Mitsuko Yamada, Feb. 10, 1950; children: Shigeru, Haruyo, Mari. BS, Nagoya U., Japan, 1945; DSc, U. Tokyo, 1954. Asst. prof. U. Tokyo, 1959-62; vis. asst. prof. Duke U., Durham, NC, 1963-65; asst. prof. physics U. Ala., Tuscaloosa, 1965-66, assoc. prof., 1966-70, prof., 1970-80, Univ. Research prof. physics, 1980-92, prof. emeritus, 1992—. Contbr. articles to profl. jours. Recipient Samuel Ullman award, 1998; USPHS grantee; EPA grantee; NIH grantee. Fellow Am. Phys. Soc.; mem., AAAS, Sigma Xi. Home: 6434 Misty Ridge Dr Birmingham AL 35235- *Finding truth in any work or in any matter, however simple, is rewarding, although painful in many cases. Successful people in every spectrum of society are master discoverers of truth.*

**MIYAKE, ISSEY,** fashion designer; b. Hiroshima, Japan, Apr. 22, 1938; BA in Graphic Design, Tama Art U., Tokyo, 1959—64; studies at, La Chambre Syndicale de la Couture Parisienne, Paris, 1965—68. Began making clothing, 1962; presented first collection in, 1963; asst. designer Guy Laroche, Paris, 1965—68, Hubert de Givenchy, Paris, 1968-69; designer Geoffrey Beene, NYC, 1969-70; founder Miyake Design Studio, NYC, 1970—, Issey Miyake, Inc., NYC, 1971—. Started working on the pleats series, 1988; launched the line Pleats Please Issey Mikake, 93; presented A-POC line (A Piece of Cloth), 98; established Mikake Issey Found., 2004. Exhbns. of work include: exhbns. in NY and Paris in 1971-73, Issey Miyake and a Piece of Cloth Seibu Mus. Art, Tokyo, 1977, East Meets West, Internat. Design Conf., Apsen, Colo., 1979, Musee des Arts Decoratifs, Paris, 1978, Costumes for Maurice Béjart's ballet, Casta Diva, performed at IRCAM, Centre Pompidou, Paris in collaboration with Tomio Mohri, 1980, MIT, Cambridge, 1982, San Francisco Mus. Modern Art, 1983, Issey Miyake Bodyworks, Victoria and Albert Mus., London, 1985, Energies exhbns. Stedelijk Mus., Amsterdam, 1990, Touko Mus. of Contemporary Art, Tokyo, 1990, Costume for the Loss of Small Details William Forsythe & Frankfurter Ballet, 1991, Issey Miyake Making Things exhbn., found. Cartier pour l'art contempo-rain Paris, ACE Gallery, NY, Mus. Contemporary Art, Tokyo, 1998-2000, A-POC Making Issey Miyake & Dai Fujiwara exhbn. Vitra Design Mus. Berlin, 2001, Big Bang exhbn. Centre Pompidou Paris, 2005; represented in permanent collections: Met. Mus. Art, NYC, Victoria and Albert Mus., London. Author: Issey Miyake: East Meets West, 1978, Issey Miyake: Bodyworks, 1983. Named Person of Cultural Merit, Japan Govt., 1998; recipient Japan Fashion Editor's Club award, 1974, Mainichi Design award, 1977, 1984, 1996, Pratt Inst. NY award for Creative Design, 1980, Internat. award, Coun. Am. Fashion Designers, 1984, Neiman-Marcus award, 1984, Best Collection presented by a Fgn. Designer award of Les Oscars 1985 de la Mode, Paris, 1985, award of the Japanese mag. for the textile industry Senken Shimbun, 1986, Asahi award, 1992, Chevalier de l'ordre Nat. de la Légion d'Honneur, 1993, Georg Jensen award, Denmark, 1999, Wexner prize, U. Ohio, 2004, Praemium Imperiale award for sculpture, Japan Art Assn., 2005, Kyoto prize (Arts and Philosophy Category), Inamori Found., 2006. Office: Issey Miyake USA Corp 3 W 18th St Fl 7 New York NY 10011-4610 Address: Miyake Design Studio 1-23 Ohyama-cho Shibuya-ku Tokyo 151 Japan*

**MIYAKE, STEPHANIE ANN,** psychology professor, director, marriage and family therapist; b. Tulsa, Okla., Feb. 8, 1953; d. Thomas Wayne and Thelma Ann Shank; m. Thomas Masami Miyake, Mar. 19, 1988; children: Jan, Amber, Diann, Chris, Lance. BA, U. Ark., 1988; MA, Phillips Grad. Inst., 1994. Lic. marriage and family therapist Calif., Tex. Bus. mgr., therapist Angeles Cmty. Counseling Ctr., Monrovia, Calif., 1994—2002; marriage and family therapist self employed, 1994—; PsyD program admin. Azusa Pacific U., Azusa, Calif., 1999—2003, dir. MA clin. psych. program, 2001—05, dir. clin. training, 2005—. Trea., bd. mem. Angeles Cmty. Counseling Ctr., Monrovia, Calif., 1998—2002; adv. So. Calif. Consortium of Marriage and Family Therapist Educators, Encino, Calif., 2002—. Editor: Skilled Empathy, 2004; author: Clinical Placement Manual, 2000. Chairperson Claremont HS Grad. Night 2000, Claremont, Calif., 1999—2000; bd. mem. San Gabriel Valley Choral Co., Monrovia, Calif., 1997—99, bd. sec., 2000—03; 1st. v.p. Parent Faculty Assn., Claremont, Calif., 1998—99. Recipient Pres. award, Phillips Grad. Inst., 1994. Mem.: Calif. Assn. of Marriage and Family Therapists, Am. Assn. of Marriage and Family Therapists, Phi Kappa Phi. Achievements include built MA program to be nationally recognized in a 3 year period. Avocations: gardening, singing. Office: Azusa Pacific U Dept of Grad Psych 701 E Foothill Blvd Azusa CA 91702 Office Fax: 628-815-5015. Business E-Mail: smiyake@apu.edu.

**MIYAKE, YASUJI,** computer science educator; b. Nagoya, Aichi Pref, Japan, Nov. 28, 1936; m. Sugako Yamada, Apr. 29, 1971; 1 child, Shigemitsu. B in Engring., Nagoya U., 1960, M in Engring., 1962, DEng, 1968. Rsch. assoc. Nagoya U., 1965-68, asst. prof., 1968-69, assoc. prof., 1969-78; prof. engring. Mie U., Japan, 1978-2000, prof. emeritus, 2000—; prof. computer sci. dept. engring. Chubu U., Japan, 2000—, chairperson computer sci. dept. engring., 2000—03, chairperson computer sci. dept. Grad. Sch., 2004—. Dir. Computation Ctr. Mie U., 1982-87, counselor, 1997-99. Inventor, patentee in field; contbr. articles to profl. jours. Recipient 1st prize Inst. for character recognition technique contests, Inst. Posts and Telecom., Ministry of Posts and Telecom. Japan, 1992, 93, 94, commendation from dir. Tokai Elec. Comm. Control, 1997. Mem. Inst. Electronics, Info. Comm. Engrs. Japan, Info. Processing Soc. Japan, Japanese Soc. Med. Electronics Biol. Engring. Buddhist. Avocations: photography, collecting cameras, driving. Office: Chubu U 1200 Matsumoto-cho Kasugai 487-8501 Japan Office Phone: 81-568-51-9104. Business E-Mail: miyake@cs.chubu.ac.jp. E-mail: y-miyake@u01.gate01.com.

MIYAMORI, KEIKO, artist; b. Yokohama, Kanagawa, Japan, Jan. 14, 1964; arrived in U.S., 1998; d. Yukio and Yuriko Miyamori. BFA, U. Tsukuba, Japan, 1993, MFA, 1995. Adj. faculty Pa. Acad. Fine Arts, Phila., 2000—. Artist-in-residence U. Pa., Phila., 1998—99, Soc. Contemporary Craft, Pitts., 2003. Recipient Sculpture Competition award, Frederik Meijer Gardens and Sculpture Park, 2004; grantee, Leeway Found., 2003. Office: PO Box 11771 Philadelphia PA 19101 Office Phone: 215-888-3245. Business E-Mail: info@princewoods.com.

MIYAMOTO, RICHARD TAKASHI, otolaryngologist; b. Feb. 2, 1944; s. Dave Norio and Haruko (Okano) Miyamoto; m. Cynthia VanderBurgh, June 17, 1967; children: Richard Christopher, Geoffrey Takashi. BS cum laude, Wheaton Coll., 1966; MD, U. Mich., 1970; MS in Otology, U. So. Calif., 1978; D Engring. (hon.), Rose Hulman Inst. Tech., 2001. Diplomate Am. Bd. Otolaryngology. Intern Butterworth Hosp., Grand Rapids, Mich., 1970—71, resident in surgery, 1971—72; resident in otolaryngology Ind. U. Sch. Medicine, Indpls., 1972—75; fellow in otology and neurotology St. Vincent Hosp. and Otologic Med. Group, L.A., 1977—78; asst. prof. Ind. U. Sch. Medicine, Indpls., 1978—83, assoc. prof., 1983—88, prof., 1988—, chmn., 1987—; chief otology and neurotology dept. otology, head and neck surgery, 1982—, chmn. dept. otolaryngology, 1987—, Arilla DeVault prof. otolaryngology, 1991; chief otolaryngology, head and neck surgery Wishard Meml. Hosp., 1979—2002. Mem. editl. bd.: Laryngoscope, Am. Jour. Otology, Otolaryngology - Head and Neck Surgery, European Archives of Oto-Rhino-Laryngology, Anales de Otorrinolaringologia Mexicana; contbr. articles tto profl. jours. Mem. adv. coun. Nat. Inst. Deafness and other Commication Disorders, 1989—94, 2002—; mem. adv. bd. Alexander Graham Bell Assn. for the Deaf, The Ear Found., St. Joseph Inst. Deaf, chmn., 2004—. Maj. USAF, 1975—77. Fellow: ACS, Am. Auditory Soc. (mem. exec. com. 1985—2003), Am. Otological, Rhinological and Laryngological Soc. (v.p. mid. sect. 2002—03), Am. Acad. Otolaryngology (gov. 1982—); mem.: Assn. Acad. Depts. in Otolaryngology-Head and Neck Surgery (sec.-treas. 2002—04, pres.-elect 2004—06), Deafness Rsch. Inst. (bd. dirs., pres. Centurion group, comm. com.), Inst. of Medicine of NAS, Am. Neurotology Soc. (pres.-elect 1999—2000, pres. 2000—01), Collegium Oto-Laryntologicum Amecitiae Sacrum, Royal Soc. Medicine London, Assn. Rsch. Otol. (pres.-elect 2000—01, pres. 2001—), Am. Otol. Soc. (coun. 1992—), Otosclerosis Study Group (coun. 1993—), NY Acad. Scis., Am. Acad. Pediats., Marines Meml. Assn., Cosmos Club of Washington, Alpha Omega Alpha (pres. Ind. chpt. 2003—), Wheaton Coll. Scholastic Honor Soc., Psi Iota Xi. Office: Ind U Sch Med 702 Barnhill Dr Indianapolis IN 46202-5128

MIYASAKI, GEORGE JOJI, artist; b. Kalopa, Hawaii, Mar. 24, 1935; BFA, Calif. Coll. Arts and Crafts, 1957, MFA, 1958. Asst. prof. art Calif. Coll. Arts and Crafts, Oakland, 1958-64; mem. faculty dept. art U. Calif., Berkeley, 1964-94, prof. emeritus. Grantee John Hay Whitney fellow, 1957—58; Tamarind printing fellow, 1961, Guggenheim fellow, 1963—64, Nat. Endowment for Arts fellow, 1980—81, 1985—86. Mem.: NAD. Home: 2844 Forest Ave Berkeley CA 94705-1309

MIYASAKI, SHUICHI, lawyer; b. Paauilo, Hawaii, Aug. 6, 1928; s. Torakichi and Teyo (Kimura) M.; m. Pearl Takeko Saiki, Sept. 11, 1954; children: Joy Michiko, Miles Tadashi, Jan Keiko, Ann Yoshie. BSCE, U. Hawaii-Honolulu, 1951; JD, U. Minn., 1957; grad., Army War Coll., 1973. Bar: Minn. 1957, Hawaii 1959, U.S. Supreme Ct. 1980. Examiner U.S. Patent Office, 1957-59; dep. atty. gen. State of Hawaii, 1960-61; mem., dir., sec./treas. Okumura Takushi Funaki & Wee, Honolulu, 1961-90; pvt. practice Honolulu, 1991—; atty. Hawaii Senate, 1961, chief counsel ways and means com., 1962, chief counsel judiciary com., 1967-70; civil engr. Japan Constrn. Agy., Tokyo, 1953-54; staff judge adv., col. USAR, Ft. DeRussy, Hawaii, 1968-79. Local legal counsel Jaycees, 1962; lectr. Nat. Assn. Pub. Accts. Hawaii Chpt. Ann. Conf., 1990, 94, Mid Pacific Inst. Found., Honolulu, 1990, Econ. Study Club of Hawaii, 1990, Meiji Life Ins. Co. Japan, 1992, Cent. YMCA, 1992, City Bank Honolulu, 1997. Legis. chmn. armed services com. C. of C. of Hawaii, 1973; instnl. rep. Aloha council Boy Scouts Am. 1963-78; exec. com., sec., dir. Legal Aid Soc. Hawaii, 1970-72; state v.p. Hawaii Jaycees, 1964-65; dir., legal counsel St. Louis Heights Community Assn., 1963, 65, 73, 91—; dir., legal counsel Citizens Study Club for Naturalization of Citizens, 1963-68; advisory bd. Project Dana Honolulu, 1991—, vice chair, 1991, 92; bd. dirs. Omote Senke Found., 1999—; life mem. Res. Officers Assn. U.S. Served to 1st It. AUS, 1951-54. Decorated Meritorious Service medal with oak leaf cluster. Mem. ABA, Hawaii Bar Assn., U.S. Patent Office Soc., Hawaii Estate Planning Council, Rotary, Central YMCA Club, Waikiki Athletic Club, Army Golf Assn., Elks, Phi Delta Phi. Office: 1001 Bishop St Ste 1030 Honolulu HI 96813-3408 Personal philosophy: Study hard, work hard, play hard, love hard, have time for nonsense, help others and be fair to all concerned.

MIYATA, KEIJIRO, culinary arts educator; b. Tokyo, Mar. 8, 1951; came to U.S., 1967; s. Yataro Miyata and Hekkiken (Liu) Choy; m. Connie Joyce Nelson, Mar. 8, 1976; children: Michelle, Kelly, Adam. Assoc. in Occupational Study, Culinary Inst. Am., Hyde Park, N.Y., 1972, cert. of nutrition, 1991; cert., Seattle Wine Sch., 1991. Cert. exec. chef; culinary educator. Garde mgr. Mid-Pacific Country Club, Kailua, Hawaii, 1972; working chef Waikiki Yacht Club, Honolulu, 1972-74; Sagano Japanese Restaurant, New Rochelle, N.Y., 1974-76; asst. pastry chef Rye Town (N.Y.) Hilton Hotel, 1976-77; working chef The Explorer, Everett, Wash., 1977-79; exec. chef Holiday Inn, Everett, 1979-81, Mill Creek (Wash.) Country Club, 1981; culinary art instr. Everett Community Coll., 1981-85, North Seattle (Wash.) Community Coll., 1985-90, Seattle Cen. Community Coll., 1990—. Cons. Chalon Corp., Redmond, Wash., Chiang-Mai Restaurant, Mukilteo, Wash., 1988, Holiday Inn Crown Plaza, Seattle, Satsuma Japanese Restaurant, 1996; USA rep. Winterlude Crystal Garden Ice Masters Invitational, Ottawa, Can. Participant Nagano Winter Olympic Ice Sculpture Festival, Karuizawa, Japan, 1998. Recipient Gold awards Am. Culinary Fedn., Oreg. State Chef's Assn., Portland, 1983, Gold and Bronze medals World Culinary Olympic, Frankfurt, Germany, 1984, 1988, Grand Champion award U.S. Nat. Ice Carving Contest, N.Y.C., 1986, 2d place award, All Japan Ice Carving Assn., Asahikawa, 1988, Ednl. Excellence award Oreg. and Wash. Community coll. Couns. Wash. Fedn. of Tchrs./Am. Fedn. of Tchrs./AFL-CIO, 1988, 1989, ACF Seafood Challenge State finalist, Charlotte, N.C., 1989, New Orleans, 1990, 1st place, Pacific Rim Invitational World Ice Sculpting Classic, 1989, Seymour Ice Sculpting Competition, 1991, 3d Ann. Internat. Ice Sculpting Competition, Lake Louise, Alta., Can., 1993, award of Excellence, Wash. Fedn. Tchrs./Am. Fedn. Tchrs./AFL-CIO, 1993, 1st place, Wash. State Seafood Festival Recipe Contest, Shelton, Wash., 1993, Grand Champion, 1994, 1st place, ICE ART'94 Ice Sculpting Competition, Fairbanks, Alaska, 1994, Most Artistic award Asahikawa Internat. Ice Sculpting Competition, 1996, 1st place Ice Carver's Choice, People's Choice Awards--8th Internat. Ice Carving Championship, Anchorage, Alaska, 1997, selected as Snow Sculpting Team Mem. of Sister City of Portland, Internat. Snow Sculpting Competition, Sapporo, Japan, 1997, participant, Nagano Winter Olympic Ice Sculpture Festival, Karuizawa, Japan, 1998, NICA, Gold Medal Ice Carver's Choice Awd., People's awd., Crystal Gall. of Ice, Internatl. Carving Comp., Alaska, 1999, 1st place, People's Choice Awards--7th Annual Internat. Ice Sculpting Competition, Lake Louise, Alberta, Canada, 2000, 2d Place Hokkaido Newspaper award, Asahikawa Internat. Ice Sculpting competition, 2000, 3rd place team, Ice Alaska, Ice Art, Fairbank, Alaska, 2001, 1st place, People's Choice Award, 9th Ann. Internat. Ice Sculpting Competition, Lake Louise, Alta., 2002, Trustees Lifelong Learning award, Seattle CC, 2003—04. Mem. Wash. State

Chefs Assn. (bd. dirs. 1982, 83, 86, 87, 88, cert. chmn. 1986-92, Chef of Yr. 1986), Am. Acad. Chefs, Nat. Ice Carving Assn. Office: Seattle Ctr Cmty Coll 1701 Broadway Seattle WA 98122-2413 Business E-Mail: kmiyat@sccd.ctc.edu.

MIYAZAKI, KOICHI, economics professor; b. Yokohama, Japan, Dec. 7, 1949; s. Yoshikazu and Teruko (Inukai) M.; m. Mizuyo Muto, Jan. 16, 1993. BA, Yokohama Nat. U., 1972; MA, U. Tokyo, 1974. Prof. dept. econs. Hosei U., Tokyo, 1986—. Author: Elucidating the Hellish Trap of Commodity Futures - A Proposal of a Fundamental Reform to Rescue Victims and Revitalize the Japanese Economy, revised edit., 2006; contbr. articles to profl. jours. Mem. Am. Econ. Assn., Tokyo Ctr. for Econ. Rsch., Japanese Econ. Assn. Avocation: tennis. Home: 350-1-108 Katakura-Machi Hachioji 192-0914 Japan Office: Hosei U Dept Econs 4342 Aihara-Machi Machida 194-0298 Japan E-mail: koichi@m.email.ne.jp.

MIYOSHI, MASAO, literature educator, writer; b. Tokyo, May 14, 1928; came to U.S., 1952; s. Katsunai Miyoshi and Hisae Takahama; m. Elizabeth Ann Lester, July 27, 1953 (div. 1977); m. Martha L. Archibald, Apr. 8, 1977 (dec. Sept. 2003); children: Kathy Michele, Owen Malcolm, Melina Cybele. BA, U. Tokyo, 1951; MA, NYU, 1955, PhD, 1963. Instr., lectr. Gakushin U., Tokyo, 1951-52, 54-55; from asst. prof. to assoc. prof. to prof. English U. Calif., Berkeley, 1963-87; Edwin O. Reischauer prof. Japanese studies Harvard U., Cambridge, Mass., 1984-85; Hajime Mori prof. lit. U. Calif., San Diego, 1986—. Vis. prof. U. Chgo., 1978-81; dir. regional seminar, Japanese studies U. Calif., Berkeley, 1980-86, dir. Japanese studies, San Diego, 1989-95; dir. council on East Asian studies, 1997-2000. Author: The Divided Self, 1969, Accomplices of Silence, 1975, As We Saw Them, 1979, Off Center, 1991; editor: Postmodernism and Japan, 1989, Japan in the World, 1993, The Cultures of Globalization, 1998, Learning Places, 2002, (book series) Asia-Pacific: Culture, Politics, and Society. Guggenheim fellow, 1971-72, 75-76. Mem. MLA, Assn. for Asian Studies, Internat. Comparative Lit. Assn. Office: U Calif 9500 Gilman Dr La Jolla CA 92093-5004

MIZE, DAVID M., marine corps officer; b. Detroit, May 4, 1947; m. Elizabeth Jane Irzyk; children: Stacey, Jeff. Degrees in fgn. affairs, gen. engring., U.S. Naval Acad., 1969 and 2d lt. USMC, 1969, advanced through grades to major gen., 1994; reported to 2nd Bn., 1st Marines, nr. Da Nang, Vietnam, 1970-71; asst. chief of staff 9th Marine Amphibious Brig., Okinawa, Japan, 1978-79; midshipman co. officer U.S. Naval Acad.; mem. performance evaluation task force USMC Hdqrs., sr. aide, USMC aide to chief of naval ops.; tng. officer 1st Marine Divsn., 1987; commdg. officer 1st Bn., 9th Marines, 1987-89; officer in charge spl. ops. tng. group I MEF, 1989-90, State Dept. Sr. Seminar, 1990-91; mil. fellow Coun. on Fgn. Rels., N.Y.C., 1991-92; dep. dir. plans, dept. plans, policies and ops. USMC Hdqrs., Washington, 1992-93, exec. asst. to dep. chief of staff plans, policies and ops., 1993-94; dep. dir. ops. U.S. European Command, Stuttgart, Germany, 1994-96; asst. dep. chief of staff manpower and res. affairs USMC Hdqrs., Washington, 1996-98; comdg. gen. Marine Forces Res., 1998—. Comdr., Marine Forces Res., New Orleans. Decorated Def. Disting. Svc. Medal, Legion of Merit, Bronze Star.

MIZE, GERALD L., JR., lawyer; b. Atlanta, Ga., Aug. 14, 1958; Student, Phillips Universität, Marburg an der Lahn, W. Germany, 1978, Ludwig Maximillans Universität, Munich, 1979; AB in Polit. Sci. and German, Univ. Ga., 1980, JD, 1984. Bar: Ga. 1984. Ptnr. in charge, internal com. Alston & Bird LLP, Atlanta, co-chair, bus. devel. com. Office: Alston & Bird LLP One Atlantic Ctr 1201 W Peachtree St NW Atlanta GA 30309-3424 Office Phone: 404-881-7579. Office Fax: 404-881-7777. Business E-Mail: gmize@alston.com.

MIZE, JOE HENRY, industrial engineer, educator; b. Colorado City, Tex., June 14, 1934; s. Kelly Marcus and Birtie (Adams) M.; m. Betty Bentley, Mar. 16, 1966; 1 dau., Kelly Jean. BS in Indsl. Engring. Tex. Tech. Coll., 1958; MS (Research Found. grantee) in Indsl. Engring, Purdue U., 1963, PhD, 1964. Registered profl. engr., Ala., Okla. Indsl. engr. White Sands Missile Range, N.Mex., 1958-61; grad. research asst. Purdue U., Lafayette, Ind., 1961-64; assoc. prof. engring. Auburn (Ala.) U., 1964-69; dir. Auburn (Ala.) U. (Computer Center), 1965-66; prof. engring. Ariz. State U., Tempe, 1969-72; prof., head Sch. Indsl. Engring. and Mgmt. Okla. State U., Stillwater, 1972-80, dir. Univ. Ctr. for Energy Research, 1980-83, Regents prof., 1982-94; v. Hong Kong U. of Sci. and Tech., 1994-98; prof., v.p. Hong Kong U. Sci. & Tech., 1994-98; rsch. affiliate engring. sys. divsn. MIT, 1998—, Cons. to Air War Coll., 1968-69, U.S. Army, Ops. Analysis Standby Unit, U. N.C., 1965-69, various mfg. firms, 1964—; program adv. Office of Mgmt. and Budget, Exec. Office of the President, Washington, 1974-79; adv. to NSF, 1974-94, Nat. Center for Productivity and Quality of Work Life, 1973-78; chmn. tech. adv. council So. Growth Policies Bd., 1975-77; accrediting visitor Engrs. Council for Profl. Devel., 1973-80 Author: (with J.G. Cox) Essentials of Simulation (translated into Japanese 1970), 1968, Prosim V.: Instructor's Manual, 1971, Student's Manual, 1971, (with C.R. White and George H. Brooks) Operations Planning and Control, 1971, (with J.L. Kuester) Optimization Techniques with Fortran, 1973, (with W.C. Turner and K.E. Case) Introduction to Industrial and Systems Engineering, 3d edit., 1993 (named Book of Yr., Am. Inst. Indsl. Engrs. 1979), Guide to Systems Integration, 1991; contrbr. articles to profl. jours., more. Recipient Disting. Engring. Alumnus award Purdue U., 1978 Mem. Am. Inst. Indsl. Engrs. (exec. v.p. 1978-80, pres. 1981-82, H.G. Maynard Innovative Achievement award 1977, Gilbreth Indsl. Engring. award 1990), Am. Soc. for Engring. Edn. (sec. govt. rels. com. 1975-76), Nat. Soc. Profl. Engrs., Okla. Soc. Profl. Engrs. (Outstanding Engring. Achievement award 1977, Outstanding Engr. in Okla. 1981), Inst. Mgmt. Scis., Coun. Indsl. Engring. Acad. Dept. Heads (chmn. 1975-76), NAE, Nat. Rsch. Coun., Sigma Xi, Tau Beta Pi, Alpha Pi Mu. Office: Oklahoma State U Dept Indsl Engring Stillwater OK 74078-0001

MIZEL, LARRY A., housing construction company executive; b. 1942; married BA, U. Okla., 1964; JD, U. Denver, 1967. Founder, dir. MDC Holdings Inc., Denver, 1972—, pres., 1996—99, chmn. bd., CEO, 1999—. Past trustee Marsico Investment Fund; dir. Richmond Am. Homes. Chmn. bd. Simon Weisenthal Ctr., 2003—. Office: MDC Holdings Inc 4350 S Monaco St Denver CO 80237-1867*

MIZELLE, ALAN KEITH, minister; b. Windsor, NC; m. Brenda Leigh Anders, June 9, 1984; children: Christopher Benjamin, Shari Morgan. Ordained to ministry So. Bapt. Conv., 1996. Pastor Connaritsa Bapt. Ch., Aulander, NC, 1996—2001, Hortons Bapt. Ch., 1996—. Divsn. capt. USCG Aux., 2001—02. Home: 114 Williford Ave Windsor NC 27983

MIZER, JOYCE TAYLOR, music educator; b. Staunton, Va., June 16, 1945; d. Wilson and Evelyn Taylor; m. Darryl E. Mizer; children: David Scott, Carol Lynn. MusB Edn., James Madison U., 1966, MusM Edn., 1972. Cert. tchr. Suzuki Assn. of the Americas. Elem. and H.S. band instr. Augusta County Pub. Schools, Fishersville, Va., 1967—84; founder, dir. instr. Suzuki Inst. Sch. of Music, Inc., Sarasota, Fla., 1984—. Guest organist Pentagon, Washington, 1969; guest cond. USAF Band, Washington, 1976. Sec. Va. Band and Orch. Dirs., Charlottesville, 1972—84. Named to Va. Honor Band, 1984. Mem.: Suzuki Assn. of the Americas (assoc.). Avocations: travel, adjudicating musical events. Home: 8951 Huntington Pointe Dr Sarasota FL 34238-3207 Office: Suzuki Inst Sch Music Inc 3100 S Tamiami Trail Sarasota FL 34239 Personal E-mail: drmizer@comcast.net.

MIZGALA, HENRY F., physician, consultant, retired medical educator; b. Montreal, Can., Nov. 28, 1932; s. Louis and Mary (Ropeleski) M.; m. Pauline Barbara Delaney, Oct. 26, 1957; children: Paul Stephen, Cynthia Louise, Liane Mary Mizgala Sizemore, Melanie Frances Mizgala Dressler, Nancy Elizabeth Mizgala Lewis. BA magna cum laude, Loyola Coll., Montreal, 1953; MD, CM, McGill U., 1957. Rotating intern, then resident in medicine St. Mary's Hosp., Montreal, 1957—59, asst. physician, 1963—66; resident in medicine Royal Victoria Hosp., Montreal, 1959—60; Dazian fellow cardiol-

ogy Mt. Sinai Hosp., NYC, 1960—61, USPHS fellow cardiology, 1961—62; resident in cardiology Montreal Gen. Hosp., 1962—63, assoc. physician, 1966—74; asst. physician, cons. cardiology Lachine Gen. Hosp., Que., 1964—80; mem. faculty McGill U. Med. Sch., Montreal, 1968—74, assoc. prof. medicine, 1973—74; assoc. prof., then prof. Montreal U. Med. Sch., 1974—81; cardiologist Montreal Heart Inst., also dir. CCU, 1974—80; prof. medicine U. B.C., 1980—87, prof. medicine, head divsn. cardiology, 1980—87, prof. medicine emeritus, 1998—; hon. attending med. staff, cardiologist Vancouver Hosp. and Health Scis. Ctr. Cons. Centre Hosp. Baie des Chaleurs, Gaspe, Que., 1975—80, B.C. Cancer Agy., Vancouver, 1981—; cons. staff Univ. Hosp., U. B.C. site, 1981—94; hon. cons. Montreal Heart Inst., 1980—. Mem. editl. bd. Can. Jour. Cardiology, 1988-99, Jour. Am. Coll. Cardiology, 1992-95; contbr. articles to profl. jours. Fellow Royal Coll. Physicians and Surgeons Can., Am. Coll. Cardiology, Am. Heart Assn. (coun. clin. cardiology); mem. Can. Med. Assn., Can. Cardiovasc. Soc. (treas. 1974-90), Que. Med. Assn., B.C. Med. Assn., B.C. and Yukon Heart and Stroke Found. (bd. dirs., B.C. Med. Assn.), Alpha Omega Alpha. Office: U BC Divsn Cardiology Dept Med 865 W 10th Ave Vancouver BC Canada V5Z IL7 Office Phone: 604-875-4755. Business E-Mail: mhenry@interchange.ubc.ca.

MIZRAHI, ABRAHAM MORDECHAY, retired health products executive, pediatrician; b. Jerusalem, Apr. 16, 1929; came to U.S., 1952, naturalized, 1960; s. Solomon R. and Rachel (Haliwa) M.; m. Suzanne Eve Glasser, Mar. 15, 1956; children: Debra, Judith, Karen. BS, Manchester Coll., 1955; MD, Albert Einstein Coll. Medicine, 1960. Diplomate: Am. Bd. Pediatrics, Nat. Bd. Med. Examiners. Intern U. N.C., 1960-61; pediatric resident Columbia-Presbyn. Med. Center, N.Y.C., 1961-63, NIH fellow in neonatology, 1963-65; assoc. dir. Newborn Service Mt. Sinai Hosp., N.Y.C.; also dir. Newborn Service Elmhurst Med. Center, 1965-67; staff physician Geigy Pharm. Corp., N.Y.C., 1967-69, head cardio-pulmonary sect., 1969-71; sr. v.p. corp. med. affairs USV Pharm. Corp., Tuckahoe, NY, 1971-76; v.p. health and safety Revlon, Inc., N.Y.C., 1976-89, sr. v.p. human resources, 1989-94; ret., 1994. Assoc. in pediatrics Columbia U., 1963-67; cons. in neonatology Misericordia-Fordham Med. Ctr., 1967-89; clin. affiliate N.Y. Hosp.; clin. asst. prof. Cornell U. Med. Coll., 1982—. Contbr. articles to profl. jours. Trustee Westchester (N.Y.) Jewish Center. Mem. AMA, N.Y. State and County Med. Soc., Am., N.Y. acads. medicine, Am. Soc. Clin. Pharmacology and Therapeutics, Am. Pub. Health Assn., Am. Occupational Med. Assn. Home: 7 Jason Ln Mamaroneck NY 10543-2108 The principles that have guided my life are old Biblical concepts. Firstly, that God had created Adam and Eve and all Men are, therefore, brothers and sisters. Secondly, God created Man and, therefore every human being has a spark of God in him. It, therefore, follows that killing diminshes God's presence on earth and saving of a human being increases His presence.

MIZRAHI, EDWARD ALAN, allergist; b. Tyler, Tex., Aug. 24, 1945; BS in Econs., U. Pa., 1967; MD, U. Fla., 1972. Diplomate Am. Bd. Internal Medicine, Am. Bd. Allergy and Immunology. Intern Med. Coll. Ga., Augusta, 1972-73, resident, 1973-75; fellow Nat. Jewish Hosp., U. Colo., Denver, 1975-77; pvt. practice Jacksonville, Fla., 1977—. Physician Bapt. Med. Ctr., Jacksonville, Meml. Med. Ctr., Jacksonville, St. Luke's Med. Ctr., Jacksonville, St. Vincent's Med. Ctr., Jacksonville, Meth. Hosp., Jacksonville, Orange Park (Fla.) Med. Ctr. Mem. Am. Coll. Allergy, Asthma and Immunology, Am. Acad. Allergy, Asthma and Immunology, Fla. Med. Assn., Fla. Allergy, Asthma and Immunology Soc., Duval County Med. Soc., Southeastern Allergy Assn. Office: Ste A3 3636 University Blvd S Jacksonville FL 32216-4223

MIZRAHI, ISAAC, fashion designer; b. Bklyn., Oct. 14, 1961; s. Zeke and Sarah M. Attended, Parsons Sch. Design, 1982. Design asst. Perry Ellis, 1982-84, Jeffrey Banks, 1984-85, Calvin Klein, 1985-87; founder, ready-to-wear line Isaac Mizrahi, 1987—98, added menswear line, added eyewear, 1990—98; designer, Isaac Mizrahi for Target Target Corp., 2002—; designer, Isaac By Isaac Mizrahi. Subject: (documentaries) Unzipped, 1995; costume designer Twyla Tharp's Ballet Brief Fling, Am. Ballet Theatre.; costume designer The Women, Roundabout Theatre Co., 2002 (Costume Design, Drama Desk award, 2002), Barefoot In the Park, Cort Theatre, NYC, 2006, The Threepenny Opera, Roundabout Theatre Co., 2006, English National Opera's-King Arthur, 2006, creator (series of comic books) The Adventures of Sandee the Supermodel, 1997, one man show (off broadway) Les Mizrahi, host The Isaac Mizrahi Show, Oxygen Network, 2001—03, Isaac, Style Network, 2005—. Recipient Perry Ellis new fashion talent award Coun. Fashion Designers Am., 1989; named Best Womenswear Designer 1989 Coun. Fashion Designers Am., 1990. Office: 876 Centennial Ave Piscataway NJ 08854-3917*

MIZRUCHI, MARK SHELDON, sociology professor, business administration professor; b. New Haven, Dec. 10, 1953; s. Ephraim Harold and Ruth (Trachtenberg) M.; m. Katherine Teves, June 1981 (div. June 1995); 1 child, Joshua. BA, Washington U., 1975; MA, SUNY, Stony Brook, 1977, PhD, 1980. Statis. analyst Albert Einstein Coll. of Medicine, Bronx, NY, 1980-83, asst. prof. psychiatry, 1981-87, supr. statis. svcs., 1983-87; asst. prof. sociology Columbia U., N.Y.C., 1987-89, assoc. prof. sociology, 1989-91; prof. sociology and bus. adminstrn. U. Mich., Ann Arbor, 1991—. Author: The American Corporate Network, 1904-1974, 1982, The Structure of Corporate Political Action, 1992; editor (with M. Schwartz) Intercorporate Relations, 1987. Recipient Presdl. Young Investigator award NSF, 1988-93; grantee NSF, 1987-88, 93-95, 99-2000, 2002-03; invited fellow Ctr. for Advanced Study in the Behavioral Scis., 1989. Mem. Am. Sociol. Assn., Acad. Mgmt., Internat. Network for Social Network Analysis, Sociol. Rsch. Assn. Office: Dept Sociology Univ Mich Ann Arbor MI 48109-1382 Office Phone: 734-764-7444. Office Fax: 734-763-6887. Business E-Mail: mizruchi@umich.edu.

MIZUMURA, MEGUMI, conservator; b. Tokyo, May 4, 1968; BA in Conservation, Camberwell Coll. Arts, London, 1998; MA in Conservation of Fine Art, Northumbria U., Newcastle upon Tyne, U.K., 2000. Paper conservator Tokyo Restoration and Conservation Ctr., 2000—01; asst. conservator Nishio Conservation Studio, Washington, 2001—04; paper conservator Bergen Art Mus., Norway, 2004; Kress intern paper conservator NE Document Conservation Ctr., Andover, Mass., 2004—05; Mellon fellow paper conservator Conservation Ctr. Art and Hist. Artifacts, Phila., 2005—. Contbr. articles to profl. jours. Fellow, Kress Found., 2004—05. Mem.: Inst. of Conservation, Am. Inst. Conservation (Christa Gaehde award 2005), Japan Soc. Conservation of Cultural Property. Home: 135 S 20th St #1104 Philadelphia PA 19103 Personal E-mail: megumimizumura@aol.com

MLINAR, JOHN R., mechanical engineer; b. St. Paul, Minn., Sept. 19, 1959; s. Russell John and Evelyn Jean Mlinar. PhD, U. Minn., St. Paul, Minn., 1997. Sr. engring. specialist 3M, St. Paul, 1984—. Recipient Engring. Achievement award, 3M, 2006. Mem.: ASME. Achievements include 11 patents in field. Office: 3M Company 3M Center Bldg 42-3E-03 Saint Paul MN 55144-1000 Office Phone: 651-778-5721. Personal E-mail: john_r_mlinar@yahoo.com. Business E-Mail: jrmlinar@mmm.com.

MNOOKIN, ROBERT HARRIS, law educator; b. Kansas City, Mo., Feb. 4, 1942; s. I.J. and Marion (Sittenfeld) Mnookin; m. Dale Seigel, June 16, 1963; children: Jennifer Leigh, Allison Heather. AB in Economics, Harvard U., 1964, LLB, 1968. Bar: DC 1970, Calif. 1971: Law clk. to Judge Carl McGowan US Ct. Appeals DC Cir., 1968—69; law clk. to Justice John M. Harlan US Supreme Ct., 1969—70; assoc. Howard, Prim, Smith, Rice & Downs, San Francisco, 1970-72, of counsel, 1972-93; lectr. U. Calif., Berkeley, 1972, dir. childhood & govt. project, 1972—74, acting prof., 1973—75, prof., 1975—82; vis. prof. Stanford U. Sch. Law, 1980-81, prof. law, 1982—87, Adelbert H. Sweet prof. law, 1987—93, dir. ctr. conflict & negotiation 1989—93; Samuel Williston prof. law Harvard Law Sch., Cambridge, Mass., 1993—; dir. Harvard negotiation rsch. project Harvard U., 1993—. Vis. prof. Harvard Law Sch., 1990-91; arbitrator IBM-Fujitsu Arbitration, 1985-87. Author: Child, Family and State, 1978, 3rd edit, 1995, In the Interest of Children, 1985, Barriers to Conflict Resolution, 1995,

Negotiating on Behalf of Others, 1999; co-author: Dividing the Child, 1992, Beyond Winning, 2000; contbr. articles to profl. journals. Mem. overseer's com. to visit Law Sch., Harvard U., 1972-78; trustee Berkeley Pub. Libr., 1973-80, chmn., 1975-77, vice chmn., 1978-80. Fellow Wolfson Coll. & Ctr. Socio-Legal Studies, Oxford, Eng., 1978, Ctr. Advanced Study in Behavioral Sciences, Stanford, Calif., 1981—82; Fulbright Scholar, Econometric Inst., Netherlands Sch. Economics, Rotterdam, 1964—65. Fellow Am. Acad. Arts and Sciences; mem. ABA, Am. Law Inst., Calif. Bar Assn. Office: Harvard Law Sch 1563 Massachusetts Ave Cambridge MA 02138 Office Phone: 617-495-9201. Office Fax: 617-496-3777. Business E-Mail: mnookin@law.harvard.edu.

**MNUCHIN, STEVEN T.,** investment company executive; m. Heather Mnuchin. BA, Yale Univ. Various mgmt. positions Goldman Sach, 1985—2001, exec. v.p., chief info. officer, 2001—02; vice chmn. ESL Investments Inc., 2003; CEO SFM Capital Mgmt. LP, 2004—04; chmn., co-CEO Dune Capital Mgmt. LP, 2004—. Mem. Yale Devel. Bd.; trustee Whitney Mus. Am. Art, Hirshhorn Mus. & Sculpture Garden, Riverdale Country Sch.; bd. dir. Kmart (now Sears Holding Corp.); bd. trustees NY Presbyn. Med. Ctr., 2004—. Office: Dune Capital Mgmt LP 30th Fl 623 Fifth Ave New York NY 10022

**MO, LUKE WEI,** physicist, researcher; b. Shangtung, China, June 3, 1934; s. Si-leng and Shu-feng (Lo) M.; m. Doris Chang, Dec. 31, 1960; children: Curtis L., Alice. BSEE, Nat. Taiwan U., 1955; MS in Physics, Nat. Tsinghua U., 1959; PhD, Columbia U., 1963. Rsch. assoc. Columbia U., N.Y.C., 1963—64; rsch. physicist Stanford Linear Accelerator, Calif., 1965—69; asst. prof. physics U. Chgo., 1969—76; prof. physics Va. Poly. Inst. and State U., Blacksburg, 1976—. Contbr. articles to profl. jours. Served with Taiwan Air Force, 1955-56. Recipient Alumni Research Excellence award Va. Poly. Inst. and State U., 1980, Guggenheim fellow, 1981. Fellow Am. Phys. Soc. Office: Va Poly Inst Dept Physics Blacksburg VA 24061-0435 Business E-Mail: lmo@vt.edu.

**MOAG, RODNEY FRANK,** language educator, country and bluegrass singer, musician, record producer; b. Warsaw, NY, Oct. 15, 1936; s. Hugh Alexander and Imogene (Hodges) Moag; m. Rachel Ann Foley, Feb. 9, 1964 (div. Aug. 1974); children: Robin Gray, Hugh Daniel, Jeffrey Lee. BS, Syracuse U., 1961; MA, U. Wis., 1966, PhD, 1973. Instr., asst. prof. U. Mo., Columbia, 1968—74, dir. college preparatory program for visually impaired, 1974; vis. Fulbright prof. U.S. Pacific, Suva, Fiji, 1975-78; vis. assoc. prof. U. Mich., Ann Arbor, 1978-80, adj. prof., 1981, vis. assoc. prof., 1982; sr. lectr. U. Tex., Austin, 1981, 83-90, assoc. prof., 1990—2004, prof. emeritus, 2004—. Author: (reference grammar) Fiji Hindi, 1977, Malayalam, 1986, singer (country music artist) 5 albums. Mng. dir. Amateur Radio Repeaters Washtenaw, 1984—86; pres. Mich. Repeater Coun., 1985—88; vol. programmer KO-OP, 1995—. Mem. Austin Repeater Orgn., Tex. VHF FM Soc., Ctrl. Tex. Bluegrass Assn., Austin Amateur Radio Club (v.p. 1993—94). Avocations: amateur radio, music. Home: 6909 Miranda Dr Austin TX 78752-3119 Office Phone: 512-467-6825. Personal E-mail: rodmoag@texas.net.

**MOALES, YVONNE EDWARDS,** school psychologist; d. Solomon and Della Mae Edwards; 1 child, April M. Dunson. BA in Psychology, Ga. State U., 1978, MEd in Psychology, 1979, EdS in Sch. Psychology, 1984. Med. lab. technologist Park City Hosp., Bridgeport, Conn., 1967—76; sch. psychologist DeKalb County Sch. Sys., Decatur, Ga., 1979—. Edn./psychol. cons. Gainesville (Ga.) Regional Detention Ctr., 2000—; edn. del. to China People to People Am. Program, 2002. Named one of Outstanding Young Women of Am., 1980; recipient Civic/Cmty. Svc. award, The Ross Report, Atlanta, 1995. Mem.: Nat. Assn. Sch. Psychologists, Ga. Assn. Sch. Psychologists. Avocations: golf, swimming, reading, spiritual development. Office: DeKalb County Schs East DeKalb Campus 5839 Memorial Dr Stone Mountain GA 30083-3487 Office Phone: 678-676-1964. Personal E-mail: ymoales@aol.com.

**MOALLEM, MAHNAZ,** educational researcher; arrived in U.S., 1987; m. Mahmoud Boddoohi; children: Maziar Boddoohi, Milad Boddoohi. Student, Tchr. Edn. Coll., Tehran, 1971; BA, Coll. of Translatio, Tehran, 1976; PhD, Fla. State U., 1993. Cert. program evaluation Fla. State U., tchr. U. N.C.-Wilmington. Program evaluator U. N.C., Wilmington, 1980—, instrnl. designer, tech. cons., 1993—. Tchr. educator Tchr. Edn. Coll., Tehran, 1978—87. Contbr. tchg. performance (Chancellor's Tchg. Excellence award, 2001); author: (book chpt.) Designing and managing student assessment in online learning environment, Communicating and collaborating in the Online Classroom: Examples and Applications; contbr. articles to profl. jours. Recipient tech. grant, Dept. of Edn., 2001—04; Sch. Rsch. award, Design of Web-Course Devel. award, Outstanding Faculty award for contbn. to U. N.C.-Wilmington, Faculty R&D award, Tchg. Excellence award. Mem.: Assn. for Ednl. Comm. and Tech. D-Liberal. Office: U NC 601 S College Rd Wilmington NC 28403 Office Phone: 910-962-4183. Office Fax: 910-962-3609. E-mail: moallemm@uncw.edu.

**MOATES, G. PAUL (PAUL MOATES),** lawyer; b. May 26, 1947; s. Guy Hart and Virginia Rose (Mayolett) Moates; m. Constance A. Sadler. BA cum laude, Amherst Coll., 1969; JD, U. Chgo., 1975. Bar: Ill. 1975, DC 1976, US Ct. Appeals (DC cir.) 1976, US Supreme Ct. 1980, US Ct. Appeals (6th cir.) 1984, US Ct. Appeals (3d cir.) 1991, US Ct. Appeals (7th cir.) 1993. Assoc. Sidley & Austin (now Sidley Austin Brown & Wood LLP), Washington, 1975—82; ptnr. and head transp. practice Sidley Austin LLP, 1982—, mem. exec. com. and worldwide co-chair acctg. and fin. com. Contbr. articles to profl. jours. With White House Comm. Agy. U.S. Army, 1971—73, Washington, DC. Mem.: ABA, DC Bar Assn., Ill. Bar Assn. Office: Sidley Austin LLP 1501 K Street NW Washington DC 20005 Office Phone: 202-736-8175. Office Fax: 202-736-0711. E-mail: pmoates@sidley.com.

**MOAVENZADEH, FRED,** engineering educator; BS, Teheran U., 1958; MS, Cornell U., 1960; PhD, Purdue U., 1962. Asst. prof. Mass. Inst. Tech., Cambridge, Mass., 1965—66, assoc. prof., 1966—72, prof., 1972—, dir. ctr. tech., policy and indsl. devel., 1998—, James Mason Crafts prof. systems engring. Cons. in field; mem. rsch. ctr. coun. CII, 1992—. Author: (book) Future Cities: Dynamics and Sustainability, 2002, Global Construction and the Environment: Strategies and Opportunities, 1994; author: (with David Geltner) Transportation, Energy and Economic Development: A Dilemma in the Developing World, 1984; author: over 300 profl. publs. and reports; editor: Concise Encyclopedia of Building & Construction Materials, 1990, Proceedings of the Conference on Science, Technology and Development in Latin America, 1986; editor-in-chief: Construction Business Review, mem. editl. bd.: Jour. Urban Tech. Recipient deFleury Medal, U.S. Army Corps Engrs., 2001. Mem.: NAE (transp. rsch. bd.), ASCE (mem. editl. bd. Jour. Infrastructure Systems), AAAS, Soc. Internat. Devel. Soc. Office: Mass Inst Tech 77 Massachusetts Ave Bldg E40-231 Cambridge MA 02139-4307 Office Phone: 617-253-8973. Office Fax: 617-253-7140. Business E-Mail: ctpidcom@mit.edu.

**MOAWAD, ATEF,** obstetrician, gynecologist, educator; b. Beni Suef, Egypt, Dec. 2, 1935; came to U.S., 1959; s. Hanna and Baheya (Hunein) M.; m. Ferial Fouad Abdel Malek, Aug. 22, 1966; children: John, Joseph, James. Student, Cairo U. Sch. Sci., 1951-52; MB, BCh, Cairo U. Sch. Medicine, 1957; MS in in Pharmacology, Jefferson Med. Coll., 1963. Diplomate Am. Bd. Ob-Gyn; licentiate Med. Coun Can. Rotating intern Cairo U. Hosp., 1958-59, Elizabeth (N.J.) Gen. Hosp., 1959-60; resident in ob-gyn. Jefferson Med. Coll. Hosp., Phila., 1961-64; lect. dept. pharmacology U. Alta., Can., 1966; asst. prof. dept. ob-gyn. and pharmacology U. Alta., Can., 1967-70, assoc. prof., 1970-72; assoc. prof. dept. ob-gyn. and pharmacology U. Chgo., 1972-75, prof. dept. ob-gyn. and pediatrics, 1975—, co-dir. perinatal ctr., 1974-80; obstetrician-gynecologist, chief obstetrics, co-dir. perinatal ctr. The Chgo. Lying-in Hosp. U. Chgo., 1980—, Blum Riese prof. ob-gyn., chief maternal fetal medicine, 2001—, interim chair dept. ob-gyn., 2002—. Vis. investigator dept. ob-gyn. U. Lund, Sweden, 1969. Co-author book chpts.,

jour. articles. Mem. perinatal adv. com. Chgo. March of Dimes, 1977—, health profl. adv. com., 1983—; mem. perinatal adv. bd. com. State of Ill., 1978—; mem. Chgo. Maternal Child Health Adv. Com., chmn., 1991—; mem. Mayor's Adv. Com. on Infant Mortality, 1991—. Fellow Jefferson Med. Coll., 1960-61, Case Western Res. U., 1964-65; grantee Brush Found., 1966-67, Maternal Fetal Medicine Units Network NIH, 1994; recipient award Phila. Obstet. Soc., 1964, Disting. Tchg. award Am. Profs. Gynecology and Obstetrics, 1993, DeLee Humanitarian award, 2003. Fellow Am. Coll. Ob-Gyn. (Purdue-Frederick award 1978), Royal Coll. Surgeons (Can.); mem. Soc. for Gynecol Investigation, Pharmacol. Soc. Can., Am. Gynecol. and Obstet. Soc., Soc. Perinatal Obstetricians, N.Y. Acad. Scis., Chgo. Gynecol. Soc., Can. Med. Assn., Christian Med. Soc., Edmonton Obstetrics Soc. Office: U Chgo Dept Ob-Gyn 5841 S Maryland Ave MC 2050 Chicago IL 60637-1463 E-mail: amoawad@babies.bsd.uchicago.edu.

**MOAZED, KHOSROW L.,** retired engineering educator; b. Meshed, Iran, Sept. 14, 1930; arrived in U.S., 1943; s. Mohammed and Forough Moazed; m. Carolyn Turner Green, Nov. 14, 1953; children: David Charles, Steven Darius, Elizabeth Ashraf, Maryam Leela. BSc, Rensselaer Poly., 1953, MSc, 1956, Carnegie Mellon U., 1958, PhD, 1959. Registered profl. engr., N.C. Rsch. assoc. Rensselaer Poly. Inst., Troy, NY, 1955—56; GE fellow Carnegie-Mellon U., Pitts., 1956—59; asst. prof. Ohio State U., Columbus, 1959—65, assoc. prof., 1965—68; prof. N.C. State U., Raleigh, 1968—91, prof. emeritus, 1991—, chmn. faculty senate, 1982—83. Prin. sci. officer Nat. Phys. Lab., Teddington, England, 1966; vis. prof. Naval Ocean Sys. Ctr., San Diego, 1985—90. Contbr. scientific papers to profl. jours. Capt., mission pilot CAP, 1995—2002. Grantee, NSF, USAF Office Sci. Rsch., U.S. Army Rsch. Office, Office Naval Rsch. Avocations: flying, art, writing, skiing

**MOBERG, DENNIS,** director; s. Donald and Gladys Moberg; m. Kathleen Kiehl; children: Analise children: Carl, Christiaan. DBA, U. So. Calif., LA. Exec. dir. Markkula Ctr. Applied Ethics, Santa Clara, Calif., 2000—01, Ignatian Ctr., 2004—06. Contbr. articles to profl. jours., chapters to books. Mem.: Soc. Bus. Ethics (pres. 2004—06). Avocations: travel, cooking. Office: Leavey School of Business Santa Clara U 500 El Camino Real Santa Clara CA 95053 Office Phone: 408-554-4713.

**MOBLEY, CUTTINO RASHAWN,** professional basketball player; b. Sept. 1, 1974; Student, U. R.I. Guard Houston Rockets, 1998—2004, Orlando Magic, 2004—05, Sacramento Kings, 2005, LA Clippers, 2005—06. Participant Schick Rookie Challenge, 2000. Named to Schick All-Rookie Second Team, 1998-99; named Atlantic 10 Player of Yr., 1997-98. Office: LA Clippers Staples Center 1111 S Figueroa St Los Angeles CA 90015*

**MOBLEY, EMILY RUTH,** library director, educator, dean; b. Valdosta, Ga., Oct. 1, 1942; d. Emmett and Ruth (Johnson) M. AB in Libr., U. Mich., 1964, AM in Libr. Sci., 1967, postgrad., 1973-76. Tchr. Ecorse (Mich.) Pub. Schs., 1964-65; adminstrv. trainee Chrysler Corp., Highland Park, Mich., 1965-66, engring. libr., 1966-69; libr. II Wayne State U., Detroit, 1969-72, libr. III, 1972-75; staff asst. GM Rsch. Labs. Libr., Warren, Mich., 1976-78, supr. reader svcs., 1978-81; libr. dir. GMI Engring. & Mgmt. Inst., Flint, Mich., 1982-86; assoc. dir. for pub. svcs. & collection devel., assoc. prof. libr. sci. Purdue U. Librs., West Lafayette, Ind., 1986-89, acting dir. librs., assoc. prof. libr. sci., 1989, dean librs., prof. libr. sci., 1989—2004; Esther Ellis Norton Disting. Prof. Libr. Sci. Purdue U., West Lafayette, Ind., 1997—. Adj. lectr. U. Mich. Sch. Libr. Sci., Ann Arbor, 1974-75, 83-86; grants reader Libr. of Mich., 1980-81; project dir. Mideastern Mich. Region Libr. Cooperation, 1984-86; cons. Libr. Coop. of Macomb, 1985-86, Clark-Atlanta U., 1990-91; search com. for new dir. of libr. Smithsonian Instn., 1988; mem. GM Pub. Affairs Subcom. on Introducing Minorities to Engring.; presenter in field. Author: Special Libraries at Work, 1984; mem. editl. bd. Reference Svcs. Rev., 1989-2004, Infomanage, 1993-97. Corp. vis. com. for librs. MIT, 1990-2004, Carnegie-Mellon U., 1998—; mem. Ind. Statewide Libr. Automation Task Force, 1989-90; state tech. strategy subcom. on info. tech. and telecomms. Ind. Corp. for Sci. & Tech., 1989; nat. adv. com. Libr. of Congress, 1988; trustee Libr. of Mich., 1983-86, v.p., 1986, long range plan com., 1979-82, task force on document access and delivery, 1977-79; info. project mem. Rep. Nat. Conv., 1980; bd. dirs. Small Farms Assn., Southfield, Mich., Lafayette Symphony Orch., YWCA. Recipient Bausch & Lomb award, 1960, Cert. for Outstanding Performance in Acad. Achievement State of Mich. Ho. of Reps., 1976, Spl. Tribute for Outstanding Contbns. Libr. of Mich. Bd. Trustees, 1986, Disting. Alumnus award U. Mich. Sch. Info. & Libr. Studies, 1989; U. Mich. Regents Alumni scholar, 1960-64; CIC doctoral fellow in libr. sci., 1973-76. Mem. ALA (com. on accreditation, subcom. to rev. 1972, standards for accreditation 1988-89, OLOS minority internship com. 1988-89, nominating com. 1992-93, mem. coun. resolutions com. 1993-97), Assn. Coll. & Rsch. Librs. (task force on libr. sch. curriculum 1988-89, com. on predict com. 1990-92), Libr. Adminstrn. & Mgmt. Assn., Assn. Rsch. Librs. (bd. dirs. 1990-93), Spl. Librs. Assn. (pres. 1987-88, fellow 1991, com. mem.), Alpha Kappa Alpha, Phi Kappa Phi, Sigma Xi, Iron Key. Office: Purdue U Librs Stewart Ctr Lafayette IN 47907 Business E-Mail: emobley@purdue.edu.

**MOBLEY, JOHN HOMER, II,** lawyer; b. Shreveport, La., Apr. 21, 1930; s. John Hinson and Beulah (Wilson) Mobley; m. Sue Lawton, Aug. 9, 1958; children: John Lawton(dec.), Anne Davant. AB, U. Ga., 1951, JD, 1953. Bar: Ga. 1952, US Dist. Ct. D.C. Ptnr. Kelley & Mobley, Atlanta, 1956-63, Gambrell & Mobley, Atlanta, 1963-83; sr. ptnr. Sutherland, Asbill & Brennan, Atlanta, 1983—. Founding chmn. Cmtys. in Schs. of Ga.; mem. Nat. Cmtys. in Schs.; former mem. bd. visitors Emory U.; trustee emeritus Canterbury Ct. Episcopal Retirement Home of Atlanta; trustee Episcopal Diocese of Atlanta Fund; twice sr. warden All Saints Episcopal Ch. Capt. JAGC USAF, 1953—55. Recipient Disting. Svc. Scroll, U. Ga. Law Sch. Mem. ABA, D.C. Bar, State Bar Ga., Atlanta Bar Assn., Am. Judicature Soc., Atlanta Lawyers Club, Atlanta Athletic Club, Atlanta Country Club, Commerce Club, Piedmont Driving Club, Georgian Club, N.Y. Athletic Club, Met. Club of Washington, Phi Delta Phi. Home: 4348 Sentinel Post Rd NW Atlanta GA 30327-3910 Office: Sutherland Asbill & Brennan 999 Peachtree St NE Ste 2300 Atlanta GA 30309-3996 Office Phone: 404-853-8128. Business E-Mail: john.mobley@sablaw.com.

**MOBLEY, KAREN RUTH,** art director; b. Cheyenne, Wyo., Aug. 26, 1961; d. David G. and Marlene G. (Franz) M. BFA, U. Wyo., 1983; MFA, U. Oka., 1987. Sales assoc. Morgan Gallery, Kansas City, Mo., 1984-85; grad. asst. U. Okla. Mus. Art, Norman, 1985-87; dir. Univ. Art Gallery N.Mex. State U., Las Cruces, 1988-93; exec. dir. Nicolaysen Art Mus., Casper, Wyo., 1993-96; dir. Spokane Arts Com., 1997—. Guest artist Oklahoma City C.C., 1986. Exhbns. include Phoenix Triennial, 1990, New Am. Talent, Laguna Gloria Art Mus., Austin, Tex., 1992, Adair Margo Gallery, El Paso, 1992-94, Wyo. Arts Coun. Gallery and Casper Coll., 1995, Mont. State U., 1996, Whitworth Coll., 2004, Good Works Gallery, 2005 Trustee Westminster Congl. Ch.; bd. dirs. Spokane Pub. Radio. Wyo. Arts Coun. Individual Artist grantee 1994, Lit. fellow, 1995-96; named Outstanding Young Women Am. Mem. Am. Assn. Mus., Coll. Art Assn., Wash. State Arts Alliance, Rotary 21, Phi Beta Kappa, Phi Kappa Phi. Office: Spokane Arts Com 808 W Spokane Falls Blvd Spokane WA 99203 Office Phone: 509-625-6050. Business E-Mail: kmobley@spokanecity.org.

**MOBLEY, STACEY J.,** lawyer, consumer products company executive; b. Chester, Pa., Nov. 19, 1945; s. James Otis and Retha B. (Hollis) M.; m. Joan Thompson, Aug. 28, 1970; children: Michele. BS in Pharmacy, Howard U., 1968, JD, 1971. Bar: Pa. 1972, D.C. 1979, U.S. Supreme Ct. 1979; registered pharmacist. Sr. v.p., chief admin. officer, gen. counsel DuPont Co., Wilmington, Del., 1972—83, dir. fed. affairs Washington, 1983—86, v.p. fed. affairs, 1986—92, sr. v.p. comm. in external affairs Wilmington, Del., 1992—99, chief admin. officer, gen. counsel, 1999—, sr. v.p., 2001—. Bd. dirs. Wilmington Trust Co. State chmn. Del. United Way campaign, 1998; chair Del. Strategic Econ. Coun., 2001. Named one of Am. Top Black Lawyers, Black Enterprise mag.; recipient LexisNexis Corp.egal Times Disting. Legal

Svc. award, Alumni award for disting. postgrad. achievement in law, Howard U., 2002. Mem. Wilmington Club, Carlton Club. Avocations: tennis, golf. Office: DuPont Co 1007 Market St Wilmington DE 19898-0001

**MOBLEY, TONY ALLEN,** foundation administrator, former dean, recreation educator; b. Harrodsburg, Ky., May 19, 1938; s. Cecil and Beatrice (Bailey) M.; m. Betty Weaver, June 10, 1961; 1 child, Derek Lloyd. BS, Georgetown Coll., 1960; MS, Ind. U., 1962, D Recreation, 1965; MRE, So. Sem., Louisville, 1963. Chmn. dept. recreation and pks. Western Ill. U., Macomb, 1965-72, Pa. State U., University Park, 1972-76; prof., chmn. recreation and pks., dean Sch. Health, Phys. Edn. and Recreation Ind. U., Bloomington, 1976—; exec. dir. Ind. U. Found., Bloomington, 2002—. Chair health adv. coun. White River Park Commn., State of Ind., 1979—; v.p Ind. Sports Corp., Indpls., 1983-89; bd. dirs. Nat. Inst. for Fitness and Sport, Indpls., 1984-93; J.B. Nash scholar, lectr. Am. Assn. Leisure and Recreation, Reston, Va., 1985. Contbr. over 50 articles to profl. jours. Bd. dirs. Monroe County YMCA, Bloomington, 1984-88, United Way, Bloomington, 1994—; mem. Gov.'s Coun. for Phys. Fitness and Sport, 1991—. Am. Coun. Edn. adminstrv. internship fellow, N.C. State U., 1970-71. Fellow Am. Acad. Pk. and Recreation Adminstrn. (pres. 1985-86); mem. Nat. Recreation and Pk. Assn. (pres. 1978-79, Nat. Disting. Profl. award 1981), Assn. Rsch., Adminstrn., Profl. Couns. and Socs. (pres. 1986-87, award 1987), Am. Alliance Health, Phys. Edn., Recreation and Dance (Coll. and Univ. Adminstrs. Coun. Honor award 1986, R. Tait McKenzie award 1996), Soc. Pk. and Recreation Edn. (pres. 1974-75, award 1978), Ind. Pk. and Recreation Assn. (Outstanding Profl. award 1985). Avocations: golf, travel. Office: Ind U Found PO Box 500 Bloomington IN 47402

**MOBLEY, WILLIAM HODGES,** finance educator, researcher, writer; b. Akron, Ohio, Nov. 15, 1941; BA, Denison U., 1963; PhD, U. Md., 1971. Registered psychologist, Hong Kong. Mgr. employee rels. rsch. PPG Industries, Pitts., 1971-73; prof. U. S.C., Columbia, 1973-80; head dept. of mgmt. Tex. A&M U., College Station, 1980-83, dean. Coll. of Bus. Adminstrn., 1983-86, exec. dep. chancellor, 1986-88, pres., 1988-93; chancellor Tex. A&M U. Sys., College Station, 1993-94; prof. mgmt. Tex. A&M U., College Station, 1980-96, China Europe Internat. Bus. Sch., Shanghai, 2002—; pres. Legend Global Pacific Ltd., Hong Kong, 2003—, Mobley Group Pacific, 2001—. Vis. fellow Cornell U., 1994, vis. prof. Hong Kong U. Sci. and Tech., 1995-97, U. Hong Kong, 1998. Author: Employee Turnover, 1982, Advances in Global Leadership, vol. I, 1999, vol. II, 2001, vol. III, 2003. Bd. dirs. Internat. Food and Agrl. Devel. and Econ. Coop., U.S. AID, 1992-94; mem. tri-lateral task force on N.Am. Higher Edn. Coop., USIA, 1993-95; trustee SIOP Found., 1998-2001, AMMA Found., Denison U., 2000-2002; mem. Pres. Bush's Commn. on Minority Bus. Devel., 1990-92, U.S. Com. of the Pacific Econ. Coop. Coun., 1995—. Sr. Fulbright scholar Found. for Scholarly Exchange, Republic China, 1978-79; recipient DAAD, Rep. Germany, 1984; Fellow NDEA U.S. Dept. of Edn., 1968-71. Fellow APA, Am. Psychol. Soc.

**MOBY, (RICHARD MELVILLE HALL),** musician; b. NYC, Sept. 11, 1965; Founder Little Idiot Collective, 1982, Area:One Festival, 2001; owner TeaNY, 2001—; performs benefit concerts for Inst. for Music & Neurologic Function. Musician: (albums) Instinct Dance, 1991, The Story So Far, 1993, Ambient, 1993, Everything is Wrong, 1995, Animal Rights, 1996, The End of Everything, 1996, Play, 1999, Play: The B Sides, 2000, 18, 2002 (Billboard top electronic album, 2002), 18 B-Sides, 2003, Baby Monkey, 2004, Hotel, 2005, (singles include) Go, 1991, Move, 1993, Why Does My Heart Feel So Bad?, 1999 (VIVA Comet award, best internat. video, 2000), Natural Blues, 2000, South Side, 2000 (MTV Music Video award, best male video, 2001, VH1/Vogue Fashion award for visionary video, 2001), We Are All Made of Stars, 2002 (MTV Video award, best cinematography, 2002), Lift Me Up, 2005; performer: (TV series) Senor Moby's House of Music, 2002. Named Best Dance/DJ Artist of the yr., Rolling Stone, 2001, Best Dance Artist, 2002. Mem.: Amend.org (bd. dirs.), MoveOn.org, PETA. Avocation: activism. Office: c/o MCT Mgmt No 1003 333 W 52nd St New York NY 10019*

**MOCEANU, DOMINIQUE,** retired Olympic athlete; b. Hollywood, Calif., Sept. 30, 1981; Mem. Nat. Team, 1992—93, 1993—94, 1995—96, 1999; coach Gymnastics World, Ohio, 2002—. Competitions include U.S. Classic, 1991, 92, 93, U.S. Gymnastics Championships, 1992, Am. Classic, 1993, U.S. Olympic Festival, 1993, Coca-Cola Nat. Championships, 1993, 94, 95, 96, Am. Classic/World Championships, 1994, Am. Classic/Pan Am. Games, 1995, World Team Trials, 1995, U.S. Olympic Trials, 1996, John Hancock U.S. Gymnastics Championships, 1997, 98; mem. U.S. Olympic Team, Sydney, 2000. Named 1st pl. balance beam, U.S. Classic, Salt Lake City, 1991, 2d pl. in balance beam jr. divsn., U.S. Gymnastics Championships, Columbus, 1992, 2d pl. in all around, 1st team vault, uneven bars and floor exercise, Jr. Pan Am. Games, 1992, 1st pl. in team and balance beam, 3d pl. in uneven bars, Internat. Tournament of Jr. Women's Gymnastics, Charleroi, Belgium, 1993, 1st pl. in all around, vault and team floor exercise, 3d in uneven bars and balance beam jr. divsn., Coca-Cola Nat. Championships, Nashville, 1994, 1st pl. in team all around, 1st pl. in vault, 3d pl. in balance beam and floor exercise, Am. Classic-Pan Am. Games Trials, Oakland, Calif., 1995, 1st pl. in all around, 2d pl. in floor exercise, 3d pl. in vault, Coca-Cola Nat. Championships, New Orleans, 1995, 1st pl. in all around, World Team Trials, Austin, 1995, 1st pl. in uneven bars, 2d pl. in balance beam, Reese's Internat. Gymnastics Cup, Portland, 1995, 1st pl. in all around, team and floor exercise, 3d pl. in vault and balance beam, 2d pl. in uneven bars, Visa Challenge, Fairfax, Va., 1995, 3d pl. all around for team, 2d pl. team balance beam, World Championships, Sabae, Japan, 1995, ISOC SportsWoman of Month (2), 1995, individual all-around finalist, World Championship Team, 1997; recipient Silver and Bronze medals, World Championships, 1995, Gold medal team competition, Atlanta Olympic Games, 1996, Gold medal Goodwill Games, 1998. Avocations: swimming, reading, music. Office: Gymnastics World 6630 Harris Rd Cleveland OH 44147

**MOCH, KENNETH IAN,** entrepreneur; b. White Plains, N.Y., Sept. 11, 1954; s. Gerald Marvin and Joan Shirley (Kahn) Moch; m. Ellen Gray Stolzman, July 27, 1987; children: Jonathan Manley, Stephen Bettmann. AB in Biochemistry, Princeton U., 1976; MBA, Stanford U., 1980. Cons. Channing, Weinberg & Co., Inc., N.Y.C., 1976-78; Sr. cons. McKinsey & Co., Inc., Chgo., 1980-82; v.p. Liposome Co., Inc., Princeton, N.J., 1982-88; mng. gen. ptnr. Catalyst Ventures, Ltd., Balt., 1988-90; pres., CEO Biocyte Corp., 1985—90; sr. v.p. Acteon, 1995—98; pres., CEO Alteon, Inc., 1998—. Mem. Stanford Bus. Sch. Alumni Assn. (pres. N.Y. chpt. 1990—). Avocations: theater, soccer. Office: Alteon Inc 6 Campus Dr Parsippany NJ 07054-4406

**MOCK, BEVERLY A.,** geneticist, researcher; m. Richard P. Nordan (dec. June 7, 1998); children: Alex, Chris. MS, U. Md., 1980, PhD in zoology, 1983. Studies on the genetics of susceptibility to parasitic diseases Dept. Immunology Walter Reed Army Inst. Rsch.; assoc. dir. sci. planning Ctr. Cancer Rsch., Nat. Cancer Inst., 1999—2004, chief Lab. Genetics, 2004—, head Cancer Genetics Sect., Lab. Genetics. Office: Lab Genetics Ctr Cancer Rsch 37 Convent Dr Bldg 37 Rm 3146 Bethesda MD 20892-4258 Office Phone: 301-496-2360. Office Fax: 301-402-1031. E-mail: bev@helix.nih.gov.

**MOCK, DAVID CLINTON, JR.,** internist; b. Redlands, Calif., 1922; s. David Clinton and Eithel (Benson) Mock; m. Marcella Enriqueta Fellin, 1952. AB, U. So. Calif., 1944; MD, M.H.D., Hahnemann Med. Coll., 1948. Intern Hahnemann Hosp., Phila., 1948-49; resident San Mateo (Calif.) County Hosp., 1949-51, 54, VA Hosp., Oklahoma City, 1954-55; research fellow in exptl. therapeutics U. Okla., Oklahoma City, 1956-57, L.N. Upjohn fellow, 1958, dir. exptl. therapeutics unit, 1959-62; dir. preceptorship program, 1968-76; assoc. prof. medicine U. Okla., Oklahoma City, 1963-72, prof., 1972-84, prof. emeritus medicine, 1984—, assoc. dean student affairs, 1970-76, assoc. dean postdoctoral edn., 1976-82, dir. continuing med. edn., 1980-83, dir. Transitional Yr. program, 1980-84, dir. History of Medicine program, 1982-84. Chief med. svc., Navajo Base Hosp., Ft. Defiance, Ariz., 1951-53; assoc. faculty homeopathy Royal London Homeopathic Hosp. Capt. USPHS, 1951-99, res.; now ret. Fellow: ACP; mem.: N.Y. Acad. Scis., Am. Fedn. Medical Rsch. Unitarian Universalist. Home: 570 Alameda Blvd Coronado CA 92118-1617

**MOCK, FRANK MACKENZIE,** lawyer; b. South Bend, Ind., May 17, 1944; s. Frank Carlton and Julia (Baughmann) M.; m. Virginia Johns, Dec. 31, 1974 (div. Feb. 1991); children: Shannon, John, Bridget; m. Christine Mall, June 1995; 1 child, Mackenzie Ann. BA, Duke U., 1966, JD, 1969. Bar: Fla. 1969. Assoc. Mahoney, Adams, Criser, Jacksonville, Fla., 1969-74, ptnr., 1977-92; gen. counsel Builders Investment Group, Valley Forge, Pa., 1974-77; ptnr. Baker & Hostetler, Orlando, Fla., 1992—, Ruden McClosky, Orlando, Fla. Mem. ABA, Am. Coll. Mortgage Lawyers, Duval County Bar Assn., Orange County Bar Assn., Dade County Bar Assn., Palm Beach County Bar Assn., Turnaround Mgmt. Assn. Republican. Episcopalian. Avocations: hiking, fishing, reading. Home: 2147 Santa Antilles Rd Orlando FL 32806-1533 Office Phone: 407-244-8001. Business E-mail: frank.mock@ruden.com.

**MOCK, JOAN BODET,** music educator; b. Houston, Dec. 3, 1937; d. Edward Bodet and Dorothy Crawford; m. Donald P. Garrett, 1966 (dec. 1985); children: William Clifford Garrett, Christopher Paul Garrett; m. Raymond Cecil Mock, July 7, 2002; 1 child from previous marriage, Charles H. Edwards II. B Music Edn., Ind. U., 1960; postgrad., U. N.Mex. Cert. tchr. N.Mex. Tchr. Espanola (N.Mex.) H.S., 1963-64, Hope H.S., Albuquerque, 1978—79; tchr. group piano lessons Piano Store Orgn., Colorado Springs, 1969—70; pvt. tchr. Garrett's Sch. Piano and Voice, Albuquerque; substitute tchr. Albuquerque Pub. Schs. Soloist for Ed Sullivan, Houston, 1956. Performer: Houston Little Theater, 1954—56, Acola Theater, 1970—79, The Ballad Hunter TV Program, 1954—56; dir.: O.P.E.R.A., 1978; contbr. poems to lit. publs. Soloist Christ Unity Ch., Albuquerque, 1988—92. Inst. Work scholar, Ind. U., 1957—60. Mem.: Albuquerque Music Tchrs. Assn., Nat. Music Tchrs. Assn., Nat. Fedn. Music Clubs. Home and Office: 10401 Crosscut Dr NW Albuquerque NM 87114 Office Phone: 505-350-7612.

**MOCK, MELINDA SMITH,** orthopedic nurse specialist, consultant; b. Austell, Ga., Nov. 15, 1947; d. Robert Jehu and Emily Dorris (Smith) Smith; m. David Thomas Mock, Oct. 20, 1969. ASN, DeKalb Coll., 1972. RN Ga., orthop. nurse specialist, cert. orthop. nurse; life care planner. Nursing technician Ga. Bapt. Hosp., Atlanta, 1967, staff nurse, 1979; asst. corr. Harcourt, Brace & World Pub. Co., Atlanta, 1968-69; receptionist, sec. Goodbody & Co., Atlanta, 1969-70; nursing asst. DeKalb Gen. Hosp., Decatur, Ga., 1970-71; staff nurse Drs.' Meml. Hosp., Atlanta, 1972-73; staff nurse, relief charge nurse Shallowford Cmty. Hosp., Atlanta, 1973, charge nurse, 1973-76, head nurse, 1976-79, orthop. nurse specialist emergency rm., 1979; rehab. specialist, sr. rehab. specialist Internat. Rehab. Assocs., Inc., Norcross, Ga., 1981, rehab. supr., 1981-82; cons., founder, propr. Healthcare Cost Cons., Inc., Alpharetta, Ga., 1982-83; cons., founder, pres., 1983—. Legis. com. adv. coun. Ga. Bd. Nursing, Atlanta, 1984—85; adv. coun. Milton HS Coop. Bus. Edn., 1986—89; task force profl. liability ins. Nat. Fedn. Splty. Nursing Orgns., 1987—89; mem. Congressman Patrick Swindall Sr. Citizen Adv. Coun., 1988, Congressman Ben Jones Vets. Affairs Adv. Coun., 1989—92, White Ho. Conf. Small Bus., 1995, Congressman Newt Gingrich Small Bus. Adv. Coun., 1997—99; apptd. Congl. Small Bus. Summit, 1998; apptd. Congressman Tom Price Health Delivery & Care Advisory Coun., 2005—. Parliamentarian Cherokee County Rep. Women, 2004; atl. del.-at-large Nat. Rep. Conv., 1996; dep. voter registrar Fulton County, Ga., 1983—87; Rep. treas. 23d House Dist.; active various coms. and positions Fulton County Rep. Party, 1989—2001; Rep. treas. 41st House Dist., 1993—97; mem. state exec. com. Ga. Rep. Party, 1997—99; 1st vice chairwoman Rep. 6th Congl. Dist., 1993—97, chmn., 1997—99; vice chair 7th Congl. Dist. Ga. Rep. Party, 2003—05, 7th Dist. GOP com., 2005; del. various convs., 1993—; mem. Chattahoochee Rep. Women, 1989—2001, chmn. campaign com., 1992—94, rec. sec., 1995—2001; chmn. nominating com. House Dist. 23, 1990; mem. steering com. Re-Elect State Rep. Tom Campbell, 1990; mem. campaign staff Re-Elect State Senator Sallie Newbill, 1990, 1992, 1994; mem. election adv. campaign Elect Matt Towery for Lt. Gov., 1990, Elect Bob Barr U.S. Senate, 1991—92; mem. election com. Mark Burkhalter for State Rep.; vol. campaign staff Re-Elect Congressman Newt Gingrich, 1992, 1994, 1996, 1998; mem. Cherokee County Rep. Party, 2001—; asst. poll mgr. Cherokee County Elections, 2004; rules com. mem. Ga. Fedn. Rep. Women; county co-chmn. Price for Congress, 2006; vol. campaign staff Elect Tom Price to State Senate, 1996, Re-Elect Tom Price to U.S. Congress. Recipient Nat. Disting. Svc. Registry award, 1987, Outstanding Alumni award Ga. Perimeter Coll., 2006; named Outstanding Young Women Am., 1984. Mem. Nat. Assn. Orthop. Nurses (nat. policies com. 1981-82, chmn. govt. rels. com. 1987-90, nat. treas. 1991-95, nat. pres. elect 1998-99, pres. 1999-2000, Nurse in Washington intern 1987, 99, legis. contbr. editor news 1989, chmn. legis workshop 1989, co-chmn. legis. workshop 1990, guest editl. Orthop. Nursing Jour. 1988, Ann. Congress del. 1982, 91-94, 96, 98-2001, 2003, 2005, Pres.'s award 1992, Outstanding Contbn. to NAON award 1996, chmn. budget and fin. com. 1991-95, nat. bylaws and policies com. 1995-98, bylaws and policies com. Atlanta chpt. 1994-96, pres-elect Atlanta chpt. 1996-97, 2004-05, pres. 1997-98, 2005-06, program dir. 2002-04), Orthop. Nurses Assn. (nat. bd. dirs. 1977-79, nat. treas. 1979-80), Coun. Splty. Nursing Orgns. Ga. (nominating com. 1976-77), Assn. Rehab. Nurses (bd. dirs. Ga. chpt. 1980-81, del. people-to-people program to China 1981, 2006, 2006), Nat. Fedn. Ind. Bus. (guardian 1988—, leadership coun. 1990—, healthcare task force chmn. 1992-2005, vice-chmn./fed. liaison Ga. adv. coun. 1995-2005), Am. Bd. Nursing Specialities (chmn. nominating com. 1993-95, chmn. com. on splty. bd. rev. 1993-95), Ga. Jaycees (dist. 4C rep. Ga. Jaycee Legis. 1984-85), Ga. Seatbelt Coalition, Orthop. Nurses Cert. Bd. (bd. dirs. 1991-96, pres. 1992-93, task force on advanced practice cert. 1991-92), Nurth Fulton C. of C. (vice chmn. health svc. effectiveness alliance 1984-85, chmn. 1985-86, co-chmn./editor periodical 1985, 3rd Quarter Workhorse award 1985), Alpharetta Jaycees (adminstrv. v.p. 1984-85, internal v.p. 1985-86), Alpharetta Jaycee Women (bd. dirs. 1983), Ga. Perimeter Coll. Nursing Alumni Assn. (dir. 2000-05, pres. 2005—), Ga. Perimeter Coll. Alumni Assn. (bd. dirs. 2005—, Outstanding Alumni award 2006), Nat. Assn. Orthopadic Nurses Found. (trustee, treas. 2005—06, pres. 2006—). Baptist. Avocations: reading, community service activities, scrapbooking. Office: Healthcare Cost Cons Inc PO Box 466 Alpharetta GA 30009-0466 Office Phone: 770-475-9454.

**MOCK, THEODORE JAYE,** finance educator; b. Traverse City, Mich., May 28, 1941; s. Raymond Doris and Georgeann (Lardie) M.; m. Mary Jo Icenhower, Mar. 25, 1962; children: Christopher, Cameron BS in Math., Ohio State U., 1963, MBA in Fin., 1964; PhD in Bus. Adminstrn., U. Calif.-Berkeley, 1969. Dir. AIS Research Ctr. UCLA, 1969-73; dir. Ctr. Acctg. Research, Arthur Andersen Alumni prof. acctg. U. So. Calif., 1982—. Vis. prof. Norwegian Sch. Econs. and Bus., Bergen, 1988, Bond U., Gold Coast, Australia, 1990, 92, So. Cross U., Lismore, Australia, 1994, Australia Nat. U., 2002—; adj. prof. U. Maastricht, The Netherlands, 1991—; hon. prof. Hong Kong City U., 1995-98; bd. dirs. Maastricht (The Netherlands) Acctg. Rsch. Ctr., U. Limburg, 1991—; Shaw prof. Nanyang Tech. U., Singapore, 1997, Tang Peng Yeu; vis. prof. Nat. U. Singapore, 2000. Author: (monographs) Risk Assessment, 1985, Internal Accounting Control (Am. Acctg. Assn. Wildman medal), 1983, Measurement and Accounting Information Criteria, 1976, Impact of Future Technology on Auditing, 1988, Auditing and Analytic Review, 1989, Belief Functions in Business Decisions, 2002; mem. editorial bd. Auditing: A Jour. of Practice & Theory, 1983-86, 88-93, 99—, editor, 1993-96; mem. editorial bd. The Acctg. Rev., 1972-78, Internat. Jour. Auditing, 1998—. Recipient CPA Faculty Excellence award Calif. CPA Found. for Edn. and Rsch., 1983; Fulbright scholar U. Otago, Dunedin, New Zealand, 1988, U. Limburg, Maastricht, The Netherlands, 1993. Mem. Acctg. Orgns. and Soc. (editorial bd. 1978-93), Am. Acctg. Assn. (dir. rsch. 1982-84, acad. vice chmn. auditing sect. 1990-91, chair auditing sect. 1996, Collaboration award with AICPA, 1998, Outstanding Auditing Educator award 2003). Office: U So Calif Sch Acctg Los Angeles CA 90089-0001

**MOCKER, HANS WALTER,** physicist; b. Teplice, Czech Republic, Feb. 22, 1929; came to U.S., 1960; s. Emil and Marie (Schubert) M.; m. Carol Virginia Vines, Feb. 13, 1981; children: Peter, Nancy. MS in Physics, Inst. Tech., Darmstadt, Germany, 1954; PhD in Physics, U. Innsbruck, Austria, 1959. Sr. rsch. scientist rsch. dept. Honeywell, Mpls., 1960—65, prin. rsch. scientist sys. and rsch., 1965—69, sect. chief sys. and rsch., 1969—78, prin. rsch. fellow sys. and rsch., 1978—93; fellow Tech. Ctr. Alliant Tech. Sys., Mpls., 1991—93; cons. Electro-Optics Laser Sys., Dothan, Ala., 1994—. Physicist Farbenfabriken Bayer, Krefeld, Germany, 1959-60; mem. advanced group on electronic devices Undersec. of. Def., Washington, 1977-78; presenter in field. Co-author: Design of Infrared and Laser Systems, 1981; contbr. articles to profl. jours. including Laser Focus, Applied Optics, Applied Physics Letters, IEEE Jour. Quant. Electr. Coach Minn. Soccer Assn., Mpls., 1981-83. Recipient H.W. Sweatt award, 1968, ir-100 award Indsl. Rsch. Mag., 1969, 77, Excellence in Oral Presentation, Soc. Automotive Engrs., 1993; named one of 7 Wonders of Engring., Minn. Soc. Profl. Engrs., 1970. Achievements include patents for apparatus for supervising proportion of magnetically active component in a fluid, for ring laser biased to permit two equal intensity transition frequencies to be generated in opposite directions, for optical system for laser doppler homodyne detection, for relaxation laser synchronizer for pulsed laser operation, for rapidly tunable laser, for method and means for removing claddings from optical fibers, for rapid wavelength switching of IR lasers with Bragg Cells, for laser doppler velocimeter using stable semiconductor or solid-state lasers, for scanning laser helmet mounted sight, for laser cavity helmet mounted sight, for solid-block homodyne interferometer, for look-ahead windshear detector by filtered Raleigh-scattered light. Home: 204 Westbrook Rd Dothan AL 36303-2952

**MOCKLER, ESTHER JAYNE,** state senator; b. Jackson, Wyo., Sept. 21, 1957; d. Franklin and Nancy (Fisher) Mockler. BA in Polit. Sci., Wellesley Coll., 1980. Legal asst., 1981-84; legal adminstr., 1984-87; tchr., cons., 1987—; exec. dir. Wyo. Dem. Party, 1993-95; mem. from Dist. 44 Wyo. Ho. of Reps., Cheyenne, 1992—96; mem. from Dist. 8 Wyo. Senate, Cheyenne, 1996—. Mem. Audubon Wyo. Bd. Office: PO Box 1857 Cheyenne WY 82003-1857 Office Phone: 307-632-5883.

**MOCKLER, JOLEE MARIE,** art educator; b. Kenosha, Wis., June 21, 1957; d. Frank A. and Josephine (Pavelich) Bobusch; m. John R. Mockler, Feb. 20, 1982. BA in art edn., Carthage Coll., 1979; MS secondary edn., U. Wis., 2000. Lic. Art Edn. K-12 Wis. Elem. art tchr. Kenosha Unified Sch., Kenosha, Wis., 1979—80; adj. prof. Edgewood Coll., Art Edn. Dept., Madison, Wis., 2003—; art instr. chairperson Reedsburg Area HS, Wis., 1988—; bus. owner Homeworks Furniture and Accents, Reedsburg, Wis., 1991—98. Supr. student tchrs. Edgewood Coll., Madison, Wis., 1996—, Luther Coll., Decorah, Iowa, 2000; art dept. chairperson Reedsburg Sch. Dist., Reedsburg, Wis., 1998—; judge art shows Sauk County Art Assn., Baraboo, 2006. Co-author: Reedsburg Sch. Dist., K-12 Art Curriculum, 1988—89. Judge for rep. Tammy Baldwin's Congressional Art Competition 2nd Congressional, Madison, Wis., 2003; active Sauk County Basset Hound Rescue. Recipient Top Notch Tchr. award, Wis. TV Channel 3, 2003, Excellence in Edn. award, Reedsburg BOE, 1999, Tchr. of Month award, Reedsburg Area HS, 1998, 2003, Outstanding Am. Tchrs. award, Nat. Honor Roll, 2005—06. Mem.: NEA, Sauk County Art Assn., Reedsburg Edn. Assn., Wis. Edn. Assn. Home: PO Box 243 La Valle WI 53941 Office: Reedsburg Area HS 1100 S Albert Ave Reedsburg WI 53959 Office Phone: 608-524-4327 ext. 1134. Business E-Mail: jmockler@rsd.k12.wi.us.

**MOCKO, GEORGE PAUL,** minister; b. Little Falls, N.Y., Feb. 15, 1934; s. George and Anna (Swancara) M.; m. Elizabeth Carol Davidson, Sept. 2, 1956 (dec); children: David (dec.), Paul, Kristopher, Elissa; m. Delores Hay, Oct. 16, 2004. BA, Hartwick Coll., 1956; BD, Phila. Sem., 1959, STM, 1972; DD (hon.), Gettysburg Coll., 1978. Ordained to ministry Evang. Luth. Ch. in Am., 1959. Pastor Jacob's and Outwood Chs., Pine Grove, Pa., 1959-62; assoc. pastor St Mark's Ch., Wilmington, Del., 1962-65, sr. pastor, 1965-78, Ascension Evang. Luth. Ch., Towson, Md., 1978-91; bishop Del.-Md. Synod Evang. Luth Ch. in Am., Towson, 1991-2000, ret., 2000. Author books; contbr. articles to profl. jours. Mem. Evang. Luth. Ch. Home: 501 Sussex Rd Baltimore MD 21286-7609 Personal E-mail: GPmocko@aol.com. *Colossians speaks of Christ as the one in whom "all things hold together". I know that Christ is the one who holds me together. Proclaiming and living his life, the church holds our society together.*

**MODABBER, ZIA F.,** lawyer; b. Jan. 9, 1962; BA, U. Calif., Berkeley, 1984; JD, Loyola Law Sch., 1988. Bar: Calif. 1988, U.S. Dist. Ct. (ctrl. dist.) Calif., U.S. Dist. Ct. (no. dist.), U.S. Ct. Appeals (9th cir.). Assoc. Wyman Bautzer Kuchel & Silbert, LA; ptnr. Katten Muchin Zavis Rosenman, LA. Mem.: ABA, LA County Bar Assn., St. Thomas More Law Honor Soc. Office: Katten Muchin Zavis Rosenman Ste 2600 2029 Century Park E Los Angeles CA 90067 Office Phone: 310-788-4627. Office Fax: 310-712-8462. E-mail: zia.modabber@katterlaw.com.

**MODAK, JAYANT PANDURANG,** mechanical engineer, consultant; b. Surat, India, Apr. 18, 1942; s. Pandurang Narayan and Nalini Pandurang Modak; m. Suhasini Jayant Marathe, July 14, 1967; children: Amit, Sarika. B of Engring., SVNIT, Surat, India, 1964, B of Engring., 1965; M of Engring., VNIT, Nagpur, India, 1973, PhD, 1980. Mech.-elect engr. MCC Ltd., Mumbai, India, 1966—67; assoc. lectr. mech. dept. VNIT, Nagpur, India, 1967—73; lectr. mech. dept., 1973-81, asst. prof. mech. dept., 1981—90, prof. mech. dept., 1990—99, dean, 1994—96; prof., dean PCE&A, Nagpur, India, 1999—. Cons. in field. Contbr. articles to profl. jours. Sec. Mukund Apt. Flat Owners Soc., Nagpur, India, 2000—02, pres., 2005—. Mem.: Indian Soc. for Tech. Edn. (life). Achievements include inventor, patentee in field. Home: A/6 Mukund Appts Shradhanand Peth Nagpur 440022 India Office: Priyadarshini Coll Engring and Arch CRPF Campus Nagpur 440019 India Office Phone: 91-07104-236381, 237307. Office Fax: 91-07104-237681. E-mail: jayant.modak@radiffmail.com.

**MODANO, MIKE (MICHAEL MODANO),** professional hockey player; b. Livonia, Mich., June 7, 1970; Right wing/ctr. Minn. North Stars, 1988—93, Dallas Stars, 1993—. Mem. US Olympic Hockey Team, Nagano, Japan, 1998, Salt Lake City, 2002, Torino, Italy, 06, Team USA, Canada Cup, 1991, Team USA, World Cup of Hockey, 1996, 2004. Named to NHL All-Star Game, 1993, 1998—2000, 2003, 2004. Achievements include being a member of World Cup Champion Team USA, 1996; being a member of Stanley Cup Champion Dallas Stars, 1999; being captain of USA Olympics Hockey Team, 2006. Office: c/o Dallas Stars 2601 Avenue of the Stars Frisco TX 75034*

**MODE, CHARLES J.,** mathematician, educator; b. Bismarck, N.D., Dec. 29, 1927; s. Charles and Fannie E. (Hansen) M.; m. Eleanore L. Perdelwitz; 1 dau., Martha Lisa. BS in Genetics, N.D. State U., 1952; MS in Genetics, Kans. State U., 1953; PhD in Genetics, U. Calif., Davis and Berkeley, 1956; postgrad. in stats. (Univ. fellow), N.C. State U., 1956-57. Asst. prof. math. Mont. State U., 1957-59, asso. prof., 1960-62, prof., 1963-66, mem. genetics group, 1957-66; asso. prof. math. stats. SUNY, Buffalo, 1966-70; prof. math. Drexel U., 1970—. Cons. to industry. Author: (books) Multitype Branching Processes - Theory and Applications, 1971, Stochastic Processes in Demography and Their Computer Implementation, 1985, Stochastic Processes in Epidemiology, HIV/AIDS, Other Infectious Diseases and Computers, 2000; contbr. articles to profl. publs.; editor (assoc.): (jour.) Math. Biosci., 1975—. Mem. Inst. Math. Stats., Biometric Soc., Am. Math. Soc., AAAS, Population Assn. Am., Sigma Xi, Phi Kappa Phi, Pi Mu Epsilon. Home: 502 Balsam Rd Cherry Hill NJ 08003-3202 Office: Drexel Univ Dept Math Philadelphia PA 19104 Business E-Mail: cmode@math.drexel.edu.

**MODELL, JEROME HERBERT,** anesthesiologist, educator; b. St. Paul, Sept. 9, 1932; s. William and Frieda (Singer) M.; m. Shirley Graves, Nov. 25, 1977; children: Charles, Jack, Julie. BA, U. Minn., 1954, BS, MD, 1957; DSc (hon.), U. Fla., 2004. Intern U.S. Naval Hosp., St. Albans,

NY, 1957-58, resident, 1958-60; practice medicine specializing in anesthesiology Gainesville, Fla., 1969—; attending staff U.S. Naval Hosp., St. Albans 1960-61, chief anesthesiology Pensacola, Fla., 1961-63; asso. prof. dept. anesthesiology U. Miami (Fla.) Sch. Medicine, 1963-69; prof., chmn. dept. anesthesiology U. Fla. Coll. Medicine, Gainesville, 1969-92; sr. assoc. dean clin. affairs, 1990-95; exec. assoc. dean, 1996-97, interim dean, 1997; assoc. v.p. U. Fla. Health Sci. Ctr. Affiliations, 1992-96. Assoc. v.p. U. Fla. Health Sci., 1998-2000, emeritus prof. 2000—, courtesy prof. large animal scis., 1999—. Author: The Pathophysiology and Treatment of Drowning and Near-Drowning, 1971, (with others) Introduction to Life Support, 1973; also numerous scientific articles. Served to lt. comdr. USN, 1957-63. Recipient Rsch. Career Devel. award, NIH, 1967—69, Lifetime Achievement award, Am. Soc. Critical Care Anesthesiologists, 1991. Mem. AMA, AAAS, Assn. U. Anesthetists, Am. Soc. Anesthesiologists (Disting. Svc. award, 2005), N.Y. Acad. Scis., Am. Soc. Chest Physicians. Home: PO Box 14347 Gainesville FL 32604-2347 Office: U Fla Coll Medicine PO Box 100254 Gainesville FL 32610-0254 Office Phone: 352-265-8076.

**MODELL, STEPHEN MARK,** medical researcher, educator; b. Detroit, June 22, 1958; s. Richard Martin and Sola Jane (Hamburger) M.; m. Wanpen Prasoptham, Jan. 14, 1988; 1 child, Marrisa Lynne. AB in Philosophy, Stanford U., 1980; MD, Med. Coll. Ohio, 1984; MS in Clin. Rsch. Design/Statis. Analysis, U. Mich., 1991. Asst. coord. The Resource for Pub. Health Policy U. Mich. Sch. Pub. Health, Ann Arbor, 1987-89; rsch. asst., dept. psychiatry U. Mich., Ann Arbor, 1989-90, Genome Ethics Com. rsch. assoc., 1992-94, Coun. Genetics and Soc. rsch. assoc. dept. health mgmt. and policy, 1995-98; rsch. dir. genetics policy dept. health mgmt. and policy, 1999—2001; dir. dissemination pub. health Mich. Ctr. for Genomics and Pub. Health, 2001—. Mem. pres.'s coun. Med. Coll. Ohio, 1992—. Genome studies sect. editor Ultimate Reality and Meaning, 1995—; editor Studies in Biophilosophy, 1997, Studies in Medicine and Health, 2006. Recipient honorable mention Nellie Westerman prize competition in clin. rsch. ethics, Am. Fedn. Clin. Rsch., 1995. Mem. AMA, Am. Fedn. Med. Rsch., N.Y. Acad. Scis., Maimonides Soc., Internat. Soc. Study of Human Ideas on Ultimate Reality and Meaning (bd. dirs. 1994—, treas. 1999-2000, v.p. 2001-02, pres. 2003-04), Rotary (hon.). Avocations: book discussion groups, water sports, jogging, hiking, travel. Office: U Mich Sch Pub Health SPH-II CBPH M4157 109 S Observatory St Ann Arbor MI 48109-2029 E-mail: mod@umich.edu.

**MODEN, JOLEEN,** communications executive; B in Bus. Adminstr. and Acctg., Kans. State U. CPA. Ptnr. Coopers & Lybrand; v.p., CFO, treas. Signature Home Care Grp.; dir. corp. audit PepsiCo Inc.; asst. contr. internal audit GTE, 1998—2000; sr. v.p. internal auditing Verizon Comm. Inc., NYC, 2000—. Office: Verizon Comms Inc Verizon Ctr VC44E227 One Verizon Way Basking Ridge NJ 07920-1997 E-mail: joleenmoden@verizon.com.

**MODERACKI, EDMUND ANTHONY,** music educator, conductor; b. Hackensack, N.J., July 18, 1946; s. Edmund Joseph and Helen Theresa (Fisher) Moderacki; m. Brenda Wing Moderacki. BA, Montclair State Coll., 1968, postgrad., 1970—71; MA, Hunter Coll., 1970, postgrad., 1970—72, Newark State Coll., 1969—70, Seton Hall U., 1970, Rutgers U., 1976—78, Ctr. for Understanding Media, 1973. Tchr. music pub. schs., River Vale, NJ, 1968—; asst. condr. Ridgewood Symphony Orch., NJ, 1969—, trustee, pres., 1986—87, 1994—95; artistic dir. Ridgewood Symphony, 2001—; asst. condr. Adelphi Chamber Orch., 1994—95; condr. Project Symphony, 2003. Tuba soloist Rutherford Cmty. Band, Ridgewood Village Band, Waldwick Band, Ridgewood Concert Band, 1978—, trustee, 1985-2000, guest condr., 1985, 86, 88, 93; mgr. All Bergen High Sch. Band, 1994; condr. All Bergen County High Sch. Band, 2001 Author: Images of America: River Vale. Town historian River Vale; mem. steering com. Bergen County Teen Arts, 1991—; mem. River Vale Hist. Preservation Commn., 2004—. Recipient County Exec. Vol. award, 1991, Tchr. Recognition award Gov. of State of N.J., 1990; Bergen County PTA fellow, 1976. Mem. NEA, Music Educators Nat. Conf., N.J. Orch. Assn. (trustee 1981-85), N.J. Edn. Assn. (alt. del. assembly 1983-93, mem. state membership com. 1986—), Music Educators Bergen County (bd. mem. at-large 1995-97, treas. 1997-2000, pres.-elect 2000-02, pres. 2002-04, treas. 2004—), River Vale Edn. Assn. (pres. 1981-83, 88-91, 2000-03), Brigade Am. Revolution (bd. dirs. at large 1991-95, info. officer 1989-95, adj. 1996-2000, editor Brigade Press 2002-05), Phi Mu Alpha Sinfonia, Kappa Delta Pi. Home: 740 White Birch Rd Township Of Washington NJ 07676 Office: Woodside Sch Rivervale NJ 07675 Office Phone: 201-358-4000 ext. 2801.

**MODERY, RICHARD GILLMAN,** marketing executive, sales executive; b. Chgo., Sept. 20, 1941; s. Richard Gustave Modery and Betty Jane (Gillman) Modery Perok; m. Kay Francis Whitby, July 31, 1966 (div. July 1977); children: Stacey Lynn, Marci Kay; m. Anne-Marie Lucette Arsenault, Feb. 27, 1979. Student, Joliet Jr. Coll., 1959—61, Aurora Coll., 1963—65, Davenport Bus. Coll., 1969—71, Northwestern U., 1987. Engr., projects engr., projects mgr., mktg. products mgr. Rapistan, Inc., Grand Rapids, Mich., 1964—75; mgr. estimating, project mgmt., customer svc. E.W. Buschman Co., Cin., 1975—78; v.p. distbg. sales, v.p. engring. and sales, exec. v.p. Metzgar Conveyor Co., Grand Rapids, 1979—84; mng. dir. Metzco Internat (Ctrl. and S.Am.), Grand Rapids, 1981—84, Transfer Technologies, Inc., Grand Rapids, 1984—87; gen. ptnr., pres., CEO Nat. Monument Co., Grand Rapids, 1986—89; v.p. Translogic Corp., Denver, 1987—88; corp. officer, v.p. mktg., field ops. and sales S.I. Handling Systems, Inc., Easton, Pa., 1988—91; pres Handling Concepts, Inc., Chgo., 1993—, Modery Sys., Inc., Chgo., 1997—2004; ret., 2004. Agt. Muratic-Murata Automated Sys., Inc., 1997—2000. Bd. dirs. Naperville Humane Soc., Ill., 2001—05, mem. fin. and revenue generating com.; commr. Traffic Commn. City of East Grand Rapids, Mich., 1983—86. With U.S. Nat. Guard, 1963—69. Mem. Internat. Material Mgmt. Soc., Am. Mgmt. Assn., Material Handling Inst. Am., Material Handling Inst. (spkr. nat. confs.), Am. Mktg. Assn., Conveyor Equipment Mfrs. Assn., Material Handling Equipment Distbrs. Assn., Mason (32 degree). Achievements include patents in field. Avocations: golf, photography, power walking, computers. Home: 2255 Palmer Cir Naperville IL 60564-5672 Office: Handling Concepts Inc 2255 Palmer Cir Naperville IL 60564-5672 also: Modery Sys Inc 2255 Palmer Cir Naperville IL 60564-5672 Office Phone: 630-904-4642. Personal E-mail: dickmodery@sbcglobal.net.

**MODESITT, CAROL ANN,** vocalist, music educator, opera director; b. Mar. 6, 1947; BA, Utah State U., Logan, 1968; MusM, Ea. Ky. U., Richmond, 1973. Asst. prof. Utah State U., Logan, 1978-84; vis. artist Plymouth (N.H.) State Coll., 1990-93; assoc. prof. voice and opera So. Utah U., Cedar City, 1993—2006, chair music dept., 2005—06, prof., 2006—. Author: (ednl. software) Reindeer Ednl. Network, 1999; book reviewer: Nat. Opera Assn. Jour., 1998—; performer (debut recital): Carnegie Hall, 2002. Pres. Cedar City (Utah) Music Arts, 1999—2002, Cedar City Arts Coun., 2002—05. Recipient Contribution to Arts award, Cedar City C. of C., 2001. Mem.: NOW, Nat. Opera Assn. (west ctrl. region gov. 1997), Music Tchrs. Nat. Assn. (pres. Cedar City 1997—), Nat. Assn. Tchrs. of Singing (pres. Las Vegas chpt. 2005—). Home: 255 Sunnyview Rd Cedar City UT 84720-2897 Office Phone: 435-865-8166. Home Fax: 435-865-1732. Business E-Mail: modesitt@suu.edu.

**MODESITT, LELAND EXTON, JR., (L.E. MODESITT JR.),** consultant, writer, poet; b. Denver, Oct. 19, 1943; s. Leland Exton and Nancy Lila (Evans) M.; m. Virginia Dale Eschenburg, Sept. 16, 1964 (div. 1977); m. 2d, Christina Alma Gribben, Oct. 22, 1977 (div. 1991); children— Leland Exton, Susan Carnall, Catherine Grant, Nancy Mayo, Elizabeth Leanore, Kristen Linnea; m. Carol Ann James Hill, Jan. 4, 1992; step-children: Lara Beth Hill, Kevin L. Hill. B.A., Williams Coll., 1965; postgrad. U. Denver, 1970-71. Rsch. analyst C.A. Norgren Co., Littleton, Colo. 1969-70; assoc. Koelbel & Co., Denver, 1970-72; rsch. dir. Armstrong for Congress, Aurora, Colo., 1972; legis. asst. US Rep. William Armstrong, Washington, 1973-78; adminstrv. asst. US Rep. Ken Kramer, Washington, 1979-81; dir. legislation US EPA, Washington, 1981-84, spl. asst. external affairs, 1984-85; mem. Multinat. Bus. Svcs., 1985—91; instr. Georgetown U., 1980-81; lectr. Plymouth State U., 1990-93. Author novels: The Fires of Paratime, 1982 (main selection Sci.

Fiction Book Club, May, 1982), The Hammer of Darkness, 1985, The Ecologic Envoy, 1986, Dawn For a Distant Earth, 1987, The Silent Warrior, 1987, In Endless Twilight, 1988, The Magic of Recluce, 1991, The Towers of the Sunset, 1992, The Magic Engineer, 1994, The Order War, 1995, The White Order, 1998, Scion of Cyador, 2000, Legacies, 2002, Scepters, 2004, Flash, 2004, Wellspring of Chaos, 2004, Ordermaster, 2005, Alector's Choice, 2005, The Eternity Artifact, 2005, Cadmian's Choice, 2006; author short stories and poetry; contbr. articles to profl. jours. Served with USN, 1965-69, SE Asia. Home: 255 Sunnyview Rd Cedar City UT 84720-2897 Personal E-mail: lmodesitt@aol.com.*

**MODESTO, VICTOR L.,** surgeon; b. N.Y.C., Dec. 26, 1955; s. Arturo Colon and Eddy (Padilla) M.; m. Marianne Derby, July 1, 1978; 1 child, Victor Andrew. BA in Biology, State U. Coll. Buffalo, 1977; MD, N.Y. Medical Coll., 1981. Diplomate Am. Bd. Colorectal Surgery, Am. Bd. Surgery. Commd. col. U.S. Army, 1981; internship Walter Reed Army Medical Ctr., Washington, 1981-82, resident, 1983-87; fellow St. Luke's Roosevelt Medical Ctr., N.Y.C., 1993-94; general surgery Womack Army Medical Ctr., Fort Bragg, N.C., 1994-95, chief dept. surgery, 1996—; deputy comdr. clinical svcs. 44th Medical Brigade, Fort Bragg, N.C., 1998—. Cons. Fayetteville (N.C.) Veteran's Adminstrn. Medical Ctr., 1997—. Author: (with others) Selected Topics in Colon and Rectal Surgery, 1994, The Surgical Clinics of North America, 1994, Clinical Decision Making in Colorectal Surgery, 1995, Surgery of the Colon, Rectum, and Anus, 1995; contbr. articles to profl. jours. including Surgical Laparoscopy and Endoscopy, JAMA, Military Med., Am. Jour. Surgery. Decorated Army Commendation medal with three oak leaf clusters, Army Achievement medal with one oak leaf cluster, Meritorious Svc. medal with one oak leaf cluster; scholar Henry J. Kaiser Family Found., 1981. Fellow Internat. Coll. Surgeons, Am. Coll. Surgeons, Am. Soc. Colon Rectal Surgeons; mem. AMA, Soc. Am. Gastrointestinal Endoscopic Surgeons (resident edn. com. 1992-94), Soc. Laparoendoscopic Surgeons, Assn. Military Surgeons, 38th Parallel Medical Soc., Alpha Omega Alpha. Office Phone: 407-678-7557.

**MODIN, FREDRIK,** professional hockey player; b. Sundsvall, Sweden, Oct. 8, 1974; Left wing Brynas IF, Toronto Maple Leafs, 1996—99, Tampa Bay Lightning, 1999—2006, Columbus Blue Jackets, 2006—. Player NHL All-Star Game, 2001. Achievements include being a member of Stanley Cup Champion Tampa Bay Lightning, 2004; being a member of gold medal winning Swedish Hockey Team, Torino Olympics, Italy, 2006. Office: Columbus Blue Jackets Nationwide Arena 200 W Nationwide Blvd Columbus OH 43215*

**MODINE, MATTHEW AVERY,** actor; b. Loma Linda, Calif., Mar. 22, 1959; s. Mark and Dolores Modine; m. Caridad Rivera, Oct. 31, 1980; 2 children: Bowman, Ruby. Appeared in films Baby, Its You, 1983, Private School, 1983, Streamers, 1983 (Best Actor award, Venice Film Festival 1983), The Hotel New Hampshire, 1984, Mrs. Soffel, 1984, Birdy, 1984, Vision Quest, 1985, Full Metal Jacket, 1987, Orphans, 1987, Married to the Mob, 1988, Gross Anatomy, 1989, Memphis Belle, 1990, Pacific Heights, 1990, La Partita, 1991, Wind, 1992, Equinox, 1992, Luck, Trust and Ketchup, 1993, And the Band Played On, HBO, 1993 (Emmy nominee for Lead Actor in a Special, 1994), Short Cuts, 1993, The Browning Version, 1994, Bye Bye, Love, 1995, Fluke, 1995, Cutthroat Island, 1995, The Real Blonde, 1997, The Blackout, 1997, The Maker, 1997, If...Dog...Rabbit, 1998, Any Given Sunday, 1999, Very Mean Men, 2000, Nobody's Baby, 2001, In the Shadows, 2001, The Shipment, 2001, Hollywood North, 2003, Funky Monkey, 2004, Transporter 2, 2005, Mary, 2005, Opa!, 2005; TV films: Amy and the Angel, 1981, Jacob: A TNT Bible Story, 1994, What the Deaf Man Heard, 1997, Flowers of Algernon, 2000, The American, 2001, Jack and the Beanstalk: The Real Story, 2001, Redeemer, 2002, Hitler: The Rise of Evil, 2003, The Winning Season, 2004; TV miniseries: Into the West, 2005; numerous TV commls.; dir. short films Smoking, 1994, Jacob, 1992; dir., writer When I Was a Boy, 1993, ECE Pirate, 1997, Full Metal Jacket Diary, 2005; theatre appearances include Finishing the Picture, 2005, Resurrection Blues, 2006; theatre dir. 12 Angry Men.*

**MODISETT, JEFFREY A.,** lawyer, former state attorney general; b. Windfall, Ind., Aug. 10, 1954; s. James Richard and Diana T. Modisett; m. Jennifer Ashworth; June 9, 1990; children: Matthew Hunter Ashworth, Haden Nicholas. BA, UCLA, 1976; MA, Oxford (Eng.) U., 1978; JD, Yale U., 1981. Bar: Ind., Calif., D.C. Clk. to Hon. R. Peckham U.S. Dist. Ct. (no. dist.) Calif., San Francisco, 1981—82; asst. U.S. atty. Office U.S. Atty. (ctrl. dist.) Calif., L.A., 1982—88; issues dir. Evan Bayh for Gov., Indpls., 1988; exec. asst. to gov. State of Ind., Indpls., 1988—90; prosecutor Marion County, Indpls., 1991—94; sr. counsel Ice Miller Donadio & Ryan, Indpls., 1995—96; atty. gen. State of Ind., 1997—2000; dep. CEO, gen. counsel Dem. Nat. Conv., 2000; co-CEO TechNet, Palo Alto, Calif., 2000—01; ptnr. Manatt Phelps & Phillips LLP, 2001—02; mng. ptnr. Bryan Cave LLP, LA, 2002—. Chmn. Gov. Commn. for Drug Free Ind., Indpls., 1989—, Gov. Coun. on Impaired and Dangerous Driving, Indpls., 1989—; pres. Family Advocacy Ctr., Indpls., 1991—94, Hoosier Alliance Against Drugs, Indpls., 1993—96; dir. Cmty. Couns. of Indpls., 1991—93; chmn. Ind. Criminal Justice Inst., Indpls., 1989—90, dir., 1989—; vice chmn. Juvenile Justice and Youth Gang Study Com., Indpls., 1992—94; legal analyst Sta. WTHR-TV, Indpls., 1995—96. Author: Prosecutor's Perspective, 1991—94; editor-in-chief: Yale Jour. Internat. Law, 1980—81. Co-chair Ind. State Dem. Coordinated Campaign, Indpls., 1996. Named Top Lawyer, Indpls. Monthly mag., 1993; named to Sagamore of Wabash, State of Ind., 1995; recipient Spl. Enforcement award, U.S. Customs, 1988, Child Safety Adv. award, Automotive Safety for Children, 1997, STAR Alliance Impact award, 1998, Spirit of Ind. award, Am. Lung Assn., 1999. Mem.: Indpls. Bar Assn., Ind. Bar Assn. Democrat. Avocation: bicycling. Office: Bryan Cave LLP 120 Broadway, Ste 300 Santa Monica CA 90401 Office Phone: 310-576-2370. Office Fax: 310-576-2200 E-mail: jamodisett@bryancave.com

**MODLIN, HOWARD S.,** lawyer; b. NYC, Apr. 10, 1931; s. Martin and Rose Modlin; m. Margot S. Modlin, Oct. 18, 1956; children: James, Laura, Peter. AB, Union Coll., Schenectady, 1952; JD, Columbia U., 1955. Bar: N.Y. 1956, D.C. 1973. Assoc. Weisman, Celler, Spett & Modlin, P.C., N.Y.C., 1956-61, ptnr., 1961-76, mng. ptnr., 1976-95, pres., 1996—. Chmn. bd. dirs., sec. Gen. DataComm Industries, Inc., Naugatuck, Conn.; bd. dirs. Am.-Book-Stratford Press, Inc., N.Y.C., Fedders Corp., Liberty Corner, NJ, Trans-Lux Corp., Norwalk, Conn. Chmn. bd. dirs. Daus. of Jacob Geriat. Ctr., Bronx, N.Y. Mem. ABA, Assn. of Bar of City of N.Y., D.C. Bar Assn. Office: Weisman Celler Spett & Modlin PC 445 Park Ave New York NY 10022-2606 Office Phone: 212-371-5400.

**MODNY, CYNTHIA JEAN,** dermatologist; b. Jan. 23, 1945; d. Michael Theodore and Mary (Tabaka) M. BA, Mt. Holyoke Coll., 1967; MD, U. Va., Charlottesville, 1971. Diplomate Am. Bd. Dermatology. Intern Lenox Hill Hosp., N.Y.C., 1971-72; resident N.Y. Hosp./Cornell Med. Ctr., N.Y.C., 1972-75, instr. dermatology, 1976—81; practice medicine specializing in dermatology Montclair, N.J., 1976-92, Phoenix, 1994—. Pvt. practice cons. undersea medicine, Montclair, 1982-92; clin. instr. dermatology Skin and Cancer Unit, NYU Med. Ctr., N.Y.C., 1981-92; participant Physicians' Undersea Medicine Tng., NOAA, Miami, Fla., 1982; dir. Skin Cancer Inst., Montclair, 1984. Med. editor Dive Travel Report (monthly), 1983-92; contbr. article to Skin Diver mag. Bd. dirs. Montclair Sr. Citizens, 1984. Fellow Am. Acad. Dermatology; mem. Undersea Med. Soc., Am. Dermatologic Surgery, Princeton Club, Mt. Holyoke Club (N.Y.C.). Office: 1277 E Missouri Ave Ste 114 Phoenix AZ 85014-2916 Office Phone: 602-266-6556. Personal E-mail: moddoc@cox.net.

**MODRICH, PAUL L.,** biochemistry professor; b. Raton, N.Mex., June 13, 1946; BS in Biology, MIT, 1968; PhD in Biochemistry, Stanford U., 1973; postgrad., Harvard U., 1973-74. Asst. prof. chemistry U. Calif.; Berkeley, 1974; asst. prof. biochemistry Duke U., 1976, assoc. prof. biochemistry, 1980, prof. biochemistry, 1984; dir. program in genetics, 1989-92, investigator Howard Hughes Med. Inst., 1994—, James B. Duke prof. biochemistry.

Contbr. articles to profl. jours.; assoc. editor: Biochemistry, 1992-94, mem. editl. adv. bd., 1986-91, 95—; mem. editl. bd. Nucleic Acids Rsch., 1980-82, Jour. Biol. Chemistry, 1982-83. Recipient award in enzyme chemistry Pfizer, 1983, NAS, 1993, Mott prize in cancer rsch. GM, 1996, Medal of Honor for basic rsch., Am. Cancer Soc., 2005, Pasarow Found. award in cancer rsch. Fellow: Am. Acad. Arts & Sci.; Mem. NIH (mem. biochemistry study sect. 1980-84, NIH NIGMS merit award 1986), Am. Soc. Biochemistry and Molecular Biology (councillor 1989-92, 97—, mem. publs. com. 1995-97), Inst. Medicine. Office: Department of Biochemistry Nanaline H Duke Box 3711 DUMC Durham NC 27710 Office Phone: 919-684-2775.*

**MOE, ANDREW IRVING,** veterinarian; b. Tacoma, Jan. 2, 1927; s. Ole Andrew and Ingeborg (Gordham) M.; m. Dorothy Clara Becker, June 25, 1950 (dec. Nov. 30, 2001); children: Sylvia Moe McGowan, Pamela Moe Barker, Joyce. BS in Biology, U. Puget Sound, 1949; BA, Wash. State U., 1953, DVM, 1954. Meat cutter Art Hansen, Tacoma, 1943—48; gen. practice as vet. Baronti Vet. Hosp., Eugene, Oreg., 1956-57; vet. regulatory Calif. Animal Health br., resident vet. II Calif. Dept. Food & Agr., Modesto, 1957-64, acting vet.-in-charge Modesto Dist. office, vet. III, 1976-77, ret., 1990—. Watersafety instr. ARC, 1958-61. Capt. Vet. Corps., 1954-56, 62; lt. col. Biomed Scis. Corps. USAF, ret., 1982. Recipient Chief Vet. badge, 1975. Mem. VFW (life, comdr. post 4144 1998-2001, quartermaster 2000-02, trustee post 3199, 2004-06), No. San Joaquin Vet. Med. Assn. (pres. 1979), Calif. Acad. Vet. Medicine (charter), Mil. Officers Assn. of Am. (charter), Res. Officers Assn. (life), Ret. Officers Assn. (life), Assn. Mil. Surgeons U.S. (life), Sons of Norway, Am. Legion (life), Shriners (bd. dirs. Modesto Shrine 1995), Masons (life), (Illustrious Master Modesto chpt. 1983, Allied Masonic degrees, pres. Modesto Masonic Luncheon Club 1991, 98, Meritorious Svc. medal 1992, Man of Yr. award 1991), Scottish Rite (pres. Ctrl. Valley 1997, bd. dirs. 1998-2006), Presido Yacht Club Sausalito, Theta Chi, Alpha Psi. Lutheran. Home: 161 Norwegian Ave Modesto CA 95350-3542

**MOE, JANET ANNE,** elementary school educator, church organist; b. Sacramento, May 24, 1946; d. Joseph Robert and Virginia Lou (Jones) Mangan; m. Edward Earl Moe, Aug. 23, 1969 (dec. Aug. 2002); children: Erik John, Erin Jean Moe Mitchell. BA, Calif. Luth. U., 1968; std. secondary tchg. credential, Calif. State U., Sacramento, 1969, crosscultural, lang. and acad. devel. cert. (CLAD), 1996; cert. in Orff Schulwerk Levels I, II and III, U. Calif. Santa Cruz, 1987; MS, Nat. U., Sacramento, 2001, preliminary adminstrv. credential, 2001. Elem. tchr. Gloria Dei Luth. Sch., Sacramento, 1969—73; elem. music specialist Sacramento City Unified Sch. Dist., 1982—. All-city elem. choir coord. Sacramento City Unified Sch. Dist., 1999—2001; chorus dir. Sierra Mt. Music Camp, 2001; facilitator Calif. dept. edn. model arts project Sacramento City Unified Sch. Dist. Singer: Sacramento City Coll. Choir, 1998—2006. Touring choir Sacramento City Coll., Italy, 1998, Ireland, 2004, Scotland, 2004; touring choir So. Calif. and Hawaii Calif. Luth. U., 1967—68; task force to restore music and the fine arts Sacramento City Unified Sch. Dist., 1999—2000; organist Gloria Dei Luth. Ch., 1970—2002, Luth. Ch. of Good Shepherd, 2003—. Recipient Hon. Svc. award, PTA Bear Flag Sch., Sacramento, 1992, VH1 Save the Music grant, 2002, 2005. Mem.: NEA, Sacramento Cmty. Concerts Assn. (bd. dirs. 2006), Calif. Music Educators Assn. (bd. dirs. 2006, elem. rep., mem. bd. Capitol Sect., Outstanding Music Educator award 1996, 2003), Nat. Audubon Soc. Republican. Lutheran. Avocations: birdwatching, travel, yoga, reading, hiking. Home: PO Box 109 Elk Grove CA 95759-0109 Personal E-mail: janetmoe46@yahoo.com.

**MOE, MICHAEL,** diversified financial services company executive; BA in Polit. Sci. and Econs., U. Minn. Cert. fin. analyst. Sr. mng. dir., dir. growth strategy Montgomery Securities; dir. global growth stock rsch., mng. dir. Merrill Lynch, 1998; founder ThinkEquity Ptnrs., San Francisco, chmn., CEO. Advisor Ctr. for Innovation; adv. bd. Edn. Industry Report. Named Best on St., The Wall St. Jour.; named to All American Rsch. Team, Instl. Investor. Mem.: San Francisco (Calif.) Analyst Soc., N.Y. Soc. Security Analysts. Office: Thinkequity Partners 600 Montgomery St # 8 San Francisco CA 94111-2702

**MOE, ORVILLE LEROY,** racetrack executive; b. Spokane, Wash., Nov. 26, 1936; s. Clarence Orville and Georgia Maria (Lombard) M.; m. Deonne Wesley Schultz, Jan. 11, 1953; children: Kathleen June, Susan Marie, Terry Ann. Co-owner Moe's Sudden Svc. Fuel Co., Spokane, Wash., 1956-74; sec. Gold Res. Mining Corp., Spokane, 1973-89, Bonanza Gold Corp., Spokane, 1973-85; pres., founder Spokane Raceway Park, Inc., 1971—. Regional v.p. Am. Hot Rod Assn., Kansas, Mo., 1968-84, mktg. dir., 1978-84; co-producer Internat. Car Show Assn., Spokane, 1969-90. Co-producer Spokane Auto Boat Speed Show, 1964—. Mem. Nat. Rep. Senatorial Com., 1984—; mem., trustee Rep. Presdl. Task Force, mem. 1992 Presdl. Trust Rep. Nat. Com. Mem. ISCA, Eagles, Am. Hot Rod Assn. (exec. v.p. Spokane, Wash. 1986—), Internat. Footprint Assn., Am. Auto Racing Assn. (regional v.p.). Republican. Avocations: auto racing, mining, collecting and rebuilding autos, fishing, ice hockey. Office: Spokane Raceway Park Inc 102 N Hayford Rd Spokane WA 99224-9510 Office Phone: 509-244-3663. Business E-Mail: srp@spokaneracewaypark.com

**MOE, RICHARD PALMER,** lawyer; b. Duluth, Minn., Nov. 27, 1936; s. Russell James and Virginia Mary (Palmer) M.; m. Julia Neimeyer, Dec. 26, 1964; children— Eric Palmer, Andrew Neimeyer, Alexandra Julia. BA, Williams Coll., 1959; LL.B., U. Minn., 1966. Bar: Minn. 1967, D.C. 1979, N.Y. 1991. Adminstrv. asst. to mayor, City of Mpls., 1961-62; lt. to gov. Minn., 1963-66; fin. dir. Minn. Democratic Farmer-Labor Party, 1967-69, chmn., 1969-72; adminstrv. asst. to Sen. Walter F. Mondale of Minn., Washington, 1972-76; chief of staff Vice Pres. Walter F. Mondale, 1977-81; counsel Davis Polk & Wardwell, Washington, 1981-85; ptnr., 1985-92; pres. Nat. Trust for Hist. Preservation, Washington, 1992. Trustee Ford Found., 1998—. Office: Nat Trust for Hist Preservation 1785 Massachusetts Ave NW Washington DC 20036-2117

**MOE, RONALD CHESNEY,** public administration researcher; b. San Diego, May 28, 1937; s. Chesney R. and L. Bernice (Weston) M.; m. Carolyn Carr, May 18, 1962 (div. Feb. 1974); children: Steven, Cynthia; m. Grace Tyler, Apr. 30, 1976. BA, Claremont Coll., 1959; MA, Columbia U., 1962, PhD in Pub. Law and Govt., 1968. Asst. prof. San Diego State U., 1967-70; sr. policy advisor Office of Econ. Opportunity, Exec. Office of the Pres., Washington, 1970-71, Cost of Living Coun., Exec. Office of the Pres., Washington, 1971-73; specialist govt. orgns. and mgmt. Congl. Rsch. Svc. Libr. of Congress, Washington, 1973—2002. Cons. OECD, Paris, 1996—, Brookings Instn., Washington, 2003—; Congl. Rsch. Svc., 2003—; adj. prof. George Washington U., 2003—. Contbr. chpts. in books, articles to profl. jours. Mem. exec. bd. Congregational, Ch. of Am., Milw., 1985-89. Capt. U.S. Army Res., 1961-63. Ctr. Study of Am. Govt. fellow Johns Hopkins U., Washington, 1993—; recipient ASPA Louis Brownlow award, 1988, 91, 95-96. Fellow Nat. Acad. Pub. Adminstrn.; mem. Acad. Polit. Sci., Cosmos Club (Washington), Phi Beta Kappa. Republican. Home: 4700 Connecticut Ave NW Apt 407 Washington DC 20008-5609 Office: Congl Rsch Svc Libr Of Congress Washington DC 20540-0001 E-mail: rmoe@crs.loc.gov.

**MOE, STANLEY ALLEN,** architect, consultant; b. Fargo, ND, May 28, 1914; s. Ole Arnold and Freda Emily (Pape) Moe; m. Doris Lucille Anderson, July 25, 1937 (dec. 2000); children: Willa Moe Crouse, Myra Moe Galther; m. Reiko Izuno, Nov. 11, 2001. BArch, U. Minn., 1936; DEng (hon.), U. ND Grand Forks, 1993. lic. arch. several states; cert. Nat. Coun. Archtl. Registration Bds. Project arch. various firms, 1936—42, U.S. Army Corps Engrs., Africa, 1942—43; ptnr. H.S. Starin, Archs. & Engrs., Duluth, Minn., 1943—47; sr. ptnr. Moe & Larsen, Archs. & Engrs., LA, 1947-54; ptnr., gen. mgr., exec. v.p. Daniel, Mann, Johnson & Mendenall, LA, 1954-71, corp. v.p., 1972-79; ptnr. Stanley A. Moe, AIA, LA, 1979—. Dir. design of major mil. projects in Eritrea, Sudan, Egypt, Yemen for Allied Forces, 1942-43; chmn. control com. DMJM & Assocs., dir. design prototype, tng. & operational facilities Titan I Intercontinental Ballistic Missiles Program USAF, 1958-63; project dir. Space Shuttle facilities Kennedy Space Ctr., 1973; project dir. for

design of aircraft maintenance complex Iranian Aircraft Industries, 1978; project mgr. for design of major med. facility program Min. of Def. and Aviation, Saudi Arabia, 1975-76; project mgr. design of Boufarik Internat. Airport, Algeria, 1983. Pres. San. Fernando Valley Young Reps., 1952, Van Nuys (Calif.) Jaycees, 1950. Recipient Disting. Svc. award for cmty. svc., Van Nuys Jaycees, 1949, Sioux award, U. ND Alumni Assn., 1985, Trustees Soc. award, U. Minn., 1992; inducted into ND Entrepreneur Hall of Fame, 2000. Mem. AIA (Calif. coun.), Rotary, Delta Tau Delta. Republican. Presbyterian. Avocations: world travel, hunting, fishing, historic restoration, woodworking. Home and Office: 447 S Plymouth Blvd Los Angeles CA 90020-4706 E-mail: stanmoe@sbcglobal.net.

**MOE, VIDA DELORES,** civic worker; b. Ryder, ND, Feb. 29, 1928; d. John Nelson and Inga Marie (Lewis) Ahlgran; m. Placido Ferdinand, July 28, 1950 (dec. 1997); children: Terrence Paul, Star Marie; m. Edgar Louis Moe, May 24, 1970 (dec. 1983). Student, Minot State U., ND, 1964-66; diploma in interior decorating, LaSalle Ext. U., 1976. Sec. Raleigh Ins., Tacoma, 1949-50; clk. stenographer Army Transp. Office, San Francisco, 1951-52; clk.-typist Base Supply, Minot AFB, N.D., 1960-61; clk.-stenographer Base Housing, Minot AFB, 1961-62, 74; sec MIADS Direction Ctr., Minot AFB, 1962-63; sec. QC Br., Minot AFB, 1963-64, dept. acctg. and fin., Minot AFB, 1964-65; med. sec. USAF Regional Hosp., 1965-66; sec. Minuteman AFSC, 1966-67, 74-75, 5th Bomb Wing, 1967-70, 1st Missile Wing, 1973-74, dept. mil. pers., 1975-76, disaster preparedness (NORAD), 1987-93; ret., 1993; sec., salesperson Allen Realty, Minot, 1980-85. Pres. City Art League, 1977-79, 86-87; chmn. Carnegie Restoration and Art Ctr. Project, 1980-87; bd. dirs. Patrons of Libr., Minot, 1978-87, sec., 1979-80, v.p., 1981, pres., 1982-83; v.p. 40/50 Rep. Women Minot, 1982, chair decorations com., 1983; historian Minot Rep. Women, 1984-86; vol. ARC, 2002-03; quilters com. 1st Lutheran Ch., 2003—; vol. Trinity Hosp Arts and Crafts Ctr., 2005 Recipient Superior Performance award 5th Bomb Wing, Minot AFB, 1968, Devotion to Vol. Duty award USAF Regional Hosp., Minot, 1983, 86, Superior Performance Cash award Dept. of Air Force 857 Combat Support Group, 1989-91. Mem. AARP (bd. dir. 1996-97, treas. Ward County chpt. 1996-2000, v.p. 2001-2002, pres. 2002-04), AVMETS, Nat. Assn. Ret. Fed. Employees (chaplain, 2002-04), ND Bus. and Profl. Women's Club (rec. sec. 1978-79, 81-82), Minot Bus. and Profl. Women's Club (pres. 1981-82), Am. Legion Aux. (judge jr. art posters contest 1980-82, pres. 1982-84, chaplain 2006—), Minot Shrine Hosp. Aux. (v.p. 1984-85, pres. 1986-87, 97), Beta Sigma Phi (v.p. Laureate Epsilon chpt. 1981-82, pres. 1983-85, Valentine Queen 1985, Girl of Yr. 1985, preceptor Eta chpt., Girl of Yr. 1985, life), MidState Porcelain Artists Guild (v.p. 1983, 89, pres. 1984, treas. 1997), Order Ea. Star (ND Grand chpt., grand rep. 1979-81, dist. rep. 1982-83, chair credentials com. 1983-84, Grand Martha 1984-85, Grand Electa 1985-86, chmn. registration com. 1986-87, assoc. Grand Conductress 1987-88, Grand Conductress 1989-90, assoc. Grand Matron 1990-91, Worthy Grand Matron 1991-92, Past Worthy Grand Matron, 1992-, Worthy Matron Minot Venus chpt. 1976, 87-89, sec. 1993-94, chaplain 1994-95, assoc. conductress 1995-96, conductress 1996-97, assoc. matron, 1997-98, Worthy Matron 1998-99), Elketts (2d v.p. 1988-89, sec. 1993-94), Sons Norway (social dir. 1993-94, chmn. social dirs. 1994), Eagles Aux. (conductor 1993-94, chaplain 1994-95, v.p. 1995-96, pres. 1996-97, jr. past pres. 1997, past pres. 1997-, chaplain 2006—), Swedish Heritage Soc. (pres. 2001-02). Lutheran. Avocations: porcelain painting, oil painting, sewing, candlemaking, embroidery. Home: 705 25th St NW Minot ND 58703-1733

**MOECK, PETER,** crystallographer, materials scientist; s. Adelinde and Erich Moeck; life ptnr. Svoboda Dimitrova; 1 child, Georg Jurkschat. PhD in Crystallography, Humboldt U. of Berlin, Germany, 1991. Cert. Adult Edn. Tchr. 2000. Rschr. Inst. for Semiconductor Physics, Frankfurt/Oder, Germany, 1983—86; rsch. asst. Humboldt U. of Berlin, 1987—91; rschr. Tech. U. of Berlin, 1991—92; post doctoral rschr. Humboldt U. of Berlin, 1992—93; forensic scientist, pub. analyst Ctrl. Forensic Sci. Labs. of the German State Brandenburg, 1993—94; sr. rsch. asst. U. of Durham, England, 1994—97; rsch. assoc. Imperial Coll. London, 1997—98; rsch. fellow U. of Oxford, England, 1998—2000; asst. rsch. prof. U. of Ill., 2000—02; asst. prof. physics Portland State U., Oreg., 2002—. Contbr. over 100 articles to profl. jours. Recipient Rsch. Innovation award, Rsch. Corp., 2003. Mem.: Internat. Ctr. Diffraction Data, Am. Phys. Soc., Materials Rsch. Soc., German Soc. for Crystallography. Achievements include invention of goniometry of direct and reciprocal lattice vectors in transmission electron microcopy; patents pending for process for forming semiconductor quantum dots with superior structural stability and nanometrology device standards for scanning proble microcrops; development of direct crystallographic analyses in transmission electron microscopy and image based nanocrystallography.

**MOEHLMAN, MICHAEL SCOTT,** lawyer; b. Columbus, Ohio, Apr. 11, 1938; s. Arthur Henry and Marguerite Caroline M.; m. Carol Jean Shafer, Sept. 28, 1963; 1 son, Matthew. Ba, Harvard U., 1960; LLB, U. Tex., 1963. Bar: Tex. 1963. With Strasburger & Price, Houston. Bd. dirs. St. Martin's Episcopal Children's Ctr. Fellow Tex. Bar Found.; mem. ABA (com. bank securities), Internat. Bar Assn., Tex. Bar Assn. (com. revision corp. law), Houston Bar Assn. (judicature com.), Tex.-Mex. Bar Assn., Am. Judicature Soc., Houston Bar Found. (chmn. bd. dirs.), Phi Delta Phi. Clubs: Houston (chmn. fin. com., bd. dirs., pres.), Houston Racquet, Houston Yacht, Harvard (Boston), Harvard (NYC), St. Charles Bay Hunting. Episcopalian. Office: Strasburger & Price 1401 McKinney St Ste 2200 Houston TX 77010-4035 Office Phone: 713-951-5684. Business E-Mail: michael.moehlman@strasburger.com.

**MOEHRING, FRED ADOLF,** wholesale distribution executive; b. Bklyn., Nov. 4, 1935; s. Fred Henry Christian and Elsa Marta (Klein) M.; m. Marilyn Agnes Rieber, June 7, 1958; 1 child, Donna. Grad. H.S., Jamaica NY. Salesman Miller Charles and Co., Mineola, NY, 1956-65, Century Fasteners Corp., Elmhurst, NY, 1963-65; gen. mgr. Stewart Air Industries, Syosset, NY, 1965-70; salesman Supreme Lake Mfg. Co., Plantsville, Conn., 1971, Allmetal Screw Products Inc., Garden City, NY, 1971-72; cab driver Scull's Angels, Flushing, NY, 1972-74; gen. mgr. Empire Fasteners, Long Island City, NY, 1974-83, Mar-Lin Sales, Bklyn., 1983-97, Fred A. Moehring, Inc., Bklyn., 1998—. Mem. ASME, ASTM, NRA, ASM Internat., Soc. Automotive Engrs., Met. Fastener Distbrs. Assn. (pres. 1991-92), Steuben Soc. Am., United German-Am. Com. of U.S.A., Inc., German-Am. Steuben Parade Com. Republican. Lutheran. Avocations: golf, travel. Office: Fred A Moehring Inc 208 N 8th St Brooklyn NY 11211-2008 Office Phone: 718-963-2220. Business E-Mail: fred35@iwon.com.

**MOEHRINGER, J. R.,** writer; b. NYC, Dec. 7, 1964; BA in History, Yale Coll., 1986. News asst. NY Times, 1986—90; gen. assignment reporter Rocky Mountain News, Denver, 1990—94; reporter, Orange County edit. Los Angeles Times, 1994—97, bur. chief Atlanta, 1997, corr. Denver. Author: (memoir) The Tender Bar, 2005. Finalist Pulitzer Prize for Feature Writing, 1998; named Scripps Howard Nat. Non-Deadline Writer of Yr., 1992; recipient Feature Writing award, AP News Exec. Coun., 1997, Lit. award, Penn Ctr. USA West, 1997, Livingston award for Young Journalists, 1997, Pulitzer Prize for Feature Writing, 2000; grantee Niemann Fellow, Harvard Univ. Home: Denver CO Office: c/o Mort Janklow Janklow & Nesbit Assoc 13th fl 445 Park Ave New York NY 10022*

**MOELHMAN, AMY JO,** social worker; b. Lafayette, Ind., Mar. 18, 1954; d. Charles and Marian (Young) Moelhman. BS, Ball State U., 1976; MSW, U. Denver, 1979. Lic. clin. social worker, Ind. Social worker Adolescent Crisis Team, Adams County Social Svc., Denver; counselor adolescent boys prog. Pleasant Run Children's Home, Indpls.; group therapist Mothers of Victims of Sexual Abuse, Mid-Town Mental Health, Indpls.; supr. foster care and counseling prog. Children's Bur., Indpls.; mgr. Family Connection Ctr., 1989-90; dir. family programs Vis. Nurse Svc., Indpls., 1990-96; dir. Holy Family Svcs., Cath. Social Svcs., Indpls., 1996—2001; couns. Brown County Family Access Ctr., 1999—; supr. cmty. programs Indpls. Transition Ctr. Casey Family Programs, 2001—03; dir. Alliance Human Svcs., 2004— Chair Ind. Coalition of Family-based Svcs., 1992-94; co-chair family preservation com. Marion County Stepahead; part-time faculty masters in social work program Ind. U.-Purdue U., Indpls. Contbr. articles to profl. jours. Mem. NASW, Acad. Cert. Social Workers. Home: 818 E 53rd St Indianapolis IN 46220-3104 Office Phone: 317-603-6866. Personal E-mail: amoelhman@aol.com.

**MOELING, WALTER GOOS, IV,** lawyer; b. Quantico, Va., Feb. 16, 1943; s. Walter Goos III and Dorothy M.; m. Nell Frances Askew, Aug. 27, 1965; children: Charles H., Christine E. BA, Duke U., 1965, JD, 1968. Bar: Ga. 1968. Assoc. Powell Goldstein, Atlanta, 1968-75, ptnr., 1975—. Bd. dirs. So. Banking Law and Policy Conf., 1989-96, Southeastern Conf. for Bank Dirs., 1996—, Children's Rehab. Ctr., Atlanta, 1982—; Gatchell Home, Atlanta, 1983-99; bd. dirs. Frazer Ctr., 1989—, chmn. bd. dirs., 1993. Mem. ABA (mem. banking com. 1986—), Ga. C. of C. (bd. dirs. 1998-2000), Ga. Bar Assn., Ga. Bankers Assn. (assoc., chairperson bank counsel sect. 1992-95, bd. dirs. 1998-2000), Cmty. Bankers Assn. (assoc.), Capital City Club, Willow Point Country Club. Democrat. Unitarian Universalist. Avocations: golf, fly fishing. Office: Powell Goldstein LLP One Atlantic Ctr 1201 W Peachtree St Atlanta GA 30309-1740 Office Phone: 404-572-6629. Business E-mail: wmoeling@pogolaw.com.

**MOELLEKEN, BRENT RODERICK WILFRED,** surgeon; b. Vancouver, B.C., Can., Apr. 19, 1960; BA, Purdue U., 1979; MD, Yale U., 1985; postgrad., Harvard U., 1980-81. Diplomate Am. Bd. Surgery, Am. Bd. Plastic Surgery. Intern U. Calif., San Francisco, 1985-86, resident in gen. surgery, 1986-92, rsch. fellow in plastic surgery, 1988-90, resident in plastic surgery, 1992-94; fellow in aesthetic surgery UCLA, 1994-95; pvt. practice Beverly Hills, Calif., 1995—, Santa Barbara, Calif., 1995—. Attending surgeon UCLA Hosp., Cedars-Sinai Hosp., L.A.; asst. clin. prof. UCLA; surgeon ABC-TV Extreme Makeover. Plastic surgery before and after lead surgeon: (TV series) Discovery Health Channel; contbr. over 120 articles to profl. jours.; appeared in: over 60 TV shows. Fellow ACS; mem. Am. Soc. Plastic Surgeons, Am. Soc. Aesthetic Plastic Surgery. Achievements include invention of livefill graft; superficial cheek lift operation; hybrid alidominoplasty 360 facelift. Office: 120 Spalding Dr Ste 340 Beverly Hills CA 90212 Office Phone: 310-273-1001. Business E-mail: info@drbrent.com. E-mail: drbrent@drbrent.com.

**MOELLER, AUDREY CAROLYN,** retired energy company executive, retired corporate secretary; b. Pitts., May 10, 1935; d. Nicholas William and Edith Tecla (Russman) M. Grad. high sch., Pitts. Legal sec. Equitable Resources Inc., Pitts., 1955-72, asst. corp. sec., 1972-80, corp. sec., 1980-86, v.p., corp. sec., 1986-99; also corp. sec. Equitable Resources Inc. subs.; ret., 1999. Com. mem. United Way Allegheny County, Pa., 1978, United Way Southwestern Pa., 1984. Mem.: Pa. Assn. Notaries, Am. Soc. Corp. Secs. (chmn. membership and asst. sec. Pitts. chpt. 1995, treas. 1996, v.p. and program chmn. 1997, pres. 1998), Loyal Christian Benefit Assn. (nat. coun. 1993, pres. br. 331 2000, nat. auditor 2001—04). Democrat. Roman Catholic. Avocations: singing, golf, travel. Home: 1003 Cherry Hill Dr Presto PA 15142

**MOELLER, DADE WILLIAM,** environmental engineer, educator; b. Grant, Fla., Feb. 27, 1927; s. Robert A. and Victoria (Bolton) M.; m. Betty Jean Radford, Oct. 7, 1949 (dec. Oct. 1998); children: Garland Radford, Mark Bolton, William Kehne, Matthew Palmer, Elisabeth Anne. BSCE, Ga. Inst. Tech., 1947, MS in Environ. Engring., 1948; PhD in Nuc. Engring., N.C. State U., 1957. Commd. jr. asst. san. engr. USPHS, 1948, advanced through grades to san. engr. dir., 1961; rsch. engr. Los Alamos (N.Mex.) Sci. Lab., 1949-52; staff asst. Radiol. Health Program, Washington, 1952-54; rsch. assoc. Oak Ridge Nat. Lab., 1956-57; chief radiol. health tng. Taft San. Engring. Ctr., Cin., 1957-61; officer charge Northeastern Radiol. Health Lab., Winchester, Mass., 1961-66; assoc. dir. Kresge Ctr. Environ. Health, Harvard Sch. Pub. Health, 1966-83, prof. engring. in environ. health, head dept. environ. health scis., 1968-83, dir. Office of Continuing Edn., 1982-84, assoc. dean continuing edn., 1985-93; environ. cons., 1993—; pres. Dade Moeller & Assocs., Inc., 1993—2003, chmn. bd., 2005—. Cons. radiol. health. Author: (textbook) Environmental Health, 3rd edit., 2005; contbr. articles to profl. jours. Chmn. Am. Bd. Health Physics, 1967-70; mem. com. 4 Internat. Commn. on Radiol. Protection, 1978-85; chmn. nat. air pollution manpower devel. adv. com. U.S. EPA, 1972-75; mem. adv. com. reactor safeguards U.S. NRC, 1973-88, chmn., 1976, chmn. adv. com. nuc. waste, 1988-93; chmn. sci. and tech. rev. panel Office of Civilian Radioactive Waste Mgmt., U.S. Dept. Energy, 2003-. Named to Ga. Inst. Tech. Engring. Hall of Fame, 1999; recipient Disting. Engring. Alumnus award, N.C. State U., 2001, Disting. Prof. Emeritus award of merit, Sch. Pub. Health, Harvard U., 2006. Fellow Am. Pub. Health Assn., Am. Nuc. Soc.; mem. AAAS, Am. Acad. Environ. Engrs., Nat. Coun. Radiation Protection and Measurements (hon.), NAE, Am. Acad. Health Physics Soc. (pres. 1971-72, Robley D. Evans Commemorative medal 2003, William McAdams Outstanding Svc. award 2005). Home and Office: 257 River Island Rd New Bern NC 28562-3669 Office Phone: 252-633-3352.

**MOELLER, JOSEPH W.,** forest products company executive; b. Holdenville, Okla., 1943; m. Mary Moeller; 3 children. BS in Bus. Adminstrn., Aarhus U., Denmark; Degree in Petroleum Mktg., Tulsa, 1966. Joined Koch Industries, Wichita, Kans., 1966, v.p. refined products group, 1980, pres. petroleum group, 1992—95, pres. Koch Industries Internat., 1995—98, pres. Koch Ventures, 1998—99, pres., COO, 1999—2005, also bd. dirs.; pres., CEO Georgia-Pacific Corp., Atlanta, 2005—, also bd. dir. 2005—, chmn., 2006—. Trustee U. Tulsa; mem. 25 Yr. Club Petroleum Industry. Named Outstanding Alumnus, U. Tulsa Coll. Bus. Adminstrn., 1995—96. Office: Georgia-Pacific 133 Peachtree Street NE Atlanta GA 30303 Office Phone: 404-652-4000.*

**MOELLER, LAURA LEE,** retired retail executive, library and information consultant; b. St. Louis, Feb. 20, 1927; d. Edwin Charles and Henrietta Maude (Schelp) Luedde; m. Gerald Herbert Moeller, June 25, 1949; children: Dereck John, Dori Lee, Merry Cay. AB, Harris Tchrs. Coll., St. Louis, 1948; sch. libr. cert., Washington U., St. Louis, 1965. Elem. tchr. Howard Sch., St. Louis, 1948-50, Bay View Sch., Norfolk, Va., 1951; libr. East Ladue Jr. High Sch., St. Louis, 1965-77; mgr., buyer Wornall House Mus. Shop, Kansas City, Mo., 1978-79; co-owner Crabtree & Evelyn London on Plaza, Kansas City, 1979—94. V.p. Women's Coun. U. Mo., Kansas City, 1984—85; active Ch. Libr. Guild, 1990—. Mem.: DAR (state regent 1994—96, regent 1996—98), AAUW, Plaza Mchts. Assn. (nominating com. 1981, bd. dirs. 1991—94), Mo. Assn. Sch. Librs. (pres. 1976—77), Rotary Aux., Conservative Capitalists Investment Club (sec. 2002—03), Carriage Club. Presbyterian. Avocations: reading, tai chi, line dancing. Home: 6247 Rosewood Shawnee Mission KS 66205 Personal E-mail: lmoeller@kc.rr.com.

**MOELLER, PHILIP D.,** commissioner; BA, Stanford U. Staff coord. com. energy, utilities and telecom. Washington State Senate; energy policy advisor to Senator Slade Gordon U.S. Senate, 1997—2000; dir. fed. rels. Capline Corp., Wash.; commr. Fed. Energy Regulatory Commn., Washington, 2006—. Head fed. office Alliance Energy Corp. Office: Fed Energy Regulatory Commn 888 First St NE Washington DC 20426 Office Phone: 202-347-8133. Office Fax: 202-208-0064.*

**MOELLER, SUSAN ELAINE,** artist; b. Akron, Ohio, Jan. 27, 1949; d. Guy Raymond and June Elaine (Inherst) Walker; m. Robert Allen Moeller, Aug. 13, 1984. BFA, BA in Edn., Akron U., 1972. Art tchr. dept. head Manchester Sch. Sys., Akron, 1972-79; ad exec. The Repository, Canton, Ohio, 1979-81; art dir. Vic & Walt's, Akron, 1981-85; illustrator Collector's Marketplace Mag., Atwater, Ohio, 1983-85; freelance artist, graphic designer Akron, 1985-94; fine artist, co-owner Creative Images Studio, Cuyahoga Falls, Ohio, 1994-98, Nogal, N.Mex., 1998—; owner Paz de Nogal Gallery and Studio, Nogal, 1998—. Co-owner Creative Images Studio, Cuyahoga Falls, 1986-98; Nogal, N. Mex., 1998—; graphic cons. Advanced Analytical and Computational Solutions, Inc., Cleve., 1996-97, Akron Chess Club, 1989-97;

art juror Cuyahoga Falls H.S., 1997; owner, organizer Paz de Nogal Fine Art Shows, 1998—. Artist, designer: (bd. game) Barnes Publishing, 1984; contbr. poetry and drawing to Cat Fancy Mag., 1994; illustrator: (mag.) Collector's Marketplace, 1983-85, (newspaper) Canton Repository, 1979-81; exhibited N.E. Ohio Fine Art Guild shows, 1996-97. Donor of fine art to various charities, Akron, 1996-98. Recipient Hon. Mention award Kent (Ohio) Art-in-the-Park Com., 1996. Mem. ASPCA, Humane Soc. U.S., Humane Soc. Summit County, Pet Ptnrs. Rescue City (Pet Angel 1997), Lincoln County Humane Soc., Creative Connection, Ohio Arts and Crafts Guild, Cuyahoga Valley Soc. Fine Arts, Lincoln County Soc. Artists. Avocations: antiques, lapidary arts, gardening, writing. Studio: Paz de Nogal PO Box 190 Nogal NM 88341-0190

**MOELLERING, JOHN HENRY,** aviation maintenance company executive; b. Ft. Wayne, Ind., Feb. 4, 1938; s. Robert Charles and Irene Pauline (Nolde) M.; m. Karla Louise Fritzsche, Dec. 21, 1963; children: John Henry, Matthew C., Ann Elizabeth. BS, U.S. Mil. Acad., 1959; MS, U. Calif., Berkeley, 1962; postgrad., Army Command and Gen. Staff Coll., 1971-72, Army War Coll., 1976-77. Registered profl. engr., La. Commd. 2d lt. U.S. Army, 1959, advanced through grades to lt. gen., 1985; aide de camp Combat Devel. Command, 1961-63; command and staff 24th Inf. Div., Fed. Republic Germany, 1964-67; ops. officer Engr. Group, Vietnam, 1967-68; instr. civil engring., asst. prof. history U.S. Mil. Acad., 1968-71; with Office Army Chief of Staff, Pentagon, 1972-73; White House staff, 1973-74; bn. comdr. 101st Airborne Div., 1974-76; dist. engr. Vicksburg, Miss., 1977-79; exec. to Army Chief of Staff, Pentagon, 1979-81; asst. div. comdr. 9th Inf. Div., Ft. Lewis, Wash., 1981-82; commandant West Point, NY, 1982-84; comdg. gen. Ft. Leonard Wood, Mo., 1984-85; asst. to chmn. Joint Chiefs of Staff, Pentagon, Washington, 1985-87; corp. v.p. Automatic Data Processing, Inc., San Ramon, Calif., 1987-90; pres., chief exec. officer Lear Siegler Mgmt. Svcs. Corp., Oklahoma City, 1990-93; pres. UNC Aviation Svcs., Annapolis, Md., 1993-97; pres., CEO Lear Siegler Svcs., Inc., Annapolis, Md., 1997—2002, JM Assocs., Chapel Hill, NC, 2002—. Bd. dirs. USAA Ins. Co., Lear Sigeler Svcs., Inc., Indsl. Coll. of the Armed Forces; frequent lectr. Nat. Def. U.; mem. adv. bd. Sch. Bus. Adminstrn. The Citadel. Editor, contbr.: Evolution of Modern Warfare, 1969, Battalion Commanders Speak Out, 1977. Mem. Sci. Def. Bd., The Pentagon; chmn. Class of '59 fund com. U.S. Mil. Acad., 1984—89. Decorated Def. DSM, Army DSM, Legion of Merit, Bronze Star; White House fellow, 1973-74. Mem.: Nat. Def. Indsl. Assn. (bd. dirs.), Phi Kappa Phi. Office: 50130 Manly Chapel Hill NC 27517-8565 E-mail: johnmoellering@hotmail.com.

**MOELLERING, ROBERT CHARLES, JR.,** internist, educator; b. Lafayette, Ind., June 9, 1936; s. Robert Charles and Irene Pauline (Nolde) M.; children: Anne Elizabeth, Robert Charles, Catherine Irene; m. Mary Jane Ferraro, July 11, 1987. BA, Valparaiso U., 1958, DSc, 1980; MD cum laude, Harvard U., 1962; DPH (hon.), St. Elizabeth U., 2005. Diplomate: Am. Bd. Internal Medicine. Intern Mass. Gen. Hosp., Boston, 1962-63, resident, 1963-64, postdoctoral fellow in infectious diseases, 1967-70, resident, 1966-67, mem. infectious disease unit and asst. physician, 1970-76, assoc. physician, 1976-83, hon. physician, 1983—, cons. bacteriology, 1972-87; instr. medicine Harvard U. Med. Sch., Boston, 1970-72, asst. prof., 1972-76, assoc. prof., 1976-80, prof., 1980—; chmn. dept. medicine, physician-in-chief New Eng. Deaconess Hosp., 1981-96; pres., CEO Deaconess Profl. Practice Group, 1995-98; Shields Warren-Mallinckrodt prof. rsch. Harvard U. Med. Sch., Boston, 1981-89, Shields Warren-Mallinckrodt prof. med. rsch., 1989-99, 2005—, Herrman Blumgart prof. medicine, 1999—2005; assoc. physician-in-chief Beth Israel Deaconess Med. Ctr., 1996—98, physician-in-chief, 1998—2005, pres., CEO, Harvard Med. Faculty physician, 1998—2003, chmn. bd. dirs., trustee, 2003—05. Mem. subcom. on susceptibility testing Nat. Com. for Clin. Lab. Standards, 1976-88; mem. subcom. on antimicrobial agts. and chemotherapy, 1978-80; subcom. on antimicrobiol disc. diffusion susceptibility testing, 1980-88; chmn. data safety monitoring bd. Nat. Inst. Allergy and Infections Disease, NIH, 1997—2002; trustee Caregroup, 1998-2005, BIDMC, 1998-2005. Mem. editl. bd. Antimicrobial Agts. and Chemotherapy, 1977-81, editor, 1985-88, editor-in-chief, 1985-95; editor European Jour. Clin. Microbial Infectious Diseases, 1990—; consulting. editor Infectious Disease Clinics N.Am., 1986—; editor Les Infections, 1983; editl. bd. New Eng. Jour. Medicine, 1977-81, European Jour.Clin. Microbiology, 1981—, Jour. Infectious Diseases, 1981-85, 89-93, Infectious Disease Alert, 1981-92, Pharmacotherapy, 1982—, Antimicrobial Agts. Ann., 1984-87, Zentralblatt Fur Bacteriologie, Microbiologie and Hygience, 1984—, Jour. of Infection, 1986—, Innovations, 1986-90, Residents Forum in Internal Medicine, 1988-90, Diagnostic Microbiology and Infectious Disease, 1989-90, Internat. Jour. Antimicrobial Agts., 1990—, Infectious Diseases in Clin. Practice, 1991-92, Jour. Infection and Chemotherapy, 1995—, Clin. Infectious Disease, 1999-2004. Served with USPHS, 1964-66. Grantee USPHS, NIH. Master ACP, Am. Acad. Microbiology, Infectious Diseases Soc. Am. (v.p. 1988-89, pres. elect 1989-90, pres. 1990-91, past pres. 1991-92); fellow Royal Coll. Physicians (hon.); mem. Am. Soc. Microbiology, Am. Clin. and Climatol. Assn., Internat. Soc. Chemotherapy, Am. Soc. Clin. Investigation, Assn. Am. Physicians, European Soc. Clin. Microbiology, Am. Fedn. Clin. Rsch., Assn. Profs. Medicine, Roxbury Clin. Records Club, Mass. Med. Soc. (councilor), Brit. Soc. Antimicrobial Chemotherapy, Coun. Biology Editors, Alpha Omega Alpha, Phi Kappa Psi. Home: 49 Longfellow Rd Wellesley MA 02481-5220 Office: Beth Israel Deaconess Med Ctr Dept Medicine 110 Francis St Boston MA 02215-5501 E-mail: rmoeller@bidmc.harvard.edu.

**MOELY, BARBARA E.,** psychologist, educator; b. Prairie du Sac, Wis., July 17, 1940; d. John Arthur and Loretta Ruth (Giese) M.; children: John Jacob Moely Wiener, David Andrew Moely Wiener. Student, Carroll Coll., 1958-60; BA, U. Wis., 1962, MA, 1964; PhD, U. Minn., 1968. Asst. prof. U. Hawaii, Honolulu, 1967-71; rsch. psychologist UCLA, 1971-72; asst. prof. Tulane U., New Orleans, 1972-75, assoc. prof. psychology, 1975-85, prof., 1985—2004, prof. emerita, 2004—, dept. chmn., 1992-96, dir. Office of Svc. Learning, 1999—2004. Contbr. articles to profl. jours. Grantee U.S. Office Edn., Handicapped Pers. Preparation, 1977-80, Tulane U., 1973, 75, 77-78, 83-84, Inst. for Mental Hygiene, City of New Orleans, 1983-84, 2000, Nat. Inst. Edn., 1983-84, La. Edn. Quality Support Fund, 1988-89, 91-92, 96, HUD, 1997-2003, Annenberg, 1997, HHS, 1997-2002, US Dept. Edn. 1999-2002, Fund for Improvement Post-Secondary Edn., 2000-03, Corp. Nat. and Cmty. Svc., 2003-. Mem. AAUP (v.p. La. conf. 1992-93, sec. 1993-97, v.p. 1998-2000, pres. Tulane 1992-94), Am. Ednl. Rsch. Assn., Southwestern Soc. for Rsch. in Human Devel. (pres. 1986-88), Phi Beta Kappa (pres. Alpha chpt. La. 1981-82, sec. 1995-99). Office: Tulane Univ Ctr for Pub Svc New Orleans LA 70118 Business E-Mail: moely@tulane.edu.

**MOENSSENS, SANDRA BIRKELBACH,** marriage and family therapist, counselor, consultant; d. Carl Max Birkelbach and Diane Judith Pery; m. Noel Moenssens; children: Nicole, Sophia. BA, Am. U., DC, 1987; MS, Barry U., Orlando, Fla., 2006. Cert. advocate domestic violence Fla. Case mgr., child specialist Mental Health Svcs. Orange County, Orlando, 1988—89; admissions officer Orlando Coll., 1990—94; leaders-in-tng. Lake Sumpter CC, Leesburg, Fla., 2006—. Cons. various day care ctrs., Clermont, Fla., 2006—. Author: (book) Brain and Body Basics for Better Testing, 2005. Bd. mem. BETA Ho., Orlando, 1997; sustaining mem., advisor, bd. mem. Jr. League Greater Orlando, 1998—99; founding sponsor Martin Luther King Jr. Nat. Meml., 2006. Recipient Wall of Tollerence honoree, So. Poverty Law Ctr, 2002. Mem.: Assn. Play Therapy, Am. Sch. Counseling Assn., Am. Counseling Assn., Am. Assn. Marital & Family Therapists. Avocations: travel, swimming, surfing.

**MOERBEEK, STANLEY LEONARD,** lawyer; b. Toronto, Ont., Can., 1951; arrived in U.S., 1953; s. John Jacob and Mary Emily Moerbeek; m. Carol Annette Mordaunt, Apr. 17, 1982; children: Sarah, Noah. BA magna cum laude, Calif. State U., Fullerton, 1974; student, U. San Diego-Sorbonne, Paris, 1977; JD, Loyola U., 1979. Bar: Calif. 1980; cert. in internat. bus. transactions, bankruptcy and bus. rehab., and civil trial practice. From law clk. to assoc. McAlpin Doonan & Seese, Covina, Calif., 1977-81; assoc.

Robert L. Baker, Pasadena, Calif., 1981-82, Miller Bush & Minnott, Fullerton, 1982-83; prin. Law Office of Stanley L. Moerbeek, Fullerton, 1984—. Notary pub. lt. gov. 9th cir. law student divsn. ABA, 1979; judge pro tem Orange County Superior Ct., 1984—96. Mem. Heritage Found., Washington, 1989—. Recipient plaque of Appreciation, Fullterton Kiwanis, 1983; Calif. Gov.'s Office scholar, 1970. Mem.: Orange County Bar Assn. (Coll. Trial Advocacy 1985), Calif. Assn. Realtors (referral panel atty. 1985—), Phi Kappa Phi. Roman Catholic. Avocations: history, politics, sports. Office: 1370 N Brea Blvd Ste 210 Fullerton CA 92835-4128 Office Phone: 714-773-5396. Personal E-mail: slmlaw@sbcglobal.net.

**MOERDLER, CHARLES GERARD,** lawyer; b. Paris, Nov. 15, 1934; came to the U.S., 1946, naturalized, 1952; s. Herman and Erna Anna (Brandwein) M.; m. Pearl G. Hecht, Dec. 26, 1955; children: Jeffrey Alan, Mark Laurence, Sharon Michele. BA, L.I.U., 1953; JD, Fordham U., 1956. Bar: NY 1956, U.S. Supreme Ct. 1962. Assoc. Cravath, Swaine & Moore, N.Y.C., 1956-65; spl. counsel coms. City of N.Y. and judiciary N.Y. State Assembly, 1960-61; commr. bldgs. City of N.Y., 1966-67; sr. ptnr., chmn. litigation dept. Stroock & Stroock & Lavan, N.Y.C., 1967—. Bd. dirs., gen. counsel, dir. N.Y. Post Co., Inc., 1987-92; cons. housing, urban devel. and real estate to Mayor of N.Y.C., 1967-73; mem. com. on character and fitness of applicants for admission to Bar, Appellate divsn. 1st Dept., N.Y., 1977—, vice chmn. 1998—; mem. disciplinary com. appellate divsn. 1st Dept., N.Y., 1998—2004, 06—, commr. N.Y. State Ins. Fund, 1978-97, vice chmn., 1986-94, chmn., 1995-97; mem. Mayor's Com. on Judiciary, 1994-2001; mem. N.Y.C. Housing Devel. Corp., 1997—; bd. dirs. N.Y.C. Residential Mortgage Ins. Corp., 1997—; chmn. bd. dirs. Bank Austria Creditanstalt LLC, 1999-2001; mem. N.Y.C. Bd. Collective Bargaining, 2000—. Mem. editorial bd. N.Y. Law Jour., 1985—; assoc. editor Fordham Law Rev., 1956. Asst. dir. Rockefeller nat. presdl. campaign com., 1964; adv. bd. Sch. Internat. Affairs Columbia U., 1977-80; bd. govs. L.I.U., 1966, trustee, 1985-91; chmn. Cmty. Planning Bds. 8 and 14, Bronx County, 1977-78; sr. v.p., mem. exec. com. Am. Jewish Congress, 2005—; bd. overseers Jewish Theol. Sem. Am., 1993-95; trustee St. Barnabas Hosp., Bronx, N.Y., 1985—. Recipient Walker Metcalf award L.I. U., 1966. Mem. Am. Bar Assn., N.Y. State Bar Assn., N.Y. County Lawyers Assn., Internat. Bar Assn., Assn. of Bar of City of N.Y., Free Sons of Israel, Metro. Club. Home: 7 Rivercrest Rd Bronx NY 10471-1236 Office: Stroock Stroock & Lavan 180 Maiden Ln New York NY 10038 Office Phone: 212-806-5648. E-mail: cmoerdler@stroock.com.

**MOESCHL, STANLEY FRANCIS,** electronics engineer, electrical engineer, management consultant; b. Cin., Mar. 14, 1931; s. Stanley F. and Matilda F. (Trenkamp) M.; m. Kathleen K. Koebel, Aug. 21, 1954; children: Stanley, Melissa, Deborah, Karen. BSEE, Purdue U., 1957. Engr. Honeywell Space Div., St. Petersberg, Fla., 1957-60, engring. mgr., 1960-69, program mgr., 1969-77; dir. engring. Honeywell Avionics Div., Mpls., 1977-80; v.p. gen. mgr. Honeywell Space Div., St. Petersberg, 1980-82, Honeywell Avionics Div., Mpls., 1982-88; pres. Sundstrand Data Control, Redmond, Wash., 1988-92. Bd. mem. com. of 100, St. Petersberg, 1980-82, Wash. Round Table, Seattle, 1989-92. Bd. dirs. Jr. Achievement, Mpls., 1983-86, Seattle, 1989-92. With USCG, 1951—54, Korea. Mem.: IEEE, Am. Assn. Individual Investors, Tau Beta Pi, Eta Kappa Nu. Home: 12826 Yacht Club Cir Fort Myers FL 33919-4635 Personal E-Mail: sfmoeschl@aol.com.

**MOESER, JAMES CHARLES,** academic administrator; b. Colorado City, Tex., Apr. 3, 1939; s. Charles Victor and Virginia (James) M.; m. Jesse Kaye Edwards, Jan. 26, 1963 (div. July 1984); children: James Christopher, Kathryn Carter; m. Susan Kay Smith Dickerson, June 21, 1987. B.Mus., U. Tex., 1961, M.M., 1964; postgrad. (Fulbright grantee), Hochschule fur Musik, Berlin, 1961-62; D.MA (Univ. fellow), U. Mich., 1966. Chmn. dept. organ, asst. prof. organ U. Kans., 1966-69, assoc. prof., 1969-74, prof., 1974-86, dean Sch. Fine Arts, 1975-86, Carl and Ruth Althaus disting. prof. organ, 1985-86; organist, choirmaster Plymouth Congl. Ch., Lawrence, Kans., 1967-86; organist nat. conf. Music Tchrs. Nat. Assn., Portland, Oreg., 1972, L.A., 1974; dean Coll. Arts and Architecture, Pa. State U., State College, 1986—91; v.p., academic affairs & provost Univ. S.C., 1991—96; chancellor U. Nebr., Lincoln, Nebr., 1996—2000, U.N.C. - Chapel Hill, 2000—. Concert organist, on tour, W. Ger., 1977, Lisbon (Portugal) Festival, 1978, 81, recitals for, Musica Festiva da Costa Verde, Portugal, 1981; organist concerts, W. Ger., 1982, 86, 87; world premier Paul Creston's 3d Symphony for Organ and Orchestra, Kennedy Ctr., Washington, 1982. Bd. govs. Josephson Inst. Ethics, 1998-2002; trustee N.C. Symphony Soc., Inc., 2001—; mem. vis. com. Meml. Ch., Harvard U. Recipient Palmer Christian award U. Mich., 1981, Disting. Alumnus awrd Grad. Sch. U. Tex., 2001; Kent fellow Danforth Found.; Danforth Assoc. Mem. Am. Guild Organists (past dean chpt., nat. dir. student groups 1973-75, nat. chmn. com. on profl. edn. 1983—, chmn. 2d nat. conf. on organ pedagogy 1984, 3d nat. conf. 1986, v.p. 1986—). Episcopalian. Home: 1000 Raleigh Rd Chapel Hill NC 27517-4415 Office: UNC Office of the Chancellor PO Box 9100 Chapel Hill NC 27599-0001 E-mail: james_moeser@unc.edu.*

**MOESSNER, HAROLD FREDERICK,** allergist; b. Lincoln, Nebr., Mar. 29, 1945; s. Samuel Frederick and Helen Lucy (Larson) M.; m. Linda McLeod, Apr. 30, 1972; children: Annie Larson, John Christopher, Sarah Elizabeth. BS with distinction, U. Nebr., 1967; MD, U. Minn., 1971. Diplomate Am. Bd. Pediatrics, Am. Bd. Allergy and Immunology. Intern VA Hosp., Dallas, 1971-72; resident in pediatrics Children's Med. Ctr., Dallas, 1972-74; commd. 2d lt. U.S. Army, 1974-78, advanced through the grades to col., 1980-87; pediatrician Fort Ritchie, Md., 1974-75, U.S. Army Hosp, Augsburg, Germany, 1975-78; fellow in adolescent medicine U. Tex. Health and Sci. Ctr., Dallas, 1978-79; asst. prof. pediatrics Uniformed Svcs., U. Health Scis., Bethesda, Md., 1980-83; fellow allergy and immunology Walter Reed Army Med. Ctr., Washington, 1983-85; chief allergy immunology svc., chief dept. medicine Blanchfield Army Hosp., Fort Campbell, Ky., 1985-87; pvt. practice Nashville, 1987—. Assoc. staff Williamson Med. Ctr., Franklin, Tenn. Contbr. to profl. jours. Fellow Am. Bd. Pediats., Am. Bd. Allergy and Immunology; mem. Am. Acad. Allergy and Immunology, Williamson County Med. Soc., Tenn. Soc. Allergy, Tenn. State Med. Assn., Phi Beta Kappa. Home: 5304 Otter Creek Ct Brentwood TN 37027-4126 Office: 1909 Mallory Ln Ste 308 Franklin TN 37067-8230 also: 251 Hillcrest Dr Ste 101 Clarksville TN 37043- Office Phone: 615-771-8800.

**MOFFAT, MARYBETH,** consulting company executive; b. Pitts., July 25, 1951; d. Herbert Franklin and Florence Grafe (Knerem) M.; m. Brian Francis Soulier, Nov. 30, 1974 (div.). BA, Carroll Coll., 1973. Indsl. engring. technician Wis. Centrifugal Co., Waukesha, Wisc., 1976-77; indsl. engr. Utility Products, Inc., Milw., 1977-79; mgr. indsl. engring. Bear Automotive (divsn. SPX Corp.), Bangor, Pa., 1980-90; program mgr. Toyota Johnson Controls, Inc. Automotive Systems Group, 1990-2001; pres., CEO Moffat Enterprises, Inc., 2001—. Group home house parent Headwaters Regional Achievement Ctr., Lake Tomahawk, Wis., 1974. Mem. Am. Inst. Indsl. Engrs., MTM Assn. for Standards Rsch., Indsl. Mgmt. Soc., Alpha Gamma Delta (standards chmn. 1971-72). Republican. Methodist. Avocations: skiing, horseback riding, swimming, reading. Office Phone: 859-272-0056. Personal E-mail: m.moffat@insightbb.com.

**MOFFATT, JOYCE ANNE,** performing company executive; b. Grand Rapids, Mich., Jan. 3, 1936; d. John Barnard and Ruth Lillian (Pellow) M. BA in Lit., U. Mich., 1957, MA in Theatre, 1960; HHD (hon.), Profl. Sch. Psychology, San Francisco, 1991. Stage mgr., lighting designer Off-Broadway plays; costume, lighting and set designer, stage mgr. stock cos., 1954-62; nat. subscription mgr. Theatre Guild/Am. Theatre Soc., N.Y.C., 1965-67; subscription mgr. Theatre, Inc.-Phoenix Theatre, N.Y.C., 1963-67; cons. N.Y.C. Ballet and N.Y.C. Opera, 1967-70; asst. house mgr. N.Y. State Theater, 1970-72; dir. ticket sales City Ctr. of Music and Drama, Inc., N.Y.C. 1970-72; prodn. mgr. San Antonio's Symphony/Opera, 1973-75; gen. mgr. San Antonio Symphony/Opera, 1975-76, 55th St. Dance Theater Found., Inc., N.Y.C., 1976-77, Dallas Theater Found., Inc./Am. Ballet Theatre, Inc., 1977-81; v.p. prodn. Radio City Music Hall Prodns., Inc., N.Y.C., 1981-83; artist-in-residence CCNY, 1981—; propr. mgmt. cons. firm for performing arts N.Y.C., 1983—; exec. dir. San Francisco Ballet Assn., 1987-93; mng. dir. Houston Ballet Assoc., 1993-95; gen. mgr. Chgo. Music and Dance Theater, Inc., 1995—2004. Cons. Ford Found., NY State Coun. on Arts, Kennedy Ctr. Performing Arts., Lensic Performing Arts Ctr., Santa Fe, Bloomington Cultural Dist., Ill., Sheboygan (Wis.) Theater Found., The Arts Partnership Spartanburg, SC; mem. dance panels NY State Coun. on Arts, 1979-81; mem. panels for Support to Prominent Orgns. and Dance, Calif. Arts Coun., 1988-92. Appointee San Francisco Cultural Affairs Task Force, 1991; chmn. bd. dir. Tex. Inst. Arts in Edn., 1994—; trustee Internat. Alliance of Theatrical Stage Employees Local 16 Pension and Welfare Fund, 1991-94; bd. dir. Rudolf Nureyev Dance Found., Chgo., 1998—. Mem. Assn. Theatrical Press Agts. and Mgrs., Actors Equity Assn., United Scenic Artists Local 829, San Francisco Visitors and Conv. Bur. (bd. dirs.), Argyle Club (San Antonio). Office Phone: 864-457-4575.

**MOFFATT, KATY (KATHERINE LOUELLA MOFFATT)**, musician, lyricist, vocalist; b. Ft. Worth, Nov. 19, 1950; d. Lester Huger and Sue-Jo (Jarrott) M. Student, Sophie Newcomb Coll., 1968, St. John's Coll., 1969-70. Rec. artist Columbia Records, 1975-79, Permian/MCA Records, 1982-84, Enigma Records, L.A., 1985, Wrestler Records, L.A., 1987-88, Red Moon Records, Switzerland, 1988-93, Philo/Rounder Records, 1989-96, Round Tower Music, U.K., Ireland, Europe, 1993-96, Watermelon Records, U.S., 1994-96, Panther City Records, New Zealand, 1998, Hightone/HMG Records, 1998-2001, Western Jubilee/Dualtone Records, 2001—, Demon/Westside Records, 2002, Fuel Records/Universal Records, 2005. Folksinger, Ft. Worth, 1967-68; musician, vocalist, songwriter, rec. artist: (films) Billy Jack, 1970, Hard Country, 1981, The Thing Called Love, 1993; prodn. asst. film, Sta. KIII-TV, Corpus Christi, 1970, audio engr., Sta. KRIS-TV, Corpus Christi, 1970; receptionist, bookkeeping asst., copywriter, announcer, Sta. KFW I, Ft. Worth, 1971, musician, vocalist, songwriter, Denver, 1971-72, on tour, 1973, 75—, Denver, 1974, on tour, 1976-79, European tour, 1977, Can. tour, 1984-85, on tour in Europe, U.S., Can., Asia and Australia, 1985—; albums include Katy, 1976, Kissin' In The California Sun, Am. release, 1977, internat. release, 1978, A Town South of Bakersfield, 1985, Walkin' on the Moon, European release, 1988, U.S. release, 1989, Child Bride, 1990, (duet album with brother Hugh) Dance Me Outside, 1992, (Switzerland only) Indoor Fireworks, 1992, The Greatest Show On Earth A.K.A. The Evangeline Hotel, 1994, Hearts Gone Wild, 1994, Tulare Dust, 1995, (duet album with Kate Brislin) Sleepless Nights, 1996, Midnight Radio, 1996, Angel Town, 1998, Loose Diamond, 1999, Cowboy Girl, 2001, (reissue on CD) Katy/Kissin' in the California Sun, 2002, Up Close & Personal, 2005; songs include The Magic Ring, 1971; Gerry's Song, 1973, Kansas City Morning, 1974, Take Me Back To Texas, 1975, (Waitin' For) The Real Thing, 1975, Didn't We Have Love, 1976, Kissin' in the California Sun, 1977, Walkin' on the Moon, 1989. Recipient Record World Album award, 1976; named one of 4 Top New Female Vocalists, Cashbox Singles Awards, 1976; nominee for Top New Female Vocalist, Acad. Country Music, 1985; winner best singer-songwriter category Ft. Worth Weekly Mag. Music awards, 1997. Mem. AFTRA, SAG, NARAS, Am. Fedn. Musicians.

**MOFFETT, DAVID MCKENZIE**, bank executive; b. Daytona Beach, Fla., Feb. 22, 1952; s. James Denny Jr. and Dorothy McCall (McKenzie) M.; m. Cynthia Ann Daugherty, Aug. 25, 1973 (div. Oct. 1977); m. Katherine Ann Martin, May 26, 1979; children: Jeffrey Martin, Layne McCall, Hilary Marie. BA, Okla. U., 1974; MBA, So. Meth. U., 1975; grad. Stonier Sch. Banking, Rutgers U., 1981. Planning analyst First Nat. Bank & Trust Co., Tulsa, 1975-76, fin. analyst, 1978, v.p., 1978-80, sr. v.p., 1981-86, exec. v.p., 1987—93; CFO Star Banc Corp. (merged with Firstar Corp.), 1993—98; CFO, vice chmn. Firstar Corp. (merged with US Bancorp), Milw., 1998—2001; CFO, vice chmn., dir. US Bancorp, Mpls., 2001—. Faculty grad. sch. banking U. Wis., 1986; adj. prof. U. Tulsa. Bd. dirs. Leadership Tulsa, Inc., 1985-87, Arts & Humanities Council, Tulsa, 1986, Salvation Army, 1986, St. John's Episc. Ch., Tulsa, 1987. Recipient Chmn.'s award bd. dirs. First Nat. Bank, 1980. Mem. Nat. Asset/Liability Mgmt. Assn. (charter), Bank Adminstrn. Inst. (treasury mgmt. com. 1984, investment banking com. 1987). Republican. Episcopalian. Clubs: Tulsa, Cedar Ridge Country (Tulsa). Avocations: running, golf, skiing, scuba diving, bicycling. Office: Us Bank 800 Nicollet Mall Ste 1500 Minneapolis MN 55402-7014*

**MOFFETT, JAMES ROBERT**, mining executive; b. Houma, La., Aug. 16, 1938; s. Robert E. and Mary G. (Pollack) M.; m. Louise C. Hohmann, June 5, 1960; children: Crystal Louise, James R. BS, U. Tex., 1961; MS, Tulane U., 1963. Cons. geologist oil and gas industry, New Orleans, 1964-69; v.p. founding ptnr. McMoRan Exploration Co., New Orleans, 1969-74; pres., chief exec. officer McMoRan Oil & Gas Co., New Orleans, 1974-81, 81-85, chmn., chief exec. officer, 1985—97, dir., from 1974; vice-chmn. Freeport McMoRan Inc., New Orleans, 1981-85, chmn., chief exec. officer, 1984—97, chmn., 1997—; co-chmn. McMoRan Exploration Co. Mem. Nat. Petroleum Council, Washington, 1979, Commn. on the Future of South, 1986; bd. dirs. La. Energy Nat. PAC, Metairie, La., 1979, World Trade Ctr., New Orleans, Am. Cancer Soc. Greater New Orleans, Bus. Task Force Edn., Inc.; chmn. bd. La. Coun. Fiscal Reform; chmn. bus. coun. New Orleans and River Region, 1985-87. 2nd lt. U.S. Army, 1961-68, capt. Res. ret. Recipient T award Ex Students Assn. U. Tex., 1960, Hornblower Yr. award Pub. Relations Soc. Am., 1986, Vol. Yr. award Urban League Greater New Orleans, 1987; Minnie Stevens Piper Found. scholar U. Tex., 1960, Jacques E. Yenni, S.J. award Loyola U. of New Orleans for Outstanding Community Svc., Jr. Achievement Bus. Hall of Fame award, 1987, Loyola U. of New Orleans' Integritas Vitae award, 1988; named One of Ten Outstanding Persons of 1985 Inst. for Human Understanding, New Orleans. Mem. All Am. Wildcatters, New Orleans Geol. Soc., Petroleum Club New Orleans, Greater New Orleans Mktg. Com. (exec. com. 1987), Geology Found U. Tex. (adv. council 1972-85), Devel. bd. U. Tex., La. Ind. producers Royalty Owners Assn. South La. Mid-Continent Oil Gas Assn. (v.p.), Dinner Steering Com. (Disting. Citizen award 1983, 85 Boy Scouts Am., New Orleans div.), Green Wave Club. Republican. Mailing: Freeport-McMoRan Copper & Gold Co PO Box 61119 New Orleans LA 70161*

**MOFFITT, CHARLES WILLIAM**, art gallery director; b. Altoona, Pa., Mar. 24, 1932; s. Charles William and Beatrice Jeanette (Shellenberger) Moffitt; m. Virginia Colyer, July 26, 1956 (dec.); m. Marianne Foley Potter, May 23, 1980 (dec.); children: Michelle Ann Hunt, Charles William III, Deborah K. Moffitt Russell; m. Mary Lou Herold, Nov. 24, 2001; stepchildren: Sherry Marshall, Heather Clayton, Kristin Pfauser. BA, Pa. State U., 1957. Examiner Pa. R.R., Buffalo, 1957-62; asst. to pres. White Cross Stores, Inc., Monroeville, Pa., 1962-65, sec., 1965-70, v.p. adminstrn., sec., 1970-72; dir. labor relations and legal affairs Revco D.S., Inc., Cleve., 1972-75, asst. v.p. personnel, 1974-75; pres. Fashion Wearhouse, Inc., Altoona, Pa., 1975-87; dir., ptnr. Servello Gallery Art, 2002—. Owner Omega Advt. Co.; pres. Olympus I, Inc., 1980-87; agt. Prin. Fin. Group, 1988-90, Variable Annuity Life Ins. Co., 1990-2001. Co-author: Mincemeat Cartoons, Altoona Mirror Newspaper. Bd. dirs. Bedford Springs Music Festival, 1984-87, Blair County Arts Found., 1987-91, Blair Concert Chorale, 2005—. Republican. Roman Catholic. Home: RR 5 Box 2324 Altoona PA 16601 Office Phone: 814-946-8922. E-mail: monkmoffitt@aol.com.

**MOFFITT, RAY**, social worker, consultant; b. Moline, Ill., Sept. 1, 1937; s. Ernest R. and Ida G. (Wiggins) M. BS, U. Ill., 1959, MSW, 1966; postgrad. child welfare tng. program, 1995. Cert. social worker, Ill. Social work trainee, grad. sch. field worker various Ill. agencies, 1963-66; social worker, program adminstr. Ill. Soldiers' and Sailors' Children's Sch., Normal, Ill., 1966-73; co-founder, dir. Kaleidoscope, Inc., Bloomington, Ill., 1973-74; pres., dir. Browndale/Kaleidoscope, Inc., various, 1974; field instr. Jane Addams Coll. Social Work U. Ill. at Chgo., 1975-77; social worker Village of Maywood (Ill.), 1977-82, cmty. rep., dir. cmty. rels., 1982-87; founder, dir. Explosonic Rockers Street Jazz Theatrical Troupe, 1987-92; founder, exec. prodr. MWAH! Performing Arts Troupe, 1993—; social worker DuPage County Sheriff's Dept., Wheaton, Ill., 1995—. Collaborator Chgo. Area Project and DuPage County Area Project. Mem. NASW, Acad. Cert. Social Workers, U.

Ill. Alumni Assn., Child Care Assn. of Ill., Ill. Alcoholism and Drug Dependence Assn., Boy Scouts Am. (former Explorer advisor), Mental Health Assns. in Ill., Ill. Drug Edn. Alliance, Ill. Assn. Student Assistance Profls., Du Page Intergenerational Village, Alpha Zeta Alumni Assn. Home: 159 Cottage Hill Ave Apt 215 Elmhurst IL 60126-3347

**MOFFITT, WILLIAM BENJAMIN**, lawyer; b. NYC, Jan. 16, 1949; s. William Benjamin and Victoria Lucinda Moffitt; 1 child, Pilar. BA, U. Okla., 1971; JD, Am. U., 1975. Bar: Va. 1976, US Dist. Ct. (ea. dist.) Va. 1976, US Ct. Appeals (4th cir.) 1980, US Ct. Appeals (5th cir.) 1981, US Ct. Appeals (11th cir.) 1982, US Ct. Appeals (6th cir.) 1988, US Ct. Appeals (1st cir.) 1991, US Dist. Ct. Md. 1994, US Ct. Appeals (3rd cir.) 1994. Ptnr. Lowe, Mark & Moffitt, Alexandria, Va., 1976-81, Mark & Moffitt, Alexandria, Va., 1981-85, Moffitt, Keats & Jones, Alexandria, Va., 1985-87, Moffitt & Jones, Alexandria, Va., 1987-89, William B. Moffitt & Assocs., Alexandria, Va., 1989-91, Moffitt, Zwerling & Kemler, Alexandria, Va., 1991-96, Asbill, Junkin & Moffitt, Chartered, Washington, 1996—2004; ptnr., criminal def. Asbill Moffitt & Boss (acquired by Cozen O'Connor), Washington, 2004—. Mem. Legal Svcs. Bd. No. Va., 1982; pres. Va. Coll. Criminal Def. Lawyers, 1983. Contbr. article to profl. jour. Bd. dirs. ACLU, 1981. Named one of Am. Top Black Lawyers, Black Enterprise Mag., 2003. Fellow Am. Bd. Criminal Lawyers; mem. Alexandria Bar Assn., Nat. Assn. Criminal Def. Lawyers (bd. dirs. 1988—, white first v.p. 1997-98, pres.-elect 1998-99, pres. 1999-2000); Internat. Assn. Criminal Def. Lawyers, va. Criminal Def. Lawyers. Office: Cozen O Connor Ste 500 1667 K St NW Washington DC 20006 Office Phone: 202-912-4816, 800-540-1355. Office Fax: 202-912-4830. Business E-mail: wmoffitt@cozen.com.

**MOFFLY, JOHN WESLEY, IV**, magazine publishing executive; b. Phila., Aug. 5, 1926; s. John W. III Moffly and Audrey (Kane) Chancellor; m. Donna Jeanette Clegg, July 11, 1959; children: Jonathan Wesley, Audrey Kane Lkotz. BA, Woodrow Wilson Sch., Princeton U., 1949. NY advt. mgr. House & Home Mag. Time Inc., NYC, 1962-66, NY advt. exec. LIFE Mag. 1967-73, v.p. selling areas mktg. divsn., 1973-87; pres., owner Moffly Publs., Inc., 1987—; pubs. Greenwich, Westport, New Canaan and Darien mags. Bd. dirs. Boys and Girls Club Greenwich, United Way, Greenwich Emergency Med. Svc., Greenwich Adult Day Care; mem. Amb.'s Round Table-Forum, World Affairs. With USAAF, 1944-45. Mem. Greenwich C. of C. (chmn. bd. dirs. 1999-2000, Small Businessman of Yr. 1991), Riverside Yacht Club, Cruising Club Am., Indian Harbor Yacht Club. Republican. Episcopalian. Avocations: sailing, tennis, clay bird shooting, skiing, international studies. Home: 100 Meadow Rd Greenwich CT 06878-2520 Office: Greenwich Mag 39 Lewis St Greenwich CT 06830-5558

**MOFORD, CRAIG S.**, prosecutor; b. Schenectady, NY; BA, Hope Coll.; JD, Valparaiso U. Atty. IRS, Cleveland, 1984—87; first asst. US atty. No. Dist., Ohio, 1987—2004; interim US atty. Eastern Dist., Mich. 2004—. Achievements include chief prosecutor, corruption trial of former Congressman James Traficant.

**MOGABGAB, ROSE-WARREN BERRYMAN**, academic administrator, writer; b. Richmond, Va., Mar. 13, 1940; d. Maynard Warren Berryman and Bessie Virginia Edwards; m. William Joseph Mogabgab, July 15, 1988 (dec.); children: Robert Mogabgab Berryman, William Joseph Mogabgab Berryman. AB, Randolph-Macon Woman's Coll., 1962. From mgr. lab. Sch. Medicine to rsch. assoc. Tulane U., New Orleans, 1965—81, rsch. assoc. Sch. Medicine, 1981—92; freelance med. writer and cons. New Orleans, 1993—. Presenter in field. Contbr. articles to profl. jours. Recipient 25 Yr. Svc. award, Tulane U. Sch. Medicine, 1980, Civc award, Mayor New Orleans, 1982. Mem.: Women for a Better La., Randolph Macon Woman's Coll. Alumnae (pres. New Orleans chpt. 1990—2001), Kingsmill Yacht Club, Kappa Alpha Theta. Avocations: antiques, gardening, travel. Home: 1220 Brookhaven Park Pl NE Atlanta GA 30319 Office Phone: 404-848-0162.

**MOGEL, WILLIAM ALLEN**, lawyer; b. NYC, Mar. 7, 1942; s. Harry H. and Therese M.; m. Judith; children: Elisabeth, Andrew. BA cum laude, Hobart Coll., 1963; LLB, U. Pa., 1966. Bar: DC 1967, Md. 1971. Ptnr. Saul Ewing, 2005. Adj. instr. Am. U., Washington, 1982—; active Washington Bd. Trade: Transportation & Marketing of Natural Gas, 1985, 86, Natural Gas: Current Federal and State Developments, 1987; editor: Natural Gas Yearbook, 1988-92; co-editor: Energy Law & Transactions; editor-in-chief Energy Law Jour., 1980—; contbr. articles to profl. jours. Trustee Hobart Coll., 1983-88. Capt. U.S. Army, 1966-69. Mem. Fed. Energy Bar Assn. Home: 5812 Madaket Rd Bethesda MD 20816-3201 Office: Saul Ewing 1025 Thomas Jefferson Pl Washington DC 20007 Office Phone: 202-245-6612. E-mail: wmogel@saul.com.

**MOGENSEN, CHARLES RAY, JR.**, retired food service executive; b. Elizabeth, N.J., May 7, 1946; s. Charles Ray, Sr. and Helen Oakley (Holland) Mogensen; m. Linda Diane Friezer, Apr. 25, 1970; children: Charles Ray III, Jason C., Eric S., Lindsey H. Student, Middlesex County Vocat. Coll., 1972. Cert. food exec., lic. real estate agt. NJ. Chef St. Elizabeth Hosp., Elizabeth, N.J., 1969-70; dir. food svcs. Cornell Hall Conv. Ctr., Union, N.J., 1970-96; dir. food svc. Corrections Corp. Am., Elizabeth Detention Ctr., 1996—2006; ret., 2006. Pres. C.R.M. Food Enterprises, Ltd., Kenilworth, NJ, 1971—89; real estate agt. Real Estate Cons., Short Hills, NJ; owner C.R. Mogensen Antiques, Ltd., Red Bank, NJ; cons. in field. Author: (recipes) Escargots Without Shells, 1979 (citation merit, 1979). Mem. adv. bd. Episcopalian Program Homeless, Elizabeth, 1990, Union County Coalition Homeless, NJ, 1991; mem. Rep. Nat. Com., Washington, 1988. With USMC, 1964—68, Vietnam. Named N.Y. Dist. winner, Gen. Foods Corp., 1981; recipient cert. of Appreciation, Roselle Park (N.J.) First Aid Squad, 1986, award of Merit, USNR, 1990, citation and medal commemorating Vietnam War Svc., State of N.J. Mem.: VFW, Am. Correctional Food Svc. Assn., Internat. Food Svc. Exec. Assn. (pres. 1977, 1979, 1985, 1986, bd. dirs. 1989—91, Royal Order of Skillet 1987, Humanitarian award 1987, Disting. Svc. medal N.J. 2004, Fed. Exec. Bd. Disting. Svc. award 2004), Asia Soc., Masons, Am. Legion (cert. of appreciation 1999), Vets. Vietnam War (life). Avocations: antiques, coin collecting/numismatics, oriental art. Home: The Harbour Club 708 Sunshine Ct Parlin NJ 08859 E-mail: mogen708@verizon.net.

**MOGG, JIMMY W.**, gas industry executive; B in Math., Southwestern Okla. State U., 1971; grad. advanced mgmt. program, Harvard U. With gas supply dept. Panhandle Ea. Pipe Line Co., Liberal, Kans., 1973—80; mgr. forcasting and ops. Panhandle Ea., Kansas City, 1980—86; gen. mgr. gas supply Trunkline Gas Co., Houston, 1986—88; gen. mgr. contracts and ops., gas supply Panhandle Ea., Trunkline, 1988; v.p. gas supply Panhandle Ea., Trunkline, Tex. Ea. Transmission Corp., 1989—91; sr. v.p. Panhandle Ea., 1991; pres. Centana Energy Corp., 1992—94; pres., CEO Duke Energy Field Svcs. LP, Denver, NC, 1999—, chmn., pres., CEO, 1999—2004, group v.p. Charlotte, NC, 2004—, chief devel. officer, 2004—. Chmn. bd. dirs. TEPPCO Ptnrs. LP. Bd. dirs. Rocky Mountain chpt. Jr. Achievement. Mem.: Gas Processors Assn. (past pres.), Soc. Petroleum Engrs. Office: Duke Energy Corp 526 S Church St Charlotte NC 28202-1803

**MOGGE, HARRIET MORGAN**, educational association executive; b. Cleve. d. Russell VanDyke and Grace (Wells) Morgan; m. Robert Arthur Mogge (div.); 1 child, Linda Jean. BME, Northwestern U.; postgrad., Ill. State U. Instr. piano, Evanston, Ill., 1954-58; instr. elem. music pub. schs., Evanston, 1959; editl. asst. archivist Summy-Birchard Co., Evanston, 1964-66, asst. to editor-in-chief, 1966-67, cons., 1968-69, ednl. dir., 1969-74, also historian, 1973-74; supr. vocal music jr. high sch., Watseka, Ill., 1967-68; asst. dir. profl. programs Music Educators Nat. Conf., Reston, Va., 1974-84, dir. meetings and convs., 1984-94, mgr. direct mktg. svc., 1981-89; sr. cons. Conv. Cons. Svc., 1993—2003, ret., 2003—. Mng. editor Am. Suzuki Jour., 1972-74, Gen. Music Today 1987-91; mgr. display advt. Model T Times, 1971—2006; vice chair editl. bd. Exposition Mgmt., 1991-93. Active various cmty. drives; parish bd. clerk, United Christian Parish, 2001-. Mem. Music

Educators Nat. Conf., Am. Choral Dirs. Assn., In and About Chgo., Music Educators Assn. (bd. dirs.1973-74), Suzuki Assn. Ams. (exec. sec. 1972-74, Disting. Svc. award 1996), Internat. Assn. Exposition Mgmt. (cert., mem. edn. com. 1979-88, chmn. edn. com. 1985-87, bd. liaison edn. com. 1987-88, bd. dirs. Washington chpt. 1983-85, nat. bd. dirs. 1986-91, nat. v.p. 1989, nat. pres. 1990, Disting. Svc. award 1996), Bus. and Profl. Women's Club Watseka (bd. dirs. 1968-70), Antique Automobile Club (registrar ann. meeting 1961-86), Model T Ford Club Internat. (v.p. 1971-72, 76-77, pres. 1981, treas. 1983-87, bd. dirs. 1971-87), Mu Phi Epsilon, Kappa Delta (province pres. 1960-66, 72-76, regional chpts. dir. 1976-78, nat. dir. scholarship 1981-84). Republican. Presbyterian. Home and Office: 1919A Villaridge Dr Reston VA 20191-4824 Office Phone: 703-201-1281.

**MOGILNY, ALEXANDER**, professional hockey player; b. Khabarovsk, Russia, Feb. 18, 1969; With Buffalo Sabres, 1988—99, capt., 1993—95; right wing Vancouver Canucks, 1995—99, NJ Devils, 1999—2001, 2005—, Toronto Maple Leafs, 2001—05. Mem. USSR Olympic Team, 1988; player NHL All-Star Game, 1992—94. Named to Sproting News All-Star 2d Team, 1992—93, NHL All-Star 2d Team, 1992—93; recipient Gold medal, USSR Olympic Hockey Team, 1988. Achievements include being a member of Stanley Cup Champion, NJ Devils, 2000. Office: NJ Devils PO Box 504 50 Rte 120 N East Rutherford NJ 07073*

**MOGK, JOHN EDWARD**, law educator, association executive, consultant; b. Detroit, Feb. 10, 1939; s. Clifford Anthony and Evelyn Lenore (Paselk) M.; m. Lylas Heidi Good, Aug. 23, 1964; children: Marja, Tenley, Matthew. BBA, U. Mich., 1961, JD with distinction, 1964; diploma in comparative law, U. Stockholm, 1965. Bar: N.Y. 1966, Mich. 1970. Assoc. atty. Shearman & Sterling, N.Y.C., 1964 68; mem. faculty Wayne State U. Sch. Law, 1968—, dir. grad. studies, 1990-95. Pres. MERRA Rsch. Corp., 1974-94; cons. econ. and urban devel., arbitrator; vis. prof. U. Utrecht, The Netherlands, 2000. Editor Michigan International Lawyer and Utilities Law Rev.; contbr. articles to profl. jours. Chmn. Mich. TOP Task Force, 1972; vice chmn. Mich. Constrn. Code Commn., 1973; mem. exec. com. Southeastern Mich. Coun. Govts., 1970; chmn. Detroit Sch. Boundary Commn., 1970, Downtown Detroit Vacant Bldg. Com., 1991-93; mem. Detroit Bd. Edn., 1970; mgr. Detroit Empowerment Zone Proposal, 1994; project exec. New Detroit Stadium, 1995; pres. Habitat for Humanity Detroit, 1999-2006. Named Outstanding Wayne State U. Assoc. Prof., 1971, Outstanding Wayne Law Sch. Prof., 1977, 83, 93, 97, 2003, Outstanding Young Man in Detroit, 1972, One of Ten Outstanding Young Men in U.S., 1973, One of Four Outstanding Vols. in U.S., 1974; recipient Presdl. citation Wayne State U., 1977, State of Mich., 1988, 94; Am.-Scandinavian fellow, 1965; vis. fellow U. Warwick, Eng., 1985-86. Mem. ABA, Mich. Bar Assn. (Outstanding Achievement award Internat. Law Sect. 2001). Home: 1000 Yorkshire Rd Grosse Pointe Park MI 48230-1432

**MOGLEN, EBEN**, law educator; b. New Haven, July 13, 1959; s. Sig and Helene (Rosenbaum) M. AB, Swarthmore (Pa.) Coll., 1980; MPhil, JD, Yale, 1985, PhD in History, 1993. Bar: N.Y. 1988. Law clk. to hon. judge Edward Wemfeld US Dist. Ct. NYC, NYC, 1985-86; law clk. to justice Thurgood Marshall US Supreme Ct., Washington, 1986-87; assoc. prof. law to prof. law Columbia U., NYC, 1987—. Mem. ABA, Am. Soc. for Legal History, Phi Beta Kappa. Office: Columbia U Law Sch 435 W 116th St, Rm 642 New York NY 10027-7297 Office Phone: 212-854-8382. E-mail: moglen@columbia.edu.

**MOGLEWER, SARAH ANNE**, music educator; b. Canoga Park, Calif., July 12, 1958; d. Sidney and Edna Moglewer. MusB in Performance, Cath. U. Am., 1982, MM in Performance, 1984. Pvt. piano tchr., Torrance, Calif. 1987—2002, Prescott, Ariz., 2002—; substitute tchr. Prescott Schs. & tri-city area, 2002—. Editor: (book) Etudes for Piano-Louise Farrenc, 2002. Mem.: Sigma Alpha Iota (sec. 1981).

**MOGLIA, JOSEPH H.**, brokerage house executive; m. Amy Jardine; 4 children from previous marriage. BA, Fordham U., 1971; MA, U. Del., 1974. Def. coord. Dartmouth Coll. football team, 1981—83; with Merrill Lynch, 1983—97, head global fixed income inst. sales, head mcpl. div., sr. v.p., head investment performance & product group, 1997—2001; CEO Ameritrade Holding Corp., 2001—. Author: Perimeter Attack Offense, 1981. Bd. dir. Creighton Univ., Nat. Italian Am. Found., 2005—, AXA Fin., 2002—. Office: Ameritrade Holding Corp 4211 S 102nd St Omaha NE 68127-1031 Mailing: Ameritrade Holding Corp PO Box 2760 Omaha NE 68103-2760 Office Phone: 402-331-2744. Business E-mail: jmoglia@ameritrade.com.

**MOGREN, PAUL ANDREW**, librarian; b. Fort Collins, Colo., Aug. 31, 1950; s. Edwin W. and Arle Mae (Arnason) M.; m. Ann Marie Breznay, Aug. 16, 1980; 1 child, Christian Andrew. BA, Colo. State U., 1972; MA, U. Denver, 1973; PhD, U. Utah, 1980. Reference libr. Marriott Libr., U. Utah, Salt Lake City, 1973-82, head of reference, 1982-96, collection specialist, 1996—. Cons. Gov.'s Mansion Libr., Salt Lake City, 1995—, Dixie Coll. Libr., St. George, Utah, 1990; adj. prof. Emporia (Kans.) State U., 1996—; mem. Ogden Union Sta. Libr., 1998—. Mem. AAUP (pres. U. Utah chpt. 1986-89), ALA (coun. 1992-96, RUSA History Libr. of Yr. award 2000), Utah Libr. Assn. (pres. 1988-89). Avocations: gardening, travel. Office: U Utah Marriott Libr 295 S 15th East Salt Lake City UT 84112-0860 Business E-Mail: paul.mogren@utah.edu.

**MOHAIDEEN, A. HASSAN**, surgeon, consultant, health products executive; b. Ramanathapuram, India, Aug. 14, 1940; s. Abdul and Mariam (Pitchai) Kader; m. Zarina M. Meera, May 30, 1965 (dec. July 1986); children: Ahamed, Mariam, Najeeba, Azeema; m. Laurie J. Kucich, June 23, 1989; children: Yasmin Sara, Leila Jahan. MD, U. Madras, India, 1965; MBA, Wagner Coll., 1996. Diplomate Am. Bd. Surgery, Am. Bd. Quality Assurance and Utilization; cert. physician exec. Am. Coll. Physician Execs. Intern Govt. Stanley Hosp., Madras, 1965-66, Good Samaritan Hosp., West Islip, NY, 1967-68; resident in gen. and vascular surgery L.I. Coll. Hosp., Bklyn., 1968-73, asst. attending surgeon, 1973-76, assoc. attending surgeon, 1976-78, attending surgeon, 1978—, chief divsn. vascular surgery, 1980-93, dir. vascular lab., 1981-93; v.p. Bklyn.-Caledonian Hosp. Ctr. (affiliate of NYU), 1994-95; sr. v.p., managed care and exec. vice-chmn. dept. surgery The Bklyn.-Caledonian Hosp. Ctr. (affiliate of NYU), 1995-96; pres., CEO, Health Plan Systems, Inc., Rochelle Park, NJ, 2001—. Asst. surgeon G.H.Q. Hosp., Ramnad, India, 1966-67; assoc. attending surgeon Meth. Hosp., Bklyn., 1982-90, attending surgeon, 1991-97; asst. attending surgeon Bklyn. Caledonian Med. Ctr., 1973-85, mem. courtesy staff, 1985-94, 97—, attending surgeon, 1994-96; attending surgeon Victory Meml. Hosp., Bklyn., 1982—; vis. physician Kings County Hosp. Ctr., Bklyn., 1973-94; clin. instr. in surgery Downstate Med. Ctr., SUNY, Bklyn., 1973-78, clin. asst. prof. surgery, 1978—; mem. exec. com. of med. staff L.I. Coll. Hosp., Bklyn., 1979-93, treas. med. staff, 1982-85, pres., 1985-87, med. chmn. Guild Ball com., 1981, mem. quality assurance com. dept. surgery, 1988-94, chmn. credentials com., 1990-93, quality assurance and risk mgmt. com., 1990-93; bd. dirs. Aetna Health Plans of N.Y., AIDS adv. com., 1987-93, stds. com., 1986-94, quality assurance com.; bd. dirs. Aetna-U.S. Healthcare, 1997; mem. credentials com. Prucare, 1988-92; sr. v.p. managed care Bklyn. Hosp., 1995-96; mem. quality mgmt. com. Oxford Health Plans, 1995-2002; mem. quality improvement com. Chubb Health, N.Y., 1994-96, Cigna (Health-Source), 1997-2003; mem. credentials com. United Healthcare, 1997—; exec. dir. Mayan Health, PPO, Atlantic Med. Assocs. IPA; pres. Health Plan Sys., Inc. Contbr. articles to med. jours. Fellow ACS (com. on Long Island dist. applicants, 1988-99, bd. dirs. Bklyn.-L.I. chpt.), Royal Coll. Physicians and Surgeons Can. (cert.), Internat. Coll. Surgeons; mem. AMA (Physician's Recognition award), AAAS, Am. Coll. Physician Execs., Med. Soc. of State of N.Y., N.Y. State Soc. of Surgeons, N.Y. Acad. of Scis., Med. Soc. of County of Kings (mediation com., 1979-85), Bklyn. Surg. Soc., Soc. for Non-Invasive Vascular Technicians, Kings Physicians I.P.A. (pres./med. dir., 1985-95), Bklyn. Physicians I.P.A. (v.p. 1985-96, pres.). Avocations: photography, computers, walking. Office Phone: 201-556-9430. E-mail: hassan@mohaideen.com.

**MOHAJER, DINEH,** cosmetics company executive; b. Bloomfield Hills, Mich., Sept. 2, 1972; d. Reza and Shahnaz Mohajer. Student, U. So. Calif. Founder, CEO Hard Candy, Inc., Beverly Hills, Calif., 1996—. Office: Hard Candy 729 Farad St Costa Mesa CA 92627-4304

**MOHAM, CARREN,** music educator, singer; b. Checotah, Okla. d. Charley Moham and Shirley Moham Stidham. BA in Edn., Northeastern State U., Tahlequah, Okla.; MusM in Voice, U. Okla.; DMA in Vocal Pedagogy and Black Music History, Ohio State U., 1997. Cert. Am. Inst. Musical Studies, Graz, Austria. Singing therapist, counselor Washington Cancer Inst., 1997—98; assoc. prof. music Ill. Wesleyan U., Bloomington, 1998—. Singer: (CD) Sonnets on Love, Rosebuds and Death: Songs by African-American Women. Recipient Artists' award, Nat. Assn. Tchrs. Singing; grantee, Ill. Wesleyan U., 2001. Mem.: Alpha Kappa Mu, Pi Kappa Lambda, Phi Kappa Phi, Sigma Alpha Iota (faculty social advisor 1999). Office: Ill Wesleyan Univ 1210 Park St Bloomington IL 61702 Office Phone: 309-556-3076. Office Fax: 309-556-3121. E-mail: cmoham@iwu.edu.

**MOHAMED, FEROZE B.,** radiology professor, director; s. Mohamed and Subaidha Ali; m. Shaila Prabhakar, Oct. 11, 1998; 1 child, Amar. PhD, Drexel U., Phila., 1996. Asst. prof. Drexel U., Phila. 1998—2004; assoc. prof. radiology Temple U., Phila., 2004—. Assoc. dir. Functional Brain Imaging Ctr. Temple U., Phila., 2004—. Achievements include research in non invasive brain mapping during truth and deception. Office: Temple Univ 3401 N Broad St Philadelphia PA 19140 Home: 1246 Lombard St Philadelphia PA 19107

**MOHAMED, JOSEPH, SR.,** real estate broker, real estate developer, farmer; b. Omar, W.Va., Mar. 19, 1928; s. Mose and Minnie Elizabeth (Martin) M.; m. Shirley Ida Medeiros; children: Joseph Jr., John W., James R., Leslie Louise. BBA Personnel, Sacramento State U., 1952; postgrad., U. Pacific, U. Calif., Davis, Am. River Coll. Farmer, 1949—; founder comml. trucking operation Calif., 1949-52; founder Mexican Co. of Agr. and Livestock Ltd., Ensenada, Baja, Calif., Mexico, 1953-57; owner Quintair, Inc., Calif., 1954—; contractor, real estate developer, 1949—; owner Joseph's Landscape Svc., Sacramento, 1952—, Joseph Mohamed Enterprises, 1971—. Pest control adviser, Calif., 1970—. Mem. Rep. Nat. Com., Rep. Presdl. Task Force, 1965—; Govs.' Emergency Drought Task Force, 1977, Civil Affairs Assn., Calif. Rental Assn., 1975—, Sacramento Apartment Assn., Calif. Apt. Assn., Nat. Apt. Assn.; dir. McClellan Aviation Museum Found., Sacramento County Sheriff's Mounted Posse, 1961—; pres. First Spiritual Enlightenment Ctr., 1994-. With U.S. Army, 1946—48, col. USAR, 1978, ret. Decorated Legion of Merit; recipient Master Aviator Badge. Mem. Sacramento U. Alumni Assn., Sacramento State U. Horseman's Assn., Calif. State Horseman's Assn., Sacramento Metro. C. of C., Navy League of U.S., Res. Officer's Assn., Assn. of U.S. Army, Mil. Civil Affairs Assn., Sacramento Bd. Realtors, Calif. Assn. Realtors, Nat. Assn. Realtors, Masons, Shriners.

**MOHAMED, MUSTAFA A.,** management educator; b. Arusha, Tanzania, Dec. 26, 1950; arrived in U.S., 1979; s. Mohamed Fiay and Aziza Kassim; m. Ruth Kiefson, Oct. 5, 1996; children: Karim, Aziza. BA, Inst. Devel. Mgmt., Morogoro, Tanzania, 1976; MS in Mgmt., Mgmt. Edn. Inst., Cambridge, Mass., 1980. Asst. lectr.I Inst. Devel. Mgmt., Morogoro, 1976—79; prof. mgmt. Roxbury C.C., Boston, 1983—. Avocations: travel, crisis hotline. Home: 194 Sherman St Cambridge MA 02140 Office: Roxbury C C 1234 Columbus Ave Cambridge MA 02140

**MOHAMMED, ABDUL K.,** chemist, educator; s. Abdul-Kadir and Wosilat Aduke Mohammed; m. Tinu Ottun, Aug. 3, 1991; children: Hassan Ekundayo, Abdul-Qadir Ayodeji, Adam Adebayo. BSc, U. Benin, Benin-City, Nigeria, 1983; PhD, La. State U., Baton Rouge, 1992. Asst. prof. N.C. A&T State U., Greensboro, NC, 1993—99, assoc. prof., 1999—2004; assoc. prof., chairperson Winston-Salem State U., NC, 2004—. Fullbright scholar Sultan Qaboos U., Muscat, Oman, 2003—04. Contbr. articles to profl. jours. Pres. Oduduwa Unity Club, Greensboro, NC, 1999—2000. Recipient Citation Faculty award, Coll. of Arts and Scis., N.C&T State U., 2001; Mem.: N.C. Acad. of Sci., Am. Chem. Soc. (Vol. of Yr. award Ctrl. N.C. sect. 2001), Phi Lambda Upsilon. Achievements include research in Inorganic chemistry research: reading, travel. Office: Winston-Salem State Univ 601 S Martin Luther King Jr Dr Winston Salem NC 27110 Office Phone: 336-750-2543.

**MOHAMMED, NAZR,** professional basketball player; b. Sept. 5, 1977; BA, Univ. Ky., 1999. Center Phila. 76ers, Pa., 1999—2001, Atlanta Hawks, Ga., 2001—03, New York Knicks, NY, 2003—04, San Antonio Spurs, Tex., 2004—05. Achievements include member, NBA Championship Team. Office: San Antonio Spurs One SBC Ctr San Antonio TX 78219*

**MOHAN, JOHN J.,** lawyer; b. St. Louis, May 22, 1945; s. John Joseph and Virginia Loretta (Durkin) M.; m. Elaine Bronwyn Lipe, May 29, 1982; children: Bryn Elizabeth, John Burke. BS Indsl. Engring., St. Louis U., Sch. Engring. and Earth Scis., 1967; JD, St. Louis U., 1971. Bar: Mo. 1971, U.S. Dist. Ct. (we. dist.) Mo. 1971, U.S. Dist. Ct. (ea. dist.) Mo. 1980, U.S. Dist. Ct. (so. dist.) Ill. 1981, U.S. Ct. Appeals (8th cir.) 1987. Asst. prosecuting atty. St. Louis County, 1971-72; asst. cir. atty. St. Louis Cir. Atty's. Office, 1972-74; spl. asst. state's atty. St. Clair County Atty's. Office, Belleville, Ill., 1974—; assoc. Lashley, Caruthers, Theis, Rava & Hamel, St. Louis, 1979-80; ptnr. Schreiber, Tueth & Mohan, Clayton, Mo., 1981-83, Danis, Reid, Murphy, Tobben, Schreiber & Mohan, Ladue, Mo., 1983-87, Hinshaw & Culbertson, St. Louis, 1987-97, Blackwell, Sanders, Peper, Martin, St. Louis, 1998-2000, Tueth, Keeney, Cooper, Mohan & Jackstadt, P.C., 2000—; mcpl. judge City Wildwood, Mo., 2004—. Mem. U. Mo. Law Sch. Found. Scholarship. Mem. ABA, Am. Arbitration Assn. (cert. mediator, arbitrator 1988—), Ill. State Bar Assn., Mo. Bar, Bar Assn. Met. St. Louis, St. Clair County Bar, St. Louis County Bar, Def. Rsch. Inst., Mo. Orgn. Def. Lawyers, Pinnacle Arbitration and Mediation Svcs. (cert. mediator, arbitrator 1997—), Phi Delta Phi. Home: 529 Big Horn Basin Ct Wildwood MO 63011-4818 Office: Tueth Keeney Cooper Mohan Jackstadt PC 425 S Woods Mill Rd Ste 300 Saint Louis MO 63017

**MOHAN, RAM S.,** chemistry professor; s. Rajan and Seetha Mohan. BSc with honors in Chemistry, Hansraj Coll., New Delhi, 1985; MS in Organic Chemistry, U. Delhi, 1987; PhD in Chemistry, U. Md., Balt., 1992. Vis. asst. prof. Coker Coll., Hartsville, SC, 1994—96, Ill. Wesleyan U., Bloomington, 1996—98, asst. prof., 1998—2001, assoc. prof., 2002—. Recipient Henry Dreyfus Tchr. Scholar award, 2001, Disting. Alumni award, U. Md. Balt., 2002. Mem.: Coun. on Undergrad. Rsch, Am. Chem. Soc., Royal Soc. Chemistry.

**MOHAN, TUNGESH NATH,** television and film producer, film educator; b. Lucknow, India, Oct. 30, 1949; arrived in U.S., 1979; s. Bhola Shanker and Saraswati P. (Devi) Nath; m. Annette Gonsalves Mohan; 1 child, Lathika. BS, Kampur (India) U., 1969; diploma in Cinema, Film and TV Inst. India, Poona, 1972; MA, Roanoke, Va. 1990. Prodr. Bombay TV, 1972-75, 77-79; asst. prof. Film and TV Inst. India, Poona, 1975-77; TV prodr. 700 Club, Virginia Beach, Va., 1980-82; prodr. spl. projects Christian Broadcasting Network, Virginia Beach, 1982-86, Christian Broadcasting Network Cable Prodns., Inc., Virginia Beach, 1986-87; dir. Internat. CBN Prodrs. Group, 1987-89, Internat. NorthStar Entertainment Group, LA, 1989-92; mgr. Adventist Comm. Network, Silver Spring, Md., 1992-93; pres. TriAngel Media Corp., Thousand Oaks, Calif., 1992-94; dir. Digital Video Ctr., Samford U., Birmingham, Ala. Adj. prof. Film and TV Inst. India, Poona, 1975—79; Spacer Coll., Poona, 1975—79, Hampton (Va.) U., 1980—92; pres. Prodrs. Unit One, Virginia Beach, 1982—. L.I.F.E. Inc., 1993—; cons. Global Comm. Assocs., Virginia Beach, 1987—88, Global TV Syndication, 1998—; dir. Telecom. Ctr., Huntsville, Ala., 1998—2005. Prodr. dir.: (films) Even So, 1972; Dishantar, 1975 (cert. Proficiency, 1975); Raktajeevee, 1977 (Golden Lion award, 1977); (documentaries) Afghanistan: Under the Iron Claw, 1982; Here I Stand, 2001; In the Footsteps of Martin Luther, 2001; Revolution of Conscience, 2001;

prodr., dir., writer: (films) U-Turn, 1973 (Garima award, 1973); exec. prodr.: Stand at Ease, 1989—90, A Father of Preachers, 2001; co-exec. prodr.: Rin Tin Tin K-9 Cop, 1988—89; prodr.: Touching the Supernatural, 1992, Midnight Cry, 1994, Master Control, 1994, The Way We Were, 1995, Bought at a Price, 1996, Hanged on a Twisted Cross, 1996 (Chris award for best film, Bronze medal for screenplay Columbus Film Festival, 1996), Inn Keeper, 1996, The Invitation, 1997, The Gift, 1997 (Bronze Plaque for 2d pl. Columbus Internat. Film Fest, 1997), (dir.): Reaalizing the Vision, 2001, The Hymnmaker, 2002, For One English Officer, 2002, The Dawning, 2002, Thank You, Mr. Hodges, 2003, The Invitation, 2003, Truth to Tell, 2003, Christianity & Islam: A Dialogue, 2004, The 51st State, 2006, Born With a Wooden Spoon, 2006. Mem.: NATAS, Dirs. Guild Am., Writers Guild Am., Lions. Mem. Seventh-Day Adventist. Avocation: Avocations: collecting stamps, music, camping, travel, tennis. E-mail: lifeincva@aol.com.

**MOHAN IYENGAR, RAJ,** automotive executive, researcher; b. Tiruchirapalli, India; s. Krishnaswamy and Rajalakshmi Rengarajan; m. Gayatri Mohan Iyengar; children: Nikitha, Anitha. BE, Madras U., India, 1980; ME, Indian Inst. Sci., Bangalorre, 1982; MS, Rutgers U., New Brunswick, N.J., 1985; ScM, Brown U., Providence, 1986; PhD, Brown U., 1990. Rsch. assoc. Brown U., Providence, 1990, U. Pa., Phila., 1990—91; rsch. scientist Battelle Meml. Inst., Columbus, 1991—99; sr. engr. Rouge Steel Co., Dearborn, Mich., 1999—2001, mgr. auto. platforms, 2001—. Editor: (ASME Jour.of EMT - Special Issue) Integration of Scientific and Engineering Aspects of Structural Materials in High Temperature Applications, 2000, (ASME Journal of PVP - Special Issue) Challenges and Resolution in Structural Life Prediction, 2001, (Fatigue and Fracture of EM&S -Jour.) Materials and Mechanics Issues in Structural Life Prediction, 1998, (ASME - Bound Volume PVP 413) Understanding and Predicting Material Degradation, 2000, (ASME Bound Volume - PVP 391) Advances in Life Prediction Methodology, 1999; assoc. editor Jour. of Pressure Vessel Tech., 2001—; contbr. over 40 articles to profl. jours.; editor (assoc. tech.): Jour. of Pressure Vessel Tech., 2002—. Mem.: ASME, SAE (com. mem. ferrous 2001—), Am. Soc. Metals (Com. mem.- Materials Divsn. nd PVP Divsn. 1997—, Achievement Certificates 1998, 1999, 2000, 2001). Office: Rouge Steel Company PO Box 1631 3001 Miller Rd Dearborn MI 48121 Business E-Mail: rmohan@rougesteel.com.

**MOHANTY, CHRISTINE ANN,** retired language educator, actress; b. Coaldale, Pa., Jan. 4, 1945; d. Warren Russell and Helen Hargraves; 1 child, Kasmira. BA, Queens Coll., Flushing, N.Y.; MS Edn., Queens Coll., 1972; PhD English Lit., SUNY, Stony Brook, 1986. Tchr. fgn. langs. Three Village Ctrl. Sch. Dist., Setauket, NY, 1969—2000; assoc. prof. Suffolk County C.C. Selden, NY, 1994—2004, SUNY, Stony Brook, —. Dir.: (plays) Death-trap, 1992, Snow Queen, 1995; actor: Stepping Out, 1992, Prelude to a Kiss, 1998, Three Blind Mice, 1999, Social Security, 1999, Arsenic and Old Lace, 2000, Phantom of the Opera, 2000, Wuthering Heights, 2001, The Corn is Green, 2002, The Uninvited, 2002, Little Women, 2002, I Hate Hamlet, 2003, Noel Coward One Acts, 2003, Jekyll & Hyde, 2003, Dancing at Lughnasa, 2004, Shadow of a Doubt, 2004, Doll's House, 2005; contbr. articles to profl. jours.; Exhibited in groups shows at Bayport Pub. Libr., N.Y., 2001—02. Recipient Educator of Week award, NY55 WLNY-TV, 2000; U. Salamanca scholarship, N.Y. State Edn. Dept., 1990. Mem.: AAUW, Am. Assn. Tchrs. French (pres. Suffolk County 1990—93, scholarship to France 1982), L.I. Lang. Tchrs., Phi Beta Kappa. Avocations: travel, tennis, creative writing, painting. Home: 790 Bretton Woods Dr Coram NY 11727 Personal E-mail: christinemohanty@excite.com.

**MOHANTY, MANOJ K.,** mineral engineer, educator; b. Bhubaneswar, Orissa, India, Mar. 9, 1965; arrived in U.S., 1991; s. Surendra Nath Mohanty, Pramila Mohanty; m. Pragyan "Sheela" P. Mohanty; children: Aadansh children: Anjalika. BS in Mining Engring., REC, Rounkela, India, 1985; PhD, So. Ill. U., 1997. Under mgr. Coal India Ltd., Brajraj Nagar, Orissa, India, 1985—91; asst. Scientist So. Ill. U., Carbondale, 1994—97, asst. prof., 2000—05, assoc. prof., 2005—; sr. process engr. Richwood Industries, Huntington, W.Va., 1998—99. Contbr. articles to profl. jours. Grantee Coal Cleaning Tech. Rsch. grants, Ill. Dept. Commerce and Cmty. Affairs; Clean Coal Rev. Bd., 2000, 2001, US Dept. of Energy, 2002—03. Mem.: Soc. Mining, Metallurgy and Petroleum Engrs. (chmn. coal preparation com 2003—, editl. bd. Coal Preparation jour.). Office: So Ill Univ Mining and Mineral Resources Engring Carbondale IL Business E-Mail: mmohanty@siu.edu.

**MOHANTY, SARAJU P.,** computer scientist, educator; B Tech Elec. Engring., Coll. Engring. and Tech., Bhubaneswar, Orissa, India, 1995; ME Systems Sci. and Automation, Indian Inst. Sci., Bangalore, 1999; PhD in Computer Sci. and Engring., U. South Fla., 2003. Asst. prof. U. North Tex., Denton, 2004—. Contbr. over 40 articles to profl. jours.; author conf. procs. Mem.: ACM, IEEE. Achievements include research in synthesis and optimization for low power VLSI circuits; VLSI architecture for copyright protection and security. Office Phone: 940-565-3276. Business E-Mail: smohanty@cs.unt.edu.

**MOHANTY, SITAKANTA,** petroleum engineer; b. Bhubaneswar, Orissa, India, Dec. 9, 1958; came to U.S 1982; s. Radhamohan and Hemaprava M. B.Tech., Indian Sch. Mines, Dhanbad, India, 1982; MS, U. Ala., 1985, PhD, 1991. Teaching asst., rsch. asst. U. Ala., Tuscaloosa; teaching asst. U. Tex., Austin, rsch. asst. 1985-90. Vol. United Action for Elderly, Austin, 1989-90. Mem. Soc. Petroleum Engrs., Sigma Gamma Epsilon (pres. 1984). Hindu. Avocations: volleyball, photography, medication, penfriendship. Home: Sanfarapur Bhubanesway India 751002

**MOHANTY, SUNIL K.,** finance educator, researcher; b. Cuttack, Orissa, India, Oct. 28, 1958; arrived in came to U.S., 1985; s. Biswanath and Khyana Prava Mohanty; m. Tamera Lyn Bach; children: Rani, Raj. B of Tech., Indian Inst. Tech., Kharagpur, India, 1981; MBA, Minn. State U., 1989; D of Bus. Adminstrn., Cleve. State U., 1995. Sr. engr. Engrs. India Ltd., New Delhi, 1981—83, asst. engr., 1983—85; bus. cons. Small Bus. Devel. Ctr., Mankato Minn., 1986—87; instr. dept. of mktg. Minn. State U., Mankato 1988—89; vis. asst. prof. of fin. Hofstra U., Hempstead, NY, 1994—95, assitant prof. of fin., 1995—2001; asst. prof. of fin. U. St. Thomas, Mpls., 2001—, assoc. prof. fin., 2004—. Mem. editl. bd.: Acad. Fin. Studies, 2000—, Acad. Comml. Banking and Fin., 2001—; contbr. articles to profl. jours. (ANBAR Citation of Highest Quality Rating, 1997). Recipient Outstanding Rsch. award, Acad. of Acctg. and Fin. Studies, 2002. Mem.: Allied Acads. Inc (Outstanding Rsch. award 2002), Fin. Mgmt. Assn. Internat. (assoc.), Ea. Fin. Assn. (assoc.), Am. Fin. Assn. (assoc.), Beta Gamma Sigma, Phi Kappa Phi. Avocations: tennis, swimming, travel. Office: U St Thomas 1000 Lasalle Ave Minneapolis MN 55403 Office Phone: 651-962-4416.

**MOHAPATRA, SURYA N.,** laboratory executive; PhD in Med. Physics, U. London; MS electrical engring., Sambalpur Univ., India. Sr. v.p. Picker Internat., 1981—99; sr. v.p., COO Quest Diagnostics, Teterboro, NJ, 1999, pres., COO, 1999—2004, chmn., pres., CEO, 2004—. Bd. dirs. Vasogen Inc., 1999—. Contbr. articles to profl. jours. Mem.: Royal Coll. Surgeons Eng. (hon.) Achievements include patents in field. Office: Quest Diagnostics One Malcolm Ave Teterboro NJ 07608*

**MOHIELDIN, AHMED NADER,** electrical engineer; b. Cairo, Feb. 23, 1974; arrived in US, 1999; s. Nader Mohieldin Rizk and Inas Hassan Abuzaid; m. Marwa Aly Mahmoud Aly, Sept. 24, 2003; 1 child, Abdelrahman Ahmed Nader. BS, Cairo U., 1996, MS, 1998; PhD in Elec. Engring., Tex. A&M U., 2003. Tchg. asst. Cairo U., 1996—98; rsch. asst. Tex. A&M U., Coll. Sta., Tex., 1999—2003; integrated circuits design engr. Tex. Instruments Inc., Dallas, 2003—. Reviewer Transactions on Cirs. and Sys., 2001—06. Contbr. articles to profl. jours. Mem.: IEEE. Achievements include patents

pending for digital compensation of continuous-time sigma-delta converter; digital blockers detection for wireless receiver; patents for high frequency tunable filter. Office Phone: 214-480-3817. Personal E-mail: anader2000@yahoo.com.

**MOHIUDDIN, SYED MAQDOOM,** cardiologist, educator; b. Hyderabad, India, Nov. 14, 1934; came to U.S., 1961, naturalized, 1976; s. Syed Nizamuddin and Amat-Ul-Butool Mahmoodi; m. Ayesha Sultana Mahmoodi, July 16, 1961; children: Sameena J., Syed R., Kulsoom S. MB, BS, Osmania U., 1960; MS, Creighton U., Omaha, 1967; DSc, Laval U., Que., Can., 1970. Diplomate in internal medicine and cardiovasc. disease Am. Bd. Internal Medicine. Intern Altoona (Pa.) Gen. Hosp., 1961-62; resident in cardiology Creighton Meml. Hosp., also St. Joseph Hosp., Omaha, 1963-65, mem. staff, 1965—; prof. adjoint Laval U. Med. Sch., 1970; practice medicine specializing in cardiology Omaha, 1970—; prof. Creighton U. Med. Sch., 1977—, assoc. dir. div. cardiology, 1983-96; prof. pharmacy practice Creighton U. Sch. Pharmacy, 1986—, dir. divsn. cardiology, 1994—, assoc. chair for acad. affairs dept. medicine, 1998—, Richard W. Booth MD prof. cardiology, 2005—. Vice chmn. dept. medicine Creighton U., Omaha, 2003—; cons. Omaha VA Hosp. Rsch. fellow Med. Rsch. Coun. Can., 1968; grantee Med. Rsch. Coun. Can., 1970, NIH, 1973, 2000-03. Fellow ACP, Am. Coll. Cardiology (gov. for Nebr. 1987-90), Am. Coll. Clin. Pharmacology, Am. Coll. Chest Physicians; mem. AAAS, Am. Heart Assn. (fellow coun. clin. cardiology, bd. dirs. 1973-75), Am. Fedn. Clin. Rsch., Nebr. Heart Assn. (chmn. rsch. com. 1974-76, dir. 1973—), Gt. Plains Heart Com. (Nebr. rep. 1976-84, pres. 1977-78), N.Y. Acad. Scis., Nebr. Cardiovasc. Soc. (pres. 1980-81), Creighton Med. Assn. (v.p. 2005—). Democrat. Moslem. Home: 12531 Shamrock Rd Omaha NE 68154-3529 Office: Cardiac Ctr Creighton U 3006 Webster St Omaha NE 68131-2027 Office Phone: 402-280-4566. Business E-Mail: smm@cardiac.creighton.edu.

**MOHL, ALLAN S.,** social worker; b. Passaic, N.J., Feb. 10, 1933; s. Milton and Ruth (Meisler) M.; m. Judith Klein, Dec. 31, 1958; children: Barbara, Eric, Adam. BA, NYU, 1954, MA, 1956, MSS, 1960; PhD, Columbia Pacific U., 1991. Diplomate Clin. Social Work. Dir. residential social svcs., adminstr. Queens (N.Y.) Soc. for Prevention of Cruelty to Children, NY, 1977-80; cons., dir. family svcs. Tip Neighborhood House, Bronx, NY, 1980-84; sch. social worker Com. on Spl. Edn., Dist. 28, N.Y.C., 1984—2002, Project Liberty, 2003—04; psychotherapist in pvt. practice Dobbs Ferry, NY, 1966—2004—. Condr. workshop on incestuous families and child sexual abuse; unit dir. Children's Village, Dobbs Ferry, N.Y., 1971-77; cons. Parents Anonymous, South Bronx, N.Y., 1983-84; com. mem. Crisis Intervention Dist. 28, 1995-2002; mem. Queens regional staff devel. com., 1995-98; mem. Queens regional social work awards com., 1996-98. Contbr. articles to profl. jours. Former chmn. Gen. Social Svcs. Adv. Coun. # 6, 1982-83; active participant Bronx Task Force on Child Abuse and Neglect; group leader Project Enable, South Bronx, N.Y., 1965-67; sponsor Parents' Anonymous group, Bronx, 1982-84; vol. White Plains Med. Hosp. Ctr., 1991—; conduct sing-a-longs various sr. care facilities, 2002—. With U.S. Army, 1956-58. NIMH grantee; recipient Editor's Choice award Internat. Libr. Poetry, 1999, 2000, 02. Mem.: NASW (awards com. Queens, NY chpt.), NY Acad. Scis., Internat. Psychohist. Assn., Am. Group Psychotherapy Assn. (assoc. clin. mem.), Internat. Assn. Counselors and Therapists, NY State Soc. Clin. Social Work Psychotherapists, Am. Orthopsychiat. Assn., Am. Assn. Marriage and Family Therapy, Internat. Soc. Poets (disting. mem.). Home: 14-16 Rockledge Ave Scarborough NY 10510 Office Phone: 914-923-1060. E-mail: mo9al@aol.com.

**MOHL, PAUL CECIL,** psychiatrist, educator; b. Washington, June 5, 1944; s. Emanuel Israel and Grace Baker Mohl; m. Judith Ann Lynn Cohen, Apr. 16, 1978; children: Rachel Grace, Evan Noah. MD, Duke U., Durham, NC, 1971. Diplomate psychiatry Am. Bd. Psychiatry and Neurology, 1978. Residency tng. dir. U. Tex. Southwestern Med. Ctr., Dallas, 1989—, vice chair for edn., 2001—. Maj. U.S. Army, 1974—76. Recipient Irma Bland award, Am. Psychiat. Assn., 2006. Office: Univ Texas Southwestern Medical Ctr 5323 Harry Hines Blvd Dallas TX 75390-9070 Office Phone: 214-648-7312. Business E-Mail: paul.mohl@utsouthwestern.edu.

**MOHLER, BRIAN JEFFERY,** diplomat; b. Niskayuna, N.Y., May 28, 1948; s. Donald and Rosemary (Brown) M. BA, Johns Hopkins U., 1970, MA, 1972. Economist Congl. Rsch. Svc. Libr. of Congress, Washington, 1973-74; commd. fgn. svc. officer U.S. Dept. State, 1974, staff asst. Bur. Econ. Affairs Washington, 1974-76, economist Bur. Econ. Affairs, 1979-82, desk officer European cmty. affairs Bur. European Affairs, 1982-84, desk officer Japanese affairs Bur. East Asian and Pacific Affairs, 1984-86, dep. dir. of econs. for Japanese affairs Bur. East Asian and Pacific Affairs, 1993-95, dir. econ. sanctions policy Bur. Econ. Affairs, 1999-2001, dir. Japanese affairs Bur. East Asian and Pacific Affairs, 2001—03, sr. adviser for Iraq Econ. Reconstrn. Bur. Econ. Affairs, 2003—04, sr. insp. Office of the Insp. Gen., 2004—05; consul Am. Consulate Gen., Strasbourg, France, 1976-78; petroleum attache Am. Embassy, Riyadh, Saudi Arabia, 1986-88, counselor for econ. affairs, 1988-90, dep. chief of mission Abu Dhabi, United Arab Emirates, 1990-93; counselor for econ affairs Am. Embassy, Tokyo, 1995-99; minister counselor econ. affairs Am. Embassy, Ottawa, Canada, 2005—. 2d lt. U.S. Army, 1972, capt. USAR, 1972-85. Recipient Superior Honor award Dept. of State, 1993, 98, 2003, 04, Meritorious Honor award, 1987, 2004, award Sec. of Transp., 1998. Mem.: Japan-Am. Soc. of Washington DC, Am. Fgn. Svc. Assn., Can. Club Ottawa, Sigma Nu. Roman Catholic. Home: 18 Maple Lane Ottawa ON K1M 1G7 Canada Office Phone: 613-688-5214. Personal E-mail: bjmohler@hotmail.com. Business E-Mail: mohlerbj@state.gov.

**MOHLER, MARY GAIL,** magazine editor; b. Milaca, Minn., Dec. 15, 1948; d. Albert and Deane (Vedders) M.; m. Paul Rodes Trautman, June 5, 1976 (div. 1994); children: Elizabeth Deane, David Albert Rodes, Theodore DeForest Lloyd. BA, U. Calif.-Davis, 1974; MA in Lit., SUNY-Stony Brook, 1976. Asst., then editor-reporter Family Circle Mag., N.Y.C., 1979-81; editorial coordinator Ladies' Home Jour., N.Y.C., 1981, assoc. articles editor, 1982, mng. editor, 1982-93, sr. editor, 1994-98; editor in chief Ladies' Home Jour. Parent's Digest; mng. editor Parents Mag., 1999—2001, editor at large, freelance writer, 2001—. Co-author: Those Who Can...Teach, 1999. Medieval philosophy fellow SUNY-Binghamton, 1978 Mem. MLA, Am. Soc. Mag. Editors, Phi Beta Kappa Clubs: Medieval; Overseas Press. Office: Parents Mag 375 Lexington Ave New York NY 10017-5514

**MOHLER, RICHARD ALBERT, JR.,** academic administrator, theologian; b. Lakeland, Fla., Oct. 9, 1959; s. Richard Albert Sr. and Janet Rae (Johnson) M.; m. Mary Ann Kahler, July 16, 1983; children: Mary Katherine, Christopher Albert. BA magna cum laude, Samford U., 1980; MDiv, So. Bapt. Theol. Sem., Louisville, 1983, PhD, 1989; postgrad., St. Meinrad Sch. Theology, 1985, Oxford (Eng.) U., 1986. Ordained min. So. Bapt. Ch. Pastor Union Grove Bapt. Ch., Bedford, Ky., 1982-87; asst. to pres., coord. found. support, dir. capital funding So. Bapt. Theol. Sem., Louisville, 1983-89, pres., 1993—; editor The Christian Index, Atlanta, 1989-93, prof. christian theology, 1996—, Joseph Emerson Brown prof. Christian theology, 2005—. Assoc. dir. The So. Sem. Found., 1983-89; rsch. fellow Ethics and Religious Liberty Commn., 1998—; bd. dirs. Focus on the Family; lectr. in field. Assoc. editor Preaching, 1985-93, contbg. editor, 1993—; gen. editor: The Gods of the Age of the God of the Ages?, 1993; editor-in-chief The So. Bapt. Jour. Theology, 1997—; columnist Religious News Svc., 1998—; sr. corr. World Mag., 1997—; mem. editl. bd. Salem Broadcasting, 1999—; host (radio programs) Truth On the Line, 2001—, The Albert Mohler Program; author daily Crosswalk Commentaries; contbr. articles to profl. jours. Pres., chmn. Coun. of Sem. Pres. of So. Bapt. Conv., 1996—, chmn., Greater Louisville Billy Graham Crusade, 2001. Named one of 40 Rising Evang. Leaders, Christianity Today, 1996, one of 96 Southerners to Watch, Atlanta Jour. and Constitution, 1996, one of 50 Young Leaders Under 40 years of age TIME Mag., one of Emerging Leaders in Edn. CHANGE Mag., 1998. Mem. Am. Acad. Religion, Soc. Biblical Lit., Evang. Theol. Soc., Evang. Philos. Soc., So. Bapt. Hist. Soc., Bapt. Pub. Rels. Assn., So. Bapt. Press Assn., Evang. Press Assn., Nat.

Assn. Evangs., Ga. Bapt. Hist. Soc., Rotary Internat., Phi Kappa Phi, Omicron Delta Kappa. Achievements include being named one of 50 young leaders under 40 years of age TIME Mag. Office: So Bapt Theol Sem 2825 Lexington Rd Louisville KY 40280-0001 Office Phone: 502-897-4121. Personal E-mail: mail@albertmohler.com. Business E-Mail: presoffice@sbts.org, mohler@sbts.edu.

**MOHLER, RONALD RUTT,** electrical engineering educator; b. Ephrata, Pa., Apr. 11, 1931; s. David Wealand and Elizabeth (Rutt) M.; m. Nancy Alice Strickler, May 6, 1950; children: Curtis Gene, Pamela Louise, Susan Lynn, Anita Marie, John Scott, Andrew Thomas, Jennifer Lee, Lisa Nancy. BS (scholarship), Pa. State U., 1956; MS, U. So. Calif., 1958; PhD, U. Mich. 1965. Designer, trainee Textile Machine Works, Rockwell Internat. Corp., Reading, Pa., 1949-56; staff mem. Hughes Aircraft Co., Culver City, Calif., 1956-58, Los Alamos Sci. Lab., 1958-65; asso. prof. elec. engring. U. N.Mex., Albuquerque, 1965-69; prof. elec. engring./aerospace, mech. and nuclear engring. U. Okla., 1969-72; prof., chmn. info. and computing scis., 1970-72; dir. Systems Research Center, 1969-72; adj. prof. elec. engring. and nuclear engring. U. N.Mex., Los Alamos Grad. Center, 1959-65; cons. Sandia Corp., Albuquerque, 1966-69, Aerojet-Gen. Corp., Sacramento, 1966; vis. assoc. prof. system sci. UCLA, 1968-69; cons. community health project OEO, Oklahoma City, 1970-71; prof. elec. and computer engring. Oreg. State U., Corvallis, 1972-98, prof. emeritus, 1998—, head dept., 1972-79, 90; pres. Pace Tech., Inc., 1982-97. Vis. prof. U. Rome, 1973, 75, Imperial Coll., London, 1978-79, U.S. Naval Postgrad. Sch., 1983-85, Australian Nat. U., 1988, Sydney U., 1995, 98; cons. Optimization Software, L.A., 1973—, Bonneville Power Adminstrn., 1975—, Internat. Inst. Applied Systems Analysis, 1988—. Author: Optimal Control of Nuclear Reactors, 1970, Bilinear Control Processes, 1973, Nonlinear Systems: Dynamics and Control, vol. 1, 1991, Applications to Bilinear Control, vol. II, 1991, Disease Dynamics, 1993; editor: Theory and Application of Variable Structure Systems, 1972, Variable Structure Systems with Application to Biology and Economics, 1975, Recent Developments in Variable Structure Systems, Economics and Biology, 1979, Nonlinear Time Series and Signal Processing, 1988, assoc. editor Annals of Nuclear Energy, 1973-97; contbr. jours. Chmn. St. Stephens Sch. Bd., Norman, 1970-72. Recipient NATO award, 1979; rsch. grantee NSF, 1966-99, Sandia Labs., 1966-68, 96-97, ONR, 1981-92, NASA, EPRI, BPA, 1990-97; AEC fellow, 1961-65, Hughes fellow, 1956-58; Acad. Sci. exch. scientist to USSR and China, 1980, US-CIS (USSR) Commn. on Engring. Edn., 1991—. Fellow IEEE (life, local chmn. 1975); mem. Control System Soc., Sigma Xi, Tau Beta Pi, Pi Tau Sigma. Democrat.

**MOHLER, STANLEY ROSS,** preventive medicine physician, educator; b. Amarillo, Tex., Sept. 30, 1927; s. Norton Harrison and Minnie Alice (Ross) M.; m. Ursula Luise Burkhardt, Jan. 24, 1953; children: Susan Luise, Stanley Ross, Mark Hallock. BA, MA, U. Tex., 1953, MD, 1956. Diplomate Am. Bd. Preventive Medicine. Intern USPHS Hosp., San Francisco, 1956-57; med. officer Center Aging Research, NIH, Bethesda, Md., 1957-61; dir. Civil Aeromed. Rsch. Inst., FAA, Oklahoma City, 1961-66, chief aeromed. applications divsn. Washington, 1966-78; prof., vice chmn. dept. community medicine, dir. aerospace medicine Wright State U. Sch. Medicine, Dayton, Ohio, 1978—. Rsch. assoc. prof. preventive medicine and pub. health U. Okla. Med. Sch., 1961—; vice-chmn. Am. Bd. Preventive Medicine, 1978—, sec.-treas., 1980—. Co-editor: Space Biology and Medicine (5 vols.), 1995 (Life Scis. Book award Internat. Acad. Astronautics); contbr. articles to profl. jours. Bd. dirs. Sr. Citizens Assn. Oklahoma City, 1962—, Flying Physicians Assn., 1961—. Served with AUS, 1946-48. Recipient Gail Borden Rsch. award, Boothby award Aerospace Med. Assn., 1966, FAA Meritorious Svc. award, 1974, Cecil A. Brownlow Publ. award Flight Safety Found., 1998, Marie Marvingt award French Soc. Aerospace Medicine and Aerospace Med. Assn., 2006; co-recipient Life Scis. Book award in space, biology and medicine Internat. acad. Astronautics, 1995. Fellow Geriatrics Soc., Aerospace Med. Assn. (pres. 1983, Harry G. Moseley award 1974, Lyster award 1984, Louis H. Bauer Founders award 1998), Am. Coll. Preventive Medicine, Gerontol. Soc.; mem. AMA, Aircraft Owners and Pilots Assn. (Sharples award 1984, Hubertus Strughold award 1991), Alpha Omega Alpha. Home: 6539 Reigate Rd Dayton OH 45459-3214 Office: Wright State U Sch Medicine PO Box 927 Dayton OH 45401-0927

**MOHN, LOUIS,** publishing executive; b. 1956; married; 2 children. BA, Miami Univ., Oxford, Ohio. Acct. mgr., dir. mktg. McGraw-Hill Cos., Pitts.; various sr. level positions including v.p. sales BusinessWeek (a McGraw-Hill pub.), NYC; sr. v.p. Real Names Corp.; pres. consumer auto group Primedia pub., NYC, 2001—06; pub. Playboy mag., NYC, 2006—; and v.p., pub. group Playboy Enterprises, NYC, 2006—. Office: Playboy Enterprises 730 Fifth Ave New York NY 10019 Office Phone: 212-261-5000.*

**MOHN, MELVIN PAUL,** anatomist, educator; b. Cleve., June 19, 1926; s. Paul Melvin and Julia (Jacobik) M.; m. Audrey Faye Lonergan, June 28, 1952; children— Shorey Faye, Andrew Paul AB, Marietta Coll., 1950; Sc.M., Brown U., 1952, PhD in Biology, 1955. Instr. SUNY Downstate Med. Ctr., Bklyn., 1955-59, asst. prof., 1959-63; asst. prof. anatomy U. Kans. Sch. Medicine, Kansas City, 1963-65, assoc. prof., 1965-72, prof., 1972-89, prof. emeritus, 1989—. Cons. Nat. Med. Audiovisual Ctr., Atlanta, 1972; vis. lectr. U. Miami Sch. Medicine, Fla., 1966. Bd. dirs. U. Kans. Med. Ctr. Credit Union, 1968-77, Kansas City Youth Symphony, 1972-77; mem. U.S. Pony Club, 1964-71, Med. Arts Symphony, 1965-71, 90—, Spring Hill Chorale, 1990-96, Spring Hill Hist. Soc., 1997—. Served with USN, 1944-46, PTO. McCoy fellow, 1950, Arnold biology fellow, 1954 Fellow AAAS; mem. Am. Soc. Zoologists, Am. Assn. Anatomists, Am. Inst. Biol. Sci., Masons, Lions, Rotary, Ruritan, Olathe Trail Riders, Phi Beta Kappa, Sigma Xi, Beta Beta Beta. Republican. Methodist. Home: Yankee Bit Farm 23595 W 223rd St Spring Hill KS 66083-4029 Office: U Kans Med Ctr Dept Anatomy 39th and Rainbow St Kansas City KS 66103

**MOHOLY-NAGY, HATTULA,** archaeologist; b. Berlin, Oct. 11, 1933; arrived in U.S., 1937; d. László and Sibyl Pietzsch Moholy-Nagy; m. Roger G. Schneggenburger, June 21, 1987; m. Hans-Rudolf Hug June 1965 (div. Mar. 1979); children: Claudine Laszlo Hug, Daniel Claude Hug. AB in History, U. Mich., 1955, PhD in Anthropology, 1994; AM in Anthropology, U. Chgo., 1958. Field lab. head Joint Casas Grandes Project of Amerind Found., Dragoon, Ariz., 1958—59; Tikal project rschr. U. Pa. Mus., Phila., 1960—, Tikal project field lab., 1960, field lab. dir., 1961-64; lectr. U. Zurich, 1971—78; rsch. assoc. U. Pa. Mus., 1994—. Reviewer anthropol. books and jours., 1960—; participant profl. meetings, 1974—; lectr. and cons. in field, 1995—. Contbr. articles and monographs to profl. jours. and conf. procs. Mem.: Catalogue Raisonné Scholars Assn., Archaeol. Inst. Am., Soc. for Am. Archaeology, Am. Anthropol. Assn. Home and Office: 1204 Gardner Ann Arbor MI 48104-4321 E-mail: hattula@sprynet.com.

**MOHR, BECKY J.,** elementary school educator; b. Sioux Falls, S.D. Aug. 6, 1958; d. Merle and Marilyn Swenson; m. Brian Dean Mohr, May 20, 1978; children: Jessica Hunsaid, Matt. B in Elem. Edn., Sioux Falls Coll., S.D., 1986; M in Ednl. Leadership, Southwest State U., Marshall, Minn., 2000. Tchr. 6th grade Brandon Valley Mid. Sch., SD, 1987—. Named to Hall of Fame for Performing Arts, Brandon Valley, S.D. 2006; recipient S.D. Mid. Level Educator of Yr., 2006. Home: 47960 257th St Garretson SD 57030

**MOHR, CHRISTINA,** retired economist; b. San Diego, Calif., June 1, 1949; d. Lloyd Crowell and Joan Watkins, Oliver Watkins (Stepfather); m. Peter Joseph Mohr, July 13, 1989; stepchildren: Robert, Tracie 1 child, Oliver Wise. BS in Polit. Sci, U. Pa., Phila., 1971; MA in Internat. Affairs, George Washington U., Washington, DC, 1979; PhD in Econs., U. Md., College Park, 1993. Cons. World Bank, Washington, 1982; analyst sci. resource Nat. Sci. Found., Washington, 1983—86, speech writer for dir., 1987—93; sci. analyst Nat. Sci. Found., Washington, 1996—2001; retired, 2001. Commr. People with Disabilities Commn., Montgomery County, Md., 1994—96. Home: 2932 Woodstock Ave Silver Spring MD 20910 Business E-Mail: mohr@nist.gov.

**MOHR, JAY PRESTON,** neurologist, educator; b. Mar. 5, 1937; s. John G. and Marguerite F. Mohr; m. Joan L. Seal, Mar. 10, 1962; children: Thea, Gregory. AB, Haverford Coll., 1958; MS, MD, U. Va., 1963. Diplomate Am. Bd. Neurology and Psychiatry. Intern then asst. resident Mary Imogene Bassett Hosp., Cooperstown, NY, 1963-65; asst. resident N.Y. Neurol. Inst., Columbia-Presbyn. Med. Ctr., N.Y.C., 1965-66; instr. neurology Johns Hopkins U. Med. Sch., U. Md. Med. Sch., 1969-71; assoc. neurologist Mass. Gen. Hosp., Boston, 1972-78; asst. prof. Harvard U. Med. Sch., 1972-78; prof. neurologi, chmn. dept. U. South Ala. Med. Sch., Mobile, 1978-83; Sciarra prof. clin. neurology Columbia U. Coll. Physicians & Surgeons, N.Y.C., 1983—. Dir. cerebrovascular research N.Y. Neurol. Inst., N.Y.C., 1983—; dir. Doris and Stanley Tananbaum Stroke Ctr., 2003—. Contbr. articles to med. jours. Mag. M.C., U.S. Army, 1969-72. Neurology fellow Mass. Gen. Hosp., 1966-69. Fellow Am. Acad. Neurology; mem. Am. Neurol. Assn., Am. Heart Assn. (Stroke coun.), Sigma Xi. Democrat. Mem. Soc. Of Friends. Office: Doris & Stanley Tananbaum Stroke Ctr NY Neurol Inst 710 W 168th St New York NY 10032-2603 also: Presbyn Hosp Columbia-Presbyn Med Ctr New York NY 10032-3784 Office Phone: 212-305-8033. Business E-Mail: jpm10@columbia.edu.

**MOHR, JEFFREY THOMAS,** lawyer; b. Fond du Lac, Wis., June 10, 1950; s. James William and Doris Jean (Tetzlaff) M.; m. Kathy Denise Shaw, July 13, 1974; children: Alex, Michael. BA in Math with honors, U. Wis., 1973, JD with honors, 1978. Bar: Wis. 1978, U.S. Dist. Ct. (ea. and we. dists.) Wis. 1978. Assoc. Foley & Lardner, Madison, Wis., 1978-80; corp. atty. Trane Co., LaCrosse, Wis., 1980-83; corp. counsel, chief legal officer Charter Co. Jacksonville, Fla., 1983-86; corp. counsel Plastics Engring. Co., Sheboygan, Wis., 1986-88, sec., gen. counsel, 1988—. Mem. ABA, State Bar Wis., Sheboygan County Bar Assn., Am. Corp. Counsel Assn., Order of Coif, Phi Beta Kappa. Avocations: golf, making beer. Office: Plastics Engring Co 3518 Lakeshore Rd Sheboygan WI 53083-2903

**MOHR, JOHN LUTHER,** biologist, environmental consultant; b. Reading, Pa., Dec. 1, 1911; s. Luther Seth and Anna Elizabeth (Davis) M.; m. Frances Edith Christensen, Nov. 23, 1939; children: Jeremy John, Christopher Charles. AB in Biology, Bucknell U., 1933; student, Oberlin Coll., 1933-34, Marine Biol. Lab., Woods Hole, Mass., 1934; PhD in Zoology, U. Calif., Berkeley, 1939; postgrad., Am. U., 1963. Research asso. Pacific Islands Research, Stanford, 1942-44; rsch. assoc. Allan Hancock Found., U. So. Calif., 1944-46, asst. prof., 1946-47, asst. prof. dept. biology, 1947-54, asso. prof., 1954-57, prof., 1957-77; chmn. dept., 1960-62; prof. emeritus, 1977—; vis. prof. summers U. Wash. Friday Harbor Labs., 1956, '57. Rsch. assoc. history and philosophy of sci., NSF, Am. U., 1963, vertebrate zoology Natural History Mus., Los Angeles County, 1996-2003; marine borer and pollution surveys harbors So. Calif. Dept. of Fish and Game, 1948-51, arctic marine biol. rsch., 1952-71; chief marine zool. group U.S. Antarctic rsch. ship Eltanin in Drake Passage, 1962, in South Pacific sector, 1965. Mem. Biol. Stain Commn., 1948-80, trustee, 1971-80, emeritus trustee, 1981—, v.p., 1976-80; bd. dirs. Calif. Natural Areas Coord. Coun., 1981-90. Guggenheim fellow, 1957-58. Fellow AAAS (coun. 1964-73, Sr. Scientists and Engrs. Nat. Network), So. Calif. Acad. Scis., Sigma Xi (life, exec. coun. 1964-67, 68, 69, chpt.-at-large bd. 1968-69); mem. Marine Biol. Assn. Eng. (life). Achievements include research in problems with American English leading to dyslexia. Home: 3819 Chanson Dr Los Angeles CA 90043-1601 Office Phone: 323-295-5664. Personal E-mail: jmohr10000@aol.com.

**MOHR, LAWRENCE CHARLES,** physician; b. S.I., N.Y., July 8, 1947; s. Lawrence Charles Sr. and Mary Estelle (Dawsey) M.; m. Linda Johnson, June 14, 1970; 1 child, Andrea Marie. AB with highest honors, U. N.C., 1975, MD, 1979. Diplomate Am. Bd. Internal Medicine. Commd. 2d lt. U.S. Army, 1967, advanced through grades to col., 1989; med. intern Walter Reed Army Med. Ctr., Washington, 1979-80, resident in medicine, 1980-82, chief resident, 1982-83, attending physician, 1984-86, pulmonary fellow, 1986-87; command surgeon 9th Inf. Div., Ft. Lewis, Wash., 1983-84; med. cons. Madigan Army Med. Ctr., Tacoma, 1983-84; White House physician Washington, 1987-93; asst. prof. medicine Uniformed Svcs. U. of the Health Scis., Bethesda, Md., 1984-91; assoc. prof. medicine Uniformed Svcs. U. Health Scis., Bethesda, Md., 1991-94; assoc. clin. prof. medicine George Washington U., Washington, 1990-94; prof. medicine Med. U. S.C., Charleston, 1994—, dir. environ. bioscis. program, 1995—. Attending physician Med. U. Hosp., Charleston, 1994—; Charleston Meml. Hosp., 1994—; mem. Working Group on Disability in U.S. Presidents, 1995—. Editor: International Case Studies in Risk Assessment and Magagement, 1997, Biomarkers, Medical and Workplace Applications, 1998; contbr. articles to profl. jours. and books. Bd. dirs. Internat. Lung Found., Washington; mem. adv. bd. Nat. Mus. Health and Medicine, Washington; mem. sci. adv. bd. Consortium in Environ. Risk Evaluation; prin. investigator Consortium in Molecular Epidemiology and Biomarker Rsch. Decorated Silver Star, Bronze Star with 2 V devices and 3 oak leaf clusters, Purple Heart, Meritorious Svc. medal with oak leaf cluster, Air medal, Army Commendation medal with oak leaf cluster, D.S.M.; recipient Erskine award Walter Reed Army Med. Ctr., 1982; named Outstanding Med. Resident, 1982. Fellow ACP, Am. Coll. Chest Physicians; mem. AMA, Army and Navy Club, Order Mil. Med. Merit, Harbour Club, Phi Beta Kappa. Episcopalian. Avocations: mountain climbing, skiing. Home: 673 Lake Francis Dr Charleston SC 29412-4345 Office: Med U S C Environ Bioscis Program 171 Ashley Ave Charleston SC 29425-0001

**MOHR, ROGER JOHN,** retired advertising agency executive; b. Milw., Sept. 8, 1931; s. Reinhold and Clara (Meissner) M.; m. Pauline Spicuzza, Oct. 18, 1958; children: Gregory, Mary Margaret, Kristin, Thomas, Kathleen. BS in Speech, Marquette U., 1953; postgrad. radio and TV, Northwestern U., 1955-56. Staff announcer radio sta. WBKB, West Bend, Wis., 1952, WCAN, Milw., 1952-54; with Arthur Meyerhoff Assos., Inc., Chgo., 1956-80, pres., 1965-80, BBDO, Chgo., 1980-82, chmn. 1982-90, vice chmn. internal 1991-93, ret., 1993. Chmn. Lake Bluff (Ill.) Plan Commn., 1972-75; mem. Lake Forest (Ill.) Plan Commn., 1994-2000, chmn., 1999-2000; bd. dirs. Chgo. City Ballet, 1982-84, Off the Street Club, 1976-78; mem. adv. coun. Marquette U. Sch. Comm., 1993-99; alderman Lake Forest City Coun., 2000—06. Served with AUS, 1954-55. Mem. Am. Assn. Advt. Agys. (chmn. Chgo. coun. 1966-67, sec., treas., nat. bd. dirs. 1976-77), Evans Scholars Alumni Assn. (pres. 1964-65), Western Golf Assn. (bd. dirs. 1980-2000), v.p. 1994-2000, trustee 2000—), Knollwood Club (bd. govs. 1980-85, 89-92), Tavern Club (bd. govs., v.p. 1988-94). Home: 2000 Knollwood Rd Lake Forest IL 60045-1137 Personal E-mail: rjpmmohr@sbcglobal.net.

**MOHRAZ, JUDY JOLLEY,** foundation administrator; b. Houston, Oct. 1, 1943; d. John Chesler and Mae (Jackson) Jolley; m. Bijan Mohraz; children: Andrew, Jonathan. BA, Baylor U., 1966, MA, 1968; PhD, U. Ill., 1974. Lectr. history Ill. Wesleyan U., 1972-74; asst. prof. history So. Meth. U., Dallas, 1974-80, coord. women's studies, 1977-81, assoc. prof. history, 1980-94, asst. provost, 1983-88, assoc. provost for student academics, 1988-94; pres. Goucher Coll., Towson, Md., 1994-2000, Virginia G. Piper Charitable Trust, Scottsdale, Ariz., 2000—. Cons. Ednl. Testing Svc., Princeton, NJ, 1984-93, Nat. Park Svcs., Seneca Falls, NY, 1992-93; bd. dirs. Balt. Equitable Soc., 1996-00, The Assocs. First Capital, 1999-00, Coun. Foundations, 2005-; bd. visitors US Naval Acad., 1996-01. Trustee St. Mark's Sch. Tex., 1993-94; adv. bd. U. Tex. Southwestern Med. Sch., 1992-94; active Leadership Dallas, 1994; bd. dirs. Nat. Assn. Ind., The Balt. Cmty. Found., Coun. of Founds., 2005—; pres. Ariz. Grantmakers Forum, 2003-05; mem. Ariz. State Sch. Readiness Bd., 2003—; bd. dirs. Greater Phoenix Leadership, 2005—. Recipient Disting. Alumni award Baylor U., 1993; named Woman of Merit, Omicron Delta Kappa, 1993. Office: Virgina G Piper Charitable Trust 6720 N Scottsdale Rd Ste 350 Scottsdale AZ 85253 Office Phone: 480-948-5853. Business E-Mail: jmohraz@pipertrust.org.

**MOHRFELD, RICHARD GENTEL,** marketing professional; b. Camden, N.J., Dec. 30, 1945; s. Herbert Henry and Elizabeth Weldon (Gentel) M.; m. Ann Bacon, June 20, 1971 (div. 1975); m. Janice Lee Strickland, July 1, 1978; children: Kathryn Elizabeth, Christopher Hall. BSc in Geology, Dickinson Coll., 1971. Staff geologist Temple U., Phila., 1971-74; pres. Mohrfeld Inc.,

Collingswood, NJ, 1974—2002; sr. mktg. exec. Quest Environ. & Engring. Svcs., Inc., Clinton, 2002—05; environ. specialist Salem County Health Dept., 2006—. Bd. dirs. South Jersey Savs. & Loan Assn., Turnersville, N.J., 1984-2000. Bd. dirs. Boy Scouts Am., Camden County, N.J., 1985—; trustee Knight Park Trustees, Collingswood, 1986—, Health Care Support Found., Inc., 1994—. Sgt. USAF, 1969-71. Mem. ASHRAE, Air Conditioning Contractors Am. (pres. 1986-88), Fuel Mchts. Assn. N.J. (pres. 1992-94), Rotary (pres. Collingswood 1980-81). Episcopalian. Avocations: travel, photography. Home and Office: 314 Auburn Rd Pilesgrove NJ 08098-2602 Office Phone: 856-935-7510. Personal E-mail: m-fuel@comcast.net.

**MOHRMAN, HENRY JOE, JR.,** lawyer, investment manager; b. St. Louis, Jan. 28, 1948; s. Henry Joseph and Mavis Claire (Lynch) M.; m. Mary Beth Mohrman, Aug. 26, 1969; children: Aaron Henry, Anna Rose. BA, Yale U., 1969; JD, U. Chicago, 1973. Bar: Mo. 1973, Ill. 1974, U.S. Supreme Ct. 1997. Assoc. Greenfield & Davidson, St. Louis, 1973-76; asst. gen. counsel LaBarge, Inc., St. Louis, 1976-77; tax mgr. Ernst & Young, St. Louis, 1977-81; pvt. practice St. Louis, 1982—. Gen. counsel Miss. Valley Equipment Co., St. Louis, 1982—, MKT Mfg., Inc., St. Louis, 1986—, Ronald Coase Inst., 2000—, Whisler Farms LLC, 2002—; prin. Mohrmanlaw LC, 2004—. Mem. ABA, U. Chicago Law Sch. Alumni Assn. (pres. St. Louis chpt. 1986—). Avocations: horsemanship, literature, theater, mathematics. Office: 7751 Carondelet Ave Ste 805 Clayton MO 63105-3369 Office Phone: 314-721-3626.

**MOHRMAN, KATHRYN J.,** academic administrator; BA, Grinnell Coll., 1967; MA, U. Wis., 1969; PhD, George Washington U., 1982. Dean undergrad. studies U. Md., College Park 1988—93; pres. The Colo. Coll., Colorado Springs, 1993—2002; exec. dir. Hopkins-Nanjing Ctr. for Chinese and Am. Studies, Johns Hopkins U., 2003—. Office: 1619 Massachusetts Ave NW Washington DC 20036 Office Phone: 202-663-5801.

**MOHS, FREDERIC EDWARD,** lawyer; b. Madison, Wis., Mar. 16, 1937; s. Frederic E. and Mary Ellen Reynolds M.; m. Mary M. Mohs, June 14, 1959; children: Paula A., Nicole L. BS, U. Wis., 1959, JD, 1964. Bar: Wis. 1964. Assoc. Axley, Brynelson, Madison, Wis., 1964-67; ptnr. Mohs, MacDonald, Widder & Maradise, Madison, 1967—. Bd. dirs. Madison Gas and Electric Co., Madison. Regent U. Wis., Madison, 1997-2004. Mem. Downtown Madison Rotary. Republican. Office: Mohs MacDonald Widder & Paradise 20 N Carroll St Madison WI 53703 Office Phone: 608-256-1978. E-mail: fred@mmwp-law.com.

**MOHTADI, HAMID,** economics professor, researcher; M in Physics, Columbia U., NYC, 1976; PhD in Econs., U. Mich., Ann Arbor, 1982. Vis. asst. prof. Columbia U., NYC, 1982—83; prof. econs. U. Wis., Milw., 2003—. Rsch. fellow Econ. Rsch. Forum, 1994—; vis. prof. U. Minn., St. Paul, 2006—, acting co-dir. Food Industry Ctr., 2006—; co-editor Internat. Economic Jour. Contbr. articles to profl. jours. Mem.: Am. Econ. Assn., Phi Beta Kappa. Avocations: reading, tennis, music. Office: 612-625-8241. Business E-Mail: mohtadi@uwm.edu.

**MOIR, CHRISTOPHER ROBERT,** surgeon; b. Montréal, Can., Jan. 5, 1954; came to U.S., 1994; BS, U. Brit. Columbia; MD, U. Brit. Columbia, Vancouver, B.C., Can., 1979. Diplomate Am. Bd. Surgery, Am. Bd. Surg. Critical Care, Am. Bd. Ped. Surgery. Intern, general surgery Dalhousie U. Program, 1979-80; resident, pediatric surgery U. Brit. Columbia, Vancouver, BC, Canada, 1980-86; fellow, pediatric surgery McGill U., Montreal, QC, Canada, 1986-88; divsn. chmn. surgery Mayo Found., Mayo Clinic Coll. Medicine, Rochester, Minn., 1994—; assoc. prof., surgery Mayo Clinic Coll. Medicine, Rochester, Minn., 1994—. Contbr. articles to profl. jours. Fellow Royal Coll. Surgeons (Can.); mem. ACS, Royal Coll. Pediatric Surgeons Can., Physicians and Surgeons B.C. (Can.), Am. Pediatric Surgeons Assn. lead surgeon for a team of doctors who separated conjoined twin girls in 2006. Office: Mayo Clinic Dept Ped Surg 200 First St SW Rochester MN 55905 Business E-Mail: moir.christopher@mayo.edu.*

**MOIZE, JERRY DEE,** lawyer, federal official; b. Greensboro, NC, Dec. 19, 1934; s. Dwight Moody and Thelma (Ozment) M.; m. Margaret Ann Wooten, Aug. 13, 1976; 1 child, Jerry Dee Jr. AB cum laude, Elon (N.C.) Coll., 1957; JD, Tulane U., New Orleans, 1960; diploma, Army Command & Gen. Staff Sch., USAR, 1981. Bar: Colo. 1961, US Dist. Ct. Colo. 1961, US Ct. Mil. Appeals 1962, US Supreme Ct. 1965, NC 1965. Legal clk. Air Def. Commd., Colo. Springs, Colo., 1960-61, assistance officer, 1962-63; chief legal assistance divsn. 2nd Army, Ft. Meade, Md., 1964-65; staff JAG, Indiantown Gap Mil. Reservation, 1965; law clk. to hon. Eugen Gordon U.S. Dist. Ct. (mid. dist.) NC, Winston-Salem, 1965-66; dir. Legal Aid Soc. Forsyth County, Winston-Salem, 1966-69; exec. dir. Forsyth Bail Project, Winston-Salem, 1968-69, Lawyer Referral Svc. of Bar of 21st Jud. Dist., Winston-Salem, 1968-69; staff atty. office of gen. counsel FAA, Washington, 1969-70, acting chief admin. & legal resources, 1970-71; staff atty. office of gen. counsel Dept. HUD, Washington, 1971, counsel Jackson area office Miss., 1971-83, chief counsel Jackson field office Miss., 1983-94; chief counsel Office Gen. Counsel Miss., Jackson, 1994—; HUD del. Miss. Fed. Exec. Assn. 1997—2000. Lectr. U. W.Va. Conf. on Poverty Law, 1968; HUD program svc. adviser, 2000—. Editor NC Legal Aid Reporter, 1968-69; NC Legal Aid Directory, 1968, Avlex Legal Index (2nd supplement), 1971, developed Miss. low income housing financing mechanism 1975-76; contbr articles to profl. jours., articles to splty. mags. Dem. candidate NC Ho. of Reps., Guilford County, 1964; mem. mil. com. Forsyth County NC Red Cross, 1967-68; pack leader Andrew Jackson coun. Boy Scouts Am., 1986-92; active Project Adv. Group US Office Econ. Opportunity Legal Svc. Program, 1968-69, Am. Com. on Housing & Urban Devel., Miss., Law Rsch. Inst., 1980-81, Pilot Mountain Preservation & Park Com., Winston-Salem, 1968-70; mem. Race Com Whitworth Hunt Races, 1975-76; Am. Master of Foxhounds Assn., 1976-79; adv. Order DeMolay, 1997—; mem. Miss Scottish Games, 1999, v.p. 2000, pres. 2001. Capt. AUS, 1960-65; ret. lt. col. USAR, 1966-87. Decorated Meritorous Svc. medal, Army Commendation medal with oak leaf cluster, Army Res. Forces Achievement medal with three oak leaf clusters, Nat. Def. Svc. medal, Armed Forces Res. medal; named Hon. Knight Mason, 1999; recipient Legion of Honor, Order of De Molay, 2000. Mem.: KT, NRA, Miss. Opera Assn., NC State Bar, Fed. Bar Assn., Sons of Confederate Vets., Caledonian Soc. Miss., The Austin Hunt (joint master of foxhounds 1976—79), Iron Bridge Hunt (v.p. 1964—65), Miss. Hist. Assn., Miss. Track Club, Whitworth Hunt (founder, master of foxhounds 1975—76), Capital Club (Jackson, Miss.), Rosicrucian, Masons (32 degree), Shriners, Order Ea. Star, Pi Gamma Mu. Republican. Episcopal. Avocations: running, book collecting. Office: Miss State Dept Housing & Urban Devel Fed Bldg 100 W Capitol 9th Flr Jackson MS 39269 Home: 120 Highland Cove Ridgeland MS 39157-4719 Office Phone: 601-965-4700 ext. 2325.

**MOJER-TORRES, LISA NAN,** lawyer; b. Queens, N.Y., Dec. 1, 1956; d. Joseph Raymond and Gwendolyn Emma Mojer; m. Rolando Torres, Oct. 24, 1987; children: Matthew Roland Torres, Liam Joseph Torres. BA, Boston U., 1978; JD, NYU, 1991. Bar: N.J. 1994, N.Y. 1994. Atty. at law Lisa Mojer-Torres, Esq., Lawrenceville, NJ, 1994—; spl. svcs. consumer adv. State of NJ, Dept. HHS, Divsn. of Addiction Svcs., Trenton, 2005—. Coun. mem. Dept. HHS, SAMHSA, Ctr. for Substance Abuse Treatment Nat. Adv. Coun., Rockville, Md., 1999—2001; com. mem. Dept. HHS, FDA, Ctr. for Drug Evaluation and Rsch. Drug Abuse Adv. Com., Rockville, Md., 1993—96; cons., expert witness, atty., consumer adv. Lisa Mojer-Torres, Esq., Lawrenceville, NJ, 1995—; panel mem. and expert witness nat. treatment plan initiative of the ctr. for substance abuse treatment Dept. HHS, SAMHSA, Ctr. for Substance Abuse Treatment, Rockville, Md.; nat. policy panelist JoinTogether (Boston U. Sch. of Pub. Health) in collaboration with the ABA (Standing Com. on Substance Abuse), Washington, 2002—03. Mem. editl. bd. Jour. Maintenance in the Addictions; author (rschr.): NJ Gov.'s Study Commn. on Discrimination in Pub. Contracting. Recipient Pub. Svc. award, Nat. Inst. of Drug Abuse, 1995. Mem.: NY Bar Assn., NJ Bar Assn. Democrat-Npl. Avocation: figure skating. Home: 9 Whitemarsh Dr Lawrenceville NJ 08648 Office: NJ DHS Divsn of Addiction Svcs PO Box

362 Trenton NJ 08648 Office Phone: 609-292-5050. Home Fax: 609-671-1994; Office Fax: 609-292-3816. Personal E-mail: rtorres605@aol.com. Business E-Mail: lisa.mojer-torres@dhs.state.nj.us.

**MOJICA, AGNES,** academic administrator; Chancellor Inter Am. U. of PR, San German, P.R. Past chair governing bd. Hispanic Assn. Colls. and Univs., 1995-96, co-chair leadership group; chair governing bd. Intercollegiate Athletic League, 2001-02. Pres., Consortium of Presidents and Chancellors for the Prevention of the Use and Abuse of Drugs and Alcohol, 1998-02; co-chair Am. Cancer Assn. Relay for Life Event, PR, Rsch. Area-Polit. Violence PR. Mem., Assn. Industrialists of P.R., Western C. of C., Am. Assn. Higher Edn., Assn. Profl. Women, Altrusa, Rotary (hon.), Alpha Delta Kappa, Phi Delta Kappa. Office: Inter Am U PO Box 5100 San German PR 00683-9801 Office Phone: 787-264-1912 ext. 73. Business E-Mail: amojica@sg.inter.edu.

**MOJICA, PABLO,** surgeon; b. San Juan, Jan. 29, 1971; s. Julio Mojica and Angela Manosa; m. Lisa Winchester, Mar. 4, 1999; 1 child, Diego Javier. BS, U. PR, 1993, MD, 1997. Resident U.D.H. and Affiliated Hosps., San Juan, 1997—2003; head and neck surgeon Roswell Park Cancer Inst., Buffalo, 2003—05; oncology surgeon City of Hope, Duarte, Calif., 2005—. Contbr. chapters to books. Avocations: soccer, sailing. Office: City Hope Nat Med Ctr 1500 East Duarte Rd Duarte CA 91010 Business E-Mail: pmojica-manosa@coh.org.

**MOJTABAI, ANN GRACE,** author, educator; b. N.Y.C., June 8, 1937; d. Robert and Naomi (Friedman) Alpher; m. Fathollah Mojtabai, Apr. 27, 1960 (div. 1966); children: Chitra, Ramin. BA in Philosophy, Antioch Coll., 1958; MA in Philosophy, Columbia U., 1968, MS in Libr. Sci., 1970. Lectr. philosophy Hunter Coll., CUNY, 1966-68; libr. CCNY, 1970-76; fellow Radcliffe Inst. Study, Cambridge, Mass., 1976-78; Briggs-Copeland lectr. on English Harvard U., 1978-83; writer-in-residence U. Tulsa, 1983—2005, Yaddo Found., Saratoga, NY, 1975, 76. Author: Mundome, 1974, The 400 Eels of Sigmund Freud, 1976, A Stopping Place, 1979, Autumn, 1982, Blessed Assurance, 1986, Ordinary Time, 1989, Called Out, 1994, Soon: Tales From Hospice, 1998. Recipient Richard and Hinda Rosenthal award Am. Acad. and Inst. Arts and Letters, 1983, Lillian Smith award So. Regional Coun., 1986, Lit. Acad. award AAAL, 1993; Guggenheim fellow, 1981-82 Mem.: PEN, Mark Twain Soc., Tex. Inst. Letters, Phi Beta Kappa. Home: 2329 Woodside Drive Amarillo TX 79124-1036 Personal E-mail: agmojtabai@aol.com.

**MOK, CARSON KWOK-CHI,** structural engineer; b. Canton, China, Jan. 17, 1932; came to U.S., 1956, naturalized, 1962; s. King and Chi-Big (Lum) M.; m. Virginia Wai-Ching Cheng, Sept. 19, 1959. BSCE, Chu Hai U., Hong Kong, 1953; M.C.E., Cath. U. Am., 1968. Registered profl. engr., Md., D.C. Structural designer Wong Cho Tong, Hong Kong, 1954-56; bridge designer Michael Baker Jr., Inc., College Park, Md., 1957-60; structural engr., chief design engr., assoc. Milton A. Gurewitz Assocs., Washington, 1961-65; ptnr. Wright & Mok, Silver Spring, Md., 1966-75; owner Carson K.C. Mok, Cons. Engr., Silver Spring, 1976-81, pres., 1982—. Facility engring. cons. Washington Met. Area Transit Authority, 1985-86; pres. Transp. Engring. and Mgmt. Assocs., P.C., Washington, 1986-2002; adj. asst. prof. Howard U., Washington, 1976-79, adj. assoc. prof., 1980-81. Contbr. articles to profl. jours. Bd. dirs. U.S. Pan Asian Am. C. of C. Sec.; N.Am. trustee China Grad. Sch. Theology, Wayne, Pa., 1972-74, pres., 1975-83, v.p., 1984-91, dir., 1992—; elder Chinese Bible Ch. Md., Rockville, 1978-80; chmn. Chinese Christian Ch. Greater Washington, 1958-61, 71, elder, 1972-76; dir. Evergreen Family Friendship Svc., Inc., A Pub. Benefit Corp., Colorado Springs, 1993—. Recipient Outstanding Std. of Tchg. award Howard U., 1980, Nat. Merit award U.S. Dept. Transp., 2000. Mem. ASCE, ASTM, Nat. Assn. Corrosion Engrs., Concrete Reinforcing Steel Inst., Am. Inst. Steel Constrn., Am. Concrete Inst., Am. Welding Soc., Prestressed Concrete Inst., Post-Tensioning Inst., Soc. Exptl. Mechanics, Internat. Assn. Bridge and Structural Engring., Pui Ching Mid. Sch. Alumni Assn. (pres. nation's capital chpt. 1991-97). Home: 4405 Bestor Dr Rockville MD 20853-2137 Office: 9001 Ottawa Pl Silver Spring MD 20910-2257 Office Phone: 301-587-3448. E-mail: ckm9001@aol.com.

**MOK, SAMUEL TINSING,** federal agency administrator; m. Nancy Mok; 2 children. BS in Acctg., Fordham U., 1968; MA in Auditing, Cath. U., Washington, 1982; grad., US Army Inst. of Administration, Fort Benjamin Harrison, US Foreign Svc. Inst., Rosslyn, Va. Cert. Internal Auditor, Govt. Fin. Mgr. Former dep. mayor Chinatown, Washington; dir. acctg. Time-Life Books, 1976—82; corp. treasurer U.S. News & World Report, 1982—86; foreign svc. officer Bureau of East Asian and Pacific Affairs, U.S. Dept. of State, 1986; mem. fed. sr. exec. svc. U.S. Dept. of State; chief fin. officer, comptroller U.S. Treasury Dept., 1988—92; CEO GL Assocs., 1992—96; mng. mem. Condor Cons., LLC, 1996—2002; chief fin. officer U.S. Dept. Labor, Washington, 2002—. With U.S. Army. Decorated Meritorious Unit Citation, Meritorious Svc. medal; recipient James Saylor award Outstanding Svc., Assn. Govt. Accts., Washington. Office: US Dept Labor 200 Constitution Ave NW Washington DC 20210

**MOKHOV, NIKOLAI V.,** physicist, researcher; b. Saratov, Russia, Dec. 13, 1946; arrived in U.S., 1992; s. Veniamin S. and Elena S. Mokhov; m. Lyudmila V. Mokhov, Nov. 12, 1971; children: Dmitri, Oleg. MS, Moscow Inst. Physics Engring., 1971, PhD, 1976. Lab. head Inst. High Energy Physics, Protvino, Russia, 1976—92; group leader Superconducting Supercollider Lab., Dallas, 1992—94; scientist II and group leader Fermi Nat. Accelerator Lab., Batavia, Ill., 1994—. Mem. Sci.-Tech. Coun. Inst. High Energy Physics, Protvino, Russia, 1989—93. Author: Passage of High-Energy Particles Through Matter, 1989; contbr. scientific papers. Recipient employee awards, Inst. High Energy Physics, 1976—92, Fermilab, 2000. Fellow: Am. Physical Soc.; mem.: Am. Nuc. Soc. (mem. exec. com.). Avocation: fly fishing. Office: Fermilab MS 220 Kirk & Wilson PO Box 500 Batavia IL 60510 Office Phone: 630-840-4409. Business E-Mail: mokhov@fnal.gov.

**MOKOTOFF, MICHAEL,** pharmaceutical sciences educator; b. Bklyn., Jan. 23, 1939; s. Jack Israel and Pauline (Hochberg) M.; m. Bonnie Faith Arieff, Apr. 22, 1967; children: Jeffrey David, Naomi Joy, Jay Daniel BS in Pharmacy, Columbia U., 1960; MS, U. Wis., 1963, PhD, 1966. Cert. pharmacist, N.Y. Fellow NIH, Bethesda, Md., 1966—68; asst. prof. U. Pitts., 1968—72, assoc. prof. medicinal chemistry, 1972—85, assoc. prof. pharm. scis., 1985—95, prof. pharm. scis., 1995—2006, prof. emeritus pharm. scis. 2006—. Vis. scientist Weizmann Inst. Sci., Robovot, Israel, 1978; mem. Pa. Drug, Device and Cosmetic Bd., Harrisburg, 1990-98 Editor, author: (with others) Pharmaceutical and Pharmacodynamics Vol. 3: Peptides, Peptoids and Proteins, 1991; mem. editl. bd. Jour. Peptide Rsch., 1997-2004; contbr. articles to Jour. Protein Rsch., Jour. Medicinal Chemistry, Jour. Peptide Rsch.; contbr. chpt. to Principles of Medicinal Chemistry fourth edit., 2002 Fellow Agy. Indsl. Sci. Tech., Tokyo, 1997 Mem. Am. Assn. Colls. Pharmacy, Am. Peptide Soc., European Peptide Soc. Achievements include patent for novel peptidyl amino steroids. Office: U Pitts 512 Salk Hall Pittsburgh PA 15261-0001 E-mail: moagie@pitt.edu.

**MOKRASCH, LEWIS CARL,** neurochemist, educator; b. St. Paul, May 9, 1930; s. Lewis and Anna (Dvorak) M.; m. Jane Carolyn Church, Apr. 20, 1974. BS magna cum laude, Coll. St. Thomas, 1952; PhD, U. Wis., 1955. Rsch. assoc. dept. psychiatry and neurology La. State U. Med. Center, New Orleans, 1956-57, assoc. prof. dept. biochemistry, 1971-76, prof., 1976-92 prof. emeritus, 1992—; acting head dept., 1978-79. Instr. medicine U. Kans. Med. Center, Kansas City, 1957-59, assoc. in medicine, dir. neurochemistry lab., 1959-62; asst. biochemist McLean Hosp., Belmont, Mass., 1960-64 assoc. biochemist, 1964-71; assoc. prof. biol. chemistry Harvard Med. Sch. Boston, 1964-67; asst. prof., 1967-71; adj. assoc. prof. biology Hellenic Coll., Brookline, Mass., 1969-71; staff scientist Neurosciences Research Programs, Brookline, 1970-71; vis. prof. neurology Duke U. Med. Center, 1981-82;

lectr. in field Author book written on myelin; contbr. articles to profl. jours.; reviewer: jours. Sci., FASEB. Pres. Belmont Preservation Soc., 1969; candidate Bd. Selectman, Belmont, 1969; active Forsyth County Adult Care Home Cmty. Adv. Com., Hospice, Sr. Fin. Care, Winston-Salem, Reynolda Ho. Mus. Am. Art, Reynolda Gardens, Sr. Svcs. Program, Winston Salem, Citizens Quality Nursing Home Care, 1991-92; sr. leader Duke Long Term Care Program Edn. Com.; mem. edn. com. Shepherd Ctr. Grantee NIMH, 1973-74, Nat. Inst. Neurol. Disability and Blindness, 1957-90, Schlieder Found., 1971-72, 83-84, La. Bd. Regents, 1986-88. Fellow Am. Assn. Clin. Chemists; mem. Am. Soc. Neurochemistry (local chmn. 1974), Am. Soc. Biol. Chemists, Soc. Neurosci. (founder, pres. local chpt. 1974-75), Soc. Rsch. Adminstrs. (membership chmn. New Eng. sect.), Nat. Citizens Coalition Nursing Home Reform, Am. Assn. Individual Investors (founder, past pres., sec. Piedmont chpt.), Libertarian. Achievements include first demonstration of adaptive enzyme regulation in animals and allosteric control of fructose bisphosphatase, of incorporation of hydrouracil into transfer RNA, of thermogenic mechanism for arousing hibernators, of metabolic control in hibernation, of altered hydrophobic proteins in neurological disorders, of biosynthesis of hydrophobic proteins and mitochondrial proteins in brain in vitro, of altered transport processes in cells of neurological disease victims, of defective transport of acetylcholine precursors into cells of Alzheimer's victims and that such transport is modulatable; development of coestimation method for ketoses, aldoses, and pentoses; first isolation in pure form of receptor hydrophobic proteins from mammalian brain. Home: 2711 Pilgrim Ct Winston Salem NC 27106 E-mail: drlewmokasch@aol.com. *Before I entered Science, I regarded it as a Priesthood of individuals dedicated to the service of humanity, whose common goal was the enhancement of human life and the remedying of its ills. After 30 years in Science, I hold this thesis more strongly and have found many colleagues who agree with it. I am certain now that the failures and abuses of Science derive from the use of it for the goals of wealth, fame and power.*

**MOKRZECKI, LECH MARIAN,** history of education educator; b. Warsaw, Apr. 5, 1935; s. Justyn and Irena (Druhowino) M.; m. Aleksandra Maria Horbowska, Aug. 20, 1983. MA, U. Toruń, Poland, 1956; dipl. cellist, Acad. Music, Gdańsk, Poland, 1962, MA, 1964; PhD, Higher Sch. Pedagogy, Gdańsk, Poland, 1967; DrHabil, U. Gdańsk, Poland, 1975; PhD (hon.), Linköping U., 1998. From asst. to prof. extraordinary Gdańsk U., Poland, 1966, prof. ordinary, 1993—2006. Author: Three Centuries of Gdansk Learning, 1969, 2d edit., 1976, The Study of the Teaching of History, 1973, In the Sphere of the Work of Gdansk Historians in XVII Century, 1974 (Min. of Edn. award 1976), The Beginning of the Knowledge of the Sea in the Former Kingdom of Poland, 1983, The Fortress Vistulamouth, 1978, Traditions of Teaching History to the Close of XVI Century-Selected Countries and Problems, 1992 (Min. of Edn. award 1993), From the Tradition of Teaching History to the End of 16th Century, 1992, Science and Education in Polish Lithuanian Commonwealth, 2001, The History of Gdansk University, 2006, co-author, editor: In the Sphere of Culture, Music, Ballet, 1971 (Min. of Culture award 1972), Scientific Copy Books of Gdansk University, Pedagogy History of Education, 1993, 97; co-author: A Significant Social Revolution, 1994. Head, History of Social Sci. Commn., Policy Acad. Sci. Mem. Assn. Internat. pour History of Edn. Belgium, Com. Internat. Scis. History, Commn. History of Historiography Italy, Polish Acad. Scis. (History of Sci. and Tech. com.). Roman Catholic. Avocations: travel, reading poetry. Home: Biała 6-28 80-435 Gdansk Poland Office: Gdansk Higher Pedagogie School Biskupia 24A 80-875 Gdansk Poland

**MOL, GRETCHEN,** actress; b. Deep River, Conn., Nov. 8, 1972; d. Janet Mol; m. Tod Williams, June 1, 2004. Grad., Am. Musical & Dramatic Acad. Actor: (films) Girl 6, 1996, The Funeral, 1996, Donnie Brasco, 1997, The Last Time I Committed Suicide, 1997, The Deli, 1997, Bleach, 1998, Too Tired to Die, 1998, Rounders, 1998, New Rose Hotel, 1998, Celebrity, 1998, Finding Graceland, 1998, Music from Another Room, 1998, The Thirteenth Floor, 1999, Cradle Will Rock, 1999, Sweet & Lowdown, 1999, Forever Mine, 1999, Just Looking, 1999, Attraction, 2000, Get Carter, 2000, The Shape of Things, 2003, Heavy Put-Away, 2004, The Notorious Bettie Page, 2005, Puccini for Beginners, 2006; (TV films) Calm at Sunset, 1996, Subway Stories: Tales from the Underground, 1997, Picnic, 2000, Freshening Up, 2002, The Magnificent Ambersons, 2002; (TV miniseries) Dead Man's Walk, 1996; (TV series) Girls Club, 2002. Office: c/o William Morris Agy 1 William Morris Pl Beverly Hills CA 90212 Office Phone: 310-859-4000.*

**MOLAEI, GOUDARZ,** research scientist; s. Hojjatollah Molaei and Gilandoust Nosrati; m. Rita Molaei; 1 child, Ashkan. PhD, U. Toronto, Canada, 1998—2004. Cert. vector biology expert WHO, 2002. Faculty U. Tehran, Iran, 1991—94; rsch. assoc. and tchg. asst. U. Toronto, 1995—2004; postdoctoral scientist Conn. Agr. Exp. Sta., New Haven, 2004—06, rsch. scientist, 2006—. Biology exec. com. U. Toronto, Mississauga, Ontario, 2001—02. Contbr. articles to profl. jours. Achievements include research in the role of Culex mosquitoes in the epidemiology of the West Nile virus; discovery and characterization of genes involved in neurotransmission; a new mosquito species involved in malaria transmission; development of the sterile insect technique to control a major agricultural pest. Office: Conn Agr Exp Sta 123 Huntington St New Haven CT 06504 Office Fax: 203-974-8502. Business E-Mail: goudarz.molaei@po.state.ct.us.

**MOLAY, HILARY S.,** lawyer; b. 1954; BA, Brandeis U.; JD, U. Miami. Bar: 1980. Law clerk to Judge Rita C. Davidson Md. Ct. of Appeals; trial atty. civil div. US Dept. Justice, Washington; assoc. Shank, Irwin & Conant, Finley, Kumble, Wagner, Heine, Underberg, Manley, Myerson & Casey; counsel J.C. Penney Co., Inc.; v.p., gen. counsel, sec. Zale Corp., Irving, Tex., 2000—05, sr. v.p., gen. counsel, corp. sec., 2005—. Mem. adv. bd. corp. counsel symposium Southern Methodist U., 2004; mem. gen. counsel forum Nat. Retail Federation. Mem.: ABA, Am. Soc. of Corp. Secretaries (mem. corp. practices comm.). Office: Zale Corp 901 W Walnut Hill Ln Irving TX 75038

**MOLDENHAUER, JUDITH A.,** graphic design educator; b. Oak Park, Ill., Feb. 28, 1951; d. Raymond L. and Jean Marie (Carqueville) M. BFA, U. Ill., 1973; MA, Stanford U., 1974; MFA, U. Wis., 1977. Design supr. N.E. Mo. State U., Kirksville, Mo., 1977-79; asst. prof. design Kansas City Art Inst., Mo., 1979-83; asst. prof. art, graphic design Sch. Art U. Mich., Ann Arbor, 1983-92; vis. lectr. Wayne State U., 1990-92, asst. prof. graphic design, 1992-98, assoc. prof. graphic design, 1998—, area coord. graphic design, 1992—. Free-lance designer The Detroit Inst. Arts, Toledo (Ohio) Mus. Art, Burroughs Corp. (Unisys) Detroit, Detroit Focus Gallery; vis. designer N.S. Coll. Art and Design, 1986; juror Ohio Mus. Assn., 1986, Collaborator Presdl. Initiative "Healthy Start": prenatal and pre-conceptional booklets and infl. modules designs, 1992-1995; mem. organizing group health info. design Design Forum; presenter Congress Women's Health Issues, 1997, 98, Internat. Inst. Info. Design, Schwarzenberg, Austria, 1998, Vienna, 2005, Read Me exhbn., Bern, Switzerland, 1999, Expert Forum Manual Design, Malardalen U., Eskilstuna, Sweden, 2000, Vision Plus II, Internat. Inst. for Info. Design, 2005, others; co-chair info. design edn. Internat. Inst. Info. Design, 2004, faculty/vis. expert Summer Acad., Bolzano, Italy, 2005, co-dir. Summer Acad., Chgo., 2006, Health Comm. Forum, Boston, 2006 Contbr. articles to profl. jours. Recipient award of distinction, merit award Am. Assn. Museums, 1985, 86, Excellence Design award Beckett Paper Co., 1991, gold award for softcover books Printing & Pub. Competition, 1994, Am. Graphic Design award, 1996, 98; Rackham grantee U. Mich., 1987, grantee Nat. Endowment for Arts, 1988; US-EU FIPSE grantee U.S. Dept. Edn. student and faculty exch. info. design, 2003. 19th Internat. Bi-Ann. Graphic Design Czech Republic, 2001; Fulbright fellow, Sweden, 2006—. Mem. Wood Engraving Network, Univ. and Coll. Designers Assn. (merit award 1979, gold award 1979), Coll. Art Assn. (chmn. panel 1991), Women's Caucus for Art (panel chmn. 1987), Amnesty Internat., Women in Design (excellence award Chgo. 1985, Sierra Club, Audubon Soc., Nat. Inst. Design. Lutheran. Office: Wayne State U Dept Art and Art History 150 Art Bldg Detroit MI 48202 Office Phone: 313-993-8165, 313-577-2980. Personal E-mail: FrogBoggd@aol.com.

**MOLDENHAUER, KERMIT GENE,** music educator; b. Fond du Lac, Wis., Oct. 24, 1949; s. Warren Herbert Moldenhauer and Verona Elsie Noldenhauer; m. Laura Jean Smith, June 20, 1971; children: Amy, Aaron, Rachel, Philip. BS in Edn., Dr. Martin Luther Coll., 1971; M Church Music, Concordia U., 1988; PhD in Theology and Ministry, Internat. Sem., 2005. Tchr. St. Stephen's Luth. Sch., Beaver Dam, Wis., 1971—75, Martin Luther Acad., New Ulm, Minn., 1975—79, Martin Luther Prep. Sch., Prairie du Chien, Wis., 1979—90; music editor Northwestern Pub. House, Milw., 1990—95; prof. music Martin Luther Coll., New Ulm, 1995—. Adv. mem. WELS Commn. on Worship, Milw., 1990—. Composer numerous settings in Christian Worship and other publs.; co-editor: Christian Worship: Manual, 1993. Mem.: Music Educators Nat. Conf., Am. Choral Dirs. Assn. Avocations: woodworking, fishing. Home: 41524 593d Ave New Ulm MN 56073 Office: Martin Luther Coll 1995 Luther Ct New Ulm MN 56073

**MOLDENHAUER, SUSAN,** museum director, curator; BFA, No. Ill. U., 1974; MFA, Pa. State U., 1982. Gallery mgr. Sch. Visual Arts, Pa. State U.; exec. dir. Second Street Gallery, Charlottesville, Va.; curator mus. progs. U. Wyo. Art Mus., Laramie, 1991—96, asst. dir., 1996—2000, interim dir., 2000—02, dir., chief curator, 2002—. Office: U Wyo Art Mus 2111 Willett Dr Laramie WY 82071-3807 Office Phone: 307-766-6620. E-mail: uwartmus@uwyo.edu.

**MOLDENHAUER, WILLIAM CALVIN,** soil scientist; b. New Underwood, S.D., Oct. 27, 1923; s. Calvin Fred and Ida (Killam) M.; m. Catherine Ann Maher, Nov. 26, 1947; children— Jean Ann, Patricia, Barbara, James, Thomas BS, S.D. State U., 1949; MS, U. Wis., 1951, PhD, 1956. Soil surveyor S.D. State U., Brookings, 1948-54; soil scientist U.S. Dept. Agr., Big Spring, Tex., 1954-57, Ames, Iowa, 1957-72, Morris, Minn., 1972-75; rsch. leader Nat. Soil Erosion Rsch. Lab., Agrl. Rsch. Svc. U.S. Dept. Agr., West Lafayette, Ind., 1975-85; prof. dept. agronomy Purdue U., West Lafayette, 1975-85, prof. emeritus, 1985—. Contbr. articles to profl. jours. Served with U.S. Army, 1943-46 Fellow Am. Soc. Agronomy, Soil Sci. Soc., Soil Conservation Soc. Am. (pres. 1979), World Assn. Soil and Water Conservation (pres. 1983-85, exec. sec. 1985-2003). Home and Office: 2400 Sunrise Ridge Cir #107 Brookings SD 57006 Business E-Mail: moldwc@itctel.com.

**MOLDOFF, WILLIAM MORRIS,** retired lawyer; b. Phila., Jan. 1, 1921; s. David and Pauline (Arcusin) Moldoff; m. Doris Elaine Johnson (dec.); children: Phillip Douglas, Laura Ellen, Janet Susan Sayers, Allan William. BA, U. Iowa, 1943; JD cum laude, U. Miami, 1950; LLM, U. Mich., 1955. Law editor Lawyers Coop. Pub. Co., Rochester, N.Y., 1952-54, 57-60; instr. Ohio No. U. Coll. of Law, 1955-57; proofreader N.Y. Codes, Rules and Regulations State of N.Y., 1960, adminstrv. asst. to exec. dep. Sec. of State, 1961-63; pvt. practice Nassau, N.Y., 1963-66; vets. claims examiner, rating bd. VA Regional, N.Y.C., 1966-85; ret., 1985. Lt (jg) USNR, 1943—46. Republican. Jewish. Home: 2 Phillips St Nassau NY 12123

**MOLDOW, SUSAN,** publishing executive; m. Bill Shinker. Various positions to exec. editor Avon Books, 1976—82; editor in chief Dell Books, 1982; editorial dir. Penguin Books, 1988—90; v.p. Viking Penguin Inc., 1988—90; editor in chief Doubleday Publishers, 1990—91; v.p. assoc. pub. and editor in chief, adult trade book div. HarperCollins, 1991—94; pub., v.p. Scribner (Simon & Shuster), N.Y.C., 1994—. Office: Scribner Simon & Shuster 1230 Ave Of The Americas New York NY 10020-1513

**MOLEKO, LEBOHANG KENNETH,** ambassador; b. Lesotho, Oct. 15, 1950; married; 3 children. BS in Mathematics & Physics, U. Botswana; MS in Physics, U. Cincinnati; PhD in Condensed Matter Physics, U. Ottawa. Assoc. prof. physics Nat. U. Lesotho, 1977—91, prof. & lecturer physics, 1991—98; amb. to numerous countries including Mexico, U.S., China, Indonesia, Republic of Korea, Thailand, Japan Lesotho, 1994—2000, high commr. to New Zealand, Singapore, Australia, Malaysia, India, 1995—99, perm. rep. designate to UN, 2001; perm. amb. Perm. Mission of Kingdom of Lesotho to UN, 2002—. Mem. hon. com. Africa-Am. Inst.; mem. Canadian Assn. of Physicists, Am. Physical Soc.; pres. exec. bd. UNICEF, 2003—. Office: Permanent Mission of Kingdom of Lesotho 204 E 39 St New York NY 10016

**MOLEN, JOHN KLAUMINZER,** lawyer; b. Gary, Ind., June 13, 1952; s. Franklin B. and Jane Anne (Klauminzer) M.; m. Susan Wilson Blair, Aug. 10, 1985; children: Mary Wilson, Elisabeth Blair. AB with honors, U. N.C., 1974, MBA, 1978, JD with honors, 1978. Bar: Ala. 1978. Assoc. Bradley Arant Rose & White LLP, Birmingham, Ala., 1978-84, ptnr., 1984—. Mem. Rotary Club Birmingham-Sunrise. Presbyterian. Avocations: sailing, swimming. Office: Bradley Arant Rose & White LLP One Federal Pl 1819 5th Ave N Birmingham AL 35203-2104 Office Phone: 205-521-8238. E-mail: jmolen@bradleyarant.com.

**MOLER, EDWARD HAROLD,** retired lawyer; b. Oklahoma City, May 26, 1923; s. Harold Stanley and Rosemary (Callahan) M.; m. Donna Blocksom Cram, Sept. 12, 1964; children: John Frederick, Shelley Elizabeth, Christopher Bryan. BA, U. Okla., 1947, LLB, 1948. Bar: Okla. 1948, U.S. Supreme Ct. 1951. Pvt. practice law, Oklahoma City, 1948-52, 61—; asst. mcpl. counselor, 1952-59; mcpl. counselor, 1959-61; spl. justice Okla. Supreme Ct., 1977. Trustee Oklahoma City Mcpl. Improvement Authority, 1960-61; bd. dirs. Mummers Theatre, Inc., 1969—; bd. dirs. Greater Oklahoma City YMCA, 1981-91. 2d lt. USAAF, 1943-45. Mem. ABA, Okla. Bar Assn., Oklahoma County Bar Assn. (bd. dirs. 1963-67, pres. 1968), Rotary, Phi Delta Phi, Phi Gamma Delta (pres. local chpt. 1946, pres. Nu Omega Housing Assn. 1963-65). Home: 2540 NW Grand Blvd Oklahoma City OK 73116-4110 Office Phone: 405-232-3566.

**MOLER, ELIZABETH ANNE,** lawyer; b. Salt Lake City, Jan. 24, 1949; d. Murray McClure and Eleanor Lorraine (Barry) M.; m. Thomas Blake Williams, Oct. 19, 1979; children: Blake Martin Williams, Eleanor Bliss Williams. BA, Am. U., 1971; postgrad., Johns Hopkins U., 1972; JD, George Wash. U., 1977. Bar: D.C. 1978. Chief legis. asst. Senator Floyd Haskell, Washington, 1973-75; law clk. Sharon, Pierson, Semmes, Crolius & Finley, Washington, 1975-76; profl. staff mem. com. on energy and natural resources U.S. Senate, Washington, 1976-77, counsel, 1977-86, sr. counsel, 1987-88; commr. FERC, Washington, 1988-93, chair, 1993-97; dep. sec. Dept. of Energy, Washington, 1997-98, acting sec., 1998; ptnr. Vinson & Elkins, Washington, 1998-99; sr. v.p. Exelon Corp., 2000—02, sr. v.p., 2002—. Mem. ABA, D.C. Bar Assn. Democrat. Office: Exelon Corp Suite 400 East 101 Constitution Ave NW Washington DC 20001 Home: 1537 Forest Ln Mc Lean VA 22101-3317

**MOLEY, KEVIN EDWARD,** ambassador; Asst. sec. mgmt. and budget U.S. Dept. Health & Human Services, Washington, 1989—92, dep. sec., 1992—93; sr. advisor to Dick Cheney Bush/Cheney Presdl. Campaign, 2000; U.S. permanent rep. to the UN & other internal orgn. in Geneva U.S. Dept. State, Geneva, 2001—. Dir. Pres. Edn. Summit with U.S. Govs., Charlottesville, Va., 1989; vice chmn. Pres.'s Coun. on Mgmt. Improvement, 1989—92; exec. dir. U.S./Pacific Islands Nations Summit, Honolulu, 1990. USMC, 1965—71.

**MOLHO, EMANUEL,** publisher; b. NYC, Jan. 27, 1936; s. Isaac Emanuel and Alvira (Altchek) M.; m. Brenda Nadel, Sept. 25, 1965; children— Deborah Rochelle, Brian Emanuel. BA, NYU, 1957; MBA, Wharton Sch., U. Pa., 1960. Pres. French & European Publs., N.Y.C., 1961—; French & Spanish Book Corp., 1967—. Pres. Librairie de France, Inc., 1961—. Recipient Orden de Merito Civil Spain, 1975 Mem. Am. Booksellers Assn., French-Am. C. of C. in U.S. (exec. com.), Paris Am. Club. Office: Librairie de France Rockefeller Center Promenade 610 5th Ave New York NY 10020-2497 E-mail: livresny@aol.com.

**MOLHO, ERIC STEVEN,** neurologist, researcher; b. NYC, Nov. 6, 1961; s. Roeben and Roslyn Molho. AB, Vassar Coll., Poughkeepsie, NY, 1983; MD, Albany Med. Coll., NY, 1987. Intern Albany Med. Ctr., 1987—88, resident in neurology, 1988—91, fellow in movement disorders, 1991—92, asst. prof. neurology, 1992—98, assoc. prof., 1998—, Rilay family chair in Parkinson's Disease, 2005—. Fellow: Am. Acad. Neurology. Avocation: birdwatching. Office: Albany Med Ctr Parkinsons Disease and Movement Disorder 215 Washington Ave E Albany NY 12205

**MOLHOEK, KERRINGTON RAMSEY,** research scientist; d. Carlton Lee and Linda Ford Ramsey; m. Charles Conrad Molhoek, June 12, 2004. PhD, U. Va., Charlottesville, 2004. Rsch. faculty U. Va. Sch. Medicine, Charlottesville, 2004—. Mem.: U. Va. Alumni Assn. (life), Colonnade Club (life), Nat. Soc. Collegiate Scholars (life), Delta Delta Delta (life). Office: Univ Va 409 Lane St MR-4 Rm 3038 Charlottesville VA 22908 Office Phone: 434-924-2129. Business E-Mail: klr5w@virginia.edu.

**MOLHOLM, KURT NELSON,** retired federal agency administrator; b. Denver, June 24, 1937; s. Ervin Maurice and Helen Pauline (Nelson) M.; m. Sonja Dell Williams, Aug. 17, 1967; children: Kevin William, Paul Nelson. BS, U. Oreg., 1959; MS, George Washington U., 1974; grad., Indsl. Coll. Armed Forces, 1974. Computer specialist D.L.A. Adminstrv. Support Ctr., Alexandria, Va., 1963-65; with Hdqrs. Def. Logistics Agy., Alexandria, 1965-85, chief planning and policy office, 1975-76, chief ADP/T tech. div., 1984-85; adminstr. Def. Tech. Info. Ctr., Alexandria, 1985—2005; ret., 2005. Pres. Nat. Fedn. Abstracting and Info. Svcs., Phila., 1993-94, treas., 1990-93; del. Va. Govs. Conf. Librs. Info. Svcs., 1990, Fed. Libr. Pre-White House Conf. On Librs. Info. Sci., 1990; vice chmn. Fed. Libr. and Info. Ctr. Com., 1992-93, 2002-03; chmn. CENDI Group, 1991-94, 99-2001; mem. NATO Agard Tech. Info. Panel, 1985-91, Internat. Coun. Sci. and Tech. Info., 1993—, treas., 1998-2001, chair editl. bd., 1999-2001, pres. 2001—04; mem. Info. Infrastructure Task Force, 1993-97; chair panel 2 U.S. Nat. Commn. on Librs. and Info. Sci. Comprehensive Assessment of Pub. Info. Dissemination, 2000; NFAIS Conrad Meml. lectr., 2003. 1st lt. U.S. Army, 1960-63. Recipient Meritorious award William A. Jump Meml. Found., 1973, Civilian Svc. award, Def. Logistics Agy., 1991, Exceptional Civilian Svc. award, DLA, 1985, Exceptional Civilan Svc. award, Def. Info. Systems Agy., 2005. Methodist. Personal E-mail: kmolholm@aol.com. E-mail: kurt@molholm.com.

**MOLINA, ALFRED,** actor; b. London, 1953; m. Jill Gascione. Grad., Guildhall Sch. Music and Drama. Film appearances include Raiders of the Lost Ark, 1981, Meantime, 1983, Number One, 1984, Eleni, 1985, Ladyhawke, 1985, Water, 1985, Letter to Brezhnev, 1986, Prick Up Your Ears, 1987, Manifesto, 1988, Not Without My Daughter, 1991, Enchanted April, 1992, American Friends, 1993, The Trial, 1993, Maverick, 1994, White Fang 2: Myth of the White Wolf, 1994, The Steal, 1994, Species, 1995, Scorpoin Spring, 1995, Hideaway, 1995, Dead Man, 1995, Drowning in the Shallow End, 1989, When Pigs Fly, 1993, White Fang II: Myth of the White Wolf, 1994, Maverick, 1994, The Steal, 1994, Hideaway, 1995, The Perez Family, 1995, Dead Man, 1995, Species, 1995, Nervous Energy, 1995, Before and After, 1996, Mojave Moon, 1996, Anna Karenina, 1997, Scorpion Spring, 1997, Further Gesture, 1997, Boogie Nights, 1997, The Man Who Knew Too Little, 1997, Impostors, 1998, The Treat, 1998, Pete's Meteor, 1998, Dudley Do-Right, 1999, Magnolia, 1999, Chocolat, 2000, Texas Rangers, 2001, Frida, 2002, Plots with a View, 2002, Ape, 2002, My Life Without Me, 2003, Identity, 2003, Coffee and Cigarettes, 2003, Luther, 2003, (TV movies) The Accountant, 1990, Virtuoso, 1991, Angels, 1992, Ashenden, 1992, A Year in Provence, 1993, The Marshal, 1993, Requiem Apache, 1994, The Place of Lions, 1997, Rescuers: Stories of Courage: Two Couples, 1998, Miracle Maker (voice), 2000, Murder on the Orient Express, 2001; (Broadway shows) Art, 1998, Fiddler on the Roof, 2004- (Tony nom. best actor in a musical, 2004); other stage appearances include Destiny, 1977, Troilus and Cressida, 1977, Bandits, 1977, The Bundle, 1977, Frozen Assets, 1977, That Good Between Us, 1977, King Lear, 1977, Dingo, 1978, Irish Eyes and English Tears, 1978, Willie, 1978, Accidental Death of an Anarchist, 1979 (Plays and Players award for most promising new actor), Destry Rides Again, 1982, Dreyfus, 1982, Viva, 1985, The Night of the Iguana, 1992, Molly Sweeney, 1995 (Theatre World award, 1996, Drama Desk award, 1996), True West, 2001, The Cherry Orchard, 2002. Office: William Morris Agy 151 S El Camino Dr Beverly Hills CA 90212-2775

**MOLINA, GLORIA,** municipal official; b. Montebello, Calif., May 31, 1948; d. Leonardo and Concepcion Molina; m. Ron Martinez, 1 child, Valentina Student, East L.A. Coll., 1968, Calif. State U., L.A., 1970-75. Staffing specialist Office Presdl. Pers., Washington, 1977-79; dir. intergovtl and congl. affairs region IX US Dept. Health & Human Services, San Francisco, 1979-81; So. Calif chief dep. Calif. State Rep. Willie L. Brown Jr., 1981; mem. Calif. State Assembly, 1982—86, L.A. City Coun., 1987—91, L.A. County Bd. Supervisors, 1991—, chair, 2005—. Mem. Revenue & Taxation, Labor & Employment, Utilities & Comm. Coms., Select Com. on Small Bus., 1982—, Consumer Protection, 1984—; chairwoman Subcom. Mental Health & Devel. Disabilities, 1984—. Named Hispanic of the Yr. Caminos mag., 1982, Dem. of the Yr. L.A. County Dem. Cent. Com., 1983, Woman of the Year Mexican-Am. Opportunity Found., 1983, MS mag, 1984, Woman of the Yr. Hispanic Bus. mag., 2006 Mem. Comision Femenil Mexicana Nacional. Office: LA County 500 W Temple St Ste 856 Los Angeles CA 90012-2723*

**MOLINA, J. ERNESTO,** thoracic surgeon, educator; s. Ernesto and Maria N. Molina; m. Carmen Aida Mendez, Oct. 15, 1960; children: Patricia M. Anderson, Ernesto, Francisco Javier, Luis Alfonso, Jorge Roberto. MD, Universidad San Carlos, Guatemala City.Guatemala, 1960; PhD, U. Minn., Mpls., 1978. Diplomate Am. Bd. Surgery, Am. Bd. Thoracic Surgery Clin instr. U. of Minn., Mpls., 1972—74, clin. assoc. prof. 1ex. Technol. U., Amarillo, Tex., 1974—76; assoc. prof. of surgery U. of South Fla., Tampa, Fla., 1976—78, U. of Minn., Mpls., 1979—91, prof. of surgery, 1991—, Contbr. articles to profl. scientific publs. (First award Gold Medal (Graduation thesis), 1961). Grantee Exptl. Rsch. projects, Medtronic, 1999, 2001; Rsch. grantee, Am. Heart Assn., 1984, Minn. Med. Found., 1980, 1984, 1998, 2001. Mem.: ACS, AMA (corr.; mem.), Am. Heart Assn., Soc. of Thoracic Surgeons, Am. Assn. for Thoracic Surgery (assoc.). Independent-Republican. Roman Catholic. Achievements include invention of Defibrillator lead; design of Heart Preservation Device; Cardiac Cannula; patents for Implantable Defibrillator lead; first to New operation for subclavian vein thrombosis; New operation fro Thoracic Outlet Syndrome. Avocations: swimming, kayaking and canoeing, hunting, hiking, bicycling. Office: U Minn 420 Delaware St S E MMC 182 Minneapolis MN 55455 Office Phone: 612-625-6911. E-mail: molin001@umn.edu.

**MOLINA, JOSE,** scriptwriter, television producer; b. San Juan, Puerto Rico, 1971; Writer (TV series) Strange World, 1999, Dark Angel, 2000—01, Firefly, 2002, 2004, writer and prodr. Law & Order: Spl. Victims Unit, 2004—06 (Nat. Coun. La Raza ALMA award (Am. Latin Media Arts), outstanding script for TV drama or comedy, 2006).*

**MOLINA, JOSEFA MARIA,** psychologist, marriage and family therapist; b. Tucson, Oct. 28, 1959; d. David Molina and Susan Lynne Stockton; life ptnr. Annamarie Giron, Oct. 18, 1990; children: Ramon Ocelotl Giron-Molina, Cristina Ixchel Giron-Molina. BA, U. Calif., Berkeley, 1981; MA, John F. Kennedy U., 1984; PhD, Calif. Inst. Integral Studies, 1996. Lic. psychologist Ariz., marriage and family therapist Bd. Behavioral Sciences, Calif., 1989. Core faculty, dir. trg. New Coll. Calif., San Francisco, 1995—98, John F. Kennedy U., Orinda, Calif., 1998—2001; dir. behavioral health Pascua Yaqui Tribe, Tucson, 2001—04; sch. psychologist Tucson Unified Sch. Dist., 2004—05; clin. team mgr. New Leaf Services for Our Cmty., San Francisco, 2005—. Author: (cookbook) Comida: Mexican American Home Cooking, poetry. Scholar, U. Calif., 1978—81, Calif. Inst. Integral Studies, 1991—96; Dissertation fellow, Soroptomist Internat., 1995, 1996,

AAUW, 1995, 1996. Mem.: NASP. Democrat. Avocations: writing, animals, travel, computers. Office Phone: 415-626-7000. Personal E-mail: josefa@dramolina.com. Business E-Mail: jmolina@newleafservice.org.

**MOLINA, JOSEPH MARIO (MARIO MOLINA),** medical administrator; b. Long Beach, Calif., May 16, 1958; s. C. David and Mary R. (Salandini) M.; m. Therese Ann Flynn; children: Carley, Colleen, David, Mary Clare. BA, Calif. State U., Long Beach, 1980; MD, U. So. Calif., 1984. Diplomate Am. Bd. Internal Medicine. Intern and residency Johns Hopkins U., 1984—87; assoc. investigator VA, San Diego, 1988-90; asst. clin. prof. U. So. Calif., LA, 1990-91; med. dir. Molina Healthcare, Inc., Long Beach, 1991-94, v.p. HMO, 1994—96, chmn., pres., CEO, 1996—. Bd. dirs. New Am. Alliance. Nat. trustee Boys and Girls Club Am. Named one of Top 10 Latinos in Healthcare, LatinoLeaders mag., 2004, 25 Most Influential Hispanics, Time Mag., 2005; named to Hall of Fame, Long Beach Cmty. Coll., 2002; recipient Ernst & Young Gr. L.A. Entrepreneur of Yr. award, 2002. Mem. ACP, Am. Coll. Physician Execs., Am. Diabetes Assn., Calif. Med. Assn. Avocation: collecting antique medical books. Office: Molina Healthcare Inc 1 Golden Shore St Long Beach CA 90802-4202 Office Phone: 562-435-3666. Business E-Mail: mario.molina@molinahealthcare.com.

**MOLINA, MARIO JOSE,** physical chemist, educator; b. Mexico City, Mar. 19, 1943; arrived in U.S., 1968; s. Roberto Molina-Pasquel and Leonor Henríquez; m. Luisa Y. Tan, July 12, 1973; 1 child, Felipe. Bachillerato, Acad. Hispano Mexicana, Mexico City, 1959; Ingeniero Químico, U. Nacional Autónoma de México, 1965; postgrad., U. Freiburg, Fed. Republic Germany, 1966—67; PhD, U. Calif., Berkeley, 1972. Asst. prof. U. Nacional Autónoma de México, 1967—68; research assoc. U. Calif.-Berkeley, 1972—73, U. Calif. Irvine, 1973—75, asst. prof. phys. chemistry, 1975—79, assoc. prof., 1979—82; sr. rsch. scientist Jet Propulsion Lab., 1983—89; prof. dept earth, atom and planet sci.. dept. chemistry MIT, Cambridge, 1989—96, Martin prof. atmospheric chemistry, 1997—2004, Inst. prof., 1997—2004; prof., chemistry and biochemistry Univ. Calif., San Diego, 2004—; faculty, Ctr. for Atmospheric Sci. Scripps Inst. of Oceanography, 2004—. Bd. dirs. MacArthur Found. Named a Trailblazer in Sci., Sci. Spectrum Mag., 2005; named one of 50 Most Important Hispanics in Govt., Edn., Hispanic Engineer and Info. Tech. mag., 2005; recipient Tyler Ecology award, 1983, Esselen award for chemistry in pub. interest, 1987, Max-Planck-Forschungs-Preis, Alexander von Humboldt-Stiftung, 1994, Nobel Prize in Chemistry, 1995, Sasakawa award, UNEP, 1999. Mem.: NAS, Pontifical Acad. Sci., Inst. of Medicine, Am. Geophys. Union (Pres.'s Com. on Advisors on Sci. and Tech. 1994—2000), Am. Phys. Soc., Am. Chem. Soc. Achievements include discovery of the theory that fluorocarbons deplete ozone layer of stratosphere. Office: Dept Chem & Biochem UCSD 2040 Urey Hall Addn 9500 Gilman Drive La Jolla CA 92093-0332 *We have to understand our environment to find out if we are tampering with it. One of our accomplishments has been to call attention to society's potential altering of the atmosphere.**

**MOLINA, RAFAEL EVENCIO,** retired urologist; b. Havana, Cuba, July 6, 1923; came to U.S.; 1961; s. Joseph M. and Maria H. Molina; m. Maria T. Rodriguez (div.); children: Louis R., Maria T., Manuel E., Rafael E. BA, BS, Colegio de Belen, Havana, 1941; MD, U. Havana, 1949. Diplomate Am. Bd. Urology. Resident U. Miami, Fla., 1963-66; physician Hoffman Urol., Huntington, W.Va., 1966—2002; ret., 2004. Contbr. articles to med. jours. Mem. AMA, ACS, Am. Urodynamic Soc., Am. Urol. Assn., Am. Soc. Nephrology, Cuban Med. Soc. in Exile, Rotary Club, Elks Club, Huntington Area C. of C. Republican. Roman Catholic. Avocations: tennis. Home: 1695 Holderby Rd Huntington WV 25701-4127 also: PO Box 7052 Huntington WV 25774-7052

**MOLINA, RON JOSEPH,** music educator; b. Antioch, Calif., Sept. 17, 1947; s. Joe Guerrero and Dorothy Mildred Molina; m. Darcy Lauck, Feb. 14, 2003; 1 child, Joseph Michael. A, Diablo Valley Coll., 1966; BA, San Jose State U., 1971. Tchr. vocal music Hollister (Calif.) H.S., 1974—79; regional v.p. Am. Internat., Marina Del Rey, Calif., 1979—82; drama tchr. Bella Vista H.S., Sacramento, 1983—; vocal music tchr. Folsom (Calif.) H.S., 1983—87; dir. choral activities Antioch (Calif.) H.S., 1987—. Dir. Internat. Antioch High Sch. Music Masters, 1988—2003. Named Man of Yr., Antioch Civic Arts Commn., 1988, Antioch C. of C., 1991, Hon. Mayor, Rosas, Spain, 2000; recipient Outstanding Cmty. Arts Person, 1991. Mem.: Music Educators Nat. Conf., Am. Choral Dir. Assn., Calif. Music Educators Assn. Avocations: golf, fishing. Office: Antioch High Sch 700 @ 18th St Antioch CA 94509 Office Phone: 925-756-5607. Office Fax: 925-753-1835. Business E-Mail: ronmolina@antioch.k12.ca.us.

**MOLINA, TANYA E.,** school librarian; b. Hamilton, New Zealand, June 2, 1971; arrived in U.S.; 1973; d. Cyril Alfred and Karen Dawn Call; 1 child, Christian Michael. BS, No. Ariz. U., 1997, MEd, 1998; MA, U. Ariz., 2000. Tchr. Safford (Ariz.) Unified Sch. Dist., 1997—2001; libr. King City (Calif.) Elem. Sch. Dist., 2001—02; libr. media specialist Avondale (Ariz.) Elem. Sch. Dist., 2002—. Cons. in field. Mem.: ALA, Internat. Reading Assn., Ariz. Libr. Assn. Republican. Lds Ch. Avocations: writing, reading, scrapbooks. Office: Centerra Mirage Sch Goodyear AZ 85338

**MOLINARI, SUSAN,** former congresswoman; b. Staten Island, NY, Mar. 27, 1958; d. Guy V. and Marguerite (Wing) Molinari; m. Bill Paxon; 2 children. BA, SUNY, Albany, 1980, MA, 1982. Former intern for State Senator Christopher Mega; former rsch. analyst N.Y. State Senate Fin. Com.; former fin. asst. Nat. Rep. Gov.'s Assn.; ethnic community liaison Rep. Nat. Com., 1983-84; minority leader N.Y.C. Council, 1986-90; mem. 101st-104th Congresses from 14th (now 13th) N.Y. dist., 1990-97, vice-chair House Rep. Conf.; anchor CBS News Sat. Morning, N.Y.C., 1997-98; Chairman, CEO The Washington Group, 2001—. Author: (book) Representative Mom: Balancing Budgets, Bill and Baby in the U.S. Congress, 1998. Roman Catholic. Office: c/o The Washington Group 1401 K Street NW Ste 1000 Washington DC 20005

**MOLINARO, JAMES P.,** city manager; b. NYC, Mar. 11, 1931; m. Carol E. Molinaro (dec.); 2 children. Chief of staff to Congressman Guy. V. Molinari 14th Congl. Dist., NY; dep. borough pres. Staten Island, NY, 1990—2001; borough pres., 2002—. With NY State Conservative Party, 1964—, chmn. Richmond County, 1974—89, exec. vice chair, 1989—. Bd. dirs. Heart Inst. Staten Island, Sisters of Charity Health Care Corp.; founder Staten Island AIDS Day Care Ctr. and AIDS med. care facility; chmn. St. Elizabeth Anne's Health and Rehab. Ctr., 1993—99. Office: Borough Pres 120 Borough Hall Staten Island NY 10301*

**MOLINARO, JOSEPH DANIEL,** dentist; b. Phila., May 4, 1969; s. Daniel Joseph and Antoinette Marie (Napolio) Molinaro; m. Ellen Catherine Frank, June 14, 2003. BS in biology, Villanova U., Pa., 1987—91; DMD, Temple U. Sch. of Dentistry, Phila., 1991—95; MS in oral biology, The George Wash. U., Washington, 1999—2001. Cert. of residency Nat. Naval Dental Ctr., Bethesda, MD, 2001, diplomate The Fed. Services Bd. of Gen. Dentistry, 2002, Am. Bd. of Gen. Dentistry 2002. Gen. dentist U.S. Naval Dental Ctr. USN, Agana, Guam, 1995—97, dental clinic divsn. officer, 1996—97, gen. dentist USS George Washington CVN 73 Norfolk, Va., 1997—99, dental clinic divsn. officer, 1998—99, resident, comprehensive dentistry Nat. Naval Dental Ctr. Bethesda, Md., 2001—, comprehensive dentist, dental clinic dept. head dental annex br. Indian Head, Md., 2001—04, dep. sr. dental surgeon personnel exchange program Portsmouth, 2004—. Contbr. articles to profl. jours. Lt. comdr. Dental Corps USN, 1995—, Dental Corps. Decorated Navy and Marine Corps Commendation medal Sec. of USN, Navy and Marine Corps Achievement medal, Humanitarian Svc. medal USN; recipient Martin I. Munin award, Temple U. Sch. of Dentistry, 1995, Commdg. Officer's award for excellence, Commdg. Officer, Nat. Naval Dental Ctr., 2000, Chief of the Dental Corps award, Chief U.S. Naval Dental Corps, 2001; Health Professionals scholarship, USN, 1991—95. Fellow: Acad. of Gen. Dentistry; mem.: ADA, Seminar of Restorative Dentistry (sec. 2000—01, Excellence in Operative Dentistry 2001), Acad. of Operative Dentistry,

Edward C. Penick Endodontic Study Club. Roman Catholic. Achievements include completed a study comparing the influence of various dental restorative materials on tooth cusp stiffness. Avocations: travel, reading, sports. E-mail: joeandellen@molinaro.us.

**MOLINARO, SAMUEL L.,** investment company executive; b. Binghamton, N.Y., Dec. 30, 1957; m. Lisa Melino; children: Danielle Anne, Alexa Nicole. BBA in Acctg., St. Bonaventure U., Olean, N.Y., 1980. CPA, N.Y. Mgr. Price Waterhouse, N.Y.C., 1980-86; sr. v.p. fin. Bear, Stearns & Co. Inc., N.Y.C., 1986-96, CFO, 1996—. Office: Bear Stearns Companies Inc 245 Park Ave New York NY 10167-0002 Home: 413 Ponus Rdg New Canaan CT 06840-6025

**MOLINA-WALTERS, DEBI ANN,** education educator; b. Antioch, Calif., Aug. 16, 1959; d. Joe Guerrero and Dorothy Mildred Molina; m. Daniel Wade Walters, Sept. 6, 1997. AA, Los Medanos Jr. Coll., Pittsburg, Calif., 1979; BA, Sonoma State U., Rohnert Park, Calif., 1983; MS, Hayward State U., Calif., 1995; MA, Chapman U., Concord, Calif., 1997; EdD, U. of the Pacific, Stockton, Calif., 2004. Adminstrv. credential Chapman U., PPS - sch. counseling credential Chapman U., elem. tchr. credential Sacramento State U., astronomy Sonoma State U. Tchr. 6th grade elem. sch. Marsh Elem. Sch., Antioch, 1989—91; tchr. mid. sch. sci. and leadership Pk. Mid. Sch., Antioch 1991—2000; lectr. Chapman U., Concord, 1998—2004; tchr. h.s. sci. Antioch H.S., 2000—01; tchr. 6th grade sci. and leadership Bidwell Elem., Antioch, 2001—03; lectr. Hayward State U., 2002—04; mid. sch. sci. tchr. Dallas Ranch Mid. Sch., Antioch, Calif., 2003—04; clin. asst. prof. Ariz. State U., Mesa, 2004—. Chair sci. dept. Antioch Unified Sch. Dist., 1998—2004, mem. leadership team, 1998—2004, mentor tchr, 1992—2004; sci. club adviser Pk. Mid. Sch., Antioch, 1991—2000; cons. Antioch Unified Sch. Dist, 1998—2004. Contbr. articles to profl. jours Named Tchr. of Yr., 1991Contra Costa County Jaycees, 1991; recipient Tchg. Recognition award, Ariz. State U., 2004, svc. award, PTSA, 1991. Mem.: ASCD, Am. Soc. Quality, Ariz. Assn. for Environ. Edn., No. Am. Assn. for Environ. Edn., Nat. Sci. Educators Leadership Assn., Calif. Sci. Tchrs. Assn., Am. Edn. Rsch. Assn., Ariz. Sci. Teachers Assn., Nat. Sci. Tchr. Assn. (assoc.), Phi Delta Kappa. Office: Ariz State Univ Bldg 140 7001 E Williams Field Rd Mesa AZ 85212 Office Phone: 480-727-1510. Office Fax: 480-727-1964. E-mail: drmo@asu.edu.

**MOLINDER, JOHN IRVING,** engineering educator, consultant; b. Erie, Pa., June 14, 1941; s. Karl Oskar and Carin (Eklund) M.; m. Janet Marie Ahlquist, June 16, 1962; children: Tim, Karen. BSEE, U. Nebr., 1963; MSEE, Air Force Inst. Tech., 1964; PhD EE, Calif. Inst. Tech., 1969. Registered profl. engr., Calif. Project officer Ballistic Systems Div., Norton AFB, Calif., 1964-67; sr. engr. Jet Propulsion Lab., Pasadena, Calif., 1969-70; prof. engring. Harvey Mudd Coll., Claremont, Calif., 1970—; prin. engr. Qualcomm Inc., 1996-97, part-time, 1997—; contractor Boeing Satellite Systems, 2000—02. Part-time lectr. Calif. State U., L.A., 1970-74; mem. tech. adv. panel Kinemetrics, Pasadena, 1985-86; part-time mem. tech. staff Jet Propulsion Lab., Pasadena, 1974-97; rep. NASA Hdqrs., Washington, 1979-80; vis. prof. elec. engring. Calif. Inst. Tech., 1982-83. Contbr. articles to profl. jours. Served to capt. USAF, 1963-67. Mem.: IEEE (sr.). Avocations: bicycling, reading, computers. Office: Harvey Mudd Coll Dept Engring 301 Platt Blvd Claremont CA 91711-5901 Business E-Mail: John_Molinder@hmc.edu.

**MOLINEAUX, CHARLES BORROMEO,** lawyer, arbitrator, columnist, poet; b. N.Y.C., Sept. 27, 1930; s. Charles Borromeo and Marion Frances (Belter) M.; m. Patricia Leo Devereux, July 2, 1960; children: Charles, Stephen, Christopher, Patricia, Peter, Elizabeth. BS cum laude, Georgetown U., 1950; JD, St. Johns U., 1959. Bar: N.Y. 1959, Mass. 1981, D.C. 1988. From assoc. to ptnr. Nevius, Jarvis & Pilz and successor firms, N.Y.C., 1959-77; ptnr. Gadsby & Hannah, N.Y.C., 1978-80; v.p., gen. counsel Perini Corp., Framingham, Mass., 1980-87; pvt. practice Washington, 1987—. Adj. faculty Internat. Law Inst., Washington, 1989—. Author numerous poems. Mem. adv. bd. Inst. for Transnat. Arbitration; committeeman Rep. Party, Nassau County, NY, 1965—71, mem. exec. com., committeeman Fairfax County, Va., 1969. 1st lt. U.S. Army, 1954—56. Fellow Am. Bar Found.; mem. ASCE, Am. Arbitration Assn. (constrn. ADR task force 1994—), Chartered Inst. Arbitrators, Fedn. Internat. Engrs.-Conseils (Assoc. Gen. Contractors del. constrn. contract com., Louis Prangey award for svc. to profession com. engring. 1996), Soc. Constrn. Arbitrators London, Del. Hist. Soc., London Ct. Internat. Arbitration, Fellowship Cath. Scholars. Roman Catholic. Home: 8321 Weller Ave Mc Lean VA 22102-1717 Office: 1660 International Dr Ste 400 Mc Lean VA 22102 Office Phone: 703-287-4232. Personal E-mail: cmlnx@aol.com.

**MOLINI, BARBARA SYMONDS,** retired elementary school educator; b. San Francisco, Dec. 15, 1941; d. Percival Lionel and Margaret Lena (Karsten) Symonds; children: Jennifer Nicole, Justin Karsten. BA in Elem. Edn. cum laude, San Francisco State U., 1965; postgrad., Calif. State U., Sonoma, U. Calif., Davis, Pepperdine U. Cert. reading specialist, Calif. Tchr. grade 7 Ctrl. Sch., San Carlos, Calif., 1965-70; tchr. grade 6 Burns Valley Sch., Clearlake, Calif., 1971-72; tchr. grades 7-8 Lower Lake (Calif.) Jr. High Sch., 1972-84, Oak Hill Middle Sch., Clearlake, 1984—2002; ret., 2002. Tchr. pilot program San Carlos Elem. Sch. dist., Calif., 1968-70; mentor in art Konocti Unified Sch. Dist., Clearlake, 1990-93, cons. program quality rev., 1994; judge Odyssey of the Mind, Calif., 1992-94; mem. numerous adv. coms. Named Outstanding Educator, Calif. League Middle Schs. Region I, 1995, Tchr. of Yr., Konocti Unified Sch. Dist., 1997 Mem.: Calif. Ret. Tchrs. Assn. Avocations: travel, gardening, photography, reading, art. E-mail: bmolini@aol.com.

**MOLITOR, GRAHAM THOMAS TATE,** lawyer; b. Seattle, Apr. 6, 1934; s. Robert Franklin and Louise Margaret (Graham) M.; m. Carlotta Jean Crum, July 30, 1960; children: Graham Thomas Tate, Anne Therese, Christopher Robert. BS, U. Wash., 1955; LLB, Am. U., 1963. Bar: D.C. 1963. Rsch. asst. U. Wash., Seattle, 1957; bailiff U.S. Criminal Ct. D.C., 1958-59; legis. counsel U.S. Ho. of Reps., Washington, 1961-63; dir. candidate rsch. Rockefeller for Pres. Com., 1963-64, 68; D.C. counsel, asst. dir. govt. rels. Nabisco, Inc., Washington, 1964-70; dir. govtl. rels. Gen. Mills, Inc., Washington, 1970-77; pres., CEO Pub. Policy Forecasting, Inc., Potomac, Md., 1977—2004; prin. ptnr. Pub. Policy Communicators, 1989-91. Prin., ptnr. Pub. Policy Action Inst., Potomac; adv. bd. Creative Bus. Strategies, Inc.; adj. prof. Grad. Sch. Bus. Am. U., Washington, 1969—75, Washington, 1979—85, Montgomery Coll., Rockville, Md., 1987—88; dir. rsch. White House Conf. on Indsl. World Ahead, 1971—72; mem. White House Adv. Com. on Social Indicators, 1975—76; chmn. Commn. on the Future of Montgomery County, 1986—88; guest lectr. numerous univs.; mem. White House Confs. on Food, Nutrition and Health, 1969—71, White House Conf. on Youth, 1970; bd. dirs. First Global Conf. on the Future, Inc., Can., 1980—; organizing com. Found. for the Future, 1997—, bd. advisors, 1999—; mem. scholar adv. bd., 2001—. Contbg. editor Food Tomorrow Newsletter, 1976-77; co-editor, chmn. editl. bd. Ency. of the Future, 1991-96; cons. editor Hist. Guide to Am. Govt., 1995-97, McMillan Compendium of the Twenty-First Century, 1998-99; editor Technol. Forecasting and Social Change, 1999—; chmn. editl. bd. Future Survey, 1995-97, World Ency. of Police Forces and Correctional Systems, 2003-05; mem. editl. bd. editors Hudson Inst. Study of World Food Problems, 1975-77; mem. editl. bd. Bus. Tomorrow Newsletter, 1977-79, Jour. of Futures Studies, 2001—; mem. bd. advisors New Mktg. Techs. Monitor, 1983-85; polit. editor On the Horizon, 1993-95; contbr. articles to profl. jours. Mem. Food Adv. Bd., N.Y.C., 1980-86. Served to 1st lt. U.S. Army, 1958-61. Recipient Disting. Service award Grocery Mfrs. Am., 1973-74, Disting. Service award Nat. Consumer Info. Center, 1974, Disting. Service award Am. Mgmt. Assn., 1975. Fellow: World Acad. Art and Sci. (mem. bd. trustees); mem.: World Future Soc. (gen. chmn. 2d Gen. Assembly 1975, v.p., dir. 1981—94, v.p., legal counsel 1994—2004, Disting. Svc. award 1975, 2004), E.D. Export Coun., Washington Indsl. Roundtable, Washington Bus.-Govt. Rels. Coun. (mem. exec. com. 2000—), chmn. commn. on Yr. 3000 2001—), Univ. Club, Phi Alpha Delta, Phi Kappa Sigma. Republican. Presbyterian. Home and office: 6343 Saucon Valley Dr Fayetteville PA 17222-9242 Office Phone: 717-352-4288. E-mail: gmolitor@earthlink.net.

**MOLITOR, MICHAEL A.,** entrepreneur, consultant; b. Bklyn., Nov. 7, 1965; s. Henry J. and Janet A. (Monti) M.; m. Michele A. Emery, July 8, 1995; 1 child, Michael. BS, Siena Coll., 1987; MBA, Columbia U., 2000. CFP. Fin. aid counselor Janet's Coll. Tuition Aid, Massapequa Park, N.Y., 1987-92; income tax acct. Michael A. Molitor, Massapequa, N.Y., 1988—; owner, fin. aid counseling svc. Molitor Coll. Aid Counseling, Massapequa, 1992—; money mgr. Molitor Money Mgmt., Massapequa, 1992—. Cons. Alive-To-Thrive, Inc., Westchester, N.Y., 1992—; cons., adv. bd. Orphan's Aid Soc., Douglaston, N.Y., 1994—; cons. in field. Author: You Can Afford A College Education, 1992; contbr. articles to profl. jours., various TV talk shows. Con. to Guidance Dept. Massapequa Sch. Dist., Massapequa, 1995-98, mem. Long Island Assn., Hauppauge, N.Y., 1990-92. Recipient Top Producer-Pres. Club Transamerica Funds, Houston, 1993-94, mem. signature Club Oppenheimer Funds, Denver, 1995. Mem. Internat. Assn. Fin. Planning, N.Y. Fin. Air Adminstr. Assn., NAt. Assn. Fin. Aid Adminstr., BMW Car Club Am., Porsche Club Am. Mem. Christian Ch. Avocations: golf, drumming, track driving.

**MOLITOR, STEVEN JOHN,** lawyer; b. May 19, 1962; BA, Franklin and Marshall Coll., 1984; JD, Cornell U., 1987. Bar: N.Y. 1988, Pa. 1996. Assoc. Morgan, Lewis & Bockius LLP, NYC and Phila., 1992-95, ptnr., 1995—2004; ptnr. fin. and real estate practice group Dechert LLP, Phila., 2004—. Home: 1701 Market St Philadelphia PA 19103-2903 Office: Dechert LLP Cira Centre 2929 Arch St Philadelphia PA 19104-2808 Office Phone: 215-994-2777. Office Fax: 215-994-2222. E-mail: steven.molitor@dechert.com.*

**MOLITORIS, BRUCE ALBERT,** nephrologist, educator; b. Springfield, Ill., June 26, 1951; s. Edward and Joyce (Tomasko) M.; m. Karen Lynn Wichterman, June 16, 1973; children: Jason, Jared, Julie. BS, U. Ill., 1973, MS in Nutrition, 1975; MD, Wash. U., 1979. Resident Sch. Medicine U. Colo., Denver, 1979-81, nephrology fellow, 1981-84, asst. prof. medicine, 1984-88, assoc. prof. medicine, 1988-93, prof., 1993; dir. nephrology Ind. U. Med. Sch., Indpls., 1993—; vis. scientist U. Colo., MCDB, Boulder, 1989-90; Max Planck Inst., Federal Republic of Germany, 1984-85; dir. Ind. Ctr. Biol. Microscopy, 2002—. NIH reviewer, 1991-94; dir. home dialysis Denver VA Ctr., 1984-93; vis. scientist dept. molecular biology Colo. State U., Ft. Collins, 1998. Mem. editl. bd. Am. Jour. Physiology, 1989-2000, Am. Jour. Kidney Diseases, 1991—; assoc. editor Jour. Investigative Medicine, 1994-99; contbr. articles to profl. jours. Pres. Cherry Creek Village South Homeowners Assn., 1989-90, Pickwick Commons Home Owners Assn., 1999; v.p. Our Father Luth. Ch., Denver, 1989-90; coun. mem. King of Glory Luth. Ch., Indpls., 1999-2002; coach Cherry Creek Soccer Assn., Greenwood Village, 1988-91, Centennial Little League Titans Basketball; bd. dirs. CSSA, 1993. Recipient Upjohn Achievement award, 1979, Liberty Hyde Bailey award, 1973. Mem. Am. Assn. Physicians, Am. Soc. Nephrology (program chmn. 2002-03), Internat. Soc. Nephrology, N.Y. Acad. Sci., Am. Soc. Clin. Investigation, Am. Fedn. for Clin. Rsch. (nat. counselor 1991-94), Western Assn. Physicians. Avocations: bridge, fishing, antiques, hiking. Office: Indiana U Med Ctr R-2 202C 950 W Walnut St Indianapolis IN 46202-5135

**MOLL, DAVID CARTER,** civil engineer; b. Ames, Iowa, Aug. 5, 1948; s. Dale Curtis and Virginia (Carter) M.; m. Margaret E. Newman (div. 1989); 1 child, Megahn Elizabeth; m. Melanie G. Harding, 2004. BSCE, Iowa State U., 1971; cert. advanced study, Am. Grad. Sch. Internat. Mgmt., 1983; MBA with distinction, U. Mich., 1984; advanced masters cert. in project mgmt., George Washington U., 1006. Cert. project mgmt. profl. George Washington U. Engr. in tng., Iowa; field engr. Chgo. Bridge & Iron Co., 1971; subcontract supr., field engr. Morrison-Knudsen Internat. Co., Inc., Surinam and Panama, 1976; site supt. engring., asst. supt. constrn. Fluor Corp., Saudi Arabia, 1977-82; group mgr. Cummins Engine Co., Columbus, Ind., 1984-85; mgr. spl. projects Kerr-McGee Coal Corp., Oklahoma City, 1985-88; project mgr. Kerr-McGee Corp., Oklahoma City, 1989, 1993—98, London, 1989-90, Saudi Arabia, 1990—92, Kerr-McGee Environ. Mgmt. Corp., Oklahoma City, 1998—2004; pres. Integrated Solutions Inc., 2005—. Lt. USN, 1971—75. Mem. ASCE, AGSIM (leadership circle), Civil Engr. Corps (Meritorious Svc. medal), Am. Soc. Quality Control (constrn. tech. com.), N.Y. Acad. Scis., Am. Legion, Order of the Knoll (Campanile Guild), Marston Club, Project Mgmt. Inst. (Red Earth chpt. dir. fin.), Chi Epsilon. Avocations: cross country skiing, jogging, golf, travel.

**MOLL, DEBORAH ADELAIDE,** lawyer; b. Wilmington, Del., Jan. 19, 1946; BA, St. John's Coll., Annapolis, Md., 1969; MA, U. Tex., 1972, JD 1975. Bar: N.Mex 1977. Law clk. Tex. Ct. Criminal Appeals, Austin, 1975-76, U.S. Ct. Appeals (10th cir.), Santa Fe, 1977-78; asst. atty. gen. N.Mex Atty. Gen., Santa Fe, 1978-84; asst. appellate defender N.Mex Pub. Defender Dept., Santa Fe, 1984-87; staff atty. N.Mex Taxation and Revenue Dept., Santa Fe, 1987-92; shareholder Kemrer-Hayes & Moll, P.A., Albuquerque, 1992; gen. counsel N.Mex Gen. Svcs. Dept., Santa Fe, 1993—. Mem.: N.Mex. State Bar (bd. dirs. bankruptcy sect. 1992, adv. opinion com. 1993—96, bd. dirs. pub. law sect. 1996—, chair pub. law sect. 1997—98, bd. dirs. employment law sect. 1999—2003, chair ad hoc com. 2001, com. establish legal specialization constrn. and pub. contracts 2002—). Avocation: photography. Office: NMex Gen Svcs Dept 715 Alta Vista St Santa Fe NM 87505-4108 Office Phone: 505-827-2000. E-mail: Deborah.Moll@state.nm.us.

**MOLL, GEORGE WILLIAM,** pediatrician, educator; b. Milw., Nov. 23, 1947; s. George William, Sr. and Laverne Delores (Klein) M.; m. Susana Valdez Ramos, June 24, 1978; children: Christina, Teresa. BA in Chemistry cum laude, Carleton Coll., 1969; PhD in Biochemistry, U. Chgo., 1975, MD, 1977. Diplomate Nat. Bd. Med. Examiners; diplomate in pediatrics and pediat. endocrinology Am. Bd. Pediatrics; cert. PALS, CPR. Pediatric resident Mott Children's Hosp., U. Mich., Ann Arbor, 1977-79; pediatric endocrinology fellowship Wyler Children's Hosp., U. Chgo., 1979-81; asst. prof. pediatrics U. Chgo., 1981-85, Emory U. Sch. Medicine, Atlanta, 1985-87; assoc. prof. pediatrics U. Miss. Med. Ctr., Jackson, 1987-93, prof. pediatrics, 1993—; assoc. staff pediatric endocrinology Little Co. of Mary Hosp., Evergreen Park, Ill., 1981-85, The Meth. Hosps., Gary and Merrillville, Ind., 1981-85; staff pediatric endocrinologist The Emory Clinic, Atlanta, 1985-87, Henrietta Egleston Hosp. for Children, Atlanta, 1985-87, Grady Meml. Hosp., Atlanta, 1985-87; staff Emory Univ. Hosp., 1987, dir. pediatric endocrinology; staff U. Miss. Med. Ctr., Jackson, 1987—. Contbr. articles to profl. jours. Active Diabetes Found. of Miss., Inc., 1998, Juv. Diabetes Found. Internat. 1998, Filipino-Am. Assn. of Miss., 1990—, Chronic Disease Coalition of Miss., 1996—. Recipient med. scientist NIH scholarship/grant U. Chgo., 1970-77, Andrew Mellon Found. fellowship, 1981-82, Med. Excellence award So. Med. Assn., 1995; grantee Am. Lung Assn., 1987-89, Eli Lilly Co., Mobil Oil Co., 1991, Diabetes Rsch. and Edn. Found., Inc., 1992, Pharmacia & Upjohn, 1998, others. Fellow Am. Acad. Pediatrics, Am. Coll. Endocrinology; mem. AAAS, Nat. Bd. Med. Examiners (comprehensive task force for reprodn./endocrinology 1989-90), Chgo. Endocrine Club (sec 1984-85), N.Y. Acad. of Sci., Am. Fedn. for Med. Rsch., Lawson Wilkins Soc. for Pediat. Endocrinology, Midwest and So. Soc. for Pediatric Rsch., Miss. State Med. Assn., Cen. Miss. Med. and Pediatric Soc., The Endocrine Soc. (regional rep. U.S. Pharmacopeia Quinquennial), Am. Diabetes Assn., Juv. Diabetes Found., Sigma Xi, others. Achievements include isolation of a bovine brain protein kinase and establishment of a protein kinase assay employing a novel PEI-cellulose thin-layer system as part of a PhD Biochemistry; established a novel modified flow-dialysis system for steady state hormone action studies; assisted the delineation of a LH-receptor defect related to precocious puberty and a novel genetic mutation in thyroid binding globulin in males. Avocations: carpentry, general handicrafts, electronics, computer repair work. Office: Univ Miss Med Ctr 2500 N State St Jackson MS 39216-4500 E-mail: gmoll@ped.umsmed.edu.

**MOLL, JOHN LEWIS,** retired electronics engineer; b. Wauseon, Ohio, Dec. 21, 1921; s. Samuel Andrew and Esther (Studer) M.; m. Isabel Mary Sieber, Oct. 28, 1944; children: Nicolas Josef, Benjamin Alex, Diana Carolyn. B.Sc., Ohio State U., 1943, PhD, 1952; Dr. h.c., Faculty Engring., Katholieke U.

Leuven, (Belgium), 1983. Elec. engr. RCA Labs., Lancaster, Pa., 1943-45; mem. tech. staff Bell Telephone Labs., Murray Hill, N.J., 1952-58; mem. faculty Stanford U., 1958-69, prof. elec. engring., 1959-69; tech. dir. optoelectronics Fairchild Camera and Instrument Corp., 1969-74; dir. integrated circuits labs. Hewlett-Packard Labs., Palo Alto, Calif., 1974-80, dir. IC structures research, sr. scientist, 1980-87, dir. Superconductivity Lab., 1987-90, mem. tech. staff, 1990-96; ret., 1996. Author: Physics of Semi Conductors, 1964; co-author Computer Aided Design and VLSI Device Development, 1985, rev. edit., 1988; inventor (with Ebers) first analytical transistor model, 1953, still valid and useful for circuit design. Recipient Howard N. Potts medal Franklin Inst., 1967, Disting. Alumnus award Coll. Engring., Ohio State U., 1970, Benjamin C. Lamme medal Coll. Engring., Ohio State U., 1988, Vladimir Karapetoff award Eta Kappa Nu, 1995; Guggenheim fellow, 1964, C&C Award, NEC Fund Integration Comm. and Computers, 1997. Fellow IEEE (Ebers award 1971, Thomas A. Edison medal 1991), Am. Acad. Arts and Scis.; mem. Am. Phys. Soc., Nat. Acad. Engring., Nat. Acad. Scis. Home: 600 Sand Hill Rd Apt 232h Palo Alto CA 94304-2635 E-mail: John1Moll@aol.com.

**MOLL, LLOYD HENRY,** retired bank executive; b. Reading, Pa., June 26, 1925; s. Lewis J. and Katie (Rothermel) M.; m. Luise G. Keiper, Oct. 25, 1947; children: Lloyd E., Darryl M. BA, Albright Coll., Reading, 1952. Aircraft engine installer War Dept., 1942-47; tire inspector Firestone Tire & Rubber Co., Pottstown, Pa., 1947-48; asst. mgr. Household Fin. Corp., Reading, Pa., 1952—57; v.p. Meridian Asset Mgmt. Inc. and Meridian Trust Co. (formerly Am. Bank & Trust Co. of Pa.), Reading, 1957—94; v.p. sales and mktg. Investors Trust Co., Wyomissing, Pa., 1995—2005; ret., 2005. Co-founder, past dir. Estate Planning Council of Berks County. Served with AUS, 1945-47. Mem. Am. Inst. Banking. (dir., chmn. bank relations Berks County chpt., pres. 1972-73), Toastmasters (pres. Reading club 1992) Optimists (pres. Reading club 1978-79). Democrat. *Although it has been known to fail me on occasion I try to live by my understanding of the "Golden Rule". When it does fail me I'm usually able to discount such failure by recounting in my mind the many times it has been a two-way street or by convincing myself that I didn't try hard enough in this particular instance. All too often it comes to me much later that the other fellow's interpretation of the "Golden Rule" was far superior to mine. When this happens I have added to my learning. When it does not happen, it forces me to try that much harder to avoid "PERFECTION".*

**MOLL, MARYANN ELIZABETH,** education educator; b. Buffalo, Apr. 1, 1943; d. Bernard John and Jean Margaret Moll; children: Mark D. Szczepanik, Nancy J. Szczepanik. AA, Erie CC, Buffalo, 1998; BA, SUNY, 2000. Cert. social studies tchr. Ariz., 2001. Copyright asst. U. Buffalo, 1998—2000; sub. tchr. Mesa Pub. Schs., Ariz., 2001—03; tchr. County Gardens Charter Sch., Laveen, Ariz., 2003—04, Ombudsman Ednl. Svcs., Phoenix, 2004—. Vol. Make A Difference, Phoenix, 2003—. Roman Catholic. Avocations: embroidery, sewing, reading.

**MOLLAND, MARIA U.,** Internet company executive; b. 1974; BA, Northwestern U.; MBA, Harvard U. With Disney Internet Group, Volpe Brown Whelan; bus. devel. mgr. Yahoo Finance, 2002—05; gen. mgr. MarketWatch, Inc. Dow Jones & Co., San Francisco, 2005—. Office: MarketWatch Inc 825 Battery St San Francisco CA 94111 Office Phone: 415-733-0500. Office Fax: 415-680-1635.*

**MOLLARD, JOHN DOUGLAS,** engineering and geology executive; b. Regina, Sask., Can., Jan. 3, 1924; s. Robert Ashton and Nellie Louisa (McIntosh) M.; m. Mary Jean Lynn, Sept. 18, 1952; children: Catherine Lynn, Jacqueline Lee, Robert Clyde Patrick. BCE, U. Sask., 1945; MSCE, Purdue U., 1947; PhD, Cornell U., 1952; LLD (hon.), U. Regina, 1995. Registered profl. engr., profl. geologist Sask., Alta. and B.C., Can. Resident constrn. engr. Sask. Dept. Hwys. and Transp., 1945; grad. asst. Purdue U., West Lafayette, Ind., 1946-47; rsch. engr. sch. civil engring. Cornell U., Ithaca, NY, 1950-52; air surveys engr., soil and water conservation and devel. Prairie Farm Rehab. Adminstrn., Govt. of Can., 1947-50, chief, airphoto analysis and engring. geology divsn. Regina, 1953-56; pres. J.D. Mollard and Assocs. Ltd., Regina, 1956—. Aerial resource mapping surveys tech. adv. Colombo plan, Govts. Ceylon and Pakistan, 1954-56; adv. Shaw Royal Commn. on Nfld. Agr.; lectr. in field. Author: Landforms and Surface Materials of Canada, 8 edits.; co-author: Airphoto Interpretation and the Canadian Landscape, 1986; contbr. over 100 articles to profl. jours. Organizer, canvasser United Appeal campaigns; bd. dirs. Regina Symphony Orch., 2002; gov. gen. Can. Adrian Clarkson Rideau Hall. Decorated officer Order of Can.; named to Engring. Alumni Wall of Distinction, U. Sask., 2000; recipient First Meritorious Achievement award, Lt. Gov. Sask., 2002, Engring. Achievement award, Assn. Profl. Engrs. Sask., 1984, Massey medal, Royal Can. Geog. Soc., 1989, Allied Arts medal, Royal Archtl. Inst. Can., 1998, Sask. Geotech. Achievement award, Sask. Geotech. Group, 2002, Sask. Centennial medal, Govt. of Sask., 2005, Roger Brown award, Can. Geotechnical Soc., 2006. Fellow: ASCE, Engring. Inst. Can. (Keefer medal 1948, Julian C. Smith medal 1999), Internat. Explorers Club, Can. Acad. Engring., Geol. Soc. Can., Geol. Soc. Am., Am. Soc. Photogrammetry and Remote Sensing (award for contbns. airphoto interpretation and remote sensing 1979); mem.: Can. Soc. Petroleum Engrs., Geol. Soc. Can., Saskatchewan Geol. Soc., Can. Geotech. Soc. (1st R.M. Hardy Meml. Keynote lectr. 1987, Thomas Roy award with engring. geology divsn. 1989, R.F. Legget award 1992), Assn. Cons. Engrs. Can., Regina YMCA (former dir.), Rotary (former dir. Regina club). Mem. United Ch. of Can. Avocations: jogging, reading, golf, tennis, nature study. Office: 810 Avord Tower 2002 Victoria Ave Regina SK Canada S4P 0R7 Office Phone: 306-352-8811 8855. Office Fax: 306-352-8820. Business E-mail: mollard@jdmollard.com.

**MOLLEN, EDWARD LEIGH,** pediatrician, allergist, clinical immunologist; b. Richmond, Va., May 13, 1946; s. Irving Roth and Ruth (Damsky) M.; m. Mary Viola Jeffrey, Dec. 14, 1975; children: Shawn, Michael, Eric, Christopher. BS in Chemistry, Coll. William and Mary, 1968; MD, Med. Coll. Va., 1972. Diplomate Am. Bd. Pediatrics, Am. Bd. Allergy and Immunology. Resident in pediatrics Med. Coll. Va., Richmond, 1972-75, fellow in allergy and immunology, 1975-77; practice allergy and pediatric allergy and clin. immunology Allergy Assocs. of Richmond, 1977-85; pvt. practice allergy/pediatric allergy and clin. immunology Richmond, 1985—. Fellow Am. Acad. Allergy, Asthma and Immunology, Am. Acad. Pediatrics; mem. Med. Soc. Va., Richmond Acad. Medicine, Asthma and Allergy Soc. Va. Avocations: bicycling, running, gardening. Office: 5855 Bremo Rd Ste 702 Richmond VA 23226-1926 Office Phone: 804-288-5216. E-mail: elmollenmd@aol.com.

**MOLLENAUER, LINN FREDERICK,** retired physicist, writer; b. Washington, Pa., Jan. 6, 1937; B of Engring. Physics, Cornell U., 1959; PhD in Physics, Stanford U., 1965. Asst. prof. physics U. Calif., Berkeley, 1965—72; rsch. staff Bell Labs./Lucent Techs., Holmdel, NJ, 1972—2003; ret., 2003. Prof. dept. applied math. U. Ariz., Tucson. Author (with J.P. Gordon): Solitons in Optical Fibers: Fundamentals and Applications, 2006; co-editor (with J.C. White): Tunable Lasers, 1987. Recipient Ballantine medal, Franklin Inst., 1986, Rank prize in Photonics, 1991; fellow, Bell Labs., 2000. Fellow: IEEE (LEOS Disting. Lectr. award 1991, LEOS Quantum Electronics award 2001), AAAS, Optical Soc. Am. (R.W. Wood prize 1982, Charles Hard Townes award 1997); mem.: NAE. Achievements include first to demonstrate optical soliton propagation, leading to the realization of soliton-based, ultra-high-capacity lightwave communication. Personal E-mail: linnm@optonline.net.

**MOLLENKOTT, VIRGINIA RAMEY,** English literature and language educator, writer, guest lecturer; b. Phila., Jan. 28, 1932; d. Robert Franklin and May (Lotz) Ramey; m. Frederick H. Mollenkott, June 17, 1954 (div. July 1973); 1 child, Paul F. BA, Bob Jones U., 1953; MA, Temple U., 1955; PhD, NYU, 1964; D in Ministry (hon.). Samaritan Coll., 1989. Chair English dept. Shelton Coll., Ringwood, NJ, 1955—63, Nyack Coll., NY, 1963—67; prof. English William Paterson U. N.J., Wayne, 1967—97, chair English

dept., 1972—76, prof. emeritus, 1997—. Asst. editor Seventeenth Century News, N.Y.C., 1965-75; stylistic cons. New International Version of the Bible, Am. Bible Soc., 1970-78; translation com. An Inclusive Language Lectionary, Nat. Coun. Chs., 1980-88; bd. dirs. Pacem in Terris, Warwick, N.Y., Kirkridge Conf. Ctr., Bangor, Pa., 1980-91, Upper Room AIDS Ministry, Harlem, N.Y.C., 1989-94; adv. bd. Program on gender and soc. Rochester (N.Y.) Divinity Sch., 1993—; manuscript evaluator Jour. Feminist Studies in Religion, Cambridge, Mass., 1994—; contbg. editor The Witness, 1994-2000, 2002—, The Other Side, 2003-05; lectr. in field. Author: Adamant and Stone Chips, 1967, In Search of Balance, 1969, Women, Men and the Bible, 1977 1st rev. edit. 1988, Korean translation, 1981, Speech, Silence, Action, 1980, (with others) Is the Homosexual My Neighbor? A Positive Christian Response, 1978, rev. edit. 1994 (Integrity award 1979), The Divine Feminine: Biblical Imagery of God as Female, 1983, in German 1985, French, 1990, Italian, 1993; (with others) Views from the Intersection, 1984, Godding: Human Responsibility and the Bible, 1987, Sensuous Spirituality: Out from Fundamentalism, 1992 (N.J. Lesbian and Gay Achievement award 1992), Omnigender: A Trans-Religious Approach, 2001 (Lambda Literary award 2002, Ben Franklin award 2002), (with others) Transgender Journeys, 2003; editor: Women of Faith in Dialogue, 1987, Adam Among the Television Trees, 1971; editl. bd. Studies in Theology & Sexuality, 1997—. Recipient Lifetime Achievement award, Sr. Action in a Gay Environment, 1999. Mem. MLA (exec. com. religion and lit. 1976-80), Women's Inst. for Freedom of Press (assoc.), Milton Soc. Am. (exec. com. 1974-76). Democrat. Episcopalian. Avocations: travel, gardening. Home and Office: 11 Yearling Trl Hewitt NJ 07421-2510 Office Phone: 973-853-4287. Business E-mail: jstvrm@warwick.net.

**MOLLER, JAMES HERMAN,** pediatrician, educator; b. Fresno, Calif., Aug. 12, 1933; s. Leonard Hansen and Eloise Jean (Hunter) M.; m. Carol Suzanne Eymann, Sept. 8, 1957; children: James, Elizabeth. AB, Stanford U., 1954, MD, 1958. Instr. pediat. U. Minn., Mpls., 1965-66, asst. prof., 1966-70, assoc. prof., 1970-73, prof., 1973—, Dwan prof., 1975—, interim head pediat., 1976-78, 97-99, chief pediat., 1976-78, head pediat., 1999—2003; chief of staff U. Minn. Hosp., Mpls., 1984-89. Vis. prof. Nat. Heart & Lung Inst., London, 1989-90, Inst. Child Health, London, 1989-90. Bd. dirs. U. Minn. Hosp., 1984-89, Mpls. Children's Health Ctr., 1975-78, Children's Hosp., St. Paul, 1975-78, Minn. Assn. Pub. tchg. Hosps., Mpls., 1984-89, Variety Club Heart Assn., Mpls., 1980-83. Capt. U.S. Army, 1961-63. Fellow Am. Acad. Pediat. (exec. bd. 1991-92, dist. chmn. 1991-92, alternate dist. chmn. 1985-91, Ross Edn. award 1989), Am. Coll. Cardiology; mem. Am. Heart Assn. (pres. 1993-94, v.p. 1988-89, bd. dirs. 1986-95, award of Merit 1989), Am. Fedn. Clin. Rsch., Am. Pediatric Soc., Am. Bd. Pediat. Nat. Bd. Med. Examiners, Midwest Soc. Pediatric Cardiology Soc., Minn. Med. Assn. (intersplty. coun. 1979-82, resource group child health 1980-82), Minn. Acad. Medicine, Mpls. Met. Pediatric Soc, No. Pediatric Cardiology Soc. (pres. 1978-79), Midwest Soc. Pediatric Rsch., Soc. Pediatric Rsch., Hennepin County Med. Soc. (bd. dirs. 1986-89), Irish Am. Paediatric Soc., British Paediatric Cardiac Assn., Coun. Med. Splty. Socs. (bd. dirs. 1991—), Sub-bd. Pediatric Cardiology (chmn. 1992-94), Internam. Heart Found. (pres. 1997-98), World Heart Fedn. (bd. dirs. 1999). Independent. Congregationalist. Avocations: gardening, travel, oriental carpets, reading. Home: 4816 Sheridan Ave S Minneapolis MN 55410-1917 Office: U Minn 420 Delaware St SE Minneapolis MN 55455-0374 Office Phone: 612-626-2790. Business E-Mail: molle002@umn.edu.

**MOLLER, PATRICIA LYNN,** language educator; b. Bryn Mawr, Pa., Feb. 15, 1961; d. Charles Windom and Betty Frances Hevenor; m. Eric George Moller, Aug. 11, 1984; children: Stephen Charles, Kevin Stuart. Student, U. Valencia, Spain, 1982; BA in Spanish and Secondary Edn., Albright Coll., Reading, Pa., 1983; MA in Spanish, Linguistics and Pedagogy, Pa. State U., State College, 1985. Permanent tchg. cert. Spanish NJ. Grad. tchg. asst. Pa. State U., State College, 1983—85; Spanish tchr. Pascack Hills H.S., Montvale, NY, 1985—90; ch. adminstr. Grace Cmty. Ch., Washingtonville, NY, 1998—2000; H.S. Spanish tchr. Pine Bush Sch. Dist., NY, 2003—. Bldg. leadership team Pine Bush H.S., NY, 2004—. Worship team leader Harmony Bapt. Ch., Middletown, NY, 2004—06. Recipient Spanish award, Albright Coll. Spanish Dept., 1983. Mem.: NY State Assn. Fgn. Lang. Tchrs., Am. Coun. Fgn. Lang. Tchrs. Avocations: reading, quilting, music.

**MOLLET, EMILY A.,** secondary school educator; B, Ea. Ill. U., 1975; M of Adminstrn., U. Ill., 1990. Tchr., coach Glenbard West High Sch., Glen Ellyn, Ill., 1975—79; tchr., coach, dept. chair Downers Grove North High Sch., 1980—. Mem.: AAHPERD, Ill. AHPERD (waiver response coord. 2006). Home: 729 Medford Dr Carol Stream IL 60188 Office Phone: 630-795-8161.

**MOLLICA, JOSEPH A.,** pharmaceutical executive; b. 1940; Various positions, sr. v.p. drug devel. Ciba-Geigy, Ardsley, NY, 1966—86; v.p. med. products E.I. Du Pont de Nemours & Co., Inc., Wilmington, Del., 1987—90; CEO Du Pont Merck Pharm. Co., Wilmington, Del., 1991—93; CEO, chmn. Pharmacopeia, Princeton, NJ, 1994—2004, chmn., 2004—. Office: Pharmacopeia Inc Po Box 5350 Princeton NJ 08543-5350 Business E-mail: mollica@pcop.com.

**MOLLICK, ANDRE VARELLA,** economics professor, researcher; b. Natal, Brazil, June 9, 1967; arrived in US, 1996, permanent resident, 2005; s. Hildebrando and Maria das Gracas Varella Mollick; m. Carolina Avila Avila Campos, Apr. 13, 1996; children: Sofia, Isabella. BA in Econs., U. Brasilia, Brazil, 1987; MSc in Econs., U. Tsukuba, Japan, 1994, PhD in Econs., 1996. Fgn. exch. and funds trader Bank of Tokyo-Mitsubishi, Miami, Fla., 1997—98; treasury mgr. SONY Capital Corp., NYC, 1998—2000; asst. prof. Monterrey's Tech. Inst., Monterrey, Nuevo Leon, Mexico, 2000—03, assoc. prof., 2003—04, U. Tex.- Pan Am., Edinburg, 2004—. Presenter in field. Contbr. articles to profl. jours. Scholar Undergraduate Sch., Brazilian Ministry Edn. and Culture, 1985—87, Japanese Govt. (Monbusho), 1989—96. Mem.: Am. Econ. Assn. Avocations: swimming, reading. Office: University of Texas - PanAm Economics 1201 W University Dr Edinburg TX 78541-2999

**MOLLMAN, JOHN PETER,** publishing executive; b. Belleville, Ill., Feb. 8, 1931; s. Kenneth John and Maurine (Farrow) M.; m. Carol J. Piper, Apr. 4, 1998; children: Sarah Chase Underhill, Eric Cleburne. BA, Washington U., St. Louis, 1952. Advt. specialist Gen. Electric Co., Schenectady and Boston, 1952-54; mgr. Enterprise Printing Co., Millstadt, Ill., 1956-66; dir. prodn. Harper & Row Pubs., N.Y.C., 1967-74; pub. Harper's Mag. Press, N.Y.C., 1971-74; v.p. prodn. Random House Inc., N.Y.C., 1974-81; sr. v.p. World Book-Childcraft Inc., Chgo., 1981-88; pres. World Book Pub., 1988-91; pub. cons., 1991-92; dir. intellectual property devel. Multimedia Publishing Microsoft, 1992-96; cons. in electronic pub. Carmel, Calif., 1996—. Mem. vis. com. Washington U.; mem. pub. com. Art Inst. Chgo.; bd. dirs. Yerba Buena Ctr. for the Arts, San Francisco; pres. Internat. ebook Award Found., N.Y. Mem. Golf Club at Quail Lodge, Phi Delta Theta, Sigma Delta Chi, Omicron Delta Kappa. Unitarian Universalist. Home: 25340 Vista Del Pinos Carmel CA 93923-8804 Office Phone: 831-622-7532. Personal E-mail: pmollman@msn.com.

**MOLLOFF, FLORENCE JEANINE,** speech and language therapist; b. St. Louis, Aug. 28, 1959; d. Lawrence Allan and Rietta Gertrude (Fiegenbaum) M. BS, Fontbonne Coll., St. Louis, 1983; MEd summa cum laude, Nat. Louis U., St. Louis, 1989; student, Project ACCESS Inst., 1992, Judevine Ctr. Autistic Children Tng., 1992. Cert. speech correctionist, Mo. Intern St. Louis State Sch. for Profoundly Retarded, 1983-84; speech therapist St. Louis Pub. Schs., 1984—; Judvine Ctr. for Autistic Children Tng., 1992; speech/lang. therapist St. Louis Pub. Schs./Autism Program, 1992-93, 97—; speech/lang. therapist Michael Sch. Medically Fragile and Multiply Handicapped Michael Sch. Medically Fragile and Multiply Handicapped, 1993-96; speech and lang. pathologist autism program Buder, 1996—, Buder and Fanning, 1997—2000. Speech, lang. therapist St. Louis Pub. Schs./Michael Sch. for Medically Fragile and Multiply Handicapped, 1990—; ednl. cons. program devel. Mo. Coalition for Environ., St. Louis, Columbia, Kansas City, 1990—; cons., trainer in puppetry Kids on the Block, St. Louis Pub. Schs., 1988—; vol. grant writer West End Restoration Corp.; speech/lang. therapist Mid. Sch. for Medically Fragile and Multiply Handicapped, 1993-96. Author: (pseudonym F.J. Molotschnikov) 91 Seconds to Armageddon, 1999; author, creator transition curriculum: Consultative Resource Program, 1989; creator puppet program: Save Our Astonishing Planet, 1990; ednl. cons. program devel. young St. Louis audiences (adapted program for severe to profoundly handicapped children "Arabian Nights", 1994; editor: Strides Newsletter, St. Louis, 1996-98; contbr. artist St. Louis Internat. Jazz Mus.; vol. grant writer West End Restoration Corp. Educator, lobbyist Coalition for the Environ., St. Louis, 1990, newsletter editor, 2000-01; activist, lobbyist Housing Now!, St. Louis, 1989; foster parent Christian Children's Fund, 1986—; activist Habitat for Humanity Internat., 1994—; fundraiser Gateway I Have a Dream Found., 1995—; hon. nat. steering com. Pres. Clinton's Re-election, 1995; contbg. mem. Dem. Nat. Com., 1995—; vol. grant writer West End Restoration Corp.; active Emily's List, Cross-Cultural Solutions Project, New Delhi, India, 1998, World Affairs Coun., St. Louis, Mo.. 2002 Mem. AAUW, ASCD, Coun. Exceptional Children (state rep. Mo. divsn. for children with communicative disorders 1988-89, presenter nat. conv. 1989), Internat. Platform Assn., Am. Fedn. Tchrs. (bldg. rep. 1992), Nat. Arbor Day Found., Nat. Parks and Conservation Assn., Nat. Women's Polit. Caucus, Mo. Assn. for Augmentative Comm. Systems, Met. St. Louis Women's Polit. Caucus, Emily's List, Am. Med. Writers Assn., Soc. for Tech. Com., NEA (editor Strides newsletter 1996-97, grantee Internet project, sec. St. Louis 1997-99), Mo. NEA, Amnesty Internat., World Affairs Coun. St. Louis. Democrat. Avocations: puppetry, international affairs, running, films. Home: 10116 Thorpe Ave Saint Louis MO 63114 Personal E-mail: jeanine.molloff@yahoo.com.

**MOLLOHAN, ALAN BOWLBY,** congressman; b. Fairmont, W.Va., May 14, 1943; s. Robert H. and Helen (Holt) Mollohan; m. Barbara Whiting, Aug. 7, 1976; children: Alan, Robert, Andrew, Karl, Mary Kathryn. AB in Polit. Sci., Coll. William and Mary, 1966; JD, W.Va. U. Coll. Law, 1970. Assoc. law firm, 1970-82; mem. US Congress from 1st W.va. dist., 1983—; mem. appropriations com., ranking minority mem. sci., state, justice, commerce and related agencies subcommittee. Served in USAR, 1970—83. Mem.: ABA, W.va. Bar, Elks, Moose. Democrat. Baptist. Office: US Ho Reps 2302 Rayburn Ho Office Bldg Washington DC 20515-0001 Office Phone: 202-225-4172.*

**MOLLOY, DAVID SCOTT, JR.,** labor relations educator; b. Providence, Aug. 17, 1946; s. David Scott and Miriam Virginia (Handy) Molloy; children: Kelsey Allende Molloy, Cady Larkin Molloy. BA, R.I. Coll., Providence, 1970; MA, U. N.H., Durham, 1972; PhD, Providence Coll., 1991. Bus driver R.I. Pub. Transit Authority, Providence, 1973-81; bus. agt. Amalgamated Transit Union, Providence, 1981-84; chief-of-staff U.S. Congresswoman Schnieder, Cranston, RI, 1984-86; prof. U. R.I., Kingston, 1986—. Lectr. various labor unions, 1980—; intern dir. Labor Rsch. Ctr., U. R.I., Kingston, 1986—; radio commentator Voice of America, Washington, 1992—. Author: (book) Trolley Wars, 1996; contbr. articles to profl. jours.; contbg. editor: Two-Volume Historical Encyclopedia of American Labor, 2004. Mem. exec. bd. Providence Heritage Commn., 1982—92, Leadership R.I., Providence, 1987—90, R.I. Heritage Hall of Fame, 1998—, v.p., 2005; bd. dirs. R.I. State Humanities Coun., Providence, 1985—95; chmn. Libr. R.I. Hist. Soc., Providence, 1987—93. Named RI Prof. of Yr., Carnegie Found. and CASE, 2005; recipient Achievement medal, City of Providence, 1986, Scott Molloy Labor Collection award, Smithsonian Instn., 1990, Tchg. Excellence award, Indsl. Rels. Rsch. Assn., 2000, Inst. Labor Studies, 2001. Mem.: AAUP (U. R.I. chmn. PAC 1994—96), AFL-CIO (R.I. adv. exec. bd. 1981—84, Achievement award 1995), Inst. Labor Studies (bd. dirs. 1987—), R.I. Indsl. Rels. Assn. (pres. 1995—96), Blackstone Valley Heritage Corridor (commr. 1988—98), R.I. Labor History Soc. (founder, 1st pres. 1987—2000). Avocations: collecting labor and industrial artifacts, weightlifting. Home: 550 Usquepaugh Rd West Kingston RI 02892-1924 Office: Labor Rsch Ctr 36 Upper College Rd Kingston RI 02881-2005 Office Phone: 401-874-2569. Business E-Mail: molloy@uri.edu.

**MOLLOY, DONALD WILLIAM,** federal judge, lawyer; b. Butte, ID, July 18, 1946; BA, U. Mont., 1968, JD with honors, 1976. Bar: Mont. 1976, U.S. Dist. Ct. Mont. 1976, U.S. Ct. Appeals (9th cir.) 1977, U.S. Supreme Ct. 1984. Law clk. to Hon. James F. Battin U.S. Dist. Ct., Billings, Mont., 1976-78; ptnr. Berger, Anderson, Sinclair & Murphy, Billings, Mont., 1978-81, Anderson, Edwards & Molloy, Billings, Mont., 1981-90, Anderson & Molloy, Billings, Mont., 1990-91; ptnr., sr., owner The Molloy Law Offices, Billings, Mont., 1991-96; judge US Dist. Ct. Mont., Missoula divsn., 1996—, chief judge, 2001—. Lawyer rep. 9th Cir. Jud. Conf., San Francisco, 1989-92. Aviation It. USNR, 1968—72. Mem. ABA, Yellowstone County Bar Assn. (pres. 1984-95), Mont. Trial Lawyers Assn. (Trial Lawyer of Yr. 1993), Am. Trial Lawyers, Am. Bd. Trial Advocates, Am. Judicature Soc., Mont. Bar Assn., Pa. Trial Lawyer's Assn., Tex. Trial Lawyers Assn., Am. Law Inst. Roman Catholic. Avocations: aviation, pilot. Office: US Dist Ct Dist Mont PO Box 7309 Missoula MT 59807-7309

**MOLLOY, SYLVIA,** language educator; b. Buenos Aires, Aug. 29, 1938; came to U.S. 1967; d. Herbert Edward and Margarita Berta (Chasseing) M. Licence es Lettres, U. Paris, 1960, Diplome D'Etudes Superieures, 1961, Doctorat de U. Paris, 1967. Asst. prof. Spanish SUNY, Buffalo, 1967-69; asst. prof. Spanish Vassar Coll., Poughkeepsie, NY, 1969-70, Princeton U., Princeton, NJ, 1970-73, assoc. prof., 1973-81, Emory L. Ford prof., 1981-86; prof. Spanish Yale U., New Haven, 1986-90; Albert Schweitzer prof. of Humanities NYU, 1990—. Author: La Diffusion de la Litterature Hispanoamericaine en France, 1972, Las Letras de Borges, 1979, En Breve Carcel, 1981, At Face Value: Autobiographical Writing in Spanish America, 1991; co-author Women's Writing in Latin America, 1991, Hispanisms and Homosexualities, 1998, El Común Olvido, 2002, Varia Imaginación, 2003; author short stories and contbr. articles to profl. jours.; cons., editorial bd. Revista Iberoamericana, 1979-81, 1985-89, Latin Am Literary Rev, 1985—, Revista de Filología, Buenos Aires, 1985— Fellow Am. Philos. Soc., 1970, NEH, 1976; Social Sci. Research Council grantee, 1983; Guggenheim Found. fellow, 1986-87 Mem. MLA (pres.), Asociacion Internacional de Hispanistas, Instituto Internacional de Literatura Iberoamericana

**MOLMENTI, ERNESTO P.,** surgeon; b. Feb. 5, 1964; BA summa cum laude, Boston U., 1985, MD, 1989. Intern Barnes Hosp.-Washington U. Sch. Medicine, St. Louis, 1989-90, chief resident, 1995—96; instr. dept. anatomy and neurobiology Washington U. Sch. Medicine, St. Louis, 1992-96; fellow, instr., transplant surgeon U. Pitts., 1996-98; asst. prof. surgery S.W. Med. Ctr., U. Tex., Dallas, 1999—2001; transplant surgeon Children's Med. Ctr., Baylor U. Med. Ctr., Dallas, 1999-2001; assoc. prof. surgery Johns Hopkins U., 2001—, surg. dir. kidney-pancreas transplantation, 2001—. Author: Atlas of Liver Transplantation, 2002; contbg. author Washington University Manual of Surgery, 1997, Laparoscopic Surgery: Principles and Procedures, Computed Body Tomography with MRI Correlation, 1997, Surgical Clinics of North America, 2000, Clinics in Liver Disease, 2000, Textbook of Critical Care, 2000; contbr. articles to profl. jours. Named Harold C. Case scholar, Boston U., 1984, Internat. scholar, 1984; recipient Avelino Gutierrez Biannual award, Nat. Acad. Medicine Argentina, 1987, Hist. Sci. award, Nat. Acad. Scis. Argentina, 1989, 1990, Excellence in Tchg. award, Washington U. Sch. Medicine, 1991, 1992, Hounsfield award, Soc. Computed Body Tomography Magnetic Resonance, 1995, Young Investigator award, Transplant Soc., 1998, Travel award, Internat. Assn. for the Study of Liver Disease, 1998, Young Investigator award, AST/Am. Soc. Transplant Surgeons, 2000; fellow Abbott Labs. and Crohns and Colitis Found., 1993—94, Faculty Rsch. fellow, ACS, 2002. Mem.: Mem. Argentine Med. Assn. (fgn. corr.), Phi Beta Kappa. E-mail: emolmen1@jhmi.edu.

**MOLNAR, ANDREA KATALIN,** anthropology professor; d. Istvan Steve Molnar and Margit Vonnak. BA, U. of Alta., Edmonton, Can., 1987, MA, 1990, BSc, 1986; PhD, Australian Nat. U., Canberra, 1994. Transl. German lang. ethnographies Athabasca U., Alta., 1989—90: rsch. assist. in ecology U. of Alta., Edmonton, Alta., 1989, anthropology lectr., 1995—96, rsch. asst. in anthropology, 1995—96; anthropology cons. on Asia devel. bank project

CHEMONICS Internat., Biodiversity Project Flores, Nusa Tenggara Timur, Indonesia, 1994; ASEAN course designer, text writer Grant McEwan C.C., Edmonton, 1995, anthropology lectr., 1995—96, lang. lectr. in Indonesian, 1995; faculty assoc. Ctr. for S.E. Asian Studies No. Ill. U., DeKalb, 1996—, asst. prof., 1996—2002, assoc. prof. anthropology, 2002—; internat. election observer democracy program Carter Ctr., East Timor, 1999, 2001. Recipient Anthropology Rsch. grant, Wenner-Gren Found. for Anthrop. Rsch., 1997, Cultural Anthropology Rsch. grant, NSF, 1997, SUGR-Cultural Anthropology grant, 2000. Mem.: Royal Inst. of Linguistics and Anthropology, Netherlands, Am. Anthrop. Assn., Assn. of Asian Studies (chair Indonesian studies com. 2001—03). Avocations: reading, travel, painting, opera, art. Office: No Ill U Anthropology Dept Dekalb IL 60115 Office Phone: 815-753-8578. Office Fax: 815-753-7027. Business E-Mail: akmolnar@niu.edu.

**MOLNAR, LAWRENCE,** lawyer; b. Czygand, Hungary, Apr. 14, 1927; came to U.S., 1954; s. Alexander and Marie (Vavra) M.; m. Virginia Hampton Broome, July 16, 1999. Juris Utriusque Candidatus, Charles U., Prague, Czechoslovakia, 1951; JD, NYU, 1962; LLM, LLD (hon.), Charles U., 1991. Bar: N.Y. 1962, U.S. Dist. Ct. (so. and ea. dists.) N.Y. 1970, Czech Republic, 1991. With U.S. Intelligence, Berlin, 1951-54, Lansen, Naeve Corp., NY, 1955-56; asst. mgr. export traffic Intra-Mar Shipping Corp., NY, 1957-58; mgr. export traffic Melchior, Armstrong, Ridgefield, NJ, 1958-59; assoc. Hamburger, Weinschenk, N.Y.C., 1963-69; ptnr. Hamburger, Weinschenk, Molnar & Fisher, N.Y.C., 1969—2001; counsel Hamburger, Weinschenk & Fisher, N.Y.C., 2001—. Mem. ABA, Assn. of Bar of City of N.Y., Consular Law Soc. (v.p. 1980—), Fgn. Law Assn., Queens Bar Assn. Office: Hamburger Weinschenk Molnar & Fisher 36 W 44th St New York NY 10036-8102

**MOLNAR, VIOLET,** mental health nurse; b. Budapest, Hungary; arrived in U.S., 1960; d. Janos Molnar and Erzsebeth Krekacs. ADN, Atlantic Union Coll., 1967; BSN, Walla Walla Coll., 1973. RN Mass., Calif. Staff nurse New Eng. Meml. Hosp., Stoneham, Mass., 1968—70; IV therapist Loma Linda U. Med. Hosp., Calif., 1970—72; psychiat. nurse St. Bernardines Med. Ctr., San Bernardino, Calif., 1974—89, Corona Regional Med. Ctr., San Bernardino, 1990—. Pub. spkr. Pres. Lady's Club Friendly Cir., Loma Linda, 1997—99, pres., 2006—; elder, deaconess, greeter Seventh Day Adventist Ch. Loma Linda U., 1975—. Mem.: Rotary Club San Bernardino/Highland (Paul Harris fellow 2001). Avocations: travel, reading, church activities. Home: 11422 Benton St Loma Linda CA 92354 Personal E-mail: imolnar@juno.com.

**MOLNAU, CAROL,** lieutenant governor; b. Minn., Sept. 17, 1949; m. Steven F. Molnau; 3 children. Attended, U. Minn. Mem. Minn. Ho. of Reps., 1992—2003; commr. Minn. Dept. Transportation; lt. gov. State of Minn., St. Paul, 2003—. Active Corn Growers, Farm Bur., Soybean Growers, Norseland Ch. Mem. Agrl. Com., Econ. Devel., Infrastructure & Regulation Fin.-Transportation Fin. Divsn., Fin. Inst. & Ins.: Internat. Trade & Economic Devel. Republican. Office: Office Lt Governor 130 State Capitol 75 Rev Dr Martin Luther King Jr Blvd Saint Paul MN 55155 Office Phone: 651-296-3391. Office Fax: 651-296-2089.

**MOLOFF, ALAN LAWRENCE,** retired military officer, physician; b. Bklyn., Sept. 29, 1954; s. Louis and Muriel Moloff. BS, U. Vt., 1976; DO, U. N.J., 1983; MPH, Harvard U., 1988; student, U.S. Army Command/Gen. Staff Course, 1994-95. Diplomate Am. Bd. Preventive Medicine, bd. cert. aerospace medicine, bd. cert. undersea medicine. Commd. platoon leader U.S. Army, 1976, advanced through grades to col., 1999; intern Fitzsimons Army Med. Ctr., Aurora, Colo., 1983—84; med. officer 1st Battalion 10th Spl. Forces Group, Bad Tolz, Germany, 1984—87; resident in aerospace medicine Harvard U., Boston, 1987—89; chief spl. ops. forces divsn. Acad. Health Scis., San Antonio, 1989—91; command surgeon Spl. Forces Command, Ft. Bragg, NC, 1992—93; dep. surgeon U.S. Army Spl. Ops. Command, Ft. Bragg, 1993—94; with command and gen. staff coll. U.S. Army, 1994—95; dep. surgeon 30th Med. Brigade, Heidelberg, Germany, 1995—96; SETAF surgeon, 1995—97; dep. U.S. Army Europe Fwd Surgeon, Hungary, 1995—96; surgeon V Corps, Germany, 1996—97; comdr. 212th M.A.S.H., Wiesbaden, Germany, 1997—99; fellow environ. policy inst. Army War Coll., 1999—2000; comdr. U.S. Army Aeromed. Ctr., 2000—02, Def. Med. Readiness Tng. Inst., 2002—06; ret., 2006. Lectr. in field. Contbr. articles to profl. jours. Active in civic activities. Decorated Legion of Merit, Meritorious Svc. medal with 4 oak leaf clusters, Joint Svc. Commendation medal, S.W. Asian Svc. medal, Army Commendation medal with oak leaf cluster, Joint Army Achievement medal, Armed Forces Svc. medal, Armed Forces Expeditionary medal, NATO medal, Kuwait Liberation medal, Kosovo Campaign medal, German Paratrooper badge, Pathfinder badge, Expert Field Med. badge, Order of Mil. Med. Merit, Master Parachutist award, Ranger, Spl. Forces Qualified Master Flight Surgeon badge, Navy Dive Med. Officer badge, Order of Aeromed. Merit, Def. Superior Svc. medal. Fellow: Aerospace Med. Assn., Am. Coll. Preventive Medicine; mem.: Spl. Ops. Med. Assn. (pres.), Soc. U.S. Army Flight Surgeons (life), Assn. Mil. Osteo. Physicians and Surgeons, Assn. Mil. Surgeons U.S. Avocations: skiing, scuba diving, weightlifting, military history, rock climbing. E-mail: moloffa@hotmail.com.

**MOLONEY, CHRISTOPHER XAVIER,** multi-media specialist, marketing executive; s. James Charles and G. Elise Sears Moloney. BS in Bus., Mo. State U.; MBA, Lindenwood U.; student in Mktg. and Comms., St. Louis U., 2001—. Dir. consumer mktg. programs Meridian Enterprises, Inc., St. Louis, 1995—99; dir. U.S. market strategy Maritz Loyalty Mktg., St. Louis, 1999—2004; v.p., gen. mgr. Loyalty Mktg. Divsn. Parago, Inc., Dallas, 2004—05; corp. v.p. mktg. Charter Comm., St. Louis, 2005—. Adj. prof. mgmt. Lindenwood U., St. Charles, Mo., 2003—; spkr. in field. Author: (chpt.) Strategic Database Marketing, A.M. Hughes. Marshall Fair St. Louis and The VP Parade, 2000—06; contbr. The Inst. of Interesting People, Dallas, 2004—06; bd. dirs. The 500 Inc. (Tor the Arts), Dallas, 2004—05. Named to Industry Innovator Hall of Fame, CRM Exec. Mag., 2005; fellow, St. Louis U., 1990. Mem.: Direct Mktg. Assn., Am. Mktg. Assn. (spkr. 2002, conf. leader 2002), Cable TV Mktg. Assn. Achievements include research in attitudinal-behavioral loyalty model; first to the customer advocacy matrix; advanced dialogue marketing model. Home: 984 Burgundy Lane Ballwin MO 63011 Office: Charter Communications US Headquarters 12405 Powerscourt Drive Saint Louis MO 63131 Office Phone: 972-543-5883'. Business E-Mail: chris.moloney@chartercom.com.

**MOLONEY, DANIEL M.,** electronics executive; BSEE, U. Mich.; MBA in Mgmt., U. Chgo. Joined Gen. Instrument Corp., 1983; sr. v.p., gen. mgr. broadband IP sys. group Motorola, Inc., exec. v.p., pres., CEO broadband comm. sector, 2002—. Contbr. articles to profl. jours.

**MOLONEY, HERBERT W., III,** advertising executive; Retail advt. mgr. The Miami Herald; sales mgr. WPRI-TV; sr. v.p. advt. Phila. Inquirer/Daily News; with Knight-Ridder, Inc., 1973—84; exec. v.p., mktg. and sales TC Advt. (now Vertis), 1994—2000; chief oper. officer Vertis, 2000—. Bd. dirs. Lee Enterprises, Inc. Office: Vertis 250 W Pratt St Baltimore MD 21201

**MOLONEY, THOMAS E.,** lawyer; b. Rockville Ctr., N.Y., Jan. 9, 1949; BS, U. Dayton, 1971; JD, U. Notre Dame, 1974. Bar: Ohio 1974. Prin. Am. Energy Svcs., Inc., Columbus, Ohio. Office: Am Energy Svcs Inc 1105 Schrock Rd Ste 602 Columbus OH 43229-1174 Office Phone: 614-885-1901.

**MOLONEY, THOMAS JOSEPH,** lawyer; b. Bklyn., Oct. 14, 1952; s. Thomas J. and Grace (Nelson) M.; m. Molly K. Heines, Dec. 26, 1976. AB, Columbia U., 1973; JD cum laude, NYU, 1976. Bar: N.Y. 1976, U.S. Dist. Ct. (so. dist.) N.Y. 1977, U.S. Dist. Ct. (ea. dist.) N.Y. 1978, U.S. Ct. Appeals (2d cir.) 1981, U.S. Dist. Ct. (no. dist.) N.Y. 1988, U.S. Ct. Appeals (4th cir.) 1989, U.S. Supreme Ct. 1991. Assoc. Cleary, Gottlieb, Steen & Hamilton, N.Y.C., 1976—84, ptnr., 1984—. Bd. dirs. N.Y. Lawyers for Pub. Interest, N.Y.C., 1986-91; mediator U.S. Bankruptcy Ct. for So. Dist. N.Y., 1995. Asst. counsel Gov.'s Jud. Nominating Com., N.Y.C., 1981-85; chmn. bus. adv. coun. Washington Irving H.S., 1994—. Mem. ABA, Am. Bankruptcy Inst.,

Assn. of Bar of City of N.Y. (bankruptcy, corp. reorganization coms. 1983-86, chair com. legal assistance 1995-97), Order of Coif. Avocations: chess, golf, dance, travel, wine. Office: Cleary Gottlieb Steen & Hamilton 1 Liberty Plz Fl 38 New York NY 10006-1470

**MOLONEY, THOMAS WALTER,** management consultant; b. N.Y.C., Feb. 8, 1946; s. Thomas Walter and Anne (Heney) M. BA, Colgate U., 1967; MA, Columbia U., 1970, MPH, 1973, MBA, 1975. Program dir. Nat. Ctr. for Deaf-Blind, New Hyde Park, N.Y., 1971-72; spl. asst. to dir. and dean N.Y. Hosp., N.Y.C., 1973-74; asst. v.p. Robert Wood Johnson Found., 1975-80; sr. v.p. The Commonwealth Fund, N.Y.C., 1980-97; dir. pub. policy and health programs The Inst. for Future, 1992-99; ptnr., owner S/B Futures Inc., Palm Beach, Fla., 1997—. Vis. lectr. Princeton (N.J.) U., 1975-80; bd. dirs. Grantmakers in Health, N.Y.C., 1984—, chmn. bd., 1984-88; mem. health adv. com. GAO, 1987—; mem. health adv. coun. Johns Hopkins U. Sch., Hygiene and Pub. Health, Balt., 1989-91; bd. dirs. Found. Health Svcs. Rsch., Washington, 1985-92; mem. bd. visitors Med. Sch., U. Calif. at Davis, 1988—; mem. vis. com. Grad. Sch. Mgmt. and Urban Policy New Sch. for Social Rsch., N.Y.C., 1988-92; mem. Nat. Bd. Examiners, 1986-90; mem. sr. adv. bd. global leadership program U. Mich. Grad. Sch. Bus., Ann Arbor, 1988—; mem. press. com. The N.Y. Acad. Scis., 1987-90; policy scholar The Eisenhower Ctr. Columbia U., N.Y.C., 1992—, Inst. Health Policy Studies U. Calif., San Francisco, 1992—. Author books; editor: New Approaches to the Medicaid Crisis, 1983; contbr. articles to profl. jours. Bd. dirs. New Eng. Med. Ctr., Boston, 1982-89. Policy scholar Inst. Health Policy Studies U. Calif., San Francisco, 1992—, Eisenhower Ctr. Columbia U., 1992—. Fellow AAAS; mem. Inst. Medicine, Nat. Acad. Scis., Nat. Acad. Social Ins., N.Y. Acad. Medicine, N.Y. Acad. Scis. (pres'. com. 1987-90). Office: S/B Futures Inc Fl 8 1170 N Ocean Blvd Palm Beach FL 33480-3244

**MOLONEY, WILLIAM J.,** school system administrator; BA in History and Polit. sci., MA in History and Polit. sci., Harvard U.; PhD in ednl. mgmt., Harvard U., Cambridge, Mass.; postgrad. studies in Slavic History, Oxford and U. of London. Supt. Calvert county pub. schools, Prince Frederick, Md., 1993—97; commr. edn. Colo. Dept. Edn., Denver, 1997—; sec. Colo. bd. edn., 1997—. Chmn. Edn. Leaders Coun., Washington; adj prof. Various Univs.; bd. dirs. Bds. of the Ctr. for Workforce Preparation, Ednl. Excellence Network. Co-author: (Books) The Content of America's Character, Education Innovation: An Agenda to Frame the Future; newspaper columnist:. Office: Colo Dept Education 201 E Colfax Ave Rm 500 Denver CO 80203 E-mail: moloney_w@cde.state.co.us.

**MOLONY, MICHAEL JANSSENS, JR.,** lawyer, arbitrator, mediator; b. New Orleans, Sept. 2, 1922; s. Michael Janssens and Marie (Perret)M.; m. Jane Leslie Waguespack, Oct. 21, 1951; children: Michael Janssens III (dec.), Leslie, Megan, Kevin, Sara, Brian, Ian, Duncan. JD, Tulane U., 1950. Bar: La. 1950, D.C. 1979, U.S. Dist. Ct. (ea. and mid. dists.) La. 1951, U.S. Ct. Appeals (5th cir.) 1953, U.S. Supreme Ct. 1972, U.S. Dist. Ct. (we. dist.) La. 1978, U.S. Ct. Appeals (11th and D.C. cirs.) 1981. Ptnr. Molony & Baldwin, New Orleans, 1950; assoc. Jones, Flanders, Waechter & Walker, New Orleans, 1951-56; ptnr. Jones, Walker, Waechter, Poitevent, Carrere & Denegre, New Orleans, 1956-75, Milling, Benson, Woodward, Hillyer, Pierson & Miller, New Orleans, 1975-91, Chaffe, McCall, Phillips, Toler & Sarpy, New Orleans, 1991-92, Sessions & Fishman, New Orleans, 1993-2000, Molony Law Firm, New Orleans, 2000—. Instr., lectr. Med. Sch. and Univ. Coll. Tulane U., 1953-59; mem. Eisenhower Legal Com., 1952. Bd. commrs. Port of New Orleans, 1976-81, pres., 1978; bd. rev. Assoc. Br. Pilots, 1990—2003; bd. dirs. La. World Expn. Inc., 1974-84; bd. dirs., exec. com. New Orleans Tourist and Conv. Commn., 1971-74, 78, chmn.; family attractions com. 1973-75; chmn. La. Gov.'s Task Force on Space Industry, 1971-73; chmn. La. Gov.'s Citizens' Adv. Com. Met. New Orleans Transp. and Planning Location of new Miss. River Bridge, 1971-77; mem. La. Gov.'s Task Force Natural Gas Requirements, 1971-72; mem. La. Gov.'s Production Commn. for Higher Edn., 1995; mem. Goals Found. Coun. and ex-officio mem. Goals Found., Met. New Orleans, 1969-73; vice chmn. Port of New Orleans Operation Impact, 1969-70, mem. Met. Area Com., New Orleans, 1970-84; trustee Pub. Affairs Rsch. Coun. La., 1970-73, mem. exec. com. Bus./Higher Edn. Coun., La. Partnership for Tech. and Innovation, 1989—; emeritus, 2000—, v.p., 1986-88, pres., 1988-90, chmn. Task Force on Pub. Higher Edn. Funding, 1990-95, chmn. govtl. affairs, 1995-2000, Task Force on Edn./Econ. Devel. Alliances, 1993-95; mem. Mayor's Coun. on Internat. Trade and Econ. Devel, 1978; mem. Mayor's Transition Task Force Econ. Devel., 1994; bd. dirs. La. Partnership for Tech. and Innovation, 1989—; Acad. Sacred Heart, 1975-77, Internat. House, 1985-86, adv. coun., 1985—; vis. com. Sch. Bus. Adminstrn., Loyola U., New Orleans, 1981-2001, trustee Loyola U., 1985-91, vice chmn. bd. trustees, 1990-91; deans coun. Tulane U. Law Sch., 1988-96, vice chmn. bldg. com., 1991-95; bd. dirs., exec. com. Internat. Trade Mart, chmn. internat. bus. com., 1983-85; bd. dirs. U. New Orleans Found., 1991-2003, World Trade Ctr.-New Orleans, 1983—, port activity com. 1985-91, transp. com. 1991-95, 2000—, govt. affairs com. 1996-99; chmn. Task Force on Internat. Banking, 1982, mem. Mayor's Task Force on Drug Abuse, 1989-90. With USAAC, 1942-46, PTO; capt. JAGDR, USAF, 1950-. Recipient Leadership award AIAA, 1971, Yenni award Loyola U., New Orleans, 1979, New Orleans Times Picayune Loving Cup, 1986, First Citizen of the Learning Soc. Dean's award UNO Met. Coll., 1992; also various civic contbn. awards; co-recipient Silver Anvil award New Orleans chpt. Pub. Rels. Soc. Am., 1991. Fellow Coll. Labor and Employment Lawyers (5th cir. credentials com. 2004-06); mem. ABA (labor and employment law and litig. sects., com. equal opportunity law, chmn. regional EEO com. liaison with equal opportunity commn., office of fed. contract compliance programs), D.C. Bar Assn., Fed. Bar Assn., La. Bar Assn. (past sec.-treas., bd. govs. 1957-60, editor your 1957-59, sec. spl. supreme ct. com. on drafting code jud. ethics), New Orleans Bar Assn. (dir. legal aid bur. 1954, chmn. standing com. legis 1968, vice chmn. standing com. publ. rels. 1970-71), Am. Judicature Soc., La. Law Inst. (asst. sec.-treas. 1958-70), Am. Arbitration Assn. (bd. dirs.), 1995-98, chmn. reg. adv. coun., chmn. reg. adv. coun. employment law cases, mem. panels-employment, employee benefits, large complex employment and comml. arbitration/mediation cases, Whitney North Seymour Sr. award 1991), So. Inst. Mgmt. (founder), AIM, U.S.C. of C. (urban and regional affairs com. 1970-73), La. C. of C. (bd. dirs. 1963-66), New Orleans and Rural Regional C. of C. (v.p. met. devel. and urban affairs 1969, past chmn. labor rels. coun., bd. dirs. 1970-78, pres. 1971, dir., exec. com. 1972, ex officio mem., bd. dirs. 1979—), Mil. Order Fgn. Wars (vice comdr. La. Commandery 2000-02, comdr. 2003-04, Comdr. Gen. Disting. Svc. award 2004), Nat. Arbitration Forum, Panel Arbitrators, Bienville Club, Pickwick Club, Plimsoll Club, Serra Club, So. Yacht Club, Sigma Chi (pres. alumni chpt. 1956). Roman Catholic. Office: Molony Law Firm 201 Saint Charles Ave Ste 3500 New Orleans LA 70170-3500 Office Phone: 504-582-1552. Office Fax: 504-582-1553. E-mail: mjm@mmolony-law.com.

**MOLSON, ERIC H.,** brewery company executive; b. Montreal, Sept. 16, 1937; s. Thomas Henry Pentland and Celia Frances (Cantlie) Molson; m. Jane Mitchell, Apr. 16, 1966; 3 children. AB in Chemistry, Princeton U., 1959. With Molson Inc., Montreal, 1960—, chmn. bd., 1988—2005; chmn. Molson Coors Brewing Co., Denver, 2005—; chancellor Concordia U., Montreal, 1993—. Bd. dirs. Montreal Gen. Hosp. Corp. and Found., Canadian Irish Studies Found., Vie des Arts. Office: Molson Coors Brewing Co 1555 Notre Dame St E Montreal PQ Canada H2L 2R5 also: Molson Coors Brewing Co 1225 17th St Denver CO 80202 Office Phone: 514-521-1786.

**MOLTENI, AGOSTINO,** pathology professor; b. Como, Lombardy, Italy, Nov. 12, 1933; came to U.S., 1963; s. Enrico and Antonia (Signorini) M.; m. Loredana Brizio, Sept. 5, 1963; children: Claudio Enrico, Ronald Stephen. MD, U. Milan, Italy, 1957; PhD in Pathology, SUNY, Buffalo, 1970. Lic. Italian Bd. Internal Medicine, 1963. Intern and resident in internal medicine U. Milan (Italy), 1957-62; asst. prof. U. Milan, 1957-63; chief rsch. sect. Farmitalia Drug Co., Milan, 1963-65; rsch. assoc. SUNY, Buffalo, 1965-69, asst. prof., 1969-71; assoc. prof. U. Kans., Kansas City, 1971-76; prof. pathology Northwestern U., Chgo., 1976-96, prof. emeritus, 1996—; prof. pathology and pharmacology U. Mo., Kansas City, 1996—, adj. prof. basic med. scis. Vis. prof. Harvard U., 1983-84; dir. med. students rsch. program U. Mo. Kansas City, 2004. Editor, author: Endocrinology and Thermal Trauma, 1990, Menopause Update, 1992; exec. editor Current Pharmaceutical Design, 2000—, Nutrition Rsch., 2003, PPAR Rsch., 2005; contbr. articles to profl. jours., chpts. to books. Recipient Sharer in Lasker award Lasker Found.: N.Y.C., 1983, Rsch. Career Devel. award NIH, Washington, 1970, award Am. Heart Assn., Chgo., 1982. Fellow Am. Acad. Clin. Biochemistry; mem. Am. Acad. Pathology, Am. Soc. Investigative Pathology, Clin. Chemistry Soc., Endocrine Soc. (emeritus), Am. Assn. Clin. Chemistry (emeritus). Achievements include patent for captopril as a cancer chemo-preventive agent; research on hypertension and hormonal regulation of cancer. Office: U Mo Truman Med Ctr 2301 Holmes St Kansas City MO 64108-2640 Office Phone: 816-235-5604. Business E-mail: moltenia@umkc.edu.

**MOLTZON, RICHARD FRANCIS,** data processing executive; b. Bklyn., Nov. 20, 1941; s. Arthur G. and Joan (Paladino) M.; m. Susan A. Anderson, Feb. 15, 1981; children: Paige, Kimberly, Michael, Keir. BS in Info. Systems Mgmt., U. Md., 1970. With IBM Corp., various locations, 1965—70; plant mgr. Telex Terminal Communications, Inc., Raleigh, NC, 1970—75, Carnes Co. div. Wehr Steel, Sanford, NC, 1975—76; dir., gen. mgr. Modular Computer Systems, Inc., Ft. Lauderdale, Fla., 1980—87; v.p. ops. Profile Corp., Pompano Beach, Fla., 1987—88; dir. mfg. AMF, Inc., Herndon, Va., 1976—79, Documation, Inc., Melbourne, Fla., 1979—90, Concurrent Computer Corp., Oceanport, NJ, 1988—89; v.p. mfg. Internat. Tech. Corp., Clearwater, Fla., 1989—90; pres. The Realty Authority, Inc., 1990—92; v.p. ops. Combustion TEC, Divsn. of Eclipse Combustion, Inc., Orlando, Fla., 1992—99; sr. v.p. ops. Control Tec LLC, Orlando, 1999—2001; v.p. product sourcing and mgmt. Environ. Lighting Concepts, Inc., Tampa, Fla., 2002—. With U.S. Army, 1961-64. Mem.: KC, Omicron Delta Kappa. Roman Catholic. Avocations: golf, jogging, writing. Office: Environ Lighting Concepts Inc 1214 W Cass St Tampa FL 33606 Office Phone: 813-621-0058. Business E-Mail: rickm@ott-lite.com. E-mail: rick.moltzon@terpalum.umd.edu.

**MOLYNEAUX, DAVID GLENN,** newspaper travel editor; b. Marion, Ind., Oct. 16, 1945; s. Glenn Ingersol and Barbara Wingate (Draudt) M.; children: Miles David, Rebecca Susan; m. Judi Dash, May 15, 1994. BS in Econs., Miami U., Oxford, Ohio, 1967. Reporter The Plain Dealer, Cleve., 1967-75, city editor, 1976-78, assoc. editor, 1979-80, editorial page editor, 1980-82, travel editor, 1982—. V.p. bd. trustees Soc. Am. Travel Writers Found., 2002—04, pres. bd. trustees, 2004—. Editor: 75 Years-An Informal History of Shaker Heights, 1987. Trustee Shaker Heights Pub. Libr., 1987—95. With U.S. Army, 1968-70. Mem. Cleve. Press Club. Office: Plain Dealer 1801 Superior Ave E Cleveland OH 44114-2198 Office Phone: 216-999-4560. E-mail: travel@plaind.com.

**MOLZ, REDMOND KATHLEEN,** public affairs educator; b. Balt., Mar. 5, 1928; d. Joseph T. and Regina (Barry) M. BS, Johns Hopkins U., Balt., 1949, MA, 1950; MALS, U. Mich., Ann Arbor, 1953; DLS, Columbia U., N.Y.C., 1976. Librarian I and II Enoch Pratt Free Library, Balt., 1953-56; pub. relations officer Free Library of Phila., 1958-62; editor Wilson Library Bull. H.W. Wilson Co., Bronx, NY, 1962-68; chief planning staff Bur. Libraries and Learning Resources U.S. Office Edn., Washington, 1968-73; prof. library sci. Sch. Library Service Columbia U., N.Y.C., 1976-80, Melvil Dewey prof., 1980-93; prof. pub. affairs Sch. Internat. and Pub. Affairs, Columbia U., N.Y.C., 1993-99, prof. emeritus, 2000—. Cons. U.S. Nat. Commn. Librs. and Info. Sci., Washington, 1974-75, U.S. Adv. Commn. Intergovtl. Relations, Washington, 1979-80; mem. nat. adv. coun. The Sheridan Librs., Johns Hopkins U., 1997—. Author: Federal Policy and Library Support, 1976 (Ralph R. Shaw award 1977), National Planning for Library Service, 1935-75, 1984, Library Planning and Policy Making: The Legacy of the Public and Private Sector, 1990, The Federal Roles in Support of Public Library Services, 1990, The Federal Roles in Support of Academic and Research Libraries, 1991; co-author (with Phyllis Dain) Civic Space/Cyberspace: The American Public Library in the Information Age, 1999; co-editor: The Metropolitan Library (anthology), 1972; author TV script Portraits in Print, 1959. Recipient Leadership Tng. award Fund for Adult Edn., 1956-57; recipient Disting. Alumnus award Sch. Library Sci. U. Mich., 1969, George Virgil Fuller award Columbia U., 1975, Johns Hopkins U. scholar, 1949-50, Horace H. Rackham fellow U. Mich., 1952-53, Columbia U. scholar, 1974-76, Tangley Oaks fellow, 1975-76; Council Library Resources Inc. Officers' grantee, 1974 Mem. ALA (councilor 1972-74, 76-80, exec. bd. 1976-80, chmn. legis. com. 1985-86), Freedom to Read Found. (dir. 1972-79, pres. 1977-79) Business E-Mail: rkm2@columbia.edu.

**MOMAH, ETHEL CHUKWUEKWE,** retired women's health nurse; b. Iyi-Enu, Ogidi, Nigeria, May 28, 1934; d. Zaccheus C. and Victoria U. (Orizu) Obi; m. Christian Chike Momah, Nov. 21, 1959; children: Chukwudi, Adaora, Azuka. SRN, Harrow Hosp., Middlesex, U.K., 1956; SCM, Mothers Hosp., London, 1957; MTD, Midwife Tchrs. Coll., Surrey, U.K., 1964; BS, Upsala Coll., 1988. Cert. inpatient obstetric nurse Nat. Cert. Corp. Nurse-midwife Guy's Hosp., London, 1959; nursing sister, head nurse labor/delivery Univ. Coll. Hosp., Ibadan, Nigeria, 1960-62; midwife tutor Lagos (Nigeria) Island Maternity Hosp., 1963-66; nurse-midwife Brit. Hosp., Paris, 1966, Hosp. Cantonal, Geneva, 1967-78; staff nurse Univ. Hosp., St. Peter's Med. Ctr., New Brunswick, NJ, 1980—85, patient care coord., 1985-90, antenatal testing nurse, 1990—2005; ret., 2005. Recipient Disting. Svc. award, NNEWI Union NY Tri-State Inc., 2000, Cultural Performance award, Anambra Enugu States Assn. N.J., 2001, Disting. Svc. award, Anambia Enugu States Assn., 2002, Cmty Leadership award, Assocs. Mental Health Devel. Disabilities, NJ, 2004, Legion of Honor award, Chapel of Four Chaplains, 2005, Courageous Leadership award, Anambra State Assn. N.J., 2006, Invaluable and Devoloped Svc. award, Nnewi N.Y. Tri-State, 2006. Mem.: Nnewi USA, Inc. (v.p. 2003—), Assn. Women's Health, Obstetric and Neonatal Nurses, Anambra-Enugu States Assn. N.J., Nne-Egwu (dance mother 1990—2006). Personal E-mail: nnanne@sbcglobal.net.

**MOMAND, ELIZABETH BLANTON,** singer, music educator; b. Miss., Oct. 10, 1963; d. Dorothy Case and Clarence Hix Blanton; m. Mohammad Isa Momand, June 21, 1986; children: Maleka Elizabeth Rosella, Bilal Hassan. MusB, Miss. Coll., Clinton, 1986; MusM, Miss. Coll., 1991; D of Musical Arts, U.Tex., Austin, 2001. Dir. vocal studies Power Academic and Performing Arts Complex, Jackson, Miss., 1990—97; dir. fine arts Lanier H.S., Austin, Tex., 2001—03; assoc. prof. music U. of Ark., Ft. Smith, 2003—; Fulbright Hays fellowship, Fulbright Assn., 1994, German Exch. scholarship, Miss. Coll., 1985. Mem.: Nat. Assn. of Teachers of Singing, Fulbright Assn. Avocations: travel, music. Office: Univ of Ark 5210 Grand Ave Fort Smith AR 72903 Office Phone: 479-788-7540. Personal E-mail: elimom@hotmail.com.

**MOMBOULI, SERGE,** ambassador; b. Pointe-noire, Republic of Congo, 1959; married; 6 children. Dr. pub. Pointe-noire and B. Pointe-noire. Career: corp. sales Air Afrique, Paris; v.p. A.W.E. Group, Houston; v.p. internat. ops. and project devel. Transworld Consortium Corp., Houston, 1995—97; Congolese presdl. spokesman in U.S., 1997; chargé d'affaires Embassy of Republic of Congo, 1997—2001; Congolese amb. to the U.S., 2001—. Office: Embassy of Republic of Congo 4891 Colorado Ave NW Washington DC 20011 Office Phone: 202-726-5500. E-mail: smombouli@hotmail.com.

**MOMENI, REZA,** plastic surgeon; BA, Haverford Coll., 1990—94; MD, Med. Coll. of Pa., 1994—98. Diplomate Am. Bd. Plastic Surgery. Resident in gen. surgery Yale U., New Haven, 1998—2001, resident in plastic surgery, 2001—04, chief resident in plastic surgery, 2003—04; plastic, reconstructive, & hand surgeon Summit Med. Group, Summit, NJ, 2004—. Cons. MedSN-.com, Santa Monica, Calif., 1998—2000; sci. reviewer Med. Sci. Monitor, Old Westbury, NY; med. illustration J/B Woolsey, Conshohocken, Pa., 1998—99. Nat. splty. rep. Am. Assn. of Med. Colleges - Orgn. of Resident Representatives, Washington, 2003—. Recipient 1st Pl., U.S. Pharmacopaeia Competition, 1996, Alpha Omega Alpha, Med. Coll. of Pa., 1998, Phi Beta Kappa, Haverford Coll., 1994, Nat. Pathology Honor Soc., Med. Coll. of Pa., 1996; scholar Class of 1934 scholarship, Haverford Coll., 1992; Yale Plastic

Surgery Scholastic award, Yale Univ., 2002, William Goldman scholarship, William Goldman Found., 1996—98, Howard Hughes Med. Inst. Rsch. scholarship, Howard Hughes Inst., 1993, Med. Coll. of Pa., Haverford Coll., 1995, Class of 1910 scholarship, Med. Coll. of Pa., 1995, Huldah Kerner scholarship, 1996, Ruth Weil Meml. scholarship, 1997, Weston Ellsworth scholarship, 1997. Mem.: AMA, Union County Med. Soc., NJ Med. Soc., Phi Beta Kappa, Alpha Omega Alpha, Yale Surg. Soc. Achievements include research in cranial reconstruction after dural complications; pulse oximetry in melanoma sentinel node dissection may be false; frontal sinus fractures: an institutional review. Avocations: travel, sailing, skiing, snowboarding. Office: Summit Plastic Surgery 1 Diamond Hill Rd Berkeley Heights NJ 07922 Office Phone: 908-277-8759.

**MOMMSEN, KATHARINA,** retired literature and language professor, foundation administrator; b. Berlin, Sept. 18, 1925; came to U.S., 1974, naturalized, 1980; d. Hermann and Anna (Johannsen) Zimmer; m. Momme Mommsen, Dec. 23, 1948. DPhil, U. Tübingen, 1956; Dr. habil., Berlin Free U., 1962. Collaborator Acad. Scis., Berlin, 1949—61; assoc. prof. Free U., Berlin, 1962—70; prof. German Carleton U., Ottawa, Canada, 1970—74; Albert Guerard prof. lit. Stanford U., 1974—94, ret., 1995. Vis. prof. U. Giessen, Tech. U. Berlin, 1965, State U. N.Y., Buffalo, 1966, U. Calif., San Diego, 1973; pres. Mommsen Found. Author over 200 publs. on 18th-20th century German and comparative lit.; editor: Germanic Studies in America. Mem. Goethe Soc., Schiller Soc. Home: 980 Palo Alto Ave Palo Alto CA 94301-2223 Office Phone: 650-326-6637. E-mail: k.mommsen@comcast.net, katmom@stanford.edu.

**MON, KEVIN G.,** research scientist; s. Kendra A. Mon. BS, U. of Calif., Berkeley, 1984—88, MS, 1988—93, PhD, 1993—96. Scientist Duke Engring. and Services, Las Vegas, Nev., 1997—2000; sr. scientist Framatome ANP, Las Vegas, Nev., 2000—05, sci. supr., 2005—. Session co-chmn. 10th Internat. Conf. on Math. and Computer Modeling and Sci. Computing, 1995. Recipient Corp. award, Framatome ANP, 2003; James Monroe McDonald scholar, U. Calif., Berkeley, 1995—96, Internat. Bus. Machines fellow, 1995—96. Mem.: Nat. Assn. of Corrosion Engineers. Office: Framatome ANP 1180 Town Ctr Dr Las Vegas NV 89144 Business E-Mail: kevin.mon@areva.com.

**MONACELLI, GIANFRANCO,** publishing executive; b. Milan; came to U.S., 1965; s. Rodolfo and Isabella (Paolillo) M.; m. Eugenia Hyman; children: Nurit, Fausto, Alexander. Dr., U. Turin, Italy, 1963, Acad. Santa Cecilia, 1964; BS, Mannes Coll., 1967; postgrad., Columbia U., 1969. Gen. mgr. Rizzoli Internat. Bookstore, N.Y.C., 1969-72; v.p. 1972-75; exec. v.p. Rizzoli Internat., Milan, 1975-78; pres., chief exec. officer Rizzoli Internat. Publs., Inc., N.Y.C., 1975-93, Rizzoli Internat. Bookstores, Inc., N.Y.C., 1975-92, Rizzoli Editore Corp., N.Y.C., 1975-89; sr. v.p. RCS Rizzoli Corp., N.Y.C., 1989-93; pres. USITAL Ltd., N.Y.C., 1993—, The Monacelli Press, Inc., N.Y.C., 1994—; v.p. Epikos Security Printing S.A., N.Y.C., 1997—. Trustee Mannes Coll., N.Y.C., 1979-81; pres. Weathersfield Music Festival, Vert., 1993—; mem. vis. com. U. Miami, Coral Gables, Fla., 1988-89. Recipient Met. Home Design 100 award, 1997, collaborative achievement award AIA, 1999; named Pub. of Yr., AIA, 1996. Mem. Century Assn., Am.-Italy Soc. (pres. 1993-94).

**MONACO, ANNE CATHERINE,** music educator; b. Binghamton, N.Y., Oct. 8, 1978; d. John M. and Dorothyann M. Rush; married, Aug. 7, 2004. MusB magna cum laude, Marywood U., 2000; MA in Music Edn., Maywood U., 2005. Cert. tchr. Pa., N.Y. Tutor in music theory Marywood U., Scranton, Pa., 1997—2000; music tchr. Gilbertsville-Mount Upton Ctrl. Sch. Dist., NY, 2000—, choreographer, 2001—, dir. grades 7-12 musical, 2005. Choir dir. St. Thomas Aquinas Ch., Binghamton, NY, 2001. Mem.: Otsego County Music Educators Assn. (adjudicator flute all-county auditions 2001—02, chmn. All County Band 2003, adjudicator low woodwinds 2003—, chmn. All County Band 2006), N.Y. State Sch. Music Assn., Kappa Delta Pi, Delta Epsilon Sigma, Kappa Gamma Pi. Avocations: dance, choreography, performing with music groups, Irish stepdancing.

**MONACO, ANTHONY JOHN,** retired health facility administrator, writer; b. Steubenville, Ohio, Oct. 26, 1926; s. Antonio Monaco and Maria Concetta Di Crescentis; m. Wilna Mae Dellinger, Apr. 11, 1953; children: Gregg Anthony, Carol Ann Dawley, Susan Lorraine. BS, Duquesne U., 1949; MPH, U. Pitts., 1958. Exec. dir. So. Ill. Med. Ctr., Mt. Vernon, 1972—79; pres., CEO Healthcare Coun. Nca, Washington, 1980—96. Adminstr. Berwick Hosp., Pa., 1956—72. Author: The Songs and Wisdom Of David And Solomon, 2003, Scriptures From The Orient, 2003, The Spirit Is in the Form, 2003, The Challenge of Moses, 2004, The Mission of Jesus and John, 2004, The Recitations of Mohammed, 2004, The Testimony of the Major Prophets, 2004, The Truth of Nanak and the Sikhs, 2004, The Real Holy Grail, 2004, Living in the Light Above the Line, 2005, God The Intelligent Designer Man The Intelligent Design, 2006. With U.S. Army, 1944—45. Home: 13062 Gorham Way Woodbridge VA 22192-2948 Personal E-mail: therealholygrail@yahoo.com.

**MONACO, CHRIS,** historian, writer, documentary filmmaker; b. Ann Arbor, Mich., June 7, 1950; s. John Monaco and Marilyn Hermine Meeks; life ptnr. Rose Widman. BA, U. of Fla., 1973; MFA, U. of South Fla., 1977. Adv. bd. mem. Conservation Trust for Fla., 2001—. Editor: (book) A Plan for the Abolition of Slavery; dir./writer/prodr. (films) The Far Frontier (Outstanding Achievement, Fla. Trust for Hist. Preservation, 1999), (TV series) Education Showcase (Beacon Award, Nat. Cable TV Pub. Affairs Assn., 1994); author: Moses Levy of Florida: Jewish Utopian and Antebellum Reformer (Presdl. Award of Distinction, Fla. Hist. Soc., 2006). Bd. mem. Plan Bd., Micanopy, Fla., 1997—99. Recipient Hampton Dunn award, Fla. Hist. Soc., 1998, Flori award, Fla. Ind. Filmmakers Festival, 1979, Award of Excellence, Nat. Cable TV Advt. and Mktg., 1986—87; Faculty-Staff scholarship, U. of South Fla., 1976—77, Individual Artist fellowship, Fla. Fine Arts Coun., 1978. Mem.: So. Jewish Hist. Soc., Fla. Hist. Soc., Orgn. of Am. Historians. Achievements include discovery of the earliest and most important antislavery publication by an American Jew; identifying the earliest Jewish communal settlement in the United States, M. E. Levy's Pilgrimage Plantation (1822-1835); establishing Moses Elias Levy as one of the most significant figures in early American Jewish history. Avocations: graphic arts, photography. Personal E-mail: csmonaco@cs.com.

**MONACO, DANIEL JOSEPH,** lawyer; b. Easton, Pa., May 12, 1922; s. Federico and Maria (Romano) M.; m. Margaret P. Monaco, June 26, 1953 (div.); children: Denise E., Mimi D. AB with honors, Lafayette Coll., 1943; postgrad., U. Mich., 1944—45; MA, U. Chgo., 1946; JD, Stanford U., 1950. Bar: Calif. 1951, U.S. Dist. Ct. (no. dist.) Calif. 1951, U.S. Supreme Ct. 1961. Mem. faculty U. Miami, Fla., 1946-47; founder, of counsel Monaco, Anderlini & Finkelstein, San Mateo, Calif., 1953—; probate judge State of Calif., 1963-67. Real estate broker, Calif., 1957-67; judge pro tem Calif. Mcpl. and Superior Cts. Chmn. San Mateo County Dem. Ctrl. Com., 1960-61, Citizen World Ct.; mem. Calif. State Dem. Exec. Bd.; founder, pres. Circlon Internat., 1978-81; chmn. World Peace Through Law Ctr. com. to establish a Citizens' World Ct.; pres. peninsula com. UN Ednl. Sci. & Cultural Orgn., 1955-59; mem. No. Calif. Coun. Fgn. Affairs; San Mateo County Hosp. Found. Bd. With U.S. Army, 1943-46, It. USAR, 1946-50. Recipient Gentry Mag. Cmty. Stars award, 1997. Mem. ABA, ATLA, UN Assocs.-U.S.A. (pres. San Mateo County chpt. 1958-65), Calif. State Bar Assn., Calif. Trial Lawyers Assn. (bd. govs.), San Mateo County Trial Lawyers Assn. (pres.), World Jurist Assn. (2d v.p. 1995-97, 1st v.p. 1997-99, pres. 1999-2001, hon. pres. 2003—), Am. Bd. Trial Advs., Internat. Law Assn. World Citizens, Gorbachev Found., The Commonwealth Club, Peninsula Golf and Country Club, U. Chgo. dist. speaker series, 2004. Democrat. Avocations: travel, international law. Home: 295 Darrell Rd Hillsborough CA 94010-7109 Office: 400 S El Camino Real Ste 700 San Mateo CA 94402-1744 Office Phone: 650-348-0102. Office Fax: 650-348-0962. Personal E-mail: dukemonaco@aol.com.

**MONACO, ROBERT ANTHONY,** radiologist; b. NYC, July 5, 1945; s. Edmond V. and Jean M.; m. Susan Margaret Thompson; children: Kevin, Robert, Christopher, Sarah. BS, Siena Coll., 1967; MD, N.J. Coll. Medicine, 1971. Diplomate Am. Bd. Radiology, Am. Bd. Nuclear Medicine. Radiology resident N.J. Coll. Medicine, Newark, 1971-75; fellow in nuclear medicine med. ctr. NYU, N.Y.C., 1975-76; attending radiologist Med. Ctr. Ocean County, Point Pleasant, NJ, 1976-87, dir. dept. radiology, 1987—, sec. med. staff, 1998-2000. Gen. ptnr Point Pleasant Radiology Group, 1987—; sec. bd. dirs. Found. Med. Ctr. Ocean County, Mid-Coastal IPA, 1997; mng. ptnr. Open MRI of Wall, 1999—. Capt. USAR, 1972-76. Mem. Am. Coll. Radiology, Am. Coll. Nuc. Medicine, Radiol. Soc. NJ (exec. com. 2005-). Roman Catholic. Avocations: tennis, fishing, swimming. Home: 13 Bretwod Dr Colts Neck NJ 07722 Office: Open MRI of Wall Rt 34 Wall NJ 07719 Office Phone: 732-974-8060. E-mail: rammdo1@aol.com.

**MONAGHAN, CRAIG THOMAS,** automotive executive; b. Phila. m. Mary Lou Murphy, Jul. 25, 1981; children: Shannon, Connor, Rand. BS industrial engr., Lehigh U., 1980; MBA in fin., Wharton U. Pa., 1985. Cert. mgmt. acct. Financial analyst General Motors, NYC, 1985-87, mgr. overseas fin., 1987-88; dir. corp. fin. Squibb, Princeton, NJ, 1988-90; dir. internat. fin. Bristol-Myers Squibb, NYC, 1990-91; asst. treas. Reader's Digest, Pleasantville, NY, 1991-92, controller europe, 1992—98; CFO iVillage.com, 1998-2000, AutoNation, Inc., Fort Lauderdale, Fla., 2000—, exec. v.p. Capt. U.S. Army, 1980—83. Mem.: Inst. Mgmt. Accts. Avocations: fishing, golf, reading. Office: AutoNation Inc 110 SE 6th St Fort Lauderdale FL 33301*

**MONAGHAN, DOMINIC,** actor; b. Berlin, Dec. 8, 1976; Actor: (TV series) Hetty Wainthropp Investigates, 1996—98, Lost, 2004— (Outstanding Performance by an Ensemble in a Drama Series, Screen Actors Guild award, 2006); (TV films) Hostile Waters, 1997, This Is Personal: The Hunt for the Yorkshire Ripper, 2000; (TV miniseries) Monsignor Renard, 2000; appeared: I Love the 90's, 2005; I Love the 90's: Part Deux, 2005; actor: (films) The Lord of the Rings: The Fellowship of the Ring, 2001, The Lord of the Rings: The Two Towers, 2002, The Lord of the Rings: The Return of the King, 2003, An Insomniac's Nightmare, 2003, Spivs, 2004, The Purifiers, 2004, Shooting Livien, 2005. Office: c/o ABC 77 W 66th St New York NY 10023*

**MONAGHAN, THOMAS STEPHEN,** philanthropist; b. Ann Arbor, Mich., Mar. 25, 1937; m. Marjorie Zybach, Aug. 25, 1962; children— Mary, Susan, Margaret, Barbara Student, Ferris State Coll., U. Mich.; PhD (hon.), Cleary Coll., 1982, Madonna Coll., 1983, Eastern Mich. U. Also St. Fla. U., 1985. Ptnr. Dominick's Pizza, Ypsilanti, Mich., 1960-65; pres., chmn. bd., founder, CEO Domino's Pizza, Inc., Ann Arbor, Mich., 1960-98; ret., 1998; founder Ave Maria Sch. Law, 2000—, Ave Maria Univ., Fla., 2003—. Owner Detroit Tigers, 1983-92. Author: (autobiography) Pizza Tiger. Founder Mater Christi Found. (now Ave Maria Found.), 1983—; bd. dirs. Cleary Coll., Ypsilanti, Henry Ford Hosp., Detroit, U. Steubinville, Ohio, St. Joseph's Hosp. Devel. Bd., Ann Arbor. Served USMC, 1956—59. Named Entrepreneur of Yr. Harvard U. Bus. Sch., 1984, Pizzaman of Yr. Nat. Assn. Pizza Owners, 1984; recipient Golden Plate award Am. Acad. Achievement, 1984, Golden Chain award Multi Unit Franchise Svc. Orgn., 1986, Horatio Alger award, 1986, Restaurant Bus. Leadership award, 1986, Pope John Paul II Family Fidelity award 1988, Pine Mission's Knights of Charity award, 1990, Semper Fidelis award USMC, 1990. Mem. Internat. Franchise Assn. (Entrepreneur of Yr. 1986), Nat. Restaurant Assn. (Silver Plate award 1985), Mich. Restaurant Assn., Ypsilanti C. of C., U. Mich. Pres.'s Club, Ann Arbor Pres.'s Assn., Missionary Vehicle Assn. (bd. dirs.), AIA (hon.), Mich. Soc. Architects (hon.). Clubs: Barton Hills Country (Ann Arbor). Lodges: K.C. Roman Catholic. Avocations: collecting Frank Lloyd Wright furniture and memorabilia, classic cars. Office: Ave Maria Univ 1025 Commons Circle Naples FL 34119*

**MONAHAN, JOHN MICHAEL,** lawyer; b. Syracuse, Mar. 2, 1969; d. James Paul Monahan Sr. and Linda Lou Monahan; m. Gena Marie Mattiaccio, Sept. 4, 2004. Student, U. Sheffield, Eng., 1989; BA in Polit. Sci. (hon.), Hobart Coll., Geneva, NY, 1991; JD, George Mason U., Arlington, Va., 1996. Bar: N.Y. 1997, U.S. Dist. Ct. (no. dist.) N.Y. 2001, U.S. Dist. Ct. (we. dist.) N.Y. 2003, N.J. 2005. Intern White House, Washington, 1991; clk. to Hon. William F. O'Brien III N.Y. Supreme Ct., Madison County, 1996—2000; atty. Hancock & Estabrook, LP, Syracuse, NY, 2000—03, Phillips Lytle LLP, Buffalo, 2003—04, Jaeckle Fleischmann & Mesel, LLP, Buffalo, 2004—. Spkr. in field. Contbr. articles to profl. jours. Mem.: ABA, Soc. Human Resources, Erie County Bar Assn., N.Y. State Bar Assn. Republican. Roman Catholic. Avocations: golf, guitar, travel. Home: 57 5th Ave Williamsville NY 14221 Office: Jaeckle Fleischmann & MuselLLP 12 Fountain Plaza Buffalo NY 14202 Office Phone: 716-856-0060, 716-856-0432. Business E-Mail: jmonahan@jaeckle.com.

**MONAHAN, JOHN T.,** law educator, psychologist; b. NYC, Nov. 1, 1946; s. John Joseph and Dorothy (King) M.; m. Linda Costa, Aug. 24, 1969; children: Katherine, John. BA, SUNY, Stony Brook, 1968; PhD, Ind. U., 1972; LLD (hon.), CUNY, 1997. Assst. prof. social ecology U. Calif., Irvine, 1972—78, assoc. prof., 1978—80; prof. U. Va. Sch. Law, Charlottesville, 1980—, now Henry L. and Grace Doherty Charitable Found. prof. law, Class of 1941 rsch. prof., prof. psychology and psychiat. medicine. Dir. mental health law MacArthur Found., Chgo., 1988-98, dir. Rsch. Network on Mandated Cmty. Treatment, 2000-. Editor: Who is the Client? The Ethics of Psychological Intervention in the Criminal Justice System, 1980; co-editor: Prevention in Mental Health: Research, Policy and Practice, 1980, Mentally Disordered Offenders: Perspectives from Law and Social Science, 1983, Children, Mental Health, and the Law, 1984, Violence and Mental Disorder: Developments in Risk Assessment, 1994, Coercion and Aggressive Community Treatment: A New Frontier in Mental Health Law, 1996, Mental Disorder, Work Disability, and the Law, 1997, Research in Community and Mental Health, Vol. 10: Coercion in Mental Health Services - International Perspectives, 1999; author: The Clinical Prediction of Violent Behavior (reprinted as Predicting Violent Behavior: An Assessment of Clinical Techniques), 1981; co-author: Social Science in Law: Cases and Materials, 1985, 1990, 1994, 1998, 2002, Rethinking Risk Assessment: The MacArthur Study of Mental Disorder and Violence, 2001, Adjudicative Competence: The MacArthur Studies, 2002. Recipient Disting. Contbn. to Rsch. in Pub. Policy Award, APA, Washington, 1990, Isaac Ray Award, APA, NY, 1996; Ind. U. Fellow, Harvard U., 1976-77; fellow Stanford U., 1978-79, Oxford U., 1992. Mem. APA (founding pres. divsn. psychology and law), Inst. of Medicine Office: U Va Sch Law 580 Massie Rd Charlottesville VA 22903-1789 Office Phone: 434-924-3632. E-mail: jmonahan@virginia.edu.

**MONAHAN, MATTHEW,** artist; b. Eureka, Calif., 1972; BFA, Cooper Union, 1990—94; attended, Gerit Rietveld Acad., Amsterdam. One-man shows include Anton Kern Gallery, NY, 1997, Fools Gold, The Bank of Netherlands, 1998, Artist is Proof, Buro Leeuwarden, NH, 1999, Gozaimas, Bur. Stedelijk, 2000, Nameless man for Not-Even-Anywhere, Galeries Fons Welters, Amsterdam, 2002, Civilized Spl. Zone, Chinese European Art Ctr., Xiamen, 2002, Container, Art Basel Miami, 2003, exhibited in group shows at Night at Life, NY, 1997, Exterminating Angel, Galerie Ghislaine Hussenot, Paris, 1998, Subreal/ The Human Condition, LA Internat. Biennial, Inmo Gallery, LA, 1999, I Love NY, Anton Kern Gallery, 2001, Mean Mercy, Tent, Rotterdam, 2001, Free-standing, Beaver Coll. Art Gallery, Phila., 2001, To Be Recycled, Six Months, LA, 2004, Remembering, U. Calif. Riverside Gallery, 2004, Whitney Biennial: Day for Night, Whitney Mus. Am. Art, 2006. Fellow De Ateliers, Amsterdam, 1994—96; grantee Fonds BK Grant, Kitaysuhu, Japan, 2000, Chinese European Art Ctr, Xiamen, China, 2002. Mailing: c/o Anton Kern Gallery 532 West 20th St New York NY 10011*

**MONAHAN, PATRICK,** singer; 2 children. Lead singer Train, 1994—. Singer: (albums) Train, 1998, Drops of Jupiter, 2001 (Song "Drops of Jupiter" won Grammy award for Best Rock Song, 2001), My Private Nation, 2003 (Song "Calling All Angels" won for Grammy award for Best Rock Vocal Performance by a Duo or Group, 2004), (songs) Meet Virginia, 1999, I Am, 1999, (from Spider-Man 2 soundtrack) Ordinary, 2004.

**MONAHAN, THOMAS PAUL,** accountant; b. Pitts., Feb. 27, 1951; s. Thomas Andrew and Patricia (Tompkins) M.; m. Ellen McKeithan Easterby, Aug. 2, 1975; children: Kelley Kathleen, Thomas Patrick, Kyle Easterby, Tessa Elizabeth. BS in Acctg., U. S.C., 1073. CPA SC. Staff acct. Rogers, Brigman, Peterson & Co., Columbia, S.C., 1972-75, ptnr., 1975-82; chmn., treas., prin. GMK Assocs., Columbia, 1982—. Chmn., bd. dirs., treas. Devel. Properties, Inc.; trustee, pres. Town Theater Trust, 2000—. Mem. bus. coun. S. Dems., 1986—; bd. dirs. Cultural Coun. of Richland and Lexington Counties; pres. Town Theatre Trust; active Com. of 100. Mem. AICPA, S.C. Assn. CPAs, Columbia Stage Soc. (trustee, bd. dirs.), Spring Valley Country Club, Capital City Club, Palmetto Club, Zeta Beta Tau (trustee emeritus). Home: 1117 Adger Rd Columbia SC 29205-1942 Office: GMK Assoc Ste 2100 1201 Main St Columbia SC 29201-3263 Office Phone: 803-256-0000. Business E-Mail: tmonahan@gmka.com.

**MONAJEMI, PEZHMAN,** computer engineer; s. Ahmad and Mehrangiz Monajemi. PhD in Elec. and Computer Engring., Ga. Inst. Tech., Atlanta, 2006. Micro electro-mech. sys. engr. Silicon Clocks, Inc., Fremont, Calif.; sr. RF design engr. Jacket Micro Devices, Inc., Atlanta, 2005—. Trainer Ga. Inst. Tech., Atlanta, 2002—05. Contbr. scientific papers in MEMS engring. Recipient Best Trainer award, Microelectronics Rsch. Ctr., Atlanta, 2003. Mem.: IEEE (Sensor Coun. Best Paper award 2004). Achievements include development of wafer-level metal-organic MEMS packaging using decomposable polymers.

**MONAT, WILLIAM ROBERT,** university official; b. Biwabik, Minn., Oct. 9, 1924; s. William Stephen and Milda Aleta (Sundby) M.; m. Josephine Ann Sclafani, Sept. 9, 1951; children: Lise Ann, Kathryn, Margaret, William Michael, Eric. AA, Virginia Jr. Coll., Minn., 1947; BA magna cum laude, U. Minn., 1949, PhD, 1956; postgrad., Wayne U., 1949-50. Asst. prof. Wayne U., 1954-57; exec. asst. to Gov. Mich., 1957-60; assoc. prof. Pa. State U., 1960-65, prof. polit. sci., 1965-69; asst. dir. Inst. Pub. Adminstrn., 1962-69; majority budget dir. Pa. Ho. of Reps., 1968-69; prof., chmn. dept. polit. sci. No. Ill. U., De Kalb, 1969-71, provost, 1976-78, Regency prof., 1986-92; Regency prof. emeritus, 1992—; pres. No. Ill. U., De Kalb, 1978-84; chancellor Ill. Bd. Regents, 1984-86; prof., dean faculties Baruch Coll., City U. N.Y., 1971-74, v.p. acad. affairs, 1974-76. Cons. USPHS, 1958, Office of Sec. Dept. Labor, 1963-64, Bur. Labor Stads., 1966, Office of Gov. Pa., 1968; bd. dirs. 1st Nat. Bank DeKalb, Castle Bancgroup, Inc. Author: Labor Goes to War, 1965, The Public Library and its Community, 1967, Politics, Poverty and Education, 1968; Editor: Public Adminstration in Era of Change, 1962, The Achieving Institution, 2000; contbr. articles to profl. jours. Mem. Gov.'s Commn. on Sci. and Tech., 1983-87; trustee Grad. Sch. Polit. Mgmt., NY, 1986-95; chmn. City of Dekalb Plan Commn.; trustee DeKalb Sanitary Dist., 2005. With AUS, 1943-46. Recipient Outstanding Achievement award U. Minn., 1981; decorated Bronze Star medal. Mem. Am. Polit. Sci. Assn., Am. Soc. Pub. Adminstrn., Phi Beta Kappa. Home: 1605 Mayflower Dr Dekalb IL 60115-1723 Business E-Mail: wmonat@niu.edu.

**MONATH, NORMAN,** publishing company executive; b. Toronto, Ont., Can. came to U.S., naturalized, 1944; m. Pauline K. Farber, Aug. 30, 1952 (dec. Feb. 1972); children— Richard, Robert, Bruce. Dir. subsidiary rights Simon & Schuster, Inc., 1957-59; now cons.; founding pres. Cornerstone Library, Inc., N.Y.C., 1960—. Composer (with Walt Kelly) Songs of the Pogo, 2003; author: Know What You Want And Get It!, rev. edit., 2002; How To Play Popular Piano, 1984, How To Play Popular Guitar, 1994, (with William Cole) Folk Songs of England, Ireland, Scotland and Wales; editor (with Bobby Short) unpublished songs of Cole Porter; songwriter with Hal David, Sammy Cahn; recs. by Dionne Warwick, Supremes, Mitch Miller, Jerry Vale, Burns and Allen, Burl Ives. With signal corps U.S. Army, 1942-45. Mem. ASCAP. Inventor Bali word game, 1954. Home: 3545 S Ocean Blvd Apt 101 Palm Beach FL 33480-5716 E-mail: monath@bellsouth.net.

**MONATH, THOMAS PATRICK,** physician; b. Hewlett Harbor, N.Y., Aug. 13, 1940; s. Paul E. and Elizabeth (Burger) M.; m. Jennifer Sanderson Mills, Sept., 25, 1964 (div. 1981); 1 child, Andrea; m. Margaret Blake Garvan, June 25, 1988; 1 child, Nicholas. AB, Harvard U., 1962, MD, 1966. Diplomate Am. Bd. Internal Medicine. Intern, resident Peter Bent Brigham Hosp., Boston, 1966-68, 73-74; med. officer Ctr. Disease Control, Atlanta, 1968-72, dir. div. Vector-Borne Diseases Ft. Collins, Colo., 1974-88; chief virology div. U.S. Army Med. Rsch. Inst. Infectious Diseases, Frederick, Md., 1988-92; chief sci. officer Acambis Inc., Cambridge, Mass., 1992—2006; ptnr. Kleiner Perkins Caufield & Byers, Menlo Park, Calif., 2006—. Cons. WHO, Geneva, 1974—; chmn. panel on virus diseases Am. Inst. Biol. Scis., Washington, 1978-88; mem. U.S.-Japan Coop. Med. Sci. Program, 1974-78; vis. rsch. fellow U. Ibadan, Nigeria, 1970-72; sr. sci. and tech. adv. to dir. CIA, 1989—. Author, editor: St. Louis Encephalitis, 1980, The Arboviruses, 1988, Field's Virology, 1990, 95, The Flaviviruses, 2003; assoc. editor Human Vaccines, Vector-Brose, Zoonotic Diseases, Acta Tropica, Jour. Virol. Methods; contbr. more than 350 articles to sci. jours. Capt. USPHS, 1968-88, col. U.S. Army, 1988-92. Recipient Presidential Citation, Med. Amateur Radio Coun., 1974, Nat. Young Meml. award Am. Com. on Anthropod-Borne Viruses, 1986, Meritorious Svc. medal UPSHS, 1978. Fellow ACP, Royal Soc. Tropical Med. Hygiene; mem. Am. Soc. Tropical Med. Hygiene (councillor 1976-80, pres. 2004-05, Richard M. Taylor award, 2002, Walter Reed medal 2002), Am. Com. on Arthopod-Borne Viruses (chmn. 1980-82), Am. Soc. Virology, Internat. Soc. Infectious Diseases. Democrat. Home: 21 Finn Rd Harvard MA 01451-1925 Office Phone: 978-456-3290. E-mail: t.monath@kpcb.com.

**MONCK, MARY C.,** science educator; b. Trenton, NJ, Nov. 15, 1961; d. Philip W. Sr. and Irene H. Monck. BS, Ursinus Coll., Collegeville, Pa., 1983; MS, Villanova U., Pa., 1985. Tchg. asst. Villanova U., 1983—85; tchr. Norwood Fontbonne Acad., Phila., 1988—91, Acad. Notre Dame, Villanova, 1991—; prof. Holy Family U., Phila. 1991—. Office: Acad Notre Dame 560 Sproul Rd Villanova PA 19085

**MONCK, MAUREEN F.,** psychoanalyst; b. N.Y.C., Dec. 12, 1938; d. Lawrence Finnerty and Mary Henrietta Crean-Lynch; m. Robert A. Monck, June 16, 1962 (dec. Jan. 1983); children: Merritt Monck-Rowley, Erinna Monck Bernstein, Caitlin Monck-Marcellino. BS, Georgetown U., 1960; PhD, NYU, 1968; MA in Art History, Cooper Hewitt-New Sch., 1999; postdoctoral cert. in adult psychoanalysis, Derner Inst.; postdoctoral cert. in child and adolescent psychotherapy, Adelphi U. Pvt. practice psychoanalyst, Oyster Bay, NY, 1968—; pres. Oyster Bay (N.Y.) Hist. Soc., 2004; supr. of psychotherapy Metro. Ctr. for Mental Health, N.Y.C., 1997—; dir. psychotherapy trg. program L.I. Inst. for Psychoanalysis, East Meadow, NY, 1985—93; dir. nursing program C.W. Post - L.I. U., Brookville, NY, 1972—75. Office Phone: 516-922-6125.

**MONCREIFF, ROBERT P.,** lawyer; b. Evanston, Ill., Mar. 26, 1930; s. W. Philip and Maxine E. M.; m. Elisabeth M.; children: Anne, Philip, Jane. BA, Yale U., 1952; MA, Oxford U., Eng. 1954; LLB, Harvard U., 1957. Bar: Mass. 1957. Assoc. Edwards, Angell, Palmer & Dodge, Boston, 1957-62, ptnr., 1963-95, of counsel, 1995—. City councillor, Cambridge, Mass., 1970-74. Office: Edwards Angell Palmer & Dodge LLP 111 Huntington at Prudential Ctr Boston MA 02199-7613 Office Phone: 617-239-0290. E-mail: rmoncreiff@palmerdodge.com.

**MONCRIEF, MICHAEL JOSEPH,** mayor, former state legislator; b. Houston, Sept. 5, 1943; s. Richard Barto Sr. and Mary Daisy (Wiley) M.; m. Rosemary Brewer, Dec. 31, 1980; children: Troy L., Mitchell K. BS, Tarleton State U., 1968. Ind. oil prodr., Ft. Worth, 1969—; mem. Tex. Ho. of Reps., 1971—72, mem. appropriations com., 1970-72; judge Tarrant County, Tex., 1974—86; mem. Tex. State Senate, 1991—2003; pres. pro tempore Tex. Senate, 2001; mayor City of Ft. Worth, 2003—. Past mem. Tarrant County Drug Abuse Bd., Lone Star Transp. Authority, N. Central Tex. Council of Govts., Appropriations Com.; mem. Gov.'s Blue Ribbon Commn. on Criminal Justice, many other groups. Bd. dirs. Assn. Retarded Citizens (hon. chmn.), chmn. Neighborhood Resources Devel. Coun., Tarrant County Med.,

Edn. and Rsch. Found., Tarrant County Mental Health Assn., Drug Treatment Ctr., Tarrant County Juvenile Bd., Ft. Worth State Sch., Inst. Pub. Svc. Tarleton State U., Tex. Affiliate Adv. Com., AHA, Alliance for Children (hon.), Paul Quinn Coll., Tex. Preservation Bd., US Olympic Com., and several others; pres. Neighborhood Health Horizons; past bd. dirs. Gill Children Svcs., Inc., Ft. Worth Infar. Bd., Longhorn Coun. Boy Scouts Am., Tex. Soc. for Prevention of Blindness, North Tex., many others; dir. North Tex. Commn., 2003-; affiliated with Ft. Worth C. of C., Tex. Arts Alliance, Muscular Dystrophy Assn., Inc. and several others. Named Outstanding Cmty. Leader Am., 1970, Outstanding Young Man Am., 1971, Newsmaker of Yr., 1974, 78, Freshman Legislator of Yr., Tex. Legislature, 1971, AARP award, 1997, Common Cause Star of Tex. Pub. Svc. award, 2000, Kiwanis Club ' Community Builder" award, 2002, many other honors. Mem. Tarleton Alumni Assn. (Disting. Alumni 1977), Ind. Petroleum Assn. Am., Am. Judicature Soc., Nat. Coll. Probate Judges, Ft. Worth Res. Police Officers, other profl. orgns. Avocations: skiing, tennis, golf, hunting rattlesnakes and alligators. Office: Office of Mayor 1000 Throckmorton St Fort Worth TX 76102 Business E-Mail: Mayor@fortworthgov.org.*

**MONCRIEF, RICHARD W.,** oil industry executive; s. William Alvin Moncrief Jr. and Elizabeth (Bright) Moncrief; m. Marsland Moncrief. BS, U. Tex. Prin. Moncrief Oil Interests, Ft. Worth; owner Moncrief Oil Internat.; gen. ptnr. Moncrief Oil Europe and Asia Holdings Partnership. Bd. trustees US Azerbaijan C. of C., Amon Carter Mus., William A. and Elizabeth B. Moncrief Found. Mem.: All-Am. Wildcatters. Office: Moncrief Oil 9th and Commerce St Fort Worth TX 76102

**MONCRIEF, WILLIAM ALVIN, JR.,** oil and gas producer; b. Little Rock, Mar. 27, 1920; d. William Alvin and Elizabeth (Bright) Moncrief; m. Deborah Beggs, Jan. 30, 1947; children: William A. III, R.W., C.B., T.O. BS in Petroleum Engring., U. Tex., Austin, 1942. Registered profl. engr., Tex. Ptnr. Moncrief Oil, Ft. Worth, 1945—; dir. First Republic Bank, Dallas. Regent, U. Tex. sys. Served to ensign USNR, 1944-45, PTO. Named Disting. Engring. Grad. U. Tex.-Austin, 1983; named one of 400 Richest Am. Forbes mag., 2006. Mem.: Shady Oaks of Ft. Worth (pres.); Eldorado (Indian Wells, Calif.); Brookhollow (Dallas). Republican. Episcopalian. Office: Moncrief Oil Moncrief Bldg 950 Commerce St at 9th Fort Worth TX 76102*

**MONCTON, DAVID,** physicist; PhD in Physics, MIT, 1975. Assoc. lab. dir. Argonne Nat. Lab., 1987—2001; exec. dir. Spallation Neutron Source project Oak Ridge Nat. Lab., Oak Ridge, Tenn., 1999—2001; dir. Nuclear Reactor Lab. MIT, 2004—. Recipient E.O. Lawrence award, U.S. Dept. of Energy, 1987. Fellow: Am. Physical Society (Leo Szilard Lectureship award 2005). Office: MIT 77 Massachusetts Ave Cambridge MA 02139

**MONCURE, ASHBY CARTER,** surgeon, educator; b. Richmond, Va., Dec. 27, 1934; s. Powhatan and Maude Leah (Carley) M.; m. Patricia Juanita Leighton, June 21, 1960 (dec. Oct. 2003); children: Diana, Ann Marie, Ashby, Elizabeth; m. Margot Graham Lord, June 21, 2004. MD, U. Va., 1960. Diplomate Am. Bd. Surgery, Am. Bd. Thoracic Surgery, Am. Bd. Vascular Surgery. Intern Mass. Gen. Hosp., Boston, 1960-61, resident, 1961-62, 64-68; practice medicine specializing in surgery Boston, 1969—. Instr. surgery Harvard Med. Sch., Boston, 1969-71, asst. prof. surgery, 1971-77, asst. clin. prof. surgery, 1977-86, assoc. clin. prof. surgery, 1986—2000, clin. prof. surgery, 2000-03, clin. prof. surgery emeritus, 2003; assoc. vis. surgeon Mass. Gen. Hosp., Boston, 1973-79, vis. surgeon, 1980—2003, sr. surgeon, 2003—. Editor: MGH Textbook of Emergency Medicine, 1978, 2d edit., 1983, 3d edit., 1989, Complex Operations at the Mass. Gen. Hospital, 1983. Capt. U.S. Army, 1962-64. Fellow ACS; mem. New Eng. Surg. Soc. (pres. 2000), Ea. Surg. Soc. (pres. 2004), Am. Surg. Assn., Soc. Thoracic Surgeons, Internat. Cardiovascular Soc., Am. Assn. Thoracic Surgery, Soc. Vascular Surgery, Boston Surg. Soc. (pres. 1995). Clubs: Union Boat, Weston Golf. Episcopalian. Home: 3 Glen Oak Dr Wayland MA 01778

**MONCURE, JOHN LEWIS,** lawyer; b. Houston, Nov. 4, 1930; s. Walter Raleigh Daniel and Margaret (Atkins) M.; m. Norma Steed, Dec. 29, 1954 (dec. June 1982); children: John Carter, Michael Lewis, Douglas Lee, Stuart Richard, Mary Margaret; m. Margaret Edmonston, Nov. 12, 1983. BBA, U. Houston, 1953; JD, U. Tex., 1956. Bar: Tex. 1956. Assoc. Butler, Binion, Rice, Cook & Knapp, Houston, 1956-68; ptnr. Prappas, Moncure & Eidman, Houston, 1969-86, John L. Moncure and Assocs., Houston, 1987—. Lectr. bus. law U. Houston, 1958-59, 68-69 Mem. sch. bd. St. Thomas Episcopal Sch., Houston, 1965-78; mem. vestry St. Thomas Episc. Ch., 1975-78. Named Distinguished Alumni Coll. Bus., U. Houston, 1968 Fellow Am. Coll. Probate Counsel; mem. Am., Tex., Houston bar assns., Assn. Christian Schs. (trustee), Coll. Bus. Alumni Assn. U. Houston (pres., dir.), U. Houston Alumni Fedn. (treas., dir.), Sigma Alpha Epsilon. Republican. Home: 1220 W Clay Houston TX 77019 Office: 1200 River Oaks Tower 3730 Kirby Dr Houston TX 77098-3905 Office Phone: 713-831-6821.

**MONDALE, JOAN ADAMS,** wife of former Vice President of United States; b. Eugene, Oreg., Aug. 8, 1930; d. John Maxwell and Eleanor Jane (Hall) Adams; m. Walter F. Mondale, Dec. 27, 1955; children— Theodore, Eleanor Jane, William Hall. BA, Macalester Coll., 1952. Asst. slide librarian Boston Mus. Fine Arts, 1952-53; asst. in edn. Mpls. Inst. of Arts, 1953-57; weekly tour guide Nat. Gallery of Art, Washington, 1965-74; hostess Washington Whirl-A-Round, 1975-76; ambassador to Japan, 1993-96. Author: Politics in Art, 1972, Letters from Japan, 1998. Bd. govs. Women's Nat. Dem. Club; hon. chmn. Fed. Coun. on Arts and Humanities, 1978-80; bd. dirs. Associated Coun. of Arts, 1973-75, Reading Is Fundamental, Am. Craft Coun., NYC, 1981-88, J.F.K. Ctr. Performing Arts, 1981-90, Walker Art Ctr., Mpls., 1987-93, Minn. Orch., Mpls., 1988-93, 97-2003, St. Paul Chamber Orch., 1988-90, Northern Clay Ctr., 1988-93; bd. dirs. St. Paul, 1988-93, Nancy Hauser Dance Co., Mpls., 1999-93, Minn. Landmarks, 1991-93, Walker Art Ctr., Mpls., 1997-2003; trustee Macalester Coll., 1986—; mem. commn. Nat. Portrait Gallery, 1997—; chair Hiawatha Light Rail Transit Pub. Art and Design com., 2000-04; active Walker Art Ctr., 2003—, Minn. Orch., 1997—; citizen's stamp adv. com. US Postal Svc., 2005— Mem.: Phi Beta Kappa Epsilon. Democrat. Presbyterian. Home: 2116 Irving Ave S Minneapolis MN 55405-2541 E-mail: joan.mondale@mac.com.

**MONDALE, S. JANIECE,** librarian; b. Lubbock, Tex., Mar. 24, 1958; d. Jon Frank Mondale and Sarah Louise Hiatt; m. Thomas E. Daniels, May 9, 1989; children: Claire, Lily. BA in Polit. Sci., Utah State U., 1981; MA in Internat. Rels., Boston U., 1993; MLS, U. Md., 2001. Intelligence officer USAF, 1998—2001; chief of libr. Nat. Reconnaissance Office, Chantilly, Va., 2001—. Maj. USAF, 1981—2001. Mem.: Assn. Info. Sci. and Tech., Spl. Libr. Assn., Intelligence Cmty. Libr. Consortium (chair-elect 2005—06). Democrat. Episcopalian. Avocations: reading, quilting, medieval studies. Home: 12403 Sexton Ln Bowie MD 20715 Office Phone: 703-808-5756. E-mail: jmondale@mac.com.

**MONDALE, WALTER FREDERICK,** former Vice President of United States, lawyer, diplomat; b. Ceylon, Minn., Jan. 5, 1928; s. Theodore Sigvaard and Claribel Hope (Cowan) M.; m. Joan Adams, Dec. 27, 1955; children: Theodore, Eleanor, William. BA cum laude, U. Minn., 1951, LLB cum laude, 1956. Bar: Minn. 1956. Law clk. Minn. Supreme Ct.; pvt. practice law, 1956-60; atty. gen. State of Minn., 1960-64; U.S. senator from Minn., 1964-77; v.p. served under Pres. James Carter U.S., 1977-81; mem. Nat. Security Council, 1977-81; mem. firm Winston & Strawn, 1981-87; U.S. amb. to Japan Tokyo, 1993-96; presdl. envoy Indonesia, 1998; ptnr. Dorsey & Whitney, Mpls., 1987—93, ptnr., internat. corp. practice group, sr. counsel, 1997—. Chmn. Nat. Democratic Inst. for Internat. Affairs, 1986—93. Author: The Accountability of Power*Toward a Responsible Presidency, 1975; mem. Minn. Law Rev. Dem. nominee for Pres. U.S., 1984. With U.S. Army, 1951-53. Named Disting. Univ. Fellow in law and pub. affairs, Hubert H. Humphrey Inst. of Pub. Affairs, Univ. Minn. Presbyterian. Democrat. Office: Dorsey & Whitney 50 S 6th St Ste 1500 Minneapolis MN 55402-1498 Office Phone: 612-340-2600. Office Fax: 612-340-2868.

**MONDAVI, ROBERT GERALD,** winery executive; b. Virginia, Minn., June 18, 1913; s. Cesare and Rosa (Grassi) Mondavi; m. Marjorie Declusin, 1940 (dec.); children: Robert, Timothy, Marcia; m. Margrit Biever, 1980. BA in Econs. & Bus. Adminstrn., Stanford U., 0196; Hon. Degree, Cornell U., 1995; Degree in Fine Arts Honoris Causa, Calif. Coll. Arts & Crafts, 2002. Dir. Sunny St. Helena Wine Co., St. Helena, Calif., 1937—45; v.p., gen. mgr. Charles Krug Winery, St. Helena, 1943—66; pres. Robert Mondavi Winery, Oakville, Calif., 1966—91; chmn. bd. Robert Mondavi Winery (acquired by Constellation Brands), Oakville, Calif., 1991—2004. Chmn. Wine Inst. Author: (autobiography) Harvests of Joy: My Passion for Excellence, 1998. Benefactor Copia: The Am. Ctr. for Wine, Food and the Arts, 2001—. Named Winemaker of Yr., Am. Wine Soc., 1982, Commandeur de Bordeaux, Grand Conseil du Vin de Bordeaux, 1983, Man of Yr., Wines and Vines mag., 1986, Decanter mag., 1988, Wine & Spirits Profl. of Yr., James Beard Found., 1990, Beverage Industry's Man of Yr., Christerman Found., 1991, Hon. Master of Wine, Inst. of Masters of Wine, 1993, Bus. Leader of Yr., Harvard Bus. Sch. Assn. No. Calif., 1997, US House Reps., Disting. Hon. Mem. of the Agrl. Leadership Alumni, 2003; named to Nat. Bus. Hall of Fame, Jr. Achievement, Inc., 1991, Bay Area Bus. Hall of Fame, Bay Area Coun., 1995, Internat. Food & Beverage Hall of Fame, Doctor of Oenology, Honoris Causa, Bd. Trustees, Johnson & Wales U., 2000, Hall of Fame-Distinguished Restaurants of N.Am., 2000; recipient Hall of Fame award, Calif. Restaurant Assn. Edni. Found., 1988, Merit award, Am. Soc. of Enology and Viticulture, 1990, Ambassador and Master of Aesthetics of Gastronomy award, Culinary Institute of Am., 1991, Calif. State Fair Lifetime Achievement award, 1997, Wine Spectator's Reader's Choice award, 1997, Internat. Achievement award, World Trade Club, 1997, Lifetime Achievement award, European Wine Coun., 1998, Patron of the Arts award, Songwriter's Hall of Fame, 1999, Ellis Island Family Heritage award, Statue of Liberty-Ellis Island Found., Inc., 2005, F. Norman Clark Entrepreneur of Yr. award, Calif. Travel Industry Assn., 2000, Wine Industry Integrity award, 2000, Lifetime Achievement Recognition from:, Calif. State Assembly, 2002, Am. Food and Entertainment award by Bon Appetit mag. and TV Food Network and Wine Enthusiast mag. Wine awards, 2002, Presdl. Citation, U. Calif. Davis, 2002, Order of Merit of the Republic of Italy, Govt. Italy, 2002, Award of Merit-Winemaker of the Century, Confrerie de la Chaine des Rotisseurs, 2003, Legion d'Honneur award, Govt. France, 2003, Lifetime Achievement award, Vinexpo, 2003. Mem.: Am. Inst. of Wine and Food, Calif. State Polytechnic U. Pomona (hon. life chmn. 1992, Winemaker of Yr. 1992), Cornell Soc. of Hotelman (assoc.). Achievements include donated gift with wife to the Univ. of Calif. to establish the Robert Mondavi Inst. for Wine and Food Science and to name in honor of Robert and Margrit Mondavi Ctr. for the Performing Arts; torch bearer International Olympic Committee in 1996. Office: Robert Mondavi Winery PO Box 106 Oakville CA 94562-0106 Address: Robert Mondavi Winery Hwy 29 Oakville CA 94562

**MONDELLO, JOHN PAUL,** financial consultant; b. N.Y.C., Aug. 9, 1948; s. Salvatore Carmelo and Mary (Monaco) M.; m. Catherine Mary Seyfried, Sept. 12, 1970; children: Lynn Marie, Timothy. BA in Econs., LeMoyne Coll., Syracuse, N.Y., 1971; MS in Fin. Svcs., Am. Coll., Bryn Mawr, Pa., 1986. CLU, Chartered Fin. Cons. Fin. cons. Signator Fin. Network, Westbury, NY, 1972—. Instr. estate planning Am. Soc. CLU & ChFC, Garden City, 1990-96, Empire State Coll., 1997-02. 1st lt. U.S. Army N.G., 1971-77. Recipient Victor Goldberg Svc. award, Nassau Assn. of Ins. and Fin. Advisors, 1989. Mem. Nassau Assn. of Ins. and Fin. Advisors, John Hancock Chmn.'s Coun., Million Dollar Round Table (life), John Hancock Pres.'s Cabinet, John Hancock Hall of Fame. Avocations: golf, reading, spectator sports. Office: Signator Adv Group 1025 Old Country Rd Ste 325 Westbury NY 11590 Office Phone: 516-794-9696 x13. Business E-Mail: jmondello@jhnetwork.com.

**MONDELLO, LISETTE MCSOUD,** federal agency administrator; BA, Trinity Coll. Dir. comm. office of Sen. Alfonse D'Amato U.S. Senate, Washington, dir. comm. office of Sen. Kay Bailey Hutchison; sr. advisor office comm. and outreach US Dept. Edn.; asst. sec. pub. & intergovernmental affairs US Dept. Veterans Affairs, 2005—. Office: US Dept Veterans Affairs 810 Vermont Ave NW Rm 900 Washington DC 20420 Office Phone: 202-273-5750. Office Fax: 202-273-5717.

**MONDELLO, MARK T.,** manufacturing executive; BSME, U. South Fla. Former project mgr. on comml. and def.-related aerospace programs Moog, Inc.; prodn. line supr. Jabil Cir., St. Petersburg, Fla., 1992—93, project mgr., 1993—97, v.p. bus. devel., 1997—99, sr. v.p. bus. devel., 1999—2002, COO, 2002—. Bd. dirs. All Children's Hosp. Office: Jabil Cir 10560 9th St N Saint Petersburg FL 33716

**MONDINI-RUIZ, FRANCO,** artist; b. San Antonio, Tex., 1961; s. Gino and Stella Mondini. BA in English, St. Mary's U., San Antonio, Tex., 1982, JD, 1985. Atty. USAA; owner Infinito Botanica and Gift Shop, San Antonio, 1995—98; ArtPace Artist in Residency Program, 1996; Tryon Ctr. Artist Residency Program Charlotte, NC, 2003. Solo exhibitions include, Infinito Botanica, ArtPace, San Antonio, 1996, Tableau Vivant, The Alamo, San Antonio, 1998, New Painting y Mas, Galeria Ortiz, San Antonio, 1999, Infinito Botanica: New York, Ctr. Curatorial Studies, Bard Coll., 1999, Mexique, El Museo del Barrio, NYC, 2000, Untitled Grid No. 7, New Mus. Contemporary Art, NYC, 2001, Infinito Botanico: St. Louis, Des Lee Gallery, Wash. U., 2001, SHOP, Jessica Murray Projects, Bklyn., 2001, Dust in the Wind, NY Pub. Art Fund, 2002, Market Squared, Galeria Ortiz, San Antonio, 2002, Nacho de Paz (and Other TexMex Miracles), Frederieke Taylor Gallery, NYC, 2002, Pan in the Pk., Laumeier Sculpture Pk., St. Louis, 2003, Infinito Botanico: LA, UCLA Fowler Mus. Cultural History, 2004—05, group exhibitions include, San Antonio Sculpture Symposium, 1989, Planta de Arte Nuclear, San Antonio, 1990, Tex. Dialogues, Arlington Mus. Art, 1991, Shrines, Milagros Contemporary Art Gallery, San Antonio, 1992, El Impacto de Dos Mundos, Art Space Gallery, New Haven, Conn., 1992, Closets: Queer Experience, Esperanza Peace and Justice Ctr., San Antonio, 1993, Hispanic Artists of 1993, Guadalupe Cultural Arts Ctr., San Antonio, 1993, The Illusive Object, Diverse Works, Houston, 1993, Blue Star VIII, Blue Star Art Space, San Antonio, 1994, Synthesis and Subversion: A Latino Direction in San Antonio Art, Art Gallery U. Tex. San Antonio, 1995, Double Trouble: Mirrors/Pairs/Twins/Lovers, Blue Star Art Space, San Antonio, 1995, Tres Proyectos Latinos, Laguna Gloria Art Mus., Austin, 1997, Simply Beautiful, Contemporary Art Mus., Houston, 1997, The Bus. of Art, Institute Cultural de Mex., San Antonio, 1998, Collective Visions, San Antonio Mus. Art, 1998, Material World, Austin Mus. Art, 1998, Trade, Salon 300, Bklyn., 1998, The Ecstatic, Trans-Hudson Gallery, NYC, 1999, Yard Sale, Downtown Arts Project, NYC, 2000, Texans in the Whitney, Arthur Roger Gallery, New Orleans, 2000, Infinito Botanico, Downtown Arts Project, NYC, 2000, City Lights: Art Walk, Comite Colbert, NYC, 2000, Whitney Biennial, Whitney Mus. Am. Art, NYC, 2000, Ultrabaroque: Aspects of Post-Latin Am. Art (traveling exhbn.), 2000—03, Hopscotch, Gallery Art, Kean U., NJ, 2001, Lost in Space, Gary Tatinsian Gallery, NYC, 2001, Caribbean Biennial, Santo Domingo, Dominican Republic, 2001, ARS01-KIASMA, Mus. Contemporary Art, Helsinki, Finland, 2001, Infinito Botanica: Spain, ARCO, Madrid, 2002, Parklife, MetroTech Ctr., Bklyn., 2002—03, Dreamspaces/Entresuenos, Deutsche Bank, NYC, 2003, Ballroom Marfa, Tex., 2004. New Forms Regional Initiative Grant, 1994, ArtPace Gen. Grant, 1999, Pollock-Krasner Found. Grant, 2000, Joan Mitchell Found. Grant, 2001, Creative Capital Found. Grant, 2001, Creative Capital Found. Supplemental Grant, 2002, Penny McCall Found. Fellowship, 2002, Jules Guerin Rome Prize Fellowship for Visual Arts, Am. Acad. in Rome, 2004—05.

**MONDINO, BARTLY J.,** ophthalmologist; b. Sacramento, May 24, 1945; married; children: Kara, Kristen. BA in Med. Scis., Stanford U., 1967, MD, 1971. Diplomate Am. Bd. Ophthalmology. Intern Stanford (Calif.) U. Hosp., 1971-72; ophthalmology resident N.Y. Hosp., Cornell U., N.Y., 1972-75; fellow in cornea, external disease U. Pitts. Sch. Medicine - Eye and Ear Hosp., Pitts., 1975-76, asst. prof. ophthalmology, 1976-79, assoc. prof. ophthalmology, 1979-82; dir. Charles T. Campbell Microbiology Lab. Eye and Ear Hosp., Pitts., 1978-82; assoc. prof. ophthalmology UCLA - Jules

Stein Eye Inst., L.A., 1982-83, prof. ophthalmology, 1983—, Wasserman Endowed chair dept. ophthalmology, 1988—; chief cornea-external disease divsn. UCLA, 1991-99, chmn. dept. ophthalmology, 1994—; dir. UCLA - Jules Stein Eye Inst., 1994—; with exec. program for acad. healthcare mgmt. The John E. Anderson Grad. Sch. Mgmt./UCLA, 1992. Bd. dirs. Charles R. Drew U. of Medicine and Sci., L.A., Braille Inst., L.A.; mem. adv. com. Rsch. Study Club, Murrieta, Calif., 1994—, scientific adv. panel on ophthalmology Calif. Med. Assn., San Francisco, 1994—. Editl. bd.: Am. Jour. Ophthalmology, Chgo., 1992—, ophthalmic Surgery and Lasers, 1995—, Ophthalmology Times, 1996—, Ophthalmic Practice (Can.), 1996—; editor-in-chief: EYE Newsletter, 1994—; co-chair corneal diseases program planning panel of Nat. Eye Inst.'s Vision Rsch. Program Planning Subcom., Bethesda, Md., 1997—, others. Recipient scholarship Stanford U. Sch. Medicine, Rsch. to Prevent Blindness Manpower award 1983-84, Rsch. to Prevent Blindness Sr. Scientific Investigator's award 1994, various lectureships, others. Mem. AMA, Assn. for Rsch. in Vision and Ophthalmology, Assn. Univ. Profs. of Ophthalmology, Am. Acad. Ophthalmology, Assn. Ophthalmology, Calif. Cornea Club, Calif. Med. Assn., Contact Lens Assn. of Ophthalmologists, Eye Bank Assn. of Am., L.A. County Med. Assn., L.A. Soc. Ophthalmology, Ophthalmology Rsch. Found., Ophthalmic Surgery and Laser Therapy, Rsch. Study Club. Office: 100 Stein Plz # 2-142 Los Angeles CA 90095-7000 E-mail: mondino@jsei.ucla.edu.

**MONDLIN, MARVIN,** retail executive, rare book dealer; b. Bklyn., July 1, 1927; s. Samuel and Thelma (Schultz) M.; m. Phyllis Grossman, Oct. 23, 1962 (div. 1968); 1 child, Gerri; m. Irene Szmulewicz, Sept. 4, 1970. Student, Cornell U., 1945; student of Aesthetic Realism, with Eli Siegel, 1945—68; student, CCNY, 1948, Bklyn. Coll., 1969—71. Ptnr. Amory Books, N.Y.C., 1953-59; clk. Strand Book Store, N.Y.C., 1951, estate book buyer, 1959-71, 74-76, sr. exec. v.p., 1976—2004; proprietor Am. Sunbeam Pub., NYC, 1996—. Bus. mgr. Definition Press., N.Y.C., 1957; cataloger U. Cath. de Louvain, Belgium, 1972. Author: Appraisals: A Guide for Bookmen, 1997; co-author: Book Row, An Anecdotal and Pictorial History of the Antiquarian Book Trade, 2003; proofreader, copy editor Dover Publs., N.Y.C., 1958; editor Yearbook of Internat. Assocs., 1974; pub. Robert Clairmont's Quintillioins, 2006. Mem.: Typophiles, Ephemera Soc. Am., European Soc. History of Phtography, Am. Photog. Hist. Soc., Bibliog. Soc. London, Bibliog. Soc. Am., Appraisers Assn. Am., Camera Club. Avocation: photography. Home and Office: 889 Broadway Apt 3C New York NY 10003-1219 Office Phone: 212-982-8189. E-mail: marvinmondlin@verizon.net.

**MONDRY, DIANE,** secondary school educator; b. Reginas, Sask., Can. 3 children. Career and tech. edn. tchr. Cmty. H.S., Grand Forks, ND. Part-time instr. dept. info. sys. and bus. edn. U. N.D. Recipient Outstanding Tchr. award, Nat. Assn. Vocat. Edn. Spl. Needs Pers. Mem.: NEA, Assn. for Career and Tech. Edn. (immediate past pres. 2001—02), Nat. Bd. for Profl. Tchg. Stds. (bd. mem.). Office: Cmty High Sch 500 Stanford Rd Grand Forks ND 58203-2748*

**MONDUL, DONALD DAVID,** patent lawyer; b. Miami, Fla., Aug. 24, 1945; s. David Donald and Marian Wright (Heck) M.; children: Alison Marian, Ashley Megan; m. Anna Marie Towle, Oct. 12, 1996. BS in Physics, U.S. Naval Acad., 1967; MBA, Roosevelt U., 1976; JD, John Marshall Law Sch., 1979. Bar: Ill. 1979, Fla. 1980, Tex. 1998; U.S. Patent Office 1980; U.S. Ct. Appeals (fed. cir.) 1982; U.S. Supreme Ct. 1990. Commd. ensign USN, 1967, advanced through grades to comdr., 1977; mktg. rep. Control Data Corp., Chgo., 1977-79; patent atty. Square D Co., Palatine, Ill., 1979-81; group patent counsel Ill. Tool Works Inc., Chgo., 1981-87; assoc. Cook, Wetzel & Egan, Chgo., 1987-89; ptnr. Foley & Lardner, Chgo. and Milw., 1989-95; sr. patent atty. IBM, East Fishkill, NY, 1995-96; gen. patent counsel Ericsson, Inc., Richardson, Tex., 1996-99; pvt. practice Dallas, 1999—. Comdr., USNR, 1967-87. Achievements include patents for Electrical Encoding Device; Method and Apparatus for Determining the Product of Two Numbers; Apparatus for Providing Power to Selected Portions of a Multiplying Device; Method and Apparatus for Multiplying a Plurality of N Numbers; Method and for Establishing an Operating Parameter for a Power Supply Device; Apparatus and Method for Locating Objects in a Three-Dimensional Space; Air Baffle Apparatus. Office: 3060 Bonsai Dr Plano TX 75093 Office Phone: 972-758-1955, 972-662-9378. Personal E-mail: dmondul@aol.com.

**MONE, MICHAEL EDWARD,** lawyer; b. Brockton, Mass., May 15, 1942; s. Edward Patrick and June Elizabeth (Kelliher) M.; m. Margaret E. Supple, Sept. 11, 1965; 1 child, Michael Edward. BA, Middlebury Coll., 1964, LLB (hon.), 2000; JD, Boston Coll., 1967; LLB (hon.), Suffolk U., 1999. Bar: Mass. 1967, U.S. Dist. Ct. Mass. 1968, U.S. Ct. Appeals (1st cir.) 1968. Trial atty. Schneider & Reilly, Boston, 1967-73, ptnr., 1969-73; trial lawyer Esdaile, Barrett & Esdaile, Boston, 1973—, ptnr., 1976—. Instr. Boston Coll. Law Sch., 1981; U.S. Supreme Court, 1996. Chmn. Zoning Bd. Appeals, Brockton, 1976-78. Fellow Am. Coll. Trial Lawyers (bd. regents 1995-2001, sec. 1997-98, pres. 1999-2000); mem. ABA, ATLA (bd. govs. 1975-78), Mass. Bar Assn. (pres. 1993-94), Mass. Acad. Trial Lawyers (pres. 1981-84, joint bar com. on jud. nominations 1986-90). Office: Esdaile Barrett & Esdaile 75 Federal St Boston MA 02110-1913 Office Phone: 617-482-0333. Business E-Mail: mone@ebelaw.com.

**MONEGRO, FRANCISCO,** alternative medicine consultant, psychology professor; b. La Vega, Dominican Republic, Apr. 20, 1949; s. Francisco Monegro-Fdez and Ana A. (Pena) Monegro. Grad. cum laude, Pontifical U., Santiago, Dominican Republic, 1973; grad. psychology, Autonomous U. Santo Domingo, 1978, MD, 1986; MA in Ednl. Psychology, Tech. Inst. Santo Domingo, 1981; PhD in Nutrition, LaSalle U., Mandeville, La., 1993. Cert. natural health profl.; hypnotherapist, profl. biofeedback profl.; diplomate in behavioral medicine, diplomate in pain mgmt.; lic. in psychology Autonomous U. Santo Domingo, 1978. Tchr. Peace H.S., Santo Domingo, Dominican Republic, 1975-76; dir. dept. psychology Holy Trinity Ednl. Ctr., Santo Domingo, 1978-80; prof. Sch. Medicine Tech. Inst. Santo Domingo, 1986-87; dir. dept. psychology Interam. U. Santo Domingo, 1988-89; prof. psychology and medicine Autonomous U. Santo Domingo, 1978-89, psychologist, counseling dept., 1979-84; staff mem. spl. edn. Bd. Edn. Dist. X, Bronx, NY, 1991-93; founder, chmn. N.Y. Inst. for Holistic Life, N.Y.C., 1991—; prof. psychology CUNY at HCC, Bronx, 1990—. Founder, pioneer in behavioral medicine Behavioral Medicine Clinic, Santo Domingo, 1987-94. Author: Biofeedback-Bio-retroalimentacion, 1988, Holistic Behavioral Medicine, 1993, Biomagnetic Medicine: Secrets and Power of Magnetic Energy, 1996, Psychology and Life Mind, Body and Society, 1997, Commonly Prescribed Psychiatric Drugs. A Guide for Clinicians and Care Takers, 2003, A Guidebook for Behavioral Evaluators, 2003, (interactive CD-ROMs) Psychology and Life, 2000, Developmental Aphasia, 2002, Commonly Prescribed Psychiatric Drugs. A Guide for Clinicians and Care Takers, 2003, A Guide for Behavioral Evaluators, 2003; editor, pub.: BOEST, 1978, Dominican Bull. Behavioral Medicine, 1987, Holistic Life/Vida Holistica, 1991, others. Mem. Dominican Psychol. Assn. (treas. 1978-79), Soc. Behavioral Medicine, Assn. for Advancement of Behavior Therapy, Am. Acad. Pain Mgmt., Assn. for Applied Psychophysiology and Biofeedback. Democrat. Roman Catholic. Avocations: computers, golf, basketball, swimming, travel. Home: PO Box 302 Bronx NY 10458-0302 Office: NY Inst for Holistic Life 976 Mclean Ave Ste 370 Yonkers NY 10704-4105 Office Phone: 718-364-2202. Personal E-mail: holisticlife@msn.com.

**MONEO, JOSÉ RAFAEL,** architecture educator; b. Tudela, Navarra, Spain, May 9, 1937; s. Rafael and María Teresa (Vallés); m. Belén Feduchi; children: Belén, Teresa, Clara Matilde. Degree in architecture, Madrid, 1961, DArch, 1963. Fellow Spanish Acad., Rome, 1963-65; prof. arch. Barcelona, Spain, 1970-80, Madrid, 1981-85, Sch. Design, Harvard U., Cambridge, Mass. 1985—, chmn. dept. arch., 1985-90, Josep Lluís Sert prof. arch., 1991—. Prin. works include Bankinter, Madrid, Logroño Hall, Mérida Roman Art Mus., Atocha Sta., Madrid, Seville (Spain) Airport, Auditorium of Barcelona, Kursaal Auditorium and Congress Ctr., Thyssen-Bornemesza Mus., Madrid Davis Mus. Wellesley Coll., Miro Found., Mus., Mallorca, Diagonal Bldg., Barcelona, Museums of Modern Art and Architecture, Stockholm, 1994-98,

City Hall Extension, Urcia, 1998, Barcelona Concert Hall & Cultural Ctr., 1999, Kursaal Concert Hall & Cultural Ctr., San Sebastian, 1999, Audrey Jone Beck Bldg., Mus. Fine Arts, Houston, 2000. Recipient Arnold W. Brunner Mem. prize in Architecture, Am. Acad. Arts and Letters, 1993, Pritzker Arch. prize, 1996, Gold medal Internat. Union of Archs., 1996, Antonio Feltrinelli prize, 1998.

**MONESKEY, TABITHA JEAN,** assistant principal; b. Akron, Ohio, Jan. 8, 1979; d. Richard Andrew Moneskey. BSBA, U. Akron, Ohio, 2000, MS in Edn., 2003. Cert. edn. Ohio, 2002. Tchr. Life Skills Ctr., Akron, 2002—03, asst. adminstr. Canton, Ohio, 2003—. Vol. Democrats, Akron, 2000—06. Recipient Life Saver award, Life Skills Ctr. Student Body, 2003. Democrat. Methodist. Office Phone: 330-456-4490.

**MONEYPENNY, EDWARD WILLIAM,** retail executive; b. Long Branch, NJ, Jan. 18, 1943; s. Edward Henry and Eleanor Kathleen (O'Hagan) M.; m. Connie Wills, Feb. 19, 1966; children: Matthew, Jonathan, Christopher. BS in Acctg., St. Joseph's U., 1964; MS in Acctg. Sci., U. Ill., 1967. CPA, Pa. Audit mgr. Coopers & Lybrand, Phila., 1970-76; mgr. corp. acctg. Sun Co., Inc. Radnor, Pa., 1976-78; v.p. fin. adminstrn. Sun Prodn. Co., Dallas, 1978-81; v.p. fin., CFO Oryx Energy Co. (formerly Sun Exploration and Prodn. Co.), Dallas, 1981-91; sr. v.p. fin., CFO Oryx Energy Co., Dallas, 1992-94, exec. v.p. fin., CFO, bd. dirs., 1994-99; sr. v.p. fin., CFO Fla. Progress Corp., St. Petersburg, Fla., 1999-2000; exec. v.p. fin., CFO Covanta Energy Corp., Fairfield, NJ, 2001; sr. v.p. fin., CFO 7-Eleven, Inc., Dallas, 2002—05. Chmn. dean's bus. coun. U. Ill. Sch. Bus., 2000-01, mem. exec. com., dean's bus. coun., 2002-; bd. dirs., mem. audit com. The Timberland Co., Stratham, NH, 2006—, NY and Co., N.Y.C., 2006—. 1st lt. U.S. Army, 1967-70. Home: 4712 Stonehollow Way Dallas TX 75287-7524

**MONG, ROBERT WILLIAM, JR.,** publishing executive; b. Fremont, Ohio, Jan. 22, 1949; s. Robert William and Betty (Dwyer) M.; m. Candace Beth Sweet, July 25, 1975 (div. 1979); m. Diane Elizabeth Reischel, Jan. 23, 1988; children: Eric Robert, Elizabeth Diana. BA, Haverford (Pa.) Coll., 1971; graduate exec. bus. program, Stanford U., 1997. Reporter Cin. Post, 1973-75, Capital Times, Madison, Wis., 1975-77; city editor Madison Press Connection, 1977-79; asst. city editor Dallas Morning News, 1979-80, bus. editor, 1980-81, projects editor, 1981-83, asst. mng. editor, 1983-88, dep. mng. editor, 1988-90, mng. editor, 1990-96; pub. Owensboro Messenger-Inquirer, 1996-97; exec. v.p. A.H. Belo Corp., Dallas, 1997-98; pres., gen. mgr. The Dallas Morning News, Dallas, 1998-2001, pres., editor, 2001—. Recipient J.B. Buck Marryat award for meritorious svc., Dallas Press Club, 2005. Mem. Am. Soc. Newspaper Editors, Newspaper Assn. Am., Southern Newspaper Pubs. Assn., Am. Press Inst. (bd. dirs.). Office: The Dallas Morning News PO Box 655237 508 Young St Dallas TX 75202-4828 Office Phone: 214-977-8222. Business E-Mail: bmong@dallasnews.com.

**MONGAN, JAMES JOHN,** healthcare system administrator; b. San Francisco, Apr. 10, 1942; s. Martin and Audrey Vera (Cunningham) M.; m. Jean Trotter Holmes, Apr. 22, 1972; children: John Holmes, Sarah Holmes. Student, U. Calif., Berkeley, 1959-62; BA, Stanford U., 1963, MD, 1967. Intern Kaiser Found. Hosp., San Francisco, 1967-68; med. officer USPHS, Denver, 1968-70; profl. staff mem. U.S. Senate Fin. Com., Washington, 1970-77; dep. asst. sec. for health HEW, Washington, 1977-79; assoc. dir. human resources Domestic Policy Staff, White House, 1979-81; asst. surgeon gen. USPHS, 1979-81; exec. dir. Truman Med. Center, U. Mo., Kansas City, 1981-96; dean sch. medicine U. Mo., Kansas City, 1987-96; pres. Mass. Gen. Hosp., 1996—2002; pres., CEO Partners HealthCare Sys. Inc, Boston, 2003—. Prof. healthcare policy, prof. medicine Harvard Med. Sch.; mem. com. on consequences of uninsured Inst. Medicine; chair adv. com. Commonwealth Fund Task Force; mem. Kaiser Commn. on Medicaid and the Uninsured. Trustee Kaiser Family Found., 1993—2001; chmn. Greater Boston C. of C., 2004—. Mem. NAS, Inst. Medicine, Am. Hosp. Assn. (trustee 1988-91), Am. Assn. Teaching Hospitals. (bd. dirs. coun. tchg hospitals. 1984-90). Office: Partners HealthCare Sys Inc Prudential Tower 800 Boylston St Ste 1150 Boston MA 02199-8001*

**MONGE, JAY PARRY,** lawyer; b. N.Y.C., Mar. 15, 1943; s. Joseph Paul and Dorothy Emma (Oschmann) M.; m. Julia T. Burdick, 1966 (div. 1994); children: Justin Parry, Lindsay Newton; m. Elizabeth Ann Tracy, 1994. AB, Harvard U., 1966; LLB, U. Va., 1969. Bar: Ill. 1969, N.Y. 1981, N.C. 2003. Assoc. Mayer, Brown, Rowe & Maw, LLP, Chgo., 1969-75, ptnr., 1976-79, N.Y.C., 1980-99, mng. ptnr., 1981-94, ptnr. Charlotte, NC, 2000—. Contbr. legal commentaries Ill. Inst. Continuing Legal Edn., 1974, 78, 81, 84, 87, 93, 96, 2002. Trustee Wagner Coll., 1996-2002. Mem. ABA, Assn. Bar City N.Y., Chgo. Club, Onwentsia Club, Sky Club, Westchester Country Club, Charlotte City Club, Carmel Country Club, LLP, Quail Hollow Club. Office: Mayer Brown Rowe & Maw LLP 214 N Tryon St Ste 3800 Charlotte NC 28202 E-mail: jmonge@mayerbrownrowe.com.

**MONHEIT, ALAN CRAIG,** economist, educator; BA with honors in Econs., CUNY, Flushing, 1968, MA in Econs., 1970; PhD in Econs., CUNY, 1975. Rsch. assoc. health econs. Health Policy Inst. Boston U., 1976—77, rsch. assoc. health econs. health svcs. rsch. sect. Sch. Medicine, 1977—78; pub. health svc. rsch. fellow Nat. Ctr. Health Svcs. Rsch., Hyattsville, Md., 1978—83, sr. economist. nat. health care expenditure survey, Intramural Rsch. Divsn. Rockville, Md., 1983—91; sr. rsch. mgr. Divsn. Med. Expenditure Studies, Ctr. Gen. Health Svcs. Intramural Rsch. Agy. Health Care Policy and Rsch., Rockville, 1991—95; dir. Divsn. Social and Econ. Rsch., Ctr. Cost and Financing Studies Agy. Healthcare Rsch. and Quality, Rockville, 1995—2001; prof. health economics Dept. HealthSys. and Policy Sch. Pub. Health U. Medicine and Dentistry N.J., Piscataway, NJ, 2001—, dir. PhD Program Sch. Pub. Health, 2002—, assoc. dir. Ctr. Health Econs. and Health Policy New Brunswick, NJ, 2005—. Fellow Employee Benefits Rsch. Inst., Washington, 2002—; rsch. assoc. Nat. Bur. Econ. Rsch., Cambridge, Mass., 2005—; rsch. prof. Rutgers U., New Brunswick, 2001—. Editor: Informing American Health Care Policy: The Dynamics of Medical Expenditure and Insurance Surveys 1977-1996, State Insurance Market Reform: Toward Inclusive and Sustainable Health Insurance Markets; contbr. Recipient Administrator's Health Svcs. Rsch. award, Agy. Health Care Policy and Rsch., 1993, Sr. Biomedical Rsch. Svc. award, U.S. HHS, 2000. Mem.: Nat. Acad. Social Ins., Am. Econ. Assn., Acad. Health, Am. Soc. Health Economists, Internat. Health Econs. Assn. Office: Sch Public Health U Medicine Dentistry NJ 683 Hoes Lane West Piscataway NJ 08854-5635 Office Phone: 732-235-2865.

**MONHEIT, ALAN GOODMAN,** obstetrician, gynecologist; b. Phila., Apr. 5, 1949; s. Richard S. and Jane G. Monheit; m. Deborah Monheit; children: Robin, Jeffrey, Daniel. BSc, Muhlenberg Coll., 1971; MD, U. Pa., 1975. Intern U. Calif., San Diego, 1975-76, resident physician dept. ob-gyn., 1975-79, fellow, maternal/fetal medicine, 1979-81; attending physician U. Hosp., Stony Brook, 1981—; clin. assoc. prof. SUNY, Stony Brook, 1981—. Tchr. medicine, specialist in high risk pregnancy SUNY, Stony Brook, 1981—. Contbr. articles to profl. jours. Asst. coach Three Village Soccer Club, Stony Brook, 1991. Recipient Tchg. award Coun. on Resident Edn. in ob-gyn., 1997. Mem. ACOG, Assn. Profs. Ob-Gyn., Soc. Perinatal Obstetricians (poster prize 1987), L.I. Perinatal Soc., Suffolk County Ob-Gyn. Soc., Phi Beta Kappa. Avocations: bicycling, hiking, space exploration, meteorology, tennis. Office: SUNY Dept Obstetrics Gynecology HSC T-9 Rm 20 Stony Brook NY 11794*

**MONHEIT, MOLLY JANE,** artist; b. Yakima, Wash., Aug. 5, 1922; d. Laurel LaVergne and Edna (Bracewell) Lugar; m. John Palmer Ruckel (dec. 1952); children: Gail Ruckel, Andrew Ruckel; m. George Monheit, Dec. 7, 1952; 1 child, William. Student, Art Ctr. Sch., Calif., 1942; BA magna cum laude, Wash. State U., 1944; MA, Mills Coll., 1947. Clk., artist, cons. Papyrus, Lafayette, Calif., 1976-97; ret., 1997. Exhibited paintings in Wash., Tex., and Calif.; prin. works represented in permanent collections in pvt. homes and museums in 38 countries; contbr. articles to Bird Watchers Digest.

Precinct chmn. Reps., Lafayette, 1954-70; social chmn. Valley View Estates, Lafayette, 1954-80. Recipient fellowship Aurelia Reinhart, 1945-47. Mem. Soc. Western Artists, Am. Women Artists, East Bay Watercolor Soc., Audubon Soc., Am. Field Svc. (pres. 1970), Diablo Art Assn. (pres.), Alpha Gamma Delta. Presbyterian. Avocations: birding trips, track and field.

**MONICAL, ROBERT DUANE,** engineering company executive; b. Morgan County, Ind., Apr. 30, 1925; s. William Blaine and Mary Elizabeth (Lang) M.; m. Carol Arnetha Dean, Aug. 10, 1947 (dec. 1979); children: Mary Christine, Stuart Dean, Dwight Lee; m. Sharon Kelly Eastwood, July 13, 1980; 1 stepson, Jeffrey David Eastwood. BSC.E., Purdue U., 1948, MSC.E., 1949. Engr. N.Y.C. R.R., Cin., 1949-51, So. Rwy., Cin., 1951; design engr. Pierce & Gruber (Cons. Engrs.), Indpls., 1952-54; founder, partner Monical & Wolverton (Cons. Engrs.), Indpls., 1954-63, Monical Assocs., Indpls., 1963—, pres., 1975—; v.p. Zurwelle-Whittaker, Inc. (Engrs. and Land Surveyors), Miami Beach, Fla., 1975-90; pres. Monical Engring., Inc., 2004—. Mem. Ind. Adminstrv. Bldg. Council, 1969-75, chmn., 1973-75; mem. Meridian St. Preservation Commn., 1971-75, Ind. State Bd. of Registration for Profl. Engrs. and Land Surveyors, 1976-84, chmn., 1979, 83 Served with USNR, 1943-46, USAR, 1948-53. Mem. ASCE (Outstanding Civil Engr. award Ind. sect. 1987), Cons. Engrs. Ind. (pres. 1969, Cons. Recognition award 1986), Am. Cons. Engrs. Council (pres. 1978-79), Ind. Soc. Profl. Engrs. (Engr. of Yr. 1980), Nat. Soc. Profl. Engrs., Am. Concrete Inst., Am. Inst. Steel Constrn., Indpls. Sci. and Engring. Found. (pres. 1992-93), Am. Legion, Lions, Masons, Shriners. Mem. Christian Ch. Home and Office: 18831 Whitcomb Pl Noblesville IN 46062-8130 Office Phone: 317-770-1266. Personal E-mail: rduane1@sbcglobal.net.

**MONIN, BENOIT,** psychology professor; b. Neuilly sur Seine, France, Dec. 22, 1972; s. Claude and Veronique (Morandat) Monin; m. Lauren Calderon, Aug. 19, 2006. Diploma, ESSEC, Cergy-Pontoise, France, 1991—94; MSc in Social Psychology, London Sch. Econs. and Polit. Scis., 1995; PhD in Psychology, Princeton U., NJ 2001. Asst. prof. Stanford U. Psychology, Calif., 2001—. Office: Stanford U Psychology Jordan Hall Bldg 420 Stanford CA 94305 Business E-Mail: monin@stanford.edu.

**MONISMITH, CARL LEROY,** civil engineering educator; b. Harrisburg, Pa., Oct. 23, 1926; s. Carl Samuel and Camilla Frances (Geidt) M. BSCE, U. Calif., Berkeley, 1950, MSCE, 1954; D of Engring. (hon.), Carleton U., Ottawa, 2004. Registered civil engr., Calif. From instr. to prof. civil engring. U. Calif., Berkeley, 1951—, chmn. dept. civil engring., 1974-79, Robert Horonjeff prof. civil engring., 1986—, prof. emeritus, 1996. Cons. Chevron Rsch. Co., Richmond, Calif., 1957-93, U.S. Army CE Waterways Expt. Sta., Vicksburg, Miss., 1968-00, B.A. Vallerga, Inc., Oakland, Calif., 1980-98, ARE, Austin, Tex. and Scotts Valley, Calif., 1978-92; cons. Bechtel Corp., San Francisco, 1982-86. Contbr. numerous articles to profl. jours. Served to 2d lt. C.E., U.S. Army, 1945-47. Recipient Rupert Myers medal U. NSW, 1976; named Henry M. Shaw Lectr. in Civil Engring., N.C. State U., 1993; sr. scholar Fulbright Found., U. NSW, 1971, Nat. Asphalt Pavement Assn. R.D. Kenyon Rsch. and Edn. award for Outstanding Contbns. for Hot Mix Asphalt Tech., 2002, Hall of Fame, 2005; named Disting. Engring. Alumnus, Coll. Engring., U. Calif., Berkeley, 1996 Fellow: AAAS; mem.: ASTM, NAE, NRC (assoc.), NAS (assoc.), ASCE (hon.; pres. San Francisco sect. 1979—80, ednl. activities com. 1989—91, State of Art award 1977, James Laurie prize 1988), Nat. Assn. of the Nat. Acads., Asphalt Inst. (Roll of Honor 1990), Calif. Asphalt Pavement Alliance (award 2002), Am. Soc. Engring. Edn., Internat. Soc. Asphalt Pavements (hon.; chmn. bd. dirs. 1988—90, Disting. Lectr. 2004), Assn. Asphalt Paving Technologists (hon. W.J. Emmons award 1961, 1965, 1985), Transp. Rsch. Bd. (assoc.; chmn. pavement design sect. 1973—79, K.B. Woods award 1972, 1st disting. lectureship 1992, Roy W. Crum award 1995). Avocation: stamp collecting/philately. Office: U Calif Dept Civil Engring 215 Mclaughlin Hall Berkeley CA 94720-1712 Office Phone: 510-665-3560. Business E-Mail: clm@maxwell.berkeley.edu.

**MONIZ, ERNEST JEFFREY,** physics professor; b. Fall River, Mass., Dec. 22, 1944; s. Ernest Perry and Georgina (Pavao) M.; m. Naomi Hoki, June 9, 1973; 1 child, Katya BS, Boston Coll., 1966; PhD, Stanford U., 1971. Prof. physics MIT, Cambridge, 1973-97, dir. Bates Linear Accelerator Ctr. Middleton, 1983-91, head physics dept., 1991-95, 97; under sec. U.S. Dept. Energy, Washington, 1997—2001; prof. physics and engring. systems MIT, 2001—. Cons. Los Alamos Nat. Lab., 1975-95; assoc. dir. for sci. Office of Sci. and Tech. Policy, Exec. Office of the Pres., 1995-97. Contbr. articles to profl. jours. Fellow: AAAS, Am. Phys. Soc., Humboldt Found. Office: 77 Massachusetts Ave Bldg E40-451 Cambridge MA 02139-4307 Office Phone: 617-253-7517. E-mail: ejmoniz@mit.edu.

**MONJAN, ANDREW ARTHUR,** health facility administrator; b. NYC, Feb. 9, 1938; s. Victor Momjian and Sonia (Sherinian) Batchahar; m. Susan Vollenweider, July 1961 (div. Nov. 1965); m. Usha Bose, Aug. 14, 1969; children: Matthew, Vanessa. BSc, Rensselaer Poly. Inst., 1960; PhD, U. Rochester, 1965; MPH, Johns Hopkins U., 1970. Rsch. asst. Sterling-Winthrop Rsch. Inst., Rensselaer, NY, 1960; USPHS rsch. fellow Ctr. for Brain Rsch. U. Rochester, NY, 1964-66; asst. prof. depts. psychology and physiology U. Western Ont., London, Canada, 1966-69; from asst. prof. to assoc. prof. dept. epidemiology Sch. Hygiene and Pub. Health Johns Hopkins U., Balt., 1971-83; expert epidemiology extramural programs br. NIH, Bethesda, Md., 1983-85, chief neurobiology/immunology programs physiology aging br., 1985-87, acting assoc. dir., 1987, chief neurobiology, 1987—; exec. sec. Nat. Commn. on Sleep Disorders Rsch., 1990-92. Presenter in field. Contbr. articles to profl. jours. N.Y. State Regents scholar, 1955-59; N.Y. State Regents Grad. Tchg. fellow, 1960-62, USPHS rsch. fellow, 1962-64, 69-70. Mem. Soc. for Neurosci., Sigma Xi. Office: Nat Inst Aging 7201 Wisconsin Ave Msc9205 Ste 350 Bethesda MD 20892-9205 Office Phone: 410-496-9350. E-mail: am39m@nih.gov.

**MONK, ALLAN JAMES,** baritone; b. Mission City, BC, Can., Aug. 19, 1942; m. Marlene Folk; 3 children. Student, Elgar Higgin and Boris Goldovsky. Operatic debut in Old Maid and the Thief, San Francisco, 1967; joined touring co., later main co. San Francisco Opera; appeared in Tulsa Opera, Pitts. Opera, Edmonton Opera, Vancouver Opera, So. Alta. Opera, Chgo. Opera, Balt. Opera, Miami Opera, Colo. Opera, Mont real Opera, Hawaii Opera Theatre, Portland Opera.; 1976. Met. Opera debut as Schaunard in La Boheme, 1976, sang title role in Wozzeck, Wolfram in Tannhauser, Dr. Malatesta in Don Pasquale, Rodrigo in Don Carlo, Sharpless in Madame Butterfly, Herald in Lohengrin; sang with Can. Opera Co. as Abelard in Heloise and Abelard, Macbeth, Rigoletto, Belcore in L'Elisir D'Amoure, Jago in Otello, as Ford in Falstaff, four villains in Les Contes d'Hoffman; with Nat. Arts Ctr. Opera Festival, Ottawa, Ont., Can., title role in Don Giovanni, Almaviva in Le Nozze Di Figaro, gulielmo in Cossi Fan Tutti, Tomsky in Pique Dame, Marcello in La Boheme; Carnegie Hall debut as Vladislav in Dalibor, 1977; European debut as Wozzeck, 1980; solo recitalist; toured with Nat. Arts Ctr. Orch. in USSR, Poland, Italy, 1975; movie debut as Baron Douphol in La Traviata, 1983. Named Artist of Yr. Can. Music Council, 1983, laureat Order of Can., 1985. Office: 14415 Parkland Blvd SE Calgary AB Canada T2J 4L5 Office Phone: 403-281-9640.

**MONK, DEBRA,** actress; b. Middletown, Ohio, Feb. 27, 1949; Grad., Frostburg State U. Stage appearances include (Broadway) Ah, Wilderness!, Steel Pier Company, Nick & Nora, Prelude to a Kiss, Pump Boys and Dinettes (also co-author), Redwood Curtain (Tony award featured actress in play 1993), Picnic (Tony nomination featured actress 1994), (theatre) Death Defying Acts, 3 Hotels (Helen Hayes award leading actress 1994), Assassins, Oil City Symphony (co-author, Drama Desk award Best Ensemble 1988), Laughing Wild, 2005, Chicago, 2005, Curtains, 2006; TV appearances include Women & Wallace, 1990, Loving, 1994, Redwood Curtain, 1995, Ellen Foster, 1997, NYPD Blue, 1998-2001 (Emmy award for Outstanding Guest Actress in a Drama Series 1999), The Music Man, 2003, Eloise at the Plaza, 2003, Eloise at Christmastime, 2003, Show People, 2006; films include: Prelude to a Kiss, 1992, For Love or Money, 1993, Fearless, 1993, Quiz Show, 1993, Reckless, 1995, Bridges of Madison County, 1995, Jeffrey,

1995, First Wives Club, 1996, Bed of Roses, 1996, Mrs. Winterbourne, 1996, Substance of Fire, 1996, Devil's Advocate, 1997, Extreme Measures, 1996, In and Out, 1997, Bulworth, 1998, Center Stage, 2000, Briar Patch, 2003, Milwaukee, Minnesota, 2003, Palindromes, 2004, Dark Water, 2005. Office: Gage Group care Steve Unger 315 W 57th St Ste 4H New York NY 10019-3158*

**MONK, DIANA CHARLA,** small business owner; b. Visalia, Calif., Feb. 25, 1927; d. Charles Edward and Viola Genevieve (Shea) Williams; m. James Alfred Monk, Aug. 11, 1951; children: Kiloran, Sydney, Geoffrey, Anne, Eric. Student, U. Pacific, 1946-47, Sacramento Coll., 1947-48, Calif. Coll. Fine Arts, San Francisco, 1948-51, Calif. Coll. Arts & Crafts, Oakland, 1972. Art tchr. Mt. Diablo Sch. Dist., Concord, Calif., 1958-63; pvt. art tchr. Lafayette, Calif., 1963-70; gallery dir. Jason Aver Gallery, San Francisco, 1970-72; owner, mgr. Monk & Lee Assocs., Lafayette, 1973-80; stable owner, mgr. Longacre Tng. Stables, Santa Rosa, Calif., 1989—. One-person shows include John F. Kennedy U., Orinda, Calif., Civic Arts Gallery, Walnut Creek, Calif., Vallery Art Gallery, Walnut Creek, Sea Ranch Gallery, Gualala, Calif., Jason Aver Gallery, San Francisco; exhibited in group shows at Oakland (Calif.) Art Mus., Crocker Nat. Art Gallery, Sacramento, Le Salon des Nations, Paris. Chair bd. dirs. Walnut Creek (Calif.) Civic Arts, 1972-74, advisor to dir., 1968-72; exhibit chmn. Valley Art Gallery, Walnut Creek, 1977-78; juror Women's Art Show, Walnut Creek, 1970, Oakland Calif. Art. Home and Office: Longacre Tng Stables 1702 Willowside Rd Santa Rosa CA 95401-3922 Office Phone: 707-544-7030. Personal E-mail: longacrestables@msn.com.

**MONK, MEREDITH JANE,** artistic director, composer, choreographer, filmmaker; b. NYC, Nov. 20, 1942; d. Theodore G. and Audrey Lois (Zellman) Monk. BA, Sarah Lawrence Coll., 1964; ArtsD (hon.), Bard Coll., 1988, U. of the Arts, 1989, Juilliard Sch. Music, 1997, San Francisco Art Inst., 1998, Boston Conservatory, 2001, Bennington Coll., 2002, Cornish Coll. Arts, 2002. Artistic dir., founder Ho. Found. Arts, N.Y.C., 1968—. Bd. dirs. Am. Music Ctr., The Kitchen. Prin. works include 16 Millimeter Earrings, 1966, Vessel, 1971, Quarry, 1976, Recent Ruins, 1979, Turtle Dreams, 1983, The Games, 1983, Book of Days, 1988, Facing North, 1990, Atlas, 1991, Three Heavens and Hells, 1992, Volcano Songs, 1994, American Archeology, 1994, The Politics of Quiet, 1996, Magic Frequencies, 1998, Mercy, 2001, Possible Sky, 2003, Impermanence, 2004, Stringsongs, 2005, exhibitions include Libr. of Performing Arts, Lincoln Ctr., 1996, Walker Art Ctr., Mpls., 1998, Whitney Mus. Art, 2002, Exit Art, 2002. Recipient Obie award, Village Voice, 1972, 1976, 1985, Creative Arts award, Brandeis U., 1974, Villager award, 1980, 1983, Deutches Kritiker preis, 1981, 1986, Bessie award, 1985, Nat. Music Theatre award, 1986, Dance Mag. award, 1993, John D. and Catherine T. MacArthur award, 1995, Sarah Lawrence Disting. Alumna award, 1996, Samuel Scripps award, 1996, Sigma Phi Omega award, 1987; fellow Guggenheim, 1972, 1982, Norton Stevens, 1993—94, MacDowell Colony. Fellow: Am. Acad. Arts and Scis.; mem.: ASCAP (award 1980—2000, Concert Music award 2005, Bessie award 2005). Office: House Found for Arts 306 W 38th St Ste 401 New York NY 10018

**MONK, SUSAN MARIE,** pediatrician, educator; b. York, Pa., May 7, 1945; d. John Spotz and Mary Elizabeth (Shelly) M.; m. Jaime Pacheco, June 5, 1971; children: Benjamin Joaquin, Maria Cristina. AB, Colby Coll., 1967; MD, Jefferson Med. Coll., 1971. Diplomate Am. Bd. Pediatrics. Pediatrician Children's Med. Ctr., Dayton, Ohio, 1975—; asst. clin. prof. pediat. Wright State U., Dayton, 1976—83, assoc. clin. prof. pediat., 1983—2000, asst. prof. pediatrics, 2000—. Mem. bd. dirs. Children's Med. Ctr., Dayton, 1991-96, chief-of-staff, 1992-94. Mem. Am. Acad. Pediatrics, We. Ohio Pediatric Soc., Pediatric Ambulatory Care Soc. Avocations: reading, gardening, travel, movies, theater. Office: Childrens Health Clinic 730 C Valley St Dayton OH 45404-1845 Office Phone: 937-641-5355.

**MONK KIDD, SUE,** writer; b. 1949; m. Sandy Monk Kidd; 2 children. BS in Nursing, Tex. Christian U., Fort Worth, 1970; studied writing, Emory Univ., Atlanta. Nurse St. Joseph's Hosp., Fort Worth, Tex., Med.Coll. Ga. Contbg. editor: Guideposts; author: God's Joyful Surprise, 1988, When the Heart Waits: Spiritual Direction for Life's Sacred Questions, 1990, The Dance of the Dissident Daughter: A Woman's Journey from Christian Tradition to the Sacred Feminine, 1996, The Secret Life of Bees, 2002 (SEBA Book of Yr. award, 2003, Publishers Weekly Bestseller list, 2003, 2004), The Mermaid Chair, 2005 (Publishers Weekly Bestseller list, 2005, Quills award for gen. fiction, 2005); contbr. essays to mags. Recipient Katherine Anne Porter Second prize in fiction, Nimrod/Hardman Awards, 1993, S.C. Fiction Projectaward, S.C. Arts Commn., 1993, 1995, 1997, Isak Dineson Creative Non-Fiction award, 1994, Literal Latte Creative Non-Fiction Third prize, 1999, Bread Loaf scholar, Bread Loaf Writers Conf., 1995; fellow, S.C. Arts Commn., 1993—94, S.C. Acad. Authors, 1994, 1996. Office: c/o Carolyn Coburn Viking Penguin 375 Hudson St New York NY 10014

**MONMONIER, MARK,** geographer, writer; b. Balt., Feb. 2, 1943; s. John Carroll and Martha Elizabeth (Mason) M.; m. Margaret Janet Kollner, Sept. 4, 1965; 1 child, Jo Kerry. BA, Johns Hopkins U., 1964; MS, Pa. State U., 1967, PhD, 1969. Asst. prof. U. Rhode Island, Kingston, 1969-70, SUNY, Albany, 1970-73; assoc. prof Syracuse U., NY, 1973-79, prof. NY, 1979-98, Disting. prof. geography NY, 1998—. Cons. N.Y. State, Albany, 1974-93, Nat. Geog. Soc., 1987, Microsoft Corp., 1993-99, Belmont Rsch., 1995, AT&T Rsch., 1996-97, George Philip Ltd., England, 1996-97; rsch. geographer U.S. Geol. Survey, Reston, Va., 1979-84; dep. dir. N.Y. Ctr. for Geographic Info. and Analysis, 1989-90; Robinson vis. fellow George Mason U., 1985; Ida Beam Disting. vis. prof. U. Iowa, 1985; mem. adv. bd. GIS Law and Policy Inst., 1994-98; adv. bd. Philip Lee Philips Soc.; cons. and expert witness various law firms, 1995—; co-editor History of Cartography in the Twentieth Century, 1999-2004, editor 2004—; mem. mapping sci. com. NRC, 2000—05; mem. com. on planning for catastrophe, 2005-06. Author: Maps, Distortion and Meaning, 1977; co-author: The Study of Population: Elements, Patterns, Processes, 1982; author: Computer-assisted Cartography, 1982, Mapping it Out, 1993, Technological Transition in Cartography, 1985, Maps with the News, 1989, How to Lie with Maps, 1991, French edit., 1993, Japanese edit., 1995, 2nd edit., 1996, German edit., 1996, Korean edit., 1998, Czech edit., 2000, Drawing the Line, 1995, Cartographies of Danger, 1997, Air Apparent, 1999, Bushmanders and Bullwinkles, 2001, Spying with Maps, 2002, Rhumb Lines and Map Wars, 2004; co-author: Map Appreciation, 1988; co-editor: History of Cartography Project, 1997—; assoc. editor The American Cartographer, Falls Church. Va., 1977—82; editor: The American Cartographer, 1982—84; assoc. editor Mapping Scis. and Remote Sensing, 1987—97, contbg. editor Cartographica, 1984—, mem. editl. adv. bd. Mercator's World, 1997—2003; author: From Squaw Tit to Whorehouse Meadow, 2006. Statistician, Police Dept, Syracuse, 1978-80. Fellow John Simon Guggenheim Meml. Found., 1984, centennial fellow Pa. State U. Coll. Earth & Mineral Scis., 1996; recipient Chancellor's citation for Disting. Acad. Achievement, 1993, Disting. Geographer award Pa. Geog. Soc., 2000, O.M. Miller Cartographic medal Am. Geog. Soc., 2001, Excellence in Grad. Edn. Faculty Recognition award, 2005 Fellow: Am. Congress on Surveying and Mapping; mem.: Philip Lee Phillips Soc., N.Am. Cartographic Info. Soc. (editl. bd. 1998—2001), Can. Cartographic Assn. (Award of Distinction 2002), Authors Guild, Am. Cartographic Assn. (pres. 1983—84), Assn. Am. Geographers (Media Achievement award 2000, Globe Book award 2004), Tau Beta Pi, Pi Tau Sigma, Sigma Xi (pres. Syracuse chpt. 2001—02). Roman Catholic. Home: 302 Waldruff Pky Syracuse NY 13224-2240 Office: Syracuse U Dept Of Geography Syracuse NY 13244-1020 Business E-Mail: mon2ier@maxwell.syr.edu.

**MONNIER, JOHN R.,** chemical engineering educator; b. Quincy, Ill., Feb. 5, 1948; s. John E. and Bonnye Gayle Monnier; m. Pamela A. Lucey, Oct. 18, 1975; children: Susanne M., Philip A., Stephen A. BS in Chemistry, St. Ambrose U., Davenport, Iowa, 1970; MS in Phys. Chemistry, U. Wis., Milw., 1972, PhD in Phys. Chemistry, 1978. Engr. Bendix Corp., Davenport, 1969—70; sr. rsch. chemist Eastman Kodak Co., Rochester, NY, 1972—76, sr. rsch. assoc., 1978—93; rsch. fellow Eastman Chem. Co., Kingsport, Tenn.,

1993—2004; prof. dept. of chem. engring. U. of S.C., Columbia, 2004—. Mem. profl. adv. bd. Clemson U., SC, 2001—03; mem. catalysis adv. bd. Los Alamos (N.Mex.) Nat. Labs. 1995—98. Contbr. articles to profl. jours. (F.C. Ciapetta Lectureship in Catalysis, 2002, Outstanding Indsl. Innovator award Am. Chem. Soc., 1998). Recipient Tailoring Solid Catalysts for Selective Reaction of Multifunctional Molecules grant, NSF, 2006—09, Use of Ionic Liquids to Mediate Chem. Oxidation Reactions grant, 2005—08, Herman Pines award for discovery and devel. of non-allylic olefin epoxidation processes, 2000, C.E.K. Mees award for discovery of the direct epoxidation of butadiene using suported silver catalysts, Eastman Kodak. Mem.: AIChE, N.Am. Catalysis Soc., Am. Chem. Soc. Republican. Roman Catholic. Achievements include discovery of Gas phase epoxidation of butadiene to 3, 4-epoxy-1-butene using Cs-promoted, silver catalysts; Catalytic Process For Isomerization Of 3, 4-Epoxy-1-Butene To 2, 5-Dihydrofuran; Catalytic Process For Isomerization Of 2, 5-Dihydrofuran To 2, 3-Dihydrofuran; Catalytic Hydrogenation Of 3, 4-Epoxy-1-Butene To 1, 2-Epoxybutane; Catalytic Process For Conversion Of Coal-Derived Gases To Useful Chemicals. Avocations: sailing, travel, cooking, gardening. Office: U SC Swearingen Engineering Center Columbia SC 29208 Office Phone: 803-777-6813. Office Fax: 803-777-0973. Business E-Mail: monnier@engr.sc.edu.

**MONOS, DIMITRIOS,** medical educator, researcher; BS in Biology, U. Patras, Greece, 1975; PhD in Biochemistry and Immunology, Georgetown U., 1981. Vis. fellow lab. tumor immunology & biology Nat. Cancer Inst. NIH, Bethesda, Md., 1982—84; immunopathology fellow dept. pathology & lab. medicine U. Pa., Phila., 1984—86, rsch. assoc. immunology, 1986—88, asst. prof., 1990—96, assoc. prof. dept. pediat., 1996—. Vis. scholar dept. biochemistry & molecular biology Harvard U., 1988—90; prof. human biology and genetics Democritus U. of Thrace Med. Sch., Alexandroupolis, Greece, 1991—; dir. immonogenetics lab. dept. pathology Children's Hosp. Phila. 1996; lectr. in field. Mem. editl. bd.: Clin. and Diagnostic Lab. Clin. Immunology and Immunopathology, ad hoc reviewer: Cancer Rsch., Diabetes, Human Immunology, Jour. Immunology, New Eng. Jour. Medicine; contbr. articles to profl. jours. Recipient New Investigator Rsch. award, NIH, 1986, rsch. award, Am. Diabetes Assn., 1995, Fogarty Internat. fellowship, NIH, 1992; grantee, 1986—, U. Pa., 1987—88, 1995, rabetes Rsch. & Edn. Found, 1990, Juvenile Diabetes Found., 1990—92, Nat. Marrow Donor Program, 1992—94, ADA, 1995—96, 1997—. Mem.: Acad. Clin. Lab. Physicians and Scientists, Am. Soc. Histocompatibility and Immunogenetics, Am. Assn. Immunologists, Sigma Xi.

**MONOSSON, IRA HOWARD,** physician; b. N.Y.C., Mar. 23, 1937; adopted s. Henry M.; s. I. Easer Rosenfield and Yetta Malvin; m. Aviva May Sokol, Sept. 20, 1970; children: Elana, Danielle, Ari. BA, Stanford U., 1959, MD, 1962. Diplomate Am. Bd. Preventive Medicine; cert. in occupational medicine. Intern Montefiore Hosp., Bronx, NY, 1962—63; resident L.A. County Gen. Hosp., 1963-64, Cedars of Lebanon Hosp., L.A., 1964-65; fellow Scripps Clinic and Rsch. Found., La Jolla, Calif., 1965-66; resident U. Calif., Irvine, 1976-77; pvt. practice San Diego, 1966-68, Southington, Conn., 1968-69, Ctrl. Med. Group, L.A., 1969-71; prin., owner Mid-City Med. Group, L.A., 1971-73; ptnr., physician Foley Med. Group, L.A., 1973-74; pub. health physician City of L.A., 1975; chief pub. health med. officer Calif. State Divsn. Occupational Safety & Health, L.A., 1976-82; pvt. practice various, Calif., 1982—. Asst. clin. prof. medicine UCLA Sch. Medicine; asst. clin. prof. preventive medicine U. So. Calif. Sch. Medicine; com. mem. UCLA Inst. Biosafety Com., 1982—; adv. bd. Hazardous Substances Task Force, City of L.A., Calif. State Divsn. Indsl. Accidents, 1984-86, Occupl. Medicine Calif. Med. Assn., 1985-88; cons. in field; spkr. house of delegates Am. Coll. Occupl. & Environ Medicine, 1995; mem. state regulatory bd. Calif. Indsl. Med. Coun., 1990-2003, chmn. 1990-93. Mem. Environ. Occupl. Health com. Am. Lung. Assn. Calif., 1986-89; steering com. of L.A. 2000 project, 1980-81; adv. com. Del Amo/Montrose Superfund Site, 1995—, Permanent Disability Study, Calif. State Commn. Health and Safety and Workers Compensation; mem. L.A. Unified Sch. Dist. Bd. Edn. Ind. Commn. regarding The Belmont Learning Ctr., 1999—. Author: (with others) A Practical Approach to Occupational and Environmental Medicine, 1994; contbr. articles to profl. jours. Fellow Am. Coll. Preventive Medicine, Am. Coll. Occupl. Environ. Medicine (bd. dirs. 1993-95), Royal Soc. Medicine, Am. Acad. Occupl. Medicine; mem. AMA, Calif. Soc. Indsl. Medicine and Surgery (pres. 1995, bd. dirs.). Office: Ste 300 7230 Med Ctr Dr West Hills CA 91307 Office Phone: 818-704-0886. Personal E-mail: imonosson@gmail.com.

**MONROE, BRYAN,** publishing executive, trade association administrator; m. Tahirah Monroe; children: Seanna, Jackson. BA, U. Wash. Photographer The Seattle Times, Roanoke Times, Va., World News and United Press Internat.; dir. photography and design Myrtle Beach Sun, SC; asst. project dir. 25/43 Project Knight Ridder; joined Mercury News, San Jose, 1991, asst. mng. editor, reporter, asst. city editor, design dir.; asst. v.p. news Knight Ridder; v.p., editl. dir. EBONY and JET Mags., Johnson Pub. Co., Inc. Picture editor, photo book coord. Songs of My People, assoc. prodr. Tom Dowd & The Language of Music, 2003. Mem. San Jose Leadership Coun.; bd. dirs. Silicon Valley Children's Discovery Mus., San Jose. Named one of 20 top Am. journalists, Presstime mag., nation's Media Elite, MediaWeek mag., 10 Most Influential African Americans in Bay Area, CityFlight mag., 2003, Most Influential Black Americans, Ebony mag., 2006; Nieman Fellow, Harvard U., 2003. Mem.: 100 Black Men of Silicon Valley, Inc., Bay Area Black Journalists Assn., Unity: Journalists of Color, Nat. Assn. of Black Journalists (v.p., pres. 2005—). Office: NABJ U Md 8701-A Adelphi Rd Adelphi MD 20783-1716*

**MONROE, CRAIG,** professional baseball player; b. Texarkana, Tex., Feb. 27, 1927; Outfielder Tex. Rangers, 2001, Detroit Tigers, 2002—. Office: Detroit Tigers Comerica Pk 2100 Woodward Ave Detroit MI 48201*

**MONROE, FREDERICK FALES,** geologist, oceanographer; b. Washington, May 3, 1936; s. Sheldon McKinley and Fredericka Fales Monroe; m. Lori Rose Farquharson, June 11, 1988; m. Patricia Ann Lynch, July 11, 1971 (dec.); m. Sue Ellen Reeves, Oct. 7, 1963 (div. Oct. 7, 1970); children: Elizabeth Carmela. Patricia Alexis(dec.), Calli Grace, Victoria Michelle. John Scott, Lisa Diane Buyan, Christina Lee. BA, Amherst Coll., 1958; MS, The Am. U., 1970; MA, U. Miami, 1977; PhD, The Am. U., 1989. Profl. geologist Va., 1983. Geologist King & Gavaris, Cons. Engrs., N.Y.C., 1960-62; phys. sci. aide U.S. Geol. Survey, Denver, 1962; oceanographer U.S. Army Corps Engrs., Washington, 1962—67; ass't. prof ocean engring. Fla. Atlantic U., Boca Raton, 1967—71; oceanog. cons. Arthur Strock, Inc., 1971—75; fgn. affairs officer U.S. Dept. State, Washington, 1975—. Adj. asst. prof. No. Va. C.C., Alexandria, 2002—05; professorial lectr. The Am. U., Washington, 1989—93. Recipient Meritorious Honor award, U.S. Dept. State, 1983, Career Achievement medal, 2001. Fellow: The Explorers Club; mem.: Marine Tech. Soc. (founding). Achievements include research in marine resource potential of U.S. Exclusive Economic Zone; co-founded U.S. Army Corps of Engrs. Coastal Engring Rsch. Ctr. Underwater Ops. Group; provided tech. support on deep seabed mining to U.S. delegation to the UN Law of the Sea Convention; wrote Coastal State Control and the Global Ocean Harvest UMI, Ann Aarbor, 1989. Office Phone: 703-534-0738. Personal E-mail: ffmonroe@hotmail.com.

**MONROE, HASKELL MOORMAN, JR.,** retired history professor, retired dean, chancellor emeritus; b. Dallas, Mar. 18, 1931; s. Haskell M. and Myrtle Marie (Moorman) Monroe; m. Margaret Joan Phillips, June 15, 1957; children: Stephen, Melanie, Mark, John. BA, Austin Coll., Tex., 1952, MA, 1954; PhD, Rice U., Houston, 1961; D (hon.), Austin Coll., 1984. From instr. to prof. Tex. A&M U., 1959-80, asst. dean Grad. Sch., 1965-68, asst. v.p. acad. affairs, 1972-74, dean faculties, 1974-80, assoc. v.p. acad. affairs, 1977-80, dean faculties emeritus College Station, 1997—; pres. U. Tex., El Paso, 1980-87; chancellor U. Mo., Columbia, 1987-91, profl. history, 1987-97, chancellor emeritus, prof. history, 1997—. Instr. Schreiner Inst., Kerrville, Tex., 1959; vis. lectr. Emory U., 1967, 72; faculty lectr. Tex. A&M U., 1972; alumni lectr. Austin Coll., 1980; bd. dirs. City Nat. Bank, Southwestern Bell Corp., Boone

County Nat. Bank, SBC Comms., Inc.; history adv. com. Sec. Air Force, 1987; orientation com. Dept. Def.-Joint Chiefs, 1986. Contbr. articles, revs. to profl. jours.; editor: Papers of Jefferson Davis, 1964—69; adv. editor: Texana, 1964—71; mem. bd. editl. advisers Booker T. Washington Washington Papers, 1965—85. Bd. dirs. Brazos Valley Rehab. Ctr., 1975-77, Salvation Army, El Paso, 1984-87, Columbia, Mo., 1988-97, Crime Stoppers of El Paso, United Way Columbia, 1988-94, Keep Brazos Beautiful, 1999-2003, Washington-on-the-Brazos State Park Assn., 2002-; trustee Bryan Hosp., 1976-79, chmn. 1979; bd. ch. visitors Austin Coll., 1977-78; deacon First Presbyn. Ch., Bryan, 1961-63, elder, 1965-67, 69-71, 73-74, clk. of session, 1973-74, chmn. pulpit nominating mem., 1971-72; mem. presbytery's coun. Presbytery of Brazos, 1969-71, mem. resources for the 80s steering com. 1978-80; elder 1st Presbyn. Ch., El Paso, 1984-87, 1st Presbyn. Ch., Columbia, 1994-96; mem. exec. bd. Great Rivers coun. Boy Scouts Am. 1990-97; mem. Pres. Coun. NCAA, 1986-87; chmn. Jefferson Davis award com. Confederate Mus., 1996-97; bd. dirs. Salvation Army, 1989-97, Schreiner U., 1999—. Recipient Citation of Appreciation, LULAC, 1982, Honor award Salvation Army, 1997, Faculty Disting. Achievement award Tex. A&M U., 1964, U. Mo. Alumni award for tchg., 1995, also numerous achievement awards; grantee Social Sci. Rsch. Coun., Tex. A&M U., Huntington Libr., Intrafraternity and Sorority Outstanding Tchr. award, 1997; named Ky. Col., 1967; named to Legends of Aggieland, 1998. Mem. Am. Hist. Assn., Orgn. Am. Historians, So. Hist. Assn. Hist. Found. Presbyn. and Reformed Chs. (pres. 1970-72), Coll. Football Assn. (chmn. bd. 1989-90, bd. dirs.), Truman Scholarship Panel, Soc. Conf. Deans Faculties and Acad. V.P.s (pres. 1978), Rotary (El Paso, hon. Columbia, Mo., Bryan, Tex., Paul Harris fellow 1986, 2005 Sonoma Cir College Station TX 77845-7907 Office: Tex A&M U 6B15 Evans Libr College Station TX 77843 Office Phone: 979-324-4546. Business E-Mail: hmonroe@tamu.edu.

**MONROE, JAMES WALTER,** retired corporate financial executive; b. Fairfax, SD, Feb. 13, 1936; s. Sherman William and Frances (Burnett) M.; m. Dorothy Lou Gillette, Apr. 1, 1961; children—Steven James, David Walter, Melody Anne, Andrew Scott. Student, Huron Coll., SD, 1954-56, U. Nebr., 1956-57; BA, Nebr. Wesleyan U., 1960. Mgr. Belleville (Kans.) C. of C., 1960-61, Concordia (Kans.) C. of C., 1961-62; asst. chief Div. Nebr. Resources, 1962-65; dir. S.D. Indsl. Devel. Expansion Agy., 1965-67, Nebr. Dept. Econ. Devel., 1967-71; sec. Nebr. Resources Found., 1967-71; exec. dir. Omaha Econ. Devel. Council, 1971-76; pres. Kansas City (Mo.-Kans.) Area Devel. Council, 1976-90; pres., chief exec. officer New Orleans and the River Region C. of C., 1990-96. Metrovision Found., Econ. Devel. Coun. Metro, New Orleans; ret., 1996. Mem. Am. Indsl. Devel. Council, 1965—, chmn. certification bd., 1981-82; sec. labor mgmt. council Greater Kansas City, 1979-90; mem. exec. com. Gov.'s Econ. Devel. Adv. Council, 1979-81. Bd. dirs. Am. Econ. Devel. Coun., 1992—. Served with AUS, 1957-59. Democrat. Congregationalist. Home: 413 12th Pl N Edmonds WA 98020-2970

**MONROE, JANE D.,** federal agency administrator; Probation officer; police officer; spl. agt. FBI, Abuquerque, 1985, Tampa, Fla., Washington; spl. agt. criminal divsn. FBI Hdqs., Washington; spl. agt. behavioral sci. unit FBI Acad., Quantico, Va.; supr. white collar crime and pub. corruption squad FBI, San Diego, 1995, coord. hostage negotiation and evidence response teams, 1995—99, asst. spl. agt. in charge Denver, 1999, spl. agt. in charge L.A., 2002, asst. dir. cyber divsn. Washington, 2002—. Office: Fed Bur Investigation J Edgar Hoover Bldg 935 Penn Ave NW Washington DC 20535-0001

**MONROE, KENDYL KURTH,** retired lawyer; b. Clayton, N.Mex., Sept. 6, 1936; s. Dottis Donald and Helen (Kurth) Monroe; m. Barbara Sayre, Sept. 12, 1956; children: Sidney, Dean, Loren. AB, Stanford U., 1958, LLB, 1960. Bar: N.Y. 1961, Calif. 1961. Assoc. Sullivan & Cromwell, N.Y.C., 1960-67, ptnr., 1968-94; ret., 1994. Chmn. TEB Charter Svcs., Inc., Teterboro, NJ, El Valle Escondido Ranch Ltd. Co., Seneca, N.Mex., Eklund Assn. Clayton, N.Mex., Union County Med. Found., Clayton, N.Mex. Chmn. adv. coun. Mandala Ctr., Des Moines, N.Mex.; adv. com. Cornerstones Cmty Partnerships, Santa Fe; bd. dirs. N.Mex. Water Dialogue, Corrales, N.Mex. Heritage Preservation Alliance, Santa Fe, NY Chamber Soloists, N.Y.C. Mem.: Assn. Bar City of N.Y., State Bar Calif., Met. Club. Home: 189 Sayre Rd Seneca NM 88415 Office Phone: 505-451-7454. Personal E-mail: kkmonroe@bacavalley.com.

**MONROE, LEONORA,** surgeon; b. Hazleton, Pa., Apr. 11, 1940; d. James and Ruth Monroe; 1 child, Franc. RN, U. Pa., 1960, BA, 1973; MD, Med. Coll. Pa., 1980. Bd. cert. in surgery Am. Bd. Surgery. Head nurse oper. rm. Columbia Presbyn. Hosp., N.Y.C., 1960-62; head nurse med.-surg. U. Pa. Grad. Hosp., Phila., 1963-68, head nurse emergency rm., 1972-75; head nurse labor and delivery Pa. Hosp., Phila., 1968-72; surg. resident Hahnemann U. Hosp., Phila., 1980-83, Polyclinic Med. Ctr., Harrisburg, Pa., 1983-86; attending surgeon Guiffré Med. Ctr., Phila., 1986-88; attending surgeon, instr. surgery Wyckoff Heights Med. Ctr., Bklyn., 1990—. Oper. rm. com. Wyckoff Heights Med. Ctr., Bklyn., 1992-96, med. records com., 1994—, autopsy com., 1996, utilization com., 2000—. Fellow ACS; mem. Am. Soc. Gen. Surgeons, Soc. Laparoendoscopic Surgeons. Avocations: skiing, squash, racquetball. Office: Family Health Ctr Ridgewood 68-52 Fresh Pond Rd Ridgewood NY 11385

**MONROE, MELROSE,** retired bank executive; b. Flowery Branch, Ga., Apr. 13, 1919; d. Willis Jeptha and Leila Adell Cash; m. Lynn Austin, June 14, 1942. AB in Edn., Ga. State U., 1968. Negotiator Trust Co. Bank, Atlanta, 1962-89, ret., 1989. Mem. Nat. Women's C. of C. (pres. 1987-88), Atlanta Women's C. of C. (dir. 1965-66, pres. Fidelis SS class 1962-63), Nat. Am. Legion Aux. (so. divsn. chmn. aux. Americanism 1995-96, so. divsn. chmn. aux. emergency fund 1996-97 cmty. svc. com.), Am. Legion Aux (pres 5th dist. 1988 87, Ga. state chaplain 1989-90, state historian 1991-92, state 2d v.p. 1992-93, 1st v.p. 1993-94, pres. 1994-95, Americanism chmn. so. divsn. 1995-95, chmn. emergency fund 1996-97, mem. cmty. svc. com. 1997-98, nat. historian 1999-00, v. chmn. nat. poppy com. 2000-01), Order Ea. Star (worthy matron 1951-52). Democrat. Home and Office: 6250 Spout Springs Rd Flowery Branch GA 30542-5031

**MONROE, ROBERT RAWSON,** national security consultant; b. Oakland, Calif., Sept. 25, 1927; s. Robert Ansiey and Muriel Estelle (Burnham) M.; m. Charlotte Boies Anderson, Oct. 16, 1951; children: Robert Anderson, Nancy Lynn Monroe Sims, Susan Leslie Monroe Gordon. BS in Naval Sci., U.S. Naval Acad., 1950; MA in Internat. Rels., Stanford U., Calif., 1962. Commd. ensign USN, 1950, advanced through grades to vice-admiral, 1977: dir. Navy Systems Analysis, 1972-73; comdr. South Atlantic Force, 1973-74; comdr. Operational Test and Evaluation Force USN, 1974-77; dir. Def. Nuclear Agy., 1977-80; dir. Navy Rsch., Devel., Test and Evaluation, 1980-83; ret., 1983; joined Bechtel Nat., Inc., San Francisco, 1984, mgr. def. and space, 1984-89, v.p., 1985, sr. v.p., ptnr., 1987, mgr. mktg. and govt. ops., 1989-91, mgr. spl. projects, 1992-93, mgr. govt. ops. Washington, 1993—2002, sr. counselor, 2002—05; ret., 2005; nat. security cons. pvt. practice, 2006—. mem. nat. security adv. bd. Los Alamos (N.Mex.) Nat. Lab., 1983—88; mem. tech. evaluation panel U.S. Dept. Energy, 1983—88; mem. engring. adv. com. Oak Ridge Nat. Lab., 1986—89, Rensselaer Poly. Inst., 1990—91; mem. bd. advisors Office Tech. Assessment, Washington, 1987—89, Nat. Contract Mgmt. Assn., 1986—91; mem. task force Def. Sci. Bd., Washington, 1983—89; corp. mem. Charles Stark Draper Lab., Cambridge, Mass., 1983—; affiliate mem. Ctr. for Internat. Security and Cooperation, Stanford U., 1989—93; chmn. space transp. subcom. NASA's Adv. Coun., 1995—2001; mem. strategic adv. bd. Nev. Test Site, 1995—99; mem. Nat. Security adv. panel Sandia Nat. Labs., 1996—; mem. threat reduction adv. com. (nuc. panel) Dept. Def., 1998—; mem. Enhanced Test Readiness External Rev. Group, 2002—03; mem. threat reduction adv. com. (sci. & tech. panel) Dept. Def., 2004—; mem. U.S. Nuc. Strategy Forum, 2004—; mem. mil. com. Ctr. for Security Policy, 2004—; mem. adv. bd. arms control nonproliferation State Dept., Washington, 2005—, chmn. task force nat. strategy combat weapons of mass destruction, 2006—. Decorated DSM, Def. DSM, Legion of Merit, Bronze Star medal with combat device, Joint Svcs.

Commendation medal, USN Commendation medal with combat device; Legion of Honor (France). Avocations: tennis, golf, hiking, reading. Home: 2313 Sawdust Rd Vienna VA 22181-3044 E-mail: rrmonroe@cox.net.

**MONROE, STEPHANIE JOHNSON,** federal agency administrator; BA, U. Md., 1980; JD, U. of Baltimore, 1985. Legis. asst. to senator of NH US Senate; chief counsel, staff dir. Com. on Labor & Human Resources, Children, Families, Drugs & Alcoholism Subcommittee, US Senate, 1989—2001; chief counsel Com. on Health, Education, Labor & Pensions, US Senate, 2001—05; profl. staff mem. US Senate Budget Com.; asst. sec. Office for Civil Rights US Dept. Edn., Washington, 2005—. Head Start Quality & Expansion adv. com. US Dept. Health & Human Svcs., 1993—. Office: Office for Civil Rights US Dept Education Potomac Ctr 6th Fl 550 12th St SW Washington DC 20202-1100 Office Phone: 202-245-6700. Office Fax: 202-205-9862.*

**MONROE, THOMAS EDWARD,** business and financial executive; b. Ironton, Mo., Nov. 19, 1947; s. Donald Mansfield and Edwina Frances (Carr) M.; children: Thomas Edward II, Katherine Jenna. BA, Drury Coll., 1969; postgrad., Washington U. Sch. Bus. Adminstrn., St. Louis, 1970. Acctg. mgr., asst. contr. Am. Transit Corp., St. Louis, 1970-74; mgr. corp. devel., asst. treas. Chromalloy Am. Corp., St. Louis, 1974-77, v.p. fin., 1977-78, exec. v.p., 1978-82; dir. Chromalloy Fin. Corp., 1976-82, Am. Universal Ins. Co., 1978-82; chmn. Capital Assocs. Corp., 1982—, Fed. Air Ambulance, The Safe Deposit Co., CompuVault, Inc., James Flying Svc., Inc., Lindbergh Leasing, Inc., Vault II, LLC. Trustee Kingsbury Place Assn., Second Presbyn. Ch. Mem. Algonquin Club. Presbyterian. Office: Capital Assocs Corp 515 S Lindbergh Blvd Saint Louis MO 63131-2731 Office Phone: 314-991-3130.

**MONROE, WILLIAM LEWIS,** human resources executive; b. Detroit, May 11, 1941; s. Lewis Stewart and Ada Jeanette (Williams) Monroe; m. Sharon Lynne Kahal, June 30, 1967; children: Andrea M. Dunk, William J. BA, Western Mich. U., 1963, MA, 1964. Rsch. analyst Chrysler Corp., Detroit, 1965-72, labor economist, 1972-77, mgr. retirement, savs. and unemployment benefit plans, 1977-81; dir. employee benefits W. R. Grace & Co., N,Y.C., 1981-87, v.p. human resources, 1987-2001, bd. trustee, v.p. cons. on employee benefits, 1989-2001, pres. coun. on employee benefits, 1995-96; cons. AON Cons./ASA, Boca Raton, 2001—02. Adj. prof. mgmt. FAU Univ., Boca Raton, 2001; corp. bd. dirs. Internat. Found. Employee Benefits, 1986—88; mem. bus. rsch. adv. coun. U.S. Dept. Labor/Bur. Labor Stats., 1987—96; mem. Human Resources Policy Inst. Boston U., 1993—96. Co-chmn. closing com. PTSA Sch., Birmingham, Mich., 1977; chmn. pers. com. Wilton Presbyn. ch., Wilton, Conn., 1982—86; officer, bd. dirs. Forest Hills Property Owners Assn., Birmingham, 1974—80; mem. exec. bd. Gulf Stream coun. Boy Scouts Am., 1993—99. Served USAR, 1965—71. Mem.: Soc. for Human Resources & Mgmt., Boca Raton Resort and Club. Republican. Presbyterian. Avocations: tennis, golf. Office: PO Box 810851 Boca Raton FL 33481-0851 Personal E-mail: bmonroe10@aol.com.

**MONROY, GLADYS H.,** lawyer; b. NYC, Aug. 29, 1937; d. Henry B. and Leonora E. (Low) Chu; m. Jaime L. G. Monroy (div.); m. C. Lawrence Marks, Nov. 29, 1980. BA, Hunter Coll., N.Y., 1957; MS, NYU, 1968, PhD, 1973; JD, U. San Francisco, 1986. Bar: Calif.; registered U.S. Patent and Trademark office. Lab. technician Sloan-Kettering Inst., N.Y., 1957-60, Pub. Health Rsch. Inst., N.Y., 1960-63, rsch. asst., 1963-68; post doctoral fellow Albert Einstein Coll. Medicine, Bronx, NY, 1973-77; asst. prof. N.Y. Med. Coll., Valhalla, 1977-79; acquisitions editor Acad. Press, Inc., 1979-81; reseach assoc. U. Calif., San Francisco, 1981-83; atty. Irell & Manella, Menlo Park, Calif., 1986-90, ptnr., 1990-91, Morrison & Foerster, Palo Alto, Calif., 1991—, co-leader patent practice group. Co-chair I.P. Group, 1997—2002, Life Scis. Group, 1997—. Contbr. articles to profl. jours. Mem. bd. dirs. Project Hogar De Los Ninos, Menlo Park, Calif., 1987, 89, mem. Profl. Women's Network, San Francisco, 1988—90; mem. bd. dirs. Child Advocates of Santa Clara and San Mateo Counties, 1995—99. Mem. ABA, Am. Intellectual Property Law Assn., Am. Soc. Human Genetics, Am. Chem. Soc., Calif. Bar Assn., San Francisco Intellectual Property Law Assn. (chair patent com. 1992-94), Peninsula Patent Law Assn. (program chair 1993-94, treas. 1994-95, sec. 1995-96, v.p. 1996-97, pres. 1997—98), Am. Soc. Microbiology, Phi Alpha Delta. Avocations: swimming, bicycling, skiing, reading, opera. Office: Morrison & Foerster LLP 755 Page Mill Rd Palo Alto CA 94304-1018 Office Phone: 650-813-5600. Office Fax: 650-494-0792. Business E-Mail: gmonroy@mofo.com.

**MONSELL, THOMAS OLIVER,** secondary school educator, writer; b. Greenport, N.Y., Aug. 26, 1933; s. Harry Monroe and Amy Adelle Monsell. BA, Ithaca Coll., 1952—56; MS, SUNY, Albany, 1959—60. Prodn. asst. Robbins Music Corp., N,Y.C., 1957—58; English tchr., drama coach, libr. Lindenhurst Pub. Sch., NY, 1960—88. Founder, dir. Stirling Players Cmty. Theater, Greenport, NY, 1972—; textbook contbr. Henry Holt & Co., Harcourt, Brace, N,Y.C., 1989—94; film & theater critic New York Guardian, 1993—96. Author: (explication) Shakespeare in Perf: Hamlet, 1990, (media criticism) Nixon on Stage and Screen, 1998; co-author (with Antonia Booth): (regional history) Greenport, 2003. Village historian (with James Monsell) City of Greenport, NY, 2000—. Mem.: Shaw Soc, Ibsen Soc. Am., Eugene O'Neill Soc., James Jones Lit. Soc., Soc. Mayflower Descendants. Avocations: reading, writing, travel, theater, directing plays for charity benefits. Home: 525 First St Greenport NY 11944

**MONSEN, ELAINE RANKER,** nutritionist, educator, editor; b. Oakland, Calif., June 6, 1935; d. Emery R. and Irene Stewart (Thorley) Ranker; m. Raymond Joseph Monsen, Jr., Jan. 21, 1959; 1 dau., Maren Ranker Grainger-Monsen. BA, U. Utah, 1956; MS (Mead Johnson grad. scholar), U. Calif., Berkeley, 1959, PhD (NSF fellow), 1961; postgrad. NSF sci. faculty fellow, Harvard U., 1968-69. Dietetic intern Mass. Gen. Hosp., Boston, 1956-57; asst. prof. nutrition, lectr. biochemistry Brigham Young U., Provo, Utah, 1960-63; mem. faculty U. Wash., 1963—, prof. nutrition, adj. prof. medicine, 1976-84, prof. nutrition and medicine, 1984—2004, prof. emeritus, 2004—, chmn. div. human nutrition, dietetics and foods, 1977-82, dir. grad. nutritional scis. program, 1994-99, mem. Council of Coll. Arts and Scis., 1974-78; chmn. Nutrition Studies Commn., 1969-83. Vis. scholar Stanford U., 1971-72; mem. sci. adv. com. food fortification Pan-Am. Health Orgn., São Paulo, Brazil, 1972; tng. grant coordinator NIH, 1976-97. Editor-in-chief Jour. Am. Dietetic Assn., 1983-2003; Editor Emeritus, Jour. Am. Dietetic Assn., 2003—; mem. editorial bd. Coun. Biology Editors, 1992-96; author rsch. papers on lipid metabolism, iron absorption. Bd. dirs. A Contemporary Theatre, Seattle, 1969-72; trustee, bd. dirs. Seattle Found., 1978-95, vice chmn., 1987-91, chmn., 1991-93; mem. Seattle bd. Santa Fe Chamber Music Festival, 1984-85; mem. Puget Sound Blood Ctr. Bd., 1996-99. Grantee Nutrition Found., 1965-68, Agrl. Rsch. Svc., 1969-84; recipient Disting. Alumnus award U. Utah, F. Fischer Meml. Nutrition Lectr. award, 1988, L.F. Cooper Meml. Lectr. award, 1991, L. Hatch Meml. Lectr. award, 1992, Goble Lectr. award Purdue U., 1997. Fellow: Am. Soc. Clin. Nutrition (sec. 1987—90), Am. Inst. Nutrition; mem.: Wash. Heart Assn. (nutrition coun. 1973—76), Am. Soc. Parenteral and Enteral Nutrition, Soc. Nutriton Edn., Am. Dietetic Assn. Office: U Wash PO Box 353410 Seattle WA 98195-3410

**MONSKY, JOHN BERTRAND,** investment company executive; b. Montgomery, Ala., May 17, 1930; s. Harry and Belle (Golding) M.; m. Joan Gilbert, June 8, 1952; children: Leslie Joy, John Richard, Harry Robert. BA, Yale, 1952; MBA, Harvard, 1954. Sec. Devoe & Raynolds Co., Inc., Louisville, Ky., 1956-65; v.p., dir. Universal Marion Corp., Jacksonville, Fla., 1965-69, pres., chmn. bd., chief exec. officer, 1969-71, cons., 1971—; vice chmn. ServAmerica, Inc., Jacksonville, 1972-74, co-chmn. bd. dirs., 1974-80, chmn. bd. dirs., 1980—; pres., chmn. bd. dirs. First Fla. Capital Corp., 1985—. Dir. Fla. Wire & Cable Co., Jacksonville, 1975-82 Past pres. bd. trustees Jacksonville Country Day Sch.; bd. dirs. Jacksonville Art Mus.; trustee Bolles Sch., Jacksonville, Jacksonville Symphony Assn. Served with USAF, 1954-56. Mem. Jacksonville Area C. of C. (com. of 100), Jackson County Citizen Involvement Clubs, Harvard Bus. Sch. Club of Ky. (exec. com. 1964-65), Phillips Acad. Andover Alumni Club of Ky. (pres. 1963-64),

Epping Forest Cmty. Master Assn. (bd. dirs. 1994—), Yale Club N.E. Fla. (bd. dirs. 1984—), Yale Club of NYC, Harvard Club (Jacksonville), Assn. Yale Alumni (del. 1996—, schs. com.), River Club, Ponte Vedra Club, Epping Forest Yacht Club, Harvard Bus. Sch. Alumni Club (Jacksonville, bd. dirs.) Home: Epping Forest 7015 Gaines Ct Jacksonville FL 32217-2672 Office: 300 Wharfside Way # B Jacksonville FL 32207-8153 Office Phone: 904-396-0348. Personal E-mail: jbmonsky@aol.com. Business E-Mail: jbmonsky@firstfloridacapital.com.

**MONSON, CAROL LYNN,** osteopath, psychotherapist; b. Blue Island, Ill., Nov. 3, 1946; d. Marcus Edward and Margaret Bertha (Andres) Monson; m. Frank E. Warden, Feb. 28, 1981. BS, No. Ill. U., 1968, MS, 1969; D.O., Mich State Coll. Osteo. Medicine, 1979. Lic. physician Mich., diplomate Am. Bd. Osteo., Am. Bd. Family Physicians, Am. Bd. Osteo. Gen. Practice, MSU-COM. Expeditor-psychotherapist H. Douglas Singer Zone Ctr., Rockford, Ill., 1969—71; psychotherapist Tri-County Mental Health, St. Johns, Mich., 1971—76; pvt. practice psychotherapy East Lansing, Mich., 1976—80; intern Lansing Gen. Hosp., Mich., 1979—80, residency dir. family practice, 1988—; pvt. practice osteo. medicine Lansing, 1980—; mem. staff Ingham Regional Med. Ctr., chmn. family practice, 1987—89. Field instr. Sch. Social Work U. Mich., 1973—76; clin. instr. Ctrl. Mich. Dept. Psychology, 1974—75; clin. prof. Mich. State U., 1988—88, asst. prof., 1988—, tng. supr. family medicine residency, 1988—97; faculty devel. fellow, 1994—95, residency dir. family medicine, 1994—97; mem. adv. bd. Substance Abuse Clearinghouse, Lansing, 1983—85, Kelly Health Care, Lansing, 1983—85, Americor Health Svcs., Lansing, 1984—88, Lansing Home Care, Lansing, 1988—94. Fellow: Am. Coll. Family Practice (osteo.); mem.: Am. Coll. Family Physicians (residency insp. 1991—), Mich. Assn. Osteo. Family Physicians (pres.-elect 1994, pres. 1995—96), Nat. Assn. Career Women (conv. com. 1984—), Ingham County Osteo. Assn. (pres. 1993—95, 1996—97), Mich. Osteo. Assn. (program com. 1992—, governance coun. 1996—97, bd. trustees 1997—, pres.-elect 2001—2002, pres. 2002—), Internat. Transactional Analysis Assn., Am. Acad. Family Practice, Am. Osteo. Assn. (del. 1994—, health policy fellow 1997—98), Mich. Coun. Grad. Med. Edn. (appointee 1998—, pres. 1999—2002), Lansing Assn. Career Women, Soc. Tchrs. of Family Medicine, Zonta (chmn. service com. Mid Mich. Capital Area chpt.). Avocations: gardening, orchid growing, antique collecting. Office: 2445 Jolly Rd Ste 200 Okemos MI 48864-4572

**MONSON, CINDY LOU,** music educator; b. Minocqua, Wis., Nov. 26, 1957; d. Elroy Vernon and Adeline I. Kriehn; children: Isaac V., Aaron A., Ruth L. Attended, U. Wis., River Falls, 1976—78. Mem. faculty The Studio Grand, Edina, Minn., 1987—93; music educator Monson Music Studio, Mpls., 1993—2002; mem. faculty MacPhail Ctr. for Music, Mpls., 2002—; dir. MacPhail Ctr. for Music, Suzuki Piano Inst., 2006. Mem.: Suzuki Assn. of Minn., Nat. Guild of Piano Teachers, Suzuki Assn. of Am. Avocations: reading, gardening, antiques. Office: MacPhail Center for Music 1128 LaSalle Ave Minneapolis MN 55403 Office Phone: 612-321-0100 461. Business E-Mail: monson.cindy@macphail.org.

**MONSON, DAN,** college basketball coach; b. Spokane, Wash., Oct. 6, 1961; BS in Math., U. Idaho, 1985; MS in Athletic Adminstrn., U. Ala., 1988. Asst. coach Oregon City H.S., 1985-86; grad. asst. U. Ala., Birmingham, 1986-88; asst. coach Gonzaga U., Spokane, 1988-94, assoc. head coach, 1994-97, head coach, 1997-99, U. Minn., 1999—. Dir. Gopherball Basketball Camp, Mpls.; asst. coach World Univ. Games, 1999, USA Basketball's 20-and-under team, 2004. Named Coach of Yr., 1998, Nat. Rookie Coach of Yr., Basketball Times, 1998. Achievements include West. Coast Conf. Champions, 1998; reached NCAA Sweet 16, 1998-99. Office: Univ of Minn Student Devel & Athletics 141 BFAB Minneapolis MN 55455-0100

**MONSON, DAVID CARL,** school system administrator, state legislator, farmer; b. Langdon, N.D., July 30, 1950; s. Carl Arthur and Shirley Jean (Klai) M.; m. Mary Kathryn Greutman, July 8, 1972; children: Cordell Carl, Cale David, Jared Arthur. Cert. tchr., adminstr., N.D. Sci. tchr. Hankinson (N.D.) Pub. Sch., 1972-75; tchr. Nekoma (N.D.) Pub. Sch., 1975-76; tchr., prin. NeKoma (N.D.) Pub. Sch., 1976-79; tchr., supt. Nekoma (N.D.) Pub. Sch., 1979-80; tchr., prin. Milton (N.D.)-Osnabrock H.S., 1981-84; supt. Adams (N.D.) Pub. Schs., 1984-88; ins. agt. N.Y. Life, Fargo, ND, 1988-95; self-employed ins. agt., Osnabrock, 1988—2003; farmer, 1975—; mem. N.D. Ho. of Reps., Bismarck, 1993—, asst. majority leader, 1998—; supt. Edinburg (N.D.) Pub. Schs., 1995—. Dir. Cavalier County Mut. Ins. Co., Osnabrock, N.D., 1990-98, Northeast Mut. Ins. Co., Cando, N.D., 1998—, N.Am. Indsl. Hemp Coun., 1999—. Leader Bobcats 4-H Club, 1988—2001; pres. Dovre Luth. Ch., Osnabrock, 2002—; mem. sch. bd. dirs. Osnabrock Sch. Bd., 1989—2001. Mem. N.D Farm Bur., N.D. Coun. Sch. Adminstrs., Eagles, KP (grand sec. N.D. and Sask. 1985-93, award 1990). Republican. Lutheran. Avocations: skiing, gardening, hunting, coin collecting/numismatics. Business E-Mail: dmonson@nd.gov.

**MONSON, DIANNE LYNN,** literacy educator; b. Minot, ND, Nov. 24, 1934; d. Albert Rachie and Iona Cordelia (Kirk) M. BS, U. Minn., 1956, MA, 1962, PhD, 1966. Tchr. Rochester (Minn.) Pub. Schs., 1956-59, U.S. Dept. Def., Schweinfurt, West Germany, 1959-61, St. Louis Park (Minn.) Schs., 1961-62; instr. U. Minn., Mpls., 1962-66; prof. U. Wash., Seattle, 1966-82; prof. literacy edn. U. Minn., Mpls., 1982-97, prof. emeritus, 1997—. Chmn. curriculum and instrn. U. Minn., 1986—89. Co-author: Scott Foresman Reading, 2000, New Horizons in the Language Arts, 1972, Children and Books, 6th edit., 1981, Experiencing Children's Literature, 1984, Language Arts: Teaching and Learning Effective Use of Language, 1988, Reading Together: Helping Children Get A Good Start With Reading, 1991; assoc. editor: Dictionary of Literacy, 1995; mem. editl. bd. Five Owls Mag., 1997-2005. Bd. adv. Kerlan Collection, 2001—04, Minn. Humanities Commn., 2004—05; bd. dirs. Friends of Kerlan Collection, 2000—04. Recipient Outstanding Educator award U. Minn. Alumni Assn., 1983, Alumni Faculty award U. Minn. Alumni Assn., 1991. Fellow Nat. Conf. Rsch. in English (pres. 1990-91); mem. ALA, Nat. Coun. Tchrs. English (exec. com. 1979-81), Internat. Reading Assn. (dir. 1980-83, Arbuthnot award 1993, Reading Hall of Fame 1997), U.S. Bd. Books for Young People (pres. 1988-90). Lutheran. Home: 515 S Lexington Pkwy # 604 Saint Paul MN 55116 Business E-Mail: monso001@tc.umn.edu.

**MONSON, JAMES EDWARD,** electrical engineer, educator; b. Oakland, Calif., June 20, 1932; s. George Edward and Frances Eleanor M.; m. Julie Elizabeth Conzelman, June 25, 1954; children: John, Jamie, Jennifer BSEE, Stanford U., 1954, MSEE, 1955, PhD in Elec. Engring., 1961. Mem. tech. staff Bell Telephone Labs., Murray Hill, NJ, 1955-56; devel. engr. Hewlett-Packard Co., Palo Alto, Calif., 1956-61; Robert C. Sabini prof. engring. emeritus Harvey Mudd Coll., 1961—. Governing bd. Claremont Unified Sch. Dist., 1966-71, pres., 1969-70; pres. Claremont Civic Assn., 1974-75; bd. dirs. Claremont YMCA, 1978-82, Coastal Health Alliance, 1999-. Fellow NSF, 1954-55, Japan Soc. Promotion Sci., 1984; Fulbright Rsch. grantee, 1975-76; Fulbright sr. lectr., 1980. Fellow IEEE (life); mem. Phi Beta Kappa, Sigma Xi. Home: PO Box 1029 Point Reyes Station CA 94956-1029 Office: Harvey Mudd Coll 301 E 12th St Claremont CA 91711-5901 Personal E-mail: j.monson@ieee.org.

**MONSON, JOHN RUDOLPH,** lawyer; b. Chgo., Feb. 4, 1941; s. Rudolph Agaton and Ellen Louise (Loeffler) M.; m. Susan Lee Brown, May 22, 1965; children: Elizabeth Louisa, Christina Lee, Donald Rudolph. BA with honors, Northwestern U., 1963; JD with distinction, U. Mich., 1966. Bar: Ill. 1966, N.H. 1970. Mass. 1985. Atty. assoc. Chapman & Cutler, Chgo., 1966-68, Levenfeld, Kanter, Baskes & Lippitz, Chgo., 1968-70, Highswander, Martin & Mitchell, Laconia, NH, 1970-71; mem., ptnr. Wiggin & Nourie, PA, Manchester, NH, 1972—, pres., 1991—94. Sec., gen. counsel Rock of Ages Corp., 1996-2000. Mem. N.H. Fish and Game Commn., Concord, 1980-94, chmn., 1983-93; sr. bd. dirs. Brown-Monson Found., 1991—; incorporator Cath. Med. Ctr., 1988-95, Optima Health, 1994-99; commr. N.H. Land and Cmty. Heritage Commn., 1998-2000. Fellow Am. Coll. Trust and Estate Counsel, Safari Club Internat. (v.p. 1999-2001, dir.-at-large 1997-99, treas.

2001-02, pres. elect 2002-04, pres. 2004—05). Republican. Avocations: skiing, hunting, running. Home: 24 Wellesley Dr Bedford NH 03110-4531 Office: Wiggin & Nourie PA 670 N Commerical St Ste 305 Manchester NH 03105 Office Phone: 603-669-2211.

**MONSON, LARRY LEE,** music educator; b. Grand Island, Nebr., Oct. 17, 1942; s. Owen H. and Glenna Imojene Monson; m. LaVonne Elise Havekost, Mar. 21, 1964; children: Martin Laurence, Ann Elise, Eric Lee. BA, Midland Luth. Coll., 1964, MA, U. Iowa, 1966. Cert. tchr. Iowa. Dir. music 1st Luth. Ch., Cedar Rapids, Iowa, 1964—67; dir. music and youth Kountze Meml. Ch., Omaha, 1967—69; dir. music 1st Luth. Ch., Sioux Falls, SD, 1969—72, St. Paul Luth. Ch., Davenport, Iowa, 1972—79; choral dir. City HS, Iowa City, 1979—89; dir. choral activities Doane Coll., Crete, Nebr., 1989—, ret. prof. choral music, 2004. Chair music cert. Nebr. State Edn., Lincoln, 1990—93. Bd. dirs. Polley Music Libr., Lincoln, 1989—95. Recipient Outstanding Alumni Achievement award, Midland Luth. Coll., 2001. Mem.: Soc. Preservation and Encouragement of Barbershop Quartet Singing, Internat. Fedn. Choral Music, Am. Choral Dirs. Assn. Avocations: biking, travel, coaching quartets, gardening. Home: 204 Wedgewood Dr Lincoln NE 68510 E-mail: larry.monson@doane.edu.

**MONSON, THOMAS SPENCER,** religious organization administrator, retired publishing executive; b. Salt Lake City, Aug. 21, 1927; s. George Spencer and Gladys (Condie) M.; m. Frances Beverly Johnson, Oct. 7, 1948; children— Thomas L., Ann Frances, Clark Spencer. BS with honors in mktg., U. Utah, 1948; MBA, Brigham Young U., 1974, LLD (hon.), 1981. With Deseret News Press, Salt Lake City, 1948-64, mgr., 1962-64; mem. Coun. Twelve Apostles, Ch. of Jesus Christ of Latter-day Saints, 1963-85, bishop, 1950-55; pres. Canadian Mission, 1959-62; mem. first presidency Ch. of Jesus Christ of Latter-day Sts., 1985—; chmn. bd. Deseret News Pub. Co., 1977-96. Vice chmn. Deseret Mgmt. Corp.; pres. Printing Industry Utah, 1958; bd. dirs. Printing Industry Am., 1958-64; mem. Utah exec. bd. U.S. West Communications. Mem. Utah Bd. Regents; mem. nat. exec. bd. Boy Scouts Am.; trustee Brigham Young U. With USNR, 1945-46. Recipient Recognition award, 1964, Disting. Alumnus award U. Utah, 1966; Silver Beaver award Boy Scouts Am., 1971; Silver Buffalo award, 1978; Bronze Wolf award World Orgn. of the Scout Movement, 1993. Mem. Utah Assn. Sales Execs., U. Utah Alumni Assn. (dir.), Salt Lake Advt. Club, Alpha Kappa Psi. Clubs: Exchange (Salt Lake City). Mem. Lds Ch. Office: LDS Ch 47 E South Temple Salt Lake City UT 84150-9701

**MONTAG, JOHN JOSEPH, II,** librarian; b. Omaha, Jan. 8, 1948; s. John Joseph and Ruth Helen (Johnston) M.; m. Linda Kay Lubanski, Apr. 8, 1971; children: Nicole Elizabeth, Megan Kristine. BA, Midland Luth. Coll., 1970; postgrad., Wash. State U., 1970-74; MA, U. Iowa, 1976; postgrad., U. Nebr., 1982-84. English tchr. pub. schs., Nebr., Iowa, 1972-75; reference libr. Concordia Coll., Moorhead, Minn., 1976-81; asst. prof. libr. sci. U. Nebr., Lincoln, 1981-84; dir. Office of Info. State Libr. Iowa, Des Moines, 1984-86, state libr., 1986-87; dir. Thomas Libr. Wittenberg U., 1987-95, Cochrane-Woods Libr. Nebr. Wesleyan U., Lincoln, 1995-97, dir. libr. and computer svcs., 1997-99, univ. libr., 1999—. Trustee Bibliog. Ctr. for Rsch., Denver, 1986-87; adv. bd. No. Lights Libr. Network, Detroit Lakes, Minn., 1980-81; chair Southwest Ohio Consortium Higher Edn. Libr. Coun., 1991-94; mem. exec. com. Nebr. Inst., 1998—; cons. U.S. Dept. of Energy. Contbr. articles to profl. jours. Co-founder Nebr. Found. for Oral History, 2001—. Univ. Found. libr. improvement grantee, U. Nebr., 1983; Challenge grantee NEH, 1992; Tchg. Am. History grantee Lincoln Pub. Schs., 2002-. Mem. ALA, Assn. Coll. and Rsch. Librs., Nebr. Ind. Coll. Libr. Consortium (chmn. libr. dirs. 2000—). Office: Cochrane Woods Libr Nebr Wesleyan U 5000 Saint Paul Ave Lincoln NE 68504-2760 Office Phone: 402-465-2401. E-mail: jmontrag@nebrwesleyan.edu.

**MONTAGUE, ANN HOOD,** veterinarian; b. Lansdale, Pa., Aug. 25, 1973; d. John Edmund and Diann Gray Montague. BA in Math., Coll. St. Benedict, 1997; DVM, U. Minn., 2003. Nurse Banfield: The Pet Hosp., St. Paul, 1996—2001, veterinarian, 2003—. Vet. sch. rep. Twin Cities Student Union Bd. Govs., St. Paul, 2002. Del. Rep. Party Minn., 1991—97. Mem.: Minn. Vet. Med. Assn., Am. Animal Hosp. Assn. Avocations: Karate, tai chi, photography, writing. Home: 4100 N Marine Dr # 14C Chicago IL 60613 Office: Banfield The Pet Hospital 5484 Touhy Ave Skokie IL 60077 Office Phone: 847-675-2080. Personal E-mail: karatevet2003@yahoo.com.

**MONTAGUE, BRIAN JOHN,** consulting company executive; b. Washington, Oct. 9, 1951; s. H.C. and Dorothy (Brand) M.; m. Kathryn Valente, Oct. 2, 1993. BA, Bridgewater Coll., 1973; student, St. Mary's Coll., Md., 1975, George Washington U., 1980, Miss. State U., 1981. Toxicology technician Hazelton Labs., Vienna, Va., 1973-74; asst. mgr. Chesapeake Sea Farms, Ridge, Md., 1974-76; tng. instr., program coord. Natural Resources Dept., Annapolis, Md., 1976-77; fishery biologist Nat. Aquarium, U.S. Fish and Wildlife Svc., Washington, 1977-82, curator aquarium, 1982-88; pres. Aquatic Images, Annapolis, 1989—. Lectr. local interest groups, 1990—; fisheries biologist, ecol. risk assessment specialist U.S. EPA, Washington. Office: Aquatic Images 3527 Jamestown Rd Davidsonville MD 21035-2009

**MONTAGUE, DROGO K.,** urologist; b. Alpena, Mich., Dec. 11, 1942; s. Frank Wright and Susan Alice (Kidder) M.; children: Mark Andrew, Lisa Joy. Student, U. Mich., 1960—63, MD cum laude, 1968. Diplomate Am. Bd. Urology. Intern Cleve. Clinic Hosp., 1968-69, resident in gen. surgery, 1969-70, resident in urology, 1970-73; assoc. staff urologist Cleve. Clinic Found., 1973-75, staff urologist, 1975—, head sect. prosthetic surgery, 1981—, urology residence program dir., 1985—, dir. Ctr. for Sexual Function, 1987—; prof. surgery Cleve. Clinic Lerner Coll. Medicine Case Western Res. U., 2004—. Trainee cardiovascular rsch. tng. program NIH, 1962-68; trustee Am. Bd. Urology, 1989-95, mem. examination com., 1975-80, examiner cert. exam., 1980-88, rep. to Am. Bd. Med. Specialties, 1989-95. Reviewer various publs. in field; contbr. numerous articles to profl. publs., chpts. to books; editor: Disorders of Male Sexual Function, 1988, Surgical Treatment of Erectile Dysfunction, 1993; author audiovisual tapes in field; mem. editl. bd. Jour. Urology. James B. Angell scholar, 1961, 62, Nat. Found. scholar, 1963-68; recipient Russell and Mary Hugh Scott Edn. award, 1989, Iowa Rsch. award, 1967. Fellow ACS; mem. Am. Urologic. Assn. (chmn. sci. exhibits com. North Cen. sect. 1977, mem. residency edn. com. 1979-83, vice chmn. audio visual com. 1989-95, mem. various coms., editor Am. Urologic. Assn. Video Libr. 1995-2000, chmn. audio visual com. 1996-2002, chmn. erectile dysfunction guidelines panel 1999—), Am. Assn. Genitourinary Surgeons, Cleve. Urologic. Soc. (sec.-treas. 1978-80, v.p. 1980-81, pres. 1981-82, 94-95), Soc. for Study of Impotence (pres. 1995). Office: Cleve Clinic Found Urol Inst 9500 Euclid Ave Cleveland OH 44195-0001 Office Phone: 216-444-5590. Business E-Mail: montagd@ccf.org.

**MONTAGUE, EDGAR BURWELL, III, (MONTY MONTAGUE),** industrial designer; b. Charlotte, N.C., Aug. 6, 1958; s. Edgar B. Jr. and Mary Sue (Calhoun) M.; m. Nancy Oliver Stallworth, Feb. 25, 1984; children: Nancy Lea, Edgar Eubank. B Environ. Design cum laude, N.C. State U., 1980. Indsl. designer Design/Joe Sonderman, Inc., Charlotte, 1980-85; design prin. Bolt (formerly Machen Montague, Inc.), Charlotte, N,Y.C., 1985—, BOLT, Charlotte, 1994—. Holder over 15 design and/or utility patents; work published in Product Design 1-6, Design for Humanity. Designer corp. identity program Habitat for Humanity, Charlotte, 1987 (logo design used throughout world). Recipient ann. design award Internat. Design mag., 1988-93, ID-40 ID Mag., 1994, Disting. Alumni award N.C. State U., 1999. Mem. Indsl. Designer Soc. Am. (co-founder Carolina chpt., program chmn. 1981-83, vice chmn. 1984, 93, Kudo award for chpt. svc. 1982, Indsl. Design Excellence awards 1989-94). Avocations: travel, art, coaching soccer. Office: BOLT 1415 S Church St Ste 3 Charlotte NC 28203-4124 Office Phone: 704-372-2658. Business E-Mail: monty@boltgroup.com.

**MONTAGUE, RAE-ANNE,** assistant dean; b. Halifax, Nova Scotia, Canada, June 20, 1969; d. Terrence Roy and M. Grace Montague; m. J. Antonio Castro Marquez, Feb. 14, 1992; children: Roy Antonio Castro-Montague, John Alexander Castro-Montague, Elisa Rebeca Castro-Montague. MEd, St. Mary's U., Halifax, 1994; MS, U. Ill., Urbana-Champaign, 2000. Libr., tchr. Am. Sch. of Torreon, Coahuila, Mexico, 1995—2000; leep coord. U. Ill., Champaign 2000—05, asst. dean for student affairs, 2005—. Contbr. chapters to books. E-learning group convener Internat. Fedn. of Libr. Assns and Instns., Seoul, 2005—05; multicultural, ethnic, and humanistic concerns sig convener Assn. Libr. and Info. Sci. Edn., Boston, 2004. Grantee Provost's Initiative on Tchg. Advancement, U. Ill., 2002; Diversity Rsch. Grant, ALA, 2003, Grad. Coll. Travel Grant, U. Ill., 2003.

**MONTANARO, ANTHONY,** medical educator; m. Karen Thornquist, Sept. 15, 1973. MD, U. Wash., Seattle, 1978. Prof. medicine OHSU, Portland, Oreg., 1983—. Office Phone: 503-494-8531.

**MONTANEZ-JOHNER, NANCY,** federal agency administrator; With profl. ptnrs. program region III behavioral health svcs. Health and Human Svcs. Sys. State of Nebr., 1995—99, admistrt. S.W. svc. area, 1999—2001, CEO We. svc. area, 2001—04, dir., 2004—05; under sec. agr. food, nutrition & consumer services USDA, Washington, 2006—. Bd. dirs. Commodity Credit Corp. USDA, 2006—. Office: USDA Adminstrn Bldg 1400 Independence Ave SW Rm 240-E Washington DC 20250 Office Phone: 202-720-7711. Office Fax: 202-690-3100.*

**MONTAVON, VICTORIA A.,** university librarian, dean; b. Cin. m. James M. Myers; 3 children Libr. Rider U., Temple U., Lindenwood Coll., Carlow Coll., Notre Dame Coll., Ohio; univ. libr. St. Joseph 's U. Libr., Phila., 1990—96, Wright State U., 1996—2001; dean, univ. libr. U. Cin., 2001—. Recipient Pres. Quality Svc. Award, 2003. Office: U Cin U Librs PO Box 210033 Cincinnati OH 45221-0033 E-mail: Victoria.Montavon@uc.edu.*

**MONTE, BONNIE J.,** performing arts company executive, director, educator; b. Stamford, Conn., Nov. 27, 1954; d. Eugene N. and Ruth M. (Thompson) M. BA, Bethany Coll., 1976; diploma, Hartman Conservatory, Stamford, 1978; LHD (hon.), Drew U., 2005. Assoc. artistic dir. Williamstown (Mass.) Theatre Festival, 1981-89; casting dir. Manhattan Theatre Club, N.Y.C., 1989-90; artistic dir. The Shakespeare Theatre of NJ, Madison, 1990—. Mem. faculty Drew U., 1991-96; guest artist-in-residence U. Notre Dame, The New Sch.-Eugene Lang. Coll., U.S.C. Recipient Nat. Soc. of Arts and Letters award, N.J., 1997, Alumni Achievement award for arts mgmt. Bethany Coll., 1999; grantee Lotte Crabtree Found., Boston, 1977. Democrat. Avocations: bicycling, archery, writing, travel. Office: Shakespeare Theatre NJ 36 Madison Ave Madison NJ 07940-1434

**MONTEAU, NORMAN KEITH,** gemologist; b. Balt., Dec. 20, 1957; s. Milton Keith and Vieva Regina (Williams) M.; m. Sandra Lynn Staub, Dec. 7, 1987. Cert. diamond grading, Gemol. Inst., 1981, cert. colored stone grading, 1982, cert. gem identification, 1982. Numerous certs. fro Gemol. Inst. Am. Gemol., founder Monteau Gemol. Svcs., Woodland Hills, Calif., 1987-91, pres., 1992—; owner, pres. Am. Internat. Gemologists, Beverly Hills, Calif., 1993—; mng. ptnr. The William Staub Co., L.A., 1994—. V.p. bd. dirs. Lynn Meadows, 1999-2000, pres. 2000-2001; appraiser to Archdiocese of L.A., Cath. Ch., 1993—; arbitrator State Farm Ins. Co., 1993—, lectr. nat. retail jewelry stores, insurance cos. others on gemology and values, 1992—; advisor to ins. cos. in Calif. for earthquake property damage assessment, 1994, expert witness L.A. Mcpl. Ct., 1995; jewelry appraiser County of Los Angeles, 1996—; mem. Ptnrs. for Internat. Edn. and Tng./U.S. AID, 1996. Contbr. articles to profl. jours. Recipient Excellence award Aetna Ins. Co., 1992; honored guest of bd. govs. Gemol. Inst. Am., Carlsbad, Calif., 1996. Mem. Nat. Assn. Jewelry Appraisers, Am. Soc. Appraisers, Gemol. Inst. Am. (mem. Pres.'s Cir. 1992—), Calif. Jewelers Assn., Alumni Assn. Gemol. Inst. Am. (charter), Jewelers Bd. of Trade, Woodland Hills C. of C. Avocations: racquetball, mountain climbing, water-skiing, jet car racing, white water rafting. Home: 2715 Edgeview Ct Newbury Park CA 91320-3883

**MONTEDONICO, JOSEPH,** lawyer; b. Washington, May 30, 1937; s. Joseph and Linda (Love) M.; m. Lynne Morrell, Nov. 12, 1979; 1 child, Maria. BA, U. Md., 1962, JD, 1965. Bar: Md. 1965. DC 1965, admitted to practice: U.S. Dist. Ct. DC 1965, U.S. Dist. Ct. Md. 1965, U.S. Supreme Ct. Law clk. to justice, Rockville, Md., 1965-66; assoc. Donahue, Ehrmantraut Mitchell, Rockville, 1966-78; ptnr. Donahue, Ehrmantraut, Montedonico, Washington, 1978-88, Montedonico & Mason, Rockville, 1988-91, Montedonico, Hamilton & Altman, PC, Chevy Chase, Md., 1991—2001, Montedonico, Belcoure & Tazzara, Washington, 2001—. Cons., lectr. in field. Author: Medical Malpractice and Health Care Care, 1987, Legal Consideration of Outpatient Anesthesia, Anesthesiology Clinics, 1987, Medical and Legal Principles of Surgical Pathology, Textbook of Surgical Pathology, 1989. With U.S. Army, 1956-58. Named one of Best Lawyers in Am., Washingtonian Mag., 1989—96, Best 75 Lawyers in Washington, 2002. Mem.: Nat. Italian Am. Found., Internat. Acad. Trial Lawyers, Washington Trial Advocates, Montgomery County Bar Assn., ABA, DC Bar Assn., Md. Bar Assn., Internat. Acad. Trial Lawyers, Am. Bd. Trial Lawyers (pres. DC chpt.), Omicron Delta Kappa, Phi Alpha Delta, Inns of Ct. Republican. Avocations: scuba, skiing, photography. Office: Montedonico Belcoure & Tazzara PC 1020 19th St NW Ste 420 Washington DC 20036 Office Phone: 202-296-1322. Office Fax: 202-296-0985. E-mail: Joseph.Montedonico@mbt_legal.com.

**MONTEGUT, ALAIN J.,** physician, consultant; b. N.Y.C., Feb. 4, 1951; s. Philippe J. and Simone R. Montegut; m. Kathleen Cotter Montegut, May 23, 1981; children: Sara K., Daniel W. BA, Ohio Wesleyan U., Delaware, Ohio, 1973; Grad. Med. Sch., U. Lausanne, Switzerland, 1973 75, MD, UCLA, L.A., 1977. Diplomate Am. Bd. Family Medicine, 1981. Solo practice family medicine Alain J. Montegut, MD, Topsham, Maine, 1981—95; med. dir. Bowdoin Med. Group, Brunswick, 1995—2001; dir. divsn. internat. health improvement Maine Med. Ctr., Portland, 1996—, dir. family medicine residency program, 2001—. Cons. Ministry of Health, Moscow, 1990—95, Hanoi, Vietnam, 1995—, Phnomh Penh, Cambodia, 2003—, Vientiane, Laos, 2004—, Capital U. Med. Scis., Beijing, 2005—; John J. Cunningham, MD vis. prof. and lectr. Dept. Family Medicine Brown U. and RI Acad. of Family Physicians, 2005; mem. bd. dir. Am. Bd. Family Medicine, Lexington, Ky. Contbr. articles to profl. jours. Recipient Ben Sichey award, U. Rochester Sch. Medicine, 2001, Gabe Smilkstein Meml. award, Soc. Tchrs. Family Medicine, 2005, Power to Change Our World award, North East Soc. Tchrs. Family Medicine, 2006. Fellow: Am. Acad. Family Physcians (Humanitarian of Yr. 2001). Office: Maine Medical Ctr 22 Bramhall S Portland ME 04102 Office Phone: 207-662-2875. Office Fax: 207-662-6055. E-mail: montea@mmc.org.

**MONTEIRO, GEORGE,** language educator, writer; b. Cumberland, R.I., May 23, 1932; s. Francisco José and Augusta (Temudo) M.; m. Lois Ann Hodgins, Aug. 14, 1958 (div. 1992); children: Katherine, Stephen, Emily; m. Brenda Murphy, Mar. 25, 1995. AB, Brown U., 1954; AM, Columbia U., 1956; PhD, Brown U., 1964; DHL (hon.), U. Mass., Dartmouth, 1993. From instr. to assoc. prof. Brown U., Providence, 1961-72, prof. English, 1972-99, prof. Portuguese, 1984-99, adj. prof., 1999—; prof. U. Mass., Dartmouth, 2006. Vis. prof. Providence Coll., 1967-68; Fulbright prof. Am. lit. U. Sao Paulo, 1969-71. Author: Henry James and John Hay: The Record of a Friendship, 1965, The Coffee Exchange: Poems, 1982, Robert Frost and the New England Renaissance, 1988, Double Weaver's Knot: Selected Poems, 1989, The Presence of Camões, 1996, The Presence of Pessoa, 1998, Stephen Crane's Blue Badge of Courage, 2000, Fernando Pessoa and Nineteenth-Century Anglo-American Literature, 2000; editor: The Man Who Never Was: Essays on Fernando Pessoa, 1982, The Correspondence of Henry James and Henry Adams, 1877-1941, 1992, Critical Essays on Ernest Hemingway's Farewell to Arms, 1994, Conversations with Elizabeth Bishop, 1996; translator: In Crete with the Minotaur and Other Poems, 1980, The Sea Within, 1983, Fernando Pessoa: Self Awareness and Thirty Other Poems, 1988, A

Man Smiles at Death with Half a Face, 1991, Iberian Poems, 2005. Decorated Order of Prince Henry the Navigator (Portugal). Office: Brown U Portuguese & Brazil Studies Providence RI 02912-0001 Office Phone: 401-863-3042. Personal E-mail: georgemonteiro23@yahoo.com.

**MONTEIRO, LOIS ANN,** nursing educator; b. Central Falls, R.I., Mar. 22, 1934; d. William Henry and Martha Mae (Leach) Hodgins; m. George Monteiro, Aug. 14, 1958 (div. Feb. 1992); children: Katherine, Stephen, Emily. RN, Roger Williams Hosp., Providence, 1954; BA, Brown U., k1958, PhD, 1970; MS, Boston U., 1960. Asst. prof. Boston U., 1960-65, Brown U., Providence, 1971-77, assoc. prof., 1978-82, prof., 1983—, chmn. dept., 1985—, assoc. dean medicine, 1991—. Vis. prof. U. Va., 1990, U. Miss., 2002; bd. dirs. Harvard Cmty. Health Plan, 1990-95, Harvard Pilgrim Health Care Plan, New Eng., 1995—. Author: Mentoring Health Status, 1976, Cardiac Rehabilitation, 1980; contbr. articles to profl. jours. Mem. Commn. State of R.I., Providence, 1989—. NSF grantee, 1969, Robert W. Johnson Found. grantee, Princeton, N.J., 1983, NIH grantee, 1987; Bunting Inst. fellow, Cambridge, Mass., 1981, Congrl. fellow House Vets. Affairs Commn., 1998; recipient Am. Sociol. Assn. Spivack award, 1998. Mem. Am. Sociol. Assn., R.I. State Nurses Assn. (pres. 1974-76), Women in Medicine/Assn. Am. Med. Colls. Democrat. Presbyterian. Avocation: collecting books on nursing history. Office: Brown U Dept Med Sci PO Box G-a413 Providence RI 02912-0001 E-mail: lois_monteiro@brown.edu.

**MONTEITH, LARRY KING,** chancellor emeritus; b. Bryson City, N.C., Aug. 17, 1933; s. Earl and Essie (King) M.; m. Nancy Alexander, Apr. 19, 1952; children: Larry, Carol, Steve. BSEE, N.C. State U., 1960; MSEE, Duke U., 1962, PhD in Elec. Engring., 1965. Registered profl. engr., N.C. Mem. tech. staff Bell Tel. Labs., Durlington, NC, 1960-62, Rsch. Triangle Inst., Raleigh, NC, 1962-66, group leader rsch. sect., 1966-68; adj. asst. prof. elec. engring. N.C. State U., Raleigh, 1965-68, assoc. prof., 1968-72, prof., 1972—, head dept. elec. engring., 1974-78, dean of engring., 1978-89, interim chancellor, 1989-90, chancellor, 1990-98, chancellor emeritus, 1998—. Contbr. articles to profl. jours. With USN, 1952-56. Recipient Disting. Engring. Alumnus award Duke U., 1984, Outstanding Engring. Achievement award N.C. Soc. Engrs., 1990, Disting. Engring. Alumnus award N.C. State U., 1999. Fellow IEEE, Am. Soc. for Engring. Edn.; mem. NSPE (edn. adv. group), Raleigh C. of C. (bd. dirs.), Rotary Internat. (Paul Harris fellow Rotary Found. 1991), Phi Beta Kappa, Sigma Xi, Sigma Iota Rho, Phi Kappa Phi, Eta Kappa Nu, Tau Beta Pi, Sigma Beta Delta. E-mail: lmonteith@nc.rr.com.

**MONTELEONE, PATRICIA L.,** dean; MD, St. Louis U., 1961; MBA, MHA. V.p. med. affairs Cardinal Glennon Children's Hosp., 1986—93; prof. pediatrics St. Louis U. Sch. Medicine, 1967—, dean, 1994—. Office: St Louis U Sch Medicine 1402 S Grand Blvd Saint Louis MO 63104-1004

**MONTELONGO, MICHAEL,** federal agency administrator, military officer; b. NYC; m. Debra Tenison; 1 child, Amanda. BS in Gen. Engring., U.S. Mil. Acad.; MBA in Corp. Strategy and Fin., Harvard U., 1988; grad., Command and Gen. Staff Coll., 1992. Commd. 2d lt. U.S. Army, 1977, advanced through grades to lt. col.; with U.S. Mil. Acad., West Point, NY, 1991, asst. prof. social scis. dept., 1988; adviser, spl. asst. to comdr.-in chief U.S. So. Command, 1989; bn. exec. officer, bn. and brigade ops. officer U.S. Army, 1993, spl. asst. to U.S. Army chief of staff Washington, 1994; legis. asst. U.S. Senate, 1995; dir. BellSouth Small Bus. Svcs., 1996; sales exec. and cons. Cap Gemini Ernst & Young, 1998; asst. sec. Air Force fin. mgmt. and comptr. U.S. Dept. Def., Washington, 2001—. Trustee Unite El Paso, 1993; mem. Leadership El Paso Program, 1999. U.S. Army Advanced Civil Schooling fellow, 1986, Inter-Univ. Seminar on Armed Forces and Soc. fellow, 1990, Congl. Hispanic Caucus Inst. fellow, 1992, Army Congl. fellow, 1995. Mem.: Am. Soc. Mil. Comptrollers (pres. 2004), Nat. Soc. Hispanic MBAs (sec.), Assn. West Point Grads. (minority outreach com. 1999—, bd. dirs. Ga. Hispanic voter registration campaign 2000). Office: US Air Force Asst Sec Air Force Fin Mgt & Comptroller 1130 Air Force Pentagon Washington DC 20330-1130*

**MONTEMARANO, WILLIAM J.,** accountant; BS in Acctg., CUNY; MBA, Boston U. CPA NY. Acct. Coopers & Lybrand (now Pricewaterhouse-Coopers), NY; autdit mgr. Bristol-Myers Squibb Co., NY; with Comcast, Phila., 1993—, v.p. internal audit.

**MONTER, E. WILLIAM,** retired history professor; b. Cin., Sept. 22, 1936; s. Edward W. and Florence S. Monter; m. Barbara Heldt, June 18, 1963 (div. Aug. 2, 1976); children: Andrea, Gustav C. Heldt, Elizabeth A. Heldt(dec.); m. Rosellen E. Engstrom, July 23, 1978. BA, Wabash Coll., Crawfordsville, Ind., 1958; PhD, Princeton U., 1963. Prof. of history Northwestern U., Evanston, Ill., 1972—2002, prof. emeritus, 2002—. Sec., program on cultural exch. in Europe, 1400-1700 European Sci. Found., Strasbourg, 1997—2004; cons. 2000 papal jubilee Office of Papal Theologian, Vatican City, 1998; mem. editl. bd. Ency. of Witchcraft ABC-Clio Pub., Santa Barbara, Calif., 1999—; vis. prof. history U. Chgo., 2005—06. Author: Calvin's Geneva (also Japanese ed.), 1967, (book) Witchcraft in France and Switzerland, 1976, Ritual, Myth and Magic (also Italian ed.), 1983, Frontiers of Heresy (Spanish ed.), 1990, Judging the French Reformation, 1999. Fellow, NEH, 1974-75, 1992-93, 1999-2000, Camargo Found. (France), 1994, 2001; grantee, Am. Coun. of Learned Societies, 1969, 1972;, Social Sci. Rsch. Coun., 1966—67, Guggenheim fellow, 1994, Richardson fellow, Inst. for Advanced Study, 1987—88, CIES (Fulbright) fellow, CCHN, Spain, 1985—86. Mem.: Am. Hist. Assn. (com. on coms. 1984—87), Am. Soc. for Reformation Rsch. (pres. 1980), Soc. d'Histoire de Genève (corr.). Home: 829 Linden Ave Wilmette IL 60091 Personal E-mail: monter@northwestern.edu.

**MONTERO, SYLVIA,** pharmaceutical executive; b. PR, BA, Columbia U. Barnard Coll., 1972; MA, CUNY Queens Coll., 1976. HS tchr. Spanish and bilingual studies, NYC; prof. lit. Interamerican U., PR; with Pfizer Puerto Rico, 1978—82, Pfizer, Inc., NYC, 1982—, v.p. human resources Animal Health Grp., 1994, sr. v.p. human resources Global Rsch. and Devel., 2003, sr. v.p. human resources, 2005, head worldwide talent devel. and human resources, head human resources leadership team. Bd. mem. Grand St. Settlement. Named one of Top 50 Hispanic Bus. Women, Hispanic Bus. Mag., 2001, 80 Elite Women, 2001, 20 Corp. Elite in US, 2006; recipient Orgullo Latino award, 100 Hispanic Women orgn., 2005. Mem.: Hispanic Fedn. Office: Pfizer Inc 235 E 42nd St New York NY 10017*

**MONTES, LEOPOLDO FELICIANO,** dermatologist, educator; b. Buenos Aires, Nov. 22, 1929; came to U.S., 1955, naturalized, 1974; s. Leopoldo A. and Celia (Gaztambide) M.; m. Maria Mercedes Pfeiffer, Nov. 25, 1961; children: Carolina, Mercedes, Ana, Leopoldo, Teresa, William. MD, U. Buenos Aires, 1954; MS, U. Mich., 1959. Intern City of Buenos Aires Hosps., 1954-55; resident in dermatology Pa. Hosp., Phila., 1955-56; resident in dermatology, then instr. U. Mich. Med. Center, Ann Arbor, 1956-60; practice medicine specializing in dermatology Buenos Aires, 1960-63, 82—, Houston, 1963-66, Birmingham, Ala., 1966-81; dermatologist U. Ala., Eye Found.; asst. prof. Baylor U. Coll. Medicine, Houston, 1963—66; mem. faculty U. Ala. Med. Ctr. and Med. Coll. Ala., Birmingham, 1966—, prof. dermatology, 1969—81, assoc. prof. microbiology, 1968—91, prof. emeritus, 1982—; dermatologist Birmingham Dermatology Ctr., 1985—; clin. prof. dermatology U. South Ala., 2002—03; dermatologist Inst. Argentino de Diagnostico & Tratamiento, 1995—. Adj. prof. anatomy Coll. Medicine, U. South Ala., Mobile, 1981-89; adj. prof. large animal surgery and medicine Auburn U. Sch. Veterinary Medicine, 1977—; dir. Dermatology Rsch. Structural Rsch. Ctr., Mobile, 1990—, Vitiligo Unit, 1990; cons. Johnson & Johnson, Del-Ray Lab., Procter & Gamble, Upjohn Co., Delbay Co., Bayer, Warner, Lambert, Westwood Pharms., Tex. Pharm., Alcon, Owen Lab., Hoffman-La Roche, 1963—; CEO Westhoven Press. Author: Atlas of Skin Diseases of the Horse, 1983, Vitiligo-Nutritional Therapy, 1999, Scanning Electron Microscopy of Normal and Abnormal Skin, 1985, Vitiligo-Current Knowledge and Nutritional Therapy, 2006; founding editor Jour. Cutaneous Pathology, 1973-83.

Mem. internat. adv. bd. Nat. Vitiligo Found., 2002—. Recipient Rsch. Career Devel. award USPHS, 1965-70; grantee USPHS, NSF, Kresge Found., John A. Hartford Found., NASA. Fellow Am. Acad. Dermatology, Am. Acad. Microbiology, Royal Coll. Physicians and Surgeons Can. (life); mem. AAAS, Am. Soc. Microbiology, Soc. Investigative Dermatology, Histochem. Soc., Am. Soc. Cell Biology, Am. Fedn. Clin. Rsch., Electron Microscope Soc. Am., Internat. Soc. Tropical Dermatology (Asst. sec. gen. 1969-74), Am. Dermatol. Assn., Am. Soc. Dermatopathology, Jockey Club Argentina (life), Sigma Xi. Achievements include patents in field. Home: Suipacha 1308 1011 Buenos Aires Argentina Office: Paraguay 2302 1121 Buenos Aires Argentina also: Structural Rsch Ctr 120 Novatan Rd Mobile AL 36608 Fax: 5411.4314.4328. Office Phone: 011-5411-4962-4684. E-mail: leopoldo_montes@hotmail.com. *While taking care of a patient I always considered it indispensable to study and research as much as I could about the disease I was treating, for I felt I was perhaps the only one in a position to help, to put myself-as Lord Lister said- in the patient's place.*

**MONTGOMERY, ANN D.,** federal judge, educator; b. Litchfield, Minn., May 9, 1949; m. Theodore Smetak; 2 children; 1 stepchild. BS, U. Kans., 1971; JD, U. Minn., 1974. Bar: Minn. 1974, US Dist. Ct. Minn., US Ct. Appeals (8th cir.), US Supreme Ct. Law clk. DC Ct. Appeals, Washington, 1974-75; asst. US atty. Dist. Minn., Mpls., 1976-83; mcpl. judge Hennepin County, 1983-85; judge Hennepin County Dist. Ct., 1985-94, US Magistrate Ct., 1994-96; federal judge US Dist. Ct., Mpls., 1996—. Adj. prof. U. Minn. Law Sch., Mpls., 1988—; steering com. mem., dir. criminal divsn. Minn. Jud. Coll., 1990-94. Recipient Trial Judge of Yr. award Am. Bd. Trial Advocates, 1996. Mem. FBA, Minn. Dist. Judges Assn., Minn. Bar Assn., Minn. Women Lawyers (Myra Bradwell award 2000), Hennepin County Bar Assn. (Professionalism award 1993), Eighth Cir. Dist. Judges Assn. (pres. 2003-04). Office: US Dist Ct 300 S 4th St Minneapolis MN 55415-1320 Fax: 612-664-5097. E-mail: admontgomery@mnd.uscourts.gov.

**MONTGOMERY, ANNA FRANCES,** elementary school educator; b. Spokane, Wash., Nov. 5, 1945; d. Carl Jacob and Edna Frances (Evans) Kuipers; m. William Lee Montgomery Jr., Oct. 7, 1989. AA, Mid. Ga. Coll., 1965; BS Elem. Edn., Woman's Coll. Ga., 1966; MEd, Ga. Coll., 1969, specialist Edn., 1973; studied Brit. ednl. sys., London, 1978. Cert. elem. tchr., Ga. Classroom tchr. Muscogee County Sch. Dist., Columbus, Ga., 1966—2002, tchr. reading Title 1 tutorial program, 1975, instr. staff devel. program, 1977—80; lead tchr. social sci. Wesley Heights Elem. Sch., Columbus, 1992—2002, chmn. mgmt. team, 1997—98; ret., 2002. Instr. tennis and athletics Camp Tegawitha, Tobyhanna, Pa., 1970; judge Columbus Regional Social Sci. Fair, 1977, 93-96; presenter in field Editor: Muscogee County School District's Handbook for Beginning Teachers, 1979 Vol. Med. Ctr. Aux., Columbus, 1975-79; pres. pastor's Bible study class St. Luke United Meth. Ch., 1993-94, 96-98, mem. Sarah Cir. 211, 1969-71, 78-80, co-chmn., 1974-76, 1996-76, 78; mem. Bessie Howard Ward Handbells Choir. Recipient Valley Forge Tchrs. medal Freedoms Found. at Valley Forge, 1975, Outstanding Tchr. of Yr. award Wesley Hts. Elem. Sch., 1975, Muscogee County Sch. Dist., 1979; named Very Important Lady award Girl Scouts U.S., Columbus, 1976, Outstanding Young Woman Am., 1982 Mem. AAUW (devel. chmn. Ga. state centennial fellowship com. Columbus br. 1973-76), Ga. PTA (hon. life), Profl. Assn. Ga. Educators (life, bldg. rep. Muscogee County chpt. 1983-2002, sec. 1992-94, treas. 1994-98, pres.-elect 1998-2000, Muscogee County's sys. rep. to the state 2000-02, social chmn. 2002-03), Nat. Coun. Social Studies (hostess and registration coms. ann. meeting 1975), Ga. Coun. Social Studies, Ga. Sci. Tchrs. Assn., Atlanta Alumni Club, Valley Area Sci. Tchrs. (corr. sec. 1996-98), Ga. Coll. Alumni Assn., Mid. Ga. Coll. Alumni Assn., Order of Amaranth (charity 1991-93, 95, truth 1994, assoc. conductress 1996, conductress 1997, assoc. matron 1998, royal matron 1999), Scottish Rite Ladies Aux., Ga. Ret. Educators Assn., Muscogee Ret. Educators Assn., Alpha Delta Kappa (Rho chpt., sec. 1975-76, pres.-elect 1976-78, pres. 1978-80, chaplain, 1996-98, 2006—, chmn. ways and means com. 2005—), Delta Kappa Gamma (Beta Xi chpt., pres. 1980-82, chmn. pubs. and publicity 1976-78, chmn. profl. affairs 1978-80, chair nominations com. 1980-82, chmn. world fellowship and fund raising 1984-86, 96-2004, chmn. fin. 1990-92, chmn. membership 1994-96, 2000-04), Order Internat. Fellowship in Edn. (life), Wesley Heights Elem. Sch. PTA (treas. 1983-86), Phi Delta Kappa, Phi Theta Kappa (life) Avocations: reading, gardening, travel, fishing, clarinet. Home: 5134 Stone Gate Dr Columbus GA 31909-5573

**MONTGOMERY, BETTY DEE,** state auditor, former state attorney general, former state legislator; b. Apr. 3, 1948; BA, Bowling Green State U.; JD, Coll. Law U. Toledo, 1976. Former criminal clk. Lucas County Common Pleas Ct.; former asst. pros. atty. Wood County, Ohio, 1977—78, former pros. atty. Ohio, 1980—88, City of Perrysburg, Ohio, 1978—81; former mem. Ohio Senate, 1988—95; former atty. gen. State of Ohio, Columbus, 1994—2002, auditor, 2002—. Former mem. Econ. Devel. Tech. & Aerospace, Agr. & Ways & Means Com.; former vice-chmn. Judiciary Com. Mem. bd. dirs. Ohio Sch. Bd. Atty. Assn. Recipient Women of Achievement award, Toledo Women in Comms., 1984, Govt. Leaders Against Drunk Drivers, MADD, 1990, Senator of the Year, Ohio Hospice Assn., 1991, Disting. Svc. award, Ohio State Bar Assn., 1992, Ohio Women Hall of Fame award, 1996, Public Svc. award, Ohio Assn. of Big Brothers/Big Sisters, 1999, Advocacy award, Ohio Soc. Healthcare Consumer Advocacy, 1999, Child Adv. of the Year, Ohio Ct. Appointed Spl. Advs./Guardian Ad Litem Assn., 1999, Toledo YWCA Milestones award, Women in Govt., 2001, Presdl. award for Pro Bono Svc., The Ohio Legal Assistance Found., 2002, ABA Pro Bono award, to the Office of the Atty. Gen., 2002, Disting. Alumnus award, Bowling Green State Univ., 2003. Mem.: Ohio Prosecuting Atty. Assn. (mem. 1984), Legis. Com., Internat. Prosecutors Assn., Wood County Bar Assn., Alternative Edn. Adv. Com. (former chmn.), Wood County Child Abuse & Neglect Adv. Bd. (former vice-chmn., chmn.), Sexual Abuse Prevention Project, Wood County Sch. (mem. 1981 ), Bowling Green C. of C. Republican. Office: Auditor of State 88 E Broad St 5th Fl Columbus OH 43215

**MONTGOMERY, BRIAN D.,** commissioner; BS, U. Houston, 1986. Comm. dir. Tex. Dept. Housing & Cmty. Affairs, & Tex. Dept. Econ. Develop., Austin, 1995—99; dir. of advance Bush Cheney 2000 Presdl. Campaign; chief dep., dir. spl. events & ops. 2001 Presdl. Inaugural Com.; dep. asst. to the Pres., dir. of advance White House, 2001—03, dep. asst. to the Pres. and a cabinet sec. Washington, 2003—05; asst. sec. for housing, fed. housing commr. US Dept. HUD, Washington, 2005—. Office: Robert C Weaver Federal Bldg Stop S Room 9100 451 Seventh St SW Washington DC 20410 Office Phone: 202-708-2601. Office Fax: 202-708-2580.

**MONTGOMERY, C. MICHAEL,** lawyer; b. Radford, Va., Jan. 7, 1947; s. Carl Ford and Margaret Painter Montgomery; children: Michael A., Jennifer M. McLees, Alexander S., Catherine R. BA, U. Va., Charlottesville, 1969; JD, U. Va., 1972. Bar: Va. 1972, Colo. 1984, Wyo. 1991. Atty./ptnr. Seawell McCoy Winston & Dalton, Norfolk, Va., 1972—84; ptnr., shareholder Montgomery, Green & Jarvis, Denver, 1984—96; ptnr. Montgomery Kolodny, 1996—. Mem.: ABA, Assn. Def. Trial Attys., Am. Bd. Trial Advocates, Colo. Def. Lawyers Assn (pres. 1989—90). Avocations: golf, skiing, guitar, banjo. Office: Montgomery Kolodny et al 475 17th St #1600 Denver CO 80202

**MONTGOMERY, CHARLES BARRY,** lawyer; b. Latrobe, Pa., Apr. 17, 1937; BA cum laude, Muskingum Coll., 1959; JD, U. Mich., 1962. Bar: Ill. 1962, U.S. Dist. Ct. (no. dist.) Ill. 1982. U.S. Supreme Ct. 1971. Atty. Jacobs & McKenna, 1962-67; founder, ptnr. Jacobs, Williams and Montgomery, Ltd., 1967-85; sr. ptnr., comml. and class action litig. and profl. liability litig. Williams Montgomery & John Ltd., Chgo., 1985—. Instr. advocacy inst. U. Mich., Ann Arbor, 1985, advanced program Nat. Inst. Trial Advocacy 1986, trial acad. Internat. Assn. Def. Counsel, 1987, law inst. program Def. Rsch. Inst.; pub. spkr. litigation. Contbr. articles to profl. jours. Fellow Internat. Acad. Trial Lawyers, Internat. Soc. Barristers; mem. ABA (vice-chair medicine and law com. 1989-90), Am. Bd. Trial Advs., Am. Arbitration Assn., Chgo. Bar Assn., Def. Rsch. Inst., Ill. Assn. Def. Trial Counsel, Ill. Assn.

Hosp. Attys., Ill. State Bar Assn., Internat. Assn. Def. Counsel, Soc. Trial Lawyers, Legal Club of Chgo., Trial Lawyers Club of Chgo. Office: Williams Montgomery & John Ltd Ste 2100 20 N Wacker Dr Chicago IL 60606-3094 Office Phone: 312-443-3200. Office Fax: 312-630-8542. Business E-Mail: cbm@willmont.com.

**MONTGOMERY, CHARLES HARVEY,** lawyer; b. Spartanburg, S.C., Jan. 28, 1949; s. Dan Hugh and Ann Louise (Gasque) M.; m. Renée Jean Gubernot, Mar. 27, 1971; children: Charles Scott, Marie Renée. BA, Duke U., 1971; JD, Vanderbilt U., 1974. Bar: N.C. 1974, U.S. Dist. Ct. (ea. dist.) N.C. 1974, U.S. Supreme Ct. 1979, U.S. Dist. Ct. (mid. dist.) N.C. 1991; cert. family law specialist, N.C., 1995. Assoc. Jordan Morris & Hoke, Raleigh, NC, 1974-75; atty. Wake County Legal Svcs., Raleigh, 1975-76; pvt. practice, Raleigh, 1977; ptnr. Montgomery & Montgomery, Cary, NC, 1978-79, Sanford Adams McCullough & Beard, Raleigh, 1979-86, Adams McCullough & Beard, Raleigh, 1986-88, Toms Reagan & Montgomery, Cary, 1989-92, Toms & Montgomery, Cary, 1992-93; pvt. practice, Cary, 1993—. Bd. dirs. Br. Bank and Trust, Cary; pres. Family Law Mediation, Inc. Councilman Town of Cary, 1977-81, 83-87; vice-chmn. Wake County Dem. party, Raleigh, 1991-92; commr. Wake County, Raleigh, 1992; bd. dirs. East Cen. Cmty. Legal Svcs., Inc., 1997-2003, State Capitol Found., 1994—. Mem.: ABA, Cary Bar Assn. (organizer 1993—), N.C. Acad. Trial Lawyers (chair family law sect. 1996—98), Wake County Bar Assn. (bd. dirs. 1999—2001), N.C. Bar Assn. (chmn. pub. info. com. 1994—96, dir. family law coun. 1994—97, 2006—). Methodist. Avocation: sailing. Office: PO Box 1325 Cary NC 27512-1325 also: 590 New Waverly Pl Ste 110 Cary NC 27512-1325 Office Phone: 919-816-9002. Business E-Mail: charles@montylaw.com.

**MONTGOMERY, CHARLES HOWARD,** retired bank executive; b. Bloomington, Ill., Mar. 23, 1930; s. Dewey H. and Madeline (Wonderlin) M.; m. Diane Dickerson Cohen, Aug. 30, 1978 (dec. Oct. 1996); children: Alison, Douglas; m. Katharine Yang, Oct. 4, 1997. AB, Ill. Wesleyan U., 1951; MS, U. Ill., 1960. CPA, Ill. Auditor Lybrand Ross Bros. & Montgomery, Rockford, Ill., 1955-59; with Abbott Labs., North Chicago, Ill., 1959-67, controller, 1965-67; v.p. finance Anchor Coupling Co., Libertyville, 1968-69; v.p., comptroller First Nat. Bank Chgo., 1969-73, sr. v.p., 1973-75, exec. v.p., 1976-88, comptroller, 1973-88, First Chgo. Corp.; ret. Past chmn. Inter-Assn. Com. Bank Acctg. Served with AUS, 1952-53. Mem. Fin. Execs. Inst., AICPA, Ill. Soc. CPAs, Tau Kappa Epsilon, Phi Kappa Phi, Univ. Club (Chgo.) Home: 6321 N Avers Ave Chicago IL 60659-1001 also: 824 Georgia St Key West FL 33040 Personal E-mail: chmonty@att.net.

**MONTGOMERY, CHRISTINA LYNN,** music educator; b. Oil City, Pa., July 30, 1951; d. Arthur Robert Montgomery and Joanne Guy (Heffernan) Wilson; children: Pamela Fellner, Michelle Kunkel. BSE in Music Edn., Clarion U., 1987; M in Secondary Guidance, Edinboro U., 1994. Cert. in music edn. Pa., 1993. Music educator Warren County Sch. Dist., Pa., 1988—. Named Tchr. of Yr., Philomel Club, 1993. Mem.: Warren County Educators Assn., Pa. Music Educators Assn. (exec. bd., CI/mid. sch. 2000—), Music Educators Nat. Conf. Avocations: reading, fishing, cooking, carpentry. Home: RD 1 Box 219H Youngsville PA 16371 Office: Youngsville Mid/Sr High Sch 227 College St Youngsville PA 16371

**MONTGOMERY, CLEOTHUS,** minister; b. Henderson, Tex., Dec. 6, 1926; s. Lewis and Amanda (Waters) M.; m. Emma Agusta Tinch (dec. Aug. 23, 1987); children: Michael Dennis, Debra Marie, Pamela Key, Diane Renea, Anthony Cleothus (dec.). BS in Drafting, Calif. Coll., 1951; B in Theology, Union Bapt. Theol. Sem., 1962; M in Theology, Inter Bapt. Theol. Sem., 1965, DD, 1973; D in Sacred Theol. (hon.), Mt. Hope Bible Coll., 1973; M in Ministry, Trinity Theol. Sem., 1990, D in Ministry, 1993. Cert. christian counselor, Tex. Minister Northside Missionary Bapt. Ch., Houston, 1962—. Counselor Chemical Dependency, Houston, 1989-97, Internat. Christian Isnt., 1990-97; invited pastor by Campus for Christ to Israel, 1987, Africa, 1990, Russia, 1995-97. Pres. World Christian Tng. Ctr., Houston, 1985-90, Houston Minister Christian Fellowship, 1992-97; chmn. Minister Network Life Gift, Houston, 1988-90, Ministers Against Crime, Houston, 1989-97; treas. Life Investment for Tng., Houston, 1990-97; v.p. Ministerial Adv. to Mayor, Houston, 1995-97; trustee bd. of regency, adv. bd. Coll. of Biblical Studies. With U.S. Army, 1945-46. Mem. NAACP, Am. Assn. Christian Counselors (chemical dependency counselor 1993-97). Democrat. Baptist. Avocations: reading, devotional writings, bowling, travel, jogging. Home: 1407 Laurentide St Houston TX 77029-3411 Office: Northside Missionary Bapt Ch 3202 Bennington St Houston TX 77093-9222

**MONTGOMERY, CLIFF WILSON,** journalist, writer, researcher; b. Cumberland, Md., Aug. 13, 1965; s. Clifford Ray and Elizabeth Ann Montgomery. European Lit. Hous.] U. Ed. by pvt. tutor, Charlotte, NC, 1983—91, Am. Lit. (hon.), 1994—98. East coast polit. corr. 3 A.M. Mag., Kirkland, Wash., 2000—. Media cons. Sierra Club, Charlotte, NC, 1998. *One of the first journalists to debunk the principal rationale behind the second Iraq War, showing the country no longer possessed stores of chemical and biological weapons or their weapon agents, and was not an immediate nuclear threat. Believes it is the job of any journalist to, "tell truth to power," however unpopular the truth.* Freelance journalist Washington Spectator, In These Times, Working for Change, Alternet and Political Affairs. Active Nat. Trust for Hist. Preservation, 1999—, Archaeol. Inst. Am., 1999—2000; activist Amnesty Internat., 1992—96; active Pub. Concern Found., 1994—. Independent. Avocations: history, travel, motorcycling. Personal E-mail: clifmn@aol.com.

**MONTGOMERY, CONNIE ROGER,** writer; b. Radford, Va., Apr. 11, 1945; s. Hobart Leamon and Gladiese Buckner Montgomery; m. Susie Fisher Montgomery, Dec. 31, 1966; children: Darrell, Rhonda, Mark, Beth. AAS in Instrumentation, New River Cmty. Coll., 1978, AAS in Indsl. Elec., 1979. Procedure writer, instrumentation Duke Power, Charlotte, NC, 1996—2000, writer Seneca, SC, 1998—2001, Bridgman, Mich., 2002, maintenance procedure writer Seneca, SC, 2003—. E-5 U.S. Army, 1965—68, Vietnam. Avocations: writing, photography, fishing. Home: PO Box 852 Clover SC 29710 E-mail: info@rogermontgomerypoems.com.

**MONTGOMERY, DAVID BRUCE,** marketing educator; b. Fargo, ND, Apr. 30, 1938; s. David William and Iva Bernice (Trask) Montgomery; m. Toby Marie Franks, June 11, 1960; children: David Richard, Scott Bradford, Pamela Marie. BSEE, Stanford U., 1960, MBA, 1962, MS in Stats., 1964, PhD in Mgmt. Sci., 1966; D honoris causa, Limburgs U. Centrum, Belgium, 1998. Asst. prof. mgmt. MIT, 1966-69, assoc. prof., 1969-70; assoc. prof. mktg. and mgmt. sci. Stanford U., 1970-73, prof., 1973-78, Robert A. Magowan prof. mktg., 1978-92, Sebastian S. Kregge prof. mktg. strategy, 1992-99, prof. emeritus, 1999—; dean Sch. Bus. Singapore Mgmt. U., 2003—05. Prin. The MAC Group Inc., 1969-91; mem. adv. bd. LEK Partnership, London; mem. sci. adv. bd. Univ. Connection, Bonn, Germany; acad. trustee Mktg. Sci. Inst., 1994-2000, exec. dirs. 1995-97. Author: (with Glen L. Urban) Management Science in Marketing, 1969, (with Massy and Morrison) Stochastic Models of Buying Behavior, 1970, (with Day et al) Planning: Cases in Computer and Model Assisted Marketing, 1973, (with others) Consumer Behavior: Theoretical Sources, 1973, (with G. J. Eskin) Data Analysis, 1975; editor 5 books; cons. editor Jour. Internat. Mktg., 2000-03; mem. editl. bd. Mgmt. Sci., Jour. Mktg., Jour. Mktg. Rsch., Mktg. Sci., Jour. acad. of Mktg. Sci., Jour. Internat. Mktg.; contbr. more than 100 articles and tech. reports to sci. and profl. jours. Trustee Family Service Assn. of Mid Peninsula, 1972-73. Recipient citation for outstanding contbns. to use of computers in mgmt. edn. Hewlett Packard, 1977, Best Paper award Strategic Mgmt. Soc., 1996. Mem.: Am. Mktg. Assn. (Mahajan award 2002, Contribution to Mktg. Strategy award 2002), Inst. Mgmt. Sci., Tau Beta Pi. Presbyterian. Home: 960 Wing Pl Stanford CA 94305-1028 Office: Stanford U Grad Sch Bus Stanford CA 94305 Business E-Mail: montgomery_david@gsb.stanford.edu.

**MONTGOMERY, DAVID CAMPBELL,** retired physics professor; b. Milan, Mo., Mar. 5, 1936; s. Merrill Edward and Ruth E. (Campbell) Montgomery; m. Shirley Arlene Imig, July 20, 1957; children: Kathleen Montgomery Sutton, Elizabeth. Student, U. Mo., 1953-55; BS, U. Wis., 1956; MA, Princeton U., 1958, PhD, 1959; D honoris causa (hon.), Eindhoven U. Tech., The Netherlands, 1996. Research assoc. Princeton U., 1959-60; instr. U. Wis., 1961-62; asst. prof. U. Md., 1962-65; assoc. prof. U. Iowa, Iowa City, 1965-70, prof., 1970-77; prof. physics Coll. William and Mary, Williamsburg, Va., 1977-84; prof. Dartmouth Coll., Hanover, NH, 1984—2004, rsch. prof., prof. emeritus, 2004—. Vis. prof., rschr. U. Colo., 1966, U. Alaska, 1968, U. Calif., Berkeley, 1969—70, Bell Labs., 1971; lectr. Internat. Summer Sch. Theoretical Physics, Les Houches, France, 1972, U. Wis., Madison, 1973, vis. prof., rschr., 89; vis. prof. Hunter Campus CUNY, 1973—74, U. Nagoya, Japan, 1983, Columbia U., NYC, 1985, Tech. U., Eindhoven, Netherlands, 1992; vis. scientist Nat. Ctr. Atmospheric Rsch., Boulder, Colo., 1975, Boulder, 76, Boulder, 79, Boulder, 87, Boulder, 2002, Boulder, 04, Boulder, 05, Boulder, 06, Riso Nat. Lab., Roskilde, Denmark, 2001; cons. NASA Hdqs., Washington, 1977—82, JET Joint Undertaking, Culham, England, 1991; vis. rsch. prof. U. Md., 1977—84; mem. vis. staff Los Alamos Sci. Lab., 1977, 78, 79, 80, 81, 86, 91, 92, 94, cons., collaborator, vis. staff; former cons. Oak Ridge Nat. Lab., NASA; vis. rschr. Los Alamos Nat. Lab., 1987—88, cons., 1998—2000; J. M. Burgers prof. Eindhoven Tech. U., Netherlands, 1995—96, Netherlands, 1997, Netherlands, 98, Netherlands, 2000, Netherlands, 01, U. Md., 1997; vis. rschr. Courant Inst. NYU, 1997. Former assoc. editor: Physics of Fluids, Internat. Jour. Engring. Sci.; contbr. articles to profl. publs. and monographs. Fellow: Am. Phys. Soc.; mem.: NY Acad. Scis., Sigma Xi, Phi Beta Kappa, Phi Mu Alpha, Pi Mu Epsilon. Achievements include introduction of modern fluid turbulence methods into space and controlled fusion theory; development of maximum entropy, or "most probable" states, method of describing coherent structures achieved as a product of turbulent relaxation. Office: Dartmouth College Physics Dept Hanover NH 03755 Office Phone: 603-646-3219. Business E-Mail: david.c.montgomery@dartmouth.edu.

**MONTGOMERY, DENISE KAREN,** nurse; b. N.Y.C., Dec. 23, 1951; d. Thomas Cornell and Dorothy Marie (Castine) Simons; m. Timothy Bruce Montgomery, July 19, 1974 (div. Feb. 1981); m. Joseph Samuel Montgomery, Aug. 20, 1983. A in Nursing, San Jacinto Coll., 1971. RN, Tex. Charge nurse Aarons Womens Clinic, Houston, 1977; rsch. asst. dept. ob-gyn. Baylor Coll. Medicine, Houston, 1977-81, nursing supr., 1979-81, program coord. population control program, 1979-81; nurse Dr. Eric J. Haufrect, Houston, 1982-83; office mgr., supr. Dr. Samuel Law, Houston, 1983-84, Dr. J.S. Montgomery III, 1987—. Contbr. articles to profl. jours. Recipient Disting. Pub. Svc. award Am. Heart Assn., 1976; numerous rsch. grants. Mem. Nat. Assn. Coll. Ob-Gyn. Republican. Christian. Home: 8202 N Tahoe Dr Houston TX 77040-1256 Office Phone: 281-955-5330. E-mail: denmnt@houston.rr.com, denmnt@hotmail.com.

**MONTGOMERY, DILLARD BREWSTER,** musician, educator; b. Memphis, Jan. 1, 1936; s. Mary Joyce Montgomery; m. Joyce Helena Beale, Dec. 9, 1965; 1 child, Lisa Jenean. BS, Tenn. State U., 1962, MA, 1968. Profl. musician Nashville Assn. Musicians, 1958—; band dir., keyboardist The New Imperials, Nashville, 1962—; tchr. Met. Nashville Schs., 1962-94, ret., 1994; asst. prin. W.A. Bass Middle Sch., 1984-93, prin., 1993-94. Choir dir. John Wesley United Meth. Ch., Nashville, 1958—, Dixon United Meth. Ch., 1970-71, Braden United Meth. Ch., 1985-2002; profl. model Terrance Hurd Agy., 1999—. Served with USAF, 1955-58. Mem. NEA, Tenn. Edn. Assn., Met. Nashville Edn. Assn., Nat. Musicians Union, Tenn. State U. Alumni Assn. (life), Alpha Phi Alpha (life). Democrat. Methodist. Avocations: computers, collecting old music, collecting old movies, recording and transferring old albums and tapes to CD, recording old movies to video and DVD. Home: 638 W Nocturne Dr Nashville TN 37207 Office Phone: 615-650-3232. E-mail: dmontgo1@bellsouth.net.

**MONTGOMERY, HENRY IRVING,** financial planner; b. Dec. 18, 1924; s. Harry Biggs and Martha Grace (Wilkinson) M.; m. Barbara Louise Hook, Aug. 14, 1948; children: Priscilla Ann, Barbara Ruth, Michael Henry, Kelly Anne, Andrew Stuart. Student, U. Iowa, 1942-43, 47-48; BBA, Tulane U., 1952; postgrad., U. Minn., 1976. CFP, Colo. Field agt. OSS, SSU, CIG, CIA, Cen. Europe, 1945-47; pres. Nehi Bottling Co., Decorah, Iowa, 1952-64; prin. Montgomery Assocs., Mktg. Cons., Trieste, Italy and Iowa, 1965-72; cons. Planners Fin. Svcs., Inc., Mpls., 1972-95, chmn., 1992—2005. Prin. Montgomery Investment Mgmt., 1992—. Author: Race Toward Berlin, 1945. With U.S. Army, 1943-46, ETO. Decorated Bronze Star; recipient P. Kemp Fain Profl. Svc. award, 1998. Mem. DAV, VFW, Inst. CFPs (bd. dirs. 1977-82, pres. 1980-81, chmn. 1981-82, CFP of Yr. 1984, chmn. profl. products stds. bd. 1984-88), Nat. Assn. Securities Dealers (dist. 8 com. 1988-91, vice-chmn. 1990), Internat. Assn. Fin. Planning (internat. dir. 1976-81, govrl. rels. com. 1991-2005, Minn. chpt. Henry and Andrew Montgomery scholarship co-named in his honor), Investment Co. Inst. (investment adviser com. 1982—), Mpls. Estate Planning Coun., Met. Tax Planning Group (pres. 1984-87), Twin City Fin. Planners (pres. 1976-78), Twin Cities Soc. CFPs, Am. Legion, Elks, DAV, Beta Gamma Sigma. Avocation: languages (Italian, German). Office: Planners Fin Svcs Inc 7710 Computer Ave Ste 100 Minneapolis MN 55435-5417 Office Phone: 952-835-3130.

**MONTGOMERY, HUBERT THERON, JR.,** physician, health care administrator; b. Birmingham, Ala., July 29, 1935; s. Hubert Theron and Edna M. (Morrison) M.; m. Sarah Diane Bryans, Sept. 19, 1969; children: Alfred Peter, Melanie Anne, Laurel Elaine, Amy Diane. AB, Samford So. Coll., 1957; MD, Tulane U., 1961. Diplomate Am. Bd. Surgery, Am. Bd. Plastic Surgery. Rotating intern St. Vincent Hosp., Birmingham, 1961-62; resident surgery Lloyd Noland Hosp., Fairfield, Ala., 1964-68; pvt. practice, Montgomery, Ala., 1968-73, 75—; resident plastic surgery U. Tenn., Memphis, 1974-75; pres., CEO Med One Inc., Montgomery, 1983—96; exec. v.p., chief exec. officer Central Ala. Preferred Provider, Inc., Montgomery, 1984-96; sec.-treas. Montgomery Surg. Ctr., Inc., 1984-85; pres. Bodegas de Mendoza, Inc., 2001—; pres., CEO Crux Imports, Inc., 2005—. Sect. chief plastic surgery Bapt. Med. Ctr., Montgomery, 1976-78, St. Margaret's Hosp., Montgomery, 1987-89; sec.-treas. Ala. Soc. Plastic Surgeons, 1990-92; pres. 1994-96; mem. Hitchcock Award Com., Montgomery, 1985. Maj. U.S. Army, 1963-69. Named New Bus. of Yr., Ala. Bus. Rev., Montgomery, 1985. Fellow: ACS; mem.: Soc. Latin Am. Plastic Surgeons (treas. 1997—98, v.p. 1999—2001, pres. 2002—04), Am. Cancer Soc. (dir. Montgomery chpt. 2002—), Newcomen Soc. N.Am., Wynn Lakes Country Club, Montgomery Country Club, Capitol City Kiwanis (dir. 1987—88). Baptist.

**MONTGOMERY, JAMES FISCHER,** savings and loan association executive; b. Topeka, Nov. 30, 1934; s. James Maurice and Frieda Ellen (Fischer) M.; m. Diane Dealey; children: Michael James, Jeffrey Allen, Andrew Steven, John Gregory. BA in Acctg., UCLA, 1957. With Price, Waterhouse & Co., C.P.A.'s, LA, 1957-60; controller Conejo Valley Devel. Co., Thousand Oaks, Calif., 1960; asst. to pres. Gt. Western Fin. Corp., Beverly Hills, Calif., 1960-64; fin. v.p., treas United Fin. Corp., LA, 1964—69, exec. v.p., 1971—74, pres., 1974—75; chmn., CEO Great Western Financial Corp., Chatsworth, Calif., 1975-96, chmn. bd. dirs., 1996—97; founder, CEO Frontier Bank, Park City, Utah, 1998—2002, chmn., 1998—. Pres. Citizens Savs. & Loan Assn., Los Angeles, 1970-75. Served with AUS, 1958-60. Office: Frontier Bank 1245 Deer Valley Dr PO Box 981180 Park City UT 84098-1180

**MONTGOMERY, JOEL ROBERT,** communications executive, consultant; b. Lexington, Sept. 9, 1946; s. Joseph Gwinn and Lucille O'Hair Montgomery. AA, U. Fla., 1966; BA, Fla. State U., 1968; MEd, EdD, Fla. Internat. U., 1992. Cert. group leader educator MATC, 1978, orgnl. develop. MATC, 1979. Mgmt. cons. Coopers & Lybrand (now Price Waterhouse Coopers), L.A., 1979—80; regional cons. interaction mgmt. Develop. Dimensions Internat., L.A., 1981—82; pres., cons. coach Resources Inst., Hollywood, Fla., 1982—93; mgr. learning arch. Andersen Cons. (now Accenture), St. Charles, Ill., 1993—98; sr. lead bus. cons. orgnl. change Origin Tech. in Bus. (now

Atos-Origin), Dallas, 1999—2000; CEO, performance coach MetaLearning .com, LLC, Geneva, Ill., 2000—02; pres. Meta Corp., 2001—; bilingual educator East Aurora H.S., Aurora, Ill., 2004—05; author, pub., on-line educator, cons. Joelmonty.net, Geneva, 2005—. With Internat. Inst. Develop. of Human Resources, Bogota, Colombia, 1982; adj. instr. Fla. Internat. U., Miami, 1989—90; performance coach, spkr., cons. Practical Bus. Assessments, Geneva, 2001—02; rep. Primerica Fin. Svcs., Carol Stream, Ill., 2002—; bilingual educator Larkin HS, Elgin, Ill., 2003, Meadowdale Elem. Sch., Carpentersville, Ill., 2003—04, East Aurora (Ill.) H.S., 2004—05; pub., on-line educator, cons. Joelmonty.net, Geneva, 2005—. Author: (book) Catalog of Workshop-Seminar Materials for The Resources Institute and INDER-HU, 1983, Human Relations Workbook--The Human Side of Teaching, 1990, (Book) The Development, Application and Implications of a Strategy for Reflective Learning from Experience, 1992; contbr. articles to profl. jours. Mem. ARC, Washington, 1964—, chmn. bd. dirs. Fox River chpt. St. Charles, 1993—96, bd. dirs. Broward County chpt. Ft. Lauderdale, 1990—92. Capt. U.S Army, 1969—79. Recipient Joint Svc. Commendation medal, U.S. Army, 1975. Mem.: Ednl. Soc. Resource Mgmt., Am. Soc. Tng. & Develop., Orgnl. Develop. Network, Internat. Found. Action Learning (leadership team U.S. chpt. 1995—2002), Acad. Human Resources Develop. (bd. dirs. 1997—99). Avocations: swimming, travel. Office: 717 Anderson Blvd Geneva IL 60134-1246 Office Phone: 630-208-0988. Personal E-mail: joelmonty@usa.net.

**MONTGOMERY, JOHN A.,** physicist; b. Memphis, Jan. 2, 1944; s. John and Mary Emma (Pittman) Montgomery; m. Cathi Montgomery. B in Physics, North Tex. State U., 1967, M in Physics, 1969; PhD, Catholic U. Am., 1982. Rsch. physicist advanced techniques br. electronic warfare divsn. Naval Rsch. Lab., 1968—80, head off-board countermeasures br., 1980—85, superintendent Tactical Electronic Warfare Divsn. (TEWD), 1985—2002, dir. rsch, 2002—. U.S. nat. leader Tech. Cooperation Program Multinat. Group on Electronic Warfare, 1987—. Mem.: Sr. Exec. Svc. (Presdl. Rank Meritorious Exec. award 1988, Presdl. Rank. Disting. Exec. award 1991, Presdl. Rank Meritorious. Exec. award 1999, Presdl. Rank. Disting. Exec. award 2002), Sigma Xi. Achievements include development of new electronic warfare technologies; more than 80 systems approved for operational use by the Navy and other services. Office: Naval Rsch Lab 4555 Overlook Ave SW Washington DC 20375

**MONTGOMERY, JOHN HAROLD,** psychiatrist; s. Joseph and Jane Montgomery; m. Heather Montgomery, July 17, 1999; children: Abigail, Blake, Zachary. DO, Nova Southeastern U., 1998. Diplomate Psychiatry and Forensic Psychiatry, Am. Bd. Psychiatry and Neurology. Forensic psychiatrist Miss. State Hosp., Whitfield, 2003—, svc. chief female line, 2004—. Asst. clin. prof. dept. psychiatry U. Miss. Med. Ctr., Jackson, 2003—. Contbr. articles to profl. jours. Recipient Young Investigator award, Am. Acad. of Psychiatry and the Law, 2003, Rosner award, Am. Acad. Forensic Scis., 2004; Steinberg Fellowship in Psychiatry and the Law, U. Rochester Sch. Medicine and Dentistry, 2002—03. Office: MS State Hospital Whitfield MS 39193 Office Phone: 601-351-8000. Personal E-mail: jmontgo651@yahoo.com. Business E-Mail: montgjo@msh.state.ms.us.

**MONTGOMERY, JOHN RICHARD,** pediatrician, educator; b. Burnsville, Miss., Oct. 24, 1934; s. Guy Austin and Harriet Pauline (Owens) M.; m. Dottye Ann Newell, June 26, 1965; children: John Newell, Michelle Elizabeth. BS, U. Ala., 1955, MD, 1958. Cert. Am. Bd. Pediat. Intern U. Miss., Jackson, 1958-59, resident in pediat., 1959-60, Baylor Coll. Medicine, Houston, 1960-61, fellow in pediat. infectious diseases and immunology, 1964-66, asst. prof. pediat., 1966-70, assoc. prof., 1970-75; chief pediat. programs U. Ala. Sch. Medicine, Huntsville, 1975-95, prof., 1975-97, prof. emeritus, 1997—. Bd. dirs. State Bd. Health, Ala. Bd. Med. Examiners; adv. com. Ala. EMS for Children. Contbr. articles to books and profl. jours. With AUS, 1961—62, Korea, ret. col. USAR, 1999. Mem. Soc. Pediat. Rsch., Am. Assn. Immunologists, Infectious Diseases Soc., N.Y. Acad. Scis., Am. Acad. Pediats. (pres. Ala. chpt. 1991-93), Sigma Xi, Phi Beta Kappa. Achievements include assisting in development of germ-free environmental bubble to protect patient with no natural immunity (patient later subject of movie The Boy in the Plastic Bubble, 1976 and PBS documentary on American Experience, 2006). Office Phone: 256-551-4600. Personal E-mail: dnjrmont@bellsouth.net.

**MONTGOMERY, JOHN T.,** lawyer; BA, Univ. Mich., 1969; JD, Boston Coll., 1975. Bar: Mass. 1975, US Dist. Ct. (Mass., ea. Mich.), US Ct. Appeals (1st, 2d, 3d, 4th & D.C. cir.). Asst. atty. gen. Commonwealth of Mass.; assoc. Ropes & Gray, Boston, 1982—85, ptnr. litigation dept., 1985—90; first asst. atty. gen. Commonwealth of Mass., 1990—92; ptnr. litigation dept. Ropes & Gray, Boston, 1992—; mng. ptnr. & mem. mgmt. com. Named one of Top Ten Lawyers, Mass. Lawyers' Weekly, 1998. Fellow: Am. Coll. Trial Lawyers; mem.: New England Legal Found. (dir.). Office: Ropes & Gray 1 International Pl Boston MA 02110-2624 Office Phone: 617-951-7565. Office Fax: 617-951-7050. Business E-Mail: john.montgomery@ropesgray.com.

**MONTGOMERY, JOHN WARWICK (BARON OF KILTARTAN AND LORD OF MORRIS, COMTE DE ST. GERMAIN DE MONTGOMERY),** law educator, theologian; b. Warsaw, NY, Oct. 18, 1931; s. Maurice Warwick and Harriet (Smith) M.; m. Lanalee de Kant, Aug. 26, 1988; 1 adopted child, Jean-Marie. AB in Philosophy with distinction, Cornell U., 1952; BLS, U. Calif., Berkeley, 1954, MA, 1958; BD, Wittenberg U., 1958, MST, 1960; PhD, U. Chgo., 1962; Docteur de l'Université, mention Théologie Protestante, U. Strasbourg, France, 1964; LLB, LaSalle Extension U., 1977; diplôme cum laude, Internat. Inst. Human Rights, Strasbourg, 1978; MPhil in Law, U. Essex, Eng., 1983; Dr. (hon.), Inst. Religion and Law, Moscow, 1999; LLM, Cardiff U., Wales, 2000; LLD, Cardiff U., 2003. Bar: Va. 1978, Calif. 1979, D.C. 1985, Wash. 1990, U.S. Supreme Ct. 1981, Eng. 1984, Paris 2003; lic. real estate broker Calif.; cert. law librarian; advanced cert. Heraldry Soc.; diplomate Med. Library Assn.; ordained to ministry Luth. Ch., 1958. Librarian, gen. reference service U. Calif. Library, Berkeley, 1954-55; instr. Bibl. Hebrew, Hellenistic Greek, Medieval Latin Wittenberg U., Springfield, Ohio, 1956-59; head librarian Swift Libr. div. and Philosophy, mem. federated theol. faculty U. Chgo., 1959-60; assoc. prof., chmn. dept. history Wilfred Laurier U. (formerly Waterloo Luth. U.), Ont., Can., 1960-64; prof., chmn. div. ch. history, history of Christian thought, dir. European Seminar program Trinity Evang. Div. Sch., Deerfield, Ill., 1964-74; prof. law and theology George Mason U. Sch. Law (formerly Internat. Sch. of Law), Arlington, Va., 1974-75; theol. cons. Christian Legal Soc., 1975-76; dir. studies Internat. Inst. Human Rights, Strasbourg, France, 1979-81; founding dean, prof. jurisprudence, dir. European program Simon Greenleaf U. Sch. Law, Anaheim, Calif., 1980-88; lic. disting. prof. theology and law, European program Faith Evang. Luth. Sem., Tacoma, 1989-91; from prin. lectr. to reader in law Bedfordshire U., England, 1991-93, prof. law and humanities, dir. Ctr. Human Rights, 1993-97, emeritus prof., 1997—; disting. prof. apologetics, law, and history of Christian thought, v.p. acad. affairs U.K. and Europe Trinity Coll. and Theol. Sem., Newburgh, Ind., 1997—, provost, 2005—; disting. prof. law Regent U., Va., 1997-99; sr. counsel European Ctr. Law and Justice, 1997-2001; founding dir. Internat. Acad. of Apologetics, Evangelism and Human Rights, Strasbourg, France, 1997—. Vis. prof. Concordia Theol. Sem., Springfield, Ill., 1964-67, DePaul U., Chgo., 1967-70, Concordia U., Irvine, Calif., 2006; hon. fellow Revelle Coll., U. Calif., San Diego, 1970; rector Freie Fakultaten Hamburg, Fed. Republic Germany, 1981-82; lectr. Rsch. Scientists Christian Fellowship Conf., St. Catherines Coll., Oxford U., 1985, Internat. Anti-Corruption Conf., Beijing, China, 1995; Pascal lectr. on Christianity and the Univ., U. Waterloo, Ont., Can., 1987; A. Kurt Weiss lectr. biomed. ethics U. Okla., 1997; adj. prof. Puget Sound U. Sch. Law, Tacoma, 1990-91; founding dir. Internat. Acad. Apologetics, Evangelism and Human Rights, Strasbourg, France, 1997—; Worldwide Adv. Conf. lectr. Inns of Ct. Sch. Law, London, 1998; law and religion colloquium lectr. U. Coll. London, 2000; hon. chmn. academic bd. Internat. Inst. Religious Freedom, World Evangel. FEllowship, 2005-. Author: The Writing of Research Papers in Theology, 1959, A Union List of Serial Publications in Chicago Area Protestant Theological Libraries, 1960, A Seventeenth-Century

View of European Libraries, 1962, 1962, Chytraeus on Sacrifice: A Reformation Treatise in Biblical Theology, 1962, The Shape of the Past: An Introduction to Philosophical Historiography, 1962; author: (rev. edit.), 1975; author: The Is God Dead Controversy, 1966; author: (with Thomas J.J. Altizer) The Altizer-Montgomery Dialogue, 1967; author: Crisis in Lutheran Theology, 2 vols., 1967; author: (rev. edit.), 1973; author: Es confiable el Christianismo?, 1968, Ecumenicity, Evangelicals, and Rome, 1969, Where is History Going?, 1969, (Romanian edit.) 2004, History and Christianity, 1970, Damned Through the Church, 1970, The Suicide of Christian Theology, 1970, Computers, Cultural Change and the Christ, 1970, In Defense of Martin Luther, 1970, La Mort de Dieu, 1971; author: (with Joseph Fletcher) Situation Ethics: True or False?, 1972; author: The Quest for Noah's Ark, 1972; author: (rev. edit.), 1974; author: Verdammt durch die Kirche, 1973, Christianity for the Toughminded, 1973, Cross and Crucible, 2 vols., 1973, Principalities and Powers: The World of the Occult, 1973, (rev. edit.), 1975, (Romanian edit.), 2004, How Do We Know There is a God?, 1973, Myth, Allegory and Gospel, 1974, God's Inerrant Word, 1974, Jurisprudence: A Book of Readings, 1974; author: (4th edit.), 1992; author: The Law Above the Law, 1975, Cómo Sabemos Que Hay un Dios?, 1975, Demon Possession, 1975, The Shaping of America, 1976, Faith Founded on Fact, 1978, Law and Gospel: A Study for Integrating Faith and Practice, 1978; author: (3rd edit.), 1994; author: Slaughter of the Innocents, 1981, The Marxist Approach to Human Rights: Analysis & Critique, 1984, Human Rights and Human Dignity, 1987, (Romanian edit.) 2004, Wohin marschiert China?, 1991, Evidence for Faith: Deciding the God Question, 1991, Giant in Chains: China Today and Tomorrow, 1994, Law and Morality: Friends or Foes?, 1994, Jésus: La Raison Rejoint L'Histoire, 1995; author: (with C.E.B. Cranfield and David Kilgour) Christians in the Public Square, 1996; author: Conflicts of Law, 1997, The Transcendent Holmes, 2000, The Repression of Evangelism in Greece, 2001, Tractatus Logico-Theologicus, 2002, Christ Our Advocate, 2002, History, Law and Christianity, 2002, Heraldic Aspects of the German Reformation, 2003, The Church: Blessing or Curse?, 2004; editor: Lippincott's Evangelical Perspectives, 7 vols., 1970-72, 1970—72, International Scholars Directory, 1973, Simon Greenleaf Law Rev., 7 vols., 1981—88, Global Jour. Classical Theology, 1998—; contbg. editor: Christianity Today, 1965—84, New Oxford Review, 1993—95; author: (films) Is Christianity Credible, 1968, In Search of Noah's Ark, 1977, Defending the Biblical Gospel (11 videocassette series), 1985, (TV series) Christianity on Trial, 1987—93; contbr. articles to acad., theol., legal encys. and jours., chapters to books . Nat. Luth. Ednl. Conf. fellow, 1959-60; Can. Council postdoctoral sr. research fellow, 1963-64; Am. Assn. Theol. Schs. faculty fellow, 1967-68; recipient Angel award Nat. Religious Broadcasters, 1989, 90, 92, Patriarch's Medal, Romanian Orthodox Church, 2003. Fellow Trinity Coll. (Newburgh, Ind.), Royal Soc. Arts (Eng.), Victoria Inst. (London) (hon. v.p., essay prize 2003-04), Soc. Advanced Legal Studies (U.K.), Acad. Internat. des Gourmets et des Traditions Gastronomiques (Paris), L.G. Affiliation (nat. philosophy sci. and history sci. commn. 1966-70); mem. ALA, European Acad. Arts, Scis. and Humanities (corr. mem., Paris), Acad. Lit. France (titulary mem.), Lawyers' Christian Fellowship (hon. v.p. 1995—), Nat. Conf. U. Profs., Calif. bar Assn. (human rights commn. 1980-83), Internat. Bar Assn., World Assn. Law Profs., Mid. Temple and Lincoln's Inn (barrister mem.), Am. Soc. Internat. Law, Union Internat. des Avocats, Nat. Assn. Realtors, Tolkien Soc. Am., N.Y. C.S. Lewis Soc., Am. Hist. Assn., Soc. Reformation Rsch., Creation Rsch. Soc., Tyndale Fellowship (Eng.), Stair Soc. (Scotland), Presbyn. Hist. Soc. (North Ireland), Heraldry Soc. (advanced cert.), Soc. Genealogists, Irish Geneaol. Soc., Am. Theol. Libr. Assn., Bibliog. Soc. U. Va., Evang. Theol. Soc., Internat. Wine and Food Soc., Soc. des Amis des Arts (Strasbourg), Chaîne des Rôtisseurs (commandeur), Athenaeum (London), Players' Theatre Club (London), Sherlock Holmes Soc. London, Soc. Sherlock Holmes de France (hon.), Club des Casseroles Lasserre (Paris), Club Prosper Montagné (Paris), Ordre des chevaliers du Saint-Sepulcre Byzantin (commandeur), Freeman of City of London, Freeman and Liveryman of Scriveners' Co., Phi Beta Kappa, Phi Kappa Phi, Beta Phi Mu. Mailing: 2 rue de Rome 67000 Strasbourg France Office: No 9 4 Crane Ct Fleet St London EC4A 2EJ England Office Phone: 33-3-88610882. Office Fax: 33-3-8860572940882. Personal E-mail: 106612.1066@compuserve.com.

MONTGOMERY, KAREN E., retired library and information scientist; b. Madison, Wis., May 25, 1939; d. Guerdon Morris and Mildred Nelson Matthews; m. William Darrell Montgomery, June 17, 1961; children: Anne Elizabeth, Jon Nelson. BA in English Edn., St. Olaf Coll.; postgrad., U. Wis., River Falls, 1977—79. Cataloging asst. U. Calif. Libr., Berkeley, 1962; circulation supr. U. Minn. Libr., Mpls., 1963—64; libr. St. Paul (Minn.) Pub. Schs., 1964—65; libr. asst. Am. Bankers Assn., N.Y.C., 1965—66; choir dir. Ezekiel Luth. Ch., River Falls; owner, technician Piano Works, River Falls, 1980—95; asst. cataloger U. Wis. Libr., River Falls, 1989—2005; ret., 2005. Mem. River Falls Pub. Libr. Found. Bd., 2002—, v.p., 2005—. Mem., treas. River Falls Pub. Sch. Band Boosters, 1982—87; treas. St. Croix Valley Summer Theatre Friends, River Falls; mem. Cmty. Arts Base, River Falls, 1999—. Mem.: AAUW (pres. River Falls Br. 1995—97, Wis. state bd. 1995—97, treas. River Falls Br. 1997—2002, Wis. state bd. 2003—04, pres. River Falls Br. 2005—07, fin. v.p. Wis. 2006—), Wis. Assn. Acad. Librs., Wis. Libr. Assn. Democrat. Evangelical Lutheran. Avocations: gardening, reading, volunteering, antiques, interior decorating. Home: 75 Woodridge Dr East River Falls WI 54022

MONTGOMERY, KATHRYN SUZAINNE, elementary school educator; b. Meridian, Miss., Nov. 23, 1978; d. Manuel Lee and Suzainne Frederick Montgomery. BS in Elem. Edn., Miss. State U., Meridian, 2002; postgrad., Miss. State U. Tchr. 5th grade West Lauderdale Mid. Sch., Collinsville, Miss., 2002—. Mem.: Houghton Mifflin Tchr.'s Club. Home: 15330 Hwy 486 Philadelphia MS 39350

MONTGOMERY, KEITH NORRIS, SR., insurance agent, military officer; b. Natchez, Miss., Sept. 22, 1931; s. Charles Norris Jr. and Miriam (Marron) M.; m. Joan Marie Bishop (div.); children: Keith Jr., Mason, Brenton BBA, U. Miss., 1974. Sales rep. Boyle-Midway, Monroe, La., 1975-77, Am. Nat. Ins., Jackson, Miss., 1977-79; owner Exec. Benefits, Clinton, Miss., 1979—; state rep. Miss. Ho. of Reps., Jackson, 1993—2003; asst. inspector gen. US Army, 2005—. City councilman City of Clinton, 1985-93. Master sgt. USNG, 1972—. Mem.: Clinton C. of C. Republican. Methodist. Home: 104 Countrywood Cir Clinton MS 39056-5717 Personal E-mail: montykn@yahoo.com.

MONTGOMERY, KEVIN, information technology executive; D, U. Calif., Santa Cruz, 1996. Tech. dir. Biocomp Ctr./NASA Ames Rsch. Ctr., Moffett Field, Calif., 1991—98, Nat. Biocomputation Ctr./Stanford U., Stanford, Calif., 1998—. CEO Intelesense Tech., Milpitas, Calif., 2005—. Recipient Smithsonian Award, Aircraft Telemedicine Project. Office: Nat Biocomputation Ctr/Stanford 701A Welch Rd Ste 1128 Palo Alto CA 94305 Office Phone: 650-498-6978. Office Fax: 650-498-5626.

MONTGOMERY, LARRY DALE, biologist; b. Longview, Wash., Feb. 24, 1950; s. Edward Dale and Wanda Lea (Collins) M.; m. Linda Fay Hensley, Nov. 17, 1978 (div. Dec. 1980). BA in Biol. Scis., Cen. Wash. State Coll., 1973. Lic. fissionable material handler; cert. pool/spa operator. Radiochemistry technician Westinghouse Hanford, Richland, Wash., 1974-76; research asst. Pacific Northwest Labs., Richland, 1976-81; prin. code enforcement officer Municipality of Anchorage, 1982-83, environ. sanitarian, 1985-86; engring. tech. Alaska Environ. Control Services, Anchorage, 1983, dir. environ. service, 1984-85; sanitarian dist. Municipality of Anchorage, 1986-87; with dept. Health Services Environ. Health Services, Albany, Ore. 1988—. Contbr. articles to profl. jours. Mem. Internat. Assn. Milk, Food, and Environ. Sanitarians, AAAS, Am. Pub. Health Assn., Nat. Environ. Health Assn. (registered sanitarian), Nat. Geog. Soc., N.Y. Acad. Scis., Conf. for Food Protection. Democrat. Baptist.

MONTGOMERY, LYNN MARIE, educational consultant; b. Faribault, Minn., July 13, 1955; d. Wilford G. and Marian Margaret Campbell; m. Daniel Blaine Montgomery, June 12, 1976; children: Kristi Lynn, Ryan Lee. BS, Coll. of St. Benedict, St. Joseph, Minn., 1976; MA, U. St. Thomas, St.

Paul, 1994. Elem. tchr. Anoka-Hennepin # 11, Coon Rapids, Minn., 1977-98; exec. dir. Assn. Tchr. Educators, Reston, Va., 1998—2003; tchg. and learning specialist Anoka-Hennepin, Coon Rapids, Minn., 2003—. Greater Minn. facilitator Destination Imagination, 1999-2000, Odyssey of the Mind, 1986-98; chair Adams Environ. Edn. Com., Minn., 1994—. Mem. AAUW, ASCD, Assn. Tchr. Educators (pres. 1998-99, Disting. Clinician 1995, Pres.'s Svc. award 1997), Minn. Assn. Tchr. Educators (bd. dirs. 1990-2000). Anoka-Hennepin Edn. Found. (bd. dirs. 1999-2002). Office: Anoka Hennepin 11 11299 Hanson Blvd Minneapolis MN 55433

MONTGOMERY, MICHAEL DAVIS, research and development company executive, real estate investor; b. San Luis Obispo, Calif., June 4, 1936; s. Harold Ray and Elva Dee (Davis) M.; m. Rita Martin, Dec. 28, 1957 (div. Sept. 1975); children: Jeanne, Gwen, Michele. MSEE, Stanford U., 1959; PhD, U. N.Mex., 1967. Group leader Max Planck Inst. for Astrophysics, Munich, 1974-76; group leader advanced concepts Los Alamos (N.Mex.) Nat. Labs., 1976-83; program mgr. for simulation Maxwell Labs. Inc., San Diego, 1983-84, dep. for DNA programs, 1984-85, v.p. rsch. and devel., 1986-91, sr. v.p. applied tech., 1991-92, sr. cons., 1992—97; owner Casa Del Mar Inn, Santa Barbara, Calif., 1991-97; real estate investor Montgomery Investments, LLC, 1997—. Owner and cons. All Santa Fe Reservations Assoc., 1999—2005. Assoc. editor Jour. Geophys. Research; contbr. articles to sci. jours. Served to lt. comdr. USN, 1959-62. Recipient (charter) Sr. Scientist award Alexander Von Humboldt Found., 1972. Mem. AAAS, Am. Phys. Soc., Phi Beta Kappa, Sigma Xi, Tau Beta Pi. Avocations: amateur radio, w5mgt. Home and Office: 735 Foxridge Dr Providence UT 84332-9693 Personal E-mail: mikedmont@comcast.net.

MONTGOMERY, MIKE, professional basketball coach; b. Long Beach, Calif., Feb. 27, 1947; m. Sarah Montgomery; children: John, Anne. BA in Phys. Edn., Calif. State U., Long Beach, 1968; MS in Phys. Edn., Colo. State U., 1976. Coach U. Fla., The Citadel, Colo. State U., USCG Acad.; asst. coach Boise State U.; head basketball coach U. Mont., Missoula, 1978-86, Stanford (Calif.) U., 1986—2004; head coach Golden State Warriors, 2004—. Named Head Coach of Yr. USA Men's 22 and Under Select Team, U.S. Basketball Men's Collegiate Com., 1996, U.S. Basketball Devel. Coach of Yr., 1996, U.S. Olympic Com. Basketball Devel. Coach of Yr., 1996. Office: c/o Golden State Warriors 1011 Broadway Oakland CA 94607

MONTGOMERY, R. LAWRENCE, retail executive; b. 1949; Pres., CEO Black's divsn. Allied Store Corp., 1985-87; sr. v.p., dir. stores, gen. mdse. mgr. Softlines L.S. Ayres divsn. May Dept. Stores, 1987-88; sr. v.p., dir. stores Kohl's Corp., Menomonee Falls, Wis., 1988-93, exec. v.p., 1993-96, vice chmn., 1996—, CEO, 1999—, also bd. dirs., chmn., 2002—. Office: Kohl's Corp N56 W17000 Ridgewood Dr Menomonee Falls WI 53051-5660*

MONTGOMERY, REX, biochemist, educator; b. Halesowen, Eng., Sept. 4, 1923; came to U.S., 1948, naturalized, 1963; s. Fred and Jane (Holloway) M.; m. Barbara Winifred Price, Aug. 9, 1948 (dec.); children: Ian, David, Jennifer, Christopher. BSc, U. Birmingham, Eng., 1943, PhD, 1946, DSc, 1963. Rsch. assoc. U. Minn., 1951-55; mem. faculty U. Iowa, Iowa City, 1955—2005, prof. biochemistry, 1963—2005, assoc. dean U. Iowa Coll. Medicine, 1974-95, v.p. rsch., 1989-90, prof. emeritus, 2005—. Vis. prof. Nat. Australian U., 1969-70; mem. physiol. chemistry study sect. NIH, 1968-72; mem. drug devel. contract rev. com., 1975-87; chmn. com. biol. chemistry NAS, 1961-64; pesticide and fertilizer adv. bd. Iowa Dept. Agr., 1990-91; bd. dirs. Wallace Tech. Transfer Found., 1989-93; chmn. bd. dirs. Neurotron Inc., 1990-95; mem. rsch. com. Iowa Corn Promotion Bd., 1995-2001; rsch. dir. Biotech. Byproducts Consortium, 1989—; cons. in field. Author: Chemical Production of Lactic Acid, 1949, Chemistry of Plant Gums and Mucilages, 1959, Quantitative Problems in Biochemical Sciences, 2d edit., 1976, Biochemistry: A Case-Orientated Approach, 6th edit., 1996; mem. editl. adv. bd. Carbohydrate Rsch., 1968-80; mem. editl. bd. Molecular Biotherapy, 1988-92; contbr. articles to profl. jours. Postdoctoral fellow Ohio State U., 1948-49; fellow Sugar Research Found., Dept. Agr., 1949-51 Fellow: Royal Soc. Chemistry. Home: 701 Oaknoll Dr Iowa City IA 52246-5168 Office: U Iowa Coll Medicine Dept Biochemistry Iowa City IA 52242 Office Phone: 319-335-7897. Business E-Mail: rex-montgomery@uiowa.edu.

MONTGOMERY, ROBERT K., lawyer; b. Dec. 22, 1938; AB, Williams Coll., 1961; LLB with honors, Duke Univ., 1964. Bar: Calif. 1965. Joined Gibson Dunn & Crutcher LLP, LA, 1964—, now ptnr. corp. transactions and securities. Mem. exec. com. Gibson & Crutcher, chair, fin. com.; sr. v.p. LA Olympic Organizing Com., 1983; bd. gov. Lowe Inst. of Polit. Economy, Claremont McKenna Coll.; bd. visitors Duke Univ. Law Sch. (past chmn.). Mem.: ABA, LA County Bar Assn. Office: Gibson Dunn & Crutcher LLP 2029 Century Pk E Los Angeles CA 90067-3026 Office Phone: 310-557-8022. Office Fax: 310-552-7021. Business E-Mail: rmontgomery@gibsondunn.com.

MONTGOMERY, ROBERT MOREL, JR., lawyer; b. Birmingham, Ala., June 9, 1930; s. Robert Morel and Ella Bernice (Smith) M.; m. Mary Lemerle McKenzie, Mar. 6, 1953; 1 child, Courtnay Elizabeth. BS, U. Ala., 1952; LL.B., U. Fla., 1957. Bar: Fla. 1957; diplomate Acad. Fla. Trial Lawyers. With Howell & Kirby Attys at Law, Jacksonville, Fla., 1957-59; ptnr. Howell, Kirby, Montgomery, Sands & D'Aiuto, Jacksonville, Fla., 1959-66, Howell, Kirby, Montgomery, D'Aiuto, Dean & Hallowes, West Palm Beach, Fla., 1966-75, Montgomery, Lytal, Reiter, Denny & Searcy, West Palm Beach, Fla., 1976-85, Montgomery Searcy & Denny, West Palm Beach, Fla., 1986-89; sr. ptnr. Montgomery & Larson, LLP, West Palm Beach, Fla., 2001—05, Robert M. Montgomery Jr. & Assoc. PL, 2006—. Civil trial adv. Nat. Bd. Trial Advocacy; lectr. Princeton U., U. Oxford Law Sch. Chmn. Palm Beach Opera; chmn. emeritus Palm Beach Cultural Coun.; co-chmn. Children's Place at Home Safe, Inc.; trustee Nat. Pub. Radio. 1st lt. AUS, 1952-54. Named Alumnus of Yr. U. Fla. Law Rev., 1983, Philanthropist of Yr. Nat. Assn. Fund Raising Execs., 1990, Honoree for Yr. City of Hope, 1991, Victim Adv. of Yr., Palm Beach County Sheriff's Office, 1997, Child Advocate of the Yr., 1996; recipient Learned Hand award Am. Jewish Com., 1985, Humanitarian award Albert Einstein Coll., 1990, Pub.'s award honor for contbg. most to improving quality of life in Broward and Palm Beach counties, 1992, Great Am. Traditions award B'nai B'rith, 1996, Humanitarian award Albert Einstein Coll. Medicine, 1999, Haym Solomon award Anti-Defamation League, 2000, Palm Beach C.C. Leadership award, 2002, Man of Yr. award Lake Worth Cultural Spotlight Com., 2002, Heartland award Lawton Chiles Found., 2003, Fla.'s Children First!, Inc. award, 2003, Dr. Martin Luther King Jr. Disting. award NAACP, 2004, Lifetime Achievement award Urban League, 2005, Disting. Cmty. Svc. award Alexis de Toqueville Soc. Palm Beach United Way, 2006. Mem. ABA, Fla. Bar Assn. (lectr. continuing edn.), Palm Beach County Bar Assn., Trial Lawyers Assn. Am., Inner Circle Advs. Home: 1800 S Ocean Blvd Palm Beach FL 33480-5104 Office: PO Box 3086 West Palm Beach FL 33402-3086 Office Phone: 561-832-2880. Business E-Mail: rmm@rmmjr.com.

MONTGOMERY, ROY DELBERT, retired gas industry executive; b. Indpls., Apr. 24, 1926; s. Lloyd Sipes and Nona Mae (Brummett) M.; m. Barbara Ann Reno, Apr. 21, 1949 (dec. 1983); children: Stephanie, Rebecca, Jeffrey, Laura. Student, Purdue U., 1950-51; M.E., Internat. Corr. Schs., 1953; A.S. in Mgmt. and Adminstrn., Ind. U., 1973. Registered profl. engr. Ind. Engr. Citizens Gas & Coke Utility, Indpls., 1952-59, supt., 1959-60, dir., 1960-73, exec. dir., 1973-78, v.p., 1978-82, sr. v.p., 1982-86, cons., 1986-88. Mem. adv. bd. AdvancedMgmt. Conf., I.U. Grad. Sch. Bus., 1974—78. Contbr. articles to profl. jours. Vice pres. exploring Crossroads of Am. Coun. Boy Scouts Am., Ind., 1978; corp. rep. Jr. Achievement Ind., 1970-82; pres. Fairway Trace at Pendia I, 1994—; Fairway Trace Home Owners Assn., 1995—. Recipient Bronze Big Horn award Boy Scouts Am. Explorer Div., Ind., 1978 Mem. Am. Gas Assn. (merit award 1966), Ind. Gas Assn., Scientec Club Ind., Kiwanis. Republican. Avocations: painting, golf, genealogy.

MONTGOMERY, SUSAN BARBIERI, lawyer; b. New Haven, Nov. 11, 1949; BFA, RISD, 1971, MAE, 1978; JD, Northeastern U., 1986. Bar: Mass. 1986, U.S. Dist. Ct. Mass. 1987, U.S. Ct. Appeals (D.C. cir.) 1988. Tchr., dept. chmn. Westport (Mass.) Pub. Schs., 1976-83; freelance artist Westport, 1971—; law clk. to Justice J. Harold Flannery Mass. Superior Ct., Boston, 1986; assoc. Foley Hoag LLP, Boston, 1986-94, ptnr., 1995—. Adj. prof. Suffolk U. Law Sch., 1999—; advisor in field. Co-editor: Worldwide Trademark Transfer, 1992—2006. Trustee Vol. Lawyers for Arts, Boston, 1992—; chmn. bldg. com. Westport Arts Group, Inc.; advisor Am. Law Inst. Mem. ABA (chair elect IPL sect., mem. UCITA working group, past chair bus. baw & IPL sect. joint task force), Mass. Bar Assn. (coms. 1987—), Boston Bar Assn. (coms. 1987—), Internat. Trademark Assn. (chmn. publs. com., dir. 1995-97), Copyright Soc. (mem. 1991—), Lex Mundi (chair intellectual property practice group). Office: Foley Hoag LLP Seaport World Trade Center West 155 Seaport Blvd Boston MA 02210-2600 Office Phone: 617-832-1222. Business E-Mail: smontgomery@foleyhoag.com.

MONTGOMERY, SUZANNE HOWARD, psychologist; b. Atlanta, Apr. 19, 1949; d. Douglas Leighton and Patricia Jean (Younkins) Howard; m. William McKinley Copley III, June 14, 1985. BA, U. Fla., 1971, PhD, 1982; MSW, Mich. State U., 1973. Lic. psychologist, Fla. Dir. aftercare svcs. Mental Health ctr. Univ. Hosp., Jacksonville, Fla., 1976-77; dir. mental health cons. and edn. Mental Health ctr., 1977-80, dir. tng. and devel., 1981-85; owner, cons. psychologist Montgomery, Copley & Assocs., Inc., Jacksonville, 1985—. Mem. allocation panel United Way Fund, 1988; chair Open Campus adv. com. Fla. C.C., Jacksonville, 1982—; bd. dirs. Mental Health Resource Ctr., Jacksonville, 1985-90, pres., 1989-91; mem. Jacksonville Women's Network, 1983—; bd. dirs., tng. chmn. Jacksonville Jr. League, 1985-87; bd. dirs. YWCA, 1992-94, Leadership Jacksonville, 1996—, Leadership devel. team, 2000-; bd. dirs., pres. Leadership Jacksonville Alumni, 1992-94, Leadership USA, 1995-96; bd. dirs. Episc. Child Svcs., 2005—. Mem. APA, Fla. Psychol. Assn., South Jacksonville Rotary, Jacksonville Women's Network, Phi Kappa Phi, Phi Alpha. Home: 4055 Cordova Ave Jacksonville FL 32207-6020 Office: Montgomery Copley & Assocs 1812 Atlantic Blvd Jacksonville FL 32207-3404

MONTGOMERY, THEODORE ASHTON, physician; b. L.A., Oct. 27, 1923; s. Wayne A. and Hazel (Osmer) M. MD, U. So. Calif., 1947; MPH cum laude, Harvard U., 1955. Diplomate: Am. Bd. Preventive Medicine, Am. Bd. Pediatrics. Intern Los Angeles County Gen. Hosp., 1946-48; intern L.A. Children's Hosp., 1948, resident, 1950-51, St. Louis Children's Hosp., 1951-52; asst. in pediatrics Washington U., St. Louis, 1951-52; instr. pediatrics U. So. Calif., 1952-55; practice medicine specializing in pediatrics, L.A., 1952-54; lectr. pub. health U. Calif., Berkeley, 1960-83. Cons. child health Calif. Dept. Pub. Health, 1954-60, chief maternal and perinatal health, 1960-61, acting chief bur. maternal and child health, 1961-63, asst. chief Fla. preventive med. services, 1963-66, chief, 1966-68, chief preventive medicine program, 1968-69, dep. dir., 1969-73; mem. mental retardation projects rev. com. USPHS, 1965-66, charter mem. surgeon gen.'s adv. com. on immunization practices, 1964-66; mem. task force on alcoholism, drug and narcotic abuse Calif. Commn. on Criminal Justice, 1968-70; chief div. disease control Alameda County Health Care Svcs. Agy., 1973-74; cons. maternal and child health Calif. Dept. Health, Berkeley, 1974-78; chief maternal and child health br. No. Calif. Regional Office, Calif. Dept. Health Svcs., 1978-83; WHO fellow med. care adminstrn., Europe, 1966; co-chmn. Calif. Inter-agy. Council on Tb, 1966-72; vice chmn. Calif. Drug Rsch. Adv. Panel, 1969-70; participant White House Conf. Mental Retardation, 1963, White House Conf. on Mental Retardation Cmty. Ctrs., 1965; Gov's. chmn. Calif. Regional Hemodialysis Rev. Com., 1968-73; exec. sec. Gov.'s Population Study Commn., 1966; mem. com. on Tb, Calif. Lung Assn., 1973-74 Author: (with others) Standards and Recommendations for Public Prenatal Care, 1960, Guide to Hearing Testing of School Children, 1961; contbr. articles to med. jours. Bd. dirs. Calif. Interagy. Coun. on Family Planning, 1970-73; chmn. Calif. State Interdepartmental Com. on Food and Nutrition, 1977-79, pres. Clan Montgomery Soc. Internat., 1981-84, regional commr., 1985-91. With M.C. AUS, 1948-50. Fellow Am. Acad. Pediatrics (chmn. Calif. com. Indian health 1973-76, mem. nat. com. on Indian health 1963-79, vice chmn. 1977-79), Am. Pub. Health Assn. (chmn. task force on population policy 1971-72); mem. Alpha Epsilon Delta, Delta Omega. Home: 85 Wildwood Gdns Piedmont CA 94611-3831 E-mail: tmontgo458@aol.com.

MONTGOMERY, THOM MATHEW, health program administrator, counselor; b. Delaware, Okla., Dec. 30, 1942; s. Francis Thomas and Ellen Grace (Whelan) M.; m. Dinah Lee Hicks, Feb. 4, 1961 (div. 1964); children: Laura Diane, Raymond Hunter; m. A.N.D. de Vermandois. Degree, Highlands U., 1966; student, Tulsa U., 1961-64, U. Calif., Irvine, 1980-81, Glenn U., Dublin, Ireland, 1993—2002. Brokerage mgr. John Hancock Life Ins. Co., Boston, 1964-70; mng. editor Renown Publs., Reseda, Calif., 1970-77; publs. dir. Am. Pub. Health Found., Corona Del Mar, Calif., 1977-79; program adminstr. Life Plus Martin Luther Hosp., Anaheim, Calif., 1979-92; dir. rsch. Brookside Inst., Irvine, Calif., 2001—. Pres. Montgomery Counseling Assocs., Fullerton, 1986—. Author: Ennobled Blood: The Heiresses of Monkstown Castle, 2002, Naltrexone: Pulling Back the Curtain, 2004; contbr. articles to profl. jours. Founding mem. Task Force on Alcohol & Drug Abuse for Disabled, Orange County, 1981, Sobriety Faire, Orange County, 1982; bd. dirs. Mid Valley Cmty. Police Coun., San Fernando Valley Employee Assistance Programs. Fellow Am. Pub. Health Found.; mem. Nat. Assn. Alcohol and Drug Abuse Counselors, Internat. Assn. Alcohol and Drug Abuse Counselors, Calif. Assn. Alcohol and Drug Abuse Counselors. Republican. Presbyn. Avocations: chess, hiking, swimming, poetry, drama. Home: 35167 El Diamante Dr Wildomar CA 92595 Office: 213 N Pomona Fullerton CA 92832 Office Phone: 310-413-4672.

MONTGOMERY, WILL S., lawyer; b. Dallas, Jan. 8, 1950; BA, Stanford U., 1980, MA, 1981; JD, U. Chgo., 1984. Bar: Tex. 1984. Shareholder Jenkens & Gilchrist, P.C., Dallas, 1992—; firm leader litig. practice group. Mem.: ABA, Dallas Bar Assn., Tex. State Bar. Office: Jenkens & Gilchrist PC Ste 3200 1445 Ross Ave Dallas TX 75202-2799 Office Phone: 214-855-4725. Office Fax: 214-855-4300. Business E-Mail: wmontgomery@jenkens.com.

MONTGOMERY, WILLIAM ADAM, lawyer; b. Chgo., May 22, 1933; s. John Rogerson and Helen (Fyke) Montgomery; m. Jane Fauver, July 28, 1956 (div. Dec. 1967); children: Elizabeth, William, Virginia; m. Deborah Stephens, July 29, 1972; children: Alex, Katherine. AB, Williams Coll., 1955; LLB, Harvard U., 1958. Bar: D.C. 1958, Ill. 1959, U.S. Ct. Appeals (7th cir.) 1959, U.S. Supreme Ct. 1977. Atty. civil divsn., appellate sect. Dept. Justice, Washington, 1958—60; assoc. Schiff Hardin LLP, Chgo., 1960—68, ptnr., 1968—93, 1999—; v.p., gen. counsel State Farm Ins. Cos., Bloomington, Ill., 1994—97, sr. counsel, 1997—99. Author: (39 corp. practice series) Tying Arrangements, 1984; co-author: Insurance Antitrust and Unfair Trade Practices Law, 2002; contbr. articles to profl. jours. Fellow: Am. Coll. Trial Lawyers; mem.: ABA (coun. antitrust sect. 1989—92), Seventh Cir. Bar Assn. (pres. 1988—89), Chgo. Bar Assn., Lawyers Club Chgo. Avocations: skiing, woodturning. Office: Schiff Hardin LLP 6600 Sears Tower Chicago IL 60606 Business E-Mail: wmontgomery@schiffhardin.com.

MONTGOMERY, WILLIAM D., former ambassador; b. Carthage, Mo., Nov. 8, 1945; m. Lynne Germain Montgomery; children: Alexander, Amelia, Katarina. BA, Bucknell U.; MA, George Washington U.; student, Nat. War Coll., 1986-87. With Fgn. Svc., 1974, econ. officer Belgrade, Yugoslavia, 1975-78, comml. then polit. officer Moscow, 1979-81; line officer, secretariat staff then exec. asst. to under sec. polit. affairs Dept. State, 1981-84, exec. asst. to dep. sec., 1991-93; dep. chief mission Dar es Salaam, Tanzania, 1984-85, Sofia, Bulgaria, 1989-91; U.S. ambassador Bulgaria, 1993-96; spl. advisor to Pres. and sec. state for Bosnia peace implementation of the Bosnia peace plan, 1996-97; U.S. amb. to Republic of Croatia, 1998-2000; chief of mission U.S. Embassy, Belgrade, Yugoslavia, 2000—01; U.S. amb. to Yugoslavia US Dept. State, Belgrade, 2001—04. With U.S. Army, 1967-1970. Decorated Bronze Star, Commendation medal with V device, Combat Infantry Men's badge; Parachute badge; decorated Order of the Horseman of the Madara, Order of the Stara Planina (Bulgaria), Order of Price Trpimir (Croatia); recipient ABA-Ctrl. and East European Law Initiative award for promotions rule of law in Cen. and Ea. Europe. Mem. Am. Fgn. Svc. Assn.

**MONTGOMERY-DOWNS, HAWLEY EVELYN,** psychologist, researcher; PhD, U. Conn., Mansfield, Conn., 2001. Postdoctoral fellow U. Louisville, 2001—05; asst. prof. W.Va. U., Morgantown, W.Va., 2005—. Grantee Nat. Rsch. Svc. Award, NIH, 2003—05, 2003—06. Mem.: Sleep Rsch. Soc. (assoc.). Office: West Virginia University POBox 6040 Morgantown WV 26506-6040 Office Phone: 304-293-2001. Office Fax: 304-293-6606. Business E-mail: hawley.montgomery-downs@mail.wvu.edu.

**MONTIEL, ALFONSO,** data processing executive; JD, Universidad del Zulla, Venezuela; MBA, Columbia Univ., NYC. With ICG Commerce, A.T. Kearny, Am. Express, Interocean; v.p. supply mktg., Bus. Process Outsourcing EDS, Plano, Tex., pres. procurement outsourcing svc. line, 2005—. Adv. bd. Edn. is Freedom; pres. Dallas chpt. Columbia Univ. Bus. Sch. Alumni Assn. Named one of 50 Most Important Hispanics in Tech. & Bus., Hispanic Engr. & Info. Tech. mag., 2004, 2005. Office: EDS 5200 Legacy Dr Plano TX 75024 Office Phone: 972-378-0824.*

**MONTO, ARNOLD SIMON,** epidemiology educator; b. Bklyn., Mar. 22, 1933; s. Jacob and Mildred (Kaplan) M.; m. Ellyne Gay Polsky, June 15, 1958; children: Sarah D. Monto Maniaci, Jane E., Richard L., Stephen A. BA in Zoology, Cornell U., Ithaca, N.Y., 1954; MD, Cornell U., N.Y.C., 1958. Diplomate Am. Coll. Epidemiology. Intern, asst. resident in medicine Vanderbilt U. Hosp., Nashville, 1958—60; USPHS postdoctoral fellow in infectious disease Stanford U. Med. Ctr., Palo Alto, Calif., 1960—62; mem. staff virus diseases sect. mid. Am. rsch. unit Nat. Inst. Allergy and Infectious Disease, Panama, 1962—65; assoc. prof. U. Mich. Sch. Pub. Health, Ann Arbor, 1965—76, prof., 1976—, chmn. dept. population planning and internat. health, 1993—97, dir. Ctr. for Population Planning, 1993—97, dir. U. Mich. Bioterrorism Preparedness Initiative, 2002—04. Vis. scientist Clin. Rsch. Ctr., Northwick Park Hosp., Harrow, Eng., 1976; scholar-in-residence bd. on sci. and tech. for internat. devel. NAS and Inst. Medicine, Washington, 1983-84; vis. scientist div. communicable diseases WHO, Geneva, 1986-87; mem. pulmonary diseases adv. coun. Nat. Heart, Lung and Blood Inst., Bethesda, Md., 1979-83; mem. nat. adv. coun. Nat. Inst. Allergy and Infectious Diseases, Bethesda, 1989-93, Contbr. articles to med. jours. Recipient career devel. award NIH. Fellow Am. Coll. Epidemiology, Infectious Diseases Soc. Am.; mem. APHA (governing coun. 1978-80), Am. Epidemiol. Soc. (pres. 2004-05). Achievements include research on respiratory viral infections in the community; demonstration of effectiveness of influenza vaccine in severe disease in the elderly; prevention of spread of influenza virus and treatment of illness, occurrence, causes and treatment of common cold. Office: U Mich Sch Pub Health 109 Observatory St Ann Arbor MI 48109-2029 Office Phone: 734-764-5453. Business E-Mail: asmonto@umich.edu.

**MONTONI, RICHARD A.,** management consultant; BS, Boston U.; MS, Northeastern U. Audit ptnr. KPMG LLP; CFO, exec. v.p. CIBER, Inc., Englewood, Colo., 1996—2000, Managed Storage Internat., Inc., Broomfield, Colo., 2000—01; CFO, treas. MAXIMUS, Inc., Reston, Va., 2002—06, CEO, 2006—. Office: MAXIMUS Inc 11410 Sunset Hills Rd Reston VA 20190-5207 Office Phone: 703-251-8500. Office Fax: 703-251-8240.*

**MONTOYA, JUAN PABLO,** professional race car driver; b. Bogota, Colombia, Sept. 20, 1975; m. Connie Montoya; 1 child, Sebastian. Indy/cart race car driver, 1999—; with Team McClaren Mercedes, 2006—. Named Rookie of Yr. in Cart Racing, 1999, also Winner Cart Racing Series; winner Indy 500, 2000 (first attempt at Indy); 7 Career Formula One Grand Prix Wins, 29 podium appearances. Office: c/o Target/Chip Ganassi Racing 7777 Woodland Dr Indianapolis IN 46278-1794*

**MONTOYA, MALAQUIAS,** art educator, artist; b. Albuquerque, N.M., June 21, 1938; BA with hon., Univ. Calif. Berkeley, 1970. Comml. artist, silkscreener, 1962—68; foreman silkscreen dept. Circo Inc., 1963—66; art instr. Laney Coll., Berkeley, 1969—70, Contra Costa Coll., Richmond, Calif., 1971; art workshop dir. Alameda Co. Neighborhood Arts Program, 1974—81; lectr. Chicano Studies Dept. Univ. Calif, Berkeley, 1960—74, full prof., 1990—, now cooperating faculty, 1996—. Spkr. in field. Exhibitions include several galleries and mus. including Whitney Mus. Am. Art, NYC, 2006. Office: PO Box 6 Elmira CA 95625*

**MONTOYA, REGINA T.,** association executive, lawyer; b. Tucumcari, N.Mex., Dec. 25, 1953; d Fred and Rosa (Meraz) M.; m. Paul E. Coggins, June 12, 1976; 1 child, Jessica. BA, Wellesley Coll., 1975; JD, Harvard U., 1979. Bar: Tex. 1979. Law clk. to U.S. Dist. Judge Sarah T. Hughes, Dallas, 1979-80; ptnr. Akin, Gump, Strauss, Hauer & Feld, Dallas, 1980-90; shareholder Godwin, Carlton & Maxwell, Dallas, 1990-93; asst. to pres., Office of Intergovernmental Affairs, Washington D.C., 1993; v.p. Westcott Comm., 1994—95; panelist Between the Lines KERA-TV, 1994; public delegate UN Gen. Assembly, 1998; pres. WORKRules, 1995—2005; CEO New Am. Alliance, 2005—. Bd. dirs. Wash. Mut., 2006—. Trustee Wellesley Coll., 1990—; bd. dirs. Dallas Theater Ctr., 2004—, Parkland Found., 2005—. Mem. Student Loan Mktg. Assn. (bd. dirs. 1994-2001). Democrat. Roman Catholic. Office: New America Alliance 1050 Connecticut Ave NW 10th Fl Washington DC 20036 Office Phone: 202-772-1872. Business E-Mail: rmontoya@naaonline.org.

**MONTOYA, VELMA,** economist, consultant; b. LA, Apr. 9, 1938; d. Jose Gutierrez and Consuelo (Cavazos) Montoya; m. Earl A. Thompson; 1 child, Bret L. Thompson. BA in Diplomacy and World Affairs, Occidental Coll., 1959, MA in Internat. Rels., 1960; MS in Econs., Stanford U., 1965; PhD in Econs., UCLA, 1977. Asst. prof. econs. Calif. State U., L.A., 1965-68; vis. assoc. prof. U. So. Calif., 1979; instr. UCLA, 1981-82; staff economist The Rand Corp., Santa Monica, Calif., 1973-82; asst. dir. for strategy, White House Office of Policy Devel. Exec. Office of the Pres., 1982-83; expert economist Office Regulatory Analysis, OSHA, U.S. Dept. of Labor, 1983-85; dir. of Studies in Pub. Policy and Assoc. Prof. of Political Economy, Sch. of Bus. Mgmt. Chapman U., 1985-87; adj. prof. Sch. Bus. Mgmt. Pepperdine U., 1987-88; pres. Hispanic-Am. Pub. Policy Inst., 1984-90; assoc. prof. fin. Sch. Bus. Adminstrn., Calif. State Poly. U., Pomona, 1988-90; mem. Occupl. Safety and Health Rev. Commn., 1990-97; cons. on regulatory and econ. policy, 1997—. Cons. Urban Inst., 1974, Mexican-Am. Study Project UCLA, 1966, Grad. and Profl. Fellowships to the Office of Post Secondary Edn., U.S. Dept. Edn.; editl. referee Contemporary Policy Issues, Economic Inquiry, Policy Analysis, Jour. Econ. Lit.; discussion leader Am. Assembly on Rels. Between the U.S. and Mex.; pres. del. White House Conf. on Aging, 1981; reader of 1988 proposals for the U.S. Dept Edn. for the Improvement and Reform of Schs. and Tchg.; rsch. participant U.S. Dept. Edn. Delphi Assessment of Drug Policies for Use in Minority Neighborhoods, 1989; mem. Hispanic adv. panel Nat. Commn. for Employment Policy, 1981-82; lectr. Brookings Inst. Seminars for U.S. Bus. Leaders; bd. adv. Close-Up Found., 1982-83; discussant Western Econ. Assn. Meetings, 1985, 93; bd. adv. Nat. Rehab. Hosp., 1991-94; nat. exec. adv. bd. Harvard Jour. Hispanic Policy, 1993-95; reader proposals for Hispanic Serving Instns., U.S. Dept. Edn., 2001-2004; regional panel to select White House Fellows, 2002— Mem. census adv. com. on hispanic population for 1990 census, 1988—93; mem. adv. com. Senate Rep. Conf. Task Force on Hispanic Affairs, Washington, 1991—; bd. regents U. Calif., 1994—2005; program rev. com. Los Alamos (N.Mex.) Nat. Lab.; mem. steering com. GetSmarter.org, 1998—99; mem. outreach adv. bd. U. Calif., 1998—2005, mem. coun. friends Bancroft Libr. Berkeley, 2005—; commr. Calif. Postsecondary Edn. Commn., 2000—01, 2004—05; coun. trustees, alumni Inst. Effective Governance Adv. Bd., 2003—. Named One of the 100 U.S. Hispanic Influentials Hispanic Bus. Mag., 1992, 96, 97, Woman of the Yr. Mex.-Am. Oportunity Found., 1983, The East L.A. Com. Union, 1979, one of 80 Elite Hispanic Women, Hispanic Bus. Mag., 2002, 03; recipient Freedom Found. at Valley Forge Honor Econ.

Edn. Excellence Cert., 1986, Profl. Achievement award S.E. L.A. Lincoln Club, 2002, Hispanic Leadership award Minorities in Bus. Mag., 2001; Univ. fellow Stanford U., Internat. Rels. fellow Calif. PTA, John Hay Whitney Opportunity fellow; Calif. State Univ. Found. Faculty Rsch. grantee; Marshall scholar, Fulbright scholar. Mem. ASTM (com. on rsch. and tech. planning 1985-87), Am. Econ. Assn. (session chair ann. meetings 1995), Nat. Coun. Hispanic Women (pres. 1997—), Am. Soc. Hispanic Economists, State Bar of Calif., Calif. State Bar Ct. (exec. com. 1987-89, disciplinary bd. 1986-89), Western Econ. Assn., Indsl. Rsch. Inst. for Pacific Nations (adv. bd. 1988-89), Salesian Boys and Girls Club (bd. dirs. 1989—), Vets. in Com. Svc. (adv. com. 1989-94), Phi Beta Kappa, Omicron Delta Epsilon, Phi Alpha Theta Home: 6970 Los Tilos Rd Los Angeles CA 90068-3107 Office Phone: 213-427-8048. Personal E-mail: velmamontoya@earthlink.net.

**MONTROLL, ANDREW H.,** lawyer, councilman; b. Washington, Apr. 11, 1957; s. Elliott W. and Shirley A. Montroll; m. Barbara Anne Komons, July 7, 1996; children: Sarah D., Elliott G. BS in Optics, U. Rochester, 1975—80, MS in Optics, 1980—81; JD summa cum laude, Vt. Law Sch., 1986—89. Bar: Vt. Supreme Ct. 1990. Engr. MRJ, Inc, Oakton, Va., 1981—86; jud. law clk. Vt. Supreme Ct., Montpelier, 1989—90; atty. Burak & Anderson, Burlington, 1990—96; counsel Riser Mgmt. Systems, Burlington, Vt., 1997—2004; atty. Law Offices of Andrew H. Montroll, Burlington, 2004—. Editor in chief The Vermont Law Review, 1988—89. Author: (book) Critical Connections, Wired for Profit. Mem. Chittenden County Met. Planning Orgn., 2005—; pres. Burlington City Coun. 2001—05, city councilor, 1994—; mem. Bd. Civil Authority, Burlington, 1994—; examiner Vt. Bd. Bar Examiners, Montpelier. Recipient Vt. Legal Scholar, Vt. Law Sch., 1989. Achievements include patents for Monolithic semiconductor laser and optical amplifier; semiconductor laser and optical amplifier. Avocation: photography. Office: Law Offices Andrew H Montroll 200 Church St Burlington VT 05401 Office Phone: 803-383-0730.

**MONTRONE, PAUL MICHAEL,** scientific instruments company executive; b. Scranton, Pa., May 8, 1941; s. Angelo H. and Beatrice M. (Giancini) M.; m. Sandra G. Gaudenzi, May 30, 1963; children: Michele Marie Cogan, Angelo Henry, Jerome Lawrence. BS in Accounting magna cum laude, U. Scranton, 1962; PhD in Fin., Econs. and Ops. Research, Columbia U., 1965. Ops. analyst Office Sec. Def., Washington, 1965-67; exec. v.p., chief fin. officer Wheelabrator-Frye Inc., Hampton, NH, 1970-83; exec. v.p. Signal Cos., Inc., La Jolla, Calif., 1983-85, pres. Engineered Products Group Hampton, NH, 1983-85; exec. v.p. fin. and adminstrn. AlliedSignal Inc., Morristown, NJ, 1985-86; pres. The Henley Group Inc., Hampton, NH, 1986-92, bd. dirs.; chmn., CEO Wheelabrator Techs. Inc., Hampton, NH, 1987-90; pres., co-owner The Gen. Chem. Group Inc., 1989-94, chmn. bd., 1994-96; vice chmn. Abex Inc., 1992-95; pres. Fisher Sci. Internat., Inc., Hampton, NH, 1991—98, CEO, 1991—, chmn., 1998—. Bd. dirs. Waste Mgmt.; mem. adv. bd. Sintokogio, Ltd. Pres. emeritus Met. Opera Assoc.; bd. dir. Wang Ctr. for Performing Arts; dir. & treas. Found. for NIH; trustee Healthcare Leadership Council; mem. bd. overseers The Bus. Roundtable, Bus. Sch. Columbia U., N.Y.C.; adv. com. Consumer Protection and Quality in the Health Care Industry, Washington. Capt. U.S. Army, 1965-67. Mem.: Brook, University (N.Y.C.); Bald Peak Colony (Melvin Village, N.H.); Lyford Cay (Nassau, Bahamas). Roman Catholic. Office: Fisher Sci Internat Liberty Ln Hampton NH 03842*

**MONTY, LOUIS HAROLD,** psychiatrist; b. L.A., Calif., May 20, 1958; s. Philip and Esther (Kousnetz) Monty. BS with hon. in Psychobiology, USC, 1980; MD, Tel Aviv U., Israel, 1985. Diplomate Am. Bd. Psychiatry & Neurology, 1991, Am. Bd. Gen. Adult Psychiatry, Am. Bd. Adolescent Psychiatry, 1993, Am. Bd. Child and Adolescent Psychiatry, 1993. Intern Duke U. Med. Ctr., Durham, NC, 1985—86, resident in psychiatry, 1986—89; fellow USC Med. Ctr., L.A., 1989—91; psychiatric cons. Pacific Clinics, Pasadena, Calif., 1991—93, L.A.Child Guidance Clinic, L.A., 1991—94; mem. staff San Bernardino County Dept. Behavioral Health, San Bernardino, Calif., 1994—99, Arrowhead Regional Med. Ctr., Colton, Calif., 1999—2004. Clin. asst. prof. Westen U. Osteo. Medicine, Pomona, Calif., 2001—. Mem.: Am. Acad. Child and Adolescent Psychiatry, Alpha Epsilon Delta (life). Avocations: classical music, piano, literature, painting, sketching. Office: We Youth Svcs 140 E Commonwealth Ave Ste 101 Fullerton CA 92832 Office Phone: 714-871-5646.

**MONZON, CARLOS MANUEL,** physician; s. Carlos Manuel and Amparo (Letona) Monzon; children: Carlos Rodolfo, Juan Pablo. MD, U. San Carlos, Guatemala, 1976; MSc, U. Minn., 1982. Diplomate Am. Bd. Pediat., Am. Bd. Pediat. Hematology and Oncology. Resident in pediat. U. San Carlos, 1976-77, U. Mo., Columbia, 1977-80; fellow in pediat. hematology and oncology Mayo Grad. Sch. Medicine, Rochester, Minn., 1980-82; instr. pediat. U. Mo., Columbia, 1982-83, asst. prof. child health, 1983-89; clin. asst. prof. in pediatrics Kansas U. Sch. Medicine, Kansas City, 1992—. Contbr. articles to med. jours. Recipient Fritz Kenny Meml. award in pediat. rsch. Midwest Soc. Pediat. Rsch., 1981. Fellow Am. Acad. Pediat. Home: 14201 Melrose St Overland Park KS 66221 Office: 20375 W 151st St Olathe KS 66061-7218

**MOOD, FRANCIS P., JR.,** lawyer, utilities executive; BA, The Citadel, 1960; LLB, Univ. Va., 1963; LLD (hon.), The Citadel, 1985, Univ. S.C., 2004. Bar: SC 1963. Ptnr. Haynsworth Sinkler Boyd, Columbia, SC, 1967—2004, pres., 1984—92; sr. v.p., gen. counsel, asst. sec. SCANA Corp., Columbia, SC, 2005—. Permanent mem. Judicial Conf., US Ct. Appeals (4th cir.); interim dean Univ. SC Sch. Law, 2003; chmn. SC Bd. Law Examiners, 1973—82. Mem. bd. vis. The Citadel, 1973—79, 1994—2000, chmn., 1997—2000; bd. dir. The Citadel Develop. Found., 1980—88, 1990—94, 2001—, pres., 1982—86; mem. Univ. SC Sch. Law Partnership Bd., 1991—94, pres., 1991—93; mem. Ctrl. Carolina Cmty. Found., 1992—98, pres., 1995—97; bd. dir. Liberty Fellowship, 2004—; Columbia Urban League. Served U.S. Army, 1964—66. Mem.: ABA, State Bar SC, Richland County Bar Assn. Office: SCANA Corporation 1426 Main St Columbia SC 29218

**MOODY, BARBARA KELLER,** systems administrator; b. Chesapeake, Va., June 21, 1952; d. Clarence Matthew and Jennie Jenkins Keller; m. Larry Eugene Moody, June 19, 1975; children: Clinton Eugene, Melissa Julia. Photographic printer Del-Mar Studios, Chesapeake, Va., 1978—79; adminstrv. asst. Norfolk Naval Shipyard, Portsmouth, Va., 1980—83, supply clk., 1983—86, br. head requirements, 1986—87, supply sys. analyst, 1987—. Co-founder Relative Praise Book Honor, Chesapeake, 2005—, dir. ministry, 2005—. Singer: (Christmas album) Christmas Jive!. Cmty. group leader Western Br. Cmty. Ch., Chesapeake, 2000—. Recipient Beneficial Suggestion award, Supply Dept. Norfolk Naval Shipyard, 1984, Sustained Superior Performance award, Norfolk Naval Shipyard, 1986, Notable Achievement award, 1990, Notable Achievement Award, 1997—99, Individual Performance award, 1992, 1994, 1995, 1997, 2000—02, Group Performance award, 2001—06. Baptist. Avocations: creative writing, arts & crafts, scrapbooks. Office: Norfolk Naval Shipyard Bldg 1500 Portsmouth VA 23709-5000 Office Phone: 757-396-9886.

**MOODY, DIXON MCGUIRE,** radiologist; b. Tyler, Tex., Jan. 12, 1937; s. Dwight Lyman Moody and Helen Blaine McGuire; m. Lucinda L. Blitz, Aug. 15, 1964; children: Abigail Ann (Moody) Sinwell, Susan Eloise (Moody) Prieto, Sarah Katherine. MD, U. of Tex. Southwestern, Dallas, 1963. Diplomate Diagnostic Radiology Am. Bd. of Radiology, 1971, Neuroradiology Am. Bd. of Radiology, 1995. Resident physician Stanford U. Sch of Medicine, Palo Alto, Calif., 1963—70; asst. physician Cornell U. Sch of Medicine, N.Y.C., 1970—71; asst. prof. U. of N.Mex Sch Medicine, Albuquerque, 1971—73; prof. and chief of neuroradiology Wake Forest U. Sch. Medicine, Winston-Salem, NC. Mem. Nat. Adv. Coun. NINDS, NIH, Bethesda, Md., 1994—97, Ctr. for Sci. Rev., NIH, Bethesda, Md., 1998—2004; mem., sci. program com. Radiol. Soc. of N.Am., Oak Brook, Ill. Capt. U.S. Army, 1966—67. Decorated Bronze Star Medal US Army; recipient Established Investigator, Clin. Sci. Award, Wake Forest U. Sch. of

Medicine, 2002; grantee Jacob K Javits Neurosci. Investigator, NIH, 1984—2004, Clin. Hypotheses in Neuroscience Imaging Rsch., Charles A Dana Found., 1996-1999. Fellow: Am. Coll. of Radiology; mem.: Am. Soc. of Neuroradiology (Outstanding Contributions in Rsch. award 2005), Soc. for Neurosci., Radiol. Soc. of N.Am. (Outstanding Rscher award 2005), Forsyth Country Club, Hillsboro Club, Alpha Omega Alpha. Achievements include research in Brain injury during heart surgery due to fat emboli; brain hemorrhage in neonates due to rupture of veins; dementia due to obstruction of veins and loss of capillaries; significant vascular disease in Alzheimer's brains; cause and prevention of brain injury during cardiopulmonary bypass. Avocation: tennis. Office: Wake Forest University School Medicine Medical Center Blvd Winston Salem NC 27157-1088 Office Phone: 336-716-2485. Business E-Mail: dmmoody@wfubmc.edu.

**MOODY, FRANK G.,** surgeon; b. Franklin, NH, May 3, 1928; BA, Dartmouth Coll., 1953; attended, Dartmouth Med. Sch., 1952—54; MD, Cornell Univ., 1956. Cert. FACS, 1967, Am. Bd. Surgery, 1980. Asst. prof. Univ. Calif. Med Sch., San Francisco, 1965—66; assoc. prof. through prof. Univ. Ala. Med. Sch., 1966—71; prof., chmn. dept. surgery Univ. Utah Sch. Med., 1971—82; staff surgeon Vet. Adminstrn. Hosp., Salt Lake City, 1971—82; chmn. dept. surgery Univ. Tex. Med. Sch., Houston, 1982—94, Denton A. Cooley prof. surgery, 1982—. Recipient Sci. Achievement award AMA, 1995. Mem.: AMA, Am. Gastroenterological Assn., Am. Pancreatic Assn. (pres. 1979), Am. Physiological Soc., Am. Surgical Assn., Phi Beta Kappa, Alpha Omega Alpha. Office: U Tex Med Sch Dept Surgery 6431 Fannin St Houston TX 77030-1501 Office Phone: 713-500-7241. Business E-Mail: frank.g.moody@uth.tmc.edu.

**MOODY, GENE BYRON,** engineering executive, small business owner, minister; b. Calhoun, Ga., Aug. 29, 1933; s. Denzel Elwood and Mary Edna (Hughes) M.; m. Willie Earline Chauncey, Sept. 1, 1955; children: Byron Eugene, Iva Marie Levy. BSCE, U. Tenn., 1956. Registered profl. engr., Ala., Ark., Ga., La., Miss., Tex. V.p. S.I.P. Engring. Corp., Baton Rouge, 1968-70; project engr. S.I.P., Inc., Houston, 1970-73; dir. of engring. Jacus Assoc., Mpls., 1972-73; dir. of civil engring. Barnard & Burk, Baton Rouge, 1973-79; project mgr. Process Svcs., Baton Rouge, 1979-80, Salmon & Assoc., Baton Rouge, 1980-81; chief engr. Minton & Assoc., Lafayette, La., 1982; mgr. Assoc. Engr. Cons., Baton Rouge, 1982-86; owner Gene B. Moody, P.E., Baton Rouge, 1986—. Author: Deliverance Manual, 1989; contbr. articles to profl. jours. Tchr. Lake Hamilton Bible Camp, Hot Springs, Ark., 1981—. With U.S. Army, 1957. U. Chattanooga scholar, 1951, U. Tenn. scholar, 1953. Fellow ASCE; mem. Am. Soc. Safety Engrs., La. Soc. Profl. Surveyors, Soc. Automotive Engrs., Inst. Transp. Engrs., La. Engring. Soc., Transp. Res. Rsch. Bd., others. Home and Office: 14930 Jefferson Hwy Baton Rouge LA 70817-5217 E-mail: gbmoody@bellsouth.net.

**MOODY, KATHRYN CURRIER,** communications executive, educator; b. Chgo. d. George Edson and Dorothy (Cleveland) C.; children: William Scott, John Currier. BA, U. Mich., 1961, MA, 1970; MEd, Columbia U., 1990, EdD, 1993. Dir. corp. devel. Nickelodeon, N.Y.C., 1981-82; dir. nat. program Sta. WQED, N.Y.C., 1983-84; exec. v.p. Framework II, N.Y.C., 1987-88; pres. Currier Moody Communications, Larchmont, NY, 1988—93; spl. asst. to pres. U. Tex. Med. Sch., Galveston, 1995—2001, dir. Open Gates programs, 1995—2001, asst. prof. neurology, 1995—2001; dir. Ctr. for Understanding Media, 1994—. Editor: Television Awareness Training, 1979, Growing Up on Television, 1980; author: The Children of Telstar, 2000; contbg. author: N.Y. Times Encyclopedia of Television; contbr. articles to profl. jours.; spkr. in field Trustee Larchmont Hist. Soc., 1977-78. Woodrow Wilson fellow Smithsonian Instn., 1978. Mem. Nat. Acad. TV Arts and Scis., N.Y. Women in Communications. Avocations: competitive tennis, poetry, jogging, raising dogs.

**MOODY, MARILYN DALLAS,** retired librarian; b. Little Rock, Aug. 28; d. Corbin Luther and Marian Dallas; m. W.I. Moody Jr., June 1, 1970 (div. 1987); m. Jeffry Baumann, 1988 Student, Hendrix Coll, Conway, Ark., 1959, U. Ark., 1960, Drexel U., 1964. Libr. Free Libr. Phila., 1964—70, cons. libr., 1971—76, coord. dist. libr. ctr. svcs., 1976—82, chief ext. svcs. divsn., 1982—91; exec. dir. Bucks County Free Libr., Doylestown, Pa., 1991—2003; ret., 2003. Recipient Cert. of Merit, 1981 Mem. ALA (councilor 1983-86), Pub. Libr. Assn. (legis. com. 1989-93), Pa. Libr. Assn. (legis. com. 1989-90, chair legis. com. 1980-82, coord. Legis. Day 1980-82, 87, 92, pres. pub. libr. divsn. 1995-96, chair scholarship com., treas. 2000-02), Assn. Pa. Pub. Libr. Sys. (chair 2002), Pa. Citizens for Better Librs. (bd. dirs., chair membership com. 2006) Avocations: reading, travel.

**MOODY, RICK (HIRAM FREDERICK MOODY III),** writer; b. NYC, Oct. 18, 1961; s. Hiram Frederick Jr. and Margaret Maureen Flynn M.; married. BA, Brown Univ.; MFA, Columbia Univ., 1986. Editl. asst. Simon & Schuster, NYC; line editor Farrar Straus & Giroux, NYC, 1988—91. Bd. dir. Corp. Yaddo; instr. SUNY, Purchase, Bennington Coll. Writing Seminars, Fine Arts Work Ctr., Provincetown, Mass., New Sch. Social Rsch. Author: (short story collections) The Ring of Brightest Angels Around Heaven, 1994 (Aga Khan award Paris Rev., 1994), Demonology, 2001, (travel memoir) The Black Veil: A Memoir with Digressions, 2002 (NAMI/Ken Book award, 2003, PEN/Martha Albrand prize for excellence in the memoir, 2003), (novels) Garden State, 1991 (Pushcart Press Editors' Choice Book award, 1991), The Ice Storm, 1994 (made into feature film, 1997), The Diviners, 2006; co-editor: (anthology) Joyful Noise: The New Testament Revisited, 1997; performer: (albums) Rick Moody and One Ring Zero, 2004. Co-founder Young Lions Book award NY Pub. Libr. Recipient Addison Metcalf award, Am. Acad. Arts and Letters, 1998; grantee Guggenheim fellowship, 2000. Mem.: PEN Am. Ctr. (sec.). Mailing: Author Mail Little Brown & Co 1271 Ave of the Americas New York NY 10020*

**MOODY, ROBERT ADAMS,** neurosurgeon; b. Swampscott, Mass., Oct. 1, 1934; s. George F. and Florence P. M.; m. Claudia; children: Robert Adams, II, Cathy, Paul, Lisa, Sherri. BA, U. Chgo., 1955, BS, 1956, MD, 1960. Intern Royal Victoria Hosp., Montreal, Que., Canada, 1960-61; resident in neurosurgery U. Vt. Affiliated Hosps., 1961-66; fellow Lahey Clinic, Boston, 1963-64; asst. prof. neurol. surgery U. Chgo. Med. Sch., 1966-71; sr. clin. instr., then asst. clin. prof. Tufts U. Med. Sch., 1972-74; prof. neurosurgery Abraham Lincoln Med. Sch., U. Ill., Chgo., 1975-81; chmn. div. neurosurgery Cook County Hosp., Chgo., 1974-81, assoc. chmn. dept. surgery, 1976-81; clin. prof. neurosurgery SUNY-Binghamton, 1983—2005; chmn. neurosurgery Guthrie Clinic, Sayre, Pa., 1981-95; ret., 1995. Contbr. articles med. jours. USPHS fellow, 1957-58 Mem. ACS, Am. Assn. Neurol. Surgeons, Pa. Neurosurg. Soc. (councillor 1986-87, pres.-elect 1988, pres. 1989), Mid-Atlantic Neurosurg. Soc., Ctrl. Neurosurg. Soc. (pres. 1978-79), Alumni Assn. Lahey Clinic Found., Sigma Xi. Office: Guthrie Clinic Guthrie Sq Sayre PA 18840 Business E-Mail: rcmoody@cqservices.com.

**MOODY, ROBERT LEE,** insurance company executive; b. 1936; Chmn., chief exec. officer Nat. Western Life Ins. Co., Austin, Tex., also bd. dirs.; pres. Am. Nat. Ins. Co., Galveston, Tex., 1995—2000, chmn., CEO, also bd. dirs.; also pres. Moody Bankshares, Inc., Galveston. Pres. Moody Investments, Galveston. Office: Am Nat Ins Co 1 Moody Plz Galveston TX 77550

**MOODY, RON,** actor, writer; b. London, Jan. 8, 1924; s. Bernard and Kate (Ogus) Moodnick. BSc in Econs., U. London, 1953. Appeared in plays: 6 Years Revue, 1959, Candide, 1960, Oliver, as Shylock in Merchant of Venice, 1967, as Polonius in Hamlet, 1972, as Richard in Richard III, 1978, Iago in Othello, 1981, as Harpagon in Moliere's The Miser, Peter Pan, 2000, 05, The Sunshine Boys, 2001, Comedians, 2001, Oliver, 2003, Peter Pan, Malvern, 2005; (films) Oliver, 1967, Twelve Chairs, 1970, Dogpound Shuffle, 1973, Wrong is Right, 1981, Where is Parsifal?, 1983, Ghost in Monte Carlo, 1989, Kid at King Arthur's Court, 1995, The Three Kings, 1999, Paradise Grove, 1999, Chopsticks, 2000, Steps, 2000, Revelation, 2001, Lost Dogs, 2004, Moussaka and Chips, 2005, The Lizard Boy, 2006; stage musicals: USA tour HMS Pinafore, 1987, Sherlock Holmes, 1989, Streets of Dublin, 1992, Bertie,

1993, Peter Pan, 1995, The Canterville Ghost, 1998; on TV as Inspector Hart in Nobody's Perfect, ABC-TV, 1980, Dial M for Murder, 1981, Keen Eddie, 2003, The Bill, 2003, Holby City, 2005, Celebration of Oliver, 2005, The Lizard Boy, 2006; dir. (play) Kafka In Love, 1991; author-composer musical comedies Joey, 1966, Saturnalia, 1970, Move Along Sideways, 1971, The Showman, 1976, Nine Lives, 1991; touring Move Along Sideways, 1991, Monologues, 2003; author: (books) The Devil You Don't, 1980, Very Very Slightly Imperfect, Off the Cuff, 1987, The Amazon Box, 1998. Served with RAF, 1943-48. Recipient Golden Globe award, 1968, Moscow Golden Bear award as best actor, 1970, Coco Trophy award, Clowns Internat., 1999; nominated Oscar, 1968. Mem. Am. Acad. Motion Picture Arts and Scis., Variety Club of Great Brit., Actors Equity, Screen Actors Guild, Clowns Internat. (life pres.), Performing Rights Soc. Writers, Soc. Authors. Home: Ingleside 41 The Green Southgate London N14 6EN England Office: Eric Glass Ltd 25 Ladbroke Crescent Notting Hill London WII IP5 England also: The Barry Freed Co 468 N Camden Dr Ste 201 Beverly Hills CA 90210 Office Phone: 0207 229 9500.

**MOODY, SHERYL L.,** educational association administrator; b. Kokomo, Ind., Feb. 26, 1949; d. Donald E.C. and Ima Ruth Leicht; children: Michael, Alexander. BA with honors in English, Purdue U., West Lafayette, Ind., 1966; JD, St. John's U., Jamaica, N.Y., 1977; PhD in Edn., Capella U., Mpls., 2006. Bar: N.Y., U.S. Dist. Ct. (ea. and so. dist.) N.Y. Hearing examiner Family Ct. of Nassau County, Westbury, NY, 1985—87; gen. counsel and counsel N.Y. Inst. Tech., Old Westbury, 1987—2003; v.p., gen. counsel Ross U. divsn. DeVry Inc., Edison, NJ, 2004—05; exec. dir. Accrediting Coun. for Independent Colls. and Schs., Washington, 2006—. Lectr. in field. Dir., treas. Harbor Day Care, NY, 1995—2003; dir., pres. West Gilgo Beach Assn., NY, 1988—99; dir. Nassau County Sports Commn., NY, 1996—99. Named Woman of the Yr., Town of Babylon, N.Y., 1992. Mem.: Nat. Assn. of Coll. and Univ. Attys., Bar Assn. of Nassau County (dir., com. chair 1978—2004, Pres.'s award 1996). Avocations: sailing, kayaking, reading. Office: ACICS 750 First St NE Ste 980 Washington DC 20002

**MOOERS, CHRISTOPHER NORTHRUP KENNARD,** physical oceanographer, educator; b. Hagerstown, Md., Nov. 11, 1935; s. Frank Burt and Helen (Miner) M.; m. Elizabeth Eva Fauntleroy, June 11, 1960; children: Blaine Hanson MacFee, Randall Walden Lincoln. BS, U.S. Naval Acad., 1957; MS, U. Conn., 1964; PhD, Oreg. State U., 1969. Postdoctoral fellow U. Liverpool, Eng., 1969-70; asst. prof. U. Miami, Fla., 1970-72, assoc. prof. Fla., 1972-76, U. Del., Newark, 1976-78, prof., 1978-79; prof. chmn. dept. oceanography Naval Postgrad. Sch., Monterey, Calif., 1979-86; dir. Inst. for Naval Oceanography, Stennis Space Ctr., Miss., 1986-89; sci. advisor to dir. Inst. for Naval Oceanography, 1989; rsch. prof. U. N.H., Durham, 1989-91; prof., chmn. divsn. applied marine physics U. Miami, 1991-93, dir. Ocean Pollution Rsch. Ctr., 1992—2002, dir. Ocean Prediction Exptl. Lab., 1993—. Coord. Coastal Ocean Sci. Program, 1991—. Editor Jour. Phys. Oceanography, 1991-96; mng. editor Coastal and Estuarine Studies, 1978-99. With USN, 1957-64. NSF fellow, 1964-67; NATO fellow, 1969-70; Sr. Queen Elizabeth fellow, 1980 Mem.: AAAS, Estuarine Res. Fedn., Marine Tech. Soc., Am. Meteorol. Soc. (chmn. sci.and tech. com. meterology and oceanography of Coastal Zone 1996—2002), U. Nat. Oceanog. Lab. Sys./Fleet Improvement Com. (chair 1994—97), U.S. Nat. Com. Internat. Union Geodesy and Geophysics (chmn. 1995—99), Ea. Pacific Oceanic Conf. (chmn. 1979—86), Am. Geophys. Union (press. ocean sci. sect. 1982—84), The Oceanography Soc. (interim councilor 1987—88), Sigma Xi. Achievements include pioneering direct observation of transient coastal ocean currents and fronts plus mesoscale and coastal ocean prediction rsch. Home: 2521 Inagua Ave Coconut Grove FL 33133-3811 Office: U Miami Divsn Applied Marine Physics OPEL/RSMAS 4600 Rickenbacker Causeway Miami FL 33149-1031 Office Phone: 305-421-4088. Business E-Mail: cmooers@rsmas.miami.edu. *My central goal is to understand the ocean as a physical system by combining the interpretation of observations with dynamical theory and numerical models. Special emphasis has been on the dynamics of coastal oceans (continental shelf regions), now the scientific basis for practical mesoscale ocean prediction applied to marginal and semi-enclosed seas and pioneering the development of operational oceanography.*

**MOOG, MATTHEW,** Internet company executive; b. 1970; Bus. devel. exec. Microsoft Corp., 1992—96; v.p. sales CoolSavings, Inc., Chgo., 1996—98, exec. v.p. sales, mktg., 1998—2001, pres., 2001—, COO, 2001, now CEO, 2001—. Named one of 40 Under Forty, Crain's Bus. Chgo., 2005. Office: CoolSavings Inc Ste 1900 360 N Michigan Ave Chicago IL 60601 Office Phone: 312-224-5000. Office Fax: 312-224-5001.*

**MOOK, SARAH,** retired chemist; b. Bklyn., Oct. 29, 1929; d. Wong and Lie Won (Woo) M. BA, Hunter Coll., N.Y.C., 1952; postgrad., Columbia U., N.Y.C., 1954—57, postgrad., 1962—65, U. Hartford, Conn., 1958—59; grad., N.Y.C. Citiznes Police Acad., 2001. Cartographic aide U.S. Geol. Survey Dept. of Interior, Washington, 1952-54; rsch. asst. Mineral Beneficiation Lab. Columbia U., NYC, 1954-57; analytical chemist nuc. divsn. Combustion Engring., Inc., Windsor, Conn., 1957-59; rsch. scientist Radiations Applications Inc., Long Island City, NY, 1959-62; chemist Marks Polarized Corp., Whitestone, NY, 1962-64; sr. chemist NRA Inc. subs. Nuc. Rsch. Assoc., Inc., New Hyde Park, NY, 1964-75; clin. chemist Coney Island Hosp., Bklyn., 1974-84, cmty. bd., 1978-80; assoc. chemist Bellevue Hosp. Ctr., 1984-89, prin. chemist, 1989-95; ret., 1995; instr. ESL, 1999—2005. Contbr. articles to profl. jours. Mem. adv. com. to state assemblyman State of NY, 1970-72; trustee Park Ave. Christian Ch., 1973-82, sec., 1973-80, vice-chair, 1980-81, chair bd. trustees, 1981-82, pres. Christian Women's Fellowship, 1962-65, elder, 1983—; mem. Neighborhood Adv. Bd. for Cmty. Devel., 1996—, sec., 1996-99, chair 2000-02; mem. Cmty. Bd., 2002-04; mem. cmty. adv. bd. Coney Island Hosp., 2004—. Named Woman of Yr., N.Y.C. Coun., 2004; recipient Margaret M. McCord Woman of Yr. Meml. award, Sheepshead Bay Hist. Soc., 2004, Woman of Yr. Humanitarian award, NY State Senate, 2004; Disting. Leadership in Cmty. award, NYC Office of Comptr. Mem. Am. Assn. Clin. Chemistry (sec. NY Met. sect. 1999—), AAAS, Am. Chem. Soc., NY Acad. Sci., Van Slyke Soc., Citizens Police Acad. Alumni Assn. (publicity com. 2004—). Republican. Home: 2042 E 14th St Brooklyn NY 11229-3314

**MOON, BARBARA G.,** lawyer; d. Thomas Hassell Cook and Mable Ruth Head; children: Shane Brock, Angie Moon Eidschun. BA in Polit. Sci., Ga. State U., Atlanta, 1985, JD, 1988. Bar: Ga. 1991, South Fulton County 1991, Atlanta 1991, Fayette 1991, DC 1991, US Dist. Ct. (no. and mid. dists.) Ga. 1989, US Ct. Appeals (11th cir.) 1989, US Ct. Appeals (DC cir.) 1992, Ga. Supreme Ct. 1989, US Supreme Ct. 1992. Pvt. practice, def. atty. Barbara G. Moon, Esq., Jonesboro, Ga., 1992—. Spkr. in field; pro hac magistrate judge Clayton County Magistrate Ct., 1993—97. Mem.: Assn. Nat. Criminal Def. Lawyers. Ga. Assn. Criminal Def. Attys. (v.p. 1995—97), Henry County Bar Assn., Clayton County Bar Assn., Atlanta Bar Assn. Family Law, Criminal Law Sects., South Fulton Bar Assn. (v.p. 1993—94, pres. 1995—97), Phi Alpha Delta. Baptist. Avocations: swimming, skiing, reading, exercise. Office Phone: 770-471-9000. E-mail: bgm2001@earthlink.net.

**MOON, CRAIG A.,** publishing executive; b. Jamestown, NY; m. Patricia Moon; children: Kelly, Jeffrey, Taylor. Student, Tampa St. Petersburg Coll., U. South Fla. Mgmt. positions in adv. and circulation Tampa Tribune, Phila. Inquirer, Yakima Herald-Republic, Wash.; advt. dir. Modesto Bee, Calif.; v.p. advt. The Cin. Post, 1985—88, The Cin. Enquirer, 1985—88; pres. & pub. The News-Press, Ft. Myers, Fla., 1988—89, Ark. Gazette, Little Rock, 1989—91; pres. The Tennessean, Nashville, 1991—2002, pub., 1992—2002; pres. Piedmont Newspaper Group Gannett Co., Inc., 1999—2002, exec. v.p. Newspaper Divsn. McLean, Va., 2002—03, pres. & pub., USA Today, 2003—. Office: USA Today 7950 Jones Branch Dr Mc Lean VA 22108*

**MOON, DAVID A.,** manufacturing executive; b. Washington, Aug. 2, 1956; d. Arthur Ray and Lillian (Baker) Moon. PhD in Comm., U.Ill., 1978. Cert.: Police/Nev. (three superiors); industrial employer Ind. Certifications Releases Corp./E Rochell, Nev. Owner,mgr. Indsl. Arts Svc. Firm, Henderson, Nev.,

---

1977; with N.L.R.B., 1977; industrialist I.C.R. Corp., Henderson, Nev., 1980; indusl. authority I.C.R. Corp. TM, Henserson, Nev., 1991—; pres., CEO Teledyne Inc., Ctr. City, 1996; judge US Superior Ct., 1956; owner Ind. Arts Systems Firm, 1972; ind. employer US Gov. Owner (magazines) 25,000 law publ. Recipient 9 First Pl. Blue Ribbon (no. 1) patent and trademark, 1969—72. Mem.: office of Bd. of Gov. Election. Baptist. Office: Indsl Arts Systems Firm 140 E Rochell Rd Henderson NV 89015 Office Phone: 702-564-3104.

**MOON, DAVID C.,** information technology executive; Bachelors in Computer Sci., Brigham Young U., 1983. From software engr. to chief tech. officer, sr. v.p. devel. WordPerfect Corp. (acquired by Novell), 1982—94; sr. v.p. development, applications group Novell, Inc., 1994—95; chief info. officer, mem. gov.'s cabinet State of Utah; gen. ptnr. EsNet, Ltd., Provo, Utah, 1996—; chmn. bd. dirs. Myfamily.com, Inc., Provo, 2001—. Bd. dirs. Rappore Techs., Manzanita Holdings, Found, O2 Blue; mem. Technol. Initiative Advisory Bd. Utah State Bd. of Regents; mem. Technol. Entrepreneurship Advisory Bd. Westminster Coll. Mem.: Utah Information Technologies Assn. (trustee, mem. exec. com.). Office: Myfamily dot com 360 W 4800 N Provo UT 84604

**MOON, DAVID TURNER, JR.,** history educator, researcher; b. Loganville, Ga., July 10, 1979; s. David Turner and Brenda Wells Moon; m. April Faye Clay, Oct. 28, 2006. AA, Gainesville Coll., 1999; BA, U. Ga., 2001; MA, Ga. State U., 2004. Student asst. spl. collections Ga. State U. Libr., Atlanta, 2001—03; grad. rsch. asst. history Ga. State U., Atlanta, 2002—04; adj. prof. history Ga. Perimeter Coll., Dunwoody, Ga., 2004—. Mem. So. Hist. Assn., Athens, Ga., 2002—, Ga. Hist. Soc., Savannah, Ga., 2001—, Bapt. History and Heritage Soc., Brentwood, Tenn., 2002—, Ga. Bapt. Hist. Soc., Macon, Ga., 2002—, Am. Hist. Assn., Washington, 2004—. Contbr. articles to profl. jours. Min. Pleasant Hill Baptist Ch., Conyers, Ga., 1999—. Recipient Hope scholarship, Ga. Student Fin. Commn., 1997—2001. Mem.: Assn. Ga. State Univ. Historians, Rockdale County Geneal. Soc., Atlanta History Ctr., Am. Hist. Assn., So. Hist. Assn., Bapt. History and Heritage Soc., Ga. Bapt. Hist. Soc., Ga. Hist. Soc. R-Consevative. Baptist. Avocations: reading, writing, researching history, watching movies.

**MOON, DEOK HYUN,** research scientist; arrived in U.S., 1991; s. Dae Ju Moon and Chun Ja Go; m. Mun Jung Kang, Aug. 4, 1968. BE in Environ. Engring., Chosun U., 1991; ME in Environ. Engring., Stevens Inst. Tech., 1994; PhD, Stevens Inst. Tech., 2003. Postdoctoral rsch. assoc. Stevens Inst. of Tech., Hoboken, 2003—. Office: Stevens Inst Tech Castle Point on Hudson Hoboken NJ 07030 Office Phone: 201-216-8097. Office Fax: 201-216-8212. E-mail: dmoon@stevens.edu.

**MOON, FLETCHER FROE,** college librarian, multi-media artist, minister; s. James Lawrence and Lakie Clarice Moon, Dorothy Sawyer Moon (Stepmother); m. Marilyn Nadine Braden, Aug. 14, 1976; 1 child, Maikaia Althea. BA (cum laude), Fisk U., 1972—76; MLS, Vanderbilt U. (Peabody Coll.), 1978—79. Lic. Born Again Ch., 2000. Ordination as Ch. Elder Born Again Ch., 2002; Librarianship N.J. Dept. of Edn., 1980. Libr. asst., spl. collections Fisk U. Libr., Nashville, 1973—76; cameraman/fl. dir./prodn. asst./courier WSM-TV, Nashville, 1975—77; creative/music dir. Larry Sonn Advt. Agy., Nashville, 1977—78; sr. libr. asst., ext. services Nashville Pub. Libr., Nashville, 1977—80; sr. reference libr./adult programming coord. Montclair Pub. Libr., NJ, 1980—83; instr./reference libr. Tenn. State U., Nashville, 1983—88, asst. prof./reference libr., 1988—98, asst. prof./head reference libr., 1998—. Musician (freelance), Nashville, 1972—; prodr., radio/tv commercials Larry Sonn Advt. Agy., Nashville, 1977—78; facilitator, project aero-scan Nashville Pub. Libr., 1978—79; project participant Atlanta U. SLIS Grant, Atlanta, 1985—87; presenter Coun. on Libr. Resources, Fisk U., Nashville, 1989; grant writer Tenn. State U., Nashville, 1990—, grant adminstr./project dir., 1991—94; presenter FIPSE/USDE Project Directors Conf., Wash., 1992—93, Black Caucus of the ALA Conf., Milw., 1994. Musician: (jazz performance) Fisk U. concerts featuring Duke Ellington, Billy Taylor, Eubie Blake, Milt Jackson, Julian Cannonball Adderley, et al, (syndicated TV prodn.) I Owe It All to the Songs That I Sing, (concert tours) The Orchestrated Crowd, Modern Black Mass Choir, other musical groups (Alumni Guest Artist award, 1979); prodr.(facilitator): (heritage tourism drama production) Freedom Trek III; recording artist: documentary film soundtrack The Gift of Black Folk; actor: (plays) Beatrice du Congo; composer (performer): (music/dance collaboration) Ring Dance; singer: (musical revue) The Cotton Club Remembered, editor libr. newsletters and pubs. Performer/supporter Black Expo, Nashville, 1974—76; charter mem. N.J. Black Librs. Network, Montclair, 1980—83; contbr. United Way of Mid. Tenn., Nashville, 1985—2000; campaign vol. Montclair Town Coun., NJ, 1980—82; vol. Howard Gentry vice-mayoral campaign, Nashville, 2002—03; elder Born Again Ch., Nashville, 1972—, trustee, 1996—; facilitator When Men Pray, Nashville, 1998. Recipient Harvard Book Award, Harvard Club of Nashville, 1970, Music award, Fisk U. Jazz Ensemble, 1979, Artist's Portrait, Kay Kato, Newark (NJ) Star-Ledger, 1982, Judge's award, Pride of Tenn. Elks Lodge, 2002—03; grantee Fund for the Improvement of Post Secondary Edn., U.S. Dept. Edn., 1991—94; Presdl. Scholarship, Fisk U., 1973—76, Title II-B Fellowship, Peabody Coll. (Vanderbilt U.), 1978—79. Mem.: ALA (mem. Black Caucus), Tenn. Libr. Assn., Assn. Vanderbilt Black Alumni, Nashville Fisk Club. Mem. Christian Ch. Avocations: reading, creative writing, prayer, walking/light exercise, travel. Office: Tenn State U 3500 John A Merritt Blvd Nashville TN 37220-2336 Office Phone: 615-963-5205. E-mail: fmoon@tnstate.edu.

**MOON, HOJIN,** statistician; m. Elizabeth (Hyunju) K., Apr. 5, 1988; children: Mark (Ki Sung), Christopher K. PhD, SUNY, Stony Brook, 1999. Instr. U. Tex., M. D. Anderson Cancer Ctr., Houston, 1999—2003; math. statistician Nat. Ctr. for Toxicological Rsch., U.S. FDA, Jefferson, Ark., 2003—. Scientist Instl. Animal Care and Use Com., Nat. Ctr. for Toxicological Rsch., U.S. FDA, Jefferson, Ark., 2004—. Author: (book chpt.) Encyclopedia of Biostatistics; contbr. articles to profl. jours. Recipient Disting. Student Paper award, Internat. Biometric Soc., Ea. NAm. Region, 1999, award, Nat. Ctr. for Toxicological Rsch., U.S. FDA, 2004, Outstanding Svc. awards, U. S. FDA, 2004, Employee of Month, Nat. Ctr. for Toxicological Rsch., U. S. FDA, 2004; scholar Academic Excellence award, Han Yang U., 1987. Mem.: Soc. for Risk Analysis, Am. Statis. Assn. (Ctrl. Ark. chpt. rep. 2004—), FDA Statis. Assn. (ctr. rep. 2005—), Am. Assn. for Cancer Rsch. Internat. Biometric Soc. Achievements include research in Attribution of tumor lethality for occult tumors in the absence of cause-of-death information; Development of Improved Survival-Adjusted Tests for Animal Carcinogenicity/Tumorigenicity Data; Estimation of Lag Time Between Onset of and Death from an Occult Tumor via Attribution of Tumor Lethality; Dose-Response Modeling for Microbial Risk Assessment; Optimal Tree-Based Ensemble Methods for Class Prediction and Classification by Ensembles from Radom Partitions. Office: US Food and Drug Adminstrn Jefferson Lab 3900 NCTR Rd Jefferson AR 72079 Office Phone: 870-543-7931. Business E-Mail: hojin.moon@fda.hhs.gov.

**MOON, JAMES RUSSELL,** technology education educator; b. St. Cloud, Minn., Apr. 12, 1950; s. Glenn Howard and Audrey Katherine (Berg) M.; m. Corrine Mae St. Aubin, July 14, 1978; children: Sheri Ann, Brian Michael. BS, St. Cloud State U., 1972; MS, Bemidji State U., 1975. Tech. edn. tchr. Minnetonka (Minn.) Pub. Schs., 1972—2005, dist. dept. chmn. tech. edn., 1993-95. Voc. standards com. Minn. Dept. Edn., 1995; mem. State Planning Com., 1989-2005. Designer/engr.: Row Crop Tractor, 1975; contbr. articles to profl. jours. Recipient Anchor award Minn. Pub. Schs., 1991, Tchr. Excellence award Internat. Tech. Edn. Assn., 1994, Disting. Tech. Educator Citation, 2002, Minnetonka Co-curricular Advisor of Yr., 2001, Tchr. of Yr. Optimist Club of Glen Lake, 2005; named Disting. Tech. Educator, Internat. Tech. Edn. Assn., 2002. Mem. Minn. Valley Tech. Edn. Assn. (sec. 1974), Minn. Tech. Edn. Assn. (mem. supermileage state competition com. 1989-2005, Tech. Edn. Tchr. of Yr. 1993, Disting. Svc. award 1991, 92, 94, Joyce Gustafson Meml. award, 2003). Presbyterian. Avocations: auto restoration,

---

outdoor activities. Home: 2037 20th St SE Buffalo MN 55313-4813 Office: Minn H S 18301 Highway 7 Minnetonka MN 55345-4114 Office Phone: 952-401-5915. Business E-Mail: jmoon@minnetonka.k12.mn.us.

**MOON, JOHN ELLIS VAN COURTLAND,** retired historian; b. Geneva, Oct. 25, 1929; arrived in U.S., 1940; s. Carlyle van Courtland and Marie Edmée (Choisy) Moon; m. Palma Roberge (div.); children: John Albert van Courtland, Margaret Hames, Laurelle Conte; m. Joan Mary Farrell, July 24, 1971. AB History and Lit., Harvard U., 1952, PhD Am. Civilization, 1968; MA English and Comparative Lit., Columbia U., 1953. Instr. English Merrimack Coll., North Andover, Mass., 1953—55, Boston U., 1957—58; from instr. to prof. history Boston State Coll., 1958—82; prof. Fitchburg State Coll., Mass., 1982—93, prof. emeritus, 1993—. Chmn. com. Coun. Pres., Mass. State Coll. Sys., 1990; vis. prof. Kings Coll., U. London, 1994—95; presenter in field. Author: Confines of Concept: American Strategy in World War II, 1988; co-editor: Biological and Toxin Weapons: Research, Development and Use from the Middle Ages to 1945, 1999; contbr. articles to profl. jours. Grantee, John Kittredge Fund, 1994, John D. and Catherine MacArthur Found., 1994. Mem.: Mass. State Coll. Assn. (pres., Boston State Coll. chpt. 1980—82), Am. Assn. Univ. Profs. (pres., Boston State Coll. chpt. 1970—72, pres. Mass. state conf. 1982—84, William S. Tacey award 1998). Avocations: mountain climbing, book collecting, trekking, travel. Home and Office: 11 Monmouth Ct Brookline MA 02446 Office Phone: 617-739-5475. Personal E-mail: jevcm@comcast.net.

**MOON, JOHN HENRY, SR.,** banker; b. Van Buren, Ark., Aug. 19, 1937; s. B.R. and Alma (Witte) M.; m. Agnes Rose Dickens, Aug. 16, 1958; children: John Henry, Randall Allen. AA, Delmar Coll., Corpus Christi, Tex., 1956; BBA cum laude, Tex. A&M U., Kingsville, 1958. Sr. acct. Tex. Eastern Transp. Co. and subs., 1958-63; exec. v.p., dir. Houston Rsch. Inst., 1963-68; sr. v.p., asst. to chmn. bd., dir. Main Bank, 1968—69; vice chmn. bd., dir. N.E. Bank, 1969; CEO, chmn. bd., dir. Pasadena (Tex.) Nat. Bank, 1970-81; gen. ptnr. Moon and Assocs., Ltd., 1977—. Chmn. bd., pres. Interservice Life Ins. Corp., Phoenix, Cmty. Bank, Houston, 1975-81, Interstate Bank, Houston, 1977-81, Moon Credit Corp., Pasadena, 1975—, Peoples Bank, Houston, 1983-93; chmn. bd. Cmty. Nat. Bank, Friendswood, Tex., 1981-93, Peoples Nat. Bank. Pasadena, Tex., 1984-93; chmn., pres. Sam Houston Pky. Transp. Corp., 1991-93; bd. dirs. Quality Wire Rope Corp., chmn., 1999-2005; pres. Sure Found. Inc., 1987—. Past bd. dirs. Pasadena Heart Assn., Salvation Army, Tex. Assn. Prevention of Blindness; past chmn. City of Pasadena Bd. Devel.; past chmn. adv. bd. Pasadena Civic Ctr.; past dir. S.E. Econ. Devel. Inc.; bd. dirs. San Jacinto Coll. Found., 2000-03, chmn., 2002-03. Named Outstanding Young Man of Yr., Pasadena Jr. C. of C., 1973; named to Pasadena Hall of Fame, 1988. Mem. AICPA, Pasadena C. of C. (bd. dirs. S.E. Econ. Devel., "C" Club, Citizen of Yr. 1994), Tex. Soc. CPAs, Tex. Bankers Assn., Rotary (pres. Pasadena Rotary found. 2001—). Home: 310 Del Monte Dr Friendswood TX 77546 Office: PO Box 3487 Pasadena TX 77501 Office Phone: 713-943-7777. Business E-Mail: johnhmoonsr@aol.com.

**MOON, JULIE ANN,** elementary school educator; b. Fort Dodge, Iowa, Dec. 3, 1956; d. Kenneth Lee and Marlene Lois Knutson; m. Kevin Michael Moon, Nov. 7, 1981; children: Ryan, Eric, Jacob. BA, Wartburg Coll., Waverly, Iowa, 1975—79; MS in Elem. Edn., U. Mo., St. Louis, 2001—04. K-5 elem. spl. edn. tchr. Eldon Pub. Schs., Iowa, 1979—83, 3d grade tchr., 1984; pre-1st grade tchr. Keokuk Pub. Schs., Iowa, 1985—86, 1st grade tchr., 1986—98, Ft. Madison Pub. Schs., Iowa, 1998—2004, Title I Reading tchr., 2004—. Named Tchr. of Yr., Ft. Madison Cmty. Schs., 2001; recipient First in the Nation award, Gov. of Iowa, 1997. Mem.: Beta Sigma Phi (pres. 1997—98, Woman of Yr. 1998). Avocations: boating, reading, travel. Home: 2175 W Point Rd West Point IA 52656 Office: Ft Madison Cmty Schs 3301 Ave L Fort Madison IA 52627 Personal E-Mail: moontime@interl.net.

**MOON, KIMBERLE IRENE,** voice educator; b. Dayton, Ohio, Feb. 3, 1952; d. Cratty Andrew and E. Janell Moon; m. Robert Bruce McKee, May 8, 1981; children: Maison Andrew. MusB, Ohio U., 1974, MusM, 1976, D of Music, 1984. French tchr. Miamisburg H.S., Ohio, 1977—78; german tchr. Dayton Stebbins H.S., Dayton, 1978—79; theater dir. Chipola Jr. Coll., Marianna, Fla., 1980—81, voice instr., 1986—87; singing voice specialist Tallahasse Profl. Voice Clinic, 1997—; voice prof. Bapt. Coll. Fla., Graceville, 1998—. Pres., treas. Tallahassee Cmty. Chorus, 1993—98; trustee Tallahassee C.C., 2005—. Mem.: Voice and Speech Trainers Assn.; Nat. Assn. Teachers of Singing, Phi Kappa Phi. Office: Bapt Coll Fla 5400 Coll Dr Graceville FL 32440 Office Phone: 850-263-3261.

**MOON, MARC R.,** cardiac surgeon; MD, Wayne State U., Detroit, 1988. Cert. in gen. surgery/thoracic surgery Bd. Surgery/Bd. Thoracic Surgery, 1996. Prof. surgery Wash. U., Saint Louis, Mo., 1998—2006. Editl. bd. Jour. Thoracic and Cardiovascular Surgery. Office: Washington Univ Sch Medicine 3108 Queeny Tower Saint Louis MO 63110-1013 Office Phone: 314-362-0993. Office Fax: 314-362-0328.

**MOON, MARILYN LEE,** economist; b. El Dorado, Kans., July 7, 1947; d. Jesse Morris and Shirley Lois M.; m. Douglas Gomery, Jan. 13, 1973. BA in Econs., Colo. Coll., 1969; MS in Econs., U. Wis., 1972, PhD in Econs., 1974. Rsch. assoc. Inst. for Rsch. on Poverty U. Wis., Madison, 1973-74; asst. prof. econs. U. Wis., Milw., 1974-80, assoc. prof. econs., 1980-81; sr. analyst human resources and cmty. devel. divsn. The Congl. Budget Office, Washington, 1981-83; sr. rsch. assoc. Health Policy Ctr. The Urban Inst., Washington, 1983-86; dir. pub. policy inst. AARP, 1986-89; sr. rsch. assoc. The Urban Inst., 1989-94, sr. fellow, 1994—2003; v.p. Am. Insts. for Rsch., 2003—, dir. health program. Cons. The Pepper Commn., 1989. Author: The Meaurement of Economic Welfare: Its Application to the Aged, 1977, Medicare Now and in the Future, 1993, 2d edit., 1996, Medicare: A Policy Primer, 2006, co-author: Balancing Access, Cost and Politics. The American Context for Health System Reform, 1991, Entitlements and the Elderly: Protecting Promises, Recognizing Realities, 1995; editor: Economic Transfers in the United States, vol. 49, 1984; co-editor: Improving Measures of Economic Well-Being, 1977; columnist The Washington Post, 1993-00; contbr. articles to profl. jours. Pub. trustee social security and Medicare trust funds, 1995-00. Ford Found. fellow, 1971-73. Mem. Nat. Acad. Social Ins. (bd. dirs. 1993-00, pres. 2005-), Medicare Rights Ctr. (bd. dirs. 1998, pres. 2005-), Inst. Medicine, Phi Beta Kappa. Avocations: photography, hiking, reading. Office: Am Insts for Rsch 10720 Columbia Pike Silver Spring MD 20901 Office Phone: 301-592-2101. E-mail: mmoon@air.org.

**MOON, NORMAN K.,** judge; BA, U. Va., 1959, JD, 1962, LLM, 1988. Bar: (Va.) 1962. With firm Edmunds & Williams (formerly Williams, Robertson & Sackett), Lynchburg, Va., 1962—74; judge 24th Jud. Cir., 1974—84, chief judge, 1982—85; judge Ct. of Appeals of Va., 1985—93, chief judge, 1993—97; judge U.S. Dist. Ct. (we. dist) Va., 1997—. Vis. lectr. U. Va. Law Sch., Charlottesville, 1975—88. Office: PO Box 657 Lynchburg VA 24505-0657

**MOON, RICHARD EUGENE,** secondary school educator; b. Carbondale, Pa., June 10, 1952; s. John and Grace Moon; m. Kay Scolere, July 5, 1991. EdD, Temple U., Phila., 1988. Cert. tchr. instructional II, biology Pa., 1977. Tchr. Sch. Dist. of Phila., 1975—. Recipient George Walk award, Temple U., 1988. Avocations: travel, golf, theater. Office: School District of Philadelphia 901 S Broad St Philadelphia PA 19147 Office Phone: 215-952-2462. E-mail: rmoon@phila.k12.pa.us.

**MOON, RONALD LESLIE,** materials scientist; b. July 15, 1939; s. Leslie H. and LaVonne Moon; 1 child, Gregory D. BS in Chem. Engring., U. Calif., Berkeley, 1962, MS in Chem. Engring., 1963, PhD in Materials Sci., 1967. Cert. gemologist. Rsch. fellow Imperial Coll., London, 1967-69; rsch. engr. Varian Assn., Palo Alto, Calif., 1969-79; rsch. scientist, project mgr., dept. mgr. Hewlett-Packard, Palo Alto, Calif., 1979-2000; dept. mgr. materials tech. dept. Agilent Labs., 2000—. Contbr. to devel. of photocathodes, growth techs., LEDs, lasers, organic LEDs; chmn., com. various confs. Contbr.

articles on solar cells, semiconductors, crystal growth and organic LEDs to various publs.; patentee in field. Mem. AIME, IEEE, Materials Rsch. Soc., Sigma Xi. Home: 152 Selby Ln Menlo Park CA 94027-3960 Office: Agilent Labs 3500 Deer Creek Rd Palo Alto CA 94304-1317

**MOON, RONALD T.Y.,** state supreme court chief justice; b. Sept. 4, 1940; m. Stella H. Moon. B in Psychology and Sociology, Coe Coll., 1962, LLD (hon.), 2001; LLB, U. Iowa, 1965; LLD (hon.), Inha U., Incheon, Korea, 2003. Bailiff, law clk. to Chief Judge Martin Pence U.S. Dist. Ct., 1965-66; dep. prosecutor City and County of Honolulu, 1966-68; assoc. Libkuman, Ventura, Ayabe, Chong & Nishimoto (predecessor firm Libkuman, Ventura, Moon & Ayabe), Honolulu, 1968-72, ptnr., 1972-82; judge 9th div. 1st cir., Cir. Ct., State of Hawaii, Honolulu, 1982-90; assoc. justice Hawaii Supreme Ct., Honolulu, 1990-93, chief justice, 1993—. Bd. dirs. Nat. Consortium on Racial and Ethnic Fairness in Ctr., 2004—; adj. prof. law U. Hawaii, 1986—88; lectr., guest spkr. numerous events. Recipient Disting. Svc. award, Nat. Ctr. for State Cts., 2003, Grand Prize award, Kyungmin Mission Schs., Korea, 2003. Mem. ATLA, ABA, Hawaii Bar Assn. (Golden Gavel award 2001), Am. Bd. Trial Advocates (pres. 1986-93, nat. sec. 89-91), Am. Inns of Cts. IV (bencher 1983—, bd. trustees 2004—), Am. Judicature Soc., Hawaii Trial Judges' Assn., Conf. Chief Justices (bd. dirs.). Office: Supreme Ct Hawaii 417 S King St Honolulu HI 96813-2902 Office Phone: 808-539-4700. Business E-Mail: ronald.t.moon@courts.state.hi.us.*

**MOON, WARREN,** professional football player; b. Los Angeles, Nov. 8, 1956; Graduated, Univ. Wash. Quarterback houston oilers, 1984—93, Minn. Vikings, 1994—96, Seattle Seahawks, 1997—98, Kansas City Chiefs, 1999—2000. Named to NFL Pro Bowl, 1988—95, 1997, NFL Pro Football Hall of Fame, 2006. Office: c/o Pro Football Hall of Fame 2121 George Halas Dr NW Canton OH 44708*

**MOON, WILLIAM NEAL,** music educator; b. Balt., Feb. 2, 1976; s. Thomas Ray and Barbara Ann Moon. BS in Music Edn., Frostburg State U., Md., 1999; MS in Curriculum and Instrn., McDaniel Coll., Westminster, Md., 2006. Gen. music tchr., choral dir. Cecil County Pub. Sch., Elkton, Md., 2000—. Dir. all-county elem. honors chorus Cecil County Pub. Schs., 2000—. Mem.: Md. Music Educators Assn. (rep. for Cecil County 2006—), Md. Tchrs. Assn. (assoc.), Music Educators Nat. Conf. (assoc.). Methodist. Avocations: bowling, singing. Office: Leeds Elem Sch 615 Deaver Rd Elkton MD 21921 Office Phone: 410-996-5070.

**MOONEY, ALLAN W.,** management consultant, foundation administrator; BS in Polit. Sci. and Pub. Svc., Abilene Christian U., Tex., 2002, MS in Rsch. and Gerontology, 2004; post grad., Capella U., 2004—. Asst. mgr. to regional mgr. McDonald's Sys. of West Germany, Fuerth, 1975—85; franchise ops. cons. and expansin mgr. Burger King, San Diego, 1985—88; regional supr. and corp. tng. supr. Pollo West, Inc., Anaheim Hills, 1988—91; operating ptnr. Green Diamond Landscaping, Simi Valley, 1990—91; CEO C&A Sys. Internat., Abilene, Tex., 1991—95; ind. computer cons. Ovalo, Tex., 1995—2002; founder and chmn. Young Seniors, 1999—; CEO Apex Design Rsch. and Cons., Abilene, 2005—. Presenter in field; rsch. asst. Pruett Gerontology Ctr. Abilene Christian U., 2002—04; grad. asst. and tech. cons. Nonprofit Mgmt. Ctr. Abilene Christian U., Tex., 2003—04, program dir., 2004—05; mng. dir. Hodges Found., 2004—; dir. Angel Smiles, Inc., Tex., 2004—; bd. dir. Neighborhoods in Progress, I-CAN. Sgt. U.S. Army, 1974—78, Germany. Jack Pope Fellow, Abilene Christian U., 2002. Mem.: Phi Sigma Alpha. Address: 624 FM 614 Ovalo TX 79541

**MOONEY, BETH,** bank executive; BA, U. Tex.; MBA, So. Meth. U. Sec. First Republic Bank, Dallas, bank mgr., 1980, Citicorp; head banking group AmSouth Bank, Tenn., No. La., 2000—04, sr. exec. v.p., CFO Birmingham, 2004—06; vice chairwoman KeyCorp, 2006—. Bd. dir. United Way Met. Nashville, 2001—, Vanderbilt Univ. Med. Ctr. Named one of 25 Most Powerful Women in Banking, USBanker Mag., 2005, Top 10 CFOs in Banking, 2006. Office: KeyCorp 127 Public Sq Cleveland OH 44114 Office Phone: 615-748-2214. Office Fax: 205-326-4072.*

**MOONEY, CHARLES WILLIAM, JR.,** law educator; b. Shawnee, Okla., Aug. 13, 1947; s. Charles W. and Mary Jane (Jones) M.; m. Christina Eager Anderson, Dec. 31, 1973; children: Mia Elizabeth, Natasha Lea. BA with high honors, U. Okla., 1969; JD cum laude, Harvard U., 1972. Bar: Okla. 1972, Pa. 1988, US Dist. Ct. (we. dist.) Okla. 1972, NY 1982, US Ct. Appeals (10th cir.) 1973. Assoc. Crowe & Dunlevy, Oklahoma City, 1972-77, ptnr., 1977-81, Shearman & Sterling, NYC, 1981-86; assoc. prof. law U. Pa. Law Sch., Phila., 1986—90, interim dean, 1999—2000, assoc. dean for academic affairs 1998—2000, prof., 1990—2004, Charles A. Heimbold Jr. prof. law, 2004—. Assoc. bar examiner Okla. Bd. Examiners, Oklahoma City, 1978-81; del. US Dept. State Internat. Inst. for Unification of Pvt. Internat. Law, Conv. on Internat. Fin. Leasing, Rome, 1986-87, Ottawa, 1988—; visiting scholar Bank of Japan, 1988. Contbr. articles to profl. jours. Mem. ABA (mem. council bus. law sect. 1987—, chmn. on uniform comml. code bus. law sect. 1982-87), Okla. Bar Assn., N.Y. State Bar Assn., Assn. of Bar of City of N.Y., Am. Law Inst. (advisor to permanent edit. bd. for uniform comml. code 1987—, Article 2 study com. 1988—), Phi Beta Kappa. Republican. Office: U Pa Law Sch 3400 Chestnut St Philadelphia PA 19104-6204 Office Fax: 215-573-2025. E-mail: cmooney@law.upenn.edu.

**MOONEY, EDWARD FISKE,** religious studies educator; b. Schenectady, NY, Feb. 25, 1941; s. David Alfred and Eleanor Fiske Mooney; m. Marcia Coleen Robinson, May 31, 1999; 1 child, Kailen Andrew. PhD, U. Calif., Santa Barbara, 1968. Prof. philosophy Calif. State Sonoma, Rohnert Park, 1968—2002; prof. religion Syracuse U., NY, 2002—. Contbr. articles and poetry to publs. Mem. Sacred & Profane, a Chorus, Berkeley, Calif., 1987—94. Recipient Friends of Libr. award for Outstanding Scholarship, Calif. State Sonoma, 1986, Henry Bugbee Meml. Lecture award, U. Mont., 1996, Glenn Gray Meml. Lecture award, Colo. Coll., 2006; fellow, NEH, 1976, 1993. Mem.: Soc. for Existential and Phenomenological Philosophy, Soc. for Advancement Am. Philosophy, Am. Assn. Religion, Am. Philos. Assn., Kierkegaard Soc. Office: Syracuse University 501 Hall of Languages Syracuse NY 13244 Office Phone: 315-443-3861. Business E-Mail: efmooney@syr.edu.

**MOONEY, HAROLD ALFRED,** plant ecologist; b. Santa Rosa, Calif., June 1, 1932; s. Harold Walter and Sylvia Anita Stefany; m. Sherry Lynn Gulmon, Aug. 15, 1974; children—Adria, Alyssa, Arica. AB, U. Calif., Santa Barbara, 1957; MA, Duke U., 1958, PhD, 1960. Assoc. prof. UCLA, 1960—68, Stanford U., Calif., 1968—75, prof. biology, 1975—, Paul S. Achilles prof. environ. biology, 1976—, sr. fellow, Inst. Internat. Studies, 2000—03. Author: Mediterranean-type Ecosystems, 1973, Convergent Evolution in Chile and California, 1977, Components of Productivity of Mediterranean Climate Regions, 1981, Disturbance in Ecosystems, 1983, Physiological of Plants in the Wet Tropics, 1984, Physiological Ecology of North American Plant Communities, 1985, Ecology of Biological Invasions of North America and Hawaii, 1986, Biological Invasions, A Global Perspective, 1989, Biodiversity and Ecosystem Function, 1993, Seasonally Dry Tropical Forests, 1995, CO2 and Terrestrial Ecosystems, 1995, Functional Roles of Biodiversity, 1996, Principles of Terrestrial Ecology, 2002. Served with AUS, 1953-55. Recipient Humboldt award, 1989, Max Planck Forscgungs Preis award Alexander von Humboldt Soc., 1992, Inst. Ecology prize, 1990, Nev. Medal of Sci. award, 2000, Blue Planet prize, 2002; Guggenheim fellow, 1974, Nat. Acad. Scis. fellow, 1982. Fellow AAAS, Am. Acad. Arts and Scis., Am. Philos. Soc.; mem. Ecol. Soc. Am. (pres. 1988-89, Mercer award 1961, Eminent Ecologist 1996), Brit. Ecol. Soc. (hon. mem.), Nat. Inst. Biol. Scis. (pres. 1994), Internat. Coun. Sci. Unions (sec. gen. 1996-2002), Botanical Soc. Am. (Merit award 1983). Office: Dept Biol Scis Stanford Univ Stanford CA 94305-1926 Office Phone: 650-723-1179.

**MOONEY, JAMES DAVID, JR.,** aerial photographer; b. Anderson, Ind., May 20, 1921; s. James David and Jane (Watson) M.; m. Christine Mott, Dec. 29, 1944 (div. 1957); children: Barbara, James II, Richard; m. Gloria van Bomel Schoninger, Dec. 8, 1972. Student, U.S. Naval Acad., 1940-43; naval aviator, USN Flight Sch., 1943; BS in Engring., Princeton U., 1947. Cert. protection profl. Am. Soc. for Indsl. Security; lic. comml. pilot FAA. Supply mgr. Willys-Overland Motors, Inc., Maywood, Calif., 1947-50; contr. F.L. Jacobs Co. Inc., Detroit, 1953-55; spl. rep. U.S. Steel Export Co., Washington, 1956-61; mgr. internat. ops. Armour Rsch. Found., Chgo., 1962-65; v.p. CDC Sys., Elizabeth, N.J., 1972-74; pres. Cash Control Corp., Mineola, N.Y., 1974-77; cons. J.D. Mooney Assoc., Oyster Bay, N.Y., 1978-98; pres. Aerial Photos by JDM, Inc., 1998—. Author: Long Range Planning, 1967. Police commr. Village of Centre Island, Oyster Bay, 1979-83, mayor, 1983-89. Lt. USN, 1940-45, 51-53. Mem.: N.Y. State Conf. Mayors, Internat. Assn. Chiefs of Police, Aircraft Owners and Pilots Assn., Seawanhaka Corinthian Yacht Club, Piping Rock Club, Cove Neck Tennis Club. Roman Catholic. Avocations: tennis, sailing. Home: 527 Centre Island Rd Oyster Bay NY 11771-5015

**MOONEY, JAMES F.,** telecommunications industry executive; With IBM Corp., 1980—99; COO Baan Co.; CEO, COO Tradeout Inc.; exec. v.p., COO Nextel Comms.; non-exec. chmn. NTL Inc., N.Y., 2003—. Bd. dir. NTL Europe. Office: NTL Europe Inc 22 Suffolk St London SW1Y 4HG England also: Ntl 909 3rd Ave Rm 2800 New York NY 10022-4790*

**MOONEY, JAMES HUGH,** newspaper editor; b. Pitts., Aug. 18, 1929; s. James H. and Kathryn A. (Hall) M.; m. Eileen Jane Casey, July 30, 1960; children: Mark Hall, Sean Francis, Annina Marie, James Matthew, Lorelei Jane, Paul Adam, Kathryn Celeste. BA in Journalism, Duquesne U., Pitts., 1957. With advt. dept., then editorial dept. Pitts. Post-Gazette, 1953—61; writer-editor Nat. Observer, 1961—77, Nat. Geographic, 1977—79; editor Found. News mag., Washington, 1979—81; press sec. Congressman Mickey Edwards of Okla., Washington, 1982; asst. nat. editor Washington Times, 1982—83; editor Status Report, 1983—92; dir. info. resources Ins. Inst. for Hwy. Safety, 1992—93; editor Western Pa. Medicine, Johnstown, 1993—95, Embassy Flash, Aspen Hill, Md., 1995—96; pres. Mooney Comms., 1997—. Former mem. editl. adv. bd. Nat. Study Ctr. Trauma and Emergency Med. Systems. Served with AUS, 1951-53. Personal E-mail: jekmooney@erols.com.

**MOONEY, JOHN BRADFORD, JR.,** oceanographer, consultant, engineer; b. Portsmouth, N.H., Mar. 26, 1931; s. John Bradford and Margaret Theodora (Akers) M.; m. Martha Ann Huntley, Dec. 25, 1953 (dec. May 1990); children: Melinda Jean, Pamela Ann, Jennifer Joan; m. Jennie Marie Duca, Nov. 24, 1990. BS, US Naval Acad., 1953; postgrad., George Washington U., 1970, 71, 76; grad. sr. execs. nat./internat. security, Harvard U., 1980. Commd. ens. USN, 1953, advanced through grades to rear adm., 1979; chief staff officer Submarine Devel. Group 1, 1971-73; commdr. Bathyscaphe Trieste II, 1964-66, Submarine Menhaden, 1966-68; commdg. officer Naval Sta., Charleston, SC, 1973-75; dep. dir. Deep Submergence Systems Div., Office Chief Naval Ops., Washington, 1975-77; commdr. Naval Tng. Ctr., Orlando, Fla., 1977-78; dir. Total Force Planning Div., Office Chief Naval Ops., Washington, 1978-81; oceanographer USN, 1981-83, chief naval rsch., 1983-87, ret., 1987; pres. Harbor Br. Oceanographic Instn., Inc., Ft. Pierce, Fla., 1989-92, marine bd., 1991-94. Mem. marine programs adv. coun. Grad. Sch. Oceanography, U. R.I., Narragansett, 1989—; chmn. study panel on undersea vehicles and nat. needs NRC, 1993—96, mem. adv. com. for postdoctoral and sr. rsch. associatship programs, 1995—2001; mem. panel to visit the former Soviet Union to evaluate undersea tech. for U.S. govt., 1993; chair, 95. At controls of Trieste II when hull of Thresher was found on floor of Atlantic, 1964; coordinated deep search and recovery of hydrogen bomb lost off coast of Spain, 1966; condr. recovery operation from depth of 16,400 feet in Mid-Pacific, 1972. Decorated Legion of Merit with 1 gold star; recipient spl. citation Armed Forces Recreation Assn., 1975, Dist. Eagle Scout award, 1986. Fellow Marine Tech. Soc. (pres. 1991-93), Explorers Club; mem. NAE, Am. Soc. Naval Engrs., Soc. Naval Architects and Marine Engrs., U.S. Naval Inst., Nat. Geog. Soc., Smithsonian Assocs., Masons, Shriners, Order of DeMolay (Legion of Honor), Tau Beta Pi. Avocations: swimming, grandchildren. Home and Office: 2313 Windswept Dr Austin TX 78738 Office Phone: 512-263-2799. Personal E-mail: jbradmooney@prodigy.net.

**MOONEY, JOHN JOSEPH,** chemical engineer; b. Paterson, N.J., Apr. 6, 1930; s. Denis and Mary Ellen (Hegarty) M.; m. Claire Josephine Ververs, Dec. 19, 1954; children: John, Mary Beth, Noreen, Susan, Kathleen, Elizabeth. BS in Chemistry, Seton Hall U., 1955; MS in Chem. Engring., Newark Coll. Engring., 1960; MBA in Mktg., Fairleigh Dickenson U., 1991. Project engr. Engelhard Corp., East Newark, 1960-64, chief process engr. Newark, 1965-70, sect. head auto rsch., 1970-72, mgr., 1972-74, tech. dir. Menlo Park, NJ, 1974-81, new ventures mgr., 1981-84, mgr. tech. svc., 1984-90, mgr. technology and new applications Iselin, NJ, 1991—2003; pres., founder Environ. and Energy Tech. Policy Inst., 2002—. Pres. Mfrs. of Emissions Controls Assn. (MECA), 1999—2002. Contbr. articles to profl. jours. With U.S. Army, 1954-56. Recipient Nat. Medal Tech., US Dept. Commerce, 2002. Fellow Soc. Automotive Engrs. Democrat. Roman Catholic. Achievements include patents in combustion and automobile emission catalysts, polyfunctional catalysts and methods of use which describe the catalysts introduced on the 1977 Volvo and now are used on all U.S. passenger cars and light trucks. Office: Environ & Energy Tech & Policy Inst Ste 1100 1660 L St, NW Washington DC 20036

**MOONEY, JUSTIN DAVID,** motel executive, consultant; b. Kansas City, Mo., Feb. 21, 1932; s. J.L. and Phoebe (Lighton) M.; m. Alayne I. Kohn, June 15, 1958; children: Jo Ann, David Alan. BBA, U. Mich., 1954, MBA, 1957. Mgr. Woolf Bros., Kansas City, 1958-66, asst. to pres., 1967-70; pres. Mission Inn Motel, Inc., Overland Park, Kans., 1970-90, J & A Ventures, Inc., Leawood, Kans., 1990—. Bd. dir. Nat. Fedn. of Ind. Bus., 1989-95; vice chmn. State of Kans., 1994-95. Chmn. Hwy. 56 Bus. Dist., 1984-87, bd. dir., 1984-90; bd. dir. hospitality divsn. Johnson County C.C., 1982-2005, chmn. bd., 1986-2005; bd. dir. Overland Park Conv. and Visitors Bur., 1983-90, v.p., 1987-90; bd. dir. Temple B'nai Jehudah, 1972-83, 86-93, bd. dir., 1968-1990, hon. bd. dir. 1995-, pres. Men's Club, 1972-74; bd. dir., pres. Catalina Bay, 1990-95, Heart Am. Jewish Hist. Soc., 1991-93, treas., 1991-93; bd. dir., exec. com., pres. Spindrifter, 1990-95; bd. mem. Pavilions Property, 2004—, treas 2005—; exec. bd., treas. Nat. Coun. Jewish Women, 2003—. Recipient Lifetime award Jewish Chatauqua, 1979, life mem. Temple Sisterhood, 1990, Hannah G. Solomon award Nat. Coun. Jewish Women, 2003; inductee Men's Club Hall of Fame, 1983. Mem. Am. Hotel and Motel Assn. (bd. dir. 1983-88, small properties adv. com., 1985-88, chmn. small prpoerties adv. com., 1988-89, exec. com. 1987, 89, vice-chmn. small properties adv. com. 1985-88, chmn. 1988-89), Kansas City C. of C. (Hall of Fame Man of Yr. 1971), Kans. Hotel Motel Assn. (bd. dir. 1972-84, pres. 1982-84, Hotel Man of Yr. 1981,82), Greater Kansas City Hotel/Lodging Assn. (bd. dir. 1973—, pres. 1982-84, chair 1985, Life Time Achievement award 1997, 98), Greater Kansas City Hotel and Lodging Found. (bd. dir. 2000—), Kans. Lodging Assn. (bd. dir. 1984, 1990, Hotel Man of Yr. 1983-84), Kansas City Athletic Club (treas. 1971-72, bd. dir. 1969-72). Avocations: antiques, sports. Home and Office: J&A Ventures Inc 14701 Delmar Shawnee Mission KS 66224-9545 E-mail: jdalayne@kc.rr.com.

**MOONEY, KAILEN ANDREWS,** ecologist, educator; b. San Francisco, Oct. 24, 1969; s. Edward Fiske Mooney and Barbara Andrews DeWind; m. Kathryn Lynn Thomas, Sept. 23, 2000; 1 child, Aeven Thomas. PhD, U. Colo., Boulder, 2004. Policy analyst Natural Resources Def. Coun., San Francisco, 1991—94; instr. Nat. Outdoor Leadership Sch., Lander, Wyo., 1995—2006; rschr. Cornell U., Ithaca, NY, 2005—. Green Party. Office: Cornell University Corson Hall Ithaca NY 14850 Office Phone: 607-255-8050.

**MOONEY, KENNETH FRANK,** design educator; b. Peterboro, N.H., Feb. 7, 1961; s. Frank Ernest and Anita Catherine Mooney. BFA, Ctrl. Conn. State U., New Britain, 1986; MFA, U. Tex., Austin, 1989. Asst. prof. Mass. Coll. of Liberal Arts, North Adams, 1991—2003, Cen. Conn. State U., New Britain, 2003—. Dir. of prodn. Oldcastle Theatre Co., Bennington, Vt., 1989—2004. Costume design, La Ronde (nat. finalist Am. Coll. Theatre Festival, 1986), Revenge of the Space Pandas (nat. finalist Am. Coll. Theatre Festival, 1988); artist, theatrical designer (Broadway): Wicked-The Musical (Tony award for costume design, 2004); How To Succeed in Business, Night of the Iguana, The Red Shoes. Recipient study grant for scene painting technique, Cen. Conn. State U., 2005. Avocations: tennis, travel. Office: Cen Conn State U 1615 Stanley St New Britain CT 06050 Office Phone: 860-832-3154. E-mail: mooneyk@ccsu.edu.

**MOONEY, KRISTA MICHELE,** academic administrator; b. Tallahassee, Fla., Jan. 4, 1973; d. Dennis Robert and Mary Ann Mooney. Student, Auburn U., 1990—91; AA, Tallahassee CC, 1990, AA, 1992; BA in Psychology, Fla. State U., 1995, JD, 1998, PhD in Higher Edn., 2005; Cert. of Completion law program, Oxford U., Eng., 1996. Head coach all-star squad Fla. Cheer Gyms, Inc., Tallahassee, 1993—94; instr. Nat. Cheerleaders Assn., Tallahassee, 1993—95; Fla. Supreme Ct. cert. legal intern Leon County Attorney's Office, Tallahassee, 1997; dir. alumni devel. Fla. State U. Coll. Law, Tallahassee, 1998—99; rsch. asst., academic and student affairs, bd. regents State U. Sys. Fla., Tallahassee, 1999—2000, sr. ednl. policy analyst, academic student affairs, bd. govs., 2003—06, assoc. dir. bd. gov., 2006—; cons. MGT Am., Inc., Tallahassee, 2000—02; sr. ct. analyst Office of State Courts Adminstr., Supreme Ct. Fla., Tallahassee, 2002—03. Participant and grad. Opportunity Tallahassee, 2005—05; vol. Guardian ad Litem, Tallahassee, 1995—99, Ronald McDonald Ho., Tallahassee, 1992—2002, Habitat for Humanity, Tallahassee, 1992—98, Meals on Wheels, Tallahassee, 1992—2002, Children's Miracle Network, Tallahassee, 1992—95; sec. Tallahassee 25, 2004—05, internat. v.p., 2005—06; tutoring/mentoring chmn., 2003—04, pres., 2006—; vol. fundraiser and booster Seminole Boosters, Tallahassee, 1992—2006. Named one of Top Twenty-Five Instr., Nat. Cheerleaders Assn., 1993—94; recipient Follow the Leader Leader Vol. of the Yr., Tallahassee 25, 2004, Disting. Pro Bono Svc. award, Fla. State U. Coll. Law, 1998; scholar, Auburn U., 1990—94. Mem.: ASTD, So. Assn. Coll. Student Affairs, Nat. Assn. Student Pers. Adminstrs., Nat. Assn. Grad.-Profl. Students, Hardee Ctr. Women in Higher Edn., Edn. Law Assn., Am. Ednl. Rsch. Assn., Fla. State U. Alumni Assn. (life), U. Ctr. Club, Capital Tiger Bay Club, Fla. State U. Varsity Club (life), Seminole Torchbearers (life), Alpha Delta Pi Alumni Assn., Phi Alpha Delta. Home: 2958 Foxcroft Dr Tallahassee FL 32309 Office: Florida Bd Govs 325 West Gaines Street Suite 1601-A Tallahassee FL 32399-0400 Office Phone: 850-245-9700. Personal E-mail: fsujdphd@aol.com.

**MOONEY, MARILYN,** lawyer; b. Pitts., July 29, 1952; d. James Russell and Mary Elizabeth (Cartwright) M. BA summa cum laude, U. Pa., 1973, JD. 1976. Bar: Mass. 1977, D.C. 1985, Pa. 1990, U.S. Dist. Ct. D.C. 1985, U.S. Ct. Appeals (D.C. cir.) 1985, U.S. Supreme Ct. 1986. Atty. E. I. du Pont de Nemours & Co., Wilmington, Del., 1976-84, Washington, 1985; assoc. Fulbright & Jaworski L.L.P., Washington, 1985—89, ptnr., 1990—, ptnr. in charge corp. and securities practice Washington Office, 2005—. Contbr. articles to profl. jours. Mem. ABA (fed. regulation securities com.), D.C. Bar (corp. fin. and securities law and internat. sections), Internat. Bar Assn. (issues and trading in securities com.), Am. Soc. Corp. Secs. (securities law com.). Office: Fulbright & Jaworski LLP 801 Pennsylvania Ave NW Washington DC 20004-2615 Office Phone: 202-662-4678. E-mail: mmooney@fulbright.com.

**MOONEY, MICHAEL EDWARD,** lawyer; b. Beloit, Wis., Jan. 21, 1945; s. William C. and Edith (Slothower) M. BA in Econs., St. Norbert Coll., 1966; JD, Boston Coll., 1969. Bar: Mass. 1969, Maine 1969, U.S. Tax Ct. 1975, U.S. Ct. Internat. Trade 1986. Assoc. Nutter, McClennen & Fish, LLP, Boston, 1969—77, sr. ptnr., 1976—, now mng. ptnr. V.p., exec. dir. Fed. Tax Inst. New Eng.; spkr., lectr. numerous seminars. Co-editor: Considerations in Buying or Selling a Business, 1985; mem. bd. editors Accounting and Financial Planning for Law Firms, 1988—. Co-chmn. Metro One Divsn. United Way, 2003—06; vice chmn. Artery Bus. Com.; bd. dirs. Filene Found., Jobs for Mass., Music Lives Found. Fellow Am. Coll. Tax Counsel; mem. Boston Bar Assn. (chmn. tax highlights com. 1986-95, fin. com. 1990-92, founder, chmn. summer jobs program), Boston Tax Forum. Office: Nutter McClennen & Fish World Trade Ctr West 155 Seaport Blvd Boston MA 02210-2604 Office Phone: 617-439-2000. Personal E-mail: mmooney@nutter.com.

**MOONEY, MICHAEL JOSEPH,** university professor; b. Evansville, Ind., Dec. 15, 1942; s. Joseph Thomas and Marie Louise (DeJean) Mooney; children: Susanne, Julia. AB summa cum laude, St. Meinrad Coll., 1964; STL magna cum laude, Univ. Innsbruck, Austria, 1968; M in Philosophy, Columbia U., 1973, PhD, 1982; DHL (hon.), Kyoto U. Fgn. Studies, 1991, Waseda U., 1999. Lectr. dept. religious studies, St. Mary's U., Halifax, Nova Scotia, Canada, 1968-70; project coord. Columbia U., NYC, 1973-74; preceptor dept. religion, 1975-76, spl. asst. to exec. v.p. for acad. affairs, 1976-77, asst. provost, 1977-79, assoc. provost, 1979-82, dep. provost, 1982-89; pres. Lewis and Clark Coll., Portland, Oreg., 1989—2003; prof. Waseda U., Tokyo, 2003—. Bd. dirs. Reid Hall, Inc., NYC and Paris, 1977—89, v.p., 1983—89; trustee Tour. Philosophy, 1982—; bd. dirs. Roothbert Fund, 1980—92; visitor Inst. for Advanced Study, Princeton, NJ, 1984; trustee Oreg. Ballet Theater, 1992—2004; mem. Portland Opera Assn., 1992—93; bd. dirs. Nat. Assn. Ind. Colls. and Univs., 1995—99, mem. exec. com., 1997—99, sec., 1998—99; mem. commn. on internat. edn. Am. Coun. Edn., 1993—95, mem. com. women in higher edn., 1997; mem. Truman Scholarship Finalists Selection Com., 2001—04; bd. adv. Music Performance Trust Fund, 2002—04. Author: Vico in the Tradition of Rhetoric, 1985 (Gottschalk prize Am. Soc. 18th Century Studies 1985); editor: Renaissance Thought and Its Sources, 1979; co-editor: Toward a Theology of Christian Faith: Readings in Theology, 1968, Vico and Contemporary Thought, 1976, Small Comforts for Hard Times: Humanists on Public Policy, 1977. Trustee Scuola d'Italia, NYC, 1986—89, World Affairs Coun., Oreg., 1992—2001, pres., 1999—2000. Recipient Rome prize Am. Acad. in Rome, 1989, Internat. Citizen award Oreg. Consular Corps., 2002; Roothbert Fund fellow, 1972, Kent fellow Danforth Found., 1972, Woodrow Wilson fellow, 1972, Presdl. fellow Columbia U., 1972, F.J.E. Woodbridge Disting. fellow Columbia U., 1973; NEH grantee, 1984; Cavaliere Ufficiale, Order Merit, Republic of Italy, 1991. Fellow Italian Acad. for Advanced Studies in Am. (sr.); mem. Phi Beta Kappa (hon.).

**MOONEY, RICHARD EMERSON,** writer; b. Plainfield, NJ, Mar. 31, 1927; s. Wandell M. and Alice (Joy) M.; m. Elizabeth B. Coleman, Oct. 30, 1954; children: James C., Stephen E., John B. BA, Yale U., 1947; postgrad. (Nieman fellow), Harvard U., 1955-56. Writer United Press, N.Y.C., 1948-51, econ. reporter Washington, 1951-56, N.Y. Times, Washington, 1957-63, econ. reporter Washington, Paris, 1963-67, econ. reporter N.Y.C., 1967, European econ. correspondent Paris, 1963-67, econ. reporter N.Y.C., 1967, asst. to exec. editor, 1968, asst. to mng. editor, 1969, dep. fgn. editor, 1970-72, asst. fin. editor, 1972-76, mem. editl. bd., 1982; contbg. editor, 1995-96; v.p. Hartford Courant, 1976-81, exec. editor, 1976-81, dir., 1977-81. Author: (with Edwin L. Dale, Jr.) Inflation and Recession, 1959. Trustee Hartford Courant Found., 1977-81. Served with USNR, 1944-48. Mem. Soc. Silurians (bd. govs. 1994-2002), Yale Club, The Coffee House, Century Assn., Cosmopolitan Club. Home and Office: 130 E 67th St New York NY 10021-6136 Personal E-mail: remooney@aol.com.

**MOONEY, TED (EDWARD COMSTOCK MOONEY),** editor, art critic, writer; b. Dallas, Tex., Oct. 19, 1951; s. Booth and Elizabeth (Comstock) M. Student, Columbia U., 1969-71; BA, Bennington Coll., 1973. Mng. editor Fiction mag., N.Y.C., 1975-77; sr. editor Art in Am. mag., N.Y.C., 1977—. Author: (novels) Easy Travel to Other Planets, 1981 (Sue Kaufman prize for 1st fiction AAAL 1981), Traffic and Laughter, 1990, Singing Into the Piano, 1997; contbr. short stories in Esquire, Am. Rev., Granta, articles to L.A. Times, Vogue, Harper's Bazaar, Artforum; lectr. in field. Fellow Creative Artists Pub. Svc. Award, 1977, Ingram Merrill Found., 1978, 80, Guggenheim fellow, 1983. Fellow N.Y. Inst. for Humanities; mem PEN Am. Center. Democrat. Episcopalian. Office: Art in Am 575 Broadway New York NY 10012-3230 Office Phone: 212-941-2800. Office Fax: 212-941-8885.

**MOONEY, THOMAS T.,** history educator, geography educator; b. Albany, N.Y., Sept. 12, 1954; s. Donald J. and Marguerite A. Mooney; m. Deborah Schneider, 1988; 1 child, Leilah; m. Virginia Rhodes (div.); 1 child, Ruairi Rhodes. BA, Antioch Coll., 1973. Cert. comprehensive social studies tchg. cert. Ohio, 1973. Tchr. Cin. Pub. Schs., 1974—79; pres. Cin. Fedn. Tchrs., 1979—2000; v.p. Am. Fedn. Tchrs., Washington, 1992—; pres. Ohio Fedn. Tchrs., Columbus, 2000—. Bd. dirs. Albert Shanker Inst., Washington, 1998—, Holmes Partnership, Waco, 1996—2000, Nat. Bd. Profl. Tchg., Arlington, 2000—. Mem. Cincinnatus Assn., Cin., Gay, Lesbian, Straight Educators Network, Washington. Democrat. Avocations: travel, music, Irish, Latin Am. and Caribbean history.

**MOONEY, TIMOTHY,** playwright, actor, theater director; b. Elgin, Ill., Nov. 4, 1959; s. James Arthur and Shirley Louise Mooney; 1 child, Isaac Arthur. BA, So. Ill. U., 1981; MFA, U. Nebr., 1985. Editor, founder The Script Rev., Arlington Heights, Ill., 1989—94; artistic/exec. dir. Stage Two, Waukegan, Ill., 1993—98; author, adaptor Moliere for the People, Prospect Heights, Ill., 1998—; author, actor, dir. Timothy Mooney Repertory Theatre, Prospect Heights, 2004—. Guest dir. U. Wis., Whitewater, 2001—, The Beck Ctr., 2005. Author: Tartuffe, The Imaginary Invalid and Thirteen Other Plays, 2005; author: (actor, dir.) (plays) Moliere Than Thou (Best Adapted Work award San Franciso Fringe Festival, 2004), Criteria (Artistic Picks Finalist, Seattle Fringe Festival, 2003), Karaoke Knights, a One-Man Rock Show. Mem.: AFTRA. Office: Timothy Mooney Repertory Theatre PO Box 638 Prospect Heights IL 60070 Office Phone: 847-757-3648 E-mail: tim_mooney@earthlink.net.

**MOONEY, WILLIAM PIATT,** actor; b. Bernie, Mo., May 2, 1936; s. Lowell E. and Louise S. M.; m. Valorie Shaw Goodall, Jan. 13, 1962; children: Sean Goodall, William Norvell. Student Am. theater wing, U. Colo. Pres. William Mooney Assocs., cons. to industry for exec. presentations Appeared in continuing role of Paul Martin on TV series All My Children, 1972-85 (2 Emmy nominations); one-man show Half Horse, Half Alligator & Damn Everything But the Circus, They All Wanted in the Act (The Lindbergh Kidnapping and Trial), Tonight! Buffalo Bill!; stage appearances: Brownsville Raid, We, A Man for All Seasons, Lolita; films: The Next Man, Network, A Flash of Green, Beer, Second Sight, C.A.T. Squad; author/star mus. play Banjo Reb and the Blue Ghost; co-author: ASAP-The Fastest Way to Create a Memorable Speech, 1992, Ready-to-Tell Tales, 1994, A Storyteller's Guide, 1995, Spiders in the Hairdo, 1999, (Grammy nominee 1998), (PBS) With a Dog's Eyes, 1997; recording artist: Why the Dog Chases the Cat, 1997 (ALA Notable Children's Choice Gold and Naird awards), Spiders In The Hairdo, 1997, More Ready-To-Tell Tales From Around The World, 2000, The Exploding Toilet, 2004. Dir. jazz mus. Jam, 8 yrs. Colo. Univ. Opera Theater, others. Grammy nominee, 1995, 98. Address: 2879 Shadow Creek Dr #105 Boulder CO 80303

**MOONVES, LESLIE,** broadcast executive; b. NYC, Oct. 6, 1949; s. Herman and Josephine (Schleifer) Moonves; m. Nancy Wiesenfeld, Dec. 17, 1978 (div.); children: Adam, Sara, Michael; m. Julie Chen, Dec. 23, 2004. BA, Bucknell U., 1971. Devel. exec. Catalina Prodns., Burbank, Calif., 1980—81; v.p. devel. Saul Ilson Prodns. Columbia Pictures TV, Burbank, 1981—82; v.p. movies and mini-series 20th Century Fox, L.A., 1982—85, Lorimar, Inc., Culver City, Calif., 1985—88; exec. v.p. creative affairs Lorimar-Telepictures, Culver City, 1988—90; pres. Lorimar TV, Burbank, 1989—93, Warner Bros. TV, Burbank, 1993—95, CBS Entertainment, L.A., 1995—97; exec. v.p. CBS/Broadcast Group, 1995—97; pres., CEO CBS TV, 1998—2003, chmn., CEO, 2003—04; co-pres., co-COO Viacom Inc., NYC, 2004—06; pres., CEO CBS Corp., 2006—. Bd. dirs. KB Home, 2004—. Developer, prodr. (TV series) Dallas, Dark Justice, Guns of Paradise, Knots Landing, Midnight Caller, Sisters, Family Matters, Full House, Perfect Strangers, Family Man, I'll Fly Away, Reasonable Doubts, Step by Step, Hangin' with Mr. Cooper, The Jackie Thomas Show, Crossroads, Homefront, Going to Extremes, Shaky Ground, It Had To Be You, Time Trax, Against the Grain, Lois & Clark: The Adventures of Superman, Cafe Americain, How'd They Do That, Living Single, Family Album, Getting By. Bd. dirs. L.A. Free Clinic; co-chair LA bd. govs. Mus. TV and Radio; bd. trustees Entertainment Industries Coun.; trustee Nat. Coun. for Families and TV, Am. Film Inst.; mem. adv. bd. NCAA. Named Showman of Yr., Variety, Most Powerful Man in Hollywood, Entertainment Weekly; recipient Gold Medal Award, Internat. Radio and TV Soc., 2003, Career Achievement award, Casting Soc. Am., Sherrill Corwin award, Am. Jewish Com. Mem.: NATAS (exec. com.), Hollywood Radio & TV Soc. (bd. dirs. 1988—91, pres. 1991). Democrat. Jewish. Office: CBS Corp 51 W 52nd St New York NY 10019-6188*

**MOONWALKER, TU,** minister, counselor, artist; b. Feb. 9, 1948; BA, Calif. State U., Sacramento, 1972; BS, U. Calif., Davis, 1973; MA, Tex. Tech. U., 1978, MS, 1979; postgrad., So. Meth. U., 1979. Chef Fairmont Hotel, San Francisco, 1971—72; rsch. and biopsy technician Tex. Tech. U. and Med. Ctr., Lubbock, 1974—78; Native Am. artist Santa Fe, 1979—87; cons. Am. Indian art Wheelwright Mus., Santa Fe, 1984—87; spiritual counselor, tchr. Ctr. for Universal Beingness, Moriarty, N.Mex., 1988—; min., canon Brigade of Light Ch., Cedar Mountain, NC, 1991—. Tech. advisor Am. Playhouse PBS Spl., Crestone, Colo., 1987; chmn. bd. dirs. Crystal Found., Denver, 1988—92, Profit from the Sun, Moriarity, 1999—2001; co-founder Ctr. for Universal Beingness; spkr. in field. Dir.(writer): (performances) Karen Lee Dance Theater, 2000—02. Chairperson bd. dirs. Ednl. Opportunity Program Calif. State U., Sacramento, 1971; mem. art com. chair, bd. dirs. YWCA, Lubbock, 1976—77; coun. mem. Sacramento Indian Ctr., 1971; vol. Talking Talons Youth Group, Tijeras, N.Mex., 2000. Named Outstanding Young Woman Am., 1987, recipient Humanitarian award, Friends for Life, Albuquerque, 1996; Wetlands Devel. Fed. grant, U.S. Wildlife, N.Mex., 1999. Mem.: Inst. Noetic Scis., Astron. Soc. Pacific, N.Y. Acad. Scis., Defenders of Wildlife (Wildlife Guardian), Acad. Am. Poets. Achievements include more than 20 years of consulting work to beginning businesses for their startup structures and management procedure. Avocations: arts and crafts, woodworking, stained glass, poetry and song writing. Office: 30-A Steeldust Ave Moriarty NM 87035

**MOORADIAN, ARSHAG DERTAD,** internist, educator; b. Aleppo, Syria, Aug. 20, 1953; arrived in U.S., 1981; s. Dertad and Araxi (Halajian) Mooradian; m. Deborah Lynn Miles, June 25, 1985; children: Arshag Dertad, Jr., Ariana Araxie. BS, Am. U., Beirut, 1976, MD, 1980. Diplomate Am. Bd. Internal Medicine. Asst. prof. medicine UCLA, 1985-88; assoc. prof. U. Ariz., Tucson, 1988-91; prof. St. Louis U., 1991. Contbr. articles to profl. jours. Grantee VA, 1985—97. Mem. Diabetes Assn. (chmn. task force micronutrients 1990—91, chmn. coun. nutrition and metabolism 2000—02), Endocrine Soc., Gerontol. Soc. Am., Am. Fedn. Clin. Rsch. Mem. Armenian Orthodox Ch. Achievements include identification of a potential biomarker of aging; research on age-related changes in the blood-brain barrier; on age-related changes in thyroid hormone action; on diabetes related changes in the central nervous system. Office: Saint Louis U Med Sch 1402 S Grand Blvd Saint Louis MO 63104-1004 Business E-Mail: mooradad@slu.edu.

**MOORADIAN, GEORGE T.,** lawyer; BA with high distinction, U. Mich., 1976; JD, U. Mich. Law Sch., 1978; LLM, NYU, 1980. Bar: DC 1979, Mich. 1979, Calif. 1983. Ptnr.-in-charge Baker & Hostetler, Costa Mesa, Calif., coord., tax, personal planning and employee benefits. Office: Baker & Hostetler 600 Anton Blvd Ste 900 Costa Mesa CA 92626-7221 Office Phone: 714-754-6600. Office Fax: 714-754-6611. Business E-Mail: gmooradian@bakerlaw.com.

**MOORE, ALBERT CUNNINGHAM,** lawyer, insurance company executive; b. Miami, Fla., May 31, 1931; s. Elias Richard and Virginia Adelaide (Thompson) Moore; m. Anne Cambreleng Bonynge, Aug. 24, 1957; children:

Emily Robinson French, Barbara Raffield, Catherine Anne Bonygne Wells. AB, U. N.C., 1953; JD, U. Va., 1959. Bar: N.Y. 1960. Atty. White & Case, N.Y.C., 1959-69; corporate sec. Studebaker-Worthington, Inc., N.Y.C., 1969-72; sr. v.p., gen. counsel Crum & Forster, 1973-87. Former trustee N.J. Shakespeare Festival; former bd. dirs. DeBordieu Property Owners Assn., DeBordieu Arch. Rev. Bd. With USNR, 1953—56. Mem.: Wilton Ctr. Tennis Club (NH), Chi Phi, Phi Alpha Delta. Home: 529 Cedar Club Cir Chapel Hill NC 27517

### MOORE, ALECIA B. See PINK

**MOORE, ALICIA JANE,** art educator; BA in Art Edn., Sam Houston State U., 1980. Art tchr. Levi Fry Mid. Sch., Texas City, Tex., 1980—85; art tchr. sch. supr. Desisto Sch., Howey-in-the-Hills, Fla., 1985—87; lead art tchr. League City Intermediate, Tex., 1989—90; tchr., chair dept. fine arts Clear Brook H.S., Friendswood, Tex., 1990—. Co-workshop organizer State Visual Arts Scholastic event, 2005—. Mem.: Tex. Classroom Tchrs. Assn., Tex. Art Edn. Assn. Avocations: art, travel, scuba diving. Office: Clear Brook HS 4607 FM 2351 Friendswood TX 77546 Office Phone: 281-284-2100.*

**MOORE, ALMA DONST,** writer, lyricist; Clk. domestic and juvenile ct., spl. dep. county clk. Warren County Bd. Freeholders Ct. Ho., Belvidere, NJ, 1948—58. Lectr. Sen. Garrett W. Hagedorn NJ State Hosp. Contbg. writer: Soul Food, 1999—; founder The Spotlight, 1948; editor: The Spotlight, 1948, Warren Jour., 1948; author: (lyrics) Lifetime; contbr. articles to profl. jour. Cultural arts dir. Hunterdon County, 2005—06; coun. mem. Rambai Mukti Mission, Clinton, NJ, 1998—. Recipient Sliver Poet, World Poetry, 1999, Gold Poet, 1999, Homer Diamond, Famous Poets Soc., 1999, Outstanding Achievement in Poetry, Silver Cup, Internat. Soc. Poets, 2003. Mem.: Inter. Soc. of Poets.

### MOORE, AMANDA LEIGH See MOORE, MANDY

**MOORE, AMY NORWOOD,** lawyer; b. Durham, NC, Sept. 24, 1953; AB summa cum laude, Mt. Holyoke Coll., 1976; MA in English, U. Va., 1978, JD, 1983. Bar: DC 1984, registered: US Ct. Appeals, DC 1985, US Ct. Appeals (6th cir.) 1985, US Tax Ct. 1998. Law clk. to Frank M. Coffin, U.S. Ct. Appeals (1st cir.), 1983-84; ptnr., Employee Benefits Practice Group Covington & Burling, Washington. Articles editor Va. Law Rev., 1982—83. Mem.: Phi Beta Kappa. Office: Covington & Burling 1201 Pennsylvania Ave NW Washington DC 20004-2401 Office Phone: 202-662-5390. Office Fax: 202-662-6291. Business E-Mail: anmoore@cov.com.

**MOORE, ANDREW TAYLOR, JR.,** banker; b. Tarboro, N.C., June 17, 1940; s. Andrew Taylor and Mary Dare (Allsbrook) M. BA in History, Duke U., 1962; LLB, U.Va., Charlottesville, 1965. Asst. sec. Signet Banking Corp., Richmond, 1965-71, asst. v.p., corporate sec., 1971-75, v.p., corporate sec., 1975-82, sr. v.p., corporate sec., 1982-94. Bd. dirs. Theatre IV, Richmond, Va., 1981-97, Va. State YMCA adv. coun., Lynchburg, 1988—; trustee Hist. Richmond Found., 1993-98; mem. presidents coun. Va. Hist. Soc., 1996-2004. Presbyterian (elder 1996—). Avocations: jogging, gardening, travel. Home: 2011 Hanover Ave Richmond VA 23220-3539 Office Phone: 804-353-5039. Personal E-mail: atmjr01@aol.com.

**MOORE, ANN ROY,** school system administrator; b. Florence, Ala. BA, Hampton U., Va.; MA, EdS, U. No. Ala.; EdD in Curriculum Leadership Pers. and Early Childhood Edn., Vanderbilt U., 1986; cert. in ednl. adminstrn., 1986, cert. in ednl. adminstrn., 1987; cert. supt., Ala. A&M, 1992. Former tchr. pre-sch. and elem. sch. Huntsville (Ala.) City Schs., curriculum specialist, 1978—80, former prin., mgr. elem. edn., dep. supt., 1999—2001, supt., 2001—; former asst. supt. Florence Sch. Sys. Office: Huntsville City Schs 200 White St Huntsville AL 35801

**MOORE, ANN S.,** publishing executive; b. McLean, Va.; 1950; d. Monty and Bea Sommovigo; m. Donovan Moore; 1 son, Brendan. BA in Polit. Sci., Vanderbilt U., 1971; MBA, Harvard U., 1978. With Time, NYC, 1978—; gen. mgr. Sports Illustrated, 1983—89; founding publisher Sports Illustrated for Kids, 1989-91; publisher People mag., 1991—93, pres., 1993—98, People Mag. Group (renamed People/In Style Mag. Group, 2001), 1999—2001; exec. v.p. Time, Inc., 2001—02, chmn., CEO, 2002—. Bd. dirs. Avon Products Inc., 1993; public spkr. bus. and women's issues. Hon. bd. mem. Gilda's Club, N.Y.C.; founder Time to Give Back; bd. dirs. Wallace Found. Named Pub. Exec. of Yr., Adweek, 1998, 2004 Bus. Statesman, Harvard Bus. Sch.; named one of The 50 Most Powerful Women in Am. Bus., Fortune mag., 100 Most Powerful Women, Forbes mag., 2005—06, 50 Women to Watch, Wall Street Journal, 2005; recipient AOL Time Warner Civic Leadership award, 2003. Achievements include guiding People magazine to spin off several popular titles including In Style (domestic and international), Teen People, People en Español, and Real Simple. Office: Time Warner Cable 1 Time Warner Ctr New York NY 10019-6038*

**MOORE, ANNE,** physician; b. N.Y.C., Apr. 28, 1944; d. John D.J. and Mary Foote Moore; m. Arnold L. Lisio, Sept. 6, 1969; children: Philip Moore, Mary Foote. BA, Smith Coll., 1965; MD, Columbia U., 1969. Diplomate Am. Bd. Internal Medicine, Am. Bd. Hematology (medicine 1996), Am. Bd. Oncology. Intern dept. medicine N.Y. Hosp., N.Y.C., 1969-73, assoc. attending physician, 1981-95, attending physician, 1996—; postdoctoral fellow Rockefeller U., 1972-73, hematology-oncology fellow, 1973-75; asst. prof. medicine Cornell U. Med. Coll., N.Y.C., 1975-91, assoc. prof. clin. medicine, 1981-95, prof. clin. medicine, 1996—. Cons. Strang Cancer Prevention Ctr.; lectr., cons., in field. Author: Patient's Guide to Breast Cancer Treatment, 1992, rev edit., 1997; ad hoc reviewer Am. Jour. Clin. Oncology, 1994, New Eng. Jour. Medicine, 1994, 96, 97; contbr. articles to profl. jours., chpts. to books. Trustee fr David's 9th., 1983-89, HealthCare Chaplaincy, Inc., 1991—; bd. dirs. Camilli Found., 1990—, Cure Myeloma Fund, 1988-98, N.Y. Community Trust. Recipient award SHARE, 1992, Wholeness of Life award Hosp. Chaplaincy, 1992, Alumnae award Oak Knoll Sch., 1994, Eileen Dreyer Meml. Lectureship award Sass Found. for Med. Rsch., 1996, Commendation award Office of Exec. Nassau County, 1996, award Artists for Breast Cancer Survival, Inc., 2000. Mem. Am. Bd. Internal Medicine (bd. dirs. 1996—), Am. Soc. Hematology, Am. Soc. Clin. Oncology, N.Y. Acad. Scis., Soc. for Study of Blood (membership chmn. 1979-80), N.Y. Met. Breast Cancer Group (membership chmn. 1992-93, sec.-treas. 1993-95, v.p. 1995-96, pres. 1997—), Soc. for Study of Breast Disease, N.Y. Cancer Soc., N.Y. Acad. Medicine (trustee 1998—). Office: Weill-Cornell Med Ctr 428 E 72nd St New York NY 10021-4635

**MOORE, BARBARA C.,** fraternal organization administrator; V.p. institutional advancement Benedict Coll., Columbia, SC. Bd. mem. Midlands YWCA, Richland County Nat. March of Dimes Found. Named one of Most Influential Black Americans, Ebony mag., 2006. Mem.: Nat. Polit. Congress of Black Women, Inc., Coun. for the Advancement and Support of Edn., Nat. Assn. of Female Execs., Nat. Coun. of Negro Women (Living the Legacy Award 1983), Top Ladies of Distinction, Inc., Zeta Phi Beta Sorority (life: nat. first v.p., chair nat. exec. bd., chmn. Nat. Capital Campaign, Grand Basileus, nat. pres. 2002—). Office: Zeta Phi Beta Sorority, Inc 1734 New Hampshire Ave, NW Washington DC 20009 also: 2nd Fl 145 Kennedy St, NW Washington DC 20011*

**MOORE, BEATRICE,** religious organization administrator; b. Somerville, Mass., Oct. 6, 1928; d. George and Christina Turner; m. Wendell Moore, May 9, 1953; children: Karl C., Linda Moore Flewelling, Diane Pearl, Larry. BA in Theology and English, Berkshire Christian Coll., Lenox, Mass., 1950. Pres. The Woman's Home and Foreign Mission Soc., Loudon, NH, past nat. pres. Charlotte, NC, 1987—96, nat. spiritual life chmn., 1997—2005. Sunday sch. tchr., deaconess Loudon Ridge Family Bible Ch.; chair Concord Christian Women's Club, 2002-03, 05-06; prayer coord. Ladies Bible Study leader, 1998-05, Concord Christian Women's Club, 2003-04; active Women's Home and Fgn. Mission Soc., Loudon, past pres. NH Soc., past pres. ea. region;

hostess, contact chmn., prayer adv., Bible club guide Stonecroft Ministries, Friendship Bible Study Guide; past leader 4-H Club. Mem.: Concord Christian Womens Club (chair 2005—). Office: Woman's Home & Foreign Mission 845 Loudon Ridge Rd Loudon NH 03307-1712

**MOORE, BETTY JO,** legal assistant; b. Medicine Lodge, Kans., July 10, 1921; d. Joseph Christy and Helen Blanche (Hubbell) Sims; m. Harold Frank Moore, June 19, 1941 (dec.); children: Terrance C., Harold Anthony, Trisha Jo. Cert., U. West L.A., 1978; student, Wichita (Kans.) U., 1940-41. Cert. legal asst./escrow officer. Sec. UCLA, 1949-59; escrow officer Security Pacific Nat. Bank, L.A., 1959-62, Empire Savs. & Loan Assn., Van Nuys, Calif., 1962-64; escrow supr. San Fernando Valley Bank, Van Nuys, 1964; escrow officer Heritage Bank, Westwood, Calif., 1964-66; escrow coord. Land Sys. Corp., Woodland Hills, Calif., 1966-67; escrow officer/asst. mgr., real estate lending officer Security Pacific Nat. Bank, 1967-80; real estate paralegal Pub. Storage, Pasadena, 1980-81; asst. mgr. escrow dept. First Beverly Bank, Century City, Calif., 1982-84; escrow trainer/officer Moore's Tng. Temps Inc., Canoga Park, Calif., 1984—92, legal asst., 1992—. Participant People to People Amb. Program/Women in Mgmt. to USSR, 1989; observer Internat. Fedn. Bus. and Profl. Women's Congress, Washington, 1965, 81, Nassau, Bahamas, 1989, Narobi, Kenya, 1991, Havana, Cuba, 2004. Adv. bd. escrow edn. Pierce Coll., Woodland Hills, Calif., 1968-80. Recipient Cert. of Appreciation, Pierce Coll., 1979, Calif. Fedn. Bus. and Profl. Women, 1989, Nat. Women's History Project, 1995. Mem. Nat. Fedn. Bus. and Profl. Women's Clubs, Calif. Fedn. Bus. and Profl. Women (pres. dist. 1987-88, Calif. Found. chmn. 1988-89, internat. coordination chmn. 1996-97, 2003), Woodland Hills Bus. and Profl. Women ((pres. 1991-92, 94-95), Valley/Sunset Dist. BPW (v.p. legislation/pub. policy 1997-98, 2001-02, 03, Cert. of Appreciation 2002), Tri Valley Dist. Bus. and Profl. Women (legis. chair 1992-93, exec./corr. sec. 1993-94, 94-95), Internat. Fedn. Bus. and Profl. Women, Nat. Women's Polit. Caucus (coord., sec. San Fernando Valley caucus 1986-87, sec. 1990-2003, legis. co-chair 1991-93), Women's Orgn. Coalition San Fernando Valley (exec. com. L.A. Women's Equality Day 1995, pres. 2002—), San Fernando Valley Escrow Assn. (bd. dirs. 1962-61), L.A. Women's Family Equity Coalition, U. West L.A. Alumni Assn., Rotary, U.N. Assn. (v.p. San Fernando Valley), League of Women Voters. Democrat. Methodist. Avocations: reading, musical theater.

**MOORE, BILLIE JO,** minister; b. Centerpoint, Ark., Aug. 15, 1929; d. Willie Corn Henry and Irene Ruby Bevill; m. Warner Conrad Moore, Aug. 14, 1948 (div. Sept. 1967); children: Mark Glenn, Janice Marie Baudat. Student, Maranatha Inst., Inc., Calif., 1995. Ordained minister Rhema Bible Tng. Ctr., Okla., 1984. Clk. City of Long Beach, Calif., 1968—79; missionary to Philippines Billie Moore Ministries, Cypress, Calif., 1984—85; self-employed Calif., 1982—2006; minister Rhema, Broken Arrow, Okla., 1984—2006; prayer coord. Ch. of Claremore, Okla., 1986—87. Area coord. Nat. Day of Prayer, Oakley, Antioch, Calif., 1990—99, Auburn, Calif., 2000—02; dir. jail ministry Billie Moore Ministries, Contra Costa County, Calif., 1995—; tchr./facilitator various chs., Calif., 1979—; chaplain Placer County Chaplaincy, Calif., 2000—05. Area facilitator Traditional Values Coalition, Placer County, Calif., 2003—06; vol. Bread of Life Ministry, Antioch, 1990—94, Friendship Manor Ch. Svc., Antioch, 1993—99. Mem.: Foothills Christian Writers, Rhema Ministerial Assn. Internat., Christian Minsterial Assn. of the Foothills, Women's Aglow Internat. (spkr.), Christian Coalition Am. Republican. Avocations: writing, charity work. Office: Billie Moore Ministries Inc PO Box 71 Auburn CA 95604 Mailing: PO Box 71 Auburn CA 95604

**MOORE, BILLY DON,** scriptwriter, film producer; b. Oklahoma City, Dec. 26, 1956; s. Orval L. and Mary E. (Perry) M.; m. Donna M. Lovelace; stepchildren: Derek, Ryan. BA in Journalism, U. Okla., 1979, MA in Journalism, 1993. Prodn. asst. FAA, Oklahoma City, 1979-81; media technician, supr. Oklahoma City, 1985-99; motion picture and broadcast archivist Okla. Hist. Soc., Oklahoma City, 1999—. Owner BVC Video. Editor, photographer (cable series) Connecting, 1983-85; prodr. pub. svc. announcements, (aviation video mag.) Okla. Approach, 1995-99; prodr. documentaries Okla. Pub. TV; prodr., editor, photographer: (TV) Yesterday; author: (book) The Oklahoma Aviation Story, 2005, Norick: The Mayors of Oklahoma City, 2006. Recipient Crystal award The Communicator, 1998, Telly award excellence, 1998, Aegis award, 1999, Videographer award excellence, 1999; 20th Anniversary Classic Telly award, 1999, Disting. Alumni award Okla. U. Coll. Journalism, 2003. Democrat. Baptist. Avocation: writing. Office: Okla Hist Soc 2401 N Laird Ave Oklahoma City OK 73105-4907 Office Phone: 405-522-6307. E-mail: bdmoore@okhistory.org.

**MOORE, BOB STAHLY,** communications executive; b. Pasadena, Calif., July 3, 1936; s. Norman Hastings and Mary Augusta (Stahly) M. Student, U. Mo., 1954-58, MIT, 1958-62. Dir. news WPEO, Peoria, Ill., 1958—60, KSST, Davenport, Iowa, 1960—62, WIRE, Indpls., 1962—64, WCFL, Chgo., 1964—67; White House corr. Metromedia, Inc., Washington, 1967—71; dir. news Gateway Comm., Altoona, Pa., 1972—74; chief Washington Bur. MBS, 1974—76, v.p. news Arlington, Va., 1976—78, White House corr., 1978—81; dir. comm. Fed. Home Loan Bank Bd., Washington, 1981—85; spl. asst. to bd. govs. Fed. Res. Sys., Washington, 1985—. Active ARC. Served with USAF, 1961-63. Recipient profl. awards News Broadcasters, 1963, Ill. News Broadcasters, 1965, UPI, 1960, 63, 65, AP, 1956, 58, 61, 65, 67, Mo. News Broadcasters, 1956, 61. Mem. Radio and TV News Dirs. Assn. (bd. dirs. 1970-72), White House Corrs. Assn., State Dept. Corrs. Assn., Radio-TV Corrs. Gallery (U.S. Capitol), Chgo. Coun. on Fgn. Rels., Pub. Rels. Soc. Am., Nat. Press Club, Washington Press Club, Chgo. Press Club, Mo. C. of C., Ill. C. of C., Sigma Delta Chi. Presbyterian. Home: 114 W Arlington Ave Vandalia MO 63382 Office: 20th And Constitution NW Washington DC 20551-0001

**MOORE, BRET A.,** psychologist, military officer; b. Hazelhurst, Miss., Oct. 20, 1971; s. David and Brynda Moore. BS in Social and Rehab. Services, U. So. Miss., 1994; MA in Counseling Psychology, Western Mich. U., 1997; D of Psychology, Adler Sch. Profl. Psychology, 2004. Lic. Ala. Bd. Examiners in Psychology, Ala., 2005. Clin. psychology resident Dwight D. Eisenhower Army Med. Ctr., Augusta, Ga., 2003—04; clin. psychologist U.S. Army 85th Med. Detachment, Ft. Hood, Tex., 2004—05; clin. psychologist, officer in charge U.S. Army, Kirkuk, Iraq, 2005—06; clin. psychologist Darnall Army Med. Ctr., Ft. Hood, 2006—. Contbr. book, articles to profl. jours. and mags. Capt. U.S. Army, 2003, Ft. Hood, TX. Decorated Army Commendation Medal U.S. Army, Army Achievement Medal, Iraqi Campaign Medal, Global War on Terrorism Medal. Mem.: APA (corr.; clin. com. mem. 2005—06), Nat. Acad. Neuropsychology (corr.), Silver Caduceus Soc. (life). R-Consevative. Christian. Achievements include first to study the effectiveness of Imagery Rehearsal Therapy for the treatment of acute nightmares in a combat environment. Avocations: writing, travel. Home: 201 Lookout Ridge Blvd #730 Harker Heights TX 76548 Office: 85th Med Detachment Fort Hood TX 76544 Office Phone: 281-743-5214. Business E-Mail: bret.moore@us.army.mil.

**MOORE, BRIAN EDWARD,** mathematics professor; b. Denver, Feb. 17, 1975; s. Herman Edward and Freda Kathleen Moore; m. Wendy Renee Edwards, Sept. 7, 1975. BS, Colo. Christian U., Lakewood, 1997; MS, Colo. Sch. Mines, Golden, 1999; PhD, U. Surrey, Guildford, Eng., 2003. Postdoctoral fellow McGill U., Montreal, Que., Canada, 2003—05; vis. asst. prof., math. rschr., math. lectr. U. Iowa, Iowa City, 2005—. Rschr. instr. McGill U., Montreal, 2003—05. Contbr. articles to profl. jours. Recipient Overseas Rsch. Student award, UK Univs., 1999; Colo. Rsch. fellow, Colo. Sch. Mines, 1998, Postgrad. rsch. fellow, U. Surrey, 1999. Avocations: coin collecting/numismatics, snowboarding, running, travel, church activities. Office: Univ Iowa Dept Math 14 MacLean Hall Iowa City IA 52242 Business E-Mail: bemoore@math.uiowa.edu.

**MOORE, C. BRADLEY,** chemistry professor; b. Boston, Dec. 7, 1939; s. Charles Walden and Dorothy (Lutz) Moore; m. Penelope Williamson Percival, Aug. 27, 1960; children: Megan Bradley, Scott Woodward. BA magna cum laude, Harvard U., 1960; PhD, U. Calif., Berkeley, 1963. Predoctoral fellow NSF, 1960-63; asst. prof. chemistry U. Calif., Berkeley, 1963-68, assoc. prof., 1968-72, prof., 1972-2000, vice chmn. dept., 1971-75, chmn. dept. chemistry, 1982-86, dean Coll. Chemistry, 1988-94, prof. grad. sch., 2000—; v.p. rsch. Ohio State U., Columbus, Disting. prof. math. and phys. sci., prof. emeritus, 2000—03; prof. emeritus, 2003—; Assoc. prof. Faculty Scis., Paris, 1970, 75; Miller Rsch. Prof. U. Calif., Berkeley, 1972-73, 87-88; vis. prof. Inst. for Molecular Sci., Okazaki, Japan, 1979, Fudan U., Shanghai, 1979, adv. prof., 1988—; vis. fellow Joint Inst. for Lab. Astrophysics, U. Colo., Boulder, 1981-82; faculty sr. scientist (Chemical Sci. Div.) Lawrence Berkeley Nat. Lab., 1974-2000, divsn. dir., 1998-2000: mem. editl. bd. Jour. Chem. Physics, 1973-75, Chem. Physics Letters, 1980-85, Jour. Phys. Chemistry, 1981-87, Laser Chemistry, 1982—; mem. Basic Energy Scis. adv. com. Office Sci. U.S. Dept. Energy, 2000-03. Editor: Chemical and Biochemical Applications of Lasers; assoc. editor Annual Review of Physical Chemistry, 1985-90; contbr. articles to profl. jours. Trustee Sci. Svc., 1995—, Sci. and Tech. Campus, 2000-03; mem. bd. govs. Ohio Supercomputer Ctr., 2000-03; rsch. officer Coun. of Ohio Bd. of Regents 2000-03; pres., chmn. bd. Ohio State U. Rsch. Found., 2000-03; mem. governing bd. Argonne Nat. Lab. 2005—, mem. sci. policy coun., 2005—. Recipient Coblentz award, 1973, E.O. Lawrence Meml. award U.S. Dept. Energy, 1986, Lippincott award, 1987, 1st award Inter-Am. Photochem. Soc., 1988; nat. scholar Harvard U., 1958-60; fellow Alfred P. Sloan Found., 1968, Guggenheim Found., 1969, Humboldt Rsch. award for Sr. U.S. Scientists, 1994. Fellow AAAS, Am. Acad. Arts and Scis., Am. Phys. Soc. (Plyler award 1994); mem. NSF adv. com. for education and human resources directorate, chair subcom. policy and planning 1997-99, NAS (chmn. com. undergrad. sci. edn. 1993-97, class I membership com. 1998-2000, 2002, 2000 nominating com.), Am. Chem. Soc. (past chmn. divsn. phys. chemistry, Calif. sect. award 1977). Avocation: bicycling. Office: Northwestern U Crown 2-223 633 Clark St Evanston IL 60208 Office Phone: 847-491-3485. E-mail: moorecb@northwestern.edu.

**MOORE, CAROL A.,** academic administrator; b. Newark, N.J., Dec. 8, 1945; d. James Clifford and Helen Mohan Brierley; m. Thomas Eric Moore, Nov. 25, 1967; 1 child, Kimberly Ann. BS in Biology, Montclair St. Coll., N.J., 1967; MA in Biology, Monclair State Coll., N.J., 1972; PhD in Biology, Northeastern Univ., Boston, Mass., 1981. Sci. tchr. H.S. and Jr. H.S., 1967—71; asst. prof. biology Massasoit C.C., Brockton, Mass., 1972—83, divsn. chairperson sci. and tech., asst. prof. biology, 1979—83, asst. dean academic affairs, asst. prof. biology, 1983—84; dean academic affairs, chief acadamic officer, asst. prof. biology Lasell Coll., Newton, Mass., 1984—88; dean undergraduate sch., chief acadminc officer, prof. biology Lesley Coll., Cambridge, Mass., 1988—91; provost & v.p. academic affairs, chief academic officer, prof. biology Mercy Coll., Dobbs Ferry, NY, 1992—98; pres. Lyndon State Coll., Lyndonville, Vt., 1998—. Vis. scientist Marine Sci. Inst., Northeastern Univ., Nahant, Mass., 1991—. Contbr. scientific papers to numerous conf., chapters to books, articles to profl. jour. Mem., Vt. higher edn. coun. rep. New Eng. Higher Edn. Bd., 1991—; mem., adv. bd. Vt. Telecom Advancement Ctr. USDA Grant, 2002—; Office of Nursing Workforce Rsch., Planning and Develp., Univ. Vt., 2001—; mem., Vt. bd. dirs. Girl Scout Coun., 2001—; mem. Am. Coun. Edn. Commn. on Women in Higher Edn., 2002—03; mem. Vt. Higher Edn. Coun., 1998—; rep. New Eng. Bd. of Higher Edn., 2002—, pres., 2001—02, v.p. 2000—01, exec. com. 1999—, sec.-treas., 1999—2000, com. on cert. & accreditation, 1998—; bd. dirs. Northeastern Vt. Devel. Assn., 2000—, Northeast Kingdom Learning Svc., 2000—. Grantee Title III Retention Grant, 1995, AAC Cirriculm Devel. Grant, 1990, NSF, 1983. Mem.: Soc. of Devel. and Comparative Immunology, Soc. for Invertebrate Pathology, Nat. Shellfisheries Soc., Am. Soc. of Zoologists (travel award), New Eng. Estuarine Rsch. Soc., Nat/ Assn. for Women Deans, Adminstr., and Counselors, Assn. of Tchr. Educators, Am. Coun. of Edn./ Nat. Identification Program, Nat. Assn. of Academic Affairs Adminstr., Sigma Xi, Phi Sigma. Office: Lyndon State Coll 1001 Coll Rd Lyndonville VT 05851

**MOORE, CAROLE IRENE,** librarian; b. Berkeley, Calif., Aug. 15, 1944; AB, Stanford U., 1966; MLS, Columbia U., 1967. Reference libr. Columbia U., N.Y.C., 1967-68, U. Toronto, Can., 1968-80, head cataloging, 1980-85, assoc. libr., 1985-86, chief libr., 1986—. Mem. nat. adv. bd. Nat. Libr. Can., Ottawa, 1991-94; bd. dirs. Rsch. Libr. Group. 1994-2000, U. Toronto Press, 1994—. Recipient Disting. Alumni award Columbia U., 1989. Mem. ALA, Can. Libr. Assn., Can. Assn. Rsch. Librs. (pres. 1989-91, bd. dirs. 1996-98). Avocation: gardening. Office: U Toronto Libr 130 Saint George St Toronto ON Canada M5S 1A5

**MOORE, CASSANDRA CHRONES,** real estate broker; b. Oneonta, N.Y., June 14, 1935; d. Constantine John and Antonia (Laskaris) Chrones; m. Thomas Gale Moore, Dec. 28, 1958; children: Charles Godwin, Antonia Laskaris. BA summa cum laude, Radcliffe Coll., Cambridge, Mass., 1956; MA, Harvard U. 1958; PhD, U. Mich., 1975. Lic. real estate broker Calif. Lectr. Duquesne U., Pitts., 1962-65, Mich. State U., East Lansing, 1966-68; broker, owner Moore Assocs., Palo Alto, Calif., 1983-85; dir. state and mcpl. legislation Nat. Assn. Realtors, Washington, 1985-87; exec. dir. Fed. Interregl. Coun. on Homeless, Washington, 1987-89; adj. scholar Competitive Enterprise Inst., Washington, 1989—, mem. adv. bd., 1995—; adj. scholar Cato Inst., Washington, 1996—. Author: Haunted Housing, 1997. Co-chmn. Radcliffe Alumnae Lectureship Com., Palo Alto and San Francisco, 1984-2000; mem. nat. com. Radcliffe Alumnae Professorship Fund, 2001-02. Recipient Fulbright fellowship U.S. Govt., Washington, 1956-57. Mem.: Calif. Assn. Scholars (mem. adv. bd. 2005—), Palo Alto Bd. Realtors (dir. 1984, 1985), Tsintzinian Soc. (bd. mem. 1999—, alt. bd. mem. 2001—02), Am. Assn. Small Property Owners (bd. mem. 1997—), Radcliffe Club Peninsula (pres. 1980—82), Phi Beta Kappa. Avocations: hiking, swimming, skiing. Office: 415 Cambridge Ave Palo Alto CA 94306 Office Phone: 650-853-0798. Personal E-mail: ccmassoc@comcast.net.

**MOORE, CHARLES HEWES, JR.,** manufacturing executive; b. Coatesville, Pa., Aug. 12, 1929; s. Charles Hewes and Jane Richards (Scott) M.; m. Judith L. McClellan, June 23, 1971; children: Charles Hewes III, James, David, Susan, Kevin, Christopher, Margery, Brian, Amanda. BME, Cornell U., 1952. With Lenape Forge Co. div. Gulf & Western Industries, West Chester, Pa., 1952-73; pres. Lapp div. Interpace Corp., Le Roy, NY, 1973—78; pres., chief exec. officer Allied Thermal Corp. subs. Interpace, 1978-79; sr. v.p. dir. Interpace, 1979-80; exec. v.p. dir. Interpace Corp., Parsippany, NJ, 1980-81; pres., chief exec. officer, dir. Clevepak Corp., 1981-83, 84-86, chief exec. officer, vice chmn. bd., dir., 1983-84; mng. dir. Peers & Co., 1987-88; chief exec. officer Peers Mgmt. Resources Inc., 1987-88; pres., chief exec. officer Ransburg Corp., Indpls., 1988-92; pres. ITW Finishing Systems and Products, Indpls., 1990-92; exec. v.p. Ill. Tool Works Inc., Glenview, 1991-92; vice-chmn. Advisory Capital Ptnrs., Inc., Greenwich, Conn., 1992—94; chmn. bd. dirs. Xpander Pak Inc., 1994—2000; dir. athletics Cornell U., 1994—99. Dep. to chairs Com. to Encourage Corp. Philanthropy, NY, 1999—2000, exec. dir., NY, 2000—; mem. Pres. Coun. on Physical Fitness & Sports, 2002—. Commr. Smithsonian Am. Art Mus., 2000—; chmn. audit com., pub. sector dir. U.S. Olympic Com., 1992—2000; mem. nat. bd. Smithsonian Instn., 2001—. Recipient Gold medal in 400 meter hurdles, 1952 Olympics, Herbert Adams Meml. award for advancement of Am. sculpture, Nat. Sculpture Soc., 1985. Mem. Pine Valley Golf Club (N.J.), Royal and Ancient Golf Club St. Andrews (Scotland), Cosmos Club (Washington), Blind Brook Golf Club (N.Y.). Republican. Episcopalian. Office: Com to Encourage Corp Philanthropy 110 Wall St Ste 2-2 New York NY 10005 Office Phone: 212-825-1254.

**MOORE, CHARLES LOYD,** lawyer; b. El Paso, Tex., Aug. 14, 1944; s. Charles McKinney and Alice Adeline (Loyd) M.; m. Peggy Jo Ball, Dec. 20, 1969; children: Kirk, Julie. BS in Mil. Engring., U.S. Mil. Acad., West Point, N.Y., 1966; MSME, Calif. Inst. Tech., 1968; JD summa cum laude, So. Meth. U., Dallas, 1975. Bar: N.Mex. 1975, U.S. Dist. Ct. 1975. Commd. 2d lt. U.S. Army, 1966, advanced through grades to capt., 1968, resigned, 1972; assoc. Keleher & McLeod, P.A., Albuquerque, 1975-79, mem. firm, 1979—2005;

---

assoc. gen. counsel PNM Resources, Inc., Albuquerque, 2005—. Asst. Bd. Bar Examiners, Santa Fe, 1990—2004. Contbr. articles to profl. jours. Dist. co-chmn. ann. fund campaign McMurry U., Abilene, Tex., 1988, trustee, 1989—92, Hatton W. Sumners Found., Dallas, 1999—; dir. Robert O. Anderson Schs. Mgmt. Found. Bd., U. N.Mex., 2003—; co-chair N.Mex. Lawyers for Gen. Wesley Clark for Pres. campaign, 2003—04. Decorated Vietnam Svc. medal, Vietnam Campaign medal, Bronze Star, Joint Svc. Commendation medal; named N.Mex. Bus. Lawyer of Yr., 2005; named one of Best Lawyers of Am., 1989—90, 1991—92, 1993—94, 1995—96, 1997—98, 1999—2000, 2001—02, 2003—04. Mem. ABA, State Bar of N.Mex. (v.p. young lawyers divsn. 1977-78, chair bus. law sect. 2001, N.Mex. Lawyer of Yr. 2005), Albuquerque Bar Assn., Phi Delta Phi (Internat. Grad. of Yr. Biennial Conv. 1975), Phi Kappa Phi. Avocations: running, reading. Home: 7929 American Heritage Dr NE Albuquerque NM 87109-3103 Office Phone: PNM Resources Inc Alvarado Sq MS 1200 Albuquerque NM 87158 Business E-Mail: cmoore1@pnm.com.

**MOORE, CHERYL JEROME (CHERYL MILKES JEROME),** lawyer; b. Dallas, Jan. 10, 1951; d. Dean and Marjorie (Wolens) Milkes; m. Edward Jerome, Aug. 21, 1976 (div. 1986); 1 child, Elizabeth Milkes; m. David Moore, Feb. 25, 1995. Student, Tulane U., 1969-70; BA and BSW, Syracuse U., 1972, JD, 1976. Bar: N.Y. 1977, Tex. 1978, U.S. Dist. Ct. (no. dist.) N.Y., U.S. Dist. Ct. (all dists.) Tex., U.S. Ct. Appeals (5th cir.). Law clk. Bogart & Andrews, Syracuse, NY, 1975-76; assoc. Law Office Louis Tarantelli, Horseheads, NY, 1976-78, Glast, Miller & Allen, Dallas, 1985-86; sr. planner, adminstrn. asst. County of Dallas, 1977—78, chief commr. fraud, Dist. Atty.'s Office, 1979-85; ptnr. Hewitt, Jerome & Armstrong, Dallas; ptnr., Securities, Oil & Gas Law, Comml. & Transactional Litigation Patton Boggs LLP, Dallas, dep. chmn. litigation dept., mem. mgmt. com. Adj. prof. So. Meth. U. Coll. Law, Dallas, 1986-2000; tchg. staff Nat. Inst. Trial Advocacy. Contbr. articles to profl. jours. Bd. dirs., legal counsel Cmty. Homes Adults, Inc., Dallas, 1987-2004; bd. dirs. Jewish Fedn. Dallas; chair Legacy Sr. Communities Inc., 2004—. Mem. N.Y. Bar Assn., Dallas Bar Assn. Democrat. Jewish. Office: Patton Boggs LLP Suite 3000 2001 Ross Ave Dallas TX 75201-8001 Office Phone: 214-758-3504. Office Fax: 214-758-1550. Business E-Mail: cmoore@pattonboggs.com.

**MOORE, CHRISTOPHER HUGH,** writer; b. Stoke-on-Trent, Eng., June 9, 1950; arrived in Can., 1954; s. M. Vincent and Kathleen A. (Lennox) M.; m. Louise A. Brophy, May 7, 1977; children: Elizabeth, Kate. BA with honors, U. B.C., Vancouver, 1971; MA, U. Ottawa, Ont., Can., 1977. Staff historian Nat. Historic Pks. Svc., Louisbourg, N.S., Can., 1972-75; sec. to bd. Heritage Can. Found., Ottawa, 1977-78; writer, historian Toronto, Ont., 1979—; dir. Access Copyright Licensing Agy., 2001—. Author: Louisbourg Portraits, 1982, 2000, The Loyalists, 1984, 94, Eighteen Sixty-Seven, 1997, The Big Book of Canada, 2002; co-author: Illustrated History of Canada, 1987, The Story of Canada, 1992, Canada: Our Century, 1999. Recipient Gov. Gen.'s Lit. award Can., 1983, Sec. of State Prize Govt. Can., Ottawa, 1985, Mr. Christie's Prize Christie-Brown Ltd., Toronto, 1993. Mem. Writers' Union of Can. (chair contracts com. 1990-94, mem. nat. coun. 1995-97, nat. chair, 1999-00), Can. Hist. Assn. Office: 70 Woodside Ave Toronto ON Canada M6P 1M1 E-mail: cmed@sympatico.ca.

**MOORE, CHRISTOPHER M.,** lawyer; b. L.A., Oct. 12, 1938; s. Prentiss Elder and Josephine (French) M.; m. Gillian Reed, Sept. 29, 1965; children: Stephanie Kia Conn, Carrie Christine McKay. AB, Stanford U.; JD, Harvard U. Dep. county counsel L.A. County Counsel, 1965-66; ptnr. Burkley & Moore, Torrance, Calif., 1969-74; pvt. practice Law Offices of Christopher Moore, Torrance, 1974-81; ptnr. Burkley, Moore, Greenberg & Lyman, Torrance, 1981-90; prin. Christopher M. Moore & Assoc., Torrance, 1990-2000, Moore, Bryan & Schroff, Torrance, 2000—. Mem. bd. edn. Palos Verdes (Calif.) Peninsula Unified Sch. Dist., 1972—77. Fellow: Am. Acad. Matrimonial Lawyers, Am. Coll. Trust and Estate Counsel; mem.: Palos Verdes Golf Club, L.A. Yacht Club. Avocations: sailing, golf. Office: Moore Bryan & Schroff Ste 490 21515 Hawthorne Blvd Torrance CA 90503-6525 Office Phone: 310-540-8855. E-mail: chris@mbslawcorp.com.

**MOORE, CORNELL LEVERETTE,** financial services executive, lawyer; b. Tignall, Ga., Sept. 18, 1939; s. Jesse Lamar and Luetta (Leverette) M.; m. Wenda Lee Weekes, June 27, 1965; children: Lynne M., Jonathon C. Meredith L. AB, Va. Union U., 1961; JD, Howard U., 1964. Bar: Minn. 1964, U.S. Dist. Ct. Minn. 1977. Atty. U.S. Treasury, various locations, 1965-68; asst. v.p., legal officer N.W.N. Bank, Mpls., 1968-70; pres. Leverette, Weekes, Mpls., 1970—; exec. v.p. Shelter Mfg. Co., Mpls., 1970-74; pres., chief exec. officer Lease Moore Equipment, Inc., Mpls., 1977-86; sr. v.p., gen. counsel Miller and Shroeder Fin. Inc., Mpls., 1987—. Bd. dirs. Golden Valley (Minn.) Bank, Ward & Assocs., Inc., Atlanta. Trustee Mpls. Soc. Fine Arts, 1986, Va. Union U., Richmond, 1986, Dunwoody Inst. Mpls. 1986, chmn. bd. vis., John H. Johnson Sch. Comm. Howard Univ. Democrat. African Methodist Epicopal. Club: Minneapolis. Office: Miller and Schroeder Fin Inc 7900 Xerxes Ave S Minneapolis MN 55431-1106*

**MOORE, DAN STERLING,** insurance executive, sales trainer; b. Lincoln, Nebr., June 27, 1956; s. Jack Leroy and Carolyn Marie (Bachman) M.; m. Marla Janine Collister, June 2, 1979; children: Tyler David, Anna Rose. Student, Red Rocks Coll., 1977. Lic. ins. exec. mgr. European Health Spa, Englewood, Colo., 1975-78; sales mgr. Colo. Nat. Homes, Westminster, 1979-80; sales assoc. Dale Carnegie, Denver, 1981; sales mgr. Paramount Fabrics, Denver, 1981-84; sales assoc. Mighty Distbg., Arvada, Colo., 1984-87; divsn. mgr. Nat. Assn. for Self Employed/United Group Assn., Englewood, Colo., 1987—; agt. Mega Life and Health Ins. Divsn. mgr. Communicating for Agr. Assn., 1993-98, Am. Bus. Coalition, 1997-2000, Am. for Financial Security, 1999—; owner Capital City Landscaping LLC, Capital City Equipment, LLC, Paradise Properties, LLC; master gardener U. Wyo. Ext.; agt. Mega Life and Health Ins. Co. Leader, trainer Alpine Rescue Team, Evergreen, Colo., 1971-74; minister Jehovah's Witnesses, 1972—. Avocations: golf, skiing, backpacking, scuba diving, tennis. Home: 1412 Sherman Mountain Loop Cheyenne WY 82009 Office: Nat Assn Self Employed/United Group Assn 6002 US Hwy 30 Cheyenne WY 82001 Office Phone: 307-637-5296. Personal E-mail: sterlingmoore@att.net.

**MOORE, DANIEL ALTON, JR.,** retired state supreme court justice; b. 1933; BBA, U. Notre Dame, 1955; JD, U. Denver, 1961. Dist. ct. magistrate judge, Alaska, 1961-62; pvt. practice law, 1962-80; judge 3d Jud. Dist. Superior Ct., 1980-83; justice Alaska Supreme Ct., Anchorage, 1983-92, chief justice, 1992-95; ret., 1995. Mediator for J.A.M.S./Endispute, 1996—.

**MOORE, DANIEL CHARLES,** retired anesthesiologist; b. Cin., Sept. 9, 1918; s. Daniel Clark and May (Strebel) M.; m. Betty Maxine Tobias, Aug. 5, 1945 (div. 1988); children: Barbara, Nancy, Daniel, Susan. Grad., Amherst Coll., Mass., 1940; MD, Northwestern U., 1944. Diplomate Am. Bd. Anesthesiologists. Intern Wesley Meml. Hosp., Chgo., 1944, resident, 1945; dir. anesthesia Va. Mason Hosp., Seattle, 1947-72; anesthesiologist (Mason Clinic), 1947-72, sr. cons. in anesthesia, 1972-83. Clin. prof. U. Wash. Sch. Medicine, 1963—89. Author: Regional Block, 1953, Stellate Ganglion Block, 1954, Complications of Regional Anesthesia, 1955, Anesthetic Techniques for Obstetrical Anesthesia and Analgesia, 1964, also papers. Served as capt. M.C. AUS, 1945-47. Recipient Ralph M. Waters award III. Soc. Anesthesiologists, Carl Koller Gold medal European Soc. Regional Anaesthesia, 1995, Eagle Scout, 1930. Mem. Am. Soc. Anesthesiologists (1st v.p. 1953-54, 2d v.p. 1954-55, pres. 1958-59, distinguished service award 1976), AMA (sec. anesthesiology sect. 1956-58), Am. Acad. Anesthesiology, Am. Soc. Regional Anesthesia (adv. bd., Gaston Labat award 1977), Wash. Soc. Anesthesiologists (pres. 1949-50), Wash. Med. Soc., King County Med. Soc., Faculty Anaesthetists Royal Coll. Surgeons (hon.), Northwest Forum, Beta Theta Pi, Nu Sigma Nu. Home: Madison Park Pl # 103 2000 43rd Ave E Seattle WA 98112-2704 Office: PO Box 900 Seattle WA 98111-0900 Office Phone: 206-223-6980. Fax: 206-223-6982. E-mail: daniel.moore@vmmc.org.

---

**MOORE, DANIEL MICHAEL,** lawyer; b. Detroit, June 12, 1954; s. Richard Edgar and Evelyn (Geromin) M.; m. Katherine Suzuki, Aug. 8, 1980; children: Brandon, Megan, Sara. BA cum laude in Acctg., Mich. State U., 1976; JD magna cum laude, Detroit Coll. Law, 1979. Bar: Mich., U.S. Dist. Ct. (ea. and we. dists.) Mich., U.S. Ct. Appeals (6th cir.), U.S. Supreme Ct. Rsch. atty. Mich. Ct. Appeals, Lansing, 1979-80, law clk. to presiding ct. of appeals judge, 1980-81; pvt. practice Lansing, 1981-87; sr. corp. counsel, v.p. Comerica Inc., Detroit, 1987-96; gen. counsel, sec., v.p. Syntel, Inc., Troy, Mich., 1996-98, chief adminstrv. officer, gen. counsel, 1998—. Oakland County cir. ct. mediator, Oakland County dist. ct. mediator. Assoc. mem. Cranbrook Sci. Mus.; patron Detroit Inst. Arts. Fellow Mich. State Bar Found. (life); mem. Mich. Bar Assn. (bd. commrs. 1989-91, rep. 30th Dist. Assembly 1986, editor Inter Alia Jour. 1987-88, young lawyers sect. sec., treas. 1986-87, vice chairperson 1987-88, chairperson 1989-90, exec. coun. 1989-92), Oakland County Bar Assn. (co-chair in-house counsel com. 1995-96, chair in-house counsel com. 1996-97), North Fairview Farms Homeowners Assn. (v.p. 1989-90, pres. 1990-92), Classic Boosters Club (bd. dirs. 1992-95, pres. 1995-97, chair 2002-04), Alpha Kappa Psi (life, dist. dir. 1978-79). Office: Syntel Inc # 300 525 E Big Beaver Rd Troy MI 48083-1364 Office Phone: 248-619-3508. E-mail: daniel_moore@syntelinc.com.

**MOORE, DARLA D.,** investment company executive; b. Lake City, S.C. d. Eugene and Lorraine Moore; m. Richard Rainwater, Dec. 13, 1991. BA, U. S.C.; MBA, George Washington U., 1981. Summer intern Sen. Strom Thurmond; rschr. Rep. Nat. Com., 1976; with Chem. Bank, N.Y.C.; pres., CEO Rainwater, Inc., Atlanta, 1994—. Office: Magellan Specialty Health 6950 Columbia Gateway Dr Columbia MD 21046-2706

**MOORE, DAVID GENE,** academic administrator; b. Tonasket, Wash., Oct. 2, 1938; s. Leonard W. and Peggy (Furst) M.; m. Diane Russell, June 15, 1965 (div. 1984); children: John, Kathy, Alan, m. Kathryn Welsch, Nov. 24, 1999. BA in Polit. Sci., Seattle U., 1960; MBA, U. Puget Sound, 1973; MS in Computer Sci., Kans. State U., 1978; postgrad., U. Mich., 1978—. Commd. 2d lt. U.S. Army, 1960, advanced through grades to col., 1979, ret., 1980; dean mgmt. info. systems Mott Community Coll., Flint, Mich., 1980-82, dean mgmt., 1982-84, pres., 1985-92; pres DeVry Inst. Tech., Los Angeles, Calif., 1992-94; pres. Nat. Edn. Centers, Inc., 1994-95; founder, chmn., pres and CEO Corinthian Colleges, Inc., Santa Ana, 1995—. Bd. dirs. Greater Flint Edn. Consortium. Contbr. articles to profl. jours. Mem. exec. com. Orange County Performing Arts Ctr., Opera Pacific. Decorated Silver Stars (2), Legion of Merit (2); recipient numerous civic and profl. awards. Mem. Soc. Automotive Engrs. (chmn. robotics sect. 1986—), Data Processing Mgmt. Assn. Avocations: skiing, woodworking. Office: Corinthian Colleges Inc 6 Hutton Centre Dr Ste 400 Santa Ana CA 92707-5764 E-mail: dmoore@cci.edu.

**MOORE, DAVID J.,** media company executive; Grad., Northwestern U. Sales rep. Turner Broadcasting, 1979-82; with Viacom, 1982; founder on-line svc. for physicians, 1993-94; co-founder Petry Interactive, NYC, 1995-98; founder 24/7 Media (formerly Petry Interactive), NYC, 1998—. Bd. dir. Internet Advt. Bur. Mem. Network Advt. Initiative, NE Ill. U. Alumnae Assn.; bd. dir. Nassau and Suffolk Svcs. for Autism. Mem. Internat. Radio and TV Soc., Responsible Electronic Comm. Assn. Achievements include helping launch the Cable Health Network, which eventually became Lifetime; developing and running Medical Television, which was targeted to physicians; developing HealthLink Television, a waiting room service for patients. Office: 24/7 Media Inc 1250 Broadway Fl 28 New York NY 10001-3791 Business E-Mail: David.Moore@247RealMedia.com.

**MOORE, DAVID ROBERT,** lawyer; b. San Diego, Oct. 28, 1953; s. Raymond Richard and Goldie Rosealie Moore; m. Sherryl Anne Sheehan, June 16, 1990; children: David Robert II, Bridget Nicole. BA cum laude, U. So. Calif., 1975; JD cum laude, Calif. Western Sch. Law, 1980. Bar: Calif. 1980, U.S. Dist. Ct. (so. dist.) Calif. 1980, U.S. Ct. Appeals (9th cir.) 1987. Assoc. Fredman, Silverburg & Lewis, San Diego, 1980-81, Marvin, Huiskamp & Black, Rancho Santa Fe, Calif., 1981-84; ptnr. Marvin & Moore, Encinitas, Calif., 1984-91, Moore & Skiljan, Carlsbad, Calif., 1991—. Com. on mandatory fee arbitration State Bar, San Francisco, 1991—94, chmn. com., 1993—94, asst. presiding arbitrator, 2000—03. Bd. dirs. Solana Recyclers, Encinitas, 1987-97; spkr. SCORE divsn. SBA, Vista, Calif., 1985—. Mem. North San Diego County Bar Assn. (bd. dirs. 1992-94, chmn. com. on fee arbitration and mediation 1989-97, chmn. legis. com. 1990-99, conf. on dels. 1991-2003, chmn. conf. of dels. 1991-2006, Pres.'s award 1992), San Diego County Bar Assn. (vice-chmn. fee arbitration com. 1997-2002). Home: 2810 Jacaranda Ave Carlsbad CA 92009-9216 Office: Moore & Skiljan 7700 El Camino Real Ste 207 Carlsbad CA 92009-8505 Office Phone: 760-944-7700.

**MOORE, DAYTON,** professional sports team executive; m. Marianne Moore. Former profl. baseball scout Atlanta Braves, asst. gen. mgr., 2001—06; sr. v.p., gen. mgr. baseball ops. Kansas City Royals, 2006—. Office: Kansas City Royals PO Box 419969 Kansas City MO 64141-6969

**MOORE, DEANNA CASH,** music educator, musician; b. Jacksonville, Fla., June 18, 1975; m. Michael William Moore. Piano faculty mem. Bob Jones U., Greenville, SC, 1999—.

**MOORE, DEBRA,** lawyer; Grad., U. Utah, 1983. Shareholder Watkiss & Saperstein; employment sect. chief litigation divsn. Utah Atty. Gen.'s Office, 1991—. Instr. legal writing U. Utah Coll. Law, 1993—96; rep. Utah Jud. Coun. Mem.: Utah State Bar (commn. 1994—2000, pres.-elect 2002—03). Office: Atty Gens Office PO Box 140856 160 E 300 S Fl Salt Lake City UT 84114-0856

**MOORE, DEMI (DEMI GUYNES, DEMETRIA GENE GUYNES),** actress; b. Roswell, N.Mex., Nov. 11, 1962; d. Danny and Virginia Guynes; m. Freddy Moore, 1980 (div. 1984), m. Bruce Willis, Nov. 21, 1987, div. 2000; 3 daughters: Rumer Glenn, Scout LaRue, Tallulah Belle; m. Ashton Kutcher, Sept. 24, 2005. Studies with Zina Provendie. Owner Moving Pictures. Actress: (feature films) Choices, 1981, Parasite, 1981, Young Doctors in Love, 1982, Blame it on Rio, 1984, No Small Affair, 1984, Master Ninja 1, 1984, St. Elmo's Fire, 1985, About Last Night..., 1986, Wisdom, 1986, One Crazy Summer, 1987, The Seventh Sign, 1988, We're No Angels, 1989, Ghost, 1990, Mortal Thoughts, 1991 (also co-producer), The Butcher's Wife, 1991, Nothing But Trouble, 1991, A Few Good Men, 1992, Indecent Proposal, 1993, Disclosure, 1994, The Scarlet Letter, 1995, Now and Then, 1995 (also prodr.), Undisclosed, 1996, Striptease, 1996, The Juror, 1996, G.I. Jane, 1997 (also prodr.), Deconstructing Harry, 1997, Passion of Mind, 2000, Charlie's Angels: Full Throttle, 2003; (TV series) General Hospital, 1982-83; (TV movies) If These Walls Could Talk, 1996 (also exec. prodr.); (voice) Beavis and Butt-Head Do America,1996, The Hunchback of Notre Dame, 1996, The Hunchback of Notre Dame II, 2002; Producer: Austin Powers: International Man of Mystery, 1997, Austin Powers: The Spy Who Shagged Me, 1999, Austin Powers in Goldmember, 2002; guest appearances on Saturday Night Live (host), 1988, Moonlighting, 1989, Tales of the Crypt, 1990, Will & Grace, 2003. Named one of 50 Most Beautiful People in the World, People, 1996. Office: Creative Artists Agy Inc 9830 Wilshire Blvd Beverly Hills CA 90212-1825

**MOORE, DENNIS,** news correspondent; Grad. Mich. State U. From assoc. prodr. to prodr. Wall St. Week, Nightly Bus. Report, Washington, corr. bus. and econ., sr. Washington corr.; dep. mng. editor USA Today, Arlington, Va. Polit. sci. fellow NSF, MIT. Mem. Phi Beta Kappa. Office: USA Today 7950 Jones Branch Dr Mc Lean VA 22108-0001

**MOORE, DENNIS,** congressman; b. Anthony, Kans., Nov. 8, 1945; m. Stephene; 7 children. BS, U. Kans., 1967; JD, Washburn U., 1970. Bar: Kans. 1970. Asst. atty. gen. State of Kans., 1971-73; pvt. practice, 1973-76; dist. atty. Johnson County, 1977-89; ptnr. Erker & Moore, LLC, 1991-98, Smith,

Gill, Fisher & Butts, 1989-91; mem. U.S. Congress from 3d Kans. dist., 1999—. Mem. House Com. on Fin. Svcs. Sci. and the Budget. Elected to Johnson County C.C. bd. trustees, 1993; re-elected, 1997; bd. dirs. Johnson County Safehome, Coalition for Prevention of Child Abuse, Kans. Child Abuse Prevention Coun., CASA (Ct. Appointed Spl. Advocate), United Cmty. Svcs., Cmty. Corrections Adv. Bd.; unsuccessful Dem. candidate for state atty. gen., 1986. With U.S. Army, U.S. Army Res. Democrat. Achievements include personally prosecuting more than 25 felony jury trials; led Consumer Protection Divsn. in the investigation and successful prosecution of a nat. oil co. charged with rigging gas pumps to cheat consumers; established a victim assistance unit; was cited by an ind. cons. hired by the Johnson County Bd. Commrs. as running the most efficient office in Johnson County govt.; served as pres. Kans. County and Dist. Atty.'s Assn. Office: US Ho Reps 1727 Longworth Ho Office Bldg Washington DC 20515-1603

**MOORE, DERRICK LANIER,** military officer; b. Buffalo, Jan. 6, 1960; s. Willis Carl Moore and Catherine Hill; m. Jacqueline Lewis (div.). BS in Criminal Justice, Grambling State U., LA, 1983; MS in Pub. Adminstrn., Chaminade U., 1987; AS in Criminology, C.C. of the Air Force, Cheyenne, Wyo., 1999. Flight chief-security forces USAF, Washington, 1984—, manpower and orgn. project mgr. Panama City, Fla., 2000—03; min. Full Gospel Bapt. Ch. Fellowship, Howell, NJ, 1998—. Asst. flight chief, dir. deployed forces USAF, FE Warren AFB, Wyo., 1998, flight chief, dir. deployed forces, Tyndall AFB, 2004—05, lead mil. war planner, 2000—03; security coord. Russian START treaty 90th Space Wing, FE Warren AFB, 1999. Actor: (movie) The Sitting Place, 2000. Project coord. Ronald McDonald Ho., Pensacola, Fla., 2002—04; lay min., coord. Tyndall AFB Chapel, Panama City, 2003—; v.p. Tyndall Parish Coun., 2003—05. Master sgt. USAF, 1984—. Decorated Commendation medals (6) USAF. Mem.: VFW, Am. Legion, Wyo. Buffalo Soldier Assn. (pres.). Democrat. Avocations: military history, sports memorabilia, Biblical history, singing, songwriting. Home: 2203 Beck Ave # B6 Panama City FL 32405 Office: Tyndall AFB 515 Suwannee Rrd Panama City FL 32403-5438 Office Phone: 850-283-4407. Office Fax: 850-283-2509. E-mail: derrick.moore@tyndall.af.mil.

**MOORE, DONALD EMERSON, III,** zoological park administrator, curator, wildlife biologist; b. Syracuse, N.Y., Jan. 9, 1954; s. Donald Emerson and Ruth Hodge (Steinhilber) M.; m. Adrienne Rose Whiteley (div.); children: Jessie Rose, Caitlin Grace; m. Suzanne L. Daley. BS in Environ. Sci. and Forestry, SUNY, Syracuse, 1976; MPA, Syracuse U., 1997; PhD, SUNY, Syracuse, 2001. Cert. biologist. Edn. asst. Burnet Park Zoo, Syracuse, 1976-77, technician animal care, 1977-79, zoologist, 1980-83, curator mammals, 1984-93; dir. Thompson Park Conservancy, 1993-95; curator Wildlife Conservation Soc., N.Y.C., 1997—2002, dir., 2003—; vis. assoc. prof. Hunter Coll. Animal Behavior and Conservation Focus, 2005—. Sci. adviser Thompson Park Zoo, Watertown, N.Y., 1984—; mem. master plan team A New Breed of Zoo, 1980-86, Springdale Farm Park, 1985-88; exploring adviser, 1989-96. Author: (mgmt. format) Species Mgmt. Plan, 1978, Disney's Wonderful World of Animals, 2006; contbr. articles to sci. jours. Instr. ARC, Syracuse, 1978-87; mem. master plan team Millbrook Sch., 1988-89. Fellow: Am. Zoo and Aquarium Assn. (prof.); mem.: NY Acad. Sci., Internat. Soc. Behavioral Ecology, Soc. Conservation Biology, Internat. Union Conservation Nature and Natural Resources (deer specialist group, mustelid/viverrid specialist group, reintroduction specialist group), Wildlife Soc., Am. Soc. Mammalogists, Explorers Club (resident fellow), Sigma Xi. Presbyterian. Avocations: skiing, hiking, canoeing, canning jams and jellies, photography. Office: Wildlife Conservation Soc 2300 Southern Blvd Bronx NY 10460

**MOORE, DONALD FRANCIS,** lawyer; b. NYC, Dec. 14, 1937; s. John F. and Helen A. (McLoughlin) M.; m. Alice L. Kalmar; children: Christina M., Marianne, Karen L., Alison A. AB, Fordham U., 1959; JD, St. John's U., Bklyn., 1962. Bar: NY 1962, DC 1970, US Supreme Ct. 1993. Assoc. Paul Weiss, Rifkind, Wharton & Garrison, NYC, 1962-70, ptnr., 1970-97, of counsel, 1998—. Editor in chief St. John's U. Law Rev., 1962. Served to Capt. U.S. Army, active 1962-64. Mem. NY State Bar Assn., Assn. of Bar of City of NY Roman Catholic. Avocation: fishing. Home: 7 Wedgewood Ct Glen Head NY 11545-2229 Office: Paul Weiss Rifkind Wharton & Garrison Ste 4200 1285 Avenue Of The Americas Fl 21 New York NY 10019-6065 E-mail: dfxm@aol.com.

**MOORE, DONALD WALTER,** retired academic administrator; b. Culver City, Calif., June 9, 1942; s. Raymond Owen and Jewel Elizabeth (Young) M.; m. Dagmar Ulbrich, Mar. 28, 1968; 1 child, Michael. AA, L.A. Valley Coll., 1967; BA in History, Calif. State U., Northridge, 1970; MA in Learning Disability, Calif. State U., 1973; MLS, U. So. Calif., 1974. Asst., adj. prof. L.A. Pierce Coll. Libr., 1974—; instr. reading L.A. Trade Tech. Coll., 1978—80, pres.'s staff asst., 1983—87; instr. learning skills L.A. City Coll. 1987—88, dir. amnesty edn., 1988—92, dir. English and citizenship program, 1992—2003, ret., 2003. Adj. instr. computer sci. L.A. (Calif.) Trade-Tech. Coll., 1983—. Author: A Guidebook to U.S. Army Dress Helmets, 2000; contbr. fiction, articles, revs. to various publs. Mem. Little Big Horn Assn. The Co. Mil. Historians, Horror Writers Assn., Mystery Writers Am. Republican. Roman Catholic. Avocations: writing, collecting military memorabilia, reading. *Personal philosophy: To survive in this world you must believe in yourself and know what's worth fighting for and what's not. But never despair, despair is the greatest sin.*

**MOORE, DUNCAN THOMAS,** optics scientist, educator; b. Biddeford, Maine, Dec. 7, 1946; s. Thomas Fogg Moore and Virginia Robinson Wing; m. Gunta Liders, July 1995. BA in Physics, U. Maine, 1969, DSc (hon.), 1995; MS in Optics, U. Rochester (N.Y.), 1970, PhD in Optics, 1974. Dir. U. Rochester, 1974-78, assoc. prof., 1978-86, prof., 1986—, Kingslake prof., 1993—, dean engring. and applied sci., 1995-97, prof. biomed. engring. 2001—, prof. bus. adminstrn., 2005—; pres. and founder Gradient Lens Corp., Rochester, 1980—97; dir. N.Y. State Ctr. Advanced Optical Tech Rochester, 1987—94; assoc. dir. technology White House Office Sci. & Technology Policy, Washington, 1997—2000; CEO Infotonics Tech. Ctr. Inc., 2002—04. Vis. scientist Nippon Schlumberger, Tokyo, 1983; Congl. fellow Am. Phys. Soc., Washington, 1993—94; sci. advisor Sen. John D. Rockefeller IV, W.Va., 1993—94; exec. dir. Univ. Industry and Govt. Partnership Advanced Photonics, 2001—02; mem. environ. and energy sec. rev. com. Idaho Nat. Engring. and Environ. Lab., 2001—02; mem. bd. assessment for Nat. Inst. Stds. and Tech. programs NRC, 2001—05, mem. panel for physics, 2001—05, chmn. panel for physics, 2002—05, chmn., 2002—05; mem. engring. vis. com. NASA-Goddard Space Flight Ctr., 2002—, chair applied engring. and tech. directorate vis. com., 2002—, mem. James Webb Space Telescope integrity team, 2002—; mem. nat. innovation initiative Coun. on Competitiveness, 2004—; mem. com. sci. engring. and pub. policy AAAS, 2005—; lectr. in field. Contbr. articles to profl. jours. Chmn. Hubble Ind. Rev. Panel, 1990—91. Named Engr. of the Yr., Rochester Engring. Soc., 1999; recipient Disting. Inventor of Yr. award, Rochester Intellectual Property Law Assn., 1993, Grin Optics award, Japanese Applied Physics Soc., 1993, Sci. and Tech. award, Greater Rochester C. of C., 1992, Gold medal, Internat. Soc. Optical Engring., 2006. Mem.: NAE, IEEE Lasers and Electro-Optics Soc. (govt. fellows selection com. 2005—), Am. Inst. Physics (state dept. fellowship selection com. 2001—02), Coalition Photonics and Optics (chair 1996—97), Forum Physics and Soc. (exec. com. 1996—97), Coun. Sci. Soc. (co-chair govt. affairs com. 1996—97), Materials Rsch. Soc., Am. Assn. Engring. Soc. (bd. govs. 1995—97, Nat. Engring. award 1999), Optical Soc. Am. (bd. dirs. 1987—89, editor Applied Optics 1990—92, bd. dirs. 1992—97, v.p. 1994, pres. 1996, adv. coun. homeland security 2004—, Leadership award 2001), Am. Soc. Precision Engring., Am. Ceramic Soc. (Edward Orton, Jr. Meml. lectr 2002). Achievements include patents in field. Home: 4 Claret Dr Fairport NY 14450-4610 Office: The Inst Optics University of Rochester Rochester NY 14627-0186 Office Phone: 585-275-5248. Business E-Mail: moore@optics.rochester.edu.

**MOORE, EDWARD, JR.,** career officer; b. Little Rock, Ark. s. Edward M., Sr.; m. Deborah Marcia Cooper; children: Kimberly, Erica, Stacey. Grad., So. Ill. U., 1968, MBA, Naval Postgrad. Sch., 1974. Commd. ensign USN, 1968;

advanced through grades to rear admiral; gunnery and comms. officer, navigator USS Severn; from comms. officer to ops. officer PRECOMMUNIT-LANG USS Lang; weapons officer USS Sterett; exec. officer USS Buchanan; commdg. officer USS Lewis B. Puller; 1st commdg. officer USS Cowpens, 1993; comdr. Carl Vinson task group, cruiser-destroyer group three, 1996; jr. officer assignment officer, coord. shore assignments Bur. Naval Personnel; opd. analyst mem. staff of Comdr. in Chief U.S. Pacific Cmd.; asst. chief of staff manpower, personnel mem. staff Comdr. in Chief US Pacific Fleet; commandant naval dist. Washington; dir. strategy and policy divsn. (N51); asst. dep. chief naval ops. (plans, policy ops., N3/N5B) Washington, 1997-98; vice admiral Com. Naval Surface Force, U.S. Pacific Fleet, San Diego, 1998—. With USNR, 1963-68. Decorated Legion of Merit with three gold stars, Navy Achievement medal. Mem. Nat. Naval Officers Assn., Kappa Alpha Psi. Office: 830 D Avenue Coronado CA 92118

**MOORE, EDWARD WARREN,** lawyer; b. Odessa, Tex., July 21, 1959; s. Edward Warren and Gloria (Schroeter) M.; m. JoAnne Bisso; children: Peggy, Barbara. BA in Econs., Princeton U., 1981; JD, So. Meth. U., 1984. Bar: Tex. 1984, US Dist. Ct. (no. dist.) Tex. 1984, U.S. Ct. Appeals (5th cir.) 1984, U.S. Ct. Appeals (10th cir.) 1985. Assoc. Ravkind, Kuehne & Biesel, Dallas, 1984-85; ptnr. Kuehne & Moore, Dallas, 1984-96; pvt. practice, 1996-2000, 2003—; mng. ptnr. Moore & Anderson, 2000—03; v.p., gen. counsel Tissue Gen, Inc. Dir. Rsch. Group Tex., Inc.; mentor North Tex. Enterprise Ctr. for Med. Tech. Fellow Am. Bar Found.; mem. AAAS, ABA (litigation sect., bus. law sect. and com., intellectual property sect.), State Bar Tex., Dallas Bar Assn., Tex. Trial Lawyers Assn., Dallas Country Club, Safari Club Internat. (life), Dallas Safari Club (life), DSC 100 (vol.), Order of Flags. Catholic. Home: 7044 Turtle Creek Blvd Dallas TX 75205-1254 Office Phone: 214-706-9040. E-mail: eddymoore@ewmpllc.net.

**MOORE, EMMETT BURRIS, JR.,** physical chemist, educator; b. Bozeman, Mont., June 14, 1929; s. Emmett Burris and Iris Marie (Brown) M.; m. Diane Elizabeth Girling, Oct. 1, 1960; children: Karen Elizabeth, Robin Diane. BS in Chemistry with honors, Wash. State U., 1951; PhD in Phys. Chemistry (Shell fellow), U. Minn., 1956. Teaching asst. U. Minn., Mpls., 1951-55, asst. prof. physics Duluth, 1957-59; staff scientist Boeing Sci. Research Labs., Seattle, 1959-73. Lectr. chemistry Seattle U., 1973; dir. power plant siting Minn. Environ. Quality Bd., St. Paul, 1973-76; gen. mgr. Richland (Wash.) Olympic Engring. Corp., 1976-78; staff scientist Pacific N.W. Nat. Lab., 1978-96; mem. environ. engring. rev. panel EPA, 1989-95; alt. mem. Hanford Adv. Bd., 1995-2000; adj. prof. environ. sci. Wash. State U., 1990—. Author: (book) The Environmental Impact Statement Process and Environmental Law, 1997, 2d edit., 2000, An Introduction to the Management and Regulation of Hazardous Waste, 2000; contbr. articles to profl. jours. Trustee Mid-Columbia Symphony Soc., 1978-85, v.p., 1980-81, pres., 1981-83; trustee Richland Light Opera Co., 1984-88, bus. mgr., 1984-88. Recipient Land Grant Faculty Excellence award Wash. State U., 1999. Fellow AAAS; mem. Am. Phys. Soc., Am. Chem. Soc. (chmn. Pauling award com. 1971, sec. Puget Sound sect. 1971-73, mem. energy panel of com. on chemistry and pub. affairs 1983-86), Am. Assn. Physics Tchrs. (v.p. Wash. sect. 1965-66, pres. 1966-67), Phi Beta Kappa, Phi Kappa Phi, Phi Eta Sigma, Alpha Chi Sigma, Phi Lambda Upsilon, Sigma Alpha Epsilon (v.p. province 1972-73) Episcopalian (vestryman 1967-69, 76-79, 91, sr. warden 1969, del. diocesan conv. 1969-72). Home: 2323 Greenbrook Blvd Richland WA 99352-8427 Office: Wash State U 2710 University Dr Richland WA 99354-1671 Office Phone: 509-372-7276. Business E-Mail: ebmoore@wsu.edu.

**MOORE, ERNEST EUGENE, JR.,** surgeon, educator; b. Pitts., June 18, 1946; s. Ernest Eugene Sr. and Mary Ann (Burroughs) M.; m. Sarah Van Duzer, Sept. 2, 1978; children: Hunter Burroughs, Peter Kitrick. BS in Chemistry, Allegheny Coll., 1968; MD, U. Pitts., 1972. Surg. resident U. Vt., Burlington, 1972-76; chief of trauma Denver Health Med. Ctr., 1976—, chief dept. surgery, 1984—. Prof. surgery, vice chmn. dept., U. Colo., 1985-95; dir. facilities Colo. Trauma Inst., Denver, 1984-95. Editor: Critical Decisions in Trauma, 1987, Trauma, 1988, rev. edits., 1991, 96, 00, 05, Early Care of the Injured, 1989, Surgical Secrets, 1996, rev. edit., 2002, 05, Trauma Manual, 2003, World of Emergency Surgery; assoc. editor Jour. Trauma, Am. Jour. Surgery, World of Surgery, Surgery-Problem Solving Approach, 2d edit., 1994, others; patentee retrohepatic vena cava shunt. Fellow ACS (com. on trauma, vice chair 1990), Soc. Univ. Surgeons (pres. 1989), Am. Assn. Surgery of Trauma (pres. 1993), Internat. Assn. Surgery of Trauma and Surg. Intensive Care (pres. 1998-99), Pan Am. Trauma Assn. (pres. 1991), Southwestern Surg. Congress (pres. 1998), Western Trauma Assn. (pres. 1989). Republican. Avocations: skiing, mountaineering, hunting, ultramarathons, fishing. Home: 2909 E 7th Avenue Pky Denver CO 80206-3839 Office: Denver Health Med Ctr Dept Surgery Denver CO 80204 Office Phone: 303-436-6558. Business E-Mail: ernest.moore@dhha.org.

**MOORE, GEORGE C.,** manufacturing executive; BA in Acctg., Loyola Coll. CPA. Acct. Arthur Andersen, 1977—87; pres., CFO Yield House, 1987—97; group fin. officer Tanaher Tools, Tool Products, Safety and Aviation and Automotive Danaher Corp., 1997—2003, group v.p. fin., 2000—03; exec. v.p. Maytag, Newton, Iowa, 2003—, CFO, 2003—. Office: Maytag 403 West 4th St N Newton IA 50208

**MOORE, GEORGE CRAWFORD JACKSON,** lawyer; b. Tenn. BA, U. Fla., 1963; PhB in Soviet Law, U. St. Andrews, Scotland, 1966; MA in English Law with honors, Cambridge U., Eng., 1968, LLM in Internat. Law, 1969. Bar: Eng. (Barrister, Inner Temple) 1970, Jamaica 1971, Fla. 1973, Turks & Caicos Islands 1974, U.S. Supreme Ct. 1976, Antigua and Barbuda, Brit. V.I., Grenada, Montserrat, St. Lucia 1977, Anguilla 1999. Legis. asst. to U.S. sen., Washington, 1970-72; asst. pub. defender Palm Beach County, Fla., 1973; pvt. practice West Palm Beach, Fla., 1973—. Founding pres. World Trade Coun. of Palm Beach County, 1981 ; chmn. Fla. Coun. Internat. Devel., 1983—84, 2000—03, Fla. Gov.'s Conf. on World Trade and Investment, 1989, Fla. Export Coun. of U.S. Dept. Commerce, 1991—92, Free Trade Agreement of Americas. Editor spl. issues Fla. Bar Jour., 1982, 87, chmn. editorial bd., 1988-89; mem. editorial bd. The Internat. Lawyer jour. of ABA, 1979-84; contbr. articles to profl. jours. Chmn. Fla. Econ. Growth and Internat. Devel. Commn., 1989-90. Fellow: Ctr. Internat. Legal Studies, Soc. Internat. Bus. Fellows (v.p.); mem.: ABA, Fla. Bar (chmn. internat. law sect. 1994—95, bd. cert. specialist in internat. law 1999—, chmn. internat. law cert. bd. 2004—). Office: 105 S Narcissus Ave Ste 812 West Palm Beach FL 33401-5530 also: 11 King's Bench Walk, Temple London EC4Y 7EQ England Office Phone: 561-833-9000, 44-20-7632-8500. Office Fax: 561-833-9990. Business E-Mail: barrister@barrister.law.com.

**MOORE, GEORGE EMERSON, JR.,** geologist, educator; b. Lebanon, Mo., Jan. 2, 1914; s. George Emerson and Dorothea Louisa (Niewohner) M.; m. Wilma Corrine Leonard, May 20, 1939; children: George E. III, Dana Corinne, Craig G. AB, U. Mo., 1936, MA, 1938; PhD, Harvard U., 1947. Instr. U. Mo., 1938-39; teaching asst. Harvard U. 1940-42, 1946-47; geologist A.P. Green Fire Brick Co., Mexico, Mo., 1942-46; instr. Ohio State U. at Columbus, 1947-48, asst. prof., 1948-57, assoc. prof., 1957-64, prof., 1964-84, prof. emeritus, 1984—. Geologist U.S. Geol. Survey, 1952-83 Fellow Geol. Soc. Am.; mem. Phi Beta Kappa, Sigma Xi. Home: 58 Mulberry Dr Wakefield RI 02879-1416

**MOORE, GEORGE W.,** electronics executive; BSEE, Clemson U.; MBA, Duke U. Elec. engr. IBM, Research Triangle Park, NC, 1978, various engring. and mgmt. positions, program mgr. strategic planning, 1986—88, mgr. electronic card assembly, 1988—89, mgr. ABS sys. prodn. mgmt. 1993—1998, gen. mgr. info. products, 1994—97, v.p. corp. mfg. staff, 1997—2000; corp. officer, exec. v.p. Solectron Corp., Milpitas, Calif., 2000—. Mem.: Nat. Assn. Mfrs. (bd. dirs.). Office: Solectron Corp 777 Gibraltar Dr Milpitas CA 95035

**MOORE, GORDON E.,** electronics executive, researcher; b. San Francisco, Jan. 3, 1929; s. Walter Harold and Florence Almira (Williamson) Moore; m. Betty I. Whittaker, Sept. 9, 1950; children: Kenneth, Steven. BS in Chemistry,

U. Calif., Berkeley, 1950; PhD in Chemistry and Physics, Calif. Inst. Tech., 1954. Tech. staff Shockley Semicondr. Lab., 1956—57; mgr. engring. Fairchild Camera & Instrument Corp., 1957—59, dir. R & D, 1959—68; co-founder Intel Corp., Santa Clara, Calif., 1968, exec. v.p., 1968—75, pres., CEO, 1975—79, CEO, 1979—87, chmn., 1979—97, chmn. emeritus, 1997—. Bd. dirs. Varian Assocs. Inc., Transamerica Corp., Gilead Sciences, Inc. Founder, chmn. Gordon & Betty Moore Found.; bd. trustee Calif. Inst. Tech., 1995—2001, sr. trustee, 2001—. Named one of Forbes' Richest Americans, 2006; recipient Nat. Medal Tech., President George Bush, 1990, Fellow award, Computer History Mus., 1998, Bower award for Bus. Leadership, Franklin Inst., 2002, Perkin medal, Soc. Chem. Industry, 2004. Fellow: IEEE (Founders medal 1977); mem.: Am. Phys. Soc., NAE. Office: Intel Corp 2200 Mission College Blvd Santa Clara CA 95054-1549 also: Betty & Gordon Moore Library Wilberforce Rd Cambridge CB3 0WD England*

**MOORE, GREGORY E.,** lawyer; b. Annapolis, Md., Mar. 4, 1952; SB, MIT, 1973; JD, Harvard Univ., 1976. Bar: Mass. 1977. Assoc. Ropes & Gray, Boston, 1976—85, ptnr. corp. dept., 1985—, co-head venture capital & emerging companies practice group. Chmn. MIT Alumni Fund Bd., 2000—02; mem. MIT Corp., 2003—; bd. dir. Lexington Montessori Sch. Mem.: ABA (chmn. Com. on Tech. & Intellectual Property 1988—92), Mass. Bar Assn., Boston Bar Assn., Computer Law Assn. (former bd. dir.). Office: Ropes & Gray 1 International Pl Boston MA 02110-2624 Office Phone: 617-951-7370. Office Fax: 617-951-7050. Business E-Mail: gregory.moore@ropesgray.com.

**MOORE, GREGORY I.,** editor; Reporter Dayton Journal Herald, 1976—80, Cleveland Plain Dealer, 1980—83, political editor, 1983—86; asst. metro editor Boston Globe, 1986—94, mng. editor, 1994—2002; editor Denver Post, 2002—. Office: The Denver Post 1560 Broadway Denver CO 80202-1577 E-mail: gmoore@denverpost.com.

**MOORE, GUY WILL,** retired public information officer, historian, writer; b. Retta, Okla., June 19, 1922; s. Guy Thomas Moore and Pearl Grace Glasgow; m. Hazel Avenell Cartwright, Aug. 31, 1948 (dec. June 18, 1986); children: Anne Elizabeth Tarquinio, March Victoria Dodge. BA in Journalism, U. Okla., 1950, MA in History, 1952. News writer Office of the Army Surgeon Gen., Washington, 1956—57, info. specialist, 1957—59; info. specialist (first) U.S. Army Rsch. and Devel. Command, Washington, 1959—60; dep. info. officer, divsn. gen. med. scis. NIH, Bethesda, Md., 1960—61, staff asst., office of dir. pub. affairs, 1961—64, chief pub. info. sect. office of rsch info., chief supervisory pub. info. specialist, news br., office of comm., 1967—79; ret., 1979. Chmn. pub. info. intern recruitment tng. com. NIH, 1961—79, spkr. grants assoc. seminar, 1971—72; spkr. Am. Coll. Pub. Rels. Assn., Washington, 1970. Author: The Case of Mrs. Surratt, 1954, The NIH: How it Works, 1981; contbg. author: The Surratt Society's In Pursuit of..., 1990; contbr. articles to astronomy jours. Contr. project feeder watch Cornell Lab of Ornithology, 1987—. Mem.: No. Va. Astronomy Club, Nat. Capitol Astronomers, Surratt Soc. Avocations: astronomy, birdwatching. Home: 224 N Nelson St Arlington VA 22201

**MOORE, GWENDOLYNNE S. (GWEN MOORE),** congresswoman; b. Racine, Wis., Apr. 18, 1951; 3 children. BA in Polit. Sci., Marquette U., Milw., 1978. Mem. Wis. State Assembly, 1989—92, Wis. State Senate from 4th dist., Madison, 1992—2004, US Congress from 4th Wis. dist., 2005—, mem. small bus. com., mem. fin. svcs. com. Named one of Most Influential Black Americans, Ebony mag., 2006. Democrat. Office: US Ho Reps 1408 Longworth Ho Office Bldg Washington DC 20515-4904 Office Phone: 202-225-4572.*

**MOORE, H. LOUIS,** agricultural economics education; b. Cumberland, Md., Mar. 22, 1930; s. Harry Paul and Esther (Shaffer) M.; m. Mary Jane Horner, Dec. 17, 1952; children: Roger, Randall, Rex, Rory. Assoc. degree, Potomac State U., 1950; BS, Pa. State U., 1952, MS, 1956. Mktg. agy. Pa. State U., University Park, 1955-58, asst. prof., 1958-67, assoc. prof., 1967-73, prof., 1973—. Presenter and cons. in field. Contbr. articles to profl. jours. Com. person Boy Scouts Am., Centre County, Pa., 1967-85; treas. Coll. Twp. Ind. Devel. Authority, Centre County, 1974-90. Cpl. U.S. Army, 1952-54. Recipient Extension award Pa. Dairymen's Assn., 1990, Gamma Sigma Delta Extension award Pa. State U., University Park, 1991; named Communicator of Yr., Atlantic Dairy Cooperation, 1990. Mem. Am. Agrl. Econ. Assn., N.E. Agrl. and Resource Econs. Assn., Antique Auto Club Am., Rolls Royce Owners Club, Pa. State Alumni Assn. (life). Republican. Methodist. Avocations: restoration of classic cars, bicycling, jogging. Home: 1700 Linden Hall Rd Boalsburg PA 16827-1719 Office: Pa State Univ 202 Armsby Bldg University Park PA 16802-5601

**MOORE, HAL G.,** mathematician, educator; b. Vernal, Utah, Aug. 14, 1929; s. Lewis Henry and Nora (Gillman) M.; m. D'On Empey, July 20, 1956; children: David, Nora (Mrs. Bret C. Hess), Alison (Mrs. Samuel M. Smith). BS, U. Utah, 1952, MS, 1957; PhD, U. Calif., Santa Barbara, 1967. Tchr. Salt Lake City Pub. Schs., 1952-53; instr. math. Carbon Jr. Coll., also Carbon H.S., Price, Utah, 1953-55, Purdue U., Lafayette, Ind., 1957-61, adminstrv. asst. dept. math, 1960-61; from asst. prof. math. to assoc. prof. math. Brigham Young U., Provo, Utah, 1961-71, prof., 1971-95, prof. emeritus, 1995—, assoc. chmn. dept. math., 1986-89. Author: Precalculus Mathematics, 2d edit, 1977, (with Adil Yaqub) Elementary Linear Algebra With Applications, 1980, College Algebra and Trigonometry, 1983, A First Course in Linear Algebra, 1992, 3d edit., 1998; contbr. articles to profl. jours. Mem. High Coun., LDS Ch., 1985-91, MTC br. pres., 1991-94, Bishop, 1958-61, 78-82. NSF faculty fellow, U. Calif., Santa Barbara, 1964—66. Mem. Am. Math. Soc., Math. Assn. Am. (bd. govs. 1989-92), Utah State Math. Coalition (planning dir. 1990, bd. dir. 1991-92), Sigma Xi (dir. 1974-80, 82-85, com. chmn. 1982-90), Phi Kappa Phi. Home and Office: 631 W 650 S Orem UT 84058-6027 Personal E-mail: mooreh@math.byu.edu. *Revelation and reason can work together to bring human beings closer to the truth of their existence and place in the universe. But charity and love and dedication are as necessary to the success of this union as they are to all others.*

**MOORE, HELENE DARLAK,** psychologist, consultant; arrived in Germany, 2001; d. Joseph Stephen and Helen Ann Darlak; m. Wayne Lee Moore, Aug. 10, 1996. BA in Psychology, Loyola U., 1988; MA in Psychology, Pepperdine U., 1992; MA in Clin. Psychology, Calif. Sch. Profl. Psychology, 1995, PhD in Clin. Psychology, 1998. Lic. clin. psychologist N.Y., 1999, Hesse, Germany, 2001. Intern U. So. Calif. Family Residency Program Calif. Hosp. Med. Ctr., L.A., 1994—95; intern Hillside Hosp. Glen Roberts Child Study Ctr., Glendale, Calif., 1995—97; intern L.I. Jewish Med. Ctr., Glen Oaks, NY, 1997—98; asst. mgr. N.Y. Presbyn. Hosp. Weill Med. Coll. Cornell U., White Plains, NY, 1998—99; clin. psychologist Columbia U. N.Y., 1999—2000; clin. psychologist Johann Wolfgang Goethe U. Inst. Psychology U. Frankfurt, Germany, 2001—. Adj. prof. Berkeley Coll., N.Y., 1999; cons. in field. Author: Sick & Tired, The Biopsychological Facets of Chronic Fatigue and Immune Dysfunction, 1996; contbr. articles to profl. jours. Vol. Red Cross, Chgo., 2005—06. Mem.: APA, Psi Chi. Independent. Avocations: travel, cooking, reading, art history, piano.

**MOORE, HERFF LEO, JR.,** management educator; b. San Antonio, Jan. 24, 1937; s. Herff Leo Moore Sr. and Constance (Benesh) Wold; children: Terri Lynn, Christopher Scott, Kimberly Anne. BSBA, Ohio State U., 1964; MBA, U. Tex., 1968; MS in Cmty. Svcs., U. Rochester, 1976; PhD, U. Tex. Arlington, 1980. Cert. sr. profl. in human resources (life). Prodn. mgmt., quality assurance officer Sacramento Air Logistics Ctr. USAF, 1964—67; pers. mgmt., adminstrv. cons. Aero. Sys. Divsn. Wright-Patterson AFB, Dayton, Ohio, 1968—73; pers. mgmt. and quality assurance cons. Defense Contract Adminstrv. Svcs. Dist. Hdqrs., Rochester, NY, 1973—76; lectr. in mgmt. and doctoral student U. Tex. Arlington, 1976—79; asst. prof. bus. adminstrn. Ea. Ky. U., Richmond, 1979—81; assoc. prof. mgmt. East Tex. State U. Texarkana, 1981—83, Saint John Fisher Coll., Rochester, 1983—85,

U. Ctrl. Ark., Conway, 1985—99, ret., 1999. Pres. H.M.C.C. Mgmt. Group, Conway, 1988-2005, H.M. Merchandising Internat., Inc., 2006—; participant Leadership Texarkana Leadership Tng., 1981-82; mgmt. cons., devel. trainer, Calif., N.Y., Ark., Ohio, N.J., Fla., Ga., Tex., 1964—. Author: (with others) Language, Customs and Protocol: A Guidebook for International Students and Employees, 1992; contbr. numerous articles to profl. jours. Capt. USAF, 1964—76. Recipient Significant Performance Contbr. award Def. Supply Agy., 1975; Nat. scholar Phi Kappa Phi, 1968; named Honor Grad. USAF Officers Tng. Sch., 1964. Mem. Soc. for Human Resource Mgmt. (tng. and devel. com. 1989-94, select panel on edn. 1989-91, coll. rels. com. 1989-92, bd. dirs. area IV 1987-91, sec., treas. Ark. coun. 1986-87), Ark. Human Resources Assn. (pres. 1991-92, bd. dirs. 1991-93), Acad. Mgmt., Soc. Human Resource Mgmt. (superior merit awards student chpt. U. Ctrl. Ark. 1985-90, 93), Alpha Kappa Psi, Phi Kappa Phi, Sigma Iota Epsilon. Mem. Assembly Of God Ch. Avocations: golf, chess, political buttons. Home: 1248 Valentine St Hurst TX 76053-4532 Office Phone: 888-205-4820. E-mail: herffmoore@hotmail.com.

**MOORE, HUBERT, JR.**, retired addictions counselor, consultant; b. Oklahoma City, Jan. 2, 1932; s. Hubert and Goldie Edith Moore; m. Mary Alene Jarnet, Dec. 9, 1958 (div. Oct. 1959); 1 child, LeAnne; m. Shirley M. Mumchuck, Apr. 1978 (dec. Nov. 8, 1985); children: Peggy, JoAnn, Lisa, Sharon. AA in Counseling, U. Alaska, 1986, BA in Human Svcs., 1992, BA in Psychology, 1992, BA in Sociology, 1996; MA in Anthropology, U. Mindanao, Philippines, 1998. Cert. addictions counselor II Alaska, Nat. Assn. Alcohol and Drug Abuse Counselors, master forensic counselor and criminal justice specialist Nat. Assn. Forensic Counselors, Nat. Register Addiction Counselors, Calif. Registry Addiction Specialists. Substance abuse counselor II No. Regional Ctr. for Addictions, Fairbanks, Alaska, 1977—85; forensic counselor Fairbanks Correction Facility, 1995—96; addictions cons. Soldotna, Alaska, 1991—2005; owner, operator (daycare ctr.) Papa's Playhouse, Soldotna, 1998—2006; ret., 2006. Campaign vol. Rep. Caucus, Soldotna, 1991—. Republican. Moslem. Avocations: philosophic studies, demographic research, motorcycling, moutain climbing, social research. Home: PO Box 1057 Soldotna AK 99669 Business E-Mail: altcounselingconsult@lycos.com.

**MOORE, J. STUART**, information technology executive; married; 5 children. Degree in Computer Scis., U. Calif., Berkeley. With Cambridge Technology Inc.; co-founder, co-chmn., co-CEO Sapient Corp., Cambridge, Mass., 1991—. Office: Sapient Corp 25 First St Cambridge MA 02141

**MOORE, JACKSON WATTS**, bank executive; b. Birmingham, Ala., Nov. 2, 1948; s. Joseph Watts and Shellye Louise (Jackson) M.; m. Elizabeth Wilson, June 12, 1971; children: Jackson Jr., Wilson, Shellye. BS, U. Ala., 1970; JD, Vanderbilt U., 1973. Assoc. Martin, Tate, Morrow and Marston, Memphis, 1973-77; mng. ptnr. Wilman, Harrold, Allen, Dixon and McDonnell, Memphis, 1977-89; pres., COO Union Planters Corp., Memphis, 1989, also bd. dirs., chmn., CEO, 2000—04; pres. Regions Financial Corp., 2004, CEO, 2005—, chmn., 2006—. Bd. dirs. Union Planters Nat. Bank, Mid-South Pub. Commn. Network, Memphis Devel. Found., PSB Bancshares, Clanton, Ala. Bd. dirs. Boy Scouts Am., Memphis Emmaus Comty.; trustee Vanderbilt Univ.; chmn. bd. Vanderbilt Law Sch.; bd. trustees pres.'s cabinet U. Ala. Capt. U.S. Army, 1973. Mem. Memphis Country Club, Memphis Hunt and Polo Club. Republican. Methodist. Avocations: golf, tennis, reading. Office: Regions Financial Corp 417 N 20th St Birmingham AL 35202*

**MOORE, JACQUELYN CORNELIA**, retired labor union administrator, editor; b. Dec. 25, 1929; d. James C. and Harriette I. Thomas; m. Clarence Carbin Moore, Jan. 19, 1947 (dec. Feb. 1970); children: Clarence Joseph, Janet Elizabeth Moore Marshall. Mail clk. U.S. P.O., Phila., 1966—93; editor Local 509 Newsletter Nat. Alliance of Postal and Fed. Employees, Washington, 1969—74, editl. newsletter chmn., 1969—74, sec. dist. 5, 1972—74, nat. editor Nat. Alliance, 1974—2004, mem. exec. bd., 1974—, union photographer, 1974—2005, ret., 2005. Dir. 202 Housing for Elderly Corp. bds., Chattanooga, New Orleans, 1981—2004, Atlanta, 1988—2004; sec. supervisory com. Nat. Fed. Credit Union, 1977—82, 1984—94, chair, 1994—. Vol. D.C. Voting Rights Corp., Washington, 1979—2004; sustaining mem. Dem. Nat. Com., 1977—2004. Mem.: Nat. Alliance Postal and Fed. Employees. Roman Catholic. Home: 1640 11th St NW 202 Washington DC 20001 E-mail: jacmar5362@aol.com.

**MOORE, JAMES CONKLIN**, lawyer; b. Albany, NY, Dec. 20, 1939; s. James Alexander and Doris Virginia (Conklin) M.; m. Shirley Jean Mitchell, June 17, 1961; children: James, Jennifer, David, Eliza. BS, Cornell U., 1961, LLB, 1964. Bar: N.Y. 1964, U.S. Dist. Ct. (we. dist.) N.Y. 1966, U.S. Dist. Ct. (mid. dist.) Pa. 1981, U.S. Dist. Ct. (no. dist.) N.Y. 1980, U.S. Ct. Mil. Appeals 1965. Assoc. Wiser, Shaw, Freeman, VanGraafeiland, Harter & Secrest, Rochester, NY, 1966-74; ptnr. Harter, Secrest & Emery, Rochester, 1974—2003, mediator, arbitrator, counsel, 2004—. Bd. dirs. Empire Justice Ctr. Contbr. articles to profl. jours., chapters to books. Trustee, pres. Friends of Rochester (N.Y.) Pub. Libr., 1993—98; trustee Nat. Equal Justice Libr., 2006—; bd. dirs., vice chmn. Geva Theater, Inc., 2002—06; pres. Legal Connection, Inc., 2002—04; coun. mem. Cornell U., 1997—2002; active Monroe County Bar Found., bd. dirs., 2002—04; chmn. bd. trustees NY Lawyer Assistance Trust, 2001—04. Capt. U.S. Army, 1964—66, Vietnam. Mem. adv. bd. Rochester Area Edni. TV, 1981-87; elder, trustee Third Presbyn. Ch., Rochester. Fellow: ABA (ho. of dels. 1998—, standing comm. on legal assistance to indigent defendants), N.Y. Bar Found. (bd. dirs. 1997—2000), Am. Coll. Trial Lawyers; mem.: Am. Arbitration Assn., Nat. Conf. Bar Pres. (exec. com. 1999—2002), Monroe County Bar Assn. (chmn. judiciary com. 1982—85, trustee 2004—, chmn. com. on lawyer advt. 2006), N.Y. State Bar Assn. (chmn. ins. sect. 1984—85, ho. del. 1984—87, chmn. task force on liability ins. 1986—87, 1986—87, chmn. com. ins. programs 1988—94, exec. com. 1992—2000, ho. del. 1993—, v.p. 1994—97, pres. 1998—99, chmn. nominating com. 2001, chmn. com. on ADR 2006—, com. on jud. nominations 2006—), Am. Inst. Law (elected). Republican. Avocations: history, restoring old furniture. Home: 251 Windemere Rd Rochester NY 14610-1342 Office: Harter Secrest & Emery 1600 Bausch & Lomb Pl Rochester NY 14604-2711 Office Phone: 585-231-1124. Business E-Mail: jmoore@hselaw.com.

**MOORE, JAMES E.**, state supreme court justice; b. Laurens, SC, Mar. 13, 1936; s. Roy Ernest and Marie (Hill) M.; m. Mary Alicia Deadwyler, Jan. 27, 1963; children: Erin Alicia, Travis Warren. BA, Duke U., 1958, JD, 1961; D of Humanities (hon.), Lander Univ., 1997. Bar: S.C. 1961, U.S. Dist. Ct. S.C. 1961. Pvt. practice, Greenwood, S.C., 1961-76; mem. SC Ho. of Reps., Columbia, SC, 1968—76; cir. judge 8th Jud. Cir. SC, Greenwood, 1976-91; assoc. justice SC Supreme Ct., 1992—. Supreme ct. liaison S.C. Bd. of Law Examiners, Bd. of Commn. on Jud. Conduct, Bd. of Commn. on Atty. Conduct; chmn. Chief Justice's Commn. on Profession. Recipient Outstanding Contribution to Justice award, S.C. Trial Lawyers Assn., 1996. Mem. S.C. Bar Assn., ABA, Am. Judicature Soc.; First Baptist Church of Greenwood. Baptist. Home: 148 Amherst Dr Greenwood SC 29649-8901 Office: SC Supreme Ct PO Box 11330 Columbia SC 29211 Office Phone: 864-942-8559.*

**MOORE, JAMES L., JR.**, beverage company executive; b. 1942; BA, Davidson Coll., 1964; MBA, Univ. N.C., 1968. Dist. mgr. Pepsi-Cola Co., 1972-74, mgr. market planning Pepsi-Cola Bottling group, 1974-75, v.p., area mgr. Houston, 1975-76; v.p., gen. mgr. Atlantic Soft Drink, Knoxville, Tenn., 1977-82, v.p. mktg., 1982-83, pres., chief exec. officer, 1983-87, Coca-Cola Bottling Co. Consolidated, 1987—, also dir. 1st lt. U.S. Army, 1972-76. Office: Coca-Cola Bottling Co Consolidated PO Box 31487 Rd Charlotte NC 28231-1487

**MOORE, JAMES LAYNE**, neurologist, educator; b. Huntington, W.Va., Sept. 4, 1960; s. James Lawrence and Theodora Ann Moore; m. Anna E. Kincheloe, Aug. 17, 2003; children: James Lucas, Galen Lewis. BS in biology, Ohio No. U., 1982; MD, Wright State U., 1987; MPH, Ohio State U.,

2004. Diplomate Am. Bd. Psychiatry and Neurology. Asst. prof. neurology Ohio State U. Coll. Medicine, Columbus, 1993—2000; assoc. prof. neurology Ohio State U. Coll. Medicine and Pub. Health, 2000—; Richard J. and Martha D. Denman Prof. Clin. Rsch. in Epilepsy, 1996—; assoc. prof. Coll. Pharmacy Ohio State U. Dir., comprehensive epilepsy program Ohio State U. Hosps., 1995—. Contbr. articles to profl. jours. Mem.: APHA (licentiate), Am. Acad. Neurology (licentiate), Am. Epilepsy Soc. (licentiate), Phi Kappa Phi, Alpha Omega Alpha. Office: Ohio State U 1654 Upham Dr 4th Floor Columbus OH 43210 Office Phone: 614-293-4882. Office Fax: 293-4688. E-mail: moore.537@osu.edu.

**MOORE, JAMES R.**, lawyer; b. Longview, Wash., Sept. 14, 1944; s. James Carlton and Virginia (Rice) M.; m. Patricia Riley, Aug. 25, 1967 (div. 1978); 1 child, Katherine M.; stepchildren: Amy McKenna, John McKenna; 1 foster child, Zia Sunseri; m. Kathryn Lindquist, Aug. 26, 1996; stepchildren: Matthew Elggren, Adam Elggren, Erin Elggren, David Heilner. BA, Whitman Coll., 1966; JD, Duke U., 1969. Bar: Wash. 1970, U.S. Ct. Appeals (4th cir.) 1972, U.S. Supreme Ct. 1973, U.S. Ct. Appeals (9th cir.) 1974, D.C., 1995. Law clk. to Hon. J. Barnes U.S. Ct. Appeals (9th cir.), L.A., 1969-70; trial atty. pollution control, land/natural resources div. U.S. Dept. Justice, Washington, 1970-74; asst. U.S. atty. U.S. Atty.'s Office, Seattle, 1974-82; regional counsel U.S. EPA Region 10, 1982-87; counsel Perkins Coie, 1987-88, ptnr., 1989-98; sr. environ. counsel, v.p. Huntsman Corp., Salt Lake City, 1999—; dep. gen. counsel Huntsman Internat., 2002—04, Huntsman LLC, Salt Lake City, 2004—, Huntsman Corp., Salt Lake City, 2005—. Spkr. in field. Contbr. articles to profl. jours. Bd. dirs. Environ. Law Inst., 1995-2000; chmn. audit com. Whitman Coll., 1994—, bd. overseers 2003—; mem. Athlete's Hall of Fame Com., 2003—; ethics com. Bd. Environ. Auditors Cert., 1998—. Mem. ABA (sect. environment, energy and resources 1987—, vice chmn. in-house counsel com., 2003-04, chmn. 2004—), Wash. State Bar Assn. (environ. and land use sect. 1974—, spl. atty. coun. 1988-95). Democrat. Office: Huntsman Corp 500 Huntsman Way Salt Lake City UT 84108-1235 Office Phone: 801-584-5828. Business E-Mail: jim_moore@huntsman.com.

**MOORE, JANE ROSS**, librarian, educator; b. Phila., Apr. 24, 1929; d. John William and Mary M. Ross; m. Cyril Howard Moore, Jr., June 1, 1956 (div. Mar. 1967). AB, Smith Coll., 1951; MLS, Drexel U., 1952; postgrad., Columbia U.; MBA with distinction, NYU, 1965; PhD, Case Western Res. U., 1974. Cataloguer Yale U. Libr., 1952-54; chief tech. processes libr. Lederle Labs., Am. Cyanamid Co., Pearl River, NY, 1954-58; chief serials catalog libr. Bklyn. Coll. Libr., 1958-65, asst. chief, chief catalog divsn., 1965-70, assoc. prof., chief catalog divsn., 1971-73, assoc. prof., assoc. libr. adminstrv. svcs., 1973-76; prof., chief libr. Mina Rees Libr., Grad. Ctr., CUNY, 1976-91, prof., chief libr. emerita, 1991—. Lectr. Syracuse U. Grad. Sch. Libr. Sci., 1967, 69, Queens Coll. Grad. Sch. Libr. and Info. Studies, 1967—69, adj. assoc. prof., 1974—76, adj. prof., 1977—86; HEW Title IIB fellow Case Western Res. U. Sch. Libr. Sci., 1970—72; mem. chancellor's task force librs. CUNY, 1979—81; trustee N.Y. Met. Reference and Rsch. Libr. Agy., 1984—93, 2d v.p., 1985—88, v.p., 1988—90, treas., 1991—93. Elder Presbyn. Ch., clk. session, pres. corp.; bd. dirs. Vis. Nurse Assn. Bklyn., 1984—2006, mem. exec. com., 1987—2006, vice chmn., 2001—06; bd. dirs., mem. exec. com., sec. Vis. Nurse Regional Health Care Sys., Inc., 2001—06. Mem.: AAUW, AAUP, ALA (life; membership com. 1967—71, chmn. coun. regional groups, resources and tech. svcs. divsn. 1968—69, dir. divsn. 1968—70, 1975—76, chmn. divsn. cataloging and classification sect. 1975—76), The Typophiles (sec.-treas. 1996—2006), N.Y. Tech. Svcs. Librs. (pres. 1963—64), Spl. Librs. Assn., Am. Printing History Assn., OCLC Users Coun. (SUNY del. 1981—85), Assn. Coll. and Rsch. Librs. (chmn. univ. librs. sect. 1983—84), N.Y. Libr. Assn. (pres. resources and tech. svcs. sect., councilor 1966—67, sec.-treas. acad. and spl. librs. sect. 1973—75, councilor 1975—76, 1978—81, pres. 1979—80), Chartered Inst. Libr. and Info. Profl. Gt. Britain (life), NYU Grad. Sch. Bus. Adminstrn. Alumni Assn. (rec. sec. 1967—69, dir. 1969—70, 1975—79), Princeton Club N.Y., Smith Coll. Club Bklyn. (pres. 1966—68, class treas. 1976—81), N.Y. Libr. Club (sec. 1964—66, coun. 1966—70, 1973—77, 1979—82, pres. 1980—81), Smith Coll. Club N.Y., Archons of Colophon, Phi Kappa Phi. Home: 103 Kendal Dr Oberlin OH 44074-1905

**MOORE, JEAN E.**, social worker, academic administrator, educator, radio personality; d. Hugh Huriel and Theodora H. Buchanan Campbell; m. Robert M. Moore, Jr.; children: Robert M. III, Doreen R. Moore Closson. BA, Hunter Coll., 1947; M of Social Svc., Bryn Mawr Coll., 1949; EdD, Temple U., 1978. Cert. social worker Acad. Cert. Social Workers, LCSW Pa., 1989. Social worker Children's Svc., Inc., Phila., 1949—52; asst. chief clin. social work svcs. Region 10 U.S.A. Phila., 1952—60; social work specialist Ctrl. Relocation Bur., Phila. Redevel. Authority, 1962—67; social work/human svcs. adviser for Model Cities Region III U.S. Dept. Housing and Urban devel. for 6 states and D.C., 1967—69; assoc. prof., grad. faculty, dir. new career ladders Temple U., Phila., dir. program devel. Office of Rsch. and Program Devel., 1969—89, assoc. prof. emerita, 1989—; exec. asst. to pres. Cheyney U. of Pa., 1985—91; v.p. instnl. advancement U. Md. Ea. Shore, Princess Anne, Md., 1991—97; host, exec. prodr. Univ. Forum Temple U. Pub. Radio, Phila., 1997—. Mem. internat. bd. advisors Radio for Peace Internat.; bd. dirs., club dir. Gundaker Found., Inc.; coun., spkr., presenter, lectr. Contbr. articles to profl. publs. Past bd. trustees Lackawanna Jr. Coll., C.C. of Phila.; past pres. Fair Housing Coun. Suburban Phila.; chair vis. accreditation teams Mid. States Assn. Colls. and Schs. Commn. on Higher Edn.; past bd. pres. Spectrum Health Svcs., Inc.; chair State Bd. Pvt. Corresp. Schs.; elder Lansdowne First Presbyn. Ch.; bd. dirs. Children's Svc., Inc. Named Paul Harris fellow, Rotary Found., 2005, Guy Gundaker fellow, Gundaker Found. Rotary Internat. Dist. 7450, 2006; named to Hall of Fame, Hunter Coll., 1999; recipient Documentary Gold award, Internat. Assn. Audio Visual Communs., 1999, Crystal award of Excellence, The Communicator Awards, 1999, 2000, 2002, 2003, 2004, 2005, 1st pl. radio/ednl., Broadcast Edn. Assn., 2000, Documentary award, 2000, Achievement in Radio award, March of Dimes, 2000—04, Gold Cindy award, Internat. Assn. Audio Visual Communicators, 2000, 2002, 2003, Media award, Kelly Anne Dolan Meml. Fund, 2003, Martin Luther King Jr. Humanitarian award, Upper Merion, 2004, Mayor's Fire Prevention medal, City of N.Y., Outstanding Contbn. in Edn. award, Theta Nu Sigma, Image award, Black Women in Sport Found., Radio Program awards, Best Coverage Maternal Health Issues/Problems Risk Pregnancies, numerous academic awards. Mem.: NASW (Golden Membership Disting. Svc. award 2005), Broadcast Pioneers of Phila., Inc., Pa. Abolition Soc. (bd. mgrs.), Rotary Club Upper Darby-Lansdown (bd. dirs. 2001—05), Phi Delta Kappa, Alpha Chi Alpha, Phi Beta Kappa, Delta Sigma Theta. Avocations: international travel, writing, poetry. Office Phone: 215-204-4376.

**MOORE, JEANNETTE AILEEN**, animal nutrition educator; b. Bellflower, Calif., Jan. 6, 1957; d. Harry Joseph Jr. and Alba Aurora (Celaya) M.; m. Matthew Henry Poore, Oct. 2, 1982. BS in Animal Scis., Calif. State Polytechnic U., 1980; MS in Animal Scis., U. Ariz., 1983, PhD in Nutritional Scis., 1987. Cert. nutrition specialist. Postdoctoral rsch. assoc. U. Ariz., Tucson, 1988-90, N.C. State U., Raleigh, 1990-92, coord. Spend-A-Day-At-State program, 1994-97, mem. coll. acad. computing adv. com., 1996—, undergrad. tchg. coord. dept. animal sci., 1997—, mem. coll. courses and curriculum com., 1998—, mem. univ. courses and curriculum com., 2000—05, chair, 2002. Vis. asst. prof. NC State U., Raleigh, 1992—98, asst. prof., 1998—2004, assoc. prof., 2004—; faculty advisor Animal Sci. Club, 1992—2004, advisor Rodeo Club, 1994—2003, World Wide Web coord. Dept. Animal Sci., 1994—. Author: (computer spreadsheet) Ruminant Animal Diet Evaluator, 1993; mem. editl. bd. Jour. Animal Sci., 1995-2001. Supt. jr. ewe show, N.C. State Fair, Raleigh, 1992-98; vol. N.C. Sci. and Math Partnership, Wake county, N.C., 1991—. Mem.: Equine Sci., Coun. Agrl. Sci. and Tech. (bd. dirs. 2004—06), Nat. Assn. Colls. and Tchrs. Agr. (tchg. fellow 2001), Am. Coll. Nutrition, Am. Soc. Animal Sci., Am. Soc. Nutritional Scis., Phi Kappa Phi, Gamma Sigma Delta, Alpha Zeta. Avocations: horseback riding, reading, travel, walking. Office: NC State U Dept Animal Sci PO Box 7621 Raleigh NC 27695-7621

**MOORE, JERRY A., III**, lawyer; b. Washington, Dec. 1, 1946; BA, Univ. Minn., 1968; MA, Univ. Wis., 1970; JD, Georgetown Univ., 1975. Bar: DC 1975. Law clerk, Hon. Barrington D. Parker US Dist Ct, 1975—76; dir., programs Greater Washington Bd. of Trade; ptnr., real estate practice group Venable LLP, Washington. Past trustee Nat. Urban League; chmn. of bd. Washington Urban League; vice chmn. of bd, treas. Children's Hospital; chmn. (two terms) DC United Way. Lt. USN, 1968—73. Office: Venable LLP 575 Seventh St NW Washington DC 20004 Office Phone: 202-344-4763. Office Fax: 202-344-8300. Business E-Mail: jamoore@venable.com.

**MOORE, JERRY JAY**, sales executive, retired archaeologist; b. Ft. Sam Houston, Tex., Jan. 29, 1960; s. Richard Vernal and Irmgard Ludwiga Ottilia (Bennewitz) Moore. Student, Ea. Ill. U., 1980—83. Lab. asst. Archaeol. Investigations Ctr. So. Ill. U., Carbondale, 1979; field/lab. technician Ill. State Mus. Soc., Springfield, 1980; asst. lab. supr. Ill. State Mus. Soc., Dickson Mounds Mus., Havana, 1980—81, Am. Resources Group, Ltd., Carbondale, 1983—86; archaeol. technician Midwestern Archaeol. Rsch. Ctr. Ill. State U., Normal, 1986—93; archaeol. asst. U. Ill., Urbana, 1993—94; archaeol. asst. Inst. Archaeology and Anthropology U. S.C., Columbia, 1993—94; merchandising asst. J.C. Penney Co., Champaign, Ill., 1994—2000; sales profl. Bergner's/Saks Inc., Urbana, 2000—02, Dick's Sporting Goods, Inc., Champaign, 2002—. Co-author: monographs; contbr. articles to profl. jours. Scholar, State of Ill., 1978—82. Mem.: SAR, Soc. Collegiate Journalists, Iroquois County Hist. and Geneal. Soc., Soc. of the War of 1812 (U.S. Army Mil. Uniform Ft. Dearborn, Ill. Project 1999—2000, sgt. at arms 2000—), Sons of the Revolution, Sons of Union Vets. of the Civil War (dept. of Ill. genealogist 1998—, Ill. dept. ordnance assessment 2004—05), Phi Theta Kappa. Republican. Roman Catholic. Avocations: history, antiques, genealogy. Home: 590 S Park St Paxton IL 60957 Office: 2113 N Prospect Ave Champaign IL 61822 Office Phone: 217-352-4173.

**MOORE, JOHN EDDY**, lieutenant governor; b. Charleston, W.Va., July 13, 1943; s. George Roy and Alvaretta (Hoskins) M.; m. Martha Clay Spangenberg, Aug. 7, 1966; children—Brian Clay, Stacia Hoskins BS in Comemrce, Washington and Lee U., 1965; JD, U. Ky., 1968. Group dir. Rockwell Internat., Cedar Rapids, Iowa, 1974-80, v.p. Dallas, 1980-81; v.p., ptnr. Korn/Ferry Internat., Dallas, 1981-82; sr. v.p. Cessna Aircraft, Wichita, Kans., 1982—2002; lt. gov. State of Kansas, 2003—. Dir. Health Care Plus, Wichita, Kans., Riverside Hosp., Wichita; former mem. Spl. Commn. on Pub. Agenda for Kans.; sec. Kans. Foodbank Warehouse, Wichita; bd. dirs. Booth Meml. Residence, Wichita Mem. Midwest Aerospace Indsl. Relations Council, Machinery and Allied Products Inst. (human resources council), Wichita C. of C. (chmn. state legis. com.), Kans. C. of C. and Industry (bd. dirs.) Republican. Methodist. Avocation: golf. Office: Office Lt Governor State Capitol 300 SW Tenth Ave Ste 222S Topeka KS 66612-1590 Office Phone: 785-296-2213. Office Fax: 785-296-5669. E-mail: Lt.Governor@gov.state.ks.us.*

**MOORE, JOHN HAMPTON**, academic administrator; b. Grand Forks, ND, Apr. 19, 1935; s. Charles Harold and Marie (Lindberg) M.; m. Barbara Sue Corbett, Feb. 23, 1963; children: John Randolph, Matthew Corbett BS in Engring., U. Mich., 1958, MBA, 1959; PhD in Econs., U. Va., Charlottesville, 1966. Rsch. chemist Procter & Gamble Co., 1959-63; asst. prof. econs. U. Va., Charlottesville, 1966-70, assoc. prof. econs., 1970-77; assoc. dir., rsch. prof. Law and Econs. Ctr. U. Miami, Fla., 1977-80; assoc. dir., prof. econs. Law and Econs. Ctr. Emory U., Atlanta, 1981; assoc. dir., sr. fellow Hoover Instn. Stanford U., Calif., 1981-85, acting dep. dir. Hoover Instn. Calif., 1983-84; dep. dir. NSF, Washington, 1985-89; dir. Internat. Inst., George Mason U., Washington, 1990-95. Disting. Svc. prof., 1995-96; pres. Grove City (Pa.) Coll., 1996—2003. Sr. assoc. St. Antony's Coll. Oxford (Eng.) U., 1973; mem. Nat. Sci. Bd., Washington, 1982-85; dir. George C. Marshall Inst., 1993—. Author: Growth With Self-Management: Yugoslav Industrialization, 1952-75, 80; co-translator, co-editor: Stalinist Planning for Economic Growth, 1933-52, 1980; editor: To Promote Prosperity, 1984, Legacies of the Collapse of Marxism, 1994; contbr. articles to profl. jours. Bd. dirs. Thomas Jefferson Ctr. Found., 1972-85, Civilian R&D Found., 1995—; chmn. standing fin. com. Internat. Coun. Sci. Unions, 1992-96; trustee Earhart Found., 1993—; Am. Council Science Health, 2000—; NASA fellow, 1963-66, Hoover Instn., Stanford U. fellow, 1975-76. Mem. AAAS, Am. Econ. Assn., Mont Pelerin Soc. (bd. dirs. 1992-96, v.p. 1994-96), Raven Soc. So. Econ. Assn., Phila. Soc., (bd. dirs. 2003—, dir., 2004-), Sigma Xi (chmn. internat. com. 1991-97, exec. com. 1995-2000, pres. 1998-99), Phi Eta Sigma, Tau Beta Pi, Omicron Delta Kappa. Home: 7254 Marlow Pl Bradenton FL 34201 E-mail: jhmoore1@comcast.net.

**MOORE, JOHN HARTWELL**, anthropology educator, consultant; b. Williston, Nd, Feb. 27, 1939; s. William Andrew and Mary Montgomery Moore; m. Shelley Ann Arlen, June 6, 1981; children: Jeremiah, Jessica, Alexandra. BS, U. of Ark., Fayetteville, AR, 1962; Ph.D, NYU, New York, NY, 1974. Anthropology educator U. of Okla., Norman, Okla., 1977—93, U. of Fla., Gainesville, Fla., 1993. Cons. Native Am. Rights Fund, Boulder, Colo., 1979—, Sand Creek Massacre Descendants Trust, Anadarko, Okla., 1991—, Sawridge Indian Band, Slave Lake, Alberta, Canada, 1992—. Author: (book) The Cheyenne; editor: Political Economy of North American Indians; editor-in-chief: Macmillan Ency. Race and Racism: Del. to state conv. Dem. Party, Oklahoma City, 1991—91; chpt. pres. Vietnam Veterans Against the War, West Orange, NJ, 1968—69; state com. Rainbow Coalition, Oklahoma City, 1987—93. Second Lt. U.S. Army, 1962—64, East Asia. Decorated Armed Forces Expeditionary Medal U.S. Army, UN Peacekeeping Medal UN; recipient Governor's Cmty. Svc. Award, State of Okla., 1990. Fellow: Ctr. for Advanced Study in the Behavioral Sciences, Am. Assn. for the Advancement of Science (chair of anthropology sect. 1997—98); mem.: Human Genome Diversity Project (chair north am. cmty. 1998). Democrat. Ethical Culture. Achievements include research in Role of ethnogenesis in human evolution; Rates of gene flow from ethnic inter-marriage. Home: 3328 North West 18 Avenue Gainesville FL 32605 Office: University of Florida 1112 Turlington Gainesville FL 32611 E-mail: moojohn@anthro.ufl.edu.

**MOORE, JOHN NORTON**, lawyer, educator, diplomat; b. NYC, June 12, 1937; s. William Thomas and Lorena (Norton) M.; m. Barbara Schneider, Dec. 12, 1981; children: Victoria Norton, Elizabeth Norton. AB in Economics, Drew U., 1959; LLB with honors, Duke U., 1962; LLM, U. Ill., 1965; postgrad., Yale U., 1965-66. Bar: Fla. 1962, Ill. 1963, Va. 1969, D.C. 1972, U.S. Supreme Ct. 1972. Tchg. fellow U. Ill., 1962—63; asst. prof. U. Fla., 1963—65, assoc. prof., 1965—66, asst. dean, Hon. mem.; assoc. prof. U. Va. Sch. Law, Charlottesville, 1966—69, prof., 1969—76, Walter L. Brown prof. law, 1976—, dir. grad. program, 1968—93, dir. Ctr. Oceans Law and Policy, 1976—, dir. Ctr. Nat. Security Law, 1984—. Counselor on internat. law Dept. State, Washington, 1972-73; chmn. Nat. Security Coun. Task Force on Law of Sea and dep. spl. rep. of Pres. and amb. Law of Sea Conf., 1973-76; fellow Woodrow Wilson Internat. Ctr. for Scholars, Washington, 1977; adj. prof. Georgetown Law Ctr., 1978—; mem. Nat. Adv. Com. on Oceans and Atmosphere, 1984-85; mem. U.S. del. Conf. Security and Coop. in Europe, 1984; spl. counsel, dep. agt. for U.S. to World Ct.; former cons. to the Pres.'s Intelligence Oversight Bd., Arms Control and Disarmament Agy., U.S. Info. Agy.; chmn. U.S. Inst. Peace, 1985-91; co-chmn. with the U.S. dep. atty. gen. Moscow Seminar on the Rule of Law, 1990; legal advisor during Gulf crisis Kuwait's Amb. to U.S., Kuwait Rep. to UN Boundary Commn., 1991-94. Author: Law and the Indo-China War, 1972 (Phi Beta Kappa award); editor: Law and Civil War in the Modern World, 1976, Readings in International Law, 1979, The Arab-Israeli Conflict, 3 vols., 1976, 4th vol. 1991, Nat. Security Law, 1990, 2d edit., 2005, Crisis in the Gulf, 1992, Nat. Security Law Documents, 1995, Treaty Interpretation, The Constitution and the Rule of Law, 2001, The National Law of Treaty Implementation, 2001, Solving the War Puzzle, 2003; editor: The Real Lessons of the Vietnam War, 2002, Civil Litigation Against Terrorism, 2003; mem. editl. bd. Am. Jour. Internat. Law; contbr. articles to profl. jours. Sesquicentennial assoc. Ctr. Advanced Studies, U. Va., 1971-72; adv. bd. law of sea State Dept., 1977-80, adv. bd. internat. law, 1982; chmn. bd. dirs. U.S. Inst. Peace, 1986-89, 89-91; chmn. oceans policy com. Rep. Nat. Com.; com. on exploration of the seas

Nat. Acad. Nat. Rsch. Coun., 2002; active Consortium on Intelligence. Recipient Alumni award in arts Drew U., 1976; Compass Disting. Achievement award for significant contbns. to art and sci. of oceanography and marine tech., 1994; NIH fellow Yale U., 1965-66. Mem. ABA (past vice-chmn. sect. internat. law, past 5-term chmn. com. on law and nat. security), Am. Law Inst., Am. Oceanic Orgn. (past exec. coun.), Marine Tech. Soc. (past exec. coun.), Rhodes Acad. Oceans Law and Policy (founding dir.), Coun. Fgn. Rels., Order of Coif, Cosmos Club, N.Y. Yacht Club, Freedom House (bd. dirs.), Phi Beta Kappa. Republican. Episcopalian. Office: U Va Sch Law 580 Massie Rd Charlottesville VA 22903-1789 Office Phone: 434-924-7441. E-mail: jnm9s@virginia.edu. *Life offers opportunity to pursue many worthwhile interests. In selecting among them it has seemed most useful to focus on those issues of sufficiently broad general significance as to justify the efforts of a lifetime. For me that has meant focus on promoting democracy and the rule of law, improving the functioning of government, controlling and reducing war, and the policy choices of the ocean frontier.*

MOORE, JOHN PLUNKETT DENNIS, publisher; b. Mexico, Mo., Mar. 2, 1931; s. Dennis Talmage and Vona Mae (Vance) M.; m. Lydia Benz Ahern, Aug. 15, 1959; children: Alison Ahern, Lydia Benz, John Talmage, Maude Ahern, Meredith Coleman. Student, Princeton U., 1948-51, U.S. Naval Acad., 1951-53; BA, U. Mo., Columbia, 1953; postgrad., Harvard Law Sch., 1955-56. Coll. traveler The Dryden Press, Inc., N.Y.C., 1957-59; coll. traveler The Macmillan Co., N.Y.C., 1959-60, editor, 1960-67; assoc. exec. editor Columbia U. Press, N.Y.C., 1968-74, editor in chief, 1974-80, pres., 1980-97, also bd. dirs. Bd. dirs., pres. Columbia U. Music Press; bd. dirs. Univ. Presses of Calif., Columbia and Princeton, Chichester, West Sussex, Eng., 1979-97, chmn., 1981-83, 85-87, 96-97; trustee Composer's Recordings, Inc., 1984-97. Author: Columbia University Press: A Historical Sketch, 1893-1993; mem. editl. bd. N.Y. Acad. Scis., 1993-01. Bd. dirs. Greenwich (Conn.) Health Assn., 1970-75; bd. dirs. assoc. Family Centers, Greenwich, Stamford, 1975—; trustee Princeton Libr. in N.Y.C., 1984—; mem. vestry St. Barnabas Ch., Greenwich, 1995-98. With U.S. Army, 1953-55. Mem. Assn. Am. Univ. Presses (chair internat. com. 1994-96, bd. dirs. 1996-97). Clubs: Publishers Lunch (admissions com. 1996-99), Princeton Club N.Y., Faculty House Columbia U., Century Assn.; Nassau, the Book Table, The Ch. Club N.Y., Princeton Club So. Calif., The English Speaking Union, The Mystery Club (pres. 2006-). Episcopalian. Home: 321 Riversville Rd Greenwich CT 06831-3228 Home (Winter): 1912 Kelton Ave Los Angeles CA 90025 E-mail: jdm123@aol.com.

MOORE, JOHN RONALD, manufacturing executive; b. Pueblo, Colo., July 12, 1935; s. John E. and Anna (Yesberger) M.; m. Judith Russelyn Bauman, Sept. 5, 1959; children: Leland, Roni, Timothy, Elaine. BS, U. Colo., 1959; grad. advanced mgmt., Harvard Grad. Sch. Bus., 1981. Mgmt. trainee Montgomery Ward & Co., Denver, 1960-65; distbn. mgr. Midas Internat. Corp., Chgo., 1965-71; v.p., gen. mgr. Midas, Can., Toronto, Ont., 1972-75; pres. Auto Group Midas Internat. Corp., Chgo., 1976-82, pres., chief exec. officer, 1982-98; ret., 2005. Bd. dirs. Keystone Automotive Industries, Inc. Bd. dirs. Lake Forest Grad. Sch. Mgmt., U. Colo. Found.; mem. bus. adv. coun. U. Colo. Sch. Bus.; trustee U. Colo. Found. Mem. Harvard Bus. Sch. Alumni Assn., U. Colo. Alumni Assn., Chgo. Coun. Fgn. Rels., Econ. Club Chgo., Comml. Club Chgo. Republican. *There is very little we accomplish in our lifetime that results from effort we alone expend. All of us should have the wisdom to express our appreciation to our families and associates who have helped us attain our goals and accomplishments— for failure to do so tarnishes our successes and breeds selfishness.*

MOORE, JOYCE KRISTINA, financial planner, director; b. Phila., June 19, 1955; d. Oscar Herbert Hariu and Virginia Wilson (Guss) Leas; m. William Burns Moore, June 20, 1980 (div. 1990); children: William Patrick, Kristofer Sean. Student, Beloit Coll., 1973-74, U. Pa., 1974-75, Lafayette Coll., 1984-88, Am. Coll., 1991—. ChFC. Photographer Clair Pruett Studios, Drexel Hill, Pa., 1977-80; photographic cons. Dan's Camera City, Allentown, Pa., 1980-81; contr., co-founder BioService, Inc., Bethlehem, Pa., 1985-89; contr. Mega Video Inc., Easton, Pa., 1989-91; spl. rep. John Hancock Fin. Svcs., Allentown, 1990-93; prin. Joyce Moore Fin. Svcs., Macungie, Pa., 1993—. Co-editor: Estate Planning Success for Pennsylvania Residents, 2002. Bd. dirs. Spring Garden Children's Sch., Easton; den leader Cub Scout Pack 31, Williams, Pa., 1991—95, scout leader, 1995—97; mem. Lehigh Valley Estate Planning Coun., 2001—; trustee United Friends Sch., Quakertown, Pa., 2004—; former mem. Warren County Dem. Com., Phillipsburg, NJ, 1981—83; councilwoman Glendon Borough, 1992—97, coun. v.p., 1996—97; overseer Religous Soc. Friends, 1986—92. Mem.: LWV (bd. dirs. Easton area 1987—91, pres. 1989—90), Pa. Assn. Ins. and Fin. Advisors (bd. dirs. 2002—), First Affirmative Fin. Network, Progressive Asset Mgmt., Social Investment Forum, Lehigh Valley Assn. Ins. Fin. Advisors (bd. dirs. 1995—, pres. 2000—01). Avocations: needlecrafts, folk music, canoeing. Office: Joyce Moore Fin Svc PO Box 175 Macungie PA 18062-0175 Office Phone: 610-966-6127. Business E-Mail: joyce@jmfs.com.

MOORE, JUEL ANN, retired elementary school educator; d. Lucy Mae Giddens; m. Gene Paul Moore, Mar. 31, 1962; children: Dr. Gina LuChrista Moore-Sanders, Richard Vernon. BA, Fisk U.; PhD, San Diego State U. and Claremont U., 1998. Cert. reading specialist Calif. Tchr. Met. Nashville, 1962—67, Travis Unified Schs., Fairfield, Calif., 1967, San Diego City Schs. 1969—81, prin. coach, 1981—2002, literacy cons. Charter Sch., 2002—. Author: (book chpt.) Black English. Recipient Svc./Cmty. award, Women's Inc., 2003. Master: Assn. African Am. Educators (pres. 2002—03). Presbyterian. Achievements include research in Language Registers of African Americans. Avocations: travel, reading, writing, research, discussion groups. Personal E-mail: gnjamoore@yahoo.com.

MOORE, JULIANNE (JULIE ANNE SMITH), actress; b. Fayetteville, N.C., Dec. 3, 1960; m. Sundar Chakravarthy, Nov. 21, 1983 (div. Oct. 12, 1985); m. John Gould Rubin, May 3, 1986 (div. Aug. 25, 1995); m. Bart Freundlich, Aug. 23, 2003; 2 children. BFA, Boston Univ. With The Guthrie Theater, 1988-89. Actress: (theatre) Serious Money, 1987, Bone-the-Fish, 1988, Ice Cream with Hot Fudge, 1990, Uncle Vanya, (TV soap operas) As the World Turns (Emmy award outstanding ingenue in daytime drama series 1988), The Edge of Night, (TV movies) Money, Power, Murder, 1989, Lovecraft, 1991, (feature films) The Hand That Rocks the Cradle, 1992, The Gun in Betty Lou's Handbag, 1992, Body of Evidence, 1993, Benny & Joon, 1993, The Fugitive, 1993, Short Cuts, 1993, Vanya on 42nd Street, 1994, Roommates, 1995, Nine Months, 1995, Safe, 1995, Assassins, 1995, Surviving Picasso, 1996, The Myth of Fingerprints, 1997, The Lost World: Jurassic Park, 1997, Hellcab, 1997, Boogie Nights, 1997, Chicago Cab, 1998, The Big Lebowski, 1998, Psycho, 1998, Map of the World, 1999, Magnolia, 1999, Cookie's Fortune, 1999, An Ideal Husband, 1999, The End of the Affair, 1999, Hannibal, 2001, Evolution, 2001, The Shipping News, 2001, Far From Heaven, 2002, The Hours, 2002, Marie and Bruce, 2004, Laws of Attraction, 2004, The Forgotten, 2004, The Prize Winner of Defiance, Ohio, 2005, Freedomland, 2006. Office: Creative Artists Agy care Kevin Huvane 9830 Wilshire Blvd Beverly Hills CA 90212-1825*

MOORE, JULIE L., bibliographer, librarian; b. Sioux City, Iowa, Sept. 11, 1941; d. Mabel (DeRaad) Rude. BA, U. Denver, 1962, MS, 1963. Indexer Conservation Libr., Denver, 1965-67; head libr. Gerontology Libr., U. So. Calif., LA, 1968-85; owner, mgr. Wildlife Info. Svc., La Cruces, N.Mex., 1971—. Compiler: Thesaurus of Sport-Fish and Wildlife, 1968, Bibliography of Wildlife Theses, 1950-1968, 1970, Bibliography of Reported Biological Phenomena...Attributed to Microwave and Radio-Frequency Radiation, 1984; indexer: Updata Index to U.S. Dept. Agriculture Handbooks, 1980; editor: Abstracts in Social Gerontology, 1989-95; co-producer CD-ROM Wildlife Worldwide, 1990-95, Bibliography of Evapotranspiration with special emphasis on riparian vegetation, 2004 . Office Phone: 505-527-2547. E-mail: julmoore@nmsu.edu.

MOORE, JUSTIN EDWARD, information technology executive; b. West Hartford, Conn., June 17, 1952; s. Walter Joseph and Victoria Mary (Calcagni) M. BS in Mgmt. Sci., Fla. Inst. Tech., 1974. Systems assoc. Travelers Ins., Hartford, Conn., 1974-77; data processing programmer R.J. Reynolds Inc., Winston-Salem, N.C., 1977-78; programmer/analyst Sea-Land Svc., Elizabeth, NJ, 1978-79, mgr. market analysis Oakland, Calif., 1979-82; asst. v.p., dir. application systems Fox Capital Mgmt. Corp., Foster City, Calif., 1982-86; mgr. bus. svcs. dept mktg. and pricing Am. Pres. Cos., Ltd., Oakland, 1987-88, dir. mktg. and pricing systems, 1988-89; dir. systems devel. The Office Club, Concord, Calif., 1989-91; dir. MIS Revo, Inc., Mountain View, Calif., 1992-93; account mgr. Imrex Computer Systems, Inc., South San Francisco, 1993-94; project mgr. Exigent Computer Group, Inc., San Ramon, Calif., 1994—. Democrat. Roman Catholic. Avocations: golf, personal computing, investment mgmt. Home: 5214 Jomar Dr Concord CA 94521-2343 Office: Exigent Computer Group Inc 4000 Executive Pky Ste 275 San Ramon CA 94583-4257 Office Phone: 925-866-1692. E-mail: justin_moore@prodigy.net. *Personal philosophy: Strive always to do the right things, at the right time, the right way for the right reasons.*

MOORE, KAREN NELSON, judge; AB magna cum laude, Radcliffe Coll., 1970; JD magna cum laude, Harvard U., 1973. Bar: DC 1973, Ohio 1976, U.S. Ct. Appeals (DC cir.) 1974, U.S. Supreme Ct. 1980, U.S. Ct. Appeals (6th cir.) 1984. Law clk. to Hon. Malcolm R. Wilkey U.S. Ct. Appeals (DC Cir.), Washington, 1973—74; law clk. to Hon. Harry A. Blackmun U.S. Supreme Ct., Washington, 1974—75; assoc. Jones, Day, Reavis & Pogue, Cleve., 1975—77; asst. prof. Case Western Res. Law Sch., Cleve., 1977—80, assoc. prof., 1980—82, prof., 1982—95; judge U.S. Ct. Appeals (6th cir.), Cleve., 1995—. Vis. prof. Harvard Law Sch., 1990—91. Mem. Harvard Law Rev., 1971—73, contbr. articles to profl. jours. Trustee Lakewood Hosp., Ohio, 1978—85, Radcliffe Coll., Cambridge, 1980—84. Fellow: Am. Bar Found.; mem.: Harvard U. Alumni Assn. (bd. dirs. 1984—87), Am. Law Inst., Phi Beta Kappa. Office: US Ct Appeals 6th Cir Carl B Stokes US Courthouse 801 W Superior Ave Cleveland OH 44113-1831*

MOORE, KENNETH CAMERON, lawyer; b. Chgo., Oct. 25, 1947; s. Kenneth Edwards and Margaret Elizabeth (Cameron) M.; m. Karen M. Nelson, June 22, 1974; children: Roger Cameron, Kenneth Nelson, Kristin Karen. BA summa cum laude, Hiram Coll., 1969; JD cum laude, Harvard U., 1973. Bar: Ohio 1973, U.S. Dist. Ct. Md. 1974, U.S. Ct. Appeals (4th cir.) 1974, D.C. 1975, U.S. Dist. Ct. (no. dist.) Ohio 1976, U.S. Ct. Appeals (6th cir.) 1977, U.S. Ct. Appeals (D.C. cir.) 1979, U.S. Supreme Ct. 1980. Law clk. to judge Harrison L. Winter U.S. Ct. Appeals (4th cir.), Balt., 1973-74; assoc. Squire, Sanders & Dempsey LLP, Washington, 1974—75, Cleve., 1975-82, ptnr., 1982—; profl. ethics ptnr., 1996—; mem. fin. com., 1990—, chair profl. ethics com., 2003—. Chmn. Ohio Fin. Com. for Jimmy Carter presdl. campaign, 1976; del. Dem. Nat. Conv., 1976; chief legal counsel Ohio Carter-Mondale Campaign, 1976; trustee Hiram Coll., 1997—, mem. exec. com., 1999, chair audit com., 1999, vice chair bd. trustees, 2000—, chair faculty and acad. affairs com., 2000—, mem. bd. Laurel Sch., mem. exec. com., sec. With AUS. 1970-76 Mem. ABA, Fed. Bar Assn., Cleve. Bar Assn., Cleve. City Club. Home: 15602 Edgewater Dr Cleveland OH 44107-1212 Office: Squire Sanders & Dempsey LLP 4900 Key Ctr 127 Public Sq Ste 4900 Cleveland OH 44114-1304 Office Phone: 216-479-8500.

MOORE, KENNETH G., foundation administrator, former manufacturing executive; b. Los Altos Hills, Calif. BA in Bus. Admin. Trustee Gordon & Betty Moore Found., 1986—; various positions in ops. planning and control, computer systems develop., supply chain and logistics mgmt. Signetics Corp., Sunnyvale, Calif., 1978—94, Philips Semiconductors, 1995—2002; dir. evaluation & IT Gordon & Betty Moore Found., 2003—. Bd. dirs. Exploratorium. San Francisco; sch. bd. Bullis Charter Sch. Office: Gordon & Betty Moore Found Presidio of San Francisco PO Box 29910 San Francisco CA 94129-0910*

MOORE, KENNETH JAMES, agronomist, educator; b. Phoenix, June 6, 1957; s. George Taylor and Barbara Joyce (Amy) M.; m. Gina Marie McCarthy Aug. 11, 1979; children: Ellyn Elizabeth, David Taylor, Mark Daniel. BS in Agr., Ariz. State U., 1979; MS in Agronomy, Purdue U., 1981, PhD in Agronomy, 1983. Asst. prof. agronomy U. Ill., Urbana, 1983-87; assoc. prof. N.Mex. State U., Las Cruces, 1988-89; rsch. agronomist Agrl. Rsch. Svc., USDA, Lincoln, Nebr., 1989-93; prof. Iowa State U., Ames, 1993—. Adj. assoc. prof. U. Nebr. Lincoln, 1989-93, prof., 1993-96; sr. rsch. fellow Ag Rsch. Grasslands, New Zealand, 1998; dir. MS in Agronomy Distance Edn. program Iowa State U., 1995—, dir. Crop Advisor Inst., 2000—. Founding editor Crop Mgmt., 2001-02; assoc. editor Agronomy Jour., 1989-93, tech. editor, 1994-97; assoc. editor Crop Sci., 1994; editor: Forages: An Introduction to Grassland Ag, 2003, Native-Warm Season Grasses: Research Trends and Issues, 2000, Post-Harvest Physiology and Preservation of Forages, 1995; contbr. chpts. to books. Bd. dirs. Lincoln Children's Mus., 1991-93, Children's Svcs. of Ctrl. Iowa, 1996-97; bd. dirs. Children's Mus. Ctrl. Iowa, 1997-2002, pres., 2000-01; mem. mgmt. com. N.E. YMCA, Lincoln, 1991-93; mem. youth policy forum Lincoln YMCA, 1991-92. Recipient Point of Light award USDA, 1991. Fellow Am. Soc. Agronomy (bd. dirs. 2002-05), Crop Sci. Soc. Am. (divsn. chmn. 1990-92, pres. 2003-04, exec. com. and bd. dirs. 2002-05, Young Crop Scientist award 1993); mem. Am. Forage and Grassland Coun. (Outstanding Young Scientist award 1982, merit award 1991). Republican. Presbyterian. Avocations: swimming, fishing, music. Office: Iowa State U Agronomy Dept 1567 Agronomy Hl Ames IA 50011-0001 Office Phone: 515-294-5482. Business E-Mail: kjmoore@iastate.edu.

MOORE, KENT ROSS, music educator; b. Saskatoon, Can., 1963; arrived in U.S., 1981; s. Lyall Keith and Eileen Moore; m. Sachiye Jeannette Hirasawa, June 5, 1993; children: Darren, Shawna. MusB summa cum laude, Temple U., 1985; MusM, Eastman Sch. Music, 1987; MusD, Temple U., 1997. Asst. prof. bassoon Baylor U., Waco, Tex., 1995—2001; sr. lectr. bassoon and theory No. Ariz. U., Flagstaff, 2001—. Prin. bassoon Waco Symphony Orch., 1995—2001, Flagstaff Symphony Orch., 2001—; bassoon Kokopelli Woodwind Quintet, Flagstaff, 2001—; judge in competitions. Performer: (CD) Music for Wind Ensemble by Steven Stucky. Mem. players com. Flagstaff Symphony Orch., 2002—. Grantee, Temple U., 1995; scholar, 1985. Mem.: Chamber Music Am., Internat. Double Reed Soc., Pi Kappa Lambda. Avocations: hiking, photography, astronomy. Office: No Ariz Univ Sch Music Coll Arts and Letters PO Box 6040 Flagstaff AZ 86011 Office Phone: 928-523-0869. Office Fax: 928-523-5111. Business E-Mail: kent.moore@nau.edu.

MOORE, KIMBERLY ANN, federal judge, law educator; b. Baltimore, Md., 1968; BS in Electrical Engring., MIT, 1990, MS, 1991; JD, Georgetown U., 1994. Bar: Md. 1995, DC. Assoc. Kirkland & Ellis LLP, DC & L.A., 1994—95; law clk. to Hon. Glenn L. Archer Jr. US Ct. Appeals (Fed. Cir.), 1995—97; asst. prof. law Chgo.-Kent Coll. Law, 1997—99, assoc. dir., Intellectual Property Law Program, 1998—99; assoc. prof. law U. Md. Sch. Law, 1999—2000; counsel Morgan, Lewis & Bockius LLP, 2000—03; assoc. prof. law George Mason U. Sch. Law, 2000—04, prof. law, 2004—. Assoc. editor Fed. Cir. Bar Journ., 1997—98, editor-in-chief, 1998—2006. Office: US Ct Appeals Fed Cir 717 Madison Pl NW Washington DC 20439

MOORE, KRISTEN L., marketing professional; BA, U. Calif., Santa Barbara. Mktg. Signetics/Philips Semiconductors; mem. chmns. council Conservation Internat. Bd. mem. Bullis-Purissima Elementary Sch. Found.; trustee Moore Family Found., Gordon & Betty Moore Found. Avocations: scuba diving, tennis, travel, photography. Office: Gordon & Betty Moore Found Presidio of San Francisco PO Box 29910 San Francisco CA 94129-0910*

MOORE, LAURENCE JOHN, business educator; b. Greeley, Colo., May 7, 1938; s. John Harold and Ruth Anderson M.; m. Nancy Kay Hibbert, Aug. 31, 1963 (div. Apr. 1996); children: Rebecca Ann, John Andrew, Stefani Ruth. BA in Econs., Monmouth Coll., Ill., 1962; MS in Econs., Ariz. State U., 1965, DBA in Mgmt. Sci., 1970. Dist. mktg. rep. Standard Oil Co. (Ind.), Chgo., 1962-63; sr. analyst long range and capital planning, 1964-66; head quantitative studies Continental Ill. Bank, Chgo., 1966-67; mem. faculty dept. mgmt. sci. Coll. Bus. Va. Poly. Inst. and State U., Blacksburg, 1970—, prof. Coll. Bus., 1977-85, C&P Disting. prof. bus., 1985-96, head dept. Coll. Bus., 1976-83, dir. univ. fin. planning and analysis, 1983-84, dir. univ. planning, 1988-89, Bell Atlantic-Va. prof. of bus., 1996—2002, Verizon prof. bus., 2002—. Cons. in field. Author: (with S.M. Lee, B.W. Taylor) Management Science, 1981, 4th edit. 1993, (with S.M. Lee) Introduction to Decision Sciences, 1975, (with E.R. Clayton) GERT Modeling and Simulation: Fundamentals and Applications, 1976. Served with U.S. Army, 1957-59. Recipient Disting. Service award SE region Am. Inst. Decision Scis., 1977 Fellow Am. Inst. Decision Scis. (pres. 1983-84, Disting. Svc. award 1986); mem. Inst. Mgmt. Sci. (Disting. Svc. award SE region), Inst. for Ops. Rsch. and Mgmt. Sci., Alpha Iota Delta, Beta Gamma Sigma, Omicron Delta Epsilon, Sigma Iota Epsilon. Presbyterian. Home: 1013 Chateau Ct Blacksburg VA 24060-3676 Office: Va Poly Inst and State U Dept Bus Info Tech 1007 Pamplin Hall Blacksburg VA 24061-5102 Office Phone: 540-231-5887. Business E-Mail: ljmoore@vt.edu.

MOORE, LEON, JR., social studies educator; b. Seoul, Apr. 2, 1970; arrived in U.S., 1970; s. Leon Sr. and Suk Hyon Moore. BA, Wichita State u., Kans., 1993, EdM, 2004. Cert. tchr. comprehensive social studies Kans. Tchr. social studies Unified Sch. Dist. 259, Wichita, Kans., 1993—2006. Volleyball coach Wichita Cath. Diocese, 2003—05. Mem.: Unified Tchrs. Wichita. Democrat. Roman Catholic. Avocations: reading, writing. Home: 1951 N Burns Wichita KS 67203 Office Phone: 316-973-1100.

MOORE, LEROI, musician; b. Durham, N.C., Sept. 7, 1961; Student, James Madison U. Mem. (saxophone, flute, whistle, keyboards, clarinet, horn, background vocals) Dave Matthews Band, 1991—. Musician (with Dave Matthews Band): (albums) Remember Two Things, 1993, Crash, 1996, Live at Red Rocks 8.15.95, 1997, Before These Crowded Streets, 1998, Don't Drink the Water, 1998, Everyday, 2001, Busted Stuff, 2002, Central Park Concert, 2003, Gorge, 2004; musician: Best of Columbia Records Radio Hour, Vol. 2, Various Artists, 1996, Code Magneta, Code Magenta, 1996, Live on Letterman: Music from the Late Show, Various Artists, 1997, Scream 2 Original Soundtrack, 1997, Musical Chairs, Hootie & The Blowfish, 1998, In November Sunlight, Soko, 2000, Great Day in C'Ville: Jazz from the Piedmont, Various Artists, 2001, Superfastgo, Peter Griesar, 2003, Toe 2 Toe, Vol. 6, Elephant Man/Vybz Cartel, 2004. Recipient (with Dave Matthews Band) Grammy award for Best Rock Performance by a Duo or Group with Vocal for So Much to Say, 1996, Chmns. award, NAACP Image Awards, 2004. Office: RCA Records 1540 Broadway New York NY 10036

MOORE, LINDA ANDERSON, art dealer, curator; b. Janesville, Wis., Aug. 2, 1947; d. Evert August Frederick and Helen Marilyn Anderson; m. Terry Douglass Moore, Mar. 22, 1969; children: Adrienne Jean, Craig William. Fgn. study program, U. Madrid, 1968; BA magna cum laude, U. of Calif., Santa Barbara, 1969; MA, Stanford U., Palo Alto, 1970; MHA, U. of Wash., 1976. Adminstr. U. of Calif. Student Health Svc., Irvine, 1972—75; v.p. Children's Hosp. and Health Ctr., San Diego, 1976—78; asst. hosp. adminstr. Kaiser Permanente, San Diego, 1978—83, asst. med. group adminstr., 1983—88; owner Linda Moore Gallery, San Diego, 1983—. Bd. dirs. Mus. of Photographic Arts, San Diego; adv. bd. Lux Art Inst., San Diego, 2004—; mem. Latin Am. arts com. San Diego Mus. of Art, 1990—. Contbr. book; author: (exhbn. catalogue) Iturria (Best Art Catalogue, Cleo Design award, 1992), Drowned Ophelia, Lo Maravilloso. Mem. Presidio Pk. Adv. Coun., San Diego, 2005—06, Patrons of the Prado, Balboa Pk., San Diego, 2005—06. Recipient TWIN - honoring Women Profls. award, YWCA, 1979, Top Women Hosp. Adminstrs., Calif. Hosp. Forum Mag., 1980, grad. study grant, Kellogg Found., 1975—76; fellow, Ford Found., 1969—70. Mem.: Francis Parker Sch. (bd. mem., chair ann. fund 1988—89), Young Hosp. Adminstrs. of San Diego (pres. 1981—82), Am. Coll. of Health Care Adminstrs. (chair young adminstrs. forum 1980—81), Jeanie Anderson Meml. Fund (bd. mem. 1972—2006), LEAD San Diego (bd. mem. 1986—87), ZLAC Rowing Club, Jr. League of San Diego (bd. mem. 1984—85, Best Project Video Employer Sponsored Child Care Project award 1986), Rotary Club 33 of San Diego, Phi Beta Kappa. Avocations: travel, writing, bridge. Office: Linda Moore Gallery 4244 Altamirano Way San Diego CA 92103 Office Phone: 619-260-1101. Personal E-mail: lmooregal@aol.com.

MOORE, LINDA LEA LACROIX, literature educator, art educator; b. Enid, Okla., Jan. 29, 1953; d. Jack Alfred and Novella Harrison La Croix; m. David Frank Moore, June 8, 1974; children: Jennifer Marie, Keeven David. BA, Northwestern Okla. State U., Alva, 1975; MEd, Southwestern Okla. State U., Weatherford, 1982. Cert. tchr. Okla. Instr. art Guymon (Okla.) Pub. Schs., 1975—77; tchr. libr. media and English Morrison (Okla.) Pub. Schs., 1977—78; tchr. Eldorado (Okla.) Pub. Sch., 1978—79; tchr. libr. media and art edn. Cement (Okla.) Pub. Sch., 1979—81; tchr. English Enid Pub. Schs., Enid, Okla., 1987—. Dir. Mother's Day Out, 1986—87; Methodist youth dir., 1981—83; moderator for deacons First Presbyn. Ch. Enid, Okla., 2003—04. Mem.: Philanthropic Ednl. Orgn. (corr. sec.), Enid Edn. Assn., Delta Zeta Sorority (historian 1973—74), Phi Delta Kappa. Presbyterian. Avocations: travel, cooking, playing cards. Office: Emerson Junior High School 700 West Elm Street Enid OK 73703 Business E-Mail: llmoore@enidk12.org.

MOORE, LINDY A., librarian; m. James E. Moore. BA in Mass Comm., U. West Ga., Carrollton, Ga., 2002; MLS, Fla. State U., Tallahassee, Fla., 2005. Cert. libr. Ga. State Bd. Librs., 2006. Br. libr. Lithia Springs (Ga.) Pub. Libr., 2002 . Presenter in field Mem. ALA, Ga. Libr. Assn. Office: Lithia Springs Public Library 7100 Junior High Drive Lithia Springs GA 30122 Office Phone: 770-944-5931. Office Fax: 770-944-5932. Business E-Mail: lindy@wgrl.net.

MOORE, LOIS JEAN, health science facility administrator; married; 1 child. Grad., Prairie View Sch. Nursing, Tex., 1957; BS in Nursing, Tex. Woman's U., 1970; MS in Edn., Tex. So. U., 1974. Nurse Harris County (Tex.) Hosp. Dist., 1957—; pres., chief exec. officer Harris County Hosp.; adminstr. Jefferson Davis Hosp., Houston, 1977-88, exec. v.p., chief ops. officer, 1988—2001; chief adminstr. U. Tex. Harris County Psychiat. Hosp., Houston, 2001—. Mem. adv. bd. Tex. Pub. Hosp. Assn. Contbr. articles to profl. jours. Mem. Mental Health Needs Council Houston and Harris County, Congressman Mickey Leland's Infant Mortality Task Force, Houston Crackdown Com., Gov.'s task force on health care policy, 1991; chairperson Tex. Assn. Pub. and Nonprofit Hosps., 1991, subcom. of Gov.'s task force to identify essential health care svc., 1992; bd. dirs. ARC, 1991—, Greater Houston Hosp. Coun., March of Dimes, United Way. Recipient Pacesetter award North-East C. of C., 1991; named Nurse of Yr. Houston Area League Nursing, 1976-77, Outstanding Black Achiever YMCA Century Club, 1974, Outstanding Women in Medicine YWCA, 1989. Mem. Am. Coll. Hosp. Adminstrs., Tex. Hosp. Assn. (chmn. pub. hosp. com.), Young Hosp. Adminstrs., Nat. Assn. Pub. Hosps. (bd. dirs., mem. exec. com. Tex. assn.), License Vocat. Nurses Assn., sigma Theta Tau. Home: 3730 S Macgregor Way Houston TX 77021-1506 Office: Univ Texas Harris County Psychiatric Ctr 2800 S Macbryor Way Houston TX 77021 Office Phone: 713-741-7803.

MOORE, LORRIE, writer, English professor; b. Glens Falls, NY, Jan. 13, 1957; BA summa cum laude, St. Lawrence U., 1978; MFA, Cornell U., 1982. Now prof. English, U. Wis., Madison. Author: Self-Help, 1985, Anagrams, 1986, The Forgotten Helper, 1987, Like Life, 1990, Who Will Run the Frog Hospital?, 1994, Birds of America, 1998 (Nat. Book Critics Cir. award finalist, Irish Times Internat. Prize for Lit.); editor: I Know Some Things: Stories About Childhood by Contemporary Writers, 1992, The Best American Short Stories 2004; contbr. fiction reviews and essays to NY Times, Harper's, Paris Rev., New Yorker, others. Recipient Nat. Endowment Arts award, 1989, Rea award achievement in short story, 2004, PEN/Malamud award short fiction, 2005; Rockefeller fellow, 1989, Guggenheim fellow, 1991, Lannan Found. fellow, 2001. Mem.: Am. Acad. Arts and Letters. Office: 7187 Helen C White Hall Univ Wis Dept English 600 N Park St Madison WI 53706

**MOORE, MALCOLM FREDERICK,** manufacturing executive; b. Kankakee, Ill., Sept. 19, 1950; s. Robert Dunham and Josephine Frances (Jones) M.; m. Patricia Claudine Bennert, June 13, 1971; children: Michael Dunham, Emily Woodhull, Marjorie Nicoll. BSBA, Am. U., 1972; M of Mgmt., Northwestern U., 1982. Internat. mktg. mgr., product mgr. FMC Corp., Chgo., 1973-84, mktg. and engring. mgr., 1985-90; cons. Frank Lynn & Assoc., Chgo., 1984-85; v.p., gen. mgr. Lindberg unit of Gen. Signal, Watertown, Wis., 1990-93; pres. Abar Ipsen Industries, Inc., Bensalem, Pa., 1993-96; Centorr Vacuum Industries, Nashua, N.H., 1993-96, Linac Holdings, Inc., Rockford, Ill., 1994-96; pres., CEO Pangborn Corp., Hagerstown, Md., 1996-98; pres., COO Gehl Co., West Bend, Wis., 1999—. Inventor material handling equipment. Episcopalian.

**MOORE, MANDY (AMANDA LEIGH MOORE),** actress, singer; b. Nashua, NH, Apr. 10, 1984; d. Don and Stacy Moore. Host MTV show, Mandy, 2000. Actor: (films) Street Rats, 1996, (voice only) Dr. Doolittle 2, 2001, The Princess Diaries, 2001, A Walk to Remember, 2002 (MTV Movie award breakthrough performance-female, 2002, Teen Choice awards choice breakout performance-actress, with Shane West Teen Choice awards choice chemistry, 2002), Try Seventeen, 2002, How to Deal, 2003, Saved!, 2003, (voice only) Racing Stripes, 2005, Chasing Liberty, 2004, First Daughter, 2004, Romance & Cigarettes, 2005, American Dreamz, 2006; (TV films) Summer Music Mania 2001, 2001, (TV appearances) Entourage, 2005; singer: (albums) So Real, 1999, I Wanna Be With You, 2000, Mandy Moore, 2001, Coverage, 2003, The Best of Mandy Moore, 2004, Candy, 2005. Office: William Morris Agy One William Morris Pl Beverly Hills CA 90212*

**MOORE, MARC ANTHONY,** retired academic administrator, writer, retired military officer; b. Dallas, July 15, 1928; s. Edward Clark and Mary Cathrine (Spake) M.; m. Mary Joan Donahue, Sept. 5, 1953; children—Daniel, Mary Ellen, Virginia, Andria. BA, So. Meth. U., 1951; MA, George Washington U., 1970; grad., Amphibious Warfare Sch., 1960, Nat. War Coll., 1974; LHD (hon.), Philippine Women's U., 1987. Enlisted man U.S. Marine Corps, 1946-48, commd. 2d lt., 1951, advanced through grades to maj. gen., 1978; regtl. comdr. Camp Pendleton, Calif., 1971; regtl. exec. officer, infantry bn. comdr. Vietnam, 1970; with Joint Chief Staff Ops., Washington, 1977-78; asst. div. Marine Command and Staff Coll., 1972-73; div. div. English and history U.S. Naval Acad., 1974-76; comdg. gen. 4th Marine Div., New Orleans, 1978-80; chief of staff U.S. Forces, Japan, from 1980, now ret.; former chancellor San Diego campus, v.p. for devel. Nat. U., 1990-91. Teaching asst. dept. psychology George Washington U., 1974; instr. dept. behavioral sci. U.S. Naval Acad., 1975-76; adj. faculty Nat. U., 1983 Co-founder Leadership 2000; mem. pres. council Calif. State U., San Marcos, 1993-96, 98-2000; mem. bd. advisors Marine Mil. Acad., 1983-95; founder and council advisors mem., Command Mus. and Warfare Leadership Ctr., Marine Recruit Depot, San Diego, 1984—. Decorated Def. Superior Svc. medal, Legion of Merit with combat V, Bronze Star with combat V with oak leaf cluster, Air medal, Def. Meritorious Svc. medal, Order Sacred Treasure (Japan); recipient Disting. Alumni award So. Meth. U., 1981. Mem. Marine Corps Assn., Phi Delta Theta. Roman Catholic. Home: 3611 Lago Sereno Escondido CA 92029-7902

**MOORE, MARGARET D.,** human resources specialist; b. New Haven, 1948; BA, Smith Coll., 1970; MBA, Columbia U., N.Y.C., 1974. Treasury analyst PepsiCo, 1973-77, asst. treas., 1977-87, v.p. investor rels., 1987-99, sr. v.p. human resources, 1999—; sr. v.p., treas. Pepsi Bottling Group, 1998-99, bd. dirs. Bd. dirs. Michael Foods; mem. corp. adv. coun. Fin. Acctg. Stds. Bd.; spkr. in field. Office: Pepsico Inc 700 Anderson Hill Rd Purchase NY 10577

**MOORE, MARK HARRISON,** criminal justice and public policy educator; b. Oak Park, Ill., Mar. 19, 1947; s. Charles Eugene and Jean (McFeely) M.; m. Martha Mansfield Church, June 15, 1968; children— Phoebe Sylvina, Tobias McFeely, Gaylen Williams. Student, Phillips Acad., 1962-65; BA, Yale U., 1969; M.Public Policy, Harvard U., 1971, PhD, 1973. Teaching fellow, instr. public policy J.F. Kennedy Sch. Govt., Harvard U., Boston, 1971-73, asst. prof., 1973-74, 75-76, assoc. prof., 1976-79, Guggenheim prof. criminal justice policy and mgmt., 1979—; dir. Hauser Ctr. Non-Profit Orgns. Harvard U., 1998—. Spl. asst. to administr., chief planning officer Drug Enforcement Adminstrn., U.S. Dept. Justice, Washington, 1974-75; cons. U.S. Dept. Justice, 1975-76, 81 Author: Buy and Bust: The Effective Regulation of an Illicit Market in Heroin, 1977, Creating Public Value: Strategic Management in Government, 1995, (with others) Dangerous Offenders, 1985, From Children to Citizens: Vol. 1, The Mandate for Juvenile Justice, 1987, (with Malcolm K. Sparrow) Ethics in Government, 1990, (with Malcolm K. Sparrow and David Kennedy) Beyond 911: A New Era for Policing, 1991; editor: (with Joel Fleishman and Lance Leibman) Public Duties, 1980, (with Dean Gerstein) Alcohol and Public Policy, 1981. Dir. Hauser Ctr. for Non Profit Orgns. Mem. Assns. Schs. Public Policy and Mgmt., Phi Beta Kappa Home: 331 Waverley St Belmont MA 02478-2418 Office: JF Kennedy Sch Govt Harvard U 79 Jfk St Cambridge MA 02138-5801 Office Phone: 617-795-1113. Business E-Mail: mark_moore@harvard.edu.

**MOORE, MARSHA LYNN,** retired elementary school educator, counseling administrator; b. Washington, May 19, 1946; d. Marshall Alexander and Doris Virginia (Diggs) Moore. BA, Howard U., 1967; MEd, U. Md., 1975. Sch. counseling K-12, cert. tchr. grades 1-6, sci. resource tchr. grades 1-6. 1st grade demonstration tchr. Anne M. Goding Sch. D.C. Pub. Schs., 1967—72; counselor Balt. County Schs., Towson, Md., 1972—77; fashion coord., mgr. Wallach's Ladies' Store, Nanuet, NY and Livingston, NJ, 1977—80; adult edn. cons., counselor East Orange (N.J.) Adult High Sch., 1980—83; coord. lang. arts Faith Hope Christian Sch., 1983—84; minority counselor Essex County C.C., Newark, 1984—85; equal opportunity fund counselor, instr. Kean Coll., Union, NJ, 1985—87; tchr. 5th grade Randle Highlands Elem. Sch., 1987—90; tchr. 5th and 6th grade Brookland Sch., Washington, 1990—98; 5th grade tchr., math. and sci. resource tchr. Shepherd Elem. Sch., Washington, 1998—2002; tchr. 6th grade math. and sci. Bertie Backus Mid. Sch., Washington, 2002—03; tchr./coord. 6th grade math. Friendship-Edison Pub. Charter Sch., Wash., 2004—05; ednl. cons., 2005—. Coord. counselor Summer Youth Program, East Orange, 1982; career fair coord. East Orange Adult H.S., 1981, Essex County C.C., 1985; mem. discipline com. PTA Shepherd Sch., Washington, 1998—2002; liaison, exec. bd., hospitality com., multicultural com. PTA, 2000—02; math.-a-thon coord. St. Jude's, 2000, coord. parent math. workshop, 2000—02; coord. Sci. Careers Expo and 1st Sci. Bee, 2001; co-sponsor Student Coun., 2001—02; facilitator DCACTS, 2001—02; math. tutor, 2000—01; sgt.-at-arms WT Union Sch. Orgn., 2002—03. Editor: Sci. newsletter. Chmn. Teen Lift, NJ, Delteens, Washington; 2d v.p. Washington Pan-Hellenic Coun., 1994—96, fin. sec., 1996—98, co-chair Greek Forum, 1996—98; mentor Best Friends, Inc. Mem.: NAACP, AFT, Internat. Soc. Poets, Washington Tchrs. Union, Nat. Coun. Negro Women, Howard U. Alumni Assn. (reunion planning com. 1967, N.J. coord. 1980—87, v.p. Washington 1989—91, pres. 1991—93, parliamentarian Washington chpt. 1999—2001, chair membership com. Wash. chpt. 2003—04, nat. rec. sec. 2004—, chair fundraising com. 2005—, co-chair pub. rels. com. 2005—, life mem. Washington chpt., co-chair spl. events com. 2005—), Friends of Andrew Rankin Chapel (adj. sec. 1994—97, newsletter co-chair, fundraising and archives coms.), U.S. Tennis Assn., Kennedy Ctr. for Performing Arts, Delta Sigma Theta (Diamond Life mem.). Episcopalian. Avocations: tennis, gardening, landscape designing, swimming, travel. Office Phone: 202-526-5537. E-mail: marsh6793@msn.com.

**MOORE, MARVELENE C.,** music educator; b. Franklin, Tenn., Sept. 13, 1944; d. Frank and Sadie Gibson Moore. BA, Talladega Coll., 1966; M in Music Edn., George Peabody Coll., 1970, edn. specialist, 1971; PhD, U. Mich., 1977. Music specialist Decatur Pub. Sch., Ala., 1966—69; prof., music edn. U. Tenn., Knoxville, 1978—; asst. prof., music edn. Savannah State

Coll., Ga., 1977—78; admin. asst. U. Mich., Ann Arbor, 1974—77. Chair, music in sch. and tchr. edn. Internat. Soc. for Music Edn., Nedlands, Australia, 2004—; mem. Jour. for Arts Edn., Hong Kong. Author: Making Music Series, 2002—05, The Music Connection Series, 1995—, Making Music with Movement and Dance, 2005—, Classroom Managment in the General Choral and Instrumental Programs, 2002—. Instr., children's classes in movement U. Tenn., Knoxville, 1985—95; min. of music United Methodist Ch., Knoxville, 1980—87, Redemption Internat. Ctr., Knoxville, 1987—95; adv. bd. Tenn. Alliance for Arts Edn., Nashville. Recipient James A. Cox Endowed Chair, U. Tenn., 2002—05, Hall of Fame, Tenn. Music Edn. Assn., 2005. Mem.: Internat. Assn. Jazz Edn. Resource Team, Music Educators Nat. Conf. (gen. music chair 1998—2000). Presbyterian. Home: 1256 Halifax Rd Knoxville TN 37922 Office: U Tenn 1741 Vol Blvd Knoxville TN 37922 Office Phone: 865-974-7515. Business E-Mail: mmoore7@utk.edu.

**MOORE, MARY FRENCH (MUFFY MOORE),** potter, advocate; d. John and Rhoda French; m. Alan Baird Minier, 1982; children: Jonathan Corbet, Jennifer Corbet, Michael Corbet. BA cum laude, Colo. U., 1964. Ceramics mfg., Wilson, Wyo., 1969-82, Cheyenne, Wyo., 1982—. Commr. County Teton (Wyo.), 1976-83, chmn. bd. commrs., 1981, 83, mem. dept. pub. assistance and social svc., 1976-82, mem. recreation bd., 1978-81, water quality adv. bd., 1976-82. Bd. dirs. Teton Sci. Sch., 1968-83, vice chmn., 1979-81, chmn., 1982; bd. dirs. Grand Teton Music Festival, 1963-68, Teton Energy Coun., 1978-83, Whitney Gallery of Western Art, Cody, Wyo., 1995—, Opera Colo., 1998—, Opera Colo. Found., 2005-06; mem. water quality adv. bd. Wyo. Dept. Environ. Quality, 1979-83; Dem. precinct committeewoman, 1978-81; mem. Wyo. Dem. Ctrl. Com., 1981-83; vice chmn. Laramie County Dem. Ctrl. Com., 1983-84, Wyo. Dem. nat. committeewoman, 1984-87; chmn. Wyo. Dem. Party, 1987-89; del. Dem. Nat. Conv., 1984, 88, mem. fairness commn. Dem. Nat. Com., 1985, vice-chair western caucus, 1986-89; chmn. platform com. Wyo. Dem. Conv., 1982; mem. Wyo. Dept. Environ. Quality Land Quality Adv. Bd., 1983-86; mem. Gov.'s Steering Com. on Troubled Youth, 1982, dem. nat. com. Compliance Assistance Commn., 1986-87; exec. com. Assn. of State Dem. Chairs, 1989; mem. Wyo. Coun. on the arts, 1989-95, chmn., 1994-95, Dem. Nat. Com. Jud. Coun., 1989—; legis. aide for Gov. Wyo., 1985, 86; project coord. Gov.'s Com. on Childrens' Svcs., 1985-86; bd. dirs. Wyo. Outdoor Coun., 1984-85; polit. dir., dep. mgr. Schuster for Congress, 1994-95; adminstrv. dir. Freudenthal for Gov., 2002, pers. coord., 2002; mem. pres.' adv. com. on the performing arts John F. Kennedy Ctr. for the Performing Arts, 1999-2001. Recipient Woman of Yr. award Jackson Hole Bus. and Profl. Women, 1981, Dem. of Yr. Nellie Tayloe Ross award Wyo. Dems., 1990. Mem. Alden Kindred of Am., Jackson Hole Art Assn. (bd. dirs., vice chmn. 1981, chmn. 1982), Assn. State Dem. Chairs, Soc. Mayflower Descendents, Pi Sigma Alpha. Home: 8907 Cowpoke Rd Cheyenne WY 82009-1234

**MOORE, MARY JOHNSON,** nurse; b. West Point, N.Y., Feb. 8, 1940; d. Robert Phillip and Edith Virginia (Carr) Johnson; m. Prentis Monroe Moore, Dec. 28, 1960 (dec. Jan. 1990); children: Carol Edith, Tracey Marie. Diploma, Boston City Hosp. Sch. Nursing, 1960. RN. Clinic nurse in pediat. and obstetrics Harris County Health Dept./Lyons Clinic, Houston, 1982—85; clinic nurse Tex. Sch. for Deaf, Austin, 1986—87; staff nurse pediat. Ben Taub Hosp., Houston, 1989—92; telephone triage nurse, ob-gyn. McGregor Clinic, Houston, 1992—93; staff nurse pediat. Grant Hosp., Chgo., 1994—96; clinic nurse Columbus-Maryville Hosp., Chgo., 1996—2002; travel nurse Star-Med Profl. Staffing, 2002—03; case mgr. Brockton Neighborhood Health Ctr., Mass., 2003—04. Mem. vol. choir St. Chrysostoms Episcopal Ch., 1997—2002. George Monks Meml. scholar, 1960. Democrat. Avocations: art, music, history, collecting unicorns, angels and lighthouses. Home: 72 Pine St Brockton MA 02302 Personal E-mail: mryjrn@yahoo.com.

**MOORE, MARY TYLER,** actress; b. Bklyn., Dec. 29, 1936; d. George and Marjorie Moore; m. Richard Meeker, 1955 (div. 1961); 1 child, Richard (dec.); m. Grant Tinker, 1963 (div. 1981); m. Robert Levine, 1983. Chmn. bd. MTM Enterprises, Inc.. Studio City, Calif. Stage appearances include (Broadway debut) Breakfast at Tiffany's, 1966, Whose Life Is It, Anyway?, 1980, Sweet Sue, 1988, The Players Club Centennial Salute, 1989, Rose's Dilemma, 2003; appeared in TV series Richard Diamond, Private Eye, 1957-59, Dick Van Dyke Show, 1961-66, Mary Tyler Moore Show, 1970-77, Mary, 1978, Mary Tyler Moore Hour, 1979, Mary, 1985, Annie McGuire, 1988, New York News, 1995, Mary and Rhoda, 1998; miniseries Gore Vidal's Lincoln, 1988, New York News, 1995; in TV movies Love American Style, 1969, Run a Crooked Mile, 1969, First You Cry, 1978, Heartsounds, 1984, Finnegan Begin Again, 1984, The Last Best Year, 1990, Thanksgiving Day, 1990, Stolen Babies, 1993 (Emmy award, Outstanding Supporting Actress in a Miniseries or Special, 1993), Payback, 1997, Mary and Rhoda, 2000, Like Mother, Like Son: The Strange Story of Sante and Kenny Kimes, 2001, Miss Lettie & Me, 2002, The Gin Game, 2003, Blessings, 2003; films: X-15, 1961, Thoroughly Modern Millie, 1967, Don't Just Stand There, 1968, What's So Bad About Feeling Good?, 1968, Change of Habit, 1969, Ordinary People, 1980 (Acad. Award nominee for best actress 1981), Six Weeks, 1982, Just Between Friends, 1986, Keys to Tulsa, 1996, Flirting with Disaster, 1996, Reno Finds Her Mom, 1997, Labor Pains, 1999; appeared on Broadway in Whose Life Is It Anyway?, 1980, Sweet Sue, 1987, Labor Pains, 2000, Cheats, 2002; in TV spl. How to Survive the Seventies, 1978, How To Raise a Drug Free Child; author: After All, 1995. Chair Juvenile Diabetes Found., 1985—. Recipient Emmy award Nat. Acad. TV Arts and Scis. 1964-65, 73-74, 76, Golden Globe award 1965, 81, Star on the Hollywood Walk of Fame, 1992; named to TV Hall of Fame, 1985. Office: William Morris Agy care Betsy Berg 151 S El Camino Dr Beverly Hills CA 90212-2775

**MOORE, MATTHEW SCOTT,** publishing executive, writer; b. Indpls., Dec. 31, 1958; s. Scott Moore and JoNelle (Painter) Giegerich. BA in Social Work, Rochester Inst. Tech., 1983. Founder, pres. MSM Prodns., Ltd., Rochester, NY, 1984—; pub., co-editor-in-chief Deaf Life, Rochester, 1986—. Flying Words Project, Rochester, 1989—; lectr., spkr. in field; organizer confs. Co-author: For Hearing People Only, 1992, Great Deaf Americans, 2nd edit., 1996; launched several websites Founder Deaf Rochesterians' Cmty. Ctr. Core Team, 1992; chmn. Third N.Y. State Conf. for Sign-Lang. Instrs., Rochester, 1992; coord. Am. Sign-Lang. Tchrs. Assn. 1st Nat. Profl. Devel. Conf., Rochester, N.Y., 1999. Recipient Recognition cert. World Recreation Assn. of Deaf, 1990, Humanitarian award Delta Sigma Phi, 1991, Pres. award Am. Sign Lang. Tchrs. Assn. Lilac chpt., 1993, Outstanding Alumni award NTID, 1993, Tex. Deaf Caucus award, 1993, Alice Cogswell award Gallaudet U., 1994, Printing Week award, 1995, Disting. Alumni Modern Era award Ind. Sch. Deaf, 1997, Georgianna Elliott award Dallas Deaf Celebration, 1998. Avocations: writing, performing, theater, collecting birdhouses. Office: MSM Prodns Ltd PO Box 23380 Rochester NY 14692-3380 Office Fax: 585-442-6371. Business E-Mail: msmoore@as14.us.com.

**MOORE, MCPHERSON DORSETT,** lawyer; b. Pine Bluff, Ark., Mar. 1, 1947; s. Arl Van and Jessie (Dorsett) M. BS, U. Miss., 1970; JD, U. Ark., 1974. Bar: Ark. 1974, Mo. 1975, U.S. Patent and Trademark Office 1977, U.S. Dist. Ct. (ea. dist.) Mo. 1977, U.S. Ct. Appeals (8th, 10th and fed. cirs.). Design engr. Tenneco, Newport News, Va., 1970-71; assoc. Rogers, Eilers & Howell, St. Louis, 1974-80; ptnr. Rogers, Howell, Moore & Haferkamp, St. Louis, 1981-89, Armstrong, Teasdale, Schlafly & Davis, St. Louis, 1989-95, Polster, Lieder, Woodruff & Lucchesi, St. Louis, 1995—. Engr. City of Ladue, Mo., 1998-2000; mem. intellectual property adv. bd. Washington U. Bd. dirs. Legal Svcs. Ea. Mo.; mem. Ladue Zoning and Planning Commn., 1998—. With USAR, 1970-76. Mem. ABA, Bar Assn. Met. St. Louis (chmn. young lawyers sect. 1981-82, sec. 1984-85, v.p. 1985-86, chmn. trial sect. 1986-87, pres. 1988-89), Ark. Bar Assn., St. Louis Bar Found. (sec. 1984-85, v.p. 1988-89, pres. 1989-90), The Mo. Bar (chmn. patent, trademark and copyright law com. 1992-94, co-chmn. 1994-95), St. Louis County Bar Assn., Women Lawyers Assn., Am. Intellectual Property Law Assn., Mound City Bar Assn., Phi Delta Theta Alumni (treas. St. Louis chpt. 1987-88, sec. 1988-89, v.p. 1989-90), Racquet Club (St. Louis). Home: 3 Mayfair Rd Saint Louis MO 63124 Office: Polster Lieder Woodruff & Lucchesi Ste 200 12412 Powers Ct Dr Saint Louis MO 63131-3615 Office Phone: 314-238-2400.

**MOORE, MECHLIN DONGAN,** communications executive, management consultant; b. N.Y.C., May 21, 1930; s. Albere Ethier and Pamela (Robinson) M.; m. Elizabeth Ann Tonkin, Feb. 11, 1956 (dec. 1992); children: Lansing, Pamela; m. Valery Ann Shields, July 14, 1995. AB, Harvard U., 1952. Reporter Washington Post, 1955-59; dir. build Am. better com. Nat. Assn. Real Estate Bds., D.C., 1960-64; dir. info. Urban Land Inst., D.C., 1964-66; exec. v.p. Ctrl. Assn. Seattle, 1966-70; asst. to pres. United Airlines, Inc., Chgo., 1971-72; sr. v.p. external affairs, 1972-74, group v.p. mktg., 1975-76, sr. v.p. pub. affairs, 1976-79; pres. Ins. Info. Inst., N.Y.C., 1979-91; chmn., CEO Informatrix Worldwide SuperSite Devel., 1996-98; pvt. practice Naples, Fla., 1991—; advisor Vertical Net, Inc., 1998-2001; project planning dir. Fla. Gulf Coast Univ. Found., 2004—05. Pres. Eagles Mere Water Co., 1993-96; bd. electors Ins. Hall of Fame; bd. govs. Internat. Ins. Seminars Contbg. author publs. Nat. Assn. Real Estate Bds.; assoc. editor Jour. Property Mgmt. Adv. bd. mem. Traffic Inst. Northwestern U.; past mem. St. George's Vestry, N.Y.C. 1st lt. U.S. Army, 1952-54. Recipient Commendation Ribbon with Metal Pendant U.S. Army, 1954, Disting. Svc. award Central Assn. Seattle, 1972 Mem. Univ. Club, Pelican Marsh Golf Club, Shenorock Shore Club. Republican. Episcopalian. Home: 750 Vistana Cir Naples FL 34119 Office Phone: 239-777-1595. E-mail: mmoore7412@aol.com.

**MOORE, MELBA (MELBA HILL),** actress, singer; b. N.Y.C., Oct. 29, 1947; d. Teddy and Melba (Smith) Hill; m. Charels Huggins (div.); 1 child. BA, Montclair State Tchrs. Coll., NJ, PhD in Arts & Letters, 1990. Broadway debut in Hair 1968-72, Purlie, 1970-71 (Drama Desk award Outstanding Performance, 1970, Theatrw World award, 1970, Tony award Best Featured Actress in a Musical, 1970), Timbuktu!, 1978, Inacent Black, 1981, Les Misérables, 1987-2003, Brooklyn, 2006—; off-Broadway autobiographical play Songs My Mother Taught Me; also nightclub performer;(films) include Pigeons, 1971 Lost in the Stars, 1974, Hair, 1979, All Dogs Go to Heaven (voice), 1989, Def by Temptation, 1990, The Fighting Temptations, 2003; (TV series) The Melba Moore-Clifton Davis Show, 1972, Melba, 1986, (TV films) Opryland, 1973, The American Women: Portraits of Courage, 1976, Purlie, 1981, Charlotte Forten's Mission: Experiment in Freedom, 1985, Seasonal Differences, 1987, Mother's Day, 1989; appeared in TV miniseries Ellis Island, 1984; guest appearances The Love Boat, 1979, The Tim Conway Show, 1980, Hotel, 1985, Falcon Crest, 1987, The Cosby Show, 1988, Monsters, 1989, Loving, 1992; albums include Look What You're Doing to the Man, 1971, Living to Give, 1972, Peach Melba, 1975, Melba, 1976, This is It, 1976, Melba, 1978, A Portrait of Melba, 1978, Burn, 1979, Dancin' with Melba, 1979, Closer, 1980, What a Women Needs, 1980, The Other Side of the Rainbow, 1982, Never Say Never, 1983, Read My Lips, 1985, A Lot of Love, 1987, I'm in Love, 1988, Soul Exposed, 1990, Official African-Am. Nat. Anthem, 1990 (Lift Every Voice and Sing), The Greatest Feeling, 1991, Happy Together, 1996, Solitray Journey, 1999, A Very Special Christmas Gift, 2001, I'm Still Here, 2002, A Night in St. Lucia, 2002, Nobody But Jesus, 2004. Advocate Melba Moore Found. for Abused & Neglected Children.*

**MOORE, MICHAEL,** film director, writer; b. Flint, Mich., Apr. 23, 1954; m. Kathleen Glynn; 1 stepchild, Natalie. Former editor Flint Voice, Mich. Dir., wrote, prodr. Roger and Me, 1989 (Ten Best Films of Yr. list), 1992 Bowling for Columbine, 2002 (Academy award Best Documentary Feature, 2003), Fahrenheit 9/11, 2004 (Palme d'Or, Cannes Film Festival, 2004); actor, dir. prodr., wrote Canadian Bacon, 1994; dir., creator, host TV Nation, 1994-1995 (Outstanding Informational Series Emmy award, 1995); dir.: (films) Two Mikes Don't Make a Wright, 1992, The Big One, 1997, (TV) The Awful Truth, 1999; Acted only: EdTV, 1999, Lucky Numbers, 2000; Author: Downsize This! Random Threats from Unarmed America, 1996, Adventures in a TV Nation, 1998, Stupid White Men and Other Sorry Excuses for the State of the Nation!, 2002, Dude, Where's My Country?, 2003, Will They Ever Trust Us Again? Letters From the War Zone, 2004, The Official Fahrenheit 9/11 Reader, 2004. Named one of Time Mag. 100 Most Influential People, 2005. Office: Creative Artists Agy c/o David Tenzer 9830 Wilshire Blvd Beverly Hills CA 90212-1804

**MOORE, MICHAEL JAMES,** information technology executive; b. Rochester, N.Y., Mar. 13, 1969; s. Susan Ann Moore. BS, Embry-Riddle Aero. U., 1997; MBA, U. Nev., Las Vegas, 2004. Cert. adminstr. Novell, 1999, sys. engr. Microsoft, 2003, desktop technician Apple Computer, 2004. Pres., cons. Digital Mechanics, Inc., Las Vegas, 1993—; microcomputer sys. specialist Clark County Sch. Dist., Las Vegas, 1995—99, mis/dp tech. specialist, 1999—. Prodr.: (radio show) Computer Guys Radio Show. With U.S. Army, 1987—90. Decorated Army Achievement medal U.S. Army, Good Conduct medal. R-Consevative. Achievements include research in indentification and management of known and unknown risks to a information system. Avocations: scuba diving, boating, bicycling. Home: 6067 Dewberry Ct Las Vegas NV 89110 Office: Digital Mechanics Inc 450 N Nellis Blvd #113 Las Vegas NV 89110 Office Phone: 702-434-9765.

**MOORE, MICHAEL ROBERT,** music educator, band director; s. Michael Ruben and Rosa Lee Moore; m. Janie Lynn Creech, June 12, 1993. MusB in Edn., Bowling Green State U., 1994. Cert. tchr. K-12 Dept. Edn., Ohio. Instr. marching band Hamilton (Ohio) H.S. Marching Band, 1988—2001; dir. of music Stephen T. Badin H.S., Hamilton, 2001—. Deacon West Side Bapt. Ch., Hamilton, 2002—06, chair structure reform com., 2003—04, tchr. adult theology, 2002—06, tchr. team kids, 2002—06. Recipient Educator of Distinction award, Nat. Soc. H.S. Scholars, 2004. Mem.: Music Educator's Nat. Conf. Republican. Southern Baptist. Avocations: model railroading, photography, music. Office: Stephen T Badin H S 571 New London Rd Hamilton OH 45013 Office Phone: 513-863-3993. Business E-Mail: mmoore@mail.badinhs.org.

**MOORE, MICHAEL WATSON,** musician, educator; b. Cin., May 16, 1945; s. Clarence Watson and Jeannette Elizabeth (Gardner) M.; m. Renee Allyn White, Oct. 23, 1993; children: Benjamin Butler, Mathew Satyavan. Attended, Cin. Coll. Conservatory of Music, 1964-65. Bass instr. Summer Stage Bank Clinic, 1969, Eastman Sch. of Music, Rochester, NY, 1974-87, U. Bridgeport, Bridgeport, Conn., 1981-83, L.I. U., Bklyn., 1993-96, William Patterson U., Wayne, NJ, 1994-95. String bass player with Cal Collins Trio, Cin., 1965, Woody Evans Trio, Cin., 1965, Woody Herman Band, USO, Africa, Ea. Europe, 1966-67, Marion McPartland Trio, N.Y.C., 1968, Freddie Hubbard Quintet, N.Y.C., 1969-70, Jack Wilkins Trio, N.Y.C., 1971, Chet Baker Quartet, N.Y.C., 1972-73, Phil Woods Quartet, N.Y.C., 1972, Gene Bertoncini Duo, N.Y.C., 1972—, Stan Getz Quartet, N.Y.C., 1973, Tony Bennett, N.Y.C., 1973, Ruby Braff, George Barnes Quartet, N.Y.C., 1973-75, Gerry Mulligan Quartet, N.Y.C., 1974, Benny Goodman Sextet, N.Y.C., 1974-76, Lee Konitz Quartet, N.Y.C., 1975, Teddy Wilson Duo, N.Y.C., 1977, Jim Hall Trio, N.Y.C., 1977, Bill Evans Trio, N.Y.C., 1978, Bob Brookmeyer Quintet, N.Y.C., 1978, Mike Abene, Michael Moore Quintet, N.Y.C., 1978, Zoot Sims Quartet, N.Y.C., 1979, Gary Burton Quartet, N.Y.C., 1981-82, Louis Belson Quartet, N.Y.C., 1982, Roger Kellaway Duo and Trio, N.Y.C., 1980s, Jimmy Rowles Duo, N.Y.C., 1980s, Jon Scoffield Duo and Quartet, N.Y.C., 1980s, Lew Tabackin Trio, N.Y.C., 1980s, Hank Jones Trio, N.Y.C., 1980s, Shelly Mann Trio, N.Y.C., 1980s, Pepper Adams Quartet, N.Y.C., 1980s, Lou Levy Duo, N.Y.C., 1980s, Al Cohen Trio, N.Y.C., 1980s, Jake Hanna Quartet, N.Y.C., 1980s, Rosemary Clooney, N.Y.C., 1987-88, Louis Stewart Trio, Ireland and U.K., 1990, Howard Alden Trio, N.Y.C., 1990s, Warren Vache Trio, N.Y.C., 1990s, Harry Allen Trio, N.Y.C., 1990s, Ken Peplowski Trio, N.Y.C., 1990s, Charlie Byrd Quartet, N.Y.C., 1990s, Dave Brubeck Quartet, 2001—; co-leader duo with Rufus Reid, 1995, with Chris Potter, 1995; leader duo with Bill Charlap, 1995; tour Japan with Harry Allen, 1997; leader trio with Ken Peplowski and Tom Melito, 1998—. Dave Brubeck Quartet, 2001—; composer: Rio Pindare, 1986, Make Me When It's Over, 1988, The Lilter, 1989, The Old New Waltz, 1992, Zoot's Suite, 1995, Just Me, Just Me, 1995, When I Wage Battle Next, 1999, Moon Dog, 1999; recs. Michael Moore Trio Plays Gershwin, 1993, Michael Moore/Bill Charlap, 1995 (One of the Best Jazz CDs of 95, The New Yorker, 1996), Michael Moore/Rufus Reid Doublebass Delights, 1996 (One of the Best Jazz CDs of 96, The New Yorker, 1997), Michael Moore/Rufus Reid The Intimacy of the Bass, 1999, Michael Moore and His Trio The History of Jazz: Vol. 1, 2000,

The Michael Moore Trio The History of Jazz Vol. 2 Dedication, 2002 (One of Best Jazz CDs of 2002, The New Yorker), Video with Rufus Reid, 1998; author: Melodic Improvising in the Thumb Position: Method for Improvisation for the String Bass, 1986, (with Clem Derosa) The Michael Moore Bass Method, 2002; performer: (with Weslia Whitfield) The White House, 1996. Councilman Borough of Bangor, Pa., 1987-88. Mem. ASCAP. Avocation: piano. Home and Office: 5 E 22d St Apt 15M New York NY 10010-5325

**MOORE, MICHELE CLAIRE,** physician; b. Watertown, N.Y., Sept. 15, 1942; d. Arthur Clair and Jeanne Marilyn (Keib) M.; m. Marcus Christian Hansen, Nov. 27, 1976; children: Martin C., Anneke K. BS, Le Moyne Coll., 1964; MD, Royal Coll. Surgeons Ireland, Dublin, 1974. Sci. tchr. Jamesville-DeWitt Ctrl. Sch., DeWitt, N.Y., 1964-65; rsch. asst. St. Luke's Hosp., N.Y.C., 1965-69; pvt. practice Crown Point, N.Y., 1976-82; town health officer, 1977-82; physician Valley Family Physicians, Charlestown, N.H., 1982-84; physician, owner holistic health practice Keene, NH, 1984—2001; contract physician Indian Health Svc., 2002—; physician Alamo Navajo Health Ctr., Magdalena, N.Mex., 2003—04. Clinician So. Adirondack Planned Parenthood, Crown Point, 1976-82; clin. instr. SUNY Upstate Med. Sch., Syracuse, 1980-90; adj. assoc. prof. Dartmouth Med. Sch., Hanover, N.H., 1990-2002; cons. physician PMS/ACT, Bow, N.H., 1991—; speaker in field. Author: The Only Menopause Guide You'll Need; Cesarean Section: Understanding and Celebrating Your Baby's Birth; DICK: A guide to the penis for men and women, Do You Really Need Surgery: a Sensible Guiide to Hysterectomies and Other Procedures, A Woman's Guide to Common Medical Tests, Pregnancy and Parenting After Thirty Five: Mid Life, New Life; contbr. articles to profl. jours. Steering com. Hospice of Sullivan County, Claremont, N.H., 1983-84; trustee N.E. Coll. Healing Arts and Sci., Bellows Falls, Vt., 1993-97; mem. adv. coun. Vt. Healing Tools Project, Brattleboro, 1996—. Fellow Am. Acad Family Physicians; mem. Am. Acad. Environ. Medicine, Am. Med. Women's Assn., N.Am. Menopause Soc., New Eng. Soc. Clin. Hypnosis, N.H. Med. Soc., Am. Cancer Soc. (bd. dirs. Essex County, N.Y. chpt. 1976-82), N.H. Writers' Project. Avocations: reading, knitting, cooking, gardening, sewing. Home: PO Box 248 Alstead NH 03602-0248 E-mail: micheleclaire42@hotmail.com.

**MOORE, MIKE,** former state attorney general; m. Tisha Moore; 1 child, Kyle. Grad., Jackson County Jr. Coll., 1972; BA, U. Miss., 1974, JD, 1976. Asst. dist. atty. State of Miss., 1977—78, dist. atty., 1979, atty. gen., 1988—2003; atty. Phelps Dunbar, 2004—. Democrat. Office: Phelps Dunbar 111 East Capitol St Ste 600 Jackson MS 39201 Office Phone: 601-352-2300. Office Fax: 601-360-9777.

**MOORE, MILO ANDERSON,** banker; b. Orange, N.J., Aug. 26, 1942; s. Milo H. and Helen M.; m. Judith J. Colosimo, May 4, 1968; children: Milo Robert, Matthew Wiley, Marykate Bartlett BS, Ithaca Coll., 1964; MBA, Rutgers U., 1971. Traffic supt. N.Y. Tel. Co., N.Y.C., 1964-71; trust officer Midlantic Nat. Bank, Newark, 1971-76; v.p. Shearson Loeb Rhoades, N.Y.C., 1976-80; sr. v.p. Donaldson Lufkin & Jenrette, N.Y.C., 1980-85; sr. mng. dir. Bear, Stearns & Co., 1985-92; v.p. JP Morgan Pvt. Bank, Morristown, NJ, 1992—2004. Advisor Jr. Achievement, Bronx, N.Y., 1967-68; pres. Chatham Jaycees, N.J., 1974; big bros. Morris County Big Bros., Morristown, 1971-81; pres. Stanley Congl. Ch., Chatham, N.J., 1995-97; trustee SAGE Solutions, 1994-2004, pres., 2002. Mem. Securities Industry Assn. (tax shelter com. 1982-85), Glenburnie Club (pres. 1989—), Canoe Brook Country Club (Summit, N.J.), Beta Gamma Sigma. Office: JP Morgan Chase Pvt Banking 225 South St Morristown NJ 07960-5336 Office Phone: 973-285-2256. E-mail: milo.moore@jpmorgan.com.

**MOORE, NATHAN P.,** lawyer; b. Arlington, 1967; m. Joy Moore; children: Grant, Trey. BBA, Tex. A&M U.; JD, St. Mary's U., 1992. Bar: Tex. 1992. Assoc. Underwood, Wilson, Berry, Stein and Johnson, Amarillo, Tex.; with Mary Kay Inc., 1995—, gen. counsel, v.p., sec., 2003—. Bd. dirs. Direct Selling Assn. Mem.: State Bar Tex., Dallas Bar Assn. (mem. intellectual propery sect., corp. counsel sect.). Office: Mary Kay Inc 16251 Dallas Pkwy PO Box 799045 Dallas TX 75379-9045*

**MOORE, OLIVER SEMON, III,** publishing executive, consultant; b. Jersey City, July 26, 1942; s. Oliver S. and Ann Loy (Spies) M.; m. Dina Downing DuBois, Feb. 23, 1961 (div. 1974); 1 child, Deborah; m. Christine Laine Meyers, May 12, 1990; 1 child, Kathryn Laine. BA, U. Va., 1964. Chief bur. Richmond (Va.) Times-Dispatch, Time mag., N.Y.C., 1966-67, contbg. editor, 1967-68; assoc. editor Newsweek, N.Y.C., 1969-71; freelance writer, 1972-75; mng. editor Motor Boating and Sailing, N.Y.C., 1976-78, editor, 1980-82; exec. editor US Mag., N.Y. Times Co., 1978-80; dep. editor Town & Country Mag., N.Y.C., 1982-84; editor Sci. Digest Mag., N.Y.C., 1984-86; pub. dir. Yachting Mag., N.Y.C., 1986-95; editorial dir. Outdoor Life, N.Y.C., 1993-95; v.p. The Outdoor Co., N.Y.C., 1994-95; editor-at-large Motor Boating & Sailing, 1995—2001; pres. Alamo Pub. Svcs., Inc., Detroit, 1995—. Co-founder, chmn. bd. Corp! (Mag.), 1998. Author: (poems) Voices International, 1969; contbg. editor Sports Afield, 1996—; photographer (mags.) Motor Boating and Sailing, Yachting, Working Woman Corp! (books) Lines to a Little Girl, Rancho Paradiso. Recipient Merit award Art Dirs. Club, 1981, award of merit Soc. Publ. Designers, 1981, Excellence in Media award Nat. Arbor Day Found., 1985. Mem. Am. Soc. Mag. Editors, Mag. Pubs. Assn. (nat. mag. award 1995), N.Y. Yacht Club, Grosse Pointe (Mich.) Club, Bayview (Mich.) Yacht Club, Wyndemere Country Club (Fla.). Republican. Episcopalian. Avocations: sailing, antique cars. Personal E-mail: omoore@comcast.net.

**MOORE, PAT HOWARD,** engineering and construction executive, educator; b. Laredo, Tex., Sept. 16, 1930; s. Howard Warren and Odette Evelyn (Bunn) M.; m. Elsie Mae Crossman, Mar. 23, 1954; children: Linda Marie Ford, Margaret Ann, Andrew Patrick. BA, Rice U., 1952, BS in Civil Engring., 1953; postgrad, Tulane U., 1956 58. Registered profl. engr., Tex., La. Div. engr. McDermott Inc., Morgan City, La., 1956-58; pres., dir. Navasota Tel. Co., Tex., 1958-63; project mgr. Brown & Root, Inc., Houston, 1963-67, exec. v.p., dir., 1990-95; pres., dir. Fluor Ocean Svcs., Houston, 1968-80; sr. v.p. Raymond Internat., Inc., Houston, 1980-86; pres., dir. Martin Moore Inc., Bellaire, Tex., 1986-90; mgmt. cons. Bellaire, 1996—2003. Adv. dir. Tex. Commerce Bank, Houston, 1979-86, Third Tech. Inc., Ft. Worth, 2004-06; bd. govs. Rice U., 1984-88, lectr. ethics 1996-2003, adj. prof. civil and environ. engring., 2003—; bd. dirs. SGB, Inc., Houston, 1986-90, Charter Builders, Inc., Dallas, 1988-90, Versar Inc., Springfield, Va., 1998-2002, XServ, Inc., Houston, 1997—. Spl. investigator US Army Counter Intelligence, 1954—56, hon. discharge, 1962. Named Outstanding Engring. Alumnus, Rice U., 2005. Fellow ASCE(life mem. 1995); mem. Chi Epsilon (hon. mem. 1995), Kiwanis (pres. 1960). Methodist. Home: 124 Chuckwagon Trail Georgetown TX 78628 E-mail: moore@rice.edu.

**MOORE, PATRICK J.,** paper company executive; b. Sept. 7, 1954; m. Beth Moore; 3 children. BSBA, DePaul U., Chgo. Asst. treas. Jefferson Smurfit Corp., St. Louis, 1987-90, treas., 1990-93, v.p., treas., 1993-94; v.p., gen. mgr. Indsl. Packaging divsn. Indsl. Packaging divsn., St. Louis, 1994-96; v.p., CFO Jefferson Smurfit Corp., St. Louis, 1996—98, Smurfit-Stone Container Corp., Chgo., 1998—2002, pres., CEO, 2002—, chmn., 2003—. Serves on NAS-DAQ CEO Coun.; bd. dir. Am. Forest & Paper Assn., JP Morgan Nat. Adv. Bd., Intern. Corrugated Case Assn., Archer Daniels Midland. Mem. Civic Progress, St. Louis, comml. Club, Chgo., Wash. U. John M. Olin Sch. Bus. Nat. Coun.; bd. dir. Met. YMCA, St. Louis, Boys Hope/Girls Hope, Big Shoulders Fund, Chgo. Office: Smurfit-Stone Container Corp 150 N Michigan Ave Chicago IL 60601-7568*

**MOORE, PATRICK S.,** epidemiologist, researcher, educator; m. Yuan Chang, 1989. MD, U. Utah. With field sta. Ctr. Disease Control and Prevention, Ft. Collins; dep. commr. Health City N.Y., 1992; rschr. Columbia U. Sch. Pub. Health, 1993; prof. dept. molecular genetics and biochemistry U. Pitts. Sch. Medicine, 2002—; dir. molecular virology program U. Pitts. Cancer Inst., 2002—. Mem. editl. bd. Virus Research, Emerging Infectious

Diseases and the Epstein-Barr Virus Report; contbr. articles and revs. in med. lit. Recipient Meyenburg Found. award cancer rsch., Robert Koch prize, N.Y.C. Mayor's award excellence in sci. and tech., Charles S. Mott prize, GM Cancer Rsch. Found., 2003. Achievements include discovery of and characterized the causative agent of Kaposi's Sarcoma-associated Herpes virus (KSHV) or human herpes virus 8 (HHV8), also is linked to other disorders that involve a compromised immune system.*

**MOORE, PATSY SITES,** food service consultant; b. San Marcos, Tex., Mar. 29, 1939; d. Sam W. and Hilda (Wiede) Sites. BS in Home Econs. Edn., S.W. Tex. State U., 1970. Owner, operator Westoner Kindergarten and Nursery Sch., San Marcos, 1965-68; food svc. dir. San Marcos Consol. Ind. Sch. Dist., 1975-97; cons. to food svc. industry, San Marcos, 1997—. Cons. in field, 1997—. Mem. steering com. Play Scape/Children's Park, San Marcos, 1992, co-chair Hays County Parks Meml. tree program, 2005-; mem. Hays County Pks. Adv. Bd., City of San Marco Sr. Citizens Adv. Coun.; sr. adv. bd. City of San Marcos, 2000—; adv. bd. Hays County Parks, 1998—; vice chmn. Hays Rep. Club, 2001-2002, sec., 2003, pres. 2006. Mem. Am. Sch. Food Svc. Assn., Tex. Sch. Food Svc. Assn., Ctrl. Tex. Sch. Food Svc. Dir. Assn. (founder, past pres.), Heritage Assn. (mem. bd. dir. 2003-), Order Eastern Star, San Marcos Fedn. Rep. Women (pres.), Pres. Hays Rep. Club, Spring Lake Garden Club (sec. 1999, 2000, pres. 2002-03). Lutheran. Avocations: gardening, painting, lapadary. Home and Office: 285 Hilliard Rd San Marcos TX 78666-8905 Office Phone: 512-392-4848. Personal E-mail: pmoore@sanmarcos.net.

**MOORE, PEARL B.,** nursing educator; b. Pitts., Aug. 25, 1936; d. Hyman and Ethel (Antis) Friedman; 1 child, Cheryl. BS in Nursing, U. Pitts., 1968, M in Nursing, 1974. Staff nurse Allegheny Gen. Hosp., Pitts., 1957-60; instr. Liliane S Kaufman Sch. Nursing, Pitts., 1960-70, asst. dir., 1970, dir., 1970-72; cancer nurse specialist Montefiore Hosp., Pitts., 1974-75; coord. Brain Tumor Study Group, Pitts., 1975-83; adj. asst. prof. U. Pitts. 1983—. Contbr. articles in field to profl. publs. Fellow Am. Acad. Nursing; mem. ANA, Oncology Nursing Soc. (exec. dir. 1983—, CEO 1999, Disting. Svc. award 1995), Am. Soc. Clin. Oncology, Am. Soc. Assn. Execs., Nurses Alumnae U. Pitts., Sigma Theta Tau. Home: 5701 Centre Ave Pittsburgh PA 15206 Office: 125 Enterprise Dr Pittsburgh PA 15275

**MOORE, POWELL ALLEN,** former federal agency administrator; b. Milledgeville, Ga., Jan. 5, 1938; s. Jere N. and Sarah (Allen) Moore; m. Pamla Hill Prochnow, Sept. 29, 2001; children: Frances Moore Preston, Powell Allen Jr. BA in Jounalism, U. Ga., 1959. Press sec. to Senator Richard Russell US Senate, Washington, 1966-71; dep. dir. pub. info. US Dept. Justice, Washington, 1971-72; dep. spl. asst. to Pres. for legis. affairs The White House, Washington, 1973-75, cons. pub. affairs, 1975-81, dep. asst. to Pres. for legis. affairs, 1981-82; asst. sec. for congl. rels. US Dept. State, Washington, 1982-83; v.p. legis. affairs Lockheed Corp., Washington, 1983-85, Ginn, Edington, Moore and Wade, Washington, 1985-90; pres. ASL Internat., Washington, 1990-93; sr. prin., mng. dir. Capitoline, MS&L, Washington, 1993-98; chief of staff Office of Sen. Fred Thompson, Washington, 1998-2001; asst. sec. for legis. affairs US Dept. Def., Washington, 2001—05; mng. dir., fed. govt. relations McKenna Long & Aldridge LLP, Washington, 2005—. Dir. press Com. to Re-elect the Pres., Washington, 1972; cons. Pres. Ford Com., 1976, Reagan-Bush Com., 1980. Served to capt., inf. U.S. Army, 1959-62. Recipient Def. Dept.'s medal for Disting. Pub. Svc., 2005. Mem. Belle Haven Country Club, Republican. Episcopalian. Office: McKenna Long & Aldridge LLP 1900 K St NW Washington DC 20006 E-mail: pmoore@mckennalong.com.

**MOORE, RACHEL SUZANNE,** performing company executive, dancer; b. Davis, Calif., Feb. 19, 1965; d. Charles Vincent and Patricia (Dudley) M. BA, Brown U., 1992; MA, Columbia U., 1994. Dancer Am. Ballet Theatre II, N.Y.C., 1982-84, 1984—88; devel. officer Nat. Cultural Alliance, Wash., 1994—95; dir., coord. Center for Cmty. Devel. & Arts Americans for the Arts, Wash., 1995—97; mng. dir. Ballet Theater of Boston, Boston, 1998; exec. dir. Project STEP, Boston, 1998—2001; dir. Boston Ballet Center for Dance Ed., Boston, 2001—04; exec. dir. Amer. Ballet Theatre, NYC, 2004—. Adjunct dance prof. Emerson Coll., Boston U. Presidential scholar U.S. Dept. of Edn., Washington, 1982. Mem. Am. Guild of Mus. Artists. Democrat. Unitarian Universalist. Office: Am Ballet Theatre 890 Broadway Fl 3D New York NY 10003-1211

**MOORE, RICHARD ALAN,** landscape architect, b. St. Louis, Jan. 17, 1930; s. Ira Mack and Helen Adoline (Fakes) M.; m. Patricia Ruth Burke, Mar. 15, 1952 (div. 1967); children: Sheryl Louise, Richard Dennis, Sara Lynn, Sandra Lee. BS, U. Mo., 1951; MLA, U. Oreg., 1957. Registered landscape architect, Calif., Hawaii. Asst. prof. landscape architecture Calif. State Poly. Coll., Pomona, 1957-61; assoc. prof., head dept. landscape architecture N.C. State U., Raleigh, 1962-67; pvt. practice landscape architecture Pomona, Calif., 1957-61; dir. land devel. and planning Oceanic Properties Inc., Honolulu, 1967-69; pvt. practice Honolulu, 1969-70, 79—; dir. ops. Eckbo, Dean, Austin & Williams, Honolulu, 1970-71, v.p. ops., 1971-73; pres. EDAW, Inc., San Francisco, 1973-76, chmn. bd., 1976-78; prof. landscape architecture Tex. A&M U., Bryan, 1977-79. Prin. works include Whispering Pines Motor Lodge, N.C., 1964 (award of merit N.C. chpt. AIA 1964), North Shore Devel. Plan, Kauai, Hawaii, 1973, Comprehensive Zoning Ordinance, County of Kauai, 1973 (Am. Soc. Landscape Architects honor award 1973, HUD honor award 1974); Lihue Devel. Plan, Kauai, 1975, Koloa, Poipu, Kalaheo Devel. Plan, Kauai, 1978, Gen. Plan Update, Kauai, 1982, Mililani Town Plan, 1967-69 (Am. Soc. Landscape Architects merit award 1970), Lanai Land Mgmt. and Devel. Study, 1969 (Am. Soc. Landscape Architects merit award 1970), Wailea Master Devel. Plan, 1971, Kukuiula Devel. Plan, 1983, Lanai Project Dist. Master Plan, 1983-89, Maliu Ridge Devel. Plan, North Kohala, 1985, Mililani Mauka Devel. Plan, 1988 Devel. Plan, Lanai City Consol. Dist., 1990, Dandan Golf Course, Guam, 1991. Fst lt. U.S. Army, 1951-53, Korea. Fellow Am. Soc. Landscape Architects; mem. Masons. Avocations: sports, drawing, painting.

**MOORE, RICHARD KERR,** electrical engineering educator; b. St. Louis, Nov. 13, 1923; s. Louis D. and Nina (Megown) M.; m. Wilma Lois Schallau, Dec. 10, 1944 (dec. 1999); children: John Richard, Daniel Charles. BS, Washington U. at St. Louis, 1943; PhD, Cornell U., 1951. Test equipment engr. RCA, Camden, NJ, 1943-44; instr. elec. engring. Washington U., St. Louis, 1947-49; rsch. assoc. Cornell U., 1949-51; rsch. engr., sect. supr. Sandia Corp., Albuquerque, 1951-55; prof., chmn. elec. engring. U. N.Mex., 1955-62; Black and Veatch prof. U. Kans., Lawrence, 1962-94; prof. emeritus, 1994—; dir. remote sensing lab. U. Kans., 1964-74, 84-93. Pres. Cadre Corp., Lawrence, 1968-87; cons. U.S., govt. agys. Author: Traveling Wave Engineering, 1960; co-author: (with Ulaby and Fung) Microwave Remote Sensing, Vol. I, 1981; Vol. II, 1982, Vol. III, 1986; contbr. to profl. jours. and handbooks. Lt. (j.g.) USNR, 1944-46. Recipient Achievement award Washington U. Engring. Alumni Assn., 1978, Outstanding Tech. Achievement award IEEE Geosci. and Remote Sensing Soc., 1982, Louise E. Byrd Grad. Educator award U Kans., 1984, Irving Youngberg Rsch. award U. Kans., 1989, Australia prize, 1995. Fellow AAAS, IEEE (sect. chmn. 1960-61, Outstanding Tech. Achievement award coun. oceanic engring. 1978); mem., NAE, AAUP, Am. Soc. Engring. Edn., Am. Geophys. Union, Internat. Sci. Radio Union (chmn. U.S. commn. F 1984-87, internat. vice chmn. commn. F 1990-93, chmn. 1993-96), Kiwanis, Sigma Xi, Tau Beta Pi. Presbyterian (past elder). Achievements include research in submarine communications, radar altimetry, radar as a remote sensor, radar oceanography; patent for polypanchromatic radar. Home: 1712 Carmel Dr Lawrence KS 66047-1840 Office: U Kans R S & Remote Sensing Lab 2335 Irving Hill Rd Lawrence KS 66045-7612 Personal E-mail: rmoore@sunflower.com.

**MOORE, RICHARD LAWRENCE,** structural engineer, consultant; b. Rocky Ford, Colo., Feb. 7, 1934; s. Lawrence and Margaret Kathryn (Bolling) M.; m. Donna St. Clair, Mar. 26, 1972 (div. 1983); 1 child, Andrew Trousdale; m. Margaret Ann Guthrie, May 4, 1984. BSCE, U. Colo., 1957; MS,

Princeton U., 1963; PhD, Calif. Western U., Santa Ana, 1975. Registered profl. engr., Mass., Maine, Colo., Pa., Iowa, Nebr., N.Mex., Wyo., Ill., Ark., Mo., ND, Mich., Okla., Mont., N.H. Structural engr. Cameron Engrs., Denver, 1964-66; v.p. Moore Internat., Jeddah, Saudi Arabia, 1967-78; asst. to pres. C.H. Guernsey Co., Oklahoma City, 1979-82; pres. R.L. Moore Co., Boston, 1983—; v.p., dir. Isolink Ing., Basel, Switzerland, 1990—. Nat. chmn. Roof Cons. Inst., Raleigh, N.C., 1988-92; prof. Episcopal Sch. Theology, Denver, 1967-71. Patentee in field. Member Mound City (Mo.) Libr. Bd., 1963-64; pres. Dist. Rep. Party, Boston, 1984—; sr. warden St. John Chrysostom Epis. Ch., Denver, 1966-71. Danforth Found. scholar, 1962. Mem. ASCE, NSPE, Am. Concrete Inst., Nat. Forensic Ctr. Avocations: golf, travel, antique pocket watch collecting. Home and Office: RL Moore Co 534 E Broadway Boston MA 02127-4407

**MOORE, RICHARD WAYNE,** electric power industry executive, former prosecutor; b. Bartow, Fla., Dec. 5, 1952; s. James Ferrell and Mary Etta (Carlisle) M.; m. Elizabeth Ann Mitchell, Sept. 1, 1984; children: Michaelan Susan, John Mark. BS summa cum laude, Spring Hill Coll., 1974; JD, Samford U., 1977. Bar: Ala. 1977, U.S. Dist. Ct. Ala. 1977. Assoc. Marr & Friedlander, Mobile, Ala., 1977-79; ptnr. Sherling, Drinkard & Moore, Mobile, Ala., 1979-81; assoc. Gibbs & Craze, Cleve., 1981-85; sr. litigation counsel U.S. Atty.'s Office, Mobile, 1985—2003; insp. gen. TVA, Knoxville, Tenn., 2003—. Atlantic fellow in Pub. Policy U.K., Oxford, Eng., 1997. Mem. Mobile County Bar Assn., Paul Brock Mobile Inn of Ct. Anglican. Avocation: hunting. Office: TVA E Tower 400 W Summit Hill Dr Rm 4C Knoxville TN 37902

**MOORE, ROBERT E.,** college president; BA in Secondary Edn., Shepherd Coll , 1970; MS in Edn. and Phys. Edn., W.Va. U., 1972, EdD in Curriculum and Instrn., 1976. Chair, divsn. phys. edn. and recreation Bluefield (W.Va.) State Coll., 1974-77, asst. dean tech. edn., 1977-81, dean of curriculum, 1981-89, v.p., dean acad. affairs, 1989-91, vice-pres./dean cmty. and tech. coll., 1991-93, pres., 1993—2002. Mem. W.Va. Joint Commn. on Vocat., Tech. and Occpl. Edn.; mem. numerous civic exec. bds. Mem. Am. Assn. Colls. for Tchr. Edn., W.Va. Assn. Cmty. Colls. for Tchr. Edn., W.Va. Assn. Cmty. Colls. (exec. bd., award 1992), Am. Assn. Cmty. Colls., Phi Delta Kappa, others. Office: Bluefield State Coll 219 Rock St Bluefield WV 24701-2100

**MOORE, ROBERT ERIC,** artist; b. Manchester, N.H., Oct. 13, 1927; s. George Anthony and Verna Winona (Blaisdell) M.; m. Margaret Doherty, June 2, 1950; children: Deirdre, Bridget, Michael O'Doherty. Student, New England Sch. Art, 1949-51, U.N.H. 1963-64. One-man shows include Allerbescht Gallery, Telford, Pa., Bayberry Art Gallery, Southern Pines, N.C., Benbow Gallery, Newport, R.I., Copley Soc., Boston, Doll and Richards, Boston, Frost Gully Gallery, Portland, Maine, The Gallery, Spartenburg, S.C., Guild of Boston Artists, Hancock Coll. Art, Santa Maria, Calif., Hobe Sound Galleries North, Portland, John Black Gallery, Cold Spring Harbor, N.Y., Loft Gallery, Princeton, N.J., Munson Gallery, New Haven, Conn., Ogunquit (Maine) Gallery, and others; exhibited in numerous group shows; represented in several permanent collections. Juror Audubon Artists 49th Annual Exhbn., N.Y.C., 1991, Annual New England Watercolor Exhbn., Boston, 1989, Audubon Artists 47th Annual Exhbn., N.Y.C., 1989, Adirondacks Nat. Exhbn Am. Watercolor, 1988; nat. juror 118th Annual Am. Watercolor Soc. Exhbn., N.Y.C., 1985. Recipient Cavanaugh award Springfield Mus. Art, 1962, Copley prize Copley Soc. Boston, 1967, Yankee Mag. award, 1967, Arches Paper award, 1977, Griffey's TV award Nat. Watercolor Soc., 1978, Watercolor award N.Mex. Art League, 1978, St. Vincent's Hosp. award Watercolor Soc. Ala., 1981, William Kowalsky prize, 1983, High Winds medal 118th Annual Am. Watercolor Exhbn., 1985, Pulsifer award, 1987, Dick Blick award La. Watercolor Soc., 1987, Garnet award Adirondacks Nat. Exhbn. Am. Watercolors, 1991, 1st prize Transparent Watercolor Soc. Am., 2005, and others. Fellow Am. Watercolor Soc. (Winsor and Newton award 1984, Dale Myers Cooper medal 1985, Internat. Waters travel exhbn. award 1991-92); mem. Nat. Acad. Design (assoc. 1991, Adolph and Clara Obrig prize 1991), Allied Artists Am. (David Soloway Meml. award 1989, Dr. Clifford W. Mills award 1986, Orion Nova Ltd. award 1982, Grumbacher Artists Materials Co. silver medal 1982), Audubon Artists (Grumbacher Gold medallion 1987). Avocations: hunting, fishing.

**MOORE, ROBERT HENRY,** writer, editor, communications consultant; b. Madisonville, Ky., Sept. 16, 1940; s. William Lee Moore and Robbie (Pritchett) Ruby; m. Diana Churchill, Aug. 17, 1963 (div. 1978); children: Randall Lee, Robin Churchill; m. Patricia Mary George, Oct. 4, 1981; 1 child, Christopher Robert. BA, Davidson (N.C.) Coll., 1962; MA, U. N.C., 1964; PhD, U. Wis., 1972. Asst. dir. admissions Davidson Coll., 1963-64; teaching asst. U. Wis., Madison, 1965-68; staff and faculty U.S. Mil. Acad., West Point, NY, 1968-70; lectr. asst. prof. U. Md., College Park, 1970-76, assoc. prof., 1976; cons. U.S. Congress, Washington, 1976-77; emerging issues coordinator The Conf. Bd., N.Y.C., 1977-79; dir. govt. relations Benefacts, Inc., Washington, 1977-78; v.p. Alexander & Alexander, Inc., Washington, 1978-81, Alexander & Alexander Svcs., Inc., N.Y.C., Washington, 1981-85, sr. v.p. corp. rels., 1985-95, sr. v.p. (inactive), 1995-97; chmn., pres. A & A Govt. and Industry Affairs Inc., Washington, 1990-94, Aon Corp., Vienna, Va., 1997—2005. Del. Nat. Security Affairs Conf., Washington, 1978-82; mem. adv. bd. Career Opportunities Inst., U. Va., Charlottesville, 1982-86, Ctr. for New Am. Work Force, 1992-96; mem. corp. adv. bd. Queens Coll., CUNY, 1985-96; mem. V.P.'s Forum, 1989-94; mem. coun. Conf. Bd. Com. Execs., 1990-94; mem. Pub. Rels. Sem., 1993-97; editl. advisor Ctr. for Mind-Body Medicine, Washington, 1998-2000; adv. coun. Mindfulness Practice Ctr. of Fairfax, 1998—; bd. visitors Dictionary of Am. Regional English, 1999—; adv. to chmn. NEH, 1999-2001. Co-author: (with others) School for Soldiers: West Point and the Profession of Arms, 1974 (NYT award 1974), Spreading the Risks: Insuring the American Experience, 2000 (Washington Book Pubs. award 2003), Risk Management, 2004 (Book of the Year), Revised Edit., 2005; contbr. articles to profl. jours.; contbr. interviews to nat. mags., newspapers, radio and TV. Mem. kitchen cabinet Points of Light Found., 1991-95. With U.S. Army, 1968-70, capt. USAR, 1970-72. Ops. Crossroads Africa fellow, 1960; U. Md. rsch. grantee, 1972, 76. Mem. Nat. Assn. Ins. Brokers (exec. com., bd. dirs., pres. 1985-86, chmn. past presidents adv. coun. 1989-93).

**MOORE, ROBERT LOWELL, JR., (ROBIN MOORE),** author; b. Boston, Oct. 31, 1925; s. Robert Lowell Sr. and Eleanor (Turner) M.; m. Barbara Luther, 1948 (div.1949); 1 child, Lacy; m. Joan Friedman, Sept. 15, 1952 (div. 1955); 1 child, Margo Joan; m. Mary Olga Troshkin, Feb. 17, 1973 (dec. April 2, 2005); m. Helen Edelston, June 29, 2005. AB, Harvard U., 1949. European corr. Boston Globe, 1947; ind. TV prodr. N.Y.C., 1949-52; dir. pub. rels. Sheraton Corp., Am., Boston, 1952- 54, dir. advt. and pub. rels., 1954-56, bd. dirs., 1954-62. Author: Pitchman, 1956, The Devil to Pay, 1961, The Green Berets, 1965, The Country Team, 1967, Fiedler, 1968, The French Connection, 1969, Court Martial, 1970, The Khaki Mafia, 1971, The Fifth Estate, 1974, Compulsion, 1982; (with Xaviera Hollander) The Happy Hooker, 1972, The Treasure Hunter, 1975, Dubai, 1976, Mafia Wife, 1977, The Banksters, 1977, Rhodesia, 1978, The Big Paddle, 1978, Search and Destroy, 1978, The Washington Connection, 1979; (with Milt Machlin) The Family Man, 1985, Force nine, 1987, The Man Who Made It Snow, 1990, The White Tribe, 1991, The Moscow Connection, 1994, the Hunt for Bin Laden (N.Y.Times Bestseller), 2003, Hunting Down Saddam, 2004; co-author: (with Raymond Flynn) Accidental Pope, 2000; screenwriter: The Green Berets, 1967, The French Connection, 1971, The Happy Hooker, 1973, Hocovn, 1979, Hoffa, 1985, The Sparrowhook Curse, 1996. With USAAF, 1944-46, ETO. Decorated Air medal with two bronze oak leaf clusters. Mem. Met. Club (N.Y.C.). Achievements include developing pvt. TV closed circuit network for hotels. Personal E-mail: rmoore31@aol.com.

**MOORE, ROBERT MADISON,** food products executive, lawyer; b. New Orleans, June 21, 1925; s. Clarence Greer and Anna Omega (Odendahl) M.; m. Evelyn Eileen Varva, Apr. 11, 1953; children: Eileen Alexandria Moore Wynne, John Greer. BBA, Tulane U., 1947; JD, U. Va., 1952; LLM (Food

Law Inst. fellow), NYU, 1953. Bar: La. 1956, Calif. 1972. Asst. to pres., gen. counsel Underwear Inst., N.Y.C., 1953-55; pvt. practice law New Orleans, 1955-56; asst. gen. atty., dir. Legal services, sec. and gen. atty. Standard Fruit & Steamship Co., New Orleans, 1957-72; v.p., gen. counsel Castle & Cooke Foods, 1972-81, Castle & Cooke, Inc., 1973-81, sr. v.p. law and govt., 1981-82; pres. Internat. Banana Assn., 1983-98; acting exec. dir. Pan Am. Devel. Found., 1999. Dir. Ferson Optics of Del., Inc., 1958-69, Baltime Securities Corp., Pan American Devel. Found. Asst. atty. gen., La., 1960-66. Served with AUS, 1943-46. Mem. ABA, Calif. Bar Assn., La. Bar Assn., SAR (sec. 1960-61), KM, Cosmos Club, Phi Delta Phi, Alpha Tau Omega. Democrat. Roman Catholic. Home: 3323 R St NW Washington DC 20007-2310 E-mail: rmevmoore@aol.com.

**MOORE, ROBERT WILLIAM,** professional organization executive; b. Claysburg, Pa., June 4, 1924; s. Frank B. and Sarah A. (Edelbute) M.; m. Helen Lingenfelter, July 17, 1948; children: Thomas R., Priscilla Jane. BA, Pa. State U., 1948. With Price Waterhouse & Co., Pitts., 1948-62, mgr., 1955-62; asst. contr. Con-Gas Svc. Corp., Pitts., 1962-65, Consol. Natural Gas Svc. Co., Inc., Pitts., 1966-72, contr., 1972-78, Consol. Natural Gas Co., Pitts., 1972-78; pres. Fin. Execs. Inst., Morristown, NJ, 1978-89, pres. emeritus, 1989—. Mem. Fin. Acctg. Standards Adv. Coun., 1978-89. Bd. dirs. Central Blood Bank, Pitts., 1960-78, treas. corp., 1962-68, chmn. finance com., 1962-68, chmn. bd., 1969-72; mem. exec. bd. Pa. State U. Alumni Council, 1975-83; mem. exec. com. Campaign for Pa. State U., bd. vis.; pres. Pa. State Coll. Bus. Adminstrn. Soc., 1981-83. Served with AUS, 1943-45. Mem. Am., Pa. insts. C.P.A.s, Inst. of Mgmt. Acct., Fin. Execs. Inst., Pa. State U. Alumni Assn., Pa. Soc., Beta Alpha Psi (nat. forum), Delta Tau Delta. Clubs: University (dir., pres. 1975-76), Valley Brook Country (dir. 1968-70, v.p. bd. 1970), Duquesne (Pitts.), University, St. Clair Country. Episcopalian. E-mail: rmoorepgh@msn.com.

**MOORE, ROBERT YATES,** neuroscience educator; b. Harvey, Ill., Dec. 5, 1931; s. Raymon Irwin and Marie Louise (Fischer) M.; children: Elizabeth Allen, Matthew McCormick, Joshua Gilbert, Thomas Douglas. BA magna cum laude, Lawrence U., 1953; MD with honors, U. Chgo., 1957, PhD, 1962; MD (hon.), Lund U., Sweden, 1974. Diplomate: Am. Bd. Psychiatry and Neurology. Intern Univ. Hosp., Ann Arbor, Mich., 1958-59; resident U. Chgo., 1959-64, asst. prof. neurology and anatomy, 1964-66, assoc. prof., 1966-70, prof., 1970-74; prof. neurosci. U. Calif., San Diego, 1974-79; prof., chmn. dept. neurology SUNY, Stony Brook, 1979-90; prof. psychiatry, neurology and neurosci. U. Pitts., 1990—, chmn. dept. neurology, 1992-2000. Cons. Contbr. numerous articles to profl. jours. Recipient numerous grants. Fellow Am. Acad. Neurology; mem. Am. Neurol. Assn., Soc. Neurosci., Internat. Brain Research Orgn., Am. Assn. Anatomists. Office: U Pitts Dept Neurology 3471 5th Ave Ste 811 Pittsburgh PA 15213-3232

**MOORE, ROGER ADDISON,** pediatrician, anesthesiologist; b. Portsmouth, Va., 1948; MD, U. Va., 1973. Diplomate: Am. Bd. Pediatrics, Am. Bd. Anesthesiology. Intern Colo. Affil. Hosps., Denver, 1974-75, resident in pediatrics, 1975-77; resident in anesthesiology Hosp. U. Pa., Phila., 1977-79; fellow in pediat. anesthesiology, CCM Children's Hosp., Phila., 1979; chmn. anesthesiology dept. Deborah Heart - Lung Ctr., Browns Mills, NJ, 1993—2004, chair emeritus, 2004—; assoc. prof. anesthesiology U. Pa., 1988-97, clin. assoc. prof. anesthesiology, 1998—. Mem. AMA, Am. Assn. Pediatrics, Am. Soc. Anesthesiologists (treas. 2003—), Soc. Cardiovasc. Anesthesiologists (pres. 2001-03), Alpha Omega Alpha, others. Office: Deborah Heart & Lung Ctr Browns Mills NJ 08015 Address: Soc Cardiovascular Anesthesiologists PO Box 11086 Richmond VA 23230-1086 Office Phone: 609-893-6611. Personal E-mail: rogermoore435@yahoo.com.

**MOORE, ROY DEAN,** retired judge; b. Chickasha, Okla., Jan. 15, 1940; s. Frank B. and Delia Pauline (Morgan) M.; m. Carolyn Kaye Wood, Aug. 10, 1962; children—Darla Kaye, Jared Dean, Amy Darise. BA, Central State U., 1962, M. Teaching. 1966; JD, Oklahoma City U., 1970; grad., Nat. Coll. State Trial Judges, 1972. Bar: Okla. 1970. Coach debate, instr. dramatics Kingfisher (Okla.) High Sch., 1962-67; instr. English and journalism, head dept. lang. arts. Jarman Jr. High Sch., Midwest City, Okla., 1967-70; pros. atty. City of Lawton, Okla., 1970; spl. dist. judge 5th Jud. Dist. Okla., 1971-72; pvt. practice law Lawton, 1972; dist. judge 5th Jud. Dist. Okla., 1990—2002. Pres. Swinney PTA, 1975-76; Editor: Problems in Teaching in the Secondary School, 1966. Pres. Comanche County Mental Health Assn., 1973-74, bd. dirs., 1972-76; co-chmn. Kingfisher County Reps. for Congressman James V. Smith, 1966; mem. state exec. com. Okla. Republican Com., 1973-74, chmn. auditing com., 1977-78; del. Rep. Nat. Conv., 1976; chmn. cts. com. Assn. South Central Okla. Govts. Crime Commn.; chmn. Comanche County Reps. for Reagan for Pres., 1973-83; mem. adv. bd. Jim Taliferro Mental Health Center, 1977-78; del. Nat. Mental Health Conv., 1975; bd. dirs. Lawton Campfire Girls; elder N.W. Ch. of Christ, 1977—; dir. Back to Bible Campaigns, 1976-2002. Named Outstanding Dist. Judge in State of Okla., Okla. Trial Lawyers Assn., 1999. Mem. Am., Okla., Comanche County bar assns., Okla. Trial Lawyers Assn., Lawton Antique Auto Club, Ford Retractible Club Am., Alpha Psi Omega, Delta Theta Phi. Republican. Mem. Ch. of Christ (elder). Clubs: Fraternal Order of Police, Lion. Home: 2114 NW Atlanta Ave Lawton OK 73505-3923 Personal E-mail: voka1@sbcglobal.net.

**MOORE, ROY S.,** former state supreme court chief justice; m. Kayla Moore; children: Heather, Roy, Caleb, Micah. BS, U.S. Mil. Acad., 1969; JD, U. Ala., 1977. Dep. dist. atty. Etowah County, Ala., 1977—82; pvt. practice Gadsden, Ala., 1982—92; cir. judge 16th Judicial Cir., Gadsden, 1992—2001; chief justice Ala. Supreme Ct., 2001—03. Captain Military Police Corps U.S. Army. Recipient George Washington Honor medal, Nat. Freedom Found., 1995, Bill of Rights award, 1997, God and Country award, Am. Family Assn., 1997, Spirit of Am. Founders award, 1997, Liberty & Union award, N.H. Ctr. for Constitutional Studies, 1998, Nat. Spirit of Life award, African Am. Family Assn., 1999, Nat. Hero of Faith award, Vision Am. Houston, 2002, Stonewall Jackson award, Vision Forum, 2003, Warriors Medal of Valor, Native Am. Nations of the U.S., 2004. Republican. Baptist.

**MOORE, SALLY FALK,** anthropology educator; b. NYC, Jan. 18, 1924; d. Henry Charles and Mildred (Hymanson) Falk; m. Cresap Moore, July 14, 1951; children: Penelope, Nicola. BA, Barnard Coll., 1943; LL.B., Columbia U., 1945, PhD, 1957. Asst. prof. U. So. Calif., Los Angeles, 1963-65, assoc. prof., 1965-70, prof., 1970-77, UCLA, 1977-81; prof. anthropology Harvard U., Cambridge, Mass., 1981—, Victor Thomas prof. anthropology, 1991—, dean Grad. Sch. Arts and Scis., 1985-89. Author: Power and Property in Inca Peru, (Ansley Prize 1957), 1958, Law as Process, 1978, Social Facts and Fabrications, 1986, Moralizing States, 1993, Anthropology and Africa, 1994, Law and Anthropology, 2005. Trustee Barnard Coll., Columbia U., 1991-92; master Dunster House, 1984—89. Grantee Social Sci. Rsch. Coun., 1968-69, NSF, 1972-75, 79-80, Wenner Gren Found., 1983; Guggenheim fellow, 1995-96. Fellow Am. Acad. Arts & Scis., Am. Anthrop. Assn., Royal Anthrop. Inst. (Huxley medallist, lectr. for 1999); mem. Am. Philos. Soc., Assn. Polit. and Legal Anthropology (pres. 1983), Am. Ethnological Soc. (pres. 1987-88), Assn. Africanist Anthropologists (pres.-elect 1995, pres. 1996-98), Law and Soc. Assn. (Kalven prize 2005) Democrat. Office: Harvard U 350 William James Hall Cambridge MA 02138

**MOORE, SCOTT,** former state official; b. York, Nebr., 1960; m. Danene Tushar, 1989. BA in Polit. Sci., U. Nebr. Legis. aide Nebr. Legislature, 1981-86, mem., 1986-94, chair appropriations com., 1991-94; sec. of state State of Nebr., 1995—2000; dir. gov. affairs Union Pacific R.R., 2000—. With Moore & Sons. Office: Union Pacific RR 1416 Dodge St Room 801 Omaha NE 68179 Home: 664 N 56th St Omaha NE 68132-2118

**MOORE, SHEMAR,** actor; b. Oakland, Calif., Apr. 20, 1970; B in communications, Santa Clara Univ. Actor: (TV series) Living Single, 1995, The Jamie Foxx Show, 1996, Arli$$, 1997, Chicago Hope, 1998, Moesha, 1999, For Your Love, 1999, Malcolm & Eddie, 1999, The Young and the Restless, 1994—2002 (Outstanding Supporting Actor Daytime Emmy award,

2000), 2004—05 (Outstanding Actor in Daytime Drama Series, NAACP Image award, 2006), Birds of Prey, 2003, Half & Half, 2004, Criminal Minds, 2005—; (TV films) Mama Flora's Hope, 1998, How To Marry a Billionaire: A Christmas Tale, 2000, Reversible Errors, 2004; (films) Hav Plenty, 1997, Butter, 1998, Box Marley, 2000, The Brothers, 2001, Motives, 2004, The Seat Filler, 2004, Greener, 2004, Diary of a Mad Black Woman, 2005. Mailing: c/o CBS Television City 7800 Beverly Blvd Los Angeles CA 90036*

**MOORE, SHERRY MILLS,** lawyer; b. 1951; m. Tim Moore; 2 children. BA, Beloit Coll.; JD, Univ. ND, 1979. Pvt. practice, Bismarck, ND. Bd. mem. Mental Health Assn. of ND, Prevent Child Abuse ND; pres. Bismarck Library Bd.; chair Mayor's Task Force on Methamphetamine. Named Vol. Lawyer of Yr., Big Muddy Bar Assn., 2000. Mem.: State Bar Assn. of ND (pres. 2004). Avocations: photography, reading, jetskiing. Office: 300 N 4th St PO Box 4144 Bismarck ND 58502-4144

**MOORE, STANLEY WAYNE,** political science professor; b. Camden, N.J., Feb. 11, 1937; s. Frank Stafford and Alma Beatrice (Law) M.; m. Nancy Joan Crawford, Sept. 1, 1961; children: David Crawford, Andrea Katrina, Stanley Edward Stafford Moore, Sonia Elizabeth. AB magna cum laude, Wheaton Coll., 1959; MA and PhD in Govt., Claremont Grad. U., 1971. Asst. prof. polit. sci. Calif. State U.-Stanislaus, Turlock, 1967—69, Monterey Inst. for Internat. Studies, Calif., 1969—72; vis. assoc. U. Redlands, Calif., 1972—73; assoc. prof. Pepperdine U., Malibu, Calif., 1973—79, prof. polit. sci., 1979—. Pres. Calif. Ctr. for Edn. in Pub. Affairs, Inc., 1991-2002. Author: A Child's Political World: A Longitudinal Perspective, 1985; contbr. articles to profl. jours. Scoutmaster troop 761 Boy Scouts Am., 1982-92, adv. bd. L.A. Area Coun., 1993—, chair advancement com., 1994-98; vice chmn. Ventura County Air Pollution Control Bd., 1981-92; mem. Ventura County Beyond the Yr. 2000 Commn., 1988-90, Nat. Dem. Com., Calif. Dem. Com., Christians in Polit. Sci.; bd. dirs. Calif. Bicentennial Found. for U.S. Constn. 1987-91; moderator Camps and Conf. Ministry Bd., 1998-2004; bd. dirs. L.A. chpt. Christians for Biblical Equality, Staff of Hope, Christians Empowering for Reconciliation with Justice; elder Presbyn. Ch., USA, del. Gen. Assembly, 2000; elected to Hist. Highland Pk. Neighborhood Coun., 2002—; mem. senate Congress L.A. Neighborhood Couns., 2006—. Recipient Medal of Honor, Boy Scouts Am., 1989; grantee Spencer Found. Chgo., 1979, 81. Fellow Am. Sci. Affiliation; mem. Am. Polit. Sci. Assn., W. Polit. Sci. Assn., So. Calif. Polit. Sci. Assn., Boat Owners Assn. So. Calif., Audubon Soc., Nat. Wildlife Fedn., Highland Pk. C. of C. (bd. dirs., sec. 2005—), Kiwanis (bd. dirs. 2003—). Presbyterian (elder). Avocations: backpacking, fishing, photography, reading, ch. activities. Office: Pepperdine U Dept Polit Sci Malibu CA 90263 Office Phone: 323-256-1024, 310-505-4372. Personal E-mail: revdrmoore@sbcglobal.net.

**MOORE, STEPHEN JAMES,** lawyer; b. Kansas City, Mo., Aug. 9, 1947; s. James Stephen and Frances Clare (Kennedy) M. BSBA, Rockhurst U., 1969, BA. 1975; JD, U. Mo., Kansas City, 1977, LLM, 1997. Bar: Mo. 1978, U.S. Dist. Ct. (we. dist.) Mo. 1978, U.S. Ct. Appeals (8th cir.) 1980, U.S. Ct. Appeals (10th cir.) 1981, U.S. Ct. Fed. Claims 1991, U.S. Ct. Appeals (6th cir.) 1997. Law intern Mo. Atty. Gen.'s Office, Kansas City, 1976-77, asst., 1978; assoc. Popham, Conway, Sweeny, Fremont & Bundschu PC, Kansas City, 1978-84, Freilich, Leitner & Carlisle, PC, Kansas City, 1985, Herrick, Feinstein, Kansas City, 1985-86, Freilich, Leitner, Carlisle & Shortlidge, Kansas City, 1986-90; ptnr. Freilich, Leitner + Carlisle, Kansas City, Dallas, L.A., 1987-2000, Aspen, Colo., 1997-2000, Peters, Moore & Jones, LLC, Kansas City, Mo., 2001—02, Peters & Moore LLC, 2002—04; pvt. law firm Stephen J. Moore, PC, 2005—. Adj. prof. law U. Mo., Kansas City, 1995—. Mem. Friends of Art, Nelson-Atkins Mus. Art, Kansas City, 1988—, Smithsonian Inst., Washington, 1985—, Nat. Trust for Historic Preservation, Washington, 1988—, Libr. of Congress Assocs., The Federalist Soc., Nat. Audubon Soc. Mem. ABA, Assn. Trial Lawyers Am., Kansas City Metro Bar Assn., Sports Car Club Am., Am. Mus. Nat. History, Porsche Club Am., Lake Ozarks Yacht Assn., Boat Owners Assn. U.S., Ancient Order of Hibernians, Delta Theta Phi, Tau Kappa Epsilon. Roman Catholic. Avocations: vintage sportscars, boating. Home: 5840 McGee St Kansas City MO 64113-2132 Office: 1500 Traders on Grand Bld 1125 Grand Ave Kansas City MO 64106 Office Phone: 816-777-1012. Business E-mail: stephen@moorelandlaw.com.

**MOORE, STEVEN E.,** energy executive; Various positions including gen. counsel, v.p., sr. v.p. law & pub. affairs, bd. dirs. OGE Energy Corp., Oklahoma City, 1974—95, pres., COO, 1995-96, chmn., pres., CEO, 1996—. Bd. dir. BOK Fin. Corp., Integris Health. Office: Okla Gas and Elec Co 321 N Harvey Oklahoma City OK 73102*

**MOORE, STEVEN E.,** foundation administrator; b. Palo Alto, Calif. s. Gordon and Betty Moore. BS in Bus. Mgmt., Santa Clara U., 1983. Exec. dir., trustee Gordon & Betty Moore Found., 1986—. Mem. environment council Tech Museum. Avocations: camping, hiking, scuba diving, fishing, skiing, travel. Office: Gordon & Betty Moore Found Presidio of San Francisco PO Box 29910 San Francisco CA 94129-0910*

**MOORE, SUSANNA,** writer; b. Bryn Mawr, Pa., Dec. 9, 1948; d. Richard Dixon and Anne (Shields) M.; 1 child, Lulu Lenane Sylbert. Author: My Old Sweetheart, 1982 (Am. Book award nomination for best first novel 1983, Sue Kaufman prize for first fiction Am. Acad. Inst. Arts and Letters 1983), The Whiteness of Bones, 1989, Sleeping Beauties, 1993, In the Cut, 1995, One Last Look, 2004. Recipient Literary Lion award N.Y. Pub. Libr., 1993, PEN/Ernest Hemingway citation, Sue Kaugman prize, 1983.

**MOORE, SUZAN E.,** lawyer; b. Richlands, Va., Apr. 27, 1960; d. Farrel Ray Moore and Sandra R. Campbell; m. Scott W. Mullins, Dec. 23, 1989. BA with highest honors, U. Tenn., 1982; JD, U. Va., 1985. Bar: Va. 1985, Ky. 1991, W.Va. 1991, US Dist. Ct. (we. dist. Va.) 1985, US Dist. Ct. (so. dist. W. Va.) 1991, US Dist. Ct. (ea. dist. Va.) 1996, US Ct. Appeals (4th cir.) 1985. Assoc. Penn, Stuart, Eskridge & Jones, Abingdon, Va., 1985—89; assoc. gen. counsel Westmoreland Coal Co., Big Stone Gap, 1989—91, asst. gen. counsel, 1991—95; assoc. gen. counsel Pittston Coal Mgmt. Co., Lebanon, 1995—2002, Alpha Natural Resources, LLC, 2003—, asst. v.p. legal, 2003—. Moot ct. explorer post leader Boy Scouts Am., 1988; team diabetes fundraising mem. Walt Disney World Marathon, 2003; bd. dirs. S.W. Va. Legal Aid Soc., 1987—89, United Way S.W. Va., 1992—93, Client Centered Legal Svcs., 1995—2001; bd. trustees William King Regional arts Ctr., 2004—, sec., 2005—. Mem.: ABA, Va. State Bar, Energy & Mineral Law Found. Avocations: fly fishing, mountain biking, hiking, canoeing, skiing. Office: Alpha Natural Resources LLC 406 W Main St Abingdon VA 24210

**MOORE, T. JUSTIN, III,** lawyer; b. Richmond, Va., Nov. 26, 1956; BA cum laude, Princeton U., 1979; MBA, JD, U. Va., 1983. Co-head, Global Capital Markets, Mergers, Acquisitions Team Hunton & Williams LLP, Richmond, Va., 1983—91, ptnr., 1991—, mem. exec. com., 2004—. Bd. dir. Valentine Mus., 1999—; chmn., prof. divsn. United Way, Richmond, 1997—98; bd. trustees Historic Richmond Found., 1984—95, pres., 1991—93; bd. gov. St. Christopher's Sch., 1994—, chmn., 2002—. Mem.: ABA, Va. Bar Assn. Office: Hunton & Williams LLP Riverfront Plz East Tower 951 E Byrd St Richmond VA 23219-4074 Office Phone: 804-788-8464. Office Fax: 804-788-8218. Business E-mail: jmoore@hunton.com.

**MOORE, THOMAS ANDREW,** former medical communications company executive; b. Cambridge, Mass., Jan. 28, 1951; s. Leo B. and Christine (Banios) M.; m. Avril Barton, Nov. 8, 1975; children: Thomas, Diana, Juliet. BA in History, Princeton U., 1973. Brand asst. Procter & Gamble Co., Cin., 1973-84, advt. mgr. Beauty Care, 1984-86, gen. mgr. Vidal Sassoon L.A. 1986-88, v.p. Health Care Cin., 1988-91; pres. Procter & Gamble Can., Toronto, Ont. Can., 1991-92; pres. Health Care Procter & Gamble USA, Cin., 1992-96; group v.p Procter & Gamble Co., Cin., 1992-96; pres., CEO Nelson Communications, 1996—2002, Biopure Corp., Cambridge, Mass., 2002—04. Treas. Alliance Drug Free Can., Toronto, 1991, 92; chmn. Cin. Ballet Co.,

1986-91; bd. dirs. Am. Health Found., N.Y.C., 1989—2004, Mercy Hosp., Anderson, Ohio, 1993—. Mem. Non Prescription Drug Mfrs. Assn. (vice chmn. 1992—96), Princeton Club, Union Club, Jasna Polana. Avocations: fly fishing, wine collecting, consumption. Office Phone: 617-331-4872. Business E-Mail: mooringsLLC@aol.com.

**MOORE, THOMAS DAVID,** academic administrator; b. Rochester, NY, July 26, 1937; s. Robert Franklin and Hilda (Kennedy) M.; m. Virginia Muller, June 13, 1959; children: Kathleen Mary, Michael David, Thomas David. BSS, St. John Fisher Coll., 1959; MS, SUNY, Brockport, 1962; EdD, Rutgers U., 1966. Tchr. Rochester City Schs., 1959-62; grad. asst. Rutgers U., New Brunswick, NJ, 1963-65; from asst. to full prof. Kent (Ohio) State U., 1965-93, asst. v.p. acad. affairs, 1976-83, v.p. faculty affairs and personnel, 1984-86, provost, v.p. acad. and student affairs 1987-91, prof. emeritus ednl. philosophy, 1991—; provost, v.p. acad. affairs Ctrl. Washington U., 1993-97, prof. edn. and philosophy, 1997—. Roman Catholic. Avocations: sports, films, public affairs, music. Office Phone: 330-524-0688. Personal E-mail: vmoore4860@sbcglobal.net.

**MOORE, THOMAS EDWIN,** biologist, educator, museum director; b. Champaign, Ill. s. Gerald E. and Velma (Lewis) M.; m. E. Eleanor Sifferd, Feb. 4, 1951; children: Deborah S., Melinda S. BS, U. Ill., 1951, MS, 1952, PhD, 1956. Tech. asst. Ill. Natural History Survey, Urbana, 1950-56; instr. zoology U. Mich., Ann Arbor, 1956-59, asst. prof. zoology, 1959-63, assoc. prof. zoology, 1963-66, prof. biology, 1966—2000, curator insects, 1956—2000, dir. exhibit mus., 1988-93. Vis. prof. Orgn. for Tropical Studies, San Jose, Costa Rica, 1970, 72; bd. dirs. Orgn. Tropical Studies, San Jose, 1968-79; mem. steering com. tropical biome U.S. Internat. Biol. Program, 1969-72; mem. conf. planning com. Nat. Inst. for Environment, 1991-92; mem. steering com. Univ. Colloquium on Environ. Rsch. and Edn., 1991-93, grievance com. U. Mich., 1997-98, faculty handbook com., 1997-98. Co-editor: Lectures on Science Education, 1991, 92, 93; Cricket Behavior and Neurobiology, 1989; author movie 17-Year Cicadas, 1975, TV. 1998; co-author: Singing Insects of N.Am. Website, 2003—. County rep. Huron River Watershed Coun., Ann Arbor, 1987-95; mem. Mich. H.S. Accreditation Adv. Com., Ann Arbor, 1988-92; mem. U. Mich. Senate Adv. Com. on Univ. Affairs, 1993-96, vice chair, 1995-96; bd. mem. U. Mich. Acad. Freedom Lecture Fund, 1995—, treas., 1995-98; vol. Kempf House Ctr. for Local History, Ann Arbor, Mich.; cons. NSF Visual Tech. in Environ. Curricula, 1994-97; cons. Misery Bay exhibits ParksCanada, 2003-06. Rsch. grantee NSF, 1963-66, 66-69, 96-97, rsch. equipment grantee, 1984-86, rsch. grantee Def. Advanced Rsch. Project Agy./Office of Naval Rsch. 1998-2001 Fellow AAAS, AAUP (pres. U. Mich. chpt. 1996-99, exec. bd. Mich. conf. 1996-98), Royal Entomol. Soc. London, Linnaen Soc. London; mem. Assn. Tropical Biology (pres. 1973-75), Sigma Xi (pres. U. Mich. chpt. 1994-96, coun. 1993-98) Home: 4243 N Delhi Rd Ann Arbor MI 48103-9485 Office: Mus of Zoology U Mich Ann Arbor MI 48109-1079 Office Phone: 734-763-4766. Business E-Mail: temoore@umich.edu.

**MOORE, THOMAS GALE,** economist, educator; b. Washington DC, Nov. 6, 1930; s. Charles Godwin and Beatrice (McLean) M.; m. Cassandra Chrones, Dec. 28, 1958; children: Charles G., Antonia L. BA, Geroge Washington U., 1957; MA, U. Chgo., 1959, PhD, 1961. Fgn. research analyst Chase Manhattan Bank, N.Y.C., 1960-61; asst. prof. econs. Carnegie Inst. Tech., 1961-65; assoc. prof., then prof. econs. Mich. State U., East Lansing, 1965-74; sr. staff economist Council Econ. Advisers, 1968-70; hon. research fellow Univ. Coll., London, 1973-74; adj. scholar Am. Enterprise Inst., 1971—, CATO Inst., 1982—; sr. fellow Hoover Inst. on War, Revolution and Peace-Stanford U., 1974—, dir. domestic studies program, 1974-85; mem. Council Econ. Advisers, Washington, 1985-89. Mem. Nat. Critical Materials Council, 1985-89; mem. econ. adv. bd. Dept. Commerce, 1971-73; mem. adv. com. RANN, 1975-77, NSF, 1975-77; cons. Dept. Transp., 1973-74, 81-83; mem. adv. panel Synthetic Fuels Corp., 1982; mem. adv. bd. Reason Found., 1982—; dir. Stanford Savs. & Loan, 1979-82, chmn., 1982. Author: The Economics of American Theater, 1968, Freight Transportation Regulation, 1972, Trucking Regulation: Lessons from Europe, 1976, Uranium Enrichment and Public Policy, 1978, Climate of Fear: Why We Shouldn't Worry About Global Warming, 1998; co-author: Public Claims on U.S. Output, 1973; contbr. articles to profl. jours. Served with USN, 1951-55, Korea. Fellow Earhart Found., 1958-59; fellow Walgreen Found., 1959-60, Hoover Instn., 1973-74 Mem. Am. Econ. Assn., Mont. Pelerin Soc., Chevy Chase Club. Home: 3766 La Donna Ave Palo Alto CA 94306-3150 Office: Stanford U Hoover Instn Stanford CA 94305 Office Phone: 650-723-1411. Business E-Mail: moore@hoover.stanford.edu.

**MOORE, THOMAS JOSEPH,** finance company executive; b. Kalamazoo, Jan. 5, 1943; s. John Joseph and Bernita (Ryan) M.; m. Laura Leigh Johnson, Aug. 1, 1975; children: Ryan Michael, Janelle Marie, Darcie Kathleen. BBA, Western Mich. U., 1965; MBA, So. Meth. U., 1990. Various sales and mktg. positions IBM Corp., Southfield, Mich., 1966-78; exec. v.p., owner Carsonville (Mich.) Metal Products Corp., 1976-79; assoc. prof. Oakland Coll., Farmington Hills, Mich., 1977-78; group mgr. industry mktg. Recognition Equipment Inc., Dallas, 1979-81; mgmt. cons. APC Skills div. Alexander Proudfoot Co., Palm Beach, Fla., 1982-83; pres., chief exec. officer Lumentech of Am., Inc., Dallas, 1983-85; v.p., prin. Capital Alliance Corp., Dallas, 1985-2001; ptnr. EquiCap Ptnrs., LLC, Dallas, 2001—; mgr. EquiCap Investments, LLC, Dallas, 2003—; ptnr. Cunningham Partnership LLP, Houston, 2003—. Chmn., CEO, Laura Leigh Stores, Inc. Plano, Tex., 1993—; chmn. Luxury Baths by Arrow, Houston, 2003—; vis. lectr. Baylor U., Waco, Tex., 1986-89, sponsor, CEO roundtable, 1989-93; bd. dirs. MJ Designs, Inc., Coppell, Tex., 1997-98; co-CEO Designer Bath and Kitchen, LLC, 2005—, Luxury Baths of San Antonio, LLC, 2005—; Luxury Baths of Dallas, LLC, 2005—. Pres. Bent Tree Homeowners Assn., Dallas, 1981-83; co-chair Jesuit Coll. Prep. Sch. Challenge Dr., 1992-95; chair car raffle Ursuline Acad. of Dallas, chmn. maj. donor campaign, 1994-95, co-chair bridge the gap campaign, 1995-96, chair underwriting, 1996; chmn. adv. coun., chmn. fin. com. John Paul II H.S., Plano, Tex., 2004. Mem. M&A Internat., So. Meth. U. Exec. MBA Alumni Assn. (bd. dirs. 1990-92). Republican. Roman Catholic. Avocations: running, reading, racquetball, cooking, wine tasting. Home: 4402 Cobblers Ln Dallas TX 75287-6732 Office: EquiCap Ptnrs LLC Park Central III Ste 514 12700 Park Central Dr Dallas TX 75251 Office Phone: 972-233-8282. E-mail: tmoore@equicappartners.com.

**MOORE, THOMAS PAUL,** retired broadcast executive; b. Danville, Ill., Feb. 29, 1928; s. Lester Rufus and Mabel Ellen (Jackson) M.; m. Jean LaVonne Sather, Aug. 31, 1952; children: Randyl Ellen, Patricia Kay, Gregory Sather. BA, North Cen. Coll., Naperville, Ill., 1952; postgrad., Denver U., 1952-53. Newscaster Sta. KFEL-AM-FM-TV, Denver, 1952-54; sales rep. Sta. KGMC, Englewood, Colo., 1954-56; sales mgr. Sta. KDEN-AM-FM, Denver, 1956-62; pres. Stas. WBCO, WQEL, Bucyrus, Ohio, 1962-98; ret., 1998. Hon. dir. First Fed. Cmty. Bank, 2001—. Lay leader, mem. program coun. Ohio Sandusky Conf., United Meth. Ch., 1966-69 (pres. gen. laity bd. and laymen's found. 1968-72); mem. Gen. Coun. on Ministries, 1980-84, N.W. Ohio Water Devel. Adv. Com., 1967-69, Sandusky River Basin Water Pollution Study Com., 1968-69; v.p., bd. mgrs. EUB Men, Evang. United Brethren Ch., 1958-68; pres. Rocky Mountain Conf., 1957-61; mem. gen. bd. Nat. Coun. Christian Chs. Am., 1968-72; charter pres. Bucyrus Bratwurst Festival, Inc., 1968; adv. bd. Bucyrus Salvation Army, 1964-68; mem. planning com. East Ohio Conf., 1972-76 (chmn. commn. on minimum salaries, 1968-72, lay reader, 1972-76); vice chmn. coun. ministries, mem. episcopal com., 1972-76, head. del. to gen. conf., Portland, Oreg., 1976, Balt., 1984; head del. to Jurisdictional Conf., Sioux Falls, 1976, Duluth, Minn., 1984; mem. United Meth. Comms., 1972-76, mem. gen. coun. fin. and adminstrn., 1976-80; mem. comms. on Nat. Coun. Chs., 1972-76; mem. comms. con. Ohio Coun. Chs.; mem. Episc. com.; chmn. New Vision Task Group, both East Ohio Conf., North Cen. Jurisdiction, United Meth. Ch.; mem. exec. com. Coun. on Ministries 1980-86; mem. World Meth. Coun., 1986-91, World Meth. Conf., 1996; trustee United Theol. Sem., 1972-80, trustee Ohio No. U., 1986—, mem. exec. com., 1991-2003, chair student affairs com., 1991-95, chair, 1995—; mem. exec. com. East Ohio del. to United Meth. Gen. Conf. and Jurisdictional Conf., 1987-91; sec. Cmty. Improvement Corp., Bucyrus, 1989-91; mem. Overall Econ. Devel. Com. of Crawford County, 1992-96; chmn. Crawford County Traffic Safety Coun., 1979-89, 96-98; pres. Crawford County Econ. Devel. Adv. Coun., 1992-96; mem., sec. Crawford County Devel. Bd., Inc., 1997-2000; mem. exec. com. of del. to 1988 Gen. Conf. United Meth. Ch., St. Louis; bd. dirs. Bucyrus Cmty. Hosp., 1992, mem. fin. com., 1993-96, chmn., 2004—, chmn. nominating com., 1993-96, campaign dir., chair fundraising com., 1993-96, v.p. bd. dirs., 1994-96; chmn. North Ctrl. Ohio Health Sys., 1996-98; mem. Crawford County Rep. Ctrl. Com., 1998-2001; mem. City of Bucyrus Bd. of Zoning Appeals, 1998-2001; pres. Crawford County Devel. Bd., 2000—; chmn. City of Bucyrus Bd. Zoning Appeals, 2000-01; sec. Bucyrus Pub. Libr Bd., 2004—. Served with USN, 1946-48. Named a Civic Leader of Am., 1968. Mem. Nat. Assn. Broadcasters (legis. liaison 1984-91, mem. small market radio com.), Ohio Assn. Broadcasters (pres. 1982-85), North Ctrl. Ohio Broadcasters Assn. (pres. 1983-84, 96-98, v.p. 1985), Bucyrus Area C. of C. (chmn. airport study com. 1967-68, bd. dirs. 1964-67, pres. 1989-91), Rotary (pres. Bucyrus chpt. 1992-93). E-mail: tommoore@wavelinc.com.

**MOORE, THOMAS RONALD (LORD BRIDESTOWE),** lawyer; b. Duluth, Minn., Mar. 27, 1932; s. Ralph Henry and Estelle Marguerite (Hero) M.; m. Margaret C. King, Sept. 10, 1955 (dec. May 10, 2003); children: Willard S., Clarissa, Charles R.H. BA magna cum laude, Yale U., 1954; JD, Harvard U., 1957. Bar: N.Y. 1958, U.S. Supreme Ct. 1965. Instr. Harvard Law Sch., 1956-57; with Dewey Ballantine, N.Y.C.; ptnr. Breed, Abbott & Morgan, N.Y.C., Finley Kumble & Wagner, N.Y.C., Law Offices of Thomas R. Moore, N.Y.C. Lectr. Harvard U. Law Sch., Cornell Law Sch., NYU Law Sch., Practising Law Inst., NYC, Las Vegas, New Orleans; lectr. Oxford U. Author Plantagenet Descent, 31 Generations from William the Conqueror to Today, 1995; co-author: Estate Planning and the Close Corporation; editor-in-chief: Gastronome, bd. editors: The Tax Lawyer; contbr. articles to profl. jours.; numerous interviews in popular press and TV commentaries. Bd. dirs. exec. com. Citymeals on Wheels; pres. bd. dirs. Nat. Soc. to Prevent Blindness; sec.-treas., trustee A.D. Henderson Found., Del., trustee, Fla.; bd. dirs. Phoenix Theatre Inc., Inst. Aegean Prehistory, Found. Future of Man, Am. and Internat. Friends of Victoria and Albert Mus., London; conservator NY Pub. Libr.; trustee Found. for Renaissance of St. Petersburg (Russia), Malcolm Wiener Found.; pres. bd. dirs. Laurence Levine Charitable Fund., Inc.; vice chmn. NY Hist. Soc.; bd. dirs. Gov.'s Commn. on Scholastic Achievement; constl. advisor to Pres. George Bush; advisor to King Michael of Romania. Decorated Knight, Queen Elizabeth II; recipient Coat of Arms, Order of Crown of Charlemagne, Order of Plantagenet, Order of Barons of Magna Charta, Order of Descendants Knights of the Garter, Thomas R. Moore Disting. Pub. Servant award, Nat. Soc. to Prevent Blindness; scholar of House, Class Marshall, Yale. Mem.: St. Andrews Soc., St. George Soc., Confrerie de la Chaine des Rotisseurs (nat. pres., dir., exec. com. world coun. Paris), Robert Burns Soc., Nat. Wine Coalition (bd. dirs.), Chevalier du Tastevin, The Pilgrims, Church Club, Univ. Club, Delta Sigma Rho. Republican. Episcopalian. Office: 590 Madison Ave Ste 2100 New York NY 10022 Office Phone: 212-333-8630.

**MOORE, THURSTON ROACH,** lawyer; b. Memphis, Dec. 10, 1946; s. Richard Charlton Moore and Halcyon Hall (Roach) Lynn; m. Corell Luckhardt Halsey, Sept. 26, 1998. BA with distinction, U. Va., 1968, JD, 1974. Bar: Va. 1974. Rsch. analyst Scudder, Stevens & Clark, N.Y.C., 1968—71; ptnr. Hunton & Williams LLP, Richmond, Va., 1974—91, mng. partner, 1991—2006, chmn., 2006—. Mem.: ABA (chmn. ptnrs. com. 1992—96, bus. law sect., fed. regulation security com., bus. law coun.), Richmond Bar Assn., Va. State Bar, Va. Bar Assn., Va. Commwealth U. Sch. Bus. Found. (trustee, bd. dirs.), Mary Morton Parsons Found. (trustee, bd. dirs.), Nature Conservancy Va. (chmn., trustee, bd. dir.), Va. Mus. Fine Arts (trustee), Va. Found. Ind. Coll. (trustee, bd. dirs.), Met. Bus. Found. (pres. 1995—2001, dir.), Phi Beta Kappa. Office: Hunton & Williams Riverfront Plz E Tower 951 E Byrd St Richmond VA 23219-4074 Office Fax: 804-788-8218. Business E-Mail: tmoore@hunton.com.

**MOORE, TIM,** lawyer; b. Lafayette, La., Sept. 4, 1957; BS in geology, Stephen F. Austin State U., 1979; JD summa cum laude, U. Houston, 1990. Bar: Tex. 1990. Geologist Placid Oil Co., New Orleans, 1980—84, Jackson, Miss., 1980—84; regional geologist Gulf Coast Kaiser Energy Inc., New Orleans, 1984—87; assoc. Weil, Gotshal & Manges, Houston, 1990—94; gen. counsel - corp. TransTex. Gas Corp., 1994—2000; v.p., gen. counsel, sec. Plains Resources, 2000—01, Plains All Am. Pipeline, Houston, 2000—. Mem.: Am. Corp. Counsel Assn., State Bar Tex., Order of the Barons, Order of the Coif, Omicron Delta Kappa. Office: Plains All Am Pipeline 333 Clay St Ste 1600 PO Box 4648 Houston TX 77210-4648

**MOORE, TIMOTHY ISAAC,** photographer, protective services official; b. Wilmington, Ohio, July 17, 1953; s. Clarence Wayne and Evelyn Josephine Moore; m. Roseann Chesnut Moore, May 7, 1988. BS in Physics and Math., Ohio State U., Columbus, Ohio, 1975. Cert. tech. accident investigator NorthWestern U., 1990. Pvt. practice profl. photographer, Wilmington, Ohio, 1975—; sgt. police Wilmington Police, Ohio, 1983—93. Mem.: KC (4th Degree), Mensa (assoc.). Republican. Roman Catholic. Avocations: travel, computers, reading, firearms and weaponry, art. Home: 368 Darbyshire Dr Wilmington OH 45177-2410 Personal E-mail: tm368@msn.com.

**MOORE, TIRIN,** neuroscientist, educator; b. Oakland, Calif., June 12, 1969; s. Walter Peter Moore and Mary Lucille Salmon; m. Giovanna Ceserani, June 21, 2003; 1 child. Emilia T. PhD, Princeton U., NJ, 1995. Asst. prof. neurobiology Stanford U., Calif., 2003—. Recipient Nat. Rsch. Svc. award, NIH, 1999—2002, Early Career award, NSF, 2006—; scholar Pew Charitable Trust, 2004—, McKnight Endowment Fund Neurosci., 2006—; NSF fellow 1990—93 MIT fellow, 1995—99, Princeton U. fellow, 1999—2003, Alfred P. Sloan Found. fellow, 2004—06. Mem.: Soc. Neurosci. Achievements include research in neurophysiology of vision, movement and cognition. Avocations: travel, movies. Office Phone: 650-725-8712.

**MOORE, TOM,** film and theater director; b. Meridian, Miss., Aug. 6, 1943; s. Heustis T. and Maryanne (Moody) M. BA, Purdue U., 1965; M.F.A., Yale U., 1968; DFA, Purdue Univ., 1995. Tchr. Am. Dramatic Inst., U. London, 1968. Guest dir. SUNY-Buffalo, 1968, Brandeis U., Boston, 1968; artistic dir. Peterborough Players (N.H.), 1971; lectr. Seminar Am. Studies, Salzburg, Austria, 1974 Dir. Broadway plays: Grease (one of the longest-running shows in history of Broadway), 1972-80, Over Here, 1974-75, Once in a Lifetime, 1978, Division Street, 1980, Frankenstein, 1981, 'night Mother, 1983 (Pulitzer Prize) (dir. film by same name 1986), The Octette Bridge Club, 1985, A Little Hotel on the Side, Nat. Actors Theatre, 1992, Moon over Buffalo, 1995-96; off-Broadway play: Welcome to Andromeda, 1973; regional theatre: The Lady with All the Answers, 2005; plays Am. Conservatory Theatre, San Francisco, 1977-81, Williamstown (Mass.) Theatre Festival, 1976, 79, 93, Mark Taper Forum, Los Angeles, 1980, 82, 83, 84, 86, 91, Tyrone Guthrie Theatre, Mpls., 1975, Arena Stage, Washington, 1975, Old Globe Theatre Festival, San Diego, 1982, 85, Ahmanson Theatre, Los Angeles, 1983, Am. Repertory Theatre, Cambridge, Mass., 1982, 84, La Jolla (Calif.) Playhouse, 1990; film Journey, 1972; co-dir. Fridays, ABC-TV; dir. thirtysomething, ABC-TV, LA Law, NBC-TV (Emmy nominee 1991), Almost Grown, CBS-TV, Wonder Years, ABC-TV (Humanitas prize for Square Dance episode, 1990), Cheers, NBC-TV, Northern Exposure, CBS-TV, Picket Fences, CBS-TV, Civil Wars, ABC-TV, Class of '96, Fox TV, Mad About You, NBC-TV; TV movies Maybe, Baby, and Fine Things, NBC, 1990; TV pilots The Flamingo Kid, 50 Minute Man. Recipient Tony award nomination 1974, 83, Golden Knight award Malta Film Festival, 1973, Cine Golden Eagle award, 1973, 6 Dramalogue awards, 1981-86, Emmy nominee, 1993. Fellow Am. Film Inst.

**MOORE, VERNON JOHN, JR.,** pediatrician, consultant, lawyer; b. Chgo., Mar. 18, 1942; s. Vernon John Moore; m. Rutheva de Vera Dizon, Feb. 27, 1979; children: Christopher, Joseph. BS, Loyola U., Chgo., 1964, JD, 1986;

MD, U. Ill.-Chgo., 1968. Bar: Ill. 1986, U.S. Dist. Ct. (no. dist.) Ill. 1986. Intern St. Joseph Health Care Ctrs. and Hosp., Chgo., 1968-69, resident in pediat., 1971-74, chief resident, 1972-74, mem. med. staff, 1974-76, 78-86; pvt. practice Chgo., 1974-76, 97—; mem. med. staff Naval Hosp. Great Lakes, 1976-78; med. officer Chgo. Mil. Entrance Processing Sta., 1996—2002, Midwest Ctr. for Youth and Families, Kouts, Ind., 1997—2006; mem. med. staff Ill. Masonic Med. Ctr., Chgo., 1997—2005, Swedish Covenant Hosp., Chgo., 1998—2005, Luth. Gen. Hosp., Park Ridge, Ill., 1998—2005, Alexian Bros. Med. Ctr., Elk Grove Village, Ill., 2000—02. Asst. dir. pediat. edn. St. Joseph Health Care Ctrs. and Hosp., 1974—76, co-dir., 1978—86, acting chmn. dept. pediat., 1985—86; clin. assoc. prof. pediat. Loyola U., Maywood, Ill., 1981—87; med. cons. CNA Ins. Cos., Chgo., 1987—94; pediat. med. cons. Hartgrove Hosp., Chgo., 1996—, Alexian Bros. Behavioral Health Hosp., Hoffman Estates, Ill., 1999—2001. Part-time staff Senator Everett M. Dirksen, Chgo., 1961—64. With med. corps USNR, 1969—2002, ret. as capt. USNR, 2002. Mem.: U. Ill. Pres. Coun., Alumni Assn. Coll. Medicine U. Ill. (alumni councillor 1989—92), U. Ill. Alumni Assn. (bd. dirs. 1983—89). Republican. Roman Catholic. Home: 146 Park Ave River Forest IL 60305-2040

**MOORE, VIRGINIA BRADLEY,** librarian; b. Laurens, S.C., May 13, 1932; d. Robert Otis Brown and Queen Esther (Smith) Bradley; m. David Lee Moore, Dec. 27, 1957 (div. 1973). BS, Winston-Salem State U., 1954; MLS, U. Md., 1970. Cert. in libr. sci. edn. Tchr. John R. Hawkins H.S., Warrenton, NC, 1954-55, Happy Plains H.S., Taylorsville, NC, 1955-58, Young and Carver elem. schs., Washington, 1958-65; libr. Davis and Minor elem. schs., Washington, 1965-72, Ballou Sr. H.S., Kramer Jr. H.S., Washington, 1972-75, 78-80, Anacostia Sr. H.S., Washington, 1975-77, 80 95; libr. I, adult svcs. Greenbelt (Md.) Br. Libr., 1997—. Dir. ch. libr. workshops Asbury United Meth. Ch., Washington, 1972—74, 1976; spkr., presenter Ch. and Synagogue Libr. Assn., 1975, 80, 83, spkr. spring workshop, 99, presenter, 2000; mem. serials com. Prince George's County Meml. Libr. Sys., 2000—05; chair-competency based curriculum D.C. pub. schs., 1978—93; chair local arrangements launching Nat. Sch. Libr. Media Month U.S. Capitol, 1985; mem. 1st libr. and info. sci. del. to People's Republic China, 1985; mem. faculty 1st established pub. svc. acad. in nation Anacostia Sr. H.S., 1990—95; coord. Nat. Libr. Week workshop Greenbelt Libr. Prince George's County Meml. Libr. Sys., 2002; presenter in field; host ch. chair Asbury United Meth. Ch., 2004. Author: (bibliography) The Negro in American History, 1619-1968, 1968; (with Helen E. Williams) Books By African-American Authors and Illustrators for Children and Young Adults, 1991; TV script for vacation reading program, 1971, sound/slide presentation D.C. Church Librs.' Bicentennial Celebration, 1976; video script and tchr.'s guide for Nat. Libr. Week Balloon Launch Day, 1983; bibliography Black Literature/Materials, 1987; contbr. articles to profl. jours. Co-chmn. nat. libr. involvement com. Martin Luther King, Jr. Fed. Holiday Commn., 1990—99, chmn., 1996—99; trustee LeRoy C. Merritt Humanitarian Fund, 2002—06; libr. Mt. Carmel Bapt Ch., Washington, 1984, chair ch. libr. com., 2000—05, ad hoc com. for churchwide programs, 2001—05, libr. Sunday Sch. Mother's Day coord., 1990—94, jr. ch. pianist, 1994—97, Sunday Sch. adult dept. pianist, 1984—, co-chmn. African-Am. History Mo. commn., 1996—, chmn. publicity com., 1996—99, com. renovation of Rev. Arthur H. Pace Libr. Multipurpose Rm., vice-chair publicity liaison com., 1999—2005, soprano sanctuary choir, 1995—, soprano soloist women's day and tribute commemoration, 1998, music com., 1998—2005; chmn. social responsibilities roundtable Martin Luther King Jr. holiday task force Am. Libr. Assn., 1999—; rec. sec. Washington Pan-Hellenic Coun., 1975. Named outstanding educator, Mt. Carmel Bapt. Ch., 1984; recipient Outstanding Congl. Libr. Ch. and Synagogue Libr. Assn., 2001, certs. of award, D.C. Pub. Librs., 1980, D.C. Pub. Schs., 1983; fellow Grad. fellow, U. Md., 1969; scholar NDEA scholar, Central State Coll. Edmond, Okla., 1969, U. Ky., 1969, Ball State U., 1969. Mem. ALA (councilor-at-large 1983-91, 96—, com. on coms. 2005, Freedom to Read Honor Roll, 1999, chmn.), LWV (sec. Prince George's County, Md. 1997-99, v.p. 1999-2000, pres. 2000-05, mem. lobby corps. 2004-, nominations chair Nat. Capital area 2005—2006), AARP, Internat. Assn. Sch. Librs., NEA (life), Am. Assn. Sch. Librs. (coms. 1973-83, 1987—), D.C. Assn. Sch. Librs. (pres. 1971-73, citation 1973, newsletter editor 1971-75, 83), Intellectual Freedom Com. (chmn. 1983-99), Freedom to Read Found., Soc. Sch. Librs. Internat. (charter), Intellectual Freedom Roundtable (bd. dirs. exec. com. 1989-91), D.C. Libr. Assn., Md. Libr. Assn., Md. Ednl. Media Orgn., Internat. Platform Assn., S.E. Neighbors Club, Am. First Day Cover Soc., Nat. Coun. Negro Women, Zeta Phi Beta (v.p. chpt. 1972-74), Delta Kappa Gamma (v.p. Alpha chpt. 1990-92, pres. 1992-95, Nu State D.C. membership chmn. 1991-92, 2002-, rec. sec. 1994-95, v.p. 1995-97, liaison U.S. Forum 1995-97, 99—, spkr., state pres. 1997-99, steering com. spkr. Soc. Internat. Legis. seminar 1998, D.C. state del. Nat. Legis. Seminar 2006). Democrat. Achievements include being First Lady Laura Bush's guest at White House to launch Nat. Libr. Week, 2003. Home: 2100 Brooks Dr apt 721 Forestville MD 20747-1016 Office: Prince Georges County Meml Libr Sys Greenbelt Br Libr 11 Crescent Rd Greenbelt MD 20770-1891 E-mail: vbmoore_99@yahoo.com.

**MOORE, VIRGINIA LEE SMITH,** elementary school educator; b. Middletown, NY, May 13, 1943; d. James William and Anna Van Alst (Suydam) Smith; m. Thomas J. Moore, Oct. 16, 1965 (div. Apr. 1980); 1 child, Christian Thomas. AA in Liberal Arts, Orange County C.C., 1963; BA in Sociology magna cum laude, SUNY, Buffalo, 1965; MS in Edn., SUNY, New Paltz, 1980; MS in Edn. of Gifted, Coll. New Rochelle, 1990. Cert. sch. staff devel., 1994; cert. sch. administrn., 1994. Cert. elem. tchr., N.Y. Spl. edn. tchr. The Devereux Found., Glen Loch, Pa., 1965-66; elem. tchr. Harris Sch., Coatesville, Pa., 1967, Pine Bush (N.Y.) Cen. Schs., 1967-70, 78-00, substitute tchr., 1970-71; nursery sch. tchr. Olivet Meth. Nursery Sch., Coatesville, Pa., 1976-78; profl. devel. coord. Pine Bush Sch. Dist., 1998. Participant math. sci. and tech on elem. level program NSF, 1997—2000, presenter edni. workshops in various sch. dists. and for orgns. and instns. Contbr. articles to profl. jours. Pres. Redtown Residents' Assn., Middletown, 1988—. Recipient Dean's Acad. Excellence award Coll. of New Rochelle, 1991, Orange County Conservation Tchr. of Yr., 1993, NY State Conservation Tchr. of Yr., 1993, Presdl. award for Excellence in math. and sci. tchg. NY State, 1997; Partnership in Edn. grantee Area Fund Orange County, NY, 1991, Energy grantee Orange and Rockland Utilities, 1995, Tech. grantee Mid-Hudson Tchr. Ctr., 1997-98, Energy grantee NY State Electric and Gas, 1998. Mem. NSTA, DAR, Internat. Tech. Edn. Assn., N.Y. State Elem. Sch. Tchr. Excellence award 1998-99), N.Y. State United Tchrs., Sci. Tchrs. Assn. N.Y. State (Outstanding Sci. Tchr. award 1992, Excellence in Sci. Tchg. award 1995), N.Y. State Tech. Edn. Assn. (Tech. grantee 1999), Orange County Geneal. Soc., Phi Beta Kappa. Baptist. Achievements include development of interactive science museum exhibits. Avocations: piano, reading, genealogy, history. Home: 177 Benedict Rd Montgomery NY 12549 Personal E-mail: vlsmoore@frontiernet.net.

**MOORE, WARD WILFRED,** medical educator; b. Cowden, Ill., Feb. 12, 1924; s. Cecil Leverett and Velma Leona (Frye) M.; m. Frances Laura Campbell, Jan. 29, 1949; children: Scott Thomas, Ann Gail, Brian Dean, Kevin Lee. AB, U. Ill., 1948, MS, 1951, PhD, 1952; DSc (hon.), Mahidol U., Bangkok, 2001. Instr., rsch. assoc. U. Ill., 1952-54; asst. prof. Okla. State U., Stillwater, 1954-55, Ind. U., Bloomington, 1955-59, assoc. prof., 1959-66, prof. physiology, 1966-89, prof. physiology and biophysics emeritus, 1989—, acting chmn. dept. anatomy, 1971-73, assoc. dean basic med. scis., 1971-89, assoc. dean, dir. med. scis. program, 1976-89. Vis. prof. Postgrad. Med. Center, Karachi, Pakistan, 1963-64; staff mem. Rockefeller Found., 1968-71; vis. prof., chmn. dept. physiology, faculty sci. Mahidol U., Bangkok, Thailand, 1968-71 Served with U.S. Army, 1943-46. Mem. Am. Physiol. Soc., Endocrine Soc., Am. Soc. Nephrology, Soc. Study Reproduction, Am. Assn. Anatomists, Soc. Exptl. Biology and Medicine, Am. Assn. Med. Colls., AAAS, Am. Inst. Biol. Scis., AAUP, Ind. Acad. Sci., Ind. Hist. Soc., Shelby County (Ill.) Hist. Soc., Monroe County (Ind.) Hist. Soc., Am. Revolution, Sigma Xi, Phi Sigma. Home: 3500 E Bradley St Bloomington IN 47401-4201 Office: Indiana U Jordan Hall # 105 Bloomington IN 47405 Business E-Mail: moorew@indiana.edu.

**MOORE, WELDON LESLIE,** lawyer; b. Dallas, Dec. 15, 1957; s. Weldon L. and Catherine (Robinson) M. BBA, U. Tex., Arlington, 1980; JD, Tex. Tech U., 1982. Bar: Tex. 1983, U.S. Dist. Ct. (no. dist.) Tex. 1985, U.S. Ct. Appeals (5th cir.) 1987, U.S. Dist. Ct. (ea., we. and so. dists.) Tex. 1988; cert. Tex. Bd. Legal Specialization in Bus. Bankruptcy Law, Consumer Bankruptcy Law. Pvt. practice, Dallas, 1983-87; assoc. and subsequently shareholder Creel and Atwood, P.C., 1987—96; counsel Malouf, Lynch, Jackson, Kessler, Collins, P.C., 1996—98; prin. Creel, Sussman & Moore, LLP, Dallas, 1998—. Mem. ABA, State Bar Tex., Coll. of State Bar of Tex. Avocations: bicycling, films, exercise, reading. Office: Creel Sussman & Moore LLP 8235 Douglas Ave Ste 1100 Dallas TX 75225-6011 Office Phone: 214-378-8270. Business E-Mail: wmoore@csmlaw.net.

**MOORE, WENDY LEIGH,** anthropology professor; b. Ft. Walton Beach, Fla., Aug. 2, 1967; d. David Clay and Donna Elaine Moore. PhD, U. Tenn., Knoxville, 2006. Tutor Students in Stats. Ronald McNair Program, Knoxville, 1996; adj. faculty Pellissippi State Tech. CC, Knoxville, 1998—; grad. tchg. assoc. U. Tenn., Knoxville, 2001—02, with ext. faculty night sch., 2001. Mem-at-large subcom. SACS Ednl. Self-Study Programs, Knoxville, 2000—02; part-time instr. anthropology U. Tenn., 2000—; presenter posters in field of anthropology. Participant Winston-Salem (N.C.) / Forsyth County Coalition on Alcohol and Drug Problems, Winston-Salem, 1991—92; vol. Fair Tax, Knoxville, 2006. Recipient dept. scholarship, anthropology dept., U. of Tenn., 1995. Mem.: Am. Assn. of Phys. Anthropologists. Libertarian. Achievements include research in archaeological shell midden collection from Escambia Bay; test of the two species hypothesis in the Levant using a clusteranalysis of mandibular measurements; Neandertal allometry. Avocations: computers, reading, knitting, news junkie. Office: Pellissippi State Tech C C 10915 Hardin Valley Rd Knoxville TN 37933-0990 Office Phone: 865-694-6685. Office Fax: 865-539-7062. E-mail: wlmoore@pstcc.edu.

**MOORE, WILLIAM GROVER, JR.,** management consultant, retired military officer; b. Waco, Tex. s. William Grover and Annie Elizabeth (Pickens) Moore; m. Marjorie Y. Gardella, Jan. 18, 1943; 1 child, Allyson. Student, Kilgore Coll., Tex., 1937—39, Sacramento State Coll., 1951, George Washington U., 1962; grad., Air War Coll., Air U., 1957, Nat. War Coll., 1962. Enlisted U.S. Army Air Force, 1940, commd. 2d lt., 1941, advanced through grades to gen., 1977; comdr. 777th Squadron, 15th AF, Italy, 1944—45, 3535th Maintenance and Supply Group, Mather AFB, Calif., 3d Bomb Group, Korea, 1952; chief bases and units divsn. Hdqrs. USAF, 1952—56; asst. dep. chief of staff ops. Hdqrs. USAF Europe, 1957—61; comdr. 314th Troop Carrier Wing, Stewart AFB, Tenn., 1962—63, 839th Air Divsn., 1963—65; asst. J3 U.S. Strike Command, 1965—66; comdr. 834th Air Divsn., Vietnam, 1966—67; dir. operational requirements Hdqrs. USAF, 1967—70; comdr. 22d AF, 1970—73, 13th AF, 1973; chief of staff Pacific Command, 1973—76; asst. vice chief of staff Hdqrs. USAF, 1976—77; comdr. in chief Mil. Air Lift Command, 1977—79; ret., 1979; pres., COO Emery Air Freight Corp., Wilton, Conn., 1981—83; bus. cons., 1983—. Pres. Met. Nashville Airport Authority, 1984—. Decorated Def. D.S.M., Air Force D.S.M. with 2 oak leaf clusters, Legion of Merit with 4 oak leaf clusters, Silver Star, D.F.C. with oak leaf cluster, Air Medal with 9 oak leaf clusters, Air Force Commendation medal with 10 oak leaf clusters (U.S.), Croix de Guerre with palm France, Armed Forces Honor medal 1st class Vietnam, Republic of China Cloud and Banner, Legion of Honor Republic of the Philippines; named to Minuteman Hall of Fame, 1979; recipient L. Mendel Rivers award of excellence; fellow Jimmy Doolittle fellow in aerospace edn., 1978. Mem.: Am. Ordnance Assn., Nat. Def. Transp. Assn., Air Force Assn. Home: 932 W Main St Franklin TN 37064-2730 Office: Nashville Internat Airport 1 Terminal Dr Ste 501 Nashville TN 37214-4110

**MOORE, WILLIAM HENRY,** radiologist; b. Pompton, NJ, Dec. 6, 1973; m. Rebecca Anne Case, May 30, 1999; 1 child, Charlotte Catherine. MD, Albany Med. Coll., NY, 1999. Diplomate Am. Bd. Radiology. Intern Albany Med. Ctr., 1999—2000; resident in internal medicine U. Hosp., Stony Brook, NY, 2000—04, chief thoracic imaging, 2004—; vis. fellow thoracic imaging NYU, NYC, 2003—04. Contbr. articles to profl. jours. Named Tchr. of Yr., 2005, Outstanding Tchr., Stony Brook Med. Sch., 2006; recipient Roentgen Rsch. award, 2003. Mem.: Soc. Thoracic Radiologist (assoc.), Alpha Omega Alpha, A3CR2 (assoc.; vice chair problem solving 2002—03). Office: Univ Hosp 100 Nicolls Rd Stony Brook NY 11794 Office Phone: 631-444-7955. Office Fax: 631-444-7538. Business E-Mail: william.moore@stonybrook.edu.

**MOORE, WILLIAM LEROY, JR.,** career officer, internist; b. Savannah, Ga., June 1, 1934; s. William Leroy Sr. and Helen Louise (Robbins) M.; m. Anna Elizabeth Ballard, Mar. 15, 1958; children: William L., Christopher A., Mary Beth. Student, Ga. Inst. Tech., 1951-52; AB, Emory U., 1955; MD, Med. Coll. Ga., 1959; postgrad. mil. tng. courses, 1962-94. Diplomate Am. Bd. Internal Medicine, Am. Bd. Infectious Diseases. Commd. capt. U.S. Army, 1962, advanced through grades to maj. gen., 1991; intern Floyd Hosp., Rome, Ga., 1959-60; pvt. practice Rome, 1960-61; resident in internal medicine Brooke Gen. Hosp., Ft. Sam Houston, Tex., 1965-68; rsch. fellow in infectious diseases U. Tex. Southwestern Med. Sch., Dallas, 1968-70; resident in internal medicine Parkland Meml. Hosp., Dallas, 1968-70; gen. med. officer Martin Army Hosp., Ft. Benning, Ga., 1962, 5th Spl. Forces Group, Spl. Warfare Ctr., Ft. Bragg, N.C., 1962-63; gen. internist, group surgeon, commdg. officer 1st Spl. Forces Group, Spl. Action Force, Okinawa, Japan, 1963-65; asst. chief to chief infectious disease svc. Brooke Gen. Hosp., Ft. Sam Houston, Tex., 1970-74; chief internal medicine svc., chief dept. medicine, chief profl. svcs. Eisenhower Army Med. Ctr., Ft. Gordon, Ga., 1978-83; comdr. Frankfurt (Germany) Army Regional Med. Ctr., 97th Gen Hosp., 1983-86; project mgr. Office of Surgeon Gen., Washington, 1986-88; adj. faculty Nat. Def. U., Ft. Lesley J. McNair, Washington, 1986-88; vice comdr. Joint Mil. Med. Command, Randolph AFB, Tex., 1988-91; comdr. Brooke Army Med. Ctr., Ft. Sam Houston, Tex., 1988-91, U.S. Army Med. Dept. Ctr. & Sch., Ft. Sam Houston, Tex., 1991-94; state epidemiologist, dir. communicable & environ. disease Tenn. Dept. Health, 1995-2001; prof. medicine divsn. infectious diseases Vanderbilt U. Sch. Medicine, Nashville, 1994—; chief of staff VA Med. Ctr., Nashville, 2001—02; dir. bur. epidemiology Nashville Davidson Met. Health Dept., 2002—. Clin. assoc. in medicine U. Tex. Southwestern Med. Sch., 1969-70; clin. assoc. prof. medicine U. Tex. Med. Sch., 1970-74: chief. sect. of infectious diseases Med. Coll. Ga., 1974-75, assoc. prof., 1974-78, clin. prof. 1978-83; prin. investigator infectious disease rsch. VA Hosp., Augusta, Ga., 1974-78, asst. chief med. svc., 1974-75; dir. clin. microbiology lab., 1974-78, epidemiologist, 1974-78; head internal medicine infectious disease 97th gen. Hosp., Frankfurt, 1983-86, Walter Reed Army Med. Ctr., 1986-88; clin. prof. medicine U. Tex. Health Sci. Ctr., San Antonio, 1989-94; mem. ref. panel on Am. Hosp. Formulary Svc. of Am. Soc. Hosp. Pharmacists, 1974-78; faculty Advisor Lane-Walker AMSA Free Clinic, Augusta, 1975-78; mem. various coms. and bds., VA Hosp., Augusta, 1974-78. Contbr. articles to profl. jours. Mem. Army Comty. Coun. San Antonio, 1988-94; dir., bd. dirs Army Med. Dept. Mus. Found. Inc., 1989-94; bd. dirs. San Antonio Area chpt. ARC, 1989. Decorated Army Commendation medal, Meritorious Svc. medal (3), Legion of Merit with three oak leaf clusters, Disting. svc. medal Army Med. Dept. Regiment, 1994, Order of Mil. Med. Merit; recipient Scholastic Excellence award C.V. Mosby Co., 1959, Laureate award, Am. Coll. Physician, 1996, Dirs. Commendation VA Hosp., Augusta, 1978. Fellow ACP, Infectious Diseases Soc. Am.; mem. NAS (nat. rsch. coun. 1995-96), Assn. Mil. Surgeons U.S. (mem.-at-large exec. coun. Alamo chpt. 1989), Soc. Med. Cons. to Armed Forces (chmn. com. on cons. activities 1977-79), Am. Heart Assn. (bd. dirs. San Antonio divsn. 1988-89), San Antonio Rsch. Club (sec., pres. 1970-74), Tenn. Med. Assn., Nashville Acad. Medicine, Tenn. Pub. Health Assn., Coun.State and Territorial Epidemiologists. *Strict adherence to moral and ethical principles, willingness to work hard, use all of one's talents to benefit others and take advantage of all of the opportunities one finds to improve one's self while serving others are the elements of success in this life.*

**MOORE, WILLIAM THEODORE, JR.,** federal judge; b. Bainbridge, Ga., May 7, 1940; s. William T. and Mary (Talbert) M.; m. Jane Hodges, July 18, 1964; children: Sarah S., Mary T. William T III. AA, Ga. Military Coll., 1960; JD, U. Ga., 1964; Law (hon.), Ga. Mil. Coll., 1978; LLM, U. Va., 2001. Bar: Ga. 1964, U.S. Dist. Ct. (so. dist.) Ga. 1964, U.S. Ct. Appeals (5th and 11th cirs.) 1979, U.S. Supreme Ct. 1980. US atty. US Dist. Ct. (So. Dist.) Ga., Savannah, 1977-81; ptnr. Corish, Smith, Remler & Moore, Savannah, 1967-77, Sparkman, Harris & Moore, Savannah, 1981-87, Oliver Maner & Gray, Savannah, 1988-94; judge US Dist. Ct. (So. Dist.) Ga., Savannah, 1994—2004, chief judge, 2004—. Atty. Savannah-Chatham County Bd. Pub. Edn., 1975-77, mem. U.S. Atty. Gen's. Adv. com D.C. 1978-81. Recipient Spl. Appreciation award Ga. Bur. of Investigation, 1980, U.S. Dept. Treasury Bur. of Alcohol, Tobacco & Firearms, D.C., 1980; Extraordinary Svc. award Savannah Chapt. Fed. Bar Assn., 1980. Fellow Am. Bd. Criminal Lawyers (pres. 1993); mem. NACDL, Nat. Assn. Former U.S. Attys. (bd. dirs. 1984—), Jud. Conf. U.S. (com. on criminal law, sentencing subcommittee), Ga. Assn. Criminal Def. Lawyers (v.p. 1986—), Ga. Bar Assn. Democrat. Episcopalian. Avocations: jogging, weight training, golf, reading. Office: US Dist Courthouse 125 Bull St PO Box 10245 Savannah GA 31412-0445

**MOORE, WISTAR,** cardiovascular surgeon; b. Feb. 16, 1959; BA, U. N.C., 1981, MD, 1985. Bd. cert. gen. surgery, thoracic surgery. Gen. surgery resident Mass. Gen. Hosp., 1985-90; cardiothoracic resident The Emory Clinic, 1990-93; cardiovasc. surgeon Watson Clinic, Lakeland, Fla., 1993-2000; chief divsn. cardiovasc. thoracic surgery Lakeland Regional Med. Ctr., 1996-2000; cardiovasc. surgeon Cardiovasc. Surgeons, Orlando, Fla., 2000—04, Leesburg-Ocala Heart Inst., 2004—. Fellow ACS, Am. Coll. Chest Physicians; mem. Fla. Soc. Thoracic and Cardiovasc. Surgeons, So. Thoracic Surg. Assn., Soc. Thoracic Surgeons. Office: 700 Doctors Ct Leesburg FL 34748 Office Phone: 352-787-9830.

**MOOREHEAD, DONALD V.,** lawyer; b. Balt., Apr. 10, 1943; BA, Univ. Va., 1965; JD with honors, George Washington Univ., 1968. Bar: DC 1968, Calif. 1982, U.S. Ct. Appeals, DC cir. 1969, U.S. Tax Ct. 1971. Chief Rep. counsel U.S. Senate Fin. Com., 1975—76; v.p. & gen. counsel Kaiser Aluminum & Chem. Corp., 1981—84; ptnr., Public Policy, Tax Law, Bus. Tranactions practices, mem. exec. com. Patton Boggs LLP, Washington. Adj. prof. Georgetown Univ. Law Sch., 1974—80. Mem.: ABA. Office: Patton Boggs LLP 2550 M St NW Washington DC 20037-1350 Office Phone: 202-457-5212. Office Fax: 202-457-6315. Business E-Mail: dmoorehead@pattonboggs.com.

**MOORES, JOHN,** professional sports team executive; b. July 9, 1944; m. Becky Moores, 1963; children: Jennifer, John Jr. With IBM, Shell Oil; founder, CEO BMC Software, 1980-89, chmn., 1980-92, Peregrine Sys., Inc., Del Mar, Calif., 1990—2000, 2002; founder, chmn. JMI Services, San Diego, 1992—; chmn., co-owner San Diego Padres, 1994—. Mem. adv. bd. San Diego Hall of Champions; bd. dirs. Scripps Rsch., Inc. Trustee Carter Ctr. of Emory U.; founder, chmn. River Blindness Found.; founder Padres Found., 1995—, Padres Scholars Program, 1995—; mem., bd. regents U. Houston, 1991-1994, U. Calif, 1999—, chmn. 2002—. Office: San Diego Padres PO Box 2000 San Diego CA 92112-2000 also: JMI Services 12680 High Bluff Dr Suite 200 San Diego CA 92130

**MOORE-VICULIN, CHARLOTTE ANNE,** artist, musician; d. Harry and Virginia Longworth (Dyer) Moore; m. Richard Jerry Viculin, Oct. 15, 1977. Grad., Detroit Conservatory of Music; BFA, postgrad., Wayne State U. Self-employed portrait artist, mural painter; tchr., performer piano, vocalist Detroit, Livonia and Plymouth, Mich.; music arranger, profl. music judge. Fundraiser Plymouth Symphony League, 1980—95; bd. dirs., former sec. Plymouth Symphony, 1991—96. Named Nat. Career Woman of Yr., Nat. Assn. Career Women, 1991. Mem. Am. Soc. Portrait Artists, Portrait Soc. Am., Nat. Guild Piano Tchrs., Nat. Music Tchrs. Assn., Mich. Music Tchrs. Assn., Nat. Fedn. Music Clubs, Mich. Fedn. Music Clubs (officer), Ann Arbor Area Piano Tchrs. Guild (officer), Livonia Area Piano Tchrs. Forum (officer) Home: 27265 Canfield Dr W Dearborn Heights MI 48127-1044 Office: Charlotte Moore-Viculin Studios of Music and Art 352 N Main St Ste 4 Plymouth MI 48170-1270 Office Phone: 734-459-1112.

**MOORHEAD, GERALD LEE,** architect; b. Davenport, Iowa, Feb. 18, 1947; s. Wayne Lee and Marilou (George) M. BA, Rice U., 1969, BArch, 1971. Arch. Middleton & Statton, El Paso, Tex., 1967, MA Floyd Assocs., Houston, 1968, CRS Design Inc., Houston, 1969-70, Phillips & Peterson AIA, Houston, 1969-73; arch., v.p. Charles Tapley Assocs., Houston, 1973-83; propr. Lloyd Jones Fillpot Assocs., 1986-87, Gerald Moorhead, Arch., 1983-98; sr. assoc. Bailey Archs., 1998—. Photography exhibited in group shows at Galveston Arts Coun., Tex., 1976, Jewish Cmty. Ctr., Houston, 1977, Cronin Gallery, Houston, 1977; one-man photog. exhbns. include Autry Ho. Gallery, Houston, 1979; editor, photographer: Houston Architectural Guide, 1999, Buildings of Texas; editor: Houston Architectural Ballade, 2000; contbg. editor Tex. Arch., Arthl. Record; contbr. articles on architecture to profl. publs.; exhbn. curator Houston Mus. Natural Sci., 1990, Mus. Fine Arts, Houston, 1991, FotoFest, Houston, 1996. Treas. Houston Ctr. for Photography, 1985-87. Recipient Spl. award Houston AIA/Houston Home & Garden, 1979, Internat. prize Union Archs. Kazakstan, 1991; named Arch. Laureate of Kazakstan, 1992. Fellow AIA (Honor award Houston chpt. 1979, Young Arch. award Houston chpt. 1985); mem. Soc. Archtl. Historians, Nat. Trust for Hist. Preservation, Tex. Soc. Archs. (1st Honor award 1976, Interiors award 1986, Flowers Journalism award 1995), Rice Design Alliance. Home: 1755 W Main Ave Houston TX 77098-3607

**MOORHEAD, GLEN W. (WALLY), III,** career officer; b. Smackover, Ark. Student, USAF Acad. Prep. Sch., 1965; BS in Engring. Scis., USAF, 1969; student pilot tng., Columbus AFB, Miss., 1970-71; student combat crew tng., England AFB, La., 1971, 72-73, Myrtle Beach AFB, S.C., 1972-73; student, Squadron Officer Sch., 1975, Fighter Weapons Sch., 1978, Air Command and Staff Coll., 1982, Air War Coll., 1987, U.S. Army War Coll., 1991. Commd. 2d lt. USAF, 1969, advanced through grades to lt. gen., 1998; pilot 8th Spl. Ops., Bien Hoa Air Base, S. Vietnam, 1971-72, various squadrons, Korat Royal Thai AFB, Thailand, 1973-75, 80-82; operational test pilot, A-10 joint test force 4486th Test Squadron, Edwards AFB, Calif., 1975-76; stationed at Davis-Monthan AFB, Ariz., 1976-77, Nellis AFB, 1977-82; A-10 squadron comdr. 356th Tactical Fighter Squadron, Myrtle Beach AFB, 1986-89; dep. dir. fighter tactics and tng. Hdqs. Tactical Air Command, Langley AFB, Va., 1989-90; various comdr. assignments, 1991-94, 96-97; spl. asst. to Supreme Allied comdr., Mons, Belgium, 1994-96; chief of staff Joint Task Force Provide Promise, Naples, Italy, 1994-96; comdr. Space Warfare Ctr., Falcon AFB, Colo., 1997-98, Air Warfare Ctr., Nellis AFB, 1998-2000; asst. dep. chief of staff USAF Hdqs. Air & Space Ops., Washington, 2000; vice commander US Air Forces in Europe, Ramstein AB, Germany, 2000—02; commander Allied Air Forces Southern Europe, Stabilization Force Air Component and Kosovo Force Air Component, Naples, Italy, and Commander 16th Air Force, USAFE, Aviano AB, Italy, 2002—. Decorated Legion of Merit with oak cluster, D.F.C., Purple Heart, Air medal with 12 oak leaf clusters.

**MOORHEAD, NANCY B.,** elementary school educator; d. Marvin and Geanice Bell; children: Mark, Lindsay, Jeff. BS in Elem. Edn., U. Tex.-Austin, 1973. Tchr. Old Town Elem., Round Rock, Tex., 1988—97; math. tchr. Cedar Valley Mid. Sch., Austin, Tex., 1998—; campus coord. Pub. Edn. Cedar Valley Mid. Sch., 2000—. Recipient Tchr. of Yr., Cedar Valley Mid. Sch., 2002—03. Mem.: Austin Area Council Tchrs. Math., Tex. Council Tchrs. Math., Nat. Council Tchrs. Math. Avocations: hiking, travel, scrapbooks.

**MOORHEAD, SYLVESTER ANDREW,** retired education educator; b. Denver, Feb. 23, 1920; s. Roy Redwing and Cora Margaret (Payne) M.; m. Katherine May Schlessman, July 21, 1945; children: Rodney A., Sylvia Kay, Kent A., Pamela Ann. BA, U. No. Colo., 1942; PhD, Stanford U., 1950. Tchr.

---

secondary sch., Redwood City, Calif., 1947-48, Sunnyvale, Calif., 1948-49; mem. faculty U. Miss., 1949—, prof. edn., 1955—, dean U. Sch. Edn., 1961-85, dean emeritus, 1985—. Contbr. articles profl. jours. Served with USAAF, 1942-45. Mem. NEA (life), Kappa Delta Pi, Phi Delta Kappa. Lodges: Rotary. Baptist. Home: 211 Vivian St Oxford MS 38655-2719

**MOORING, F. PAUL,** physics editor; b. Pitt County, N.C., Feb. 6, 1921; s. Benjamin Arthur and Amanda Elizabeth (Congleton) M.; m. Jean Louise Carpenter, Aug. 28, 1948; children: Cecily Hamm, Carol Larson, Margaret Calderon. BA, Duke U., 1944; PhD, U. Wis., 1951. Instr. Duke U., Durham, NC, 1943-46; teaching asst. U. Wis., Madison, 1946-50, rsch. asst., 1950-51; physicist Argonne (Ill.) Nat. Lab., 1951-83; editor, cons. Am. Inst. Physics, Argonne, 1983—. Adj. prof. St. Louis U., 1966-83. Contbr. articles to profl. jours. Pres. The Ill. Prairie Path, Wheaton, Ill., 1971-93, Ill. Audubon Soc., Wayne, Ill., 1978-81. Fulbright Rsch. fellow U. Helsinki, 1962-63. Mem. AAAS, Am. Phys. Soc., DuPage County Environ. Commn. Democrat. Home: 295 Abbotsford Ct Glen Ellyn IL 60137-4803 E-mail: fmooring@aol.com

**MOORMAN, CHARLES W.,** transportation executive; b. Hattiesburg, Miss. Grad., Ga. Tech. Univ., Harvard Bus. Sch. With Norfolk Southern Corp., 1970—, v.p. employee rels., 1992—93, v.p. info. tech., 1993—99; pres. Thoroughbred Tech. & Telecommunications, 1999—2003; sr. v.p. corp. planning & svc. Norfolk Southern Corp., 2003—04, pres., 2005—, CEO, 2005—, chmn. 2006—. Office: Norfolk Southern Corp 3 Commercial Pl Norfolk VA 23510-2191

**MOORMAN, DONALD WAYNE,** surgeon, healthcare administrator; b. Leon, Iowa, Aug. 16, 1951; s. Virgil Glen and Dorothy Ann (Coon) Moorman. BS, Iowa State U., Ames, 1973; MD, U. Iowa, Iowa City, 1976. Diplomate Am. Bd. Surgery, cert. investigator Nat. Cancer Inst. Intern in surgery Univ. Akron Gen. Med. Ctr., Ohio, 1976—77, resident in surgery, 1976—81; ICU rotation Jackson Meml. Hosp., Miami, Fla., 1979; patient safety leadership fellow Health Forum, 2003—04; clin. instr. surgery Northeastern Ohio U. Coll. Medicine, Rootstown, 1980—83, assoc. prof., 1986—91, prof., 1991—93; sr. staff dept. surgery Akron Gen. Med. Ctr., 1981—92, surgery clerkship dir., 1981—89, program dir. gen. surgery residency program, 1987—92, dir. nutritional support team, 1982—92; dir. clin. divsn., sr. staff scientist, chmn. Human Gene Therapy Rsch. Inst., 1993—2000; mem. courtesy surg. med. staff Clarke County Hosp., Osceola, Iowa, 1998—2000; sect. chief dept. surgery Iowa Meth. Med. Ctr., Des Moines, 1998—2000; vice chair edn., assoc. surgeon in chief Beth Israel Deaconess Med. Ctr., Boston, 2000—, program dir. residency in gen. surgery, 2000—01, acting chief surgery, 2001, attending trauma surgery, dir. Trauma Ctr., 2003—04, faculty dir. Clin. adv. bd. Critical Care Am., 1983—88; clin. assoc. prof. U. Iowa, Iowa City, 1993—2000, mem. adv. com., 1996—2000; collaborating prof. zoology and genetics Iowa State U., Ames, 1993—; lectr. surgery Harvard Med. Sch., 2000—01, assoc. prof., 2000—; gen. surgery cons. VA Med. Ctr., Des Moines, mem. dean's com.; mem. courtesy gen. surgery staff Iowa Luth. Hosp., Des Moines; mem. gen. staff Broadlawns Med. Ctr., Des Moines; dir. surg. edn. Iowa Meth. Med. Ctr., Des Moines, dir. clin. divsn. Human Gene Therapy Rsch. Instn., chief sect. gen. surgery, chair surgery edn. com., mem. med. staff, ATLS instr.; sr. scholar Carl J. Shapiro Inst. Edn. and Rsch. Harvard Med. Sch. and Beth Israel Deaconess Med. Ctr., 2000—; mem. anatomical gift pub. awareness adv. com. State of Iowa Dept. Pub. Health, 1997—, team leader physician Iowa trauma sys. verification, 2000—. Contbr. articles to profl. jours. Named Tchr. of the Yr., Akron Gen. Med. Ctr., 1986, Disting. Alumni, 2005, Surgery Tchr. of the Yr., Iowa Meth. Med. Ctr., 2000; named to Hall of Distinction, Indianola HS, Iowa, 2005; recipient Dean's Spl. award, Northeastern Ohio U. Coll. Medicine, 1992, Harold Benloff award Humanism in Edn., Beth Israel Deaconess Med. Ctr., 2001. Fellow: ACS (chair Iowa dist. #2 1996—99); mem.: AMA, Eastern Cooperative Oncology Group, Iowa Oncology Rsch. Assn. (v.p., bd. dirs. 1994—), Polk County Med. Soc. (pres. elect 1999, pres. 2000), Boston Surg. Soc., Ctrl. Surg. Assn., Iowa Acad. Surgery (chair resident rsch. competition, mem. program com. ann. meeting), Assn. Hosp. Med. Edn. (mem. project adv. panel 1988—89), Soc. Critical Care Medicine, Assn. Program Dirs. Surgery (mem. edn. com. 1992, bd. dirs. 1994—99), Midwest Surg. Assn. (treas. 1998—2001, pres. elect 2002—03, pres. 2003—04, chair nominating com. 2004—06), Phi Eta Sigma, Alpha Omega Alpha. Office: Beth Israel Deaconess Med Ctr 110 Francis St 9B Boston MA 02215

**MOORMAN, JOHN A.,** librarian; b. Humboldt, Nebr., Sept. 15, 1947; m. Ileen Mary Geiger, Dec. 20, 1968; children: Johanna, Jessica Trinoskey, John A. Moorman Jr. AB, Guilford Coll., Greensboro, N.C., 1969; MSLS, U. N.C., 1972; postgrad., U. N.C., Greensboro, 1974-75; PhD, U. Ill., 2002. Pub. svcs. and circulation libr. Guilford Coll., 1972-75; dir. Elbert Ivey Meml. Libr., Hickory, NC, 1975-80, Brazoria County Libr. System, Angleton, Tex., 1980-86, Oak Lawn (Ill.) Pub. Libr. 1986-88; exec. dir. Cumberland Trail Libr. System, Flora, Ill., 1989-92; city libr. Decatur (Ill.) Pub. Libr., 1992-2000; dir. Williamsburg (Va.) Regional Libr., 2000—. Adj. faculty Cath. U., 2003—. Author: Managing Small Library Collections in Businesses and Community Organizations: Advice for Non-Librarians, 1989, Running a Small Library: A How-To-Do-It Manual, 2006. Grad. Decatur Leadership Inst., 1993, Leadership Hist. Triangle, 2003. Mem.: ALA, Va. Libr. Assn. (legis. com.). Mem. Soc. Of Friends. Avocations: travel, reading, woodworking, sports. Home: 8216 Old Mill Ln Williamsburg VA 23188-1135 Office: Williamsburg Regional Libr 7770 Croaker RD Williamsburg VA 23188 Office Phone: 757-259-7777. E-mail: jmoorman@mail.wrl.org.

**MOORMAN, RICHARD HAL, IV,** lawyer; b. Waco, Tex., Mar. 2, 1950; s. George R. and Billie (Scoggin) M.; m. Lucy Baker, May 24, 1974; children: Theodore Clark, Lydia Anne, Peter Baker. BCE, MIT, 1971; JD, So. Meth. U., 1976. Bar: Tex. 1976, U.S. Dist. Ct. (so. dist., we. dist., ea. dist.) Tex. 1976, U.S. Ct. Appeals (5th cir.) 1976; Bd. Cert. Civil Trial Law and Estate Planning and Probate Law, Tex. Bd. of Legal Specialization. Engr. Turner Collie & Braden, Houston, 1971-72, P.G. Bell Co., Houston, 1972-75; ptnr. Moorman Tate Moorman Urquhart & Haley L.L.P., Brenham, Tex., 1976—. Bd. dirs. Washington County Abstract Co., Brenham; bd. mem. Trinity Med. Ctr. Hosp.; past examiner (2002) Tex. Bd. of Legal Specialization; course dir. State Bar of Tex. Advanced Estate Planning and Probate Seminar. Mem. Tex. Air Control Bd., Austin, 1980-86; past pres. Washington on Brazos State Pk. Assn., Brenham, Brenham Downtown Assn. Named one of Tex. Superlawyers. Fellow Am. Coll. Trust and Estate Counsel, Tex. Bar Found.; mem. ABA (estate gift tax com.), State Bar of Tex. (coun. mem. real estate probate and trust sect.), Washington County C. of C. (pres.); Main Street Bd.; Elder: Brenham Bible Ch. Avocations: antiques, hunting, fishing, theology. Office: Moorman Tate Moorman Urquhart Haley LLP 207 E Main St Brenham TX 77833-3754 Office Phone: 979-836-5664. Business E-Mail: hmoorman@moormantate.com.

**MOORMAN, WILLIAM A.,** federal judge, retired career military officer; b. Chgo. BA in History and Econs., U. Ill., 1967, JD, 1970; Grad., Air Command & Staff Coll., Maxwell AFB, 1980; student Nat. War Coll., 1988—89. Commd. 2d lt. USAF, 1970, advanced through grades to maj. gen., 1999, ret., 2002; chief of contracts Air Force Comm. Svc., Richards-Gebaur AFB, Mo., 1971—74; chief of claims 475th Air Base Wing and 5th Air Force, Yokota AB, Japan, 1974-77; dep. staff judge advocate then staff judge advocate 31st Tactical Fighter Wing, Homestead AFB, Fla., 1977-79; staff judge advocate 832nd Air Divsn., Luke AFB, Ariz., 1980-83; chief preventive law and legal air group, then chief Office of the Judge Advocate Gen., Washington, 1983-88; staff judge advocate 12th Air Force/U.S. Southern Command Air Forces, Bergstrom AFB, Tex., 1989-91; dep. staff judge advocate Strategic Air Command, Offutt AFB, Nebr., 1991-92; staff judge advocate, 1992-93, Hdqs. USAF Europe, Ramstein AB, Germany, 1993-95; comdr. Air Force Legal Svcs. Agy., Bolling AFB, D.C., 1995-96; staff judge advocate Hdqs. Air Combat Command, Langley AFB, Va., 1996—99; judge JAG Hdqs., USAF, Washington 1999—2003, US Ct. Appeals Vets. Claims, Washington, 2004—. Decorated Legion of Merit with oak leaf cluster. Office: US Ct Appeals Vets Claims 625 Indiana Ave NW Ste 900 Washington DC 20004

---

**MOOS, H. WARREN,** physicist, educator, astronomer, director; b. NYC, Mar. 26, 1936; s. Henry H. and Dorothy E. (Warren) M.; m. Doris Elaine McClure, July 13, 1957; children: Janet, Paul, Daniel, David. BS, Brown U., 1957; MA, U. Mich., 1959, PhD, 1962. Rsch. assoc. Stanford (Calif.) U., 1961-63; acting asst. prof. Johns Hopkins U., Balt., 1963-64, asst. prof., 1964-68, assoc. prof., 1968-71, prof., 1971—, dir. Ctr. for Astrophys. Scis., 1988-93, chmn. Physics & Astronomy, 1993-96. Cons. in field; mem. com. on planetary and lunar exploration NRC/Nat. Acad. Sci., Washington, 1982-86; mem. space and earth sci. adv. com. NASA, Washington, 1984-87; vis. fellow Joint Inst. for Lab. Astrophysics, 1972-73, 80-81. Editor: Optical Properties of Ions in Crystals, 1967; contbr. over 300 articles to profl. jours. Trustee Associated Univs., Inc., 2002—, chair bd. trustees, 2004—. Sloan Found. fellow, 1965-69. Fellow Am. Phys. Soc.; mem. Am. Astron. Soc., Internat. Astron. Union. Achievements include prin. investigatorof far ultraviolet spectroscopic explorer; co-investigator of Apollo 17 ultraviolet spectrometer, of Hopkins Ultraviolet Telescope, of Voyager ultraviolet spectrometer, of space telescope imaging spectograph; research on ultraviolet astronomy and fusion plasma diagnostics. Office: Johns Hopkins U Dept Physics & Astronomy 34th & Charles Sts Baltimore MD 21218

**MOOS, RUDOLF H.,** psychologist, researcher; b. Berlin, Sept. 10, 1934; s. Henry R. and Herta M. (Ehrlich) M.; m. Bernice Schradski, June 9, 1963; children: Karen, Kevin. BA in Psychology, U. Calif. at Berkeley, 1956; PhD, U. Calif.-Berkeley, 1960. Mem. faculty psychiatry Stanford (Calif.) U., 1962—, dir. psychiatry research tng. program, 1967-92, prof. psychiatry, 1972—, dir. social ecology lab., 1967-92; sr. rsch. career scientist VA Med. Center, Palo Alto, Calif., 1981—, dir. Ctr. for Health Care Evaluation, 1984—2002, dir. Program Evaluation and Resource Ctr., 1990-99. Vis. prof. Inst. Psychiatry, also Maudsley and Royal Bethlem Hosp., London, 1969-70 Author: Issues in Social Ecology, 1974, Evaluating Treatment Environments, 1974, Health and the Social Environment, 1974, Evaluating Correctional and Community Settings, 1975, Human Adaptation Coping with Life Crises, 1976, The Human Context, 1976, Environment and Utopia, 1977, Coping with Physical Illness, 1977, Evaluating Educational Environments, 1979, Coping with Physical Illness: New Perspectives, 1984, Coping with Life Crises: An Integrated Approach, 1986, Alcoholism Treatment: Content, Process and Outcome, 1990, Group Residential Facilities for Older Adults, 1994, Evaluating Residential Facilities, 1996; mem. editl. bd. Jour. Behavioral Medicine, 1984-04, Internat. Jour. Therapeutic Cmtys., Prevention in Human Svcs., Psychosomatic Medicine, Evaluation and Program Planning, 1977-99, Jour. Personality and Social Psychology, 1985-91, Health Psychology: An Internat. Jour., 1985-97, Violence, Agression, and Terrorism, 1985-94, Jour. Substance Abuse, 1986-2001, Jour. Applied Gerontology, 1988-2005, Jour. Cmty. and Applied Social Psychology, Psychology and Aging, 1986-91, Environ. and Behavior, 1987-91, Indian Jour. Clin. Psychology, 1996-2002, Jour. Studies Alcohol, 1997, Am. Jour. Cmty. Psychology, 1998—, Pakistan Jour. Psychol. Rsch., 2005, Internat. Jour. Clin. and Health Psychology, 2006; assoc. editor: Ency. of Psychological Assessment. Fellow APA, Acad. Clin. Psychology, Acad. Behavioral Medicine, Soc. Behavioral Medicine, Am. Orthopsychiat. Assn., Nat. Inst. on Alcohol Abuse and Alcoholism (mem. coun.); mem. Am. Sociol. Assn., Am. Psychosomatic Assn. (mem. coun.). Home: 25661 W Fremont Rd Los Altos CA 94022-1600 Office: Stanford U Dept Psychiatry MC 5550 Palo Alto CA 94305

**MOOS, WALTER HAMILTON,** pharmaceutical company executive; AB in Chemistry cum laude, Harvard U., 1976; PhD in Chemistry, U. Calif., Berkeley, 1982. Scientist Parke-Davis Rsch. Divsn. Warner Lambert Co., Ann Arbor, Mich., 1982-83, sr. scientist, 1984, rsch. assoc., 1984-86, sr. rsch. assoc., 1986-87, sect. dir. chemistry, 1987-89, dir. chemistry, 1989, sr. dir. chemistry, 1990, v.p. neuroscis. and biol. chemistry, 1990-91; v.p. rsch. devel. Chiron Corp., Emeryville, Calif., 1991-97; chmn., CEO MitoKor, San Diego, 1997—2004; v.p. bioscience div. SRI Internat., Menlo Park, Calif., 2005—. Adj. asst. prof. dept. medicinal chemistry Coll. Pharmacy, U. Mich., 1990, adj. assoc. prof., 1990-91; adj. prof. dept. pharm. chemistry U. Calif., San Francisco, 1992—; bd. dirs. Migenix, Rigel Pharm., Biotech. Industry Orgn.; Alnis, Anterion, Axiom, Keystone Symposia, Mimotopes, Oncologic, Onyx; presenter to numerous sci. confs. Co-editor: Drug Discovery Technologies, 1990, Cognitive Disorders: Pathophysiology and Treatment, 1991; editor-at-large Medicinal Chemistry, 1988-2004; cons. editor Bio-Organic and Medicinal Chemistry Letters. Mem. Am. Peptide Soc. (charter mem.), U. Mich. Enzyme Discussion Group (co-founder), ACS Divsn. Medicinal Chemistry (chmn. membership com. 1989, councilor 1990), Am. Chem. Soc. Office: SRI Internat 333 Ravenswood Ave Menlo Park CA 94025

**MOOSAZADEH, KIOOMARS,** orthopedist, educator, physiatrist, researcher; b. Tehran, Iran, Apr. 27, 1956; arrived in U.S., 1998; s. Yakhazghel Moosazadeh and Mohtaram Banayee; m. Katayoun Ooriel, Apr. 5, 1989; children: Pegah, Kiarash. MD, Shahid Beheshti U., 1989. Cert. med. dr. 2001. Orthopaedic surgeon Emdad Hosp. Health and Med. Scis., Shahrood, Semnan, Iran, 1989—98; fellow in advanced orthopedic surgery A-O Internat., Switzerland, 1996; asst. prof. Azad U. Shahrood, 1996—98; fellow Hosp. Joint Disease Orthopedic Inst., N.Y.C., 1999—2000; vis. fellow in joint disease orthopedics NYU Hosp., 2000—01; intern Bklyn. Hosp. Ctr., 2001—02; clin. assoc. State U. Hosp., Bklyn., 2002—. Permanent mem., cons., med. com. retirement and impairment Social Welfare Orgn., Divsn. of Health Ministry, Shahrood, 1991—98; cons. physician Jewish Charity Hosp., Tehran. With Iranian Mil., 1982—84. Mem.: AMA (assoc.). Achievements include research in Bone Reimplantation Technique. Avocations: carpentry, music. Home: 26 Coolidge Ave Roslyn Heights NY 11577 Office: State Univ Hosp 445 Lenox Rd Brooklyn NY 11203 E-mail: kioomarsmd@hotmail.com.

**MOOSE, CHARLES A.,** former protective services official; b. Aug. 11, 1953; BA in U.S. History, U. N.C., 1975; MA in Pub. Adminstrn., Portland State U., 1984, PhD in Urban Studies and Criminology, 1993; grad., FBI Nat. Acad. Patrol officer Portland Police Dept., 1975-81, sergeant, 1981-84, lieutenant, 1984-91, capt. of No. Precinct, 1991-92, dep. chief of Ops. Branch, 1992-93, chief of police, 1993—99, Montgomery County, Md., 1999—2003. Co-author (with Charles Fleming): Three Weeks in October, 2003. Bd. dirs. Boys and Girls Club of Portland, Comprehensive Options for Drug Abusers; mem. funding allocation com. Black United Fund Oreg.; mem. Multnomah County Cmty. Action Commn., Police Exec. Rsch. Forum, Bd. Pub. Safety Standards and Tng., Gov.'s Drug and Violent Crime Policy Bd., Gov.'s Juvenile Justice Task Force; bd. dirs. Portland State U. Mem. Am. Soc. Criminology, Nat. Orgn. of Black Law Enforcement Execs., Soc. of Police Futurists Internat., Internat. Assn. Chiefs of Police. Home: Oahu HI

**MOOSE, SANDRA OHRN,** management consultant; b. Boston, Jan. 17, 1942; d. Fritz Andrew and Esther Helen (Bastey) Ohrn. Student, U. Vienna, Austria, 1962; BA summa cum laude, Wheaton Coll., 1963; MA, Harvard U., 1965, PhD, 1968. Tutor Harvard U., Cambridge, Mass., 1964-65; cons. FDIC, Washington, 1966-68; sr. v.p. The Boston Cons. Group, Boston, 1968-81, 84-89, 1993—2003, mng. ptnr. N.Y.C., 1988-98; pres. Strategic Advisory Services. Dir. GTE Corp., Rohm & Haas, New Eng. Life Mut. Funds, Verizon Comm. Inc., AES Corp. Contbr. articles to profl. jours. Trustee, Wheaton Coll., Norton, Mass., 1981-91; bd. dirs., treas. Arts Boston, 1976-88; mem. Dana Farber Cancer Inst.; corporator New Eng. Deaconess Hosp., Boston, 1981—; trustee Hampshire Coll., 1976-83; bd. dirs. Theatre Devel. Fund, N.Y., 1988-92, Boston Pub. Libr. Found., Ctr. for Cancer Prevention, Harvard U., Alfred P. Sloan Found.; overseer Mus. Fine Arts, Boston; mem. vis. com. Harvard Sch. Pub. Health, 1996—. Recipient 100th Anniversary award Wheaton Coll. Alumnae Assn., 1970. Mem. Am. Econs. Assn., Com. of 200, Women's Forum, Union Club, Harvard Grad. Sch. Alumni Assn. (bd. dirs.). Office: Strategic Advisory Services 3 Altarinda Rd Ste 205 Orinda CA 94563*

**MOOSHAGIAN, MARK NISHAN,** education educator; b. Worcester, Mass., Dec. 8, 1960; s. Madieros and Mary Mooshagian; 1 child, John Samuel. BS, U.S. Naval Acad., Annapolis, 1982; MA, U. R.I., Kingston, 2006. Cert. Secondary Math. Tchr. U.S. Naval Acad. Tchr. R.I., 1998, Commonwealth of Mass., 2003. Owner, operator Subway Sandwiches, Bristol, RI, 1994—97; math tchr. Commonwealth of Mass., Fall River, 2001—05, Newport (R.I.) Pub. Schs.

Mem. Friends of Sheffield PTO, Newport, RI, 2005—06. Lt. USN, 1982—93. Decorated Surface Warfare Officer USN, Armed Forces Expeditionary medal, Nat. Def. Svc. medal, Master Tng. Specialist. Mem.: Mensa, VFW (life), DAV (life), Nat. Honor Soc., U.S. Naval Acad. Alumni Assn. (life). Conservative. Armenian Apostolic. Home: 3 Bedlow Pl Newport RI 02840 Office: Home 3 Bedlow Pl Newport RI 02840 Office Phone: 401-847-9549. Business E-Mail: mooshagian@teachers.org.

**MOOSSA, A. R.,** surgeon, educator; b. Port Louis, Mauritius, Oct. 10, 1939; s. Yacoob and Maude (Rochecoute) M.; m. Denise Willoughby, Dec. 28, 1973; children: Pierre, Noel, Claude, Valentine. BS, U. Liverpool, Eng., 1962, MD (hon.), 1965; postgrad., Johns Hopkins U., 1972—73, U. Chgo., 1973—74. Intern Liverpool Royal Infirmary, 1965-66; resident United Liverpool Hosps. and Alder Hey Children's Hosp., 1966-72; from asst. prof. surgery to assoc. prof. U. Chgo., 1975-77, prof., dir. surg. rsch., chief gen. surgery svc., vice chmn. dept., 1977-83; chmn. dept. surgery U. Calif.-San Diego Med. Ctr., 1983—2004, prof., surgery, emeritus chmn., assoc. dean, spl. counsel for clin. affairs, 2004—. Litchfield lectr. U., Oxford, Eng., 1978; praelector in surgery U. Dundee, Scotland, 1979; Hampson Trust vis. prof. U. Liverpool, 1992, G.B. Ong. vis. prof. U. Hong Kong, 1993, Philip Sandblon vis. prof. U. Lund, Sweden. Editor: Tumors of the Pancreas, 1982, Essential Surgical Practice, 1983, 4th edit., 2000, Comprehensive Textbook of Oncology, 1985, 2d edit., 1991, Gastrointestinal Emergencies, 1985, Problems in General Surgery, 1989, Operative Colorectal Surgery, 1993. Fellow Royal Coll. Surgeons (Hunterian prof. 1977); mem. ACS, Am. Surg. Assn., Soc. Univ. Surgeons, Am. Soc. Clin. Oncology, European Surg. Assn. Office: U Calif San Diego Thornton Hosp 9300 Campus Point Dr 7212 La Jolla CA 92037 Office Phone: 858-657-6112. Business E-Mail: amoossa@ucsd.edu.

**MOOSSY, JOHN,** neurologist, consultant, pathologist; b. Shreveport, La., Aug. 24, 1925; s. John Yazbeck and Rose (Ferris) M.; m. Yvonne Reese, Mar. 15, 1951; children: John Jefferson, Joan Marie. MD, Tulane U., 1950. Intern Charity Hosp. of New Orleans, 1950-51, neurology resident, 1951-53; neuropathology fellow Columbia U. Coll. of Physicians and Surgeons, N.Y.C., 1953-54; assoc., lectr. in neuropathology Tulane U. Sch. Medicine, New Orleans, 1954-57; asst. to prof. in pathology, neurology La. State U., New Orleans, 1957-65; prof. pathology, grad. faculty U. Pitts., 1965-67; prof. pathology neuropathology Bowman Gray Sch. of Medicine, Winston-Salem, NC, 1967-72; prof. pathology and neurology, dir. div. neuropathology U. Pitts., 1972-93, emeritus prof., 1993—. Dir. Cerebrovascular Disease Study, World Fedn. of Neurology, Antwerp, Belgium, 1960-61; cons. Armed Forces Inst. of Pathology, Washington, 1977—, mem. sci. adv. bd., Washington, 1984-86. Editor: Cerebral Vascular Disease Seventh Conference, 1970, Cerebrovascular Diseases 12th Research Conference, 1981; editor-in-chief Jour. Neuropathology and Exptl. Neurology, 1981-91; mem. editorial bd. Archives Neurology, 1982-92. Recipient Excellence in Teaching award U. Pitts. Sch. of Medicine, 1987-88; named Commencement Speaker U. Pitts. Sch. of Medicine, 1989. Mem. Am. Acad. Neurology (sec.-treas. 1963-655), Am. Neurol. Assn. (v.p. 1977-78), Am. Assn. Neuropathologists (pres. 1974-75, Neuropathology award 1992), Internat. Soc. Neuropathology, Coun. Biology Editors.

**MOOTE, A. LLOYD,** history professor; b. Hamilton, Ont., Can., Mar. 22, 1931; s. Stanley Alanson and Esther Grace (Wood) M.; m. Barbara Brown, Dec. 27, 1956 (div. 1982); children: Karen, Peter, Daphne, Robert; m. Dorothy Carter May, May 30, 1986. BA, U. Toronto, 1954; MA, U. Minn., Mpls., 1956, PhD, 1958. Tchg. asst. U. Minn., Mpls., 1955-58; lectr. U. Toronto, 1958-61; asst. prof. U. Cin., 1961-62; from asst. prof. to prof. history U. So. Calif., L.A., 1962-92, prof emeritus, 1993—. Vis. prof. Queen's U., Kingston, Ont., 1965-66; chmn. gen. edn. program U. So. Calif., 1978-81; mem. Inst. Advanced Study, Princeton, 1988-89; affiliated prof. Rutgers U., 1994—. Author: The Seventeenth Century, 1970, The Revolt of the Judges, 1971, The World of Europe: The Seventeenth Century, 1973, 2d edit., 1979, Louis XIII: The Just, 1989, paperback edit., 1991, (with Dorothy C. Moote) The Great Plague: The Story of London's Most Deadly Year, 2004, paperback edit., 2006 (nominated Pulitzer prize); co-editor, contbr. issue of French hist. studies on biography, 1996; mem. editl. bd. French Hist. Studies, 1971-74; internat. adv. bd. European History Quar., 1983—. Founder, convener So. Calif. Early Modern French Studies Group, 1980-93, Rutgers, Princeton and Phila. Early Modern History Group, 1994—. Recipient William Koren prize Soc. French Hist. Studies, 1962, creative scholarship award U. So. Calif. Assocs., 1973, faculty book award U. So. Calif. chpt. Phi Kappa Phi, 1990; younger scholar NEH, 1969; grantee Am. Philos. Soc., 1962, Haynes Found., 1973, Wellcome Inst. for History Medicine, 1993-94, Burroughs-Wellcome Fund, 1996; Guggenheim fellow, 1976, fellow U. Essex, Eng., 1993-94, Rutgers Ctr. for Hist. Analysis, 1995-97. Mem. Am. Hist. Assn., Soc. French Hist. Studies (pres. 1984-85), Soc. for Study French History (U.K.), Sixteenth-Century Studies Conf. Home: 149 Meaowbrook Dr Princeton NJ 08540-3664 Personal E-mail: dlmoote@verizon.net.

**MOOTHA, VAMSI KRISHNA,** biomedical researcher, educator; BS, Stanford U., 1993; MD, Harvard U, 1998; internship and residency in Internal Med., Brigham and Women's Hospital, 1998—2001; postdoctoral fellowship, Whitehead and Broad Institutes, 2004. Asst. prof. sys. biology Harvard Med. Sch.; also asst. prof. med. Mass. Gen. Hosp., Boston. Author: numerous articles in jour. such as Proceedings of the Nat. Acad. of Sci. USA, Cell, and Nature Genetics. Named a MacArthur Fellow, 2004. Achievements include pioneering powerful, adaptable computational strategies for mining data collected in laboratories throughout the world, as well as for fundamental insights in seritochondrial biology. Office: Dept Systems Biology Broad Inst 2 Cambridge Ctr Cambridge MA 02142-1401 Address: Ctr for Human Genetic Rsch Simches Rsch Bldg 185 Cambridge St Boston MA 02114 Office Phone: 617-252-1672. Office Fax: 617-252-1902. E-mail: vamsi@hms.harvard.edu.

**MOOTY, JOHN WILLIAM,** lawyer; b. Adrian, Minn., Nov. 27, 1922; s. John Wilson and Genevieve (Brown) M.; m. Virginia Nelson, June 6, 1952 (dec. 1964); children: David N., Bruce W., Charles W.; m. Jane Nelson, Jan. 15, 1972. BSL, U. Minn., 1943, LLB, 1944. Bar: Minn. 1944. Ptnr. Gray, Plant, Mooty & Bennett, Mpls., 1945—. Bd. dirs. Internat. Dairy Queen, Inc., Bur. of Engraving, Inc., Riverway Co. and subs.; chmn. Rio Verde Svcs., Inc., Ariz. Author (with others): Minnesota Practice Methods, 1956. Chmn. Gov.'s Task Force on Edn., 1981; pres. Citizens League Mpls., 1970; acting chmn. Republican Party of Minn., 1958. Named to Minn. Bus. Hall of Fame, 2003. Mem. ABA, Minn. Bar Assn., Hennepin County Bar Assn., U. Minn. Alumni Assn. (pres. 1982), Tonto Verde Country Club, Minikahda (Mpls.) Club, Mpls. Club. Home: 8106 Highwood Dr Apt Y232 Bloomington MN 55438-1054 Office Phone: 612-632-3200. Business E-Mail: john.mooty@gpmlaw.com.

**MOR, GOPAL KUMAR,** materials scientist, researcher; arrived in U.S., 2002; s. Kapoor Singh and Rammurti Mor; m. Rashmi Joon, June 27, 2003; 1 child, Nishant. BS, Devi Ahilya U., Indore, India, 1994, MS, 1996; PhD, Indian Inst. Tech. Delhi, New Delhi, 2002. Jr. research fellow Indian Inst. Tech. Delhi, New Delhi, 1996—99, sr. rsch. fellow, 1999—2001, project asst., 2001—02; postdoctoral scholar Material Rsch. Inst., Pa. State U., University Park, 2002—. Recipient Young Scientist award, Dept. Sci. and Tech., Govt. India, 2001; fellow, Indian Inst. Tech. Delhi, 1996—2001. Mem.: AAAS, Materials Rsch. Soc., Am. Chem. Soc. Achievements include research in enhanced photocleavage of water using titania nanotubes; self cleaning capability of titania nanotubes sensing hydrogen gas at room temperature; fabrication of dye sensitized solar cell by utilizing titania nanotubes array grown on conducting glass; patent in field. Avocations: cricket, volleyball. Home: 10 Vairo Blvd Apt 16A State College PA 16803 Office: Material Rsch Inst Hasting Road 212 MRL University Park PA 16802 Office Phone: 814-865-6780. Office Fax: 814-865-6780. Business E-Mail: gkm1@psu.edu.

**MORA, ALBERTO J.,** retail executive, lawyer; b. Boston, 1952; BA with honors, Swarthmore Coll., 1974; JD, U. Miami, 1981. Bar: Fla., D.C. Fgn. svc. officer US Dept. State, 1975—78; gen. counsel USIA, 1989—93, mem.

broadcasting bd. govs., 1995—2001; counsel internat. law Greenberg Traurig LLP, Washington; gen. counsel, dept. of Navy US Dept. Def., Washington, 2001—05; v.p., gen. counsel, internat. divsn. Wal-Mart Stores, Inc., 2006—. Bd. dirs. Nat. Coun. for Internat. Visitors, Radio Free Asia, Radio Free Europe/Radio Liberty. Editor-in-chief: Law of the Ams.: U. Miami Jour. of Internat. Law. Recipient John F. Kennedy Profile in Courage award, John F. Kennedy Library Found., 2006; fellow, Orgn. of Am. States. Mem.: Coun. Fgn. Rels. Office: Wal-Mart Stores Inc 702 SW 8th St Bentonville AR 72716 Office Phone: 479-204-9027.

**MORA, ANTONIO GONZALEZ, III,** broadcast journalist; b. Havana, Cuba, Dec. 14, 1957; came to U.S., 1960; s. Antonio Gonzalez Jr. and Natalia (Sandoval) M.; m. Julie Good, Aug. 27, 1994; children: Clara, Antonio Daniel. JD, U. Catolica Andres Bello, Caracas, Venezuela, 1980; LLM, Harvard U., Cambridge, Mass., 1981; DHL, Our Lady of Holy Cross, New Orleans, 2000; PhD (hon.), Ursinus Coll., 2001. Assoc. Debevoise & Plimpton, N.Y.C., 1981-88; anchor Sta. WXTV, Secaucus, NJ, 1990-91, Sta. WNJU, Teterboro, NJ, 1991; anchor Nightside NBC, Charlotte, NC, 1992; reporter, anchor Sta. WTVJ-TV, Miami, 1992-93; host Good Day LA Tv Sta. KTTV, L.A., 1993—94; host Good Morning America Sunday ABC, N.Y.C., 1994-95; correspondent ABC News, N.Y.C., 1995-99; news anchor Good Morning America ABC, N.Y.C., 1999—2002; evening news anchor TV Sta. WBBM, Chgo., 2002—. Recipient Nat. Emmy award, 2000, Peabody award, 2000-01, Edward R. Murrow award, 2000, 5 Local Emmy awards, 2004-05. Mem.: Coun. Fgn. Rels.

**MORA, JIM, JR.,** professional football coach; b. Los Angeles, Nov. 19, 1961; m. Shannon Mora; children: Cole, Lillia, Ryder, Trey. Grad., U. Wash., 1983. Asst. coach U. Wash., 1984; pro. pers. San Diego Chargers, 1985, asst. coach, 1986—91; secondary coach New Orleans Saints, 1992—96; asst. coach San Francisco 49ers, 1997—2003; head coach Atlanta Falcons, Flowery Br., Ga., 2004—. Office: Atlanta Falcons 4400 Falcon Pkwy Flowery Branch GA 30542

**MORA, PAT,** writer, speech professional; b. El Paso, Tex., Jan. 19, 1942; d. Raul Antonio and Estella (Delgado) M.; m. William H. Burnside, July 27, 1963 (div. Aug. 1981); children: William Burnside, Elizabeth Burnside, Cecilia Burnside; m. Vernon L. Scarborough, May 25, 1984. BA, Tex. Western Coll., 1963; MA, U. Tex., El Paso, 1967. Lectr. English U. Tex., El Paso, 1979-81; asst. to v.p. for acad. affairs, 1981-89, mus. dir., asst. to pres., 1987-89; cons. W.K. Kellogg Found., Battle Creek, Mich., 1989-91. Advisor Kellogg Nat. Fellowship Program, 1991-93. Author: (poetry) Chants, 1984 (SW Book award 1985), Borders, 1986 (SW Book award 1987), Communion, 1991, Agua Santa: Holy Water, Aunt Carmen's Book of Practical Saints, 1997; (nonfiction) Nepantla: Essays from the Land in the Middle, 1993, House of Houses, 1997; (children's books) Confetti: Poems for Children, Uno, Dos, Tres: One, Two, Three, Listen to the Desert: Oye al Desierto, The Race of Toad and Deer, The Gift of the Poinsettia: El regalo de la flor de nochebuena, The Desert Is My Mother: El desierto es mi madre, Agua, Agua, Agua, Pablo's Tree, A Birthday Basket for Tía, 1992 (SW Book award 1993), Tomás and the Library Lady, 1997, A library for Juana: The World of Sor Juana Inés, 2002 (Tomás Rivera Mexican American Children's Book award, 2002), Dona Flor: A Tall Tale About a Giant Woman with a Great Big Heart, 2005 (Am. Libr. Assn. Pura Belpre Author Honor Book, 2006). Kellogg nat. fellow W.K. Kellogg Found., 1986; Nat. Endowment Arts Creative Writing fellow, 1994; recipient poetry award Conf. Cin. Women, 1990; named to El Paso Herald Post Writers Hall of Fame, 1988. Mem Tex. Inst. Letters, Acad. Am. Poets, Nat. Coun. Tchrs. English, Soc. Children's Book Writers, Poetry Soc. Am. Democrat. Avocations: reading, walking, travel.*

**MORA, PHILIPPE,** screenwriter, producer, director, painter; b. Paris, Aug. 8, 1949; s. Georges and Mirka Madeleine (Zelik) M.; m. Pamela Mai Krause, Aug. 1, 1980; children: Madeleine Mai, Georges Ritchie Maximillian, Dominic Marceau. Student, La Trobe U., Melbourne, Australia, 1967. Screenwriter, dir., producer, 1969—. Founder Cinema Papers mag., Melbourne, 1967. Dir., writer, prodr. (films) Trouble in Molopolis, 1969, The Howling III: The Marsupials, 1987, Snide and Prejudice, 1997, According to Occam's Razor, 1999, Project 65, 2002, Gertrude Stein, 2006; co-writer (film) Double Headed Eagle, 1971; dir., writer (films) Swastika, 1972 (Blue Ribbon award 1974), Brother Can You Spare a Dime, 1975, Mad Dog, 1976 (John Ford Meml. award 1976), According to Occam's Razor, 2000, I Love You Gertrude Stein, 2006; dir. (films) The Beast Within, 1980, The Return of Captain Invincible, 1981, A Breed Apart, 1983, The Howling II, 1984, Death of a Soldier, 1985, Back in Business, 1996; dir. prodr. Communion, 1990, Art Deco Detective, 1994, Pterodactyl Woman from Beverly Hills, 1994, Precious Find, 1995, Burning Down the House, 1996, Thick and Thin, 1997, Joseph's Gift, 1999, The Times They Ain't A Changin', 2005, The Vatican Tapes, 2005; dir., prodr. (film) Hamlet, 2001; exhibited in one-man and group shows at Argys Gallery, Melbourne, 1967, Clytie Jessop Gallery, London, '1968-71, Sigi Kraus Gallery, London, 1970-71, Camden Arts Centre, London, 1970, Richard Demarco Gallery, Edinburgh, 1971, Tolarno Gallery, Melbourne, 1971, Watters Gallery, Sydney, Australia, 1972, William Mora Gallery, Melbourne, 1987, Caz Gallery, L.A., 1990, Larrikins in London, 2003, Coll. Fine Arts, Sydney, 2003; represented in permanent collection Nat. Gallery Collection, Canberra, Australia, 1982, Mus. Modern Art Australia; English Lit. exhbn. Victorian Edn. Authority, Victoria, Australia, 1966; contbr. articles to mags Mem. Dirs. Guild Am., Acad. Motion Picture Arts and Scis., Australian Film Dirs. Assn. Office: Michael Blaha Esq 2530 Wilshire Blvd Santa Monica CA 90403-4616 Personal E-Mail: cinepamela@aol.com. E-mail: moracyber@juno.com.

**MORACA-SAWICKI, ANNE MARIE,** oncology nurse; b. Niagara Falls, N.Y., Sept. 28, 1952; d. Joseph R. and Joan (Forgione) Moraca; m. Richard L. Sawicki, Sept. 15, 1979. BSN, D'Youville Coll. 1974; MS in Nursing, SUNY in Buffalo, 1971. Asst. prof. nursing D'Youville Coll., Buffalo, 1977-81; clin. editor Springhouse (Pa.) Corp., 1981-82; charge nurse Mt. St. Mary's Hosp., Lewiston, N.Y., 1982-84; surg. coord., adminstrv. asst. Dr. Richard L. Sawicki, Niagara Falls, N.Y., 1983—. Clin. cons., externship site supr. Niagara County C.C., Sanborn, N.Y.; bd. dirs. Health Assn. Niagara County, Inc., adult day care program Health Assn. Niagara County Inc. Contbr.: Nurses Legal Handbook, 1985, Pharmacotherapeutics: A Nursing Process Approach, 1986, 2d edit., 1990, 3rd edit., 1994, 4th edit., 1998; clin. editor, contbr. Nurses Ref. Libr. Series Vols. on Drugs, Definitions, Procedures and Practices; clin. reviewer Manual of Med./Sug. Nursing, 1995, contbr., 1996; clin. reviewer Critical Care Handbook and IV Drug Handbook, 1995; clin. cons. Critical Care Plans, 1987, Taber's Cyclopedic Med. Dictionary, 16th edit., 1989; grant writer LaSalle Bus. and Profl. Assn. Mem. Niagara Falls Cmty. Devel. Bd.; bd. dirs. Barbara Zimmer Holiday Wish Show, Barbara Zimmer Holiday Wish Breast Cancer Fund Raiser; co-chairperson LaSalle Bus. and Profl. Cmty. Devel. Fund Raising Com. Recipient Cert. of Appreciation Niagara County C.C., 1988, 91, 92, Cmty. Svc. award Am. Cancer Soc., 1978, Miss Hope award, 1977, Am. Cancer Soc. Nursing Fellowship Grant, 1977, Good Neighbor award Niagara Falls Meml. Med. Ctr., 2003, LaSalle Bus. and Profl. Assn. Cmty. Svc. award, 2003, Pres.'s award, HANEI, 2004; Grad. fellow SUNY, Buffalo, 1976-77; grantee mulitple grants for cmty. devel., beautification and health and safety, LaSalle. Mem. AAUP, N.Y. State Nurse's Assn., Health Assn. Niagara County (chairperson 1995—, bd. dirs. adult day care program), LaSalle Bus. and Prof. Assn. (publicity chairperson), Am. Bus. Women's Assn., Sigma Theta Tau. Home: 4658 Vrooman Dr Lewiston NY 14092-1049 E-mail: ams928@webtv.net.

**MORADI, AHMAD F.,** software company executive; b. Tehran, Persia, Mar. 21, 1955; arrived in US, 1973; s. Akbar and Afsar (Mokaram) M.; m. Lourdes Pernas; 1 child, Aimee. AS, Broward Community Coll., 1978; BA, Fla. Atlantic U., 1980; PhD, LaSalle U., 1989. Advisor restaurant industries, Miami, Fla., 1974-78; pres. Octa-8, Inc., Ft. Lauderdale, Fla., 1980-82; mgmt. cons. MGI-MCG, Boca Raton, Fla., 1982-83; dir. ops. Datamation, Hollywood, Fla., 1983-85; pres. Software Intelligence Corp., Ft. Lauderdale, 1985—; with ARM Financial Corp., 1987-89; MIS dir., CIO Churchill Tech.,

Inc., Davie, Fla., 1992—; MIS dir. Westmack Group Holding Co., Delray Beach, 1995—; prin. G4, Inc., Ft. Lauderdale, 1992—; CEO Futuretrak Internat. OTC BB:FTRK, 1998-99, Worldcast Interactive Inc.; with Biomed. Rsch. Techs., 1997—, Interchange Med., Inc., 1999—, Maxwell Rand Inc., 1999—, Netstairs.com, 2000—. Lectr. South Fla. Bus. Jour., 1984-85, Victoria Hosp., Miami, Fla., 1985, Mt. Sinai Hosp., Miami, Fla., 1985, U. Miami, Fla., 1986, Chiropractic Today, 1989; cons., mus. adv., internat. mktg. and telemarketing mgmt. Software Intelligence Corp., 1985—; systems analyst Softway, Inc., Ft. Lauderdale, 1986; hon. co-chmn. bus. adv. coun. Nat. Leadership Coun. and Nat. Rep. Bus. Commn.; hon. chmn. U.S. Presdl. Bus. Commn., 2002. Named Businessman of Yr., U.S. Presdl. Bus. Commn., 2003; recipient Gold medal, 2002. Mem. Data Processing Mgmt. Assn., Small Bus. Inst. Office Phone: 954-229-0900. E-mail: inquiry@g41.com.

**MORAGNÉ E SILVA, MICHÈLE LOWE,** language educator; b. White Plains, N.Y., May 23, 1955; d. John Hutchins and Catherine Theresa (Kelley) M.; m. Amandio Silva, June 25, 1983; children: Marisa, Sabrina. BA, Bucknell U., 1977; MEd, R.I. Coll., 1981; PhD, U. Tex., 1991. Instr. Am. Language Inst., Porto, Portugal, 1978-79; instr., cons. R.I. Coll., Providence, 1980-83; asst. instr. U. Tex., Austin, 1984-85; asst. prof., dir. English for internat. students St. Edward's U., Austin, 1985—. Mem. com. on ESL, conv. presenter Conf. on Coll. Composition and Communication, 1987, 91, 92, 2004. Pub. (composition textbook) Authentic Writing; mem. editl. bd. Jour. Second Lang. Writing; contbr. articles to profl. jours., articles to The World Edn. Ency., 2001. Mem. MLA, Tchrs. English to Speakers of Other Langs. (conv. presentor 1981-88, 92), Nat. Coun. Tchrs. English, Fgn. Lang. Edn. Ctr. Student Assn. (sec., v.p.). Democrat. Roman Catholic. Avocations: travel, music, art, languages, swimming. Office: St Edwards U 3001 S Congress Ave Austin TX 78704-6489 Office Phone: 512-448-8653. E-mail: michelem@admin.stedwards.edu.

**MORAHAN, JOHN KELLY,** social studies educator; b. Scranton, Pa., Dec. 31, 1957; s. Joseph Paul and Dorothy Theresa Morahan; m. Kristen Mary Walsh, Dec. 23, 1988; children: Sean Kelly, Caitlin Mary. BA in Social Studies, U. Scranton, Pa., 1980; MS in Secondary Sch. Adminstrn., U. Scranton, 1995. Cert. tchr. Pa. Tchr. social studies, coach, athletic dir. Pocono Ctrl. Cath. HS, Cresco, Pa., 1981—88; tchr. social studies, coach Notre Dame HS, East Stroudsburg, Pa., 1988—89; tchr. social studies Elk Lake HS, Dimock, Pa., 1989—. V.p. Susquehanna Little League, Rush/Lawton, Pa., 2001—02; pres. Elk Lake Youth Soccer, Dimock, 1998—2004; PIAA ofcl. Soccer Orgn. Fellow, Northeastern Pa. Diversity Edn. Consortium, 2004—. Democrat. Roman Catholic. Avocations: golf, basketball.

**MORAHAN-MARTIN, JANET MAY,** psychologist, educator; b. N.Y.C., Jan. 13, 1944; d. William Timothy and May Rosalind (Tarangelo) Morahan; m. Curtis Harmon Martin, June 2, 1979; 1 child, Gwendolyn May. AB, Rosemont (Pa.) Coll., 1965; MEd, Tufts U., 1968; PhD, Boston Coll., 1978. Asst. mkt. rsch. analyst Compton Advt. Co., N.Y.C., 1965-67; mkt. rsch. analyst Ogilvy & Mather Advt., N.Y.C., 1967; ednl. rsch. asst. Tufts U., Medford, Mass., 1968-69; counselor Psychol. Inst. Bentley Coll., Waltham, Mass., 1971-72; dir. counseling svcs. Bryant U., Smithfield, RI, 1972-75, psychology instr., 1972-76, asst. prof. psychology, 1976-81, assoc. prof. psychology, 1981-91, prof. psychology, 1991—. Bd. dirs. Multi-Svc. Ctr., Newton, Mass., 1980-82. Contbr. articles to profl. jours., chpts. to books; reviewer APA Conv., 1985—, Teaching of Psychology Jour., 1988—, Collegiate Micro-Computer Jour., 1991, 93, Nat. Soc. Sci. Jour., 1991; mem. editl. bd., spl. editl. editor Cyber Psychology and Behavior. Bd. dirs. Wellesley (Mass.) Community Children's Ctr., 1986-90, Coun. for Children, Newton, Mass., 1984-86. NIMH fellow, 1967-68; NSF grantee, 1974-76, U.S. Office Edn. grantee, 1980. Mem. APA, Mass. Audubon Soc., Internat. Soc. for Online Mental Health (founding mem.), Soc. for Tchg. of Psychology, Soc. Computers in Psychology. Avocations: photography, antiques, gardening, literature. Home: 17 Fuller Brook Rd Wellesley MA 02482-7108 Office: Bryant U 1150 Douglas Pike Smithfield RI 02917-1291 Business E-Mail: jmorahan@bryant.edu.

**MORALES, CARLOS,** director, educator; s. Carlos E. Morales and Elsie Irizarry; m. Amarilis Morales, June 28, 1997; children: Ricardo Morales Conty, Arelys Morales Conty. BS in Biology/Microbiology, Interamerican U. P.R., 1994, MA in Edn., 1997; postgrad., Capella U. Cert. online instr. Walden U., 2001; distance learning adminstr. Tex., 2002. Instr. U. Metropolitana, Aguadilla, PR, 1999—2001, EDP Coll. P.R., San Sebastian, PR, 1999—2001; instrnl. designer N.J. City U., Jersey City, 2001—; biology instr. Seminole C.C., Sanford, Fla., Colegio Tecnologico y Comercial de PR, Aguada, PR. Instrnl. design/ednl. tech. cons. Rutgers U., New Brunswick, NJ, 2005. Trustee Consortium Distance Edn. CODE, Mt. Laurel, NJ, 2004—; mem. EDUCAUSE, Washington, 2005—; pres. IDOL Learners Group, Kirksville, Mo., 2005—06; peer reviewer Project MERLOT.org, Calif., 2004—05; mem. Copyright Statewide Com., Newark, 2004—06. Mem.: Inter-American Distance Edn. Consortium, Assn. for the Advancement of Computing in Edn. (corr.), Internat. Soc. for Tech. in Edn. (corr.). Office: New Jersey City University 2039 Kennedy Blvd P117 Jersey City NJ 07305 Office Phone: 201-200-2572. Office Fax: 201-200-2360. Business E-Mail: crmorales@njcu.edu.

**MORALES, DIANE K.,** former federal agency administrator; b. Houston, July 11, 1946; d. Arthur Clement and Helen Mary (Araiza) Morales, Louie Welch (Stepfather); m. James Neal Glerum. BA, U. Tex.-Austin, 1968. Account exec. Goodwin, Dannenbaum, Littman & Wingfield, Houston, 1968—70; pub. rels. rep. Gittings, Inc., Dallas, 1970—71; asst. buyer, mgr. Neiman-Marcus, Dallas, 1971—80; sr. assoc., mktg. mgr. 3/D Internat., Houston, 1980—81; dep. asst. sec. policy U.S. Dept. Interior, Washington, 1981—83; bd. dirs. CAB, Washington, 1983—86; v.p. govt. rels. Earth Tech. Corp., Washington, 1986—88, pres. Morales Consulting Svc. Co., Washington, 1988—90; dep. asst. sec. def. for logistics U.S. Dept. Def., Washington, 1990—93, dep. under sec. logistics and material readiness, 2001—04; pres. DMS, Inc., Washington, 1993—2001, DMG Enterprises, LLC, Washington, 2004—. Mem. logistics mgmt. com. Nat. Def. Industry Assn., 1995—2001. Pres. Downtown Rep. Women's Club, Dallas, 1975-80; bd. dirs. Dallas County Men's Rep. Club, 1978-80, Dallas Coun. Women's Rep. Club, 1978-80, Houston Interam. C. of C., 1980-81, Christian Embassy, 1990-93, Am. Cancer Soc./NOVA, 2000-04, Wolf Trap Found., 2005—, Nat. Job Corps Assn., 2005—; Project Nehemiah, 1996—, Tex. State Soc., 1996-2001; mem. Rep. Women's Fed. Forum, Rep. Nat. Hispanic Assembly, Conservative Rep. Network, 1985-89. Mem.: Women in Def. Industry. Republican. Presbyterian.

**MORALES, EMMITT,** mechanical engineer, consultant; s. Emilio and Alice Morales; m. Virginia Eilene Lopez, Nov. 27, 1951; children: David, Michael. Grad. h.s., Port Arthur, Tex. Co-owner Tool Tech, Beaumont, Tex., 1999—. With U.S. Army, 1969—71. Church Of Christ. Achievements include patents for stud removal and fastening tool. Avocation: golf. Home: 5260 Stardust Beaumont TX 77706 Office: Tool Tech 5420 Gorman Rd Beaumont TX 77705

**MORALES, HECTOR E., JR.,** bank executive, lawyer; BA, Columbia Coll.; JD, U. Tex. Pvt. practice Graves, Dougherty, Hearon & Moody, Austin, Tex., Crain, Caton, & James, Houston; atty. internat. law Reliant Energy, Houston, 1993—97; pres., gen. mgr. Reliant Energy Argentina, 1997—2000; sr. v.p. Viamericas Corp.; fin. svcs. cons.; alt. exec. dir. U.S. Inter-Am. Devel. Bank, 2003, acting exec. dir., 2003—04, exec. dir., 2004—. Office: US Dept Treasury 1300 NY Ave NW Rm NE1101 Washington DC 20577 Office Phone: 202-623-1075. Office Fax: 202-623-3096.

**MORALES, HUGO,** broadcast executive; BA with honors, Harvard Coll.; JD, Harvard Law Sch.; D (hon.), Calif. State U., Fresno. Founder, exec. dir. Radio Bilingüe, Inc., Fresno, 1976—. Bd. dirs. Calif. Endowment, 2004—, Central Calif. Legal Services, Nat. Alliance for Hispanic Health; bd. mem. Calif. Postsecondary Ed. Commn., Accrediting Commn. for Sr. Coll. and U., We. Assn. of Sch. and Coll., Rosenberg Found., San Francisco Found., Calif.

Tomorrow, Calif. Wellness Teen Pregnancy Prevention Initiative Adv. Comm., Fresno Arts Council Folk Arts Program Adv. Comm., Alliance for Calif. Traditional Arts. Recipient Edward R. Murrow award, Corp. for Public Broadcasting, 1999, Susan Hadden award, Alliance for Public Tech., Cesar Chavez award, Assn. of Mexican-Am. Educators; fellow MacArthur Found., 1994. Office: Radio Bilingue Inc 5005 E Belmont Ave Fresno CA 93727*

**MORALES, JOHN PAUL,** television services producer; b. Menard, Tex., May 17, 1963; s. Herb Morales; m. Karen Elain Cox-Morales, Aug. 14, 1993. BAS, Tex. Tech U., 1986. On-air promotion mgr. KTVD-UPN 20, Englewood, Colo., 1996—99; TV svcs. prodr. Denver Police Dept., 2000—. Owner HEDZUP Prodns., Denver, 2000—. Videographer, editor (training video) Intro to Krav Maga (Gold Classic Telly award, 2004). Recipient Telly award, 2002. Mem.: Law Enforcement Video Assn. (Gold Shield and award of honor 2003). Office: Denver Police Acad 8895 Montview Blvd Bldg # 58 Denver CO 80220 Office Phone: 303-370-1522.

**MORALES, JOSE,** psychotherapist, writer; b. Hatillo, P.R., May 27, 1930; s. Polonio and Marciala (Dorta) M.; m. Ramona Velez, Oct. 24, 1954 (div. Mar. 1976); 1 child, Jose R. Jr.; m. Carmen Iris Lopez, Apr. 12, 1976; 1 child, Delia. BA in Edn., U. P.R., 1960; MSW, NYU, 1968; PhD, U. Calif., Santa Barbara, 1985. Cert. social studies tchr., P.R., N.Y.; cert. social worker, N.Y. Tchr. P.R. Bd. Edn., Arecibo, 1960-63; ednl. counselor Puerto Rican Migration Dept., N.Y.C., 1964; case worker Lincoln Hall, N.Y.C., 1964-66, social worker, 1968-70; social worker, supr. Greenpoint Hosp., Bklyn., 1970-76; social worker VA Hosp., Phila., 1977-80; social work supr. Kings County Hosp., Bklyn., 1981-93; psychotherapist CCM, Bklyn., 1993—. Cons./supr. N.Y. PCC, Bklyn. Author: Puerto Rican Spiritism, 1977 (Meritorious award 1981), Pepito, 1998, El Morro, 1998, Galeria de Heroes de Puerto Rico, 1997 (Meritorious award 1999); freelance journalist Eco Latino, 1993, El Latino Americano, 1997. Co-founder CILI, Bklyn., 1973, ACCEPIA, Bklyn., 1993. Mem. NASW, Am. Psychology Soc., Latin Am. Assn. Poets and Writers (co-founder, sec. 1997—, leadership com. 1998), N.Y. Acad. Scis. Avocations: reading, writing, researching geneology. Home: Bay Ridge Sta PO Box 234 Brooklyn NY 11220-0234 Office: CCM 185 Montague St Fl 9 Brooklyn NY 11201-3608 E-mail: JMora52825@aol.com.

**MORALES, MARCIA PAULETTE MERRY,** language educator, archaeologist; b. Denver, Dec. 10, 1946; d. Paul Robert Merry and Berneice Roberta Lyddon; m. Jorge Bernardo Morales, Dec. 28, 1977; children: Marcia Paloma, Elisa Berenice, Andrea Paul-Etta. BA, U. Denver, 1969; MA cum laude, U. Am., 1975. Rsch. asst. dept. anthropology U. Ill., Puebla, Mexico, 1972—75; tchr. Eng., art history Escuela Preparatoria, Cuautla, Morclos, Mexico, 1975—76; tchr., coord. Eng. Colegio Oquetza, Cuautla, 1982—91; tchr. anthropology, Eng. Centro Cultural Iberoamericano, Cuernavaca, Mexico, 1992—95; tchr. Spanish Aztec (N.Mex.) HS, 1996—. Instr. Spanish Fort Lewis Coll., Durango, Colo., 1997—. Contbr. chapters to books Ancient Chalcatzingo, 1987. Fellow: Durango Heartbeat (pres. 1997—), San Juan Audubon Soc. (treas. 1996—). Methodist. Avocations: hiking, birdwatching, travel.

**MORALES, MYRON RUSSELL,** lawyer; b. Victoria, Tex., June 1, 1974; s. Steve A. and Hope Morales; m. Dolores Gonzales, Aug. 8, 1998. BA, U. Tex. at Austin, 1996; JD, South Tex. Coll. Law, 2000. Bar: Ky. Supreme Ct. 2002, DC Ct. Appeals 2003. Atty. Law Offices of Myron R. Morales, Louisville, 2002—03, Law Offices of Allen E. Kaye, P.C., NYC, 2003—04; ptnr. Lee Ln. Smith LLP, 2004—. Content editor LeapLaw, Boston, 2002—03; contract author Bender's Immigration Bull., Newark, 2001—04; contract editor Lexis-Nexis, 2003—04. Contbr. articles to profl. jours. Mem.: Am. Immigration Lawyers Assn. Catholic. Avocations: travel, astronomy, coin collecting/numismatics. Office: Lee Lane Smith LLP 67 Wall Street Suite 2211 New York NY 10005 Office Phone: 212-709-8296. E-mail: m.morales@mlls.co.uk.

**MORALES-RAMOS, JUAN ALFREDO,** entomologist, researcher; s. Alfredo Morales and Hortencia Ramos De Morales; m. Maria Guadalupe Rojas, Sept. 15, 1985. BS, Autonomous U. Nuevo Leon, Mex., 1977; MS, Higher Coll. of Tropical Agr., Mex., 1982; PhD, Tex. A&M U., 1991. Rschr., lectr. Colegio Superior de Agricultura Tropical, Cardenas, Tabasco, Mexico, 1978—84; rsch. technician Tex. A&M U., Coll. Sta., Tex., 1985—86; rsch. entomologist U.S. Dept. Agrl.-Agrl. Rsch. Svc. Subtropical Agrl. Rsch. Ctr., Weslaco, Tex., 1992—98, U.S. Dept. Agrl.-Agrl. Rsch. Svc. So. Regional Rsch. Ctr., New Orleans, 1998—2004, U.S. Dept. Agrl.-Agrl. Rsch. Svc. Nat. Biol. Cont. Lab., New Orleans, 2004—. Author: Natural Enemies and Pest Control: An Integrated Pest Management Concept, 2003; mem. editl. bd.: Biopesticides International, 2006—; contbr. articles to prof. jours. Recipient Scientist of the Yr. award, USDA-ARS, 2002, Excellence in Tech. Transfer award, Fed. Lab. Consortium, 2004. Mem.: Fla. Entomol. Soc., Am. Inst. of Biol. Scis., Soc. Mex. de Control Biologico, Entomol. Soc. of Am., The Mars Soc., The Planetery Soc. Achievements include research in mass dissemination an release technology of the boll weevil parasitoid Catolaccus grandis; development of artificial diet for the boll weevil parasitoid Catolaccus grandis; patents for artificial diet for Ectoparsitoid Insects; first to first biological control of a primary insect pest (the boll weevil) in an annual crop (cotton); first biological control of a primary insect pest by mass propagating a natural enemy using an artificial diet; patents for bait matrix for control of subterranean termites; first to the use of chemical analysis of food sources for the development of artificial diets and baits for beneficial insects and pests: 5 US patents; development of nutritionally balanced bait matrixes to deliver toxics to socialinsect pests such as termite and ants. Avocations: astronomy, music. Office: USDA-Agrl Rsch Svc Nat Biol Control Lab 59 Lee Rd Stoneville MS 38776 Business E-mail: jmorales@msa-stoneville.ars.usda.gov.

**MORAN, ANNE E.,** lawyer; b. Rockville Centre, NY, July 9, 1953; BA, Wellesley Coll., 1975; JD, Harvard U., 1978. Bar: DC 1978, NY 1979. Law clk. to Hon. Philip Nichols US Ct. Appeals (Fed. cir.); ptnr. Miller & Chevalier Chartered, Washington, Steptoe & Johnson LLP, Washington. Mem. ERISA adv. coun. US Dept. Labor, 1992-94; tax counsel fin. com. US Senate. 1983-86; adj. prof. LLM prog. Georgetown U. Contbr. articles to profl. jours. Mem. ABA (chmn. joint com. on employee benefits 1989-90), DC Bar (chmn. com. on employee benefits), Phi Beta Kappa. Office: Steptoe & Johnson 1330 Connecticut Ave NW Washington DC 20036-1704 E-mail: amoran@steptoe.com.

**MORAN, BARBARA BURNS,** librarian, educator; b. Columbus, Miss., July 8, 1944; d. Robert Theron and Joan (Brown) Burns; m. Joseph J. Moran, Sept. 4, 1965; children: Joseph Michael, Brian Matthew. AB, Mount Holyoke Coll., S. Hadley, Mass., 1966; MLS, Emory U., Atlanta, 1973; PhD, SUNY, Buffalo, 1982. Head libr. The Park Sch. of Buffalo, Snyder, NY, 1974-78; prof. Sch. Info. and Libr. Sci. U. N.C., Chapel Hill, 1981—, asst. dean, 1987-90, dean, 1990-98, prof. and dir. internat. programs, 1999—. Bd. govs. U. N.C. Press, 1998—; Fulbright sr. specialist Charles U., Prague, 2006; participant various seminars; evaluator various edn. progs.; cons. in field. Author: (book) Academic Libraries, 1984; author: (with Robert D. Stueart) Library Information Center Management, 6th edit., 2002; contbr. articles to profl. jours., chapters to books; mem. editl. bd.: Jour. Acad. Librarianship, 1992—94, Coll. and Rsch. Librs., 1996—2002, Jour. Edn. Info. and Libr. Sci. 2001—. Grantee Univ. Rsch. Coun., 1983, 1989, Coun. Libr. Resources, 1985, IMLS, 2004; others, Fulbright sr. specialist, Charles U., Prague, 2006. Mem.: ALA, N.C. Libr. Assn., Assn. Libr. And Info. Sci. Edn., Popular Culture Assn. Beta Phi Mu. Home: 1307 Leclair St Chapel Hill NC 27517-3034 Office: Univ NC Sch Info & Libr Sci Chapel Hill NC 27599-0001 Office Phone: 919-962-8062. Business E-mail: moran@ils.unc.edu.

**MORAN, CHARLES, JR.,** consumer products company executive; BA, Canisius Coll. From v.p. fin. CA One Svcs. to pres., COO Del. North Cos. Buffalo, 1992—2003, pres., COO, 2004—. Office: Delaware North Companies 40 Fountain Plaza Buffalo NY 14202

**MORAN, CHARLES A.,** security firm executive, educator; b. Chgo., Feb. 7, 1943; s. Charles W. and Rose B. (Sutcher) M.; m. Donna L. Orbach, Sept. 3, 1967; children: Scott Alan, Erin Lizabeth. AB, Princeton U., 1964; JD, U. Mich., 1967; postgrad. advanced mgmt., Harvard U., 1982. CFP CFP Bd. Stds., 1996, cert. employee benefit specialist Internat. Found. and Wharton Sch. U Pa., 2003. Fellow Chase Manhattan Bank, NYC, 1967-70; pension trust officer, adminstrv. officer, officer in charge new bus. devel., pension div. Mfrs. Hanover Trust Co., NYC, 1970-87, sr. v.p.; officer-in-charge employee benefit trust div., 1979-80; chmn. bd., pres., CEO, MH/Edie Investment Counsel (formerly Lionel D. Edie & Co.), NYC, 1980-82, officer-in-charge corp. trust div., 1982-83, officer in charge-global securities group, 1983-87; pres. Govt. Securities Clearing Corp., NYC, 1987-96, Strategic Fin. Adv. Montclair, NJ, 1996—. Asst. prof., faculty fellow, faculty senate, Coll. of NJ, Trenton, 1996-99; prof. Harvard U., Cambridge, Mass., summers, 1997—; asst. prof., residential coll. adv. bd., Bucknell U., 1989-2003; prof., dir. fin. planning program SUNY, Cobleskill, 2003—, dir. Ctr. for Collaborative Sustainability, NYU, 2006-; chmn. bd. dirs. Inform, Inc.; cons. Urban Vol. Cons. Group, Inc.; adv. coun. US Dept. Labor; adv. bd. BNA Pension Reporter; mem. Employees Retirement Income Security Act of 1974 Roundtable; industry adv. com. Future Electronic Funds Payments Svcs. Fed. Res.; pres. Acad. Legal Studies in Bus., chair Bus. and Environment Section; lectr. in field. Adv. bd. mem., Jour. Fin. Planning; contbr. articles to profl. jours. Mem. Am. Inst. Banking, Am. Employee Benefits Inst. (treas. 1976-79), NY State Bankers Assn. (employees trust com.), Assn. Pvt. Pension and Welfare Plans (dir., mem. exec. com.), ERISA Industry Com. (pres., dir., mem. exec. com., treas.), Am. Bankers Assn. (chmn. employee benefit trust com. 1977-82), Internat. Found. Pension and Welfare Plans, Bank Adminstrn. Inst. (mem. tech. commn.), NY C. of C. (task force on pub. pensions), Fin. Planning Assn. (dir., chmn. govt. rels. com., ethics com.), The Inst. of Cert. Fin. Planners (bd. dirs., com. on career devel.), NJ Soc. Inst. Cert. Fin. Planners (bd. dirs., sec., treas.), World Future Soc., Internat. Soc. Cert. Employee Benefit Specialists, Am. Acad. Mgmt., Am. Soc. Fin. Svcs. Profls., Strategic Mgmt. Soc., Internat. Soc. Cert. Employee Benefit Specialist, Princeton Club, Harvard Bus. Sch. Club NY-Cmty. Ptnrs. (cons.).

**MORAN, ELIZABETH AMES,** library director; b. Camden, Maine, June 22, 1940; d. Robie Frank and Dorothy Dyer Ames; m. Andrew Jackson Moran, Dec. 3, 1966; children: Heather Elizabeth, Melissa Ames. BA, U. Maine, 1962; MA in Law & Diplomacy, Fletcher Sch. Law & Diplomacy, 1964; MLS, U. S.C., 1997. Intelligence officer CIA, Washington, 1964-68; sch. libr. Fairfax (Va.) County Schs., 1981-87; libr. Camden (Maine) Pub. Libr., 1988-90, libr. dir., 1990—. Bd. dirs. Camden Tech. Coll., 1997-98; chair Maine Libr. Commn., 2000—. Mem. ALA, Maine Libr. Assn. (pres. 1998-2000), Pub. Libr. Assn. Small Pub. Libr. Assn., Camden Garden Club, Phi Beta Kappa. Republican. Episcopalian. Avocations: sailing, needlecrafts. Home: 32 Atlantic Hwy Northport ME 04849-3010 Office: Camden Pub Libr 55 Main St Camden ME 04843-1794

**MORAN, JAMES BYRON,** federal judge; b. Evanston, Ill., June 20, 1930; s. James Edward and Kathryn (Horton) M.; children: John, Jennifer, Sarah, Polly; stepchildren: Katie, Cynthia, Laura, Michael. AB, U. Mich., 1952; LLB magna cum laude, Harvard U., 1957. Bar: Ill. 1958. Law clk. to judge U.S. Ct. of Appeals (2d cir.), 1957-58; assoc. Bell, Boyd, Lloyd, Haddad & Burns, Chgo, 1958-66, ptnr., 1966-79; judge U.S. Dist. Ct. (no. dist.) Ill., Chgo., 1979—. Dir. Com. on Ill. Govt., 1960-74, chmn., 1968-70; vice chmn., sec. Ill. Narcotic Drug Adv. Coun., 1967-74; dir. Gateway Found., 1969—; mem. Ill. Ho. of Reps., 1965-67; mem. Evanston City Council, 1971-75. Served with AUS, 1952-54. Mem. Chgo. Bar Assn., Chgo. Council Lawyers, Lawyers Club, Phi Beta Kappa. Home: 117 Kedzie St Evanston IL 60202-2509 Office: US Dist Ct 219 S Dearborn St Chambers 1846 Chicago IL 60604-1800 Office Phone: 312-435-5572. Personal E-mail: jbm117@aol.com.

**MORAN, JAMES JOSEPH, JR.,** insurance company executive; s. James J. and Marilyn A. (Sullivan) M.; m. Mary Therese Stevens, Oct. 6, 1979; children: Sean M., James E., Matthew S. AB cum laude, Boston Coll., 1975. JD, 1978. Bar: Mass. 1978, U.S. Ct. Appeals (1st cir.) 1979, U.S. Dist Ct. Mass. 1979, U.S. Tax Ct. 1979, U.S. Supreme Ct. 1982; CPCU; Assoc. in reins. Assoc. Haussermann, Davison & Shattuck, Boston, 1978-84, Morrison, Mahoney & Miller, Boston, 1984—87, ptnr., 1988—98; pres. Eastern Casualty Ins. Co., Marlborough, Mass., 1998—2001; sr. v.p, sec., gen. counsel Quincy (Mass.) Mutual Fire Ins. Co., 2001—. V.p., gen. counsel Ind. Property-Casualty Insurers Mass. Inc., 1991-98; bd. dirs. R.I. Insurers Insolvency Fund, 2003—, Mass. Insurers Insolvency Fund, 2004—; counsel Mass. Assn. Ins. Agts., 1985-96; ins. broker, Mass.; New Eng. regional regulatory counsel Alliance Am. Insurers, 1994-98; trustee New Eng. Coll. Fin., 1998-2000. Bd. dirs. (gubernatorial appointee) Mass. Pollution Liability Reinsurance Corp., 1988-90. Recipient Econ. Leadership award Orgn. New Equality, 1997. Mem. Internat. Assn. Def. Coun., CPCU Soc. (pres. Boston chpt. 1993-94), Fedn. Ins. Corp. Coun., Ins. Libr. Assn. Boston (trustee 1983-2004, pres. 1989-90), Liquor Liability Joint Underwriting Assn. Roman Catholic. Home: 15 Bramel Cir Walpole MA 02081-2043 Office: Quincy Mutual Fire Ins Co 57 Washington St Quincy MA 02169-9155

**MORAN, JAMES M.,** automotive sales executive; b. 1918; married. Owner Courtesy Motor Sales Inc. (formerly Hudson Motor Franchise Inc.), Chgo., 1947-68; chmn.. now hon. chmn. JM Family Enterprises Inc. Deerfield Beach, Fla., 1969—. Named one of Forbes' Richest Americans, 2006. Office: JM Family Enterprises 100 NW 12th Ave Deerfield Beach FL 33442-1702*

**MORAN, JAMES MICHAEL, JR.,** astronomer, educator; b. Plainfield, N.J., Jan. 3, 1943; s. James Michael and Martha (Algermissen) M.; m. Barbara Putney Smith. Nov. 30, 1974; children: Susan Harrison, Michael Putney. BS, U. Notre Dame, 1963; SM, MIT, 1965, PhD, 1968. Mem. staff MIT Lincoln Lab., Lexington, 1968-70; sr. radio astronomer Smithsonian Astrophys. Obs., Cambridge, Mass., 1970—; prof. practice of astronomy Harvard U., Cambridge, 1979-89, Donald H. Menzel prof. astrophysics, 2001—; assoc. dir. Harvard-Smithsonian Ctr. Astrophysics, Cambridge, 1987-92, dir. Submillimeter Array Project, 1996—2005. Jansky lectr. Nat. Radio Astronomy Obs., 1996; trustee N.E. Radio Obs. Corp., Cambridge, 1983—. Contbr. numerous articles on radio astronomy to profl. publs. Co-recipient Rumford prize Am. Acad. Arts and Scis., 1971; recipient Sr. award Alexander von Humboldt Soc., 1993. Fellow AAAS, IEEE; mem. NAS, Am. Astron. Soc. (Pierce prize 1978), Explorers Club. Achievements include development of technique of very long baseline interferrrometry; research in study of black holes. Home: 93 Anson Rd Concord MA 01742-5704 Office: Harvard-Smithsonian Center for Astrophysics 60 Garden St Cambridge MA 02138-1516 Office Phone: 617-495-7477. Business E-Mail: moran@cfa.harvard.edu.

**MORAN, JEFFREY W., JR.,** county surrogate; b. Winfield Park, NJ, Dec. 23, 1946; m. Patricia Kennedy, 1969; children: Collenn, Tricia, Alma White Coll., Newark State Coll., 1970, MA. Assemblyman dist. 9 N.J. State Assembly, 1986—2003; Ocean county surrogate, 2003—. Councilman Beachwood, N.J.; chmn. higher edn. & regulated profls. com. N.J. State Assembly, mcpl. govt. com., sr. citizens com., tourism com., N.J. Hist. Commn.; asst. dir. handicapped svcs. Toms River (N.J.) Sch. Planning bd. Beachwood City Coun.; mem. utilities authority Ocean County, N.J.; mem. Selective Svc. Bd.; trustee New Lisbon Devel. Ctr. Awarded Nat. Def. Medal. Mem. Beachwood Civic Improvement Assn., Taxpayers Assn., N.J. State Sch. Prins. Assn., Ocean County Sch. Prins. Assn. Office: PO Box 2191 Toms River NJ 08754-2191

**MORAN, JERRY,** congressman; b. Great Bend, Kans., May 29, 1954; m. Robba A. Moran; 2 children. BS, Kansas U., 1976, JD, 1981. Senator dist. 37 State of Kans., 1989—96, sen. majority leader, 1994—96; mem., asst. majority whip US Congress from 1st Kans. dist., 1997—, mem. agr., transp., infrastructure, vets. affairs coms., chmn. subcom. on gen. commodities; chmn.

Rural Health Care Coalition. Republican. Office: US House Reps 1519 Longworth House Office Bldg Washington DC 20515-1601 Office Phone: 202-225-2715. Office Fax: 202-225-5124.

**MORAN, JIM (JAMES PATRICK MORAN JR.),** congressman, stock broker; b. Buffalo, May 16, 1945; s. James Patrick and Dorothy (Dwyer) Moran; m. Mary Craig, Dec. 27, 1967 (div. 1974); children: Jimmy, Mary; m. Mary Howard; children: Michael, Patrick, Dorothy. BA in Econs., Coll. Holy Cross, Worcester, Mass., 1967; postgraduate student, CUNY, 1967-68; MPA, U. Pitts., 1970. Comptr., budget analyst US Dept. Health, Edn. and Welfare, Washington, 1968—74; budget and fiscal policy specialist Congl. Rsch. Svc. Libr. Congress, Washington, 1974-76; sr. staff mem. appropriations com. US Senate, Washington, 1976-79; investment broker A.G. Edwards & Sons, Alexandria, Va., 1979; mem. City Coun., Alexandria, Va., 1979—82; vice mayor Alexandria, Va., 1982-84; mayor, 1985—90; mem. US Congress from 8th Va. dist., 1991—, mem. appropriations com. Chmn. No. Va. Transp. Bd., 1988, United Way, 1977-79; vice chmn. Mental Health Retard and Substance Abuse Bd., 1976-78, vice chmn. D.E.O., 1976-78; dir. Met. Area Coun. Govts., dir. No. Va. Transp. Commn., 1985. Recipient Outstanding Citizenship award, YMCA, 1983. Mem. C. of C. (dir. 1985-86). Democrat. Roman Catholic. Office: US House Reps 2239 Rayburn House Office Bldg Washington DC 20515-4608 Office Phone: 202-225-4376.*

**MORAN, JOHN BERNARD,** retired government official; b. Saginaw, Mich., Nov. 26, 1936; s. Leo Lewis and Marie Katherine (Langley) M.; m. Diann Marie Markey, May 20, 1963 (div.); m. Barbara Jane Livingston, Aug. 18, 1978; children— Leslie Marie, Leanne Rene, Jeffrey John BS in Metall. Engring., Ill. Inst. Tech., 1959. Sr. automotive specialist Dow Chem. Co., Midland, Mich., 1962-71; program dir. research EPA, Research Triangle Park, N.C., 1971-75, dir. monitoring tech. div. Washington, 1975-76; dir. div. safety research Nat. Inst. for Occupational Safety and Health, Ctrs. for Disease Control, USPHS, HHS, Morgantown, W.Va., 1976-77, 83-88; dir. research and devel. safety products div. Am. Optical Corp., Southbridge, Mass., 1977-80; v.p., dir. ops. Geomet, Inc., Rockville, Md., 1980-83; program dir. Hartford Engring. Tech., Inc., Windsor, Conn., 1988; assoc. dir. health and safety laborers Associated Gen. Contractors, 1988-89; dir. safety and health Laborers Health and Safety Fund, 1989-95; spl. asst. to dep. asst. sec. Worker Health and Safety U.S. Dept. Energy, Washington, 1995; dir. policy OSHA, U.S. Dept. Labor, Washington, 1996; expert cons. to asst. sec. OSHA, Washington, 1996—; expert cons. to CDC Chem./Bioagts., 1996-99, ret.; now cons. in field. Mem. Nat. Mine Health Rsch. Adv. Com., Atlanta, 1980-84; govt. del. ILO, Geneva, 1985; mem. Nat. Adv. Com. on Constrn. Safety and Health, 1985-88, 92-95, Bur. Labor Stats. Rsch., 1991-95, hazardous material transp. info. com. NAS, 1991-93, Hazardous Materials Control Rsch. Inst.; chmn. lead subcom. Bldg. Constrn. Trades Dept., 1991-95; adj. asst. prof. mech. engring. W.Va. U., 1985-88; vis. ext. prof. U. Conn., Storrs, 1988-90; mem. Fed. Facilities Environ. Restoration Com., constrn. com. A 10 Am. Nat. Stds. Inst.; co-chair EPA-Labor Superfund Task Force, 1990-95, 96—; mem. nat. lead task force HUD, 1993-95; cons., expert witness. Patentee; contbr. articles to profl. jours, chpts. to books. Mem. Task Force on Hazardous Materials, Rockville, Md., 1983. mem. Tech. Workshops on Safety and Health Issues. Served to capt. USMC, 1959-65 Recipient Bronze medal for commendable service EPA, 1974, Commitment to Life award Nat. Safe Workplace Inst., 1988. Mem. Internat. Soc. Respiratory Protection (pres. 1985-87, bd. dirs. 1987-89), Am. Conf. Govtl. Indsl. Hygienists. Roman Catholic. Home: 107 Galemist Ct Brunswick GA 31523-7143

**MORAN, JOHN FRANCIS,** cardiologist; b. Chgo., Sept. 5, 1938; MD, Loyola U., Stritch Sch. Medicine, 1964. Cert. cardio. disease 1973. Office: Loyola U Med Ctr 2160 S 1st Ave Maywood IL 60153 Office Phone: 708-327-2784.

**MORAN, JULIETTE M.,** retired chemicals executive; b. NYC, June 12, 1917; d. James Joseph and Louise M. BS, Columbia U., 1938; MS, NYU, 1948. Research asst. Columbia U., 1941; jr. engr. Signal Corps Lab., U.S. Army, 1942-43; with GAF Corp. (formerly Gen. Aniline & Film Corp.), 1943-82; from jr. chemist process devel. dept. to exec. v.p. and dir. GAF Corp., 1953—80, vice chmn., 1982—2002, cons., 1982—95; ret., 1982. Bd. dirs. N.Y. State Sci. and Tech. Found. Recipient Greater N.Y. Advt. award for excellence in communications N.Y. chpt. Assn. Indsl. Advertisers, 1972, Alumni Achievement award N.Y. U. Grad. Sch. Arts and Scis., 1977 Fellow AAAS, Am. Inst. Chemists; mem. Am. Chem. Soc., Comml. Devel. Assn. Home: 10 W 66th St New York NY 10023-6206

**MORAN, KATE,** sculptor, photographer; b. Langhorne, Pa., Dec. 27, 1958; BA in Visual Arts, Antioch Coll., 1982; cert., Pa. Acad. Fine Arts, Phila., 1988; MFA, U. N.C., 1992. Grad. faculty Pa. Acad. Fine Arts, 2002; instr. Acad. Fine Arts, Phila., 2004, Arcadia U., Glenside, Pa., 2004; bd. artistic advisors Creative Arts Network, Phila., 2002. One-woman shows include Fleisher Art Meml., Phila. 1992, Westby Art Gallery, Rowan Coll. N.J., Glassboro, 1992, More Gallery, Phila., 1995, Lafayette Coll., Williams Ctr. for Arts, Easton, Pa., 1995. John Michael Kohler Arts Ctr., Shebyoyan, Wis., 1996, U. N.C., Chapel Hill, 1997 (also vis. artist, lectr.), Steinbaum Krauss Gallery, N.Y.C., 1997, 98, List Gallery, Swarthmore (Pa.) Coll., 1997, Mangel Gallery, Phila., 1998, Mus. Am. Art, Pa. Acad. Fine Arts, 1998, Bernice Steinbaum Gallery, Miami, Fla., 2000. Olin Gallery, Kenyon Coll., Gambier, Ohio, 2000, Gallery Joe, Phila., 2004; 2 woman shows SPACES, Cleve., 1996, Suzanne H. Arnold Art Gallery, Lebanon Valley Coll. Pa., Annville, 1996; exhibited in group shows, 1991—, including Del. Art Mus., Wilmington, 1991, 93, 96, Print Club, Phila., 1991, New Orleans Mus. Art, 1992. Phila. Art Alliance, 1992, 94, Nexus Gallery, Phila., 1993, Stuart Levy Gallery, N.Y.C., 1993, 94, More Gallery, 1993, 94, Beaver Coll., Glenside, Pa., 1994, Snug Harbor Cultural Ctr., S.I. N.Y., 1995, Woodmere Art Mus., Phila., 1996, Phila. Mus. Art, 1996, 98, Rosenwald-Wolf Gallery, U. Parts, Phila., 1996; represented in permanent collections Mus. Am. Art at Pa. Acad. Fine Arts, Phila. Mus. Art. Woodmore Art Mus., New Orleans Mus. Art, State Mus. Pa.. Harrisburg, CIGNA Mus. art Collection, Phila., Bryn Mawr (Pa.) Coll. Library; work represented in various pubs. Recipient award Friends of Beaver Coll., 1991, purchase award New Orleans Mus. Art, 1992; John Michael Kohler Arts-Industry Residency, 1997, Works on Paper award Pa. Coun. on the Arts, 2000; fellow Pa. Coun. on Arts, 1992-93, 95-96, photography fellow PEW Fellowships in Arts, 1993-94; grantee Leeway Found., 1996-97, 2000; Works on Paper fellow Pa. Coun. Fine Arts, 2002. Home: 357 Leverington Ave Philadelphia PA 19128 Office: The Bernice Steinbaum Gallery 3550 N Miami Ave Miami FL 33127 E-mail: kmor@erols.com.

**MORAN, KEVIN PAUL,** lawyer; BSME, U. Wis., 1986, JD, 1992. Bar: Wis. 1992, Colo. 1992, Minn. 1995. Engr. Trek Bicycle Corp., Waterloo, Wis., 1986—89; assoc. Sheridan, Ross & McIntosh, Denver, 1992—95; assoc./ptnr. Michael Best & Friedrich LLP, Milw., 1995—. Lectr. in field; chmn. intellectual property practice group Michael Best & Friedrich, 2005—. Contbr. articles to profl. jours. Office: Michael Best & Friedrich LLP N19 W24133 Riverwood Dr Waukesha WI 53188

**MORAN, LESLIE MASON,** music educator; b. Scranton, Pa., Aug. 27, 1970; d. Barry C. and Barbara A. Mason; m. Patrick M. Moran, Aug. 16, 1997; children: Liam Patrick, Quinn Catherine. MusB in Edn., U. Hartford, 1993. Tchr. music Lackawana Trail Sch. Dist., Factoryville, Pa., 1997—98, Mid Valley Sch. Dist., Throop, 1998—; tchr. voice Marywood U. Sch. Continuing Edn., Scranton, 2000—, Wilkes U., Wilkesbarre, 1994—; condr., tchr., accompanist children's and youth choirs Choral Soc. N.E. Pa., Scranton, 1994—. Soprano Lyric Consort, Scranton, 1993—, St. Lukes Ch., 1993—2003; guest condr. PMEA Songfest Marywood U., 2001; presenter in field. Mem.: Music Educators Nat. Conf., Am. Choral Dirs. Assn., Pa. State Educators Assn. Democrat. Episcopalian. Avocations: calligraphy, bicycling, cooking. Home: 909 Grandview St Scranton PA 18509 Office: Mid Valley Sch Dist 52 Underwood Rd Throop PA 18512

**MORAN, LEWIS TERRILL,** architect; b. Cin., May 20, 1952; s. John Robert and Ruth Haubrock Moran; m. Margaret Kathleen Cottrell, June 8, 1984; children: Max Frances, Samuel Lewis, Joseph Terrill. BA, U. Minn., 1978, MArch, 1982. Dir. campus corp. KKE, Mpls., 1996—99; dir. arch. Atkins Benham, St. Paul, 1999—2002; prin., v.p. HGA, Ltd., Mpls., 2002—. Chmn. bd. Ramsey Site Based Mgmt., Mpls. Trustee Minn. State Coll. and Univs., St. Paul; trustee, chmn. Sobriety HS, St. Paul. Home: 2912 W 42nd St Minneapolis MN 55410 Office: HGA Ltd 701 Washington Ave N Minneapolis MN 55401

**MORAN, MARTIN JOSEPH,** fundraising company executive; b. Bklyn., Nov. 3, 1930; s. Dominick and Mary (Lydon) Moran; m. Mary Therese Schofield, June 5, 1954; children: Martin Joseph, John P., Maureen M., Thomas S., Robert P., William M., Maria M. BA, St. John's U., 1952. Profl. fundraising cons., 1956—; founder Martin J. Moran Co., Inc., NYC, 1964, pres., 1964—74, chmn. bd., 1974—. Mem. Am. Revolution Bicentennial Commn., Oyster Bay, NY, Massapequa Park Ethics Commn., 1969—72; trustee Notre Dame Coll., S.I, NY, 1969—72, La Salle Acad., NYC, 1971—87; mem. pres.'s coun. Cath. U. P.R., Ponce, 1966—71; mem. Cardinal's Com. for Edn., NYC, 1970—79, Cardinal's Com. for Laity Archdiocese NY, 1979—98, Massapequa Park (NY) Bd. Zoning Appeals, 1972—84, chmn., 1978—84; bd. councilors, sec., treas. Equestrian Order Holy Sepulchre of Jerusalem, 1990—, sec.-treas., 1990—93, pres., 1993—. Served as aviator USNR, 1952—56. Decorated knight Grand Cross Order Holy Sepulchre, Pope Paul VI, Knight of Malta Pope Paul VI, papal Knight of Order of St. Gregory the Gt. Pope John Paul II, knight comdr.; recipient Pietas medal, St. John's U., NY, 1988. Mem.: Am. Assn. Fundraising Counsel (bd. dirs. 1970—75), Navy Hist. Assn., Navy League, Friendly Sons of St. Patrick, Nassau County Hist. Soc., St. John's U. Alumni Assn. (pres. 1987—94), Old Port Yacht Club, Lost Tree Club (N. Palm Beach, Fla.), KC. Home: 1300 Lakeshore Dr Massapequa Park NY 11762-1764 Office: Martin J Moran Company 11 Penn Plz Fl 5 New York NY 10001-2003 Personal E-mail: mjmmarty@aol.com.

**MORAN, MITCH,** lawyer; b. Houston, Tex. BA, Northwestern U.; JD, Miss. Coll., 1996. Farmer, La.; atty. Tribal Chief Phillip Martin Miss. Band of Choctaw Indians, 1996; solo practice Moran Law Firm, Carthage, Miss., 1998—. Achievements include defense atty. for Edgar Ray Killen, convicted of the 1964 manslaughter of 3 civil rights workers, Andrew Goodman, James Chaney and Michael Schwerner in June 2005. Office: Moran Law Firm 119 N Pearl St Carthage MS 39051 Office Phone: 601-298-2000.

**MORAN, NANCY A.,** ecologist, educator; b. Dallas, Dec. 21, 1954; BA in biology, U. Tex., 1976; MS in zoology, U. Mich., 1978, PhD in zoology, 1982. Asst. prof. entomology U. Ariz., 1986—91, assoc. prof. ecology and evolutionary biology, 1991—96, prof. ecology and evolutionary biology, 1996—2001, regent's prof. ecology and evolutionary biology, 2001—. NSF postdoctoral fellow, No. Ariz. U., 1984-1986, NAS postdoctoral fellow, Inst. Entomology, Czech, 1984. MacArthur Fellow, John D. and Catherine T. MacArthur Found., 1997. Mem. NAS, Soc. Study Evolution (pres. 2002), Am. Naturalists Soc. (v.p. 2001, Pres. award, 1988); fellow Am. Acad. Arts & Sciences Office: U Ariz Dept Ecology and Evolutionary Biology PO Box 210088 Biosciences W 310 1041 E Lowell St Tucson AZ 85721 Office Phone: 520-621-3581. Office Fax: 520-621-9190. E-mail: nmoran@email.arizona.edu.*

**MORAN, PATRICIA,** lawyer; b. Wilmington, Del., 1959; BS, U. Scranton, 1981; JD, Villanova U., 1984. Bar: Del. 1984. Atty. Skadden, Arps, Slate, Meagher & Flom LLP, N.Y., ptnr., 1994—. Office: Skadden Arps Slate Meagher & Flom LLP Four Times Square New York NY 10036

**MORAN, PATRICIA GENEVIEVE,** corporate financial executive; b. Evanston, Ill., July 26, 1945; d. James Moran; children: Christine Coyle, Thomas Beddia, Donald Beddia. Student, Marquette U. Dir. corp. transp. JM Family Enterprises, Inc., 1984, corp. assoc. rels. dir., 1985, v.p., 1985-88; group v.p. sales Southeast Toyota, Deerfield Beach, Fla., 1988-89; pres., CEO JM Family Enterprises, Inc., Deerfield Beach, Fla., 1989—2000, chmn., 2000—. Bd. dirs. Am. Heritage Life Ins. Co. Bd. dirs. Take Stock in Children, Boca Raton Resort and Club. Named One of Top 50 Working Women by Working Woman's Mag. Mem. Nat. Assn. Automobile Dealers, Am. Internat. Automobile Dealers Assn., Fla. Council of 100, Com. of 200. Office: JM Family Enterprises 100 NW 12th Ave Deerfield Beach FL 33442

**MORAN, PAUL JAMES,** journalist, columnist; b. Buffalo, July 20, 1947; s. Paul James and Frances (Sciortino) M.; m. Kim Maldiner, Mar. 17, 1975 (div. July 1979); m. Colette Stass (div. Jan. 1997). Student, SUNY, Buffalo, 1965-67, Millard Fillmore Coll., 1971-73. Sports editor Tonawanda News, North Tonawanda, NY, 1972-75; writer/columnist Fort Lauderdale (Fla.) News/Sun Sentinel, 1975-85, N.Y. Newsday, Melville, 1985—. Cons. Green Country Racing News., Tulsa, 1983-85. Author: (with others) Crown Jewels of Thoroughbred Racing; contbr. articles to mags. and newspapers. Sgt. USAF, 1967-71. Recipient Eclipse award Thoroughbred Racing Assn., 1985, 90, Disting. Writing award Am. Soc. Newspaper Editors, 1990, Deadline Writing award Soc. Silurians, 1990, Deadline Reporting award L.I. Press Club, 1991, Disting. Sports Writing award N.Y. Newspaper Pubs. Assn., 1992, (with others) Journalism collection Best Newspaper Writing 1991, Media award L.I. Vet. Med. Assn., 1997, excellence in continuing feature Fla. Mag. Assn., 1999, Best of Manhattan award N.Y. Press, 2002. Mem. N.Y. Turf Writers' Assn. (pres. 1990-92, sec.-treas. 1992-94), Nat. Turf Writers' Assn. (bd. dirs. 1987-90). Avocations: photography, art collecting. Home: 40 Carnation Ave Floral Park NY 11001-1730 Office: Newsday 235 Pinelawn Rd Melville NY 11747-4250 Personal E-mail: pmoran1686@aol.com.

**MORAN, PHILIP DAVID,** lawyer; b. Lynn, Mass., June 3, 1937; s. J. Francis and Margaret M. (Shanahan) M.; m. Mary Carol A. Regan, May 12, 1962; children: Maura F., Philip David. AB, Holy Cross Coll., 1958; EdM, Salem State Coll., 1961; JD, Suffolk U., 1968. Bar: Mass., 1968, U.S. Dist. Ct. Mass., 1972, U.S. Supreme Ct., 1988, U.S. Ct. Appeals (1st cir.), 1993. House counsel Viatron Computer Systems Corp., Burlington, Mass., 1968-71; ptnr. Kane & Moran, Lynn, Mass., 1972-78; pvt. practice law Salem, Mass., 1978—; propr. Law Offices of Philip D. Moran P.C., 1993—. Asst. dist. atty. Essex County (Mass.), 1974-78; mem. pres.'s coun. Holy Cross Coll., 1985—, Nat. Inst. Trial Advocacy U. Colo., 1973; gen. chmn. bicentenary com. Maynooth Coll., Boston, 1994-96. Contbg. author: Encyclopedia of Biomedical Policy, 1995. Bd. dirs. Nat. Right to Life Inc., 1977-83, 87—, treas., 1981-83; bd. dirs. Citizens for Life, 1975—, pres. 1979-80, chmn. 1991-93; chmn. Salem Con Con, 1982-89; active Salem Bd. Voter Registration, 2005; pastoral coun. Archdiocese Boston, 2004—. With U.S. Army, 1960-66. Recipient Ignatius O'Connor Pro Life award, 1994, Gold medatl St. Patrick Maynooth Coll., Irelnd, 1996, Knight of Malta, 1997, Family, Faith and Freedom award Family Rsch. Coun., 1997, Citizenship award Mass. Family Inst., 1997, Leadership award, Rep. Nat. Cong. Com., 2003. Mem. Mass. Bar Assn., Salem Bar Assn., Lynn Bar Assn., Am. Trial Lawyers Assn., Nat. Acad. Elder Law Attys., Murray Inn of Ct., Pro Life Legal Def. Fund (pres. 1997), Hibernian Civil Rights Coalition (bd. dirs. 1997, pres. 1997), Irish Am. Partnership, Nat. Coalition of Pro Life Dems. (bd. dirs., treas. 1999-2001), Dem State Com., Catholic Alliance (bd. dirs., gen. coun. 1999-2001), Internat. Soc. Photographers. Roman Catholic. Avocations: swimming, reading, gardening, boating, photography. Home: 415 Lafayette St Salem MA 01970-5337 Office: 265 Essex St Salem MA 01970-3419 Office Phone: 978-745-6085. Personal E-mail: philipmoranesq@aol.com.

**MORAN, RACHEL,** law educator; b. Kansas City, Mo., June 27, 1956; d. Thomas Albert and Josephine (Portillo) Moran. AB, Stanford U., 1978; JD, Yale U., 1981. Bar: Calif. 1984. Assoc Heller, Ehrman, White & McAuliffe, San Francisco, 1982-83; prof. law U. Calif., Berkeley, 1984—, Robert D. and Leslie-Kay Raven prof. law, 1998—. Vis. prof. UCLA Sch. Law, 1988, 2002, Stanford (Calif.) U. Law Sch., 1989, NYU Sch. Law, 1996, U. Miami Sch.

Law, 1997, U. Tex. Law Sch., 2000, Fordham Law Sch., 2005; chair Chicano/Latino Policy Project, 1993—96; dir. Inst. for Study Social Change, 2003—. Contbr. articles to profl. jours. Recipient Disting. Tchg. award, U. Calif. Mem.: ABA, Calif. Bar Assn., Am. Law Inst., Phi Beta Kappa. Democrat. Unitarian Universalist. Avocations: jogging, aerobics, reading, listening to music. Office: U Calif Sch Law Boalt Hall Berkeley CA 94720 Office Phone: 510-643-6351. Business E-Mail: moran@law.berkeley.edu.

**MORAN, REBECCA ANN,** secondary school educator; d. Charles William Moran and Dorothy Ann Irby. BA, U. North Tex., Denton, 1977. Tchr. Dallas ISD, 1977—. Curriculum writer Belo Corp., Dallas, 1996—2006. Author: (curriculum writer) Teacher's Guide for the Tex. Almanac. Rec. sec. Tex. Coun. for Social Studies, 2004—05. Recipient Tchr. of Yr., Seagoville Mid. Sch., 1992—93. Mem.: Nat. Coun. for Social Studies, Tex. Coun. for Social Studies (rec. sec. 2004—05). Avocations: travel, reading. Office: Seagoville Mid Sch 950 Woody Rd Dallas TX 75253 Office Phone: 972-892-7121. E-mail: rmoran@dallasisd.org.

**MORAN, TERRY,** news correspondent; BA, Lawrence U., 1982. Writer New Republic; reporter, asst. mng. editor Legal Times; corr., anchor Court TV, 1992—97; joined ABC News, 1997, corr. assigned to US Supreme Ct., 1998—99, chief White House corr. Washington, 1999—, anchor World News Tonight Sunday, 2004—, co-anchor Nightline, 2005—. Contbr. NY Times, Washington Post. Recipient Lucia R. Briggs Disting. Achievement Award, Lawrence U., 2003, Merriman Smith award, White House Corrs. Assn., 2006. Office: ABC News Nightline 1717 Desales St NW Washington DC 20036 Office Phone: 202-222-7700. Office Fax: 202-222-7686. E-mail: terry.moran@abc.com.*

**MORAN, THOMAS HARRY,** retired academic administrator; b. Milw., Oct. 21, 1937; s. Harry Edward and Edna Agnes Moran; m. Barbara Ellen Saklad, June 10, 1969; children: David Thomas, Karen Ellen. BS, U. Wis., Madison, 1964, MA, 1972, PhD, 1974. Dir. capital budgeting Wis. Dept. Adminstrn., 1962-64; exec. dir. Wis. Higher Ednl. Aids Bd., 1964-69; spl. cons. tax policy Wis. Dept. Revenue, 1973-74; dep. dir. Wis. Manpower Coun., Office of Gov., 1974-76; v.p. bus. and fin. affairs U. Detroit, 1976-78; exec. assoc. v.p. health affairs U. So. Calif., LA, 1979-87, v.p. bus. affairs, 1988—2002, v.p. emeritus, 2002—. USN fellow, 1957-59, U.S. Office Edn. rsch. fellow, 1973. Mem. Am. Assn. Higher Edn., Phi Kappa Phi. Personal E-mail: thmoran@adelphia.net.

**MORAN, THOMAS J.,** insurance company executive; BS mathematics, Manhattan Coll.; JD (hon.), Nat. Univ. Ireland. Pension underwriter Mutual of America Life Ins. Co., 1975, COO, 1992, CEO, pres., 1994. Mem. bd. dir. Life Ins. Coun. NY, United Way NYC, Nat. Ctr. Disability Svcs., Nat. Com. Am. Foreign Policy, Manhattan Coll.; chmn. Concern Worldwide. Recipient Medal of Honor, Cavalry Hospital, Humanitarian Award, NYC Fire Dept., Concern Worldwide. Office: Mutual of America Life Ins Co 320 Park Ave New York NY 10022 Office Phone: 212-224-1600. Office Fax: 212-224-2539.*

**MORAN, WENDI K,** biology educator; d. Walter Paul and Karen Gay Wolfram; m. Gerald Raymond Moran, Jan. 27, 1997; 1 child, Matthew Tyler. BS in biology, Hardin-Simmons U., Abilene, Texas, 2002, MS in Environ. Mgmt., 2004. Customer svc. BodyBilt Seating, Navasota, Tex., 1993—95; profl. placement - mktg. cons. Interim Pers., Abilene, Tex., 1995; property mgmt. - asst. mgr. Ea. Oaks II Apartments, Abilene, Tex., 1995—98; ins. claims processor - claims technition Blue Cross and Blue Shield of Tex. FEP, Abilene, 1998—2000; undergraduate student Hardin-Simmons U., Abilene, 2000—02, adj. prof. and biology lab coord., 2002—. Exec. dir., founder Conservation Tng. Rsch. Edn. Ctr., Abilene, 2005—. Spl. events com. chair PDBC Women's Ministry, Abilene, Tex., 2004—06; sc. U. Women, Abilene, 2004—06. Recipient Grad. Dean's Award of Excellence - Nominee, Hardin-Simmons U., 2004, Travel award, Tex. Acad. of Sci., 2004; Rsch. grant, 2005, Grad. Dean scholarship, Hardin-Simmons U., 2002—04. Mem.: Am. Soc. of Mammologists, Bot. Soc. of Am., Tex. Acad. of Sci. Bapt. Avocations: reading, outdoor recreation, wildlife photography. Office Phone: 325-671-2134. Personal E-mail: wkmoran@aol.com. E-mail: wkmoran@hsutx.edu.

**MORAN, WENDY JACQUELINE,** music educator, musician; b. Chappaqua, N.Y., Jan. 16, 1952; d. Edward Albert and Gladys (Dildarian) Hamilton; m. Brian Vincent Moran, Aug. 5, 1979; children: Melissa Kathleen, Kevin William. Attended, U. N.C., Greensboro, 1970—72; MusB Edn., Westminster Choir Coll., Princeton, N.J., 1975; grad. student in Musicology, NYU, 1978—80. Cert. music specialist Pre-K-12 Dept. Edn. Mass., 2000, N.J., 1975. Music specialist Westminster Choir Coll. (Conservatory divsn.), Princeton, 1975; pvt. instrn. (voice/flute/recorder/eurhythmics) Holliston, Mass., 1975—; music specialist Montessori Children's Rm., Armonk, N.Y., 1975—83, various Montessori schs., music schs., pub. schs., pvt. schs., Md., Mass., N.Y., 1983—89, Christian Family Montessori Sch., Holliston, 1989—, Hopkinton Pub. Schs., Mass., 1996—. Flute soloist in field, 1975—; soprano soloist in field, 1975—; student Kodaly Music Tchrs. Workshops, Princeton, 1975; participant/student Music Educator Workshops/Chamber Music Workshops:Dalcroze Sch. of Music/Mannes Coll. of Music, N.Y., 1978—89; participant master class with Jean-Pierre Rampal, N.Y., 1979, Montessori Music Teacher's Workshop Whitby Sch., Greenwich, Conn., 1980; flutist Southeastern Mass. Concert Band, Medway, Mass., 1990—; singer Berkshire Choral Inst., Sheffield, Mass., 1996—; profl. devel. mgr., exec. bd. New Eng. chpt. Am. Orff-Schulwerk Assn., Lexington, Mass., 1999—2003; singer Heritage Chorale, Framingham, 1999—, chorus rep. bd. dirs., 2003—; singer/flutist Composer's Conf.: Chamber Music Ctr. and Singer's Workshop, Wellesley, Mass., 2003—. Author (co-author): (guidebook) Curriculum Guide for Hopkinton Mass Dept Music; singer (concerts) choral concerts under the direction of Leonard Bernstein, Pierre Boulez, Antal Dorati, (concert) under Robert Shaw in Mostly Mozart Festival, Lincoln Ctr. Music specialist, volunteered classes in music to support funding for town playground Town of Annapolis, Md., 1988; membership chmn. Medway Newcomer's Club, Mass., 1988—89. Recipient numerous monetary awards given to Hopkinton Edn. Found. in name of Ms. Moran for fostering excellence in edn., Hopkinton, Mass., 1999 - 2005. Mem.: Gone with the Winds woodwind quintet, Cmty. Orch., Arundel Vocal Arts Soc. (Md.), Westchester Choral Soc., Somer's Chorale, Bach Choral Soc., Pleasantville Cantata Singers (N.Y.), Broadmoor Chamber Singers. Achievements include developing a system for music education based upon Kodaly/Orff/Dalcroze methods; researching and developing methods for ear-training and pitch understanding for young children; thirty years of studying and implementing creative approaches of music education based upon the Dalcroze, Kodaly, Orff methods of music learning. Avocations: yoga, swimming, cross-country skiing, hiking, dance. Home: 267 Norfolk St Holliston MA 01746 Office: Hopkinton Public Schools Haydn Rowe St Hopkinton MA 01748 Personal E-mail: wenmora@aol.com. Business E-Mail: wmoran@hopkinton.k12.ma.us.

**MORANO, FRANK,** radio producer, talk show host; b. Staten Island, NY, May 29, 1984; s. Carmine Anthony and Elizabeth Morano (Stepmother), Stephanie Morano. BA, NYU, 2005. Prodn. coord. Bklyn. Cyclones, 2001—03; videographer, editor Li-Da Video, NYC, 2000—05; tv talk show host Time Warner Cable, NYC, 2000—; prodr. WABC Radio, NYC, 2004—. Pres. NY Soc. Neighborhoods, NYC, 2005; exec. com. mem. Richmond County Independence Party, Staten Island, NY, 2002; state exec. com. mem. Independence Party, NYC, 2005; founder Draft Tom Golisano for Gov., NYC. Independent. Roman Catholic. Avocations: movies, air hockey. Office: WABC Radio 2 Penn Plz 17th Fl New York NY 10121 Office Fax: 212-613-3823. Personal E-mail: frank@moranovision.com. Business E-Mail: frank.morano@abc.com.

**MORANO, GERARD JOHN,** marketing executive; b. Mount Vernon, N.Y., Oct. 23, 1944; s. Gerard Anthony and Pauline (Ungaro) M.; m. Allison Lenore Folz, June 28, 1975; 1 child, Steven Christopher. BS in Fin., CUNY, 1974;

BA in Mktg., Pace U., Pleasantville, N.Y., 1981; MBA, Pace U., White Plains, N.Y., 1982. From fin. planner to mgr. sales promotion ITT Continental, Rye, NY, 1968—84; from dir. mktg. to sr. v.p. mktg. and comm. Quality Bakers Am., Greenwich, Conn., 1984—2000; exec. v.p. QBA, Advt., Inc., Greenwich, Conn., 1992—2000, Solutions Mktg. LLC, Darien, Conn., 2001—. Alumni mentor Pace U., 1988—; fundraiser Vietnam Vets. Meml. Com., Washington, 1980-82; bd. dirs. Vets. Bus. Network, 2001—. With U.S. Army, 1966-68, Vietnam. Decorated Bronze Star; recipient Conspicuous Silver Svc. Star and Order of Merit, State of NY, 2001. Mem.: Promotional Mktg. Assn., Am. Film Inst., 199th Inf. Assn., Ellis Island Found., Vietnam Vets. Am., Wildlife Conservation Soc. Avocations: photography, videography. Office: Solutions Mktg LLC 30 Old Kings Hwy S Darien CT 06820 Office Phone: 203-655-2614. Personal E-mail: jmorano2000@aol.com.

**MORANO, KEVIN R.,** mining company executive; b. June 28, 1953; m. Ellen Dooley. BS magna cum laude, Drexel U., 1977; MBA, Rider Coll., 1983. Audit supr. Coopers & Lybrand, Newark, N.J.; with contr. dept. ASARCO Inc., N.Y.C., 1978-88, treas., 1989, gen. mgr. Ray Copper Mining and Smelting Complex, 1991, v.p., CFO, 1993-98, exec. v.p., COO, 1999, also bd. dirs.; exec. v.p., CFO Exide Tech., 1999—2001, Lumiens Ltd., 2002—. Bd. dirs. Apex Silver Ltd., Datatwatch Corp., Bear Creek Mining Corp. Mem. AICPA, N.J. Soc. CPA.

**MORANT, BRENDA WHITE,** publishing executive, small business owner, investor; b. Balt., May 5, 1944; BS, U. Md., 1973; MPA, Cen. Mich. U., 1974. Founder, chief exec. officer Women's Econ. Enterprises, 1988—; publisher Networking Mag., 1990—; bus. devel. The BES Co., 1988—; owner Market Rsch. Cons., Atlanta, 1994—. Cons. U.S. Air Force, Oscodo, Mich., 1977, Greater Mt. Calvery Bapt. Ch., Jackson Miss., 1991—, Options & Opportunities Career Ctr., Greenville, N.C., 1991—. Inventor electro thermo engineered insulated refrigeration container system for heat sensitive products. Organizer Battered Women's Ctr., 1979, Juneteen Celebration in Miss., 1980, Commn. on Women, 1986, Industrial Energy Sec., 1984. With USMC, 1962-64. Named 1st Businesswoman on the front Cover of Miss. Official State Mag., 1987; recipient Innovation award U.S. Dept of Energy, 1985, Governor Miss., 1985. Mem.: NAFE, Alumni Assn. Ctrl. Mich. U. (pres. Atlanta chpt.), Assn. Female Vets. (bd.). Avocations: dance exercising, boating, travel, painting, reading. Office: BES Techs PO Box 162125 Atlanta GA 30321-2125

**MORANT, RICARDO BERNARDINO,** psychology professor; b. New Britain, Conn., Feb. 13, 1926; s. J. Ramon and Rosario (Ciscar) M.; m. G. Francisca Giner, Dec. 26, 1955; children— Ramon, Francisca, Dolores, Ricardo. AB, Harvard, 1948; postgrad., Wesleyan Coll., Middletown, Conn., 1948-49; MA, Clark U., 1950, PhD, 1952. From faculty to prof. Brandeis U., Waltham, Mass., 1952—91, Minnie and Harold L. Fierman prof. psychology, 1991—2005, emeritus, 2005—, prof. Volen Nat. Ctr. for Complex Sys., 1994—2005. Prin. investigator NIMH, Spencer Found., Rothman Found. 1960—; spl. research space perception, body orientation. Bd. dirs. Coun. Pub. Schs., 1970-73; mem. steering com. Sensory Aid Eval. and Devel. Ctr., MIT, 1963-67; chmn. bd. trustees Hiatt Ednl. Programs, 1982-94. Served with USNR, 1946-48. Fellow APA; mem. Psychonomic Soc. Home: 35 Cliff Rd Wellesley MA 02481-3001 E-mail: morant@brandeis.edu.

**MORARI, MANFRED,** chemical engineer, educator; b. Graz, Austria, May 13, 1951; came to U.S., 1975; s. Manfred and Hilde M.; m. Marina Korchynsky, May 12, 1984. Diploma Chem. Engring., Eidgenoessische Technische Hochschule, Zurich, Switzerland, 1974; PhD in Chem. Engring., U. Minn., 1977; Dr h c, Babes Bolyai U., 2003. Asst. prof. U. Wis., Madison, 1977-81, assoc. prof., 1981-83; prof. chem. engring. Calif. Inst. Tech., Pasadena, 1983-94, McCollum-Corcoran prof., 1991-94, exec. officer, 1990-93, prof. control and dynamical sys., 1993-94; exec. officer, 1993-94; head automatic control lab. ETH. Gulf vis. prof. chem. engring. Carnegie Mellon U., 1987. Contbr. articles to profl. jours. Recipient D.P. Eckman award Am. Automatic Control Coun., 1980. Fellow: NAE, AIChE (A.P. Colburn award 1984, Profl. Progress award 1995, Computing in Chem. Engring. award 2002), IEEE (George S. Axelby Outstanding Paper award 1990, Control Sys. Field award 2005), Am. Soc. Engring. Edn. (Curtis W. McGraw rsch. award 1989), Am. Chem. Soc. Home: Laerchentobelstrasse 22 CH-8700 Kusnacht Switzerland Office: Automatic Control Lab ETH-Z ETL I 29 CH-8092 Zurich Switzerland Business E-Mail: morari@control.ee.ethz.ch.

**MORARIU, CORINA,** professional tennis player; b. Detroit, Michigan, Jan. 26, 1978; d. Albin and Rodica Morariu; m. Andrew Turcinovich. Grad., St. Andrews H.S., 1996. Mem. U.S. Nat. Tennis team. Won Jr. Championship Australian, French and U.S. Opens, 1995, Australia, 1994, Wimbledon, doubles, 1999 (with Lindsay Davenport), Australian Open Mixed Doubles (with E. Ferreira), 2001; winner 1 Career Singles Title, 10 Career Doubles Titles, WTA Tour. Office: USTA 70 W Red Oak Ln White Plains NY 10604-3602 also: ATP Tour 201 Atp Tour Blvd Ponte Vedra Beach FL 32082-3211

**MORATH, MAX EDWARD,** entertainer, composer, writer; b. Colorado Springs, Colo., Oct. 1, 1926; s. Frederic Palmer and Gladys Hester Nancy (Ramsell) M.; m. Norma Loy Tackitt, Oct. 23, 1953 (div. 1992); children: Kathryn, Christine, Frederic; m. Diane Fay Skomars, May 24, 1993. BA in English, Colo. Coll., 1948; postgrad., Stanford NBC-Radio-TV Inst., Palo Alto, Calif., 1951; MA in Am. Studies, Columbia U., 1996. Touring nationally in concerts and theater, 1961-04; writer: (radio series) Ragtime to the Max, 2006; recs. on Epic RCA Vanguard SoloArt Omega Premier; author: The Road to Ragtime, 1999, The NPR Curious Listener's Guide to Popular Standards, 2002; playwright, prodr., composer (musical play) Trust Everybody...But Cut the Cards, 2003. Mem. Broadcast Music, Inc. Home and Office: 463 Hartley Place Duluth MN 55803 Office Phone: 218-724-5886. Personal E-mail: rathmo@gmail.com.

**MORATZ, KAREN EVANS,** musician; b. Pasadena, Calif., Apr. 7, 1963; d. Hermann and Anna Lore Moratz; m. George Henry Evans, Apr. 7, 2004. MusB, Johns Hopkins U., 1984; orch. diploma, Musikhochschule Freiburg im Breisgau, Germany, 1986. Prin. flute player Indpls. Symphony Orch., 1989—; artist-in-residence Jordan Coll. Fine Arts Butler U., Indpls., 1989—. Mem. speakers bur. and guild The Julian Ctr. Domestic Violence Shelter, Indpls., 2003. Mem.: Nat. Flute Assn. (young artist competition coord. 2004—, 1st Place Cadenza Competition 1990). Achievements include first use of the orchestral model flute in the US. Home: 5933 Washington Blvd Indianapolis IN 46220 Office: Indpls Symphony Orch 32 E Washington St Ste 600 Indianapolis IN 46204 Personal E-mail: kmoratz@butler.edu.

**MORAVEC, PAUL,** composer; b. Buffalo, 1958; Attended, Am. Acad., Rome; BA in music composition magna cum laude, Harvard U., 1980; MusM in music composition, Columbia U., 1982, D Musical Arts in music composition, 1987. Tchg. asst. Columbia U., 1980—84; preceptor, 1985—87; dir. Columbia U. Composers' Colloquium, 1985—87; asst. prof. Dartmouth Coll., 1987—93, assoc. prof., 1993—96; prof. chmn. Adelphi U., 1993—; Vis. assoc. prof. Columbia U., 1996—98; adj. assoc. prof. Hunter Coll., 1998. Composer over seventy orchestral, chamber, choral, and lyric compositions including, (orchestral) Spiritdance, 1989, Adelphony, 1997, Ancient Lights, 1994, Northern Lights Electric, 2000, Tempest Fantasy, 2003, (chamber) The Kingdom Within, 1989, Circular Dreams, 1991, Quintessence, 1999, Octocelli, 2000, (piano solo) Music Remembers, 1983, Piano Triptych, 1991, Characteristics, 1995, (choral) Ave Verum Corpus, 1979, Three Anthems, 1983, A Spirit of Power, 1996, Personals, 1999. Fellow in Music Composition, Nat. Endowment Arts, Rockefeller Found., Goddard Lieberson; Rome Prize Fellowship, Am. Acad. Rome, residency fellowship, Carnargo Found., Charles Ives Fellowship, Am. Acad. Arts Letters. Office: Adelphi U Dept Music Post Hall Second Fl Garden City NY 11530

**MORAWETZ, CATHLEEN SYNGE,** mathematician; b. Toronto, Ont., Can., May 5, 1923; arrived in U.S., 1945, naturalized, 1950; d. John Lighton and Elizabeth Eleanor Mabel (Allen) Synge; m. Herbert Morawetz, Oct. 28, 1945; children: Pegeen Morawetz Rubinstein, John Synge, Lida Morawetz Jeck, Nancy. BA, U. Toronto, 1945; SM, MIT, 1946; PhD, NYU, 1951; degree (hon.), Ea. Mich. U., 1980, Smith Coll., 1982, Brown U., 1982, Princeton U., 1986, Duke U., 1988, N.J. Inst. Tech., 1988, U. Waterloo, 1993, U. Dublin, 1996, U. Toronto, 1996. Research assoc. Courant Inst., NYU, 1952—57, asst. prof. math., 1957—60, assoc. prof., 1960—65, prof., 1965—, assoc. dir., 1978—84, dir., 1984—88. Chmn. bd. Sch. Theoretical Physics Dublin Inst. for Advanced Studies, 1990—2000. Contbr. articles to profl. jours. Trustee Princeton U., 1973—78, Sloan Found., 1980—94. Recipient Nat. medal of Sci., NSF, 1998; fellow Guggenheim, 1967, 1979; grantee Office of Naval Rsch., 1975—90. Fellow: AAAS, Royal Soc. Can.; mem.: NAS, London Math. Soc., Royal Irish Acad., Soc. Indsl. and Applied Math., Am. Philos. Soc., Am. Acad. Arts and Scis., Am. Math. Soc. (term trustee 1975—85, pres. 1995—97, George David Birkhoff prize in Applied Math. (awarded jointly) the Am. Math. Soc. and Soc. for Indsl. and Applied Math.) 2006, Steele prize 2004). Achievements include research in applications of partial differential equations, especially transonic flow and scattering theory. Office: CIMS 251 Mercer St New York NY 10012-1110 Office Phone: 212-998-3297. Business E-Mail: morawetz@cims.nyu.edu.

**MORBY, JACQUELINE,** venture capitalist; b. Sacramento, June 19, 1937; d. Junior Jennings and Bertha (Backer) Collins; m. Jeffrey L. Morby, June 21, 1959; children: Andrew Jennings, Michelle Lorraine. BA in Psychology, Stanford U., 1959; M in Mgmt., Simmons Grad. Mgmt. Sch., Boston, 1978. Assoc. TA Assocs., Boston, 1978-81, gen. ptnr., 1982-89, mng. dir., 1989—2002, prin., 2003—. Bd. dirs. HVL, Inc., Pitts., Softmed Sys. Inc., Bethesda, Md., Ansys, Inc., Canonsburg, Pa., Pacific Life Corp., Newport Beach, Calif., J&B Software, Inc., Bluebell, Pa. Trustee Simmons Coll., Warholl Mus. Mem. Nat. Venture Capital Orgn. Avocations: theater, reading, art, skiing, travel. Office: TA Assocs 125 High St Boston MA 02110-2704 E-mail: jmorby@ta.com.

**MORDECAI, MONICA MYERS,** anesthesiologist; d. Larry Daniel and Ann Hoffman Myers; m. Mark Mordecai, Mar. 2, 1996; children: Dylan Myers, Mia Danielle. MD, U. of Fla., 1991. Lic. physician Fla. Anesthesiologist U. of Fla., Jacksonville, 1995—2000, Mayo Clinic, Jacksonville, Fla., 2000—. Office: Mayo Clinic 4500 San Pablo Blvd Jacksonville FL 32224 Office Phone: 904-953-2000.

**MORDEN, ANNETTE SONJA KNUDSON,** retired education educator; b. Phoenix, Mar. 17, 1940; d. Maynard Wold and Mertie Lucille Knudson; m. Robert Dean Morden, Aug. 5, 1962; children: Kristina, Shauna. BA, U. No. Iowa, 1962, MA in edn., 1966. Math tchr. Rockford Roosevelt, Ill., 1962—65; benthic biologist U. Wis., 1972, 1975, sr. lectr. and dir. math tutoring lab, 1982—2005. Unit leader and budget, audit and fin. com. League of Women Voters, 1971—73; brownie and girl scout leader Girl Scouts Am., 1963—64, 1977—82; bd. dirs. and exec. bd. YMCA, 1976—81; mem. founding com. and exec. bd. Habitat for Humanity, 1991—94. Mem.: Assn. U. Wis. Profls. Lutheran. Avocations: reading, travel, snorkeling. Home: 1422 N 21st St Superior WI 54880

**MORDEN, JOHN REID,** security-business intelligence consultant; b. Hamilton, Ont., Canada, June 17, 1941; s. Warren Wilbert and Isabelle Gemmell (Reid) M.; m. Margaret Keens, June 27, 1964; children: Michael, Geoffrey. BA, Dalhousie U., 1962; postgrad., Dalhousie Law Sch., 1962-63; LLD (hon.), Dalhousie U., 2003. With Can. Dept. External Affairs, various worldwide cities, 1963-84; asst. dep. min. native claims Dept. Indian & Northern Devel., Canada, 1984-85; trade and econ. policy Can. Dept. External Affairs, 1985-86; asst. sec. to cabinet Fgn. and Def. Affairs, Can., 1986-87; dir. Can. Security Intelligence Svc., 1987-91; dep. min. fgn. affairs Govt. Can., 1991-94; pres, CEO, Atomic Energy of Can., Ltd., Ottawa, Ont., Canada, 1994-98; mng. dir. Kroll Asocs. Can., Toronto, 1999-2000; chmn. KPMG Corp. Intelligence Inc., Toronto, 2000—02; pres. RM & A, Inc., 2002—; exec. dir. Independent Inquiry UN Iraq Oil for Food Programme, 2004—06. Mem. Inst. for Study Violence and Terrorism; chair bd. govs. Trent U.; chair coun. of chairs Ont. Univs.; fellow Can. Def. and Fgn. Affairs Inst. Internat. adv. coun. York U.; Can. com. Coun. for Security and Cooperation in Asia and Pacific. Decorated Order of Can.; Order of So. Cross (Brazil); recipient Ian L. Macrae award, 1998. Mem. Toronto Hunt Club, Nat. Club. Avocations: photography, music, ballet, reading. Office Phone: 416-486-3520. Business E-Mail: reidmorden@rogers.com.

**MORDY, JAMES CALVIN,** lawyer; b. Ashland, Kans., Jan. 3, 1927; s. Thomas Robson and Ruth (Floyd) M.; m. Marjory Ellen Nelson, Nov. 17, 1951; children: Jean Claire Mordy Jongeling, Rebecca Jane Mordy King, James Nelson. BA in Chemistry, U. Kans., 1947; JD, U. Mich., 1950; postgrad., George Washington U., 1952—53. Bar: Kans. 1950, Mo. 1950, cert.: Am. Bankruptcy Bd. (in bus. bankruptcy law). Assoc., Morrison, Hecker, Buck, Cozad & Rogers, Kansas City, Mo., 1950—59; ptnr. Morrison & Hecker LLP, Kansas City, 1959—96, sr. counsel, 1996—97, of counsel, 1997—2000; ret., 2000. Contbg. author: Missouri Bar Insurance Handbook, 1968, Missouri Bar Bankruptcy Handbook, 1991, also supplements; contbr. articles to profl. jours. Chmn. bd. Broadway United Meth. Ch., Kansas City, 1964-70, chmn. bd. trustees, chmn. fin. com., 1988-90, 94, 2000-2002; bd. dirs. Broadway Child Enrichment Ctr., 1980-2006; bd. dirs., exec. com. Della Lamb Neighborhood House, Kansas City, 1973-80; bd. dirs., treas. Friends of Sacred Structures, Kansas City, 2000—; coun. mem. St. Paul Sch. Theology, Kansas City, 1986-; bd. dirs. Kingswood Sr. Living Cmty., Kansas City, 2004—, vice chmn., 2005-; del. 17th World Meth. Conf., Rio de Janeiro, 1996; ranger Rocky Mountain Nat. Park, 1948-1949. With USN, 1945-46, 51-53, comdr. USNR, ret. Recipient Shepherd of the Lamb award, Della Lamb Neighborhood House, 1980; Summerfield scholar, 1943—47. Fellow Am. Coll. Bankruptcy, Am. Bar Found. (life); mem. ABA, Am. Judicature Soc., Am. Bankruptcy Inst., Mo. Bar Assn., Kansas City Met. Bar Assn. Lawyers Assn. Kansas City, Workout Profs. Assn. Kansas City, Univ. Club (v.p., bd. dirs. 1983, 86), Barristers Soc., Phi Beta Kappa, Delta Tau Delta (pres. Kansas City alumni chpt. 1965-72, pres. U. Kans. House Corp. 1966-72), Alpha Chi Sigma, Phi Alpha Delta. Avocations: travel, geography (maps), history, music, theology. Home: 8741 Ensley Ln Leawood KS 66206-1615 Office: Stinson Morrison Hecker LLP 1201 Walnut St Kansas City MO 64106-2150

**MORE, DOUGLAS MCLOCHLAN,** lawyer; b. N.Y.C., Apr. 21, 1926; s. Morgan Berkeley and Lucinda (Bateson) M.; m. Pamela Bennett Marr, Aug. 6, 1954; children— Robin Maclachlan More Eddy, Alison Marr More Davies. Grad., Phillips Exeter Acad., 1943; BA, Harvard U., 1947; LL.B., Columbia U., 1950. Bar: N.Y. State bar 1951, Conn. bar 1981, Fla. bar 1983. With N.Y. Trust Co., 1950-51; asso. firm Bigham, Englar, Jones & Houston, N.Y., 1951-53; fin. analyst Johns-Manville Corp., 1953-54; assoc. firm Kissam & Halpin, N.Y., 1954-59; assoc. counsel Hooker Chem. Corp., 1959-63, gen. counsel, 1963-72, v.p., 1967-72; v.p. law Airco, Inc., 1972-75; gen. counsel Beker Industries Corp., 1975-81, v.p., 1975-78, sr. v.p., 1978-81; ptnr. firm More Phillips & Duncan, P.C., Greenwich, Conn., 1981-88, of counsel, 1988—. Served to It. (j.g.) USNR, 1943-46. Mem. ABA, Conn. Bar Assn., Greenwich Bar Assn., Phi Delta Phi, Phoenix S-K Club, Hasty Pudding Inst. 1770 (Harvard). Home and Office: 27 Skylark Rd Greenwich CT 06830-4624 Office Phone: 203-869-0663.

**MORE, JOSÉ,** photojournalist; Bur. chief United Press Internat., Kans., Mo.; chief photographer Palm Beach Post, Fla.; photographer Chgo. Tribune, 1980—, chief photographer, 1991—94. Co-recipient George Polk award for internat. reporting, 2006. Office: Chicago Tribune 435 N Michigan Ave Chicago IL 60611 E-mail: jmore@tribune.com.*

**MORE, PHILIP HARVEY BIRNBAUM,** business administration educator; b. San Diego, Jan. 21, 1944; s. Louis and Ruth Laureen (Bay) B.; m. Marlin Sue Van Every, Dec. 26, 1964; 1 child, Brian Philip. BA, U. Calif., Berkeley, 1965; PhD, U. Wash. 1975. Internal cons./analyst Los Angeles County Civil Svc. Commn., 1965-67; tchg. assoc. U. Wash., Seattle, 1972-74; asst. prof. bus. adminstrn. Ind. U., Bloomington, 1975-80, assoc. prof., 1980-85, prof., 1986—. Resident dir. J.F.K. Int., Tiburg U., The Netherlands; vis. scholar Polish Acad. Scis., Hungarian Acad. Scis., Tokyo U., SDA Bocconi, Milan, Italy, Seoul Nat. U., Korea, Dartmouth Coll. Co-author: Organization Theory: Structural and Behavioral Analysis, Modern Management Techniques for Engineers and Scientists, International Research Management: Studies in Interdisciplinary Methods From Business, Government and Academics, 1990; assoc. editor IEEE Transaction on Engring. Mgmt. jour.; contbr. articles to profl. jours., book revs., sects. to books, invited papers Germany, Poland, Eng., Can., Thailand, Hong Kong, Korea. With USAF, 1967—71. NSF fellow, 1974-75, N.Y. Acad. Scis. fellow, 1981; U. Hong Kong Sr. Fulbright scholar, 1981-82. Mem. Acad. Mgmt. (pres. tech. and innovation mgmt. divsn. 1989-90), Engring. Mgmt. Soc., Inst. Ops. Rsch. and Mgmt. Scis., Internat. Assn. for Study of Interdisciplinary Rsch., Beta Gamma Sigma, Beta Alpha Psi, Sigma Iota Epsilon, Sigma Chi. Methodist. Office: Univ So Calif Marshall Sch Bus Los Angeles CA 90089-0808 Office Phone: 213-740-0744, 213-740-0744. Business E-Mail: phbmore@marshall.usc.edu.

**MOREAN, WILLIAM D.,** manufacturing executive; s. William E. Morean and Audrey Peterson; m. Kelly Morean; 4 children. Student in Aviation, Western Mich. U. With Jabil Circuit, St. Petersburg, Fla., 1977—, v.p., pres., bd. dirs., 1978—, chmn. bd. dirs., 1988—, CEO, 1988—2000. Bd. dirs. Eagle's Wing Found., St. Petersburg. Named one of 400 Richest Ams., Forbes mag., 2006. Office: Jabil Circuit 10560 Dr Martin Luther King Jr St N Saint Petersburg FL 33716*

**MOREAU, ROBERT DANIEL, JR.,** art educator; b. Port Arthur, Tex., Dec. 19, 1965; s. Robert Daniel Moreau and Susan Ann Robison. BFA, Lamar U., 1998, MA, 2000; MFA, Stephen F. Austin. 2003. Asst. prof. Northwestern State U., Natchitoches, La., 2003—. Juror Argus Mag., Natchitoches, 2003, 04, Yaca State Art Exhbn., Alexandria, La., 2004. Recipient 1st pl. award, Beawcarts Ball, 1994. Mem.: Phi Kappa Phi. Avocations: reading, writing, films, music, cuisine. Home: 402 Elvira Dr Natchitoches LA 71457 Office Phone: 318-357-6013. E-mail: moreaur@usula.edu.

**MOREFIELD, MICHAEL THOMAS,** financial executive; b. Chgo., Aug. 13, 1956; s. Preston Thomas and Geraldine Judith Morefield BA Acctg., Lewis U., 1978; M Fin., Loyola U., Chgo., 1987. Mgr. gen. acctg. Gen. Binding Corp., Northbrook, Ill., 1980, dir. corp. acctg., 1981—83, dir. corp. fin. planning, 1983, asst. corp. contr., 1984—86, corp. contr., 1986—88; sr. v.p. fin. and adminstrn., CFO Toyoda Machinery USA, Inc., Arlington Heights, Ill., 1988—93; v.p. fin., CFO Schmalbach-Lubeca Holdings, Inc., Downers Grove, Ill., 1993—99; v.p., CFO United Plastics Group, Inc., Westmont, Ill., 1999—2002; v.p. fin., CFO Exelon Svcs. Inc., Westchester, Ill., 2002—03; sr. exec. v.p., CFO Portola Packaging, Inc., Batavia, 2004—. Bd. dirs. Cap Snap Europe; gen. mgr. White Cap Mex. S.A. de C.V., Cuatitlan, 1996-99 Active Friars Civic Orgn., Romeoville, Ill., 1976-78 Mem. Nat. Machine Tool Builders Assn. (fin. com. 1988-90); Arlington Heights C. of C Avocations: scuba diving, music, skiing, basketball, baseball. Home: 6836 Bantry Ct Darien IL 60561-3688 Office: 951 Douglas Rd Batavia IL 60510 Office Phone: 630-326-2074.

**MOREHEAD, ANDREW TURNER, JR.,** chemistry professor; b. Santiago, Chile, Feb. 7, 1967; s. Andrew Turner and Katherine Wren Morehead; children: Erin, Griffin, Aidan. BA in Chemistry, Harvard U., Cambridge, Mass., 1985—89; PhD, Duke U., Durham, N.C., 1991—96. NIH postdoctoral rschr. Calif. Inst. Tech., Pasadena, 1996—98; asst. prof., chemistry U. Md., College Park, 1998—2003, E. Carolina U., Greenville, NC, 2003—. Recipient Outstanding Academic Advisor, U. Md. Parents' Assn. 2002. Mem.: Am. Chem. Soc. (sec., local sect. 2004—06), Sigma Xi. Office: Dept Chemistry E Carolina Univ Greenville NC 27858 Office Phone: 252-328-9798. Office Fax: 252-328-6210. Business E-Mail: moreheada@ecu.edu.

**MOREHOUSE, LAWRENCE GLEN,** veterinarian, educator, academic administrator; b. Manchester, Kans., July 21, 1925; s. Edwy Owen and Ethel Merle (Glenn) M.; m. Georgia Ann Lewis, Oct. 6, 1956; children: Timothy Lawrence, Glenn Ellen. BS in Biol. Sci., Kans. State U., 1952, DVM, 1952; MS in Animal Pathology, Purdue U., 1956, PhD, 1960. Lic. vet. medicine. Veterinarian County Animal Hosp., Des Peres, Mo., 1952-53; supr. Brucellosis labs. Purdue U., West Lafayette, Ind., 1953-60; staff veterinarian lab. svcs. USDA, Washington, 1960-61; discipline leader in pathology and toxicology, animal health divsn. USDA Nat. Animal Disease Lab., Ames, Iowa, 1961-64; prof., chmn. dept. vet. pathology U. Mo. Coll. Vet. Medicine, Columbia, Mo., 1964—69, 1969—86, dir. Vet. Med. Diagnostic Lab., 1968-88, prof. emeritus, 1986—. Cons. USDA, to comdg. gen. U.S. Army R&D Command, Am. Inst. Biol. Scis., NAS, to Surg. Gen., Miss. State U., St. Louis Zoo Residency Tng. Program, Miss. Vet. Med. Assn., Okla. State U., Pa. Dept. Agr., Ohio Dept. Agr. Co-editor: Mycotoxic Fungi, Mycotoxins, Mycotoxicoses: An International Encyclopedic Handbook, 3 vols., 1977; contbr. articles on diseases of animals to profl. jours. Active Trinity Presbyn. Ch., Columbia, 1964-2002; bd. dirs. Mo. Symphony Soc., Columbia, 1989-92. Pharmacists mate second class USNR, 1943-46, PTO; 2d. lt. U.S. Army, 1952-56. Recipient Outstanding Svc. award USDA, 1959, merit cert., 1963, 64, Disting. Svc. award U. Mo. Coll. Vet. Medicine, 1987, Dean's Impact award, 1996, Kans. State U. Alumni award, 2004. Fellow Royal Soc. Health London; mem. AAAS, Am. Assn. Vet. Lab. Diagnosticians (E.P. Pope award 1976, chmn. lab. accreditation bd. 1972-79, 87-90, pres. 1979-80, sec.-treas. 1983-87), World Assn. Vet. Lab. Diagnosticians (bd. dirs. 1984-94, dir. emeritus 1994—), N.Y. Acad. Sci., U. S. Animal Health Assn., Am. Assn. Lab. Animal Sci., Mo. Soc. Microbiology, Am. Assn. Avian Pathologists, N.Am. Conf. Rsch. Workers in Animal Diseases, Mo. Univ. Retirees Assn. (pres. 1996-99). Presbyterian. Avocations: classic cars, boating, genealogy. Home: 916 Danforth Dr Columbia MO 65201-6164 Office: U Mo Vet Med Diagnostic Lab PO Box 6023 Columbia MO 65205-6023 E-mail: lmorehou@coin.org, gmoreho@att.global.net.

**MOREHOUSE, SARAH MCCALLY,** retired political science professor; b. Boston, Jan. 15, 1927; d. Ralph Dewey and Eugenia Whitehead (Norris) Powell; m. W. Bradley Morehouse, Nov. 8, 1969 (div. Nov. 1986); children: Richard, John, Catherine, David; m. Malcolm Edwin Jewell, Dec. 28, 1991. BA in Polit. Sci., Wellesley Coll., 1948; PhD in Polit. Sci., Yale U., 1964. Instr. Conn. Coll., New London, 1964-66; lectr. Hunter Coll., Bronx, N.Y., 1966-69; assoc. prof. Manhattanville Coll., Purchase, N.Y., 1969-75; prof. U. Conn., Stamford, 1976-92, prof. emerita, 1992—. Univ. senator U. Conn., 1982-85, assoc. dir., 1990-91. Author: State Politics, Parties and Policy, 1981, The Governor as Party Leader, 1998; contbr. various articles to profl. jours. Sec. Charter Revision Commn. Fairfield, Conn., chmn. Ethics Commn., Fairfield, 1984-88; pres. LWV, 1996-98; state LWV sec. bd. dirs. 1998-2001; political parties/elections, 2001. Vis. professorship for women NSF, 1991; fellow Danforth Found., 1960; rsch. grantee Russell Sage Found., 1983; vis. scholar U. Calif, Berkeley, 1991-92. Mem. Wellesley Club. Home: 242 Somerset Ave Fairfield CT 06824-4935 Personal E-mail: macsarahj@worldnet.att.net.

**MOREHOUSE, WARD, III,** theater critic, writer, playwright; b. N.Y.C., Aug. 11, 1945; s. Morehouse Ward, II and Joan Marlowe Rahe; m. Elizabeth Haggard, Feb. 10, 1979; 1 child, William. Student, Am. Acad. Dramatic Art, N.Y.C., 1965—66. Male-up editor, reporter N.Y. Post, N.Y.C., 1969—73; staff reporter, staff corr. Christian Sci. Monitor, Boston, 1973—77, N.Y.C. 1977—82; press rep. NBC News, N.Y.C., 1983—84; freelance drama critic Christian Sci. Monitor, N.Y.C., 1984—2002; Broadway columnist Reuters, N.Y.C., 1993—95, N.Y. Post, N.Y.C., 1994—98; reporter, writer People Mag., People.com, N.Y.C., 1998—2000; drama critic, feature writer Christian Sci. Monitor, N.Y.C., 2000—02; Broadway columnist N.Y. Sun, N.Y.C., 2002—04, AM New York, N.Y.C., 2004—. Author: (book) The Waldorf-Astoria: America's Gilded Dream, 1991, Inside the Plaza: An Intimate Portrait of the Ultimate Hotel, 2001, (plays) The Actors, 1986—87, If It Was Easy, 2001 (Best Play nomination Am. Critics Assn.), The Caedmon School, 2003. Mem.: Drama Desk, Lambs Club. Home: 12 E 86th St Apt 938 New York NY 10028-0514

**MORELAN, PAULA KAY,** choreographer; b. Lafayette, Ind., Nov. 24, 1949; d. Dickie Booth and Marian Maxine (Fetterhoff) M.; m. Kerim Sayan, Aug. 10, 1974. Student, U. Utah, 1968-69; BFA, Tex. Christian U., 1972; postgrad., El Centro Coll., 1969-70. Tchr. Rosello Sch. Ballet, Dallas, 1972-74; mgr., tchr. Ballet Arts Ctr., Dallas, 1974-76; owner, tchr. Ballet Classique, Garland, Tex., 1976-87, Garland Ballet Acad., 1977-87; resident choreographer Garland Civic Theatre, 1986—, lifetime mem., 1998. Asst. to Mythra Rosello Tex. Civic Ballet, Dallas, 1972—74; assoc. artistic dir. Dance Repertory Theatre Dallas, 1974—75, artistic dir., 1975—76, Garland (Tex.) Ballet Assn., 1977—90, Classical Ballet Acad., Performing Arts Sch., 1987—90; artistic dir. musical theatre dept. KD Actors Conservatory, 2005—; founder, chairperson Act IV Guild, 2002—05. Bd. dirs. Garland Civic Theatre, 2000—05. Recipient Leon Rabin award for Best Choreography, Dallas Theatre League, 1996, 1998, 2000, 2001, 2004, Column award, 2004, Best Choreographer award, 2003, Choreographer of Yr. award, 2001, 2002, 2003, 2004. Personal E-mail: pkm@worldnet.att.net.

**MORELAND, DONALD EDWIN,** physiologist; b. Enfield, Conn., Oct. 12, 1919; s. Albert Sinclair and Ruth (Cowan) M.; m. Verdie Brown Stallings, Nov. 6, 1954; 1 child, Donna Faye; stepchildren: Frank C., Paul Ziglar. BS in Forestry, N.C. State U., 1949, MS in Plant Physiology, 1950, PhD in Plant Physiology, 1953. Plant physiologist SUNY Coll. Forestry, Syracuse, 1952-53, USDA-Agrl. Rsch. Svc., Raleigh, NC, 1953-71, rsch. leader, 1972-78, sr. exec., 1979-95, collaborator, 1996—; asst. prof. to prof. N.C. State U., Raleigh, 1953-95, prof. emeritus, 1996—. Mem. toxicology study sect. NIH, USPHS, Bethesda, Md., 1963-67. Editor: Biochemical Responses Induced by Herbicides, 1982; mem. editorial bd. Pesticide Biochemistry and Physiology, 1971-97, Pesticide Sci., 1987-96; contbr. articles to profl. jours. 1st lt. U.S. Army, 1941-46. AEC predoctoral fellow, 1950-52. Fellow AAAS, Weed Sci. Soc. Am. (outstanding rsch. award 1973); mem. Am. Chem. Soc., Plant Growth Regulator Soc. Am., Am. Soc. Plant Physiologists, So. Weed Sci. Soc., Sigma Xi. Avocations: woodworking, surf fishing, square dancing. Home: 1508 Pineview Dr Raleigh NC 27606-2562 Office: NC State U USDA-Agrl Rsch Svc Dept Crop Sci 3127 Ligon St Raleigh NC 27607-5376

**MORELAND, ROBERT LYLE,** minister; b. Fairmont, W. Va., Feb. 6, 1921; s. James Rogers and Ethel Bernice (Finnicum) Moreland; m. Martha Bamford Smith, Dec. 18, 1943; children: John Rogers, Mary Ellen Robertson, Sarah Jeanne Conyer, Sue Anne Eason. BA, Coll. of Wooster, 1943; BD, Princeton Theol. Seminary, 1945; MA, Mich. State U., 1968. Ordained Minister Presbytery of Grafton Presbyn. Ch., 1945. Asst. pastor First Presbyn. Ch., Joplin, Mo., 1945—47, pastor Harrison, Ark., 1947—51, Emporia, Kans., 1951—57, Eastminster Presbyn. Ch., East Lansing, Mich., 1957—68; stated clerk, treas. Presbytery of Detroit, 1968—75; controller Synod of the South, Atlanta, 1975—78; v.p., corp. sec. Bd. of Pensions, Phila., 1978—87; ret., 1987. Chmn. Human Rels. Commn., East Lansing, Mich., 1965—68; pres Kiwanis Club, East Lansing, 1967—68; treas. Gibbons Home, Springfield, Pa., 1991—2001. Mem.: Rotary Club of Swarthmore. Presbyn. Home: 801 Yale Ave Apt 1210 Swarthmore PA 19081

**MORELL, MICHAEL JOHN,** actuary; b. Concord, Mass., Jan. 3, 1974; s. Roy Kelly and Mary Ellen Theresa Morell; m. Elen Yakovleva, Nov. 30, 2001; children: Victor, Natalie. BA, Harvard Coll., Cambridge, Mass., 1995. F.S.A. Soc. of Actuaries, 2002, M.A.A.A. Am. Acad. of Actuaries, 2001. V.p. Bankers Trust Co., N.Y., 1995—99; co-founder, CEO Make Us An Offer, Inc., Lawrenceville, NJ 1999—2000; actuary Am. Skandia, Inc., Shelton, Conn., 2000—02; dir., product devel. AEGON Structured Products, Louisville, 2002—. Christian. Achievements include patents for Internet haggling character. Avocations: hiking, fast food, real estate. Office: AEGON Structured Products 400 West Market St Louisville KY 40202 Office Phone: 502-560-2069. E-mail: mmorell@ucgonusa.com.

**MORELL, WILLIAM NELSON, JR.,** foreign trade association executive, government agency administrator; b. July 13, 1920; s. William N. and Louise (Cox) M.; m. Patricia Leonhard, Apr. 3, 1943; 1 child, Lynn Noble. Student, Coll. William and Mary, 1938—40; AB, George Washington U., 1942; MA, U. Pa., 1948; postgrad., Am. U., 1950—51; grad., Nat. War Coll., 1956. Jr. economist Bur. Labor Stats., 1941; asst. to prof. fin. George Washington U., 1941; naval mem. U.S. mil. mission to Moscow, 1944-46; asst. prof. Drexel Inst. Tech., 1946-48; instr. U. Pa., 1947-48; with CIA, 1949-68, staff mem. Office Nat. Est., 1950-52, mng. dir. U.S. econ. intelligence com., 1955-65, chmn., 1966-67; chmn. spl. study group NSC Planning Bd., 1960; econ. counselor Am. Embassy, Moscow, 1960-61; dir. office rsch. and reports CIA, 1962-66, dir. Office Econ. Rsch., 1966-67; mem. U.S. econ. def. adv. com., adv. com. export policy, 1966-67; lectr. on Communist econs., 1960-68; faculty Nat. War Coll., 1968; econ. counselor Am. Embassy, Taipei, Taiwan, 1968-73, spl. asst. to sec. treasury, 1973-77; treasury mem. U.S. Nat. Intelligence Bd., 1973-77; mng. dir. USA-ROC Econ. Coun., Crystal Lake, Ill., 1977-95, pres., 1979-90; cons. U.S. Taiwan Trade, 1979-94, ret., 1994. Author, lectr. on Taiwan economy. Eucharistic min. Episc. ch. Lt. USNR, 1942-46. Decorated Order Brilliant Star Taiwan, Order Brilliant Star with Violet Grand Cordon; recipient Superior Achievement award, medal of merit CIA, Exceptional Svc. medal Treasury Dept., U.S. Nat. Intelligence Disting. Svc. award, Taiwan Econ. Ministry medal. Mem. Artus, Econ. Soc. (hon.). Home: 340 S Berkshire Dr Lake Forest IL 60045-4823

**MORELLA, CONSTANCE ALBANESE,** ambassador, former congresswoman; b. Somerville, Mass., Feb. 12, 1931; d. Salvatore and Mary Christine (Fallette) Albanese; m. Anthony C. Morella, Aug. 21, 1954; children: Paul, Mark, Laura; guardians of: Christine, Catherine, Louise, Rachel, Paul, Ursula. AA, Boston U., 1950, AB, 1954; MA, Am. U., 1967, D of Pub. Svc. (hon.), 1988, Norwich U. and Dickinson Coll., 1989, Mt. Vernon Coll., 1995, U. Md. U. Coll., 1996, USUHS, 1997, U. Md., 1997, Elizabethtown Coll., 1999. Tchr. Montgomery County (Md.) Pub. Schs., 1956-60; instr. Am. U., 1968-70; prof. Montgomery Coll., Rockville, Md., 1970-86; mem. Md. Ho. Dels., Annapolis, 1979-86, U.S. Congress from 8th Md. dist., 1987—2003; mem. sci. com., tech. subcom., basic rsch. subcom., govt. reform com., chair D.C. subcom., mem. civil svc. subcom.; visiting fellow Kennedy School, Harvard, 2003; U.S. permanent rep. to Orgn. for Econ. Co-operation & Devel. U.S. Dept. State, Paris, 2003—. Mem. civil svc., adv. bd. Am. Univ., Washington Mem. adv. coun. Montgomery County Hospice Soc.; hon. bd. mem. Nat. Kidney Found; active Human Rights Caucus; Congressional Women's Caucus, Older Ams. Caucus, Population and Devel. Caucus; mem. Bd. Cafritz Found. Named Glamour Woman of Yr. Glamour mag. 1995, Washingtonian of Yr. 1991; named to Md. Women's Hall of Fame, Md. Women's Hall of Fame, 1994. Republican. Avocations: theater, tennis, reading. Home: USOECD PSC 116 APO AE 09777

**MORELLO, CELESTE ANNE,** historian, criminologist; b. Norristown, Pa., July 22, 1958; d. Ann M. Morello. Student, Loyola U., Rome, 1978; BA in Classics cum laude, BA in Art History magna cum laude, Chestnut Hill Coll., Phila., 1980; cert. in Paralegal Studies, Villanova U., Pa., 1986; MS in Criminology, St. Joseph's U., Phila., 1994; MA in History, Villanova U., Pa., 2000; grad., Civilian Police Acad., Phila., 2000. Cert. paralegal Villanova U., 1986. Tchr. history, social studies, sci. Archdiocese of Phila., 1977-84; lectr. on ancient history of Sicily, 1982—; cons. criminologist in Mafia and LCN history Phila. Police and U.S. Atty.'s Office, 1993—. Pioneer in criminal and Mafia history; petitioner, originator over 25 Phila. hist. marker sites Pa. Hist. and Mus. Commn. Hist. Marker Program, 1993—; lectr. in field. Author: Beyond History: The Times and Peoples of St. Paul's R.C. Church, 1843-1993, 1992; writer, dir. History of the Mafia and LCN in Philadelphia 1880-1959 for Dept. of Justice, FBI, Phila, 1997, History of South Philadelphia, Introduction, Institute for Service Learning, 1996, Survey of Illicit Narcotics Use in Philadelphia 1900-45 for Dept. of Justice, High Intensity

Drug Traffic Area, Philadelphia/Camden, The Phenomenon of the Mafia, 1997, Oral Histories of Three Men: All Mafiosi Before 1930, 1998, The Early Sicilian American Mafia Before 1930, 1998, Case Study of A Western Sicilian Colony in Suburban Philadelphia, 1998, The Philadelphia Italian Market Cookbook, 1999, Before Bruno: The History of Philadelphia's Mafia, Book I 1880-1931, 1999, Book II 1931-1946, 2001, Book III 1946-1959, 2005, The Philadelphia Police's Homicide Records: The First Decades of Investigating and Advancement, 2003, Philadelphia's Italian Foods: A History of Over 200 Years with Recipes from the City's Best Italian Cooks, 2006; contbr. articles to profl. jours., chpts. to books. Founder Sicilian Culture Collection, Hist. Soc. Pa., Phila. Mem. Moyamensing Hist. Soc. (founder), Pa. Hist. Assn. Roman Catholic. Office: 1234 S Sheridan St Philadelphia PA 19147-4820 Office Phone: 215-334-6008.

**MORELLO, JOSEPH ALBERT,** musician, educator; b. Springfield, Mass., July 17, 1928; s. Joseph Charles and Lilia (LaPalme) M.; m. Jean Ann Mehnert. Grad. high sch., Springfield. Ind. drummer, Springfield, 1945-49; drummer Gil Melé, Stan Kenton, Tal Farlow, Johnny Smith, N.Y.C., 1953-55, Dave Brubeck Quartet, touring worldwide, 1955-68; clinician Selmer Ludwig Drum Co., Elkhart, Ind., 1957-92; leader Joe Morello Quartet, 1979—; clinician DW Drums, Oxnard, Calif., 1993—; rec. artist Digital Music Products Inc., 1993—. Rec. artist Savoy, Capitol, Norgran, Blue Note, Columbia, RCA labels; innovator finger control in jazz drumming; author: Joe Morello Drum Method, The Natural Approach to Technique, 1993, Joe Morello Drum Method 2, 1994, also New Directions in Rhythm, Rudimental Jazz, Off the Record, Master Studies, Master Studies II, 2006; releases include (with Joe Morello Quartet) Going Places, 1993, Morello's Standard Time, 1994, Marion Mc Partland's Hickory House Trio, 1999, Marion McPartland Trio with Joe Morello, 2002, Rufus Reid Live at Shanghai Jazz, 2002. Named to Hall of Fame, Modern Drummer mag., 1988, Percussive Arts Soc. Hall of Fame, 1993, Am. Jazz Hall of Fame, 2001, Trumpets Jazz Hall of Fame, 2002; recipient New Star award, Downbeat mag., 1955, Melody Maker mag. award, 1963—67, Jazz mag. award, 1964—67, Thomas A. Edison Lifetime Achievement award, 1990, Lifetime Achievement award, Jersey Shore Jazz and Blues Found., 1996, Recognition of Outstanding Leadership award, Kosa Internat. Percussion Workshops, 2002, Lifetime Achievement award, Montreal Drum Festival, 2002, poll winner, Downbeat mag., 1963—65, Playboy mag., 1963—67, Lifetime Achievement award, Sabian Ltd., 2003. Mem.: N.J. Jazz Soc. Avocation: photography.

**MORELLO, STEVEN JOHN,** lawyer; b. Saginaw, Mich., Sept. 17, 1952; m. Francia S. Morello, Apr. 8, 1978; children: Steven Jr., Rebecca. BS in Fgn. studies, Georgetown U., 1974; JD, U. Detroit Mercy Sch. Law, 1977; MBA, Boston Coll. Law Sch., Heidelberg, Fed. Republic Germany, 1980; MA in Pastoral studies, Sacred Heart Major Seminary. Bar: Mich. 1977, Ill. 1984; cert. profl. contracts mgr., Nat. Contract Mgmt. Assn. (Fellow). Staff asst. U.S. Senator Philip A. Hart, Washington; mng. atty. regional office Digital Equipment Corp., Arlington Heights, Ill., 1984; atty. contract Northrop Corp. Def. Sys. Divsn., Rollings Meadows, Ill., 1982-84; v.p., gen. counsel Prechter Holdings Inc., Southgate, Mich.; gen. counsel, Dept. Army U.S. Dept. Def., Washington, 2001—05; gen. counsel Sault Ste. Marie Tribe of Chippewa Indians. Mem. Sault Ste. Marie Tribe of Chippewa Indians. Capt. JAGC U.S. Army, 1978—85, trial counsel 21st Support Command, first mem. Trial Def. Svc., Karlsruhe, Germany, legal asst., adminstrv. law officer, Berlin Recruiting Command, Ft. Sheridan, Ill., contract atty., 86th Army Reserve Command USAR, Ft. Sheridan, Ill. Fellow Nat. Contract Mgmt. Assn. (pres. Chgo. chpt. 1985-86). Office: Sault Tribe Legal Dept 523 Ashmun St Sault Sainte Marie MI 49783

**MORENCY, PAULA J.,** lawyer; b. Oak Park, Ill., Mar. 13, 1955; AB magna cum laude, Princeton U., 1977; JD, U. Va., 1980. Bar: Ill. 1980, U.S. Dist. Ct. (no. dist.) Ill. 1980, U.S. Ct. Appeals (7th cir.) 1981, U.S. Ct. Appeals (5th cir.) 1990, U.S. Dist. Ct. (ctrl. dist.) Ill. 1999, U.S. Dist. Ct. (ea. dist.) Wis. 2000. Assoc. Mayer, Brown & Platt, Chgo., 1980-86, ptnr., 1987-94; Schiff Hardin & Waite, Chgo., 1994—. Adj. prof. trial advocacy Northwestern U. Sch. Law, Chgo., 1997—; faculty Midwest Regional, Nat. Inst. for Trial Advocacy, 1988—; mem. pres.'s coun. Dominican U., 1998-2002. Author: Cross-Examination of a Franchise Executive, 1995, Insurance Coverage Issues in Franchise and Intellectual Property Litigation, 1996, Re-Emergence of Franchise Class Actions, 1997, Judicial and Legislative Update: ABA Forum on Franchising, 1999, How to Find, Use and Defend Against the Expert Witness, 2000, Dealing With System Change in a High-Tech World, 2001, A Decade After Daubert, 2004. Mem. ABA (forum franchising, governing com. 2001-04, litig. sect., antitrust sect., intellectual property sect., bd. dir.), Chgo. Coun. of Lawyers (bd. govs. 1989-93), Constnl. Rights Found. Chgo. (chair 2001). Office: Schiff Hardin LLP 6600 Sears Tower Chicago IL 60606 Office Phone: 312-258-5549.

**MORENO, ALBERT F.,** apparel executive, lawyer; b. Dec. 1943; BA in economics, San Diego State U., 1966; M in L.Am. econ. studies, U. Madrid, 1967; JD, U. Calif., Berkeley, 1970. Bar: Calif. 1970. Regional dir. Legal Svcs. Corp., San Francisco; asst. gen. counsel Levi Strauss & Co., San Francisco, 1978—81, assoc. gen. counsel, 1981—85, dep. gen. counsel, 1985—94, chief counsel Levi Strauss N.Am., 1994—96, sr. v.p., gen. counsel, 1996—. Bd. dirs. New Century Energies Inc., 1999—2000, Xcel Energy Inc., 2000—. Dean's adv. coun. San Diego State U. Coll. Arts and Letters; chmn. bd. trustees Rosenberg Found., 2003—. Recipient Monty Alumni Award, San Diego State U., 2001. Office: Levi Strauss & Co 1155 Battery St San Francisco CA 94111

**MORENO, ARTURO (ARTE MORENO),** major league baseball team owner, former advertising executive; b. Tucson, Aug. 1947; m. Carol Moreno, 1986; 3 children. BS in Mktg., Univ. Ariz., 1973. With Eller Outdoor, 1973—84; pres., COO Outdoor Systems Inc., 1984—99; former owner Salt Lake Trappers minor league baseball club; former minority owner Arizona Diamondbacks baseball club, Phoenix Suns basketball club; owner & pres. Los Angeles Angels of Anaheim baseball club, 2003—. Dir. Nelnet. Cofounder (with Carol Moreno) Moreno Family Found. Served U.S. Army, 1966—68, Vietnam. Named one of Forbes' Richest Americans, 2004. Office: Los Angeles Angels of Anaheim 2000 Gene Autry Way Anaheim CA 92806*

**MORENO, BARRY,** historian, writer; b. LA; s. Rafael S. and Eva Maria Moreno. BA in History, Calif. State U., L.A., 1985. Libr., historian Statue of Liberty and Ellis Island, N.Y.C., 1988—. EEO counselor Nat. Park Svc., NYC, 1988—96. Author: The Statue of Liberty Encyclopedia, 2000, Italian Americans, 2003, Images of America: Ellis Island, 2003, Encyclopedia of Ellis Island, 2004, Images of America: The Statue of Liberty, 2004, Children of Ellis Island, 2005, Manhattan Street Scenes, 2006; (foreword) Ellis Island Interviews, 1997; (bibliography) Statue of Liberty Revisited, 1994; cons. for, appeared on numerous film, TV and radio documentaries including Ellis Island: Everyman's Monument, 1991, On the Inside: The Statue of Liberty, 1999, Building a Colossus: The Statue of Liberty, 2001, The Sweetest Sound, 2001, Lady By the Sea: The Statue of Liberty, 2004, How to Start Your Own Country, BBC, 2005; contbr. chpts. to books, articles to profl. jours Recipient EEO Counseling award Statue of Liberty Nat. Monument, 1994. Mem. Mus. Coun. N.Y., Am. Immigration and Ethnic History Soc., Calif. Hist. Soc., Monarchist League, Am. Vaudeville Soc., English-Speaking Union, Orgn. Am. Historians. Roman Catholic. Avocations: writing, studying foreign languages, reading. Office: Statue of Liberty Nat Monument and Ellis Island Liberty Island New York NY 10004 E-mail: barry_moreno@nps.gov.

**MORENO, CARLOS R.,** state supreme court justice; b. LA, Nov. 4, 1948; m. Christine Moreno; children: Keiko, Nicholas. BA in Polit. Sci., Yale U., 1970; JD, Stanford U., 1975. Dep. city atty. L.A. City Atty.'s Office; atty. with Mori & Ota (now known as Kelley, Drye & Warren), 1979; apptd. justice Mncpl. Ct., 1986—93; justice L.A. County Superior Ct., 1993—97, US Dist. Ct. (ctrl. dist.) Calif., 1998—2001; assoc. justice Supreme Ct. Calif., 2001—. Bd. visitors Stanford Law Sch.; bd. advs. Assns. Yale Alumni. Avocation: air. Arroyo Vista Family Health Ctr. Recipient Criminal Justice Superior Ct. Judge of Yr. award, L.A. County Bar Assn., 1997, For God, For Country and For Yale

award, Yale U., 2001. Mem.: Municipal Ct. Judges Assn., Presiding Judges Assn., Calif. Judges Assn., Mexican Am. Bar Assn. (past pres.). Avocations: theater, opera, crossword puzzles. Office: Calif Supreme Ct 350 McAllister St San Francisco CA 94102-4783*

**MORENO, CHRISTINE MARGARET,** lawyer; b. Miami, Fla., Sept. 7, 1960; d. Arthur and Christine Moreno. BS magna cum laude, Barry U., 1981; JD cum laude, U. Miami, Coral Gables, Fla., 1984. CPA Fla.; bar: Fla. 1984, D.C. 1985, U.S. Dist. Ct. (so. dist.) Fla. 1985, U.S. Dist. Ct. (mid. dist.) Fla. 1987, U.S. Tax Ct. 1987, U.S. Supreme Ct. 1988, U.S. Ct. Appeals (11th cir.) 1988. Law intern U.S. Securities Exch. Commn., Miami, Fla., 1984; assoc. atty. Ruden, Barnett, McCloskey, Ft. Lauderdale, Fla., 1984-85, Koppen, Watkins, Ptnrs. & Assocs., Miami, 1985-89; mayor City of North Miami, 1989-91; owner, atty., CPA Law Offices of Christine M. Moreno, North Miami, Stuart, Fla., 1989—; commr. Jensen Beach (Fla.) Cmty. Redevelopment Agy., 1994-98, Martin County Environ. Control Bd., 1999—; legal counsel to Ambassador Ray Cantillo, rep. to U.N. Miccosukee Nation, 1998—. Bd. dirs. North Miami Energy Adv. Bd.; life time dir. Mayor's Econ. Task Force, North Miami, 1989—. Co-author: Senior Citizens Handbook, 1990; staff mem.: U. Miami Law Rev., 1982—84. Bd. dirs. Nat. League of Cities, Washington, 1990—91; v.p. polit. action Miami Dade C.C. Alumni, 1991—98, sec., 1998—. Mem.: AICPA, North Dade Bar Assn. (bd. dirs. Gold Coast chpt.), Fla. Inst. CPA (treas. Gold Coast chpt.), North Miami Jaycees (Jaycee of Yr. 1993), Dade County Rep. (com. woman 1990—94), Martin County Rep. Club (exec. com.), Phi Alpha Delta, Internat. Law Fraternity (Miami alumni chpt. justice 1985—). Office: 4450 SE Federal Hwy Stuart FL 34997-

**MORENO, DONNA MARIE,** communications executive; b. Amesbury, Mass., July 25, 1957; d. Robert and Marie Doris (Lucier) Mezrigian; m. Carlos Moreno, Nov. 17, 1999. BS Math., U. Lowell, 1979, MBA Ops., 1983. Analyst material control AVCO Corp., Wilmington, Mass., 1979—81; analyst ops. Blue Cross & Blue Shield, Boston, 1981—83, analyst risk, 1983—84; analyst sys. Bell Atlantic Corp., Bethesda, Md., 1984—86, cons. internal, 1986—89, mgr. project, 1989—91, mgr. new tech. strategic planning, 1992—97, sr mgr. sales channel devel., 1997—2001; sr. mgr. mktg. Verizon, 2001—04, sr. cons. sales incentive compensation, 2004—. Spkr. FUSE Nat. and Regional Confs., 1988, 91; mem. Verizon Hispanic Orgn Inventor (software) User-assisted Adhoc Reporting, 1988, Natural English Report Access, 1988 Vol. Montgomery County Vol. Assn., Md., 1983—, PALS Montgomery County, 1984—; chair spl. events New Mem. Svcs. John F. Kennedy Ctr. Performing Arts, Washington, 1985—, mem. vol. adv. com., 1991, 92; chair vol. adv. com. Kennedy Ctr., 1992—; bd. dirs. Sister City Corp., Rockville, v.p., 1993-95, pres.-elect, 1994-95, pres., 1995—; Geissenbier mem. Jr. Chamber Internat. Found., 1996—; Geissenbier mem. U.S. Jr. C. of C. Found., 1997—; mem. Montgomery County Ethnic Affairs Commn., 2005—; bd. dirs. U.S. Jaycees Found., sec., 2003, 04; dir. Women's Assn. Verizon Employees Mid Atlantic Mentoring Program, 2003-04, Mid Suburban Program, 2005- Recipient Internat Tng. Fellow, JCI, 2001—. Mem. NAFE, Ops. Rsch. Soc., Intelligent Comput Rsch. Inst., Verizon User Group (co-chmn. artificial intelligence group 1989, leader, coord. spl. interest groups for Nat. Com., 1989, nat., regional spkr. 1988, 91), Women's Assn. Verizon Employees (bd. dirs.), Native Am. People of Verizon (pres. 2006), Rockville Jr. C. of C. (sec. 1992-93), Md. Jr. C. of C. (program mgr. internat. involvement 1992-93, dir. 1993-94, cmty. devel. v.p. 1994-95, U.S. Jr. C. of C. internat. affairs commn. 1995-98, JCI individual devel. commn. 1996, spl. asst. to world pres. 1997—), Internat. Spkrs. Platform, Jr. C. of C. Republican. Roman Catholic. Avocations: photography, travel. Office: Verizon 13100 Columbia Pike Silver Spring MD 20902 Office Phone: 301-236-2834. Personal E-mail: dmenzigian@aol.com.

**MORENO, JAIME,** professional soccer player; b. Santa Cruz, Bolivia, Jan. 19, 1974; Grad. Tahuichi Acad., Santa Cruz. Mem. Middlebrough, English Premier League, 1995—96, DC United Major League Soccer, 1996—2002, NY/NJ MetroStars, Major League Soccer, 2003; forward DC United, Washington, 2004—, Bolivia Nat. Soccer Team, 1999—. Named Most Valuable Player, Major League Soccer, 1999, AT&T Best XI, 1999. Mem. DC United, Major League Soccer Cup Champions, 1996, 1997, & 1999; mem. DC United, Major League Soccer, US Open Cup Champions, 1996; mem. DC United, Major League Soccer, CONCACAF Champions Cup Winners, 1998; Winner, Golden Boot award, Major League Soccer (16 goals), 1997. Mailing: RFK Stadium 2400 East Capital St, SE Washington DC 20003

**MORENO, JONATHAN,** bioethicist; b. Poughkeepsie, NY, June 11, 1952; B., Hofstra U., 1973, PhD (hon.), 1998; PhD, Washington U., 1977. Prof. Swarthmore Coll., Pa., U. Tex., Austin, George Washington U., Washington, U. Penn., Philadelphia, 1995—97, Health Sci. Ctr., SUNY Brooklyn, 1997—98; Emily Davie and Joseph S. Kornfeld prof. Biomedical Ethics U. Va., Charlottesville, 1998—, dir. Ctr. for Biomedical Ethics; sr. fellow Ctr. for Am. Progress, Washington. Faculty affiliate Kennedy Inst. Ethics, Georgetown U.; advr. bd. Howard Hughes Med. Inst.; bd. Health Sciences Policy Inst. Medicine, com. on prison rsch.; com. biodefense analysis & countermeasures Nat. Academies; accreditation coun. Assn. Accreditation of Human Rsch. Protection Programs; sr. cons. Nat. Bioethics Adv. Commn.; sr. policy & rsch. analyst President's Adv. Com. on Human Radiation Experiments, Washington; ethics commentator ABCNews.com. Author: Ethics in Clinical Practice, 1994, Deciding Together: Bioethics & Moral Consensus, 1995, Arguing Euthanasia, 1995, Undue Risk: Secret State Experiments on Humans, 2001, In the Wake of Terror: Medicine & Morality in a Time of Crisis, 2003, Ethical & Regulatory Aspects of Clinical Research, 2003, Is There an Ethicist in the House?, 2005; contbr. articles, chapters to books. Fellow: NY Acad. Medicine, Hastings Ctr.; mem.: Am. Soc. Bioethics & Humanities (former pres.), Inst. Medicine ((in conjunction w/NRC) mem. adv. com. Human Embryonic Stem Cell Rsch. 2006—). Office: Ctr Biomedical Ethics UVA PO Box 800758 Charlottesville VA 22908 Office Phone: 434-924-0274. E-mail: jdm8n@virginia.edu.*

**MORENO, RITA (ROSITA DOLORES ALVERIO),** actress; b. Humacao, P.R., Dec. 11, 1931; m. Leonard I. Gordon, June 18, 1965; 1 child, Fernanda Luisa. Spanish dancer since childhood, night club entertainer; appeared on Broadway in The Sign in Sidney Brustein's Window, 1964-65, Gantry, 1969-70, The Last of the Red Hot Lovers, 1970-71, The National Health, 1974, The Ritz, 1975, Wally's Cafe, 1981, The Odd Couple, 1985; (off Broadway) After Play, 1995, (London prodn.) Sunset Blvd., 1996; motion picture debut, 1950, and appeared in numerous films including West Side Story, Carnal Knowledge, The King and I, Singing in the Rain, The Four Seasons, I Like It Like That, 1994, Angus, 1995, Wharf Rat, 1995, Slums of Beverly Hills, 1998, Carlo's Wake, 1999, Blue Moon, 2000, Pinero, 2001, King of the Corner, 2004, Lolo's Cafe, 2006, Play It By Ear, 2006, (TV) The Rockford Files: If It Bleeds...It Leads, 1999, Strong Medicine, 2003, The Guardian, 2003, Copshop, 2004, Law and Order, 2005, (series) American Family, 2002. Recipient Acad. Award for best supporting actress, 1962; Grammy award for best rec., 1973; Antoinette Perry award for best supporting actress Broadway play, 1975; Emmy award, 1977, 78, award Nat. Osteoporosis Found., 2000. Achievements include being in the Guinness Book of World Records as the only female performer to win Acad., Grammy, Tony and Emmy awards. Address: care Agency for Performing Arts 9200 W Sunset Blvd Los Angeles CA 90069-3502*

**MORENO, VERONICA,** food products executive; m. Eduardo Moreno. Co-founder Olè Mexican Foods, Norcross, Ga., 1987—. Named Nat. Hispanic Businesswoman of Yr., U.S. Hispanic C. of C., 2001, Latina Entrepreneur of Yr., Hispanic Bus. Mag., 2004. Office: Ole Mexican Foods Inc 6585 Crescent Dr Norcross GA 30071

**MORENO-CABRAL, CARLOS EDUARDO,** cardiac surgeon; b. Zacatecas, Mex., Nov. 4, 1951; s. Manuel Julio Moreno and Dominga Cabral; m. Elaine Nakumara; children: Rodrigo, Iza, Daniel. MD, Nat. U. Mex., 1976. Diplomate Am. Bd. Thoracic Surgery. Resident in gen. surgery U. Hawaii, 1977-80, Mich. State U., 1980-82; fellow in cardiac surgery Stanford (Calif.)

U., 1982-84, 86-88; tng. in thoracic surgery SUNY, Bklyn., 1984-86; dir. cardiac transplant program St. Francis Hosp., Honolulu, 1989—. Author: Postoperative Management in Adult Cardiac Surgery, 1988. Fellow ACS; mem. Soc. Thoracic Surgeons, European Assn. Cardio-Thoracic Surgery. Avocation: photography. Office: 1380 Lusitana St Ste 912 Honolulu HI 96813-2448 E-mail: cemoreno@aol.com.

**MORESCO, ROBERT,** scriptwriter, film and television producer; 1 child, Amanda. Actor: (films) Winter Kills, 1979, Turk 182!, 1985, Men of Respect, 1991; writer: One Eyed King, 2001; co-prodr.: Million Dollar Baby, 2004; prodr., writer Crash, 2004 (Southeastern Film Critics Assn. award for Best Original Screenplay, 2005, Broadcast Film Assn. award for Best Writer, 2006, Original Screenplay, British Acad. Film and TV Arts, 2006, Best Original Screenplay award, Acad. Motion Picture Arts and Sciences, 2006, Best First Feature, Independent Spirit award, 2006), dir., writer 10th & Wolf, 2005; co-prodr.: (TV series) Millennium, 1996, EZ Streets, 1996; exec. prodr., co-writer Falcone, 2000.*

**MOREST, DONALD KENT,** neuroscientist, educator; b. Kansas City, Mo., Oct. 4, 1934; s. F. Stanley and Clara Josephine (Riley) M.; m. Rosemary Richtmyer, July 13, 1963 (dec. 2002); children: Lydia, Claude. BA, U. Chgo., 1955; MD, Yale U., 1960. Sr. asst. surgeon USPHS, Bethesda, Md., 1960-63; asst. prof. U. Chgo., 1963-65; asst. to assoc. prof. Harvard Med. Sch., Boston, 1965-77; prof., dir. Ctr. for Neurol. Scis. U. Conn. Health Ctr., Farmington, 1977—; prof. commn. scis. U. Conn., Storrs, 2002—. Cons. NIH, Bethesda, 1975—, European Commn. Contbr. articles to profl. jours. and books. Recipient Loeser award U. Conn. Health Ctr., Farmington, 1982; Career Devel. awardee NIH, 1971; named Javits neurosci. investigator NIH, 1984, Claude Pepper awardee, 1990. Mem. Am. Assn. Anatomists (C. Judson Herrick award 1966), Soc. for Neurosci., Assn. for Rsch. in Otolaryngology, Conn. Acad. Sci. and Engring. (elected), Cajal Club (pres. 1980). Avocations: flute, badminton. Home: 18 Shady Ln West Simsbury CT 06092-2232 Business E-mail: kentmorest@revron.uchc.edu.

**MORETTI, AUGUST JOSEPH,** pharmaceutical executive, lawyer; b. Elmira, NY, Aug. 18, 1950; s. John Anthony and Dorothy M. (De Blasio) M.; m. Audrey B. Kavka, Nov. 8, 1981; children: David Anthony, Matthew Alexander. BA magna cum laude, Princeton U., 1972; JD cum laude, Harvard U., 1975. Assoc. Heller, Ehrman, White and McAuliffe, San Francisco, 1976-82, ptnr., 1982-2000; CFO, gen. counsel Surro Med, Inc., 2001—05; CFO Alexza Pharms., 2005—. Lectr. bus. adminstrn. U. Calif. Berkeley, 1977-79; bd. dirs. AviGenics. Bd. dirs. Ann Martin Children's Ctr.; mem. adv. panel U. Calif. Berkeley Entrepreneur Program. Mem. ABA.

**MORETTI, FRANCO,** professor of comparative literature; Ed., Universita' di Roma Laurea, 1972. Prof. Ctr. for Study of the Novel, Stanford U., 2000—, Danily C. and Laura Louise Bell prof., prof. English and Comparative Lit. Calif. Scientific adv. Ministry of Rsch., France; lectr. Gauss seminars Princeton U.; lectr. Beckman lectr. UCLA, Berkeley. Author: Signs Takes for Wonders, 1983, The Way of the World, 1987, Modern Epic, 1996, Atlas of the European Novel 1800-1900, 1998, Graphs, Maps and Trees, 2005; chief editor The Novel, 2006; contbr. articles News Left Rev. Fellow: Wissenschaftskolleg zu Berlin; mem.: Am. Acad. Arts and Sciences. Office: Dept Comparative Lit Stanford Univ Margaret Jacks Hall Bldg 460 Rm 417 Stanford CA 94305-2087 Office Phone: 650 723 4590. Office Fax: 650 725 0755. E-mail: moretti@stanford.edu.*

**MOREWITZ, STEPHEN JOHN,** behavioral scientist, consultant, sociologist, educator; b. Newport News, Va., May 14, 1954; s. Burt M. and Ruth (August) M., Lora Friedman (stepmother). BA, Coll. William and Mary, 1975, MA, 1978; PhD, U. Chgo., 1983. Rsch. asst. Michael Reese Hosp., Chgo., 1979-84; asst. social scientist Argonne (Ill.) Nat. Lab., 1984-85; asst. to dean, asst. prof. U. Ill., Chgo., 1988-92, sr. rsch. splst., 1991-92; vol. rsch. staff San Francisco Gen. Hosp., 1993-97; pres. S. Morewitz, PhD & Assocs., Chgo. and Buffalo Grove, Ill., 1988—, San Francisco, 1992—. Part-time sociology faculty DePaul U., Chgo., 1985—; mem. faculty St. Elizabeth's Hosp., 1987—88; assoc. prof. Calif. Sch. Podiatric Medicine, 1997—2000, prof., rsch. dean, 2000—02; adj. prof. Calif. Sch. Podiatric Medicine, 2003—; cons. in field; lectr. Calif. State U., 2004. Co-author: Medical Malpractice, 1996; author: Sexual Harassment and Social Change, 1996, Stalking and Violence, 2003, Domestic Violence and Maternal Child Health, 2004; contbr. articles to profl. jours., chapters to books. Vol. docent Garfield Farm Mus., LaFox, Ill., 1979—; curator Saving of S.S. Quanza, Chgo., 1991—. Mem. Am. Pub. Health Assn. (Top 10 Injury Poster award 2000), Am. Diabetes Assn. (profl. sect.), Assn. for Behavioral Scis. and Med. Edn., Am. Sociol. Assn. (cert., nat. finalist med. sociology), Soc. Behavioral Medicine, Generalist in Med. Edn., Sociol. Practice Assn., Soc. Study Social Problems (divsn. chmn., Outstanding Scholar award 2003). Avocations: theater, museum design, swimming, environmental preservation, farming. Office: S Morewitz PhD & Assocs PMB M858 28 E Jackson Blvd 10 Fl Chicago IL 60604

**MOREY, CARL REGINALD,** musicologist; b. Toronto, Ont., Can., July 14, 1934; s. Reginald Donald and Julia Beatrice (Mabey) M.; m. Lorna Ann Dalton, June 2, 1960 (dec.); 1 child, Rachel Adriana MusB, U. Toronto, 1957; MusM, Ind. U., 1961; PhD, 1965. Asst. prof. Wayne State U., Detroit, 1962-63; assoc. prof. U. Windsor, Ont., 1964-70; prof. music U. Toronto, 1970-2000, dean faculty of music, 1984-90, Jean A. Chalmers prof., dir. Inst. for Can. Music, 1991-2000. Author: Music in Canada: A Research and Information Guide, 1997; MacMillan On Music, 1997, An Opera Sampler, 1998, Opera Viva, 2000; editor: (musical) Works of Glenn Gould (Schott), 1995, 96, 97, 99, 2004. Avocation: swimming. Office: U Toronto Faculty of Music Toronto ON Canada M5S 2C5 Home: 907 77 Carlton St Toronto ON Canada M5B 2J7 Business E-mail: carl morey@utoronto.ca

**MOREY, CHARLOTTE ANN,** elementary school educator, music educator; b. Dickinson, N.D., Dec. 1, 1949; d. Clarence William Hartman and Catherine Sills; m. Michael Scott Morey, June 19, 1971; children: Christopher Michael, Melissa Kay. BS, Dickinson State Coll., 1971. Elem. music specialist Slope County Schs., Amidon, ND, 1971—72, New England Pub. Schs., 1972—75, 1980—80; jr. high sch. music specialist McKenzie County Pub. Schs., Watford City, 1976—78; elem. music specialist Hettinger Pub. Sch., 1985—2000, Lincoln Elem. Sch., Fargo, 2000—. Contbr. articles to profl. jours. Flutist cmty. bands, Hettinger, Bismark, Fargo, 1981—; organist Luth. Ch., Regent, New England, Watford City, Hettinger, 1965—2000. Named N.D. Music Educator of Yr., 2001; recipient Disting. Svc. award, Internat. Misic Camp, 1999, Alumni Fellows award, Dickinson State U., 2004. Mem.: Music Educators Assn. N.D. (clinician & adjudicator 1971—), Orgn. Am. Kodaly Educators (clinician 1995—, pres. North Plains chpt.), N.D. Music Educators Assn. (state chair, bd. dirs., exec. bd., Music Educator of Yr. 2001), N.D. Am. Choral Dirs. Assn. (state pres. 2001—, past repertoire & stds. chair). Avocations: cross stitch, gardening, cooking, reading. Office: Lincoln Elem Sch 2120 9th St S Fargo ND 58103

**MOREY, ROBERT HARDY,** communications executive; b. Milw., Sept. 5, 1956; s. Lloyd W. and Ruby C. (McElhaney) M. AA, Ricks Coll., 1978; BA, Brigham Young U., 1983. Program dir. Sta. KABE-FM, Orem, Utah, 1982-83, sales mgr., 1983; nat. mgr. ops. Tiffany Prodns. Internat., Salt Lake City, 1983-84; account exec. Osmond Media Corp., Orem, 1984; exec. sec., bd. dirs. Positive Communications, Inc., Orem, 1984—87, chief exec. officer, 1987—; gen. mgr. Sta. KSRR, Orem, 1985—; pres. K-Star Satellite Network, Orem, 1986—89, Broadcast Media Svcs., Orem, 1987—; gen. mgr. Sta. KMGR, Salt Lake City, 1993; ops. mgr. KQMB-FM, Salt Lake City, 1994-95; gen. mgr., 1995-98; gen. mgr. KCFM, 1998—. With Ams. Freedom Festival at Provo, 2002—; guest lectr. various colls. and univs. Chmn. Rep. voting dist., Orem, 1984. Recipient Community Service award Utah Valley Community Coll., 1983; named one of Outstanding Young Men in Am. U.S. Jaycees, 1983. Mem.: Utah Broadcasters Assn. (bd. dirs. 2005—). Avocations: reading, collecting stamps. Home: PO Box 828 Orem UT 84059-0828 Office Phone: 801-224-1400.

**MOREYRA, ABEL E.,** medical educator; b. Mar del Plata, Argentina, Dec. 2, 1941; came to U.S., 1972; s. Genaro and Emilia (Basso) M.; m. Maria Elena Moreyra; children: Maria Eugenia, Maria Evelina, Fernando Abel. MD, U. Nacional de La Plata, Argentina, 1967. Fellow Cleve. Clinic Found., 1972-75; asst. prof. medicine UMDNJ-Robert Wood Johnson Med. Sch., New Brunswick, NJ, 1975-83, assoc. prof., 1983-95, prof., 1995—. Fellow ACP, Am. Coll. Cardiology; mem. Am. Coll. Angiology. Office: UMDNJ-RW Johnson Med Sch CN-19 Rm 582A New Brunswick NJ 08903 Office Phone: 732-235-7851. E-mail: moreyra@umdnj.edu.

**MORFOPOULOS, V.,** metallurgical engineer, materials engineer; b. Athens, Greece, Oct. 22, 1937; BS, Purdue U., 1958; MS, Columbia U., 1961, ScD in Engring. Sci., 1964. Rsch. assoc. metall. engring. Purdue U., 1957-60; rsch. engr. U.S. Steel Corp., 1961; instr. chem. CUNY, 1961-63; rsch. engr. Argonne Nat. Lab., 1963, Am. Iron & Steel, Columbia U., 1964-65, sr. metall. sci., 1965-66; tech. dir. R&D testing Am. Standards Testing Bur., 1966—. Cons. govt. and industry, 1966—; mem. Int. Commn. Chem. Thermodyn. & Kinetics; mem. Transp. Rsch. Bd., Nat. Rsch. Coun. Mem. AAAS, Am. Inst. Mining, Metall. Petroleum Engrs., Am. Soc. Engr. Edn., Assn. Cons. Chemists and Chem. Engrs., N.Y. Acad. Sci. Achievements include research and consulting in fields of corrosion and oxidation phenomena. low and high temperature thermodynamics, liquid metals and compounds, surface phenomena, electrometallurgy and electrode phenomena, electrical and magnetic properties of matter, failure and stress analysis, metal finishing, joining and working. Office Phone: 212-943-3160. Personal E-mail: worldteck@aol.com.

**MORFORD, CRAIG S.,** prosecutor; BA, Hope Coll., 1981; JD, Valparaiso U. Sch. Law, 1984. Trial atty. dist. counsel IRS, 1984—86; with US Dept. Justice, 1986—, trial atty. organized crime prosecution, 1986—89, asst. U.S. atty. (no. dist.) OH, mem. organized crime strike force, 1989—2002, interim U.S. atty. (ea. dist.) Mich., 2004—05, spl. atty. to U.S. atty. gen. heading investigation into first major U.S. post Sept. 11 trial, 2004—. Office: US Attys Office 211 W Fort St Ste 2001 Detroit MI 48226 Office Phone: 313-226-9100. Office Fax: 313-226-2311.

**MORFORD, JOANN (JOANN MORFORD-BURG),** state senator, investment company executive; b. Miller, S.D., Nov. 26, 1956; d. Darrell Keith Morford and Eleanor May Morford-Steptoe. BS in Agrl.-Bus., Comml. Econs., S.D. State U., 1979; cert. in personal fin. planning, Am. Coll., 1992. CLU; chartered fin. cons. Agrl. loan officer 1st Bank System, Presho, SD, 1980-82, Wessington Springs, SD, 1982-86, Am. State Bank, Wessington Springs, 1986; investment rep. ARM Fin. Svcs. Inc., Wessington Springs, 1986-96, Capital Financial Svcs., Inc., Miller, 1997—; mem. S.D. State Senate, Wessington Springs, 1990-96, majority whip, 1993-94, minority whip, 1995-96, mem., 1990-97, Miller, 1997-98; ins. agt. Western Fraternal Life Assn., 2001—03. Mem. transp. com., commerce com., taxation com. S.D. State Senate, Pierre, 1990—92, mem. appropriations com., 1993—98, chair ops. and audit com., 1993—94, mem. ops. and audit com., 1995—98; mem. fed. issues environ. com. Nat. Conf. State Legislators' Assembly, 1994—98, vice chair, 1996—97. Mem. midwestern-Am. task force Midwest Conf., 1990—94; treas. twp. bd. Wessington Springs, 1990—92; bd. dirs. Nyoda Coun. Girls Scouts U.S.; mem. fin. com. United Meth. Ch., Miller, 2001—04. Fleming fellow, Ctr. Policy Alternatives, 1996. Mem.: S.D. Farmers Union, Bus. and Profl. Women (2nd v.p. 2002), Alumni Coun. Young Polit. Leaders (China delegation 1996, host El Salvador delegation 1999), Future Farmers Am. (adv. bd. Wessington Springs chpt. 1984—96), S.D. State U. 4-H Alumni Assn., Quter Ea. Star (various offices 1980—). Democrat. Home and Office: 1510 N Parkview Pl Miller SD 57362-0021

**MORFORD, THOMAS,** health facility administrator; b. May 11, 1946; BA, Canisius Coll., 1968; MA, Syracuse U., 1971. Dir. office survey & cert. health stds. & quality bur. Health Care Fin. Adminstrn., 1979-82, deputy dir. health stds. & quality bur., 1982-86, dir. health stds. & quality bur., 1986-92; deputy dir. office rsch. integrity Office of Asst. Sec. for Health, 1992-95; assoc. adminstr. ops. & mgmt. Health Resources & Svcs. Adminstrn., Rockville, Md., 1995-97; dep. adminstr., 1997—2001; dep. dir. Johns Hopkins U. Urban Health Inst., Balt., 2001—. Contbr. articles to profl. jours. Office: Johns Hopkins U Urban Health Inst 111 Market Pl Ste 850 Baltimore MD 21202 Office Phone: 410-895-1100. Business E-Mail: tmorford@jhsph.edu.

**MORGA BELLIZZI, CELESTE,** editor; b. N.Y.C., Mar. 8, 1921; d. Louis and Emma (Macari) Morga; m. John J. Bellizzi, Sept. 1, 1942; children: John J., Robert F. Student, Columbia U., 1940-41, SUNY, Albany, 1970. Cert. med. lab. technician. Medical lab. technician USMC Hosp., N.Y.C., 1942, Woman's Hosp., N.Y.C., 1952-62; spl. investigator N.Y. State Atty. Gen.'s Office, Albany, 1958-65; editor Internat. Drug Report publ., The Narc Officer publ. Internat. Narcotic Enforcement Officers Assn., Albany, 1965—. Dir. Albany Inst. History and Art. 1988-90. N.Y. State Press Women, Albany, 1987; advisor UN Non-govtl. Orgns. Drug Com., N.Y.C., 1980-90. White House Conf. Drug Free Am., Washington, 1987; mem. com. Bethlehem Drug Prevention Program, Delmar, N.Y., 1987-90, Action Commn. Narc Edn., Delmar, 1984-90; v.p. Women's Rep. Party Albany, 1972 Recipient Pres.'s award INEOA, 1982, Disting. Svc. award Houston Police Dept., 1981. Mem. Nat. Fedn. Press Women, Nat. Press Club, Univ. Club, Albany Country Club, Aberdeen Country Club. Avocations: painting, golf, tennis. Office: Internat Narcotic Enforcement Officers Assn 112 State St Albany NY 12207-2005 Office Phone: 518-463-6232.

**MORGAN, ALAN VIVIAN,** geologist, educator; b. Barry, Glamorgan, Wales, Jan. 29, 1943; emigrated to Can., 1964, naturalized, 1977; s. George Vivian Williams and Sylvia Nesta (Atkinson) M.; m. Marion Anne Medhurst, June 14, 1966; children: Siân Kristina, Alexis John. B.Sc. with honors in Geology and Geography, U. Leicester, Eng., 1964; M.Sc. in Geography, U. Alta., Calgary, Can., 1966; PhD in Geology, U. Birmingham, Eng., 1970. Postdoctoral fellow U. Western Ont. and U. Waterloo, Ont., Canada, 1970-71; asst. prof. earth scis. and man-environ. studies U. Waterloo, 1971-78, assoc. prof. earth scis., 1978-85, prof., 1985—, assoc. dir. Quaternary Scis. Inst. Ont., Canada, 1992-97, dir. Quaternary Scis. Inst., 1997—2004. Mem. Brit. Schs. Exploring Soc. Ctrl. Iceland Expdn., 1960; rep. Can. Geosci. Coun., 1977-83, exec. dir., 1988-94, adminstrv. dir., 1996-2001, edn. dir., 2003-; mem. com. on global change Royal Soc. Can., 1988-91, mem. com. on pub. awareness of sci., 1989-94; coord. global change Geol. Survey Can., 1990-92; sr. officer Internat. Geosci. Edn. Orgn., 2000—, sec.-treas., 2003—; dir. Can. Prize Awards Found., 2000—, Can. Prize Found., 2001-; chair Can. Geosci. Edn. Network, 2003—. Author 6 field guides; editor newsletter OYEZ, 1990-94; contbr. articles to numerous profl. publs.; dir., prodr. documentary film The Heimaey Eruption, 1974. Recipient award for MS thesis Can. Soc. Petroleum Geologists, 1967, Bancroft award Royal Soc. Can., 1994, John H. Moss award Nat. Assn. Geology Tchrs., 1995, J. Willis Ambrose medal Geol. Assn. Can., 1997. E.R.W. Neale medal Geol. Assn. Canada, 1998, Civic award City of Waterloo, 2004; Charles Lapworth scholar, 1970; grantee Nat. Scis. and Engring. Rsch. Coun. Can., 1971— Fellow Geol. Assn. Can. (hon. life, sec.-treas. 1975-83, disting. fellow), Geol. Soc. Am.; mem. Am. Quaternary Assn. (pres. 1990-92), Can. Quaternary Assn. (pres. 1987-89), Brit. Quaternary Research Assn., Internat. Union Quaternary Research (sec. gen. XII congress 1983-87). Office: U Waterloo Dept Earth Scis Waterloo ON Canada N2L 3G1 Office Phone: 519-888-4567 ext. 3029. Business E-Mail: avmorgan@uwaterloo.ca.

**MORGAN, ALFRED VANCE,** management consulting company executive; b. Liberal, Kans., Apr. 13, 1936; s. Forest Francis and Gertrude Irene (Henning) M.; m. Peggy Ann Riley, June 29, 1960; children: Trudie Marie, Vance Riley, Allen Forest, Bradley Augustus, Kelly James. BBA, U. Kans., 1958; MBA, U. So. Calif., 1966; postgrad., Am. Inst. Banking, 1965. Asst. mgr. Fruehauf Trailer Co., L.A., Calif., 1960-61; asst. mktg. dir. Security Pacific Nat. Bank, 1961-65; mktg. exec. Doyle, Dane, Bernbach Advt., 1965-66; cons. Harbridge House, Inc., Boston, 1966-71; pres. Morgan Bus. Assocs., Inc., Santa Barbara and Boston, 1971—; instr. bus. L.A. City Coll., 1971-72; instr. mgmt. Santa Barbara City Coll., 1973. Pres. Exptl. in Internat.

Living. 1980-81. Contbr. articles to profl. publs. Mem. Lobero Theatre Bd., 1984-88; mem. vestry All Saints Espiscopal Ch., 2003—, jr. warden, 2006; v.p. El Escorial Condo Assn., 2003—. With AUS, 1958-60. Mem. ASTD, Am. Mktg. Assn. L.A., Am. Soc. Profl. Cons., U. So. Calif. Grad. Sch. Bus. Alumni Assn. Office: Morgan Bus Assocs 136 La Mar Cir Santa Barbara CA 93103 Office Phone: 805-963-7765. E-mail: almorgan@morganba.com.

**MORGAN, ALLEN B., JR.,** securities executive; b. 1942; BA, U. N.C., 1965. Branch mgr. Courts & Co., Memphis, Tenn., 1965-69; founder Morgan Keegan & Co., Inc., Memphis, 1969, now chmn. bd. dirs. Vice chmn. Regions Fin. Corp.; chmn. Regions Morgan Keegan Select Funds, Securities Industry Assn., 2002. Office: Regions Fin PO Box 10247 Birmingham AL 35202-0247

**MORGAN, ANDREW LANE,** urologist, educator; b. May 13, 1920; s. James Albert and Elsie Edna (Johnson) M.; m. Miriam Cleary, June 9, 1951; children: Andrew Lane, Christine, Martha, James. Exch. fellowship, St. John's U., Shanghai, China, 1939—40; BA, Dartmouth Coll., 1942; MD, Cornell U., 1945. Diplomate Am. Bd. Urology. Intern Lenox Hill Hosp., N.Y.C., 1945—46; resident Queen's Med. Ctr., Honolulu, 1948—50, Yale U., 1950—52; practice medicine, specializing in urology Honolulu, 1952—87; ret., 1987. Chmn. dept. surgery Queen's Med. Ctr., 1979; clin. prof. urology John Burns Sch. Medicine, U. Hawaii; mem. renal transplant team St. Francis Med. Ctr.; past pres. Hawaii Med. Libr., 1957-58 Served to capt., AUS, 1946-48 Fellow ACS; mem. AMA, Am. Urol. Assn. (past pres. We. sect.), Hawaii Med. Assn., Societe Internationale d'Urologie, Honolulu County Med. Soc. (bd. govs. 1970-76, treas. 1978-79), Pacific Club Honolulu Episcopalian. Home: 44 Puako Beach Dr Kamuela HI 96743-9707

**MORGAN, ANN MARIE,** psychologist; b. Fresno, Calif., Mar. 8, 1949; d. Charles and Cassie Alvena (Armey) McMurray; m. Stephen Charles Morgan, Sept. 6, 1969; 1 child, Kesley Suzanne. BA, U. LaVerne, 1971, MEd, 1973; MS in Marriage and Family Counseling, U. Laverne, 1999; MA in Psychology, Calif. Sch. Profl. Psychology, 1999, PsyD in Clin. Psychology, 2001. Tchr. Ontario (Calif.)-Montclair Sch. Dist., 1971-78, Cabrillo Unf. Sch. Dist., Half Moon Bay, Calif., 1978-85; project coord. U. La Verne, Calif., 1986—94; dir. program Ctr. Aging Resources, 2004; pvt. practice, 2004. Exec. com. Camp Fire Boys and Girls, Inc., Mount Baldy Region, Claremont, Calif., 1989—, bd. dirs., 1987—; mem. Children's Home Soc., Claremont, 1987-2004; bd. dirs. Ctr. Aging Resources, 2004. Mem.: Pi Gamma Mu. Mem. Ch. of the Brethren. Avocations: reading, gardening, exercise, skiing. Office: 428 W Harrison Ave Ste 101A Claremont CA 91711 Office Phone: 909-399-3402.

**MORGAN, ANNE MARIE G.,** broadcast journalist, educator; b. Paducah, Ky., Apr. 23, 1955; d. Ralph Edward and Vera Christine Gill; m. Michael William Morgan, Nov. 19, 1977; children: Deborah, Jon, James. BA in Govt. and Psychology, Coll. William and Mary, 1976; MA in Polit. Sci., U. Richmond, 1997; postgrad. in Pub. Policy, Va. Commonwealth U., 1998. HS tchr. James-City County Sch., Williamsburg, Va., 1977, Colonial Hts. Sch., Va., 1977-79; TV and radio journalist Capitol News, Richmond, Va., 1984—, Va. Pub. Broadcasting, Richmond, Va., 1987—, WRIC-TV. Richmond, 1994—96, WTVR-TV. Richmond, 1996—2000; broadcast news anchor Va. News Network, Richmond, Va., 2000—02; journalist WVTF Radio, Roanoke, 2002—, Va. Pub. Radio, 2002—; assoc. prof. polit. sci. U. Richmond, Va., 1998—. Author: (with others) Controversies in American Public Polity, 1999, Opposing Viewpoints Series, 1991. Sec. Parents' Guidance/Pupil Pers. Guidance Com., Powhatan, Va., 1996—98; state bd. dirs. Va. Pub. Broadcasting, Richmond, 2000—02; bd. dirs. Va. Adv. Coun. Adult Edn. and Literacy, Richmond, 1999—2002, Coun. Child Care and Early Childhood Devel., Richmond, 1995—96; chair bd. dirs. State Bd. for Cmty. Colls., Richmond, 1997—2002; chair Va. Coun. Status of Women, Richmond, 1994—2002. Recipient Meritorious award, Va. Assoc. Press Broadcasters, 2002, Disting. Faculty award, U. Richmond Sch. Contg. Studies, 2005, 1st Pl. award, Nat. Fedn. Press Women, 2005; Gov. proclamation Anne Marie Morgan Day in Commonwealth Va., Gov. Va., 1997. Mem.: Soc. Profl. Journalists, Soc. Profl. Journalists (Va. profl. chpt.), Nat. Fedn. Press Women (1st Pl. Prepared Radio Report award 2005), Va. Press Women (1st Pl. award 2005, 1st Pl. award spl. programming radio 2006, 1st Pl. award on the scene report radio 2006, 1st Pl. award prepared report radio 2006), Capitol Corrs. Assn., Am. Polit. Sci. Assn., Pi Sigma Alpha. Avocations: music, singing, mentoring.

**MORGAN, ARDYS NORD,** school improvement consultant; b. South Bend, Ind., Nov. 1, 1946; d. Arthur August and Janet Ardis (Eide) Nord; children: Elizabeth Elayne, Matthew Richard. BS in Elem. Edn., Ind. U., Bloomington, 1968; MS in Elem. Edn., Ind. U., Indpls., 1972; reading cert., Ind. U. South Bend, 1982; EDS, Ind. U., Bloomington, 1992; adminstr. lic., Ind. U.-Purdue U., Indpls., 1989; EdD in Curriculum and Sch. Adminstrn., Ind. U., 1994. Tchr., South Bend, 1968-69, 73-87; adminstr. dept. instrn. and curriculum, 1987-90; tchr. Indpls., 1969-70; resident lectr. Ind. U./Purdue U., Indpls., 1970-73, adminstr., 1989; mem. adj. faculty Ind. U., South Bend, 1985-90, acting program dir. elem. and secondary edn., 1990-92; asst. supt. schs. Michigan City (Ind.) Area Schs., 1992-94; supt. Union North United Schs. Corp., 1994-96; ednl. cons., tech. and staff devel. in curriculum Lightspan Partnership, San Diego, 1997-99; pres. Sch. Improvement Partnership, Inc., Granger, Ind., 1999—. Cons. on implementation of tech., mid. grades and effective teaching strategies, elem. curriculum, reading and lang. arts, fed. and state projects, staff devel. Recipient Disting. Alumni award div. edn. Ind. U., South Bend, 1990. Lilly Endowment fellow, 1987. Home: 51550 Stratton Ct Granger IN 46530-8342 Office: Sch Improvement Partnership 51550 Stratton Ct Ste 300 Granger IN 46530-8342

**MORGAN, ARLENE NOTORO,** university administrator; b. Phila., July 27, 1945; d. James Vincent and Mary Rose (Actis-Grande) Notoro; m. David J. Morgan, Mar. 3, 1948; children: Elizabeth, Lauren. BS in Journalism, Temple U., 1967. Reporter Delaware County Daily Times, Chester, Pa., 1967-69, Phila. Inquirer, 1969—, dep. metro editor, 1990-91, sr. editor, asst. mng. editor, 1991-2000, reader advocate columnist, 1998-2000; assoc. dean prizes and programs Columbia U. Grad. Sch. Journalism, N.Y.C., 2000—05; treas. Scattergood Behavioral Health Found., Phila., 2005—. Author: The Authentic Voice: The Best Reporting on Race and Ethnicity, 2006. Bd. dirs. Friends Hosp., Phila., 1978—2005, Scattergood Behavioral Health Found., 2005—; mem. adv. bd. Temple U., La. State U.; mem. diversity com. Am. Soc. Newspaper Editors; dir. Columbia Race Project; mem. centennial com. Corpus Christi Ch., Manhattan. Recipient Phila. Newspapers Inc. Employee Recognition award, 1987, Excellence in Diversity award Knight Ridder, 1995; Media Studies Ctr. fellow Freedom Forum, 1996-97. Mem. Soc. Profl. Journalists., Newspaper Assn. Am. (diversity com.). Roman Catholic. Avocations: ballet, travel, opera and art appreciation, advocate to the mentally ill. Office Phone: 212-854-5377. E-mail: am494@columbia.edu.

**MORGAN, BARBARA M.,** psychotherapist, educator; b. Biloxi, Miss., June 18, 1960; m. Franklyn C. Morgan, Dec. 15, 1991; children: Rachel E. McCauley, Erin L. McCauley, Brittany N. McCauley. PhD, Coll. of William and Mary, 1998. Lic. profl. counselor Va., 1998, marriage and family therapist Va., 1998, cert. counselor Nat. Bd. for Cert. Counselors, 1998. Prof. of psychology Richard Bland Coll., Petersburg, Va., 1997—; pvt. practice psychotherapist Barbara M. Morgan, Ph.D., Colonial Heights, Va., 1998—; pres. Relationship Intelligence, LLC, Colonial Heights, Va., 2005—. Contbr. articles to profl. jours. Adult edn. leader Christ and Grace Episcopal Ch., Petersburg, Va., 2000—06; pres. Va. Assn. of Marriage and Family Counselors, Charlottesville, 1998—99; bd. mem. Southside Regional Med. Ctr. Ethics Bd., Petersburg, Va., 1999—2006, Coll. of William and Mary Sch. of Edn. Adv. Bd., Williamsburg, Va., 2005—06. Recipient Acad. award, Va. Commonwealth Univ. Coll. of Humanities and Scis., 1994, Helen C. Hopper Meml. scholarship for family counseling, Coll. of William and Mary, 1995, Dean's award for student scholarship on women, 1996—98, Award of excellence, Coll. of William and Mary Sch. Edn., 1998. Mem.: Va. Assn. of Marriage and Family Counselors, Va. Counselors Assn., Am. Counselors Assn. Avocations: running, horseback riding, gardening, playing the piano.

Office: Barbara M Morgan PhD 320C Charles Dimmock Pky Colonial Heights VA 23834 Office Phone: 804-520-4166. Home Fax: 804-520-6475; Office Fax: 804-520-6475. Personal E-mail: barbmorgan@rcn.com.

**MORGAN, BETSY STELLE,** lawyer; b. Terre Haute, Ind., Mar. 15, 1963; BA, DePauw U., 1985; JD, John Marshall Law Sch., 1988. Bar: Ill. 1989. With Baker & McKenzie, Chgo., 1988—, counsel, 1997—2002, ptnr., 2002—. Co-chair N.Am. Pro Bono Initiative Baker & McKenzie, Chgo. Author: United States Business Immigration Manual, 2003. Office: Baker & McKenzie One Prudential Plz 130 E Randolph Dr Chicago IL 60601

**MORGAN, BEVERLY CARVER,** pediatrician, educator; b. NYC, May 29, 1927; d. Jay and Florence (Newkamp) Carver; children: Nancy, Thomas E. III, John E. MD cum laude, Duke U., 1955. Diplomate Am. Bd. Pediat. (oral examiner 1984-90, mem. written examination com. 1990—), Nat. Bd. Med. Examiners. Intern, asst. resident Stanford U. Hosp., San Francisco, 1955-56; clin. fellow pediat., trainee pediatric cardiology Babies Hosp.-Columbia Presbyn. Med. Ctr., NYC, 1956-59; rsch. fellow cardiovasc. diagnostic lab. Columbia-Presbyn. Med. Ctr., NYC, 1959-60; instr. pediat. Coll. Physicians and Surgeons, Columbia U., NYC, 1960; dir. heart sta. Robert B. Green Meml. Hosp., San Antonio, 1960-62; lectr. pediat. U. Tex., 1960-62; spl. rsch. fellow in pediatric cardiology Sch. Medicine, U. Wash., Seattle, 1962-64, from instr. to prof. pediat., 1962-73, chmn. dept. pediat., 1973-80; mem. staff U. Wash. Hosp.; chief of staff, 1975-77; mem. staff Harborview Med. Ctr., Children's Orthop. Hosp. and Med. Ctr., dir. dept. medicine, 1974-80; prof., chmn. dept. pediat. U. Calif., Irvine, 1980-88, prof. pediat. and pediatric cardiology, 1980—; pediatrician in chief Children's Hosp. Orange County, 1988. Mem. pulmonary acad. awards panel Nat. Heart and Lung Inst., 1972-75; mem. grad. med. edn. nat. adv. com. to sec. HEW, 1977-80; mem. Coun. on Pediatric Practice; chmn. Task Force on Opportunities for Women in Pediat., 1982; mem. nursing rev. com. NIH, 1987-88. Contbr. articles to profl. jours.; mem. editl. bd. Clin. Pediat., Am. Jour. Diseases of Children, Jour. of Orange County Pediatric Soc., Jour. Am. Acad. Pediat., LA Pediatric Soc. Recipient Women of Achievement award Matrix Table, Seattle, 1974; Disting. Alumnus award Duke U. Med. Sch., 1974; Ann. award for Bd. Med. Coll. Pa., 1977; Career Devel. award USPHS, 1966-71; Moseby scholar, 1955. Mem. Am. Acad. Pediat. (chmn. com. on pediat. manpower 1984-86), Am. Coll. Cardiology, Soc. for Pediat. Rsch., Am. Fedn. Clin. Rsch., Am. Pediat. Soc., Assn. Med. Sch. Pediat. Dept. Chmn. (sec.-treas. 1981-87), Western Soc. for Pediat. Rsch., Alpha Omega Alpha. Office: U Calif Irvine Med Ctr Dept Pediatrics 101 The City Dr S Orange CA 92868-3201 Office Phone: 714-456-6483. Business E-Mail: bcmorgan@uci.edu.

**MORGAN, BEVERLY HAMMERSLEY,** elementary school educator, artist; b. Wichita Falls, Tex. d. Vernon C. and Melba Marie (Whited) Hammersley; m. Robert Lewis Morgan, Sept. 21, 1957 (div. 1972); children: Janet Claire, Robert David. BA, So. Meth. U.; MA, U. Ala., 1980, AA certification, 1982; postgrad., U. Tex., 1991—. Cert. art tchr., Tex., Ala.; cert. elem. tchr., Ala. Tchr. art Ft. Worth Pub. Schs., 1955-60; tchr. English, Lincoln County Schs., Fayetteville, Tenn., 1961-62; elem. tchr. Huntsville (Ala.) Pub. Schs., 1960-61, 62-68, tchr. art, 1972-92, 93-94. One-woman shows include U. Ala., 1980, Huntsville Art League, 1981, and various other art gallerys, art shows and exhbns. Mem. HAL Gallery, Huntsville, Madison County Sr. Art Gallery. Mem. Huntsville Mus. Art, Am. Contract Bridge League. Republican. Avocations: bridge, travel, collecting Hammersley English bone china. Home: 12027 Chicamauga Trl SE Huntsville AL 35803-1544

**MORGAN, BRUCE RAY,** management consultant; b. LA, Oct. 29, 1932; s. Francis Raymond and Rose Hall (Black) M.; m. Bette Jeanne Moore, Oct. 7, 1957; children: Michael John, Brian Leo, Jeanne Anne. AA, Sacramento Jr. Coll., 1952; BS, U. Calif.-Berkeley, 1954, LL.B., 1957. Bar: Calif. 1957. Judge adv. USAF, Saudi Arabia and Morocco, 1958-61; atty. firm Tebbs, Marrin, Johnson & Bridges, San Francisco, 1961-67; dep. dir. Peace Corps, Nepal, 1967-68, dir, 1968-70; exec. dir. Center Research and Edn., Denver, 1971-75; dir. U.S. representation to Saudi Arabia-U.S. Joint Commn. on Econ. Coop., Riyadh, 1975-76; pres. Bruce Morgan Assocs., Inc., Washington, 1976—. Editor: Calif. State Bar Jour. Legis. Rev, 1957. Served with USAF, 1958-61. Mem. U.S., Calif. bars. Office: Bruce Morgan Assocs 4201 Cathedral Ave NW Apt 823W Washington DC 20016 Business E-Mail: bmorgan@bmainc.com.

**MORGAN, CATHERINE MARIE,** psychologist, writer; b. Duluth, Minn., Mar. 27, 1947; m. Ralph Morgan, 1967; 1 child, Andrew. BS, U. Nebr., 1968; MEd, U. Okla., 1973; PhD, Okla. State U., 1987; postgrad. Menninger Found., Psychotherapy Tng. Program, 1987-89. Child devel. specialist Southwest Guidance Ctr., Wheatland, Okla., 1973-74; pvt. practice Family Counseling Assocs., San Antonio, 1974-75; psychol. asst. Edmond Guidance Ctr., Okla., 1975-82; psychol. asst. supr. Southeast Guidance Ctr., Del City, Okla., 1982-86; psychol. intern Cleve. County Health Dept., Moore, Okla., 1986-87; psychologist Cen. State Hosp., Norman, Okla., 1987-89; pvt. practice assocs. in psychology Edmond, Okla.; vice chair bd. mgrs. Integris Mental Health; pres. Assocs. in Psychology, 1988—. Mem. AAUW, APA, Okla. Psychol. Assn., Am. Bus. Women's Assn., P.E.O., Kappa Delta Pi. Avocations: writing, reading, knitting, racquetball. Office: 9636 N May Ave Ste 200 Oklahoma City OK 73120

**MORGAN, CHARLES RUSSELL,** lawyer; b. New Orleans, La., Oct. 15, 1946; s. Charles and Marian E. (Wetzel) M.; children: Charles Bradford, William Russell, Elizabeth Anne. BA, U. N.C., 1968; JD, Columbia U., 1973. Bar: N.Y. 1973, Ill. 1981, Ohio 1994. Law clk. to cir. judge US Ct. Appeals, Washington, 1971-72; atty. Davis Polk & Wardwell, NYC, 1972-80; sr. staff counsel Household Internat., Inc., Prospect Heights, Ill., 1980-83; v.p., asst. gen. counsel Kraft., Glenview, Ill., 1983-85, v.p., sr. corp. counsel, 1985-88; v.p., gen. counsel, sec. Chiquita Brands Internat., Cin., 1988-95; ptnr. Mayer Brown & Platt, Chgo., 1995-98; exec. v.p., gen. counsel BellSouth Corp., Atlanta, 1998—2004. V.p., sec., dir. John Morrell & Co., Inc. Contbg. editor The Corp. Counselor, 1986—. The Environmental Corporate Counsel Report. Recipient Spirit of Excellence Award, Am. Bar Assoc., Corp. Legal Diversity Award, Am. Corp. Counsel Assoc., 2000, Nat. Diversity Leadership Award, Coalition of fBar Assoc. of Color, Diversity 2000 Award, Minority Corp. Coun. Assoc. Mem. ABA (chmn. corp. counsel com. 1983-86, chmn. comm. com. 1986—), Am. Law Inst., Am. Corp. Counsel Assn. (bd. dirs.), Am. Arbitration Assn. (bd. dirs.), Legal Club Chgo., Army-Navy Club of Washington. In Nov., 2000, Morgan was appointed by the Chief Justice of the Supreme Court of Ga. as Chair of the Supreme Court's Blue Ribbon Commission on Indigent Defense.

**MORGAN, CLYDE NATHANIEL,** dermatologist; b. Bell County, Tex., Nov. 2, 1923; s. Xenophen William and Rhoda Ella (Deck) M.; m. Birdie Joyce Rich, Mar. 3, 1951; children: Clyde Nathaniel Jr., Reinette Jean, Nancy Elaine. *Dr. Morgan is a descendant of Morgan ap Morgan, the first white settler in West Virginia, of Captain David Morgan, Indian fighter and Captain in the American Revolution, and of James Morgan who assisted in establishing American independence while acting in the capacity of private and Indian spy under Captain James Brenton and Colonel John Evans in 1778. Family tradition has it that Captain David Morgan taught George Washington how to survey. Wife, Birdie Morgan, was a delegate to the Republican National Convention in 1964.* BS, Abilene Christian Coll., 1948; MD, U. Tex., Galveston, 1953. Assoc. prof. biology Abilene (Tex.) Christian Coll., 1954-56; pvt. practice Abilene, 1954-67; dermatologist, 1969—. *Presented research papers on the development of special techniques in the cryosurgical treatment of benign and malignant lesions of the skin before the American College of Cryosurgery meetings in New Orleans and New York City; before the Southern Medical Association meeting in San Antonio; before the World Congress of cryosurgery meetings in San Remo, Italy, and Manila, Philippines; and before the Indian Cryogenics Council in Calcutta. Invited guest lecturer at the Jadavpur University Medical School in Calcutta, India.* Contbr. articles to profl. jours. Mem. AMA, SAR (chpt. pres. 1997-99, award 1995), Am. Coll. Cryosurgery, Internat. Soc. Cryosurgery, Tex. Med. Assn., So. Med. Assn., Tex. Dermatologic Soc., Taylor-Jones-Haskell County Med.

Soc. Republican. Mem. Ch. Of Christ. Avocations: golf, fishing, hunting, cryogenics research. Home: 1718 Cedar Crest Dr Abilene TX 79601-3228 Office: 1166 Merchant St Abilene TX 79603-5014 Office Phone: 325-673-4242. Personal E-mail: cnmorgan@cox.net, clybird@juno.com.

**MORGAN, COLBY SHANNON, JR.**, lawyer; b. Marshalltown, Iowa, Mar. 29, 1949; s. Colby Shannon and Elizabeth Perkinson (Robertson) M.; m. Leslie Marmon, Apr. 5, 1975; children: Colby Shannon III, Jeffrey Michael, Sarah Elizabeth. AB cum laude, Dartmouth Coll., 1971; JD, Vanderbilt U., 1974. Bar: NY 1975, U.S. Dist. Ct. (so. and ea. dists.) NY 1976, Tenn. 1977, U.S. Dist. Ct. (we. dist.) Tenn. 1978, U.S. Ct. Appeals (6th cir.) 1980, U.S. Dist. Ct. (ea. and we. dists.) Ark. 1983, U.S. Ct. Appeals (8th cir.) 1987, U.S. Dist. Ct. (no. dist.) Calif. 1994, U.S. Ct. Appeals (3d cir.) 1995, U.S. Ct. Appeals (9th cir.) 1996, U.S. Ct. Appeals (4th cir.) 1996, U.S. Supreme Ct. 1998, U.S. Dist. Ct. (no. dist.) NY 1998, U.S. Dist. Ct. (we. dist.) Mich. 2001, U.S. Dist. Ct. (ctrl. and no. dists.) Ill. 2001, U.S. Ct. Appeals (2d cir.) 2004. Assoc. Crowe, McCoy, Agoglia & Zweibel, Mineola, N.Y., 1974-78, Rosenfield, Borod & Kremer, Memphis, 1978-83, Apperson, Crump, Duzane & Maxwell, Memphis, 1983-86, Shuttleworth, Smith, Young & Webb, Memphis, 1986; sr. atty. Holiday Inns, Inc., Memphis, 1986-91; assoc. Petkoff & Lancaster, Memphis, 1991-92; sr. counsel Fed. Express Corp., Memphis, 1992. Chancellor, bd. dirs. Memphis Boys Town, 1979-86; chmn. Memphis Civil Svc. Commn., 1980-83; bd. dirs., chmn. bd. dirs. Memphis Emmaus Cmty., 1983—; bd. dirs. Christ Meth. Adminstrv. Bd., Memphis, 1984-86; Leadership Memphis, 1984—; cubmaster Pack 241 Boy Scouts Am., Memphis, 1992-93; treas., bd. dirs. Memphis Symphony Chorus, 1981-85. Mem. ABA, FBA, Assn. Corp. Counsel, Dartmouth Lawyers Assn., Order of the First Families of Tenn., Gen. Soc. Colonial Wars, N.Y. Sons of the Revolution, Mil. Order of the Stars and Bars (lt. comdr. 1994—), Tenn. Geneaol. Soc., Jamestowne Soc., Clan Donnachaidh Soc., Mensa, SAR (chancellor, past pres. Memphis chpt., v.p. West Tenn. 1992—, chancellor, bd. govs. Tenn. chpt. 1994—), Scottish Rite. Republican. Methodist. Avocations: genealogy, marathon runner, tennis, golf, reading. Home: 5521 Fiesta Dr Memphis TN 38120-2826 Office: Fed Express Corp 3620 Hacks Cross Rd Memphis TN 38125 Office Phone: 901-434-8545. E-mail: csmorgan@fedex.com.

**MORGAN, CONSTANCE LOUISE**, real estate company executive; b. Denver, July 24, 1941; d. Willis Stephen and Evelyn (Rutar) Claus; m. Robert M. Morgan, Jan. 3, 1963; children: Stephen, Melayne. BS, U. N. Mex., 1963. Lic. real estate broker, Fla. master gardener, 1996. Realtor, assoc. Investors Realty, Tallahassee, 1980-82, br. mgr., 1982-83; pres., broker Connie Morgan Realty, Inc., Tallahassee, 1983-96, Constance L. Morgan, Broker, Tallahassee, 1996—; founder Network for Ind. Brokers, 1989-93. Chmn. docents Fla. Gov.'s Mansion, Tallahassee, 1979-80; pres. Newcomers-Univ. Women, Tallahassee, 1968, Hunters Crossing Homeowners Assn., 1998-99; bd. dirs. Tallahassee Symphony Orch., 1990-96; bd. dirs. Rotary Youth Camp, Inc., 1995—, Tallahassee United Way. Mem. Nat. Assn. Realtors, Fla. Assn. Realtors, Tallahassee Bd. Realtors (chmn. Multiple Listing Svc. 1984, 94), Tallahassee Cmty. Realty Group, Tallahassee C. of C. (bd. dirs. 1984-86, 89-92), Rotary, Chi Omega (treas.), Phi Gamma Nu (pres. 1962). Home and Office: 144 Bellevalley Ln Columbia SC 29229 E-mail: clmorgan@sc.rr.com.

**MORGAN, CURTIS FRANKLIN**, history professor; b. Baltimore, Md., Nov. 13, 1960; s. Curtis Franklin and Anne Thelma Morgan; m. Katherine Elizabeth Powell, Feb. 21, 1987; 1 child, Elizabeth Xiangbing. BA in Hist. and English, Ctrl. Wesleyan Coll., 1983; MA in Hist., Clemson U., 1985; PhD in Modern European Hist., U. SC., 1998. Info. officer, fgn. broadcast CIA, Wash., DC, 1987—91; adj. prof. hist. Midlands Tech. Coll., Columbia, SC, 1995—2000; prof. hist. Lord Fairfax C.C., Middletown, Va., 2000—. Author: James F Byrnes, Lucius Clay and American Policy in Germany, 1945-1947. Mem.: So. Hist. Assn. (chair, program com., European hist. sect. 2004—05), World Hist. Assn. Office: Lord Fairfax CC 173 Skirmisher Ln Middletown VA 22645 Office Phone: 540-868-7064. Business E-Mail: cmorgan@lfcc.edu.

**MORGAN, DAHLIA**, museum director, art educator; BA, McGill U., Montreal, 1958; postgrad., Sir George Williams U., Montreal, 1968-69, U. Miami, Fla., 1974. Lectr. Mus. of Fine Arts, Montreal, 1965-70; lectr./rschr. Sir George Williams U., Montreal, 1968-70; grad. asst. dept. art and art history U. Miami, Fla., 1971-74; adj. prof. visual arts dept. Fla. Internat. U., Miami, 1975-77, vis. rof. visual arts dept., 1978-79, faculty visual arts dept., 1979—, dir. Art in State Bldgs. Program, 1984—, dir. Art Mus., 1980—. Lectr. in field; curator numerous exhbns.; panelist NEA Mus. Grants, 1993, Cultural Advancement Grants, 1990, 92; cons. Fed. Gen. Svcs. Adminstrn., 1992, Metro-Dade Art in Pub. Places Program, 1992. Prodr. numerous catalogues to exhbns. Juror South Miami Art Fair Photo Group; bd. dirs. Nat. Found. for Advancement in the Arts, 1984—; founder Friends of the Frost Art Mus. Support Group at Fla. Internat. U., 1984—; chmn. State of Fla. Art in Bldgs., 1984—; chmn. Art in Pub. Places, Dade County, Fla., 1980-84. Recipient 3d Ann. MAXIE award Miami Arts Exchange, 1990; grantee Fla. Endowment for Humanities, 1986, Metro Dade County Cultural Affairs Coun., 1986, Fla. Internat. U., 1990, 91; U. Miami-Coral Gables merit scholar, fed. scholar. Mem. Assn. Coll. and Univ. Mus. and Galleries, Am. Assn. Mus., Coll. Art Assn. Am., Fla. Mus. Dirs. Assn., Fla. Higher Edn. Arts Network, Internat. Coun. Mus. (fine arts com.), Miami Cultural execs. Coun., Southeastern Mus. Assn., Fla. Cultural Action Alliance, Phi Kappa Phi. Office: Frost Art Mus Fla Internat U University Park PC # 110 11200 SW 8th St Miami FL 33199-0001

**MORGAN, DANIEL LOUIS**, lawyer, educator; b. Newark, Oct. 17, 1952; s. A. Henry and Eunice (Neubauer) M. BA in History, Tufts U., 1974; JD, U. Conn., 1977; LLM, Georgetown U., 1981. Bar: Conn. 1977, D.C. 1978. Atty., advisor, chief counsel IRS, Washington, 1977-81; assoc. Tucker, Flyer & Lewis P.C., Washington, 1981-85, prin., 1985-99; prtr., bus. planning, employment law Venable LLP Washington, 2000—. Adj. prof. Cath. U. Law Sch., Washington, 1984-96; profl. lectr. in law George Washington U. Law Sch., 1997-2000; charter fellow Am. Coll. Employee Benefits Counsel. Co-author: The 401(K) Handbook, 1991, Employees and Independent Contractors, 1990; contbr. articles to profl. jours. Fellow Am. Coll. Employee Benefits Counsel (charter); mem. ABA (chmn. tax sect. com. on employment taxes 1986-88), D.C. Bar Assn. (sect. taxation and employee benefits com., chmn. employee benefits com. 1998-2000). Office: Venable LLP 575 7th St NW Washington DC 20004-1601 Office Phone: 202-344-8550. Office Fax: 202-344-8300. Business E-Mail: dlmorgan@venable.com.

**MORGAN, DAVID FORBES**, minister; b. Toronto, Ont., Can., Aug. 3, 1930; came to U.S., 1954; s. Forbes Alexander and Ruth (Bamford) M.; m. Delores Mae Storhaug, Sept. 7, 1956; children: Roxanne Ruth, David Forbes II. BA, Rocky Mt. Coll., 1960; ThB, MDiv, Coll. of the Rockies, 1970; postgrad., Bishop's Sch. Theology; LittD Nat. Coll., 1954, D.C. Nat. Coll., 1954, Temple Coll., 1956. Ordained priest. Pres. Coll. of the Rockies, Denver, 1960-73; founder, rector Prior Order of Christ Centered Ministries, Denver, 1973—; canon pastor St. John's Cathedral, Denver, 1982-96, canon at large, 1996—. Bd. dirs. Internat. Contemplative Outreach, Ltd., mem. internat. faculty. Author: Christ Centered Ministries, A Response to God's Call, 1973, Songs with a Message, 1956. Mem.: Oratory of the Good Shepherd, Toronto. Home: 740 Clarkson St Denver CO 80218-3204 Office: 740 Clarkson St Denver CO 80218-3204

**MORGAN, DENNIS KEITH**, lawyer; b. St. Louis, Dec. 12, 1947; s. Charles Gustave and Justine Estelle (Picarelli) M.; children: James, Elizabeth, Rebecca. BJ, U. Mo., 1970, JD, 1972; LLM, Washington U., St. Louis, 1978. Bar: Mo. 1972, U.S. Dist. Ct. (we. dist.) Mo. 1972, Ill. 1978, U.S. Dist. Ct. (ea. dist.) Mo. 1978, U.S. Ct. Appeals (8th cir.) 1978, Tex. 1981, U.S. Tax Ct. 1981, U.S. Ct. Mil. Appeals 1981., Pa. 2003. Atty. Office Spl. Counsel for Compliance U.S. Dept. Energy, 1979—80; with So. Union Co., Austin, Tex., 1981—, exec. v.p. adminstrn., 2001—04, gen. counsel, corp. sec., 2001—, exec. v.p. regulatory and litig., 2004—. Mem. exec. com. Austin Visual Arts Assn., 1999—2002; bd. dirs. Austin Symphony Orch., 2000—02; trustee

Everhart Mus. Maj. JAGC USAR, 1970—86. Mem. ABA, Tex. Bar Assn., Mo. Bar Assn., Pa. Bar Assn., Am. Gas Assn. (legal com.), So. Gas Assn. (legal com.). Lutheran. Avocations: teaching, history, travel, art. Office Phone: 713-989-7507. E-mail: dmorgan@southernunionco.com

**MORGAN, DENNIS RICHARD**, lawyer; b. Jan. 3, 1942; s. Benjamin Richard and Gladys Belle (Brown) Morgan. BA, Washington and Lee U., 1964; JD, U. Va., 1967; LLM in Labor Law, NYU, 1971. Bar: Ohio 1967, Va. 1967, U.S. Ct. Appeals (4th cir.) 1968, U.S. Ct. Appeals (6th cir.) 1971, U.S. Supreme Ct. 1972. Law clk. to chief judge U.S. Dist. Ct. (ea. dist.) Va. 1967—68; mem. Marshman, Snyder & Seeley, Cleve., 1971—72; dir. labor rels. Ohio Dept. Adminstrv. Svcs., 1972—75; asst. city atty. Columbus, Ohio, 1975—77; dir. Ohio Legis. Reference Bur., Columbus, 1979—81; assoc. Clemans, Nelson & Assocs., Columbus, 1981; pvt. practice Columbus, 1978—92. Lectr. in field; guest lectr. Cen. Mich. U., 1975; judge moot ct. Ohio State U. Sch. Law, 1981, 83, grad. divsn., 73, 74, 76; guest lectr. Baldwin-Wallace Coll., 1973; legal counsel Dist. IV Comms. Workers Am., 1982—88; pers. dir. Pub. Utilities Commn., Ohio, 1989—91; asst. atty. gen. State of Ohio, 1991—2003. Negotiator Franklin County United Way, 1977—81; regional chmn. ann. alumni fund-raising program U. Va. Sch. Law; mem. Greater Hilltop Area Commn., 1989—2006; pres. Woodbrook Village Condominium Assn., 1985—2005, v.p., 2005—; vice-chmn. Franklin County Dem. Party, 1976—82; dem. com. person Ward 58, Columbus, 1973—; chmn. rules com. Ohio State Dem. Conv., 1974; co-founder, trustee Greater West Side Dem. Club; bd. dirs. Hilltop Civic Coun., Inc., 1997—99. Capt. U.S. Army, 1968—70. Recipient Am. Jurisprudence award, 1967; scholar Robert E. Lee Rsch., 1965. Mem.: Am. Judicature Soc., Fed. Bar Assn., Indsl. Rels. Rsch. Assn., Pi Sigma Alpha. Roman Catholic. Home: 1261 Woodbrook Lane G Columbus OH 43223-3243 E-mail: dmorga15@columbus.rr.com.

**MORGAN, DONNA EVENSEN**, lawyer; b. Bklyn., Feb. 28, 1957; d. Edward Ivar and Judith (Larsen) Evensen; m. Charles S. Morgan, Sept. 3, 1988. BA, Colgate U., 1979; JD, U. Mich., 1984. Bar: Ill. 1985. Assoc. Chapman and Cutler, Chgo., 1985-86, Kirkland and Ellis, Chgo., 1987-89, Mayer Brown Rowe & Maw LLP, Chgo., 1989—. Office: Mayer Brown Rowe & Maw LLP 71 S Wacker Dr Chicago IL 60606-4637 Office Phone: 312-701-7138. Business E-Mail: dmorgan@mayerbrownrowe.com.

**MORGAN, EDMUND SEARS**, retired history professor; b. Mpls., Jan. 17, 1916; s. Edmund Morris and Elsie Sears (Smith) M.; m. Helen Theresa Mayer, June 7, 1939; children: Penelope, Pamela; m. Marie Caskey, June 22, 1983. AB, Harvard U., 1937, PhD, 1942. Instrument maker Radiation Lab., MIT, 1942-45; instr. U. Chgo., 1945-46; asst. prof. Brown U., 1946-49, asso. prof., 1949-51, prof., 1951-55, acting dean grad. sch., 1951-52; prof. Yale U., 1955-65, Sterling prof., 1965-86, prof. emeritus, 1986—. Rsch. fellow Huntington Libr., 1952-53; Johnson rsch. prof. U. Wis., 1968-69 Author: The Puritan Family, 1944, Virginians at Home, 1953; author: (with Helen M. Morgan) The Stamp Act Crisis, 1953; author: The Birth of the Republic, 1956, The Puritan Dilemma, 1958, The Gentle Puritan, 1962, Visible Saints, 1963, Roger Williams, 1967, So What About History, 1969, American Slavery American Freedom, 1975, The Challenge of the American Revolution, 1976, The Meaning of Independence, 1976, The Genius of George Washington, 1980, Inventing the People, 1988, Benjamin Franklin, 2002, The Genuine Article, 2004, Not Your Usual Founding Father, 2006; mem. editl. bd.: N.E. Quar.; contbr. articles and revs. to hist. jours. Trustee Smith Coll., 1984-89. Recipient Nat. Humanities medal, 2000. Mem.: Am. Acad. Arts and Scis., Orgn. Am. Historians (pres. 1971—72), Royal Hist. Soc., Brit. Acad., Am. Philos. Soc., Am. Antiquarian Soc., Mass. Hist. Soc., Colonial Soc. Mass.

**MORGAN, ELAINE R.**, hematologist, oncologist, medical educator; b. Phila., May 22, 1946; d. Bernard and Sadie Jean (Blackman) Morgan; children: Brandon, Kerry David, Ari, Erin, Katelyn. BA, U. Pa., Phila., 1967, MD, 1971; cert. in Clin. Bioethics, Med. Coll. Wis., Milw., 2001. Cert. hosp. palliative medicine 2006. Resident pediat. Children's Hosp. of L.A., 1971—74; fellow pediat. oncology Children's Hosp.·Med. Ctr., Boston, 1974—75; attending physician Children's Meml. Hosp., Chgo., 1976—. Co-dir. pediat. hospice Palliative Care North Shore, Evanston, Ill., 1999—, Horizon Hospice Midwest Palliative Care Ctr.; med. advisor Make A Wish Found., Ill.; med. dir. Parent to Parent Children's Meml. Hosp., Chgo., 1995—; mem. faculty Feinberg Sch. Medicine, Northwestern U., 1978—, prof. pediat., 2005—. Contbr. articles to profl. jours. Recipient Tchr. of Yr., Children's Meml. Hosp., 1987; grantee, Leukemia Rsch. Found., 1978—79. Fellow: Am. Acad. Pediat.; mem.: Am. Soc. Bioethics and Humanities, Am. Acad. Pediat. Hematology-Oncology, Am. Soc. Clin. Oncology, Am. Soc. Hematology, Phi Beta Kappa. Avocations: reading, children's issues, crafts. Office: Children's Meml Hosp 2300 Children's Plz Chicago IL 60614 Office Phone: 773-880-4562. Business E-Mail: emorgan@northwestern.edu.

**MORGAN, ELIZABETH**, plastic surgeon; b. Washington, July 9, 1947; d. William James and Antonia (Bell) Morgan; 1 child, Elena. BA magna cum laude, Harvard U., 1967; postgrad. (fellow), Oxford U., 1967, 70; MD, Yale U., 1971; PhD in Psychology, U. Canterbury, Christchurch, New Zealand, 1995. Diplomate Am. Bd. Surgery, Am. Bd. Plastic Surgery. Intern Yale-New Haven Hosp., 1971-72, resident, 1972-73, 76-77, Tufts-New Eng. Med. Center, Boston, 1973-76, Harvard-Cambridge Hosp., Mass., 1977-78; columnist Cosmopolitan mag., 1973-80; pvt. practice specializing in cosmetic plastic surgery Washington, 1978-87, McLean, Va., 1998—, Chevy Chase, Md., 1998—. Faculty dept. psychology U. Md., 1995; assoc. faculty Am. U. Dept. Law, Justice and Soc., 1998. Author: The Making of A Woman Surgeon, 1980, Solo Practice, 1982, Custody, A True Story, 1986, The Complete Book of Cosmetic Surgery for Men, Women and Teens, 1988. Fellow: ACS, Am. Soc. Aesthetic Plastic Surgeons, Am. Soc. Plastic Surgeons; mem.: APA. Episcopalian. Office: 333 S Doheny Dr 202 Los Angeles CA 90048-3527 Office Phone: 240-687-2590. Business E-Mail: mail@drelizabethmorgan. E-mail: morgan52650@gmail.com.

**MORGAN, ELIZABETH ANN**, lawyer; d. Cyril Charles and Ann Howard Morgan; m. Matthew J. Bokor, May 1984 (div. Feb. 1999). BA, U. Fla., 1979; JD, Emory U., 1990. Bd. cert. bus. litigation: Fla. Ptnr. Powell Goldstein Frazer & Murphy LLP, Atlanta, 2000—03, Hunton & Williams LLP, Atlanta, 2003—06, Epstein Becker and Green PC, Atlanta, 2006—. Vice chair litigation com. U.S. Intellectual Property Owners Assn., Washington, 2003—; vice chair bus. litig. certification com. Fla. Bar, Tallahassee, 1998—2005; mem. Fla. Bar Standing Com. on Professionalism, 1993—2002. Mem. Leadership Atlanta, 2002; dir. ACLU of Ga., Atlanta, 2003—05. Named one of Top 50 Women Attys. in Atlanta, Atlanta Mag. and Ga. Super Lawyers Mag., 2005, Ga.'s Legal Elite, Ga. Trend Mag., 2003, 2004, 2005, Top 5% Ga. Intellectual Property Litig. Attys., Atlanta Mag. and Ga. Super Lawyers Mag., 2004, 2005, 2006. Master: Bleckley Inn of Ct.; mem.: FBA, ATLA (chair bus. torts 2005—06), ABA, Fla. Assn. for Women Lawyers (pres. Miami chpt. 1995), Internat. Trademark Assn. (chair U.S. legis.subcom. 2002—03, chair polit. action com. 2003—, mem. USPTO subcom. 2004—), Licensing Execs. Soc., Nat. Assn. for Women Lawyers, Ga. Assn. for Women Lawyers, Atlanta Bar Assn., Copyright Soc. of U.S., Am. Intellectual Property Law Assn. (vice chair trademark legis. com., women in intellectual property law com.), Acad. of Fla. Trial Lawyers, Atlanta Lawyer's Club. Office: Epstein Becker and Green PC Resurgence Plaza 945 E Paces Ferry Ste 2700 Atlanta GA 30326-1380 Office Phone: 404-869-5315. Office Fax: 404-869-5415. Business E-Mail: eamorgan@ebglaw.com.

**MORGAN, ELIZABETH SEYDEL**, writer, educator, retired writer; b. Atlanta, Ga, Feb. 19, 1939; d. John Rutherford and Jane Reynolds Seydel; children: Matthew, John, Elizabeth Borkey. BA, Hollins College, Roanoke, Va, 1956—60; MFA, Virginia Commonwealth University, Richmond, Va, 1983—86. Teacher, english and creative writing St. Catherine's School, Richmond, Va., 1960—93. Author: (poet,book,) Parties, 1988, (book) The Governor of Desire, 1993, On Long Mountain, 1998 (finalist, Lib. Va. prize, 1999); translator: (part of penn greek drama series) "Electra" by Euripides, 1998; author: (short fiction) "Economics", 1991 (Emily Clark Balch Prize, 1992); contbr. essay Wild In The City: the James River in Richmond, 1999;

author: (screenplay) Queen Esther, 1993 (Govs. award, Fa. Film Fest., 1993), (short fiction anthologies) New Stories From The South, 1993. Bd. dir. Richmond Pub. Libr. Found., Richmond, 1999—. Mem.: Fellows Council, Virginia Center for the Creative Arts. Home: 504 Honaker Avenue Richmond VA 23226

**MORGAN, EVAN**, retired chemist; b. Spokane, Wash., Feb. 26, 1930; s. Evan and Emma Anne (Klobucher) M.; m. Johnnie Lu Dickson, Feb. 14, 1959; 1 child, James. BS, Gonzaga U., 1952; MS, U. Wash., 1954, PhD, 1956. Staff chemist IBM Corp., Poughkeepsie, NY, 1956-60; group supr. Olin Mathieson Co., New Haven, 1960-64; assoc. prof. chemistry High Point (N.C.) Coll., 1964-65; sr. rsch. chemist Reynolds Metals Co., Richmond, Va., 1965-72; chemist Babcock & Wilcox, Lynchburg, Va., 1972-95, Lynchburg Tree Steward, Lynchburg, 1995—2002; ret., 2002—. Mem. Am. Chem. Soc. Home: 5128 Wedgewood Rd Lynchburg VA 24503-4208 E-mail: emorgan@worldnet.att.net.

**MORGAN, EVELYN BUCK**, retired nursing educator; b. Phila., Nov. 3, 1931; d. Kenneth Edward and Evelyn Louise (Rhineberg) Buck; m. John Allen McGeary, Aug. 15, 1958 (div. 1964); children: John Andrew, Jacquelyn Ann McGeary Keplinger; m. Kenneth Dean Morgan, June 26, 1965 (dec. 1975). Grad., Muhlenberg Hosp. Sch. Nursing, Plainfield, N.J., 1955; BSN summa cum laude, Ohio State U., 1972, MS, 1973; EdD, Nova U., 1978. RN, N.J., Ohio, Fla., Calif.; cert. clin. specialist ANCC; cert. advanced RN practitioner, Fla. Staff nurse Muhlenburg Hosp., 1955-57; indsl. nurse Western Electric Co., Columbus, Ohio, 195-59; supr. Mt. Carmel Hosp., Columbus, 1960-65; instr. Grant Hosp. Sch. Nursing, Columbus, 1965-72; cons. Ohio Dept. Health, Columbus, 1972-74; prof. nursing Miami (Fla.)-Dade C.C., 1974-96, prof. emerita, 1996—; pvt. practice family therapy, Ft. Lauderdale, Fla., 1982—. Family therapist Hollywood Pavilion Hosp., 1977-82; founder Elder Reach, Inc., care mgmt. co., 1998. Sustaining mem. Dem. Nat. Com., 1975—. Mem. ANA, Nat. Guild Hypnotists, Am. Nurses Found., Am. Holistic Nurses Assn., Fla. Coun. Psychiat. and Mental Health Clin. Specialists, Sigma Theta Tau. Roman Catholic.

**MORGAN, FRANK**, mathematics professor; BS, MIT, 1974; MA, Princeton U., 1976, PhD, 1977; ScD (hon.), Cedar Crest Coll., 1995. Moore instr. to assoc. prof., Green prof. MIT, Cambridge, 1977-87; chmn. Dept. Math. Williams Coll., 1988—94, Meenan 3d Century prof., chmn. dept. math., 1997—2003. Vis. prof. Rice U., Houston, 1982-83, Stanford U., 1986-87; mem. Inst. Advanced Study, Princeton, N.J., 1990-91; vis. prof. disting. tchg. Princeton U., 1997—; adj. prof. U. Mass., 1992—. Author: Geometric Measure Theory, 1988, 3d edit., 2000, Riemannian Geometry, 1993, revised edit., 2001, Calculus Lite, 1995, 2d edit., 1997, The Math Chat Book, 2000; contbr. over 100 articles to profl. jours. Recipient Haimo award for disting. coll. or univ. tchg. of math. Math. Assn. Am., 1993; grantee NSF, 1977—. Mem.: Math. Assn. Am. (2d v.p. 2000—02). Office: Williams College Dept of Mathematics Williamstown MA 01267

**MORGAN, FRANK EDWARD, II**, corporate financial executive; b. Burlington, Vt., May 16, 1952; s. Robert Griggs and Ruth (Jepson) M. First Class Cert. Merit, U. Edinburgh, Scotland, 1973; AB with honors, Brown U., 1974; LLM, Cambridge U., Eng., 1976; JD, U. Va., 1978. Bar: Mass. 1978, N.Y. 1990. Assoc. Gaston & Snow, Boston, 1978—82; v.p., gen. counsel Madison Fund, Inc. and Adobe Resources Corp., N.Y.C., 1982—87; ptnr. Gaston & Snow, N.Y.C., 1987—91, Mayer, Brown & Platt, N.Y.C., 1991—96, Dewey Ballantine, N.Y.C., 1996—2003; pres., COO Coller Capital, Inc., N.Y.C., 2003—. Bd. mem. ABS Ventures, Annex Capital, Capitol Health Ptnrs., New Venture Ptnrs. and Washington and Congress, Cambridge in Am. Republican. Congregationalist. Home: 14 Sutton Pl S New York NY 10022-3071 Office: Coller Capital Inc 410 Park Ave Ste 740 New York NY 10022 Office Phone: 212-644-8500. Business E-Mail: frank.morgan@collercapital.com.

**MORGAN, FRED**, lawyer, state representative; b. St. Louis, Mo., Feb. 9, 1954; s. George P. Jr. and Charoletta (Goff) Morgan; m. Page Price; children: Megan, Dan. BA, St. Louis U., 1976; JD, Okla. City U., 1980. Bar: Okla. 1980. Lawyer Sole Practice, Okla. City; rep Ho. Reps., State of Okla., Okla. City, 1995—. Mem. banking and fin., energy and utility regulation, pub health and rules coms. Ho. Reps. Okla., Okla. City, 1995—, mem. subcom. on pub. safety and judiciary to the appropriations and budget com., 1995—, minority fl. leader, 1998—2002, chmn. judiciary com., 2004—. Mem. Leadership Okla. City; alumni leadership Okla. Mem.: Rotary Club Okla. City (pres. 1995—96). Republican. Office: 2300 N Lincoln Blvd Rm 542 Oklahoma City OK 73105 Home and Office: PO Box 1121 Oklahoma City OK 73101 Office Phone: 405-232-8131. E-mail: morganfs@rrvmla.com.

**MORGAN, GREGORY PAUL**, financial investment advisor; b. Cocoa Beach, Fla., Sept. 9, 1958; s. Paul Leo and Mickey Maxine (Cooper) M. BS in Psychology magna cum laude, Pepperdine U., 1980. Cert. fin. planner. Fin. analyst Williams & McCombs, Inc., Arlington, Tex., 1980-83; fin. advisor Balanced Fin., Dallas, 1983-86; ptnr. Strategic Fin. Group, Arlington, 1986—. Chmn. coun. Lowry Fin. Svcs.; pres. Strategic Fin.Mgmt., 1989; lectr. numerous orgns. Big Bros. Am. United Way, Dallas, 1986—. Named Best Fin. Planners, Dallas Mag., 2003, 2004, 2005; named to Bloomberg Top 200 Wealth Mgrs., 2003, 2004, 2005. Mem.: Fin. Planners Assn. Avocations: tennis, running, snow-skiing. Office: 5310 Harvest Hill Rd Ste 146 Dallas TX 75230-5893 Home: 403 Rockcrest Dr Coppell TX 75019 Office Phone: 972-960-6460 Ext.2. Business E-Mail: gmorgan@sfmgadvisors.com.

**MORGAN, GWYN**, oil and gas executive; b. Carstairs, Alta., Can., Nov. 4, 1945; BSc in Mech. Engring., U. Alta., 1967; postgrad., Cornell U. Enginon engr. Alta. Energy Resources Conservation Bd.; mgr. ops and engring. Consolidated Natural Gas Ltd., Consolidated Pipelines Ltd., Norlands Petroleums Ltd., with Alta. Energy Co., Ltd., Calgary, 1975—2002; pres., CEO En Cana Corp., Calgary, 2002—. Bd. dirs. HSBC-Bank N.Am.; mem. adv. bd. Accenture Energy. Trustee Fraser Inst.; dir. Inst. of the Ams.; vice-chair Can. Coun. Chief Execs.; gov. Coun. for Can. Unity. Mem.: Am. Petroleum Inst. Avocations: sailing, hiking, skiing, physical fitness, bicycling. Office: EnCana Corp 1800-855 2d St SW Calgary AB Canada T2P 2S5

**MORGAN, HENRY COKE, JR.**, judge; b. Norfolk, Va., Feb. 8, 1935; s. Henry Coke and Dorothy Lea (Pebworth) M.; m. Margaret John McGrail, Aug. 18, 1965; children: D. Robertson Hanckel Jr., Catherine Morgan Stockwell, Coke Morgan Stewart. BS, Washington and Lee U., 1957, JD, 1960; LLM in Jud. Process, U. Va., 1998. Bar: Va. 1960, U.S. Dist. Ct. (ea. dist.) Va. 1961, U.S. Ct. Appeals (4th cir.) 1964. Asst. city atty. City of Norfolk, 1960-63; ptnr. Pender & Coward, Virginia Beach, Va., 1963-92; vice chmn., gen. counsel Princess Anne Bank, 1986-92; judge U.S. Dist. Ct. (ea. dist.) Va., 1992—2004, sr. judge, 2004—. Served with U.S. Army, 1958-59. Episcopalian. Office: US Dist Ct Eastern Dist Va Walter E Hoffman US Courthouse 600 Granby St Ste 307 Norfolk VA 23510-1915 E-mail: henry_morgan@vaed.uscourts.gov.

**MORGAN, HOLLY GUTHRIE**, elementary school educator; d. Donald Ray and Patricia Gale Guthrie; m. Joshua Shane Morgan, May 29, 2004. BS in Edn., U. Ala., Tuscaloosa, 2001; MA in Edn., U. Ala., Birmingham, 2003; postgrad., U. Ala., 2005—. Cert. early childhood elem. edn. Ala., reading edn. Ala. First grade tchr. West Jasper (Ala.) Elem., 2001—03; reading coach Meml. Pk. Elem. Sch., Jasper, 2003—05; reading coach trainer Ala. Reading Initiative, Jasper, 2005—. Master coach-summer reading acad. Ala. State Dept. of Edn., 2004—; peer rev. team mem. SACS, Ala., 2005—; reading and math tutor, Jasper, 2004—. Upward basketball coach Abundant Life Ch., Carbon Hill, Ala., 1999—2005, ch. choir mem./soloist, 1997—2005. Recipient Disting. Undergrad. Scholar award, U. Ala. Coll. of Edn., 2001, New Tchr. award, U. Ala., Birmingham, 2004; Alumni Honors scholar, U. Ala., 1997—2001, Wind Ensemble scholar, 1997—99, Edn. scholar, U. Ala. Coll. of Edn., 1999—2001. Mem.: NEA, Jasper Edn. Assn., NAEYC, Internat. Reading Assn. (Exemplary Reading award State of Ala. 2005), Kappa Delta

Pi (Kappa Delta Pi Disting. Undergraduate Scholar Award 2001), Mortar Bd., Alpha Delta Kappa (com. mem. 2004—05). Avocations: reading, walking. Office: Memorial Park Elementary 800 10th Ave Jasper AL 35501 Office Phone: 205-384-6461.

MORGAN, HUGH JACKSON, JR., retired bank executive, retired energy executive; b. Nashville, Aug. 10, 1928; s. Hugh Jackson and Robert Ray (Porter) M.; m. Ann Moulton Ward, Aug. 28, 1954; children— Ann, Grace, Caroline, Hugh AB, Princeton U., N.J., 1950; LL.B., Vanderbilt U., Nashville, 1956; A.M.P., Harvard Bus. Sch., 1976. Bar: Tenn. 1956. Practice law Miller & Martin, Chattanooga, 1956-60; atty. So. Natural Gas Co., Birmingham, Ala., 1961-65, gen. atty., 1966-70, v.p., 1971-78, pres., 1982-84, comm. bd., 1984-87; v.p. Sonat Inc., Birmingham, Ala., 1973-78, sr. v.p., 1979-84, exec. v.p., 1984, vice chmn. bd., 1984-87; vice chmn. Nat. Bank of Commerce, Birmingham, Ala., 1987-90, chmn., 1990—2003. Bd. dirs. Atrion Corp. Chmn. Birmingham Airport Authority, 1986-2000; trustee Children's Hosp. Ala., Birmingham, 1974—. Served to lt. (j.g.) USN, 1950-53. Recipient Bennett Douglas Bell Meml. prize Vanderbilt Law Sch., 1956 Mem. Order of the Coif. Clubs: Mountain Brook (pres. 1972), Redstone, (Birmingham); Belle Meade (Nashville); Linville Golf (N.C.). Lodges: Rotary. Home: 3121 Brookwood Rd Birmingham AL 35223-2016 Office: 1927 1st Ave N Birmingham AL 35203-4058

MORGAN, JACQUI, illustrator, painter, art educator, writer; b. NYC, Feb. 22, 1939; d. Henry and Emily (Cook) Morganstern; m. Onnig Kalfayan, Apr. 23, 1967 (div. 1972); m. Tomás Gonda, Jan. 1983 (dec. 1988). BFA with honors, Pratt Inst., Bklyn., 1960; MA, CCNY, 1978. Textile designer M. Lowenstein & Sons, N.Y.C., 1961-62, Fruit of the Loom, N.Y.C., 1962; stylist-design dir. Au Courant, Inc., N.Y.C., 1966—; assoc. prof. Pratt Inst., Bklyn., 1977—. Guest lectr. U. Que., Syracuse U., Warsaw TV & Radio, Poland, NYU, Parsons Sch. Design, N.Y.C., Sch. Visual Arts, N.Y.C., Va. Commonwealth U., Fashion Inst. of Tech., others; mem. profl. juries; curator Tomás Gonda retrospective exhbn.; adj. profl. Fashion Inst. Tech., N.Y.C.; condr. workshops. One-person shows include Soc. Illustrators, N.Y.C., 1977, Art Dirs. Club, N.Y.C., 1978, Gallerie Nowe Miasto, Warsaw, 1978, Gallerie Baumeister, Munich, W.Ger., 1978, Hansen-Feuerman Gallery, N.Y.C., 1980, Krannert Mus./U. Ill., 1998, Art Gallery at Marywood U., Scranton, Pa., 1998, Soc. Illustrators N.Y., 2005; group shows include Mus. Contemporary Crafts, N.Y.C., 1975, Smithsonian Instn., Washington, 1976, Mus. Warsaw, 1976, 78, Mus. Tokyo, 1979, Nat. Watercolor Soc., 1989, Salmagundi Club, 1990, New Eng. Watercolor Soc. Open, 1990, Miss. Watercolor Grand Nat., 1990, Illustration West 29, 1990, Adirondack Nat., 1990, Die Verlassenen Schuhe, 1993, N.Y. restaurant Sch., 1994, Lizan-Tops Gallery, 1996, The Art Club, 2000, Museum at Fashion Inst. Am., 2003, Soc. Jelust, N.Y.C., 2005, Spring Studio, N.Y.C., 2006; represented in permanent collections: Smithsonian Instn., Mus. Warsaw; author, illustrator: Watercolor for Illustration; produced 3 instrnl. watercolor videos; series of prints pub., 1995; series of plates publ., 1995; co-curator Tomas Gonda Retrospective, Va. Commonwealth U., Rutgers U., Carnegie Mellon U., others in U.S., Museo Del Arte Moderno, Buenos Aires, Ulmer Mus., Ulm, Germany; illustrator Lights Along the Path, 1999, The Healing Garden, 1999; contbr. articles to profl. jours. Recipient more than 200 awards from various orgns. including Soc. Illustrators, Fed. Design Coun., Comm. Arts Mag., Am. Inst. Graphic Arts, N.Y. Art Dirs. Club, Print Design Ann. Mem.: Graphic Artists Guild (dir. 1975—79), Soc. Illustrators, Women Artists of the West, Pa. Watercolor Soc. Studio: 6940 Yellowstone Blvd 515 Forest Hills NY 11375-3400 I understand that it's the pleasure of the process and the satisfaction of improvement that gives satisfaction.

MORGAN, JAMES C., manufacturing executive; b. 1938; BSME, MBA, Cornell U.; DEng (hon.), De Anza Coll., 1994. Corp. staff Textron Inc., 1963—72; sr. ptnr. West Ven Mgmt., San Francisco, 1972—76; pres. Applied Materials, Inc., Santa Clara, Calif., 1976—87, CEO, 1977—2003, chmn. bd., 1987—, vice chmn. pres. export coun., 2003—. Apptd. by Pres. Clinton to Commn. U.S.-Pacific Trade and Investment Policy, 1996; mem. Nat. Adv. Com. Semiconductors, 1988—92; bd. dirs. Cisco Sys.; apptd. to U.S-Japan Sector Govt. Commn., 2002; adv. bd. mem. Ctr. Sci. Tech. &: Soc. Santa Clara U., Calif. Co-author: Cracking the Japanese Market: Strategies for Success in the New Global Economy. Bd. gov. Nature Conservancy; trustee Nature Conservancy Calif. Named Internat. Citizen of Yr., World Forum of Silicon Valley, 1995; named to Jr. Achievement Hall of Fame, 1991; recipient Cmty. Svc. award, NCCJ, 1995, Nat. Medal of Tech., Pres. Clinton, 1996, Global Humanitarian Award, Tech. Mus. Innovation, Cmty. Svc. Award, Nat. Conf. Cmty. & Justice. Mem.: Semiconductor Equipment and Materials Internat. (dir. emeritus, past pres.), Pacific Basin Econ. Coun. (chmn.'s circle), Coun. Competitiveness, Nat. Ctr. Asia-Pacific Econ. Cooperation (bd. dirs.), Congrl. Econ. Leadership Inst. (bd. dirs.), World Presidents Orgn., Semiconductor Equipment and Materials Internat/SEMATECH (past bd. dirs., Global Pioneer Award), Am. Electronics Assn. (past bd. dirs.). Office: Applied Materials Inc 3050 Bowers Ave Santa Clara CA 95054-3298*

MORGAN, JAMES DURWARD, retired computer company executive; b. N.Y.C., Sept. 10, 1936; s. Durward Field and Harriet (Airey) M.; m. Ruth Ann Dobson, Jan. 14, 1967; children: Jennifer, Andrew. BEE, Yale U., 1961, MEE, 1962. Systems engr. Calspan Corp., Buffalo, 1962-68; v.p. Comptek Rsch. Inc., Buffalo, 1968—83, 1990—2001, also bd. dirs.; v.p. Barrister Info. Systems Corp., Buffalo, 1983-90, also bd. dirs., 1983—. Former mem. adv. coun. Erie C.C., Amherst, N.Y., 1985-2000, past chmn.; bd. dirs Yale Alumni Bd., Buffalo, 1987-2001. Served with USN, 1959-61. Mem.: IEEE, ACM.

MORGAN, JAMES EARL, librarian, administrator; b. Wheeling, W.Va., June 30, 1941; s. James H. L. and Ethel Irene (Goodwin) M.; m. Carman H. Head, Dec. 23, 1966; 1 child, Scott Andrew BS in Edn., Ariz. State Coll., 1965; MSLS, Fla. State U., 1966. Reference asst. social scis. Fla. State U., Tallahassee, 1965-66; head pub. services Ga. Coll., Milledgeville, 1967-69; dir. pub. services U. Tex. Med. Br., Galveston, 1969-73; dir. libraries U. Conn. Health Ctr., Farmington, 1973-76, Oreg. Health Sci. U., Portland, 1976—. Contbr. articles to profl. jours. Grantee Nat. Library Medicine, 1974-76, 78-81 Mem. ALA (life), Med. Libr. Assn. (chmn. Pacific N.W. chpt. 1981), Oreg. Health Scis. Librs. Assn., Pacific N.W. Libr. Assn., Spl. Libr. Assn., Oreg. Libr. Assn., Portland Area Spl. Librarians Assn., Assn. Coll. and Rsch. Librs., Am. Med. Informatics Assn., Nat. Rural Health Assn. Democrat. Office: Oreg Health & Sci U 3181 SW Sam Jackson Park Rd Portland OR 97239-3098 E-mail: morgan@ohsu.edu.

MORGAN, JAMES JOHN, environmental engineering educator; b. NYC, June 23, 1932; s. James and Anna (Treanor) M.; m. Jean Laurie McIntosh, June 15, 1957; children— Jenny, Johanna, Eve, Michael, Martha, Sarah BCE, Manhattan Coll., 1954; MSCE, U. Mich., 1956; postgrad., U. Ill., 1956-60 PhD, Harvard U., 1964; ScD (hon.), Manhattan Coll., 1989. Instr. civil engring. U. Ill., Urbana, 1956-60; assoc. prof. U. Fla., Gainesville, 1963-65, Calif. Inst. Tech., Pasadena, 1965-69, prof. environ. engring., 1969-87, Marvin L. Goldberger prof. environ. engring. sci., 1987—, dean of students, 1972-75, dean grad. studies, 1981-84, v.p. student affairs, 1980-89; exec. officer environ. engring. sci., 1993-96. Mem. environ. studies bd., NRC, 1974-80, Abel Wolman lectr., 2004; chmn. Acid Deposition Sci. Adv. Com., Calif., 1983-98; chmn. Gordon Rsch. Conf. on Environ. Sci.; Water, 1970. Author: (with Werner Stumm) Aquatic Chemistry, 1970, 2d edit., 1981, 3rd edit. 1996; editor Environ. Sci. and Tech., 1966-74; contbr. articles to profl. jours. Recipient Stockholm Water prize, 1999, Clarke Water prize, 1999. Mem. ASCE (award 1997), Am. Chem. Soc. (award 1980), AAAS, Am. Soc. Limnology and Oceanography (editorial bd. 1977-80), Nat. Acad. Engring., Assn. Environ. Engring. Profs (award 1981, 83, 94), Am. Water Works Assn. (award 1963), Sigma Xi, Chi Epsilon. Democrat. Roman Catholic. Avocations: tennis, music. E-mail: morgan_j@caltech.edu.

MORGAN, JAMES PHILIP, pharmacology and cardiology educator; b. Cin., Jan. 13, 1948; s. James Weldon and Dorcas Adele (Meyer) M.; m. Kathleen Greive, Dec. 22, 1973; children: James Patrick, Jonathan Michael. BS, U. Cin., 1970, PhD, 1974, MD, 1976. Diplomate Am. Bd. Internal

Medicine, Am. Bd. Cardiovascular Disease. Fellow internal medicine Mayo Clinic, Rochester, Minn., 1976—79, fellow cardiovascular disease, 1979—83; asst. medicine Beth Israel Hosp., Boston, 1983—. Instr. pharmacology U. Cin., 1975—76; asst. prof. pharmacology, instr. medicine Mayo Clinic, 1981—83; asst. prof. medicine Harvard U., Boston, 1983, assoc. prof., 1988—96, Herman Dana prof. medicine, 1996—2005; affiliate faculty, dept. pharmacology Harvard Med. Sch., 1986—2000; chief and prgram dir. cardiovascular divsn. Beth Israel Hosp., 1994—2001, vice chmn. medicine, 2000—05; chief cardiovasc. medicine St. Elizabeth's Med. Ctr., Boston, 2005—, dir. Caritas Christi Cardiovasc. Ctr., 2005—, Contbr. articles to profl. jours. Recipient Young Investigators award Am. Coll. Cardiology, 1982, Balfour award Mayo Clinic, 1983, Advanced Cardiac Life Support Spl. Recognition award Mayo Clinic, 1983, Rsch. Career Devel. award NIH, 1985-90. Mem. AMA, Am. Heart Assn., Biophys. Soc. Am. Soc. Pharmacology and Exptl. Therapeutics, Masons. Avocation: philatelics. Office: Caritas St Elizabeth's Med Ctr 736 Cambridge St Boston MA 02135-2997 Office Phone: 617-789-2226. Business E-Mail: james.morgan@caritachristi.org.

MORGAN, JANE HALE, retired library director; b. Dines, Wyo., May 11, 1926; d. Arthur Hale and Billie (Wood) Hale; m. Joseph Charles Morgan, Aug. 12, 1955; children: Joseph Hale, Jane Frances, Ann Michele. BA, Howard U., 1947; MA, U. Denver, 1954. Staff Detroit Pub. Libr., 1954-87, exec. asst. dir., 1973-75, dep. dir., 1975-78, dir., 1978-87; ret., 1987. Mem. Mich. Libr. Consortium Bd.; exec. bd. Southeastern Mich. Regional Film Libr.; vis. prof. Wayne State U., 1989—. Trustee New Detroit, Inc., Delta Dental Plan of Mich., v.p. Delta Dental Fund, Delta Dental Plan of Ohio; v.p. United Southwestern Mich.; pres. Univ.-Cultural Ctr. Assn.; bd. dirs. Rehab. Inst., YWCA, Met. Affairs Corp., Literacy Vols. Am., Detroit, Mich. Ctr. for the Book, Interfaith Coun.; bd. dirs., v.p. United Comty. Svcs. Met. Detroit; chmn. Detroiters for Adult Reading Excellence; chmn. adv. coun. libr. sci. U. Mich.; mem. adv. coun. libr. sci. U. Mich., mem. adv. coun. libr. sci. Wayne State U.; dir. Met. Detroit Youth Found.; chmn. Mich. LSCA adv. coun.; mem. UWA Literacy Com., Attys. Grievance Com., Women's Commn., Mich. Civil Svc. Rev. Com.; vice-chair Mich. Coun. for Humanities; v.p. Commn. for the Greening of Detroit; adv. com. Headstart; mem. Detroit Women's Com., Detroit Women's Forum, Detroit Exec. Svc. Corps.; sec., treas. Delta Dental Fund, pres. 1999. Recipient Anthony Wayne award Wayne State U., 1981, Summit award Greater Detroit C. of C.; named Detroit Howardite of Year, 1983 Mem. ALA, AAUW, Mich. Libr. Assn., Women's Nat. Book Assn., Assn. Mcpl. Profl. Women, NAACP, LWV, Women's Econ. Club (bd. dirs.), Sorosis Club (v.p.), Alpha Kappa Alpha (pres.). Democrat. Episcopalian.

MORGAN, JOE LELAND, physician, psychiatrist; b. Augusta, Ga., June 5, 1955; s. Robert Leland and Jozette Morgan; m. Debra Baily Morgan, July 10, 1993; children: Robert, David 1 stepchild, Tonya. BS, Valdosta State Coll., Valdosta, Ga., 1976; MS, Univ. Ga. Vet Sch., Athens, Ga., 1979; MD, Med. Coll. of Ga., Augusta, Ga., 1987. Cert. Am. bd. of Psychiatry and Neurology, 1993. Rsch. asst. Med. Coll. of Ga., Augusta, Ga., 1979—83, med. sch., 1983—87, med. resident, 1988—89, psychiatry resident, 1989—90, chief resident psychiatry, 1990—91, asst. prof. psychiatry, 1991—95; pvt. practice Valdosta Psychiatric Assoc., Valdosta, Ga., 1995—. Chief psychiatry svc. South Ga. Med. Ctr., Valdosta, Ga., 2000—, Parkwood Devel. Ctr., Valdosta, Ga., 1999—. Contbr. chapters to books, articles pub. to profl. jour. Recipient Vet. Adminstrn. Special Performance Award, 1993; grantee Dean's Summer Rsch. Grant, Med. Coll. og Ga., 1984. Mem.: APA, Med. Ass. of Ga., Ga. Psychiatric Physicians Assn. (sec. 2005, Psychiatrist of Yr. 2004). Republican. Meth. Avocations: fishing, tennis, snorkeling, scuba diving, baseball. Office: Valdosta Psychiatric Asso PO Box 3229 Valdosta GA 31604-3229 Office Phone: 229-244-4200. Business E-Mail: 244200@bellsouth.net.

MORGAN, JOHN DAVIS, government agency administrator, consultant; b. Newark, Feb. 14, 1921; s. John Davis and Caroline Frommel (Schaller) M.; m. Leta Maude Bretzinger, June 27, 1953; children: John Davis III, Bret Zinger. BS, Pa. State U., 1942, MS, 1947, PhD, 1948, E.M.; 1950; grad. extension course, Indsl. Coll. of Armed Forces, Washington, 1953. Asst. for materials and stockpile policies Nat. Security Resources Bd., Washington, 1948-51; dir. materials rev. div. DPA, Washington, 1951-53; materials expert ODM, Washington, 1953-56; mem. staff President's Cabinet Com. on Mineral Policy, 1953-54; cons. bus. and def. problems in metals, minerals and fuels Washington, 1956-71; mem. nat. def. exec. res. for ODM, 1956-58, OCDM, 1958-61, Office Emergency Planning, 1961-71, Emergency Minerals Adminstrn., 1972-95; mem. spl. stockpile advisory com. to ODM, 1957-58; com. on scope and conduct of materials research NAS, 1959-60, then, mem. com. on mineral sci. and tech., 1966-70; mem. NAS.eng. Adv. Com. on Mining and Mineral Research, 1977-95. Head dept. sci. and math. Daytona Beach C.C., Fla., 1961-71; asst. dir. mineral position analysis U.S. Bur. Mines, Dept. Interior, Washington, 1971-74, acting dir. bur., 1973-74, 77-78, assoc. dir. mineral and materials supply/demand analysis, 1974-79, chief staff officer, 1979-95, Interior Dept. liaison to Com. Internat. Econ. Policy Staff, 1973-77, to Econ. Policy Bd. Staff, 1974-77, to Dept. Def. Materials Steering Group, 1975-78, to FPA-FEMA Stockpile Com., 1975-88, to Winter Energy Emergency Planning Group of Dept. of Energy, 1977-81; alt. Interior rep. Trade Policy Rev. Group, 1975-81; chmn. minerals rev. com. Non-Fuel Minerals Policy Study, 1978; chmn. materials supply task force NSC Stockpile Study, 1983-87; liaison to Dept. Def. Stockpile Com., 1988-95; mem. Def. Logistics Agy. Market Impact Com., 1988-95; mem. Def. Dept. Adv. Com. Operation and Modernization of Stockpile, 1993-95; U.S. rep. UN Sci. Conf. on Resources, 1949; lectr. numerous univs. including Nat. Def. U., War Coll., Indsl. Coll., Def. Intelligence Coll., Army War Coll., 1949—; hon. prof. Indsl. Coll., 1983—; invited spkr. nat. meetings sci. and engring. socs., 1949—. Author: Domestic Mining Industry of the U.S. in World War II, 1949; contr. Mining Ann. Rev., London, 1958-95; contbr. articles to profl. jours. Served from 2d lt. to maj. Corps Engrs. AUS, 1942-46. Decorated Bronze Star; recipient Distinguished Service gold medal Interior Dept., 1976; named Meritorious Exec. Sr. Exec. Service, 1983 Fellow Soc. Am. Mil. Engrs.; mem. Sci. Research Soc. Am., Soc. Mining Engrs. (Disting. mem.), AIME (nat. Krumb lectr. 1973, Legion of Honor 1989), Sigma Xi, Tau Beta Pi, Sigma Tau, Pi Mu Epsilon, Phi Lambda Upsilon, Phi Kappa Phi, Phi Eta Sigma, Sigma Gamma Epsilon. Clubs: Cosmos (Washington). Home: 5013 Worthington Dr Bethesda MD 20816-2748

MORGAN, JOHN DERALD, electrical engineer; b. Hays, Kans., Mar. 15, 1939; s. John Baer and Avis Ruth (Wolf) M.; m. Elizabeth June McKneely, June 23, 1962; children: Laura Elizabeth, Kimberly Ann, Rebecca Ruth, John Derald. BSEE, La. Tech. U., 1962; MS, U. Mo., Rolla, 1965, Degree in Elec. Engring. (hon.), 1987; PhD, Ariz. State U., 1968. Registered profl. engr., forensic engr., Mo., N.Mex., Ala. Elec. engr. Tex. Eastman div. Eastman Kodak Co., 1962-63; instr. U. Mo., Rolla, 1963-65, Ariz. State U., 1965-68; asso. prof. elec. engring. U. Mo., Rolla, 1968-72, Alcoa Found. prof. elec. engring., 1972-75, chmn. elec. engring., 1978-85, assoc. dir. Ctr. Internat. Programs, 1970-78, Emerson Electric prof., 1975-85; dean engring. N.Mex. State U., 1985-99; v.p. univ. advancement U. Ala. in Huntsville, 1999—; exec. sec. U. Ala. Huntsville Found., 1999—; pres. J. Derald Morgan and Assoc., Inc.; ptnr. Morgan-Morris Devel. Co. LLC; mng. ptnr. Morgan Travel, LLC. Nat. adv. com. Engring. Exploring; cons. to industry. Author: Power Apparatus Testing Techniques, 1969, Computer Monitoring and Control of Electric Utility Systems, 1972, Control and Distribution of Megawatts Through Man-Machine Interaction, 1973, Electromechanical and Electromagnetic Machines and Devices, 1986, Wolf Brethren, 2003, Macy Friends, vols. I and II; also articles. Pres. bd. trustees First United Meth. Ch., Rolla, 1971-73, pres. adminstrv. bd., 1978-79; v.p., mem. bd. adminstrn. People to People, 1976; bd. dirs., cubmaster Ozarks dist. Boy Scouts Am., 1968-79, asst. dist. commr., 1971-73, cubmaster Yucca coun., 1986-90, coun. commr., 1989-90, asst. scout master, 1990-99, dist. com. Sunshine Dist., dist. chmn. Meramec dist., 1978-80, engring. exploring nat. com.; chmn. Creek Dist., 2000—05, bd. dirs Greater Ala. Coun. No. Svc. Dist., 2000—; bd. dirs Mo. Ptnrs. of the Americas. Recipient Scouters Key award and Scouter Tng. award Ozarks coun., Boy Scouts Am., 1971, Dist. award of merit 1977, Silver Beaver award, 1982, Cub Leader award, Webelos Leader award, Dist. Com. Key award, James West Soc. award, Sunshine Dist. Yucca coun.; T.H. Harris

scholar, 1959-61; John H. Horton scholar, 1961-62. Fellow: IEEE (chmn. internat. practices subcom. 1972—79, chmn. ednl. resources subcom. 1973—78, chmn. 1979—85, sec. PSE com., vice chmn., Centennial award 1984, award of Merit St. Louis sect., Educators award St. Louis sect., honor award St. Louis sect.), Nat. Acad. Forensic Engrs.; mem.: PSI, ASTM, Order of the Engr. (nat. bd. govs. 1996—, sec.), Am. Soc. Engring. Edn. (chair bylaws com. 1999—2001), N.Mex. Soc. Profl. Engrs. (N.Mex. Engr. of Yr. 1993), NSPE (bd. govs., nat. dir., vice chmn., S.W. chmn. Profl. Engrs. in Edn. v.p., mem. Steinman Coun.), SAR (Tenn. Valley chpt. sec.), Rotary Internat. (Paul Harris fellow 1997), Phi Kappa Phi, Omicron Delta Kappa, Eta Kappa Nu, Tau Beta Pi, Sigma Xi, Epsilon Gamma (grand master, grand procurator), Kappa Sigma (faculty and alumni advisor, Hall of Fame Beta Cptr.). Home: 113 Lansdowne Dr Madison AL 35758-7613 Office: U Ala in Huntsville Alumni House 102 Huntsville AL 35899-0001 Office Phone: 256-824-6127. E-mail: jdm@knology.net.

MORGAN, JOHN K., chemicals executive, electronics executive; BS in Engring. Tech., Purdue U.; MBA, Ind. U. From mgmt. to pres., chief devel. officer Acuity Brands Inc., Atlanta, 1979—2004, pres., 2004—, chief devel. officer, 2004—. Office: Acuity Brands Inc 1170 Peachtree St NE Atlanta GA 30309

MORGAN, KATHRYN LAWSON, retired historian, educator; 1 child, Susan Morgan Crooks MA, Howard U., 1952, U. Pa., 1967, PhD, 1970. Asst. prof. U. Del., Newark, 1970-71; lectr. Swarthmore Coll., Pa., spring 1970, prof. history and folklore Pa., 1972—95, Sara Lawrence Lightfoot Prof. History emerita Pa., 1995. Vis. assoc. prof. Bryn Mawr Coll., 1972-75, Haverford Coll., 1972-74, U. Calif.-Berkeley, winter 1975; cons. Research for Better Schs., Phila., 1968-69, Black History Mus., Phila., 1966-76, Smithsonian Instn., 1974-76, Ednl. Film Service, 1977 Author: Children of Strangers; Stories of a Black Family, 1980, transl. Brazilian-Portuguese, 2002, Books Across the Seas, Selected for Youth, 1981; contbr. articles to profl. jours., mags. Grantee Smithsonian Instn.-Am. Philos. Soc., 1983; Danforth Found. fellow, 1968—70, sr. rsch. scholar, Swarthmore Coll., 2003. Avocations: travel, storytelling, theater, music. Office: Swarthmore Coll Dept Hist Swarthmore PA 19081

MORGAN, KERMIT JOHNSON, lawyer; b. Wales-Henderson, Iowa, Feb. 13, 1914; s. Samuel Jr. and Jennie Amelia Morgan; m. Georgina R. Morgan, Oct. 12, 1940 (dec. 1978); children: Georgina Morgan Street, Wilson S.; m. Ortrud Impol, Dec. 9, 1960. BA, U. Iowa, 1935; JD, U. So. Calif., 1937. Bar: Calif. 1939. Pvt. practice, L.A., 1940—45, 1971—80, 1991—; ptnr. McBain & Morgan, L.A., Calif., 1945—58, McBain, Morgan & Roper, L.A., 1965—71, Kermit J. Morgan, L.A., 1940—45, 1971—80, Morgan & Armbrister, L.A., Calif., 1980—91. Mem. ABA, Am. Bd. Trial Advs. (diplomate, nat. pres. 1973, pres. L.A. 1972), Assn. Def. Trial Attys. (bd. dirs. 1982-85), Internat. Assn. Ins. Counsel, Hon. Order of Blue Goose, Calif. State Bar, Assn. So. Calif. Def. Counsel (bd. dirs. 1966-67), L.A. Bar Assn. Republican. Congregationalist. Avocation: golf. Home: 2108 Stradella Rd Los Angeles CA 90077-2325 Office: 3420 Ocean Pk Blvd Santa Monica CA 90405 Office Phone: 310-314-4764.

MORGAN, LARRY RONALD, minister; b. Springhill, La., Mar. 12, 1936; s. Woodrow Wilson Morgan and Alma Elizabeth (Dunn) Burch; m. Elizabeth Dianne Baker, May 24, 1958; children: Elizabeth Denise Morgan Davis, Dennis Kevin. ADiv, Bapt. Missionary Assn. Theol. Sem., Jacksonville, Tex., 1990. Ordained to ministry Bapt. Ch., 1971. Clk., carrier U.S. P.O., Springhill, La., 1956-71; assoc. pastor Webb Chapel Bapt. Ch., Dallas, 1971-72, pastor, 1972-99, First Bapt. Ch., Springhill, La., 1999—. Clk., trustee Bapt. Missionary Assn. Sem., Jacksonville, 1983-86; chmn. bd. trustees Bapt. Progress, Dallas, 1984-87. Pres PTA Browning Elem. Sch., Springhill, 1969-70. With USAR. 1959-66. Mem. Bapt. Missionary Assn. Am. (v.p. hdqrs. Little Rock 1985-86, pres. 1986-88, v.p. Am. 1996-98, pres. 1998-2000), Dallas County Bapt. Assn. (moderator 1982-84), Bapt. Missionary Assn. of La. (moderator 2000—), Springhill Baptist Assn. (moderator 2001-). Baptist. Home: 611 Butler St Springhill LA 71075-2519 Office Phone: 318-539-2610. Personal E-mail: ronaldmorgan1@juno.com.

MORGAN, LEON ALFORD, retired utilities executive; b. Washington, Dec. 29, 1934; s. Albert Lewis and Alice Viets (Alford) M.; children: David Richard, Sherry Alice; m. Jacqueline Jamieson, Feb. 14, 1993. BSEE, Worcester Poly. Inst., Mass., 1957. Registered profl. engr., Conn. With United Illuminating Co., New Haven, 1957-94, gen. ops. mgr., then v.p. ops., 1973-76, exec. v.p., 1976-83, sr. v.p. fin., 1984-94. Republican. Episcopalian. Home: 43 Forest Brook Rd Guilford CT 06437-2245

MORGAN, LEON TERRELL, environmental health services specialist; b. Spartanburg, S.C., Oct. 9, 1957; s. Leon W. and Helen K. Morgan; m. Susan Elaine Morgan, Aug. 28, 1999. AA, Anderson Coll., 1960; BS, East Tenn. State U., 1982. Registered environ. health specialist, reg. sanitarian Nat. Environ. Health Assn., 2001. Environ. health officer USPHS, Rockville, Md., 2001—03; investigator/ life safety surveyor SC. Dept. of Health & Environ. Control, Columbia, 2005—. State dir. US Jr. C. of C., Spartanburg, SC, 1990—95, v.p.-cmty. devel. Boiling Springs, SC, 1995—97; fire fighter Seneca Fire Dept., SC, 1978—84; firefighter/med. first responder North Spartanburg Fire Dept., SC, 1990—95. Lt. USPHS, 2001—03. Decorated Nat. Def. medal USAF. Mem.: Nat. Environ. Health Assn. (licentiate), Am. Soc. of Safety Engrs. (assoc.). Home: 13 Lawrence St Lyman SC 29365

MORGAN, LINDA F., director; d. Nadine Fishel; m. Howard L. Morgan, Mar. 11, 1948; children: Laura Leigh, Lindy Nicole. BA in Journalism/Pub. Rels., U. Okla., Norman, 1979; MEd in Bus. Southeastern Okla. State U., Durant, 1987. Instr., dept. chair Ea. Okla. State Coll., Wilburton, 1986—2006, dir. GEAR UP grant, 2006—. State advisor Okla. FBLA-PBL. Pianist First Bapt. Ch., Red Oak, Okla., 2005—06. Named Outstanding Local Chpt. Advisor, Phi Beta Lambda, 1993, Post-Secondary Tchr. of the Yr., Mountain Plains Bus. Edn. Assn., 1994—95, Tchr. of Yr., Ea. Okla. State Coll., 1994; recipient Excellence in Tchg. award, Nat. Inst. for Staff and Orgnl. Devel., 2006; grantee Fed. GEAR UP grantee, U.S. Dept. Edn., 2006—. Mem.: Mountain Plains Bus. Edn. Assn. (assoc.; ISBE rep, pres. elect, pres., past pres. 1995—99), Nat. Bus. Edn. Assn. (assoc.; bd. mem. 1997—98), Profl. Divsn. FBLA-PBL (life). Democrat. Baptist. Office: Eastern Oklahoma State College 1301 W Main Wilburton OK 74578 Office Phone: 918-465-1722. Business E-Mail: lmorgan@eosc.edu.

MORGAN, LINDA GAIL, theater producer; b. Tallahassee, May 14, 1952; d. Thomas Mitchell Morgan Sr. and Helen Frances (Rives) Stokes. BS, Fla. State U., 1974. Prodn. mgr. Valley Forge Ballet-5th World Peace Youth Culture Festival, Honolulu, 1985, Salute to Lady Liberty, Madison Square Gardens, 1986, U.S. Consm. 200 Yr. Anniversary Parade, Phila., 1986-89, Columbus Day Parade, N.Y.C., 1988, Gift of the White Bird Parade-Landmark Entertainment, Oita, Japan, 1990-91, 1996 Olympic Opening and Closing Ceremonies-Centenniel Events, Inc., Olympic Stadium, Atlanta, 1996, Super Bowl XXXI Half Time Show, New Orleans, 1997, N.Y. Jets Halftime Show, Meadowlands Stadium, N.J., 1997; prodn. state mgr. Walt Disney Bus. Prodns., 1998; coordinating prodr. (musical) This Is America, The New World, Freedom Music, Santa Monica, Calif., 1989, California Traditional Music Festival, Human Rights Lectr. Series, Soka U. Am., L.A., 1992-95, The Genius and the Great, L.A., 1993, Every Child Deserves a Chance, L.A., 1994, A Tribute to Burt Reynolds, L.A., 1994, Celebrate the Garnet and Gold IV Honoring Charles Nelson Reilly, L.A., 1995, Leisure Quest Internat./Entertainment Devel. Group, Burbank, Calif., 1997; artist agt., co. gen. mgr. Zoli Mgmt., Inc., N.Y.C., 1986-89; orch. prodn. mgr. All Am. Gen. Meeting, Spectrum, Phila., 1987; asst. prodn. mgr. 8th World Peace Culture Festival, Fukuoka, Japan, 1987, This Is America, Madison Square Gardens, 1988, 1991 Olympic Festival Opening Ceremonies Radio City Spl. Events, Dodger Stadium, L.A., 1991; prodn. staff Inauguration Mayor of Atlanta, Civic Ctr., Atlanta, 1998; event mgr. Coke on Ice World of Coca Cola, Atlanta, 1997-98, Disney Events Productions, 1998-2003, Tribeca Film

Fest., 2004; prodr. Anheuser-Bush Creative Svcs., 2001-. Mem. Soka Gakkai Internat. (arts divsn. culture dept. 1995-99), Fla. State U. So. Calif. Alumni Assn. (bd. dirs. 1991-95, Garnet/Gold award 1995), Internat. Spl. Event Soc., Alpha Chi Omega. Democrat. Buddhist. Avocations: arts, needlepoint, antiques, piano, gardening. Personal E-mail: lgailmorgan@cs.com.

MORGAN, LINDA JOAN, former federal agency administrator, lawyer; b. Chester County, Pa., May 19, 1952; m. Michael E. Karam; 1 child, Meredith Lyn. AB in Hispanic Studies, Vassar Coll., 1973; JD, Georgetown U., 1976; postgrad., Harvard U., 1991. Bar: DC 1976. Assoc. Welch & Morgan, Washington, 1976-78; staff counsel US Senate Com. on Commerce, Sci. and Transp., 1978-86, gen. counsel, 1987-94; mem. ICC, Washington, 1994-96, chmn., 1995-96, Surface Transp. Bd., Washington, 1996—2003; ptnr. Covington & Burling, Washington, 2003—, chmn., Trasp. Practice Group. Named Alumna of Yr., Georgetown U. Law Ctr., 1999, Person of Yr. in Transp., Robert H. Smith Sch. Bus., U. Md., 2003; named one of 5 People to Watch, Washington Post, 1998; recipient Woman of Yr. award, Women's Transp. Seminar. Mem.: Women's Transp. Seminar, Women's Bar Assn., Bar Supreme Ct. US, DC Bar Assn. Democrat. Office: Covington & Burling 1201 Pennsylvania Ave NW Washington DC 20004-2401 Office Phone: 202-662-6291, 202-662-5214. Business E-Mail: lmorgan@cov.com.

MORGAN, LUCY WARE, news correspondent, journalist; b. Memphis, Oct. 11, 1940; d. Thomas Allin and Lucile (Sanders) Keen; m. Alton F. Ware, June 26, 1958 (div. Sept. 1967); children: Mary Kathleen, Andrew Allin; m. Richard Alan Morgan, Aug. 9, 1968; children: Lynn Elwell, Kent Morgan AA, Pasco Hernando C.C., New Port Richey, Fla., 1975; student, U. South Fla., 1976-80. Reporter Ocala Star Banner, Fla., 1965-68, St. Petersburg Times, Fla., 1967-86, capitol bur. chief, 1986—2006, sr. corr., 2006—. Assoc. editor and bd. dirs. Times Pub. Co., 1991—2006. Recipient Paul Hansel award Fla. Soc. Newspaper Editors, 1981, First in Pub. Service award Fla. Soc. Newspaper Editors, 1982, First Place award in pub. service Fla. Press Club, 1982, Pulitzer award for investigative reporting Columbia U., 1985, First Place award in investigative reporting Sigma Delta Chi, 1985; named to Kappa Tau Alpha Hall of Fame, 1992, Fla. Women's Hall of Fame, 2006; named Fla. Senate Press Gallery in Morgan's honor, 2005. Home: 7030 Spencer Dr Tallahassee FL 32312-3548 Office: St Petersburg Times 336 E College Ave Tallahassee FL 32301-1551 Office Phone: 850-224-7263. Personal E-mail: lucytimes@aol.com.

MORGAN, LYLE WARNER, II, medical educator; b. Fremont, Nebr., Apr. 5, 1947; s. Lyle W. and Ione E. Morgan. AB, Doane Coll., 1969; MEd, Fla. State Christian U., 1970; MA in Edn., Wayne State Coll., Nebr., 1973, MS in Edn., 1976; PhD, U. Nebr., 1980; D in Homeopathic Medicine, Internat. U., Brussels, Belgium, 1984. Prof. Pittsburg (Kans.) State U., 1984—, chmn. pre-medicine & health scis. program, 2000—03. Dir. composition Pittsburg (Kans.) State U., 1984—, dir. English edn., 1984—, chmn. pre-medicine and health scis., 2000—03; sachem Tribe of Mic-O-Say, 1980; chieftain Tribe of Lone Bear, Mo., 2005. Author: Homeopathic Treatment of Sports Injuries, 1988, Homeopathic Medicine: First-Aid & Emergency Care, 1989, Treating Sports Injuries the Natural Way, 1990, Homeopathy and Your Child, 1992. Mem. Ozark Trails Coun. Boy Scouts of Am., Springfield, Mo., 1984—, exec. bd. mem., v.p., 1984—. Recipient Vigil Honor award, Order of the Arrow, 1979, Silver Beaver award, Boy Scouts Am., 1983, Distinguished Eagle Scout award, 1995, Silver Antelope award, 1997; fellow, Coll. Preceptors, UK, 1993. Mem.: SAR, Commn. Religious Counseling and Healing (licentiate), Rockefeller Family and Assocs. Republican. Office: Pitts State U 1701 S Broadway Pittsburg KS 66762-7515 Office Phone: 620-235-4691. E-mail: lmorgan@pittstate.edu.

MORGAN, LYNN, sports association executive; BS in Mktg., U. Ga. Dir. sales devel., Olympic mktg. mgr. Cox Enterprises, Inc., Atlanta, 1991—2001; pres., CEO Women's United Soccer Assn., N.Y.C., 2001—03. Bd. dirs. Atlanta Sports Coun., Atlanta Thunder; gen. mgr. Atlanta Beat Women's United Soccer Assn. Bd. dirs. Salvation Army, Atlanta Ad Club, Atlanta Arts and Bus. Coun.

MORGAN, M. JANE, computer systems consultant; b. Washington, July 21, 1945; d. Edmond John and Roberta (Livingstone) Dolphin (dec.); 1 child, Sheena Anne. Student, U. Md., 1963-66, Montgomery Coll., 1966-70; BA in Applied Behavioral Sci with honors, Nat.-Louis Univ., 1987, MS in Mgmt., 1991; postgrad. diploma in info. resource mgmt, Am. U., 1995; cert., USDA Grad. Sch., 2000; postgrad. diploma, State U. Calif., Northridge, 2002. With HUD, Washington, 1965-84, computer specialist, 1978-84; pres., CEO Systems and Mgmt. Assocs., 1983-97, dir. systems engring. Advanced Tech. Systems, Inc., Vienna, Va., 1984-86, sr. cons., 1989; chief tech. staff Tech. and Mgmt. Svcs., Inc., 1986-89; sr. computer scientist Integrated Systems divsn. Computer Scis. Corp., 1989-90; computer systems specialist gen. svcs. adminstrn. U.S. Govt., 1991—2001; divsn. dir. U.S. Gen. Svcs. Adminstrn. 2001—06. Mgmt. cons. author: Rapid Identification of Critical Staff, 1991. Bd. dirs. PL Active. Mem. Federally Employed Women (life, webmaster, 1996-, nat. exec. v.p. 1998-2000), Order Eastern Star. Episcopalian. E-mail: webwoman@jmorgan.net.

MORGAN, MARABEL, writer; b. Crestline, Ohio, June 25, 1937; d. Howard and Delsa (Smith) Hawk; m. Charles O. Morgan, Jr., June 25, 1964; children— Laura Lynn, Michelle Rene. Student, Ohio State U. Pres. Total Woman, Inc., Miami, Fla., 1970—. Pub. speaker. Author: The Total Woman, 1973, Total Joy, 1976, The Total Woman Cookbook, 1980, The Electric Woman, 1985, The Home on the Range Cookbook, 1995. Office: c/o Total Woman Inc 1300 NW 167th St Ste 3 Miami FL 33169-5738

MORGAN, MARY ANN, lawyer; b. Orlando, Fla., Mar. 12, 1955; d. Charles Clayburn and Eileen Louise (Mutzbauer) M.; m. Patrick Thomas Burke, Dec. 12, 1992. BS in Criminology, Fla. State U. 1978, JD 1986. Bar: Fla. 1986, U.S. Dist. Ct. (mid. dist.) Fla. 1986, U.S. Supreme Ct. Investigator Auditor Gen.'s Office State of Fla., Orlando, 1979-83; staff analyst criminal justice com. Fla. Ho. of Reps., Tallahassee, 1985-86; ptnr. Billings, Cunningham, Morgan & Boatwright, Orlando, 1986—2005, mng. ptnr., 2005—. Chmn. renovation com. Orange County Hist. Mus., Orlando, 1995—; spkr. Physician/Lawyer Drug Awareness Program, Orange County Schs., Orlando, 1997. Mem. ABA, ATLA, Fla. Bar Assn. (spkrs. bur. 1997, chair grievance com. 1993-96, vice chair 9th jud. cir. fee arbitration com.), Orange County Bar Assn. (exec. coun. 1991—, chmn. renovation com. 1995—, del. ABA 1989, 90, pres. young lawyers sect. 1990-91, pres. 2001-02), Acad. Fla. Trial Lawyers, Ctrl. Fla. Assn. for Women Lawyers (bd. dirs. 1990-92), Fla. State U. Alumni Assn. (bd. dirs. 1996—), Orange County Legal Aid Soc. (bd. dirs. 1997—, pres.-elect 1998-99, pres. 1999-2000), Nat. Assn. Women Lawyers, Am. Inns of Ct., Tiger Bay Club, Million Dollar Advs. Club. Avocations: waterskiing, golf, boating. Office: Billings Morgan Boatwright & Herandez LLC 399 Carolina Ave Winter Park FL 32789 Office Phone: 407-679-9900. Business E-Mail: maryann@billingslawfirm.com.

MORGAN, MARY DAN, librarian; b. Tallulah, La., Nov. 30, 1943; d. Daniel Boone and Mary Louise (McLeod) M.; m. William Jefferson Day (div. Dec. 1995); 1 child, Forrest Jefferson Day. BA, La. Coll., 1965; MLS, La. State U., 1968; MA Edn., Murray State U., 1976; MSW, U. Louisville, 1992. Cert. social worker, Ky., Ind. Libr. Ascension Parish Schs., Donaldsonville, La., 1966—68, Jefferson County Schs., Louisville, 1968—75; tchr. Webster County Schs., Dixon, Ky., 1975—79, Hardin County Schs., Elizabethtown, Ky., 1979—82, dir. media ctr., 1982—87, tchr. day and residential juvenile facilities, 1987—91, tchr. mid. and sr. high alt. schs., 1991—93; social worker Hospice of Ctrl. Ky., Elizabethtown, 1993—2000, Gentiva Health Svcs. Louisville, 1995, Lincoln Trail Dist. Home Health, Elizabethtown, 1997—98; libr. Luther Luckett Correctional Complex, La Grange, Ky., 2000—. Pres. Webster County Tchrs. Assn., Dixon, Ky., 1977-78; sec. Ky. Libr. Network Bd., Frankfort, 1986-87. Mem.: ALA, NASW, NEA (life), Filson Hist. Soc. Office: Luther Luckett Correctional Complex PO Box 6 La Grange KY 40031 Office Phone: 502-222-0363.

MORGAN, MARY E., publishing executive; married; 1 child. B, SUNY Binghamton. Adv. dir. Fitness Mag., 1992—94; assoc. group pub. Parents and Child Mag., 1994—95; assoc. pub. Ladies Home Journal, 1995—97; v.p., pub. Health Mag., 1997—2003, Redbook, 2003—. Mem. editl. bd. Pharmaceutical Executive Magazine. Mem.: Nat. Assn. of Chain Drug Stores, Cosmetic Exec. Women (philanthropy com.), Advt. Women of N.Y. (mem. bd. dirs.), Advt. Club of N.Y. Office: Redbook 224 West 57th St New York NY 10019 Home: Chatham MA Office Phone: 212-649-3450.*

MORGAN, MARY JO, school system administrator; b. West Point, N.Y., Aug. 19, 1948; d. William Burbridge and Phyllis VanderFehr Yancey; m. Joe Howard Morgan, Nov. 25, 1976; children: Phyllis Ruthann(dec.), Marian Amanda, Elizabeth Darbonne. Master's degree, George Wash. U., 1972; PhD, U. ND, 1993. H.s. prin. Norman County West Schs., Halstad, Minn., 1993—98; chief ops. officer Little Falls (Minn.) Cmty. Schs., 1999—. Asst. dir. Bur. of Ed Rsch., U. N.D., Grand Forks, 1990—93. Mem.: AAUW (pres. 2004), ASCD, Soc. for Human Resource Mgmt. Dfl. Roman Catholic. Avocation: community theater. Home: 1109 Celebration Dr Sartell MN 56377 Office: Little Falls Comty Schs 1001 5th Ave SE Little Falls MN 56345 Office Phone: 320-632-2005. Home Fax: 320-632-2010; Office Fax: 320-632-2010. Business E-Mail: mjmorgan@lfalls.k12.mn.us.

MORGAN, MARY LOU, retired education educator, volunteer; b. Chgo., Mar. 5, 1938; d. William Nicholas and Esther Lucille (Galbraith) Wanmer; m. James Edward Morgan, May 30, 1963. BA in Bus. Edn. and Econs., Wichita State U., 1971, MEd in Student Pers. and Guidance, 1974; postgrad., Kans. State U., 1986. Cert. bus. tchr., Kans. Reservationist Braniff, Wichita, Kans., 1961—62; stenographer, fin. analyst, clk.-typist Boeing Co., Wichita, 1962—68, tng., pers. and records positions, 1979—93; pers. cons. Rita Pers. Svc., Wichita, 1974—75; adminstrv. aide, manpower specialist, job developer City of Wichita, 1975—76; account exec., employment counselor Mgmt. Recruiters, 1976—77; pers. mgr., patient cons. Women's Clinic, 1977; vocat. rehab. counselor State of Kans., Parsons, 1977—79; pvt. detective Investigation Svcs., Wichita, 1981—84; instr. career devel. Wichita State U., 1988—90. Paralegal asst. Turner & Hensley, Wichita, 1975. Coord. funding Women's Crisis Ctr., Wichita, 1975; docent Carver Mus., Hoover Mus.; vice chmn. Hist. Preservation Commn.; founder, coord. Ann. Women's Chautauqua; Precinct committeewoman Wichita Dem. Com., 1992—94; pres. Jasper County-Newton County Dems., 1998; sub., co-chair then chmn. precinct walkers voter registration Grover Beach Dems., 2004—, assembly dist. mem., 2005—, chmn. equal rights com., del. to state; mem. 22,000 Club Calif. State Dem. Coun., 2006—; vol. Dem. Party, San Luis Obispo; bd. dir. City of Wichita Commn. on Status of Women, 1988—91. Mem.: AARP, NOW (founder, 1st pres. and v.p. program chmn. Wichita chpt. 1969—93, asst. state coord. polit. action com. Wichita chpt. 1993—95, at-large state bd. Joplin chpt. 1994—95, 1997—98, 1999—2000, at-large state mem. 2001—04, mem. Grover Beach chpt. 2005—, del. nat. convention 2006), LWV (v.p. issues study Joplin area league 1998—2000, Grover Beach league 2001—06, off board dir. 2002—03, bd. dir. 2003—04), AAUW (bd. dir. edn., equity, women's issues Joplin br. 1999—2000, mem. Grover Beach br. 2001—, pres. Grover Beach br. 2002—04, mem. state pub. policy com. 2003—04, br. pub. policy chair 2004—05, v.p. membership 2004—), Alliance Ret. Persons, Dem. Women United, Century Club. Avocations: water-skiing, boating, travel.

MORGAN, MARY LOUISE FITZSIMMONS, fund raising executive, lobbyist; b. NYC, July 22, 1946; d. Robert John and Mary Louise (Gordon) Fitzsimmons; m. David William Morgan, Aug. 7, 1971; children: Mallory Siobhan, David William. BA, Marquette U., 1964; MA, Cath. U., 1966; postgrad., Columbia U., 2005. Assoc. prof. Monmouth U., West Long Branch, NJ, 1966-69; campaign dir. United Way, NYC, 1969-80; pres. Morgan Communications, NYC, 1980-82; capital campaign dir. YMCA of Greater NY, 1982-85; dir. devel. NY Med. Coll., Valhalla, 1985-88; counsel Challenger Ctr., Va., 1988-89; v.p. Ctr. Molecular Medicine & Immunology, Newark, 1989-92, Garden State Cancer Ctr., Newark, 1989-92; chief devel. and pub. affairs officer Mental Health Assn., White Plains, NY, 1993-95; dir. external affairs St. Vincents Svcs., 1996—, mng. dir., 2006—. Adj. prof. Iona Coll., New Rochelle, NY, 1994-95; dir. Meth Ch. Home for Aged, Riverdale, NY, Casita Maria Inc., NYC, 1975-95; pres., founding dir. Achievement Rewards for Coll. Scientists Inc., 1978-80. Sec. Darien (Conn.) Dem. Town Com., 1984—, vice chmn. Darien nominating com. 1986—. Recipient 50th Anniversary award Casita Maria Inc., N.Y.C., 1984, Iris award Bus. Communicators of Am., 1991, Nat. Depression Awareness Campaign award NMHA, 1994, Am. Graphic Design award, 2002. Mem. Nat. Soc. Fund Raising Execs., Nat. Soc. Hosp. Adminstrn., Spring Lake (NJ) Bath and Tennis Club. Democrat. Roman Catholic. Avocations: golf, gardening, tennis. Office: 66 Boerum Pl Brooklyn NY 11201-5705 Office Phone: 718-422-2255. E-mail: MaryL.Morgan@svs.org.

MORGAN, MICHAEL B., retired music educator; b. Muncie, Ind., Oct. 24, 1948; s. Betty J. Morgan; children: Stacie Lynn Carpenter, Tricia Michelle. BS in Music performance, Excelsior Coll., Albany, N.Y., 1999; MEd, Northwestern State U., La., 2002. Cert. tchr. La., 2002. Sr. instr. Armed Forces Sch. of Music, Norfolk, Va., 1980—85; NATO band leader Supreme Hdqs. Allied Powers Europe, Mons, Belgium, 1985—90. SACS facilitator La. State Bd. of Edn., Baton Rouge, 2002—. Composer: (military march) Major International March, numerous jazz and combo arrangements. 1st sgt. U.S. Army, 1966—2001. Mem.: Dist. V Band Dirs. Assn. (assoc.; pres. 2002—04), La. Band Dirs. Assn. (assoc.), La. Music Educators Assn. (assoc.; asst. state jazz chmn. 2002—03), MENC (assoc.). Achievements include organized first NATO international band for the Supreme Command of Europe; development of rehearsal techniques manual for the Military School of Music.

MORGAN, MICHAEL BREWSTER, publishing executive; b. LA, Dec. 30, 1953; s. Brewster Bowen and Eleanor (Royson) M.; m. D. Jna (Tunte), July 20, 1986. BA, Conn. Coll., 1975. Coll. sales rep. Addison Wesley Pub. Co., Chapel Hill, NC, 1977—81, sponsoring editor Reading, Mass., 1981—84; CEO Morgan Kaufmann Pubs., San Francisco, 1984—2002, Morgan and Claypool Pubs., San Rafael, Calif., 2002—. Mem. Am. Assn. Artificial Intelligence, Assn. Computing Machinery. Office: Morgan and Claypool Pubs 40 Oak View Dr San Rafael CA 94903 Business E-Mail: morgan@morganclaypool.com.

MORGAN, MICHAEL LYNN, music educator, foundation director; b. Birmingham, Ala., July 7, 1955; s. Willie L. and Katie M. Morgan; m. Ann D. Morgan. BS in Music Edn., Hampton U., Va., 1977. Founder / dir. African Am. Music Found., San Diego, 2002—; music tchr. Warren-Walker Mid. Sch., San Diego, 2003—. Singer various symphonies, orchs., Calif., 1989—. Composer: African Am. spirituals. Ex-officio bd. mem. Spreckles Organ Soc., San Diego, 1989—92. Mem.: Music Educators Nat. Conf. Office Phone: 858-846-0361. E-mail: aamuf@sbcglobal.net.

MORGAN, OWAIN DAVID, investment company executive; b. Bristol, Gloucestershire, England, Jan. 4, 1971; s. David Morgan and Helen Frances Bates. MA in Physics with honors, St. John's Coll. Oxford U., Eng., 1992. Pvt. pilot cert. Head trading rsch. JP Morgan, London, 1994—98, head core European strategy rsch., 1996—98, emerging markets proprietary trader, 1998—99, proprietary credit investment mgr. N.Y.C., 1999—2002; dir. risk mgmt. The Rohatyn Group, 2002—. Editor rsch. Global Markets Outlook and Strategy. Editor. Mem.: Global Assn. Risk Mgmt. Professionals. Office Phone: 212-984-2933. E-mail: owain.morgan@rohatyngroup.com.

MORGAN, PATRICIA, financial consultant, former Republican party chairman; Chairwoman Rep. Party, East Providence, RI Rep. State Ctrl. Com., West Warwick, 2001—03; fin. cons. Smith Barney, Providence, 2003.

MORGAN, PETER MONROE, religious organization administrator, minister; b. N.Y.C., Mar. 16, 1939; s. Fonso Monroe Morgan and Mildred Estelle Manley; m. Lynne Rollins, Aug. 26, 1961. AB, Bethany Coll., W.Va., 1961,

HHD (hon.), 1996; MDiv, Lexington Theol. Sem., Ky., 1964. Ordained Christian Ch. in Ohio, 1964. Assoc./interim min. Belmont Christian Ch., Roanoke, Va., 1964—65; pastor Marion (Iowa) Christian Ch., 1965—75; program dir. Divsn. of Homeland Ministries, Indpls., 1975—95; pres. Disciples of Christ Hist. Soc., Nashville, 1995—2004; historian in residence Nat. City Christian Ch., Washington, 2004—. Founder Order of Andrew, Linn Haven, Inc.; Oreon E. Scott lectr. Bethany Coll., W.Va., 1982; Roy Griggs lectr. First Christian Ch., Tulsa, Okla., 2001; guest faculty in liturgy Lexington Theol. Sem., 1990; Forrest H. Kirkpatrick lectr. Disciples of Christ Hist. Soc. presented at Bethany Coll., 1992; Founders Day spkr. Bethany Coll., 1996; Peter Ainslie lectr. Coun. on Christian Unity presented in Wash., DC, 2004; interim sr. pastor Nat. City Christian Ch., Washington, 2005. Author: Disciples Eldership/A Quest for Identity and Ministry, 1983, rev. edit., 2003, Story Weaving/Using Stories to Transform Your Congregation, 1986, Leaders for Such a Time as This, 1990; author: (with Hilda E. Koontz) Miracles in the Cathedral: A History of the National City Christian Church, 2005; contbr.: hymnbook Chalice Hymnal, 1995, Chalice Hymnal/Worship Leader's Companion, 1998, The Tennessee Encyclopedia of History and Culture, 1998, Walter Scott, A Nineteenth Century Evangelical, 1999, The Stone Campbell Encyclopedia, 2004; editor: Disciples Family Album, 1990, One Diaconate, 1977, Becoming a Guest of the Holy, 1978; prodr.: (audio tape) Eldership Voices, 1984 (DeRose Hinkhouse award, 1984), (video tape series (four) Leading the People of Word and Table, 1990; prodr., writer (video tape) Disciples at Worship and Prayer, 1988. Named to Christian Unity Honor Roll, Restoration Forum, Joplin, Mo., 2004; recipient spl. recognition as founder of Linn Haven, Inc., Marion Christian Ch., 1977, spl. award as founder of Order of Andrew, Divsn. of Homeland Ministries, Indpls., 1999. Mem.: N.Am. Acad. Liturgy (assoc.), Disciples of Christ Hist. Soc. (life). Disciples Of Christ. Avocations: travel, reading. Office Phone: 202-232-0323. Personal E-mail: morganpm@aol.com.

MORGAN, RAYMOND F., plastic surgeon; b. Pitts., Apr. 24, 1948; s. Edwin J. and Alberta (Hirt) M.; m. Sue Ann; children: Ryan Frederic, Alexander Evan, Elizabeth Anne. BS, U. Pitts., 1969, MEd, DMD, U. Pitts., 1972; MD, W.Va. U., 1976. Diplomate Am. Bd. Plastic Surgery, Am. Bd. Hand Surgery. Intern Johns Hopkins U. Hosp., Balt., 1976-77, resident surgery, 1977-80, resident plastic surgery, 1980-82; resident hand surgery Union Meml. Hosp., Balt.; staff U. Va. Health Scis. Ctr., Charlottesville, M.T. Edgerton prof., chmn. dept. plastic surgery, 1988—. Mem. ACS, Soc. Univ. Surgeons, So. Surg. Assn., Am. Soc. for Surgery of the Hand, Am. Assn. Plastic Surgeons. Office: U of Va Dept Of Plastic Surgery Charlottesville VA 22908-0001

MORGAN, RAYMOND FRANKLIN, education educator; b. Crisfield, Md., Dec. 19, 1943; s. Raymond Franklin and Anna Marie (Evans) M.; m. Susan Morgan, July 1, 1978; children: Jonathan, Christopher. BA, Randoph-Macon Coll., 1966; MEd, U. Va., 1970, EdD, 1974. Tchr. English and reading Chesterfield Pub. Schs.; English tchr. York Acad. and Miller Sch. of Albemarle; asst./assoc. prof. adult grad. program dir. in reading, then prof. edn. Old Dominion U., Norfolk, Va., 1974—. Presenter, spkr., cons. in field. Co-author: Reading for Success, 1996, Reading to Learn in the Content Areas, 6th edit., 2006, others; co-author: The Psychology of Human Development, 2d edit., 1985, 3rd edit., 1993, Critical Reading-Thinking Skills for the College Student, 1985, 2d edit., 1986; mem. editl. bd. Reading in Va., Reading Improvement; contbr. over 60 articles to profl. jours Recipient Tonelson award Darden Coll. Edn. Mem.: Nat. Soc. for the Study of Edn., Coll. Reading Assn., Assn. Lit. Scholars Critics, Internat. Reading Assn., Phi Kappa Phi. Avocation: golf. Home: 5298 W Valleyside Ct Virginia Beach VA 23464-2606 Office Phone: 757-683-4181. Personal E-mail: rmorgvbva@aol.com. Business E-Mail: rmorgan@odu.edu.

MORGAN, RAYMOND VICTOR, JR., mathematics professor; b. Brownwood, Tex., May 10, 1942; s. Raymond Victor and Lovey Lucile (Tate) M.; m. Mary Jane Folks, Aug. 13, 1967; children: Jason Wesley (dec.), Jeremy Victor. BA, Howard Payne U., 1965; MA, Vanderbilt U., 1966; PhD, U. Mo., 1969. Asst. prof. So. Meth. U., Dallas, 1969-75; assoc. prof. Sul Ross State U., Alpine, Tex., 1975-82, math. dept. chmn., 1976-85, prof., 1982—, dean of scis., 1979-86, exec. asst. pres., 1985-90, pres., 1990—. Bd. dirs. Tex. Internat. Edn. Consortium. Author textbook: Agricultural Mathematics, 1978; author articles. Bd. dirs. Texas Rural Cmtys., 1998—, chair, 2003—04; Marfa Pub. Radio, 2005-; founder regional commr. Alpine Soccer League, 1984; v.p. coach Alpine Baseball League, 1983; pres. Alpine PTA, 1982-83; founder, pres. So. Meth. U. Faculty Club, 1973-75; mem. exec. com. Tex. Assn. Coll. and Univ. Student Pers. Adminstrs., 1990-92; mem. commn. on colls. class of 2003 So. Assn. Colls. and Schs. NSF grantee, 1979. Mem. Am. Assn. Higher Edn., Tex. Assn. Coll. Tchrs. (chpt. v.p. 1978-79), Math. Assn. Am. (chmn. Tex. sect. 1985-86), Chihuahuan Desert Rsch. Inst. (bd. dirs.), Lions Club (pres. 1979-80, Lion of Yr. 1980, 83), Alpine Country Club. Republican. Mem. Ch. Of Christ. Avocations: motocycling, golf, shooting. Home: PO Box 1341 Alpine TX 79831-1341 Office: Sul Ross State U E Highway 90 PO Box C114 Alpine TX 79831-0114 Office Phone: 432-837-8032. Business E-Mail: rvmorgan@sulross.edu.

MORGAN, RICHARD J., dean, law educator; JD, UCLA, 1971. Bar: Calif. Assoc., ptnr. Krueger & Marsh, L.A., 1972-80; dean, prof. U. Wyo. Coll. Law, 1987-89; assoc. dean Ariz. State U. Coll. Law, Tempe, 1983-87, dean, prof., 1990-97; dean, prof. William S. Boyd Sch. Law U. Nev., Las Vegas, 1997—. Office: U Nev William S Boyd Sch Law 4505 S Maryland Pkwy Las Vegas NV 89154-9900 Office Phone: 702-895-3671. E-mail: morgan@ccmail.nevada.edu.*

MORGAN, ROBERT, writer, poet, educator; b. Hendersonville, NC, 1944; BA, U.N.C., 1965; MFA, U.N.C., Greensboro, 1968; LittD (hon.), U. N.C., Chapel Hill, 2006. Tchg. asst. U.N.C., Greensboro, 1967—68; instr. Salem Coll. Winston Salem, NC, 1968—69, lectr. Cornell U., Ithaca, NY, 1971—73, asst. prof., 1973—78, assoc. prof., 1978—84, prof. English, 1984—, Kappa Alpha prof. English, 1992—. Author: (poetry) Zirconia Poems, 1969, The Voice in the Crosshairs, 1971, Red Owl, 1972, Land Diving, 1976, Trunk and Thicket, 1978, Groundwork, 1979, Bronze Age, 1981, At the Edge of the Orchard Country, 1987, Sigodlin, 1990, Green River: New and Selected Poems, 1991, Topsoil Road, 2000, The Strange Attractor: New and Selected Poems, 2004, (novels) The Blue Valleys, 1989, The Mountains Won't Remember Us, 1992, The Hinterlands, 1994, The Truest Pleasure, 1995, Gap Creek, 1999 (So. Book award), This Rock, 2001, Brave Enemies: A Novel of the American Revolution, 2003, (essays) Good Measure, 1993. Recipient N.C. award for lit., James G. Hanes Poetry award, Jacaranda Rev. Fiction prize, Enniu Tictjcus prize, 1979, O. Henry award, 1997; fellow, Nat. Endowment for the Arts, 1968, 1974, 1981, 1987, Guggenheim Found., 1988—89; Bellagio fellow, Rockefeller Found. Mem.: Fellowship of So. Writers. Office: Goldwin Smith Hall Dept English Cornell U Ithaca NY 14853 also: c/o Algonquin Books PO Box 2225 Chapel Hill NC 27515-2225 Office Phone: 607-255-3503. Business E-Mail: rrm4@cornell.edu.

MORGAN, ROBERT ARTHUR, accountant; b. Decatur, Ill., Oct. 23, 1918; s. Robert Howard and Katherine (Massey) M.; m. Julia Ann Franklin, June 28, 1941; children: Robert A., Susan Ruth. BS, U. Ill., 1941. Acct. Pure Oil Co., 1941, Caterpillar Tractor Co.: Peoria, Ill., 1945-56, controller, 1956-78; mem. Fin. Acct. Standards Bd., Stamford, Conn., 1978-82; cons. Morton, Ill., 1982—. Contbr. articles to acctg. periodicals. Past mem. fin. acctg. standards adv. coun. Fin. Acctg. Found.; pres. bd. edn. Morton Twp. High Sch., 1960-61. Civilian auditor AUS, 1942-44. Mem. Nat. Assn. Accts. (nat. dir., nat. v.p. 1965-66, chmn. mng. practices 1974-75), Machinery and Allied Products Inst. (fin. coun. II 1956-78), Fin. Execs. Inst. (mem. com. corp. reporting 1977-78), Internat. Fedn. Accts. (chmn. com. fin. and mgmt. acctg. 1983).

MORGAN, ROBERT MARION, educational research educator; b. Ponca City, Okla., Feb. 5, 1930; s. Perry Harrison and Velma Beatrice (Stowe) M.; m. Constance Louise Claus, Jan. 3, 1963; children— Stephen, Melayne. BS, Okla. State U., 1955, MS, 1956; PhD, Ohio State U., 1958; LLD, Dongah U.,

Pusan, Korea. Asst. prof. U. N.M., 1958-62; pres. Gen. Programmed Tchg. Corp., Palo Alto, Calif., 1961-64; v.p. Ranchers Corp., Albuquerque, 1962-64; dir. ednl. systems Litton Industries, College Park, Md., 1964-66; dep. dir. divsn. vocational rsch. U.S. Office Edn., Washington, 1966-68; prof.. head dept. ednl. rsch. Fla. State U., Tallahassee, 1968-74; dir. Center for Ednl. Tech., 1968-75, Learning Systems Inst., 1975—2003, prof. emeritus, 2003. Lectr. Catholic U. Am., 1966-68, Seoul (Korea) Nat. U., 1970-71; cons. AID, Republic of Brazil, Korea, Italian Air Force, Navy Dept., U.S. Naval Acad.; Chmn. Fla. R & D Council, 1969—; sch. bd. U. Sch., Tallahassee, 1969-74. Author: Programmed Instruction-A Concept of Learning, 1963, An Educational Systems Analysis for the Republic of Korea, 1970; contbr. articles to profl. jours. Bd. dirs. U.S. Coalition for Edn. for All, 1992—; trustee Aerospace Ednl. Found. Found. With AUS, 1949-52. Fellow Royal Soc. Arts; mem. Am. Ednl. Research Assn., Am. Psychol. Assn., Nat. Soc. for Programmed Instrn., Am. Mgmt. Assn., Rotary, Sigma Xi. Republican. Presbyterian. Office: Fla State Univ C4605 University Ctr Tallahassee FL 32306 Home: 144 Belevalley Ln Columbia SC 29223 Office Phone: 850-644-2570. Business E-Mail: rmorgan@lsi.fsu.edu. E-mail: rmorgan32@sc.rr.com.

**MORGAN, ROBERTA DIANE,** music educator; b. Jeffersonville, Ind., Aug. 2, 1965; d. Beryl and Betty Lou Hensley; m. Mark Earl Morgan, July 8, 1989; children: Curtis Earl, Kyle Lee, Courtney Diane, Clay Everett. MusB in Edn., U. Louisville, 1987; MS in Elem. Ed, Ind. U., New Albany, 1991. Music tchr. Christ the King Sch., Louisville, 1987—88, Louisville Deaf Oral Sch., 1987—89, Clarksville Cmty. Sch. Corp., Ind., 1989—92; choir dir., music tchr.; theater tchr. Parkview Mid. Sch., Jeffersonville, Ind., 1992—. Festival coord. Clark County Jr. Choral Festival, Jeffersonville, Ind., 2001—; state coord. Ind. Music Educators Assn., Muncie, 2004—. Mem. Right to Life of So. Ind., Jeffersonville, 2000—06. Mem.: Ind. Music Educators Assn. (corr.). Home: 20916 Charlestown-Bethlehem Rd Charlestown IN 47111 Office: Parkview Mid Sch 1600 Brigman Ave Jeffersonville IN 47130 Office Phone: 812-288-4844. Office Fax: 812-288-2849. Personal E-mail: mnrmorgan@insightbb.com. Business E-Mail: rmorgan@gcs.k12.in.us.

**MORGAN, ROBIN EVONNE,** poet, writer, journalist, editor; b. Lake Worth, Fla., Jan. 29, 1941; 1 child, Blake Ariel. Grad. with honors, The Wetter Sch., 1956; student, pvt. tutors, 1956-59, Columbia U.; DHL (hon.), U. Conn., 1992. Free-lance book editor, 1960-69; editor Grove Press, 1967-70; editor, columnist World column Ms. Mag., NYC, 1974-87, editor in chief, 1989-93, cons. editor, 1993—, columnist, 2003—04, global editor, 2004—. Vis. chair and guest prof. women's studies New Coll., Sarasota, Fla., 1973; disting. vis. scholar, lectr. Ctr. Critical Analysis of Contemporary Culture, Rutgers U., 1987, U. Canterbury, Christchurch, New Zealand, 1989, U. Denver Grad. Sch. Internat. Affairs, 1996-97; invited spl. mem. UN Com. UN Conv. to End All Forms Discrimination Against Women, Sao Paulo and Brasilia, Brazil, 1987; adv. bd. ISIS (internat. network women's internat. cross-cultural exch.); spl. advisor gen. assembly conf. on Gender UN Internat. Sch., 1985-86; free-lance journalist, lectr. cons., editor, 1969—; presenter, spkr. in field Author, compiler, editor: Sisterhood Is Powerful: An Anthology of Writings from the Women's Liberation Movement, 1970, Swedish edit., 1972, Sisterhood Is Global: The International Women's Movement Anthology, 1984, U.K. edit., 1985, Spanish edit., 1994, Feminist Press edit., 1996, Sisterhood Is Forever:The Women's Anthology for A New Millennium, 2003; author: (nonfiction) Going Too Far: The Personal Chronicle of a Feminist, 1978, German edit., 1978, The Anatomy of Freedom: Feminism, Physics and Global Politics, 1982, 2d edit., 1994, fgn. edits. UK, 1984, Germany, 1985, Argentina, 1986, Brazil, 1992, The Demon Lover: On the Sexuality of Terrorism, 1989, UK edit., 1989, Japanese edit., 1992, Italian edit., 1998, rev. US edit., 2002, The Word of a Woman: Feminist Dispatches 1968-91, 1992, 2d edit., 1994, UK edit., 1992, Chinese edit., 1996, A Woman's Creed, English, Arabic, French, Italian, Sanskrit, Hindi, Russian, Spanish, Portuguese, Chinese and Persian edits., 1995, Saturday's Child: A Memoir, 2000, Fighting Words, 2006, (fiction) Dry Your Smile: A Novel, 1987, UK edit., 1988, The Mer-Child: A New Legend, 1991, German edit., 1995, Korean edit., 2000, The Burning Time, 2006, (poetry) Monster: Poems, 1972, Lady of the Beasts: Poems, 1976, Death Benefits: Poems, 1981, Depth Perception: New Poems and a Masque, 1982, Upstairs in the Garden: Selected and New Poems, 1968-88, 1990, A Hot January: Poems 1996-1999, 1999, (plays) In Another Country, 1960, The Duel, 1979; editor: The New Woman: Anthology, 1969; author numerous poems; contbr. articles to proff. jours Mem. 1st women's liberation caucus CORE, 1965, Student Nonviolent Coordinating Com., 1966; organizer 1st feminist demonstration against Miss Am. Pageant, 1968; founder, pres. Sisterhood is Powerful Fund, 1970, NY Women's Law Ctr., 1970; founder NY Women's Ctr., 1969; co-founder, bd. dirs. Feminist Women's Health Network, Nat. Battered Women's Refuge Network, Nat. Network Rape Crisis Ctr.; bd. dirs. Women's Fgn. Policy Coun.; adv. trustee Nat. Women's Inst. for Freedom of Press; founding mem. Nat. Mus. Women in Arts; founder Sisterhood is Global Inst., 1984, officer, 1989-97, chair adv. bd., 1997-2004, pres., 2004—; co-founder Nat. Women's Media Ctr., 2005, Womens Radio Network, 2006; co-organizer, U.S. mem. ofcl. visit Coalition of Philippines Women's Movement, 1988; chair NY state com. Hands Across Am. Com. for Justice and Empowerment, 1988; adv. bd. Global Fund for Women, Equality Now Recipient Front Page award for disting. journalism, Wonder Woman award for internat. peace and understanding, 1982, Feminist of Yr. award Fund for Feminist Majority, 1990; Human Rights Activism Award from Equality NOW, 2002, Feminist Press award, 2003; writer-in-residence grantee Yaddo, 1980; grantee Nat. Endowment for Arts, 1979-80, Ford Found., 1982-84 Mem. Nat. Mus. Women in Arts, Feminist Writers' Guild, Media Women, N.Am. Feminist Coalition, Pan Arab Feminist Solidarity Assn. (hon.), Israeli Feminists Against Occupation (hon.). Office: c/o Edite Kroll Literary Agency 20 Cross St Saco ME 04072

**MORGAN, RONALD BRIAN,** retired aerospace engineer, advocate, writer, lecturer; b. Jamaica, N.Y., Nov. 12, 1935; s. Raymond Edward and Gladys Irene Morgan; m. Eileen Marie Crowley, Dec. 19, 1959 (dec.); children: Glen, Genevieve, Mary, Mark, Brian. EE, Manhattan Coll., Bronx, N.Y., 1955. Design engr. Douglas Aircraft Co., Santa Monica, Calif., 1955-58; lead engr. and group leader McDonnell Douglas Corp., Kennedy Space Ctr., Fla., 1968—75; supr. Planning Rsch. Corp., Cocoa Beach, 1975—83; sec.-treas. Exec-Invest, Inc., 1979—83; prin. engr. McDonnell Douglas Corp., Merritt Island, 1983—91; author and lectr. self-employed, Cocoa Beach, 1998—2001; owner and pres. Ronald B. Morgan Publ., Merritt Island, 2001—; founder, pres. Am. Millennium Found., Inc., 2004—. Bd. dirs. McDonnell Douglas Mgmt. Assn., Kennedy Space Ctr., 1969—74; co-founder and 2nd pres. PRC Mgmt. Assoc., Cocoa Beach, Fla., 1975—82; co-founder and by-laws chmn. Profl. Businessmen's Assn., 1970—72; bd. mem. Brevard County Bicentennial Com., 1973—76. Author: The Am. Spirit in the New Millenium, 2001, (play) No Time for Planners, 1970—72. Season pres. Fla. Silver-Haired Legislature, Merritt Island, Fla., 2001—, CEO, 2004; chmn. Brevard County Pub. Guardianship Funding Task Force, 2004—05; bd. dirs. commn. on aging Brevard County, 2005—; dept. elder affairs adv. coun. Sate of Fla., 2005—; bd. dirs. Joe Realino Meml. Fund, Cocoa Beach, Fla., 2001—; Sr. Resource Alliance Advocacy Coun., 2000—, chmn., 2005; bd. dirs. Brevard County TRIAD, Inc., 2005; chmn. bd. dirs. Found. Indigent Guardianship, Inc., 2005—; adv. coun. Dept. Elder Affairs, Fla., 2005—. Recipient Apollo Program Honoree, NASA, 1969, Space Shuttle Return to Flight Group Achievement award, NASA, Kenedy Space Ctr., 1989, Congressional Record citation, 2001. Mem.: AARP Avocacy Team (Fla. coord. 2002—03), Brevard Tomorrow/Leadership Brevard (mem. govt. working group 2000—04). Roman Catholic. Achievements include invention of electrical "T" connector; design of first aircraft emergency lighting system used on commercial aircraft; first series of hand-held elec./electronic test equipment for commercial aircraft; first integrated logistics system for all NASA Kennedy Space Ctr. facilities, systems and equipment; integrated logistics system for the mirror fusion project at the Lawrence Livermore Labs; first integrated data system used for configuration mgmt. of Spacelab payloads flown on the Space Shuttle at Kennedy Space Ctr. Avocations: historical research, law research, legislative bills, senior issues. Office Phone: 321-720-3220.

**MORGAN, RUTH PROUSE,** academic administrator, educator; b. Berkeley, Calif., Mar. 30, 1934; d. Ervin Joseph and Thelma Ruth (Prcesang) Prouse; m. Vernon Edward Morgan, June 3, 1956; children: Glenn Edward, Renée Ruth. BA summa cum laude, U. Tex., 1956; MA, La. State U., 1961, PhD, 1966. Asst. prof. Ark. Polytech. Inst., 1966-70; asst. prof. So. Meth. U., Dallas, 1966-70, assoc. prof., 1970-74, prof., 1974-95; prof. emeritus, 1995—; asst. provost So. Meth. U., Dallas, 1978-82, assoc. provost, 1982—86, provost ad interim, 1986-87, provost, 1987-93, provost emerita, 1993—; v.p. Chem. Abatement Tech., Inc., 1995—. Tex. state polit. analyst ABC, N.Y.C., 1972-84. Author: The President and Civil Rights, 1970, Governance By Decree: The Impact of the Voting Rights Act in Dallas, 2004; mem. editl. bd. Jour. of Politics, 1975-82, Presdl. Studies Quar., 1980-2006; contbr. articles to profl. jours. Mem. Internat. Women's Forum, 1987—, City of Dallas Redistricting Commn., 2001, Greater Dallas Planning Coun, 1997—; mem. adv. bd. Maguire Ctr. for Ethics and Pub. Responsibility; trustee Hockaday Sch., 1988-94, The Kilby Awards Found., 1993-95; bd. dirs. United Way, Met. Dallas, 1993-99; adv. com. U.S. Army Command and Gen. Staff. Coll., 1994-97; founder Archives of Women of the Southwest, 1992, chmn. adv. com. 1995-99; mem. Dallas Women's Found.; adv. bd. Cary M. Maguire Ctr. for Ethics and Pub. Responsibilty, 1998—, The Women's Mus., Dallas, 1999— Mem. Am. Polit. Sci. Assn., So. Polit. Sci. Assn. (mem. exec. coun. 1979-84), Southwestern Polit. Sci. Assn. (pres. 1982-83, mem. exec. coun. 1981-84), The Dallas Assembly, The Dallas Forum of Internat. Women's Forum (pres. 1996-97), Charter 100 Club (pres. 1991-92), Ctr. for the Study of the Presidency, The Women's Mus (charter), Dallas Summit Club (pres. 1992-93), Phi Beta Kappa, Pi Sigma Alpha, Phi Kappa Phi, Theta Sigma Phi. Avocations: photography, travel. Office Phone: 214-691-5944. Personal E-mail: morgan_ruth@yahoo.com.

**MORGAN, SAMUEL P(OPE),** physicist, applied mathematician; b. San Diego, July 14, 1923; s. Samuel Pope and Beatrice Marie (Summers) M.; m. Mary Caroline Annin, Jan. 23, 1948; children: Caroline Gail, Lesley Anne, Alison Lee, Diane Elizabeth. BA, Calif. Inst. Tech., 1943, MS, 1944, PhD in Physics, 1947. Mem. tech. staff AT&T Bell Labs., Murray Hill, NJ, 1947-59, head dept. math. physics, 1959-67, dir. computing tech., 1969-70, dir. computing sci. research center, 1967-82, disting. mem. tech. staff, 1982-95, Lucent Tech./Bell Labs., 1996-98, ret., 1998. Research, publs. on electromagnetic theory, applied math., queueing theory; patentee in field. Fellow IEEE (life); mem. AAAS, Am. Phys. Soc., Sigma Xi. Home: 4113 Fellowship Rd Basking Ridge NJ 07920-3906

**MORGAN, STEPHEN CHARLES,** academic administrator; b. Upland, Calif., June 2, 1947; s. Thomas Andrew and Ruth Elizabeth (Miller) M.; m. Ann Marie McMurray, Sept. 6, 1969; 1 child, Kesley Suzanne. BA, U. La Verne, 1968; MS, U. So. Calif., 1971; EdD, U. No. Colo., 1979. Devel. officer U. La Verne, Calif., 1968-71, asst. to pres. Calif., 1971-73, dir. devel. Calif., 1973-75, v.p. devel. Calif., 1975-76, pres. Calif., 1985—; dir. devel. U. So. Calif., L.A., 1976-79; exec. dir. Ind. Colls. No. Calif., San Francisco, 1979-85. Dir. Ind. Colls. So. Calif., L.A., 1985—. Bd. dirs. Mt. Baldy United Way, Ontario, Calif., 1988-98, McKinley Children's Ctr., San Dimas, Calif., 1989-99, LeRoy Haynes Ctr. for Family and Children's Svcs., 2000—; chair nat. com. on higher edn. Ch. of Brethren, Elgin, Ill., 1988-90; dir. Pomona Valley Hosp. Med. Ctr., 1992-98, 99—, Inter Valley Health Plan, 1992-97, PFF Bank and Trust, 2001—. Mem. Assn. Ind. Calif. Colls. and Univs. (exec. com. 1989—, vice-chmn. 1996-2000, chmn. 2000-2002), L.A. County Fair Assn. (bd. dirs., chmn. 2002—), Western Coll. Assn. (exec. com. 1992-98, pres. 1996-98), Western Assn. Schs. and Colls. (sr. accrediting commn. 1996-2001), Pi Gamma Mu. Avocations: orchid culture, fly fishing. Home: 2518 N Mountain Ave Claremont CA 91711-1579 Office: U LaVerne Grad Pres 1950 3rd St La Verne CA 91750-4401 E-mail: morgans@ulv.edu.

**MORGAN, TED (LE COMTE SANCHE ARMAND GABRIEL DE GRAMONT),** writer; b. Geneva, Mar. 30, 1932; naturalized, US, 1977; s. Gabriel Antoine Armand Comte de Gramont. Student, Yale Univ. Reporter NY Herald Tribune. Author: (as Sanche de Gramont) The Secret War: The Story of International Espionage Since 1945, 1962, The French: Portrait of a People, 1969, Epitaph for Kings, 1969, The Strong Brown God: The Story of the Niger River, 1977, (as Ted Morgan) On Becoming American, 1978, Maugham, 1980 (finalist, Nat. Book award, 1982), Churchill: A Young Man in a Hurry, 1982, FDR: A Biography, 1985 (finalist, Pulitzer prize, 1982), Literary Outlaw: The Life and Times of William S. Burroughs, 1990, An Uncertain Hour: The French, the Germans, the Jews, the Barbie Trial, and the City of Lyon, 1940-1945, 1989, Wilderness at Dawn, 1944, Shovel of Stars, 1996, A Covert Life: Jay Lovestone: Communist, Anti-Communist and Spymaster, 1999, Reds: McCarthyism in Twentieth Century America, 2003, (memoir) My Battle of Algiers, 2006. 2nd lt. French Army. Recipient (as Sanche de Gramont) Pulitzer prize for local reporting, 1961. Mailing: Author Mail HarperCollins Pub 10 East 53rd St New York NY 10022

**MORGAN, THOMAS I.,** manufacturing executive; With Genuine Parts Co., 1975—97; CEO U.S. Office Products Co., Washington, 1997—99, Value America, 1999, enfoTrust Networks, 2000—01; pres., COO Hughes Supply Inc., Orlando, Fla., 2001—03; pres., CEO, 2003—. Office: Hughes Supply Inc Corp Office One Hughes Way Orlando FL 32805*

**MORGAN, THOMAS ROWLAND,** retired marine corps officer; b. Allentown, Pa., Jan. 6, 1930; s. Harry Campbell and Olwen (Pierce) M.; m. Barbara A. Croze, June 29, 1957; children— Lynn A., Susan E., Beth E. BA in History, Colgate U., 1952; student, Marine Corps Command and Staff Coll., 1965-66; MA in Edn., U. Va., 1973. Commd. 2d lt. USMC, 1952, advanced through grades to gen., 1986; naval aviator Naval Air Sta., Pensacola, Fla., 1953-54; asst. maintenance officer 3d Marine Aircraft Wing, El Toro, Calif., 1954-55; personnel officer Marine Aircraft Group Western Pacific, 1954-55; aide to comdg. gen. 1st Marine Aircraft Wing, Pacific, 1955; asst. ops. officer Marine Aircraft Group, Kaneohe Bay, Hawaii, 1956-57; squadron pilot, ground tng. officer Marine Attack Squadron, Hawaii, 1957-59; flight instr. Naval Air Sta., Olathe, Kans., 1959; personnel officer, aircraft maintenance officer Marine Fighter Squadron, Beaufort, SC, 1959-61; exec. officer Hdqrs. and Maintenance Squadron, Atsugi, Japan, 1961-62; fleet liaison officer Marine Corps Air Sta., Yuma, Ariz., 1962-65; comdr. Marine Fighter Attack Squadron, Beaufort, 1966-67; group ops. officer, officer-in-charge DaNang DASC, Vietnam, 1968-69; exec. officer Marine Corps Air Sta., Quantico, Va., 1969-71; exec. officer Naval ROTC unit U. Va., 1971-73; chief war plans br. J-5 U.S. European Command Hdqrs., Stuttgart, Fed. Republic Germany, 1973-76; asst. to dep. chief of staff requirements and programs Hdqrs. U.S. Marine Corps, Washington, 1976-77; asst. div. comdr. 3d Marine Div., Okinawa, Japan, 1977-78; asst. chief of staff C-5 Combined Forces Command, Seoul, 1978-80; dep. comdr. FMF Pacific, Camp Smith, Hawaii, 1980-81; dep. chief of staff for requirements and programs Hdqrs. Marine Corps, Washington, 1981-85; dep. chief staff for plans, policies and ops, acting Chief of Staff, 1985-86, asst. commandant, 1986-88, ret. Decorated D.S.M., Def. Superior Service medal, Legion of Merit, Bronze Star medal, Meritorious Service medal, Air medal; Order of Nat. Security medal, Cheonsu medal (Korea) Mem. Am. Legion Avocations: golf, skiing, water sports. E-mail: tmorgva@cox.net.

**MORGAN, VICTORIA,** performing company executive, choreographer; BFA, U. Utah, 1973, MFA magna cum laude, 1976. Prin. dancer Ballet West, 1969-78. San Francisco Ballet, 1978-87; resident choreographer San Francisco Opera, 1987—97; artistic dir. Cin. Ballet, 1997—. Dancer with lead roles in numerous classical, neoclassical and modern ballets including works by George Balanchine, Forsythe, and Kudelka, lead roles for TV and films, choreographer creating over 40 works for 20 ballet and opera cos. across U.S. including Utah Ballet, Pacific Northwest Ballet, Glimmerglass Opera, N.Y.C. Opera and Cin. Opera; creator, prodr. Ballet CD-ROM, choreography featured in documentary The Creation of O.M.O. Office: Cincinnati Ballet 1555 Central Pkwy Cincinnati OH 45214-2863*

**MORGAN, VIRGINIA MATTISON,** judge; b. 1946; BS, Univ. of Mich., 1968; JD, Univ. of Toledo, 1975. Bar: Mich. 1975, Federal 1975, U.S. Ct. Appeals (6th cir.) 1979. Tchr. Dept. of Interior, Bur. of Indian Affairs, 1968-70, San Diego Unified Schs., 1970-72, Oregon, Ohio, 1972-74; asst. prosecutor Washtenaw County Prosecutor's Office, 1976-79; asst. U.S. atty. Detroit, 1979-85; magistrate judge U.S. Dist. Ct. (Mich. ea. dist.), 6th circuit Detroit, 1985—. Mem. bd. Fed. Jud. Ctr., 1997-2001; mem. jud. conf. U.S. Com. on Long Range Planning, 1993-96. Recipient Spl. Achievement award Dept. of Justice, Disting. Alumni award U. Toledo, 1993. Fellow Mich. State Bar Found.; mem. FBA (chpt. pres. 1996-97), Fed. Magistrate Judges Assn. (pres. 1995-96). Office: US Courthouse 231 W Lafayette Blvd Detroit MI 48226-2700

**MORGAN, WILLIAM BRUCE,** naval architect; b. Fairfield, Iowa, Dec. 20, 1926; s. Orville Burns and Mary Verle (Balderson) M.; m. Mary Maxine Gillam, June 21, 1950; children: Margaret Ann, Ann Elise. BS in Marine Engring., U.S. Mcht. Marine Acad., 1950; MS in Hydraulic Engring., U. Iowa, 1951; DEng in Naval Architecture, U. Calif., 1961. Hydraulic engr. David Taylor Model Basin, Bethesda, Md., 1951-52, naval architect, 1952-58, naval architect supr., 1958-62, head propeller br., 1962-70; head hydromechanics div. David Taylor Naval Ship R&D Ctr. (formerly David Taylor Model Basin), Bethesda, 1970-79, head hydromechanics directorate, 1979—2001; ret. Chmn. exec. com. Am. Towing Tank Conf., 1983-86; mem. exec. com. Internat. Towing Tank Conf., 1984-90. Co-inventor ventilated propeller, supercavitating propeller with air ventilation; contbr. articles to profl. jours. Recipient Navy Disting. Civilian Svc. award USN, 2000, Navy Superior Civilian Svc. award, 1974, Navy Meritorious Svc. award, 1967, Meritorious Exec. award Office of Pres., 1987, William Froude medal Royal Instn. Naval Architects, 1989, Capt. Robert Dexter Conrad award USN, 1993, Gibbs Bros. medal NAS, 1997; named to U. Iowa Disting. Engring. Alumni Acad., 1999. Fellow Soc. Naval Architects and Marine Engrs. (hon. life; exec. com. 1985—, Davidson medal 1986), ASME (chmn. fluids engring. div. 1981-82); mem. NAE, Schiffbautechnische Gesellschaft, Am. Soc. Naval Engrs. (Gold Medal award 1993), Chinese Soc. Naval Architects and Marine Engrs. (hon.), Sigma Xi. Presbyterian. Home: 110 Upton St Rockville MD 20850-1836 Personal E-mail: wbmorgan@erols.com.

**MORGAN, WILLIAM J.,** accounting company executive; b. Bklyn., Jan. 12, 1947; s. William J. and Emma T. (Kraft) M.; m. Patricia A. Maltz, Mar. 23, 1968; children: Michele, Jennifer. BS, St. John's U., 1968. CPA, NY Conn., NJ. Prin. KPMG LLP, Stamford, Conn., audit staff, 1968—72, audit supr., 1972—74, audit mgr. 1974—77, ptnr.-in-charge pvt. bus. adv. svc. N.Y.C., 1977—79, nat. office, ptnr.-in-charge recruiting, 1979—82, ptnr. comml. health care practice Short Hills, NJ, 1982—91, ptnr.-in-charge N.J. audit practice, 1989—91, mng. ptnr. Fairfield/Westchester counties practice, 1991—94, ptnr. in charge met. N.Y. area mfg., retail and distbn. practice, 1993—96, ptnr. in charge global accts., 1996—98, mng. ptnr. Stamford office, 1996—2003, chmn. audit quality coun., mem. audit and risk adv. svcs. leadership team, 2004—06. Mem. Bus. Unit Planning Task Force, 1987—90, compensation com., 1990—91, chmn. profit distbn. com., 1991—95, future direction com., 1991—93, pension task force, 1991—92, chmn. compensation com., 1997—2003, bd. process com., 1997—2002, nominating com., 2002—03; independence disciplinary com. KPMG Americas, 2002—06. Acctg. adv. bd. Grad. Sch. Bus. Fordham U., 1979—82; mem. standardization com. Nat. Retail Mchts. Assn., 1979; trustee Tri County Scholarship Fund, 1984—91; v.p., exec. com., adv. bd. Fairfield coun. Boy Scouts Am., 1993—95; bd. dirs. Stamford Symphony, 1995—99; bd. dirs., chmn. bus. ops. com. heritage affiliate Am. Heart Assn., 1997—2000; chmn. Fairfield County Info. Exch., 1992—94; chmn. bd. SACIA, the Bus. Coun. of Fairfield Co., 2001—03, bd. dirs., 1993—2004, Inroads Fairfield and Westchester County chpt., 1992—95; mem. Bus. Execs. for Nat. Security, 1995—99, Ambs. Roundtable, 1995—99; exec. com. Conn. Policy and Econs. Coun., 1998—2003. Recipient Stamford Good Scout award, 1999, Walter H. Wheeler Disting. Leadership award, 2000, KPMG-Walter E. Hanson Lifetime Achievement award, 2004. Mem. AICPA (small bus. devel. com. 1979-81, acctg. lit. awards com. 1983-86), N.J. Soc. CPA (chmn. acctg. and auditing stds. com. 1988-90, trustee 1990-92, pub. rels. task force, 1987, subcom. health care acctg. 1983-86), N.Y. State CPA (retail acctg. com. 1975-78, com. on edn. in coll. and univs. 1978-82), Nat. Assn. Accts. (dir. manuscripts 1975-77, v.p. N.Y. chpt. 1977-81, pres. N.Y chpt. 1981-82, nat. publs. com. 1982-83, com. acad. rels. 1983-84, nat. dir. 1983-86, Disting. Svc. award 1975), Health Care Fin. Mgmt. Assn. (NJ chpt. chmn. auditing com. 1982-83, legis. task force com. 1985-86, chmn. joint ventures com., 1987-88), Swedish Am. C. of C. (bd. dirs., exec. com. 1995—), Fairmount Country Club (bd. govs., treas. 1987-90), Woodway Country Club, Conn. Golf Club (bd. govs. 2003-06). Roman Catholic. Office: KPMG LLP 3001 Summer St Stamford CT 06905-4317

**MORGAN, WILLIAM JASON,** geophysics educator; b. Savannah, Ga., Oct. 10, 1935; married; 2 children. BS, Ga. Inst. Tech., 1957; PhD in Physics, Princeton U., 1964. Rsch. assoc. Princeton U., 1964-66, from asst. prof. to assoc. prof., 1966-77, prof. geophysics, 1977—. Recipient Japan prize, 1990, co-Recipient James b. Macelwane Young Investigator medal Am. Geophysical Union, 1995, Nat. Medal of Science award, 2002. Mem. NAS, 1982-, Am. Geophys. Union, European Union Geol. Sci. Achievements include research in mantle convection, heat flow, plate tectonics, marine geophysics. Office: Princeton U Dept Geosciences 417 Guyot Hall Princeton NJ 08544-0001 E-mail: wjmorgan@princeton.edu.

**MORGAN, WILLIAM NEWTON,** architect, educator; b. Jacksonville, Fla., Dec. 14, 1930; s. Thomas and Kathleen (Fiske) M.; m. Bernice E. Leimback, July 31, 1954; children: William Newton, Dylan Thomas. AB magna cum laude, Harvard Coll., 1952, MArch Grad. Sch. of Design, 1958. Pres. William Morgan Architects, P.A., Jacksonville, Fla., 1961—. Critic various archtl. schs.; lectr. in field; adj. prof. of art history Jacksonville U., 1995-96, U. North Fla., 1997; Beinecke-Reeves Disting. Prof. Architecture, U. Fla., 1999-99. Prin. works include Fla. State Mus., Jacksonville Police Meml. Bldg., Pyramid Condominium, Ocean City, Md., Fed. Cts. and Offices, Ft. Lauderdale, Fla., Westinghouse World Hdqs., Orlando, Fla., Neiman-Marcus store, Ft. Lauderdale, 1st Union St. Ct. Appeal, Tallahassee, Fla., Conf. Ctr., Tallahassee, U.S. Embassy, Khartoum, Sudan, U.S. Courthouse, Tallahassee; author: Prehistoric Architecture in the Eastern United States, 1980, Prehistoric Architecture in Micronesia, 1988, Ancient Architecture of the Southwest, 1994, Precolumbian Architecture in Eastern North America, 1999. Subject of The Architecture of William Morgan (Paul Spreiregen) 1987, Images Master Architect Series: William Morgan (Robert McCarter), 2002; Fulbright grantee to Italy, 1958-59; grantee Graham Found. Advanced Studies Arts, 1973; Lehman fellow Harvard U., 1957, Wheelwright fellow 1964-65, fellow NEA, 1991; Sam Gibbons Eminent scholar Fla. A&M U. and U. South Fla.; recipient numerous nat. and regional awards for excellence in design. Fellow AIA (past chmn. com. design) AIA Inst. honor for rsch. into the beginnings of archtl. creativity 1998, Fla. 2000 Millenium award honor for design 2000). Office: William Morgan Architects 220 E Forsyth St Jacksonville FL 32202-3328 Office Phone: 904-356-4195. Personal E-mail: wnmorgan@aol.com.

**MORGAN, WILLIAM RICHARD,** mechanical engineer; b. Cambridge, Ohio, Mar. 27, 1922; s. Wilbur Alfred and Treva Beatrice (Minto) M.; m. Marjorie Eleanor Stevens, Feb. 17, 1946; children: Carol M. Morgan Dingleby, William R., Jr. BSME, The Ohio State U., 1944; MSME, Purdue U., 1950, PhD in Mech. Engring., 1951. Registered profl. engr., Ohio. Power plant design engr. Curtiss Wright Corp., Columbus, Ohio, 1944-47; instr., rsch. fellow Purdue U., West Lafayette, Ind., 1947-51; supr. exptl. mech. engring. GE, Cin., 1951-55, mgr. controls analysis, devel. Aircraft Gas Turbine Divsn., 1955-59, mgr. XV5A vertical take-off and landing aircraft program, 1959-65, mgr. acoustic engring. Flight Propulsion Divsn., 1965-69, mgr. quiet engine program Flight Propulsion Divsn., 1969-71; pres. Cin. Rsch. Corp., 1971-73; v.p., COO SDRC Internat., Cin., 1973-79; engring. and mgmt. cons. Cin., 1979—. Contbr. articles to profl. jours. Lt. j.g. USNR, WWII. Westinghouse Rsch. fellow Mem. ASME, Masons, Sigma Xi, Pi Tau

Sigma, Pi Mu Epsilon. Achievements include patents in Humidity Detection and Indicating Instrument, Stall Prevention/Acoustic Tip Treatment, Acoustic Treatment, Inlet Noise Reduction Configuration; research in geometric configuration factors in radiant heat transmission. Home and Office: 312 Ardon Ln Cincinnati OH 45215-4102

MORGANROTH, MAYER, lawyer; b. Detroit, Mar. 20, 1931; s. Maurice Jack Morganroth and Sophie (Reisman) Blum; m. Sheila Rubinstein, Aug. 16, 1958; children: Lauri, Jeffrey, Cherie. JD, Detroit Coll. Law, 1954. Bar: Mich. 1955, US Dist. Ct. Mich. 1955, Ohio 1958, US Dist. Ct. (no. dist.) Ohio 1958, US Dist. Ct. DC 2002, US Ct. Appeals (6th cir.) 1968, US Supreme Ct. 1971, NY 1983, US Dist. Ct. NY 1985, US Tax Ct. 1985, US Ct. Appeals (4th cir.) 1985, US Ct. Claims 1986, US Ct. Appeals (2d cir.) 1986, US Ct. Appeals (fed. cir.), US Ct. Appeals (8th cir.) 1994, US Dist. Ct. Wash. DC, 2002. Sole practice, Detroit, 1955—, NYC, 1983—; ptnr. Morganroth & Morganroth, PLLC, 1989—. Cons. to lending instns.; lectr. on real estate NYU, 1980—, bus. entities and structures Wayne State U., 1981—; trial atty. in fed. and state jurisdictions, nationwide. Served with USN, 1948-50. Mem. ATLA, ABA, FBA, NY State Bar Assn., Southfield Bar Assn., Oakland Bar Assn., Assn. Trial Lawyers Mich., Am. Judicature Soc., US Supreme Ct. Hist. Soc., Nat. Assn. Criminal Def. Attys., West Bloomfield (Mich.) Club, Fairlane Club (Dearborn, Mich.), Knollwood Country Club, Edgewood Athletic Club (pres. 1963-65). Democrat. Jewish. Office: 3000 Town Ctr Ste 1500 Southfield MI 48075-1186 also: 156 W 56th St Ste 1101 New York NY 10019-3800 Office Phone: 248-355-3084. Business E-Mail: mmorganroth@morganrothlaw.com

MORGANS, BOB D., minister; b. Claremore, Okla., June 29, 1956; s. John Henry Morgans and Rhodana Mae Sutherland; m. Barbara Kay Carter, May 8, 1976; adopted children: Tim Isaah, Dalton John children: Bobby Dean, Deana Marie. BS, Tarkio Coll., Mo., 1986. Pastor United Pentecostal Ch., Trenton, Mo., sr. pastor Athens, Ohio, 1998—2005, pastor Liberty, Mo., 2005—. Home missions dir. sect. eight United Pentecostal Ch., Kans. City, Mo., 1991—97. Author: (book) How to Pray with a Child to Receive the Holy Ghost (Best Seller, 2001), How to Pray with an Adult to Receive the Holy Ghost, No Fear, Just Believe, How to Receive Your Miracle, (video) Worldwide Children's Crusades. Coord. for ann. walk Multiple Sclerosis Soc., Trenton, Mo., 1990—94. Mem.: Children's Evangelist Assn. Avocation: travel. Home: 1300 Wellington Way Liberty MO 64068 Personal E-mail: bmorgans@frognet.net.

MORGANTE, JOHN-PAUL, human resources specialist; b. Yonkers, NY, June 26, 1962; s. Enzo and Teresa (DellaToffola) M.; m. Ellen Rothberger, May 26, 1984; children: Camden Anne, Bethany Nicole, Hailee Marie. BA, U. So. Calif., L.A., 1984; MBA, Open U. Bus. Sch., England, 2004. Ordained to ministry Christian Ch., 1987; cert. profl. in human resources; sr. profl. human resources. Adminstrv. dir. MCM Internat., Lomita, Calif., 1984-87; dir. human resources, 1987-91; exec. dir. Champions for Christ, Austin, Tex., 1991-93; pres. Annimar Assocs., Austin, 1991—95; OD and tng. officer Tex. Dept. Health, Austin, 1995-97; mgr. human resources The TFE Group, Augusta, Ga., 1997-99, sr. mgr., 2000; corp. human resources mgr. Morris Comms. Corp., Augusta, Ga., 2000—01, asst. dir. corp. human resources, 2001—03; dir. human resources and adminstrn. Talla-Com Industries, Talla-hassee, 2003—. Contbr. articles to profl. jours. Ctrl. com. Orange County (Calif.) Reps., 1988-89; intern U.S. Rep. Robert Badham, Washington, 1983, campaign worker, 1984; intern Assemblyman Curt Pringle, Garden Grove, Calif., 1988; campaign worker U.S. Senator Chic Hecht, 1982, U.S. Rep. Robert Dornan, 1984, Reagan-Bush, 1984, Tex. State rep. Terry Keel, Austin, 1996, Leadership Austin program Austin C. of C., 1994; solicitation bd. City of Austin, 1996-97; del. Dist. 14 Rep. Conv., Austin, 1999; nat. nominating com. Outstanding Young Ams., 1996-2001; peer moderator Nat. Issues Conv., Phila., 1996; campaign work George W. Bush, 2000; moderator, Mayor's Initiative on Race, Tallahassee, 2003. Recipient Rep. Presdl. Legion of Merit, Tallahasse Cmty. Coll., 2006, Presdl. Commemorative Honor Roll, 1991, Staff Mem. of Yr., 1987; commd. Hon. Texan by Gov. George Bush, 1995. Mem. ASTD, Soc. for Human Resource Mgmt. (Area II bd. dirs. 2002-03), Augusta-Aiken Soc. for Human Resource Mgmt. (sec. 2000, pres. elect, 2001, pres. 2002), Big Bend Soc. Human Resource Mgmt. (exec. bd. 2004, sec. 2005-), Acad. of Mgmt., World at Work, Rotary Club Tallahassee, Sister City Com. Tallahassee. Avocations: golf, travel, contemporary jazz. Office: Talla-Com Industries 1721 W Paul Dirac Dr Tallahassee FL 32310 Business E-Mail: jpmorgante@annimar.com.

MORGENROTH, EARL EUGENE, entrepreneur; b. Sidney, Mont., May 7, 1936; s. Frank and Leona (Ellison) M.; m. Adrienne Smith; children: Dolores Roxanna, David Jonathan, Denise Christine BS, U. Mont., 1961. From salesman to gen. mgr. Sta. KGVO-AM Radio, Missoula, Mont., 1958-65; sales mgr. Stas. KGVO-TV, KTVM-TV and KCFW-TV, Missoula, Butte, Kalispell, Mont., 1965-66, gen. mgr., 1966-68, Sta. KCOY-TV, Santa Maria, Calif., 1968-69; v.p., gen. mgr. Western Broadcasting Co., Missoula, 1966-69, gen. mgr., pres., 1969-81, numerous cos. in Mont., Calif., Idaho, PR, Ga., 1966-84; pres., chmn. Western Broadcasting Co., Missoula, 1981-84, Western Comm., Inc., Reno, 1984-90; prin. Western Investments, Reno, 1984—. Chmn. Western Fin., Inc., Morgenroth Music Ctrs. Inc., Mont. Band Instruments, Inc., E&B Music Inc., Times Square, Inc., Rio Plumas Ranches, LLC; mem. presdl. adv. coun. U. Mont., 1994—, mem. biol. scis. adv. coun., 1999—. Mem. Mont. Bank Bd., Helena; commencement spkr. U. Mont., 1988, mem. pres.' adv. coun., 1992—, mem. biol. scis. adv. coun., 2001—; bd. dirs. U. Mont. Found., 1985-95. With. U.S. Army, 1954-57. Named Boss of Yr. Santa Maria Valley J.C.s, 1968, Alumnus of the Yr., U. Mont. Bus. Sch., 1998. Mem. U. Mont. Century Club (pres.), Missoula C. of C. (pres.), Rocky Mountain Broadcasters Assn. (pres.), Craighead Wildlife-Wildlands Inst. (bd. dirs. 1991-97), Boone and Crockett Club (pres. 2001-02), Grizzly Riders Internat. (bd. dirs., v.p. 1991—, pres. 2005-), Bldg. A Scholastic Heritage (bd. dirs. 1987-97, pres. 2006). Republican. Methodist.

MORGENSEN, JERRY LYNN, construction company executive; b. Lub-bock, Tex., July 9, 1942; s. J. J. and Zelline (Butler) Morgensen; m. Linda Dee Austin, Apr. 17, 1965; children: Angela, Nicole. BS in Civil Engring., Tex. Tech U., 1965. Area engr. E.I. Dupont Co., Orange, Tex., 1965-67, div. engr. La Place, La., 1967-73; project mgr. Hensel Phelps Constrn. Co., Greeley, Colo., 1973-78, area mgr., 1978-80, v.p., 1980-85, pres., CEO, 1985—, chmn. bd. Mem. bd. trustees UNC; Member Constn. Indus. Devel. Coun. CSU; mem. Tex. Tech. Civil Engring. Acad. Office: 420 6th Ave Greeley CO 80631-2332*

MORGENSON, GRETCHEN C., reporter; b. State College, Pa., Jan. 2, 1956; married; 1 child. BA in English and History, Saint Olaf Coll., Northfield, Minn., 1976. Asst. editor to writer, fin. columnist Vogue Mag. 1976—81; stock broker Dean Witter Reynolds, NYC, 1981—84; staff writer Money Mag., 1984—86; editor, investigative bus. writer Forbes Mag., 1986—93, press sec. for Forbes for President campaign, 1995—96, asst. mng. editor, 1996—98; sr. editor Worth Mag., 1993—95; asst. bus. and fin. editor NY Times, NYC, 1998, now Market Watch columnist, Sunday Money and Bus. section. Author: Forbes Great Minds of Business, 1997; co-author: The Woman's Guide to the Stock Market, 1981; author: (with Campbell R. Harvey) The New York Times Dictionary of Money and Investing: The Essential A-to-Z Guide to the Language of the New Market, 2002; co-author: (with Allen R. Myerson (editor), Floyd Norris) The New Rules of Personal Investing: How to Prosper in a Changing Economy, 2001. Recipient Gerald Loeb award, 1998, 2002, Pulitzer Prize for beat reporting, 2002, TJFR Group/MasterCard Internat. Bus. News Luminaries award, 2003, Fin. Journalism prize for lifetime achievement, Women's Econ. Round Table, 2003. Office: NY Times 229 W 43d St New York NY 10036*

MORGENSTEIN, WILLIAM, shoe company executive; b. Bklyn., Jan. 11, 1933; s. Samuel and Jeanne Marie (Mittentag) M.; m. Sylvia Dove, June 8, 1952; children: Lee Brian, David Barry. BS in Fin., U. Ala., 1955. Salesman Greenwald Shoe Co., Birmingham, Ala., 1954-56; sr. buyer Melville Shoe Corp., NYC, 1958-67; pres. Kitty Kelly Shoe Co., NYC, (1967-70; exec. v.p. A.S. Beck Shoes, NYC, 1970-71, Sandia Internat., Englewood Cliffs, NJ,

1971-75; pres., chief exec. officer Marquesa Internat. Corp., Englewood, NJ, 1975-95; sr. acct. mgr. Signature Group divsn. Montgomery Ward, 1995—99; v.p. Advanceme.com Inc., 1999—; sr. v.p., nat. sales dir. Sterling Funding Corp., 2005—. Internat. cons. footwear exporting, 1965—. Served with U.S. Army, 1956-58. Mem. Footwear Distrbs. and Retailers Am. (vice-chmn., bd. dirs., exec. com.), Internat. Footwear Assn. (vice-chmn., exec. com. 1986—, chmn. 1989—, pres.), 210 Assn. (Pres.' Circle 1987), Toastmasters (past pres. Teaneck, NJ chpt.). Republican. Jewish. Avocations: history, golf. Office Phone: 866-486-5638 ext. 161, 866-456-5638 161. Personal E-mail: bmorgens@aol.com. Business E-Mail: bill.morgenstein@sterlingfunding.com.

MORGENSTERN, JOE, film critic; b. NYC, Oct. 3, 1932; s. Mark E. and Mollie (Fisch) M.; m. Rosetta Jacobs, Jan. 21, 1962 (div. Apr. 1981); 1 child, Anna. BA in English magna cum laude, Lehigh U., 1953. Film critic Newsweek mag., NYC, 1965-72; columnist LA Herald Examiner, 1982-87; film critic Wall Street Jour., NYC, 1995—. Co-founder Nat. Soc. Film Critics. Author: World Champion, 1968 (TV scripts) Boy in the Plastic Bubble, Law & Order, 10,000 Black Men Named George. Recipient Pulitzer Prize for criticism, 2005. Mem. Phi Beta Kappa, NY Film Critics Cir., LA Soc. Film Critics. Office: Wall Street Jour PO Box 1946 Santa Monica CA 90406-1946 E-mail: joe.morgenstern@wsj.com.

MORGENSTERN, KENNETH E., plastic surgeon; s. Stephen and Nina Morgenstern; m. Jennifer Lynne Morgenstern; children: Grayson, Thatcher, Addison. BS, Emory U., Atlanta, Ga., 1991; MD, Hahnemann U., Phila. 1995. Ophthalmology Am. Bd. of Ophthalmology, 2005, Orbital and Plastic Surgery Am. Soc. of Ophthalmic Plastic and Reconstructive Surgery, 2005. Categorical gen. surgery resident Med. Coll. of Pa., Hahnemann U., 1995—99; ophthalmology resident W.Va. U., Morgantown, 1999—2002, chief resident, 2001—02; asst/ clin. prof Ohio State U., Columbus, 2002—04; pediatric orbital and reconstructive surgery Children's Hosp. of Columbus, Ohio, 2002—04; facial cosmetic surgery Ctr. for Facial Rejuvination, Columbus, Ohio, 2003—04; asst. clin. prof Va. Commonwealth U., 2004—05, U. Pa., Phila., 2005—06; pres. Morgenstern Ctr. for Orbital and Facial Plastic Surgery, Phila., 2006—; dir. of orbital and facial plastic surgery Veterans Adminstrn. Med. Ctr., Phila., 2006—. Rsch. Morgenstern Ctr. for Orbital and Facial Plastic Surgery, Phila., 2002—; assoc. fellowship preceptor U. Pa., Phila., 2006—; Childrens Hosp. of Pa., Phila., 2006—; editl. com. BioMed Ctrl., Opthalmic Plastic and Reconstructive Surgery; resident rev. com. Am. Coll. of Gen. Med. Edn.; bd. mem. Resident Coun. of ACGME; pres. Honor Ct. of Med. Coll. of Pa. Dir.: (educational course) Ophthalmology for the Internist; contbr. educational course; dir.: (educational program) Talking with Patients in Difficult Situations; contbr. scientific papers, chapters to books. Recipient W.va. U. Resident Rsch. award, Dept of Opthalmology, W.Va. U., 2002, Resident Rsch. Aaward, W.Va. Acad. of Opthalmology, 2002, Physician Humanitarian award, County Med. Soc. of Phila., 1998, Intern of Yr., Med. Coll. of Pa. and Hahnemann U., 1995—96, Cheif Resident, W.Va. U., 2002; grant, Nat. Inst. of Health, 1997—99, Am. Thyroid Cancer Assn. Rsch. grant, Am. thyroid Cancer Assn., 2002—04, Departmental grant, Dept Ophthalmology, W.Va. U., 2000—02, Rsch. Devel. grant, W.Va. U., 2000—01. Fellow: Am. Soc. of Ophthalmic Plastic and Reconstructive Surgery, Am. Bd. of Ophthalmology; mem.: AMA, Assn. Rsch. in Vision and Ophthalmology, Pa. Med. Soc., ARVO, W.va. Acad. of Ophthalmology, Va. Acad. of Ophthalmology. Achievements include patents for blocking agent for I131 induced lacrimal injury. Office Phone: 610-687-8771. E-mail: kmorgenstern@pol.net.

MORGENSTERN, LEON, surgeon; b. Pitts., July 14, 1919; s. Max Samuel and Sarah (Master) M.; m. Laurie Mattlin, Nov. 27, 1967; 1 son, David Ethan. Student, CCNY, 1936—37; BA magna cum laude, Bklyn. Coll., 1940; MD, N.Y. U., 1943. Diplomate: Am. Bd. Surgery. Intern Queens Gen. Hosp., Jamaica, NY, 1943—44, fellow, asst. resident in pathology, 1947—48, resident in surgery, 1948—52; practice medicine, specializing in surgery LA, 1953—, Bronx, NY, 1959—60; dir. surgery Cedars of Lebanon Hosp., LA, 1960—73, Cedars-Sinai Med. Ctr., LA, 1973—88, emeritus dir. surgery, 1989—; dir. bioethics program, 1995—; prof. surgery UCLA Sch. Medicine, 1973-90, prof. surgery emeritus, 1990—. Asst. prof. surgery Albert Einstein Coll. Medicine, N.Y.C., 1959-60; adj. prof. bioethics U. Judaism, L.A., 1996—; dir. Ctr. Health Care Ethics Cedars-Sinai Med. Ctr., 1998-2004, emeritus dir. 2004-. Assoc. editor Mount Sinai Jour. Medicine, 1984-88, Surg. Innovation, 2004-; contbr. articles to profl. publs. Served to capt. M.C. U.S. Army, 1944-46. Mem. Soc. for Surgery Alimentary Tract, Soc. Am. Gas-trointestinal Endoscopic Surgeons (hon.), Am. Gastroent. Assn., L.A. Surg. Soc. (pres. 1977), ACS (sec.-treas. 1976-77, pres. 1978, bd. dirs. So. Calif. chpt. 1976-84, gov.-at-large), Internat. Soc. Surgery, Western Surg. Assn., Pacific Coast Surg. Assn., AMA, Calif. Med. Assn., L.A. County Med. Assn., Am. Surg. Assn., others. Home: 5694 Calpine Dr Malibu CA 90265-3812 Office Phone: 310-423-1630. Business E-Mail: morgenstern@cshs.org.

MORGENSTERN, MATTHEW, computer scientist; b. N.Y.C. BSEE, Columbia U., 1968, MSEE and Computer Sci., 1970; MS in Computer Sci. and Mgmt., MIT, 1975, PhD in Computer Sci., 1976. Asst. prof. computer sci. Rutgers U., New Brunswick, NJ, 1976-82; research computer scientist Info. Scis. Inst., U. So. Calif., Los Angeles, 1982-84; sr. computer scientist SRI Internat., Menlo Park, Calif., 1984-90; dir. R & D programs advt. info. tech. divsn. Xerox, Cambridge, Mass., 1990-92; prin. scientist Xerox Design Rsch. Inst./Cornell U. Ithaca, NY, 1992—. Cons. Hewlett-Packard Corp., Palo Alto, Calif., 1990, Cornell U., 1996—; prin. investigator U.S. Govt. DARPA projects on heterogeneous databases and metadata repositories, 1992—. Co-author: Database Security VIII, 1994; contbr. articles to profl. jours. Mem. IEEE, Am. Assn. Artificial Intelligence, Assn. Computing Machinery, Sigma Xi, Tau Beta Pi. Eta Kappa Nu Office: Xerox Design Research Inst Cornell Univ 605 Rhodes Hall Theory Ctr Ithaca NY 14853-3801 E-mail: mmorgen@alum.mit.edu.

MORGENSTERN, SHELDON JON, symphony orchestra conductor; b. Cleve., July 1, 1938; s. Irwin Arthur and Harriet Sue Morgenstern; m. Patricia Lou Bradshaw; 1 child, Sali Sharpe Hagan. MusB, Northwestern U., 1961; MusM, New Eng. Conservatory, 1966; DMA (hon.), Greensboro (N.C.) Coll., 1986. Mem. conducting staff New Eng. Conservatory, 1965-66; music dir. Greensboro Symphony Orch., 1967-74; prin. guest condr. Betica Philharm., Seville, Spain, 1978-82, Polish Radio Orch., Warsaw, 1990—. Music advisor Miss. Symphony Orch., 1985-86; bd. mem. Istanbul Internat. Festival, Turkey, 1975—, Company for Televised Theatre; mus. coms. U.S. Dept. Interior for Wolf Trap Farm Park, 1972; mem. adv. bd. Avery Fisher Award, 1978—; music dir. Ea. Music Festival, Greensboro, 1962-98, music dir. emeritus, 1998—; artistic dir. Arts Sans Frontieres, 2005-; adv. coun. mem. Kent/Blossom Music Festival, 2006-. Author: No Vivaldi in the Garage, 2001. Mem. adv. bd. Blossom Cleve. Orch. Festival, 2006—. Recipient O'Henry award City of Greensboro, 1980, Long Leaf Pine award State N.C., 1989, Nat. Alumni award Northwestern U., 1990. Home: Airans/Farges Ch des Charmys 01550 Collonges France E-mail: shellymorgenstern@yahoo.fr.

MORGENTHALER, DAVID TURNER, venture capitalist; b. Chester, S.C., Aug. 5, 1919; s. Henry W. and Elizabeth (Taylor) M.; B.S. in Mech. Engring., M.S., Mass. Inst. Tech., 1941; m. Lindsay Anne Jordan, May 17, 1945; children— David T., Gary J., Todd W., Gaye Elizabeth. Sales mgr. Ervite Corp., 1945-47; mech. engr. Copes Vulcan div. Blaw-Knox Co., 1947-50; v.p., dir. sales Delavan Mfg. Co., Des Moines, 1950-57; pres. Foseco, Inc., Cleve., 1957-68; chmn. bd. Foseco Technik Ltd., Birmingham, Eng., 1964-68; chmn. bd. API Instruments Co., 1968-70, dir., 1963-70; chmn. bd. Mfg. Data Systems, Inc., Ann Arbor, Mich., 1969-81; chmn. exec. com. dir. LFE Corp., Waltham, Mass., 1970-85; founding ptnr. Morgenthaler Assos.; mng. ptnr. Morgenthaler Ventures, 1981—; dir. Hauserman, Inc., Cleve., Tartan Labs., Inc., Pitts., Three Phoenix Co.; bd. dirs. Ribozyme Pharmaceuticals, 1992-02, chmn., 1995-02; cos. Brentwood Assocs.; trustee Cleve. Clinic Found.; bd. overseers Case Western Res. U. Served to capt., AUS, 1941-45. Mem. Nat. Venture Capital Assn. (past pres.), Chief Execs.

Orgn., Inc. (past pres.), Young Pres. Orgn. (sr. v.p., bd. dirs.), Sigma Nu. Clubs: Westwood Country, Union, Pacific Union, Lyford Cay. Home: 13904 Edgewater Dr Cleveland OH 44107-1416 Office: 50 Public Sq Ste 2700 Cleveland OH 44113

MORGENTHALER-LEVER, ALISA, lawyer; b. St. Louis, June 3, 1960; d. Gerald Thomas and Mary Louise (Neece) M. BA, S.W. Mo. State U., 1982; JD, Cornell U., 1985. Bar: N.Y. 1986, D.C. 1988, Calif. 1990. Law clk. City of Springfield, Mo., 1981; atty. bd. govs. Fed. Res. Sys., Washington, 1984, staff atty., 1985-86; assoc. Kirkpatrick & Lockhart, Washington, 1986-88, Stroock & Stroock & Lavan, Washington, 1988-89; ptnr. Christensen, Glaser, Fink, Jacobs, Weil & Shapiro, L.A., 1989—. V.p., sec., bd. dirs. L.A. Retarded Citizens Found.; v.p., bd. dirs. Malibu Riviera III Homeowners Assn., 2000—04. Named one of So. Calif. Super Lawyers, Martindale-Hubbel A-V Rating. Mem. ABA, Calif. Bar Assn. (del. to com. on adminstrn. justice), D.C. Bar Assn., N.Y. Bar Assn., L.A. County Bar Assn. (jud. appts. com.), Beverly Hills Bar Assn., Century City Bar Assn., Women Lawyers assn. of L.A. (bd. dirs.), 3019 Third St. Owners Assn. (v.p. bd. dirs. 1991-2000), Order of Omega, Phi Alpha Delta, Rho Lambda, Phi Kappa Phi, Pi Sigma Alpha, Gamma Phi Beta. Office: Christensen Miller Fink Jacobs Glaser Weil & Shapiro 10250 Constellation Blvd 19th Fl Los Angeles CA 90067-5010 E-mail: amorgenthaler@chrisglase.com.

MORGENTHAU, ROBERT MORRIS, prosecutor; b. NYC, July 31, 1919; s. Henry Jr. and Elinor (Fatman) M.; m. Martha Pattridge (dec.); children: Joan, Anne, Elinor, Robert P., Barbara; m. Lucinda Franks, Nov. 19, 1977; children: Joshua, Amy. BA, Amherst Coll., 1941, LLD (hon.), 1966; LLB, Yale U., 1948; LLD (hon.), NY Law Sch., 1968, Syracuse Law Sch., 1976, Albany Law Sch., 1982, Colgate U., 1988. Bar: N.Y. 1949. Assoc. firm Patterson Belknap & Webb, N.Y.C., 1948-53, ptnr., 1954-61; U.S. atty. So. Dist. N.Y., 1961-62, 62-70; dist. atty. New York County, 1975—. Former pres. N.Y. State Dist. Attys. Assn.; lectr. London Sch. Econs., 1993. Chmn. Police Athletic League; trustee Baron de Hirsch Fund; chmn. Gov.'s Adv. Com. on Sentencing, 1979; counsel N.Y. State Law Enforcement Coun.; chmn. A Living Meml. to the Holocaust-Mus. of Jewish Heritage; Dem. candidate for Gov. of N.Y., 1962; trustee Temple Emanu-El, N.Y.C.; bd. dirs. P.R. Legal Def. and Edn. Fund. Lt. comdr. USNR, 1940—45. Recipient Emory Buckner award Fed. Bar Coun., 1983, Yale Citation of Merit, 1982, Fordham-Stein prize, 1988, Thomas Jefferson award in law U. Va., 1991, Brandeis medal U. Louisville, 1995, Omanut award Yeshiva U., 1995, Trumpeter award Nat. Consumers League, 1995, Frank S. Hogan award N.Y. State Dist. Atty.'s. Assn., 2000, Lone Sailor award USN Meml. Found., 2000; named Man of Yr., Fed. Law Enforcement Assn. Found., 2004; Matheson-Morgenthau Disting. Professorship in Law named in his honor, Va. Law Sch. Fellow Am. Bar Found.; mem. ABA, N.Y. State Bar Assn. (award for Excellence in Pub. Svc. 2001), Assn. of the Bar of the City of N.Y., N.Y. County Lawyers Assn. (Disting. Pub. Svc. award 1993), Amherst Alumni Assn. (hon. pres. 2001), Phi Beta Kappa. Office: Office Dist Atty 1 Hogan Pl New York NY 10013-4311

MORGESE, VINCENT JOHN, neurosurgeon; b. Whippany, N.J., Apr. 23, 1961; s. Albert Nicholas and Irma Nittoli Morgese; m. Victoria C. Morgese, Apr. 1, 1990; children: Elizabeth, Albert. BA in Biophysics, Johns Hopkins U., 1983; MD, Brown U., 1987. Diplomate Am. Bd. Neurologic Surgery. Resident neurosurgery Loma Linda (Calif.) U., 1987-93; pvt. practice neurosurgeon Napa, Calif., 1993—. Recipient Good Citizenship award DAR, N.J., 1979. Mem. AMA, Am. Assn. Neurol. Surgeons, Congress Neurol. Surgeons, Calif. Assn. Neurol. Surgeons, Calif. Med. Assn., Napa County Med. Assn. Office: 980 Trancas St Ste 12 Napa CA 94558-2933

MORGISON, F. EDWARD, investment broker; b. Clay Center, Kans., Oct. 4, 1940; s. Fred and Lena Edna (Chaput) M.; m. Karen Lorene Herdman, Nov. 21, 1964; 1 child. Diana Michelle. BA in Math., Emporia State U., 1963; MSBA, U. Mo., Columbia, 1964; postgrad., U. Mo., Kansas City. Cert. purchasing mgr.; registered securities agt., Mo., Kans., Ill., 2001. Computer programmer U. Mo. Med. Ctr., Columbia, 1964-65; adminstrv. and budget analyst Urban Renewal Project, Independence, Mo., 1965-66; acct. exec., bank broker Stifel Nicolaus & Co., Kansas City, Mo., 1966-73; pres., CEO Will-Mor Investment Sys., Kansas City, Mo., 1973-75; br. mgr. Edward Jones & Co., Kansas City, 1975; editl. and exec. asst. to Morgan Maxfield for U.S. Congress, Kansas City, 1976; sr. acct. exec., merger and acquisitions specialist Rowland & Co., Kansas City, 1976-77; chmn. bd., pres., CEO Mo. Securities, Inc., Kansas City, 1977-78; v.p., regional mgr. Charles Schwab & Co., Kansas City, 1978-79; v.p. Profl. Assistance, Kansas City, 1979-81; exec. v.p. J. Penner & Assocs., Kansas City, 1981-82; pres. J. Penner & Co., Kansas City, 1982-83; acct. exec., registered broker Lowell H. Listrom & Co., 1981-84; pres., CEO First Allen Securities, Inc., 1983-89, Venture House, Kansas City, 1989—. Agt. Offerman & Co., Kansas City, 1979-81, CEO Morgison & Assoc., Kansas City, 1979-81; fiscal dir. Housing Authority of Kansas City, 1981; dir., sec. Hubach Group, Inc., 1987-88; treas. Skytrader Corp., 1986-89, Emergency Svcs., 1986-87, Internat. Tex. Industries, Inc., San Antonio, 1986-88; chmn. bd., treas. Masters Mark, Inc., 1986-89; CFO Am. Utilicraft Corp., 1992-97. v.p. purchasing, 1997—; acct. exec. N.Y. Stock Exch., Am. Exch., 1986-89. Recipient Bausch and Lomb Sci. award, 1959, Sci. award Lambda Delta Lambda, 1962. Mem. NRA (life), U. Mo. Alumni Assn. (life), Emporia State U. Alumni Assn. (life), U.S. Chess Fedn. (life), Mensa (life). Home: 1000 NE 96th Ter Kansas City MO 64155-2145

MORGNER, AURELIUS, economist, educator; b. NYC, May 23, 1917; s. Oscar A. and Anna G. (Hoffmeister) M. BS in Bus. Adminstrn., U. Mo., 1938, MA in Econs., 1940; PhD, U. Minn., 1955. Investigator Dept. Labor, 1941; project dir. Employment Stblzn. Research Inst., 1941-42; instr. bus. adminstrn. U. Minn., 1942-46; lectr. Northwestern U., 1946-47; assoc. prof. Tex. A&M U., 1947-50, prof., 1950 51; vis. prof. U. Sao Paulo, Brazil, 1958-60, dir. grad. social studies, 1959-60; prof. econs. U. So. Calif., L.A., 1960—, chmn. dept., 1962-69; prof. internat. econs. Sch. Internat. Relations, 1960—. Pub. panel mem. Chgo. Regional War Labor Bd., 1943-45; pub. rep. minimum wage com. Dept. Labor, 1942,43; cons. Govt. Ecuador, 1965-68, Govt. Guyana, 1968, state Nev., 1970, Philippines, 1971-72, Yemen Arab Republic, 1974-75; U.S. State Dept. vis. lectr., Brazil, summer 1966 Co-author: Local Labor Markets, 1948, Problems in Economic Analysis, 1948, Problems in the Theory of Price, 1954 (trans. Spanish 1965, Portuguese 1967). Ford faculty fellow Columbia U., 1954-55 Mem. So. Calif. Econ. Assn. (pres. 1965-66), Am. Econs. Assn., Western Econ. Assn., Am. Arbitration Assn., Internat. Studies Assn. Office: U So Calif Dept Econs Los Angeles CA 90089-0001

MORGRIDGE, JOHN P., computer systems network executive; b. Elm-hurst, Ill., July 23, 1933; m. Tashia F. Morgridge; three children. BBA in Mktg. & Fin., U. Wis., 1955; MBA, Stanford U., 1957; DSc (hon.), U. Wis. 1994; LLD (hon.), Carleton U., 2002; LHD, Lesley Coll., No. Ill. U. Mktg. profl. Honeywell Info. Systems, 1960-80; v.p. mkgt., sales and svc. Stratus Co., Inc., 1980-86; pres., chief ops. officer GRiD Systems (now part of Tandy Corp.), 1986-88; pres., CEO Cisco Systems Inc., San Jose, Calif., 1988-95, chmn., 1995-98. Lectr. Stanford U. Bus. Sch., 1997—. Bd. dirs. Cisco on Competiveness, CARE, The Cisco Found., The Cisco Learning Inst., Inter-plast, The Nature Conservancy, Wis. Alumni Rsch. Found.; trustee Stanford U., 2002—. Capt. USAF, 1957—60. Recipient Leadership in Tech. award Tech. Corps, 1988, Ernest C. Arbuckle award, Stanford U., 1998, Philanthro-pist of the Yr., Ctr. for Excellence in Nonprofits, 1999, Devenek Humani-tarian award, Hidden Villa, 1999; named one of 400 Richest Americans, Forbes, 2006. Office: Cisco Systems Inc 170 W Tasman Dr San Jose CA 95134-1700*

MORHOUSE, SANFORD W., lawyer; b. Keene Valley, N.Y., Dec. 13, 1944; BA, Williams Coll., 1966; JD, Columbia Univ., 1969. Bar: N.Y. 1969, US Dist. Ct. so. N.Y. Assoc. to ptnr. Dewey Ballantine LLP, N.Y.C., 1969—, co-chmn. mgmt. com., mem. exec. com. & chmn. private equity group. Dir. Damon Runyon Cancer Rsch. Found., Broad Hollow Estates Inc. Mem.: ABA, N.Y. State Bar Assn., Assn. of the Bar City of N.Y., Am. Coll. Real

Estate Lawyers. Office: Dewey Ballantine LLP 1301 Ave of the Americas New York NY 10019-6092 Office Phone: 212-259-8400. Office Fax: 212-259-8499. Business E-Mail: smorhouse@dbllp.com.*

**MORI, ALLEN ANTHONY,** academic administrator, consultant; b. Hazleton, Pa., Nov. 1, 1947; s. Primo Philip and Carmella (DeNoia) M.; m. Barbara Epoca, June 26, 1971; 1 child, Kirsten Lynn. BA, Franklin and Marshall Coll., Lancaster, Pa., 1969; MEd, Bloomsburg U. Pa., 1971; PhD, U. Pitts., 1975. Spl. edn. tchr. White Haven (Pa.) State Sch. and Hosp., 1969-70, Hazleton Area Sch. Dist., 1970-71, Pitts. Pub. Schs., 1971-74; supr. student tchrs. U. Pitts., 1974-75; prof. spl. edn. U. Nev., Las Vegas, 1975-84; dean coll edn. Marshall U., Huntington, W.Va., 1984-87; dean coll. edn. Calif. State U., L.A., 1987—2003, provost, v.p. acad. affairs Dominquez Hills, 2003—. Hearing officer pub. law 94-142 Nev. Dept. Edn., Carson City, 1978—; mem. Nev. Gov.'s Com. on Mental Health and Mental Retardation, 1983-84; cons. Ministry Edn., Manitoba, Can., 1980-82; pres. Tchr. Edn. Coun. State Colls. and Univs., 1993-94. Author: Families of Children with Special Needs, 1983; co-author: Teaching the Severely Retarded, 1980, Handbook of Preschool, Special Education, 1980, Adapted Physical Education, 1983, A Vocational Training Continuum for the Mentally and Physically Disabled, 1985, Teaching Secondary Students with Mild Learning and Behavior Problems, 1986, 93, 99; author numerous articles, book revs. and monographs. Bd. dirs. Assn. Retarded Citizens San Gabriel Valley, ElMonte, 1989—94. Recipient grants U.S. Dept. Edn., 1976-91, Nev. Dept. Edn., W.Va. Dept. Edn., Calif. State U. Chancellor's Office. Mem. Assn. Tchr. Educators, Coun. for Exceptional Children (div. on Career Devel. exec. com. 1981-83), Nat. Soc. for Study of Edn., Phi Beta Delta, Phi Delta Kappa, Pi Lambda Theta, Phi Kappa Phi. Avocations: wine collecting, travel. Office: Calif State U Dominguez Hills 1000 E Victoria Carson CA 90747 Office Phone: 310-243-3307. Business E-Mail: amori@csudh.edu.

**MORI, MARIKO,** artist; b. Tokyo, 1967; Student, Bunka Fashion Coll., Tokyo, 1986-88, Byam Shaw Sch. Art, London, 1988-89, Chelsea Coll. Art. 1989-92, Whitney Mus. Am. Art, 1992-93. One-woman shows include Geneva Project Room, N.Y.C., 1993, Shiseido Gallery, Tokyo, 1995, Am. Fine Arts Co., N.Y., 1995, Galerie Emmanuel Perrotin, Paris, 1996, Ctr. Nat. D'Art Contemporain Grenoble, Italy-Nordic Pavilion Venice Biennale, 1997, L.A. County Mus. Art, 1998, Mus. Contemporary Art, Cgo., 1998, Serpentine Gallery, London, 1998, Andy Warhol Mus., Paris, 1998, Bklyn. Mus. Art, Kunstmus. Wolfsburg, 1999, Fondazione Prada, Milan, 1999, Ctr. Pompidou, Paris, Ctr. Nat. Photography, 2000, Mus. Contemporary Art, 2002, Tokyo, 2004.

**MORI, TOSHIKO,** architecture educator; Student, Cooper Union, 1970—71, BArch, 1976: AM (hon.), Harvard U., 1996. Registered Arch., Fla., Maine, N.Y., NCARB cert. Arch. Edward Larrabee Barnes and Assocs., 1976—81, Toshiko Mori Arch., 1981—; prof. architecture Grad. Sch. Design Harvard U., 1995—2001, Robert P. Hubbard prof. arch. Grad. Sch. Design, 2002—, chair dept. architecture Grad. Sch. Design, 2002—. Arch. Tod Williams and Assocs., 1972—73, ELS Design Group Urban Design, 1973—74; vis. critic Grad. Sch. Design Harvard U., 1989, 94; Eero Saarinen vis. prof. Yale U., 1992, vis. critic Sch. Architecture, 93, Columbia U., 1994; lectr. in field. Advisor Greenwich Village Soc. Historic Preservation; mem. adv. bd. Montreal Mus. Decorative Art McDonald Stewart Found. Recipient prize for urban design, Abraham Kazan Fund, 1976, Henry Adams Cert. of Achievement, AIA, 1976, The One Show Merit award, 1981, N.Y.C./AIA Design Award Citation Interior Architecture, 1988, N.Y.C./AIA Design award in interior architecture, Internat. Assn. Lighting Designers, 1989, 11th Ann. Interiors award for best retail design, Shinkenchiku/Ctrl. Glass Internat., 1990, Renovation award, C. of C., Rockport, Rockland, Maine, 1995, Silver medal in exhbn. design at MOMA, Art Dirs. Club, 1999, N.Y.C./AIA Design award, 1998, 2000. Office: Harvard Design Sch Room 207 Gund Hall 48 Quincy St Cambridge MA 02138

**MORI, YOSHIKO,** language educator; b. Tokyo; children: Misa, Mina. AA, Nanzan Jr. Coll., Japan, 1980; BA, Nanzan U., Japan, 0198; MA, Ohio U., Athens, 1991; PhD, U. Ill., Urbana-Champaign, 1996. Cert. second language acquistion, tchr. edn. U. Ill. at Urbana-Champaign, 1996. Tchr. Hikarigaoka Girls' HS, Okazaki, Japan, 1983—84, Tokyo Met. Edn. Bd., 1984—89; tchg. asst. Ohio U., Athens, 1989—91; tchg., rsch. asst. U. Ill., Urbana-Champaign, 1991—96; assoc. prof. Georgetown U., Washington, dir. Japanese lang. program; vis. prof., Japanese pedagogy Columbia U., N.Y.C. Bd. mem. Assn. for Tchrs. of Japanese, 2005—; editl. bd. mem. Japanese Assn. Second Lang. Acquisition (JASLA), Tokyo, 2006—. Contbr. articles various profl. jours. Recipient Acknowledged Academic Excellence by the Internat. Student Union award, Ohio U., 1990; grantee, Georgetown U., 2003-2004, Fund for Improvement of Post Secondary Edn., 1999, Japanese Tchg. Material Donation Program, Japan Found., 2000; Competitive grants-in-Aid, Georgetown U., 1997, Summer Academic grant, Grad. Sch. of Arts and Sci., 1999, Nanzan U. Exch. Student fellowship, DePauw U., Nanzan U., 1981-1982, Faculty of Lang. and Linguistics (FLL) Summer Rsch. grant, Georgetown U., 1997, 2002, Workshops Conf. grant, Japan Found., 1999, Jr. Faculty Rsch. fellowship, Georgetown U., 2000. Mem.: Internat. Reading Assn., Assn. Tchrs. of Japanese, Am. Coun. on Tchg. of Fgn. Lang., Am. Ednl. Rsch. Assn. Office: Georgetown U ICC 306 O & 37 St Washington DC 20057-1052 Office Phone: 202-687-5098. Office Fax: 202-687-2408. Business E-Mail: moriy@georgetown.edu.

**MORIAL, MARC HAYDEL,** association executive, former mayor; b. New Orleans, Jan. 3, 1958; s. Ernest and Sybil M.; m. Michelle Miller; 1 child, Mason; 1 child from previous marriage, Kemah. Bar: La. Legis. intern U.S. Sen. Russell Long, Washington, 1979; dir. U. Pa. Office of Supportive Svcs., Phila., 1979-80; summer assoc. U.S. Atty. U.S. Dist. Ct. (so. dist.) N.Y., 1982; legis. asst. U.S. Rep. George T. Leland, Washington, 1983; atty. Barham & Churchill, New Orleans, 1983-85; pvt. practice New Orleans, 1985—; mem. La. Senate, Baton Rouge, 1991-93, mem. revenue and fiscal affairs com., commerce com., labor and indsl. rels. com., select com. crime & drugs, intergovtl. rels. com., Pres. Clinton's action com. on crime & drugs, senate select com. on econ. devel.; mayor City of New Orleans, 1993—2002; ptnr. Adams & Reese, 2002—03; pres. Nat. Urban League, NYC, 2003—. Adj. prof. law, polit. sci. Xavier U. La., New Orleans, 1988-90. Del. Nat. Rainbow Coalition Conv., 1986, La. State Dem. Conv., 1986, Dem. Nat. Conv., Atlanta, 1988; cooperating atty. NAACP Legal Def. Fund, mem. nat., New Orleans br.; gen. counsel La. Assn. Minority and Women Owned Businesses, Inc., La. Voter Registration/Edn. Crusade; cooperating atty. Minority Bus. Enterprise Legal Def. and Edn. Fund; divestment coord., legal advisor New Orleans Anti-Apartheid Coalition, 1983—; bd. dirs. La. ACLU, La. Spl. Olympics, Milne Boys Home; mem. project steering com. Voting Rights Law Reporter; mem. Young Leadership Coun., Friend of New Orleans Ctr. for Creative Arts. Recipient Chmns. award Congl. Black Caucus, 1989, Outstanding Svc. award Lutcher H.S., 1990, La. NAACP Cmty. Svc. award, 1988; named Legis. Rookie of Yr. Baton Rouge Bus. Report, 1992, All Rookie Team by polit. columnist John Maginnis, 1993, Legis. Newcome of Yr., 1992; named one of Most Influential Black Americans, Ebony mag., 2006 Mem. ABA (standing com. on world order under law 1982-83), Nat. Bar Assn., La. State Bar Assn. (Pro Bono Pub. award 1988), La. Assn. Criminal Def. Attys., Nat. Conf. Black Lawyers, Amnesty Internat. USA, Transafrica, Louis A. Martinet Legal Soc. New Orleans, La. Trial Lawyers Assn. Nat. Black Law Students Assn. (nat. bd. dirs. 1981-83), US Conf. Mayors (pres. 2001-02), Alpha Phi Alpha. Office: Nat Urban League 120 Wall St 8th Fl New York NY 10005*

**MORIARTY, DONALD WILLIAM, JR.,** bank executive; b. Amarillo, Tex., Sept. 15, 1939; s. Donald William and Lorraine Julia (Walck) Moriarty; m. Rita Ann Giller, Nov. 28, 1964; children: Mary Kathleen, Jennifer Ann, Anne Marie, Kerry Lee, Erin Teresa. Student, St. Benedict's Coll., 1957-59, 60-61; BSc, Marquette U., 1962; MSc, St. Louis U., 1965, PhD, 1970. Cost acct. Emerson Electric, St. Louis, 1959-63; grad. fellow in econs. St. Louis U., 1963-65, instr., 1965-68; asst. prof. U. Mo., St. Louis, 1968-70; with Fed. Res. Bank of St. Louis, 1968-83, v.p., 1971-74, sr. v.p., controller, 1974-77,

1st v.p., 1977-83; sr. v.p. Gen. Bancshares Corp., 1983-86; exec. v.p. Commerce Bancshares, Inc., 1986-87; bank cons., 1987-89; pres., CEO, bd. dirs. Duchesne Bank, St. Peters, Mo., 1989-95; sr. cons. Universal Fin. Group, Inc., 1996—2003; assoc. prof. bus. Fontbonne U., St. Louis, 1998—2005; bus. cons., 2005—. Vis. instr. Webster Coll., 1975—82; adviser City of Des Peres, Mo., chmn. fin. com., 1976—78, chmn. mgmt. com., 1978—81, mem. pers. commn., 1978—81, mem. planning and zoning com., 1981—83; bd. dirs. Mid-Am. Payments Exch., Duchesne Bank; arbitrator N.Y. Stock Exchange, 2006—. Mem. parent's coun. Creighton U., Omaha, 1995—97; mem. adv. bd. St. Joseph Acad., 1982—86; mem. pres.'s coun. St. Louis U. 1983—; dist. chmn. Boy Scouts Am., 1991—93, vice chmn., 1994—2001; trustee, chmn. St. Joseph Hosp., 1982—93; bd. dirs. ea. Mo. region NCCJ, 1987—93. Recipient Alumni Merit award, St. Louis U., 1979. Mem.: Nat. Assn. Securities Dealers (arbitrator 2006—), Alhpa Kappa Psi, Beta Gamma Sigma.

**MORIARTY, GEORGE MARSHALL,** lawyer; b. Youngstown, Ohio, Sept. 16, 1942; s. George Albert Moriarty and Caroline (Jones) Bass; m. Elizabeth Bradley Moore, Sept. 11, 1965 (div. 1986); children: Bradley Marshall, Caroline Walden, Sarah Cameron; m. Phyllis A.N. Thompson, May 2, 1998. BA magna cum laude, Harvard U., 1964, LLB magna cum laude, 1968. Bar: Mass. 1969, U.S. Dist. Ct. Mass. 1973, U.S. Ct. Appeals (1st cir.) 1976, U.S. Ct. Appeals (D.C. cir.) 1984, U.S. Claims Ct. 1983, U.S. Supreme Ct. 1976, U.S. Ct. Appeals (2d cir.) 1997. Law clk. to Hon. Bailey Aldrich U.S. Ct. Appeals (1st cir.), Boston, 1968-69; law clk. to Hon. Warren Burger, Hon. Hugo Black, Hon. Potter Stewart, Hon. Byron White U.S. Supreme Ct., Washington, 1969-70; spl. asst. to Hon. Elliot L. Richardson, Dept. Health, Edn. & Welfare, Washington, 1970-71, exec. asst., 1971-72; assoc. Ropes & Gray, Boston, 1972-77, ptnr., 1977—. Bd. dirs. Ptnrs. Healthcare Sys. Pres. Boston Athenaeum; chmn. Brigham and Women's Hosp. Mem. ABA, Am. Law Inst., Boston Bar Assn., Somerset Club, Tavern Club, Met. Club. Office: Ropes & Gray 1 Internat Pl Boston MA 02110

**MORIARTY, JOHN,** opera administrator, artistic director; b. Fall River, Mass., Sept. 30, 1930; s. John J. and Fabiola Marie (Ripeau) M. MusB summa cum laude, New Eng. Conservatory, 1952, DM, 1992. Artistic adminstr. Opera Soc. of Washington, 1960-62, Santa Fe Opera, 1962-65; dir. Wolf Trap Co., Vienna, Va., 1972-77; chmn. opera dept. Boston Conservatory, 1973-89, New Eng. Conservatory, 1989—. Prin. condr. Central City Opera, Denver, 1978—, artistic dir., 1982-98, artistic dir. emeritus, 1998—; panelist Nat. Inst. Music Theater, 1985, 86, 87, Conn. Arts Coun., 1982, 84; adjudicator various contests including Met. Opera auditions, 1965—. Author: Diction, 1975. Bd. dirs. Wm. Matheus Sullivan Found.; trustee Boston Concert Opera; recs. on Cambridge Records, Newport Classics, Parnassus Records; adv. bd. Shoshana Found. Recipient Frank Huntington Beebe award, Boston, 1954, Disting. Alumni award New Eng. Conservatory Alumni Assn., 1982, Gold Chair award Central City Opera House Assn., 1988. Mem. Nat. Opera Assn., Sigma Alpha Iota, Delta Omicron, Pi Kappa Lambda. Office: New Eng Conservatory 290 Huntington Ave Boston MA 02115-5018 also: Central City Opera House Assn 400 S Colorado Blvd Ste 530 Denver CO 80246-1255 Office Phone: 617-585-1100.

**MORIARTY, JOHN KLINGE,** electrical engineer, consultant; b. Washington, Feb. 6, 1956; s. John Klinge and Mary (Cozart) M.; m. Elizabeth Rouse, Dec. 31, 1987; children: Maire Elizabeth, John Lank, Harris James. BS in Physics, Va. Poly. Inst. and State U., 1981; M of Engring. in Elec. Engring., Clemson U., 1996. Project engr. Delco Electronics divsn. G.M.C., Kokomo, Ind., 1981-84; staff engr. Hekimian Labs., Gaithersburg, Md., 1984-85; sr. LSI design engr. Case Comms., Inc., Columbia, Md., 1985-86; ind. electronics cons. Gaithersburg, 1986-88; mem. tech. staff Bell Labs., Reading, Pa., 1988-97; ind. electronics cons. Reading, 1997—. Cons. Squire Comms., Miami, Fla., 1986, Delco Electronics Corp., Kokomo, 1986—88, Mfg. Networks Inc., San Francisco, CPClare Corp., Beverly, Mass., Wireless Sys. Techs., Inc., San Jose, Calif.; mem. tech. adv. bd. SOMA Networks, Inc., San Francisco; tutorial presenter West Med. Design and Mfg. Conf., Anaheim, Calif., 1991, East Med. Design and Mfg. Conf., N.Y.C., 1991; sen. mem Tech. Staff Legerity Luc, 2003—. Contbr. articles to profl. jours. including IEEE Jour. Solid State Cirs., Procs. IEEE Custom Integrated Cirs., Cons. Record of IEEE Indsl. Applications Soc., Cancer Treatment Reports. Recipient Supplier Recognition award Hughes Aircraft Corp., 1992. Mem. IEEE, IEEE Electron Device Soc., IEEE Solid State Cirs. Soc., IEEE Cirs. and Sys. Soc. Achievements include patents in field. Home: 2557 River Rd Reading PA 19605-2840 Office Phone: 610-929-7223. Personal E-mail: jmoriarty@ieee.org.

**MORIARTY, JOHN TIMOTHY,** transportation consultant, writer; b. Cleve., Jan. 23, 1939; s. James Joseph and Margaret (Healy) Moriarty; m. Angela Marie Veneziano, June 29, 1968; children: Patrick J., Sean Gerald. Student, John Carroll U., 1957, Cleve. State U., 1964—67. Traffic analyst, Cleve., 1957—82; transp. cons. Norfolk So. R.R., Cleve., 1982—. Author: One Square Mile of Mayhem, 1998, Honest John, 1998, The Phantom Employee, 1998, Sister Mommy, 1999, Thin Ice, 2001, Streets of Gold, 2001. With U.S. Army, 1961—63. Mem.: Ill. Internat. Freight Coun. Roman Catholic. Avocations: basketball, billiards, reading. Home: Apt 2615 1111 Independence Ave Akron OH 44310-1896

**MORIDANI, MAJID Y.,** research scientist, educational consultant; s. Moridani and Heibati; children: Arian, Sina. PharmD, Tehran Med. U., Iran, 1993; PhD in Pharm. Chemistry and Medicinal Chemistry, U. London, 1996; postdoctoral diploma in clin. chemistry, U. Toronto, Can., 2003. Cert. pharmacist Pharm. Soc., clin. chemistry Am. Bd. of Clin. Chemistry. Posdoctoral rschr. in biochem. toxicology and drug metabolism faculty pharmacy U. Toronto, Ont., 1999—2001; clin. chemistry fellow Sch. Medicine, 2001—03; asst. prof. in pharm. scis. Sch. Pharmacy Tex. Tech. U. Health Scis. Ctr., Amarillo, 2004—. Recipient Allan Pollard Postdoctoral Clin. Chemistry prize, U. Toronto Sch. Medicine, 2003. Mem.: Am. Assn. Colls. Pharmacy, Can. Soc. Clin. Chemists, Internat. Soc. for the Study Xenobiotics, Proteome Soc., Melanoma Rsch. Found., Am. Assn. Pharm. Scientists, Am. Assn. Cancer Rsch., Am. Soc. Clin. Chemists. Achievements include research in drug metabolism and drug toxicology, pharmacogenetics, drug design and drug discovery and clinical chemistry. Office: Sch Pharmacy 1300 Coulter Dr Amarillo TX 79106 Office Phone: 806-356-4015. Business E-Mail: majid.moridani@ttuhsc.edu.

**MORIE, G. GLEN,** lawyer, manufacturing executive; BA, Bowdoin Coll., 1964; LLB, U. Pa., 1967. Bar: Wash. 1968. Pvt. practice law, Wash., 1970-73; asst. counsel PACCAR, Inc., Bellevue, Wash., 1973-79, asst. gen. counsel, 1979-82, gen. counsel, 1983-85, v.p., gen. counsel, 1985—. Office: PACCAR Inc PO Box 1518 Bellevue WA 98009-1518

**MORIMOTO, MASAHARU,** chef, television personality; b. Hiroshima, Japan, May 26, 1955; Trained in Sushi and traditional Kaiseki cuisine, Hiroshima. Exec. chef Sony Club, NYC, 1993—98, Nobu Restaurant, NYC, 1998—2001; chef, owner Morimoto Restaurant, Phila., 2001—, NYC, 2004—, Wasabi, Mumbai, India. Iron chef Japan Iron Chef (Food Network), 1995—99, Iron Chef America, 2005—. Office: Morimoto Restaurant 723 Chestnut St Philadelphia PA 19102*

**MORIN, JOYANN HAUGE,** education educator; d. Harry Adrian and Anna (Barnec) Hauge; m. Dale Arthur Morin, May 21, 1954; children: David Dale, Angelique Marie, Debra Kay(dec.). AA, ElCamino Coll., 1967; BA in History, Calif. State U., Dominguez Hills, 1969, MA, 1977; EdD in Curriculum and Instrn., U. So. Calif., 1986. Elem. tchg. credential Commn. on Tchr. Credentialing, Calif. Elem. tchr. St. Catherine Laboure Sch., Torrance, Calif., 1969—71, LA. Unified Sch. Dist., 1971—77; curriculum coord. L.A. Sch. Dist., 1977—84; prof. Calif. State U., Northridge, 1984—93, L.A., 1993—, prof. emeritus, 2002. Presenter in field. Author: Social Education Instruction, 2003; contbr. articles to profl. jours. Recipient Spl. Merit award, Edn. Jour., 1996; Innovative Tchg. grant, Calif. State U., L.A.,

1994. Mem.: AAUP, Calif. Coun.on the Edn. Tchrs., Nat. Coun. for the Social Studies. Avocations: creative writing, researching. Office: Calif State Univ 5151 State University Dr Los Angeles CA 90032-8140 Home: PO Box 875 Wolf Point MT 59201

**MORIN, LOUIS,** lawyer; b. Que., Can., Sept. 29, 1941; s. Paul-Emile and Jeanne Dechene) M.; m. Marthe Champoux, Sept. 12, 1970; children: Francois, Antoine, Brigitte. BA, Coll. Jesuites, 1962; LLL, U. Laval, 1965. Atty. Grondin LeBel Morin, Que., Canada, 1966—77; judge Que. Labor Ct., 1977—2002, chief judge, 1990—98; pres. Que. Labour Rels. Bd., 2002—04; atty. Grondin Poudrier Bernier, Québec, Canada, 2004—. Mem. Que. Jud. Coun., Montreal, 1992-96; tchr. labor law U. Laval, Que., 1989. Mem. Can. Bar Assn., Que. Bar Assn., Que. Young Bar Assn. (pres. 1975-76), Que. Judge's Assn. (pres. 1989-90). Avocations: skiing, bicycling. Office: Grondin Poudrier Bernier 500 Grande Allée Est Bur 900 Quebec City PQ Canada G1R 2J7 Office Phone: 418-683-3000. Business E-Mail: lmorin@grondinpoudrier.com.

**MORIN, LYNN P.,** music educator, director, secondary school educator; d. Marjorie Huber. BA in Voice and Theatre Performance, Rocky Mountain Coll., 1995; BA in Music Edn., U. Mont., 1996. Dir. band and choir St. Regis (Mont.) Sch., 1996—2001; dir. choral Richland (Wash.) H.S., 2001—04; choral dir. Torrington (Conn.) H.S., 2004—. Dir. Mineral County Choir, St. Regis, Mont., 1999—2001; soprano Mont. Chorale, Great Falls, Mont., 1998—2001, Hartford (Conn.) Chorale, 2004—05; vocal dir. Richland (Wash.) Light Opera Co., 2003—04. Actor: (plays). Praise team Southside Ch., Richland, 2001—04; bd. dirs. Richland (Wash.) Cmty. Concerts, 2002—03. Schieffelin scholar, Rocky Mountain Coll., 1992—95. Mem.: NEA, Music Educator's Nat. Conf., Am. Choral Dirs. Assn. (assoc.). Republican. Avocations: travel, acting, theater, scrapbooks.

**MORIN, PIERRE JEAN,** retired management consultant, social services administrator; b. Quebec City, Que., Can., Aug. 5, 1931; s. Augustin Norbert and Yvonne (Gaudry) M.; m. Colette Poulin, Apr. 3, 1954; children: Anne, Gilles, Louis. BS, Concordia U., Montreal, 1964; MS, Laval U., Que., 1970, D.Sc., 1973. Quality control technician Dow Brevery, Montreal, Que., 1952-56; research assoc. Royal Victoria Hosp., Montreal, 1957-67; coordinator of research Que. Heart Inst., 1967-73; dir. research labs. Laval Hosp., Que., 1973-80, lectr. dept. medicine Que., 1973-77; dir. gen. Community Service Ctr., 1980-88; mgmt. cons., 1988-91; ret., 1991. Cons. Que. Minister of Environ., 1975-84. Contbr. articles to profl. jours. Schering Travelling fellow, 1971 Mem. AAAS Roman Catholic. Home: 336 Rg Castor Leclercville PQ Canada G0S 2K0 *Well assumed failure may be a must towards later success.*

**MORING, JOHN FREDERICK,** lawyer; b. Farmville, Va., Oct. 30, 1935; s. Scott O'Ferrall and Margaret Macon (Mitchell) M.; m. Margaret Ann Clarke, Mar. 30, 1959; children: Martha, Elizabeth, Scott, Lee. BS, Va. Poly. Inst., 1957; JD, George Washington U., 1961. Bar: Va. 1961, D.C. 1962, U.S. Supreme Ct. 1964; cert. mediator civil disputes Supreme Ct. Va. 2004, U.S. Dist. Ct. Va., 2004, U.S. Cir. Ct., 2004. Assoc. Morgan, Lewis & Bockius, Washington, 1961-68, ptnr., 1969-78, Jones, Day, Reavis & Pogue, Washington, 1978-79; founding ptnr. Crowell & Moring, Washington, Irvine, London, Brussels, 1979—2000. Sec. Associated Gas Distbrs., Inc., 1977-2000. Local gas utility columnist: Nat. Gas Jour., 1989—2000; mem. editl. bd. Natural Gas Contracts, 1994—2001. Mem. nat. panel neutrals Am. Arbitration Assn., 2003—; chmn. bd. dirs. Washington Legal Counsel for Elderly, 2000—01; Rep. candidate 23d Dist./Va. Gen. Assembly, Alexandria, 1973; mem. bd. govs. St. Stephen's and St. Agnes Sch., Alexandria, 1989—95; pres. St. Stephen's Found., Inc., 1990—93; sr. warden Immanuel Ch. on the Hill, Alexandria, 1988, 1989; trustee Ch. Schs. of Diocese of Va., 1996—; mem. found. bd. Shrine Mont Conf. Ctr. Episc. Diocese Va., Orkney Springs, Va., 2001—; mem. bd. govs. St. Margaret's Sch., Tappahannock, Va., 2002—. 2d lt. U.S. Army, 1958. Mem.: ABA (natural resources law sect. 1982—86, coun.), Am. Arbitration Assn., Fed. Energy Bar Assn. (sec. 1963—66, pres. 1982—83), Indian Creek Yacht and Country Club (Alleykannock, Va.). Episcopalian. Avocations: golf, fishing, canoeing. Home: PO Box 224 White Stone VA 22578 Office: Crowell & Moring 1001 Pennsylvania Ave NW Fl 10 Washington DC 20004-2595 also: 3 Park Plaza 20th Fl Irvine CA 92614-8505 also: 11 Pilgrim St London EC4V 6RN England also: 71 Rue Royale B 1000 Brussels Belgium Business E-Mail: fredmoring@rivnet.net.

**MORIOKA, BRENNON T.,** engineering executive, political organization worker; b. Hawaii; BS in Civil Engring., MS in Civil Engring., U. Calif.; PhD in Civil Engring., U. Hawaii, 1999. Sr. geotechnical engr. URS Corp., Honolulu. Chmn. Rep. Party, Hawaii. Mem.: ASCE (chmn. geotechnical com.), Hawaii Soc. Profl. Engrs. (named Young Engr. of Yr.).

**MORIS, LAMBERTO GIULIANO,** architect; b. Siena, Tuscany, Italy, Mar. 29, 1944; came to U.S., 1972; s. Gualtiero Luigi and Giovanna (Avanzati) M.; m. Tracy P. Schilling, 1970 (div. 1985); children: Giacomo, Stefano; m. Beverly Chiang, Mar. 28, 1986; 1 child, Christopher. MA in Arch., U. Florence, Italy, 1970. Assoc. Marquis Assocs., San Francisco, 1972-78, prin., 1978-85, Simon Martin-Vegue Winkelstein Moris, San Francisco, 1985—2005, Moris/Marino and Assoc., San Francisco, 2005—. Tchr. San Francisco City Coll., 1982—84; juror DuPont Antron Design Awards, 1989, AIA Hon. Awards, 1995, AIA Interior Architecture Awards, Chgo. chpt., 1997; mem. interior design adv. coun. Acad. Art Coll., San Francisco, 1992—2001; lectr. AIA Nat. Conf., 1996, Aircraft Interiors Expo, Cannes, France, 2000, Aircraft Interiors Conf. and Exhbn., Long Beach, Calif., 2001, AIA- Italy Summit, San Francisco, 2003. Mem. design com. Clairmont Pines Task Force, 1991; charter mem. Forecast 21 Principals Roundtable, 1993; mem. Bldg. Industry Conf. Bd. (BICB), 2001—; mem. bd. dirs. ItaLingua Inst., 1984—. Mem.: FAIA (mem. selection com. 2003), AIA (mem. internat. com. 2003), Interior Architecture, No. Calif. chpt., Am. Inst. Architects, Coll. Fellows, Am. Inst. Architects (corp. mem. 1979—), Am. C. of C. in Italy, Oakland Met. C. of C., Accademia Italiane della Cucina, Cath. Prof. Bus. Club, San Francisco Opera Assn., Il Cenacolo (bd. dirs. 1991), San Francisco Heritage Assn., Engr. Club. Roman Catholic. Avocations: coin collecting/numismatics, skiing, travel. Office: Page and Moris 48 2d St San Francisco CA 94105 Office Phone: 510-381-5083. Personal E-mail: lgmoris@mindspring.com.

**MORISCO, JERID SIMON,** music educator, conductor; b. Rockmart, Ga., Nov. 18, 1967; s. Ann Floyd and Gary Dewayne Galloway. MusB, Shorter Coll., Rome, Ga., 1990; MusM, Sam Houston State U., Huntsville, Tex., 1992; degree in Edn. Specialist, Lincoln Meml. U., Harrogate, Tenn., 2001; post grad. in Musical Arts, Shenandoah U., Winchester, Va., 2001. Cert. tchr. Ga., 1998. Tenor Atlanta Symphony Orch. Chorus, 1989—90; asst. prof. music Gulf Coast C.C., Panama City, 1993—97; dir. choral studies Mt. Eden H.S., Hayward, 1997—98; adj. prof. Shorter Coll., Marietta, Ga., 1999—; music specialist Marietta City Schs., Ga., 1999—; artistic dir. / founding condr. The Marietta Master Chorale, Inc., Ga., 2001—. Recipient Going the Extra Mile award, Marietta Kiwanis Club, 1999. Mem.: Internat. Kodaly Soc., Orgn. Am. Kodaly Educators, Internat. Soc. for Music Edn., Music Educators Nat. Conf., Ga. Music Educators Assn., Am. Choral Dirs. Assn., Conductors Guld, Phi Theta Kappa, Pi Kappa Lambda, Phi Mu Alpha. Eposcopalian. Office: The Marietta Master Chorale 105 Park St Marietta GA 30060 Personal E-mail: jerid_morisco@hotmail.com.

**MORISHITA, AKIHIKO,** manufacturing executive; b. Osaka, Japan, Oct. 14, 1941; came to U.S., 1981; s. Sueyoshi and Toshiko Morishita; m. Fumiko Okamura; children: Shizuko, Kumiko, Okamura. BA in Econs., Wakayama U., Wakayama, Japan, 1965. Mgr. Hanwa & Co. Ltd., Osaka, 1965-80; cons. oil dept. Pacific Southwest Trading Co., San Diego, 1981-82; exec. Pacific Marine Bunkering, Inc., L.A., 1982—. Mem.: Club Leconte. Home: 4610 Don Pio Dr Woodland Hills CA 91364-4205

**MORISSEAU, FAY EDWIN,** lawyer; b. Jan. 1951; BS with hon. in petroleum engring., U. Oklahoma, 1973; JD magna cum laude, U. Houston, 1978. Lic.: U.S. Patent & Trademark Office. Petroleum engr. Shell Oil Co.; ptnr.-in-charge Orange County Office McDermott Will & Emery LLP, Irvine, Calif., 1998—. Mem.: Tex. State Bar, Calif. State Bar. Office: McDermott Will & Emery LLP 18191 Von Karman Ave Ste 500 Irvine CA 92612-0187 Home: 77 Montecito Dr Corona Del Mar CA 92625-1018 Office Phone: 984-851-9348. Office Fax: 984-757-7115. Business E-Mail: fmorisseau@mwe.com.

**MORISSEAU, NAN KRUGER,** television personality; b. Oklahoma City; d. Albert William and Lillie Mae (Kubala) K.; m. Fay Edwin Morisseau Esq., III, June 8, 1974; children: Katherine, Paul. BS, U. Okla., 1972; postgrad., U. Houston, 1986-90. Fashion designer Charm of Hollywood, L.A., 1972-74, Jackson Sq., New Orleans, 1974-75; buyer Federated Dept. Stores Foleys Houston, 1975-80; stockbroker Prudential Securities, Houston, 1980-86; pres. The Newport Beach (Calif.) Recital Series, 1995-99, also bd. dirs.; pres. Cachet' Prodns. Internatl., Newport Beach, 1994—, Golden Girl Jewelry, Newport Beach, 1997—; TV talk show host Rise & Shine with Nancy Morgan Pacific Family Entertainment, Fountain Valley, Calif., 1997—, also bd. dirs., 1996-97. Author (plays) White Russian, 1988, Meyerhold, 1990, (screenplay) Triumph of The Spirit, 1992; actor (situation comedy) Student Union, 1992, (play) Charon Unleashed, 1993. Hostess Chamber Music Salons, 1995-99; pres. Friends of Newport Beach Recital Series, 1995—; bd. dirs. Orange County Philharm. Soc., Big Canyon, Calif., 1996-97. Vol. Ctr. devel. grantee, 1996; recipient Bronze medal Nastar Downhill Skiing, 1996. Mem. AAUW (chair classical music sect. 1997), Womens Diversity Forum, North Orange County Computer Club, Arts Orange County. Avocations: skiing, surfing, computer graphics, music, ballet. Home and Office: Cachet Prodns Internatl 77 Montecito Dr Corona Del Mar CA 92625-1018

**MORISSETTE, ALANIS NADINE,** singer; b. Ottawa, ON, Canada, June 1, 1974; d. Alan and Georgia Morissette. Singer: (albums) Alanis, 1991, Now is the Time, 1992, Jagged Little Pill, 1995 (Grammy award for Album of Yr., Best Female Rock Vocal Performance, Best Rock Song, Best Rock Album, 1996), Supposed Former Infatuation Junkie, 1998, Space Cakes, 1998, Alanis Unplugged, 1999, Under Rug Swept, 2002, Feast On Scraps, 2002, So-Called Chaos, 2004, Jagged Little Pill Acoustic, 2005, Alanis Morissette: The Collection, 2005; actor: (films) Anything for Love, 1993, Dogma, 1999, Jay and Silent Bob Strike Back, 2001; (TV films) The Great Warming, 2003; (TV series) You Can't Do That on Television, 1986; actor, prodr., writer (TV series) We're with the Band, 2006; actor: (TV appearances) Sex and the City, 2000, American Dreams, 2004, Degrassi: The Next Generation, 2005; (plays) The Exonerated, 2003. Recipient BRIT award for Best Internat. Newcomer, 1996, MTV European Music award for Best Female Artist, 1996, Juno award for Prodr. of the Yr., 2003. Achievements include inducted into Canadian Walk of Fame, 2005. Office: Third Rail Entertainment 9169 Sunset Blvd Los Angeles CA 90069*

**MORISUE, GLENN T.,** graphics designer; b. San Francisco, Nov. 22, 1940; BA, Art Inst. Pitts., 1962; BFA, Cleve. Inst. Art, 1964. Greeting card designer Am. Greetings Corp., Cleve., 1965—69; art dir. Schuckert Studio, Cleve., 1970—73; creative dir. Hauser King Marford Co., Cleve., 1974—76; v.p., design dir. Copper K Industries, Cleve., 1977—79; dean edn. Cooper Sch. Art, Cleve., 1980—82; free-lance illustrator, 1983—93. Recipient numerous Best of Show awards, Nat. Drawing Competition award winner, Am. Artist Drawing Mag., 2004. Mem.: Pastel Soc. Am., Am. Soc. Portrait Artists, Meadville Coun. on the Arts. Home: 6201 1/2 Lake Rd W Ashtabula OH 44004-9757

**MORITA, RICHARD YUKIO,** microbiology and oceanography educator; b. Pasadena, Calif., Mar. 27, 1923; s. Jiro and Reiko (Yamamoto) M.; m. Toshiko Nishihara, May 29, 1926; children— Sally Jean, Ellen Jane, Peter Wayne BS, U. Nebr., 1947; MS, U. So. Calif., 1949; PhD, U. Calif., 1954. Microbiologist Mid-Pacific Expdn., 1950, Danish Galathea Deep-Sea Expdn., 1952, Trans-Pacific Expdn.; Postdoctoral fellow U. Calif., Scripps Inst. Oceanography, 1954-55; asst. prof. U. Houston, 1955-58; asst. prof., assoc. prof. U. Neb. 1958-62; prof. microbiology and oceanography Oreg. State U., Corvallis, 1962-89, prof. emeritus microbiology and oceanography, 1989—. Prog. dir. biochemistry NSF, 1968-69; Disting. vis. prof. Kyoto Univ.; cons. NIH, 1968-70; researcher in field. Contbr. articles to sci. lit. Patentee in field. Served with U.S. Army, 1944-46 Grantee NSF, 1962—, NIH, 1960-68, NASA, 1967-72, Office Naval Research, 1966-70, Dept. Interior, 1968-72, NOAA, 1975-82, Bur. Land Mgmt., 1982, EPA, 1986—; recipient awards including King Fredericus IX Medal and Ribbon, 1954, Sr. Queen Elizabeth II Fellowship, 1973-74, Hotpack lectr. and award Can. Soc. Fellow Japan Soc. for Promotion Sci.; Am. Soc. Microbiology (Fisher award). Home: 1515 NW 14th St Corvallis OR 97330 Personal E-mail: dickmorita@aol.com.

**MORITSUGU, KENNETH PAUL,** internist, federal official; b. Honolulu, Mar. 5, 1945; s. Richard Yutaka and Hisayo Joan (Nishikawa) M.; children: Erika Lizabeth, Vikki Lianne (deceased), Emily Renee. Student, Chaminade Coll. Honolulu, 1963-65; BA in Classical Langs. with honors, U. Hawaii, 1967; MD, George Washington U., 1971; MPH, U. Calif., Berkeley, 1975; DSc (hon.), Coll. Osteopathic Medicine, U. New Eng., 1988, Midwestern U., 1993, Des Moines U., Iowa, 2005; DSC (hon.), Still U., 2005; D Pub. Svc. (hon.), U. North Tex., 1994; DHL (hon.), Western U. Health Scis., 2002, Alliant Internat. U., 2002; DDL (hon.), Phila. Coll. Osteo. Medicine; DHL (hon.), Campbell U., 2003, Nova Southeastern U., 2004. Diplomate Am. Bd. Preventive Medicine (fellow); cert. correctional health profl. Intern USPHS Hosp., San Francisco, 1971-72, resident, 1972-75; commd. USPHS, 1968, advanced through grades to med. dir., 1979; promoted to rank of rear adm., asst. surgeon gen., 1988; staff med. officer USPHS Hosp., San Francisco, 1972-73; regional cons. med. manpower planning and devel. HEW, San Francisco, 1976-78, chief internat. edn. programs br. Washington, 1978, dep. dir. divsn. medicine, 1978; dir. Bur. Health Professions, div. medicine HHS, Rockville, Md., 1978-83, dir. Nat. Health Service Corps, 1983-87, dep. dir. Bur. Health Professions, 1987; med. dir. Fed. Bur. Prisons Dept. Justice, Washington, 1987-98; dep. surgeon gen. USPHS, Rockville, Md., 1998—; acting surgeon gen., 2002. Decorated D.S.M., knight grand cross Mil. and Hospitaller Order St. Lazarus of Jerusalem; named Disting. Alumnus, George Washington U., 2002; recipient Commendation medal, Meritorious Svc. medal, Outstanding Svc. medal, Surgeon Gen.'s medallion, Surgeon Gen.'s medal, Dirs. award, U.S. Marshal's Svcs., John D. Chase award, AMSUS, Nathan Davis award, AMA, Disting. Svc. award, ACHSA, DSM award, U.S. Dept. Justice, Fed. Bur. Prisons, Health Leader of Yr., Commd. Officers Assn. Fellow Am. Coll. Preventive Medicine, Royal Soc. Health, Royal Soc. Medicine; mem. APHA, Assn. Tchrs. Preventive Medicine, Assn. Mil. Surgeons U.S., Res. Officers Assn., Mensa, Am. Guild Organists, Am. Acad. Physicians Assts. (hon.), Delta Omega, Omicron Delta Kappa. Office: USPHS Office of Surgeon Gen 5600 Fishers Ln Ste 18-67 Rockville MD 20857-0001 Personal E-mail: 1samurai@cox.net.

**MORITZ, CHAD HENRY,** research scientist; Grad. magna cum laude, U. Wis., 1977. Diagnostic radiographer Aurora Health Care, Milw., 1991—93, Covenant Health Care, Milw., 1993—94; MRI rsch. technologist Med. Coll. Wis., Milw., 1994—96; rsch. assoc. Dartmouth Coll., Hanover, NH, 1996—98; rsch. program mgr. radiology dept. U. Wis. Med. Sch., Madison, 1999—. Presenter in field. Contbr. chapters to books, articles to profl. jours. Recipient award for Excellence, St. Luke's Sch. Radiol. Tech., 1993; Profl. devel. grantee, U. Wis. 2003. Mem.: Am. Soc. Functional Neuroradiology, Soc. for Magnetic Resonance Technologists, Am. Soc. Radiol. Technologists (cert. radiologic technologist), Orgn. for Human Brain Mapping, Internat. Soc. for Magnetic Resonance in Medicine. Avocations: bicycling, accordion. Business E-Mail: ch.moritz@hosp.wisc.edu.

**MORITZ, DANA DEE,** language educator; b. Moravia, Iowa, June 16, 1939; d. Fern William and Vivien Agnes (Wilson) Wright; m. Glenn Garnett Moritz, June 3, 1961; children: Henry Warren, Andrew William. BS in English Edn., Truman State U., 1960, MA in English Edn., 1970; AAS in

Computer Programming, Indian Hills C.C., 2004. Cert. choice theory, reality therapy and lead mgmt. William Glasser Inst. Tchr. secondary English Sanborn Cmty. Schs., Iowa, 1960—64, Centerville Cmty. Schs., Iowa, 1978—2002, dir. drama, 1980—89. Negotiator Centerville Edn. Assn., Iowa, 1980—2002, pres., 1992—93. Dir. Cmty. Theater, Centerville, Iowa, 1983, 1985, 1996; mem. Mcpl. Housing Authority, Centerville, Iowa, 2005—, chair, 2006. Recipient Ctrs. of Excellence award, Nt. Coun. Tchrs. of English, 1987. Mem.: NEA, PEO, DAR. Democrat. United Methodist. Avocations: reading, sewing, walking, computer programming. Home: 511 W Grand St Centerville IA 52544 E-mail: dmoritz@mchsi.com.

**MORITZ, DONALD BROOKS,** mechanical engineer, consultant; b. Mpls., June 17, 1927; s. Donald B. and Frances W. (Whalen) M.; m. Joan Claire Betzenderfer, June 17, 1950 (dec. Dec. 21, 2004); children: Craig, Pamela, Brian. BS in Mech. Engring., U. Minn., 1950; postgrad., Western Res. U., 1956-58. Registered profl. engr., Ill. Minn., Ohio. V.p., gen. mgr. Waco Scaffold Shoring Co., Addison, Ill., 1950-72; group v.p. Bliss and Laughlin Industries, Oak Brook, Ill., 1972-83; sr. v.p. AXIA Inc. (formerly Bliss and Laughlin Industries, Oak Brook, 1983-84, exec. v.p., chief operating officer, 1984-88; cons. Exec. Svc. Corps Chgo., 1988—; pres. Image-A-Nation, Unltd., 1988—. Bd. dirs. Am. Photographic Acad. Patentee in field. Served with USN, 1945-46. Mem. ASME, Scaffold and Shoring Inst. (founder, past pres.), Mensa, Five Seasons Country Club. Office: Moritz and Assocs PO Box 305 Clarendon Hills IL 60514-0305

**MORITZ, MILTON EDWARD,** security consultant; b. Reading, Pa., Sept. 5, 1931; s. Edward Raymond and Anna May M.; m. Elizabeth Ann Walls, June 6, 1952; children: Betsy Ann Moritz Koppenhaver, Stephen Edward, Sandra E. Student, U. Md., 1950-51, Fla. State U., 1959-60. Enlisted U.S. Army, 1949, chief warrant officer 3, 1968, sgt. M.I.; ret., 1970; safety and security dir. Harrisburg (Pa.) Hosp., 1970-72; security mgr. Sprint, Carlisle, Pa., 1972-94; prin. Moritz Assocs., Harrisburg, 1994—. Lectr., instr. Harrisburg Area Community Coll.; mem. Indsl. Security Adv. Coun. Assoc. editor: Protection of Assets Manual. Pres. Greater Harrisburg Crime Clinic, 1974. Decorated Bronze Star with oak leaf cluster. Mem. Am. Soc. Indsl. Security (past pres., chmn. bd. dirs.), Assn. Former Intelligence Officers, Internat. Narcotic Enforcement Officers Assn., Pa. Crime Prevention Assn. (bd. dirs). Republican. Lutheran. Home and Office: 7723 Avondale Ter Harrisburg PA 17112-3805 Office Phone: 717-545-6551. Business E-Mail: mickmoritz@cs.com.

**MORITZ, TIMOTHY BOVIE,** psychiatrist; b. Portsmouth, Ohio, July 26, 1936; s. Charles Raymond and Elisabeth Bovie (Morgan) M.; m. Joyce Elizabeth Rasmussen, Oct. 13, 1962 (div. Sept. 1969); children: Elizabeth Wynne, Laura Morgan; m. Antoinette Tanasichuk, Oct. 31, 1981; children: David Michael, Stephanie Lysbeth. BA, Ohio State U., 1959; MD, Cornell U., 1963. Diplomate Am. Bd. Psychiatry and Neurology. Intern in medicine N.Y. Hosp., N.Y.C., 1963-64, resident in psychiatry, 1964-67; spl. asst. to dir. NIMH, Bethesda, Md., 1967-69; dir. Community Mental Health Ctr., Rockland County, NY, 1970-74, Ohio Dept. Mental Health, Columbus, Ohio, 1975-81; med. dir. psychiatry Miami Valley Hosp., Dayton, Ohio, 1981-82; med. dir. N.E. Ga. Community Mental Health Ctr., Athens, Ga., 1982-83, Charter Vista Hosp., Fayetteville, Ark., 1983-87; clin. dir. adult psychiatry Charter Hosp., Las Vegas, Nev., 1987-94; pvt. practice psychiatry Las Vegas, 1987—; med. dir. Problem Gambling Cons., Las Vegas, 2000—. Prof. Wright State U., Dayton, Ohio, 1981-82; asst. prof. Cornell U., N.Y.C., 1970-73; mem. human subjects biomed. scis. rev. com. U. Nev., Las Vegas, 2000-2001; cons. NIMH, Rockville, Md., 1973-83. Author: (chpt.) Rehabilitation Medicine and Psychiatry, 1976; mem. editorial bd. Directions in Psychiatry, 1981-1993. Dir. dept. mental health and mental retardation Gov.'s Cabinet, State of Ohio, Columbus, 1975-81. Recipient Svc. award Ohio Senate, 1981, Svc. Achievement award Ohio Gov., 1981. Fellow Am. Psychiat. Assn. (disting. life, Disting. Svc. award 1981); mem. AMA, Nev. Assoc. Psychiat. Physicians, Nev. State Med. Assn., Am. Assn. Chronic Fatigue Syndrome, Clark County Med. Soc., Cornell U. Med. Coll. Alumni Assn., Ohio State U. Alumni Assn. (life). Office: 2330 Paseo del Prado Ste C-109 Las Vegas NV 89102-4336 Office Phone: 702-363-3633.

**MORIUCHI, K. DEREK,** secondary school educator; b. LA, 1958; BA, UCLA, 1981; MA, Calif. State U., 1982; MA in Ednl. Adminstrn., Calif. State U., L.A., 2005. Cert. single subject tchg. credential in math., cross cultural lang. acquisition devel., nat. bd. cert. tchr., lic. in adminstrv. svcs. Tchr. math. Marshall Mid. Sch., 1986—90, Ganesha H.S., 1991—93; tchr. history Stevenson Middle Sch., L.A., 1993—2003, chairdept. math.; secondary math. expert L.A. Unified Sch. Dist., L.A., 2003—. Spkr. in field. Mem.: Calif. Math. Coun. (spkr. 2000—03), Nat. Bd. for Profl. Tchg. Stds. (bd. mem. 2001—), Pi Lambda Theta. Office: Local Dist 5 LA Unified Sch Dist 2151 N Soto St Los Angeles CA 90032 Office Phone: 323-224-3132. Personal E-mail: k12536@aol.com. E-Mail: derek.moriuchi@lausd.net.

**MORIYAMA, IWAO MILTON,** statistician, consultant; b. San Francisco, Jan. 26, 1909; s. Saburo and Reki Moriyama; m. Toshiko Kako Moriyama; children: Halley Isao, Ken. BS, U. Calif., Berkeley, 1931; MPH, Yale U., 1934, PhD, 1937. Chief mortality analysis Nat. Office of Vital Stats. USPHS, Washington, 1946—61, dir. Office of Health Stats., Nat. Ctr. for Health Stats. Rockville, Md., 1961—74, assoc. dir. internat. stats. Nat. Ctr. Health Stats. 1974—75; chief epidemiology and stats. dept. Radiation Effects Rsch. Found., Hiroshima, Japan, 1975—78; dep. exec. dir. Internat. Inst. for Vital Registration and Stats., Bethesda, Md., 1978—86, pres. and exec. dir., 1986—; chief epidemiology and stats. dept. Atomic Bomb Casualty Commn., Hiroshima, 1971—73. Vis. prof. faculty of medicine U. Tokyo, Japan, 1988; collaborator program for accelerated improvement of civil registration and vital stats. in developing countries UN/WHO; mem. expert panel on health stats. WHO, Geneva, 1950—75, head US delegation Internat. Conf. for 9th Decennial Revision of Internat. Classification of Diseases, 1975; lectr. Am. U., Washington, 1965; vis. lectr. biostatistics U. Calif., Berkeley, 1967; project officer Longitudinal Study of Survival and Outcome of a Birth Cohort, Safdarjung Hosp., New Delhi, 1969—89, Longitudinal Studies in Human Reprodn., Christian Med. Coll., Vellore, India, 1973—89; biostatistician vital stats. divsn. Bur. of Census, US Dept. Commerce, 1940—46; exec. sec. US Nat. Com. on Vital and Health Stats., 1949—75; editl. cons. Demography, 1966—75; cons. in field. Recipient Disting. Svc. award, US Dept. HEW, Halbert L. Dunn award, Nat. Assn. Pub. Health Stats. and Info. Sys. Fellow APHA, Population Assn. Am., AAAS, Am. Statis. Assn.; mem.: Internat. Epidemiol. Assn., Am. Epidemiol. Soc., Cosmos Club, Sigma Xi, Delta Omega. Home: 7120 Darby Rd Bethesda MD 20817-2914 E-mail: imoriyama@comcast.net.

**MORIYAMA, KAREN ITO,** educational association administrator; d. Sadamu and Sumiko Honma Ito; children: Ryan M., Kristel S. BEd with high honors, U. Hawaii, Manoa, 1970, MEd, 1975. Lic. sch. adminstr. Dept. Edn., Hawaii, sch. counselor Dept. Edn., Hawaii, psychol. examiner Dept. Edn., Hawaii, cert. elem. tchr. Dept. Edn., Hawaii. Tchr. Red Hill Elem., Honolulu, 1971—73, Kipapa Elem. Sch., Mililani, Hawaii, 1973—82; counselor Solomon Elem. Sch., Wahiawa, Hawaii, 1982—85; counseling resource tchr. Dept. Edn., Central District, Hawaii, 1985—87; vice prin. Wheeler Intermediate Sch., Wahiawa, 1987—89; prin. Leihoku Elem. Sch., Waianae, Hawaii, 1989—94, Kanoelani Elem. Sch., Waipahu, Hawaii, 1995—2002; dep. supt. Leeward Dist., Waipahu, 2000—02; complex area supt. Nanakuli-Pearl City, Waipahu, 2002—. Adv. mem. U. Hawaii Counseling and Guidance Adv. Com., Honolulu, 1986. Mem., sec. Waianae Mil./Civilian Adv. Coun., 1991—94; bd. dirs. Joint Venture Edn. Forum, Honolulu, 2002—05, YMCA, Mililani, Hawaii, 1997—2001. Mem.: NAESP (assoc. Leeward Dist. Disting. Prin. award 1994, 1999), Hawaii Assn. Supervision and Curriculum Devel. (assoc.), Delta Kappa Gamma (Beta chpt.) (assoc. pres., pres., v.p. 1996—2000). Office: Leeward District Dept Edn Rm 418 601 Kamokila Blvd Kapolei HI 96707 Office Phone: 808-692-8000. Office Fax: 808-692-7899. E-mail: karen_moriyama@notes.k12.hi.us.

**MORK, GORDON ROBERT,** historian, educator; b. St. Cloud, Minn., May 6, 1938; s. Gordon Matthew and Agnes (Gibb) Mork; m. Dianne Jeannette Muetzel, Aug. 11, 1963; children: Robert, Kristiana, Elizabeth. BA, Yale U., 1960; MA, U. Minn., 1963; PhD, 1966. Instr. history U. Minn., Mpls., 1966; lectr., asst. prof. U. Calif., Davis, 1966-70; mem. faculty Purdue U., West Lafayette, Ind., 1970—, assoc. prof., 1973-94, prof. history, 1994—, dir. honors program humanities, 1985-87, dir grad. studies history, Am. studies, 1987-93, mem. Jewish studies com., 1980—, head dept. history, 1998—2003; resident dir. Purdue U.-Ind. U. Program, Hamburg, Germany, 1975-78. Rsch. fellow in humanities U. Wis., Madison, 1969—70; mem. test devel. com. advanced placement European history Ednl. Testing Svc., 1993—99, chair, 1995—99; cons. Coll. Bd. and Ednl. Testing Svc., 1999—. Author: Modern Western Civilization: A Concise History, 3d edit., 1994; editor: The Homes of Ober-Ammergau, 2000; mem. adv. bd. Teaching History, 1983—, History Teacher, 1980—2002. Mem. citizens task force Lafayette Sch. Corp., 1978—79; bd. dirs. Ind. Humanities Coun., 1986—89; elder Ctrl. Presbyn. Ch., Lafayette, 1973—75, deacon, 1996—99, trustee, 2001—04; bd. dirs., sec. Murdock-Sunnyside Bldg. Corp., 1980—2000. Mem.: Soc. History Edn., German Studies Assn., Am. Hist. Assn., Internat. Soc. History Didactics (v.p. 1991—95, 1996—2000), Mortar Bd., Phi Beta Kappa (mem. mortar bd.). Home: 1521 Cason St Lafayette IN 47904-2642 Office: Purdue U Dept History 672 Oval Dr West Lafayette IN 47907-2087 Office Phone: 765-494-4138. Business E-Mail: gmork@purdue.edu.

**MORKOÇ, HADIS,** electrical engineer, educator; b. Senkaya, Erzurum, Turkey, Oct. 2, 1947; came to U.S., 1971; s. Mustafa and Saadet (Metin) M.; m. Amy C. Ahlberg, Sept. 5, 1975; 1 child, Erol Taner. MS, Tech. U., Istanbul, 1969; PhD, Cornell U., 1975. Postdoctoral fellow Cornell U., Ithaca, NY, 1975-76; mem. tech. staff Varian Assocs., Palo Alto, Calif., 1976-78; prof. elec. engring. U. Ill., Urbana, 1978-97, Va. Commonwealth U., 1997—. Disting. vis. scientist Calif. Inst. Tech., Pasadena, 1987-88; cons., Motorola, IBM, AT&T, others. Author: Principles and Technology of ModFETs, 1991, Nitride Semiconductors and Devices, 1999, 2d edit., 2006, Advanced Semiconductor and Organic Nano-techniques, 2004; contbr. chpts. to books, articles to profl. jours. Scholar, Va. Commonwealth U., 2002. Fellow IEEE, AAAS, Am. Phys. Soc.; mem. Math. Rsch. Soc., Optical Soc. Am., Sigma Xi, Eta Kappa Nu, Sigma Phi Sigma. Achievements include invention of fastest transistor in world. Home: 2403 Lake Loreine Ln Richmond VA 23233-2523 Office: Va Commonwealth U PO Box 843072 601 W Main St Richmond VA 23284-9052 Office Phone: 804-827-3765. Business E-Mail: hmorkoc@vcu.edu.

**MORLAN, MERWYN EUGENE,** retired music educator; b. Indpls., Oct. 25, 1917; s. Willard Merwyn Morlan and Edna Eugenia Collins; m. Betty B. James, June 8, 1940; children: John Allan, Beth Ann Schill, Michelle Mary St. Clair children: Richard Eugene, Ann Christine Bayba, Steven Collins, Mary Eugenis Howell. BA, Ind. State U., Terre Haute, 1939; Masters, George Peabody Coll., Nashville, 1945, EdD, 1966. Music and social studies tchr. Westfield (Ill.) Twp. HS, 1939—41; supr. music Shenandoah County Va. Pub. Schs., Woodstock, 1941—54; dir. profl. programs Music Educators Nat. Conf., Washington, 1955—85. Pres. Lions Internat., Westfield, Ill., 1939—40, Woodstock, Va., 1948—49, Shenandoah Co. Chpt. for Crippled Children, Woodstock, Va., 1946—48; condr. Woodstock (Va.) Cmty. Chorus, 1946—52, McLean (Va.) Choral Soc., 1992—94; min. of music Luth. Ch. of the Redeemer, McLean, Va., 1958—71; condr. McLean (Va.) Ward I Choir, 1971—2001; condr., musical dir. The Mormon Choir of Wash. (DC), 1980—2000; chmn., condr. Interfaith Conf. of Met. Wash. (DC), Washington, 1987—97; condr. emeritus Mormon Choir of Wash. (DC), 2000; condr. McLean (Va.) Handbell Choir, 1971. Sgt. U.S. Army, 1945—46. Recipient Disting. Music Alumni Achievement award, Ind. State U., 1995. Mem. Ch. Of Jesus Christ Of Lds. Avocations: music, ornithology. Home: 6933 Espey Ln Mc Lean VA 22101-5456 Personal E-mail: satb@cox.net.

**MORLEY, HARRY THOMAS, JR.,** real estate executive; b. St. Louis, Aug. 13, 1930; s. Harry Thomas and Celeste Elizabeth (Davies) M.; m. Nelda Lee Mulholland, Sept. 3, 1960; children: Lisa, Mark, Marci. BA, U. Mo., 1955; MA, U. Denver, 1959. Dir. men's student activities Iowa State Tchrs. Coll., 1955-57; dir. student housing U. Denver, 1957-60; pvt. practice psychol. consulting St. Louis, 1960-63; dir. adminstrn. County of St. Louis, Mo., 1963-70; regional dir. HUD, Kansas City, Mo., 1970-71, asst. sec. adminstrn., 1971-73; pres. St. Louis Regional Commerce and Growth Assn., 1973-78, Taylor, Morley, Inc., St. Louis, 1978—2005, Morley Investments, Inc., 2005—. Teaching cons., lectr. Washington U., St. Louis, 1962-70; bd. dirs. Mid-Am. Alliance Corp., Life Ins. Co. Bd. dirs., exec. com. St. Louis Coll. Pharmacy; past chmn. Better Bus. Bur.; chmn. Mo. Indsl. Devel. Bd., Mo. State Hwy. Commn.; bd. dirs. St. Luke's Hosps., St. Johns Hosp., Downtown St. Louis, Inc., Laclede's Landing Redevel. Corp. With USN, 1951-53. Mem. Am. Nat. Assn. Homebuilders, St. Louis Homebuilders Assn. (pres.), St. Louis Advt. Club, Mo. Athletic Club, St. Louis Club, Noonday Club, Castle Oak Country Club, Round Table Club, Sunset Country Club. Republican. Methodist. Home: 14238 Forest Crest Dr Chesterfield MO 63017-2818 E-mail: morleyh@charter.net.

**MORLEY, JAMES EVERITT, JR., (JAY MORLEY JR.),** retired academic administrator, former educational association administrator; b. Middletown, NY, Dec. 23, 1940; s. James Everitt and Helen Scott (Fiero) Morley; m. Elizabeth Chadwell Wyman, Dec. 8, 1962; children: Margaret, Scott, Sarah, Sarah, James Everitt III. BME, Rensselaer Poly. Inst., 1962; MS in Acctg., Syracuse U., 1969. Mgmt. cons. Ernst & Ernst, NYC, 1969—72; comptroller Syracuse U., 1972—76; v.p. Rider Coll., Lawrenceville, NJ, 1976—78, Rensselaer Poly. Inst., Troy, NY, 1978—85; v.p., treas. Cornell U., Ithaca, NY, 1985—87, sr. v.p., 1987. Contbr. Mem. Troy Indsl. Devel. Authority, 1979—85; dir. Capital Regional Tech. Devel. Coun., Albany, NY, 1983—85, Tompkins County Area Devel., NY, 1985—. Served to col USMC, 1962—. Mem.: Eastern Assn. Coll. and U. Bus. Officers, Nat. Assn. Coll. and U. Bus. Officers (bd. dir. 1984—, pres., CEO). Office Phone: 202-861-2510. Office Fax: 202-861-2583. E-mail: james.morley@nacubo.orr.*

**MORLEY, JOHN EDWARD,** physician; b. Eshowe, Zululand, South Africa, June 13, 1946; came to U.S., 1977; s. Peter and Vera Rose (Phipson) M.; m. Patricia Morley, Apr. 4, 1970; children: Robert, Susan, Jacqueline. MB, BCh, U. Witwatersrand, Johannesburg, South Africa, 1972. Diplomate Am. Bd. Internal Medicine, subspecialty cert. endocrinology and geriatrics. Asst. prof. Mpls. VA Med. Ctr. and U. Minn., 1979-81; assoc. prof. U. Minn., Mpls., 1981-84; prof. UCLA San Fernando Valley, 1985-89; dir. GRECC Sepulveda (Calif.) VA Med. Ctr., 1985-89; Dammert prof. gerontology, dir. div. geriatric medicine St. Louis U. Med. Ctr., 1989—; dir. geriatric rsch. edn. and clin. ctr. St. Louis VA Med. Ctr., 1989—. Author: (with others) Nutritional Modulation of Neuronal Function, 1988, Neuropeptides and Stress, 1988, Geriatric Nutrition, 1990, 2d edit., 1995, Medical Care in the Nursing Home, 1991, 2d edit., 1997, Endocrinology and Metabolism in the Elderly, 1992, Memory Function and Aging Related Disorders, 1992, Aging and Musculoskeletal Disorders, 1993, Aging, Immunity and Infection, 1994, Sleep Disorders and Insomnia in the Elderly, 1993, Quality Improvement in Geriatric Care, 1995, Focus on Nutrition, 1995, Applying Health Services Research to Long-Term Care, 1996, Cardiovascular Disease in Older People, 1997, Hydration and Aging, 1997, Advances in Care of Older People with Diabetes, 1999, Endocrinology of Aging, 1999, Science of Geriatrics, 2000, Subacute Care, 2000, Anti-Aging, 2004, Principles and Practices of Geriatric Medicine, 4th edit., 2006; mem. editl. bd. Peptides, 1983—, Internat. Jour. Obesity, 1986-89, Jour. Nutritional Medicine, 1990—, Clinics in Applied Nutrition, 1990-92; editor geriatrics sect. Yearbook of Endocrinology, 1987-2001, Nursing Home Medicine, 1992-97, Clin. Geriatrics, 1992-97, Sandwich Generation, 1997, others; editor Jour. Gerontology: Med. Scis., 2000-04 Mem. adv. bd. Alzheimer's Assn., St. Louis, 1990-92; mem. adv. com. for physicians Mo. Divsn. Aging, Jefferson City, 1990-2001; bd. dirs. Mo. Assn. Long Term Care Physicians, 1991—, Long Term Care Ombudsman Program, St. Louis, 1992, Fund for Psychoneuroimmunology, 1990-2001, Hamilton Hts. Health Resource Ctr., 1992—. Recipient Mead Johnson award, Am. Inst. Nutrition, 1985, Cmty. Svc. award, BREM, 1997, Robert H. Bollinger

Disting. Acad. award, U. Kans., 1997, Longevity prize, Ispen Found., 1999, Circle award, Am. Dietetics Assn., 2001, Ralph T. Freeman award, Gerontology Soc. Am., 2004, Marsha Goodwin-Beck Interdisciplinary award for excellence in geriatric leadership, Dept. Vets. Affairs, 2005. Mem. ACP (geriatrics subcom. 1991-92), Am. Geriatric Soc. (Nasher/Manning award 2002), Internat. Soc. Study-Aging Male, Am. Soc. Clin. Investigation, Endocrine Soc., Am. Fedn. Clin. Rsch., Am. Acad. Behavioral Sci., Gerontology Soc. Am. (Freeman award, 2004), Am. Diabetes Assn., Am. Soc. Pharmacy and Therapeutics, Am. Soc. for Neurosci., La Asociacion de Gerontologica y Geriatrica, A.C. (hon.), Assn. Dirs. Geriatric Acad. Programs, Internat. Soc. Study Male Aging, Phi Beta Kappa. Office: Saint Louis U Sch Medicine 1402 S Grand Blvd Rm M238 Saint Louis MO 63104-1004 Office Phone: 314-977-8462. E-mail: marley@slu.edu.

**MORLEY, LAWRENCE WHITAKER,** geophysicist, consultant; b. Toronto, Feb. 19, 1920; s. George Whitaker and Mary Olive (Boyd) M.; divorced; children; Lawrence, Patricia, Chris, David (dec.); m. Beverly Anne Beckworth; step-children: Sandra Wellman, Stephen Burdett, Richard Burdett. BA, U. Toronto, 1946, MA, 1949, PhD, 1952; DSc (hon.) (hon.) York U., Toronto, 1974; Dr Environ. Studies (hon.), U. Waterloo, 2001. Dir. geophysics div. Geol. Survey Can., Ottawa, 1952-71; founding dir. gen. Can. Centre for Remote Sensing, Ottawa, 1971-80; founding exec. dir. Inst. for Space and Terrestrial Sci., Toronto, 1987-91; pres. Teledetection Internat. 1991—. Sci. counselor Can. High Commn., London. Lt. Can. Navy, 1941-45. Decorated Order of Can. Fellow Royal Soc. Can., Can. Aeronautics and Space Inst., Royal Can. Geog. Soc.; mem. Can. Soc. Remote Sensing (founding pres. 1971-74), Am. Geophys. Union, Am. Soc. Phototogrammetry and Remote Sensing, Soc. Exploration Geophysicists, Can. Geophys. Union, Can. Geomatics Inst. Home and Office: 16 Raglan St Ste 307 Collingwood ON Canada L9Y 4Y2 Office Phone: 705-443-8998. E-mail: l.mrley@rogers.com.

**MORLEY, LLOYD ALBERT,** electrical engineering educator; b. Provo, Utah, Oct. 28, 1940; s. John Jr. and Dorothea (Nielsen) M.; m. Jo Ann Bryant, Feb. 22, 1975; 1 child, Paul Loring. BS in Mining Engring., U. Utah, 1968, PhD in Mining Engring., 1972. Tchg. asst., rsch. assoc. U. Utah, Salt Lake City, 1968-71; asst. prof. mining engring. Pa. State U., University Park, 1971-75, assoc. prof., 1975-80, prof., 1980-85; prof., head dept. mineral engring. U. Ala., Tuscaloosa, 1985-93, endowed chair mining engring., 1993-99, prof. elec. engring., 1996—, assoc. dept. head elec. and computer engring., 1997-99, interim head, 1999-2000, head, 2000—04. Cons. Jim Walter Resources, Inc., Brookwood, Ala., 1987-98, Pitts. and Midway Coal Mining Co., Englewood, Colo., 1990-98, Drummond Co., Inc., Birmingham, Ala., 1991-98. Author: Mine Power Systems, 1990; contrb. articles to profl. jours. Staff sgt. USNG, 1958-66. Recipient Wilson Outstanding Tchg. award Pa. State U., 1980; Outstanding Rsch. Report awards U.S. Bur. Mines, 1983-84, Hackney Faculty Leadership award, U. Ala., 2000, HKN Outstanding Tchg. award, U. Ala., 2004. Fellow IEEE (bd. dirs. 1991-92, 94, 97-99, v.p. publs. 1994, 99, v.p. tech. activities 1997, 98, Richard M. Emberson award 2005); mem. Industry Applications Soc. IEEE (Mining Best Paper awards 1984, 88, 90, pres. 1988, Disting. lectr. 1991, Disting. Svc. award 1995), Power Engr. Soc., Computer Soc., Phi Kappa Phi, Eta Kappa Nu. Avocations: high-fidelity systems, classic sports cars, rose growing, music. Office: U Ala Dept Electrical and Computer Engring PO Box 870286 Tuscaloosa AL 35487-0286 Office Phone: 205-348-0672. Business E-Mail: lmorley@eng.ua.edu.

**MORLEY, MALCOLM A.,** artist, b. London, 1931, arrived in NYC, 1958, permanent resident. Student, Camberwell Sch. Arts & Crafts, London, 1952—53, Royal Coll. Art, 1954-57. Tchr. Royal Coll. Art, London, from 1956; mem. faculty Ohio State U., Columbus, 1965-66, Sch. Visual Arts, N.Y.C., 1967-69, SUNY, Stony Brook, 1972. Asso. Royal Coll. Art. London. Exhibited in one-man shows Kornblee Gallery, N.Y.C., 1964, 67, 69, Xavier Fourcade, N.Y.C., 1986, Temerance Hall Gallery, Bellport, N.Y., 1988, Pace Gallery, N.Y.C., 1988, 89, Anthony D'Offay Gallery, London, 1990, Pace Gallery, N.Y.C., 1991; group shows include Bienal de Sao Paulo, Brazil, 1957-67, Guggenheim Museum, N.Y.C., 1966, Am. Fedn. Arts, N.Y.C., 1968, Milw. Art Center, 1969, Whitney Mus. Am. Art, 1970, 72, Kunst des 20 Jahrhunderts, Stadtische, Kunsthalle, Dusseldorf, 1970, Documenta V, Kassel, Germany, 1972, Projekt 74, Cologne, Germany, 1974, Xavier Fourcade, N.Y.C., 1982, 83/84, 86, Akron Art Mus. (Ohio), 1982, Tate Gallery, London, 1983, 84, Mus. Modern Art, N.Y.C., 1984, 88, Museo Rufino Tamayo, Mexico City, 1984, Fabian Carlsson Gallery, London, 1985, Pace Prints, N.Y.C., 1986, Mus. Contemporary Art, L.A., 1989; touring retrospective show Basel Kunsthalle, 1983, Rotterdam Mus., 1983, White Chapel, London, 1983, Corcoran Mus. Art, Washington, 1983, Mus. Contemporary Art, Chgo., 1983-84, Bklyn. Mus., 1984, Bonnefanten Mus., Maastrich, 1991, Kunsthalle Basel, 1991, Mus. de Marseille, 1991, The Tate Gallery, Liverpool, 1992, Parish Art Mus., Southampton, N.Y., 1992; represented in numerous pub. collections. First recipient Turner prize, London, 1984 Mem.: NAD (academician). Mailing: c/o Gemini GEL at Joni Moisant Weyl 21B 58 W 58th St New York NY 10019-2509

**MORLEY, MARTIN L.,** musician; b. Longview, Wash., Nov. 6, 1956; s. Laurence S. and Alice C. Morley. MusB, U. Kans., Lawrence, 1978, MusM, 1981. Cert. church musician Presbyn. Assn. Musicians, 1987. Organist, music dir. West Side Presbyn. Ch., Lawrence, Kans., 1974—83; dir. music First Presbyn. Ch., Mesquite, Tex., 1983—95; dir. worship, music, and the arts Resurrection Luth. Ch., Plano, Tex., 1997—2004, Our Savior's Luth. Ch., Lafayette, Calif., 2004—. Freelance pianist, 1976—. Musician: Schumann Concerto with North Dallas Symphony; touring accompanist: Columbia Artists Mgmt.; contrb. articles to jour. Mem.: Greater Dallas Handbell Assn. (bd. dirs. 1985—88), Am. Guild Organists, Assn. Luth. Ch. Musicians, Presbyn. Assn. Musicians, Am. Choral Directors Assn., Am. Guild English Handbell Ringers (chair area IX, Tex. and Okla. 1998—2000, sec./treas. 1988—92) Choristers Guild Mensa Pi Kappa Lambda Mu Phi Epsilon Independent. Elca. Avocations: cooking, travel, contract bridge. Office Phone: 925-283-3722. Personal E-mail: martbar56@comcast.net.

**MORLOK, EDWARD KARL,** engineering educator, consultant; b. Phila., Nov. 3, 1940; s. Edward Karl and Anna Marie (Kurtz) M.; m. Ottilia Angela Husz, Dec. 14, 1968 (div. July 1983); 1 child, Jessica Angela; m. Patricia Campbell Conboy, Mar. 23, 1991. BE, Yale U., 1962; PhD, Northwestern U., 1967; MA (hon.), U. Pa., 1973. Civil engr., transp. U.S. Dept. Commerce, Washington, 1966-67; from asst. prof. civil engring. to assoc. prof. Northwestern U., Evanston, Ill., 1967-73, asst. dir. rsch., transp. ctr., 1969-73; 1907 Found. assoc. prof. U. Pa., Phila., 1973-75, chmn., transp. grad. group, 1983-86, 91-95, UPS found. prof. transp., 1975—, prof. systems engring., 1986—, chair systems grad. program, 1988-91, emeritus, 2004—. Cons. nat. transp. policy study commn., Washington, 1978-79. Author: Analysis Transportation Technology and Network Structure, 1969, Introduction to Transportation Engineering and Planning, 1978; assoc. editor Transp. Rsch. Jour., 1975-2004; consulting editor series in transp. for McGraw-Hill Publ. Co., 1980-98; contrb. more than 80 articles to profl. jours. Mem. Nat. Assembly Engring. panel on innovation in transp., Washington, 1979-80, panel on hazardous material transp., Washington, 1980-81. Recipient U.S. Sr. Scientist award Alexander von Humboldt Found., 1980-81; Rsch. grantee Commonwealth of Pa., Consol. Rail Corp., K-Line Am., U.S. Dept. Transp., NASA, NSF. Mem. ASCE, Transp. Rsch. Forum (v.p. 1974-75, pres. 1975-76, bd. disting. mems. 1983—, Disting. Transp. Rsch. award 1998), Transp. Rsch. Bd. (rev. com. of coun. of univ. transp. ctrs. 1985-88, coun. mem. 1988-90, chair freight transp. planning and logistics com. 1994-99, chair com. on policy options for intermodal freight trans. 1996-98). Lutheran. Office: U Pa Dept Elec and Systems Engring 220 S 33rd St Philadelphia PA 19104-6315 Business E-Mail: morlok@seas.upenn.edu.

**MORMAN, DEAN SMITH,** accountant, consultant; b. Owosso, Mich., Jan. 4, 1936; s. Cornelius Frank and Alliene Delight Morman; m. Christine Marie Paletta, Oct. 26, 1985; m. Betty Ann Branham, Aug. 7, 1954 (div. Oct. 21, 1985); 1 child, Dawn Denise Bogert. BBA, Kettering U. (GMI), Flint, Mich.,

1959. Acctg. mgr. Ctrl. Foundry Divsn., GMC, Saginaw, Mich., 1954—63; mgr. of material control Midland-Ross Corp., Cleveland, Ohio, 1963—66; various mgmt. and exec. positions IBM Corp., Armonk, NY, 1966—88; pres. Self Funded Svcs., Ocean City, NJ, 1989—2009; bus. controls mgr. Atlantic City Coin and Slot Svc. Co., Pleasantville, NJ, 1999—2002. Author: (poem) The Living Sea, 2003, (essay) Pets, 2003. Treas. South Jersey Cancer Fund, Brigantine, NJ, 1991—2000, St. Andrew by-the-Sea Luth. Ch., Atlantic City, 1988—99. R-Conservative. Lutheran. Avocations: travel, reading, creative writing. Personal E-mail: dmor136@aol.com.

**MORNEAU, WILLIAM,** pension and benefits company executive; BA, U. Western Ontario; MSc, London Sch. Econs.; MBA, INSEAD, France. Pres., CEO Morneau Sobeco, Toronto. Apptd. bd. dirs. AGF Mgmt. Ltd., 2000. Involved with numerous charitable and community organizations. Named one of Canada's Top 40 under 40, 2001. Office: Morneau Sobeco 895 Don Mills Rd Ste 700 Toronto ON Canada M3C 1W3

**MORNEWECK-FULD, LYNN E.,** music educator; b. Plainfield, N.J., Aug. 19, 1968; m. Steven Jay Fuld, Apr. 20, 2002; 1 child, Morgan Jay Fuld. BA, Oberlin Coll., Ohio, 1990; MAT, Rutgers U., New Brunswick, NJ, 1993. Vocal/gen. music tchr. Belmar (N.J.) Elem. Sch., 1993—95; choral dir. No. Valley Regional H.S., Old Tappan, NJ, 1995—96, Indian Hills H.S., Oakland, NJ, 1996—97, Mahwah (N.J.) H.S., 1997—. Condr. CantaLyrica Singers, Glen Rock, NJ, 1997—2004, YouthSong Voices, Ramsey, NJ, 2004—05, Bergen County Chorus, 2004; singer West Side Pres. Ch. Chancel Choir, Ridgewood, NJ, 1996—. Treas. CantaLyrica, 1998—2001, pres., 2001—04. Mem.: ACDA, MENC. Office: Mahwah High School 50 Ridge Rd Mahwah NJ 07430 Office Phone: 201-684-1127. Business E-Mail: lmorneweck@mahwah.k12.nj.us.

**MORNING, JOHN,** graphic designer; b. Cleve., Jan. 8, 1932; s. John Frew and Juanita Kathryn (Brannan) M.; m. Carole Ann Coleman, Jan. 24, 1964 (div. July 1984); children: Ann Juanita, John Floyd. BFA, Pratt Inst., 1955. Art dir. McCann-Erickson, Inc., N.Y.C., 1958-60; pvt. practice design N.Y.C., 1960—. Bd. dirs. Dime Savings Bank N.Y. Trustee com. on edn. Mus. Modern Art; chmn. bd. trustees Pratt Inst., Bklyn., 1988—92; vice chmn. NYC Cultural Affairs Adv. Commn., 1994—2000; dir. NY Coun. for Humanities, 1999—; trustee CUNY, 1997—, Rockefeller Bros. Fund, 1999—, Charles Stewart Mott Found., 2000—, Wilberforce U., 1986—, Mott Found.; bd. dirs. N.Y. Landmarks Conservancy; bd. dirs., co-chair Mus. African Art, NYC, 1991—94; bd. dirs. Charles E. Culpepper Found., 1990—, Bklyn. Acad. Music, 1993, 1993, Lincoln Ctr. Inst., 1993, Vivian Beaumont Theater, 1993—; bd. dirs., chmn. Henry St. Settlement, 1979—86. With U.S. Army, 1956—58. Recipient Alumni medal Pratt Inst., 1972, Presdl. Recognition award Pres. of U.S., 1984, Lillian D. Wald Humanitarian award, 1992. Mem.: Assn. Governing Bds. Colls. and Univs. (bd. dirs., chmn. 1998—2000), Am. Acad. Dramatic Arts (trustee 1988—95). Republican. E-mail: 110733.3622@compuserve.com.

**MORNINGSTAR, COLIN JON,** physicist, researcher; b. Fort Erie, Canada, Mar. 7, 1962; arrived in U.S., 2005, permanent resident; s. Robert Baker and Katherine Caroline Morningstar; m. Mary Louise Linton; children: Amberly Joyce, Solana Bree, Jocelyn Paige. BS, U. Toronto, 1985, MD, 1987, PhD, 1991. Postdoctoral rsch. assoc. Stanford (Calif.) Accelerator Ctr., 1991—93; postdoctoral rsch. fellow U. Edinburgh, Scotland, 1993—95; postdoctoral rsch. assoc. U. Calif., San Diego, 1995—99; asst. prof. physics Fla. Internat. U., Miami, Fla., 1999—2000, Carnegie Mellon U., Pitts., 2000—. Grantee, NSF, 1999—2006. Mem.: Am. Physics Soc. Achievements include research in comprehensive determination of the mass spectrum of glueballs using Monte Carlo computations in lattice gauge theory. Office: Carnegie Mellon University 5000 Forbes Avenue Pittsburgh PA 15213 Office Phone: 412-268-2728. Office Fax: 412-681-0648. Business E-Mail: colin_morningstar@cmu.edu.

**MOROF, JEFFREY W.,** lawyer; AB, U. Mich, 1976; JD, Washington U., St. Louis, 1979. Mng. ptnr., mem. exec. com. Bryan Cave LLP, Chgo. Office: Bryan Cave LLP 161 North Clark, Ste 4800 Chicago IL 60601 Office Phone: 312-602-5045. E-mail: jwmorof@bryancave.com.

**MORONEY, JAMES M., III,** publishing executive; m. Barbara Moroney; 5 children. BA in Am. Studies, Stanford U., 1978; MBA, U. Tex., 1983. With Belo Corp., 1978—; asst. exec. WFAA-TV, FKDM-TV, Beaumont, Tex., 1978—84; nat. sales position Petry TV, NY; named local sales mgr. WFAA-TV, 1985; controller Belo Corp., Dallas, 1989, asst. to pres. broadcast divsn., 1990—92; v.p., gen. mgr. KOTV, 1992—93, pres., gen. mgr., 1993; v.p. broadcast divsn. Belo Corp., 1994—95, exec. v.p. TV Group, 1995—97, pres. TV Group, 1997—98, exec. v.p., 1998—99; founding pres. Belo Interactive, Inc., 1999—2001; pub., CEO Dallas Morning News, 2001—. Mem. Dallas Citizens Coun.; mem. bd. dirs. TV Bur. Adv., Goodwill Industries, Dallas, Tulsa, United Way Tulsa, Cath. Charities Tulsa, Jr. Achievement Tulsa, Gilcrease Mus. Tulsa, Cistercian Perp. Sch. Dallas, Greater Dallas Chamber, State Fair Tex.; mem. bd. dirs. Coll. Center U. Tex. Austin. Named Pub. of TV, Editor & Pub. mag., 2004. Office: Dallas Morning News PO Box 655237 508 Young St Dallas TX 75265-5237 Business E-Mail: jmoroney@dallasnews.com.*

**MORONEY, JOHN RODGERS,** economist, educator; b. Dallas, Jan. 29, 1939; s. John Rodgers and Irene (Lewis) M.; m. Margaret Cecil Kearny, May 30, 1959; children: John Rodgers, Stephen Kearny, Helen, Michael Edward; m. Carmen Lambert, May 22, 1993 BA, So. Meth. U., 1960; PhD, Duke U., 1964. Asst. prof. econs. Fla. State U., 1964—66; assoc. prof. econs. Mich. State U., 1966—69; mem. exec. com. Inst. Pub. Utilities, 1968—69; prof. econs., chmn. dept. Tulane U., New Orleans, 1969—81; prof., head dept. econs. Tex. A&M U., College Station, 1981—. Vis. prof. econs. M.I.T., 1975 76; Schmidt internat. prof. A.D. Freeman Sch. Bus., Tulane U., New Orleans, 1998—; pres. Moroney Econ. Rsch. Assocs., 1992— Author: The Structure of Production in American Manufacturing, 1972, Exploration, Development, and Production: Texas Oil and Gas, 1997, editor, contrb.: Income Inequality: Trends and Internat. Comparisons, 1979, Economic Aspects of New Technology, 1980, Formal Energy and Resource Models, 1982; editor: Econometric Models of the Demand for Energy, 1984, Energy and Sustainble Development in Mexico, 2005; editor, contrb.: Energy, Capital, and Technological Change, 1987, Energy, Growth, and the Environment, 1992, Energy Prices and Production, 1994, Sustainable Economic Growth, 1995, Energy Supply and Demand, 1997, Fuels for the Future, 1999; mem. editl. bd. Bus. Topics, 1968-69, So. Econ. Jour, 1975— Social Sci. Rsch. Coun. faculty rsch. fellow, 1969; NSF rsch. fellow, 1975-76, 77-79 Mem. Am. Econ. Assn., So. Econ. Assn. (exec. com. 1975—, v.p. 1980), Royal Econ. Assn., Econometric Soc., Phi Beta Kappa Home: 210 Fireside Cir College Station TX 77840-1877 Office: Dept Econs Tex A&M U College Station TX 77843-4228 Office Phone: 979-845-1363. Business E-Mail: jmoroney@econmail.tamu.edu.

**MOROOKA, HIROSHI,** neurosurgeon; b. Kurashiki, Okayama, Japan, Aug. 28, 1946; s. Shigeru and Akiko (Kobayashi) M.; m. Michiko Ninomiya, June 6, 1976; children: Takatoshi, Hanako, Teruko. MD, U. Okayama, 1971, PhD, 1978. Diplomate Japanese Bd. Neurol. Surgery. Clin. asst. neurosurgery U. Okayama Med. Sch., 1972-77; instr. neurosurgery, 1980-83, asst. prof. neurosurgery, 1984-86; rsch. assoc. neurology U. Miami Med. Sch., Fla., 1977-79; chief neurosurgery Okayama Rousai Hosp., 1987-92, Bizen City Hosp., 1993-95, Okayama Saidaiji Hosp., 1996—. Author: Cytoprotection & Cytobiology, 1995-97, Medical Biochemical & Chemical Aspects of Free Radicals, 1989, Intracranial Pressure VII, 1989, Brain Edema IX, 1993. Recipient Disting. Prof. award, BWW Soc., Inst. Advancement of Positive Global Solutions, Calif., 2003, Legion of Honor award, United Cultural Conv., NC, 2005, Leading Health Profls. of World award, IBC, Cambridge, Eng., 2005; Nat. Rsch. grantee, 1981. Mem. AAAS, Japan Neurol. Soc., Societas Neurologica Japonica, N.Y. Acad. Scis., Am. Heart Assn., Am. Chem. Soc. Liberal Dem. Christian. Avocation: golf. Home: 880-165 Minato

703 8266 Okayama Japan Office: Okayama Saidaiji Hosp 8-41 Saidaiji Nakano Honmachi Okayama 704-8192 Japan Office Phone: 086-943-2211. Business E-Mail: morooka@okym.enjoy.ne.jp.

**MOROWITZ, HAROLD JOSEPH,** biophysicist, educator; b. Poughkeepsie, N.Y., Dec. 4, 1927; s. Philip Frank and Anna (Levine) M.; m. Lucille Rita Stein, Jan. 30, 1949; children: Joanna Lynn, Eli David, Joshua Alan, Zachary Adam, Noah Daniel. BS, Yale U., 1947, MS, 1950, PhD, 1951. Physicist Nat. Bur. Stds., 1951-53, Nat. Heart Inst., Bethesda, Md., 1953-55; mem. faculty Yale U., 1955-88, assoc. prof. biophysics, 1960-68, prof. molecular biophysics and biochemistry, 1968-88, master Pierson Coll., 1981-86; mem. faculty George Mason U., Fairfax, Va., 1988—, Robinson prof. biology and natural philosophy, 1988—; dir. Krasnow Inst. for Advanced Study, 1993-98. Chmn. com. on models for biomed. rsch. NRC, 1983-85, mem. bd. on basic biology, 1986-92. Author: Life and the Physical Sciences, 1964, (with Waterman) Theoretical and Mathematical Biology, 1965, Energy Flow in Biology, 1968, Entropy for Biologists, 1970, (with Lucille Morowitz) Life On The Planet Earth, 1974, Ego Niches, 1977, Foundations of Bioenergetics, 1978, The Wine of Life, 1979, Mayonnaise and the Origin of Life, 1985, Cosmic Joy and Local Pain, 1987, The Thermodynamics of Pizza, 1991, Beginnings of Cellular Life, 1992, (with James Trefil) The Facts of Life, 1992, Entropy and the Magic Flute, 1993, The Kindly Dr. Guillotin, 1997, The Emergence of Everything, 2002; editor Complexity, 1994 2002; contrb. articles to profl. jours. Mem. nat. adv. bd. Search Fo Inst., 1991-97, co-chmn. sci. adv. bd., 2000—06. Recipient Biol. Scis. award, Washington Acad. Scis., 2004. Mem. Biophys. Soc. (exec. com. 1965), Nat. Ctr. for Rsch. Resources (coun. 1987-92). Office: George Mason U Mail Stop 2A1 Krasnow Inst Advanced Study Fairfax VA 22030 Office Phone: 703-993-4334.

**MOROZ, PAVEL EMANUEL,** retired research scientist; b. Leningrad, Russia, 1928; came to U.S., 1976. Degree in Medicine, Pavlov Med. Inst., Leningrad, 1952, MD in Cytology and Biophysics, 1960. Rsch. scientist various insts., Leningrad, 1952-75, ret., 1975. Author: (in Russian) A Book of Aphorisms, 2002, Balding in the Spheromobile, 2005, The Fever, 2006; contrb. articles articles to profl. jours. Mem. N.Y. Acad. Scis. Achievements include development of centrifuge microscope; analysis of the physical limits of biological evolution, particularly of the vertical posture in man; research in the effects of the force of gravity and centrifugal force on the cell. Home and Office: 15-17 Willet St Apt 3K New York NY 10002 Personal E-mail: pavel15-17@yahoo.com.

**MOROZOVA, IRINA,** musician, music educator; arrived in U.S., 1990; d. Michael Brainin and Maria Morozova; 1 child, Gary Dennis Linkevich. MusB, St. Petersburg Conservatory, Russia, 1990; MusM, Manhattan Sch. Music, 1995. Piano faculty Mannes Coll. Music, N.Y.C., 1995—; piano assoc. faculty Manhattan Sch. Music, N.Y.C., 1995—; piano faculty Spl. Music Sch. Am., N.Y.C., 1996—. Musician: (performances) Solo Appearances, Recitals, Chamber Music. Named Prize winner, New Orleans Internat. Piano Competition, 1994, San Antonio Internat. Piano Competition, 1997, Winner, Artists Internat. Auditions, 1996. Home: 2464 Hammett Ave Fort Lee NJ 07024 Personal E-mail: irinapiano@att.net.

**MORPHEW, DOROTHY RICHARDS-BASSETT,** artist, real estate broker; b. Cambridge, Mass., Aug. 4, 1918; d. George and Evangeline Booth Richards; children: Jon Eric Bassett, Marc Alan Bassett, Dana Kimball Bassett. Grad., Boston Art Inst., 1949. Draftsman United Shoe Machinery Co., 1937—42; blueprinter, advt. artist A.C. Lawrence Leather Co., Peabody, Mass., 1949—51; propr. Studio Shop and Studio Potters, Beverly, Mass., 1951—53; tchr. ceramics and art Kingston, NH, 1953—; real estate broker, 1965—81; two-man exhbn. Topsfield (Mass.) Libr., 1960; owner, operator Ceramic Shop, West Stewartstown, NH. With USNR, 1942—44. Recipient Profl. award, New Eng. Ceramic Show, 1975, also numerous certs. in ceramics. Mem.: Englewood (Fla.) Art Guild.

**MORPHY, JAMES CALVIN,** lawyer; b. Pitts., Jan. 16, 1954; s. Robert Samson and Autumn (Phillips) M.; m. Priscilla Winslow Plimpton, July 11, 1981; children: Calvin, Katherine, Victoria. BA, Harvard U., Cambridge, Mass., 1976, JD, 1979. Bar: NY 1980. Assoc. Sullivan & Cromwell, NYC, 1979-86, ptnr., 1986—, mng. ptnr. com., 1992, mng. ptnr. M&A group, 1995—. Vice chmn. Tulane Mea Law Inst.; guest lectr. Harvard Law Sch. Author (contbg.): (treatise) New York and Delaware Business Entities: Choice Formation, Operation, Financing, and Acquisition, 1997, Transactional Lawyer's Deskbook, 2001. Trustee Greenwich Acad. Mem. ABA (com. on fed. securities law 1992—), Assn. Bar of City of NY, Wianno Club (bd. govs.), Greenwich Country Club, Harvard Club NY, Wianno Yacht Club, Phi Beta Kappa. Office Phone: 212-558-4000. Office Fax: 212-558-3588. Business E-Mail: morphyj@sullcrom.com.

**MORPHY, JOHN,** manufacturing executive; b. Rochester, N.Y., Aug. 14, 1947; s. John and Mary (Kelleher) M.; m. Marcia Price, June 5, 1971; children: Jaime, Matthew. BS in Acctg., Le Moyne Coll., Syracuse, N.Y., 1969. CPA, N.Y. Mgr. Arthur Andersen & Co., Rochester, 1969-76; v.p., controller Computer Consoles Inc., Rochester, 1976-85; v.p., CFO Goulds Pumps Inc., Seneca Falls, N.Y., 1985; group v.p. Gould's Pumps, Inc., 1992-95; v.p., dir. of fin. Paychex, Inc., Rochester, N.Y., 1996—. Office: Paychex Inc 911 Panorama S Rochester NY 14625-0397

**MORREALE, JOSEPH CONSTANTINO,** academic administrator, educator, economist, consultant; b. Bronx, N.Y., Oct. 26, 1944; s. Joseph Vincent Morreale and Grace (Soricelli); m. Barbara McAdorey; children: Gwenn F., Margaret I., Adam J.; stepchildren: Neil J., Michael D., John D. BA, Queens Coll. CUNY, 1967; MA, SUNY, Buffalo, 1969. PhD in Econs., 1972; MS in Higher Ednl. Adminstrn., SUNY, Albany, 1989. Asst. prof. econs. Western Mich. U. (Kalamazoo), 1970-74, sabbatical U. Wis. (Madison), 1974-75 asst. to assoc. prof. health svcs. adminstrn., econs. Grad. Sch. Pub. Health U. Pitts., 1975-79; assoc. to prof. econs., environ. studies Bard Coll., Annandale-On-Hudson, NY, 1979-88; vis. rsch. fellow Grad. Sch. Edn., H.E. Adminstrn. SUNY, Albany, 1988-89; prof., chmn. dept. edn. adminstrn. Grad. Sch. Pace U., White Plains, NY, 1989-96; vice provost for planning assessment and instnl. rsch. Pace U., N.Y.C., Westchester, 1996-98, v.p. planning, assessment, rsch. and acad. support, 1998—, sr. assoc. provost, v.p., 2001—. Health care and govt. fin. cons. to fed. agencies, state and local govts., pvt. firms, 1979—; adj. prof. law Pace U., 1990-96; adj. prof. pub. adminstrn. Grad. Sch. Pub. Affairs, SUNY-Albany, 1990-96; vis. prof. U. Lancaster, Eng., 1984-85; rsch. assoc., bd. dirs. Hudsonia Environ. Rsch., Annandale, 1985-95; fin. planner Prudential Fin. Svcs., Newburgh, N.Y., 1987-89. Author: Health Care Economics, 1977, Post Tenure Review and Renewal: Experienced Voices, 2002; editor: The U.S. Medical Care Industry, 1974, Post-tenure Review: Policies, Practices, Precautions, 1997; contrb. articles to profl. jours. Appoint pub. rep. Westchester County Deferred Compensation Bd., Mt. Kisco Planning Bd. Recipient NDEA fellowship, 1967-70, Pharm. Mfg. Assn. fellowship, 1969-70, post-doctoral fellowship Health Econ. Rsch. Ctr. U. Wis., 1974-75, rsch. fellowship SUNY-Albany, 1988-89, ACE fellowship UNC, Charlotte, 1995-96, sr. rsch. fellow Harvard IEM Inst., 2000. Mem. Am. Soc. Pub. Adminstrn., Am. Econ. Assn., Am. Ednl. Fin. Assn., Assn. Instl. Rsch., Am. Assn. Higher Edn., Am. Coun. Edn. (fellow 1995-96), N.Y. State Govt. Fin. Officers Assn. (bd. dirs. 1990-95). Mem. Soc. Of Friends. Avocations: photography, tennis, music. Office: Pace U VP 1 Pace Plz New York NY 10038-1598

**MORREIM, E. HAAVI,** medical ethics educator; b. July 21, 1950; d. Paul Eugene and Florence Morreim. BA in Philosophy, St. Olaf Coll., 1972; MA in Philosophy, U. Va., 1976, PhD, 1980. Med. philosopher program in human biology and soc. U. Va. Sch. Medicine, Charlottesville, 1980-82, asst. prof. philosophy in medicine, 1982-84; from asst. to assoc. prof. dept. human values and ethics U. Tenn. Coll. Medicine, Memphis, 1988—93, prof. dept. human values and ethics, 1993—. Adj. prof. philosophy Va. Commonwealth U., Richmond, 1980; vis. prof. philosophy St. Olaf Coll., Northfield, Minn.,

1982; Andrew Mellon vis. asst. prof. humanities and medicine Georgetown U. Sch. Medicine, Washington, 1983; sr. vis. rsch. scholar Kennedy Inst. Ethics, Georgetown U., 1983; manuscript reviewer; presenter and lectr. in field. Author: Balancing Act: The New Medical Ethics of Medicine's New Economics, 1991, Holding Health Care Accountable: Law and the New Medical Marketplace, 2001; mem. editl. adv. bd. Jour. Medicine and Philosophy; bd. editors: Jour. Law, Medicine and Ethics, IRB: Ethics and Human Research; contbr. articles to profl. jours. Active Hastings Ctr. Mem. Am. Health Lawyers Assn., Am. Soc. Law, Medicine, and Ethics, Am. Soc. for Bioethics and Humanities, Phi Beta Kappa. Avocations: running, high-performance automobile driving, photography, skiing. Office: Univ Tenn Coll Medicine 956 Court Ave Ste B328 Memphis TN 38163-2814 Office Phone: 901-448-5725. Business E-Mail: hmorreim@utmem.edu.

**MORRELL, GENE PAUL,** gas industry executive, consultant; b. Ardmore, Okla., Oct. 4, 1932; s. Paul T. and Etta L. (Weaver) M.; m. Jan A. Foster, Aug. 20, 1954; children: Jeffrey T., Kelly Ann, Rob Redman. BS in Geology, U. Okla., 1954, LLB, 1962. Bar: D.C. 1973. Geologist Gilmer Oil Co., Ardmore, Okla., 1957-59, atty.-geologist, 1962-63; pvt. practice Ardmore, 1963-69; ofcl. Dept. Interior, Washington, 1969-72; v.p. Lone Star Gas Co., Washington, 1972-76; sr. v.p. United Energy Resources, Inc., Houston, 1976-86; vice chmn. Petro United Terminals, Inc., Houston, 1986-98; cons. on investments, 1998—. Contbr. articles to profl. jours, Commr. City of Ardmore. 1967-69 vice-mayor, 1968. Mem. D.C. Bar Assn., Am. Assn. Petroleum Geologists, River Oaks Country Club (Houston), Phi Alpha Delta, Sigma Alpha Epsilon. Episcopalian.

**MORRICE, BRAD A.,** diversified financial services company executive; b. 1956; MBA, Stanford U., 1982; JD, U. Calif., Berkeley. Atty. Manatt, Phelps & Phillips LLP, Fried, King Holmes & August; ptnr. King, Purtich & Morrice LLP, 1990—93; exec. v.p., chief adminstrv. officer Plaza Home Mortgage, Inc., 1993—94, pres., COO, 1994—95; co-founder, pres., gen. counsel, sec. New Century Fin. Corp., Irvine, Calif., 1995—96, vice chmn., pres., 1996—2001, vice chmn., pres., COO, 2001—06, pres., CEO, 2006—. Office: New Century Fin Corp Ste 1000 18400 Von Karman Ave Irvine CA 92612*

**MORRILL, BILLIE ALBERTA,** librarian; b. Hartford, Conn., Aug. 25, 1942; d. Clifford Kenneth Worland and Alberta Molly Schwartz; m. Richard Melvin Morrill, June 11, 1966; 1 child, Celeste. AS in Gen. Studies, Three Rivers C.C., Norwich, Conn., 1998. Asst. editor Travelers Bull. Travelers Ins. Co., Hartford, 1970—73, head spkrs. bur., 1973—75; copywriter G. Fox & Co., Hartford, 1979—83; freelance writer, 1983—87; circulation clk., 1987—90; reference libr. East Lyme Pub. Libr., Niantic, Conn., 1987—1994—, head circulation svcs., 1990—94. Author poetry; contbr. articles to profl. jours. Charter mem., pres. Travelers Toastmistress Club, Hartford, 1970—75. Recipient Trustee's medallion, Three Rivers C.C., 1998. Mem.: Poets of the Sound (facilitator 1998—), Conn. Poetry Soc., LTA Alumni Assn., Phi Theta Kappa. Methodist. Avocations: writing, reading, walking. Office: East Lyme Pub Librr 39 Society Rd Niantic CT 06357-1100

**MORRILL, KELLI RAE,** secondary school educator; b. Wakeeney, Kans., Apr. 4, 1965; d. Leon and Ginger Fabrizius; m. James Morrill, June 8, 1991; children: Jackson, Easton. BA, Ft. Hays State U., Hays, Kans., 1988; MA, Pitts. State U., Pitts., Kans., 1991. Tchr. Ft. Scott H.S., Ft. Scott, Mo., 1988—91, Ctr. H.S., Kans. City, Mo., 1991—93, Sumner Acad. Arts and Sci., Kans. City, 1993—98, Raytown South H.S., Mo., 1998—. Coach speech and theatre Raytown South H.S., 2000—. Named Tchr. of Yr., Raytown South H.S., 2006. Mem.: NEA, Nat. Forensic League (named Triple Diamond Coach 2003), Psi Kappa Delta, Alpha Psi Omega. Luth. Office: Raytown South Sr High Sch 8211 Sterling Ave Raytown MO 64138-2690

**MORRILL, PENNY CHITTIM,** art historian; b. San Antonio, Feb. 4, 1947; d. Jack Robert and Dorothy Born (Sutherland) Chittim; m. James Agrippa Morrill, July 12, 1969; children: Jackson Forrest, Julia Chiltipin BA with honors, Tulane U., 1969; MA, U. Pa., 1971; PhD, Md., 2001. Program coord. Cancer Rsch. Found. Am., Alexandria, Va., 1990—95; adj. prof. Md. Inst. Coll. Art, Balt., 2000, Corcoran Coll. Art, Washington, 2003, Georgetown U., 2004—05, Hood Coll., Md., 2006—. Author: Silver Masters of Mexico, 1996, Mexican Silver, 1994; curator Carlyle Ho. Mus., Alexandria, 1980; curator, catalogue author traveling exhbn. Maestros de Plata: William Spratling and the Mex. Silver Renaissance, San Antonio Mus. Art., 1998-2004; contbr. articles to profl. jours. Vol. teen pregnancy prevention Nat. ARC, Washington, 1986-98; participant Core Women in Leadership, Washington, 1988; mem. adv. com. Betty Ford Breast Health Ctr., Washington, 1997-98, adv. bd.; bd. dirs. Nat. Rehab. Hosp., Washington, 1991-2006, pres., 1991-2006; mem. alumnae bd. Newcomb Coll./Tulane U., 1990-94, v.p., 1992-97; v.p. Lyceum Mus., Alexandria, 1992-97, bd. mem., pres.; bd. mem., editor, pres. Hist. Alexandria Found., 1980-89; curator exhbn. Carlyle House Mus., Alexandria, 1980; mem. alumnae bd., v.p. Newcomb Coll. Tulane U., 1991-2006; bd. dirs., pres. Lyceum Mus., Alexandria, 1992-97, Hist. Alexandria Found., 1980-89, editor, 1980-89. Recipient Achievement award Jr. League Phila., 1985, RAP and AMAZE award, Nat. ARC, 1988, Spirit Volunteerism award Jr. League Washington, 1992, Recognition award Nat. Rehab. Hosp., 1997, Bd. Dir. award, 2005 Mem. Coll. Art Assn., Am. Soc. Jewelry Historians Episcopalian. Avocations: knitting, gardening.

**MORRIN, PETER PATRICK,** museum director; b. St. Louis, Oct. 31, 1945; s. Kevin Charles and Helen Louise (Clanton) M.; m. Carolyn Brooks, Oct. 5, 1974; children: Matthew, Rebecca. AB, Harvard U., 1968; MFA, Princeton U., 1972. Asst. prof., dir. art gallery Vassar Coll., Poughkeepsie, NY, 1974-78; curator 20th century art High Mus. Art, Atlanta, 1979-86; dir. Speed Art Mus., Louisville, 1986—. Panelist Nat. Endowment Arts. Contbr. articles to profl. publs. Served with USAR, 1968-74. Mem.: Assn. Art Mus. Dirs. (pres. 2003—04). Office: Speed Art Mus 2035 S 3rd St Louisville KY 40208-1812 Office Phone: 502-634-2700. Business E-Mail: pmorrin@speedmuseum.org

**MORRIS, ALBERT JEROME,** health products executive; b. N.Y.C., Jan. 3, 1919; s. Peter and Minnie (Miller) M.; Barbara McLeod, Feb 6, 1943; children: Peter A., Lee Ellen Morris Guenther, Lisa Ann Morris Rasche. BS in Electronics, U. Calif., Berkeley, 1941; MS in Electronics, Stanford U., 1948, Degree of Engr., 1950. Registered profl. engr., Calif. Founder Morris Defibrilator Co., 1949; sr. v.p., co-founder Levinthal Elec. Products, Palo Alto, Calif., 1953-60; pres., dir. Radiation at Stanford, Palo Alto, 1960-63; pres., chief exec. officer Energy Systems Inc., Palo Alto, 1963-66, Genesys Systems Inc., Palo Alto, 1967-84, Biosys, Palo Alto, 1983-88, chmn. bd., 1989; also chmn. bd. TurboEnergy Systems, Phoenix, 1989-90; chmn. bd., chief exec. officer Neural Systems Corp., Palo Alto, 1991—. Cons. to schs. of engring., Stanford U. and 18 other major univs.; chmn. San Francisco coun. Western Electronics Mfrs. Assn., 1965; chmn. bd. Western Electronics Show and Conv., Calif., 1961, Neural Sys. Corp. Author over 50 papers on high stabilization, high power electronics, med. electronics and continuing edn. Recipient Best Paper award IEEE/ASEE Frontiers in Edn. Conf., 1978. Fellow IEEE, Sigma Chi Iota; mem. AAAS. Avocations: tennis, golf.

**MORRIS, ALVIN LEONARD,** retired dentist, academic administrator; b. Detroit, July 2, 1927; s. Frank and Lulu (Cornett) M.; m. Arlene Teschler, Feb. 1, 1947 (dec. Apr. 1974); children: Jeffry, Gregg, Beth; m. Beverly Hackman, 1975. Student, Ill. Tech., 1944-45; D.D.S., U. Mich., 1951; PhD, U. Rochester, 1957; D.Sc. (hon.), U. Md., 1983. Intern Letterman Army Hosp., San Francisco, 1951-52; postdoctoral research fellow NIH, 1954-57; head dept. oral diagnosis U. Pa. Sch. Dentistry, 1957-61; dean U. Ky. Coll. Dentistry, Lexington, 1961-68; asst. v.p. U. Ky. Coll. Dentistry (Med. Center), 1968-69, v.p. adminstrn. univ., 1970-75; exec. dir. Assn. for Acad. Health Centers, Washington, 1975-79; prof. dental care systems Sch. Dental Medicine, assoc. v.p. health affairs U. Pa., 1979-87; sr. assoc. Leonard Davis Inst. Health Econs., Wharton Grad. Sch., 1980-87, prof. emeritus, 1987-89; research prof. Health Services Research Ctr./Sch. of Dentistry, U. N.C., Chapel Hill, 1987-89. Cons. Dental Corps, U.S. Army, 1960-70, VA, 1962-75, U.S. Dept.

Def., 1969-72; pub. health service cons. dental study sect. USPHS, 1963-67; also chmn.; cons., lectr. USN Dental Sch.; cons. Army Med. Service Adv. Com. Preventive Dentistry, 1967-71; mem. Nat. Adv. Council Edn. Health Professions, 1968-72; bd. dirs. Nat. Center Health Edn., 1977-84; adv. com. Ednl. Testing Service, 1977-82; chmn. adv. com. Nat. Preventive Dental Demonstration Program, 1976-83 Served with inf. AUS, 1944-46; to 1st lt. Dental Corps 1951-54. Recipient Pierre Fauchard medal, 1974, Henry Spenadel medal, 1982, Callahan medal, 1991. Fellow Internat., Am. colls. dentists; mem. ADA (Disting. Svc. award 1985), Inst. Medicine of NAS, AAAS, Internat. Assn. Dental Rsch., So. Conf. Dental Deans and Examiners (pres. 1964-65), Sigma Xi. Presbyterian (deacon, trustee). Home: 302 Briarcliff Ln Danville KY 40422

**MORRIS, ASHLEY,** information scientist, educator; b. DeFuniak Springs, Fla., Oct. 20, 1963; s. Kenneth Eugene and Dorothy Morris; m. Hana Zizková, May 15, 1999; children: Katerina, Annabel Lee, Rey d'Orleans. BS, U. So. Miss., 1985, MS, 1995; PhD, Tulane U., 1999. Software specialist Digital Equipment Corp., Culver City, Calif., 1987—89; cons. Ashley Morris Cons., LA, 1989—93, AT&T, Seattle, 1993—94; instr. Oracle, Redwood Shores, Calif., 1997—98; prof. U. Idaho, Moscow, 1998—2000, DePaul U., Chgo., 2000—. Cons. H.A. Morris, Inc., New Orleans, 1994—, Oracle, Atlanta, 1997—98; rschr. Naval Rsch. Lab., Stennis Space Ctr., Miss., 1997—98. Contbr. articles to profl. articles. Grantee, Oracle, 1999, U. Idaho, 1999, Inst. Mus. & Libr. Svcs., 1998, U. Idaho, 1999, NATO, 2005—06; Cobase grant, NAS, 2003—04. Mem.: AAUP, IEEE Computer Soc., Assn. Computing Machinery, Internat. Fuzzy Sets Assn., N.Am. Fuzzy Info. Processing Soc., Upsilon Pi Epsilon. Avocations: music, hockey, travel. Office: DePaul Univ 243 S Wabash Ave Chicago IL 60604 Office Phone: 312-362-8252. Office Fax: 312 362 6116. Personal E-mail: ashley@ashleymorris.com. Business E-Mail: amorris@acm.org.

**MORRIS, BRENDA DENISE,** music educator, director; b. Kansas City, Mo., Mar. 27, 1952; d. Clyde Edward and Irene Perdue; m. Casey Thomas Morris, June 1, 1991; m. Walter Edward Freeman; children: Kerri, Michelle, Derek, Jamie. At, U. Mo. Music Conservatory, Kansas City. Pvt. music tchr., 1967—2006; prin. tchr. Prodigy Sch. MusicArts, 2006—. Ch. musician First Assembly of God Ch., 1961—70; condr. 12th grade Lee's Summit H.S., 1969—70; music dir. Longview Christian Ch., 1989—99, Longview Bapt. Ch., 2000—02, One Spirit Meth. Ch., Kansas City, 2004—, Aldersgate Meth. Ch., Olathe, Kans.

**MORRIS, BRIAN,** advertising executive; m. Cindy Morris; 2 children. Graduate, So. Meth. Univ., Dallas; M in Personnel Svcs., Miami Univ., Ohio. Pres. Dailey & Assoc., LA, CEO. Named Leader of Yr., LA Advt. Agencies Assn.; recipient Silver Medal award, Am. Advt. Fedn. Office: Dailey & Assoc 8687 Melrose Ave Ste G300 West Hollywood CA 90069-5725

**MORRIS, BRIAN,** state supreme court justice; b. Butte, Mont., Sept. 5, 1963; m. Cherche Prezeau; 3 children. BA in Economics, Stanford U., 1986, MA in Economics, 1987; JD, Stanford Law Sch., 1992. Law clerk for Judge John T. Noonan, Jr. U.S. Ct. of Appeals for Ninth Circuit, 1992—93; law clerk for Justice William H. Rehnquist U.S. Supreme Ct., 1993—94; legal asst. Iran-U.S. Claims Tribunal, The Hague, 1994—95; prtnr. Goetz, Gallik, Baldwin & Dolan, 1995—99; sr. legal officer UN Compensation Commn., 2000—01; state solicitor Mont. Dept. of Justice, 2001—04; justice Mont. Supreme Ct., 2005—. Author several law review and professional jour. articles. Office: Mont Supreme Ct PO Box 203003 Helena MT 59620-3003*

**MORRIS, DAVID S.,** publishing executive; Grad., St. Anselm Coll. From NY adv. mgr. Entertainment Weekly to assoc. pub. Time Inc., NYC, 1991—2000, pres., pub., Entertainment Weekly, 2000—03, 2005—, pres., pub., Sports Illustrated, 2003—05. Office: Time Inc Entertainment Weekly 1675 Broadway 30th Fl New York NY 10019*

**MORRIS, DESMOND (JOHN),** zoologist, writer, artist; s. Harry Howe Morris and Dorothy Marjorie (Hunt) Fuller; m. Ramona Joy Baulch, July 30, 1952; 1 son, Jason. BSc, Birmingham U., Eng.; DPhil, Oxford U., Eng.; DSc (hon.), Reading U., Eng., 1998. Rsch. worker zoology U. Oxford, Eng., 1954-56; head Granada T.V. and Film Unit, Zool. Soc. London, 1956-59, curator mammals, 1959-67; dir. Inst. Contemporary Arts, London, 1967-68; rsch. fellow Wolfson Coll., Oxford, 1973-81. Author: Biology of Art, 1962, Apes and Monkeys, 1965, Big Cats, 1965, Mammals: A Guide to the Living Species, 1966, The Naked Ape, 1968, The Human Zoo, 1969, Intimate Behavior, 1971, Manwatching: A Field Guide to Human Behavior, 1977, The Soccer Tribe, 1981, The Book of Ages, 1983, The Art of Ancient Cyprus, 1985, Bodywatching: A Field Guide to the Human Species, 1985, The Illustrated Naked Ape, 1986, Catwatching, 1986, Dogwatching, 1986, The Secret Surrealist, 1987, Catlore, 1987, The Animals Roadshow, 1988, The Human Nestbuilders, 1988, Horsewatching, 1988, The Animal Contract, 1990, Animalwatching, 1990, Babywatching, 1991, Christmas Watching, 1992, The World of Animals, 1993, The Human Animal, 1994, Body Talk, A World Guide to Gestures, 1994, The Naked Ape Trilogy, 1994, Illustrated Cat Watching, 1994, Illustrated Babywatching, 1995, Illustrated Dogwatching, 1996, Catworld: A Feline Encyclopedia, 1996, The Human Sexes, 1997, Illustrated Horsewatching, 1998, Cool Cats: The 100 Cat Breeds of the World, 1999, Body Guards, 1999, Dogs: A Dictionary of Dog Breeds, 2001, Peoplewatching, 2002, The Nature of Happiness, 2004, The Naked Woman, 2004, Watching: Encounters With Humans and Other Animals, 2006, others; co-author: (with Ramona Morris) Men and Snakes, 1965, Men and Apes, 1966, Men and Pandas, 1966, The Giant Panda, 1981, Gestures: Their Origins and Distribution, 1979; autobiography Animal Days, 1979, The Naked Eye, 2000; editor Primate Ethology 1969, (fiction) Inrock, 1983; number numerous articles to zool. jours.; one-man shows include Mayor Gallery, London, 1997, Pub. Art Gallery, Buxton, 1997, Keitelman Gallery, Brussels, 1998, Rossaert Gallery, Antwerp, 1998, Witteveen Gallery, Amsterdam, 1999, Mus. Modern Art, Ostend, 2002, others. Address: care Jonathan Cape RandomCH 20 Vauxhall Bridge Rd London SWIV 2SA England Business E-Mail: dmorris@ukstudio.org.

**MORRIS, DIANE L.,** mathematics professor; d. Donald H. and Jean F. Owens; m. Jerry L. Morris, Dec. 16, 1972; 1 child, Nathan L. BS in Edn., Ohio U., Athens, 1973; MS, Wheeling Jesuit Coll., W.Va., 1991. Tchr. math. St. Clairsville H.S., Ohio, 1975—85; prof. math. Belmont Tech. Coll., Ohio, 1985—. Foster mother Belmont County Dept. of Job and Family Svcs., St. Clairsville, Ohio, 2001—06; vol. litter collector Ohio Dept. Transp., New Philadelphia, 1991—2006; mem. Wheeling Civic Garden Ctr., Oglebay Good Zoo, Am. Mensa, Ltd., Farm Bur. Mem.: Am. Math. Assn. of 2-Yr. Colls. Avocations: quilting, gardening, hiking, bicycling. Home: 65250 Barkcamp Park Rd Belmont OH 43718 Office: Belmont Tech Coll 120 Fox Shannon Pl Saint Clairsville OH 43950 Office Phone: 740-695-9500 ext. 1191. Business E-Mail: dmorris@btc.edu.

**MORRIS, DICK,** columnist, political consultant; b. NY, 1952; s. Eugene Morris; m. Eileen McGann. BA, Columbia U. Polit. cons. Bill Clinton's Campaign for Gov., Ark., 1977, Ark., 1982, Bill Clinton's Re-Election Campaign for Gov., Ark., 1984, Ark., 1986, Ark., 1990; chief strategist for Argentina Pres. Fernando de la Rua Campaign for Pres., 1999, for Uruguay Pres. Jorge Battle Campaign for Pres., 1999, for Mexican Reformer Vicente Fox's Campaign, 2000; commentator FOX News Channel; weekly columnist New York Post, The Hill Mag., Nat. Post, Canada. Founder Vote.com, 1999, co-founder (with Eileen McGann) Legalvote.com, 2000. Author: Bum Rap on Am. Cities - The Real Causes of Urban Decay, 1977, Behind the Oval Office: Getting Re-Elected Against All Odds, 1998, The New Prince: Machiavelli Updated for the 21st Century, 1999, Vote.com - A Guide to the Internet basted politics of the future, 2000, Power Plays: Win or Lose - How History's Great Polit. Leaders Play the Game, 2003, Off With Their Heads: Traitors, Crooks & Obstructionists in Am. Politics, Media & Bus., 2003, Rewriting History,

2004, Because He Could, 2004. Achievements include working as polit. cons. for winning campaigns of more than 30 senators or governors. Office: New York Post 1211 Avenue Of The Americas New York NY 10036

**MORRIS, DONALD,** tax specialist; b. Chgo., Oct. 13, 1945; s. Donald Charles and Cathleen (Lautner) M.; children: Keith, Sarah. BA, Calif. State U., L.A., 1968; MA, De Paul U., 1972, MS in Taxation, 1987; PhD, So. Ill. U., 1978. CPA Ill., N.Mex.; CFP, cert. fraud examiner. Prof. philosophy John A. Logan Coll., Carterville, Ill., 1972-79; tax mgr. Evans-Gries & Co. CPAs, Addison, Ill., 1980-83; sr. tax advisor Alexander Grant, CPA, Chgo., 1983-84; tax mgr. Evans & Co., Itasca, Ill., 1984-87; pvt. practice Addison, 1987—88, Bloomingdale, 1988—93, Roselle, Ill., 1993—97; prof. acctg. E. N.Mex. U., Portales, 1997—2006, chmn. Dept. Acctg., Fin. and CIS; prof. acctg. U. Ill., Springfield, 2006—. Author: Dewey and the Behavioristic Context of Ethics, 1995, Opportunity: Optimizing Life's Chances, 2006; co-author: Accounting Desk Book, 2006. Libertarian candidate for comptroller State of Ill., 1986. Mem. AICPA, N.Mex. Soc. CPAs, Am. Philos. Assn., Am. Acctg. Assn., Assn. Cert. Fraud Examiners, Soc. for Bus. Ethics, Assn. Informal Logic and Critical Thinking, Delta Mu Delta. Avocations: distance running (4 marathons), tennis, woodworking. Home: 1516 Saltcedar Ct Springfield IL 62712 Office: U Ill at Springfield Dept Accountancy UHB 4064 4900 Shephard Rd Springfield IL 62703 Business E-Mail: don.morris@uis.edu.

**MORRIS, DONALD GEORGE,** engineering company executive; s. Donald and Betty (Lewis) Morris; m. Anita M. Janicek; children: Suzanne, Mary Ellen, Catherine, Donald III. BSBA, North Ga. Coll. and State U., 2000, MS in Pub. Adminstrn., 2001. Various to engr. Goetze Corp. of Am., LaGrange, Ga., 1986—89; plant mgr. Jakes Mfg., Greenwood, Miss., 1989—92; CEO Morris & Assocs., Gainesville, Ga., 1992—. Contbr. articles to profl. jours. Recipient Leadership award, Wall Street Jour., 2000. Mem.: Fabricators and Mfrs. Assn., Soc. Die Cast Engrs. Business E-Mail: dgmorr@consultant.com.

**MORRIS, DOUGLAS PETER,** recording company executive; b. Far Rockaway, N.Y., Nov. 23, 1938; s. Walter and Mary (Lerner) Morris; m. Monique Jequel, Mar. 20, 1964; children: Walter, Peter. BA, Columbia Coll., 1960. Gen. mgr. Robert Mellin, Inc., N.Y.C., 1964—65; writer. producer Laurie Records, Inc., NYC, 1965—69, v.p., gen. mgr.; owner Big Tree Records (acquired by Atlantic Records), NYC, 1970—78; pres. ATCO Records, Swan Song and Rolling Stones Records (subs. of Warner Music), 1978, Atlantic Records, NYC, 1980—90; co-chmn., co-CEO Atlantic Recording Group, NYC, 1990—94; chmn., COO, pres. Warner Music-U.S., 1994—95; chmn., CEO Universal Music Group (formerly MCA Music Ent.), NYC, 1995—. Cons. Ampex Records, 1968. Composer: (songs) Sweet Talkin Guys, 1968, Smoking in the Boys' Room, 1970; prodr.: (song) Wave on Wave, 2003. With U.S. Army, 1962—64. Named Man of Yr. in Record Industry, United Jewish Appeal, 1981; scholar, Paragon Oil, 1954, Columbia Coll., 1960. Mem.: ASCAP. Office: Universal Music Group 1755 Broadway Fl 7 New York NY 10019-3743

**MORRIS, EARLE ELIAS, JR.,** retired state official; b. Greenville, S.C., July 14, 1928; s. Earle Elias and Bernice (Carey) M.; m. Jane L. Boroughs, Apr. 12, 1958; children: Lynda Lewis, Carey Mauldin, Elizabeth McDaniel, Earle Elias III; m. Carol Telford, Oct. 4, 1972; 1 son, David Earle (dec.). BS, Clemson Coll., 1949, LLD; D.Pub. Svc. (hon.), U. S.C., 1980, S.C. State Coll., 1990; Dr. Med. Sci., U. S.C.; LLD (hon.), The Citadel, Cen. Wesleyan Coll.; HHD (hon.), Lander Coll., Francis Marion Coll., 1984, U. Charleston, 1992; DHL, Winthrop U., 1996. V.p., dir. Pickens Bank, 1956-69, Bankers Trust S.C., Pickens, 1968-75; pres. Gen. Ins. Agy., Pickens, 1970—; ptnr. Morris Realty Co., Pickens; mem. S.C. Ho. of Reps., 1950-54, S.C. Senate, 1954-70; lt. gov. State of S.C., 1971-75, comptr. gen., 1976-99. Bd. dirs. S.C. Bus. Alliance for Transp; dir. Brunswick Worsted Mills, S.C. Devel. Corp., Pickens Savs. & Loan Assn.; hon. consul Republic of Korea. Pres. Clemson U. Found., 1984-85; state dir. Selective Svc. Sys. Served to brig. gen. S.C. N.G., maj. gen. S.C. S.G. Decorated Legion of Merit, Meritorious Svc. medals; recipient Algernon Sydney Sullivan award, 1980, Donald L. Scantlebury award, 1985, Nations Most Valuable Pub. Ofcl. award, 1993, Pub. Svc. award Am. Legion, 1993, Living Legend award S.C. Hist. Found., 1997, Clemson Medallion award 1997, Order of the Palmetto; named Disting. Alumnus, Clemson Coll. Mem. Nat. Assn. State Comptrollers (pres. 1982), Nat. Assn. State Auditors, Comptrollers and Treasurers (pres. 1988-89), S.C. Nat. Guard Assn. (pres. 1980-81), S.C. Jr. C. of C., S.C. Rehab. Assn. (v.p.), Govtl. Acctg. Standards Adv. Coun. (chmn. 1989-96), Fin. Acctg. Found. (trustee 1985-88, 96—, v.p. 2000-01), S.C. Retirees Assn. (pres.), Blue Key, Palmetto Club, Faculty Club (Columbia), Poinsett Club (Greenville), Masons, Shriners, Lions (hon., life), Order of Saint Stanislas (grand chancellor, Knight Grand Cross), Order of white Eagle of Saint Stanislas, Sovereign Mil. Order Swabia, Order of Polonia Restituta (knight comdr., 2d class), Knights of Malta. Presbyterian (elder, former deacon, synod trustee). Home: 159 Lake Murray Ter Lexington SC 29072-9103 *In my personal, public and professional life I have tried to follow the Biblical admonition of "loving mercy, doing justly, and walking humbly."*.

**MORRIS, G. MICHAEL,** science educator; BS with spl. distinction in engring. physics, U. Okla., 1975; MS in elec. engring., Calif. Inst. of Tech., 1976, PhD, 1979. Scientist U. Rochester, Inst. of Optics, 1979—82; prof. of optics U. Roch., Inst. of Optics, 1982—2001; adj. prof. of optics U. Rochester, Inst. of Optics, 2001—; co-founder Rochester Photonics Corp. (RPC), 1989—. CEO Apollo Optical Systems LLC, Rochester Photonics Corp., 1989—. Recipient Rochester C. of C. Civic award for sci. and tech., 1997. Fellow: Optical Soc. of Am. (pres. 2003); mem.: Optical Soc. of Am., Rochester Sect. (hon.). Office: Optical Society of America 8SCR Lane Victor NY 14564

**MORRIS, G. RONALD,** automotive executive; b. East St. Louis, Ill., Aug. 30, 1936; s. George H. and Mildred C. M.; m. Margaret Heino, June 20, 1959; children: David, Michele, James. BS in Metall. Engring. U., 1959. Metall. engr. Delco-Remy divsn. Gen. Motors Corp., 1959-60; factory metallurgist Dubuque Tractor Works, John Deere Co., Iowa, 1960-66; with Fed.-Mogul Corp., 1966-79, v.p., group mgr. ball and roller bearing group, 1979; pres. Tenneco Automotive divsn. Tenneco, Inc., Deerfield, Ill., 1979-82; pres., CEO PT Components, Inc., Indpls., 1982-88; vice-chmn. Rexnord Corp., Indpls., 1988-89; chmn., pres., CEO CTP Holdings Inc., 1986-88; chmn. Integrated Technologies, Inc., Indpls., 1990-92, also bd. dirs.; pres., CEO Western Industries, Inc., Milw., 1991-99. Bd. dirs. NN, Inc., Erwin, Tenn., Hines Hort, Inc., Irvine, Calif. Mem. Pres.'s Coun., U. Ill., mem. sr. adv. bd. Sch. Materials Sci. and Engring; mem. U. Ill. Found. Mem. ASM, SAE, U. Ill. Alumni Assn. (bd. dirs.), The Landings Club (Savannah, Ga.), Masons, Scottish Rite, Kiwanis Internat. Republican. Presbyterian. E-mail: savannahronm@yahoo.com.

**MORRIS, GERALD MICHAEL,** lawyer, educator; b. Endicott, NY, July 17, 1951; s. John Philip and Rita Cathrine Morris; m. Lynn Carol (Baker), Apr. 12, 1980; children: David, Kathrine, Mary. BA in History, LeMoyne Coll., 1973; JD with honors, Nova So. Ea. U. Law Ctr., 1977; LLM, U. Houston Law Ctr., 2002. Cert.: Fla. Bar (health law) 1995, bar: Fla. 1977, US Dist. Ct. (so. dist.) Fla. 1977, US Dist. Ct. (mid. dist.) Fla. 1983, US Ct. Appeals (5th cir.) Fla. 1981, US Ct. Appeals (11th cir.) Fla. 1981, US Supreme Ct. 1981. Law clk. Saunders, Curtis, Ginestra & Gore, Ft. Lauderdale, Fla., 1975—77, assoc., 1977—82, ptnr., 1982—86; sr. assoc. Finley, Kumble, Wagner, Heine, Underberg, Manley, Myerson & Casey and successor firm Tew, Jordon & Schulte, 1986—88, Heinrich, Gordon, Batchelder, Hargrove, Weihe & James, 1989, ptnr., 1990—92; gen. coun. Holy Cross Hosp., Inc., 2002—. Mem. Fla. Bar Young Lawyers, 1977—80, bd. governors rep., 1984—87; mem. Fla. Bar Health Law Com. 1983—87, Fla. Bar Health Law Sect., 1989—; grievance com. mem. Fla. Bar 17th cir., 1987—90, grievance chmn., 1990; mem. bd. govenors Shepard Broad Law Ctr. Nova So. Ea. U., 1990—, adj. prof., 1992—; spkr. various seminars, 1989—2004. Bd. dirs. Boys and Girls Club Broward County, 1987—2001; mem. FDA Instl. Review Bd., Holy Cross Hosp., Fla., 1986—92; profit magazine editl. bd.

mem. Greater Ft. Lauderdale C. of C., Fla., 1987—88, selection com. mem. Youth Leadership Broward, 1988—90, mem. 1988—92, chmn. legis. action sub-com., 1989—91, co-chmn. A1A Beach Redevel. Task Force, 1990, chmn., 1991, vice-chair com. affairs, 1992, exec. com. mem., 1992—93, chmn. Health Care Com., 1992—94, bd. govs., 1992—94; lector, extraordinary min. St. David Catholic Ch., Davie, Fla., 1974—2001. Recipient Vision Broward award, Greater Ft. Lauderdale C. of C., 1990. Mem.: Bioethics & Health Law Consortium of South Fla., Am. Soc. Law Medicine and Ethics, Am. Health Lawyers Assn., Broward County Bar Assn. (Young Lawyers Sect.) (exec. com. 1983—88, sec., treas. 1985—86, pres.-elect 1986—87, pres. 1987—88), Broward County Bar Assn. (law day com. 1985—88, chmn. 1986—87, exec. com. 1986—88, legal/medical com. 1997—99, President's award 1987), Phi Alpha Delta (legal frat.) (chpt. vice justice 1976—77). Office: Holy Cross Hosp Inc Legal Affairs Dept 4725 N Fed Hwy Fort Lauderdale FL 33308 Office Phone: 954-229-8500. Office Fax: 954-776-3177. Business E-Mail: gerald.morris@holy-cross.com.

**MORRIS, GORDON JAMES,** financial company executive, consultant; b. Mt. Vernon, Ohio, Oct. 6, 1942; s. R. Hugh and Betty Jane (Roberts) M.; m. Janet Ann Swanson, Aug. 28, 1965 (div. 1971); m. Nancy Joan Meyfarth, July 26, 1975 (div. Oct. 1998); 1 child, Lawrence Hugh; m. Phyllis J. Hersha, Jan. 1, 2000. Student, Ohio State U., 1960-61; BA, Otterbein Coll., 1966; postgrad. in law, Capital U., Bexley, Ohio, 1967-68; postgrad., Coll. Fin. Planning, Denver, 1983-90, Inst. Cert. Fund Specialists, 1991. Registered investment advisor; cert. fin. planner; cert. fund specialist; lic. loving trust advisor; cert. divorce planner; life lic., Fla., 1974—; security lic. NASD, 1976—; real estate lic., Fla., 1986—. Asst. to pres. Jaeger Machine Co., Columbus, Ohio, 1968-73; rep. Equitable Fin. Svcs., Sarasota, Fla., 1974-81; pres. Beacon Wealth Mgmt. (formerly Morris & Assocs., P.A.), Sarasota, 1981—; co-gen. ptnr. Beacon Bridge Loan Pool, Ltd., 1994-97. Chmn. bd. dirs. MAP Fin. Group, Inc., Sarasota, 1985-89; co-owner U.S.I.S.L. West Fla. Fury Soccer Team, 1996-98; bd. dirs., v.p. Soccer Resource Group, Sarasota, 1997-99, Radyx Capital Ptnr., Tampa, 1999-2003, seminar lectr. High Mark Ins. Svcs., Inc., Beacon Wealth Mgmt., 2003—. Past columnist The Creative News. Past chmn. West Coast chpt. March of Dimes, Bradenton, Fla., bd. dirs., 1986-88; v.p. All Sch. Kids, Inc., 1998-99; pres. Epilepsy Found. S.W. Fla., Inc., 1986-87. Mem. Inst. Cert. Fin. Planners, Million Dollar Roundtable, Sertoma (pres. local club 1979-80). Republican. Methodist. Home and Office: 3822 Countryside Ln Sarasota FL 34233-2122 Personal E-mail: striker.five@comcast.net. Business E-Mail: beaconl@sigmarep.com.

**MORRIS, GRANT HAROLD,** law educator; b. Syracuse, NY, Dec. 10, 1940; s. Benjamin and Caroline Grace (Judelson) Morris; m. Phyllis Silberstein, July 4, 1967; children: Joshua, Sara. AB, Syracuse U., 1962, JD, 1964; LLM, Harvard U., 1971. Bar: N.Y. 1964. Atty. NY Mental Hygiene Law Recodification Project, Inst. Public Administrn., N.Y.C., 1964-66; from asst. prof. to assoc. prof. Wayne State U. Law Sch., 1967—70, prof., 1970-73, dean acad. affairs, 1971-73; prof. U. San Diego Law Sch., 1973—, Univ. prof., 1996-97, acting dean, 1977-78, 88-89, assoc. dean grad. legal edn., 1978-81, interim dean, 1997-98; prof. law in psychiatry Wayne State U. Med. Sch., 1970-73; adj. prof. U. Calif.-San Diego Med. Sch., 1974-84; clin. prof. dept. psychiatry U. Calif. Med. Sch., San Diego, 1984—. Legal counsel Mich. Legis. Com. to Revise Mental Health Statutes, 1970-73; organizer law and psychiatry sect. Assn. Am. Law Schs., 1973, chmn., 1973-74; patients advocate, San Diego County, 1977-78; cons. Criminal Code Commn., Ariz. Legis., 1974; reporter task force on guidelines governing roles of mental health profls. in criminal process Am. Bar Assn. standing com. on assn. standards for criminal justice, 1981-84; cert. rev. hearing officer San Diego Superior Ct., 1984-90, ct. commr./judge pro tem, 1990-92, mental health hearing officer, 1992-97; hearing officer San Diego Housing Commn., 1988-92; mem. exec. com. law and mental disability Assn. Am. Law Schs., 1990-97. Author: The Insanity Defense: A Blueprint for Legislative Reform, 1975; co-author: Mental Disorder in the Criminal Process: Stan Stress and the Vietnam/Sports Conspiracy, 1993; editor, contbr.: The Mentally Ill and the Right to Treatment, 1970. Mem. Atascadero State Hosp. adv. bd., 2000—, chair, 2003—. Mem. Phi Alpha Delta (faculty adv. 1970-73, 75-92). Office: U San Diego Law Sch 5998 Alcala Park San Diego CA 92110-2492 Office Phone: 619-260-2321. Business E-Mail: gmorris@sandiego.edu.

**MORRIS, GREGORY K.,** minister, consultant; s. Carroll R. and Murelene H. Morris; m. Sandra E. Cottle, June 26, 1982; children: Joshua C., Caleb K., Elizabeth-Anne. BA, U. Akron, Ohio, 1973—77; MRE, Trinity Evang. Div. Sch., Deerfield, Ill., 1977—79; PhD, La. Bapt. U., Shreveport, 2003—05; ThM, Christian Bible Coll., Rocky Mount, NC. Ministerial ordination Lakeside Bapt. Ch., 1985. Pres. Leadership Dynamics, Lakeland, Fla., 2000—. Author: (book) In Pursuit of Leadership: Principles and Practices From the Life of Moses. Office: Leadership Dynamics PO Box 7354 Lakeland FL 33807-7354 Personal E-mail: gregmorrisministries@earthlink.net. Business E-Mail: mail@leadershipdynamics.org.

**MORRIS, HENRY MADISON, III,** minister, writer, speech professional, consultant; b. El Paso, Tex., May 15, 1942; s. Henry Madison and Mry Louis (Beach) M.; m. Janet Deckman, July 25, 1965; children: Henry M., Scotta Marie. BA summa cum laude, Immanuel Heritage Coll., 1976; MDiv, Luther Rice Sem., 1977; DMin, 1978; MBA, Pepperdine U., 1989. Ordained to ministry Bapt. Ch., 1968. Regional mgr. Integon Ins. Co., Greenville, SC, 1969-75; pastor Hallmark Bapt. Ch., Greenville, SC, 1969-75; assoc. prof. Bible Christian Heritage Coll., El Cajon, Calif., 1977-78; adminstrv. v.p., 1978-80; pastor First Bapt. Ch., Canoga Park, Calif., 1980-86; chief adminstrv. officer, CFO SunGard Fin. Sys. Inc., Canoga Park, 1986-94; v.p. sales and mktg., 1994-96; adminstrv. pastor Ch. at Rocky Peak, Chatsworth, Calif., 1996-99; regional sales mgr. SunGard Ins. Sys., 2000—01; exec. v.p. Inst. for Creation Rsch., Santee, Calif., 2002—. Lectr. in field; cons. World Pubs., 1995; commr. Transitional Assn. Christian Colls. and Schs., 2003—. Author: Baptism: What is It?, 1977, Explore the Word, 1978, Churches: History and Doctrine, 1980, After Eden, 2003; co-author: Many Infallible Proofs, 1996, Sampling the Psalms, 1999; contbg. editor: The Defenders Bible, 1995. Served with U.S. Army, 1959-66. Republican. Office: Inst for Creation Rsch 10996 Woodside Ave N Santee CA 92091 Office Phone: 972-506-3035. Business E-Mail: hmorrisiii@icr.org.

**MORRIS, HOWARD HENDERSON,** protective services official; b. Oneida, Tenn., Dec. 16, 1948; s. Raymond Warren and Ida Lee Morris; 1 child, Kelcy Meighan. BSc in Criminal Justice Administrn., Mid. Tenn. State U., Murfreesboro, Tenn., 1975; MPA, Golden Gate U., San Francisco, Calif., 2004. Cert. police officer standards and tng. Tenn. POST Commn., 1998. Pub. safety officer Tenn. Vets. Affairs, Gallatin, Tenn., 1976—77; investigator Wilson Law Office, Oneida, Tenn., 1978—79; capt. Atlantic Undersea Testing and Evaluation Ctr., Andros, Bahamas, 1979—80; spl. agent Tenn. Bur. Investigation, Nashville, 1981—90, coord., 1990—98; dir. Tenn. Dept. Revenue, Nashville, 1990—93; chief police LaVergne Police Dept., Tenn., 1998—2001, Bethel Police Dept., Bethel, Alaska, 2002—04; capt. DeKalb County Sheriff's Dept., Smithville, Tenn., 2004—. Mem. exec. bd. Rutherford County E-911 Bd., Murfreesboro, Tenn., 1998—2001; bd. dirs. 13th J.D. Domestic Violence Coalition, Murfreesboro, 1998—2001. Petty officer 2nd USN, 1969—72, Vietnam. Decorated Vietnam Cross Gallentry USN, Accomodation medal, Achievement medal, Vietnam Svc. medal, Nat. Def. medal; recipient Outstanding Drug Enforcment award, U.S. Drug Enforcement Administrn., 1982, Humanitarian medal, Bethel Police Dept., 2003. Mem.: Tenn. Narcotics Assn., Nat. Drug Enforcement Assn., Alaska Chiefs Police Assn., Tenn. Assn. Chiefs of Police, Smithville Internat. Assn. Chiefs of Police, Mu Tau Sigma. Roman Cath. Avocations: winter sports, water sports. Home: PO Box 1213 Cookeville TN 38503 Office: DeKalb County Sheriff's Department 100 Public Square Smithville TN 37166 Office Phone: 615-597-4044.

**MORRIS, IAIN,** information technology executive; b. Scotland; B in Tech. and Bus. Studies, U. Strathclyde, Glasgow, Scotland. With Motorola, 1978—2001; pres. embedded and personal sys. orgn. Hewlett Packard Co.,

2001—02, sr. v.p. mobility and emerging techs., 2002—03; sr. v.p. personal connectivity solutions group Advanced Micro Devices, Sunnyvale, Calif., 2004—. Office: Advanced Micro Devices ONe AMD Pl PO Box 3453 Sunnyvale CA 94088-3453

**MORRIS, JACK G.,** architecture educator, writer; b. Clark County, Wash., June 1, 1920; s. Thomas Frank and Hazel Ann (Ditmer) Morris; m. Rosalind Vallens, Mar. 16, 1945 (dec. Nov. 1990); children: Jane, Wendy, Virginia, Thomas. Jr. cert., U. Oreg., 1942; BA, Stanford U., 1948; Calif. tchg. credential, UCLA, 1950; cert. in environ. design, U. Calif., Irvine, 1981. Tchr. Union H.S., Perris, Calif., 1950—53, LaPuente, Calif., 1953—76; archtl. designer, draftsman, craftsman various cos. and contractors, Calif., 1976—86; tchr. archtl. drafting and rendering various cmty. colls., Orange County, Calif., 1986—91; freelance writer Calif., 1994—2002. Bd. mem. ext. program in environ. design U. Calif. Irvine Ext., 1978—83. Author: (memoir) One Angel Left, 2001. Chmn. Orange County Stanford Annual Fund, Stanford U., 1980—85, Stanford Alumni Assn., Stanford Club, 1985—86; art therapy vol. Spring Lake Village, Santa Rosa, Calif., 2002—05. Capt. USMC, 1942—46, PTO. Mem.: Stanford Assocs., Stanford Faculty Club (assoc.). Democrat. Avocation: watercolor painting. Home: 5555 Montgomery Dr C-205 Santa Rosa CA 95409 Personal E-mail: jackguy@sonic.net.

**MORRIS, JAMES CARL,** architect; b. Richmond, Va., Sept. 2, 1930; s. James Carl and Florence Virginia (Hey) M.; m. Frances Parrott Wooten, June 9, 1952; children: James Carl Jr., David Palmer. Student, N.C. State U., 1948-50; BS in Bldg. Constrn., Va. Polytechnic Inst., 1952. Cert. Nat. Coun. Archtl. Registration Bds. Archtl. draftsman Va. Electric & Power Co., Richmond, Va., 1955-56, Marcellus, Wright & Son, Richmond, 1956-57; architect C.W. Huff, Jr., Richmond, 1957; ptnr. to prin./owner Huff-Morris Architects, Richmond, 1966—. Pres. Point of Rocks Devel. Corp., Chesterfield, Va., 1986—; ptnr. Rivermont Assocs., Chesterfield, 1987—, JCM Partnership, Chesterfield, 1988—. Contbr. articles to profl. jours. Bd. dirs. Chesterfield Preservation Commn.; deacon Branch's Ch., Richmond, 1986-90; chmn. Va. Bapt. Extension Bd., Richmond, 1991-2001, 2004-; mem. 250th anniversary com. Chesterfield County, 1999. With U.S. Army, 1953-54. Recipient award of Merit S.S. Bd. of So. Bapt., Nashville, Excellence in Masonry Design award Va. Masonry Coun., Richmond. Mem. AIA (past pres. Richmond chpt.), Constrn. Specifications Inst., Interfaith Forum on Religion, Art & Architecture, Commonwealth Club of Va. Avocations: woodworking, fishing, hunting. Office: Huff-Morris Arch PC 400 E Grace St Richmond VA 23219-2102 Home: 5907 Village Lake Ct Richmond VA 23234-6945 Office Phone: 804-343-1505. Business E-Mail: architecture@huffmorris.com.

**MORRIS, JAMES E.,** lawyer, judge, educator; b. Rochester, N.Y., Nov. 20, 1942; s. Ira H. and Hortense Morris; m. Ruth J. Myers, June 15, 1965 (div. Oct. 1977); children: Kim I. Gayler, Deborah M. Field; m. Virginia B. Morris, Aug. 22, 1983; children: Katelyn E., Eric W. BS, Syracuse U., 1964, LLB, 1967. Bar: N.Y. 1967. Asst. dist. atty. County of Monroe, Rochester, NY, 1968-72; Brighton Town justice Town of Brighton, NY, 1972—2005; ptnr. Morris and Morris, Rochester, NY, 1967—. Adj. prof. Monroe C.C., Rochester, 1975-2005; mem. criminal procedure law adv. bd. N.Y. State Office Ct. Adminstrn., 1980-86. Author: You Can Win Big in Small Claims Court, 1981, 2002, Victim Aftershock, 1983; co-author: New York Village, Town and District Courts Guide, 1995. Mem., past pres. Med. Motor Svc. at Al Sigl Ctr., Rochester, N.Y., 1971—; Brighton Fire Dept., 1985—; mem. Convalescent Hosp. for Children, Rochester, 1980s. Named to, best Lawyers Am., 2000—. Mem. N.Y. State Bar Assn., N.Y. State Trial Lawyers Ass., N.Y. State Magistrates Assn. (past pres.), Am. Soc. Writers on Legal Subjects, Monroe County Bar Assn.; fellow Am. Coll. Civil Trial Mediators. Republican. Office: Morris and Morris Attorneys 120 Corporate Woods #240 Rochester NY 14623-1455

**MORRIS, JAMES MALACHY,** lawyer; b. Champaign, Ill., June 5, 1952; s. Walter Michael and Ellen Frances (Solon) M.; m. Mary Delilah Baker, Oct. 17, 1987; children: James Malachy Jr., Elliot Rice Baker, Walter Michael, Nicholas Aidan. Student, U. Eng., 1972; BA, Brown U., 1974; JD, U. Pa., 1977. Bar: N.Y. 1978, U.S. Dist. Ct. (so. and ea. dists.) N.Y. 1978, Ill. 1980, U.S. Tax Ct. 1982, U.S. Supreme Ct. 1983; admitted to Barristers Chambers, Manchester, Eng., 1987. Assoc. Reid & Priest, N.Y.C., 1977-80; sr. law clk. Supreme Ct. Ill., Springfield, 1980-81; assoc. Carter, Ledyard & Milburn, N.Y.C., 1981-83; sole practice N.Y.C., 1983-87; counsel FCA, Washington, 1987—; acting sec., gen. counsel FCS Ins. Corp., McLean, Va., 1990-98, exec. asst., bd. chmn., 2005—. Cons. Internat. Awards Found., Zurich, 1981—2002, Pritzker Architecture Prize Found., NYC, 1981—2002, Herbert Oppenheimer, Nathan & VanDyck, London, 1985—2004. Contbr. articles to profl. jours. Mem. ABA, Ill. Bar Assn., N.Y. State Bar Assn., N.Y. County Lawyers Assn., Assn. Bar City N.Y., Brit. Inst. Internat. and Comparative Law, Am. Inst. Parliamentarians, Lansdowne Club (London), Penn Club (N.Y.C.), Casanova (Va.) Hunt Club. Office: PO Box 1407 Mc Lean VA 22101-1407

**MORRIS, JAMES T.,** insurance company executive; BA, UCLA, 1982. With Pacific Life Ins. Co., Newport Beach, Calif., 1982—, asst. v.p. product rsch. & develop., 1986—87, 2d v.p. product design & develop., 1987—90, v.p. product design, 1990—93, v.p. m-ops., 1993—96, sr. v.p. m-ops., 1996—2002, exec. v.p. life ins. div., 2002—05, exec. v.p. chief ins. officer, 2005—06, COO, 2006—. Fellow: Soc. Actuaries; mem.: Am. Acad. Actuaries, LA Actuarial Club. Office: Pacific Life Ins Co 700 Newport Ctr Dr Newport Beach CA 92658-9030*

**MORRIS, JAMES VICTOR,** secondary school educator; b. Enterprise, West Va., Nov. 20, 1913; s. Vinson Mile and Maude Fernriver Morris. BA, Fairmont State U., 1936; MA, W.Va. U., 1947. Tchr. Harrison County Bd. Edn., Clarksburg, W.va.; ednl. rep. W.va. Dir. Bank of Shinnston, W.Va. Lt. USN, 1942—45. Named James V. Morris scholarship fund, W. Va. U., 1986, Crystal Miller scholarship fund, Fairmont State U., 1967, James V. Morris scholarship fund, Waynesburg Coll., 1995; named to Shinniston Lincoln Hall of Fame, 1997, 4-H All Stars Hall of Fame, 1995. Mem.: NEA, W. Va. Edn. Assn., Kiwanis Club. Democrat. Meth. Home: Rte 1 Box 27 AAA Enterprise WV 26568

**MORRIS, JAMES WATSON, III,** lawyer; b. Richmond, Va., Oct. 29, 1932; s. James Watson Morris Jr. and Annie Florence Browder; m. Jane Carolyn Mallory; children: James Watson IV, Carolyn Morris O'Connor. Student, Va. Mil. Inst., 1951-52, Randolph Macon Coll., 1952-54; LLB, T.C. Williams Sch. of Law, 1957. Bar: Va. 1958, U.S. Dist. Ct. (ea. dist.) Va. 1958, U.S. Dist. Ct. (we. dist.) Va. 1959, U.S. Ct. Appeals (4th cir.) 1959. Assoc. Lehman, Browder & Russell, Richmond, 1958-61; ptnr. Browder, Russell & Morris, Richmond, 1961-63; ptnr., mem. exec. com. Browder, Russell, Little, Morris & Butcher, Richmond, 1964-76; ptnr., mem. exec. com., chmn. Browder, Russell, Morris & Butcher, Richmond, 1977-89; ptnr., chmn. Morris and Morris, P.C., Richmond, 1989—. Spkr. in field. Contbr. articles to profl. publs. Pres., founder Va. Assn. Def. Attys., 1973-76; bd. dirs. Product Liability Adv. Coun., Detroit, 1989-92, Lawyer for Civil Justice, 1989-92; trustee Supreme Ct. Hist. Soc., exec. com., 2005—; bd. dirs., v.p. John Marshall Found. 1st lt. JAG, US Army, 1957-63. Recipient Award for Excellence in Civil Litigation Va. Assn. Def. Attys.; named to Top 30 Ind. Def. Lawyers in USA, Nat. Law Jour., 1991, Hunter W. Martin Professionalism award, 2005, Top 10 Super Lawyers Va., 2006. Fellow Am. Coll. Trial Lawyers (regent 1997-01, treas. 2001-03, pres.-elect 2003-04, pres. 2004-05), Am. Bar Found., Trial Attys. Am., internat. Acad. Trial Lawyers, Va. Law Found.; mem. ABA, Va. State Bar Assn., Va. Bar Assn., Richmond Bar Assn. (pres. 1998-99, Professionalism award), Internat. Assn. Def. Counsel (chmn. civil rights com.), 4th U.S. Cir. Ct. Jud. Conf., Va. Assn. Def. Attys. (pres. 1973-76), Def. Rsch. Inst. (pres. 1988-89, chmn. bd. 1989-90). Democrat. Episcopalian. Avocations: reading, contract bridge. Home: 6130 St Andrews Cir Richmond VA 23226-3209 Office: Morris and Morris PC 1200 Wytestone Plaza PO Box 30 801 E Main St 12th Fl 23219 Richmond VA 23218-0030 Office Phone: 804-344-8200.        Office        Fax:        804-344-8359.        Business        E-Mail: jmorris@morrismorris.com.

**MORRIS, JANINE ELAINE,** psychologist; b. Rochester, NY, Dec. 9, 1970; d. Robert John and Carol Wilsey (Stepmother), Stephen Michael Matties (Stepfather) and Sondra Kay Jones; m. Creighton Josiah Morris, July 1, 2001; children: Lauren Elizabeth, Alyson Melody. BA, SUNY, Plattsburgh, NY, 1992; MSc, Rochester Inst. of Tech., 1995. Pupil Personnel ServicesS chool Psychologist NY, 2005, Nationally Certified School Psychologist Nat. Assn. Sch. Psychologists, 2006. Sch. psychologist Montrose County Sch. Dist. RE-1J, Colo., 1995—98, Douglas County Sch. Dist., Castle Rock, Colo., 1998—2000, Escondido Union H.S. Dist., Calif., 2000—05, NYC Bd. Edn., Bklyn., 2006—. Mem.: NY Assn. Sch. Psychologists, Nat. Assn. Sch. Psychologists, Psi Chi (life), Phi Eta Sigma (life). R-Consevative. Meth.

**MORRIS, JEFFREY BRANDON,** law educator; b. NYC, Jan. 8, 1941; s. Richard B. and Berenice (Robinson) M.; m. Dona Gene Baron, July 9, 1972; children: David Brandon, Deborah Helaine. AB, Princeton U., 1962; JD, Columbia U., 1965, PhD in Polit. Sci., U. Va., 1972. Bar: N.Y. 1967, U.S. Supreme Ct. 1970, D.C. 1978, U.S. Dist. Ct. D.C. 1978. Lectr., instr., asst. prof. CUNY, N.Y.C., 1968-74; spl. asst. to provost Columbia U., N.Y.C., 1974-76; jud. fellow U.S. Supreme Ct., Washington, 1976-77, rsch. assoc. adminstry. asst. chief justice, 1977-81; asst. prof. polit. sci. U. Pa., Phila., 1981-88; vis. assoc. prof. Bklyn. Law Sch., N.Y.C., 1988-90; from assoc. prof. to prof. law Touro Law Sch., Huntington, NY, 1990—. Rapporteur Nat. Conf. on Causes Population Dissatisfaction, with Popular Dissatisfaction Adminstrn. of Justice, St. Paul, 1976; cons. bicentennial exhibitions Independence Nat. Hist. Park, 1986. Author: Federal Justice in the Second Circuit, 1988, U.S. District Court Eastern District N.Y., 1965-90, 1992, Making Sure We are True to Our Founders, 1997, Brooklyn Law School: The First Hundred Years, 2001, Calmly to Poise the Scales of Justice, 2001; co-author: A Pocket History of the United States, 9th rev. edit., 1992; editor: Encyclopedia of American History, 1982, 7th edit., 1996; assoc. editor Yearbook, Supreme Ct. Hist. Soc., 1979-83. Mem. Brookings Conf. on Interbr. Rels., Williamsburg, Va., 1980, 81. Jewish. Avocations: opera, dance, theater. Home: 234 Forest Rd Flushing NY 11363-1303 Office: Touro Law Sch 300 Nassau Rd Huntington NY 11743-4346 E-mail: jeffreym@tourolaw.edu.

**MORRIS, JOHN,** composer, conductor, arranger; b. Elizabeth, N.J. s. Thomas Arthur and Helen (Sherratt) M.; m. Francesca Bosetti; children: Evan Bosetti, Bronwen Helen. Student, Julliard Sch. Music, 1946-48, U. Wash., 1947, New Sch. Social Research, 1946-49. Composer (film) The Producers, The Twelve Chairs, The Gamblers, Blazing Saddles (nominated Acad. award 1976), The Bank Shot, Young Frankenstein, Sherlock Holmes Smarter Brother, Silent Movie, The Last Remake of Beau Geste, The In-Laws, The World's Greatest Lover, In God We Trust, High Anxiety, The Elephant Man (nominated Acad. award 1981), Table for Five, History of the World Part I, Yellowbeard, The Doctor and the Devils, Clue, To Be or Not To Be, Woman in Red, Johnny Dangerously, Haunted Honeymoon, Dirty Dancing, Spaceballs, Ironweed, The Wash, Stella, Life Stinks; (Broadway stage plays) My Mother, My Father and Me, Doll's House, Camino Real; (mus.) A Time for Singing; (off-Broadway) Take One Step, Young Andy Jackson, N.Y. Shakespeare Festival Much Ado About Nothing, Peer Gynt, Richard III, Love's Labor's Lost, Electra, As You Like It, Comedy of Errors, Titus Andronicus, Henry IV Parts 1 and 2, Romeo and Juliet, Hamlet, The Cherry Orchard, Stratford Connecticut Shakespeare Festival The Tempest, Julius Caesar, Antony and Cleopatra, Measure for Measure, Twelfth Night, Lincoln Ctr. King Lear; (TV) Fresno, Katherine Anne Porter, Ghost Dancing, The Firm, The Mating Season, Splendor in the Grass, The Electric Grandmother, The Scarlet Letter, The Adams Chronicles, Georgia O'Keeffe, The Franken Project, The Tap Dance Kid (Emmy award 1986), Make Believe Marriage, ABC After Sch. Spl. Theme, Making Things Grow Theme, The French Chef Theme, The Desperate Hours, The Skirts of Happy Chance, Infancy and Childhood, The Fig Tree, The Little Match Girl, Our Sons, The Last to Go, The Last Best Year, The Sunset Gang, Coach Theme, Favorite Son, Journey Into Genius, When Lions Roared, Scarlett Mini Series, With God On Our Side, Ellen Foster, Murder in a Small Town, The Lady in Question, Tribute to Julie Harris, Only Love, Blackwater Lightship, documentary films; mus. supr., condr., arranger numerous TV spls., Broadway and off-Broadway shows and recs. including Anne Bancroft Spl. #1 (Emmy award), 'S Lemmon 'S Gershwin 'S Wonderful (Emmy award), Hallmark Christmas Spls.; (Broadway) Peter Pan, Bells Are Ringing, Bye-Bye Birdie, All-American, Wild Cat, Kwanmina, Baker Street, Mack and Mabel, Much Ado About Nothing; (off-Broadway) Hair; (records) Wildcat, All-American, Bells Are Ringing, First Impressions, Bye-Bye Birdie, Kwamina, Baker Street, Rodgers and Hart, George Gershwin vols. I and II, Jerome Kern, Lyrics of Ira Gershwin, Cole Porter, others. Mem. ASCAP, Acad. Motion Picture Arts and Scis., Soc. Composers and Lyricists, Am. Fedn. Musicians. Personal E-mail: jmorris319@hotmail.com.

**MORRIS, JOHN SELWYN,** philosopher, educator, retired academic administrator; b. Tonypandy, Wales, July 2, 1925; came to U.S., 1954, naturalized, 1993; s. Jenkin and Hannah M. (Williams) M.; m. Enid Elry Walters, Apr. 10, 1954; 1 child, Paul John. BA, Univ. Coll. South Wales and Monmouthshire, 1951; MA, Cambridge U., Eng., 1953; student, Union Theol. Sem., 1957-60; MA, Colgate U., 1961; PhD, Columbia U., 1961; LL.D. (hon.), Hartwick Coll., 1979; LHD (hon.), Elmyra Coll., 1990; DLitt, Skidmore Coll., 1991. Ordained to ministry Presbyterian Ch., 1954; minister Vernon (N.Y.) and Vernon Center Presbyn. chs., 1954-57; instr. Colgate U., Hamilton, NY, 1960-63, asst. prof., 1963-66, assoc. prof., 1966-70, prof. philosophy and religion, 1970-79, dir. div. humanities, 1970-72, dir. div. univ. studies, 1972-73, provost, dean of faculty, 1973-79, acting pres., 1977; prof. philosophy Union Coll., Schenectady, 1979-90, pres., 1979-90; chancellor Union U., 1979—90; pres. emeritus, rsch. prof. philosophy Union Coll., Schenectady, 1990—. Leverhulme vis. fellow U. Exeter, Eng., 1968-69; chmn. Commn. Ind. Colls. and Univs., 1984-86; trustee Cazenovia Coll., N.Y. Trustee Skidmore Coll. With RAF, 1943-47. Recipient Disting. Svc. award Colgate U. Alumni Corp., 1978, Schenectady Patroon award, 1989, Union Coll. Founders Medal, 1990; fellow Cardiff U. Mem. AAUP, Am. Philos. Assn., Am. Acad. Religion, Royal Inst. Philosophy, Soc. for Study Theology, Nat. Welsh Am. Found. (bd. advisors). Office: Union Coll Humanities Ctr Schenectady NY 12308

**MORRIS, JOHN WOODLAND, II,** retired engineering consultant, retired military officer; b. Princess Anne, Md., Sept. 10, 1921; s. John Earl and Allice (Cropper) M.; m. Geraldine Moore King, May 12, 1947; children: Susan K., John Woodland III, BA, U.S. Mil. Acad., 1943; MS, U. Iowa, 1948; postgrad., Army War Coll., 1961—62, U. Pitts., 1966. Commd. 2d lt. U.S. Army, 1943, advanced through grades to lt. gen., 1976; dep. dist. engr. Savannah, Ga., 1952-54; resident engr. Goose Bay, Labrador, 1955-57; staff officer Office Chief Engrs., 1957-60; comdg. officer 8th Engr. Bn., Korea, 1960-61; dist. engr. Tulsa, 1962-65; dep. comdt. U.S. Mil. Acad., 1965-67; dep. chief legis. liaison Office Sec. Army, Washington, 1967-69; comdg. gen. 18th Engr. Brigade, Vietnam, 1969-70; div. engr. Missouri River Div., Omaha, 1970-72; dir. civil works Office C.E., Washington, 1972-75; dep. chief engr. U.S. Army, 1975-76, chief engr., 1976-80; ret., 1980; exec. dir. Royal Volker Stevin, 1980-84; pres. J.W. Morris Ltd., 1981—2006; ret., 2006; prof. U. Md., 1983-86; chmn. bd., CEO PRC Engring., 1986-88. Engr. advisor, cons. Zorc, Rissetto, Weaver & Rosen, 1988-92; engr. advisor Seltzer & Rosen, 1992-98; bd. dirs. Air Water Tech., Morganti Constrn. Co., Search Techs. Inc., Thaco Rsch. Inc., Dutra Corp.; mem. adv. bd. AMEC Ltd. Mem. Indian Nations coun. Boy Scouts Am., 1962-65; chmn. Water Resources Congress, 1988-90; trustee U.S. Mil. Acad. Assn. Grads, 1986—; advisor dean engring. and math. U. Vt., 1990-96. Decorated Legion of Merit with three oak leaf clusters, Army D.S.M., Def. D.S.M.; recipient Merit award Am. Cons. Engrs. Council; Palladium medal Audubon Soc.; award of excellence Constrn. Industry Inst., 1997. Fellow ASCE (Disting. Constructor award 2000); mem. AIA (hon.), Internat. Navigation Congress (v.p.), U.S. Soc. Mil. Engrs. (pres.), Nat. Acad. Engrs. (Founders award 1996), U.S. Com. on Large Dams (past chmn. environ. effect com., named Constrn. Man of Yr. 1977, Navigation Hall of Fame 1990, Golden Beaver award for engring. 1995, Golden Eagle award, 1998, Acad. of Dist. Eng. U. Iowa, 1998, Dist. Grad. of U.S. Mil. Acad., 1998). Episcopalian. E-mail: morrisJ@aol.com.

**MORRIS, JOSEPH ANTHONY,** retired health science association administrator; b. Marboro, Md., Mar. 6, 1918; s. Charles Lafayette and Essie (Stokes) M.; m. Ruth Savoy, Nov. 1, 1942; children: Carol Ann, Marilyn T., Joseph A., Larry A. BS, Cath. U. Am., 1940, MS, 1942, PhD, 1947. Asst. scientist Josiah Macy, Jr. Found., N.Y.C., 1943-44; virologist Depts. Agr., Interior, Laurel, Md., 1944-47; virologist, chief hepatitis virus rsch. Walter Reed Army Inst. Rsch., Washington, 1947-56; virologist, asst. chief, dept. virus and rickettsial dis. U.S. Army Med. Command, Japan, 1956-59; virologist chief sect. respiratory diseases divsn. biologics stds. NIH, Bethesda, Md., 1959—2003; ret. Dir. slow, latent and temperate virus br. FDA, Bethesda, 1972-76; lectr. dept. microbiology U. Md., College Park, 1977-79; vice-chmn. Bell of Atri, Inc., College Park, 1979-82, chmn., 1983; cons. Commn. on Influenza, Armed Forces Epidemiologic Bd., 1960—, Nat. Inst. Neurol. Diseases and Blindness, 1962—. Mem. Soc. Tropical Medicine and Hygiene, Soc. Am. Microbiologists, Soc. Exptl. Biology and Medicine, Am. Assn. Immunologists, N.Y. Acad. Scis. Achievements include discovery of respiratory sycytial virus; research on infectious hepatitis, respiratory diseases of virus etiology and zoonosis. Home: 23E Ridge Rd Greenbelt MD 20770-0714

**MORRIS, JOSEPH RAYMOND,** finance educator; b. Stuckey, Ga., May 29, 1939; s. Joseph Alton and Ora Lou (Hinson) M.; m. Joyce Marilyn Speiller, Mar 17, 1984; children from previous marriage: Theresa, Marianne, Jennifer. BA, Nova U., 1986, M of Internat. Bus. Adminstrn., 1988. Sales profl. Dixie Pllywood Corp. Inc., Miami, Fla., 1964-68; sales mgr. Bradley Plywood Corp. Inc., Savannah, Ga., 1968-73; mgr. City Motel Inc., Franklin, NC, 1973-78; pres., owner Coweee Gem Shop, Franklin, 1973-78; with Eastern Airlines Inc., Miami, 1978-90; adj. prof., then full-time/part-time prof. Broward C.C., Ft. Lauderdale, Fla., 1989—. Adj. prof. Palm Beach C.C., Boca Raton, Fla., 1995, Fla. Internat. U., Miami,1990—, Lynn U., Boca Raton, 1998—; instr. part-time Nova Southeastern U., Ft. Lauderdale, 1996—, Johnson & Wales U., 2000—. With USN, 1956-64. Recipient Enterpreneurship Inst. Svc. award, 1998, Fla. Inernat. U. Cmty. Svc. award, 1997. Mem. Am. Inst. Econ. Rsch., Acad. Internat. Bus., Franklin Gem and Mineral Soc.,, Lions (pres. Franklin chpt. 1976-77, v.p 1973-75, chmn. western counties 1977-78), Civitans (treas. 1982-83), Toastmasters, Masons, Shriners. Republican. Baptist. Avocations: golf, swimming, community service, time with students. Home and Office: PO Box 292104 Davie FL 33329-2104

**MORRIS, JUSTIN ROY,** food scientist, consultant; b. Nashville, Ark., Feb. 20, 1937; s. Roy Morris; m. Ruby Lee Blackwood, Sept. 5, 1956; children: Linda Lee, Michael Justin. BS, U. Ark., 1957, MS, 1961; PhD, Rutgers U., 1964. Instr. Rutgers U., New Brunswick, NJ, 1964-67; ext. horticulturist U. Ark., Fayetteville, 1964-67, from asst. to assoc. prof., 1967-75, prof., 1975-85, univ. prof., 1985-97, disting. prof., 1997—, dir. Inst. Food Sci. and Engring., Ctr. Food Processing and Engring., 1995—. Cons. viticulture sci. program Fla. A&M U., Tallahassee, 1979—81; cons. viticulture and enology program Grayson City Coll., Denison, Tex., 1987—97; cons. J. M. Smucker Co., 1982—91. Assoc. editor: Am. Jour. Enology and Viticulture, 1985; co-author: (book) Small Fruit Crop Management, 1990, Quality and Preservation of Fruits, 1991, Modern Fruit Science Text Book, 1995; contr. chapters to books; publ. over 365 rsch. articles to sci. jours. Apptd. by gov. Ark. Wine Prodrs. Coun., 2002—. Named to Ark. Hort. Hall of Fame, 2005; recipient Rsch. award, Nat. Food Processors Assn., 1982, Food Processors 49er Leadership award, 1998, Food Sci Rsch. award, 1998, award of merit, Am. Wine Soc., 1999, John White Outstanding Team award, 2002, So. Region Grape Rsch. award, 2003, Outstanding Alumnus award, U. Ark. Horticulture Dept., 2003, Disting. Alumni award, U. So. Ark., 2004; Spitze Land grantee, 1997. Fellow: Inst. Food Technologists (co-organizer fruit and vegetable divsn. 1987—), Am. Soc. Hort. Sci. (assoc. editor 1985, Gourley award 1979, Outstanding Rsch. award 1983); mem.: Am. Soc. Enology and Viticultures (chairperson 1996—97, Disting. Achievement award ea. sect. 1995, Nat. Merit award 1996), Food Processors Guard Soc. (life Grape Team Rsch. award 2002, Outstanding Grape and Wine Rsch. award So. Region 2003, Ark. Hort. Hall of Fame 2005), Coun. Agrl. Sci. and Tech. (chmn. nat. concerns 1987—93, pres.-elect 1993, pres. 1994, 1995), Ozark Food Processers Assn. (exec. v.p. 1988—), Gamma Sigma Delta. Achievements include development of mechanical cane fruit harvester; mechanical strawberry harvester; modified grape harvester for wine grapes; mechanical shoot positioner for grapes; patents for mechanized systems for the production, harvesting, handling and utilization of grapes. Office: U Ark Inst Food Sci and Engring 2650 N Young Ave Fayetteville AR 72704-5690 Office Phone: 501-575-4040, 479-575-4040. Business E-mail: jumorris@uark.edu.

**MORRIS, LEIGH EDWARD,** mayor, retired health facility administrator; b. Hartford City, Ind., Dec. 26, 1934; s. Fredus Orlando and Martha (Malott) M.; m. Marcia Renee Meredith, Oct. 7, 1967; children: Meredith Anne, Curtis Paul. BS in Commerce, Internat. Coll., 1954; BSBA, Ball State U., 1958; M in Health Adminstrn., U. Minn., 1972. Mem. labor relations staff Borg-Warner Corp., Muncie, Ind., 1961-64; various positions then personnel mgr. Internat. Harvester Co., Ft. Wayne, Ind., 1964-70; pres. Huntington (Ind.) Meml. Hosp., 1972-78, La Porte (Ind.) Hosp., 1978-2000; ret.; mayor City of LaPorte. Bd. dirs. First of Am. Bank of Ind., Am. Hosp. Svcs., Inc., Health Forum, Inc.; chmn., bd. dirs. Am. Hosp. Pub. Co.; chmn. La Porte Devel. Corp., 1980-81. Chmn. LaPorte chpt. ARC, 1984-86; bd. dirs. John G. Blank Ctr. for the Arts, Lubeznik Ctr. for the Arts, LaPorte County Symphony Orch. With U.S. Army, 1958-60. Recipient Disting. Alumni award Ball State U., Muncie, Ind., 1968, James A. Hamilton award U. Minn., Mpls., 1972, Trustees award Am. Hosp. Assn., 1996. Fellow Am. Coll. Healthcare Adminstrn. (life), Health Care Fin. Mgmt. Assn.; mem. APHA, Am. Hosp. Assn. (trustee, regional chmn. 1985-89), Soc. for Healthcare Planning and Mktg. (bd. dirs. 1980 81), La Porte C. of C. (chmn. 1981-82). Republican. Presbyterian. Avocations: classic cars, civic affairs. Home: 424 Lake Shore Dr La Porte IN 46350-2917 Office Phone: 219-362-8220. Personal E-mail: lmorris@csinet.net. Business E-mail: leighmorris@cityoflaporte.com.

**MORRIS, LISA KAPLAN,** engineering educator, physics professor, mathematics professor; d. Robert B. and Audrey A. Kaplan; m. Robert E. Morris; children: Matthew, Benjamin. BA in Physics, U. Calif., Santa Barbara, 1981; MS in Geol. Sci., U. So. Calif., L.A., 1985. Instr. physics Mont. Coll. Mineral Sci. and Tech., Butte, 1987—91, Wash. State U., Pullman, 1991—2000, Whitworth Coll., Spokane, Wash., 2001—01; instr. math. Wash. State U., Pullman, 2001—05, instr. civil engring., 2003—. Mem.: Am. Soc. Engring. Edn., Am. Assn. Physics Tchrs. Office: Wash State Univ PO Box 642910 Pullman WA 99164-2910 Office Phone: 509-335-3227. E-mail: lisa_morris@wsu.edu.

**MORRIS, LOIS LAWSON,** retired education educator; b. Antoine, Ark., Nov. 27, 1914; d. Oscar Moran and Dona Alice (Ward) Lawson; m. William D. Morris, July 2, 1932 (dec.) 1 child, Lavonne Morris Howell (dec.). BA, Henderson U., 1948; specialist degree, U. Ark., 1956, MS, 1951, MA, 1966; postgrad., U. Colo., 1954, Am. U., 1958, U. N.C., 1968. History tchr. Delight H.S., Ark., 1942-47; counselor Huntsville Sch. 1947-48; guidance dir. Russellville Pub. Sch. Sys., Ark., 1948-55; asst. prof. edn. U. Ark., Fayetteville, 1955-82, prof. emeritus, 1982—. Ednl. cons. Ark. Pub. Schs., 1965—78. Author: Biographical Essays, 2000; contr. book reviews and articles to mags. and profl. jours. including Ga. Hist. Quar., 1998, Ark. Biography, 2000. Mem. Hist. Preservation Alliance Ark.; pres. Washington County Hist. Soc., 1983-85, Pope County Hist. Assn.; mem. Ark. Symphony Guild; charter mem. Ark. Mus. in Arts; bd. dirs. Potts Inn Mus. Found. Named Ark. Coll. Tchr. of Yr., 1972; recipient Plaque for Outstanding Svcs. to Washington County Hist. Soc., 1984. Mem. LWV, AAUW, NEA, Washington County Hist., Soc. (exec. bd. 1977-80), Ark. Edn. Assn., Ark. Hist. Assn., Pope County Hist. Assn. (pres. 1991-92), The Ga. Hist. Soc., U. Ark. Alumni Assn., Sierra Club, Nature Conservancy, Ark. River Valley Arts Assn., Phi Delta Kappa, Kappa Delta Pi, Phi Alpha Theta. Democrat. Episcopalian. Address: 1601 W 3d St Russellville AR 72801-4725

**MORRIS, MAC GLENN,** advertising executive; b. Bessemer City, N.C., Jan. 24, 1922; s. Manly T. and Erin C. (Cline) M.; m. Janelle Conneyey, July 27, 1946; children— Robert S., Janelle C., Patricia A., John Logan. AB, Davidson Coll., 1942. Space salesman Progressive Farmer mag., N.Y.C., 1946-52; exec. v.p., advt. dir. This Week mag., 1952-68; pres. Newspaper One, N.Y.C., 1968-71; sr. v.p. nat. sales Newspaper Advt. Bur., N.Y.C., 1972-87; proprietor MGM Assocs., Princeton, NJ, 1987—. Bd. dirs. Princeton Bank & Trust Co. divsn. Chem. Bank N.J., N.A., now owned by P.N.C. Bank, N.Y.C. Served to 1st lt., pilot USMCR, World War II. Decorated D.F.C. (2), Air medal (7). Mem. Newcomen Soc. in N. Am., Pi Kappa Phi. Presbyn. (deacon). Club: Springdale Golf (Princeton, N.J.) (bd. govs.). Home and Office: 383 Herrontown Rd Princeton NJ 08540 *I am always an optimist at my work, with friends, and with my family.*

**MORRIS, MALCOLM STEWART,** title company executive, lawyer; b. Houston, May 8, 1946; s. Carloss M.; m. Rebecca Ann Simmons, June 14, 1969; children: Matthew William, Andrew James. BBA, So. Meth. U., 1968; JD, U. Tex., 1970, MBA, 1972. Bar: Tex. 1970. Legis. aid State of Tex., Sen. Charles Wilson, Austin, 1969-70; examiner Stewart Title Austin Inc., 1970-71; analyst Bank of the S.W., Houston, 1973-74; bus. mgr. Richard Hogue Evangelism, Inc., Houston, 1974-75; cons. Morris, Lendais, Hollrah & Snowden, Houston, v.p. ops. Stewart Title Guaranty Co., Houston, 1975-87, sr. exec. v.p., asst. chmn., 1987-91, pres., CEO, 1991—; chmn. Stewart Title Co.; chmn., co-CEO Stewart Info. Services Corp., Houston. Mem. bd. Stewart Title Ins. Co., N.Y.C., Stewart Title Ins. Co. U.K.; past mem. Tex. Land Title Assn., Am. Land Title Assn. Past chmn. Deacons, 1st Bapt. Ch., Houston; past chmn. Living Water Internat.; chmn. Millennium Water Alliance. Fellow Am. Bar Found., Houston Bar Assn.; mem. ABA, State Bar Tex., Houston Bar Assn., Phi Delta Phi. Baptist. Office: 1980 Post Oak Blvd Ste 800 Houston TX 77056-3826 also: Stewart Info Services Corp 1980 Post Oak Blvd Houston TX 77056

**MORRIS, MARGARET ELIZABETH,** marketing professional, small business owner; b. NYC, Nov. 1, 1962; d. John Daniel and Jean Bingham (MacCollom) M. BA in English, Georgetown U., 1984. Cert. Rubenfeld Synergy Method, 1997; cert. scuba diver: openwater, rescue diver, divemaster, emergency first responder instr., PADI. Mem. staff mktg. programs AT&T Nat. Fed. Mktg., Arlington, Va., 1985; mktg. tech. cons. AT&T Nat. Fed. Systems, Washington, 1985-87; tech. cons. computer mktg. Cin. Bell Tel. Co., 1987-89, mktg. tech. cons., 1989-95; sr. acct. exec.-strategic accts., 1995—. Tutor (vol.) Ptnrs. in Edn. Editor: (newsletter) District Action Project RAP, 1981-82; contbr. chpt. to book. Intern Citizens' Complaint Ctr., Washington, 1981—82; asst. coach River City Volleyball Club; coach CYO Girls Volleyball; vol. tech. amb. Corryville Cath. Sch.; vol. coord. SPCA Cin.; participant Leukemia and Lymphoma Soc. Am. Team in Tng., Suzuki Rock n Roll Marathon, San Diego, 2000, Walt Disney World Marathon, Orlando, Fla., 2001, Flying Pig Marathon, Cin., 2001, Mayor's Midnight Sun Marathon, Anchorage, 2002, Las Vegas Internat. Marathon, 2003, Marine Corps Marathon, 2003, NYC Marathon, 2004, Rock N Roll Arix. Half Marathon, 2004, Flying Pig Half Marathon, 2006. Named Salesperson of Yr., 1997, Corp. Vol. of Yr., SPCA Cin., 2001. Mem.: Telephone Pioneers Am. (Pioneer Vol. of Yr. 2000). Office: Cin Bell Tech Solutions Rm 346-500 4600 Montgomery Rd Cincinnati OH 45212

**MORRIS, MARK WILLIAM,** choreographer; b. Seattle, Aug. 29, 1956; s. William and Maxine (Crittenden) Morris. Studied with, Verla Flowers and Perry Brunson; D (hon.), Boston Conservatory of Music, Juilliard Sch., L.I. U., Pratt Inst., Bowdoin Coll. Artistic dir. Mark Morris Dance Group, N.Y.C., 1980—, Théâtre Royal de la Monnaie, Brussels, 1988—91; co-founder White Oak Dance Project, 1990; owner Mark Morris Dance Ctr., Bklyn., 2001—. Performed with Lar Lubovitch Dance Co., Hannah Kahn Dance Co., Laura Dean Dancers and Musicians, Eliot Feld Ballet, Koleda Balkan Dance Ensemble. Choreographer Esteemed Guests, Joffrey Ballet, 1986, Nixon in China, Houston Grand Opera, 1987, L'Allegro, il Penseroso ed il Moderato, 1988, Drink to Me Only With Thine Eyes, Am. Ballet Theatre, 1988, Orféo et Euridice, Seattle Opera, 1988, Dido and Aeneas, 1989, Ein Herz, Paris Opera Ballet, 1990, The Death of Klinghoffer, Théâtre de la Monnaie, 1991, The Hard Nut, 1991, Great Performances/Dance in Am. The Hard Nut, 1992, Maelstrom, San Francisco Ballet, 1994, The Office, 1994, Lucky Charms, 1994, Pacific, San Francisco Ballet, 1995, Platée, Royal Opera Covent Garden, 1997, Sandpaper Ballet, San Francisco Ballet, 1999, Four Saints in Three Acts, 2000, Sang-Froid, 2000, A Garden, San Francisco Ballet, 2001, Gong, Am. Ballet Theatre, 2001; dir.: Die Fledermaus, 1988, Falling Down Stairs, 1997 (Emmy award, 1997), The Capeman, Kolam, 2002. Recipient Dance and Performance award, 1984, 1990; fellow, Guggenheim Found., 1986, MacArthur Found., 1991. Office: Mark Morris Dance Group 3 Lafayette Ave Brooklyn NY 11217 Office Phone: 718-624-8400. E-mail: info@mmdg.org, barbie@mmdg.org.*

**MORRIS, MARTHA MARNEL,** music educator; b. Trenton, N.J., Aug. 25, 1948; M Music, American Conservatory, 1977; B Music Edn., St Mary of the Woods Coll., 1972. Co-founder/dir. Flutes Unlimited, Chgo., 1997—; music exec. Saint Xavier U., Chgo., 1984—96; conductor St. Xavier U. Orch., Chgo., 1983—; assoc. prof. music St. Xavier U., 1977—. Presenter in field. Musician: (CD) An Art Song Excursion, 2004, Wind and Song, 2000; arranger (flute, music and voices). Recipient various grants, St. Xavier U.; scholar, 2005. Achievements include research in application of vocal tract resonance in achieving optimum tone quality in woodwind and brass players. Office Phone: 773-298-3420. E-mail: morris@sxu.edu.

**MORRIS, MARY ELIZABETH,** pastor; b. Schenectady, N.Y. d. William and Kathryn Dilkes (Wilkins) Simpson; m. David John Stevens, Sept. 10, 1966 (dec. Dec. 1975); children: Jeffrey David, Wendy Elizabeth; m. Gerald Douglas Morris, Apr. 15, 1977; stepchildren: Laura Louise, Douglas Owen. BS with cert. in phys. therapy, Simmons Coll., 1966; MDiv, Boston U. Theology, 1988. Ordained min. 1993. Pvt. phys. therapist Muscular Dystrophy Assn., Dedham, Mass., 1971—93; vicar Holy Trinity Luth. Ch., North Easton, Mass., 1988—89; interim pastoral asst. Zion Luth. Ch., Plymouth, Mass., 1989—91; interim chaplain Symmes Hosp., Arlington, Mass., 1990—91; phys. therapist South Shore Vis. Nurse Assn, Braintree, Mass., 1991—93; pastor Bethany Luth. Ch., Orange, Mass., 1993—98, St. Mark Evangelical Luth. Ch., Woonsocket, RI, 1999—. Dean R.I. Conf. of New Eng. Synod of Evangelical Luth. Ch. in Am., 2002—05; ecumenical rep. R.I. State Coun. Chs., 2001—. Mem. Evangelical Luth. Ch. in Am. Office: St Mark Evangel Luth Ch 871 Harris Ave Woonsocket RI 02895 Office Phone: 401-769-8320.

**MORRIS, MATTHEW CHRISTIAN,** professional baseball player; b. Middletown, N.Y., Aug. 9, 1974; Attended, Seton Hall Univ. Played Team USA, 1994; pitcher St. Louis Cardinals, 1997—. Named All-Am. Office: St Louis Cardinals 250 Stadium Plz Saint Louis MO 63102*

**MORRIS, MICHAEL DAVID,** chemistry professor; b. N.Y.C., Mar. 27, 1939; s. Melvin M. and Rose (Pollock) M.; m. Leslie Tuttle, June 5, 1961; children: Susannah, David, Rebecca, Ari. BA in Chemistry, Reed Coll., 1960; PhD in Chemistry, Harvard U., 1964. Asst. prof. Pa. State U., University Park, Pa., 1969; assoc. prof. U. Mich., Ann Arbor, 1987-92; prof., 1982—. Assoc. chmn. U. Mich., Ann Arbor, 1992-97. Editor: Spectroscopic and Microscopic Imaging of the Chemical State, 1993; mem. editorial bd. Applied Spectroscopy, 1994— (Gold medal N.Y. sect. 1993), Spectrochim Acta Rev., 1987-92, editor, 1993. Recipient Anachem award Assn. Analytical Chemists, 1997. Mem. Am. Chem. Soc. (award in Spectrochemical Analysis Divsn. Analytical Chemistry 1995), Soc. Applied Spectroscopy (Strock award 1995), Microbeam Analysis Soc. Office: Univ Mich Dept Chemistry Ann Arbor MI 48109 E-mail: mdmorris@umich.edu.

**MORRIS, MICHAEL G.,** utilities executive; b. Fremont, Ohio, Nov. 11, 1946; married, Linda Lindstrom, 1970; two children. BS, Ea. Mich. U., MS, 1973; JD cum laude, Detroit Coll. Law, 1981. With environ. dept. Commonwealth Assocs., Jackson, Mich., 1973—76; pres. ANR Gathering Co.; exec. v.p. mktg., transp. and gas supply ANR Pipeline Co., 1982—87; pres. Colo. Interstate Gas Co., 1987—88; exec. v.p., natural gas & mktg. Consumers Energy subsidiary of CMS Energy Corp., 1988—92, COO, 1992—94, pres., CEO, 1994—97; chmn., pres., CEO Northeast Utilities, Berlin, Conn., 1997—2003; pres., CEO Am. Electric Power Co., Springfield, Mass., 2004—, chmn., 2004—. Past chmn. Conn. Bus. & Industry Assn.; chmn. Edison Electric Inst.; bd. dir. Nuclear Electric Ins. Ltd., Flint Ink Corp., Cincinnati Bell, Hartford Fin. Svc. Group Inc. Exec. com., trustee Inst. Gas Tech.; trustee Ea. Mich. U. Found.; trustee Detroit Coll. Law, Delta Sigma Phi Found.; mem. Olivet Coll. Leadership Adv. Coun.; US Dept. Energy, Electricity Adv. Bd.; Task Force Electricity Infrastructure, Nat. Gov. Assn.; Inst. Nuclear Power Ops.; Bus. Roundtable; Columbus Downtown Devel. Corp.; bd. dirs. Libr. Mich. Found.; bd. regents Ea. Mich. U., 1997—. Recipient Disting. Alumnus award Ea. Mich. U., 1995. Mem. Mich. Bar Assn., Delta Sigma Phi (pres.). Office: Am Electric Power Co 1 Riverside Plz Columbus OH 43215-2372*

**MORRIS, OWEN GLENN,** engineering corporation executive; b. Shawnee, Okla., Feb. 3, 1927; s. Vestus and Myrtle (Lindsey) M.; m. Joyce Gast; children: Deborah Morce, Janine Inez. BS in Mech. Engring, U. Okla., 1947, M.Aero. Engring., 1948; postgrad., U. Va., 1952-53, Va. Poly. Inst., 1955-56, Coll. William and Mary, 1957-58. Aero., research scientist NASA, Langley Field, Va., 1948-61, mgr. mission engring. Apollo to mgr. sys. integration space shuttle Houston, 1961—74, mgr. sys. integration space shuttle, 1974—80; pres. Eagle Engring., 1980-86; pres., chief exec. officer Eagle Aerospace, Houston, 1987-90, chmn., chief exec. officer, 1990-93, chmn. bd., 1992—. Served with USNR, 1943-46. Recipient U.S. Medal of Freedom, 1972, NASA Distinguished Service medal, 1973, NASA Exceptional Service medal, 1969, Outstanding Leadership medal NASA, 1979. Asso. fellow Am. Inst. Aeros. and Astronautics; mem. Am. Astronautical Soc., Acad. Model Aeros., Tau Beta Pi, Tau Omega. Presbyterian (elder 1964—). Club: Rotary. Home: 14914 Timberland Ct Houston TX 77062-2922

**MORRIS, QUINTON ILANDO,** music educator, director; b. Springfield, Ill., Sept. 7, 1977; s. Henry Smiley and Viesta Eileen Morris. MusB, NC Sch. Arts, Winston-Salem, 2002; MusM, The Boston Conservatory, 2004. Tchr. Austin Chamber Music Ctr., Tex., 2004—; instr. Texas U., Austin, 2006—. Artistic/exec. dir. The Young Eight String Octet, Austin, Tex., 2002—; tchr. The Young Eight String Seminar, Austin, 2003—; guest lectr. Huston-Tillotson U., Austin, 2005—. Prodr., artistic dir. (ensemble performances), Seattle Symphony. Mem. Chamber Music Am., NYC, 2003—; vice-chair King Country Children & Family Commn., Seattle, 1994—96; sec. Youth-N-Action, Seattle, 1994—97; pres., found. The Young Eight, Seattle, 2003—. Recipient Black History Resolution award, Wash. State Ho. Reps., 1994, Outstanding Cmty. Svc. award, Black Child Devel. Inst., 1997, Second Place award, Seattle Philharm. Orch., 2002, Chamber Music prize, The Boston Conservatory, 2004, Proclamation & Key to Wash. State, King County Coun., 2005, Outstanding Leadership award, The Links, Inc., Seattle Chpt., 2005, Best New Chamber Music Ensemble award, Seattle Symphony, 2005. Mem.: NAACP. Office: The Young Eight PO Box 301197 Austin TX 78703-0020 Office Phone: 512-374-1631. Office Fax: 512-374-1631. Business E-mail: qimorris@theyoungeight.com

**MORRIS, RALPH WILLIAM,** chronopharmacologist; b. Cleveland Heights, Ohio, July 30, 1928; s. Earl Douglas and Viola Minnie (Mau) M.; m. Carmen R. Mueller; children: Christopher Lynn, Kirk Stephen, Timothy Allen and Todd Andrew (twins), Melissa Mary. BA, Ohio U., Athens, 1950, MS, 1953; PhD, U. Iowa, 1955; postgrad., Seabury-Western Theol. Sem., 1979-81, McHenry County Coll., 1986-88. Research fellow in pharmacology, then teaching fellow U. Iowa, 1952-55; instr. dept. pharmacology Coll. Medicine, 1955-56; asst. prof. dept. pharmacognosy and pharmacology Coll. Pharmacy, 1956-62, assoc. prof., 1962-69; prof. Med. Center, U. Ill., Chgo., 1969-98, prof. emeritus, 1998, adj. prof. dept. pharmacodynamics, 1998-2000. Mem. adv. com. 1st aid and safety Midwest chpt. ARC, 1972-83; cons. in drug edn. to Dangerous Drug Commn., Ill. Dept. Pub. Aid, Chgo., Ill. Dept. Profl. Regulataions, Ill. Dept. Corrections and suburban sch. dists.; adj. prof. edn. Coll. Edn., U. Ill., Chgo., 1976-85; vis. scientist San Jose State U., Calif., 1982-83, St. George Med. Sch., Grenada, 1994. Referee and contbr. articles to profl. and sci. jours., lay mags., radio and TV appearances. Trustee Palatine (Ill.) Pub. Libr., 1967-72, pres., 1969-70; trustee North Suburban Libr. System, 1968-72, pres. 1970-72, mem. long-range planning com., 1975-81; chmn. Ill. Trustees, 1970-72, intellectual freedom com.; mem. Title XX Ill. Citizens Adv. Coun., 1981-83; trustee McHenry (Ill.) Pub. Libr. Dist., 1987-89, pres., 1987-89; trustee St. Gregory's Abbey, Three Rivers, Mich., 1989-96; bd. dirs. North Suburban Libr. Found., Wheeling, Ill., 1998-99; bd. dirs. United Campus Ministry U. Ill. at Chgo., 1983-87; pres. R.W. Morris & Assocs., 1988—; v.p. Lake Barrington Shores Condo X Assn., bd. dirs., 1999—; mem. archit. commn. Lake Barrington Shores Master Bd., 1999—. Recipient Golden Apple Teaching award U. Ill. Coll. Pharmacy, 1966; cert. of merit Town of Palatine, 1972 Mem. AAAS, Am. Assn. Coll. Pharmacists, Internat. Soc. Chronobiology, European Soc. Chronbiology, Am. Soc. Pharmacology and Exptl. Therapeutics, Am. Library Trustee Assn., Ill. Library Trustee Assn. (v.p. 1970-72, dir. 1969-72), Sigma Xi, Rho Chi, Gamma Alpha. Episcopalian. Home and Office: 584 Shoreline Dr Lake Barrington IL 60010-3883 Office Phone: 847-304-0605. Personal E-mail: raphaelmor@aol.com.

**MORRIS, RICHARD IDES,** retired petroleum engineer, science educator; b. Tulsa, Okla., Sept. 14, 1930; s. Ides Virgil Morris and Frances Geneva Casey; m. Glenda Claire Walker, June 26, 1954 (div. 1985); adopted children: Holly Jean, Paul Casey. BS in Geol. Engring. with distinction, U. Okla., Norman, 1957. Petroleum exploration Carter Oil Co., Tulsa, Okla., 1957—60; geophysicist Humble Oil Co., Houston, 1960—62, New Orleans, 1963—65, Esso Iberia, Spain, 1962—63; regional field engr. west Dresser Industries, Hibbing, Minn., 1965—70; tchr. sci. Norman Pub. Schs., Okla., 1972—80; petroleum geophysicist Exxon, Oklahoma City, 1981—86; ret. 1986. Vol. fossil storage preparation Okla. Mus. Natural History, Norman, 1998—; state treas. Common Cause, 2000—; mem. planning bd. East Main Pl., 1995—2002; mem. rev. com. Sierra Club, 2000—2001. Staff sgt. USAF, 1949—54, Korea. Democrat. Unitarian Univesalist. Achievements include development of process to determine drill rates in differing rock types. Home: 1511 Sunrise Cir Norman OK 73071-2630

**MORRIS, RICHARD L.,** information technology executive; Information technology positions US Healthcare, Fidelity Bank, Combustion Engring., Pitney Bowes; chief information officer East Coast, Wellspring Resources, BetzDearborn, Perkin Elmer; mng. dir. Xernon Technology Solutions; v.p., chief information officer CSS Industries, Inc., Phila., 2005—. Office: CSS Industries Inc 1845 Walnut St Philadelphia PA 19103 Office Phone: 215-569-9900. Office Fax: 215-569-9979.

**MORRIS, ROBERT,** songwriter, musician, music educator; b. Memphis, Dec. 12, 1951; s. Ray and Mable Morris; m. Irene Morris, June 11, 1990; 4 stepchildren. Cameo appearance: (Finnish movie) Leningrad Cowboys Go America, 1989; songwriter: (gold) Trucker's Last Ride, 1995, Trucker's Last Ride (German transl.), songwriter: over 600 songs, co-writer with: Rick Christian, Irene Morris, Cliff Hutchinson, Joe Berry, Cordell (Rockin' Grandma) Jackson, Eva Jo Hensley, Charlie Louvin, performer with: Charlie Feathers, John The Baptist, Capt'n Blue, Ma Rainey, Little Laura Dukes, Cordell Jackson; musician: (shared show billings with) Billie Jo Spears, Justin Timberlake, David Frizzell, Dale Street, Mike Crews, Nika Vann, (album) Robert Morris Greatest Hits, Trucker's Last Ride And Other Trucking Songs. Named a Col., State of Tenn., 2000; named to, Rockabilly Hall of Fame, 2000, Traditional Country Music Hall of Fame, 2002; recipient Pioneer Lifetime Achievement award, United Music Heritage Inc., 1999, Gov.'s award, Tenn. Gov. Don Sundquist, 1999, Miss. Gov. Don Musgrove, 2000, Key to City of Memphis, Promoter of Large Events award, Tex. River Best of Country Award Show, 2004.

**MORRIS, ROBERT CRANE,** management training executive; b. El Centro, Calif., July 22, 1937; s. George Howser Morris and Lillian Cauthen Barnhouse; m. Susanne Rockne, Feb. 17, 1968. BS, U. Calif., Davis, 1961, MS, 1972; PhD, Mich. State U., 1984. Vol. U.S. Peace Corps, Lyallpur, Pakistan, 1961-63, asst. dir. Lahore, Pakistan, 1963-64; cons. Swedish Internat. Devel. Agy., Stockholm, 1965; dir. overseas ops. sch. partnership program U.S. Peace Corps, Washington, 1966-68; dir. info. ctr. Internat. Secretariate Vol. Svc., Washington, 1968-69; fellow Social Sci. Rsch. Coun., Colombia, 1972-74; faculty dept. comm. Mich. State U.; U.S. Embassy, Bogota, Colombia, 1972-74; faculty dept. comm. Mich. State U.; U.S. Embassy, Bogota, Mgmt. Tng. and Devel. Inst., Washington, 1978—. Chmn. Mgmt. Tng. & Devel. Inst., Singapore, 1995—97; cons. Cross-Cultural Connection, 2005—. Author: Overseas Volunteer Programs; guest editor Rural Africana, 1977; editor, mgmt. comm. series SUNY Press, Albany, 1994—. Adv. com. Indus Found., 1997—. Mem. ASTD, Soc. Internat. Devel., Assn. Internat. Educators. Avocation: guitar. Home: 1230 4th St SW Washington DC 20024-2302 Office Phone: 202-484-7999. E-mail: rands.morris@verizon.net.

**MORRIS, ROBERT GEMMILL,** retired foreign service officer; b. Des Moines, July 20, 1929; s. Robert William and Iva May (Gemmill) M.; m. Beverly Schupfer, July 3, 1955; children: Robert William II, John Schupfer, Richard Edward. BS, Iowa State U., 1951; postgrad, Charles Francis U., Graz, 1951—52; MS, Calif. Inst. Tech., 1954; PhD, Iowa State U., 1957. Asst. prof. S.D. Sch. Mines and Tech., Rapid City, 1958-59, assoc. prof., 1959-62, prof., head dept. physics, 1962-68; phys. sci. officer Office of Naval Research, Washington, 1968-73, dir. electronics program, 1973-74; U.S. fgn. service officer U.S. Dept. State, Washington, 1974-78; counselor for sci. and technol. affairs U.S. Mission to OECD, Paris, 1978-82, U.S. Embassy, Bonn, Fed. Republic Germany, 1982-85; dep. asst. sec. of state for sci. and tech. affairs Washington, 1985-87; fgn. svc. officer U.S. Embassy, Buenos Aires, 1987-90, Madrid, 1990-92. Contbr. articles to profl. jours. Fulbright scholar, Austria, 1951; Swiss govt. fellow, Zurich, 1957. Fellow APS; mem. Am. Fgn. Service Assn.

**MORRIS, ROBERT LOUIS,** management consultant; b. Phila., Aug. 24, 1932; s. Joseph Aloysius and Philomena Mary Ellen (Clauser) M.; m. Elizabeth Marie Smyth, Sept. 10, 1955; children: Robert L., Thomas J., Lawrence F., Elizabeth M., Mary Ellen, Richard B. BS, Drexel U., 1955; MS, U. Pa., 1957; postgrad., U. Cin., 1965-66, U. Chgo., 1969-71. Group leader Proctor & Gamble Co., Miami Valley Labs., 1958-68; dir. computing svcs. rsch. & devel. divsn. Kraft, Inc., Glenview, Ill., 1968-71; dir. rsch. and process devel. Continental Baking Co., St. Louis and Rye, NY, 1971-77, v.p. tech. affairs, 1978-92; tech. dir. food and chem. products ITT, Inc., N.Y.C., 1977-78; pres. Regu-Tech. Inc., Williamsburg, Va., 1992—, Regu-Tech Assocs., Inc., Lightfoot, Va., 1997—. Patentee in field. Bd. dirs. Fundacion Chile, Santiago, 1978-79, 83-85; mem. Greenwich Rep. Town Meeting, 1977; bd. dirs. Olde Towne Med. Ctr., Williamsburg, 2000-05, vice chair, 2003-05. With AUS, 1957 NSF fellow, 1955-56, Wilson S. Yerger fellow, 1956-57. Fellow AIChE.; mem. Assn. Rsch. Dirs., Indsl. Rsch. Inst. (bd. dirs. 1988-91), Am. Assn. Cereal Chemists, Ford's Colony Golf Club. Roman Catholic. Office: MTI Group PO Box 6506 Williamsburg VA 23188-6506 Office Phone: 757-258-9105. Personal E-mail: rlmatmti@cox.net.

**MORRIS, RONALD ANTHONY,** county official; b. Wilmington, Del., Nov. 8, 1946; s. Elwood and Sophia (Ptak) M.; m. Barbara Marie Szostkowski, July 16, 1976. BS, U. Balt., 1970; MBA, Widener U., 1975. Cert. govt. fin. mgr. Cost acct. Atlas Chem. Industries, New Castle, Del., 1966-67; sr. cost acct. Bethlehem Steel Corp., Balt., 1967-70; sr. acct. J.K. Lasser & Co., CPAs, Wilmington, 1970-71; dep. dir. fin. City of Wilmington, 1971-74; acctg. supr. New Castle County, 1974-75, controller, 1975-80, budget and acctg. mgr., 1980-97, CFO, 1997—. Recipient Achievement award Nat. Assn. Counties, 1990, 92, 94, EXSL award Nat. Ctr. for Pub. Productivity, 1990, Award of Excellence, Nat. Assns. County Info. Officers, 1989. Mem. Del. Assn. Govtl. Fin. Officers (v.p. 1990-94), Am. Soc. Pub. Adminstrn., Del. Assn. for Pub. Adminstrn. (coun. mem. 1980-82), Govt. Fin. Officers Assn., U.S. and Can. (com. mem. 1989—, Fin. Reporting Achievement award 1981-2002, Disting. Budget Presentation award 1991-2002, award for Excellence 2004, Achievement award 2004), Am. Acctg. Assn., Nat. Assn. Accts., ICMA, New Castle County Econ. Devel. Coun., Rotary Club of Wilmington (Del.). Avocations: beach, classic cars, coins, currency. Business E-Mail: rmorris@co.new-castle.de.us.

**MORRIS, RONALD LEW,** management consultant, oil and gas industry executive, petroleum engineer; s. Joel and Lillian Morris; m. Lynda Lea Johnson, Jan. 1967 (div. Oct. 2000); children: Adria Jenny, Adam Polf; m. Yan Wang, Feb. 2001; children: Oliver Wang, Mattie Wang. BSc in Aero. Engring., U. Okla., 1970; MSc in Mech. Engring., Colo. State U., 1972. Project coord. Danish Undergrounds Consortium, Copenhagen, 1979-83; mgr. planning and econs. Texaco Ltd., London, 1983-84; drilling mgr., dist. engr. Texaco North Sea UK, Aberdeen, Scotland, 1984-89; portfolio evaluations mgr. Texaco USA, Midland, Tex., 1989-91; asst. gen. mgr. Texaco-Angola, Luanda, 1991-96; v.p., mng. dir. Texaco Exploration Myanmar Inc., Yangon, 1996-98; mng. dir. CACT-Ops. Group, Shekou, China, 1998—2001; gen. mgr. Ori Ox Energy Assocs. Ltd., Hong Kong, Beijing, 2002—06; dir. engring. and constrn. Momentum Energy Group LLC, Durango, Colo., 2006—. Chmn. bus. mgmt. seminar 7th Oil & Gas Conf., Beijing, 2000. Contbr. articles to profl. jours. Instr. Jr. Achievement and Young Astronauts, Midland, 1990-93; cub scout leader Boy Scouts Am., Aberdeen, 1986-88. Recipient Provencial Friendship award, Guangdong, China, 2001, Regional Svc. award, Soc. Petroleum Engrs. Asia Pacific, 2003. Mem. AIAA, Aircraft Owners and Pilots Assn., Am. C. of C., Soc. Petroleum Engrs. Avocations: golf, travel, pilot. Mailing: PO Box 1549 Durango CO 81302 Office Phone: 970-769-6538. Personal E-mail: rlmorrischina@yahoo.com.

**MORRIS, SANDRA K.,** computer company executive; b. Paxtang, Pa., 1954; BS with honors and distinction, U. Del., 1976, MS, 1981; postgrad., U. Pa. Faculty mem. U. Del.; with RCA Corp. David Sarnoff Rsch. Ctr.; product mgr. Intel Corp., 1985, v.p. e-bus. group, 1999—2002; CIO, and V.P. Intel Corp, 2002—. Co-author: Multimedia Application Development Using Indeo video and DVI Technology, 1982. Office: Intel Corp PO Box 58119 2200 Mission College Blvd Santa Clara CA 95052-8119

**MORRIS, SANDRA N.,** elementary school educator; b. Holton, Kans., Nov. 27, 1951; d. L. Scott and Betty J. Nelson; m. Timothy B. Morris, Jan. 3, 1970; children: Stephanie, Katherine, Erin Lea. BSEd, Washburn U., Topeka, Kans., 1973; MS in Curriculum and Edn., Emporia State U., Kans., 1979; cert. reading specialist, Emporia State U., 1986. Cert. tchr. Kans. 2d grade tchr. Royal Valley Sch. Dist., Mayetta, Kans., 1973—75, kindergarten tchr., 1975—85, 1st grade tchr., 1985—93, Title 1 reading tchr., 1993—2004, literacy coach, 2004—. Field supr. Emporia (Kans.) State U., 1985—93; presenter in field. Recipient Innovator in Edn. award, Alliance for Bus. and Edn., Emporia, 1989, Tchr. of Yr. award, Region 2 Kans., 1999, Fulbright Meml. Fund Program award, Govt. of Japan, 2001; grantee, Martin Outdoor Co., Topeka, 1985, Quaker Oats, Topeka, 1987, Goodyear Tire and Rubber Co., Topeka, 1993; Excellence in Edn. grantee, Southwestern Bell, Topeka, 1988, 1994. Mem.: NEA, Kans. Nat. Educators Assn., Topeka Area Reading Coun. (sec. 1975—77, v.p. 1993—94, pres. 1994—95, Outstanding Reading Educator award 1996), Kans. Reading Assn. (chmn. R.E.A.D. Week 1994—95, v.p.-elect 1994—95, v.p. 1995—96, pres. 1996—97, mem. exec. bd. 1997—98), Internat. Reading Assn., Delta Kappa Gamma. Republican. Methodist. Avocations: bicycling, reading, golf. Home: 23318 P Rd Holton KS 66440 Office: USD 337 Royal Valley Elem Sch 1st and Highland Hoyt KS 66440 Office Phone: 785-986-6286. Business E-Mail: morris@rv337.k12.k12.ks.ms. E-mail: snmorris@holtonks.net.

**MORRIS, SCOTT STEPHEN,** musician, educator; b. Wichita, Kans., July 21, 1970; s. Stephen Neal and Roberta Diane Morris; m. Casey Wen Xiao-Morris. BMus, U. So. Calif., 1994; MusM, Yale U., New Haven, Conn., 1997; D in Musical Arts, Claremont Grad. U., 2004. Music prof. Cal. State U. Dominguez Hills, Carson, 2004—. Musician: (recording) Invocation, Holly-

wood Guitar Duo; author: (guitar teaching method) The Guitarist's Path. Fellow, Claremont Grad. U., 2000; Performance scholar, Yale U., 1996—97, Aspen Music Sch., 1996. Achievements include Carnegie Hall debut in 1998. E-mail: scottmorris@aya.yale.edu.

**MORRIS, STEPHEN BURRITT,** marketing information company executive; b. Morristown, N.J., Aug. 13, 1943; s. Grinnell and Cornelia (Kellogg) M.; m. Victoria Ann French, Feb. 18, 1967; children: Christopher Jackson, Robin Taylor. BA, Yale U., 1965; MBA, Harvard U., 1969. With product mgmt. Gen. Foods Corp., White Plains, NY, 1969—83, gen. mgr. Maxwell House Coffee div., 1983-85, v.p., 1983-87, pres. Maxwell House div., 1986-87; founder, pres. Spectra Mktg. Systems Inc., Chgo., 1987-90; pres., CEO Vid Code Inc., Waltham, Mass., 1990-92; pres., CEO, Arbitron Inc., N.Y.C., 1992—. Bd. dirs. John B. Stetson Co. Trustee N.Y. Theatre Workshop, 1995; bd. dirs. Advt. Rsch. Found.; trustee David Parsons Dance Co., 2003. Served to 2d lt. USMCR, 1965-66. Avocations: tennis, gardening. Home: 300 Mt Holly Rd Katonah NY 10536-3546 Office: Arbitron Inc 142 W 57th St Fl 11 New York NY 10019-3397

**MORRIS, STEVEN LYNN,** engineering consultant, retired military officer; b. Dallas, Dec. 7, 1952; s. William Ira and Alta Faye (McCarley) M.; m. Jacqueline Ann Fenter, July 30, 1977; children: Steven Sean, Michael Wayne. BS in Engring. Scis., USAF Acad., 1975; MS in Aero. Engring, Air Force Inst. Tech., 1980; PhD in Aerospace Engring., Tex. A&M U., 1989. Registered profl. engr., Tex., Colo. Commd. 2d lt. USAF, 1975, advanced through grades to lt. col., 1991, ret., 1999; assoc. prof., dep. head dept. aeronautics USAF Acad., Colo., 1989-99; engring. specialist SRS Techs., Colorado Springs, Colo., 1999-2000; sr. cons. Engring. Systems, Inc., 2000—. Named to Outstanding Young Men in Am., 1981. Fellow AIAA (assoc., flight mechanics tech. com. 1991-94, 98-01, mem. applied aerodynamics tech. com. 2003-06, dir. for edn. region V 1992-94, dep. dir. for precoll. outreach region V 1998-02 Sustained Svc. award 2005, Summerfield Book award 2006); mem. USAF Acad. Assn. Grads., Soc. Automotive Engrs. (mem. aircraft icing subcom.), Air Force Assn., Tex. A&M U. Assn. Former Students, Tau Beta Pi, Sigma Gamma Tau. Baptist. Avocations: running, photography, hiking. Home: 5331 Wells Fargo Dr Colorado Springs CO 80918 Office: Engring Systems Inc Ste 106 4775 Centennial Blvd Colorado Springs CO 80919 Office Phone: 719-535-0400. E-mail: slmorris@esi-co.com.

**MORRIS, STEVLAND See WONDER, STEVIE**

**MORRIS, STEWART, JR.,** title insurance company executive; b. Houston, Oct. 14, 1948; s. Stewart Sr. and Joella (Mitchel) M. BA, Rice U., 1971; MBA, U. Tex., 1973. With Stewart Title Co., 1973—, v.p. Houston, 1975-87, sr. exec. v.p., asst. to pres., 1987-91, chmn., pres., 1991—; advisory dir. Stewart Information Services Corp., 1997—2000, bd. dirs., pres., co-CEO, 2000—. Bd. dirs. Southern Nat. Bank, Houston. Bd. dirs. Houston chpt. Cystic Fibrosis Found., 1985—. Mem. Am. Land Title Assn., Am. Driving Soc. (bd. dirs. 1984—), Houston Area Carriage Assn. (pres. 1995—), Carriage Assn. Am. (pres. 1995—). Office: 1980 Post Oak Blvd Ste 800 Houston TX 77056-3826*

**MORRIS, SYLVIA JUNE BURBANK,** retired physician; b. Le Roy, Iowa, June 18, 1921; d. Dean Stanley and Myra G. (Douglas) Burbank; m. John Thomas Morris, Jan. 1, 1948 (div.); children: Thomas Dean, Richard Lee, John Douglas. BA in Chemistry, Grinnell Coll., 1942; MD, U. Iowa, 1945; MPH, U. Ala., 1981. Intern Balt. City Hosp., 1945—46; pediat. intern. Johns Hopkins Hosp., 1946—47; pvt. practice Pleasantville, Iowa, 1947—48, Hanceville, Ala., 1949—53; asst. med. dir. Tri-County Health Dept., Decatur, 1972—88, epidemiologist, 1981—88; ret., 1988. Asst. prof. health policy U. Ala. Sch. Pub. Health, Birmingham, 1983—88; mem. children's policy coun. Juvenile Ct., Cullman, Ala., 1994—. Author: Jerome-Civil War Letters, 1994, Doctoring, 1996, Jennifer, 1999, Jennifer Again, 2003, Piggy Flu & Lil' Sam Too: Medical Adventures in Appalacia, 2003, Beth's Song, 2005; editor: Doctoring in Cullman County Before 1900, 1996, Jennifer-A Cat Tale, 2003; contbr. articles to profl. publs. Mem. Cullman County Hist. Soc., Ala. Hist. Assn. Mem.: AMA, Med. Assn. State of Ala. (dist. counselor 1999—), Ala. Writer's Conclave, Ala. Hist. Assn., Cullman County Hist. Soc., Symphony Club. Home: PO Box 305 Cullman AL 35056-0305

**MORRIS, THOMAS BATEMAN, JR.,** lawyer; b. Columbus, Ohio, Aug. 11, 1936; s. Thomas Bateman and Margaret (O'Shaughnessy) M.; m. Ann Peirce, Feb. 23, 1963; children: Lauren, Thomas III, Richard. AB, Princeton U., 1958; JD, Harvard U., 1962. Bar: Pa. 1962. Sr. ptnr. Dechert LLP, Phila., 1962—2001, chmn., 1990-96. Bd. dirs. Berwind Corp., Phila., AstenJohnson, Inc., Charleston, S.C., Envirite Corp., Plymouth Meeting, Pa., Peirce-Phelps, Inc., Phila., The Contributionship Cos. Co-chmn. Greater Phila. First, 1996-2000; trustee Princeton U., 1975-80; bd. trustees Thomas Jefferson U., 1989—. Hon. Consul King of Belgium, Phila., 1974-89. Mem. ABA, Pa. Bar Assn., Phila. Bar Assn. (chmn. city tax policy com.), Internat. Bar Assn. (chmn. com. on structure and ethics of law practice), Phila. Club. Princeton Club, Sunnybrook Golf Club, Pine Valley Golf Club, NY Athletic Club. Office: Dechert LLP 4000 Bell Atlantic Tower Philadelphia PA 19103-2793 E-mail: tmorris@dechert.com.

**MORRIS, THOMAS ROBBINS,** political scientist, educator, academic administrator; b. Roanoke, Va., July 28, 1944; s. Robert Vaughan and David (Robbins) M.; m. Barbara-lyn Belcher, July 23, 1966; children: Sheila Dawn (dec.), Tabbitha Lyn, Sharon Robbins, Rosa-Lyn Vaughan. BA in History, Va. Mil. Inst., 1966; MA, U. Va., 1969, PhD in Govt., 1973; postgrad., Princeton Theol. Sem., 1966-67. Asst. prof. U. Richmond, Va., 1971-78, assoc. prof. polit. sci. Va., 1978-87, prof. Va., 1987-92, chair dept. Va., 1981-84; polit. analyst WTVR-Channel 6 TV Richmond, 1981-95, WDBJ-Channel 7 TV Roanoke, Va., 1998—; pres. Emory & Henry Coll., 1992—. Vis. scholar U. Utah, 1986-87; chmn., commn. Va.'s State and Local Tax Structure for The 21st Century, 1999-2000; mem. Va. Gov.'s Commn. Efficiency and Effectiveness, 2002. Author: The Virginia Supreme Court: An Institutional and Political Analysis, 1975, Virginia Government and Politics: Readings and Comments, 4th edit., 1998. Bd. dirs. Housing Opportunities Made Equal, Richmond, Va., 1982-92. Liberal arts fellow Harvard Law Sch., Cambridge, Mass., 1976-77, NEH fellow U. Wis.-Madison, 1979-80; named Disting. Educator. U. Richmond, Va., 1982. Mem. Am. Polit. Assn., Omicron Delta Kappa. Methodist. Office: Emory & Henry Coll Office of Pres Emory VA 24327 Office Phone: 276-944-6107. Business E-Mail: trmorris@ehc.edu.

**MORRIS, THOMAS WILLIAM,** symphony orchestra administrator; b. Rochester, N.Y., Feb. 7, 1944; s. William H. and Eleanor E. M.; m. Jane Allison. Aug. 7, 1965; children: Elisa L., Charles A., William H. AB, Princeton U., 1965; MBA, Wharton Sch. U. Pa., 1969. Adminstrv. asst., Ford Found. fellow for adminstrv. interns in arts Cin. Symphony, 1965-67; payroll clk. bus. office Boston Symphony Orch., 1969-71, asst. mgr. bus. affairs, 1971-73, mgr., 1973-78, gen. mgr., 1978-86, v.p. spl. projects and planning, 1986; pres. Thomas W. Morris and Co., Inc., Boston, 1986-87; exec. dir. Cleve. Orch., 1987—2004; artistic dir. Ojai Music Festival, 2004—. Chmn. policy com. Maj. Orch. Mgrs., 1977-79; chmn. orch. panel Nat. Endowment for Arts, 1979-80. Chmn. Cleve. Cultural Coalition, 1992-95; mem. Cleve. Bicentennial Comm., 1993-97; mem. bd. overseers Curtis Inst. Music, 1998—. Mem. Am. Symphony Orch. League (dir. 1977-79) Office: 2533 Fairmount Blvd Cleveland OH 44106

**MORRIS, VICTOR FRANKLIN, JR.,** retired meteorology educator; b. Hyannis, Mass., Mar. 1, 1947; s. Victor Franklin and Florence Muriel (Rund) M. Student, MIT, 1965-66; BS in Atmospheric Scis., U. Wash., 1969; MS in Meteorology, U. Hawaii, 1975; MA in Environ. Geography, San Diego State U., 1979. Cert. community coll. instr. earth scis., Calif.; cert. advanced and instrument ground instr. FAA. Rsch. asst. U. Hawaii, Honolulu, 1973-75; teaching asst., lectr. San Diego State U., 1976-80; instr. San Diego Community Colls., 1976-80; prof. aero. sci. in meteorology Embry-Riddle Aero. U.,

Daytona Beach, Fla., 1981-94; pres. Caribbean Weather Svc., Rincon, PR, 1994—2001, ret., 2001. Cons. meteorologist Surfer Publs., Dana Point, Calif., 1980—2001; chief East Coast meteorologist Surf Line, Huntington Beach, Calif., 1987—2001. Author: The Weather Surfer, 1977, Meteorology: A Study Guide, 1985; writer monthly newsletter Sea Watch, 1980—2001; contbr. articles to profl. jours. and mags. Lt. USN, 1970-72. Mem. Am. Meteorol. Soc., Phi Kappa Phi. Avocations: surfing, distance running, gardening, beachcombing, amateur radio. Home: PO Box 384874 Waikoloa HI 96738-4874

**MORRIS, WILLIAM CHARLES,** investor; b. St. Louis, Apr. 15, 1938; s. Barney Lockhart and Kathryn (Evers) M.; m. Susan VanAvery Follett, Aug. 26, 1961; children: Edward F., David L., Kenneth V. SB in Chem. Engring., MIT, 1960; MBA, Harvard U., 1963. Assoc. Mobil Chem. Co., N.Y.C., 1963-66; with Lehman Bros., NYC, 1967-84; chmn. Carbo Ceramics Inc., Dallas, 1987—, J&W Seligman & Co., Inc., N.Y.C., 1988—. Chmn. Tri-Continental Corp., N.Y.C., 1988—, Seligman Group of Investment Cos., NYC, 1988—. Mng. dir. Met. Opera Assn., NY, 1995—, pres., CEO NY, 2003—; trustee Woods Hole (Mass.) Oceanog. Instn., 2001—. Ensign USCGR, 1961. Office: J & W Seligman & Co Inc 100 Park Ave New York NY 10017-5598 Office Phone: 212-850-1864.

**MORRIS, WILLIAM OTIS, JR.,** lawyer, educator; b. Fairmont, W.Va., Dec. 2, 1922; s. William Otis and Flora Helois (Preston) M.; m. Hazel Irene Kolbus, May 28, 1948; children: Barbara Ann, Melinda Lou. Student, Fairmont State Coll., W.Va., 1940—41; AB, Coll. William and Mary, 1944; LLB, U. Ill., Champaign/Urbana, 1946; JD, U. Ill., 1968; HDC, Nicholas Copernicus U., Torun, Poland, 1992; LLD, Fairmont State U., W.Va., 2003. Bar: Va. 1945, Ill. 1946, U.S. Supreme Ct. 1949. Prof. bus. law U. Ill., 1947-55; assoc. prof. law Stetson U., 1955-58; prof. law W.Va. U., Morgantown, 1958-94, prof. emeritus law, 1994—. Vis. U. Vienna, Austria, Nat. U. Singapore, Nat. U. Seoul, Korea, U. Sydney, Australia, East China Inst. Law and Politics, U. Thessaloniki, Greece; vis. prof. U. Tex., U. Miss., Baylor U., U. San Diego, Samford U., Stetson U., George Washington U., others. Author: Dental Litigation, 1972, 2d edit., 1977, The Law of Domestic Relations in West Virginia, 1975, Veterinarian in Litigation, 1976, Revocation of Professional License, 1985, Handbook of Dental Law, 1994, The Dentist's Legal Advisor, 1994; mem. bd. editors Jour. Law and Ethics in Dentistry, Med. Malpractice Prevention, Clin. Jour.; contbr. articles to profl. jours. Decorated Merit medal (Poland); recipient Spl. award Nat. U. Seoul, Old Guard Medallion Coll. William and Mary, 1994, Lifetime Achievement Award Dentistry, 1994. Fellow Cleve. Clinic Med. Inst.; mem. ATLA, Va. Bar, Ill. Bar, W.Va. Trial Lawyers Assn., Order of Coif, Order of White Jackets, Sir Robert Boyle Soc. Republican. Lutheran. Home: 644 Bellaire Dr Morgantown WV 26505-2421 Office Phone: 304-599-2664. Personal E-mail: bajrmig@webtv.net, wmillini@aol.com.

**MORRISEY, MARENA GRANT,** art museum administrator; b. Newport News, Va., May 28, 1945; BFA in Interior Design, Va. Commonwealth U., 1967, MA in Art History, 1970. With Orlando (Fla.) Mus. Art, 1970—, exec. dir., 1976—. Former v.p., chmn. mus. svcs. com., mem. ad hoc com. on collections sharing and long range planning com., past chmn. exhbns. and edn. com. Am. Fedn. Arts; former mem. nat. adv. coun. George Washington U. Clearinghouse on Mus. Edn.; former mem. accreditation com. Nat. Found. for Interior Design Edn. Rsch. Former mem. strategic planning adv. coun. Orange County Sch. Dist.; former mem. advt. rev. bd. BBB; former mem. Orlando Pub. Art Adv. Bd., Orlando Leadership Coun., Orlando Hist. Bldg. Commn.; mem. art selection com. Orlando Internat. Airport, former chmn.; former mem. bd. dirs. Sta. WMFE-TV; bd. dirs. New World Sch. of Arts; vol. Sister Cities of Orlando; mem. internat. arts and culture com. Metro Orlando Internat. Affairs Commn.; pub. art review com. Orange County; exec. com. Uptown Dist. Named Orlando's Outstanding Woman of Yr. in Field of Art; recipient Fla. State of Arts award. Mem. Am. Assn. Mus. (former mem. governing bd., accreditation commn., profl. stds. and practices com., internat. coun. of mus.), Assn. Art Mus. Dirs. (comm. and publs. com.), Southeastern Mus. Conf. (past pres.), Fla. Art Mus. Dirs. Assn. (past pres.), Fla. Assn. Mus. (former bd. dirs.), Greater Orlando C. of C. (past mem. steering com. Leadership Orlando), Jr. League Orlando-Winter Park, Rotary Club Orlando (Paul Harris fellow). Office: Orlando Museum of Art 2416 N Mills Ave Orlando FL 32803-1483 Office Phone: 407-896-4231. Business E-Mail: mgmorrisey@omart.org.

**MORRISEY, MICHAEL A.,** health economics educator; b. Crookston, Minn., Mar. 20, 1952; s. Charles Arthur and Eleanor E. (LaFleur) M.; m. Elaine M. Mardian, Aug. 26, 1972; children: Michelle Ann, David Michael. BA, No. State U., Aberdeen, S.D., 1974; MA in Econs., U. Wash., 1975, PhD in Econs., 1979. Rsch. asst., specialist Battelle HARC, Seattle, 1976—79; sr. economist Am. Hosp. Assn., Chgo., 1979-85; sr. economist, asst. dir. Hosp. Rsch. & Ednl. Trust, Chgo., 1983-85; vis. scholar Northwestern U., Evanston, Ill., 1984-85; assoc. prof. U. Ala., Birmingham, 1985-88, prof., 1988—; disting. faculty investigator, 1999-2000; dir. Lister Hill Ctr. for Health Policy, Birmingham, 1990—. Dep. editor Med. Care, Cleve., 1987—96; mem. Pa. Mandates Benefits Rev. Panel, Harrisburg, 1987—, Ala. Task Force on Rural Health Care Crisis, 1989; mem. health svcs. devel. grants rev. com. Agy. for Health Care Rsch. and Quality, Rockville. Md., 1992—96; cons. in field. Author: Price Sensitivity in Health Care, 1992, 2d edit., 2005, Cost Shifting in Health Care, 1994, Managed Care and Changing Health Care Markets, 1998; mem. editl. bd. Health Svcs. Rsch., 1985-94, Health Affairs, 1998—. Jour. Gerontology, 1998-2001, Health Svcs. and Outcomes Rsch. Methodology, 1999—, Health Adminstrn. Press, 1999-2002, 2005—. Med. Care Rsch. and Rev., 2000—; contbr. more than 130 articles to profl. jours. Recipient John D. Thompson prize in health svc. rsch., Assn. Univ. Programs in Health Adminstrn., 1991, UAB Pres. award for excellence in tchg., 2000—01; fellow, Employee Benefits Rsch. Inst.; grantee, Nat. Ctr. Health Svcs. Rsch., NIH, Agy. for Health Care Rsch. and Quality, Robert Wood Johnson Found.; Adj. scholar, Am. Enterprise Inst., 2002—. Mem.: Am. Soc. Health Economists (adv. bd. 2004—), Internat. Health Econs. Assn. (treas. 1994—2000, sec.-treas. 2000—04), Acad. Health (chmn. com. 2000), Am. Econ. Assn. Republican. Roman Catholic. Office: UAB Sch Pub Health Birmingham AL 35294-0022 Office Phone: 205-975-8966. Business E-Mail: morrisey@uab.edu.

**MORRISH, THOMAS JAY,** golf course architect; b. Grand Junction, Colo., July 6, 1936; s. Wilbur Merle and Margaret Beula (Cronk) M.; m. Louise Ann Dunn, Apr. 2, 1965; children: Carter J., Kimberly L. Coder. AA, Mesa Coll., Grand Junction, 1956; BS in Landscape and Nursery Mgmt., Colo. State U., 1964. Golf course arch. Robert Trent Jones, Montclair, N.J., 1964-67. George Fazio, Jupiter, Fla., 1967-69, Desmond Muirhead, Newport Beach, Calif., 1969-72, Jack Nicklaus, North Palm Beach, Fla., 1972-83; prin. Jay Morrish & Assocs., Flower Mound, Tex., 1983—. Prin. golf course designs include: Troon Golf & Country Club, Scottsdale, Ariz., Las Colinas Sports Club, Irving, Tex., Mira Vista, Ft. Worth, Foothills Golf Course, Phoenix, Forest Highlands, Flagstaff, Ariz. (One of 100 Top Golf Courses in World, Golf mag., Golf Digest), Bentwater on Lake Conroe, Houston, Shadow Glen Golf Club, Olathe, Kans. (Best New Private Course, Golf Digest 1989), Troon North Golf & Country Club, Scottsdale (One of 100 Top Courses in U.S., Golf mag.), Harbor Club on Lake Oconee, Greensboro, Ga., Loch Lomond, Scotland, The Country Club of St. Albans, Mo., Broken Top, Bend, Oreg., Dauble Eagle Club, Galena, Ohio (one of Top 100 Courses in World, Golf Mag.), Buffalo Creek Golf Course, Rockwall, Tex., La Cantera, San Antonio (Best New Pub. Course of 1995, Golf Digest Mag.), numerous others. Edn. grantee State of Colo., 1961-64; Trans-Miss. golf scholar, 1962-64; named Architect of Yr. Golf World Mag., 1996. Mem. Am. Soc. Golf Course Archs. (pres. 2002), Dallas Safari Club. Republican. Avocation: hunting. Office: PO Box 271559 Flower Mound TX 75027-1559

**MORRISON, ALAN,** musician, educator; b. Atlanta, Ga., Nov. 29, 1968; s. Don T. and Jeannine Romer Morrison; life ptnr. Angelo Marabella. BMus, MMus, Curtis Inst. of Music, Phila., 1993; profl. studies, Juilliard Sch., N.Y.C., 1996. Coll. organist Ursinus Coll., Collegeville, Pa., 1995—; chmn.

organ dept. Curtis Inst. of Music, Phila., 2002—. Artist-in-residence, disting. vis. prof. Rollins Coll., Winter Park, Fla., 2001—. Musician concerts. Recipient Silver Medal, Calgary Internat. Organ Festival Competition, 1994, 1st Prize, Artur Poister Nat. Organ Competition, 1991, Mader Nat. Organ Competition, 1991, GMEA Concerto Competition, 1985. Mem.: Leschetizky Assn., Am. Guild of Organists. Office: Curtis Inst Music 1726 Locust St Philadelphia PA 19103 Office Phone: 215-893-5252. Personal E-mail: alan.morrison@curtis.edu.

**MORRISON, ANNE DEINLEIN,** law librarian; b. Balt., Md., July 3, 1962; d. John Frederick and Mary Katherine Kress Deinlein; m. Jeffrey Morrison, Nov. 7, 1992; children: Ian, Katherine. BA in English, Towson State U., 1980—84; MA in Legal & Ethical Studies, U. of Balt., 1990—94. Asst. libr. Piper & Marbury Law Firm, Balt., 1984—93; law libr. Semmes, Bowen & Semmes, Balt., 1994—95, Prince George's County Law Libr., Upper Marlboro, Md., 1997—. Pres. Law Libr. Assn. of Md., 1994—95. Editor: (newsletter) Law Libr. Assn. of Md. Newsletter. Coord. Girl Scouts of Ctrl. Md., Shipley's Choice, 2002—03. Mem.: State Ct. and County Law Libraries SIS (exec. bd. mem. 2003—), Law Libr. Assn. of Md., Spl. Libraries Assn., Am. Assn. of Law Libraries. Office: Prince George's County Law Libr 14735 Main St Rm 172 Upper Marlboro MD 20772 Office Phone: 410-544-4000 x 268. Business E-Mail: admorrison@co.pg.md.us. E-mail: anne.morrison@longnandfoster.com.

**MORRISON, ASHTON BYROM,** retired pathologist, medical school official; b. Northern Ireland, Oct. 13, 1922; came to U.S., 1955; s. Samuel and Henrietta (Good) M.; m. Claire Morris, M.D.; 1 dau., Mary Claire. MB, Queen's U, Belfast, No. Ireland, 1946; PhD, Queens U., Belfast, No. Ireland, 1950, MD (hon.), 1988; MD, Duke U., 1946. Intern Royal Victoria Hosp., Belfast, 1947; asst. lectr. Queens U., 1947-52; registrar dept. exptl. medicine Cambridge U., 1952-55, dir. med. studies Corpus Christi Coll., 1954-55; assoc. Duke U., N.C., 1955-58; asst. prof. pathology U. Pa. Sch. Medicine, 1958-61; assoc. prof. U. Rochester Sch. Medicine, 1961-65; prof. pathology, chmn. dept. Rutgers U. Med. Sch., 1965-80; v.p. acad. affairs Eastern Va. Med. Authority, 1980-83; dean Eastern Va. Med. Sch., 1980-83; prof. pathology Robert Wood Johnson Med. Sch.-U. Medicine and Dentistry N.J., Camden, 1983-93; assoc. dean in charge Robert Wood Johnson Med Sch.-U. Medicine and Dentistry N.J., Camden, 1983-89, prof. pathology emeritus, 1993-96, prof. pathology and lab. medicine emeritus, 1997—; prof. pathology Ea. Va. Med. Sch., 1994—. 22nd Scott Heron lectr. Royal Victoria Hosp., Belfast, No. Ireland, 1978. Recipient Disting. Alumnus award Duke U. Med. Sch., 1987. Mem. Am. Assn. Investigative Pathologists (emeritus), Am. Physiol. Soc. (emeritus), Soc. Exptl. Biology and Medicine (emeritus), Am. Soc. Nephrology (emeritus). Home: 3518 Rue De Fleur Columbus OH 43221

**MORRISON, BRUCE ANDREW,** federal official, public information officer; b. NYC, Oct. 8, 1944; s. George and Dorothea A. (Meyer) M.; m. Nancy A. Wanat, Sept. 22, 1991; 1 child, Drew. S.B., MIT, 1965; MS, U. Ill., 1970; JD, Yale U., 1973; LittD (hon.), Quinnipac Coll.; LLD (hon.), U. Coll. Dublin. Staff atty. New Haven Legal Assistance Assn., 1973-74, mng. atty., 1974-76, exec. dir., 1976-82; mem. 98th-101st Congresses from 3d Conn. dist., 1983-91; chmn. L.I. Sound Caucus, chmn. Third World Debt Caucus. Chmn. judiciary subcom. on immigration, refugees, and internat. law U.S. Ho. of Reps.; chmn. Fed. Housing Fin. Bd., 1995-2000; co-chmn. ad hoc com. on Irish affairs; mem. U.S. commn. on immigration reform, 1991 97; chair Irish Ams. for Clinton-Gore, 1992, 96; chair Ams. for a New Irish Agenda, 1993-95; vice chmn. GPC Internat., 2000-2001; chmn. Morrison Pub. Affairs Group, 2001-. Mem. Nat. Dem. Ethnic Coordinating Com., Nat. Dem. Ethnic Leadership Coun.; bd. dirs. Alliance for Responsible Cuba Policy. Mem. ABA, Conn. Bar Assn., Am. Immigration Lawyers Assn. Democrat. Lutheran. Office: 6004 Onondaga Rd Bethesda MD 20816 Office Phone: 301-263-1142. Personal E-mail: b.a.m@att.net.

**MORRISON, CHARLES E.,** think-tank executive; b. Billings, Mont., 1944; m. Chieko Hayashi; children: Karen, Erica, Kenneth, Douglas. BA in Internat. Studies, Johns Hopkins U., MA, PhD, Johns Hopkins U. Legis. asst. U.S. Senate, 1972-80; part-time sr. rsch. assoc. Japan Ctr. for Internat. Exch., 1980-92; asst. to pres. East-West Ctr., 1986-92, dir. program on internat. econs. and politics, 1992-95, pres., 1998—; chair U.S. Consortium of APEC Study Ctrs., 1996-98; internat. chair Pacific Econ. Cooperation Coun., 2006—. Editor: Asia-Pacific Security Outlook books, 1997—; author: wide range of books, papers and analyses; widely quoted by major news media on issues of regional cooperation, internat. rels., U.S. Asia policy and trade policies. Mem.: U.S. Asia Pacific Coun. (founding mem. 2003). Office: East West Ctr 1601 E West Rd Honolulu HI 96848-1601 Office Phone: 808-944-7111.

**MORRISON, CHERYL LYNN,** petroleum engineer, information technology manager; b. Galveston, Tex., Mar. 12, 1953; d. John Lipuscek and Dorothy Eloise (Weed) Morrison. BS in Biology, U. Ala., Tuscaloosa, 1975, BS in Petroleum Engring., 1979. Assoc. ops. engr. Getty Oil Co., Mobile, Ala., 1979—82, prodn. engr. Kilgore, Tex., 1982—85; drilling engr. Mobil Oil Co., Lafayette, La., 1985—87, Houston, drilling supr., 1987—89; drilling rep. Chevron USA, Lafayette, 1989—90, Bakersfield, Calif., 1990—96, petroleum engr., 1996—99, project mgr., 1999—2000, Chevron Texaco, San Ramon, Calif., 2000—. Mem. Soc. Petroleum Engrs. (sec., treas., bd. dirs. 1979-), Tex. State Profl. Engrs. Methodist.

**MORRISON, CRAIG O.,** chemicals executive; Grad., Ea. Ky. Univ.; MBA, Harvard Univ., 1987. Cons. Bain & Co., 1987—90; sr. operational and bus. mgmt. pos. GE Co., 1990—93; pres. gen. mgr. Van Leer, Inc., 1993—98, Alcan Pharm. and Cosmetic Packaging, divsn. Alcan, Inc., Millville, NJ, 1998—2002; pres., CEO Hexion Specialty Chemicals Inc, Columbus, Ohio, 2002—, chmn., 2005—. Office: Hexion 180 E Broad St Columbus OH 43215*

**MORRISON, DAVID,** science administrator, researcher; b. Danville, Ill., June 26, 1940; s. Donald Harlan Morrison and Alice Lee (Douglass) Guin; m. Nancy Dunlap, June 19, 1966 (div. 1977); m. Janet L. Irick, Aug. 23, 1981. BA, U. Ill., 1962; PhD, Harvard U., 1969. Prof. astronomy U. Hawaii, Honolulu, 1969-88, vice chancellor rsch., 1983-85, dir. IRTF telescope, 1985-88; dep. assoc. administr. NASA Office Space Sci., Washington, 1981; chief space sci. divsn. NASA Ames Rsch. Ctr., Moffett Field, Calif., 1988-96, dir. astrobiology and space rsch., 1996—2001, chief scientist NASA Astrobiology Inst., 2001—. Pres. Astron. Soc. of the Pacific, San Francisco, 1982-84; chmn. Divsn. for Planetary Scis., Washington, 1980-81; councillor Am. Astron. Soc., Washington, 1982-85; pres. Internat. Astron. Union Commn. on Planets, 1991-94. Author: Exploration of the Universe, 1987, 91, 95, The Planetary System, 1988, 96, Cosmic Catastrophes, 1989, Exploring Planetary Worlds, 1993, Voyages Through the Universe, 1996; editor: Satellites of Jupiter, 1982; contbr. articles to profl. jours. Fellow AAAS, 1982, Com. for Sci. Investigation of Claims of Paranormal, 1983, Calif. Acad. Sci. Achievements include advanced research for Voyager and Galileo planetary exploration missions. Home: 14660 Fieldstone Saratoga CA 95070 Office: NASA Ames Rsch Ctr MS 240-1 Moffett Field CA 94035 Office Phone: 650-604-5094. Business E-Mail: dmorrison@arc.nasa.gov.

**MORRISON, DONALD FRANKLIN,** statistician, educator; b. Stoneham, Mass., Feb. 10, 1931; s. Daniel Norman and Agnes Beatrice (Packard) M.; m. Phyllis Ann Hazen, Aug. 19, 1967; children: Norman Hazen, Stephen Donald. BS in Bus. Adminstrn, Boston U., 1953, AM, 1954; MS, U. N.C., 1957; PhD, Va. Poly. Inst. and State U., 1960; MA (hon.), U. Pa., 1971. Mem. staff Lincoln Lab., M.I.T., 1956; cons. math. statistician NIMH, Bethesda, Md., 1956-63; mem. tech. staff Bell Labs., Holmdel, NJ, 1967; mem. faculty, dept. stats. Wharton Sch. U. Pa., 1963-99, prof. stats., 1973-99, chmn. dept., 1978-85, prof. emeritus, 2000—. Author: Multivariate Statistical Methods, 4th edit., 2005, Applied Linear Statistical Methods, 1983; editor The Am. Statistician, 1972-75; assoc. editor Biometrics, 1972-74; contbr. articles to profl. jours. Served with USPHS, 1956-58. NSF grantee, 1966 Fellow Am.

Statis. Assn., Inst. Math. Stats.; mem. Internat. Statis. Inst., Royal Statis. Soc., B&M R.R. Hist. Soc., Nat. R.R. Hist. Soc., R.R. and Locomotive Hist. Soc., N&W Hist. Soc., Bridge Line Hist. Soc., N.E. Elec. Rwy. Hist. Soc. Democrat. Lutheran. Home: 118 E Brookhaven Rd Wallingford PA 19086-6327 E-mail: donaldm@wharton.upenn.edu.

**MORRISON, DONALD GRAHAM,** business educator, consultant; b. Detroit, Feb. 26, 1939; s. Roderick and Ethelyne (Murray) M.; m. Sherie Leaver, Sept. 12, 1964; children: Heather Margaret Felix, Tracey Michelle Oliva. BSM.E., MIT, 1961; PhD in Ops. Research, Stanford U., 1965. Instr. Stanford U., Calif., 1965-66, vis. prof. Calif., 1982-97; mem. faculty Columbia U., N.Y.C., 1966-87, prof., 1973-87, Armand G. Erpf prof. bus., 1985-87; William E. Leonard prof. Anderson Grad. Sch. Mgmt., UCLA, 1987—. Vis. prof. U. Calif., Berkeley, 1970-71; cons. in field, UCLA faculty athletic rep. to NCAA. Editor in chief Mgmt. Sci., 1983-90; founding editor Mktg. Sci., 1980-82. Elder Hitchcock Presbyn. Ch., Scarsdale, N.Y., 1978-84, Westwood Presbyn. Ch., L.A., 1991-94, 95-98; treas. Scarsdale Jr. H.S. PTA, 1977-78; acad. trustee Mktg. Sci. Inst., 1986-92; mem. Decision, Risk and Mgmt. Sci. rev. bd. NSF, 1989-91. Recipient Lifetime Achievement in Mktg. Rsch. Award, AMA, 2001, Disting. Educator of Yr. Award, McGraw-Hill/Irwin, 2002. Mem. Inst. Mgmt. Sci. (pres. 1990-92), Ops. Rsch. Soc., Am., Am. Statis. Assn. Presbyterian. Avocations: golf, jogging, bridge. Office: UCLA Anderston Grad Sch Mgmt 110 Westwood Plz Los Angeles CA 90095-0001 Business E-Mail: donald.morrison@anderson.ucla.edu.

**MORRISON, DONALD NICK,** surgeon; s. Donald Newton and Alvera Alma Morrison; m. Therese Ellen Morrison, May 20, 1972; children: Kelly Lorenzen, Briana, Patrick. BS in Pre-Med. Studies, Gonzaga U., Spokane, Wash., 1968; MD, Creighton U., Omaha, Nebr., 1972. Diplomate Am. Bd. Surgery, 1978. Intern St. Joseph's Med. Ctr., Phoenix, 1972—73; resident gen. surgery Maricopa County Gen. Hosp., Phoenix, 1973—77; pvt. practice Phoenix, 1977—; dir. Morrison Vein Inst., Tempe, Ariz., 1998—, Scottsdale, Ariz., 1998—, Morrison Tng. Inst., Tempe, 2003—, Scottsdale, 2003—. Contbr. chapters to books. Dir. Charitable Med. Care Found., 1990—. Mem.: AMA, ACS (pres. Ariz. chpt. 1986—88), Am. Coll. Phlebology (bd. dirs., mem. ethics com., chmn. annual symposium program, chmn. regional symposium program), Phoenix (Ariz.) Surg. Soc. (pres. 1991, mem. exec. coun.). Avocations: travel, bicycling, skiing. Office: Morrison Vein Inst 8575 E Princess Dr Ste 223 Scottsdale AZ 85255

**MORRISON, DONALD WILLIAM,** lawyer; b. Portland, Oreg., Mar. 31, 1926; s. Robert Angus and Laura Calista (Hodgson) M.; m. Elizabeth Margaret Perry, July 25, 1953; children: Elizabeth Laura, Carol Margaret. BSE.E., U. Wash., 1946; LL.B., Stanford U., 1950. Bar: Oreg. 1950, Calif. 1950, N.Y. 1967, Ill. 1968, Ohio 1974. Assoc. Pendergrass, Spackman, Bullivant & Wright, Portland, 1950-57, ptnr., 1957-60; gen. atty. Pacific N.W. Bell, Portland, 1960-66; atty. AT&T, N.Y.C., 1966-68; counsel Ill. Bell Telephone Co., Chgo., 1968-74; v.p., gen. counsel Ohio Bell Telephone Co., Cleve., 1974-91; of counsel Arter & Hadden, Cleve., 1992—2003. Trustee Archael. Inst. Am., Cleve. Archaeol. Soc., Cleve. Chamber Music Soc.; mem. adv. com. Cleve. Play House, Cleve. Bot. Garden; mem. Ohio adv. bd. Trust for Pub. Land. With USN, 1943—50. Recipient various bar and civic appreciation awards. Mem. ABA, Ohio State Bar Assn., Bar Assn Greater Cleve., Oreg. State Bar Assn., Calif. Bar Assn., Rowfant Club.

**MORRISON, FRED LAMONT,** law educator, dean; b. Salina, Kans., Dec. 12, 1939; s. Earl F. and Madge Louise (Glass) M.; m. Charlotte Foot, Dec. 27, 1971; children: Charles, Theodore, George, David. AB, U. Kans., 1961; BA, Oxford (Eng.) U., 1963, MA, 1968; PhD, Princeton U., 1966; JD, U. Chgo. 1967. Bar: Minn. 1973. Asst. prof. law U. Iowa, Iowa City, 1967-69; counselor on internat. law U.S. State Dept., Washington, 1982-83; assoc. prof. law U. Minn., Mpls., 1969-73, prof. law, 1973-90, Oppenheimer Wolff and Donnelly prof., 1990-97, acting dean, 1994-95, Popham Haik/Lindquist & Vennum prof., 1998—, interim co-dean, 2006—. Of counsel Popham, Haik, Schnobrich & Kaufman, Mpls., 1983-97. Mem. adv. com. on internat. law U.S. Dept. State, Washington, 1987-89; mem. internat. adv. bd. Inst. on Internat. Law, Kiel, Germany, 1989—. Home: 1412 W 47th St Minneapolis MN 55419-5204 Office: U Minn Law Sch 229 19th Ave S Minneapolis MN 55455-0400 Office Phone: 612-625-0321. Business E-Mail: morrison@umn.edu.

**MORRISON, GAIL,** internist, nephrologist, educator; BA in Biology, Chemistry magna cum laude, Boston U., 1967; MD, U. Pa., 1971. Diplomate Am. Bd. Med. Examiners, Am. Bd. Internal Medicine, Am. Bd. Nephrology. Instr. dept. continuing edn. Boston U., 1966-67; clin. fellow Harvard U., Boston, 1971-72; intern Beth Israel Hosp., Boston, 1971-72; jr. asst. resident Georgetown U. Hosp., Washington, 1972-73; staff physician clin. ctr. NIH, Bethesda, Md., 1973-74; staff assoc. Nat. Heart & Lung Inst., 1973-74; fellow in nephrology renal electrolyte sect. U. Pa. Hosp., Phila., 1974-76, rsch. fellow in nephrology renal electrolyte sect. NIH, 1975-76, asst. prof. medicine 1982-83; from asst. prof. to assoc. prof. medicine U. Pa. Sch. Medicine, Phila., 1976-94, prof. medicine, 1994—, vice dean edn., 1995—, dir. acad. programs, 1995—; attending Phila. Vets. Adminstrn. Med. Ctr., 1976-77, U. Pa. Health Sys., 1996—. Asst. dir. dialysis unit U. Pa. Hosp., Phila., 1976-77, assoc. dir., 1977-82, dir. renal outpatient prog., 1976-82, dir. outpatient dialysis unit, 1979-84, acting dir. dialysis prog. for inpatient and outpatient dialysis units, 1981-82, dir., 1982-86; acad. coord. dept. medicine U. Pa. Hosp., Phila., 1985-96; assoc. chmn. dept. medicine for student edn. U. Pa. Sch. Medicine, Phila., 1986-96, acting assoc. dean for clin. curriculum, 1991, assoc. dean for clin. curriculum, 1991-95, vice dean for edn., dir. acad. prog., 1995 ; mem. numerous acad., search, planning, steering, alumni, budget, nutrition coms., others; cons.; advisor in field; presenter, co-dir., tchr., leader workshops, symposiums, confs. Author: (with A. Goroll) Core Medicine Clerkship: A Curriculum Guide, Manual for Curriculum 2000, 1996; editor: (with others) Introduction to Clinical Medicine, 2d rev. edit., 1995, Concepts in Basic Science, 1995, Essentials of Nutrition: A Case-Based Approach, 1995; mem. editorial bd. Am. Jour. Medicine, 1996-99; author papers, reviews, abstracts, chpts. to books; contbr. articles to profl. jours. Recipient Daniel C. Tosteson award for leadership in med. edn., Disting. Alumni Svc. award U. Pa.; grantee Pa. Sch. Nursing, 1989-90, Heinz Endowment Fund, 1990-95, U. Pa. Sch. Medicine, 1993-95, 93-96, 97-98. Fellow ACP, Coll. Physicians of Pa. (mem. sect. on pub. health and preventive medicine 1995—); mem. AAAS, Internat. Soc. Nephrology, Am. Soc. Nephrology, Am. Fedn. for Clin. Rsch., Am. Assn. Med. Colls. Women's Liaison Officer, Pa. Soc. Nephrology (coun. mem. network #24 federally funded end-stage renal disease orgn. 1978-83, mem. facility planning bd. 1979-80, chmn. 1980-82, mem. exec. com. 1980-82, ad-hoc mem. med. review bd. 1980-82, mem. nomination and credential com. 1982-83), Southeastern Nat. Kidney Found. (bd. dirs. 1984-88), Phi Beta Kappa, Sigma Xi, Alpha Omega Alpha. Home: 1040 Stony Ln Gladwyne PA 19035-1136 Fax: 215-573-4289. Office Phone: 215-898-8034. Business E-Mail: morrisog@mailmed.upenn.edu.

**MORRISON, GLENN,** neurosurgeon; b. Phila., June 16, 1940; married, 3 children. AB, Colgate U., 1962; MD, Case Western Reserve U., 1967; postgrad., Nat. Comm. Disease Ctr., 1968. Diplomate Am. Bd. Neurological Surgery, Am. Bd. Pediatric Neurological Surgery. Intern Cleve. Met. Hosp., 1968; resident in neurosurgery Univ. Hosps. Cleve., 1970—74; with Neurosurg. Assocs., Coral Gables, Fla., 1974—85, Baptist Hosp., Miami, 1974—; U. N. Miami, 2000—; chief pediatric neurosurgical surgery Miami Children's Hosp., 1986—; pvt. prac. Coral Gables, 1985—2000. Prof. dept. neurological surgery, U. Miami Sch. Med., dir. pediat. neurosurg. alliance; cons. divsn. children's med. svcs. state of Fla. Lt. Cmdr. USPHS, 1968-70. Recipient Nat. Found. award, 1967. Fellow ACS (sec., treas. greater Miami chpt. 1979-83, pres. 1983-85, interview com. 1980—); mem. Am. Assn. Neurol. Surgeons, Congress Neurol. Surgeons, Am. Acad. Pediats., Neurol. Soc. Am., Internat. Soc. Pediat. Neurosurgery, So. Neurosurg. Soc. (v.p. 1989-90, treas.

1992-95, pres. 1996-97), Fla. Neurosurg. Soc. (pres. 1982), Greater Miami Neurosurg. Soc. (pres. 1978), numerous others. Office: Miami Children's Hosp 3200 SW 60th Ct Ste 301 Miami FL 33155-4071 Office Phone: 305-662-8386.

**MORRISON, GLENN LESLIE,** minister; b. Cortez, Colo., Feb. 26, 1929; s. Ward Carl Morrison and Alma Irene (Butler) Anderson; m. Beverely Joanne Buck, Aug. 26, 1949; children: David Mark, Betty Jo Morrison Mullen, Gary Alan, Judith Lynn Morrison Oltmann, Stephen Scott. Student, San Diego State U., 1948-49, Chabot Coll., 1968-69. Ordained ministry Evang. Ch. Alliance, 1961. Dir. counseling follow-up Oakland (Calif.) Youth Christ, 1954-56; pres. Follow Up Ministries, Inc., Castro Valley, Calif., 1956—. Assoc. pastor 1st Covenant Ch., Oakland, 1956-58; exec. dir. East Bay Youth Christ, Oakland, 1964-66; supervising chaplain Alameda County (Calif.) Probation Dept., 1971-90; vol. chaplain Alameda County Sheriff's Dept., 1971—; founder, dir. God Squad Vol. Program Prison Workers, 1972—; seminar leader Calif. Dept. Corrections, Sacramento, 1978—, mem. chaplains coordinating com., 1988—. Author: Scripture Investigation Course, 1956, Tired of the Same Ol' Same Ol'? There is a Better Way, 1978. Mem. Am. Correctional Assn., Am. Protestant Correctional Chaplains Assn. (regional pres., sec. 1980-86, nat. sec. 1986-88, nat. 2nd v.p. 1996-98). Office: Follow Up Ministries Inc PO Box 2514 Castro Valley CA 94546-2514 Personal E-mail: fumi2000@msn.com.

**MORRISON, GORDON MACKAY, JR.,** investment company executive; b. Boston, Jan. 18, 1930; s. Gordon Mackay and Alice (Blodgett) M.; m. Barbara J. Lee, June 15, 1954; children: Lee (dec.), Leighton, Faith. AB, Harvard U., 1952, MBA, 1954. Regional mgr. Bankers Leasing Corp., Boston, 1965-68; portfolio mgr. Loomis, Sayles and Co., Boston, 1969-71; sr. v.p. Ft. Hill Investors Mgmt., Boston, 1972-75; chmn. bd. Bradford Gordon Inc., Boston, 1977—2001; gen. ptnr. Bradford Gordon Ptnrs., Boston, 1977—. Trustee East Boston Savs. Bank, 1962-91; trustee Meridian Fin. Svcs., Inc., 1991-2002, hon. trustee, 2002—. Bd. dirs. The New Eng. Hosp., 1961-96, emeritus, 1996—. Republican. Congl. Club: Harvard. Lodge: Masons. Home: 5 Neptune Ln Biddeford ME 04005-9594 Office: Bradford Gordon Ptnrs 50 Congress St Boston MA 02109-4027

**MORRISON, GREGORY BERNARD,** information scientist; b. Washington, Dec. 19, 1959; s. Carl Edward and Evelyn Patricia (Goodwin) M.; m. Patrice Hinton, May 20, 1981 (div. June 1989); children: Krystina, Michael, Matthew; m. Debra Dobson, 1993. BS in Math. and Physics magna cum laude, S.C. State U., 1982; MS in Indsl. Engring., Northwestern U., 1987. Mgr. info. svcs. Prudential Ins. Co. Am., Newark, 1989-90, dir. and group systems exec., 1990-93, dir. info. svcs. Roseland, NJ, 1993—2000, v.p. info. svcs., 2000—02; COO RealEstate.com, 2000; v.p., chief info. officer Cox Enterprises, Inc., Atlanta, 2002—. Bd. dirs. Met. YMCA, West Orange, N.J., 1990—. Minority Interchange, Inc., Newark, 1989-93. Capt. U.S. Army, 1982-89. Fellow U.S. Army, 1986. Mem. Ops. Rsch. Soc. Am., 100 Black Men N.J., Masons, Phi Beta Sigma. Avocations: golf, gardening. Home: 2718 Bonar Hall Path Duluth GA 30097-7462 Office: Cox Enterprises Inc 6205 Peachtree Dunwoody Rd Atlanta GA 30328

**MORRISON, HARRY,** chemistry professor; b. Bklyn., Apr. 25, 1937; s. Edward and Pauline (Semmers) M.; m. Harriet Thurman, Aug. 23, 1958; children: Howard, David, Daniel. BA, Brandeis U., 1957; PhD, Harvard U., 1961. NATO-NSF postdoctoral fellow Swiss Fed. Inst., Zurich, 1961-62; rsch. assoc. U. Wis., Madison, 1962-63; asst. prof. chemistry Purdue U., West Lafayette, Ind., 1963-69, assoc. prof., 1969-76, prof., 1976—, dept. head, 1987-92, dean Sch. Sci., 1992—2000. Mem. acad. adv. com. Indsl. Rsch. Inst., 1993-96. Contbr. numerous articles to profl. jours. Bd. fellows Brandeis U. Mem. Am. Chem. Soc., Am. Soc. Photobiology, Inter-Am. Photochem. Soc., Coun. for Chem. Rsch. (chmn. 1995), Phi Beta Kappa Office: Purdue Univ Dept Chemistry Brown Bldg West Lafayette IN 47907-2084 Office Phone: 765-494-5246. Business E-Mail: hmorrison@purdue.edu.

**MORRISON, JAMES FRANK,** optometrist, state legislator; b. Colby, Kans., Apr. 11, 1942; s. Lloyd Wayne and Catherine Louise (Beckner) M.; m. Karen Jean Carr, Aug. 25, 1963; children: Mike, Jeff, Scott. Student, U. Kans., 1960-64; BS, OD, So. Coll. Optometry, 1967. Pvt. practice, 1969-75; founder, chief staff N.W. Kans. Ednl. Diagnostic and Referral Ctr. Children, Inc., Colby; asst. chief engr. Sta. KXXX-FM, 1977-80, chief engr., 1980-82; prof. vision dept. Colby Community Coll., 1979-84; mem. Kans. Ho. Reps., Topeka, 1992—. Cubmaster pack 140 Cub Scouts Am., 1970-80, dist. chmn., 1977-79. Fellow Am. Acad. Optometry, Coll. Optometrists in Vision Devel.; mem. Am. Optometric Assn., Am. Soc. Broadcast Engrs., Kans. Soc. Broadcast Engrs. (founder, pres. 1970-71), Kans. Optometric Assn., Kans. Assn. Children with Learning Disabilities, Mo. Optometric Assn., Thomas County Assn. Retarded Children, Rotary, Lions, Kiwanies (pres. 1971-72), Masons, Shriners. Rotary. Mem. Assemblies of God. Ch. Avocations: amateur radio, photography, astronomy. Home: 3 Cottonwood Dr Colby KS 67701-3902 Office: Morrison Optometric Assocs 180 W 6th St Colby KS 67701-2315

**MORRISON, JAMES V.,** biology professor; s. James V. and Mary E. Morrison; m. Louise V. Mottashed, Aug. 5, 1968; children: Jennifer Forte, James. BA in Biology, Kans. State U., Manhattan, 1968, MS in Zoology, 1971; MPH in Epidemiology, Loma Linda U., Calif. 1978. Assoc. prof. biology Riverside CC, Calif., 1971—. Mem.: Phi Kappa Phi, Delta Omega (life). Avocations: sailing, scuba diving, travel. Office: Riverside CC 2001 Third St Norco CA 92860-2600 Office Phone: 951-372-7169. Home Fax: 951-372-7050; Office Fax: 951-372-7050.

**MORRISON, JOHN HADDOW, JR.,** engineering company executive; b. Bozeman, Mont., Aug. 24, 1933; s. John Haddow Sr. and Rosalie (Lehrkind) M.; m. Shirley Easbey, Sept. 11, 1954; children: Robert, Richard; m. Minh Le, Apr. 25, 2001. BS, Mont. State U., 1955. Registered profl. engr., Mont., Ariz., Calif.; registered land surveyor, Mont. Project engr. Morrison-Maierle, Inc., Helena, Mont., 1957—64, chief airport design, 1964—73, chief exec. officer, 1973—88, chmn., 1998—2000, dir. emeritus, 2000—; pres. Morrison-Maierle Ariz. Inc., Tempe, 2000—02. Bd. dirs. Mont. State U. Found., Inc., 1983-2004, chmn. 1992-94; exec. trustee Helena YMCA, 1977-80. With U.S. Army 1955-57. Mem. ASCE (pres. Mont. sect. 1971-72), NSPE (pres. Helena chpt. 1968-69, Outstanding Young Engr., Helena chpt. 1965), Cons. Engrs. Council Mont. (past sec., past v.p., pres. 1986-87). Lodges: Kiwanis, Masons. Methodist. Avocations: golf, photography. Home: 2415 E Windsong Dr Phoenix AZ 85048 Office: Morrison-Maierle Inc Ste 201 80 E Rio Salado Pkwy Tempe AZ 85281-9108 E-mail: jmorrison@m-m.net.

**MORRISON, JOHN HENRY,** neuroscientist, educator, lab administrator; b. Cleve., July 17, 1952; s. Malcolm Gray and Leonie Johnson Morrison; m. Abbie Ruth Pollack, Dec. 4, 1954; children: Kelsey Ilana, Alexander Malcolm. BA, Johns Hopkins U., 1974, PhD, 1979. Postdoctoral fellow Salk Inst., La Jolla, Calif., 1980—83; from asst. to assoc. prof. Scripps Rsch. Inst., La Jolla, Calif., 1983—89; Johnson Prof. of Geriat. and Adult Devel., Mt. Sinai Sch. of Medicine, N.Y.C., 1989—, prof. and co-dir. neurobiology, 1991—2002, prof. and dir. neurobiology, 2002—04, prof. and chmn. dept. of neurosci., 2004—. Dir. Am. Fedn. for Aging Rsch., N.Y.C., 1990—2002; mem. Dana Alliance for Brain Initiatives, Dana Found., N.Y.C., 1993—; sci. adv. bd. Bachman-Straus Dystonia and Parkinson Found., N.Y.C., 1996—; co-founder and dir. Neurome, Inc., La Jolla, Calif., 2000—. Editor (sect. editor): (sci. jour.) Neuroscience, Exptl. Neurology; contbr. articles to profl. jours. Recipient Faculty/Scholar award, Alzheimer's Assn., 1984-1987; grantee, NIH, 1991-current. Mem.: N.Y. Acad. of Sci. (co-chair sect. of neurosci. 2000—02), Soc. for Neurosci. (mem. chair 2003—05), Shenorock Shore Club, Cajal Club (pres. 2002—04). Achievements include research in Elucidated key elements of neuropathology in Alzheimer's disease and their relationship to dementia. In addition, discovered several key characteristics of normal brain aging. Avocations: cycling, enology, fishing. Office: Mt Sinai Sch Medicine Box 1065 One Gustave L Levy Pl New York NY 10029-6574 Office Phone: 212-659-5985.

**MORRISON, JOHN HORTON,** lawyer; b. Sept. 15, 1933; BBA, U. N.Mex., 1955; BA, U. Oxford, 1957; JD, Harvard U., 1962. Bar: Ill. 1962, US Supreme Ct. 1966. Assoc. Kirkland & Ellis, Chgo., 1962-67, ptnr., 1968-99. Named Hon. Officer Most Excellent Order Brit. Empire, 1994; Rhodes scholar. Mem. ABA, Internat. Arbitration (arbitrator, mediator London Ct.), Internat. Bar Assn., Assn. Am. Rhodes Scholars (pres. 1998-2006), Chgo. Internat. Dispute Resolution Assn. (dir.). Home: 2717 Lincoln St Evanston IL 60201-2042 Personal E-mail: johnhmorrison@post.harvard.edu. Business E-Mail: jmorrison@kirkland.com.

**MORRISON, JOHN JAMES,** lawyer; b. Chgo., Apr. 16, 1949; BS with high honors, U. Ill., Chgo., 1971, MS, 1973; JD with honors, DePaul U., 1978. Bar: Ill. 1978, U.S. Tax Ct. 1978, U.S. Dist. Ct. (no. dist.) Ill. 1978, U.S. Dist. Ct. (ea. dist.) Mich. 1993, U.S. Ct. Appeals (7th cir.) 1982, U.S. Supreme Ct. 1985, U.S. Ct. Claims 1985, U.S. Dist. Ct. (ea. dist.) Wis. 1988. Sr. atty. Office of Chief Counsel IRS, Chgo., 1978-84; pvt. practice Chgo., 1984—. Contbg. author in field. Ill. State scholar, 1967-71; U. Ill. fellow, 1971; recipient Chief Counsel's award, IRS, Chgo., 1984. Mem. ABA, Fed. Bar Assn. (bd. dirs. Chgo. chpt. 1990-99, jud. selection com. 1996-98), Ill. State Bar Assn., Chgo. Bar Assn. (chmn. fed. taxation procedure and adminstrn. div. 1986-88, law and lit. com., 2003-05). Office Phone: 312-641-3484. E-mail: morrison@taxlawchicago.com.

**MORRISON, JOHN M.,** bank executive; Owner, CEO Ctrl. Bank Group, Golden Valley, Minn.; interim chmn., CEO Allina Health Sys., 2001—02, bd. chmn., 2004—. Mem. Fairview U. Med. Ctr. Bd., Fairview Health Sys. Corp. Bd.; chmn. exec. com. bd. trustees U. St. Thomas; former mem. bd. govs., chmn. bd.'s fin. com. U. Minn. Acad. Health Ctr.; former mem. Johns Hopkins Medicine bd. visitors Johns Hopkins U. Mem.: U. St. Thomas Sch. Law (mem. bd. govs., founder John. M. Morrison Ctr. Entrepreneurship). Office: Allina Hosps and Clinics 710 E 24th St Minneapolis MN 55404

**MORRISON, JOSEPH YOUNG,** transportation executive, consultant; b. Flushing, N.Y., Jan. 4, 1951; s. William Barrier and Barbara Helen (Lowe) Morrison; children: Susan Parker, Travis Barrier. AS, Montreat (N.C.)-Anderson Coll., 1971; BA, Oglethorpe U., 1989. Dept. head J.C. Penny & Co., Atlanta, 1971-74; uniform patrol officer City of Atlanta, 1974-80; spl. agt. U.S. Dept. Transp., Atlanta, 1980-82; group dir. safety and ins. Western Express, Atlanta, 1982-85; dir. safety Taylor Maid Transp., Albany, Ga., 1985-86; v.p. risk mgmt. Burlington Motor Carriers, Inc., Daleville, Ind., 1986-96; pres. Motor Carrier Safety Cons. Inc., Noblesville, Ind., 1996-97, Nat. Transp. Cons., Inc., Noblesville, Ind., 1997—. Co-author: Guide to Handling Hazardous Material, 1986. Mem.: Am. Soc. Safety Engrs., Am. Trucking Assn. (mem. hazardous materials com. 1982—86, mem. safety mgmt. coun. 1982—, chmn. injury control com. 1984—88, mem. interstate carrier conf. 1985—, mem. nat. freight claims and security coun. 1985—, Safety Improvement award, Accident Reduction award, Injury Reduction award), Sertoma Club, Kenilworth Civic Club (treas. Stone Mountain Ga. chpt. 1981—83, pres. 1983—84), Sigma Alpha Epsilon. Methodist. Avocations: home remodeling, restoring old cars. Home: 7111 Oakview Cir Noblesville IN 46062-9419 Office: Nat Transp Cons 1109 S 10th St PO Box 2067 Noblesville IN 46061-2067 Office Phone: 317-770-0953. E-mail: jmorrison@ntconsult.com.

**MORRISON, K. JAYDENE,** education counseling firm executive; b. Cherokee, Okla., Aug. 22, 1933; d. Jay Frank and Kathryn D. (Johnson) Walker; m. Michael H. Morrison, July 11, 1955 (dec. 1991); children: Jay, Mac. BS, Okla. State U., 1955, MS, 1957; postgrad., U. Colo., 1965, Ctrl. State U., 1967—70, postgrad., 1984, U. Denver, 1981—82. Lic. coun. Okla., marriage and family therapist, cert. sch. psychologist, counselor. Psychologist Cushing Pub. Schs., Okla., 1955—57, Indpls. Pub. Schs., 1958—59; counselor, tchr. spl. edn. Helena-Goltry Pub. Schs., Okla., 1965—73; psychometrist Okla. State Title III Program, Alva; sch. psychologist Okla. State Dept. Edn., Enid, 1977—85; pres., dir. Ventures in Learning, Inc., Helena 1984—. Career counselor, Oklahoma City, 1985—86; rural specialist Okla. Conf. Chs. AG LINK, 1986—88; v.p., sec./treas. Okla. Made, Inc., Oklahoma City, 1988—89; sch. psychologist Okla. City Pub. Schs., 1988—93; therapist and pub. sch. liason Chisholm Trail Counseling Svc., 1993—95; coord. Statewide Farm Stress Program, 1994—95; therapist Greenleaf Drug/Alcohol Rehab., 1988—89; sec., treas. Pure; part-time counselor Clayton Clinic, 1987—89; cons. Okla. Family Inst., 1990—93; with Dept. Behavior Mgmt. Ctrl. Dist., Hawaii, 1995—. Author: Coping with ADD/ADHD, 1995; co-author: Coping With a Learning Disability, 1992; author: I'm Not Sick, Society Is--A 5 Step Drug-Free Parent/Teacher Guide, 2006. Chmn. Alfalfa County Excise and Equalization Bd., Cherokee, 1979—83; asst. state coord. Okla. Am. Agr. Movement, Oklahoma City, 1982—83; co-chmn. Alfalfa County Dem. Party, Cherokee, 1976—83; sec./treas. 6th Dist. Okla. Dem. State Exec. Bd., 1983—87; counselor United Meth. Counseling Ctr., 1987—88; mem. Elder Christian Ch. Named Citizen of Yr., Okla. chpt. Nat. Assn. Social Workers, 1988; recipient Tchr. of Yr. award, Helena Masonic Lodge, 1967, Spl. award, Okla. Women for Agr., 1979. Mem.: Okla. Assn. Learning Disabilities, Garfield County Interagy. Task Force, Okla. Sch. Psychologists Assn., Nat. Assn. Sch. Psychologists, Okla. Soc. Advancement Biofeedback, Biofeedback Soc. Am., Chi Omega Alumni, Delta Kappa Gamma. Office: PO Box 917 Nederland CO 80466-0917 Office Phone: 303-258-3976. Business E-Mail: JaydeneMor@aol.com.

**MORRISON, KENDRA ANN,** environmental scientist; b. Hugo, Colo., June 8, 1970; d. Kenneth Patrick and Judy Ann Morrison. BS in Environ. Health, Colo. State U., 1993; MS in Environ. Scis., U. Colo., 1999. Specialist consumer health and protection Colo. at Denver Dept. Pub. Health and Environ., 1993; specialist environ. health Tri-County Health Dept., Commerce City, Colo., 1993—98; scientist U.S. Environ. Protection Agy., Denver, 1998—. Rsch. asst. U. Colo., Denver, 2001; mem. adv. bd. Engrs. Without Borders, Longmont, Colo., 2003—05; intern, lab. and rsch. asst. MIT, Honolulu, 1994. Named Environ. Pub. Health Emerging Leader, U.S. Dept. Health and Human Svcs. Ctrs. Disease Control and Prevention, 2003. Mem.: Colo. Hazardous Waste Mgmt. Soc., Air and Waste Mgmt. Assn., Nat. Environ. Health Assn. (registered environ. health specialist 2000, registered sanitarian 2000, Merit award 2004, scholar 1999). Avocations: tropical plants, tai chi, travel. Home: 180 Poplar St Unit G Denver CO 80220 Office: US EPA Region 8 999 18th St Ste 200 8P-HW Denver CO 80202

**MORRISON, KENNETH DOUGLAS,** writer, columnist; b. Mpls., Apr. 1, 1918; s. Kenneth Mortimore and Florence Myrtle (Sutton) M.; m. Helen Curtis, Feb. 25, 1943; children: Kenneth D., Sally, Steven C., Mary. AB, Carleton Coll., 1940; postgrad., U. Miami, 1940—41, U. Minn., 1941. Free lance writer, Mpls., 1941; editor publs. Minn. Dept. Conservation, 1942-47; Minn. rep. to Nat. Audubon Soc., 1947-49, dir. pub relations, editor Audubon mag., 1949-56, v.p., 1955-56; dir. Mountain Lake Sanctuary and Singing Tower Am. Found., 1956-80, dir. environ. concerns 1980-82, fellow, 1982-83; syndicated nature-conservation newspaper columnist 4 papers, 1985—95. Audubon tour lectr., 1958-63; interviewer naturalists Wildlife Unltd., TV sta. WOR-TV, N.Y.C., 1951- 52; Mem. Minn. Bird Commn., 1951-54; trustee emeritus Fla. Nature Conservancy; trustee Fla. Conservation Found.; v.p., trustee Conservation 70's; mem. Gov. Fla. Natural Resources Com., State Parks Adv. Council, 1971-79. Author: Favorite Birds of America, 1951, Favorite Animals of America, 1951, Mountain Lake Almanac, 1984, Tonic of Wiloness, 2006; Compiler: (with Mrs. M. E. Herz) Where to Find Birds In Minnesota, 1950. Bd. dirs. Defenders Wildlife. Recipient Gov. Fla. Wildlife Conservation award, 1960, Gulf Oil Conservation award, 1982, Feinstone Environ. award SUNY, 1987, Carleton Coll. Disting. Achievement award, 1990, Grassroots Leadership award Fla. Nature Conservancy, 1996. Mem. Wilson Ornithol. Soc., Wilderness Soc., Greenpeace, Native Plant Soc., Fla. Audubon Soc. (pres., Award of Merit 1964, Cruickshank Conservation award

1993), Hawk Mountain Sanctuary Assn. (bd. sponsors), Nature Conservancy (lifetime Conservation award, 2006, Sierra Club, Friends of Earth, Green Horizon Land Trust (bd. dirs. 1999—), Pi Delta Epsilon. Methodist. Home: 1351 Hollister Rd Babson Park FL 33827-9684 *We ought to keep in mind that we are mammals and that we need to renew regularly our contact with the basic, simple life of soil, sun, water, animals and trees.*

**MORRISON, MALCOLM CAMERON,** engineering management professional; b. Pitts., Apr. 12, 1942; s. Malcolm Smith and Floy Alphine (Sample) M.; m. Julia Gertrude Collette, Dec. 30, 1960 (div. oct. 1972); 1 child, Malcolm Paul; m. Lois Roxane Florian, July 27, 1974; 1 child, Rachel Floy. BS, Caltech, Pasadena, Calif., 1964, PhD, 1969. Sr. scientist Havens Internat., San Diego, 1969-71; group leader Calgon Corp., San Diego, 1971-72; v.p. Chem. Systems, Irvine, Calif., 1972-79; Purolator Puropore, Tustin, Calif., 1979-82, Puropore, Inc., Tustin, 1982-85; dir. Microgon, Laguna Hills, Calif., 1985-95, Spectrum Cos., Laguna Hills, 1996-98; v.p. Spectrum Labs., Rancho Dominquez, Calif., 1998—2002; sr. process engr. Santa Fe Sci. and Tech., 2004—. Cons. in field, 1985—; v.p./owner OMMS Engrs., Inc., Santa Ana, Calif., 1982-2005. Contbr. articles to profl. jours. Dir. Santiago Sanitation Dist., Silverado, Calif., 1978-80. Mem. Am. Inst. Chem. Engrs., Orange County CAER (sec./treas. 1990-2005), Am. Filtration Soc. (pres. Golden State chpt. 1985-91), The Nature Conservancy. Republican. Roman Catholic. Avocations: horseback riding, gardening, birding, church activities. Home: Box 810 El Rito NM 87530-0810 Office: Santa Fe Sci and Tech 3216 Richards Ln Santa Fe NM 87507 Office Phone: 505-474-3500 ext. 22. Business E-Mail: morrison@sfst.net.

**MORRISON, MARTIN,** writer; b. Oakland, Calif., Mar. 28, 1947; s. Raymond Earl and June (Cabral) M. AB with distinction, U. Calif., Berkeley, 1967, MA, 1969, postgrad., 1969-73. Certified (life) nat. tournament dir.; cert. jr./community coll. tchr. (life), Calif. Instr. classics and English composition U. Calif. at Berkeley, 1967; instr. legal argument Boalt Hall Law Sch., 1972; with exec. office CF Air Freight, Inc., 1979-83, asst. to traffic mgr. for spl. projects, 1982-83, computer systems mgr., 1982-83; computer systems analyst Qantel Bus. Computers, 1983-86, sr. computer systems analyst, 1986-92; sr. tech. writer Shared Med. Systems, 1992-96, supr. tech. writing, 1996-98, mgr. tech. writing, 1998—2000; lead tech. writer Kaiser Permanent, 2001—. Mem. Amateur Chamber Music Players, 1978—. Author: Writing Argument, 1972, USCF Yearbooks, 1974-76, Official Rules of Chess, 1975, 77, Chess Competitor's Handbook, 1980, Latin Works for Transparent Language Computer Program, 1992-93; editor: Chess Voice, 1968-73, Keeping Ancient Rome Alive, 1987-89; contbg. author: Fundamentals of Management, 3d edit., 2000; chess editor: Oakland Tribune, 1965-66; columnist Via Lorenzo, 1987-88, Metric Today, 1985—; mgr. Chess Life & Rev., 1977-78, Bancroft Music Sch., 1958-60. Asst. concertmaster Berkeley Chamber Chorus and Orch., 1980-83; concertmaster Oakland Philharm., 1987-90, bd. dirs., corp. sec., 1988-90; 1st violin Albany Trio, 1987-91, Mostly Baroque Ensemble, 1999-2000; vol. staff Chabot Sci. Ctr., 1981-84, chmn. computer system mgmt. staff; sec., treas. AstroSoft, 1983-87. Schola Gregoriana San Francisco, 1989-92, Schola Cantemus, 1992-95; dir. St. John Schola, 1995—. Fellow U.S. Metric Assn. (life, chmn. consumer edn. com. 1984—), Spl. Citation 1986, cert. advanced metrication specialist 1987); mem. Am. Philol. Assn., Am. Classical League, Eastbay Astron. Soc. (bd. dirs. 1981-84, v.p. 1983-84), Internat. Assn. Chess Press (v.p. 1973-77), Soc. for Tech. Comm. (sr.), Chess Journalists Assn. (pres. 1972-75), World Chess Fedn. (internat. life arbiter, mem. rules com. 1973-78, chmn. 1976-78), U.S. Chess Fedn. (bd. dels. 1968-78, 1st v.p. Pacific Region 1972-73, nat. sec. 1972-75, tech. dir. 1973-76, exec. dir. 1976-78, Disting. Vol. award, 1982, Spl. citation, 1984, Disting. Svc. award 1995), Calif. Alumni Assn. (life, scholarship com., chmn. 1987-93, Disting. Chmn. award 1990), San Lorenzo Garden Homes Assn. (v.p./sec. 1985-86, pres. 1986-92), Mensa, Friends of the Alameda Free Library, Phi Beta Kappa.

**MORRISON, MICHAEL DEAN,** lawyer, law educator; BA with high honors, Okla. U., 1971, JD, 1974. Bar: Okla. 1975, Tex. 1981, U.S. Ct. Appeals (5th cir.) 1980, U.S. Dist. Ct. (ea., no. and so. dists.) Tex. 1983, U.S. Dist. Ct. (we. dist.) Tex. 1980, U.S. Dist. Ct. (we. dist.) Okla. 1975, U.S. Supreme Ct. 1979. Pvt. practice, Wichita, Kans., 1974-75; asst. dir. Law Ctr. Okla. U., 1975-77, asst. prof., 1977-80, assoc. prof., 1980-82, prof. law, 1982-90, William J. Boswell chair of law, 1990—2005; chief of staff to pres. Baylor U., 2005—06. Mayor City of Waco, 1996—2000; ordained elder 1st Presbyn. Ch. Waco, stated clk. of session, 1996—98. Mem. Order of Coif, Phi Beta Kappa. Office: PO Box 97288 Waco TX 76798-7288

**MORRISON, MICHAEL GORDON,** academic administrator, clergyman, history professor; b. Green Bay, Wis., Mar. 9, 1937; s. Gordon John and Gertrude (Crilly) M. AB, St. Louis U., 1960, MA, Ph.L., St. Louis U., 1965, S.T.L., 1969; PhD, U. Wis., 1971. Ordained priest Roman Catholic Ch., 1968. Joined S.J., 1955; asst. v.p. acad. affairs Marquette U., Milw., 1974-77; v.p. acad. affairs Creighton U., Omaha, 1977-81, acting pres., 1981, pres., 1981-2000, dir. Mem. governing bd. Creighton Prep. Sch., 1993-99. Bd. dirs. Health Future Found., 1983-2000, Xavier U., 1992-98; mem. cons. com. SAC, 1988-99; mem. adv. bd. Salvation Army, 1992-2000; trustee Duchesne Acad. of Sacred Heart, 1995-2000; bd. dirs. Red Cloud Indian Sch., 1997-2000; bd. trustees, Loyola U., Chgo., 1998-2000. Recipient Human Rights award Anti-Defamation League, 1982, Humanitarian award Nat. Conf. Christians and Jews, 1989. Mem. Assn. Jesuit Colls. and Univs. (bd. dirs.), Assn. Ind. Colls. and Univs. Nebr. (bd. dirs. 1981-2000), Nat. Assn. Ind. Colls. and Univs. (bd. dirs. 1993-2000), Greater Omaha C. of C. (bd. dirs 1993-2000), Alpha Sigma Nu, Beta Alpha Psi.

**MORRISON, NANCY ANNE,** public affairs consultant; b. New Haven, May 7, 1953; d. Edward John and Lena (Lobudek) Wanat; m. Bruce A. Morrison, Sept. 22, 1991. AA in Nursing, Norwalk Community Coll., 1978; BS in Biology, So. Conn. State U., 1981; MPA, NYU, 1988. RN, Conn. Asst. head nurse Coronary Care Unit/Yale New Haven Hosp., 1978—84; health systems cons. The Travelers Health Network, Hartford, Conn., 1985—87; legis. dir. govt. affairs Travelers Ins. Co., Hartford, 1987—88; mgr. issues analysis customer cons. Aetna Ins. Co., Middletown, Conn., 1988—89; asst. dir. product mgmt. Travelers Ins. Co., Hartford, 1989—91; adminstrv. dir. Morrison, Sheehan & Swaine, New Haven, 1991—95; adminstrv. dir. Ctr. for Congl. and Presdl. Shediel, Am. U., Washington, 1997—99; exec. dir. Nat. Women's Party/Sewell-Belmont House, Washington, 2000—2001; ptnr. Morrison Pub. Affairs Group, 2001—. Campaign ops. Congressman Bruce Morrison Re-election Campaign, New Haven, 1984; scheduler Gloria Sandillo for Mayor Campaign, Hamden, 1985; field coord. Bruce Morrison for Gov. Campaign, New Haven, 1990. Scholarship NYU, 1986. Democrat. Home: 6004 Onondaga Rd Bethesda MD 20816-2152 Office Phone: 301-263-1142.

**MORRISON, PATRICE BURGERT,** lawyer; b. St. Louis, July 8, 1948; d. Frank J. and Loretta (S.) Burgert; m. William Brian Morrison, Aug. 12, 1969; 1 child, W. Brett. AB, U. Miami, 1971, MA, 1972; JD, Am. U., 1975; LLM in Taxation, Georgetown U., 1978. Bar: Fla. 1975, DC 1977, NY 1983. Atty. US Dept. Treas., Washington, 1975-79; atty., ptnr. Nixon Hargrave Devans & Doyle, LLP, Palm Beach County, Fla., 1980-89, Nixon Peabody LLP (formerly Nixon, Hargrave, Devans & Doyle), Rochester, NY, 1989—. Bd. dirs. Rochester Friendly Sr. Svcs., Inc., 1996—. Bd. dirs Alzheimer's Assn., Rochester, 1990-95, Nat. Women's Hall of Fame, 1990-92; mem. Rochester Women's Network; mem. exec. com. Estate Planning Coun. Rochester, 1992-95; dir. Cloverwood Sr. Living, Inc., 2000—. Mem. Am. Immigration Lawyers Assn. Republican. Office: Nixon Peabody LLP PO Box 31051 Rochester NY 14603-1051

**MORRISON, PATRICIA B.,** information technology executive; BA in Math. & Stats. summa cum laude, Miami Univ., BS in Secondary Edn. Sys. mgmt., IT positions Procter & Gamble; CIO GE Indsl. Sys. Gen. Electric,

1997—2000; CIO Quaker Oats Co., Chgo., 2000—02, Office Depot, Inc., Delray Beach, Fla., 2002—05; sr. v.p., chief info. officer Motorola Inc., 2005—. Bd. dir. Jo-Ann Stores, Inc. Office: Motorola Inc 1303 E Algonquin Rd Schaumburg IL 60196*

**MORRISON, PORTIA OWEN,** lawyer; b. Charlotte, NC, Apr. 1, 1944; d. Robert Hall Jr. and Josephine Currier (Hutchison) M.; m. Alan Peter Richmond, June 19, 1976; 1 child, Anne Morrison. BA in English, Agnes Scott Coll., 1966; MA, U. Wis., 1967; JD, U. Chgo., 1978. Bar: Ill. 1978. Ptnr. DLA Piper Rudnick Gray Cary U.S. LLP, Chgo., 1978—. Lectr. in field. Past pres. Girl Scouts of Chgo. Mem.: ABA, CREW Chgo., Chgo. Fin. Exch., Pension Real Estate Assn., Chgo. Bar Assn. (real property com., subcom. real property fin., alliance for women), Am. Coll. Real Estate Lawyers (past pres. bd. govs., bd. govs.). Office: DLA Piper Rudnick Gray Cary US LLP 203 N La Salle St Ste 1800 Chicago IL 60601-1210 Office Phone: 312-368-4013. Business E-Mail: portia.morrison@dlapiper.com.

**MORRISON, RAY LEON,** library director, education educator; b. Boise, Idaho, Sept. 17, 1952; s. Duane Alton and Wilma Lucille (Bybee) M.; m. Barbara Ann Derrenbacher, Apr. 2, 1977; children: Eric, Shawn. BJ, San Jose State U., Calif., 1974, MA in Library Sci., 1975; CAS in Library Sci., U. Ill., 1984; EdD, U. Ark., 1992. Reference librarian Olivet Nazarene Coll., Kankakee, Ill., 1975-80; Bibl. Inst. librarian Pittsburg State U., Kans., 1980-85; library dir. Mid-Am. Nazarene U., Olathe, Kans., 1986—. Adj. prof. edn. Mid Am. Nazarene U. Author: Library Skills Workbook, 1981, 2d rev. edit., 1983; contbr. articles to profl. jours., book revs. to pubs. Pres. bd. dirs. Olathe Libr.; dist. commr. Boy Scouts Am. Mem. ALA, Kans. Libr. Assn., Christian Librarians Fellowship, Nazarene Librarians Fellowship, Kans. Libr. Network Bd., Kansas City Met. Libr. Network. Republican. Mem. Ch. of Nazarene. Avocations: cross country skiing, NASCAR, olympic games, track and field, reading. Home: 1904 S Parkwood Dr Olathe KS 66062-2806 Office: Mid-Am Nazarene U PO Box 1776 Olathe KS 66051-1776 Office Phone: 913-971-3561. Business E-Mail: rmorriso@mnu.edu.

**MORRISON, RICHARD A.,** lawyer; b. Miami, Fla., Feb. 2, 1959; BA, Vanderbilt U., 1981; JD, U. Fla. Coll. Law, 1984. Bar: Fla. 1984. Mng. ptnr., head pub. fin. Weil, Gotshal & Manges, LLP, Miami, Fla., 1988—. Mem.: ABA, Nat. Assn. Bond Lawyers, Fla. Bar. Office: Weil Gotshal & Manges 1395 Brickell Ave Ste 1200 Miami FL 33131 Office Phone: 305-577-3125. Office Fax: 305-374-7159. Business E-Mail: richard.morrison@weil.com.

**MORRISON, ROBERT CLIFTON,** artist; b. Billings, Mont., Aug. 13, 1924; s. Lloyd Clifton and Elsie Genevive (Talgo) M.; m. Berta Frances McPike, June 16, 1948; children: James, Barbara, Judith, Bruce. BA, Carleton Coll., Northfield, Minn., 1949; MA, U. N.Mex., 1951. Arts supr. Billing Pub. Schs., 1957-67; prof. art Rocky Mt. Coll., Billings, 1967-87, acad. dean, 1985-86; artist, 1965—. One-person shows and invitational exhibits include U. Oreg. Art Gallery, Eugene, 1960, Mont. Hist. Soc., Helena, 1962, Mus. of the Plains Indian, Browning, Mont., 1969, Western Art Gallery, Albuquerque, 1972, JPL Gallery, London, 1975, Yellowstone Art Mus., Billings, Mont., 1978, Waterworks Gallery, Miles City, Mont., 1986, The Billings Clinic Gallery, 1988, Paris Gibson Art Mus., Great Falls, Mont., 1995, Carbon County Arts Guild, Red Lodge, Mont., 1996, 98, Smithsonian Instn., Washington, 1996, 97; represented in pvt. and pub. collections in U.S., Eng., Denmark and Norway. Bd. dirs. Western Heritage Ctr., Billings, 1982-91; mem. Mont. Arts Coun., Helena, 1977-82, 1997-2002. With inf. AUS, 1943-46, ETO.

**MORRISON, ROBERT SCHECK,** former manufacturing executive, former food marketing processing company executive; b. Chgo., Apr. 4, 1942; s. Forrest John Morrison and Grayce Morrison (Scheck) Hopkins; m. Susan E. Brennan, Oct. 1, 1988; children: R. Scott, Stephen L., James F., Emily E., Catherine A. BS in English, Coll. Holy Cross, 1963; MBA, U. Pa., 1969. Asst. brand mgr. Procter & Gamble, Cin., 1969-72, brand mgr., 1972-75, assoc. advt. mgr., 1975-81, divsn. mgr., 1981-83; v.p. mktg. Kraft Inc., Glenview, Ill., 1983-85, group v.p., pres. refrigerated products group, 1985-89; pres. Kraft Gen. Foods Can., Toronto, Ont., 1989-91, Gen. Foods U.S.A., White Plains, NY, 1991-95; chmn., CEO Kraft Foods, Inc., Northfield, Ill., 1994-97; chmn., pres. CEO Quaker Oats Co., Chgo., 1997—2001; vice chmn. PepsiCo., Inc., Purchase, NY, 2001—03; interim chmn., CEO 3M Co., St. Paul, 2005. Bd. dir. Aon Corp., 2000—, Tribune Co., 2001, 3M Corp., 2002—, Ill. Tool Works Inc., 2003—, Econ. Club of Chgo., Grocery Manufacturers of Am. Mem. bd. trustees Lyric Opera of Chgo., Ravinia Festival, Highland Park, Ill., Chgo. Urban League. Decorated Silver Star, Purple Heart. Mem.: Stanwich Club Greenwich, Conn., Glen View Golf Club, Comml. Club Chgo., Chgo. Club. Avocations: golf, tennis, skiing.*

**MORRISON, ROGER BARRON,** geologist; b. Madison, Wis., Mar. 26, 1914; s. Frank Barron and Elsie Rhea (Bullard) M.; m. Harriet Louise Williams, Apr. 7, 1941 (dec. Feb. 1991); children: John Christopher, Peter Hallock and Craig Brewster (twins). BA, Cornell U., 1933, MS, 1934; postgrad., U. Calif., Berkeley, 1934—35, Stanford U., 1935—38; PhD, U. Nev., 1964. Registered profl. geologist, Wyo. Geologist U.S. Geol. Survey, 1939-76; vis. adj. prof. dept. geoscis. U. Ariz., 1976-81, Mackay Sch. Mines, U. Nev., Reno, 1984-86; cons. geologist; pres. Morrison and Assocs., Morrison Cons. Corp., 1978—. Prin. investigator 2 Landsat-1 and 2 Skylab earth resources investigation projects NASA, 1972-75. Author 3 books; co-author 1 book; co-editor 2 books; editor Quaternary Nonglacial Geology, Conterminous U.S., Geol. Soc. Am. Centennial Series, vol. K-2, 1991; mem. editl. bd. Catena, 1973-88; contbr. over 250 articles to profl. jours. Fellow Geol. Soc. Am.; mem. AAAS, Internat. Union Quaternary Rsch. (mem. Holocene and paleopedology commns., chmn. work group on pedostratigraphy), Am. Soc. Photogrammetry and Remote Sensing, Internat. Soil Sci. Soc., Am. Quaternary Assn. Achievements include research in on Quaternary geology and geomorphology, hydrogeology, environmental geology, neotectonics, remote sensing of Earth resources, paleoclimatology, pedostratigraphy; technology for converting waste wood, garbage, municipal solid waste, natural gas, landfill gas, etc. to mixed-alcohol motor fuel; development of forest and range land and a new town in western Paraguay; research in nuclear waste issues at Yucca Mtn., Nev. Home and Office: 7500 N Calle Sin Envidia Apt 8104 Tucson AZ 85718-7361 Office Phone: 520-531-8820. E-mail: rbmorrison@comcast.net.

**MORRISON, SARAH LYDDON,** author; b. Rochester, N.Y., May 19, 1939; d. Paul William and Winifred (Cowles) Lyddon. BA, U. Vt., 1961. Sec. asst. Glamour mag., N.Y.C., 1961-63, Vogue mag., N.Y.C., 1963-65; asst. editor Venture mag., N.Y.C., 1966-71; dir. pub. rels. for tourism Commonwealth of P.R., N.Y.C., 1971-75; asst. Am. Legion, Washington, 1988-98; owner Sarah Lyddon Morrison Pub. Rels., Washington, 1999—. Author: The Modern Witch's Spellbook, 1971, Book II, 1983, The Modern Witch's Dream Book, 1985, The Modern Witch's Book of Home Remedies, 1991, The Modern Witch's Book of Symbols, 1997, Modern Witch's Guide to Magic and Spells, 1998 Advisor to nat. security coord. John Kerry Presdl. Campaign, 2003—04. Mem. Washington Club, DAR (Emily Nelson chpt.), Colonial Dames XVII Century (refreshment chmn., nat. def. chmn.). Avocations: travel, reading, swimming, rock music, cooking. Office Phone: 202-966-2981. Personal E-mail: sarahlyd@verizon.net.

**MORRISON, SCOTT DAVID,** management consultant, small business owner; b. Duluth, Minn., May 8, 1952; s. Robert Henry and Shirley Elaine (Tester) M. (dec. 1990); m. Jana Louise Bergeron, May 29, 1976; chilren: Robert Scott (dec. 1999), Matthew John. Cert. in welding, Duluth Area Inst. Tech., 1971; student, U. Wis.-Superior, 1976-77; A in Mfg. Mgmt., N. Hennepin C.C., 1985; BA, Concordia Coll., St. Paul, 1988; MBA, St. Thomas U., St. Paul, 1991. Cert. in quality tech., Am. Soc. Quality, 1985, Dell Computer, Inc. instr. Six Sigma; lic. vocat. instr., Minn. Cert. welder Litton Ship Systems, Pascagoula, Miss., 1971-72, Barko Hydraulics, Superior, Wis., 1972-76, Am. Hoist and Derrick Co., Mpls., 1977-79, cert. level II nondestructive exam. insp., 1979-80; quality supr. Colight Inc., Mpls., 1980,

Tol-O-Matic, Inc., Mpls., 1980-82; quality assurance engr. ADC Telecomm., Mpls., 1982-84, design assurance engr., 1985-86, product assurance engr., 1986-87, sr. product assurance engr., quality improvement facilitator, 1987-88, product engr. supr., 1988-90, mgr. design assurance, quality assurance, component engring., 1990-92; dir. quality and reg. affairs Waters Instruments, Inc., 1992-96, sr. quality engr., 1996, corp. quality sys. mgr., 1996-98; corp. mfg. and quality Compaq Computer Corp., Houston, 1996-98; sys. engr., sr. cons. Dimension Product Group, 1998—2001, Dell Computer Corp., Austin, Tex., 1998—, quality engr., sr. cons. Transactional Line of Bus., 1999—2000, mgr. quality sys. application team project, 2000, supplier quality engr., sr. cons., 2000—01; sr. cons. ABS Cons. Mgmt. Sys. divsns., Houston, 2001—03; mgr. Mgmt. Sys. Cons., 2002—03; owner Dimensions in Quality, LLC, 2003—; contract mgmt. sys. auditor Moody Internat., 2004—, auditor quality, environ. and health and safety mgmt. sys., 2006—. Judge U.S. Amateur Boxing Fedn., Mpls., 1978-87, 95-97; examiner Minn. Quality Award Minn. Coun. for Quality, 1993, 95, Tex. Quality Award, 1997; mem. quality coun. Am. Electronics Assn., 1994-95; mem. bd. dirs. Rochester Quality Coun., 1994-95; examiner Malcolm Baldridge Nat. Quality award Nat. Inst. Standards and Technology, 1994-95, sr. examiner, 1996-97, alumni examiner, 1999-2000; reviewer fellowship grant applications ASQ, 1996; adj. instr. Riverland Tech. Coll., Rochester, Minn., 1995; lic. profl. boxing judge Tex. Dept. Licensing and Regulation, 1996—; cert. lead quality auditor Brit. Standards Internat., 1996, cert. lead environ. sys. auditor, 2001; facilitator Malcolm Bridge Nat. Quality Award Regional Conf., 1997; cons. in field. Recipient Tech. Excellence award ADC Telecoms., 1987, 88. Mem. ASTM, Am. Soc. Quality (cert. quality engr. cert. quality auditor, cert. quality mgr., cert. six sigma black belt, chmn. host and attendance subcom. 1986-87), Am Welding Soc., Soc. Mfg. Engrs., Internat. Platform Assn. Roman Catholic. Home and Office: 18 Seneca Pl The Woodlands TX 77382-5353 Office Phone: 281-419-1253. Personal E-mail: diminq@houston.rr.com.

**MORRISON, SHELLEY,** actress; b. NYC, Oct. 26, 1936; d. Maurice Nissim and Hortense Mitrani; m. Walter R. Dominguez, Aug. 11, 1973. Student, L.A. City Coll., 1954—56. Presenter Alma awards, 2001—02, Imagan Awards, 2001, Nosotros Golden Eagle awards, 2002. Actress: (films) Interns, 1962, The Greatest Story Ever Told, 1964, Castle of Evil, 1965, Divorce, American Style, 1965, How to Save a Marriage, 1966, Funny Girl, 1967, Three Guns for Texas, 1969, Man and Boy, 1971, Blume in Love, 1972, McKenna's Gold, 1967, Breezy, 1973, People Toys, 1973, Rabbit Test, 1975, Max Dugan Returns, 1982, Troop Beverly Hills, 1988, Fools Rush In, 1996, Shark Tale, 2004, others, (TV movies) The Girl Who Came Giftwrapped, Three's a Crowd, 1969, Once an Eagle, 1974, The Night That Panicked America, 1975, Kids Don't Tell, 1984, Cries From the Heart, 1999, Columbo: It's All In the Game, Lassie: A New Beginning, others, (TV series) Laredo, 1965-67, The Flying Nun, 1966-70, First and Ten, 1987, I'm Home, 1990, The Fanelli Boys, 1990, Love, Lies and Murder, 1990, Playhouse 90, Dr. Kildare, The Fugitive, Gunsmoke, Marcus Welby, General Hospital, and many others, 1960-70, Man of the People, Sisters, 1991, 92, Murder She Wrote, 1992, Johnny Bago, 1993, Columbo, 1993, L.A. Law, 1994, Live Shot, 1995, Courthouse, Home Improvement, 1997, Nothing Sacred, 1997, Prey, 1997, Nearly Yours, 1998; recurring role in Will & Grace, 1998–, series regular 1999-06 (Diversity award 2004, People's Choice award 2005, nominee Golden Globe award 2005, nominee SAG award 2005); TV guest appearances include Prey, Nothing Sacred, L.A. Law, Busting Loose, Marcus Welby, M.D., Occasional Wife, Between the Lines, Home Improvement, Murder, She Wrote, The Bold Ones, Divorce Court, Soap, The Streets of San Francisco, Dr. Kildare, Man of the People, The Partridge Family, My Favorite Martian, The Outer Limits, The Robert Taylor Show, numerous others; (voice over animated cartoon comml.) Handy Manny, 2006 (voice animated cartoon series), (A&E) Letters, 2003, numerous others, (stage prodns.) Pal Joey, 1956, Bus Stop, 1956, Only in America, 1960, Orpheus Descending, 1960, Spring's Awakening, 1962, over 65 other prodns., 1956-1970, also appeared in The Mikado, Pal Joey, Anastasia, Orpheus Descending, A Streetcar Named Desire, Sweet Bird of Youth, The Crucible, Zoo Story, Rashomon, Desk Set, Pygmalion, The Would-Be Gentleman, Comedy of Errors, Tiger at the Gates, The Rose Tattoo, Orpheus Descending, Come Back Little Sheba, The Odd Couple, Only in America, El Camino Real, Hamlet, Country Girl, Romeo and Juliet, Cotton Candy, Point of View, Coney Island of the Mind, Last of the Aztecs, numerous others; prodr., writer, 1975—; prodr. (with husband Walter Dominguez) documentary Mexican culture, 2003. Condr. seminars (with husband Walter Dominquez) about Native Americans to keep traditions and ceremonies flourishing. Honored (with husband Walter Dominguez) for work with homeless City of LA, 1985, for work during LA riots, 1992, Bronx Walk of Fame, 2004, Diversity award Women's Theater Group, 2004; nominated for Alma awards SAG, 2000, 01, 02, 06; recipient Emmy award Best Comedy for Will and Grace, 2000, SAG award for Will and Grace, 2002, Halo award, 2003, People's Choice award for Will and Grace ensemble, 2004, Gladd award for Will and Grace ensemble, 2004, Diversity award for Will and Grace ensemble, 2004. Mem. SAG, AFTRA, Actors Equity Assn. Democrat.

**MORRISON, SHERIE LEAVER,** microbiologist, educator; b. New Eagle, Pa., July 5, 1942; d. James Elsworth and Lillian Collard Leaver; m. Donald Graham Morrison; children: Heather M. Felix, T. Michelle Oliva. BA, Stanford U., Calif., 1963, PhD, 1966. Post doctoral fellow Columbia U., N.Y., 1966–74; postdoctoral fellow Albert Einstein Coll. Medicine Yeshiva U., N.Y., 1966–74; prof. Columbia U., 1974—88, U. Calif., L.A., 1988—. Fellow: AAAS; mem.: Am. Assn. Microbiologists, Am. Assn. Immunologists. Home: 258 Denslow Ave Los Angeles CA 90044 Office: Dept Microbiol Immunol and Molec Genetics UCLA Los Angeles CA 90095

**MORRISON, SHERRIE CRAWFORD,** secondary school educator; b. Charleston, S.C., Aug. 26, 1944; d. Burdette Boughner and Sarah Etta (Hoover) Crawford; children: Laura Gail Morrison Scaggs, Murdoch Warren Morrison. BA in English, St. Andrews Presbyn. Coll., Laurinburg, N.C., 1965; MA in Secondary Edn., U. N.C., Charlotte, 1989; postgrad., U. S.C., Columbia, 1991—. Cert. mentor Kings Mountain Dist. Schs.; cert. tchr., gifted/talented tchr., S.C. Nat. Bd. Cert. Adolescence and Young Adulthood English Lang. Arts Nat. Bd. for Tchg. Profl. Standards, 2003. English tchr. Whiteville (N.C.) H.S., 1965-66, Lumberton (N.C.) H.S., 1966-67; tchrs. aide Marian Elem. Sch., Shelby, N.C., 1973-76; sec., bookkeeper Gilliatt's Gifts and Flowers, Shelby, 1978-84; English tchr. Kings Mountain (N.C.) Jr. H.S., 1984-90; tchr. English and journalism Lexington (S.C.) H.S., 1990-96, tchr. English and drama, 1996—. Sec., bd. dirs. S.C. Scholastic Press Assn., Columbia, 1993-96; mem. N.C. Writing Project, U. N.C., Charlotte, 1986, N.C. Lit. Project, 1987; cooperating tchr. Gardner-Webb Coll., N.C.; adj. supr. for Coll. Edn., U. N.C., Charlotte, 1989; mem. Lexington Dist. Tchr. Forum, 2001–; fine arts mag. advisor White Knoll H.S., 2005. Sec., Crisis Pregnancy Ctr., Shelby, 1980-83; pub. awareness coord. grassroots conservation group, Shelby, 1975; mem. transp. coun. County Food Bank, Charlotte, 1970-72; funding drive assoc. Am. Cancer Soc., Columbia, 1996—; cmty. vol. Mothers March of Dimes, 1996—; mem. tchr. forum Lexington Sch. Dist. Named Dist. Tchr. of Yr., Lexington Dist. 1, 1995. Mem. Palmetto State Tchrs. Assn. Republican. Mem. Assemblies Of God Church. Avocations: poetry, cooking, gardening, Karate (black belt), yoga. Office: Lexington HS 2463 Augusta Hwy Lexington SC 29072-2215 Home: 105 Wilmington Ln Lexington SC 29072-7336 Office Phone: 803-359-5565. Personal E-mail: msmo5@hotmail.com. Business E-Mail: smorrison@lexington1.net.

**MORRISON, STACY LYNNE,** magazine editor; b. Jenkintown, Pa., Jan. 17, 1969; d. Robert Isaac and Sharon Lee (Wiley) Morrison; m. Christopher Cole Shannon, Oct. 1, 1994. BA, Washington & Lee U., 1990. Editl. asst. Mirabella mag., NYC, 1991-92, asst. editor, 1992-93, assoc. features editor, 1993-95; mng. editor J. Crew Group Inc., NYC, 1995, Time Out New York, NYC, Conde Nast Sports for Women; editor-in-chief Modern Bride, 1998—2000, ONE, 2000—01; exec. editor Marie Claire, NYC, 2001—04; editor-in-chief Redbook, NYC, 2004—. Office: Redbook 224 W 57th St New York NY 10019*

**MORRISON, STEPHEN GEORGE,** lawyer; b. Pasadena, Calif., Aug. 10, 1949; s. Ira George and Virginia Lee (Zimmer) M.; m. Gail Louise Moore, June 10, 1972; 1 child, Gregory Stephen. BBA, U. Mich., 1971; JD, U. S.C., 1975. Ptnr. Nelson, Mullins, Riley & Scarborough, Columbia, S.C., 1975—. Adj. prof. U. S.C., Columbia, 1973-75, 82—; pres. Defense Rsch. Inst., 1995-96; exec. v.p., gen. counsel, sec., chief adminstrv. officer Policy Mgmt. Sys. Corp.; presenter in field. Author/editor: Products Liability Pretrial Notebook, 1989, South Carolina Appellate Practice Handbook, 1986. Bd. dirs. S.C. Com. Humanities, Columbia, 1986—, S.C. Gov. Sch. Arts, Columbia, 1988-95; pres., bd. dirs. Richland County Pub. Defender Assn., Columbia, 1991-95. Fellow S.C. Bar Found.; mem. Internat. Assn. Defense Coun., Lawyers for Civil. Justice (bd. dirs. 1995—, pres. elect 1997—). Democrat. Episcopalian. Avocations: fishing, country music, chamber music, physics, history. Home: 2626 Stratford Rd Columbia SC 29204-2342 Office: Nelson Mullins Riley & Morrison 1330 Lady St Fl 3 Columbia SC 29201-3300

**MORRISON, TONI (CHLOE ANTHONY WOFFORD),** writer, educator, editor; b. Lorain, Ohio, Feb. 18, 1931; d. George and Ella Ramah (Willis) Wofford; m. Harold Morrison, 1958 (div. 1964); children: Harold Ford, Slade Kevin. BA in English, Howard U., 1953; MA in Am. Lit., Cornell U., 1955; degree (hon.), Harvard U., U. Pa., Sarah Lawrence, Oberlin, Dartmouth, Yale, Georgetown, Columbia U., Brown U., U. Mich., Universite Paris 7-Denis Diderot. Instr. English Tex. So. U., 1955-57, Howard U., 1957-64; assoc. editor Random House, Syracuse, NY, 1965—67, sr. editor NYC, 1967—83; assoc. prof. English SUNY, Purchase, 1971-72, Albert Schweitzer Prof. in the Humanities Albany, NY, 1984-89; Robert F. Goheen Prof. in the Humanities Princeton U., Princeton, NJ, 1989—, dir. Princeton Atelier, 1994—. Vis. lectr. Yale Univ., 1976-77, Bard Coll., 1986-88, Obert C. Tanner Lectr. U. Mich., Ann Arbor, 1988, Jeannette K. Watson Disting. Prof., Syracuse U., 1988; delivered the Clark lectures, Trinity Coll., Cambridge, 1990, Massey Lectures, Harvard U., 1990; Internat. Cordorcet Chair, Ecole Normale Superieure and College de France, 1994. Author: (novels) The Bluest Eye, 1969, Sula, 1973 (National Book Award nomination 1975, Ohioana Book Award 1975), Song of Solomon, 1977 (National Book Critics Circle Award 1977, American Acad. and Inst. of Arts and Letters Award 1977), Tar Baby, 1981, Beloved, 1987 (Pulitzer Prize for fiction 1988, Robert F. Kennedy Meml. Book Award 1988, Melcher Book Award Unitarian Universalist Assn. 1988, National Book Award nomination 1987, National Book Critics Circle Award nomination 1987, Best American Fiction of Past 25 Years, NY Times, 2006), Jazz, 1992, Paradise, 1998, Love, 2003, (children's book) Remember: The Journey to School Integration, 2004 (Coretta Scott King Award ALA, 2005), (play) Dreaming Emmett, 1986, (non-fiction) Playing in the Dark: Whiteness and the Literary Imagination, 1992, (speech) The Dancing Mind, 1996; co-author (with son Slade Kevin) (children's books) The Big Box, 1999, The Book of Mean People, 2002, The Lion or the Mouse?, 2003, The Ant or the Grasshopper?, 2003, The Poppy or the Snake?, 2003; editor: The Black Book, 1974, Race-ing Justice, En-Gendering Power: Essays on Anita Hill, Clarence Thomas, and the Construction of Social Reality, 1992, To Die for the People: The Writings of Huey P. Newton, 1995; co-editor Birth of a Nation'Hood: Gaze, Script, Spectacle in the O.J. Simpson Case, 1997; lyricist: Honey and Rue, 1992. Recipient NY State Governor's Art Award, 1986, Elizabeth Cady Stanton Award National Orgn. Women, Nobel Prize in Literature, 1993, Nat. Book Found. Medal for Disting. Contbn. to Am. Letters, 1996, Nat. Humanities Medal, 2000. Mem. Am. Acad. Arts and Letters, Author's Guild (coun.), Nat. Coun. Arts. Achievements include being first African American woman to win the Nobel Prize in Literature.*

**MORRISON, VAN,** musician, songwriter; b. Belfast, Ireland, Aug. 31, 1945; s. George and Violet Morrison; 1 child, Shana. Founder, lead singer rock group Them, 1964-67, albums include Them, 1965, Them Again, 1966, Them featuring Van Morrison, 1972; solo career, 1967—; albums include Blowin' Your Mind, 1967, Astral Weeks, 1968, Moondance, 1968, Best of Van Morrison, 1970, His Band and Street Choir, 1970, Tupelo Honey, 1971, St. Dominic's Preview, 1972, Hard Nose the Highway, 1973, It's Too Late To Stop Now, 1974, TB Sheets, 1974, Veedon Fleece, 1974, This Is Where I Came In, 1977, A Period of Transition, 1977, Wavelength, 1978, Into the Music, 1979, Common One, 1980, Beautiful Vision, 1982, Inarticulate Speech of the Heart, 1983, Live at the Grand Opera House Belfast, 1984, A Sense of Wonder, 1985, No Guru, No Method, No Teacher, 1986, Poetic Champions Compose, 1987, (with The Chieftains) Irish Heartbeat, 1988, Live for Ireland, 1988, Avalon Sunset, 1989, Enlightenment, 1990, The Best of Van Morrison, 1990, Hymns to the Silence, 1991, Bang Masters, 1991, The Best of Van Morrison, 1993, Too Long in Exile, 1993, A Night in San Francisco, 1994, Days Like This, 1995, The Healing Game, 1997, Tell Me Something, 1997, The Philosopher's Stone, 1998, Brown Eyed Girl, 1998, Brown Eyed Beginnings, 1998, The Masters, 1999, Super Hits, 1999, New York Sessions '67: Bang Demos, 1999, Back On Top, 1999, The Skiffle Sessions: Live in Belfast 1998, 2000, You Win Again, 2000, Brown Eyed Handsome Man, 2001, The Essential Van Morrison, 2001, Down The Road, 2002, What's Wrong With This Picture, 2003, Madame George, 2004, Magic Time, 2005; composer numerous hit singles including Gloria, 1965, Brown Eyed Girl, 1967, Moondance, 1968, Domino, 1970, Wild Night, 1971; composer TV film Drei Amerikanische LP's, 1969, films Dusty and Sweets McGee, 1971, Slipstream, 1974, Lamb, 1986, Moondance, 1995, Beyond the Clouds, 1995; actor films The Day the Music Died, 1977, The Last Waltz, 1978, Van Morrison in Ireland, 1980, Ready Steady Go, 1983, TV series (voice) Irish in America: The Long Journey Home, 1998. Inducted into Rock and Roll Hall of Fame, 1993, Songwriters Hall of Fame, 2003; recipient Grammy award for Best Pop Collaboration With Vocals, 1995, 97.

**MORRISON, WILLIAM DAVID,** lawyer; b. Aug. 19, 1940; s. Maxey Neal and May Fuller (Chew) M.; m. Barbara Heath, Aug. 25, 1962 (div.); children: David Conrow, Stephen Munro, John Pomeroy; m. Sandra Elizabeth Butter, Mar. 16, 1983; children: Charles Nicholas, Sophie Natasha. BA, Princeton U., 1962; LLB, Yale U., 1965. Bar: N.Y. 1966, Calif. 1975. Assoc. Winthrop, Stimson, Putnam & Robert, N.Y.C., 1965-74; ptnr. Erickson & Morrison, and predecessor firms, L.A., 1974—79, LeBoeuf, Lamb, Leiby & Macrae, N.Y.C., 1979-88, Bryan Cave, St. Louis, 1988-97, Sidley, Austin, Brown & Wood, N.Y.C., 1997—2002; sr. cons. MEC Internat. Ltd., London, 2002—; sr. legal advisor The Trinity Group, London, 2003—. Lectr. on Saudi Arabian law; active Royal Inst. Internat. Affairs (Chatham House). Mem. ABA, Calif. Bar Assn., Internat. Bar Assn., Royal Geog. Soc., Internat. Inst. for Strategic Studies, The Pilgrims, Brooks, City of London Club, Marks Club, Annabel's, RAC Club, Princeton Club, Calif. Club. Home: 34 Norland Sq London WII4PU England Office: The Trinity Group 22 Upper Grosvenor St London W1K 7PE England Office Phone: (+44) (0) 20 7229 5187. Business E-Mail: wd.morrison@btinternet.com.

**MORRISON, WILLIAM FOSDICK,** business educator, retired electrical company executive; b. Bridgeport, Conn., Mar. 14, 1935; s. Robert Louis and Helen Fosdick (Mulroney) M.; m. E. Drake Miller, Dec. 14, 1957 (div. Sept. 1972); children: Donna Drake, Deanne Fosdick, William Fosdick; m. Carol Ann Stover, Nov. 20, 1972. BA in Econs., Trinity Coll., 1957. Mgr. purchasing dept. Westinghouse Electric Co., Lima, Ohio, 1960—68, mgr. mfg. Upper Sandusky, Ohio, 1969, gen. mgr. Gurabo, Puerto Rico, 1970—71, mgr. tng. Pitts., 1972—84, program mgr. Sunnyvale, Calif., 1984—89, procurement project dir., 1990—94; prof. San Jose State U., Calif., 1993—, Golden Gate U., San Francisco, 1995—; lead negotiator Advanced Micro Devices, Santa Clara, Calif., 1995—97; prof. U. Calif., Berkeley, 1996—2002, Menlo Coll., 1998—2001; faculty adv. Beta Gamma Sigma, 2002—. Negotiation cons. and trainer, 1969—; lead negotiator ReSound Corp., 1998-99; mgr. renovation project San Jose State U., 1999-2000. Author: The Pre-Negotiation Planning Book, 1985, The Human Side of Negotiations, 1994; contbr. articles to profl. jours. Bd. dirs. Valley Inst. of the Theatre Arts, Saratoga, Calif., 1986-90, Manhattan Playhouse, 1989-94; chmn. Sensory Access Found. Golf Tournament, 1995-96. Served to capt. USAFR, 1958-64; mem. protocol office World Cup USA, 1994. Named Man of the Yr. Midwest Lacrosse Coaches Assn., 1983, recipient Service award U.S. Lacrosse Assn., 1982. Mem.: Nat. Assn. Purchasing Mgmt. (pres. Lima

chpt. 1966—67, dir. nat. affairs 1967—68, dist. treas. 1968—70), The Propeller Club (sec., San Francisco port 2002—), Circumnaviagators Club (founder, pres. San Francisco chpt. 2001—), Sunnyvale Golf Assn. (vice-chmn. 1985, chmn. 1986, handicap scorer 1992—93, chmn. 1993), Elks. Avocation: golf. Home: 3902 Duncan Pl Palo Alto CA 94306-4550 Office: San Jose State U Coll of Bus 1 Washington Sq San Jose CA 95112-3613 E-mail: wfmorrison@earthlink.net.

**MORRISS, FRANK,** writer, educator; b. Pasadena, Calif., Mar. 28, 1923; s. B. Gerard Morriss and Regina Spann; m. Mary Rita Moynihan, Feb. 11, 1950 (dec. Oct. 23, 1996); children: Patricia, Mary Ellen Hill, Regina Sister M John, OSF(dec.); Gerard. BS in Philosophy magna cum laude, Regis Coll., Denver, 1943; JD, Georgetown U., 1948. Editor Register Newspapers, Denver, 1949—61, 1963—67; assoc. editor Vt. Cath. Tribune, Burlington, 1961—63; contbg. editor The Wanderer, St. Paul, 1967—; educator Colorado Cath. Acad., Wheat Ridge, Colo., 1971—83. Bd. dirs. Wanderer Forum Found., St. Paul, 1969—; policy expert Heritage Found., 1995—. Author: Saints in Verse, Two Chapels, The Divine Epic, The Catholic as Citizen, The Conservative Imperative, Boy of Philadelphia, Alfred of Wessex, The Adventures of Broken Hand, Submarine Pioneer, (lectrs. on CD) Saints Speak to Modern World. Founder Colo. Cath. Acad., Wheat Ridge, 1970—2002. Sgt. U.S. Army, 1943—45, PTO. Recipient Frederic Ozanam award, Soc. Cath. Social Scientists, 2003. Mem.: Fellowship of Cath. Scholars, VFW. Republican. Roman Catholic. Home: 3505 Owens Street Wheat Ridge CO 80033 Office Fax: 303-422-1475.

**MORRISS, FRANK HOWARD, JR.,** pediatrics educator; b. Birmingham, Ala., Apr. 20, 1940; s. Frank Howard Sr. and Rochelle (Snow) M.; m. Mary J. Hagan, June 29, 1968; children: John Hagan, Matthew Snow. BA, U. Va., 1962; MD, Duke U., 1966. Diplomate Am. Bd. Pediatrics, Am. Bd. Perinatal and Neonatal Medicine. Intern Duke U. Med. Ctr., Durham, NC, 1966-67, resident in pediatrics, 1967-68, fellow in neonatology, 1970-71, U. Colo., Denver, 1971-73; asst. prof. to prof. U. Tex. Med. Sch., Houston, 1973-86; prof. U. Iowa Coll. Medicine, Iowa City, 1987—, chmn. dept., 1987—2004. Editor: Role of Human Milk in Infant Nutrition and Health, 1986; contbr. numerous articles to profl. jours, chpts. to books. Lt. comdr. USN, 1968-70. Grantee, NIH, 1977—87, 1990—2004. Mem. Am. Pediatric Soc., Soc. Pediatric Rsch., Am. Acad. Pediatrics, Soc. Gynecol. Investigation, Midwest Soc. Pediatric Rsch. Office: U Iowa Hosps & Clinics Dept Pediatrics Iowa City IA 52242 Office Phone: 319-384-6530.

**MORRISSETTE, JASON WILLIAM,** theater educator, actor, director; b. Saginaw, Mich. m. Ann Marie Bulley, June 6, 2001; children: Miranda Ann, Olivia Marie. BFA, Otterbein Coll., Westerville, Ohio, 1995; MFA, U. Ilinois, Champaign-Urbana, 1999; MA, U. Ill., Urbana-Champaign, 2001. Faculty Parkland Coll., Champaign, Ill., 1997—. Home: 410 N Elm St Champaign IL 61820 Personal E-mail: jwmorris@uiuc.edu.

**MORRISSEY, EDMOND JOSEPH,** philologist; b. N.Y.C., June 5, 1943; s. William J. and Anne K. (Gaffney) M.; m. Patricia M. Hanlon, Oct. 11, 1987; children: William, Edmond, Kathleen, Patrick, Jennifer, Lisa, Paula. AB summa cum laude, Boston Coll., 1965; BA, U. Oxford, 1967, MA, 1971, Harvard U., 1969, PhD, 1974. Seminarian Pope John XXIII Nat. Sem., Weston, Mass., 1974-77; collaborator prof. Sterling Dow Harvard U., Cambridge, Mass., 1977-95. Cons. in pub. and photoreprodn. Author: Studies in Inscriptions Listing the Agonistic Festivals, 1974, A Quinquagesimal History of the Church of St. Bernadette, 1987; contbr. articles to profl. jours. Pres., chmn. adminstrn. fin., St. Bernadette's Ch., Archdiocese of Boston, 1980—; founding dir. Theol. Lectures Series, Randolph, Mass., 1978—, Randolph Hist. Commn., 1988—; staff vol. Cardinal Medeiros Program for Handicapped, 1980-82; treas., bd. dirs. Randolph Community Food Pantry, 1994—. Marshall scholar, 1965—67, Wilson scholar, 1965—, Gen. Motors scholar, 1962—65, Ford Found. fellow, 1967—69, Harvard U. fellow, 1969—71. Mem. Am. Inst. Archaeology, Am. Philol. Assn., Alumni Assn. Harvard, Oxford U. Alumni Assn., Boston Coll. Alumni Assn. Democrat. Roman Catholic. Home: 4 Bennington St Randolph MA 02368-2106 Personal E-mail: EdmondusM@msn.com.

**MORRISSEY, EDWARD T., II,** conservative political blogger, nationally-syndicated radio co-host, columnist; b. Apr. 1963; m. Marcia A. Morrissey; 1 child, David. Polit. blog writer Captainsquarters.blog.com, 2003—. Invited spkr. Contbr. essays to NY Sun, NY Post, and the Daily Standard; co-host (weekly talk-radio show), Mpls., 2004—, guest appearances TV and radio shows in the US and Canada, regular contbr. (online, Daily Standard). Mem. Northern Alliance, Minn. E-mail: captain@captainsquartersblog.com.*

**MORRISSEY, J. RICHARD,** lawyer; b. LA, Jan. 8, 1941; BA, Santa Clara Univ., 1963; JD, Univ. Calif., Berkeley, 1966. Bar: Calif. 1966, US Ct. Mil. Appeals 1967, US Supreme Ct. 1980. Ptnr., co-leader Product Liability practice, head LA Litigation sect. Pillsbury Winthrop Shaw Pittman, LA. Mem.: ABA, LA County Bar Assn. Office: Pillsbury Winthrop Shaw Pittman Suite 2800 725 S Figueroa St Los Angeles CA 90017 Office Phone: 213-488-7525. Office Fax: 213-629-1033. Business E-Mail: richard.morrissey@pillsburylaw.com.

**MORRISSEY, JOHN CARROLL, SR.,** lawyer; b. NYC, Sept. 2, 1914; s. Edward Joseph and Estelle (Caine) M.; m. Eileen Colligan, Oct. 14, 1950; children: Jonathan Edward, Ellen (Mrs. James A. Jenkins), Katherine, John, Patricia, Richard, Brian, Peter. BA magna cum laude, Yale U., 1937, LLB, 1940; JSD, N.Y. U., 1931; grad., Command and Gen. Staff Sch., 1944. Bar: N.Y. State 1940. Dist. C3. 1953, Calif. 1954, U.S. Supreme Ct. 1944. Asso. firm Dorsey and Adams, 1940-41, Dorsey, Adams and Walker, 1946-50; counsel Office of Sec. of Def., Dept. Def., Washington, 1950-52; acting gen. counsel def. Electric Power Adminstrn., 1952-53; atty. Pacific Gas and Electric Co., San Francisco, 1953-70, assoc. gen. counsel, 1970-74, v.p., gen. counsel, 1975-80; individual practice law San Francisco, 1980-2000. Dir. Gas Lines, Inc. Bd. dirs. Legal Aid Soc., San Francisco; chmn. Golden Gate dist. Boy Scouts Am., 1973-75; commr. Human Rights Commn. of San Francisco, 1976-89, chmn., 1980-82; chmn. Cath. Social Svc. of San Francisco, 1966-68; adv. com. Archdiocesan Legal Affairs, 1981—; regent Archdiocesan Sch. of Theology, St. Patrick's Sem., 1994-99; dir. Presidio Preservation Assn., 1995-99. Served to col. F.A. U.S. Army, ETO, 1941-46. Decorated Bronze star, Army Commendation medal. Mem. NAS, AAAS, ABA, Calif. State Bar Assn., Fed. Power Bar Assn., N.Y. Acad. Scis., Calif. Conf. Pub. Utility Counsel, Pacific Coast Electric Assn., Pacific Coast Gas Assn., Econ. Round Table of San Francisco, World Affairs Council, San Francisco C. of C., Calif. State C. of C., Harold Brunn Soc. Med. Rsch., Electric Club, Serra Club, Commonwealth Club, Yale Club of San Francisco (pres. 1989-90), Pacific-Union Club, Sometimes Tuesday Club, Sovereign Mil. Order Malta, Phi Beta Kappa. Roman Catholic. Home: 2030 Jackson St San Francisco CA 94109-2840 Office: 1661 Pine St # 1135 San Francisco CA 94105 Personal E-mail: dadjcm@aol.com.

**MORRISSEY, MICHAEL JOSEPH,** investment banker; b. Mount Holly, NJ, June 26, 1947; s. Edward Francis and Winifred (Monahan) M.; m. Jeanne Stone, June 5, 1982; children: Scott Christopher, Nathanial Joseph Cake. AB, Boston Coll., 1969; MBA, Dartmouth Coll., 1971; grad. Corp. Fin. Mgmt. Program, Harvard U., 1979. Security analyst Philo Smith & Co., Inc., Stamford, Conn., 1971-73, Kidder Peabody & Co., Inc., N.Y.C., 1973-74, asst. v.p., 1974-76, v.p., 1976-77, Dean Witter Reynolds, Inc., N.Y.C., 1977-78, Crum and Forster, Morristown, NJ, 1978-80, sr. v.p., 1980-83; pres. Firemark Investments, Morristown, NJ, 1983-85, chmn. bd., 1985—; exec. v.p. Manhattan Nat. Corp., N.Y.C., 1985, pres., chief operating officer, 1985-86; mng. ptnr. Firemark Tiger Fund, 2005. Bd. dir. Fin. Pacific Ins. Group, Calif., CGA Group Ltd., Bermuda. Vice chmn. Rep. Party Santa Fe County; bd. dirs. Boys & Girls Club, Santa Fe. Recipient CFA award, 1977.

Mem. Internat. Ins. Soc., Young Pres.' Orgn., Dartmouth Club (N.Y.C.), Spring Brook Country Club. Republican. Episcopalian. Office: FireMark Investments 200 W De Vargas St Santa Fe NM 87501 E-mail: mjm@firemarkinv.com.

**MORRISSEY, PATRICIA A.,** federal agency administrator; AA in Liberal Arts, Hartford CC, 1964; BA in Psychology, Stetson U., 1966; M.Ed. in Spl. Edn., Pa. State U., 1971, PhD in Spl. Edn., 1974. Positions with US Ho. of Reps. Com. on Edn. and Labor, Senate Com. on Health, Edn., Labor, and Pensions; sr. assoc. Booz Allen Hamilton, McLean, Va.; commr. Adminstrn. Devel. Disabilities Adminstrn. Children and Families, HHS, 2001—. Republican. Office: Adminstrn Children and Families Adminstrn Devel Disabilities 370 L'Enfant Promenade SW Washington DC 20447 Office Phone: 202-690-6590. Business E-Mail: pmorrissey@acf.hhs.gov.*

**MORRISSEY, THOMAS A.,** publishing executive; Pub. Entertainment Weekly. Office: Entertainment Weekly 1675 Broadway New York NY 10019 Office Phone: 212-522-5600. Office Fax: 212-522-6104.

**MORRIS-TYNDALL, LUCY,** construction executive; married; 2 children. From sec. to cost engr. Swinerton & Walberg, San Francisco, 1977—92, asst. project mgr., 1992—94, with mgmt. and consulting br., 1994—97, v.p., ops. mgr., 1997—99; chief info. officer Swinerton Inc. (formerly Swinerton & Walberg), San Francisco, 1999—. Recipient Julia Morgan award, YWCA of Oakland, 1996, Medal of Excellence, Women at Work, 2002. Mem.: AGC of Calif. (info. tech. task force), Constrn. Info. Execs. Office: Swinerton Inc 260 Townsend St San Francisco CA 94107

**MORRONE, FRANK,** electronics executive; b. Marano Marchesato, Cosenza, Italy, May 13, 1949; s. Luigi and Emma (Molinaro) M.; m. Katherine Ann Kuehn, Feb. 1, 1975; children: Louis H., Cecilia E., Joseph V. BSEE, U. Wis., 1972; MBA, Northwestern U., 1993. Project engr. 3M Co., St. Paul, 1972—73; product engr., mgr. Eaton Corp., Kenosha, Wis., 1973—79; chief elec. engr. Tree Machine Tool, Racine, Wis., 1979—80; v.p. engring. MacPower divsn. Manu-Tronics, Inc., Kenosha, 1980—84, exec. v.p., 1984—99, sec., 1988—99; v.p. ops. Sanmina Corp., 1999—2001, sr. v.p., 2001—. Mem. exec. bd. southeast coun. Boy Scouts Am., Racine, 1987—; bd. dirs. Kenosha Libr., 1987-98. U. Wis.-Parkside Benevolent Found., 2000—; mem. mgmt. coun. Lakeview Tech. Acad., 1997-99. Mem. IEEE, Kenosha County Club (bd. dirs.). Office: Sanmina-SCI Corp 8701 100th St Pleasant Prairie WI 53158-2202 Office Phone: 262-947-7700.

**MORROW, BARRY NELSON,** screenwriter, producer; b. Austin, Minn., June 12, 1948; s. Robert Clayton and Rose Nell (Nelson) M.; m. Beverly Lee McKenzie, Mar. 3, 1969; children: Clayton McKenzie, ZoeAnna Rachel. BA, St. Olaf Coll., 1970; DHL (hon.), U. La Verne, Calif., 1990. Media specialist U. Iowa, Iowa City, 1974-81; freelance screenwriter Los Angeles, 1981-90; pres. Morrow-Heus Prodns., 1990-00. Storywriter (TV film) Bill, 1981 (Emmy award 1982); screenwriter: (TV films) Bill: On His Own, 1983, Conspiracy of Love, 1987, Silent Victory, 1988, The Karen Carpenter Story, 1989, (feature film) Rain Man, 1988 (co-recipient Acad. award Best Original Screenplay 1989); screenwriter, exec. prodr.: Christmas on Division Street, 1991; exec. prodr.: Switched at Birth, 1991 (Emmy nomination), Gospa, 1995, The Fifties, 1997, Behind the Mask, 1999; screenwriter, prodr. Race the Sun, 1996; monologist: Bill for Short, 1992. Recipient Pres.'s award Am. Acad. for Devel. Medicine, 1978, Outstanding Contbn. award Mid-Am. Congress on Aging, 1983, SI award NASW, 1991, Pope John XXIII award Viterbo Coll., 1992. Mem. Writers Guild Am. West, Acad. TV Arts and Scis., Acad. Motion Picture Arts and Scis., Motion Picture Screen Cartoonists Guild.

**MORROW, BILL,** state legislator; b. Monterey Park, Calif., Apr. 19, 1954; married; 1 child. BA, U. Calif., L.A., 1976; JD, Pepperdine U., 1979. Commd. officer, mil. judge adv. USMC, 1979-87; civil litig. atty., 1987—; mem. Calif. State Assembly, 1993-98, Calif. State Senate, 1998—, vice chmn. judiciary com., mem. coms. on bus., edn., chmn. vet. Active Spl. Olympics, Boys and Girls Club, Salvation Army. Named Legislator of Yr. Orange County League of Cities., Legislator of Yr. Pro-Life PAC Orange County, 1995, Civil Justice Reform Legislator of Yr. Orange County Citizens Against Lawsuit Abuse, 1996, Legislator of Yr., Calif. Rep. Assembly, 1996, Legislator of Yr. Golden State Mobilehome Owners League Calif., 1997, Small Bus. Legislator of Yr. Calif. Rep. Assembly, 2002, Legislator of Yr. Calif. Rifle and Pistol Assn., 2002. Mem. NRA, Am. Legion, Marine Corps League, Gun Owners Calif., Ducks Unlimited, Calif. Waterfowl Assn., Oceanside C. of C., San Juan C. of C., North County Armed Forces, Amvets, Kiwanis, YMCA. Republican. Protestant. Office: State Capitol Rm 4048 Sacramento CA 95814 also: 27126A Paseo Espada # 1621 San Juan Capistrano CA 92675-2725 also: 2755 Jefferson St Ste 101 Carlsbad CA 92008-1714 E-mail: bill.morrow@assembly.ca.gov.

**MORROW, BRUCE WILLIAM,** academic administrator, management consultant; b. Rochester, Minn., May 20, 1946; s. J. Robert and Frances P. Morrow; m. Jenny Lea Morrow. BA, U. Notre Dame, 1968, MBA in Mgmt. with honors, 1974, MA in Comparative Lit., 1975; grad., U.S. Army Command and Gen. Staff Coll., 1978. Cert. project mgmt. profl. Project Mgmt. Inst., 2003. Chmn. elem. German U. Notre Dame, 1973—75; co-mgr. Wendy's Old Fashioned Hamburgers, South Bend, Ind., 1973-76; adminstrn. mgr. Ea. States Devel. Corp., Richmond, Va., 1977; v.p. JDB Assocs., Inc., Alexandria, Va., 1976—78; sr. cons. Data Base Mgmt., Inc., Springfield, Va., 1979—80; owner Aardvark Prodns., Alexandria, Va., 1980—82; sys. analyst, staff officer Hdqrs., Dept. Army, Washington, 1980—84; chmn. bd. Commonwealth Dominion Corp., Sierra Vista, Ariz., 1982— Strategic planner, dep. comdr. Fort Pickett, Blackstone, Va., 1986—89; dir. continuing edn. Southside Va. C.C., Alberta, 1989—91; co-founder S.W. Bus. Group, Tucson, 1995—99; pres. Sierra Vista Golf, Inc., Ariz., 1994—95; Cochise County team leader Ariz. Coun. Econ. Conversion, 1994—95; mem. com. Ariz. Small Bus. Initiative, 1994—99; internet webmaster, 1996—; exec. dir. Southea. Ariz. Contrs. Assn., 1997—98; corp. adminstr. Garcia Cos., Sierra Vista, Tucson, Phoenix, 1997—99; property adminstr. Brown & Root Svcs., Ft. Huachuca, Ariz., Land Between the Lakes, Ky., 1999—2000, logistics coord., 2000—02; dir. assessment ctr. Transport Security Agy. NCS Pearson, Nashville and Fresno, 2002; project advisor Dyncorp Internat., Irving, Tex., 2004. Author: (radio series) Survival in the Computer Jungle, 1986, (classroom text) Introduction to Computers, 1988, 2d edit., 1993, Defense Conversion Handbook, 1995, Business Assessment Manual, 1996, Employee Manual Guide, 1996, Business Plan Guide, 1996, Marketing Plan Guide, 1996, (screenplay) Gray Rock, 2000; contbg. columnist Notre Dame mag., 1974—86; exec. prodr.: (motion picture) Beneath the Law, 1995—96; composer songs. Active Boy Scouts Am., 1960—69; firefighter Roanoke Wildwood Vol. Fire Dept., 1991—93. Lt. col. USAR, ret. Decorated Bronze Stars, Army commendation medals, Army Achievement medal, Meritorious Svc. medals, Parachutist's badge, Army Gen. Staff badge. Mem. VFW (life), Nat. Eagle Scout Assn., Lake Gaston C. of C. (bd. dirs.), Am. Legion, Sierra Vista Area C. of C., Lions (v.p. local club), Friends Internat. (Am. v.p. 1969-71, Boeblingen, Germany), Order of DeMolay, Beta Gamma Sigma, Delta Phi Alpha. Office: Commonwealth Dominion Corp 334 Landing Strip Rd Hardin KY 42048-9413 E-mail: cdc@theriver.com.

**MORROW, CAROLINE DONOVAN,** retired social worker; b. Houston, Tex., Dec. 11, 1937; d. Ira and Verda Ree Donovan; m. Leonard Emery Morrow, June 17, 1967; children: Emery Donovan, April Antionette. BS, Wiley Coll., 1960; MSW, Atlanta U., 1962. LCSW Colo. Counselor Ansel Rd. Golden Age Ctr., Cleve., 1962—67; vol. counselor Rhine Main AFB, Frankfurt, Germany, 1967—69; adminstr. Job Corp. YWCA, Denver, 1970—75; med. social worker Rose Med. Ctr., Denver, 1976—2003, ret. 2003. Cons. in field. Vol. Village East Elem. Sch., Aurora, Colo., 2002—04; vol. presdl. election Dem Com., Denver, 2004; vol. food bank Mt. Gilead Bapt. Ch., Denver, sec., 1999. Recipient Appreciation cert., USAF, 1978, Wall

Tolerance, 2004, Recognition cert., NAACP, 2004. Mem.: Order Ea. Star, Alpha Kappa Alpha. Democrat. Avocations: reading, writing, puzzles, collecting recipes, decorating. Home: 1358 So Oswego Ct Aurora CO 80012

**MORROW, DONALD L.,** lawyer; b. Inglewood, Calif., Apr. 14, 1951; BA cum laude, U. So. Calif., 1972, JD, 1975. Bar: Calif. 1975. Ptnr. Paul, Hastings, Janofsky & Walker, Costa Mesa, Calif., mem. policy com., chmn. profl. devel. com. Lawyer rep. 9th Cir. Jud. Conf., 1989, 91-92. Dir. Pacific Symphony Orch., 1990-91. Fellow Am. Coll. Trial Lawyers; mem. Orange County Bar Assn. (dir. 1992—), Orange County Bar Found. (pres. 1993, dir. 1990—), Robert A. Banyard Am. Inn of Ct. (master bencher 1987-92). Office: Paul Hastings Janofsky & Walker 17th flr 695 Town Center Dr Costa Mesa CA 92626-1924 Office Phone: 714-668-6291. Office Fax: 714-668-6391. Business E-Mail: donaldmorrow@paulhastings.com.

**MORROW, ELIZABETH HOSTETTER,** sculptor, museum director, farmer, educator; b. Sibley, Mo., Feb. 28, 1947; d. Elman A. and Lorine H. Morrow; married, 1970 (div. 1979); children: Jan Pawel, Lorentz Arthur. Student, William Jewell Coll., 1958-59, Colo. Coll., 1959-60, U. Okla., 1960-62; BFA, U. Kans., 1964, MFA, 1967; postgrad., U. Minn., 1965, U. Kans., 1968. Pres. E. Morrow Co., Kansas City, Mo., 1966-67; head dept. art U. Hawaii, Honolulu, 1968-69, Tarkio (Mo.) Coll., 1970-74; exec. dir. Pensacola (Fla.) Mus. Art, 1974-76; pres., owner Blair-Murrah Exhbns., Sibley, Mo., 1980—. Pres. bd. trustees, CEO Blair-Murrah, Inc., 1991—; sec.-treas. Coun. for Cultural Resources, 1995—. Del. White House Conf. on Small Bus., 1986. Lew Wentz scholar U. Okla., 1960-62. Mem. Internat. Coun. of Mus., Internat. Coun. Exhbn. Exch., Internat. Soc. Appraisers, Am. Assn. Mus., Canadian Assn. Mus., Internat. Trade Club of Greater Kansas City, Nat. Assn. Mus. Exhibitions, Ft. Osage Hist. Soc., Hist. Six MileCemetery Bd., Friends Art, Internat. Com. Fine Arts, Internat. Com. Conservation, Internat. Sculpture Ctr., DAR, UDC, Delta Phi Delta. Independent. Avocations: historical and cultural activities, antique cars, midwest farm auctions, genealogy. Home: RR # 1 Sibley MO 64088 Office: Blair-Murrah Vintage Hill Orch Sibley MO 64088 also: 7 rue Muzy PO Box Nr 554 1211 Geneva Switzerland Office Phone: 816-650-3000.

**MORROW, HUBERT W.,** retired minister, retired theology studies educator, writer, educator; b. Mt. Pleasant, Ark., Nov. 30, 1922; s. James R. and Myrtle Edith (Dawson) Morrow; m. Virginia Sue Williamson, June 21, 1952; children: Mary Sue, David Marvin. BA magna cum laude, Bethel Coll., McKenzie, Tenn., 1944; BD, Vanderbilt U., Nashville, 1948, MA, 1959, PhD, 1965. Pastor Cumberland Presbyn. Ch., Calico Rock, Ark., 1948—49, exec. sec. bd. missions Memphis, 1950—54, pastor Goodlettsville, Tenn., 1955—56; prof. Bethel Coll., McKenzie, Tenn., 1957—74; pastor First Morningside Cumberland Presbyn. Ch., Evansville, Ind., 1975—79; prof. Memphis Theol. Sem, 1981—88; ret., 1988; writer and lectr., 1988—. Moderator, gen. assembly Cumberland Presbyn. Ch., 1956; chmn. Caribbean and N. Am. area World Alliance of Ref. Ch., 1972—73; dean emeritus Memphis Theol. Sem., 1988—. Author: (books) The Holy Spirit Comes, 1974, We Are Empowered by the Spirit, 1990, Covenant of Grace, 1996; contbr. articles to rel. jours. Sec. Rotary Club. Named Founder's medalist, Vanderbilt U. Div. Sch., 1948; fellow faculty, So. Fellowship Fund, 1960. Mem.: Presbyn. Hist. Soc. of S.W. Democrat. Avocations: fishing, gardening, golf.

**MORROW, JAMES FRANKLIN,** lawyer; b. Shenandoah, Iowa, Oct. 23, 1944; s. Warren Ralph and Margaret Glee (Palm) M. BS, Kans. State U., 1967; JD, U. Ariz., 1973. Bar: Ariz. 1973, U.S. Dist. Ct. Ariz. 1973. Ptnr. Bilby, Shoenhair, Warnock & Dolph, Tucson, 1973-83, Quarles & Brady Streich Lang LLP, Tucson, 1984—. Mng. editor U. Ariz. Law Rev., 1972-73. Past chmn. bd. trustees Palo Verde Mental Health Svcs.; past pres. U. Ariz. Alumni Assn.; past chmn. bd. Palo Verde Hosp., Ariz. Tech. Devel. Corp.; past pres. bd. Cath. Cmty. Svcs.; past chmn. bd. dirs. U. Ariz. Found. Capt. U.S. Army, 1967-70. Mem. Am. Coll. Real Estate Lawyers, Am. Coll. Mortgage Attys., State Bar Ariz. (cert. real estate specialist, adv. com. real estate specialists, past chmn. real estate property sect.), Pima County Bar Assn., Calif. Bar Assn. Democrat. Roman Catholic. Avocation: golf. Office: Quarles & Brady Streich Lang LLP Ste 1700 One South Church Ave Tucson AZ 85701

**MORROW, JAMES THOMAS,** energy executive; b. Seattle, Apr. 24, 1941; s. James Elroy and Helen Margaret (Helzer) M.; 1 child, Shannon F. BSEE, BS Gen. Sci., Oreg. State U., 1964; MBA, U. Santa Clara, 1966, PhD, 1973. Registered investment advisor, SEC; profl. engr., Calif. Engr. GE Co., San Jose, Calif., 1964—66; mgr. engring. Beckman Instruments, Inc., Palo Alto, Calif., 1966—69; pres. MSA Cons., Inc., Portland, Oreg., 1969—75; mgr. A.T. Kearney, Inc., San Francisco, 1975—78; v.p. mktg. Pierce Pacific Mfg., Portland, 1978—79; chmn., CEO Lanco Internat., Inc., Clackamas, Oreg., 1979—81; regional mgr., v.p. Case & Co., Portland, 1981—82; chmn. bd., exec. v.p. Morley Fin. Svcs. Inc., 1982—94; chmn., pres., CEO Capital Devel. Group, Inc., Portland, 1994—96; chmn., CEO Apollo Fin. Group, N.Y.C., 1996—98, Olympic Healthcare Tech., Inc., Portland, N.Y.C., 1998—2002; sr. v.p. El Rincon Resort, Cabo San Lucas, Mexico, 2002—03; pres., CEO, dir. Naanovo Energy, Inc., Calgary, Alta., Canada, 2003—; pres., CEO Naanovo Energy USA, Inc., Lincoln City, Oreg., 2003—, Naanovo Internat. Free Zone N.V., Oranjestad, Aruba, 2005—, Naanovo Internat. FZC, Dubai, United Arab Emirates, 2005; mgr. T Squared LLC, Newport, Oreg., 2005—. Chmn. bd. dirs. Ship Harbor Resort and Marina, Inc., 1998-2004, Turtle Cove Resort, Inc., 1998, Olympic Capital, Inc., 1998-2003; bd. dirs. Naanove Energy, Accucom Data Network, Inc., Pierce Pacific Mfg., Lanco Internat., Energy Guard, Inc., G&R Devel. Co., Inc., MSA Cons., Inc.; sec.-treas. Everybody's Record Co., Inc. Contbr. articles to profl. jours., chpts. to textbooks Bd. dirs. Found. for Oreg. Rsch. and Edn., Jr. Achievement, First August Fin., Inc., Met. Youth Symphony; chmn. steering com. R.S. Dow Neurol. Scis. Inst.; mem. Russian ANT-25 Aviation Com. Mem. Oreg. Pilots Assn. (pres. Beaverton chpt.). Republican. Congregationalist. Achievements include patents for waste to energy technology; biojector needleless syringe. Home: 3721 NW Port Ave Lincoln City OR 97367 Office Phone: 971-223-0628. Business E-Mail: tmorrow@naanovo.com.

**MORROW, JASON DREW,** pharmacologist, educator; b. St. Louis, Mar. 30, 1957; s. Ralph Ernest and Vera Rowena (Cummings) M.; m. Lisa Lee Hyman, Mar. 26, 1983; children: Jeremy Nash, Stephanie Rose. BA magna cum laude, Vanderbilt U., 1979; MD, Washington U., St. Louis, 1983. Diplomate Am. Bd. Internal Medicine, Am. Bd. Infectious Diseases. Med. intern, resident Vanderbilt U. Hosp., Nashville, 1983-86, Hugh J. Morgan chief med. resident, 1987-88, rsch. fellow in clin. pharmacology, 1988-91; sr. rsch. fellow dept. pharmacology Vanderbilt U., Sch. Medicine, Nashville, 1991-94, asst. prof. pharmacology and medicine, 1994-95; assoc. prof. Vanderbilt U., Nashville, 1995-99, F. Tremaine Billings prof. medicine, 1999—, dir. Eicosanoid Core Lab. dept. pharmacology, 1992—; clin. fellow in infectious diseases Barnes Hosp./Washington, 1986-87; staff physician in medicine and infectious diseases VA Med. Ctr., Nashville, 1991—; dir. med. scholars program Vanderbilt Med. Sch., 1997—2003, assoc. dean, 2003—03, chief divsn. clin. pharm., 2004—. Mem. internat. adv. com. 9th Internat. Conf. on Prostglandins and Related Compounds, Florence, Italy, 1994, 10th Conf.. Vienna, Austria, 1996; dir. Rsch. Ctr. Pharm. and Drug Toxicology, Vanderbilt Med. Sch., 1999—. Contbr. over 450 articles, revs. and papers to sci. jours., chpts. to books; mem. editl. bd. numerous sci. and med. jours. Physician Nashville Union Rescue Mission, 1988-00. Recipient Physician-Scientist award NIH, 1990-91, grantee; recipient Rsch. Found. Devel. award Internat. Life Scis. Inst., 1992-96, Centennial Clin. Pharmacology fellow Boehringer-Ingelheim, 1990-91, Howard Hughes Med. Inst. Physician rsch. fellow, 1991-94; grantee Liddle Med. Rsch., 1996, Stanley Cohen Rsch. award, 2006, Stanley Cohen Med. Rsch. award Vanderbilt U., 2006. Mem. AMA, ACP, AAAS, Am. Fedn. Clin. Rsch., Am. Soc. Clin. Investigation, So. Soc. Clin. Investigation, Soc. Free Radiol. Biol. MEdicine (bd. dirs., Discovery award 2006), Infectious Diseases Soc. Am., Am. Fed. Med. Rsch., Am. Soc. Pharmacology Exptl. Therapeutics, Am. Soc. Biochemistry and

Molecular Biology, Phi Beta Kappa. Avocations: running, fishing, outdoors. Home: 6408 Eastbourne Dr Brentwood TN 37027-4802 Office: Vanderbilt U Dept Clin PHarmacology 532 RRB 23d and Pierce Nashville TN 37232-6602 Office Phone: 615-322-4785. E-mail: jason.morrow@vanderbilt.edu.

**MORROW, JENNIFER LEIGH See LEIGH, JENNIFER**

**MORROW, JOHN E.,** lawyer; b. L.A., Mar. 17, 1943; s. Charles Henry and Lillian (Harmon) M.; m. Sue C. Taylor, June 28, 1989. BS, U. Southern Calif., 1965; JD, U. Chgo., 1968; postgrad., U. Munich, 1969. Bar: Calif. 1969, Ill. 1971. Law clk. to judge U.S. Dist. Ct. (cen. dist.) Calif., 1969-70; ptnr. Baker & McKenzie, Chgo., 1970-73, 75-76, 83—, Zurich, Switzerland, 1974-75, Hong Kong, 1976-82. Mem. ABA (subcom. on internat. bus. law com. corp. sect.). Office: Baker & McKenzie One Prudential Plz 130 E Randolph St Fl 32 Chicago IL 60601-6207 E-mail: john.e.morrow@bakernet.com.

**MORROW, LANCE,** journalist, educator, writer; b. Phila., Sept. 21, 1939; s. Hugh M. and Elise Vickers; m. Susan Brind, Oct. 29, 1988; children: James Michael, Justin Thomas. BA, Harvard U., 1963. Reporter Washington Star, 1964-65; writer, essayist Time Mag., N.Y.C., 1965—; univ. prof. Boston U., 1996—. Mem. usage panel Am. Heritage Dictionary. Author: The Chief, 1984, Fishing in the Tiber, 1988, America, A Rediscovery, 1989, Safari, 1992, Heart, 1995, Evil, 2003, The Best Year of Their Lives: Kennedy, Johnson, and Nixon in 1948, 2005. Recipient Nat. Mag. award Columbia U., 1981, 01. Mem. Harvard Club (N.Y., Boston). Office: Time Time-Life Bldg Rockefeller Plz New York NY 10020-2002 E-mail: lmorrow1@aol.com.

**MORROW, MONICA,** medical educator; b. Abington, Pa., Sept. 16, 1953; d. James Robert and Maxine Cooper Morrow; m. Virgil Craig Jordan, OBE, PhD, DSc. BS magna cum laude, Pa. State U., 1974; MD, Jefferson Med. Coll., 1976. Diplomate Am. Bd. of Surgery. Fellow in surg. oncology Meml. Sloan Kettering Cancer Ctr., New York, NY, 1981—83; asst. prof. of surgery SUNY Health Sci. Ctr. at Bklyn, Brooklyn, NY, 1983—88; assoc. prof. of surgery U. of Chgo., Chicago, Ill., 1988—93, Northwestern U., Chicago, Ill., 1993—97, prof. of surgery, 1997—2004; chmn. dept. surgical oncology and G. Willing Pepper chair cancer rsch. Fox Chase Cancer Ctr., Phila., 2004—. Dir., cancer dept. ACS, Chgo., 1999—2001; exec. dir. Am. Joint Com. on Cancer, Chgo., 1999—2001; mem. Nat. Cancer Policy Bd., Inst. of Medicine, Washington, 1999—2002; co-chair Joint Com. of the ACS, Am. Coll. of Radiology, and Coll. of Am. Pathologists on Standards for Breast Conservation, 2000—02, 2005. Editor: (book) Managing Breast Cancer Risk, American Joint Committee on Cancer Staging Manual, sixth edition, Diseases of the Breast, Breast Diseases: A Problem Based Approach. Named Distingushed Alumni, Pa. State U., 2002; Co-Principal Investigator, Specialized Program Rsch. Excellence in Breast Cancer grantee, Nat. Cancer Inst., 2000—05, Avon Found. Ctr. Excellence grantee prin. investigator, 2000—06. Fellow: Royal Coll. Physicians and Surgeons Glasgow (hon.); mem.: Am. Surg. Assn., Am. Soc. Clin. Oncology (bd. dirs. 1998—2001), Soc. Surg. Oncology (exec. com. 1993—96, 2003—06). Avocations: travel, history, wine. Office: Fox Chase Cancer Ctr 333 Cottman Ave Philadelphia PA 19111-2497 Office Phone: 215-728-3096.

**MORROW, NANA KWASI SCOTT DOUGLAS,** choreographer, director, writer, filmmaker, educator; b. NYC, Jan. 29, 1954; s. Alfredo and Lorraine (Lopez) Morro. BFA in Dance, SUNY, Purchase, 1976; MA in Choreography, UCLA, 1986. Ordained interfaith min. 2004. Prin. instr. Phil Black Dance Studio, N.Y.C., 1969—77; dir. dance divsn. No. Ill. U., DeKalb, 1976—78; artistic dir., resident choreographer No. Ill. Repertory Dance Co., 1976—78; artistic dir. Scott Morrow Dance Theatre Co. and Sch., L.A., 1978—85; prin. instr. Mary Tyler Moore Los Angeles Dance Ctr., 1979—80; resident dance master South Coast Repertory Acting Conservatory, Calif., 1979—82; vis. prof. Wright State U., Ohio, 1981; ballet master, resident choreographer Empire State Ballet, Buffalo, 1984—85; asst. prof. U. Kans., Lawrence, 1985—88. Choreographer Morrow Dance Theatre-in-Residence, U. Kans., 1985-88, 92d St. Dancer Ctr., YMHA and YWHA, NYC, 1989, Morrow Dance Theater Co., Sch. and Summer Inst., NYC, 1990-2002; founder, dir. Jazz Dance Ministry for Racial Reconciliation, Peace and Healing, N.Y.C., 1988—; assoc. dir., edn. pub. sch. dance programs K-12, Bronx Dance Theatre Performing Arts Ctr., NYC, 1990-93; faculty Internat. Summer Sch. Royal Acad. Dancing, NYC, 1991-92, Calif. State U. Sys. Summer Inst. for Tchg. and Learning, 1994; sr. faculty Lilly Conf. on Coll. Tchg., Miami U., Ohio, 1991-2001; dance specialist State Edn. Dept. Summer Inst. on Assessment in Arts, NY, 1992; founder, dir. in chief Inst. Advancement Edn. Dance, NYC, 1992-02; adv. bd. Internat. Found. for Performing Arts Medicine, 1992—; adv. Performing Arts Medicine Ctr., Kessler Inst. Rehab., NJ, 1995—; Walter H. Annenberg disting. vis. artist-scholar The Renaissance Sch., NYC, 1995-96; cons. presenting and commissioning program Nat. Endowment for Arts, 1993-95; peer rev. panel Fund for Innovation in Edn. US. Edn. Dept., 1993-94; co-chmn. dance edn. com. World Dance Alliance: Americas Ctr., 1993-97; internat. artistic advisor Noyam Exptl. Dance Co. and Rsch. Project, Ghana, 1998—; founder, min. in chief Embassy of Sekyere Kwaming Traditional Area, Asante Nation, Ghana to the U.S.A., 1998—; internat. adv. bd. Ctr. for Nat. Culture, Kumasi, Asante Nation, Ghana, 2001—; co-founder and co-pastor Of One Blood Ministries, N.Y.C., 2004—. Choreographer: (mus. theater) Broadway Musical Classics on International Tour, (musical stage rev) Bebop Hot! Celebrating the Music of Dizzy Gillespie & Charlie Parker, (vaudeville revue) Horn & Hardart Mid-Broadway Cafeteria, NYC; (film musical) Chestnuts, Rainbows Edn.; (documentary film) Broadway Babies: Long Forgotten Performers of the Vaudeville Era, (teleseries) Adventures of Hans Christian Andersen, (telespecial) Rapsodia Afrikiko: A Celebration in Dance, (indsl. show) Le Parfum Salvador Dali, (nightclub) The African Room, NYC; (fashion show) Abraham & Straus, NYC; choreographer, asst. Broadway musical Safari 300: A Musical Experience of 300 Years of Black Culture, Song & Dance, NYC; film dir., editor Of One Blood: Returning Home to Africa, 1999 (Best Documentary Film award Black Internat. Cinema Festival); co-author, dir., choreographer, co-star (nat. stage prodn.) Realizing the Dream: Celebrating the Enduring Spirit of Rev. Dr. Martin Luther King Jr.; world premieres presented at festivals including Morningside Dance Festival, NYC, Mid Am. Dance Festival, L.A. Dance Kaleidoscope Festival, Middfest Internat., Ohio, Smithsonian Instn's Duke Ellington Festival, Washington, Marche Internat. de Disque et de l'Edition Musicale, Cannes, France, Anokyekrome Festival, Kumasi, Asante Nation, Ghana, Royal Performance King Nana Barimah Abeyie Ntori Nimpah II, Sekyere Kwamang, Asante Nation, Ghana, Black Internat. Cinema Festival, Berlin; creator over 40 ballets; contbr. to profl. publs. including African Profiles USA Mag., African Personality Mag., African Press. Nat. Festival for the Performing Arts Choreographers fellow, 1989; Josephine & Randolph Stewart African Heritage Fund Edn. and Rsch. grantee, 1997; named Master Educator and Disting. Fellow, Am. Bd. Master Educators, 1987; Alvin Ailey scholar, Sch. Am. Ballet scholar, Harkness House for Ballet Arts scholar; recipient Grand Prize for Choreography, Ann. Internat. Artistic Impression Competition, 1991, citation U.S. Edn. Dept., 1993, Contbns. to Growth and Advancement of Performing Arts award U.S. Arts Coun. Co-op, 1993; named Traditional Chief and Spl. Advisor in Edn. and Human Devel. to King, Sekyere Kwamang, Asante Nation, Ghana, 1997, Pan-African and Humanitarian Vision award African Profiles USA mag., 2001. Office: Embassy Sekyere Kwamang Trad Area Asante Nation Ghana to US The Belvedere 84-12 35th Ave Jackson Heights NY 11372 E-mail: nanasmorrow@hotmail.com.

**MORROW, RICHARD MARTIN,** retired oil company executive; b. Wheeling, W.Va., Feb. 27, 1926; B.M.E., Ohio State U., 1948. With Amoco Corp., 1948-91; v.p. Amoco Prodn. Co., 1964-66; exec. v.p. Amoco Internat. Oil Co., 1966-70, Amoco Chem. Corp., 1970-74, pres., 1974-78, Amoco Corp., 1978-83, chmn. chief exec. officer, 1983-91; ret. 1991. Trustee U. Chgo. and Rush U. Med. Ctr. Office: 200 E Randolph Dr Ste 6952 Chicago IL 60601-7704

**MORROW, ROB,** actor; b. New Rochelle, NY, Sept. 21, 1962; s. Murray and Diane Francis (Markowitz) M; m. Debbon Ayer, 1988; 1 child. Mem. Ensemble Studio Theatre. Actor (TV series) Tattingers, 1988, Northern Exposure, 1990-94 (Lead Actor in TV Drama Emmy award nominee 1991, 92, 93, Lead Actor in TV Drama Golden Globe nominee 1991, 92, 93), Nearly Yours, 1999, Street Time, 2002-03, Numb3rs, 2005-, (TV films) The Day Lincoln Was Shot, 1998, Only Love, 1998, The Thin Blue Lie, 2000, Jenifer, 2001, (films) Private Resort, 1985, Quiz Show, 1994, Last Dance, 1996, Mother, 1996, Into My Heart, 1998, Other Voices, 2000, Maze, 2000, Sam the Man, 2000, Labor Pains, 2000, The Guru, 2002, The Emperor's Club, 2002, Night's Noontime, 2002, Going Shopping, 2004; dir. (TV series) Oz, 2002, Street Time, 2003, Joan of Arcadia, 2004, (TV films) The Silent Alarm, 1993, (films) Maze, 2000; Stage appearances include Escape from Riverdale, 1984, The Return of Pinnochio, 1988, The Chosen, 1987-88, The Substance of Fire, 1990. Bd. dirs. Project ALS. Mem. Naked Angels (co-founder). Jewish.

**MORROW, SANDRA KAY,** librarian; b. Levelland, Tex., Jan. 6, 1944; d. Oran Eiland and Martha Jane Johnson; m. Troy Leon Morrow; children: Paul, Kile. AA, Lubbock Christian U., 1964; BS in Edn., Abilene Christian U., 1966. Cert. libr. sci. U. Tex., 1973. Tchr. Andrews Sch. Dist., Andrews, Tex., 1966—68, New Deal Sch. Dist., New Deal, Tex., 1970—71, Ector County Sch., Odessa, Tex., 1971—72; libr. Austin Sch. Dist., Austin, Tex., 1974—77; tchr. Brentwood Christian Sch., Austin, 1984—. Originator Christian Librarians' Conf., Searcy, Ark., 1996—2003; presenter in field; dir. Yearly Booklist for primary, intermediate and Jr. H.S., 1992—. Creator Children's Crown award, 1992, Lamplighter award, 1996, Children's Crown Gallery award, 2000; ministry leader Westover Hills Ch. of Christ, Austin, 1977—2002, nursery dir., 1975—85. Recipient Disting. Alumni award, Lubbock Christian U., 2002, Abilene Christian U., 2005—. Mem.: Nat. Christian Sch. Assn. (awards dir. 1996—, Christian Educator of Yr. award 2001), Tex. Christian Schools Assn. (Tchr. of Yr. award 2001), Tex. Libr. Assn. Republican. Mem.Church Of Christ. Avocations: reading, gardening, jogging, music. Home: 8308 Grayledge Drive Austin TX 78753 Office: National Christian School Association 11908 North Lamar Boulevard Austin TX 78753 Business E-Mail: smorrow@brentwoodchristian.org.

**MORROW, WALTER EDWIN, JR.,** electrical engineer, lab administrator; b. Springfield, Mass., July 24, 1928; s. Walter Edwin and Mary Elizabeth (Ganley) M.; m. Janice Lila Lombard, Feb. 25, 1951; children: Clifford E., Gregory A., Carolyn F. S.B., M.I.T., 1949, S.M., 1951. Mem. staff Lincoln Lab., MIT, Lexington, Mass., 1951-55, group leader, 1956-65; head div. communications MIT Lincoln Lab., 1966-68, asst. dir., 1968-71, assoc. dir., 1972-77, dir., 1977-98, dir. emeritus, 1998—. Contbr. articles to profl. publs. Recipient award for outstanding achievement Pres. M.I.T., 1963, Edwin Howard Armstrong Achievement award IEEE Communications Soc., 1976 Fellow IEEE, Nat. Acad. Engring. Achievements include patent for synchronous satellite, electric power plant using electrolytic cell-fuel cell combination. Office: MIT Lincoln Lab PO Box 73 Lexington MA 02420-9108

**MORROW, WILLIAM CLARENCE,** judge, lawyer, arbitrator; b. Austin, Tex., Aug. 9, 1935; s. Theodore Faulkner and Gladys Lee (Ames) M.; m. Sheila Beth Pfost, June 29, 1973; children: Scott Fitzgerald Morrow, Elizabeth Ann Rettig, Shana Lynn Peterson. BA, Baylor U., 1957; JD, So. Meth. U., 1962. Bar: Tex. 1962. Trial atty. SEC, Ft. Worth, 1963-65; former ptnr. Cotton, Bledsoe, Tighe, Morrow & Dawson, Lynch, Chappell and Alsup; v.p. Magnatex Corp., Midland, 1980-86; v.p., gen. counsel, sec. Elcor Corp., Midland, 1986-88; county judge Midland County, Tex., 1999—. Mem. Tex. Jail Standards Commn., Austin, Tex., 2002—. Mem. Midland City Coun., 1992-95, Tex. Jail Commn., 2002-, mayor pro tem, 1994-95; former vice chmn. Tex. Rehab. Commn.; pres. Found. Mental Health and Mental Retardation Permian Basin; pres. United Way of Midland, 1985, Indsl. Found. Midland, 1987; trustee Midland Cmty. Theatre, 1980—, chmn., 1995-96; elder First Presbyn. Ch., Midland. Mem. Coll. of State Bar Tex., Tex. Bar Assn., Midland County Bar Assn., Tex. Coll. of Probate Judges, Phi Delta Phi. Home: 3110 Gulf Ave Midland TX 79705-8205 Office: 200 W Wall Ste 006 Midland TX 79701-4512

**MORROW, WILLIAM EARL,** retired government official, retired law educator; b. Perryopolis, Pa., Oct. 22, 1923; s. Robert Ferguson and Daisy (Johnson) M.; m. Danna Katunaric, Apr. 26, 1958; children: Jamie Johnson, Tammara Marie, Kim Ina, William Joseph, Geoffrey Sean. BS in Psychology, Waynesburg Coll., 1948; MA, U. Pitts., 1953; LLD (hon.), U. Zagreb, 1958; postgrad., U. Md., 1969, Indsl. Coll. Armed Forces, 1969-70. With Survey Rsch. Ct. U. Mich., 1947; auditor, employment interviewer, then asst. dir. pers. Jones & Laughlin Steel Corp., 1944-54; exec. coord. Peoples Cab Co., 1954; labor-mgmt. adviser, policy coord. Arabian Am. Oil Co., Saudi Arabia, 1954—57; pers. expert UN/ILO, Switzerland, Yugoslavia, Zagreb, 1957—58; cons., 1958—59; ing./program officer AID U.S. Dept. State, 1959—65; adminstrv. officer Bur. Internat. Labor Affairs U.S. Labor Dept., 1965—68; dep. division. chief Bur. Internat. Labor Affairs Labor Dept., 1968—72, projects dir. L.Am., Caribbean, 1973—80; asst. dir. Office Fgn. Rels., 1980—86; exec. sec. Employee Retirement Income Security Act Office of Sec. Labor U.S. Dept. Labor, 1986—95; ret., 1995. Guest prof. U. Coll. W.I., 1960-64; lectr. Prince George's Community Coll., 1965-97; lectr. U. Md., 1967-97; adj. prof. U. Md., 1997-2003. Mem. Tantallon (Md.) Citizens Assn. With USAF, 1942-44. Mem. Indsl. Rels. Rsch. Assn., Prince George's County Bd. Realtors, Am. Fedn. Govt. Employees, Am. Soc. Tng. Dirs., Am. Legion, D.A.V., Masons, Scottish Rite, Shriners, U. Md. Faculty Club, Dominion Valley Golf and Country Club, Tantallon-On-The-Potomac Golf and Country Club, Psi Chi Iota, Phi Alpha Theta, Delta Sigma Phi. Methodist. Home (Winter): Village Walk on Palmer Ranch 8308 Jesolo Ln Sarasota FL 34238 Home (Summer): Dominion Valley Golf and Country Club 5726 Wheelwright Way Haymarket VA 20169 Personal E-mail: willmorrow@aol.com

**MORROW, WINIFRED BRYANT,** artist, educator; b. Duluth, Ga., Oct. 27, 1946; d. Frank Winfred and Lucy Virginia (Dillard) Bryant; m. James David Williams, July 24, 1966 (div. Dec. 1974); m. Richard Lewis Morrow, Aug. 10, 1991; 1 stepchild, Charles Richard. Student, Young Harris (Ga.) Coll., 1964-65; BFA, U. Ga., 1969, postgrad., 1977, 78; MEd, West Ga. Coll., Carrollton, 1976; edn. specialist degree, Berry Coll., 1999. Cert. tchr. Ga. Tchr. art Haralson County Bd. Edn., Buchanan, Ga., 1969-72; tchr. art, sci. and phys. edn. Floyd County Bd. Edn., Cave Spring, Ga., 1972-78, tchr. art Coosa, Ga., 1978-84, Lindale, Ga., 1984-89, Bartow County Bd. Edn., Cartersville, Ga., 1989-99; ret., 1999. Co-founder, trustee Alton Holman Heritage Arts, Inc., Cave Spring, 2004—. Watercolor artist. Chair investigating com. State Sch. for Arts, Cave Spring, 1987; bd. dir. Cave Spring Hist. Soc., 1975—96, 2002—, chmn., 1975—85, arts festival juror, 1976—97, arts festival judges coord., 1985—, arts festival coord., 1987, 1988; CEO Cave Spring Area History Mus., 2004—; pianist Cave Spring United Meth. Ch., 1975—97, trustee, 1993—, choir mem., 1997—2003. Mem.: NEA, Rome Area Coun. Arts, Ga. Art Edn. Assn., Ga. Assn. Educators, Nat. Art Edn. Assn., Ga. Ret. Tchrs. Assn., NEA Ret. Tchrs. Assn. Avocations: copper enameling, piano, poetry, dulcimer. Home: 7385 Rome Rd Cave Spring GA 30124 Office: Alton Homan Heritage Arts Inc 30 Alabama St PO Box 390 Cave Spring GA 30124

**MORROW, WINSTON VAUGHAN,** financial executive; b. Grand Rapids, Mich., Mar. 22, 1924; s. Winston V. and Selma (von Egloffstein) M.; m. Margaret Ellen Staples, June 25, 1948 (div.); children: Thomas Christopher, Mark Staples; m. Edith Burrows Ulrich, Mar. 2, 1990. AB cum laude, Williams Coll., 1947; JD, Harvard U., 1950. Bar: R.I. 1950, U.S. Dist. Ct., U.S. Supreme Ct. Assoc. atty. Edwards & Angell, Providence, 1950-57; exec. v.p., asst. treas., gen. counsel, bd. dirs. Avis, Inc. and subs., 1957-61; v.p., gen. mgr. Rent A Car div. Avis, Inc., 1962-64, pres., bd. dirs. 1974-75; chmn., chief exec. officer, bd. dirs. Avis, Inc. and Avis Rent A Car System, Inc., 1965-77; chmn., pres., bd. dirs. Teleflorists Inc. and subs., 1978-80; pres. Westwood Equities Corp., L.A., 1981-95, CEO, 1984-95, also bd. dirs.; chmn., pres., chief exec. officer Ticor Title Ins. Co., 1982-91, also bd. dirs.; chmn. TRTS Data Svcs. Inc., 1985-91; bd. dirs. AECOM Tech. Corp., L.A., 1990-99. Mem. Pres.'s Industry and Govt. Spl. Travel Task Force, 1968,

travel adv. bd. U.S. Travel Svcs., 1968-76, L.A. City-wide Airport Adv. Com., 1983-85; co-chmn. L.A. Transp. Coalition, 1985-91. Mem. juvenile delinquency task force Nat. Coun. Crime and Delinquency, 1985-86, L.A. Mayor's Bus. Coun., 1983-86, Housing Roundtable, Washington, 1983-85, Calif. Bus. Roundtable, 1985-90; chmn., pres. Spring St. Found., 1991—; bd. dirs. Police Found., Washington, 1983-91; trustee Com. for Econ. Devel., Washington, 1987-91; trustee Adelphi U., 1970-75. Decorated Stella Della Solidarieta Italy, Gold Tourism medal Austria. Fellow The Huntington; mem. R.I. Bar Assn., Car and Truck Rental Leasing Assn. (nat. pres. 1961-63), Am. Land Title Assn. (bd. govs. 1989-90), L.A. Area C. of C. (bd. dirs. 1983-90), Calif. Club, Williams Club, L.A. Tennis Club, Phi Beta Kappa, Kappa Alpha. Home: 4056 Farmouth Dr Los Angeles CA 90047-1314 also: Meadowview Farm 286 Cushing Corner Rd Freedom NH 03836-0221 Personal E-mail: wvm4291@aol.com.

**MORSCH, THOMAS HARVEY,** law educator, lawyer; b. Oak Park, Ill., Sept. 5, 1931; s. Harvey William and Gwenodyne (Maun) M.; m. Jacquelyn Casey, Dec. 27, 1954; children: Thomas H. Jr., Margaret, Mary Susan, James, Kathryn, Julia. BA, Notre Dame U., 1953; BSL, Northwestern U., 1953, JD, 1955. Bar: Ill. 1955, D.C. 1955. Assoc. Crowell & Leibman, Chgo., 1955-62; ptnr. Leibman, Williams, Bennett, Baird & Minow, Chgo., 1962-72, Sidley & Austin, Chgo., 1972-97, counsel, 1998-2000. Bd. dirs. Chgo. Lawyers Com. for Civil Rights Under Law, chmn., 1982-83; bd. dirs. Pub. Interest Law Initiative, pres., 1993-95; No. Dist. Ill. Civil Justice Reform Com., 1991-95, Ill. Equal Justice Commn., 1999—2003; mem. vis. com. Law Sch. Northwestern U., 1989-90, dir. Small Bus. Opportunity Ctr., 1998—, assoc. clin. prof., 1998-2003, clin. prof., 2003—; mem. adv. bd. Kellogg Ctr. for Nonprofit Mgmt., 2001—. Pres. Republican Workshops of Ill., 1970; gen. counsel Ill. Com. to Re-elect the Pres., 1972; mem. LaGrange Plan Commn., Ill., 1972-80, LaGrange Fire and Police Commn., 1968-72; trustee LaGrange Meml. Hosp., 1983-89; mem. adv. bd. Cath. Charities of Chgo., 1985—. Fellow Am. Coll. Trial Lawyers; mem. Ill. State Bar Assn., Chgo. Bar Assn. (bd. mgrs. 1979-81), DC Bar, 7th Cir. Bar Assn., Northwestern Law Sch. Alumni Assn. (pres. 1988-89), Chgo. Bar Found. (bd. dirs., pres. 1995-97), Univ. Club (Chgo.), LaGrange Country Club, Palisades Park Country Club (Mich.), Point O'Woods Country Club (Mich.). Roman Catholic. Home: 301 S Edgewood Ave La Grange IL 60525-2153 Office: Northwestern U Sch Law 357 E Chicago Ave Chicago IL 60611 E-mail: tmorsch@law.northwestern.edu.

**MORSE, ABRAHAM NICHOLAS,** obstetrician, gynecologist, educator; b. 1965; BA, Swarthmore Coll., 1988; MD, Harvard U., Cambridge, Mass., 1993. Diplomate Am. Bd. Ob-Gyn., 2001. Intern and resident Johns Hopkins Hosp., Balt., 1993—97; fellow in urogynecology Mayo Clinic, Scottsdale, Ariz., 1997—2000; asst. prof. ob-gyn. Med. Sch. U. Mass. Meml. Med. Ctr., Worcester, 2000—. Dir. female pelvic medicine and reconstructive surgery fellowship Med. Sch. U. Mass. Fellow: Am. Coll. Ob-Gyn.; mem.: Am. Urogynecologic Soc. Office: U Mass Meml Health Care Dept Ob Gyn 119 Belmont St Worcester MA 01605 Office Phone: 508-334-8454. Business E-Mail: morsea@ummhc.org.

**MORSE, EDWARD LEWIS,** petroleum industry executive; b. NYC, Jan. 5, 1942; s. Jonah Benjamin and Rebecca (Freiberg) M.; m. Linda Kasle Jones, Aug. 15, 1965; children: Michael Ari, Molly Rachel. BA, Johns Hopkins U., Balt., 1963; MA, Johns Hopkins U., Washington, 1966; PhD, Princeton U., 1969. Asst. prof. internat. politics Woodrow Wilson Sch. Princeton (N.J.) U., 1969-75; sr. rsch. fellow Coun. on Fgn. Rels., N.Y.C., 1975-78; exec. asst. to undersec. econ. affairs U.S. Dept. State, Washington, 1978-79; dep. asst. sec. for internat. energy policy, 1979-81; dir. internat. affairs Phillips Petroleum Co., Bartlesville, Okla., 1981-84; mng. dir. Petroleum Fin. Co., Ltd., Washington, 1984-96; pres., publisher Petroleum Intelligence Weekly, N.Y.C., 1988-99, The Oil Daily Co., N.Y.C., 1996-99; exec. Hess Energy Trading Co., N.Y.C., 1999—. Author: Foreign Policy and Interdependence in Gaullist France, 1973, Modernization and the Transformation of International Relations, 1976; contbr. articles to various publs. Office: HETCO 1185 Avenue Of The Americas New York NY 10036-2601 E-mail: elmorse@hess.com, edmorse@aol.com.

**MORSE, JOHN B., JR.,** corporate financial executive; From product dir. to chmn., CEO Johnson & Johnson, 1953—89; ptnr. Price Waterhouse, 1972; v.p., CFO Washington Post Co., Washington, 1989—, v.p., contr., 1989—. Mem.: AICPA, Inst. Newspaper Fin. Execs. Office: Washington Post Co 1150 15th St NW Washington DC 20071

**MORSE, JOSEPH GRANT,** chemistry educator; b. Colorado Springs, Colo., Oct. 16, 1939; s. Grant Addison and Faris Ellen (Winninger) M.; m. Karen Dale Williams, Apr. 6, 1963; children: Robert Grant, Geoffrey Easton. BS, S.D. State Coll., 1961; MS in Chemistry, U. Mich., 1963, PhD, 1966. Instr. U. Mich., Ann Arbor, 1965-66; asst. prof. Utah State U., Logan, 1968-74, assoc. prof., 1974-82, prof. Western Wash. U., Bellingham, 1993-2000, dir. sci. edn., 1996-2000. Councilman Cache County, Utah. Capt. U.S. Army, 1966-68. Fellow AAAS; mem. Am. Chem. Soc. Office: Western Wash U Chemistry Dept Bellingham WA 98225 E-mail: mjkaren@qwest.net.

**MORSE, KAREN WILLIAMS,** academic administrator; b. Monroe, Mich., May 8, 1940; m. Joseph G. Morse; children: Robert G., Geoffrey E. BS, Denison U., 1962; MS, U. Mich., 1964, PhD, 1967; DSc (hon.), Denison U., 1990. Rsch. chemist Ballistic Rsch. Lab., Aberdeen Proving Ground, Md., 1966-68; lectr. chemistry dept. Utah State U., Logan, 1968-69, from asst. to assoc. prof. chemistry, 1969-83, prof. chemistry dept., 1983-93, dept. head Coll. Sci., 1981-88, dean Coll. Sci., 1988-89, univ. provost, 1989-93; pres. Western Wash. U., Bellingham, 1993—. Mem., chair Grad. Record Exam in chemistry com., Princeton, N.J., 1980-89, Gov.'s Sci. Coun., Salt Lake City, 1986-93, Gov.'s Coun. on Fusion, 1989-91, ACS Com. on Profl. Tng., 1984-92; cons. 1993; nat. ChemLinks adv. com. NSF, 1995; bd. advisor's orgn. com. 2008 summer Olympic Games, Seattle, 1995; faculty Am. Assn. State Colls. and Univs. Pres.'s Acad., 1995, 96; chair Wash. Coun. of Pres., 1995-96; bd. dirs. Whatcom State Bank; NCAA Divsn. II Pres.'s Coun., 1999—, CHEA bd., 2000—; Nat. Rsch. Coun. Chem. Svcs. Roundtable, 1999—. Contbr. articles to profl. jours. Mem. Cache County Sch. Dist. Found., Cache Valley, Logan, 1988-93; swim coach, soccer coach; trustee First United Presbyn. Ch., Logan, 1979-81, 82-85; adv. bd. Sci. Discovery Ctr., Logan, 1993, KCTS-TV, Bellingham, 1996—, Seattle Opera Bd., 1999—; mem. bd. dirs. United Way, Whatcom County, 1993—; exec. com. Bellingham-Whatcom Econ. Devel. Com., 1993—. Recipient Disting. Alumni in Residence award U. Mich., 1989, Francis P. Garvan and John M. Olin medal, 1997. Fellow AAAS; mem. Am. Chem. Soc. (Utah award Salt Lake City and Cen. dists. 1988, Garvan-Olin medal 1997), Am. Assn. State Colls. and Univs. (mem. policy and purposes com. 1995, chair 1996), Bus. and Profl. Women Club (pres. 1984-85), Philanthropic Edn. Orgn., Phi Beta Kappa, Sigma Xi, Phi Beta Kappa Assocs., Phi Kappa Phi, Beta Gamma Sigma. Avocations: skiing, bicycling, photography. Office: Office of the Pres Western Washington U 516 High St Old Main 450 MS 9000 Bellingham WA 98225-5946

**MORSE, LARRY EUGENE,** botanist, conservationist; b. Dayton, Ohio, Nov. 15, 1947; s. Carson Clark and Dorothy Virginia (Clum) Morse. BS, Mich. State U., East Lansing, 1970; AM, Harvard U., Cambridge, Mass., 1971, PhD, 1979. Staff botanist Dayton Mus. of Natural History, Ohio, 1966—69; rsch. asst. Smithsonian Instn., Washington, 1971—72, N.Y. Bot. Garden, Bronx, 1976—73; chief botanist The Nature Conservancy, Arlington, Va., 1979—2000; N.Am. botanist NatureServe, Arlington, Va., 2001—06; ind. cons. L.E.M. Natural Diversity, 2006—. Founder, convener Plant Conservation Roundtable, Washington, 1981—88. Author: Computer Programs for Specimen Identification; co-editor: Rare Plant Conservation: Geographical Data Organization; contbr. chapters to books, articles to profl. jours. Fellow, NSF, 1970, Woodrow Wilson Fellowship Found., 1970. Mem.: New Eng. Bot. Club, Mich. Bot. Club, Bot. Soc. Washington (pres. 1985—86, mem. centennial symposium com. 2001, chair field trip com. 2006—), Ottawa Field-Naturalists' Club (life), So. Appalachian Bot. Soc. (life), Internat. Assn.

for Plant Taxonomy (life). Achievements include development of a methodology for plant specimen identification with computers, a methodology for conservation status ranking, guidelines for conservation status reports, a methodology for invasiveness assessment of non-native plants; design of central scientific databases. Avocations: nature photography, paleontology, stamp collecting/philately, contra dancing. Home: 1306 Corbin Pl NE Washington DC 20002 Office: LEM Natral Diversity PO Box 77157 Washington DC 20013 Business E-Mail: larry.e.morse@lem-natural-diversity.com.

**MORSE, LEONARD J.,** epidemiologist, public health service officer; MD, U. Md., 1955. Intern infectious diseases U. Md. Med. Sys., resident infectious diseases; fellow internal medicine New Eng. Med. Care Hosps.; pvt. practice Worcester, Mass.; ret., 1996; med. dir. New Bedford Cmty. Health Ctr., 1996—2001; prof. clin. medicine, family medicine, cmty. health U. Mass. Med. Sch., Worcester; pub. health commr. Worcester, 2001—. Mem.: AMA Found. (immediate past chair Coun. Ethical and Jud. Affairs, Pride in Profession award 2004), Am. Soc. History Medicine, Am. Med. Writers Assn., Am. Soc. Microbiology, Infectious Diseases Soc. Am., Am. Soc. Internal Medicine, Mass. Med. Soc. (pres. 1993—94, past chmn. Com. Ethics and Discipline, Lifetime Achievement award 1997, Grant V. Rodkey award 1997), Am. Coll. Physicians (Named Internist of Yr. Mass. chpt. 1998). Office: Worcester Pub Health 25 Meade St Worcester MA 01610 Office Phone: 508-799-8533. Business E-Mail: lmorsemd@massmed.org.*

**MORSE, M. HOWARD,** lawyer; b. Louisville, May 30, 1959; s. Marvin Henry and Betty Anne (Hess) M.; m. Laura E. Lean, Apr. 17, 1988; children: Elizabeth L., Marni L. AB summa cum laude, Dartmouth Coll., 1981; JD cum laude, Harvard U., 1984. Bar: D.C. 1984, U.S. Ct. of Internat. Trade 1985, U.S. Ct. Appeals (fed. cir.) 1985, U.S. Dist. Ct. D.C. 1986, U.S. Ct. Appeals (D.C. cir.) 1986, U.S. Ct. Appeals (4th cir.) 1987. Assoc. Arnold & Porter, Washington, 1984-88; atty. FTC Bur. Competition, Washington, 1988-91, dep. asst. dir. for policy, 1991-93, asst. dir., 1993-97; ptnr., co-chair, antitrust group Drinker, Biddle & Reath LLP, Washington, 1998—. Adj. prof. law Georgetown Law Ctr., Washington, 1995—2000. Dist. enrollment dir. Dartmouth Coll., 2004—. Mem.: ABA (chair computer industry com. 1996—99, chair intellectual property com. 1999—2002, coun. 2002—05, chair exemptions and immunities com. 2006—, mem. antitrust sect.), D.C. Bar Assn., Intellectual Property Owners Assn. (vice chair antitrust and competition law com.), Phi Beta Kappa. Office: Drinker Biddle & Reath LLP 1500 K St NW Ste 1100 Washington DC 20005-1209 Office Phone: 202-842-8883. Office Fax: 202-842-8465. E-mail: howard.morse@dbr.com.

**MORSE, MARVIN HENRY,** retired judge; b. Mt. Vernon, NY, July 19, 1929; s. Frank Irving and Lillian (Seeger) M.; m. Betty Anne Hess, Dec. 27, 1953; children: Martin Albert, Michael Howard, Lee Anne. AB, Colgate U., 1949; LLB, Yale U., 1952. Bar: N.Y. 1952, Ky. 1956, Md. 1964, U.S. Supreme Ct. 1960, U.S. Ct. Appeals (6th cir.), U.S. Dist. Ct. (we. dist.) Ky., U.S. Ct. Mil. Appeals, U.S. Ct. Claims, U.S. Ct. Appeals (D.C. cir.), U.S. Ct. Appeals (fed. cir.), U.S. Dist. Ct. (no. dist.) Tex., U.S. Dist. Ct. Hawaii. Pvt. practice, Louisville, 1956-62; asst. counsel Office of Gen. Counsel Dept. Navy, Washington, 1962-65, Office of Gen. Counsel Office Sec. Def., Washington, 1965-68; asst. gen. counsel GSA, Washington, 1968-70, U.S. Postal Svc., Washington, 1970-73; adminstrv. law judge Fed. Energy Regulatory Commn., Washington, 1973-75, Postal Rate Commn., Washington, 1975-77, CAB, Washington, 1977-80; dir. adminstrv. law judges Office Pers. Mgmt., Washington, 1980-82; chief adminstrv. law judge SBA, Washington, 1982-87, asst. adminstr. hearings and appeals, 1985-87; adminstrv. law judge Exec. Office of Immigration Rev. Dept. Justice, Washington, 1987—2002; temp. mem. Bd. of Immigration Appeals, 1998—2002; ret., 2002. Mem. Adminstrv. Conf. of U.S., 1980-84, govt. mem., 1985-86, 87-95, liaison mem.; faculty and faculty coord. The Nat. Jud. Coll., 1977, 79-80. Author: (with S. Groner) ABA Handbook chpt. on adminstrv. law, 1981, (with Lucy Moran) Troubling the Waters: Human Cargos, 2002. Trustee Washington area chpt. Am. Digestive Disease Soc., 1976-87. With JAGC, USAF, 1952-56, to col. USAFR, ret. 1979. Decorated USAF Legion of Merit; recipient Disting. Svc. award Am. Digestive Disease Soc., 1980. Mem. ABA (exec. com. 1977-82, 84-87, chmn. 1980-81, conf. adminstrv. law judges, del. ho. of dels. 1984-87, lawyers in govt. com. 1985-86, jud. selection, tenure and compensation com. 1987-93, govt. pub. sect. lawyers divsn., coun. 1990-92), Fed. Bar Assn. (nat. coun. 1976—, chmn. career svc. sect. 1983-86, chmn. judiciary sect. 1986-88, sect. coord. 1988-90, sec. 1991-92, del. to ABA ho. of dels. 1992-93, 97-99, v.p. 1993-94, pres.-elect 1994-95, pres. 1995-96), Am. Law Inst., Fed. Adminstrv. Law Judges Conf. (exec. com. 1975-77, 82-96, 2000-01), Nat. Assn. Adminstrv. Law Judges (hon.), Fed. Am. Inn of Ct. (coun. 1990-92, pres. 1992-94).: 2425 Gulf of Mexico Dr Longboat Key FL 34228-3287 Personal E-mail: bhmmhm@comcast.net.

**MORSE, RICHARD JAY,** human resources specialist, consultant; b. Detroit, Mich., Aug. 2, 1933; s. Maurice and Belle Rosalyn (Jacobson) M. BA, U. Va., 1955; MA in Clin. Psychology, Calif. State U., L.A., 1967. Area pers. adminstr. Gen. Tel. Co. of Calif., Santa Monica, 1967-83; sr. v.p. human resources The Bekins Co., Glendale, Calif., 1967-83; pvt. cons. human resources and orgn. devel. Cambria, 1983—. Contbr. articles to profl. jours. Fund raiser various orgns., So. Calif., 1970—. Mem. Internat. Soc. Performance Improvement (founding mem. 1958—). Republican. Jewish. Avocations: travel, tennis, walking, swimming. Home and Office: 6410 Cambria Pines Rd Cambria CA 93428-2009 Office Phone: 805-927-3457. Personal E-mail: dickmorse@earthlink.net.

**MORSE, ROBERT HARRY,** lawyer; b. Bklyn., May 25, 1941; s. Soll and Rachel Morse; m. Sandra Goldstein, July 22, 1967; children: Lisa Jennifer, Eric Jeffrey. BSEE with honors, MIT, 1963, MSEE with honors, 1964; JD, Harvard U., 1967. Bar: N.Y. 1968, D.C. 1978, Md. 1985. Assoc. Kenyon & Kenyon, Reilly, Carr & Chapin, N.Y.C., 1967-71; trial atty. antitrust divsn. Dept. Justice, Washington, 1971-74; sr. trial atty., 1974-78; ptnr. Peabody, Lambert & Meyers, Washington, 1978-82, Galland, Kharasch, Morse & Garfinkle, Washington, 1982-96, Ropes and Gray, Washington, 1997-2000; pres., CEO Esrom Consulting LLC, Rockville, Md., 2000—; ptnr. Farkas & Morse LLC, Washington, 2003—05. Dir. Earle Palmer Brown Cos., 1984-98. Mem. nat. capital area coun. Boy Scouts Am.; gen. counsel, 1991-94, exec. bd. dirs., 1990—, pres. 2001-02, chmn., 2002-2003. Recipient Spl. Achievement award Dept. Justice, 1973, Meritorious award Dept. Justice, 1976, Silver Beaver award Boy Scouts Am., 1999. Mem.: ABA, Patent Bar, D.C. Bar Assn., Nat. Alumni Assn. MIT (bd. dirs. 1986—88), MIT Club Washington (sec. 1981—82, pres. 1983—84), Eta Kappa Nu, Tau Beta Pi, Sigma Xi. Office Phone: 301-929-1010. E-mail: courtmaven@alum.mit.edu.

**MORSE, ROBERT PARKER,** investment company executive; b. Nyack, N.Y., May 8, 1945; s. Robert Willard Parker and Julia (Larson) M.; m. Sarah Morgan Cumings, Sept. 23, 1978; children: Robert Bradley St. Clair, Barber Morgan, Sarah Spencer. BS in Econs., U. Pa., 1967; student in advanced currency theory, Adelphi Suffolk U., 1970-71. V.p. Am. Express/W.H. Morton Divsn., N.Y.C., 1970-74; sr. v.p., ptnr. William G. Campbell & Co., Inc., N.Y.C., 1975-80; chmn., CEO Morse, Williams & Co., Inc., N.Y.C., 1981—. Bd. dirs. Dialogic Comm. Corp., eLottery Inc. Gov. emeritus Soc. Mayflower Descs., N.Y., 1993-98; trustee Plimoth Plantation, Mass., 1994-2000, Bermuda Biol. Sta. Rsch., 1983-2000, Gen. Svc. Bd. N.Y., 1981-93, trustee, chmn. fin. English Spkg. Union, 1998—, U.S. del. internat. coun., English Spkg. Union, London, 2002; bd. assocs. The Whitehead Inst., 1995—; bd. dirs. Arlington Inst., 1995-2001; chmn. bd. The Wall Street Fund, 1984—. Lt. USNR, 1967-78. Mem. Am. Def. Preparedness Assn., Pilgrims of U.S., River Club, Bond Club N.Y., U.S. Naval Inst., Union Club, N.Y. Yacht Club, Links Club, River Club. Episcopalian. Avocations: sailing, skiing, reading, golf, tennis, squash. Office: Morse Williams & Co Inc 230 Park Ave Rm 1635 New York NY 10169-1602 Office Phone: 212-856-8200. Business E-Mail: rpm@morsewilliams.com.

**MORSE, STEARNS ANTHONY,** science educator; b. Hanover, N.H., Jan. 3, 1931; s. Stearns Morse and Helen Ward Field Morse; m. Dorothy Garrett Forbes, June 25, 1960; children: Elise, Anne, Sophia. AB, Dartmouth Coll., 1952; MS, McGill U., 1958, PhD, 1962. Mineralogist U.S. Army Cold Regions Rsch., Hanover, NH, 1961—62; asst. prof., assoc. prof. Franklin & Marshall Coll., Lancaster, Pa., 1962—71; assoc. prof. U. Mass., Amherst, 1971—98, rsch. prof., 1998—. Dir. Nain Anorthosite Project, Labrador, 1971—81; vis. scientist Geol.-Mineralogical Mus., Oslo, 1977—78, U. Cambridge, Dept. Earth Scis., England, 1984—85, 1992, 95, 99, 2003. Author: Kiglapait Layered Intrusion Labrador, 1969, Basalts & Phase Diagrams, 1994; co-author: Crystal Identification with the Polarizing Microscope, 1994; contbr. scientific papers to profl. pubs. With U.S. Army, 1952—54. Recipient Peacock Meml. prize, Walker Mineralogical Club, Toronto, 1961; fellow, Carnegie Inst., Washington, 1967—68; grantee, NSF, 1963—2003. Fellow: Mineralogical Soc. Am., Am. Geophys. Union (section pres. 1992—94). Democrat. Episcopalian. Avocations: skiing, horseback riding. Office: Dept Geoscis 611 N Pleasant St Amherst MA 01003-9297 Business E-Mail: tm@geo.umass.edu.

**MORSE, STEPHEN J.,** law educator; b. 1945; AB, Tufts U., 1966, EdM, JD, Tufts U., 1970; PhD, Harvard U., 1973. Bar: Mass. 1972. Teaching fellow Social Rels. Dept. Harvard U., 1969-73; prin. investigator Ctr. for Law and Health Scis., Boston U., 1973-74, asst. prof. psychology, 1973-74; asst. prof. So. Calif. U., 1974-76, assoc. prof., 1976-79, assoc. dean, 1979-80, prof., 1979-82, Orrin B. Evans prof. law. psychology and behavior scis., 1982-88; Ferdinand Wakeman Hubbell prof. U. Pa., 1988—. Cons. Ctr. for Law and Health Scis. Boston U., 1974-76. Author: (with R.I. Watson Jr.) Psychoterapies: A Comparative Casebook, 1977. Cons. MacArthur Found. Program on Mental Health and the Law, 1988—. Mem. Am. Psychol.-Law Soc. (pres. 1981-82, bd. dirs. 1977), Am. Psychol. Assn. (div. 41, pres. 1986-87). Office: U Pa Law Sch 3400 Chestnut St Philadelphia PA 19104-6204 Office Phone: 212-898-2562. Office Fax: 212-573-2025. E-mail: smorse@law.upenn.edu.

**MORSE, STEPHEN SCOTT,** virologist, epidemiologist, immunologist, educator; b. NYC, Nov. 22, 1951; s. Murray H. and Phyllis Morse; m. Marilyn Gewirtz, Feb. 1991. BS, CCNY, 1971; MS, U. Wis., 1974, PhD, 1977. NSF trainee dept. bacteriology U. Wis., Madison, 1971-72, rsch. asst., 1972-77; Nat. Cancer Inst. rsch. fellow Med. Coll. Va./Va. Commonwealth U., Richmond, 1977-80, instr. microbiology, 1980-81; asst. prof. microbiology Rutgers U., New Brunswick, NJ, 1981-85; rsch. assoc. Rockefeller U., NYC, 1985-88, asst. prof., 1988-96, adj. faculty, 1996—; program mgr. Def. Advanced Rsch. Projects Agy., 1996-2000; asst. prof. to assoc. prof. epidemiology, Mailman Sch. Pub. Health, Columbia U., 1996—, dir. Ctr. Pub. Health Preparedness, Mailman Sch. Pub. Health, 2000—05. Cons. U.S. Congress Office Tech. Assessment, Washington, 1989; chair conf. on emerging viruses NIH, 1989; mem. com. microbial threats to health, chair subcom. on viruses Inst. Medicine-NAS, 1990—92, steering com. forum on emerging infections, 1996—, com. future biothreats, 2003—05; chair program for monitoring emerging diseases (ProMED) Fedn. Am. Scientists, 1993—; mem. com. on biodef. analysis and countermeasures NAS-NRC, 2005—. Author: Emerging Viruses, 1993, Evolutionary Biology of Viruses, 1994; editor-in-chief Pasteur Inst. Jour., 1996—99; sect. editor: Ctr. for Disease Control and Prevention Jour., Emerging Infectious Diseases, 1995—2002, mem. editl. bd.: Emerging Infectious Diseases, 2003—, Biosecurity and Bioterrorism, 2003—. Fellow: NY Acad. Medicine, Am. Coll. Epidemiology, NY Acad. Scis. (vice chair microbiology sect. 1994—96, chair 1996—98), Am. Acad. Microbiology; mem.: Marine Biology Lab., Am. Assn. Immunologists, Am. Soc. Microbiology, Coun. on Fgn. Rels., Sigma Xi. Office: Columbia U Mailman Sch Pub Health 722 W 168th St New York NY 10032-3722 Business E-Mail: ssm20@columbia.edu.

**MORSE-MCNEELY, PATRICIA,** poet, writer, retired secondary school educator; b. Galveston, Tex., Apr. 2, 1923; d. Bleecker Lansing Sr. and Annie Maud (Pillow) Morse; m. Chalmers Rankin McNeely, Mar. 22, 1949 (div. Aug. 1959); children: David Lansing McNeely, Timothy Ann McNeely Caldwell, Patricia Grace McNeely Dragon, Abigail Rankin McNeely. BS in Edn., U. Tex., 1972; MA in Ednl. Psychology/Spl. Edn., U. Tex. at San Antonio, 1976, MA in Ednl. Psychology/Counseling, 1981. Cert. tchr. Tex., profl. counselor. Sec. various cos., Galveston & Austin, Tex., 1945-49, 60-70; dep. clk. Ct. of Civil Appeals, Galveston, 1947-48; police stenographer Austin Police Dept., 1970-74; history and spl. tchr. N.E. Ind. Sch. Dist., San Antonio, 1974-76; spl. edn. tchr. S.W. Ind. Sch. Dist., San Antonio, 1978-81; vocat. adjustment coord. East Ctrl. Ind. Sch. Dist., San Antonio, 1981-82; counselor, tchr. Stockdale (Tex.) Ind. Sch. Dist., 1982-84; clinic sec. Humana Hosp., Dallas, 1985-87; tchr. history, spl. edn. and lang. arts Dallas Ind. Sch. Dist., 1987-2000; ret., 2000. TSTA/NEA assn. rep. Hill Mid. Sch., Dallas, 1990—91, E.B. Comstock Mid. Sch., Dallas, 1991—2000. Author: (poetry) Texas City, 1947, A Gift of Love, 1978, The Key, 1991, The House Part I, 1995, The Gull's Quill, 2001, 2d edit., 2005, Pat's Portfolio, 2002, 2d edit., 2005, The House Parts I and II, 2002, From Mother's Writings, 2005, numerous poems in lit. pubs. and anthologies; contbr. articles to newspapers and profl. jours. V.p. zone, corr. sec., libr., various coms. Parents Without Ptnrs., Inc., Austin, 1965—74, 1976—78, chmn. internat. ad hoc com. for writing leadership tng. program, 1968, newsletter editor, 1967—72. Recipient award for poetry. Mem.: AARP, NEA (life), San Gabriel Writers League, Soc. Children's Book Writers and Illustrators, Nat. Trust for Edn. (trustee), U. Tex. Austin Alumni Assn. (First Bernice Milburn Moore scholarship award 1972), Internat. Libr. Poetry (Hall of Fame 1997), Assn. Am. Poets, Tex. Ret. Tchrs. (life), Tex. State Tchrs. Assn. (life; del. to Tex. State Tchrs. Assn. Conf. 1978—81, 1991—97), Internat. Soc. Poets (life). Episcopalian. Avocations: reading, music, sewing/handcrafts, book collecting. Personal E-mail: pmmcneely@netzero.net.

**MORSHED, MOQBUL MONTY,** civil and environmental engineer; b. Rajshahi, Bangladesh, July 17, 1962; came to U.S., 1986; s. M. Rahman and Khojesta Fasiha (Akhter) Sarkar; m. Tahmina Rahman, Jan. 3, 1991. BSCE, Bangladesh U., 1984; MSCE, Wayne State U., 1987. Registered profl. engr., Fla., Pa., Oreg. Asst. engr. Bur. Cons. Engrs. Ltd., Dhaka, Bangladesh, 1984-86; civil/environ. engr. CH2M Hill, Phila., 1987-92; sr. environ. engr. Oreg. Dept. of Environ. Quality, Portland, 1992—2001; sr. project engr., project mgr. SCS Engrs., Tampa, Fla., 2001—03; sr. project mgr. Santa Ana Watershed Project Authority, Riverside, Calif., 2003—06; indep. assoc. Pre-Paid Legal Svcs., Inc., Ada, Okla., 2004—. Recipient 1st grade Merit scholarship Rajshahi, Bangladesh Bd. edn., 1977-84. Mem. ASCE, NSPE, Chi Epsilon. Home: 28937 Golden dawn Dr Menifee CA 92584 Office Phone: 951-232-7613. Personal E-mail: montymorshed@yahoo.com.

**MORT, PETER J.,** lawyer; b. Guilford, Conn., 1947; BA with high honors, Univ. Calif., Riverside, 1974; JD, Univ. Conn., 1978. Bar: Conn. 1978, US Dist. Ct. (conn. dist.) 1978, bar: Calif. 1982, US Dist. Ct. (ctrl., so. dists.) Calif. 1985, US Supreme Ct. 1990, US Dist. Ct. (no., ea. dists.) Calif. 1991, US Ct. of Appeals (9th cir.) 1991, US Dist. Ct. (Ariz. dist.) 1999. Legis. intern Sen. John V. Tunney, Calif.; mng. ptnr. Thomas, Mort, Prosser & Knudsen LLP, Riverside, Calif.; mng. ptnr., head advocacy and litig. practice, Calif.; Akin Gump Strauss Hauer & Feld LLP, LA and Riverside, Calif., 1998—. Capt. U.S. Army, 1966—70, with USMC, Vietnam. Mem.: ABA, Leo A Deegan Inn of Ct. (pres. 1997—98), State Bar of Calif., Riverside County Bar Assn. Office: Akin Gump Strauss Hauer & Feld LLP ste 2400 2029 Century Pk E Los Angeles CA 90067-3012

**MORTENSEN, CHRIS,** sports analyst, reporter; b. Nov. 7, 1952; Student, El Camino Coll. Reporter South Bay (Calif.) Daily Breeze, 1969-83; reporter Atlanta Braves Atlanta-Jour. Constn., 1983-85; reporter Atlanta Falcons, 1985-86; reporter NFL, 1987-89; The Nat., 1989-90; analyst NFL draft ESPN, 1991, 92, reporter NFL Game Day, NFL Prime Monday, SportsCenter, 1991—, reporter Outside the Lines series, 1991—. Author: Playing for Keeps: A True Story about Football, Playoffs and the Mob; NFL columnist The Sporting News; contbg. writer Sport mag. Served with U.S. Army. Recipient

George Polk award for reporting, 1987, 18 awards in journalism. Nat. Headliner award for investigative reporting, 1978; nominated for two Pulitzer Prizes. Office: c/o ESPN ESPN Pla Bristol CT 06010*

**MORTENSEN, FRED N.,** engineer; b. Ft. Worth, Tex., 1945; BS in mech. engring., U. N.Mex, 1967, MS in mech. engring., 1968, PhD in numerical fluid dynamics, 1972. Co-op student arming and fusing branch Air Force Weapons Lab., Kirtland AFB; staff mem. Los Alamos Nat. Lab. (LANL), 1972—, small weapons design group, 1972—76, tech. staff mem. applied physics divsn. thermonuclear applications (X-2), 1976—. Mem. strategic advy. group Blue Ribbon Plane, US Strategic Command. Recipient seven Nuclear Weapons Tech. Recognition of Excellence awards, US Dept. Energy, Ernest Orlando Lawrence award, 2004, R&D 100 Team award, R&D Mag. Mem.: JASONS. Office: Los Alamos Nat Lab PO Box 1663 Los Alamos NM 87545

**MORTENSEN, GORDON LOUIS,** artist, printmaker; b. Arnegard, N.D., Apr. 27, 1938; s. Gunner and Otillia Ernestine (Reiner) M.; m. Phoebe Hollis Hansen, Apr. 10, 1965 (div. 1968); m. Linda Johanna Sisson, Dec. 7, 1969. BFA, Mpls. Coll. Art and Design, 1964; postgrad., U. Minn., 1969-72. One-man shows include Minn. Mus., St. Paul, 1967, Concept Art Gallery, Pitts., 1981, 1983, 1985, 1987, 1989, 1991, 1993, C.G. Rein Galleries, Mpls., 1978, 1980, 1985, 1989, 1991, 1993, others, exhibited in group shows at Miami U., Oxford, Ohio (1st pl. award, 1977), Phila. Print Club (George Bunker award, 1977), 12th Nat. Silvermine Guild Print Exhbn., New Canaan, Conn., 1976, 1978, 1980, 1983, 1986, 1994, 1996 (Hearsch Mag. award, 1978, Purchase award, 1983, 1986), 4th Miami Internat. Print Biennial (4th pl. award, 1980), Rockford Internat., 1981, 1985 (Juror's award, 1981), Boston Printmakers Nat. Exhbn., 1977, 1979, 1980, 1981, 1983, 1997, 2003 (Purchase award, 1977, 1979, 1983, Juror's Accomodation), others, Represented in permanent collections Achenbach Found. Graphic Arts at Palace Legion of Honor, San Francisco, Bklyn. Mus., Phila. Mus. Art, Libr. of Congress, Minn. Mus. Art, Met. Mus. and Art Ctr., Miami, Fla., Mus. Am. Art, Washington, Art Inst. Chgo., Mus. Art at Carnegie-Mellon Inst., Pitts., Walker Art Ctr., Mpls., Dulin Gallery Art, Knoxville, Tenn., Phila. Mus. Art, Tokyo Fuji Art Mus., numerous corp. collections; profiled in numerous art jours. Served with USMC, 1957-60. Mem. Boston Printmakers, Phila. Print Club, L.A. Printmaking Soc., Albany Print Club, Am. Print Alliance. Home and Office: 4153 Crest Rd Pebble Beach CA 93953-3052 Office Phone: 831-625-0960.

**MORTENSEN, ROBERT HENRY,** landscape architect, golf course architect; b. Jackson, Mich., June 9, 1939; s. Henry and Charlotte Marie (Brown) Mortensen; m. Linda McGinnis, 2005; children: Phillip, Paul, Susan, Julia. B in Landscape Architecture, Ohio State U., 1961; M in Landscape Architecture, U. Mich., 1965. Registered landscape arch., Va., Md. Landscape arch. various firms, Louisville, 1960, 61-63; with Ohio Divsn. Pks., Columbus, 1960-61; landscape arch. various firms, Toledo, 1963, 65-67; pvt. practice Ann Arbor, Mich., 1963-65; ptnr. firms Toledo, 1967-78; pres. Harvey Jones and Assocs., Clearwater, Fla., 1979-81; owner Mortensen Assocs., Toledo and Falls Church, Va., 1979-85; prin. Mortensen, Lewis & Scully, Inc., Vienna, Va., 1985-93; owner Mortensen Assocs., McLean, Va., 1985—. Assoc. prof. U. Mich. Grad. Sch., 1973; vis. lectr. Ohio State U., 1965—, Bowling Green (Ohio) State U., 1969—, U. Mich., 1971, Purdue U., 1971, Mich. State U., 1973—, U. Mass., 1986—; mem. archtl. environ. rev. com. Ohio Arts Coun., 1974-78; adj. prof. Dept. Landscape Architecture, U. Md., 1992—; chmn. Merrifield Master Plan Task Force, 1998-2001. Editor: Handbook of Professional Practice, 1972, Marketing Landscape Architectural Services to the Federal Government, 1974. Mem. Ohio Bd. Unreclaimed Strip Mined Lands, 1973-76; mem. Lucas County facilities rev. com. Health Planning Assn. N.W. Ohio, 1972-76, chmn. maternal and child health subcom., 1972-74; bd. dirs. No. Va. Cmty. Appearance Alliance, 1988—2002, chair, 1991, pres., 1994. Recipient Disting. Svc. award Health Planning Assn. N.W. Ohio, 1973, Disting. Alumni award U. Mich. Sch. Natural Resources, 1985, Disting. Alumnus award Ohio State U. Coll. Engring., 1985. Fellow Am. Soc. Landscape Architects (trustee 1977-82, v.p. 1982-83, pres.-elect 1983-84, nat. pres. 1984-85, del. to Internat. Fedn. Landscape Architects 1987-92, del. Internat. Landscape Alliance 1994-2000); mem. Ohio Soc. Landscape Architects (pres. 1969-74), Landscape Inst. U.K. (hon. corr.), Toledo C. of C. (chmn. sts. and hwys. transit com. 1972-73), Greater Merrifield Bus. and Profl. Assn. (bd. dirs. 1993-2002, chmn. bd. dirs. 1998, pres. 1997), Nat. Bldg. Stone Inst. (mem. advy. bd.), Washington Golf and Country Club (officer, bd. dirs. 1999-2003, pres. 2002-03), Sigma Phi Epsilon. Home: 6843 Churchill Rd Mc Lean VA 22101-2822 Office: Mortensen Assocs 6843 Churchill Rd Mc Lean VA 22101 Office Phone: 703-917-1515. Personal E-mail: rhmort@aol.com. *One of the best continuing educational experiences for a practising professional is to teach students what you have learned. They respond in a critical and ever-so-fresh "so what" atmosphere, and demand more of you sometimes than you demand of yourself. Thus, there is learning on both sides of the lectern.*

**MORTENSEN, VIGGO,** actor; b. NYC, N.Y., Oct. 20, 1958; BA in Govt. and Spanish, St. Lawrence U., 1980, ArtsD (hon.), 2006. Actor: (TV miniseries) George Washington, 1984; (TV films) Once In a Blue Moon, 1990; (films) Witness, 1985, Salvation!, 1987, Fresh Horses, 1988, Prison, 1988, Leatherface: Texas Chainsaw Massacre III, 1990, Young Guns II, 1990, Reflecting Skin, The, 1990, Tripwire, 1990, Indian Runner, The, 1991, Boiling Point, 1993, Ruby Cairo, 1993, Carlito's Way, 1993, Young Americans, The, 1993, Ewangelia wedlug Harry'ego, 1993, Desert Lunch, 1994, Floundering, 1994, Crew, The, American Yakuza, 1994, Crimson Tide, 1995, Black Velvet Pantsuit, 1995, Prophecy, The, 1995, Gimlet, 1995, Albino Alligator, 1996, Portrait of a Lady, The, 1996, Daylight, 1996, G.I. Jane, 1997, Pistola de mi hermano, La, 1997, Perfect Murder, A, 1998, Psycho, 1998, Walk on the Moon, A, 1999, 28 Days, 2000, Lord of the Rings: The Fellowship of the Ring, 2001, Lord of the Rings: The Two Towers, 2002, Lord of the Rings: The Return of the King, 2003, Hidalgo, 2004, A History of Violence, 2005. Office: Creative Artists Agy 9830 Wilshire Blvd Beverly Hills CA 90212-1825

**MORTENSEN-SAY, MARLYS,** retired school system administrator; b. Yankton, S.D., Mar. 11, 1924; d. Melvin A. and Edith L. (Fargo) Mortensen; m. John Theodore Say, June 21, 1951; children: Mary Louise, James Kenneth, John Melvin, Margaret Ann. BA, U. Colo., 1949, MEd, 1953; Adminstrv. Specialist, U. Nebr., 1973. Tchr. Huron (S.D.) Jr. H.S., 1944-48, Lamar (Colo.) Jr. H.S., 1950-52, Norfolk Pub. Sch., 1962-63; sch. supr. Madison County, Madison, Nebr., 1963-79; ret., 1979. Mem. ASCD, NEA (life) AAUW, Am. Assn. Sch. Adminstrs., Dept. Rural Edn., Nebr. Assn. County Supts., N.E. Nebr. County Supts. Assn. Assn. Sch. Bus. Ofcls., Nat. Orgn. Legal Problems in Edn., Nebr. Edn. Assn., Nebr. Sch. Adminstrs. Assn. Republican. Methodist. Home: 1222 W S Airport Rd Norfolk NE 68701-1349

**MORTENSEN, JANICE GAYLE MILLS,** business owner, accountant; b. Chgo., Apr. 25, 1949; d. Richard Thomas and Elizabeth Ruth (Sanders) Mills; m. LeRoy A. Mortenson, Apr. 16, 1983 (dec. May 1987); m. James Richard White, Dec. 18, 1993. BA, U. Minn., 78, 75, 1976; MBA, Seattle U., 1987. CPA Wash. Co-owner Mortenson Co., Kirkland, Wash., 1984—87; contr. NW Composites, Marysville, Wash., 1987—93; owner Postal Boxes Plus, Bothell, Wash., 1993—2001, Woodsilk (JMW Enterprises, Inc.), Seattle, 1993—2001; acct. Cottle & Swanson, CPA, 2002—04; pvt. practice Bothell, 2004—05; with Paul A. Hense, CPA, PC, Grand Rapids, Mich., 2005—. Mem. Wash. State CPA Soc. (bus. and industry com. 1993-94), Mich. Assn. CPA Presbyterian. Office Phone: 616-949-5555. Personal E-mail: janicemortenson@hotmail.com.

**MORTENSEN, KRISTIN OPPENHEIM,** musician; b. San Antonio, Tex., July 14, 1964; d. Russell E. and Martha Kunkel Oppenheim; m. Gary Curtiss Mortenson; children: Leah Marie, Sarah Grace. Attended, U. Tex., 1984; MusB, La. State U., 1986, MusM, 1988. Violinist Austin Symphony Orch., Austin, Tex., 1981—84, Baton Rouge Symphony, Baton Rouge, 1985—89, Wichita Symphony Orch., Wichita, Kans., 1991—93, Des Moines Symphony, Des Moines, 1993—2001; assoc. concertmaster Topeka Symphony Orch.,

Topeka, 2001—; instr. music Kans. State U., 2004—. Assistant editor The International Trumpet Guild Jour., 2001—, violinist (live performances with) Ray Charles, Dionne Warwick, Bob Hope, Shirley Jones, Marvin Hamlisch, Rich Little. Mem. Lee Sch. Site Coun., Manhattan, Kans., 2000—02; pres. Lee Sch. PTO, Manhattan, Kans., 2000—01, 2005—06, treas., 2004—05. Mem.: Am. String Tchrs. Assn. (state pres. La. 1988—89), Sigma Alpha Iota (life; pres. U. Tex. 1983—84, Coll. Honor award, Sword of Honor 1984). Home: 522 Westview Dr Manhattan KS 66502

**MORTENSON, THOMAS THEODORE,** health products executive, management consultant; b. Hallock, Minn., Dec. 18, 1934; s. Theodore William and Esther (Hanson) M.; m. Alice L. Girdvain, June 27, 1958; children: Kim M., Laura Dee Mortenson Pavlides. BSBA, U. ND, 1956, postgrad., 1957—58. Sales rep. Johnson & Johnson, Detroit, 1960-66, tng. and product dir. New Brunswick, NJ, 1968—70; market devel. C.R. Bard, Murray Hill, NJ, 1973-75; gen. mgr. MacBick, Murray Hill, 1976-78; dir. mktg. Bard Med. Systems, Murray Hill, 1979-81, dir. sales, 1982; dir. sales/mktg., bd. dirs. Bac-Data Med. Info. Systems, Totowa, NJ, 1983-84; v.p. mktg. and sales United Med. Corp., Haddonfield, NJ, 1985—86; exec. v.p. Daltex Med. Scis., West Orange, NJ, 1987-92; dir. ConMed Corp., Utica, NY, 1993—2005; ret., 2005. Guest lectr. Am. Mgmt. Assn., 1971, Mktg. Scis. Inc., NYC, 1978. Internat. Novel Drug Delivery Techs., Tustin, Calif., 1987. With U.S. Army, USMC reserves, 1953—58. Mem. Am. Mgmt. Assn. (instr. 1971), Berkeley Swim Club (Berkeley Heights, NJ, pres. 1979-82, bd. dirs. 1974-84). Avocations: auto model collecting, woodworking, gardening, WWII history. Home: 29169 Irons Lane Dagsboro DE 19939

**MORTHAM, SANDRA BARRINGER,** former state official; b. Erie, Pa., Jan. 4, 1951; d. Norman Lyell and Ruth (Harer) Barringer; m. Allen Mortham, Aug. 21, 1950; children: Allen Jr., Jeffrey. AS, St. Petersburg Jr. Coll., 1971; BA, Eckerd Coll. Cons. Capital Formation Consultants, Inc., Bellair Bluffs, Fla., 1972-74; commr. City of Largo, Fla., 1982-86, vice mayor Fla., 1985-86; mem. Fla. Ho. of Reps., 1986-94, Rep. leader pro tempore, 1990-92, Rep. leader, 1992-94; Sec. of State State of Fla., 1995-98; pub. affairs dir., CEO, exec. v.p. Fla. Med. Assn., 1999—. Bd. dirs. Performing Arts Ctr. & Theatre, Clearwater, Fla.; exec. com. Pinellas County Rep. Com., Rep. Nat. Com. Named Citizen of Yr., 1990; recipient Tax Watch Competitive Govt. award, 1994, Bus. and Profl. Women "Break the Glass Ceiling" award, 1995, Fla. League of Cities Quality Floridian award, 1995, also numerous outstanding legislator awards, achievement among women awards from civic and profl. orgns. Mem. Am. Legis. Exch. Coun., Nat. Rep. Legislators Assn., Largo C. of C. (bd. dirs. 1987—, pres.), Largo Jr. Woman's Club (pres., Woman of Yr. award 1979), Suncoast Community Woman's Club (pres., Outstanding Svc. award 1981, Woman of Yr. award 1986), Suncoast Tiger Bay, Greater Largo Rep., Belleair Rep. Woman's, Clearwater Rep. Woman's, Tallahassee Rep. Woman's Club (pres. 1999-2000), Fla. Fedn. Rep. Women (2d v.p.). Republican. Presbyterian. Home: 6675 Weeping Willow Way Tallahassee FL 32311-8795 Office Phone: 850-224-6496. E-mail: smortham@aol.com.

**MORTIMER, RICHARD WALTER,** mechanical engineer, educator; b. Phila., Dec. 7, 1936; s. Horace and Almira Duffield (Matthews) M.; m. Doris Claire Ridler, June 29, 1957; children: Patrick Lee, David Walter, James Matthew, Daniel Scott. BSME, Drexel U., 1962, MSME, 1964, PhD, 1967. Prof. Drexel U., Phila., 1967—2002, assoc. dean grad. sch., 1974-76, head dept. mech. engring., 1976-85, assoc. v.p. acad. affairs, 1985-89. Mem. exec. com. Engring. Accreditation Com., N.Y.C., 1986-91. Contbr. over 40 articles to profl. jours. Pres. Haverford (Pa.) Twp. Sch. Dist., 1980-83. With U.S. Army, 1958—60. Recipient Achievement award Am. Soc. Nondestructive Testing, 1973, Best Tech. Paper award, 1973; fellow NASA, 1967, 68; grantee numerous orgns. including NASA, USAF, NSF, 1967-87; Fellow Members awd., Am. Soc. for Engineering Education, 1992. Fellow Am. Soc. Engring. Educators; mem. ASME (mem. numerous coms., bds. and chairs 1976-92). Republican. Episcopalian. Achievements include research in fields of structural dynamics and composite materials. Personal E-mail: dickmortimer@earthlink.net.

**MORTIMER, WENDELL REED, JR.,** judge; b. Alhambra, Calif., Apr. 7, 1937; s. Wendell Reed and Blanche (Wilson) M.; m. Cecilia Vick, Aug. 11, 1962; children: Michelle Dawn, Kimberly Grace. AB, Occidental Coll., 1958; JD, U. So. Calif., L.A., 1965. Bar: Calif. 1966. Trial atty. Legal div. State of Calif., L.A., 1965-73; assoc. Thelen, Marrin, Johnson & Bridges, L.A., 1973-76, ptnr., 1976-93; pvt. practice San Marino, Calif., 1994-95; judge L.A. Superior Ct., 1995—, mem. complex litigation panel, 2000—. With U.S. Army, 1960-62. Mem. ABA, Internat. Acad. Trial Judges, Los Angeles County Bar Assn., Calif. Judges Assn., Am. Judicature Soc., Am. Judges Assn., Legion Lex., Irish-Am. Bar Assn., Am. Bd. Trial Advocacy (nat. bd. dirs., exec. com. L.A. chpt.), San Marino City Club (bd. dirs., pres.), Pasadena Bar Assn., Balboa Yacht Club Home: 1420 San Marino Ave San Marino CA 91108-2042

**MORTLOCK, ROBERT PAUL,** microbiologist, educator; b. Bronxville, N.Y., May 12, 1931; s. Donald Robert and Florance Mary (Bellaby) M.; m. Florita Mary Welling, Sept., 1954; children: Florita M., Jeffrey R., Douglas P. BS, Rensselaer Poly. Inst., N.Y., 1953; PhD, U. Ill., Urbana, 1958. Asst. prof. microbiology U. Mass., Amherst, 1963-68, assoc. prof. microbiology, 1968-73, prof. microbiology, 1973-78, Cornell U., Ithaca, NY, 1978-99, prof. emeritus, 2000. Editor: Microorganisms as Model Systems for Studying Evolution, 1984, The Evolution of Metabolic Function, 1992. Served to 1st lt. U.S. Army, 1959-61 Fellow Am. Acad. Microbiology; mem. AAAS, Am. Soc. Microbiology, Northeastern Microbiologists, Physiology, Ecology and Taxonomy (pres. 1984-91). Office: Cornell U Dept Microbiology Wing Hall Ithaca NY 14852 Business E-Mail: rpm2@cornell.edu.

**MORTON, BRIAN,** writer, editor; b. N.Y.C., July 8, 1955; s. Richard Paul and Tasha (Brisman) Morton. BA, Sarah Lawrence Coll., 1978. Instr. grad. dept. English, NYU, N.Y., 1992-94, 98—, acting dir. Grad. Creative Writing Program, 2003—04, acting assoc. dir. Grad. Creative Writing ProgramN, 2004—05; tchr. 92d St. YMCA, N.Y., 1993-98; instr. New Sch. Social Rsch., N.Y.C., 1995-97; exec. editor Dissent Mag., N.Y.C., 1994-99; instr. Sarah Lawrence Coll., Bronxville, NY, 1998—. Author: (novels) The Dylanist, 1991, Starting Out in the Evening, 1998, A Window Across the River, 2003; book rev. editor: Dissent Mag., 1988—2000. Finalist PEN/Faulkner award, 1999; recipient Koret Jewish Book award for fiction, 1998, Acad. Lit. award, Am. Acad. Arts and Letters, 2000; fellow Guggenheim, 2001. Office: Sarah Lawrence Coll One Mead Way Bronxville NY 10708

**MORTON, CRAIG RICHARD,** real estate investor; b. Mpls., Dec. 8, 1942; s. William Charles and Patricia Louise (Hare) M.; m. Barbara Jean Larsen, 1998; children: Kelly McCall, Bradley Winslow; step-son Thomas Paul Caspers. Student, U. Philippines, Quezon City, 1961-62; BA in Geography of Southeast Asia, U. Minn., 1966; postgrad., St. John's Coll., Annapolis, 1966. Vol. U.S. Peace Corps, Philippines, 1966-68; v.p. Rent Mgmt., Inc., Mpls., 1970-80; pres. Diversified Hawaiian Investments, Inc., Mpls., 1981-99, Craig R. Morton & Assoc., Inc., Mpls., 1980-2000. No. Am. Land Corp., 1992—. Founder 49 real estate ltd. partnerships, Minn., N.Mex., Hawaii, Tex.; real estate developer Enchanted Lakes, Minn., 1990; pres. Am. Forex Corp., 1995-98, Sweet Magnolia HOA, 2001—, Royal Palms HOA, 2002—, Ashby Cove HOA, 2003—, Space Coast Barter, 2003—. Am. Field Svc. scholar to Pakistan, 1960. Mem. Soc. Mayflower Descs., Jaguar Club Minn., Country Classics Car Club, Rotary (Paul Harris fellow), Order of DeMolay, Boy Scouts Order of Arrow, Loyal Order of Moose, Internat. Arabian Horse Assn., U.S. Space Walk of Fame Found. (life). Republican. Avocations: Jaguar automobiles, reading, stamp collecting/philately, woodsmanship, raising arabian horses. Home: 3569 Muirfield Dr Titusville FL 32780 Office Phone: 321-264-1615. E-mail: craig@spirithollow.us.

**MORTON, D. HOLMES,** physician; m. Caroline S. Morton. Individualized degree program, Trinity Coll., 1979; MD, Harvard Med. Sch., 1983. Resident Children's Hosp. Boston; conducted biochemical genetics rsch. John Hopkins U., Children's Hosp. Phila.; country doctor, rsch. physician, clinic dir., co-founder Clinic for Spl. Children, Strasburg, Pa., 1989—. Contbr. articles to Nature Genetics, American Journal of Medical Genetics, Pediatrics and others. MacArthur Fellow, John D. and Catherine T. MacArthur Found., 2006. being co-founder with wife of a non-profit medical and diagnostic service for children with inherited metabolic disorders in Lancaster County, Pennsylvania. The clinic was established to provide comprehensive medical care for children with chronic, complex medical problems due to inherited disorders. Office: Clinic for Special Children 535 Bunker Hill Rd Strasburg PA 17579*

**MORTON, DAVID RAY,** sales and marketing executive; b. Rockford, Ill., Dec. 7, 1948; s. Raymond Thomas and Nathalie Ilene (Hendricks) Morton; m. Carol Lynn Pott, Apr. 1, 1972; children: Rebecca Lynn, Eric David. BS in Forestry, U. Ill., 1971; MBA, Ohio State U., 1983. Field svc. rep. So. Forest Products Assn., New Orleans, 1972-73; sales rep. chem. divsn. Ga. Pacific Corp., Columbus, Ohio, 1973-76; lumber broker Fireside Forest Industries, Columbus, 1976-77; sr. tech. sales & svc. rep. chem. divsn. Ga. Pacific Corp., Columbus, 1977-84; dir. mktg. Monitronix Corp., Columbus, 1984-85; dir. mktg. & sales Freeman Mfg. & Supply Co., Cleve., 1985-88; nat. sales and mktg. mgr. Hexcel Corp.-Resins Group, LA, 1988-95; sales mgr. Hapco, Inc., Hanover, Mass., 1995-96; nat. sales mgr. Conap, Olean, NY, 1996-99; sr. market devel. mgr. H.B. Fuller Co., N.Am. ASC Group, Assembly Group, St. Paul, 1999—2003; owner Rezolin, LLC, Ormond Beach, Fla., 2003—05; Polaris Polymers LLC, Avon Lake, 2006—. Del.-at-large Rep. Platform Planning Com., Avon Lake, Ohio, 1992. Sgt. maj. N.G. U.S. Army, 1971—99. Mem.: Polyurethane Mfr. Assn. (del. 1990—95), Am. Foundrymen's Soc. (publ. chmn. 1992—99), Soc. Mfg. Engr. (treas. 1982—84), Enlisted Assn. N.G. US, Ohio State Alumni Assn., U. Ill. Alumni Assn., Ohio N.G. Enlisted Assn., Phi Kappa Sigma. Avocations: sailing, handball, tennis, woodworking. Home: 296 Chestnut Ct Avon Lake OH 44012-2141 Office Phone: 440-933-7196. Fax: 440-930-8685. Personal E-mail: mort296@aol.com.

**MORTON, DONALD CHARLES,** astronomer; b. Kapuskasing, Ont., Can., June 12, 1933; s. Charles Orr and Irene Mary (Wightman) M.; m. Winifred May Austin, Dec. 12, 1970; children: Keith James, Christine Elizabeth. BA, U. Toronto, 1956; PhD, Princeton U., 1959. Astronomer U.S. Naval Rsch. Lab., Washington, 1959-61; from rsch. assoc. to sr. rsch. astronomer with rank of prof. Princeton (N.J.) U., 1961-76; dir. Anglo-Australian Obs., Epping and Coonabarabran, Australia, 1976-86; dir. gen. Herzberg Inst. Astrophysics, NRC of Can., Ottawa and Victoria, 1986—2001; rschr. emeritus NRC of Can., 2001—. Contbr. numerous articles to profl. jours. Fellow Australian Acad. Sci.; mem. Internat. Astron. Union, Royal Astron. Soc. (assoc. 1980), Astron. Soc. Australia (pres. 1981-83, hon. mem. 1986), Royal Astron. Soc. Can., Am. Astron. Soc. (councilor 1970-73), Can. Astron. Soc. Can. Assn. Physicists, U.K. Alpine Club, Am. Alpine Club, Alpine Club Can. Avocations: mountain climbing, rock climbing, ice climbing, marathon running. Office: Herzberg Inst Astrophysics NRC Can 5071 W Saanich Rd Victoria BC Canada V9E 2E7

**MORTON, DONALD JOHN,** librarian; b. Bklyn., Jan. 11, 1931; s. Ellwood Stokes and Gladys (Hassler) M.; m. Ann Mayo Tilden, Aug. 16, 1958; children—Saundra Kay, Donald John, Mary Ann. BS, U. Del., 1952; MS, La. State U., 1954; PhD, U. Calif. at Berkeley, 1958; MS in Libr. Sci., Simmons Coll., 1969, Dr. Arts in Library Sci, 1976. Asst. prof. botany N.M. State U., Las Cruces, 1957-58; asst. prof. plant pathology N.D. State U., Fargo, 1959-61; plant pathologist Agr. Dept., Tifton, Ga., 1961-65; asso. prof. plant pathology U. Del., Newark, 1965-68; librarian Northeastern U., Boston, 1968-70; head librarian, asst. prof. history of medicine U. Mass. Med. Sch., Worcester, 1970-74, dir. libr., assoc. prof. libr. sci., 1974-94, libr. cons., 1994—; tchr. med. librarianship Worcester State Coll., 1974-94; libr. cons., 1994—; computer cons. Hampton Hist. Soc., 1995—2006; libr. advisor Exeter Hosp., NH, 1996—2006; libr. vol. Maine Med. Ctr., 2006—. Cons. in field; mem. adv. com. med. librarianship Simmons Coll., 1972-94; mem. task force com. New Eng. Regional Libr. Svc., 1971-94; mem. cooperating staff Worcester Found. Exptl. Biology, 1972-94; chmn. Coun. Developing Med. Librs., 1974; pres. North Atlantic Health Scis. Librs., 1974-75, Worcester Area Coop. Librs., 1974-75. Contbr. articles to profl. jours. Mem. Oliver Wendell Holmes endowment com. Boston Med. Libr., 1973-74, U. Mass. Bicentennial Com., 1973-75. Mem. Am. Assn. Univ. Administrs., Simmons Coll. Libr. Sch. Alumni Assn. (pres. 1975-76), Worcester Art Mus., Worcester Hist. Soc., Northboro Hist. Soc., Hampton Hist. Soc., N.H. Hist. Soc., Am. Soc. Info. Sci., ALA, Mass. Libr. Assn., Med. Libr. Assn. (chmn. New Eng. group 1974-75), Mycol. Soc. Am., Spl. Librs. Assn., New Eng. Coll. Librarians, Piscataqua Pioneers Hereditary Soc., Sigma Xi, Phi Kappa Phi, Phi Sigma, Delta Tau Delta, Alpha Zeta. Personal E-mail: atmdjm@maine.rr.com.

**MORTON, EDWARD JAMES,** insurance company executive; b. Ft. Wayne, Ind., Nov. 8, 1926; s. Clifford Leroy and Clara Marie (Merklein) M.; m. Jean Ann McClernon, Apr. 30, 1949; children: Marcia Lynn, Anne; m. Matthild Schneider, Sept. 19, 1986; 1 child, Katherine. BA, Yale U., 1949. With John Hancock Mut. Life Ins. Co., Boston, 1949—, v.p., then sr. v.p., 1967-74, exec. v.p., 1974-82, pres., chief operating officer, 1982-86, chmn., chief exec. officer, 1987-92, also bd. dirs. Trustee Gettysburg Coll. 1990-2002, trustee emeritus, 2002—; hon. life overseer Children's Hosp. Fellow Soc. Actuaries; mem. Actuaries Club Boston, Comml. Club Boston, Phi Beta Kappa. Office: John Hancock Life Ins Co PO Box 111 C-01-03 Boston MA 02117-0111 Personal E-mail: ejmorton@potomacnet.com.

**MORTON, FREDERIC,** author; b. Vienna, Oct. 5, 1924; s. Frank and Rose (Ungvary) M.; m. Marcia Colman, Mar. 28, 1957; 1 dau., Rebecca. BS, Coll. City N.Y., 1947; MA, New Sch. Social Research, 1949. Author: The Hound, 1947, The Darkness Below, 1949, Asphalt and Desire, 1952, The Witching Ship, 1960, The Schatten Affair, 1965, Snow Gods, 1969, An Unknown Woman, 1976, The Forever Street, 1984, Crosstown Sabbath, 1987, (biography) The Rothschilds, 1962, A Nervous Splendor-Vienna 1888/9, 1979, Thunder at Twilight-Vienna 1913/14, 1989, Runaway Waltz--A Memoir From Vienna To New York, 2005; books translated into 14 langs.; actor (documentary) Crosstown Sabbath, 1995; contbg. editor: Vanity Fair; contbr. to publs. including Best Am. Short Stories, 1965, Best Am. Essays of 2003, and other anthologies, N.Y. Times, Harper's mag., Atlantic mag., Nation, Playboy, Esquire, N.Y. Mag., Hudson Rev., Wall Street Jour., Vanity Fair, L.A. Times, others; columnist Village Voice, Conde-Nast Traveler, Wall Street Jour.3.2 Recipient Author of Year award Nat. Anti-Defamation League, B'nai B'rith; Hon. Professorship award Republic of Austria, 1980, Tom Osborne Disting. lectureship U. Nebr., 1989; Dodd, Mead Intercollegiate Lit. fellow, 1947; Yaddo residence fellow, 1948, 50; Breadloaf Writers' Conf. fellow, 1947; Columbia U. fellow, 1953; recipient Golden Merit award City of Vienna, 1986, City of Vienna medal of honor in gold, 2001, Cross of Honor for Achievements in Arts, Republic of Austria, 2003. Mem. Author's Guild (exec. coun.), P.E.N. Home: 110 Riverside Dr New York NY 10024-3715 Office: Sandra Diskstra Agy PMB 515 1155 Camino Del Mar Del Mar CA 92014 *As a writer I'm trying to tell the truth interestingly.*

**MORTON, HUGH WESLEY,** television producer, television director; b. Pasadena, Calif., Dec. 8, 1931; s. Hugh Wesley Morton and Timey Delacey Hopper; m. Paula Dozois, Nov. 30, 1951 (dec. May 1954); m. Norma Antonia Daloisio, Apr. 22, 1965 (div.); 1 adopted child, Wil Guido. BA, Northwestern U., 1954; BS, U. Mont., 1959; MA, U. Oreg., 1961. Mailboy, prodn. office clk. Paramount Prodns., Hollywood, Calif., 1962-64; dir., rschr. Profl. Theatre Workshop, Desilu Studios, Hollywood, 1964-66; asst. to contbr. Columbia Pictures TV, Hollywood, 1966-68, asst. to exec. v.p. TV prodn., 1968-75; asst. to studio pres. The Burbank (Calif.) Studios, 1975-78; dir. Hollywood Central, Glendale, Calif., 1978-82; spl. events prodr., dir. studio facilities Fox Studios/News Corp., L.A., 1982-97; vol. oncology, sr. peer counseling Providence St. Joseph Hosp., Burbank, Calif., 1997—; cons. on call IV Prodns., L.A., 1997—. Prodr. 400 TV episodes, 50 films; author: Assistant

Director's Handbook, 1973. Mem. Mus. of Arts, City of Hope, L.A.; libr. assoc. Coll. Canyons; prodr. Ciba Geigy, L.A.; prodr. various spl. events. Named Vol. of Yr. Providence St. Joseph Hosp., 1998; recipient Outstanding Support award White House Comms. Agy., 1994, Outstanding Svc. award C. of C., 1983, Award of Merit Media Workshop Found. Mass Comm. and Educating Am. Youth; Fulbright scholarship Alternate Royal Acad. Mem. Acad. of TV Arts and Scis., Screen Actors Guild, Am. Fedn. of TV and Radio Artists, Internat. Alliance of Theatrical State Employees Artists and Allied Crafts of the U.S., Calif. State Sheriff's Assn., Canyon Theatre Guild, Met. Mus. of Art (assoc.), Wildlife Sta., Calif. State Parks Assn., L.A. County Mus. of Arts, L.A. Natural History Mus., The Colony Playhouse. Avocations: hiking, gardening, singing, reading. Office: IV Prodns PO Box 2517 Toluca Lake CA 91610

**MORTON, JAMES CARNES, JR.,** automotive executive; b. Duncan, Okla., May 8, 1945; s. James Carnes and Syble Lyda (Looney) Morton; m. Susan Phillips, May 25, 1968; children: James III, Terrissa Anne, Scott Thomas. BA, Westminster Coll., 1967; JD, U. Mo., 1972. Bar: Mo. 1972. Tax acct. Arthur Andersen Co., St. Louis, 1972—74; tax atty. Gen. Dynamics Corp., St. Louis, 1974—76; asst. gen. counsel Michelin Tire Corp., Greenville, SC, 1976—86; gen. counsel Michelin Tire Corp. and Michelin Tires (Can.) Ltd., Greenville, 1990—92; dir. pub. rels and govt. affairs Michelin Tire Corp., Greenville, 1986—92; exec. dir. external rels. Michelin N.Am., Inc., Greenville, 1992—96, v.p. pub. rels. and govt. rels., 1996—2000; sr. v.p. fin. and adminstrn., bd. dirs., mem. mgmt. com. Nissan North Am., Inc., Gardena, Calif., 2000—06, vice chmn., 2006—. Bd. dirs. Nissan Can., Inc.; adv. bd. Hollings Cancer Ctr. Med. U. SC, 2005—. Bd. dirs. Greenville Symphony Orch., 1986—89, United Way Greenville, 1987—88, Greenville YMCA, 1988—89; mem. S.C. Reorganization Commn., 1985—98; trustee S.C. Gov.'s Sch. Sci. and Math., 1996—99; mem. sch. bd. Christ Ch. Episcopal Sch., Greenville, 1997—2000; vice chmn. S.C. Ports Authority, 1999—2000; pres. Nissan Found., 2003—. Lt. U.S. Army, 1967—70, capt. Mo. N.G., 1970—72. Recipient Alumni Achievement award, Westminster Coll., 2003. Mem.: ABA, Mo. Bar Assn. (non-resident), Alliance Automobile Mfrs. (bd. dirs. 2000—03), Rubber Mfrs. Assn. (bd. dirs. 1995—2000, govt. affairs com., tire mgmt. com.), Assn. Internat. Automobile Mfrs. (exec. com. 2000—, chmn. bd. dirs. 2005—), Nat. Urban League (trustee 2004—), S.C. C. of C. (exec. com. 1981—84, 1986—95, pres. 1993—94, chmn. 1994—95, bd. dirs.), Greater Greenville C. of C. (bd. dirs. 1990—93, chmn. legis. affairs com. 1996—98), L.A. Urban League (bd. dirs. 2001—05), Calif. C. of C. (bd. dirs. 2001—04), Kiawah Island Club, Greenville Country Club. Presbyterian. Avocation: golf. Office: Nissan NAm Inc PO Box 685001 Franklin TN 37068-5001 Office Phone: 615-725-5550. Business E-Mail: jim.morton@nissan-usa.com.

**MORTON, JOE,** actor; b. NYC, Oct. 18, 1947; m. Nora Chavooshian, Oct. 1984; children: Ara, Seta. Student, Hofstra U. Actor Actors Theatre of Louisville, 1984-85. Dir. play: Honeymoon Bouquet; film appearances include Between the Lines, 1977, ...And Justice for All, 1979, The Killing Hour, 1981, The Brother From Another Planet, 1984, Crossroads, 1985, Trouble in Mind, 1985, Zelly and Me, 1988, The Good Mother, 1988, Tap, 1989, City of Hope, 1991, Judgment Day, 1991, Of Mice and Men, 1992, Forever Young, 1992, The Walking Dead, 1994, The Inkwell, 1994, In the Hands of the Enemy, 1994, Speed, 1994, Executive Decision, 1996, Lone Star, 1996, Toubles on the Corner, 1997, The Pest, 1997, Speed 2: Cruise Control, The Astronaut's Wife, 1998, Blues Brother's 2000, 1998, APT Pupil, 1998, What Lies Beneath, 2000, Ali, 2001, Dragonfly, 2002, Crossing, 2003, Thoughtcrimes, 2003, Paycheck, 2003, Lenny the Wonder Dog, 2004, Breaking Dawn, 2004, Back in the Day, 2005, Stealth, 2005, The Night Listener, 2006; TV appearances include Feeling Good, 1974-75; Grady, 1975-76; Watch Your Mouth, 1978, Equal Justice, 1990, A Different World, 1991-92, Tribeca, 1993, The Great Depression, 1993, Under One Roof, 1995, New York News, 1995, Mercy Point, 1998, also on daytime series Search for Tomorrow, 1973-74, Prince Street, 1997, Another World, 1983-84, All My Children, 2002, on TV movies, This Man Stands Alone, 1979, Death Penalty, 1980, A Good Sport, 1984, Alone in the Neon Jungle, 1988, burnout, 1988, Terrorist on Trial: The United States versus Salim Ajami, 1988, Howard Beach: Making the Case for Murder, 1989, Legacy of Lies, 1992, In the Shadow of Evil, 1995, Miss Ever's Boys, 1997, Mutiny, 1999, Y2K, 1999, Ali: An American Hero, 2000, Jasper, Texas, 2003, Gone But Not Forgotten, 2004; also episodes and spls.; numerous stage appearances including, Raisin, Honky Tonk Nights, 1986, King John, 1988, Elektra, 1988, Crumbs from the Table, 1995, Hair, A Midsummer Night's Dream, Crazy Horse, Electra, Julius Caesar, The Tempest; recordings include Days of Grace, 1993, God's Trombones: Seven Negro Sermons in Verse, 1993, Possessing the Secret of Joy, 1993, The Autobiography of Malcolm X, 1993. Avocation: magic. Office: Judy Schoen and Assocs 606 N Larchmont Blvd Ste 309 Los Angeles CA 90004-1309*

**MORTON, JOHN DOUGLAS,** retail executive; b. 1951; With Wolfe's Sporting Goods, 1972-80; dist. mgr. sporting goods divsn. Malone and Hyde, 1980-86; divsn. mgr. Utah region Gart Sports Co., Denver, 1986-88, divsn. v.p. Utah region, 1988-90, v.p. ops., 1990-94, exec. v.p., 1994-95, pres., CEO, chmn. bd., 1995—2003; vice chmn., CEO The Sports Authority, Englewood, Colo., 2003—04, chmn., pres., CEO, 2004—. The Sports Authority 1050 W Hampden Ave Englewood CO 80110 Fax: 303-829-1511.

**MORTON, JOSEPH,** school system administrator; BS, Auburn U.; MS, U. Ala., PhD in Ednl. Adminstrn. Supt. of edn. Sumter County Schs., Ala., Sylacauga City Schs., Ala.; dep. state supt. edn. Ala. Dept. Edn., interim state supt. edn., 2004, state supt. edn., 2004—. Founder Sylacauga City Schs. Found. Office: Ala Dept Edn 50 N Ripley St PO Box 302101 Montgomery AL 36104 Office Phone: 334-242-9700. E-mail: jmorton@alsde.edu.

**MORTON, LINDA JUNE,** academic administrator; b. Nashville, Jan. 21, 1943; d. William Taylor Morton and Ruby Grayson (Maiden name-Page) Morton. BA, George Peabody Coll., 1964; MS, 1976; PhD, Vanderbilt U., 1981. Cert. ednl. adminstr. Tenn., 1981; tchr. English 7-12 Tenn., 1964; tchr. music K-12 Tenn., 1964; career ladder III tchr. Tenn., 1985. Tchr. high sch. English, music Metro Nashville Pub. Schs., 1964—67, tchr. mid. sch. tchr. music, 1967—89, asst. prin., 1989—2000. Chair, McGavock cluster prins. Metro Nashville Pub. Schools, 1990—91, spl. edn. prins. adv. com. mem., 1992—94; chair curriculum com. 10 yr. sacs evaluation McGavock H.S., 1992—92. Wrote and compiled (7th grade music curriculum outline) 7th Grade Music Curriculum Outline. Dir. Jr. Dept. Woman's Club Nashville, 1972—74; vice-moderator, bd. trustees Memphis Theol. Sem., 1998—2003; mem. bd. dirs. Kidney Found. Mid. Tenn., 1981—83. Mem.: Fla. Oceanographic Soc., Aerospace Edn., Internat. Soc. Music Edn., U. Club Nashville, Woman's Club Nashville (life), Phi Delta Kappa, Alpha Delta Kappa. Avocations: photography, swimming, travel, music, scuba diving. Home: 6740 Currywood Dr Nashville TN 37205 Office Phone: 772-225-1599. Personal E-mail: laquarius@aol.com.

**MORTON, LOUIS GEORGE,** retired social sciences educator; b. St. Louis, May 21, 1928; s. Louis George and Helen (Kesl) Morton; children: Robert, David, James. *Emma Morton Ginsburg (1865-1953), the wife of the "Wandering Jew in Brazil," was a great female Baptist Missionary. Born to Mary and Henry Morton, a Presbyterian, she joined the Second Baptist Church, and at twenty-two she was baptized. The Foreign Mission Board approved Emma as a missionary. In Brazil, she met Dr. Solomon Ginsburg, a young widower missionary, married him, and worked collaboratively with him, moving from one location to another, building self-supporting churches. Dr. Ginsburg died in 1927 and Emma moved to America as a speaker in demand. In Pernambuco, the Solomon Ginsburg Institute Schools stand as a memorial to Dr. and Mrs. Ginsburg. BS in Edn., Mo. U., 1953; MA, Western State Coll., Gunnison, Colo., 1966, cert. in edn. specialist, 1971. Tchr. history Ctrl. HS, Grand Junction, Colo., 1961—66; prof. polit. sci. Mesa State Coll., Grand Junction, 1966—95, prof. emeritus, 1995—, pres. faculty senate, 1988—90, dept. chmn. social scis., 1991—92. Pres. Ctrl. CEA, Grand Junction, 1965—66. After retiring from Mesa State College in 1993, where he specialized in Constitutional Law and Political Theories, the Mesa State*

*College Alumni Relations office invited Mr. Morton to attend the 2006 Distinguished Alumni Banquet for recognition of his services and contributions to the college and student body. It was an honor for him to participate in Mesa State College's activities and to contribute to the students as Faculty Advisor for the Student Body Association. As Director of the Mesa State College Model United Nations for over fifteen years, he supervised over 200 High School students each Spring utilizing the college's facilities for their annual debates.* Author: A Student's Guide to the U.S. Constitution, 1987, A Citizen's Guide to the U.S. Constitution, 1993, The First 75 Years History Mesa State College, 2003, E Mail Humor, 2005, E Mail Humor Revisited, 2006. 1st lt. USAF, 1946—53. NSF grantee, U. Mo., 1966, U. Tex., 1975. Mem.: Nat. Ret. Tchrs. Assn. (nat. guidance com.), Mesa State Coll. Emeriti Assn. (pres. 1997—98), Colo. Ret. Sch. Employees Assn. (pres. 2004—06), Mesa County Ret. Sch. Employees Assn. (pres. 2000—01), Am. Legion. Democrat. Methodist. Avocations: coin collecting/numismatics, stamp collecting/philately, writing. Home: 1111 Horizon Dr # 403 Grand Junction CO 81506 Office Phone: 970-257-1658. Personal E-mail: lmorton22@msn.com.

**MORTON, MARILYN MILLER,** retired genealogy educator, researcher, retired history professor, travel company executive; b. Water Valley, Miss. Dec. 2, 1929; d. Julius Brunner and Irma Faye (Magee) Miller; m. Perry Wilkes Morton Jr., July 2, 1958; children: Dent Miller Morton, Nancy Marilyn Morton Driggers, E. Perian Morton Dyar. BA in English, Miss. U. for Women, 1952; MS in History, Miss. State U., 1955. Cert. secondary tchr. Tchr. English, speech and history Starkville (Miss.) H.S., 1952-58; part-time instr. Miss. State U., 1953-55; spl. collection staff Samford U. Libr., Birmingham, Ala., 1984-92; lectr. genealogy and history, instr. Inst. Genealogy & Hist. Rsch., Samford U., Birmingham, 1985-93, assoc. dir., 1985-88, exec. dir., 1988-93; founding dir. SU Brit. and Irish Inst. Genealogy & Hist. Rsch. Samford U., Birmingham, 1986-93; owner, dir. Marilyn Miller Morton Brit-Ire-U.S. Genealogy, Birmingham, 1994—95, British Virgin Islands, 1994—95. Instr. genealogy classes Samford U. Metro Coll., 1986-94; former lectr. nat. conf. Fedn. of Geneal. Soc. Contbr. articles to profl. jours. Miss. state pres. Future Homemakers Am., 1947-48; active Birmingham chpt. Salvation Army Aux., 1982-87. Named to Miss. U. for Women Hall of Fame, 1952. Fellow Irish Geneal. Rsch. Soc. London; mem. Nat. Geneal. Soc. (mem. nat. program com. 1988-92, lectr. nat. meetings), Antiquarian Soc. Birmingham (sec., 2d v.p. 1982-84), DAR (regent Cheaha chpt. 1977-78), Daus. Am. Colonists (regent Edward Waters chpt. 1978-79), Nat. League of Am. Penwomen, Phi Kappa Phi (charter mem. Samford U. chpt. 1972). Avocations: reading, research, travel, bridge, chess. Home: PO Box 660562 Birmingham AL 35266-0562

**MORTON, R. STEVEN,** lawyer; b. Atlanta, Dec. 3, 1958; BS in Environ. Studies, Allegheny Coll., 1980; grad. studies in Hydrogeology, U. Tex.; JD, Vanderbilt U., 1984. Bar: Tenn. 1985, Tex. 1986. Ptnr. Brown McCarroll & Oaks Hartline, Austin; shareholder Jenkens & Gilchrist, P.C., Austin, 1995—, firm leader environ. & adminstrv. advocacy practice group. Office: Jenkens & Gilchrist PC Ste 2500 401 Congress Ave Austin TX 78701 Office Phone: 512-499-3856. Office Fax: 512-499-3810. Business E-Mail: smorton@jenkens.com.

**MORTON, RICHARD ALBERT DUNLAP,** physician; b. El Paso, Tex., Sept. 6, 1932; s. Richard Albert Dunlap and Julie Ann (More) M.; children: Priscilla, Richard Albert Dunlap III, Maria, Margaret, Andrew, Arthur. Student, Tex. Western Coll., 1950-53, U. Colo., 1953; MD, Tulane U., 1957. Diplomate Am. Bd. Otolaryngology. Physician Drs. Morton and Blumenfeld, PA, El Paso; pvt. practice otolaryngology, 1963—. Bd. dirs. Tex. Liability Trust, Austin, 1981-87, 91-94; bd. dirs. Tex. State Bd. Med. Examiners, Austin, 1988-91, pres., 1990-91. Mem. governing bd. Sierra Med. Ctr. Hosp., 1981-82; bd. mem. El Paso Ind. Sch. Dist., 1970-76. Capt. USAF, 1961-63. Fellow ACS, Am. Acad. Otolaryngology; mem. AMA (del. 1980-85), Tex. Med. Assn. (del. 1970-80), Tex. Surg. Soc., Tex. Otolaryngological Assn. (pres. 1980-81), Rotary Club El Paso. Republican. Avocations: hunting, fishing, tennis. Office: Drs Morton Blumenfeld and Nanez PA 1733 Curie Dr Ste 110 El Paso TX 79902-2909 Address: 10470 Vista del Sol Ste 110 El Paso TX 79925 Office Phone: 915-533-5461.

**MORTON, SALLIE W.,** music educator; b. Columbus, Ohio, Nov. 5, 1947; d. William Waldo Waters and Lillianne Stewart Rudisill; m. Charles Ward Morton, July 1, 1989; children: Ari Shawn Williams, Tara Danielle Sutter, Christy Lyn Winkler. B in Music Edn., Denison U., Granville, Ohio, 1968; MA in Christian Edn., Scarritt Coll., Nashville, 1970. Cert. elem./intermediate, advanced piano tchr. Ohio, Orff level I and II. Dir. Scarritt Coll. Singers Scarritt Coll., Nashville, 1969—70; dir. music Brentwood United Meth. Ch., Nashville, 1971—76; dir. Christian Edn., music and youth Brooksville United Meth. Ch., Fla., 1976—80; band dir. Rittman H.S., Ohio, 1980—81; tchr. music Chippewa Local Schs., Doylestown, Ohio, 1981—. Pvt. piano, flute tchr., 1963—. Vocal judge MacDowell Club of Wooster, Ohio, 2002—06; tone chime dir. Dalton Presbyn. Ch., 2004—06. Recipient Sallie Williams Day, Brooksville United Meth. Ch., 1978. Mem.: Nat. Guild Piano Tchrs., Ohio Music Educators Assn., MacDowell Music Club Wooster. Republican. Methodist. Avocations: camping, swimming, crafts. Home: 3472 Tamarack Ln Wooster OH 44691 Office: Hazel Harvey Elementary Sch 165 Brooklyn Ave Doylestown OH 44230

**MORTON, SAMANTHA,** actress; b. Nottingham, Eng., May 13, 1977; d. Peter and Pamela; 1 child, Esme. Actor: (TV miniseries) Band of Gold, 1995, The History of Tom Jones, a Foundling, 1997; (TV series) Soldier Soldier, 1991, Max and Ruby, 2002; (TV films) The Token King, 1993, Emma, 1996, Jane Eyre, 1997; (films) The Future Lasts a Long Time, 1996, Under the Skin, 1997, This Is the Sea, 1998, Sweet and Lowdown, 1999 (Acad. award nomination for best supporting actress, 2000), Jesus' Son, 1999, The Last Yellow, 1999, Eden, 2001, Morvern Callar, 2002, Minority Report, 2002, In America, 2002 (Acad. award nomination for best actress, 2004), Code 46, 2003, The Libertine, 2004, River Queen, 2005, Lassie, 2005. Mailing: c/o Creative Artists Agy 9830 Wilshire Blvd Beverly Hills CA 90212*

**MORTON, STEPHEN DANA,** chemist, consultant; b. Madison, Wis., Sept. 7, 1932; s. Walter Albert and Rosalie (Amlie) M. BS, U. Wis., 1954, PhD, 1962. Asst. prof. chemistry Otterbein Coll., Westerville, Ohio, 1962-66; postdoctoral fellow water chemistry, pollution control U. Wis., Madison, 1966-67; water pollution rsch. chemist WARF Inst., Madison, 1967-73, head environ. quality dept., 1973-76; mgr. quality assurance Raltech Sci. Svcs., 1977-82; pres. SDM Cons., 1982—. Author: Water Pollution-Causes and Cures, 1976. 1st lt. Chem. Corps, AUS, 1954-56. Mem. AAAS, Am. Chem. Soc. Home and Office: 1126 Sherman Ave Madison WI 53703-1620

**MORTON, WILLIAM GILBERT, JR.,** stock exchange executive; b. Syracuse, NY, Mar. 13, 1937; s. William Gilbert and Barbara (Link) M.; m. Margaret Halleron, Nov. 26, 1982; children: Andrew Baker, William Gilbert III, Sarah Ellsworth, Kate Spencer. BA, Dartmouth Coll., 1959; MBA, NYU, 1965. Asst. v.p. Discount Corp. N.Y., 1960-67; co-mgr. trading, sr. v.p., dir. Mitchell Hutchins Inc., 1967-79; mng. stock rsch. divsn., sr. v.p., dir. Dean Witter Reynolds Inc., 1979-85; chmn., CEO Boston Stock Exch. Inc. 1985-2001, chmn. emeritus, 2001—02. Chmn. allocation com. NY Stock Exch., floor ofcl., 1976—81, com. mem., 1970—85; bd. dirs. Radio Shack Corp., Ft. Worth, The Griswold Co., NY; J.P. Morgan Funds. Bd. dirs. Vt. Acad., Saxton's River, 1984-90, Boston 2000 Commn., 1998-2001, Nat. Football Found. and Coll. Hall of Fame, N.Y.; trustee search com. Dartmouth Alumni Coun., 1988-91; trustee Berklee Coll. Music, Stratton Mountain Sch., Stratton, Vt. With USMC, 1959-65. Mem. NASD (nominating com. 2003—), Boston Econ. Club, Mass. Bus. Roundtable, Nat. Orgn. Investment Profls., Racquet and Tennis Club N.Y.C., Stratton Mt. Country Club (Vt.), Colo. Arlberg Club (Winter Park), Brae Burn Country Club (Newton), Ekwanok Country Club (Vt.), Royal Poinciana Club (Fla.), Stock Exch. Luncheon Club N.Y.C., Theta Delta Chi. Republican. Presbyterian. Office: 304 Newbury St #560 Boston MA 02115

**MORTVEDT, JOHN JACOB,** soil scientist, researcher; b. Dell Rapids, SD, Jan. 25, 1932; s. Ernest R. and Clara (Halvorson) M.; m. Marlene L. Fodness, Jan. 23, 1955; children: Sheryl Mortvedt Jarratt, Lori Mortvedt Klopf, Julie Mortvedt Stride. BS, SD State U., 1953, MS, 1959; PhD, U. Wis., 1962. Soil chemist TVA, Muscle Shoals, Ala., 1962-87, sr. scientist, 1987-92, regional mgr. field programs dept., 1992-93; ext. soils specialist Colo. State U., Ft. Collins, 1994-95, ext. environ. and pesticide edn. specialist, 1996. Agr. cons. U.S. Borax, 1997—. Co-author: Fertilizer Technology and Application, 1999; editor: Micronutrients in Agriculture, 1972, 2d edit., 1991; contbr. articles to profl. jours. 1st lt. U.S. Army, 1953-57. Fellow AAAS, Soil Sci. Soc. Am. (pres. 1988-89, editor-in-chief 1982-87, Profl. Svc. award 1991, Disting. Svc. award 1996), Am. Soc. Agronomy (exec. com. 1987-90, Agronomic Svc. award 2003); mem. Internat. Union Soil Sci., Colombian Soil Sci. Soc. (hon.), Exch. Club (pres. Florence, Ala. chpt. 1987-88), Toastmasters (pres. Florence chpt. 1964-65), Phi Kappa Phi. Avocations: photography, golf. Office: Colo State U Dept Soil And Crop Scis Fort Collins CO 80523-1170

**MORVANT, BARBARA L.,** nursing administrator; Exec. dir. La. State Bd. Nursing, Metairie. Recipient R. Louise McManus award, Nat. Coun. State Bds. Nursing, 2005. Office: La State Bd Of Nursing 5207 Essen Ln Ste 6 Baton Rouge LA 70809-3565 Office Phone: 504-838-5332. Office Fax: 504-838-5433. E-mail: norvant@lsbn.state.la.us.

**MORVILLO, ROBERT GUY,** lawyer; b. NYC, Jan. 22, 1938; s. M. Victor and Marie (Santeramo) M.; m. Catherine A. Shields, Apr. 20, 1963; children: Christopher, Gregory, Edward, Robert. AB, Colgate U., 1960; JD, Columbia U., 1963. Bar: N.Y. 1964, U.S. Dist. Ct. (so. dist.) 1966, U.S. Ct. Appeals (2nd cir.) 1964, U.S. Ct. Appeals (3rd cir.) 1979, U.S. Ct. Appeals (10th cir.) 1983, U.S. Supreme Ct. 1982. Law clk. to Hon. William B. Herlands U.S. Dist. Ct. (so. dist.), N.Y.C., 1963-64, asst. U.S. atty., 1964-68, chief trial counsel fraud unit, 1970-71, chief criminal div., 1971-73; assoc. Reavis & McGrath, N.Y.C., 1968-70; prin. Morvillo, Abramowitz & Grand, P.C. and predecessors, N.Y.C., 1973—. Lectr. Columbia Law Sch., N.Y.C., 1974-85. Columnist, N.Y. Law Jour., N.Y.C., 1982—; editor, White Collar Crime: Business and Regulatory Offenses, 1990. Bd. dirs. South Nassau Cmty. Hosp., 2005—. Fellow Am. Coll. Trial Lawyers; mem. ABA, Assn. of Bar of City of N.Y., N.Y. State Bar Assn., N.Y. Coun. of Def. Lawyers (bd. dirs. 1987—91). Office: Morvillo Abramowitz Grand Iason Anello & Bohrer PC 565 Fifth Ave New York NY 10017 Office Phone: 212-880-9400. E-mail: rmorvillo@magislaw.com.

**MOSALLAEI, HOSSEIN,** science educator; s. Keramatollah Mosallaei and Sedigheh Moradi; m. Afsaneh Ghanavati, Apr. 20, 1995; 1 child, Ali. PhD, UCLA, 1997—2001. Postdoctoral rsch. fellow UCLA, 2001—02; asst. rsch. scientist U. of Mich., 2002—05; asst. prof. Northeastern U., Boston, 2005—. Recipient Young Scientist award, URSI, 2001, Raj Mittra Travel grant, AP-S and URSI, 2002; Grad. fellowship, UCLA, 1997—98. Mem.: IEEE, URSI. Achievements include first to advanced meta-materials for RF/wireless and micro-nano-scale front-ends.

**MOSBACHER, GEORGETTE PAULSIN,** cosmetics executive; b. Hammond, Ind., Jan. 16, 1947; d. George Michael and Dorothy (Bell) Paulsin; m. Robert Mosbacher Sr., Mar. 1, 1985. BS, Ind. U., 1969; DFA (hon.), Internat. Fine Arts Coll., 1990; DBA (hon.), Bryant U., 1992. V.p. lic. Faberge, Inc.; CEO La Prairie, Inc., NYC, 1987—95; pres., CEO Borghese, NYC; chair, CEO Georgette Mosbacher Enterprises. Author: Feminine Force, It Takes Money Honey. Bd. dirs. Houston Grand Opera Exec. Com., Am. Hosp. in Paris, Ind. U. Found., Statute of Liberty/Ellis Island Commn., Am. Art Alliance, M.D. Anderson Hosp., United Negro Coll. Fund, Child Help U.S.A., Hudson River Park Trust; mem. adv. bd. Ctr. Strategic Internat. Studies; presdl. appointment Advocate Com. for Trade and Internat. Negotiations; Republican Nat. Committeewomen, State NY. Mem. Women's Econ. Alliance. Avocations: scuba diving, sailing. Office: Borghese 10 E 34th St New York NY 10016*

**MOSBACHER, ROBERT A.,** investment company executive; BA, Georgetown U., 1973; JD, So. Methodist U., 1977. Chmn. Tex. Welfare Reform Task Force, 1998; chmn. bd. Tex. Dept. Human Svcs., 1989—91; pres., CEO Moasbacher Energy Co., Houston, 1986—2005, Overseas Pvt. Investment Corp. (OPIC), 2005—. Immediate past-chmn. Greater Houston Partnership, chmn. health care advisory com., mem. edn. and workforce advisory com.; founder, co-chmn. Rebuilding Together Houston; bd. dirs. South Tex. Coll. Law, Soc. Performing Arts. Office: Overseas Pvt Investment Corp 1100 NY Ave NW Washington DC 20527 Office Phone: 202-336-8400. Office Fax: 202-408-9859.*

**MOSCATO, JOSEPH LOUIS, JR.,** health facility administrator, military officer; b. Erie, Pa., Feb. 25, 1948; s. Joseph Louis and Anna Mae Moscato; m. Kimberly Lynn Williams, July 5, 1991; children: Jack McKinney, Joseph III, Rachel, Kelly. BA, BS in Biology, Oglethorpe U., 1971; BBA, Kennesaw State U., 1982; MBA, Brenau U., 1984; Masters in Healthcare Adminstrn., Mercer U., 1996. Commd. 2d lt. USAF, 1972—, advanced through grades to maj.; v.p. bus. devel. Am. Outpatient, Ft. Lauderdale, Fla., 1996; v.p. sales and mktg. Med Lab Specialist, Atlanta, 1998; ea. mgr. Gambro Lab, Ft. Lauderdale, 2003—04; mkt. adv. bd. Atlanta Dialysis Ctr. Mem.: Res. Officers Assn. (jr. v.p. USAF 2001, pres.). Republican. Roman Catholic. Avocations: golf, tennis, basketball, theater, hiking. Home: 3122 Hudson Pond Ln Marietta GA 30062 Office Phone: 954-585-1100. Office Fax: 770-578-0406. Personal E-mail: jlmoscato@aol.com.

**MOSCHELLA, SAMUEL L.,** dermatology educator; b. East Boston, Mass., Apr. 22, 1921; BS, Tufts U., 1943, MD cum laude, 1946. Diplomate Am. Bd. Dermatology. Intern in medicine Boston City Hosp., 1946-47; resident in dermatology U.S. Naval Hosp., Phila., 1948, St. Albans, 1951; postgrad. in skin and cancer Bellevue Hosp., N.Y.C., 1952-53; chief dermatology U.S. Naval Hosp., Phila., 1953-54, chief dermatology, asst. chief medicine, Guantanamo Bay, Cuba, 1948-51, chief dermatology, Chelsea, Mass., 1956-62, chmn. dept. dermatology, Phila., 1962-67; chmn. dept. dermatology Lahey Clinic Med. Ctr., Burlington, Mass., 1969-82; clin. prof. dermatology Harvard U. Med. Sch., Boston, 1980-91, prof. emeritus, 1991—. Cons. U.S. Naval Hosp., Phila., 1967-72, U. Pa. Grad. Sch., 1962-67, Harvard Sch. Tropical Medicine, 1975-2002, Nat. Hansen's Disease Ctr., Baton Rouge, 2002—. Author/editor: (with otherw) Dermatology, 3d edit., 1992; contbr. articles to profl. jours.; also papers, book chpts. Fellow ACP; mem. Am. Acad. Dermatology, Am. Dermatol. Assn., Am. Soc. Dermapathology, Internat. Leprosy Assn., Internat. Soc. Dermatology, New Eng. Dermatologic Soc., Soc. Investigative Dermatology. Home: 887 Commonwealth Ave Newton MA 02459-1036 Office: Lahey Clinic Med Ctr 41 Mall Rd Burlington MA 01805-0002 E-mail: samuel.l.moschella@lahey.org.

**MOSCHELLA, WILLIAM EMIL,** federal agency administrator; b. 1968; BA, U. Va.; JD, George Mason Univ. Sch. of Law. Gen. coun. House Commn. on Rules, 1999, chief investment coun., 1999—2001; chief legis. counsel, parliamentarian House Com. on the Judiciary, 2001—03; asst. atty. gen. Office Legis. Affairs U.S. Dept. of Justice, Washington, DC, 2003—. Office: US Dept Justice Rm 1145 950 Pennsylvania Ave NW Washington DC 20530 Office Phone: 202-514-2141.

**MOSCHOPOULOS, PANAGIS,** science educator; BS, U. Athens, Greece, 1969; MS, McGill U., Montreal, Que., Can., 1977; MA, PhD, U. Rochester, NY, 1981. Prof. U. Tex., El Paso, 1981—. Office: U Tex at El Paso 500 W University Ave El Paso TX 79968 E-mail: peter@math.utep.edu.

**MOSCHOVAKIS, YIANNIS NICHOLAS,** mathematics professor; b. Athens, Greece, Jan. 18, 1938; s. Nicholas Yiannis and Ismene Nicholas Moschovakis; m. Joan Rand, Aug. 26, 1963; children: Nicholas Rand, Anna Elizabeth. BS in Math., MS in Math., MIT, Cambridge, 1960; PhD, U. Wis., Madison, 1963; PhD (hon.), U. Athens, Sofia U., Bulgaria. Instr. Benjamin Peirce Harvard U., Cambridge, Mass., 1963—64; prof. math. U. Calif., LA,

1964—, U. Athens, 1996—2005. Dir. Grad. Program Logic and Algorithms, Athens, 1997—. Author: (research monograph) Descriptive set theory, Elementary induction on abstract structures. Fellow, Guggenheim Found., 1968—69, Sloan Found., 1971—72. Mem.: Acad. of Athens (corr.). Office: UCLA Dept Mathematics 520 Portola Plz Los Angeles CA 90095-1555 Business E-mail: ynm@math.ucla.edu.

**MOSCO, SCOTT MORRIS,** small business owner; b. Park Ridge, Ill., Oct. 7, 1962; s. Owen Nathaniel Mosco and Barbara Joyce (Ordman) Palermo; m. Marcela Madeline Apolo, Dec. 13, 1986; children: Nathaniel, Daniel. Student, Harry S. Truman City Coll., De Paul U. Trading fl. phone clk. Lind Waldock & Co., Chgo., 1982-84, Chgo. Corp., 1984; trading fl. mgr. Chgo. RSch. & Trading Group, 1984-87; trading fl. phone clk. Merrill Lynch Commodities, Chgo., 1987, Mocatta Metals Inc., Chgo., 1987-88; rsch. analyst asst. G.N.P. Commodities Inc., Chgo., 1988-89; pres. Jewelry As Art Inc., Valparaiso, Ind., 1989—. Republican. Avocations: investing, reading books and newsletters. Office: Jewelry As Art Inc 1304 Gibralter Ct Valparaiso IN 46383-4013 Office Phone: 219-477-5394. Personal E-mail: smmosco@comcast.net.

**MOSCOWITZ, TODD,** music company executive; b. 1970; Various positions Rush Comm., 1991—2000, pres. Def Jam Music Publishing, Def Jam Interactive Gaming; ptnr. Violator Mgmt., 2000—04; pres. Asylum Records Warner Music Group, 2004—; pres. Independent Label Group, 2006—. Office: Warner Music Group Corp 75 Rockefeller Plz New York NY 10019 Office Phone: 212-275-2000. Office Fax: 212-757-3985.*

**MOSEBACH, MICHAEL,** education educator; s. James and Lorraine Doucette Mosebach; m. Janet Ellen Berger; 1 child, Michael Robert. PhD, U. Okla., Norman, 1996. CPA Calif., 1976. Asst. prof. U. Ark., Fayetteville, 2001—, Old Dominion U., Norfolk, Va. Home: 200 East Parks St Prairie Grove AR 72753 Office: Univ of Ark Business Bldg Fayetteville AR 72701 Home Fax: 479-575-2252. Personal E-mail: mmosebach@walton.uark.edu.

**MOSELEY, CHRIS ROSSER,** marketing executive; b. Balt., Apr. 13, 1950; d. Thomas Earl and Fern Elaine (Coleman) Rosser; m. Thomas Kenneth Moseley. BA with honors, The Coll. of Wooster, 1972. Asst. dir. advt. and promotion Sta. WBAL-TV, Balt., 1972-74; dir. pub. rels. Mintz & Hoke Advt. Inc., Hartford, Conn., 1974-75; promotion mgr. Sta. WFSB-TV, Hartford, 1975-77; audience promotion mgr. Sta. WTVJ-TV, Miami, Fla., 1977-78; pres. CMA Mktg. Cons., Hyde Park, NY, 1979-82; promotion mgr. Ind. Network News-Sta. WPIX-TV, N.Y.C., 1982-84; sr. v.p., mgmt. supr. Christopher Thomas Muller Jordan Weiss, N.Y.C., 1984-89, Earle Palmer Brown/N.Y., N.Y.C., 1989-90; sr. v.p. advt., promotion Discovery Networks, U.S., Bethesda, Md., 1990-99; exec. v.p. mktg. ABC, Inc., N.Y.C., 1999—2000; exec. v.p., chief mktg. officer Hallmark Channel, Studio City, Calif., 2000—. Bd. dirs. Promax/BDA, Cable Positive, WICT, CTAM. Recipient Best Bus.-to-Bus. award Art Direction mag., 1984, achievement award in media rels. and edn. Nat. Resources Coun. Am. 1991, Best Editorial Excellence award Mag. Age, 1992, Best Overall Mktg. Campaign award MIP/MIPCOM, 1994, 1st Place Print award: Media Promotion, London Internat. Advt. awards, 1993, Gold award Broadcast Designers, 1993, Mktg. 100 award Ad Age, 1995, Cable Marketer of Yr. award Ad Age, 1995. Mem.: Advt. Women N.Y., Nat. Cable TV Assn. (conv. com. 1995, 1996, named one of Multichannel News' Wonderwomen of Yr. 2002, Vanguard award 1996), Cable and Telecom. Assn. Mktg. (chair Mark award 1995, bd. dir. 1996, co-chair 1997, bd. dir. 1997). Avocations: horticulture, travel. Home: 5224 Los Encantos Way Los Angeles CA 90027 Office: Hallmark Channel 12700 Ventura Blvd Ste 100 Studio City CA 91604-6201 Office Phone: 818-755-2587. E-mail: chrismoseley@hallmarkchannel.com.

**MOSELEY, CLIFFORD WAYNE,** writer, poet; b. Odessa, Tex., Aug. 10, 1947; s. Leylon Ivan and Josephine Opal Moseley; m. Cathryn Lualice Brotherton, Oct. 11, 1968; children: Clifford Wayne Jr., Patrick Lee. AAS, Odessa Coll., 1989; B in Bus. Mgmt., U. Tex. Permian Basin, Odessa, 1994. Enlisted U.S. Army, 1968, advanced through grades to SFC, 1982; ret., 1985; with Ready Reserves, 1985—89. Writer tech. manuals, Dover, NJ, 1971—75. Contbr. poems to Tomorrow's Dreams, 1995. Decorated Bronze Star, 1971; nominee Tex. Scout of Yr., Boy Scouts Am., 1966. Republican. Avocation: collecting military paraphernalia. Home and Office: 4280 Bonham Ave Odessa TX 79762 E-mail: Cliff_Moseley@yahoo.com.

**MOSELEY, JAMES FRANCIS,** lawyer; b. Charleston, S.C., Dec. 6, 1936; s. John Olin and Kathryn (Moran) M.; m. Anne McGehee, June 10, 1961; children: James Francis Jr., John McGehee. AB, The Citadel, 1958; JD, U. Fla., 1961. Bar: Fla. 1961, U.S. Supreme Ct. 1970. Pres. Moseley, Prichard, Parrish, Knight & Jones, Jacksonville, Fla., 1963—. Chmn. jud. nominating com. 4th Jud. Cir., 1978-80 Assoc. editor: American Maritime Cases; contbr. articles on admiralty, transp. and ins. law to legal jours. Pres. Jacksonville United Way, 1979; chmn. bd. dirs. United Way Fla., 1992-93, S.E. regional coun. United Way, 1992-96; trustee Jacksonville Cmty. Found.; chmn. bd. trustees Jacksonville Pub. Libr.; trustee Libr. Found., sec., 1987-91; trustee CMI Am. Found.; chmn. Jacksonville Human Svcs. Coun., 1989-91; chmn. bd. trustees United Way N.E. Fla., 1995-97; bd. govs. United Way Am., 1996-2002. Recipient Meritorious Pub. Svc. award/medal U.S. Dept. Transp./USCG, 1998. Fellow Am. Coll. Trial Lawyers, Am. Bar Found.; mem. ABA (ho. of del. 2002—), Jacksonville Bar Assn. (pres. 1975), Fla. Coun. Bar Pres. (chmn. 1979), Maritime Law Assn. U.S. (exec. com. 1978-81, chmn. navigation com. 1981-88, v.p. 1992-96, pres. 1996-98), Comm. Maritime Internat. (titulary), Com. on Collision (Lisbon Rules), Fed. Ins. Corp. Counsel (chmn. maritime law sect.), Internat. Assn. Def. Counsel (chmn. maritime com. 1994), Inns of Ct. (master of bench), Assn. of Citadel Men (bd. dir. 1989-93, exec. com. 1994, Man of Yr. award 1992, S.C. Palmetto medal and award 2001, Citadel Inn of Ct. sr. bencher), Deerwood Club, River Club, India House (N.Y.C.), Army Navy Club (Washington), St. John's Dinner Club (pres. 1988). Office: Moseley Prichard Parrish Knight & Jones 1887 West Rd Bay St Jacksonville FL 32202 Office Phone: 904-356-1306. Office Fax: 904-354-0194. Business E-Mail: jfmoseley@mppjk.com.

**MOSELEY, JAMES R.,** former federal agency administrator, farmer; b. Peru, Ind., June 2, 1948; s. Donald and Violet (Love) Moseley; m. Kathryn Lynn Maple, 1969; children: Jeff, Jennifer, Bethany, Amanda, Neil, Brandon, Kyle. BS in agriculture, Purdue U., 1980. Owner Ag Ridge Farms, Clarks Hill, Ind.; mng. ptnr. Infinity Pork LLC, Clarks Hill; asst. sec. agr. natural resources and environ. USDA, 1990—92; dir. agrl. svcs. and regulations State of Ind., Purdue U., West Lafayette, 1992—95; dep. sec. USDA, Washington, 2001—05. Agrl. advisor to adminstr. U.S. Environ. Protection Agy., 1989—90; chmn. industry negotiating team Am. Clean Water Found. Nat. Environ. Dialogue on Pork Prodn., 1997; cons. Nat. Assn. State Depts. Agr., 1995. Past mem. editl. bd. Farm Jour. Pub., past polit. analyst.

**MOSELEY, JOHN TRAVIS,** academic administrator, physicist, researcher; b. New Orleans, Feb. 26, 1942; s. Fred Baker and Lily Gay (Lord) M.; m. Belva McCall Hutson, Aug. 11 1964 (div. June 1978); m. Susan Diane Callow, Aug. 6, 1979; children: Melanie Lord, John Mark, Stephanie Marie, Shannon Eleanor. BS in Physics, Ga. Inst. Tech., 1964, MS in Physics, 1966, PhD in Physics, 1969. Asst. prof. physics U. West Fla., Pensacola, 1968-69; sr. physicist SRI Internat., Menlo Park, Calif., 1969-75; program mgr., 1976-79; vis. prof. U. Paris, 1975-76; assoc. prof. U. Oreg., Eugene, 1979-81, dir. chem. physics inst., 1980-84, prof. physics, 1984—, head physics dept., 1984-85, v.p. rsch., 1985-94, v.p. acad. affairs, provost, 1994-2001, sr. v.p., provost, 2001—06. Mem. exec. com., coun. on acad. affairs NASULGC, 1994-2000, chair, 1996-97; bd. dirs. Oreg. Resource and Tech. Portland; mem. com. on Atomic and Molecular Sci., 1983-85. Contbr. numerous articles to profl. jours. Mem. So. Willamette Rsch. Corridor, Eugene, 1990-00, Lane Econ. Devel. Com., Eugene, 1988-94; bd. dirs. Eugene/Springfield Metro Partnership, 1985-01, Oreg. Bach Festival, Eugene, 1987-94, Eugene Arts Found., 1995-97. Recipient Doctoral Thesis award Sigma Xi, 1969; Fulbright fellow, 1975; numerous rsch. grants, 1969—. Fellow AAAS, Am.

Physical Soc.; mem. AAUP, Am. Chem. Soc. Avocations: skiing, backpacking. Home: 2140 Essex Ln Eugene OR 97403-1851 Office: U Oreg Office of Sr VP and Provost Eugene OR 97403-1258 Business E-Mail: jtm@uoregon.edu.

**MOSELEY, JULIA W.,** music educator, preservationist; b. Tampa, Fla., Mar. 21, 1919; d. Hallock Preston and Ruby Winifred Moseley. BA, Agnes Scott Coll., Decatur, Ga., 1940. Nat. cert. music tchr. Asst. food and fashion editor Atlanta Constn., 1940-41; credit report typist, publicist, fund raiser Mchts. Assn. Tampa, 1942-43; teletype operator, writer/editor, commodities marketer USDA, Atlanta, 1943-47; self-employed music tchr. Atlanta, 1945-47; hist. rschr. New Orleans, 1947—48; self-employed music tchr. Fla., 1948—; also cattle raiser, citrus grower; preservationist Moseley Homestead, Brandon, Fla., 1948—. Author, editor: Come to My Sunland, 1997; co-author: Internet Lake Atlas, 1999, Recipes and Remembrances, 1999-2004; composer song Brandon, Brandon. Mem. Brandon Citizens Adv. Com.; established Timberly Trust, Inc., 1994; worked with Historic Tampa/Hillsborough Cunty Preservation Bd., 1983-92; spokesperson to Hillsborough County Bd. Commrs. on land use and preservation, 1966-99; mem. Brandon Task Force involved with county devel. issues; mem. hist. com. Brandon Centennial Celebration, 1990. Elizabeth Ordaway Dunn Found. grantee, 1998. Mem.: Fla. State Music Tchrs. Assn. (past officer), Limona Acad. Arts, Letters and Scis. (past officer and dir.), Art Publ. Soc. (Guild tchr.), Nat. Music Clubs, Nat. Guild Piano Tchrs., Music Tchrs. Nat. Assn., Tampa Music Tchrs. Assn. (officer), Fla. Breeding Bird Atlas, Tampa Preservation, Inc., Nature Conservancy, Fla. Trust for Historic Preservation, Nat. Trust for Historic Preservation, Friday Morning Musicale Club. Avocations: bird watching, reading, walking, photography, star gazing. Personal E-mail: ttland@hotmail.com.

**MOSELEY, MARC ROBARDS,** sales executive; b. L.A., July 14, 1954; s. Thomas Robards and Doris Cecile (Tye) M.; m. Laura Hoon Hamilton, 1999. Student, U. Ky., Lexington, 1972-74, U. Ga., Athens, 1977-78; BA, La. Tech. U., 1985; postgrad., Western Mich. U. Kalamazoo, 1986. Svc. rep. Ky. Mortgage Co., Lexington, 1973; loan rep. Templan Fin. Co., Atlanta, 1975-77; sr. cons. Co-Ordinated Planning Assocs., Atlanta, 1979-80; sales rep. Nat. Starch & Chem. Corp., Monroe, La., 1980-84; v.p. sales Ednl. Funding Svc., Monroe, 1984-85; tech. sales rep. polymer divsn. Ralston Purina, St. Louis, 1985-87; account mgr. Protein Techs. Internat. Polymer Group subs. Ralston Purina, St. Louis, 1988-90, sr. account mgr., 1990-92, area dir. market ops., 1992-96; dir. industry mgmt. and bus. devel. Polymer Group subs. Dupont Ag Enterprise, 1996-98; dir. strategic accounts Polymer Group Dupont Soy Enterprise, 1999—2002; reg. sales mgr. Phila. Mixing Solutions, Palmyra, Pa., 2004—. V.p. sales and mktg. RANA Enterprises, Inc., Atlanta, 1991-98; dir. Radiant Chem., Atlanta, 1992-2001; v.p., dir. Bishop Pharm. Co., Inc., West Monroe, La., 1994-96. Mem. TAPPI Greater Atlanta, U. Ky. Alumni Assn. (bd. dirs. 1991-97, exec. v.p. Ga. sect. 1992-94). Avocations: water and snow skiing, basketball, music, golf. Home: 12220 Brookfield Club Dr Roswell GA 30075-1265 Office: Philadelphia Mixing Solution 1221 E Main St Palmyra PA 17078 Office Phone: 770-552-5257. E-mail: mrmosley@mindspring.com.

**MOSELEY, T. MICHAEL (TEED MICHAEL MOSELEY),** career military officer; BA in Polit. Sci., Tex. A&M U., 1971, MA in Polit. Sci., 1972; grad., Squadron Officer Sch., Maxwell AFB, Ala., 1977, U.S. Navy Fighter Weapons Sch., 1979, Fighters Weapons Instr. Course, 1981, Air Command, Staff Coll, 1984, USAF Jt. Sr. Battle comdr. Cos, Hurlbut Field, Fla., 1988, Nat. War Coll., Ft. Lesley J. McNair, 1990; grad, Combined Forces Air Component Combat. Course, Maxwell AFB, Ala. & Hurlbert Field, Fla., 2000. Commd. 2d. lt. USAF, 1971, advanced through grades to gen., 2003; undergrad. pilot tng. Webb AFB, Tex., 1972-73; T-37 instr. pilot, spin flight test pilot, flight test pilot, standardization and evaluation flight examiner 3389th Flying Tng. Squadron, 78th Flying Tng. Wing, Webb AFB, Tex., 1973-77; F-15 instr. pilot, flight lead mission comdr. 7th Tactical Fighter Squadron, Holloman AFB, N.M., 1977-79; F-15 weapons tactics officer, instr. pilot, flight lead and mission comdr., standardization and evaluation and flight examiner 44th Tactical Fighter Squadron, 12th Tactical Fighter Squadron, Kadena Air Base, Japan, 1979-83; course officer Air Command & Staff Coll., Maxwell AFB, Ala., 1983—84; chief, Tactical Fighter Branch, Tactical Forces Divsn., Directorate of Plans, Dep. Chief of Staff for Plans & Ops. USAF, Washington, 1984—87; comdr. F-15 divsn. & instr. pilot, fighter weapons instr. course USAF Fighter Weapons Sch., Nellis AFB, Nev., 1987—89; course officer Nat. War Coll., Washington, 1989-90, chief staff, 1990-92; comdr. 33rd Ops. Group, Englin AFB, Fla., 1992-94; chief Hdqs. USAF, Washington, 1994-96; comdr. 57th Wing, Nellis AFB, Nev., 1996-97; dep. dir. polit.-mil. affairs Joint Chiefs Staff, Washington, 1997-99; dir. legis. liaison, Office Sec. Air Force USAF, Washington, 1999—2001; comdr. 9th Air Force & US Ctrl. Command Air Force, Shaw AFB, SC, 2001—03; vice chief of staff USAF, Washington, 2003—05, chief of staff, 2005—. Decorated Def. Disting. Svc. Medal, Disting. Svc. Medal, Def. Superior Svc. medal with oak leaf cluster, Legion of Merit award with oak leaf cluster, Meritorious Svc. medal with three oak leaf clusters, Air medal, Joint Svc. Commendation medal, Air Force Commendation medal, Air Force Achievement medal, Global War on Terrorism Expeditionary medal, French Nat. Order of Merit, United Arab Emirates Military medal, 1st Class; recipient H.H. Arnold award, Air Force Assn., 2003. Office: USAF 1670 Air Force Pentagon Washington DC 20330*

**MOSEMANN, LLOYD KENNETH, II,** research and development company executive; b. Lancaster, Pa., May 16, 1936; s. Lloyd Kreider and Beatrice Elizabeth (Frey) M.; m. Arlene K. White, Sept. 6, 1957; children: Gigi Renee Mosemann Falke, Lloyd Kenneth III, Douglas Lamar, Holly Joy. AB in Social Sci., U. Chgo., 1957, AM in Internat. Rels., 1959. Gen. supply officer Navy Electronics Supply Office, Great Lakes, Ill., 1958-62; inventory mgmt. specialist Def. Electronics Supply Ctr., Dayton, Ohio, 1962-63; head integrated-retail supply and support br. Naval Supply Systems Command, Washington, 1963-69; dep. chief logistics support analysis office Def. Logistics Agy., Alexandria, Va., 1969-71; dep. for supply and maintenance Office Sec. of Air Force, Washington, 1971-74; dep. asst. sec. for logistics and communications Dept. Air Force, Washington, 1974-91, dep. asst. sec. for comm., computers and logistics, 1991-93, dep. asst. sec. for comm., computers and support systems, 1993-96; software and acquisition cons., 1996-97; sr. v.p. corp. devel. Sci. Applications Internat. Corp., McLean, Va., 1997—. Mem. Air Force Exec. Resources Bd., 1981—95. Author: AntiChrist in the Midst, 2006. Decorated DSM; recipient Meritorious Svc. medal Sec. Air Force, 1977, Exceptional Civilian Svc. medal sec. Air Force, 1979, 81, 82, 87, 96, Meritorious Sr. Exec. award Pres. of U.S., 1982, 87, Def. Meritorious Civilian Svc. medal, 1985. Mem. Soc. Logistics Engrs. (bd. advisers 1983—, Founders medal 1983, H. Mark Grove award for excellence in software mgmt. 1996, Govt. Computer News Hall of Fame 1996, Fed. Computer Week "100" award 1996), Am. Def. Preparedness Assn. (bd. dirs. 1974-83), Nat. Inst. for Urban Search and Rescue (exec. bd. dirs. 1990-2005). Home: 10013 Blake Ln Oakton VA 22124

**MOSENA, DAVID R.,** museum administrator; M in City Planning, U. Tenn. Dir. rsch. Am. Planning Assn., Chgo.; mem. staff City of Chgo., 1984-89, planning commr., 1989-91, chief of staff 1991-92, aviation commr., 1992-96; pres. CTA, 1996—97; chmn. bd. dirs., CEO Museum of Science and Industry, Chicago, 1997—. Chmn. bd. dirs. Oreg. Museum of Science and Industry 5700 S Lake Shore Dr Chicago IL 60637

**MOSER, BARRY,** artist; b. Chattanooga, Tenn., Oct. 15, 1940; Student, Auburn U., U. Tenn., Chattanooga; postgrad., U. Mass. Owner, pub. Pennyroyal Press, 1970—; resident RI Sch. Design, 1991—98; prof. in residence, printer to the coll. Smith Coll., 2001—. Illustrator: The Divine Comedy, 1980, Scarlet Letter, 1984, A River Runs Through It, 1989, Appalachia, the Voices of Sleeping Birds, 1991 (Boston Globe-Horn Book award), And Still the Turtle Watched, 1991, Tales of Edgar Allan Poe, 1991, Ariadne, Awake!, 1994, Call of the Wild, 1994, Cloud Eyes, 1994, Farm Summer 1942, 1994, Pilgrim's Progress, 1994, What You Know First, 1995, When Birds Could

Talk and Bats Could Sing, 1996, Earthquack!, 2002, Voices of Egypt, 2003; represented in permanent collections: Met. Mus., British Mus., Harvard U., Princeton U., Libr. of Congress, Victoria & Albert, Vatican Libr.; prin. works include (illustrator) Alice in Wonderland, 1993 (Nat. Book award for Design and illustration, 1993) (publisher, illustrator) Pennyroyal-Caxton Bible, 1999. Mem.: NAD (academician 1994—). Business E-mail: sales@moser-pennyroyal.com.

**MOSER, C. THOMAS,** lawyer; b. Seattle, Aug. 10, 1947; s. Carl Thomas and Helen Louise (Felton) M.; m. Deborah J. St. Clair, Sept. 25, 1976; children: Nicole, Lauren. BA, Cen. Wash. U., 1972; M in Pub. Adminstrn., George Washington U., 1974; JD, Gonzaga U., 1976. Bar: Wash. 1977; U.S. Dist. Ct. (we. dist.) Wash. 1977, U.S. Dist. Ct. (ea. dist.) Wash. 1980, U.S. Ct. Appeals (9th cir.) 1980, U.S. Supreme Ct. 1981. Dep. pros. atty. Skagit County Pros. Atty., Mount Vernon, Wash., 1976-77, chief civil dep., 1979-80, pros. atty., 1980-86, San Juan County Pros. Atty., Friday Harbor, Wash., 1977-79; pvt. practice Mount Vernon, 1987—. Hearing examiner pro tem Skagit County, 1992—. Author: Gonzaga Law Review, 1975. Bd. dirs. Wash. Environ. Coun., Seattle, 1971-72, Padilla Bay Found., Skagit County, Wash., 1988; bd. trustees Wash. Assn. County Ofcls., Olympia, 1983; exec. bd. North Pacific Conf. Evang. Covenant Ch., vice sec. 1991-96; bd. trustees Skagit Valley Coll., 2000—. Sgt. U.S. Army, 1967-69, Korea. Recipient Silver Key award ABA Student Law Div., 1976, Legion of Honor award Internat. Order DeMolay, Kansas City, Mo., 1982, Chevalier award 1982. Mem. ATLA, Nat. Coll. Advocacy (advocate), Wash. State Trial Lawyers Assn. (bd. govs. 1990-92, 96-97), Wash. Assn. Pros. Attys. (bd. dirs. 1983-85), Skagit County Bar Assn. (pres. 1995-96, Professionalism award 2004), Kiwanis Club Mt. Vernon, Affiliated Health Svc. (ethics com.), Christian Legal Soc. Democrat. Evangelical. Avocations: skiing, golf, woodworking. Office: 411 Main St Mount Vernon WA 98273-3837 Office Phone: 360-428-7900. E-mail: tom@tomoser.com.

**MOSER, DON,** writer; s. Charles Frank Moser and Mildred Clementine Balavitch; children: Zachary August, Nicholas Sher. BA in Philosophy, U. Tex., Austin, 1975, BS in Radio, TV, Film, 1977; MA in Philosophy, U. Houston, 1979—80. Cert. in Secondary Teaching Tex., 1985. Author: (screenplays) On the Bus, 1979, (teleplay) Down Routes, 1988, (of poems) For Women Only, 2004. Home: PO Box 3824 Houston TX 77253 Office Phone: 877-734-8218.

**MOSER, HUGO WOLFGANG,** physician; b. Switzerland, Oct. 4, 1924; came to U.S., 1940, naturalized, 1943; s. Hugo L. and Maria (Werner) M.; m. Ann Boody, Dec. 28, 1963; children— Tracey, Peter, Karen, Lauren. MD, Columbia U., 1948; A.M. in Med. Sci, Harvard U., 1956. Intern Columbia-Presbyn. Med. Center, N.Y.C., 1948-50; asst. in medicine Peter Bent Brigham Hosp., Boston, 1950-52; research fellow dept. biol. chemistry Harvard U., 1955-57; asst. resident, resident in neurology Mass. Gen. Hosp., 1957-59, asst. neurologist, 1960-67, assoc. neurologist, 1967-69, neurologist, 1969-76. Teaching fellow neuropathology Harvard Med. Sch., 1959-60, instr. neurology, 1960-64, assoc. in neurology, 1964-67, asst. prof., 1967-69, asso. prof., 1969-72, prof., 1972-76; dir. research and tng. Walter E. Fernald State Sch., 1963-68, asst. supt., 1968-73, acting supt., 1973-74, supt., 1974-76; dir. Center for Research on Mental Retardation and Related Aspects of Human Devel., dir. univ. affiliated facilities for mentally retarded, 1965-74; co-dir. Eunice Kennedy Shriver Center for Mental Retardation, Inc., 1969-74; pres. John F. Kennedy Inst., Balt., 1976-88; prof. neurology and pediatrics Johns Hopkins U., 1976—. Author: (with others) Mental Retardation: An Atlas of Diseases with Associated Physical Abnormalities, 1972; Contbr. (with others) articles to med. jours. Served with AUS, 1943-44; to capt. U.S. Army, 1952-54. Recipient Hower award Child Neurology Soc., 1994, Becker award German Soc. for Neuropediats., 1999, Frank Ford award Internat. Child Neurology Assn., 2002. Mem. Am. Acad. Neurology, Am. Assn. Mental Deficiency, Am. Assn. Neuropathologists, Am. Neurol. Assn., Internat. Soc. Neurochemistry, Am. Pediatrics Soc., Sigma Xi, Alpha Omega Alpha. Home: 100 Beechdale Rd Baltimore MD 21210-2209 Office: Kennedy Inst 707 N Broadway Baltimore MD 21205-1832 Office Phone: 443-923-2750. Business E-Mail: moser@KennedyKrieger.org.

**MOSER, JEFFERY RICHARD,** real estate manager; b. Miller, S.D., Feb. 8, 1961; s. Richard and Aressa Joan (Yost) M. Student, U. Minn., 1979—84, Duke U., 1995, Northwestern U., 1997, U. Denver, 2005—. Cert. lay minister; cert. in pub. policy and pub. fin.; cert. CPR, Am. Red Cross. Lab asst., intern U. Minn. Dept. Limnology, Mpls., 1980-81; exec. intern pub. affairs dept. Target Corp., Mpls., 1982, Nat. Farmers Union, Nat. Youth Adv. Coun., Denver, 1980-81; intern/asst. for legis. and policy Minn. Agri-Growth Coun., Bloomington, 1984-85; field office asst. US Congressman Thomas A. Daschle, Aberdeen, SD, 1986; pvt. cons. to non-profit groups. Huron, SD, 1986—89; notary pub. State of SD, 1986-99; acting camp dir. SD Farmers Union Edn. Program, 1987-88; small bus. owner Westangrove, SD, 1986—2002; exec. dir. SD Towns and Twps., 1990-95; dep. state treas. to treas. Richard D. Butler State of SD, Pierre, 1995-99; dir. econ. and coop. devel. Nat. Farmer's Union, Greenwood Village, Colo., 1999—. Participant 4-H/UN/USAID Presdl. young adult exch. program to Kenya and Botswana, Africa, summer 1985. Vol. U. Minn. Hosps., 1979-83, U. Minn. Dept. Minn. Unions, Mpls., 1983-84; gen. election poll watcher Hand County Rural precincts, 1988; past mem. Beadle County Dems., Hand County Dems., Brown County Dems., Hughes County Dems., v.p., 1997-98, Arapahoe County Dems., 1999—; del. State Dem. Conv., 1990, 92, 94; alt. del. Nat. Dem. Conv., Chgo., 1996, Clinton for Pres., 1992; nom. Dem. candidate State Auditor, 1994, US House, 1998; donor SD Dems., Dem. Nat. Com.; Dem. Nat. Senate Task Force; Dem. Congl. Campaign Com.; chair, del. Selection/Affirmative Action Com., 1996; Clinton-Gore, mem. State Adv. Com., 1996, at. del. Dem. Nat. Conv., 1996; mem. Hughes County Steering Com. to Re-Elect Senator Tom Daschle, 1997-98; dem. candidate SD at-large dist. US Ho. of Rep., 1998; vol. leader, advisor, and state fair judge SD 4-H Program, 1981-94; bd. dirs. SD Rural Devel. Coun., 1993-95, SD State Adv. Com. for Green Thumb, Inc., 1993-95; mem. task force Nat. Urban Comparative Risk Environ., 1994, Common Cause SD, 1991-94; dist. edn. dir. SD Farmers Union, 1988-93; dir. Minn. Union Coordinating Bd., U. Minn., 1982-84; bd. dirs. Golden Razor Hair Salon, Inc., Mpls., 1983-84, bd. dirs. Internat. Study & Travel Assn., Mpls., 1982-83; mem. Rose Hill Presbyn. Ch., Clan Campbell Soc. (N.Am.), E. River Sierra Club, Rocky Mountains/Hi Plains Group Sierra Club, SD AG Heritage Mus., SD Com. for World Food Day, SD Bread for the World, Dakota Rural Action, SD Project Prosperity Coalition, SD Farmers Union, SD Horticulture Soc., Dakota Rural Action, South Dakotans For the Arts, Wilson Ctr., Am. Mus. Nat. Hist., Smithsonian Assocs., Lib. Congress, Oscar Howe Art Ctr., Siouxland chpt. Alzheimer's Assn., SD Health Care Reform Coalition, SD Artists Network, SD Hist. Soc., Colo. Pub. Radio/TV (donor), Nat. Farmers Union Found. (donor), Cmty. Shares of Colo. (donor), 9th Jud. Circuit Ct. Assn., Nat. Resource Defense Coun., Nat. Audubon Soc., Internat. 4-H Programs; host family Botswana Agr. Exch. Program, 1992, Presbytery of S.D., sec. Congl. Devel. Ministry, 1988-91, Advocacy Devel. Ministry unit, 1992-93, ch. camp dean, moderator Soc. Witness and Action Com., 1995-99, mem. com. representation, 1995-99, mem. com. Self-Devel. People, 1995-99; exec. Presbytery Search com., 1995-96, active Am. Heart Assn. Pierre Area Heart Walk, 1995, 97; vol. coord. Bread for the World Human Hunger Awareness event, Huron, 1993; mem. planning com. 1993 Regional 4-H Leaders Forum, Sioux Falls; past del. rep. SD Nat. 4-H Congress, 1981; past del. rep. Nat. Farmers Union Nat. conf., Presbyn. Ch. USA Gen. Assembly, 1990, Presbyn. Ch. USA Consultation on Sustainable Devel., 1995, Nat. 4-H Coun. Master Communicators Conf., Albuquerque, Presbyn. Ch. USA Synod Lakes and Prairies Workshop on Representation and Nominations, Rochester, Minn., 1997, Common Cause Nat. Leadership conf., Washington, 1993, Sharing Global Harvests Nat. Tng., Nat. Assn. Towns and Twps. Am.'s Town Meeting, Washington, 1992, strategic leadership for state execs. course Duke U., 1995, Inst. Pub. Fin. Northwestern U., 1997; bd. co-chair Huron Postal Customer Adv. Bd., 1993-95; bd. dirs. SD Peace and Justice Ctr., sec.-treas., 1994, v.p., 1995, dir. 1994-97; copywriter Minn. Ag. Manual, 1985; active Fed. Credit Union; vol. comty. data reporter US Census Bur., 2000-2002; participant

Future Coop Leaders program N.C.B.A., Washington, 2002; mem. Nat. Grants Rev. panel USDA, CSREES, 2001-03, 05; vol. Population, Employment and Labor Survey Reporting, US Census Bur., 2001-02; mem. Nat. Trust for Hist. Preservation; sec. Mich. Farmers Union Found., 1999—; mem. Colo. Criminal Justice Reform Coalition, Bread for the World, Cmty. Alliance with Family Farmers 2003—. Mem. Nat. Audubon Soc., Nat. Coop. Bus. Assn., Assn. of Coop. Educators, Phi Beta Kappa, Omicron Delta Kappa, Mortar Bd., Golden Key, Sierra Club. Democrat. Avocations: piano, painting, poetry. E-mail: jeff.moser@nfu.org.

**MOSER, JONATHAN R.,** music educator; b. Pitts., Sept. 25, 1974; s. Frank D. and Rosemary C. Moser; m. Mary A. Uribe, Dec. 4, 1993. MusB, Shenandoah U., Winchester, Va., 2001; MusM, Ariz. State U., Tempe, 2003. Dir. music ministries U. Presbyn. Ch., Las Cruces, N.Mex., 2003—04; Providence Presbyn. Ch., Robinson Township, Pa., 2004—; violin instr. Grove City Coll., Pa., 2004—06, Westminster Coll., New Wilmington, Pa., 2006—. Conservative. Reformed Protestant. Avocations: mountain biking, hiking, fishing. Office: Westminster Coll Dept Music 319 S Market St New Wilmington PA 16172 Office Phone: 724-946-7271. Business E-Mail: moserjo@westminster.edu.

**MOSER, KENNETH ALLEN,** lawyer; b. Rowan County, NC, Sept. 8, 1942; BA, Wake Forest U., 1965, JD cum laude, 1968. Bar: NC 1968. Mng. mem. Winston-Salem office Womble Carlyle Sandridge & Rice PLLC. Mem. faculty Grad. Sch. Banking of South, Baton Rouge, La., 1987-89. Assoc. editor: Wake Forest Law Rev., 1967-68. Mem.: ABA (chair loan practices and lender liability com. 1988—93, mem. books and media com. 1995—99, real estate, probate and trust law sect.), Am. Counsel Assn., Forsyth County Bar Assn., NC Bar Assn., Am. Coll. Mortgage Attorneys, Am. Coll. Real Estate Lawyers. Office: Womble Carlyle Sandridge & Rice PLLC One West Fourth St Winston Salem NC 27101 Office Phone: 336-721-3504. Office Fax: 336-733-8323. Business E-Mail: kmoser@wcsr.com.

**MOSER, M(ARTIN) PETER,** lawyer; b. Balt., Jan. 16, 1928; s. Herman and Henrietta (Lehmayer) M.; m. Elizabeth Kohn, June 14, 1949; children— Mike, Moriah, Jeremy AB, The Citadel, Charleston, S.C., 1947; LLB, Harvard U., 1950. Bar: Md. 1950, U.S. Supreme Ct., U.S. Ct. Appeals (4th cir.). Asst. states atty. City of Balt., 1951, 53-54; assoc. Blades Rosenfeld, Balt., 1950, 53-54; ptnr. Frank, Bernstein, Conaway & Goldman and predecessor firms, Balt., 1955-90, co-chmn. firm, 1983-86; counsel, 1991-92; of counsel DLA Piper Rudnick Gray Cary US LLP, 1992—. Instr. U. Balt. Law Sch., 1954-56, 86, U. Md. Law Sch., 1986-87. Contbr. articles to profl. jours. Del., chmn. local govt. com. Md. Constl. Conv., 1967-68; mem. Balt. City Planning Comm., 1961-66, Balt. Regional Planning Council, 1963-66, Md. Common. to Study Narcotics Laws, 1965-67, Mayor's Task Force on EEO, 1966-67, Met. Transit Authority Adv. Council, 1962, Com. to Revise Balt. City Planning Laws, 1962, Com. to Revise Balt. City Charter Provision on Conflicts of Interest, 1969-70; mem. Citizens Adv. Com. on Dist. Ct., chmn., 1971, Dist. Adv. Bd. for Pub. Defender System for Dist. 1, 1973-85; mem. Atty. Grievance Commn. of Md., 1975-78, chmn. 82-86; chmn. Md. State Ethics Commn., 1987-89; bd. dirs. Sinai Hosp., 1983-2004, Lifebridge Health Sys., 1998—, Ct. of Appeals Comm. to Study the Model Rules, 1983-86, 2002-05. Served with JAGC, U.S. Army, 1951-53. Fellow: Balt. Bar Found., Md. Bar Found., Am. Bar Found. (pres. 2002—04); mem.: ABA (ho. of dels. 1978—2002, bd. govs. 1984—87, 1992—96, treas. 1993—96), Balt. Bar Assn. (pres. 1970—71), Md. State Bar Assn. (pres. 1979—80), Wednesday Law Club, Lawyers' Roundtable. Democrat. Jewish. Office: DLA Piper Rudnick Gray Cary 6225 Smith Ave Baltimore MD 21209-3600 Office Phone: 410-580-4218. Business E-Mail: peter.moser@DLApiper.com.

**MOSER, MARVIN,** physician, educator; b. Newark, Jan. 24, 1924; s. Sol and Sophia (Markowitz) M.; m. Joy Diane Lipez, July 1, 1954; children: Jill, Stephen, John. AB, Cornell U., 1943; MD, Downstate Coll. Medicine, N.Y.C., 1947. Diplomate: Am. Bd. Internal Medicine, subdd. cardiovascular disease; cert. specialist in hypertension Am. Soc. Hypertension. Intern univ. div. Kings County Hosp., N.Y.C., 1947-48, resident in medicine, 1948-49, Montefiore Hosp., N.Y.C., 1949-50; Nat. Heart Assn. fellow Mt. Sinai Hosp., N.Y.C., 1950-51; charge vascular service Walter Reed Army Hosp. Med. Centre, Washington, 1951-53; practice medicine specializing in cardiology White Plains NY, 1953-95; assoc. physician cardiology Montefiore Hosp., 1953-75, in charge hypertension sect., 1960—74. Attending physician cardiology White Plains Hosp., 1968-95, chief cardiology, 1969-78; adj. physician in cardiology Grasslands Hosp., Valhalla, NY, 1953-60; attending physician in medicine in charge Hypertension Clinic, Westchester County Med. Center, Valhalla, 1974-84; asst. clin. prof. medicine Albert Einstein Coll. Medicine, 1965-75; clin. prof. medicine NY Med. Coll., 1974-84, Yale U. Sch. Medicine, 1984—; sr. med. cons. nat. high blood pressure program NIH, 1975-2002, mem. nat. high blood pressure coordinating com., 1976-2005; chmn. Joint Nat. Com. Hypertension, 1977, vice-chmn., 1979, mem., 1984-88, 92, 96, 2003; exec. com. Nat. Citizens for Treatment High Blood Pressure, 1976-78, vice-chmn., 1978-88; mem. NY State Adv. Com. on Hypertension, 1977-84; chmn. Nat. Conf. on High Blood Pressure Control, 1979; mem. select panel on hypertension in Am. Congl. Subcom. on Aging, 1978-79; cons. cardiology NY State Dept. Health, Gen. Hosp., Saranac Lake, NY, 1980-90; med. dir. Westchester County Hypertension Program, NY, 1979-88. Author: (with A.M. Master, M. Moser. H. Jaffee) Cardiac Emergencies and Heart Failure, 2d edit., 1955; (with A. Goldman) Hypertensive Vascular Disease, 1967, Hypertension, A Practical Approach, 1975, Lower Your Blood Pressure and Live Longer, 1988; co-editor, contbr. Yale University School of Medicine Heart Book, 1992, Week by Week to a Strong Heart, 1992, Heart Healthy Cooking for all Seasons, 1996, Clinical Management of Hypertension, 1996, 7th edit., 2004, Myths, Misconceptions and Heroics, the Story of the Treatment of Hypertension, 1997, 2002, (with J. Sowers) Management of Cardiovascular Risk Factors in Diabetes, 2001, 2d edit., 2005; mem. editl. bd. Preventive Cardiology, 1998—, Jour. Medicine and Sports, 1999-2004; assoc. editor Angiology, 1976-85; bd. editors Primary Cardiology, 1975-78, assoc. editor-in-chief, 1978-96; editor-in-chief Jour. Clin. Hypertension, 1999—; sr. editor Jour. of Cardio Metabolic Syndrome, 2006—. Chmn. Narcotics Guidance Coun., Scarsdale, 1968-72; trustee Scarsdale Bd. Edn., 1970-73, Trudeau Inst. 1990-2004, Nat. Hypertension Found., 1992-2001, Nutrition 21, 1997—, Comprehensive Neuroscience; bd. dirs. Third Ave. Value and Small Cap Funds, 1994—; pres. Hypertension Edn. Found., 1977—. Served U.S. Army, 1941-46; capt. M.C. USAF, 1951-53. Recipient Achievement awards Nat. High Blood Pressure Edn. Program, 1985, 97, award Internat. Soc. Hypertension, 2004, 06, award Am. Soc. Hypertension, 2006; grantee Nat. Inst. Health, 1958-62. Fellow: ACP, Am. Heart Assn. ((various offices): pres. coun. geriatric cardiology 1996-97, others)), Am. Coll. Cardiology, Royal Coll. Physicians and Surgeons (hon.); mem.: Am. Soc. Hypertension, Century Country Club. Home and Office: 13 Murray Hill Rd Scarsdale NY 10583 Personal E-Mail: moserbp@aol.com.

**MOSER, ROBERT HARLAN,** internist, educator, writer; b. Trenton, NJ, June 16, 1923; s. Simon and Helena (Silvers) Moser; m. Linda Mae Salsinger, Mar. 18, 1989; children from previous marriage: Steven Michael, Jonathan Evan. BS, Loyola U., Balt., 1944; MD, Georgetown U., Washington, DC, 1948. Diplomate Am. Bd. Internal Medicine. Commd. 1st lt. U.S. Army, 1948, advanced through grades to col., 1966, intern D.C. Gen. Hosp., 1948—49, fellow pulmonary disease D.C. Gen. Hosp., 1949—50, bn. surgeon Republic of Korea, 1950—51; asst. resident Georgetown U. Hosp., 1951—52; chief resident Georgetown U. Hosp. U.S. Army, 1952—53, chief med. service U.S. Army Hosp. Salzburg, Austria, 1953—55, Wurzburg, Germany, 1955—56, resident in cardiology Brooke Gen. Hosp., 1956—57, asst. chief dept. medicine Brooke Gen. Hosp., 1957—59, chief Brooke Gen. Hosp., 1967—67, fellow hematology U. Utah Coll. Medicine, 1959—60, asst. chief U.S. Army Tripler Gen. Hosp., 1960—64, chief William Beaumont Gen. Hosp., 1965—67, chief Walter Reed Gen. Hosp., 1968—69, ret., 1969; chief of staff Maui (Hawaii) Meml. Hosp., 1969—73, chief dept. medicine, 1975—77; assoc. prof. medicine U. Coll. Physicians, Phila., 1976—86; v.p. med. affairs The NutraSweet Co., Deerfield, Ill., 1986—91. Assoc. prof. medicine Baylor U., 1958—59; clin. prof. medicine Hawaii U., 1969—77, Washington U.,

1970—77, Abraham Lincoln Sch. Medicine, 1974—75; adj. prof. medicine U. Pa., 1977—86, Northwestern U., 1987—91; adj. prof. Uniformed Svcs. U. Health Scis., 1979—97; clin. prof. medicine U. N.Mex. Coll. Medicine, 1992—96, emeritus, 1996—; flight contr. Project Mercury, 1959—62; cons. mem. med. evaluation team Project Gemini, 1962—66; cons. Project Apollo, 1967—73, Tripler Gen. Hosp., 1970—77, Walter Reed Army Med. Ctr., 1974—86; sr. med. cons. Canyon Cons. Corp., 1991—2004; mem. cardiovascular and renal adv. com. FDA, 1978—82; chmn. life scis. adv. com. NASA, 1984—87, mem. adv. coun., 1983—88; chmn. gen. med. panel Hosp. Satellite Network, 1984—86; mem. adv. com. NASA Space Sta., 1988—93; mem. Dept. Def. Com. on Grad. Med. Edn., 1986—87, Life Scis. Strategic Planning Study Group, 1986—88; mem. space studies bd. NRC, 1988—93, space exploration initiation study, 1990; mem. NASA Space Sta. Commn., 1992—93, mem. com. adv. tech. human supp. space, 1996—97; mem. med. adv. bd. the patient channel GE Healthcare, 2001—. Editor, chief divsn. sci. publs. Jour. AMA, Chgo., 1973—75, contbg. editor Med. Opinion and Rev., 1966—75, chmn. editorial bd. Diagnosis mag., 1986—89, mem. editorial bd. Hawaii Med. Jour., Family Physicians, Archives of Internal Medicine, 1967—73, Western Jour. Medicine, 1975—87, Chest, 1975—80, Med. Times, 1977—84, Quality Rev. Bull., 1979—91, The Pharos, 1991—, book rev. editor. 2000—05, mem. editorial bd. Travel Medicine, 1994—96; contbr over 200 articles to med. sci. jours. and med. books; author: Diseases of Medical Progress, 1955, 1969, House Officer Training, 1970, Decade of Decision, 1992, Past Imperfect A Personal History of Life In and Around Medicine, 2003; co-author Adventures in Medical Writing, 1970, editor chief divsn. sci. publs. Jour. AMA, Chgo., 1973—75, contbg. editor Med. Opinion and Rev., 1966—75, chmn. editl. bd. Diagnosis mag., 1986—89; contbr. articles to med. sci. jours. and med. books. Master: ACP (exec. v.p. 1977—86); fellow: Am. Clin. and Climatol. Assn., Am. Coll. Cardiology, Royal Coll. Physicians and Surgeons Can. (hon.); mem.: AMA (adv. panel registry of adverse drug reactions 1960—67, coun. on drugs 1967—73), Soc. Med. Cons. to Armed Forces, Coll. Physicians Phila., Chgo. Soc. Internal Medicine, Nat. Assn. Physician Broadcasters, Inst. Medicine-NAS, Am. Osler Soc., Am. Therapeutic Soc., Am. Med. Writers Assn., Alpha Omega Alpha, Alpha Sigma Nu. Democrat. Jewish. Avocations: hiking, international travel, distance bicycling. Home and Office: 943 E Sawmill Canyon Pl Green Valley AZ 85614 Office Phone: 520-399-2526. Personal E-Mail: rhmoser@earthlink.net.

**MOSER, ROBERT LAWRENCE,** pathologist, health facility administrator; b. Passaic, N.J., Mar. 22, 1952; s. Robert George and Marjorie Ann (Frankenberg) M.; m. Rosemarie Scolaro, June 16, 1978; children: Rachel Ann, Alexander Robert. BA in Biology magna cum laude, Lafayette Coll., 1974; MD Microbiology/Internal Med. with honors, Hahnemann Med. Coll., 1978. Diplomate Am. Bd. Pathology, Am. Bd. Anatomic Pathology, Am. Bd. Clin. Pathology, Am. Bd. Forensic Pathology. Intern, fellow dept. pathology The Johns Hopkins Hosp., Balt., 1978-79, resident, fellow dept. pathology, 1979-81, chief resident, fellow dept. pathology, 1981-82, resident, fellow dept. lab. medicine, 1982-84; cons. pathologist Perry Point (Md.) VA Med. Ctr., 1983-84; pathologist Helene Fuld Med. Ctr., Trenton, N.J., 1984-88; med. dir. St. Francis Med. Ctr., Trenton, 1988—; dir. clin. info. sys., 1995—, Franciscan Health Sys., 1995-96, Cath. Health Initiatives, 1996—2000. Pres. Pathology Assocs., Lawrenceville, N.J., 1981—. Contbr. articles to profl. jours. Fellow Coll. Am. Pathologists, Coll. Physicians of Phila.; mem. Am. Med. Informatics Assn., Med. Soc. N.J., Mercer County Med. Soc., Clin. Jersey Ind. Physician Assn. (v.p. 1994-95, sec.-treas. 1995-96, exec. v.p. 1997—), Ea. Pathology Assn. (v.p. 1996-2003), Phi Beta Kappa. Avocations: golf, gardening, skiing.

**MOSER, ROYCE, JR.,** preventive medicine physician, educator; b. Versailles, Mo., Aug. 21, 1935; s. Royce and Russie Frances (Stringer) M.; m. Lois Anne Hunter, June 14, 1958; children: Beth Anne Moser McLean, Donald Royce. BA, Harvard U., Cambridge, Mass., 1957, MD, 1961; MPH, Harvard Sch. Pub. Health, Boston, 1965. Diplomate Am. Bd. Preventive Medicine (trustee 1989-98). Commd. officer USAF, 1962, advanced through grades to col., 1974; resident in aerospace medicine USAF Sch. Aerospace Medicine, Brooks AFB, Tex., 1965-67; chief aerospace medicine Aerospace Def. Command, Colorado Springs, Colo., 1967-70; comdr. 35th USAF Dispensary Phan Rang, Vietnam, 1970-71; chief aerospace medicine br. USAF Sch. Aerospace Medicine, Brooks AFB, 1971-77; comdr. USAF Hosp., Tyndall AFB, Fla., 1977-79; chief clin. scis. divsn. USAF Sch. Aerospace Medicine, Brooks AFB, 1979-81, chief edn. divsn., 1981-83, sch. comdr., 1983-85, ret., 1985; prof. dept. family and preventive medicine U. Utah Sch. Medicine, Salt Lake City, 1985—, vice chmn. dept., 1985-95; dir. Rocky Mountain Ctr. for Occupl. and Environ. Health, Salt Lake City, 1987—2003. Cons. in occupl., environ. and aerospace medicine, Salt Lake City, 1985—; presenter in field. Author: Effective Management of Occupational and Environmental Health and Safety Programs, 1992, 2d edit, 1999; contbr. book chpts. and articles to profl. jours. Past pres. 1st Bapt. Ch. Found., Salt Lake City, 1987-89, moderator, 2006; chmn. numerous univ. coms., Salt Lake City, 1985—; bd. dirs. Hanford Environ. Health Found., 1990-92; preventive medicine residency rev. com. Accreditation Coun. Grad. Med. Edn., 1991-97; ednl. adv. bd. USAF Human Sys. Ctr., 1991-96; chmn. long-range planning com. Am. Bd. Preventive Medicine, 1992-95; mem. alumni coun. Harvard Sch. Pub. Health, 2003—, chair alumni award of merit com., 2005—. Decorated Legion of Merit (2); recipient Harriet Hardy award New Eng. Coll. Occupl. and Environ. Medicine, 1998, Rutherford T. Johnstone award Western Occupl. and Environ. Med. Assn., 2002. Fellow Aerospace Med. Assn. (pres. 1989-90, chair fellows group 1994-97, Harry G. Mosely award 1981, Theodore C. Lyster award 1988, Eric Liljencrantz award 2001, Pres.'s citation, 2006), Am. Coll. Preventive Medicine (regent 1981-82), Am. Coll. Occupl. and Environ. Medicine (v.p. med. affairs 1995-97, Robert A. Kehoe award 1996); mem. Internat. Acad. Aviation and Space Medicine (selector 1989-91, chancellor 1994-98), Soc. of USAF Flight Surgeons (pres. 1970-79, George E. Schafer award 1982), Phi Beta Kappa. Avocations: photography, fishing. Home: 664 Aloha Rd Salt Lake City UT 84103-3329 Office: Rocky Mountain Ctr Occupl & Environ Health 391 Chipeta Way Ste C Salt Lake City UT 84108 Office Phone: 801-581-8719. Business E-Mail: Royce.Moser@hsc.utah.edu.

**MOSER, SANDRA KAY,** secondary school educator; b. LaPorte, Ind., Aug. 16, 1940; d. Richard Wayne and Elizabeth Frances Prentiss; divorced; children: Stacy Karen, Shae Kimberly, Jae Emmert. BS, Ball State U., 1958—62; MA, Purdue U., 1977—80; postgrad., Ind. U., 1990—95. Tchr. Barker Jr. H.S., Michigan City, Ind., 1962—69, Wanatah (Ind.) Pub. Sch., 1977—, tech. dir., 1996—. Author poetry. Mem.: NEA, Ind. State Tchr. Assn. Roman Catholic. Avocation: travel. Home: 2 Ave B Westville IN 46391 Office: Wanatah Pub Sch 309 School Dr Wanatah IN 46390

**MOSER, WILLIAM OSCAR JULES,** mathematics professor; b. Winnipeg, Can., Sept. 5, 1927; s. Robert and Laura (Fenson) M.; m. Beryl Rita Pearlman, Sept. 2, 1953; children— Marla, Lionel, Paula. B.Sc., U. Man., 1949; MA, U. Minn., 1951; PhD, U. Toronto, 1957. Lectr. U. Sask., 1955-57, asst. prof., 1957-59; asso. prof. U. Man., 1959-64, McGill U., 1964-66, prof., 1966-97, prof. emeritus, 1997—. Author: (with H.S.M. Coxeter) Generators and Relations for Discrete Groups, 1957, 4th edit., 1980, (with R. Barbeau, M. Klamkin) 500 Mathematical Challenges, 1995, (with P. Brass and J. Pach) Research Problems in Discrete Geometry, 2005, also rsch. papers; editor: Can. Math. Bull., 1962-70, Can. Jour. Math., 1982-85. NRC fellow, 1951-53; Can. Coun. leave fellow, 1971. Mem.: Math. Soc., Can. Math. Soc. (pres. 1975—77), Math. Assn. Am. Office: McGill U Dept Math 805 Sherbrooke St W Montreal PQ Canada H3A 2K6 Office Phone: 514-398-3820. E-mail: moser@math.mcgill.ca.

**MOSES, ABE JOSEPH,** financial planner, consultant; b. Springfield, Mass., July 15, 1931; s. Mohammed Mustapha and Fatima (Merriam) M.; m. Donna C. Moses (dec. 1987); children: James Douglas, John C, Peter J.; m. Mary Jo Morris, Aug. 25, 2001. BA, Amherst Coll., 1955; MA in Internat. Affairs, Johns Hopkins U., 1957. Legis. aide Sen. J.F. Kennedy, 1955-57; fgn. service officer Dept. State, 1960-65; v.p. gen. mgr. Libyan Desert Oil Co., Texfel Petroleum Corp., Tripoli, Libya, 1965-67; v.p. adminstrn., fin. Occidental

Petroleum Corp., Libya, 1967-70; v.p. fin., dir. Northrop Corp., 1970-74; chmn. Transworld Trade Ltd., Washington, 1971—; v.p., mng. dir. world adv. group Chase Manhattan Bank, 1974-80; pres. Berkshire Properties, 1976-95; pres., COO, Grolier Internat., Inc. Danbury, Conn., 1980-82; CEO, dir. Galadari Bros., Dubai, United Arab Emirates, 1982-86; internat. bus. and fin. cons. Traxol, Dubai, 1986—; fin. cons. Govt. Costa Rica, 1986-89. Chmn. Aviation Sys. Corp., Northampton, Mass., 1974, Dillon Internat., Akron, Ohio, 1986—; mng. dir. Sheraton Suites Akron, Cuyahoga Falls, Ohio, 1990—; owner's dep. Monarch Sheraton Hotel, Springfield, Mass., 1993-95; bd. dirs., v.p. Morgan Freeport Co., Hudson, Ohio; bd. dirs. Seeds of Peace, Washington; gen. ptnr. BPM Ltd. Partnership, 1995—; bd. dirs. owners adv. bd. Starwood Hotels and Resorts, 2005—. Pres., bd. dirs. Riverside Comty. Urban Redevel. Corp.; mem. exec. com., bd. dirs. Near East Found., N.Y.C., 1978—; pres. Riverfront Ctr. Assn., Cuyahoga Falls, 1992-95; bd. dirs. Gulfcoast Radio Ptnrs., 1997-99, Capitol City Radio Ptnrs., 1998-2000, Ind. Radio Ptnrs., Monroe (La.) Radio mems., LLC, Commonwealth Opera Co., Northampton, Mass., 2002—. Capt. USAF, 1957-60. Ford Found. fellow Johns Hopkins U., 1955, Barr Found. fellow, 1955-57. Mem.: Assn. Starwood Franchise Owners N.Am. (bd. dirs. 2006—), Assn. Sheraton Franchise Owners N.Am. (bd. dirs. 2004—). Democrat. Home: 16 Highmeadow Rd Northampton MA 01062-2625 Office: Riverside CURC 1989 Front St Cuyahoga Falls OH 44221-3811 Office Phone: 330-920-7502. Personal E-mail: abejmoses@comcast.net.

**MOSES, ALFRED HENRY,** lawyer, writer, diplomat; b. Balt., July 24, 1929; s. Leslie William and Helene Amelia (Lobe) Moses; m. Carol Whitehill, Nov. 24, 1955 (dec.); children: Barbara, Jennifer, David, Amalie; m. Fern Magonet Schad, Aug. 28, 2005. BA, Dartmouth, 1951; postgrad., Woodrow Wilson Sch., Princeton U., 1951-52; JD, Georgetown U., 1956. Bar: D.C. 1956. Assoc. Covington & Burling, Washington, 1956-65, ptnr., 1965—94, 1997—99, of counsel, 1999—. Co-founder, vice-chmn., gen. coun. Promontory Fin. Group LLC and affiliates; legal advisor minority rights Dem. Nat. Com., Washington, DC Commn. Urban Renewal; commr. Pub. Housing, Fairfax County, Va., 1971—72; chmn. UN Watch, Geneva, 2001—; chmn. nat. bd. Hebrew Coll., Newton Ctr., Mass., 2002—; spi. advisor, spl. counsel Pres. Jimmy Carter, Washington, 1980—81; amb., Romania, 1994—97; spl. Presdl. emissary for Cyprus Conflict, 1999—2001; lectr. in field; bd. chair Project on Ethnic Rels., Inc., Princeton, NJ, 2006—. Contbr. articles to profl. jours. Pres. Am. Jewish Com., 1991—94, chmn. centennial com., 2004—, chmn. adv. coun., 1997—; bd. dirs. Paralysis Cure Rsch. Found., 1978—81; trustee Phelps Stokes Fund, N.Y.C., 1978—84, Jewish Publ. Soc., 1989—94, Haifa U., 1988—90; co-chmn. legal divsn. United Givers Fund, Washington, 1975—76; active Coun. Fgn. Rels., NYC, 1977—; pres. Nat. Children's Island, Washington, 1975—76, Golda Meir Assn., 1986—88, nat. chmn., 1988—93; bd. regents Georgetown U., 1986—92. Mem.: ABA, D.C. Bar Assn., Met. Club. Democrat. Jewish. Home: 7710 Georgetown Pike Mc Lean VA 22102-1431 Office: 1201 Pennsylvania Ave NW Washington DC 20004-2401

**MOSES, GREGORY H., JR.,** health services administrator; m. Johnella Moses. Lead engagement ptnr. Sister Mercy Health Corp.; ptnr.-in-charge Healthcare Consulting Group, N.Y., N.J.; ptnr. Coopers & Lybrand; pres., COO United Am. Healthcare Corp., Detroit, 1998—. Office: United American Health Care 300 River Place Dr Ste 4700 Detroit MI 48207-5069 Office Phone: 313-393-7944.

**MOSES, HAMILTON, III,** hospital administrator, neurologist; s. Hamilton Jr. and Betty Anne Moses; m. Elizabeth Lawrence Hormel, 1977 (dec. 1988); m. Alexandra McCullough Gibson, 1992. BA in Psychology, U. Pa., 1972; MD, Rush Med. Coll., Chgo., 1975. Clk. Nat. Hosp. for Nervous Diseases, London, 1974; intern in medicine Johns Hopkins Hosp., Balt., 1976-77, resident in neurology, 1977-79, chief resident, 1979-80, assoc. prof. neurology, 1986-94, vice chmn. neurology and neurosurgery, 1980-88, v.p., 1988-94, dir. Parkinson's Ctr., 1984-94; dir. neurol. inst., prof. neurology and neurosurgery and mgmt. U. Va., Charlottesville, 1994-97; sr. advisor Boston Cons. Group, 1995—; prof. Darden Sch. Bus. U. Va., Charlottesville, 1994-98; cons. neurologist Mass. Gen. Hosp., Boston, 1997—; vis. prof. neurology and psychiatry Harvard U. Sch. Medicine, Boston, 1997-99; chmn. The Alerion Inst., 2002—. Sr. advisor Ptnrs. Healthcare, Boston; spl. advisor Nat. Health Svc., Eng., 1988-91; dir. various tech. companies. Editor, major author: Principles of Medicine, 1985-96; editor newsletter Johns Hopkins Health, 1988-94; contbr. articles to profl. jours. Com. on med. ministries Episcopal Diocese Md., Balt., 1987; bd. dirs. Valleys Planning Ct.; trustee McLean Hosp., Belmont, Mass., 1997—. Fellow Am. Acad. Neurology (sec. 1989-91), Royal Soc. Medicine (UK); mem. Am. Neurol. Assn., Md. Neurol. Soc. (pres. 1984-86), Movement Disorders Soc. Avocations: photography, sailing. Office: PO Box 150 North Garden VA 22959-0150

**MOSES, HAROLD L.,** oncologist; MD, Vanderbilt U., 1962. Rschr. NIH, 1965—68; faculty Vanderbilt U., Nashville, 1985—, prof. cancer biology, the Benjamin F. Byrd Jr. prof. of clin. oncology, prof. pathology and prof. medicine, 1993—, dir. Vanderbilt-Ingram Cancer Ctr., 1999—, chair dept. cell biology, 1985—98. Dir. Frances Williams Preston Rsch. Labs. T.J. Martell Found., 1993—; clin. oncologist Mayo Clinic, Rochester, Minn., 1973—85; mem. nat. dialogue on cancer, vice chair cancer rsch. team, chair parent com. Nat. Cancer Inst., mem. bd. sci. counselors, co-chair breast cancer progress rev. group. Recipient Outstanding Investigator award, Nat. Cancer Inst., 1986, 1993. Mem.: Am. Assn. for Cancer Rsch. (past pres.), Assn. of Am. Cancer Insts. (pres.), Inst. Medicine. Office: Vanderbilt-Ingram Cancer Ctr 691 Preston Bldg Nashville TN 37232 Office Phone: 615-936-1782.*

**MOSES, HARRY ELECKS,** physicist, mathematician; b. Canton, Ohio, Aug. 30, 1922; s. David and Amelia Moses; m. Barbara Fischeer, Jan. 6, 1957; 1 child, Celia Ellen Moses Stanger. PhD, Columbia U., N.Y., 1951. Rsch. math. physicist Inst. Math. Sci., N.Y. U., N.Y.C., 1950—60; with Lincolkn Lab, MIT, Mass., 1960—70. Contbr. scientific papers to profl. jours. Avocation: travel. Home: 150 Tappan St Brookline MA 02445 Personal E-mail: b.moses@rcn.com.

**MOSES, JEFFREY WARREN,** cardiologist, educator; b. Bklyn., May 12, 1948; s. Julian and Mildred Moses; m. Laurie Levinberg, Nov. 4, 1982; children: Ariel, Jarret, Chandler, Harrison. BA, Yale U., 1970; MD, U. Pa., 1974. Intern Presbyn.-U. Pa., Phila., 1974—75, resident in medicine, 1975—77, fellow in cardiology, 1978—80; asst. instr. U. Pa., Phila., 1975—77; med. adv. staff Blue Cross/Blue Shield Greater N.Y., 1977—78; asst. med. dir. Equitable Life Soc., N.Y.C. 1977—78; asst. attending physician N.Y. Hosp., N.Y.C., 1980—87, asst. dir. adult cardiac catheterization lab., 1980—83, dir. clin. electrophysiology, 1981—87, assoc. dir. adult cardiac catheterization lab., 1983—87, assoc. attending physician, 1987; instr. medicine Cornell U. Med. Coll., N.Y.C., 1980—81, asst. prof., 1981—87, assoc. prof. clin. medicine, 1987; chief interventional cardiology Lenox Hill Hosp., N.Y.C., 1987—2005, assoc. attending physician, 1987—88, sr. attending physician, 1988—2005; clin. assoc. prof. medicine NYU Sch. Medicine, N.Y.C., 1993—96, clin. prof. medicine, 1996—; interventional cardiologist NY-Presbyterian Hosp./Columbia U. Med. Ctr., 2005—. Fellow: ACP, Soc. Cardiac Angiography and Intervention, Am. Coll. Cardiology. Office: 16 East 60th ST New York NY 10022 also: 161 Fort Washington Ave New York NY 10032 Office Phone: 212-305-7060. Office Fax: 212-305-4825, 212-342-3660.

**MOSES, JOEL,** computer scientist, educator; b. Petach Tikvah, Israel, Nov. 25, 1941; came to U.S., 1954, naturalized, 1960; s. Bernhard and Golda (Losner) M.; m. Margaret A. Garvey, Dec. 27, 1970; children: Jesse, David. BA, Columbia U., 1962, MA, 1963; PhD, MIT, 1967. Asst. prof. dept. elec. engring. and computer sci. MIT, Cambridge, 1967-71, assoc. prof., 1971-77, prof., 1977—, assoc. dir. Lab for Computer Sci., 1974-78, assoc. head computer sci. and engring., dept. elec. engring. and computer sci., 1978-81, head dept., 1981-89, D.C. Jackson prof., 1989-99, dean Sch. Engring., 1991-95, provost, 1995-98, prof. engring. sys. divsn., 1999—, Inst. prof., 1999—, acting dir., engring. sys. divsn., 2006, acting. dir. Ctr. Tech., Policy

and Indsl. Devel., 2006—. Vis. prof. Harvard Grad. Sch. Bus. Adminstrn., 1989-90; vis. adj. sr. rsch. scientist Columbia U. FU Found. Sch. Engring. and Applied Sci., 1998. Editor: The Computer Age: A Twenty Year View, 1979; co-originator Knowledge Based System Concept; developer MACSYMA system for formula manipulation. Recipient Achievement award MIT Lab. for Computer Sci., 1985. Fellow IEEE, AAAS, Am. Acad. Arts and Scis.; mem. NAE, Assn. for Computing Machinery, Am. Soc. Engring. Edn. (Centennial cert.). Office: MIT Computer Sci Artificial Intelligence Lab 32-249 Cambridge MA 02139 Office Phone: 617-253-8592. E-mail: moses@mit.edu.

**MOSES, MARJORIE,** elementary school educator; b. Delaware, Ohio, Feb. 15, 1949; d. Joe Miller and Janet Moses. BS in Heath & Phys. Edn., Bowling Green U., Ohio, 1970. Cert. tchr., health & phys. edn. Ga. Dept. Edn. Phys. edn. tchr. Hawthorne Jr. High, Lorain, Ohio, 1970—72, Hayes HS, Delaware, 1972—80, Sedalia Pk. Elem., Marietta, Ga., 1982—2004, Arnold Mill Elem., Woodstock, 2004—. Cheerleader adv. Hawthorne Jr. High, 1970—72; basketball coach Ohio Wesleyan U., 1972—73, Rutherford B. Hayes HS, 1972—80, cheerleader adv., 1972—73, field hockey coach, 1973—75, varsity softball coach, 1973—80; mem. UPI Basketball Coaches Bd. Ctrl. Ohio, 1977—80. Recipient Tchr. of Yr., Elizabeth Elem., Cobb County, Ga., 1984—85, Sedalia Pk. Elem., Cobb County, Ga., 2003—04. Mem.: Profl. Assn. Ga. Educators. Office: Arnold Mill Elem Sch 710 Arnold Mill Rd Woodstock GA 30188

**MOSES, MICHAEL JAMES,** insurance company executive, small business owner; b. Roaring Spring, Pa., Apr. 13, 1956; s. William E. and Carol J. (Berkey) M.; m. Laura L. Bishop, June 7, 1980 (div. 1990); children: J'aime Lee, Justin Michael. BA, Williamson Trade Sch. Salesman 84 Lumber, Cresson, Pa., 1977-78; area mgr. Nat. Home Life Ins., Valley Forge, Pa., 1978-80; regional v.p. A.L. Williams Agy. (name changed to Primerica), Duluth, Ga., 1981—; owner Luigetta's Restaurant, Altoona, Pa., 2003—. Republican. Mem. Pentecostal Ch. Avocations: basketball, golf, tennis. Office Phone: 814-942-6167.

**MOSES, ORAL,** music educator; s. Otis Moses and Elveta Lewis-Moses. D, U. Mich., 1984. Opera singer Mich. Opera Theater, Detroit, 1983—84; prof. voice Kennesaw State U., Ga., 1984—. Vis. prof. U. Cape Coast, Ghana, 2003; part-time recitalist, 1984—. Performer: (albums) Deep River: Art Songs and Spirituals, 1995, Amen-African American Composers of 20th Century, 2001, Spirituals in Old Zion, 2001, Third Day-A Worship Album, 2001. Artistic dir. Cobb County Choir, Marietta, Ga., 1988—. With U.S. Army, 1966—69. Recipient Achievement award, NAACP, 1990; grantee, Harvard U., 1986, Boston Coll., 1992; Salzburg fellow, Salzburg Sem., Austria, 1976, Thomas J. Watson fellow, Fisk U., Munich, Germany, 1975—76. Mem.: Soc. Am. Music, Nat. Assn. Tchrs. Singing. Avocations: gardening, music.

**MOSES, SAMUEL B.,** accountant, consultant; s. Alfred J. and Alice R. Moses. BA, Calif. State U., Fullerton, 1985. CPA Calif., 1990. Auditor Arthur Andersen & Co., Costa Mesa, Calif., 1985—86; tax sr. cpa BDO Seidman, Orange, Calif., 1987—90; owner Samuel B. Moses, Santa Monica, Calif., 1991—. Western dir. Intertel (Top 1% IQs), L.A., 2002—03. Recipient Peat Marwick award, Beta Alpha Psi Chpt., 1985. Mem.: Mensa (licentiate; chmn. Greater L.A. area chpt. 1996—2000). Office: Samuel B Moses CPA Ste 1800 100 Wilshire Blvd Santa Monica CA 90025 Office Phone: 310-395-9922. Business E-mail: smosescpa@aol.com.

**MOSES, SHEILA JOHNSON,** nurse, bookkeeper; b. Darlington, SC, June 22, 1965; d. Elijah Johnson Jr. and Inez Williams Johnson; m. Donnie Moses, June 5, 1993; 1 child, Donte Jevon. A in Acctg. and Data Processing, Sumter Tech. Coll., SC, 1985; A in Health Sci. in Nursing, Ctrl. Carolina Tech. Coll., Sumter, 1997. EMT SC. Bd. EMS; RN State Bd. Nursing for SC Dept. of Labor, Licensing and Regulations. Nurse Tuomey Hosp., Sumter, SC, 1997—99; nurse supr. Springdale Nursing Home, Camden, SC, 1999—2003; dialysis nurse Lee County Dialysis, Bishopville, SC, 2002—; bookkeeper Johnson and Johnson Constrn., Camden, SC, 1988—; sch. nurse Lee county Sch. Dist., Bishopville, 2003—. EMT Lee Rescue Squad, Bishopville, 1989—95; com. mem. Lee County Health Connection for Sch. Success, SC; team capt. Lee County Cancer Soc.; bd. mem. Lee County First Steps, Bishopville; rep. Avon, 1987—, unit leader, 2004—. Notary pub., 1988—. Recipient Mem. of the Future Bus. Leaders, Lee County Vocat., 1981-1882, Honors Soc., Bishopville. Mem.: Nat. Assn. of Sch. Nurse, Lee County Health Ministry, Lee County First Step. Baptist. Avocations: meeting people, travel, cooking, basketball. Office Phone: 803-484-5386.

**MOSES, SHELIA P.,** writer, poet, playwright, producer; b. Rich Square, NC, 1961; Author: So They Burned the Black Churches, 1996, One More River to Cross, The Legend of Buddy Bush, 2004 (Nat. Book Award finalist, 2004), I, Dred Scott, 2005; co-author (with Dick Gregory): Callus on My Soul: A Memoir, 2000; co-author: (plays) Ain't No God in Hollywood. Recipient Coretta Scott King Honor Book award, 2005.

**MOSESSO, VINCENT NICHOLAS, JR.,** emergency physician, health facility administrator; b. Pitts., Pa., Sept. 28, 1957; s. Vincent Nicholas and Jean Lois Mosesso; m. Janet L. Mosesso, June 17, 1983; children: Jennifer Moss, Chadwick. BA, Duquesne U., Pitts., 1979; MD, U. of Pitts., 1988. Lic. emergency medicine Am. Bd. of Emergency Medicine. Assoc. prof. of emergency medicine U. of Pitts. Sch. of Medicine, 1991—. Asst. med. dir. dept. of pub. safety City of Pitts., 1993—; med. dir. prehospital care U. Pitts. Med. Ctr., 1996—; mem. nat. BLS subcom. Am. Heart Assn., Emergency Cardiac Care Com., Dallas, 2001—; med. dir. advanced med. life support Nat. Assn. of Emergency Med. Technicians, Clinton, Miss., 2002—. Mem. editl. bd.: med. jours. Prehospital Emergency Care. Mem. Allegheny divsn. Am. Heart Assn., Pitts., 1993—; bd. dirs., med. dir. Sudden Cardiac Arrest Assn., Washington, 2005—06. Named Emergency Physician of the Yr., Pa. Emergency Health Svcs. Coun., 1998; grantee, Medtrionic Found., 2000—02. Fellow: Am. Coll. of Emergency Medicine; mem.: Nat. Assn. of EMS Physicians (bd. dirs. 2004). Avocations: golf, travel, sports, exercise. Office: U Pitt Ste 911 230 McKee Pl Pittsburgh PA 15213 Office Phone: 412-647-1103. E-mail: mosessovn@upmc.edu.

**MOSHER, DANIEL LEE,** music educator; b. Hornell, N.Y., Apr. 4, 1956; s. Wayne Adelbert Mosher Sr. and Jacquelyn Marie Mosher; m. Sandra Lynn Scozzari, Aug. 20, 1977; children: Ryan Daniel, Erin Ann. BMus. Ithaca Coll., 1979; MusM, Crane Sch. Music, 1984. Cert. music tchr. N.Y. 1984. Tchr. music Edwards Ctrl. Sch., NY, 1979—85, Gouverneur Ctrl. Sch., NY, 1985—94, Carthage Ctrl. Sch., NY, 1994—. Coord. music and theater Carthage Ctrl. Sch., 2003—. Trustee Village of Gouverneur, 1988. Named Citizen of Yr., Gouverneur VFW, 1992. Mem.: N.Y. State Sch. Music Assn. (2d v.p. 2004—), exec. coun. 1995—97, state assigner of adjudicators 1999—2004), Music Educators Nat. Conf., Am. Musicians Assn. Democrat. Methodist. Avocations: reading, woodworking, snowshoeing. Home: 34638 Schwendy Dr Carthage NY 13619

**MOSHER, DONALD ALLEN,** artist; b. Malden, Mass., Oct. 11, 1945; s. Allen M. and Florence C. (Post) M.; m. Christine Ann Crivello, Feb. 15, 1969; 1 child, Heather Ann. Cert., Vesper George Sch. Art, Boston. Comml. artist Stop & Shop Corp., Boston, 1971-75, Rich's Dept. Store, Salem, Mass., 1975-81; profl. artist Rockport, Mass., 1972—. Exhibited Am. Watercolor Soc. and NAD, Butler Inst., Chgo., Cleve. Meml. Gallery, SUNY, Mystic Seaport Mus., New Bedford Whaling Mus., Mint Mus. Fine Arts, Tuskegee Inst., numerous others. Recipient more than 150 awards from various art assns. Mem. Rockport Art Assn. (v.p. 1988-92, curator 1988-94), New Eng. Watercolor Soc., Guild of Boston Artists, Copley Soc., Salmagundi Club, Am. Artists Profl. League, North Shore Art Assn., Whiskey Painters Am., Am. Soc. Marine Artists, Acad. Artists Assn., Hudson Valley Arts Assn. Home: 13 Main St Rockport MA 01966-1512

**MOSHER, SALLY EKENBERG,** lawyer, musician; b. N.Y.C., July 26, 1934; d. Leslie Joseph and Frances Josephine (McArdle) Ekenberg; m. James Kimberly Mosher, Aug. 13, 1960 (dec. Aug. 1982). MusB, Manhattanville Coll., 1956; postgrad., Hofstra U., 1958-60, U. So. Calif., 1971-73, JD, 1981. Bar: Calif., 1982. Musician, pianist, tchr., 1957-74; music critic Pasadena Star-News, 1967-72; mgr. Contrasts Concerts, Pasadena Art Mus., 1971-72; rep. Occidental Life Ins. Co., Pasadena, 1975-78; v.p. James K. Mosher Co., Pasadena, 1961-82, pres., 1982—; Oakhill Enterprises, Pasadena, 1984—; assoc. White-Howell, Inc., Pasadena, 1984-94; real estate broker, 1984-96. Harpsichordist, lectr., composer, 1994—; pub. Silver Wheels Pub., ASCAP. Musician (CD recs.) William Byrd: Songs, Dances, Battles, Games, 1995, From Now On: New Directions For Harpsichord, 1998, Sally Mosher Plays English Renaissance Harpsichord Music, Images and Moods, (with Patrick Lindley, Scott Frasier, Justin Weaver) Towards the Light; author: People and Their Contexts: A Chronology of the 16th Century World; contbr. articles to various pubs. Bd. dirs. Jr. League Pasadena, 1966-67, Encounters Concerts, Pasadena, 1966-72, U. So. Calif. Friends of Music, L.A., 1973-76, Calif. Music Theatre, 1988-90, Pasadena Hist. Soc., 1989-91, I Cantori, 1989-91; bd. dirs. Pasadena Arts Coun., 1986-92, pres., 1989-92, chair adv. bd., 1992-93; v.p., bd. dirs. Pasadena Chamber Orch., 1986-88, pres., 1987-88; mem. Calif. 200 Coun. for Bicentennial of U.S. Constn., 1987-90; mem. Endowment Adv. Commn., Pasadena, 1988-90; bd. dirs. Foothill Area Cmty. Svcs., 1990-95, treas., 1991, vice chair, 1992-94, chair, 1994-95; sec., bd. dirs. Piano Spheres, 2001-02, pres., 2002—. Manhattanville Coll. hon. scholar, 1952-56. Mem. ABA, Calif. Bar Assn., Assocs. of Calif. Inst. Tech., So. Calif. Baroque Assn. (bd. dirs., 2004—), Athenaeum, Kappa Gamma Pi, Mu Phi Epsilon, Phi Alpha Delta. Home: 1260 Rancheros Rd Pasadena CA 91103-2759 Fax: 626-795-3146. E-mail: sally@cyberverse.com.

**MOSHIER, DAVID IRWIN,** church administrator; b. Roanoke, Va., Sept. 14, 1954; s. Emery Irwin (dec.) and Evelyn Mae (Kunkel) M.; m. Bonnie Sharon Dailey, Feb. 13, 1982. STD, Am. Bible Inst., 1991; DD, World Christianship Mins., 1997; ThB, Sch. Christian Min., 1998; ThM, Greensburg Bible Coll. & Sem., 1998. Ordained to ministry Am. Evang. Christian Chs., 1992, Reformed Presbyn. Ch., 1995, World Christianship Ministries, 1997, St. Thomas-A-Becket Mins., 1998, Can. Evangel. Christian Chs., 1997, Gen. Conf. Evang. Protestant Chs., 2000. Rsch. asst. mktg. dept. Clarendon Bank & Trust, Arlington, 1974, collection agt., installment loan dept., 1974-75; loan collection officer George Washington U., Washington, 1975-77, sr. loan collection officer, 1977-79; student loan collection coord. Hahnemann Med. Coll. and Hosp., Phila., 1979-80; prin. account clk. George Washington U., Washington, 1980-83; pastor The Wesleyan Ch., Waldorf, Md., 1983-86; asst. pastor Floor Meml. Wesleyan Ch., Arlington, 1986-89; pastor First Wesleyan Ch., Alexandria, Va., 1989-91; dir. govt. rels. Am. Evang. Christian Chs., Alexandria, 1992-93, moderator Mid-Atlantic region, 1992-95, nat. exec. dir., 1993; pastor Fredericksburg (Va.) Area Reformed Presbyn. Mission, 1995; stated clk. Reformed Presbyn. Ch., Hanover, 1996-99; v.p., prof. homiletics Greensburg (Ind.) Bible Coll. and Theol. Sems., 1998-99; special counsel to pres. Sch. Christian Ministry and Theological Seminary, 1999—. Coord. Conf. Confessing Presbyn. Chs., 1996-98; bd. dirs. Rate Wave Tariff Svcs., Falls Church, Va.; ops. mgr., 1999; sec. ext. and evangelism Capital Dist. Wesleyan Ch., Great Falls, Va., 1986-88; spl. asst. Office Army Chief of Chaplains, Arlington, 1987-90, cemetery rep. Arlington Nat. Cemetery, 1996-97; alumni coun. Flint Hill Sch., Oakton, Va., 1991-98; supply pastor Cmty. Ch./Am. Rescue Workers, Capitol Heights, Md., 1992; ch. resls. cons. WABS Radio, Arlington, 1992-94; mem. adv. bd. Covered Bridge Ministries, St. Paul, Ind., 1993—, others. Contbr. articles to profl. jours. Officer of election Electoral Bd., Alexandria, 1991-92, Arlington, 1992-93. Recipient Cert. of Commendation, Army Chief of Chaplains, Washington, 1988, 89, 90, Cert. of Civil Svc., Desert Shield-Storm/Hqrs. U.S. Army, Washington, 1992, Knight Grad Collar, Order of St. Oswald, 1995; fellow in philosophy of religion St. Aidan's Acad., 1995; created Baron of Mesta, Byzantine Dynastic House of Polanie-Patrikios, 1998. Mem. George Washington U. Gen. Alumni Assn. Republican. Home and Office: 5810 Kingstowne Ctr Alexandria VA 22315-5711

**MOSHMAN, JACK,** statistical consultant; b. Richmond Hill, N.Y., Aug. 12, 1924; s. Morris and Sadye (Posner) M.; m. Annette Gordon, Aug. 10, 1947; children: Gordon, Marc, Sherri, Ira. BA, NYU, 1946; MA, Columbia U., 1947; PhD, U. Tenn., 1953. Instr. Queens Coll., Flushing, NY, 1946-47, U. Tenn., Knoxville, 1947-53; statistician AEC, Oak Ridge, Tenn., 1948-50; sr. statistician Oak Ridge (Tenn.) Nat. Labs., 1950-54; mem. tech. staff Bell Tel. Labs., Murray Hill, NJ, 1954-57; v.p. C-E-I-R Inc., Washington, 1957-66; mng. dir. EBS Mgmt. Cons., Washington, 1966-68; sr. v.p. Leasco Systems & Rsch., Bethesda, Md., 1968-69; pres. Moshman Assocs. Inc., Bethesda, Md., 1970—. Adj. prof. Rutgers U., 1963-66; professorial lectr. George Washington U., 1959-62; chmn. Inst. for Safety Analysis, Rockville, Md., 1975-89, mem. office of mgmt. and budget adv. com. on statistical policy. Editor: Faith, Hope & Parity, 1967; author Ency. sect. Computers & Politics, 1985, 90, 93; contbr. articles to profl. jours. Trustee Babbage Found., St. Paul, 1983-87; pres. Moshman Charitable Found., Bethesda, 1996—; v.p. Eleanor & George Kokiko Sr. Found., Bethesda, 1997—. With U.S. Army, 1943-46, ETO. Fellow Am. Statis. Assn. (coun. 1956, 58); mem. Am. Fedn. Info. Processing Soc. Am. (bd. dirs. pres. 1986-87), Assn. for Computing Machinery (sec. 1956-64, v.p 1965), Inst. for Math. Stats., Inst. for Mgmt. Scis., Ops. Rsch. Soc. Am., Biometrics Soc. Avocation: genealogy. Office: Moshman Assocs Inc 4340 East West Hwy Bethesda MD 20814-4411 Office Phone: 301-229-3000. Personal E-mail: jmoshman@aol.com.

**MOSHOLDER, ANDREW DONALD,** psychiatrist; b. Washington, Sept. 25, 1957; s. Donald and Mary Mosholder; m. Janet Marie Rauch, Aug. 5, 1989; 1 stepchild, Erik Harrison. BA, Haverford Coll., Pa., 1979; MD, U. Va., 1983; MPH, Johns Hopkins U., 2001. Diplomate Am. Bd. Psychiatry and Neurology, 1988, lic. in child and adolescent psychiatry Am. Bd. Psychiatry and Neurology, 1991, psychiatrist Va., 1985. Resident psychiatry Med. Coll. Va., Richmond, 1983—87; resident child and adolescent psychiatry U. Va., Charlottesville, 1987—89; psychiatrist Ctrl. Va. Cmty. Svcs., Lynchburg, Va., 1989—92; med. officer FDA, Rockville, Md., 1992—. Recipient Frances Kelsey Drug Safety Excellence award, FDA Ctr. for Drug Evaluation and Rsch., 2005. Mem.: APHA, Am. Acad. Child and Adolescent Psychiatry. Mem. Soc. Of Friends. Avocation: bass guitar. Office: FDA 10903 New Hampshire Ave Mail Stop 3411 Silver Spring MD 20993-0002 Office Phone: 301-796-0508. Business E-mail: andrew.mosholder@fda.hhs.gov.

**MOSICH, ANELIS NICK,** accountant, writer, educator, consultant; b. Croatia, Aug. 30, 1928; came to U.S., 1939, naturalized, 1951; s. Dinko and Josephine (Ursich) M.; m. Dorothy V. Rasich, June 15, 1958; children: Lori, Lisa, Jeffrey. BS, UCLA, 1951, MBA, 1953, PhD, 1963. CPA, Calif. Mem. faculty UCLA, 1955-63, Calif. State U., Northridge, 1963-64; examiner for Calif. State Bd. Accountancy, 1964-70; prof. acctg. U. So. Calif., LA, 1964-74, William C. Hallett prof. acctg., 1974-81, Ernst & Young prof., 1981-90, chmn. acctg. dept., 1970-74, 77-78, prof. emeritus, 1993. Cons. various bus. orgns., 1953—; expert witness; guest spkr. various profl. and bus. groups in Calif., Oreg., NY, Tex., Fla., Hawaii, Mex., 1963—95; bd. dirs. Metro-Goldwyn-Mayer, Inc., 2003—05. Author: Intermediate Accounting, rev. 6th edit., 1989, Financial Accounting, 1970, 75, Accounting: A Basis for Business Decision, 1972, Modern Advanced Accounting, 4th edit., 1988, The CPA Examination: Text, Problems and Solutions, 1978; editor: Education column Calif. CPA Quar., 1965-66; contbg. editor: Education and Professional Training column Jour. Accountancy, 1971-77; contbr. numerous articles to jours. and acctg. mem. productivity commn. City of L.A., 1993—94; bd. dirs. Bill Hannon Found. With U.S. Army, 1953—55. Fellow UCLA, 1963; recipient Dean's award Sch. Bus. Adminstrn., U. So. Calif., 1973, 78, Fred B. Olds Support Group award U. So. Calif., 1994, Disting. Svc. award for Leventhal Sch. Acctg., 1999, Mosich Endowment Chair award, U. So. Calif., 2006 Office: U So Calif Leventhal Sch Acctg University Park Los Angeles CA 90089-1425

**MOSIER, ARVIN RAY,** chemist, researcher; b. Olney Springs, Colo., June 11, 1945; s. Isaac James Ellen Rena (Ross) M.; m. Susan Minnick, Dec. 30, 1965; children: Andrew, Katherine. BS, Colo. State U., 1967, MS, 1967-68, PhD, 1974. Chemist agr. rsch. svcs. USDA, Ft. Collins, 1967—2004, with global environ. change and food sys. program Gainesville, Fla., 2005—. Contbr. papers and book chpt. to profl. publ. Mem. AAAS, Am. Soc. Agronomy, Soil Sci. Soc. Am., Internat. Soil Sci. Sco., Council Agrl. Sci. Tech., Phi Kappa Phi, Sigma XI, Gamma Sigma Delta. Republican. Methodist. Avocations: tennis, soccer. Home: 7555 NW 47th Way Gainesville FL 32653 Office: Agrl and Biol Engring Dept U Fla 281 Frazier Rogers Bldg Gainesville FL 32611 Office Phone: 352-392-1864 281. E-mail: armosier@ufl.edu.

**MOSIER, WILLIAM ARTHUR,** psychiatrist, psychotherapist, director, medical educator, researcher; b. Richmond, Calif., Oct. 21, 1946; s. William Nathaniel and Violet Olga (Luzum) M.; m. Virginia Rondero (div. Apr. 1992); children: Robert Carlos, Cristina Dominique; m. Gloria Sifuentes (div. 1998); 1 child, William Nathaniel; m. Gabriela Pickett; children: Gabriela, Diana. BA, Webster U., 1971, MA in Tchg., 1973; MD, U. Ctrl. del Este, Dominican Republic, 1986; EdD, U. So. Calif., 1987; BS with distinction, U. Okla., 1991; MPAS in Psychiatry, U. Nebr., 1997. Diplomate Am. Bd. Forensic Medicine, Am. Bd. Med. Psychotherapists, Am. Bd. Psychol. Specialties, lic. physician asst. Tex., Fla., N.Y., Va.; marraige and family therapist, chem. dependency counselor Tex.; marriage and family therapist Ohio. Tchr. St. Louis Pub. Schs., 1971—74; tchr., ctr. dir. Project Head Start, Vallejo, Calif., 1975—77; dir. rsch. Ctr. for Study of Child Devel., Sacramento, 1977—95; physician asst. U.S. Army, Ft. Hood/Ft. Sam Houston, Tex., 1989—91; assoc. prof. U. Mary Hardin-Baylor, Belton, Tex., 1991—92; psychotherapist pvt. practice, Tex., 1993—95; mem. adj. faculty dept. psychiatry Barry U., Miami Shores, Fla., 1997—2000; med. dir. Fla. Inst. Neuro Devel., Vero Beach, Fla., 1995—2000; clin. assoc. prof. psychiatry Nova Southeastern U., Ft. Lauderdale, Fla., 1997—99; asst. prof. medicine, dir. acad. curriculum George Washington U., 2000—01; assoc. prof. psychiatry Kettering Coll. med. Arts Kettering (Ohio) Med. Ctr., 2001—02; dir. physicians asst. program; child devel. cons., marriage and family therapist, 2001—; asst. prof., child devel. Wright State U., Dayton, Ohio, 2002—. Mem. test writing com. Nat. Assn. Cert. Physicians Assts., 1995—, Nat. Bd. Med. Examiners; bd. dir. Ohio State Counselor, Social Worker and Marriage and Family Therapist Regulatory Bd. Newspaper columnist:, mem. editl. adv. bd.: Advance for PAs; contbr. articles to profl. jours., chapters to books. Lt. col. USAF, 1967-68, Vietnam, maj. USAFR, 1987—. Decorated Bronze Star, Air medal. Fellow: APA (mem. adv. bd. 1997—, editl. adv. bd. Annals of Am. Psychotherapy Assn.), Am. Assn. Surg. PAS, Am. Acad. Physician Assts., Assn. Mil. Surgeons U.S. (life), Aerospace Med. Assn. (life), Am. Coll. Forensic Examiners (life); mem.: Ohio Assn. Marriage and Family Therapy (bd. dir.), Am. Assn. Marriage and Family Therapy (del. regulatory bd. Ohio), Assn. of Psychiat. PAs (founding mem., pres.), Soc. PAs in the Addiction Medicine (exec. bd., pres.). Democrat. Mem. Soc. Of Friends. Avocations: musical composition, piano, guitar, swimming, yoga. Office: 649 Greenlawn Ave Dayton OH 45403-3356 E-mail: drwillmosier@yahoo.com.

**MOSIMAN, RITA ESTHER,** music educator; children: Theresa, Mark, Brian. B in Music (hon.), U. Ariz., 1963. Lic. secondary tchg. Ariz., 1963. English, speech tchr. Dreux Am. H.S., France, 1964—65; adminstrv. asst. U.S. Dept. Def., Supt. Sch. Office, Orleans, France, 1965—66; choral dir. Los Lunas Consol. Sch., N.Mex., 1980; pvt. voice and piano tchr. Albuquerque, 1980—. Guest conductor, choral clinician Am. All Spain H.S. Music Festival, Zaragoza, Spain, 1979. Guest solo vocalist: U. N.Mex., 1982, U. Ariz., 1985, Whitworth Coll., 1988; prodr.(vocalist, pianist): America's Best Kept Secret-Rita M., 2004; dir.(soloist): La Gran Via, 1988,: Santa Fe Spirit, 1989. Vol. Concert for Humanity, Albuquerque, 1984; dir., pianist benefit concert Pennies for the Homeless, Albuquerque, 1998. Named Outstanding Ind. Woman, U. Ariz., 1963; recipient Solo Artist, Northern Ariz. Symphony, 1962, Leadership award, Sigma Alpha Iota, we. dist., 1963. Mem.: Nat. Assn. Tchrs. Singing. Avocations: hiking, photography, travel, birdwatching. Office Phone: 505-294-6018.

**MOSJIDIS, JORGE,** agricultural studies educator, researcher; b. Santiago, Chile; arrived in U.S., 1976; d. Georgios and Aliky Mosjidis; m. Cecilia O'Hara Mosjidis, Mar. 23, 1986; children: Christina Zoe Wood, Alexis Georgios. B in Agronomy, U. Chile, Santiago, 1970; PhD, U. Calif., Riverside, 1981. Asst. prof. Auburn (Ala.) U., assoc. prof., 1986—96, prof., 1996—. Chair clover crop germplasm com. USDA, 2005—, sec., 2002—05; assoc. editor Crop Sci., 1995—2000. Contbr. articles to profl. jours. Bd. dirs. Annunciation Greek Orthodox Ch., Montgomery, Ala. Recipient Dir.'s Rsch. award, Ala. Agr. Exptl. Sta., 2005; grantee, USDA-CSREES-NRI, 2003—06, CSREES, Integrated Organic Program, 2005—, So. Region SARE, 2005—, 2005—. Mem.: Am. Forage and Grassland Coun., Am. Genetic Assn., Am. Soc. Agronomy, Crop Sci. Soc. Am. (assoc. editor 2000), Gamma Sigma Delta, Sigma Xi. Greek Orthodox. Achievements include patents pending for utilization of a plant to control gastrointestinal parasites in ruminants; obtained a certificate of plant variety protection for 18 years for a sericea lespedeza cultivar. Avocations: yoga, flower and vegetable gardening, tai chi, qi kung. Office: Auburn Univ 202 Funchess Hall Auburn University AL 36849-5412 Office Phone: 334-844-3976.

**MOSK, RICHARD MITCHELL,** judge; b. LA, May 18, 1939; s. Stanley and Edna M.; m. Sandra Lee Budnitz, Mar. 21, 1964; children: Julie, Matthew. AB with great distinction, Stanford U., 1960; JD cum laude, Harvard U., 1963. Bar: Calif. 1964, U.S. Supreme Ct. 1970, U.S. Ct. Mil. Appeals 1970, U.S. Dist. Ct. (no., so., ea., and cen. dists.) Calif 1964, U.S. Ct. Appeals (9th dist.) 1964. Staff Pres.'s Commn. on Assassination Pres. Kennedy, 1964; rsch. clk. Calif. Supreme Ct., 1964-65; ptnr. Mitchell, Silberberg & Knupp, L.A., 1965-87; prin. Sanders, Barnet, Goldman, Simons & Mosk, PC, L.A., 1987-2000; justice Calif. Ct. Appeal, 2nd Dist., 2001—. Spl. dep Fed. Pub Defender, L.A., 1975 76; instr. U. So Calif Law Sch. 1978; judge Iran-U.S. Claims Tribunal, 1981—84, 1997—2001, substitute arbitrator, 1984—97; mem. L.A. County Jud. Procedures Commn. 1973—82, chmn., 1978; chmn., co-chmn. Motion Picture Assn. Classification and Rating Adminstrn., 1994—2000; mem. panel Ct. Arbitration for Sport-Geneva, 1998—2001; lectr. internat. law Hague Acad., 2003. Contbr. articles to profl. jours. Mem. L.A. City-County Inquiry on Brush Fires, 1970; bd. dirs. Calif. Mus. Sci. and Industry, 1979-82, Vista Del Mar Child Ctr., 1979-82; trustee L.A. County Law Libr., 1988-91; bd. govs. Town Hall Calif., 1986-91; mem. Christopher Commn. on L.A. Police Dept., 1991; mem. Stanford U. Athletic Bd., 1991-95. With USNR, 1964-75. Hon. Woodrow Wilson fellow, 1960; recipient Roscoe Pound prize, 1961. Mem.: ABA (coun. internat. law sect. 1986—90), Am. Law Inst., L.A. County Bar Assn., Beverly Hills Bar Assn., Am. Bar Found., Phi Beta Kappa. Office: Ct Appeal 300 S Spring St Los Angeles CA 90013

**MOSKAL, ANTHONY JOHN,** retired dean, management consultant, educator; b. South Amboy, N.J., May 31, 1946; s. Anthony Joseph and Jennie (Salamon) M.; m. Kathryn Jean Coakley, July 8, 1978; 1 child, Nicole Elizabeth. AB, Villanova (Pa.) U., 1968, MA, 1972; MEd, Ga. State U., 1974; PhD, Columbia Pacific U., San Rafael, Calif., 1987. Prin. instr. U.S. Army, Ft. Benning, Ga., 1969-71; research mgr. Blue Cross and Blue Shield, Columbus, Ga., 1972-74; sales rep. J.C. Penney Co., Parlin, N.J., 1974-76; dean of students Alliance Coll., Cambridge Springs, Pa., 1976-77; tchr. Sayreville (N.J.) pub. schs., 1977-79; county 4-H agt. Rutgers U., New Brunswick, 1979-86; pres. Eagle Assocs., South Amboy, N.J., 1985—; dir. Burning Bush Prodns., 1986—. Adj. faculty Georgian Ct. Coll., Lakewood, NJ, 1987—; U.S. Army Command and Gen. Staff Coll., Ft. Leavenworth, Kans., 1989—2000, Nat. Def. U., Washington, 1991—2000; cons.-dir. Union County Ednl. Svcs. Commn., 2000—; spl. liaison to Mcpl. Bd. Edn., Sayreville, 1991—95, Sayreville, 2000—; area admissions rep. U.S. Mil. Acad., 1984—91; bd. dirs. Burning Bush Prodn.; mem. Environ. Commn., Sayreville, 2004—; cons. in field. Contbr. articles to profl. jours. Active Boy Scouts Am.; counselor, mem. dist. com. Ctrl. N.J. Coun. Boy Scouts Am., 1982—; pres., bd. dirs. Vol. Action Ctr., Middlesex County, NJ, 1979—87;

pres. Sayreville War Meml. H.S. Band Parents Assn., 1994—96, NJ 4-H Agts. Assn., 1985—86; commr. Environ. Commn., Sayreville, 2004—; county committeeman Middlesex County, 1990—94, 2000—; dir. religious edn. Sacred Heart Parish, South Amboy, NJ, 1988—91. With U.S. Army, 1969—71, with U.S. Army, 1990—92, lt. col. USAR. Decorated Meritorious Svc. medal, Army Commendation medal (2), Mil. Outstanding Vol. Svc. medal; recipient Order of the Arrow award Boy Scouts Am., 1960, 20th Century award of Achievement, Nat. Assn. Chiefs of Police, Desert Shield/Desert Storm medal State of N.J., Disting. Svc. medal State of N.J.; United Way of Ctrl. Jersey grantee, 1984, others. Mem.: ASCD, Holy Name Soc., U.S. Army Officer Candidate Alumni Assn., Am. Fedn. Police (award of merit 1989, legion of honor 1990, J. Edgar Hoover Meml. medal 1991, St. Michael the Archangel award 1992, patriotism award 1993), Nat. Assn. Ext. 4-H Agts. (regional contact 1981—83, profl. devel. chmn. 1984—86, cert. appreciation 1983), Res. Officers Assn., Mil. Police Regtl. Assn., N.J. Assn. 4-H Agts. (pres. 1985—86, outstanding svc. citation 1981, 1987), Vietnam Vets. of Am. (life; rec. sec., honor guard), Nat. Infantry Assn. (life), Nat. Eagle Scout Assn., Am. Legion, K. of C. (3d degree Dep. Grand Knight, program dir., degree team capt., color corps commdr., diocesan degree team, vol. coord. fife and drum corps, dist. degree team, 4th degree aide to Dist. Master, 3d degree Dist. Warden, 4th degree Past Faithful Navigator, family of mo., Knight of mo. (3), 4th degree family of yr., Assembly Color Corps man of yr.(2), Dist. Color Corps man of yr., 3d degree family of yr., Assembly Color Corps man of yr.) Kiwanis, Pi Gamma Mu, Epsilon Sigma Phi, Alpha Phi Omega. Republican. Roman Catholic. Avocations: reading, music, recreational camping, travel, woodworking. Office: Eagle Assocs 166 Luke St South Amboy NJ 08879-2231 Office Phone: 908-317-8634. E-mail: ajmoskal@verizon.net.

**MOSKAL, BARBARA M.,** engineering educator, mathematics professor; d. Stanley L. and Barbara A. Moskal; m. Brian E. Field, July 5, 1997; 1 child, Tori Elizabeth Field. BS in Math. Edn., Duquesne U., 1989; EdD, U. Pitts., 1997. Grad. tchg. asst., grad. rsch. asst. U. Pitts., 1989—91, adj. faculty, 1995—97, Duquesne U., Pitts., 1995—97; lectr. Colo. Sch. of Mines, Golden, 1997—99, asst. prof., 1999—2004, assoc. prof., 2004—. Assoc. dir. for the Ctr. for Engring. Edn. Colo. Sch. of Mines, 1999—2000. Contbr. articles to profl. jours. Named Outstanding Faculty Mem. in Math. and Computer Scis., Colo. Sch. of Mines Alumni Assn., 2001; recipient Gen. Excellence in Secondary Edn. award, Duquesne University's Sch. Edn., 1989, Superior Academic Performance award, U. Pitts. Sch. Alumni Assn., 1996—97, Tchg. award, Colo. Sch. of Mines Alumni Assn., 2003, Burton W. Jones award for Disting. Tchg., 2006, William; grantee NSF, 2000—, Eisenhower Colo. Commn. on Higher Edn., 2003, Commn. on Higher Edn., 2004, Colo. Dept. Edn., 2004—; New Faculty fellow, Frontiers in Edn. Conf., 2000, Alfred E. Jennie fellow, Colo. Sch. of Mines, 2004. Mem.: IEEE (chair learning module assessment com. 2003—05), Nat. Coun. Tchrs. Math., Colo. Coun. Tchrs. Math., Am. Ednl. Rsch. Assn. Math. Assn. Am. (Burton W. Jones Disting. Tchg. award 2006), Nat. Coun. Measurement in Edn., Am. Soc. Engring. Edn. (assoc. Wilson Elgin Wickenton award 2006), Sigma Xi. Avocations: hiking, travel, bicycling. Office Phone: 303-273-3867. Business E-mail: bmoskal@mines.edu.

**MOSKIN, JOHN ROBERT,** editor, writer; b. N.Y.C., May 9, 1923; s. Morris and Irma (Rosenfeld) M.; m. Doris Marianne Bloch, Oct. 7, 1948 (div. 1978); children: Mark Douglas, David Scott, Nancy Irma; m. Lynn Carole Goldberg, Apr. 10, 1986. Grad., Horace Mann Sch., 1940; BS, Harvard U., 1944; MA, Columbia U., 1947. Reporter Boston Post, 1941-42, Newark News, 1947-48; asst. to gen. mgr. N.Y. Star, 1948-49; editor Westport (Conn.) Town Crier, 1949; med. editor Look mag., N.Y.C., 1950-51, articles editor, 1951-53, sr. editor, 1956-66, fgn. editor, 1966-71; mng. editor Woman's Home Companion, 1953-56; sr. editor Collier's, 1956; editor at large Saturday Rev., 1972-75; sr. editor World Press Rev., 1976-87, contbg. editor, 1987-93; editl. dir. Aspen Inst., 1977-83. Editl. dir. Commonwealth Fund, 1984-87, sr. editl. advisor, 1987-93. Author: (with others) The Decline of the American Male, 1958, Morality in America, 1966, Turncoat, 1968, The U.S. Marine Corps Story, 1977, 82, 87, 92, Among Lions, 1982, (with Julia Vitullo-Martin) The Executive's Book of Quotations, 1994, Mr. Truman's War, 1996, 2002; editor: The Marines, 1998; mem. editl. adv. com. Dimensions mag, 1970-71, Present Tense, 1973-90. Trustee Scarsdale Adult Sch., 1965—72, chmn., 1969—70; mem. comm. screening com. Coun. Internat. Exch. Scholars, 1974—77, Pres.'s Coun. Heritage U., 1995—; bd. dirs. SIECUS, 1972—80, Jerusalem Found., 1977—2003, Marine Corps Hist. Found., 1979—82, 1989—95, Faculty for Continuing Med. Edn., 1983—86, Authors Guild Found., 2000—; bd. dirs., sec. Lotos Club Found., 2000—; mem. Dana Reed Prize com. Harvard U., 1947—2000, mem. com. Class of 1944, 1943—. With AUS, 1943—46. Recipient Benjamin Franklin Gold medal for pub. svc. Woman's Home Companion, 1955, Page One award Newspaper Guild N.Y., 1965, Sidney Hillman Found. award, 1965, National Headliners award, 1967, Overseas Press Club award, 1969, citation for excellence, 1971, Disting. Svc. award Marine Corps Combat Corrs. Assn., 1978, 99, Nat. Jewish Book award, 1983, Disting. Svc. award Marine Corps Hist. Found., 1996, Gen. O.P. Smith award Marine Corps Heritage Found., 1999. Mem.: PEN, Nat. Press Club (Washington), Fgn. Editors Group (chmn. 1970—71), Am. Hist. Assn., Soc. Mil. History, Authors Guild, Lotos Club (bd. dirs. 1988—90, pres. 1991—94, bd. dirs. 1994—2002, historian), Harvard Club (N.Y.C.), The Century Assn., Overseas Press Club (gov. 1975—79), Sigma Delta Chi (nat. freedom of info. com. 1964). Home: 945 5th Ave New York NY 10021-2666 also: 157 Jerusalem Rd Tyringham MA 01264 E-mail: jrmedit@att.net.

**MOSKIN, MORTON,** lawyer, director; b. NYC, Mar. 28, 1927; s. Barnett and Sonia (Burr) M.; m. Rita Lee Goldberg, June 15, 1952; children: Tina, Ilene, Jonathan. BA, Pa. State Coll., 1947; LLB, Cornell U., 1950. Assoc. White & Case, N.Y.C., 1950—61, ptnr, 1962—94, cons., 1995—. Chmn. exec. com. Mallinckrodt, Inc. (formerly IMCERA, previously Internat. Minerals and Chem. Corp.), St. Louis, 1988-91, chmn. corp. governance com., 1993 97; nnu. BT Mortgage Investors, Garden City, NY, 1973-82; bd. dirs. NY County Lawyers' Assn. Found., Inc., 2004, 05, 06. Author (with E. Carolan Berkley): Third Party Legal Opinions, 2005; editor (with Field): New York and Delaware Business Entities: Choice, Formation, Operation, Financing, Acquisitions, 1997, Transactional Lawyer's Deskbook: Advising Business Entities, 2001; editor: Commercial Contracts: Strategies for Drafting and Negotiating, 2002. Bd. dirs. Fedn. Employment and Guidance Svcs.; bd. dirs., pres. Henry M. Blackmer Found., N.Y.C.; bd. dirs. Achievement Found., Stamford, Conn., pres., 1988-94; bd. dirs. Jewish Cmty. Svcs. L.I., 1974-93, pres., 1984-87. Fellow Am. Bar Found.; mem. ABA, NY County Lawyers Assn. Found. Inc. (bd. dirs. 1981-86, 99-02, 04, 05, 06), N.Y. County Lawyers Assn. Found. Inc. (bd. dirs. 2004-06), Norfolk (Conn.) Country Club, Cornell Club. Home: 1160 Park Ave Apt 15B New York NY 10128-1212 Office: White & Case 1155 Ave of Americas New York NY 10036-2711 Business E-Mail: mmoskin@whitecase.com.

**MOSKOS, CHARLES C.,** social studies educator; b. Chgo., May 20, 1934; s. Charles and Rita (Shukas) M.; m. Ilca Hohn, July 3, 1966; children: Andrew, Peter. BA cum laude, Princeton, 1956; MA, UCLA, 1961, PhD, 1963; LHD (hon.), U. Norwich U., 1992, Towson U., 2002. Asst. prof. U. Mich., Ann Arbor, 1966-69; assoc. prof. sociology Northwestern U., Evanston, Ill. 1966-70, prof., 1970—. Fellow Progressive Policy Inst., 1992—; mem. Presdl. Commn. on Women in the Mil., 1992. Author: The Sociology of Political Independence, 1967, The American Enlisted Man, 1970, Public Opinion and the Military Establishment, 1971, Peace Soldiers, 1976, Fuerzas Armadas y Sociedad, 1984, The Military--More Than Just A Job?, 1988, A Call to Civic Service, 1988, Greek Americans, 1989, Soldiers and Sociology, 1989, New Directions in Greek American Studies, 1991, The New Conscientious Objection, 1993, All That We Can Be, 1996, Reporting War When There Is No War, 1996, The Media and the Military, 2000, The Postmodern Military, 2000. Chmn. Theodore Saloutos Meml. Fund; mem. Archdiocesan Commn. Third Millenium, 1982-88; mem adv. bd. Vets. for Am., 1997—; mem. Congl. Commn. on Mil. Tng. and Gender-Related Issues, 1998-99, Nat. Security Study Group, 1998-2001. Served with AUS, 1956-58. Decorated D.S.M., Fondation pour les Etudes de Def. Nat. (France), S.M.K. (The

Netherlands); named to Marshall rsch. chair ARI, 1987-88, 95-96; Ford. Found. faculty fellow, 1969-70; fellow Wilson Ctr., 1980-81, guest scholar, 1991; fellow Rockefeller Found. Humanities, 1983-84, Guggenheim fellow, 1992-93, fellow Annenberg Washington Program, 1995; grantee 20th Century Fund, 1983-87, 92-94, Ford Found., 1989-90; recipient Nat. Educator Leadership award Todd Found., 1997, Book award Washington Monthly, 1997, Honored Patriot award Selective Svc. Sys., 1998; Pub. Policy fellow Wilson Ctr., 2002; Eisenhower chair Royal Mil. Acad. Netherlands, 2002. Mem. Am. Sociol. Assn., Internat. Sociol. Assn. (pres. rsch. com. on armed forces and conflict resolution 1982-86), Am. Polit. Sci. Assn., Inter-Univ. Seminar on Armed Forces and Soc. (chmn. 1987-99), Am. Acad. Arts and Scis. Greek Orthodox. Address: 1040 4th St #309 Santa Monica CA 90403 Business E-Mail: c-moskos@northwestern.edu.

**MOSKOS, HARRY,** columnist, editor; b. Chgo., Oct. 8, 1936; m. Victoria Marie Poulos; 3 children. BA, U. N.Mex., Albuquerque, 1958. With Albuquerque Tribune, 1953-59; editor Grants (N.Mex.) Daily Beacon, 1959-60; newsman AP, Albuquerque, 1960, state editor, 1961-63, chief of bur. Honolulu, 1963-69; city editor Albuquerque Tribune, 1969-73, mng. editor, 1973—80; editor El Paso Herald-Post, 1980—84, Knoxville News-Sentinel, 1984—2001; columnist, letters editor Albuquerque Jour., 2001—. Office: 7777 Jefferson St NE Albuquerque NM 87109 Office Phone: 505-823-3837. Business E-Mail: hmoskos@abqjournal.com.

**MOSKOVITZ, ELISA MCMILLAN,** music educator, musician; b. Columbia, S.C., Nov. 29, 1953; d. William Gooding and Elizabeth Anne McMillan; m. Barry L. Moskovitz, Apr. 5, 1980 (div. Dec. 1982); m. Finnbarr T. Dunphy, Nov. 19, 2000. B of Music Edn., Winthrop U., 1976, MMus, 1977; D of Musical Arts, U. S.C., 1989. Tchr. gen. music and chorus Lexington (S.C.) Sch. Dist. 1, 1977—89, program specialist for fine arts; tchr. music theory Lexington H.S., 1990—2002; choral dir. White Knoll H.S., 2002—06. Organist, choirmaster St. Timothy's Episcopal Ch., Columbia, 1985—2002; pianist So. Arts Trio, Columbia, 1994—; adj. prof. U. S.C., Columbia, 1990—2004, Limestone Coll., Columbia, 1990, Columbia, 96; coord. music Tri-Dist. Arts Consortium, Columbia, 1997—99; organist, choirmaster Centennial Presbyn. Ch., Columbia, 2004—, Centennial Assoc. Reformed Presbyn., 2004—; coord. SC State Choral Festival, 2004—. Author: The American Music Teacher, 1990, Yemassee, 2001, JRME, 0992. Coord. A Little Summer Music concert series St. Timothy's Ch., Columbia, 1995—; mem. People to People Ambassadorial Program, 2003—. Fellow, NEH, 1992; grantee, Nat. Music Edn. Project, 1991. Mem.: S.C. Music Educators Assn., Am. Guild Organists, Pi Kappa Lambda, Delta Kappa Gamma. Episcopalian. Avocations: golf, poetry, literature. Office Phone: 803-996-4558. Office Fax: 803-996-4558.

**MOSKOVITZ, JACKOB,** biology professor; arrived in U.S., 1992; s. Raphael and Zipora Moskovitz. BA in Biology, Technion, 1985, MS in Biology, 1988, DS in Medicine, 1992. Asst. prof. U. Kans., Lawrence, 2004—. Cons. Amgen, Thousand Oaks, Calif., 2000, UBI, Lake Placid, NY, 2004—. Contbr. articles to profl. jours. Fellow, Roch Inst. Molecular Biuology, Nutley, NJ, 1992—95, NIH, Bethesda, Md., 1996—2004. Mem.: Neurosci. Assn. Avocations: piano, painting, sports, travel.

**MOSKOW, MICHAEL H.,** bank executive; b. Paterson, N.J., Jan. 7, 1938; s. Jacob and Sylvia (Edelstein) M.; m. Constance Bain, Dec. 18, 1966; children: Robert Bain, Eliot Marc, Lisa Danielle. AB, Lafayette Coll., Easton, Pa., 1959; MA in Econs., U. Pa., 1962, PhD, 1965. Instr. econs. Lafayette Coll., 1964—65; asst. prof. mgmt. Drexel Inst. Tech., Phila., 1963-64, 65-67; assoc. prof. econs., dir. Bus. Econ. and Bus. Research, Temple U., Phila., 1967-69; sr. staff economist Coun. Econ. Advisers The White House, Washington, 1969-70; exec. dir. Constrn. Industry Collective Bargaining Commn., 1970-71; dep. under sec. U.S. Dept. Labor, 1971-72, asst. sec. for policy, evaluation and research, 1972-73, under-sec. labor, 1976-77; asst. sec. for policy devel. and research US Dept. Housing & Urban Devel., 1973-75; dir. Council on Wage and Price Stability, 1975-76; cons. Com. for Econ. Devel., 1977; dir. corp. devel. and planning Esmark, Inc., 1977-78, v.p. corp. devel. and planning, 1978-80; exec. v.p. Estronics, Inc. div. Esmark, Inc., 1980-82; pres. Velsicol Chem. Corp. div. N.W. Industries, Inc., Chgo., 1982-84; v.p. corp. devel. Dart & Kraft, Inc., Northbrook, Ill., 1985-86; v.p. strategy and bus. devel. Premark Internat. Inc. (spinoff from Dart & Kraft), Deerfield, 1986-90; dep. U.S. Trade Rep. Exec. Office Pres., Washington, 1991-93; prof. strategy and internat mgmt. Northwestern U. Kellogg Grad. Sch. Mgmt., Evanston, Ill., 1993-94; pres. Fed. Res. Bank Chgo., 1994—. Bd. dirs. Conrail, Inc., 1994. Author: Teachers and Unions, 1966, Labor Relations in the Performing Arts: An Introductory Survey, 1970; co-author: Collective Negotiations for Teachers, 1966, Collective Bargaining in Public Employment, 1970, Strategic Planning in Business and Government, 1978; co-editor: Readings on Collective Negotiations in Public Education, 1967, Employment Relations in Higher Education, 1969, Women and Work, 1987; contbr. articles to profl. jours. Bd. trustees Lafayette Coll; mem. Coun. Foreign Location; dir. Chgo. Coun. Foreign Rels., Coun. Fgn. Rels. NYC, Northwestern Meml. Found., World Bus. Chgo., Chicagoland C. of C.; mem. governing bd. Ill. Coun. Econ. Edn.; 1st lt. AUS, 1959-60. Fellow Nat. Acad. Pub. Adminstrn.; mem. Indsl. Rels. Rsch. Assn. (pres. 1987), Nat. Bur. Econ. Rsch. (chmn. 2002-05), Comml. Club Chgo. (civic com.), Econs. Club Chgo. (chmn. 2001-03). Home: 400 Sheridan Rd Winnetka IL 60093-2628 Office: Fed Reserve Bank Chgo 230 S La Salle St Chicago IL 60604-1496 Office Phone: 312-322-5001.*

**MOSKOWITZ, DAVID K.,** lawyer; b. Glen Burnie, Md., Apr. 24, 1958; m. Hallie A. Moskowitz. BA summa cum laude, Western Md. College, 1980; JD with honors, George Washington U., 1983. Corp. counsel MDC Holdings Inc., 1986—90; with Echostar Communications, Englewood, Colo., 1990, exec. v.p., gen. counsel, sec., dir. Mem.: Am. Corp. Counsel Assn., Denver Bar Assn., Colo. Bar Assn., ABA. Office: Echostar Communications 9601 S Meridan Blvd Englewood CO 80112 Home: 7 Waterside Ter Englewood CO 80113-4141 Office Phone: 303-723-1040. Office Fax: 303-723-1699. Business E-Mail: david.moskowitz@echostar.com.

**MOSKOWITZ, DEBORAH LYNN,** lawyer; b. Orlando, Fla., Sept. 24, 1972; d. George Richard and Marsha Fay Moskowitz. BS in Comm., U. of Miami, Coral Gables, Fla., 1994; JD, Samford U., Birmingham, Ala., 1997. Asst. state atty. Eighteenth Jud. Circuit of the State of Fla., Sanford, Fla., 1997—99; counsel CNA Ins., Maitland, Fla., 1999; assoc. Bobo Spicer Ciotoli Fulford Bocchino DeBevoise & Romaguera, Orlando, 1999—2001; ptnr./shareholder Quintairos, Prieto, Wood, & Boyer, P.A., Orlando, 2001—. Mem.: ABA. Republican. Jewish. Office: 9766 Poplar Pl Orlando FL 32827 Office: Quintairos Prieto Wood & Boyer PA 8427 South Park Cir Ste 100 Orlando FL 32819 Office Phone: 407-903-9205. Office Fax: 407-903-9206. E-mail: dmoskowitz@qpwblaw.com.

**MOSKOWITZ, HAROLD J.,** lawyer; b. NYC, Oct. 8, 1940; BS, CUNY, 1962; JD, St. John's U., 1965. Bar: NY 1966, DC 1972, US Dist. Ct. Ea. Dist. NY, US Dist. Ct. So. Dist. NY. Founding ptnr. Wilson, Elser, Moskowitz, Edelman & Dicker LLP, NYC. Mem.: assoc. com. Mem.: ABA, Profl. Liability Underwriting Soc., DC Bar Assn., Internat. Bar Assn., NY State Bar Assn., Def. Rsch. Inst. Assn. of the Bar of the City of NY. Office: Wilson Elser Moskowitz Edelman & Dicker LLP 23rd Fl 150 E 42nd St New York NY 10017-5639 Office Phone: 212-490-3000 ext. 2230. Office Fax: 212-490-3038. Business E-Mail: moskowitzh@wemed.com.

**MOSKOWITZ, HERBERT,** management educator; b. Paterson, NJ, May 26, 1935; s. David and Ruth (Abrams) Moskowitz; m. Heather Mary Lesgnier, Feb. 25, 1968; children: Tobias, Rebecca, Jonas. BS in Mech. Engring., Newark Coll. Engring., 1956; MBA, U.S. Internat. U., 1964; PhD, UCLA, 1970. Rsch. engr. GE, 1956-60; systems design engr. Gen. Dynamics Convair, San Diego, 1960-65; asst. prof. Purdue U., West Lafayette, Ind., 1970-75, assoc. prof., 1975-79, prof., 1979-85, Disting. prof. mfg. mgmt., 1985-87, James B. Henderson Disting. prof., 1987-91, Lewis B. Cullman

Disting. prof. mfg. mgmt., 1991—, dir. Dauch Ctr. Mgmt. Mfg. Enterprises. Cons. AT&T, Inland Steel Co.; adv. panelist NSF, 1990—. Author: Management Science and Statistics Texts, 1975—90; assoc. editor Decision Scis. Jour., 1984—90, Jour. Behavioral Decision Making, 1986—90; contbr. articles to jours. in field. Bd. dirs. Sons of Abraham Synagogue, Lafayette; mem. Lafayette Klezmorem, 1973—. Capt. USAF, 1956—60. Recipient Disting. Doctoral Student award, UCLA Alumni Assn., 1969—70; Fulbright Rsch. scholar, 1985—86. Fellow: Decision Scis. Inst. (sec. 1985—87, v.p. 1978—80); mem.: Ops. Rsch. Soc. Am/Inst. Mgmt. Sci. (liaison officer 1977—, panelist, advisor NSF and Fulbright Scholar program 1993—), Pi Tau Sigma, Tau Beta Pi. Jewish. Avocations: jewish music, tennis. Home: 1430 N Salisbury St West Lafayette IN 47906-2420 Office: Purdue U West Lafayette IN 47907-2056

**MOSKOWITZ, JAY,** health science association administrator, educator, dean; b. NYC, Jan. 9, 1943; s. Murray and Helene Moskowitz; m. Joanne Cathy Schindelheim, Dec. 27, 1970; children: Michael Bradley, Andrew Cory. BS, Queens Coll., 1964; postgrad., CUNY, 1965; PhD, Brown U., 1969. From research assoc. in pharmacology to dep. dir. NIH, 1969—93, dep. dir. for sci. policy & tech. transfer, prin. dep. dir., 1993; various positions Nat. Heart, Lung and Blood Inst., 1976-86; acting dir. Nat. Inst. on Deafness and Other Communication Disorders, 1988-90, dep. dir., 1993-95; sr. assoc. dean for rsch. devel., prof. pub. health scis. Wake Forest U. Sch. Medicine, Winston-Salem, NC, 1995—2001, sr. assoc. dean, 1997—2001; assoc. v.p. health sci. rsch. Pa. State U., 2002—, vice dean rsch. coll. medicine, 2002—, prof. medicine, 2002—. Contbr. articles to profl. jours. Served to lt. comdr. USPHS. Recipient Meritorious award William A. Jump Meml. Found., 1977, Dir.'s award NIH, 1978, Superior Svc. award USPHS, 1980, performance awards Sr. Exec. Svc., Presdl. Meritorious Exch. Rank award 1989, Disting. Svc. award HHS, 1991, Disting. Svc. award Nat. Inst. on Deafness and Other Comm. Disorders, 1994. Mem. AAAS, Soc. Exptl. Biology and Medicine, N.C. Inst. Medicine. Jewish. Home: 1760 Adeline Dr Mechanicsburg PA 17050 Office: Penn State College Medicine 500 University Hershey PA 00033 Office Phone: 717-531-7199. Business E-mail: jmoskowitz@psu.edu.

**MOSKOWITZ, JOEL STEVEN,** lawyer; b. NYC, Jan. 14, 1947; s. Jack I. and Myra (Shor) M.; m. Anna Boucher; children: David, Michael, Ellen. BA, UCLA, 1967, JD, 1970. Bar: Calif. 1971, U.S. Ct. Appeals (9th cir.) 1971, U.S. Ct. Appeals (D.C. cir.) 1975, U.S. Supreme Ct. 1975, U.S. Ct. Appeals (2d cir.) 1979. Dep. atty. gen. Calif. Dept. Justice, Sacramento, 1970-83; dep. dir. Calif. Dept. Health Svcs., Sacramento, 1983-85; of counsel Gibson, Dunn & Crutcher, L.A., 1985-88, ptnr., 1988-96, Moskowitz, Brestoff, Winston & Blinderman LLP, 1996—. Author: Environmental Liaibility in Real Property Transactions, 1995; contbr. articles to legal publs. Mem. Phi Beta Kappa. Office: 1880 Century Park E Ste 300 Los Angeles CA 90067-1631 Office Phone: 310-373-9790. Personal E-mail: joel_s_moskowitz@yahoo.com. Business E-Mail: joel@moskowitzhq.com.

**MOSKOWITZ, MICHAEL ARTHUR,** neuroscientist; b. NYC, May 26, 1942; s. Irving Lawrence and Clara (Dranoff) M.; m. Mary Henderson, May 18, 1991; 1 child, Jenna Rachel. AB, Johns Hopkins U., 1964; MD, Tufts U., 1968; MSc (hon.), Harvard U., 1992. Diplomate Am. Bd. Psychiaty and Neurology, Am. Bd. Internal Medicine. Intern Yale U. Dept. Medicine, 1968-69, resident, 1969-71; resident in neurology Peter Bent Brigham Children Hosp., 1971-74; asst. prof. Med. Sch., Harvard U., Boston, 1975-79, assoc. prof., 1979-92; prof. divsn. health sci. and tech. Harvard-MIT, Boston, 1992—. Established investigator Am. Heart Assn., 1980-85; neurophysiologist and assoc. neurologist Mass. Gen. Hosp., Boston, 1981—; H.J. Barnett lectr. Canadian Heart Assn., Queens U., Kingston, Ont., 1993—; Witter lectr. U. Calif., San Francisco, 1994—, Barraquer-LaFora lectr. Spanish Neurol. Soc., Barcelona, Spain, 1994—, Decade of the Brain lectr. Am. Acad. Neurology, 1995, Briggs lecture dept. pharmacology U. Tex., San Antonio, 1995, Richardson lectr. Canadian Neurol. Assn., 1998, John Graham lectr. Am. Assn. Study Headache, Merck Sharpe Dohme Neurosci. lectr. Birmingham, Eng., 2000, Soriano lectr. Am. Neurol. Assn., 2003, Dr. Chaim Mayman lectr. Beth Israel Hosp., Boston, 2003, others; chmn. sci. adv. bd. Max Plank Inst., Köln; program project dir. stroke and migraine NIH program projects, NIH rev. study sect. mem. 1982-85, 88-91, 97—; 2nd internat. hon. lectr. European Stroke Conf., 1997; cons. pharm. industry; chmn. sci. adv. bd. Max Planck Inst., U. of Ottawa, Can., Queen's Neurosc. Inst.; mem. sic. adv. bd. Queen's Med. Ctr., Honolulu, U. Ottawa. Editl. bd. Stroke, Acta Neurol. Scandinavica Cephalgia, Jour. Cerebral Blood Flow & Metabolism, Cerebrovascular Disease; editor: Animal Models of Headache, 1996; basic sci. editor Stroke (AHA jour.); contbr. numerous articles to jours; patentee in field. HIT postdoctoral fellow, 1974-76, Alfred Sloan Found. fellow, 1978-80; recipient Enrico Greppi award Italian Neurology Soc., 1986, 88, Tchr.-Investigator award Nat. Inst. Neurol. Disease and Stroke, 1975-80, Zülch prize Max-Planck Soc./Inst., 1996, John Graham award AASH, 1998, Arnold Friedman award Am. Headache Soc., Thomas Willis award Am. Stroke Assn., 2006, C. Miller Fisher award Am. Stroke Assn. N.E. affiliate, 2005, Top 200 Most Highly Cited in Neurosci., Info. Svcs. Inst.; rsch. grantee Bristol-Myers Squibb, 1993—; MGH Interdepartmental Stroke Ctr. Mem. Am. Heart Assn. (nat. rsch. com. 1991-96, exec. com. stroke coun. 1991-96), Am. Neurol. Assn. (Soriano lectr., 2003, 04), Am. Heart and Stroke Assn. (co-chair program com. 2001—), Am. Acad. Neurology, Am. Pain Soc., Soc. Neurosci., Internat. Soc. for Cerebral Blood Flow and Metabolism (bd. dirs., pres. 2001—), Internat. Symposium Pharm. of Cerebral Ischemia, Can. Neurol. Soc. (hon.). Achievements include research in neuroscientific, neurology literature including stroke and migraine. Office: Mass Gen Hosp Charleston Navy Yard 149 13th St Charlestown MA 02129-2020 Office Phone: 617-726-8442.

**MOSKOWITZ, RANDI ZUCKER,** nurse; b. N.Y.C., Oct. 19, 1948; d. Seymour and Gertrude (Levy) Zucker; m. Marc N. Moskowitz, July 11, 1976. RN, Jewish Hosp. and Med. Ctr., 1969; BA, Marymount Manhattan Coll., 1975; MS, Hunter Coll., 1979; MBA, Columbia U., 1990. Gen. staff nurse neurosurgery unit N.Y. Hosp., N.Y.C., 1969—71, sr. staff nurse recovery rm., 1971—76, nurse coord. utilization rev., 1976—79; health educator Office of Cancer Commn. Meml. Sloan-Kettering Cancer Ctr., N.Y.C., 1979—81, adminstr. Surg. Day Hosp., 1990—98; adminstrv. nurse oncologist Bklyn. Cmty. Hosp. and Meth. Hosp., 1981—83, grants coord. radiotherapy dept., 1983—86; adminstr. Ambulatory Oncology Ctr. Columbia-Presbyn. Med. Ctr., N.Y.C., 1986—89; mgr. Oncology Svcs. St. Vincent Cath. Med. Ctrs., Jamaica, NY, 1999—2006; adminstr. pediat. oncology Columbia U. Med. Ctr., N.Y.C., 2006—. Masters prof. oncology Columbia U. Sch. Nursing. Co-editor Oncology Nursing: Advances, Treatments and Trends into the Twenty-first Century; contbr. articles to profl. jours. Mem. N.Y. Assn. Ambulatory Care, Oncology Nursing Soc. (sec. N.Y. chpt. 1983-87, pres. 1988-89). Home: 446 E 86th St Apt 5F New York NY 10028-6474 Office: Columbia Univ Med Ctr 161 Ft Washington Ave New York NY 10032 Office Phone: 212-342-3455. Personal E-mail: rm2505@columbia.edu.

**MOSKOWITZ, RICHARD,** physician; b. Passaic, N.J., Dec. 16, 1938; s. Harry and Sylvia (Margoles) M.; m. Carol Ann Dukes, Feb. 15, 1963 (div. 1965); 1 child, Michael; m. Linda Ruth Reissman, Oct. 20, 1984; 1 child, Jennifer. BA, Harvard U., 1959; MD, NYU, 1963; fellow in philosophy, U. Colo., 1963-65. Diplomate Am. Bd. Homeotherapeutics. Intern St. Anthony's Hosp., Denver, 1966-67; staff physician Beth Israel Hosp., Denver, 1967-68, West Side Neighborhood Health Ctr., Denver, 1968-69, Red Hook Neighborhood Health Ctr., Bklyn., 1969-70; pvt. practice, 1971. Mem. faculty Nat. Ctr. Homeopathy, Washington, 1978—, bd. dirs., 1980-87, pres., 1985-86; mem. faculty Internat. Found. Homeopathy, Seattle, 1992—. Author: Dissent in Medicine (with others), 1989, Homeopathic Medicines in Pregnancy and Childbirth, 1992, Resonance: The Homeopathic Point of View, 2001; contbr. articles to Jour. Am. Inst. Homeopathy, Brit. Homeopathic Jour., others. Mem. ACLU, Am. Inst. Homeopathy, Am. Holistic Med. Assn., Amnesty Internat., Phi Beta Kappa. Democrat. Jewish. Achievements include investigation of

homeopathy as a species of medical reasoning, malpractice as a subspecies of iatrogenic illness and injury, vaccinations as a hidden source of chronic diease. Office: 173 Mount Auburn St Watertown MA 02472-4005 Office Phone: 617-923-4604.

**MOSKOWITZ, ROLAND WALLACE,** internist; b. Shamokin, Pa., Nov. 3, 1929; MD, Temple U., 1953. Intern Temple U. Hosp., Phila., 1953-54; fellow in internal medicine Mayo Clinic, Rochester, Minn., 1954-55, 57-60; mem. staff U. Hosps. Cleve.; prof. medicine Case Western Res. U. Sch. Medicine, Cleve. Mem.: ACR, Alpha Omega Alpha. Office: Parkway Med Ctr 3609 Park East Dr STe 307N Beachwood OH 44122

**MOSKOWITZ, ROSS F.,** lawyer; b. NYC, Feb. 8, 1959; BA, George Washington Univ., 1981; JD, NY Law Sch., 1984. Bar: NY 1985. Exec. dir. NYC Indsl. Devel. Agy., 1994—98; exec. v.p. NYC Econ. Devel. Corp., 1994—98; with real estate practice group Stroock & Stroock & Lavan LLP, NYC, 1998—, now also hiring ptnr. Bd. dir. Lawyers Alliance for NY, 1991—95; mem., econ. devel. com and zoning and esign com. Real Estate Bd., NYC, 1999—; tech. adv. com. mem. Group of 35, Schumer task force on NYC comml. space, 2000—01; bd. dir. Bklyn. Navy Yard Devel. Corp., 2002—. Office: Stroock & Stroock & Lavan LLP 1809 Maiden Ln New York NY 10038-4982 Office Phone: 212-806-5550. Office Fax: 212-806-6006. Business E-Mail: rmoskowitz@stroock.com.

**MOSKOWITZ, STANLEY ADAM,** finance company executive; b. NYC, June 8, 1956; s. Sol and Kate (Mermelstein) M.; m. Eve Kronenberger, Sept. 20, 1981 (div Apr. 2003); children: Alana, Kate. BA, Queens Coll., 1978; MBA in Fin., St. John's U., 1980. Sr. credit analyst Mfrs. Hanover Leasing Corp., N.Y.C., 1979-81; gen. ptnr. Execu. Leasing Co., N.Y.C., 1981-83; pres. Execulease Corp., Elmont, NY, 1983-97; pres., CEO QuesTech Fin. LLC, Danbury, Conn., 1998—. Treas. UFA/Fedn. of Greenwich, Conn., 1997-2003. Named finalist, Ernst & Young Entrepreneur of Yr., 2001. Mem. Ea. Assn. Equipment Lessors (chmn. pub. rels. 1985-90, bd. dirs. 1988-92, Meretorious Svc. award 1986-87, chmn. ethics com. 1991-92), Omicron Delta Epsilon. Republican. Jewish. Avocations: reading, bicycling. Office: QuesTech Fin LLC 33 Mill Plain Rd Danbury CT 06811-6101 Office Phone: 203-778-1000. E-mail: sammy@qtfc.com.

**MOSKUS, JERRY RAY,** retired academic administrator; b. Springfield, Ill., Dec. 10, 1942; s. Raymond Charles and Jean (Riley) M.; children: Elizabeth, Jane. BS in English, Ill. State U., 1965, MS in English, 1968, PhD in Edn. Adminstrn., 1983. Tchr. English Saybrook (Ill.) Arrowsmith High Sch., 1966-69; instr. Lincoln Land CC, Springfield, 1969-71, asst. to pres., 1971-73, dir. rsch., 1973-75, dean, 1975-84, v.p. acad. svcs., 1984-85; exec. v.p. Des Moines Area CC, Ankeny, Iowa, 1985-90; pres. Lane CC, Eugene, Oreg., 1990—2001, Metro. CC, Omaha, 2001—05; ret. Mem. Am. Assn. C.C.s (bd. dir. 1999-2001), Phi Delta Kappa, Sigma Tau Delta. Home: P15 1100 County Road Arlington NE 68002-5621 Business E-Mail: jmoskus@mccneb.edu.

**MOSLER, BRUCE E.,** real estate company executive; Grad., Duke U., 1980. Exec. v.p. Cushman & Wakefield, Inc., NYC, pres. U.S. ops., 2000—, CEO, 2005—, also bd. dirs. Bd. mem. Modell Found., Urban Tech.; mem. bd. govs., exec. com. Real Estate Bd. N.Y.; mem. profl. svcs. adv. coun. Lower Manhattan Devel. Corp. Bd. mem. Fisher Ctr. Alzheimer's Rsch. Found., Fuqua Bus. Sch. Duke U., Bowery Residents Com., Intrepid Mus. Found., Achilles Track Club. Named Property Svcs. Exec. of Yr., Comml. Property News, 2002, Brokerage Exec. of Yr., 2004; named one of 40 Under 40, Crain's N.Y. Bus., 1994; recipient Deal of the Yr. award, Real Estate Bd. N.Y, 1999, 2000, Kenneth R. Gerrety Humanitarian award, 2003. Office: Cushman & Wakefield Inc 51 W 52nd St New York NY 10019-6178

**MOSLEY, DANIEL LYNN,** lawyer; b. Birmingham, Ala., Nov. 2, 1956; s. Lynn Houston and Phyllis (Stanley) M.; m. Heather Stanton, Jan. 26, 1991. BA, U. Ala., 1977, JD, 1980; LLM, NYU, 1981. Assoc. Sullivan & Cromwell, N.Y.C., 1981-84; Cravath, Swaine & Moore, N.Y.C., 1984-87, ptnr., 1987—. Bd. dirs. Greenwich Hosp., Pinkerton Found., William S. Paley Found., William E. Simon Found., Edward J. Noble Found., Thomas J. Watson Found. Mem. Ala. Bar Assn., N.Y. State Bar Assn., Assn. of Bar of City of N.Y. Office: Cravath Swaine & Moore 825 8th Ave Fl 38 New York NY 10019-7475 Office Phone: 212-474-1696. Office Fax: 212-474-3700. Business E-Mail: dmosley@cravath.com.

**MOSLEY, GLENN RICHARD,** religious organization administrator, minister; b. Akron, Ohio, May 23, 1935; s. James Garfield and Viola Mildred (Wiseman) M.; m. Martha Lorella Mitchell, July 17, 1952; children: Glenn R. Jr., Tracey, Susan, Kristin, Robert. BA, Wayne State U., 1974; PhD, Walden U., 1976; MS in Adminstrn., Cen. Mich. U., 1991; DD (hon.), Unity Sch. Christianity, Kansas City, Mo., 1976. Ordained to ministry Unity Ch. 1961. Letter writer, student min. Silent Unity Prayer Soc., Kansas City, Mo., 1957-59; min. Unity Ch., Flushing, N.Y., 1959-64, Des Moines, 1964-65, co-min. N.Y.C., 1965-68; min. Unity Temple, Detroit, 1968-75, Unity Ch., Akron, 1975-85; pres., CEO Assn. Unity Chs., Lee's Summitt, Mo., 1985—. Author, co-author of nine books; mem. editl. staff Jour. Thanatology, 1966-76; contbr. numerous articles and monographs to profl. jours. Mem. AAAS, John Templeton Found. (Sewanee, Tenn., judge for Templeton prize for progress in religion), Rep. Presdl. Coun. Office: Assn Unity Chs 401 SW Oldham Pkwy Lees Summit MO 64081-2747 *The Religious Truth message we teach is eternal, and the techniques for teaching it work best for me when I develope new ways to teach which meet a great diversity of learning styles. There are almost zero days left in the current millennium; what an exciting period in which to live and teach.*

**MOSLEY, MARY MAC,** retired librarian; b. Rome, Ga., Nov. 11, 1926; d. William McKinley and Mary (Caldwell) H.; m. Samuel A. Mosley, June 12, 1946 (div. 1964); children: Samuel A. Jr., Pamela Ann, James Irwin. Student, Ga. State Coll. for Women, 1943-45; BS, Auburn U., 1947; cert. in teaching, Athens Coll., 1963; M in Library, Emory U., 1968. Tchr. sci. Rome City Schs., 1964-66; extension libr. Tri-County Regional Libr., 1966-67; libr. Shorter Coll., 1967-68, assoc. prof. libr. sci., 1968-76, dir. libr. svcs., 1968-93. Ch. linr., Decaon, Instruction Christian Women's Fellowship, 1st Christian Ch., 1998—; corr. sec. Rome Symphony Women's Assn., v.p., 1996-99, pres., 1999-2001; vol. Good Neighbor Ministry, Rome Floyd County Libr. Mem. ALA, AAUW (pres. Rome br. 1974-1976, v.p 2002-2004, 2006), Delta Kappa Gamma. Democrat. Mem. Christian Ch. Avocations: piano, reading, gardening, bridge. Home: 205 Benton Dr Rome GA 30165-1703 E-mail: marymacmo@earthlink.net.

**MOSLEY, TIMOTHY Z. See TIMBALAND**

**MOSLEY, WALTER,** writer; b. LA, Jan. 12, 1952; s. LeRoy and Ella Mosley; m. Joy Kellman (div.), 1987. Student, Goddard Coll., 1971; BA, Johnson State Coll., 1977; student, City Coll., CUNY, 1985—89. Artist in residence Africana Studies Inst., NYU, NYC, 1996—. Bd. dir. Full Frame Documentary Film Festival. Author: Devil in a Blue Dress, 1990 (Shamus award Private Eye Writers Am. 1990, Edgar award nomination Mystery Writers Am. 1990), A Red Death, 1991, White Butterfly, 1992, Black Betty, 1994, RL's Dream, 1995, A Little Yellow Dog, 1996, Gone Fishin', 1997, Always Outnumbered, Always Outgunned: The Socrates Fortlow Stories, 1998, Blue Light, 1998, Walkin' the Dog, 1999, Workin' on the Chain Gang: Shaking Off the Dead Hand of History, 2000, Fearless Jones: A Novel, 2001, Futureland: Nine Stories of an Imminent Future, 2001, Bad Boy Brawley Brown, 2002, What Next: An African American Initiative Toward World Peace, 2003, Six Easy Pieces, 2003, Fear Itself: A Mystery, 2003, The Man in My Basement, 2004, Little Scarlet, 2004, Cinnamon Kiss, 2005, 47, 2005, Life Out of Context, 2006, The Wave, 2006, Fortunate Son, 2006, Fear of the Dark, 2006; writer, prodr. (films) Devil in a Blue Dress, 1995. Recipient John Creasey Meml. award, Black Caucus of the Am. Library Assn. Literary award, O. Henry award, 1996, Anisfield-Wolf Book award, 1996, TransAf-

rican Internat. Literary prize, 1998, Risktaker award Sundance Inst., 2004. Mem.: Mystery Writers Am. (past pres.), Manhattan Theater Club, Poetry Soc. Am. (bd. dir.), Nat. Book Found., TransAfrica (bd. dir.). Mailing: c/o Nation Books 8th fl 33 Irving Place New York NY 10003*

**MOSMAN, MICHAEL W.,** federal judge, former prosecutor; b. Eugene, Ore. BA, Utah State U., 1981; JD, Brigham Young U., 1984. Law clk. U.S. Ct. Appeals, 1984-85, U.S. Supreme Ct., 1985—86; assoc. Miller, Nash, Portland, Oreg., 1986—88; asst. U.S. atty. Dist. Oreg. U.S. Dept. Justice, 1988—2001, U.S. atty. Dist. Oreg., 2001—03; judge U.S. Dist. Ct., Oreg., 2003—. Office: 1000 SW 3rd Ave Portland OR 97204-2902

**MOSNER, LAWRENCE J.,** retired financial administration company executive; BA, Midland Coll., Fremont, Nebr.; MBA, Roosevelt Univ. With Sears Roebuck & Co.; exec. v.p., COO Hanover Direct; pres. Deluxe Direct, Shoreview, Minn., 1995—97, Deluxe Fin. Svcs., Shoreview, Minn., 1997; exec. v.p. Deluxe Corp., Shoreview, Minn., 1997—2001, vice chmn., 1999—2001, chmn., CEO, 2001—05. Office Phone: 651-483-7111.

**MOSORA-STAN, FLORENTINA IOANA,** physics professor; b. Cluj, Romania, Jan. 7, 1940; arrived in Belgium, 1968; d. Oprea and Cornelia (Stanescu) M.; m. Stephan Stan, Jan. 22, 1977; 1 child, Guy Bart. B in Biol. Sci. with highest distinction, U. Bucharest, Romania, 1961, B in Phys. Sci. with highest distinction, 1967, PhD in Biophysics cum laude, 1971. Cert. biologist and physicist. Rsch. fellow U. Bucharest, 1967-71, U. Liege, Belgium, 1971-74, maitre de conferences, 1974-75; head rsch. fellow Inst. Physics, U. Liege, Belgium, 1975-79, lectr., 1979-88, prof., 1988—. Author: Elements of General Physics and Biophysics, vol. 1, 1974, vol. 2, 1975, Introduction to the Mechanics of Physiologic Fluids, 1984-85, Mechanics of Microcirculation, 1990; Editor: Biomechanical Transport Processes, 1991. Mem. European Med. Rsch. Coun. Devel. of Resch. in Nutrition and Stable Isotopes, 1991—. Decorated officer Ordre of Loopold II, (Belgium), 1981, comdr. Ordre de la Couronne (Belgium), 1992; recipient Agathon de Potter prize Royal Acad. Belgium, 1982. Mem. Stareso Oceanographic Rsch. Calvi (sci. coun. 1987—), Isotopes Stables (v.p. 1987—), Inst. Recherches Marines et Interactions Air-Mer (pres. 1989—), Hemo Liege (founder), Belgian Soc. Biophysics, Internat. Soc. Rsch. Circulation and Environ. Diseases, N.Y. Acad. Scis. Roman Catholic. Avocations: swimming, gymnastics. Home: Residence Verdi Av Blonden 7 4000 Liège Belgium Office: U Liege Inst Physics B5 4000 Liège Belgium

**MOSPAW, KATHAN J.,** retired social studies educator; b. Woonsocket, R.I., Dec. 29, 1945; d. George Harold and Dorothy Wilson Moroney; m. Jeffrey G. Mospaw (div.); children: Jennifer Mospaw Wilson, Elizabeth Mospaw Schaafsma. AB, Syracuse U., N.Y., 1967; MEd, R.I. Coll., Providence, 1977; JD, So. New Eng. Sch. Law, New Bedford, Mass., 1994. Bar: Mass. 1994; cert. tchr. R.I. Tchr. social studies Burrillville Sch. Dept., Harrisville, RI, 1969—2000; ret. 2004. Exec. bd. NEA R.I., Cranston, 1990—2000; pres. Burrillville Tchrs. Assn., Harrisville, 1990—2000. Chair No. R.I. Coun. Arts, Woonsocket, 1986—90, Burrillville Orgn. Substance Abuse Prevention, Pascoag, RI, 1990—2005; vol. local schs.; sec. Burrillville Dem. Town Com., Harrisville, 2005—; bd. dir. R.I. Legal - Ednl. Partnership, Providence, 1992—2000. Named R.I. Law Related Tchr. of Yr., R.I. Legal - Ednl. Partnership, 1992. Mem.: Sr. Citizens Assn. (sec. 2004—).

**MOSQUEIRA, IGNACIO,** astronomer, writer; s. Jose Mosqueira and Alicia Lobera. PhD, Cornell U., Ithaca, N.Y., 1989—95; BSc in Physics, Moravian Coll., Bethlehem, Pa., 1988. Nrc assoc. NASA Ames Rsch. Ctr., Moffett Field, Calif., 1995—98; postdoctor U. Calif., Santa Cruz, 1998—2000; prin. investigator SETI Inst., Mountain View, Calif., 2000—. Author (director, actor): (play) Flying with Ana; author: The Cannery, Aguirre: Prince of the New World. Recipient Ames cert. of Achievement, NASA, 1996, Reviewer of Yr. award, Icarus, 1996. Achievements include first to numerically verify the presence of a fluid instability pertaining to dense planetary rings, which is the likely cause of the observed structure in Saturn's outer B ring; introduced a scaling technique that speeds up the simulation of global ring dynamics by several orders of magnitude without loss of fidelity; development of unified models for the formation of the regular satellites of the giant planets. Office Phone: 650-604-2797. Personal E-mail: igmos00@yahoo.com.

**MOSS, ADAM WENDER,** editor; b. Bklyn., May 6, 1957; s. Paul and Abigail (Wender) M. BA, Oberlin Coll., 1979. Assoc. editor Rolling Stone Collected Papers, N.Y.C., 1979-81; asst. editor, assoc. editor, sr. editor, mng. editor, dep. editor Esquire mag., N.Y.C., 1981-87; editor in chief 7 Days, N.Y.C., 1987-90; cons. editor N.Y. Times, N.Y.C., 1991—93; editorial dir. The N.Y. Times Mag., N.Y.C., 1993—98, editor, 1998—2003; assoc. mng. editor N.Y. Times, 2002—03; asst. mng. editor N.Y. Times, features, N.Y.C., 2003—04; editor N.Y. Mag., N.Y.C., 2004—. Named Editor of the Yr., Advt. Age, 2001. Office: NY Mag 444 Madison Ave New York NY 10022

**MOSS, AMBLER HOLMES, JR.,** lawyer, educator, former ambassador; b. Balt., Sept. 1, 1937; s. Ambler Holmes and Dorothea Dandridge (Williams) M.; m. Serena Welles May 6, 1972; children: Ambler H., Benjamin Sumner, Serena Montserrat, Nicholas George Oliver. BA, Yale U., 1960; JD, George Washington U., 1970. Bar: D.C., Fla. Joined Fgn. Svc., Dept. State, 1964; vice consul Barcelona, 1964—66; adviser U.S. del. to OAS, 1966—69; Spanish desk officer Dept. State, Washington, 1968—70; assoc. Coudert Bros., Washington, 1971—73, resident atty. Brussels, 1973—76; mem. U.S. Negotiating Team for Panama Canal treaties, 1977; dep. asst. Sec. of State, Washington, 1977—78; amb. to Panama Am. Embassy, Panama City, 1978—82; of counsel Greenberg, Traurig, LLP, Miami, 1982—87, 1995—; prof. U. Miami, Fla., 1984—, dean Grad. Sch. Internat. Studies, 1984—94. Bd. dirs. Espirito Santo Bank of Fla., Caucedo Investments Inc. Mem. Panama Canal Consultative Com., 1995-2000. With USN, 1960-64. Mem. ABA, Am. Soc. Internat. Law, Inter-Am. Bar Assn., Am. Fgn. Svc. Assn., Coun. Fgn. Rels., Am. Legion, Inter-Am. Dialogue (Washington), Navy League, Greater Miami C. of C. (gov. 1983-86), Royal Inst. Internat. Affairs (London), Internat. Inst. Strategic Studies (London), Army and Navy Club, Order of the Coif. Home: 5711 San Vicente St Coral Gables FL 33146-2724 Business E-Mail: ahmoss@miami.edu.

**MOSS, ANNA LEE,** construction executive, music educator; b. Canton, Ga., Oct. 31, 1954; d. Howard Leslie and Marie Johnson Collins; m. Ronnie J. Moss, Oct. 17, 1976; children: Christina Moss Rodriguez, Ashley Ellen, Benjamin Joseph Collins, Amy Danielle, Charity Anne, Tabitha Moss Scott, Tonya Michelle. BA, Mercer U., 1976. Mgr. R J Moss Constrn. Co., Jasper, Ga., 1979—; authorized agt., mgr. Bridgeway Solutions, LLC, Jasper, 2002—. Tchr. piano Anna Moss Studio, Jasper, 1976—. Composer: (songs) Shepherd's Song, 1979. Poll mgr. Pickens County Elections, Jasper, 2004—05. Mem.: Am. Coll. Musicians. Avocations: reading, writing, travel. Home and Office: R J Moss Construction Co 142 Cornett Lane S Jasper GA 30143 Office Phone: 706-692-0339. E-mail: almhome@alltel.net.

**MOSS, ARTHUR HENSHEY,** lawyer; b. Reading, Pa., July 26, 1930; s. John Arthur and Christine Bracken (Henshey) M.; m. E. Leslie Fritz, Feb. 1982; 1 child by previous marriage, John Arthur. AB, Williams Coll., 1952; JD, U. Pa., 1955. Bar: Pa. 1956. Assoc. Montgomery, McCracken, Walker & Rhoads, Phila., 1960-69, ptnr., 1969-2000, of counsel, 2000—. Editor U. Pa. Law Rev., 1953-55; contbr. articles to profl. jours. Pres. Wayne Civic Assn., 1964—65; commr. gen. assembly Presbyn. Ch. (U.S.A.), 1985; steward deacon Wayne Presbyn. Ch., 1966—72, 1979—84, 1989—95, ruling elder, 1966—72, 1979—84, 1989—95, clk. of session, 1973—74, 1978—89, trustee, 1987—93, Presbytery of Phila., 1984, 1994—2001, treas., 1996—2001; chmn. Radnor-Haverford-Marple Sewer Authority, 1968—83; bd. dir. John Bartram Assn., 1987—2002, treas., 1989—2002, president, 2002—; trustee Radnor Twp. Meml. Libr., 2001—. Lt. JAGC USN, 1956—60. Mem. Radnor Hist. Soc. (dir., sec. 1978-90), Broadacres Trouting Assn., Athenaeum of Phila., Merion Golf Club, Edgemere Club. Home: 200

Walnut Ave Wayne PA 19087-3423 Office: Montgomery McCracken Walker & Rhoads 123 S Broad St Philadelphia PA 19109-1030 Office Phone: 215-772-1500. E-mail: wwww.esq@verizon.net.

**MOSS, ARTHUR JAY,** physician; b. White Plains, NY, June 21, 1931; s. Abraham Loeb and Ida (Bank) M.; m. Joy Folkman, June 23, 1957; children: Katherine, Deborah, David. BA, Yale U., 1953; MD, Harvard U., 1957. Resident Mass. Gen. Hosp., 1957-58, 60-61; fellow in cardiology med. ctr. U. Rochester, NY, 1961-65, from asst. to assoc. prof. sch. medicine and dentistry, 1966-71, clin. assoc. prof., 1971-82, clin. prof., 1982-91, prof. medicine, 1991—, clin. heart rsch. follow-up program med. ctr., 1971—. Mem. cardiology adv. com. Nat. Heart, Lung, and Blood Inst., NIH, 1980-82, chmn., 1982-84, mem. epidemiology and disease control study sect., 1998—. Author: Antiarrhythmic Agents, 1973; editor: Clinical Aspects of Life-threatening Arrhythmias, 1984, QT Prolongation and Ventricular Arrhythmias, 1992, Noninvasive Electrocardiology, 1995; editor-in-chief Ann. Noninvasive Electrocardiology, 1996—; mem. editl. bd. Am. Jour. Cardiology, 1988—, Jour. Am. Coll. Cardiology, 1997-2001, 2005—. Lt. USNR, 1958—60. Mem. Assn. Am. Physicians, Alpha Omega Alpha. Home: 581 Claybourne Rd Rochester NY 14618-1224 Office: Univ Rochester Med Ctr PO Box 653 Rochester NY 14642-8653 Office Phone: 585-275-5391. Business E-Mail: heartajm@heart.rochester.edu.

**MOSS, BEN FRANK, III,** art educator, painter; b. Phila., Feb. 28, 1936; s. B. Frank Jr. and Helen Charlotte (Figge) M.; m. Jean Marilyn Russel, Aug. 26, 1960; children: Jennifer Kathleen, Benjamin Franklin IV. BA, Whitworth Coll., 1959; postgrad., Princeton Theol. Seminary, 1959-60; MFA, Boston U., 1963; MA (hon.), Dartmouth Coll., 1993; studied with Walter Murch, Karl Fortess and Herman Keys. Instr. Gonzaga U., Spokane, Wash., 1964-65; assoc. prof., dir. MFA and vis. artist program Fort Wright Coll., Spokane, 1965-72; acting dean, co-founder Spokane Studio Sch., 1972-74; prof. painting and drawing Sch. Art and Art History U. Iowa, Iowa City, 1975-88; George Frederick Jewett prof. art Dartmouth Coll., Hanover, NH, 1993—. Chmn. studio art dept. Dartmouth Coll., Hanover, 1988-94, Vt. Studio Ctr., Johnson, 1990; area head painting U. Iowa, 1985; artist-in-residence Queens Coll., U. Melbourne, Australia, 1993-94; vis. artist, lectr. Northwest Mo. State U., Maryville, 1996, Houghton (N.Y.) Coll., 1996, Gordon Coll., Wenham, Mass., 1996, Northwestern U., Evanston, Ill., 1997, Colo. State U., Ft. Collins, 1997, Ravenscroft Sch. Raleigh, N.C., 1997, Coe Coll., Cedar Rapids, Iowa, 1998, Seattle Pacific U., 2002, Bowling Green U., Ohio, 2003, Williams Coll., Williamstown, Mass., 2003, numerous others. Represented by Pepper Gallery, Boston, Francine Seders Gallery, Ltd., Seattle, Susan Conway Galleries, Washington; one-man shows include Susan Conway Galleries, 1990, Dartmouth Coll., 1989, 94, Kraushaar Galleries, 1981, 83, 87, Swarthmore Coll., Pa., 1984, Stony Brook (N.Y.) Sch., 1982, Saint-Gaudens, Picture Gallery, Cornish, N.H., 1981, Kans. State U., 1980, Francine Seders Gallery, Seattle, 1979, 82, 99, Hudson D. Walker Gallery, Fine Arts Work Ctr., Provincetown, Mass., 1978, Arnot Art Mus., Elmira, N.Y., 1977, Kirkland Coll., Clinton, N.Y., 1977, Juniper Tree Gallery, Spokane, 1975, Middlebury (Vt.) Coll., 1971, Seligman Gallery, Seattle, 1967, 69, Cheney Cowels Meml. Mus., Spokane, 1967, Loomis Chaffee Sch., 1995, Tasis England Am. Sch., 1994, Queens Coll., U. Melbourne, 1994, Houghton Coll., 1996, Gordon Coll., 1996, N. W. Mo. State U., 1996, Princeton Theol. Sem., 2001, Taylor U., Upland, Ind., 2002, Bedford Art Mus., Mass., 2003, Brattleboro Mus. and Art Ctr., 1995, Nat. Acad. and Design, 1995, Messiah Coll., 1995, 97, 99, 2001, 2003, Phillips Exeter Acad., 1995, Susan Conway Galleries, 1993, 96, Chase Gallery City Hall, Spokane, 1993, Colby-Sawyer Coll., New London, N.H., 1992, Pepper Gallery, Boston, Mass., 1998, 2000, Idaho State U., Pocatello, 1972, Kouros Gallery, N.Y.C., 2001, Augustana Coll., Rock Island, Ill., 2002, New England Coll., Henniker, N.H., 2003, others; exhibited in group shows at Blair Acad., Blairstown, N.J., 1996, Albright Knox Gallery, Buffalo, N.Y., 1995-96, Smith Coll., North Hampton, Mass., 1996, Nat. Acad. Design, N.Y.C., 1995, Boston U., 1995, Brattleboro (Vt.) Mus. and Art Ctr., 1995, Susan Conway Galleries, 1989—, Middlebury Coll. Mus. Art, Babcock Galleries, N.Y.C., Albany Inst. History and Art, Owensboro (Ky.) Mus. Fine Art, Westmoreland Mus. Art, Greenburg, Pa., Md. Inst. & Coll. Art, 1993-94, Gallery 68, 1992, Vt. Studio Ctr. Visiting Critics, Vergennes, 1992, 79th Ann. Maier Mus. Art, Randolph, Macon Women's Coll., Lynchburg, Va., 1990, Del. Ctr. Contemporary Arts, Wilmington, 1988, U. Iowa, 1976, 78, 80, 82, 84, 86, 88, Bladen Meml. Mus., Fort Dodge, Iowa, 1987, Phila. Mus. Art, 1986, Union League Club, N.Y.C., 1986, Blackfish Gallery, Portland, 1986, Columbia (S.C.) Mus. Art, 1985, Columbus Mus. Art, 1982-86, Paine Art Ctr., Oshkosh, Wis., 1985, Burpee Art Ctr., Rockford, Ill., 1985, Ill. State U., Normal, 1985, Wilkes Coll., Wilkes-Barre, Pa., 1985, Albright-Knox Mus., Buffalo, N.Y., 1984, Ark. Art Ctr., Little Rock, 1984, Millersville (Pa.) U., 1983, Fairfield (Conn.) U., 1983, Marion Koogler McKay Inst., San Antonio, 1983, Boston City Hall Gallery, 1983, Cedar Rapids (Iowa) Mus. Art, 1982, Montclair (N.J.) Jr. League, 1981, Iowa Arts Coun., Des Moines, 1980-81, Pepper Gallery, Boston, 1997-98, Spheris Gallery Fine Art, 1997, The Art Spirit Gallery of Fine Art, Walpole, N.H., 1997, Coeur d' Alene, Ind., 1998, numerous others. Sr. Faculty fellow Va. Ctr. for Creative Arts, 1996, Dartmouth Coll., 1993, MacDowell Colony, 1992, Devel. grant U. Iowa, 1980, 86; Summer fellowship U. Iowa, 1979, Rsch. and Travel grantee Ford Found., 1979-80, Yaddo Found., 1965, 72, Travel grantee U. Iowa Found., 1986,; recipient Disting. Alumni award Boston U., 1988 Mem. NAD (academician mem., 1994), Coll. Art Assn. Independent. Presbyterian. Avocations: music, poetry, travel, tennis. Office: Dartmouth Coll Hb 6081 Studio Art Hanover NH 03755 Office Phone: 603-646-2285. Business E-Mail: ben.moss@dartmouth.edu.

**MOSS, BERNARD,** virologist, researcher; b. NYC, July 26, 1937; s. Jack and Goldie (Altman) M.; m. Toby Frima Lieberman, Dec. 25, 1960; children: Robert, Jennifer, David. BA, NYU, 1957, MD, 1961; PhD, MIT, 1967. Diplomate Am. Bd. Med. Examiners. Intern Children's Hosp., Boston, 1961-62; investigator, sect. head NIH, Bethesda, Md., 1966—, lab. chief, 1984—. Mem. adv. bd Virus Rsch., 1984 ; Current Opinion Biotech., 1989—. Assoc. editor Virology Jour., 1976-92, editor, 1992—; mem. editorial bd. Jour. of Virology, 1972—, Antimicrobial Agts. and Chemotherapy, 1973-79, Jour. Biol. Chemistry, 1982-87; AIDS rsch. Human Retroviruses, 1989—; contbr. more than 600 articles to profl. jours. Mem. adv. com. Am. Cancer Soc., N.Y.C., 1983-86; bd. dirs. Found. Advanced Edn. in Scis., Bethesda, 1985-91; mem. NIH AIDS vaccine selection com., 1989—. Served as med. dir. USPHS, 1966-98. Named one of 100 Most Innovative Scientists of 1986, Sci. Digest; recipient Solomon A. Berson Alumni Achievement award Sch. Medicine, NYU, Meritorious Svc. medal USPHS, Disting. Svc. medal USPHS, Dickson prize in medicine, Invitrogen award for eukaryotic gene expression, ICN Internat. prize in Virology, Taylor Internat. prize in medicine, Bristol-Myers Squibb Award, Distinguished Achievement in Infectious Disease Research, 2000. Fellow AAAS; mem. Am. Soc. for Biochemistry and Molecular Biology, Am. Acad. Microbiology, Am. Soc. Microbiology, Am. Soc. Virology (pres. 1995), Nat. Acad. Sci., Phi Beta Kappa, Sigma Xi, Alpha Omega Alpha. Office: NIH 4 Center Dr Bethesda MD 20892-0445 E-mail: bmoss@nih.gov.

**MOSS, BILL RALPH,** lawyer; b. Amarillo, Tex., Sept. 27, 1950; s. Ralph Voniver and Virginia May (Atkins) M.; 1 child, Brandon Price. BS with honors, West Tex. A&M U., 1972, MA, 1974; JD, Baylor U., 1976; cert. regulatory studies program, Mich. State U., 1981. Bar: Tex. 1976, U.S. Dist. Ct. (no. dist.) Tex. 1976, U.S. Dist. Ct. (we. dist.) Tex. 1976, U.S. Dist. Ct. 1979, U.S. Ct. Appeals (5th cir.) 1983. Briefing atty. Ct. Appeals 7th Supreme Jud. Dist. Tex., Amarillo, 1976-77; assoc. Culton, Morgan, Britain & White, Amarillo, 1977-80; hearings examiner Pub. Utility Commn. Tex., Austin, 1981-83; asst. gen. counsel State Bar Tex., Austin, 1983-87; founder, owner Price & Co. Publs., Austin, 1987-97; asst. gen. counsel Tex. Ethics Commn., Austin, 1997—2004; asst. atty. gen. antitrust and civil medicaid fraud div. Office Atty. Gen., Tex., 2004—. Instr., lectr. West Tex. State U., Canyon, Ea. N.Mex. U., Portales, 1977-80; spkr. in field. Active St. Matthew's Episcopal Ch.; election inspector State of Tex., 1998—. Mem. ABA, Tex. Bar Assn., Nat. Orgn. Bar Counsel, Internat. Platform Assn., Capitol of Tex. Rotary Club, Alpha Chi, Lambda Chi Alpha, Omicron Delta Epsilon, Phi Alpha

Delta, Sigma Tau Delta, Pi Gamma Mu. Home: 506 Explorer St Lakeway TX 78734-3447 Office: Office of Atty Gen William P Clements Bldg 300 W 15th St 9th Fl Austin TX 78701 Business E-Mail: bill.moss@oag.state.tx.us.

**MOSS, CARL ARTHUR,** psychologist; b. Port Huron, Mich., Aug. 12, 1940; s. August Carl and Frances Elizabeth Moss; m. Patricia Elizabeth Howe, Feb. 13, 1965; children: Miriam, Anne Elizabeth. AA, Port Huron Jr. Coll., Mich., 1960; BS, Ea. Mich. U., 1966, MS, 1973. Cert. sch. psychologist Mich. Psychologist Port Huron Area Schs., 1967—. Trustee Port Huron Mus., 1970—76, bd. pres., 1974—76; founding mem. Riverside Heritage Assn., Port Huron, 1972—78; active Olde Town Dist. Com., Port Huron, 2000—; mem. Port Huron Hist. Dist. Commn.; sec. bd. dirs. Wills Sainte Claire Automobile Mus., Marysville, Mich. With U.S. Army, 1963—69. Recipient Spirit of Port Huron award for civic involvement, 2002. Episcopalian. Avocations: civil war history, antiques. Home: 1617 Military St Port Huron MI 48060

**MOSS, CARRIE-ANNE,** actress; b. Vancouver, British Columbia, Can., Aug. 21, 1967; Actress in films: Flashfire, 1993, The Soft Kill, 1994, Terrified, 1995, Sabotage, 1996, Secret Life of Algernon, 1997, Lethal Tender, 1997, New Blood, 1999, The Matrix, 1999, Memento, 2000, The Crew, 2000, Red Planet, 2000, Chocolat, 2000, The Matrix Reloaded, 2003; tv movies: Doorways, 1993; television appearances: L.A. Law, 1986, Daywatch, 1989, Dark Justice, 1991, Silk Stalkings, 1991, Street Justice, 1992, Nightmare Cafe, 1992, Forever Knight, 1992, Matrix, 1993, Models Inc., 1994, Nowhere Man, 1995, Nowhere Man, 1996, F/X: The Series, 1996, Viper, 1997.

**MOSS, CHARLES BRITT,** economics educator; b. Elk City, Okla., Sept. 30, 1960; s. Charles Eual Moss and Linda Joy (Courtney) Kennedy; m. Susan Diane Steritz, Dec. 28, 1985; 1 child, Alexander Charles. AS, Sayre (Okla.) Jr. Coll., 1980; BS in Agr., Okla. State U., 1982, MS, 1984; PhD, Purdue U., 1987. Grad. rsch. asst. Okla. State U., Stillwater, 1982-84; grad. asst. Purdue U., West Lafayette, Ind., 1984-87; asst. prof. econs. U. Fla., Gainesville, 1987—. Mem. Am. Agrl. Econs. Assn., Am. Econs. Assn., Am. Fin. Assn., Econometric Soc., Royal Econs. Soc., So. Agrl. Econs. Assn. Home: 2001 NW 31st Ter Gainesville FL 32605-3720 Office: U Fla Dept Food and Econs G097 McCarty Hall Gainesville FL 32611

**MOSS, DAVID,** music company executive; Cert., Musician's Inst. in Hollywood, 1985; B of commerce in mktg and fin., Concordia U., 1989. Dir., sch. of fine arts Saidye Bronfman Ctr. for the Arts, 1994—96, exec. dir., 1996—2003; gen. dir. Montreal Opera, 2003—. Founding mem., mem. exec. com. Culture Montreal; apptd. to Groupe Conseil pour la Politique Culturelle de Montreal, 2002; appt. to bd. La Vitrine Culturelle de Montreal, 2003. Office: L'Opera de Montreal 260 Maisonneuve Blvd W Montreal PQ H2X 1Y9 Canada Office Phone: 514-985-2222.

**MOSS, DOUGLAS,** architectural firm executive; BArch, Tex. Tech. U. Assoc. Hardy, Holzman, Pfeiffer Assocs. LLP, N.Y.C., prin., 2002—03, ptnr., 2003—, mng. dir. Co-founder internet co.; lectr. in field. Mem.: AIA (mem. profl. practice com., com. on edn. N.Y. chpt.). Office: HHPA 19th Fl 902 Broadway New York NY 10010

**MOSS, ELIZABETH LUCILLE (BETTY MOSS),** retired transportation executive; b. Ironton, Mo., Feb. 13, 1939; d. James Leon and Dorothy Lucille (Russell) Rollen; m. Elliott Theodore Moss, Nov. 10, 1963 (div. Jan. 1984); children: Robert Belmont, Wendy Rollen. BA in Econs. and Bus. Adminstrn., Drury Coll., 1960. Registrar, transp. mgr. Cheley Colo. Camps, Inc., Denver and Estes Park, 1960-61; office mgr. Washington Nat. Ins. Co., Denver, 1960-61; sec. White House Decorating, Denver, 1961-62; with Ringsby Truck Lines, Denver, Oakland, Calif., and L.A., 1962-67, System 99 Freight Lines, L.A., 1967-69, terminal mgr. Stockton, Calif., 1981-84; with Yellow Freight System, L.A., 1969-74, Hayward, Calif., 1974-77, ops. mgr. Urbana, Ill., 1977-80; sales rep. Calif. Motor Express, San Jose, 1981; regional sales mgr. Schneider Nat. Carriers, Inc., No. Calif., 1984-86; account exec. TNT-Can., Nev. and Cen. Calif., 1986-88; mgr. Interstate-Intermodal Divs. HVH Transp., Denver, 1988-89; regional sales mgr. MNX, Inc., Northern Calif., 1989-91; sales dir., nat. accts. mgr., terminal mgr. Mountain Valley Express, Manteca, Calif., 1992—2003; ret., 2003. Chmn. op. coun. for San Joaquin and Stanislaus Counties Calif. Trucking Assn., 1983-84, Truck Accident Reduction Projects, San Joaquin County, 1987-88. Mem. Econ. Devel. Coun. Stockton C. of C., 1985-86; active Edison High Sch. Boosters, 1982-88. Mem.: Calif. Trucking Assn. (tri county unit steering com. 2001—03), So. Calif. Round Table (bd. dirs. 1993—2001), Coun. Logistics Mgmt., Oakland Traffic Club, Ctrl. Valley Traffic Club, Stockton Traffic Club (bd. dirs. 1982—84, Trucker of Yr.), Nat. Def. Transp. Assn. (bd. dirs. 1986—87), Delta Nu Alpha (bd. dirs. Region 1 1982—84, v.p. chpt. 1984—85, pres. chpt. 1985—86, chmn. bd. 1985—87, regional sec. 1987—88, Outstanding Achievement award 1986, 1988). Methodist. Avocation: reading. Home: One Parkway Pl 2A 350 S John Q Hammons Pkwy Springfield MO 65806 E-mail: MossBetty@sbcglobal.net.

**MOSS, GARY CURTIS,** lawyer; b. Taylorville, Ill., Feb. 17, 1944; s. William Gary and Sophronia Irene (McClellan) M.; m. Judith K. Jones, April 14, 1945; children: Gary Curtis, Kristin Suzanne. B.A., U. Ill.-Champaign, 1966; J.D., U. Iowa-Iowa City, 1969. Bar: Iowa 1969, Calif. 1970, U.S. Dist. Ct. (cen. dist.) Calif. 1972, Nev. 1991, U.S. Ct. Appeals (9th cir.) 1974, U.S. Dist. Ct. (so. and no. dists.) Calif. 1981, U.S. Dist. Ct. Nev. 1991. Assoc., O'Melveny & Myers, Los Angeles, 1969-75; assoc. Seyfarth, Shaw, Fairweather & Geraldson, Los Angeles, 1975-78, ptnr., 1978-87; judge pro tem West Los Angeles Mcpl. Ct., 1981-83, Pasadena Mcpl. Ct., 1983—; ptnr.-in-charge Las Vegas office, DLA Piper Rudnick Gray Cary, Las Vegas. Mem. ABA, State Bar Calif. (hearing referee, arbitrator mandatory fee arbitrations), State Bar Iowa, Los Angeles County Bar Assn. Republican. Club: Athletic (Los Angeles). Office: DLA Piper Rudnick Gray Cary Ste 400 3960 Howard Hughes Pkwy Las Vegas NV 89109-0993 Office Phone: 702-737-3433, 702-737-1612. Business E-Mail: gary.moss@piperrudnick.com.

**MOSS, JEROME (JERRY) S.,** recording industry executive; b. Bronx, NY, May 8, 1935; s. Irving and Rose Moss; m. Ann Moss. BA, Brooklyn Coll. Record promoter, NYC, LA; co-founder Carnival Records, 1961; owner, co-founder A&M Records, 1962—94; co-founder Almo Sounds, 1994—2002; co-founder, chmn. Rondor Music Inc., 1994—. Founding mem. UCLArts Bd. of Visitors; bd. mem. Calif. Horse Racing Bd., 2004—. With U.S. Army. Recipient Lifetime Achievement award, Rock and Roll Hall of Fame, 2006. Avocation: owns racehorse Giacomo, winner of the 131st Kentucky Derby, 2005. Office: 2540 Sepulveda Blvd Los Angeles CA 90064 also: 1010 Hurley Way Ste 300 Sacramento CA 95825

**MOSS, KATE,** model; b. Croydon, England, Jan. 16, 1974; 1 child, Lila Grace. With Storm Agy., England, Women Model Mgmt., N.Y.; model Calvin Klein Jeans, Yves Saint Laurent, Prada, Versace, Burberry, Celine, Gucci, Louis Vuitton, Chanel, Dior. Appeared in films Unzipped, 1995, Catwalk, 1995, Beautopia, 1998, Blackadder Back and Forth, 1999, Original Copies, 1999, (TV films) Inferno, 1992, Naomi Conquers Africa, 1998, Astley's Way, 2001, We Know Where You Live, 2001, Terry & Liz, 2004, (TV series) French and Saunders, 1987. Recipient Lifetime Achievement award, Coun. Fashion Designers Am., 2005 Office: Storm Model Mgmt 5 Jubilee Pl 1st Fl London SW3 3TD England

**MOSS, LESLIE OTHA,** homeland security specialist; b. Detroit, Mar. 8, 1952; s. Lonnie and Emma (Robinson) M. BA, U. Mich., 1982, postgrad., 1990—. Cert. protection officer, security supr. Dept. Homeland Security, protection profl., security specialist 2005. Technician oper. rm. Sinai Hosp., Detroit, 1972-75; nurses' technician Detroit Osteo. Hosp., 1976-83; supr. Southfield Placement Ctr., Mich., 1983-85; rsch. technician Wayne County Commr.'s Office, Detroit, 1985-86; fin. aid counselor Wayne State U., 1986-87; probation officer Dept. Corrections State of Mich., 1988—; exec. asst. Human Rights Dept., City of Detroit; rsch. asst. Law Dept. City of Detroit, 1990; asst.

pers. mgr. Detroit Osteo. Hosp., 1991-93; Highland Pk. C.C., 1991-93; mental health worker Mich. Health Ctr.-Adult Mental Health and New Ctr. Hosp., 1992-94; legal technician Ptnrs. Against Crime, Detroit, 1994; social work technician, 1994. Sgt. of arms Detroit Police Res., 1987—; intern, assoc. prodr. local TV sta., Detroit, 1993; mem. bd. advisors, mem. bd. govs. Am. Biog. Rsch. Inst., dep. gov., 1994; exec. cons. in field., 1993—; asst. pers. mgr., 1993—. Mem. re-election com. Mayor Coleman A. Young, Detroit, 1989-93; patient care counselor; adv. various causes, including industrialized Am., higher edn., automotive quality. Recipient Twentieth Century Achievement award Biog. Centre, 1994, Spl. Recognition award Detroit Pub. Sch. Sys., 1992, Internat. Man of Yr. award, 1992-93; award for mass media svc. participation Barden Cable Vision, Detroit, 1991, Man of the Yr. award, 1996, Disting. Alumni Award Mumford H.S. Detroit, 1996, Most Outstanding Men of the Twentieth Century award, 1999; named Most Admired Man of Decade, 1994, Disting. Alumnus, Detroit Pub. Schs. Mich., 1995, Most Admired Man of the Yr., State of Mich., 1998; named to Internat. Honors Hall of Fame, 1998, Millenium Hall of Fame, 1998; inducted 500 Leaders of Influence Pub., 2000. Mem. NAFE, NAACP (advisor 1989), Internat. Order of Merit, Assn. Pre-Med Students (cons. 1988—), Assn. Psychologists, Am. Biog. Rsch. Inst. Assn. (mem. bd. govs. 1993, dep. gov.), Internat. Platform Assn., U. Mich. Alumni Assn., Golden Key Internat. Honor Soc. (life), Kappa Alpha Psi, Phi Theta Kappa. Home and Office: 1190 Seward St Apt 306 Detroit MI 48202 2336

**MOSS, LOGAN VANSEN,** lawyer; b. Atlanta, Apr. 17, 1957; s. Joseph Henry Moss and Elsie Louise (McCown) Daniels. BA, Bates Coll., Lewiston, Maine, 1979; JD, U. Tulsa, Okla., 1982; MTS, Ave Maria U., 2003; certificate of Advanced Study Bioethics and Health Policy, Loyola U. Med. Sch., 2006. Bar: Okla. 1982, U.S. Dist. Ct. Okla. 1982, Maine 1984, U.S. Dist. Ct. Maine 1984, U.S. Supreme Ct. 1986, Tex. 1991. Law clk. to presiding justice Okla. Ct. Appeals, Tulsa, 1982—84; assoc. Strout, Payson et al, Rockland, Maine, 1984—87, Joseph M. Cloutier & Assocs., Camden, Maine, 1987—88, Armstrong & Assocs., Tulsa, 1988—91; asst. gen. counsel Temple-Inland Forest Products Corp., Diboll, Tex., 1991—2002; gen. counsel litig. Temple-Inland, Austin, 2003—. Republican. Roman Catholic. Avocation: catholic studies. Office: Temple Inland 1300 S Mopac Expy Austin TX 78746 Office Phone: 512-434-8050. Business E-Mail: loganmoss@templeinland.com.

**MOSS, MADISON SCOTT,** editor; b. Charlotte, N.C., May 23, 1948; s. James Madison and Nellie Lee (Jenkins) M. BA in English, U. N.C., 1970. Editl. aide NASW, Inc., Washington, 1974, promotions specialist, 1974-79, assoc. editor, 1979-80, editor, 1980-90, mng. editor, 1990—. Campaign coord. Eugene McCarthy for Pres., Rutherford County, N.C., 1968. Recipient award for Pub. Excellence Comms. Concepts, 1993, 94, 95, 96, 97, 98, Bronze award newspaper gen. excellence Soc. Nat. Assn. Publs., 1996, Silver award, 1997, Bronze awards, 2005, 06. Mem. Am. Assn. Ret. Persons, U. N.C. Gen. Alumni Assn., Am. Found. AIDS Rsch. Democrat. Office: NASW Inc 750 1st St NE Ste 700 Washington DC 20002-4241 Business E-Mail: Smoss@naswdc.org.

**MOSS, MARCIA LYNN,** retired biochemist; d. Frank and Loretta Moss; m. Fred Harold Rasmussen; 1 child, Alden Rasmussen. PhD, U. Wis., 1989. Organic chemist U. Mich., Ann Arbor, 1980—84; postdoctoral U. Wis. Sch. Pharmacy, Madison, 1990—92; postdoctoral dept. physiology U. Wis., Madison, Wis., 1989—90; rsch. investigator I and II Glaxo, Research Triangle Park, NC, 1992—99, ret., 1999; sr. project leader Cognosci, Research Triangle Park, NC, 2001—02; dir. rsch. BioZyme Inc., Apex, NC, 2003—04. Author (primary investigator): (identification of novel metalloprotease) Cloning of a disintegrin metalloproteinase that processes precursor tumour-necrosis factor-alpha; author: (graduate student) (mechanism of enzyme) The role of S-adenosylmethionine in the lysine 2, 3-aminomutase reaction; author: (co-investigator) (mechanistic studies on finasteride) Mechanism of time-dependent inhibition of 5 alpha-reductases by delta 1-4-azasteroids: toward perfection of rates of time-dependent inhibition by using ligand-binding energies; author: (senior investigator) (phage display) Substrate specificity of human collagenase-3 assessed using a phage display library, (novel enzyme in tgf alpha processing) Multiple Metalloproteinases Process ProTransforming Growth Factor- (ProTGF-.; prin. author: rev. articles Shedding Membrane Proteins by ADAM Family Proteases, Therapeutic Benefits from Targeting of ADAM Family Members; contbr. articles to profl. jours. Ch. mem. New Horizons, Apex, NC. Grantee, NIH, 2001, 2002, 2002-2005, 2004—; Procter and Gamble fellowship, U. Wis., 1988, 1989, Fellowship grant, NIH, 1989, 1990. Mem.: ACS, Internat. Proteolysis Soc., Jour. Biol. Chemistry. Achievements include patents pending for Assays to measure matrix metalloproteinases. Home: 1513 Old White Oak Church Rd Apex NC 27523 Office: Duke Univ Research Dr 242 Nanaline Durham NC 27710 Office Phone: 919-668-5376. Personal E-Mail: mmoss@biozyme-inc.com. E-mail: moss120@bellsouth.net.

**MOSS, MYRA ELLEN (MYRA MOSS ROLLE),** philosophy educator; b. LA, Mar. 22, 1937; m. Andrew Rolle, Nov. 5, 1983. BA, Pomona Coll., 1958; PhD, The Johns Hopkins U., 1965. Asst. prof. Santa Clara (Calif.) U., 1968-74; prof. Claremont McKenna Coll., 1975—, chmn. dept. philosophy, 1992-95. Assoc. dir. Gould Ctr. for Humanities, Claremont, Calif., 1993-94; adv. coun. Milton S. Eisenhower Libr./Johns Hopkins U., 1994-96, 2001—; vis. scholar Am. Acad. Rome, 2005. Author: Benedetto Croce Reconsidered, 1987, Mussolini's Fascist Philosopher: Giovanni Gentile Reconsidered, 2004, Italian edit., 2006; translator: Benedetto Croce's Essays on Literature & Literary Criticism, 1990; co-author: Values and Education, 1998; assoc. editor Special Issues: Journal of Value Inquiry, 1990-95 (Honorable Mention, Phoenix award); cons. editor Jour. Social Philosophy, 1988—; assoc. editor: Value Enquiry Book Series, 1990-95; editor: The Philosophy of José Gaos, by Pio Colonnello, Value Inquiry Book Series, 1997. Bogliasco fellow, Liguria, Italy, 2000; vis. scholar Am. Acad. Rome, 2005. Mem. Am. Philos. Assn., Am. and Internat. Soc. for Value Inquiry, Soc. for Aesthetics, Internat. Ctr. for the Arts, Humanities and Value Inquiry (assoc.), Collingwood Soc. (life), Phi Beta Kappa. Avocations: gardening, horseback riding. Office: Claremont McKenna Coll 850 Columbia Ave Claremont CA 91711-3901

**MOSS, PATRICIA L.,** bank executive; m. Greg Moss; children: Jennifer, Jeffrey. BS in bus. adminstrn., Linfield Coll., Oreg.; masters studies Portland State U.; certification ABA Comml. Banking Sch., U. Okla. From mem. staff to pres., CEO Cascade Bancorp, Bend, Oreg., 1977—99, pres., CEO, 1998—; CEO Bank of the Cascades, Bend, Oreg., 1998—. Bd. dirs. Cascade Bancorp, Bank of the Cascades, Aquilla Tax-Free Trust of Oreg., Ctrl. Oreg. Ind. Health Svcs., MDU Resources Group Inc., 2003—. Adv. bd. Oreg. State U. Cascade Campus. Named Disting. Citizen of Yr., Bend C. of C., Ctrl. Oreg. Bus. Woman of Yr. Mem.: Ind. Cmty. Bankers Assn. Am., Oreg. Bankers Assn. (bd. dir.), Oreg. Women's Forum. Office: Cascade Bancorp 1100 NW Wall St Bend OR 97701*

**MOSS, RANDY,** professional football player; b. Feb. 13, 1977; 2 children. Student, Marshall U. Wide receiver Minn. Vikings, 1998—2005, Oakland Raiders, 2005—. Named Rookie of Yr., NFL, 1998, Most Outstanding Player, NFL Pro-Bowl, 2000; named to NFL Pro-Bowl, 1998—2000, 2002—03; recipient Espy Award for Breakthrough Athlete of the Yr., 1999. Achievements include first round draft pick NFL, 1998; led NFL in recieving touchdowns, 1998, 2000, 2003; holds NFL record for receptions in first five seasons (414), holds NFL record for fewest games to reach 5,000 career receiving yards (59 games); holds every receiving record at Marshall Univ. Office: Oakland Raiders 1220 Harbor Bay Pkwy Alameda CA 94502*

**MOSS, RICHARD B.,** pediatrician; b. NYC, Oct. 30, 1949; MD, SUNY, Downstate Medical Ctr., Brooklyn, 1975. Cert. Am. Bd. Allergy/Immunology, Am. Bd. Pediatrics. Intern Children's Meml. Hosp., Chgo., 1975-76, resident, 1976-77; fellow Stanford (Calif.) U. Med. Sch., 1977-79, 80-81; now pediatrician Lucile Salter Packard Children's Hosp., Palo Alto, Calif. Prof. pediats. Stanford U. Med. Sch. Office: Pediatric Pulmonary Medicine Dept Lucile Packard Children's Hospital 701 Welch Rd #3328 MC 5786 Palo Alto CA 94304 Office Phone: 650-723-5191.*

**MOSS, RICHARD SPENCER,** communications executive; b. Portland, Oreg., May 26, 1949; s. Harry and Mary Louise (Ruckdeschel) M.; divorced; children: Emily Anne, Paul Spencer, Kathryn Elizabeth, Brian Richard. AA, Mount Hood C.C., 1975; BA in Comm., U. Portland, 1977. Publs. mgr. First Nat. Bank Oreg., Portland, 1977; mgr. employee comm. Ga.-Pacific Corp., Portland, 1977–80; dir. alumni and cmty. rels. U. Portland, 1980-84; dir. employee comm. NERCO Inc., Portland, 1984-87; pres. R.S. Moss & Assocs., Corp. Comms, Portland, 1987—. Bd. dirs. Vietnam Vets. of Oreg. Meml. Fund, Inc. With USN, 1969-73; Vietnam. Recipient Arnold's Admirables award The Ragan Report, 1982, Award of Excellence Annual Reports, Comm. Arts mag., Design Annual, 1989-90, Excellence award Soc. for Tech. Comms., 1989. Mem. Pub. Rels. Soc. Am., Internat. Assn. Bus. Communicators (chpt. dir., chpt. pres. 1985-86, Gold Quill award 1979, 83), Portland Advt. Fedn., Vietnam Vets. Am. (chpt. dir., state coun. dir.), bd. dirs. Vietnam Vets. of Oregon Meml. Fund. Republican. Roman Cath. Home and Office: 716 Smith Ave Lebanon PA 17042-7138

**MOSS, ROGER WILLIAM,** historian, writer, administrator; b. Zanesville, Ohio, Jan. 31, 1940; s. Roger William and Dorothy Elizabeth Moss; m. Gail Caskey Winkler, 1981; children: Elizabeth Moss McQuiston, Victoria Stiles. BS in Edn., Ohio U., 1963, MA, 1964; postgrad., Attingham, Eng., 1966; PhD, U. Del., 1972. Staff Peace Corps, Cameroon, 1962-63; curator of rare books Ohio U., 1962-64; lectr., dept. history U. Del., 1966-68, U. Md., 1967-68; exec. dir. Athenaeum of Phila., 1968—. Lectr. to adj. prof. architecture U. Pa., Phila., 1981–2004. Publs. include Master Builders, 1972, Century of Color, 1981, Biographical Dictionary of Philadelphia Architects, 1985, Victorian Interior Decoration, 1986, Victorian Exterior Decoration, 1987, Lighting for Historic Buildings, 1988 (Joel Polsky prize 1989), The American Country House, 1990, Philadelphia Victorian, 1998, Historic Houses of Philadelphia, 1998, Historic Sacred Places of Philadelphia, 2004; editor: Paint in America, 1994; contbr. articles to profl. jours. Assoc. mem. Nat. Preservation Inst., 1982—93; sec. Christopher Ludwick Found., 1969—, bd. dirs., 1969—; sec.-treas. Brit. Cathedrals and Hist. Chs. Found., 1996—2001, pres., 2002—04, bd. dirs.; sec. Victorian Soc. in Am., 1969—88, treas., 1969—88, bd. dirs., 1969—88; treas. Phila. Area Cultural Consortium, 1977—82, bd. dirs., 1977—82; sec. Hopkinson House Coun., 1982—93, Cliveden Coun., Nat. Trust Hist. Preservation, 1974—81, 1984—86; exec. com. Phila. Area Consortium Spl. Coll., 1988—93; sec. Friends of Laurel Hill, 1978—83; bd. dirs. Conservation Ctr. for Art and Hist. Artifacts, 1984—96, chmn., 1993—95; sec. Harrington House, 1969—81, bd. dirs., 1969—81, Hist. House Assn. Am., 1978—83, Com. Preservation of Archtl. Records, 1978—80, Mus. Coun. Phila., 1976—78, Woodlands Cemetery Co., 1990—99, Rsch. Librs. Group, 1993—96, Abraham Lincoln Found., 1996—2005, Am. Friends Attingham Summer Schs., 2006—. NEH grantee, 1983-85; recipient Biddle award Preservation Alliance, 2004. Mem. Carpenters' Co. (hon.), Soc. Archtl. Historians, Hist. New Eng., Castine Yacht Club, Phila. Club. Club: Office: Athenaeum of Phila 219 S 6th St Philadelphia PA 19106-3794 Office Phone: 215-925-2688. E-mail: rwmoss@philaathenaeum.org.

**MOSS, SANTANA,** professional football player; b. Miami, Fl., June 1, 1979; s. Lloyd, Natalie; children: Santana Jr., Saniya. BA in Liberal Arts, Univ. Miami, 2000. Wide receiver NY Jets, 2000–04, Wash. Redskins, 2005—. Named to NFC ProBowl Team, 2005; recipient BIG East Offensive and Special Teams Player Yr. awards, 2000. Achievements include holding all-time receiving yards record at Univ. Miami. Office: Washington Redskins 21300 Redskin Park Dr Ashburn VA 20147*

**MOSS, SARA E.,** delivery service executive, lawyer; b. NYC, Nov. 13, 1946; BA magna cum laude, U. Mass., 1968; JD, NYU, 1974. Bar: N.Y. 1975, U.S. Dist. Ct. (so. dist.) N.Y. 1976, U.S. Ct. Appeals (2d cir.) 1975, U.S. Tax Ct. 1983, U.S. Supreme Ct. 1983. Law clk. to Hon. Constance Baker Motley U.S. Dist. Ct. (so. dist.) N.Y., 1974-75, asst. U.S. atty., 1978-81; law clk. Davis Polk & Wardell, 1975-78, 80-84; ptnr. Howard Smith & Levin, 1984-96; v.p., gen. counsel Pitney Bowes, Inc., Stamford, Conn., 1996—2003; sr. v.p., gen. counsel, sec. Estée Lauder, NYC, 2003—. Instr. Nat. Inst. Trial Advocacy. Contbr. articles to profl. jours. Mem. ABA, Fed. Bar Coun. (trustee 1996—), Am. Arbitration Assn. (bd. dirs.), N.Y. Coun. Def. Lawyers (bd. dirs. 1994-96), Assn. Bar City of N.Y. (mem. fed. cts. com., mem. litig. com.), Phi Beta Kappa. Office: Estee Lauder 767 Fifth Ave New York NY 10153 Home: 325 Central Park W Apt 3N New York NY 10025-7686 Office Phone: 212-572-4200. Business E-mail: emoss@estee.com.

**MOSS, STEPHEN BRUCE,** lawyer; b. Jacksonville, Fla., July 14, 1943; s. Rudy and Betty (Sobel) M.; m. Rhoda Goodman, Nov. 24, 1984; children: Kurt, Shannon. BA, Tulane U., 1964; JD, Cumberland Sch. Law, 1968. Bar: Fla. 1968, U.S. Dist. Ct. (So. Dist.) Fla., U.S. Tax Ct. 1971. From assoc. to ptnr. Heiman & Crary, Miami, Fla., 1971-74; pvt. practice law So. Miami, Fla., 1974-75; ptnr. Glass, Schultz, Weinstein & Moss P.A., Coral Gables, Fla., 1975-78, Ft. Lauderdale, Fla., 1978-80, Holland & Knight, LLP, Ft. Lauderdale, 1980—, mem. dir. com. Lectr. in the field. Mem. pro bono com. 17th Jud. Cir., 2000; co-founder, co-chair Broward County Child Welfare Initiative, 2001. Capt. U.S. Army, 1968-70, Vietnam. Named Outstanding Kiwanian, Miami, Fla., 1974, Child Advocate of the Yr., Broward County, Fla., 2003, Role Model, 2004, Legal Elite, Fla. Trend Mag., 2004; named an Olympic torchbearer, 1996. Fellow: Am. Bar Found., Fla. Bar Found.; mem.: ABA (mem. real property, probate and trust sect.), Internat. Law Moot Ct., Broward County Bar Assn., Legal Aid Svc. of Broward County (bd. dirs. 2000), Fla. Bar Assn. (mem. real property, probate and trust law sect.), Greater Ft. Lauderdale C. of C. (gen. counsel 1991—92, chmn. bd. dirs., bd. govs. 1995, trustee rep. 2005, past chair, Chmn.'s award 1991, 2000, Sr. Exec. Alumni of Year 2003), Tower Forum (pres. 1993—94, bd. dirs. 1995—2005), Tower Club, Phi Alpha Delta. Democrat. Jewish. Avocations: baseball, travel, child welfare. Office: Holland & Knight LLP 1 E Broward Blvd Ste 1300 Fort Lauderdale FL 33301-1845 Office Phone: 954-468-7857. Business E-mail: stephen.moss@hklaw.com.

**MOSS, SUSAN HECHT,** artist, writer; b. Chgo., May 6, 1944; d. Benjamin Franklin and Amy (Hecht) Moss; m. Glen Galloway, Jan. 15, 1964 (div. Sept. 1974). BA in Art/Psychology with honors, U. Nev., 1966; MFA, Otis Art Inst., 1970. Spkr. World Conf. on Breast Cancer, Canada. Author: Keep Your Breasts! Preventing Breast Cancer the Natural Way (in German, Dutch and English), 1994, 6th edit., 2002; contbr. poetry to profl. publs.; exhibitions include David Findlay Jr. Gallery, N.Y., Albright-Knox Mus., Forum Gallery, N.Y., Represented in permanent collections L.A. County Mus. Art, Skirtball Mus., L.A., Laguna Mus. Art. Mem.: Cancer Ctrl. Soc. (spkr. 1996, 2002, 2003). Democrat. Jewish. Avocations: swimming, weightlifting, hiking, filmmaking. Studio: 4767 York Blvd Los Angeles CA 90042-1648 Home: 1879 Montiflora Ave Los Angeles CA 90041-2016 Office Phone: 323-255-3382. Personal E-mail: susanbc@aol.com.

**MOSS, THOMAS E.,** prosecutor; b. 1937; BA, U. Idaho; JD, U. Idaho Coll. Law, 1965. Prosecuting atty. Bingham County Dist. Ct., 1967—71, 1979—99; ptnr. Moss, Cannon and Romrell, Blackfoot, Idaho; mem. ID Ho. Reps., 2001; US atty. dist. ID US Dept. Justice, Boise, 2001—. Faculty mem. Nat. Advocacy Ctr., Columbia, SC; adv. coun. U. Idaho Coll. of Law; mem. Attn. Gen. Adv. Ctr., 2005—; Atty. Gen. Exec. Working Grp. Pres. Blackfoot Chamber of Commerce, Blackfoot Rotary Club; mem. Governor's Coordinating Coun. for Families and Children. Fellow: Am. Coll. Trial Lawyers; mem.: Idaho Prosecuting Attorneys' Assn. (pres.), Seventh Jud. Dist. Bar Assn. (pres.), Idaho State Bar Assn. (pres.), Idaho Ho. of Reps. Office: US Attys Office MK Plaza IV Ste 600 800 Park Blvd Boise ID 83712-9903*

**MOSS, THOMAS HENRY,** science foundation director, physicist; b. Cleve., June 27, 1939; s. Joseph Harold and Elsa Margaret (Lemkau) M.; m. Kathleen Goddard, May 31, 1966; children: Ellen, Joseph, Cheryl, David. AB Harvard U., 1961; PhD, Cornell U., 1965. Cons. analyst govtl. sci. policy U.S. Govt. Office Mgmt. and Budget, Washington, 1963-67; research physicist IBM

Corp., Yorktown, NY, 1967-74, 75-76; staff dir., sci. advisor Office of Congressman George E. Brown, Washington, 1976-79; staff dir. subcom. sci., research and tech. Ho. of Reps., Washington, 1979-82; prof. physics, dean grad. studies and research Case Western Res. U., Cleve., 1982-96; exec. dir. Govt.-U.-Industry Roundtable, 1996—2001; with Nat. Acad. Scis, Washington; dir. U. relations Ohio Aerospace Inst., 2001—03. Adj. prof. physics Columbia U., NYC, 1966-76; mem. nat rev. com. Office of Nuclear Waste Isolation, Columbus, 1983-87; bd. dirs. U. Tech. Inc., Cleve., G. Mason U. Intellectual Properties, Inc., 2004—; bd. dirs. Ctr. Great Lakes, Chgo., 1985-89; v.p. Edison Poymer Innovation Corp., Independence, Ohio, 1986-90. Editor: The Three Mile Island Nuclear Accident-Lessons, 1981; asst. editor Environ. Profl. mag.; cons. editor Sci, Tech. and Human Values Environ. mag.; contbr. articles to profl. jours. Treas. Lake Bancroft Cmty. Assn., Falls Church, Va., 1980; mem. adv. bd. Small Bus. SBIR Program, Cleve., 1983-85; mem., v.p. Shaker Heights Bd. Edn., Ohio, 1989-96; chmn. NE Region Ohio Systemic Statewide Initiative in Sci. and Math. Edn., 1992-95. ASME fellow, 1995-96, NSF fellow Nobel Instn., 1966-67. Fellow Am. Phys. Soc. (chmn. forum on physics and soc. 1990-91), Nat. Coun. U. Rsch. Adminstrs. (Nat. Innovation Program award 1987), Scientists Inst. Pub. Info. (Disting. Svc. award Harlem Prep. Sch. 1971), AAAS (chmn. com. on sci., engring. and pub. policy 1989-91, chmn. sect. X 1998-99, exec. com. sect. P 2004—). Avocations: gardening, camping. Office Phone: 703-914-2854. Personal E-mail: tomhmoss@verizon.net.

**MOSSAVAR-RAHMANI, BIJAN,** oil and gas company executive; b. Tehran, Iran, June 14, 1952; arrived in U.S., 1978; s. Morteza and Fatemeh (Mohtashem-Nouri) Mossavar-R.; m. Sharmin Batmanghelidj, Oct., 1980. BA, Princeton U., 1974; MS, U. Pa., 1975; MPA, Harvard U., 1982. Oil and energy columnist Kayhan Group of Newspapers, Iran, 1975-78; energy policy analyst Govt. of Iran, 1976-78; vis. rsch. fellow The Rockefeller Found., N.Y., 1978-80; rsch. coord. internat. natural gas study Harvard U., Mass., 1982-85, asst. dir. Energy and Environ. Policy Ctr. Mass., 1985-87; pres. Apache Internat., Inc., Houston, 1988-96; chmn. bd. Mondoil Corp., N.Y.C., 1996—, Foxtrot Internat. LDC, Abidjan, Cote d'Ivoire, 1999—. Author: Energy Policy in Iran, 1981; co-author: OPEC and the World Oil Outlook, 1983, World Natural Gas Outlook, 1984, The OPEC Natural Gas Dilemma, 1986, Energy Security Revisited, 1987, Natural Gas in Western Europe, 1987, Lower Oil Prices: Mapping the Impact, 1988, Competition and Realignment in Global Energy Markets, 1997, Energy Policies and Markets: New Trends or Old Cycles, 2001, Energy Liberalization and Regulation Revisited, 2002, Thinking the Unthinkable, 2003; mem. editl. adv. bd. Offshore mag., 1992-94. Bd. dirs. U.S.-Angola C. of C., 1990-92, Persepolis Found.; mem. coun. Internat. Exec. Svc. Corps, 1991-96; mem. vis. com. Dept. Islamic Art Met. Mus. Art, 2003-; mem. internat. coun. Belfer Ctr. for Sci. and Internat. Affairs, Harvard U., 2004-. Decorated Comdr. de l'Ordre Nat. de Cote d'Ivoire. Mem. Denver U. Club, Nassau Club, Harvard Club of N.Y. Address: 953 Fifth Ave New York NY 10021 Office Phone: 212-535-9930.

**MOSSAWIR, HARVE H., JR.,** retired lawyer; b. Morton, Miss., Aug. 9, 1942; s. Harve H. and Madeline (Price) M.; children: Anna Christine, Karen Elyse; m. Judy S. Bardugo, Aug. 5, 1985; 1 child, Leigh Sarah. BA with honors, U. Ala., 1964; MA in Econs., U. Manchester, 1965; JD with honors, U. Chgo., 1968. Bar: Calif. 1970. Asst. prof. U. Ala. Law Sch., Tuscaloosa, 1968-69; assoc. Irell & Manella, L.A., 1969-74, ptnr., 1974-94, of counsel, 1994-96. Mem. bd. editors U. Chgo. Law Rev., 1966-68; contbr. articles to profl. jours. Fulbright scholar, 1964-65, Floyd Russell Mecham scholar, 1965-68. Republican. Presbyterian. E-mail: labard1@yahoo.com.

**MOSSBERG, WALTER,** columnist; b. Warwick, RI; m. Edith Mossberg; children: Steven, Jonathan. B in Politics, Brandeis U.; MA, Columbia U.; LLD (hon.), U. RI, 2001. Reporter, editor Wall St. Jour., NYC, 1970—; dep. Washington bur. chief, 1983-87, sr. contr., asst. news editor, 1987-91, creator, author personal tech. column, 1991—. Author: The Wall Street Journal Book of Personal Technology, (weekly column) Jour., Mossberg's Mailbox, The Mossberg Solution, The Mossberg Report; contbg. editor SmartMoney, The Wall Street Journal Mag. Personal Bus.; co-editor Labor Letter. Named Most Influential Computer Journalist in Nation, Mktg. Computers Mag., Most Influential Journalist Writing About Computers, Tech. Mktg. mag., 1995—2001; recipient Loeb award for Commentary, 1999, Nat. Headliner award, 2001. Office: Dow Jones & Co World Fin Ctr 200 Liberty St New York NY 10281

**MOSSE, PETER JOHN CHARLES,** financial services executive; b. Mtarfa, Malta, Sept. 8, 1947; arrived in US, 1977; s. John Herbert Charles and Barbara Haworth (Holden) M.; m. Christine Marielle St. Preux, Oct. 17, 1994. BA, Oxford U., 1969; MBA, U. Pa., 1971; MA, Oxford U., 1989. Bank officer N.M. Rothschild & Sons Ltd., London, 1971-76; spl. projects officer banking Bumiputra Malaysia Bankers Berhad, Kuala Lumpur, Malaysia, 1976-77; v.p., treas., sec. NMR Metals Incorp., N.Y.C., 1977-79, exec. v.p., 1979-83; sr. v.p. Rothschild, Inc., N.Y.C., 1983-90; v.p., CFO, The Arista Group Inc., N.Y.C., 1991-93; U.S. rep. Travelex Fin. Svcs. Ltd., London, 1994-95; ptnr. Creelman Fine Arts, NYC, 1995—2003; chmn. 2nd Ave. Physician Practice, 2005—. Treas. Circumnavigators Found., 2004—05. Fellow Royal Soc. Arts.; mem. Pilgrims of the U.S., St. George's Soc. N.Y. (life, bd. dirs. 2006—), Oxford U. Alumni Soc. (exec. com. 1994-96), Gold Inst. (co. rep., bd. dirs. 1985-90), Silver Inst. (co. rep., bd. dirs. 1989-90), Copper Club, Commodity Exch., Inc. (co. rep. 1979-90), Circumnavigators Club (bd. govs. 2006—), Travelers Century Club. Episcopalian. Avocations: travel, trains, railroad art. Home and Office: 353 E 72nd St Apt 33D New York NY 10021-4622

**MOSSELMANS, CAREL MAURITS,** investment banker; b. East Knoyle, Wiltshire, Eng., Mar. 9, 1929; s. Adriaan Willem and Nancy Henriette (Van der Wyck) M.; m. Prudence Fiona McCorquodale, Jan. 4, 1962; children: Michael Lodowick Stewart, Julian Frederick Willem. MA, Trinity Coll., Cambridge, Eng., 1952. With Sedgwick Collins & Co., 1952-63; dir. Sedgwick Collins & Co. Ltd., 1963-71; dir. mng. dir. Sedgwick Collins (Underwriting) Ltd., 1971, 72-73; chmn. Sedgwick Lloyd's Underwriting Agts., 1974-89, Sedgwick Forbes Marine Ltd., 1974-78, Sedgwick Forbes Svcs. Ltd., 1978-81, Sedgwick Ltd., 1981-84, Sedgwick Group Plc., 1984-89, The Sumitomo Marine & Fire Ins. Co. (Europe) Ltd., 1981-90; Coutts & Co., 1981-95; chmn. Rothschild Asset Mgmt. Ltd., 1989-99, Rothschild Int. Asset Mgmt., 1989-96. Chmn. Exco Plc, 1991-96, Janson Green Holdings Spl. Trust Ltd., 1993-96, Rothschild Fund Mgmt. Ltd., 1990-96; chmn. Janson Green Ltd., 1993-96, non-exec. dir., 1997-98. Avocations: shooting, fishing, music, golf. Home: 15 Chelsea Sq London SW3 6LF England

**MOSSINGHOFF, GERALD JOSEPH,** lawyer, educator; b. St. Louis, Sept. 30, 1935; m. Jeanne Carole Jack, Dec. 29, 1958; children: Pamela Ann Jennings, Gregory Joseph, Melissa M. Ronayne. BSEE, St. Louis U., 1957; JD with honors, George Washington U., 1961. Bar: Mo. 1961, DC 1965, Va. 1981. Project engr. Sachs Electric Corp., 1954-57; dir. congl. liaison NASA, Washington, 1967-73, dep. gen. counsel, 1976-81; asst. Sec. Commerce, commr. patents and trademarks U.S. Patent Office, 1981-85; pres. Pharm. Rsch. and Mfrs. Am., Washington, 1985-96; Cifelli prof. intellectual property law George Washington U., Washington, 1996—; sr. counsel Oblon, Spivak, McClelland, Maier & Neustadt, Arlington, Va., 1997—. Amb. Paris Conv. Diplomatic Conf.; adj. prof. George Mason U. Law Sch. Named Disting. Alumnus, George Washington U., 1996, presdl. rank of meritorious exec., 1980; recipient Exceptional Svc. medal, NASA, 1971, Disting. Svc. medal, 1980, Outstanding Leadership medal, 1981, Jefferson medal, 2000, Disting. Pub. Svc. award, Sec. of Commerce, 1983. Fellow: Am. Acad. Pub. Adminstrn.; mem.: Reagan Alumni Assn. (bd. dirs.), Cosmos Club, Knights of Malta, Order of Coif, Pi Mu Epsilon, Eta Kappa Nu. Home: 1530 Key Blvd Penthouse 28 Arlington VA 22209-1532 Office: Oblon Spivak McClelland Maier and Neustadt 1940 Duke St Alexandria VA 22314 Personal E-mail: gmossing@aol.com.

**MOSS-SALENTIJN, LETTY (ALEIDA MOSS-SALENTIJN),** anatomist, educator; b. Amsterdam, The Netherlands, Apr. 14, 1943; arrived in U.S., 1968; d. Ewoud and Johanna Maria (Schoonhoven) Salentijn; m. Melvin Lionel Moss, Apr. 17, 1970. DDS, State U. Utrecht, Netherlands, 1967, PhD, 1976. Asst. prof. histology State U. Utrecht, 1967-68; asst. prof. Columbia U., N.Y.C., 1968-74, assoc. prof., 1974-86, prof., 1986—, Edwin S. Robinson prof., 1999—, dir. dental radiology, 1980-86, dir. grad. program dental sci., 1986—, dir. postdoctoral affairs, 1987-90, asst. dean postdoctoral programs, 1990-94, assoc. dean acad. affairs, 1994—2005, sr. assoc. dean acad. affairs, 2005—. Author: Orofacial Histology & Embryology, 1972; Dental and Oral Tissues, 1980, 2d edit., 1984, 3d edit., 1990; contbr. chpts. to books, articles to profl. jours. Fellow Royal Microscopical Soc., Am. Coll. Dentists, NY Acad. Dentistry; mem. Am. Assn. Anatomists, Internat. Assn. Dental Rsch., Am. Soc. Biomechs., Sigma Xi (chpt. sec. 1980-87, pres. 1987-89, 98-99), Omicron Kappa Upsilon (pres. local chpt. 1987). Avocation: stained glass art. Home: 560 Riverside Dr Apt 20K New York NY 10027-3239 Office: Columbia U/SDOS Sr Assoc Dean Acad Affairs 630 W 168th St New York NY 10032-3702 Office Phone: 212-305-8334. Business E-mail: lm23@columbia.edu.

**MOSTAGHIMI, MEHDI,** economist, educator; arrived in U.S., 1975; s. Abolfazle Mostaghimi and Toba Rashidzadeh; m. Du D Cheng, Aug. 28, 1991; children: Darius, Alexander. BA in Econs., Nat. U. Iran, 1975; PhD in Sys. Engring., U. Va., 1987; MS in Ops. Rsch., We. Mich. U., 1999. Sr. mgr. portfolio and decision analysis group Pfizer Pharm., N.Y.C., 1997—99; prof. economics and decision scis. Sch. of Bus. So. Conn. State U., New Haven, 1984—. Chmn. internat. chapts. subcom. Inst. of Ops. Rsch. and Mgmt. Scis., 2001—03; Grad. Rsch. Fellowship panel NSF, 2006. Co-author: Analysis of Bus. Cycles, 2004; contbr. articles to profl. jours. Fellow: Inst. of Ops. Rsch. and the Mgmt. Scis. (chmn. internat. chapts. subcommittee 2001—02); mem.: Am. Statis. Assn. (com. on internat. rels. 1994—98, pres. Conn. chpt. 1994—96). Achievements include research in modeling combining information and forecasts; predicting a turning point in economy; strategic and policy decision making. Home: PO Box 569 Madison CT 06443 Office: Southern Connecticut State Univ 501 Crescent Street New Haven CT 06515 Office Phone: 203-392-5625. Personal E-mail: mostaghimi@yahoo.com.

**MOSTELLER, DARLA BROOKS,** singer; d. Thomas Jefferson and Sue Osborne Brooks; m. Paul Mosteller, July 5, 2000. MusB, Birmingham-Southern Coll., Ala., 1977. Young artist Lyric Opera Chgo., 1980—81; leading soprano Lucerne (Switzerland) Opera, 1984—85, Würzburg (Germany) Opera, 1985—86, Cologne (Germany) Opera, 1987—96; pvt. voice tchr. Birmingham, Ala., 2000—. Guest artist Dortmund (Germany) Opera, 1990—96; guest soloist Vienna (Austria) State Opera, 1991—96; artist Schwetzingen (Germany) Festival, 1993—95; soloist Trondheim (Norway) Symphony, 1993—95, Bergen (Norway) Symphony, 1995; guest artist Opera Bonn, Bonn, Germany, 1986—87, Mannheim (Germany) Opera, 1986—95, German Opera on the Rhine, Düsseldorf, Germany, 1989—96, Gran Teatre del Liceu, Barcelona, 1991—96, Mozart Festival, Prague, Czech Republic, 1991, Bavarian State Opera, Munich, 1993—94, Deutsche Oper, Berlin, 1993—95, Min-On Concert Assn., Tokyo, 1993, Salzburg (Austria) Festival, 1995—96; tchr. voice Birmingham (Ala.) So. Coll., 1997—2000. Singer (actor): (TV films) LIncoronazione di Poppea, 1991, (films) Falstaff (Salieri), 1993. Finalist, Met. Opera Nat. Coun., 1976, 1977, 1978, 1980, 1983, 1984; scholar, Am. Inst. Musical Studies, 1981; Singer's scholar, Norman Treigle Scholarship Fund, 1980. Mem.: Nat. Assn. Tchrs. Singing. Office: Private Voice Studio 3308 Brookview Trace Birmingham AL 35216 Office Phone: 205-249-7464.

**MOSTELLER, JAMES WILBUR, III,** data processing executive; b. Ft. Riley, Kans., June 21, 1940; s. James Wilbur Jr. and Ruth Renfro (Thompson) M.; m. Sandra Josephine Stevenson, Oct. 13, 1962; children: Margaret, Steven, Michael. BS in Econs., Rensselaer Poly. Inst., 1962; MBA, Temple U., 1971. Cert. in data processing. Data processing sys. analyst Philco-Ford, Ft. Washington, Pa., 1966-69; data processing analyst and supr. Merck Sharp & Dohme, West Point, Pa., 1969-75; dir. mgmt. info. sys. KELCO divsn. Merck and Co., San Diego, 1975-87; dir. info. mgmt. Advanced Sys. divsn. United Technologies, San Diego, 1987-88; computer scientist Navy Personnel Research and Devel. Ctr., San Diego, 1988-97; head prodn. sys. Navy SPAWAR Sys. Ctr., 1997—. Bd. dirs. New Horizons Montessori Sch., Ft. Washington, 1974-75; leader youth programs North County YMCA, 1977-81; mem. San Diego Rsch. Park Com., 1978-86; 1st v.p., mem. exec. com. San Diego Space and Sci. Found., 1985-92; trustee emeritus Reuben H. Fleet Sci. Ctr., 2003—. With USN, 1962-66, capt. Res., 1966-93. Mem. Data Processing Mgmt. Assn., Assn. Sys. Mgmt., Naval Res. Assn. (life), U.S. Naval Inst. (life), Royal Scottish County Dance Soc. (chmn. San Diego br. 2001-03), La Playa Yacht Club, Beta Gamma Sigma, Sigma Alpha Epsilon (chpt. pres. 1961-62). Office: Navy SPAWAR Sys Ctr 2641 San Diego CA 92152-5001 Personal E-mail: jim.mosteller@cox.net.

**MOSTELLER, ROBERT P.,** law educator; b. 1948; BA, U. N.C., 1970; MA, Harvard U., 1975; JD, Yale U., 1975. Bar: N.C. 1975, D.C. 1976. Law clk. to Hon. Braxton Craven U.S. Ct. Appeals (4th cir.), Asheville, NC, 1975-76; atty., chmn. trial div., tng. dir. D.C. Pub. Defender Svc., 1976-83; assoc. prof. Duke U., Durham, NC, 1983-87, prof., 1987-2001, Harry R. Chadwick, Sr. prof., 2001—, sr. assoc. dean, 1989-91, chair acad. counsel, 1998-2000. Mem. Phi Beta Kappa (pres. 1969-70).

**MOSTER, MARY CLARE,** public relations executive; b. Morristown, NJ, Apr. 7, 1950; d. Clarence R. and Ruth M. Moster; m. Louis C. Williams, Jr., Oct. 4, 1987. BA in English with honors, Douglass Coll., 1972; MA in English Lit., Univ. Chgo., 1973. Accredited pub. rels. counselor. Editor No. Trust Bank, Chgo., 1973-75, advt. supr., 1975-77, communications officer, 1977-78; account exec. Hill & Knowlton, Inc., Chgo., 1978-80, v.p., 1980-83, sr. v.p., 1983-87, sr. v.p., mng. dir., 1987-88; staff v.p. comms. Navistar Internat. Corp., Chgo., 1988-93; v.p. corp. comms. Comdisco, Inc., Rosemont, Ill., 1993—2002; sr. v.p. L.C. Williams and Assocs., Chgo., 2002—. Adj. prof. Integrated Mktg. Comm. Medill Sch., Northwestern U., 2000-05 Author poetry, poetry translation. Bd. govs. Met. Planning Coun., Chgo., 1988-94; fellow Leadership Greater Chgo., 1989-90; bd. dirs. New City YMCA, Chgo., 1986-92; corp. devel. bd. Steppenwolf Theatre Co., Chgo., 1988-90; active Chgo. Network, 1994—, dirs., 1996-99. Mem. Nat. Investor Rels. Inst. (bd. dirs. 1988-89, 90-99, pres. Chgo. chpt. 1998-99), Arthur W. Page Soc., Pub. Rels. Soc. Am., Internat. Women's Forum. Avocations: sailing, cross country skiing, book groups, biking. Office: L C Williams & Assocs 150 N Michigan Ave Ste 3800 Chicago IL 60601

**MOSTERT, PAUL STALLINGS,** retired mathematician; b. Morrilton, Ark., Nov. 27, 1927; s. Johannes F. T. and Lucy (Stallings) Mostert; m. Barbara Bond; children: Paul Theodore, Richard Stallings, Kathleen, Kristina. AB, Rhodes Coll., 1950; MS, U. Chgo., 1951; PhD, Purdue U., 1953. Mem. faculty Tulane U., 1953-70, prof. math., 1962-70, chmn. dept., 1968-70; prof. U. Kans., 1970-91, prof. emeritus math., 1991—, chmn. dept., 1970-73. Vis. prof. U. Tubingen, Germany, 1962—63; mem. Inst. Advanced Study, Princeton, 1967—68; vis. prof. math. U. Ky., 1984—85; chmn. Rhodes Coll. Sci. Initiaitve Task Force, 1989—90; pres. Equix Inc., 1984—85, Pennfield Biomechanics Corp., Inc., 1985—89, Equix Biomechanics, 1989—97, Equix Rsch. Corp., 1989—2005; proprietor Mostert Group, 1997—2003; dir. rsch. Mostert-Group LLC-Equix Biomechanics, 2004—06; mng. MSRCO, LLC, 2004—. Co-author: Splitting in Topological Groups, 1963, 3d edit., 1993, Elements of Compact Semigroups, 1966, The Cohomology Ring of Finite and Compact Abelian Groups, 1974; editor: Proc. Conf. Transformation Groups at New Orleans, 1969, Questiones Mathematicae, 1973—95; co-founder, editor: Semigroup Forum, 1970—85, mng. editor; 1967—85; editor, 1985—88; creator 9 software programs. Mem. Ky. Statewide Exptl. Program Stimulate Competitive Rsch. Com., 1994—96. With USN, 1945—46. Recipient Rsch. award, Small Bus. Innovative Rsch.; 2000—05; Sr. postdoctoral fellow, NSF, 1987—88. Mem.: AAAS, Assn. Computing Machinery, Assn. Mem. Inst. Advanced Studies, Am. Math. Soc. (mem. at large coun. 1972—75, chmn. com. acad. freedom, tenure and employment security 1973—76), Thoroughbred Owners and Breeders Assn. Achievements include patents for methods and computer-readable medium for tracking motion and for navigating between a plurality of discrete images. Office: 3298 Roxburg Dr Lexington KY 40503-3432 Office Phone: 859-223-1490. E-mail: pmostert@windstream.net.

**MOSTILLO, RALPH,** medical association administrator; s. Joseph and Antoinette Mostillo. BA in Chemistry magna cum laude, Rutgers U., Newark, 1972; MA in Biochemistry, Princeton (NJ) U., 1974, PhD in Biochemistry, 1978. Rsch. fellow Princeton U., 1972-78; sr. scientist drug regulatory affairs Hoffmann-La Roche, Inc., Nutley, NJ, 1979-85; founder, chmn., CEO Am. Cancer Assn., Nutley, 1986—. With USN, 1962—66, Vietnam. Fellow, NIH, 1972—78. Mem.: NY Acad. Scis., Am. Mktg. Assn., Am. Mgmt. Assn., Am. Chem. Soc., Vietnam Vets. Am., Am. Legion, Phi Beta Kappa, Sigma Xi. Achievements include research in molecular transport systems in E. coli as general models for drug delivery into cells. Home: PO Box 505 Nutley NJ 07110-0505 Office: Am Cancer Assn PO Box 87 Nutley NJ 07110-0087

**MOST-LEVIN, CAROL LYNN,** physician, geriatrician; b. Long Island, N.Y., Sept. 1, 1959; d. Herbert Jules and Jean (Friedman) Most; m. Ronald Mitchell Levin, June 17, 1979; children: Jay Samuel, Marc Andrew, Eric Brian. BA magna cum laude, La Salle Coll., Phila., 1981; MD, Med. Coll. Pa., 1985. Diplomate Nat. Bd. Med. Examiners; diplomate in internal medicine and geriatric medicine. Am. Bd. Internal Medicine. Intern and resident Abington (Pa.) Meml. Hosp., 1985-88; pvt. practice, 1988—95; internist Abington Meml. Hosp., 1995-2001, mem.-at-large med. exec. com., 1999—2002; pvt. practice, 2001—03; staff physician W.G. (Bill) Hefner VA Med. Ctr., Salisbury, NC, 2003—06, West Palm Beach Va. Med. Ctr., Fla., 2006—. Med. dir. U.S. Homecare, Phila., 1991-94; clin. instr. Temple U., Phila. 1995-96; instr. Jefferson U., 1996-2003, med. sch. interviewer Alleghany U., 1995-97; spkr. in field. Contbr. articles to mag., jours. Recipient First prize Eleanor Dixon Writing/Rsch. Competition, 1988; named Clin. Employee of Yr., VA Med. Ctr., 2004. Fellow ACP; mem. AMA (Physician's Recognition award 1991, 94, 97, 2000, 03, 06), Am. Geriatrics Soc. Avocations: travel, cooking, decorating. Office: West Palm Beach Va Med Ctr 7305 N Military Trail West Palm Beach FL 33410 Home: 7912 Sonoma Springs Cir Apt 101 Lake Worth FL 03463 Personal E-mail: cmlmdfacp@aol.com.

**MOSTOFF, ALLAN SAMUEL,** lawyer, consultant; b. NYC, Oct. 19, 1932; s. Morris and Ida (Goldman) M.; m. Alice Tamara Popelowskuy, July 31, 1955; children: Peter Alexander, Nina Valerie. BS, Cornell U., 1953; MBA, NYU, 1954; LLB, N.Y. Law Sch., 1957. Bar: N.Y. 1958, D.C. 1964. Assoc. Olwine Connelly Chase O'Donnell & Weyher, N.Y.C., 1958-61; atty. SEC, Washington, 1962-66, asst. dir., 1966-69, assoc. dir., 1969-72, dir. divsn. investment mgmt. regulation, 1972-76; ptnr. Dechert Price & Rhoads, Washington, 1976—2002, Dechert, Washington, 2000—03; ptnr. emeritus, sr. counsel Dechert LLP, Washington, 2002—03, of counsel, 2004—; pres. Mut. Fund Dirs. Forum, 2002—. Adj. prof. Georgetown U. Law Ctr., 1972-82; mem. Fin. Acctg. Standards Adv. Bd., 1982-86; mem. adv. bd. Investment Lawyer, 2000—, BNA Securities Regulation and Law Report, 1977-87. Mem. ABA, Assn. of Bar of City of N.Y., Fed. Bar Assn. (past chmn. exec. coun. securities regulation com. 1990-92), Am. Law Inst. Home: 6417 Waterway Dr Falls Church VA 22044-1325 Office: 1255 23rd St NW Ste 200 Washington DC 20037 Business E-Mail: allan.mostoff@mfdf.com.

**MOSTOW, GEORGE DANIEL,** mathematics professor; b. Boston, July 4, 1923; s. Isaac J. and Ida (Rotman) M.; m. Evelyn Davidoff, Sept. 1, 1947; children: Mark Alan, David Jechiel, Carol Held, Jonathan Carl. BA, Harvard U., 1943, MA, 1946, PhD, 1948; DSc (hon.), U. Ill., Chgo., 1989. Instr. math. Princeton U., 1947-48; mem. Inst. Advanced Study, 1947-49, 56-57, 75, mem. bd. of trustees, 1982-92; asst. prof. Syracuse U., 1949-52; asst. prof. math. Johns Hopkins U., 1952-53, assoc. prof., 1954-56, prof., 1957-61; prof. math. Yale U., 1961-66, James E. English prof. math., 1966-81, Henry Ford II prof. math., 1981-98, chmn., 1971-74, prof. emeritus, 1998—. Vis. prof. Conselho Nat. des Pesquisas, Inst. de Matematica, Rio de Janiero, Brazil, 1953-54, 91, U. Paris, 1966-67, Hebrew U., Jerusalem, 1967, Tata Inst. Fundamental Rsch., Bombay, 1970, Inst. des Hautes Etudes Scientifiques, Bures-Sur-Yvette, 1966, 71, 75, Japan Soc. for Promotion of Sci., 1985, Eidgenossische Technische Hochschule, Switzerland, 1986; chmn. U.S. Nat. Com. for Math, 1971-73, 83-85, Office Math. Scis., NRC, 1975-78; mem. sci. adv. coun. Math. Scis. Rsch. Inst., Berkeley, Calif., 1988-91; mem. sci. adv. com., bd. govs. Weizmann Inst., Israel, 1987—2003; bd. govs. Tel Aviv U., 1990-2000; mem. Harvard Grad. Coun., 1988-91; mem. vis. com. dept. math. Harvard U., 1975-81, MIT, 1981-84; Ritt lectr. Columbia U., 1982, Bergman lectr. Stanford U., 1983, Sachar lectr. Tel Aviv U., 1985, Karcher lectr. U. Okla., 1986, Markert lectr. Pa. State U., 1993. Assoc. editor Annals of Math., 1957—64, Trans. Am. Math. Soc., 1958—65, Am. Scientist, 1970—82, Geometriae Dedicata, 1985—90, bd. cons. Jour. D'Analyse Mathématique, 1994—; editor: Am. Jour. Math., 1965—69; assoc. editor Am. Jour. Math., 1969—79; author rsch. articles:. Fulbright rsch. scholar, France, 1966; Conselho Nat. des Pesquisas, Brazil, 1953-54; Guggenheim fellow, 1957-58 Mem. AAAS, NAS (chmn. sect. math. 1982-84), Am. Math. Soc. (pres. 1987-88, Steele prize for Paper of Lasting Importance 1993), Internat. Math. Union (chmn. U.S. del. to Gen. Assembly Warsaw 1982, exec. coun. 1983-86), Phi Beta Kappa, Sigma Xi. Home: 25 Beechwood Rd Woodbridge CT 06525-1309 Office: Yale Univ Dept Mathematics New Haven CT 06520 E-mail: george.mostow@yale.edu.

**MOSZKOWSKI, NEAL,** health products executive; Degree, Amherst Coll.; MBA, Stanford Univ. Grad. Sch. Bus. Vice-pres., exec. dir. principal investment area Goldman, Sachs & Co.; co-head, ptnr. Soros Private Equity Partners, LLC, 1998, chmn. bd. dir., 2002—. Dir. Bluefly, Inc., Day Internat Group, Inc., Jet Blue Airways Corp., Integra LifeSciences Holding Corp. Office: WellCare Health Plans Renaissance 1 8725 Henderson Rd Tampa FL 33634 Office Phone: 813-290-6200. Office Fax: 813-262-2802

**MOTCH, MARJORIE MCCULLOUGH,** service organization executive; b. Cin., July 12, 1923; d. Robert Stedman and Mildred (Rogers) McCullough; m. Homer E. Lunken, Apr. 15, 1944 (dec. 1970); children: Karen Lunken-(dec.), Kathryn Lunken Summers, Margo Lunken Yesner; m. William McLeod Ittmann, Mar. 17, 1972 (dec. 1982); m. Harold Hiatt, Apr. 14, 1984 (dec. 1999); m. Graham E. Marx, Jan. 4, 2003 (dec. 2003); m. Arthur E. Motch Jr., Sept. 18, 2004 (dec. 2005). Student, U. Cin., Ohio, 1941—43, DFA (hon.), 2003. Active Girl Scouts U.S., 1962—, comm. vice com., 1972, del. world convs., 1969, 72, 75, 78, 81, 84, 87, 93, chmn. pub. relations com., 1963-66, mem. com., 1963-75, mem. nat. bd., 1962—, 44th v.p., 1966-69, 1st v.p., 1969-72, nat. pres., 1972-75, chmn. nat. adv. council, 1975-82, mem. birthplace adv. com., 1980-97. Vice chmn. world conf., Orleans, France, 1981; world com. World Assn. Girl Guides and Girl Scouts, 1978-87, vice chmn., 1984-87; trustee emeritus U. Cin. Found. Regional dir. Assn. Jr. Leagues Am., 1958—60, nat. pres., 1960—62; mem. br. Nat. Assembly for Social Policy and Devel., 1968—71; mem. exec. com. Coun. Nat. Orgns. for Children and Youth, 1960—62, 1968—72; mem. br. Jr. League Cin., 1944—58, Nat. Tng. Labs., 1963—66; mem. policy com. Ctr. Vol. Soc., 1971—72; mem. Ohio Citizens Coun., 1956—58; mem. bd. advisors U. Cin. Coll. Nursing, 2000—; bd. dirs. 7th Presbyn. Ch., 1967—74, 1985—, ruling elder, 1976—78, 2000—, chmn. bd. trustees, 1992—94; sr. warden St. Martin's in the Field, Biddeford Pool, Maine; bd. dirs. United Way Am., 1962—67, sec., 1965—66, v.p., 1966—67, 1989—; bd. dirs. Fine Arts Fund, 2002—, Coll. Prep. Schs., Cin., 1962—69, pres., 1964—69; bd. dirs. Cin. Speech and Hearing Ctr., 1955—56, v.p., 1958—62, pres., 1963—66, trustee emeritus 1966—; mem. bd. Children's Theatre, Cin., 1948—58, pres., 1948—50; bd. dirs. Cmty. Health and Welfare Coun. Cin., 1957—63, Hamilton County (Ohio) Plng. Found., 1963—65, Cancer Family Care, Cin., 1971—72, Boys Clubs Greater Cin., Marjorie P. Lee Home for the Aged, Ctrl. Psychiat. Clinic, Music Hall Assn., Cin. Symphony Orch., Beechwood Home for Incurables, 1975—87, St. Margaret Hall, 1991—, Cin. Civic Garden Ctr., 1992—95, Greater Cin. Found., 1979—87, Ctrl. Clinic, 2000—; YWCA, 1998—, Fine Arts Fund, 2002—. Recipient Mary Herriman award, 2000, Mardee Wachs Vol. Svc. award, Hearing, Speech, and Deaf Ctrs., 2006. Mem.

**MOTCHAN, DENNIS GLENN,** physician; b. St. Louis, Apr. 6, 1950; s. Harold Lloyd and Radine (Goldman) M.; m. Nancy Helene Shulman, Jan. 26, 1975; children: Randall Kenneth, Katherine Rae. BS, Northwestern U., 1972, MD, 1974. Diplomate Am. Bd. Internal Medicine. Intern St. John's Mercy Med. Ctr., Creve Coeur, Mo., 1974-75, resident in internal medicine, 1975-77, chief resident in internal medicine, 1977-78, attending physician, instr. internal medicine, 1978—; practice medicine specializing in internal medicine Northway Internists, Inc., Bridgeton, Mo., 1978—2005; pvt. practice Maryland Heights, Mo., 2006—. Mem. AMA (Physician's Recognition award in continuing med. edn. 2000), St. Louis County Met. Med. Soc. Office: Concentra Med Ctr 83 Progress Pkwy Maryland Heights MO 63043 Office Phone: 314-434-8174.

**MOTE, CLAYTON DANIEL, JR.,** academic administrator, mechanical engineer, educator; b. San Francisco, Feb. 5, 1937; s. Clayton Daniel and Eugenia (Isnardi) M.; m. Patricia Jane Lewis, Aug. 18, 1962; children: Melissa Michelle, Adam Jonathan. BSc, U. Calif., Berkeley, 1959, MS, 1960, PhD, 1963; Doctorate (hon.), Tashkent State Tech. U., 2001; DSc, Ohio State U., 2001; Dr Sci. and Tech. (hon.), Carnegie Mellon U., 2004. Registered profl. engr., Calif. Asst. specialist U. Calif. Forest Products Labs., 1961-62, asst. mech. engr., 1962-63; lectr. mech. engring. U. Calif., Berkeley, 1962-63, asst. prof., 1967-69, asst. research engr., 1967-69, assoc. prof., assoc. research engr., 1969-73, prof., 1973-98, vice chmn. mech. engring. dept., 1976-80, 83-86, chmn. mech. engring. dept., 1987-91, vice chancellor univ. rels., FANUC chair mech. systems, 1991-98; research fellow U. Birmingham, Eng., 1963-64; asst. prof. Carnegie Inst. Tech., 1964-67; Glen L. Martin Inst. prof. engring. U. Md., College Park, 1998—, pres., 1998—. Vis. prof. Norwegian Inst. Wood Tech., 1972—73, vis. sr. scientist, 1976, 78, 80, 84, 85; cons. in engring., design and analysis; cons. in engring. NAE, 1988, Nat. Acad. Arts and Sci., 2004; sr. scientist Alexander Von Humboldt Found., Germany, 1988, Japan Soc. for Promotion of Sci., Japan, 1991. Mem. editl. bd. Soma Jour. Sound and Vibration, Machine Vibration; contbr. articles to profl. jours.; patentee in field. NSF fellow, 1963-64, Sr. Scientist fellowship Japan Soc. Promotion Sci., 1991, Berkeley fellow, 2001; recipient Disting. Teaching award, U. Calif., 1971, Pi Tau Sigma Excellence in Teaching award, U. Calif., 1975, Humboldt Prize, Fed. Republic Germany, 1988, Disting. Engring. Alumnus award U. Calif., 2001, Frederick W. Taylor Rsch. medal. Soc. Mfg. Engrs., 1991, Hetenyi award Soc. Exptl. Mechanics, 1992, Eagle award Met. Washington chpt. ARCS, 2000. Fellow: Am. Acad. Arts & Sci. (coun. del. Sect M 2003—), NAE (coun. 2002—, former program com., peer com., Founder's award 2005), ASME (hon.; chmn. San Francisco sect. 1978—79, nat. chmn. noise control and acoustics 1980—84, v.p. environ. and transp. 1986—90, Blackall award 1975, Disting. Svc. award 1991, Charles Russ Richards award 1994, Rayleigh lectr. 1994, Applied Mechanics award 2001, Den Hertog award 2005), Acoustical Soc. Am., Internat. Acad. Wood Sci.; mem.: ASTM (com. on snow skiing F-27 1984—87), AAAS, Orthopaedic Rsch. Soc., Am. Soc. Biomechanics, Am. Acad. Mechanics, Am. Soc. Engring. Edn. (Ralph Coast Roe award 1997), Internat. Soc. Skiing Safety (hon.; sec. 1977—85, bd.dirs. 1977—, chmn. coun. 1985—, v.p.), Nat. Soc. Collegiate Scholars, Golden Key Nat. Honor Soc., Phi Kappa Phi, Omicron Delta Kappa, Tau Beta Pi, Pi Tau Sigma, Sigma Xi. Office: Office of Pres U Md Main Adminstrn Bldg College Park MD 20742-5025 Office Phone: 301-405-5803. Business E-mail: president@umd.edu.

**MOTE, CLYDE A,** retired lawyer; b. Vernon, Tex., Feb. 12, 1926; s. Neven and Lona (May) M.; m. Jean Henderson, Apr. 26, 1952 (dec. May 1998); children— Terron, Bruce, Douglas; m. Roxann Evans, Jan. 21, 1999. J.D., Baylor U., 1950. Bar: Tex. 1950, Okla. 1960. Ptnr. Cummings & Mote, Abilene, Tex., 1950-52; asst. city atty. City of Lubbock, Tex., 1952-54; ptnr. Napier & Mote, Lubbock, 1954-59; atty. Amoco Prodn. Co., Houston, 1959-86, regional atty., New Orleans Region, 1986—89. Served to sgt. U.S. Army, 1943-46, ETO. Mem. Am. Petroleum Inst. (subcom. on exploration and prodn. law), Interstate Oil Compact Commn., Phi Alpha Delta. Republican. Baptist. Home: 244 N Bay Dr Bullard TX 75757-8917

**MOTES, CARL DALTON,** lawyer; b. May 31, 1949; s. Carl Thomas and Orpha Jeanette (McGauley) M.; m. Maria Eugenia Aguirre, Apr. 19, 1975. AA with honors, St. Johns River Jr. Coll., 1969; BA, Fla. State U., 1971, JD with honors, 1974. Bar: Fla. 1974, U.S. Dist. Ct. (cen., no. and so. dists.) Fla. 1975, U.S. Ct. Appeals (11th cir.) 1980. Assoc. Maguire, Voorhis & Wells P.A., Orlando, Fla., 1975-79, ptnr., 1979-97, Motes & Sears P.A., Winter Park, Fla., 1998-99, Motes & Carr, P.A., Orlando, 1999—2005; asst. to pres. Fla. Bar, Tallahassee, 1974-75; ptnr. Arnold, Matheny & Eagan, PA, Orlando, Fla., 2005—. Dir. Legal Aid Soc., Orlando, 1979-83, pres., 1983-84; lectr. at various Bar Assns. and ednl. insts. Mem. editl. bd. Jour. Trial Advocate Quar., 1981-91, chmn., 1989-91; contbr. articles to profl. jours. Active in Planning & Zoning Bd., Altamonte Springs, Fla., 1977-79, Capital Funds Project Rev. Com., Cen. Fla., 1983; bd. dirs. Cen. Fla. coun. Boy Scouts Am., mem. exec. bd., v.p. adminstrn. 1993-94. Mem. Internat. Assn. Def. Counsel, Fla. Def. Lawyers Assn. (bd. dirs. 1989-94, sec., treas. 1991-92, pres.-elect 1992-93, pres. 1993-94), Fla. Bar, Fedn. of Def. and Corp. Counsel, Orange County Bar Assn. (sec. 1979-80, exec. coun. 1980-83, named Outstanding Mem. 1981-82, Outstanding Com. Chmn. 1977), Fla. State U. Coll. Law Alumni Assn. (bd. dirs. 1975-78, pres. 1979), Def. Rsch. Inst. (state chair 1994), Phi Delta Phi. Republican. Office: Arnold Matheny + Eagan PA 605 E Robinson St Ste 730 Orlando FL 32801 Office Fax: 407-841-8746. Business E-Mail: cmotes@amerorl.com.

**MOTHERWAY, NICHOLAS J.,** lawyer; b. Chgo., Jan. 21, 1940; s. Daniel Lawrence and Margaret Ann Motherway; m. Kathleen Elizabeth Butler, Dec. 23, 1967; children: Daniel, Nicholas, Carolyn, Brian. BSc, Loyola U., 1961; JD, DePaul U., 1965. Bar: Ill. 1965, U.S. Dist. Ct. (no. dist.) Ill. 1965, U.S. Ct. Appeals (7th cir.) 1996. Assoc. states atty. Cook County States Atty., Chgo., 1966—73; assoc. Philip H. Corboy, Chgo., 1973—82; prin. Motherway and Napleton, Chgo., 1982—. Lt. USAR, 1961—67. Fellow: Am. Coll. Trial Lawyers; mem.: ATLA (bd. govs. 1990—95), Am. Bd. Trial Adv. (pres. Ill. chpt. 1995—96, nat. bd. dirs. 1996—). Office: Motherway and Napleton 100 W Monroe St Chicago IL 60603 Office Phone: 312-726-2699. Business E-Mail: nmotherway@mnlawoffice.com.

**MOTHKUR, SRIDHAR RAO,** radiologist; b. Mothkur, India, Oct. 5, 1950; arrived in U.S., 1975, naturalized; s. Venkat Rao and Laxmi Bai (Gundepally) Mothkur; m. Sheila Rama Rao Paga, Nov. 30, 1973; children: Swathi, Preethi, Venkat Krishna. Student, Coll. Arts and Sci. Osmania U., Hyderabad, India, 1966; MB, BS, Osmania U., Hyderabad, India, 1972, DPH, 1974; MPA, Ind. U.N.W., 2000. Diplomate Am. Bd. Radiology. Rotating intern Osmania Gen. Hosp., Hyderabad, 1972-73, internal medicine intern, 1973, resident in surgery, 1974-75; resident Resurrection Hosp., Chgo., 1975-76; resident in radiology Luth. Gen. Hosp., Park Ridge, Ill., 1976-79, chief resident radiology, 1978-79; with rotations in nuclear medicine, angiography and neuroradiology Rush-Presbyn. St. Luke's Med. Ctr., Chgo., 1978; chmn. and med. dir. dept. radiology Louise Burg Hosp., Chgo., 1979-85, Shriner's Hosp., Chgo., 1986-88; fellow in ultrasound and computerized tomography U. Ill., Chgo., 1988-89; fellow in magnetic resonance imaging, 1988-89; staff radiologist St. Anthony Hosp., Michigan City, Ind., 1989—, med. dir. MRI Ctr., 1989—; pvt. practice, Michigan City, 1989—; staff radiologist Kingwood Hosp., Michigan City, 1989-94, Charter Hosp., Behavioral Health Sys. Ind., Michigan City, 1994-96; pres. Michigan City Radiologists, Inc., Michigan City, 1998—2003; med. dir. dept. diagnostic imaging St. Anthony Meml. Med. Ctr., Michigan City, 2004—. Cons., radiologist Med. Group Michigan City, 1989—98, Franklin Clin. and Med. Watch, Michigan City, 1989—; spl. staff radiologist Christ hosp. Med. Ctr., Oak Lawn, Ill., 1988—89, Jasper County Meml. Hosp., Rensselaer, Ind., 1994—, United Diagnostic Svcs., Westchester, Ill., 1979—2000; dir. MRI Ctr. Meml. Hosp., 1989—97; med. dir. interventional radiology St. Anthony and Meml. Hosp., Michigan City,

1989—93; clin. asst. prof. radiology U. Ill., Chgo., 1990—2004; cons. radiologist Health Partners Medical Group, St. Francis, 2004—; others in field. Mem. Chinmaya Mission, Vishva Hindu Parishad. Fellow: Internat. Coll. Angiology, Am. Coll. Angiology, Am. Coll. Internat. Physicians; mem.: AMA, AmAm. Assn. Therapeutic and Interventional Neuroradiology, La Porte County Med. Soc., Telugu Assn. Greater Chgo., Chgo. Med. Soc., Ind. Med. Soc., Ill. Med. Soc., Ind. Assn. Physicians Indian Origin, India Med. Assn. N.W. Ind. (bd. dirs. 1999—2001), Am. Assn. Radiologists Indian Origins, Ind. Interventional Radiol. Assn., Tristate Telugu Assn., Indian Radiol. and Imaging Assn., Ind. Assn. Physicians from India, Soc. Magnetic Resonance in Medicine, Soc. Cardiovascular and Interventional Radiology, Soc. Magnetic Resonance Imaging, Am. Coll. Healthcare Execs., Am. Telugu Assn., Am. Soc. Head and Neck Radiology, Am. Coll. Emergency Physicians, Am. Diabetes Assn., Am. Assn. Physicians of Indian Origin, Am. Roentgen Ray Soc., Telugu Assn., Radiol. Soc. N.Am., Am. Assn. Andhra Brahmins, Internat. Soc. Krishna Consciousness, Pi Alpha Alpha. Republican. Home: 1481 Nelson Dr Chesterton IN 46304-3393 Office: Michigan City Radiologists Inc 8865 W 400 N Ste 115 Michigan City IN 46360-9223 Office Phone: 219-872-7268.

**MOTIPALLI, V. V. SATISH KUMAR,** mechanical engineer, researcher; s. Gopala Krishna Murthy and Sarada Devi Motipalli; m. Sunitha Kopparthi, Aug. 21, 2002. B of Engring. in Mech. Engring., SIR C. R. Reddy Coll. of Engring., Eluru, Andhra Pradesh, India, 2000; M in Mech. and Nuc. Engring., Kans. State U., Manhattan, 2002, D in Mech. and Nuc. Engring., 2003, M of Software Engring., 2006. Grad. rsch. asst. Kans. State U., Manhattan, 2001—04, grad. tchg. asst., 2001—04; grad. rsch. intern Advanced Mfg. Inst., Manhattan, Kans., 2004—05; summer rsch. asst. Kans. State U., Manhattan, 2005—05, grad. rsch. asst. Nat. Gas Machinery Lab., Manhattan, Kans., 2005—. Reviewer 24th ASME Internat. Design Engring. Tech. Conf., Salt Lake City, 2004, session co-chair, 04; reviewer 25th ASME Internat. Design Engring. Tech. Conf., Long Beach, Calif., 2005, 26th ASME Internat. Design Engring. Tech. Conf., Phila., 2006. Contbr. papers to sci. confs., articles to profl. jours. Recipient Mech. and Nuc. Engring. Outstanding TA/Instr. award, Kans. State U., 2004; Best Rsch. Paper scholarship, Kans. Biosci. Orgn., 2006. Mem.: ASME, Indian Student Assn., Soc. for Appreciation of Bharatiya Arts and Culture (corr.; sec. 2002—03). Avocations: badminton, tennis, listening to music. Office: Kans State Univ 3014 Rathbone Hall Manhattan KS 66506 Office Phone: 785-532-2620.

**MOTL, LUBOS,** physics professor, researcher; b. Pilsen, Czech Republic, Dec. 5, 1973; s. Miloslav Motl and Jana Motlova. Magister, Charles U., Prague, 1997; PhD, Rutgers U., New Brunswick, N.J., 2001. Ist fellow Harvard U., Cambridge, Mass., 2001—04, asst. prof., 2004—. Translator: The Elegant Universe; author: We grow linear algebra; contbr. to weblogs, articles to profl. jours. Recipient 1307 Hist. Signet of the City of Pilsen, City of Pilsen, 1992, Jaroslav Heyrovsky award, Charles U., 1997, Rutgers U. Grad. Sch. Rsch. award, Rutgers U., 2002, Richard J. Plano Dissertation prize, 2002. Avocation: music. Office: Harvard Univ 17 Oxford St Cambridge MA 02138 Office Phone: 617-384-9488. Home Fax: 801-454-1858; Office Fax: 617-496-0110. E-mail: motl@feynman.harvard.edu.

**MOTLEY, JOHN PAUL,** psychiatrist, consultant; b. Carbondale, Pa., July 5, 1927; s. Joseph Adrian and Lillian (McCormick) M.; BS, Georgetown U., 1951; MD, Hahnemann Med. Coll., Phila., 1955; children: Marianne, Patricia, Kathleen, John Paul, Elizabeth, Joseph A. III, Grace, Michael. Intern, Hahnemann Med. Coll. Hosp., Phila. 1955-56; resident in psychiatry Inst. of Living, Hartford, Conn., 1956-59; practice medicine specializing in psychiatry, Point Pleasant, N.J., 1961—; mem. staff Jersey Shore Med. Ctr., 1961-72, chief of psychiatry, 1970-72; mem. staff Point Pleasant Hosp., 1961—, chief of psychiatry, 1961—; cons. in forensic psychiatry to various cts. and agys. Served with U.S. Army, 1944-47, ETO. Diplomate Am. Bd. Psychiatry and Neurology. Fellow Am. Psychiat. Assn. (disting. life); mem. AMA, Speakslake Golf Club. Republican. Roman Catholic. Office: 1738 Hwy 35 D-61 Wall NJ 07719 Office Phone: 732-449-7961.

**MOTOC, MIHNEA IOAN,** international organization official; b. Bucharest, Nov. 11, 1960; married; 1 child. JD, U. Bucharest Sch. of Law; LLM in Pub. Internat. and Comparative Law, George Washington U., Washington, DC; post-graduate studies in Pub. and Private Internat. Law, Nice U., France. Worked as magistrate; dir.-gen. of the Directorate General European and Euro-Atlantic Orgns.; joined Ministry Foreign Affairs, 1991, dep. dir., human rights dept., 1994, dir., European Union dept., 1996; appointed amb. Romania to the Netherlands and permanent rep. to the Organization for Prohibition of Chemical Weapons, 1999; state sec. European Integration and Multilateral Affairs, 2001—03; permanent rep. of Romania UN, NY, 2003—. Participated in political treaty talks with neighbouring countries, 1992—96; permanent secretariat Inter-ministerial Committee for European Integration, 1996—98; mem. Internat. Humanitarian Fact Finding Commn., 1996—2000; vice-chmn. Exec. Coun. of the Orgn. for Prohibition of Chemical Weapons, 2000; pres. of the Inter-departmental Commn. for Romania's Accession to NATO, 01; nat. coordinator South-East Europe Stability Pact, 2001; pres. Nat. Security Authority, 2001, 02; head of the Romanian Delegation for Accession Talks to NATO, 03; headed Romanian delegations to international meetings of the United Nations, Council of Europe, OSCE and the European Union. Office: UN Hdqs First Ave at 46th St New York NY 10017*

**MOTRONI, HECTOR JOHN,** manufacturing executive; b. Havana, Cuba, Dec. 2, 1943; came to U.S., 1956; s. Marco Antonio and Lilia Ines (Suarez) M.; m. Myra Helene Egan, Aug. 9, 1969; children: Marcus Alan, Melissa Aimee. BA, Dartmouth Coll., 1966, BE, 1967, ME, 1968. Engr. USPHS, Bethesda, Md., 1969-71; various positions Xerox Corp., Stamford, Conn., 1971-99, corp. sr. v.p., chief staff officer, 1999—2002, corp. sr. v.p., chief staff and ethics officer, 2003—. Bd. dirs. Prep for Prep. Trustee Temple Israel, Westport, Conn., 1981-84; bd. adv. Outward Bound USA, 1998; bd. dirs. Nat. Action Coun. Minorities in Engring., Horizons at Green Farms Acad., 2005; chmn. bd. trustees Xerox Polit. Action Com., 2001—. Named Hispanic Achiever of Yr., Hispanic Corp. Achievers, 1997; named one of 50 Most Important Hispanics in Bus. and Tech., Hispanic Engrs. and Info. Tech. Mag., 2003, 2004, 2005, 2006, 25 Top Hispanic Execs., Hispanic Trends Mag., 2005, 100 Most Important Hispanics of 2005, Hispanic Bus. Mag.; recipient Eagle award, Nat. Eagle Inst., 1997. Mem. Nat. Policy Assn. (bd. dirs., chmn. com. New Am. realities 1996-2002), Dartmouth Soc. Engrs. (pres. 1977-85), Dartmouth Coll. Alumni Coun. (chmn. communications 1983-88), Coun. of the Ams. (adv. bd. 1983-89), Forum for World Affairs (bd. dirs. 1996-2001). Avocation: running. Office: Xerox Corp PO Box 1600 Stamford CT 06904-1600

**MOTSENBOCKER, REX ALAN,** construction company executive; b. Norman, Okla., Dec. 14, 1962; s. Rex Albert and Nondace Nadine (Bonner) M.; m. Karla Doreen Miller, Nov. 14, 1992. BS in BA, Calif. State U., Sacramento, 1984; BS in Constrn. Engring., Ariz. State U., 1986; MBA in Fin. magna cum laude, Western Internat. U., Phoenix, 1994; postgrad., So. Calif. U., Newport, 1994—. Cert. fin. cons. Project coord. Tibshraeny Bros., Mesa, Ariz., 1986; project mgr. Joe E. Woods, Tempe, Ariz., 1986-87; project engr. Sundt Corp., Phoenix, 1987—; pres. Master Investments, Phoenix, 1994—; CFO Master Builders Devel., LLC, Las Vegas, Nev., 1994—; mgr. CFO Remington Estates Devel. L.L.C., Phoenix, 1995—. Bd. dirs. bullion Recovery Sys., Inc., Phoenix. Author: Financial Aspects of Investing in Mexico, 1994. Team leader Senator McCain Re-election Campaign, Phoenix, 1992-94; project dir. Christmas in April, Phoenix, 1989-93. Mem. Project Mgrs. Inst. (v.p. membership 1990—), Am. Mgrs. Assn., Constrn. Mgmt. Assn., Phoenix C. of C., Nat. Asbestoc Council, Ariz. State U. Alumni Assn. (v.p. bd. 1994—), Delta Mu Delta (v.p. 1993—). Republican. Avocations: triathlons, singing. Home: 15833 N 7th Dr Phoenix AZ 85023-4435

**MOTSETT, CHARLES BOURKE,** sales, marketing and leadership executive; b. Peoria, Ill., Jan. 13, 1949; s. William James and Matilda (Robb) M.; m. Mary T. Werner, Aug. 26, 1972; children: Jon Bourke, Jill Suzanne, Brian Werner. BA in Polit. Sci., Econs. and Mktg., U. So. Fla., 1974. Product support mktg. analyst Caterpillar Tractor Co., 1974-75; parts and service sales rep. Caterpillar Ams. Co., Mexico City, 1976-79; product support rep. Caterpillar Tractor Co., Vancouver, B.C., Can., 1979-80, group prodn. mgr. remanufactured products Peoria, 1981-84, dist. mgr. parts and service sales Jacksonville, Fla., 1984-85; v.p. sales, customer svc. and mktg. Multi Media Productions of Am., Inc., Jacksonville, 1985-86; v.p. sales and mktg. Consol. Indsl. Skills Corp., Jacksonville, 1987—, corp. officer, 1988-92; v.p. and gen. mgr. Ogden CISCO Inc., Jacksonville, 1992—94; v.p. sales and mktg. CompuTower Technologies Corp., Miami, 1994—95, Shred All, 1995—96; pres. and CEO Bus. Devel. Specialists, Inc. and the Alternative Bd., Jacksonville, 1996—2006. Participant Exec. Coach Summit, 2001, 02, 03, 04, 05; edtl. bd. Internat. Jour. Coaching Orgns. Author: If It Wasn't for the People...This Job Would Be Fun (Coaching for Buy-in and Results, 1998; co-author: How To Find a Qualified Corporate or Executive Coach, 2001; contbr. articles to profl. jours.; mem. editl. bd.: Internat. Jour. Coaching in Orgns. V.p. PTO, Dunlap, Ill., 1981—82; mem. adv. coun. Sch. Bd. Vocat. Edn., 1991—92; pres. bd. dirs. N.E. Fla. Jr. Achievement, Jr. Achievement Fla. First Coast, Inc.; vice chmn. St. Anthony's Ch., Vancouver, 1979—80; chmn. St. Jude Ch., Dunlap, 1982—83, Bishop Kenny H.S. PTO Polit. Action Com., 1989; pres. bd. dirs. Cath. Charities Housing Assn. Capt. U.S. Army, 1967—70. Decorated Silver Star, Air medal with V device, Bronze Star with V device and oak leaf cluster, Purple Heart with 2 oak leaf clusters, Army Commendation medal with V device, Good Conduct medal, Combat Infantryman's badge. Mem. ASTD, Internat. Coach Fedn., Internat. Consortium Coaching in Orgns. (founding mem.), Assn. Facilities Engring., Soc. Automotive Engrs., Am. Soc. Naval Engrs., Soc. Naval Architects and Marine Engrs., Am. Nuclear Soc., Assn. Nuclear Plant Engrs., U.S Army Spl. Forces Assn., Worldwide Assn. Bus. Coaches (bd. dir., chmn. credentialing com., exec. coach summit 2002-03), Spl. Ops. Assn., Internat. Coach Fedn., Propellor Club. Republican. Roman Catholic. Avocations: scuba diving, sailing, reading, golf. Home: 4457 Barrington Oaks Dr Jacksonville FL 32257-5092 Office Phone: 904-730-0654. Personal E-mail: cork130@comcast.net.

**MOTT, FREDERICK B., JR.,** publishing executive; b. Miami, 1947; m. Shirlene Mott; children: Jaimie, Alissa. B. in Acctg., Fla. State U., 1972. CPA Deloitte & Touche LLP; with Knight Ridder, 1979—2005; gen. mgr. Tallahassee Democrat, Fla., 1984—91; pub. Post-Tribune, Gary, Ind., 1991—95; pres., pub. The State, Columbia, SC, 1995—2002; pres., gen. mgr. Philadelphia Newspapers Inc., 2002—05; pub., CEO ANG Newspapers, Oakland, Calif., 2006—. Avocations: golf, saltwater fishing. Office: ANG Newspapers 401 13st St Oakland CA 94612*

**MOTT, PEGGY LAVERNE,** sociologist, educator; b. Stephenville, Tex., Mar. 23, 1930; d. Artemis Victor Dorris and Tempie Pearl (Price) Hickman; m. J.D. Mott, Sept. 11, 1947 (dec. Apr. 1988); children: Kelly A. Wilcoxson, Kimberly S. Mott. BA, Southwest Tex. State U., 1980, MA, 1982. Cert. instr. ceramic arts Nat. Ceramic Art Inst., 1972. Instr. ceramics Arts & Crafts Ctr. Lackland AFB, San Antonio, 1969-72, dir. sales Arts & Crafts Ctr., 1972-77; asst. instr. S.W. Tex. State U., San Marcos, 1980-82; instr. sociology Palo Alto Coll., San Antonio, 1991—. Author: Screaming Silences, 1994, (poem) Concho River Rev., 1993, Inkwell Echos, 1989-95, Lucidity, The T.O.P. Hwupp, 1994-95, Hwap, Patchwork Poems, 1995; co-author: Activities, Field Studies for Students. Vol. coord. Fisher Houses, Inc., Lackland AFB, 1992—; parliamentarian Artistic Expressions, 1996—. Named Vol. of Month, USAF, 1976, 77, 78, Vol. of Quarter, 1976, 77, 78, 84, Vol. of Yr., 1980. Mem. Internat. Soc. Poets, Clipper Ship Poets, San Antonio Poets Assn. (v.p. 1991-92, pres. 1992-93, Poet Laureate 1994-95), San Antonio Ethnic Arts Soc., San Antonio Poetry Festival. Avocations: reading, writing, needlecrafts. Home: 1307 Canyon Ridge Dr San Antonio TX 78227-1727 E-mail: profpurple@msn.com.

**MOTT, RANDALL D. (RANDY MOTT),** computer company executive; b. 1956; BS in Math., U. Ark., Fayetteville, 1978. Various positions Wal-Mart Stores, Inc., 1978—94, sr. v.p., chief info. officer, 1994—97, mem. exec. com., 1997; sr. v.p., chief info. officer Dell, Inc., Round Rock, Tex., 2000—05; exec. v.p., chief info. officer Hewlett-Packard Co., Palo Alto, Calif., 2005—. Mem. Pres. Info. Tech. Adv. Com., 2003—. Named Chief Info. Officer of Yr., Info. Week mag., 1997, Disting. Alumni, Fulbright Coll. Alumni Acad., 2005. Office: Hewlett-Packard Co 3000 Hanover St Palo Alto CA 94304*

**MOTT, RODNEY B.,** metal products executive; BS in Indsl. Engring., Northeastern U., 1974; MSc in Mgmt., Trenton State Coll., 1978. Various mgmt. positions US Steel, Fairless Hills, Pa., 1974—86; supt. ops. Lone Star Steel, 1986—88; v.p., gen. mgr. South Carolina plant, Arkansas plant, Crawfordsville plant Nucor Steel, 1988—2000; pres., CEO Pechiney Rolled Products, 2000—01, Internat. Steel Group, Richfield, Ohio, 2002—05; cons. Tricap Mgmt. Ltd.; pres, CEO Steleco Inc., Hamilton, Ont., 2006—. Named Mgr. of Yr., New Steel Mag., 1995. Mem.: Am. Iron and Steel Engrs. (pres. 1998). Office: Stelco Inc PO Box 2030 Hamilton ON L8N 3T1 Canada*

**MOTT, STEWART RAWLINGS,** food products executive, political organization worker; b. Flint, Mich., Dec. 4, 1937; s. Charles Stewart and Ruth (Rawlings) M.; m. Kappy Wells, Oct. 13, 1979 (div. Mar. 1999); 1 child, Samuel Apple Axle. BS in Bus. Adminstrn, Columbia, 1961, BA in Comparative Lit, 1961, postgrad. English lit., 1961-62. Exec. trainee various cos., 1956-63; English instr. Eastern Mich. U., 1963-64; corp. dir. U.S. Sugar Corp., Clewiston, Fla., 1965—98. Investor various diversified cos., 1968—. Founder Flint Cmty. Planned Parenthood, 1963; pres. S.R. Mott Charitable Trust, 1968—; pres., founder Spectemur Agendo, N.Y.C. and Flint, 1965—; bd. dirs. Fund For Peace, N.Y.C. 1967-90, Nat. Com. for Effective Congress, N.Y.C., 1968-, Planned Parenthood Fedn. Am., 1964-81, Am. Commn. on U.S.-Soviet Rels., 1977-92, Citizens Research Found., 1977-97, Ams. for Dem. Action, 1978-90, Friends of Family Planning, 1979-84, Voters for Choice, 1979-89; bd. dirs., founder Fund Constl. Govt., 1974-; bd. dirs. Population Action Council, 1978-82; maj. donor McCarthy, McGovern, Anderson campaigns. Mem. Phi Beta Kappa. At age 18 I realized that two problems confront planet earth that dwarf and aggravate all conventional problems: namely the threat of nuclear war and the continuing worldwide population explosion. Coming to grips with these realities, I decided to dedicate my life to help find solutions to these two problems through public service in philanthropy and politics.

**MOTT, THOMAS CHARLES,** science educator; b. Chgo., May 9, 1946; s. Joseph August and Margaret Ann Mott; m. Pamela Joyce Pindras (dec.); children: Thomas Charles, Christine Ann; m. Peggy Ann Deichstetter, June 25, 1988. BS in Edn., No. Ill. U., DeKalb, 1967; MS in Tchg. Physics, Roosevelt U., Chgo., 1972; postgrad., U. Mich., Ann Arbor, 1981—83, Rochester U., N.Y. Cert. tchr. Ill. Tchr. biology, phys. sci. and physics Glenbard East H.S., Lombard, Ill., 1967—2001. Roundtable commr. Boy Scouts Am., DuPage County, Ill., 1984—87, asst. dist. commr., 1981—84, mem. troop com. Glen Ellyn, Ill., 1983—2000, Webelos leader, 1982—83. Named Scouter of the Yr., DuPage Area coun. Boy Scouts Am., 1985; recipient Dist. Award of Merit, Chanonee dist. Boy Scouts Am., 1986. Mem.: Ill. Sci. Tchrs. Assn. (exec. bd. 1978—79), Ill. Assn. Biology Tchrs. (pres. 1976—77), Nat. Assn. Biology Tchrs. (conv. com. 1978). Avocations: scuba diving, fishing, camping, travel. Home: 4N610 Wescot Ln West Chicago IL 60185

**MOTTELSON, BEN ROY,** physicist; b. Chgo., July 9, 1926; naturalized Danish citizen, 1971. s. Goodman and Georgia (Blum) M.; m. Nancy Jane Reno, 1948 (dec. 1975); 3 children; m. Britta Marger Siegumfeldt, 1983. BSc, Purdue U., 1947; PhD, Harvard U., 1950; degree (hon.), Purdue U., U. Heidelberg, Fed. Republic Germany, Lund U., Sweden, Liverpool U., Eng. Sheldon traveling fellow Inst. Theoretical Physics, Copenhagen, 1950—51, U.S. AEC fellow, 1951—53; with theoretical study group CERN, Copenhagen, 1953—57; prof. Nordic Inst. for Theoretical Atomic Physics, Copenhagen, 1957—; dir. European ctr. Theoretical Studies in Nuc. Physics and Related Areas, Trento, Italy, 1980—87. Physicist Neils Bohr Inst., Copenhagen; bd. dir. Nordita; vis. prof. U. Calif., Berkeley, 1959, Berkeley, 84; adj.

prof. Niels Bohr Inst., Copenhagen, 1994; Feshbach lectureship, 96. Author: Nuclear Structure, vol. 1, 1969, vol. 2 (with A. Bohr), 1975; numerous other publications in field. Recipient Nobel prize for physics, 1975. Mem.: Norwegian Acad. of Sci. and Letters, Polish Acad. of Sci., Kroatian Acad. Sci. (fgn. assoc.), Finnish Soc. Sci. and Letters, European Acad. of Arts, Sci., and Letters, Kgl. Fys. Graf, Lund, Sweden, Am. Acad. Arts and Letters, Royal Dan. Acad. Sci. and Letters, Nat. Acad. Sci. (fgn. assoc.). Address: NORDITA and The Niels Bohr Inst Blegdamsvej 17 DK-2100 Copenhagen Denmark Business E-Mail: mottelson@nordita.dk.*

**MOTTER, THOMAS FRANKLIN,** medical products executive; b. Modesto, Calif., June 27, 1948; s. Thomas Dean and Beverley June (Mosier) M.; m. Wanda Lenice Parker, Feb. 9, 1968 (div. Jan. 1972); children: Eric Franklin (dec.), Katrina Lenice; m. Jerry Ann Averill, Oct. 24, 1976; children: Heidi Marika, Courtney Averill. AA, Cabrillo Jr. Coll., Santa Cruz, Calif., 1968; BA, Stephens Coll., 1970; MBA, Pepperdine U., 1975. Social worker County of Santa Cruz and Amador, 1970-77; nat. dir. mktg. Humphrey Instruments/SmithKline, San Leandro, Calif., 1978-88; internat. gen. mgr. HGM Med. Lasers, Salt Lake City, 1988-89; pres., CEO Paradigm Med. Industries Inc., Salt Lake City, 1989—. Mem. Nat. Ski Patrol, Stockton, 1973-79; v.p. Sandy (Utah) Pony Baseball, 1994-95; coach Kearns (Utah) Am. Legion Baseball, 1995-96. Capt. U.S. Army, 1970-76. Named Mem. Nat. Adult Baseball Assn. (mem. Nat. Championship team), Am. Legion, Sons of the Am. Revolution Utah State Chpt., Knight Orthodox Order of the Knights of the Hosp. of St. John of Jerusalem. Episcopalian. Avocations: skiing, hardball baseball, coaching, fly fishing, hunting. Office: Paradigm Med Industries Inc 2355 S 1070 W Salt Lake City UT 84119-1552

**MOTTO, DAVID M.,** music educator, writer; b. Modesto, Calif., Aug. 24, 1964; s. Rodney E. and Freda A. Motto; m. Stephanie T. Railsback, Aug. 15, 1992. BA in Humanities, with high honors, U. of Calif., Berkeley, 1986. Lectr., electric bass San Francisco State U., San Francisco, 1996—; owner Molto Music Pub. Co., Oakland, Calif., 1999—; electric bass instr. Pvt. Tchg. Studio, 1985—; bassist: live performances and rec. sessions Various, 1985—. Clinician Am. String Tchrs. Assn., 2005, Nat. Flute Assn., 2004—05, Ind. Music Educators Assn., 2005, Tex. Music Educators Assn., 2005, Calif. State U. Summer Arts Program, Long Beach, Calif., 2000. Author: (book) Musician's Practice Planner; musician: (compact disc) Handsome Poets: Rebirth, Bill Meyer: Rooted, (audio recording) Keltia: The Dirty Linen Sampler, vol. 1, (compact disc) Jack Gates: New Geography, Jack Gates: Earth Messenger, Big Skin: Moon Over Tuesday, Big Skin: Sandancer; author: (book, with audio cd) Essential Sightreading Studies for Electric Bass, volume 1, Essential Sightreading Studies for Electric Bass, volume 2, Essential Sightreading Studies for Electric Bass, volume 3; software developer (webware) Musician's Online Practice Planner; musician: (compact disc) Phoenyx: Keepers of the Flame, Jessie Turner: Here and There. Mem.: Nat. Assn. of Music Merchants, Retail Print Music Dealers Assn., Music Educators Nat. Conf., String Industry Coun. of Am. String Tchrs. Assn., Internat. Assn. of Jazz Edn., NARAS (voting mem.). Avocations: swimming, canoeing, hiking. Office: San Francisco State Univ SMD 1600 Holloway Ave San Francisco CA 94132-1740 Personal E-mail: david@moltomusic.com.

**MOTTO, JEROME ARTHUR,** psychiatrist, educator; b. Kansas City, Mo., Oct. 16, 1921; MD, U. Calif., San Francisco, 1951. Diplomate Am. Bd. Neurology and Psychiatry. Intern San Francisco Gen. Hosp., 1951-52; resident Johns Hopkins Hosp., Balt., 1952-55; sr. resident U. Calif., San Francisco, 1955-56, from instr. to prof., 1956—91, prof. emeritus, 1991—. Pres. Am. Assn. Suicidology, 1972—73; sec. gen. Internat. Assn. Suicide Prevention, 1977-93. Contbr. articles to profl. jours. With AUS, 1942-46, ETO. Fellow: Am. Psychiatric Assn. (life; disting. fellow).

**MOTTOLA, EMIL,** physicist, researcher; b. Bronx, Oct. 13, 1953; s. Emil Anthony and Sylvia Mottola; m. Sharon Marie Krieg, Apr. 29, 1989; 1 child, Emil Joseph. PhD, Columbia U., NYC, 1979. Mem. Inst. Advanced Study, Princeton, NJ, 1979—82; rsch. assoc. Inst. Theoretical Physics, U. Calif., Santa Barbara, 1982—86; staff mem. Los Alamos Nat. Lab., N.Mex., 1986—. Contbr. articles to profl. jours. Mem.: Am. Phys. Soc. (life), Phi Beta Kappa (life). Home: 20 Vista Herrera Santa Fe NM 87506 Office: Los Alamos National Laboratory Theoretical Division T-8 MS B285 Los Alamos NM 87545 Office Phone: 505-667-7646. Office Fax: 505-665-3700.

**MOTTOLA, TOMMY (THOMAS D. MOTTOLA),** recording industry executive; b. Bronx, NY, July 14, 1949; m. Lisa Clark, 1971 (div. 1990); 2 children; m. Mariah Carey, June 5, 1993 (div. Mar. 5, 1998); m. Thalía Sodi, Dec. 2, 2000. Attended, Hofstra U. Pres., CEO Sony Music Entertainment Inc, NYC, chmn., CEO, 1998—2003; pres. Casablanca Records, 2004—.

**MOTTS, WARREN EARL,** museum director; b. Bremen, Ohio, Nov. 10, 1940; s. Wilbur Ernest and Mabel Marie Motts; m. Daisy Nell Blair, July 1, 1966; children: Wayne Earl, Lori Lynn. M in photography, Profl. Photographers of Am., 1977; MS in photography, Brooks Inst. Sch. of Profl. Photography, 1990; M, China, 1990, Mexico, 1990. Photo lab tech. Battelle Meml. Inst., Columbus, Ohio, 1960—62; med. photographer Ohio State Hosp., Columbus 1962—64; photographer Columbus and Southern Electric, Columbus, 1964—67; commercial photographer Columbus Art, Columbus, 1967—69; v.p. Moor Photography, Columbus, 1969—72; pres., owner Motts Photographic Ctr., Columbus, 1972—97; founder, dir. Motts Mil. Mus., Groveport, Ohio, 1988—. Pres. Profl. Photo of Am., Atlanta, 1990—91, Mil. Vets Edn., Columbus, Ohio, 1999—2000; bd. dirs. Veterans Meml., Columbus, 2001—; lectr. Mathew Brady: Civil War Photographer, 1994. Creator: (films) American Freedom Train, 1976; Gettysburg: A Portrait in Red, Gray, and Blue; contbr. articles various profl. jours. Pres. Groveport Lions Club, Groveport, Ohio, 1999—2000, Columbus Civil War, Columbus, Ohio, 1967; chmn. of bd. Brice United Meth. Ch., Brice, Ohio, 1981—; 32nd Mason Masonic Order, Columbus, Ohio, 1981. With Ohio Nat. Guard, 1959—68. Named Communicator of Yr., Communicatings Arts, 1991; recipient Patriotic, Daughters of Am. Revolution, 1982, Dist. Svc. award, PP of Am., 1991. Mem.: Ohio Hist. Mus., Am. Mus. Assoc., Advance Assn. (life). Republican. Meth. Avocation: antiques. Office: Motts Mil Mus 5075 S Hamiton Rd Groveport OH 43125 Office Phone: 614-836-1500. Office Fax: 614-836-5110.

**MOTULSKY, ARNO GUNTHER,** internist, geneticist, educator; b. Fischhausen, Germany, July 5, 1923; arrived in U.S., 1941; s. Herman and Rena (Sass) Molton; m. Gretel C. Stern, Mar. 22, 1945; children: Judy, Harvey, Arlene. Student, Cen. YMCA Coll., Chgo., 1941—43, Yale U., 1943—44; BS, U. Ill., 1945, MD, 1947, DSc (hon.), 1982, MD (hon.), 1991. Diplomate Am. Bd. Internal Medicine, Am. Bd. Med. Genetics. Intern, fellow, resident Michael Reese Hosp., Chgo., 1947—51; staff mem. charge clin. investigation dept. hematology Army Med. Service Grad. Sch., Walter Reed Army Med. Ctr., Washington, 1952—53; research assoc. internal medicine George Washington U. Sch. Medicine, 1952—53; from instr. to assoc. prof. dept. medicine U. Wash. Sch. Medicine, Seattle, 1953—61, prof. medicine, prof. genetics, 1961—; head div. med. genetics, dir. genetics clinic Univ. Hosp., Seattle, 1959—89; dir. Ctr. for Inherited Diseases, Seattle, 1972—90. Attending physician Univ. Hosp., Seattle; cons. Pres.'s Commn. for Study of Ethical Problems in Medicine and Biomed. and Behavioral Rsch., 1979—83; cons. various coms. NRC, NIH, WHO, and others. Editor: Am. Jour. Human Genetics, 1965—75, Human Genetics, 1969—97. Follow Commonwealth Fund in human genetics, Univ. Coll., London, 1957—58, Ctr. Advanced Study in Behavorial Scis., Stanford U., 1976—77, Inst. Advanced Study, Berlin, 1984; scholar John and Mary Markle in med. sci., 1957—62. Fellow: AAAS, ACP; mem.: NAS, Am. Philos. Soc., Am. Acad. Arts and Scis., Inst. of Medicine, Am. Assn. Physicians, Am. Soc. Clin. Investigation, Am. Soc. Human Genetics, Western Soc. Clin. Rsch., Genetics Soc. Am., Am. Fedn. Clin. Rsch., Internat. Soc. Hematology. Home: 4347 53rd Ave NE Seattle WA 98105-4938 Office: U Wash Medicine and Genome Scis PO Box 357730 Seattle WA 98195-7730 Business E-Mail: agmot@u.washington.edu.

**MOTZ, DIANA GRIBBON,** federal judge; b. Washington, July 15, 1943; d. Daniel McNamara and Jane (Retzler) Gribbon; m. John Frederick Motz, Sept. 20, 1968; children: Catherine Jane, Daniel Gribbon. BA, Vassar Coll., 1965; LLB, U. Va., 1968. Bar: U.S. Dist. Ct. Md. 1969, U.S. Ct. Appeals (4th cir.) 1969, U.S. Supreme Ct. 1980. Assoc. Piper & Marbury, Balt., 1968—71; asst. atty. gen. State of Md., Balt., 1972—81, chief of litigation, 1981—86; ptnr. Frank, Bernstein, Conaway & Goldman, Balt., 1986—91; judge Md. Ct. of Special Appeals, 1991—94, U.S. Ct. Appeals (4th Cir.), 1994—. Mem.: ABA, Fed. Cts. Study Com., Lawyers Round Table, Md. Bar Found., Am. Bar Found., Am. Law Inst., Balt. City Bar Assn. (exec. com. 1988), Md. Bar Assn., Wranglers Law Club. Roman Catholic. Office: 920 US Courthouse 101 W Lombard St Ste 920 Baltimore MD 21201-2611

**MOTZ, JOHN FREDERICK,** federal judge; b. Balt., Dec. 30, 1942; s. John Eldered and Catherine (Grauel) M.; m. Diana Jane Gribbon, Sept. 20, 1968; children: Catherine Jane, Daniel Gribbon. BA, Princeton U., Conn., 1964; LLB, U. Va., 1967. Bar: Md. 1967, U.S. Ct. Appeals (4th cir.) 1968, U.S. Dist. Ct. Md. 1968. Law clk. to Hon. Harrison L. Winter U.S. Ct. Appeals (4th cir.), 1967-68; assoc. Venable, Baetjer & Howard, Balt., 1968-69; asst. U.S. atty. U.S. Atty.'s Office, Balt., 1969-71; assoc. Venable, Baetjer & Howard, Balt., 1971-75, ptnr., 1976-81; U.S. atty. U.S. Atty.'s Office, Balt., 1981-85; judge U.S. Dist. Ct. Md., Balt., 1985—, chief judge, 1994—2001. Trustees Friends Sch., Balt., 1970-77, 1981-88, Sheppard Pratt Hosp., 1987-97, 99—. Mem.: ABA, Am. Coll. Trial Lawyers (mem. bd. editors. Manual of Complex Litigation (4th), mem. Judicial Panel on Multidist. Litigation), Am. Law Inst., Am. Bar Found., Md. State Bar Assn. Republican. Mem. Soc. Of Friends. Office: US Dist Ct 101 W Lombard St Rm 510 Baltimore MD 21201-2605

**MOUAWAD, JAD,** reporter; Energy reporter NY Times. Office: NY Times 229 West 43rd St New York NY 10036 Office Phone: 212-556-8094. Office Fax: 212-556-1445. E-mail: jad@nytimes.com.*

**MOUCHARAFIEH, RAMZI CHARIF,** orthopedist, surgeon; b. Beirut, Dec. 1, 1959; s. Charif Hamid and Violette Richard Moucharafieh; m. Ruth Margret Jones, Dec. 24, 1992; children: Matthew Charif, Grace Ffion. BSc, Am. U. Beirut, 1976, MD, 1988. Cert. orthopaedics, hand and microvascular surgery Robert Jones and Agnus Hunt Orthopaedic Hosp., Bermingham, 1991. Prof. orthopaedics hand and microvascular surgery St George U. Hosp., Balamand U., Beirut, 1991—. Recipient JK Rose award, Robert Jones Orthopaedic Hosp., UK, 1990. Fellow: Am. Coll. Surgeons (life). Avocations: swimming, golf, fishing, soccer, tennis. Home: Cairo St Salamoun Bld 6th floor Beirut 113-5622 Lebanon Office: St Georges Univ Hosp Achrafieh Beirut 166378 Lebanon Office Phone: 009611575700. Home Fax: 009611738666; Office Fax: 009611582560. Business E-Mail: admin@stgeorgehospital.org.

**MOUGH, SCOTT THOMAS,** chemist; s. John Charles and Virginia Rose Mough; m. Rhonda Bloom, Aug. 26, 2000. BS in Chemistry, U. Pitts., 1997; postgrad., Georgetown U., 2001—. Chemist Aristech Chem. Corp., Pitts., 1997—99, RJ Lee Group, Inc., Monroeville, 2000—01. Auditor Aristech Chem. Corp., Pitts., 1998—99. Fellow, Achievement Rewards Coll. Scientists, 2003—05; Espensheid fellow, Georgetown U., 2002, Mary Louise Theodore scholar, U. Pitts., 1997. Mem.: Am. Crystallographic Assn., Am. Chem. Soc. Avocations: travel, swimming, tennis. Office: Georgetown U 37th and O St NW Washington DC 20057 Office Phone: 202-687-4353. Office Fax: 202-687-6209. Personal E-mail: stm6@georgetown.edu.

**MOUL, BRIAN E.,** music educator; b. Gettysburg, Pa., July 10, 1958; s. Henry Edgar and Betty Jane Moul; m. Anne Denney. BS in Music Edn., West Chester U., Pa., 1980. Instrumental music tchr. Easton (Md.) HS, 1980—81, Penn Wood HS, Lansdowne, Pa., 1981—84, Dover (Pa.) HS, 1984—92, Dover Sch. Dist., 1992—. Brass instr. Lancers Drum and Bugle Corps, Hanover, Pa., 1989—; pvt. trombone instr.; arranger band music and drum and bugle corps music. Treas. Emmanuel United Ch. of Christ, 1992—; mem. Phoenix Vocal Ensemble, York, Pa., 1991—2005, Wheatland Chorale, Lancaster, Pa., 2005—. Mem.: Internat. Trombone Assn., Pa. State Edn. Assn., Pa. Music Educators Assn., Music Educators Nat. Conf. Republican. Avocations: golf, singing, drum and bugle corps. Home: 3045 Brookfield Dr York PA 17404 Office: North Salem Elem Sch 5161 N Salem Church Rd Dover PA 17315 Office Phone: 717-292-3671 ext 346. Fax: 717-292-4388. E-mail: golfnband@suscom.net.

**MOUL, WILLIAM CHARLES,** lawyer; b. Columbus, Ohio, Jan. 12, 1940; s. Charles Emerson and Lillian Ann (Mackenbach) M.; m. Margine Ann Tessendorf, June 10, 1962; children: Gregory, Geoffrey. BA, Miami U., Oxford, Ohio, 1961; JD, Ohio State U., 1964. Bar: Ohio 1964, U.S. Dist. Ct. (so. dist.) Ohio 1965, U.S. Ct. Appeals (2d cir.) 1982, U.S. Ct. Appeals (6th cir.) 1984, U.S. Ct. Appeals (3d cir.) 1985. Assoc., ptnr. George, Greek, King, McMahon & McConnaughey, Columbus, 1964-79; ptnr. McConnaughey, Stradley, Mone & Moul, Columbus, 1979-81; ptnr.-in-charge Thompson, Hine & Flory, Columbus, 1981-89, exec. com., 1989-98. Chmn. Upper Arlington Civil Svc. Commn., Ohio, 1981-86. Mem. ABA, Ohio State Bar Assn. (labor sect. bd. dirs. 1983—), Columbus Bar Assn. (chmn. ethics com. 1980-82), Lawyers Club Columbus (pres. 1976-77), Athletic Club, Scioto Country Club, Wedgewood Country Club, Masons. Lutheran. Home: 2512 Danvers Ct Columbus OH 43220-2822 Office: Thompson Hine LLP 10 W Broad St Ste 700 Columbus OH 43215-3435 Office Phone: 614-469-3220. Business E-Mail: william.moul@thompsonhine.com.

**MOULAISON, HEATHER LEA,** librarian, educator; d. Nancy Rosalie Idoux and Robert L. Moulaison. MA in French, U. Ill., Urbana, 1997—2001; MSLS, U. Ill., Champaign, 2001—02. Lectr., dept. English U. Burgogne à Dijon, France, 1998—2000; instr. Soc. English Protection, Dijon, France, 1998—2000; instr., dept. French U. Ill., Urbana, 1997—2001; indexer, abstractor Rare Books and Spl. Collections Libr., U. Ill., Champaign, 2001; cataloging libr., asst. prof. full. sci. Mo State U., Springfield, 2002—05, mem. faculty, dept. modern and classical langs., 2003—04; cataloging/modern langs. libr. The Coll. of N.J., Ewing, 2005—. Part-time lectr. Rutgers Sch. Comm. and Libr. Studies, 2005, 06; translator, interpreter, radio announcer Autoroute Info Radio Sta., Le réseau des Autoroutes Paris-Rhin-Rhone, Dijon, France, 1999; bilingual svc. Burgundy Region's Registry for Digestive Cancers, U. Bourgogne à Dijon Med. Sch., France, 2000. Contbr. articles to profl. jours.; translator. Vol. Humane Soc., Springfield, Mo., 2002, NPR/PBS, Springfield, Mo., 2002; coord. Club de Cuentos Early Childhood Literacy Program, Springfield, Mo., 2002; mem., vol. Spay/Neuter Assistance Program, Springfield, Mo., 2004. Mem.: ALA, Online Audiovisual Catalogers, Assn. Coll. and Rsch. Librs., Mensa, Beta Phi Mu, Pi Delta Phi, Phi Beta Kappa. Avocations: travel, puzzles, kickboxing, yoga, ballet.

**MOULD, JEREMY RICHARD,** astronomer; b. Bristol, Eng., July 31, 1949; s. Michael Thomas and Sheila Patricia (Pickering Clarke) Mould; m. Joan Mary Milesi, Dec. 11, 1971; children: Helen, Kate. BSc with honors, U. Melbourne, Australia, 1971; PhD, Australian Nat. U., 1975. Rsch. fellow Royal Greenwich (Eng.) Obs., 1976; postdoctoral fellow Kitt Peak Nat. Obs., Tucson, 1976—78, asst. astronomer, 1980—82; Carnegie fellow Hale Obs., 1978—79; prof. Calif. Inst. Tech., Pasadena, 1982—93, exec. officer for astronomy, 1987—90; prof. Australian Nat. U., Canberra, 1993—2001; dir. Mt. Stromlo & Siding Obs., Weston, Australia, 1993—2001, Nat. Optical Astronomy Obs., Tucson, 2001—. Mem. Anglo Australian Telescope Bd., 1993—2001, chair, 1999; mem. Australia Telescope Steering Com., 1995—2000; mem. space sci. adv. com. NASA. Mem.: Australian Acad. Sci., Assn. Univ. Rsch. Astronomy (bd. dirs. 1997—2001), Astron. Soc. Pacific, Astron. Soc. Australia, Am. Astron. Soc. Office: NOAO Mail Stop DODP 950 N Cherry Ave Tucson AZ 85726-6732 Business E-Mail: jmould@noao.edu.

**MOULDER, RETHA RAY,** retired librarian, retired media specialist, freelance/self-employed educational consultant; b. Shelbyville, Tenn., May 31, 1943; d. Dolphus and Louise (Shearin) Knox; m. William Moulder, Aug.

17, 1967; children: Marion Moulder Soward, Lou Lynn. BS in Elem. Edn. and Social Sci., Mid. Tenn. State U., 1964, MA in Curriculum and Instrn., 1967, postgrad., 1983-84, Vol. State U., 1983, Tex. Women's U., 1992. Tchr. Tullahoma (Tenn.) City Schs., 1964-65, Shelbyville City Schs., 1965-67; tchr., libr. Ft. Benning (Ga.) Dependent Schs., 1968, 69-71; curriculum coord., dir. reading lab., team leader Suffolk (Va.) City Schs., 1971-74; tchr. reading Fairfax County Pub. Schs., Fairfax, Va., 1974-75; asst. tchr. to learning disabled, tchr. lang. arts Ft. Knox (Ky.) Dependent Schs., 1975-77; tchr. Baumholder Elem. Sch., Germany, 1978-80; elem. tchr. Grace Luth. Sch., Huntsville, Ala., 1980-82; libr., elem. tchr. St. Paul Christian Acad., Nashville, 1982-84; tchr. Mt. Auburn Elem. Sch., Dallas, 1985-89, Kramer Elem. Sch., 1989—99; reading specialist Dallas Reading Ctrl., 1989—2004, ret., 2004; pvt. practice cons. Richardson, Tex., 2005—. Ednl. cons. Retha's Enterprise. Named Tchr. of Yr., Mt. Auburn Elem. Sch., 1989. Mem. ALA, Tex. Libr. Assn., Tex. Storytelling Assn., Dallas County Libr. Assn., U.S. Golf Assn., Canyon Creek Country Club, Delta Rho Avocations: golf, reading, bicycling, crafts, sewing. E-mail: rrmbirdie@comcast.net.

**MOULDER, T. EARLINE,** musician; b. Buffalo, Mo., Oct. 11; d. Earl Young and Ruby M. (Phillipot) M.; m. R. David Plank, Dec. 21, 1980; children: Jeannine Stanton, Jon Stanton, Timothy Stanton. AB in Biology and French, Drury Univ., 1973; studied piano with Soulima Stravinsky, 1961; M in Music, Ind. U., 1963; D in Musical Arts, U. Kansas, 1991; pvt. organ study, Andre Marchal, Paris, France, 1971. Concert organist, US, Europe, Middle East, Australia, Eng., South Am., Wales, Ireland, 1964—; exec. editor Drury Coll. Mirror, Springfield, Mo., 1971-73; rschr. Am. U., Beirut, 1973; journalist U.S. Naval Res., Springfield and Treasure Island, Calif., 1975-77; chair organ dept. Drury U., Springfield, Mo., 1968—, univ. organist, 1991—. Translator, Profl. documents, 1990—; guest artists Liszt Acad. Music, Budapest, Hungary, 2006; lectr. in field. Author: Organ Works of Elsa Barraine, 1995, Music of Alice Jordan, 1998; composer organ composition The Crucifixion, 1995; musician (organ recital series) Queen's Golden Jubilee, London, Eng., 2002; contbr. articles to profl. jours. Charter mem. Nat. Mus. Am. Music, 1994—. Recipient Teaching fellow U. Kans., Drury Mirror award Rank I Mo. Coll. Newspaper Assn. Mem. Mortar Bd., Sigma Alpha Iota, Alpha Lambda Delta, Pi Delta Phi, Beta Beta Beta, Pi Kappa Lambda, Organ Hist. Soc., Am. Guild Organist. Home: 3563 E Linwood Dr Springfield MO 65809-2131 Office: Drury Univ 900 N Benton Ave Springfield MO 65802-3712 Address: 95 rue de Seine 75006 Paris France Office Phone: 417-873-7376. Personal E-mail: dplank@msn.com. Business E-Mail: emoulder@drury.edu.

**MOULDS, ERIC SHANNON,** professional football player; b. Lucedale, Miss., July 17, 1973; BS in Edn. Psychology, Miss. State U. Wide receiver, kickoff return Buffalo Bills, 1996—2006, Houston Texans, 2006—. Named to Pro-Bowl, 1998, 2000, 2002. Achievements include first round draft pick NFL, 1996. Office: Houston Texans Two Reliant Park Houston TX 77054

**MOULDS, JOHN F.,** judge; m. Elizabeth Fry, Aug. 29, 1964; children: Donald B., Gerald B. Student, Stanford U., 1955-58; BA with honors, Calif. State U., Sacramento, 1960; JD, U. Calif, Berkeley, 1963. Bar: U.S. Supreme Ct., U.S. Dist. Ct. (no. dist.) Calif., U.S. Dist. Ct. (ea. dist.) Calif. 1968, U.S. Ct. Claims 1982, U.S. Ct. Appeals (9th cir.) 1967, Calif. Rsch. analyst Calif. State Senate Fact-Finding Com. on Edn., 1960-61; adminstrv. asst. Senator Albert S. Rodda, Calif., 1961-63; staff atty. Calif. Rural Legal Assistance, Marysville, 1966-68, dir. atty. Marysville field office and Sacramento legis. adv. office, 1968-69; staff atty. Sacramento Legal Aid, 1968-69; ptnr. Blackmon, Isenberg & Moulds, 1969-85, Isenberg, Moulds & Hemmer, 1985; magistrate judge U.S. Dist. Ct. (ea. dist.) Calif., 1985—, chief magistrate jduge, 1988-97. Moot ct. and trial practice judge U.C. Davis Law Sch., 1975—, U. of Pacific McGeorge Coll. Law, 1985—; part-time U.S. magistrate judge U.S. Dist. Ct. (ea. dist.) Calif., 1983-85; mem. 9th Cir. Capital Case Com., 1992—, U.S. Jud. Conf. Com. on the Magistrate Judge Sys., 1992—, Adv. Com. to the Magistrate Judges' Divsn. Adminstv. Office of U.S. Jud. Conf., 1989—. Author: (with others) Review of California Code Legislation, 1965, Welfare Recipients' Handbook, 1967; editor: Ninth Circuit Capital Punishment Handbook, 1991. Atty. Sacramento Singlemen's Self-Help Ctr., 1969-74; active Sacramento Human Relations Commn., 1969-75, chair, 1974-75; active community support orgn. U. Calif. at Davis Law Sch., 1971—; mem., atty. Sacramento Community Coalition for Media Change, 1972-75; bd. dirs. Sacramento Country Day Sch., 1982-90, Sacramento Pub. Libr. Found., 1985-87; active various polit. orgns. and campaigns, 1960-82. Mem. ABA, Fed. Bar Assn., Nat. Coun. Magistrates (cir. 1986-88, treas. 1988-89, 2d v.p. 1989-90, 1st v.p. 1990-91), Fed. Magistrate Judges Assn. (pres.-elect 1991, pres. 1992-93), Calif. State-Fed. Jud. Coun. Conf. (panelist capital habeas corpus litigation 1992), Fed. Jud. Ctr. Training Conf. for U.S. Magistrate Judges (panel leader 1993), Milton L. Schwartz Inns of Ct. Office: 8240 US Courthouse 501 First St 16th Fl Ste 1640 Sacramento CA 95814-7300

**MOULDS, WILLIAM J.,** retired aeronautical engineer; b. Newton, Kans., Mar. 7, 1933; s. William J. and Edith M. (Cox) Moulds; m. Myra Teresa Cummins, Dec. 28, 1955; children: Michael J., Robert W., Barbara L., Anne T. Moulds-Laughlin, Patrick L., Margaret L. Moulds-Vittitow. BSME, U. N.Mex., 1957; MSME, N.Mex. State U., 1970. Registered profl. engr., N.Mex. Rsch. engr. rsch. lab. Allis-Chalmers, Cin., 1956—57; supr. aero. engr. Air Force Spl. Weapons Ctr., Albuquerque, 1958—63; sr. aero. rsch. engr. Air Force Weapons Lab., Albuquerque, 1963—72, theoretical rsch. engr., 1972—79, chief tech. svcs. divsn., staff rsch. engr. to comdr., 1979—89; ret., 1989. Contbr. articles to profl. jours.; patentee in field. Vol. Barrett House; founder, 1st pres. U. N.Mex. Sch. Engring Alumni Assn.; bd. dirs. N.Mex. State Bd. Registration for Profl. Engrs. and Land Surveyors, 1990—95, chmn. com. on rules, regulations and statues, 1992; com. mem. Barrett Found. Named to Sociedad de Ingenieros as Ingeniero Eminente, New Mex. State U., 1993; recipient Honor award, U. N.Mex. Sch. Engring., 2000. Republican. Roman Catholic. Home: 1401 Cardenas NE Albuquerque NM 87110 6623

**MOULITSAS ZÚNIGA, MARKOS,** former military officer, blog writer; b. Chgo., Sept. 11, 1971; married; 1 child. B in Philosophy, Polit. Sci. and Journalism, Northern Ill. U.; JD, Boston U. Sch. Law. writer dailykos.com, 2002—. Former cons.; writer The Guardian, 2005; co-founder SB Nation (Sport Blog Nation), SportsBlogs, Inc. Writer, performer (several piano compositions); co-author: Crashing the Gate: Netroots, Grassroots, and the Rise of People Powered Politics, 2006. MLRS/Lance Fire Direction Specialist (artillery) U.S. Army, 1989—92. Avocations: music, piano.*

**MOULTHROP, REBECCA LEE STILPHEN,** retired elementary school educator; b. Lubbock, Tex., Mar. 5, 1944; d. Lee Edward and Geraldine (Lansford) Stilphen; m. John Stephen Martin Moulthrop, June 1967 (div. 1968); 1 child, Paul Martin. BS in edn., U. New Mex., 1966; MS in reading edn., Calif. State U., Fullerton, 1971; postgrad., U. LaVerne. Elem. tchr. Arnold Heights Elem. Sch., Moreno Valley, Calif., 1966-67, Hawthorn Elem. Sch., El Monte, Calif., 1968-69; chap. I reading specialist Posey Elem. Sch., Lubbock, 1971-72; elem. tchr. Arnold Heights Elem. Sch., Moreno Valley, 1972-74, Sunnymead Elem. Sch., Moreno Valley, 1974-80, Moreno Elem. Sch., Moreno Valley, 1980-88; chap. I program coord. Edgemont Elem. Sch., Moreno Valley, 1988-91; elem. tchr. Sunnymeadows Elem. Sch., Moreno Valley, 1991—2005, ret., 2005. Assertive discipline coach Moreno Valley (Calif.) Unified Sch. Dist., 1979-85, mentor/tchr., 1985-89, adminstrm. designee/trainee, 1988-95; effective tchg/supervision coach Riverside (Calif.) County Sch. Office, 1984-87. Recipient Tchr. of Yr., Moreno Valley Unified Sch. Dist., 2005. Mem. NEA, Calif. Reading Assn., Internat. Reading Assn., Reading Edn. Guild, Delta Kappa Gamma, Phi Delta Kappa. Avocations: travel, dance, painting. Home: 23820 Ironwood Ave Unit 56 Moreno Valley CA 92557-8109

**MOULTON, EDWARD QUENTIN,** civil engineer, educator; b. Kalamazoo, Mich., Nov. 16, 1926; s. Burt Frederick and Esther (Fairchild) M.; m. Joy Wade, Jan. 2, 1954; children: Jennifer Fairchild, Charles Wade, David

Frederick II, Alison Joy. BS, Mich. State U., 1947; MS, La. State U., 1948; PhD, U. Calif., Berkeley, 1956; DSc (hon.), Wittenberg U., 1980; LLD (hon.), Xavier U., 1983, Wilmington Coll., 1983. Registered profl. engr., Ohio. Instr. civil engring Mich. State U., 1947; hydraulic engring. fellow La. State U., 1947-48; engr. U.S. Waterways Expt. Sta., Vicksburg, Miss., 1948; rsch. fellow U. Wis., 1948-49; asst. prof. civil engring. Auburn U., 1949-50; lectr. civil engring. U. Calif., Berkeley, 1950-54; asst. prof. civil engring. Ohio State U., 1954-58, assoc. prof., 1958-64; asst. dean Ohio State U. (Grad. Sch.), 1958-62, assoc. dean Grad. Sch., Coll. Arts and Scis., chmn. geodetic sci., 1962-64; dean off-campus edn., asso. dean faculties for personnel budget, prof. engring. mechanics Ohio State U. Grad. Sch., Columbus, 1964-66; dir. Coll. Sci. and Engring. Dayton campus Miami U.-Ohio State U., 1963-66; pres. U. S.D., 1966-68; exec. asst. to pres. Ohio State U., 1968-69, sec. bd. trustees, 1968-79, prof. civil engring., 1968-79, v.p. adminstrv. ops., 1969-70, exec. v.p. adminstrv. ops., 1970-71, exec. v.p., 1971-73, v.p. bus. and adminstrn., 1973-79, v.p., sec. emeritus, 1984—; chancellor Ohio Bd. Regents, 1979-84, chancellor emeritus, 1984—; exec. v.p. Cranston Securities Co., 1984; pres. Lake Erie Coll., 1985-86; pres., gen. mgr. Columbus Symphony Orchestra, 1986-88, mem. trustees cir., 2000—. Cons. civil engring. 1954—. Author articles, reports, bulls. on environ. engring. and edn. Trustee Blue Cross Ctrl. Ohio, 1971-77, 80-82, Columbus Symphony Orch., 1980-85, Riverside Meth. Hosp., 1979-95, chmn. fin. and assets com., 1983-94, treas., 1988-94, vice-chmn., 1994-95, chmn., 1995-96; nat. adv. coun. for small bus. to U.S. Sec. Treasury, 1975-76, steering com. Devel. Com. Greater Columbus, 1970-1980, chmn., 1978-79; nat. adv. coun. SBA, 1973-76; bd. dirs. Columbus Safety Coun., 1970-79; bd. mem. Greater Columbus Arts Coun., 1970-78, Mid-Ohio Health Planning Commn., 1973-74, Am. Univs. for Rsch. in Astronomy, 1972-79, Ohio Transp. Rsch. Ctr., 1979-83, U.S. Health Corp. (now Ohio Health), 1995-97; chmn. Grant/Riverside Meth. Hosps., 1995-97, mem. trustees' coun., 1998—, trustee emeritus, 1999—; vice-chmn. Ohio Higher Edn. facilities Commn., 1979-83; mem. Ohio Sch. and Coll. Bd. Registration, 1979-83, Ohio Ednl. TV Commn., 1979-83, Midwest Edn. Commn., 1979-85; chmn. Columbus Symphony Grand Ball, 1983; chmn. judging Internat. Sci. and Engring. Fair, 1984. With USN, 1945-46, PTO. Fellow ASCE; mem. Ohio Hist. Soc. (bd. dirs. 1979-83), State Higher Edn. Exec. Officers (exec. com. 1981-83), Meml. Soc. Columbus Area (pres. 1999-2000, bd. mem.), Ohio Commodore, Scioto Country Club, Faculty Club (Columbus), Athletic Club Columbus, Sigma Xi, Tau Beta Pi, Pi Mu Epsilon, Chi Epsilon, Delta Omega, Romophos, Sigma Alpha Epsilon. Congregationalist. Home: 1303 London Dr Columbus OH 43221-1541

**MOULTON, GRACE CHARBONNET,** retired physicist; b. New Orleans, Nov. 1, 1923; d. Wilfred J. and Louise A. (Hellmers) Charbonnet; m. William Gates Moulton, June 1, 1947; children: Paul Charbonnet Moulton, Nancy Gates Moulton. BA, Tulane U., 1944; MS, U. Ill., 1948; PhD, U. Ala., 1962. Asst. prof. physics U. Ala., Tuscaloosa, 1962-65, Fla. State U., Tallahassee, 1965-74, assoc. prof. physics, 1974-80, prof. physics, 1980-91, prof. emerita, 1991. Cons. State Bd. Regents, 1985-90, Fla. Univ. System, 1985, 90. Referee jour. articles Jour. Chem. Physics, Radiation Rsch.; contbr. many sci. rsch. articles to profl. jours. Scholar, U. Ill.; Four Yr. Undergrad. scholar, Tulane U., rsch. grantee, NIH. Mem. Am. Phys. Soc., (mem. coun. southeastern sect. 1988-92). Avocations: gardening, music (classical and folk), birding. Office: Fla State U Dept Physics Tallahassee FL 32306 Business E-Mail: gmoulton@phy.fsu.edu.

**MOULTON, LAWRENCE HALE,** statistician, educator; b. Des Moines, Mar. 23, 1956; s. Phillips Prentice and Mary (Cochran) Moulton; m. Ann Patricia Riley, Oct. 16, 1988; children: Tyler Lynch, Carine Hale Riley. BA, SUNY Buffalo, 1976; MS, U. Tex. Sch. Pub. Health, 1978; PhD, Johns Hopkins U. Sch. Hygiene and Pub. Health, 1987. Vol. and adj. prof. Nat. U. Benin U.S. Peace Corps, Cotonou, Benin, 1979—80; vis. scientist INSERM, Villejuif, France, 1984—85; asst. prof. U. Mich., Ann Arbor, 1986—91; asst. prof. Sch. Hygiene and Pub. Health Johns Hopkins U., Balt., 1991—96, assoc. prof. Sch. Hygiene and Pub. Health, 1996—2003, prof. Bloomberg Sch. Pub. Health, 2003—. Co-dir. Inst. for Vaccine Safety, Balt., 1997—; chair-elect stats. sect. APHA, Washington, 2004—; mem. anthrax vaccine expert com. Health Resources and Svcs. Adminstrn., 1999—2003; cons. WHO, Geneva, 1994—; dir. Biostats. Core CREATE Consortium, Balt., 2004—. Contbr. articles to profl. jours. Grantee FIRST Award, NIH, 1992—98; Chateaubriand Scholarship, Govt. of France, 1984—85. Mem.: Delta Omega, Phi Beta Kappa. Avocation: sport parachuting. Office: Dept Internat Health 615 N Wolfe St Baltimore MD 21205 Office Phone: 410-955-6370. E-mail: lmoulton@jhsph.edu.

**MOULTON, LYNN,** chef; Pastry cook Radius, Boston, Ambrosia, Boston; pastry chef L'Etoile, Martha's Vineyard, Mass., Rialto, 2002—04; stage Helene Darroze, Paris, 2005; pastry asst. Blu, Boston, pastry chef. Tchr., design course New England Culinary Inst., 2002. Named one of Boston's Rising Stars, StarChefs.com, 2006. Office: Blu 4 Avery St Boston MA 02111 Office Phone: 617-375-8550.*

**MOULTON, RICHARD WAY,** minister; b. Norfolk, Va., June 11, 1948; s. Robert Eugene and Betsy (Babcock) M.; m. Nancy Neal, Dec. 29, 1967; children: Richard Way, Angela, Paul, Mindy, Randall, Angel, Annie. BS in Math., Rose-Hulman Inst. Tech., Terre Haute, Ind., 1970; MS in Computer Sci., Northwestern U., Evanston, Ill., 1972; MDiv, Trinity Luth. Sem., Columbus, Ohio, 1977, DMin, Reformed Theol. Sem., Maitland, Fla., 1994. Ordained to ministry Am. Luth. Ch., 1977. Mem. tech staff Bell Telephone Labs., Naperville, Ill., 1970-72; staff engr. GTE Automatic Elec., Melrose Park, Ill., 1972-73; pastor Christ Luth. Ch., Harrisburg, Ill., 1977-78, Faith Luth. Ch., Orlando, Fla., 1979-81, Hosanna! Ch., Orlando, 1981-86; engring. mgr. Stromberg-Carlson Corp., Lake Mary, Fla., 1979-89; cons. Moulton Rsch. Inc., Altamonte Springs, Fla., 1989-90; pastor Northland Community Ch., Longwood, Fla., 1990-96; engring. mgr. Siemens Info. and Comm. Networks, Lake Mary, 1997—2005; engring. section mgr. Gen. Dynamics C4 Sys., Orlando, 2005—. Cons. Martin-Marietta Corp., Orlando, 1990. Avocations: music composing, guitar, keyboards, basketball, reading. Office: 12001 Research Pky Orlando FL 32826

**MOULTON, SARA,** chef, magazine editor; m. Bill Moulton; children: Ruth, Sam. Grad., U. Mich., 1974, Culinary Inst. Am., 1977; postgrad. stagaire with a master chef, Chartres, France, 1979. With Julia Child and More Co., 1979; mem. test kitchen Gourmet mag., 1984—88, exec. chef, 1988—, Good Morning Am., food corr., 1997, food editor; sous chef La Tulipe, NY; instr. Peter Kump's NY Cooking Sch. Co-founder NY Women's Culinary Alliance. Host Cooking Live, Food Network, 1996—2002, Sara's Secrets, 2002—; co-author (with Jean Anderson): (cookbooks) Good Morning America Cut the Calories Cookbook, 2000; author: Sara Moulton Cooks at Home, 2002, Sara's Secrets for Weeknight Meals, 2005. Office: Sara Moulton Enterprises Inc 130 W 24th St 3B New York NY 10011 Business E-Mail: sara@saramoulton.com.*

**MOULTON REGER, SARA JONENE,** global management executive; b. Rapid City, S.D., Dec. 11, 1958; d. Harold William and Ora Mae (Hoffman) Moulton. BBA with honors, Colo. State U., Ft. Collins, 1981; MBA, U. North Colo., Greeley, 1987. Cert. mgmt. acct. Intern Solar Energy Rsch. Inst., Golden, Colo., 1980; retail acct. Western Grocers, Inc., Denver, 1981-82, acctg. mgr., 1982; office mgr. Trivest Corp., Denver, 1982-83; contract adminstr. Storage Tech. Corp., Louisville, 1984-85, sr. fin. analyst, 1985-86, fin. mgr., 1986-88; mgmt. cons. Deloitte & Touche, Denver, 1988-90; mgmt. cons., mgr. Ernst & Young, Denver, 1990-95; prin. IBM, Denver, 1995—, global practice exec., 2000—. Presenter in field. Author: Can Two Rights Make a Wrong?; contbr. articles to profl. publs. Cellist Arapahoe Philharm., Denver, Jefferson Symphony. Mem. Inst. Mgmt. Accts., Am. Prodn. and Inventory Control Soc., CAM-I, Beta Gamma Sigma (v.p. 1980-81), Phi Kappa Phi. Republican. Avocations: cello, skiing, hiking, musical and cultural events, church activities. Office: IBM 2929 N Central Ave Phoenix AZ 85012 Home: 6938 E Lomas Verde Dr Scottsdale AZ 85262 Office Phone: 602-217-2754. Business E-Mail: moulton@us.ibm.com.

**MOULTRIE, FRED,** geneticist, researcher; b. Albertville, Ala., Apr. 18, 1923; s. Walter Louis and Minnie Alma (Bodine) M.; m. Frances Grace Aldridge, May 28, 1947; children: Marilyn R. Moultrie Phillips, Elizabeth Anne Moultrie Becker, Janet Carol Moultrie Gauger. BS, Auburn U., 1948, MS, 1949; PhD in Genetics, Kan State U., 1953. Asso. prof. Auburn U., 1951-55, prof., 1955-56; geneticist Arbor Acres Farm, Inc., Glastonbury, Conn., 1956-59, research coordinator, 1959-62, v.p., dir. research, 1962-64, exec. v.p., 1964-72, pres. domestic div., 1972-73; pres. Corbett Breeders, Westover, Md., 1973-81; v.p. dir. research Corbett Enterprises, Inc., 1973-81, Kennebec Internat., 1981-84; geneticist Perdue Farms, Salisbury, Md., 1984-88; genetics cons., 1988—. Served with USCGR, 1942-46. Mem. World's Poultry Sci. Assn., Am. Poultry Sci. Assn., Poultry Breeders Am. (pres. 1967-68), Sigma Xi, Phi Kappa Phi, Alpha Zeta, Gamma Sigma Delta. Clubs: Masons. Home and Office: 30390 Southampton Bridge Rd Salisbury MD 21804-2497

**MOUNCE, CAROLYN P.,** retired school librarian; b. Ecru, Miss., Dec. 18, 1938; d. Walter Gerald and Mary Ozelle Mounce. BA, Blue Mountain Coll., 1960; MA in Libr. Sci., George Peabody Coll., 1963. Asst. libr. Guyton Libr, Blue Mountain Coll., Miss., 1960—70, head libr., 1971—2004; ret., 2004. Libr. sci. instr. Blue Mountain Coll., 1967—87. Mem.: AAUW (officer, Branch Woman Achievement award 1990), Blue Mountain Coll. Alumnae Assn., Pontotoc Fed. Woman's Club (officer), Woodmen of World Lodge (Fraternal Spirit award 2005). Democrat. Baptist. Avocation: sports. Home: 785 North Rd Ecru MS 38841

**MOUNT, WILLIE LANDRY,** state legislator; b. Lake Charles, La., Aug. 25, 1949; d. Lee Robert and Willie Veatrice (McCullor) Landry; m. Benjamin Wakefield Mount, Aug. 19, 1976. BS, McNeese State U., 1971. Geophys. asst. La. Land and Exploration, Lake Charles, La., 1971-76; pharm. rep. Lederle, Lake Charles, 1976-80; realtor Mary Kay Hopkins, Lake Charles, 1976-87; co-owner Paper Place, Lake Charles, 1991-95; mayor City of Lake Charles, 1993—2000; mem. La. State Senate, 2000—, mem. select com. on consumer protection, mem. jud. C, health and welfare, legis. audit adv. commn., bond commn., mem. state tech. adv. commn., joint juvenile justice commn., millennium port com., sch. fin. rev. commn., mem. edn. comm., vice chair joint legis. com. on capital outlay, chmn. revenue and fiscal affairs com. Gov. Violent Crime & Homicide Task Force, Baton Rouge, 1993—95; mem. steering com. La. conf. Mayors bd. pres. La. Asset Mgmt. Pool Bd., 1997. Guest condr. Lake Charles Symphony, 1992; active La. Mcpl. Assn., Baton Rouge, 1995-98; pres. Jr. League of Lake Charles, mem. state interagy. coordinating coun. Dyslexia Study Com.; mem. adv. bd. S.W. La. Literacy Coalition; mem. adv. coun. Pet Overpopulation; active First United Meth. Ch., La. Meth. Conf., McNeese State U. Found., Prevent Child Abuse bd. Micro-Enterprise Devel. Alliance of La. Bd., McNeese State U. Found. Bd., St. Patrick Hosp. Bd. Councillors, Coastal Plain Conservancy Bd., United Way, Children's Miracle Network; exec. com. Coun. for a Better La. Recipient Spiritual Aims award Kiwanis Club, 1991, Cmty. Svc. award, 1995, Citizen of Yr. 1996-97, Dorthea Combre award NAACP, 1994, La. Mcpl. Assn. Cmty. Achievement award, 1995-97, Disting. Citizen award Boy Scouts Am., 1999, Patron Architecture, 2000, Disting. Alumni award Mc-Neese State U., 2000, Golden Apple award Delta Kappa Gamma, 2002, Disting. Svc. award La. Restaurant Assn., 2002, Spl. Friend of La. Mcpl. Assn. award, 2003, Wilton Bellard Jr. award S.W. La. Ctr. for Health Svcs., Ron Schroeder award MEDAL; named Woman of Yr., Quota Club, 1991, Citizen of Yr., Women's com. S.W. La., 1992, Woman of Yr., Pub. Ofcl. of Yr. Msgr. Cramers KC, Pub. Ofcl. of Yr., NASW, 1997, Legislator of Yr., La. Orthopaedic Assn., Champion for Children, Prevent Child Abuse. Mem.: LWV, S.W. La. Mayor's Assn. (chmn. 1993—94). Home: 205 Shell Beach Dr Lake Charles LA 70601-5933 Office: PO Box 3004 Lake Charles LA 70602-3004 Business E-Mail: lasen27@legis.state.la.us.

**MOUNTAIN, CLIFTON FLETCHER,** surgeon, educator; b. Toledo, Apr. 15, 1924; s. Ira Fletcher and Mary (Stone) M.; m. Merel Ann Grey; children: Karen Lockerby, Clifton Fletcher, Jeffrey Richardson. AB, Harvard U., 1946; MD, Boston U., 1954. Diplomate Am. Bd. Surgery. Dir. dept. statis. rsch. Boston U., 1950-57; cons. rsch. analyst Mass. Dept. Pub. Health, 1951—53; intern U. Chgo. Clinics, 1954, resident, 1955—58, instr. surgery, 1958—59; sr. fellow thoracic surgery Houston, 1959. Mem. staff U. Tex. Anderson Cancer Ctr.; asst. prof. thoracic surgery U. Tex., 1960-73, assoc. prof surgery, 1973-76, prof., 1976-94, prof. emeritus, 1995—, prof. surgery Sch. Medicine, 1987—, chief sect. thoracic surgery, 1970-79, chmn. thoracic oncology, 1979-84, chmn. dept. thoracic surgery, 1980-85, cons. dept. thoracic and cardiovascular surgery, 1996—, chmn. program in biomath. and computer sci., 1962-64, Mike Hogg vis. lectr. in S. Am., 1967; prof. surgery U. Calif., San Diego, 1996—; pres., chmn. Mountain Found. for Lung Cancer Rsch. and Edn., 1997—; mem. sci. mission on cancer USSR, 1970-78, and Japan, 1976-84; com. health, rsch. and edn. facilities Houston Cmty. Coun., 1964-78; cons. Am. Joint Com. on Cancer Staging and End Result Reporting, 1964-74, Tex. Heart Inst., 1994-96; mem. Am. Joint Com. on Cancer, 1974-86, chmn. lung and esophagus task force; working party on lung cancer and chmn. com. on surgery Nat. Clin. Trials Lung Cancer Study Group, NIH, 1971-76; mem. plans and scope com. cancer therapy Nat. Cancer Inst., 1972-75, mem. lung cancer study group, 1977-89, chmn. steering com., 1973-75, mem. bd. sci. counselors divsn. cancer treatment, 1972-75; hon. cons. Shanghai Chest Hosp. and Lung Cancer Ctr., Nat. Cancer Inst. of Brazil; sr. cons. Houston Thorax Inst., 1994-96. Editor The New Physician, 1955-59; mem. editl. bd. Yearbook of Cancer, 1960-88, Internat. Trends in Gen. Thoracic Surgery, 1984-91; contbr. articles to profl. jours., chpts. to textbooks. Chmn. profl. adv. com. Harris County Mental Health Assn.; bd. dirs. Harris County Chpt. Am. Cancer Soc. Lt. USNR, 1942-46. Recipient award Soviet Acad. Sci., 1977, Garcia Meml. medal Philippine Coll. Surgeons, 1982, Disting. Alumni award Boston U., 1988, Disting. Achievement U. Tex. M.D. Anderson Cancer Ctr., 1990, Disting. Svc. award Internat Assn. for the Study of Lung Cancer, 1991, Disting. Alumnus award Boston U. Sch. of Medicine, 1992, ALCASE Internat. award for excellence, 1997, Rudolf Nissen medal German Soc. Cardiovascular and Thoracic Surgery, 1998, named hon. pres. First Internat. Congress on Thoracic Surgery, 1997; Fellow ACS Am. Coll. Chest Physicians (chmn. com. cancer 1967-75), Am. Thoracic Surgery, Inst. Environ. Scis. N.Y. Acad. Sci., Assn. Thoracic and Cardiovascular Surgeons of Asia (hon.), Hellenic Cancer Soc. (hon.), Chilean Soc. Respiratory Diseases (hon., hon. pres. 1982). Mem. AAAS, AMA, Am. Assn. Cancer Rsch., So. Med. Assn., Am. Thoracic Soc., Soc. Thoracic Surgeons, Soc. Biomed. Computing, Am. Fedn. Clin. Rsch., Internat. Assn. Study Lung Cancer (pres. 1976-78), Am. Radium Soc., European Soc. Thoracic Surgeons, Pan-Am Med. Assn., Houston Surg. Soc., Soc. Surg. Oncology, James Ewing Soc., Sigma Xi. Achievements include conception and development of program for application of mathematics and computers to the life sciences, of resource for experimental designs, applied statistics and computational support; concept and implementation of multidisciplinary, site specific cancer mgmt. clinics; first clinical use of physiological adhesives in thoracic surgery; demonstration of clinical behavior of undifferentiated small cell lung cancer; first laser resection of lung tissue at thoracotomy; development of internat. system for staging of lung cancer at thoracotomy. Office Phone: 858-454-6028. Business E-Mail: cmountain@ucsd.edu.

**MOUNTAIN, JANET,** foundation administrator, former computer company executive; BBA, U. Tex., Austin; MBA, Harvard Bus. Sch. Former sr. consultant Andersen Consulting, Houston; v.p. & gen. mgr., US consumer div. Dell, Inc., 1993—2003; exec. dir. Michael & Susan Dell Found., 2003—. Named a Young Global Leader, Forum of Young Global Leaders, 2006. Office: Michael & Susan Dell Found One Dell Way Round Rock TX 78682*

**MOUNTCASTLE, VERNON BENJAMIN,** retired neuroscientist; b. Shelbyville, Ky., July 15, 1918; s. Vernon and Anne-Francis Marguerite (Waugh) Mountcastle; m. Nancy Clayton Pierpont, Sept. 6, 1945; children: Vernon Benjamin III, Anne Clayton, George Earle Pierpont. BS in Chemistry, Roanoke Coll., Salem, Va., 1938, DSc (hon.), 1968; MD, Johns Hopkins U., 1942; DSc (hon.), U. Pa., 1976, Northwestern U., 1985, U. Minn., 1995; MD (hon.), U. Zurich, 1983, U. Siena, 1984, U. Santiago, Spain, 1990. House officer surgery Johns Hopkins Hosp., 1942—43; mem. faculty Johns Hopkins Sch. Medicine, 1946—, prof. physiology, 1959, dir. dept., 1964—80, prof. neurosci., 1980—92, prof. emeritus, 1992—; dir. Bard Labs. Neurophysiology Johns Hopkins U., Balt., 1981—91. Spl. rsch. physiology brain; chmn. physiology study sect., mem. physiology tng. com. NIH, 1958—61; adv. coun. Nat. Eye Inst., 1971—74; vis. prof. Coll. de France, Paris, 1980. Author: Perciptual Neuroscience: The Cerebel Cortex, 1996, The Sensory Nand. Neural in Somatic Srnsation, 2005; editor-in-chief: Jour. Neurophysiology, 1961—64, editor, contbr.: Med. Physiology, 12th edit., 1968, Med. Physiology, 13th edit., 1974, Med. Physiology, 14th edit., 1980; contbr. articles to profl. jours. Lt. (s.g.) M.C. USNR, 1943—46. Recipient Lashley prize, Am. Philos. Soc., 1974, F.O. Schmitt prize and medal, MIT, 1975, Sherrington prize and Gold medal, Royal Acad. Medicine, London, 1977, Horowitz prize, Columbia U., 1978, Helmholtz prize, 1982, Fyssen Internat. prize, Paris, 1983, Lasker award, 1983, Nat. Medal Sci. 1986, Zotterman prize and medal, Swedish Physiol. Soc., 1989, award in neurosci., Fidia Fedn., 1990, Australia prize, 1993. Mem.: AAAS (McGovern prize and medal 1990), NAS (chmn. sect. on physiology 1971—74, award in neurosci. 1998), Acad. Sci. (Finland, fgn.), Royal Soc. London (fgn.), Acad. Scis. (France, fgn.), Nat. Inst. Medicine, Am. Philos. Soc. (councillor 1979—82), Soc. Neurosci. (pres. 1970—72, Gerard prize 1980), Harvey Cushing Soc., Am. Acad. Arts and Scis., Am. Physiol. Soc., Physiol. Soc. London (hon.), Am. Neurol. Assn. (hon. Bennett lectr. 1978), Sigma Xi, Phi Chi, Alpha Omega Alpha, Phi Beta Kappa. Home: 6605 Walnutwood Cir Baltimore MD 21212 Business E-Mail: mountcastle@mbi.mb.jhu.edu.

**MOUNTCASTLE, WILLIAM WALLACE, JR.,** philosophy and religion educator; b. Hanover, N.H., July 10, 1925; s. William Wallace and Grace Elizabeth (Zottarelli) M.; m. Ila M. Warner (div.); children: Christine, Susan, Gregory, Eric; m. Barbara Kaye Griffin, Oct. 19, 1979; 1 child, Cathleena; stepdaughter, Dasha. BA, Whittier Coll., 1951; STB, Boston U., 1954, PhD, 1958. Ordained to ministry United Meth. Ch. Asst. prof. philosophy and religion High Point Coll., NC, 1958—60; mem. So. Calif. Ann. Conf. United Meth. Ch., 1954—60; assoc. prof., head dept. philosophy Nebr. Wesleyan U., Lincoln, 1960—63, prof., head dept. philosophy, 1963—67; mem. Nebr. Ann. Conf. United Meth. Ch. 1960—95; prof. philosophy Fla. So. Coll., Lakeland, 1967—68; assoc. prof. philosophy and religion U. West Fla., Pensacola, 1968—79, prof. philosophy and religion, 1979—, M.L. Tipton prof. philosophy and religion, 1980—2003, emeritus M.L. Tipton prof., 2003. Author: Religion in Planetary Perspective, 1979, Science Fantasy Voices and Visions of Cosmic Religion, 1996; contbr. articles to profl. jours. Fighter pilot USAAF, 1942-48, PTO. Mem. NEA/United Faculty Fla., Am. Assn. Religion, Am. Philos. Assn., Democrat. Home: 2526 Bayou Blvd Pensacola FL 32504 Office: U West Fla Dept Phil-Religious Studies Pensacola FL 32514

**MOUNTJOY, DENNIS LEE,** state official; b. Pasadena, Calif., Feb. 12, 1957; children: Tammy, Nicholas. Grad. h.s., Monrovia. V.p., gen. mgr. Mountjoy Constrn., 1978—88; owner constrn. co., 1988—; mem. Calif. State Assembly, 2000—, mem. ins. com., transp. com. Mem. Calif. Rep. Assembly. Mem. San Gabriel Valley Caucus. Mem.: Inland Empire Caucus, Gov. Organization Com., Lincoln Club. Republican. Mailing: PO Box 942849 Sacramento CA 94249 Office: CA State A 135 W Lemon Ave Monrovia CA 91016 Office Phone: 916-319-2059. Business E-Mail: assemblymember.mountjoy@assembly.ca.gov.

**MOUNTS, L. DAVID,** food products executive; married; 3 children. BSBA in fin. and Mgmt. Info., U. Nev.; MBA, U. Pa. Wharton Sch. Bus. Joined UPS Inc., 1983, v.p. mergers and aquisitions, 1999—2002, CFO Supply Chain Solutions Group, 2002—05; exec. v.p., CFO Domino's Pizza Inc., 2005—, also bd. dirs. Bd. dirs. The Genesis Shelter. Office: Dominos Pizza 30 Frank Lloyd Wright Dr Ann Arbor MI 48106*

**MOUNTS, NANCY,** secondary school educator; Tchr. home econs. North High Sch., Sioux City, Iowa; tech. prep. specialist Cen. Campus, Sioux City, 1995—; dir. Northwest Iowa Ctr. Teaching and Learning Morningside Coll. Recipient State Tchr. of Yr. Home Econs. award Iowa, 1992. Office: Cen Campus 1121 Jackson St Sioux City IA 51105-1434

**MOUNTZ, WADE,** retired healthcare executive; b. Winona, Ohio, Nov. 19, 1924; s. Lowell J. and Ethel M. (Coppock) M.; m. Betty G. Wilson, June 3, 1946; children: David John, Timothy Wilson. BA, Baldwin-Wallace Coll., 1948; MHA, U. Minn., 1951; LHD (hon.), Ky. Wesleyan Coll., 1991. With Norton Meml. Infirmary, Louisville, 1951-69, adminstr., 1958-69; pres. Norton-Children's Hosps., Inc., Louisville, 1969-81, NKC, Inc., Louisville, 1981-85, vice chmn., 1985-87; pres. emeritus Norton Healthcare, 1987—. Vice chmn. Comprehensive Health Planning Council Ky., 1968-73, chmn., 1973-79; bd. dirs. Louisville chpt. ARC, 1961-74; trustee Blue Cross Hosp. Plan, 1959-72; trustee Am. Hosp. Assn., 1971-76, chmn. bd., 1975. Served with A.C., USNR, 1943-45. Recipient Disting. Service award Ky. Hosp. Assn.; Disting. Layman award Ky. Med. Assn. Fellow Am. Coll. Hosp. Healthcare Execs. (life, gold medal), Masons. Home and Office: 9 Muirfield Pl Louisville KY 40222-5074 Office Phone: 502-412-9210. Personal E-Mail: wmountz@insightbb.com.

**MOURNING, ALONZO,** professional basketball player; b. Chesapeake, Va., Feb. 8, 1970; m. Tracy Mourning; children: Alonzo III, Myka. Student, Georgetown U. Player Charlotte Hornets, SC, 1992—95, Miami Heat, 1995—2003, NJ Nets, 2003—04, Miami Heat, 2005—. Mem. Dream Team II, 1994; player All-Star Game, 1994. Named to NBA All-Rookie 1st team, 1993.

**MOURNING, PAUL W.,** lawyer; b. Hattiesburg, Miss., Dec. 21, 1957; BA magna cum laude, Dartmouth Coll., 1980; JD, Univ. Va., 1983. Bar: N.Y. 1984. Ptnr. Health Corp. dept., recruiting ptnr. Cadwalader Wickersham & Taft, NYC. Editor (in chief): Va. Jour. Internat. Law. Mem.: ABA, N.Y. State Bar Assn., Phi Beta Kappa. Office: Cadwalader Wickersham & Taft LLP 1 World Fin Ctr New York NY 10281 Office Phone: 212-504-6216. Office Fax: 212-504-6666. Business E-Mail: paul.mourning@cwt.com.

**MOUROKH, LEV GRIGORIEVICH,** physicist, researcher; b. Nizhny Novgorod, Russia, Mar. 23, 1968; came to U.S., 1998. s. Grigory Lvovich and Serafima Maksovna (Mil'ner) M. Diploma in Engring., N. Lobachevsky State U., Nizhny Novgorod, 1991, PhD, 1996. Engr. Tech. Rsch. Inst., Nizhny Novgorod, 1991-92; asst. prof. physics N. Lobachevsky State U., 1995-98. Vis. asst. physics City Coll. of CUNY, 1998-99; vis. rsch. asst. prof. physics, Stevens Inst. Tech., Hoboken, N.J., 1998-2001, rsch. asst. prof. physics, 2001-05; rsch. scientist Bklyn. Coll. of CUNY, 1999-2001; vis. rsch. asst. prof. physics Queens Coll. CUNY, 2005—. Contbr. articles to profl. jours. Swedish Royal Acad. Sci. fellow, 1995. Mem.: Am. Phys. Soc. Home: 1751 67th St Apt E11 Brooklyn NY 11204-4361 E-Mail: levmour@prodigy.net.

**MOUSER, LES (LYMAN MOUSER),** advertising executive; Pres., COO Campbell Mithun Esty, Mpls., 1999—; CEO Campbell Mithun, Mpls., 2001—04, chmn. Office: Campbell Mithun Esty 222 S 9th St Minneapolis MN 55402-3389 Office Phone: 612-347-1000. Office Fax: 612-347-1515.

**MOUTARI, OUSMANE,** permanent representative to UN Niger; b. 1952; married; 2 children. Degree in Pub. Law, Faculty Law and Econs., Cameroon, 1979; degree, Inst. Internat. Administrn. Pub., 1984; MS in Pub. and Non-Profit Mgmt. and Policy, NYU, 2004. Mem. delegation Niger to security coun., 1979—87; first sec. Permanent Mission of Niger to UN, NYC, 1979—87; dir. Office Political and Cultural Affairs, Min. Foreign Affairs and Cooperation of Niger, 1979—87; amb. Niger to former Soviet Union/Commonwealth Ind. States, 1990—93; first counsellor Embassy of Niger to Fed. Rep. Germany, 1987—90; dir. cabinet of sec. gen. Orgn. of Islamic Conf., Jeddah, Saudi Arabia, 1993—95, rep. of sec. gen. to King of Morocco, 1995—97; sec. gen. Ministry African Integration and Citizens of

Niger Abroad, 1997; spl. advisor diplomatic affairs Office of Pres., 1998; permanent rep. Niger UN, 1999—. Office: NY Permanent Mission 417 E 50th St New York NY 10022 Office Phone: 212-421-3260. E-mail: ousmanez@aol.com.

**MOUTTET, JANE ELIZABETH,** school librarian, educator; b. Grand Rapids, Mich., Mar. 23, 1961; d. Roger Willis and Celia Driesens; m. David Frederick Mouttet, June 4, 1988; 3 children. BA, Calvin Coll., 1983. Cert. elem. tchr. ACSI. Tchr., libr. Hilltop Christian Sch., Window Rock, Ariz., 1983—2004. Contbr. column to Christian Libr. Jour., 2002. Mem.: ALA, Soc. Children's Book Writers and Illustrators, Nat. Coun. Tchrs. English, N.Mex. Libr. Assn. E-mail: jane@mouttetfamily.com.

**MOW, ROBERT HENRY, JR.,** lawyer; b. Cape Girardeau, Mo., Dec. 10, 1938; s. Robert H. Sr. and Ann Elise (Beck) M.; m. Jody K. Boggs, Aug. 29, 1987; children: Robert M., Brynn A., W. Brett, Rebecca M., W. Kirk, Allison M. Student, Westminster Coll., 1956-57; AB with distinction, U. Mo., 1960; LLB magna cum laude, So. Meth. U., 1963. Bar: Tex. 1963, U.S. Dist. Ct. (no. dist.) Tex. 1965, U.S. Dist. Ct. (so. dist.) Tex. 1969, U.S. Dist. Ct. (ea. and we. dists.) Tex. 1976, U.S. Ct. Claims 1973, U.S. Ct. Appeals (5th cir.) 1972, U.S. Ct. Appeals (11th cir.) 1981, U.S. Ct. Appeals (fed. cir.) 1994, U.S. Supreme Ct. 1978. Assoc. Carrington, Johnson & Stephens, Dallas, 1963-69; ptnr. Carrington, Coleman, Sloman & Blumenthal, Dallas, 1970-85, Hughes & Luce, LLP, Dallas, 1985, mng. ptnr., 2003—. Editor-in-chief Southwestern Law Jour., 1962-63. Trustee First Bapt. Acad., chair, 1999-2002. Served to 1st lt. U.S. Army, 1963-65. Named one of Best Lawyers in Dallas, D Mag., 2005, Best Lawyers in Am., 1984—. Fellow: Am. Coll. Trial Lawyers; mem.: Dallas Bar Assn. (chair evaluation com., Com. Qualified Judiciary, Dallas Bar Trial Lawyer of Yr. 2003), ABA (chair intellectual property com. litig. sect.), State Bar Tex., Dallas Bar Fellows (chmn. 2003—04), Am. Bd. Trial Advocates (pres. Dallas chpt. 1983—84), Tex. Assn. Def. Counsel (v.p. and dir. 1981—82), Dallas Assn. Def. Counsel. Republican. Baptist. Office Phone: 214-939-5448. Business E-Mail: mowb@hughesluce.com.

**MOW, VAN C.,** engineering educator, researcher; b. Chengdu, China, Jan. 10, 1939; B. Aero. Engring., Rensselaer Poly. Inst., 1962, PhD, 1966. Mem. tech. staff Bell Telephone Labs., Whippany, NJ, 1968-69; assoc. prof. mechanics Rensselaer Poly. Inst., Troy, NY, 1969-76, prof. mechanics and biomed. engring., 1976-82, John A. Clark and Edward T. Crossan prof. engring., 1982-86; prof. mech. engring. and orthopedic bioengring. Columbia U., N.Y.C., 1986—98, chmn. dept. biomed. engring. Fu Found. Sch. Engring. and Applied Sci., 1998—; dir. Orthopedic Rsch. Lab., Columbia-Presbyn. Med. Ctr., N.Y.C., 1986—, Stanley Dicker prof. biomed. engring., 1998—. Vis. mem. Courant Inst. Math. Sci., NYU, 1967-68; vis. prof. Harvard U., Boston, 1976-77; chmn. orthopaedics and musculoskeletal study sect. NIH, Bethesda, Md., 1982-84; hon. prof. Sichuan U., 1981, Shanghai Jiao Tong U., 1987, Shanghai U., 1983, Hong Kong Poly. U., 2003, Zhejiang U., 2004, Beihang U., 2004; chmn. grants rev. bd. Orthopaedic Rsch. Edn. Found., 1992-96; bd. dirs. Hoar Rsch. Found., 1993—; chmn. adv. com. divsn. Med. Engring. Rsch. Nat. Health Rsch. Inst., Taiwan, 1999—; cons. in field. Assoc. editor Jour. Biomechanics, 1981—, Jour. Biomech. Engring., 1979-86; chmn. editorial adv. bd. Jour. Orthopedic Rsch., 1983-90; adv. editor Clin. Orthopedic Rel. Rsch., 1993—; assoc./co-editor Osteo-arthritis & Cartilage; contbr. numerous articles to profl. jours. Founder Gordon Research Conf. on Bioengring. and Orthopedic Sci., 1980. NATO sr. fellow, 1978; recipient William H. Wiley Disting. Faculty award Rensselaer Poly. Inst., 1981, ASME Van C. Mow medal for bioengring., 2004; Japan Soc. for Promotion Sci. Fellow, 1986, Fogarty Sr. Internat. fellow, 1987; Alza disting. lectr. Biomed. Engring. Soc., 1987; H.R. Lissner award ASME, 1987, Kappa Delta award AAOS, 1980, Giovani Borelli award, 1991. Fellow ASME (chmn. biomechanics divsn. 1984-85, Melville medal 1982, R.H. Thurston lectr., Van C. Mow medal for bioengring. 2004); Am. Inst. Med. Biol. Engring.; mem. Orthopaedic Rsch. Soc. (pres. 1982-83), Am. Soc. Biomechanics (founding), Internat. Soc. Biorheology, U.S. Nat. Com. on Biomechanics (sec.-treas. 1985-90, chmn. 1991-94), Nat. Acad. Engring., Inst. of Medicine, Nat. Acad. Sci., Academia Sinica. Business E-Mail: vcm1@columbia.edu.

**MOWE, GREGORY ROBERT,** lawyer; b. Aberdeen, Wash., Feb. 23, 1946; s. Robert Eden and Jeannette Effie (Deyoung) M.; m. Rebecca Louise Nobles, June 14, 1969; children: Emily, Tom. BA, U. Oreg., 1968, MA, 1969; JD magna cum laude, Harvard Law Sch., 1974. Bar: Oreg. 1974, U.S. Dist. Ct. Oreg. 1974, U.S. Ct. Appeals (9th cir.) 1974. Assoc. atty. Stoel Rives Boley Jones & Grey, Portland, Oreg., 1974-79, ptnr., 1979—. Pres. bd. dirs. Planned Parenthood of Columbia/Willamette, Portland, 1989-90. 1st lt. U.S. Army, 1969-71, Vietnam. Mem. ABA, Phi Beta Kappa. Office: Stoel Rives Boley Jones & Grey 900 SW 5th Ave Ste 2300 Portland OR 97204-1229 Office Phone: 503-294-9458. Business E-Mail: grmowe@stoel.com.

**MOWEN, JOHN C.,** business educator; b. Charlottesville, Va., Nov. 13, 1943; s. John Calvin and Hope Hopkins Mowen; m. Maryanne Myers, June 12, 1971; children: Katherine, Cara. BA, William & Mary U., 1969; PhD, Ariz. State U., 1977. Prof. in bus. Okla. State U., Stillwater, 1978—. Cons. in field; bd. dirs. Consumer Credit Counseling Svc., Oklahoma City. Pres. Payne County United Way, Stillwater, 1996; co-chair House Campaign for Dem. Legislator, Stillwater, 1976; founder, bd. dirs. Mission of Hope Shelter for Homeless, Stillwater, 1987-98. Capt. U.S. Army, 1969-73, Vietnam. Decorated Bronze Star; recipient Best Article award Jour. Personal Selling, 1992. Mem. APA, Am. Mktg. Assn. (Best Article award 1998), Soc. for Consumer Psychology, Assn. for Consumer Rsch., Stillwater C. of C. (bd. dirs. 1997—), CCCS Ctrl. Okla. (bd. dirs. 1998-99). Avocations: golf, water gardening. Office: Okla State U Coll Bus Stillwater OK 74078-0001 E-mail: jcmmkt@okstate.okway.edu.

**MOWERY, GERALD EUGENE,** publishing executive, writer; b. Buena, Wash., Mar. 7, 1927; s. Jennings Bryan and Opal Mae Mowery; children: Colleen, Theresa, Rhonda, Laura, Victoria, Charles, Peggy. Degree in bus., Kinmen's U. Lic. pub. acct., Wash. Supr. Boeing Airplane Co., Seattle, 1968-78; owner Jerry's Coin, Book and Frame Shops, Puyallup, Wash., 1978-85, Rudolph Maurer Pub., Puyallup, Wash., Tampa, Fla., 1985—. Author and pub. more than 152 books including All Matter Originates from Electrons, Positrons and Neutrinos, 1981, E=GM Squared, 1994, The Revised Periodic Table of Elements, The Four Unacknowledged Elements, 1999; co-author with Gene Buck: The Entrepreneurs Favorite Short Stories, Favorite Poems, Favorite Facts and Stuff; author, publ. Adjusted Periodic Table of Elements, 1982, 93, 97, 98, 2001; author children's books The Adventures of Alexander Smiriotes series including Alexander Simiriotes Rides his Alligator Through Tampa, Alexander Visits Athens, Greece, Chelsea Thompson Visits Seattle. Achievements include illustrating the atomic mass make up of sub atomic particles and their relationship to carbon 12; prepared (atomic mass) sub atomic particle table from the equation atomic mass squared x 938.27231 equals measured MeV Values; illustrated that elements are periodic, paired functions of Electrons, Protons, Neutrinos and .000249089 atomic mass particles; developed periodic table of elements progression law of 1+2+2+2+2; confirming the existence of six additional elements within the table and predicting their measurements, configuration, composition, charge, isotopes, and other values; established that isotopes are periodic progression and are not randomly added; established the theory and concept of compact neutrons as the basis for the periodic table; illustrated that the configuration and measurements of elements are paired with themselves, that all atoms are paired in a solid state, singular in a gas state, and both paired and unpaired in a liquid state; confirmed and illustrated how matter has a periodic atomic mass progression from the subatomic particles through the elements; put on a firm basis the theory that subatomic particles are the result of Proton Fractures at certain points in the 27 electron/proton chain and releasing energy (MeV) in the process; illustrated that the atomic number of an element should be two times its configuration plus one. Address: 203 South G St #217 Tacoma WA 98405 Personal E-mail: gemowery@msn.com.

**MOWERY, WARD FRANKLIN,** retired music educator; s. Walter James and Mary Elizabeth Mowery; m. Anita Mae Hitchcock, June 12, 1960; children: Dale Richard, Angela Denise Mowery-Bemus. BS, Ohio State U., 1962, PhD, 1993; MS, MMusic, U. Ill., 1968. Nationally registered music educator, 1991, cert. tchr. Ohio. Assn. Christian Schs. Internat. Tchr. River View Local Schs., Warsaw, Ohio, 1962—63, Lima Shawnee Local Schs., Lima, Ohio, 1963—65; instr. Wilkes Coll., Wilkes-Barre, Pa., 1968—69; tchr. Lincolnview Local Schs., Van Wert, Ohio, 1969—74; music ministry The Mowerys, Lima, 1974—85; assoc. prof. Bluffton Coll., Ohio, 1976—90, adj. prof., 1990—99; tchr. Lima City Schs., 1989—99, Christian Acad. Louisville, 1999—2002. Prin. bassist Lima Symphony Orch., Lima, 1977—99; ch. musician Lyndon Christian Ch., Louisville, 1999—, SE Christian Ch., Louisville, 1997—. Composer musical compositions. With USN, 1955—58, Hawaii. Mem.: MENC (adjudicator 1978—95). Republican. Achievements include Mowery's music ministry performed over 1600 concerts 1974-1985; Numerous former students now major teachers. Avocations: music performance, church music, physical conditioning. Home: 7215 Quail Ridge Road Louisville KY 40291-1878 Personal E-mail: wamowery@aol.com.

**MOWL, LINDA,** special education educator; m. Gary Mowl, Aug. 24, 1991. BS in Edn., Truman State U., Kirksville, Mo., 1975. Tchr. assoc., athletic coach Davenport Cmty. Schs., Walcott, Iowa, 1975—83; devel. edn. instr. Muscatine CC, Iowa, 1983—. Recipient Chancellor's award, Eastern Iowa C.C., 2000, Excellence award, Nat. Inst. for Staff and Orgnl. Devel., 2000, Outstanding Employee award, Muscatine C.C., 1998. Avocations: gardening, floral design, reading, travel. Office: Muscatine CC 152 Colorado St Muscatine IA 52761 Office Phone: 563-288-6055.

**MOWREY, KIMBERLY ALLISON,** school system administrator, editing consultant; b. DuBois, Pa., Mar. 28, 1979; d. Richard David and Lynne Crawley Mowrey. BS, Wake Forest U., Winston Salem, NC, 2002. Editing cons. Mgmt. Svc., Ltd., Punxsutawney, Pa., 1995—; mktg. and devel. intern Punxsutawney Area Hosp., Pa., 1998—98; sr. asst. to assoc. dean U. Pitts., Pa., 2003—04, 2004—. Sr. vol. Make-a-Wish Found., Punxsutawney, 1996—2003. Recipient Spkr. award, Rsch. Am., 2004. Mem. Soc. Rsch. Administrators Internat. Home: 5930 Walnut St Apt C1 Pittsburgh PA 15232 Office: Univ Pittsburgh Sch Nursing 3500 Victoria St Rm 350 Pittsburgh PA 15261 Office Phone: 412-624-8392. Office Fax: 412-624-2401. Personal E-mail: kimamowrey@yahoo.com. E-mail: kam72@pitt.edu.

**MOWREY, ROBERT D.,** lawyer; b. Cin., Sept. 27, 1963; BA summa cum laude, Wittenberg Univ., Springfield, Ohio, 1985; JD cum laude, Univ. Chgo., 1988. Bar: Ga. 1988. Ptnr., chmn., environ. and land use group Alston & Bird LLP, Atlanta. Adj. prof., environ law Emory Univ., Atlanta. Mem. Chgo. Law Rev. Office: Alston & Bird LLP One Atlantic Plz 1201 W Peachtree St NW Atlanta GA 30309-3424 Office Phone: 404-881-7242. Office Fax: 404-881-7777. Business E-Mail: bmowrey@alston.com.

**MOWRIS, GERALD WILLIAM,** lawyer; b. Grand Forks, N.D., Oct. 2, 1948; s. Robert Earl and Lillian Vivian Mowris; m. Susan Leah Sachtjen; children: Danae E., Jeffrey W. Student, Mich. State U., 1966-67; JD, U. Wis., 1973. Bar: Wis. 1973, U.S. Dist. Ct. (we. dist.) Wis. 1973, U.S. Ct. Appeals (7th cir.) 1984, U.S. Ct. Mil. Appeals 1984. Asst. dist. atty. Dane County Dist. Atty.'s Office, Madison, 1973-79; ptnr. Pellino, Rosen, Mowris & Kirkhuff, Madison, 1979—. Co-founder, mem. steering com. Wis. Criminal Justice Study Commn. Bd. dirs. YMCA of Met. Madison, 1991-94; mem. ARC Cmty. Svcs., Madison, 1980—, past pres., apptd. by gov. Wis. Sentencing Commn., 2003—. Maj. USAR, 1970-92 Mem. State Bar Wis. (co-chmn. com. for local bar leaders 1995-97, bd. govs. 1999-2000, pres. 2001-02), Dane County Bar Assn. (pres. 1994-95), Wis. Assn. Criminal Def. Lawyers (pres. 1995-96), Nat. Assn. Criminal Def. Lawyers, Wis. Acad. Trial Lawyers, Nat. Ski Patrol (patroller 1967—). Avocations: skiing, fishing, hiking, canoeing, golf. Office: Pellino Rosen Mowris & Kirkhuff SC 131 W Wilson St Ste 1201 Madison WI 53703-3243 Office Phone: 608-255-4501. Office Fax: 608-255-4345. Business E-Mail: gmowris@prmk.com.

**MOWRY, ROBERT WILBUR,** pathologist, educator; b. Griffin, Ga., Jan. 10, 1923; s. Roy Burnell and Mary Frances (Swilling) Mowry; m. Margaret Neilson Black, June 11, 1949; children: Janet Lee, Robert Gordon, Barbara Ann. BS, Birmingham So. Coll., 1944; MD, Johns Hopkins U., 1946. Rotating intern U. Ala. Med. Coll., 1946-47, resident pathology, 1947-48; sr. asst. surgeon USPHS-NIH, Bethesda, Md., 1948-52; fellow pathology Boston City Hosp., 1950-52; asst. prof. pathology Washington U., St. Louis, 1952-53; from asst. prof. pathology to prof. emeritus U. Ala. Med. Ctr., Birmingham, 1953—89; prof. emeritus U. Ala. Med. Center, 1989—2003. Sr. scientist U. Ala. Inst. Dental Rsch., 1967—72, dir. autopsy svcs., 1975—79; vis. scholar dept. pathology U. Cambridge, England, 1972—73; cons. FDA, 1975—81. Author (with J. F. A. McManus): Staining Methods: Histologic and Histochemical, 1960; mem. editl. bd. Jour. Histochemistry and Cytochemistry, 1960—75, Stain Tech., 1965—90, AMA Archives Pathology, 1967—76, Biotechnics and Histochemistry, 1991—. With USPHS, 1948—52. Mem.: Am. Assn. Univ. Profs. Pathology, Biol. Stain Commn. (v.p. 1974—76, pres. 1976—81, trustee 1966—), Internat. Acad. Pathology, Am. Soc. Investigative Pathology, Sigma Xi, Phi Beta Kappa, Alpha Kappa Kappa, Delta Sigma Phi. Presbyterian. Achievements include research in perfection of staining methods for complex carbohydrates (Alcian blue and colloidal iron) and insulin (Alcian blue-aldehyde fuchsin) and utility of these in diagnostic histopathology. Home: 9293 Poplar Ave Apt 218 Germantown TN 38138

**MOWSHOWITZ, ABBE,** computer scientist; b. Liberty, NY, Nov. 13, 1939; s. Jacob and Minnie Mowshowitz; m. Harriet Angell Hobson, Feb. 1, 1964; children: Jed Elijah, Seth Isaiah. BS, U. Chgo., 1961; MS, MA, PhD, U. Mich., 1967. Rsch. assoc. Human Scis. Rsch., McLean, Va., 1962—63; rsch. asst. U. Mich., Ann Arbor, 1963—67, lectr., 1967—68; asst. prof. U. Toronto, 1968—69, U. B.C., Vancouver, Canada, 1969—74, assoc. prof., 1974—80; prof. Grad. Sch. Mgmt., Delft, Netherlands, 1979—80, Rensselaer Poly. Inst., Troy, NY, 1982—84, CCNY, 1984—. Vis. fellow Ctr. for Study Dem. Instns., Santa Barbara, Calif., 1975; rsch. assoc. Cornell U., Ithaca, NY, 1975—76; dir. Croton Rsch. Group, Croton-on-Hudson, NY, 1980—82; pres. Tech. Impact Rsch., Inc., Larchmont, NY, 1983—94; prof. Erasmus U. Rotterdam, Netherlands, 1990—91, U. Amsterdam, 1991—93, 1994—95; Tinbergen chair Erasmus U., Rotterdam, 1990—91, prof., 2001—02; CeTim chair in tech. innovation Rotterdam Sch. Mgmt., 2001—02. Author: (book) The Conquest of Will: Information Processing in Human Affairs, 1976, Inside Information: Computers in Fiction, 1977, Human Choice and Computers, 2, 1988, Virtual Organization: Toward a Theory of Societal Transformation Stimulated by Information Technology, 2002. Mem.: IEEE (assoc.), Assn. for Computing Machinery (corr.; chmn., vice-chmn. 1983—87). Achievements include research in comprehensive analyses of the social effects of computers; structural complexity of combinatorial graphs; development of concept of virtual organization; design of method for measuring the bias of search engines. Office: CCNY Convent Ave at 138th St New York NY 10031 Office Phone: 212-650-6161. Office Fax: 212-650-6248. Personal E-mail: abbem@bestweb.net. E-mail: abbe@cs.ccny.cuny.edu.

**MOXLEY, JOHN HOWARD, III,** internist; b. Elizabeth, NJ, Jan. 10, 1935; s. John Howard Jr. and Cleopatra (Mundy) Moxley; m. Doris Banchik; children: John Howard IV, Brook, Mark. BA, Williams Coll., 1957; MD, U. Colo., 1961; DSc (hon.), Sch. Medicine Hannemann U. Diplomate Am. Bd. Internal Medicine. Intern Peter Bent Brigham Hosp., Boston, 1961—62, resident in internal medicine, 1962—66; with Nat. Cancer Inst., USPHS, 1963—65; asst. to dean, instr. medicine Harvard Med. Sch., Boston, 1966—69; dean Sch. Medicine, U. Md., 1969—73; vice chancellor health scis., dean Med. Sch., U. Calif.-San Diego, 1973—79; asst. sec. for health affairs Dept. Def., Washington, 1979—81; sr. v.p. Am. Med. Internat., Beverly Hills, Calif., 1981—87; pres. MetaMed. Inc., Playa Del Rey, Calif., 1987—89; mgr. dir. Korn/Ferry Internat., L.A., 1989—. Cons. FDA, NIH; dir. Nat. Fund for Med. Edn., 1986—94, chmn., 1993—94; dir. Henry M. Jackson Found. for Adv. Mil. Medicine. Contbr. articles to profl. jours. Dir. Polyclinic Health Svcs. Games of XXIII Olympiad. Recipient Gold and Silver award, U.

Colo. Med. Sch., 1974, commr.'s citation for outstanding svc. to over-the-counter drug study, FDA, 1977, spl. achievement citation, Am. Hosp. Assn., 1983, Sec. of Def. medal for disting. pub. svc., 1981. Fellow: ACP, Am. Coll. Physician Execs. (disting.); mem.: AMA (chmn. coun. sci. affairs 1985), Am. Hosp. Assn. (trustee 1979—81), Soc. Med. Adminstrs., Calif. Med. Assn. (chmn. sci. bd. 1978—83, councilor), Inst. Medicine NAS, San Diego C. of C., Rotary, Alpha Omega Alpha. Office: Korn Ferry Internat 1900 Ave of the Stars Ste 2600 Los Angeles CA 90067-1512 Office Phone: 310-200-1296. E-mail: moxleyj@kornferry.com.

**MOXLEY, ROY ANTHONY,** early childhood educator; b. Grosse Pointe Farms, Mich., Jan. 30, 1934; s. Roy Anthony and Anetta May (Van Alstyne) M. B.S. in Sci., U. Detroit, 1958; M.A. in English, Wayne State U., 1962; Ph.D. in Edn., U. Mich., 1972. Instr. U. Mich., Ann Arbor, 1970-71; asst. prof. edn. Ind. U., 1971-72; prof. edn. W.Va. U., Morgantown, 1972-2005, prof. emeritus 2005—. Mem. Am. Assn. Behavior Analysis. Author: (with Mary Fitch) Changing Patient Behavior: A Behavior Modification Manual for Dental Professionals, 1978, 2d edit., 1984; Writing and Reading in Early Childhood, 1982; contbr. articles to profl. jours. Home: 884 E Everly St Apt 15 Morgantown WV 26505-3454

**MOY, EDMUND C.,** federal agency administrator; b. 1957; m. Karen Moy; 1 child, Nora. Grad., U. Wis., 1979. Sales and mktg. exec. Blue Cross Blue Shield United, Wis., 1979—89; polit. appointee Health Care Financing Adminstrn. HHS, 1989—93; with Welsh, Carson, Anderson & Stowe; various positions with venture capital firms; spl. asst. to Pres. for presdl. personnel The White House, Washington; dir., US Mint US Dept. Treasury, Washington, 2006—. Bd. dirs. Christianity Today, Christianity Today Found. Office: US Mint 801 9th St NW Washington DC 20220*

**MOY, HENRY,** museum director; b. Chgo., Dec. 8, 1955; s. Fook Sing and Jennie Moy. BA, MAT, Beloit Coll., 1978. Curator collections and exhbns. Lakeview Mus. Arts Scis., Peoria, Ill., 1981—84; dir. mus., chair mus. studies program Beloit Coll., Wis., 1985—96; dir. Mus. Red River, Idabel, Okla, 1997—. Bd. mem. Okla. Museums Assn., Oklahoma City; adv. bd. mem. Chinatown Mus. Found., Chgo., 2003—; adv. panel mem. Exhibits USA, Mid Am. Arts Alliance, Kansas City, Mo., 2003—; pres. Wis. Fedn. Mus., Madison, 1988—93; v.p. Congress Ill. Hist. Socs. and Mus., Springfield, 1983—84; program cons. mus. studies U. Wis., Superior, 2001—03; grants reviewer Inst. Mus. and Libr. Svcs., Washington, 1998—2001. Editor: (exhibit catalog) Precolumbian Art in Cultural Context. Pres. Idabel Rotary Club, 2000, asst. gov., 2006—07; chair visual arts program, mem. by-laws com. Arts Coun. McCurtain County, Idabel, 1997—2001; v.p., treas. McCurtain Cmty. Fund, 2002—04; chair nominating com., mem. by-laws com. E.T. Dunlap Higher Learning Ctr. Found., Idabel, 2001—04. Mem.: Assn. Mid-west Mus. (bd. dirs. 1995—97, Midwest Mus. Conf.), Am. Assn. Mus. (com. mus. profl. tng. 1995—97), Okla. Museums Assn. (chair bylaws com., awards com., ann. program 1998—2004), Idabel Chamber Commerce and Agr. (bd. dirs., 2d v.p. 2006—). Liberal. Achievements include Von Eschen-Steele Award for Excellence in Teaching. Avocations: travel, cooking, popular culture, fencing. Home: PO Box 1574 Idabel OK 74745 Office: Mus of Red River 812 E Lincoln Rd Idabel OK 74745 Office Phone: 580-286-3616. Home Fax: 580-286-4374; Office Fax: 580-286-3616. Personal E-mail: henrymoy@usa.com. E-mail: motrr@hotmail.com.

**MOY, RICHARD L.,** virologist; BA in Biochemistry, Columbia U., 1996—2000; PhD in Microbiology, Mt. Sinai Sch. of Medicine-NYU, 2001—. Lab. technician Aaron Diamond AIDS Rsch. Ctr. (ADARC)-Rockefeller U., N.Y.C., 2000—01; ph.d. student Mt. Sinai Sch. of Medicine, N.Y.C., 2001—. Recipient Semifinalist, 55th Ann. Westinghouse Sci. Talent Search, Sci. Svc., 1996; fellow (T32) Tng. Program in Mechanisms of Virus-Host Interactions, NIH (NIH), 2001-2, Student Internship (awarded twice), Elizabeth Glaser Pediatric AIDS Found., 1999, 2001. Mem.: Am. Soc. Virology (student travel grant 2005), Am. Soc. Microbiology, AAAS, Am. Soc. for Biochemistry and Molecular Biology (assoc.). Office: Mt Sinai Sch of Medicine One Gustave L Levy Pl Box 1124 New York NY 10029 E-mail: richard.moy@mssm.edu.

**MOY, RONALD LEONARD,** dermasurgeon; b. Stuttgart, Germany, June 10, 1957; s. Howard Leonard Stephen and Jenny (Yee) M.; m. Lisa Wing Lan Lin, Aug. 10, 1986; children: Lauren, Erin. Grad., Rensselaer Poly. Inst., 1977, Albany Med. Coll., 1981. Dir. Mohs micrographic surgery div. dermatology UCLA, 1988-93, dir. dermatologic surgery div. dermatology, 1988-93, co-chief div. dermatology, 1992-93, clin. prof. David Geffen Sch. Medicine, 2005—; chief dermatologic surgery VA-West Los Angeles Med. Ctr., 1988—. Mem. Med. Bd. Calif., 2000—, pres. divsn. med. quality, 2005—. Author: Atlas of Cutaneous Flaps and Grafts, 1990, Facial Rejuvenation, 1999; editor: Principle and Practice of Dermatologic Surgery, 1993, Facial Rejuenation, 2000, Facelift, 2006, Blepharoplasty, 2006; editor-in-chief: Dermatologic Surgery, 1997—2001; mem. editl. bd. Archives Facial Plastic Surgery, Archives of Dermatology, Jour. Am. Acad. Cosmetic Surgery; contbr. articles to profl. jours. Bd. dirs. L.A. Costal unit Am. Cancer Soc., 1988. Recipient J. Lewis Pipkin award in dermatology Nat. Student Rsch. Forum, 1981, Henry Christian award Am. Fedn. Clin. Rsch., T-cell and Cytokine Patterns in Skin Cancer award NIH, 1992. Fellow: Am. Acad. Cosmetic Surgery (bd. dirs. 2004—), Am. Acad. Dermatology (Gold award 1986); mem.: Pacific Dermatol. Assn. (pres. elect 2005—06), Am. Acad. Facial Plastic Surgery, L.A. County Med. Assn. (pres. Bay dist. 1997—98), Assn. Acad. Dermatol. Surgeons (bd. dirs. 1992—95), Am. Coll. Mohs Micrographic Surgery and Cutaneous Oncology (bd. dirs. 1992—95), Am. Soc. Dermatol. Surgery (bd. dirs. 1993—96, v.p. 2001—02, pres. 2003—04). Roman Catholic. Office: 100 UCLA Med Plz Ste 590 Los Angeles CA 90024-6992 Office Phone: 310-794-7422.

**MOYA, CARLOS,** professional tennis player; b. Palma de Mallorca, Spain, Aug. 27, 1976; s. Andres and Pilar Moya. Winner Buenos Aires, 1995, Umag, 1996, L.I., 1996, U.S. Open, 1997, Copa Telmex, 2006, 17 European singles titles; winner 18 ATP singles titles. Avocations: video games, music, soccer. Office: c/o ATP Tour Internat Hdqrs 201 Atp Tour Blvd Ponte Vedra Beach FL 32082*

**MOYA, CYNTHIA ANN,** small business owner, librarian; b. L.A., Calif., Oct. 30, 1962; d. Ephraim F. and Mary A. Moya; life ptnr. Ivan Stormgart. BA, U. Calif., L.A., Calif., 1987; M of Libr. Info. Scis., U. Wash., 2001; PhD in Sexology, Inst. for Advanced Study of Human Sexuality, San Francisco, 2006. Archives cataloguer Vulcan Inc, Seattle, 2001—04; prin., owner Moya Svcs., Seattle, 2004—; pres. Alta-Glamour, Inc., 2006—. Dir. libr. Seattle (Wash.) Sex-Positive Cmty. Ctr., 2001—04. Mem.: ALA, Am. Assn. Mus., Am. Assn. Sex Educators, Counselors and Therapists, Soc. Sci. Study of Sexuality. Office: Moya Services PO Box 4632 Seattle WA 98194 Office Phone: 206-382-7282. Business E-Mail: cyndemoya@earthlink.net.

**MOYA, EVA M.,** health services executive; b. El Paso Ciudad Juarez; BA, MS, U. Tex. Exec. dir. U.S.-Mex. Border Health Commn. Sr. program coord. U.S.-Mex. Border health collaborative outreach project U. Ariz., 1995—2001, assoc. dir. health career occupation program; project dir. Cmty. Health Worker's Evaluation Tool Kit Project, 1998—2001; co-dir. Cmty. Access Program for Ariz.; pres. U.S.-Mex. Border Health Assn., 1999—2000. Contbr. articles to profl. jours. Named one of Top 10 Latinos in Healthcare, LatinoLeaders mag., 2004; recipient Adelante Mujer Hispana: Cmty. Involvement award, Tex. Cmty. Health Program award, 1990, Award for Excellence, U.S. Dept. Health & Human Services, Human Svcs. Nat. Health Svcs. Program award. Office: US Mex Border Health Commn 201 E Main Ste 1616 El Paso TX 79901 E-mail: emoya@borderhealth.net.*

**MOYA, FRANCISCO SAEZ,** consumer products company executive; b. 1951; Pres. Play by Play Toys and Novelties Europe, vice chmn., 1998—; also bd. dirs. Office: Play By Play Toys & Novelties Inc 1153 E Commerce St San Antonio TX 78205-3305 Fax: 210-824-6565.

**MOYA, PATRICK ROBERT,** lawyer; b. Belen, N.Mex., Nov. 7, 1944; s. Adelicio E. and Eva (Sanchez) Moya; m. Sara Dreier, May 30, 1966; children: Jeremy Brill, Joshua Dreier. AB, Princeton U., 1966; JD, Stanford U., 1969. Bar: Calif. 1970, Ariz. 1970, DC 1970, U.S. Dist. Ct. (no. dist.) Calif. 1970, U.S. Ct. Claims 1970, U.S. Tax Ct. 1970, U.S. Ct. Appeals (DC cir.) 1970, U.S. Supreme Ct. 1973. Assoc. Lewis and Roca, Phoenix, 1969—73, ptnr., 1973—83; sr. ptnr. Moya, Bailey, Bowers & Jones, P.C., Phoenix, 1983—84; ptnr., mem. nat. exec. com. Gaston & Snow, Phoenix, 1985—91; ptnr. Quarles & Brady LLP, Phoenix, 1991—2003, mem. nat. exec. com., 2000—02, of counsel, 2005—; exec. v.p. Insight Enterprises, Inc., Tempe, Ariz., 2002—05, chief adminstrv. officer, 2003—05, sec., 2002—05, gen. counsel, 2002—05. Instr. sch. of law Ariz. State U., 1972; bd. dirs. BIG-E Real Estate, Inc., 2000-05, Plusnet, plc., 2003-, InPlay Technologies, Inc., 2005-. Mem. Paradise Valley Bd. Adjustment, 1976-80, chmn., 1978-80; mem. Paradise Valley Town Coun., 1980-82; bd. dirs. Phoenix Men's Arts Coun., 1973-81, pres., 1979-80; bd. dirs. The Silent Witness, Inc., 1979-84, pres., 1981-83; bd. dirs. Enterprise Network, Inc., 1989-94, pres., 1991-92; bd. dirs. Phoenix Little Theatre, 1973-75, Interfaith Counseling Svc., 1973-75; precinct committeeman Phoenix Rep. Com., 1975-77; dep. voter registrar Maricopa County, 1975-76; mem. exec. bd. dirs. Gov.'s Strategic Partnership for Econ. Devel.; pres. GSPED, Inc.; mem. of Steering Com. for Sonora-Ariz. Joint Econ. Plan; mem. Gov.'s Adv. Com., Ariz. and Mex., Ariz. Corp. Commn. Stock Exch. Adv. Coun., Ariz. Town Hall. Mem. ABA, Nat. Hispanic Bar Assn., Los Abogados Hispanic Lawyers Assn., Nat. Assn. Bond Lawyers, Ariz. Bar Assn., Maricopa County Bar Assn., Paradise Valley Country Club, Univ. Club.

**MOYA, SHARON STAGGS,** language educator; b. Xenia, Ohio, May 12, 1946; adopted d. Marion Joseph and JoAnne Kalkenburg Bergin; m. Joaquin Moya, May 3, 1976; children: Nehml, Nuria Moya Lang. BA, Westhampton Coll., U. Richmond, 1968; MA, U. Fla., 1975, PhD, 1987. Cert. tchr. Ohio, 2001. Rsch. assoc. EAC, Georgetown U., Arlington, Va., 1989—90; vis. prof. Ctr. for English Tchr. Tng.; Eotvos Lorand U., Budapest, Hungary, 1993—97; adj. faculty Colo. Mountain Coll., 1999—2000, Mesa State Coll., Grand Junction, Colo., 1999—2000; English lang. learner tchr. Basalt H.S., Colo., 2000—06; English lang. learner instrn. facilitator Roaring Fork Sch. Dist., 2006—; instr. in MEd program Adams State Coll., Alamosa, Colo., 2004—05. Chair and mem., sch. bd. Am. Internat. Sch. of Budapest, 1994—96. Contbr. articles to profl. jours. Vol. Peace Corps, Nengbehn, Liberia, 1968—71; lead organizer and mem. Latino Youth Summit, Roaring Fork Valley, Colo., 2003—05. Recipient Tchr. of the Yr., Basalt H.S., 2002—03; Title VII fellow, U. S. Dept. of Edn., 1982—85, Title VI NDFL fellow, U.S. Dept. of Edn., 1976. Mem.: TESOL Internat., Phi Delta Kappa, Pi Lambda Theta. Independent. Achievements include research in the writing process of English-as-a-Second Lanuuage Learners. Avocations: gardening, reading, writing. Office: Basalt HS 600 South Side Dr Basalt CO 81621 Office Phone: 970-384-5943. Office Fax: 970-384-5955. Personal E-mail: sharonmoya@aol.com. E-mail: smoya@rfsd.k12.co.us.

**MOYA, STEVE,** health products executive; BA in Urban Affairs, U. So. Calif.; postgrad., Va. Poly. Inst. and State U. Formerly sr. v.p. Manning, Selvage and Lee, N.Y.C.; founder Moya Villanueva & Assocs.; former v.p. strategic planning and comm. LatinWorks Mktg., Austin, Tex.; former prin. Growth Strategies Consulting; sr. v.p., chief mktg. officer Humana, Inc., Louisville. Office: Humana Inc 500 W Main St Louisville KY 40202

**MOYARS-JOHNSON, MARY ANNIS,** retired history professor; b. Lafayette, Ind., July 19, 1938; d. Edward Raymond and Veronica Marie (Quigg) Moyars; m. Raymond Leon Molter, Aug. 1, 1959 (div. 1970); children: Marilyn Eileen Molter Davis, William Raymond Molter Johnson, Ann Marie Molter Guentert; m. Thomas Elmer Johnson, May 25, 1973 (div. 1989); children: Thomas Edward, John Alan, Barbara Suzanne. BS, Purdue U., 1960; MA, Purdue U., West Lafayette, Ind., 1991, postgrad., 1985—. Grader great issues Purdue U., West Lafayette, 1960-63, writer ednl. films, 1962-65, publicity dir. convocations and lectures, 1969-74, devel. officer Sch. Humanities, 1979-88, asst. to dir. Optoelectronics Rsch. Ctr., 1989-90, mgr. indsl. rels. Sch. Elec. and Computer Engring., 1990—2002, assoc. v.p. for info. tech., for comm., 2002—04; tchr. English and math. Benton Cmty. Schs., Fowler, Ind., 1966-69, ret., 1969; pub. rels. dir. Sycamore Girl Scout Coun., Lafayette, Ind., 1974-78; dir. pub. info. Ind. Senate, Majority Caucus, Indpls., 1977-78; sr. script writer Walters & Steinberg, Lafayette, 1988-89; ret., 2004. Adj. faculty Ivy Tech State Univ., 2005. Author: Colonial Potpourri, 1975, Ouiatanon--The French Post Among the Ouia, 2000; co-author: Historic Colonial French Dress, 1982, 2nd edit., 1998; contbr. articles to profl. jours. Bd. govs. Tippecanoe County Hist. Assn., Lafayette, 1981-97. Mem. Women in Comms., Inc. (Pres. award 1983, pres. Lafayette chpt. 2004-05), Ctr. for French Colonial Rsch. (dir. 1986-89, 2006—, editor 1988-89), Palatines to Am., Ind. History Assn., Ind. Hist. Soc., French Colonial Hist. Soc. Roman Catholic. Avocations: history, genealogy, embroidery. Home: 924 Elm Dr West Lafayette IN 47906-2246 Personal E-mail: mamoyars@indy.net.

**MOYER, ALAN DEAN,** retired newspaper editor; b. Galva, Iowa, Sept. 4, 1928; s. Clifford Lee and Harriet (Jacques) M.; m. Patricia Helen Krecker, July 15, 1950; children: Virginia, Stanley, Glenn. BS in Journalism, U. Iowa, 1950. Reporter, copy editor Wis. State Jour., Madison, 1950-53; reporter, photographer Bartlesville (Okla.) Examiner-Enterprise, 1953; telegraph editor Abilene (Tex.) Reporter-News, 1954-55; makeup editor Cleve. Plain Dealer, 1955-63; mng. editor Wichita (Kans.) Eagle, 1963-70; exec. editor Wichita Eagle and Beacon, 1970-73; mng. editor Phoenix Gazette, 1973-82, Ariz. Republic, 1982-89; ret., 1989. Pres. dir. Wichita Profl. Baseball, Inc., 1969-75; mem. jury Pulitzer Prizes, 1973-74, 85, 86, 88. Mem. AP Mng. Editors Assn. (dir. 1973-78), Am. Soc. Newspaper Editors, Wichita Area C. of C. (dir. 1970-72), Sigma Delta Chi. Office: Phoenix Newspapers Inc 200 E Van Buren St Phoenix AZ 85004-2238 E-mail: moyeralan@cox.net.

**MOYER, DAVID S.,** executive search consultant; BA in History, SUNY, Purchase, 1975. Spl. asst. for pub. affairs Grumman Corp., Bethpage, NY, 1975-76; instr. R.T.Y., Inc., N.Y.C. and Miami, Fla., 1976-77; exec. v.p. Wesley-Brown, Inc., N.Y.C. and L.A., 1977-83; v.p. Paul Stafford Assocs. Ltd., N.Y.C., 1983-90, Fenwick Ptnrs., Inc., N.Y.C., 1990-91, Moyer, Sherwood Assocs., Inc., Stamford, Conn., 1991-97, N.Y.C., 1997—. Contbr. articles to profl. pubs. Bd. dirs. The Helicon Found., N.Y.C., 1999—. Mem. Assn. Exec. Search Cons. (bd. dirs. 2003-05, mem. admin. coun. 2005—), Stamford Yacht Club (chmn. membership com. 1993-97). Office: 1285 Ave Americas 35th Fl New York NY 10019

**MOYER, F. STANTON,** financial executive, pharmaceutical executive; b. Phila., June 7, 1929; s. Edward T. and Beatrice (Stanton) M.; m. Ann P. Stovell, May 16, 1953; 1 child, Alice E. BS in Econs., U. Pa., 1951. Registered rep. Smith, Barney & Co., Phila., 1951-54, Kidder, Peabody & Co., Phila., 1954-60; mgr. corp. dept. Blyth Eastman Dillon & Co., Inc. (formerly Eastman Dillon, Union Securities & Co.), Phila., 1960-65, instl. sales mgr., 1965-67, gen. partner, 1967-71, 1st v.p., 1971-74, sr. v.p., 1974-80; v.p., resident officer Kidder, Peabody & Co. Inc., Phila., 1980-86; chmn. Pa. Mcht. Group Ltd., Radnor, 1987-88; exec. v.p. Rorer Asset Mgmt., Phila., 1990-92; chmn. Mercer Capital Mgmt., 1992-93, Global Mgmt. Group, Inc., 1993-95; mng. dir. Avonwood Capital Corp., 1995-97; chmn. Main Line Capital Ptnrs. Inc., 1997—. Trustee U. Pa., 1978-83, Hosp. of U. Pa., 1978-87; bd. dirs. Atwater Kent Mus., Phila., 1983—. Mem. Racquet Club (Phila.), St. Anthony Club (Phila.), Merion Cricket Club (Haverford, Pa.), Gulph Mills Golf Club (King of Prussia, Pa.), Gulf Stream Golf Club (Fla.), Gulf Stream Bath and Tennis Club, Delta Psi. Republican. Episcopalian. Home (Summer): 445 Caversham Rd Bryn Mawr PA 19010 Home (Winter): 3 Little Club Rd Gulf Stream FL 33483 Office Phone: 561-274-8378, 610-527-5015. E-mail: growthguy@aol.com.

**MOYER, GENEVIEVE J.,** counselor; b. Toledo, Ohio, Mar. 19, 1949; d. John Thomas and Genevieve Mary Bork; m. Thomas Eugene Moyer (dec.); 1 child, Eugene Thomas. BA, U. Toledo, 1977, MEd in Counseling, 1983, EdS in Counseling, 1986. Lic. counselor Mich., 1990, registered technologist

Am. Registry Radiol. Tech., 1969. Student radiol. tech. St. Vincent Med. Ctr., Toledo, 1967—69; radiol. tech. Toledo (Ohio) Hosp., 1969—70, Flower Meml. Hosp., Sylvania, Ohio, 1970—88; vocat. counselor State of Mich., Adrian, 1988—95, Saginaw, 1995—. Adj. tchr. Monroe (Mich.) C.C., 1989—95; breeder Alpaca Registry Inc., Midland, Mich., 2003—05. Represented in permanent collections Toledo (Ohio) Art Mus. Bd. dirs. Cath. Social Svcs., Monroe, Mich. Mem.: Lions Club (bd. dirs. 1998—2005, officer, 3d v.p. 2004, 2d v.p. 2005). Republican. Roman Cath. Avocations: sewing, hand spinning fleece, needlecrafts, painting, drawing. Home: 4114 N Ehlers Rd Midland MI 48642 Office: Michigan Rehabilitation Svcs 3875 Bay Rd Ste 7 Saginaw MI 48603

**MOYER, HOMER EDWARD, JR.,** lawyer; b. Atlanta, Nov. 20, 1942; s. Homer Edward and Mildred Joye (Wilkerson) M.; m. Beret Butter, July 6, 1974; children: Bronwen, Homer, Eli, Kaia Joye. BA, Emory U., 1964; LLB, Yale Law Sch., 1967. Bar: Ga. 1967, D.C. 1973. Assoc. Covington & Burling, Washington, 1973-76; from dep. gen. counsel to gen. counsel U.S. Dept. of Commerce, Washington, 1976-81; ptnr. Miller & Chevalier, Washington, 1981—. Author: The R.A.T. (Real-World Aptitude Test): Preparing Yourself for Leaving Home, 2001; co-author: Export Controls as Instruments of Foreign Policy, 1988, Justice and the Military, 1972. Bd. visitors Emory U., Atlanta, 1987-91; trustee Ctr. for Am. & Internat. Law, Council for Excellence in Govt.; past pres. Washington Council of Lawyers; chmn. Friends of CEELI Inst.; served USN JAG Corps. Mem. ABA (chmn. internat. law and practice sect. 1990-91, chmn. trade com. 1984-86, chmn. Cen. and East European Law Initiative 1990-2002, chmn. Friends of the CEELI Inst., chmn. Moscow conf. on law and bilateral econ. rels. 1990, World Order Under Law Award, 1998, CEELI Vol. award, 2002, spl. award at Runnymede, 2000), Coun. on Fgn. Rels., Phi Beta Kappa. Episcopalian. Office: Miller & Chevalier 655 15th St NW Ste 900 Washington DC 20005-5799 Office Phone: 202-626-6020. Office Fax: 202-628-0858. Business E-Mail: hmoyer@milchev.com.

**MOYER, J. KEITH,** publishing executive; b. Louisville, Ky. s. Billye Pearl (Watkins) Moyer; m. Marilyn Moyer; children: Austin, Alexis, Samantha. B in journalism, U. Fla., 1977. City hall reporter Tampa Times, Fla.; with Lakeland Ledger, Fla.; exec. editor News-Press, Fort Myers, Fla., 1986—90; named v.p., editor Ark. Gazette, Little Rock, 1990; v.p., editor Times-Union, Rochester, NY, Democrat & Chronicle, Rochester, NY; exec. editor The Fresno Bee, Calif., 1994—97, pub. Calif., 1997—2001; pub., pres. Star Tribune, Mpls., 2001—. Mem. Itasca Project; bd. mem. Capital Cities Partnership, Minn. Bus. Partnership. Bd. mem. Walker Art Mus., Mpls.; mem. nat. adv. com. Sch. Journalism and Mass Communication, U. Minn. Named Editor of Yr., Gannett Co., 1989, Alumnus of Distinction, Coll. Journalism and Comm., U. Fla., 2003. Office: Star Tribune 425 Portland Ave Minneapolis MN 55488*

**MOYER, KENNETH EVAN,** psychologist, educator; b. Chippewa Falls, Wis., Nov. 19, 1919; s. John Evan and Margaret (Lashway) M.; m. Doris Virginia Johnson, May 29, 1943; children: Robert Stephen, Cathy Lita. AB with honors, Park Coll., 1943; MA, Washington U., St. Louis, 1948, PhD, 1951. Mem. faculty Carnegie-Mellon U., Pitts., 1949—, prof. psychology, 1961—. Cons. on higher edn. Gov. Norway, 1954; mem. research adv. com. Pa. Commonwealth Mental Health Found., 1956— Author: The Physiology of Hostility, 1971, You and Your Child: A Primer for Parents, 1974, The Psychobiology of Aggression, 1976, Physiology of Aggression and Implications for Control, 1976, A Reader's Guide to Aggressive Behavior, 1977, Neuroanatomy, 1980, Bibliography of Aggressive Behavior: A Reader's Guide to the Literature, Vol. II, Violence and Aggression, 1987. Recipient Carnegie Found. award for excellence in teaching, 1954 Fellow AAAS, Am. Psychol. Assn.; mem. Psychonomic Soc., Soc. Philosophy and Psychology, Pitts. Psychol. Assn. (past dir.), Sigma Xi, Theta Kappa Theta. Achievements include research, publs. endocrinology emotion, startle response avoidance behavior, physiology aggression; demonstrated young children have capacity for prolonged attention spans if proper toys are used, that adrenal glands are not essential for effects electroconvulsive shock on behavior; devel. physiol. theory aggressive behavior. Home: 1211 Ridgewood Dr Lillian AL 36549-5303

**MOYER, R. CHARLES,** finance company executive, educator, retired dean; b. Reading, Pa., July 11, 1945; s. Ralph Charles and Jane Anne (Huls) M.; m. Sally Louise Prizer, May 19, 1973; children: Laura Prizer, Craig Prizer. BA in Econs., Howard U., 1967; MBA, U. Pitts., 1968, PhD in Fin., 1971. Asst. prof. fin. U. Houston, 1971-76; fin. economist U.S. Maritime Adminstrn., Washington, 1973-74; assoc. prof. Lehigh U., Bethlehem, Pa., 1976-77; from assoc. prof. to prof. U. N.Mex., Albuquerque, 1977-80; prof., chmn. fin. dept. Tex. Tech U., Lubbock, 1980-87; GMAC ins. chair in fin., Babcock Grad. Sch. Wake Forest U., Winston-Salem, NC, 1988—2004, dean Babcock Grad. Sch. of Mgmt., 1996—2003, dean emeritus 2003—; dir. King Pharm., Inc., Bristol, Tenn., 2000—; dean Coll. Bus. Adminstrn. U. Louisville, 2005—. Pres., founder R.O.E. Cons. Group, Lubbock, 1978; cons. Pub. Svc. Co. N.Mex., 1977—, KN Energy, Denver, 1979—, Gas Co. N.Mex., 1985—, San Diego Gas Electric Co., 1986—; mem. adv. bd. Amarr Garage Door Co., Winston-Salem, 2001-05; bd. dirs. Metacyte, Ky. Seed Capital Fund. Author: Financial Management with Lotus 1-2-3, 1986, Managerial Economics, 10th edit., 2005, Contemporary Financial Management, 10th edit., 2006, Contemporary Financial Management Fundamentals, 2d edit., 2006; contbr. numerous articles to profl. jours. Vice-chmn. Lubbock Gen. Hosp. Found., 1985-88. Capt. US Army, 1972-74. Fed. Res. Bank Cleve. fellow, 1970-71. Mem.: We. Fin. Assn., Ea. Fin. Assn., Sou. Fin. Assn. (v.p. 1990—93, pres. 1993), Am. Econs. Assn., Am. Fin. Assn., Fin. Mgmt. Assn. (bd. dir. ombudsman 1985—87, v.p. 1988—, sec.-treas. 1994—2002), Lake Forest Country Club, Louisville Boat Club, Old Town Club, Beta Gamma Sigma, Phi Beta Kappa. Avocations: tennis, golf, bicycling. Office Phone: 502-852-6443.

**MOYER, RYAN P.,** marine biologist; b. Reading, Pa., Sept. 30, 1976; s. John E and Cheryl L. Moyer; m. Aya Shinohara, Sept. 15, 2004. MS, Nova Southeastern U., Ft. Lauderdale, Fla., 2003. Pre-coll. instr. The Marine Sci. Consortium, Wallops Island, Va., 1999—2000; rsch. assoc. Nat. Coral Reef Inst., Dania Beach, Fla., 2001—04; grad. tchg. asst. The Ohio State U., Columbus, 2005—. Contbr. articles to profl. jours. Recipient Simpson award, Kutztown U. Dept. of Phys. Sci., 1999; fellow NSF Access Sci. fellow, U. of Pa., 2004—05; grantee Travel grantee, Am. Geophys. Union, 2006. Mem.: Geol. Soc. of Am., Am. Geophys. Union, Internat. Soc. for Reef Studies, Gamma Theta Upsilon. Avocations: travel, photography, surfing. Office: The Ohio State University 125 S Oval Mall Columbus OH 43210 Office Phone: 1-614-292-1434. E-mail: moyer.120@osu.edu.

**MOYER, THOMAS J.,** state supreme court chief justice; b. Sandusky, Ohio, Apr. 18, 1939; s. Clarence and Idamae (Hessler) M.; m. Mary Francis Moyer, Dec. 15, 1984; 1 child, Drew; stepchildren: Anne, Jack, Alaine, Elizabeth. BA, Ohio State U., 1961, JD, 1964. Asst. atty. gen. State of Ohio, Columbus, 1964-66; pvt. practice law Columbus, 1966-69; dep. asst. Office Gov. State of Ohio, Columbus, 1969-71, exec. asst., 1975-79; assoc. Crabbe, Brown, Jones, Potts & Schmidt, Columbus, 1972-75; judge U.S. Ct. Appeals (10th cir.), Columbus, 1979-86; chief justice Ohio Supreme Ct., Columbus, 1987—. Chair Conference of Chief Justices, 1995—96, Nat. Conf. on Ct. Security, 2005. Sec. bd. trustees Franklin U., Columbus, 1986-87; trustee Univ. Club, Columbus, 1986; mem. nat. council adv. com. Ohio State U. Coll. Law, Columbus. Recipient Award of Merit, Ohio Legal Ctr. Inst., Am. Judicature Soc. award, Disting. Service award Nat. Ctr. for State Cts., 1997, Innovative Program award Assn. Family & Conciliation Cts., 1998, Better World award Ohio Mediation Assn., 1999, Whitney North Seymour medal Am. Arbitration Assn., 2000, James F. Henry award, 2003; named Outstanding Young Man of Columbus, Columbus Jaycees, 1969. Mem. Ohio State Bar Assn. (exec. com., council dels., Ohio Bar medal 1991), Columbus Bar Assn. (pres. 1980-81, Liberty Bell award), Critchon Club, Columbus Maennerchor Club; fellow Ohio State Bar Found. (Ritter award 1996). Republican. Avocations: sailing, tennis. Office: Ohio Supreme Ct 65 S Front St Columbus OH 43215*

**MOYERS, BILL D.,** journalist, writer; b. Hugo, Okla., June 5, 1934; s. John Henry and Ruby (Johnson) M.; m. Judith Suzanne Davidson, Dec. 18, 1954; children: William Cope, Suzanne, John Davidson. BJ with honors, U. Tex., 1956; grad. student, U. Edinburgh, Scotland, 1956-57; MDiv with honors, Southwestern Baptist Theol. Sem., 1959; DFA (hon.), Am. Film Inst. Personal asst. to Senator Lyndon B. Johnson, 1960—61; assoc. dir. pub. affairs Peace Corps, 1961-62, dept. dir., 1963; spl. asst. to Pres. Johnson, 1963-67, press sec., 1965-67; pub. Newsday, Garden City, NY, 1967-70; editor-in-chief Bill Moyers Jour. (weekly pub. affairs program on pub. TV), 1971-76, 78-81; chief corr. CBS Reports, CBS-TV, 1976-78; sr. news analyst CBS News, CBS-TV, 1981-86; founder Pub. Affairs Programming, Inc., 1986—; anchor, writer NOW with Bill Moyers, 2002—04. Author; editor: Listening to America, 1971, Report from Philadelphia, 1987, The Secret Government, 1988; editor: Joseph Campbell and the Power of Myth, 1988, A World of Ideas, 1989, 2d edit., 1990, Genesis, 1996, Fooling With Words, 1999; prodr. (TV series) Creativity with Bill Moyers, 1982, Healing and the Mind, 1993. Pres. The Florence and John Schumann Found., 1991—. Recipient over 30 Emmy awards, Ralph Lowell medal for contbn. to pub. TV, George Peabody award, 1976, 80, 85-86, 88-90, 99, 2000, 04, DuPont-Columbia U. Silver Baton, 1979, 86, 88, Gold baton award, 1991, 99, George Polk award, 1981, 86, career achievement award Internat. Documentary Assn., Eric Barnouw award Orgn. Am. Historians, medal of excellence N.Y. State Bd. Regents, James Madison award Nat. Broadcasting Editl. Assn., Communicator of Decade award Religious Comm. Congress, Elmer Holmes Bibst award NYU, Religious Liberty award Am. Jewish Com., 1995, Walter Cronkite award for excellence in journalism, 1995, The Fred Friendly First Amendment award, 1995, NEH Charles Frankel prize for outstanding contbns. to cultural life, 1997; elected to TV Hall of Fame, 1995; George Polk award for career achievement, 2005. Fellow AAAS; mem. Am. Philos. Soc. Office: Pub Affairs TV Inc 450 W 33rd St New York NY 10001-2603

**MOYERS, JUDITH DAVIDSON,** television producer; b. Dallas, May 12, 1935; d. Henry Joseph and Eula E. (Dendy) Davidson; m. Bill D. Moyers; children: William Cope, Suzanne, John. BS, U. Tex., 1956; LittD (hon.), L.I. U., 1989, SUNY, 1990. Pres., exec. prodr. Pub. Affairs TV, N.Y.C., 1987—; exec. editor NOW, 2001—05. Exec. prodr. TV documentaries (Emmy 1980, 93, 98, 2001,03, DuPont 1999, Christopher 1990, Parker 1992, Gold Hugo 1991, Humanitas prize 1995); exec. editor Now with Bill Moyers, 2001-; contbr. articles to profl. jours., newspapers, mags. Trustee SUNY, 1976-90; commr. U.S. Commn. UNESCO, Washington, 1977-80, White House commn. Internat. Yr. of Child, Washington, 1978-80; mem. jud. selection com. State N.Y., 1992-93; dir. Pub. Agenda Found. Recipient Christopher award, 2004. Mem. Acad. TV Arts and Scis., Century Club. Mem. Congregational Ch. Office: Pub Affairs TV Inc 450 W 33rd St Fl 7 New York NY 10001-2603

**MOYERS, SYLVIA DEAN,** retired medical librarian; b. Independence, W.Va., Oct. 22, 1936; d. Wilkie Russell and Ina Laura (Watkins) Collins; m. Paul Franklin Moyers, June 29, 1957; children: Tammy Jeanne, Thomas Paul, Tara Sue. Student, Am. Med. Record Assn., 1977—79. Sec. Teets Lumber Co., Terra Alta, W.Va., 1954-58, Preston County News, 1958-60; med. record clk. med. record dept. Preston Meml. Hosp., W.Va., 1960-75, dir., 1975-88; sec. The Terra Alta Bank, 1990-95; ret., 1995. Charter mem., past mother advisor Order of Rainbow Girls (Terra Alta Assembly No. 26), past grand editor Mountain Echoes; vol. Preston Meml. Hosp., ARC, Salvation Army, Am. Cancer Soc., Boy Scouts Am., Muscular Dystrophy Assn.; active Kingwood Fire Dept. Aux. Mem.: Preston County Hist. Soc., Kingwood Red Hat Mamas (charter), Preston Meml. Hosp. Aux., Kingwood Civic Club. Republican. Methodist. Home: 120 Miller Rd Kingwood WV 26537-1321

**MOYES, JERRY C.,** transportation executive; b. Plain City, Utah; m. Vickie Moyes; 10 children. Grad., Weber State Coll. Co-founder Swift Transp. Co., Inc., 1966—, v.p., 1966—84, chmn., pres., CEO Phoenix 1984—; owner SME Steel. Limited ptnr. Ariz. Diamondbacks, Phoenix Suns; co-owner Phoenix Coyotes, 2001—. Mem.: Am. Trucking Assn. (v.p.), Ariz. Motor Transportation Assn. (pres. 1987—98). Office: Swift Transp Co 2200 S 75th Ave Phoenix AZ 85043-7410 also: PO Box 29243 Phoenix AZ 85038-9243 Fax: 623-907-7380.*

**MOYLAN, DOUGLAS B.,** attorney general; b. Stockton, Calif., Oct. 19, 1966; s. Richard and Jane Moylan. B in Bus. Admin., U. Notre Dame, 1988; JD, Santa Clara U., 1991. Bar: Guam Bar Admissions 92, Calif. Bar Admissions 1992, cert.: D.C. Ct. of Appeals 1993. Law clk. Judge Alberto C. Lamenora Superior Ct. Guam, 1991, staff atty., 1991—93; atty. with Robert Torres P.C. Legis. Counsel, 24th, 25th, 26th Guam Legis., 1993—96; small claims ct. referee Superior Ct. Guam, 1995—97; pvt. practice Moylan & Van de Veld Law Offices, 2001—02; atty. gen. The Justice Bldg., Guam, 2002—. Bd. mem. Guam Election Commission, 1996—2000. Bd. mem. Guam's Election Commn. Bd. Office: The Justice Bldg DM W O'Brien Dr Hagatna GU 96910 Office Phone: 671-475-3324. E-mail: dbmoylan@ite.net.

**MOYLAN, KALEO,** lieutenant governor; s. Kurt S. and Judith G. Moylan; m. Julie R. Cruz; children: Alyssa Lehua, Jada Pomaikai. BA, U. Colo., Boulder, 1988; JD, U. Puget Sound. Senator 25th and 26th Guam Legis., chmn. com. on housing, gen. govt. svcs. and fgn. affairs; chmn. on ways and means, chmn. ways and means com.; lt. gov. Ter. of Guam, Anigua, 2003—. Regional mgr. life divsn. Moylan's Inc.; exec. v.p. Netcare Life and Health Ins. Co. Mem. Tumon Bay Rotary Club, Guam C. of C. Republican. Office: Office Lt Governor RJ Bordallo Governor's Complex PO Box 2950 Hagatna GU 96932 Office Phone: 671-475-9380. Office Fax: 671-477-2007. Business E-Mail: ksmoylan@ite.net.*

**MOYLE, PETER BRIGGS,** marine biologist, educator; b. May 29, 1942; s. John Briggs and Evelyn (Wood) M.; m. Marilyn Arneson, June 11, 1966; children: Petrea Ruth, John Noah. BA, U. Minn., 1964, PhD, 1969; MS, Cornell U., 1966. Asst. prof. Calif. State U., Fresno, 1969-72; from asst. prof. to prof. U. Calif., Davis, 1972—, chmn. dept. wildlife and fisheries, 1982-87, Pres.'s chair in undergrad. edn., 2003—. Head, Delta Native Fishes Recovery Team, 1993-95. Author: Inland Fishes of California, 1976, 2d edit., 2002, Fishes: An Introduction to Ichthyology, 3d edit., 2003, Fish: An Enthusiast's Guide, 1993. Fellow Calif. Acad. Sci.; mem. Am. Fisheries Soc. (life, award of excellence West divsn. 1991, Outstanding Educator award 1995), Ecol. Soc. Am., Am. Soc. Ichthyologists and Herpetologists, Soc. Conservation Biology, Natural Heritage Inst. (v.p.). Home: 612 Eisenhower St Davis CA 95616-3031 Office: U Calif Dept Wildlife Fish & Conservation Biolog 1 Shields Ave Davis CA 95616 E-mail: pbmoyle@ucdavis.edu.

**MOYLES, PHILIP VINCENT, JR.,** financial services company executive; b. N.Y.C., July 14, 1964; s. Philip Vincent and Anne Kane Moyles; m. Beth O'Connor. BA in History, Kenyon Coll., 1986; postgrad., Dartmouth Coll. 2000. Mgmt. trainee Rollins Burdick Hunter Co., Chgo., 1986-87; assoc. Johnson & Higgins, N.Y.C., 1987-90; sr. acct. rep. Marsh & McLennan Inc., N.Y.C., 1990-91, asst. v.p., 1991-93, v.p., 1993-95, sr. v.p., 1995-96; from mng. dir., practice leader mergers and acquisitions to exec. v.p. Marsh Inc., N.Y.C., 1996—2004, exec. v.p., 2004—. Mem. Union League Club N.Y., Allegheny Country Club, Apavaaunis Clubn Hudson Nat. Golf Club Republican. Roman Catholic. Office: Marsh Inc 1166 Ave of Americas 44th Floor New York NY 10036

**MOYNA, JOHN LAWRENCE,** priest; b. NYC, Aug. 20, 1945; s. John Lawrence and Margaret Mary (Healy) Moyna. BA, St. Joseph's Sem. Coll., 1969; MDiv, Christ the King Sem., 1975. Ordained Roman Catholic Priest Diocese of Albany, 1973. Assoc. pastor St. Clare's Ch., Colonie, NY, 1973—75, St. Mary's Ch., Clinton Heights, NY, 1975—79, St. Pius X Ch., Londonville, NY, 1979—83, St. John the Evangelist Ch., Schenectady, NY, 1983—86; pastor St. Mary's Ch., Coxsackie, NY, 1986—; chaplain N.Y. State Dept. of Corrections, 1996—. Dean Suburban Albany, NY, 1982—83. Co-chmn. Ministerial Assoc., Coxsackie; mem. Presbyterian Coun., Albany, 1975—79, 1988—93, chmn., 1991—93; mem. strategic pastoral planning com. Diocese of Albany, 1990—91; mem. NY State Cath. Conf. Com. On Apostolate, 2006—. Mem.: Am. Correctional Assn., Acad. Correctional Health Profls. Roman Catholic. Achievements include development of hospice tng. for prison inmates. Home and Office: St Mary's Ch 80 Mansion St Coxsackie NY 12051 Office Phone: 518-731-8800.

**MOYNAHAN, JOHN DANIEL, JR.,** retired insurance executive; b. Chgo., Dec. 10, 1935; s. John Daniel and Helen (Hurley) M.; m. Virginia Thomas, Oct. 10, 1959; children: Laura, Mark, Tricia, Kate. BA cum laude, U. Notre Dame, 1957. With Met. Life Ins. Co., N.Y.C., 1957—, regional v.p., from 1971, with nat. div. group nat. accounts, 1979-80, sr. v.p. group life and health ops., 1980-86, exec. v.p., 1986-97; ret., 1997.

**MOYNAHAN, JULIAN LANE,** retired literature educator, writer; b. Cambridge, Mass., May 21, 1925; s. Joseph Leo and Mary (Shea) M.; m. Elizabeth Rose Reilly, Aug. 6, 1945; children: Catherine (dec.), Brigid, Mary Ellen. AB, Harvard U., 1946, A.M., 1951, PhD, 1957. Cataloguer, rare books asst. Boston Pub. Library, 1948-49, 51; teaching fellow Harvard U., 1951-53; instr. English Amherst Coll., 1953-55; instr., asst. prof. English Princeton, 1955-63; Fulbright lectr. Am. and English lit. Univ. Coll., Dublin, 1963-64; assoc. prof. English Rutgers U., 1964-66, prof., 1966-93, disting. prof., 1976-93, prof. emeritus, 1993—. Vis. prof. U. Wyo., summer 1965, Harvard U., summer 1967, Bread Loaf Sch., 1969, NYU, 1997; NEH vis. prof. Manhattanville Coll., 1972; Gauss lectr. Princeton U., 1975; vis. scholar English dept. U. Utah, spring 1980; lectr. N.J. Coun. for Humanities, 1998, 99. Author: Sisters and Brothers, 1960, The Deed of Life, A Critical Study of D.H. Lawrence, 1963, Pairing Off, 1969, Vladimir Nabokov, 1971, Garden State, 1973, Where the Land and Water Meet, 1979, Anglo-Irish: The Literary Imagination in a Hyphenated Culture, 1995; editor: (D.H. Lawrence) Sons and Lovers: Text, Criticism, Backgrounds, 1968, 77, The Viking Portable Thomas Hardy, 1977; contbr. revs. and criticism to N.Y. Times Book Rev., T.L.S., Washington Post Book World, N.Y. Rev. Books; contbr., mem. editl. bd. The Recorder, Jour. Am. Irish Hist. Soc., 1994—; contbr. poetry to jours. Bicentennial preceptorship Princeton, 1960-63, grants-in-aid Am. Coun. Learned Socs.; Am. Philos. Soc.; mem. Pulitzer Prize Fiction Jury, 1981, chmn., 1987; mem. Friends of Princeton U. Libr., 2002—. Served with AUS, 1943-44, 7500 creative writing award Nat. Found. Arts, 1966; Ingram-Merrill award, 1967; NEH fellow, 1975; Guggenheim fellow, 1983-84. Mem. MLA, PEN, Harvard Club of Princeton. Democrat. Home: 136 Bayard Ln Princeton NJ 08540-3041 Address: Apt 9B London Ter 405 W 23d St New York NY 10011 E-mail: moy@patmedia.net.

**MOYNE, JOHN ABEL,** computer scientist, linguist, educator; b. Yezd, Iran, July 6, 1920; came to U.S., 1956, naturalized, 1965; s. Abul Kasim and Sogra (Afshar) M.; m. Claudia Wienert, July 4, 1963; children: David, Nicholas, Parvin. BA, Georgetown U., Washington, D.C., 1959, MA, 1960; PhD, Harvard U., Cambridge, Mass., 1970. With Brit. Govt., Iran and India, 1943-52, market rsch. officer Tehran, 1952; linguist U.S. Govt., Cyprus, 1953-56; rsch. assoc. Georgetown U., Washington, 1960-63; mgr. applied linguistics dept. IBM Corp., Cambridge, Mass., 1963-71; prof., chmn. computer sci. dept. Queens Coll. CUNY, Flushing, 1971-81, chmn. divsn. math. and natural scis., 1978-81, univ. faculty for PhD in Computer Sci., 1978-82, exec. officer Grad. Sch. PhD Program in Linguistics, 1983-88, prof. linguistics and computer sci., 1971—91, prof. emeritus linguistics and computer sci., 1991—. Author, co-author: Hafiz of Shiraz, 1946, Life in India, 1949, Open Secret, 1984, Understanding Language: Man or Machine, 1985, Unseen Rain, 1986, Rumi: These Branching Moments, 1988, This Longing Poetry, Teaching Stories, and Letters of Rumi, 1988, LISP: A First Language for Computing, 1991, Say I Am You, 1994, The Essential Rumi, 1995, Rumi and the Sufic Tradition: Essays on the Mowlavi Order and Mysticism, 1998, The Drowned Book, 2004; contbr. articles to profl. jours., chpts. to books. Grantee EURATOM, AEC, NSF, CUNY. Mem. Linguistics Soc. Am., Brit. Inst. Engring. Tech., The Acad. Am. Poets. Democrat. Home: 40 Prospect Ave Sea Cliff NY 11579-1029 Office: CUNY PhD Program Linguistics Grad Ctr 365 5th Ave New York NY 10016-4334 E-mail: jmoyne@post.harvard.edu, jmoyne@gc.cuny.edu, jmoyne@verizon.net.

**MOYNIHAN, BRIAN T.,** finance company executive; b. 1960; m. Susan Berry; 3 children. Grad., Brown U.; JD, Notre Dame Law Sch. Dep. gen. coun. FleetBoston Fin. Corpn., 1993—94, mng. dir. corp. strategy and devel., 1994—2000, sr. v.p. 1998—99, exec. v.p. 1999, exec. v.p. brokerage and wealth mgmt., 2000; pres. global wealth & investment mgmt. Bank Am. Corpn. Bd. dirs. YouthBuild Boston; chmn. Providence Halibut Project, Inc. Office: Bank Am Corp Ctr 100 N Tryon St Fl 58 Charlotte NC 28255-0001

**MOYNIHAN, GARY PETER,** industrial engineering educator; b. Little Falls, N.Y., Mar. 5, 1956; s. Peter H. and Frances S. (Ferjanec) M.; m. Eleanor T. McCusker, Mar. 10, 1984; children: Andrew Ross, Keith Patrick. BS in Chemistry, Rensselaer Polytech. Inst., 1978, MBA in Opsl. Mgmt., 1980; PhD in Indsl. Engring., U. Ctrl. Fla., 1990. Prodn. supr. Am. Cyanamid, Bound Brook, N.J., 1978-79, Nat. Micronetics, Kingston, N.Y., 1980-81; assoc. mfg. engr. Martin Marietta Aerospace, Orlando, Fla., 1981-82, indsl. engr., 1982-85, sr. indsl. engr., 1985-87, group indsl. engr., 1987-90; asst. prof. indsl. engring. U. Ala., Tuscaloosa, 1990-96, assoc. prof., 1996—2001, prof., 2001—. Cons. in field. Contbr. articles to profl. jours. Regents scholar N.Y. State Bd. Regents, 1974-78; rsch. fellow NASA, 1992-93, 98-99; rsch. grant BellSouth Telecomm., 1994-96; recipient Outstanding Tchg. award AMOCO Found., 1993-94, Ralph R. Teetor Engring. Educator award Soc. Automotive Engrs, 2000. Mem.: IEEE (sr.), Aerospace and Def. Soc. (v.p. fin. and adminstrn. 1994—97), Inst. Indsl. Engrs. (sr.; chpt. dir. 1991—95, chpt. pres. 1996—97, regional v.p. 2004—06, Outstanding Faculty Adv. SE Region award 2004). Achievements include design and development of information systems applications for the aerospace and foundry industries; 4 software copyrights. Office: U Ala Dept Indsl Engring Tuscaloosa AL 35487-0001

**MOYNIHAN, JAMES M.,** bishop; b. Rochester, N.Y., July 16, 1932; Student, St. Bernard's Sem., Rochester, N.Am. Coll., Rome, Gregorian U. Ordained priest Roman Cath. Ch. 1957. Bishop Diocese of Syracuse, Syracuse, NY, 1995—. Office: 240 E Onondaga St Syracuse NY 13202-2608

**MOYNIHAN, JOHN BIGNELL,** retired lawyer; b. NYC, July 25, 1933; s. Jerome J. and Stephanie (Bignell) M.; m. Odilia Marie Jacques, Nov. 13, 1965; children: Blair, Dana. BS, Fordham U., 1955; JD, St. John's U., N.Y.C. 1958. Bar: Tex. 1961, U.S. Supreme Ct. 1965, U.S. Dist. Ct. (we. dist.) Tex. 1968, U.S. Ct. Appeals (5th cir.) 1973. Sole practice, Brownsville, Tex., 1961-62; asst. city atty. City of San Antonio, 1962-63; sole practice San Antonio, 1963-65; estate tax atty. IRS, San Antonio, 1965-73; dist. counsel EEOC, San Antonio, 1974-79; assn. U.S. atty. Office U.S. Atty., San Antonio, 1980-87, sr. litigation counsel, 1987-94; sole practice San Antonio, 1995-98; ret., 1998. Chmn. reform and renewal com., San Antonio Roman Cath. Archdiocese, 1968. Served with U.S. Army, 1958-60; lt. col. USAFR (ret.), 1986. Mem. San Antonio Bar Assn. (chmn. state and nat. legis. com. 1972-73, Meritorious Svc. award 1968); Fed. Bar Assn. (bd. dirs. San Antonio chpt. 1983—, pres. elect 1986, pres. 1987), KC (pres. 1967). Home: 11011 Whispering Wind St San Antonio TX 78230-3746 E-mail: jmoynihan@satx.rr.com.

**MOYNIHAN, WILLIAM J.,** museum executive; b. Little Falls, N.Y., Apr. 8, 1942; s. Bernard J. and Mary A. (Flynn) M.; m. Irene A. Sheilds, July 2, 1966; children: Patricia, Erin, Sean. BA, SUNY, Binghamton, 1964; MA, Colgate U., 1966; PhD, Syracuse U., 1973. From asst. to assoc. prof. Colgate U., Hamilton, NY, 1973—77, from asst. to assoc. dean faculty 1977—80, dean students 1980—83, dean coll., 1983—88; v.p.m. dir. Am. Mus. Natural History, NYC, 1988—95; pres., CEO Milw. Pub. Mus., 1995—2002; ret., 2002. Bd. dirs. N.Y. State Mus.; adv. com. arts and culture Congressman J. Nadler, N.Y.C., 1993-95. Adv. editor Curator jour., 1991-95. Mem. Am. Mus. Assn., Am. Assn. Museums (mem. ethics com. bd.), Wis. Acad. of Scis. Arts and Letters (councillor-at-large 1995-02), Univ. Club. Home: 84 Eaton St Hamilton NY 13346

**MOYSE, HERMANN, III,** banker; b. Baton Rouge, Dec. 28, 1948; s. Hermann Jr. and Marie Louise (Levy) M.; m. Janet Lee Doise; children: Allison Leze, David Hermann, Aaron Lewis. BA, Coll. of Emporia, 1970; MSW, La. State U., 1973. Asst. dir. Capital Area Health Planning Agy., 1973-74; research assoc. La. State U., Baton Rouge, 1974-78; trainee to v.p. City Nat. Bank, Baton Rouge, 1978—, sr. v.p., 1985-94, also bd. dirs., chmn., 1994-98; owner, pres. HM3 Corp., 1999—. Sec.-treas. Melrose Devel. Corp., Baton Rouge, 1986-87; bd. dirs. La. Cos., Charter Chambers, LLC; CEO Health Net One, 1999; adv. bd. Iberra Bank, 2004—; pres. WRKF Radio, 2003-04; chmn. La. State U. Health Care Svcs. Found., 2002—. Mem. Istrouma Council Boy Scouts Am.; mem. Capital Area United Way Agy. Svcs. Div., Baton Rouge, 1979-86, 88-91, vice chmn. 1981, bd. dirs., 1987—; chmn., 1989-90; v.p. Arts Coun. Greater Baton Rouge, 1990—; 1st v.p. La. Arts & Sci. Ctr., Baton Rouge, 1985—, pres., 1988; mem. Community Funds for Arts, 1989-90; mem. Arts & Humanities Coun., 1990—, v.p., 1991—; treas., 1992; mem. Community Funds for the Arts, 1989—, vice chmn., 1992; pres. Cath. Community Life Office, Baton Rouge, 1981, Baton Rouge Speech and Hearing Found., 1986, pres. 1983, treas., 1981; mem. St. Joseph's Acad. Adv. Bd., v.p., 1986-88, pres., 1987-88; bd. dirs. St. James Place; treas. Baton Rouge Crisis Intervention Ctr., 1984-85, v.p., 1987, pres., 1987; sec. St. Joseph's Children's Home, 1980; bd. dirs. Crime Stoppers, Inc., 1986—, v.p., 1989, pres. 1991—; pres. Mid City Devel. Alliance, 1991-93, 97—; mem. adv. bd. Tau Ctr., 1990-93; trustee Episc. High Sch., 1990-92; treas. La. Delta Svc. Corps. Inc., 1995—; bd. trustees Gen. Health Sys., Inc, 1994-98, La. Nature Conservancy, 2001—, Our Lady of Lake Coll., 2001—, sec., 2003—; mem. Baton Rouge Crimestoppers, chmn. fin. com., 1997—; chmn. First Commerce Cmty. Devel. Corp., 1993-99. Mem. La. Bankers Assn. (fed. affairs com. 1990—), La. Coun. Econ. Edn. (trustee 1987, regional v.p. 1990—, Community Vol. Activist award 1988), NCCJ (chpt. bd. dirs. 1988, treas. 1995), City Club, Baton Rouge Country Club. Democrat. Jewish.

**MOZELL, HERBERT LEE,** mental health services professional; b. Miami, Fla., Feb. 16, 1963; s. Alfonzo and Ethel Mae Mozell. BA in Psychology, A&T State U., 1988, MS in Adult Edn., 1997; postgrad., Nova Southeastern U. Habilitation tech, Greensboro, NC, 1990—96; exec. dir. Visions of N.C. Inc., Greensboro, 1997—. Mental health tech., Greensboro, 1988—97; tchr. Allen Jay Mid. Sch., Archdale, 1999—2001; cons., Greensboro, 2004—, Little Seedlings, Greensboro, 2004—, Faith House, Lexington, 2004—, Sensational Living, Raleigh, 2004—. Recipient Humanitarian award, Nova S.E. U., 2004. Mem.: Am. Mental Health Counselor Assn., Kappa Delta Pi. Democrat. Baptist. Avocations: Karate, weightlifting. Office: Visions of NC Inc 7607-A Alcorn Rd Greensboro NC 27409 Office Phone: 336-931-0432.

**MOZENTER, CYRILLA,** artist; b. Newark, N.J., June 3, 1947; d. Paul and Sophie Manas Mozenter; m. Philip David Perkis. BFA, Pratt Inst., Bklyn., 1970; MFA, Pratt Inst., 1972. Instr. Pratt Inst., Bklyn., 1985—, Parsons Sch. Design, NY, 1994—97, Cooper Union Sch. Art, NY, 2001. Panelist verbal and visual metaphor Conf. Writing the Arts/When Lang. Meets Form Pratt Inst., Bklyn., 1996; jury panelist workspace program Dieu Donne Papermill, NY, 2002; jury panelist MFA program Queens Coll. CUNY, 2002; spkr. in field. One-woman shows include Mercer Gallery, NY, 1985, William Paterson U., Wayne, NJ, 1988, Susan Schreiber Gallery, NY, 1990, JamisonThomas Gallery, 1993, Bklyn. Acad. Mus.Majestic Theater, 1996, The Drawing Ctr., 2000, Little Red Sch. House, NY, 2004, Aldrich Contemporary Art Mus., Ridgefield, Conn., 2005—06, exhibited in group shows at Adam Baumgold Gallery, NY, 2005, The Drawing Ctr., 2002, PS 122 Gallery, 2002, TheWorkspace, 2002, Neuberger Mus. Art, Purchase, NY, 2000, 1999, Bklyn. Mus. Art, 1997, Sculpture Ctr., 1996, John Michael Kohler Arts Ctr., Sheboygan, Wis., 1995, Stark Gallery, 1992, Jamison Thomas Gallery, 1991, Rotunda Gallery, Bklyn., 1986. Studio: 147 W 22d St #10N New York NY 10011

**MOZER, MARTHA K.,** music educator; MusB in Voice, Cleve. Inst. Music, 1967—71, MusM in Voice & Opera Theatre, 1971—73. Co. mgr. Goldovsky Opera Theatre, NYC, 1973—80; opera workshop stage dir. New Eng. Conservatory Music Ext. Divsn., Boston, 1979—85; music dir. Fairhope Christian Ch., Ala., 1993—; drama and chorus tchr. Fairhope Mid. Sch., 1994—. Grantee Artist in Edn.. Ala. Coun. on Arts, 1994. Mem.: MENC. Office: Fairhope Mid Sch 408 N Section St Fairhope AL 36532-2695 Office Phone: 251-928-2573. Business E-Mail: mmozer@bcbe.org.

**MOZILO, ANGELO R.,** diversified financial services company executive; BS, Fordhan U., 1960; LLD (hon.), Pepperdine U. Co-founder, vice chmn. Countrywide Fin. Corp., Calabasas, Calif., 1969—99, pres., 2000—03, CEO, 1998—99, chmn., CEO, 1999—. Bd. mem. Nat. Housing Endowment, Joint Ctr. for Housing Studies, Harvard U., Homes for Working Families; trustee Gonzaga U. Named one of 30 most respected CEOs, Barron's mag., 2005; named to Nat. Assn. of Home Builders' Hall of Fame; recipient Boy Scouts of Am. James E. West Fellowship award, Ellis Island Medal of Honor, Albert Schweitzer award, Special Achiev. award, Nat. Italian Am. Found., Horatio Alger Assn. of Disting. Am. award. Mem.: Mortgage Bankers Assn. of Am. (pres. 1991—92). Office: Countrywide Fin Corp 4500 Park Granada Calabasas CA 91302-1613*

**MOZLEY, PAUL DAVID,** retired obstetrics and gynecology educator; b. Decatur, Ala., Oct. 27, 1928; s. James Howard and Ruth Dianne (Brindely) M.; m. Mary Dale Goss, Aug. 30, 1983; children from previous marriage: Susan Ruth, Paul David Jr., Sally Robin. BA, U. Ala., 1950; MD, Med. Coll. Ala., 1955. Diplomate Am. Bd. Ob-Gyn, Am. Bd. Psychiatry and Neurology. Commd. lt. USN, 1955, advanced through grades to capt.; 1970; resident ob-gyn Corona (Calif.) and San Diego Naval Hosp., 1956-59; resident in psychiatry Bethesda, Md., 1964-66, Phila. Naval Hosp., 1969-70; staff gynecologist U.S. Naval Hosp., Yokosuku, Japan, 1959-62, chief gynecologist Memphis, 1962-64, dir. med. services Naples, Italy, 1966-68, comdg. officer, 1969; chmn. neuropsychiatry Naval Regional Med. Ctr., Portsmouth, Va., 1970-75; ret., 1975; assoc. prof. psychiatry Eastern Va. Med. Sch., Norfolk, 1975-77, prof., interim chmn. dept., 1977-78, vice chmn. psychiatry, 1978-79; prof., dir. undergrad. edn. Dept. Ob-Gyn Sch. Medicine, East Carolina U., Greenville, 1979-84; prof. ob-gyn, chmn. dept., Coll. Community Health Scis. U. Ala., Tuscaloosa, 1984-99, prof. ob-gyn, assoc. chmn. dept. Sch. Medicine, 1984-99, prof., chmn. emeritus Sch. Medicine, prof. emeritus obstetrics, 1999—; ret., 2002; obstetrician-gyn. private svcs. Norfolk Gen. Hosp., 1975-79; chmn. dept. ob-gyn DCH Regional Med. Ctr., Tuscaloosa, 1986—; obstetrician Baldwin Clinic; cons. med. liability law legal firms., Ala., Tenn., 1980—. Contbr. numerous articles to profl. jours. Mem. Regional Parental Adv. Council, Montgomery, Ala., 1986-87; sponsor Tuscaloosa Symphony Assn. Recipient Meritorious Service medal Pres. U.S., 1975, Surgeon Gen.'s Merit award, 1975, Attending of Yr. award Residents in Psychiatry, 1979, Clin. Sci. Course award Dept. Ob-Gyn grad. class, 1982, Eastern Va. Sch. Medicine; named one of Outstanding Young Men in Am., Jaycees, 1964 Fellow ACS, Am. Coll. Ob-Gyn (chmn. various programs 1974, 76, 77, Chmn.'s award clin. research 1969, life), Am. Psychiat. Assn. (Continuing Med. Edn. Standards award 1977, life); mem. AMA (Physician's Recognition award 1986), Am. Soc. Psychosomatic Ob-Gyn (founding mem., pres. 1979-80, chmn. nominating com. 1981, permanent steering com. 1982), Va. Ob-Gyn Soc., Assn. Acad. Psychiatry, Va. Med. Soc., N.C. Neuropsychiat. Assn., Pitt County Med. Soc., Med. Assn. Ala., Ala. Psychiat. Assn., LWV, Torch Club (Portsmouth), Alpha Epsilon Delta. Democrat. Mem. Ch. of Christ. Avocations: cabinetry, goldsmithing. Home: 563 N Mobile St Fairhope AL 36532-2609 Personal E-mail: pm02@bellsouth.net.

**MRACHEK, LORIN LOUIS,** lawyer; b. Fairmont, Minn., Jan. 5, 1946; s. Louis L. and Kathleen (Loring) M.; m. Elizabeth Moss, Aug. 31, 1968; children: Kathleen Elizabeth, Louis Moss. BA with honors, Fla. State U., 1968; MBA, JD, Columbia U., 1974. Bar: Fla. 1974, Va. 1977, U.S. Ct. Mil. Appeals 1977, U.S. Dist. Ct., U.S. Ct. Appeals (5th cir.), U.S. Ct. Appeals (7th cir.), U.S. Ct. (11th cir.), U.S. Supreme Ct. 1978, U.S. Bankruptcy Ct. (so. dist.) Fla., U.S. Bankruptcy Ct. (mid. dist.) Fla., U.S. Bankruptcy Ct. (no. dist.) Fla.; cert. in civil trial law, 1985-2005, bus. litigation, 1997-, Fla. Bar Bd. Certification; cert. in bus. bankruptcy law Am. Bd. Bankruptcy Certification, 1992-; cert. in civil trial advocacy Nat. Bd. Trial Advocacy, 1995-

2005. Commd. 2d lt. USMC, 1969, advanced through grades to capt., 1974, chief def. counsel Marine Corps. Recruit Depoit, Paris Island, 1975-77, resigned, 1977; spl. asst. to gen. counsel U.S. Ry. Assn., Washington, 1977-78; shareholder Gunster, Yoakley, Valdes-Fauli & Stewart, P.A., West Palm Beach, Fla., 1978-2000; founding shareholder Page, Mrachek, Fitzgerald & Rose, West Palm Beach, Fla., 2000—. Editor-in-chief Columbia Jour. Law and Social Problems, 1973-74; contbr. articles to profl. jours. Named one of Best Lawyers in Am.; Harlan Fiske Stone scholar. Fellow Am. Coll. Trial Attys.; mem. ABA, Am. Bankruptcy Inst., So. Fla. Bankruptcy Bar Assn. Avocations: travel, golf. Office: 505 S Flagler Dr Ste 600 West Palm Beach FL 33401-5941 Office Phone: 561-655-2250. Business E-Mail: lmrachek@pm-law.com.

**MRACKY, RONALD SYDNEY,** marketing executive, tourism consultant, media specialist; b. Sydney, Australia, Oct. 22, 1932; came to U.S., 1947, naturalized, 1957; s. Joseph and Anna (Janousek) M.; m. Sylvia Frommer, Jan. 1, 1960; children: Enid Hillevi, Jason Adam. Student, English Inst., Prague, Czechoslovakia, 1943-47; grad., Parsons Sch. Design, N.Y.C., 1950-53; postgrad., NYU, 1953-54. Designer D. Deskey Assocs., N.Y.C., 1952-53; art dir., designer ABC-TV, Hollywood, Calif., 1956-57; creative dir. Neal Advt. Assocs., L.A., 1957-59; pres. Richter & Mracky Design Assocs., L.A., 1959-68; pres., CEO Richter & Mracky-Bates divsn. Ted Bates & Co., L.A., 1968-73, Regency Fin., Internat. Fin. Svcs., Beverly Hills, Calif., 1974-76; sr. ptnr. Sylron Internat., L.A., 1973—, mgmt. dir. for N.Am. Standard Advt.-Tokyo, 1978-91. CEO, Std./Worldwide Cons. Group, L.A., Tokyo, 1981-87; officer, bd. dirs. Theme Resorts, Inc., Denver, 1979—; prin., officer Prodn. Travel & Tours, Universal City, 1981—, Eques Ltd., L.A., 1988-93; mng. ptnr. GO! Pubs., 1993—; cons. in field; exec. dir. Inst. for Internat. Studies and Devel. L.A., 1976-77; mng. ptnr. Africa Consult Group, 1998—. Dir. MedicusTravel.com, 2003—; mem. editl. bd., mktg. dir. The African Times and Africa Quar., 1990—; contbr. articles to profl. jours With U.S. Army, 1954-56. Recipient nat. and internat. awards design and mktg. Mem. Am. Mktg. Assn., Africa Travel Assn. (amb.-at-large, internat. secretariat, bd. dirs.), L.A. Publicity Club, Pacific Asia Travel Assn., S.Am. Travel Assn., Am. Soc. Travel Agts. Personal E-mail: africaconsult@mindspring.com.

**MRAK, ROBERT EMIL,** neuropathologist, educator; b. Oakland, Calif., Dec. 18, 1948; s. Emil Marcel and Vera Dudley (Greaves) M.; m. Paula Elizabeth North, Oct. 18, 1980; children: Lara North, Eric North, Ian North. BS in Math., U. Calif., Davis, 1970, MD, 1975, PhD in Zoology, 1976. Diplomate Am. Bd. Pathology, Am. Bd. Neuropathology. Resident in pathology Vanderbilt U. Hosp., Nashville, 1976-78, fellow in molecular biology, 1978-80; asst. prof. pathology Vanderbilt U., 1980-84; assoc. prof. U. Ark. for Med. Scis., Little Rock, 1984—87, prof., 1993—98, chief neuropathology, 1999—, dir. neuropathology core, Alzheimer Disease Core Ctr., 2001—, prof. pathology, neurobiology and devel. scis., 1998—, chief autopsy, 2003—. Chief electron microscopy VA Hosp., Little Rock, 1984-98; cons. in neuropathology Ark. Children's Hosp., Little Rock, 1984—. Editl. bd. mem. Jour. Neuropathy & Explt. Neurology, 1996-99, Human Pathology, 1996-2004; editor-in-chief Jour. Neurinflammation, 2003—; contbr. articles and abstracts to profl. jours Rsch. grantee VA, 1980-83, 86-89, Muscular Dystrophy Assn., 1981-85, NIH, 1986-90, 95—. Mem. Am. Assn. Neuropathologists, Soc. for Neurosci., U.S. and Can. Acad. Pathology. Avocations: running, skiing. Office: U Ark for Med Scis #517 4301 W Markham St Little Rock AR 72205-7101 Business E-Mail: mrakroberte@uams.edu.

**MRAZ, MARK,** education educator, researcher; b. Kittanning, Pa., July 5, 1951; s. Michael and Lena Mraz; m. Sue Mae Gittner, May 17, 1953; children: Rose Ann, Sue Leah. PhD, Pa. State U., State College, 1995. Cert. social studies tchr. Pa. Adj. prof. history U. Pitts. at Bradford, St. Marys, Pa., 1995—2002; asst. prof. edn. Slippery Rock (Pa.) U., 2002—. Cons. Tchg. Am. History Grant, St. Marys, Pa., 2002—. Adviser Secondary Edn. Club, Slippery Rock, 2002—. Mem.: NCSS (assoc.; scholarship com. 2006—). Office: Slippery Rock U 208D McKay Edn Bldg Maltby Dr Slippery Rock PA 16057 Office Phone: 724-738-2288. Office Fax: 724-738-4987. E-mail: mark.mraz@sru.edu.

**MRAZEK, DAVID ALLEN,** psychiatrist; b. Ft. Riley, Kans., Oct. 1, 1947; s. Rudolph George and Hazel Ruth (Schayes) M.; m. Patricia Jean, Sept. 2, 1978; children: Nicola, Matthew, Michael, Alissa. AB in Genetics, Cornell U., 1969; MD, Wake Forest U., 1973. Lic. psychiatrist, child psychiatrist, N.C., Ohio, Colo., D.C., Va., Md., Minn., Ariz., Fla. Lectr. child psychiatry Inst. of Psychiatry, London, 1977-79; dir. pediatric psychiatry Nat. Jewish Ctr. for Immunology and Respiratory Medicine, Denver, 1979-91; chmn. psychiatry Children's Nat. Med. Ctr., Washington, 1991-98; chair psychiatry and behavioral scis. George Washington U. Sch. Medicine, 1996-2000; dir. Children's Rsch. Inst. Neurosci., 1995-98; chair psychiatry and psychology Mayo Clinic, Rochester, Minn., 2000—; prof. psychiatry and pediatrics Mayo Sch. Medicine, Rochester, 2000—; dir. Mayo Clinic S.C. Johnson Genomics of Addictions Program, 2004—. Asst. prof. psychiatry U. Colo. Sch. Medicine, 1979-83, assoc. prof. psychiatry and pediatrics, 1984-89, prof., 1990-91; prof. psychiatry and pediatrics George Washington U. Sch. Medicine, 1991-2000, Leon Yochelson prof. psychiatry and behavioral scis.; dir. Am. Bd. Psychiatry and Neurology, 2003-. Contbr. chapters to books, articles to profl. jours. Recipient Rsch. Scientist Devel. awards NIMH, 1983-88, 88-91, Irving Phillips Meml. award for outstanding rsch. in prevention Acad. Child and Adolescent Psychiatry, 2000, Simon Wile award Am. Acad. Child and Adolescent Psychiatry, 2005 Fellow Am. Acad. Child and Adolescent Psychiatry (Simon Wile award 2005), Royal Soc. Medicine, Am. Psychiat. Assn. (chmn. coun. children, adolescents and families 2006—), Blanche F. Ittleson award 1996, Agnes Purcell McGavin award 1999), Royal Coll. Psychiatrists, Am. Coll. Psychiatrists; mem. Group for the Advancement of Psychiatry, Colo. Child and Adolescent Psychiatry Soc. (pres. 1984), Benjamin Rush Soc., Am. Bd. Psychiatry Neurology (bd. dirs. 2003—). Office: Mayo Clinic Dept Psychiatry/Pschology 200 1st St SW Rochester MN 55905 Office Phone: 507-284-0491. Office Fax: 507-266-5519. Business E-Mail: mrazek.david@mayo.edu.

**MRAZEK, ROBERT J.,** writer, former congressman; b. Newport, RI, Nov. 6, 1945; s. Harold Richard and Blanche Rose M.; m. Catherine Susan Gurick, Mar. 31, 1971; children: Susannah Rose, James Nicholas. BA in Govt., Cornell U., 1967. Spl. asst. to U.S. Senator Hartke, Washington, 1969-71; spl. projects coordinator Town of Huntington, NY, 1971; legislator Suffolk County, Hauppauge, NY, 1975-82, minority leader, 1979-82; mem. 98th-102nd Congresses from 3d NY dist., 1983—93. Author: (novels) Stonewall's Gold, 1999 (Michael Shaara award for Excellence in Civil War Fiction, 1999), Unholy Fire, 2003, The Deadly Embrace, 2006. Bd. dirs. World Devel. Assn. Huntington Village, NY, 1971-76, pres. 1972-74. With USN, 1968. Recipient Happel award for contributions to battlefield preservation, Civil War Preservation Trust, 2004. Mem. DAV. Democrat. Methodist.

**MRKVICKA, EDWARD FRANCIS, JR.,** writer, finance company executive; b. Aurora, Ill., Oct. 17, 1944; s. Edward Francis Sr. and Ruth Caroline (Phillips) M.; m. Madelyn Helen Rimnac, July 1, 1972; children: Edward Francis III, Kelly Helen. Cert. comml. pilot, U. Ill., 1965; diploma, Dept. Def., 1967. Bank Mktg. Assn., 1972, grad. cert., 1973. Mktg. officer Downers Grove (Ill.) Nat. Bank, 1964-72; asst. v.p., mktg. officer Bank of Westmont, Ill., 1972-73; v.p., cashier 1st State Bank Hanover Park, Ill., 1973-76; pres. 1st Nat. Bank Marengo, Ill., 1976-81, Reliance Enterprises, Inc., Fin. News Syndicate, Omni, Fin. Group, Eagle Publishing, Marengo, 1981—. Adv. coun. Am. Monetary Found., Fullerton, Calif., 1987; mem. panel of experts Boardroom Reports, 1990—. Pub: (newletter) Money Insider; author: Battle Your Bank-And Win!, 1984, Moving Up, 1985; (with others) The Complete Book of Personal Finance, 1987, The Bank Book, 1989, 91, 94, 1,037 Ways to Make or Save Up to $100,000 This Year Alone, 1991, The Rational Investor, 1992, Your Bank is Ripping You Off, 1997, 99, J.K. Lasser's Pick Winning Stocks, 2000, Be Not Deceived, 2006; contbr. articles to profl. jours. and newspapers. In. columnist Nat. Enquirer, 1996—. Bd. dirs. DuPage County Lung Assn., Downers Grove, 1970, Western Suburbs Combined Com.

Appeal, Downers Grove, 1971, McHenry County Easter Seals Clinic, Woodstock, Ill., 1979; v.p.; treas. Marengo/Union Chamber, 1980; Am. rep. Cans. for Constitutional Money, 1990—. Sgt. USAF, 1965-69. Mem. Nat. Writers Union. Republican. Avocations: bowling, fishing. Office: Reliance Enterprises Inc PO Box 413 Marengo IL 60152-0413 Office Phone: 815-568-8267. Business E-Mail: reliance@cin.net.

**MROCZKOWSKI, MATTHEW,** biomedical engineer; MS, Syracuse U., N.Y., 2003. Rsch. engr. Zimmer, Inc., Warsaw, Ind., 2003—05. Contbr. articles to profl. jours. Recipient Bioengineering Founder's award, Syracuse U., Dept. Bioengring., 2001. Mem.: Orthop. Rsch. Soc. Office: Zimmer 1800 W Center St Warsaw IN 46580 Office Phone: 574-267-6131. Office Fax: 574-372-4922. E-mail: matt.mroczkowski@zimmer.com.

**MROSKO, MATTHEW L.,** music educator; b. Warren, Mich., Oct. 10, 1979; s. Richard John and Marie Christina Mrosko. BA in Music Edn., Shenandoah U., 2003. Cert. tchr. Va. Band tchr. Shenandoah County Pub. Schs., Woodstock, Va., 2004—. Mem.: Music Educators Nat. Conf. Avocations: travel, hiking. Office: Peter Muhlenberg Mid Sch 1251 Susan Ave Woodstock VA 22664 Office Phone: 540-459-2941. Personal E-mail: morosoko@yahoo.com. Business E-Mail: mlmrosko@shenandoah.k12.va.us.

**MROZ, JOHN EDWIN,** political scientist; b. Lowell, Mass., May 1, 1948; s. Edwin T. and Margaret Mary (Little) M.; m. Karen Linehan, June 17, 1972; children: Jonathan E.R., Jessica, Jeffrey. BA, cert. Soviet and East European studies, U. Notre Dame, 1970; AM, Northeastern U., 1972; MA, MALD, Tufts U., 1974. Exec. sec. UN Assn. Greater Boston, 1971-73; asst. dir. Middle East Studies, Internat. Peace Acad., Inc., N.Y.C., 1976-81; pres. Inst. East West Studies, N.Y.C., 1981—; cons., U.S. Govt. intermediary in Middle East, U.S. Dept. State, 1981-82; cons. Fgn. Svc. Inst., Dept. State, 1977-81; cons. Coun. of Europe, Strasbourg, Fed. Republic Germany, 1989—, East European govts., 1990—. Author: Beyond Security: Private Perceptions Among Arabs and Israelis, 1980. Contbr. articles to profl. jours. Teaching fellow NSF, 1971-72. Decorated Officer's Cross of Order of Merit Fed. Republic of Germany, 1991. Mem. Coun. on Fgn. Rels., Internat. Inst. Strategic Studies. Republican. Avocations: travel, falconry. Office: Inst East West Studies 700 Broadway New York NY 10003-9536

**MROZEK, ERNEST J.,** customer service administrator; married; 2 children. Grad. in Acctg., U. Ill. CPA Ill. Pres., COO, Consumer Svcs., The ServiceMaster Co., Downers Grove, Ill., 1997—98, group pres. consumer and comml. svcs., 1998—2002, pres., COO, 2002—04, pres., CFO, 2004—. Mem.: AICPAs, Ill. CPA Soc. Office: ServiceMaster 3250 Lacey Rd Downers Grove IL 60515*

**MROZEK, LAWRENCE JAMES,** director; s. Mary Anna and Albin Bruno Mrozek. BS in Psychology, Mich. State U., 1984, MA in Phys. Exercise and Exercise Sci., 1989; Cert. - Alcohol and Other Drug Specialist, Calif. State Univeristy, LA, Los Angeles, CA, 1992—93; Cert. - Family Violence and Child Maltreatment, Calif. State U., LA, Los Angeles, CA, 1993—2003; PhD in Edn., Ohio State U., 2003—. Cert. alcohol and other drug specialist Calif. State U., 1993, family violence and child maltreatment specialist Calif. State U., 2003. Area coord. Whittier Coll., Calif., 1986—87; resident dir. Calif. State U., L.A., 1987—89; from asst. to dir. to asst. dir. for programs U. Student Union, L.A., 1989—92, from asst. dir. for ops. to ops. mgr. Northridge, Calif., 1992—2002. Directorate - commn. for alcohol and other drug issues Am. Coll. Pers. Assn., Washington, 1990—92, directorate - commn. on assessment for student devel., 2002—03; conf. planning com. Assn. of Coll. Unions Internat. - Region 15, L.A., 1995—95, San Bernardino, Calif., 1997—97. Del. Coun. of Grad. Students, Columbus, Ohio, 2005. Recipient Employee of Yr. award, U. Student Union - Calif. State U., Northridge, 1994-1995, Aida C. Salazar award, 1995-1996. Mem.: NEA, Am. Ednl. Rsch. Assn., Assn. for Study of Higher Edn., Nat. Assn. of Student Pers. Administrs., Am. Coll. Pers. Assn., Phi Kappa Phi, Pi Lambda Theta. Office: Ohio State Univ 47 Curl Dr Columbus OH 43210-1111 Office Phone: 614-247-6220.

**MROZOWICZ-PICKEN, MARIA M. See PICKEN, MARIA**

**MRUK, EUGENE ROBERT,** retired marketing professional, urban planner; b. Buffalo, Sept. 12, 1927; s. Stanley and Lucy Ann (Wolanski) M.; m. Florence Helen Guzy, Apr. 15, 1950; children: Linda, Lawrence, Edith, Ginny. AA in Engring., U. Buffalo, 1966, BA in Sociology, 1970; cert. sys. analysis & application admin., U. Wis., 1971; MA in Econs., U. Buffalo, 1974. Asst. dir. planning City of Buffalo, 1958-70; commr. planning Erie County, N.Y., Buffalo, 1970-74; dir. socioecon. studies Ecology and Environment, Inc., Buffalo, 1974-79, dir. transp. system studies, 1979-81, dir. bus. devel., 1981-86, v.p. sales and mktg., 1986-90, sr. v.p. sales and mktg. nat. and internat., 1990-94, cons., 1994-96; ret. 1996. Pvt. practice planning cons. Buffalo area, 1950-64; v.p. rsch. and planning coun. WNY, 1971-74; mem. indsl. adv. bd. dept. chem. engring. SUNY, Buffalo. Author various mcpl. govt. plans. Coord. Econ. Devel. program, Buffalo, 1966; exam. cons. Civil Svc. Commn. City of Buffalo, 1974; grand marshal Gen. Pulaski Parade com., Buffalo, 1972; trustee Villa Maria Coll. Buffalo, 1992-93. Named Man of Yr. in Govt. Am-Pole Eagle newspaper, 1970; gold medal sr. olympics, N.H., N.Y., 2003, 04, 05, 06. Mem. Am. Assn. Cert. Planners, Am. Planning Assn. (Disting. Leadership award N.Y. upstate chpt. 1992, dir.), Profl. Businessmen's Assn., Fr. Kolbe Soc./Polish Union of Am. (pres. 1995-2000). Democrat. Roman Catholic. Avocations: tennis, senior olympic basketball, photography, oil and acrylic painting. Home: 3 Dennis Ln Cheektowaga NY 14227-1301

**MSHANA, PAMELA MARIVA,** secondary school educator; b. Pomona Calif., Sept. 28, 1969; d. Godi Mshana and Patricia Ann Mshana-Caraway; 1 child, Mariva Jamilla Mshana-Dawes. BFA, NYU, 1991; MEd, Azusa Pacific U., 2003. Writer, rschr. Kundola Prodns., N.Y.C., 1991—93; drama/playwright instr. House of Praise Pvt. Playhouse, Moreno Valley, Calif., 1994—96; tchr. lang. arts Pomona Unified Sch. Dist., 1999—. Author: (plays) Ebony, 1990, A Toast to Leslie, 1990, Girls in Search of Cover, 2003. Finalist Young Playwrights Festival, The Dramatist Guild, 1987, Internat. Young Playwrights Festival, Sydney Opera House, 1989; recipient 3d Pl. award, NAACP Nat. Young Poets Contest, 1984. Avocations: theater, film arts, reading.

**MUBARAK, KAMAL K.,** pulmonologist; arrived in U.S., 1989; s. Ali Khan and Azra Mubarak; m. Tabinda Khan Mubarak, Dec. 20, 1995; children: Eman Azra, Izan Ali. MD, Aga Khan U., Karachi, 1988. Cert. in critical care and pulmonary medicine, diplomate Am. Bd. Internal Medicine. Asst. prof. medicine Wayne State U., Detroit, 2000—, dir. pulmonary hypertension clinic, 2001—. Fellow: Am. Coll. Chest Physicians; mem.: Am. Thoracic Soc., Internat. Soc. Philos. Enquiry. Office: Wayne State U 3990 John R 3937 Hudson Detroit MI 48201 Office Phone: 313-745-6033. Office Fax: 313-993-0562.

**MUCCI, GARY LOUIS,** lawyer; b. Buffalo, Nov. 12, 1946; s. Guy Charles and Sally Rose (Battaglia) M.; m. Carolyn Belle Taylor, May 4, 1991. BA cum laude, St. John Fisher Coll., 1968; JD, Cath. U., 1972. Bar: N.Y. 1972. Law clk. to Hon. John T. Curtin U.S. Dist. Ct., Buffalo, 1972-74; assoc. atty. Donovan Leisure Newton & Irvine, N.Y.C., 1974-75, Saperston & Day P.C., Buffalo, 1975-80, sr. ptnr., 1980—2001; ptnr. Hiscock Barclay, 2001—. Chmn. bd. Buffalo Philharm. Orch., 1985-86; pres. Hospice Buffalo, 1986-87; mem. N.Y. State Coun. on the Arts 1987-2000; chmn. Citizens Com. on Cultural Aid, Buffalo, 1992-98; trustee St. John Fisher Coll.; chmn. bd. trustees Hardin Acad., 2005—. Recipient Brotherhood award NCCJ, Buffalo, 1983; named Man of Yr. William Paca Soc., 1984. Mem. Erie County Bar Assn., N.Y. State Bar Assn. Home: 27 Tudor Pl Buffalo NY 14222-1615 Office: Hiscock Barclay 3 Fountain Plz Ste 1100 Buffalo NY 14203-1486 Office Phone: 716-566-1520. Business E-Mail: gmucci@hiscockbarclay.com.

**MUCCI, PATRICK JOHN,** financial consultant, realtor, commercial loan broker; b. Albany, N.Y., July 5, 1947; s. Philip and Angelina (Patrella) M.; m. Beverly Ann Scully, June 8, 1968; children: Philip Michael, Angelina Maria. AAS, Hudson Valley Community Coll., Troy, N.Y., 1967; BS, SUNY, Albany, 1977; MBA, Fairleigh Dickinson U., 1979. Cert. review appraiser, comml. investment mgr., real estate broker, internat. financier; registered mortgage underwriter; lic. ins. broker for life and accident ins. Adminstrv. asst. Nat. Savs. Bank, Albany, 1973-76; asst. v.p. Heritage Savs. Bank, Kingston, N.Y., 1976-78, Home Savs. Bank, Albany, 1978-81; v.p., 1981, Home & City Savs. Bank, Albany, 1981-83, sr. v.p. lending, 1983-90; pres., chmn. bd., founder Greenbush Assocs., Inc., East Greenbush, 1990—2003. Chmn. bd., founder, pres. Patrician Funding, Inc., 1997—, East Greenbush; bd. dirs. Vec Tech., Inc., Philangie Corp.; v.p., sr. comml. loan officer Provantage Funding Corp., 2000-02; v.p. govt. guaranteed lending, Key Bank, 2003-. Active Nat. Assn. Govt. Guaranteed Lenders; treas., bd. dirs. Theater Voices, 1990; bd. dirs. Albany League Arts, Discovery Ctr. Capital Region, 1990, N.Y. State Mus. Inst., Capital Affordable Housing Funding Com., Albany County Affordable Housing Corp., Grand St. Cmty. Arts; mem. Rensselaer County Com. Sewer & Water Authority, 1993-94. Staff sgt. USAF, 1969-72. Mem. Nat. Assn. Mortgage Brokers, N.Y. State Mortgage Brokers Assn., N.Y. State Assn. Comml. and Indsl. Brokers, Soc. Internat. Financiers, Worldwide Network, N.E. Assn. Mtge. Bankers. Avocations: travel, reading, photography, computers. Home: 296 Luther Rd East Greenbush NY 12061-4312 Office Phone: 518-257-9405. Business E-Mail: patrick_mucci@keybank.com.

**MUCCIA, JOSEPH WILLIAM,** lawyer; b. NYC, May 31, 1948; s. Joseph Anthony and Charlotte (Mohring) M.; m. Margaret M. Reynolds, June 29, 1985. BA magna cum laude, Fordham U., 1970, JD, 1973. Bar: N.Y. 1974, U.S. Dist. Ct. (so. dist.) N.Y. 1974, U.S. Dist. Ct. (ea. dist.) N.Y. 1974, U.S. Ct. Appeals (2d cir.) 1974, U.S. Ct. Appeals (D.C. cir.) 1980, U.S. Supreme Ct. 1980. Assoc. Cahill Gordon & Reindel, N.Y.C., 1973-82; ptnr. Conbin Silverman & Sanseverino, N.Y.C., 1983—2001, Brown Raysman Millstein Felder & Steiner LLP, N.Y.C., 2002—. Assoc. editor Fordham Law Rev., 1972-73. Mem. ABA (litigation sect.), N.Y. County Lawyers Assn., Fed. Bar Coun., N.Y. State Bar Assn. (com. litigation sect.), Phi Beta Kappa, Pi Sigma Alpha. Office: Brown Raysman et al 900 3d Ave New York NY 10022 Office Phone: 212-895-2930. Business E-Mail: jmuccia@brownraysman.com.

**MUCHA, SISTER MARLENE M.,** secondary school educator; d. John Peter and Stacia J. Mucha. BA, Coll. Our Lady of Elms, Chicopee, Mass., 1965; MA, R.I. Coll., 1974. Joined Sisters of St. Joseph; cert. English lang. tchr. Mass. Tchr. English, chmn. English dept. Marianhill H.S., Southbridge, Mass., 1965-69, Holyoke (Mass.) Cath. H.S., 1969—. Acad. standards com. Holyoke Cath. H.S., alumni bd., Cursillo retreat spiritual advisor, Nat. Honor Soc. advisor, faculty advanced placement com., advisor sr. class, chair English dept. Bd. trustees Our Lady of Coll. of Elms, 2003, Nat. Youth Leadership Forum Recognition. Recipient Galleon award in Journalism, Jostens, 1983, Golden Apple Edn. award for Excellence in Edn., Sta. WGGB-TV/McDonalds, 1991, Excellence in Tchg. award Pioneer Valley, 2004, Harold Grinspoon Tchg. award, Stonehill Coll. Cert. Recognition, Herald Grinspoon Excellence Tchg. award, 2004. Mem. Nat. Coun. Tchrs. of English, NCEA. Avocations: reading, crafts, quilling, macramé. Home: 621 Grattan St Chicopee MA 01020 Office: Holyoke Cath HS 66 School St Granby MA 01033

**MUCHMORE, DON MONCRIEF,** retired cultural organization administrator, retired museum director, foundation administrator; b. Wichita, Kans., Dec. 26, 1922; s. Floyd Stephen and Ivy Fay (Campbell) Muchmore; m. Virginia Gunn, June 18, 1949 (div. Dec. 1978); children: Melinda, Marcia. BA, Occidental Coll., Los Angeles, 1945; postgrad., U. So. Calif. Law Sch., 1945, UCLA. Intern Nat. Inst. Pub. Affairs, Washington, 1944; exec. asst. to congressman Washington, 1946-48; teaching asst. UCLA, 1949-50; mem. faculty San Diego State U., 1950-51; asst. prof., adminstr. Calif. State U., Long Beach, 1951-56; pres., CEO The Campbell Found., L.A., 1956—2002; spl. asst. to supt. pub. instrn. Calif. Dept. Edn., Sacramento, 1956-57; exec. mus. dir. Calif. Mus. Sci. and Industry, L.A., 1957-62, 82-89; exec. v.p., chief exec. officer Calif. Mus. Found., L.A., 1957-62, 82-89; dep. dir. (on loan from mus.) Calif. Dept. Fin., Sacramento, 1960; exec. vice chancellor Calif. State Colls. and Univs. System, Long Beach, 1962-64; first exec. asst. to chmn. and chief exec. officer Calif. Fed. Savs. and Loan Assn., L.A., 1964-66; sr. v.p. Calif. Fed. Savs. and Loan Assn., L.A., 1966-82; pres., CEO PE Conservation Svcs., Inc., 1990-94; ret. 2002. Chmn. bd. dirs., CEO Opinion Rsch. of Calif. Opinion Surveyors, The State Poll and Mktg. Surveys, Inc., Long Beach, 1948—71; syndicated by L.A. Times, 1961—70; also M-R Assocs. Campaigns; cons. in pub. opinion mus. mgmt. and fund raising, 1948—71; chmn., CEO, cons. DMM & Assocs., Long Beach, 1961—2002; sec., treas. EV-ENUP for the Homeless, 1994—97; mem. Inst. Mus. Svcs., 1983—88. Contbr. chapters to books. Participant in pub. opinion work Dem. and Rep. Campaigns, 1954—72; mem., chmn. 4 presdl. commns., 1970—82, Just Say No Internat., 1989—91, Reading is Fundamental, 1989—, The Buckley Sch., 1989—90; cons. overseas traveling sci. exhibit, planning mus., 1984—96; sr. adminstr., advisor, cons. PCS (South Ctrl. L.A.) Sr. Citizens, 1995—96; cons. Long Beach com. Improvement League, 1995—96; lead cons. New Solution to Homeless, 1993—98; prin. officer Peruvians Cultural Exhibit, 1988—96; prin. cons. cultural exhibit Wonders of World, 1992—95, Queensway Bay, Long Beach, 1992—98; bd. dirs. Bus. Tele Network, 1995—97; active Even up for the Homeless, 1996—98; cons. Christian Outreach Agy., 1998—99; pres. Harborplace Tower Home Owners Assn., 1999—; pres. bd. trustees East Village Cmty. Ctr., 1998—, pres., 1998—2001. Named Chpt. Advisor of Yr., Sigma Alpha Epsilon, 1999, Pollster of Yr., Newsweek, 1968; recipient Highest Mus. Edn. award, Sigma Alpha Epsilon, 1992, Citizen of Yr. award and numerous other awards from nat. and local groups, scholar Elks Nat. scholar. Mem.: AAAS, Calif. Mus. Assn. (pres. 1960, bd. dirs. 1982—88), Am. Polit. Sci. Assn., Am. Assn. Pub. Opinion Rsch., Assn. Sci. and Tech. Ctrs. (bd. dirs. 1982—88), Am. Assn. Mus.

**MUCHMORE, ROBERT BOYER,** engineering executive, consultant; b. Augusta, Kans., July 8, 1917; s. Ray Boyer and Charlotte (McPherron) M.; m. Betty Morgan, Jan. 29, 1944; children: Andrew Vaughan, Douglas Boyer. BS, U. Calif., Berkeley, 1939; degree in Elec. Engring., Stanford U., 1942. Project engr. Sperry Gyroscope Co., Garden City, NY, 1942-46; sr. mem. tech. staff Hughes Aircraft, Culver City, Calif., 1946-54; v.p., chief scientist TRW Systems, Redondo Beach, Calif., 1954-73, cons. Sonoma, Calif., 1973—. Lectr. in engring. UCLA, 1954-58. Author: Essentials of Microwaves, 1952. Fellow IEEE; mem. AAAS, Assn. Computing Machinery, Sierra Club. Home: 4311 Grove St Sonoma CA 95476-6046 E-mail: rbm@sonic.net.

**MUCHNICK, RICHARD STUART,** ophthalmologist, educator; b. Bklyn., June 21, 1942; s. Max and Rae (Kozinsky) Muchnick; m. Felice Dee Greenberg, Oct. 29, 1978; 1 child, Amanda Michelle. BA with honors, Cornell U., 1963, MD, 1967. Diplomate Am. Bd. Ophthalmology. Nat. Bd. Med. Examiners. Intern in medicine N.Y. Hosp., N.Y.C., 1967—68, now assoc. attending ophthalmologist, chief Pediatric Ophthalmology Clinic, resident in ophthalmology, 1970—73, practice medicine, specializing in ophthalmology, notably strabismus and ophthalmic plastic surgery, 1974—. Attending surgeon, chief Ocular Motility Clinic Manhattan Eye, Ear and Throat Hosp., N.Y.C.; clin. assoc. prof. ophthalmology Cornell U., N.Y.C., 1984—; clin. rschr. strabismus, ophthalmic plastic surgery, 1973—. With USPHS, 1968—70. Recipient Coryell Prize Surgery, Cornell U. Med. Coll., 1967, McLean Medal in Ophthalmology, Weill Med. Coll. of Cornell U., 2006. Fellow: ACS, Am. Acad. Ophthalmology; mem.: AMA, Manhattan Ophthal. Soc., Greater N.Y. Soc. Pediat. Ophthalmology and Strabismus (pres.), N.Y. Acad. Medicine, N.Y. Soc. Clin. Ophthalmology, Internat. Strabismological Assn., Am. Assn. Pediatric Ophthalmology and Strabismus, Am. Soc. Ophthalmic Plastic and Reconstructive Surgery, 7th Regt. Tennis, Lotos, Alpha Epsilon Delta, Alpha Omega Alpha. Office: 69 E 71st St New York NY 10021-4213 Office Phone: 212-744-1726.

**MUCINO-QUINTERO, VICTOR HUGO,** mechanical engineering educator, consultant; b. Mexico City, Jan. 2, 1952; arrived in U.S., 1985; s. Alfonso Mucino-Reyes and Marcelina Quintero-Elizondo; m. Elisabeth Sanchez, Jan. 26, 1990; children: Andrea, Veronique. BSME, Poly. Inst. Mex., Mexico City, 1974; M Engring., U. Wis., Milw., 1977, DEng, 1981. Registered profl. engr., Wis., W.Va. Rsch. assoc. J. I. Case Co., Racine, Wis., 1977-80; prof. Nat. U. Mex., Mexico City, 1981-85; prof. mech. engring. W.Va. U., Morgantown, 1985—. Dir. indsl. outreach program in Mex. W.Va. U.; indsl. cons. Contbr. articles to profl. jours., including ASME Jour. Mech. Design, Indsl. Tribology, SAE Trans., Jour. Sound and Vibrations, others. Mem.: ASME, Am. Soc. Engring. Educators, Acad. Engring. Mex., Soc. Automotive Engrs. (Ralph Teetor award 1995). Avocations: music, poetry. Office: WVa U PO Box 6106 Morgantown WV 26506 E-mail: vmucino@wvu.edu.

**MUCKENFUSS, CANTWELL FAULKNER, III,** lawyer; b. Montgomery, Ala., Apr. 25, 1945; s. Cantwell F. and Dorothy (Dauphine) M.; m. A. Angela Lancaster, June 25, 1978; children: Alice Paran Lancaster, Cantwell F. IV. BA, Vanderbilt U., 1967; JD, Yale U., 1971. Bar: N.Y. 1973, D.C. 1976. Law clk. to Hon. William E. Miller U.S. Ct. Appeals (6th Cir.), 1971-72; atty., project developer Bedford Stuyvesant D and S Corp., Bklyn., 1972-73; spl. asst. to the dir. FDIC, Washington, 1974-77, counsel to the chmn., 1977-78; sr. dep. comptroller for policy Office of the Comptroller of the Currency, Washington, 1978-81; ptnr. Gibson, Dunn & Crutcher LLP, Washington, 1981—. Mem. editorial adv. bd. Issues in Bank Regulation, Rolling Meadows, Ill., 1977-91, Electronic Banking Law and Commerce Report, 1996—; mem. bd. advisors Rev. Banking and Fin. Svcs., N.Y.C., 1985—; bd. dis. Fair Tax Edn. Fund, Washington, 1987-90. Served with USNG, 1968-70, USAR, 1970-74. Recipient Spl. Achievement award U.S. Dept. Treasury, 1979, Presdl. Rank award U.S. Govt., 1980. Mem. ABA, Fed. Bar Assn. Clubs: Kenwood Country (Bethesda, Md.); Yale (N.Y.C.). Democrat. Episcopalian. Office: Gibson Dunn & Crutcher LLP 1050 Connecticut Ave NW Ste 900 Washington DC 20036-5306*

**MUCKENHOUPT, BENJAMIN,** retired mathematics professor; b. Newton, Mass., Dec. 22, 1933; s. Carl Frederick and Sarah Joanna (Boell) M.; m. Mary Kathryn Heath, Aug. 29, 1964; children: Margaret, Carl Edward. AB, Harvard U., 1954; MS, U. Chgo., 1955, PhD, 1958. Instr. DePaul U., Chgo., 1958-59, asst. prof. math., 1959-60; faculty Rutgers U., New Brunswick, NJ, 1960-91, prof. math., 1970-91. Vis. assoc. prof. Mt. Holyoke Coll., 1963-65; visitor Inst. Advanced Study, Princeton, N.J., 1968-69, 75-76; vis. prof. SUNY-Albany, 1970-71 Contbr. articles to profl. jours. NSF rsch. grantee, 1965-88; Rutgers Rsch. Coun. fellow, 1968-69. Mem. Am. Math. Soc., Math. Assn. Am., Phi Beta Kappa, Sigma Xi. Home: 196 Woodfern Rd Neshanic Station NJ 08853-4054 E-mail: muckenho@post.harvard.edu.

**MUCKERMAN, NORMAN JAMES,** priest, writer; b. Webster Groves, Mo., Feb. 1, 1917; s. Oliver Christopher and Edna Gertrude (Hartman) M. BA, Immaculate Conception Coll., 1940, M. in Religious Edn., 1942. Ordained priest Roman Catholic Ch., 1942. Missionary Redemptorist Missions, Amazonas, Para, Brazil, 1943-53, procurator missions St. Louis, 1953-58; pastor, adminstr. St. Alphonsus Ch., Chgo., 1958-67, St. Gerard, Kirkwood, Mo., 1967-71; mktg. mgr. circulation Liguori Pubs., Liguori, Mo., 1971-76; editor Liguorian Mag., Liguori, Mo., 1977-89. Author: How to Face Death Without Fear, 1976, Redemptorists on the Amazon, 1992, Preparation for Death, 1998, Into Your Hands, 2001, From the Heart of St. Alphonsus, 2002; contbg. editor: Liguorian, 1989—95. Recipient Nota Dez award Caixa Fed. Do Para, Brazil, 1958 Mem. Cath. Press Assn. (cons. 1971-95, bd. dirs. 1976-85, pres. 1981-84, St. Francis De Sales award 1985). Avocations: reading, writing. Personal E-mail: nmuckerman@liguori.com.

**MUCKLER, JOHN,** professional sports team executive; b. Midland, Ont., Can., Apr. 3, 1934; m. Audrey Muckler; children: Karen, John, Tracy, Jenny. Coach, gen. mgr. Long Island Ducks; 1st pres. NY Jr. Met. League; coach, gen. dir. player pers., mgr. NY Rangers affiliate team, Am. Hockey League; Providence; head coach Minn. North Stars, 1968-69; asst. coach Edmonton Oilers, 1984—85, co-coach, 1987—88, head coach, 1989—91, Buffalo Sabres, 1991-94, gen. mgr. 1994-98; head coach NY Rangers, NYC, 1997—98, 1999—2000; gen. mgr. Ottawa Senators, 2002—. Office: Ottawa Senators Scotiabank Place 1000 Palladium Dr Kanata ON K2V 1A5 Canada*

**MUCZYNSKI, PAUL FRANK,** human resources specialist; b. Plains, Pa., Sept. 15, 1946; s. John J. Muczynski and Helen A. Swatski. BS in Edn., Temple U., Phila., 1977, MEd, Temple U. 1982; EdD, Hamilton U., Evanston, Ill., 2000. Cert. vocat. instr., supr. curriculum devel., supr. comprehensive vocat. edn. Vocat. instr. Wilkes Barre Area Vo-Tech. Sch., Plains, 1972—82; instr. Royal Saudi Naval Forces Sch., Jubail, Saudi Arabia, 1982—84, tng. and ops. mgr., 1984—88; curriculum specialist Saudi Aramco, Dhahran, 1988—96, supr. computer support, 1996—2000, change mgmt. coord., 2002—04. Author: (phamplet) Developing Job Task Certification Standards, 1994; actor: (phamplet) Professional On-Job-Development, 2000. Mem.: Arabian Soc. Human Resource Mgmt., Rotary. Avocations: reading, computers.

**MUDAVANHU, BLESSING,** research scientist; b. Harare, Mashonaland, Zimbabwe, May 26, 1971; s. Jackson and Gladys Mudavanhu; m. Mutsa Tongoona, July 22, 1996; children: Mandisa, Thandeka. BS in Gen. Math. and Stats., U. Zimbabwe, Harare, 1993, BS in Math., 1995; M in Fin. Engring., U. Calif., Berkeley, 2002; MS, U. Wash., 1998, PhD, 2002. Rsch. asst. U. Wash., Seattle, 1996—2001; derivatives quantitative analyst Am. Internat. Group, N.Y.C., 2002—05, v.p., 2002—05; v.p. corp. risk mgmt. Merrill Lynch & Co., N.Y.C., NY, 2005—. Book reviewer: Soc. Indsl. and Applied Math., 2003—; contbr. articles to profl. jours. Fellow U. of Zimbabwe Math. fellow, 1995; scholar Fulbright scholar, U.S. Govt., 1996—98. Mem.: Internat. Assn. for Fin. Engrs., Soc. for Indsl. and Applied Math., Am. Math. Soc., Fulbright Assn. (bd. dirs. Puget Sound chpt. 2000—02). Office Phone: 212-449-4464. Personal E-mail: blessingmudavanhu@yahoo.com.

**MUDD, ANGELA,** social worker; d. Leonard Delmar and Jane Marie (Osborn) Mudd; m. Clyde Lee Simmons, Nov. 29, 1980; children: Sarah Mudd-Simmons, William Daniel Mudd-Simmons. BA, U. Ky., 1975; MSW, U. Mich., 1979. Juvenile probation officer Lexington-Fayette Urban County Gov., Ky., 1974—78; mental health specialist III Bluegrass E. Comprehensive Care Ctr., Lexington, 1980—82; clin. social worker Charter Ridge Hosp., Lexington, 1982—84, Family Counseling Svcs., Lexington, 1984—87, St. Joseph Hosp., Lexington, 1985—86; lic. clin. social worker Angela Mudd, M.S.W., Lexington, 1984—. Sec., pres.-elect, pres. Ky. Soc. Clin. Social Work, 1983—89; instr. Ctr. Women and Children, Lexington, 1983—85. Founding mem. Montessori Mid. Sch., Lexington, 1995—; vol. Cmty. Montessori Sch., Lexington, 1987—; vol., bd. mem. Sch. Creative, Performing Arts, Lexington, 1998—2005; mem. Dem. Party, Lexington. Mem.: Nat. Soc. Clin. Social Work (state pres. 1980—), Nat. Assn. for Women. Avocations: gardening, photography, camping. Home: 629 Kastle Rd Lexington KY 40502 Office: Angela Mudd M S W 3150 Custer Dr Ste 203 Lexington KY 40502 Office Phone: 859-271-7788.

**MUDD, DANIEL H.,** finance company executive; married; 4 children. BA in History, U. Va.; MPA in Econs. and Internat. Affairs, Harvard U., 1986. V.p. bus. devel. GE Capital, 1991—93, mng. dir. internat. financing, 1993—95, pres., CEO, European Fleet Services Brussels, 1995—96, pres. Asia Pacific, 1996-99, pres., CEO Japan, 1999—2000; vice chmn., COO Fannie Mae, Washington, 2000—04, interim CEO, 2004—05, pres., CEO, 2005—. Mem. Coun. Fgn. Relations; bd. dirs. Fannie Mae, 2000—, Oriental & Gen. Fund Ltd., Fannie Mae Found., Ryder System Inc., Local Initiative Support Corp., Nat. Bldg. Museum, Hampton U., St. Patrick Sch. Officer USMC. Robert Bosch Found. fellow, 1989. Office: Fannie Mae 3900 Wisconsin Ave NW Washington DC 20016-2892

**MUDD, JOHN O.,** lawyer; b. 1943; BA, Cath. U., 1965, MA, 1966; JD, U. Mont. 1973; LLM, Columbia U., 1986; JSD of Law, 1994. Bar: Mont. 1973. Pntr. Mulroney, Delaney, Dalby & Mudd, Missoula, Mont., 1973-79; lectr. U. Mont., Missoula, 1973-74, 75-76, prof. law, dean, 1979-88; ptnr. Garlington, Lohn & Robinson, Missoula 1988—99; sr. v.p. Providence Svcs., 2000—05, also bd. dirs.; sr. v.p. Providence Health & Svcs., 2006—. Pres. Mid-Continent Assn. Law Schs., 1982—83; chmn. bd. dirs. Ascension Health, 2004—. Editor: Mont. Law Rev., 1972—73. Chmn. Mont. Commn. Future of Higher Edn.; elected Dem. candidate U.S. Senate, 1994; bd. dirs. St. Patrick Hosp., 1985—90. With U.S. Army, 1967—73. Mem.: State Bar Mont., Am. Judicature Soc. (bd. dirs. 1985—89).

**MUDD, MARY CORDELIA,** historian; b. Oak Park, Ill., July 24, 1948; d. Edward Lee and Audrey Sack Michaels; m. John Edward Mudd, Sept. 4, 1976 (dec.); 1 child; William Andrew Lewis. BA in English cum laude, U. Houston, 1969, BS in Math., 1969; MA in History, Rutgers U., New Brunswick, NJ, 1974, PhD in History, 1984. Ind. scholar Roman and Byzantine History, Wall, NJ, 1984—; med. sec. Lakewood Pathology Assoc., NJ, 1996—99, Olsten Staffing Svcs., Tinton Falls, NJ, 1999—2004; physician credentials coord. Meridian Health, Wall, 2004—. Freelance lectr. archaeology and Roman history, 1978—95. Author: I, Livia: The Counterfeit Criminal, 2005, Studies in Reign of Constantius II, 1989; contbr. articles to scholarly publs. Recording sec. Freedom Theatre Parents Group, Phila., 1993—95; environ. activist Clean Ocean Action, Highlands, NJ, 1984—. Mem.: Nat. Assn. Med. Staff Svcs., Am. Hist. Assn., PEO Sisterhood, NJ Environ. Fedn., Earthjustice. Avocations: bicycling, swimming, theater, ballet, cooking, archaeology, cats. Office: Mary Mudd PhD PO Box 1275 Wall NJ 07719 Office Phone: 732-299-8608.

**MUDD, ROGER HARRISON,** newscaster, educator; b. Washington, Feb. 9, 1928; s. Kostka and Irma Iris (Harrison) M.; m. Emma Jeanne Spears, Oct. 26, 1957; children: Daniel H., Maria M., Jonathan, Matthew M. AB, Washington and Lee U., 1950; MA, U. N.C., 1953. Tchr. Darlington Sch., Rome, Ga., 1951—52; reporter Richmond News Leader, Va., 1953; news dir. Sta. WRNL, Richmond, 1953—56; reporter radio and TV Sta. WTOP, Washington, 1956—61; corr. CBS, 1961—80; chief Washington corr. NBC, 1980—87; Congl. corr. MacNeil/Lehrer News Hour, 1987—92; prof. journalism Princeton U., 1992—94, Washington & Lee U., 1995—96. Host The History Channel, 1995-2005. Trustee Randolph-Macon Women's Coll., Lynchburg, Va., 1971-78, Robert F. Kennedy Journalism Awards Com., 1971-78, Blue Ridge Sch., Dyke, Va., 1978-84; bd. dirs. Fund for Investigative Journalism, PEN/Faulkner, 1985-92, Va. Found. for Humanities, Va. Hist. Soc., 1988-94, RIAS Berlin Commn., 1996-99, Va. Found. for Ind. Colls., Nat. Portrait Gallery Commn., Civil War Trust, 1999-01; chmn. adv. com. Mt. Vernon Ladies Assn., Eudora Welty Found., 2002—; bd. dirs. Media Gen., 1998-01. With AUS, 1945-47. Mem. Radio-TV Corr. Assn. (chmn. exec. com. 1969-70), Am. Antiquarian Soc.

**MUDGE, LEWIS SEYMOUR,** theologian, educator, university dean; b. Phila., Oct. 22, 1929; s. Lewis Seymour and Anne Evelyn (Bolton) M.; m. Jean Bruce McClure, June 15, 1957; children: Robert Seymour, William McClure, Anne Evelyn. BA, Princeton U., 1951, M Div, 1955, PhD (Kent fellow), 1961; BA with honors in Theology, Oxford U., Eng., 1954, MA (Rhodes scholar), 1958. Ordained to ministry Presbyn. Ch., 1955. Presbyn. univ. pastor Princeton, 1955-56; sec. dept. theology World Alliance Ref. Chs., Geneva, 1957-62; minister to coll. Amherst Coll., 1962-68, asst. prof. philosophy and religion, 1962-64, assoc. prof., 1964-70, prof. philosophy and religion, 1970-76, chmn. dept. philosophy and religion, 1968-69, 75-76; dean faculty, prof. theology McCormick Theol. Sem., Chgo., 1976-87, San Francisco Theol. Sem., 1987—; prof. Grad. Theol. Union, Berkeley, Calif., 1987-95; dir. Ctr. for Hermeneutical Studies, Grad. Theol. Union/U. Calif., Berkeley, 1990-97; Stuart prof. theology Grad. Theol. Union, Berkeley, Calif., 1995—. Mem. commn. on faith and order Nat. Council Chs., 1965-70; sec. spl. com. on confession faith United Presbyn Ch., 1965-67, chmn. spl. com. on theology of the call, 1968-71; chmn. theol. commn. U.S. Consultation on Ch. Union, 1977-89; co-chmn. Internat. Ref.-Roman Cath. Dialogue Commn., 1983-90; observer Extraordinary Synod Bishops, 1985. Author: One Church: Catholic and Reformed, 1963, Is God Alive?, 1963, Why is the Church in the World?, 1967, The Crumbling Walls, 1970, The Sense of a People: Toward a Church for the Human Future, 1992, The Church as Moral Community, 1998, Rethinking the Beloved Community, 2001; also numerous articles and revs.; editor: Essays on Biblical Interpretation (Paul Ricoeur), 1980, (with James Poling) Formation and Reflection: the Promise of Practical Theology, 1987, (with Thomas Wieser) Democratic Contracts for Sustainable and Caring Societies, 2000 Pres. Westminster Found. in New Eng., 1963-67; chmn. bd. Nat. Vocation Agy., 1972-75; mem. com. selection Rhodes Scholars, Vt., 1966, Wis., 1983-85, Iowa, 1986; mem. adv. com. social witness policy Presbyn. Ch., U.S.A., 2005— Mem. Phi Beta Kappa. Democrat. Home: 2444 Hillside Ave Berkeley CA 94704-2529 Office: Grad Theol Union 2905 Dwight Way Berkeley CA 94704-2514 Office Phone: 510-845-5958. E-mail: lewismudge@aol.com.

**MUDRY, MICHAEL,** pension and benefit consultant; b. Lucina, Czechoslovakia, Dec. 5, 1926; (parents Am. citizens); s. John Zaleta and Helen (Molchan) M.; m. Kendall Archer, June 17, 1960; children: F. Goodrich Archer, Benjamin Kendall. BA, U. Conn., 1951. Sr. v.p. Hay/Huggins Co. Inc., Phila., 1956-93; self-employed pension and benefit cons. Wayne, Pa., 1994—. Former actuary Ch. Pensions Conf. Contbr. articles to profl. jours. Bd. dirs., actuary Am. Coun. on Gift Annuities, Indpls., 1978—; mem. exec. bd., treas. St. Davids Condominium Assn., 2005—. Served with U.S. Army, 1945-46. Fellow: Conf. Cons. Actuaries, Soc. Actuaries; mem.: Internat. Assn. Cons. Actuaries, Internat. Actuarial Assn., Am. Acad. Actuaries, Tri-State Jazz Soc. (bd. dirs. 2001—, treas. 2001—).

**MUEGGE, UWE,** terminology professor; m. Christine Carola Muegge; children: Jule Maren, Mia Maria, Hanna Margareta. BA, U. Tuebingen, Germany, 1986; MA, U. Oreg., 1990, Monterey Inst. Internat. Studies, 1998. Corp. terminologist Medtronic, Inc., Mpls., 2004—; adj. prof. Monterey Inst. Internat. Studies, Calif., 2005—. Owner Muegge.cc - computer-driven Transl. Solutions, Tuebingen, Germany 1991—2002; terminologist Sun Microsystems, Cupertino, Calif. 1998, cons., Dublin, 99, SAP, Walldorf, Germany, 2001, DaimlerChrysler, Stuttgart, Germany, 2002; translator J.D. Edwards, Denver, 2002—04; mem. terminology sig Localization Industry Standards Assn., Romainmôtier, Switzerland, 2004—; cons. Merrill Corp., St. Paul, 2006—, U. Minn., Mpls., 2006—. Author: Translation contract: a standards-based model solution, 2005; co-author: Lokalisierung von Technischer Dokumentation, 2002. Mem.: Localization Industry Stds. Assn., The Inst. of Localization Profls. (assoc.). Achievements include development of a High-Performance Solution For Automatic Terminology Extration; the CLOUT rule set, a controlled language for authoring translation-friendly source texts; a website (muegge.cc) that enables on-the-fly automatic translation using the Google machine translation system; Processes That Result In The Availability Of Project-Specific Multilingual Terminology Before Source Texts For Translation Are Written; implementation of a machine translation program at Medtronic, the world's leading medical technology vendor. Avocation: distance running; modern art. Office Phone: 763-514-7792.

**MUEHLBAUER, JAMES HERMAN,** manufacturing and distribution executive; b. Evansville, Ind., Nov. 13, 1940; s. Herman Joseph and Anna Louise (Overfield) M.; m. Mary Kay Koch, June 26, 1965; children: Stacey, Brad, Glen, Beth, Katy. BSME, Purdue U., 1963, MS Indsl. Adminstrn., 1964. Registered profl. engr., Ind., 1970. Engr. George Koch Sons, Inc., Evansville, 1966-67, chief estimator, 1968-72, chief engr., 1973-74, v.p., 1975-81, dir., 1978—, exec. v.p., bd. dirs., 1982-98; exec. v.p., bd.dirs. Koch Enterprises, Inc., 1999—; pres. George Koch Sons LLC, Evansville, 2003—, chmn., 2003—04; pres. Koch Air LLC, 2003—. V.p., bd. dirs. Brake Supply Co., Evansville, Gibbs Die Casting Corp., Henderson, Ky., Uniseal, Inc., Evansville, George Koch Sons LLC, Evansville, Comfort Fin. Svcs. LLC, Evansville; bd. dirs. Fifth Third Bank Indiana, George Koch Sons (Europe) Ltd., Lichfield, Eng., Red Spot Paint & Varnish Co., Inc., Evansville, George Koch Sons de Mex., Monterrey, George Koch Sons GmbH, Cologne, Koch Air LLC, Evansville. Co-author: Tool & Manufacturing Engineering Handbook, 1976; patentee in paint finishing equipment. Bd. dirs., past pres. Evansville Indsl. Found., 1980—; bd. dirs., past pres., past campaign chmn. United Way S.W. Ind., Evansville, 1983—; bd. dirs., past vice-chmn. Univ. So. Ind. Found., Evansville, 1988-2001; bd. dirs. Deaconess Hosp., Evansville, 1986—, treas., 1991-96, vice-chmn., 1999-2003, chmn., 2003—; bd. dirs. Cath. Found. Southwestern Ind., 1998-2004; dir. bd. advisors U. So. Ind. Sch. Bus., 1997—, chmn., 2001-02; bd. dirs. Ind. Assn. United Ways, 2000-06, Alliance Indpls., 1993-2004, pres. 1999; mem. Brute Soc., Cath. Diocese Evansville, 1997, Equestrian Order of the Holy Sepulchre of Jerusalem, 1996—. Named Engr. of Yr. S.W. chpt. Ind. Soc. Profl. Engrs., 1983; recipient Tech. Achievement award Tri-State Coun. for Sci. and Engring., Evansville, 1984, Purdue U. Alumni Citizenship award, 1991. Mem. Soc. Mfg. Engrs. (past nat. chmn. finishing and coating tech. divsn.), ASME, NSPE, Evansville Country Club, Evansville Kennel Club (bd. dirs. 1997-2001). Republican. Roman Catholic. Home: 2300 E Gum St Evansville IN 47714-2338 Office: Koch Enterprises 14 S 11th Ave Evansville IN 47744-0001 Office Phone: 812-962-5260. Business E-mail: jmuehlbauer@kochair.com.

**MUEHLNER, SUANNE WILSON,** library director; b. Rochester, Minn., June 29, 1943; d. George T. and Rhoda (Westin) Wilson. Student Smith Coll., 1961-63; A.B., U. Calif.-Berkeley, 1965; M.L.S., Simmons Coll., 1968; M.B.A., Northeastern U., Boston, 1979. Librarian, Technische Univ. Berlin, Germany, 1970-71; earth and planetary scis. librarian MIT Libraries, Cambridge, 1968-70, 1971-73; personnel librarian, 1973-74, asst. dir. personnel services, 1974-76, asst. dir. pub. services, 1976-81; dir. libraries Colby Coll., Waterville, Maine, 1981—. Mem. ALA, New Eng. Assn. Coll. and Research Librarians (sec.-treas. 1983-85, pres. 1986-87), Maine Libr. Assn. (chmn. intellectual freedom com. 1984-88, OCLC Users Coun., 1988-95), Nelinet (bd. dirs. 1985-91, chair 1989-91). Office: Colby Coll Miller Libr Waterville ME 04901

**MUEHRCKE, DEREK DAVID,** thoracic and cardiovascular surgeon; b. Oak Park, Ill., Jan. 30, 1958; s. Robert Karl and Barbara M.; m. Jill Taylor. MD, Grinnel-Rush Coll., 1983. MD, Ohio, Fla. Intern in gen. surgery Mass. Gen. Hosp.-Harvard U. Sch. Medicine, Boston, 1983-84, resident in gen. surgery, 1984-86; registrar in gen. and vascular surgery Plymouth (Eng.) Health Authority, Nat. Health Svc., 1986-87; sr. surg. resident Mass. Gen. Hosp.-Harvard U. Sch. Medicine, Boston, 1989-91, chief resident, 1991-94; assoc. staff mem. Cleve. Clinic Found., 1994, mem. staff, 1995-96; mem. group practice Southeast Cardiovasc. Group, Jacksonville, Fla., 1996—. Rsch. fellow Cardiovasc. Rsch. Inst., U. Calif., San Francisco, 1988-89; prin. and co-investigator numerous rsch. projects. Contbr. articles to profl. jours. Fellow ACS, Am. Coll. Thoracic Surgeons Office: Southeast Cardiovasc Group 1820 Barrs St Ste 701 Jacksonville FL 32204-4730

**MUELLER, ALFRED H.,** physics professor, researcher; BS in Physics, Iowa State U., 1961; PhD, MIT, 1965. Rsch. scientist Brookhaven Nat. Lab., 1965—71; Enrico Fermi prof. physics Columbia U., 1972—. Visiting prof. NYU, Inst. for Advanced Study, Inst. for Theoretical Physics; mem. visiting com. MIT Lab. for Nuclear Sci., Werner Heisenberg Inst., Saclay; mem. sci. & tech. steering com. Brookhaven Sci. Associates. Grantee A.P. Sloan Fellowship, 1972, J.S. Guggenheim Fellowship, 1988. Fellow: Am. Acad. Arts & Sciences; mem.: Am. Physical Soc. (Sakurai prize). Office: Columbia U Physics Dept 538 W 120th St New York NY 10027

**MUELLER, BETTY JEANNE,** social work educator; b. Wichita, Kans., July 7, 1925; d. Bert C. and Clara A. (Pelton) Judkins; children— Michael J., Madelynn J. MSSW, U. Wis., Madison, 1964, PhD, 1969. Asst. prof. U. Wis., Madison, 1969-72; vis. asso. prof. Bryn Mawr (Pa.) Coll., 1971-72; asso. prof., dir. social work Cornell U., Ithaca, NY, 1972-78, prof. human svcs. studies, 1979-96, prof. policy and mgmt., 1996-98, prof. emeritus, 1998—. Nat. cons. Head Start, Follow Through, Appalachian Regional Commn., N.Y. State Office Planning Svcs., N.Y. State Dept. Social Svcs., N.Y. State Divsn. Mental Hygiene, Nat. Congress PTA, ILO; mem. internat. adv. com. Family Resources Tng. Ctr., Singapore, 1999—. Author (with H. Morgan) Social Services in Early Education, 1974, (with R. Reinoehl) Computers in Human Service Education, 1989, Determinants of Human Behavior, 1995; contbr. articles to profl. jours. Recipient Fulbright Rsch. award, 1990; grantee, HEW, 1974—76, 1979—80, State of N.Y., 1975—97, Israeli Jewish Agy., 1985—87. Mem. Leadership Am., Chi Omega. Democrat. Unitarian Universalist. Home: 412 Highland Rd Ithaca NY 14850-2216 Office: Cornell U Policy and Mgmt 108 MVR Hall Ithaca NY 14853 Personal E-mail: bjm5@cornell.edu.

**MUELLER, CARL RICHARD,** theater arts educator, author; b. St. Louis, Oct. 7, 1931; s. Anton John and Bonita Blanche (Lacey) M. BS, Northwestern U., 1954; MA, UCLA, 1960, PhD, 1967; cert., Freie U., Berlin, 1961. Prof. theater dept. Sch. Theater, Film and Television UCLA, 1967—; dramaturg New Theatre, Inc., L.A., 1975-2000. Cons. U. Calif. Press, 1972—2005. Translator plays published include Buechner: Complete Plays and Prose, 1963, Brecht: The Visions of Simone Machard, 1965, Brecht: The Measures Taken, 1977, Hauptmann: The Weavers, 1965, Hebbel: Maria Magdalena, 1962, Strindberg: A Dream Play and The Ghost Sonata, 1966, Strindberg: Five Major Plays, 2000, Schnitzler: La Ronde and Game of Love, 1964, Hofmannsthal: Electra, 1964, Wedekind: The Marquis of Keith, 1964, Wedekind: The Lulu Plays, 1967, Wedekind: Four Major Plays, 2000, Zuckmayer: The Captain of Koepenick, 1972, Horváth: Tales from the Vienna Woods, 1998, Schnitzler: Four Major Plays, 1999, Sophocles: The Complete Plays, 2000, Pirandello: Three Major Plays, 2000, Kleist: Three Major Plays, 2000, Wedekind: Four Plays, vol. 2, 2002, Strindberg: Five Major Plays, vol. 2, 2002, Aeschylus: The Complete Plays, vol. 1, Oresteia, 2002, Aeschylus: The Complete Plays, vol. 2, Four Plays, 2002, Goethe: Faust, 2004, Euripides: The Complete Plays, Vols. 1-4, 2005; translator plays produced include Anon: The Puppet Play of Dr. Johannes Faustus, Hauptmann: The Beaver Coat, Schnitzler: Dr. Bernhardi, Schnitzler: Anatol, Sternheim: The Underpants, Brecht: Mother Courage, Brecht: Caucasian Chalk Circle, Brecht: The Trial of Joan of Arc, Brecht: In the Jungle of Cities, Brecht: Man is Man, Brecht: He Who Says Yes, Brecht: He Who Says No, Brecht: The Exception and the Rule, Brecht: Round Heads, Peaked Heads, Brecht: Schweyk in the Second World War, Kleist: The Broken Jug, 1992, Lessing: Nathan the Wise, 1993, Toller, The Blind Goddess, 1993, Sophokles, Elektra, 1994, Zweig, Volpone, 1995, Sternheim, The Snob, 1996; gen. editor Visual Resources, Inc., 1976-2000; theater editor Mankind mag. 1975-82; editor New Theater/Teatro Nuevo, 1985-87; author catalogue and slides A Visual History of European Theater Arts, 1978, A Visual History of European Experimental Theater, 1983, Greek and Roman Classical Theatre Structures and Performance Iconography, 1991, Medieval Theater and Performance Iconography, 1991, The Theater of Meyerhold, 1992, Stanislavsky and the Moscow Art Theater, 1992, The Commedia dell'Arte, 1992, Russian Scene and Costume Design, vols. 1 and 2, 1993, The Baroque Stage, 1993, 18th and 19th Cen. European Theater Structures, Performance Iconography and Costume Designs, 1994, Renaissance Theater Structures, Performance Iconography and Costume Designs, 1994, The Genius of the Russian Theatre 1900-1990, 1995, 20th Century World Theater, From Appia to Dali, 1900-50, vol. 1, 1996, 20th Century World Theater, From Mother Courage to Hair,

1951-68, vol. 2, 1996, 20th Century World Theater, From Svoboda to Hockney, 1968-91, vol. 3, 1996, The Genius of the Russian Theater, From Meyerhold to the Present, 1996, Contemporary European Experimental Theater, vol. 1, Italy and Germany, 1996, The Classical Experience: The Greek Theater and Its World, 1996, The Classical Experience: The Roman Theater and Its World, 1996; dir.: (plays) Spring's Awakening, Endangered Species, Hedda Gabler, My Body, Frankly Yours, Hamlet, Macbeth, Dionysos. Served with U.S. Army, 1954-56. Recipient Samuel Goldwyn Creative Writing award Goldwyn Found., 1959; Fulbright exchange grantee Berlin, 1960-61 Mem. Internat. Arthur Schnitzler Research Assn., UCLA Center for Medieval and Renaissance Studies (mem. adv. com. 1980-83) Democrat. Office: UCLA Dept Theater Sch Theater Film TV 102 E Melnitz Box 951622 Los Angeles CA 90095-1622 Office Phone: 310-825-2707. Business E-Mail: cmueller@tft.ucla.edu. *Communication has always been the primary goal of my life. The challenge of passing on to generations of new students the life sustaining ideas of human culture is formidable; the joy of searching out new ideas and methods of thought and action is a privilege of which far too few of us take proper advantage.*

**MUELLER, CHARLES FREDERICK,** radiologist, educator; b. Dayton, Ohio, May 26, 1936; s. Susan Elizabeth (Wine) W.; m. Kathe Louise Lutterbei, May 28, 1966; children: Charles Jeffrey, Theodore Martin, Kathryn Suzanne. BA in English, U. Cin., 1958, MD, 1962. Diplomate Am. Bd. Radiology, Am. Bd. Nuclear Medicine. Asst. prof. radiology U. N.Mex., Albuquerque, 1968-72, assoc. prof. radiology, 1972-74, Ohio State U., Columbus, 1974-79, acting chmn. dept. radiology, 1975, prof. radiology, 1979—2002, prof. radiology, dir. post grad. program radiology, 1980-2000, acting chmn. dept. radiology, 1990—93, prof. emeritus, 2002—. Bd. dirs. Univ. Radiologists, Inc., Columbus, v.p., 1980—86; pres., founder Ambulatory Imaging, Inc., Columbus, 1985—2002. Author: Emergency Radiology, 1982; contbr. numerous articles to profl. jours.; edltl. bd. Emergency radiology, 1995-2002; editor Internat. Trauma, Am. Jour. Roentgenology, 1997-2004. Com. chmn. Boy Scouts Am., Columbus, 1980—84; vol. Columbus Free Clinic, 2003—, Franklin Park Conservatory, 2003—. Capt. USAF, 1966—68. Research grantee Ohio State U. 1975, Gen. Electric Co., 1986-88; Gold medalist ASER, 2001. Fellow Am. Coll. Radiologists; mem. AMA, Assn. Univ. Radiologists, Am. Roentgen Ray Soc., Am. Soc. Emergency Radiology (founder 1988, pres. 1993-94, Gold medal 2001), Radiol. Soc. N.Am., N.Mex. Soc. Radiologists (pres. 1973-74), Ohio State Radiol. Soc. (pres. 1986-87). Republican. Presbyterian. Avocations: fly fishing, hiking, model railroading. Office: Ohio State Univ Hosps Dept Radiology 410 W 10th Ave Columbus OH 43210-1240 E-mail: cmueller@columbus.rr.com.

**MUELLER, CHERONE,** religious organization administrator, writer, minister; b. The Dalles, Oreg. Diploma in Acctg., Chemeketa Coll., Oreg., 1984, diploma in Bus. Mgmt., 1984; DD (hon.), World Christianship Ministries, Calif., 2002. Ordained minister World Christianship Ministries, 2002, cert. counselor World Christianship Ministries, 2002. Founder Cherone Faith Ministry, Jacksonville, 1999—, pres., CEO, 2000—. Ordained min. A Call to Worship Ch., Jacksonville, 2001—. Author: (book) At San Jose Make a Left, Dancing Around the Throne, of numerous poems. V.p. singles group Salem UPC, 1983—91, choir Salem, 1982—91, treas. ladies aux., 1984—90, v.p. Singles Group, 1983—91; nursery caregiver First UPC, Jacksonville, 1995—97; Sunday sch. tchr. Christ Ch. Jacksonville, 1997—98, praise singer, fellowship coord., 1997—2001; dir. Daughters of Zion (praying for our children) UPC Internat., Jacksonville, 1999—2001. Named Pastor of the Month, Radio WAYR, Jacksonville, Fla. June, 2003; recipient Editor's Choice award, Internat. Libr. Poetry, 2001, 2002, 2003, 2004, 2005, 2006. Master: World Christianship Ministries (licentiate; rev. 2002). Avocations: sewing, cooking, crocheting, sign language, designing clothes. Office: Cherone Faith Ministry PO Box 47077 Jacksonville FL 32247-7077 Personal E-mail: cheronefaith@mail.com.

**MUELLER, CHRISTA,** radiologist; b. Sonthofen, Germany, June 5, 1962; d. Joachim Friedrich and Waltraud Mueller. MD, Ludwig-Maximilians U., Munich, Germany, 1994; PhD, Ludwig-Maximilians U., 1995. Physician Technic U., Munich, 1992—93, Ludwig-Maximilians U., Munich, 1994—96, Katharinen Hosp., Stuttgart, Germany, 1996—98; physician, rschr. Georg-August U., Goettingen, Germany, 1998—2002, sr. radiologist, rschr., 2002—04; radiologist Paracelsus U., Salzburg, Austria, 2004—. Contbr. articles to profl. jours. Mem.: German Roentgen Soc. Office: Paracelsus Univ Hinterreit 478 A 5084 Grossgmain Austria Office Phone: 0043-662-4482-57769. Personal E-mail: christamueller@yahoo.de. Business E-Mail: ch.mueller@salk.at.

**MUELLER, EDWARD ALBERT,** retired transportation engineer; b. Madison, Wis., May 12, 1923; s. Edward F. and Lulu (Wittl) M.; m. Margaret Wetzel, Sept. 12, 1953; children: Lynn, Karen. Student, U. Wis., 1941-43; BCE, Notre Dame U., 1947; cert. in traffic, Yale U., 1953, postgrad., 1952—53, Fla. State U., 1955-62; MCE, Catholic U. Am., 1967. Registered profl. engr., Fla. Project engr. Carl C. Crane, Inc., 1947-50; engr. Ammann & Whitney, Inc., Milw., 1950-52; rsch. asst. Yale U., 1953-55; asst. dir., dir. traffic and planning div. Fla. State Rd. Dept., Tallahassee, 1955-63; engr. traffic and ops. Transp. Rsch. Bd., Washington, 1963-70; sec. Fla. Dept. Transp., Tallahassee, 1970-72; exec. dir. Jacksonville (Fla.) Transp. Authority, 1972-80; mgr. transp. div. Reynolds, Smith & Hills, 1980-83; v.p. Morales and Shumer Engrs., Inc., 1983-95. Occasional lectr. U. Fla., 1971-76, U. N.Fla., 1974-76 Author: Steamboating on the St. Johns, 1979, Ocklawaha River Steamboats, 1983, St Johns River Steamboats, 1986, Perilous Journeys, 1990, Upper Mississippi River Ratting Steamboats, 1995, Steamships of the Two Henrys, 1996, Along the St. Johns and Ocklawaha River, 1999, Queen of Sea Routes, 2000, The Savannah Line, 2001, First Coast Steamboat Days, 2005; contbr. engring. articles to profl. jours. Mem. Fla. Com. of 100, 1970-72; bd. dirs. Luth. Social Svcs., Jacksonville, 1982-94, v.p., 1981-91; regional v.p. Fla.-Ga. dist. Luth. Laymen's League, 1982-92; curator Jacksonville Maritime Mus. 1990-99, mem. exec. com., 1990-95, pres., 1993-95, exec. dir., 1995-99. Recipient Disting. Svc. award Coll. Engring., U. Fla., 1975, Samuel Ward Stanton award for life achievement Steamship Hist. Soc. Am., 2001; named one of top 10 pub. works ofcls. in U.S., 1978. Mem. Southeastern Assn. State Hwy. Ofcls. (pres., v.p. 1971-72), Engrs. in Govt. (chmn., vice-chmn. sec.), Fla. Engring. Soc. (pres. Northeast chpt. 1982-83, Engr. of Yr. Tallahassee chpt. 1972, Jacksonville chpt. 1974, award for outstanding tech. achievement 1976, outstanding svc. to engring. profession 1989, James Shivler award 1993), Inst. Transp. Engrs. (pres. 1977, disting. svc. award Fla. sect. 1976), Fla. Transit Assn. (pres. 1974-75), Fla. Engring. Found. (sec. 1986-95). Lutheran. Home: 4734 Empire Ave Jacksonville FL 32207-2136

**MUELLER, GARY ALFRED,** software engineer; b. Denver, Oct. 6, 1950; s. Alfred Henry and Verna Mae (Ashmore) M. BS in Mineral Engring. Physics, Colo. Sch. Mines, 1972, BS in Mineral Engring. Math., 1973; BSEE and Computer Sci. with honors, U. Colo., Denver, 1975, MSEE, U. Colo., Boulder, 1995. Registered profl. engr., Colo. Computer programmer, mathematician U.S. Geol. Survey, Denver, 1977-81; mem. tech. staff AT&T Bell Labs., Denver, 1982-84; adv. software engr. Storage Tech. Corp., Louisville, Colo., 1985—2001; cons., 2002—. Mem.: Assn. for Computing Machinery, IEEE (sr.), Tau Beta Pi, Kappa Mu Epsilon, Eta Kappa Nu.

**MUELLER, GERARD,** realtor, investor, former Internet executive; b. N.Y.C., Mar. 17, 1944; s. John and Mary (Choisy) M.; m. Debra Pritt, Sept. 17, 2000. BA, St. Johns U., 1965; MBA, Adelphi U., 1970. Mktg. exec. IBM, White Plains, NY, 1967-84; pres., gen. mgr. Prodigy Network, White Plains, 1985-97; now realtor and investor. Avocations: wine collecting, golf. Home: 6738 N Ocean Blvd Ocean Ridge FL 33435 Office Phone: 561-573-2363. E-mail: muellerg@bellsouth.net.

**MUELLER, GERARDINE LILLIAN,** art educator, artist; b. Newark; d. Frank J. Mueller and Teresa B. Saalmuller. BA, Caldwell Coll., 1954; MA, U. Notre Dame, 1959, MFA, 1966; postgrad. Inst. Cultural Guadalajara, 1971; studied with, Albinas Elskus, Ken Von Roenn, Bill Cummings. Home:

Dominican Sisters. Instr. art St. Dominic Acad., Jersey City, 1954—63; from instr. to prof. Caldwell (N.J.) Coll., 1963—79, prof., chmn. dept. art, 1963—79, adj. prof., 1989—97, lectr. 1997—. Prin. works include 32 stained glass windows, Caldwell Coll., 3 stained glass windows, St. Teresa Mausoleum, Summit, N.J., 16 stained glass windows, St.Catherine Convent, Caldwell, N.J., 6 panel glass mosaic, Caldwell Coll., 2 sculptures, Sisters Chapel, Caldwell, N.J., murals, Sacred Heart Sch., Vailsburg, N.J., glass tabernacles, Cedar Grove and Fairfield, N.J., silver meml. light, L. McGinley, S.J., Fordham, 3 CD covers, A.P.I. Records, ceremonial book, Dominican Sisters, Caldwell, N.J., 2 glass panels restoration, Yale U., 5 stained glass windows, Puyo Cathedral, Ecuador. Avocations: pre Columbian art history, lettering, illumination. Business E-Mail: sgmueller@caldwell.edu.

**MUELLER, GERHARD GOTTLOB,** retired financial accounting standard setter, retired educator; b. Eineborn, Germany, Dec. 4, 1930; arrived in US, 1952, naturalized, 1957; s. Gottlob Karl and Elisabeth Charlotte (Hossack) M.; m. Coralie George, June 7, 1958; children: Kent, Elisabeth, Jeffrey. AA, Coll. of Sequoias, 1954; BS with honors, U. Calif.-Berkeley, 1956, MBA, 1957, PhD, 1962; D Econs. (hon.), Swedish Sch. Econs. and Bus. Adminstrn., 1994; D Laws (hon.), Kwansei Gakuin U., 2000. CPA (ret.), Wash. Staff acct. FMC Corp., San Jose, Calif., 1957-58; faculty dept. acctg. U. Wash., Seattle, 1960-96, assoc. prof., 1963-67, prof., 1967-96, chmn. dept., 1969-78, dir. grad. profl. acctg. program, 1979-90, sr. assoc. dean, 1990-95, acting dean, 1994, Hughes M. Blake prof. internat. bus. mgmt., 1992-95, Julius A. Roller prof. acctg., 1995-96, mem. fin. acctg. stds. bd., 1996—2001; ret., 2001. Dir. U. Wash. Acctg. Devel. Fund, Overlake Hosp. Med. Ctr., Bellevue, 1984-96, chmn. bd. trustees, 1991-93; cons. internat. tax matters U.S. Treasury Dept., 1963-68; cons. Internat. Acctg. Rsch., 1964-96; vis. prof. Cranfield Sch. Mgmt. Eng., 1973-74, U. Zurich, Switzerland, 1973-74; lectr. in field. Author: International Accounting, 1967; co-author: Introductory Financial Accounting, 3d edit., 1991, A Brief Introduction to Managerial and Social Uses of Accounting, 1975, International Accounting, 1978, 2nd edit., 1992, Accounting: An International Perspective, 1987, 4th edit., 1997; editor: Readings in International Accounting, 1969, Accounting-A Book of Readings, 2d edit., 1976, A New Introduction to Accounting, 1971, A Bibliography of Internat. Accounting, 3d edit., 1973, Essentials of Multinational Accounting— An Anthology, 1979, Frontiers of International Accounting, 1986, AACSB Curriculum Internationalization Resource Guide, 1988; contbr. chpts. to books, numerous articles to profl. jours. Recipient U. Wash. Disting. Tchg. award, 1983, Disting. Svc. award, U. Wash., 1984; Ford Found. fellow, 1958—59, Price Waterhouse Internat. Acctg. Rsch. fellow, 1962—64. Fellow Acad. Internat. Bus.; mem. AICPA (internat. practice exec. com. 1972-75, exec. coun. 1987-89, Disting. Achievement in Acctg. Edn. award 2000), Am. Acctg. Assn. (pres. 1988-89, acad. v.p. 1970-71, chmn. adv. bd. internat. acctg. sect. 1977-79, Wildman medal 1986, Nat. Outstanding Educator 1981, Disting. Internat. Lectr. in Black Africa 1987, Outstanding Internat. Acctg. Educator 1991), Wash. Soc. CPAs (pres. 1988-89, Outstanding Educator award 1985, Pub. Svc. award 1995), Acctg. Edn. Change Commn. (chmn. 1994-96), Beta Alpha Psi (Acad. Acct. of Yr. 1987), Beta Gamma Sigma (Disting. scholar 1978-79), Alpha Gamma Sigma. Home: 15794 Dovewood Ct Poway CA 92064-2282 Business E-Mail: gmueller@u.washington.edu. *It has always been important to me to associate with people and tangible and intangible things of the highest quality. I make it a practice to set clear goals and then pursue them actively. A broad world view on all aspects of life engenders more success and happiness than special interest perspectives. I welcome change in professional matters, but seek constancy in personal and family affairs. Fate has played a role in my successes. I believe in God, Protestant ethics, and the merits of classical academic scholarship.*

**MUELLER, GREG LESTER,** artist, educator; b. Minneapolis, Minn., Mar. 30, 1966; s. Lester Robert Mueller and Ramona Ann (Mueller) Steele; m. Meg Ann Koenig, June 26, 1999. MFA, Mont. St U. Sch. of Art, 2001. Sculpture instr. Bowling Green State U Sch. of Art, Ohio, 2002. Sculpture, Silent Spaces. Home: 1021 Fort Dr Bowling Green OH 43402 Office: Bowling Green State U Sch of Art 1000 Fine Arts Ctr Bowling Green OH 43403 Office Phone: 419-372-4193. Personal E-mail: g.mueller@verizon.net.

**MUELLER, HOLGER,** physicist; b. Munich, Jan. 20, 1974; arrived in U.S., 2004; s. Claus Erich Mueller and Maren Mueller-Rasmussen; m. Cornelia Sabine Becker-Weimann, Feb. 27, 2004; 1 child, Amelie Felicitas. PhD, Humboldt-U., Berlin, Germany, 2004; physics diploma, U. Konstuna, Germany, 2000. Rsch. asst. U. Konstanz, Germany, 2000—02, Humboldt-U., Berlin, 2002—04; postdoctoral rschr. Stanford U., Calif., 2004—. Cons. GW-Elektronik, Munich, 1990—; cons. (electronic design) Fritz-Haber-Institut der Max-Planck Gesellschaft, Munich, 2006—. Contbr. rsch. (Joung Rschr.'s award Conf. on Precision Electromagnetic Measurement, 2002). Fellow: Alexander von Humboldt Found. (Feodor Lynen fellowship 2004—06); mem.: AAAS. Achievements include patents for TV and Microwave technology; research in Atom Interferometry and Tests of Special Relativity. Office: Stanford Univ 382 Via Pueblo Mall Stanford CA 94305 Home: 770 Coleman Ave Menlo Park CA 94025 Office Phone: 650-725-2354. Business E-Mail: holgerm@stanford.edu.

**MUELLER, JOHN ERNEST,** political science professor, dance critic; b. St. Paul, June 21, 1937; s. Ernst A. and Elsie E. (Schleh) M.; m. Judy A. Reader, Sept. 6, 1960; children: Karl, Karen, Susan AB, U. Chgo., 1960; MA, UCLA, 1963, PhD, 1965. Asst. prof. polit. sci. U. Rochester, NY, 1965-69, assoc. prof., 1969-72, prof., 1972-2000, prof. film studies, 1983-2000, founder, dir. Dance Film Archive, 1973—; prof. polit. sci., Woody Hayes chair nat. security studies Ohio State U., 2000—. Lectr. on dance in U.S., Europe, Australia, 1973—; OP-ED columnist Wall St. Jour., 1984—, L.A. Times, 1988—, N.Y. Times, 1990—; mem. dance panel NEA, 1983-85; columnist Dance Mag., 1974 82; dance critic Rochester Dem. and Chronicle, 1974-82; mem. adv. bd. Dance in Am., PBS, 1975; mem. editl. bd. Ohio State U. Press, 2000—04. Author: War, Presidents and Public Opinion, 1973 (one of Fifty Books That Significantly Shaped Public Opinion Rsch. 1946-95 Am. Assn. Pub. Opinion Rsch. 1995), Dance Film Directory, 1979, Astaire Dancing: The Musical Films, 1985 (de la Torre Bueno prize 1985), Retreat From Doomsday: The Obsolescence of Major War, 1989, Policy and Opinion in the Gulf War, 1994, Quiet Cataclysm: Reflections on the Recent Transformation of World Politics, 1995, Capitalism, Democracy, and Ralph's Pretty Good Grocery, 1999, The Remnants of War, 2004 (Lepgold prize 2004); co-author: Trends in Public Opinion: A Compendium of Survey Data, 1989; editor: Approaches to Measurement, 1969, Peace, Prosperity, and Politics, 2000; co-editor Jour. Policy Analysis and Mgmt., 1985-89; mem. editl. bd. Pub. Opinion Quar., 1988-91, Jour. Cold War Studies, 1999—, Internat. Polit. Sociology, 2005—; prodr. 12 dance films, DVD/recorded commentator on 2nd soundtrack of laser disc edit. Swing Time, 1986, DVD edit., 2005; co-adapter (musical) A Foggy Day, 1998; prodr. Shaw Festival Niagara-on-the-Lake, Ont., 1998, 99. Grantee NSF, 1967-70, 74-75, NEH, 1972-73, 74-75, 77-78, 79-81; Guggenheim fellow, 1988. Mem. Am. Acad. Arts & Scis., Am. Polit. Sci. Assn., Dance Critics Assn. (bd. dirs. 1983-85). Home: 420 W 5th Ave Columbus OH 43201-3159 Office: Ohio State U Polit Sci Dept Columbus OH 43210-1373 Office Phone: 614-247-6007. Business E-Mail: bbbb@osu.edu.

**MUELLER, JOHN S.,** music educator; b. East Liverpool, Ohio, Aug. 4, 1927; s. Herman F. and Marjorie (Storm) Mueller; m. Margaret Ellen Mueller; 1 child, Laura Marjorie. MusB, Oberlin Coll., 1950; MusM, U. Mich., 1952; DMA, Boston U., 1968. Asst. prof. Flora MacDonald Coll., 1954—55; prof. organ dept. head Salem Coll., 1955—95. Guest lectr. Longy Sch. Mus., 1966; tchr. organ N.C. Sch. Arts, 1967—95; organist, choirmaster Harvard U., 1967; dean Am. Guild Organists; presenter in field; organ recitalist, 1954—; Program chmn. Music Tchr. Nat. Assn. With U.S. Army, 1952—54. Grantee, Salem Coll., 1970; Fulbright grant, 1960—61. Mem.: Chamber Music Soc., Coll. Music Soc. Democrat. Episcopalian. Home: 1524 Sharon Rd Winston Salem NC 27103-4186 Office: Salem Coll Salem Sq Winston Salem NC 27108

**MUELLER, KATHRYN LUCILE,** medical educator; b. Lincoln, Nebr. Feb. 14, 1951; d. Roland Fredrick and Elizabeth (Brown) Mueller; m. Rex A. Logemann, Apr. 27, 1978; children: Elizabeth C. Logemann, Alexander F. Logemann. BA, U. Nebr., 1973, MD, 1977; MPH, Med. Coll. Wis., 1994. Diplomate Am. Bd. Preventive Medicine, Am. Bd. Occupl. Medicine. Instr. Rush Med. Sch., Chgo., 1981-87; asst. prof. U. Colo. Health Scis. Ctr., Denver, 1987-98, dir. student and occupational health svcs., 1989-96, assoc. prof. surgery and preventive medicine, 1998—2004; med. dir. Colo. Divsn. Worker's Compensation, Denver, 1991—; prof. surgery and preventive medicine U. Colo. Health Scis. Ctr., Denver, 2005—. Project med. dir. Christ Hosp. EMS Program, Chgo., 1983—87; physician advisor Emergency Med. Svcs. State of Colo., Denver, 1991—92; peer reviewer Tomes Plus, 1991—; oral bd. examiner Am. Bd. Emergency Medicine, 1992—95; chair first test com. Am. Bd. Med. Ind. Med. Examiners, 1994—95. Mem. editl. bd.: Guides Newsletter AMA, 1996—. Am. Coll. Emergency Medicine fellow, 1983—2002, Robert Wood Johnson grantee, 1998—2000. Fellow: Am. Coll. Occupl. and Environ. Medicine (chair com. state legis. affairs 1996—2002, bd. dirs. 2000—04, co-chair coun. on govtl. affairs 2002—03, sec.-treas. 2004—06); mem.: Rocky Mountain Acad. Occupl. and Environ. Medicine (bd. dirs. 1992—94, pres. 1997). Avocations: cross country skiing, travel, reading. Office: U Colo Health Scis Ctr 4200 E 9th Ave B 211 Denver CO 80262-0001 Business E-Mail: kathrynmueller@uchsci.edu.

**MUELLER, LISEL,** writer, poet; b. Hamburg, Germany, Feb. 8, 1924; BA in Sociology, U. Evansville; postgrad., Ind. U. Vis. faculty Goddard Coll., 1977-80, Warren Wilson Coll. 1983, 85-86; vis. lectr. U. Chgo., 1984; disting. writer-in-residence Wichita State U., 1981. Author: Dependencies, 1965, 2d edit, 1998, Life of a Queen, 1970, The Private Life, 1976, Voices from the Forest, 1977, The Need to Hold Still, 1980, Waving from Shore, 1989, Second Language, 1986, Learning to Play by Ear, 1990, Alive Together: New & Selected Poems, 1996 (Pulitzer prize). Recipient Pulitzer prize for poetry, Nat. Book award for poetry, Carl Sandburg award, Ruth Lilly Poetry prize, 2002, Jacob Glatstein Meml. prize, Eunice Tietjens Meml. prize; NEA fellow. Mem.: Poetry Ctr. Chgo. (founding mem.). Office: La State U Press PO Box 25053 Baton Rouge LA 10894-5053

**MUELLER, MARGARET S.,** musician, educator; b. Creston, Iowa, Dec. 3, 1924; d. Homer Cowan and Pearl Callahan Snodgrass; m. John Storm Mueller, June 10, 1958; 1 child, Laura Marjorie Mueller Woods. Student, Kans. U., 1943-46; MusB, Oberlin Conservatory, 1950, MusM, 1958. Instr. piano N.D. State Tchrs. Coll., Minot, 1950-51; instr. piano and organ Iowa State U., Ames, 1951-55, Randolph-Macon Woman's Coll., Lynchburg, Va., 1957-58; prof. organ and theory Salem Coll., Winston-Salem, N.C., 1958-95, prof. emerita, 1995—. Performing artist organ various concerts throughout the U.S. and Europe, 1953—; organist St. Paul's Episcopal Ch., Winston-Salem, 1963—2001; judge André Marchal Internat. Competition, Biarritz, France, 2001. Grantee Fulbright Assn., Frankfurt, Germany, 1955-56, Aeolian grantee, Paris, 1956-57. Mem.: Nat. Guild Piano Tchrs. (judge piano and organ), Winston-Salem Profl. Piano Tchrs. Assn., Music Tchrs. Nat. Assn. (judge piano and organ), Organ Hist. Soc., Am. Guild Organists (judge state, regional and nat. competitions 1965—, performing artist organ nat. and regional convs. 1973, 1976, 1987, 1993), Pi Kappa Lambda, Mu Phi Epsilon. Democrat. Episcopalian. Home: 1524 Sharon Rd Winston Salem NC 27103-4816 Office: Salem Coll Salem Square Winston Salem NC 27108

**MUELLER, MARK CHRISTOPHER,** lawyer; b. Dallas, June 19, 1945; s. Herman August and Hazel Deane (Hatzenbuehler) M.; m. Linda Jane Reed. BA in Econs., So. Meth. U., 1967; MBA in Acctg., 1969, JD, 1971. Bar: Tex. 1971, U.S. Dist. Ct. (no. dist.) Tex. 1974, U.S. Ct. Appeals (5th cir.) Tex. 1974; CPA, Tex. Acct. Arthur Young & Co., Dallas, 1967-68, A.E. Krutilek, Dallas, 1968-71; pvt. practice law Dallas, 1971—; assoc. L. Vance Stanton, Dallas, 1971-72. Instr. legal writing and rsch. So. Meth. U., Dallas, 1970-71, instr. legal acctg., 1975; unauthorized practice of law com. Supreme Ct. Tex. Leading articles editor Southwestern Law Jour., 1970-71. Mem. NRA, Tex. Bar Assn., Tex. State Rifle Assn., Dpling Arms Coll., Tex. Soc. CPA's, Dallas Bar Assn., SAR, Sons Republic Tex., Sons of Union Vets. of Civil War, Sons Confederate Vets., Mil. Order Stars and Bars, Dallas Arms Coll., Order of Coif, Dallas Hist. Soc., Dallas County Pioneer Assn., Rock Creek Barbeque Club, Masons, Shriners, York Rite, Grotto, Scottish Rite (32 degree Knight Commdr. Ct. of Honor), Beta Alpha Psi, Phi Delta Phi, Sigma Chi. Home: 7310 Brennans Dr Dallas TX 75214-2804 Office: 6510 Abrams Rd Ste 565 Dallas TX 75231-7292 Office Phone: 214-221-6888.

**MUELLER, NANCY SCHNEIDER,** retired biology professor; b. Wooster, Ohio, Mar. 8, 1933; d. Gilbert Daniel and Winifred (Porter) Schneider; m. Helmut Charles Mueller, Jan. 27, 1959; 1 child, Karl Gilbert. AB in Biology, Coll. of Wooster, Ohio, 1955; MS in Zoology, U. Wis., Madison, 1957, PhD in Zoology, 1962. Instr. zoology U. Wis., Madison, 1958; asst. prof. poultry sci. and zoology N.C. State U., Raleigh, 1968-71; vis. prof. biology N.C. Cht. U., Durham, 1971-73, assoc. prof., 1973-79, prof., 1979-93; ret., 1993. Vis. scientist U. Vienna, Austria, 1975. Contbr. articles, abstracts to profl. publs. Mem. Soc. for Integrative and Comparative Biology, Wis. Acad. Sci., Arts and Letters, N.C. Acad. Sci., LWV, Sigma Xi. Avocations: bird migration, conservation and environmental issues. Home: 409 Moonridge Rd Chapel Hill NC 27516-5576 E-mail: hmuelle@earthlink.net.

**MUELLER, O. THOMAS,** molecular geneticist, pediatrics educator; b. Berlin, Aug. 17, 1950; arrived in U.S.; s. Heinz Carl and Gertrud (Jung) M.; m. Mary Gail Craig, April 24, 1976; children: Cara Lynne, Kyle Thomas, Eric Andreas. BA, Lehigh U., 1972; PhD in biol. chemistry, Pa. State U., 1978. Diplomate: Am. Bd. Med. Genetics in Molecular and Biochemical Genetics. Postdoctoral fellow U. Colo. Med. Ctr., Denver, 1978-80; rsch. asst. Roswell Park Meml. Inst., Buffalo, 1980-84, rsch. affiliate, 1984-87; assoc. prof. pediats. U. So. Fla., Tampa, 1987—; dir. molecular genetics All Children's Hosp., St. Petersburg, Fla., 1994—. Contbr. numerous articles to scientific jours. including Human Genetics, Am. Jour. Med. Genetics, Am. Jour. Human Genetics, Jour. Biol. Chemistry, and others. Avocations: triathlons, sailing. Home: 2001 Point Overlook Dr NE Saint Petersburg FL 33703-3435 Office: Dept Pathology All Children's Hosp 801 6th St S Saint Petersburg FL 33701-4816 Office Phone: 727-767-8985. Business E-Mail: muellert@allkids.org.

**MUELLER, PAUL HENRY,** retired bank executive; b. NYC, June 24, 1917; s. Paul Herbert and Helen (Cantwell) M.; m. Jean Bonnel Vreeland, Sept. 10, 1949; 1 child, Donald Vreeland. BS, NYU, 1940; AB, Princeton U., 1941; LittD (hon.), Heriot-Watt U., Edinburgh, Scotland, 1981; LHD (hon.), Bloomfield Coll., 1991. From page to sr. v.p. Citibank N.A., 1934—65, sr. v.p., 1965—74, chmn. credit policy com., 1974—82; chmn. Saab-Scania Am. Inc., 1982—90; ret. 1990. Joined U.S. Fgn. Svc., served in Panama, Cairo, Washington, 1941-43; asst. adminstrv. sec. UN Montary and Fin. Conf., Bretton Woods, N.H., 1944; divisional asst. Dept. State, 1946; sec. West Indian Conf., 2d session, St. Thomas, V.I., 1946; vis. lectr. U. Va., 1980-2001; founding chmn., sr. fellow Ctr. Internat. Banking Studies, 1977. Author (contbg.): Offshore Lending by U.S. Commercial Banks, 1975, 2d edit., 1981, Bank Credit, 1981, Classics in Commercial Bank Lending, 1981, Vol. II, 1985, Loan Portfolio Management, 1988, Credit Culture, 1994, Credit Risk Management, 1995; author: (with Leif H. Olsen) Credit and the Business Cycle, 1979; author: Learning from Lending, 1979, Credit Doctrine for Lending Officers, 1976, 1981, 2d edit., 1997, Credit Endpapers, 1982 Perspective on Credit Risk, 1988, Credit in a Nutshell, 2002; contbr. articles to profl. jours. Trustee Bloomfield Coll., N.J. 1965—. vice chmn., 1987-88, chmn. 1988-91, trustee emeritus; treas. Marcus Wallenberg Found. (U.S.), 1984—. Served from 2d lt. to capt. USMCR, 1944-59. Decorated Order Polar Star, Sweden; recipient Alumni award Grad. Sch. Credit and Fin. Mgmt., Dartmouth Coll., 1958, Disting. Svc. award Robert Morris Assocs., 1981. Mem. Bankers Assn. Fgn. Trade (v.p. 1976), Pilgrims, SAR, Swedish-Am. C. of C. USA (chmn. 1989-90, hon. dir.), Royal Econ. Soc. (U.K.), Univ. Club (N.Y.C.), Beta Gamma Sigma. Republican. Presbyterian. Home: 75 Rotary Dr Summit NJ 07901-3131

**MUELLER, PAULA DEUTSCH,** retired music educator; b. Chgo., Mar. 27, 1950; d. Zoltan (Bud) Robert Deutsch and Eleanor Esther Tomaszewski/Deutsch; m. Martin F. Mueller, May 5, 1973. MusB in Edn., VanderCook Coll. of Music, 1972. Cert. music tchr. Music Educators National Conference. Fine arts tchr. Elem. Sch. Dist. 2, Bensenville, Ill., 1973—2005. Handchime ensemble dir. Elem. Sch. Dist. 2, 1980—2005, fine arts dept. coord. gen. music, instrumental music, visual art, chorus, drama, 1993—; freelance handchime ensemble clinician, bassoon player, Ill., 1980—. Contbr.: gen. music chpt. Music Resource Manual for Curriculum Planning, 1993. Mem. fine arts content-area stds. panel Ill. State Bd. of Edn., Springfield, 1990, 2003—04; rep. Bensenville (Ill.) Arts Coun.; bd. dirs. Glen Ellyn (Ill.) Children's Chorus, 1993—2003, pres. bd. dirs., 1996—2002. Recipient Founder's Award for enduring contributions of exceptional quality and for sustained commitment to the educatiional well-being of the children in Bens, Elem. Sch. Dist. #2, 1990. Mem.: PTA (life), Chorus Am., Bensenville (Ill.) Edn. Assn. (pres. 1984—91, 1997—2004), Ill. Edn. Assn. (bd. dirs., chmn. region 58 1998—2005, exec. com. 2001—03), Ill. Music Educators Assn. (assoc.), Music Educators Nat. Conf. (assoc.; chmn., jr. h.s., elem. music coun. Dist. 9). Democrat. Presbyterian. Avocations: gardening, cooking, crafts. Personal E-mail: paula.mueller@ieanea.org.

**MUELLER, PEGGY JEAN,** dance educator, choreographer, rancher; b. Austin, Tex., June 14, 1952; d. Rudolph George Jr. and Margaret Jean (Locke) M.; m. John Yerby Tarlton, June 24, 1972 (div. June 1983). BS. in Home Econs., Child Devel., U. Tex., Austin, 1974. Dance tchr. Shirley McPhail Sch. Dance, Austin, 1972-75, Jean Tarlton Sch. Dance, Alpine, Tex., 1975-77, College Station, Tex., 1977-80, Sul Ross State U., Alpine, 1975-77, Tex. A&M U., College Station, 1977-80, A&M Consol. Community Edn., Coll. Station, 1977-78, Jean Mueller Sch. Dance, Austin, 1980—, U. Tex., Austin, 1980—. Dancer, contest judge Gt. Tex. Dance-Off, Austin, 1985—86; mem. equestrian com. Austin Travis County Livestock Show and Rodeo, 1980—92, chmn. trail ride, 1986—, Star Tex. Fair and PRCA Rodeo, 2000—; trial boss, pres. Austin Founders Trail Ride, 1986—; trail boss Bandera Longhorn Cattle Dr. and Trail Ride, 1990, 91; choreographer, head cheerleader Austin Texans Pro Football Team, 1981; dance tchr. Austin Ballroom Dancers, 1988, the Austin Club, 1997, 98; dancer, agt. George Strait/Bud Light Comml. Auditions, 1990; head contest judge Am.'s Ultimate Dance Contest, Austin, 1994; contest judge Two-Stepping Across Am., Austin, 1994; hon. trial boss Dream Catcher Ranch Trail Ride, Franklin, Tex., 1995, 96, Grapevine/Housgon Country Donkey, Mule and Horse Trail Ride, 1997, 2000. Dancer Oklahoma, Austin, 1969, Kiss Me Kate, Austin, 1970; choreographer, lead role Cabaret, Alpine, 1976, (mini-series) True Women, 1997. Active Women's Symphony League Austin, 1972—, Settlement Club, Austin, 1987—; recreation chmn. St. Martin's Evang. Luth. Ch., Austin, 1972—; hon. trail boss St. Jude Children's Rsch. Hosp. Trail Ride, Austin and Kyle, Tex., 1991. Recipient Outstanding Trail Rider of Yr. award Wild Horse Trail Ride, Okla., 1984; named Tex. First Lady Trail Boss, Gov. Mark White, Mayor Frank Cooksey, Austin City Coun., 1986, Judge Bill Aleshire, Travis County Commrs., 1989, Outstanding Intramural Sports Team Mgr.-Player, Tex. A&M U., 1978-79. Mem. Tex Assn. Tchrs. of Dancing, Inc., U.S. Twirling and Gymnastics Assn., Univ. Tex. Ex-Students Assn., Tex. Execs. in Home Econs., Am. Vet. Med. Assn. Aux. (v.p. 1978-79, pres. 1979-80), Am. Horse Shows Assn., Internat. Arabian Horse Assn., Austin Women's Tennis Assn. (v.p. 1985-86, pres. 1986-90, spl. events chmn. 1990-92, advisor 1990—, winner 2d ann. Harriet Crosson Outstanding Player & Community Svc. award), Women's Team Tennis of Austin Assn. (pres.-elect 1992-93, pres. 1993-94), Capital Area Tennis Assn. (membership com. 1991, 92), Houston Salt Grass Trail Ride Assn., San Antonio Alamo Trail Ride Assn., Ft. Worth Chisholm Trail Ride Assn., U. Tex. Longhorn Alumni Band, Austin C. of C., Am. Bus. Women's Assn., Austin Alumnae Panhellenic Assn. (1st v.p. 1989-90, rush forum chmn. 1990, pres. 1990-91, parliamentarian 1991-92), Lone Grove Cmty. Club (treas. 199697, v.p. 1997-99, pres. 1999—, exec. trustee 1997-99, exec. dir. 1999-2000), Omicron Nu (v.p. 1973-74), Jr. Austin Woman's Club (historian 1990-91), Austin Country Club (team tennis captain 1994-95, player 1994—, dance tchr. 1993-96), Zeta Tau Alpha (Austin Alumnae Chpt., alumnae photographer, social advisor 1982-87, treas. 1987-89, publicity chmn. 1989, Easter Seals fundraiser, Honor Cup winner 1990, pres. 1991-92, internat. convention official del. 1988, 92, nominating chmn. 1992-93, mem. yearbook com. 1992-94, 2d v.p. 1993-94). Clubs: Cen. Tex. Arabian Horse, Capitol Area Quarter Horse Assn., Jr. Austin Woman's, Austin Country. Republican. Avocations: theater, piano, drums, sports, travel. Home and Office: PO Box 5868 Austin TX 78763-5868 E-mail: aftr@USATrailRides.com.

**MUELLER, PETER STERLING,** psychiatrist, educator; b. NYC, Dec. 28, 1930; s. Reginald Sterling and Edith Louise (Welleck) M.; m. Ruth Antonia Shipman, Aug. 9, 1958; children: Anne Louise, Peter Sterling, Paul Shipman, Elizabeth Ruth. AB, Princeton U., 1952; MD, U. Rochester, 1956. Am. Cancer Soc. student fellow Francis Delafield Hosp., N.Y.C., summer 1955; intern Bellevue Hosp., Columbia U., N.Y.C., 1956-57; asst. resident in psychiatry Henry Phipps Psychiat. Clinic, Johns Hopkins Hosp., Balt., 1963-66; asst. prof. psychiatry Sch. Medicine, Yale U., New Haven, 1966-72; asso. prof. psychiatry Coll. Medicine and Dentistry of N.J., Rutgers Med. Sch., Piscataway, 1972-76, clin. prof. psychiatry, 1976-82; cons. for Rehab. Unit and Center for Indsl. Human Resources, Community Mental Health Center, 1973—; mem. courtesy staff dept. psychiatry Princeton Med. Center, 1976—. Cons. in psychotherapy Conn. Valley Hosp., Middletown, 1966-72; cons. in psychiatry Carrier Clinic, Belle Mead, N.J., 1973-82, VA Hosp., Lyons, N.J., 1975-78 Contbr. writings in field to profl. publs. U.S. and Brit., papers to profl. confs. on the use patents in U.S. and fgn. countries for direct dopamine agonists in the treatment of tobacco addiction. Served with USPHS, 1957-63. Recipient Exemplary Psychiatrist award Nat. Alliance for the Mentally Ill, 1994. Mem. Am. Psychosomatic Soc., Am. Psychiat. Assn., AAAS, Amyotrophic Lateral Sclerosis Found. (adv. bd.), Sigma Xi. Episco-palian. Achievements include patents for treatment of disorders secondary to organic impairment with sibutramine; method of treatment of Irritable Bowel Syndrome with a fibric acid. Home: 182 Snowden Ln Princeton NJ 08540-3915 Office and Ste B-3 Princeton NJ 08540-2757 Office Phone: 609-924-4061. *For some, a hyperactive learning disorder is a curse that hobbles them throughout life; but for others, including myself, this disorder has become a somewhat uncomfortable and bewildering spur for lifelong compulsive puzzle-solving. This bittersweet mandate has produced the original, serendipitous, and occasionally disconcerting ideas which have marked my life.*

**MUELLER, RICHARD L.P.,** physician; b. Jersey City, Feb. 16, 1962; BS, Brown U., 1983; MD, U. Calif., San Francisco, 1987. Diplomate in internal medicine and cardiovasc. diseases Am. Bd. Internal Medicine, cert. Nat. Bd. Echocardiography, Am. Bd. Clin. Lipidology. Internal medicine intern North Shore Univ. Hosp., Manhasset, NY, 1987—88, resident in internal medicine, 1988—90, chief resident in internal medicine, 1990—91; fellow in cardiovasc. diseases N.Y. Hosp. Cornell Med. Ctr., N.Y.C., 1991—94; pres. Med. Assocs. N.Y., N.Y.C., 1994—, Cardiovasc. Diagnostics, PC, N.Y.C., 2001—, Cardiac Imaging For Life, PC, River Edge, NJ, 2005—. Clin. instr. medicine Weill Coll. Medicine, Cornell U., 1994—; asst. attending physician N.Y. Presbyn. Hosp., 1994—. Contbr. articles to profl. jours. Fellow: ACP, Am. Coll. Chest Physicians, Am. Soc. Angiology, Am. Heart Assn., Am. Coll. Cardiology; mem.: Med. Soc. State N.Y. (heart, lung and cancer com. 2004—). Office: Cardiac Imaging for Life PC Ste 204 130 Kinderkamack Rd River Edge NJ 07661 also: Cardiovascular Diagnostics PC 401 E 55th St New York NY 10022-4103 also: Cosmetic Vein Solutions 401 E 55th St New York NY 10022 Office Phone: 212-593-9800, 212-832-7575. Office Fax: 212-593-5757.

**MUELLER, ROBERT LOUIS,** manufacturing executive; b. Denver, Aug. 25, 1927; s. George Winchester and Ruth Mabel (Cole) M.; m. Sue McCoy, July 3, 1949; children: Robert, Richard, Edward, Mark; m. Susan Galbraith, June 23, 1985. BSMechE, Yale U., 1948. Chief computer Western Geophys. Co., Mont., Wyo., Colo., Tex., 1949-50; dist. mgr. Armco Steel Corp., Colo., Ohio, N.Y., 1950-63, L.B. Foster Co., N.Y.C., 1963-66; v.p. Wheeling Pitts.

Steel Co., W.Va. and Pa., 1966-75; chmn., pres., chief exec. officer Connors Steel Co., Ala., 1975-82; pres., chief exec. officer Judson Steel Co., Calif., 1982-87; pres., COO Proler Internat., Houston, 1987-94, also bd. dirs., 1987-94, cons., 1994—; dir. Employee Solutions, Inc., 1995—; pres. Mueller Resources, Inc., Sedona, Ariz., 1993—. Co-author: Handbook of Drainage and Construction Products, 1954. With USN, 1945-46. Mem. ASCE, Assn. Iron and Steel Engrs., Duquesne Club (Pitts.), Houston City Club, Sedona Racquet Club, The Sedona 30.

**MUELLER, ROBERT SWAN, III,** FBI Director; b. NYC, Aug. 7, 1944; s. Robert Swan Jr. and Alice (Truesdale) Mueller; m. Ann Standish, Sept. 3, 1966; children: Cynthia, Melissa. BA, Princeton U., 1966; MA, NYU, 1967; JD, U. Va., 1973. Bar: Mass., U.S. Dist. Ct. Mass., U.S. Ct. Appeals (1st cir.), Calif., U.S. Dist. Ct. (no. dist.) Calif., U.S. Ct Appeals (9th cir.). Assoc. Pillsbury, Madison & Sutro, San Francisco, 1973-76; asst. U.S. atty. (No. dist.) Calif. US Dept. Justice, San Francisco, 1976-80, chief unit spl. prosecutions, 1980-81, chief criminal divsn., 1981-82, chief criminal divsn. Mass. dist. Boston, 1982-85, 1st asst. U.S. atty., 1985, U.S. atty., 1986-87, dep. U.S. atty., 1987-88; ptnr. Hill & Barlow, Boston, 1988-89; asst. to atty. gen. for criminal matters U.S. Dept. Justice, Washington, 1989-90, asst. atty. gen. criminal divsn., 1990-93; lawyer Hale & Dorr, Washington, 1993—95; sr. litigator, homicide sect.; DC US Atty's Office US Dept. Justice, Washington, 1995—98; US atty. (No. dist) Calif. U.S. Dept. Justice, 1998—2001, acting dep. atty. gen., 2001, dir. FBI, 2001—. Capt. USMC, 1967-70; Vietnam. Decorated Bronze Star, Purple Heart, Vietnamese Cross of Gallantry. Office: FBI J Edgar Hoover Bldg 935 Pennsylvania Ave NW Washington DC 20535-3404*

**MUELLER, RODNEY ALAN,** music educator; b. Oak Park, Ill., Apr. 10, 1954; s. Robert John Andrew and Alice Marie Mueller; m. Linnea Christine Danielson, Dec. 26, 1981; children: Jonathan Edward, Johanna Christine, Daniel Robert Alan, Peter Andrew. BA, Wheaton Coll., 1976; B of Music Edn., No. Mich. U., 1977, MusM, 1982; EdD, U. Ill., 1997. Cert. K-12 Music Tchr. Ill. State Bd. Edn. String tchr.,orch. dir. Grinnell Newburg Cmty. Schs., Iowa, 1978—85; faculty music Prairie Bible Coll., Three Hills, Alberta, Canada, 1985—93; string tchr., orch. dir. Champaign Cmty. Unit 4 Schs., Ill., 1996—; tchr. string pvt. practice. Sect. cellist Parkland Cmty. Orch., Champaign, 2003—; guest cellist. jr. orch. Ill. Music Educators Assn. Dist. 5 Festival, Charleston, 2004; asst. condr. Sangamon Valley Youth Orch., Springfield, 1995—96; substitute. sect. cellist Champaign-Urbana Symphony Orch., 2000—04; jr. string orch., sect. tchr. & condr. Ill. Summer Youth Music, Urbana, 1995—2001; coop. tchr. preservice string edn. students Millikin U., U. Ill., 1998—; clinician, adjudicator string edn., Ill., 1997—. Mem., musician Stratford Pk. Bible Chapel, Champaign, 2004—; v.p., pres. Grinnell Area Arts Coun., 1979—81. Named Fullbright Exch. Tchr., U.S. Dept Edn., 1982—83; recipient Exceptional Tchr. Tribute, Stanford U., 2003. Mem.: Nat. Sch. Orch. Assn., Ill. Music Educators Assn., Music Educators Nat. Conf., Am. String Teachers Assn. (Ill. Sch. Tchr. of Yr. 2002). Achievements include design of Visualized Vibrato: Multimedia program to aid in the teaching/learning of violin/viola vibrato. Avocations: swimming, bicycling, gardening, woodworking. Home: 2302 Glenoak Dr Champaign IL 61821-6220 Office Phone: 217-351-3790.

**MUELLER, SHARON LEE (SHERRY MUELLER),** educational organization executive; b. Chgo., Aug. 17, 1943; d. LeRoy Elmer Arthur and Lucille Viola (Armborst) M. BA, Am. U., Washington, D.C., 1965; MA in Law and Diplomacy, Tufts U., Medford, Mass., 1966, PhD, 1977. Group leader Experiment in Internat. Living, 1969; cross-cultural trainer Nat. 4-H Found., 1970-71; cons. U.S. Dept. State, 1972, contract escort officer, 1972-77; cons. Fletcher Sch. Law and Diplomacy, 1976-81; lectr. dept. polit. sci. U. R.I. Kingston, 1975-77; adj. prof. Sch. Internat. Svc. Am. U., Washington, 1981-87; program officer Inst. Internat. Edn., Washington, 1978-82, dir. prof. exch. programs, 1982-96; exec. dir. Nat. Coun. for Internat. Visitors, Washington, 1996—2001, pres., 2001—. Mem. editl. adv. bd. Internat. Educator, 1991-2005; bd. dir. Nat. Coun. for Internat. Visitors, 1983-88; bd. dir., trustee World Learning, 1999-, bd. mem. PUb. Diplomacy Coun.; chair Coalition for Am. Leadership Abroad. Author: Careers in International Education, Exchange, and Development, 1998; contbr. chpts. to books; guest editor, contbr. Internat. Educator, 1992. Mem. exec. com. Internat. Student House, Washington, 1992-95; usher Foundry Meth. Ch., Washington, 1990-2004; mem. The Pres.'s Cir. Coun., Am. U., Washington, 1988-98, chair, 1996-98. Recipient Alumni Recognition award Am. U., 1990, award of appreciation Nat. Coun. for Internat. Visitors, 1988, award of appreciation World Ctr. for Tng. and Devel., 1988, Disting. Alumni award Lake Park High Sch., 1995, Outstanding Svc. award U.S.I.A., 1996. Mem. Nat. Press Club (assoc.), Sch. Internat. Svc. Alumni Assn. The Am. U. (founding pres. 1981-83), Sigma Iota Rho (hon.), Cosmos Club. Home: 1317 N Lynnbrook Dr Arlington VA 22201-4918 Office: NCIV 1420 K St NW Ste 800 Washington DC 20005-2500 Office Phone: 202-842-1414.

**MUELLER, SHIRLEY ANNE,** lawyer, real estate broker; b. Miami, Fla., Aug. 25, 1950; d. Robert Peter and Arvella Gertrude (Feldkamp) M.; divorced; children: Peter, Tybe, Samantha. AA in Journalism, Miami Dade Jr. Coll., 1970; BA in Philosophy, U. Calif., Berkeley, 1972; JD, Benjamin Cardozo Sch. Law, N.Y.C., 1982. Dir. children's advt. dir. Coun. Better Bus. Bur., N.Y.C., 1973-79; assoc. Cutner & Rathkopf, N.Y.C., 1983-87; pres. Uncommon Properties, Inc., N.Y.C., 1990-94; pvt. practice, N.Y.C., 1994—; with Sotheby's Internat. Realty, N.Y.C., 2002—04; v.p. Brown Harris Stevens Residential Sales, LLC, N.Y.C., 2004—. Mem. fundraising com. Children's Air Ctr. N.Y. Hosp., N.Y.C., 1988—99, Nightingale Bamford Schl, N.Y.C., 1987—98; bd. dirs. Am. Symphony Orch., N.Y.C., 2003—. Roman Catholic. Avocations: reading, music, travel, dance. Home: 3601 S Flagler Dr West Palm Beach FL 33405 Office: 43 N Moore St New York NY 10011 Office Phone: 212-906-0561. Personal E-mail: smueller08@aol.com. Business E-Mail: smueller@bhsusa.com.

**MUELLER, SUSAN JONES,** school system administrator; b. Suffern, N.Y., Aug. 21, 1947; d. Charles Jones and Phyllis Lembo; children: Seamus, Nora. BE, Duquesne U., Pitts., 1969; MS in Ednl. Adminstrn., U. Dayton, Ohio, 2001. Tchr. Rockland County Sch. Sys., Haverstraw, NY, 1969—70; ELS tchr. Frankfurt Konstanz, Germany, 1971—91; tchr. Diocese of Toledo, Perrysburg, Ohio, 1991—98, prin. Blakeslee, Ohio, 1998—2000; supt. schs. Diocese of Pensacola-Tallahassee, 2000—05. Mem. Springfield C of C., Ohio, 2000—05. Recipient Resolution, Toledo, 2003. Mem.: NCEA. Office: Diocese Pensacola-Tallahassee 11 N B St Pensacola FL 32501 Office Phone: 850-435-3500. Business E-mail: muellers@ptdiocese.org.

**MUELLER, VICKI LYNN,** elementary school educator; d. John Stanley Zdychnec and Virginia Jea Klein; m. Charles LeRoy Mueller, June 23, 1972; children: Kevin, Andrea, Jeff. Student, Iowa State U., 1971—73; BA in Edn., Buena Vista U., 1984; MA in Ednl. Adminstrn., U. No. Iowa, 1996. Tchr. Council Bluffs (Iowa) Schs., 1984—98, Amarillo (Tex.) Schs., 1998—. Trainer, presenter workshops in field. Contbr. articles to profl. jours. Finalist Dist. Tchr. of Yr., Amarillo Schs., 2002, 2004; named Tchr. of Yr., Wilson Jr. High, Council Bluffs, 1998, Austin Mid Sch., Amarillo, 2002, 2004. Mem.: ASCD, Internat. Reading Assn., NEA, Nat. Coun. Tchrs. English. Home: 7104 Glenoak Amarillo TX 79109 Office: Austin Mid Sch 1808 Wimberly Amarillo TX 79109 Office Phone: 806-354-4450. E-mail: teach8read@hotmail.com.

**MUELLER, WAYNE DENNIS,** music educator; b. Scottsbluff, Nebr., Apr. 20, 1947; s. Roger Wayne Mueller and Lorraine Rose Marie Eisenach; m. Mitzi Marie Hummel, Aug. 22, 1969; 1 child, Robert. Bachelors in Music Edn., U. of Nebr., Lincoln, NE, 1970. Cert. Teaching Certificate, K-12 Music Nebr. 6-12 vocal / instrumental music Thedford Pub. Schools, Thedford, Nebr., 1970—70; 7-12 vocal / instrumental music Morrill Pub. Schools, Morrill, Nebr., 1970—72; 7-12 vocal music Mitchell Pub. Schools, Mitchell, Nebr., 1972—73; sales and instrumental repair Jay's Music, Scottsbluff, Nebr., 1973; 6-12 instrumental music North Platte Pub. Schools, North Platte, Nebr., 1974—. Musician Mcpl. Band, North Platte, Nebr., 1975—, Sandhills

Symphony, North Platte, Nebr., 1975—; condr. Sandhill Symphony, North Platte, Nebr., 1994—2000; musical dir. Cmty. Playhouse, North Platte, Nebr., 1995. Pres., sec., elder, choir dir. Beautiful Savior Luth. Ch., North Platte, Nebr., 1980—2002; soccer referee Am. Youth Soccer Orgn., North Platte, Nebr., 1985—90. Recipient Art Beat Award, North Platte Chamber of Commerce, 1996; Music grantee for accelerated program, North Platte Pub. Sch. Found., 2000—03. Mem.: Nebr. Music Edn. Assn., North Platte Edn. Assn. (pres. 1974—2002), Optimist Club. Lutheran. Avocations: golf, coaching football and baseball, coaching football and baseball, coaching football and baseball, community musical events. Home: 2607 West Philip Avenue North Platte NE 69101 Office: North Platte Public Schools 1000 West Second Street North Platte NE 69101

**MUELLER, WILLARD FRITZ,** economics professor; b. Ortonville, Minn., Jan. 23, 1925; s. Fritz and Adele C. (Thrmaehlen) Mueller; m. Shirley I. Liesch, June 26, 1948; children: Keith, Scott, Kay. BS, U. Wis., 1950, MS, 1951; PhD, Vanderbilt U., 1955. Asst. prof. U. Calif., Davis, 1954-57; prof. U. Wis., 1957-61, prof. agrl. and applied econs. dept. econ. Sch. Law Madison, 1969—; chief economist small bus. com. U.S. Ho. of Reps., 1961; chief economist, dir. bur. econs. FTC, 1961-68; exec. dir. Pres.'s Cabinet Com. Price Stability, 1968-69. Expert House and Senate Com., 1960—86; cons. in indsl. orgn. and pub. policy. Past bd. editors Rev. Ind. Orgn., Antitrust Law and Econ. Rev., Antitrust Bull., Jour. Reprints for Antitrust Law and Econs. Mem. Econ. Policy Inst., 1987—90. With USN, 1943—46. Recipient Disting. Svc. award, FTC, 1978. Fellow: Am. Agrl. Econs. Assn. (profl. excellence awards in policy contrib. 1980, in comm. 1985, in rsch. discovery 1988); mem.: Argus Econ. Svcs. (pres. 1985—), Indsl. Orgn. Soc. (pres. 1989—90), Assn. Evolutionary Econs. (pres. 1974—75), Am. Econs. Assn. Unitarian Universalist. Office: U Wis 427 Lorch St Madison WI 53706-1513 Home: 8625 Wood Violet Way Madison WI 53717 Personal E-mail: wfritzmueller@aol.com.

**MUENCH, KARL HUGO,** clinical geneticist; b. St. Louis, May 3, 1934; MD, Washington U., St. Louis, 1960. Diplomate Am. Bd. Med. Genetics. Intern Barnes Hosp., St. Louis, 1960-61; fellow in biological chemistry Stanford U. Sch. Medicine, 1961-65; staff mem. Jackson Meml. Hosp., Miami, Fla.; prof. medicine U. Miami Sch. Medicine. Mem. AMA, ACP, Am. Coll. Med. Genetics. Office: U Miami Sch Med Div Genetic Med PO Box 16960 Miami FL 33101-6960 Office Phone: 305-243-6653. Business E-Mail: kmuench@med.miami.edu.

**MUENDERMANN, ANNEGRET,** researcher; b. Stuttgart, Germany, Jan. 26, 1973; d. Wolfgang Josef and Ursula Irmgard Hau; m. Lars Muendermann, Aug. 5, 2000; 1 child, Kira. Staatsexamen, Universitaet Konstanz, Germany, 1997; PhD, U.Calgary, Can., 2002. Postdoctoral fellow Stanford U., Calif., 2003—05, rsch. assoc., 2005—. Recipient Chancellor's Grad. Medal, U. of Calgary, 2003; scholar Govt. of Can. award, Dept. of Fgn. Affairs and Internat. Trade Can., 2000—02. Mem.: Deutsche Gesellschaft fuer Bio-mechanik, Internat. Soc. of Biomechanics, Can. Soc. of Biomechanics, Am. Soc. of Biomechanics, Internat. Soc. of Biomechanics, Orthop. Rsch. Soc. Protestant. Office: Stanford University 496 Lomita Mall Stanford CA 94305 Office Phone: 650-724-9684.

**MUETH, JOSEPH EDWARD,** lawyer; b. St. Louis, Aug. 8, 1935; s. Joseph and Marie Clare (Reher) M.; m. Ellen Agnes O'Heron, Dec. 24, 1973; children: Erin R., Patricia A. B.Chem. Engring., U. Dayton, 1957; LL.B. Georgetown U., 1960, LL.M., 1961. Bar: Calif. 1964. Practice law, L.A.; ptnr. Wills, Green & Mueth, L.A., 1974-83; pvt. practice law Calif., 1983-94; of counsel Sheldon & Mak, Pasadena, Calif., 1994—. Adj. prof. law U. Calif. Hastings Coll. Law, San Francisco, 1972-75; lectr. Claremont Grad. Sch. 1982—. Author: Copyrights Patents and Trademarks, 1974. Chmn. bd. Rio Hondo council Camp Fire Girls Inc., 1967-72. Mem. AAAS, Am., Los Angeles County bar assns., State Bar Calif., N.Y. Acad. Scis., L.A. Athletic Club. Home: PO Box 3369 1217 Seal Way Seal Beach CA 90740-6419 Office: 225 S Lake Ave Ste 800 Pasadena CA 91101-4858 Office Phone: 626-584-0396.

**MUETHER, CHARLES ALEXANDER,** writer, educator; b. Port Jefferson, NY, Nov. 14, 1964; s. Herbert Robert and Anne Muether; m. Kristie Jo Muether, Aug. 27, 1988. MA Curriculum and Devel., Dordt Coll., Sioux Center, Iowa, 1997. BA English and Secondary Edn., 1987; postgrad., Heidelberg Theol. Sem. English and drama educator Pella Christian, Pella, Iowa, 1989—2001; prin. educator Volga Christian, Volga, SD, 1988—89. Writer Wioarey Press, Des Moines, 2000—02. Author: (book) Theatre in the Middle; editor: Assessing the Whole Child. Deacon, elder, v.p. Covenant Ref. Ch., Pella, Iowa, 2002; mem. Grace Ref. Presbyn. Ch., Covenant Ref. Ch. Recipient Walmart Tchr. of the Yr. Award, Walmart, 2000, Golden Apple Award, Who-TV, 1995. Mem.: Nat. Coun. of Teachers of English. Independent. Avocations: reading, photography, model railroading. Home: 310 Prairie Street Pella IA 50219

**MUEZZINOGLU, MEHMET KEREM,** research scientist; b. Ankara, Turkey, Feb. 22, 1976; arrived in U.S. 2003; s. Metin and Aysen Muezzinoglu; m. Tulay Muezzinoglu, Sept. 22, 2001. BS, Istanbul Tech. U., 1998, MS, 2000; PhD, Dokuz Eylul U., Izmir, Turkey, 2003. Rsch. and tchng. asst. Dokuz Eylul U., Izmir, 2000—03; Grosscurth fellow U. Louisville, 2003—06, asst. prof., 2006—. Contbr. articles to profl. jours. Scholar, Sci. and Tech. Rsch. Coun. Turkey, 2000—03. Mem.: IEEE, Eta Kappa Nu. Achievements include development of neural associative memory models. Avocations: travel, zoology. Office: U Louisville Lutz Hall Rm 407 Louisville KY 40292 E-mail: mkerem@ieee.org.

**MUFSON, MAURICE ALBERT,** infectious diseases physician, educator; b. N.Y.C., July 7, 1932; s. Max and Faye M.; m. Diane Cecile Weiss, Apr. 1, 1962; children: Michael Jeffrey, Karen Andrea, Pamela Beth. AB, Bucknell U., 1953; MD, NYU, 1957. Intern Bellevue Hosp., N.Y.C., 1957-58, resident, 1958-59; chief resident Cook County Hosp., Chgo., 1965-66; sr. surgeon USPHS Lab. Infectious Diseases, NIH, 1961-65; from asst. prof. medicine to prof. U. Ill., 1965-76; prof. Marshall U., 1976—2002, prof. emeritus, 2002—, chmn. dept. medicine, 1976—2000, chmn. emeritus, 2000—. Vis. scientist Karolinska Inst., 1984-85. Contbr. articles to profl. jours. Served with U.S. Navy, 1959-61. WHO grantee, 1967; recipient Meet-the-Scholar award Marshall U., 1986, Rector H. Yr. award Sigma Xi, Marshall U., 1989, Solomon A. Berson Alumni Achievement award in health sci. NYU Sch Medicine, 1997; co-recipient Louis Weinstein award Jour. Clin. Infectious Diseases, 1990; named to Greater Huntington Wall of Fame, 2002. Master ACP (traveling scholar 1987, Laureate award W.va. chpt.). Infectious Diseases Soc. Am.; mem. AMA, Soc. Exptl. Biology and Medicine, Ctrl. Soc. Clin. Rsch., So. Soc. Clin. Investigation, W.Va. State Med. Assn., Assn. Profs. Medicine (counselor 1992-95, pres.-elect 1995-96, pres. 1996-97, past pres. 1997-98), Alpha Omega Alpha. Office: Marshall U Sch Medicine 1600 Med Ctr Dr Ste G500 Huntington WV 25701 Personal E-mail: maurice@ezwv.com. Business E-Mail: mufson@marshall.edu.

**MUFTI, AFTAB A.,** civil engineering educator; b. Sukkur, Sind, Pakistan, Apr. 24, 1940; arrived in Can. 1963; s. Abdul Wahid D. and Shah Jahan M.; children: Javed, Alex; m. Zehra Mehdi, Sept. 22, 2000. BCE, NED Engring. U., Karachi, 1962; MCE, McGill U., Montreal, 1965, PhD, 1969. Registered profl. engr., Man.; B.C. Asst. prof. McGill U., 1969-72; assoc. prof., head dept. comp. sci. Acadia U., Wolfville, N.S., 1972-76, prof., dir. Sch. Comp. Sci., 1976-80; prof. civil engring. Dalhousie U., Halifax, 1980-2000; pres. Intelligent Sensing for Innovative Structures Can. Network of Ctrs. of Excellence U. Man., Winnipeg, Canada, 2000—, prof. structural engring., 2000—; pres. Internat. Soc. Structural Health Monitoring Intelligent Infra-structure, 2002—. Pres. Advanced Composite Materials in Bridges and Structures Network of Can., 1992-98; judge Can. Cons. Engring. Awards, 1987; earthquake cons. Lepereau Nuclear Power Plant and Confedn. Bridge. Author: Elementary Computer Graphics, 1982, Bridge Engineering, 1994; editor: Advanced Composite Materials in Bridges and Structures, 1972, Finite

Element Method in Civil Engineering, 1993, Developments in Short and Medium Span Bridge Engineering, 1994, Bridge Superstructures New Developments, 1996; contbr. numerous articles to refereed jours., also conf. papers. Vol. fireman Wolfville Fire Dept., 1976-77. Recipient award for Distinction in Engring., Assn. Profl. Engrs. of N.S., 1996, award of merit Consulting Engrs. Man., 2003, award of excellence Consulting Engrs. Man., 2003, award of recognition Natural Scis. and Engring. Rsch. Coun., 2004, award of appreciation ISIS Can. Rsch. Network, 2004, Mirko-Ros Gold medal outstanding life's work rsch. and edn. Swiss Fed. Labs. Materials, Testing and Rsch., Dubendorf, Switzerland, 2005, Merit award Assn. Profl. Engrs. and Geoscientists Man., 2005, Nat. Sci. and Rsch Found. Synergy award, 2005. Fellow Can. Acad. Engring., Engring. Inst. Can. (Phelp Johnson prize 1969), Can. Soc. Civil Engring. (Whitman Wright award 1990, Pratley award 1993, A.B. Sanderson award 2006), ASCE (Lt. Govs. award Engring. Excellence in Nova Scotia 1996, IRF award 1997, ACI design award 1998, Nova award 2000). Achievements include patents for Bridge Deck and Steel Free Bridge Deck. Office: ISIS Can Admin Ctr U Man A250-96 Dafoe Rd Winnipeg MB Canada R3T 2N2 Office Phone: 204-474-7476. Office Fax: 204-474-7519. Business E-Mail: muftia@cc.umanitoba.ca.

**MUGERAUER, ROBERT W., JR.,** architecture educator; B in Liberal Studies, U. Notre Dame, 1967; PhD in Philosophy, U. Tex., 1973. Faculty mem. Grand Valley State Coll., Mich.; 1975—80; various positions including assoc. acad. den. acad. dean, acad. v.p., acting exec. v.p St. Edward's U., Austin, Tex., 1980—84; with U. Tex., 1985—2000; Sid Richardson Centennial chair arch. and planning U. Tex. Sch. Arch., Austin, 1990—2000, assoc. prof., 1990—2000; prof. urban design and planning U. Wash., Seattle, 2000—, dean Coll. Arch. and Urban Planning, 2000—. Author: Interpretations on Behalf of Place: Environmental Displacements and Alternative Responses, 1994, Environmental Interpretations: Tradition, Deconstruction, and Hermeneutics, 1997. Named a Most Important Midcareer Rschr.-Tchr., Environ. Design Rsch. Assn., 1996; recipient Excellence Tchg. award, U. Tex. Sch. Arch., 1988—89, Outstanding Tchr. award, 1993, 2000. Mem.: Internat. Assn. for Philosophy and Environment (sec.), Internat. Assn. for Study Traditional Environments (mem. steering com.). Office: U Wash Sch Arch 224 Gould Hall Box 355726 Seattle WA 98195-5726

**MUGGENBURG, BRUCE AL,** retired veterinary physiologist; b. May 2, 1937; s. Elmer Carl and Gladys O. (Bakke) M.; m. Marianne Nordgren, June 18, 1960 (dec. 1976); m. Carolyn Seale, July 16, 1977; children: Katherine Ann, Carl Thor, Virginia Hope. BS, U. Minn., St. Paul, 1959, DVM, 1961; MS, U. Wis., 1964, PhD, 1966. Asst. prof. U. Wis. Madison, 1966-69; sr. scientist Lovelace Inhalation Toxicology Rsch. Inst., Albuquerque, 1969—2004, scientist emeritus, 2005—. Vis. prof. U. do Rio Grande dul Sol, Porto Alegre, Brazil, 1966—68; clin. rsch. prof. dept. medicine U. N.Mex., Albuquerque, 1988—2000, clin. prof. coll. pharmacy, 1993—2000. Contbr. articles to profl. jours. Mem. AVMA, Scandinavian Club of Albuquerque (pres. 1983, 87, 88). Lutheran. Home: 2805 Calle Del Rio NW Albuquerque NM 87104-3141 Office Phone: 505-348-9441. E-mail: bmuggenb@lrri.org.

**MUGGERIDGE, DEREK BRIAN,** engineering executive, consultant; b. Godalming, Surrey, U.K., Oct. 10, 1943; arrived in Can., 1956; s. Donald William and Vera Elvina (Jackson) M.; m. Hanny Meta Buurman, Dec. 4, 1965; children: Karen Julie, Michael Brent. BS in Aero. Engring., Calif. State Polytech. U., 1965; MASc in Aerospace Engring., U. Toronto, 1966, PhD in Aerospace Engring., 1970. Grad. fellow U. Toronto, 1965—66, NRC, Canada, 1967—70, indsl. post-doctoral fellow, 1971—72, Fleet Mfg. Co., Fort Erie, Ont., 1970-72; spl. lectr. U. Toronto, Ont., Canada, 1971; from asst. prof. to prof. Meml. U. of Nfld., St. John's, 1972-93, univ. rsch. prof., 1990-93; dir. Ocean Engring. Rsch. Ctr., 1982-93; dean Okanagan U. Coll., Kelowna, B.C., Canada, 1993—2003, assoc. v.p rsch., 1998—2003; pvt. practice Lake County, B.C., Canada, 2003—. Pres. Offshore Design Assocs. Ltd., St. John's, Nfld., 1980—; sec., ptnr. Nfld. Ocean Cons., St. John's, 1981-93; ptnr. LNF Joint Venture Ltd., St. John's, 1984-90; vis. prof. Norwegian Inst. Tech., Trondheim, Norway, 1976, NRC, Ottawa, Can., 1976, U. Victoria, B.C., 1988-89. Co-author: Ice Interaction with Offshore Structures, 1988; contbr. articles to profl. jours.; contbr. conf. articles, reports. Mem. Assn. Profl. Engrs. and Geoscientists of Province of B.C. Marine and Naval. Avocations: windsurfing, sailing, rock collecting. Home and Office: 16438 Carr's Landing Rd Lake Country BC Canada V4V 1C3 Office Phone: 250-766-1023. Business E-Mail: dmuggeridge@cablelan.net.

**MUGLIA, ROBERT L.,** information technology executive; BS in Computer Sci., U. Mich., 1981. Devel. mgr. ROLM Co.; with Microsoft, Redmond, Wash., 1988, v.p. enterprise storage svcs. group, 2001—03, sr. v.p., windows server div., 2003—. Mem. Sr. Leadership Team, Bus. Leadship Team, Microsoft. Office: Microsoft One Microsoft Way Redmond WA 98052-6399

**MUGNAINI, ENRICO,** neuroscience educator; b. Colle Val d'Elsa, Italy, Dec. 10, 1937; came to U.S., 1969. children: Karin E., Emiliano N.G. MD cum laude, U. Pisa, Italy, 1962; degree (hon.), U. Torino, 2005, U. Pisa, 2005, U. Salamanca, 2006. Microscopy lab. rsch. fellow dept. anatomy U. Oslo Med. Sch., 1963, asst. prof., head of electron microscopy lab., 1964-66, assoc. prof., 1967-69; prof. biobehavioral scis. and psychology, head lab. of neuromorphology U. Conn., Storrs, 1969-95; E.C. Stuntz prof. cell biology, dir. Inst. for Neurosci., Northwestern U., Chgo., 1995—. Vis. prof. Dept. Anatomy Harvard U., Boston, 1969-70; traveling lectr. Grass Found., 1986, 1990. Mng. editor USA Anatomy and Embryology Jour., 1989—; contbr. more than 200 articles to books and jours. Recipient Decennial Camillo Golgi award Acad. Nat. dei Lincei, 1981, Sen. Javits Neurosci. Rsch. Investigator grantee NIH, 1985-92, Fernndez-Lindsay Lectureship grantee U. Chgo., 2003. Mem. AAAS, Am. Assn. Anatomists, Am. Soc. Cell Biology, Internat. Brain Rsch. Orgn., Internat. Soc. Developmental Neurosci., Nouveau Inst. Anatuomists, Assn. Intel. Letters, Soc. Neurosci., Inst. Lombardo, Acad. Sci. Lettere (corr. 2005-), Cajal Club (pres. 1987-88, Campano d'Oro award, 2005). Office: U Northwestern Inst Neurosci 5-474 Searle Bldg 320 E Superior St Chicago IL 60611-3010 Office Phone: 312-503-4300. Business E-Mail: e-mugnaini@northwestern.edu.

**MUGNIER, CLIFFORD JOHN,** engineering educator, consultant; b. New Orleans, Jan. 15, 1944; s. Clifford Alphonse and Anna Irma Mugnier; children: Gaston Bennett, André Steven, Jacques Claude, Monique Marie, Theodore (Ted) John, Philippe Antoine, Alyce Marie. B, Northwestern State U., Natchitoches, La., 1967; cert. in advanced photogrammetry, George Washington U., Washington, 1970. Cert. photogrammetrist, Am. Soc. Photogrammetry and Remote Sensing, mapping scientist (GIS/LIS), Am. Soc. Photogrammetry and Remote Sensing. Cartographer, photogrammetrist USAF Aero Chart & Info Ctr., St. Louis, 1967—68; capt. topographic engr. Army Map Svc., Washington, 1968—72; chief applied photogrammetry Raytheon/Autometric Operation, Wayland, Mass., 1972—73; photogrammetry divsn. mgr. Owen & White, Inc., Baton Rouge; mem. engring. faculty U. New Orleans, 1980—2000, La. State U., 2000—. Cons. in photogrammetry and geodesy, New Orleans and Baton Rouge, 1977—. Contbr. articles to profl. jours. Capt. US Army Corps of Engrs., 1968—72. Fellow: Am. Congress Surveying and Mapping; mem.: La. Soc. Profl. Surveyors (hon., life), Am. Soc. Photogrammetry and Remote Sensing (dir. photogrammetric applications divsn. 2006—, Talbert Abrams hon. mention 1978). Republican. Roman Catholic. Avocation: conventional bullseye pistol competition. Home: 1423 Westchester Dr Baton Rouge LA 70810-5237 Office: La State U Dept Civil Engring CEBA-3223A Baton Rouge LA 70803 Office Phone: 225-578-8536. E-mail: cjmce@lsu.edu.

**MUHAMMAD, AVA,** minister and national spokesperson for the Nation of Islam; b. Columbus, Ohio, 1951; m. Darius Muhammad, 1988. JD, Georgetown U., 1975. Bar: NY 1976. Asst. DA Borough of Queens, NY; defense atty. NYC; joined Nation of Islam, 1981, min., 1985—, so. regional min., 1998, head Muhammad Mosque No. 15 Atlanta, 1998, nat. spokesperson, 2000—. Author: Queen of the Planet Earth, The Rebirth, Rise of the Original Woman.

Achievements include first woman in Islam to be given authority over a Mosque; successfully sued the NY Post for defamation of Louis Farrakhan's character, 1994. Office: Nation of Islam 734 W 79th St Chicago IL 60620

**MUHAMMAD, CLAUDETTE MARIE,** religious organization administrator; d. Travis and Ernestine Johnson; 1 child, Anthony L. Pinkins. Student, U. Abidjan, 1978—79; BA, Am. U., 1982; postgrad., UN, Geneva, 1982, U. Geneva, 1982, Johns Hopkins Sch. Advanced Internat. Studies, 1982. Tech. libr. Gen. Dynamics Astronautics, 1960—62; sec. to Congressman Lionel Van Deerlin U.S. Congress, Washington, 1963—68; spl. asst. to commrs. Pres.'s Commn. on Civil Disorders, Washington, 1968—69; dir. cmty. affairs Fed. City Coll., Washington, 1973—75; dir of mayor's call program Dep. Mayor Econ. Devel., Washington; dir. mktg. Manara Travel Agy., Washington, 1987—88; enrollment mgmt./recruitment counselor U. D.C., Washington, 1988; chief protocol to Hon. Min. Louis Farrakhan Nation of Islam, 1989—2005; commr. commn. discrimination and hate crimes Gov. Ill., 2005—. Contbr. articles to profl. jours. Model Ebony Fashion Model, 1963; pres. Jimmy Carter's Inauguration Com. Protocol; exec. bd. Millions More Movement, Inc., 2005; nat. dep. dir. Million Man March, Washington, 1995, Million Family March, Washington, 2000. Finalist 3d runner-up Miss Bronze California, 1958; recipient Women in History award, Urban League, 2002, Jerusalem 2000 Unity Day Conf. award, 2000, Jr. Achievement award, 1961—62.

**MUHAMMAD, MUSHIN,** professional football player; b. Lansing, Mich., May 5, 1973; Student, Mich. State, 1996. Wide receiver Carolina Panthers, 1996—2004, Chgo Bears, 2004—. Named to Pro Bowl, NFL, 2000, 2005. Office: Chgo Bears 1000 Football Dr Lake Forest IL 60045*

**MÜHLANGER, ERICH,** ski manufacturing company executive; b. Aug. 26, 1941; arrived in U.S., 1971, naturalized, 1975; s. Alois Mühlnager and Maria (Stückelschweiger) Mühlanger; m. Gilda V. Oliver, July 13, 1973; 1 child, Erich. A in Engring., Murau Berufsschule Spl. Trade, Austria, 1959; student, Inst. Tech. and Engring., Weiler Im Allgau, Germany, 1963—65. Salesman Olin Ski Co. (Olin-Authier), Switzerland, 1965—67, mem. mktg. dept., 1967—67, svc. and mfg., 1969—71, quality control insp. Middletown, Conn., 1971—77, supr., 1977—78, gen. foreman, 1978—83, process control mgr., 1983—88; dir. mfg. Entech Corp., 1988—89; prodn. mgr. metallizing divsn. Risden Corp., Thomaston, Conn., 1989—94, quality process engr., 1994—. Pres. Bus. Consolidating Svcs. Internat., Rocky Hill, Conn., 1989—, quality control technician, 1990—, quality process request divsn., fragrance divsn., 1993—; pres. Bus. Cons. Svcs. Internat., 2004—. Chartered mem. Presdl. Task Force, trustee; preferred mem. U.S. Senatorial Club. Served to cpl. Austrian Air Force, 1959—60. Mem.: Mgmt. Club, Am. Soc. Quality Control, Am. Mgmt. Assn., Screenprinting Assn. Am. Roman Catholic. Home: 13 Clemens Ct Rocky Hill CT 06067-3218 Office: 60 Electric Ave Thomaston CT 06787-1617 also: Bus Consolidating Svcs Internat Rocky Hill CT 06067 Office Phone: 860-416-5845. E-mail: erich.muhlanger@cox.net.

**MUHLBACH, ROBERT ARTHUR,** lawyer; b. LA, Apr. 13, 1946; s. Richard and Jeanette (Marcus) M.; m. Kerry Eldene Mahoney, July 26, 1986. BSME, U. Calif., Berkeley, 1967; JD, U. Calif., San Francisco, 1976; MME, Calif. State U., 1969; M in Pub. Adminstrn., U. So. Calif., 1978. Bar: Calif. 1976. Pub. defender County of Los Angeles, 1977-79; assoc. Kirtland & Packard LLP, Los Angeles, 1979—85, ptnr., 1986—2001, sr. ptnr., 2001—. Chmn. Santa Monica Airport Commn., Calif., 1984-87, chmn., bd. dirs. Hawthorne Airport Cmty. Assn. Inc. Served to capt. USAF, 1969-73. Mem. ABA, AIAA, Internat. Assn. Def. Counsel, Am. Bd. Trial Advs. Office: Kirtland & Packard LLP 2361 Rosecrans Ave 4th Fl El Segundo CA 90245 Office Phone: 310-536-1000. Business E-Mail: ram@kirtland-packard.com.

**MUHLBERGER, RICHARD CHARLES,** museum director, writer, educator; b. Englewood, NJ, Jan. 20, 1938; s. George Albert and Margaret Bertha (Heins) M. AA, Calif. Concordia Coll., 1958; BA, Wayne State U., 1964; MA in Art History, Johns Hopkins U., 1967. Curator mus. edn. Worcester Art Mus., Mass., 1966-72; chmn. edn. Detroit Inst. Arts, 1972-75; dir. Mus. Fine Arts and George Walter Vincent Smith Art Mus., Springfield, Mass., 1976-87; vice dir. for edn. Met. Mus. Art, N.Y.C., 1987-89; dir. Knoxville (Tenn.) Mus. Art, 1990-91; adj. prof. art history Western New England Coll., Springfield, Mass., 1991—. Guest curator Mus. Am. Folk Art, 1997-98; mem. adv. panel NEH, 1976-78, Mass. Coun. on Arts and Humanities, 1979-81; mem. policy panel, mus. program Nat. Endowment Arts, 1981-83. Author: The Bible in Art, The New Testament, 1990, The Bible in Art, The Old Testament, 1990, The Christmas Story, 1990, What Makes a Raphael a Raphael, 1993, What Make a Bruegel a Bruegel, 1993, What Makes a Rembrandt a Rembrandt, 1993, What Makes a Monet a Monet, 1993, What Makes a Degas a Degas, 1993, What Make a Van Gogh a Van Gogh, 1993, What Makes a Leonardo a Leonardo, 1994, What Makes a Goya a Goya, 1994, What Makes a Cassatt a Cassatt, 1994, What Makes a Picasso a Picasso, 1994, The Unseen Van Gogh, 1998, American Folk Marquetry, 1998, Charles Webster Hawthorne: Paintings and Watercolors, 1999, Woodrow Wilson fellow, 1965-66; recipient Outstanding Young Man award Greater Worcester Jaycees, 1970 Mem. Am. Assn. Museums (chmn. comm. on edn. 1974-76, councilor 1988-91), New England Mus. Assn. (pres. 1985-87), Phi Beta Kappa. Home: 41 Smithfield Ct Springfield MA 01108-3129 Office Phone: 413-737-9660.

**MUHLENBRUCH, CARL W.,** civil engineer; b. Decatur, Ill., Nov. 21, 1915; s. Carl William and Clara (Theobald) M.; m. Agnes M. Kringel, Nov. 22, 1939; children: Phyllis Elaine Wallace, Joan Carol Wenk. BCE, U. Ill. 1937, CE, 1945; MCE, Carnegie Inst. Tech., 1943; LLD, Concordia U., River Forest, Ill., 1995. Lic. profl. engr. Ill.; Pa. Rsch. engr. Aluminum Rsch. Labs., Pitts., 1937-39; cons. engring., 1939-50; mem. faculty Carnegie Inst. Tech., 1939-48; assoc. prof. civil engring. Northwestern U., 1948-51, lectr. in Civil Engring., 1998—; pres. TEC-SEARCH, Inc. (formerly Ednl. and Tech. Consultants Inc.), 1954-67, chmn. bd., 1967—. Pres. Profl. Ctrs. Bldg. Corp., 1961-77; lectr. civil engring., 1997—. Author: Experimental Mechanics and Properties of Materials, 1944, 2d edit., 1955; contbr. articles to profl. jours. Treas., bd. dir. Concordia Coll. Found.; dir. Mo. Luth. Synod, 1965-77, vice chmn. 1977-79. Recipient Stanford E. Thompson award, 1945. Mem. Am. Econ. Devel. Coun. (cert. econ. developer); Am. Soc. Engring. Edn. (editor Ednl. Aids in Engring.), NSPE, ASCE, Univ. Club (Evanston), Rotary (dist. gov. 1980-81, dir. svc. projects Ghana and the Bahamas), Sigma Xi, Tau Beta Phi, Omicron Delta Kappa. Home and Office: Tec-Search Inc 4071 Fairway Dr Wilmette IL 60091-1005 Office Phone: 847-256-2750.

**MUHLENBRUCK-FLEISCHER, DEBORAH LYNN,** music educator; b. Mason City, Iowa, Oct. 28, 1969; d. Robert Floyd and Jeannette Jeraldine Muhlenbruck; m. Eric Matthew Fleischer, May 22, 1999; 1 child, Julia Lynn Fleischer. MusB in Vocal Performance, No. Ariz. U., 1993; MusM in Vocal Performance, U. Nev., 1997. Pvt. voice prof. U. Nev., Las Vegas, 1997—2002, C.C. So. Nev., 1998—2001. Prodr.: (vocal instruction cd) Sing Like the Pros. Recipient Rave Rev. award, Clark County Sch. Dist., 2001—02. Mem.: Music Educators Nat. Conf., Am. Choral Dirs. Assn. (assoc.), Nat. Assn.Tchrs. Singing (life; Las Vegas chpt. v.p. 2000—01, Las Vegas chpt. pres. 2001—03), U. Nev. Alumni Assn. (life). Conservative. Presbyterian. Office: Schofield Mid Sch Choirs 8625 Spencer St Las Vegas NV 89123 Office Phone: 702-799-2290.

**MUHLENFELD, ELISABETH S.,** academic administrator, literature educator, writer; b. Washington, Nov. 12, 1944; d. Merle Roberts and Cornelia Elizabeth (Herring) Showalter; m. Edward F. Muhlenfeld, Sept. 10, 1966 (div. 1975); children: Allison Elisabeth Finch, David Edward; m. Laurin A. Wollan, Jr., June 5, 1982; stepchildren: Ann Louise Wollan Westberg, Laurin A. Wollan III. BA in Philosophy, Goucher Coll., 1966; MA in English, U. Tex., Arlington, 1973; PhD, U. S.C., 1978. With U. S.C., Columbia, 1975-78; asst. prof. English Fla. State U., Tallahassee, 1978-82, assoc. prof., 1982-87, prof. English, 1987-96, dean undergrad. studies 1984—96; pres. Sweet Briar (Va.) Coll., 1996—. Mem. ABA Commn. on Coll. and Univ. Legal Studies, 1991—94; mem. adv. com. U.S. Nat. Commn. UN Devel. Fund for Women; bd. dirs.

Employee Assistance of Ctrl. Va., United Way Ctrl. Va., chair, 2003. Author: Mary Boykin Chesnut: A Biography, 1981; editor: William Faulkner's Absolom, Absolom: A Critical Casebook, 1984, The Private Mary Chesnut: The Unpublished Civil War Diaries, 1984, Two Novels By Mary Chestnut, 2002; contbr. chpts. to books and articles to pubs. Chair Coun. Ind. Colls. in Va., 2001—02; mem. exec. com. Va. Found. Ind. Colls.; mem. commn. on colls. So. Assn. Colls. and Schs., 2001—, mem. exec. com. 2003—05, vice chair, 2005—; bd. dirs. Employment Assistance of Ctrl. Va., United Way of Ctrl. Va., chair, 2003. bd. dirs. Am. Civil War Ctr. at Tredegar. NEH Dir.'s grantee, 1983-84. Mem. MLA, St. George Tucker Soc. (charter fellow), So. Assn. Women Historians, William Faulkner Soc. (charter mem; sec.-treas. 1991-94), Phi Kappa Phi (exec. bd., pres. 1992-93). Office: Sweet Briar Coll Pres's Office Box C Sweet Briar VA 24595 Office Phone: 434-381-6210. Business E-Mail: muhlenfeld@sbc.edu.

**MUHLERT, JAN KEENE,** art museum director; b. Oak Park, Ill., Oct. 4, 1942; d. William Henry and Isabel Janette (Cole) Keene; m. Christopher Layton Muhlert, Jan. 1, 1966; 1 son, Michael Keene. BA in Art and French, Albion Coll., Mich., 1964; MA in Art History, Oberlin Coll., Ohio, 1967; student, Neuchatel U., Switzerland, Inst. European Studies, Paris, Inst. de Phonetique, Acad. Grande Chaumiere. Asst. curator Allen Meml. Art Mus., Oberlin, 1967-68; asst. curator 20th Century painting and sculpture Nat. Collection Fine Arts, Smithsonian Instn., Washington, 1968-73, assoc. curator, 1974-75; dir. U. Iowa Mus. Art, 1975-79, Amon Carter Mus., Ft. Worth, 1980-95, Palmer Museum of Art, University Park, Pa., 1996—. Author museum brochures, catalogues. Mem. Nat. Mus. Act. Adv. Coun., 1980—83; vis. com. Allen Meml. Art Mus. Oberlin Coll., Ohio, 1992—2003; chair adv. com. North Tex. Inst. Educators on the Visual Arts, U. North Tex., 1992—95. Grantee Nat. Endowment Arts-Donner Found., 1979; recipient Friend of Art Edn. award Tex. Art Edn. Assn., 1994. Mem. Assn. Art Mus. Dirs. (trustee 1981-82, 84-86, 92-93, chmn. govt. and art com. 1982-84, chmn. profl. practices com. 1990-92), Western Assn. Art Mus. (regional rep. 1978-79), Am. Assn. Mus. (commn. for new century 1981-84, gen. co-chair 1993 ann. meeting), Am. Arts Alliance (dir. 1980-86, vice-chmn. 1982-84). Office: Palmer Museum of Art Pa State U Curtin Rd University Park PA 16802-2507 Office Phone: 814-865-7673.

**MUHLESTEIN, KERRY,** educator; b. Utah; PhD, UCLA, 2003. Asst. prof. Brigham Young U. Hawaii, Laie, 2003—06, Brigham Young U., Provo, Utah, 2006—. Office Phone: 801-422-2067.

**MUHN, JUDY ANN,** psychologist, genealogist, trainer; b. Detroit, Dec. 29, 1952; d. Wilbur William and Dolores Eleanor (Sutinen) Nimer; m. Dennis James Muhn, June 6, 1975. BS, Mich. State U., East Lansing, 1975; MEd, Boston U., Mass., 1992; MA in Counseling, U. San Francisco, Calif., 1997. Lic. psychologist Mich. Legis. aide press sec. to Calif. state senator 1982—84; dir. pub. rels. Tierra del Oro coun. Girl Scouts U.S., 1984—86, mgr. mem. devel. San Antonio area coun., 1986—90; adj. faculty U. Md. Germany, 1992—94; intl. cons. Capital Enquiry, Sacramento, 1994—96; counselor Yuba City Indian Health Ctr., 1997; intervention counselor Sutter-Yuba Mental Health, 1997—98; counselor, intern White Ho. Cmty. Counseling Ctr., 1998; pvt. practice Wixom, Mich., 1998—; dep. exec. dir. U. Santo Tomas Alumni Assn., 1998—2000; therapist Brighton Hosp., 2000—01; dir. adult devel. and vol. svcs. Girl Scouts Metro Detroit, 2002—. Adj. faculty Henry Ford CC, 1998—2001, Oakland CC, 1998—2001; therapist Brighton Hosp., 2000—01, Advanced Counseling Svcs., Brighton, 2001—03; spkr. in field. Columnist: Press-Republican, 1995—98. Bd. dirs., chmn. pub. affairs com. Planned Parenthood Clinton County, NY, 1980—81; bd. dirs. Family Planning Advs., Albany, 1981, Planned Parenthood San Antonio, 1987—89; founder Women's Roundtable, Planned Parenthood, 1981; pres. Planned Parenthood Assn. Sacramento Valley, 1982—84; sec. San Antonio Coun. Native Ams., 1986—89; co-founder Womansspirit Rising, 1987—89; mem. Metis Cmty. Ea. Can. Named Bd. Mem. of Yr. Planned Parenthood Sacramento Valley, 1982; recipient Human Rights award, Sacramento Fair Housing Commn., 1983, Woman of Yr. award-Nonprofit, YWCA, Sacramento, 1984. Mem.: ASTD, Nat. Geneal. Soc., Assn. Prof. Genealogists, Metis Cmty. Ea. Can., Assn. Vol. Adminstrs., Net. Detroit Vol. Adminstrs., Assn. Univ. Women, Amnesty Internat., Greenpeace, San Antonio Women's C. of C. (bd. dirs. 1989), Assn. Girl Scout Exec. Staff. Personal E-mail: jmuhn@gsofmd.org. Business E-Mail: jmuhn@gsofmd.org.

**MUILENBURG, JOHN POWELL,** minister; b. Grand Rapids, Mich., Oct. 26, 1911; s. Teunis William and Sena Muilenburg; m. Virgina Louise Turpin, Apr. 2, 1944; children: Peter, Jonathan, Stephan, Bartholomew. BA, Hope Coll., Holland, Mich., 1933; ThM, Princeton Theology Sem., 1938; MDiv, New Brunswick Theology Sem., New Brunswick, N.J., 1936. Pastor Ref. Ch. in Am., Rocky Hill, NJ, 1938—40, asst. pastor Kingston, NY, 1940—41, missionary to China, 1942—50, missionary to Philippines, 1952—67, exec. staff nat. coun. of ch., 1967—76. Town coun. Town of Penney Farms, Fla., 1995—98, mayor Fla., 1999—2000. Recipient A.J. Muste award, New Brunswick Theology Sem., 1986. Democrat. Reformed Ch. In Am. Avocations: tennis, golf, music, sailing. Home: 4400 Ott St POB 646 Penney Farms FL 32079

**MUIR, J. DAPRAY,** lawyer; b. Washington, Nov. 9, 1936; s. Brockett and Helen Cassin (Dapray) M.; m. Louise Rutherfurd Pierrepont, July 16, 1966. AB, Williams Coll., 1958; JD, U. Va., 1964. Bar: Md., Va. D.C. 1964, U.S Supreme Ct. 1967. Asst. legal advisor for econ. and bus. affairs U.S. Dept. State, 1971-73; pvt. practice Washington, 1973—. Mem. U.S. del. to joint U.S./USSR Comml. Commn., 1972; chmn. D.C. Securities Adv. Com., 1981-84, mem. 1985-88. Bd. editors Va. Law Rev., 1963-64; contbr. articles to profl. jours. Bd. dirs. Trust Mus. Exhbns., 2001—2005, Internat. Fedn. Insts. Advanced Study, 1992—97. Lt. (j.g.) USNR, 1958—61. Mem. Am. Arbitration Assn. (panel of comml. arbitrators, 1997—), DC Bar (chmn. internat. law div. 1977-78, chmn. environ., energy and natural resources div. 1982-83), Met. Club, Washington, Chevy Chase Club, Md. Office: 1717 K St NW Ste 600 Washington DC 20036 Office Phone: 202-337-1724. Business E-Mail: jdmuir@muirlaw.net.

**MUIR, MALCOLM,** federal judge; b. Englewood, N.J., Oct. 20, 1914; s. John Merton and Sarah Elizabeth Muir; m. Alma M. Brohard, Sept. 6, 1940 (dec. 1985); children: Malcolm, Thomas, Ann Muir, Barbara (dec.), David Clay. BA, Lehigh U., 1935; LL.B., Harvard U., 1938. Sole practice, Williamsport, Pa., 1938-42, 45-49, 68-70; mem. firm, 1949-68; judge U.S. Dist. Ct. (mid.) Pa., 1970—. Active charitable orgns., Williamsport, 1939-70 Mem. ABA, Pa. Bar Assn. (pres.-elect 1970) Avocation: reading. Office: US Dist Ct Ste 401 240 W 3rd St Williamsport PA 17701-6461 Office Phone: 570-322-0287.

**MUIR, PATRICIA ALLEN,** professional association administrator; b. Dallas, Nov. 4, 1929; d. Jack Charleton Allen and Anna Patricia (Hovis) Allen Atchison; m. Lester Doyle Rader, Jr., Aug. 4, 1950 (dec. Sept. 1950); 1 child, Lester Doyle III; m. Peter James Muir, June 2, 1956 (div.); children: Edward John, Patricia Jane. Grad., Our Lady of Victory Coll., 1948; student, George Washington U., 1948-49, Washington Sch. for Sec., 1949-50. Traffic mgr. Am. Storage Co., Washington, 1960-69; asst. sec. Ind. Tele. Pioneer Assn., Washington, 1969-76; adminstrv. asst. ALA, Washington, 1977-98, staff liaison to Fed. Libr. Round Table, 1991-98, staff liaison to Armed Forces Libr. Round Table, 1991-98, staff liaison to Govt. Documents Round Table, 1991-98; office mgr. Fed. Documents Clearing House, Washington, 1998-2000; cons., 2000—. Columnist, comm. The Ind. Pioneer, 1969-76. V.p. Friendship House Child Devel. Ctr. Parents, Washington, 1978, pres., 1979—83; mem. parish coun. St. Peter's Cath. Ch., 1987—91, mem. edn. and spiritual devel. com., 1986—, chair, 1988—91, coord. Bible study, 1999—2003; mem. St. Peter's Interparish Sch. Reading Program, 2001—02. Mem. Ladies Ancient Order of Hibernians (state pres. 1991-97, nat. budget com. 1996-98, nat. elections com 1998—, nat. constn. com 1998-02, nat. rules of order com. 2000-02). Avocations: travel, genealogy, reading, writing.

**MUIR, RUTH BROOKS,** alcohol/drug abuse services professional, consultant; b. Washington, Nov. 27, 1924; d. Charles and Adelaide Chenery (Masters) B.; m. Robert Mathew Muir, Nov. 26, 1947 (dec. Feb. 20, 1996); children: Robert Brooks, Martha Louise, Heather Sue. BA in Art, Rollins Coll., Winter Park, Fla., 1947; MA in Rehab. Counseling, U. Iowa, 1979. Cert. substance abuse counselor, Iowa. Program advisor Iowa Meml. Union, Iowa City, 1959-66; counselor, coord. Mid Eastern Coun. on Chem. Abuse, Iowa City, 1976-81; patient rep. Univ. Hosp., Iowa City, 1982-85; rsch. project interviewer dept. psychiatry U. Iowa Coll. Medicine, 1985-88; pvt. practice family counselor, 1984—. Docent U. Iowa Mus. of Art, 1999—. Art exhibited at Iowa City Sr. Ctr., 1987, 92, Iowa City Art Ctr., 1989, U. Iowa Hosp., 1991, Great Midwestern Ice Cream Co., 1991, Summit St. Gallery, 1995, Iowa City C. of C., 2001, Iowa City's First Art Walk March, 2003; creator, coord. therapeutic series Taking Control, Iowa City Sr. Ctr., 1986-87, Art Walk Lorenz Boot Shop, 2003. Vol. coord. art exhibits Sr. Ctr., Iowa City, 1992-94, Iowa City Arts Exhbn. Com., 1996, Arrowmont Sch. Art, 1996—, Arrowmont Amb., 1996-98; treas. bd. dirs. Crisis Ctr., Iowa City, 1976-77; sec. coun. elders Sr. Citizens Ctr., Iowa City, 1976-78; pres. Unitarian-Universalist Iowa City Women's Fedn., 1985, mem. pastoral com., 2006; friend U. Iowa Mus. Art, docent, 1999—; active Opera Supers, Iowa City Unitarian U.N. Envoy; fgn. rels. coun., bd. dirs. annual changing family conf. U. Iowa, 1986-92; non-govtl. rep. Earth Summit Global Forum, 1992; care review bd. Mental Health Homes, 1997-99; bd. dirs., exhbn. chair Arts Iowa City, 2002—. Mem.: AAUW (state cultural rep. 1990—92, Iowa City chpt. co-chair for programs 1998—99), Health Care: Health Svcs., Nat. League Am. PEN Women (membership chair 2002—04, v.p. 2004—), Iowa City Unitarian Soc. (adult program com. 1993—94, unitarian care com. 1993—, membership com.), Nat. Soc. Colonial Dames, U. Iowa Retirees Assn. (bd. mem. 2004—, chair membership 2005—, membership chair), U. Iowa Print and Drawing Study Club (bd. dirs. 2003—04, pres. elect 2005), Pi Beta Phi (pres. alumnae club 1995—97). Home and Office: 6 Glendale Ct Iowa City IA 52245-4430 Office Phone: 319-337-7287. Business E-Mail: ruthmuir2989@inavia.net.

**MUIR, WARREN ROGER,** chemist, educator; b. N.Y., 1945; s. Ernest Roger and Phyllis (Stirn) M.; m. Jo-Ann McNally; children: Amy, Douglas, Michael, Gregory, Daniel. AB in Chemistry cum laude, Amherst Coll., 1967; MS in Chemistry, Northwestern U., Evanston, Ill., 1968, PhD in Chemistry, 1971; postgrad. in epidemiology, Johns Hopkins U., 1975-77. Sr. staff mem. environ. health Council on Environ. Quality, EPA, Washington, 1971-78; dir. Office of Toxic Substances, EPA, 1978-81; pres. Hampshire Rsch. Assocs., Inc., 1981-99, Hampshire Rsch. Inst., 1987-99; exec. dir. divsn. earth and life studies NRC/Nat. Acad. Scis., 1999—. Assoc. environ. health scis. Johns Hopkins U., 1981-99; rsch. prof. biology Am. U., 1985; sr. fellow INFORM, 1982-95; mem. Nat. Conf. Lawyers and Scientists, 1987-89; bd. environ. scis. and toxicology Nat. Rsch. Coun., 1997-99 Contbr. articles on environ. quality to profl. jours. Mem., chair several Nat. Rsch. Coun. coms.; pres. Children's Friendship Project for No. Ireland, 1997-99, bd. dirs. 1995—, chair 1997-2002, bd. dirs. HasNa, Inc., 2003-. Recpient NSF Acad. award, 1966, Howard Waters Doughty prize Amherst Coll., 1967, Forris Jewett Moore fellow, 1967; comdr., 1996, officer brother Most Venerable Order of St. John, 1992; co-recipient Adminstrs. award U.S. EPA, 1992, Cmty. Svc. award Nat. Acads., 2003. Mem.: AAAS, Am. Chem. Soc. Home: 9426 Forest Haven Dr Alexandria VA 22309-3151

**MUIR, WILLIAM KER, JR.,** political science professor; b. Detroit, Oct. 30, 1931; s. William Ker and Florence Taylor (Bodman) M.; m. Paulette Irene Wauters, Jan. 16, 1960; children: Kerry Macaire, Harriet Bodman. BA, Yale U., 1954, PhD, 1965; JD, U. Mich., 1965. Bar: N.Y. 1960, Conn. 1965. Instr. U. Mich. Law Sch., 1958-59; assoc. firm Davis Polk & Wardwell, NYC, 1959-60; lectr. in polit. sci. Yale U., 1960-64, 65-67; from assoc. to ptnr. Tyler Cooper Grant Bowerman & Keefe, New Haven, 1964-68; prof. emeritus polit. sci. U. Calif., Berkeley, 1968-98, dept. chmn., 1980-83; speechwriter v.p. U.S., 1983-85; columnist Oakland (Calif.) Tribune, 1992-93; writer Gov. of Calif., Sacramento, 1994. Sr. cons. Calif. State Assembly, Sacramento, 1975-76; cons. Oakland Police Dept., 1969-74; vis. prof. polit. sci. Harvard U., summers 1976, 79; vis. prof. Hawaii Pacific U., 2000, U. Ariz., 2002. Author: Prayer in the Public School, 1967, later republished as Law and Attitude Change, 1974, Police: Streetcorner Politicians, 1977, Legislature: California's School for Politics, 1982, The Bully Pulpit: The Presidential Leadership of Ronald Reagan, 1993, An Understanding of Democracy, 2003, Power and American Democracy, 2003, memoirs, 2003. Mem. Berkeley Police Rev. Commn., 1981-83; chmn. New Haven Civil Liberties Coun., 1965-68; Rep. candidate Calif. State Assembly, 1996. Recipient Hadley B. Cantril Meml. award, 1979, Disting. Tchg. award U Calif., Berkeley, 1974, Phi Beta Kappa No. Calif. Assoc. Excellence in Tchg. award, 1994. Mem. Am. Polit. Sci. Assn. (Edward S. Corwin award 1966). Republican. Presbyterian. Office: U Calif Dept Polit Sci Berkeley CA 94720-1950 Personal E-mail: sandymuir@aol.com.

**MUIR, WILLIAM LLOYD, III,** academic administrator; b. Norton, Kans., Mar. 20, 1948; s. John Thomas and Rosalie June (Benton) M. BBA, Kans. State U., 1977. Asst. sec. of state State of Kans., Topeka, 1971—72, fin. adminstr. atty. gen. office, 1972—79, comptr. Office of Gov., 1979—87, sec. of cabinet, 1979—87, asst. sec. adminstrn., 1986—87; dir. econ. devel. Kans. State U., Manhattan, 1987—91, asst. to v.p. for cmty. rels., 1991—2002, asst. v.p. for cmty. rels., 2002—, faculty rep., senator Student Governing Assn., 1992—, mem. union governing bd., 1997—, mem. coun. on parking ops., 2001—. Chmn. housing appeals bd. City of Manhattan, 1996—; trustee Kans. State U. Found., 1993—; mem. Leadership Kans., 1989; state officer Native Sons and Daus., 1997—2002, pres., 2001; mem. Kans. Territorial Sesquicentennial Commn., 2001—, Kans. Capitol Area Plaza Authority, 2003—; bd. dirs. United Way Riley County, 1989—99, chmn., 1992; treas. Flint Hills Regional Leadership Program, 2002—. Mem.: Nat. Geog. Soc., Friends of Cedar Crest Assn., Sierra Club, Blue Key, Masons (Scottish Rite), Alpha Kappa Psi, Alpha Tau Omega (nat. officer, bd. govs. Alpha Tau Omega Found.). Episcopalian. Avocation: travel. Home: 2040 Shirley Ln Manhattan KS 66502-2059 Office: Kansas State U 122 Anderson Hall Manhattan KS 66506-0100 Office Phone: 785-532-6269. Business E-Mail: billmuir@ksu.edu.

**MUIR-BROADDUS, JACQUELINE ELIZABETH,** psychology educator; b. Brantford, Ontario, Canada, Dec. 14, 1961; came to U.S., 1986; d. Jack Edward and Ellen Joann (MacKinnon) M. BA, U. Guelph, Can., 1984, MA, 1986; PhD, Fla. Atlantic U., 1990. Teaching asst. U. Guelph, Guelph, Ontario, Canada, 1984-86; rsch. asst. Fla. Atlantic U., Boca Raton, 1986-90, instr., 1987, 89; assoc. prof. Southwestern U., Georgetown, Tex., 1990—2002, prof., 2002—. Intern psychometrist Hosp. for Sick Children, Toronto, 1985, Wellington County Sch. Bd., 1985; adj. instr. Broward Community Coll., Coconut Creek, Fla., 1987. Author: (with others) Annals of Child Development, 1988, Interactions Among Strategies, Knowledge, and Aptitude in Cognitive Performance, 1990, Children's Strategies: Contemporary Views of Cognitive Development, 1990, Gifted Underachievers: Insights from the Characteristics of Strategic Functioning Associated with Giftedness and Achievement, 1995, The Effects of a Knowledge Base manipulation on Individual Differences in Processing Speed V Recall, 1995, Name Seven Words, 1998, Conservation as a Predictor of Individual Differences in Children's Susceptibility to Leading Questions, 1998, Neuropsychological Test Performance of Children with ADHD Relative to Test Norms and Parent Behavioral Ratings, 2002. Recipient Alma Mater scholarship, Entrance scholarship, U. Guelph, 1980, Daniel Brown Meml. scholarship, Fla. Atlantic U., 1988, Dissertation award APA, 1990; finalist Thesis Contest Ontario Psychol. Assn., 1986. Mem.: Cognitive Devel. Soc., Southwestern Psychol. Assn., Soc. Rsch. in Child Devel. Avocation: tennis. Home: 5702 Greenledge Cv Austin TX 78759-6244 Office: Southwestern U Dept Of Psychology Georgetown TX 78626 Business E-Mail: muirbroj@southwestern.edu.

**MUIRHEAD, JAMES RUSSELL,** federal judge; b. Phillipsburg, Pa., Apr. 11, 1941; BS, Cornell U., 1963, LLB, 1966. Bar: N.H. 1966. Pvt. practice, Manchester, N.H., 1966-95; magistrate judge for N.H., U.S. Fed. Ct., Concord, N.H., 1995—. Office: WB Rudman US Courthouse 55 Pleasant St Concord NH 03301-3954

**MUIRHEAD, VINCENT URIEL,** retired aerospace engineer; b. Dresden, Kans., Feb. 6, 1919; s. John Hadsell and Lily Irene (McKinney) M.; m. Bobby Jo Thompson, Nov. 5, 1943; children: Rosalind, Jean, Juleigh. BS, U.S. Naval Acad., 1941; BS in Aero. Engring, U.S. Naval Postgrad. Sch., 1948; Aero. Engr., Calif. Inst. Tech., 1949; postgrad., U. Ariz., 1962, 64, Okla. State U., 1963. Midshipman U.S. Navy, 1937, commd. ensign, 1941, advanced through grades to comdr., 1951; nav. officer U.S.S. White Plains, 1945-46; comdr. Fleet Aircraft Service Squad, 1951-52; with Bur. Aeros., Ft. Worth, 1953-54; comdr. Helicopter Utility Squadron I, Pacific Fleet, 1955-56; chief staff officer Comdr. Fleet Air, Philippines, 1956-58; exec. officer Naval Air Tng. Center, Memphis, 1958-61; ret., 1961; asst. prof. U. Kans., Lawrence, 1961-63, assoc. prof. aerospace engring., 1964-76, prof., 1976-89, prof. emeritus, 1989—, chmn. dept., 1976-88. Cons. Black & Veatch (cons. engrs.), Kansas City, Mo., 1964— Author: Introduction to Aerospace, 1972, 6th edit., 2004, Thunderstorms, Tornadoes and Building Damage, 1975. Decorated Air medal. Fellow AIAA (assoc.); mem. Am. Acad. Mechanics, Am. Soc. Engring. Edn., Tau Beta Pi, Sigma Gamma Tau. Mem. Ch. of Christ (elder 1972-96). Achievements include research on aircraft, tornado vortices, shock tubes and waves. Home: 503 Park Hill Ter Lawrence KS 66046-4841 Office: Dept Aerospace Engring Univ Kans Lawrence KS 66045-0001 Personal E-mail: vmuirhead@sunflower.com.

**MUIR-TAYLOR, DOUGLAS JAMES,** ophthalmologist; b. Edinburgh, May 4, 1932; s. Thomas William and Jane Craig Muir-Taylor; m. Lesley Elizabeth Muir-Taylor; children: Victoria Grace, Elizabeth Laura. Grad., Heriot-Watt U., Edinburgh, 1954; MB BChir, U. London, 1960. House surgeon ophthalmology Kings Coll. Hosp., London, 1960—60, house physician medicine, 1960—61; sr. house surgeon A&E Lewisham Hosp., London, 1961—62; gen. practice prin. London Redbridge, 1962; clin. assoc. ophthalmology Moorfields Hosp., London, 1962—66, Royal London Hosp., 1978—85, assoc. specialist ophthalmology, 1978—85, clin. dir. contact lens and prosthetic dept., 1991—. Clin. dir. Telephone Cables GEC, London, 1963—90, Electric Windings Ltd., London, 1970—94, F.J. Cipa Panel Craft PT Ltd., London, 1996—. Fellow: Rpyal Soc. Medicine, Brit. Optical Assn., Brit. Coll. Optometry; mem.: Contact Lens Assn. Ophthalmologists, Royal Coll. Physicians (licentiate), Am. Soc. Cataract and Refractive Surgery, Royal Coll. Ophthalmologists, Royal Coll. Surgeons. Achievements include research in photorefractive keratectomy in high myopia; photorefractive keratectomy after corneal surgery; photorefractive keratectomy in pregnancy and menopause; correction of aphakia with extended wear gas permeable contact lenses, serum markers in germ cell tumours. Avocations: fishing, winter sports, shooting, fine wines, golf. Home: 63 Plover Way London SE16 7TS England Office: Blackheath Eyecare Ctr 16 Old Dover Rd London SE16 7TS England Office Fax: 020 8858 5627. E-mail: muirtaylor@aol.com.

**MUJA, KATHLEEN ANN,** state official, consultant; b. Denver, June 24, 1965; d. Thomas Raymond and Bridget Catherine (Hirschfeld) Cramer; m. Adrian Constantin Muja, June 4, 1988 (div. Apr. 1991); 1 child, Thomas Constantin. BBA, U. Denver, 1995. Employment specialist Dept. of Labor and Employment, Colo., 1991—98, Colo., 2000—02; office mgr. Colo. Dept. Labor, Denver, 1999-2000, bus. analyst, 2002—. Contbr. poems to various publs. Vol. Mus. Natural History, Denver, 1987—; home visitor Cmty. Caring Project, Denver, 1996-2001. Mem. AAUW, U. Denver Alumni Assn. Roman Catholic. Avocations: hiking, biking, canvas cross-stitch, writing, reading. Home: 460 Washington St Denver CO 80203-3810 Office: Colo Dept Labor 251 E 12th Ave Denver CO 80203-2272 Office Phone: 303-318-9091. E-mail: katmuja@hotmail.com.

**MUJAT, MIRCEA,** optics scientist; b. Sibiu, Romania, Feb. 23, 1970; s. Ioan and Steliana Ana Mujat; m. Claudia Popa, Sept. 4, 1993; 1 child, Victor Andrei. B in Physics, U. Bucharest, Romania, 1994; MA in Physics, Temple U., 1998; MS in Optics, U. Ctrl. Fla., 2001. Rsch. asst. R&D Inst. of the Army, Bucharest, 1994—96; grad. tchg. asst. dept. physics Temple U. Coll. Arts and Scis., Phila., 1996—98; grad. rsch. asst. Ctr. Rsch. and Edn. in Optics and Lasers Sch. Optics U. Ctrl. Fla., Orlando, 1998—. Contbr. articles to profl. jours. Recipient New Focus Travel award, New Focus and Optical Soc. Am., 2001. Mem.: Am. Physics Soc., The Internat. Soc. for Optical Engring., Optical Soc. of Am. (pres. student chpt. 2000—01), Ctr. Rsch. and Edn. in Optics and Lasers Assn. Optics Students (v.p. 2000—01, pres. 2001—02). Avocations: soccer, photography, skiing. Home: 33 Washington St Apt 4 Medford MA 02155-4753 E-mail: mircea@creol.ucf.edu.

**MUJICA, BARBARA LOUISE,** language educator, writer; d. Louis and Frieda (Kline) Kaminar; m. Mauro E. Mujica, Dec. 26, 1966; children: Lillian Louise, Mariana Ximena, Mauro Eduardo Ignacio. AB, UCLA, 1964; MA, Middlebury Coll., 1965; PhD, NYU, 1974. Instr. French UCLA, 1963-64; assoc. editor modern langs. Harcourt Brace Jovanovich, N.Y.C., 1966-73; instr., asst. prof. Romance langs. CUNY, 1973-74; prof. Spanish Georgetown U., Washington, 1974—. Mem. faculty NEH Summer Inst., 1980. Author: (book) A-LM Spanish, Levels I-IV, 1969—74, Readings in Spanish Literature, 1975, Calderon's Characters: An Existential Point of View, 1980, Pasaporte, 1980, rev. edit., 1984, Aqui y ahora, 1979, Entrevista, 1982, Iberian Pastoral Characters, 1986, Texto y Espectáculo, 1987, Et in Arcadia Ego, 1990, Texto y Vida: Introduccion a la Literatura Española, 1990, Antología de la Literatura Española: La Edad Media, 1991, Renacimiento y Siglo de Oro, 1991, Siglos XVII y XIX, 1999, Texto y Vida: Introduccion a la Literatura Hispano-Americana, 1992, Looking at the Comedia in the Year of the Quincentennial, 1993, Premio Nobel, 1997, Books of the Americas, 1997, El Texto Puesto en Escena, 2000, (novels) Sanchez Across the Street, 1997, The Deaths of Don Bernardo, 1990, Far From My Mother's Home, 1999, Frida: A Novel, 2001, (book) Teresa de Jesus: Espiritualidad y feminismo, Milenio, 2002, Sister Teresa, 2006; editor: Comedia Performance Jour.; editor, pub. Verbena: Bilingual Rev. of Arts, 1979—85, sr. assoc. editor, bd. dirs. Washington Rev., mem. editl. bd. Bull. of Comediantes Hispana; editor: (book) Women Writers of Early Modern Spain: Sophia's Daughters, 2004, (jour.) Comedia Performance. Named winner, E.L. Doctorow Internat. Fiction Competition, 1992; named one of 50 Best Op Eds of Decade, N.Y. Times, 1990; recipient Pangolin prize best short story, 1998, Hoepner award for fiction, 2002, Trailblazers award, 2004; grantee, Spanish Govt., 1987, Poets and Writers of N.Y.; Penfield fellow, 1971. Mem.: MLA (pres. Golden Age sect.), Assn. Hispanic Classical Theater (pres.). Office: Georgetown U Dept Spanish Washington DC 20057-1039 Office Phone: 202-687-5778. Business E-Mail: mujica@georgetown.edu.

**MUJICA, MAURO E.,** architect; b. Antofagasta, Chile, Apr. 20, 1941; came to U.S., 1965, naturalized, 1970; s. Mauro Raul and Graciela (Parodi-Blayfus) M.; m. Barbara Louise Kaminar, Dec. 26, 1966; children: Lillian Louise, Mariana Ximena, Mauro Eduardo Ignacio III. BArch, MArch, Columbia U., 1971. Head designer Columbia U. Office Archtl. Planning, N.Y.C., 1966-71; project mgr. Walker, Sander, Ford & Kerr, Architects, Princeton, NJ, 1971-72; prin. Mauro E. Mujica, Architect, N.Y.C., 1972-74; dir. internat. divsn. Greenhorne & O'Mara, Inc., Riverdale, Md., 1974-78; ptnr. Mujica & Reddy Architects, Washington, 1978-80; prin. Mauro E. Mujica, Architect, Washington, 1980-81; ptnr. Mujica & Berlin Investment Bankers, Washington, 1982-85, Mujica Keppie Henderson Internat., Washington and Glasgow, Scotland, 1981-83, Mujica-Seifert Architects, Washington and London, 1983-87; pres.,CDEO, The Pace Group, Washington, 1987-91; ptnr. Pace/Walsh Internat., London and Washington. Chmn. bd., CEO, U.S. English Found., Washington, 1993—; mem. mem. Emmanuel Coll. Cambridge (Eng.) U., 1995; mem. adv. bd. U.S.-U.K. Fulbright Commn., 1995-2000.

**MUKADAM, ANJUM SHAGUFTA,** astronomer; d. Mohammed Taiyab and Zaheda Nahid Mukadam; m. Sivakumar Panneerselvam Mudanai, Jan. 19, 2001. MS in Physics, Indian Inst. Tech. Bombay, Mumbai, India, 1997; MS in Astronomy, U. Tex., 2000, PhD in Astronomy, 2004. Hubble postdoctoral fellow U. Wash., Seattle, 2004—. Mentor U. Wash., 2005—. Author: rsch. in field (Benfield award for Excellence in Rsch., 2002), (articles) Astrophys. Jour. Recipient award, J. N. Tata Endowment, Mumbai, India, 1998; fellow, U. Tex.-Austin, 2001—02, 2002—03, Cullen Trust Found., 2003—04, Hubble fellowship, Space Telescope Sci. Inst., 2004—. Mem.: White Dwarf Rsch. Corp. (bd. dirs. 2004—06), Am. Astron. Soc. Athiest Avocations: gardening, cooking, travel, writing. Office: Univ Washington Dept Astronomy Seattle WA 98195-1580 Office Phone: 206-543-5280. Office Fax: 206-685-0403. Business E-Mail: anjum@astro.washington.edu.

**MUKASEY, MICHAEL B.,** lawyer, former federal judge; b. Bronx, NY, 1941; AB, Columbia U., 1963; LLB, Yale U., 1967. Assoc. Webster Sheffield Fleishchmann Hithcock & Brookfield, 1967-72, Patterson, Belknap, Webb & Tyler, 1976-88; asst. U.S. atty. criminal divsn. (so. dist.) NY US Dept. Justice, 1972-76; judge US Dist. Ct. (so. dist.) NY, 1988—2006, chief judge, 2000—06; ptnr. Patterson Belknap Webb & Tyler LLP, NYC, 2006—. Lectr. in law Columbia Law Sch. Contbr. articles to profl. jour. Office: Patterson Belknap Webb & Tyler LLP 1133 Ave Americas New York NY 10036*

**MUKERJEE, PASUPATI,** chemistry professor; b. Calcutta, India, Feb. 13, 1932; s. Nani Gopal and Probhabati (Ghosal) M.; m. Lalita Sarkar, Feb. 29, 1964 (dec.); m. Mina Maitra, Nov. 14, 1998. B.Sc., Calcutta U., 1949, M.Sc., 1951; PhD, U. So. Calif., 1957. Lectr., vis. asst. prof. U. So. Calif., 1956-57; rsch. assoc. Brookhaven Nat. Lab., L.I., 1957-59; reader in phys. chemistry Indian Assn. Cultivation of Sci., Calcutta, 1959-64; guest scientist U. Utrecht, Holland, 1964; sr. scientist chemistry dept. U. So. Calif., 1964-66; vis. assoc. prof. U. Wis., Madison, 1966-67, prof. Sch. Pharmacy, 1967-94, emeritus prof., 1994—. Vis. prof. Indian Inst. Tech., Kharagpur, 1971-72; mem. commn. on colloid and surface chemistry Internat. Union Pure and Applied Chemistry Contbr. articles to profl. jours.; mem. editl. bd. Jour. Colloid and Interface Sci., 1978-80, Asian Jour. Pharm. Scis., 1978-85, Colloids and Surfaces, 1980-86. Grantee USPHS, NSF, Nat. Bur. Stds., Petroleum Rsch. Fund. Fellow AAAS, Acad. Pharm. Scis., Am. Inst. Chemistry; mem. Am. Chem. Soc. (editorial bd. Langmuir 1985-86), Am. Pharm. Assn., Acad. Pharm. Scis., Rho Chi. Home: 5526 Varsity Hl Madison WI 53705-4652 Office: 777 Highland Ave Madison WI 53705-2222 Office Phone: 608-262-7289.

**MUKERJEE, SHAIBAL,** environmental scientist; b. Lexington, Ky., Sept. 29, 1962; s. Debdas and Freny Dee (Bhaisa) M.; m. Mamta Syal, Oct. 3, 1997. BS, Xavier U., 1986; MS, U. Cin., 1988, PhD, 1991. Rsch. phys. scientist EPA, Research Triangle Park, N.C., 1991—. Guest editor Environ. Internat., 1997, Sci. Total Environment, 2001. Mem. Internat. Soc. Exposure Analysis, Air and Waste Mgmt. Assn. (chair U.S.-Mex. border air quality sessions 1999). Achievements include research in atmospheric characterization and modeling of incinerator emissions, environmental and exposure studies in U.S.-Mexico border region, wind sector analysis for source apportionment air studies, transboundary air pollution assessments, and development of risk apportionment concept; expertise in use of exposure measurements with geographic information system data to improve exposure estimations for respiratory health studies.

**MUKERJI, INDRANIL,** lawyer; b. Queens, NY; s. Bisu and Malaya Mukerji; m. Kerstin Mukerji. BS, Cornell U., M of Engring.; JD, Boston U. Mng. ptnr. Wall Marjama & Bilinski LLP, Syracuse, NY, 2004—. Mem.: Am. Intellectual Property Law Assn. Office: Wall Marjama & Bilinski LLP 101 S Salina St Ste 400 Syracuse NY 13202 Office Phone: 315-425-9000. Office Fax: 315-425-9114.

**MUKHERJEE, AMIYA K.,** metallurgy and materials science educator; PhD, Oxford (Eng.) U., 1962. Prof. U. Calif., Davis. Recipient Alexander von Humboldt award Fed. Republic Germany, 1988, Albert Easton White Disting. Tchr. award Am. Soc. Materials, 1992, Pfeil medal and prize Inst. Materials, 1993, U. Calif. prize and citation, 1993, Anatoly Bochvar medal U. Moscow, 1996, Inst. medal Max Planck Inst. for Metallforschung, 1997. Office: U Calif Davis Dept Chem Engring & Material Sci Davis CA 95616 E-mail: akmukherjee@ucdavis.edu.

**MUKHERJEE, BHARATI (MRS. CLARK BLAISE),** writer, language educator; b. Calcutta, India, July 27, 1940; d. Sudhir Lal and Bina (Banerjee) M.; m. Clark L. Blaise, Sept. 19, 1963; children: Bart Anand, Bernard Sudhir. BA, U. Calcutta, 1959; MA, U. Baroda, India, 1961; MFA, U. Iowa, 1963, PhD, 1969. Instr. in English Marquette U., Milw., 1964-65; vis. prof. in Wis., Milw., 1965; lectr. McGill U., Montreal, Que., Can., 1966-69, asst. prof. English, 1969-73, assoc. prof., 1973-78, prof., 1978-79, Skidmore Coll., Saratoga Springs, N.Y., 1979-84; assoc. prof. Montclair (N.J.) State College, 1984-87; prof. CUNY, 1987-89, U. Calif., Berkeley. Vis. prof. of writing U. Iowa, Iowa City, 1979, 82; vis. prof. Emory U., Atlanta, 1983. Author: The Tiger's Daughter, 1972, Wife, 1975, (with Clark Blaise) Days and Nights in Calcutta, 1977, Darkness, 1985, The Middleman and Other Stories, 1988 (Nat. Book Critics Circle award 1989), (with Clark Blaise) The Sorrow and the Terror, 1988, Jasmine, 1989, The Holder of the World, 1993, Leave It to Me, 1997, Desirable Daughters, 2002, The Tree Bride, 2004; contbr. short stories, essays and book revs. to several jours. Grantee McGill U., 1968, 70, Can. Arts Coun., 1973-74, 77, Shastri Indo-Can. Inst., 1976-77, Guggenheim Found., 1978-79, Can. Govt., 1982; recipient 1st prize Periodical Distbn. Assn., 1980, NEA award, 1986. Mem. PEN. Hindu. Office: U Calif Dept English 322 Wheeler Hall Berkeley CA 94720-1030

**MUKHERJEE, DEBABRATA,** cardiologist, researcher; s. Prabodh Chandra Mukherjee. MD, Govt. Med. Coll., Nagpur, India, 1988; M in Clin. Rsch., U. Mich., 2003. Med. lic. Ohio, Mich., Ky., bd. cert. in internal medicine 1996, bd. cert. in cardiovascular diseases 1999, bd. cert. in interventional cardiology 2000. Fellow in molecular cardiology Cleveland Clinic Found., 1989—92, resident in internal medicine, 1993—96, fellow in clin. cardiology, 1996—99, fellow in interventional cardiology and peripheral vascular interventions, 1999—2000, chief interventional cardiology fellow, 2000—01; dir. peripheral vascular interventions for cardiology, asst. prof. divsn. cardiology U. Mich., 2001—04; endowed prof. interventional cardiology, dir. peripheral vascular interventions, assoc. dir. cardiac catheterization lab. U. Ky., Ky., 2001—. Mem. spl. emphasis panel Nat. Heart Lung and Blood Inst., 2003; external reviewer Can. Inst. Health Rsch., 2003. Asst. editor ACC Current Jour. Review, 2002—, internat. editor The Reviews, 2004—, mem. editl. bd. Vascular Disease Prevention, 2003—, Internat. Jour. Angiology, 2005—, Am. Heart Jour., 2005—; author manual of vascular diseases; reviewer (various manuscripts); contbr. chapters to books. Finalist Astra-Zeneca Young Investigator, 1999, 2000; recipient Recognition award, Indian Coun. Med. Rsch., 1986, LN Jaiswal Gold Medal, 1988, Sadiq Vali Gold Medal, 1988, DB Jaiswal Gold Medal, 1988, Robert C. Tarazi Fellowship award for Excellence in Cardiovascular Rsch., 1990, Joseph Cash Meml. award for excellence in health outcome rsch., 2001; McKay Rsch. grant for peripheral arterial disease, U. Mich. Cardiovascular Ctr., 2003—04. Fellow: Am. Coll. Cardiology, Soc. Vascular Medicine and Biology; mem.: AAAS, AMA, ACP, Am. Heart Assn. (Rsch. fellowship 1990, 1991, Bristol-Myers Squibb Travel award 1997, Grant-in-Aid 1999—2001), Internat. Fedn. Advancement Genetic Engring. and Biotechnology, Am. Coll. Cardiology (mem. cardiac catheterization and intervention com. 2005—08, summit adv. work group 2006—09, Affiliate Travel award 1998, finalist Young Investigator award 1999, First prize for abstract 1999, Career Devel. Award 2002—03, First prize for abstract 2000, William F. Keating Career Devel. award for hypertension and peripheral vascular disease 2002—03). Achievements include research in Impact of combination evidence-based med. therapy on mortality in patients with acute coronary syndromes; Missed opportunities to treat atherosclerosis in patients undergoing peripheral vascular interventions; Risk of cardiovascular events associated with selective COX-2 inhibitors. Office: Univ Ky 326B Wethington Bldg 900 S Limestone St Lexington KY 40536-0200 Office Phone: 859-323-5630. Office Fax: 859-323-6475.

**MUKHERJEE, PRACHETA,** management educator, researcher, consultant; b. Kanpur, India, Sept. 2, 1951; came to U.S., 1984; s. Shyamapada and Gouri (Banerjee) Mukherjee; m. Krishna Chakravarty, Feb. 28, 1981. BSc with honors, Ranchi (Bihar) U., 1972; MBA, Indian Inst. Mgmt., Calcutta, West Bengal, 1975; MS, U. Kans., 1988, PhD, 1992. Trainee account rep. Hindustan Thompson Assocs., Calcutta, 1975-76; sr. acct. Calcutta Electric Supply Corp., 1976-84; grad. teaching and rsch. asst. U. Kans., Lawrence, 1984-89; asst. prof. mgmt. Slippery Rock U. Pa., 1989—95, vis. faculty Sch. Bus., 2002—04. Prin. Mukherjee Assocs., 1993—; rschr., cons. field. Mem. Acad. Mgmt. (nominee doctoral consortium U. Kans. 1987), Inst. for Ops. Rsch. and Mgmt. Scis., Beta Gamma Sigma. Avocations: photography, stamp collecting/philately, international travel. Home: 227 W Cooper St # 20 Slippery Rock PA 16057-1533 Personal E-mail: pracheta@aol.com.

**MUKHERJEE, SANDIP KUMAR,** cardiologist; b. India, Oct. 28, 1961; came to U.S. 1985; s. Tridib and Debdasi (Chatterjee) M.; m. Sholeh Moghaddam, Dec. 21, 1985; children: Mina, Alexander. BS, Tex. A&M U., 1982; MD, Tex. Tech U., 1988. Diplomate Am. Bd. Internal Medicine, Am. Bd. Cardiovascular Disease. Intern and resident in internal medicine Yale U. Sch. Medicine, New Haven, 1988-91, chief med. resident, 1991-92, fellow in cardiovascular medicine, 1992-95, asst. clin. prof. medicine, 1996—; ptnr. pvt. practice Cardiology Assocs. of New Haven, P.C. Co-dir. NIH/NHLBI study, 1996—; dir. cardiovascular workshop Yale Med. Sch.; presenter in field. Editl. fellow Med. Letter, 1997—; contbr. articles to profl. jours. Fellow Am. Coll. Cardiology; mem. AMA, ACP, Am. Heart Assn. Clin. Cardiology Coun., Beta Beta Beta. Office: Cardiology Assn New Haven 40 Temple St Ste 6A New Haven CT 06510-2715

**MUKHOPADHYAY, SHARMILA MITRA,** materials engineer, educator; d. Arun Kumar and Bani Mitra; m. Bhaskar Mukhopadhyay, June 29, 1985; 1 child, Amrita. BS, MS, Indian Inst. Tech.; PhD, Cornell U., 1989. Assoc./asst. prof. Wright State U., Dayton, Ohio, 1997—2003, prof. materials sci. and engring., 2003—. Reviewer NSF, 1994—. Editor: MPMD Fifth Global Innovations Procs: Surfaces and Interfacesin Nanostructured Materials; contbr. articles to profl. jours. Recipient cert. for nat. ranking (top 10), Indian Sch. Cert. Orgn., 1977, several scholarship awards, including Nat. Merit scholarship, Indian Inst. Tech. and W.B. Govt., 1981, rsch. awards, NSF, DOE, NASA, AFOSR, EPA, several rsch. grants, Procter & Gamble; Summer Faculty Rsch. fellow, Air Force Rsch. Lab., Propulsion Directorate. Mem.: Materials Rsch. Soc., Am. Vacuum Soc., Am. Soc. Engring. Edn., TMS (symposium organizer 2003—06), ASM Internat. (exec. com. Dayton chpt. 1998—), Am. Ceramic Soc. (exec. com. electronics divsn. 2005—). Achievements include development of thin film techniques, including fabrication of superconducting oxides from nanoparticles; research in modification of plasma interfaces in superconductors; surface activity measurements using XPS; modification of nanostructural materials. Avocations: travel, painting, poetry. Office: Wright State U Mech and Materials Engring Dept Dayton OH 45435     Office    Phone:    937-775-5092.    Business    E-mail: sharmila.mukhopadhyay@wright.edu.

**MUKOYAMA, JAMES HIDEFUMI, JR.,** security firm executive; b. Chgo., Aug. 3, 1944; s. Hidefumi James and Miye (Maruyama) M.; m. Kyung Ja Woo, June 20, 1971; children: Sumi Martha, Jae Thomas. BA in English, U. Ill., 1965, MA in Social Studies, 1966; grad. (hon.), US Army Inf. Sch., 1966; grad., US Army Command Gen. Staff Coll., 1979, US Army War Coll., 1984. Registered prin., sr. registered options prin. Nat. Assn. Securities Dealers. Commd. 2d lt. U.S. Army, 1965; advanced through grades to maj. gen. USAR, 1990, ret., 2004; asst. dept. mgr. Mitsui & Co. (USA), Inc., Chgo., 1971-74; mem. Chgo. Bd. Options Exch., 1974—75; allied mem. N.Y. Stock Exch., 1982-84; v.p. Heartland Securities Inc. & Lefta Advt., Chgo., 1976-90, Fleet Brokerage, Chgo., 1990-95; exec. v.p., COO, Regal Discount Securities, 1995—. Mem. exec. bd. Hillside Free Meth. Ch., Evanston, Ill., 1982-93, participating mem. Willow Creek Ch., 2003-; dir. Chgo. coun. Boy Scouts Am., 1993-95; bd. dirs. Nat. Japanese Am. Meml. Found., 1995-2004; patient vol. Rainbow Hospice, 2003-; vice chair adv. com. minority vets. Dept. VA, 2003-; pres. bd. dirs. Japanese Assn. Svc. Corr. Housing Corp., 2005-. Decorated Silver Star, Legion of Merit, Purple Heart, 3 Bronze Stars, Disting. Svc. medal; Vietnamese Army Cross of Gallantry; Japanese Army Parachutist badge; recipient cert. of merit Korean Army, others. Mem. VFW (life), U. Ill. Alumni Assn. (life), Assn. U.S. Army (life), U.S. Army Warr Coll. Alumni Assn. (life), Army Res. Assn. (pres., founder 1992—), Mil. Order Purple Heart (life), Am. Legion (life), Res. Officers Assn. (life), Sr. Army Res. Comdrs. Assn. (life), Nat. Infantryman's Assn. (life). Home: 4009 Tracey Ct Glenview IL 60025-2468 Office: Regal Securities 950 Milwaukee Ave Ste 101 Glenview IL 60025-3766 Personal E-mail: jhmukoyama@yahoo.com.

**MULALLY, ALAN R.,** automotive company executive, former aerospace company executive; b. Oakland, Calif., Aug. 4, 1945; m. Nicki Mulally; 5 children. BS in Aerospace Engring., U. Kans., 1968, MS in Aerospace Engring., 1969; MA in Mgmt., MIT, 1982. With Boeing Def. and Space Group, Seattle, 1969—2006, v.p. 777 engring., v.p. gen. mgr. 777 divsn., sr. v.p. airplane devel., 1994—97, pres., 1997-99; exec. v.p Boeing Co., 1997—2006; pres. Boeing Comml. Air Group, 1998—2006; pres., CEO Ford Motor Co., Dearborn, Mich., 2006—. Mem. adv. bd. NASA, U. Wash., U. Kans.; mem. sci. adv. bd. USAF. Alfred P. Sloan fellow, 1982; recipient Leadership Tomorrow Program award, Seattle C. of C., 1984, One of 25 Bus. Leaders award, Puget Sound Bus. Jour., 1985, Disting. Engring. Svc. award, U. Kans. Engring. Sch., 1994, Laurels award, Aviation Week and Space Tech. mag., 1996, Engr. of Yr. award, Design News, 1996, Robert J. Collier Trophy (on behalf of 777 team), Nat. Aero. Assn., 1996, Fellow Royal Aero. Soc. (Eng.), AIAA (Tech. Mgmt. award 1986, Reed Aeronautics award 1990); mem. NSPE (Industry Engr. of Yr. 1978), NAE. Avocations: private pilot, reading, tennis, golf. Office: Ford Motor Co 1 American Rd Dearborn MI 48126*

**MULARKEY, MIKE,** professional football coach; b. Ft. Lauderdale, Fl, Nov. 19, 1961; m. Betsy Mularkey. Degree in Kinesiology and Sociology, U. Minn. Player Minn. Vikings, 1983—88, Pitts. Steelers, 1989—91; offensive line coach Concordia Coll., 1993; quality control coach Tampa Bay Buccaneers, 1994; tight ends coach Pitts. Steelers, 1996—2000, offensive coord., 2001—03; head coach Buffalo Bills, 2004—05; offensive coord. Miami Dolphins, 2006—. Office: Miami Dolphins 7500 SW 30th St Davie FL 33314*

**MULARZ, THEODORE LEONARD,** architect; b. Chgo., Nov. 6, 1933; s. Stanley A. and Frances (Baycar) Mularz; m. Ruth L. Larson, Nov. 9, 1963; children: Anne Catherine, Mark Andrew. BArch, U. Ill., 1959. Registered arch., Colo., Oreg. Prin. Theodore L. Mularz, AIA Architects, Aspen, Colo., 1981-90; v.p. Benedict-Mularz Assocs., Inc., 1978-81; pvt. practice Ashland, Oreg., 1990—. Prin. works include numerous archtl. projects, including comml., indsl., religious, recreational, residential and hist. restoration. Vice-chmn. Pitkin County Bd. Appeals, 1972—90; mem. Colo. Bd. Examiners Archs., 1975—85, pres. 1976—80, v.p., 1978; vice-chmn. City of Aspen Bd. Appeals, 1980—90; mem. adv. com. City of Aspen Planning/Bldg. Dept., 1989; bd. dirs. Rogue Valley Symphony, Ashland, 1990—92, treas., 1991—92, chmn. fin. com., 1991—92; mem. Oreg. Bd. Examiners Archs., 1996—2000. With USCGR, 1953—55. Fellow: AIA; mem.: Colo. Soc. Archs. (Cmty. Svc. award 1975), Nat. Coun. Archtl. Registration Bds. (profl. conduct com. 1977—78, procedures/docs. com. 1978—82, chmn. Am. Council 1982—83, bd. dirs. 1982—87, chmn. 1983—84, mem. interprofessional coun. registration 1984—85, exec. com. 1984—87, internat. rels. com. 1984—89, interant. oral exam. com. 1984—89, v.p. 1985, pres. 1985, 1986, broadly experienced arch. interview com. 1987—2001), Aspen Hist. Soc. (com. chmn. 1963—64), Aspen C. of C. (past dir., pres., v.p.), Rotary (dir. Ashland Found. 2001—03, pres. 2001—02). Roman Catholic. Studio: 793 Elkader St Ashland OR 97520-3307 Personal E-mail: tmularz@aol.com.

**MULCAHY, ANNE MARIE,** printing company executive; b. Rockville Centre, N.Y., Oct. 21, 1952; d. Thomas and Anne Dolan; m. Joe Mulcahy; 2 children. BA in English & Journalism, Marymount Coll., 1974. With Chase Manhattan Bank, 1974—76; various mgmt. positions Xerox Corp., 1976—88, v.p. regional gen. mgr., 1988—91, v.p. worldwide mktg. ops. planning, 1991, dir. corp. human resources, 1991—92, v.p. human resources, 1992-95, v.p., staff officer customer ops. worldwide, 1996-97, sr. v.p., chief staff officer, 1998, pres. gen. mkts. ops. Stamford, Conn., 1999—2000, COO, 2000—01, pres., 2000—02, CEO 2001—, chmn., 2002—. Bd. dirs. Xerox Corp., 2000—, Fannie Mae, 2000—, Catalyst, Citigroup Inc., 2004—, Fuji-Xerox Co. Ltd., Target Corp. Named one of Most Powerful Women, Forbes mag., 2005, World's Best CEO, Barron's Mag., 2006, The TIME 100-The People Who Shape Our World, 2006, 100 Most Powerful Women, Forbes Mag., 2006. Mem.: Bus. Coun. Office: Xerox Corp 800 Long Ridge Rd Stamford CT 06904-1227 Office Fax: 203-968-3218.*

**MULCAHY, GABRIEL M.,** pathologist; b. Jersey City, Feb. 16, 1929; s. Joseph Alphonsus and Anna Elizabeth Mulcahy; m. Vesna Maria Mulcahy, May 24, 1958; children: Mary, Michael, Robert, Richard, Thomas, John, Gabriel Jr. AB, St. Peter's Coll., Jersey City, 1950; MD, Georgetown U., 1954. Diplomate Nat. Bd. Med. Examiners, Am. Bd. Pathology. Intern St. Michaels Hosp., Newark, 1954-55; med. officer U.S. Pub. Health Svc., Crownpoint, N.Mex., 1955-57, resident in pathology Seattle, 1957-59, Staten Island, NY, 1959-61, chief pathology svc Detroit, 1961-62; with pathology faculty Creighton U., Omaha, 1962-69; dir. pathology Jersey City Med. Ctr., 1969-78; mem. pathology faculty Univ. Medicine and Dentistry N.J., Newark, 1978-2001; chief lab. med. Univ. Hosp., Newark, 1978-2001. Mem. editl bd.: Annals of Clin. and Lab. Sci., 2000 ; contbr. articles to profl. jours. Mem. adv. bd. St. Ann's Home for the Aged, Jersey City, 1973-89, sec., 1973-83; pres. bd. edn. St. Paul's Parish Sch., Jersey City, 1973-78. Mem. AAAS, Am. Soc. Human Genetics, Am. Assn. Blood Banks, Assn. Clin. Scientists (sci. coun. 1999—), Coll. Am. Pathologists, Soc. Med. Decision Making. Roman Catholic. Avocations: history, philosophy, philology, photography. E-mail: mulcahy@comapp.org, mulcahy21@comcast.net.

**MULCAHY, ROBERT EDWARD,** management consultant; b. Cambridge, Mass., Mar. 2, 1932; s. George Frances and Hazel (Douglas) M.; m. Ethel Walworth, Nov. 14, 1953; children: Linda, Scott, Steven, Susan. BS, Lowell Textile Inst., 1953. With Allied Chem. Corp., Morristown, N.J, 1953—; from engr. to mktg. mgr. Nat. Aniline div. Allied Corp., 1953-63, from dir. indsl. mktg. to v.p.-mktg. Fibers div., 1963-69, asst. to group v.p.-corporate office, 1969, v.p. and gen. mgr.-consumer group Fabricated Products div., 1969-71, pres. Fibers div., 1971-74, group v.p., 1974-75, pres., dir., 1975-79, asst. to chmn. and dir., 1979-80; sr. assoc The Corp. Dir., Inc., N.Y.C., 1981-83; pres. Counselors to Mgmt. Inc., 1984—.

**MULCAHY, ROBERT WILLIAM,** lawyer; b. Milw., Jan. 11, 1951; s. T. Larry and Mary Margaret (Chambers) M.; m. Mary M. Andrews, Aug. 3, 1974; children: Molly, Kathleen, Margaret, Michael. BS, Marquette U., 1973, JD, 1976. Staff atty. NLRB, Milw., 1976-79; prin. Mulcahy & Wherry, S.C., Milw., 1979-90, Michael, Best & Friedrich, Milw., 1990—. Co-author: Strike Prevention and Control Handbook, 1983, 2d edit., 2006, Comparable Worth: A Negotiator's Guide, 1985, Public Sector Labor Relations in Wisconsin, 1994. Bd. dirs. Milw. Repertory Theater, 1993-97, Gateway Tech. Coll. Found., 2004—; chmn. St. Monica Parish Coun., 1988-96, Charles Allis/Villa Terrace, 1991-, Whitefish Bay Police Commn.; divsn. chmn. United Performing Arts Fund, 1993-94; co-chmn. Villa Terrace Garden Renaissance Project, 2000-04. Mem. ABA, State Bar Wis. (chair labor sect. 1986-87), Milw. Bar Assn. (co-chair labor sect. 1988-95), Nat. Assn. Counties, Nat. Pub. Employers Labor Rels. Assn., Nat. Assn. Coll. & Univ. Attys., Wis. Counties Assn., Indsl. Rels. Rsch. Assn., Mgmt. Resources Assn., Wis. Sch. Attys. Assn., Milw. Area Mcpl. Employers Assn. Office: Michael Best & Friedrich 100 E Wisconsin Ave Ste 3300 Milwaukee WI 53202-4108 E-mail: rwmulcahy@mbf-law.com, rwmulcahy@michaelbest.com

**MULCH, ROBERT F., JR.,** physician; b. Quincy, Ill., June 21, 1951; s. Robert Franklin and Martha Jo (Nisi) M.; m. Barbara Ann Best, Apr. 5, 1975; children: Matthew, Luke. BS, U. Ill., 1973; MD, Rush Med. Coll., Chgo., 1977. Diplomate Am. Bd. Family Practice; cert. in geriatrics. Intern Riverside Meth. Hosp., Columbus, Ohio, 1977-78, resident in family practice, 1978-80; family physician Hillsboro (Ill.) Med. Ctr., 1980—; ptnr., assoc. med. dir. Springfield Clin., 1998—; pres. med. staff Hillsboro Area Hosp. asst. clin. prof. family medicine So. Ill. U., Springfield, 1981—90; reviewer Ctrl. Ill. Peer Rev. Orgn.; pres. med. staff Hillsboro Area Hosp. Fellow Am. Acad. Family Practice; mem. Am. Coll. Physician Execs. Lutheran. Avocations: computers, swimming. Office: Hillsboro Med Ctr SC 1250 E Tremont St Hillsboro IL 62049-1912 Office Phone: 217-532-6911. E-mail: rmulch@consolidated.net, rmulch@springfieldclinic.com

**MULCHAHEY, TERRY S.,** human resources executive, management consultant; b. Laurium, Mich., May 3, 1948; m. Patricia Brooks Mulcahey. BA with honors, Mich. State U., 1970; MS in Indsl. and Labor Rels. Studies, Cornell U., 1973. Various human resources positions Mobil Corp., Princeton, NJ, 1976—85; mgr. employee rels. Rubbermaid, Inc., Wooster, Ohio, 1984—89; dir. human resources and labor rels. KLM Royal Dutch Airlines, Elmsford, NY, 1989—95; v.p. human resources Alper Holdings USA, N.Y.C., 1995—98, Uniscribe Profl. Services, Inc., Norwalk, Conn., 1998—99; prin. The Hyde Hazen Group, Ridgefield, Conn., 1999—. Mem.: Am. Arbitration Assn. (labor mgmt. edn. com. 1991—94), Internat. Assn. Corp. and Profl. Recruiters (nat. bd. mem., chmn. Fairfield/Westchester chpt. 1994—96), US Squash Racquets Assn. (life), Cornell Club N.Y.C. Episcopalian. Office Phone: 203-438-9676.

**MULCONREY, BRIAN GEORGE,** management consultant, futurist; b. Chgo., Ill., Oct. 19, 1953; s. George Thomas and Mary Mulconrey; m. Linda Marie Szopa, Apr. 20, 1974; children: Hailey Kathryn, Matthew George. MS in Fin. Svcs., Am. Coll., Bryn Mawr, Pa., 1985. Chartered fin. cons. Am. Coll.; cert. project mgmt. profl. Project Mgmt. Inst. Consulting prin., dir. mktg. Continuum, Inc. (now CSC Fin. Svcs.), Austin, Tex., 1983—90; mgmt. cons., futurist BG Mulconrey, Inc., Austin, 1990—. Web log host Global Bus. Network, Emeryville, Calif., 1998—. Author: (study) Role of Brands in the Digital Economy; contbr. articles to profl. jours. Fellow: Life Office Mgmt. Assn. Achievements include development of literary format for imagining the enterprises of tomorrow called enterprise poetry; detailed business model for launching the personal information management services industry; research in operational blueprints to advance organizational learning called Organizational Learning Laboratories. Office: BG Mulconrey Inc 6315 Big Cat Cove Austin TX 78750 Office Phone: 512-338-9557.

**MULDAUR, DIANA CHARLTON,** actress; b. N.Y.C., Aug. 19, 1938; d. Charles Edward Arrowsmith and Alice Patricia (Jones) M.; m. James Mitchell Vickery, July 26, 1969 (dec. 1979); m. Robert J. Dozier, Oct. 11, 1981. BA, Sweet Briar Coll., 1960. Actress appearing in: Off-Broadway theatrical prodns., summer stock. Broadway plays including A Very Rich Woman, 1963-68; guest appearances on TV in maj. dramatic shows; appeared on: TV series Survivors, 1970-71, McCloud, 1971-73, Tony Randall Show, 1976, Black Beauty, 1978; star: TV series Born Free, 1974, Hizzoner, 1979, Fitz & Bones, 1980, Star Trek: The Next Generation, 1988-89; NBC miniseries and TV series A Year in the Life, 1986; TV movie Murder in Three Acts, The Return of Sam McCloud, 1989; TV series L.A. Law, 1989-91; motion picture credits include McQ, The Lawyer, The Other, One More Train to Rob, Mati, etc. Bd. dirs. Los Angeles chpt. Asthma and Allergy Found. Am.; bd. advisors Nat. Ctr. Film and Video Preservation, John F. Kennedy Ctr. Performing Arts, 1986. Recipient 13th Ann. Commendation award Am. Women in Radio and TV, 1988, Disting. Alumnae award Sweet Briar Coll., 1988. Mem. Acad. Motion Picture Arts and Scis., Screen Actors Guild (dir. 1978), Acad. TV Arts and Scis. (exec. bd., pres. 1983-85), Conservation Soc. Martha's Vineyard Island. Office: Bauman Bedanty & Shaul 5757 Wilshire Blvd Ste 473 Los Angeles CA 90036 Office Phone: 310-454-2241.

**MULDER, DAVID S.,** cardiovascular surgeon; b. Eston, Sask., Can., July 28, 1938; s. Peter and Laura (Lovie) M.; m. Norma D. Johnston, Aug. 19, 1961; children – Scott D., Lizabeth J., John C. MD, U. Sask., 1962; M.Sc., McGill U., 1964. Intern, resident in surgery Montreal Gen. Hosp., McGill U., 1963-67; resident in cardiac surgery U. Iowa, 1967-69; surgeon-in-chief Montreal Gen. Hosp., 1977-98; prof. surgery McGill U., 1979—; chmn. dept. surgery, 1993-98. Contbr. articles to med. jours. Fellow: ACS, Royal Coll. Surgeons Can.; mem.: Soc. Thoracic Surgeons (named Order Can. 1997), Am. Assn Thoracic Surgery, Am. Assn. Trauma, Nat. Hockey League Team Physicians Assn., Soc. Univ. Surgeons. Conservative. Home: 76 Sunnyside Ave Westmount PQ Canada H34 1C2 Office: Montreal Gen Hosp Room L-512 Montreal PQ Canada H3G 1A4 Office Phone: 514-935-4888. Personal E-mail: dsmulder@sympatico.ca. Business E-Mail: david.mulder@muhc.mcgill.ca.

**MULDOON, PAUL,** poet, educator; b. Portadown, No. Ireland, 1951; came to U.S., 1987; m. Jean Hanff Korelitz; 2 children. BA in English Lang. and Lit., Queen's U., Belfast, No. Ireland, 1973. Prodr. arts programs radio BBC No. Ireland, 1973-78, sr. prodr. arts programs radio, 1978-85, TV prodr., 1985-86; Judith E. Wilson vis. fellow Cambridge U., 1986-87; creative writing fellow U. East Anglia, 1987; Roberta Holloway lectr. U. Calif., Berkeley, 1989; lectr. Princeton U., NJ, 1990—, prof., 1995, dir. creative writing program, 1993—2002, Howard G.B. Clark '21 Univ. Prof. humanities and creative writing, 1998—, founding chair Ctr. for Creative and Performing Arts, 2006—; prof. poetry U. Oxford, 1999—2004. Part-time tchr. writing divsn. Sch. of Arts, Columbia U., 1987-88; part-time tchr. creative writing program Princeton U., 1987-88, vis. prof. U. Mass., Amherst, 1989-90. Author: (poetry) Knowing My Place, 1971, New Weather, 1973, Spirit of Dawn, 1975, Mules, 1977, Immram, 1980, Why Brownlee Left, 1980, Out of Siberia, 1982, Quoof, 1983, Selected Poems 1968-83, 1986, Meeting the British, 1987, Madoc: A Mystery, 1990, Incantata, 1994, The Prince of the Quotidian, 1994, The Annals of Chile, 1994, Hay, 1998, Moy Sand and Gravel, 2002, Reverse Flannery: Magical Tales of Ireland, 2003, Medley for Morin Khur, 2005, Sixty Instant Messages to Tom Moore, 2005, Horse Latitudes, 2006, others, (criticism) To Ireland, I, 2000, The End of the Poem, 2006, (opera libretto) Shining Brow, 1993, Bandanna, 1999, (TV play) Monkeys, 1989, (translation from Irish) The Astrakhan Cloak, 1993, (children's book) The O-O's Party, 1981, The Noctuary of Narcissus Batt, 1997; editor: (poetry) The Scrake of Dawn, 1979, The Faber Book of Contemporary Irish Poetry, 1986, The Essential Byron, 1989, The Faber Book of Beasts, 1997; contbr. to anthologies. Recipient Eric Gregory award, 1972, Sir Geoffrey Faber Meml. award, 1980, 91, T.S. Eliot prize, 1994, Acad. award in lit. Am. Acad. Arts and Letters, 1996, Irish Times prize for poetry, 1997, Pulitzer Prize for poetry, 2003, Griffin Internat. prize excellence in poetry, 2003, Shakespeare prize, 2004, Aspen prize for poetry, 2005, Am. Ireland Fund Lit. award, 2004; John Simon Guggenheim Meml. fellow, 1990. Fellow Royal Soc. Lit.; mem. Am. Acad. Arts and Scis., Aosdana. Office: Princeton Univ Rm 122 185 Nassau St Princeton NJ 08544-0001 Office Phone: 609-258-4708. E-mail: muldoon@princeton.edu.

**MULDOON, ROBERT JOSEPH, JR.,** lawyer; b. Somerville, Mass., Nov. 16, 1936; s. Robert Joseph and Catherine Eileen (Hurley) M.; m. Barbara Joyce Mooney, Aug. 24, 1968; children: Andrew Robert, Catherine Lane, Timothy John. AB, Boston Coll., 1960, MA, 1961, LLB, 1965. Bar: Mass. 1965, U.S. Tax Ct. 1966, U.S. Supreme Ct. 1970. Law clk. Supreme Jud. Ct. Mass., 1965-66; assoc Withington, Cross, Park & Groden, Boston, 1966-71, ptnr., 1972-82, Sherin and Lodgen, LLP, Boston, 1982—. Mem. Bd. Bar Examiners Mass., 1974—, chmn., 2005—; chmn. Nat. Conf. Bar Examiners, 1985-86; pres. Mass. Continuing Legal Edn., Inc., 1992-94. Trustee Boston Coll. H.S., 1990-96, chmn. bd. trustees, 1995-96. Fellow Am. Coll. Trial Lawyers; mem. Am. Law Inst., Boston Bar Assn., Curtis Club, Nisi Prius Club, Tavern Club. Office: Sherin and Lodgen LLP 101 Federal St Boston MA 02110 Office Phone: 617-646-2225. E-mail: rjmuldoon@sherin.com.

**MULÉ, ANN C.,** oil industry executive; b. Phila., Oct. 22, 1956; BA magna cum laude, St. Joseph's U., 1978; JD cum laude, Villanova U., 1981. Bar: Pa. 1981, U.S. Supreme Ct. 1988. From atty. to chief governance officer Sunoco Inc., Phila., 1980—2002, chief governance officer, 2002—. Bd. dirs. Phila. Zoo; mem. adv. bd. Ctr. Corp. Governance, U. Del. Mem.: ABA, Am. Corp. Counsel Assn. (vice chmn. exec. counsel, mem. corp. and securities law com.), Phila. Bar Assn., Pa. Bar Assn. (chmn. bus. law sect., mem. bd. govs., chmn. com. securities regulation, mem. title 15 task force); Am. Soc. Corp. Secs. (bd. dir., mem. exec. steering com., mem. nat. conf. com., mem. corp. practices com.). Office: Sunoco Inc Mellon Bank Ctr 1735 Market St Ste LL Philadelphia PA 19103

**MULETA, JOHN B.,** lawyer; b. Addis Ababa, Ethiopia, Dec. 13, 1964; BS in Sys. Engring., Univ. Va., 1986, MBA, JD, Univ. Va., 1993. Bar: Va. 1993. With GTE Corp; co-founder OI Systems Inc; pres., CEO Source 1 Technologies LLC; pres. PSINet India, Middle East and Africa Divsn., PSINet's Global Facilities Divsn., PSINet Ventures, Inc., Washington, 1998—2000; with Coopers & Lybrand Consulting, LLC; dep. bur. chief, Common Carrier Bur. to chief, Enforcement Divsn. FCC, 1994—98; chief FCC Wireless Telecom. Bur.; ptnr., co-chair comm. group Venable LLP, Washington. Office: Venable LLP 575 Seventh St NW Washington DC 20004 Office Phone: 202-344-4281. Office Fax: 202-344-8300. Business E-Mail: jmuleta@venable.com.

**MULFORD, DAVID CAMPBELL,** ambassador, former finance company executive; b. Rockford, Ill., June 27, 1937; s. Robert Lewis Mulford and Theodora Henie Countryman; m. Jeannie Louise Simmons, Oct. 19, 1985; children: Robert Ian, Edward Maitland. BA in Econs, cum laude, Lawrence U., 1959; postgrad. U. Cape Town, South Africa, 1960; MA in Polit. Sci., Boston U., 1962; PhD, Oxford U., 1966; LLD (hon.), Lawrence U., 1984. White House fellow U.S. Dept. Treas., Washington, 1965-66, under asst. sec. internat. affairs, 1984-89; dir. White Weld & Co., N.Y.C. and London, 1966-74; sr. investment advisor Saudi Arabian Monetary Agy., Riyadh, 1974-84; asst. sec. internat. affairs Dept. of Treas., 1984-89; under sec. treasury internat. affairs, 1989-92; vice chmn. CS First Boston, N.Y.C., 1992—93; chmn. Credit Suisse First Boston, London, 1993-98, internat. chmn., 1998—2003; U.S. amb. to India U.S. Dept. State, New Delhi, 2004—. Author: Northern Rhodesia General Election, 1962, Zambia: The Politics of Independence, 1967. Trustee Lawrence U., 1986—. Decorated Legion d'Honneur, 1990; recipient Order of May Merit Pres. Argentina, 1993, Officers Cross of the Medal of Merit Pres. Poland, 1995; Rotary Internat. fellow Oxford U., U. Cape Town, 1961-62, Woodrow Wilson fellow Boston U., Oxford U., 1962, Ford Found. fellow St. Anthony's Coll., Oxford, 1963-65; named Disting. Alumni Boston U., 1992; Disting. scholar Ctr. Strategic and Internat. Studies, Washington, 1993—. Mem. Coun. Fgn. Rels., White House Fellows Assn., Metropolitan Club (Washington). Republican. Office: US Dept State 9000 New Delhi Pl Dulles VA 20189-9000

**MULFORD, RICHARD ALBERT,** mechanical engineer, professional society administrator; b. Phila., Dec. 1, 1930; s. William Abernathy and Jeanne Ann (Roy) Mulford. BSME, U. Pa., 1952, MS in Mech. Engring., 1957; Diploma in Bus., Dartmouth Coll., 1985. Registered profl. engr., Pa. Engr. Phila. Elec. Co., 1952-64, sr. engr., 1964-67, project mgr., 1967-85, staff engr., 1985-91; exec. dir. Engrs. Club of Phila., 1991—. Vol. Pacoli Meml. Hosp., Pa., 1991—. donor Phila. Orch. Assn., 1980—; treas., donor Phila. Engring. Found. 1991—. Recipient Disting. Svc. award, Pa. Soc. Profl. Engrs., 1991, 1998, D. Robert Yarnall award (Outstanding Engring. Alumnus), U. Pa., 1981, Alumni award of merit, 1993, Presdl. award, Phila. sect. ASCE, 2002, Outstanding Svc. award, Del. Valley Engrs. Week Coun., 2003. Fellow: Engrs. Club Phila. (sec.-treas. 1953—, George Washington medal 1988); mem.: NSPE, Union League Phila. (scholarship trustee 1963—), Racquet Club Phila. Republican. Achievements include patents in field. Avocations: classical music, antique cars, home and lawn maintenance. Home: 1231 Wisteria Dr Malvern PA 19355-9736 Office: Engrs Club of Phila 215 S 16th St Ste 36 Philadelphia PA 19102-3349 Office Phone: 215-985-5701. Business E-Mail: info@engrclub.org.

**MULHALL, KIMBERLY A.,** business manager; b. Evanston, Ill., Dec. 26, 1967; d. Michael J. and Karen A. Mulhall, Mary M. Mulhall (Stepmother). B in Bus. Adminstrn., Roosevelt U., Chgo., 1990, MBA, 1996. Acct. Network Svcs. Co., Mount Prospect, Ill., 1990—95, sr. acct., 1995—97; asst. payroll supr. Underwriters Labs. Inc., Northbrook, Ill., 1997—98, payroll supr., 1998—2000, bus. analyst, 2000—01, sr. mktg. analyst, 2001—05, US regional bus. mgr., 2005—. Vol. Children's Advocacy Ctr. N.W. Cook County. Named Vol. of Yr., Children's Advocacy Ctr. N.W. Cook County, 2003. Mem.: Am. Mktg. Assn. Roman Catholic. Office: Underwriters Labs Inc 333 Pfingsten Rd Northbrook IL 60062 E-mail: kimberly.a.mulhall@us.ul.com.

**MULHAUSER, CRAIG H.,** energy executive; BS in Aerospace Engring., MS, U. Cin. Formerly with NASA; formerly with aircraft engine and power systems group GE; sr. v.p. sales and svc. Ams., v.p. worldwide aftermarket bus. Pratt & Whitney, Conn., 1995—97; v.p. Ford Motor Co., 1997—2000; pres. Visteon Automotive Systems, 1997—2000; chmn., CEO Exide Techs., Princeton, NJ, 2000—. Mem. U. Cin. Found. Mem.: Motor Equipment Mfrs. Assn. Office: Exide Technologies 13000 Deerfield Pkwy Ste 200 Alpharetta GA 30004-6118

**MULHERN, MARTIN ROBERT,** engineer; b. New Brunswick, N.J., June 12, 1946; s. Thomas Desmond and Helen Casserly M. BS in Civil Engring., U. Calif., Berkeley, 1968; MS in Civil Engring., U. Wash., 1982. Cert. inshore/offshore hydographer Am. Congress of Surveying and Mapping; unltd. master merchant marine lic. USCG. Structures weights engr. The Boeing Co., Everett, Wash., 1968; capt. NOAA Corps., Silver Spring, Md., 1969-98; cons. Boulder, Colo., 1998-2001. NOAA rep. U. Nat. Oceanographic Lab. System, Silver Spring, 1992-96; comdg. officer NOAA ship Whiting. Recipient H. Arnold Karo award Soc. of Am. Mil. Engrs., 1980, 88. Mem. The Oceanography Soc. (charter, life mem.), Soc. Am. Mil. Engrs. (life), Am. Geophys. Union (life), The Hydrographic Soc. Achievements include conducting geodetic and hydrographic surveys with the Nat. Ocean Survey, extensive duty with labs. and hdqtrs. of the Office of Atmospheric and Oceanographic Rsch. Office: PO Box 19545 Boulder CO 80308-2545 E-mail: mmulhern@attglobal.net.

**MULHERON, MARILYNN,** family practice nurse practitioner; b. New Rochelle, Ariz., July 3, 1970; d. Patricia Ann and adopted d. Thomas Charles Mulheron, Steven John Kolk. AA, Simon's Rock Coll. of Bard, 1990, BA cum laude, 1990; ADN with honors, Berkshire C.C., 1994; BS summa cum laude, U. Mass., 1995; MS, Ariz. State U., 2003. Lic. family nurse practitioner, cert. critical care nurse. Nurse Mayo Clinic Hosp., Phoenix, 1998—2003; family nurse practitioner St. Luke's Ctr. Clinic II, Phoenix, 2003—04, Maricopa Integrated Health Sys., Phoenix, 2004—05, Foothills Family Medicine, 2005—. Med. provider Neighborhood Christian Clinic, Phoenix, 2003—05; vol. So. Berkshire Vol. Ambulance Squad, Great Barrington, Mass., 1990—98; catechist, mem. choir St. Timothy's Cath. Cmty., Mesa, Ariz., 1998—2005. Recipient Fairview Hosp. Physicians' award, Berkshire C.C. and Fairview Hosp., 1993; scholar, U. Mass., Amherst, 1995; Thomas H. Blodgett Scholar, Simon's Rock Coll. of Bard, 1990, Martin Naumann scholar. Mem.: Am. Acad. Critical Care Nurses, Am. Acad. Nurse Practitioners, MENSA, Sigma Theta Tau. Roman Catholic. Avocations: singing, travel. Home: 1820 E Bell de Mar Dr #N206 Tempe AZ 85283 Office: Foothills Family Medicine 4545 E Chandler Blvd Ste 304 Phoenix AZ 85048 Personal E-mail: marilynn_mulheron@yahoo.com.

**MULHOLLAND, NANCY W.,** state agency administrator; BA, Vassar Coll. Various info. tech. mgmt. and tech. positions GE; dir. NY State Project Mgmt. Office Office Tech.; dep. exec. dir. and chief info. officer NY State Workers' Compensation Bd., Albany, 2002—. Named one of Premier 100 IT Leaders, Computerworld, 2005; recipient Award for Excellence in Govt. Info. Services, NYS Forum, 2005. Office: NY State Workers Compensation Bd 20 Park St Albany NY 12207 Office Phone: 518-474-6670.*

**MULHOLLAND, PAUL A.,** gas industry executive; BS, Drexel U., 1975, MBA, 1978. Mgr. fin., mergers and acquisitions Sunoco Inc., Phila., 1993—97, dir. corp. fin., 1997—2000, treas., 2000—, Sunoco Logistics Ptnrs., 2002—. Office: Sunoco Inc Ten Penn Ctr 1801 Market St Philadelphia PA 19103-1699

**MULHOLLAND, TERENCE JOHN (TERRY MULHOLLAND),** professional baseball player; b. Uniontown, Pa., Mar. 9, 1963; Student, Marietta Coll. Pitcher San Francisco Giants, 1984-89, Phila. Phillies, 1989-94, NY Yankees, 1994-96, Seattle Mariners, 1996, Chgo. Cubs, 1997—99, Atlanta Braves, 1999—2000, LA Dodgers, 2001—02, Cleve. Indians, 2002—03, Minn. Twins, 2004—05, Ariz. Diamondbacks, 2006—. Mem. Nat. League All-Star Team, 1993. Pitched no-hit victory, Aug. 15, 1990. Office: Ariz Diamondbacks 401 E Jefferson St Phoenix AZ 85004-2438

**MULHOLLAND, WILLIAM DAVID, JR.,** retired bank executive; b. Albany, N.Y., June 16, 1926; s. William David and Helen E. (Flack) M.; m. Nancy Louise Booth, June 22, 1957; children: William David III, Charles Douglass, James Andrew, John Alexander, Elizabeth Helen, Madeline Louise, Sarah Alexandra, Caroline Marie, Bruce Henry. AB cum laude, Harvard U., 1950, MBA, 1952; LLD, Meml. U., 1972, Queens U., 1988. Mem. staff Morgan Stanley & Co., N.Y.C., 1952-61, gen. ptnr., 1962-69; pres., chief exec. officer Brinco Ltd., Montreal, Que., Can., 1970-74, Churchill Falls (Labrador) Corp. Ltd., 1970-74; pres. Bank of Montreal, 1975-81, chief exec. officer, 1979-89, chmn. bd., 1981-90. Bd. dirs., mem. exec. com. Bank of Montreal, Can. Pacific Ltd., Upjohn Co.; bd. dirs. Brooks Fashion Stores, Kimberly-Clark Corp., Harris Bank Corp., Chgo., Rio Tinto-Zinc Corp., London, Standard Life Assurance Corp., Consol. Edinburgh, Consol. Bathurst Corp.; chmn. exec. com. Bank of Montreal, Upjohn, Colo. Life gov. Douglas Hosp., Montreal; hon. v.p. Quebec provincial coun. Boy Scouts Can.; mem. adv. coun. Ecole des Hautes Etudes Commerciales, Montreal; mem. adv. coun. Ctr. Can. Studies Sch. Advanced Internat. Studies Johns Hopkins U.; bd. dirs. Atlantic Salmon Fedn., St. Michael's Coll. Found.; Mounted Police Found., Conf. Bd. Can., Monreal Symphony Orch.; trustee Hudson Inst., Queen's U., Kingston, Can. Olympic Trust; fin. com. Queen's U.; nat. co-chmn. Can. Coun. Christians and Jews. Served as officer, inf. U.S. Army, 1944-46, PTO. Decorated Knight Comdr.'s Cross (Badge and Star) Order of Merit, Fed. Republic of Germany, 1989, Prime Minister's medal State of Israel, 1987; recipient Human Rels. award, Good Servant's medal Can. Coun. Christians and Jews, 1985. Mem. Mount Royal Club (Montreal), Caledon Riding and Hunt Club, Toronto Club. Roman Catholic. Office: Bank of Montreal 302 Bay St Ste 400 Toronto ON Canada M5X 1A1 Office Phone: 416-867-7611.

**MULHOLLEM, PAUL B.,** agricultural products executive; m. Valerie Mulhollem; 1 child, Claire Jean. Grad., U. Minn., 1971. Mng. dir. Archer Daniels Midland Internat. Ltd., London, 1992—96; v.p. Archer Daniels Midland Co., 1996—97, group v.p., 1997—99, sr. v.p. Global Oilseeds & Cocoa Decatur, Ill., 1999—2001, sr. v.p., Global Grain Ops., 2001, pres. & CEO, 2001—. Mem. Alfred C. Toepfer Internat. Bd., Agricore United Bd., Carle Found., Champaign, Ill. Office: Archer Daniels Midland Co 4666 Faries Pkwy Decatur IL 62526

**MULKEY, JACK CLARENDON,** retired library director; b. Shreveport, La., Oct. 31, 1939; s. Jack Youmans and Hilda Lillian (Beatty) Mulkey; m. Mary Lynn Shepherd, Jan. 30, 1971; 1 child, Mary Clarendon. BA, Centenary Coll., 1961; postgrad. (Rotary scholar), U. Dijon, France, 1961-62, Duke U. Law Sch., 1962-63; MS, La. State U., 1969. Jr. exec. Lykes Bros. S.S. Co., 1964-66; asst. dir. admissions Centenary Coll. of La., 1966-67; head reference services and acquisitions Shreveport Pub. Library, 1968-71; dir. Green Gold Library System of N.W. La., 1971-73; mgmt. cons. Miss. Library Commn., 1973-74, asst. dir. 1974-76, dir., 1976-78, Jackson Met. Library System, 1978-85; assoc. dir. Ark. State Library, 1986-2000; State Librarian of Ark., 2000—05; ret., 2005. Adj. prof. U. So. Miss. Grad. Sch. Libr. Sci., 1979—

treas., bd. dirs. Southeastern Library Network (SOLINET), 1985-86; cons. in field; mem. White House Conf. Taskforce on Libraries and Info. Services, 1980—. Chmn. Miss. Govs. Conf. on Libraries, 1979; chmn. Miss. delegation White House Conf. on Libraries, 1979; hon. del. White House Conf. on Librs., 1991. Served with USAF, 1963-64. Mem. ALA (chmn. state libr. agy. sect. 1995-97), Southeastern Libr. Assn. (bd. dirs. 1994—), Miss. Libr. Assn. (pres. 1981-82), Ark. Libr. Assn. (exec. bd. dirs. 1994—), Chief Officers of State Libr. Agys., Phi Alpha Delta, Beta Phi Mu, Omicron Delta Kappa, Phi Kappa Phi. Episcopalian. Home: 1805 Martha Dr Little Rock AR 72212-3840 Office: 1 Capitol Mall Little Rock AR 72201-1049 Personal E-mail: jmulkey@webtv.net.

**MULL, GALE W.,** lawyer; b. Hillsdale, Mich., Sept. 8, 1945; s. Wayne E. and Vivian M. (Bavin) M.; m. Holly Ann Allen, Aug. 2, 1969 (div. Nov. 1983); 1 child, Carter B.; m. Jeanne Anne Haughey, Aug. 18, 1985. BA, Mich. State U., 1967; MA in Sociology, Ind. U., 1969; JD, Emory U., 1972. Bar: Ga. 1972, U.S. Dist. Ct. (no. dist.) Ga. 1972, U.S. Ct. Appeals (5th cir.) 1973, U.S. Ct. Appeals (11th cir.) 1981. Instr. sociology Clemson (S.C.) U., 1968-69, Spelman Coll. Atlanta, 1969-70; pvt. practice, Atlanta, 1972-75; ptnr. Mull & Sweet, Atlanta, 1975-81; pres. Gale W. Mull, P.C., Atlanta, 1981—. Bd. dirs. BOND Community Fed. Credit Union, Atlanta, 1975-81; directing atty. Emory Student Legal Services, Atlanta, 1975-91; Sociology instr. Clemson U., Clemson, S.C., 1968-69, Spelman Coll., Atlanta, Ga., 1969-70. Pres. Inman Park Restoration, Inc., Atlanta, 1972—74, BASS Orgn. for Neighborhood Devel., Inc., 1974—78; mem. Housing Appeals Bd., Atlanta, 1982—88, Mayor's Task Force on Prostitution, 1984—86; bd. dirs. Trinity Towers, Inc., 1999—2000; vestry St. John's Episc. Ch., 1992—99, 2003—05, sr. warden, 1998—99, 2005—06; bd. dirs. St. John's Episcopal Day Sch., 1992—97, Bethlehem Ministries, 1997—, ACLU Ga., 1981—92, sec. bd. dirs., 1983—85, cooperating atty., 1972—. Mem. ABA, Ga. Bar Assn., Atlanta Bar Assn., Lawyers Club Atlanta. Clubs: Quail Unltd. (bd. dirs., sec. 1984-86). Office: 2149 Rugby Ave Atlanta GA 30337 Office Phone: 404-761-6600. Personal E-mail: galewmull@mindspring.com.

**MULL, ROBERT W.,** filmmaker, curator; b. Great Bend, Kans., Mar. 8, 1953; s. Charles Laverne and Mary Anne Mull; m. Donna Lee Howell, May 24, 1976 (div. Jan. 1980). B in Gen. Studies, U. Kans., 1976; MA, Ea. Wash. U., 1982. Curator Yakima (Wash.) Valley Mus., 1981—85, Pacific Sci. Ctr., Seattle, 1985—88; ind. documentary filmmaker Wash., 1981—93; ind. writer Seattle, 1993—. Cons. Wash. Commn. for Humanities, Olympia, 1982—85; founder, officer Wash. State Folklife Coun., Olympia, 1983—87; mem. planning com. Wash. 1989 Centennial, Seattle, 1988—89. Author: The Lupus Kid and Other Stories, 2002; prodr.: (documentaries) When Court Adjourned, 1982 (PBS award, 1983, Sepia award (State of Wash. award) 1988), Something To Win the War, 1985 (TLC award, 1987). Grants writer Harbor Assn. Vols., Westport, Wash., 1996—2000; publicist Seattle Housing Authority, 1999—2003. Named Alumnus of Yr., Ea. Wash. U., 1996; grantee, Wash. Commn. for Humanities, 1981, Wash. Centennial Commn., 1988. Mem.: Olive Ridge Cmty. Coun., Ea. Wash. U. Alumni Assn., N.W. chpt. Lupus Found. (event chmn. 2002, bd. dirs. 2003—, pres. 2005—). Congregationalist. Avocations: travel, reading, volunteer work. Home: 1700 17th Ave #608 Seattle WA 98122

**MULLALLY, MEGAN,** actress; b. LA, Nov. 12, 1958; d. Carter Mullally, Jr. and Martha Mullally; m. Michael Katcher (div.); m. Nick Offerman, Sept. 20, 2003. Student, Northwestern U. Actor: (TV films) Rainbow Drive, 1990, Winchell, 1998, Everything Put Together, 2000, Lifetime, The Pact, 2002; (TV series) My Life and Times, 1991, Ellen Burstyn Show, 1986, Fish Police, 1992, Rachel Gunn, RN, 1992, Will and Grace, 1998—2006 (Emmy Award Supporting Actress in a Comedy, 2000, Outstanding Comedy Series award, 2000, Am. Comedy Award, 2001, Outstanding Female Actor Award, 2001, Screen Actors Guild award Oustanding Actress in a Comedy Series, 2001, 2002, 2003, Emmy award for Outstanding Supporting Actress in a Comedy Series, 2006); (Broadway plays) Grease, 1994, How to Succeed in Business Without Really Trying, 1995—96; host (talk show) Megan Mullally Show, 2006—; actor: (films) Once Bitten, 1985, Last Resort, 1986, About Last Night, 1986, Anywhere But Here, 1999, Best Man in Grass Creek, 1999, Everything Put Together, 2000, Monkey Bone, 2001, Stealing Harvard, 2002; actor, actor: (films) Speaking of Sex, 2001, (voice) Teacher's Pet, 2004, Rebound, 2005, (guest appearance): (TV series) Murder, She Wrote, 1988, China Beach, 1989, Wings, 1990, Herman's Head, 1991, Seinfeld, 1993, Frasier, 1997, Mad About You, 1997, Caroline in the City, 1997, Just Shoot Me!, 1998, 3rd Rock from the Sun, 2000; (TV series, voice) King of the Hill, 2002. Office: The Gersh Agency PO Box 5617 Beverly Hills CA 90210 also: Will and Grace KoMut Entertainment 4024 Radford Ave Studio City CA 91604*

**MULLAN, BRIAN,** medical educator; b. Chgo., Apr. 21, 1963; s. Sean F. and Vivian C. Mullan; m. Karyn Shanks; children: Sean, Aidan. BA, Johns Hopkins U., Balt., 1985; MS, Northwestern U., Evanston, Ill., 1986; MD, U. Chgo. Med. Sch., 1991. Diplomate Am. Bd. Radiology, 1996. Assoc. prof and vice-chair dept. radiology U. Iowa, Iowa City, 2003—, chair, med. edn. com. Carver Coll. Medicine, 2004—06. Author: jour. articles in field. Recipient Collegiate Tchg. Award, U. Iowa, 2004, Louis D. Holloway award for Rsch. in Health Scis. Edn., 2004, Tchr. of Yr. for Med. Student Tchg., Dept. Radiology, Carver Coll. Medicine, U. Iowa, 1997, 1998, 1999, 2005. Office: Univ Iowa Dept Radiology 200 Hawkins Dr Iowa City IA 52245 Office Phone: 319-356-3562. Business E-Mail: brian-mullan@uiowa.edu.

**MULLAN, DONALD WILLIAM,** archbishop; b. Galt, Ont., Apr. 26, 1937; s. William James and Lillian Maude (Sachs) M.; m. Cathy Templeman. Met. bishop Christ Cath. Ch. Internat.; pastor Cathedral of St. Luke, Niagara Falls, Ont. Trustee Bd. Edn., Preston, Ont., 1962-68, Waterloo County, Ont., 1969-70, Wellington County, Ont., 1971-72. Mem. Order of Noble Companions of the Swan (grand prelate), Moose, Scouts of Can. E-mail: dmullan1@cogeco.ca.

**MULLAN, FITZHUGH,** public health physician; b. Tampa, Fla., July 22, 1942; s. Hugh and Mariquita (MacManus) Mullan; children: Meghan Elizabeth, Jason Michael, Caitlin Patricia. BA, Harvard U., 1964; MD, U. Chgo., 1968; DSc, U. Osteo. Medicine, 1993; LHD, Coll. Osteo. Medicine Pacific, 1993. Intern Jacobi Hosp., Bronx, 1968—70; resident Lincoln Hosp., Bronx, 1970—72; physician Nat. Health Svc. Corps., Santa Fe, 1972—75; dir. Nat. Health Svc. Corps, Rockville, Md., 1977—81; scholar-in-residence Inst. Medicine, Washington, 1981—82; dir. pub. health history project Office of Surgeon Gen., Rockville, 1988—90; sr. med. officer NIH, Bethesda, Md., 1982—84; sec. for health and environment State of N.Mex., Santa Fe, 1984—85; assoc. prof. Johns Hopkins Sch. Hygiene and Pub. Health, Balt., 1986—88; dir. bur. health professions USPHS, Rockville, 1990—96; contbr. editor Health Affairs, Bethesda, 1996—; clin. prof. pediats. and pub. health George Washington U., 1996—; asst. physician Upper Cardozo Cmty. Health Ctr., 1996—; Asst. Atty. Gen. US Pub. Health Svc. Author: White Coat, Clenched Fist: The Political Education of an American Physician, 1976, Vital Signs: A Young Doctor's Struggle With Cancer, 1983, Plagues and Politics: The Story of the United States Public Health Service, 1989; contbr. articles to profl. jours.; contbg. editor: Health Affairs, narrative matters section. Fellow: Am. Acad. Pediats.; mem.: Inst. of Medicine of NAS, Am. Assn. for History of Medicine, APHA, AMA. Office: Health Affairs 7500 Old Georgetown Rd Ste 600 Bethesda MD 20814-6133

**MULLAN, JOHN H.,** science administrator; b. Middletown, NY, Apr. 16, 1942; BA cum laude, Johns U.; LLB, Columbia U.; LLM in Taxation, NYU. Bar: NY 1968, Calif. 1997. From staff to dep. gen. counsel Grumman Corp., LA, 1975—94; from east coast litigation counsel to sr. corp. counsel Northrop Grumman Corp., LA, 1994—99, corp. v.p., sec., 1999—. Woodrow Wilson fellow, Stanford U., 1964—65. Office: Northrop Grumman Corp 1840 Century Park E Los Angeles CA 90067-2199

**MULLANE, DENIS FRANCIS,** insurance company executive; b. Astoria, N.Y., Aug. 28, 1930; s. Patrick F. and Margaret (O'Neill) M.; m. Kathryn Mullman, June 28, 1952; children: Gerard, Kevin, Denise. BS in Mil. Engring, U.S. Mil. Acad., 1952; LHD (hon.), U. Conn., 1988, St. Joseph's Coll., 1990; LLD (hon.), U. Hartford, 1993, Trinity Coll., Hartford, Conn., 1995; MS in Fin. Svcs., The Am. Coll., Bryn Mawr, Pa., 1995. CLU. With Conn. Mut. Life Ins. Co., Hartford, 1956—, v.p., 1969-72, sr. v.p., 1972-74, exec. v.p., 1974-76, pres., 1977—, chief exec. officer, 1983-85, chmn., chief exec. officer, 1985-90, chief exec. officer, pres., 1990-93; chmn. Mulane Enterprises, Inc., Hartford, Conn., 1994—; with Mullane Enterprises, West Hartford, Conn., 1994—. Bd. dirs. Conn. Natural Gas Co.; chmn. The Am. Coll., Bryn Mawr, Pa., 1993-96; chmn. joint planning com. Am. Coll. and Soc. Fin. Svcs. Profls., 1996-99. Dir. U.S. Chamber, 1991-95. 1st Lt. C.E., U.S. Army, 1952-56. Recipient John Newton Russell award, 1987, Knight of St. Gregory award, Disting. Grad. award USMA, 2004. Mem.: Assn. Grads. U.S. Mil. Acad. (bd. dirs. 1989—93), Nat. Assn. Ins. Fin. Advisors, Am. Soc. Corp. Execs. Republican. Roman Catholic. Office: Mullane Enterprises Inc 29 S Main St Hartford CT 06107-2449 Office Phone: 860-561-7650. E-mail: dmullane52@juno.com.

**MULLANE, JOHN FRANCIS,** pharmaceutical executive; b. NYC, Mar. 10, 1937; s. John Gerald and Rita Ann (Hoben) Mullane; m. Ruth Ann Cecka, Nov. 17, 1962; children: Rosemarie, Michael, Kathleen, Therese, Thomas. MD, SUNY Med. Ctr., 1963; PhD, SUNY, 1968; JD, Fordham U., 1977. Bar: NY 1978, DC 1979. Assoc. med. dir. Ayerst Labs. div. Am. Home Products Corp., N.Y.C., 1973-75, dir. clin. research, 1975-76, v.p. clin., 1977, v.p. sci., 1978-82, sr. v.p., 1982, exec. v.p., 1983-88; pres. Mullane Health Care Cons., N.Y.C. and Sarasota, Fla., 1989—; dir. drug devel. DuPont Med. Products, Wilmington, Del., 1990; sr. v.p. DuPont-Merck, Wilmington, 1991-94; exec. v.p. Amylin Pharms., 1994-96. Contbr. articles to profl. jours. Served to lt. col. US Army, 1970-73 Recipient Upjohn Achievement award, 1970; NY Heart Assn. Crawford-Maynard fellow, 1966-68 Fellow Am. Coll. Clin. Pharmacology; mem. ABA, Am. Soc. Clin. Pharmacology and Therapeutics, Am. Assn. Study of Liver Diseases, Misty Creek Country Club (pres. 2004-2005). Roman Catholic. Avocation: golf. Home and Office: 9047 Misty Creek Dr Sarasota FL 34241-9542 Personal E-mail: jfmullane@earthlink.net.

**MULLANY, GERRY,** editor; married. BA, Binghampton U., 1984. Dep. met. editor NY Times, asst. met. editor, politics. Office: NY Times Metropolitan Desk 229 West 43rd St New York NY 10036 Office Phone: 212-556-1533. Office Fax: 212-556-3690. E-mail: gemull@nytimes.com.*

**MULLANY, KEVIN FERGUS,** music educator, director; b. N.Y.C., June 7, 1968; s. Fergus and Elaine (Sigle) M.; m. Cristina; 1 child, Meghan L. BA in English, Queens Coll. 1997; MA in Music Edn., SUNY, 2004. Cert. music, English tchr. N.Y. Tchr. Forest Hills (N.Y.) Montessori Sch., 1992-97, Harbor Consevetory, N.Y.C., 1994-96; music dir. Garden Sch., Jackson Heights, NY, 1997—98; choral dir. Flushing H.S., Queens, 1999—. Author: (novel) La Telaraña, 1997, Collection of Short Stories, 1997, I Like to Hop; composer: Collective Solos for Piano, 1996, Collective Compositions for Chorus, 2005 Choir dir. St. Lucy-St. Patrick Ch., Bklyn., 1995—, organist, 1995—; children's choir dir. St. John Evangelist Ch. Bklyn., 1996-98. Writing award Queens Coll., 1994, 96. Mem. Tri-M Music Honor Soc., Music Educators Nat. Conf., Composers Guild, Am. Choral Drs. Assn., Nat. Assn. Composers (life). Home: 11114 14th Rd College Point NY 11356-1416 Office Phone: 718-888-7500 x 155. Business E-Mail: kmullan@nycboe.net.

**MULLARKEY, MARY J.,** state supreme court chief justice; b. New London, Wis., Sept. 28, 1943; d. John Clifford and Isabelle A. (Steffes) M.; m. Thomas E. Korson, July 24, 1971; 1 child, Andrew Steffes Korson. BA, St. Norbert Coll., 1965, LLD (hon.), 1989; LLB, Harvard U., 1968. Bar: Wis. 1968, Colo. 1974. Atty.-advisor U.S. Dept. Interior, Washington, 1968-73; asst. regional atty. EEOC, Denver, 1973-75; 1st atty. gen. Colo. Dept. Law, Denver, 1975-79, solicitor gen., 1979-82; legal advisor to Gov. Lamm State of Colo., Denver, 1982-85; ptnr. Mullarkey & Seymour, Denver, 1985-87; justice Colo. Supreme Ct., Denver, 1987, chief justice, 1998—. Fellow: Colo. Bar Found., ABA Found.; mem.: ABA, Denver Bar Assn. (Jud. Excellence award 2003), Colo. Women's Bar Assn. (Mary Lathrop award 2002), Colo. Bar Assn., Thompson G. Marsh Inn of Ct. (pres. 1993—94). Office: Supreme Ct Colo Jud Bldg 2 E 14th Ave Denver CO 80203-2115*

**MULLEN, DANIEL ROBERT,** finance company executive; b. Swedesboro, N.J., Apr. 17, 1941; s. Harold Legrand and Gladys (DeVault) M.; m. Elizabeth A. Willers, Dec. 17, 1977; children: William H., Jonathan O. BS in Fin., Ariz. State U., 1966, postgrad., 1966-67. Appraiser Ariz. Dept. Revenue, 1966—68; financial analyst Amerco, 1968—70, treas., 1970—82; pres. Continental Leasing Co., 1980—; v.p. Southwest Pipe and Supply Co., 1982; treas. Talley Industries, Inc., 1982—93, v.p., 1993—98; COO Friendship Publs., 1998—99. Bd. dirs. C Myers Corp., Amerco, U-Haul Internat. Oxford Life Ins. Co. Del. Ariz. Presdl. Dem. Conv., 1972; bd. dirs. Big Sisters of Ariz., 1975, Found. for Blind Children, 1984-90, Phoenix Little Theatre, 1985-91, Kachina Country Day Sch., 1988-94, New Way Sch., 1994-2000, Interfaith Coop. Ministries, 2003-, With U.S. Army, 1959-62. Ariz. Soc. CPAs grantee, 1964-65 Mem. Fin. Execs. Internat. Home: 3627 E Medlock Dr Phoenix AZ 85018-1505 Office Phone: 602-263-6123.

**MULLEN, EDWARD JOHN, JR.,** Spanish language educator; b. Hackensack, NJ, July 12, 1942; s. Edward J. and Elsie (Powell) M.; m. Helen Cloe Braley, Apr. 2, 1971; children: Kathleen, Julie Ann. BA, W.Va. Wesleyan Coll., 1964; MA, Northwestern U., 1965, PhD, 1968. Asst. prof. modern langs. Purdue U., West Lafayette, Ind., 1967-71; assoc. prof. Spanish U. Mo. Columbia, 1971-78, prof. Spanish, 1978—. Author: La Revista Contemporáneos, 1972, Carlos Pellicer, 1977, Langston Hughes in the Hispanic World and Haiti, 1977, The Life and Poems of a Cuban Slave: Juan Francisco Manzano 1797-1854, 1981, Critical Essays on Langston Hughes, 1986, Sendas Literarias: Hispanoamerica, 1988, El cuento hispánico, 1980, 84, 89, 94, 2000, 04, Afro-Cuban Literature: Critical Junctures, 1998; editor: The Harlem Group of Negro Writers (Melvin B. Tolson), 2001; co-editor Afro-Hispanic Rev., 1987—. Recipient Diploma de Honor Inst. de Cultura Hispánica, 1964; Woodrow Wilson fellow, 1964-65; Northwestern U. fellow, 1965-67; Rsch. grant U. Mo., 1972, 76; grantee Am. Council Learned Socs., 1979 Mem. MLA, Am. Assn. Tchrs. Spanish and Portuguese, Assn. of Depts. Fgn. Langs. (pres. 1989-91). Home: 207 Edgewood Ave Columbia MO 65203-3413 Office: U Mo Dept Romance Langs 143 Arts And Sci Bldg Columbia MO 65211-0001 Office Phone: 573-882-5041. Business E-Mail: mullene@missouri.edu.

**MULLEN, EILEEN ANNE,** human resources executive; b. Phila., Feb. 14, 1943; d. Joseph Gregory and Helen Rita (Kane) M.; m. William John Raschiatore (dec.). BS in English, St. Joseph's U., 1967; MA in English, Villanova U., 1978. Cert. tchr. Pa. Tchr. St. Anastasia Sch., Newtown Square, 1960-67, West Cath. Girls H.S., 1967-74; mgr. staff tng. and devel. ASTM, Phila., 1974-96. dir. human resources, 1996—. Instr. lit., speech and communications Widener U., Chester, Pa. and Wilmington, Del. Contbg. author articles on comms. tng. program; contbr. articles to profl. jours. Mem. ASTD (pres. Phila./Del. Valley chpt. 1980-81, Outstanding Leadership as Pres. award 1981), Soc. for Human Resource Mgmt. Democrat. Roman Catholic. Office: ASTM 100 Barr Harbor Dr West Conshohocken PA 19428-0700 Office Phone: 610-832-9766. Business E-Mail: emullen@astm.org.

**MULLEN, GRAHAM C.,** judge; b. 1940; BA, Duke U., 1962, JD, 1969. Bar: NC 1969. Ptnr. Mullen, Holland, Cooper, Morrow, Wilder & Sumner, 1969-90; judge US Dist. Ct. (We. Dist.) NC, Charlotte, 1990—99, chief judge, 1998—2005, sr. judge, 2005—. Lt. USN, 1962—66. Mem.: Mecklenburg County Bar Assn., NC Bar Assn. (bd. gov. 1983—88). Office: US Courthouse 401 W Trade St Rm 230 Charlotte NC 28202-1619 Office Phone: 704-350-7450. Business E-Mail: graham_mullen@ncwd.uscourts.gov.

**MULLEN, J. THOMAS,** lawyer; b. Evanston, Ill., Aug. 27, 1940; BSE, Princeton U., 1963; JD cum laude, U. Mich., 1967. Bar: Ill. 1967. Atty. Mayer, Brown, Rowe & Maw LLP, Chgo., 1967—74, ptnr., 1974—; ptnr.-in-charge London office London, 1974-78, ptnr. Chgo., 1978—. Chmn. recruiting com. Mayer, Brown, Rowe & Maw LLP. Bd. dirs. Legal Assistance Found. Chgo., 1979-85. Mem. ABA, Chgo. Bar Assn., Chgo. Coun. Lawyers, Ill. State Bar Assn., Law Club of Chgo. Office: Mayer Brown Rowe & Maw 71 S Wacker Dr Chicago IL 60606-4637 E-mail: tmullen@mayerbrownrowe.com.

**MULLEN, JAMES C.,** biotechnology company executive; b. 1959; m. Justine Mullen; 4 children. BS in Chem. Engring., Rensselaer Polytech. Inst., 1980; MBA, Villanova U., 1984. Various positions SmithKline Beckman Corp. (now GlaxoSmithKline plc), 1984—88; dir. facilities engring. Biogen, Inc., 1989—92, v.p. ops., 1992—96, v.p. internat., 1996—99, CEO, pres., 2000—03, chmn. bd., 2002—03; pres., CEO Biogen Idec Inc., 2003—. Bd. trustees Rensselaer Polytech. Inst.; bd. dirs. Biotech. Industry Orgn., Biomed. Scis. Careers Program, Pharmaceuticals Rsch. and Manufacturers Am., PerkinElmer, Inc., 2004—. Co-chair capital campaign steering com. Cambridge Family and Children's Svc. Responsible for the manufacturing and successful launch of AVONEX (Interferon beta-la), a world leading therapy for relapsing forms of multiple sclerosis. Office: Biogen Idec Inc 14 Cambridge Ctr Cambridge MA 02142*

**MULLEN, JAMES JOSEPH, III,** lawyer; s. James Joseph and Maria Isabel Mullen; m. Nancy Ellen Ross, July 27, 1996; children: Isabella Zenovia, Olivia Rasha, Samantha Maria. BA, U. Calif., San Diego, 1988; JD, U. Calif. Hastings Coll. Law, San Francisco, California, 1997; PhD, U.Tex. Grad. Sch. of Biomedical Scis., 1994. Bar: United State Patent and Trademark Office 1999, Calif. 1998. Assoc. Knobbe, Martens, Olson and Bear, LLP, San Diego, 1997—2003, Morrison & Foerster, LLP, San Diego, 2003—06, of counsel, 2006—. Office: Morrison Foerster Llp 12531 High Bluff Dr San Diego CA 92130-3014 Office Phone: 858-720-7940. Business E-Mail: jmullen@mofo.com.

**MULLEN, MAUREEN ANN,** social worker; b. Chgo., Mar. 22, 1949; d. Robert Vincent and Mary Geraldine M. BA, U. Ill., 1971; MEd, Coll. of William and Mary, 1974; MSW, Univ. Ill., 1990; postgrad., U. Chgo., 1985, 86. Programmer Computer Task Group, N.Y.C., 1980-81; analyst, programmer Guy Carpenter, N.Y.C., 1981-82; analyst C.N.A. Ins., Chgo., 1982-84; analyst, programmer Lakeshore Nat. Bank, Chgo., 1984-85; sales support Sterling Software, Chgo., 1986; owner Mullen Designs, Chgo., 1987; dir. of social svcs. Vista Health, Fayetteville, Ark., 2002—03; employee assistance counselor Ark. Employee Assistance Program, Fayetteville, 2003—06. Prodr., host (TV show) Ozarks Live!, 2003—06. Vol. Samaritans Hotline, Chgo., 1986; adv. bd. Lakeview Mental Health Ctr., Chgo., 1986; active Chgo. Coun. on Fgn. Rels., 1986—87; chmn. fundraiser Habitat for Humanity, 1987; vol. Manic Depressive and Depressive Assn. and Nat. Alliance for Rsch. into Schizophrenia and Depression, 1988, Wilmette Sch. Bd. Caucus, 1997, endowment fund com., 1996—97; vol. Chgo. Bot. Garden, 1999; spkrs. chmn. Fayetteville Freedom Festival, 2003; nominating com. ACLU, 2005—; vol. Thomas Hynes campaign, Chgo., 1987, New Trier Dem. Orgn., 2000; alderman candidate, 2004; bd. dirs. ACLU N.W. Ark., 2005—06, N.W. Ark. Mental Health Assn., 2002—04, chmn. sch. libr. book project, 2002, 2003; bd. dirs. Cmty. Access TV, Fayetteville, 2003—. Recipient Fat Cat award, Cmty. Access TV, Fayetteville, 2003—05; Ill. State scholar, 1971. Mem.: ACLU (bd. dirs. NW Ark. chpt. 2005—06), NOW, Nature Conservancy, Sierra Club, Dem. Nat. Com., So. Poverty Law Ctr. Avocations: painting, poetry, backpacking, photography, acting. Home: 51 Grove Hill Ave Newton MA 02460 Office Phone: 617-678-3773. Personal E-mail: momoses2002@yahoo.com.

**MULLEN, MICHAEL G.,** career military officer; b. LA; m. Deborah Morgan; children: John, Michael. Graduate, U.S. Naval Acad., 1968; MSc in Ops. Rsch., Naval Postgraduate Sch., 1985. Enlisted USN, 1968, advanced through grades to adm., 2003; stationed on USS Collett, USS Blandy; comdr. USS Noxubee, 1973-75; company officer, exec. asst. U.S. Naval Acad., 1975-78; chief engr. USS Fox, 1978-80; exec. officer USS Sterett, 1981-83; comdr. USS Goldsborough, 1985-87; dir. division officer course Surface Warfare Officer's Sch., 1987-89; staff asst. for navy programs Office of the Sec. Defense, 1989-91; comdr. USS Yorktown, 1992-94; from dir. surface officer distribution divsn. to dep. dir. Bureau of Naval Personnel, 1994-96; comdr. Cruiser-Destroyer Group 2, 1996-98; dir. surface warfare divsn. Office of Chief of Naval Ops., 1998—2000; comdr. SECOND fleet/ Striking Fleet Atlantic, 2000—01; dep. chief naval ops., resources, requirements & assessments USN, 2001—03, vice chief naval ops., 2003—04, chief of naval ops. Washington, 2005—; comdr. US Naval Forces Europe, 2004—05, Regional Command South, Naples, Italy, 2004—05. Office: Office Chief Naval Oper 1200 Navy Pentagon Washington DC 20350*

**MULLEN, MICHAEL T.,** lawyer; b. Evanston, Ill., Apr. 15, 1956; s. George Martin and Marguerite (Tully) M.; m. Patricia Reilly, Apr. 24, 1987; children: Claire, Catherine, Michael, Conor. BA, Marquette U., 1978; JD, Loyola U., 1981. Bar: Ill. 1981, U.S. Dist. Ct. (no. dist.) Ill. 1981, U.S. Ct. Appeals (7th cir.) 1981, U.S. Supreme Ct., 2000. Assoc. atty. gen. Ill. Atty. Gen., Chgo., 1981—85; asst. U.S. atty. U.S. Atty., Chgo., 1985—90, 1990—92, dep. chief, 1990—92; ptnr. Mullen & Minella, Chgo., 1992—98, Paul B. Episcope, Ltd., Chgo., 1998—. Contbr. articles to profl. jours. Trustee Village of Western Springs (Ill.), 1995—. Recipient Spl. Achievement award for sustained superior U.S. Dept. Justice, 1988, performance award 1990; named to Loyola Acad. Athletic Hall of Fame. Mem. Ill. State Bar Assn., Ill. Trial Lawyers Assn., West Suburban Bar Assn. lawyer for multiple cases with multimillion dollar jury verdicts and settlements. Office: Paul B Episcope Ltd 77 W Washington St Ste 300 Chicago IL 60602-2896 Office Phone: 312-782-6636. E-mail: mtm@episcopeltd.com

**MULLEN, PETER P.,** lawyer; b. N.Y.C., Apr. 8, 1928; m. Cecilia Kirby; 5 children. AB cum laude, Georgetown U., 1948; LLB, Columbia U., 1951. Bar: N.Y. 1951. Ptnr. Skadden, Arps, Slate, Meagher & Flom LLP, N.Y.C., 1961—98, exec. ptnr., 1981—94, of counsel, 1998—. Co-chmn. Cardinal's Com. Laity Archdiocese N.Y., 1989-2003; bd. dirs., sec., treas. Eye Surgery, Inc. Formerly mem., pres. Bd. Edn. Pub. Schs., Bronxville, N.Y., 1979-81; chmn. Skadden Fellowship Found., 1988—; bd. dirs., vice-chmn. Lawrence Hosp., Bronxville, 1984-89; bd. dirs., sec. Project Orbis Internat., 1985—; Georgetown U., Washington, 1982-99, chmn., 1985-92; bd. dirs. Legal Aid Soc., 1987-93, Vols. Legal Svcs., Inc., 1988-99, United Way Bronxville, 1985-93, New Milford Hosp. Found., 1997-. Practicing Attys. Law Students, 1988-99; trustee Lawyer's Commn. Civil Rights Under Law, 1984-99; chmn. Gregorian U. Found., 1989—; bd. dirs., exec. com. Vatican Obs. Found., 1993— Named Man of Yr. Cath. Big Bros., 1987; recipient John Carroll award Georgetown U., 1984, John Carroll Medal Merit, 1988, Thomas More award Lawyers Com. Cardinal's Com. of the Laity, 1996, Elizabeth Ann Seton award Nat. Cath. Edn. Assn., 1998; named Stone scholar Columbia U. 1951. Mem. ABA, Assn. Bar City N.Y., Soc. Friendly Sons St. Patrick (N.Y., pres. 1989-90), Knight Malta. Office: Skadden Arps Slate et al LLP 4 Times Sq New York NY 10036-6522

**MULLEN, ROD,** nonprofit organization executive; b. Puyallup, Wash., Aug. 2, 1943; s. Charles Rodney and Grace Violet (Fritsch) M.; m. Lois Fern Tobiska, May 3, 1963 (div. Jan. 1977); children: Cristina, Charles, Moneka; m. Naya Arbiter, Oct. 17, 1977. Student, U. Idaho, 1961—63; AB in Polit. Sci., U. Calif., Berkeley, 1966; postgrad., San Francisco Art Inst., 1968. Dir. Oakland (Calif.) facility Synanon Found., Inc., 1971-72, dir. San Francisco facility, 1972-73, dir. Tomales Bay (Calif.) facility, 1976-78, dir. Synanon edn. programs, 1973-76; treatment dir. nat. programs Vision Quest, Inc., Tucson, 1981-82; dir. resources and devel. Amity, Inc., Tucson, 1982-84, exec. dir., 1984-95; founder, pres., CEO Amity Found., Porterville, Calif. 1995—. Mem. Nat. Adv. Com. on Substance Abuse Prevention, 1990-96; adv. bd. Ctr. for Therapeutic Cmty. Rsch., Nat. Devel. and Rsch. Insts., NYC, 1991-2002; cons. Calif. Office Criminal Justice Planning, Sacramento, 1993;

prin. investigator program Nat. Inst. on Drug Abuse, 1990-93; pres. Calif. Therapeutic Com., 2004-; editl. adv. bd. Offender Substance Abuse Report, 2000-2004. Dir.: (documentaries) Prodigal Daughters, 2002, TC Pioneers, 2003, The Therapeutic Community, 2005, Encounter Groups, 2006; contbr. chapters to books, articles to profl. jours. Mem.: Calif. Therapeutic C. (pes. 2004—06), Therapeutic Coms. of Am. (treas. 2006—), Am. Correctional Assn. Office: Amity Found 120 S Houghton Rd Ste 138 PMB 321 Tucson AZ 85748-2155 Office Phone: 520-749-8211. Business E-Mail: rmullen@amityfdn.org.

**MULLEN, RON,** insurance company executive; b. Tex., Aug. 8, 1939; s. Durward Lacy and Blanche V. (Coulson) M.; m. Carole King, Dec. 29, 1959; children: Lacy Lynne Holcomb, Misty Kay. Student, Abilene Christian Coll., 1957-58, San Antonio Coll., 1958-59; BBA, S.W. Tex. State U., 1965. C.L.U., Chartered Fin. Cons. City council mem. City of Austin, 1977-83, mayor, 1983-85; mgr. Prin. Fin. Group, Austin, 1965-98, Ron Mullen & Assocs. Inc., Austin, 1966—, InNet Fin. Group; prin. Small Employer Benefits L.P. Chmn. TML Ins. Trust Fund Com., 1983—; mem. Gov.'s Task Force on State Employees Health Ins. Benefits, Austin, 1984 Chmn. Austin Transp. Study Com., Austin, 1983—, Greater Austin-San Antonio Corridor Coun., 1984—, Social Policy Adv. Com., Austin, 1979-80, March of Dimes campaign, Austin, 1974-75; co-chmn. Consumers United for Rail Equity, Austin, 1983—; v.p. Austin Symphony Orch., 1974-75; mem. exec. com. Capital Area Planning Coun., Austin, 1976—, exec. bd. Tex. Mcpl. League, Austin, 1983—, Gov.'s Task Force on Indigent Health Care, Austin, 1984, Tex. Adv. Commn. on Intergovtl. Rels., Austin, 1981—; chmn. Infant Parent Tng. Ctr., 1985-98; bd. dirs., chmn. South MoPac Transp. Com., 1986-87; life mem. Austin Jaycees, bd. dirs., 1974-75; vice-chmn. Mental Health Mental Retardation Bd.; vice chmn. South Tex. Audio Reader Svc.; bd. dirs. BBB, Inc., Hyde Park Bapt. Sch., 1999—. Recipient Road Hand award Tex. Dept. Hwys. and Transp., 1985, award for regional statesmanship Greater Austin-San Antonio Corridor Commn.; named Boss of Yr., Treaty Oaks chpt. Am. Bus. Women's Assn., 1978, Nat. Mgr. of Yr., Bankers Life Ins. Co., 1977, 82, 84-85, Alumnus of Yr. Austin Jaycees, 1988-90. Mem. Am. Coll. Life Underwriters (pres.), Tex. Assn. Life Underwriters (pres. 1997-98), Austin Assn. Life Underwriters (pres. 1974-75), Austin Gen. Agts. and Mgrs. Assn. (pres. 1978-80), Sales and Mktg. Execs. of Austin (pres. 1972-73), Downtown Rotary (pres. 1996-97), Tex. Assn. Ins. and fin. Advisors (nat. committeeman). Baptist. Home: 6902 Mesa Dr Austin TX 78731-2822 Office Phone: 512-973-9993. Personal E-mail: ron9991@msn.com.

**MULLEN, THOMAS EDGAR,** real estate consultant; b. Hackensack, N.J., Feb. 10, 1936; s. Luke B. and Jean (Edgar) M.; m. Sarah Lee Huff, Aug. 17, 1984. BS in Engring., Va. Poly. Tech., 1954; grad mgmt. program, Harvard U., 1964. Cons. in field. Mgr. mktg. Eastern Airlines, N.Y.C., 1955—69; pres. Profl. Sprits Mktg., N.Y.C., 1969—72, Shelter Devel. Corp. Am., N.Y.C., 1972—79; supr. ops. Gen. Mills, Orlando, Fla., 1980—86; cons., exec., realtor A.H.M. Graves Co. Inc., Indpls., 1986—92; pres. Pegasus Assocs. Ltd., 1992—. Inventor TV Guider Holder, patent, 1971. Fundraiser Am. Cancer Soc., Miami, 1967-70, Westchester Hosp., N.Y.C., 1967-70; pres. Brighton Found. Mem. Met. Bd. Realtors, Builders Assn. Greater Indpls. (bd. dirs.), Ind. Builders Assn. (bd. dirs.), Nat. Assn. Realtors, Inst. Residential Mktg. (pres. sales & mktg. coun., bd. dirs.). Republican. Roman Catholic. Avocations: tennis, recreational pilot. Home: 6251 Behner Way Indianapolis IN 46250-1494 Office Phone: 317-845-8467. E-mail: t.mullen@mindspring.com.

**MULLEN, WILLIAM JOSEPH, III,** military analyst, retired army career officer; b. Plattsburg, NY, Dec. 26, 1937; s. William Joseph Jr. and Georgia (Cook) M.; m. Norma Sturgeon, Aug. 6, 1962; 1 child, William Joseph IV. BS, U.S. Mil. Acad., West Point, N.Y., 1959; MS in Internat. Affairs, George Washington U., 1971. Commd. 2d lt. U.S. Army, 1959, advanced through grades to brig. gen., 1987; various assignments in U.S., Vietnam, Korea, Panama, Germany, Saudi Arabia, 1959-92; mem. staff, faculty U.S. Mil. Acad., West Point, 1967-70; comdr. 1st Brigade, 1st Inf. Div., Ft. Riley, Kans., 1983-86; asst. div. comdr. 5th Inf. Div., Ft. Polk, La., 1986-87; comdg. gen. U.S. Army Combined Arms Tng. Activity, Ft. Leavenworth, Kans., 1987-89, 1st Inf. Div. (Forward), Germany, 1989-91; dep. dir. ops. J3 Forces Command, Ft. McPherson, Ga., 1991-92; sr. mgr. mil. tng. and analysis sys. BDM Fed., Inc., Monterey, Calif., 1992-98; sr. program mgr. tng. mgmt. sys. Northrop Grumman Mission Sys., Monterey, 1998—2004; ret., 2004; cons. Army Operations and Tng., 2004—. Co-author: Changing an Army, An Oral History of Gen. W.E. DePuy, 1979; contbr. articles, book revs. to Mil. Rev. Decorated D.S.C., D.S.M. Mem. Assn. U.S. Army, Assn. Grads. U.S. Mil. Acad. (bd. dir. West Point Soc. of Monterey Peninsula 2005-), Soc. 1st Div. (chpt. officer 1968, assoc. 1989-93, trustee found. 1989-93, bd. dir.), Legion of Valor (bd. dir. 2005-), Nat. Infantry Assn. (Order of St. Maurice). Avocations: sports, reading. *When in doubt, I have always found direction from the guidance explicit in the 1st Infantry Division's motto, "Duty First!"*

**MULLENDORE, WALTER EDWARD,** retired economist; b. Harrah, Okla., Apr. 22, 1940; s. Newton and Ida Minnie (Lohmann) M.; m. Edra Janell Havenstrite, July 4, 1963; children: Matthew Edward, Karen Kay, Mark Andrew. BS, Okla. State U., 1961, MS, 1963; PhD in Econs., Iowa State U., 1968. Grad. asst. Okla. State U., 1961-63; instr. Iowa State U., 1965-67; mem. faculty dept. econs. U. Tex., Arlington, 1968—2002, prof., 1975—2002, dean Coll. of Bus., 1980—93; ret., 2002. Contbr. articles to profl. jours. Served with U.S. Army, 1963-65. Mem. Mo. Valley Econ. Assn. (v.p. 1980-81, pres. 1982-83), Gt. S.W. Rotary (pres. 1989-90), Omicron Delta Epsilon. Methodist. Home: 8003 John T White Rd Fort Worth TX 76120-3611

**MULLENIX, LINDA SUSAN,** law educator; b. N.Y.C. Oct. 16, 1950; d. Andrew Michael and Roslyn Marasco; children: Robert Bartholomew, John Theodore. William Joseph. BA, CCNY, 1971 M Philosophy, Columbia U., 1974; PhD Pres.'s fellow, 1977; JD, Georgetown U., 1980. Bar: D.C. 1981, U.S. Dist. Ct. D.C. 1981, U.S. Ct. Appeals (D.C. cir.) 1981, U.S. Supreme Ct. 1986, Tex. 1991, U.S. Ct. Appeals (5th cir.) 1995. U. Md. European divsn. Ramstein, Germany, 1974; adj. instr. Fordham U., N.Y.C., 1975—76, adj. asst. prof., 1977; instr. N.Y. Inst. Tech., N.Y.C., 1976; assoc. prof., lectr. George Washington U., Washington, 1977-80; asst. prof. Am. U., Washington, 1979; assoc. Pierson, Ball & Dowd, Washington, 1980-81; clin. prof. Loyola U. Law Sch., L.A., 1981-82; asst. prof. Cath. U. Law Sch., Washington, 1984-86; assoc. prof., 1986-90; prof., 1990; Reuschlein disting. vis. chair Villanova Law Sch., 2000. Vis. asst. prof. CCNY, 1977, Cooper Union Advancement Sci., Art, N.Y.C., 1977, Loyola U. Law Sch., L.A., 1982-83. Cath. U. Law Sch., Washington, 1983-84; jud. fellow U.S. Supreme ct. and fed. Jud. Ctr., 1989-90; Bernard J. Ward Centennial prof. U. Tex., 1991-2001, Morris and Rita Atlas chair in advocacy, 2001—; vis. prof. Harvard Law Sch., 1994-95. Mich. Law Sch., 1996; resident scholar Rockefeller Found. Bellagio (Italy) Study Ctr., 2002. Author: Mass Tort Litigation: Cases and Materials, 1996, Civil Procedure Roadmap, 1997, Casenotes: Federal Courts, 1997, ExamPro: Civil Procedure, 1998, State Class Actions: Practice and Procedure, 2000, Civil Procedure, 2004; co-author: Understanding Federal Courts, 1998, Federal Courts in the Twenty-First Century, 1996, 2d edit., 2002; Moore's Federal Practice and Procedure, 1991, 97, and annual updates; editor bibliographies Polit. Theory, A. Jour. Polit. Philosophy, 1972-74, The Tax Lawyer Jour., 1978-80; columnist The National Law Jour., 1998—; contbr. editor preview of U.S. Supreme Ct. Cases; co-reporter Report and Plan of Civil Justice Reform Act Adv. Group, S.d., Tex., 1991; assoc. reporter ALI, Restatement of the Law Governing Lawyers; contbr. articles to profl. jours. Alt. del. Dem. State Conv., 1980. Fellow NDEA, 1971-74; N.Y. State Regents Scholar, 1967-71. Fellow Tex. Bar Found.; mem. ABA (reporter task force on class actions 1995-97), Internat. Assn. Procedural Law, Am. Law Inst., DC Bar Assn. (com. on ethics, CLE and the Model Rules 1987), Am. Assn. Law Schs. (com. sect. on civil proc. 1987-88, exec. com., sec. on conflicts of law 1991-92, chair profl. devel. com. 1990-93), Jour. Legal Edn. (editl. bd. 1997-1999), Phi Beta Kappa. Home: 722 Crystal Creek Dr Austin TX 78746-4730 Office: U Tex Sch Law 727 E Dean Keeton St Austin TX 78705-3224 Office Phone: 512-232-1375. Business E-Mail: lmullenix@law.utexas.edu.

**MULLENS, DELBERT W.,** automotive executive; b. Buffalo; children: Dorian, Mandy. BA in History and English, minor in Bus., Tenn. State U.; EdM, U. Buffalo, 1974; studied Metallurgy, Lehigh U. With Bethlehem Steel; CEO Wesley Ind., Inc., Bloomfield Hills, Mich. Trustee U. Buffalo; founder Thinking Outside the Box Scholarship award, U. Buffalo, 1992—; chmn., Campaign for U. Buffalo: Generation to Generation Com., Grad. Sch. Edn. U. Buffalo. Named Entrepreneur of Yr., Mich. Commerce Dept.; recipient Lifetime Achievement award, Nat. Black MBA Assn.

**MULLENS, WILLIAM REESE,** retired insurance company executive; b. Franklin, Tenn., Sept. 12, 1921; s. William Pope and Elizabeth (Reese) M.; m. Katherine Ann Jones, Nov. 24, 1945; children: Jo Ann Mullens Sanditz, Carol Ann Mullens Slegers. BA, Vanderbilt U., 1942. With Bus. Men's Assurance Co., Kansas City, Mo., 1947-75, exec. v.p., dir., 1969-75; pres., dir. J.C. Penney Life Ins. Co., 1975-82; pres. Gt. Am. Res. Ins. Co., 1975-84, dir., 1975-89. Dir. Nat. Fidelity Life Ins. Co., 1986-89 Served to lt. comdr. USNR, 1943-46. Fellow Soc. Actuaries; mem. Phi Beta Kappa, Alpha Tau Omega. Presbyterian. Home: One McKnight Pl Apt 118 Saint Louis MO 63124

**MULLER, CAROLYN BUE,** physical therapist, volunteer; b. Crosby, N.D., Feb. 24; d. Sigurd Christian and Eleanor (Rushfeldt) Bue; m. Willard Chester Muller, Jan. 27, 1945; children: Marolyn Jean, Barbara Anne, Nancy Eleanor. BA, St. Olaf Coll., 1940; cert. in phys. therapy, Harvard U., 1944. Assoc. dir. younger girls and phys. edn. sect. YWCA, Syracuse, N.Y., 1940-43; phys. therapist Valley Forge Hosp., Phoenixville, Pa., 1944-45; med. records libr. Trust Territory of Pacific Islands, Truk, Caroline Islands, 1951-52. Founder, prin. organizer Am. Cmty. Sch., Truk, 1952, Lincoln Sch., Katmandu, Nepal, 1956, Am. Cmty. Sch., Mogadiscio, Somali Republic, 1958, Kampala, Uganda, 1966; panelist workshop Wash. Commn. for Humanities, Yakima, 1996. Author: Living in Uganda, 1967; cartographer: Maudie - An Oregon Trail Childhood, 1993. Charter registrar Clallam County Mus. and Hist. Soc., Port Angeles, Wash., 1977-87; vol. reading tutor Port Angeles Sch. Dist., 1980—; cmty. coord. UNICEF, Port Angeles, 1982-85; rep. Target Wash. Seminar, Seattle, 1984; rep. Asia-Can. Women in Mgmt. Conf., Victoria, B.C., Can., 1985; regional judge Wash. State Nat. History Day Contest, Port Angeles, 1985-2002; selection judge Wash. State Inquiring Mind Lecture Series, Seattle, 1989, 90, 96, organizer/coord., Inquiring Mind Lecture Series 1983-2002; Wash. state judge Nat. History Day Contest, Ellensburg, Wash., 1993-2003; bd. dirs. Wash. State Friends of the Humanities, 1991-94; trustee Wash. Commn. for the Humanities, 1995-97; pres. Am. Women's Club, Katmandu, 1957-58, Mogadiscio, 1959-60; v.p. Internat. Women's Club, Saigon, South Vietnam, 1971; mem. selection com. Evergreen State Soc. Awards, 1998, 99. Recipient Women Making a Difference award Soropimist Internat., 1984, Outstanding Vol. award Citizens' Edn. Ctr. N.W., 1988, Evergreen award Evergreen State Soc., 1992. Mem. AAUW (bd. dirs. 1980-84, Edn. Found. scholarship in her name 1996). PEO (rec. sec. 1984-85, v.p. 1985-86, pres. 1987-89, chaplain 1994, Internat. Peace scholarship in her name 1990, state chmn. Internat. Peace scholarship 1989-90), Washington Athletic Club. Avocations: growing flowers, cross-country walking, painting, reading, travel. Home: 3624 S Mount Angeles Rd Port Angeles WA 98362-8910 E-mail: muller@tenforward.com.

**MULLER, DAVE,** artist; b. San Francisco, 1964; MFA, Calif. Inst. Art, 1993; attended, Fine Arts Grad. Program Sch. Visual Arts, NY, 1990—91. Founder Three Day Weekend, LA. One-man shows include Woo, Mint Gallery, Calif. Arts, 1992. A Number of Ladders (Borrowed), Broad Studio #2, Cal Arts, 1993, Studio 246, Kunstlerhaus Bethanian, Berlin, 1996, Love Is All Around, Spanish Box, Santa Barbara, Calif., 1997, L.A., L.A., L.A., L.A., L.A., L.A., Blum & Poe, Santa Monica, Calif., 1998, here & now, Four Walls, San Francisco, 1999, The Approach, London, 2002, Blum & Poe, LA, 2003, San Francisco Mus. Modern Art, 2003, Engholm Engelhorn, Vienna, 2004, exhibited in group shows at Sound Art Derby, Beyond Baroque, Venice, Calif., 1993, On the Eve of New Years: Eve A Cocktail Party, Three Day Weekend, LA, 1994, Smells Like Vinyl, Roger Merians Gallery, NY, 1995, Love's Labor's Lost, SITE, NY, 1996, Hot Coffee, Artist's Space, NY, 1997, Three Day Weekend, P-House, Tokyo, 1997, LA or Lilliput?, Long Beach Mus. Art, Calif., 1998, Standing Still and Walking in LA, Gagosian Gallery, Beverly Hills, Calif., 1999, Subtle Occupation, Murray Guy, NY, 2003, For the Record: Drawing Contemporary Life, Vancouver Art Gallery, BC, Can., 2003, It Happened Tomorrow, 7th Lyon Biennale of Contemporary Art, Lyon, 2003, Playlist, Palais de Tokyo, Paris, 2004, Whitney Biennial, Whitney Mus. Am. Art, 2004. Mailing: c/o Blum & Poe 2754 South La Cienega Blvd Los Angeles CA 90034

**MULLER, DAVID EUGENE,** mathematics professor, computer scientist, educator; b. Austin, Tex., Nov. 2, 1924; s. Hermann Joseph Muller and Jessie Marie Jacobs; m. Denise Josee Impens, Mar. 3, 1990; m. Alice Mimi Held (dec.); children: Kenneth, Chandra. BS. Caltech, Pasadena, 1947, PhD, 1951; PhD (hon.), U. Paris, 1989. Prof. U. Ill., Urbana, 1952—92, prof. emeritus, 1992—. Adj. prof. N.Mex. State U., N.Mex., 1995—. With USN, 1944—46. Fellow: AAAS. Home: 4200 Sotol Dr Las Cruces NM 88011 Personal E-mail: dmuller@cybermesa.com.

**MULLER, EDWARD ROBERT,** energy executive, lawyer; b. Phila., Mar. 26, 1952; s. Rudolph E. and Elizabeth (Steiner) M.; m. Patricia Eileen Bauer, Sept. 27, 1980; children: Margaret Anne, John Frederick. AB summa cum laude, Dartmouth Coll., 1973; JD, Yale U., 1976. Assoc. Leva, Hawes, Symington, Martin & Oppenheimer, Washington, 1977-83; dir. legal affairs Life Scis. group Whittaker Corp., Arlington, Va., 1983-84; v.p. Whittaker Health Svcs., Arlington, Va., 1984-85; v.p., gen. counsel, sec. Whittaker Corp., L.A., 1985-93, chief adminstrv. officer, 1988-92, CFO, 1992-93, bd. dirs., 1993-99; v.p., gen. counsel, sec. BioWhittaker, Inc., Walkersville, Md., 1991-93; pres., CEO bd. dirs. Edison Mission Energy, Irvine, Calif., 1993-2000; chmn., pres., CEO Mirant Corp., Atlanta, 2005—. Bd. dirs. Oasis Residential, Inc., Las Vegas, 1995—98, GlobalSantaFe Corp., Houston, 1997—, Interval, Inc., Marina del Rey, Calif., 2000—05, Strategic Data Corp., Santa Monica, Calif., 2001—05. The Keith Cos., Inc., Irvine, Calif., 2001—05, RigNet, Inc., Houston, 2002—05, RealEnergy, Inc., Woodland Hills, Calif., 2003—05, Ormat Tech., Inc., Sparks, Nev., 2004—05; mem. Brookings Task Force on Civil Justice Reform, 1988—89; chmn. U.S.-Philippines Bus. Com., 1998—2000; adv. bd. Tennenbaum Capital Ptnrs., LLC, L.A., 1997—2003; mem. Coun. on Fgn. Rels., 1998—, Pacific Coun. on Internat. Policy, 1998—; pres. chmn. Contact Energy Ltd., Wellington, New Zealand, 1999—2000. Trustee Exceptional Children's Found., L.A., 1988-94, treas., 1988-93; co-chair Internat. Energy Devel. Coun., Washington, 1993-00; bd. govs. Jr. Achievement of Orange County and the Inland Empire, 1995-96; mem. Pres. Leadership Coun., Dartmouth Coll., 2003—; trustee Riverview Sch., East Sandwich, Mass, 2004—; bd. advisors The Pathway Program UCLA Ext. LA, 2004—. Office: Mirant Corp 1155 Perimeter Ctr W Atlanta GA 30338

**MÜLLER, GENE ALAN,** historian, consultant; b. Grand Island, Nebr. Jan. 10, 1943; s. Ludwig Frederick Alex and Erma Gertrude (Gorin) M.; m. Diana June Currey; children: Michelle Nicole Müller-Mehta, Alyssa Katherine, Alexandra Mariel, Nicholas Christian. B.A. cum laude, Midland Lutheran Coll., Fremont, Nebr., 1965; NYU in Spain scholar, U. Madrid, 1963-64; Fulbright-Hays scholar, U. Nacional Tucuman, Argentina, 1965-66; M.A., U. Kans., Lawrence, 1969, Ph.D, 1982. Asst. instr. U.Kans., 1967-73; asst. prof. history Ft. Hays State U., Kans., 1973-74; bilingual prof. history, El Paso Community Coll., Tex., 1974—; project reviewer Nat. Endowment Humanities, 1978—. Author: The Church in Poverty: Bishops, Bourbons, and Tithes in Spanish Honduras, 1700-1821; A Select Bibliography on the Catholic Church in Latin America, The Status of the Clergy and the Condition of the Church Wealth in Mexico: 1800-1850, Dr. Tomas Ruiz: Founder of Univ. of Nicaragua and Precursor of C.Am. Independence, 1777-1819, John Gorin of Fairfax County, Virginia: Defender of Mt. Vernon in 1781; also articles, book revs., chpts. in books. Minister Port El Paso Council Internat. Visitors, 1982-83, pres., 1983-85; pres. So. N.Mex./El Paso br. Lutheran Brotherhood, v.p. Thrivent fraternal chpt., 2003-05; bd. dirs. Nat. Council for Internat. Visitors, Leadership El Paso, Class VIII; pres. El Paso chpt. Am. Field Service; mem.

El Paso County Coun. for the Social Studies, regional chairperson, Regional Fulbright Tchr. Exchg. Interview Com.; pres., bd. dirs. El Paso Mission Trails Assn.; moderator Nat. Issues Forums, 1985—; coordinator NCIV/USAID Midwinter Seminar, El Paso, 1983-86, NEH Summer Seminar U. Tex., El Paso, 1986; lay asst. Luth. Quad Parish of Western, Kans. Am. Field Service scholar, New Zealand, 1960; NDFL Title VI fellow U. Kans., 1969; Ford Found. grantee, Nicaragua, 1969, Central Am., 1970; OAS fellow to Guatemala, 1973; Fulbright summer grantee, Brazil, 1982, Netherlands, 1983; sr. Fulbright lectr., U. Costa Rica, 1987, Fulbright-Alfonso Gercia Robles sr. lectr., UACJ, Mex., 1992-93, Fulbright-Hays, Nepal and India, 2003; recipient Burlington No. Teaching award, 1988, Outstanding Alumni award Midland Luth. Coll., 1988, El Paso Energy Found. award, 1993-94, EPCC Faculty Achievement award, 2004, NISOD Master Tchr. Award, 2004, NCIV award, 2005. Mem. Am. Hist. Assn., Am. Cath. Hist. Assn., Latin Am. Studies Assn., Conf. Latin Am. Studies, Tex. Cath. Hist. Assn., Rocky Mountain Council Latin Am. Studies, Southwest Assn. Latin Am. Studies., Fulbright Assn. (pres. del Norte chpt. 1989—). Democrat. Home: 10708 Vista Lomas Dr El Paso TX 79935-3611 Office: El Paso Community Coll PO Box 20500 El Paso TX 79998-0500 Office Phone: 915-831-2483. Business E-Mail: genem@epcc.edu.

**MULLER, HENRY NICHOLAS, III,** retired foundation administrator; b. Pitts., Nov. 18, 1938; s. Henry N. Jr. and Harriet (Kerschner) M.; m. Nancy Clagett, June 20, 1959 (div. 1985); children: Charles T., Brook W.; m. Carol A. Cook, Jan. 4, 1986. BA, Dartmouth Coll., 1960; PhD, U. Rochester, 1968. Instr. Dartmouth Coll., Hanover, NH, 1964; lectr. Mt. Allison U., Sackville, Canada, 1964—66; asst. prof., prof. history U. Vt., Burlington, 1966—78, asst. dean Coll. Arts, Scis., 1969—70, assoc. dean Coll. Arts, Scis., 1970—73, dir. Living, Learning Ctr., 1973—78; pres. Colby-Sawyer Coll., New London, NH, 1978—85; dir. State Hist. Soc. Wis., Madison, 1985—96; pres., CEO Frank Lloyd Wright Found., Scottsdale, Ariz., 1996—2002; ret., 2002. Dir. Standex Internat. Corp., Salem, NH, 1984, chair corp. governance and nom. com., mem. pension plan investment and compensation com.; mem. Wis. State Hist. Records Adv. Bd., 1985—96, Gov. Coun. Tourism, 1997—96; chmn. Wis. Burial Sites Bd., 1988—96; trustee Nat. Trust Hist. Preservation, 1989—98; chair Wis. Submerged Cultural Resources, 1993—96. Co-author: An Anxious Democracy, 1982; co-editor: Science, Technology and Culture, 1974, In a State of Nature, 1982, The Quotable Ethan Allen, 2005; sr. editor Vt. Life mag., 1975-87; editor Vt. History, 1977-85 Fin. commn. Vt. Bicentennial Commn., 1970—77; trustee Vt. Hist. Soc., 1972—85, 2003—, v.p., 1975—82; chmn. Vt. Coun. Hist. Preservation, 1977—78; chair Bicentennial Com., Burlington, 1976; mem. NH Postsecondary Edn. Commn., 1983—85; trustee, pres. Taliesin Preservation, Inc., 1991—2001; mem. Wis. Sesquicentennial Commn., 1995—99; trustee Frank Lloyd Wright Found., 1996—2004; v.p. Ind. Coll. Univ. Coun. Ariz., 1998—2000, mem. bd., 1998—2002; interim chmn. Taliesin Archs., 2000—01; counselor Essex (N.Y.) Cmty. Fund, 2002—, Adirondack Archtl. Heritage Ctr., 2005—; bd. dirs. Wis. Preservation Fund Inc., 1989—2006, USS Wis., 1989—93; trustee Ethan Allen Homestead Trust, 2002—, treas., 2003—05; v.p., 2005—; dir., vice chmn. Essex (N.Y.) Cmty. Heritage Orgn., 2003—04; bd. dirs., vice chmn., chmn. Smith House Health Care Ctr., Willsboro, NY, 2004—, chmn., 2006—; mem. Essex Bicentennial Com., 2004—05, Essex Planning Bd., 2005—; trustee Nat. Trust CDFL, Inc., 2006—. Fellow: Ctr. Rsch. on Vt.; mem.: Am. Assn. State and Local History (councillor 1988—91), Vt. Archeol. Soc. (pres. 1971—74), Nat. Coun. Pub. History (bd. dirs. 1988—90), Madison Club.

**MULLER, JENNIFER,** choreographer, dancer; b. Yonkers, NY, Oct. 16, 1944; d. Don Medford and Lynette (Heldman) Muller. BS, Juilliard Sch. Music, 1967. Instr. in dance H.S. Performing Arts, 1967-72, Sarah Lawrence Coll., 1968-72, The Juilliard Sch., 1969-70, Nederlands Dans Theater, 1971-76, Utah rep., 1973-74, Centre Nat. de la Dance, Paris, 1998, Acad. Isola Danzo, Venice, 1999-2001, Atelier de Paris, 1999, Institut del Teatre de Barcelona, 2001, Centro Andaluz de Danza-Seville, 2003-05; commns.: Alvin Ailey Am. Dance Theatre, N.Y.C., 1977, 85, 2005, Festival d'Avignon, France, 1980, Lyon Opera Ballet, France, 1984, Aterballetto, 1988, Ballet Stagium, 1991, Dansgroep Krisztina de Chatel, 1992, Tanz-Forum Staatsoper Koln, Sachsische Staatopera-Dresden, ARTSCAPE-Balt., 1991, 95, Aterballetto, Italy, 1993, Les Ballet Jazz de Montreal, 1994, Ballet du Nord, France, 1995, White Wave Rising, 1996, Bat Dor Dance Co., Israel, Nederlands Dans Theatre 3, Ballet Contemporaneo, Argentina, Ohio Ballet, 2000, Dance Inst. U. Akron, 2003; cons. Met. Mus. Art, 1971-72. Mem. Pearl Lang Dance Co., N.Y.C. 1959-63, prin. dance, Jose Limon Dance Co., N.Y.C., 1963-71, assoc. dir., choreographer, prin. dancer, Louis Falco Dance Co., N.Y.C., 1968-74; founder, dir., choreographer: Jennifer Muller/The Works, N.Y.C., 1974-; choreographic works include: Nostalgia, 1971, Rust, 1971, Cantata, 1972, Tub, 1973, An American Beauty Rose, 1974, Biography, 1974, Speeds, 1974, Winter Pieces, 1974, Clown, 1974, Four Chairs, 1974, Wyeth, 1974, White, 1975, Strangers, 1975, Beach, 1976, Crossword, 1977, Predicaments for Five, 1977, Mondriaan, 1977, Lovers, 1978, Solo, 1979, Conversations, 1979, Chant, 1980, Terrain, 1981, Shed, 1982, Kite, 1983, Souls, 1984, The Enigma, 1986, Fields, 1986, Couches, 1986, Life/Times, 1986, Darkness and Light, 1986, Interrupted River, 1987, Occasional Encounters, 1988, City, 1988, The Flight of a Predatory Bird, 1989, Refracted Light, 1990, RIGHTeous About Passing (on the LEFT), 1990, Woman with Visitors at 3am, 1991, Regards, 1991, arm in arm in arm..., 1991, Thesaurus, 1991, Glass Houses, 1991, 2-1-1/Attic, 1992, Momentary Gathering, 1992, The Waiting Room, 1993, The Politician/Peeling the Onion, 1993, Orbs, Spheres and Other Circular Bodies, 1993, HUMAN/NATURE-A Response to the Longhouse Gardens, 1993, Pierrot, 1993, Desire-That DNA Urge, 1994, Point of View (A Case of Persimmons and Picasso), 1994, The Spotted Owl, 1995, Some Days are Like That, 1995, Promontory, 1996, Fruit, 1996, The Dinner Party, 1996, A Broken Wing, 1996, Ricochet, 1997, Degas Revisited, 1998, Dialectics Part I, 1998, Spores, Solitude & Summer Humming, 1999, Beethoven-Not Four Naught, 2000, aSOlo, 2000, Hymn for Her, 2000, Time Treading, 2000, China Project: Sagone; Suk Road; Dancing Waves, 2001, The Door, 2001, Never in The Same Room, 2002, To Live Alone..., 2002, Moon, 2002, It's a c#!* City, 2002, Prayer, 2003, Bounce, 2003, Footprints, 2003, Flowers, 2004, Ecstatic Poems, 2004, A Candle at Both Ends, 2004, Island, 2005, Sunlight and Shadow, 2005, Momentum, 2005; choreographer for theatrical prodns.: Frimbo, 1980, The Death of von Richthofen..., 1982, Fame, The Musical, 1988, Up Against It, 1989, The Seven Deadly Sins, 1990, Signature, 1990, Esther, 1993, Once Around the City, 1998, 01; dir. Le Jongleur, 2000. Recipient Best Performance award Berlin Festival, 1977, Acad. award Juilliard Sch. Music, 1967, Carbonell award, 1989; grantee Nat. Endowment for Arts, 1971-77, 80-85, 86-87, 87-88, Creative Artists Pub. Svc., 1976-77, NY State Coun. on Arts, 1976-77, 78-79, 85-93, NYC Dept. Cultural Affairs, 1978-79, 94-06, NYC Dept. Youth and Cmty. Devel., 2001-05. Mem. Am. Guild Mus. Artists, Soc. Stage Dirs. and Choreographers, World Arts Coun. (founding mem.). Home and Office: The Muller Works Found Inc 131 W 24th St New York NY 10011-1942 Office Phone: 212-691-3803. Business E-Mail: jmuller@jmtw.org, twinfo@jmtw.org.

**MULLER, JEROME KENNETH,** photographer, art director, editor; b. Amityville, NY, July 18, 1934; s. Alphons and Helen (Haberl) M.; m. Nora Marie (Nestor), Dec. 21, 1974. BS, Marquette U., 1961; post grad., Calif. State U., Fullerton, 1985—86; MA, Nat. U., San Diego, 1988; post grad., Newport Psychoanalytic Inst., 1988—90. Comml. and editorial photographer, NYC, 1952-55; mng. editor Country Beautiful mag., Milw., 1961-62, Reproductions Rev. mag., NYC, 1967-68; editor, art dir. Orange County (Calif.) Illustrated, Newport Beach, Calif., 1962-67, art editor, 1970-79, exec. editor, art dir., 1968-69; owner, CEO Creative Svcs. Advt. Mag.; Newport Beach, Calif., 1969-79. Founder, CEO, Mus. Graphics, Costa Mesa, Calif., 1978—; instr. photography Lindenhurst (NY) HS, 1952-54, comic art U. Calif., Irvine, 1979, publ. design Orange Coast Coll., Costa Mesa, Calif., 1997-2002; guest curator Fiftieth Anniversary Exhbn. Mickey Mouse, 1928-78, The Bower's Mus., Santa Ana, Calif., 1978. One-man shows include to Souk Gallery, Newport Beach, 1970, Gallery Two, Santa Ana, Calif., 1972, Cannery Gallery, Newport Beach, 1974, Mus. Graphics Gallery, 1993, White Gallery Portland State U., 1996, U. Calif., Irvine, 1997, Nat. Telephone and Comm., Irvine, Calif., 1998, Robert Mondavi Wine and Food Center, Costa

Mesa, 2000; author: Rex Brandt, 1972, Publication Design and Production, 2000; contbr. photographs and articles to mag. Mem. Cultural Arts Com., City of Costa Mesa, CA., 2000-2002. With USAF, 1956-57. Recipient, two silver medals Twentieth Ann. Exhbn. Advt. and Editorial Art in West, 1965, Inkpot award, San Diego Comic Conv., 1980. Mem.: Laguna Beach Art Mus., Met. Mus. Art, Mus. Modern Art (N.Y.C.), Orange County Mus. Art, Alpha Sigma Nu. Office: PO Box 11155 Costa Mesa CA 92627 Office Phone: 949-644-0808.

**MULLER, JOHN BARTLETT,** university president; b. Port Jefferson, NY, Nov. 8, 1940; s. Frederick Henry and Estelle May (Reeve) M.; m. Barbara Ann Schmidt, May 30, 1964 (dec. 1972); m. Lynn Anne Spongberg, Oct. 10, 1987. AB in Polit. Sci., U. Rochester, 1962; postgrad. in apologetics, Westminster Sem., Phila., 1962-63; MS in Psychology, Purdue U., 1968, PhD in Psychology, 1975. Asst. prof. psychology Roberts Wesleyan Coll., Rochester, NY, 1964-66, acting chmn. div. behavioral sci., dir. instl. research, 1967-70; vis. asst. prof. psychology Wabash Coll., Crawfordsville, Ind., 1970-71; research assoc. Ind. U.-Purdue U., Indpls., 1971-72; prof. psychology, v.p. for acad. affairs Hillsdale (Mich.) Coll., 1972-85; pres. BMW Assocs., Osseo, Mich., 1984-85, Bellevue (Nebr.) U., 1985—; pres. Nebr. Ind. Coll. Found., Omaha, Assn. Ind. Colls. Nebr., Lincoln; bd. advisors Applied Info. Mgmt. Inst., Gt. Western Bank. Contbr. articles to profl. jours. and textbooks. Bd. govs. Boys Club of Omaha; bd. dirs. Mid-American Coun. Boy Scouts Am. Nat. Inst. Mental Health fellowship Purdue U., 1963, Nat. Tchg. fellowship Fed. Govt., 1967, Townsend fellowship U. Rochester, 1962. Mem. APA, Bellevue U. C. of C. (bd. dirs. 1989-95), Phi Beta Kappa, Phi Kappa Phi. Republican. Home: 13303 Lochmoor Cir Bellevue NE 68123-3770 Office: Bellevue U Office of the Pres 1000 Galvin Rd S Bellevue NE 68005-3098 Office Phone: 402-293-3700. Business E-Mail: jmuller@bellevue.edu.

**MULLER, KATHERINE LYNN,** clinical psychologist; b. Point Pleasant, NJ, Nov. 22, 1973; d. Barbara Jean (Mahlschnee) Morey Hahn and Charles Muller; m. Simon Alexander Rego, May 18, 2003. BA, Douglass Coll., 1992—96; M in Psychology, Rutgers U., 1999, D in Psychology, 2001. Lic. psychologist State of NY, 2003, State of Pa., 2004. Rsch. asst. Rutgers U., New Brunswick, NJ, 1996—2000; psychology intern Montefiore Med. Ctr., Bronx, NY, 2000—01; clinician/rschr. U. of Pa., Ctr. for the Treatment and Study of Anxiety, 2001—03; assoc. dir. of psychology tng./dir., cognitive behavior therapy program Montefiore Med. Ctr., Bronx, 2003—; asst. prof. of psychiatry and behavioral sciences Albert Einstein Coll. of Medicine, Bronx, 2003—. Curriculum dir., cognitive behavior therapy program Montefiore Med. Ctr., Bronx, 2003—; cons. Healthcare Coun., NY, 2004—. Contbg. editor: Einstein Journal of Biology and Medicine. V.p. Fairmount Tenants Assn., Phila., 2002—03; mental health provider NY Project Liberty 9-11 Program, Bronx, 2003—04. Grad. Excellence fellowship, Rutgers U. Grad. Sch. of Applied and Profl. Psychology, 1996—2000, Agnes McDede Murray fellowship, Douglass Coll., 1996, Ocean County C. of C. scholarship, Toms River, NJ, 1996. Mem.: Assn. for Advancement of Behavior Therapy, Nat. Assn. of Cognitive Behavioral Therapists, Am. Psychol. Assn., Phi Beta Kappa. Avocations: music, theatre. Office: Montefiore Med Ctr 111 East 210th St Bronx NY 10467 Office Phone: 718-920-5024. Office Fax: 718-920-6538. Business E-Mail: kmuller@montefiore.org.

**MULLER, MERVIN EDGAR,** computer scientist, consultant, statistician, educator; b. Hollywood, Calif., June 1, 1928; s. Emanuel and Bertha (Zimmerman) Muller; m. Barabara McAdam, July 13, 1963; children: Jeffrey McAdam, Stephen McAdam, Todd McAdam. AB, UCLA, 1949, MA, 1951, PhD, 1954. Instr. in math Cornell U., 1954-56; rsch. assoc. in math Princeton (NJ) U., 1956-59; sr. scientist stats. and elec. engring., 1968-69; sr. statistician, dept. mgr. IBM, NYC, White Plains, 1956-64; prof. computer sci. and stats. U. Wis., 1964-71; prof. computer sci. George Mason U., 1985; dept. dir. World Bank, Washington, 1971-81, sr. advisor, 1981-85; Robert M. Critchfield prof. computer info. sci. Ohio State U., 1985-98, prof. emeritus, 1994-98, dept. chair, 1985-94. Chair sci. and tech. info. bd. NRC, NAS; bd. dirs. Advanced Info. Tech. Ctr., Columbus, Ohio. Mem. editl. bd. Computation and Stats., 1990, Jour. Computational and Graphical Stats., 1990; contbr. articles to profl. jours. Trustee First Unitarian Ch., Bethesda, Md., 1975—79. Rsch. grantee, AT&T, Columbus, 1987. Fellow: World Acad. Productivity Sci., Am. Statis. Assn.; mem.: Internat. Assn. Statis. Computing (sci. sec. 1979—83, pres. 1977—79), Internat. Statis. Inst. (mem. steering com. Internat. Rsch. Ctr. 1987—89). Avocations: reading, jogging, walking, bridge. Home: 4171 Clairmont Rd Upper Arlington OH 43220-4501 Office: Ohio State U Dept Computer Info Sci Rm 395 2015 Neil Ave Columbus OH 43210-1210 Office Phone: 614-292-4281. E-mail: mmuller@columbus.rr.com, muller.m@cse-ohio-state.edu.

**MULLER, PATRICIA ANN,** nursing administrator, educator; b. N.Y.C., July 22, 1943; d. Joseph H. and Rosanne (Bautz) Felter; m. David G. Smith, Mar. 19, 1988; children: Frank M. Muller III, Kimberly M. Muller. BSN, Georgetown U., 1965; MA, U. Tulsa, 1978, EdD, 1983. RN. Coord. staff devel. St. Francis Hosp., Tulsa, 1978—79, asst. dir. for nursing svc., nursing edn., 1979—82, dir. dept. edn., 1982—98, St. Francis Health Sys., 1998—2002, cons., 2002—. Mem. faculty Okla. U., Northeastern U., Tulsa U.; presenter at confs. and convs. Contbg. editor JOPAN, 1992-2001; contbr. articles to profl. jours. Mem. Leadership Tulsa, 1991; bd. dirs. Am. Heart Assn., Ronald McDonald House. Mem. ANA, Nat. League for Nursing, Am. Soc. for Nursing Svc. Adminstrs., Am. Soc. for Health Manpower Edn. and Tng., Okla. Nurses Assn., Okla. Orgn. of Nurse Execs. (pres. 1992-93), Sigma Theta Tau. Home and Office: 6203 W Utica Ct Broken Arrow OK 74011 Office Phone: 918-671-7767. E-mail: mullsmi@aol.com.

**MULLER, PETER,** lawyer, film company executive, retail executive; b. Teplitz-Sanov, Czechoslovakia, Mar. 4, 1947; came to U.S., 1949; s. Alexander and Elizabeth Rudolpha (Weingarten) M.; m. Irene Smolarski, Nov. 18, 1971 (div. 1973); children: Chloe, Aurisha; m. Esther Unterman Meisler, Jan. 4, 1987 (div. 1995). BA, NYU, 1968, JD cum laude. Entertainment editor Ambience mag., NYC, 1978-79, Women's Life mag., NYC, 1980-81; sole practice NYC, 1984—; entertainment writer Jewish Press; CEO Producers Releasing Corp., NY, 1987-88, Nev., 1987—88, pres. entertainment div. NY, 1987-88, Nev., 1987—88; pres., founder Muller Entertainment Group, NYC, 1988—, Calif., 1988—; pres., chief oper. officer ACA Joe, Inc., San Francisco and N.Y.C., also bd. dirs. Expert tech. adv. svc. for attys., Pa., 1987—; lectr. entertainment and comm. bus. to various orgns.; adj. prof. NYU, UCLA, LaGuardia CUNY, Zicklin Sch. Bus. Baruch Coll. CUNY. Author: Show Business Law, 1991, The Music Business: A Legal Perspective, 1994. Bd. dirs. NYU Coll. Arts and Sci.; vol. Lawyers for the Arts, NYC, 1987—. Mem. ABA (forum on entertainment and sports industries, forum on copyright, trademark and patent law), NY State Bar Assn., NYU Alumni Assn. (bd. dirs. 1987—, v.p. bd. dirs., chmn.), Assn. of Am. Mgmt. Assn. (pres.). Avocations: sports, history, writing, travel, hiking. Office Phone: 212-358-3406.

**MULLER, RALPH W.,** hospital administrator; b. Oct. 26, 1945; married. BA in economics, Syracuse U., NY, 1966; MA in govt., Harvard U., Cambridge, Mass., 1968. Asst. to commr. Nicholas Johnson FCC, Washington, 1967; assoc., health care consulting Orgn. for Social and Tech. Innovation, Cambridge, Mass., 1969-70; rsch. asst. to Prof. Samuel H. Beer Harvard U., 1967—68, teaching fellow, govt., and resident tutor, 1969—72; govt. instr. Suffolk U., Boston, 1972—74; budget dir., dept. of public welfare Commonwealth of Mass., Boston, 1975—78, dep. commr., dept. public welfare, 1978—80; dir. fin. planning and budget U. Chgo., 1980—83, assoc. v.p. budget, computing and info. sys., 1984, v.p., hospitals and clinics and dep. dean, divsn. biological sciences, 1985—86; pres., CEO U. Chgo. Hospitals and Health Sys., 1986—2003; CEO U. Pa. Health Sys., 2004—. Fellow: AAAS; mem.: Coun. of Tchg. Hospitals (chmn. 1997—98), Am. Assoc. of Med. Colleges (AAMC) (chmn. 1999—2000). Office: U Pa Health Sys 3400 Spruce St Philadelphia PA 19104*

**MULLER, RIANA RICCI,** musician, educator; b. Orange, Calif., July 14, 1943; d. Ruggeri Ricci and Ruth (Ricci) (Rink) Mairs; m. William Paul Muller, Aug. 17, 1968; 1 child, Christine Rae. BM with Distinction, Eastman Sch. of Music, Rochester, N.Y., 1965; MM Performance, Music Lit., 1969. Instr. Amarillo Coll. Tex., 1973—76; asst. prof. Coll. St. Benedict, St. Joseph, Minn., 1976—78; violinist Puerto Rico Symphony, San Juan, 1978—79; music tchr. (orch.) Hendrick Hudson Pub. Sch., Montrose, NY, 1984—2004; violinist freelance, Greater NY Area, 1984—2004, Pa., 2004—, Muller Duo, Lewisburg, Pa., 1979—; instr. Lycoming Coll., Williamsport, Pa. Violin study with Carrol Glenn, Joseph Knitzer, Louis Persinger and Ruggeri Ricci (my father). Author (and violinist): (DVD) Classical composers in the Foreign Language Classes, 2005; author: Ear Training Exercises for Violin Students, 2006. Decorated with medal and Diplome d'Honneur Eugene Ysaÿe Found., Brussels; recipient Cert. of Commendation for Chamber Music Tchg., Chamber Music Am., 1993. Mem.: Sigma Alpha Iota. Achievements include world premiere performance of Ysaÿe Violin Concerto No.8 (1977). Home: 1119 W Market St Lewisburg PA 17837

**MULLER, RICHARD PARTAIN,** chemist, researcher; b. Chgo., July 1, 1966; BA in Chemistry, Rice U., 1988—88; PhD in Chemistry, Calif. Inst. Tech., 1994—94. Mem. tech. staff Sandia Nat. Labs., Albuquerque, 2003—. Office: Sandia Nat Lab PO Box 5800 M/S 1110 Albuquerque NM 87185-1110

**MULLER, RICHARD STEPHEN,** electrical engineer, educator; b. Weehawken, NJ, May 5, 1933; s. Irving Ernest and Marie Victoria Muller; m. Joyce E. Regal, June 29, 1957; children: Paul Stephen, Thomas Richard. ME, Stevens Inst. Tech., Hoboken, N.J., 1955; MSEE, Calif. Inst. Tech., 1957, PhD in Elect. Engring. and Physics, 1962. Test engr. Wright Aero/Curtiss Wright, Woodridge, NJ, 1953-54; mem. tech. staff Hughes Aircraft Co., Culver City, Calif., 1955-61; instr. U. So. Calif., L.A., 1960-61; asst. prof., then assoc. prof. U. Calif., Berkeley, 1962-72, prof., 1973—. Guest prof. Swiss Fed. Inst. Tech., 1993; founder, dir. Berkeley Sensor & Actuator Ctr., 1985—; chmn. sensors electron devices NRC Army Rsch. Lab., 2003-04, chmn. microtech. adv. com. Helmholtz Assn., Germany, 2003—; chmn. steering com. Internat. Sensor and Actuator Meeting. Co-author: Device Electronics for Integrated Circuits, 1977, 3d. rev. edit., 2002, Microsensors, 1990; editor-in-chief IEEE/ASME Jour. Microelectromech. Sys., 1998—; contbr. over 200 articles to profl. jours. Pres. Kensington (Calif.) Mcpl. Adv. Coun., 1992-98; trustee Stevens Inst. Tech., 1996-2005. Fellow Hughes Aircraft Co., 1955-57, NSF, 1959-62, NATO postdoctoral fellow, 1968-69, Fulbright fellow, 1982-83, Alexander von Humboldt prize, 1993, Tech. U. Berlin, 1994; Berkeley citation, 1994, Stevens Renaissance award, 1995, Career Achievement award Internat. Conf. on Sensors and Actuators, 1997. Fellow IEEE (life, Cledo Brunetti award 1998, Millennium prize 2000); mem. IEEE Press Bd., NAE, NRC (chmn. sensors adv. bd. U.S. Army Rsch. Lab. 2003-04, liaison between NAE and NRC 2003-05), Nat. Acad. Engring., Nat. Materials (adv. bd. 1994-98), Electron Devices Soc. (adv. com. 1984-98). Achievements include patents in field; development of operating micromotor and introduction of silicon surface micromachining. Office: U Calif Dept EECS # 1770 401 Cory Hall Berkeley CA 94720-1770 Office Phone: 510-642-0614. Personal E-mail: rsmuller@pacbell.net. Business E-Mail: r.muller@ieee.org.

**MULLER, ROBERT JOSEPH,** gynecologist; b. New Orleans, Dec. 5, 1946; s. Robert Harry and Camille (Eckert) M.; m. Susan Philipsen, Aug. 22, 1974; children: Ryan, Matt. BS, St. Louis U., 1968; BS, MSc, Emory U., 1976; MD, La. State U., New Orleans, 1981; cert. in emergency mgmt., FEMA, 1998; cert. in Mgmt., Auburn U., 2001, MBA/MHA, 2003. Intern Charity Hosp., New Orleans, 1981-82; resident La. State U. Affiliate Hosp., 1982-85; resident staff physician La. State U. Med. Ctr., New Orleans, 1981-85; pvt. practice Camellia Women's Ctr., Slidell, La., 1985—; staff physician Tulane Med. Ctr., New Orleans, 1986—. Med. dir. Northshore Regional Med. Ctr., Slidell, 1987—, chief staff, 1998, vice chair governing bd., 2004; mem. adv. bd. Auburn U., 2004; med. dir. New Orleans Police Dept., 1981-95, S.W. La. Search and Rescue, Covington, La., 1986—, St. Tammany Parish Sheriff Dept., Covington, 1989—, commdr., 1990—, Camellia City Classic, Slidell, 1989—, Crawfishman Triathalon, Mandeville, La., 1988—, Res-Q-Med Laser Team, 1994—. Contbr. articles to profl. jours. Recipient Commendation Medal New Orleans Police Dept., 1986, 87, 89, Medal Valor St. Tammany Parish Sheriff Office, Covington, 1990, Cert. Valor S.E. La. Search and Rescue, Mandeville, 1990; named one of Outstanding Young Men of Am., 1984, one of Am.'s Top Gynecologists, 2005, 06. Mem. Am. Coll. Ob-Gyn. (Am.'s Top Ob-Gyn's. 2005), La. State Med. Soc., Profl. Assn. Diving Instrs. (divemaster 1991, asst. instr. 1995), So. Offshore Racing Assn. (med. dir. 1982-95), Offshore Profl. Racing Tour (med. dir. staff 1990-95), Am. Power Boat Assn. (med. staff 1984-89). Roman Catholic. Avocations: scuba diving, boating, shooting. Home: 1181 Yorktown Dr Slidell LA 70461-3023 Office: Camellia Womens Ctr 105 Smart Pl Slidell LA 70458-2039 Office Phone: 985-641-2100. Personal E-mail: rmullermd@aol.com.

**MULLER, SCOTT WILLIAM,** lawyer; b. Stamford, Conn., Feb. 15, 1950; s. Robert Sielke and Patricia (Harris) M.; m. Caroline Severance Adams, June 24, 1972; children: Christopher Adams, Robin McPherson, Peter Severance. BA cum laude, Princeton U., 1971; JD, Georgetown U. Law Ctr., 1976. Bar: NY 1976, US Dist. Ct. (so. dist.) NY 1977, US Ct. Appeals (2d. cir.) 1978, US Supreme Ct. 1978, US Tax Ct. 1984, DC 1986. Law clk. to presiding justice US Ct. Appeals (3d cir.), Phila., 1975-76; asst. atty. criminal div. US Atty.'s Office, NYC, 1978-82; assoc., litigator Davis, Polk & Wardwell, Washington, 1976-78, 82-84, mng. ptnr., 1985—2002; gen. counsel CIA, Washington, 2002—04. Adj. prof. in fed. law enforcement Georgetown U. Law Ctr. Nat. trustee Boys and Girls Clubs of Am.; mem. governing bd. St. Albans Sch.; mem. audit com. Protestant Episcopal Cathedral Found. (the Nat. Cathedral); bd. and former chmn. Ctr. for the Community Interest. Served N.G., 1971—72. Mem. ABA (vice-chmn, white collar crime com.), NY State Bar Assn., Fed. Bar Assn., Assn. of Bar of City of NY, Am. Law Inst. Republican. Episcopalian.

**MULLER, STEVEN,** international studies educator, academic administrator; b. Hamburg, Germany, Nov. 22, 1927; came to U.S., 1940, naturalized, 1949; s. Werner Adolph and Marianne (Hartstein) M.; m. Margie Hellman, June 19, 1951 (dec. July 1999); children: Julie, Elizabeth; m. Jill E. McGovern, Feb. 5, 2000. BA, UCLA, 1948; BLitt (Rhodes scholar), Oxford U., Eng., 1951; PhD, Cornell U., 1958. Assoc. then full prof. Cornell U., 1956-58; mem. faculty and adminstrn. Cornell U., 1958-71, dir. Ctr. Internat. Studies, 1961-66, v.p. pub. affairs, 1966-71; provost Johns Hopkins U., 1971-72, pres., 1972-90, pres. emeritus, 1990—, fellow Pop. Policy Inst., disting. lectr., 1993—. Cons. Dept. Def., 1962-67, ACDA, 1967-77; bd. dirs. Orgn. Resources Counselors, Inc., Atlantic Coun. of the U.S. Author: Documents on European Government, 1963; co-editor: From Occupation to Cooperation, 1992, In Search of Germany, 1996; editor: Universities in the Twenty First Century, 1996. Trustee, chmn. St. Mary's Coll., 1991—2003; trustee German Marshall Fund of the US. Decorated comdr. Order of Merit (Fed. Republic of Germany), commendatore Republic of Italy. Mem. Am. Inst. Contemporary German Studies (co-chmn. emeritus), Coun. Fgn. Rels., Am. Polit. Sci. Assn., Internat. Inst. Strategic Studies, Am. Assn. Rhodes Scholars, Phi Beta Kappa, Cosmos Club (Washington). Office: Johns Hopkins U Sch Advanced Internat Studies 1619 Massachusetts Ave NW Washington DC 20036-2213 Office Phone: 202-663-5821. Business E-Mail: smuller1@jhu.edu.

**MULLER, STEVEN JOHN,** music educator; s. Darrell Marvin and Marilyn Rose Muller; m. Catherine Brown, Dec. 16, 1978; children: Emily Ann Callendar, Alexander Skeen. BS in Music, Ea. Oreg. State Coll., 1979, BS in Secondary Edn., 1979; MS in Music, Oreg., 1985. Music tchr. Wasco (Oreg.) Sch. Dist., 1979—80, Stanfield (Oreg.) Sch. Dist., 1980—83, Pendleton (Oreg.) Sch. Dist., 1984—. Choir dir. Presbyn. Ch., LaGrande, Oreg., 1979—79, Pendleton, 1990—; orch. dir. Happy Canyon Night Show, Pendleton, 1995—. Founding mem. Oreg. East Symphony, Pendleton, 1985. Mem.: Am. Choral Dirst. Assn., Oreg. Music Educators (pres. dist. III),

Internat. Musician Union (v.p. local 560 1990—2006). Democrat. Presbyterian. Avocations: golf, running, swimming, bicycling, hunting. Office: Pendleton HS 1800 NW Carden Pendleton OR 97801

**MULLER, WILLARD C(HESTER),** writer; b. Havre, Mont., May 7, 1916; s. Chester Rudolph and Clara (Hansen) M.; m. Carolyn Elfrid Bue, Jan. 27, 1945; children: Marolyn Jean, Barbara Anne, Nancy Eleanor. BA, Stanford U., 1941; MPA, Maxwell Grad. Sch. Govt. Adminstrn., 1943; student, Nat. War Coll., 1961-62. Newspaper reporter, short story writer Bremerton (Wash.) Daily Searchlight, 1934-36; White House corr. Bremerton Daily Searchlight and Port Angeles Evening News, 1941; mgmt. analyst USDA, 1942, 46-47; mem. staff for food, agr. and forestry U.S. Dept. Army and U.S. High Commr. for Germany, Munich and Frankfurt, Fed. Republic Germany, 1948-50; dist. adminstr., Am. consul U.S. Trust Territory of Pacific Islands, Truk, Caroline Islands, 1951-55; dep. dir. ICA, U.S. Ops. Mission to Nepal, Kathmandu, 1956-58; dir. U.S. Ops. to Somali Republic, 1958-61, Office East and Southern African Affairs, AID, Dept. State, Washington, 1962-65, AID, Kampala, Uganda, 1965-70, assoc. dir. mission, rep. for land reform Saigon, Vietnam, 1970—73, ret., 1973, cons., 1974-81; free lance writer, 1973—. Author various short stories; contbr. articles to profl. jours. Chmn. steering com. 4-state program dialogue on peace Pacific NW dist. Am. Luth. Ch., Tacoma, 1983-85; mem. Clallam br. Wash. State Centennial Commn., 1986-89; mem. Food Bank Bd., Port Angeles, Wash., 1986-90. Lt. USNR, 1943-45, PTO. Mem.: Am. Fgn. Svc. Assn., Am. Soc. Pub. Adminstrn., Kiwanis. Avocation: travel. Home and Office: 3624 S Mount Angeles Rd Port Angeles WA 98362-8910 Office Phone: 360-457-1892. Personal E-mail: muller@tenforward.com.

**MULLER, WILLIAM ALBERT, III,** retired library director; b. Savannah, Ga., Jan. 1, 1943; s. William Albert Jr. and Julia Anne (Cleary) M.; m. Claudya Barbara Burkett, Dec. 12, 1965 (div. 1986); 1 child, Martha Genevieve; m. Pamela Qualls, Apr. 9, 1988; 1 child, Tabitha Wade. BS, Ga. So. Coll., 1966; MLS, Emory U., 1969. Dir. War Woman Regional Libr., Elberton, Ga., 1969-73; rsch. libr. City of Savannah, 1973-75; dir. Mason County Pub. Libr., Point Pleasant, W.Va., 1976-78; pub. rels. cons. Eastern Shore Regional Libr., Salisbury, Md., 1978-81; dir. Brooke County Pub. Libr., Wellsburg, W.Va., 1982-84, McDowell Pub. Libr., Welch, W.Va., 1984-88, Bristol (Va.) Pub. Libr., 1988—2000; ret., 2000. Dir. Albermarle Regl. Libr., Winton, N.C., 2003—; sec. So. W.Va. Libr. Automation Corp., Beckley, 1984-87, pres. 1987-88, S.W. Info. Network Group, Abindgdon, Va., 1990-91, treas. (swing) 1993—; bd. dir. Albermarle Regional Libr., Winton, NC. Fundraiser Paramount Fund, Bristol, 1989; acct. exec. United Way Fund of Bristol, 1991; vol. Murfreesboro Pub. Libr., 2004—; Sunday Sch. tchr. St. Thomas Episcopal Ch., Ahoskie, NC, 2004—; bd. dirs. Mid-Atlantic Chamber Orch., Bristol, 1988—92, treas., 1992; bd. dirs. Bristol Preservation Soc., 1988—98, Nat. Ctr. for Quality, 1992—98, Main St. Bristol, 1991—95, treas., 1994; bd. dirs. Jr. Achievement, 1992—99, pres., 1997—99; bd. dirs. Vol. Bristol, 1998; bd. dirs., vol. chair Racefest, 1998—99. Mem.: N.Y.C. Ballet Guild, Smithsonian Assocs., N.C. Mus. Art. Democrat. Avocations: gardening, cabinetry, photography, travel, model railroads. Home: 406 Holly Hill Rd Murfreesboro NC 27855 Office Phone: 252-287-9753. Personal E-mail: unclebillm@yahoo.com.

**MULLER, WILLIAM HENRY, JR.,** surgeon, educator; b. Dillon, S.C., Aug. 19, 1919; s. William Henry and Octavia Elizabeth (Bethea) M.; m. Hildwin Clare Headly, Mar. 23, 1946; children: William Henry III, Marietta John Lewis. BS, The Citadel, 1940, DS (hon.), 1972; MD, Duke U., 1943; DHL (hon.), Med. U. S.C., 1977. Diplomate Am. Bd. Thoracic Surgery, Am. Bd. Surgery (rep. conf. com. grad. tng. in surgery). Intern Johns Hopkins Hosp., Balt., 1944, asst. surgery, asst. resident, 1944-46, resident gen. surgery, instr. surgery, 1948-49, resident cardiovascular surgery, 1949; practice gen. surgery Dillon, 1947-48; asst. prof. surgery UCLA, 1949-53, assoc. prof. Sch. Medicine, 1953-54; attending specialist thoracic surgery Wadsworth VA Hosp., Los Angeles; chief sect. cardiovascular surgery Los Angeles County-Harbor Gen. Hosp., Torrance, Calif.; cons. surgery St. Johns's, Santa Monica Hosps., 1949-54; cons. cardiovascular surgery U.S. Naval Hosp., San Diego, 1953-54; Stephen H. Watts prof. surgery, chmn. dept. U. Va. Sch. Medicine, 1954-82, v.p. health affairs, 1976-88, univ. prof. surgery and health policy, 1988-90, S. Hurt Watts prof. surgery emeritus, 1990—, v.p. for health affairs emeritus; surgeon-in-chief U. Va. Hosp., 1954-82; chmn. S.E. Surg. Congress; mem. panel heart disease Pres.'s, 1972; past chmn. surgery study sect. NIH; mem. exec. com., div. med. scis. NRC. Mem. editorial bd.: Am. Jour. Surgery, Annals of Surgery, Am. Surgeon; contbr. articles to med jours. Trustee, mem. exec. com. Duke U. Served as capt. M.C. AUS, 1946-47. Named One of 10 Outstanding Young Men of Yr. U.S. Jr. C. of C., Calif. Jr. C. of C., 1952; recipient Disting. Alumni award (1st award) Duke U. Med. Ctr., 1969; Thomas Jefferson award U. Va., 1982; McCallie Sch. Alumni Achievement award, 1986; Paul Harris fellow Nat. Rotary Found., 1988. Fellow ACS (past chmn., forum com. fundamental surg. problems, regent 1971—, chmn. bd. regents 1976-78, pres.-elect 1979); mem. Internat. Soc. Surgery, Internat. Cardiovascular Soc. (past v.p.), AMA, Am. Surg. Assn. (pres. 1974-75), So. Surg. Assn. (pres. 1975), Pacific Coast Surg. Assn., Am. Assn. Thoracic Surgery, Soc. Univ. Surgeons (past pres.), Soc. Surgery Alimentary Tract, Assn. Acad. Surgeons, James IV Assn. Surgeons (v.p. U.S.), Med. Soc. Va., Albemarle County Med. Soc., Soc. Vascular Surgery (past pres.), Am. Heart Assn. (chmn. surgery research study com., mem. central research com.), Va. Surg. Soc, Halsted Soc., Johns Hopkins Soc. Scholars, Raven Soc., Sigma Xi, Alpha Omega Alpha, Phi Chi Home: 900 Flordon Dr Charlottesville VA 22901-7844

**MULLIGAN, BRIAN C.,** film company executive; BBA, U. So. Calif.; MBA, UCLA. Sr. v.p. bus. develop. & strategic planning Universal Studios, 1995—98, exec. v.p. ops. & fin., 1998—99; co-chmn. Universal Pictures, Universal City, Calif., 1999; exec. v.p., CFO Seagram Co. Ltd. 1999—2001; chmn. Fox TV Stations, Inc., 2001—02; venture capitalist, advisor to Marvin Davis, 2001; exec. adv. The Boston Consulting Group, Inc., 2002; founder, principal Universal Partners, 2002—04; sr. exec. adv. media & entertainment Cerberus Capital Mgmt. LP. Bd. mem. Roxio, 2003—. Bd. dirs. Napster, 2003—. Office: Cerebus Capital Mgmt LP 299 Park Ave New York NY 10171

**MULLIGAN, DAVID KEITH,** consulting company executive, securities arbitrator; b. Detroit, Jan. 25, 1951; s. Robert Keith and Yvonne Bette Mulligan. Student, Oakland Coll., 1973-78. Cert. data processor, quality technician, quality auditor, software quality engr.; NASD gen. securities registered rep. Pres. Atlas Prodns., N.Y.C., 1973—. Cons. info. systems, human factors, tech. and mktg. comm. Author: Human Factors in Document Design, 1982, Computer Aids to Software Engineering, 1984, Document Design and Production for the '90s, 1989, Documentation and System Maintenance, 1989, Avoiding Outsourcing and Its Demoralizing Consequences, 1990, Programmer-Analyst: Dinosaur of the '90s, 1990, Information Management: New Thinking for the '90s, 1991, Product Documentation: Key to Internat. Marketing Success, 1993, Joint Application Design Critical Success Factors, 1994, Successful Worldwide Interactive Marketing, 1995, Management Information: Lifeblood of Business, 1996, Executive Ego: Most Powerful Force in Business, 1997, Investigation Techniques in the Healthcare Industry, 1997, Oracle Data Base Adminstration: A Structured Approach, 1999, Information Management in the Entertainment Industry, 1999, Database Application Implementation in the New Millennium, 1999, Sixty Minute Methodology for Desktop Development, 2000, Broad Band Communications: A Business Blueprint, 2000, Data Design: Key To Effective Telecom Provisioning, 2001, Data Management in the Mortgage Banking Industry, 2002, Data Design: Key to Effective Mortgage Banking, 2002, Dysfunction in Corporate America, 2002, Corporate Politics: The Greatest Menace to Productivity, 2003, Automotive Information Management: Engine of Success, 2004, Accounting Controls: Key to Coherence in the Entertainment Industry, 2005, Creative Accounting Processes for the Entertainment Industry, 2005, A New Paradigm for Ocean Shipping and International Logistics, 2006, 21st Century Logistics for the Entertainment Industry, 2006; co-author: Structured Analysis and Design for the Case User, 1993. Mem. ASCAP, NARAS, Am. Soc. Quality, Am. Fedn. of Musicians, N.Y. Friars Club, Assn. Cert. Fraud

Examiners, Am. Soc. for Automation in Pharmacy, The Authors Guild, Am. Mensa, NASD (bd. arbitrators). Avocations: musical composition, music performance, photography. Office: Atlas Productions PO Box 6688 Woodland Hills CA 91365-6688

**MULLIGAN, ELINOR PATTERSON,** lawyer; d. Frank Clark and Agnes (Murphy) Patterson; m. John C. O'Connor; children: Christine Fulena, Valerie Clark, Amy O'Connor, Christopher Criffan O'Connor; m. William G. Mulligan, Dec. 6, 1975. BA, U. Mich.; JD, Seton Hall U., 1970. Bar: N.J. 1970. Assoc., Springfield and Newark, 1970—72; pvt. practice Hackettstown, NJ, 1972; ptnr. Mulligan & Jacobson, N.Y.C., 1973—91, Mulligan & Mulligan, Hackettstown, 1976—. Atty. Hackettstown Planning Bd., 1973-86, Blairstown Bd. Adjustment, 1973-95; sec. Warren County Ethics Com., 1976-78, sec. Dist. X and XIII Fee Arbitration Com., 1979-87, mem. and chair, 1987-91, mem. dist. ethics Com. XIII, 1992—; mem. spl. com. on atty. disciplinary structure N.J. Supreme Ct., 1981—; lectr. Nat. Assn. Women Judges, 1979, N.J. Inst. Continuing Legal Edn., 1988—. Contbr. articles to profl. jours. Named Vol. of Yr., Attys. Vols. in Parole Program, 1978. Fellow Am. Acad. Matrimonial Lawyers (1st woman pres. N.J. chpt. 1995-96); mem. ABA, Warren County Bar Assn. (1st woman pres. 1987-88), N.J. State Bar ASsn., N.J. Women Lawyers Assn. (v.p. 1985—), Am. Mensa Soc., Union League Club (N.Y.C.), Baltusrol Golf Club (Springfield, N.J.), Panther Valley Golf and Country Club (Allamuchy, N.J.), Kappa Alpha Theta. Republican. Home: 12 Goldfinch Way Hackettstown NJ 07840-3007 Office: 933 County Road 517 Hackettstown NJ 07840-4654 Office Phone: 908-852-0202. Personal E-mail: llp-nj@mindspring.com. Business E-mail: elinormulligan@mulliganmulligan.com.

**MULLIGAN, JEREMIAH T.,** lawyer; b. Rochester, NY, 1944; BA, St. Bernard's Seminary and Coll., 1966; JD, Fordham U., 1970. Mem. Curtis, Mallet-Prevost, Colt & Mosle, N.Y. Office: Curtis Mallet-Prevost Colt & Mosle 101 Park Ave Fl 34 New York NY 10178-0061 Office Phone: 212-696-6040. Business E-Mail: jmulligan@cm-p.com.

**MULLIGAN, JOHN J.,** corporate financial executive; Student, Holy Cross Coll.; BA in Liberal Arts, St. John's U., NYC, 1976; M in Bus. and Acctg., Fordham U., NYC, 1981. With Mfrs. Hanover Leasing Corpn., 1979—86; mgr. lease financing Philip Morris Capital Corpn., 1986—87, dir. structured fin., 1987—94, v.p. lease/structured fin., 1994—2001, pres., CEO, 2001—. Office: Altria Grp Inc 120 Park Ave New York NY 10017*

**MULLIGAN, MICHAEL DENNIS,** lawyer; b. St. Louis, Mar. 9, 1947; s. Leo Virgil and Elizabeth (Leyse) M.; m. Theresa Baker, Aug. 7, 1971; children: Brennan, Colin. BA in Biology, Amherst Coll., 1968; JD, Columbia U., 1971. Bar: Mo. 1971, U.S. Dist. Ct. (ea. dist.) Mo. 1972, U.S. Ct. Appeals (8th cir.) 1982, U.S. Tax Ct. 1985. Law clk. to judge U.S. Dist. Ct. (ea. dist.) Mo., 1971-72; assoc. Lewis, Rice & Fingersh, L.C., St. Louis, 1972-80, ptnr., 1980—. Mem. editl. bd. Estate Planning Mag., 1985—, Jour. of Taxation, BNA Estates, Gifts and Trusts Jour. Served as cpl. USMC, 1968-70. Fellow Am. Coll. Trust and Estate Counsel; mem. ABA (mem. real property, probate and trust, and taxation sects.), Mo. Bar Assn. (mem. probate and trust, taxation sects.). Office: Lewis Rice & Fingersh LC 500 N Broadway Ste 2000 Saint Louis MO 63102-2147 Office Phone: 314-444-7757. E-mail: mmulligan@lewisrice.com.

**MULLIGAN, MICHAEL K.,** headmaster; m. Joy Mulligan; 1 child. BA, Middlebury Coll.; EdM, Harvard U.; MA in English, Middlebury Coll. History and English teacher & soccer, lacrosse, and wrestling coach Gov. Dummer Acad., 1977—82, dir. coll. placement, 1982—86; dean of administration, teacher, and coach The Thacher Sch., Ojai, Calif., 1986—93, head of sch., 1993—. Mem.: Assn. of Boarding Schools. Office: Thacher Sch 5025 Thacher Rd Ojai CA 93023

**MULLIGAN, ROBERT FRANCIS, JR.,** economist, civil engineer; b. Westbury, N.Y., May 29, 1961; s. Robert F. and Helen Christine (Romano) M. BSCE, Ill. Inst. Tech., 1983; MA, SUNY, Binghamton, 1989, PhD, 1993. Advanced studies cert. Internat. Econ. Policy Rsch., Kiel Inst. World Econs., 1995. Referee Jour. Evolutionary Econs., Quar. Jour. Austrian Econs., Rev. Austrian Econs., Jour. Instnl. Econs., Econ. Sys.; lectr. SUNY, Binghamton, 1991-93; vis. asst. prof. Clarkson U., 1993-94. Contbr. articles to profl. publs. Capt. USAF, 1983-87. Mem. Am. Econ. Assn., Internat. J.A. Schumpeter Soc., Soc. for Devel. of Austrian Econs., Royal Econ. Soc., Eastern Econ. Assn., Mil. Order World Wars (v.p. Spokane chpt. 1981-82). Office: Coll Bus Dept Bus Computer Info Sys and Econs Western Carolina U Cullowhee NC 28723 Address: 60 Buzzard Roost Cullowhee NC 28723 Office Phone: 828-227-3329. Business E-Mail: mulligan@wcu.edu.

**MULLIKIN, THOMAS WILSON,** mathematics professor; b. Flintville, Tenn., Jan. 9, 1928; s. Houston Yost and Daisy (Copeland) M.; m. Mildred Virginia Sugg, June 14, 1952; children: Sarah Virginia, Thomas Wilson, James Copeland. Student, U. South, 1946-47; AB, U. Tenn., 1950; postgrad., Iowa State U., 1952-53; A.M., Harvard, 1954, PhD, 1958. Mathematician Rand Corp., Santa Monica, Calif., 1957-64; prof. math. Purdue U., 1964-93, interim v.p., dean grad. sch., 1991-93, dean grad. sch., prof. math emeritus, 1993—. Served with USNR, 1950-52. Mem.: AAAS, Am. Math. Soc. Home: 104 Club Ct Cape Carteret NC 28584-9736

**MULLIN, GENE,** state legislator; b. San Francisco, Apr. 21, 1937; m. Terri Mullin; children: Jennifer, Kevin. BA in Polit. Sci., U. San Francisco, 1960. Lifetime secondary tchg. credential U. San Francisco, 1967. Tchr. govt. South San Francisco High Sch., 1967—99; mem. planning commn. City of South San Francisco, 1972—80, mem. city council, 1995—, mayor, 1998, 2001—02; mem. Calif. State Assembly from 19th dist., 2002—. Chair negotiations com. South San Francisco CTA, 1986—90; lectr., cons. Inst. Local Self Govt., 1989—97, Ctr. Youth Citizenship, 1999—; vice chair Labor and Employment Com.; mem. Edn. Com., Housing and Cmty. Devel. Com., Human Svcs. Com., Local Govt. Com., Vets. Affairs Com.; pres. Soutn San Francisco Classroom Tchr.'s Assn., 1992—95. Author: 2 books on local govt. JAG gen. corps U.S. Army, 1959—60. Mem.: Assn. Bay Area Govts. (mem. exec. com. 1999—), San Mateo County Retired Tchrs. Assn., Young Men's Inst. Democrat. Roman Catholic. Mailing: Capitol Office PO Box 942849 Sacramento CA 94294 Office: Dist Office Ste 302 1528 S El Camino Real San Mateo CA 94402

**MULLIN, LEO FRANCIS,** airline executive; b. Concord, Mass., Jan. 26, 1943; s. Leo F. and Alice L. (Fearns) M.; m. Leah J. Malmberg, Sept. 10, 1966; children: Jessica, Matthew. AB, Harvard U., 1964, MS, 1965, MBA, 1967. Assoc. McKinsey & Co., Washington, 1967-73, prin., 1973-76; sr. v.p. strategic planning Consol. Rail Corp., Phila., 1976-78; sr. v.p. 1st Chgo. Corp., Chgo., 1981-84, exec. v.p., 1984-91, vice chmn. Am. Nat. Bank and Trust Co., 1991-93, pres., COO, 1993-95; vice chmn. Unicom/Commonwealth Edison, Chgo., 1995—97; CEO Delta Airlines, Atlanta, 1997—2003, chmn. bd. dirs, 1999—2004; sr. advisor pvt. equity group Goldman Sachs, NYC, 2004—. Bd. dirs. Johnson & Johnson, BellSouth, 1998—. Vice chmn. Chgo. Urban League, 1993—; chmn. bd. trustees Field Mus. Natural History, 1994—; bd. dirs. Chgo. chpt. Juvenile Diabetes Found., 1988—, Chgo. Meml. Planning Coun., 1983—, Children's Meml. Hosp., Chgo., 1989—, Chgo. Coun. Fgn. Rels., 1994—; mem. Chgo. Econ. Devel. Commn., 1992-95; trustee Northwestern U., 1992—. Mem. Chgo. Club, Harvard Club of Chgo., Econ. Club of Chgo.

**MULLIN, PATRICK ALLEN,** lawyer; b. Newark, Jan. 13, 1950; s. Gerard Vincent and Frances Regina (Magnanti) M. BA, William Paterson U., 1972, MEd, 1974; JD with honors, N.Y. Law Sch., 1979, LLM in Taxation, 1990; postgrad., Harvard Law Sch., 1979. Bar: NJ 1979, DC 1980, NY 1990; cert. criminal trial atty. NJ Supreme Ct. Law clk. to Hon. Dickinson R. DeBevoise, US Dist. Ct., NJ, Trenton, 1979-80; assoc. Charles Morgan Assocys., Washington, 1980-81; pvt. practice, Hackensack, NJ, 1988—; instr., 1985—. Mem. Practitioners Adv. Group US Sentencing Commn., 1995—; lectr. Seton Hall

Law Sch., 2001, 02, 04, 06, ATLA, 2003; instr. Gerry Spence's Trial Lawyers Coll., 2001—; moderator ICLE program Upheaval in Fed. and State Sentencing, 2005, with criminal trial practice, 1999-2006; lectr. criminal trial practice Seton Hall Law Sch., 2005. Contbr. articles to profl. jours. Mem. ABA. Roman Catholic. Avocations: jogging, martial arts. Address: 25 Main St # 200 Hackensack NJ 07601-7015 also: 305 Madison Ave Ste 449 New York NY 10165-0006 Office Phone: 201-488-5500. Home Fax: 201-487-2840. E-mail: mullin.law@verizon.net.

**MULLIN, WILLIAM JESSE,** physics professor; b. St. Louis, Dec. 8, 1934; s. Charles Francis and Mae Ella (Saindon) M.; m. Sandra Carole Willmering, Feb. 11, 1961; children: Paul Andrew, Christopher Michael, Carole Elizabeth. BS summa cum laude, St. Louis U., 1956; PhD, Washington U., St. Louis, 1965. Rsch. assoc. U. Minn., Mpls., 1965-67; asst. prof. U. Mass., Amherst, 1967-71, assoc. prof., 1971-79, prof., 1979—2000; sr. vis. fellow U. Sussex, Brighton, Eng., 1973, 81, 88, Ecole Normale Superieure, Paris, 1988; prof. emeritus U. Mass., Amherst, 2000. Co-author: Introduction to the Structure of Matter, 1989, Fundamentals of Sound with Applications to Speech and Hearing, 2002; contbr. articles to profl. jours. 1st lt. USAF, 1961-64. Fellow NSF, Wash. U., 1959-60; grantee ONR, NSF. Mem. Am. Phys. Soc. Home: 10 Forestedge Rd Amherst MA 01002-1534 Office: Dept Physics/Astronomy Hasbrouck Lab U Mass Amherst MA 01003 Office Phone: 413-545-0822.

**MULLINAX, PERRY FRANKLIN,** rheumatologist, immunologist, allergist; b. Quebec City, Que., Can., June 7, 1931; MD, Med. Coll. Va., 1955. Diplomate Am. Bd. Allergy and Immunology, Am. Bd. Diagnostic Lab. Immunology, Am. Bd. Internal Medicine, Am. Bd. Rheumatology. Intern Yale Med. Ctr., New Haven, 1955-56, resident in medicine, 1958-59; fellow in medicine Mass. Gen. Hosp., Boston, 1959-61; fellow in microbiology immunology Washington U., St. Louis; fellow in biology MIT, Boston, 1962-63; mem. faculty dept. internal medicine Med. Coll. Va./Va. Commonwealth U., 1963—, prof. internal medicine, 1977-2000, emeritus prof. internal medicine, 2000—. Mem. AAAS, Am. Coll. Rheumatology. Office: Med Coll Va VA Commonwealth U PO Box 980263 Richmond VA 23298-0263 Office Phone: 804-828-9685. Business E-Mail: pfmullin@hsc.vcu.edu.

**MULLINEAUX, DONAL RAY,** geologist; b. Weed, Calif., Feb. 16, 1925; s. Lester Ray and Mary Lorene (Drew) M.; m. Diana Suzanne Charais, Nov. 21, 1951; children: Peter, Lauren, Keith. Student, U. Wash., 1942, BS in Math., 1947, BS in Geology, 1949, MS in Geology, 1950, PhD in Geology, 1961. Drilling insp. U.S. Army C.E., 1948; geologist U.S. Geol. Survey, 1950-86; contracting geologist, 1987-90; scientist emeritus U.S. Geol. Survey, 1990—2005. Author articles on volcanic activity and hazards, Mt. St. Helens, other Cascade Range volcanoes, stratigraphy and engring. geology of Puget Sound Lowland, Wash. With USNR, 1943-54, active duty, 1943-46, S1-53. Rsch. fellow Engring. Expt. Sta. U. Wash., 1949-50. Fellow Geol. Soc. Am. (E.B. Burwell Jr. award 1983); mem. Colo. Sci. Soc. Home: 14155 W 54th Ave Arvada CO 80002-1513 Personal E-mail: dondiana@mullineaux.us.

**MULLINS, CHARLES BROWN,** physician, academic administrator; b. Rochester, Ind., July 29, 1934; s. Charles E. and Mary Ruth B. (Bamberger) M.; BA, N. Tex. State U., 1954; MD, U. Tex., 1958; m. Stella Churchill, Dec. 27, 1955; children: Holly, David. Diplomate Am. Bd. Internal Medicine. Intern, U. Colo. Med. Ctr., Denver, 1958-59; resident in internal medicine Parkland Meml. Hosp., Dallas, 1962-64; USPHS rsch. fellow U. Tex. Southwestern Med. Sch., Dallas, 1964-65; chief resident medicine Parkland Meml. Hosp., 1965-66; USPHS spl. rsch. fellow cardiology br. Nat. Heart Inst., Bethesda, Md., 1967-68; practice medicine specializing in cardiology, Dallas, 1966-81; sr. attending staff Parkland Meml. Hosp., dir. med. affairs, 1977-79; asst. prof. medicine U. Tex. Southwestern Med. Sch., Dallas, 1968-71, assoc. prof., 1971-75, dir. clin. cardiology, 1971-77, prof., 1975-79, clin. prof. medicine, 1979-81; prof. medicine U. Tex. Health Sci. Ctr., Dallas, 1981-; exec. vice-chancellor health affairs U. Tex. System, 1981-2001, spl. projects dir., 2001-02; CEO Dallas County Hosp. Dist., 1979-81. Contbr. articles to profl. jours. With M.C., USAF, 1959-62. Fellow ACP, Am. Coll. Cardiology (Tex. gov. 1974-77, chmn. bd. govs. 1976), Am. Heart Assn. Coun. on Clin. Cardiology; mem. AMA, Am. Fedn. Clin. Rsch., Assn. Acad. Health Ctrs., Assn. Univ. Cardiologists, Laennec Soc., Alpha Omega Alpha. Office: 5323 Harry Hines Blvd Dallas TX 75390-9166

**MULLINS, JACK ALLEN,** cardiologist, educator; b. Oklahoma City, 1952; MD, U. Okla., 1982. Diplomate in internal medicine, cardiovasc. disease, interventional cardiology Am. Bd. Internal Medicine. Intern U. Tex., Houston, 1982-83, resident in internal medicine, 1983-85; fellow in cardiology U. Okla., Oklahoma City, 1985-88; dir. cardiac cath. lab. Columbia Bayshore Med. Ctr., Pasadena, Tex.; clin. instr. cardiology Baylor Coll. Medicine, 1988—, U. Tex. Med. Sch., Houston, 1988—. Mem. ACP, Am. Coll. Cardiology. Office: Cardiovasc Ctr PA 3337 Plainview St Ste 8 Pasadena TX 77504-1924 Office Phone: 713-941-6083.

**MULLINS, ROBERT F.,** cell biologist; b. St. Louis, May 22, 1967; s. John Edward and Cora Mayo Mullins; m. Rebecca W Wang, June 10, 1989; children: Jenna M., Natalie C. BS in Biology, Wheaton Coll., Ill., 1989; MS in Biology, St. Louis U., 1991, PhD in Cell and Molecular Biology, 1998. Asst. prof. U. Iowa, Iowa City, 2001—. Grantee, Nat. Eye Inst., 2004—06. Mem.: Am. Sci. Affiliation, Assn. Rsch. Vision Ophthalmology. Office: Univ Iowa 375 Newton Rd Iowa City IA 52242 Office Phone: 319-335-8222. Personal E-mail: robert-mullins@uiowa.edu.

**MULLINS BERG, RUTH GLADYS,** nurse; b. Westville, N.S., Can., Aug. 25, 1943; came to U.S., 1949, naturalized, 1955; d. William G. and Gladys H.; m. Leonard E. Mullins Aug. 27, 1963 (dec.); children: Deborah R. Jenkins, Catherine M., Leonard III; m. Bernard J. Berg, June 19, 2004 BS in Nursing, Calif. State U., Long Beach, 1966; MSN, UCLA, 1973; PhD, Columbia Pacific U. Cert. pediatric nurse practitioner. Pub. health nurse Los Angeles County Health Dept., 1967-68; nurse Meml. Hosp. Med. Ctr., Long Beach, 1968-72; dir. pediatric nurse practitioner program Calif. State U., Long Beach, 1973-97, asst. prof., 1975-80, assoc. prof., 1980-85, prof., 1985—; coord. accelerated BSN program, 2003—. Health svc. credential coord. Sch. Nursing Calif. State U., Long Beach, chmn., 1979-81, coord. grad. programs, 1985-92; mem. Calif. Maternal, Child and Adolescent Health Bd., 1977-84; vice chair Long Beach/Orange County Health Consortium, 1984-85, chair 1985-86. Author: (with B. Nelms) Growth and Development: A Primary Health Care Approach; contbg. author: Quick Reference to Pediatric Nursing, 1984; assoc. editor Jour. Pediatric Health Care, 1985—. Tng. grantee HHS, Divsn. Nursing Calif. Dept. Health. Fellow Nat. Assn. Pediatric Nurse Assocs. and Practitioners (exec. bd., pres. 1990-91), Nat. Fedn. Nursing Splty. Orgns. (sec. 1991-93); mem. APHA, Nat. Alliance Nurse Practitioners (governing body 1990-92), Assn. Faculties Pediatric Nurse Practitioner Programs. L.A. and Orange County Assn. Pediatric Nurse Practitioners and Assocs. (treas. 1998—), Assn. Am. Univ. Faculty. Democrat. Methodist. Home: 13240 Eldorado Dr #187A Seal Beach CA 90740 Office: Calif State U Dept Nursing 1250 N Bellflower Blvd Long Beach CA 90840-0001 Office Phone: 562-985-4476. Personal E-Mail: rgmullins@sprintmail.com. Business E-Mail: rmullins@csulb.edu.

**MULLIS, KARY BANKS,** biochemist; b. Lenoir, NC, Dec. 28, 1944; s. Cecil Banks Mullis and Bernice Alberta (Barker) Fredericks; m. Richards Mullis (div.); 1 child, Louise; m. Cynthia Mullis (div.); children: Christopher, Jeremy; m. Nancy Lier Cosgrove, 1998. BS in Chemistry, Ga. Inst. Tech., 1966; PhD in Biochemistry, U. Calif., Berkeley, 1973; DSc (hon.), U. S.C., 1994. Lectr. biochemistry U. Calif., Berkeley, 1972, postdoctoral fellow San Francisco, 1977—79, U. Kans. Med. Sch., Kansas City, 1973—76; scientist Cetus Corp., Emeryville, Calif., 1979—86; dir. molecular biology Xytronyx, Inc., San Diego, 1986—88; cons. Specialty Labs, Inc., Amersham, Inc., Chiron Inc. and various others, Calif., 1988—96; chmn. StarGene, Inc. San Rafael, Calif.; v.p. Histotec, Inc., Cedar Rapids, Iowa; v.p. molecular biology chemistry Vyrex Inc., La Jolla, Calif.; disting. rschr. Children's Hosp., Rsch. Inst., Oakland, Calif. Disting. vis. prof. U. S.C. Coll. of Sci. and Math.

Author: (autobiography) Dancing Naked in the Mind Field, 1998; contbr. articles to profl. jours.; patentee in field. Bd. dir. Nat. Orgn. Reform of Marijuana Laws, 2000—. Named Scientist of Yr., R&D Mag., 1991, Calif. Scientist of Yr., 1992; named to National Inventors Hall of Fame, 1998; recipient Preis Biochemische Analytik award, German Soc. Clin. Chem., 1990, Allan award, 1990, award, Gairdner Found. Internat., 1991, Nat. Biotech. award, 1991, Robert Koch award, 1992, Chiron Corp. Biotechnology Rsch. award, Am. Soc. Microbiology, 1992, Japan prize, Sci. and Tech. Found. Japan, 1993, Nobel Prize in Chemistry, Nobel Foundation, 1993. Mem.: Inst. Further Study (dir. 1983—), Am. Acad. Achievement, Am. Chem. Soc. Achievements include invention of invention of Polymerase Chain Reaction (PCR). Avocations: astrology, surfing.*

**MULLIS, TONY RANDALL,** social studies educator; s. Don and Susan Mullis (Stepmother); m. Maureen Heller, Apr. 11, 1981; children: Sean, Seth, Scot. B. Auburn U., 1981; M, Va. Tech, 1982; PhD, U. Kans., 2002. Commd. 2d lt. USAF, 1982; acad. instr.; advisor Air Command and Staff Coll., Montgomery, Ala., 2002—05; advanced through grades to lt. col USAF; assoc. prof. Command and Gen. Staff Coll., Ft. Leavenworth, Kans., 2005—. Adj. instr. Auburn U., Montgomery, 1997—2005. Author: (book) Peacekeeping on the Plains: Army Operations in Bleeding Kansas; contbr. book. Decorated Meritorious Svc. medal Air Force; Alf Landon Rsch. grant, Kans. State Hist. Soc., 2001. Mem.: Kans. State Hist. Soc., Soc. Mil. History. Avocations: tennis, golf. Office: Command and Gen Staff Coll 1 Reynolds Blvd Fort Leavenworth KS 66027 Office Phone: 913-684-2536.

**MULLOY, PATRICK ALOYSIUS,** lawyer; b. Wilkes-Barre, Pa., Sept. 14, 1941; s. Hugh Patrick and Ellen Mary (Meagher) M.; m. Marjorie Baumer; children: Maura Alice, Daniel Patrick, Claire Ellen. BA magna cum laude, King's Coll., 1963; MA, U. Notre Dame, 1965; JD with honors, George Washington U., 1971; LLM, Harvard U., 1978. Bar: D.C. 1972, Pa. 1972, U.S. Ct. Appeals (D.C., 2d, and 9th cirs.) 1975, U.S. Supreme Ct. 1975, U.S. Ct. Appeals (5th and 9th cirs.) 1976. Fgn. service officer U.S. Dept. State, Washington, 1965-72; trial lawyer Dept. Justice, Washington, 1973-77, sr. lawyer antitrust div., 1978-82; Congl. fellow U.S. Congress, 1983; minority gen. counsel U.S. Senate Banking Com., 1984-86, gen. counsel, 1987-89, sr. counsel, internat. affairs advisor, 1989-92, chief internat. counsel, 1993-94, chief internat. coun. (minority) Washington, 1995-98; asst. sec. market access and compliance Internat. Trade Adminstrn., U.S. Dept. Commerce, Washington, 1998-2001. Apptd. asst. sec., exec. br. commn. on security and coop. in Europe by Pres. Clinton, 1999-2001; apptd. commr. Joint House Senate U.S.-China Econ. and Security Rev. Commn., Washington, 2001—; adj. prof. internat. trade law Cath. U. Law Sch., Washington, 2002—, George Mason Law Sch., Arlington, Va., 2003—; rep. Alfred P. Sloan Found., Washington, D.C., 2005—. Home: 304 W Masonic View Ave Alexandria VA 22301-2419 Office: US China Security Rev Commn Hall of States Ste 602 444 N Capitol St NW Washington DC 20001 Office Phone: 202-624-1412. Business E-Mail: pmulloy@uscc.gov. E-mail: pamulloy@aol.com.

**MULRONEY, BRIAN (MARTIN BRIAN MULRONEY),** former Prime Minister of Canada; b. Baie Comeau, Que., Can., Mar. 20, 1939; s. Benedict and Irene (O'Shea) M.; m. Mila Pivnicki, 1973; children: Caroline, Benedict, Mark, Nicolas. BA, St. Francis Xavier U., LLD, 1979; LLL, U. Laval, Que.; LLD (hon.), Meml. U. Nfld., Nfld., 1980, U. W.I., 1993, Tel Aviv U., 1994, Ctrl. Conn. State U., 1994, Barry U., 1995. Ptnr. Ogilvy Renault, Montreal, Canada, 1965-76; exec. v.p. Iron Ore Co. Can., Montreal, 1977-83, 1976-77, pres., 1977-83; mem. Parliament Can. from Ctrl. N.S., Ottawa, Ont., 1983-84; mem. Parliament Can. from Manicouagan, 1984-88; mem. Parliament Can. from Charlevoix, 1988-93; leader of Her Majesty's Loyal Opposition, 1983-84; prime min., 1984—; royal commr. Cliche Commn. investigating violence in Que. constrn. industry, 1974; sr. ptnr. Ogilvy Renault, Montreal, 1993—. Chmn. internat. adv. bd. Barrick Gold Corp., The J.P. Morgan Chase Corp.; mem. internat. adv. coun. Power Corp. Can.; mem. adv. bd. The China Internat. Trust and Investment Corp.; mem. Hicks Muse Capital Ptnrs. Ind. News and Media, PLC; mem. internat. adv. coun. Inst. Internat. Studies; bd. dirs. Archer Daniels Midland Co., Barrick Gold Corp., The Trizec Properties Inc., Power Corp., Quebecor World Inc.; chmn. Forbes, NYC. Author: Where I Stand, 1983. Trustee Montreal Heart Inst.; mem. internat. adv. coun. Les Hautes Etudes Commerciales l'Université de Montréal. Named Grand Officer, Ordre Nat. du Que.; recipient Companion of the Order of Can. Office: Ogilvy Renault 1981 McGill College Ave Ste 1100 Montreal PQ Canada H3A 3C1 Business E-Mail: bmulroney@ogilvyrenault.com.

**MULRONEY, DERMOT,** actor; b. Alexandria, Va., Oct. 31, 1963; m. Catherine Keener, 1990; 1 child, Clyde. Grad., Northeastern U., 1985; BS, Northwestern U., 1985. Appeared in films Sunset, 1988, Young Guns, 1988, Staying Together, 1989, Longtime Companion, 1989, Survival Quest, 1990, Bright Angel, 1991, Career Opportunities, 1991, Where the Day Takes You, 1992, Point of No Return, 1993, Samantha, 1993, The Thing Called Love, 1993, Silent Tongue, 1993, Bad Girls, 1994, There Goes My Baby, 1994, Angels in the Outfield, 1994, Box of Moonlight, 1996, Bastard Out of Carolina, 1996, Kansas City, 1996, The Trigger Effect, 1996, My Best Friend's Wedding, 1997, Where the Money Is, 1999, Goodbye Lover, 1999, Trixie, 2000, The Safety of Objects, 2001, Lovely & Amazing, 2001, Investigating Sex, 2001, About Schmidt, 2002, Undertow, 2004, Something Borrowed, 2004, Wedding Date, 2005, Must Love Dogs, 2005, The Family Stone, 2005; TV appearances include Fame, 1982, Sin of Innocence, 1986, Daddy, 1987, Long Gone, 1987, Unconquered, 1989, The Heart of Justice, 1993, The Last Outlaw, 1993, Friends, 2003, (mini-series) Family Pictures, 1993, (spls.) The Drug Knot, 1986; prodr. (film) Living in Oblivion, 1995. Office: Internat Creative Mgmt 8942 Wilshire Blvd Beverly Hills CA 90211 Address: PMK/KBH Ste 700 8500 Wilshire Blvd Beverly Hills CA 90211*

**MULROW, PATRICK JOSEPH,** medical educator; s. Patrick J. and Delia (O'Keefe) M.; m. Jacquelyn Pinover, Aug. 8, 1953; children: Deborah, Nancy, Robert, Catherine. AB, Colgate U., 1947; MD, Cornell U., 1951; MSc (hon.), Yale U., 1969. Intern N.Y. Hosp., 1951-52, resident, 1952-54; instr. physiology Med. Coll. Cornell U., 1954-55; research fellow Stanford U., 1955-57; instr. medicine Yale U., 1957-60, asst. prof., 1960-66, assoc. prof., 1966-69, prof. medicine, 1969-75; chmn. dept. medicine Med. Coll. Ohio, Toledo, 1975—95, prof. medicine, 1975—97, prof. emeritus, 1997—. Chmn. ednl. com. Council for high blood pressure rsch. Am. Heart Assn., 1968-70, mem. exec. com., 1986-96, vice-chmn. of coun., 1990-92, chmn. 1992-94, past chmn., 1995-96; mem. study sect. NIH, 1970-74. Editorial bd. Jour. Clin. Endocrinology and Metabolism, 1966-70, 75-79, Endocrine Rsch., 1974—; Jour. Exptl. Biology and Medicine, Hypertension, 1994-98; contbr. articles to profl. jours. With USNR, 1944-46. Mem. ACP, Am. Soc. Clin. Investigation, Assn. Am. Physicians, Am. Physiol. Soc., Endocrine Soc., Am. Fedn. Clin. Rsch., Am. Clin. and Climatol. Assn., Am. Heart Assn. (nat. rsch. com., chmn. cardiovasc. regulation rsch. study com. 1986-91), Assn. Profs. Medicine, Assn. Program Dirs. in Internal Medicine, Cen. Soc. Clin. Rsch. (pres. 1988-89), Internat. Soc. Hypertension, World Hypertension League (sec.-gen. 1995—), Inter-Am. Soc. Hypertension, Sigma Xi (pres. Yale chpt. 1965-66), Alpha Omega Alpha. Home: 9526 Carnoustie Rd Perrysburg OH 43551-3501 Office: Med Coll Ohio Dept Medicine 3120 Glendale Ave Toledo OH 43614-5809 Office Phone: 419-383-3767. Business E-Mail: pmulrow@meduohio.edu.

**MULROY, MICHAEL FRANCIS, II,** anesthesiologist; b. Alton, Ill., Mar. 24, 1944; s. James Richard and Suzanne (Sparks) Mulroy; m. Barbara Kimm, Jan. 12, 2003; children: Brian Rhodes, Lauren Elizabeth. BA, Georgetown U., Washington, 1964; MD, Cornell U., N.Y.C., 1969. Diplomate Am. Bd. Anesthiology, 1978. Staff anesthesiologist Va. Mason Med. Ctr., Seattle, 1977—, dir. anesthesia residency program, 1982—2000; clin. prof. anesthesiology U. Wash., Seattle, 1998—. Author: (Handbook) Regional Anesthesia: A Procedural Handbook, 1985. Lt. cmmdr. USNR, 1971—73, Vietnam. Democrat. Avocations: hiking, kayaking. Office: Va Mason Med Ctr 1100 Ninth Ave Seattle WA 98111 Office Phone: 206-223-6980.

**MULRYAN, HENRY TRIST,** mining executive, consultant; b. Palo Alto, Calif., Jan. 6, 1927; s. Henry and Marian Abigail (Trist) M.; m. Lenore Hoag, Aug. 25, 1948; children: James W., Carol. Student, Yale U., 1945-46; AB in Econs., Stanford U., 1948; postgrad., Am. Grad. Sch. Internat. Bus., 1949, Columbia U., 1983. V.p. mktg. Sierra Talc Co., South Pasadena, Calif., 1955-65, United Sierra, Trenton, NJ, 1965-67, v.p., gen. mgr., 1967-70, pres., 1970-77; v.p. Cyprus Mines Corp., Los Angeles, 1978-80; sr. v.p. ops. Cyprus indsl. minerals div. Amoco Minerals Co., Englewood, Colo., 1980-85; pres. Cyprus Indls. Minerals Co., Englewood, 1985-87; v.p. Cyprus Minerals Co., Englewood, 1985-87, sr. v.p. mktg., corp. adminstr., 1987-89; pres. Mineral Econs. Internat., 1989—. Vol. exec. Internat. Exec. Svc. Corps., Zimbabwe, 1998, Romania, 98, Jordan, 2000, Jordan, 01, Jordan, 02, Jordan, 04, Armenia, 03; pres. Jonathan Art Found., 2004—05. Served with U.S. Army, 1944-46. Mem.: Rotary (pres. South Pasadena club 1964—65, bd. dir. Princeton, N.J. club 1969—75), Jonathan Club. Office: 539 Muskingum Ave Pacific Palisades CA 90272-4252 E-mail: htmulryan@verizon.net.

**MULSANT, BENOIT HENRI,** psychiatrist, educator, medical researcher; b. Paris, Feb. 28, 1957; arrived in U.S., 1985; s. Henri Edmond and Francoise Emilie Mulsant; m. Sharon Jane Laufenberg, Feb. 17, 1995; children: Louise Sharon, Sophie Sharon. MD, U. Laval, Que., Can., 1983—84; MS, Carnegie Mellon U., 1989. Lic. Am. Bd. of Psychiatry and Neurology. Assoc. prof. psychiatry U. Pitts., 1996—2004, prof. psychiatry, 2004—; med. dir. ECT svc. U. Pitts. Med. Ctr., 1994—2005. Prin. investigator federally-funded and industry-sponsored clin. rsch. trials on psychiat. disorders in geriatric patients. Contbr. articles to profl. jours., chpts. to books. Recipient Jr. Investigator award, Am. Assn. for Geriatric Psychiatry, 1994, Ann. Award for Merit, Nat. Psychiat. Endowment Fund, 1990, Laughlin fellowship, Am. Coll. of Psychiatrists, 1990, NIH Career Development award. Mem.: Internat. Coll. Geriatric Neuropsychopharmacology (founding mem. 2001), Am. Psychiat. Assn. Office: U Pitts - WPIC 3811 O'Hara St Pittsburgh PA 15213

**MULTHAUP, MERREL KEYES,** artist; b. Cedar Rapids, Iowa, Sept. 27, 1922; d. Stephen Dows and Edna Gertrude (Gard) Keyes; m. Robert Hansen Multhaup, Apr. 7, 1944; children: Eric Stephen, Robert Bruce. Student, State U. Iowa, 1942—43, Rice U., 1971. Tchg. faculty Summit (NJ) Art Assn., 1956—60; art instr. studio classes Springfield, NJ, 1954—55, Bloomfield (NJ) Art Group, 1955—56, Westport, Conn., 1962—63; tchg. faculty Hunterdon Art Ctr., Clinton, NJ, 1985—92. Numerous one-woman shows including Summit Art Assn., 1955, Papermill Playhouse, NJ, 1957, 1959, 1960, 1978, 1979, Benedict Gallery, NJ, 1976, Coriell Gallery, 1995; exhibited in group shows at Nat. Assn. Women Artists, NYC, 1957-2001 (awards in figure painting), Hartford (Conn.) Athanaeum Mus., 1961 (1st prize), Highgate Gallery, NYC, Waverly Gallery, NYC, Leicester Gallery, London, Silvermine Gallery, Conn., Leicester Gallery, London, Pendut Gallery, Tex., Benedict Gallery, Sidney Rothman Gallery, NJ, Stamford (Conn.) Mus., Bridgeport (Conn.) Mus., Montclair (NJ) Mus., Newark Mus., Coriell Gallery, Albuquerque, Leicester Gallery, London; (traveling exhibit) Nat. Assn. Women Artists, 1996—, Travel USA, 1999, New World Art Ctr., NYC, 1998-99, Gallery Art 54, NYC, 1997, Atelier 14 Gallery, NYC, 2000-02; more than 30 commd. portraits, 1960—. Bd. dirs., exhbn. chmn. Summit Art Assn., 1950-60, Silvermine Guild of Art, New Canaan, Conn., 1960-64; bd. dirs. Artist's Equity of NJ, 1977-84, chmn. state-wide event, 1983, 86; artist's adv. coun. Hunterdon Art Ctr., Clinton, 1988-92; pres. Four Hills Neighbors, 1998-2000. Recipient awards in juried exhbns. in Iowa, Pa., NJ, Conn., NYC. Mem. Nat. Mus. for Women in Arts (charter mem.), Nat. Assn. Women Artists Inc. (awards for figure painting 1957, 80-89), Silvermine Nat. Portrait Group of Artists. Avocations: entertaining, singing, dance, playing the piano, reading. Home: 1321 Stagecoach Rd SE Albuquerque NM 87123-4320

**MULVA, JAMES JOSEPH,** oil industry executive; b. Oshkosh, Wis., June 19, 1946; m. Miriam Mulva; 2 children. BBA in Fin., U. Tex., 1968, MBA in Fin., 1969. Mgmt. trainee, treas. Phillips Petroleum Co., Bartlesville, Okla., 1973, asst. treas. London, 1974, mgr. fgn. exch. and investment Bartlesville, Okla., 1976, v.p., treas. Europe/Africa div. London, 1980, mgr. corp. and planning Bartlesville, Okla., 1984, asst. treas., 1985, treas., 1986, v.p., treas., 1988—90, chief fin. officer, 1990—99, pres., COO, 1994—99, vice-chmn., pres. & CEO, 1999, chmn., CEO, 1999—. Officer Navy, 1969—73. Roman Catholic. Office: Phillips Petroleum Co 18 Phillips Bldg Bartlesville OK 74003*

**MULVA, PATRICK T.,** oil industry executive; b. Green Bay, Wis. BBA, Notre Dame U.; MBA, U. Tex. Fin. analyst ExxonMobil Corp., Baton Rouge, 1976, exec. asst. to pres. U.S. affiliate, 1987, asst. contr. internat. affiliate, fin. dir. Malaysia, 1991, upstream to asst. contr., 1993; contr. Imperial Oil Ltd., 1996, sr. v.p. fin. and adminstrn., 1998—2002, contr., 2000—02; v.p. investor rels. and sec. ExxonMobil Corp., 2002, v.p., controller. With USAF, 1972—75. Office: ExxonMobil Corp 5959 Las Colinas Blvd Irving TX 75039-2298*

**MULVANEY, MARY FREDERICA,** systems analyst; b. NY, Nov. 27, 1945; d. Michael Joseph and Mary Catherine (Clapper) Mulvaney. BA, Marymount Coll., 1967; MA, U. Va., 1968; MS in Computer Sci., Marymount U., 1999. Cert. data processor Inst. Cert. Computer Profls. Computer systems analyst Dept. of Def., Ft. Meade, Md., 1968-74; sr. programmer analyst Planning Rsch. Corp., McLean, Va., 1974-83; mem. tech. staff Fed. Systems Group TRW, Inc., Fairfax, Va., 1983-90, engr., scientist, 1994—2002; sr. mem. tech. staff GTE Govt. Sys. Corp., Rockville, Md., 1990-94; software engr. Northrop Grumman, Fairfax, 2003—. Mem.: IEEE, Cath. Assn. Scientists and Engrs., Computer Measurement Group, Data Processing Mgmt. Assn. Roman Catholic. Office: Northrop Grumman Mission Sys 12900 Federal Sys Park Dr Fairfax VA 22033

**MULVANEY, MARY JEAN,** retired physical education educator; b. Omaha, Jan. 6, 1927; d. Marion Fowler and Blanche Gibons (McKee) M. BS, U. Nebr., 1948; MS, Wellesley Coll., 1951; LHD (hon.), U. Nebr., 1986. Instr. Kans. State U., Manhattan, 1948-50, U. Nebr., Lincoln, 1951-57, asst. prof., 1957-62, U. Kans., Lawrence, 1962-66; assoc. prof. U. Chgo., 1966-76, prof., 1976-90, prof. emeritus, 1990—, chmn. women's divsn., 1966-76, chmn. dept. phys. edn. and athletics, 1976-90; mem. vis. com. on athletics MIT, 1978-81, Wellesley Coll., 1978-79. Dir. athletics U. Chgo., 1980—90; mem. selection com. U. Chgo. Athletics Hall of Fame, 2006—. Recipient Honor award Nebr. Assn. Health, Phys. Edn. and Recreation, 1962, U. Nebr. Alumni Achievement award, 1998; named to U. Chgo. Athletics Hall of Fame, 2003; Office of Dir. Athletics, U. Chgo., named in honor, 2003. Mem.: AAHPERD, Univ. Athletic Assn. (sec. 1986—90, exec. com. 1986—90, dels. com. 1986—90, chmn. athletic adminstrs. com. 1986—88), Ill. Assn. Intercollegiate Athletics for Women (chmn. 1978—80), Nat. Assn. Collegiate Dirs. of Athletics (exec. com. 1976—80, Hall of Fame 1990), Midwest Assn. Intercollegiate Athletics for Women (chmn. 1979—81), Nat. Collegiate Coun. Women Athletic Adminstrs. (Lifetime Achievement award 2006), Nat. Collegiate Athletic Assn. (coun. 1983—87), Alpha Chi Omega, Mortar Bd. Home: 5821 Kennelley Ct Lincoln NE 68516-3799 Personal E-mail: maryjeanmulvany@aol.com.

**MULVEE, ROBERT EDWARD,** bishop; b. Boston, Feb. 15, 1930; s. John F. and Jennie T. Mulvee. BA, PhB, U. Sem. Ottawa, 1953; MRE, Am. Coll., Louvain, Belgium, 1957; D Canon Law, Lateran U., Rome, 1964; DD (hon.), Rivier Coll., Nashua, NH, 1979. Ordained priest Diocese of Manchester, NH, 1957; asst. chancellor Diocese, 1964—72; named monsignor, 1966; elevated to domestic prelate, 1970; named chancellor, 1972; Aux. Bishop of Manchester NH, 1977—85; Bishop of Wilmington Del., 1985—95; Coadjutor Bishop of Providence RI, 1995—97; Bishop of Providence RI, 1997—2005; ret., 2005. Trustee Nat. Shrine Imaculate Conception, Washington, 1987. Mem.: Nat. Conf. Cath. Bishops. Roman Catholic.

**MULVEY, GERALD JOHN,** meteorologist; b. Cambria Heights, N.Y., Dec. 20, 1949; s. George Patrick and Estelle Florence M.; m. Katherine Louise Strick, July 7, 1973. BS in Physics, York Coll., Jamaica, N.Y., 1971; MS in Atmospheric Sci., SUNY, Albany, 1973; PhD in Atmospheric Sci., Colo. State U., 1977. Cert. cons. meteorologist, CCM. Rsch. assoc. dept. atmospheric sci. Colo. State U., 1977—78; mgr. dept. atmospheric physics Meteorology Rsch., Inc., Altadena, Calif., 1978—80; sr. tech. engr. Lockheed Martin Missiles and Space, Sunnyvale, Calif., 1980—97; advanced programs mgr. Lockheed Martin Western Devel. Labs., 1997—99; lectr. dept. geoscis. San Francisco State U., 1995—98; advanced programs mgr. Lockheed Martin Global Telecomm., Sunnyvale, Calif., 1998—99; prin. sys. engr. DIVA Sys. Corp., Redwood City, Calif., 1999—2002; sr. mgr. NPOESS Northrop Grumman, 2002—. Co-author: Environmental Impacts of Artificial Ice Nucleating Agents, 1978; contbr. articles to profl. jours. including Analytical Chemistry and Jour. Applied Meteorology. Mem. Cupertino (Calif.) Libr. Commn., 1989—93; v.p. bd. dirs. Cupertino Libr. Found., 2000—01. Mem.: AAAS, Internat. Soc. Measurement and Control (v.p. Santa Clara Valley 1996—97), Am. Meterol. Soc. (cert. consulting meteorologist), Sigma Xi. Roman Catholic. Achievements include verifying/documenting of long range transport of active artificial cloud nucleating agents. Office: Nothrop Grumman R10/1791 Mission One Space Pk Redondo Beach CA 90278 Office Phone: 310-812-5196. Business E-Mail: gerry.mulvey@ngc.com.

**MULVIHILL, JAMES EDWARD,** periodontist, educator; b. Cleve., Sept. 24, 1940; s. John F. and Teresa J. (Carlos) M.; m. May Jane Forino, 1963; children— Karen, Kristen, Jason BA, Coll. of Holy Cross, 1962; DMD, Harvard U., 1966. Asst. dean for student affairs, coordinator Harvard-VA continuing edn. program Harvard Sch. Dental Medicine, Boston, 1970-71; dean clin. campus L.I. Jewish-Hillside Med. Ctr., Queens Hosp. Ctr. Affiliation, Jewish Inst. for Geriatric Care, Health Scis. Ctr. SUNY-Stony Brook, 1971-80; v.p. for edn. and research L.I. Jewish-Hillside Med. Ctr., New Hyde Park, NY, 1975-80; v.p., provost for health affairs, exec. dir. Health Ctr., prof. periodontics U. Conn., Farmington, 1980-92; attending periodontist John Dempsey Hosp., U. Conn. Health Ctr., Farmington, 1982-92; pres. John Dempsey Fin. Corp., Farmington, 1988-92; sr. v.p. for health policy The Travelers Corp., Hartford, Conn., 1992-94; chmn. bd. The Travelers Health Co., Hartford, 1992-93; sr. fellow in health policy Assn. of Acad. Health Ctrs., 1994; pres., CEO Managed Health, Inc., 1994, Comty. Health Plan of Queens/Nassau, New Hyde Park, NY, 1994-95, Forsyth Dental Ctr., Boston, 1995-96, Juvenile Diabetes Found. Internat., 1996-99; dir. instnl. advancement and corp. rels. Am. Dental Edn. Assn., 2000—; asst. to pres. So. Maine Med. Ctr., 2000—01; chief dept. dentistry Harvard U. Health Svcs., 2003—. Cons. in field Author: (with others) Guide to Foreign Medical Schools, 1975, Editorial Instructions for Dental Authors, 1979-80, 1979, Human Subjects Research: The Operational Handbook for IRB's, 1982, 2d edit., 1984, Japanese edit., 1987; also articles, chpt. in book Bd. dirs. William Gies Found., Nat. Fund for Med. Edn., Found. for Blood Rsch.; overseer Joslin Diabetes Ctr. Recipient Disting. Alumnus award Harvard Sch. Dental Medicine, 1982, Disting. alumnus award Holy Cross Coll., 1991. Fellow AAAS, Am. Coll. Dentistry, Internat. Coll. Dentistry; mem. ADA, Am. Acad. Periodontology, Conn. State Dental Assn. (Fones award 2004), Harvard Dental Alumni Assn., Alpha Sigma Nu, Sigma Psi. Avocations: golf, gardening, photography. Address: 117 Kings Hwy Kennebunkport ME 04046-5606 Personal E-mail: mulvi@adelphia.net.

**MULVIHILL, KEITHLEY D.,** lawyer; b. Pitts., Oct. 16, 1956; s. Bernard H. and Doris L. M.; m. Donna Colella, 1980; children: Michael, Mary Katherine. BA in History, Ind. U., Pa., 1978; JD cum laude, U. Pitts., 1981. Bar: Pa. 1981, U.S. Dist. Ct. (we. dist.) Pa. 1981, U.S. Ct. Appeals (3d cir.) 1982; CPCU. Assoc. Rose, Schmidt, Hasley & DiSalle, Pitts., 1981-88, shareholder, 1988-2001; ptnr., head litigation dept. Leech, Tishman, Fuscaldo & Lampl, Pitts., 2001—03; mng. ptnr. Pitts. office Rawle & Henderson LLP, 2003—. Spl. master Ct. of Common Pleas of Allegheny County, Pa.; commr. Municipality of Mt. Lebanon, Pa., 1999—, v.p. 2002, pres., 2003. Mng. editor U. Pitts. Law Rev., 1980—81. Mem. Allegheny County Dem. Com; rep. Mt. Lebanon South Hills Area Coun. of Govts., 2000-03; mem. St. Bernard Roman Cath. Ch. (past mem. parish coun.); bd. dirs. Med. Rescue Team Sout Authority, 2005—. Mem. ABA, Pa. Bar Assn., Pa. Def. Inst. (treas. 1998-2004), Allegheny County Bar Assn., Def. Rsch. Inst., CPCU Soc. (pub. rels. chmn. Allegheny County claims com.). Office: Rawle & Henderson LLP Ste 1000 Henry W Oliver Bldg 535 Smithfield St Pittsburgh PA 15222 E-mail: kmulvihill@rawle.com.

**MULVIHILL, WILLIAM J.,** former health science association administrator; BBA, U. Cinn.; MEd, Ohio U. V.p. Ohio River Valley chpt. Arthritis Found., 1984-87, chair, 1987-90, midwest. area vice chair, 1988-90, chair fin. devel. com., 1991-93, vice chair of couns., 1993, treas., 1994-96, sr. vice chair, 1996-98, chair, 1998—2001; mem. board Alliance for Lupus Research. Mem. com. on appointments, salary and personnel com., exec. com.; assoc. dir. athletics for external affairs U. Cinn., exec. dir. athletic team scholarships. Mem. Coun. for Advancement and Support of Edn., Nat. Assn. Collegiate Dirs. of Athletics, Nat., Assn. Athletic Devel. Dirs. Office: Alliance For Lupus Research 28 W 44th St #1217 New York NY 10036-6600

**MUMFORD, CHRISTOPHER GREENE,** corporate financial executive; b. Washington, Oct. 21, 1945; s. Milton C. and Dorothea L. (Greene) Mumford. BA, Stanford U., 1968, MBA, 1975. Cons. Internat. Tech. Resources Inc., 1974; asst. v.p. Wells Fargo Bank, San Francisco, 1975-78; asst. treas. Arcata Corp., San Francisco, 1978-82, v.p. fin., 1982-87, exec. v.p. fin., 1987-94. Gen. ptnr. Scarff, Sears & Assocs., San Francisco, 1986—95; mng. dir. Questor Ptnrs. Fund, L.P., San Francisco, 1999—98; v.p. bd. dirs. Triangle Pacific Corp., Dallas, 1986—88, Norton Enterprises Inc., Salt Lake City, 1988—90, Crown Pacific Ptnrs., Portland, Oreg., 1991—2004, Ryder TRS, Inc., Miami, Fla., 1996—98, Ockham PLC, London, 1996—98, Impco Technologies, Inc., Cerritos, Calif., 1998—2000. Office: PO Box 1340 Mill Valley CA 94942-1340 Office Phone: 415-601-6800. Personal E-mail: cgmumford@aol.com.

**MUMFORD, DAVID BRYANT,** mathematics professor; b. Worth, Sussex, Eng., June 11, 1937; came to U.S., 1940; s. William Bryant and Grace (Schiott) M.; m. Erika Jentsch, June 27, 1959 (dec. July 30, 1988); children: Stephen, Peter, Jeremy, Suchitra; m. Jenifer Moore, Dec. 29, 1989. BA, Harvard U., 1957, PhD, 1961; DSc (hon.), U. Warwick, 1983, Norwegian U. Sci.-Tech., 2000, Rockefeller U., 2001. Jr. fellow Harvard U., 1958-61, assoc. prof., 1962—67, prof. math., 1967—77, Higgins prof., 1977-97, chmn. dept. math, 1981-84; prof., divsn. applied math. Brown U., 1996—. V.p. Internat. Math. Union, 1991-94, pres., 1995-99. Author: Geometric Invariant Theory, 1965, Abelian Varieties, 1970, Introduction to Algebraic Geometry, 1976, 2 and 3 Dimensional Patterns of the Face, 1999, Indra's Pearls, 2002. Recipient Fields medal Internat. Congress Mathematicians, 1974, Longuet-Higgins prize, 2005, Shaw prize in Math. Sciences, Shaw Found., Hong Kong, 2006.; MacArthur Found. fellow, 1987-92. Fellow Tata Inst. (hon.); mem. Acad. Nazionale dei Lincei, Nat. Acad. Scis., Am. Acad. Scis., Am. Philos. Soc., Norwegian Acad. Sci. and Letters. Office: Brown U 182 George St Providence RI 02912-9056 Home: 15 Sleeper St Boston MA 02210 Office Phone: 401-863-3441. E-mail: david_mumford@brown.edu.

**MUMFORD, JEFFREY,** composer, educator; b. Washington, D.C., 1955; BA in Painting, U. Calif.-Irvine, 1977; student in composition, Aspen Music Sch., 1977—81; MA in Musical Composition, U. Calif.-San Diego, 1981. Pvt. studies in composition with Lawrence Moss, 1977—78; pvt. studies in composition with Elliott Carter, 1980—83; theory & composition instr. Settlement Music Sch., Phila., 1985—89; theory instr. Westchester Conservatory of Music, White Plains, NY, 1986—89; theory & composition instr./spl. projects coord. Washington Conservatory of Music, Washington, 1989—99; artist in residence, composition Bowling Green State U., Ohio, 1999—2000; composer-in-residence Oberlin Conservatory of Music, 2000—. Co-coord., Washington/Balt. chpt. Am. Composers Forum, 1977; asst. dir. prodn./media liaison Washington Bach Consort, 1989—90; seminar coord., program note annotator, prodn. supr. The Concert Soc. at Md., U. Md., College Park, 1990—95; mem. Pa. State Arts Coun. Music Panel (Composition), 1990, Md. State Arts Coun. Music Panel (Composition), 1991, N.C. State Arts Coun.

Music Panel (Composition), 1992, NEA Composer Fellowship Panels, 1990, 94; juror Mayor's Arts Awards, Washington, 1994; mem. NEA Chamber Music Panel, 1994; cons. Mary Flagler Cary Charitable Trust Recording Program, 1996; mem. Mass. Cultural Coun. Panel (Organizations), 1999, 2000, 05, Ill. State Arts Coun. Panel, 2001, NEA Presenters Panel, 2004, NEA Access to Artistic Excellence Panel, 2006; lectr. in field. Composer: (for piano) barbaglio dal manca, 1981, rev., 1992, 2000, for Elliott, 1983, tango variations, 1984, fragments from the surrounding evening, 1984, a flower in folding shadows, 1986, a landscape of interior resonances, 2001, four dances for Boris, 2004, (solo instrumental) linear cycles VII (cambiamenti II), 1979, rev., 1993, variazioni elegiaci, 1979, rev., 1997, morning thunder for solo flute, 1979—80, a window's gathering of clouds, 1981, variazioni elegiaci II, 1983, amid fleeting pockets of billowing radiance, 1990, the clarity of remembered springs, 1992—93, revisiting variazioni elegiaci, 2001, wending, 2001, the milliner's fancy, 2003, the mussings...revisiting memories, 2005, an expanding distance of multiple voices, 2005, (chamber) linear cycles II, 1978, string quartet no. 1 (formerly quartet no. 3), 1978, rev., 1980, numerous others, recordings, Bang on a Can Live, the focus of blue light, Dark Fires, Telling Tales, the promise of the far horizon, linear cycles II, quartet no. 3 (string quartet no. I); composer/performer: WCLV radio sta., Cleve.; composer: (interview programs) Around Noon, WCPN-FM, Cleve., Artsbeat, WPFW-FM, Washington, Desert Island Discs, WETA-FM, Washington, The Diane Rehm Show, (vocal) two haiku settings: of place and love, 2006. Recipient Meet the Composer, 2003, 2006; grantee, U. Calif., 1977, ASCAP Found., 1979, Martha Baird Rockefeller Fund for Music, Inc., 1979, 1981, Meet the Composer, 1980, 1981—82, 1983, 1985, 1987, 1989, 1991, Meet the Composer/Arts Endowment Commissioning Music U.S.A., 1996, Alice M. Ditson Fund of Columbia U., 1980, Aaron Copland scholarship, Am. Soc. Composers, Authors and Publishers, 1981, fellowship, Composers' Conf., Johnson, Vt., 1982, Am. Music Ctr., 1982, 1994, Minn. Composers' Forum, 1985—86, D.C. Commn. Arts & Humanities, 1994, small projects grant, 1997, Guggenheim fellowship, 1995—96, Recording grant, Oberlin Coll., 2001, Individual Artist fellowship, Ohio Arts Coun., 2002, Individual Excellence award, 2006, Academy Award in Music, Am. Acad. Arts & Letters, 2003. Mem.: Am. Soc. Composers, Authors and Pubs., Am. Composers Forum, League of Composers (U.S. sect., N.Y.C., bd. dirs.), Bascom Little Fund (adv. bd.). Home: 22 King Street Oberlin OH 44074-1321 Office Phone: 440-775-8034. Business E-Mail: jeffrey.mumford@oberlin.edu. E-mail: jmdc@oberlin.net.

**MUMFORD, LAWRENCE R.,** composer, educator; s. Richard W. and Mary Margaret Mumford; m. Donna L. Mumford, Mar. 9, 1996. BA in Music, George Washington U., 1975; MMus, Peabody Conservatory, Balt., 1976; DMus, U. So. Calif., L.A., 1989. Cert. tchr. Ind. U., Bloomington, 1977. Music accompanist Glendale Coll., Calif., 1990—91; music prof. The Master's Coll., Santa Clarita, Calif., 1992—2004; adj. music prof. Calif. State U., Northridge, 1993—94, Concordia U., Irvine, Calif., 2001—04; prof. music Vanguard U., Costa Mesa, 2004—. Compositions and arrangements published by 7 different cos. Recipient Composition Prize, Culver Chamber Soc., 1999. Mem.: Soc. for Music Theory, Soc. of Composers, Inc., Music Tchrs. Assn. of Calif. (branch pres. 1989—90, pres. emeritus), Pi Kappa Lambda, Phi Beta Kappa. Home: 15 Cortona Irvine CA 92614 Office: Vanguard U 55 Fair Dr Costa Mesa CA 92626 Office Phone: 714-556-3610 ext. 3102. Business E-Mail: lmumford@vanguard.edu.

**MUMFORD, STEPHEN DOUGLAS,** research scientist; b. Louisville, Aug. 28, 1942; s. Adrian Leroy and Mildred Margaret (Cardwell) M.; m. Judy Sheng Ju Lee, Dec. 26, 1966; children: Christopher Lee, Sonia Lea BS in Agr., U. Ky., 1966; MPH Internat. Health/Population Study, U. Tex., Houston, 1971, DrPH Health Svcs. Adminstrn., 1975. Indsl. hygienist Ky. State Dept. Health, Frankfort, 1966—67; rsch. asst. dept. ob.-gyn. Baylor Coll. Medicine, Houston, 1973—75; rsch. statis. aide population studies U. Tex., Houston, 1971—75, rsch. asst. reproductive biology/endocrinology, 1974—76; dir. rsch., sr. vasectomy counselor Planned Parenthood Houston, 1975—76; adminstr. Nat. Swine Flu Immunization Program/Houston/Harris County, Tex., 1976—77; from sect. leader design/analysis divsn. to scientist Internat. Fertility Rsch. Program, Research Triangle Park, NC, 1977—83; pres. Ctr. for Rsch. on Population and Security, Research Triangle Park, 1984—; CEO ISAF, Research Triangle Park, 2005—. Author: The Pope and the New Apocalypse: The Holy War Against Family Planning, 1986, American Democracy and the Vatican: Population Growth and National Security, 1984, Population Growth Control: The Next Move is America's, 1977, The Decision-Making Process that Leads to Vasectomy: A Guide for Promoters, 1977, Vasectomy Counseling, 1977, The Life and Death of NSSM 200: How the Destruction of Political Will Doomed a U.S. Population Policy, 1996; contbr. numerous articles to profl. jours., chpts. to books; contbr. editor The Churchman, 1991-98 Mem. Alan Guttmacher Inst., Assn. for Vol. Sterilization, Environ. Def. Fund, Fund for Feminist Majority, Nat. Abortion Rights Action League, Population Inst., Population Ref. Bur., Ams. United for Separation of Ch. and State, Religious Coalition for Abortion Rights. Capt. U.S. Army, 1966-70 Recipient Cert. of Appreciation for Outstanding Contbns. to Advancing the Cause of Reproductive Rights, Feminist Caucus of Am. Humanist Assn., 1986, Humanist Disting. Svc. award, 1981, Margaret Mead Leadership prize in population and ecology, 1981, Award for Outstanding Single Project in Area of Human Rels., U.S. Jaycees, 1974-75, Award for Outstanding Chmn. of a Single Project in Area of Human Rels., 1974-75 Mem. AAAS, Am. Humanist Assn., APHA (population sect.), Ams. for Immigration Control, Ams. for Religious Liberty, Fedn. for Am. Immigration Reform, Internat. Epidemiol. Assn., Negative Population Growth, Carrying Capacity Network, Soc. for Epidemiologic Rsch., Zero Population Growth, NOW Avocations: gardening, fruit growing, woodworking, fishing, running. Home: 322 Azalea Dr Chapel Hill NC 27517-8105 Office: ISAF 99 TW Alexander Dr PO Box 13067 Research Triangle Park NC 27709 Office Phone: 919-990-9099. Personal E-Mail: smumford@mindspring.com.

**MUMMA, ALBERT GIRARD, JR.,** architect b. Long Beach, Calif., July 2, 1928; s. Albert Girard and Carmen (Braley) M.; m. Janeal Thomas Woolf, Dec. 24, 1973; children: Eugenia M. Villagra, Albert Girard III, Peter Brenaman. B.Arch., U. Va., 1951. Designer McLeod & Ferrara, Architects, Washington, 1951-56; assoc. Deigert & Yerkes, Architects, 1956-62; prin. Mumma & Assocs., Washington, 1962—. Archtl. designer hotel div. Marriott Corp., 1980-82 Prin. archtl. works include Nat. Arboretum Hdqrs. Bldg, 1961, Finnmark Sq., Silver Spring, Md., 1964, Inverness townhouses, Potomac, Md., 1971, Post Office and Food Bldg., Elkins, W.Va., 1971, U.S. Trade Fairs in Spain, Finland, Japan, El Salvador, Poland 1963-72, Fallswood housing project, Falls Church, Va., 1972, Bristow Village townhouses, Annandale, Va., 1972-73, Marriott Hotel, Dayton, Ohio, 1982, Plaza Venetia, Biscayne Bay, Miami, Fla., 1983, Houston Med. Ctr. Hotel, Newark Airport Hotel, 1984, pvt. residences, No. Neck, Rappahanock River, Lancaster County, Va., 1993-2004, subdivision and townhouse projects, Washington, Md., Va., Pa., 1962—. Served with USMC, 1945-47. Recipient Design award Washington Bd. Trade, 1964; winner Newark Airport Hotel Competition, 1981. Mem. AIA (medal 1951), Rappahannock River Yacht Club, Indian Creek Yacht and Country Club, Moran Creek Yacht Club.

**MUMMA, MICHAEL JON,** research scientist; b. Lancaster, Pa., Dec. 3, 1941; s. John Henry and Violet Lyndell (Baxter) M.; m. Sage Bailey Tower, Aug. 20, 1966; children: Peter Robb, Amy Elizabeth. AB in Physics with honors, Franklin and Marshall Coll., 1963; PhD in Physics, U. Pitts., 1970. Grad. research asst. U. Pitts., 1963-70; astrophysicist NASA Goddard Space Flight Center, Greenbelt, Md., 1970-76, head br. Infrared and Radio Astronomy, 1976-84, assoc. chief Lab. Extraterrestrial Physics, 1984-85, head Planetary Systems br., 1985-90, chief scientist Lab. Extraterrestrial Physics, 1990—, dir. Goddard Ctr. Astrobiology, 2003—; adj. rsch. assoc. in physics Pa. State U., 1978—81; prof. physics, 1981-88; sr. scientist Solar Sys. Exploration Divsn., 2005—. Mem. numerous working groups and adv. coms. NASA, Nat. Bur. Standards, NSF, Nat. Acad. Scis., 1973—; adj. prof. physics U. Toledo, 2002-05; lectr. in field. Contbr. numerous articles to profl. publs., 1970—; editor: The Study of Comets, Vols. 1, 2, 1976, Vibrational-Rotational Spectroscopy for Planetary Atmospheres, vols. 1, 2, 1982, Astrophysics from

the Moon, 1990. Recipient NASA medal for Exceptional Sci. Achievement, 1988, 97; Kershner award for physics, 1962; Coll. Trustee's scholar Franklin and Marshall Coll., 1963., Asteroid 8340 named "Michael J. Mumma" by Internat. Astron. Union, 1999. Fellow Am. Phys. Soc., Washington Acad. Sci.; mem. AAAS, Am. Astron. Soc., Am. Geophys. Union, Internat. Astron. Union, Sigma Pi Sigma. Achievements include discovery of natural lasers in atmospheres of Mars, Venus, and Jupiter; first detection of water vapor in comets, discovery of formaldehyde, methanol, methane, and ethane in comets; discovery of x-rays in comets; first definitive measurements of deuterium and hydrogen on Mars and Venus; first absolute wind measurements on Venus and Mars; invention of tunable diode laser heterodyne spectrometer and other advanced instruments; development of Doppler-limited infrared spectroscopy for laboratory and astrophysical applications, of absolute calibration procedures in vacuum ultraviolet, of molecular branching ratio technique for intensity calibration in vacuum ultraviolet; measurement of many absolute cross sections in vacuum ultraviolet; research on atomic and molecular physics and chemistry, on comets, on planetary atmospheres, on infrared astronomy, on high-resolution spectroscopy, and in the field of dissociative excitation of molecules. Office: Code 690 Goddard Space Flight Ctr Greenbelt MD 20771-0001

**MUMMANENI, PADMAJA,** research scientist, educator; d. Ram Mohan Rao and Lakshmiswaramma Mummaneni. BSc in Life Scis., Delhi U., India, 1980, MSc, 1982, PhD, 1989. Postdoctoral rsch. fellow U. Ky., Lexington, 1989—96; staff fellow NIH, Bethesda, Md., 1996—2000; scientist Neuralstem Inc., Gaithersburg, Md., 2000—03; vol. consult dir. Neuronascent Inc., Md., 2004; contract RSR fellow CDER, FDA, Rockville, Md., 2004—05; adj. prof. microbiology Marymount U., Va., 2005. Guest lectr. Found. for Advanced Edn. in the Scis. NIH. Bethesda, Md., 1998—2000, juror, 1998—2000. Contbr. articles to profl./peer-reviewed jours. Fellow: AAAS, Am. Soc. of Cellular and Molecular Biology, N.Y. Acad. Scis.; mem.: Am. Women In Sci. Hindu. Avocations: painting, art. Home: 10513 Montrose Ave Bethesda MD 20814 Office: FDA 1451 Rockville Pike Rockville MD 20852 Personal E-Mail: pmummaneni@aol.com.

**MUMMERY, DANIEL R.,** lawyer; b. Miami, Fla., Mar. 4, 1959; s. Charles R. Mummery and Kathleen M. Osborne; m. Frances D. Nuelle, Oct. 11, 1997; children: Amanda F., William G., Alexander G. AB, Bowdoin Coll., 1977—81; JD, Fordham U. Sch. Law, 1985—88. Bar: Mass. 1989, NY 1989, Calif. 2002. Assoc. Milbank, Tweed, Hadley & McCloy, New York, NY, 1988—96, ptnr., 1996—2001, Cooley Godward LLP, Palo Alto, Calif., 2001—04, Latham & Watkins LLP, Menlo Park, Calif., 2004—. Editor-in-chief Fordham Urban Law Jour., 1987. Recipient Chambers and Ptnrs., 2005. Mem.: ABA (assoc.), NYC Bar. Assn. (assoc.). Avocations: tennis, wine, films. Office: Latham & Watkins 135 Commonwealth Dr Menlo Park CA 94025 Office Phone: 650-463-3069. Office Fax: 650-463-2600. Business E-Mail: daniel.mummery@lw.com.

**MUMMIDI, SRINIVAS,** veterinarian, research scientist, educator; s. Ram Mohan Rao and Lakshmi Tulasi Mummidi; m. Sridevi Allam, Nov. 21, 1993; children: Amrutha children: Adithya. DVM, Andhra Pradesh Agrl. U., Hyderabad, India, 1986; MVSc, Indian Vet. Rsch. Inst., Izatnagar, India, 1989; PhD, Iowa State U., 1996. Asst. prof. U. of Tex. Health Sci. Ctr., San Antonio, 2000—; rsch. health scientist South Tex. Veterans Health Care Sys., 2002—. Contbr. articles to profl. jours. Mem.: DNA Methylation Soc., Am. Soc. for Microbiology, Gamma Sigma Delta. Achievements include patents pending for DC-SIGN isoforms, related compositions and methods for their use in disease therapy; discovery and identification of CC chemokine receptor 5 human haplogroups/haplotypes by genotyping of CCR5/CCR2 genes; research in identification of CC chemokine receptor genotypes associated with altered rates of HIV-1 disease progression and transmission. Office: Univ of Texas Health Sci Ctr 7703 Floyd Curl Dr San Antonio TX 78229 Office Phone: 210-567-0384. Office Fax: 210-567-4654.

**MUMPOWER, JERYL L.,** academic administrator; m. Edwina Dorch; 1 child, Sarah. BA, Coll. William and Mary; PhD in Social and Quantitative Psychology, U. Colo. Dir., policy analyst NSF; assoc. dir. Rockefeller Inst. Govt.; prof. pub. adminstrn., pub. policy and info. sci. U. Albany, SUNY, 1984—, dir. Ctr. for Policy Rsch., assoc. provost, dean grad. studies, interim provost, v.p. for acad. affairs, 2004—. Contbr. chapters to books, articles to profl. jours. Office: Univ Albany SUNY UAB 400 1400 Washington AVe Albany NY 12222

**MUN, KYUNG CHUN,** finance educator, researcher; b. Young-Ahm, Chullanamdo, Republic of Korea, Oct. 20, 1953; arrived in US, 1984, naturalized, 1994; s. Dae Sik Mun and Soon Tae Kim; m. Soo Hee Bae, Apr. 13, 1980; 1 child, Thomas Sung. BS, Seoul Nat. U., Republic of Korea, 1980; MBA, Hankuk U., Seoul, 1983; MA in Econ., U. Houston, 1987; MS in Stats., Va. Poly. Inst. and State U., Blacksburg, 1991, PhD in Fin., 1991. Credit analyst Korea Credit Guarantee Fund, Seoul, 1980—81; internat. banking analyst Korea Exch. Bank, Seoul, 1981—84; prof. Truman State U., Kirksville, Mo., 1991—. Contbr. articles to profl. jours. Civic vol. KC, Kirksville, 1993—2006. Pvt. Korean Air Force, 1973—76. Outstanding Rsch. fellow, Ctr. for Options and Futures Market, 1990. Mem.: European Fin. Mgmt. Assn., Western Fin. Assn., Fin. Mgmt. Assn., Am. Fin. Assn., Beta Alpha Psi (hon.), Delta Sigma Pi (hon.). Avocations: mountain climbing, guitar, gardening. Home: 2514 N New St Kirksville MO 63501 Office: Truman State University divsn bus acctg 100 E Normal Kirksville MO 63501 Office Phone: 660-785-4367. Business E-Mail: amun@truman.edu.

**MUNARI, MICHAEL F.,** music educator, small business owner; b. Laramie, Wyo., Oct. 23, 1970; s. Anton C and Winona J Munari; m. Tonya L. Mangan, June 20, 1998. BA in music edn., U of Wyo 1990 96, MA in music edn., 1998 2001, Adminstrv. Endorsement, 2003—05. Music educator Chugwater Schools, Wyo., 1996—97, Wheatland H.S., Wyo., 1997—, Wheatland Mid. Sch./Jr. High, Wyo., 1997—. Mobile dj svc. owner M'n'M Music Factory Mobile DJ Svc., Wheatland, Wyo., 1998—. Mem. and past pres. Wheatland Kiwanis Club, Wheatland, Wyo., 1999—2005. Recipient North Platte Dist. Music Educator of the Yr., Wyo. Music Educators Assn., 2005; Arts In Edn. Tech. grants, Wyo. Arts Coun., 1998, 2001, 2003. Mem.: NEA (assoc.), Wyo. Music Educators Assn. (assoc.), Music Educators Nat. Conf. (assoc.), Platte County Edn. Assn. (assoc.; bldg. rep. 2000—01), Wyo. Edn. Assn. (assoc.). Home: 245 E Oak Wheatland WY 82201 Office: Wheatland HS 1350 Oak St Wheatland WY 82201 Office Phone: 307-322-2075. Office Fax: 307-322-9739.

**MUNASINGHE, RANJITH ARACHCHIGE,** mathematics professor, engineer; b. Galle, Sri Lanka, Jan. 16, 1957; arrived in U.S., 1985; s. Martin Silva and Roslin Munasinghe; m. Lakmalie Fernando Munasinghe, Jan. 1, 1991; children: Ranga, Malie. BS in Elec. and Electronic Engring., U. Peradeniya, Sri Lanka, 1982; MS in Math., U. Wyo., Laramie, 1987, PhD in Math., 1992. Engr. Dept. Telecomm., Colombo, Sri Lanka, 1982—83, Saudi Telecomm., Riyadh, 1985; tchg. asst. U. Wyo., Laramie, 1985—92; prof. math. W. Va. Inst. Tech., Montgomery, 1992—. Author: (articles) Houston Jour. Math., Coll. Jour. Math. Nominee Golden Apple award for Tchg., U. Wyo.; recipient Jathika Navodaya scholarship, Sri Lanka; grantee, Dept. Defense/Alton Sys., Montgomery, 2003—, SURE project, Dept. Energy, Montgomery, 2005—. Mem.: Am. Soc. Enging. Edn. Avocations: chess, camping, reading. Home: 101 Stratford Pl Charleston WV 25303 Office: W Va Inst Tech Dept Math Montgomery WV 25136 Business E-Mail: ranjith.munasinghe@mail.wvu.edu.

**MUNCH, CHRISTOPHER JOSEPH,** music educator; s. William Peter and Elise Bourg Munch. BA in Instrumental Music Edn., U. New Orleans, 1987, MusM, 1994, post grad., 1995, MEd in Ednl. Adminstrn., 2004. Tchr. Milaudon Mid. Sch. Bernard Parish Sch. Sys., La., 1988—89; tchr. P.G.T. Beauregard Mid. Sch., 1989—90; tchr. L.W. Higgins H.S. Jefferson Parish Sch. Sys., 1990—91; tchr. West Jefferson H.S., 1991—94, tchr. Helen Cox Jr.

H.S., 1993—94, tchr. Riverdale Mid. Sch., 1994—98, tchr. Riverdale H.S. 1994—. Adminstr. summer sch. Jefferson Parish Sch. Sys., 2005. Mem.: La. Music Educators Assn., Phi Delta Kappa. Avocation: music. Home: 469 Barreca St Norco LA 70079

**MUNCK, ALLAN ULF,** physiologist, educator; b. Buenos Aires, July 4, 1925; came to U.S., 1945, naturalized, 1959; s. Carl and Elisabeth (Schmidt) M.; m. Claire Brosi, Oct. 5, 1957; children— Alexander Charles, Ingrid Claire, Kirsten Tanya. BS in Chem. Engring, MIT, 1948, MS, 1949, PhD in Biophysics, 1956. Chem. engr., Ducilo, Buenos Aires, 1949-50; mem. staff Huntington Lab. Mass. Gen. Hosp., Boston, 1956-57, Worcester Found. Exptl. Biology, Shrewsbury, Mass., 1957-59; mem. med. sch. faculty Dartmouth Coll., 1959—; prof. physiology Dartmouth Med. Sch., 1967—2001, prof. physiology emeritus, 2001—. Marius Tausk prof. Leiden U., The Netherlands, 1998. Served with Argentine Army, 1949. Home: PO Box 114 Norwich VT 05055-0114 Office: Dartmouth Med Sch Dept Physiology Lebanon NH 03756 Business E-Mail: allan.u.munck@dartmouth.edu.

**MUNCY, ESTLE PERSHING,** physician; b. Tazewell, Tenn., Apr. 9, 1918; s. William Loyd and Flora Media (Monday) M.; m. Dorothy Davis, Dec. 31, 1946 (div. Apr. 1980); children: Robert H., Teresa A., Dorothy J., Estle II,James; m. Jean Marie Hayter, Mar. 19, 1985. AB, Lincoln Meml. U., 1939; MD, U. Tenn., 1943. Resident Dallas Meth. Hosp., 1948; tchg. resident Tufts Med. Sch., Boston, 1949-50; physician Jefferson City, Tenn., 1950-96. Author: The Muncys in the New World, 1988, People and Places in Jefferson County, Tennessee, 1994. Alderman Jefferson City, 1974-77; chmn. Jefferson City Planning Commn., 1976-79. Capt. M.C., U.S. Army, 1944-46. Recipient Commendation for work on Tenn. history Gov. Don Sundquist, Jefferson award Am. Inst. Pub. Svc., 1995, Covenant Health Platinum award, 2000; named to Lincoln Meml. U. Lit. and Profl. Halls of Fame, 1997. Mem. Tenn. Heart Assn. (pres. 1966-67), Hamblen County Med. Soc. (pres. 1960-61), Jefferson County Hist. Soc. (pres. 1993-94, historian 1995—). Republican. Baptist. Avocations: photography, gardening. Home: 1428 Russell Ave Jefferson City TN 37760-2216 Office Phone: 865-475-3377.

**MUNCY, TINA GRAY,** educator, educational coordinator; b. Northampton, Mass., Nov. 3, 1946; d. Austin and Marie (Hubbard) Gray; children: Elisha, Aaron. BS, SUNY, Oneonta, 1968; M in Adminstrn. and Planning, U. Vt., Burlington, 1995. Cert. tchr. Vt., prin. Vt. Prin. Wash. Village Schs., Vt.; tchr. Montpelier Schs., Vt., Brighton Schs., Mich.; sch. support coord. Vt. Dept. Edn., Montpelier, 2003—. Nat. facilitator Nat. Sch. Reform Faculty. Home: 27 Hebert Rd Montpelier VT 05602 Office: Vt Dept Edn 120 State St Montpelier VT 05620 Office Phone: 802-828-1184. Business E-Mail: tinamuncy@education.state.vt.us.

**MUND, GERALDINE,** judge; b. LA, July 7, 1943; d. Charles J. and Pearl M. BA, Brandeis U., 1965; MS, Smith Coll., 1967; JD, Loyola U., 1977. Bar: Calif. 1977. Bankruptcy judge U.S. Ctrl. Dist. Calif., 1984—, bankruptcy chief judge, 1997—2002. Past pres. Temple Israel, Hollywood, Calif.; past mem. Bd. Jewish Fedn. Coun. of Greater L.A. Mem. ABA, L.A. County Bar Assn. Office: 21041 Burbank Blvd Woodland Hills CA 91367-6606 Office Phone: 818-587-2840.

**MUND, LORRAINE G.,** English studies educator, writer; b. Glemsford, Suffolk, Eng. d. Mario and Joan Muselli; m. Joseph Mund, May 29, 1965; children: Jemine, Lorna, Kristin. BA in English, St. Josephs Coll., 1962; MA in English, Columbia U., 1964; PhD in English, La Salle U., 1997. Asst. prof. Five Towns Coll., Merrick, N.Y., 1976-78; instr. SUNY, Old Westbury, N.Y., 1978-96. Part-time instr. SUNY, Stony Brook, 1997-99; adj. prof. Nassau Coll., Garden City, N.Y., 1974—; workshop dir. East Meadow (N.Y.) Sch., 1995, 96; dir. Old Westbury Poetry Ctr., 1994-96; guest spkr. Rotary, Hicksville, N.Y., 1997, 98, 99. Author numerous short stories; author: Poetry, Like an IV..., 2000, Ring Them Bells, 2003; editor Poetry Jour. SUNY, 1994-96. Performer, singer Camcos, N.Y. chpt. Mem. Internat. Found. Freedom Women (spkr.), Women's Faculty Assn. Avocations: teaching, writing, conducting workshops. Home: 40 Alpine Ln Hicksville NY 11801

**MUNDAY, ROBERT STEVENSON,** priest, dean; b. Benton, Ill., Oct. 19, 1954; s. Robert Meade and Kathryn (McCollum) M.; m. Christina Ellen Karroll, July 31, 1976. BA, So. Ill. U., 1976; MDiv, Mid-Am. Bapt. Theol. Sem., Memphis, 1979, PhD, 1984; MLS, Vanderbilt U., 1986; postgrad., Duquesne U., U. of the South, Sewanee, Tenn. Ordained priest Episcopal Ch., 1990. Chaplain St. Jude Children's Rsch. Hosp., Memphis, 1981-84; instr. Mid-Am. Bapt. Theol Sem., Memphis, 1984-86; libr. dir. Trinity Episcopal Sch. for Ministry, Ambridge, Pa., 1986—2001, prof. systematic theology, 1986—2001, assoc. dean for adminstrn., 1987-94, assoc. dean planning and policy, 1994-97, assoc. dean for libr. and info. svcs., 1997—2001; pres., dean Nashotah House Theol. Sem., Wis., 2001—. Dep. to the gen. conv. Episcopal Ch., 1994, 97, 2000, 03, prof. Systematic Theology, 2001—. Chmn. bd. dirs. Life Choices, Memphis, 1984-86; bd. dirs. Cen. Pitts. Crisis Pregnancy Ctr., 1989-2001, pres., 1990-95; bd. dirs. Pregnancy Care Ctrs. Pitts., 1995-2001, pres., 1996-2001; bd. dirs. S.Am. Missionary Soc., 2001—. Mem. Nat. Orgn. Episcopalians for Life (bd. dirs., pres. 1991-94), Fairfax Va., Theol. Edn. Commn., Episcopal Synod Am., Am. Acad. Religion, Am. Theol. Libr. Assn., Brotherhood St. Andrew (life), Fellowship of St. Alban and St. Sergius, Oblate, Order of St. Benedict. Office: Nashotah House Theol Sem 2777 Mission Rd Nashotah WI 53058 Home: 2777 Mission Rd Nashotah WI 53058-9790 *Life is about possibility and transformation—the possibility of being lifted above mere human existence to be the creatures who are ideally in the mind of God. The possibility of that transformation is the good news of our redemption in Jesus Christ.*

**MUNDAY, STEPHEN DALE,** writer, artist; b. Haskell, Tex., Mar. 10, 1949; s. Edna Mae Moody; m. Joyce Lavern Stuteville, June 19, 1981. BA, West Tex. State U., 1970. Farm and ranch editor Abilene Reporter-News, Tex., 1971—72; field editor The Cattleman Mag. Tex. and Southwestern Cattle Raisers Assn., Fort Worth, 1972—74, editl. dir., 1976—78; info. dir. Tex. Cattle Feeders Assn. Amarillo, 1974; freelance writer Arlington, 1974—76; dir. field svcs. Simmental Shield Mag. Am. Simmental Assn., 1975; news dir. Tex. and Southwestern Cattle Raisers Found., Fort Worth, 1978—81, adminstrv. asst. media and govt. rels., 1981—85, exec. v.p., 1995—2001. Asst. sec. Tex. and Southwestern Cattle Raisers Found., Fort Worth, 1995-2001; sec.-treas. Tex. and Southwestern Cattle Raisers Assn. Ins. Svcs., Inc., Ft. Worth, 1995-2001, Tex. and Southwestern Cattle Raisers Assn. Legal Def. Fund, 1995-2001. Editor: TSCRA News Update, 1979-1995 (1st pl. gen. excellence Livestock Pubs. Coun. 1986, 88, 90-91, 2d pl., 1989). Bd. dir. Hist. Camp Bowie, Inc., Fort Worth, 2001. Capt. U.S. Army, 1971-79. Avocations: reading, painting, cartooning, collectibles. Home: 3415 Bristol Rd Fort Worth TX 76107 Office Phone: 817-878-2440. E-mail: stevemunday@sbcglobal.net.

**MUNDELL, ROBERT ALEXANDER,** economist, educator; b. Kingston, Ont., Can., Oct. 24, 1932; s. William C. and Lila (Knifton) Mundell; m. Barbara Sheff, Oct. 14, 1957 (div. 1972); children: Paul Alexander, William Andrew, Robyn Leslie; m. Valerie Sophia Natsios, Nov. 10, 1998; 1 child, Nicholas Robert. BA, U. B.C., Can., 1953; postgrad., U. Wash., 1953—54, London Sch. Econs. and Polit. Sci., 1955—56; PhD, MIT, 1956; postdoc., U. Chgo., 1956—57; PhD (hon.), Renmin U. China, 1985, U. Paris, 1992. Instr. econs. U. B.C., Vancouver, Canada, 1957—58; acting asst. prof. econs. Stanford U., Calif., 1958—59; vis. prof. econs. Sch. Advanced Internat. Studies, Johns Hopkins U. Ctr., Bologna, Italy, 1959—61; sr. economist research dept. IMF, Washington, 1961—63; vis. prof. econs. McGill U., Montreal, Que., Canada, 1963—64; Rockefeller vis. research prof. internat. econs. Brookings Instn., Washington, 1964—65; prof. Grad. Inst. Internat. Studies, Geneva, 1965—75; Ford Found. vis. research prof. econs. U. Chgo., 1965—66, prof., 1966—71; prof. econs., chmn. dept. U. Waterloo, Ont., Canada, 1972—74; prof. econs. Columbia U., N.Y.C., 1974—. Marshall lectr. Cambridge U., 1974; economist Can. Royal Commn on Price Spreads on Food Products, 1957; mem. joint fiscal mission to Peru OAS and Inter-am. Devel. Bank, 1964; cons. FRS, IBRD, 1966—, U.S. Treasury Dept.,

1969—74, EEC, 1970—73, UN, Govt. Panama; organizer, participant internat. confs.; lectr. numerous univs. and profl. orgn. meetings; hon. prof. Renmin U. China, Beijing. Author: The Internat. Monetary System- Conflict and Reform, 1965, Man and Economics, 1968, International Economics, 1968, Monetary Theory-Interest, Inflation and Growth in the World Economy, 1971; contbr. articles to profl. jours.; co-editor: Monetary Problems of the International Economy, 1969, Trade Blaance of Payments and Growth, 1971, The International Monetary System, 1977; editor: Jour. Polit. Economy, 1966—70, Global Disequilibrium in the World Economy, 1989, 1992, Building the New Europe, 1991, Debt, Deficit and Economic Importance, 1990, Inflation and Growth in China, 1996. Named Companion of Order of Can., 2003; recipient James Rueff medal, French Senate, 1983, Nobel prize in Econs., 1999; fellow, Guggenheim, 1970—71; grantee, NSF, 1967—70. Fellow: AAAS, 1998; mem.: Am. Econ. Assn. (Disting. fellow 1997). Office: Dept Econs Columbia U 1031 Internat Affairs 420 W 118th St # Mc3308 New York NY 10027-7213*

**MUNDHEIM, ROBERT HARRY,** law educator; b. Hamburg, Germany, Feb. 24, 1933; m. Guna Smitchens; children: Susan, Peter. BA, Harvard U., 1954, LLB, 1957; MA (hon.), U. Pa., 1971. Bar: NY 1958, Pa. 1979. Assoc. Shearman & Sterling, N.Y.C., 1958-61; spl. counsel to SEC Washington, 1962-63; vis. prof. Duke Law Sch., Durham, NC, 1964; prof. law U. Pa., Phila., 1965—. Univ. prof. law and fin., 1980-93, dean, 1982-89, Bernard G. Segal prof. law, 1987-89; co-chmn. Fried, Frank, Harris, Shriver & Jacobson, NYC, 1990-92; exec. v.p., gen. counsel Salomon Inc., 1992-97; sr. exec. v.p., gen. counsel Salomon Smith Barney Holdings, Inc., 1997-98; of counsel Shearman & Sterling, 1999—; gen. counsel U.S. Dept. Treasury, Washington, 1977-80, trustee, pres., 2000-6, Am. Acad. in Berlin; chmn. legal adv. bd. NASDAQ, chmn. legal adv. bd. NASD; dir. Appleseed Found., 1996-2006; trustee New Sch. U.; coun. Am. Law Inst.; bd. dirs. eCollege, 2001—, Arnhold & S. Bleichroder, 2004—; gen. counsel Chrysler Loan Guarantee Bd., 1980; mng. dir., mgmt. bd. Salomon Bros. Inc., NYC, 1992-97; overseer Curtis Inst., 2000—; mem. supervisory bd. Hypo Real Estate Holdings AG, 2004—. Author: Outside Director of the Publicity Held Corporation, 1976; American Attitudes Toward Foreign Direct Investment in the United States, 1979; Conflict of Interest and the Former Government Employee: Re-thinking the Revolving Door, 1981; chmn. adv. bd. Jour. Internat. Econ. Law, 1996-97. Trustee SEC Hist. Soc. With USAF, 1961-62. Recipient Alexander Hamilton award U.S. Dept. Treasury, 1980, Harold P. Seligson award Practicing Law Inst., 1988, Francis J. Rawle award, ABA-ALI, 1992, Anti-Defamation League Human Rels. award, 1999. Mem. ABA (task force on corp. responsibliity), Am. Law Inst., San Diego Securities Regulation Inst. (exec. com.). Office: Shearman & Sterling 599 Lexington Ave Fl 16 New York NY 10022-6069 Office Phone: 212-848-7738.

**MUNDIE, CRAIG JAMES,** computers software company executive; b. 1949; BEE, Ga. Inst. Tech., M in Info. Theory and Computer Sci. Software developer Data Gen. Corp., 1972; co-founder, CEO Alliant Computer Systems Corp., 1982—92; with Microsoft Corp., Redmond, Wash., 1992—, gen, mgr., advanced consumer tech., 1992—93, v.p., advanced consumer tech. group, 1993—96, sr. v.p., consumer platforms divsn., 1996—2001, sr. v.p. advanced strategies and policy, 2001—02, chief tech. officer, advanced strategies & policy, 2001—06, sr. v.p., advanced strategies & policy, 2001—06, chief tech. & strategy officer, 2006—. Presdl. appointee Nat. Security Telecom. Adv. Com., 2000; mem. Coun. on Fgn. Rels., 2002—; Task Force on Nat. Security in the Info. Age, 2002—; trustee Fred Hutchinson Cancer Rsch. Ctr., Seattle; adv. bd. mem. Coll. of Computing Ga. Inst. Tech., Atlanta; mem. adv. bd., Live Labs (Rsch. partnership between MSN and Microsoft Rsch.) Microsoft Corp., 2006—. Office: Microsoft Corp One Microsoft Way Redmond WA 98052-6399*

**MUNDINGER, DONALD CHARLES,** retired college president; b. Chgo., Sept. 2, 1929; s. George Edward and Bertha (Trelkenberg) M.; m. June Myrtle Grubbe, June 17, 1951; children: Debra Sue, Donald William, Mary Ruth (dec.). Student, U. Ill., 1947-48; BA, Concordia Coll., River Forest, Ill., 1951, LLD (hon.), 1982; MA, Northwestern U., 1952; PhD, Washington U., St. Louis, 1956; DH (hon.), MacMurray Coll., Jacksonville, Ill., 1984, Ritsumeikan U., Kyoto, Japan, 1992; LLD (hon.), Ill. Coll., Jacksonville, 1993; postdoctoral study, Cambridge U.Eng., 1967-68. Asst. prof. polit. sci., chmn. dept. Augustana Coll., Sioux Falls, S.D., 1956-58; asst. prof. govt. Valparaiso (Ind.) U., 1958-61, assoc. prof., 1961-65, prof., 1965-73; dean Valparaiso (Ind.) U. (Coll. Arts and Scis.), 1965-67; dir. Overseas Center, Cambridge, Eng., 1967-68, v.p. acad. affairs, 1968-73; pres. Ill. Coll., Jacksonville, 1973-93; chmn. Fedn. Ind. Ill. Colls. and Univs., 1975-78; chmn. non-public adv. com. Ill. Bd. Higher Edn., 1988-91. Postdoctoral fellow Center Study Higher Edn., U. Mich., 1964-65; chmn. bd. Council Ind. Colls., 1988-90. Contbr. articles to profl. jours. Mem. Ill. State Bar Assn. (com. on fed. judicial and related appointments 1983-89), Nat. Assn. Ind. Colls. and Univs. (commn. on new initiatives, 1988-90), Pi Sigma Alpha, Phi Eta Sigma. Home: 3803 Pheasant Walk Dr Valparaiso IN 46383-2205

**MUNDINGER, MARY O'NEIL,** nursing educator; b. Fredonia, N.Y., Apr. 27, 1937; d. Thomas Lewis and Dorothy (Hanselman) O'Neil; m. Paul C. Mundinger, Aug. 23, 1958; children: Paul Jr., Ann Mundinger Schimenti, Thomas, Elizabeth. BS, U. Mich., 1959; MA, Columbia U., 1974, PhD, 1981; LHD (hon.), Hamilton Coll., 1996. Adminstr., instr. Tchrs. Coll. Columbia U., NYC, 1975; adj. instr. Pace U., NYC, 1975-77, asst. prof., 1977-82; assoc. prof. nursing, dir. grad. program Columbia U. Sch. Nursing, NYC, 1982-83, assoc. prof. nursing, dir. grad. program, 1983-84, assoc. prof., assoc. dean adminstrv. affairs, 1984-85, assoc. prof., asst. dean faculty of medicine, 1986, dean, Centennial prof. health policy, 1986—. Bd. dirs. Conn. Hospice, Branford, UnitedHealth Group, 1997-, Cell Therapeutics, Inc., 1997-, Gentiva Health Services, 2002-, Welch Allyn Inc., 2002-; adv. group steering com. N.Y. Acad. Medicine, N.Y.C., 1992—; regional adv. com. Nat. Network Librs. of Medicine, N.Y.C., 1992—; Robert Wood Johnson health policy fellows bd. Inst. Medicine, Washington, 1990—, Health Svcs. Improvement Fund, NYC, 1992—, health policy adv. com. Sen. Edward Kennedy, Washington, 1985—, med. adv. bd. Walt Disney Imagineering (Wonders of Life), Orlando, Fla., 1988-89; charter mem. health care tech. Inst. Medicine, NAS, 1985-. Author: Home Care Controversy: Too Little, Too Late, Too Costly, 1983 (Book of Yr 1984), Autonomy in Nursing, 1980 (Book of Yr. 1981). Recipient grant W.K. Kellogg Found., 1989, grant Katzenbach Found., 1986; Nurse Practitioner Year award, The Nurse Practitioner Journal, 1998. Fellow: Am. Acad. Nursing, NY Acad. Medicine; mem.: Inst. Medicine. Avocations: skiing, reading. Office: Office of Dean of Nursing 630 W 168th St Box 6 New York NY 10032-3702 Fax: (212) 305-1116.*

**MUNDO, PAUL L.,** music educator; b. Colorado Springs, Colo., Jan. 11, 1971; s. Barbara S. Holroyd; m. Kathleen M. Boyce, Apr. 24, 1974. Student, Manhattan Sch. Music, 1994; MusB, Western Mich. U., 1994, MusM, 1997; postgrad., U. North Tex., 1997; MusB, Mich. State U., 2000. Cert. music. tchr. Mich. Band dir. Chelsea Beach Mid. Sch., Chelsea, Mich., 2000; dir. of bands Plainwell H.S., Mich., 2000—. Tchg. fellow, U. of North Tex., 1997—98, Irving S. Gilmore Emerging Artist grant, Gilmore Found., 1993. Mem.: Internat. Trombone Assn. Home: 669-120th Ave Martin MI 49070-8744 Office: Plainwell High Sch 684 Starr Rd Plainwell MI 49080 Office Phone: 269-685-9554 1586. Home Fax: 269-685-9064; Office Fax: 269-685-9064. Personal E-mail: paulworld@gtlakes.com. Business E-Mail: pmundo@plainwellschools.org.

**MUNDT, BARRY MAYNARD,** management consultant; b. San Francisco, June 28, 1936; s. Kenneth Francis and Janet (Doughty) M.; m. Sally Hanscom, June 13, 1960; children: Kevin Warren, Trevor Stevens, Stacey Corbin BS in Indsl. Engring., Stanford U., 1959; MBA, Santa Clara U., 1964. Registered indsl. engr., Calif. Statistician Aerojet-Gen., Sacramento, 1957-58; reliability engr. Lockheed Missiles, Sunnyvale, Calif., 1959-61; mgmt. engr. C-E-I-R, Inc., Los Altos, Calif., 1961-65; sr. cons. Peat, Marwick, Livingston & Co., Los Angeles, 1965-68; mgr., prin. Peat, Marwick, Mitchell & Co., Atlanta, 1968-84; ptnr.-in-charge, ops. mgmt. cons. KPMG Peat Marwick Main & Co., N.Y.C., 1984-88; internat. mgmt. cons. ptnr. KPMG Internat.,

N.Y.C. and Amsterdam, The Netherlands, 1988-92; mgmt. cons., ptnr. KPMG Peat Marwick U.S., Montvale, NJ, 1992-95; prin. The Strategy Facilitation Group, Asheville, NC, 1995—. Author-editor: Managing Public Resources, 1982; co-author II Manager Pubblico (Italy), 1986; mem. editl. bd., contbg. author Handbook of Industrial Engineering, 3rd edit., 2001; contbr. articles to profl. jours. Mem. ann. campaign Atlanta Symphony Orch., 1974-82, Atlanta Arts Alliance, 1976-81; del. to assembly United Way of Met. Atlanta, 1974-84; bd. chmn., mem. Brandon Hall Sch., Atlanta, 1980—2002. Fellow Inst. Indsl. Engrs. (treas. 1976-81, pres. 1982-83, asst. treas. 1985-92); mem. Asheville Country Club. Episcopalian. Avocations: golf, boating. Home and Office: 32 Dover St Asheville NC 28804 Office Phone: 838-254-2769. Personal E-mail: bmundt@charter.net.

**MUNERA, GERARD EMMANUEL,** manufacturing executive; b. Algiers, Algeria, Dec. 2, 1935; s. Gabriel and Laure (Labrousse) M.; m. Paule A. Ramos, July 28, 1959; children: Catherine, Philippe, Emmanuelle, Jean-Marie. M Math, M Physics, M Chemistry, Ecole Poly., Paris, 1956; CE, Ecole Ponts et Chaussees, Paris, 1959. Chief county engr. Dept. Rds. and Bridges, South Algiers, 1959-62; cons. French Ministry Fgn. Affairs, Argentina, 1962-66; sr. v.p. fin. Camea Group Pechiney Ugine Kuhlmann, Buenos Aires, 1966-70, chmn. bd., chief exec. officer, 1976-77; exec. v.p. Howmet Aluminum Corp., Greenwich, Conn., 1976-77, pres., chief operating officer, 1977-79, pres., chief exec. officer, 1980-83; corporate v.p. nuclear fuels Pechiney, Brussels, 1983-85; vice chmn., chief exec. officer Union Minière, Brussels, 1985-89; head corp. planning and devel. RTZ, London, 1989-90; pres., CEO Minorco USA, Englewood, Colo., 1990-94, also bd. dirs.; chmn. and CEO Latin Am. Gold, Inc., N.Y.C., 1994-96, Synergex Inc., 1996—. Bd. dirs. Nevsun Resources, Inc., Meridian Gold Inc., Dynamic Materials Corp., Inc., SiVault Sys., Inc., May Industries; chmn., CEO, Arcadia Inc., mng. ptnr. Synergex Group LLC. Patentee low-income housing system. Served with French Air Force, 1956-57. Decorated officer Legion of Honor (France). Roman Catholic. Office: Arcadia 60 Bonner St Stamford CT 06902-6610 Office Phone: 203-316-8000.

**MUNERA, PEDRO ANTONIO,** child and adolescent psychiatrist; b. Granollers, Spain, May 16, 1970; s. Pedro Munera and Dolores Cordoba; m. Sherry Lynn Rowlett, Mar. 7, 2003. MD, Univ. Autonoma de Barcelona, Barcelona, 1994. Cert. psychiatrist Am. Bd. Psychiatry and Neurology, 2002, in child and adolescent psychiatry Am. Bd. Psychiatry and Neurology, 2004. Child and adolescent psychiatrist Weems Cmty. Mental Health Ctr., Meridian, Miss., 2003—; clin. asst. prof. Dept. of Psychiatry, U. of Miss., Jackson, Miss., 2003—. Chmn. mems. in tng. com. Tex. Soc. of Psychiat. Physicians, Austin, 1998—2000; mem. resident and early career psychiatrist com. Am. Acad. of Child and Adolescent Psychiatry, Washington, 2002—06; chair, early career psychiatrist com., exec. coun. Miss. Psychiat. Assn., 2005—. Author: (book review) Jour. of the Am. Acad. of Child and Adolescent Psychiatry, (case report) Jour. of the Am. Acad.of Child and Adolescent Psychiatry (Resident of the Yr., Pharm. Co. grant, 2001), Jour. of Child and Adolescent Psychopharmacology. Mem.: Miss. Psychiat. Assn. (assoc.), Am. Acad. of Child and Adolescent Psychiatry (assoc.; residents and early career psychiatrists com. 2002—03), Am. Psychiat. Assn. (assoc.). Roman Catholic. Avocations: travel, reading. Office: U of Miss Med Ctr 2500 N State St Jackson MS 39216 Personal E-mail: pedromunera@comcast.net.

**MUNERLYN, LORRAINE,** foundation administrator; b. Flint, Mich., Dec. 23, 1958; d. Lurane Allen; m. Raydell Munerlyn, Sr., Nov. 16, 1979; children: Raydell, Jr., Jordan Earl, Stephanie. Deputized Correctional Chaplain Forgotten Man Min., Mich., 2002. Line worker Gen. Motors V-8 Engine, Flint, Mich., 1977—79, Gen. Motors Buick Plant, Flint, Mich., 1980—81, Gen. Motors Buick, Olds, Cadillac, Lake Orion, Mich., 1984—92; deputized chaplain Forgotten Man Ministries, Grand Rapids, Mich., 2002—; adminstrv. sec. Five Fold Outreach Ministries, Flint, Mich., 2002—. Author: (collection of poems) From God's Lips To My Ears Insp. Poems (Life As It Lay); composer: (poetry in songs) Project Song of Praise- songs Guardian Angel's Love with Amercord, (songs) America At War: Unforgettable Men & Women at War. Recipient Award of Merit in Writing, Amherst Soc., 2001, Hon. Mention, Iliad Press, 2002, Cert. of award Teacher's Tng., New Beginings Ministries, 2002—. Avocations: cooking, poetry, drawing, singing, landscaping. Home: 1101 Milbourne Ave Flint MI 48504-3367 Office: Poetess Lorraine/Inspirational Poems PO Box 4203 Flint MI 48504-3367 Office Phone: 1-810-423-2175. Home Fax: 1-810-238-9002. Personal E-Mail: lmunerlyn@prodigy.net.

**MUNGEKAR, HEMANT P.,** process engineer, researcher; s. Pralhad and Pravina Mungekar. BS, Indian Inst. of Tech., Bombay, 1994; MS, Rutgers U., 1996; PhD, U. Mich., 2001. Rsch. fellow U. Mich., Ann Arbor, 1996—2001; sr. process engr. Applied Materials, Santa Clara, Calif., 2001—. Contbr. articles to profl. jours. Recipient Disting. Achievement award, Coll. of Engring., U. Mich., 2001; Raisler fellowship, Rutgers U., 1996, Academic Excellence fellowship, U. Mich., 1998. Mem.: ASME (K-15 com. heat transfer divsn. 2003—06, conf. session chair). Achievements include research in Ability to control flame pollution and improve combustion efficiency; patents for Flow Systems in Semiconductor Equipment; Chemistry Control in Semiconductor Equipment; Process Enhancement of Semiconductor manufacturing; patents pending for Magnetic Field interaction with Plasmas; Microcontamination control in semiconductor process. Personal E-mail: mungekar@hotmail.com. Business E-Mail: hermant_mungekar@amat.com.

**MUNGER, CHARLES T.,** diversified company executive; b. Omaha, Nebr., 1924; m. Nancy Munger; 8 children. Student, U. of Mich., 1941—42, Calif. Inst. Technol., 1943; JD, Harvard Law Sch., 1948. Joined Musick Peeler & Garrett, Los Angeles, Calif.; co-founder Munger, Tolles & Olson, 1962—, ptnr., 1962—65, Wheeler Munger & Co., LA, 1962—75; chmn., CEO, Blue Chip Stamps, 1976—; vice chmn. Berkshire Hathaway, Inc., Omaha, 1978—, also chmn., CEO Wesco Fin. subs., 1983—. Chmn. Daily Jour. Corp.; bd. dirs. Costco, 1997—. Meteorological officer USAF, World War II. Named one of Forbes' Richest Americans, 2006. Office: Berkshire Hathaway Inc 1440 Kiewit Plz Omaha NE 68131-3302 also: Munger Tolles and Olson 355 S Grand Ave Los Angeles CA 90071-1560*

**MUNGER, EDWIN STANTON,** political geography educator; b. LaGrange, Ill., Nov. 19, 1921; s. Royal Freeman and Mia (Stanton) M.; m. Ann Boyer, May 2, 1970; 1 child, Elizabeth Stanton Gibson. B.Sc., U. Chgo., 1948, M.Sc., 1949, PhD, 1951. Fulbright fellow Makerere U., 1949-50; research fellow U. Chgo.; field assoc. Am. Univs. Field Staff, 1950-60; faculty Calif. Inst. Tech., Pasadena, 1961—, prof. polit. geography, 1960—. Research fellow Stellenbosch U., 1955-56; vis. prof. U. Warsaw, 1973 Author books including Afrikaner and African Nationalism, 1968, The Afrikaners, 1979, Touched by Africa: An Autobiography, 1983, Cultures, Chess and Art: A Collector's Odyssey Across Seven Continents, Vol. 1 Sub Saharan Africa, 1996, Vol. 2, Americas, 1997, Pacific Islands and the Asian Rim, Vol. 3, 1999, 10 short stories for kids--L.A. Times on Africa, 2001-02; editor books including Munger Africana Library Notes, 1969-82; contbr. chpts. to books and numerous articles to profl. jours. Evaluator Peace Corps, Uganda, 1966, Botswana, 1967; chmn. State Dept. Evalustion Team South Africa, 1971; trustee African-Am. Inst., 1956-62; acting pres. Pasadena Playhouse, 1966; chmn. bd. trustees Crane Rogers Found., 1979-82, fellow, 1950-54; mem. exec. com. NAACP, Pasadena, 1979—, nat. del., 1984, 85; trustee Leakey Found., 1968—; pres., 1971-84; pres. Cape of Good Hope Found., 1985—; pres. Internat. Vis. Coun., L.A., 1991-93, bd. dirs., 1979-93. Recipient Alumni Citation award for pub. svc. U. Chgo., 1993, Gandhi Martin Luther King-Ikeda award Morehouse U., 2002. Fellow South African Royal Soc., Royal Soc. Arts, African Studies Assn. (founding bd. dirs. 1963-66, Martin L. King Ikeda-Mahatma Gandhi award 2002); mem. PEN USA West (v.p.), Coun. Fgn. Rels., Cosmos Club, Athenaeum Club, Twilight Club, Chess Collectors Internat. (bd. dirs 1998—). Office: Calif Inst Tech Divsn Humanities & Social Scis 1201 E California Blvd Pasadena CA 91125-0001 E-mail: munger@hss.caltech.edu.

**MUNGER, ELMER LEWIS,** civil engineer, educator; b. Manhattan, Kans., Jan. 4, 1915; s. Harold Hawley and Jane (Green) M.; m. Vivian Marie Bloomfield, Dec. 28, 1939; children: John Thomas, Harold Hawley II, Jane Marie. BS, Kans. State U., 1936, MS, 1938; PhD, Iowa State U., 1957. Registered profl. engr., Nebr., Kans., Iowa, Vt.; registered pvt. land surveyor Republic of The Philippines. Rodman St. Louis-Southwestern Ry., Ark., Mo., 1937-38; engr. U.S. Engr. Dept., Ohio, Nebr., 1938-46; missionary engr. Philippine Episcopal Ch., 1946-48; engr. Wilson & Co., Salina, Kans., 1948; tchr. Iowa State U., 1948-51, 54-58; engr. C.E., U.S. Army, Alaska, 1951-54; from tchr. to dean Norwich U., Northfield, Vt., 1958-69; prof. gen. engring. U. P.R., Mayagüez, 1969-75; prof. civil engring. Mich. Tech. U., 1975-82; ret. Mem. spl. com. on engring. Inter-Am. Devel. Bank, U. W.I., 1971. Author: (with Clarence J. Douglas) Construction Management, 1970. Fellow ASCE; mem. NSPE, Vt. Soc. Profl. Engrs., Am. Soc. Engring. Edn., Phi Kappa Phi, Sigma Tau, Tau Beta Pi, Chi Epsilon. Clubs: Masons, Shriners. Episcopalian.

**MUNGER, KRISTEN A.,** school psychologist; b. Auburn, N.Y., Dec. 31, 1967; d. Creston D. and Janice Sheahen Munger. AA, Cayuga C.C., Auburn, N.Y., 1987; BA, Wells Coll., 1990; MS, SUNY, Oswego, 1993; postgrad., Syracuse U. Sch. psychologist Phelps-Clifton Springs Sch. Dist., NY, 1993—96, So. Cayuga Ctrl. Schs., Aurora, NY, 1996—2005; learning disabilities counselor N.Y. Chiropractic Coll., Seneca Falls, NY, 2000—; rsch. data mgr. Syracuse U., NY, 2005—. Ednl. cons. Tompkins-Seneca-Tioga BOCES, Ithaca, NY, 2005—. Mem. Reading Works, Ithaca, NY, 2004—05. Recipient Ann Pugh prize, Wells Coll., 1990, Faculty Alumni award, SUNY, Oswego, 1993. Mem.: NASP, Student Orgn. of Lit. Rschrs. and Educators (pres. 2005—), Phi Beta Kappa, Phi Theta Kappa. Business E-Mail: krmunger@syr.edu.

**MUNGER, MOLLY,** lawyer; b. Boston, Mass., May 14, 1948; BA cum laude, Radcliffe Coll., 1970; JD, Harvard U., 1974. Asst. U.S. atty. U.S. Dist. Ct. (cen. dist.) Calif., 1978-83; ptnr. Baird, Munger & Meyers, 1983—89, Fried, Frank, Harris, Shriver & Jacobsen, L.A., 1989—93; regional counsel NAACP Legal Defense and Educational Fund, 1994—98; ptnr. English, Munger & Rice, L.A., 1998—. Instr. Atty. Gen's. Trial Advocacy Inst., Washington, 1982, U.S.C. Law Ctr. Inst. for Trial Advocacy Skills, 1984; guest lectr. in trial advocacy Law Sch. U. SO. Calif., 1983. Bd. mem. James Irvine Found., 2002—. Mem. ABA (com. trial lawyers sect. 1985-87, judicial appts. com. 1986-88), Fed. Bar Assn., Assn. Bus. Trial Lawyers. Office: Fried Frank Harris Shriver & Jacobson 725 S Figueroa St Los Angeles CA 90017-5524*

**MUNGER, PAUL R.,** engineering educator; b. Hannibal, Mo., Jan. 14, 1932; s. Paul O and Anne M.; m. Frieda Anna Mette, Nov. 26, 1954; children: Amelia Ann Munger Fortmeyer, Paul David, Mark James, Martha Jane Munger Cox. BSCE, Mo. Sch. Mines and Metallurg, 1958, MSCE, 1961; PhD in Engring. Sci., U. Ark., 1972. Registered profl. engr., Mo., Ill., Ark. Instr. civil engring Mo. Sch. Mines and Metallurgy, Rolla, 1958-61, asst. prof., 1961-65; assoc. prof. U. Mo., Rolla, 1965-73, prof., 1973-99; dir. Inst. River Studies, U. Mo., Rolla, 1976-93; exec. dir. Internat. Inst. River and Lake Systems, U. Mo., Rolla, 1984-93, interim chmn. CE dept., 1998-99, prof. emeritics of CE, 2000—. Mem. NSPE, Mo. Soc. Profl. Engr., Am. Soc. Engring. Edn., ASCE, Nat. Coun. Engring. Examiners (pres. 1983-84), Mo. Bd. Architects, Profl. Engr. and Land Surveyors (chmn. 1978-84, 95-2002).

**MUNGUIA TAPIA, EMMANUEL,** electrical engineer, researcher, computer scientist; b. Cd. Obregon, Sonora, Mexico, Jan. 26, 1978; s. Leonardo Munguia Xochihua and Josefina Amparo Tapia Berrelleza; m. Margarita Akiyama Gutierrez, Aug. 14, 2004. BSc, Inst. Politecnico Nac., Mex., 2000; MS, MIT, Cambridge, 2002, PhD, 2006. Rschr. Intel Rsch. Seattle, Seattle, 2004, Mitsubishi Electric Rsch. Laboratories, Cambridge, Mass., 2005, MIT, Cambridge, 2006. Dir. sensing tech. design MIT PlaceLab Living Lab., Cambridge, 2005—06; cons. in field. Recipient Presdl. award, Pres. of Mex., 2000, Best Graduating Engr. Nat. award, Nat. Assn. Schs. Engring., 2000, MIT Rsch. Assistantship award, MIT, 2002—06; fellow Telmex fellow, MIT Media Lab., 2000—06; scholar, Google, 2006. Mem.: IEEE (assoc.), Assn. for Computing Machinery (assoc.). Achievements include patents for scalable activity recognition for sensor networks; research in object-based dense sensing activity recognition. Home: 540 Memorial Dr Apt 1307 Cambridge MA 02139 Office: MIT One Cambridge Center 4F Cambridge MA 02142 Office Phone: 617-710-0300. Home Fax: 617-225-0027; Office Fax: 617-225-0027. Business E-Mail: emunguia@mit.edu.

**MUNICH, MARIO ENRIQUE,** research scientist, electronics executive; Elec. Technician, Instituto Politécnico Gen. San Martín, Rosario, Argentina, 1985; Elec. Engr., U. Nacional de Rosario, Argentina, 1991; Electronic Systems Design Specialist, U. Politécnica de Madrid, 1993; MS in Elec. Engring., Calif. Inst. Tech., 1994, PhD in Elec. Engring., 2000. Rsch. scientist VocalPoint Technologies, San Francisco, 2000—01; v.p. engring., prin. scientist Evolution Robotics, Pasadena, 2001—. Contbr. articles to profl. jours. Recipient J. Walker von Brimer award, 2000, Leadership and Acad. Accomplishments award, Jr. Chamber of Rosario, 1991; Iberoam. Cooperation Inst. fellow, 1993. Mem.: ACM, IEEE. Achievements include patents for Apparatus and Method for Tracking Handwriting from Visual Input; Camera-Based Handwriting Tracking. Office: Evolution Robotics 130 W Union St Pasadena CA 91103 Office Phone: 626-535-2871. E-mail: mariomu@ieee.org.

**MUNIO, DAVID J.,** bank executive; B of Mktg., UCLA, MBA, U. Calif, 2003. With 1st Interstate Bank; exec. v.p. loan supv. Wells Fargo & Co., 1996—99, exec. v.p., dep. chief credit officer, 1999—2001, exec. v.p., CEO, 2001—. Office: Wells Fargo & Co 420 Montgomery St San Francisco CA 94163

**MUNISTERI, JOSEPH GEORGE,** construction executive; b. Rome, Sept. 24, 1930; arrived in USA, 1934; s. Peter P. and Inez Gertrude (Ziniti) Munisteri; m. Theresa Grasso, June 7, 1952 (div. Dec. 2000); children: Joanne, Robert, Laura, Stephen, James, Richard; m. Barbra Coffman, Nov. 30, 2001. BE, Yale U., 1952. With Bechtel Corp., San Francisco, 1952-59; with The Lummus Co., N.Y.C., London and Houston, 1959-67, gen. mgr., 1967—70; sr. v.p. sales Brown & Root, Inc., Houston, 1970—75, group v.p. power div., 1975-80, group v.p. corp. devel., 1980-81, also bd. dirs.; pres. Enserch Engrs. & Constructors, Inc., Houston, 1981-85; exec. v.p. Ford, Bacon & Davis, Inc., Dallas, 1985-87; chmn., pres., CEO Comstock Group, Inc., Danbury, Conn., 1987-88; pres. Joseph G. Munisteri Co., Houston, 1989—. Former chmn. bd. Pine-O-Pine. Former mem. Bd. dirs. Atomic Indsl. Forum; Bd. dirs. Am. Nuclear Energy Council. Mem. Atomic Indsl. Forum, Am. Inst. Chem. Engrs., Am. Nuclear Soc., Atomic Indsl. Forum, ASTM, Council Engring. Law, ASCE, Assoc. Iron and Steel Engring., Assoc. Builders and Contractors (dir.), Yale Club of Houston, Yale Club of N.Y. Office: 4265 San Felipe St Ste 1100 Houston TX 77027-2998 Office Phone: 713-960-1272. Personal E-mail: jmunisteri@houston.rr.com.

**MUNITZ, BARRY,** former arts and foundation administrator; b. Bklyn., July 26, 1941; m. Anne Tomfohrde. BA, Bklyn. Coll., 1963; MA, Princeton U., 1965, PhD, 1968; cert., U. Leiden, Netherlands, 1962; doctorate (hon.), Claremont U., Calif. State Univ. Sys., Whittier Coll., U. Notre Dame. Asst. prof. lit. and drama U. Calif., Berkeley, 1966-68; staff assoc. Carnegie Commn. Higher Edn., 1968-70; acad. v.p. U. Ill. System, 1971—76; v.p., dean faculties Central Campus U. Houston, 1976-77, chancellor, 1977-82; pres., COO Federated Devel. Co., 1982-91; vice chmn. Maxxam Inc., L.A., 1982-91; chancellor Calif. State U. System, Long Beach, Calif., 1991-98; prof. English lit. Calif. State U. L.A., 1991—; pres., CEO, trustee J.Paul Getty Trust, L.A., 1998—2006. P-16 Edn. Council Calif. Dept. Edn., Sacramento, 2004—. Bd. dirs. KCET-TV, SLM Holdings, KB Home; trustee Princeton U. Author: The Assessment of Institutional Leadership, also articles, monographs. Mem. art mus. vis. com. Princeton and Harvard; former chair bd. dirs. ACE; former co-chair trustees planning com. Gardner Mus.; former chair Calif. Gov. Transition Team. Recipient Disting. Alumnus award

Bklyn. Coll., 1979, U. Houston Alumni Pres.'s medal, 1981; Woodrow Wilson fellow. Fellow Am. Acad. Arts and Scis.; mem. Phi Beta Kappa. Mailing: P-16 Edn Council Calif Dept Edn 1430 N St Sacramento CA 95814 E-mail: bmunitz@getty.edu.

**MUNIZ, FRANKIE (FRANCISCO JAMES MUNIZ IV)**, actor; b. Ridgewood, NJ, Dec. 5, 1985; s. Frank and Denise Muniz. Actor: (films) Lost & Found, 1999, Little Man, 1999, My Dog Skip, 2000, It Had to Be You, 2000, (voice) Dr. Dolittle 2, 2001, Big Fat Liar, 2002, Deuces Wild, 2002, Agent Cody Banks, 2003, Agent Cody Banks 2: Destination London, 2004, (voice) Racing Stripes, 2005, Stay Alive, 2006, Danny Roane: First Time Director, 2006; (TV films) To Dance with Olivia, 1997, What the Deaf Man Heard, 1997, Miracle in Lane 2, 2000; (TV series) Malcolm in the Middle, 2000— (Young Star award for Best Young Actor/Performance in a Comedy TV Series, 2000, Young Star award for Best Young Ensemble Cast - TV, 2000, Young Artist award for Best Ensemble in a Feature Film, 2001, Young Artist award for Best Performance in a TV Comedy Series - Leading Young Actor, 2002, Young Artist award for Best Ensemble in a TV Series (Comedy or Drama), 2003, Emmy nomination for Outstanding Lead Actor in a Comedy Series, 2001), (voice) The Fairly Odd Parents, 2001—03, Moville Mysteries, 2002. Office: United Talent Agy Ste 500 9560 Wilshire Blvd Beverly Hills CA 90212*

**MUNIZ, JORGE**, composer, music educator; b. Fribourg, Switzerland, Aug. 5, 1974; s. Jose Florencio Muniz and Maria Ascension Salas; m. Jennifer Muniz, Jan. 26, 1976. MusM in Composition, Carnegie Mellon U., 2000; B in Music Composition, Royal Conservatory, Madrid, 1997; D of Musical Arts in Composition, Manhattan Sch. Music, 2004. Accompanist Conservatory of Asturias, Oviedo, Spain, 1990—95, asst. condr. Oviedo Opera Festival Chorus, Oviedo, Asturias, Spain, 1996—98; sound engr. Pitts. Digital, 1999—2000; theory faculty, coord. aural skills Manhattan Sch. Music, N.Y.C., 2002—06; prof. music theory and composition Indiana U., South Bend, 2006—. Artistic dir. composition faculty Magistralia Summer Music Festival, Gijon, Asturias, 2005—. Composer: (opera) Germinal, (symphonic) Arche (First Grand Prize European Young Composers Competition, 1998), Piano Concerto (Second Prize Spanish Soc. of Authors Composition Competition, 1999), Areiotolmos (Joaquin Turinal Prize, 1995), In Memoriam (H.G. Archer Prize of Symphonic Composition, 2000). Named Asturian of Month, Newspaper La Nueva Espana, 2005; fellow Goodwill Amb., Rotary Internat., 2000—01; grantee, Atlantic Ctr. for Arts, 2003; scholar Fulbright scholar, 1998—2000. Mem.: Coll. Music Soc., Pi-Kappa-Lambda. Home: 908 Woodside St South Bend IN 46614 Office: Ernestine Racin Sch Arts Indiana Univ 1700 Mishawaka Ave PO Box 7111 South Bend IN 46634 Business E-Mail: contact@jorgemuniz.com.

**MUNIZ, MARCO ANTONIO See ANTHONY, MARC**

**MUNK, PETER**, mining executive; b. Budapest, Hungary, Nov. 8, 1927; arrived in Can., 1948; s. Louis L. and Katherine (Adler) M.; m. Linda Gutterson; children: Anthony, Nina; m. Melanie Jane Bosanquet, 1973; children: Natalie, Cheyne, Marc David. BASc in Elec. Engring., U. Toronto, Ont., Can., 1953, LLD, 1995, Upsala Coll., N.J., 1991, U. Toronto, Que., Can., 1995, Bishops Coll., 1995, Concordia U., Montreal, Que., 1999. Chmn., CEO So. Pacific Hotel Corp., Sydney, Australia, 1969-81; chmn. Barrick Resources, Toronto, 1981-83, Am. Barrick Resources Corp. (now Barrick Gold Corp.), Toronto, 1983—, The Horsham Corp., Toronto, 1987-96; CEO Trizec Hahn Corp., Toronto, 1996—2000, chmn., 2001—; chmn., pres., CEO Trizec Can. Inc., Toronto, 2002—04, chmn., CEO, 2005—06. Chmn. Trizec Properties, Inc., 2001—. Decorated officer Order of Can. Office: Barrick Gold Corp 161 Bay St 3700 Toronto ON Canada M5J 2S1 Business E-Mail: sfennessy@barrick.com.

**MUNKVOLD, GARY P.**, plant pathologist, educator; BS in Forestry, U. Ill., 1986, MS in Plant Pathology, 1988; PhD in Plant Pathology, U. Calif., Davis, 1992. Grad. rsch. asst. Ill. Natural History Survey, Champaign, 1986-88; grad. rsch. asst. dept. plant pathology U. Calif., Davis, 1988-92; asst. prof., ext. plant pathologists dept. plant pathology Iowa State U., Ames, 1993-98, assoc. prof., ext. plant pathologist dept. plant pathology, 1998—. Recipient Novartis award Am. Phytopathol. Soc., 2000. Office: Iowa State U Dept Plant Pathology 317 Bessey Hall Ames IA 50010 Fax: 515-294-9420. E-mail: munkvold@iastate.edu.

**MUNN, CECIL EDWIN**, lawyer; b. Enid, Okla., Aug. 8, 1923; s. Cecil Edwin and Margaret (Kittrell) M.; m. Carolyn Taylor Culver, May 8, 1948; children: Franklin Culver, Charlotte Munn Forswall. BA, U. Okla., 1945; JD cum laude, Harvard U., 1947. Bar: Okla. 1948, Tex. 1956. Practice in, Enid, 1947-54, Ft. Worth, 1954—; partner firm Cantey & Hanger, Ft. Worth, 1960-91, of counsel, 1992—. With Champlin Petroleum Co., 1954-60, v.p., atty., 1958-60, dir., 1962-75. Fellow Am. Coll. Trial Lawyers, Am. Bar Found.; mem. ABA (chmn. natural resources law sect. 1970-71), Southwestern Legal Found. (past dir.), Tex. Bar Found., Phi Delta Theta, Phi Delta Phi. Presbyterian. Office: 2100 Burnett Plz 801 Cherry St Fort Worth TX 76102-6803 *Some things in life are better decided wrong than left undecided. It is amazing how much one can accomplish if unconcerned with who gets the credit.*

**MUNN, STEPHEN P.**, manufacturing executive; Pres., CEO Carlisle Co. Inc., 1988—93, chmn., pres., CEO, 1993—2001, bd. dir. Bd. dirs. Carrier Corp. N.Y. Dir. Gannett Co. Inc., 2001—. Office: Carlisle Cos Inc 13925 Ballantyne Corpo Pl Charlotte NC 28277

**MUNN, VIVIAN CAROLE**, music educator, conductor; b. Bloomington, Ill., Apr. 19, 1941; d. John G. Johnson and Alice Marie Mehlberg; m. A. Christopher Munn, Mar. 9, 1981. Bachelor of Music Edn., Wartburg Coll., 1963; Master of Music Edn., U. Tex., El Paso, 1969; Doctor of Musical Arts, U. Okla., 1990. Dir. choirs Iowa City Schs., Burges H.S., El Paso; supr. Donne Schs., Tex.; music dir. First Luth. Ch., Edinburg, Tex., 1988—; prof. music U. Tex.-Pan Am., Edinburg, 1990—. Author: Music Reading Unlimited, 1995, 1997; editor: Songs for Sight Singing, 2002, 7 books. Recipient Outstanding Tchg. award, U. Okla., 1982, U. Tex.-Pan Am., 1999. Mem. Phi Kappa Phi (treas.). Home: 1419 Post Oaks Rd Edinburg TX 78539 Office: Dept Music U Tex Pan Am 1201 W University Edinburg TX 78539 Office Phone: 956-381-2860. Business E-Mail: vivmunn@utpa.edu.

**MUNOFF, GERALD J.**, university librarian; BA in Art and Photography, Antioch Coll., Ohio; MLS, U. Ky. Past libr. Berea Coll., Ky., U. Ky.; dir. adminstrv. svc. Ky. Dept. Libr. and Archives, dep. state libr. and arch. conserv.; asst. dir. adminstrv. svc. U. Chgo. Libr., 1985—89, dept. dir., 1989—98; univ. libr. U. Calif. Irvine, 1998—. Office: 566 Main Libr U Calif Irvine PO Box 19557 Irvine CA 92623-9557 Office Phone: 949-824-5213. Office Fax: 949-824-2472. E-mail: gmunoff@uci.edu.*

**MUNOZ, ANDREA LEE**, human resources specialist; b. Inglewood, Calif., May 21, 1968; d. Lou and Alma Lou Munoz. BS in psychology, Lamar U., Beaumont, Tex., 1996, MS in indsl. orgnl. psychology, 2003. Store mgr. Merry-Go-Round, Beaumont, 1989—93; tech. svcs. cons. Helena Lab., Beaumont, 1993—2000; workforce devel. specialist Tex. Workforce Ctr., Port Arthur, Tex., 2000—02; spl. populations and disability coord. Lamar State Coll., Port Arthur, 2002—. Mem. bd. Workforce Devel. Ctr., Port Arthur, 2002—03; adv. bd. Lamar State Coll. Port Arthur, 2002—03. Bd. mem. S.E. Tex. Hispanic Cultural and Ednl. Ctr., Inc., 2002—, dir., 2002—04, Jefferson County Coun. on Alcohol and Drug Abuse. Grantee, Lamar U., 1987, Dr. Harry Starr Pre-Med scholarship, 1989, Maime McFadden-Ward Health Sci. scholarship, 1997. Mem.: Assn. on Higher Edn. and Disability, Disability Consortium of SE Tex., Psi Chi. Roman Catholic. Office: Lamar State Coll Port Arthur 1500 Procter St Port Arthur TX 77641 Office Phone: 409-984-6241.

**MUÑOZ, CARLOS RAMÓN**, retired bank executive; b. NYC, Dec. 8, 1935; s. Alejandro and Gladys Helena (Judah) Muñoz; m. Wilhelmina Elaine North, June 8, 1957 (div. 1993); children: Carla Christine, Kyle Alexander; m. Kassie Ohtaka, Sept. 23, 2000. BA, Columbia U., 1957, MA, 1961. Insp., ofcl. asst. Citibank N.A., N.Y.C., 1959-64, from asst. mgr. to mgr. Dominican Republic, P.R., 1965-70, asst. v.p. N.Y.C., 1971-72, v.p. dept. head, 1972-78; sr. v.p., regional mgr. and dir. Citicorp USA, San Francisco, 1978-81, sr. v.p. mem. credit policy com., 1982-95; exec. v.p., chief credit and risk mgmt. officer Dime Savs. Bank, N.Y.C., 1995-2000; pres., dir. Dime Consulting Group, N.Y.C., 1999-2000. Adv. coun. Credit Rsch. Ctr., 1994-2000. Mem. Columbia U. Senate, 2001—03; chmn. bd. dirs. Grace Ch. Cmty. Ctr., 2003—; v.p. Episcopal Mission Soc., 1995—2000; trustee Episcopal Diocese of NY, 1994—2001, Cathedral of St. John the Divine, 1998—2004; bd. dir. Episcopal Mission Soc., NYC, 1974—2000, Inner City Scholarship Fund, 1984—95. 1st lt. USAR, 1958—64. Recipient Productivity award State Senator Diane Watson, L.A., 1981, John Jay award for Disting. Profl. Achievement Columbia Coll., 2001; named Fairfield County Alumnus of Yr., 1989-90. Mem. Columbia Coll. Alumni Assn. (bd. dirs., treas. 1988-92, v.p., 1992-93, 1st v.p 1994-96, pres. 1996-98), Columbia Club, Westchester Hills Golf Club. Republican.

**MUÑOZ, CELIA ALVAREZ**, artist; b. El Paso, Tex., Aug. 15, 1937; d. Frank P. and Enriqueta (Limon) Alvarez; m. Andres Munoz, July 27, 1965; children: Anna Celia, Andres III. BA, U. Tex., 1964; MFA, U. North Tex., 1982. Fashion illustrator White House Dept. Store, El Paso, Tex., 1961; art instr. El Paso Pub. Schs., 1964-74, Bauder Fashion Coll., Arlington, Tex., 1984-88; lectr. U. Tex., Arlington, 1984-89. Adv. bd. Arlington Mus. Art, 1993—; mem. design team Sky Harbor Internat. Airport, 1993, N.Y. Percent for Art, P.S. 8, 1995—, Henry B. Gonzalez Convention Ctr. Expansion Project, 1995-98, Dallas Area Rapid Transit, 1998, Dallas Dept. Cultural Affairs Commn. Latino Cultural Ctr., 1999. Author: If Walls Could Speak, 1991, 95, Biennial Whitney Mus. of Am. Art.; one woman shows include Irving Arts Ctr., 1999; group shows include Arlington Mus. Art, Handley-Hicks Gallery, Tex. Tech U. NEA fellow, 1988, 91; recipient Outstanding Achievement in the Arts award Women's Caucus. Avocations: bicycling, walking, cinema, music, photography. Home: 5815 Arbor Valley Dr Arlington TX 76016-1522*

**MUNOZ, CHERYL ANN**, portfolio manager; d. Roy D. and Karen Gene Willis; m. Rick Munoz, Sept. 6, 1998. MusB, Calif. State U., 1997; postgrad., Pepperdine's Graziadio Sch. Bus., 2003—06. Chartered Financial Analyst designation CFA Inst., 2002, NASD Series 6 Nat. Assn. Securities Dealers, 1998, NASD Series 63 Nat. Assn. Securities Dealers, 1999, NASD Series 7 Nat. Assn. Securities Dealers, 2004, NASD Series 65 Nat. Assn. Securities Dealers, 2004, NASD Series 24 Nat. Assn. Securities Dealers, 2005. Gen. office clk. Marine & Roubidoux, Inc., Westlake Village, Calif., 1996—97, adminstrv. asst., 1998—99, portfolio administr., 1999—2002, portfolio mgr., strategist, 2002—05; portfolio mgr., v.p. Zephyr Investment Mgmt., Westlake Village, 2006—. Named Nat. Essay Writing Competition Winner, Big Bros./Big Sisters Orgn., 1987; Music scholar, Calif. State U. Northridge, 1991. Mem.: CFA Soc. LA, CFA Inst., Beta Gamma Sigma, Golden Key Honor Soc. Achievements include researching and creating various proprietary investment management models with the goal of reducing risk and enhancing returns. Avocations: horseback riding, skiing, clarinet, reading. Office Phone: 805-496-6810. Personal E-mail: chermunoz@yahoo.com.

**MUÑOZ, EDUARDO RAFAEL**, elementary school educator; arrived in U.S., 1961; s. Luis Alberto and Clara Luz Muñoz; m. Maria Judith Amador Muñoz, Dec. 28, 1979; children: Cristina, Rebeca. BA, U. Calif., Davis, 1974, elem. tchg. credential, secondary tchg. credential, U. Calif., Davis, 1975; MA in Edn., Santa Clara U., Calif., 1981. Elem. sch., tchr. New Haven Unified Sch. Dist., Union City, Calif., 1975—. Sch. site coord. Decoto Elem., Union City, 1975—98, summer sch. prin., 1981, Union City, 82; PTA pres. Maloney Elem., Fremont, Calif., 1991—93. Vol. Cmty. Emergency Response Team, Fremont, Calif., 1996—. Named Outstanding Individual, Union City, 1981; recipient Gold Leaf PTA Svc. award, Fremont, 1993. Mem.: NEA, AARP, KC, Calif. Tchrs. Assn. (nominee Cesar Chavez award 2006). Democrat. Roman Catholic. Avocations: soccer, golf, baseball, hiking, audio-visual programs. Office: New Haven Unified Sch Dist 34200 Alvarado-Niles Blvd Union City CA 94587

**MUÑOZ, HERALDO (HERALDO MUÑOZ VALENZUELA)**, diplomat; b. Santiago, Chile, July 22, 1948; m. Pamela Quick; 1 child. BA in Polit. sci., SUNY, Oswego; Internat. Rels. grad. with honors, Cath. U. of Chile, 1975; PhD in Internat. studies. U. of Denver, 1978; student, Harvard U.; D Honoris Causa (hon.), SUNY, 1996. Former pres. Economist Conferences, Chile, 1998—99, Latinanalyst Consultores; prof. Inst. of Internat. Studies, U. of Chile; nat. supr. People's Stores, Chile, 1973; sec. of internat. rels. Socialist Party of Chile, 1983—85; campaign chief Ricardo Lagos' senatorial race, 1989; internat. advisor of Lagos presdl. campaign and headed Internat. and Def. Commn, Chile, 1999; Chilean amb. to Brazil, 1994—98, to OAS, 1990—94; dep. fgn min. govt. of Chile, 2000—02, min. sec. gen., 2002—03; Chilean amb. and permanent rep. to UN, 2003—05. Vis. prof./lectr. several univ. and diplmatic adads. in U.S., Europe and Latin Am. Has pub. more than 20 books and dozens of essays in acad. journals. Recipient Disting. Alumnus award, Grad. Sch. of Internat. Studies, U. of Denver, 1991; fellow Resources for the Future, Ford Found., Tinker Found., Twentieth Century Fund, and MacArthur Found., PhD fellow, Brookings Inst., Washington, 1977. Achievements include founding and being dir. of fgn policy inst., Programa de Seguimiento de las Politicas Esteriores Latinoamericanas (PROSPEL), Santiago, 1983-90; co-founder of Party for Democracy. Office: Perm Mission of Chile to UN 10th Fl 305 E 47th St New York NY 10017 Business E-Mail: hmunoz@chileun.org.

**MUÑOZ, JOSEPH MARK**, education educator, consultant; b. Zamboanga, Philippines, Apr. 19, 1966; arrived in U.S., 1999; s. Jose Edgar Cabato and Charity Judith (Schuck) Munoz; m. Melanie Salazar Bragas, Oct. 18, 1995; children: Ma.Marijka, John Paolo, Ma.Markiesha, John Marko. BS, U. Philippines, 1986; MBA, U. San Jose, Philippines, 1992, PhD in Mgmt., 1997. Retail market specialist Shell Group of Co., Manila, Philippines, 1990—92; internat. sales and mktg. dir. SGAC Retail Devel. Group, Manila, Philippines, 1992—96; country mgr. Asia Kerametal Co. Ltd., Bratislava, Slovakia, 1996—99; sr. cons. Asia Enjo Bus. Clin., Cebu, Philippines, 1997—99; acctg. dir. U.S. and Asia Ploq Rsch., NJ, 1999—2001; asst. prof. internat. bus. Millikin Univ., Decatur, Ill., 2001—; mng. dir. Munoz and Assoc. Internat., Cebu, Philippines, 2001—. Mem. of the bd. De Montaigne Investment Banking, Sydney, Australia, 2001—, Monteland Group of Co., Cebu, Philippines, 1999—; presenter internat. bus. conferences, Hawaii, Greece, North Ireland, Malaysia, Philippines. Contbr. articles to profl. jour. Co-founder Breakfast for the World Found., Philippines, 2001. Comdr. Coast Guard, 1997—99, Philippines. Nominee Global Leader for Tomorrow, WEF; recipient Best Rsch., Enterprise Conf. Hawaii, 2003. Mem.: MBA Global Net-USA Internat. Coun. Small Bus., Internat. Exec. Svc. Corp., U.S. Assn. for Small Bus. and Entrepreurship. Roman Catholic. Achievements include research in travel executives' perceptions on the impact of globalization on contemporary business. Home: 56 Ridge Ave Decatur IL 62521 Office: Millikin Univ 1184 W Main St Decatur IL 62522 Office Phone: 217-420-6762. Business E-Mail: jmunoz@mail.millikin.edu.

**MUÑOZ, MARIO ALEJANDRO**, civil engineer, retired consultant; b. Havana, Cuba, Feb. 27, 1928; arrived in U.S., 1961, naturalized, 1968; s. Ramón and Concepción (Bermudo) M.; m. Julia Josephine Garrofe, Jan. 17, 1970. *Cuba-born wife Julia chose exile in 1960, and came to the U.S. in 1962, via Spain. Her volunteer and Philanthropic endeavors in Chicago are many: Board member of the Cardinal's Committee in the mid-1960's, Chicago Symphony Docent, Art Institute Docent, Board member of the Women's Association of the Chicago Symphony, Co-chair of the "Eternal Feminine" project at Ravinia Festival 2000, advisor of the "Crossing Boundaries" 2002 project for the Illinois Humanities Council. She and her husband were patrons of the St. James Steeplechase.* M.Arch., U. Havana, 1954; postgrad.,

City Colls., Chgo., 1974, U. Wis., 1974. Owner Muñoz Bermudo-Construcciones, Havana, 1954-61; designer various cos. Chgo., 1961-65; designer Chgo. Transit Authority, Mdse. Mart, 1965-69; civil engr. Dept. Water and Sewers, City of Chgo., 1969-79; supervising engr. Dept. of Sewers, 1979-85, coordinating engr., 1985-88, asst. chief engr., 1988-93. Mem. ctrl. area subway sys. utilities com. City of Chgo., 1974-93, mem. computer graphics com., 1977-78. Mem. Am. Pub. Works Assn., Western Soc. Engrs., Chgo. Architecture Found., Theodore Thomas Soc. Chgo. Symphony, Chgo. Coun. Fgn. Rels., Soc. of the shield of Loyola, The Overture soc. of the Lyric Opera, Ground Hog Club, Execs. Club (speaker's table com.), Oak Brook Bath and Tennis Club, Barrington Polo Club. Roman Catholic.

**MUÑOZ, ROMEO SOLANO**, audio visual curator; b. Daraga, Philippines, July 2, 1933; s. Maximo M. and Fe (Solano) M.; m. Soledad Roselada, Jan. 2, 1964; children: Francis Vincent, Theresa Lourdes, Romualdo Romeo, Maria Cecilia, Angela, Stephen Ignatius. BA in Psychology, Aquinas Coll., Manila, 1965; MS, Ea. Ill. U., 1968; MA, Gov's. State U., 1989; EdD, No. Ill. U., 1995; postgrad., So. Ill. U. Audio visual curator Ateneo U., Quezon City, Philippines, 1962-67; audio visual dir. Olive-Harvey Coll., Chgo., 1969—. Prof. City Coll. Chgo., 1969—, prof. emeritus; cons. adminstrv. svcs., fin. City Coll. Bd. Trustees, Chgo., 1988—; v.p. Gov.'s State U., University Park, Ill. Author: Filipino Americans: From Invisibility to Empowerment, 2002. Del. AFL/CIO, Chgo., 1989, 90; deacon Archdiocese Chgo. Roman Cath. Ch., 1976—, Professed Secular Franciscan; trustee Calumet City Libr., 1993. Recipient fellowship Ea. Ill. U., Charleston, 1967-68, So. Ill. U., Carbondale, 1968-70, Gov.'s State U., Univ. Park, Ill., 1981-2000. Mem. ALA, Gov.'s State U. Alumni (bd. dirs.), Philippine Profls. Assn. (pres.), Nat. Fedn. of Filipino-Am. Orgns., Philippine Hist. Soc., Phi Delta Kappa (pres. 2000), Philippine Educators in Am. (pres.). Avocation: physical fitness. Home: 383 Hoxie Ave Calumet City IL 60409-2330 Office Phone: 708-891-3146. E-mail: rmunoz@ccc.edu, rs-munoz@yahoo.com.

**MUÑOZ FERNÁNDEZ, MICHELA**, electrical engineer, researcher; arrived in US, 2000; d. Juan and Alicia. Diploma summa cum laude in Elec. Engring., Escuela Politécnica, U.A.H., Madrid, Spain, 1998; MS in Space Studies, Internat. Space U., Strasbourg, France, 2000; MSEE, Calif. Inst. Tech., 2001, PhD in Elec. Engring., 2005; MSEE, U. Complutense, Madrid, 2004. Registered profl. engr., Spain, 1998. Database mgmt. engr. SEMA Group Alcatel Formacion y Consultoria, Madrid, 1996; elec. engr. European Space Agy. ROSETTA mission Nat. Aerospace Inst. of Spain, Madrid, 1997—99; telecom. engr. Jet Propulsion Lab. NASA, Pasadena, Calif., 1999, rschr. Jet Propulsion Lab., 2000—06; project sys. engr. Jet Propulsion Lab., 2006—. Organizer politechnical congress Escuela Politécnica, U.A.H., Madrid, 1994—95. Contbr. articles to profl. jours. Best paper Advanced Systems for Satellite Comm. Category award). Recipient award, Caltech/JPL, 2004; fellow, U. Politécnica, 1999, Divsn. Sci. and Engring., Calif. Inst. of Tech., 2000—01; grantee, NASA, 2002—05; scholar, European Space Agy., 1999—2000; Calvo Rodés fellowship, Nat. Aerospace Inst., 1997, Amelia Earhart fellowship, Zonta Internat. Found., 2002, 2004. Mem.: IEEE, The Internat. Soc. Optical Engring., Athenaeum-Caltech Club. Achievements include first to new technology for high-rate coherent optical communications for deep space. Mailing: 158 S Madison Ave No 209 Pasadena CA 91101 Office Phone: 818-219-9306. Personal E-mail: michela@caltech.edu. Business E-Mail: michela.munoz.fernandez@jpl.nasa.gov.

**MUÑOZ-SOLÁ, HAYDEÉ SOCORRO**, library administrator; b. Caguas, PR, Dec. 27, 1943; d. Gilberto Muñoz and Carmen Haydeé (Solá) de Muñoz; m. Juan M. Masini-Soler, Jan. 8, 1966 (div. 1979); children: Juan Martín Masini-Muñoz, Haydeé Milagros Masini-Muñoz. BA in Psychology, U. P.R., Río Piedras, 1965, MLS, 1970; D in Libr. Sci., Columbia U., 1985. Asst. libr. U. P.R., Río Piedras, 1964-67; dir. libr. Interam. U., Aguadilla, PR, 1974-75; head svcs. to pub. U. P.R., Aguadilla, 1975-76; cataloguer Cath. U., Ponce, PR, 1976-79. U. P.R., Río Piedras, 1982-84, head libr. and info. sci. libr., 1984-85, prof. grad. libr. sch., 1986, 99, dir. libr. sys., 1986-93, coord. external resources libr. sys., 1994-97, dir. of libr. Ponce, PR, 1997, collection devel. officer Rio Piedras, 1998, sabbatical leave, 2000-01; compiler, editor Puerto Rican Bibliography, 2001—. Dir. P.R. Newspaper Project, Río Piedras, 1986-90; mem. Adv. Com. on Pub. Librs., San Juan, 1987-93; proposal reviewer NEH, 1990—; chmn. Puerto Rican Del. to Nat. White House Conf. on Libr. and Info. Svcs., 1991. Author: La Información y la Documentación Educativa/Informe Sobre la Situación Actual en Puerto Rico, 1991, Memorias: Segunda Pre-Conferencia de Casa Blanca Sobre Bibliotecas y Servicios de Información en Puerto Rico, 1991, Lineamientos para Colecciones Bibliograficas Nacionales, 1997, Premio por Excelencia en Investigación Aplicada y Publicación, 1997; contbr. articles to profl. jours. Mem. Ponce Sport Club, 1976—83, ARC, Ponce, 1978. Recipient plaque White House Pre-Conf. on Libr. and Info. Sci., 1990, others, Leccion Magistral Josefina del Toro Fulladosa, 2002; French Alps Study Tour scholar Assn. Caribbean Univ. Rsch. and Instl. Libr., 1989, Germany Study Tour scholar Fgn. Rels. Office, Germany, 1991, coord. So. area 1974, Lauro award 1989, Leccion Magistral Josefina del Toro Fulladosa award, 2002. Mem. ALA, Am. Mgmt. Assn., Grad. Sch. Libr. and Info. Sci. Alumni Assn. (pres. 1988-90), Seminar for Acquisitions L.Am. Libr. Materials, Iberoamerican Nat. Libr. Assn. (pres. 1992-93), Puerto Rican Libr. Soc., Assn. Caribbean U. Rsch. and Instnl. Libr. (Parchment award 1988), Asoc. para las Comunicaciones y Tecnología Educativa, Mid. States Assn. Coll. and Sch. (collaborator), Am. Women Assn., Nat. Commn. P.R. Women, Phi Delta Kappa (chair P.R. 1988-90, Kappan of Yr. 1990), Eta Gamma Delta. Roman Catholic. Avocations: reading, crewel work, embroidery, knitting, movies. Office: PO Box 23302 San Juan PR 00931-2302 Office Phone: 787-764-0000 x2707. Business E-Mail: hmunoz@uprrp.edu.

**MUNRO, ALICE**, writer; b. Wingham, Ont., Can., July 10, 1931; d. Robert Eric and Anne Clarke (Chamney) Laidlaw; m. James Armstrong Munro, 1951 (div. 1976); children: Sheila, Jenny, Andrea; m. Gerald Fremlin, 1976 BA, U. Western Ont., 1952, DLitt (hon.), 1976. Established Munro Books bookstore, 1963; writer in residence U. BC & U. Queensland, 1980. Author: (first short story) The Dimensions of a Shadow, 1950, (short story collections) Dance of the Happy Shades, 1968 (Gov. Gen.'s Lit. Award, Can. Coun. Arts, 1968), Something I've Been Meaning to Tell You, 1974, Who Do You Think You Are? (pub. outside Can. as Beggar Maid: Stories of Flo and Rose), 1978 (Gov. Gen.'s Lit. Award, Can. Coun. Arts, 1978), The Moons of Jupiter, 1982. The Progress of Love, 1986 (Gov. Gen.'s Lit. Award, Can. Coun. Arts, 1986), Friend of My Youth, 1990 (Trillium Book Award, 1991, Commonwealth Writers' Prize, 1991), Open Secrets, 1994 (WH Smith Award, 1995), Selected Stories, 1996, The Love of a Good Woman, 1998 (Giller Prize, 1998, Nat. Book Critics Circle Fiction Award, 1998, Named Fiction Book of Yr., Can. Booksellers Assn. Ex Libris awards, 1999), Hateship, Friendship, Courtship, Loveship, Marriage, 2001, Runaway, 2004 (Giller Prize, 2004), (novels) Lives of Girls and Women, 1971 (Can. Booksellers Assn. Internat. Book Yr. Award, 1972). Recipient Can.-Australia Lit. Prize 1977, Marian Engel Award, 1986, Rea Award for the Short Story, 2001; Named one of Time Mag. 100 Most Influential People, 2005. Office: William Morris Agy 16th Fl 1325 Avenue of the Americas New York NY 10019

**MUNRO, BARBARA HAZARD**, nursing educator, dean, researcher; b. Wakefield, RI, Nov. 28, 1938; d. Robert J. and Honore (Egan) Hazard; children: Karen Aimee, Craig Michael, Stephanie Anne. BS, MS, U. RI, Kingston; PhD, U. Conn. RN, Conn. Asst. prof. U. RI Coll. Nursing, Kingston; assoc. prof., chmn. doctoral prog. in nursing rsch. Yale U., New Haven; assoc. prof., asst. dir. Ctr. for Nursing Rsch. U. Pa., Phila.; dean, prof. Boston Coll. Sch. Nursing 1991—. Presenter and workshop leader various nursing confs. and seminars in U.S. Contbr. articles and rsch. to profl. pubs. Trustee St. Elizabeth's Med. Ctr. Boston, 1994—. Recipient Nat. Rsch. Svc. award. Fellow Am. Acad. Nursing; mem. ANA, Golden Key, Sigma Theta Tau, Pi Lambda Theta, Phi Kappa Phi. Office: Boston Coll Sch Nursing Cushing Hall Chestnut Hill MA 02467-3812 Office Phone: 617-552-1710. Business E-Mail: barbara.hazard.1@bc.edu.

**MUNRO, DONALD JACQUES,** philosopher, educator; b. New Brunswick, N.J., Mar. 5, 1931; s. Thomas B. and Lucile (Nadler) M.; m. Ann Maples Patterson, Mar. 3, 1956; 1 child, Sarah de la Roche. AB, Harvard U., 1953; PhD (Ford Found. fellow), Columbia U., 1964. Asst. prof. philosophy U. Mich., 1964-68, assoc. prof., 1968-73; prof. philosophy, 1973—90, prof. philosophy and Asian langs., 1990-96; prof. emeritus philosophy and Chinese, 1996—; chmn. dept. Asian langs. and cultures U. Mich., 1993-95; vis. research philosopher Center for Chinese Studies, U. Calif., Berkeley, 1969-70; assoc. Center for Chinese Studies, U. Mich., 1964—; mem. Assn. for Asian studies China and Inner Asia Coun., 1970—72; chmn. com. on studies of Chinese civilization Am. Council Learned Socs., 1979-81. Mem. Com. on Scholarly Communication with People's Republic China, NAS, 1978-82, China Coun. of Asia Soc., 1977-80, Com. on Advanced Study in China, 1978-82; Evans-Wentz lectr. Stanford U., 1970; Fritz lectr. U. Wash., 1980; Gilbert Ryle lectr. Trent U., Ont., 1983; John Dewey lectr. U. Vt., 1989; Ch'ien Mu lectr. Chinese U. Hong Kong, 2002-2003. Author: The Concept of Man in Early China, 1969, the Concept of Man in Contemporary China, 1977; editor: Individualism and Holism, 1985, Images of Human Nature: A Sung Portrait, 1988, The Imperial Style of Inquiry in Twentieth Century China, 1996, A Chinese Ethics for the New Century, 2005. Mem. exec. com. Coll. Literature, Sci. and The Arts U. Mich., 1986-89. Served to lt. (j.g.) USNR, 1953-57. Recipient letter of commendation Chief Naval Ops.; Disting. Svc. award U. Mich., 1968, Excellence in Edn. award, 1992; Rice Humanities award, 1993-94; Nat. Humanities faculty fellow, 1971-72; John Simon Guggenheim Found. fellow, 1978-79; grantee Social Sci. Rsch. Coun., 1965-66, Am. Coun. Learned Socs., 1982-83, China com. grantee NAS, 1990; vis. rsch. scholar Chinese Acad. Social Scis. Inst. Philosophy, Beijing, 1983, dept. philosophy Beijing U., 1990. Home: 14 Ridgeway St Ann Arbor MI 48104-1739 Office: Dept Philosophy U Mich Ann Arbor MI 48104 *I believe that knowledge is interrelated and that academic disciplinary boundaries are transitory conveniences. The human significance of any research task I undertake should be obvious to those inside and outside my professional group (a goal I seek but do not always achieve).*

**MUNRO, DONALD WILLIAM, JR.,** non-profit organization executive; b. Phila., Dec. 27, 1937; s. Donald William and Emily McCoy (Graham) M.; m. Joyce Eleanor Thomas, Sept. 9, 1961; children: Deborah Joy, Mark William. BS, Wheaton Coll., 1959; MS, Pa. State U., 1963, PhD, 1966. Prof. biology Houghton (N.Y.) Coll., 1966-94; exec. dir. Am. Sci. Affiliation, Ipswich, Mass., 1994—2005. Adj. prof. biology Gordon Coll., Wenham, Mass., 1995-2004; chmn. biology dept. Houghton Coll., 1972-94. Capt. U.S. Army, 1960-69. Predoctoral fellow NIH, 1964-66. Mem. Am. Philatelic Soc., Newburyport Stamp Club, Houghton Stamp Club (pres. 1988-90). Republican. Baptist. Avocations: stamps, piano, hiking, bioethics. Office: Am Sci Affiliation PO Box 668 55 Market St Ipswich MA 01938-2262 E-mail: don@asa3.org, dandjmunro@earthlink.net.

**MUNRO, ELEANOR,** writer, lecturer; b. Bklyn., Mar. 28, 1928; d. Thomas and Lucile (Nadler) Munro; m. Alfred Frankfurter (dec. 1965); children: David, Alexander (dec.); m. E.J. Kahn, Jr. (dec.). BA, Smith Coll., Northampton, Mass., 1949; MA, Columbia U., N.Y.C., 1968. Staff writer, editor Art News Mag., N.Y.C., 1952-59; freelance writer, art critic, lectr. N.Y.C., 1960—. Vis. fellow Woodrow Wilson Nat. Fellowship Fedn., Princeton, N.J., 1990—; cons., juror Bush Fdn., St. Paul, 1994; resident fellow Bellagio Study Ctr., Lake Como, Italy, 1991, Yaddo, Saratoga Springs, N.Y., 1984. Author: Encyclopedia of Art, 1961, Through the Vermilion Gates, 1971, Originals: American Women Artists, 1979 (a N.Y. Times Notable Book of Yr.), Memoir of a Modernist's Daughter, 1988, On Glory Roads: A Pilgrim's Book about Pilgrimage, 1987 (N.Y. Times Notable Book of Yr.); author articles, criticism, fiction and poetry. Bd. dirs. Truro (Mass.) Ctr. for Arts, 1979—, The Living Theater, N.Y.C., 1989—, Nat. Alliance Rsch. into Schizophrenia and Depression, N.Y.C., 1995-2000. Recipient Cleve. Arts prize, 1988, medal of honor Smith Coll., 1990, Nat. Lifetime Achievement award Women's Caucus for Art, 2003. Mem. PEN Am., Am. Internat. Assn. Art Critics, Authors Guild. Home: 176 E 71st St # 3B New York NY 10021-5159

**MUNRO, JOHN HENRY ALEXANDER,** economics professor, writer; b. Vancouver, B.C., Can., Mar. 14, 1938; s. Hector Gordon and Blanche (Almond) M.; m. Jeanette Roberta James, May 25, 1968; children: Robert Ryder, Valerie Marlene. BA with honors, U. B.C., Vancouver, 1960; MA in History, Yale U., 1961, PhD in History, 1965. Instr. in history U. B.C., 1964-65, asst. prof. history and econs., 1965-68; assoc. prof. econs. U. Toronto, 1968-73, prof., 1973—2003, prof. emeritus, 2003—; assoc. dir. Centre for Medieval Studies, U. Toronto, 1975-78. Cons. on coinage to pub. U. Toronto Press, 1973— Author: Wool, Cloth, and Gold, 1973, Bullion Flows and Monetary Policies in England and the Low Countries, 1350-1500, 1992, Textiles, Towns and Trade: Essays in the Economic History of Late-Medieval England and the Low Countries, 1994; contbr. articles to profl. jours., essays to books; mem. editl. bd. Textile History, 1980-97, Explorations in Economic History, 1998—, Medieval Clothing and Textiles, 2005; Medieval area editor Oxford Ency. of Econ. History, 1996—2003. Can. Coun. leave fellow, Belgium, 1970-71, Social Scis. and Humanities Rsch. Coun. Can. fellow, Engl. and Holland, 1979-80, Belgium, 1986-87, Eng. and Belgium, 1992-96, 96-99, 99—, Connaught Rsch. fellow, 1993-94, 2000—01. Mem. Can. Econ. Assn., Econ. History Assn. (U.K.), Econ. History Soc. (U.K.), Medieval Acad. Am. (councillor 1990-93), Instituto Internazionale di Storia Economica (sci. com. 1999—, exec. bd. 2003—), Royal Flemish Acad. Belgium for Sci. and Arts. (fgn.). Presbyterian. Home: 9 Woodmere Ct Toronto ON Canada M9A 3J1 Office: Dept Econs U Toronto 150 St George St Toronto ON Canada M5S 3G7 Office Phone: 416-978-4552. E-mail: munro5@chass.utoronto.ca, john.munro@utoronto.ca.

**MUNRO, JP,** artist; b. Inglewood, Calif., 1975; Exhibitions include Ending is Better Than Mending, Sadie Coles HQ, London, 2002, JP Munro, 2005, Morbid Curiosity, I-20 Gallery, NY, 2002, Golden, Galerie Michael Jenssen, Cologne, 2003, Drawings, Metro Pictures Gallery, NY, 2003, 100 Artists See God, Inst. Contemporary Art, London, 2004, Contemporary Art Ctr. Va., 2005, The Early Show, White Columns, NY, 2005, Whitney Biennial: Day for Night, Whitney Mus. Am. Art, 2006. Office: c/o China Art Objects Gallery 933 Chung King Rd Los Angeles CA 90012*

**MUNRO, RALPH DAVIES,** former state official; b. Seattle, June 25, 1943; s. George Alexander and Elizabeth (Troll) M.; m. Karen (Hansen), Feb. 17, 1973; one son, George Alexander. BA in History and edn. (scholar), Western Wash. U. Indsl. engr. Boeing Co., Wash., 1966-68; sales mgr. Continental Host, Inc., Wash.; asst. dir. ACTION Agy., Wash., 1971; spl. asst. to gov. State of Wash., 1970-76; gen. mgr. Tillicum Enterprises and Food Svc. Co., Wash.; dir. Found. for Handicapped, 1976-80; pres. N.W. Highlands Tree Farm; sec. of state State of Wash., 1980—2000; bd. dir. Vote Here. Chmn. cmty. svc. com. Seattle Rotary Club 4; founder 1st pres. Rotary Youth Job Employment Ctr., Seattle. Named Man of Yr. Assn. Retarded Citizens, Seattle, 1970. Mem. Nat. Assn. Sec. State (pres.), Nat. Assn. Retarded Children, Wash. Hist. Mus. (dir.), Wash. Trust Hist. Preservation (founder), Nature Conservancy. Republican. Lutheran.

**MUNROE, GEORGE BARBER,** retired mining and manufacturing company executive; b. Joliet, Ill., Jan. 5, 1922; s. George Mueller and Ruth (Barber) Munroe; m. Elinor Bunin, May 30, 1968; children from previous marriage: George Taylor, Ralph W. Taylor. AB, Dartmouth Coll., 1943; LLB, Harvard U., 1949; BA (Rhodes scholar), Christ Church, Oxford U., Eng., 1951, MA, 1956; DHL (hon.), No. Ariz. U., 1981; LLD (hon.), Dartmouth Coll., 1993. Bar: N.Y. 1949. Assoc. Cravath, Swaine & Moore, N.Y.C., 1949; atty. Office Gen. Counsel U.S. High Commn. Germany, Frankfurt and Bonn, 1951-53; justice U.S. Ct. Restitution Appeals Allied High Commn. Germany, Nuremberg, 1953-54; assoc. Debevoise, Plimpton & McLean, N.Y.C., 1954-58; with Phelps Dodge Corp. 1958-87, v.p., 1962-66, pres., 1966-75, 80-82, chief exec. officer, 1969-87, chmn. bd., 1975-87, dir., 1966-94. Trustee emeritus Met. Mus. Art; chmn. emeritus bd. dirs. Acad. Polit. Sci. Served to

---

lt. (j.g.) USNR, 1943—46. Mem. Mining and Metall. Soc. Am., Coun. Fgn. Rels., Century Assn., River Club, Univ. Club (N.Y.C.). Bridgehampton Club. Office: 444 Madison Ave Fl 19 New York NY 10022-6903 Office Phone: 212-750-4569.

**MUNSCH, MARTIN JOHN, III,** sound recording engineer, music producer; s. Martin John Munsch, Jr. and Camille M. Munsch; m. Julie E. Harvey; 1 child, Carolyn C. AA, William Paterson U., 1994. Prodr. Punk-rockrecords.com, Oakland, N.J., 1985—, owner, pres. A&R, 1985—; prodr. Atlantic Records, 1985—, MCA Records; chief master engr. Chgo., 1989—; head engr. Pipeline, Newark, 1992—97. Prodr.: (LPCD) Not Enjoyin' It (Top Ten Punk LP/CD, 1996). Named one of Top 5 Punk Music Prodrs. of 1980s, 1990s, 2000s. Home and Office: Punk Rock Records Publishing 2 June Rd Chester NY 10918 Office Phone: 845-406-2815. Business E-Mail: prnetwork@frontiernet.net.

**MUNSELL, DEBRA S.,** physician assistant, educator; b. Pt. Arthur, Tex., June 13, 1957; d. Rosemond B. and Bettie Lawrence Schoenberg; m. Lloyd Allen Foreman III, Feb. 16, 1985 (dec. Mar. 1991); m. William Peter Munsell, July 18, 1998. BS in Biology, Stephen F. Austin State U., 1979; BS in Health, U. Tex., Galveston, 1981; MPhysician Asst. Studies in Otolaryng., U. Nebr., 2000. Cert. phys. asst. Physician asst. Angleton (Tex.) Clinic, 1981-83, Tex. Dept. Corrections, Huntsville, 1983-84; physician asst. med. br. Galveston U. Tex., 1985-90, clin. instr. med. br. Galveston, 1985—; physician asst. M.D. Anderson Cancer Ctr. Houston, 1990—2005, dir. physician asst. student edn. program M.D. Anderson Cancer Ctr., 1996—2005; clin. assoc. prof. physician asst. edn. We. U. Health Sci., Pomona, Calif., 1999—; asst. prof. U. Tex. Med. Br., Sch. Allied Health Sci., Galveston, 2005—. Clin. instr. Baylor Coll. Medicine, Houston, 1999—. Author: (with others) Primary Care Oncology, 1999, Primary Care: A Collaborative Approach, 1999, Primary Care, A Collaborative Practice, 2d edit., 2003, The Physician Assistant Medical Handbook, 2d edit., 2004. Life mem. Brazoria County Fair Assn., Angleton, Tex., 1992—. Glaxo/Wellcome Leadership fellow Am. Acad. Physician Assts./Physician Asst. Found., 1997-98. Fellow: Assn. Physician Assts. in Oncology, Soc. Physician Assts. in Otolaryngology, Head and Neck Surgery (charter mem. 1991, bd. dirs. 1992—94, chair continuing med. edn 1994—96, pres. 1996—2000), Am. Acad. Otolaryngology, Head and Neck Surgery, Am. Acad. Physician Assts. (chair nominating com. 1998—2002, external liaison 2001—); mem.: Houston Yacht Club. Home: 9807 Williams Bend Ct Missouri City TX 77459-6279 Office: U Tex Med Br-Galveston SAHS 301 University Blvd Galveston TX 77553-1028 Office Phone: 409-772-9559. Business E-Mail: dsmunsel@utmb.edu.

**MUNSELL, ELSIE LOUISE,** retired lawyer; b. N.Y.C., Feb. 15, 1939; d. Elmer Stanley and Eleanor Harriet (Dickinson) M.; m. George P. Williams, July 14, 1979. AB, Marietta Coll., 1960; JD, Marshall-Wythe Coll. William and Mary, 1972. Bar: Va. 1972, U.S. Dist. Ct. (ea. dist.) Va. 1974, U.S. Ct. Appeals (4th cir.) 1976, U.S. Supreme Ct. 1980. Tchr. Norview High Sch., Norfolk, Va., 1964-69; asst. Commonwealth atty. Commonwealth Atty.'s Office, Alexandria, Va., 1972-73; asst. U.S. atty. Alexandria, 1974-79; U.S. magistrate U.S. Dist. Ct. (ea. dist.) Va., Alexandria, 1979-81; U.S. atty. Dept. Justice, Alexandria, 1981-86; sr. trial atty. Office of Gen. Counsel, Dept. Navy, Washington, 1986-89, asst. gen. counsel installations and environ. law, 1989-91; dep. asst. environ. and safety Sec. Navy, 1991-2001, ret., 2001. Mem. USEPA Clean Air Act Adv. Com., 1997—; bd. dirs. BMT Designers & Planners. Active Va. Commn. on Status of Women, 1966-74; bd. vistors Coll. William and Mary, 1972-76; active Atty. Gen.'s Adv. Com. U.S. Attys., 1981-83; bd. dirs. Carpenter's Shelter, Inc., 1990-93; vestry St. Alban's Ch., Annandale, Va., 1996-99, 2003; fed. preservation officer Dept. Navy, 1999. Presdl. Meritorious Exec., 1999; recipient Spl. Achievement award Nat. Mil. Fish and Wildlife Assn., 2001, Disting. Civilian Svc. award, 2001. Mem. Sr. Execs. Assn., Chi Omega. Episcopalian.

**MUNSELL, WILLIAM A.,** healthcare insurance company executive; With UnitedHealth Grp., 1997—; CFO UnitedHealthcare, 1997—2000, COO, 2000—03, chief adminstrv. officer, 2003—04; CEO Specialized Care Svcs., 2004—. Office: UnitedHealth Grp PO Box 1459 Minneapolis MN 55440-1459*

**MUNSEY, VIRDELL EVERARD, JR.,** retired utilities executive; b. Washington, Sept. 25, 1933; s. Virdell Everard and Mildred Lovenia (Wood) M.; m. Bernice Ann Wilson, Sept. 20, 1956; children: Wanda Louise, Allan Coll, Andrew Everard, Carolyn Jane. BA magna cum laude, Yale U., 1955; M.P.A., Harvard U., 1967. Reporter Washington Post, 1957-63; legis. asst. Rep. Henry S. Reuss, Washington, 1963-68; info. dir. United Democrats for Humphrey, Washington, 1968; asst. dir. public affairs Dem. Nat. Com., 1968; with Nat. Planning Assn., Washington, 1969-77, exec. v.p., 1974-76; dep. asst. sec. for public affairs Dept. Treasury, Washington, 1977-81; cons. World Bank, 1981; with Va. Electric and Power Co., 1981-86, mgr. corp. communications, 1982-83, exec. dir. pub. policy, 1983-86, v.p. pub. policy, 1986, Dominion Resources Inc., 1986-96; cons., 1996—2002. Mem. Va. Coal and Energy Commn., 1983-95. Chmn. Arlington County Dem. Party, 1967-69; mem. Arlington County Bd., 1972-75, chmn., 1973; vice chmn. No. Va. Transp. Commn., 1973, chmn., 1974; bd. dirs. Washington Met. Area Transit Authority, 1975; mem. transp. planning bd. Met. Washington Coun. Govts., 1973-75; treas. Competitive Power Policy Forum, 1990-96. Served with U.S. Army, 1955-57. Am. Polit. Sci. Assn. fellow, 1966-67 Mem. United Ch. Christ. Personal E-mail: everard1933@yahoo.com.

**MUNSON, ALEX ROBERT,** judge; b. L.A., Sept. 25, 1941; s. Robert Alexander and Lillian Agnus (Hamel) M.; m. Kathleen Rae Abernathey, June 29, 1968. BA, Long Beach (Calif.) State Coll., 1964, MA, 1965; EdD, U. So. Calif., L.A., 1970; JD, Loyola U., L.A., 1975. Atty. Kirtland and Packard, L.A., 1978-82; chief justice High Ct. of The Trust Terr. of The Pacific Islands, Saipan, Commonwealth of the No. Mariana Islands, 1982-88; chief judge U.S. Dist. Ct. of No. Mariana Islands, Saipan, Commonwealth of the No. Mariana Islands, 1988—. Mem. ABA, Calif. Bar Assn. Republican. Home: PO Box 5356 Saipan MP 96950-5356 Office: US Dist Ct NMI PO Box 500687 Saipan MP 96950-0687

**MUNSON, HAROLD LEWIS,** education educator; b. Windham, N.Y., Aug. 2, 1923; s. Esmond Lewis and Gladys (Disbrow) M.; m. Evelyn Claire Moore, Sept. 8, 1947; children: Michael Lewis, Jeffrey Charles. AB, Hobart Coll., 1947; MA, SUNY, Albany, 1948; Ed.D., NYU, 1961. Tchr. social studies, counselor Cairo (N.Y.) Central Sch., 1948-50; dir. guidance Williamson (N.Y.) Central Sch., 1950-54; supr. guidance N.Y. State Edn. Dept., Albany, 1954-59; prof. edn., chmn. Center for Counseling, Family and Worklife Studies, U. Rochester, NY, 1959-85, prof. emeritus, 1985—; prof. edn. Overseas Program, Boston U., 1985-87; pres. Munson Assocs., 1988—. Vocat. cons. Social Security Adminstrn., HEW, 1962-79 Author: (with H.W. Houghton) Organizing Orientation Activities, 1956, My Educational Plans, 1959, 70, Guidance Activities for Teachers of English, Social Studies, Science, Mathematics and Foreign Languages, 1965, (with Gilbert Gockley) Career Insights and Self Awareness Games, 1973; contbg. author: Ency. of Careers, 1967, Elementary School Guidance: Concepts, Dimensions and Practice, 1970, The Foundations of Developmental Guidance, 1971, Career Education for Deaf Students: An Inservice Leader's Guide, 1975, The Land In The Sky, 2004. Served with USNR, 1944-46. Mem. Am. Counseling Assn., Nat. Career Devel. Assn., Am. Sch. Counselor Assn., Phi Delta Kappa. Home: 9 Charleston Drive Mendon NY 14506 Office: U Rochester Warner Grad Sch Edn and Human Devel Rochester NY 14627 Office Phone: 585-582-3275. Personal E-mail: hmunson@rochester.rr.com. *Success is whatever you want it to be. By defining it in such personal terms, everyone should be able to experience some degree of success. From it, we have been being able to feel a measure of personal fulfillment through my accomplishments in helping others to define and examine their own existence.*

---

**MUNSON, HOWARD G.,** federal judge; b. Claremont, N.H., July 26, 1924; s. Walter N. and Helena (O'Halloran) M.; m. Ruth Jaynes, Sept. 17, 1949; children: Walter N., Richard J., Pamela A. BS in Economics, U. Pa., 1948; LL.B., Syracuse U., 1952. Bar: N.Y. With Employers' Assurance Corp., Ltd., White Plains, NY, 1949-50; mem. firm Hiscock, Lee, Rogers, Henley & Barclay, Syracuse, NY, 1952-76; judge U.S. Dist. Ct. No. Dist. N.Y., Syracuse, 1976—. Mem. pres. Syracuse Bd. Edn.; bd. dirs. Sta. WCNY-TV; chmn. ethics com. Onondaga County Legislature. Served with U.S. Army, 1943-45, ETO. Decorated Bronze Star, Purple Heart. Mem. Am. Coll. Trial Lawyers, Nat. Assn. R.R. Trial Counsel, Am. Arbitration Assn., Justinian Soc., Alpha Tau Omega, Phi Delta Phi. Office: US Dist Ct US Courthouse P O Box 7376 Syracuse NY 13261-7376 Office Phone: 315-234-8580.

**MUNSON, JOHN BACKUS,** computer scientist, retired data processing executive; b. Chgo., May 1, 1933; s. Roger and Catherine Louise (Cherry) M.; m. Anne Lorraine Cooper, July 6, 1957; children: David B., Sharon A. BA, Knox Coll., 1955. With Unisys Corp., McLean, Va., 1957-93, v.p. corp. software engring., 1977-81, v.p. tech. ops., 1981-84, v.p. gen. mgr. space transp. systems, 1984-89, 89-93, v.p., gen. mgr. Space Systems divsn., 1989-94, ret., 1994. Mem. sci. adv. bd. USAF, 1981-86, mem. USN panel on F14D issues, 1987-88. Mem. bd. advisors U. Houston, Clear Lake, 1988-93, chmn. 1990-92; bd. dirs. Bay Area YMCA, 1988-93, chmn. 1992, Clear Lake Am. Heart Assn., 1989-93; co-chmn. Bay Area United Way, 1988—, chmn., 1992; Disting. visitor IEEE Computing Soc., 1981-94. Capt. U.S. Army, 1955-57. Recipient Exceptional Civilian Svc. award USAF, 1986, Superior Pub. Svc. award USN, 1988, cert. of appreciation NATO, 1984; named to Mgmt. Assn. Hall of Fame, 1994. Fellow IEEE (editor Trans. of Software Engring. 1982-84, bd. dirs. com. software engring. 1982—); mem. AIA, Am. Astronautical Soc. (bd. dirs. S.W. sect. 1989-94), Aerospace Industries Assn. (space com. 1989-94), U.S. Army Assn., Nat. Security Indsl. Assn., Armed Forces Comm. Electronics Assn. (pres. Houston chpt. 1987-90), S.W. Regional Coun. Corp. CEOs. Home and Office: 1018 Westcreek Ln Westlake Village CA 91362-5462 E-mail: JaxG3@aol.com.

**MUNSON, JOHN CHRISTIAN,** acoustician; b. Clinton, Iowa, Oct. 9, 1926; s. Arthur J. and Frances (Christian) M.; m. Elaine Hendershot, Sept. 2, 1950; children: John Christian, Holly Elizabeth. BS, Iowa State Coll., 1949; MS, U. Md., 1952, PhD, 1962; Navy Dept. scholar, MIT, 1956. Electronic scientist Naval Ordnance Lab., Washington, 1949-66; tech. dir. navy portion Practice Nine, Naval Air Systems Command, 1967; supt. acoustics divsn. Naval Rsch. Lab., 1968-85; v.p. Engring. & Sci. Assocs., 1983-94; chmn. bd. dirs., 1994; ret. Asst. extension prof. elec. engring. U. Md., 1964-66; mem. Underwater Sound Adv. Group, 1969-75, U.S. Sonar Team, 1971-85, Mobile Sonar Tech. Com., 1972-85; cons., 1985-. Editor U.S. Navy Jour. Underwater Acoustics, 1983-91; patentee in field. Mem. exec. bd. D.C. Bapt. Conv., 1973—, chmn. fin. com., 1973, v.p., 1996-97, pres., 1997-98; trustee Midwestern Bapt. Theol. Sem., 1970-80; trustee Bapt. Sr. Adult Ministries of Washington Met. Area, 1976-91, 92—94, pres., 1981-88, CEO, 1991-92; mem. Gen. Bd. Am. Bapt. Chs. U.S.A., 1994-99; pres. Allied Silver Spring Interfaith Svcs. to Srs. Today, 1994-2000, bd. dirs. 1994-2003; bd. mgrs. Am. Bapt. Hist. Soc., 1996-2003, sec., 1997-2003; corp. mem. Am. Bapt. Homes of the West, 1999, dir., 2000-04. Fellow IEEE, Signal Processing Soc. (mem. adminstrv. com. 1974-76, chmn. underwater acoustics com. 1973-76), Acoustical Soc. Am.; mem. Sigma Xi. Home: 3118 Chartwell Crescent Ln Adamstown MD 21710-9643 E-mail: johncmunsonsr@cs.com. *I have a positive joy for life, and I am an incurable optimist: my basic attitude is that things will work out for the best— but only if we do our very best. Each of us has a responsibility to grow to our maximum capacity and to be of reasonable service to mankind. The proper balance among family, job, service to God, service to others, and attention to yourself is essential. Whatever you are doing, do it from the right motivation and with enthusiasm.*

**MUNSON, LAWRENCE SHIPLEY,** management consultant; b. N.Y.C., Jan. 10, 1920; s. Lawrence J. and Anna (Lee) M.; m. Gretchen Thannhauser, May 24, 1947; children: Catherine Anne, Shipley John. AB, Harvard U., 1942, JD, 1948. Bar: N.Y. 1948. Assoc. Willkie, Owen, Farr, Gallagher & Walton, N.Y.C., 1948-51; assoc., then partner McKinsey & Co., Inc., N.Y.C., 1953-67; pres. Loral Corp., Scarsdale, N.Y., 1967-69; v.p. Allegheny Power System, Inc., N.Y.C., 1969-72; v.p., mng. prin. Louis Allen Assocs., Inc., 1972-97; self-employed cons., 1998—. Author: How To Conduct Training Seminars, 1984, 2d edit., 1992. Pres. East Hampton Village Preservation Soc., 1982—87, trustee, 1982—2001, chmn., 1993—2001, trustee emeritus, 2000—, East Hampton Healthcare Found., 2001—; chmn. bd. Planned Parenthood N.Y.C., 1966—70; bd. dirs. Planned Parenthood Manhattan and Bronx, 1960—66, Planned Parenthood World Population, 1967—70, Gtr. N.Y. Fund., 1966—88, chmn. mgmt. assistance com., 1970—75; bd. dirs. United Way N.Y.C., 1988—89; co-founder, trustee East Hampton Healthcare Found., 1998—2000. Maj. USAAF, 1942—46, with USAF, 1951—53. Mem. ASTD (pres. N.Y. met. chpt. 1988—89, chmn. bd. dirs. 1990—93), Harvard Club (N.Y.C.). Office Phone: 978-263-5952.

**MUNSON, NANCY K.,** lawyer; b. Huntington, NY, June 22, 1936; d. Howard H. and Edna M. (Keenan) Munson. Student, Hofstra U., 1959—62; JD, Bklyn. Law Sch., 1965. Bar: NY 1966, U.S. Dist. Ct. (ea. and so. dists.) NY 1968, U.S. Supreme Ct. 1970, U.S. Ct. Appeals (2d cir.) 1971. Law clk. to Hon. E. Merritt Weidner, Huntington, NY, 1959—66; pvt. practice, 1966. Legal adv. bd. Chgo. Title Ins. Co., Riverhead, NY, 1981—; bd. dirs., legal officer Thomas Munson Found. Trustee Huntington Fire Dept. Death Benefit Fund; pres., trustee, chmn. bd. dirs. Bklyn. Home Aged Men Found.; bd. dirs. Huntington Rural Cemetery Assn., Inc.; trustee Noyac Harbor Property Owners Assn. Mem.: DAR (trustee, treas. Ketewamoke chpt.), NRA, ABA, Federalist Soc. for Law and Pub. Policy Studies, Bklyn. Bar Assn., Suffolk County Bar Assn., N.Y. State Bar Assn., Soroptimists (past pres.). Republican. Christian Scientist. Office: 197 New York Ave Huntington NY 11743-2711 Office Phone: 631-271-8161.

**MUNSON, RICHARD HOWARD,** horticulturist; b. Toledo, Dec. 20, 1948; s. Stanley Warren and Margaret Rose (Winter) M. BS, Ohio State U., 1971; MS, Cornell U., 1973, PhD, 1981. Plant propagator The Holden Arboretum, Kirtland, Ohio, 1973-76; asst. prof. Agrl. Tech. Inst., Wooster, Ohio, 1976-78, Tex. Tech U., Lubbock, 1981-84; dir. botanic garden Smith Coll., Northampton, Mass., 1984-95; exec. dir. The Holden Arboretum, Kirtland, Ohio, 1995-2000; dir. botanic garden U. Mo., Columbia, Mo., 2001—04; mgr. The Conservatory, Miami U., Hamilton, Ohio, 2004—. Ret. lt. col. USAR, 1971-99. Recipient Disting. Alumnus award Ohio State U. Coll. Agr., 1998. Fellow Internat. Plant Propagator's Soc.; mem. Am. Pub. Garden Assn. (com. chmn. 1987-92, 01-03), Sigma Xi, Pi Alpha Xi, Gamma Sigma Delta. Avocations: fishing, fly-tying, golf, woodworking, gardening. Office: Miami U-Hamilton 1601 University Blvd Hamilton OH 45011 Office Phone: 513-785-3086. Business E-Mail: munsonrh@muohio.edu.

**MUNSON, RICHARD JAY,** government agency administrator; b. Hollywood, Calif., Aug. 10, 1950; s. Jay S. and Grace P. (Palmer) M.; m. Diane MacEachern; children: Daniel, Dana. BA, U. Calif., Santa Barbara, 1971; MA, U. Mich., 1973. Instr. U. Mich., Ann Arbor, 1973-75; coord. Environ. Action Found., Washington, 1975-77; exec. dir. Solar Lobby, Washington, 1977-83, N.E.-Midwest Inst., Washington, 1986—. Author: The Power Makers, 1985, Cousteau, 1988, The Cardinals of Capitol Hill, 1993, From Edison to Enron, 2005. Office: NE Midwest Inst 218 D St SE Ste A Washington DC 20003-1917 Office Phone: 202-544-5200.

**MUNSON, WILLIAM LESLIE,** insurance company executive; b. Chgo., Apr. 28, 1941; s. David Curtiss and Leona Ruth (Anderson) M.; m. Marian Lee Blanton, July 16, 1966; children: Katherine, Sandra, Deborah. Student, U. Md., 1959-62; BBA cum laude, Coll. of Ins., 1968. CPCU, 1967. Asst. mgr. N.Y. Fire Ins. Rating Orgn., N.Y.C., 1959-69; br. mgr. CNA Ins. Co., N.Y.C., 1969-75; pres., dir. Commerce & Industry Ins. Co., N.Y.C., 1975-83; pres. Commerce & Industry of Can., 1980-83; sr. v.p., chief underwriting officer Am. Internat. Underwriters, 1983-87; exec. v.p. Home Ins. Co., 1987-93; pres., chief exec. officer Home Indemnity Ins. Co., 1987-93, also bd.

dirs.; chmn. City Internat. Ins. Co. Ltd., 1991-93; pres., COO Merc. and Gen. Reins. Co. Am., 1993-97; chmn., pres., CEO Toa-Re-Ins. Co. Am. (now Toa Reins. Co. Am.), 1993—2003. Bd. dirs. USF Ins. Co.; trustee Coll. of Ins., 1985—2001, Am. Inst. for Property Casualty Underwriters, 1996—2002; bd. overseers Sch. of Risk Mgmt., Ins. and Actuarial Sci. St. John's U., 2001—; mem. bd. visitors Drew U., 2002—; bd. dirs. Nat. Coun. Compensation Ins., 1989—92, ISO Comml. Risk Svcs., 1993, mem. comml. lines. com. Ins. Svcs. Office, 1989—92. Pres. Wyckoff (NJ) Bd. Edn., 1979-82; chmn. bd. lay leaders Grace United Meth. Ch., Wyckoff, 1989-92, trustee, 1999—, pres. bd. trustees, 2005-. Past mem. Soc. CPCUs (bd. dirs. N.Y. chpt.); mem., Conf. Spl. Risk Underwriters, Reinsurance Assn. Am. (bd. dirs. 1993-2002). Clubs: John St. (N.Y.C.). Republican. Home: 762 Albemarle St Wyckoff NJ 07481-1005 Office Phone: 201-891-7834. E-mail: wlmunson@verizon.net.

**MUNT, JANET STAPLES,** state senator; b. NYC, June 14, 1923; m. Plummer Coldwell Munt (dec.); 4 children. BA, Sweet Briar Coll., 1944; MS, Columbia U., 1948. Bd. cert. diplomate. Dir. maternal and child health divsn. Visiting Nurse Assn. Chittenden County, 1978—95; pvt. practice clin. social worker, 1995—2005. Trustee Burlington Coll. Sgt. WAC, WWII. Fellow Am. Orthopsychiat. Assn., Inc.; mem. NASW, Acad. Cert. Social Workers. Democrat.

**MÜNTER, LEILANI MAAJA,** race car driver; b. Rochester, Minn. d. Manfred and Doris Munter. BS in Biology, U. Calif., San Diego. Lic. stock car driver Nat. Assn. Stock Car Auto Racing. Former tchg. asst. cellular biology U. Calif., San Diego; race car driver Nascar Elite divsn., 2004—; competed in ROMCO Super Late Model Series, Allison Legacy Series. Spl. corr. Nascar.com, 2004—. Photo double (for Catherine Zeta-Jones films) in Traffic and America's Sweethearts. Avocations: scuba diving, snowboarding. Office: PO Box 3335 Mooresville NC 28117 also: 5315 Highgate Dr Ste 204 Durham NC 27713 Business E-Mail: marketing@leilanimunter.com.

**MUNTZ, DAVID S.,** information technology executive; Data sys. dir. of info. svc. Presbyn. Healthcare Sys., Dallas, v.p. info. svcs. and telecommunications, 1996; sr. v.p. info. svc. and tech. Texas Health Resources (formed in merger with Presbyn. Healthcare Sys., others), Arlington, 1997—. Office: SVP & CIO Texas Health Resources Ste 900 611 Ryan Plz Dr Arlington TX 76011

**MUNTZ, ERIC PHILLIP,** aerospace and mechanical engineering educator, consultant; b. Hamilton, Ont., Can., May 18, 1934; came to U.S., 1961, naturalized, 1985; s. Eric Percival and Marjorie Louise (Weller) M.; m. Janice Margaret Furey, Oct. 21, 1964; children: Sabrina Weller, Eric Phillip. BASc., U. Toronto, 1956, MASc., 1957, PhD, 1961. Halfback Toronto Argonauts, 1957-60; group leader Gen. Electric, Valley Forge, Pa., 1961-69; assoc. prof. aerospace engring. and radiology U. So. Calif., Los Angeles, 1969-71, prof., 1971-87, chmn. aerospace engring., 1987-97, A.B. Freeman prof. engring., 1992—, chmn. aerospace and mech. engring., 2000—03. Cons. to aerospace and med. device cos., 1967—; mem. rev. of physics (plasma and fluids) panel NRC, Washington, 1983-85 Contbr. numerous articles in gas dynamics, micromech. sys., and med. diagnostics to profl. publs., 1961—; patentee med. imaging, isotope separation, nondestructive testing, net shape mfg., transient energy release micromachines, microscale vacuum sys., micropropulsion sys. Mem. Citizens Environ. Avc Coun., Pasadena, Calif., 1972-76. Pilot RCAF, 1955-60. U.S. Air Force grantee, 1961-74, 82—; NSF grantee, 1970-76, 87-92; NASA grantee, 1990-94, 2001—; FDA grantee, 1980-86. Fellow AIAA (aerospace Contbn. to Soc. award 1987), Am. Phys. Soc.; mem. NAE. Episcopalian. Home: 1560 E California Blvd Pasadena CA 91106-4104 Office: U So Calif Univ Pk Los Angeles CA 90089-1191 Office Phone: 213-740-5366. Business E-Mail: muntz@spock.usc.edu.

**MUNYER, EDWARD ARNOLD,** zoologist; b. Chicago, May 8, 1936; s. G. and M. Munyer; m. Marianna J. Munyer, Dec. 12, 1981; children: Robert, William, Richard, Laura, Cheryl. BS, Ill. State U., 1958, MS, 1962. Biology tchr. MDR High Sch., Minonk, Ill., 1961-63; instr. Ill. State U., Normal, 1963-64; curator zoology Ill. State Mus., Springfield, 1964-67, asst. dir., 1981-98, asst. dir. emeritus, 1998—; assoc. prof. Vincennes (Ind.) U., 1967-70; dir. Vincennes U. Mus., 1968-70; assoc. curator Fla. Mus. Natural History, Gainesville, 1970-81. Mem. Mus. Accreditation Vis. Com. Roster, 1976—. Contbr. articles to profl. jours. Mem. Am. Assn. Mus. (bd. dirs. 1990-95), Assn. Midwest Mus. (pres. 1990-92, lifetime achievement award for disting. svc. 1998), Ill. Assn. Mus. (bd. dirs. 1981-86, lifetime profl. achievement award 1998), Wilson Ornithol. Soc. (life). Office: Ill State Mus Spring & Edward Sts Springfield IL 62706-0001

**MUNYON, WILLIAM HARRY, JR.,** architect; b. Panama City, Panama, Feb. 20, 1945; (parents Am. citizens); s. William Harry and Ruth (Hyde) M.; m. Cheryl Lynn Guess, Dec. 31, 1986 BA, Tulane U., 1967; postgrad., U. Hawaii, 1972-73; BArch with high distinction, U. Ariz., 1978; postgrad., U.S. Naval War Coll., 1984, Armed Forces Staff Coll., 1985. Elec. designer Ohlsen-Mitchell, Inc., New Orleans, 1966-67; rsch. cons. hist. preservation U. Ariz., Tucson, 1974-75; cons. hist. preservation State of Ariz., Phoenix, 1974-75; mktg. dir., programmer, designer Architecture One, Ltd., Tucson, 1975-78; mng. prin. Artistic License II, graphics and design, 1975-86; mng. ptnr. Aardvark Graphics, 1986—; dir. mktg. Hansen Lind Meyer, P.C., Iowa City and Chgo., 1978-79; v.p. John F. Steffen Assocs., Inc. (subs. Turner Constrn.), St. Louis, 1979-80; sr. assoc., dir. corp. devel. Rees Assocs., Inc., Oklahoma City, 1980-82; mktg. dir., asst. to pres., dir. planning/interior arch. SHWC, Inc., Dallas, 1982-84; dir. justice facilities program Henningson, Durham & Richardson, Inc., Dallas, 1984-87; prin., dir. justice and security facilities Kaplan/McLaughlin/Diaz Architects, San Francisco, 1987-90; prin. Silver & Ziskind Architects, San Francisco, 1990-91; founder, mng. prin., lead designer The Resource Group (now TRG Cons., Inc.), Indian Wells, Calif., 1991—; mktg. cons. TRG Cons., Inc., Fresno, 1979—. Vice-chmn., CEO Program Mgmt. Assocs. subs. Kaplan/McLaughlin/Diaz, 1987-90 mem. adv. bd. Interior Design mag., 1978-79, mem. Bldg. Energy Performance Stds. Adv. Panel, 1979-81; founder ann. archtl. history prize U. Ariz., 1979—95, ann. mil. leadership award Tulane U., 1985—95, Naval War Coll. Found., 1999—. Active U. Ariz. Fund for Athletic Devel., 1977—; sponsor Dallas 500; mem. Naval War Coll. Found. With USN, 1967-73; capt. Res. Recipient Producer's Coun. prize for design excellence, 1977, Henry Adams award 1978, Regional Design awards. Mem. AIA (architecture for justice com. 1978-92), Nat. Trust Hist. Preservation, Naval Res. Officers Assn., Soc. Archtl. Historians, Am. Planning Assn., Am. Correctional Assn., Am. Jail Assn. (stds. com. 1991-96), Am. Soc. Indsl. Security, Western States Corvette Coun., Nat. Corvette Mus. (charter), Naval Inst., Nat. Sheriffs' Assn. (life), Calif. State Sheriffs' Assn., Soc. Mktg. Profl. Svcs., Mil. Officers Assn. U.S. (life), Mensa, Lionel Collectors Club Am., Brit. Model Soldier Soc., William Britain Collector's Club, NRA, Profl. Svcs. Mgmt. Assn., Assn. Former Intelligence Officers, Navy League, Tulane U. Alumni Assn., Tulane U. "T" Club, U.S. Golf Assn., Blue Key, Scabbard and Blade, Phi Kappa Phi (life), Sigma Chi (life), 65 Roses Sports Club. Roman Catholic. Home: 74885 N Cove Dr Indian Wells CA 92210-7109 Office Phone: 559-269-3500. E-mail: whmunyon@lightspeed.net, harry@trg-consulting.com.

**MUNZNER, ROBERT FREDERICK,** biomedical engineer; s. Robert F. Munzner and Catherine E. (Appel) Gay; m. Jo Ann Goettee, Sept. 2, 1960 (div. 1980); children: Elizabeth Mae, Robert Victor, Ann Catherine; m. Karen E. Winstedt, Oct. 1, 1988. BS in Physics, Loyola Coll., Balt., 1963; PhD in Biomed. Engring., U. Va., 1976. Aerospace engr. Westinghouse Def. and Space, Balt., 1963-69; rsch. assoc. Johns Hopkins U., Balt., 1975-77; chief, neurol. devices br. U.S. FDA, Rockville, Md., 1977-91; expert sci. reviewer, 1998-99; regulatory affairs cons. Schuyler, Va., 1999—. Exec. sec. neurol. device adv. panel. U.S. FDA, Rockville, Md.; bd. standards IEEE, 1999-2001; mem. biomed. engring. adv. bd. U. N.C., Chapel Hill, 2004—. Co-author: Cerebellar Stimulation for Spasticity, 1984, The Physicians Perspective on Medical Law, 1997; contbr. articles to profl. jours. Fellow Johns Hopkins U., Balt., 1975, U. Va. Charlottesville, 1972-73, Thornton fellow, 1971. Mem. IEEE (sr., Millennium medal 2000), Biomed. Engring. Soc., Engring.

---

in Medicine and Biology Soc. (chmn. stds. com., ad com. 1999-2005), Sigma Xi. Achievements include research in atrial mechanical stimulation producing vasomotor reflex. Office Phone: 434-263-8862. Business E-Mail: robert@doctordevice.com.

**MURABITO, JOHN,** insurance company executive; BA in Econs., Augustana Coll.; MA in Indsl. Rels., U. Iowa. With The Trane Co., Symbion, Inc., Frito-Lay divsn. PepsiCo; sr. v.p. human resources and corp. svcs. Monsanto; exec. v.p. human resources and svcs. divsn. Cigna Corp., Phila., 2003—. Office: Cigna Corp 1 Liberty Pl Philadelphia PA 19192-1552

**MURAD, FERID,** physician; b. Whiting, Ind., Sept. 14, 1936; s. John and Josephine Murad; m. Carol Ann Leopold, June 21, 1958; children: Christine, Marianne, Carrie, Julie, Joseph. BA, DePauw U., 1958; MD, PhD, Case Western Res. U., 1965; Degree (hon.), Tirana U., 1999, Thomas Jefferson U., 2000, Case Western REs. U., 2000, State U. Ceara, 2000, Chinese U., Hong Kong, 2002, DePauw U., 2004, Charles U., 2005, Southeastern U., 2006. Diplomate Nat. Bd. Med. Examiners. Intern and resident Mass. Gen. Hosp., Boston, 1965—67; clin. assoc. NIH, Bethesda, Md., 1967—70; dir. clin. rsch. ctr. U. Va., Charlottesville, 1971—81, prof. internal medicine and pharmacology, 1975—81, Stanford U., Calif., 1981—88, acting chmn. dept. medicine, 1986—88; chief of medicine VA Med. Ctr., Palo Alto, Calif., 1981—88; v.p. pharm. divsn. Abbott Labs., 1988—92, CEO, pres. molecular geriatrics, 1993—95; prof. dept. medicine, chmn. dept. integrative biology and pharmacology U. Tex., Houston, 1997—, dir. Inst. Molecular Medicine, 1999—. Co-editor: The Pharmacological Basis of Therapeutics, 1985; contbr. articles to profl. jours. Recipient Ciba award, 1988, Albert and Mary Lasker Found. award, 1996, Nobel Prize for Medicine, 1998, others. Mem.: NAS, Western Assn. Physicians, Assn. Am. Physicians, Am. Soc. Clin. Investigation, Am. Soc. Physiology, Am. Soc. Biol. Chemists, Am. Soc. for Pharmacology and Exptl. Therapeutics, Am. Acad. Arts and Scis., NAS Inst. Medicine. Achievements include patents in field. Avocations: golf, carpentry. Office: U Tex Med Sch Inst Molecular Medicine PO Box 20708 Houston TX 77225-0708 Office Phone: 713-500-7509. Business E-Mail: ferid.murad@uth.tmc.edu.

**MURADIAN, VAZGEN,** violist, composer; b. Ashtarak, Armenia, Oct. 17, 1921; arrived in U.S., 1950, naturalized, 1956; s. Grigor and Arusiak (Vardanian) Muradian; m. Arpi Kirkyasharian, Aug. 29, 1964; children: Vardges, Armen Morian. Grad. professore di musica, Benedetto Marcello State Conservatory Music, Venice, Italy, 1948; studied composition with Gabriele Bianchi, studied composition with Vittoria Giannini, studied violin with Luigi Ferro, studied viola d'amore with Renzo Sabatini. Tchr. violin, solfeggio and theory of music Collegio Armeno, Venice, Italy, 1945-50. Pvt. tchr. viola d'amore. Composer numerous works including 57 symphonies, 69 concertos for all classical instruments and many non-traditional instruments, 12 suites for orch., 4 moto perpetuos for violin and orch., 7 sonatas for solo violin, 7 sonatas for violin and piano, 2 sonatas for piano, sonatas for viola d'amore, 2 quartets, 2 trios for violin, cello and piano, 56 songs with orch. and 8 songs for chorus and orch. in six languages on works of Shakespeare, Petrarch, Dante, Goethe, Hugo, others; more than 200 major works to date; compositions performed throughout the U.S. and abroad; author articles in field; debut, N.Y. Lincoln Center, 1972; violist with various U.S. orchs. including New Orleans Philharmonic, Wagner Opera Co.; appeared as viola d'amore soloist, U.S. and abroad. Recipient Tekeyan prize, Saint Mesrop, 1962, Mashdots Medal for lifetime achievement, 1996, Viola D' Amore Soc. Am. award, 2000, Saint Sahak and Saint Mesrop Medal for lifetime achievement, 2001, and numerous others. Mem.: ASCAP, Viola D'amore Soc. Am. Achievements include being the only composer to write concertos for all classical instruments and first ever concertos for many non-traditional instruments, to date 68 concertos for 39 different instruments; all major compositions are written in classical sonata form. All melodies and themes are his own originals. Home: 269 W 72nd St Apt 11A New York NY 10023-2719

**MURAI, KEVIN,** information technology executive; b. 1964; BSEE, U. Waterloo, Ontario. Former mgr. mgmt. info. svcs. Verifact, Inc., Ontario, Canada; joined Ingram Micro Inc., 1988, sr. v.p., 1997—2002, exec. v.p. Santa Ana, Calif., 2000—, officer, 2000—; v.p., operations Ingram Micro Can., Canada, 1993—97, pres., 1997—2000, joined Ingram Micro US, 2000—01, COO, 2000—02; pres., COO Ingram Micro N. Am., 2002—. Office: Ingram Micro Inc 1600 E St Andrew Pl Santa Ana CA 92705-4931 Office Phone: 714-566-1000. Office Fax: 714-566-7900.*

**MURANAKA, HIDEO,** artist, educator; b. Mitaka, Tokyo, Japan, Feb. 4, 1946; s. Nobukichi and Hisae M. BFA, Tokyo Nat. U. of Fine Arts, 1970, MFA, 1972. Calif. Community Coll.- Instr. Cred. Drawing accepted for The Pacific Coast States Collection from the v.p. house, Washington, 1980, Nat. Mus. Art, Bklyn. Mus., Achenbach Found., Calif. Palace of Legion of Hon., Yergeau-Musee Internat. d'Art (Can.), Japanese Calligraphy Book, 2000. Mem. Democratic Nat. Comm., Wash., others. Recipient second prize Iternat. Art Exhbn. Museo Hosio, Italy, 1984, V.J.'s Artist award Palm Springs Desert Mus., 1995; named to Hist. Preservation Am. Hall of Fame. Mem. Oakland Mus. Assn., The Fine Arts Mus. San Francisco, Lepidopterist's Soc. Avocations: collecting butterflies, music. Home: 179 Oak St Apt W San Francisco CA 94102-5948

**MURANE, WILLIAM EDWARD,** lawyer; b. Denver, Mar. 4, 1933; s. Edward E. and Theodora (Wilson) M.; m. Rosemarie Palmerone, Mar. 26, 1960; children: Edward Wheelock, Peter Davenport, Alexander Phelps. AB, Dartmouth Coll., 1954; LLB, Stanford U., 1957. Bar: Wyo. 1957, Colo. 1958, D.C. 1977, U.S. Supreme Ct. 1977. Assoc. then ptnr. Holland & Hart, Denver, 1961-69; dep. gen. counsel U.S. Dept. Commerce, Washington, 1969-71; gen. counsel FDIC, Washington, 1971—72; ptnr. Holland & Hart, Denver, 1972—2000. Pub. mem. Adminstrv. Conf. of the U.S., Washington, 1978-81, Bd. dirs. Ctr. for Law and Rsch. D., 1973-74, Acad. in the Wilderness, Denver, 1986—, Colo. Bus. Com. for Arts, 2002—; trustee Colo. Symphony Orch., 1994-2000; mem. bd. visitors Stanford U. Law Sch. Capt. USAF, 1958-61. Fellow Am. Coll. Trial Lawyers; mem. ABA (ho of dels. 1991-96), U. Club, Cactus Club. Republican. Avocations: fishing, classical music. Office: Holland & Hart 555 17th St Ste 2700 Denver CO 80202-3950

**MURANO, ELSA A.,** academic administrator, former federal agency administrator; b. Havana, Cuba; BS in Biol. Sci., Fla. Internat. U.; MS in Anaerobic Microbiology, Va. Polytechnic Inst.; PhD in Food Sci. and Tech., Va. State U. Asst. prof. Iowa State U., Ames, 1990—92, prof. in charge rsch. programs linear accelertor facility, 1992—95; various positions including dir. food safety Tex. A&M U., College Station, Tex., 1995—2001, assoc. prof. animal sci., 1995—2000, prof. dept. animal sci., 2000—01, vice chancellor, 2005—, dean agrl. & life sciences, 2005—; dir. Tex. Agrl. Experiment Station, College Station, Tex., 2005—; under sec. for food safety USDA, Washington, 2001—04. Chair food safety state initiative com. Tex. Agr. Ext. Sta., 1999—2001; nat. adv. com. meat and poultry inspection USDA, 2001; mem. Nat. Alliance for Food Safety Ops. Com., 1998—2001, chair, 2000—01; bd. dirs. Hormel Foods Corp., 2006—. Mem.: Intenat. Assn. Food Protection, Poultry Sci. Assn., Inst. Food Technologists, Assn. Meat Sci., Am. Soc. Microbiology. Office: Tex A&M U 109 Kleberg Bldg 2042 TAMU College Station TX 77843

**MURARKA, SHYAM PRASAD,** science and engineering educator, administrator; b. Jaynagar, Bihar, India, Mar. 13, 1940; came to U.S., 1966; s. Bihari L. and Suti Murarka; m. Saroj Murarka, May 21, 1962; children: Sumeet, Amal. BS in Chemistry with honors, Bihar U., Muzaffarpur, 1958, MS in Chemistry, 1960; PhD in Chemistry, Agra (India) U., 1970; PhD in Materials Sci. and Metals, U. Minn., 1970. Lectr., rsch. assoc. Bihar U., 1960-61; trainee Atomic Energy Est., Trombay, Maharastra, 1961-62, sci. officer, 1962-66; rsch. asst. U. Minn., Mpls., 1966-70, rsch. assoc., 1970-72; mem. tech. staff, supr. Bell Labs., Murray Hill, NJ, 1972-84; prof. Rensselaer Poly. Inst., Troy, NY, 1984—2002, dir. Ctr. for Integrated Electronics and Electronics Mfg., 1994-96, dir. Ctr. for Advanced Interconnect Sci. and Tech.,

---

1996-2000, dir. Sematech Ctr. of Excellence, 1989-96, Elaine S. & Jack S. Parker chair engring., 1997—2002, prof. emeritus, 2002—. Cons. Bell Labs., Murray Hill, N.J., 1984-89, Applied Materials, Santa Clara, Calif., 1997-99. Author: Silicides for VLSI Applications, 1983, Metallization Theory and Practice for VLSI and ULSI, 1993; (with others) Electronic Materials Science and Technology, 1989, Chemical Mechanical Planarization of Microelectronic Materials, 1997, Copper Fundamental Mechanisms for Micorelectronic Applications, 2000, Interlayer Dielectrics for Semiconductor Technologies, 2003; co-editor: Advanced Metallizations in Microelectronics, 1990, Advanced Metallization and Processing for Semiconductor Devices and Circuits II, 1992, Interface Control of Electrical, Chemical, and Mechanical Properties, 1994, Advaned Metallization for Devices and Circuits, 1994, Microelectronics Technology and Process Integration, 1994, Low Dielectric Constant Materials Synthesis in Microelectronics, 1995, Interlayer Dielectrics for Semiconductor Technologies, 2003; contbr. book chpt. Transition Metal Silicides, 1983, Handbook of Semiconductor Technology, 2000, Diffusion Processes in Advanced Technological Materials, 2005. Mem. Tri-City India Assn.'s Indian Comty. Support Group, Albany, 1996. Recipient Gold medal Bihar U., 1960; Univ. Grants Commn. scholar, 1961. Fellow IEEE, Am. Vacuum Soc., Am. Soc. Metals and Electrochem. Soc. (Thomas Callinan award 1987, Electronics Divsn. award 2001); mem. Materials Rsch. Soc., Bihar U. Chem. Soc. (hon. life). Achievements include 18 patents in field, over 560 rsch. papers and talks.

**MURARO, PAOLO A.,** immunologist, neurologist; b. Conegliano, Treviso, Italy, July 16, 1967; arrived in U.S., 2001; MD, U. Rome, 1993, PhD, 1998. Vis. fellow neuroimmunology br. NINDS, NIH, Bethesda, Md., 1995—98, vis. scientist neuroimmunology br., 2001—; resident in neurology U. G D'Annunzio, Chieti, Italy, 1998—2001. Instr. immunology residency program in clin. pathology and lab. medicine U. Chieti Med. Sch., 1998—. Contbr. articles to sci. jours. Grantee Istituto Superiore di Sanita', Italian Ministry Health, 1996, Nat. Rsch. Coun., Italy 1997, Ministry Univ. and Rsch., Italy, 1998—2002. Fellow: Italian Multiple Sclerosis Soc. (reviewer grant applications 1997—); mem.: Italian Neuroimmunology Assn., Am. Acad. Neurology. Office: NIH Bldg 10-5B16 10 Center Dr MSC1400 Bethesda MD 20892-1400

**MURASE, JIRO,** lawyer; b. N.Y.C., May 16, 1928; BBA, CCNY, 1955; JD, Georgetown U., 1958, LL.D. (hon.), 1982. Bar: D.C. 1958, N.Y. 1959. Sr. ptnr. Marks & Murase L.L.P., N.Y.C., 1971-97, Bingham McCutchen Murase, N.Y.C., 1997—. Legal counsel Consulate Gen. of Japan; mem. Pres.'s Adv. Com. Trade Negotiations, 1980-82; mem. Trilateral Commn., 1985—; apptd. mem. World Trade Coun., 1984-94; adv. com. internat. investment, tech. and devel. Dept. State, 1975. Editorial bd.: Law and Policy in Internat. Bus. Trustee Asia Found., 1979-83, Japanese Ednl. Inst. N.Y.; bd. dirs. Japan Soc., Japanese C of C. in N.Y., Inc.; hon. bd. regents Georgetown U.; bd. visitors Georgetown Law Ctr.; adv. coun. Pace U., Internat. House Japan; pres. Japanese-Am. Assn. N.Y., Inc., 1996-98—, Japan Ctr. Internat. Exch., 2001—. Recipient N.Y. Gov.'s citation for contbns. to internat. trade, 1982; named to Second Order of Sacred Treasure (Japan), 1989. Mem. ABA, Assn. of Bar of City of N.Y., N.Y. State Bar Assn., N.Y. County Lawyers Assn., Maritime Law Assn., Consular Law Soc., Fed. Bar Coun., Am. Soc. Internat. Law, World Assn. Lawyers, Japanese-Am. Soc. Legal Studies, Am. Arbitration Assn., Lic. Execs. Soc., U.S. C. of C. Clubs: Nippon (dir.); Ardsley Country; N.Y. Athletic; Mid Ocean (Bermuda). Office: Bingham McCutchen Murase 399 Park Ave New York NY 10022-4614 Office Phone: 212-705-7878. Business E-Mail: jiro.murase@bingham.com.

**MURASHIMA, KUMIKO,** artist, educator; arrived in US, 1967; d. Minoru and Michiko (Nagashima) M. BFA in Fiber Arts, Women's Coll. Fine Arts, Tokyo, 1961; MFA in Fiber Arts, Ind. U., 1970. Craftsman apprentice Serizawa Dyed Paper Inst., Tokyo, 1963-65; freelance textile designer Izumi Archtl. Design Co., Tokyo, 1965-67, Saphier, Lerner, Schindler Environetics, Inc., Chgo., 1970-71; asst. prof. art dept. Rowan U., 1971—, assoc. prof. art dept., 1974—. Artistic dir. Trio Creations, Sewell, 1987—. Author: Katazome in Contemporary Use, 1994. Recipient Malcolm Koch Mus. Purchase, Evansville (Ind.) Mus. Art, 1969, Wilber D. Peat Meml. award, 1970, Mr. and Mrs. Paul Arnold Merit award Herron Mus. Art, 1971; Craftsman's fellow N.J. State Coun. on Arts, 1985. Mem. Am. Crafts Coun., Artists Equity Assn. (Dorothy Grafly Meml. award 1981), Coll. Art Assn. Am., N.J. Designer and Craftsmen, Inc. (chairperson 1985-87), Am. Fedn. Tchrs. Avocations: reading, theater, classical music, gourmet foods, walking. Home: PO Box 515 Williamstown NJ 08094-0515 Office: Rowan Univ 201 Mullica Hill Rd Glassboro NJ 08028 Office Phone: 856-256-4023. Business E-Mail: murashima@rowan.edu.

**MURAT, WILLIAM M.,** legislative staff member; b. Stevens Point, Wis., Dec. 4, 1957; s. James L. and Rose Murat. BS, U. Wis., Stevens Point, 1980; JD, U. Wis., Madison, 1983; MBA, Columbia U., 1992. Asst. dist. atty. to dist. atty. Portage County, Wis., 1983-88, dist. atty., 1988-91; assemblyman Wis. State Dist. 71, 1995-99; chief of staff Congressman Tammy Baldwin. Vice chmn. Portage County Dem. Com., 1976-80, chmn., 1985-86; exec. dir. Wis. Young Dems., 1978-79, pres., 1982-83; mem. exec. com. Seventh Dist. Dems., Wis., 1978-80, 82-90; adminstrv. com. Wis. Dem. Com., 1982-99; mem. Dem. Nat. Com., 1997-99; 1st vice chair Dem. Wis., 1997-99. Mem. Phi Delta Phi, Pi Kappa Delta. Home: 901 N Pollard St Apt 617 Arlington VA 22203-4091

**MURAT, YUSEF J.,** plastic surgeon; b. Oaxaca, Mex., Sept. 2, 1964; arrived in U.S., 2003; s. Mateo Jiménez and Zandra Luz Murat; m. Ireri Salazar Urquiza, Nov. 29, 1997; children: Valentina, Miranda. MD, UNAM, Mexico City, 1989. Cert. plastic surgeon UNAM, 1996, Bd., 1997. Fellowship hand surgeon UNAM, Mexico City, 1997, fellowship microsurgery Hosp. Gen. Manuel Gea Gonzalez, UNAM, Mexico City, 1998, prof. plastic surgery, hand surgery, microsurgery, 1997—. Contbr. scientific papers in plastic surgery, hand surgery and microsurgery. Mem.: Assn. Dr. Ortiz-Monasterio. Avocations: tennis, golf. Office Phone: 956-544-7197. E-mail: yusmd@prodigy.net.mx.

**MURATA, TADAO,** engineering and computer science educator; b. Takayama, Gifu, Japan, June 26, 1938; arrived in U.S., 1962; s. Yonosuke and Ryu (Aomame) M.; m. Nellie Kit-Ha Shin, 1964; children: Patricia Emi, Theresa Terumi. BSE.E., Tokai U., 1962; MS.E.E., Ill., 1964, PhD in Elec. Engring., Hiss Rsch. asst. U. Ill., Urbana, 1962-66; asst. prof. U. Ill. at Chgo., 1966-68, assoc. prof., 1970-76, prof., 1977—, UIC disting. prof. 2002—; assoc. prof. Tokai U., Tokyo, 1968-70. Vis. prof. U. Calif., Berkeley, 1976-77; cons. Nat. Bur. Stds., Gaithersburg, Md., 1984-85; panel mem. NAS, Washington, 1981-82, 83-85; vis. scientist Nat. Ctr. For Sci. Rsch., France, 1981; guest rschr. Gesellschaft für Mathematik und Datenverabeitung, Germany, 1979; Hitachi-Endowed prof. Osaka (Japan) U., 1993-94. Editor IEEE Trans. on Software Engring., 1986-92; assoc. editor Jour. of Cirs., Sysems and Computers, 1990—; contbr. articles to sci. and engring. jours. Recipient C.A. Petri Disting. Tech. Achievement award Soc. Design and Process Scis., 2000; Sr. univ. scholar award U. Ill., 1990, NSF grantee, 1978—, U.S.-Spain coop. rsch. grantee, 1985-87. Fellow IEEE (life; golden core charter mem. IEEE Computer Soc., Donald E. Fink Prize award 1991), Inst. Electronics, Info. and Comm. Engrs., IEICE; mem. Assn. Computing Machinery, Info. Processing Soc. Japan, European Assn. for Theoretical Computer Sci., Upsilon Pi Epsilon. Avocations: golf, travel. Office: U Ill Dept Computer Sci m/c 152 851 S Morgan St Chicago IL 60607-7042 E-mail: t.murata@ieee.org.

**MURATOV, CYRILL B.,** mathematician, educator; b. Baku, Azerbaijan, July 20, 1971; s. Boris M. Muratov and Emma A. Svatenko; m. Maya Potapova, Nov. 28, 1992. MSc in Applied Math. and Physics, Moscow Inst. Physics and Tech., 1993; PhD in Physics, Boston U., 1997. Asst. prof. Courant Inst. Math. Scis., NYC, 1997—99; asst. prof. NJ. Inst. Tech., Newark, 1999—. Referee nat. jours. in field. Contbr. articles to profl. jours. Grantee,

NSF, 2002—05, NIH, 2005—. Mem.: Soc. Indsl. and Applied Math. Achievements include research in nonlinear sciences. Office: NJ Inst Tech University Heights Newark NJ 07102 Office Phone: 973-596-5833.

**MURAYAMA, MAKIO,** biochemist; b. San Francisco, Aug. 10, 1912; s. Hakuyo and Namiye (Miyasaka) M.; children: Gibbs Soga, Alice Myra. BA, U. Calif., Berkeley, 1938, MA, 1940; PhD (NIH fellow), U. Mich., 1953; ScD honoris causa, Open Internat. U., Sri Lanka, 1994. Rsch. biochemist Children's Hosp. Mich., Detroit, 1943, 1945—48, Bellevue Hosp., N.Y.C., 1943—45, Harper Hosp., Detroit, 1949—54; rsch. assoc. biochemistry Grad. Sch. Medicine U. Pa., Phila., 1956—58; spl. rsch. fellow Cavendish Lab. Nat. Cancer Inst., Cambridge, England, 1958; sr. rsch. biochemist NIH, Bethesda, Md., 1958—93. Author: (with Robert M. Nalbandian) Sickle Cell Hemoglobin, 1973; discovered DIPA (decompression-inducible platelet aggregation), 1975; discovered DIPA causes vascular occlusion in both acute mountain sickness and diver's syndrome, 1984. Fellow Am. Inst. Chemists; mem. AAAS, Am. Chem. Soc., Am. Soc. Biol. Chemists, Assn. Clin. Scientists, Undersea and Hyperbaric Med. Soc., Aerospace Med. Assn., Internat. Platform Assn., West African Soc. Pharmacology (hon.), N.Y. Acad. Sci., Sigma Xi. Achievements include patent for automatic amperometric titration apparatus, 1958; development of molecular mechanism of human red cell sickling and prevention of sickle cell crisis by oral prophylactic carbamide, 1972; discovery of decompression inducible platelet aggregation by means of simulation of decompression-inducible platelet aggregation of diving in frogs and mice that diver's disease and acute mountain sickness could be alleviated by piracetam and thymol, antiplatelet agents, 1986. Home: 5010 Benton Ave Bethesda MD 20814-2804 Personal E-mail: mmurayama@aol.com.

**MURBURG, THELMA D.,** retired elementary school educator; b. Illon, NY, Jan. 24, 1924; d. Horace L. and Margaret (Kruger) White; children: Michele, Michael, John(dec.). BEd, SUNY, Oneonta, 1945; MA, William Paterson Coll., NJ, 1974, MA, 1976. Cert. tchr., adminstr. NJ. Tchr. Seaford (NY) Sch., 1945—47, Franklin Sch., Englewood, NJ, 1947—52, Byram Sch., Cresskill, NJ, 1962, Roberge Sch., Rivervale, NJ, 1962—95, Woodside Sch., Rivervale, 1962—95; ret., 1995. Author curriculum materials in social studies and lang. arts. Negotiator Rivervale Tchrs. Union, 1990—95; vol. Hospice Pascack Valley Hospice Hosp., Emerson, 1998—, chaplain asst., 2003—06; facilitator Bereavement Groups, Hospice, Emerson, 2005—06; founder choral group, 2005; asst. pastor nursing home svcs. Named Vol. of Yr., P.U. Hospice, 2005. Avocations: music, painting, writing poetry, gardening, reading. Home (Summer): 300 Piermont Rd Norwood NJ 07648 Home (Winter): 4414 Northampton Dr New Port Richey FL 34653

**MURCHISON, DAVID CLAUDIUS,** lawyer; b. NYC, Aug. 19, 1923; s. Claudius Temple and Constance (Waterman) M.; m. June Margaret Guilfoyle, Dec. 19, 1946 (dec. June 2001); children: David Roderick, Brian, Courtney, Bradley, Stacy. AA, George Washington U., 1947, BA, 1949, JD with honors, 1949. Bar: DC 1949, Supreme Ct. 1955. Assoc. Dorr, Hand & Dawson, NYC, 1949-50; founding ptnr. Howrey & Simon, Washington, 1956-90, counsel, 1990—. Legal asst. under sec. army, 1949-51; counsel motor vehicle, textile, aircraft, ordinance and shipbldg. divsns. Nat. Prodn. Authority, 1951-52; assoc. gen. counsel Small Def. Plants Adminstrn., 1952-53; legal adv. and asst. to chmn. FTC, 1953-55 Chmn. So. Africa Wildlife Trust. With AUS, 1943-45, ETO. Mem. ABA (chmn. com. internat. restrictive bus. practices sect. antitrust law 1954-55, sect. adminstrv. law, sect. litigation), FBA, DC Bar Assn., NY State Bar Assn., Order of Coif, Met. Club, Chevy Chase Club, Talbot Country Club. Republican.

**MURCHISON, DAVID RODERICK,** lawyer; b. Washington, May 28, 1948; s. David Claudius and June Margaret (Guilfoyle) M.; m. Kathy Ann Kohn, Mar. 15, 1981; children: David Christopher, Benjamin Michael. BA cum laude, Princeton U., 1970; JD, Georgetown U., 1975. Bar: D.C. 1975, Fla. 1993. Legal asst. to vice chmn. CAB, Washington, 1975-76, enforcement atty., 1976-77; sr. atty. Air Transport Assn., Washington, 1977-80, asst. v.p., sec., 1981-85; sr. assoc. Zuckert, Scoutt and Rasenberger, Washington, 1980-81; v.p., asst. gen. counsel Piedmont Aviation, Inc., Winston-Salem, NC, 1985-88; v.p., gen. counsel, sec. Braniff, Inc., Dallas, 1988-89, chief exec. officer Orlando, 1990-94; fed. adminstrv. law judge Office of Hearings and Appeals, Charleston, W.Va., 1994-96, chief adminstrv. law judge Mobile, Ala., 1996-99, adminstrv. law judge, 1999—. Lectr. continuing legal edn. program Wake Forest U., Winston-Salem, 1988. Contbr. articles to legal jours. Lt. USNR, 1970-72. Mem. ABA, Met. Club Washington. Republican. Roman Catholic. Office: Hearings & Appeals Office 550 Government St #200 Mobile AL 36602 Office Phone: 251-441-5441.

**MURDOCH, AMELIA CLARA,** educational association administrator; d. Thomas Jerome and Viola Scanlan Murdoch. AB with honors, U. Pa., 1945, PhD, 1952. Instr. Juniata Coll., Huntingdon, Pa., 1950—51; linguist Nat. Security Agy., Ft. George Meade, Md., 1951—82, 1985—94; pres. and founder Nat. Mus. Lang., College Park, Md., 1998—. Mem. Tree and Landscape Bd., College Park, 1991—; chair Com. for a Better Environment, College Park, 1983—97, Vets. Meml. Improvement Com., College Park, 1991—2003. Am. Coun. Learned Socs. and Jusserand study and travel fellow, U. Pa., 1948—49. Mem.: MLA, Medieval Acad. Am., Internat. Arthurian Soc., Phi Beta Kappa (Mary Isabel Sibley fellow 1947—48). Avocations: reading, gardening. Office: Nat Museum of Language 7100 Baltimore Ave Ste 202 College Park MD 20740 Office Phone: 301-864-7071. Business E-mail: acmurdoch@languagemuseum.org.

**MURDOCH, COLIN,** academic administrator; BA summa cum laude, Case Western Reserve U.; MusM, U. Ill. Faculty mem. music Lawrence U., Appleton, Wis.; dean Lawrence U. Conservatory of Music, Appleton, Wis., 1978, San Francisco Conservatory Music, Calif., 1988—92, pres. Calif., 1992—. Mem. New Orleans Symphony. Recipient Excellence Award, Pacific Musical Soc. Mem.: Nat. Assn. Schs. Music (mem. Futures Com., Commn. on Accreditation). Office: San Francisco Conservatory Music Office Pres 1201 Ortega St San Francisco CA 94122-4411

**MURDOCH, DAVID ARMOR,** lawyer; b. Pitts., May 30, 1942; s. Armor M. and N. Edna (Jones) M.; m. Joan Wilkie, Mar. 9, 1974; children: Christina, Timothy, Deborah. AB magna cum laude, Harvard U., 1964, LLB, 1967. Bar: Pa. 1967, U.S. Dist. Ct. (we dist.) Pa. 1967, U.S. Ct. Mil. Appeals 1968, U.S. Supreme Ct. 1990, U.S. Ct. Appeals (3d cir.) 1991. Assoc. Kirkpatrick Lockhart Nicholson Graham, LLP, Pitts., 1971—78, ptnr., 1978—. Co-author: Business Workouts Manual. V.p., bd. dirs. Avonworth Sch. Dist., 1977-83; bd. dirs. Pitts. Expt., 1988-93, chmn., 1983-87; alt. del. Rep. Nat. Conv., 1980; elder Presbyn. Ch. Sewickley, 1986-92; past pres. Harvard Law Sch. Assn. W. Pa.; bd. advisors Geneva Coll., 1993-94, trustee, 1994-97; trustee Sewickley Pub. Libr., 1994-2002, vice chmn., 1997-2002; trustee World Learning, Inc., 1995-04, vice chmn., 1998-2000, chmn., 2000-04, chmn. emeritus, 2004—; dir. Allegheny County Libr. Assn., 1994-96; chair Czech Working Group, Presbyn. Ch. USA, 1995-2000; bd. visitors U. Ctr. Internat. Studies, U. Pitts., 1996—; bd. advisors Ctr. for Internat. Legal Edn., U. Pitts. Sch. Law, 1997—; mem. adv. bd. Ctr. for Internat. Legal Edn., U. Pitts. Sch. Law, 1997—; mem. Global Focus Adv. Bd., Chatham Coll., 2005—; bd. dirs., mem. exec. com., vice chmn World Affairs Coun. Pitts., 1997-; bd. dirs. Am. Coun. Germany, 1998—; hon. consul Fed. Rep. Germany in Pitts., 2002-. Capt. U.S. Army, 1968—71. Recipient Disting. Svc. award Allegheny County Libr. Assn., 2001. Fellow Am. Coll. Bankruptcy, Am. Bar Found.; mem. ABA (bus. bankruptcy com., chmn. subcom. on bankruptcy coms., trust indentures and claims trading 1991-97), Am. Law Inst. Office: Kirkpatrick Lockhart Nicholson Graham LLP Henry W Oliver Bldg 535 Smithfield St Pittsburgh PA 15222-2312 Office Phone: 412-355-6472. Business E-mail: dmurdoch@klng.com.

**MURDOCH, ELISABETH,** media company executive; b. Sydney, 1968; d. Rupert and Anna Murdoch; m. Elkin Pianim, 1993 (div.); children: Cornelia, Anna; m. Matthew Freud, 2001; 1 child, Charlotte. With News Corp.; owner, operator NBC affiliate stations, 1994—96; gen. mgr. broadcasting dept. BSkyB, 1996, dir. programming, 1996—98, mng. dir. Sky Networks, 1998—2001; founder, chmn., CEO Shine Ltd., London, 2001—. Named one of 50 Women to Watch, Wall St. Jour., 2005. Office: Shine Ltd 140 Kensington Church St London W8 4BN England*

**MURDOCH, HELEN CLAIRE,** secondary school educator; b. Ann Arbor, Mich., July 20, 1965; BA, Conn. Coll., 1987; MA, U. Calif., Santa Barbara, 1992. Cert. tchr., cross-cultural lang. and acad. devel.; tech. cert. level III mentor; nat. cert. tchr. Nat. Bd. Profl. Tchg. Standards. Tchr. Carpinteria (Calif.) H.S., 1994-95, San Marcos H.S., Santa Barbara, Calif., 1995—. Mentor tchr. Santa Barbara Sch. Dist., 1998, 99. Impact II grant Santa Barbara County Edn. Office, 1997-98, Venoco Crystal Apple Outstanding Tchr. award Santa Barbara (Calif.) County, 2005 Mem. Calif. Coun. for Social Studies, Phi Delta Kappa. Avocation: reading. Office: San Marcos High Sch 4750 Hollister Ave Santa Barbara CA 93110-1998 E-mail: hcmurdoch@yahoo.com.

**MURDOCH, JOHN,** museum director; Asst. dir. collections Victoria and Albert Mus., London; gallery dir. Courtauld Inst. Art, U. London, 1993—2002; dir. Huntington Art Collections, San Marino, Calif., 2002—. Office: Huntington Art Collections 1151 Oxford Rd San Marino CA 91108

**MURDOCH, LAWRENCE CORLIES, JR.,** retired banker, economist; b. Phila., June 3, 1926; s. Lawrence C. and Barbara (Boyd) M.; children: Lawrence C. III, Anne G.; m. 2d Eleanor M. Egan, June 16, 1970. BS Wharton Sch., U. Pa. in Econs., 1948; MBA, Wharton Sch., U. Pa., 1956. With Fed. Res. Bank Phila., 1954-92; ret., 1992. Bd. dirs. Cliveden Inc., 1981. Contbr. articles to consumer and monetary publs.; producer documentary films; spokesman (radio and TV). Lt. (j.g.) USN, 1948-54. Mem. Soc. Cin. (pres. 1990-93), Little Egg Harbor Yacht Club (Beach Haven, N.J.), Beta Gamma Sigma, Zeta Psi. Home: 115 Hilltop Rd Philadelphia PA 19118-3737

**MURDOCH, RUPERT (KEITH RUPERT MURDOCH),** multimedia company executive; b. Melbourne, Australia, Mar. 11, 1931; arrived in US, 1974, naturalized, 1985; s. Sir Keith and Dame Elisabeth Joy (Greene) M.; m. Patricia Booker, 1956 (div. 1965); 1 child: Prudence; m. Anna Maria Torv, Apr. 28, 1967 (div. June 8, 1999); children: Elisabeth, Lachlan, James; m. Wendi Deng, June 25, 1999; children: Grace Helen, Chloe. MA, Worcester Coll., Oxford, Eng., 1953. Pub. NY Post, 1976—86, 2005; CEO News Corp., 1979—, chmn., 1991—; dir. BSkyB, 1990—, chmn., DirecTV Group, 2003—. Owner, pub. numerous newspapers, mags. and TV ops. in U.S.A., Australia, U.K., Asia. Companion of the Order of Australia, 1984; Knight Order of St. Gregory the Great, 1998; named one of World's 100 Most Influential People, Time Mag. 2005, Forbes Richest Americans, 2006. Avocation: sailing. Office: News Corp 8th Fl 1211 Avenue Of The Americas New York NY 10036

**MURDOCK, CHARLES WILLIAM,** lawyer, educator; b. Chgo., Feb. 10, 1935; s. Charles C. and Lucille Marie (Tracy) Murdock; m. Mary Margaret Hennessy, May 25, 1963; children: Kathleen, Michael, Kevin, Sean. BSChemE, Ill. Inst. Tech., 1956; JD cum laude, Loyola U., Chgo., 1963. Bar: Ill. 1963, Ind. 1971. Asst. prof. law DePaul U., 1968-69; assoc. prof. law U. Notre Dame, 1969-75; prof., dean Law Sch. Loyola U., Chgo., 1975-83, 86—; dep. atty. gen. State of Ill., Chgo., 1983-86; of counsel Chadwell & Kayser, Ltd., 1986-89. Vis. prof. U. Calif., 1974; cons. Pay Bd., summer 1972, SEC, summer 1973; co-founder Loyola U. Family Bus. Program; arbitrator Chgo. Bd. Options Exch., Nat. Assn. Securities Dealers, N.Y. Stock Exch., Am. Arbitration Assn.; co-founder, mem. exec. com. Loyola Family Bus. Ctr., 1990—; bd. dirs. Plymouth Tube Co., 1993—. Author: Business Organizations, 2 vols., 1996; editor: Illinois Business Corporation Act Annotated, 2 vols., 1975; tech. editor The Business Lawyer, 1989-90. Chmn. St. Joseph County (Ind.) Air Pollution Control Bd., 1971; bd. dirs. Nat. Center for Law and the Handicapped, 1973-75, Minority Venture Capital Inc., 1973-75. Capt. USMCR. Mem. ABA, Ill. Bar Assn. (cert. of award for continuing legal edn.), Chgo. Bar Assn. (cert. of award for continuing legal edn., bd. mgrs. 1976-78), Ill. Inst. Continuing Legal Edn. (adv. com) Roman Catholic. Home: 2126 Thornwood Ave Wilmette IL 60091-1452 Office: Loyola U Sch Law 1 E Pearson St Chicago IL 60611-2055 Office Phone: 312-915-7142. Business E-mail: cmurdoc@luc.edu.

**MURDOCK, DAVID H.,** food products executive; b. Kansas City, Mo., Apr. 10, 1923; LLD (hon.), Pepperdine U., 1978; LHD (hon.), U. Nebr., 1984, Hawaii Loa Coll., 1989. Sole proprietor, chmn., chief exec. officer Pacific Holding Co., L.A.; chmn. Dole Food Co. (formerly Castle & Cooke, Inc.), L.A., 1985—, CEO, also bd. dirs. Trustee Asia Soc., N.Y.C., L.A.; founder, bd. dirs. Found. for Advanced Brain Studies, L.A.; bd. visitors UCLA Grad. Sch. Mgmt.;bd. govs. Performing Arts Coun. of Music Ctr., L.A.; bd. govs. East-West Ctr., L.A.; patron Met. Opera, N.Y.C. With USAAC, 1943-45. Named one of Forbes' Richest Americans, 2006. Mem. Regency Club (founder, pres.) Bel-Air Bay Country Club, Sherwood Country Club (founder, pres.), Met. Club (N.Y.C.). Office: Dole Food Co Inc P.O. Box 5132 One Dole Dr Westlake Village CA 91359-5132 also: Pacific Holding Co 10900 Wilshire Blvd Ste 1600 Los Angeles CA 90024-6530*

**MURDOCK, DORIS DEAN,** special education educator, program developer; b. Pacific Junction, Iowa, Feb. 7, 1913; m. Myron J. Murdock, June 28, 1933; 1 child, John Timothy. BS in Elem. Edn., So. Oreg. U., 1964; MS in Remedial Edn., U. Oreg., 1968. Primary tchr. Days Creek Elem. Sch., Oreg., 1962—66, Grants Pass Dist., 1966—67, Riddle Elem., Riddle, Oreg., 1968—71; founder, dir. Plowshare Sch., Rogue River, Oreg., 1972—78, Child Life Sanctuary, Rogue River, 1978—88; founder, dir. special education program developer Ctr. for Habilitation Living, Grants Pass, 1989—2006. Author: No Thank You! No Ritalin for Me Today!, 2003. Vol. Peace Corps, 1978—80. Mem.: Coun. for Exceptional Children (life). Republican. Seventh Day Adventist. Office: Ctr for Habilitative Living Inc 4493 Jerome Prairie Grants Pass OR 97527

**MURDOCK, PAMELA ERVILLA,** travel and advertising company executive; b. L.A., Dec. 3, 1940; d. John James and Chloe Conger (Keefe) M.; children: Cheryl (dec.), Kim. BA, U. Colo., 1962. Pres. Dolphin Travel, Denver, 1972-87; owner, pres. Mile Hi Tours, Denver, 1973—, MH Internat., 1987—, Mile Hi Advt. Agy., 1986—. Bd. dirs Rocky Mountain chpt. Juvenile Diabetes Found. Internat., 1994-2000; exec. bd. Rocky Mountain Father's Day Coun., 1998, 99. Named Wholesaler of Yr., Las Vegas Conv. and Visitors Authority, 1984; recipient Leadership award Nat. Multiple Sclerosis Soc., 1996. Mem.: NAFE, Nat. Fedn. Ind. Businessmen, Am. Soc. Travel Agts. Republican. Home: 5565 E Vassar Ave Denver CO 80222-6239 Office: Mile Hi Tours Inc 2160 S Clermont St Denver CO 80222-5007 Personal E-mail: pamelaemurdock@aol.com. Business E-mail: pamm@milehitours.com.

**MURDOCK, ROBERT MEAD,** curator; b. N.Y.C., Dec. 18, 1941; s. Robert Davidson and Elizabeth Brundage (Mead) M.; m. Ellen Rebecca Olson, Apr. 22, 1967 (div.); children: Alison Mead, Anne Davidson; m. Deborah C. Ryan, Apr. 28, 1995. BA, Trinity Coll., Conn., 1963; MA, Yale U., 1965; student, Mus. Mgmt. Inst., U. Calif., Berkeley, 1980. Ford Found. intern Walker Art Center, Mpls., 1965-67; curator Albright-Knox Art Gallery, Buffalo, 1967-70; curator contemporary art Dallas Mus. Fine Arts, 1970-78; dir. Grand Rapids (Mich.) Art Mus., 1978-83; chief curator Walker Art Ctr., Mpls., 1983-85; program dir. IBM Gallery of Sci. and Art, N.Y.C., 1985-87, 90-93; dir. exhbns. Am. Fedn. Arts, N.Y.C., 1987-88. Panelist, cons. Nat. Endowment for Arts, 1974-90. Author: (with others) Tyler Graphics: The Extended Image, 1987, A Gallery of Modern Art, 1994, Paris Modern, The Swedish Ballet 1920-1925, 1995, Works by Leland Bell, 1950's-1991, 2001; contbr. articles on David Novros, William Conlon, 1985, Bill Freeland, 1989, Nassos

Daphnis, 1990, Cai Guo-Qiang, 1998, John Evans, 2004; exhbn. catalogues Early 20th Century Art from Midwestern Museums, 1981, Berlin/Hanover: The 1920's, 1977, Richard Tuttle: Books and Prints, 1996, Lesley Dill, 1998, Jim Torok, 1999, Debra Bermingham, 2002. Nat. Endowment for Arts fellow, 1973 Home and Office: 202 1st Ave Apt 14 New York NY 10009-3726

**MURDOCH, TULLISSE ANTOINETTE (TONI MURDOCH),** academic administrator; BS, MA, N. Mex. State U.; PhD, U. Ariz.; grad. HERS, Bryn Mawr Inst. Women in Higher Edn., 1988. Adminstr. Western Wyo. Coll., faculty; asst. dean coll. arts and scis. U. Ariz.; assoc. provost of programs Seattle U., 1989—97; pres. Antioch U., Seattle, 1997—. Office: Antioch U 2326 Sixth Ave Seattle WA 98121-1814

**MURDY, JILL MARIA,** liturgy director, music director, educator; b. Havre, Mont., Apr. 20, 1963; d. Patrick James and Rosemarie Emma Murdy. BS in Music Edn., Dickinson State U., 1993; MA in Theology, Notre Dame U., 1999. Music tchr. Hebron (N.D.) Pub. Schs., 1993—97; dir. liturgy, web sister Sacred Heart Monastery, Richardton, ND, 1993—2002; dir. liturgy and music St. Frances Cabrini Parish, West Bend, Wis., 2002—; instr. Whitehouse Music, West Bend, 2004—. Archdioscan liturgy Archdiocese Milw., 2002—, mem. archbishop's abuse task force, 2004—. Contbr. chapters to books, articles to profl. jours.; author poetry. Vol. Habitat for Humanity; leader Taize Prayer Svcs., 1993—. Named Outstanding Female Grad., Dickinson State U., 1993; recipient 2nd prize nat. essay context, St. John's Ecumenical Inst. Mem.: ALMA, Nat. Pastoral Musicians. Roman Catholic. Avocations: whitewater rafting, composing, web creation, writing, cooking. Home: 1803 Hilltop Dr West Bend WI 53095 Office: St Frances Cabrini Parish 1025 S 7th ave West Bend WI 53095

**MURDY, WAYNE WILLIAM,** mining company executive, financial officer; b. LA, July 4, 1944; s. Lee Robert and Louise Marie (Kleinemas) M.; m. Diana Yvonne DeCruse, Nov. 23, 1968; children: Dawn Marie, Christopher John, Joseph William, Elizabeth Anne. AA, El Camino Coll., 1966; BS, Calif. State U., Long Beach, 1968. C.P.A., Calif. With Atlantic Richfield Co., Los Angeles, 1968-78; gen. auditor Getty Oil Co., Los Angeles, 1978-81; group v.p. Texaco Trading & Transp. Inc., Denver, 1981-87; sr. v.p., chief fin. officer Apache Corp., Denver, 1987-92, Newmont Mining Corp., Denver, 1992—99, pres., 1999—2002, CEO, 2001—, chmn., 2002—. Mem. Am. Inst. C.P.A.s Clubs: University (Denver); Village (Cherry Hills Village, Colo.). Roman Catholic. Office: Newmont Mining Corp 1 Norwest Ctr 1700 Lincoln St Denver CO 80203-4500*

**MURDY, WILLIAM F.,** diversified services executive; BS, US Mil. Acad.; MBA, Harvard U. Various positions including COO Pacific Resources, Inc., 1974—81; mng. gen. ptnr. Morgan Stanley Venture Capital Fund; pres., CEO Gen. Investment and Devel. Co., 1989-97; chmn., CEO, pres. LandCare USA, 1997-99; interim pres., CEO Club Quarters; chmn., CEO Comfort Sys. USA, Inc., Houston, 2000—. Mem. Nat. Adv. Bd. Boy Scouts of Am., Nat. Bd. of Bus. Executives for Nat. Security. With U.S. Army, Vietnam, bd. vis. U.S. Mil. Acad., West Point. Office: Comfort Sys USA Inc 777 Post Oak Blvd Ste 500 Houston TX 77056 Office Phone: 713-830-9600. Office Fax: 713-830-9696.

**MURDZA, PETER JOHN, JR.,** actuary; b. Beverly, Mass., Jan. 22, 1948; s. Peter John Murdza and Malvina Bertha Korosa; m. Barbara Ann Prince, June 28, 1986; children: Katherine, Julia, James, Robert. BA, Boston Coll., 1969; MA, U. Wis., 1972, PhD, 1979. Cert. Casualty Actuarial Soc., Soc. Of Actuaries. Actuarial analyst Liberty Mutual Ins. Co., Boston, 1979—82; asst. prof. U. Hartford, West Hartford, Conn., 1983—87; chief actuary State of NC, Raleigh, 1987—90; cons. Casualty Study Manuals, Hanover, NH, 1990—. Cons. Proposition 103 Enforcement Project, Los Angeles, 1995—97; lectr. Ariz.-Kazakhstan Partnership, 2004. Author: (study manuals) Casualty Actuarial Soc. and Soc. of Actuaries. Mem. Hanover Sch. Bd., Hanover, NH, 1996—99; auditor Dresden Sch. Dist., Hanover, 1999—2006. Fellow: Ford Found.; mem.: Am. Hist. Assn., Soc. Actuaries, Casualty Actuarial Soc., Am. Contract Bridge League (life master), Alpha Sigma Nu Nat. Jesuit Honor Soc. Avocations: bridge, travel, coaching sports. Home: 11 Ledyard Ln Hanover NH 03755 Office: Casualty Study Manuals 11 Ledyard Ln Hanover NH 03755 Office Phone: 603-643-6941. Fax: 603-643-6941. E-mail: peter.murdza@valley.net.

**MUREIKA, JONAS R.,** physics professor; s. Roman and Juanita Mureika; m. Natasha Bayus, Aug. 7, 1999. BSc, U. of Toronto, Ont., Can., 1993; MSc, U. of Waterloo, Ont., Can., 1995; PhD, U. of Toronto, Ont., Can., 2001. Asst. prof. of physics Loyola Marymount U., L.A., 2004—. Vis. asst. prof. of physics Claremont McKenna, Scripps, and Pitzer Colls., Claremont, Calif., 2001—04. Office: Loyola Marymount U MS 8227 1 LMU Dr Los Angeles CA 90045 Office Phone: 1-310-338-7809. Office Fax: 1-310-338-5816. E-mail: jmureika@lmu.edu.

**MUREN, DENNIS E.,** special effects expert; b. Glendale, Calif., Nov. 1, 1946; s. Elmer Ernest and Charline Louise (Clayton) M.; m. Zara Pinfold, Aug. 29, 1981; children: Gregory, Gwendolen. AA, Pasadena (Calif.) City Coll., 1966; student, Calif. State U., L.A. Freelance spl. effects expert, 1968-75; camera operator Cascade of Calif., Hollywood, 1975-76; visual effects dir. photography Indsl. Light & Magic, San Rafael, Calif., 1976-80, visual effects dir., 1980—. Guest speaker Berlin Film Festival, UCLA, Film Dept., U. Calif. Berkeley Film Series, Liverpool (Eng.) U. Film Program, Mill Valley Film Festival Program, Siggraph '86, Siggraph '87, Am. Film Inst., Portland Creative Conf. '89. Cameraman, photographer various films including Star Wars, 1977, Close Encounters of the Third Kind, 1977, Battlestar Galactica, 1978, The Empire Strikes Back, 1980 (Oscar award); visual effects supr. films include Dragonslayer, 1981 (Oscar nomination), ET: The Extraterrestrial, 1982 (Oscar award), Return of the Jedi, 1983 (Oscar award, Brit. Acad. of Film and TV award), Indiana Jones and the Temple of Doom, 1984 (Oscar award, Brit. Acad. of Film and TV award), Young Sherlock Holmes, 1985 (Oscar nomination), Captain Eo, 1986, Star Tours, 1986, Innerspace, 1987 (Oscar award), Empire of the Sun, 1987, Willow, 1988 (Oscar nomination), Ghostbusters II, 1989, The Abyss, 1989 (Oscar award), Terminator 2, 1991 (Oscar award, Brit. Film and TV award), Jurassic Park, 1993 (Oscar award, Brit. Film and TV award), Casper, 1995; visual effects supr. (TV program) Caravan of Courage (Emmy award); creative advisor Twister, 1995, Mission Impossible, 1995, Jurassic Park: The Lost World, 1997 (Academy award nomination), Star Wars: The Phantom Menace, 1999, (Acad. award nomination, Saturn award for best visual effects, Best Action Sequence award MTV), A.I., 2001 (acad. award nomination), Star Wars: The Attack of the Clones, 2002, The Hulk, 2003, The Day After Toorrow, 2004, War of the Worlds (Acad. award nomination, Hollywood Film Festival award for Best Visual Effects); prodr., dir. The Equinaxi, 1967. Recipient Acad. Sci./Tech. Award for the devel. of a Motion Picture Figure Mover for animation photography, 1981, Edit/VES Honors award, 2003; star on Hollywood Walk of Fame, 1999. Mem. Am. Soc. Cinematographers, Acad. Motion Picture Arts and Scis., Visual Effects Soc. (award). Office: Indsl Light & Magic Box 29909 San Francisco CA 94129-0909

**MURGATROYD, ERIC NEAL,** data processing executive; b. Ware, Mass., July 30, 1950; s. Howard E. and Jean Francis M.; m. Pamela Lee Swift, Aug. 14, 1976 (div. Dec. 1992); 1 child, Lisa Nicole; m. Donna K. Goodwin, Sept. 4, 1999. Student, U. Mass, 1968—70; BSc in Computer Sci., Almeda U., 2004. Computer operator Hammond Organ Co., Chgo., 1972—73; sys. analyst Ctrl. States Health, Welfare and Bond Prints, Chgo., 1973—78; sr. analyst sys. Gould-Fluid Components Divsn., Niles, Ill., 1978—80; project leader mfg. sys. Motorola Corp., Schaumburg, Ill., 1980—85; mgr. billing sys. Cellular Billing Sys., Inc., Park Ridge, Ill., 1985—86; dir. info. sys. Leaf, Inc., Lake Forest, Ill., 1997—98; ind. IT cons. Y2K Audit, 1998—99; mgr. IT bus. processes TeleHub Network Svcs., Gurnee, Ill., 1999—2000; mgr. data warehouse Ajilon, Inc., Itasca, Ill., 2000—01; IT bus. cons. Data Warehousing, 2000—02; IT project mgr. quality mgmt., sr. EAI sys. analyst Washington

Mut. Bank, FA, Vernon Hills, Ill., 2003—. Author computer programs and computer architecture. Mem. Project Mgmt. Inst., Mensa. Avocations: camping, swimming, coin collecting/numismatics, golf. E-mail: murgs@comcast.net.

**MURGUIA, JANET,** non-profit organization administrator; BS in Journalism, Kans. U., 1982, BA in Spanish, 1982, JD, 1985. Legis. coun. to Rep. Jim Slattery US Ho. Reps., Washington, 1987—94; various postions including dep. asst. to Pres. Clinton, dep. dir. legis. affairs, sr. liaison to Congress Washington, 1994—2000; exec. vice. chancellor univ. rels. U. Kans., 2001—04; exec. dir., COO Nat. Coun. La Raza, Washington, 2004, pres., CEO, 2005—. Bd. trustees YouthFriends. Named one of 100 Top Latinas, Hispanic mag., 100 Most Influential Hispanics, Hispanic Bus. mag., 80 Elite Hispanic Women. Office: Nat Coun La Raza 1111 19th St NW Ste 1000 Washington DC 20036 Office Phone: 202-785-1670.

**MURIEL, ANA,** education educator; PhD, Northwestern U., Evanston, Ill., 1997. Asst. prof. U. Mich., Ann Arbor, 1997—99, U. Mass., Amherst, 1999—2005, assoc. prof., 2005—. Contbr. articles to profl. jours., chapters to books. Recipient Career award, NSF, 2002—; fellow Ramon y Cajal, Ministry of Sci. and Tech. of Spain, 2004. Mem.: Prodn. and Ops. Mgmt. Soc. (Third Best Paper award 2000), Inst. for Ops. Rsch. and Mgmt. Sci (Ops. Rsch. Meritorious Svc. award 2001, 2004). Office: Univ of Mass Amherst 160 Governors Dr Amherst MA 01003 Office Phone: 413-545-4242. Office Fax: 413-545-1027. E-mail: muriel@ecs.umass.edu.

**MURILLO, JUAN A.,** civil engineer; BSc in Civil Engring., Rensselaer Poly. Inst., MSc. Cert. Prof. Engr. Tech. dir., cable-stayed, segmental bridges Parsons Brinckerhoff, San Francisco, 1986, now sr. v.p., tech. mgr, major bridges. Named one of 50 Most Influential Hispanics in Tech. & Bus., Hispanic Engr. & Info. Tech. mag., 2005; recipient Pioneer award, Hispanic Engr. Nat. Achievement awards. Achievements include design of temp. bypass structure for replacement of east spans of San Francisco-Oakland Bay Bridge following Loma Prieta earthquake. Office: Parsons Brinckerhoff Ste 700 N 303 Second St San Francisco CA 94107-1317 Office Phone: 415-243-4777. Office Fax: 415-243-9501. Business E-mail: murillo@pbworld.com.*

**MURILLO-ROHDE, ILDAURA MARIA,** marriage and family therapist, consultant, educator, retired dean; b. Garachine, Panama; came to U.S., 1945; d. Amalio Murillo and Ana E. (Diaz) de Murillo; m. Erling Rohde, Sept. 19, 1959. BS, Columbia U., 1951, MA, 1953; diploma (hon.), Escuela Nat. de Enfermeria, Guatemala, 1964; MEd, Columbia U., 1969; PhD, NYU, 1971; diploma (hon.), Centro Estudios Naturista, Barcelona, Spain, 1992. RN; lic. marriage and family therapist, N.J.; cert. mental health-psychiat. nursing, ANA; lic. sex. therapist, N.J. Instr., supr. Bellevue Psychiat. Hosp., N.Y.C. 1950-54; asst. dir. psychiat. div. Wayne County Gen. Hosp., Eloise, Mich., 1954-56; chief nurse psychiat. div. Elmhurst Gen. Hosp., Queens, N.Y., 1956-58, Met. Hosp. Med. Ctr., N.Y.C., 1961-63; psychiat. cons. to govt. of Guatemala WHO, UN, Guatemala, 1963-64; assoc. prof., chmn. psychiat. dept. N.Y. Med. Coll. Grad. Sch. Nursing, N.Y.C., 1964-69; dir. mental health-psychiatry, asst. prof. NYU, N.Y.C., 1970-72; assoc. prof. Hostos Coll., CUNY, N.Y.C., 1972-76; assoc. dean. acad. affairs, prof. U. Wash., Seattle, 1976-81; prof., dean Coll. of Nursing SUNY, Downstate Med. Ctr., Bklyn., 1981-85; dean and prof. emeritus SUNY, Bklyn., 1985—. Bd. dirs. Puerto Rican Family Inst., N.Y.C., 1983—96; dir. Latin Am. Oncological Nurses Fuld Fellowships, 1989-90; psychiat. cons. Sch. Nursing, U. Antioquia, Medellin, Colombia, 1972-73; WHO; psychiat./rsch. cons. for master program Sch. Nursing, U. Panama; Project Hope, 1986; dir., leader mental-psychiat. interdisciplinary group to study the Chinese family after 30 yrs. of communism People to People Amb. Program, 1985. Editor: National Directory of Hispanic Nurses, 1981, 2d edit., 1986, 3d edit., 1994; contbr. numerous articles to profl. nat. and internat. jours., chpts. to books in field. Bd. dirs. Nat. Coalition of Hispanic Mental Health and Human Svcs. Orgns., 1974-84, chmn. bd., 1980-84; mem. Wash. State adv. com. U.S. Commn. on Civil Rights, Seattle, 1977-81; nat. adv. com. White House Coun. on Families, Washington, D.C., 1979-81; pres. King County Health Planning Coun., Seattle, 1979-81; exec. com. Puget Sound Health Systems Agy., Seattle, 1979-81; mem. bd. advisors Marquis Who's Who, 1983-91; mem. Mosby Consumer Health's Hispanic adv. bd., 1996. Univ. Honors scholar NYU, 1972; named Citizen of the Day, Radio Sta. KIXI and N.W. Airlines, Seattle, 1979, Disting. lectr. Sigma Theta Tau, 1988-89, Woman of Yr., N.Y. Gotham Club Bus. and Profl. Women, 1989; recipient 1st Nat. Intercultural Nursing award Coun. of Intercultural Nursing, ANA, New Orleans, 1984, Women's Honors in Pub. Svc. award Minority Fellowship Programs and Cabinet Human Rights, ANA, 1986, Disting. Alumna award Divsn. Nursing, NYU Alumni Assn., 1989, 1st Nat. Dr. Hildegard Peplau award for outstanding svcs. in mental health, psychiat. nursing, edn., rsch. and practice, Las Vegas conv. ANA, 1992, Practice award Tchrs. Coll., Columbia U. Nursing Edn. Alumni, 1994; designated Living Legend for leadership in practice, edn. and rsch. Am. Acad. Nursing, 1994; inducted into Nursing Hall of Fame, Columbia U., 1999; bd. advisors Marquis Who's Who, 1991-99. Fellow Am. Assn. Marriage and Family Therapy; mem. ANA (affirmative action task force 1974-84, commn. human rights, cabinet human rights, rep. ANA at ICN Cong. Tokyo 1977, spokesperson Nat. Health Ins., conceived and designed Coun. Intercultural Nursing), Am. Orthopsychiat. Assn. (bd. dirs. 1976-79, treas. 1986-89, Presdl. nominee 1980, 93), N.Y. Assn. Marriage and Family Therapy (pres. 1973-76), Nat. Assn. Hispanic Nurses (founder, 1st pres. 1976-80), Internat. Fedn. Bus. and Profl. Women (UN rep. to UNICEF London, 1987—, del. to World UN Summit for Children N.Y.C. 1990, UN N.Y. Com. for Internat. Yr. of Family 1994, Hall of Fame for Outstanding Achievements in Field of Sci., Rsch., Mental Health-Psychiatry, 4th edit., 1995), Am. Rsch. Inst. (dep. govt. 1987), NYU Club, Gotham Bus. and Profl. Women's Club Democrat. Avocations: travel, reading, music, stamp collecting/philately, skiing. Home: 300 W 108th St Apt 12A New York NY 10025-2704 Office: SUNY Bklyn Coll Nursing Box 22 450 Clarkson Ave Brooklyn NY 11203-2056 E-mail: murillorohde@aol.com.

**MURIS, TIMOTHY JOSEPH,** former federal agency administrator, lawyer, educator; b. Massillon, Ohio, Nov. 18, 1949; s. George William and Louise (Hood) M.; children: Matthew Allen, Paul Austin; m. Pam Harmon, June 27, 1997. BA in economics, history, and polit. sci., San Diego State U., 1971; JD, UCLA, 1974. Bar: Calif. 1974, DC. Asst. to the dir. planning office FTC, Washington, 1974-76; dir. Bur. Consumer Protection, 1981-83; dir. Bur. Competition, 1983-85, chmn., 2001—04; exec. assoc. dir. Office Mgmt. and Budget, Washington, 1985—88, cons., 1988—89; law and economics fellow U. Chgo. Law Sch., 1979-80; asst. prof. antitrust and consumer law U. Miami Law Sch. and Law Economics Ctr., Fla., 1976-79, assoc. prof., 1979-81, prof., 1981-83; Found. prof. law George Mason U. Sch. Law, Arlington, Va., 1988—2001, 2005—, interim dean, 1996-97; of counsel Collier, Shannon, Rill & Scott, 1992—2000, Howrey, Simon, Arnold & White, 2000—01, O'Melveny & Myers LLP, Washington, 2004—, co-chair antitrust/competition practice. Dep. counsel Presdl. Task Force on Regulatory Relief, Washington, 1981; cons. Coun. on Wage and Price Stability, Washington, 1981; mem. Nat. Issues Forum, Brookings Inst., 1986-88; mem. adv. bd. Antitrust and Trade Regulation Report, 1990—; testified before numerous congressional committees on antitrust, consumer protection, and regulatory/budget issues. Assoc. editor, UCLA Law Review, 1973-74; editor: The Federal Trade Commission since 1970: Regulation and Bureaucratic Behavior, 1981; author and co-author of books, monographs and articles. Mem. Reagan-Bush transition team for FTC, Washington, 1980; sr. advisor Bush-Quayle transition team, 1988-89. Am. Bar Found. affiliated scholar, 1979 Mem. ABA (antitrust sect., 1983-, antitrust law spl. com. to study role of FTC 1988-89), Calif. Bar Assn., Order of Coif, Phi Kappa Phi, Phi Eta Sigma. Office: O'Melveny & Myers LLP 1625 Eye St NW Washington DC 20006 also: George Mason U Sch Law 3301 Fairfax Dr Arlington VA 22201 Office Phone: 202-383-5350. Office Fax: 202-383-5414. Business E-mail: tmuris@omm.com. E-mail: tmuris@gmu.edu.

**MURKETT, PHILIP TILLOTSON,** human resource executive; b. Chattanooga, Apr. 3, 1931; s. Philip Tillotson and Dorothy (Ingram) M.; m. Mary Jane Brewer, Dec. 10, 1960 (dec.); children: Emmette, Mary Jane Easter, Leanne. BA, Duke U., 1954; MBA, U. Pa., 1957; postgrad., Warnboro Coll., Oxford, England, 1980. Methods engr. Westinghouse Elec. Co., Staunton, Va., 1957-60; adminstrv. mgr. Vulcan Materials Co., Birmingham, Ala., 1960-68; human resources mgr. Blount. Inc., Montgomery, Ala., 1968-74; pres. Murkett Enterprises Inc., Montgomery, 1974—. Adj. instr. Auburn U., Montgomery, Ala.; with internat. affairs Yonok Coll., Lampang, Thailand; search cons. Murkett Assocs., Montgomery, 1974—; bd. advisors Digitech Inc. Author: Use & Value of References, 1957; editor (newsletter) H.R. Quar., 1983. Pres. Montgomery Mus. Fine Art, 1982, Cmty. Concert Assn., Montgomery, 1982, Montgomery Symphony Assn., 1987; pres. Am.-Thai Edn. Devel. Found. Inc., 1991, bd. dirs. 1990; bd. dirs. Ala. World Affairs Coun., 1997; jr. warden Episcopal Ch. of Ascension, 1972. Recipient Gov.'s Arts award Ala. Arts Coun., 1983, commendation from crown princess of Thailand, 1992. Mem. Montgomery C. of C. (task chair 1983), Montgomery Country Club, Capitol City Club, Kiwanis (bd. dirs. 1972), Delta Tau Delta (chpt. v.p. 1953). Avocations: gardening, swimming, music, tennis, geneology. Office: PO Box 527 Montgomery AL 36101-0527

**MURKISON, EUGENE COX,** finance educator; b. Donalsonville, Ga., July 2, 1936; s. Jeff and Ollie Mae (Shores) Murkison; m. Marilyn Louise Adams, July 3, 1965; children: James, David, Jennifer. Grad., U.S. Army JFK Spl. Warfare Sch., 1967, U.S. Naval War Coll., 1972, U.S. Army Command/Staff Coll., 1974; BS, U. Ga., 1959; MBA, U. Pa., 1957; postgrad., PhD, U. Mo., 1986. Surveyor USDA, Donalsonville, 1956—59; commd. 2d lt. U.S. Army, 1959, advanced through grades to lt. col., 1974, inf. bn. leader Vietnam, 1967—68; mechanized comdr. (G-3), ops. officer Brigade Exec. Officer, Korea, Europe and U.S., 1968—70; prof. leadership & psychology West Point, NY, 1970—73; ops. officer (J-3) Office of Chmn. Joint Chiefs of Staff, Washington, 1974—77; prof. mil. sci. and leadership Kemper Mil. Coll., 1977—81; ret. U.S. Army, 1981; instr. U. Mo., Columbia, 1981—84; asst. prof. Ga. So. U., Stateboro, 1984—89, assoc. prof., 1989—94, prof., 1995—, chair grad. curriculum & programs task force, 1996—99. Vis. prof. mgmt. and bus. U. Tirgoviste, Romania, 1994—96, 1998—2000; vis. prof. human resource mgmt. Tech. U. Romania, Cluj-Napoca, 1998—2000; chmn. grad. programs curriculum com. GSU, 1998—2002. Author (with Gheorghe Ionescu): Human Behavior in Organizations, 2000; contbr. articles to profl. jours., chapters to books. Adminstrv. bd. Pittman Pk. Meth. Ch., Statesboro, 1986—, trustee, 1992—99, chmn., trustee, 1995—96, mem. staff-Parish com., 2000—04. Decorated Bronze Star with oak leaf cluster; recipient Tchg. award, U. Mo., 1983, Devel. award, Ga. So. U., 1990, Albert Burke Rsch. award, 1992, Internat. Educator of the Yr. award, others; grantee, IREX, 1994, SOROS, 1995, 1996. Mem.: VFW, Ga. Hist. Soc., Bus. History Conf., Acad. Mgmt., Internat. Acad. Bus. (program chair 1994, 1995, Best Paper award 10th Ann. Conv.), Inst. Info. and Mgmt. Sci., So. Mgmt. Assn., Inst. Mgmt. Sci., Newcomen Soc., Scabbard & Blade, Blue Key, Alpha Zeta, Beta Gamma Sigma. Republican. Avocations: history, hiking, boating, farming. Office: Ga So U Coll Bus Adminstrn Statesboro GA 30460-8154 Office Phone: 912-681-0318. Business E-mail: murkison@georgiasouthern.edu.

**MURKOWSKI, FRANK HUGHES,** governor; b. Seattle, Mar. 28, 1933; s. Frank Michael and Helen (Hughes) M.; m. Nancy Rena Gore, Aug. 28, 1954; children: Carol Victoria Murkowski Sturgulewski, Lisa Ann Murkowski Martell, Frank Michael, Eileen Marie Murkowski Van Wyhe, Mary Catherine Murkowski Judson, Brian Patrick. Student, Santa Clara U., 1952—53; BA in Econs., Seattle U., 1955. With Pacific Nat. Bank of Seattle, 1957-58, Nat. Bank of Alaska, Anchorage, 1959-67; asst. v.p., mgr. Nat. Bank of Alaska (Wrangell br.), 1963-66; v.p. charge bus. devel. Nat. Bank of Alaska, Anchorage, 1966-67; commr. dept. econ. devel. State of Alaska, Juneau, 1967-70; pres. Alaska Nat. Bank, Fairbanks, 1971-80; senator from Alaska U.S. Senate, Washington, 1981—2002, ranking mem. Com. on Energy and Natural Resources, mem. Com. on Fin., Vets Affairs Com., Indian Affairs Com., Japan-US Friendship Com., mem. intelligence com. fgn. affairs; gov. State of Alaska, 2003—. Rep. nominee for U.S. Congress from Alaska, 1970; chmn. Can.-U.S. Interparliamentary Group. Former v.p. B.C. and Alaska Bd. Trade; mem. U.S. Holocaust Mus. Coun. Served with U.S. Coast Guard, 1955-57. Mem. AAA, AMVETS, NRA, Am. Legion, Ducks Unlimited, Res. Officer's Assn., Alaska World Affairs Coun., Coalition Am. Vets., Alaska Native Brotherhood, Am. Bankers Assn., Alaska Bankers Assn. (pres. 1973), Young Pres.'s Orgn., Alaska C. of C. (pres. 1977), Anchorage C. of C. (bd. dirs. 1966), Fairbanks C. of C. (bd. dirs. 1973-78), Pioneers of Alaska, Internat. Alaska Nippon Kai, Capital Hill Club, Washington Athletic Club, Elks, Lions. Republican. Roman Catholic. Office: Office of Gov State Capitol PO Box 110001 Juneau AK 99811 Office Phone: 907-465-3500. Office Fax: 907-465-3532.*

**MURKOWSKI, LISA ANN,** senator; b. Ketchikan, Alaska, May 22, 1957; d. Frank Hughes Murkowski & Nancy 9Gore); m. Verne Martell, Aug. 22, 1987; children: Nicholas, Matthew. BA in Economics, Georgetown U., 1980; JD, Willamette Coll., 1985. Dist. coun. atty., Anchorage, 1987-89; comml. atty. Hoge and Lekisch, 1989-96; pvt. law practice, 1989—96; mem. Alaska Ho. of Reps., Anchorage, 1999—2002, majority leader, 2002; U.S. Senator from Alaska, 2002—. Dir. First Bank; mem. Mayor's Task Force Homeless, 1990-91; state ctrl. com. Dist. 14 Rep. chair, 1993-98; commr Anchorage Equal Rights Commn., 1997-2002; citizens adv. bd. Joint Com. Mil. Bases in Alaska, 1998—. Trustee Cath. Svcs.; pres. Govt. Hill Elem. PTA; dir. Alaskan Drug Free Youth; mem. YWCA, Arctic Power. Recipient Comunity Leadership award, FBI Dir., 1993, Outstanding Volunteer award, Alaska Sch. Dist., 1998, 2000, Food Safety award, Nat. Food Processors Assn., 2003. Mem. Alaska Bar Assn., Anchorage Bar Assn., Alaska Fedn. Rep. Women (bd. dirs.), Anchorage Rep. Womens Club, Midnight Sun Rep. Women. Republican. Roman Catholic. Address: 510 L St # 550 Anchorage AK 99501 Office: US Senate 709 Hart Senate Office Bldg Washington DC 20510 Office Phone: 202-224 6665.*

**MURLEY, SUSAN W.,** lawyer; b. 1959; BA summa cum laude, Tufts Univ., 1981; JD, Univ. Va., 1986. Bar: Mass. 1986. Assoc. to ptnr., Corp. dept., mem. mgmt. com. Wilmer Cutler Pickering Hale & Dorr, Boston, 1986—. Named a Mass. Super Lawyer, Boston Mag., 2004. Mem.: Mass. Bar Assn., Boston Bar Assn., Phi Beta Kappa. Office: Wilmer Cutler Pickering Hale & Dorr 60 State St Boston MA 02109 Office Phone: 617-526-6832. Office Fax: 617-526-5000. Business E-mail: susan.murley@wilmerhale.com.

**MURNANE, MARGARET MARY,** engineering and physics educator; b. Limerick, Ireland, Jan. 23, 1959; d. Matthew and Helen (Bourke) M.; m. Henry Cornelius Kapteyn, Mar. 26, 1987. MSc, U. Coll. Cork, Ireland, 1983; PhD, U. Calif., Berkeley, 1989. Postdoctoral researcher U. Calif., Berkeley, 1990; asst. prof. Wash. State U., Pullman, 1990-95; assoc. prof. U. Mich., Ann Arbor, 1996—99; prof. Univ. U. Colo., 1999—, fellow, Joint Inst. Lab. Astrophysics. Presdl. Young Investigator awardee NSF, 1991, Sloan Found. fellow, 1992, Presdl. faculty fellow NSF, 1993, John D. and Catherine T. MacArthur fellow, 2000. Mem. NAS, Am. Phys. Soc. (Simon Ramo award 1990, Maria Goeppert-Mayer award 1997), Optical Soc. Am., Soc. Photo-Optical Instrumentation Engrs., Assn. Women in Sci.; Fellow Am. Acad. Arts & Sciences Office: Univ Colo Joint Inst Lab Astrophysics 440 UCB Boulder CO 80309-7789*

**MURNION, WILLIAM EDWARD,** philosopher; b. N.Y.C., Jan. 27, 1933; s. William Edward and Frances Annie (Canavan) M.; m. Deborah Warren Cary, June 14, 1969; children: William Cary, Gregory Thomas. BA, St. Joseph's Coll., 1954; STL, Gregorian U., Rome, 1958, PhD, 1969. Ordained priest Roman Cath. Ch., 1957. Parish priest Roman Cath. Archdiocese of N.Y., 1958—68; lectr. St. John's Sem., Little Rock, 1966-67; asst. prof. Duquesne U., Pitts., 1967-68; faculty fellow Boston Coll., Chestnut Hill, Mass., 1968-69; asst. prof. Newton (Mass.) Coll., 1969-72; prof. Ramapo Coll., Mahwah, NJ, 1972-2000; writer, lectr., counselor PhilosophyWorks, Bellvale, NY, 2000—. Dir. NEH summer seminar, 1992, 95. Author: St. Thomas's Theory of Understanding, 1969; contbr. articles to profl. jours.,

chpts. to books. Mem. Am. Philos. Assn., Am. Acad. Religion, Internat. Soc. Philosophy of Law and Social Philosophy, Am. Cath. Philos. Assn. Avocations: painting, gardening, sports. Office Phone: 845-986-5406. Personal E-mail: philosophyworks@optonline.net.

**MUROFF, LAWRENCE ROSS,** nuclear medicine physician, educator; b. Phila., Dec. 26, 1942; s. John M. and Carolyn (Kramer) M.; m. Carol R. Savoy, July 12, 1969; children: Michael Bruce, Julie Anne. AB cum laude, Dartmouth Coll., 1964, B of Med. Sci., 1965; MD cum laude, Harvard U., 1967. Diplomate Am. Bd. Radiology, Am. Bd. Nuclear Medicine. Intern Boston City Hosp., Harvard, 1968; resident in radiology Columbia-Presbyn. Med. Ctr., N.Y.C., 1970-73, chief resident, 1973; instr. dept. radiology, asst. radiologist Columbia U. Med. Ctr., N.Y.C., 1973-74; dir. dept. nuc. medicine, computed tomography and MRI Univ. Cmty. Hosp., Tampa, Fla., 1974-94, H. Lee Moffitt Cancer Hosp., Tampa, 1994—2006; pres. Edn. Symposia Inc., Tampa, 1975-2001; pres., CEO Imaging Cons. Inc., Tampa, 1994—; chmn. bd. Am. Phys. Ptnrs. Inc. (Radiologix), Dallas, 1996-98; chmn. bd. EagleEye Radiology, 2006—. Clin. assoc. prof. radiology U. South Fla., 1974-78, clin. assoc. prof., 1978-82, clin. prof., 1982—; clin. prof. U. Fla., 1988—; chmn. bd. EagleEye Radiology, Inc. Contbr. articles to profl. jours. Lt. comdr. USPHS, 1968-70. Fellow Am. Coll. Nuclear Medicine (disting. fellow., Fla. del.), Am. Coll. Nuclear Physicians (regents 1976-78, pres.-elect 1978, pres. 1979); Am. Coll. Radiology (councilor 1979-80, 91-96, 2001—06, chancellor 1981-87, chmn. commn. on nuclear medicine 1981-87); mem. Am. Assn. Acad. Chief Residents Radiology (chmn. 1973), AMA, Boylston Soc., Fla. Assn. Nuclear Physician (pres. 1976), Fla. Med. Assn., Hillsborough County Med. Assn., Radiol. Soc. N.Am., Soc. Nuclear Medicine (coun. 1975-90, trustee 1980-84, 86-89, pres. Southeastern chpt. 1983, vice chmn. correlative imaging coun. 1983), Fla, Radiol. Soc. (exec. com. 1976-91, treas. 1984, sec. 1985, v.p. 1986, pres. elect 1987, pres. 1988, gold medal 1995), West Coast Radiol. Soc., Soc. Magnetic Resonance Imaging (bd. dirs. 1988-91, chmn. ednl. program 1989, chmn. membership com. 1989-93), Clin. Magnetic Resonance Soc. (pres.-elect 1995-98, pres. 1998-2000, bd. dirs. 1995—). Office: 16804 Avila Blvd Tampa FL 33613-5220 Personal E-mail: lrmuroff@hotmail.com.

**MURPHEY, ARTHUR GAGE, JR.,** law educator; b. Macon, Miss., June 16, 1927; s. Arthur Gage and Elizabeth (Crutcher) Murphey; m. Linda Chaney, May 17, 1975; 1 stepchild, Leslie Jo Pafford;children from previous marriage: Mason Alexander, Arthur Nesbit. Student, Vanderbilt U., 1947—48; AB, U. N.C., 1951; JD, U. Miss., 1953; postgrad., London Sch. Econs., U. London, 1953—54; LLM, Yale U., 1962. Assoc. Satterfield, Ewing, Williams and Shell, Jackson, Miss., 1953; asst. prof. U. Ga., Athens, 1956-58, Emory U., Atlanta, 1958-61, U. Akron (Ohio), 1962-63, assoc. prof., 1963-67; prof. U. Ark., Little Rock, 1967-96, asst. dean Sch. Law, 1970-73, Ark. Bar Found. prof., 1996-97, Ark. Bar Found. prof. emeritus, 1997—. Vis. lectr. Case Western Res. U., Cleve., 1966; vis. prof. U. Miss., 1977. Faculty editor: Jour. Pub. Law, 1958—61; faculty advisor Ga. Bar Jour., 1958—61; contbr. articles to profl. jours. With USAAF, 1945—47. Fulbright scholar, 1953—54, Ford Found. grantee, 1964. Mem.: ABA, Phi Beta Kappa, Beta Theta Pi, Phi Delta Phi. Reformed Episcopal Ch. Home: 1918 Old Forge Dr Little Rock AR 72227-5515 Office: U Ark Sch Law 1201 McMath Ave Little Rock AR 72202-5142

**MURPHEY, MURRAY GRIFFIN,** history professor; b. Colorado Springs, Colo., Feb. 22, 1928; s. Bradford James and Margaret Winifred (Griffin) M.; children— Kathleen Rachel, Christopher Bradford, Jessica Lenoir. AB, Harvard U., 1949; PhD, Yale U., 1954. Asst. prof. U. Pa., Phila., 1956-61, assoc. prof., 1961-66, prof., 1966-2000, chmn. dept. Am. civilization, 1969-81, 87-94. Author: Development of Peirce's Philosophy, 1961, Our Knowledge of the Historical Past, 1973, (with E. Flower) A History of Philosophy in America, 1977, Philosophical Foundations of Historical Knowledge, 1994, C.I Lewis: The Last Great Pragmatist, 2005. Democrat. Home: 200 Rhyle Ln Bala Cynwyd PA 19004-2324

**MURPHEY, ROBERT STAFFORD,** pharmaceutical executive; b. Littleton, NC, Oct. 29, 1921; married; 2 children BS, U. Richmond, 1942; MS, U. Va., 1947, PhD in Organic Chemistry, 1949. Rsch. chemist in medicinal chemistry A.H. Robins & Co. Inc., Richmond, Va., 1948-53, dir. chemistry rsch., 1953-55, assoc. dir., 1955-57, dir. rsch., 1957-60, dir. internat. rsch., 1960-66, dir. sci. devel., 1966-82, asst. v.p., 1967-73, dir. sci. devel., v.p., 1973-82, v.p. sci. affairs and corp. devel., 1982-83, sr. v.p. sci. affairs and corp. devel., 1983-87, sr. v.p., dir. new bus. devel., 1983-90; sr. v.p., dir. bus. devel. E.C. Robins Internat., Inc., Glen Allen, Va., 1990—. Mem. AAAS, Am. Chem. Soc., Licensing Exec. Soc. Office: E C Robins Internat Inc 9878 Mayland Dr Richmond VA 23233

**MURPHEY, SHEILA ANN,** infectious diseases physician, educator, researcher; b. Phila., July 10, 1943; d. William Joseph and Sara Esther (Mallon) M. AB, Chestnut Hill Coll., 1965; MD, Women's Med. Coll. of Pa., 1969. Diplomate Am. Bd. Internal Medicine, Am. Bd. Infectious Diseases. Intern in internal medicine Mt. Sinai Hosp. of NY, 1969—70, resident in internal medicine, 1970—72, instr. internal medicine, 1971—72; fellow infectious diseases U. Pa. Sch. Medicine, Phila., 1972—74, instr. dept. medicine, 1974—75, asst. prof. dept. medicine, 1975—77; chief infectious diseases sect. Phila. Gen. Hosp., 1974-77; attending physician Hosp. U. Pa., Phila. Gen. Hosp., 1974—77; dir. divsn. infectious diseases, asst. prof. medicine Jefferson Med. Coll., Phila., 1977—80, clin. assoc. prof. medicine, 1980—2003; dir. divsn. infectious diseases Thomas Jefferson U., Phila., 1977—88; infection control officer, attending physician Thomas Jefferson U. Hosp., Phila., 1977—2003; br. chief infection control devices br., Office Device Evaluation Ctr. for Devices and Radiologic Health, FDA, Rockville, Md., 2005—. Contbr. articles to profl. jours. Fellow Coll. Physicians Phila.; mem. ACP, Am. Soc. Microbiology, Soc. Healthcare Epidemiology of Am., Infectious Diseases Soc. Am., Alpha Omega Alpha. Democrat. Roman Catholic.

**MURPHREE, A. LINN,** ophthalmologist; b. Houston, Miss., June 6, 1945; d. John Alan and Maxine (Linn) M. BS, U. Miss., 1967; MD, Baylor Coll., 1972. Cert. Am. Bd. Ophthalmology. Resident affiliated hosps., 1973-76, chief resident ophthalmology, 1975-76; fellow ophthalmic genetics and pediatrics The Wilmer Inst., Johns Hopkins U. Hosp., 1976-77; asst. prof. ophthalmology and pediatrics U. So. Calif., Los Angeles, 1978-83, assoc. prof., 1983—91, prof., 1991—, dir. pediatric and devel. ophthalmology Los Angeles, 1978—; head, div. ophthalmology Children's Hosp. Los Angeles, 1978—, dir. Clayton Found. Ctr. Ocular Oncology, 1978—; chief med. ops. Childrens Hosp. of Los Angeles, 1986-87. Profl. adv. com. Blind Children's Ctr., Los Angeles, 1980—; med. adv. bd. Nat. Assn. Visually Handicapped, 1980—. Contbr. numerous articles to profl. jours. Served to capt. med. corps., USAR, 1972-80. Dolly Green scholar Research to Prevent Blindness, 1984, Fulbright scholar U. Copenhagen, 1967-68; Medical Genetics fellow Baylor Coll. of Med. Affiliated Hosps., 1972-73. Mem. Calif. Assn. Ophthalmology, Calif. Med. Assn., Los Angeles County Med. Assn., Los Angeles Ophthalmol. Soc., Los Angeles Pediatric Soc., Ophthalmology Research Study Club Los Angeles, Pacific Coast Oto-Ophthalmol. Soc., Salerni Collegium, Am. Acad. Ophthalmology (honor award 1983), Am. Assn. Pediatric Ophthalmology and Strabismus, Am. Orthoptic Council, Assn. Research in Vision and Ophthalmology, Ophthalmic Genetics Study Club, Am. Bd. Ophthalmology (assoc. examiner), Internat. Soc. Genetic Eye Disease (sec. 1986—). Office: Childrens Hosp Los Angeles 4650 Sunset Blvd Mailstop 88 Los Angeles CA 90027-6016

**MURPHREE, HAROLD T.,** retired minister; b. Saint Clair, Alabama, June 22, 1917; s. Soloman Cleveland and Sadie Lucas (Gibbs) Murphree; m. Sara Beatrice Smith, Dec. 1, 1940; children: Janice Elaine, Gary Doyle, Harold Wayne. Min. Bold Springs Meth. Ch., Walton County, Ga., 1962, Philadelphia & Ebenezer Chs., Rockdale City, Ga., 1963—68, Bellmont Meth. Ch., DeKalb County, Ga., 1969—70, Anvil Block Meth. Ch., Ellenwood, Ga., 1970—73, N. Covington Meth. Ch., Covington, Ga., 1974—77, Forsyth Circuit, 1977—82, Cokes Chapel Meth. Ch., Sharpsburg, Ga., 1982—83,

Campbellton Meth. Ch., Fairburn, Ga., 1984—86; ret., 1986. Min. Carmel Meth. Ch., Gay, Ga., 1987—92. Author: Tried and Proven, 2000. Sgt. USAF, 1945—47, The Phillipines. Republican. Avocation: gardening. Home: 2532 Freemans Walk Path Dacula GA 30019-1390

**MURPHREY, ELIZABETH HOBGOOD,** history professor, librarian; b. Rocky Mount, N.C., Mar. 22, 1947; d. Isaac Green and Ernestine Ragsdale (Hobgood) Murphrey. BA, U. N.C., Greensboro, 1969; MA, Duke U., 1971, PhD, 1976; postgrad., U. Fla., 1984; MLS, U. N.C., Chapel Hill, 1993. Vis. instr. history Wake Forest U., Winston-Salem, NC, 1976; asst. prof. history N.C. A&T State U., Greensboro, 1977—81; intelligence rsch. specialist U.S. Army, Fayetteville, NC, 1982—89; adj. prof. history Fayetteville State U., 1989—90; adj. instr. history Fla. Met. U. South Campus, Orlando, 2000—03, adj. history, instr. Columbia Coll. Orlando divsn., 2005, rsch. libr., 1998—. Vis. asst. prof. of history Elizabeth City State U., NC, 1993—96; adj. instr. history Colmbia Coll., 2005. Editor (guidebook): Socialist Party of America Papers, microfilm edit., 2 vols., 1973—77. Apptd. Seminole County Disiability Adv. Coun., 2005. Recipient award, NEH, 1994, 1996, 2000. Mem.: LWV (bd. dirs. Seminole County chpt. 2001—, bd. dirs. Guilford County chpt. 1978—82), ALA, Fla. Libr. Assn., Am. Hist. Assn. Home: 424 Windmeadows St Altamonte Springs FL 32701 Office: Fla Met U South Orlando Campus 9200 Southpark Center Loop Orlando FL 32819 Office Phone: 407-851-2525. Personal E-mail: emurphrey@hotmail.com.

**MURPHY, ANN PLESHETTE,** magazine editor-in-chief; m. Steven Murphy; children: Madeleine, Nick. BA in psychology, Harvard U. Editor-in-chief Parents mag., N.Y.C., 1988—98, contributing editor, 1998—2002; parenting contributor, Am. Family segment Good Morning Am., 1998—; columnist, Mom Know How Family Circle mag. Author: The 7 Stages of Motherhood: Making the Most of Your Life as a Mom. Bd. dirs. Child Care Action Campaign, Parents as Teachers, Zero to Three; chair, bd. dirs. Greyston Family Inn. Recipient Academy of Women Achievers, YWCA, 1990.

**MURPHY, ARTHUR THOMAS,** systems engineer, consultant; b. Hartford, Conn., Feb. 15, 1929; s. Arthur T. and Mary (Beakey) M.; m. Jane M. Gamble, Aug. 16, 1952; children: Thomas, Patricia, Mary, John, Sheila, Jane, Joseph. BEE, Syracuse U., 1951; MS, Carnegie-Mellon U., 1952, PhD, 1957. Registered profl. engr., Kans. Instr. Carnegie-Mellon U., Pitts., 1952-56; asst., assoc. prof., head. elec. engring. Wichita State U., Kans., 1956-61; vis. assoc. prof. mech. engring. MIT, Cambridge, Mass., 1961-62; prof., dean engring. Widener U., Chester, Pa., 1962-71, v.p., acad. dean, 1971-75; Brown prof., head mech. engring. dept. Carnegie-Mellon U., Pitts., 1975-79; prof. industry, mgr. computer and automated systems, sr. research fellow DuPont de Nemours Co., Camp Hill, Pa., 1979-87, DuPont fellow Wilmington, Del., 1987-96, DuPont fellow emeritus, 1996—, cons., 1996—2006; acting pres. Pa. Inst. Tech., Media, 1998. Vis. rsch. fellow Sony Corp. Rsch. Ctr., Yokohama, Japan, 1991-92; Internat. Superconductivity Tech. Ctr., Tokyo, 1993; vis. prof. control engring. U. Manchester, Eng., 1968-69; cons. Boeing Co., Seattle, Wichita and Morton, Pa., 1957-68; adj. prof. Pa. State U., 1983-87; DuPont rep. Chem. Rsch. Coun., 1994-97; cons. sci. adv. com. Parlec, Inc., 2000-06; cons., chair microwave adv. com. Herley Industries., 2002-06. Author: Introduction to System Dynamics, 1967; contbr. articles to profl. jours.; editor: Pergamon Press, 1966-75; patentee thick film filter connector, substrate and ceramic package, connection method for circuit bd. (ball grid array), superconducting mixer antenna array. Former mem. adv. coun. Tex. A&M U., Swarthmore Coll.; program evaluator Accreditation Bd. Engring. and Tech., 1996—. DuPont fellow, 1987—; recipient DuPont Spl. Compensation award, 1988, Electronics Mktg. Excellence award DuPont Co., 1990. Fellow AAAS, IEEE (exec. com., treas. computer packaging), Am. Soc. Engring. Edn. (v.p. fin. 2001-05, chmn. grad. studies, instrumentation, awards com., corp. mem. coun., We. Electric Fund award 1966); mem. ASME (exec. com. control divsn.), Sigma Xi, Tau Beta Pi, Eta Kappa Nu, Sigma Pi Sigma, Pi Mu Epsilon, Phi Kappa Phi, Phi Theta Kappa. Avocations: hiking, photography, travel, genealogy. Home and Office: 535 Gradyville Rd S128 Newtown Square PA 19073-2815 Personal E-mail: artmurph@msn.com.

**MURPHY, ARTHUR WILLIAM,** lawyer, educator; b. Boston, Jan. 25, 1922; s. Arthur W. and Rose (Spillane) M.; m. Jane Marks, Dec. 21, 1948 (dec. Sept. 1951); 1 dau., Lois; m. Jean C. Marks, Sept. 30, 1954; children—Rachel, Paul. AB cum laude, Harvard, 1943; LL.B., Columbia, 1948. Bar: N.Y. State bar 1949. Asso. in law Columbia Sch. Law, N.Y.C., 1948-49; asso. dir. Legislative Drafting Research Fund, 1956, prof. law, 1963—; trial atty. U.S. Dept. Justice, 1950-52; asso. firm Hughes, Hubbard, Blair & Reed, N.Y.C., 1953-56, 57-58; partner firm Baer, Marks, Friedman & Berliner, N.Y.C., 1959-63. Mem. safety and licensing panel AEC, 1962-73; mem. spl. commn. on weather modification NSF, 1964-66; mem. Presdl. Commn. on Catastrophic Nuclear Accidents, 1980-89 Author: Financial Protection against Atomic Hazards, 1957, (with others) Cases on Gratuitous Transfers, 1968, 3d edit., 1985, The Nuclear Power Controversy, 1976. Served with AUS, 1943-46. Decorated Purple Heart. Mem. ABA, Assn. of Bar of City of N.Y. (spl. com. on sci. and law) Office: Columbia Sch of Law 435 W 116th St New York NY 10027-7297

**MURPHY, AUSTIN DE LA SALLE,** economist, educator, banker; b. NYC, Nov. 20, 1917; s. Daniel Joseph and Marie Cornelia (Austin) M.; m. Mary Patricia Halpin, June 12, 1948 (dec. May 1974); children: Austin Joseph, Owen Gerard; m. Lee Chilton Romero, Dec. 14, 1974; stepchildren: Thomas Romero, Robert Romero (dec.). AB, St. Francis Coll., Bklyn., NY, 1938; AM (Hayden fellow 1938-40), Fordham U., 1940, PhD, 1949; PhD (hon.), Canisius Coll., 1986. Instr. econ. Fordham U., 1938-41; Instr. econ. Georgetown U., 1941-42; asst. statistician, statis. controls Bd. Econ. Warfare, 1942; sr. econ. rsch. editor NY State Dept. Labor, NY, 1947-50; lectr. econ. Fordham U. Sch. Edn., 1946-55; instr. NYU Sch. Commerce, 1949-51; assoc. prof. bus. administrn. Seton Hall U., South Orange, NJ, 1950-55; Albert O'Neill prof. Am. enterprise, dean sch. bus. administrn. Canisius Coll., Buffalo, 1955-62; dir. edn. dept. NAM, 1962-63; exec. v.p. Savs. Banks Assn. NY State, 1963-70; chmn., pres. River Bank Am. (formerly East River Savs. Bank), 1970-89, vice chmn., dir., 1989-96, chmn. adv. bd., 1996-98. Charter trustee Savs. Bank Rockland County, 1965-70; dir. Bank of Charleston (SC), 1989-91; chmn. bd., trustee Savs. Bank Life Ins. Fund, 1983-87; chmn. dist. I, mem. adv. coun. Conf. State Bank Supr., 1986-93; bd. dir. MSB Fund, Inc. Author (with Fleming Frasca, and Mannion): Social Studies Review Book, 1946; author: (with Bullock & Doerflinger) Leading Problems of New Jersey Manufacturing Industries, 1953; author: Reasons for Relocation, 1955, Forecast of Industrial Expansion in Buffalo and the Niagara Frontier, 1956, Metropolitan Buffalo Perspective, 1958; editor: Handbook of New York Labor Statistics, 1950. Mem. Livingston (NJ) Charter Commn., 1954—55; mem. capital expenditures com. City of Buffalo, 1957—63; trustee Fordham U., 1973—79, NY Med. Coll., 1978—81; bd. dirs. NY coun. Boy Scouts Am., 1974—, Jr. Achievement of Buffalo, 1958—63, Invest-in-Am. 1st lt. U.S. Army, 1942—46. Named Knight of Malta, 1971. Mem. NAM (chmn. ednl. aids com. 1958-63), Am. Fin. Assn., Def. Transp. Assn. (life), Nat. Assn. Mut. Savs. Banks (bd. dir., treas. 1976-81), Friendly Sons. St. Patrick (1st v.p., 1976-77), DownTown Lower Manhattan Assn. (dir., vice chmn. 1982-93), Union League Club (pres. 1991-93), Larchmont Yacht Club, Carolina Yacht Club, KC, Alpha Kappa Psi, Pi Gamma Mu. Office: RB Asset Corp 645 5th Ave New York NY 10022-5910 Home: 2409 103 Theall Rd Rye NY 10580-1406 *Through the various happy events and the difficult and sorrowful, loss of loved ones as well as the vagaries of business life, I have found that an ongoing prayerful relationship to God brings a certain detachment and peace that overcomes life's passing problems.*

**MURPHY, BARRY AMES,** lawyer; b. Summit, N.J., Mar. 3, 1938; s. Robert Joseph and Florence C. (Ames) M.; m. Leslie Lynn Smith, June 9, 1962; children—Karen Irene, Sean Patrick, Conor Brendan, Ilana Taraleigh. BA in English, Stanford U., 1960; MBA, Harvard U., 1963; JD, U. So. Calif., 1972. Bar: Calif. bar 1973, U.S. Supreme Ct 1976, U.S. Tax Ct 1976. Fin. analyst Office of Sec. Def., 1963-65; pres. Tech. Industries Inc., Los Angeles, 1966-72; invidiual practice law San Mateo, Calif., 1972-74; corp. counsel Falstaff Brewing Co., San Francisco, 1974-77; sr. partner firm Levine & Murphy, San Francisco, 1978-81; v.p. Microvertics, Mountain View, Calif. 1981-86; pres. Murphy Law Corp., San Anselmo, 1987—. Mem. Am., Calif. bar assns., Calif. Trial Lawyers. Address: 28 Fern Ln San Anselmo CA 94960-1807 E-mail: barry@murphy-law.com.

**MURPHY, BETTY SOUTHARD (MRS. CORNELIUS F. MURPHY),** lawyer; b. East Orange, N.J. d. Floyd Theodore and Thelma (Casto) Southard; m. Cornelius F. Murphy, May 1, 1965; children: Cornelius Francis Jr., Ann Southard Murphy; m. H. Leland Hernly, Apr. 26, 2003. AB, Ohio State U.; student, Alliance Française and U. Sorbonne, Paris; JD, Am. U. Washington Coll. Law, Washington, DC; LLD (hon.), Ea. Mich. U., Ypsilanti, 1975, Capital U., Columbus, Ohio, 1976, U. Puget Sound (now Seattle U.), 1986; LHD (hon.), Tusculum Coll., Greenville, Tenn., 1987. Bar: D.C. Corr., free lance journalist, Europe and Asia, UPI, Washington; practiced in Washington, 1960—74; mem. firm McInnis, Wilson, Munson & Woods (and predecessor firm Roberts & McInnis); dep. asst. sec., adminstr. Wage and Hour Divsn. Dept. Labor, 1974-75; chmn. and mem. NLRB, 1975-79; ptnr. firm Baker & Hostetler, LLP, 1980—. Adj. prof. law Am. U., 1972-80, 99—; mem. adv. com. on rights and responsibilities of women to Sec. HHS; mem. panel conciliators Internat. Ctr. Settlement Investment Disputes, 1974-85; mem. Adminstrv. Conf. U.S., 1976-80, Pub. Svc. Adv. Bd., 1976-79; mem. human resouces com. Nat. Ctr. for Productivity and Quality of Working Life, 1976-80; mem. Presdl. Commn. on Exec. Exch., 1981-85, Ctr. for Study of the Presidency, 1998—. Trustee Mary Baldwin Coll., Staunton, Va., 1977—85, Am. U., Washington, 1980—99, 2001—, George Mason U. Found., Inc., Fairfax, Va., 1993—2000, George Mason U. Edn. Found., 1993—2000, 2001—; mem. exec com. Commn. on Bicentennial of US Constn., chmn. internat. adv. com., 1985—92; vice chmn. James Madison Meml. Fellowship Found., 1969—96; trustee Friends of Congl. Law Libr., 1992—, Friends of Dept. of Labor, 1984—; mediator World Intellectual Property Orgn., 1996—; nat. bd. dirs. Med. Coll. Pa., Phila., bd. corporators, 1976—85; bd. dirs. Ctr. for Women in Medicine, Phila., 1980—86, Meridian Internat. Ctr., 1992—98; bd. mem. Summer Opera Theatre, 2006—; bd. govs. St. Agnes Sch., Alexandria, Va., 1981—87. Recipient Ohio Gov.'s award, 1980, fellow award, 1981, Outstanding Pub. Service award U.S. Info. Service, 1987; named Disting. Fellow John Sherman Myers Soc., 1986, 96; fellow Nat. Acad. Human Resources, 1998. Fellow: ABA (chmn. labor law com. 1980—83, chmn. internat. and comparative law adminstrv. law sect. 1983—84, chmn. customs, tariff and trade com. 1988—90, employment law sect. 1990—2004, chmn. internat. com. dispute resolution sect. 1995—); mem.: Am. Inns of Ct. (Professionalism award 2006), US-Mex. Bar Assn. (US chair, com. on labor and employment law 2006—), Nat. Acad. Human Resources, Nat. Assn. Women Lawyers, Women's Bar Assn., Internat Bar Assn., Am. U. Alumni Assn. (Women's Leadership Award 2004), Supreme Ct. Hist. Soc., Union Internat. des Advocats (gov. bd. 1997—2000, 2003—), Rep. Nat. Lawyers Assn. (nat. v.p. 1990—95, nat. vice chmn. 1996—2000, 2001—03, co-chmn. 2003—, mem. exec. bd. 2003—, Rep. Lawyer of Yr. 2005), Am. Arbitration Assn. (bd. dirs. 1985—2000, mem. editl. bd. 1992, mem. exec. com. 1995—2000, mem. internat. arbitration com. 1997—, steering com. lawyers for Bush 2000, mem. exec. com. 2002—, bd. dirs. 2004—, trustee summer opera 2006—, bd. dirs. 2006—, mem. exec. com. 2006—), Bar Assn. D.C., Inter-Am. Bar Assn. (co-chmn. labor law com. 1975—83, editor newsletter, Silver medal 1967), FBA, World Peace Through Law Ctr., Mortar Bd., Kappa Beta Pi. Republican. Office: Baker & Hostetler LLP Ste 1100 1050 Connecticut Ave NW Washington DC 20036-5304 Office Phone: 202-861-1500. Office Fax: 202-861-1783. Business E-Mail: bsmurphy@bakerlaw.com.

**MURPHY, BRITTANY,** actress; b. Atlanta, Nov. 10, 1977; Actor: (films) Clueless, 1995, Freeway, 1996, Drive, 1997, The Prophecy II, 1998, Bongwater, 1998, Phoenix, 1998, Zack and Reba, 1998, Falling Sky, 1998, Drop Dead Gorgeous, 1999, Girl, Interrupted, 1999, Trixie, 2000, Angels!, 2000, Cherry Falls, 2000, The Audition, 2000, Sidewalks of NY, 2001, Summer Catch, 2001, Don't Say a Word, 2001, Riding in Cars with Boys, 2001, Spun, 2002, 8 Mile, 2002, Just Married, 2003, Uptown Girls, 2003, (voice) Good Boy!, 2003, Little Black Book, 2004, Sin City, 2005; (TV films) Double Jeopardy, 1996, David and Lisa, 1998, The Devil's Arithmetic, 1999, Common Ground, 2000; (TV series) Drexell's Class, 1991, Almost Home, 1993, Sister, Sister, 1994, (voice) King of the Hill, 1997, Pepper Ann, 1997; TV appearances include: Murphy Brown, 1991; Kids Incorporated, 1992; Parker Lewis Can't Lose, 1992; Blossom, 1993; Frasier, 1994; Party of Five, 1994; Boy Meets World, 1995; Murder One, 1995; The Marshal, 1995; SeaQuest DSV, 1995; Nash Bridges, 1996; Clueless, 1996.

**MURPHY, BRUCE ALLEN,** government educator, law educator, writer; b. Abington, Mass., Sept. 30, 1951; m. Carol Lynn Wright, June 14, 1975; children: Emily, Geoffrey. BA, U. Mass., 1973; PhD, U. Va., 1978. Fred Morgan Kirby prof. civil rights Lafayette Coll., Easton, Pa. Author: The Brandeis/Frankfurter Connection: The Secret Political Activities of Two Supreme Court Justices, 1982, Fortas: The Rise and Ruin of a Supreme Court Justice, 1988, (with Larry Berman) Approaching Democracy, 1996, 6th edit., 2006, Wild Bill: The Legend and Life of William O. Douglas, 2003. Avocations: fishing, reading, sports. Office: Lafayette Coll Dept Govt and Law 200 Kirby Hall Civil Rights Easton PA 18042 Office Phone: 610-330-5395. Business E-Mail: murphyb@lafayette.edu.

**MURPHY, CAROLYN,** model; b. Walton Bch., Fla., Aug. 11, 1975; m. Jake Schroeder; 1 child. Model IMG Agy.; spokesperson Estee Lauder, 2001—. Actor: (films) Liberty Heights, 1999. Named Model Yr., VH1 Fashion Awards, 1998. Achievements include appeared on numerous mag. covers including Vogue, Harper's Bazaar, W, Elle, Marie Claire; one of the models to appear on the cover of Vogue's "Model of the Millennium" issue; starred in Calvin Klein's "Contradiction" comml. and print ads. Mailing: 420 W 45th ST New York NY 10036

**MURPHY, CARYLE MARIE,** foreign correspondent; b. Hartford, Conn., Nov. 16, 1946; d. Thomas Joseph and Muriel Kathryn (McCarthy) Murphy. BA cum laude, Trinity Coll., 1968; M in Internat. Pub. Policy, Johns Hopkins U., 1987. Tchr. English, history St. Cecilia Tchr. Tng. Coll., Nyeri, Kenya, 1968—71; reporter Brockton (Mass.) Enterprise, 1972—73; freelance corr. Washington Post, Newsweek, Sunday Times of London, et al, Luanda, Angola, 1974—76; reporter Fairfax County Washington Post, 1976—77, fgn. corr. in South Africa, 1977—82, reporter immigration issues, 1982—85, bur. chief Alexandria, Va., 1985—89, fgn. corr. Mid. East Cairo, 1989—94, religion corr. Vol. ARC, Washington, 1984, Whitman-Walker Found., Washington, 1988—89. Recipient Courage in Journalism award, Internat. Women's Media Found., 1990, George Polk award, L.I. U., 1991, Edward Weintal Journalism award, Sch. Fgn. Svc., Georgetown U., 1991, Pulitzer Prize for internat. reporting, 1991, Edward R. Murrow fellow, Coun. on Fgn. Rels., N.Y., 1994—95. Roman Catholic. Avocations: foreign languages, hiking. Office: Washington Post Fgn Desk 1150 15th St NW Washington DC 20071-0002

**MURPHY, CATHERINE,** painter; b. Cambridge, Mass., 1946; BFA, Pratt Inst., 1967; student, Skowhegan Sch. Painting and Sculpture, 1966. One-woman shows First Street Gallery, N.Y.C., 1972, Piper Gallery, Mass., 1972, Fourcade, Droll, Inc., N.Y.C., 1975, Phillips Collection, Washington, 1976, Xavier Fourcade, Inc., N.Y.C., 1979, 85, J. Rosenthal Fine Arts, Chgo., 1988, Lennon, Weinberg, Inc., N.Y.C., 1989, 92, 95, 97, 2001; exhibited in group shows at Whitney Mus. Am. Art, N.Y.C., 1972, 73, Indpls. Mus., 1974, Inst. Contemporary Art, Boston, 1976, Mus. Contemporary Art, Chgo., 1977, Am. Acad. and Inst. Arts and Letters, N.Y.C., 1979, 87, 89, 90, 92, Xavier Fourcade, Inc., N.Y.C., 1977, 80, 83, 87, 93, (traveling exhbn.) San Francisco Mus. Modern Art, 1985, Daniel Weinberg Gallery, L.A., 1989, (traveling exhbn.) Cin. Art Mus., 1989, Lennon Weinberg, Inc., N.Y.C., 1989, 90, 91, 93, 94, 97, 98, 2000, 2003, (traveling exhbn.) Miyaqi Mus. Art, Sendai, Japan, 1991-92, Forum Gallery, N.Y.C., 1993, Koplin Gallery, Santa Monica, Calif., 1993, Tibor de Nagy Gallery, N.Y.C., 1994, Apex Art Curatorial Program, NYC, 1997, DC Moore Gallery, NYC, 1999; permanent collections Chase

Manhattan Bank, N.Y.C., Hirshhorn Mus. & Sculpture Garden, Washington, Met. Mus. Art, N.Y.C., Newark Mus., N.J. Art Mus., Trenton, Phillips Collection, Washington, Va. Mus. Fine Arts, Richmond, Weatherspoon Art Gallery, Greensboro, N.C., Whitney, Mus. Am. Art, N.Y.C. Grantee NEA, 1979, 89, Ingram Merrill Found., 1986; Guggenheim fellow, 1982; recipient AAIAL award, 1990. Mem.: NAD (academician). Mailing: c/o Lennon Weinberg Inc 514 W 25th St New York NY 10001

**MURPHY, CILLIAN,** actor; b. Douglas, Ireland, May 25, 1976; m. Yvonne McGuinness, 2004. Studied Law, U. Coll. Cork. Actor: (TV miniseries) The Way We Live Now, 2001; (films) Quando, 1997, The Tale of Sweety Barrett, 1998, Eviction, 1999, At Death's Door, 1999, Sunburn, 1999, The Trench, 1999, Filleann an Feall, 2000, On the Edge, 2001, How Harry Became a Tree, 2001, Disco Pigs, 2001, 28 Days Later, 2002, Zonad, 2003, Intermission, 2003, Girl with a Pearl Earring, 2003, Cold Mountain, 2003, Batman Begins, 2005, Red Eye, 2005, Breakfast on Pluto, 2005; (plays) The Seagull, The Shape of Things, Juno and the Paycock, The Country Boy, Much Ado About Nothing. Office: United Talent Agy 9560 Wilshire Blvd Ste 500 Beverly Hills CA 90212*

**MURPHY, CORNELIUS B., JR., (NEIL MURPHY),** academic administrator; b. July 17, 1944; m. Joanne Murphy; children: Tracy, Megan, Maureen, Michael. B in Chemistry magna cum laude, St. Michael's Coll., 1966; PhD in Chemistry, Syracuse U., 1970; DSc (hon.), Clarkson U., 1997. Joined as a lab technician O'Brien & Gere Cos., East Syracuse, NY, 1970; sr. v.p. O'Brien & Gere Engrs., Inc., East Syracuse, 1982—92, pres., 1992, chmn., chief scientist, 1998; pres. O'Brien & Gere Ltd., East Syracuse, 1996, chmn., 1999; pres. SUNY Coll. Environ. Sci. and Forestry, East Syracuse, 2000—. Mem.: AAAS, Am. Chem. Soc. Office: SUNY Coll Environ Sci and Forestry 1 Forestry Dr Syracuse NY 13210 E-mail: cbmurphy@esf.edu.*

**MURPHY, CULLEN,** writer, editor; b. New Rochelle, NY, Sept. 1, 1952; s. John Cullen M.; married. B with honors in History, Amherst Coll., 1974. Staff mem. Change Mag.; editor Wilson Quarterly, 1977; mng. editor Atlantic Monthly, Boston, 1985—2005, acting editor, 2002—05; contbr. editor Vanity Fair Mag., NYC, 2006—. Syndicated script writer Prince Valiant comic strip, 1979—; co-author (with William Rathje): Rubbish, 1992; author: Just Curious, 1995, The Word According to Eve, 1998. Office: Vanity Fair Magazine 4 Times Sq New York NY 10036*

**MURPHY, DANIEL IGNATIUS,** lawyer; b. Phila., Mar. 14, 1927; s. John Anthony Murphy and Irene Cooper Thorn; m. Jeanne B. Genetti, July 28, 1956 (div. Aug. 1978); children: Jewel A., Daniel I. Jr.; m. Barbara Ann Uncles, Jan. 1, 1979. BS in Econs., U. Pa., 1950; LLB, Yale U., 1953. Bar: Pa. 1954, U.S. Dist Ct. (ea. dist.) Pa. 1954, U.S. Ct. Appeals (3d cir.) 1954, U.S. Tax Ct. 1956, U.S. Supreme Ct. 1959. Assoc. Evans, Bayard & Frick, Phila., 1953-55; asst. city solicitor City of Phila., Pa., 1956-59; ptnr. Cavanaugh, Murphy & Kalodner, Phila., 1958-64, Shapiro, Stalberg, Cook, Murphy & Kalodner, Phila., 1964-66, Takiff, Bolger & Murphy, Phila., 1966-72, Waters, Gallagher, Collins & Masterson, Phila., 1972-80, Stradley, Ronon, Stevens & Young, Phila., 1980-92, ret., of counsel, 1993. Tchr. Am. Soc. CLUs, Villanova, Pa., 1956-57; mem. exec. com. Phila. Estate Planning Coun., 1958-60; lectr. Pa. Bar Inst., Harrisburg, 1974-92, Pa. Coll. Orphans Ct. Judges, Harrisburg, 1978, Pitts., 1991; apptd. spl. master for trial mgmt. of complex litigation Phila. County Ct. Common Pleas, 1994—; judge pro tem Philadelphia County Ct. Common Pleas, 2000—; arbitrator Nat. Assn. Securities Dealers, 2001-2002. Editor: Phila. Bar Assn. Mag. The Shingle, 1958-67; contbr. chpts. to manuals and articles to profl. jours. Chmn. Phila. Chpt. Am. Cancer Soc., 1956-63; mem. Com. of 70, Phila., 1968-2003, chmn., 1972-74; trustee Hahnemann U., Phila., 1983-86; bd. dirs. Covenant Ho. Pa., 2004—; trustee Easttown Libr. and Info. Ctr., Pa., 2004-2005. With USN, 1945-46. Fellow: Pa. Bar Found. (life); mem.: ABA, Colonial Soc. Pa. (bd. dirs. 2001—), Phila. Bar Assn. (vice chmn. com. censors 1971), Pa. Bar Assn., Pa. Soc. S.R., Soc. Colonial Wars, Phila. Country Club, Union League Phila. Democrat. Roman Catholic. Avocation: U.S. Civil War history. E-mail: dmurphyesq@comcast.net.

**MURPHY, DANIEL J., JR.,** aerospace and defense manufacturing company executive, military officer; b. Newport, RI, May 30, 1948; m. Pam Murphy; children: Dan, Kate. BS, U.S. Naval Acad., 1970; M in Law and Diplomacy, Tufts U., 1981. Exec. asst. to chief of naval ops. USN; exec. asst. to Supreme Allied Comdr. Atlantic; adminstrv. aide to Sec. of Navy; plans officer Plans and Ops. Directorate; mil. analyst Bur. Intelligence and Rsch. Dept. of State; rear adm. dir. surface warfare USN, 1996-98, vice adm., comdr. Sixth Fleet, and NATO striking & support forces So. Europe, 1998—2000; group v.p., precision systems and pres. tactical systems Alliant Techsystems (ATK), Edina, Minn., 2000—03, chmn., CEO, 2003—. Comdr. Eisenhower Battle Group and Cruiser-Destroyer Group 8, comdr. Destroyer Squadron 14, commdg. officer USS Kidd, sea tours with USS Goldsborough, USS Richard L. Page, USS Edson, USN. Office: Alliant Techsystems 5050 Lincoln Dr Minneapolis MN 55436

**MURPHY, DENNIS JOSEPH,** lawyer; b. Irvington, N.J., Oct. 8, 1946; s. Joseph J. and Mary E. (Fahey) M.; m. Deborah M. Sullivan, Dec. 29, 1978. AB, Harvard U., 1968; JD, Georgetown U., 1973. Bar: N.Y. 1974, Ohio 1981, U.S. Dist. Ct. (so. dist.) N.Y. 1976. Assoc. Shearman & Sterling, N.Y.C., 1973-81, Paris, 1977-79; ptnr. Smith & Schnacke, Cin., 1981-84, Frost & Jacobs, Cin., 1984—99; ret., 2003. Chmn. So. Ohio Dist. Export Coun., Cin., 1986-89; mem. Export Now Nat. Adv. Com., Washington, 1988-89; mem. steering com. Nat. Dist. Export Coun., Washington, 1988—. Contbr. numerous articles to profl. jours. Mem. adv. bd. Salvation Army, Cin., 1992—. Recipient E award Gov. Ohio, 1987. Mem. ABA, Internat. Bar Assn., Ohio State Bar Assn., Cin. Bar Assn., Assn. Bar of City of N.Y., No. Ky. Internat. Trade Assn. (v.p. 1992). Republican. Roman Catholic. Home: 318 Bowline Ct Fort Collins CO 80525-3116

**MURPHY, DIANA E.,** federal judge; b. Faribault, Minn., Jan. 4, 1934; d. Albert W. and Adleyne (Heiker) Kuske; m. Joseph Murphy, July 24, 1958; children: Michael, John E. BA magna cum laude, U. Minn., 1954, JD magna cum laude, 1974; postgrad., Johannes Gutenberg U., 1954—55. U. Minn., 1955—58; LLD, St. Johns U., 2000, U. St. Thomas, 2003. Bar: Minn. 1974, U.S. Supreme Ct. 1980. Assoc. Lindquist & Vennum, 1974—76; mcpl. judge Hennepin County, 1976—78, Minn. State dist. judge, 1978—80; judge U.S. Dist. Ct. for Minn., Mpls., 1980—94, chief judge, 1992—94; judge U.S. Ct. of Appeals (8th cir.), Mpls., 1994—. Chair U.S. Sentencing Commn., 1999—2004. Mem. editors: Minn. Law Rev., Georgetown U. Jour. on Cts., Health Scis. and the Law, 1989—92. Bd. dirs. Nat. Assn. Pub. Interest Law Fellowships for Equal Justice, 1992—95, Mpls. United Way, 1985—2001, treas., 1990—94, vice-chmn., 1996—97, chmn. bd. dirs., 1997—98; bd. dirs. Bush Found., 1982—2006, chmn. bd. dirs., 1986—91; organizer, 1st chmn. adv. coun. Amicus, bd. dirs., 1976—80; chair Mpls. Charter Commn., 1973—76; bd. dirs. Ops. De Novo, 1971—76, chmn. bd. dirs., 1974—75; mem., chmn. bill of rights com. Minn. Constl. Study Commn., 1971—73; regent St. Johns U., 1978—87, 1988—98, chmn. bd., 1995—98, bd. overseers sch. theology, 1998—2001; mem. Minn. Bicentennial Commn., 1987—88; trustee Twin Cities Pub. TV, 1985—94, chmn. bd., 1990—92; trustee U. Minn. Found., 1990—, chmn. bd., 2003—05; bd. dirs. Sci. Mus. Minn., 1988—94, vice-chmn., 1994—; trustee U. St. Thomas, 1991—, chair exec. com., 2006—; vice chair bd. govs. U. St. Thomas Law Sch., 2001—04, chair, 2004—06; bd. dirs. Spring Hill Conf. Ctr., 1978—84; bd. govs. Hill Mus. and Manuscript Libr., 2005—; bd. dirs. Minn. Opera, 1998—2004, 2005—. Recipient Amicus Founders' award, 1980, Outstanding Achievement award, U. Minn., 1983, YWCA, 1981, Disting. Citizen award, Alpha Gamma Delta, 1985, Devitt Disting. Svc. to Justice award, 2001, Disting. Alumnus award, U. Minn. Law Sch., 2002, Woman Who Makes a Difference award, Internat. Women's Forum, 2003, Iustitia et Lex award, 2006; scholar Fulbright. Fellow: Am. Bar Found.; mem.: ABA (ethics and profl. responsibility judges adv. com. 1981—88, standing com. on jud. selection, tenure and compensation 1991—94, standing com. on fed. jud. improvements 1994—97, Appellate Judges conf. exec. com. 1996—99, chmn. ethics and profl. responsibility judges adv. com. 1997—2000), Fed. Jud. Ctr. (bd. dirs. 1990—94, 8th cir. jud. coun. 1992—94, 1992—94, convener gender fairness task force 1993, U.S. jud. conf. com. on ct. adminstrn. and case mgmt. 1994—99, chair gender fairness implementation com. 1997—98), Hist. Soc. for 8th Cir. (bd. dirs. 1988—91), Fed. Judges Assn. (bd. dirs. 1982—2003, v.p. 1984—89, pres. 1989—91), U. Minn. Alumni Assn. (bd. dirs. 1975—83, nat. pres. 1981—82), Minn. Women Lawyers (Myra Bradwell award 1996), Nat. Assn. Women Judges (Leadership Judges Jud. Adminstrn. award 1998, Honoree of Yr. 2002), Nat. Assn. Governing Bds. Univs. Colls. (dir. 1998—, vice chair 2006—), Am. Judicature Soc. (bd. dirs. 1982—93, v.p. 1985—88, treas. 1988—89, chmn. bd. 1989—91), Am. Law Inst., Hennepin County Bar Assn. (gov. coun. 1976—81), Minn. Bar Assn. (bd. govs. 1977—81), Order of Coif, Phi Beta Kappa. Office: 11 E US Courthouse 300 S 4th St Minneapolis MN 55415-1320

**MURPHY, DONNA,** actress; b. Corona, N.Y., Mar. 7, 1959; m. Shawn Elliott, 1990. Student, NYU Sch. of the Arts. Actor: (Broadway plays) They're Playing Our Song, The Human Comedy, The Mystery of Edwin Drood, Passion (Tony award best actress in a musical, 1994, Drama Desk award, Drama League award), The King and I, 1996 (Tony award best actress in a musical, 1996, Drama League award), Wonderful Town, 2003—04 (Tony nom. best actress in a musical, 2004, Drama Desk award best actress in a musical, 2004, Drama League award, 2004); (plays) Song of Singapore, Privates on Parade, Showing Off, Birds of Paradise, Little Shop of Horrors, A...My Name Is Alice, Twelve Dreams, 1995, Hello Again, 1994; (TV series) Murder One, 1995—96, Law & Order, 1993, 1997, 2000, The Practice, 1998, Ally McBeal, 1998, What About Joan, 2001, Hack, 2002—03; (TV miniseries) LIBERTY! The American Revolution, 1997; (TV films) Tales from the Hollywood Hills: A Table at Ciro's, 1987, Power, Passion and Murder, 1987, Passion, 1996, Someone Had to Be Benny, 1996 (Cable ACE award, 1996, Daytime Emmy, 1996), The Day Lincoln Was Shot, 1998, The Last Debate, 2000; (films) Jade, 1995, October 22, 1998, Star Trek: Insurrection, 1998, The Astronaut's Wife, 1999, Center Stage, 2001, The Door in the Floor, 2004, Spiderman 2, 2004, Ira and Abby, 2006, World Trade Center, 2006. Office: Innovative Artists 235 Park Ave S New York NY 10003*

**MURPHY, EDDIE,** comedian, actor; b. Bklyn., Apr. 3, 1961; s. Vernon and Lillian Murphy Lynch; m. Nicole Mitchell, March 18, 1993; children: Bria, Myles, Shayne. Student pub. schs., Bklyn. Began performing Richard M. Dixon's White House, L.I., N.Y.; performed at various N.Y.C. clubs, including The Comic Strip; with Saturday Night Live, N.Y.C., 1980-84; host 35th Ann. Emmy Awards, 1983. Actor: (TV Special) Eddie Murphy Delirious, 1983, Eddie Murphy Raw, 1987; (films) 48 hrs., 1982, Trading Places, 1983, Best Defense, 1984, Beverly Hills Cop, 1984, The Distinguished Gentleman, 1992, Beverly Hills Cop III, 1994, The Nutty Professor, 1996, Metro, 1997, Mulan (voice), 1998, Dr. Dolittle, 1998, Holy Man, 1998, Bowfinger, 1999, Shrek (voice), 2001, Dr. Dolittle 2, 2001, Showtime, 2002, The Adventures of Pluto Nash, 2002, I Spy, 2002, Daddy Day Care, 2003, The Haunted Mansion, 2003, Shrek 2, 2004; actor, exec. prodr.: The Golden Child, 1986; The Nutty Professor II: The Klumps, 2000; Harlem Nights, 1989; actor, prodr. Life, 1999; actor, writer Beverly Hills Cop II, 1987; Coming to America, 1988; actor, writer: films Another 48 hrs., 1990, Boomerang, 1992; actor(actor, prodr.): (films) Vampire in Brooklyn, 1995; actor, exec. prodr.: (TV series) The PJ's (voice), 1999.

**MURPHY, EDWARD FRANCIS,** sales executive; b. Chgo., July 30, 1947; s. Edward F. and Marjorie (Mooney) M.; m. Kay A. Worcester, Apr. 17, 1970; 1 child, Chgn D. BA in Mktg., No. Ill. U., 1976. Dist. mgr. Midas Internat. Corp., Chgo., 1977-85; sales mgr. Raybestos, McHenry, Ill., 1985-89, Wagner Brakes, St. Louis, 1989-99; owner Displays of Distinction, Mesa, Ariz., 1998—. V.p. Associated Roof Structures, Mesa, 1999—. Author: Vietnam Medal of Honor Heroes, 1987, Heroes of World War II, 1990, Korea's Heroes, 1990, Dak To, 1993, Semper Fi-Vietnam, 1995, Khe Sahn-The Hill Fights, 2000; hist. cons. (book) Above and Beyond, 1985. Sgt. U.S. Army, 1965-68. Recipient Dist. Svc. award Congl. Medal of Honor Soc., 1989. Mem. Medal of Honor Hist. Soc. (founder, pres. 1975—). Republican. Avocations: writing, flying. Home: 2659 E Kael St Mesa AZ 85213-2363

**MURPHY, EILEEN BRIDGET,** retired mathematics professor; b. Newport, R.I., Dec. 28, 1940; d. Henry Timothy and Mary Anne (Lyne) M. BA in Teaching Math., Elms Coll., 1969; MAT in Math., Purdue U., 1971; MSA in Adminstrn., U. Notre Dame, 1981; postgrad., Nova Southeastern U., 1992—96. Cert. secondary edn., math. and adminstrn., Mass. Tchr. math. Cathedral H.S., Springfield, Mass., 1961-71; tchr. Holyoke Cath. H.S., Mass., 1971-84, dept. chair, 1975-84; asst. prof., lectr. Elms Coll., Chicopee, 1984—2006, dept. chair math. scis., 1985-90, div. chair math. and sci., 1987-89; ret., 1989. Steering com. Accreditations New Eng. Assn. Secondary Schs. and Colls., Chicopee, 1991-92. Mem. Sisters of St. Joseph of Springfield, Sisters of St. Joseph Fin. Team; co-treas. Sisters of St. Joseph Festival, 1984-86; bd. dirs. Mont Marie Health Care Ctr., 1990-2005; vol. computer tchr. Hampden County Dept. Corrections; vol. tchr. math. and computer applications Elms Coll., 2006—. Recipient Econs. of Pvt. Enterprise grant Strathmore Paper Co., Springfield Coll., Mass., 1978. Mem. Math. Assn. Am., Nat. Coun. Tchrs. Math., Assn. Computing Machinery (Western Mass. chpt. pub. rels. com. 1985-86, sec. 1986-91). Democrat. Roman Catholic. Avocations: peer support for multiple sclerosis groups, knitting, puzzle solving. Home: 414 Chestnut St Apt 1204 Springfield MA 01104-3442 Business E-Mail: murphye@elms.edu.

**MURPHY, ELLIS,** association management executive; b. Lincoln, Nebr. s. Ellis F. and Virgie (Olson) M.; m. Judy Neel, 1975; children by previous marriage: Sharon, Michael, Edward, Randall; stepchildren: Mary, Janet, Susan BS in Agr, Purdue U., 1947; MBA, Northwestern U., 1957; postgrad., Ill. Inst. Tech., 1969-81, U. Wash.: 1950-51, Mexico City Coll., 1947, U. Chgo., 1964. Assoc. editor Pacific Builder & Engr. Seattle, 1948 51; tech. editor Portland Cement Assn., 1933-55; dir. public relations Chgo. chpt. Am. Inst. Arch., 1955-56; account exec. Carrier & Jobson, Inc., Chgo., 1956-57; pres. Ellis Murphy, Inc., Chgo., 1957-73, Murphy, Tashjian & Assocs., Chgo., 1973-78; v.p. Lurie/Murphy Assocs., Inc., Chgo., 1979-83; pres. Murphy & Murphy Inc., Chgo., 1984—. Cons. mktg. communication to various bus. firms, 1970—; instr. (part-time) mktg. Ill. Inst. Tech., 1977-79; instr. (part-time) assn. mgmt. DePaul U., Chgo., 1985—; cons. to various trade assns., 1970—. Mem. Bd. Edn. Thornton Fractional HS Dist., Ill., 1961—67; trustee First Meth. Ch., Lansing, Ill., 1959—65; chmn. bd. dirs. funds Purdue Club, Chgo., 1990—95; docent dept. anthropology Field Mus., 1998—2006. Maj. USMCR, 1943—46; maj. USMCR, 1950—52. Mem.: Chgo. Assn. Execs. (Disting. Svc. award 1986), Am. Soc. Assn. Execs., Am. Mktg. Assn., Public Relations Soc. Am. (citation 1963), St. Bernard Commndery (past comdr., York Rite Cross of Honor 2003), Knights Templar, Sigma Delta Chi. Home: 32361 Wildwood Dr Dowagiac MI 49047 Personal E-Mail: emememem@aol.com.

**MURPHY, EVELYN FRANCES,** economist; b. Panama Canal Zone, May 14, 1940; d. Clement Bernard and Dorothy Eloise (Jackson) M. AB, Duke U., 1961, PhD, 1965; MA, Columbia U., 1963; degree (hon.), Regis Coll., 1978, Curry Coll., Northeastern U., Simmons Coll., Wheaton Coll., Anna Maria Coll., Bridgewater State Coll., Salem State Coll., Emmanuel Coll., Suffolk U. Pres. Ancon Assocs., Boston, 1971-72; ptnr. Llewelyn-Davies, Weeks, Forrester-Walker & Bor, London, 1973-74; sec. environ. affairs Commonwealth of Mass., Boston, 1975-79, sec. econ. affairs, 1983-86, lt. gov., 1987-91; mng. dir. Brown Rudnick Freed and Gesmer, Boston, 1991-93; exec. v.p. Blue Cross/Blue Shield of Mass., Boston, 1994-98; also bd. dirs. Blue Cross Blue Shield Mass., Boston; resident scholar Brandeis U. Women's Studies Rsch. Ctr., 1999—; founder, pres. The Wage Project, Inc., 2003—. Vice-chmn., chmn. Nat. Adv. Com. on Oceans and Atmosphere, 1979-80; bd. dirs. Citizens Energy Corp., SBLI USA Mut. Life Ins., The Commonwealth Inst., Polaris Project, Nat. Ctr. on Women and Aging, chair, 1998-2002, chmn. emeritus, 2002; pres. Health Care and Policy Inst., 1997-98; resident scholar Brandeis U., 1998—; bd. trustees Regis Coll., 2003—. Author: (books) Getting Even: Why Women Don't Get Paid Like Men & What to Do About

It, 2005. Recipient Dist. Svc. award New Eng. Coun., 1996, Nat. Sierra Club, 1978, Nat. Bd. Govs. Assn., 1978, Outstanding Citizen award Mass. Audobon Soc., 1978; Harvard U. fellow, 1979-80. Mem. Women Execs. in State Govt. (chair 1987), Internat. Women's Forum, 1993—. Democrat. Avocation: jogging. Personal E-mail: evmurphy1@aol.com.

**MURPHY, EWELL EDWARD, JR.,** lawyer; b. Washington, Feb. 21, 1928; s. Ewell Edward and Lou (Phillips) M.; m. Patricia Bredell Purnell, June 26, 1954 (dec. 1964); children: Michaela, Megan Patricia, Harlan Ewell. BA, U. Tex., 1946, LLB, 1948; DPhil, Oxford U., Eng., 1951. Bar: Tex. 1948. Assoc. Baker & Botts, Houston, 1954-63, ptnr., 1964-93, head internat. dept., 1972-89. Pres. Houston World Trade Assn., 1972-74; trustee Southwestern Legal Found., 1978—2003; chmn. Houston Com. on Fgn. Rels., 1984-85, Inst. Transnat. Arbitration, 1985-89, Internat. and Comparative Law Ctr., 1986-87; mem. J. William Fulbright Fgn. Scholarship Bd., 1991-96, vice chmn., 1992-93, chmn., 1993-95; vis. prof. U. Tex. Law Sch., 1993-97; Disting. lectr., U. Houston Law Ctr., 1996—. Contbr. articles to profl. jours. Served to lt. USAF, 1952—54. Recipient Carl H. Fulda award U. Tex. Internat. Law Jour., 1980; Rhodes scholar, 1948-51 Mem.: ABA (chmn. sect. internat. law 1970—71), Internat. Law Inst. (bd. dirs. 1994—), Houston Bar Assn. (chmn. internat. law com. 1963—64, 1970—71), Coun. on Fgn. Rels., Philos. Soc. Tex., Houston C. of C. (chmn. internat. bus. com. 1964—65), Fulbright Assn. (bd. dirs. 1999—2004, v.p. 2002—04). Home and Office: 17 W Oak Dr Houston TX 77056-2117 Office Phone: 713-622-3840. E-mail: ewellmurphyjr@sbcglobal.net.

**MURPHY, FRANCES LOUISE, II,** retired newspaper publisher; b. Balt., Oct. 8, 1922; d. Carl James and L. Vashti (Turley) M.; m. James E. Wood (div.); children: Frances Murphy Wood Draper, James E., Jr., Susan Wood Barnes, David Lloyd Campbell. BA, U. Wis., 1944; BS, Coppin State Coll., Balt., 1958; MEd, Johns Hopkins U., 1963. City editor Balt. Afro-Am., 1956-57; dir. News Bur., Morgan State Coll., Balt., 1964-71; chmn. bd. dirs. Afro-Am. Newspapers, Balt., 1971-74; assoc. prof. journalism State Univ. Coll., Buffalo, 1975-85, Howard U., Washington, 1985-91; editor Washington Afro-Am., 1951-56, pub., 1987-99; editl. page editor Afro-Am. Newspapers, Balt., 1999—. Contbr. columns in newspapers. Treas. African Am. Civil War Meml. Freedom Found.; trustee State Colls. Md., 1971-76, U. D.C., 1994-99; bd. dirs. Delta Rsch. and Ednl. Found., 1993-95; nat. bd. dirs. NAACP, 1971-76; vestry St. James' Episcopal Ch. Named one of 100 Most Influential Black Ams., Ebony mag., 1973, 74, Disting. Marylander, Gov. State of Md., 1975; recipient Ida B. Wells award Congl. Black Caucus, 1989, Public Svc. award African Methodist Episcopal Ch., 1991, Invaluable Svc. award Martin L. King Jr. Found., 1992, Black Women of Courage award Nat. Fedn. Black Women Bus. Owners, 1993, Black Awareness Ach. award Holy Redeemer Catholic Ch., 1993, Bus. of the Yr. award Bus. and Profl. Women's League, 1993, Ounstanding Svc. award Capital Press Club, 1993, Black Conscious Commitment trophy Unity Nation, 1993, Dedicated Cmty. Svc. award Ward I Cmty. and DC Pub. Schs., 1994, Women of Strength award Nat. Black Media Coalition, 1994-95, Outstanding Woman of Yr. award Alpha Gamma chpt. Iota Phi Lambda, 1994, Art Carter Excellence award Capital Press Club, 1994, Excellence in Comm. award Washington Inter-Alumni Coun. United Negro Coll. Fund, 1994, 95, Disting. Cmty. Svc. award The Questers, Inc., 1995, Outstanding Journalist award Masons, 1995, Outstanding Achievement award Beta Zeta chpt. Zeta Phi Beta, 1996, award in recognition of outstanding contbns. made to youth The Soc., 1996, Disting. Black Women award BISA, 1996, Woman of 20th Century award Nat. Pol. Congress Black Women, 1999. Mem. Nat. Newspaper Pubs. Assn. (editl. com. 1987—, Merit award 1987, 89-97, First Pl. editl. writing 2003), Soc. Profl. Journalists (Disting. Svc. in local journalism award Washington chpt. 1994), Links (pres. Balt. chpt. 2004—), Capital Press Club (exec. bd. 1987-98, Outstanding Svc. award 1993, Art Carter award 1994), Delta Sigma Theta (Frances L. Murphy II Comm. award Fed. City Alumnae chpt. 1993, Fortitude Image award Prince George's County chpt. 1994, Ethel L. Payne award 1996-97), Kiwanis Club (first woman hon. 1995), Iota Phi Lambda (hon.) Democrat. Avocation: bridge. Office: Baltimore 2519 N Charles St Baltimore MD 21218-4602 Address: 2406 Overland Ave Baltimore MD 21214-2440 Office Phone: 410-554-8200. Personal E-mail: frankielou@aol.com.

**MURPHY, FRANCES M.,** federal agency administrator; MD with honors, Georgetown U., Washington, 1979; MPH, Uniformed Svcs. U. of the Health Scis., 1993. Diplomate Am. Coll. Psychiatry and Neurology. Resident in neurology Georgetown U., Washington; staff neurologist Andrews AFB, Md., 1983—87; chief cons. occupl. and environ. medicine US Dept. Veterans Affairs, Washington, dep. under-sec. for health, 1999—2002, acting under sec. for health, 2002, dep. under sec. for health policy coord., 2002—. Adj. assoc. prof. neurology Uniformed Svcs. U. of the Health Scis. Contbr. articles to profl. jours. With USAF. Office: US Dept Veterans Affairs 810 Vermont Ave NW Washington DC 20420*

**MURPHY, FRANCIS,** language educator; b. Springfield, Mass., Mar. 13, 1932; s. Frank Edward and Sarah (O'Connor) M. BA, Am. Internat. Coll., 1953; MA, U. Conn., 1955; PhD, Harvard U., 1960; LittD (hon.), Am. Internat. Coll., 1986. Mem. faculty English lang. and lit. Smith Coll., 1959-99, assoc. prof., 1966-69, prof., 1970-99, prof. emeritus, 1999—. Vis. curator Springfield Mus. Fine Arts, 1975-76, Hudson River Mus., 1983-84. Editor: The Diary of Edward Taylor, 1964, Major Am. Poets, 1967, Form and Structure in Poetry, 1964, Edwin Arlington Robinson, 1970, Walt Whitman, 1969, The Uncollected Essays of Yvor Winters, 1973, The Complete Poems of Walt Whitman, 1975, Of Plymouth Plantation (William Bradford), 1981; author: Willard Leroy Metcalf, 1976, (with Dean Flower) A Catalogue of American Paintings, Water Colors and Drawings (to 1923) in the G.W.V. Smith Museum, 1976, The Landscape Within: J. Francis Murphy, 1982, The Book of Nature: American Painters and the Natural Sublime, 1983; co-editor: Norton Anthology of American Literature, 1979—, Mass. Rev. 1966-67.

**MURPHY, FREDERICK AUGUSTUS,** virologist, researcher; b. NYC, June 14, 1934; s. Frederick A. and Louise A. (Knizak) Murphy; m. Irene M. Warwas, July 2, 1960 (dec.); children: Frederick A., W. Timothy, John G., Terence D. BS in Microbiology, Cornell U., 1956, DVM, 1959; PhD in Comparative Pathology, U. Calif., Davis, 1964; MD (hon.), U. Turku, Finland, 1987; DSc (hon.), U. Guelph, Can., 2000. Chief viral pathology br. Ctrs. for Disease Control, Atlanta, 1964-78; assoc. dean Coll. Vet. Medicine Colo. State U., Ft. Collins, 1978-83; dir. divsn. viral & rickettsial diseases Ctrs. for Disease Control, Atlanta, 1983-87; dir. Nat. Ctr. for Infectious Diseases, 1987-91; dean Sch. Vet. Medicine U. Calif., Davis, 1991-96, disting. prof. Sch. Vet. Medicine, 1996—2005, disting. prof and dean emeritus, 2006—; prof. dept. pathology U. Tex. Med. Br., Galveston, 2006—. Program chair virology divsn. Internat. Union Microbiology Socs., 1978—87, chair virology divsn., 1981—84; adv. bds. Lawrence Livermore Nat. Lab., 1996—; v.p. Found. Human Rabies Edn. & Eradication, 1999—; com. mem. on Future Contributions to Public Health, Agr., Basic Rsch. Counterterrorism, Non-Proliferation Activities in Russia US Nat. Acad. Scis., 2001—03, co-chair Comm. on Occupational Health and Safety in Care of Non-Human primates, 2001—03, com. mem. on Food Safety and Nutrition, 2001—02; com. mem. on Emerging Microbial Threats to Health in 21st Century Inst. Medicine and US Nat. Acad. Scis., 2001—03, com. mem. on Transmissible Spongiform Encephalopathies, 2002—04. Editor: (book series) Advances in Virus Research, 1983—, (book) Virus Taxonomy, 1995; editor in chief: jour. Archives of Virology, 1984—2000; sr. author: book Veterinary Virology III, 1999; contbr. over 450 articles to profl. jours., reports, reviews, monographs, books, and chapters to books. Mem. Pew Trusts Nat. Vet. Edn. Program: Future Directions in Vet. Medicine, 1986—89; mem. Internat. Advisory Group Royal Vet. Coll., London, 2004—; mem. Secretary's Coun. Public Health Preparedness US Dept HHS, 2002—. Capt. U.S. Army, 1959—62, cmdr. USPHS, 1964—68. Named elected mem., German Acad. Nat. Scis., 1985, Inst. Medicine, US Nat. Acad. Scis., 1999, Acad. Medicine Engring. Sci. Tex., 2006; recipient K.F. Meyers Gold Headed Cane, Am. Vet. Epidemiology Soc., 1986, Davis medal, U. Calif., 1998, Pres. Rank award, US Govt., 1992, Richard Moreland Taylor award, Am. Com. Arthropod-Borne Viruses, Am. Soc. Tropical Medicine & Hygeine, 2003. Fellow:

Infectious Diseases Soc. Am., John Curtin Sch. Med. Rsch., Australian Nat. U. (hon.); mem.: Am. Soc. Virology (founding coun. mem.), Internat. Com. on Taxonomy of Viruses (life; pres. 1990—96), Am. Soc. Microbiology (com. public health 2006—, public and scientific affairs bd.). Democrat. Roman Catholic. Office: Univ Tex Med Br Dept Pathology 3.145 A Keiller Bldg 301 Univ Blvd Galveston TX 77555-0609 Business E-Mail: famurphy@utmb.edu.

**MURPHY, GERALD,** retired federal official; b. Washington, Aug. 25, 1938; s. Jeremiah T. and Jean (Curley) M.; m. Kathryn Beckman, Sept. 24, 1988; children by previous marriage: William Michael, Janet Marie, Kathleen Anne B.C.S. with honors, Benjamin Franklin U., Washington, 1960, M.C.S., 1963. C.P.A., D.C. Dep. div. dir. Dept. Treasury, Washington, 1970-71, div. dir., 1971-74, asst. commr., 1974-75, dep. commr., 1975-79, dep. fiscal asst. sec., 1979-86, fiscal asst. sec., 1986-98; sr. prin. Keane Pub. Enterprise Consulting, Washington, 1998-2000; ind. cons., 2000—. Lectr. in acctg. Southeastern U., Washington, 1965-70. Dept. Agr. Grad. Sch., Washington, 1970-76; mem. Govt. Acctg. Standards Adv. Council, 1984-89; mem. Fed. Acctg. Standards Adv. Bd., 1991-98. Served with U.S. Army, 1956 Recipient Disting. Alumni award Benjamin Franklin U., Washington, 1976. Mem. Am. Inst. C.P.A.s, Assn. Govt. Accts. (nat. pres. 1977-78, Robert W. King award 1983, Meritorious Exec. Rsch. award 1992), Sr. Execs. Assn., Fed. Exec. Inst. Alumni Assn. Roman Catholic. Personal E-mail: gmurph825@aol.com.

**MURPHY, GERARD NORRIS,** trade association executive; b. Washington, July 10, 1950; s. Maurice J. and Marguerite (Norris) M.; m. Jacqueline Franz, May 26, 1973; children: Anne Marie, Michael Jonathan, Kathleen Elizabeth. BA, U. Md., 1972, MA, 1975; JD, George Mason U., 1980. Mgmt. trainee Washington Area New Automobile Dealers Assn., 1972-74; asst. CEO, 1974-82, pres., CEO, 1982—; prodr. Washington Auto Show, 2003—. Bd. dirs. Met. Washington BBB, chmn., 1992—97; bd. dirs. Small Bus. Legis. Coun., 2000—; mem. exec. coun. Washington Workforce Investment Coun., 2000—; trustee Nat. Capital Area Transp. Fedn., Washington, 1990—2000. Co-founder, past chmn. Washington Regional Alcohol Program, Vienna, Va., 1983-86; trustee Nat. Automobile Dealers Assn. Sales Rep. Cert. Commn., 1995-99; sec. Boys and Girls Clubs Greater Washington, Silver Spring, 1987-02, v.p. 2002-05, bd. dirs., 2006—; trustee Greater Washington Bd. Trade PACs, Va., 2000—; nat. treas., 2003—; co-founder Montgomery Students Automotive Trades Found., Montgomery Pub. Schs., 1978, sec., 1990—. Recipient Govs. citation Gov. William Donald Schaefer, 1990, Silver medal Boys and Girls Clubs Am., 1997; named Automotive Trade Exec. of Yr., Northwood U., 1997. Fellow Am. Soc. Assn. Execs. (cert., com. mem. 1989-90, 96-97, 2005-06); mem. ABA, Assn. Healthcare Coalition (sec. 1995, v.p. 1996-97, pres. 1998-00), Automotive Trade Assn. Execs. (bd. dirs. 1987-88, sec., treas. 1996, v.p. 1997, pres. 1998), D.C. Bar Assn., Greater Washington Soc. Assn. Execs. (com. chmn. 1993-94, trustee Found. 1997-00, chmn. award 1994), Leadership Washington (8th class 1993-94), Rotary (sec. 1998-00, v.p. 2001-02, dist. conf. chmn. 2001, pres. 2002-03, 06, v.p. found. 2005, pres. found. 2006—, Paul Harris fellow 1990), Delta Theta Phi, Delta Tau Delta. Democrat. Roman Catholic. Office: Washington Area New Auto Dealers Assn Ste 210 5301 Wisconsin Ave NW Washington DC 20015-2015 Office Phone: 202-237-7200. Business E-Mail: gm@wanada.org.

**MURPHY, GORDON JOHN,** electrical engineer, educator; b. Milw., Feb. 16, 1927; s. Gordon M. and Cecelia A. (Knerr) M.; m. Dorothy F. Brautigam, June 26, 1948; children: Lynne, Craig. BS, Milw. Sch. Engring.; 1949; MS, U. Wis., 1952; PhD, U. Minn., 1956. Asst. prof. elec. engring. Milw. Sch. Engring., 1949-51; systems engr. A C Spark Plug divsn. GM, 1951-52, cons., 1959-62; instr. U. Minn., 1952-56, asst. prof. elec. engring., 1956-57; assoc. prof. elec. engring. Northwestern U., Evanston, Ill., 1957-60, prof., 1960-97, head dept. elec. engring., 1960-69; pres. IPC Systems, Inc., 1975—2004; dir. Lab. for Design of Electronic Systems Northwestern U., Evanston, Ill., 1987-97, prof. emeritus, 1997—; pres. CUECOA, Inc., 2006—. Cons. numerous corps., 1959—; founder, 1st chmn. Mpls. chpt. Inst. Radio Engrs. Profl. Group on Automatic Control, 1956-57, Chgo. chpt., 1959-61; pres. IPC Systems, Inc., 1975-2003; expert witness in numerous patent cases, 1997-2004. Author: Basic Automatic Control Theory, 1957, 2d edit., 1966, Control Engineering, 1959; contbr. numerous articles, papers to profl. jours.; patentee TV, electronic timers, periodontal instruments and motion control systems. Mem. indsl. adv. com. Milw. Sch. Engring., 1971-2001. Served with USN, 1945-46. Recipient ECE Centennial medal U. Wis., 1991, Outstanding Alumnus award Milw. Sch. Engring. Alumni Assn., 1974; named One of Chgo.'s Ten Outstanding Young Men Chgo. Jaycees, 1961. Fellow IEEE (for edn. and rsch. in automatic control 1967); mem. feedback control systems com. 1960-68, discrete systems com. 1962-68, adminstrv. com. profl. group on automatic control 1966-69, chmn. membership and nominating coms. 1966-67); mem. Am. Automatic Control Coun. (edn. com. 1967-69), Engr.'s Coun. for Profl. Devel. (guidance com. 1966-67), Nat. Electronic Conf. (bd. dirs. 1983-85), Am. Electronics Assn. (exec. com. M.W. coun. 1990-93), Sigma Xi, Eta Kappa Nu, Tau Beta Pi. Home: 638 Garden Ct Glenview IL 60025-4105 Office: Northwestern U Elec Engring Dept Evanston IL 60208 Office Phone: 847-491-7258.

**MURPHY, GREGORY E.,** insurance company executive; Grad., Boston Coll.; grad. Advanced Mgmt. Program, Harvard Univ.; grad., MIT Sloan Sch. Mgmt. CPA. Joined Selective Ins. Group Inc., 1980, sr. v.p. fin., 1994—95, sr. v.p., CFO, 1995—97, COO, 1997—99, pres., 1997—, CEO, 1999—, chmn., 2000—. Bd. trustees Newton Meml. Hosp. Found. Mem.: Am. Inst. for Chartered Property Casualty Underwriters (bd. trustees), Ins. Inst. of Am. (bd. trustees). Office: Selective Ins Group 40 Wantage Ave Branchville NJ 07890 Office Phone: 973-948-3000.*

**MURPHY, HAROLD LOYD,** federal judge; b. Haralson County, Ga., Mar. 31, 1977; r. James Loyd and Georgia Gladys (McBrayer) M.; m. Jacqueline Marie Ferri, Dec. 20, 1958; children: Mark Harold, Paul Bailey. Student, West Ga. Coll., 1944-45, U. Miss., 1945-46; LL.B., U. Ga., 1949. Bar: Ga. 1949. Pvt. practice, Buchanan, Ga., from 1949; ptnr. Howe & Murphy, Buchanan and Tallapoosa, Ga., 1958-71; judge Superior Cts., Tallapoosa Circuit, 1971-77; U.S. dist. judge No. Dist. of Ga., Rome, 1977—. Rep. Gen. Assembly of Ga., 1951-61; asst. solicitor gen. Tallapoosa Jud. Circuit, 1956; mem. Jud. Qualifications Commn., State of Ga., 1977 With USNR, 1945-46. Fellow Am. Bar Found.; mem. ABA, Ga. Bar Assn., Dist. Judges Assn. for 11th Cir. Bar Assn., Am. Judicature Soc., Tallapoosa Cir. Bar Assn., Old War Horse Lawyers Club, Am. Inns Ct. (past pres. Joseph Henry Lumpkin sect.), Fed. Judges Assn. Methodist. Home: 321 Georgia Highway 120 Tallapoosa GA 30176-3114 Office: US Dist Ct PO Box 53 Rome GA 30162-0053

**MURPHY, HELEN,** recording industry executive; b. Glasgow, Scotland, Oct. 2, 1962; came to U.S., 1990; d. Francis and Kathleen (Gallagher) M.; m. Michael Christopher Luksha, Apr. 1, 1989. BA in Econs. with honors, U. Guelph, Can., 1982; MBA, U. Western Ontario, Can., 1984. CFA. Asst. mgr. securities rsch. Confederation Life, Toronto, Can., 1984-86; sr. analyst entertainment & merchandising Prudential Bache Securities, Toronto, Can., 1986-89; v.p. rsch. Richardson Greenshields Can., Toronto, 1989-90; v.p. investor rels. Polygram Holding Inc., N.Y.C., 1990-91; v.p., treas. Polygram Records Inc., N.Y.C., 1991-92, sr. v.p. corp. fin., treas., 1992-95; sr. v.p. investor rels. PolyGram Internat. Inc., N.Y.C., 1995-97; sr. v.p. mergers and acquisitions PolyGram Holding, Inc., N.Y.C., 1997-99; CFO, 1997-99, Westvaco Corp., 1999; CFO & chief adminstrv. office Martha Stewart Living Omnimedia, Inc., N.Y.C., 1999—2001; exec. v.p., CFO Warner Music Group, 2001—. Lectr. U. Guelph, 1982-90. Fellow Nat. Investor Rels. Inst., N.Y. Soc. Security Analysts, N.Y. Treas. Group. Office: Warner Music Group 75 Rockefeller Plz New York NY 10019

**MURPHY, J. ANDREW,** lawyer; b. Stanford, Calif., Jan. 21, 1961; Student, Univ. Munich, Germany; BA cum laude, Harvard Univ., 1983; JD high honors, George Washington Univ., 1987. Ptnr., head, Project Devel., Fin. com. Mem.: ABA, Am. Coll. Investment Counsel. Office: Hunton & Williams LLP 1900 K St NW Washington DC 20006-1109 also: Hunton & Williams

LLP 43rd Fl 200 Park Ave New York NY 10166-0136 Office Phone: 202-955-1543, 212-309-1035. Office Fax: 202-778-2201, 212-309-1100. Business E-Mail: dmurphy@hunton.com.

**MURPHY, JAMES EDWARD,** public relations and marketing executive; Degree in Journalism, U. Ill. Sr. corp. comms. officer Owens-Corning Fiberglas, Beatrice, Merrill Lynch; exec. v.p. Burson-Marsteller, vice chmn., 1990, chmn., CEO Ams., 1991-93; chmn., CEO Murphy & Co., 1993—; chief mktg. and comm. officer Accenture (formerly known as Andersen Cons.), 1993—. Mem. bd. advisors Medill Sch. Journalism, Northwestern U.; mem. devel. bd. Coll. Comm., U. Ill. Mem. Pres., past pres., bd. dirs. Arthur Page Soc.; chmn. PR Coalition. Mem. Inst. Pub. Rels. Rsch. (trustee), Union League Club, Belle Haven Club, Woodway Country Club, Palmetto Golf Club, Preston Mountain Club. Office: Accenture 6th Fl 1345 Avenue of the Americas New York NY 10105 E-mail: james.e.murphy@accenture.com.

**MURPHY, JAMES JEFFREY,** electronics executive; b. Kenosha, Wis., Nov. 4, 1954; s. Eugene C. and Thelma M. (Jensen) M.; m. Susan M. Larson, June 10, 1978. BA in Bus. Mgmt. and Labor Econs. with honors, U. Wis., 1976. Sales rep. Inland Steel, Chgo., 1976-77, product analyst, 1977; sales rep. Joerndt & Ventura, Inc., Kenosha, 1977-78; field sales rep. Applied Power Corp., New Berlin, Wis., 1978-79; Magnavox regional mgr. Philips Consumer Electronics Co., Knoxville, Tenn., 1979-87, zone mgr., 1987-89, divsn. field sales mgr., 1989-91, natl. account dir., 1991-95, v.p. merchandising, 1995—2000; mgr. VAS Portfolio, 2004—. Mem. Lincoln Continental Owners Club (treas. 1991), Vintage Radio-Phonograph Soc. Avocations: car collecting, reading, walking. Home: 2330 Stonegate Dr Cumming GA 30041-7410 Office: Philips Consumer Electronics Co 64 Perimeter Ctr E Atlanta GA 30346-2295 Office Phone: 770-821-2922. E-mail: jmurphy54@bellsouth.net.

**MURPHY, JENNIFER MELISSA,** school psychologist; b. Allentown, Pa., Sept. 25, 1977; d. Terrence Murphy and Mary Romanzyn; m. Michael Gabovitz, July 26, 2006. BA in Psychology, Millersville U., 1999, MS in Psychology, 2003. Cert. sch. psychologist Pa. Dept. of Edn., 2003. Sch. psychologist Colonial Intermediate Unit 20, Easton, Pa., 2002—. Mem.: NASP (cert. psychologist). Achievements include 2006 Champion of Get Up, Get Healthy fitness competition.

**MURPHY, JEREMIAH T.,** professional sports team executive, construction executive; b. NYC, July 21, 1944; m. Sandra Murphy; children: Lisa, Tara, Gregory. BA, Bernard Baruch Coll. CPA Calif. Sr. ptnr. Bowman and Co., Stockton, Calif., 1971-82; CFO A.G. Spanos Companies, Stockton, Calif., 1982—; v.p. San Diego Chargers. Mem.: Calif. Soc. of CPAs, Am. Inst. of CPAs. Office: AG Spanos Companies 10100 Trinity Pky Stockton CA 95219 also: San Diego Chargers 4020 Murphy Canyon Rd San Diego CA 92123

**MURPHY, JIM,** writer; b. Newark, N.J., 1947; m. Alison Blank; children: Michael, Ben. BA in English, Rutgers U., 1970. Author: (book) Weird and Wacky Inventions, 1978, Rat's Christmas, 1979, Harold Things Big, 1980, Death Run, 1982 (SLJ Best Book of Yr.), Two Hundred Years of Bicycles, 1983, The Indy 500, 1983, Tractors: From Yesterday's Steam Wagons to Today's Supercharged Giants, 1984, Baseball's All-Time All-Stars, 1984, Guess Again: More Weird and Wacky Inventions, 1986, Custom Car: A Nuts and Bolts Guide to Building One, 1988, The Last Dinosaur, 1988, The Call of the Wolves, 1989 (Nev. Young Reader's award, 1992), The Boy's War: Confederate and Union Soldiers Talk About the Civil War, 1991 (SCBW Golden Kite award nonfiction, 1990, Sch. Libr. Jour. Best Book of Yr., Bank St. Coll. Children's Book of Yr.), Dinosaur for a Day, 1992, The Long Road to Gettysburg, 1992 (SCBWI Golden Kite award nonfiction, 1992, SLJ Best Book of Yr., ALA Booklist Editors Choice, ALA Best Book for Young Adults), Backyard Bear, 1993, Across America on an Emigrant Train, 1993 (ALA Notable Book, NCTE Orbis Pictus award, 1994, Va. Librs. Jefferson Cup, 1994), Night Terrors, 1993 (Md. Black-Eyed Susan award 1995-96), The Great Fire, 1995 (Newbery Honor Book, 1996, NCTE Orbis Dictus award), Into the Deep Forest, 1995, A Young Patriot: The American Revolution as Experienced by One Boy, 1996 (Fraunces Tavern Mus. Book award 1997, SLJ Best Book of Yr.), The Journal of James Edmond Pease: A Civil War Union Soldier: Virginia, 1863, 1998, West to a Land of Plenty: The Diary of Teresa Angelino Viscardi, 1998, Gone-A-Whaling: The Lure of the Sea and the Hunt for the Great Whale, 1998 (ALA Notable Children's Book, SLJ Best Book of Yr.), Pick & Shovel Poet: The Journeys of Pascal D'Angelo, 2000, Blizzard! The Storm that Changed America, 2000 (ALA Siebert Honor Book, 2001), My Face to the Wind: The Diary of Sarah Jane Prince, a Prarie School Teacher, Broken Bow, Nebraska, 1881, 2001, An American Plague: The True and Terrifying Story of the Yellow Fever Epidemic of 1793, 2003 (Nat. Book award nominee, 2003, ALA Siebert award, 2004, ALA Newbery Honor Book, 2004, NCTE Orbis Pictus award, 2004, Boston Globe-Horn Book award, 2004, James Madison Book award 2004), Inside the Alamo, 2003.

**MURPHY, JOANNE BECKER,** writer; b. Detroit; d. Louis Norman and Gertrude Margaret (Kornmeier) Becker; m. Joseph A. Murphy, Jr., June 24, 1961; children: Michael Ellis, Joseph A. III. BA in Journalism, Mich. State U., 1958; MA in Humanities, Wayne State U., 1975. With pub. rels. dept. WBZ TV, Boston, 1958-60; The Jam Handy Orgn., Detroit, 1960-62, Detroit Symphony Orch., 1969-70; freelance writer, editor Detroit, 1978—90, Washington, 1990—. Contbg. writer: Affecting Change, 1986, Glass: State of the Art, 1989; editor: As Parents We Will, 1985 (1st Pl. award Pub. Svc. Nat. Found. for Alcoholism Comm.); writer, editor publs. for arts and human svcs. orgns.; contbr. articles to mags., newspapers. Program bd. Grosse Pointe (Mich.) War Meml., 1987—90; bd. dirs. Detroit Artists Market, 1982—90, Mich. Metro coun. Girl Scouts USA, 1971—78, Family Svcs. Detroit and Wayne County, 1970—76, All Hallows Guild Grounds Oversight Bd., Washington Nat. Cathedral, 1993—; bd. canvassers Grosse Pointe Sch. Sys., 1986—90; DC regional bd. Nat. Capital Area United Way, Washington, 1999—. Mem.: Washington Ind. Writers, Am. News Women's Club (Washington, bd. dirs. 1996—2001), Kappa Alpha Theta. Home and Office: 2717 O St NW Washington DC 20007-3128 Office Phone: 202-337-7856. E-mail: murphy.joanne@verizon.net.

**MURPHY, JOHN B.,** portfolio manager; b. Pitts., May 30, 1947; s. John Bernard and Knolle Cordelia (Bonham) M.; m. Lauren Osa Brown, Mar. 20, 1994; children: Kira Mei Li, Lauren Osa Ba, U. New Orleans, 1970; MBA, Columbia U., 1984. CFA 1987. Dir. La. Heritage Fair, New Orleans, 1974-75, 78-80; assoc. dir. New Orleans Jazz and Heritage Festival, 1978-80; exec. dir. New Orleans Jazz and Heritage Found. Inc., 1980; assoc. editor, analyst Value Line Pubs., N.Y.C., 1984-86; equity analyst, v.p. Drexel, Burnham, Lambert, N.Y.C., 1986-90; portfolio mgr., mng. dir. Guardian, N.Y.C., 1990—. Head of convertible investments, mng. dir. Family Svc. Life and other Guardian subs., 1998—; mem. alumni counseling bd. Sch. Bus. Columbia U., N.Y.C., 1986—; prodn. cons. Newport Jazz Festival, Capitol Radio Jazz Festival, Memphis Heritage Festival, 1978-80. Recipient Mayoralty Merit award City of New Orleans, 1978. Mem. Assn. Investment Mgmt. and Rsch., N.Y. Soc. Security Analysts, Beta Gamma Sigma (scholar 1983). Avocations: poetry, photography, golf. Home: PO Box 243 Ardsley on Hudson NY 10503-0243 Office: Guardian 7 Hanover Sq New York NY 10004-2616 Office Phone: 212-598-8104. E-mail: john_murphy@glic.com.

**MURPHY, JOHN CONDRON, JR.,** lawyer; b. Mpls., May 26, 1945; s. John Condron and Elaine Anne (Wentink) M.; m. Marie Antoinette Calcara, Aug. 17, 1968; children: Justin Peter, Jonathan Patrick. AB cum laude, Georgetown U., Washington, 1967; JD cum laude, U. Pa., 1972. Bar: Calif. 1972, D.C. 1978. Assoc. O'Melveny & Myers, L.A., 1972-75; spl. counsel U.S Securities & Exch. Commn., Washington, 1975-77; assoc. Cleary Gottlieb Steen & Hamilton LLP, Washington, 1977—81, ptnr., 1982-84, 87—; gen. counsel Fed. Deposit Ins. Corp., Washington, 1984-87. Mem. bd. editors Banking Policy Report, 1988—; contbr. articles to profl. jours. Lt. (j.g.) USNR, 1968-69. Mem. ABA (subcom. chmn. banking law com., chmn.

acquisitions and dispositions subcom. 1992-95), Fed. Bar Assn. (chmn. banking law com. 1992-94), Columbia Country Club (Chevy Chase, Md.). Republican. Roman Catholic. Home: 6 Newlands St Chevy Chase MD 20815-4202 Office Phone: 202-974-1580.

**MURPHY, JOHN F.,** lawyer; b. Jersey City, May 24, 1954; s. John Francis and Helen Joan (Makowski) M.; m. Bridget Fagan, Aug. 4, 1984; children: Helen Mary, John William. BA, U. Conn., 1976; JD, Washington & Lee U., 1979. Bar: Mo. 1979, U.S. Dist. Ct. (we. dist.) Mo. 1979, U.S. Ct. Appeals (8th cir.) 1982, U.S. Supreme Ct. 1991. Assoc. Shook, Hardy & Bacon LLP, Kansas City, Mo., 1979-85, ptnr., 1985—, chmn., 2003—. Bd. dirs. Lakemary Ctr. Endowment Assn., Paola, Kans., Friends of Spl. People, Starlight Theatre, Cath. Edn. Found.; pres. Waterford Homes Assn., 1994. Mem. Fedn. Ins. and Corp. Counsel, Mo. Bar Assn., Kansas City Met. Bar Assn., Greater Kansas City C. of C. (bd. dirs.), Phi Beta Kappa, Phi Kappa Phi, Omicron Delta Kappa. Republican. Roman Catholic. Avocations: running, spectator sports. Office: Shook Hardy & Bacon LLP 2555 Grand Blvd Kansas City MO 64108 Office Phone: 816-474-6550. Office Fax: 816-421-5547. E-mail: jmurphy@shb.com.

**MURPHY, JOHN FRANCIS,** law educator, consultant; b. Portchester, NY, Apr. 25, 1937; s. Francis John and Emilie (Tourtellot) M.; m. Laura S. Murphy; children: Andrew, Robert; stepchildren: Dan, Jessie, Gabriel. BA, Cornell U., 1959, LLB in Internat. Affairs, 1962. Bar: D.C. 1963, Kans. 1970, Pa. 1987. Afro-Asia Pub. Svc. fellow, India, 1962-63; assoc. Winthrop, Stimson, Putnam & Roberts, N.Y.C., 1963-64; atty. Office Legal Adv., Dept. State, Washington, 1964-67; assoc. Kirkland, Ellis, Hodson, Chaffetz & Masters, Washington, 1967-69; assoc. prof. law U. Kans., Lawrence, 1969-72, prof. law, 1972-84, assoc. dean Sch. Law, 1975-77; vis. prof. law Villanova U., Pa., 1983-84, prof. law sch. law, 1984—. Vis. prof. law Cornell U., Ithaca, N.Y., fall 1979, Georgetown U., summer 1982, San Diego U., summer Paris, 1986, 95, Mexico City, 1988, London, 1989, La. State U. summer, Aix-en-Provence, 1990, Haifa (Israel) U., 1997; Charles H. Stockton Prof. Internat. Law, Naval War Coll., 1980-81. Author: Legal Aspects of International Terrorism: Summary Report of an International Conference, 1980, The United Nations and the Control of International Violence, 1982, Punishing International Terrorists, 1985, State Support of International Terrorism: Legal, Political and Economic Dimensions, 1989, (with Alan Swan) The Regulation of International Business and Economic Relations, 1991, Supplements, 1994, 95, 2d edit., 1999 (cert. of merit Am. Soc. Internat. Law 1992), (with James D. Dinnage) The Constitutional Law of the European Union, 1996, Supplement, 1999, The United States and The Rule of Law in International Affairs, 2004; contbr. articles, comments, book revs. to profl., popular jours.; editor (with Alona E. Evans), contbg. author: Legal Aspects of International Terrorism, 1978; bd. editors Cornell Law Quar., 1961, 62; mem. bd. editors Terrorism: An Internat. Jour., 1981-92, Terrorism and Polit. Violence, 1993-2003, The Internat. Lawyer, 1998—, Transnat. Publishers, 1999—; mem. editl. bd. Internat. Law Studies, Naval War Coll., 2003—. Mem.: ABA (alt. observor to US Mission to UN 2006), Internat. Law Assn., Am. Soc. Internat. Law. Episcopalian. Office: Villanova U Sch Law 299 N Spring Mill Rd Villanova PA 19085 Office Phone: 610-519-7065. Business E-Mail: murphy@law.villanova.edu.

**MURPHY, JOHN JOSEPH,** manufacturing executive; b. Olean, N.Y., Nov. 24, 1931; s. John Joseph and Mary M.; m. Louise John; children: Kathleen A. Murphy Bell, Karen L. Murphy Rochelli, Patricia L. Murphy Smith, Michael J. AAS in Mech. Engring., Rochester Inst. Tech., 1952; MBA, So. Meth. U., 1981. Engr. Clark div. Dresser Industries, Olean, 1952-67, gen. mgr. roots blower div. Connersville, Ind., 1967-69, pres. crane, hoist and tower div. Muskegon, Mich., 1969-70, pres. machinery group Houston, 1970-75, sr. v.p. ops. Dallas, 1980, exec. v.p., 1982, pres., 1982-92, CEO, 1983—95, chmn. bd., 1983-96; mng. dir. SMG Mgmt. L.L.C., Dallas, 1997-2000. Bd. dirs. W.R. Grace & Co., CARBO Ceramics, Inc.; emeritus mem. Bus. Coun.; dir. ShawCor Ltd. With U.S. Army, 1954—56. Office: 3838 Oak Lawn Ave Ste 224 Dallas TX 75219

**MURPHY, JOHN JOSEPH,** literature educator, critic, editor; b. NYC, Apr. 3, 1933; s. John and Margaret B. (Shadegg) M.; m. Sarah Marie McMahon, June 30, 1962; children: Sarah, Joseph, Willa, John, Emily. BA, St. John's U., N.Y.C., 1956, MA, 1961. Instr. English lit. Coll. of St. Teresa, Winona, Minn., 1960-65; assoc. prof. English lit. Merrimack Coll., North Andover, Mass., 1965-68, assoc. prof., 1969-84, chmn. dept. English, 1974—76, 1979—82; prof. English lit. Brigham Young U., Provo, Utah, 1984—2005, prof. emeritus, 2005—, chair Am. lit. sect. dept. English, 1986—89, assoc. dir. Ctr. for Study Christian Values in Lit., 1994—2004. Organizer and dir. Willa Cather and Nebr. 1st Internat. U. Nebr. Cather Seminar, Hastings and Red Cloud, Nebr., 1981; bd. govs. Willa Cather Meml., 1984—; mem. editl. bd. Willa Cather Scholarly Edit., U. Nebr. Press, 1986—; vis. prof. U. Leon, Spain, 2001, U. Santiago, Spain, 2003, U. Rome 3, 2005; presenter in field. Author: My Antonia: The Road Home, 1989; editor: Critical Essays on Willa Cather, 1984, Penguin My Antonia, 1994, Literature and Belief, 1994—2004, Death Comes for the Archbishop, 1999, Willa Cather: Family, Community, History, 1990, Willa Cather and the Culture of Belief, 2002, Shadows on the Rock, 2005; prodr.: (TV series) KTCA TV, Great Ladies of the Am. Novel, 1963, Nathaniel Hawthorne, Am. Realist, 1964; contbr. chapters to books, articles to profl. jours. With U.S. Army, 1958-60. Recipient R.E. Twitchell award N.Mex. Hist. Soc., 1982. Home: 1390 Avenida Rincon # 102 Santa Fe NM 87506-6004 Office: Brigham Young U English Dept 4198 JFSB Provo UT 84602 Office Phone: 505-820-1981. Business E-Mail: john_murphy@byu.edu.

**MURPHY, JOHN VINCENT,** financial services company executive; b. Boston, July 12, 1949; s. James Gerald and Mary Lee (Dolan) M.; m. Kathleen Ryan, Nov. 17, 1973; children: Elizabeth Ryan, Christopher John, Carolyn Holmes. BS, Boston Coll., 1971. CPA, Mass. Acct. Arthur Andersen & Co., CPA's, Boston, 1972-77; controller Continental Investment Corp., Boston, 1977-81; v.p., controller Torchmark Fin. Services Co., Boston, 1981-85; sr. v.p. fin., chief fin. officer Liberty Fin. Services, Inc., Boston, 1985—; treas. Torchmark Leasing Programs, Inc., Boston, 1981-85, Liberty Real Estate Corp., 1981—, Liberty Asset Mgmt. Co., 1985—, Copley Venture Capital Inc., 1984—; bd. dirs. Fiduciary Trust Co. of N.H., Chatham Fin. Assocs., 1983-85; chmn. Boston Coll. High Sch. Alumni Capital Campaign, 1986-87. Mem. devel. adv. com. to bd. trustees Boston Coll. High Sch. Served with AUS, 1971-72. Mem. Am. Inst. CPA's, Mass. Soc. CPA's, Fin. Execs. Inst., Fides Exec. Com.; Greater Boston C. of C. Execs. Club. Clubs: Boston Coll. Varsity (pres. 1980-82), Boston Racquet, Blue Chips, Algonquin (Boston); Charitable Irish Soc.; Shriver. Office: Liberty Fin Services Inc Federal Reserve Plz Boston MA 02210-2204

**MURPHY, JOSEPH ALBERT, JR.,** lawyer; b. Grosse Pointe, Mich., May 29, 1934; s. Joseph Albert and Isabel C. (Callahan) M.; m. Joanne Becker, June 24, 1961; children: Michael, Joseph III. BS, Georgetown U., 1956; JD, Detroit Coll. Law, Mich. State U., 1962. Bar: Mich. 1962, D.C. 1996. House counsel Blue Cross Mich., Detroit, 1964-69, gen. counsel, corp. sec., 1969-75; v.p., gen. counsel Blue Cross & Blue Shield Mich., Detroit, 1975—88; chief Washington counsel Blue Cross and Blue Shield Assn., Washington, 1989—2001; cons. eLawForum, Washington, 2002—. Chmn. Health Care Network, Southfield, Mich., 1981-85, Blue Care Inc., Southfield, 1986-88; Editl. adv. bd. Thompson Pub., 2005—. Allocations panel United Found., Detroit, 1985-88; treas. Grosse Pointe Dem. Club, 1973-75; chmn. Health and People's Polit. Action Commn., Detroit, 1978-84; fundraiser United Way of Nat. Capital Area, 2005—. With U.S. Army, 1957-59. Mem. ABA, Mich. Bar Assn., Detroit Bar Assn., DC Bar Assn., Am. Health Lawyers Assn. (pres. 1981-82), Am. Corp. Counsel Assn., Am. Arbitrators Assn. (panel of arbitrators). Roman Catholic. E-mail: 2717 O St NW Washington DC 20007-3128 Personal E-mail: jamjr5@verizon.net.

**MURPHY, JOSEPH EDWARD, JR.,** broadcast executive; b. Mpls., Mar. 13, 1930; s. Joseph Edward Murphy and Ann Hynes; m. Diana Kuske, July 24, 1958; children: Michael, John. BA, Princeton U., 1952; postgrad., U.

Minn., 1956-60. Chartered fin. analyst. Dir. investment rsch. Woodward-Elwood & Co., Mpls., 1961-67; v.p. Northwestern Nat. Bank, Mpls., 1967-83; chmn. Midwest Communications, Inc., Mpls., 1990-92; ret. Dir. Midwest Comm., Inc., 1956-89, vice chmn., 1985-89. Author: Adventure Beyond the Clouds: How We Climbed China's Highest Mountain and Survived, 1986 (Friends Am. Writers award 1986), With Interest: How to Profit From Interest Rate Fluctuations, 1987, Stock Market Probability, 1988, revised edit., 1994, South to the Pole by Ski, 1990, The Random Character of Interest Rates, 1990, To the Poles by Ski and Dogsled, 1996, Bond Tables of Probable Future Yields, 1996, The Random Character of Corporate Earnings, 1997, Why the Stock Market Rises, 1998. Vice chmn. Minn. Coun. on Quality Edn. 1971-77; trustee Macalester Coll., St. Paul, 1973-87, Mpls. Soc. Fine Arts, 1977-78, Voyageur Outward Bound, 1985-92; bd. dirs. Minn. Opera Co., 1971-80, Childrens Theater Co., 1975-80, Minn. Ctr. for Book Arts, 1987-93, Greater Mpls. coun. Girl Scouts U.S.A., 1987-93, Fund for Peace, 1988-92, Minn. Nature Conservancy, 1991-96. 2d lt. U.S. Army, 1952-55. Mem. Am. Alpine Club (life, v.p. and bd. dirs 1975-81), Himalayan Club (life), Mpls. Club. Avocations: mountain climbing, exploration. Home: 2116 W Lake Isle Minneapolis MN 55405-2425

**MURPHY, JOSEPH JAMES,** chiropractic physician; b. Newark, July 30, 1956; s. Joseph P. and Roberta (Nittolo) Murphy; children: Joseph Raymond, Alexandra Renee; m. Maria Elena Sileo, Feb. 17, 2002; 1 child, Sean Alfred. BA in Biology, Rider Coll., 1978; D in Chiropratic Medicine, Palmer Coll., 1984. Diplomate Nat. Bd. Chiropractic Examiners; cert. N.J. State Bd. Med. Examiners. Rsch. chemist Mallinkrodt, Inc., Englewood, NJ, 1979-81; staff physician Mid-Island Chiropractic, Levittown, NY, 1984; dir., chief exec. officer Suburban Chiropractic Ctr., Chatham, NJ, 1984—. Apptd. mem. N.J. Bd. Chiropractic Examiners, 2000—, sec., 2003, pres., 2006. Mem. editl. bd. Am. Chiropractor Mag., 2000—; editor-in-chief newsletter The Column. Advisor Chatham High Sch. Key Club, 1986-87; trustee Early Childhood Learning Ctr., Chatham, 1999—, sec. 2002; mem. spkrs. bur. Am. Heart Assn. D. D. Palmer scholar, 1981, 82, 83. Mem.: AAAS, APHA, Morris County Chiropractic Soc. (pres. 1987—, bd. dirs. 2006), Bd. Chiropractic Examiners (apptd. mem. State of N.J.), Internat. Soc. Food Technologists, N.Y. Acad. Sci., N.J. Chiropractic Soc. (editor-in-chief Jersey Jour. 1986—, bd. dirs. 1987—, chmn. inter profl. rels. com. 1989—, 1st v.p. 1992—95, pres. 1995—, Meritorious Svc. award 1986, Disting. Svc. award 1987—97), Am. Chiropractic Assn., Am. Assn. Cereal Chemists, Chatham C. of C. (chmn. profl. rels. com. 1988—92, pres. 1989—92, Dist. Mem. Svc. award 1996), Kiwanis (bd. dirs. Chatham club 1986—89, Disting. Svc. award 1995), Tri Beta. Republican. Presbyn. Avocations: skiing, photography, model building, automobiles, bicycling. Home: 20 Squire Ct Basking Ridge NJ 07920 Office: Suburban Chiropractic Ctr 301 Main St Chatham NJ 07928-2410 Office Phone: 973-635-0036. Business E-Mail: drmurphy@drmurphy.com.

**MURPHY, JUDITH CHISHOLM,** trust company executive; b. Chippewa Falls, Wis., Jan. 26, 1942; d. John David and Bernice A. (Hartman) Chisholm. BA, Manhattanville Coll., 1964; postgrad., New Sch. for Social Research, 1965-68, Nat. Grad. Trust Sch., 1975. Asst. portfolio mgr. Chase Manhattan Bank, N.A., N.Y.C., 1964-68; trust investment officer Marshall & Ilsley Bank, Milw., 1968-72, asst. v.p., 1972-74, v.p., 1974-75; v.p., treas. Marshall & Ilsley Invesmtent Mgmt. Corp., Milw., 1975-94; v.p. Marshall & Ilsley Trust Co., Phoenix, 1982—, Marshall & Ilsley Trust Co. Fla., Naples, 1985—; v.p., dir. instnl. sales Marshall & Ilsley Trust Co., Milw., 1994-97, sr. v.p., 1997-98, M&I Investment Mgmt. Corp., 1998—. Coun. mem. Am. Bankers Assn., Washington, 1984-86; govt. relations com. Wis. Bankers Assn., Madison, 1982-88. Contbr. articles to profl. jours. Chmn. Milw. City Plan Commn., 1986—97; commr. Milw. County Commn. on Handicapped, 1988—90; bd. dirs. Cardinal Stritch Coll., Milw., 1980—89, Children's Hosp. Wis., Milw., 1989—98, Milw. Ballet Co., 1996—2001, Milw. Ctr. for Independence, 1999—2004, Girl Scouts Milw. Area, 2002—, Milw. Symphony Orch., 2002—. Recipient Outstanding Achievement award YWCA Greater Milw., 1985, Sacajawea award Profl. Dimensions, Milw., 1988, Pro Urbe award Mt. Mary Coll., 1988, Vol. award Milw. Found., 1992; named Disting. Woman in Banking, Comml. West Mag., 1988. Mem. Milw. Analysts Soc. (sec. 1974-77, bd. dirs. 1977-80), Fin. Women Internat. (bd. dirs., v.p. 1976-80), Am. Inst. Banking (instr. 1975-78), TEMPO (charter), Profl. Dimensions (hon.), University Club, Woman's Club Wis., Rotary. Democrat. Roman Catholic. Home: 3622 N Lake Dr Milwaukee WI 53211-2644 Office: M&I Investment Mgmt Corp 111 E Kilbourn Ave Milwaukee WI 53202-3197 Business E-Mail: judith.murphy@micorp.com.

**MURPHY, KATHLEEN ANNE FOLEY,** communications executive; b. Fresh Meadows, NY, Oct. 15, 1952; d. Thomas J. and Audrey L. Finn; m. Timothy Sean Murphy, Sept. 26, 1992; 1 child, G. David. BA, Marymount Coll., 1974; postgrad., Smith Coll., 1985. V.p. acct. supr., sr. v.p. mgmt. supr., sr. v.p. group dir. Ogilvy & Mather Inc., NYC, 1974-90; sr. v.p., worldwide account dir. Young & Rubicam, San Francisco, 1990-92, sr. v.p., dir. account svcs., 1992-95, exec. v.p., dir. acct. svcs., 1995-97, exec. v.p., gen. mgr. 1997—2002, COO, 2002—03; dir. network devel. WPP, San Francisco, 2003—. Mem. Family Caregivers Alliance. Roman Catholic. Home: One Brookside Ave Berkeley CA 94705 Office: WPP 303 Second St S Tower 9th Fl San Francisco CA 94107

**MURPHY, KATHLEEN M.,** lawyer; b. Evergreen Park, Ill. BA, St. Xavier Coll., 1980; MA, Loyola U., Chgo., 1982, JD, 1985. Bar: Ill. 1985, US Ct. Appeals, 7th Cir., US Ct. Appeals, Fed. Cir., US Ct. Internat. Trade, US Dist. Ct., No. Dist Ill. Ptnr., nat. chair Customs and Internat. Trade Dept. and Global Trade Adv. Group Katten Muchin Zavis Rosenman, Chgo. Mem.: ABA, Women in Internat. Trade, Midwest Importers Trade Assn., Joint Industry Group, Customs and Internat. Trade Bar Assn., Am. Assn. of Exporters and Importers. Office: Katten Muchin Zavis Rosenman 525 W Monroe St Chicago IL 60661 Office Phone: 312-902-5364. Office Fax: 312-577-8849. E-mail: kathleen.murphy@kmzr.com.

**MURPHY, KATHLEEN MARY,** former law firm executive, alternative healing professional; b. Bklyn., Dec. 16, 1945; d. Raymond Joseph and Catherine Elizabeth (Kearney) Murphy. BA in Edn., Molloy Coll., 1971; MS in Edn., Bklyn. Coll., 1975. Ordained minister Ch. of the Loving Servant; cert. hypnotherapist; cert. elem. sch. tchr., N.Y. Elem. sch. tchr. various parochial schs., L.I., Bklyn., Queens, N.Y., 1969-80; from asst. prin. to prin. parochial schs. Queens, 1980-82; supr.-trainer Davis, Polk, Wardwell law firm, N.Y.C., 1982-88; mgr. Schulte Roth & Zabel, N.Y.C., 1988-95; Reiki master (alternative healing profl.), 1996—. Trainer program for new employees, 1984; speaker edn. topics, Bklyn., Queens, 1979-81. Mem.: NAFE, Reiki Alliance. Democrat. Roman Catholic. Avocations: psychic phenomenon, workings of mind, ancient histories, crossword puzzles, museums. Home: 290 14th St Brooklyn NY 11215 Office Phone: 347-282-4391.

**MURPHY, KENNETH F.,** human resources specialist; BS in Labor Rels., Cornell U., 1977. Mgr. human resources Gen. Foods Corp., 1981—85, mgr. human resources desserts divsn., 1985—94; v.p. human resources, mktg. and sales Philip Morris USA, N.Y.C., 1996; sr. v.p. human resources and adminstrn. Altria Group, Inc., 2003—. Office: Altria Group Inc 120 Park Ave New York NY 10017-5592

**MURPHY, KENYON W.,** lawyer; b. Rome, Ga., Nov. 28, 1956; BBA in Acctg., U. Ga., 1978; JD, Harvard U., 1981. Bar: Ga. 1981. Law clerk to Judge James C. Hill U.S. Ct. of Appeals, 11th Circuit, 1981—82; assoc. Alston & Bird, Atlanta, 1982—85; from asst. counsel to sr. v.p., gen. counsel Nat. Svc. Industries Inc., 1985—2000, sr. v.p., 2000—01, gen. coun. 2000—01; sr. v.p. Acuity Brands Inc, Atlanta, 2001—, gen. counsel, 2001—. Mem.: ABA, Am. Corp. Counsel Assn., Ga. State Bar Assn. Office: Acuity Brands Inc 1170 Peachtree St NE Atlanta GA 30309

**MURPHY, KEVIN M.,** economics professor; AB, U. Calif., 1981; PhD, U. Chgo., 1986. Asst. prof. bus. economics and indsl. rels. U. Chgo., 1986—88, assoc. prof., 1988—89, prof., 1989—93, George Pratt Schultz prof.,

1993—2002, George J. Stigler prof. economics, 2002—, George J. Stigler disting. svc. prof. economics, dept. economics and grad. sch. bus., 2005—. Faculty rsch. assoc. Nat. Bur. Econ. Rsch. Co-author: Social Economics: Market Behavior in a Social Environment, 2000; co-editor: Measuring the Gains from Medical Research: An Economic Approach, 2003; contbr. articles to profl. jours. Named MacArthur fellow, John D. and Catherin T. MacArthur Found., 2005; fellow, Earhart Found., 1980—81, 1983—84, Friedman Fund, 1981—83. Fellow: Econometric Soc.; mem.: Am. Acad. Arts and Scis. Office: Univ Chgo Grad Sch Bus 5807 S Woodlawn Ave Chicago IL 60637 Office Phone: 773-702-7280. Office Fax: 773-702-2699. E-mail: murphy@chicagogsb.edu.*

**MURPHY, KIM,** newspaper bureau chief; b. Indpls., Aug. 26, 1955; married; 2 children. BA in English Lit. magna cum laude, Minot State Univ., ND, 1977. Asst. editor North Biloxian, Miss., 1973—74; reporter Minot Daily News, ND, 1978—80, Orange Co. Register, Calif., 1980—83, asst. metro editor Calif., 1982—83; gen. assignment staff writer, Orange Co. edition LA Times, 1983—89, nat. and fgn. corr., including Moscow Bur. chief, 1990—. Named a finalist, deadline reporting, ASNE awards, 2005; recipient ND Press Women award best news story, 1979, ND Sigma Delta Chi award, 1979, Orange Co. Press Club award, 1980, 1981, 1982, 1983, 1984, Orange Co. Press Club Watchdog award, 1985, LA Sigma Delta Chi award for fgn. corr., 1993, Pulitzer Prize for internat. reporting, 2005.

**MURPHY, LEWIS CURTIS,** lawyer, former mayor; b. N.Y.C., Nov. 2, 1933; s. Henry Waldo and Elizabeth Wilcox (Curtis) M.; m. Carol Carney, Mar. 10, 1957; children— Grey, Timothy, Elizabeth. BSBA, U. Ariz., 1955, LLB, 1961. Bar: Ariz. 1961. Pvt. practice, Tucson, 1961-66; trust officer So. Ariz. Bank & Trust Co., 1966-70; atty. City of Tucson, 1970-71; mayor, 1971-87; ret., 1987. Mem. Schroeder & Murphy, Tucson, 1978-88; trustee U.S. Conf. Mayors, 1978-87, chmn. transp. com., 1984-87; pub. safety steering com. Nat. League Cities, 1973-87, transp. steering com., 1973-87; v.p. Ctrl. Ariz. Project Assn., 1978-87. Bd. dirs. Cmty. Food Bank, 1987-2000, United Way Greater Tucson, 1988-90. With USAF, 1955-58. Mem. Ariz. Bar Assn., Pima County Bar Assn., Ariz. Acad., Sigma Chi (Significant Sig award). Republican. Presbyterian.

**MURPHY, LIAM B.,** law educator; b. 1960; BA, Melbourne U., 1982, LLB, 1984; MPhil, Columbia U., 1990, PhD, 1991. Tchg. fellow Columbia U., 1990—92; jr. fellow Soc. Fellows Harvard U., 1992—94; rsch. fellow NYU Sch. Law, 1994—95, asst. prof. law, 1995—98, assoc. prof., 1998—2000, prof., 2000—; also prof. philosophy NYU. Fellow Nat. Humanities Ctr., Rsch. Triangle Pk., NC, 2000—01. Office: NYU Sch Law Vanderbilt Hall Rm 337 40 Washington Sq S New York NY 10012-1099 Office Fax: 212-995-4341. E-mail: liam.murphy@nyu.edu.

**MURPHY, MARGARET A.,** nursing educator, adult nurse practitioner; b. N.Y.C., Apr. 4, 1934; d. William J. and Margaret (Burchill) Allen; m. Raymond L.H. Murphy, Jr., July 12, 1958; children: Raymond L.H. III, Michael W., Ann Murphy Postell, Maureen D. Murphy Olsen, Alice M., Matthew D. BSN, St. Joseph Coll., West Hartford, Conn., 1955; MS, NYU, 1957; PhD, Boston Coll., Chestnut Hill, Mass., 1987. RN Mass., cert. adult nurse practitioner. Instr. Boston U. Sch. Nursing, 1971-72; pulmonary clin. nurse specialist Pulmonary Assocs., Boston, 1972-73; pulmonary nurse clinician Tufts U., Medford, Mass., 1973-76; from instr. pulmonary nursing to assoc. prof. nursing Boston Coll., 1976—2001, assoc. prof. emeritus, 2001, chmn. adult health nursing, 1988-92, dir. adult nurse practitioner program, 1987—2001, dir. Kennedy Audio Visual Resource Ctr., 1991-95, coord. MBA-MSN program, 1993-99. Rschr. in lung sound patterns in health and disease, women's attitudes toward menopause. Co-editor: Pharmacotherapeutics and Advanced Nursing Practice, 1998; co-author: (CD) Learning Lung Sounds, 2002, (CD) Learning Heart and Lung Sounds, 2005; contbr. articles to profl. jours. Fellow, USPHS, 1957—58; grantee, Uniformed Svcs. U. Health Scis., 1995—96. Fellow: Am. Coll. Nurse Practitioners; mem.: ANA, Mass. Thoracic Soc. (chmn. com. on nursing practice, counselor 1989—91), Am. Thoracic Soc., Mass. Nurses Assn. (co-chmn. cabinet on legis. 1985—88), Sigma Theta Tau (chmn. awards and scholarships com. Alpha Chi chpt. 1994—96, pres. 1996—98, newsletter editl. bd. 1998—2004, Alpha Chi chpt. Mentor award 2001). Office Phone: 617-552-4063. E-mail: murphy@bc.edu.

**MURPHY, MARGARET HACKETT,** US bankruptcy judge; b. Salisbury, N.C., 1948; BA, Queens Coll., Charlotte, N.C., 1970; JD, U. N.C., Chapel Hill, 1973. Bar: Ga. 1973, U. S. Dist. Ct. (no. dist.) Ga. 1973, U.S. Ct. Appeals (5th cir.) 1974, U.S. Ct. Appeals (11th cir.) 1982. Assoc. Smith, Cohen, Ringel, Kohler and Martin, Atlanta, 1973-79; ptnr. Smith, Gambrell & Russell (formerly Smith, Cohen, Ringel, Kohler and Martin), Atlanta, 1980-87; U.S. bankruptcy judge U.S. Dist. Ct. (no. dist.) Ga., Atlanta, 1987—. Office: 1290 US Courthouse 75 Spring St SW Atlanta GA 30303-3309

**MURPHY, MARK JOSEPH,** enterprise sales executive; b. Rockville Centre, NY, Aug. 5, 1960; s. John Stephen and Barbara Ann (Seeney) M.; m. Annamaria Martin, July 19, 1986; children: Dana Martine, Kelly Gabrielle. BS in Econs. and Fin., St. John's U., 1983. Sr. tech. clk. St. John's U., Jamaica, N.Y., 1979-83; sys. engr. Property and Liability Br. IBM Corp., N.Y.C., 1983-84; sys. engr. N.Y. Ins. Br., 1984-86, mktg. rep. Manhattan Ins. Br., 1986-89, advt. mktg. staff Ea. Area, 1989, mktg. mgr. N.Y. banking, 1990-93, sys. svcs. mgr., 1993-95, mgr. client server and internet sys. mktg. N.E. area, 1995-97, client exec. fin. industry sector, 1997—2001, software sales exec., 2001—04; v.p. sales nat. accounts fin. industry sector Siemens AG, N.Y.C., 2004—. Bd. dirs. Make-A-Wish Found., Suffolk County, N.Y., past vice-chmn., past chmn. bd. devel. com., chmn. bylaws com.; vol. Make-A-Wish Found.: Am. Mgmt. Assn. Avocations: golf, travel. Home: 134 Parkwood Rd West Islip NY 11795 3001 Office: Siemens AG 1120 Avenue of the Americas New York NY 10036 Personal E-mail: bigblue@optonline.net.

**MURPHY, MARK KENNETH,** physicist, researcher; s. Kenneth George Murphy and Dorothy Alice Murphy-Cearns; m. Kalleen Ann Reeder, Oct. 20, 1990; children: Brian Thomas, Evan Patrick Goldsmith. BS in Physics, We. Wash. U., Bellingham, 1986; MS in Environ. and Radiol. Sci., Wash. State U., Pullman, 1999. Sr. rsch. scientist Pacific NW Nat. Lab., Richland, Wash., 1986—. Cons. Sunna Sys. Corp., Richland, Wash., 2000—04, v.p., 2006—. Contbr. articles to profl. jours. Recipient Entrepreneurial award, Battelle, 1999, R&D100 award, R&D Mag., 2000, 2006, Fed. Lab. Consortium award, U.S. Dept. Energy, 2006. Mem.: ASTM. Achievements include being part of a team that discovered compound that can prevent female infertility after radiation therapy; original scientific evaluations on the new IsoRay cesium-131 medical implant seed for cancer therapy. Avocations: genealogy, writing, camping. Office: Pacific NW Nat Lab PO Box 999 Richland WA 99354 Office Phone: 509-376-7997.

**MURPHY, MARY,** retired librarian; b. Hibbing, Minn., Aug. 14, 1917; d. John Philip and Ethel Robinson Murphy. BA, St. Lawrence U., Canton, NY, 1940; BSLS, U. Ill., Urbana, 1941. Map cataloger Army Map Svc. Libr., Washington, 1943—45, acquisition specialist, 1945—46, book cataloger, reviser, 1946—52, chief reference unit, asst. chief book and periodical br., 1956—65, chief document br., 1966—68, chief info. sect. Army Topographic Command, Washington, 1968—70; chief analysis br. Def. Mapping Agy. Info. Ctr., Washington, 1970—80; ret., 1980. Spkr. in field. Contbr. articles to profl. jours. Mem.: Spl. Libre. Assn. (editor Geography and Map Divsn. Bull.), Zonta Club, Phi Beta Kappa. Democrat. Episcopalian. Avocations: reading, dance, travel, photography. Home: 8102 Birnam Wood Dr Mc Lean VA 22102-2713

**MURPHY, MATT,** information technology executive; Bus. devel. mgr. network sys. group Sun Microsystems, product line mgr.; product mgmt. NetBoost; ptnr. Kleiner Perkins Caulfield and Byer. Mem. bd. dir. IPUnity,

Kodiak Networks, RGB Networks, Stoke, XSIGO, eASIC, Oakley Networks, Scintera, Quorum Sys., Endforce, Devicescape. Office: 2750 Sand Hill Rd Menlo Park CA 94025 Office Phone: 650-233-2750. Office Fax: 650-233-0300.*

**MURPHY, MEISSA BLEU,** music educator, behaviorist; d. Raymond Edward and Delcia Lucille Spry; m. Hershel Ring Murphy, Sept. 22, 1990; m. Harry Angevin Rider (dec.); children: William Cary Rider, Tiffany Ann Rider, Sheri Kay Rider. Student, Ind. Music Sch., 1954, U. of L, 1956, La Salle Interior Design, 1972—78, Harron Art Sch., 1984—87; BA in Psychology, Purdue U., 1990. Tchr. music, Indpls., pub. schs., Indpls.; behaviorist St. Vincent Hosp., New Hope-Indpls. Vocal coach, piano tchr., Indpls.; mem. faculty Am. Coll. Music, Austin, Tex.; profl. musician, guitarist and vocalist for internat. performances. Composer: Is It Raining, 1971, Small House for Sale; composer: (music score) Christmas Mouse, 1972; composer: TV commls. Mem. Wildlife Fedn., Hist. Soc., Indpls. Zoo, Heart Drive, First Monday Symphony, Harmony Club, Symphony Womans Group. Mem.: Indpls. Matinee Musicales, Indpls. Piano Tchrs. Assn., Musician's Uniom (Local 3), Am. Mensa, Indpls. Art Mus., Psi Chi (pres. 1987—89). Avocations: flying, music, music, art. Office: Mrs Murphys Westside Piano Studio 7988 Fishback Rd Indianapolis IN 46278 Office Phone: 317-297-1139. Personal E-mail: meissableu@aol.com.

**MURPHY, MICHAEL EMMETT,** retired food company executive; b. Winchester, Mass., Oct. 16, 1936; s. Michael Cornelius and Bridie (Curran) M.; m. Adele Anne Kasupski, Sept. 12, 1959; children: Leslie Maura, Glenn Stephen, Christopher McNeil. BS in Bus. Adminstrn, Boston Coll., 1958; MBA, Harvard, 1962. Financial analyst Maxwell House div. Gen. Foods Corp., White Plains, NY, 1962-64, cost mgr. San Leandro, Calif., 1964-65, controller Jackonville, Fla., 1965-67, Hoboken, NJ, 1967-68, mgr. fin. planning and analysis, 1968-69; mgr. planning Hanes Corp., Winston-Salem, NC, 1969-70, corp. controller, 1970-72; v.p. adminstrn. Hanes Corp. (Hanes Knitwear), Winston-Salem, NC, 1972-74; v.p. fin. Ryder System Inc., Miami, Fla., 1974-75, exec. v.p., 1975-79; exec. v.p., dir. Sara Lee Corp., Chgo., 1979-93, vice chmn., 1993-97. Bd. dirs. GATX Corp., Payless Shoe Stores, Inc., CNH Global N.V., Coach Inc., Bassett Furniture Industries, Inc., No. Funds. Mgmt. adviser Jr. Achievement, 1965-66; mem. exec. com. Hudson County Tax Rsch. Coun., 1967-68; trustee Boston Coll., 1980-88; chmn. Civic Fedn. Chgo., 1984-86; bd. dirs. Jobs for Youth, Chgo., 1983-86, Lyric Opera, 1986-2002; bd. dirs. Northwestern Meml. Hosp., Chgo., 1989-2000, Big Shoulders Fund, Chgo. Ctrl. Area Com., 1995—, Chgo. Cultural Ctr. Found., 1995—, Met. Pier and Exposition Authority, 2004—, Joffrey Ballet, 2006—; prin. Chgo. United, 1995-98. Mem. Nat. Assn. Mfrs. (bd. dirs. 1989-96, dir. Big Shoulders Fund 1995—), Fin. Execs. Inst., Hoboken C. of C., Winson-Salem C. of C., Miami C. of C., Internat. Platform Assn., UN Assn., Ouimet Scholar Alumni Group, Beta Gamma Sigma. Roman Catholic. Home: 1242 N Lake Shore Dr Chicago IL 60610-2361 Office: Sara Lee Corp 3 First National Plz Chicago IL 60602 Office Phone: 312-580-7820. Personal E-mail: mebmurphy@aol.com.

**MURPHY, MICHAEL GEORGE,** actor; b. Los Angeles, May 5, 1938; s. Bearl Branton and Georgia Arlyn (Money) M.; m. Wendy Crewson, 1988; children: Maggie, John (Jack) Branton. BA, U. Ariz., 1961. Former HS tchr., 1962—64. Appeared in films The Legend of Lylan Clare, 1968, The Arrangement, 1969, MASH, 1969, Brewster McCloud, 1970, McCabe & Mrs. Miller, 1971, What's Up, Doc?, 1972, Phase IV, 1973, The Autobiography of Miss Jane Pittman, 1974, Nashville, 1975, The Front, 1976, An Unmarried Woman, 1978, Manhattan, 1978, The Class of Miss MacMichael, 1978, John Cheever's O, Youth and Beauty, 1979, Strange Behavior, 1981, The Year of Living Dangerously, 1982, Cloak and Dagger, 1983, Two Marriages, 1983, Salvador, 1986, Hard Copy, 87, The Caine Mutiny Court-martial, 1987, Tanner'88, 1988, Tailspin, 1988, Shocker, 1989, Private Parts, 1997, Magnolia, 1999, Tart, 2001, Tricks, 2004, Silver City, 2004, Childstar, 2004, Heights, 2004, X-Men: The Last Stand, 2006; (TV) The Day Reagan Was Shot, 2001, Live From Baghdad, 2002, Footsteps, 2003, In the Dark, 2003, Tanner on Tanner, 2004, H2O, 2004, Hunt for Justice, 2005, Mayday, 2005, Playing House, 2006. Served with USMC, 1956-57. Office: care Internat Creative Mgmt 3100 N Damon Way Burbank CA 91505-1015*

**MURPHY, MICHAEL R.,** federal judge; b. Denver, Aug. 1947; s. Roland and Mary Cecilia (Maloney) M.; m. Maureen Elizabeth Donnelly, Aug. 22, 1970; children: Amy Christina, Michael Donnelly. BA in History, Creighton U., 1969; JD, U. Wyo., 1972. Bar: Wyo. 1972, U.S. Ct. Appeals (10th cir.) 1972, Utah 1973, U.S. Dist. Ct. Utah 1974, U.S. Ct. Appeals (5th cir.) 1976, U.S. Tax Ct. 1980, U.S. Ct. Appeals (9th cir.) 1981, U.S. Ct. Appeals (fed. cir.) 1984. Law clk. to chief judge U.S. Ct. Appeals (10th cir.), Salt Lake City, 1972-73; with Jones, Waldo, Holbrook & McDonough, Salt Lake City, 1973-86; judge 3d Dist. Ct., Salt Lake City, 1986-95, presiding judge, 1990-95; judge U.S. Ct. Appeals (10th cir.), Salt Lake City, 1995—. Mem. adv. com. on rules of civil procedure Utah Supreme Ct., 1985—95, mem. mng. bd. dist. ct. judges, 1989—90; mem. Utah State Sentencing Commn., 1993—95, Utah Adv. Com. on Child Support Guidelines, 1989—93, Utah Child Sexual Abuse Task Force, 1989—93; mem. com. on fed.-state jurisdiction Jud. Conf. of U.S., 2001—. Recipient Freedom of Info. award, Soc. Profl. Journalists, 1989, Utah Minority Bar Assn. award, 1995, Alumni Achievement citation, Creighton U., 1997; named Judge of Yr., Utah State Bar, 1992. Fellow Am. Bar Found.; mem. ABA (editl. bd. Judges' Jour. 1997-99), Utah Bar Assn. (chmn. alternative dispute resolution com. 1985-88), Sutherland Inn of Ct. II (past pres.). Office: 5438 Federal Bldg 125 S State St Salt Lake City UT 84138-1102 Office Phone: 801-524-5955.*

**MURPHY, OTIS,** music educator; b. Milledgeville, Ga., Oct. 25, 1972; s. Otis Murphy, Sr. and Ruby Mitchell Murphy; m. Haruko Murphy, May 29, 1999; children: Kevin, Renée, Ethan. MusB magna cum laude in Eng. U, Ga., 1995, MusM in Saxophone, Ind. U., 1998, student in Music in Saxophone, 1998—; student, Conservatoire National Régional de Musique de Cergy-Pontoise, 1999—2000. Musician: Indpls. (Ind.) Symphony Orch., 2002—05, Ind. U. Festival Orch., 2002, U. North Tex. U. Symphony Orch., 2002, U. N.C. Symphony Orch., 2004, numerous solo performances. Home: 4592 Compton Blvd Bloomington IN 47401 Office: Indiana Univ School Music Bloomington IN 47405

**MURPHY, PAMELA ANN,** music educator, actress, musician; b. Cooperstown, NY, June 8, 1962; d. William John and Mary Kathryn Barrett; m. Michael Francis Murphy, II, July 11, 1987; children: Michael Francis III, Sean Patrick, Timothy Andrew. MusB, SUNY, Potsdam, 1984; MS, Western Conn. State U., 1990. Permanent tchg. lic. N.Y., cert. adjudicator NYSSMA. Music tchr. Valley Ctrl. Mid. Sch., Montgomery, NY, 1984—89, Valley Ctr. Mid. Sch., Montgomery, 1999—, Valley Ctrl. H.S., Montgomery, 1991—94, Kinry Rd. Elem. Sch., Poughkeepsie, NY, 1994—97. Guest condr. for all-county chorus Dutchess County (N.Y.) Music Educators Assn., 1994; owner, music dir. Hudson Valley Conservatory Fine Arts, Walden, NY, 1995—; profl. vocalist and keyboard player for various radio commls., weddings and bands; adjudicator state and local vocal competitions. Composer: (songs) My Love, 2002; actor: New Rose Theatre, 1996—. Facilitator fundraising activities Am. Heart Assn., Otego, NY, 1995; artistic dir. Hudson Valley Parents Performing Students, Walden, 1997—; fundraiser Muscular Dystrophy Assn., Newburgh, NY, 2003. Mem.: Orange County Music Educators Assn. (guest condr. for all-county chorus 1986, 1989, 2002, govt. rels. officer), N.Y. State Sch. Mus. Assn., Music Educators Nat. Conf., Nat. Write Your Congressman. Roman Catholic. Avocations: singing, dance, acting, flute, painting. Home: 30 Browns Rd Walden NY 12586 Office: Hudson Valley Conservatory Fine Arts PO Box 704 35 E Main St Walden NY 12586 Office Phone: 845-778-2478. Personal E-mail: murphhvc@yahoo.com.

**MURPHY, PATRICK NEIL,** lawyer; b. Wahoo, Nebr., Jan. 15, 1946; s. Albert S. and Alice B. (Daley) Murphy; m. Kathryn Ann Kearns, June 8, 1968; children: Megan, Mia, Michael. BA, U. Nebr., 1968; JD, Creighton U., 1972. Bar: Nebr. 1973, Iowa 1973, U.S. Dist. Ct. Nebr. 1973, U.S. Dist. Ct. (no. dist.) Iowa 1975, U.S. Supreme Ct. 1992. Asst atty. County of Plymouth,

Iowa, 1973—92; ptnr. Murphy & Collins P.L.C., LeMars, Iowa, 1973—. Dist. chmn. Prairie Gold coun. Boy Scouts Am., 1976—83; bd. dirs. Plains Area Mental Health Ctr., 1975—82; chmn., bd. dirs. Cath. Charities Diocese, Sioux City, 1992—98; charter dir. Plymouth County Conservation Found., 1993—; pres. LeMars Cmty. Sch. Bd. Dirs., 2000—02; pres. Plymouth County REAP Congress Plymouth County Civil Svc. Commn., 1988—2000; ctrl. committeeman Plymouth County Dems., 1974—84. Sgt. U.S. Army, 1969—71. Mem.: ATLA, ABA, Nebr. Assn. Trial Lawyers, Iowa Assn. Trial Lawyers (bd. govs. 1996—2000), Nebr. Bar Assn., Iowa Bar Assn. (mem. Am. citizenship commn. 1974—, mem. grievance commn. 1997), LeMars C. of C. (bd. dirs. 1980—83), KC, Elks, Sertoma. Roman Catholic. Home: 1517 1st Ave SW Le Mars IA 51031-2707 Office: Murphy and Collins PLC PO Box 526 Le Mars IA 51031-0526 Office Phone: 712-546-8844. Business E-Mail: murphlaw@lemarscomm.net.

**MURPHY, PAUL REGIS, JR.,** business educator; b. DC, Aug. 12, 1954; m. Sheryl Anne Booher, July 4, 1995. AB, U. Notre Dame, Ind., 1972—76; MBA, U. Md., College Park, 1976—79, PhD, 1980—85. Cert. in transportation and logistics. Prof. bus. logistics John Carroll U., Univ. Heights, Ohio, 1995—. Author: (textbook) Contemporary Logistics, 8th edit., 2004. Recipient Disting. Doctoral Alumnus award, Smith Sch. Bus., U. Md., 1998, Disting. Faculty award, John Carroll U., 2002. Mem.: Am. Soc. Transp. & Logistics (bd. mem. 2002—05). Office: John Carroll Univ 20700 N Park Blvd University Heights OH 44118 Business E-Mail: drmurphy@jcu.edu.

**MURPHY, RAMON JEREMIAH CASTROVIEJO,** physician, pediatrician; b. NYC, Feb. 12, 1944; s. William J. and Angelines (Castroviejo) M.; m. Lila, Sept. 12, 1971; children: Jessica, David. BA, U. Notre Dame, 1965; MD, Northwestern U., 1969; MPH, Columbia U., 1974. Diplomate Am. Bd. Pediats. Intern in medicine Cook County Hosp., Chgo., 1969—70; resident in pediats. Children's Meml. Hosp., Chgo., 1970—71, Babies Hosp.-Columbia-Presbyn. Med. Ctr., N.Y.C., 1971—73; resident in cmty. medicine Mt. Sinai Hosp., N.Y.C., 1973—74, clin. asst. pediatrician, 1974—75, asst. attending pediatrician, 1975—83, assoc. attending pediatrician, 1983—, assoc. instr. cmty. medicine, 1974—75, asst. prof. clin. pediats., asst. prof. cmty. medicine, 1975—83, assoc. prof. clin. pediats., 1983—; pediatrician Uptown Pediat., P.C., N.Y.C., 1976—, pres., 1990—. Co-dir. Mt. Sinai Children's Cmty. Health, 1999—, Mt. Sinai Global Health Ctr., 2005—; dir. Mt. Sinai Off-Site Pediat. Residency Tng. Program, 1999—, Mt. Sinai Pediat. Global Health Tng. Program, 2004—; vis. clin. fellow pediat. Columbia U., Coll. Physicians and Surgeons, N.Y.C., 1971-73; pediat. cons. Oxford Health Plan, 1990-94, Children's Aid Soc., 2004—; Commonwealth Fund, 1995—. Contbr. articles to profl. jours. Co-med. dir. Benito Juarez People's Health Ctr., Chgo., 1970-71; dep. co-dir. Wagner Child Health Project, N.Y.C., 1973-75; sch. physician The Day Sch., 1984—, The Trinity Sch., 1992—, trustee, 1993-99. Fellow Am. Acad. Pediat.; mem. N.Y. Pediat. Soc. (program chmn. 1986-89, pres. 1988-90). Soc. for Adolescent Medicine, Mt. Sinai Alumni Assn. Office: 1245 Park Ave New York NY 10128-1211

**MURPHY, RANDALL KENT,** writer, educator, consultant; b. Laramie, Wyo., Nov. 8, 1943; s. Robert Joseph and Sally (McConnell) M.; m. Cynthia Laura Hillhouse, Dec. 29, 1978; children: Caroline, Scott, Emily. Student, U. Wyo., 1961—65; MBA, So. Meth. U., 1983. Dir. mktg. Wycoa, Inc., Denver, 1967—70; dir. Comm. Resource Inst., Dallas, 1971—72; account exec. Xerox Learning Sys., Dallas, 1973—74; regional mgr. Systema Corp., Dallas, 1975; pres. Performance Assocs.; pres., dir. Acclivus Corp., Dallas, 1976—; founder, chmn. Acclivus Inst., 1982—. Author: Performance Management of the Selling Process, 1979, Coaching and Counseling and Performance, 1980, Managing Development and Performance, 1982, Acclivus Performance Planning System, 1983, (with others) BASE For Performance, 1983, Acclivus Coaching, 1984, Acclivus Sales Negotiation, 1985, R3 Service, 1997, BASE for Effective Presentations, 1987, BASE for Strategic Presentations, 1988, The New BASE for Excellence, 1988, Major Account Planning and Strategy, 1989, Strategic Management of the Selling Process, 1989, Building on the BASE, 1992, Negotiation Mastery, 1995, R3 Service, 1997, Co-creating R3 Value, 2002, Getting the Meeting, 2004, R3 Interaction, 2005; co-inventor The Randy-Band multi-purpose apparel accessory, 1968. Active Dallas Mus. Fine Arts, Dallas Hist. Soc., Dallas Symphony Assn.; vice chmn. bd. trustees The Winston Sch., 1994-96, chmn. bd. trustees, 1997-2000; mem. adv. bd. The Women's Ctr. of Dallas, 1995-98. With AUS, 1966. Mem. ASTD, Inst. Mgmt. Scis., Soc. Applied Learning Tech., Nat. Soc. Performance and Instrn., Assn. Mgmt. Cons., Am. Assn. Higher Edn., World Future Soc., Soc. for Intercultural Edn., Tng. and Rsch., Internat. Fedn. Tng. and Devel. Orgns., Inst. Noetic Scis., Nat. Peace Inst., Amnesty Internat., Acad. Polit. Sci., The Nature Conservancy, Theosophical Soc. Am., Children's Arts and Ideas Found., So. Meth. U. Alumni Assn., U. Wyo. Alumni Assn. Home: 11110 Lawnhaven Rd Dallas TX 75230 Office Phone: 972-385-1277. Business E-Mail: randall.murphy@acclivus.com.

**MURPHY, RICHARD WILLIAM,** retired diplomat; b. Boston, July 29, 1929; s. John Deneen Murphy and Jane (Diehl) Bonner; m. Anne Herrick Cook, Aug. 25, 1955; children: Katherine Anne, Elizabeth Drew, Richard McGill. Grad., Phillips Exeter Acad., 1947; AB, Harvard U., 1951, Cambridge U., Eng., 1953; postgrad. Arabic studies, U.S. Fgn. Service Inst., Beirut, 1959-60; LLD (hon.), New Eng. Coll., 1989, Balt. Hebrew U., 1992. Vice consul U.S. Consulate Gen., Salisbury, So. Rhodesia, 1955-58; consul Aleppo, Syria, 1960-63; polit. officer Am. Embassy, Jedda, Saudi Arabia, 1963-66, Amman, Jordan, 1966-68; pers. officer U.S. State Dept., Washington, 1968-69, dir. Office Arabian Peninsula Affairs, 1969-71, asst. sec. state for Near Ea. and South Asian affairs, 1983-89; U.S. amb. to Mauritania 1971-74, to Syria, 1974-78, to the Philippines, 1978-81, to Saudi Arabia, 1981-83; sr. fellow for Middle East Coun. Fgn. Rels., N.Y.C., 1989—2004; cons. Richard Murphy Assocs., N.Y.C., 1993—. Chmn. Fgn. Students Svc. Coun., Washington, 1989—93, Mid. East Inst., Washington, 1993—2001, Chatham House Found., 1993—2004; mem. bd. advisors Naval War Coll., 1991—94. Trustee Am. U. of Beirut, 1995—; mem. vis. com. Harvard Mid. East Ctr., 1999—, Near East Found., 2000-2003; dir. Found. for Mid. East Peace, 2000—; chmn. Friends of UN Relief and Works Agy. Assn., 2005—. Served with US Army, 1953-55. Recipient Superior Honor award, U.S. Dept. State, 1969, Pres.'s Disting. Svc. award, 1986, 88, 89. Mem. Coun. Fgn. Rels., Fgn. Svc. Assn., Century Club. Republican. Episcopalian. Avocations: tennis, scuba diving. Home: 16 Sutton Pl 9A New York NY 10022-3057 Office Phone: 212-319-6541. Home Fax: 212-421-7067. Business E-Mail: richard@rwmurphyassociates.com.

**MURPHY, ROBERT,** executive search consultant; b. Davenport, Iowa; s. James and Patricia M. BS, U. Ill., Chgo., 1963. Registered pharmacist, Ill. With Walgreen Co., Chgo., 1963—73; corp. mgr. Coll. Rels. & Recruiting Corp.; mgr. Human Resource Planning Corp.; dir. Orgn. and Human Resource Planning & Devel.; U.S. ptnr.-in-charge exec. search PricewaterhouseCoopers, Chgo., 1974—93; founder, chmn. Murphy Ptnrs. Internat., global exec. search firm, 1993—. Contbr. articles to profl. jours. including Wall St. Jour., Newsweek. Mem. Internat. Human Resource Assn., Soc. Human Resource Mgrs., Internat. Cons. Assn., Am. Soc. Pers. Adminstrs., Soc. Human Resource Profls., Kappa Psi. Office: 956 Shoreline Rd Barrington IL 60010-3815 Office Phone: 847-304-1599. Business E-Mail: bob@mpivips.com.

**MURPHY, ROBERT BLAIR,** management consulting company executive; b. Phila., Jan. 19, 1931; s. William Beverly and Helen Marie (Brennan) M.; children: Stephen, Emily, Julia, David, Catherine. BS, Yale, 1953. Indsl. engr. DuPont Corp., Aiken, SC, 1953-55; mgr. sales can divsn. Reynolds Metals Co., Richmond, Va., 1955-69; gen. mgr. corrugated divsn. Continental Can Co., N.Y.C., 1969-73; v.p. and gen. mgr. beverage divsn. Am. Can Co., Greenwich, Conn., 1973-75; assoc. Heidrick & Struggles, Inc., N.Y.C., 1976-78, v.p., 1978; v.p.; mng. dir. Stamford office Spencer Stuart & Assocs., 1978-84, ptnr., 1982-84; co-founder and CEO Sullivan-Murphy Assocs.,

1984—. Mem. Riverside Yacht Club (Greenwich), Yale Club (N.Y.C.), Merion Cricket Club (Haverford, Pa.), Bucks Harbor Yacht Club (Brooksville, Maine). Home: 11 Indian Mill Rd Cos Cob CT 06807-1315 E-mail: rblairm69@aol.com.

**MURPHY, ROBERT JAMES,** language educator, consultant, pianist, pipe organ performer; b. Decatur, Ind., Aug. 31, 1941; s. James William and Catherine Agnes (Schumacker) Murphy; m. Linda L. Nolan, June 28, 1975; 1 child, Christina Lyn. BS in Edn., Ball State U., 1963; MS in Edn., St. Francis U., 1967; postgrad., U. Denver, 1986, Ball State U., 1972. Cert. English, speech, drama and journalism tchr. Ind. Speech and drama tchr. Rochester (Ind.) H.S., 1976—78; chair dept. English Lawrenceburg (Ind.) H.S., 1978—81; Holy Family H.S., Denver, 1981—86; prin. Randall-Moore Sch., Denver, 1986—87; dir. edn. Mansfield Bus. Sch., Denver, 1987—89; prin. St. John the Bapt. Cath. Sch., Ft. Wayne, Ind., 1989—94; pres., founder Murphy Ednl. Consulting, Ft. Wayne, Ind., 1995—, D/B/A Alternative Edn. Curriculum and The Learning Kaleidoscope, Pensacola, Fla., 1995—. Cons. Am. Printing House for Blind, Louisville, 1999—2002; cons., writer, spkr. homeschooling groups, 1995—; exec. dir., co-founder The Kaleidoscope Edn. Ctr., Ft. Wayne, Ind., 2003, co-founder, dir., 03; tchr., supr. Aurora (Colo.) Evening H.S., 1986—87; tchr. U. St. Francis, Ft. Wayne, 2003—; edn. coord., tchr. M.A.Y.A. Unity Ctr., Ft. Wayne, 2003; dir. edn. Phoenix Youth Ctr., 2003—; musician Colo., Ind., Ill., 1961—. Author: All in One Big Book, 1998, The Pump Man, 1998; co-author: Teaching the Student with a Visual Impairment, 2000, author reading and writing curriculum; dir.: Firehouse Theater, 2006—. Bd. dirs. Ft. Wayne Pub. Transp. Co., 2000—, League for Blind and Disabled, Ft. Wayne, 2000—; chmn. bd. dirs. United Voice Coalition, Ft. Wayne, 2002—05; chmn. bd. dirs. State Ind. Alliance Cmty. Inclusion, 2003—05; site visitor U.S. Dept. Edn. Blue Ribbon Sch., 1991; devel. dir. Fifth Freedom Network for People with Disabilities, Ft. Wayne, 2006—; founding bd. dirs., exec. asst. dir. Phoenix Youth Ctr.-Club Unified, Ft. Wayne, 2003—06. Named Advocate of Yr., League for the Blind and Disabled, 2002; recipient Disting. Graduate award, Decatur (Ind.) Cath. Elem. and HS, 2003. Mem.: Am. Guild Organists. Avocations: gardening, hiking, swimming, piano, organ. Office Phone: 260-493-3893. Personal E-mail: murphymuse@yahoo.com.

**MURPHY, ROSEMARY,** actress; b. Munich; came to U.S., 1939; d. Robert D. and Mildred (Taylor) M. Student, Paris, France and Kansas City, Mo. Broadway appearances include Look Homeward Angel, 1958, Night of the Iguana, World premier at Spoleto (Italy) Festival of Two Worlds, 1959, Period of Adjustment, 1961, King Lear, 1963, Any Wednesday, 1964-66, Delicate Balance, 1966, Weekend, 1968, Butterflies are Free, 1970, Lady Macbeth, Stratford, Conn., 1973, Ladies of the Alamo, 1977, John Gabriel Borkman, 1980, Learned Ladies, 1982, Coastal Disturbances, 1987, The Devil's Disciple, 1988, A Delicate Balance, 1996, Waiting in the Wings, 1999; motion picture appearances include To Kill a Mockingbird, 1962, Any Wednesday, 1966, Ben, 1972, Walking Tall, 1972, You'll Like My Mother, 1972, Forty Carats, 1973, Julia, 1976, September, 1987, For the Boys, 1991, And The Band Played On, 1993, The Tuskegee Airmen, 1995, Message in a Bottle, 1998, Dust, 2001, The Savages, 2006; TV appearance Eleanor and Franklin, 1975 (Emmy award for best supporting actress 1976), George Washington, 1983 (Tony award nominations 1961, 64, 67, award Motion Picture Arts Club 1966), E-Z Streets, 1996, The Unicorn's Secret, 1998, Frasier, 1997, 99. Recipient Variety Poll award, 1961, 67. Address: 220 E 73rd St New York NY 10021-4319

**MURPHY, SANDRA ROBISON,** lawyer; b. Detroit, July 28, 1949; m. Richard Robin. BA, Northwestern U., 1971; JD, Loyola U., Chgo., 1976. Bar: U.S. Dist. Ct. (no. dist.) Ill. 1976. Assoc. Nuzzi, Craven, Mead, Maloney & Price, Chgo., 1976-78; ptnr. McDermott, Will & Emery, Chgo., 1978—. Mem. ABA (family law sect.), Ill. Bar Assn. (chair sect. family law coun. 1987-88), Chgo. Bar Assn. (chair matrimonial law com. 1988-90), Am. Acad. Matrimonial Lawyers (sec. 1990-91, v.p. 1991-92, pres. Ill. chpt. 1992-93, pres.-elect 1994-95, pres. 1995-96), Legal Club Chgo. Business E-Mail: smurphy@mwe.com.

**MURPHY, SHARON B.,** health facility administrator; b. Chgo., Oct. 19, 1943; m. Frank L. Murphy, Dec. 7, 1969 (div. 1975); 1 child, James Edward. BS, U. Wis., 1965; Med. Diplomate, Harvard U., 1969. Diplomate Am. Bd. of Pediat., 1974, Sub-Board of Pediatric Hematology, Oncology, 1974, Nat. Bd. of Med. Examiners, 1970. Asst. mem. St. Jude Children's Rsch. Hosp., Memphis, 1976—78, assoc. mem., 1979—85, full mem., 1985—88; divsn. chief Children's Meml. Hosp., Divsn. of Hematology, Oncology, Chgo., 1988—2002; dir. U. of Tex. Health Sci. Ctr. at San Antonio, Children's Cancer Rsch. Inst., 2002—. Cons. Oncology Drug Adv. Com., Ctr. for Drug Evaluation, FDA, HHS, 2004—. Recipient Return of the Child, Leukemia and Lymphoma Soc., 2002, Outstanding Achievement in Clin. Rsch., Assn. of Cmty. Cancer Ctrs., 2001, Phi Beta Kappa, U. of Wis., 1964. Mem.: Am. Cancer Soc. (bd. of directors mem. 1986—90), Am.Assoc. for Cancer Rsch. (bd. of directors 1991—94), Am. Soc. of Clinical Oncology (bd. of directors mem. 1982—85), Am. Soc. of Hematology (exec. com. mem. 2003), Texans for Advancement of Med. Rsch. (bd. dirs. 2004), Lymphoma Rsch. Found. (sci. adv. bd. 2002), Alpha Omega Alpha. Home: 13230 Hunters Lark San Antonio TX 78230 Office: Children's Cancer Rsch Inst 8403 Floyd Curl Dr MC 7784 San Antonio TX 78229 Office Phone: 210-562-9000. Office Fax: 210-562-9014. E-mail: murphysb@uthscsa.edu.

**MURPHY, SHARON MARGARET,** retired communications educator; b. Milw., Aug. 2, 1940; d. Adolph Leonard and Margaret Ann (Hirtz) Feyen; m. James Emmett Murphy, June 28, 1969 (dec. May 1983); children: Shannon Lynn, Erin Ann; m. Bradley B. Niemcek, Aug. 7, 1999. BA, Marquette U., 1965; MA, U. Iowa, 1970, PhD, 1973. Cert. K-14 tchr., Iowa. Tchr. elem. and secondary schs., Wis., 1959-69; dir. publs. Kirkwood C.C., Cedar Rapids, Iowa, 1969-71; instr. journalism U. Iowa, Iowa City, 1971-73; asst. prof. U. Wis., Milw., 1973-79; assoc. prof. So. Ill. U., Carbondale, 1979-84; dean, prof. Marquette U., Milw., 1984-94; prof. Bradley U., Peoria, Ill., 1994—2006, provost, v.p. acad. affairs, 1994-97, pres. Cmty. Career and Tech. Ctr., 1997-98, prof. emeritus, 2006. Pub. rels. dir., editor Worldwide mag., Milw., 1965—68; reporter Milw. Sentinel, 1967; Fulbright sr. lectr. U. Nigeria, Nsukka, 1977—78; Fulbright sr. scholar U. Ljubljana, Slovenia, 2002. Author: Other Voices: Black, Chicano & American Indian Press, 1971; (with Wigal) Screen Experience: An Approach to Film, 1968; (with Murphy) Let My People Know: American Indian Journalism, 1981; (with Schilpp) Great Women of the Press, 1983; editor: (with others) International Perspectives on News, 1982. Mem. Peoria Riverfront Commn., 1995—2000; co-chair Peoria Race Rels. Com., 1999—2000; mem. NCA Higher Learning Commn.; bd. dirs. Dirksen Congl. Leadership Ctr., 1994—2000, Dow Jones Newspaper Fund, NY, 1986—95, Peoria Symphony, 1996—2002. Recipient Merit medal Journalism Edn. Assn., 1976, Tchg. Excellence award Amoco, 1977, Outstanding Achievement award Greater Milw. YWCA, 1989, Paul Snider Tchg. Excellence award Bradley U., 2005; named Knight of Golden Quill, Milw. Press Club, 1977; Nat. headliner Women in Comm., Inc., 1985. Mem. Assn. Edn. in Journalism and Mass Comm. (pres. 1986-87), Soc. Profl. Journalists, Nat. Press Club, Accrediting Coun.on Edn. in Journalism and Mass Comm. (v.p. 1983-86). Democrat. Roman Catholic. Office: Bradley U Global Comm Ctr Peoria IL 61625-0001 Business E-Mail: smm@bradley.edu.

**MURPHY, SHEIGLA BRIGHID,** sociologist, researcher; b. San Francisco, Calif., July 31, 1949; children: Moira O'Neil children: Sarah M. O'Neil. PhD, U. of Calif. San Francisco, 1992. Dir. Ctr. for Substance Abuse Studies Inst. for Sci. Analysis, San Francisco 1977—. Peer reviewer Nat. Inst. of Drug Abuse, Bethesda, Md., 1992—; reviewer Jour. Ethnicity and Substance Abuse, 2004—06, Jour. Drug Issues. Author (with others): Cocaine Changes: The Experience of Using and Quitting, 1991, Pregnant Women on Drugs: Combating Stereotypes and Stigma, 1999. Mem. Harm Reduction Therapy Ctr., San Francisco, 2001—06. Recipient 11 RO1 grants, NIH, 1977—2008. Mem.: NIH Alumni Assn., Soc. for the Study of Social Problems (mem. drinking and drugs sect. 1995—97, Sr. Scholar award 2005), Am. Sociol. Assn. (chair tobacco, alcohol and drug sect. 2003—05), Am. Soc. of Criminology (chair drugs and crime divsns. 1999—2000). Democrat. Avocations: travel, reading, gardening. Office: Inst for Sci Analysis 2nd FL Ste D 390 4th St San Francisco CA 94107 Office Phone: 415-777-2352. Personal E-mail: sheigla@aol.com.

**MURPHY, STACIA,** health service association executive; BA, Talladega Coll. With Cmty. Service Soc., N.Y. City Mission Soc., NY State Divsn. Youth, Alcoholism Coun. of N.Y.; exec. dir. NYC affiliate Nat. Coun. on Alcoholism and Drug Dependence, Inc., 1990-99, pres. NYC, 1999—2005. Office: Nat Coun Alcoholism and Drug Dependence 22 Cortlandt St Ste 801 New York NY 10007-3128 Office Phone: 212-269-7797. Business E-Mail: president@ncadd.org.

**MURPHY, STEPHEN JOSEPH, III,** prosecutor; b. St. Louis, Sept. 23, 1962; s. Stephen Joseph and Mary Elizabeth Murphy; m. Amy Elizabeth Uhl, June 8, 1996. BS, Marquette U., 1984; JD, St. Louis U., 1987. Mar: Mo. 1987, Mich. 1998. Trial atty. US Dept. Justice, Washington, 1987-92, asst. U.S. atty. (ea. dist.) Mich. Detroit, 1992-2000; asst. gen. counsel Gen. Motors Corp., Detroit, 2000—05; U.S. atty. Eastern Dist. Mich., Detroit, 2005—. Adj. prof. trial practice, bus. crime U. Detroit Mercy, 1993-2000; adj. prof. evidence Ave. Maria, 2002; master of the bench Am. Inn of Ct., Detroit, 1996-99. Contbr. articles to profl. jours. Big brother Big Bros./Big Sisters of S.E. Mich., Southfield, 1993-96; co-chmn. Combined Fed. Campaign, Detroit, 1993. Recipient Commendation, Bur. ATF, 1993, Letter of Thanks from Dir. of FBI, 1996, Commendation, U.S. Secret Svc., 1998, Commendation, Detroit FBI, 1999, Commendation, Motion Picture Assn. Am., 1999. Mem. State Bar Mich. (bd. commrs. 2002-05, com. rules criminal procedure 2001-05), Fed. Bar Assn., Nat. Lawyers Assn., Pros. Attys. Assn. Mich. Roman Catholic. Office: US Attys Office 211 W Fort St #2001 Detroit MI 48226-3211 Business E-Mail: stephen.j.murphy@usdoj.gov.*

**MURPHY, TERENCE MARTIN,** biology professor; b. Seattle, July 1, 1942; s. Norman Walter and Dorothy Louise (Smith) M.; m Judith Baron, July 12, 1969; 1 child, Shannon Elaine Knotts. BS, Calif. Inst. Tech., 1964; PhD, U. Calif. San Diego, La Jolla, 1968. Sr. fellow dept. biochemistry U. Wash., Seattle, 1969-70; asst. prof. botany U. Calif., Davis, 1971-76, assoc. prof., 1976-82, prof. plant biology, 1982—, chmn. dept. botany, 1986-90. Author: Plant Molecular Development, 1988; co-author: Plant Biology, 1998, 2nd edit. 2006; N.Am. exec. editor, N.Am. office, Physiologia Plantarum, 1988-98; contbr. articles to profl. jours. Mem. AAAS, Am. Soc. Plant Biologists, Am. Soc. Photobiology, Scandinavian Soc. Plant Physiology. Home: 725 N Campus Way Davis CA 95616-3518 Office: U Calif Sect Plant Biology Davis CA 95616 Office Phone: 530-752-2413. E-mail: tmmurphy@ucdavis.edu.

**MURPHY, THELMA ARABELLA,** elementary school educator, photographer; b. Cardston, Alta., Can., June 12, 1947; arrived in U.S., 1986; d. Raymond and Isabella (Many Feathers) King; m. Laurence Patrick Murphy, May 12, 1971. EdB, U. Lethbridge, Alta., 1976. Cert. tchr. Hawaii, grad. Profl. Devel. and Svc. Program 2004. Tchr. Dept. Indian Affairs, Edmonton, Alta., 1971—80, Edmonton Pub. Sch. Bd., 1980—86; tchr. spl. edn. Highlands Intermediate Sch., Pearl City, Hawaii, 1986—87; tchr. St. Theresa Sch., Honolulu, 1987—. Profl. wedding photographer, 1980—. Author poetry. Recipient scholarship, U. Lethbridge, 1967; scholar, Dept. Indian Affairs, 1967—71. Mem.: Nat. Cath. Edn. Assn., Indian Rights for Indian Women (sec. 1971—85). Roman Catholic. Avocations: photography, writing, reading, beading, sewing. Business E-Mail: murphyf008@hawaii.rr.com.

**MURPHY, THEODORE R., II,** utilities executive; BA in Econs., Trinity Coll., 1980; MBA in Fin., Columbia U., 1986. Chartered fin. analyst. Asst. v.p., comml. loan officer Conn. Bank and Trust; dir. credit risk mgmt. Philbro Energy; v.p. power mktg. and trading AIG Trading; v.p., market risks Enron Corp., 1997—2000; sr. v.p., chief risk officer Enron Europe Ltd., 2001—02; sr. v.p. Cinergy Corp., Cin., 2002—, chief risk officer, 2002—. Mem. com. chief risk officers Cinergy Corp. Office: Cinergy Corp 139 E 4th St Cincinnati OH 45202

**MURPHY, THOMAS J., JR.,** former mayor; b. Aug. 15, 1944; m. Mona McMahon; children Shannon, Molly, and T.J. BS in Biology and Chemistry, John Carroll U., 1967; MS in Urban Affairs/Planning summa cum laude, Hunter Coll., 1973. Vol. Peace Corps, Paraguay, 1970-72; exec. dir. Perry Hilltop Citizen's Coun., 1973-76; chem. sales rep. Alcoa, 1967-70; exec. dir. North Side Civic Devel. Coun., 1976-78; state rep. 20th Legis. Dist., 1979-94; mayor City of Pitts., 1994—2006. Democrat.

**MURPHY, THOMAS JOHN,** publishing executive; b. Lockport, NY, Mar. 29, 1931; s. Matthew J. and Mary Frances (Tracy) M.; m. Maryanne Elizabeth Stadnicki, Dec. 29, 1956; children: Kevin, Janine, Peter, Thomas. BS, SUNY-Brockport, 1952; postgrad., Boston U., 1955-57, Northwestern U., 1976. Sales rep., asst. dir. advt., mgr. sales services, dir. tng., asst. dir. mktg., dir. mktg. McGraw-Hill Co., St. Louis, NYC, 1954-73; v.p., gen. mgr. sch. dept. Holt, Rinehart & Winston pub. CBS, Inc., NYC, 1973-78; sr. v.p. CBS Sch. Pub., 1978-80, pres., 1980-82; v.p. AICPA, 1982-88; ptnr. Profl. Pub. Svcs. Co., Kensington, Conn., 1988—; pres. World Book Pubs., 1991. Contbr. articles to profl. jours. Bd. dirs. Brockport Found., 1977-83, Rec. for Blind, 1980-89, Inter-Faith Housing Assn., 1991-94; mem. social concerns com. Ch. of Assumption, Westport, 2000—; docent New Britain Mus. Am. Art; mem. Commn. for Aging, Berlin, Conn., 2006—. Named to Heritage Hall of Fame, SUNY. Democrat. Roman Catholic. Home and Office: 145 Robindale Dr Kensington CT 06037-2053 Office Phone: 860-829-7266. Personal E-mail: pps2000@comcast.net.

**MURPHY, THOMAS MICHAEL,** civil engineer; b. Hubbard, Ohio, Mar. 26, 1963; s. Michael F. Jr. and Gratia Marie (Henry) M.; m. Regina Marie Quinn, Mar. 28, 1992; 1 child, Caitlin Marie. BS, Youngstown State U., 1988. Cert. asst. team leader N.Y.C. Dept. Transp., N.Y. State Dept. Transp., N.Y. State Thruway Authority. Structural engr. Marsico & Assocs., Youngstown, Ohio, 1987; constrn. inspector Adlaka & Assocs., Boardman, Ohio, 1987, Marsico & Assocs., Youngstown, 1987; structural engr. Hardesty & Hanover, N.Y.C., 1988-94, A&H Engrs., N.Y.C., 1994, Ammann & Whitney, N.Y.C., 1995-96, M.S. Cons., Youngstown, 1996; quality assurance/quality control engr. Star Aluminum Extrusions, Canfield, Ohio, 1997-99; civil engr. PSI Inc., Pitts., 1999-2000, Youngstown, Ohio, 2000—01, ACA Engring., 2001—. Mem. ASCE (affiliate mem. N.Y. met. chpt. and Youngstown State U. chpt.) Am. Soc. Cert. Engring. Technicians (mem., sec.-tres. Youngstown State U. Steel Valley chpt. 1985-86), KC (3d and 4th degree). Democrat. Roman Catholic. Avocations: photography, new technology in bridge design and construction. Office: ACA Bldg 10B 590 Western Reserve Rd Poland OH 44514 Home: 210 Christian Ave Hubbard OH 44425-2010

**MURPHY, THOMAS PATRICK,** lawyer; b. Syracuse, NY, Feb. 12, 1952; s. George Edward and Sara Eileen (Murphy) M.; m. Susan Hollis Francher, Oct. 19, 1976 (div. Oct. 1992); m. Lise M. Adkins, Aug. 6, 1994; children: Casey Marie, Matthew Thomas. BS, Clarkson U., 1974; JD, Vt. Law Sch., 1978. Bar: N.Y. 1978, D.C. 1981, Md. 1988, Va. 1989. Asst. U.S. atty. U.S. Atty.'s Office, Washington, 1982—85; assoc. Highsaw & Mahoney, Washington, 1985—87, McGuire, Woods, Battle & Boothe, Washington, 1987—90; ptnr. Reed Smith Shaw & McClay, McLean, Va., 1990—99, Hunton & Williams, McLean, 1999—. Contbr. articles to profl. jours. Chmn. bd. profl. responsibility D.C. Ct. Appeals With USN, 1978-82, USNR, 1978-90. Recipient Spl. Achievement award US Dept. Justice, 1984; named one of Best Lawyers in Am. for employment law. Mem. ABA, Fed. Bar Assn., N.Y. State Bar Assn., D.C. Bar Assn. (chmn. pro se litigants com.), Md. Bar Assn., Asst. U.S. Attys., Bd. Profl. Responsibility D.C. Ct. Appeals (hearing com.). Office: Hunton & Williams 1751 Pinnacle Dr Ste 1700 Mc Lean VA 22102-3836 Office Phone: 703-714-7533. Business E-Mail: tpmurphy@hunton.com.

**MURPHY, TIMOTHY F.,** congressman; b. Cleve., Sept. 11, 1952; s. John and Florence Murphy; m. Nanette Missign, Aug. 23, 1975; 1 child, Bevin. BS, Wheeling Jesuit U., 1974; MA, Cleve. State U., 1976; PhD in Psych., U. Pitts., 1979. Mem. Pa. State Senate from Dist. 37, Harrisburg, 1997—2002, US Congress from 18th Pa. dist., 2003—, mem. energy and commerce com., co-chair Congl. Mental Health Caucus, mem. 21st Century Healthcare Caucus. Chmn. aging and youth com. Pa. State Senate, chmn. pub. health and welfare com., comm. and high tech. com., cmty. and econ. devel. com., edn. com., health care task force; asst. prof. U. Pitts. Sch. Medicine. Author: The Angry Child, Overcoming Passive-Aggression. Bd. dirs. Head Start, Alliance for Infants, Parents Helping Parents, Korean War Vets. Western Pa. Meml. Fund; founding dir. Sr. Aides Employment Svc.; mem. St. Thomas More Ch., Bethel Park, Pa.; mem. adv. bd. Allegheny Co. Ct. of Common Pleas Family Ct. Divsn., steering com. on children's issues roundtable; mem. US Mil. Acad. Rev. Bd. Mem. Pa. Perinatal Assn. (bd. dirs.), Bethel Park C. of C., South Park C. of C., Brentwood-Baldwin-Whitehall C. of C., Greater Bridgeville C. of C., Sons of Am. Legion Republican. Roman Catholic. Office: US Ho Reps 322 Cannon Ho Office Bldg Washington DC 20515 Office Phone: 202-225-2301.*

**MURPHY, TIMOTHY JAMES,** lawyer; b. Topeka, Sept. 30, 1946; s. Miles J. and Norine D. Murphy; m. Patricia MacKinnon, Apr. 7, 1990. BA, U. Ga., 1968; JD with honors, Washington & Lee U., 1970; LLM, Harvard U., 1976. Bar: Va. 1970, Fla. 1972. Atty. Anderson, Mori & Rabinowitz, Tokyo, 1970—71, Shutts & Bowen, Miami, Fla., 1976—. Contbr. articles to profl. jours. Mem. Fla. Ho. of Reps., 1982-84; bd. dirs. Cath. Charities, Inc., 1982-97, Cath. Charities Legal Svcs., Inc., Miami, 2000—, The Barnacle soc., 1991-2002, pres. 2000-02; mem. adv. bd. Miami-Dade County Pub. Libr., 1980-2002. Col. JAG Corps USAFR, 1971-95. Mem.: Biscayne Bay Yacht Club, Army and Navy Club (Washington). Democrat. Roman Catholic. Avocation: sailing. Office: Shutts & Bowen 201 S Biscayne Blvd Ste 1500 Miami FL 33131-4308 Office Phone: 305-379-9137.

**MURPHY, TIMOTHY W.,** music educator; b. Takoma Park, Md., Oct. 2, 1969; s. Warren and Caroline Murphy. MusB, Stetson U., 1991; MusM, La. State U., 1993. Piano tchr. Stetson U., Cmty. Sch. of Arts, DeLand, Fla., 1994—. Accompanist Datyona Beach Choral Soc., Fla., 2001—; pianist New Heights Cmty. Ch., Holly Hill, Fla., 2003—. Mem.: Nat. Guild of Piano Tchrs., Fla. Fedn. of Music Clubs, Volusia County Music Tchrs. Assn. (pres. 1993—). Republican. Assembly Of God. Avocations: travel, music.

**MURPHY, WILLIAM ALEXANDER, JR.,** diagnostic radiologist, educator; b. Pitts., Apr. 26, 1945; s. William Alexander and LaRue (Eshbaugh); m. Judy Marie Lang, June 18, 1977; children: Abigail Norris, William Lawrence, Joseph Ryan. BS, U. Pitts., 1967; MD, Pa. State U., 1971. Diplomate Am. Bd. Radiology. Intern Barnes Hosp., St. Louis, 1971-72, staff radiologist, 1975-93; radiology resident Washington U., St. Louis, 1972-75, prof. radiology, 1983-93; sec. chief Mallinckrodt Inst. Radiology, St. Louis, 1975-93; cons. Office Med. Examiner City and County St. Louis, 1993—. Radiologist, prof. radiology, John S. Dunn Sr. prof., disting. chair MD Anderson Cancer Ctr. U. Tex., 1993—, v.p. hosp. and clinics, 1996-97, COO, 1997; chmn. bd. dirs. MD Anderson Physicians Network Corp., 2001—. Fellow Am. Acad. Forensic Scis., Am. Coll. Radiology; mem. Radiol. Soc. N.Am. (1st. v.p. 1997-98), Am. Roentgen Ray Soc., Am. Soc. Bone and Mineral Rsch., Internat. Skeletal Soc., Assn. Univ. Radiologists. Methodist. Home: 4808 Bellview St Bellaire TX 77401-5306 Office: U Texas Anderson Cancer Ctr Div Dx Imaging 057 1515 Holcombe Blvd Houston TX 77030-4009 Office Phone: 713-792-4916. Business E-Mail: wmurphy@di.mdacc.tmc.edu.

**MURPHY-DANIELS, KAREN ILENE,** environmental services administrator, safety engineer; b. Oak Ridge, Tenn., May 20, 1955; d. Charles Everett and Charlotte Wilson Murphy; m. Richard C. Daniels, Dec. 5, 1997. BS in Transp. and Mktg., U. Tenn, 1977; MS in Occupl. Safety & Health, U. Tenn., 1982. CSP BSCP, REM & CEA Nat. Registry Environ. Profls., CHMM Inst. Hazardous Material Mgmt., ISO 14001 environ. mgmt. systems provisional auditor, cert. AHERA asbestos bldg. inspector, fall protection component person, 501 OSHA industry instr. Project mgr., comml. market mgr. Analysas Corp./DPRA, Oak Ridge, 1988—96; owner, mgmt. cons. SAFE Systems, Seattle, 1996—97; ESH specialist Boeing, Seattle, 1997—. Vol. cons. Wash. Dept. Ecology, Lacey, 1997; chair Boeing Nat. Safety Tech. Com., Seattle. Vol. Habitat for Humanity; bd. dirs. Puget Sound IHMM, Puget Sound Habitat for Humanity, 2002—. Mem.: Am. Soc. Quality, Am. Indsl. Hygiene Assn., Am. Soc. Safety Engrs. (treas., sec. East Tenn. chpt. 1988—90, v.p. Puget Sound 2003—04, bd. dir., pres. Puget Sound). Democrat. Avocations: kayaking, snowshoeing, dog training, horseback riding. Office Phone: 253-592-0818. Business E-Mail: karen.i.murphy-daniels@boeing.com. E-mail: eshanalysis@aol.com.

**MURPHY-PILON, MONICA,** cultural organization administrator; BA in Sociology, Iona Coll., 1993. Spl. events mgr. N.Y. U. Downtown Hosp., 1994—98; dir. fund devel. Northside Ctr. Child Devel., 1998—2000; dir. instl. giving Cmty. Svc. Soc., 2001—. Scholar, USMC, 1989—92. Mem.: Women In Devel., Assn. Fundraising Profls. Conservative-R.

**MURR, JAMES COLEMAN,** retired federal agency administrator; b. Lake Charles, La., Oct. 29, 1944; m. Connie Paige Chadwell, Sept. 21, 1968; children: Christopher David, Richard Reno. BA, Tex. Tech U., 1966; MPA, Am. U., 1974. With Sears, Roebuck & Co., Tex., 1971-72, Dept. Labor, Washington, 1972-74; U.S. Customs Svc., Treasury, Washington, 1975-76; legis. analyst Office Mgmt. and Budget, Washington, 1977-81, br. chief, 1982-89, assoc. dir. administrn., 1990-93, asst. dir. legis. reference, 1994-98. Capt. USAF, 1967-70. Roman Catholic. E-mail: jcmurr@cebridge.net.

**MURRAH, ANN RALLS FREEMAN,** historical association executive; b. Gadsden, Ala., June 23, 1932; d. Oscar William Freeman, Sr. and Annie Collier (Ralls) Freeman; m. Robert Leland Murrah, Aug. 9, 1952; children: Frances Ralls Murrah Lovett, Robert Leland Murrah Jr. Grad., Brenau U., 1954. Pres. Gen. Descendants of the Signers of the Constn., Orlando, Fla., 1991—. Rep. Fla. 8th congl. dist. Congl. Sr. Intern Program, Wash., 1998; keynote spkr. Feminist Summit for Global Peace, Taipei, Taiwan, 1995; mem. protocol & hospitality coms. for equestrian events 1996 Olympics; mem. Am. com. Ball des Rosenkavaliers, Vienna, 1989—90; bd. dir. Arnold Palmer Hosp. Bd., Orlando, Fla.; founder Nat. Constn. Ctr., Phila., 2003—; spkr. in field. Mem. women's com. N.Y. U. Downtown Hosp., 1996—99; gala chmn. Winter Pk. Health Found., Winter Pk., Fla., 1996; ball chmn. Arnold Palmer Hosp. for Women & Children, Orlando, Fla., 1997—99, 2001; mem. Orlando Regional Healthcare Found., Orlando; active Coun. of 101-Orlando Mus. Art; v. chmn. dinner com. fundraiser March of Dimes, 1998. Named First Woman Knighted in her own right, Order of St. John of Jerusalem, 1992; named to Brenau U. Alumni Hall of Fame, 2001; recipient Meritorious Svc. award, Sons of the Am. Revolution, 1986, Martha Washington medal, 1988, The Rallye Saintogeais Hunt award, Foret De La Coubre, France, 1988. Mem.: DAR (1st vice-regent), Nat. Soc. Dames Am., Met. Opera Guild, Plantagenet Soc., Washington Soc., Gavel Soc., Fla. Opera Guild, Nat. Steeplechase Assn., Shakerag Hunt Club (awarded colors), Nat. Soc. of Colonial Dames, Daus. of the Cin., Sovereign Colonial Soc. Am. of Royal Descent, Sonsand Daus. of the Pilgrims (pres. in Ga. 1992—94, historian gen. of the U.S. 1994—97, first vice-gov.), Descs. of Knights of the Garter, Colonial Dames of Am., Colonial Order of the Crown, Magna Charta Dames (herald and courier), Alpha Delta Pi (province pres., dir. ritual and paraphernalia). Home and Office: Soc of Descendants of Signers of Constitution 903 Sussex Close Orlando FL 32804

**MURRAY, ALICE PEARL,** data processing company executive; b. Clearfield, Pa., Aug. 4, 1932; d. James Clifford and Leah Mae (Williams) Murray. BS, Pa. State U., Univ. Park, 1954. With IBM, 1954—, sys. svc. rep. Pitts., 1954—56, computer test ctr. rep. Endicott, NY, 1956—58, edn. devel. coord., 1958—59, adv. instr. L.A., 1959—63, staff instr., 1963—68, exec. edn. coord., 1968—74; sr. instr. Info. Sys. Mgmt. Inst. IBM, 1974—84; sr.

edn. rep. IBM Ams. Far East Corp., 1984—87; sr. staff mem. customer exec. edn. IBM, 1989, ind. cons., 1995—. Exhibit coord. Calif. State Mus. Sci. and Industry; guest spkr. civic and profl. groups; guest instr. univs. and colls.; profl. lectr. Named hon. citizen, Tex., Alaska; recipient Distinguished Educator award, IBM, 1974, Outstanding Professionalism award, 1975. Mem.: L.A. Litre. Found., L.A. County Art Mus., Assistance League So. Calif., Wilshire Country Club, Pa. State Alumni Assn., Delta Delta Delta. Republican. Home and Office: 514 S Gramercy Pl Apt 16 Los Angeles CA 90020-4969 Office Phone: 213-384-2316.

**MURRAY, ANDREW W.,** biology professor, researcher; PhD, Harvard U., 1984. Postdoctoral rschr. Harvard Med. Sch.; part-time lectr. Yale U., 1985—86; postdoctoral rschr. U. Calif., San Francisco, asst. prof. dept. physiology, 1989—94, assoc. prof., 1994—2000; prof. molecular and cell biology, dir. Bauer Ctr. Genomics Rsch. Harvard U., Cambridge, Mass., 2000—. Spkr. in field. Contbr. articles to profl. jours. Fellow, David and Lucile Packard Found., 1991. Mem.: Am. Soc. Cell Biology. Achievements include research in the function and evolution of cells; chromosome behavior during meiosis and mitosis. Office: Harvard Univ Dept Molecular and Cell Biology 16 Divinity Ave Rm 3000 Cambridge MA 02138 Office Phone: 617-496-1350. E-mail: amurray@mcb.harvard.edu.*

**MURRAY, ANNE,** singer; b. Springhill, NS, Can., June 20, 1945; d. Carson and Marion (Burke) M.; m. William M. Langstroth, June 20, 1975; children: William Stewart, Dawn Joanne. B.Phys. Edn., U. N.B., 1966, D.Litt. (hon.), 1978, St. Mary's U., 1982. Rec. artist for Arc Records, Canada, 1968, Capital/EMI Records, 1969—. Appeared on series of TV spls. CBC, 1970—81, 1988—93; star CBS spls., 1981—85; toured N. Am., Japan, Englan, Germany, Holland, Ireland, Sweden, Australia and New Zealand, 1977—82. Singer: (31 albums including) A Little Good News, 1984, (albums) As I Am, 1988, Greatest Hits, vol. I, 1981, vol. II, 1989, Harmony, 1987, You Will, 1990, Yes I Do, 1991, Croonin', 1993, The Best So Far, 1994, Now and Forever, Anne Murray, 1996, An Intimate Evening with Anne Murray-Live, 1997, What A Wonderful World, 1999, What A Wonderful Christmas, 2001, Country Croonin', 2002. Hon. chmn. Can. Save the Children Fund, 1978-80. Recipient Juno awards as Can.'s top female vocalist, 1970-81; Can.'s Top Country Female Vocalist, 1970-86; Grammy award as top female vocalist-country, 1974; Grammy award as top female vocalist-pop, 1978; Grammy award as top female vocalist-country, 1980, 83; Country Music Assn. awards, 1983-84; named Female Rec. Artist of Decade, Can. Rec. Industry Assn., 1980, Top Female Vocalist 1970-86; star inserted in Hollywood Walkway of Stars, 1980; Country Music Hall of Fame Nashville; decorated companion Order of Can.; inducted Juno Hall of Fame, 1993. Mem: AFTRA, Assn. Canadian TV and Radio Artists; Am. Fedn. Musicians. Office: Bruce Allen Talent No 500 425 Carrall St Vancouver BC Canada V6B6E3 also: Emi Music 1750 Vine St Los Angeles CA 90028-5209

**MURRAY, ANTHONY,** lawyer; b. LA, Apr. 25, 1937; s. Bernard Anthony and Frances Louise (Simpson) M.; children— Matthew Anthony, Thomas Andrew. JD, Loyola U., Los Angeles, 1964. Bar: Calif. 1965. Assoc. firm Ball, Hunt & Hart, Long Beach, Calif., 1964-68; ptnr. Hitt & Murray, 1968-79, Ball, Hunt, Hart, Brown & Baerwitz, Los Angeles, 1979-95, Loeb & Loeb LLP, 1995—. Instr. Calif. State U., 1966; adj. prof. Loyola U. Los Angeles, 1975-85; active various profl. cons.; guest lectr. and panelist various legal subjects before numerous groups. Contbr. articles to legal jours. Fellow Am. Coll. Trial Lawyers (bd. regents 1995-99, mem. Calif. jud. coun. 1983-85); mem. ABA, Chancery Club, LA County Bar Assn., Long Beach Bar Assn., State Bar Calif. (bd. govs. 1980-83, pres. 1982-83, numerous other positions). Democrat. Office: Loeb & Loeb LLP 10100 Santa Monica Blvd Ste 2200 Los Angeles CA 90067-4120 Office Phone: 310-282-2000.

**MURRAY, ANTHONY DAVID,** music educator, director; b. Metter, Ga., Dec. 22, 1979; s. Jon David and Melba Gail Murray. BA in Music Edn., Armstrong Atlantic StateU., Savannah, Ga., 2003. Dir. bands mid. sch. Effingham County Bd. Edn., Springfield, Ga., 2003—. Musician: Savannah (Ga.) Jazz Orch., 1999—. Named Star Student, Effingham County, 1998; recipient John Philip Sousa award, 1998, Louis Armstrong award, 1998; scholar, Coastal Jazz Assn. Mem.: Nat. Music Educators Assn. Avocations: fishing, baseball, football, music, camping. Home: 105 Rosewood Dr Guyton GA 31312

**MURRAY, BILL,** actor, writer; b. Wilmette, Ill., Sept. 21, 1950; s. Edward and Lucille Murray; m. Margaret Kelly, 1980 (div. 1994); children: Homer, Luke; m. Jennifer Butler, July 4, 1997; children: Jackson, Cal, Cooper, Lincoln. Student, Regis Coll., Denver, Second City Workshop, Chgo. Owner minor league baseball team the Riverdogs, Charleston, SC; co-owner Caddyshack Restaurant, Jacksonville, Fla. Performer, Second City Comedy Troupe, 1973-75; voice, Nat. Lampoon Radio Hour, 1975; actor, writer, Saturday Night Live, 1977-80; Film appearances include Next Stop, Greenwich Village, 1976, Meatballs, 1979, Mr. Mike's Mondo Video, 1979, Where the Buffalo Roam, 1980, Caddyshack, 1980, Loose Shoes, 1980, Stripes, 1981, Tootsie, 1982, Ghostbusters, 1984, The Razor's Edge, 1984, Nothing Lasts Forever, 1984, Little Shop of Horrors, 1986, Scrooged, 1988, Ghostbusters II, 1989, What About Bob?, 1991, Groundhog Day, 1993, Mad Dog and Glory, 1993, Ed Wood, 1994, Kingpin, 1996, Larger Than Life, 1996, Space Jam, 1996, The Man Who Knew Too Little, 1997, With Friends Like These, 1998, Veeck As In Wreck, 1998, Rushmore, 1998, Wild Things, 1998, The Cradle Will Rock, 1999, Scout's Honor, 1999, Hamlet, 1999, Company Man, 1999, Charlie's Angels, 2000, Speaking of Sex, 2001, The Royal Tenenbaums, 2001, Osmosis Jones, 2001, Coffee and Cigarettes, 2003, Lost in Translation, 2003 (Golden Globe for best actor in a musical or comedy, 2004, Acad. Award nomination for best actor, 2004, Screen Actors Guild Award nomination for best actor, 2004), Garfield: The Movie (voice), 2004, The Life Acquatic with Steve Zissou, 2004, Broken Flowers, 2005, The Lost City, 2005, Garfield: A Tail of Two Kitties (voice), 2006; actor, dir., prodr. Quick Change, 1990; (TV movies) The Rutles: All you Need Is Cash, 1978; (TV series) Stories from My Childhood (voice only), 1998, The Sweet Spot, 2002 Recipient Emmy award for best writing for comedy series, 1977, Sons of the Desert Comedy Performer award, 1997. Office: Creative Artists Agy care Jessica Tuchinsky 9830 Wilshire Blvd Beverly Hills CA 90212-1825*

**MURRAY, BRIAN,** publishing executive; Cons. media practice Booz Allen & Hamilton; dir. finance and analysis, adult book trade HarperCollins Publishers, 1997—98, v.p., finance and publishing operations, 1998—99, sr. v.p., mng. dir. gen. books group, 1999—2001; CEO HarperCollins Australia/New Zealand, 2001—04; group pres. HarperCollins Publishers, 2004—. Office: HarperCollins 10 E 53rd St New York NY 10022

**MURRAY, BRYAN CLARENCE,** professional hockey coach; b. Shawville, Que., Can., Dec. 5, 1942; came to U.S., 1980; s. Clarence Herbert and Rhoda (Schwartz) M.; m. Geraldine Frances Sutton, July 8, 1967; 1 dau.. Heide Alicia. Grad., McGill U., 1964. Former athletic dir., hockey coach McGill U.; athletic dir. MacDonald Coll., Ste. Anne de Bellevue, Que., 1968-72; coach tchr. Rockland Nat.-Pontiac High Sch., Rockland, Ont., 1974-76; coach Pembroke-Kings, Pembroke, Ont., 1976-79. Regina Pats, Sask., 1979-80, Hershey (Pa.) Bears, 1980-81; former coach Washington Capitals, Landover, Md., from 1981; coach, gen. mgr. Detroit Red Wings, 1990-94; gen. manager Florida Panthers, Fort Lauderdale, Fla., 1994—2001; head coach Mighty Ducks Anaheim, 2001—02, gen. mgr., 2002—04; head coach Ottawa Senators, 2004—. Recipient Jack Adams award as NHL Coach of Yr., 1983-84. Office: Ottawa Senators Scotiabank Place 1000 Palladium Dr Kanata ON K2V 1A5 Canada*

**MURRAY, CARLA MARY,** sound effects artist, artist; b. North Bay, Ont., Can., Apr. 3, 1957; d. Thomas Joseph and Laura Catherine Murray; life ptnr. Paula Kathleen Fairfield. BFA, N.S. Coll. Art and Design, Halifax, Can., 1982; MFA, York U., Toronto, Ont., 1996. Cofounder, adminstrv. dir. Women's Art Resource Ctr., Toronto, 1984—91; contract art adminstr., writer, rschr. various clients Toronto, 1992—94; sound designer, sound effects editor

MHz Sound Design Inc., L.A., 1997—. Ways and means com., adminstr. Trinity Sq. Video, Toronto, 1987; author, exhbn. co-coord. Graphic Feminism: Graphic Art of the Ont. Women's Movement 1970-1986, (catalogue) Women's Movement Archives, Toronto, 1986; founding mem. Power Up L.A., 2000, vol. sound designer, sound effects editor, 2001—03. One-woman shows include Gallery 940, Toronto, Stride Gallery, Calgary, IDA Gallery, Toronto, exhibitions include Out of the Frame, Advocate Gallery, LA; sound designer, sound effects editor: (films) Spy Kids 3D: Game Over; Terminator 3: Rise of the Machines; The Adventures of Shark Boy and Lava Girl in 3D; Assault on Precinct 13; Sin City; Lucky Number Slevin; The Black Dahlia; founding mem. editl. bd.: Matriart: A Can. Feminist Art Jour., 1990—91. Bd. dirs. A Space Gallery, Toronto, 1984; jury mem. Ont. Arts Coun., Toronto, 1994. Grantee, Ont. Arts Coun., 1984—91; Explorations grantee, Can. Coun., 1984, Photography grant, 1992. Mem.: Am. Film Inst., Nat. Mus. Women in Arts, Internat. Alliance Theatrical Stage Employees, Moving Picture Technicians, Artists and Allied Crafts of the US, Its Territories and Can., Motion Picture Editor's Guild. Office Phone: 818-980-0306.

**MURRAY, CATHERINE MARY MURPHY,** retired accountant; b. Severn, Md., July 7, 1940; d. George William Murphy and Emma May Rodgers; m. Rudolph Chesley Stanley, Dec. 21, 1963 (dec. Oct. 31, 1978); children: Kenneth Michael Stanley, Mary Ellen Stanley Fahlstrom; m. Charles Edward Murray, Nov. 22, 1988 (dec. Dec. 13, 2001). Student in Early Childhood Edn., U. Maine, 1981. Classroom asst. to coord. Coastal Econ. Devel. Corp., Boothbay Harbor/Bath, Maine, 1969—81; acct. Pvt. Contractor Constrn., 1984—89; project acct. Chesapeake Sprinkler Co., Odenton, Md., 1990—2006; ret., 2006. Proofreader, asst. editor David W. Webster FSA Scot, Livingston, Scotland, 1998—; presenter in field. Author: Through the Generations, 1999, To Honor Thy Family, 1999; co-author: The Family True, 2001. Contbr. genealogy material Ch. of Jesus Christ of LDS, Salt Lake City; sponsor Anne Arundel County Scottish Festival, Inc., Crownsville, Md.; contbr. genealogy material Amesbury (Mass.) Pub. Libr. With USN, 1958—59. Avocations: genealogy, history, reading, travel, music. Personal E-mail: catherinemmurray@comcast.net.

**MURRAY, CHARLES ALAN,** social scientist; b. Newton, Iowa, Jan. 8, 1943; s. Alan Benton and Frances Bradburn (Patrick) M.; m. Suchart Dej-Udom, Aug. 19, 1966 (div. 1980); children: Narisara, Sarawan; m. Catherine Bly Cox, July 29, 1983; children: Anna, Bennett. BA, Harvard U., 1965; PhD, MIT, 1974. Scientist Am. Insts. for Rsch., Washington, 1974-79, chief scientist, 1979-81; fellow Manhattan Inst., N.Y.C., 1981-90; Bradley fellow Am. Enterprise Inst., Washington, 1990—. Author: Losing Ground, 1984, In Pursuit of Happiness and Good Government, 1988, Apollo, 1989, Human Accomplishment: The Pursuit of Excellence in the Arts and Sciences, 800 BC to 1950, 2003, In Our Hands, 2006; co-author: The Bell Curve, 1994. Office: Am Enterprise Inst 1150 17th St NW Washington DC 20036-4603

**MURRAY, CHRISTOPHER CHARLES, III,** architect; b. Bklyn., July 6, 1950; s. Christopher Charles and Gertrude Rose (Marr) M.; m. Ann Herring, Nov. 16, 1974. BArch, U. Notre Dame, 1973; MSc in Real Estate, Johns Hopkins U., 2005. Registered arch., N.Y., Md., D.C., Va., Ga. Project arch. Hibner Archs., Garden City, NY, 1973-76; project mgr. BBM Archs., N.Y.C., 1976-79; project dir. Gensler & Assocs., N.Y.C., 1979-84; office dir., v.p., mem. nat. mgmt. com. Gensler, Washington, 1984-96, internat. practice leader profl. svc. firms, 1996—. Prin. works include interior design Sidley & Austin Worldwide, McDermott, Will & Emery, Latham & Watkins, Baker McKenzie, Covington & Burling. Asst. scoutmaster Boy Scouts Am., also NCAC dist. commr.; active Greater Washington Bd. Trade, 1986. Mem. AIA, Md. Soc. Archs., Notre Dame Club, Club at Franklin Sq. Roman Catholic. Home: 12517 Knightsbridge Ct Rockville MD 20850-3732 Office: Gensler 2020 K St NW Washington DC 20006-1806 Office Phone: 202-721-5300. Business E-Mail: christopher_murray@gensler.com.

**MURRAY, DANIEL RICHARD,** lawyer; b. Mar. 23, 1946; s. Alfred W. and Gloria D. Murray. AB, U. Notre Dame, 1967; JD, Harvard U., 1970. Bar: Ill. 1970, U.S. Dist. Ct. (no. dist.) Ill. 1970, U.S. Ct. Appeals (7th cir.) 1971, U.S. Supreme Ct. 1974. Ptnr. Jenner & Block, Chgo., 1970—. Trustee Chgo. Mo. and Western Rlwy. Co., 1988-97; adj. prof. U. Notre Dame, 1997—. Co-author: Secured Transactions, 1978, Uniform Laws Annotated—Uniform Commercial Code Forms, 2001, Illinois Practice: Uniform Commercial Code Forms, 2002, Illinois Practice: Uniform Commercial Code with Illinois Code Comments, 2006. Bd. regents Big Shoulders Fund, Archdiocese of Chgo., Bernardin Ctr., Cath. Theol. Union. Mem.: Assn. Transp. Practitioners, Transp. Lawyers Assn., Am. Coll. Comml. Fin. Lawyers, Am. Bankruptcy Coll., Am. Law Inst., Am. Bankruptcy Inst., Cath. Lawyers Guild Chgo., Lawyers' Club Chgo. Roman Catholic. Home: 1307 N Sutton Pl Chicago IL 60610-2007 Office: Jenner & Block One IBM Plz Chicago IL 60611-3605 Office Phone: 312-222-9350. Business E-Mail: dmurray@jenner.com.

**MURRAY, DAVID GEORGE,** architect; b. Tulsa, Nov. 9, 1919; s. Lee Cloyd and Marion (Bennett) M.; m. Margaret Elizabeth Oldham, Sept. 23, 1944; children: Michael Allen, Lucy Margaret (Mrs. Norman Scheer), Patrick David. BArch, Okla. State U., 1942. Registered architect, Okla. Ptnr. Atkinson & Murray, Tulsa, 1949-52; prin. David G. Murray & Assocs., Tulsa, 1952-56; pres. Murray, Jones, Murray, Inc., Tulsa, 1957-85, chmn., 1986-89. Chmn., bd. govs. Licensed Architects, Oklahoma City, Tulsa 1964-74. Prin. works include Cities Service Technology Ctr., Broken Arrow, Okla.. Terminal Bldg. Tulsa Internat. Airport, St. Patrick's Ch., Oklahoma City, Coll. of Osteopathic Medicine and Surgery, Tulsa, First Nat. Tower, Tulsa, Hillcrest Med. Ctr., Tulsa, Thomas Gilcrease Mus., Tulsa, Tulsa Civic Ctr. Bldgs. Chmn., dir. Goodwill Industries of Tulsa, 1966-87; chmn., exec. com. Downtown Tulsa United, 1975-87; v.p., exec. com. Mus. Tulsa U. of U., 1979-83. Served to 1st lt. USAF, 1942-45. Named to Hall of Fame Coll. Engring. Okla. State U., 1969. Fellow AIA (pres. Tulsa chpt. 1964, mem. com. office practice 1983-87); mem. Southern Hills Country Club (dir. 1977-80). Republican. Methodist. Avocations: travel, golf.

**MURRAY, DIANE ELIZABETH,** librarian; b. Detroit, Oct. 15, 1942; d. Gordon Lisle and Dorothy Anne (Steketee) LaBoueff; m. Donald Edgar Murray, Apr. 22, 1968. AB, Hope Coll., 1964; postgrad., Mich. State U., East Lansing, 1964-66; MLS, Western Mich. U. 1968; MM, Aquinas Coll., 1982. Catalog libr., asst. head acquisitions sect. Mich. State U. Librs., East Lansing, 1968-77; libr. tech. and automated svcs. Hope Coll., Holland, Mich., 1977-88; dir. libris. DePauw U., Greencastle, Ind., 1988-91; acquisitions libr. Grand Valley State U., Allendale, Mich., 1991—. Sec., vice chair, chairperson bd. trustees Mich. Libr. Consortium, Lansing, 1981—85. V.p. Humane Soc. Putnam County, Greencastle, 1990—91; bd. dirs. Loutit Dist. Libr., 1999—. Mem.: ALA. Methodist. Avocations: dog breeding and showing, handbell ringing. Office: Grand Valley State U Zumberge Libr Allendale MI 49401 Business E-Mail: murrayd@gvsu.edu.

**MURRAY, EDWARD ROCK,** insurance broker; b. Bklyn., Jan. 31, 1947; s. Garrett Francis and Anne M. (Rock) M.; m. Barbara Marie Robotti; children: Pamela Jean, Stephanie Elise. BA in Bus. Adminstrn., St. Bonaventure U., N.Y., 1968. Claims examiner N.Y.C., 1970-72; agt. and mgr. John Hancock Life Ins., Albany, N.Y., 1972-76; regional dir. Colonial Life Insur, Albany, 1976-80; ptnr. Murray & Zuckerman, Inc., Schenectady, N.Y., 1980—. Bd. dirs Northeast Mgmt. Forum, 1997—; treas. The Mktg. Alliance. 1st lt. U.S. Army, 1968-70, Vietnam. Mem. Mohawk Club (past chmn.), Edison Club. Roman Catholic. Avocation: golf. Office: Murray & Zuckerman Inc 128 Erie Blvd Ste 2 Schenectady NY 12305-2283 Office Phone: 518-382-5483. Business E-Mail: emurray@mandzinc.com.

**MURRAY, EILEEN K.,** investment company executive; BSc in acctg., Manhattan Coll., 1980. Formerly with Peat Marwick; with Morgan Stanley, 1984—2002; v.p. Morgan Stanley Group Inc., 1988—91, prin., 1991—94, mng. dir., 1994, controller and treas.; chief adminstrv. officer, instl. securities

group Morgan Stanley Dean Witter & Co., 1999—2002; head of global tech, ops. & product control Credit Suisse First Boston, NYC, 2002—. Bd. dirs. Omgeo LLC, 2001—. Office: Credit Suisse First Boston 11 Madison Ave New York NY 10010

**MURRAY, ELIZABETH,** artist; b. Chgo., 1940; married; 1 child, Dakota Sunseri. B.F.A., Art Inst., Chgo., 1962; M.F.A., Mills Coll., Oakland, Calif., 1964; D (hon.), Art Inst., Chgo., 1992; degree (hon.), RI School Design, 1993; D (hon.), New School U., 2001. Vis. instr. Wayne State U., 1975, Calif. Inst. Arts, 1975-76, Chgo. Art Inst., 1975-76; instr. Bard Coll., Annandale on Hudson, NY, 1974-75, 76-77, Princeton U., 1977, Yale U., 1978-79. One-woman shows, Jacobs Ladder Gallery, Washington, 1974, Paula Cooper Gallery, N.Y.C., 1975, 76, 78, 81, 83, 88, 89, Jared Sable Gallery, 1975, Ohio State U., Columbus, 1978, Phyllis Kind Gallery, Chgo., 1978, Galerie Mukai, Tokyo, 1980, Susanne Hilberry Gallery, Birmingham, Mich., 1980, Smith Coll. Art Gallery, Northampton, Mass., 1982, Daniel Weinberg Gallery, Los Angeles, 1982, Portland Ctr. Visual Arts, Oreg., 1983, Knight Gallery, Charlotte, N.C., 1984, San Francisco Mus. Modern Art, 1988, Mayor Rowen Gallery, London, 1989, Barbara Krakow Gallery, Boston, 1990, Gallery Mukai, Tokyo, 1990, John Berggruen Gallery, San Francisco, 1990, Wexner Center for the Arts, 1991, 92, Jaffe-Friede Strauss Galleries, Hanover, N.H., 2005, Mus. Modern Art N.Y.C., 2005, Maier Mus. Art, Lynchburg, Va, 2005; group shows include, Whitney Mus. Am. Art, N.Y.C., 1972, 73, 77, 79, 81, 82, 84, John Doyle Gallery Cologne, Ger., 1974, Paula Cooper Gallery, 1974, 76, 77, 78, 79, 81, 82, 83, 84, Michael Walls Gallery, N.Y., 1975, Middlebury (Vt.) Coll., 1976, Gallery of July and August, Brockport, N.Y., 1976, Susanne Hilberry Gallery, Detroit, 1976, Guggenheim Mus., N.Y.C., 1977, Sarah Lawrence Coll. Gallery, Bronxville, N.Y., 1977, Lowe Art Gallery Syracuse U., 1977, Mus. Contemporary Art, Chgo., 1977, Inst. Contemporary Art, U. Pa., 1978, Tampa Bay Art Center, Fla., 1978, Phyllis Kind Gallery, Chgo., 1979, William Patterson Coll., Wayne, N.J., 1979, Susan Caldwell Gallery, N.Y., 1979, U. N.C. Weatherspoon Art Gallery, Greensboro, 1979, Galerie Yvon Lambert, Paris, 1980, Bklyn. Mus., 1980, Dart Gallery, Chgo., 1981. Contemporary Arts Center, Cin., 1981, High Mus. Art, Atlanta, 1981, 82, Galerie Mukai, Tokyo, 1981, Va. Mus., Richmond, 1981, Boston Mus. Fine Arts, 1982, Milw. Art Mus., 1982, Art Inst. Chgo., 1982, Daniel Weinberg Gallery, Los Angeles and San Francisco, 1983, Hirshhorn Mus., Washington, 1983, Hobart and William Smith Colls., Geneva, N.Y., 1983, Mus. Art, Ft. Lauderdale, Fla., 1986, 40th Biennial Exhbn. Contemp. Am. Paintings Corcoran Gallery of Art, 1988, Mus. Modern Art, 1990, 91, numerous others; artist and curator Elizabeth Murray: Modern Art N.Y., Mus. Modern Art N.Y., 1995; represented in permanent collections: Whitney Mus. Am. Art, N.Y.C., Guggenheim Mus., Hirshhorn Mus. and Sculpture Garden, Washington, H.H.K. Found., Milw., St. Louis Art Mus., Detroit Inst. Arts, Albright-Knox Art Gallery, Buffalo, N.Y., Allen Meml. Art Mus., Oberlin Coll., Art Inst. Chgo., Baltimore Mus. Art, Carnegie Mus. Art, Pittsburgh, Pa, Cleveland Mus. Art, Dallas Mus. Art, High Mus. Art, Atlanta, Met. Mus. Art, N.Y.C., Nat. Gallery Art, Washington, Mus. Contemporary Art, L.A., Mus. Fine Arts, Boston, Nelson-Atkins Mus. Art, Kansas City, Phila. Mus. Art. Va. Mus. Fine Arts, Walker Center, Minn., Yale U. Art Gallery. Recipient Walter M. Campana award Art Inst. of Chgo., 1982, Am. Academy & Inst. of Arts & Letters award, 1984, Skowhegan prize for painting, 1986, Larry Aldrich prize in contemporary art, 1993, John D. & Catherine T. MacArthur Found. award, 1999, Nat. Artist award Anderson Ranch Art Ctr., 2002; honored by Artists Space, NYC, 2001. Mem. Am. Acad and Inst. of Arts and Letters, 1992, NAD (academician). Office: Pace Wildenstein Gallery 32 E 57 St New York NY 10001

**MURRAY, GEORGE E.,** lawyer; b. Mo., 1954; BA magna cum laude, Dartmouth Coll., 1976; JD cum laude, U. Mo., 1979. Bar: Mo. 1979. Ptnr. Bryan Cave LLP, St. Louis, group co-leader Real Estate Devel. Construction and Project Fin. Note and comment editor: Mo. Law Rev., 1978-79. Mem. ABA, Order of Barristers, Order of Coif. Office: Bryan Cave LLP One Metropolitan Square 211 N Broadway, Ste 3600 Saint Louis MO 63102 Office Phone: 314-259-2344. E-mail: gemurray@bryancave.com.

**MURRAY, GORDON FRANKLIN,** medical educator; b. Muskegon, Mich., 1939; MD, U. Mich., 1963. Intern Johns Hopkins Hosp., Balt., 1963-64, resident, 1964-66, 67-70; with W.Va. U. Hosps., Morgantown; prof. W.Va. U. Office: WVa U Dept Surgery 4061 Health Scis Ctr Morgantown WV 26506

**MURRAY, HELEN,** writer; b. Gleason, Tenn., Feb. 9, 1938; d. Velma (Kinney) Arnold; 1 child, Vicky. Student, Mayfield Graves Coll., 1989-90, Nat. Edn. Author of poems; writer (songs) included in High Country cassette album, 1997, Spring Hilltop America Songbook, 2005. Recipient Editors Choise award, Nat. Libr. Poetry, 1990. Mem. Faternal Order of Eagle. Baptist. Avocations: writing, reading, flea mkts., hiking. Home: PO Box 5038 Mayfield KY 42066-5038

**MURRAY, JAMES DOYLE,** accountant, educator; b. Rochester, N.Y., July 24, 1938; s. William Herbert and Mildred Frances (Becker) M.; m. Mary Louise Goodyear, June 22, 1962; children: William Doyle, Robert Goodyear. BS, U. Rochester, 1961. CPA, N.Y. With Ernst & Whinney, Rochester, N.Y., 1963—, ptnr., 1977-86; pvt. practice Rochester, 1986—; former mem. faculty NYSCPA. Contbr. articles to profl. jours. Treas. William Warfield Scholarship Fund, Inc.; bd. dirs. March of Dimes, Rochester chpt.; trustee B. Thomas Golisano Found.; active fund raising Boy Scouts Am., Rochester Philharm., Rochester Mus. and Sci. Ctr., U. Rochester; former bd. dirs., treas. Downstairs Cabaret; mem. Eagle bd. of rev. Boy Scouts Am.; elder Presbyn. Ch.; past pres. Egypt Vol. Fire Dept. Lt. (j.g.) USN, 1961-63. Named Acct. Adv. of Yr. for region II, SBA, 1996. Mem. N.Y. State Soc. CPAs (pres. Rochester chpt. 1992-93), Instl. Mgmt. Accts. (bd. dirs. 1978-80). Republican. Home: 42 Black Watch Trail Fairport NY 14450-3702 Office: 349 W Commercial St East Rochester NY 14445-2407

**MURRAY, JAMES JOSEPH, III,** association executive; b. Boston, Dec. 31, 1933; s. James Joseph Jr. and Anne Louise (Gurvin) M.; children: James Arthur, Paul, Douglas Joseph, Laura Anne. AB, Harvard U., 1955. Regional editor Prentice Hall, Inc., 1957-60, editor, 1960-64, v.p., exec. editor, 1964-69; pres. Winthrop Pubs., Inc. subs. Prentice Hall, Cambridge, Mass., 1969-82, also bd. dirs.; spl. mng. cons. Am. Coun. Edn., Washington, 1983-84, dir. external affairs, 1984—, v.p., 1997—. Chmn. N.J. Heart Fund; spl. cons. NEH, 1975—. Mem. editorial bd. Capitol Pub., 1992—; author, editor: American Colleges and Universities, 2000. Mem. Dem. Nat. Com. from N.J. 1968; del. Dem. Nat. Conv., 1968; mem. gov. bd. Marine Mil. Acad., 1995—. 1st lt. USMCR, 1955-57. Mem. Am. Polit. Sci. Assn., Assn. Physical Plant Adminstrs. (bd. dirs.), Am. Assn. of Higher Edn., Harvard Club, Harvard Varsity Club, Pi Eta. Office: One DuPont Circle Ste 800 Washington DC 20036

**MURRAY, JAMES MICHAEL,** librarian, lawyer; b. Seattle, Nov. 8, 1944; s. Clarence Nicholas and Della May (Snyder) M.; m. Linda Monthy Murray. MLaw Librarianship, U. Wash., 1978; JD, Gonzaga U., 1971. Bar: Wash. 1974, U.S. Dist. Ct. (we. dist.) Wash. 1975, U.S. Dist. Ct. (ea. dist.) Wash. 1985. Reference/res. libr. U. Tex. Law Libr., Austin, 1978-81; assoc. law libr. Washington U. Law Libr., St. Louis, 1981-84; law libr., asst. prof. Gonzaga U. Sch. Law, Spokane, 1984-91; libr. East Behnor County Libr., 1991-97, U.S. Cts. Libr., Spokane, 1997—. Mem. state adv. bd. Nat. Reporter on Legal Ethics and Profl. Responsibility, 1992-91; cons. in field. Author: (with Reams and McDermott) American Legal Literature: Bibliography of Selected Legal Resources, 1985, (with Gasaway and Johnson) Law Library Administration During Fiscal Austerity, 1992; editor Tex. Bar Jour. (Books Appraisals Column), 1979-82; contbr. numerous articles and revs. to profl. jours., acknowledgements and bibliographies in field. Bd. dirs. ACLU, Spokane chpt., 1987-91, Wash. Vol. Lawyers for the Arts, 1976-78. Mem. ABA, Idaho Libr. Assn., Wash. State Bar Assn. (law sch. liaison com. 1986-88). Home: 921 W 29th Ave Spokane WA 99203-1318 Office Phone: 509-353-3293. Business E-Mail: James_Murray@lb9.uscourts.gov.

**MURRAY, JAMES WILLIAM, III,** manufacturing executive, lawyer; s. James William and Betty Murray; m. Susan Todd Murray; children: James William IV, Alyssa Ashley. BS, Okla. State U., Stillwater, Okla., 1977; JD, U. Okla., Norman, Okla., 1981. Bar: Okla. 1981. Atty. Linn, Helms, Kirk and Burket, Okla. City, Okla., 1981—82, Kirk and Chaney, Okla. City, 1982—87, Cliff Wright and Assocs., Okla. City, Okla., 1987—90; v.p. LSB Industries, Inc., Okla. City, 1990—, sr. assoc. gen. counsel, 1990—. Coach youth soccer Frontier Country Soccer Assn., Okla. City, 2000—06, Mustang Youth Soccer Assn., Okla., 1989—2003. Avocations: soccer, boating. Office: LSB Industries Inc 16 S Pennsylvania Ave Oklahoma City OK 73107 Office Phone: 405-235-4546.

**MURRAY, JEANNE See STAPLETON, JEAN**

**MURRAY, JEFFREY C.,** medical educator, pediatrician; BS, MIT, 1972; MD, Tufts Med. Sch., 1978. Pediat. resident Boston Floating Hosp.; genetics fellow U. Washington; mem. faculty U. Iowa, 1984—, prof. pediatrics, pediat. dentistry, biological sciences, epidemiology, co-chair genetics doctoral program; former dir. Cooperative Human Linkage Ctr.; dir. Comprehensive Oral Health Rsch. Ctr. of Discovery. Contbr. scientific papers, chapters to books. Recipient E. Mead Johnson award, Am. Pediat. Soc., 1997, William Geis award, Internat. Assn. Dental Rsch., 1997. Mem.: Inst. Medicine. Office: University of Iowa Iowa City IA 52241 Office Phone: 319-335-6897. E-mail: jeff-murray@uiowa.edu.*

**MURRAY, JOHN PATRICK,** psychologist, educator, researcher; b. Cleve., Sept. 14, 1943; s. John Augustine and Helen Marie (Lynch) M.; m. Ann Coke Dennison, Apr. 17, 1971; children: Jonathan Coke, Ian Patrick. PhD, Cath. U. Am., 1970. Rsch. dir. Office U.S. Surgeon Gen. NIMH, Bethesda, Md., 1969-72; asst. to assoc. prof. psychology Macquarie U., Sydney, Australia, 1973-79; vis. assoc. prof. U. Mich., Ann Arbor, 1979-80; dir. youth and family policy Boys Town Ctr., Boys Town, Nebr., 1980-85; prof., dir. Sch. Family Studies and Human Svcs. Kans. State U., Manhattan, 1985-98, interim assoc. vice provost rsch., 1998—2000; vis. scholar Ctr. on Media and Child Health Harvard U. Med. Sch., 2004—. Scholar-in-residence Mind Sci. Found., San Antonio, 1996-97; mem. children's TV com. CBS, 1996-99. Author: Television and Youth: 25 Years of Research and Controversy, 1980, The Future of Children's TV, 1984, (with H.T. Rubin) Status Offenders: A Sourcebook, 1983, (with E.A. Rubenstein, G.A. Comstock) Television and Social Behavior, 3 vols., 1972, (with A. Huston and others) Big World, Small Screen: The Role of Television in American Society, 1992, (with C. Fisher and others) Applied Developmental Science, 1996, Children and Television: 50 Years of Research (with N. Pecora and E. Wartella), 2006; contbr. numerous articles to profl. jours. Mem. Nebr. Foster Care Rev. Bd., 1982-84; mem. Advocacy Office for Children and Youth, 1980-85; mem. Nat. Coun. Children and TV, 1982-87; trustee The Villages Children's Homes, 1986—, Menninger Found., 1996—; mem. children's TV adv. bd. CBS-TV, 1996-99. Fellow Am. Psychol. Assn. (pres. div. child youth and family svcs. 1990); mem. Internat. Comm. Assn., Soc. Rsch. in Child Devel., Royal Economic wealth Soc. (London), Manhattan Country Club. Home: 1731 Humboldt St Manhattan KS 66502-4140 Office: Kans. State U 303 Justin Hall Manhattan KS 66506-1304 Office Phone: 785-532-1456. E-mail: jpm@ksu.edu.

**MURRAY, JOSEPH EDWARD,** retired plastic surgeon; b. Milford, Mass., Apr. 1, 1919; s. William Andrew and Mary (DePasquale) Murray; m. Virginia Link, June 2, 1945; children: Virginia, Margaret, Joseph Link, Katharine, Thomas, Richard. AB, Holy Cross Coll., 1940, DSc, 1965; MD, Harvard, 1943; DSc, Rockford Coll., Ill., 1966, Roger Williams Coll., 1986; PhD (hon.), Anna Marie Coll., 1993, SUNY, Albany, 1993, U. Suffolk, 1993, Magill U., Montreal, 1996. Diplomate Am. Bd. Surgery, Am. Bd. Plastic Surgery. Chief plastic surgeon Peter Bent Brigham Hosp., Boston, 1951—86; chief plastic surgeon Children's Hosp. Med. Center, Boston, 1972—85; prof. surgery Harvard Med. Sch., 1970—86; ret., 1986. Chmn. Am. Bd. Plastic Surgery, 1969. Maj. M.C. U.S. Army, 1944—47. Recipient Gold medal, Internat. Soc. Surgeons, 1963, Nobel prize for medicine or physiology, 1990, Sabin award, 1994, Lifetime Achievement award, Mass. Med. Soc., 1988. Fellow: AMA, AAAS (hon.), Royal Coll. Surgeons Edinburgh, Royal Coll. Surgeons Ireland, Royal Coll. Surgeons of Eng., Royal Australasian Coll. Surgeons; mem.: NAS, ACS (regent 1970—79, v.p. 1983), Am. Acad. Arts and Scis. (Hon. award 1962), Am. Assn. Plastic Surgeons (pres. 1964—65, Hon. award 1969), Soc. U. Surgeons, Boston Surg. Soc. (pres. 1975), New Eng. Surg. Assn. (pres. 1986—87), Am. Surg. Assn. (v.p. 1979), Harvard Med. Sch. Alumni Coun. (pres. 1984), Tavern Club, Badminton and Tennis Club, Wellesley Country Club, Alpha Omega Alpha. Home: 108 Abbott Rd Wellesley MA 02481-6104

**MURRAY, JULIA KAORU (MRS. JOSEPH E. MURRAY),** occupational therapist; b. Wahiawa, Oahu, Hawaii, 1934; d. Gijun and Edna Tsuruko (Taba) Funakoshi; m. Joseph Edward Murray, 1961; children: Michael, Susan, Leslie. BA, U. Hawaii, 1956; cert. occupl. therapy, U. Puget Sound, 1958. Therapist Inst. Logopedics, Wichita, Kans., 1958; sr. therapist Hawaii State Hosp., Kaneohe, 1959; part-time therapist Centre County Ctr. for Crippled Children and Adults, State College, Pa., 1963; vice chmn. adv. bd. Hosp. Improvement Program East Oreg. State Hosp., Pendleton, 1974; v.p. Ind. Living, Inc., 1976—79; instr. job search; mem. adv. com. Oreg. Ednl. Coordinating Commn., 1979—82; mem. Oreg. Bd. Engring. Examiners, 1979—87; supr., occupl. therapist Fairview Tng. Ctr., Salem, Oreg., 1984—94; occupl. therapist U.S. Naval Hosp., Yokosuka, Japan, 1994—99, Yokosuka, Japan, 1999—. Rep. from Umatilla County Commrs. to Blue Mountain Econ. Devel. Council, 1976-78; mem. Ashland Park and Recreation Bd., 1972-73; vice chmn. adv. bd. LINC, 1978; mem. exec. bd. Liberty-Boone Neighborhood Assn., 1979-83. Decorated Meritorious Civilian Svc. medal USN. Mem. Am. Occupational Therapy Assn., Oreg. Occupational Therapy Assn., Hawaii Occupational Therapy Assn. (sec. 1960, LWV (bd. dirs. Pendleton 1974, 77-78, pres. 1975-77; bd. dirs. Oreg. 1979-81, Ashland, Wis., 1967-71, Wis. v.p. 1970). Personal E-mail: jkfmurray@hotmail.com.

**MURRAY, KATHLEEN ANNE,** lawyer; b. L.A., Feb. 14, 1946; d. Francis Albert and Dorothy (Thompson) M.; 1 child, Anne Murray Ladd; m. Arthur T. Perkins Jr., June 29, 1991. BA, U. Mich., 1967; JD, Hastings Coll. Law, 1973. Bar: Calif. 1973, U.S. Dist. Ct. (no. dist.) Calif. 1973, U.S. Ct. Appeals (9th cir.) 1973. Sr. staff atty Child Care Law Ctr., San Francisco, 1979—84, cons. child day care law and regulation, 1984—86; atty Epstein & Harris, San Francisco, 1985—86; gen. counsel Fisher Friedman Assocs., San Francisco, 1986—89; assoc. gen. counsel Calif. State Automobile Assn., San Francisco, 1989—98; sr. counsel Firemen's Fund Ins. Co., San Francisco, 1998—2002; prin. Mercer Health & Benefits, LLC, San Francisco, 2003—. Exec. dir., editl. adv. bd. Parenting Mag., 1985; chair Labor and Employment Law Com. Assn. Corp. Coun. Am., 2001-03 Editor: Child Care Center Legal Handbook; Tax Guide for California Child Care Providers; contbr. articles to profl. jours. Mem. adv. coun. Humanities West, Inc., 1986-96; vestry Episcopal Ch. of St. Mary the Virgin, 1990-92; pres. Parents' Assn., Lick-Wilmerding H.S., 1993-94; Pers. Practices Com. Episcopal Diocese of Calif., 1998-2003. Mem.: Assn. Corp. Counsel (chair labor and employment law com. 2001—03). Democrat. Episcopalian. Office: Mercer HR Cons Three Embarcadeo Ctr Ste 1500 San Francisco CA 94111-4015 Business E-mail: kathleen.murray@mercer.com.

**MURRAY, KATHLEEN SARAH-JANE,** literature and language professor; BA, Auburn U., Ala., 1996; diploma, Ecole Normale Superieure-Ish, 2001; PhD, Princeton U., NJ, 2003. Asst. prof. medieval lit. and french Honors Coll. Baylor U., Waco, Tex., 2003. Co-dir. The Charrette Project Princeton (N.J.) U. and Baylor U., 1998—2003; lectr. in field. Co-editor: Cultural History of Reading, 2005, Literature and Literary Studies on Their Way Towards the Digital Media—Where Are We?, 2005, Encyclopedia of Sex, Love and Culture in the Medieval World, 2006, Encyclopedia of World History, 2006; mem. editl. bd. Baylor Jour. Theatre and Performance, 2003—, Academic Exchange Quar., 2005—; contbr. articles to profl. jours. Named Outstanding Faculty Mem., Baylor U., 2006; recipient Lauréate du Concours Général des Lycées de France, French Ministry Edn., 1992, John Edward Wiatt prize,

---

Auburn (Ala.) U., 1997, Armstrong prize, Dept. Romance Langs. and Lit. Princeton (N.J.) U., 1998, 1999, 2000, 2001, 2002, 2003; grantee, Baylor U., 2003—04, 2005—06; Alfred Foulet fellowship, Princeton (N.J.) U., 2001, Porter Ogden Jacobus fellowship, 2002—03, Donald and Mary Hyde fellowship, 2002. Mem.: MLA, Medieval Acad. Am., Princeton (N.J.) Alumni Schs. Com., Princeton (N.J.) Club, Princeton (N.J.) Assn. Grad. Alumni, Phi Mu (spirit chmn., asst. treas., panhellenic rep.). Office: Baylor University One Bear Place 97144 Waco TX 76798 Office Phone: 254-710-7854. Business E-Mail: sj_murray@baylor.edu.

**MURRAY, LARRY,** government agency administrator; b. Stratford, Ont., Can., June 6, 1947; s. William Alexander and Ethel May (Mulholland) M.; children: Wendi, Kimberly, Jeffrey, Sean. BA in History, Carleton U., Ottawa, 1968; Cert., Casn. Forces Staff Coll., 1980. Commd. Can. Forces, advanced through grades to vice admiral., 1993; comdr. can. Destroyer Squadron Maritime Command, Halifax, N.S., 1987-88; dir. gen. maritime doctrine and ops. Nat. Defence Hdqs., Ottawa, 1989-91, assoc. asst. dep. min. policy and comm., 1991-93, dep. chief def. staff, 1993—94, vice chief def. staff, 1995-97; comdr. Maritime Command, Halifax, 1994-95; acting chief def. staff Nat. Defence Hdqs., Ottawa, 1997; assoc. dep. minister Min. Fisheries and Oceans, Ottawa, Canada, 1997—99, dep. min., 2004—, dep. minister vet. affairs Charlottetown, Canada, 1999—2004. Decorated Can. 125 medal, NATO Spl. Svc. medal, Order of Mil. Merit. Office: Fisheries & Oceans Can 200 Kent St Ottawa ON Canada K1A 0E6

**MURRAY, LAWRENCE,** management consultant; b. NYC, May 10, 1939; s. Gilbert and Edna (Blatt) M.; children: Robert, Stacy, David, Daniel, Abigail. BA, Cornell U., 1961; MBA, U. Okla., 1966; PhD, Pacific Western U., 1993. Cert. Fac. Food Mgmt. Account exec. Merrill Lynch, Paramus, NJ, 1965-69; chmn., pres. Murray, Lind & Co., Inc., Jersey City, 1969-72; dir. investor rels. IU Internat. Corp., Phila., 1972-73, dir. spl. projects, 1974-75; dir. fin. comm., mem. exec. staff, chmn. bd. ARA Svcs., Inc., Phila., 1975-78; chmn., chief exec. officer Century Mgmt. and affiliated cos., West Chester, Pa., 1976-82; chmn. bd., CEO Creative Mgmt. Corp., Bala Cynwyd and West Chester, Pa., 1982-87, Fin. Mgmt. Profl. Corp., West Chester, 1983-89; chmn. bd. dirs. Venture Frontiers Co., Denver, 1984-89; chmn. bd., CEO Fin. Intelligence Corp., West Chester, 1989-95; CEO, chmn. bd. dirs. Healthy Living Ctrs., West Chester, 1993—. Lectr. bus. orgn. and mgmt. Bergen C.C., 1971-72; chmn. bd. dirs. Med. Intelligence Corp., West Chester, 1993-95; CEO, chmn. bd. dirs. Miramax Corp.; chmn. bd. dirs., CEO, Tax Doctor Corp., West Chester, 2002-. Author: The Organized Stockbroker, 1970; A New Era in Mergers and Acquisitions, 1974; Communications: Management's Newest Marketing Skill, 1976, Powerful Tax-Saving Strategies for Honest People, 1992, Teach Your Children How to Eat Properly and Add 20 Years to Their Lives, 1999; contbr. articles to profl. jours. Pres., Congregation Beth Israel, Media, Pa., 1977-78, Parents Without Ptnrs., Valley Forge, Pa., 1982-83; v.p. Cornell U. Class of 1961, 1981-86; mem. White House Conf. on Bus. Ethics in Am., 1986; active Beth Chaim Reform Synagogue. Served to 1st lt. arty./intelligence, U.S. Army, 1963-64. Decorated U.S. Army Commendation medal. Mem. Nat. Investor Rels. Inst. (pres. Phila. chpt. 1976-78), Internat. Coun. Shopping Ctrs., Am. Health Info. Mgmt. Assn., C. of C. Greater West Chester. Home: 625 Beaumony Cir West Chester PA 19380 Office Phone: 610-436-4800. Personal E-mail: lmurray761@aol.com.

**MURRAY, LOWELL,** Canadian senator; b. New Waterford, N.S., Can., Sept. 26, 1936; s. Daniel and Evelyn (Young) M.; m. Colleen Elaine MacDonald; children: William, Colin. BA, St. Francis Xavier U., Antigonish, N.S., Can.; MA in Pub. Adminstrn., Queen's U., Kingston, Ont., Can.; LLD (hon.), St. Francis Xavier U., 2005. Chief of staff Minister of Justice and Minister of Pub. Works Can., Ottawa, Ont., Senator M. Wallace McCutcheon, Ottawa, Ont.; leader of opposition Can., Ottawa, Ont.; dep. minister Premier N.B. (Can.); mem. Senate of Can., Ottawa, Ont., 1979—, co-chmn. joint Senate-House of Commons com. ofcl. langs., 1980-84, chmn. standing Senate com. on banking, trade and commerce, 1984-86, chmn. standing senate com. on nat. fin., 1995—96, 1999—2004, chmn. standing senate com. on social affairs, sci. and tech., 1997-99. Bd. dirs. SONY Can. Inc.; trustee Inst. Rsch. Pub. Policy, 1984-86, mem. Trilateral Commn., 1985-86; mem. coun. Fedn. Adv. Panel Fiscal Imbalance, 2005-06. Sworn of the privy coun., appointed leader of Govt. in the Senate, 1986—93; Min. of State Fed.-Provincial Rels., 1986—91; min. responsible for Atlantic Can. Opportunities Agy., 1987—88, acting min. comms., 1988—89; nat. campaign chmn. gen. election Progressive Conservative Party Can., 1977—79, 1981—83. Progressive Conservative. Roman Catholic. Office: The Senate Ottawa ON Canada K1A 0A4

**MURRAY, MARK ANDREW,** food products executive, former academic administrator, economist; b. Lansing, Mich., July 6, 1954; s. John and Francoise G. (Martin) M.; m. Elizabeth J. Chapman, July 15, 1978; children: Hannah B., Laura E., Ellen T. BA, Mich. State U., 1976, M in Labor and Industrial Rels., 1979; D in Pub. Svc. (hon.), Ea. Mich. U., 2000. Economist Mich. Dept. Social Svcs., Lansing, 1978-85, Mich. Dept. Commerce, Lansing, 1985-90, dir. bus. rsch. office, 1987-90; exec. dir. Mich. Health Planning Coun., 1990-91; dep. dir. Mich. Dept. Mgmt. and Budget, 1991—94, state budget dir., 1994—98, state treas., policy advisor, 1999—2001; pres. Meijer, Inc., Grand Rapids, Mich., 2006—. Guest lectr. U. Okla. Contbr. articles to profl. jours. Named Mich. Pub. Servant of Yr., 1992; recipient Donald L. Scantlebury Award for Leadership in State Govt. Fin., 1998. Mem. Nat. Assn. Welfare Rsch. and Statistics (bd. dirs. 1984-85), Nat. Assn. State Devel. Agys. (rsch. div., bd. dirs. 1986-90), Mich. Hist. Assn., Mensa, Internat. Platform Assn., Omicron Delta Upsilon. Roman Catholic. Avocations: athletics, photography. Office: Meijer, Inc 1920 44th St SE Grand Rapids MI 49508*

**MURRAY, MICHAEL DENNIS,** pharmacist; b. Blairsville, Pa., Apr. 13, 1952; s. Howard Jacob and Elizabeth Murray; m. Jennifer Jayne Chumbler, Aug. 4, 1979; children: Ryan Michael, Kristin Elizabeth. BSc in Pharmacy, Duquesne U., 1975, D of Pharmacy, 1977; M of Pub. Health, Ind. U., 1992. Registered pharmacist, Ind., Pa. Asst. prof. Purdue U. Sch. of Pharmacy, West Lafayette, Ind., 1982-88, assoc. prof., 1988-99 prof., 1999—2001, Bucke prof. pharmacy, 2002—. Adj. asst. prof. Purdue U. Sch. of Pharmacy, West Lafayette, 1977—82; adj. assoc. prof. Ind. U. Sch. Medicine, 1992—2001, adj. prof., 2001—; dir. rsch. Ind. Drug Evaluation and Analysis Ctr., Indpls., 1995—98; faculty Health Svcs. R&D, Indpls., 1995—98; dir. healthcare data and epidemiology Regenstrief Inst., Indpls., 1996—2004; faculty scholar Purdue U., 1999; Mescal S. Ferguson disting. prof. U. NC at Chapel Hill; dir. U. NC at Chapel Hill, Ctr. Study Pharm. Outcomes, Sch. Pharm., Chapel Hill, NC. Commr. Saints Football Club, Lawrence, Ind., 1996-97; v.p. Ind. Soccer League, Carmel, Ind., 1996-97. Fellow: Internat. Soc. Pharmacoepiemiology (sci. programs 1989—2004, membership chair 1990—93, bd. dirs. 1991—94); mem.: U.S. Pharmacopia (safe medicine use and therapeutic decision expert panels 2000—05, exec. com. coun. of experts 2005—, chair safe medication use com.), Am. Soc. Clin. Pharmacology and therapeutics (pharmacoepidemiology chair 1998—2001, chair com. on coordination of sci. sects. 2001—04, bd. dirs.). Democrat. Roman Catholic. Avocations: stained glass crafts, arts, hiking, bicycling. Home: 3526 Stonegate Dr Chapel Hill NC 27516 Office: U NC Campus Box 7360 2212 Kerr Hall Chapel Hill NC 27599-7360 Business E-Mail: mick@unc.edu.

**MURRAY, MICHAEL PATRICK,** lawyer; b. Milw., Jan. 31, 1930; s. Michael James and Florence Mary M.; m. Allene Vereen, May 8, 1976; children: Bryan Patrick, Laura Renee. BA, Milton (Wis.) Coll., 1953; JD, Marquette U., 1958; LLM, John Marshall Law Sch., 1960; D of Juridicial Sci., George Washington U., 1989; M of Liberal Arts, Johns Hopkins U., 1996. Bar: Wis. 1958, Calif. 1966, U.S. Supreme Ct. 1967, U.S. Ct. Appeals (9th cir.) 1982, D.C. 1989, Va. 1989, U.S. Ct. Appeals (D.C. cir.) 1989, U.S. Ct. Appeals (4th cir.) 1990. Commd. 2d lt. USMC, 1953, advanced through grades to col., 1975, prosecutor and def. counsel, 1960—66, trial judge and SJA, 1966—69, dir. policy and research Washington, 1969—72; dir. Law Ctr. Iwakuni, Japan, 1973-74; dep. legal advisor chmn. Joint Chiefs of Staff, Washington, 1974—75; ret. USMC, 1978; trial atty. Anderson & Murphy, Milw., 1958—60; appellate judge USN Ct. of Rev., Washington, 1975—78; pvt. practice, San Diego, 1982—89; atty., counsel

---

Clary, Lawrence, Lickstein & Moore, Falls Church, Va., 1989—91; ptnr. Michael Patrick Murray & Assocs., South Riding, Va., 1991—; asst. gen. counsel NRA, Washington, 1992—95. Assoc. prof. law Pepperdine U., Malibu, Calif., 1978-80, Marquette U., Milw., 1980-81; adj. prof. law Western State U., San Diego, 1983-88, Nat. U. Coll. Law, 1988-89; pro bono vol. atty. for indigents, San Diego, 1982-89. Author: Quarter: the Warrior's Dilemma, 1967, (law study) Eichman and Major German War Criminal Trials, 1973, O'Ryans Law, 1992, Murder By Class, 1997, Law Is a Jealous Mistress, 1999, People Needing People, 2000, Love's Mirror, 2003, Judgment in NAM, 2005, Passion, Prose and Poetry, 2005. Mem. Calif. Bar Assn., Wis. Bar Assn., D.C. Bar Assn., Va. Bar Assn., Am. Legion, First and Third Marine Div. Assn., Marine Corps Assn., Marine Mustang Assn., Phi Delta Phi. Roman Catholic. Avocations: poetry, creative writing. Office: Michael Patrick Murray & Assocs 26083 Glasgow Dr South Riding VA 20152 Office Phone: 703-327-1350. E-mail: michael.p.murray@att.net.

**MURRAY, PATRICIA,** electronics company executive; b. Detroit; BA, Michigan St. U.; BS, St. Louis U.; JD, U. Mich., 1986. Nurse, intensive care unit, nursing adminstr. U. Mich. Hospitals; employment litigator Morrison & Foerster, Palo Alto, Calif., until 1990; atty. human resources legal staff Intel Corp., 1990—91, mgr. human resoures legal staff, 1992—95, dir., v.p. human resources Santa Clara, 1996—97, sr. v.p., 1997—. Chmn. Intel Found. Office: Intel Corp PO Box 58119 2200 Mission College Blvd Santa Clara CA 95052-8119 E-mail: patricia.murray@intel.com.

**MURRAY, PATRICK ROBERT,** microbiologist, educator; b. L.A., Jan. 15, 1948; married, 1970; 3 children. BS, St. Mary's Coll., Calif., 1969; MS, U. Calif., L.A., 1972, PhD in Microbiology, 1974. Rsch. fellow clinical microbiology Mayo Clinic & Mayo Found., 1974-76; asst. prof. medicine Wash. U. Sch. Med., 1976-82, assoc. dir., 1976; dir. clinical microbiology Barnes Hosp., St. Louis, 1977—, dir. postdoctoral training program, 1982—; assoc. prof. medicine Wash. U. Sch. Medicine, 1983—. Cons. St. Luke's Hosp., 1985—; mem. Nat. Com. Clinical Lab. Standards, 1980—; chmn. exam com. Am. Bd. Medical Microbiology, 1982—, mem. joint standards and exam com., 1985—; bd. dirs. Southwestern Assn. Clinical Microbiologist; chmn. Clinical Microbiologist Divsn. Am. Soc. Microbiologist. Becton Dickinson Co. Clinical Microbiology award Am. Soc. Microbiology, 1993. Fellow Am. Acad. Med. Microbiology, Infectious Disease Soc; mem. Am. Assn. Pathologist, Am. Soc. Microbiologist, Med. Mycol Soc. Am., Am. Federation Clinical Rsch., Sigma Xi. Achievements include research in new diagnostic and therapeutic tests for clinical microbiology.

**MURRAY, PATTY (PATRICIA J. MURRAY),** senator; b. Bothell, Wash., Oct. 10, 1950; d. David L. and Beverly A. (McLaughlin) Johns; m. Robert R. Murray, June 2, 1972; children: Randy P., Sara A. BA, Wash. State U., 1972. Sec. various cos., Seattle, 1972-76; citizen lobbyist various ednl. groups, Seattle, 1983-88; legis. lobbyist Orgn. for Parent Edn., Seattle, 1977-84; instr. Shoreline Community Coll., Seattle, 1984-88; mem. Wash. State Senate, Seattle, 1989-92; US Senator from Wash., 1993—. Mem. com. appropriations US Senate, com. budget, com. health, edn., labor and pensions, com. veterans affairs. Author (with Catherine Whitney): Nine and Counting: The Women of the Senate, 2000. Mem. bd. Shoreline Sch., Seattle, 1985-89; mem. steering com. Demonstration for Edn., Seattle, 1987; founder, chmn. Orgn. for Parent Edn., Wash., 1981-85; 1st Congl. rep. Wash. Women United, 1983-85. Recipient Outstanding award Washing. Women United, 1986, Recognition of Svc. to Children award Shoreline PTA Coun., 1986, Golden Acorn Svc. award, 1989; Outstanding Svc. award Wash. Women United, 1986, Outstanding Svc. to Pub. Edn. award Citizens Ednl. Ctr. NW, Seattle, 1987, Wash. State Legis. of Yr., 1990, George Falcon Spike award Nat. Assn. Railroad Passengers, 2003, Person of Yr. award Wash. State VFW, 2004. Democrat. Roman Catholic. Office: US Senate 173 Russell Senate Office Bldg Washington DC 20510-0001 also: Henry M Jackson Federal Bldg Ste 2988 915 Second Ave Seattle WA 98174-4067 Office Phone: 202-224-2621, 206-553-5545. Office Fax: 202-224-0238, 206-553-0891.*

**MURRAY, PETER,** retired metallurgist, manufacturing executive; b. Rotherham, Yorkshire, Eng., Mar. 13, 1920; came to U.S., 1967, naturalized, 1974; s. Michael and Ann (Hamstead) M.; m. Frances Josephine Glaisher, Sept. 8, 1947; children: Jane, Paul, Alexander. BSc in Chemistry with honors, Sheffield U., Eng., 1941, postgrad., 1946-49; PhD in Metallurgy, Brit. Iron and Steel Research Bursar, Sheffield, 1948. Research chemist Steetley Co., Ltd., Worksop, Notts, Eng., 1941-45; with Atomic Energy Research Establishment, Harwell, Eng., 1949-67, head div. metallurgy, 1960-64, asst. dir., 1964-67; tech. dir., mgr. fuels and materials, advanced reactors div. Westinghouse Electric Corp., Madison, Pa., 1967-74; dir. research Westinghouse Electric Europe (S.A.), Brussels, 1974-75; chief scientist advanced power systems divs. Westinghouse Electric Corp., Madison, Pa., 1975-81, dir. nuclear programs Washington, 1981-92; sr. cons. Nuc. Programs, 1992—2001. Mem. divisional rev. coms. Argonne Nat. Labs., 1968-73; Mellor Meml. lectr. Inst. Ceramics, 1963 Contbr. numerous articles to profl. jours.; editorial adv. bd.: Jour. Less Common Metals, 1968—. Recipient Holland Meml. Research prize, Sheffield U., 1949. Fellow Royal Inst. Chemistry (Newton Chambers Research prize 1954), Inst. Ceramics, Am. Nuclear Soc.; mem. Brit. Ceramics Soc. (pres. 1965), Am. Ceramic Soc., Nat. Acad. Engring. Roman Catholic. Home: 20308 Canby Ct Montgomery Village MD 20886-4014

**MURRAY, PETER See HAUTMAN, PETE**

**MURRAY, R. SCOTT,** computer software company executive; Grad., U. We. Ont. Chartered acct. Arthur Andersen, Canada; exec. v.p., CFO The Learning Co., 1994—99; pres., COO Stream Internat., 2000—01; CEO Modus Media Internat., 2002—05; pres., CEO 3Com Corp., Marlborough, Mass., 2006—. Office: 3Com Corp 350 Campus Dr Marlborough MA 01752-3064*

**MURRAY, RAYMOND HAROLD,** physician; b. Cambridge, Mass., Aug. 17, 1925; s. Raymond Harold and Grace May (Dorr) M.; children: Maureen, Robert, Michael, Margaret, David, Elizabeth, Catherine, Anne. BS, U. Notre Dame, 1946; MD, Harvard, 1950. Diplomate Am. Bd. Internal Medicine, also Sub-bd. Cardiovascular Disease. Practice medicine, Grand Rapids, Mich., 1955-62; asst. prof. to prof. medicine Ind. U. Sch. Medicine, 1962-77; prof. dept. medicine Coll. Human Medicine Mich. State U., Lansing, 1977-95, chmn. dept. medicine Coll. Human Medicine, 1977-89, emeritus, 1995—. Chmn. aeromed.-bioscis. panel Sci. Adv. Bd., USAF, 1977-81; mem. adv. coun. Office Alternative Medicine/NIH, 1997-99. Contbr. numerous articles to profl. publs. Served with USNR, 1942-45; Served with USPHS, 1950-53. Master: ACP (gov. Mich. chpt. 1994—98); mem.: Am. Fedn. Clin. Rsch., Am. Heart Assn. (fellow coun. clin. cardiology). E-mail: Raymondmur@aol.com.

**MURRAY, RICHARD BENNETT,** retired physics professor; b. Marietta, Ga., Dec. 5, 1928; s. William Moore and Ruth (Mozley) M.; m. Clella Bay, Apr. 1, 1956; children: Ada, Annette. BA, Emory U., 1947; MS, Ohio State U., 1950; PhD, U. Tenn., 1955. Rsch. asst. Gaseous Diffusion Plant, Oak Ridge, Tenn., 1947-48; rsch. physicist Oak Ridge Nat. Lab., 1955-66; vis. assoc. prof. physics U. Del., Newark, 1962-63, assoc. prof., 1966-69, prof., 1969-98, prof. emeritus, 1998—, asst. chmn. dept. physics, 1975-76, univ. coord. for grad. studies, 1979-85, assoc. provost grad. studies, 1986-88, acting provost, v/p. acad. affairs, 1988-91, provost, 1993-94, ret., 1998. Lectr. physics U. Tenn., Knoxville, 1963-66; vis. rsch. physicist U.S. Naval Rsch. Lab., 1991-92; vis. scientist Clarendon Lab., Oxford U., 1992; cons. to industry, 1957-93; councillor Oak Ridge Associated Univs., 1979-88, bd. dirs., 1983-94, vice chmn. coun., 1983-85. Contbr. chmn. 1985-88; sec.-treas. NE Assn. Grad. Schs., 1982-84; dir. U. Del. Press 1979-82. Contbr. numerous articles on exptl. nuclear and solid state physics to profl. publs., 1954-85. Trustee Sanford Sch., Hockessin, Del., 1981-85; chmn. bd. dirs. Oak Ridge Associated Univs. Found., 1989-94; bd. dirs. Del. Inst. for Med. Edn. and Rsch., 1989-91. Predoctoral fellow Oak Ridge Inst. Nuclear Studies, 1953-55;

grantee AEC, NSF, Dept. Energy, 1967-84. Fellow AAAS, Am. Phys. Soc.; mem. Southeastern Univs. Rsch. Assn. (bd. dirs. 1989-97), Phi Beta Kappa, Sigma Xi, Sigma Pi Sigma, Phi Kappa Phi, Cosmos Club. Home: 4 Bridlebrook Ln Newark DE 19711-2058 Office: U Del Dept Physics & Astronomy Newark DE 19716 Business E-Mail: rmurray@udel.edu.

**MURRAY, RICHARD M.**, engineering educator; BS with honors in elec. engring., Calif. Inst. Tech., 1985; MS in elec. engring. and computer sciences, U. Calif., Berkeley, 1989, PhD, 1991. Asst. prof. mech. engring. Calif. Inst. Tech., 1991—97, assoc. prof. mech. engring., 1997—2000, prof. mech. engring., 2000—05, chair Divsn. Engring. and Applied Sci., 2000—, prof. Control and Dynamical Sys., 2005—; dir. mechatronic systems United Technologies Rsch. Ctr., 1998—2000. Mem. info. sci. and tech. study group Def. Advanced Rsch. Projects Agy., Dept. Def., 2000—; mem. R&D strategy adv. com. Rockwell Sci. Co., 2001—; mem. Jet Propulsion Lab. adv. coun. NASA, 2001—; mem. vis. com. Dept. Mech. Engring., MIT, 2001—; chair exec. bd. Collaborative Ctr. on Control Sci., 2002—; mem. sci. adv. bd. USAF, 2002—; cons. Alphatech, Raytheon, United Technologies Rsch. Ctr., Northrop Corp. Recipient Eliahu Jury Award, U. Calif. Berkeley, 1991, Early Faculty Career Devel. Award, NSF, 1995, Young Investigator Award, Office Naval Rsch., 1995, Donald P. Eckman Award, Am. Automatic Control Coun., 1997; Richard P. Feynman-Hughes Faculty Fellowship, Calif. Inst. Tech., 1993. Achievements include patents for Actuator Bandwidth and Rate Limit Reduction for Control of Compressor Rotating Stall (with Simon Yeung), US Patent 5,984,625, Nov. 1999. Office: Control and Dynamical Systems 107-81 Calif Inst Tech MC 107-81 Pasadena CA 91125

**MURRAY, RICHARD MAXIMILIAN**, insurance company executive; b. Vienna, Nov. 21, 1922; came to U.S., 1955, naturalized, 1961; s. and Elizabeth Helen Peiker. Grad. in world commerce studies, U. Vienna; postgrad., Columbia U. Asst. sec. Sterling Offices Ltd. (reins. intermediaries), London, Toronto, N.Y.C., 1951—59; v.p. Guy Carpenter, Inc. (reins. intermediaries), N.Y.C., 1959—68, Travelers Ins. Cos., 1968—87, ret., 1987. Mng. dir. La Metropole Ins. Co., Brussels, ret., 1987; chmn. bd. Nippon Mgmt. Corp., N.Y.C., ret., 1991; chmn. bd. Travelers Marine Corp., ret., 1987; pres. Travelers Reins Co. Bermuda Ltd., ret., 1987; pres. Travelers of Asia Ltd., Hong Kong, ret., 1987; vice-chmn. bd. La Prov Corp., N.Y.C.; bd. electors Ins. Hall of Fame; bd. dirs. United Am. Inst. Co., United Am. Holdings Co., Inc.; mem. adv. bd. Firemark Global Ins. Fund, L.P.; dir. emeritus Davis Internat. Total Return Fund.; guest prof. Donau U., Krems, Austria. Contbr. articles to profl. publs. Decorated for promotion of pvt. ins. (Peru); Knight Order of St. John, Knights of Malta (ambassador at large). Mem. Internat. Ins. Coun. (chmn. 1979-81, award 1990). Home: 60 Remsen St Apt 10C Brooklyn NY 11201-3453 Office: 1 Penn Plz Ste 3600 New York NY 10119-2108 Business E-Mail: nyork@gnp.com.mx.

**MURRAY, RICHARD RUSSELL**, music educator; b. Hillsboro, Ohio, Dec. 14, 1952; s. Murray Jr. and Charlotte Elberta Russell; m. Pamela Joy Roush, Aug. 17, 1976; children: Jane, Bethany, Jordan, Katherine. BA, Cin. Christian U., 1975; MA in Music Edn., Ohio State U., Columbus, 1990. Cert. tchr. ACSI. Tchr. Tree of Life Christian Sch., Columbus, 1980—82, 1990—. Mem.: Ohio Music Edn. Assn.

**MURRAY, ROBERT FULTON, JR.**, physician; b. Newburgh, N.Y., Oct. 19, 1931; s. Robert Fulton and Henrietta Frances (Judd) Murray; m. Isobel Ann Parks, Aug. 26, 1956; children: Conin Charles(dec.), Robert Fulton III, Suzanne Frances, Dianne Akwe. BS, Union Coll., Schenectady, 1953; MD, U. Rochester, N.Y., 1958; MS, U. Wash., Seattle, 1968. Diplomate Am. Bd. Internal Medicine, Am. Bd. Med. Genetics. Intern Denver Gen. Hosp., 1958—59; resident in internal medicine U. Colo. Med. Ctr., 1959—62; staff investigator (service with USPHS) Nat. Inst. Arthritis and Metabolic Diseases, NIH, Bethesda, Md., 1962—65; NIH spl. fellow med. genetics U. Wash., 1965—67; faculty Howard U. Coll. Medicine, Washington, 1967—74, prof. pediatrics and medicine, 1974—, grad. prof., 1976, prof. oncology, 1976, chief divsn. med. genetics, 1968—; chmn. dept. genetics and human genetics Howard U. Coll. Medicine Grad. Sch., 1976—. Nat. adv. gen. med. scis. coun. NIH, 1971—75, recombinant DNA adv. com., 1988—92; ethics adv. bd. to sec. HEW, 1978—80; chmn. Washington Mayor's Adv. Com. on Metabolic Disorders, 1980—89; mem. Med. Com. Human Rights. Co-author: Genetic Variation and Disorders in Peoples of African Origin, 1990; co-editor: Genetic, Metabolic and Developmental Aspects of Mental Retardation, 1972, Genetic Counseling: Facts, Values and Norms, 1979, The Human Genome Project and the Future of Health Care, 1996; mem. editl. bd.: Am. Jour. Clin. Genetics, 1977—93, Ency. Bioethics, 1975—77, 1993—95, Jour. Clin. Ethics, 1990. Sci. adv. bd. Nat. Sickle Cell Anemia Found.; trustee Union Coll., 1972—80. Fellow Rotary Found. fellow, 1955—56; grantee Rsch. grantee, NIH, 1969—75. Fellow: AAAS, ACP, Am. Coll. Med. Genetics, Inst. Soc., Ethics and Life Scis., Inst. Medicine; mem.: Acad. Medicine Washington, Genetics Soc. Am., Am. Soc. Human Genetics, Assn. Acad. Minority Physicians, AAUP, Neighbors Inc. D.C., Alpha Omega Alpha, Sigma Xi. Unitarian Universalist. Home: 510 Aspen St NW Washington DC 20012-2740 Office: Howard U Coll Medicine PO Box 75 Washington DC 20059-0001

**MURRAY, ROBERT GRAY**, sculptor; b. Vancouver, B.C., Can., Mar. 2, 1936; U.S. citizen; s. John Gray and Vera (Meakin) M.; m. Cintra Wetherill Lofting, Jan. 23, 1971; children: Rebecca and Megan (twins), Claire, Hillary. Student, U. Sask., Can., 1956-58. One man shows Betty Parsons Gallery, N.Y.C., 1965, 66, 68, David Mirvish Gallery, Toronto, 1967, 68, 72, 73, 74, 75, Jewish Mus., N.Y.C., 1967, Hammarskjold Plaza, N.Y.C., 1971, Paula Cooper Gallery, N.Y.C., 1974, Janie Lee Gallery, Houston, 1977, Hamilton Gallery, N.Y.C., 1977, 79, 80, Klonaridis Inc., Toronto, 1979, 81, 82, Rice U., 1978, Dayton Mus., 1979, Columbus Mus., 1979, Lamont Gallery, Phillips Acad., Exeter, N.H., 1983, Art Gallery Greater Victoria, 1983, Gallery One, Toronto, 1985, Culturale Canadese Roma, 1985, Gallery 291, Atlanta, 1986, Richard Greene Gallery, N.Y.C., 1986, L.A., 1987. Del Art Mus., Wilmington, 1990, Muhlenberg Coll., Allentown, Pa., 1992, Mira Godard Gallery, Toronto, Reading (Pa.) Pub. Mus., 1994, 96, Andre Zarre Gallery, N.Y.C., 1994, 04, 05, spl. showing Hillary Ground for Sculpture, Trenton N.J., 1997, retrospective, 1997, Moore Gallery, Toronto, 1999, 2001, 03, Ericson Gallery, Phila., 1999, McLaren Gallery, Barrie, 2001, Nat. Gallery of Can., Ottawa, 1999, Winchester Galleries, Victoria, 2004, Freedman Gallery, Reading, 2004; exhibited in group shows at Whitney Mus. 1996— Am., Art, N.Y.C., 1964-66, Tibor de Nagy Gallery, N.Y.C., 1965, Musée cantonal des Beaux Arts, Lausanne, Switzerland, 1966, World House Gallery, N.Y.C., 1966, Betty Parsons Gallery, 1966, Sch. Visual Arts, N.Y.C., 1967, Los Angeles County Mus., 1967, Nat. Gallery Can., Toronto, 1967, Inst. Contemporary Art, Boston, 1967, U. Toronto, 1967, Guggenheim Mus., N.Y.C., 1967, Inst. Torcuato Di Tella, Buenos Aires, 1967, Musée d'Art Moderne, Paris, 1968, Whitney Mus., 1967, Walker Art Gallery, 1969, X Sao Paulo Biennial, Brazil, 1969, Boston City Hall, 1971, Artist and Fabricator, Amherst, Mass., 1975, Met. Mus., N.Y.C., 1983, Del. Art Mus., 1990, GrandRapids (Mich.) Mus., 1994; represented in permanent collections, Montreal Mus. Fine Arts, Nat. Gallery Can., Joseph Hirshhorn Collection, Art Gallery Ont., Larry Aldrich Mus., Ridgefield, Conn., New Brunswick Mus., Whitney Mus. Am. Art, Met. Mus., N.Y.C., Columbus Mus., Dayton Art Inst., Storm King Art Centre, Del. Art. Mus., Wilmington, Muhlenberg Coll., Allentown, Pa., others; major commns. include, Everson Mus., Syracuse, N.Y., Fredonia (N.Y.) State Coll., Canadian Dept. External Affairs, Ottawa, Ont., U. Mass., U. Toronto, Ont., State Mus., Juneau, Alaska, Honeywell Corp., Mpls., CNIB, One King West, Toronto, also others. Decorated Order of Can. Fax: 610-869-4403. Office Phone: 610-869-4636. E-mail: rmurray601@earthlink.net.

**MURRAY, ROBERT PATRICK**, music educator, musician; b. Emporia, Kans., Dec. 26, 1958; s. Robert Patrick and Gloria Jacqueline Murray; m. Lauren Baker Murray, June 26, 2001. MusB, Portland State U., 1994, MusM, 1996; Mus D, U. North Tex., 2002. Asst. dir. bands U. Wash., Seattle, 1983—87; regional tng. dir. Kay-Bee Toys, Portland, Oreg., 1988—93; prof. trumpet Murray State U., Ky., 1999—2003, U. North Colo., Greeley, Colo., 2003—. Prin. trumpet Portland Musical Theater Co., Portland, Oreg., 1990—98; trumpet Dallas Brass, Dallas, 1997—2000; prin. trumpet Portland

Opera, Portland, Oreg., 1998—99, Owensboro Symphony Orch., Owensboro, Ky., 1999—2003, Orquesta Sinfonica de Mineria, Mexico City, 2000—03; trumpet Harmonie del Sur, Evans, Colo., 1999—; first trumpet Rocky Mountain Brass Quintet, Greeley, Colo., 2003—. Musician: (trumpet soloist and clinician) World Association of Symphonic Bands and Ensembles, British Association of Symphonic Bands and Ensembles, (trumpet soloist and performer) International Trumpet Guild, (trumpet soloist) Owensboro Symphony Orchestra; author (lecture recital): (college music society) Synthesis and Integration: World and Electro-Acoustic Music in the Applied Studio, (nat. symposium on music instruction tech) A Global View: Applying World and Electro-Acoustic Music to the Intrumental Studio; author: (dissertation) A Performance Guide to Tomas Svoboda's Duo Concerto for Trumpet and Organ. V.p. prodn. programming Murray Civic Music Assn., Murray, Ky., 1999—2003. Mem.: Hist. Brass Soc., Coll. Music Soc., Music Educators Nat. Conf., Internat. Trumpet Guild. Achievements include research in The introduction of world music and electro-acoustic music into the Applied Music Studio. Office: U Northern Colorado School Music Campus Box 28 Greeley CO 80639 Office Phone: 970-351-2285. Business E-Mail: robert.murray@unco.edu.

**MURRAY, ROBERT WALLACE**, chemistry professor; b. Brockton, Mass., June 20, 1928; s. Wallace James and Rose Elizabeth (Harper) M.; m. Claire K. Murphy, June 10, 1951; children: Kathleen A., Lynn E., Robert Wallace, Elizabeth A., Daniel J., William M., Padraic O'D. AB, Brown U., 1951; MA, Wesleyan U., Middletown, Conn., 1956; PhD, Yale U., 1960. Mem. tech. staff Bell Labs., Murray Hill, NJ, 1959-68; prof. chemistry U. Mo., St. Louis, 1968-81, chmn. dept., 1975-80, Curators' prof., 1981-2000, Curators' prof. emeritus, 2001—. Vis. prof. Engler-Bunte Inst. U. Karlsruhe, Fed. Republic Germany, 1982, dept. chemistry Univ. Coll., Cork, Ireland, 1989; cons. to govt. and industry. Co-editor: Singlet Oxygen, 1979; contbr. articles to profl. jours. Mem. Warren (N.J.) Twp. Com., 1962-63, mayor, 1963; mem. Planning Com. and Bd. Health, 1962-64, Bd. Edn., 1966-68. Served with USN, 1951-54; Lt. comdr. USNR. Grantee EPA, NSF, NIH, Office of Naval Research. Fellow AAAS, Am. Inst. Chemists, N.Y. Acad. Scis.; mem. Am. Soc. Photobiology, Am. Chem. Soc., The Oxygen Soc., Sigma Xi. Home: 1810 Walnutway Dr Saint Louis MO 63146-3659 Office: Univ Mo Dept Chemistry Saint Louis MO 63121 Personal E-Mail: kinsale63@aol.com.

**MURRAY, RODERICK CHARLES**, manufacturing executive; b. Johannesburg, S. Africa, Jan. 29, 1945; came to U.S., 1987; s. Charles Victor Murray and Yvonne Margaret Sheriffs; m. Yvonne Edna Bennett, Feb. 26, 1966; children: Sandra Leigh, Stuart Charles. BS, Witwatersrand U., 1967; MBA, Calif. Coast U., 1990. Quality assurance S. African Breweries, Johannesburg, 1971-75; tech. mgr. Hens Paper, Eerbeek, Holland, 1975-80; dir. mktg. and sales Metal Box, Barlow Rand, Johannesburg, 1980-87; v.p. mktg. ARPAC L.P., Chgo., 1987-89; pres. BMI Machinery, Milw., 1990-96; v.p. Klockner Packaging, 1990—96; CEO, pres. PPi Techs., Sarasota, Fla., 1996—. Author: Label Paper Technology, 1976, Brand Introductions, 1989; contbr. articles to profl. jours. Fellow British Bottlers; mem. Inst. Packaging Profls. (chmn. 1976), Internat. Beverage Tech. (vice chmn. 1978). Republican. Anglican. Avocations: golf, tennis, boating, travel. E-mail: rcmpp@aol.com.

**MURRAY, RUSSELL, II**, aeronautical engineer, security consultant; b. Woodmere, NY, Dec. 5, 1925; s. Herman Stump and Susanne Elizabeth (Warren) M.; m. Sally Tingue Gardiner, May 22, 1954; children: Ann Tingue, Prudence Warren, Alexandria Gardiner. BS in Aero. Engring., MIT, 1949, MS, 1950. Guided missile flight test engr. Grumman Aircraft Engring. Corp., Bethpage, NY, 1950-53, asst. chief operations analysis, 1953-62; prin. dep. asst. sec. of def. for systems analysis The Pentagon, Washington, 1962-69; dir. long range planning Pfizer Internat., N.Y.C., 1969-73; dir. review Center for Naval Analyses, Arlington, Va., 1973-77; asst. sec. of def. for program analysis and evaluation Dept. of Def., The Pentagon, Washington, 1977-81; prin. Systems Research & Applications Corp., Arlington, Va., 1981-85; spl. counsellor Com. on Armed Services U.S. Ho. of Reps., 1985-89, nat. security cons., 1989—. Served with USAAF, 1944-45. Recipient Sec. of Def. Medal for meritorious civilian service, 1968; Disting. Public Service medal Dept. Def., 1981 Home: 210 Wilkes St Alexandria VA 22314-3839

**MURRAY, SABINA**, writer; BA, Mt. Holyoke Coll., Mass.; MA, U. of Tex. Writer-in-residence Phillips Acad., Andover, Mass., 2000—. Tchr. creative fiction and poetry. Author: (novels) Slow Burn, 1990, The Caprices, 2002 (PEN/Faulkner award for fiction, 2003), A Carnivore's Inquiry, 2004, (screenplays) The Beautiful Country, 2004. Michener Fellow, U. Texas, Bunting Fellow, Radcliffe Inst., Harvard U. Address: Sabina Murray c/o Houghton Mifflin Co Trade Divsn Adult Editl 8th Fl 222 Berkeley St Boston MA 02116-3764 E-mail: smurray@andover.edu.

**MURRAY, STEPHEN JAMES**, lawyer; b. Phila., Jan. 27, 1943; s. Paul Martin and Hannah (Smith) M.; m. Linda Sanders, June 20, 1970; children: Gordon Joshua, Cara Sanders. AB cum laude, Brown U., 1963; JD, Harvard U., 1966; LLM, George Washington U., 1967. Bar: N.Y. 1968, U.S. Ct. Appeals (2nd cir.) 1971, U.S. Ct. Appeals (fed. cir.) 1998, U.S. Dist. Ct. (so. and ea. dists.) N.Y. 1972, U.S. Ct. Claims 1974, U.S. Supreme Ct. 1975, Conn. 1988, U.S. Dist. Ct. Conn. 1988, U.S. Ct. Internat. Trade 1998. Spl. asst. SEC, Washington, 1966-67, Maritime Adminstrn., Washington, 1967-68; assoc. Hill, Betts & Nash, N.Y.C., 1970-76; transp. atty. Union Carbide Corp., N.Y.C., 1976-78; sr. transp. atty., 1978-85, chief transp. counsel Danbury, Conn., 1985—2001, group counsel, 1986—2001, chief real estate counsel, 1992—2001, commfl. counsel, 1993—2001, customs and internat. trade counsel, 1997—2001; of counsel Mahoney & Keane, New York City, 2001—. Spkr. in field. Contbr. articles to profl. jours. Lt. JAGC, USN, 1968-70. Mem. ABA, Conn. State Bar Assn., U.S. Naval Inst., Navy League of U.S., Maritime Law Assn., U.S. Transp. Lawyers Assn., N.Y. State Bar Assn. Am Corp. Counsel Assn. (co chair real estate com. Westchester-So. Conn. chpt.), Conn. Maritime Assn., Harvard Club, Brown Club (co-pres.), Brown Faculty Club, Brown Alumni Sch. Commn. (chmn. Fairfield County), Brown Alumni Assn. (bd. govs.). Office: Mahoney & Keane 14 Pilgrim Ln Weston CT 06883 Office Phone: 203-222-1019. Personal E-Mail: murraysj@optonline.net.

**MURRAY, STEPHEN SANFORD**, composer, lyricist, playwright; b. Putnam, Conn., Mar. 13, 1963; s. Charles Sanford and Donna Saegaert Murray; m. Ruth Werner Kaplan, Aug. 15, 1992; m. Dianne Tower, June 1982 (div. Oct. 1990); children: Daniel McCord, Benjamin Charles, Natasha Elizabeth, Jennifer Ruth. BA, Westfield State Coll., Mass., 1985; MEd, Fitchburg State Coll., Mass., 2003. Lic. tchr. Mass., 1985. Composer, lyricist, playwright: musical plays Musical! The Bard is Back! (Jackie White Meml. Nat. Children's Playwrighting award, 2000), Tortoise Vs. Hare (Anna Zornio Children's Playwriting award, 1993), Pom-Pom Zombies, Katastrophe Kate, Mother Goose, Inc. (3rd Pl. Jackie White Play Competition, 1995), The Magic Snowman. Mem.: Music Educators Nat. Conf. Personal E-Mail: stevesanmu@msn.com. E-mail: stephen_murray@wayland.k12.ma.us.

**MURRAY, THOMAS HENRY**, bioethics educator; b. Phila., July 30, 1946; s. Thomas Henry and Colomba Rita (Lucci) M.; m. Sharon Marie Engelkraut, Jan. 1968 (div. Sept. 1975); children: Kathleen Elizabeth Dominique Maria, Peter Albert; m. Cynthia Sarah Aberle, Apr. 1, 1978; 1 child, Emily Sarah Aberle. BA in Psychology, Temple U., 1968; PhD in Social Psychology, Princeton U., 1976; MD (hon.), Uppsala U., 2003. Instr. New Coll., Sarasota, Fla., 1971-75; asst. prof. Interdisciplinary Studies Miami U., Oxford, Ohio, 1975-80, assoc. prof., 1980; assoc. social behavioral studies The Hastings Ctr., Hastings-on-Hudson, NY, 1980-84; assoc. prof. Inst. Med. Humanities U. Tex. Med. Br., Galveston, 1984-86, prof., 1986-87; prof., dir. Ctr. Biomed. Ethics Case We. Res. U., Cleve., 1987-99, Susan E. Watson prof. bioethics, 1999—99; pres. The Hastings Ctr., Garrison, NY, 1999—. Mem. Nat. Bioethics Adv. Commn., 1996-2001; mem. ethical, legal and social issues working group Human Genome Project NIH/Dept. Energy, 1989-95. Author: The Worth of a Child, 1996; founder, editor Med. Humanities Rev.; mem. editl. bd. Human Gene Therapy, Cloning, Politics and the Life Scis., Hastings Cetr. Report, Jour. of Law, Medicine and Ethics; editor: Encyclo-

pedia of Ethical, Legal, and Policy Issues in Biotechnology, (with K.W.M. Fulford and D.L. Dickenson) Healthcare Ethics and Human Values: An Introductory Text with Readings and Case Studies, 2002, (with Carol Levine) The Cultures of Caregiving: Conflict and Common Ground Among Families, Health Professionals and Policy Makers, 2004, (with M. Rothstein, G.E Kaebkick and M.A. Majunder) Genetic Ties and the Family: The Impace of Paternity Testing on Parents and Children, 2005. Fellow NEH, 1977-78, 1979-80, Aspen Inst., 1989. Fellow Hastings Ctr.; mem. APHA, Assn. Practical and Profl. Ethics, Am. Soc. Law Medicine and Ethics (bd. dirs. 1993-97), Assn. Integrative Studies (bd. dirs. 1980-87, pres. 1983), Soc. Health and Human Values (chair program dirs. sect. 1989-90, faculty assn. 1989-90, SHHV program com. 1990, pres.-elect 1992-93, pres. 1993-94), Am. Soc. Human Genetics (chair social issues com. 1998-99), Am. Coll. Ob-Gyn. (com. on ethics 1996-2001), Am. Soc. Bioethics and Humanities (pres.-elect 1998-99, pres. 1999-2000), Human Genome Orgn. (ethics com.), World Anti-Doping Agy. (chair ethical issues rev. panel 2004—). Office: The Hastings Ctr 21 Malcolm Gordon Rd Garrison NY 10524-5555 Office Phone: 845-424-4040.

**MURRAY, THOMAS J.**, advertising executive; b. Bridgeport, Conn., Mar. 12, 1924; s. Thomas and Mary (Diskin) M.; m. Mary Elizabeth Cull, Feb. 22, 1945; children: Joshua Francis, Mary Elizabeth, Katherine Diskin. AB, Dartmouth Coll., 1947. Instr., Dartmouth Coll., 1947-48; with Warwick & Legler, N.Y.C., 1948-68, sr. v.p., mgmt. account supr., 1964-68; sr. v.p. group supr. Gaynor & Ducas, Inc., 1968-74, exec. v.p., 1974—, chief fin. officer and gen. mgr., 1978-87; pres. TJM & Assn., 1987—. Pres., trustee Hillcrest Gen. Hosp., N.Y.C.; Westchester Inst. for Disabled in Psychoanalysis and Psychotheraphy, Mt. Kisco, N.Y. Served as 1st lt. USAAF, 1942-45. Decorated D.F.C., Air medal with 4 oak leaf clusters. Mem. Nat. Wholesale Druggists Assn., Propriety Assn., Nat. Assn. Chain Drug Stores, Am. Mktg. Assn. Home and Office: 65 Norfield Rd Weston CT 06883-2213 Office Phone: 800-749-4254. E-mail: tjma@optonline.net.

**MURRAY, THOMAS JOHN (JOCK MURRAY)**, medical humanities educator, physician, neurologist; b. Halifax, N.S., Can., May 30, 1938; m. Janet Kathleen Pottie; children: Shannon, Bruce, Suellen, Brian. Grad. pre-med, St. Francis Xavier U., 1958, LLD (hon.), 1989; MD, Dalhousie U., 1963; DSc (hon.), Acadia U., 1991; LittD (hon.), St. Thomas U., 2004. Family physician, Nashwaaksis, N.S., 1963-65; chief medicine Camp Hill Hosp., Halifax, N.S., 1974-79; chief neurology Dalhousie U., Halifax, N.S., 1979-85, dir. multiple sclerosis rsch. unit, 1980—2003, dean medicine, 1985-92, prof. med. humanities, 1992—2003, prof. emeritus, 2003—. Mem. working group on Diability in U.S. Pres., 1994—96. Co-author: (textbook) Essential Neurology; author over 200 pub. works, including 7 books and contbns. to 14 textbooks. Bd. dirs. St. Francis Xavier U., Pictou Acad. Found., Robert Pope Found., Nat. Coun. on Bioethics and Health Rsch. Decorated officer Order Can.; recipient Neilson award Hannah Inst. for Med. History, Disting. Profl. award Discovery Ctr., 2005, 81 rsch. grants. Fellow Royal Coll. Physicians (Can. and London, Mentor of Yr. award 2002), ACP (master; gov. 1985-90, chmn. bd. govs. 1990-91, chair bd. regents 1995-97, emeritus chair, Dr. Nicholas Davies award, Laureate award, Stengel award); mem. Can. Neurol. Soc. (pres. 1982-84), Am. Acad. Neurology (v.p. 1981-83, Dr. A.B. Baker award), Can. Med. Assn., N.S. Med. Soc., Assn. Can. Med. Colls. (pres. 1991-92), Can. Med. Forum (chmn. 1992-95), Multiple Sclerosis Soc. Can. (chmn. med. adv. bd., Perkins award), Consortium of Multiple Sclerosis Ctrs. (pres. 1997-99), Can. Soc. for History of Medicine (pres. 1997-99), Rotary Internat. (Paul Harris fellow, Profl. Distinction award Diocomy Ctr.). Avocations: medical history, piano, windsurfing. Home: 16 Bobolink St Halifax NS Canada B3M 1W3 Office: Dalhousie Med Sch Clin Rsch Ctr Halifax NS Canada B3H 4H7 Office Phone: 902-422-7817. Business E-Mail: jock.murray@dal.ca.

**MURRAY, THOMAS VEATCH**, lawyer; b. Phoenix, July 17, 1947; s. Robert Morrison Jr. and Jane Veatch (Murray) Barber and Richard A. Barber; m. Cynthia Ann Burnett, June 2, 1971; children: Jane Caroline, Thomas Veatch Jr. BA, U. Kans., 1969; JD, U. Mich., 1972. Bar: Kans. 1972, U.S. Dist. Ct. Kans. 1972, U.S. Ct. Appeals (10th cir.) 1983, U.S. Supreme Ct. 1976. Assoc. Barber, Emerson, Six, Springer & Zinn, Lawrence, Kans., 1972-76; mem. Barber, Emerson, Springer, Zinn & Murray, L.C., Lawrence, Kans., 1976—2003; of counsel Lathrop & Gage L.C., Overland Park, Kans., 2004—. Adj. prof. western civilization U. Kans., 1975-77, Sch. Law., 1990-91, instr. bar rev. course, 1975-82; dir. The First Nat. Bank of Lawrence, Kans., 1980-91, The Reuter Organ Co., 1991-, Hall Ctr. for the Humanities, Lawrence, Kans., 1988-. Contbr. articles to profl. jours. Mem. adv. bd. Lawrence Consumer Affairs Assn., 1974—77, Sta. KANU, Lawrence, 1975—80; mem. Bd. Law Examiners, 1995—, chmn., 2006—; mem. Lawrence Emergency Svcs. Coun., 1998—2002; dir. Lawrence C. of C., 1993—95; treas. Louie Holcom Baseball Assn., 1972—73; trustee First Presbyn. Ch., 1975—76. Mem. ABA, Fedn. Def. and Corp. Counsel (regional v.p. 1994-97, dir. 1997-99), Kans. Assn. Def. Counsel (dir. 1993-97), Def. Rsch. Inst., Kans. Bar Assn. (pres. corporation, banking and bus. law sect. 1983), Kans. Bar Found. (trustee 1999-2005), Johnson County Bar Assn., Judge Hugh Means Inns of Ct., Douglas Co. Bar Assn., Coaches' Corner (Lawrence), Lawrence Lions Alumni Assn., The Supreme Ct. Hist. Soc., Kansas City Club, The River Club, Lawrence Country Club, The Fortnightly Club (Lawrence). Republican. Presbyterian. Avocation: classical and operatic music. Office: Lathrop & Gage LC 10851 Mastin Blvd Bldg 82 Ste 1000 Overland Park KS 66210-1669 Office Phone: 913-451-5100. Business E-Mail: tmurray@lathropgage.com.

**MURRAY, TIMOTHY P.**, mayor; m. Tammy L. Sullivan. BA in Am. Studies, Fordham U.; JD, Western New England Sch. Law. Pvt. law practice State of Mass., Worcester, Mass., councillor-at-large, mayor, 2002—. Office: 455 Main St, Rm 305 Worcester MA 01608-1821 E-mail: mayor@ci.worcester.ma.us.

**MURRAY, TODD ANTHONY**, performing company executive; b. Blackwell, Okla., Feb. 27, 1965; s. James Junior and JoAnn Louise Murray; m. Ann Elena Williams, Dec. 20, 1985; children: Ian Riley Murray, Elliot Blair. BA, U. Ctrl. Okla., Edmond, 1988; AA, No. Okla. Coll., Tonkawa, 1985. Cert. tchr. Okla. Speech, drama and debate instr. Bartlesville Pub. Schs., Okla., 1989—91; dir. forensics Jenks Pub. Schs., Okla., 1992—2000; pac dir. Owasso Pub. Schs., Okla., 2000—. Mem. Mus. Adv. Bd., Owasso, Okla., 2003—; bd. dirs. Owasso Cmty. Theatre Co., Okla. Mem.: NEA, Okla. Edn. Assn., Nat. Forensic League. Democrat. Episcopalian. Home: 102 E 24th Ct Owasso OK 74055 Office: Owasso Pub Schs 12901 E 86th St N Owasso OK 74055 Office Phone: 918-274-3420. Office Fax: 918-274-3421. Personal E-mail: toddmurray@cox.net. Business E-Mail: murrayt@owasso.k12.ok.us.

**MURRAY, WILLIAM BRUCE**, opera singer; b. Schenectady, N.Y., Mar. 13, 1935; s. John Allison and Jessie Chrystal (Gray) M.; m. Nancy Lee Adams, Mar. 1, 1958; children: John Horton, Christopher Andrew, Judith Leora. BA in Music Edn., Adelphi U., 1956; Cert. di Studio, U. Perugia, Italy, 1957; grad., Goethe Inst., 1960. Opera singer Landestheater Detmold, Germany, 1960-61, Staatstheater Braunschweig, Germany, 1961-64, Nat. Theater Mannheim, Germany, 1964-66, Staatsoper München, Germany, 1966-78, Deutsche Oper Berlin, Germany, 1969—, Houston Grand Opera, 1994—. Opera singer numerous other theaters including N.Y. State Opera, Catania, Italy, Marseille, France, L.A. Opera, Teatro Reggio Torino (Italia), 1992; voice Shepherd Sch. Music Rice U., Houston. Recordings include Salome, Die Bassariden, Hochzeit des Camacho, Schöne Müllerin, Die Totestadt. With U.S. Army, 1958-60. Named Kammersänger Senate Berlin Germany, 1980; Fulbright fellow, 1956. Mem. Lions Club. Avocations: hiking, cooking, swimming. Home: 113 Homeyer Rd Sparrow Bush NY 12780-8302 Office Phone: 845-665-9629. Business E-Mail: wbmurray@rice.edu.

**MURRAY SHAW, JULEEN,** actress; d. Marianne Polly Eileen Arnold; m. Mathew Scott Shaw, May 8, 1988; 1 child, Sophie Fay Jiaoxin Shaw. BA, Moorhead State U., Minn., 1979. Prodr. Nursery Tap, LLC, Gig Harbor, Wash., 2004—. Prodr., dir., actor (performing arts dvd's for children) Nursery Tap Hip to Toe, Vol. I (George Foster Peabody award, 2005, Parents Choice award, iParenting Media award, KIDS FIRST! Endorsement, Dr. Toy's Best Products award, Creative Child Mag. Preferred award, 2005). Recipient Award of Excellence, reviewcorner.com, Dove Found. Seal of Approval Highest Rating. Mem.: Screen Actor's Guild. D-Liberal. Office Phone: 888-855-0545. Personal E-mail: info@nurserytap.com.

**MURRELL, JAMES THOMAS,** academic administrator, botanist; b. Dickson, Tenn., Mar. 17, 1942; s. James Thomas and Vera Grear Murrell; m. Virginia Carole Melton; children: Kenneth Troy, Michelle Nicole Rogers, Amber Liane Holcomb. PhD, Vanderbilt U., Nashville, 1968. Asst. prof. biology George Peabody Coll. Tchrs., Nashville, 1969—75, Miss. U. Women, Columbus, 1975—78, dean grad. sch. 1978—81, provost, 1981—88; v.p., acad. dean Hiwassee Coll., Madisonville, Tenn., 1989—2002; v.p. acad. affairs Martin Meth. Coll., Pulaski, Tenn., 2002—. Bd. dirs. Exch. Club, Pulaski, 2002—06. Independent. Methodist. Avocations: fishing, gardening. Home: 1523 Old Elkton Pike Dellrose TN 38453 Office: Martin Meth Coll 433 W Madison St Pulaski TN 38478 Office Phone: 931-363-9823. Office Fax: 931-363-9811. Business E-mail: jmurrell@martinmethodist.edu.

**MURRELL, JILL PONGRACZ,** music educator, director; b. Lorain, Ohio, Mar. 10, 1956; d. Julius Albert and Donna Jean Pongracz; m. Richard Albert Murrell, Aug. 12, 1978 (div. Oct. 31, 1989); children: Rebekka Anne, Zachary Albert. MusB, Miami U., Oxford, Ohio, 1977; M in the Art of Tchg., Marygrove Coll., Mich., 1998. Choir dir. Lorain (Ohio) Hungarian Ref. Ch., 1978—; music tchr. Keystone Local Schs., LaGrange, Ohio, 1979—89; vocal music tchr., vocal music coord. Lorain City Schs., 1989—2001; choral dir. Southview HS, Lorain, 2002—; artistic musical dir. Ashland (Ohio) Symphonic Youth Chorus, 2004—. Music mentor Cleve. Opera on Tour. Musician (flutist) Patriots Symphonic Band. Com. chair Boy Scouts of Am., Sheffield Lake, Ohio, 1999—2003; trustee Lorain Internat. Assn., 1998—2006; officer Sheffield-Sheffield Lake (Ohio) Band Boosters, 1994—2003; music com. chair Lorain Hungarian Ref. Ch., 1978—2006. Mem.: Lorain Edn. Assn. (bldg. rep. 2001—06), Ohio Choral Dirs. Assn., Ohio Music Edn. Assn. (state curriculum com. 2004—06, pub. music rep. 2002—). Democrat. United Church Of Christ. Home: 219 Gayle Dr Sheffield Lake OH 44054 Office: Southview High Sch 2270 E 42nd St Lorain OH Office Phone: 440-277-7271 ext 114. Personal E-mail: jponmurr@hotmail.com. Business E-mail: jmurre@lorainschools.org.

**MURRELL, ROBERT GEORGE,** lawyer; b. Jan. 27, 1932; s. Samuel Edwin and Myrtle Josephine (Hailey) M.; m. Bonnie Bird Robinson, Nov. 11, 1961; children: Robert George, Michele Grace, Bonnie Melissa. BA, U. Fla., 1951, JD, 1953. Bar: Fla. 1953, N.Y. 1981, U.S. Dist. Ct. (so. dist.) Fla. 1953, U.S. Dist. Ct. (mid. dist.) Fla. 1980, U.S. Ct. Appeals (5th cir.) 1953, U.S. Ct. Appeals (11th cir.) 1981, U.S. Ct. Mil. Appeals 1958, U.S. Supreme Ct. 1958, U.S. Ct. Claims 1975, U.S. Tax Ct. 1975, U.S. Ct. Customs and Patent Appeals 1975, U.S. Ct. Appeals (D.C. cir.) 1989, U.S. Ct. Appeals (3rd, 4th, 6th, 7th, 8th, 9th, 10th cirs.) 1989, U.S. Ct. Appeals (2nd cir.) 1990, U.S. Ct. Vet. Appeals 1992; arbitrator Am. Arbitration Assn. Atty. Sam E. Murrell & Sons., Orlando, Fla., 1953—. Mem. Citrus Assocs. of N.Y. Stock Exch.; pres. Colonial Mortgage Co. Fla., Inc.; dir. Weiss Realty Corp., Lake Margaret Co. With U.S. Army, 1953—55. Mem.: ATLA, ABA, Acad. Fla. Trial Lawyers, Orange County Bar Assn., Univ. Winter Park, Elks (Orlando), Shriners, Masons. Republican. Baptist. Office: Sam E Murrell & Sons 1 N Rosalind Ave Orlando FL 32801-1682 Home: 1212 Ayrshire St Orlando FL 32803 Office Phone: 407-843-8500.

**MURRELL, SUSAN DEBRECHT,** librarian; b. St. Louis, Aug. 10, 1951; d. Edward August and Edith (Keeney) DeB.; children: Brian, Katherine. BA in History, U. Ky., 1973; MLS, U. Mo., 1976. Children's libr. Louisville Free Pub. Libr., 1974-76, talking book libr. head, 1976-83; lower/mid. sch. libr. Ky. Country Day Sch., Louisville, 1983-84; children's libr. Emmet O'Neal Libr., Mountain Brook, Ala., 1984-86, asst. dir., 1986-89, dir., 1989—. Active Jefferson County Pub. Libr.; mem. admissions com. United Way; exec. bd. Jefferson County Libr. Bd.; bd. dirs. Mountain Brook Libr. Found., 1993—. Ala. Ctr. for Book. Mem. ALA, Ala. Libr. Assn. (mem. publicity com. 1992-93, pub. libr. chair 1995-96), Rotary Internat. Roman Catholic. Office: Emmet O'Neal Libr 50 Oak St Birmingham AL 35213-4295 Office Phone: 205-879-0492.

**MURREN, JAMES JOSEPH,** recreational facility executive, hotel executive; Various positions Deutsche Morgan Grenfell, 1984—98; exec. v.p. MGM Mirage, Las Vegas, 1998—, CFO, 1998—, pres., 1999—, treas., 2001—. Office: MGM Mirage 3600 Las Vegas Blvd South Las Vegas NV 89109*

**MURRETT, ROBERT B.,** federal agency administrator, career military officer; b. Oct. 8, 1952; BA, U. Buffalo; M in Govt. and Strategic Intelligence, Georgetown U.; M. Def. Intelligence Coll. Advanced through ranks to vice admiral USN, 2006, watch stander and briefing officer, chief naval ops. intelligence plot, 1980—83, asst. intelligence officer, 1983—85; asst. naval attache U.S. Embassy, Oslo, 1986—89; ops. intelligence officer U.S. Pacific Fleet USN, 1989—92, asst. chief of staff intelligence for comdr. carrier group eight, 1992—95, asst. chief of staff intelligence for comdr. second fleet, 1995—97, exec. asst. to dir. naval intelligence, 1997—98, dir. intelligence directorate Office of Naval Intelligence Washington, 1998; comdr. Atlantic Intelligence Command, 1999; dir. intelligence U.S. Joint Forces Command, 2000—02; vice dir. intelligence Joint Staff USN, 2002—05, dir. naval intelligence Washington, 2005—06; dir. Nat. Geospatial-Intelligence Agy. US Dept. Def., Bethesda, Md., 2006—. Office: Nat Geospatial-Intelligence Agy 4600 Sangamore Rd Bethesda MD 20816*

**MURRIAN, ROBERT PHILLIP,** retired federal judge, educator; b. Knoxville, Tenn., Apr. 1, 1945; s. Albert Kinzel and Mary Gilbert (Eppes) M.; m. Jerrilyn Sue Boone, Oct. 29, 1983; children: Kimberley Ann, Jennifer Rebecca, Albert Boone, Samuel Robert. BS, U.S. Naval Acad., 1967; JD, U. Tenn., 1974, Bar: Tenn. 1974, U.S. Dist. Ct. (ea. dist.) Tenn. 1975, U.S. Dist. Ct. (mid. dist.) Tenn. 2005, U.S. Ct. Appeals (6th cir.) 1982. Law clk. to judge US Dist. Ct. (ea. dist.) Tenn., Knoxville, 1974-76, magistrate judge, 1978—2002; assoc. Butler, Vines, Babb & Threadgill, Knoxville, 1976-78; ptnr. Kramer Rayson LLP, Knoxville, 2002—. Adj. prof. U. Tenn. Coll. Law, 1990-93, 95-96, 2002; trial lawyer, arbitrator, mediator, spl. master litigation. Lt. USN, 1967-71. Green scholar, 1973-74. Nat. Moot Ct. Advocate, 1974; named to Best Lawyers in Am., 2005-06. Fellow Tenn. Bar Found.; mem. ABA, Tenn. Bar Assn., Knoxville Bar Assn. (bd. govs. 1994, 2002—), Sixth Cir. Jud. Conf. (life), Order of Coif. Am. Inn of Ct. (master of the bench, pres. 1997-98), Phi Kappa Phi. Presbyterian (Elder). Office: Kramer Rayson LLP PO Box 629 Knoxville TN 37901-0629 Address: First Tennessee Plz 800 S Gay St Ste 2500 Knoxville TN 37929 Office Phone: 865-525-5134. Business E-Mail: rpmurrian@kramer-rayson.com.

**MURRIN, MICHAEL J.,** literature educator, writer; MA, PhD, Yale U. s. David B. and Clara E. Stern prof. humanities U. Chgo.; prof. religion and literature, Divinity Sch., prof. comparative literature and English language and literature. Author: The Veil of Allegory, 1969, The Allegorical Epic, 1980, History and Warfare in Renaissance Epic, 1994. Fellow: Am. Acad. Arts and Sciences. Office: Univ Chicago Gates-Blake Halls 315 5845 S Ellis Ave Chicago IL 60637 Office Phone: 773-702-7985. Office Fax: 773-702-8223. E-mail: m-murrin@uchicago.edu.*

**MURRIN, REGIS DOUBET,** lawyer; b. Erie, Pa., June 2, 1930; s. John III and Gabrielle (Doubet) M.; m. Evelyn L. Alessio, Aug. 22, 1959; children: Catherine Shaw Murrin Hargenrader, Mary Murrin, Elizabeth Murrin Talotta, Rebecca Fielding Lamanna. BA, U. Notre Dame, 1952; JD, Harvard U.,

1959; LLM, Temple U., 1968. Bar: Pa. 1959, U.S. Supreme Ct. 1971. Assoc. Murrin & Murrin, Butler, Pa., 1959-62; atty. Housing & Home Fin. Agy., Phila., 1962-64; ptnr. Baskin & Sears, Pitts., 1964-84, Reed Smith Shaw & McClay, Pitts., 1985-95, of counsel, 1995-99, counsel, 1999—. Trustee Pitts. Oratory, 1976-97; chmn. Zoning Bd. Adjustment, City of Pitts., 1994—; bd. dirs. Ellis Sch., 1991-99. Served as lt. USNR, 1952-55, Korea, Vietnam. Mem. Allegheny County Bar Assn., Edwin Sorin Soc. Democrat. Roman Catholic. Office: Reed Smith Shaw & McClay 435 6th Ave Ste 2 Pittsburgh PA 15219-1886 Office Phone: 412-288-3352.

**MURRY, CHARLES EMERSON,** lawyer, federal official; b. Hope, ND, June 23, 1924; s. Raymond Henry and Estelle Margarete (Skeim) M.; m. Donna Deane Kane, June 20, 1948; children: Barbara, Karla, Susan, Bruce, Charles. BS, U. N.D., 1948, JD, 1950. Bar: N.D. 1950. Mem. firm Nelson and Heringer, Rugby, ND, 1950-51; dir. N.D. Legis. Council, 1951-75; adj. gen. with rank of maj. gen. State of N.D., Bismarck, 1975-84; mgr. Garrison Diversion Conservancy Dist., 1985-93. Cons. Council State Govts.; mem. res. forces policy bd. Sec. of Def. Vice-pres. Mo. Slope Luth. Home of Bismarck, 1965-66. Served with AUS, 1942-45. Decorated D.S.M., Legion of Merit, Meritorious Service medal, Bronze Star, Army Commendation medal; Fourragere Belgium; Orange Lanyard Netherlands; recipient Sioux award U. N.D., 1970; Gov.'s award of excellence, 1971; Nat. Leadership award Bismarck C. of C., 1971 Mem. Adjs. Gen. Assn. (exec. com., sec. 1983-84), Nat. Legis. Conf. (past chmn.), N.G. Assn., Am. Bar Assn., N.D. Bar Assn., Commrs. Uniform State Laws. Lodges: Elks, Masons. Lutheran. Office: 5505 Ponderosa Ave Bismarck ND 58503-9159

**MURRY, HAROLD DAVID, JR.,** lawyer; b. Holdenville, Okla., June 30, 1943; s. Harold David Sr. and Willie Elizabeth (Dees) M.; m. Ann Moore Earnhardt, Nov. 1, 1975; children: Elizabeth Ann, Sarah Bryant. BA, Okla. U., 1965, JD, 1968. Bar: Okla. 1968, D.C. 1974. Asst. to v.p. U. Okla., Norman, 1968-71, legal counsel Research Inst., 1969-71; atty. U.S. Dept. Justice, Washington, 1971-74; spl. asst. U.S. Atty., Washington, 1972; assoc. Clifford & Warnke, Washington, 1974-78, ptnr., 1978-91, Howrey & Simon, Washington, 1991-98, Baker Botts LLP, Washington, 1998—. Mem. ABA, Okla. Bar Assn., D.C. Bar Assn., Fed. Bar Assn., Met. Club (Washington), Chevy Chase Club (Md.), Phi Alpha Delta. Democrat. Office: Baker Botts LLP Ste 1300 1299 Pennsylvania Ave NW Washington DC 20004-2408 Home: 3711 Village Park Dr Chevy Chase MD 20815-5745

**MURTAGH, MICHAEL PAUL,** psychologist; b. Washington, Sept. 23, 1959; s. Hugh Hunter and Margaret (Payne) M.; m. Anne Marie Murtagh, Nov. 30, 1985. BS magna cum laude, James Madison U., 1981; MS, Villanova U., 1983; PhD, U. Mont., Missoula, 1991. Lic. psychologist, N.Y. Staff psychologist Eagleville (Pa.) Hosp., 1984-87; dir. psychol. svcs. Mont. State Prison, Deer Lodge, 1991-94; staff psychologist, coord. forensic svcs. Madison County Dept. Mental Health, Wampsville, NY, 1994-2000; asst. prof. Bridgewater State Coll., 2000—. Part-time faculty Salish-Kootenai Coll., Pablo, Mont., 1988; vis. prof. U. Mont., Missoula, 1992; adj. faculty Onondaga C.C., Syracuse, N.Y., 1998-2000; coord. graduate program in psychology Bridgewater (Mass.) State Coll., 2000—; consultant sex offender treatment program Madison County Dept. Mental Health, 2000—; lectr., presenter in field. Contbr. articles to profl. jours. Vol. crisis counselor Listening Ear Svc., Harrisonburg, Va., 1980-81. Recipient Disting. Svc. award Southea. Pa. Mental Health Assn., 1985. Mem. Am. Psychol. Assn. Avocation: baseball. Home: 57 Seymour St Berkley MA 02779 Office Phone: 508-531-2843. Business E-Mail: mmurtagh@bridgew.edu.

**MURTAGIAN, GREGORIO ROBERTO,** mechanical engineer; s. Sergio Murtagian and Victoria Kabakian; m. Veronica Lidia Ponce, Dec. 31, 2002; children: Camila Magdalena, Zoe Martina. Diploma in mech. engring., Universidad Tecnologica Nacional, Buenos Aires, 1994; MS in Materials Sci. and Tech., Universidad de Gen. San Martin, Buenos Aires, 1997; PhD in Mech. Engring., Ga. Inst. Tech., Atlanta, 2004. Rschr. Ctr. Indsl. Rsch. TENARIS, Buenos Aires, 1995—99; grad. rsch. asst. Ga. Inst. Tech., Atlanta, 1999—2004; sr. engr. Intel Corp., Phoenix, 2004—. Recipient Recognition for Contbns. on organizing the STLE/ASME 2003 Conf., STLE/ASME, 2003; Jorge A. Sabato fellow, Instituto de Tecnologia. Comision Nacional de Energia Atomica, 1994. Mem.: ASME. Achievements include research in dynamic crack propagation on pipelines; sealability of metal-to-metal seals; surface integrity of machined intermetallic compounds; invention of bimetallic contact for force modulation with temperature for CPU package and LGA socket; development of hollow sucker rods for progressive cavity pumping. Avocations: piano, piano restoration and testing. Home: 14426 S 42nd St Phoenix AZ 85044 Office: Intel Corp 5000 W Chandler Blv Chandler AZ 85226 Office Phone: 480-554-1286. Office Fax: 480-554-1521. Personal E-mail: krikorik@gmail.com. Business E-Mail: gregorio.r.murtagian@intel.com.

**MURTAUGH, CHRISTOPHER DAVID,** lawyer; b. Darby, Pa., Oct. 25, 1945; s. John Michael and Rita (Sullivan) M.; m. Nancy R. Hanauer, Nov. 30, 1968; children: Jason C., Colin M., Alison M. AB, U. Ill., 1967, JD, 1970. Bar: Ill. 1970, Fla. 1973, U.S. Dist. Ct. (no. dist.) Ill. 1975. Assoc. to ptnr. Winston & Strawn LLP, Chgo., 1974—, capital ptnr. 1987—, real estate dept. chmn., 1994—2005. Mem. Glen Ellyn (Ill.) Capital Improvements Com., 1985-89, Glen Ellyn Plan Com. 1989-96. Met. Planning Coun., 1995—; bd. visitors U. Ill. Coll. of Law, 1998-2001. bd. dirs. LifeSource Blood Svcs., 2005—; Lt. USNR, 1971-74. Mem. ABA, Am. Coll. Real Estate Lawyers, Fla. Bar Assn., Ill. State Bar Assn., Chgo. Bar Assn., Internat. Coun. Shopping Ctrs. Order of Coif. Office: Winston & Strawn LLP 35 W Wacker Dr Ste 4200 Chicago IL 60601-1695 Office Phone: 312-558-5600. E-mail: cmurtaugh@winston.com.

**MURTHA, JOHN PATRICK, JR.,** congressman; b. New Martinsville, W.Va., June 17, 1932; s. John Patrick and Mary Edna (Ray) Murtha; m. Joyce Bell, June 10, 1955; children: Donna Sue, John, Patrick. BA in Econs., U. Pitts., 1961; postgraduate student, Ind. U. Pa., 1962-65; HHD (hon.), Mt. Aloysius Jr. Coll. Mem. Pa. State Ho. Reps., 1969-73, US Congress from 12th Pa. dist., 1974—. mem. appropriations com., ranking minority mem. def. appropriations subcommittee. Author (with John Plashall): From Vietnam to 9/11: On the Front Lines of National Security, 2003. Served in USMC, as lt. 1952-55, as maj. 1966-67, USMC Res., 1955-66, 1967-90 Decorated Bronze Star, 2 Purple Hearts, Cross of Gallantry Vietnam; Recipient Pa. Disting. Svc. award, 1978, Pa. Meritorious Svc. medal, numerous service awards for work during Johnstown flood, 1977. Iron Mike award Marine Corps League, 1988, Disting. Am. award (Nation's Capital chpt.) Air Force Assn., 1989, Outstanding Vet. award Vets. Caucus of Am. Acad. Physician Assts., 1989, Man of Steel award Cold Finished Steel Bar Inst., 1989, Pa. Disting. Svc. medal & Pa. Meritorius Svc. medal, 2000, Spirit of Hope award United Svc. Orgns., Inc., 2000, Funding Hero award Breast Cancer Rsch. Found., 2002, John F. Kennedy Profile in Courage award John F. Kennedy Libr. Found., 2006; named Man of Yr. Johnstown Jaycees, 1978 Mem.: VFW, Salvation Army, Am. Legion. Democrat. Roman Catholic. Office: US Ho Reps 2423 Rayburn Ho Office Bldg Washington DC 20515-0001 Office Phone: 202-225-2065.*

**MURTHY, SANJEEVA N.,** education educator, materials scientist; b. Mysore, India, May 12, 1949; s. Narasimhaiah Ugrappa Mysore and Mahadevamma; m. Meena Sanjeeva Kumari, Feb. 18, 1979; children: Sandeep Narasimha, Praveen Giridhara. PhD, U. Conn., 1976. Rsch. scientist Honeywell Internat. Inc., Morristown, NJ, 1981—2002; assoc. prof. U. Vt., Burlington, 2002—. Author rsch. papers and 150 review articles in profl. jours. Recipient Spkr. of Yr., The Fiber Soc., 1999—2000; fellow, Internat. Ctr. for Diffraction Data, 2002. Fellow: Am. Phys. Soc.; mem.: Sigma Xi. Achievements include patents for Nanocomposites and Films. Office: Univ Vt 82 Univ Pl Burlington VT 05405 Office Phone: 802-656-0308. Office Fax: 802-656-0817. Business E-Mail: murthy@mailaps.org.

**MURTHY, UDAY,** accountant, educator; BCommerce, U. Poona, India, 1981; MBA, Drexel U., 1985; PhD, Ind. U., 1988. Chartered acct., Inst. Chartered Accts. India. Assoc. prof. Tex. A&M U., College Station, 1989—2002; prof., quinn eminent scholar Sch. Accountancy U. S. Fla., Tampa, 2002—. Home and office: 4202 E Fowler Ave BSN3403 Tampa FL 33620-5500 Office Phone: 813-974-6523. Home Fax: 813-974-6528. Personal E-mail: umurthy@coba.usf.edu.

**MUSA, JOHN DAVIS,** information technology executive, writer; b. Amityville, N.Y., June 11, 1933; s. Khan Hussein and Ione Geraldine (Ryan) M.; m. Marilyn Laurene Allred, June 24, 1959. BA, Dartmouth Coll., 1954, MSEE, 1955. With AT&T Bell Labs., Murray Hill, NJ, 1958-96, mem. tech. staff, 1958-63, supr. guidance program devel., 1963-68, supr. command and control program devel., 1968-69, supr. mgmt. control and new software tech., 1969-72, supr. human factors test, 1972-74, supr. computer graphics, 1974-80, supr. computer measurements, 1980-85, supr. software quality, 1985-90, tech. mgr. software reliability engring., 1991-96. Mem. N.J. Coun. R&D; lectr., spkr. in field. Author: Software Reliability: Measurement, Prediction, Application, 1987, Software Reliability Engineering: More Reliable Software, Faster Development and Testing, 1998, Software Reliability Engineering: More Reliable Software Faster and Cheaper, 2004; editor: (book series) Software Quality Institute; contbr. over 100 articles to prof. jours. and books. Lt. USN, 1955-58. Fellow IEEE (Third Millenium medal for outstanding achievements and contbns.); mem. IEEE Computer Soc. (2d v.p. 1986, v.p. publs. 1984-85, v.p. tech. activities 1986, chair tech com. software engring. 1982-84, founding mem. editl. bd. IEEE Software Mag., Disting. lectr. 1980-83, Meritorious Svc. award 1984, 85, 87, Golden Core award, founding officer com. on software reliability engring., mem. editl. bds. Spectrum mag., 1984-86, Proc. of the IEEE 1983-90, Technique et Science Informatiques jour., sr. editor Software Engring. Inst. book series, sr. founding editor Software Quality Inst. book series, chair steering com. Internat. Conf. on Software Engring.), IEEE Reliability Soc. (Engr. of Yr. 2004), Assn. for Computing Machinery. Achievements include internat. leader in software engring. and in creation new tech. software reliability engring.; created two software reliability models; developed concepts and practice of operational profile, software-reliability engineered testing, concept of execution time; reduced operation software (ROS), and operational development; created concept of fault exposure ratio; developed approach for choosing software development strategies to meet different reliability objectives; international leader in reducing software reliability engineering to practice. Office: 39 Hamilton Rd Morristown NJ 07960-5341 Personal E-mail: j.musa@ieee.org.

**MUSA, SAMUEL ALBERT,** university executive; m. Judith Friedman; children: Gregory, Jeffrey. BA, BSEE, Rutgers U., 1961; MS in Applied Physics, Harvard U., 1962, PhD in Applied Physics, 1965. Rsch. scientist Gen. Precision Inc., Little Falls, NJ, 1965-66; asst. prof. elec. engring. U. Pa., Phila., 1966-71; project leader Inst. for Def. Analyses, Arlington, Va., 1971-78; dep. dir. Office of Under Sec. Def., Washington, 1978-83; dir. rsch. and advanced tech. E-Systems, Inc., Dallas, 1983-86, v.p. rsch. and advanced tech., 1986-95; exec. dir. Ctr. Display Tech. and Mfg. U. Mich., 1995-99; assoc. v.p. for strategic initiative, prof. elec. and computer engring. Northwestern U., Evanston, Ill., 1999—. Mem. sci. adv. bd. USAF; mem. sci. bd. Def. Intelligence Agy., Army Sci. Bd. Contbr. articles to profl. jours. Recipient Exceptional Civilian Svc. award, Sec. of Air Force, cert. of appreciation, Sec. Def. Fellow IEEE; mem. AIA (tech. and ops. coun. 1986-95, vice chmn. 1993, chmn. 1994), Sigma Xi, Tau Beta Pi, Pi Mu Epsilon.

**MUSA, SARHAN,** electrical and computer engineering educator, mathematician; PhD, CUNY, N.Y.C., 1992. Instr. CCNY, 1996—2001; prof. Prairie View A&M U., Prairie View, Tex., 2002—. Dir.: (research and training) Communications and Networking; contbr. articles to profl. jours. Achievements include research in computing and computer communication networks. Personal E-mail: smmusa@pvamu.edu.

**MUSACCHIA, X(AVIER) J(OSEPH),** physiology and biophysics educator; b. Bklyn., Feb. 11, 1923; s. Castrense and Orsolina (Mazzola) M.; m. Betty Cook, Nov. 23, 1950; children: Joseph, Mary, Thomas, Laura Ann. BS, St. Francis Coll. Bklyn., 1944; MS, Fordham U., 1947, PhD, 1949. Instr. biology Marymount (N.Y.) Coll., 1948-49; from instr. to prof. biology St. Louis U., 1949-65; prof. physiology U. Mo., Columbia, 1965-78; prof. physiology and biophysics U. Louisville, 1978-91, prof. emeritus, 1991—, dean Grad. Sch., 1978-89, assoc. provost for rsch., 1985-89. Bd. dirs. Coun. Grad. Schs., 1986-89. Author: Depressed Metabolism, 1969, Regulation of Depressed Metabolism and Thermogenesis, 1976, Survival in Cold, 1981; also articles. Bd. govs. J. Graham Brown Cancer Ctr., Louisville, 1978-83; bd. dirs. Oak Ridge Associated Univs. Served with AUS, 1943-45. Research grantee NIH; Research grantee NASA. Fellow AAAS; mem. Am. Physiol. Soc., Am. Soc. Zoologists, Am. Soc. for Space and Gravitational Biology (v.p. 1988-89, pres. 1989-90), Soc. Exptl. Biology and Medicine, Corp. Marine Biol. Lab., Sigma Xi. (past chpt. pres.) Home: 1770 East Overland Dr Fayetteville AR 72703-5202

**MUSANTE, TONY (ANTHONY PETER MUSANTE JR.),** actor; b. Bridgeport, Conn. s. Anthony Peter and Natalie Anne (Salerno) M.; m. Jane Ashley Sparkes, June 2, 1962. BA (Baker scholar), Oberlin Coll. 1958; postgrad., Northwestern U., 1957; student, HB Studios, N.Y.C., 1961-65. Appearances include: (off Broadway prodns.) Borak, 1960, Zoo Story, Night of the Dunce, The Collection, Match-Play, Kiss Mama, L'Histoire du Soldat, A Gun Play, Falling Man, Cassatt, Grand Magic, The Big Knife, The Taming of the Shrew, Two Brothers, The Archbishop's Ceiling, Souvenir. A Streetcar Named Desire, Double Play, Dancing in the End Zone, Snow Orchid, Wait until Dark, Widows, Anthony Rose, Mount Allegro, Frankie and Johnny in the Clair de Lune, Breaking Legs, The Flip Side, Love Letters. The Sisters, Italian Funerals and Other Festive Occasions (Broadway prodns.) PS Your Cat is Dead, 1975 (N.Y. Drama Desk nomination), Memory of Two Mondays, 27 Wagons Full of Cotton, The Lady from Dubuque; films: Once a Thief, 1964, The Incident (Best Actor award Mar del Plata Internat. Film Festival), 1967, The Detective, The Mercenary, One Night at Dinner, Bird with the Crystal Plumage, Grissom Gang, Anonymous Venetian, The Last Run, Pisciotta Case, Goodbye and Amen, Break-Up, Collector's Item, The Repenter, Devil's Hill, Appointment in Trieste, Nocturne, The Pope of Greenwich Village, The Deep End of the Ocean, The Yards, Life As It Comes, Love's Promise, We Own The Night; TV appearances include Ride with Terror, 1963, star series Toma, 1973-74 (Photoplay Gold medal award 1974), scriptwriter several episodes; star HBO series Oz, A&E series 100 Centre Street; also starred in TV miniseries and movies: Pompeii, Traffic, Exiled, The Seventh Scroll, Deep Family Secrets, A Kiss In the Dark, High Ice, Breaking Up is Hard to Do, The Baron, Legend of the Black Hand, The Story of Esther, My Husband is Missing, Nowhere to Hide, The Quality of Mercy (Emmy nominee 1975), Court Martial of Lt. William Calley, Night Heat, Rearview Mirror, Nutcracker: Money, Madness and Murder, Acapulco HEAT, Nothing Sacred, American Playhouse: Weekend, Last Waltz on a Tightrope; daytime TV (guest star): Loving, ABC, 1993, As The World Turns, CBS, 2000. Mem. SAG, AFTRA, ATAS, Actors Equity Assn., Writers Guild Am. West, Acad. Motion Picture Arts and Scis.

**MUSAT, KATHERINE GADUS,** retired music educator; b. Cleve., Feb. 6, 1944; d. William Martin Gadus and Catherine Ruth Salmon; m. John George Musat, July 5, 1969; children: John William, Mary Katherine Smith, Danielle Eleanor. MusB in Edn., Baldwin-Wallace Coll., Berea, Ohio, 1966; MSc in Edn., Coll. Mt. St. Joseph, Cin., Ohio, 1988. Cert. tchr. Ohio, 1966. Dir. instrumental music Parma (Ohio) City Schs., 1967—2004; ret., 2004. Studio brass tchr. Baldwin-Wallace Coll., 1985—; prin. trumpet Parma Symphony Orch., 1967—, Hermit Club Orch., 1985—. Vol. church musician various chs., 1964—. Home: 2141 Jacqueline Dr Parma OH 44134-6858 Personal E-mail: kagy@cox.net.

**MUSCALO, DAVID,** geologist, environmental consultant; b. Lockport, NY, Feb. 9, 1943; s. Bruno and Florence Loretta (Licata) Muscalo; m. Andrea B Muscalo. BA, SUNY Buffalo, 1961—65, MA, 1965—67. Instr. geoscience Jersey City State Coll., NJ, 1969—72; sr. geologist Woodward Clyde Cons., Wayne, NJ, 1979—85; section chief NJ Dept. Environ. Protection, 1985—89; assoc. geologist Malcom Pirnie, Inc., Paramus, NJ, 1989—91; sr. project geologist HydroQual, Mahwah, NJ, 1991—94; dir. geology Vectre Corp, Lafayette, NJ, 1994—97; mng. prin. Advocate Environ. Cons., Inc., Lafayette, NJ, 1997—. V.p. Lafayette Bd. Health, 1998—; mem. Open Space Adv. Com., Lafayette, NJ, 2004—, Sussex County Water Quality, 2002—. Mem.: Assn. of Environ. and Engring. Geologists (former sect. chmn. 1989—95). Democrat. Avocations: painting, sailing, hiking, photography, winemaking. Home: 19 Voight Lane Lafayette NJ 07848 Office: Advocate Environ Cons Inc P O Box 780 Lafayette NJ 07848 Office Phone: 973-875-4685. Business E-Mail: dmuscalo@tellurian.com.

**MUSCARELLA, PETER,** physician; b. Lackawanna, N.Y., May 3, 1967; s. Peter and Madeline Antoinette Muscarella; m. Mary Angela Durgala, Feb. 3, 1996; children: Stevie Lynn, Peter Jacob, Nicholas Paul. BS in Microbiology, U. Rochester, NY, 1986—89; MD, N.Y. Med. Coll., Valhalla, 1989—93. Cert. Am. Bd. Surgery, 2001. Asst. prof., surgery Ohio State U., Columbus, 2000—. Named one of America's Top Surgeons, Consumers' Rsch. Coun. Am., 2004; fellow, Nat. Cancer Inst., 1995, Am. Cancer Soc., 1996. Fellow: ACS; mem.: The Pancreas Club, Am. Pancreas Assn., Am. Soc. for Bariatric Surgery, Am. Assn. for Cancer Rsch., The Soc. for Surgery of the Alimentary Tract, The Columbus Surg. Soc. (pres. elect 2005—), Soc. Am. Gastrointestinal Endoscopic Surgeons, Assn. for Acad. Surgery, Am. Hepato-Pancreato-Biliary Assn., Am. Soc. for Gastrointestinal Endoscopy, Assn. for Surg. Edn., Columbus Med. Assn., Ohio State Med. Assn., Alpha Delta Phi (rush chmn. 1988—89). Roman Catholic. Achievements include discovery of Mesocricetus auratus cyclin-dependent kinase inhibitor 2 mRNA, complete cds - Genbank submission; Mesocricetus auratus cyclin-dependent cell cycle inhibitor gene, exon 1 - Genbank submission; Mesocricetus auratus cyclin-dependent cell cycle inhibitor gene, exon 2 and partial cds - Genbank submission; Mesocricetus auratus cyclin-dependent kinase inhibitor 2 mRNA, complete cds - Genbank submission; Mesocricetus auratus mRNA for p15INK4b cyclin-dependent kinase inhibitor (p15INK4b gene) - Genbank submission. Office: Ohio State Univ N711 Doan Hall 410 W 10th Ave Columbus OH 43210 Office Phone: 614-293-5815. Office Fax: 614-293-4030.

**MUSCARI, JOSEPH CHARLES,** manufacturing executive; b. Jersey City, Sept. 14, 1946; s. Joseph Vincent and Anneliese (Baumberger) M.; m. Donna Marie Veneziale, Apr. 17, 1971; children: Joseph, John, Marisa. BS in Indsl. Engring., NJ Inst. Tech., 1968; MBA, U. Pitts., 1969; LLD (hon.), Salem-Teikyo U., 1994. Indsl. engr. Alcoa, New Kensington, Pa., 1969, sr. indsl. engr. Massena, NY, 1969, chief indsl. engr., supr. Cleve., 1969, controller forging divsn., 1979, group controller Engring. Product Group, 1979, gen. mgr. powder and pigments divsn. Pitts., 1979, dir. Alcoa Mgmt. Info. Svcs., quality dir. Fin. Group, 1986, group v.p. The Stolle Corp. Ohio, 1989, pres. Alcoa Asia Japan, 1992, v.p. audit Pitts., 1997, v.p. Environ., Health and Safety, Audit and Compliance, 1997, group pres. Asia and Latin Am., 2001, exec. v.p., 2002—, head Rigid Packaging, Foil and Asia Group, 2004, CFO, 2006—, mem. exec. coun. Dir. Minerals Techs., Inc.; mem. bd. overseers NJ Inst. Tech. Recipient Spkrs. award Data Processing Mgmt. Assn. and Am. Prodn. and Inventory Control Soc., 1987. Mem. Alpha Pi Mu, Tau Beta Pi, Duquesne Club. Roman Catholic. Achievements include established Alcoa's first major operation in China and developed the company's long-term strategy there. Avocations: golf, winemaking, sports. Office: Alcoa 390 Park Ave New York NY 10022-4608

**MUSCATINE, CHARLES,** language educator, writer; b. Bklyn., Nov. 28, 1920; m. Doris Corn, July 21, 1945; children: Jeffrey, Alison. BA, Yale U., 1941, MA, 1942, PhD, 1948; L.H.D. (hon.), New Sch. for Social Research, 1982; Litt.D., SUNY, 1989, Rosary Coll., 1991. Mem. faculty dept. English U. Calif., Berkeley, 1948—, prof. 1960-91, prof. emeritus, 1991—, dir. Collegiate Seminar Program, 1974-80. Vis. prof. Wesleyan U., 1951-53; Ward Phillips lectr. U. Notre Dame, 1969; mem. com. of selection J.S. Guggenheim Found., 1969-89, chmn. 1985-89. Author: Chaucer and the French Tradition, 1957, The Book of Geoffrey Chaucer, 1963, Poetry and Crisis in the Age of Chaucer, 1972, The Old French Fabliaux, 1986, Medieval Literature, Style, and Culture, 1999; co-author, editor: Education at Berkeley, 1966, (with M. Griffith) The Borzoi College Reader, 1966, 7th edit., 1992, First Person Singular, 1973; co-editor Integrity in the Coll. Curriculum, 1985. Bd. dirs. No. Calif. chpt. ACLU, 1959-62, 63-66, Assn. Am. Colls., 1979-82, Ctr. for the Common Good, 1994-99; bd. dirs. Fedn. State Humanities Couns., 1989-94, chair, 1991-93; mem. Commn. on Humanities, Rockefeller Found., 1978-79, Calif. Coun. Humanities, 1986-94. With USNR, 1942-45. Recipient Navy Commendation ribbon, 1945, Berkeley citation, 1991; Fulbright fellow, 1958, 62, ACLS Rsch. fellow, 1958, Guggenheim fellow, 1962, NEH Sr. fellow, 1968. Fellow Am. Acad. Arts and Scis., Medieval Acad. of Am.; mem. MLA, New Chaucer Soc. (pres. 1980-81), Aircraft Owners and Pilots Assn., Phi Beta Kappa. Home: 2812 Buena Vista Way Berkeley CA 94708-2016 Personal E-mail: chasm@berkeley.edu.

**MUSCATO, ANDREW,** lawyer; b. Newark, Aug. 28, 1953; s. Salvatore and Bertha (Kubilus) M.; m. Ann Marie Hughes, Aug. 19, 1978; children: Amy, Andrew Joseph, Amanda. AB magna cum laude, Brown U., 1975; JD, Seton Hall U., 1978. Bar: NJ 1978, NY 1984, US. Dist. Ct. NJ 1978, U.S. Dist. Ct. (so. and ea. dists.) NY 1984, U.S. Dist. Ct. (no. dist.) NY 1998, U.S. Ct. Appeals (3d cir.) 1981, U.S. Ct. Appeals (2d cir.) 2005. Law clk. to presiding judge, appellate div. N.J. Superior Ct., Somerville, 1978-79; staff atty Attorney Office of Coll., Trenton, NJ, 1979-80, assoc. Simon & Allen, Newark, 1980-86; ptnr. Kirsten & Simon, Newark, 1987-89, Whitman & Ransom, Newark, 1989-93, Whitman Breed Abbott & Morgan, LLP, Newark, 1993-99; counsel Skadden, Arps, Slate, Meagher & Flom LLP, Newark, 1999—2004, N.Y.C., 2004—; commr. N.J. Pub. Employee Rels. Commn., 1999—2002; mem. N.J. Banking Adv. Bd., 2002—. Atty. Irvington (N.J.) Rent Leveling Bd., 1980—. Author: Executing on a Debtor's Interest in a Tenancy by the Entirety, 1986. Mem. ABA, Essex County Bar Assn., Trial Attys. N.J., N.J. Inst. Mcpl. Attys., Def. Rsch. Inst. Republican. Roman Catholic. Home: 66 Addison Dr Basking Ridge NJ 07920-2202 Office: Skadden Arps Slate Meagher & Flom LLP 4 Times Sq New York NY 10036 Office Phone: 212-735-2217. Business E-Mail: amuscato@skadden.com.

**MUSCHENHEIM, FREDERICK,** retired pathologist; b. N.Y.C., July 9, 1932; s. Carl and Haroldine (Humphreys) M.; m. Linda Alexander, Mar. 29, 1958; children: Alexandra Lydia, Carl William, David Henry. AB, Harvard U., 1953; MDCM, McGill U., Montreal, Can., 1963. Intern Santa Clara County Hosp., San Jose, Calif., 1963—64; resident pathology U. Colo. Med. Ctr., Denver, 1964—68, chief resident clin. pathology, 1968—69; pathologist Freeman, Hanske, Munkittrick & Foley PA, Mpls., 1969—77; clin. pathologist Union-Truesdale Hosp., Fall River, Mass., 1977—78; chief pathologist St. Clare's Hosp., Denville, NJ, 1978—83, Oneida Healthcare Ctr., 1984—99, ret., 1999; cons. pathologist St. Jude Hosp., Vieux Fort, St. Lucia, West Indies, 1999—2002. Clin. asst. prof. SUNY Health Sci. Ctr., Syracuse, 1984-90, clin. assoc. prof., 1990-97, clin. prof., 1998-99, clin. prof. emeritus, 1999-2001; chief med. staff Oneida City Hosps., 1991; pres. Sunderman Fund., Bermuda Biol. Sta. for Rsch., v.p Madison County (NY) bd. health 1995-96, pres., 1997-2000. Choir 1st Presbyn. Ch. of Cazenovia, NY, 1984-2000, trustee, 1985-89; choir Wayzata (Minn.) Cmty. Ch., 2001—. Mem.: Syracuse ARC Blood Svcs. (chmn. med. adv. coun. 1995—99), Minn. Soc. Pathologists (sec. 2002—05), N.Y. State Soc. Pathologists (councilor 2d dist. 1991—2000, clin. legis. com. 1991—2000, del. to MSSNY 1998—99), N.Y. State Assn. Pub. Health Labs. (v.p. 1992—93, pres. 1993—94, edn. chmn. 1994—95), Med. Soc. Madison County (v.p. 1990—91, pres. 1991—93), Med. Soc. State N.Y. (legis. com. 1991—2000), Coll. Am. Pathologists (govt. affairs com. 1994—97, nominating com. 1995, steering

com. ho. dels. 1999—2002), Assn. Clin. Scientists (v.p. 1989, pres. 1990, rec. sec. 1995—, del. Intersoc. Pathology Coun. 2004—05, Diploma of Honor 1991). Home: 1159 Hollybrook Dr Wayzata MN 55391-1364

**MUSCO, LYNN ANN,** music educator; b. Reedsburg, Wis., Aug. 6, 1959; d. Lewis Alan and Geraldine Ann Schmidt; m. Enrico Musco III, Dec. 31, 1999; m. Bruce John Chokla, Sept. 16, 1981 (div. Nov. 1997); 1 child, Alexander Blaine Chokla. BFA, U Wis., 1984; MusM, N.Mex State U, 1986; Mus D Fla. State U, 1994. Freelance music, Fla., 1981—, Wis., 1981—; grad. asst. tchr. N.Mex State U, Las Cruces, N.Mex., 1983—86, Fla. State U. Tallahassee, 1986—88; prof. music Stetson U Sch. of Music, Deland, Fla., 1988—. Prin. clarinet Bach Festival Orch., Winter Park, Fla., 1996—. Contbr. Tres Vientos - Music of Am. Composers. Mem.: Am. Federation of Musicians, Fla. Bandmasters Assoc. (assoc.) Democrat. Meth. Avocations: reading, remodeling old homes, sewing, gardening. Office: Stetson Univeristy School of Music 421 North Woodland Blvd Deland FL 32720 E-mail: lmusco59@cfl.rr.com.

**MUSE, GAR,** architectural firm executive; b. Newark, N.J. MArch, U. Fla. Registered Ga., cert. NCARB. From retail group dir. to prin. Cooper Carry Inc., Atlanta, 1990—92, prin., 1992—. Awards juror Superior Achievement Design and Imaging. Bd. dir. Sandy Springs Revitalization Inc. Mem.: Internat. Coun. Shopping Ctrs. Office: Cooper Carry Inc 3520 Piedmont Rd NE Ste 200 Atlanta GA 30305-1595

**MUSE, JOHN R.,** investment company executive; b. Ft. Worth, Feb. 24, 1951; s. Arthur C. and Betty L. (Smith) M.; m. Lyn A. Reynolds, Aug. 10, 1975; children: Michael J., I Tyler Whitney J. BS, USAF Acad., 1973; MBA, UCLA, 1974. Commd. 2d lt. USAF, 1973, advanced through grades to capt., resigned, 1978; sr. v.p., corp. fin. dir. Schneider, Bernet & Hickman, Dallas, 1980-84; mng. dir. Prudential Bache Capital Funding, Dallas, 1984—89; co-founder, ptnr., mem. mgmt. com. Hicks, Muse, Tate & Furst Inc., Dallas, 1989—, chmn., 2005—. Bd. dirs. Dean Foods Co., 1997—, Swift & Co., 2002—. Bd. visitors UCLA Anderson Sch. Mgmt. Presbyterian. Office: Hicks Muse Tate & Furst Inc Ste 1600 200 Crescent Ct Dallas TX 75201*

**MUSE, MARTHA TWITCHELL,** foundation executive; b. Dallas, Sept. 1, 1926; d. John Blackburn Muse and Kathryn (Poole) M. BA, Barnard Coll., 1948; MA, Columbia U., 1955; D.H.L., Georgetown U., 1981. Exec. dir. Tinker Found., NYC, 1965-68, pres., 1968-95, chmn., 1975—. Bd. dirs. Americas Found., Americas Soc. Inc., Coun. of the Ams.; trustee emeritus Columbia U., N.Y.C.; vice chmn., bd. dirs. Spanish Inst.; bd. visitors Edmund A. Walsh Sch. Fgn. Svc., Georgetown U., 1973—; bd. dir. Am. Portuguese Soc.; mem. Wilson coun. Woodrow Wilson Internat. Ctr. for Scholars; mem. coun. Internat. Exec. Svc. Corps; mem. adv. coun. Luso-Am. Devel. Found. Decorated Comdr. Orden del Sol del Peru, Comdr. Ordem Nacional do Cruzeiro Do Sul (Brazil), Comdr. Order of Bernardo O'Higgins (Chile), Comdr. Orden de Mayo al Merito (Argentina), Lazo de Dama de la Orden de Merito Civil (Spain), Assoc. Dame Orde St. John Jerusalem (Great Britain); recipient Alumni award for excellence Columbia U. Grad. Faculties, 1987. Mem. Huguenot Soc., Nat. Soc. Colonial Dames. Clubs: Colony (N.Y.C.), Met (N.Y.C.). Episcopalian. Home: 3664 SE Fairway E Stuart FL 34997-6116 Office: Tinker Found Inc 55 E 59th St Rm 2102 New York NY 10022-1187

**MUSFELT, DUANE CLARK,** lawyer; b. Stockton, Calif., Sept. 14, 1951; s. Robert H. and Doris E. (Roth) M.; m. Linh T. To, Sept. 6, 1980. Student, U. Calif., Davis, 1969-71; BA in Econs., U. Calif.-Berkeley, 1973; JD, UCLA, 1976. Bar: Calif. 1976, U.S. Dist. Ct. (cen. dist.) Calif. 1977, U.S. Ct. Appeals (9th cir.) 1980, U.S. Dist. Ct. (no. dist.) Calif. 1982, U.S. Dist. Ct. (ea. and so. dists.) Calif. 1983, U.S. Supreme Ct. 1987. Assoc. Haight, Dickson, Brown & Bonesteel, L.A., 1976-77, Mori & Ota, L.A., 1977-79, Lewis, D'Amato, Brisbois & Bisgaard, L.A., 1979-82; ptnr. Lewis, Brisbois, Bisgaard & Smith, San Francisco, 1982—. Mem. State Bar Calif., Bar Assn. San Francisco. Democrat. Presbyterian. Avocations: tennis, skiing, bridge. Office: Lewis Brisbois Bisgaard & Smith One Sansome St Ste 1400 San Francisco CA 94104-4431 Office Phone: 415-362-2580. Business E-Mail: musfelt@lbbslaw.com.

**MUSGRAVE, FRANKLYN GARFIELD,** obstetrician, gynecologist; b. Basseterre, St. Kitts, 1942; s. William Franklin and Inez Lucina (Clarke) M.; children: Ian K., Franklyn G. BA in Psychology and Zoology, Sir George Williams U., Montreal, 1968; MD, Howard U., 1975. Adminstrv. asst. office of the dean of students Sir George Williams U., 1968—69; biochemistry tech. Montreal Children's Hosp., 1969—70; tchg. asst. dept. zoology Howard U., 1970—71, summer fellow, 1972—73; extern in emergency care and family practice clinic Howard U. Hosp., 1973—75; intern, resident Georgetown U. Hosp., Washington, 1975—78; pvt. practice ob-gyn. Washington, 1979—; clinician Pub. Benefit Corp., 1979—2001; gynecologist Comn. Pub. Health, Washington, 2002—. Past v.p. DC Dr.'s Coun. Mem. Physicians for DC Youth Orchestra Program. Mem.: Assn. Clin. Physicians DC (past pres.), Med. Chrirugical Soc. DC, DC Med. Soc. (mem. judiciary com., spkr.'s bur.), Nat. Med. Assn. Home: 319 Camilo Ave Coral Gables FL 33134-7208

**MUSGRAVE, MARILYN N.,** congresswoman; b. Greeley, Colo., Jan. 27, 1949; m. Steven Musgrave, 4 children. BA, Colo. State U., 1972. Co-owner Musgrave Bale Stacking; mem. Colo. Ho. Reps., 1995—99, Colo. Senate, Dist. 1, Denver, 1998—2003; chmn. transp. com.; mem. health, environment, and instns. com.; mem. state, vets. and mil. affairs com.; mem. US Congress from 4th Colo. dist., 2003—; mem. Agriculture com., Edn. & Workforce com., Resources com. & Small Bus. com. Past pres. Morgan County Rep. Women; former bd. mem. RE-3 Sch. Dist. Republican. Office: US Ho Reps 1507 Longworth Ho Office Bldg Washington DC 20515-0604

**MUSGRAVE, R. KENTON,** federal judge; b. Clearwater, Fla., Sept. 7, 1927; Student, Ga. Inst. Tech., 1945-46, U. Fla., 1946-47; BA, U. Wash., 1948; JD with distinction, Emory U., 1953. Asst. gen. counsel Lockheed Internat., 1953-62; v.p., gen. counsel Mattel, Inc., 1963-71; mem. firm Musgrave, Welbourn and Fertman, 1972-75; asst. gen. counsel Pacific Enterprises, 1975-81; v.p.; gen. counsel Vivitar Corp, 1981-85; v.p.; dir. Santa Barbara Applied Rsch., 1982-87; judge U.S. Ct. Internat. Trade, NYC, 1987—97, sr. judge, 1997—. Trustee The Dian Fossey Gorilla Fund, Dolphins of Sharks Bay (Australia); hon. trustee Pet Protection Soc.; mem. United Way, Save the Redwoods League; active Palos Verdes Community Assn. Mem. Internat. Bar Assn., Pan Am. Bar Assn., State Bar Calif. (chmn. corp. law sect. 1965-66, del. 1966-67), L.A. County Bar Assn., Fng. Trade Assn. So. Calif. (bd. dirs.). Office: US Ct Internat Trade 1 Federal Plz New York NY 10278-0001

**MUSGRAVE, STORY,** design educator, astronaut, physiologist, surgeon; b. Boston, Aug. 19, 1935; children: Lorelei Lisa, Bradley Scott, Holly Kay, Christopher Todd, Jeffrey Paul, Lane Linwood. BS in Math. and Stats., Syracuse U., 1958; MBA, UCLA, 1959; BA in Chemistry, Marietta Coll., 1960; MD, Columbia U., 1964; MS in Biophysics, U. Ky., 1966; MA in Lit. U. Houston, 1987, MA in Humanities, 1989. Surg. intern U. Ky. Med. Ctr. Lexington, 1964-65; scientist-astronaut NASA, Houston, 1967-97, backup sci.-pilot 1st Skylab mission, 1973, flew on first Challenger flight, STS-6, 1983, flew on Spacelab 2, 1985, flew on space shuttle mission STS-33, 1989, flew on STS-44, 1991, flew as payload comdr. STS61 Hubble Telescope Repair Mission, 1993, flew on STS-80 last flight, 1996; concept artist Walt Disney Imagineering, 1997—; performing artist, 1997—; designer Tupperware, Inc., 2003; prodr., dir. Lannistoria, Sydney, 2002—; innovator Applied Minds, Inc., Glendale, Calif., 2002—; landscape architect Kissimmee, Fla., 1997—. Author: numerous poems; contbr. articles to profl. jours. With USMC, 1953-56. Recipient Reese AFB Comdr.'s trophy, 1969, NASA exceptional svc. medal, 1974, 83, 90, NASA disting. svc. medal, 1992, 94, 97, NASA spaceflight medal, 1983, 85, 89, 91, 93, 96, Space award Aviation Week and Space Tech., 1997; USAF postdoctoral fellow, 1965-66, Nat. Heart Inst. postdoctoral fellow, 1966-67. Mem. AAAS, AAS, AIAA, Flying Physicians Assn. (Airman of Yr. award 1974, 83), Civil Aviation Med. Assn.,

N.Y. Acad. Sci., Nat. Geog. Soc., Soaring Soc. Am., U.S. Parachute Assn., Marine Corps Assn., Alpha Kappa Psi, Phi Delta Theta, Omicron Delta Kappa, Beta Gamma Sigma. Office Phone: 407-390-0221. Personal E-mail: storymusgrave@hotmail.com. *From subatomic particles, to the stardust from which I was created, from the forming galaxies, to the universes beyond our own, I live to participate physically and spiritually in every aspect of this cosmic creation and evolution.*

**MUSGRAVE, THEA,** composer, conductor; b. Edinburgh, Scotland, May 27, 1928; m. Peter Mark, 1971. Student MusBac, Edinburgh U.; student, Paris Conservatory. Composer: (opera) The Abbot of Drimock, 1955, The Decision, 1964-65, The Voice of Ariadne, 1972-73, Mary, Queen of Scots, 1975-77, (first performed Scottish Opera) A Christmas Carol, 1978-79 (first performed Va. Opera Assn., 1979), An Occurrence at Owl Creek Bridge, 1981, Harriet, The Woman Called Moses, 1981-84 (first performed Va. Opera 1985), Simon Bolivar, Pontalba, New Orleans Opera, 2001-03, (ballet) Beauty and the Beast, 1969. (symphony and orchestral music) Obliques, 1958, Nocturnes and Arias, 1966, Concerto for Orch., 1967, Clarinet Concerto, 1969, Night Music, 1969, Scottish Dance Suite, 1969, Memento Vitae, 1969-70, Orfeo II, 1975, Soliloquy II and III, 1980, From One to Another, 1980, Peripeteia, 1981, The Seasons, 1988, (marimba concerto) Journey through a Japanese Landscape, (bass-clarinet concerto) Autumn Sonata, (oboe concerto) Helios, Phoenix Rising, 1997, (chamber and instrumental music) String Quartet, 1958, Trio for flute, oboe and piano, 1960, Monologue, 1960, Serenade, 1961, Chamber Concerto No. 1, 1962, Chamber Concerto No. 2, 1966, Chamber Concerto No. 3, 1966, Music for horn and piano, 1967, Impromptu No. 1, 1967, Soliloquy I, 1969, Elegy, 1970, Impromptu No. 2, 1970, Space Play, 1974, Orfeo I, 1975, Fanfare, 1982, Pierrot, 1985, Narcissus, 1987, Niobe, 1987, (vocal and choral music) Two Songs, 1951, Four Madrigals, 1953, Six Songs: Two Early English Poems, 1953, A Suite O'Bairnsangs, 1953, Cantata for a Summer's Day, 1954, Song of the Burn, 1954, Five Love Songs, 1955, Four Portraits, 1956, A Song for Christmas, 1958, Triptych, 1959, Sir Patrick Spens, 1961, Make Ye Merry for Him That Is to Come, 1962, Two Christmas Carols in Traditional Style, 1963, John Cook, 1963, Five Ages of Man, 1963-64, Memento Creatoris, 1967, Primavera, 1971, Rorate Coeli, 1973, Monologues of Mary, Queen of Scots, 1977-86, O Caro M'e Il Sonno, 1978, The Last Twilight, 1980, Black Tambourine, 1985, For the Time Being, 1986, Echoes Through Time, 1988, Wild Winter for Viols & Voices, 1993, On the Underground Sets 1, 2 & 3, 1994, 95, (Robert Burns' poems for soprano & orch.) Songs for a Winter's Evening, 1995, (for orch.) Phoenix Rising, 1996-97, (for 3 flutes and percussion) Voices from the Ancient World, 1998, (for chorus and orch.) Celebration Day, 1998-99, (for 8 instruments) Lamenting With Ariadne, 1999, (orchestral work) Turbulent Landscapes, Boston Symphony, 2004, Journey into Light (soprano and orch.), 2004-05, Going North (childrens chorus and 2 clarinets), 2004. Office: Va Opera Assn PO Box 2580 Norfolk VA 23501-2580

**MUSGROVE, KATHERINE E.,** theater educator; b. Shreveport, La., Dec. 17, 1961; d. Robert J and Dorothy C Potts; m. Jj Musgrove, June 12, 1998. BA, Columbus Coll., Columbus, Ga., 1986; MFA, U of Va., Charlottesville, 1992; PhD, Tex. Tech U., Lubbock, 1996. Chair, dept. theatre Graceland U., Lamoni, Iowa, 1995—2001; chair, Barter Theatre Conservatory Emory & Henry Coll., Emory, Va., 2001—03; theatre dept. chair, assoc. prof. Columbus State U., Ga., 2003—. Guest dir. Springer Opera Ho., Columbus, Ga., 2007—, Barter Theatre, Abingdon, Va., 2001—02. Dir.: (play) Dinner with Friends, Communicating Doors, Seagulls in a Cherry Tree (World Premiere), The Trestle at Pope Lick Creek, A Doll House. Mem.: Assn. of Theatre in Higher Edn., Theatre Comm. Group, Ga. Theatre Conf., S.E. Theatre Conf., Phi Kappa Phi (life). Avocations: gardening, squash, golf, cooking. Office: Columbus State U 4225 University Ave Columbus GA 31907 Office Phone: 706-568-2048.

**MUSHAK, PAUL,** toxicologist, consultant; b. Dunmore, Pa., Dec. 9, 1935; s. Steven and Mary Mushak; m. Elizabeth Orr Walker, June 30, 1973. BS in Chemistry, U. Scranton, 1961; PhD, U. Fla., 1969; postgrad., Yale U., 1969-71. Diplomate Am. Bd. Forensic Medicine, Am. Coll. Forensic Examiners, 1996. Asst. prof. U. N.C. Sch. Medicine, Chapel Hill, 1971-77, assoc. prof., 1977-85; prin. PB Assocs., Durham, NC, 1992—. Adj. prof. U. N.C. Sch. medicine, 1986-93; vis. prof. Albert Einstein Coll. of Medicine, Bronx, N.Y., 1995—; mem. com., cons. EPA Sci. Adv. Bd., Washington, 1989-97, 2000-03, 05—; mem. com. Nat. Acad. of Sci., Washington, 1989-93, 85-87, 73-75. Author and co-author chpts. to books and 175 sci. publs. in field. Mem. Environ. Affairs Bd., Durham, NC, 1990—92, Durham Housing Appeals Bd., NC, 1990—93. Recipient Pre-doctoral fellowship, NIH, 1961-67, Postdoctoral fellowship, Yale U., 1969-71; recipient Meritorious Svc. award U.S. EPA, Cin., 1981; grantee NIH, 1971-85; Hon. Mention in Colloid Chemistry Rsch., U. of S.C., 1961 Fellow Am. Coll. Forensic Examiners; mem. Soc. for Risk Analysis, Soc. of Toxicology. Achievements include Lab. methods for testing constituents of antique textiles; research in major studies on lead poisoning in children: lead vs. IQ, lead levels in remote peoples, physical chemical and biochemical determinants of metal toxicity, paths of exposure. Office: PB Assocs 714 9th St Ste 204 Durham NC 27705-4849 Office Phone: 919-286-7193. Personal E-mail: pandbmushak@cs.com.

**MUSHAM, BETTYE MARTIN,** consumer products executive; m. William C. Musham. Diploma, Duke U. Mgr. U.S. Louis Vuitton; owner, pres. GEAR Holdings, Inc., NYC, 1977-99, chmn., CEO, 1999—. Established internship program with GEAR and R.I. Sch. Design, Cornell U., U. Va., Auburn U.; bd. dirs. Brunswick Corp., IO Electric, Peace Links, World Svc. Council of the YWCA; adv. bd. N.Y.C. Partnership, Bus. Council United Nations, Duke U. Sch. Environment, Duke U. Hosp., 1986-91; Commr. Del. and Lehigh Navigation Canal Nat. Heritage Corridor, 1989; trustee Marymount Manhattan Coll., R.I. Sch. Design, 1991-91 Recipient Mr. Entrepreneurial award Nat. Assn. Women Bus. Owners N.Y., 1983, 1994. Mem. Nat. Home Fashions, Am. Nurses Assn., Am. Women's Econ. Dev. Corp., Women's Forum, Com. of 200, Catalyst, The Fashion Group, Sierra Club, Women's City Club N.Y. Office: Gear Holdings Inc 142 E 30th St New York NY 10016-7319 Office Phone: 212-459-0050. Office Fax: 212-459-0060. Business E-Mail: gearhome@aol.com.

**MUSHEFF, TODD M.,** lawyer; AB in Econs. cum laude, Miami U., Oxford, Ohio, 1983; JD, Ohio State U., Columbus, 1986. Asst. atty. gen. Republic of Palau, Koror, 1991—96; spl. counsel Barnwell Whaley Patterson & Helms, LLC, Charleston, SC, 2001—. Office: Barnwell Whaley Patterson & Helms LLC PO Drawer H Charleston SC 29401 Office Phone: 843-577-7700. Office Fax: 843-577-7708. Business E-Mail: tmusheff@barnwell-whaley.com.

**MUSHINSKY, MARY M.,** state legislator; b. New Haven; m. Martin J. Waters; children: Martin Waters, Edward Waters. BA, So. Conn. State U., 1973; postgrad., Fla. Atlantic U., MA, Wesleyan U., Middletown, Conn., 1993. Mem. Conn. Ho. of Reps., Hartford, Conn., 1981—; mem. environ., fin. revenue and bonding com., mem. select com. on children, asst. majority leader. Democrat. Home: 158 S Cherry St Wallingford CT 06492-4016 Office: Conn House of Reps Capitol Ave Hartford CT 06106 Office Phone: 860-240-8585.

**MUSHLIN, ALVIN L,** medical educator, researcher; b. N.Y.C., Oct. 28, 1941; s. Max M.; m. Linda M.; children: Amy, Katey. BA, Vanderbilt U., Nashville, 1963, MD, 1966; ScM, Johns Hopkins U Sch. Hygiene, Baltimore, 1973. Diplomate Am. Bd. Internal Medicine. Instr. Johns Hopkins U., Balt., 1972-76, asst. prof., 1972-76; assoc. prof. medicine U. Rochester (N.Y.) Sch. Medicine, 1976-93; assoc. prof. U. Rochester Sch. Medicine, Rochester, NY, 1976-90, prof., 1993-99; Nanette Laitman disting. U. chmn. dept. pub. health Cornell U. Weill Med. Coll., N.Y.C., 1999—. With USN, 1968-70. Fax: 212-746-8544. E-mail: aim2001@mail.med.cornell.edu.

**MUSICH, ROBERT LORIN,** motivational speaker; b. Glendale, Calif., Feb. 15, 1969; s. Richard and Zola (Nickel) M. MBA, M, La Salle U. Sr. asst. mgr. Am. Gen. Fin., Upland, Calif., 1988-89; mgmt./corp. trainer Mortgage

Link, Pasadena, 1989-94; mgr. AT&T, L.A., 1994-96; owner Musich & Assocs., West Covina, Calif., 1989—. Singer (tenor) So. Calif. Mormon Choir, 1994—; cand. Calif. State Assembly, 59th Dist., 1995; vol. Am. Cancer Soc., 1994-96; coach Youth League Football, 1987-92; elder's quorum pres. LDS Ch., sec., 1992-93, 2d and 1st counselor, 1995-96, mem. stake single adult com., 1993-95, mem. regional single adult com. bi-regional chmn., 1993-95. Republican. Avocations: singing, dance, theater, volleyball, football. Office: Musich and Associates 3447 E Hillhaven Dr West Covina CA 91791-1718

**MUSICK, GERALD JOE,** retired entomology educator; b. Ponca City, Okla., May 24, 1940; s. Arlie A. and Leona (Beier) M.; m. Florene Ione Thompson, May 11, 1962; children: Linda Kaye, Mary Louise. BS, Okla. State U., 1962; MS, Iowa State U., 1964; PhD, U. Mo., 1969. Grad. asst. Iowa State U., 1962-64; instr. U. Mo., 1964-69; asst. prof. Ohio State U., Wooster, 1969-71, assoc. prof., 1971-76; dept. head U. Ga., Tifton, 1976-79; prof., dept. head U. Ark., Fayetteville, 1979-86, interium dir. agrl. exptl. sta., 1986-87, dean, assoc. v.p. agrl. rsch., 1987-93, univ. prof. entomology, 1993—2002, chmn.-elect faculty coun. Dale Bumpers Coll. Agrl., Food and Life Scis., 1997, chmn., 1998, prof. emeritus, 2002—, ret., 2002—; chmn. faculty coun. Dale Bumpers Coll. of Agrl. Food and Life Scis., 1998; gen. mgr. Razerback Pk. Golf Course, Fayetteville, Ark., 2003—. Author and co-author numerous pubs. Vice-chairperson com. Coop. States Rsch. Svc., 1993, So. Expt. Sta.; chairperson steering com. Midwest Food Safety Consortium, 1991-93; mem. U. Ark. Faculty Senate, 1994—, chair campus faculty, 1998-99, chair faculty sentate 1999-2000, faculty exec. com., 1999—; coord. Pest Mgmt. Programs, 1998—. Mem. Entomol. Soc. Am. (pres. S.E. br. 1983-84), Ark. Acad. Sci., Ctrl. States Entomol. Soc. (v.p. 1995-96, pres. 1996-97), Sigma Xi, Gamma Sigma Delta. Lutheran. Avocation: golf. Office: Razorback Park Golf Course Fayetteville AR 72704 Personal E-mail: gjmfim@cox.net.

**MUSICK, MARILYN IRENE,** retired secondary school educator; b. Springfield, Ill., Mar. 20, 1950; d. Kenneth Ray and Ida May Sampson; m. David Neil Musick, Aug. 19, 1972; children: John David, Allison Renee. B in Music Edn., Ill. Wesleyan U., 1972. Vocal music tchr. grades 5-12 El Paso-Gridley Unit II, Ill., 1972—2005; ret., 2005. Music advisor Ill. Elem. Sch. Assns., Bloomington, 2000—03; music cons. Immanuel Bible Found., Bloomington, 1996—2001. Choir dir. Evang. Free Ch., Bloomington, 1984—. Recipient Those Who Excel award of recognition, Ill. State Bd. of Edn., Springfield, 1993. Mem.: Am. Choral Dirs. Assn., Music Educators Nat. Conf. Avocation: rose gardening. Home: 217 Reitan Rd Normal IL 61761 E-mail: marilynim@yahoo.com.

**MUSIKER, REUBEN,** library director; b. Johannesburg, Jan. 12, 1931; s. Judel and Sarah Musiker; m. Naomi Measroch, Apr. 9, 1961; children: Judith, Arnon, Carmel. BSc, U. Witwatersrand, Johannesburg, 1954; MA, U. Pretoria, South Africa, 1968. Dep. univ. libr. Rhodes U., Grahamstown, South Africa, 1962-72; univ. libr. U. Witwatersrand, Johannesburg, 1973-91, prof. librarianship and bibliography, 1975-91; libr. cons. South African Jewish Bd. Dept., Johannesburg, 1999—. Recipient Reuben Musiker award for bibliography, 1986. Fellow South African Inst. Librarianship (life). Avocations: music, collecting and writing books. E-mail: NMusiker@netactive.co.za.

**MUSIL, ROBERT KIRKLAND,** educator; b. N.Y.C., Oct. 27, 1943; s. Ralph A. and Margaret Hooker (Kirkland) M.; m. Caryn Lynne McTighe, June 15, 1968; children: Rebecca M. Unruh, Emily Kirkland. BA, Yale U., 1964; MA, Northwestern U., 1966, PhD, 1970; MPH, Johns Hopkins U., 2001. Instr. Def. Info. Sch., Ft. Benjamin Harrison, Ind., 1969-71; co-dir. CCCO/An Agy. for Mil. and Draft Counseling, Phila., 1971-74; dir. mil. affairs project Ctr. for Nat. Security Studies, Washington, 1974-75; asst. prof. English and Am. studies Temple U., Phila., 1976-78; prodr., host Consider the Alternatives Radio, Phila., 1978-92; exec. dir. SANE Edn. Fund, Phila. and Washington, 1984-88, Profls. Coalition for Nuclear Arms Control, Washington, 1988-92; dir. policy and programs Physicians for Social Responsibility, Washington, 1992-95, exec. dir., CEO, 1995—2006; scholar-in-residence Am. U., 2006—. Adj. prof. Sch. Internat. Svc., Am. U., 1997—. Prodr. (documentary series) Shadows of the Nuclear Age: American Culture and the Bomb, 1980 (NEH grantee). Bd. dirs. Scoville Fellowships, Washington, 1989-92, 95—, Environ. Alliance, 2006—, 20/20 Vision, 2006—, SANE, 1978-84; mem. adv. bd. Coun. for a Livable World, 2006—. Capt. U.S. Army, 1969-71. Recipient Maj. Armstrong award for radio Armstrong Found., Columbia U., N.Y.C., 1988, 89. Mem. United Ch. of Christ. Home: 8600 Irvington Ave Bethesda MD 20817-3604 Office Phone: 202-667-4260. E-mail: bmusil@yahoo.com.

**MUSK, ELON,** aerospace transportation executive; b. South Africa, 1971; married. Student, Queen's U., Kingston, Ont.; BS in Physics, U. Pa.; BS in bus., U. Pa. Wharton Sch. Bus. With Pinnacle Rsch.; software devel. Rocket Science, Microsoft; co-founder, chmn., CEO, chief tech. officer Zip2 Corp. (sold to Compaq for $307 million), 1995—99; co-founder, chmn. CEO PayPal (acquired by eBay for $1.5 billion), 1999—2002; founder, CEO, chief tech. officer Space Exploration Tech. Corp., 2002—. Bd. dirs. The Planetary Society, 2003—. Office: SpaceX 1310 E Grand Ave El Segundo CA 90245*

**MUSMANN, LOIS S.,** conductor, music educator; d. Myron Roger and Lois MacNary Steele; m. Ronald Clapp, Sept. 6, 1959 (div. 1983); children: Mark Douglass Steele, Debra Clapp Walter, Holly Clapp Rogers; m. Klaus Musmann, Dec. 27, 1986. MusB, New Eng. Conservatory Music, 1984; MusM, U. Redlands, 1986; D in Musical Arts, U. So. Calif., 1989. Condr., founder Musica Viva, Redlands and Riverside, Calif., 1990—95; condr., artistic dir. Euterpe Opera Theatre, L.A., 1993—; condr., founder Pacifica Chamber Orch., Redlands and Palm Springs, Calif., 1995—2001; condr. U. Calif. Choral Soc., Riverside, 1997—2000; prof. Notre Dame de Namur U., Belmont, Calif., 2001—; vis. scholar U. Calif. Beatrice Bain Rsch. Group, Berkeley, 2002—; prof. San Francisco Conservatory Music, 2003—. Lectr., founder lectr. series Redlands Symphony Orch., 1991—92, 1997—2001; chair Internat. Conf. Coll. Music Soc., Vienna, 1997; chair edn. com. San Diego Chamber Orch., La Jolla, Calif., 1997—99; mem. adv. bd. Inland Empire Chamber Music, San Bernardino, 1998—2001; mem. faculty San Francisco Conservatory Music. Condr. articles to profl. jours.; composer: Closing Prayer, 1987; condr.: world premier opera Serafina y Arcangela. Exec. advisor Am. Coun. N.Am. Indians, Haywood, Calif., 2001—02. Recipient Fulbright Scholar, Sr. Specialist in Music, 2004, Baroque Concerto Competition Winner, New Eng. Conservatory Music, 1984; grantee, Riverside Arts Found., 1991, 1992; Postdoctoral Fellow, U. So. Calif., 1996—2001, Disting. Accomplishments award, Goodwill Industries, 1994. Mem.: Nat. League Am. Pen Women, Assn. Calif. Symphony Orchs., Pi Kappa Lambda. Avocations: travel, reading, gardening. Home: 975 Pizarro Ln Foster City CA 94404 Office: Notre Dame de Namur Univ 1500 Ralston Ave Belmont CA 94002

**MUSOLF, LLOYD DARYL,** political science professor, educational association administrator; b. Yale, SD, Oct. 14, 1919; s. William Ferdinand and Emma Marie (Pautz) M.; m. Berdyne Peet, June 30, 1944; children: Stephanie, Michael, Laura. BA, Huron Coll., 1941; MA, U. SD, 1946; PhD, Johns Hopkins U., 1950. Mem. faculty Vassar Coll., Poughkeepsie, NY, 1949-59, assoc. prof. polit. sci., 1955-59; chief of party adv. group Mich. State U., East Lansing, 1959-61, prof. polit. sci., 1961-63. U. Calif.-Davis, 1963-87, prof. emeritus, 1988—, dir. Inst. Govtl. Affairs, 1963-84. Vis. prof. Johns Hopkins U., Balt., 1953, U. Del., 1954, U. Mich., 1955-56; U.S. Nat. rapporteur for Internat. Congress Adminstrv. Scis., Berlin, 1983; cons., lectr. in field. Author: Federal Examiners and the Conflict of Law and Administration, 1953, Public Ownership and Accountability: The Canadian Experience, 1959, Promoting the General Welfare, Government and the Economy, 1965, (with others) American National Government-Policies and Politics, 1971, Mixed Enterprise-A Developmental Perspective, 1972, (with Springer) Malaysia's Parliamentary Systems-Representative Politics and Policymaking in a Divided Society, 1979, Uncle Sam's Private Profitseeking Corporations-Comsat, Fannie Mae, Amtrak and Conrail, 1983; editor: (with Krislov) The

Politics of Regulation, 1964, Communications Satellites in Political Orbit, 1968, (with Kornberg) Legislatures in Developmental Perspective, 1970, (with Joel Smith) Legislatures in Development-Dynamics of Change in New and Old States, 1979; contbr. monographs, chpts. to books, articles to profl. jours. Served to lt. USNR, 1942-45. Johnston scholar Johns Hopkins U., 1946-48; Faculty fellow Vassar Coll., 1954-55; sr. assoc. East-West Ctr., Honolulu, 1968-69; vis. scholar Brookings Instn., Washington, 1980. Mem. ASPA (exec. coun. 1967-70), Nat. Assn. Schs. Pub. Affairs and Adminstrn. (exec. coun. 1972-75), Western Govtl. Rsch. Assn. (exec. bd. 1966-68), Am. Polit. Sci. Assn., Nat. Assn. State Univs. and Land Grant Assn. (rsch. com. divsn. urban affairs 1980-81). Home: 844 Lake Blvd Davis CA 95616-2611 Office: U Calif Dept Polit Sci Davis CA 95616

**MUSON, HOWARD HENRY,** writer, consultant; b. Mt. Vernon, NY, Mar. 19, 1935; s. Joseph Ernest and Beatrice (Hakmaier) Muson; m. Dorothy Regina Tyor, May 21, 1967; children: Eve, Stephanie, Nickolas, Alice. AB magna cum laude, Harvard U., Cambridge, Mass., 1956; cert., Johns Hopkins Sch. Advanced Internat. Studies, Bologna, Italy, 1956-57; postgrad., U. Calif., Berkeley, 1957-58. Dir. program research CARE Inc., NYC, 1960-62; bur. chief Hartford Courant, Conn., 1962; newsman, columnist AP, Boston, 1963-66; contbg. editor Time mag., NYC, 1966-70; articles editor N.Y. Times mag., NYC, 1970-77; exec. editor Psychology Today mag., NYC, 1977-82; editor Across The Board, NYC, 1983-89; editor, pub. Family Bus. mag., Phila., 1992-2000; rsch. assoc. Lansberg Gersick & Assocs., New Haven, 1998—. Vis. lectr. in residential colls. Yale U., New Haven, 1982-83; instr. in sci. and environ. reporting program NYU, 1992; lead writer, exec. action reports, Mid-Market Series, The Conf. Bd., 2002-. Author: Triumph of the American Spirit: Johnstown, Pennsylvania, 1989, Managing Growth: Smart Strategies for Smaller and Midsize Companies, 2000, Valuing Experience: How to Motivate and Retain Mature Workers, 2002, The Family Business Growth Handbook, 2002; co-author: Generations of Giving: Leadership and Continuity in Family Foundations, 2004; contbr. articles to profl. jours., popular mags. Dir. Project Concern/No. Westchester Walk for Mankind, Mt. Kisco, NY, 1986-90; media rels. Westchester Walk for Diabetes, 2002-03. Mem. Nat. Assn. Sci. Writers Office Phone: 914-941-1881. Personal E-mail: hmuson@earthlink.net.

**MUSONE, AMY LYNN,** elementary school educator; b. New Castle, Pa., Aug. 8, 1969; d. Frank Anthony and Rudelle Carla Battista; m. John Paul Muscone, Aug. 6, 1994; children: Jacob Paul Muscone, Frances Ann Muscone. BS in Elem./Early Childhood Edn., Gannon U., 1991; M in Reading, Millersville U., 1996; M in Spl. Edn., Millersville, 2002; cert. in adminstrn., Millersville U., 2005. 1st grade tchr. Balt. City Pub. Sch., 1992—93; 3d grade tchr. Ctrl. York (Pa.) Sch. Dist., 1993—2000, spl. edn. tchr., 2000—04, 2d grade tchr., 2004—. Bd. dirs. Cmtys. That Care, York, 2005—06, vol., 2004—06, Cath. Harvest Food Pantry, York, 2005—06, YMCA Child Care, York, 2000—06. Excellence grantee, Ctrl. York Sch. Dist., 1999. Mem.: ASCD, Pa. State Edn. Assn. Home: 2851 Primrose Lane N York PA 17404 Office: Ctrl York Sch Dist 775 Marian Rd York PA 17402 Business E-Mail: amusone@cysd.k12.pa.us.

**MUSSA, MICHAEL L.,** economist, educator; b. LA, Apr. 15, 1944; AB, UCLA, 1966; MA, U. Chgo., 1970, PhD, 1974. Asst. prof. econs. U. Rochester, 1971—75, assoc. prof., 1975—76; assoc. prof. econs. U. Chgo., 1976—80, prof. internat. bus., 1980—91; mem. US Coun. of Econ. Advisers, 1986—88; econ. counselor, dir. Dept. Rsch. IMF, 1991—2001; sr. fellow Inst. Internat. Econs., Washington, 2001—. Rsch. fellow London Sch. Econs., 1975—76, Grad. Sch. Internat. Studies, Geneva, 1976—81; vis. prof. Asian Dept. IMF, 1980; vis. faculty mem. CUNY Grad. Ctr. Author: Argentina and the Fund: From Triumph to Tragedy, 2002; contbr. articles to profl. jours. Office: Inst Internat Econs 1750 Massachusetts Ave, NW Washington DC 20036-1903 Office Phone: 202-328-9000. Office Fax: 202-659-3225. E-mail: mmussa@iie.com.*

**MUSSANO, THEODORE ANTHONY,** retired court services supervisor; b. Paterson, N.J., Dec. 15, 1943; s. Theodore Anthony, Sr. and Theresa Marie Mussano; m. Susan Fay Januszewski, May 24, 1980; 1 child, Theodore Edward. BA cum laude, Seton Hall U., 1965; MA, St. John's U., 1967. Probation officer Passaic County Probation Dept., Paterson, N.J., 1971-77, sr. probation officer, 1977-83; ct. svcs. supr. Superior Ct. N.J., Paterson, 1973—2005. Tchg. fellow, 1965—67, 1967—68, Weaver fellow, 1967. Mem.: Fraternal Order of Police, Probation Assn. N.J. (pres. 1977), Soc. Ancient Numismatists, Am. Numis. Assn., Ancient Coin Collectors Guild, KC. Roman Catholic. Avocations: ancient and medieval studies, reading, coin collecting/numismatics, genealogy. Home: 17 Fenner Pl Wayne NJ 07470-2809 Office: Passaic County Probation Divsn 63-65 Hamilton St Paterson NJ 07505 Personal E-mail: tmwardo@aol.com.

**MUSSEHL, ROBERT CLARENCE,** lawyer; b. Washington, May 1, 1936; s. Chester Carl and Clara Cecelia (Greenwalt) Mussehl; m. Misook Chung, Mar. 22, 1987; 1 child, Omar;children from previous marriage: Debra Lee(dec.), David Lee. BA, Am. U., 1964, JD, 1966. Bar: Wash. 1967, U.S. Dist. Ct. (we. dist.) Wash. 1967, U.S. Supreme Ct. 1971. Sr. ptnr. Thom, Mussehl, Navoni, Hoff, Pierson & Ryder, Seattle, 1967-78, Neubauer & Mussehl, Seattle, 1978-80, Mussehl & Rosenberg, Seattle, 1980—2001, Mussehl & Khan, 2004—06. Spkr. law convs. and other profl. orgns.; chmn. bd. dirs., CEO Seattle Smashers, 1976—80; moot ct. judge Nat. Appellate Adv. Competition, San Francisco, 1987; panel mem. ABA Symposium Compulsory Jurisdiction World Ct., San Francisco, 1987. Contbr. articles to profl. jours. Mem. Wash. Vol. Lawyers Arts, 1976—80; bd. dirs. Wash. State Pub. Interest Law Ctr., 1976—81; founder, past chair Lawyers Helping Hungry Children, bd. dirs., 1991—2006; founder, past chair Wash. State Lawyers Campaign Hunger Relief, 1991—; statewide chair Lawyers for Durning for Gov., 1976; mem. task force single adult and ch. Ch. Coun. Greater Seattle, 1976—78. Recipient Jefferson award for Cmty. and Pub. Svc., State of Wash., Am. Inst. Pub. Svc., 1997. Fellow: Am. Acad. Matrimonial Lawyers, Am. Bar Found. (life); mem.: ABA (ho. dels. 1979—91, mem. assembly resolutions com. 1979—91, chair marriage and family counseling and concilliation com. 1981—83, mem. world order under law standing com. 1983—89, chair 1986—89, chair ad hoc com. assembly 1986—89, mem. blue ribbon com. world ct. 1987—88, mem. spl. adv. com. internat. activities 1989—91, mem. standing com. dispute resolution 1992—93, mem. exec. coun. sect. dispute resolution 1993—95, asst. budget officer 1995—97, budget officer 1997—99, chair 2001—02, sect. liaison commn. racial and ethnic diversity 2002—04, ho. dels. 2003—, commn. racial and ethnic diversity 2004—06, editor Goal IX newsletter 2004—), World Assn. Lawyers World Peace through Law Ctr. (founding mem.), Am. Arbitration Assn. (panel arbitrators), Seattle-King County Bar Assn. (mem. other coms. 1970—, chmn. young lawyers sect. 1971—72, mem. family law sect. 1971—90, sec. 1972—73, trustee), Wash. State Trial Lawyers Assn., Wash. State Bar Assn. (mem. exec. com. family law sect. 1973—75, chmn. internat. law com. 1974—76, sec.-treas., mem. com. world peace through law sect. 1980—, chair 1981—82, mem. editl. bd. Family Law Deskbook 1987—89), UN Assn. USA (bd. dirs. Seattle chpt. 1989—91), Heritage Club YMCA Greater Seattle (charter 1977—). Avocations: squash, bicycling, tennis, weightlifting, painting, religious studies. Home: One Pacific Tower 2000 1st Ave Apt 902 Seattle WA 98121-2167 Office: 520 Pike St Ste 2210 Seattle WA 98101 Office Phone: 206-386-7200. Personal E-mail: bobmussehl@earthlink.net.

**MUSSELMAN, ERIC,** professional basketball coach; b. Ashland, Ohio, Nov. 19, 1964; m. Wendy Musselman; children: Michael, Matthew. BS, U. San Diego, 1987. Asst. dir. scouting L.A. Clippers, 1987—90; asst. coach Minn. Timberwolves, 1990—91; gen. mgr. Fla. Beach Dogs, Continental Basketball Assn., 1990—98, head coach, 1991—98, Fla. Sharks, U.S. Basketball League, 1995—96; asst. coach Orlando Magic, 1998—2000, Atlanta Hawks, 2000—02; head coach Golden State Warriors, Oakland, Calif., 2002—04; asst. coach Memphis Grizzlies, 2004—06; head coach Sacramento Kings, 2006—. Office: Sacramento Kings Arco Arena One Sports Pkwy Sacramento CA 95834*

**MUSSELMAN, LLOYD K.,** history professor; b. Balt., June 22, 1938; s. Harold Garland and Verna Bee Musselman; m. Nancy Lee Sloan; children: David Paul, Kathryn Lee. BA in History, Western Md. U., Wesminster, 1960; MA in History, Denver U., 1961, PhD in History, 1969. Tchr. Lakewood H.S., Colo., 1963—69; prof. Oklahoma City U., 1969—, Darbeth-Whitten prof., 1978—. Author: Rocky Mountain National Park, 1965, The Federal Period, 1972; co-author: Teachers Manual for the American Revolution, 1969, Teachers Manual for the American Frontier, 1969. Named Disting. Tchr., Oklahoma City U., 2002; recipient Sears-Roebuck award, 1990. Mem.: ACLU, AAUP (Okla.state pres. 1992—93, assembly state conf. 1994—96), Sierra Club. Democrat. Avocations: reading, bicycling, coaching. Home: 6040 N Shawnee Ave Oklahoma City OK 73112 Office: Oklahoma City Univ 2501 N Blackwelder Oklahoma City OK 73106

**MUSSELMAN, RANDALL L.,** electrical engineer, educator; b. Peoria, Ill., July 27, 1958; s. Dale and Nancy Musselman; m. Kimberly Musselman; children: Alexandra, Amber. BSEE, So. Ill. U., Carbondale, 1983; MSEE, U. Colo., Colorado Springs, 1990, PhD in Elec. Engring., 1997. Cert. profl. engr., Colo., 1987; EMT Colo., 2000. Design engr. Tex. Instruments, Colorado Springs, 1983—84, 1987—90, Honeywell, 1984—87; pres. Outland Comm., 1990—92; instr. Ill. Ctrl. Coll., East Peoria, 1992—94; graduate asst. U. Colo., 1994—97; prof. elec. engring. USAF Acad., Colorado Springs, 1997—, rsch. dir. elec. engring., 1997—. Adj. faculty U. Colo., Colorado Springs; cons. RF Antenna Comm.; com. mem. Nat. Sci. Found. Contbr. 35 articles to profl. jours.; presenter to profl. socs. Vol. EMT El Paso County Search and Rescue, Colorado Springs, 1997—2006; vol. wildland firefighter El Paso County Sheriff Wildland Fire Crew. Graduate fellowship, U. Colo., 1997. Mem.: IEEE (sr.), Eta Kappa Nu, Tau Beta Pi. Achievements include recognized for accomplishments in field of electro-magnetics research. Avocations: mountain climbing, rock climbing, hunting, drums. Home: 581 Tamarron Dr Colorado Springs CO 80919 Office: USAF Acad 2354 Fairchild Dr U S A F Academy CO 80840 Office Phone: 719-333-4211. Personal E-mail: randy@ieee.org. Business E-Mail: randall.musselman@usafa.af.mil.

**MUSSELWHITE, BENETA JO,** mathematics educator; b. Lindsborg, Kans., July 15, 1948; d. Floyd Wesley and Velda W. (Roller) M. BA, Bethany Coll., 1970. Tchr. math. Bazine (Kans.) Unified Sch. Dist., 1970-72, Smoky Valley Unified Sch. Dist., Lindsborg, 1973-85, Ottawa (Kans.) Unified Sch. Dist., 1985-89, Salina (Kans.) Unified Sch. Dist., 1989—. Active local polit. campaigns. Mem. NEA (conv. del.), Kans. Edn. Assn. (bd. dirs. 199197, 2002-06, strategic planning com.), Nat. Coun. Tchrs. Math., Kans. Assn. Tchrs. Math., KSDE Math. Stds. Revision Commn. Republican. Mem. Belmont Blvd. Christian Ch.

**MUSSENDEN, GEORG ANTONIO,** electronics engineer; b. San Juan, P.R., Aug. 25, 1959; s. Gustavo Adolfo and Christa-Maria (Gotsch) M. Student, U. P.R.-Rio Piedras, 1977-79; BS in E.E. with honors, U. Fla., Gainesville, 1982; postgrad. in elec. engring., U. Fla. Electronics technician Radiotelephone Communicators of P.R. (Motorola), 1976; computer sys. programmer and operator U. P.R., Rio Piedras, 1978-79; rsch. asst. dept. physics, 1978-79; computer programmer Regional Electrocardiogram Analysis Ctr. J. Hillis Miller Health Ctr., U. Fla., Gainesville, 1981; pre-profl. engr. IBM Corp. Devel. Lab., Endicott, N.Y., 1981; sr. assoc. engr./scientist entry sys. tech. SPD, CPD and ESD design and devel. labs., Boca Raton, Fla., 1982-93; elec. hardware devel. engr. sci. Core Internat. Rsch. and Devel. Corp., Boca Raton 1993—. Contbr. articles to profl. jours. Scholar San Jose Alumni, 1973-77, Fonalledas Found., 1977-79, Procter and Gamble, 1980; U.F. Sr. Honors scholar, 1980; scholar Nat. Fund Minority Engring., 1980, Du Pont, 1981; Nat. Consortium for Grad. Degrees for Minorities in Engring. fellow, 1981. Mem. IEEE, SMPTE, AES, N.Y. Acad. Scis., Audio-Visual Club, Amateur Radio Club, Golden Key, Eta Kappa Nu, Tau Beta Pi, Phi Kappa Phi. Roman Catholic. Achievements include 12 technological invention disclosures. Home: 3815 NW 4th Ave Boca Raton FL 33431 Office Phone: 954-723-3461. E-mail: gmussen@bellsouth.net.

**MUSSINA, MICHAEL COLE,** professional baseball player; b. Williamsport, Pa., Dec. 8, 1968; BA Econs., Stanford U., 1990. Pitcher Balt. Orioles, 1990-2000, N.Y. Yankees, 2001—. Player Am. League All-Star Team, 1992-94. Named Internat. League Most Valuable Pitcher, 1991, recipient 5 Am. League Gold Gloves, 5-time Am. League All-Star. Office: The New York Yankees Yankee Stadium 161st Street and River Avenue Bronx NY 10451 E-mail: csmd12000@aol.com.

**MUSSON, WARREN R.,** investment banker; s. Richard W. and Victoria L. Musson; m. Anne Marie Flemming, May 21, 1982; children: Kelly, Kate. BA, Alma Coll., Alma, Mich., 1978. 2nd v.p. Nat. Bank of Detriot, Mich., 1978—90; pres. Massey Holdings Inc., Plymouth, Mich., 1990—92; v.p. Great Lakes Bancorp, Ann Harbor, Mich., 1992—93; sr. v.p. Peoples State Bank, Hamtramck, Mich., 1993—99; sr. v.p., head of lending Cmty. Bank of Dearborn, Dearborn, Mich., 1999—; mng. mem. Creeks Crossing, LLC. Mem.: Colony Swim Club (treas., pres. 1992—94), Wabeek Country Club, Theta Chi. Avocations: boating, skiing, golf, landscape design. Home: 8900 Quail Cir Plymouth MI 48170 Office: Cmty Bank of Dearborn 1360 Porter St Dearborn MI 48124 Office Phone: 313-565-5700.

**MUSTACCHI, PIERO,** preventive medicine physician, educator; b. Cairo, May 29, 1920; came to U.S., 1947; naturalized, 1962; s. Gino and Gilda (Rieti) M.; m. Dora Lisa Ancona, Sept. 26, 1948; children: Roberto, Michael. BS in Humanities, U. Florence, Italy, 1938; postgrad. in anatomy, U. Lausanne, Switzerland, 1938-39; MB, ChB, Fouad I U., Cairo, Egypt, 1944, grad. in Arabic lang. and lit., 1946; D Medicine and Surgery, U. Pisa, 1986; Degree (hon.), U. Aix-Marseille, France, 1988, U. Alexandria, Egypt, 1985. Qualified med. examiner, Calif. Indsl. Accident Commn., 1994. House officer English Hosp., Ch. Missionary Soc., Cairo, 1945-47; clin. affiliate U. Calif., San Francisco, 1947-48; intern Franklin Hosp., San Francisco, 1948-49; resident in pathology U. Calif., San Francisco, 1949-51; resident in medicine Meml. Ctr. Cancer and Allied Diseases, N.Y.C., 1951-53; rsch. epidemiologist Dept. HEW, Nat. Cancer Inst., Bethesda, Md., 1955-57; cons. allergy clinic U. Calif., San Francisco, 1957-70, clin. prof. medicine and preventive medicine, 1970-90, clin. prof. medicine and epidemiology, 1990-96, head occupl. epidemiology, 1975-90, head divsn. internat. health edn. dept. epidemiology and internat. health, 1985-90; médecin agréé, official physician Consulate Gen. of France, San Fransisco, 1995—; sr. cons. internat. health care U. Calif., San Francisco. Med. cons., vis. prof. numerous ednl. & profl. instns., U. Marseilles, 1981—82, U. Pisa, Italy, 1983, U. Gabon, 1984, U. Siena, Italy, 1985; cons U. Calif., 1975—, sr. cons. internat. med. care, 2000—. Contbr. chpts. to books, articles to profl. jours. Editorial bd. Medecine d'Afrique Noire, Ospedali d'Italia. Served with USN, USPHS, 1953-55 Decorated comdr. Order of Merit (Italy), officer Ordre de la Legion d'Honneur (France), Medal of St. John of Jerusalem, Sovereign Order of Malta, Order of the Republic (Egypt); Scroll, Leonardo da Vinci Soc., San Francisco, 1965; award Internat. Inst. Oakland, 1964; Hon. Vice Consul, Italy, 1971-90. Fellow ACP, Am. Soc. Environ. and Occupational Health; mem. AAAS, Am. Cancer Rsch., Calif. Soc. Allergy and Immunology, Calif. Med. Assn., San Francisco Med. Soc., West Coast Allergy Soc. (founding), Mex. Congress on Hypertension (corr.), Internat. Assn. Med. Rsch. and Continuing Edn. (U.S. rep.), Acad. Italiana della Cucina. Democrat. Avocations: music, math, languages. also: 3838 California St San Francisco CA 94118-1522

**MUSTAFA, SHAKIR,** English and Arabic language educator; b. Baghdad, Iraq, June 15, 1952; came to U.S., 1990; s. Mahmoud Mustafa and Zakiya Mahdi; m. Nawal Nasrallah, Apr. 15, 1979. BA in English Lit., Baghdad U., 1974, MA in English Lit., 1977; PhD, Ind. U., 1999. Vice chmn. English dept. Mosul (Iraq) U., 1988-90; vis. asst. prof. Ind. U., 1999-2000; asst. prof. Boston U., 2000—. Author: To the Promised Land through Gas Chambers: Zionism and the Jewish Novel in America, 1980, Literary Translation, 2 vols., 1984, 85, Seventeenth-Century English Poetry, 1988; contbr. articles to profl.

jours.; co-editor: A Century of Irish Drama, 2000; translator Arabic lit. Mem. Modern Fgn. Langs., Union of Writers in Iraq. Moslem. Office: Boston U 718 Commonwealth Ave Boston MA 02215 Office Phone: 617-353-6231. Business E-Mail: mustafa@bu.edu.

**MUSTAPHA, AZLIN,** food scientist, educator; b. Johor Baru, Malaysia; PhD, U. Nebr., Lincoln, 1993. Rschr. U. Minn., St. Paul, 1994-96; asst. prof. U. Mo., Columbia, 1996—2003, assoc. prof., 2003—. Mem.: Internat. Assn. Food Protection, Am. Soc. Microbiology, Inst. Food Technologists. Office: U Mo Food Sci Program 256 WCS Wing Eckles Hall Columbia MO 65211 Office Phone: 573-882-2649.

**MUSTARD, LEWIS WILLIAMS,** management consultant, educator; b. Durham, N.C., Sept. 4, 1942; s. Harry S. and Elizabeth (Williams) M.; divorced; children: Juliana Janice, Lewis Williams Jr. AB in English, U. NC, Chapel Hill, 1966; cert. in hosp. adminstrn., Duke U., 1970; LLB, La Salle U., Chgo., 1974; D Bus. Adminstrn., Western Coll. U., 1976; PhD in Health Adminstrn., Union Grad. Sch., Cin., 1992; MA in Humanities, Calif. State U., Dominguez Hills, 1995. Hosp. adminstr. Woodruff (S.C.) Hosp., 1968-70; exec. dir. AID, Inc., Bryn Mawr, Pa., 1970-73; sr. hosp. cons. Summerour & Assocs., Atlanta, 1975-76; regional v.p. Qualicare, Inc., New Orleans, 1976-78; regional adminstr. Triage Corp., Clearwater, Fla., 1978-80; pres. Healthcare Mgmt. Cons., Atlanta, 1980-88; mem. continuing edn. faculty Duke U., Durham, NC, 1994—96; CEO Healthcare Negligence Control, Inc., Chapel Hill, NC, 1993—. Adj. prof. Ctrl. Mich. U., Mt. Pleasant, 1993-, So. Ill. U., Carbondale, 1993-, Webster U., St. Louis, 1994—, Bellevue (Nebr.) U., 2005—, Strayer U., 2005—; assoc. prof. North Ctrl. U., Prescott, Ariz., 2004-; adj. charter Oak State Coll., 2002—, New Britain, Conn., 2003-; adj. prof. NYIT, 2004—; legal cons., sole practitioner, 1992—; adj. prof. NY Inst. Tech. MBA Program, adj. Strayer U. Raleigh, NC. Served w/ USNR Res., 1959-68. Episcopalian. Office Phone: 919-929-1885.

**MUSTELIER, MARGARITA M.,** psychologist, director; b. NYC, Oct. 10, 1967; d. Salvador Triego and Margarita M. H. Mustelier. BA in Liberal Arts, Tulane U., New Orleans, 1991, BS in Psychology, 1991; MS, Nova Southeastern U., Miami, Fla., 2000, PsyD in Clin. Psychology, 2004. Postdoctoral trainee SE Fla. Inst. Psychoanalysis and Psychotherapy, Ft. Lauderdale; grad. asst. Touch Rsch. Inst., Ft. Lauderdale, 1999—2000; predoctoral intern U. Miami/Jackson Meml. Hosp., 2003—04; postdoctoral fellow, 2005; dir. behavior health svcs. Camillus Health Concern, Miami, Fla., 2005—. Water safety instr. YMCA, Miami, 1987—90; student rsch. interviewer Fla. Internat. U., Miami, 1990; mem. staff Here's Help South, Miami, 1992—93; rschr. dept. pediat., divsn. infectious diseases and immunology U. Miami Sch. Medicine, 1993—98; rschr. Inflexxion, Newton, Mass., 2002—05; psychotherapist Children's Psychiat. Ctr., Miami, 2002—03; adj. faculty mem. Coll. Arts and Scis. Nova Southeastern U., 2005; presenter, organizer workshops, seminars in field. Contbr. articles to profl. publs. Mem.: APA, SE Fla. Assn. Psychoanalytic Psychology, Phi Beta Kappa. Office: Camillus Health Concern 336 NW 5 St Miami FL 33128

**MUSTION, ALAN LEE,** pharmacist; b. Oklahoma City, Feb. 6, 1947; s. Granville E. and Iris E. (Graham) Mustion; m. Mary Jane Bozek, Dec. 4, 1982; children from previous marriage: Jeffrey Alan, Jennifer Chere. BS in Pharmacy, Southwestern Okla. State U., 1970. Staff pharmacist VA Med. Ctr., Oklahoma City, 1970—74, dir. pharmacy Richmond, Va., 1976—77, Iowa City, 1977—90; dir. pharmacy svcs. VA Hosp., Houston, 1990—2002; pharmacy mgr. Integris Bapt. Med. Ctr., Oklahoma City, 2002—. Clin. instr. clin./hosp. divsn. U. Iowa, 1977—90; adj. assoc. prof. pharmacy practice U. Houston, 1990—2002. Contbr. articles to profl. jours. Served to lt. col. USAR. Grantee Rsch., Travenol Labs., 1980—87, VA HSR&D, 1984, 1988. Mem.: Okla. Soc. Health Sys. Pharmacists, Am. Soc. Health Sys. Pharmacists, Kappa Psi. Methodist. Office: 3300 NW Expressway Oklahoma City OK 73112 Home: 513 Winding Creek Rd Yukon OK 73099-4471 Office Phone: 405-552-0857. E-mail: alan.mustion@integris-health.com.

**MUSTO, DAVID FRANKLIN,** medical researcher, educator, historian, consultant; b. Tacoma, Jan. 8, 1936; s. Charles Hiram and Hilda Marie (Hanson) Mustoe; m. Emma Jean Baudendistel, June 2, 1961; children: Jeanne Marie, David Kyle, John Baird, Christopher Edward. BA, U. Wash., 1956, MD, 1963; MA, Yale U., 1961. Lic. physician, Conn.. Pa. Clerk Nat. Hosp. for Nervous Disease, London, 1961; intern Pa. Hosp., Phila., 1963-64; resident Yale U. Med. Ctr., New Haven, 1964-67; spl. asst. to dir. NIMH, Bethesda, Md., 1967-69; vis. asst. prof. Johns Hopkins U., 1968-69; asst. prof. Yale U., 1969-73, assoc. prof., 1973-78, sr. rsch. scientist, 1978-81, prof., 1981—, exec. fellow Davenport Coll., 1983-88; mem. adv. editorial com. Yale Edits. Private Papers James Boswell, 1975—; cons. Exec. Office of Pres., 1973-75; mem. White House Strategy Coun., 1978-81; mem. panel on alcohol policy NAS, Washington, 1978-82; cons. White House Conf. on Families, 1979-80. Vis. fellow Clare Coll., Cambridge U., 1994; mem. alcohol adv. com. Nat. Assn. Broadcasters, 1994—; DuMez lectr. U. Md.; Walter Reed meml. lectr. Richmond Acad. Medicine; Galdston lectr. N.Y. Acad. Medicine; Sirridge lectr. U. Mo. Med. Sch.; Clendening lectr. U. Kans. Med. Sch. Author: The American Disease: Origins of Narcotic Control, 1973, expanded edit., 1987, 3rd edit., 1999; co-author: (with P. Korsmeyer) The Quest for Drug Control: Politics and Federal Policy in a Period of Increasing Drug Use, 1963-1981, 2002; editor: One Hundred Years of Heroin, 2002, Drugs in America: A Documentary History, 2002. Historian Pres.'s Commn. on Mental Health, 1977-78; adv. U.S. Del. to UN Commn. Narcotic Drugs, Geneva, 1978-79; mem. nat. coun. Smithsonian Instn., Washington, 1981-90, hon. mem., 1991—; hist. cons. Presdl. Commn. Human Immuno-deficiency Virus Epidemic, 1988; mem. nat. adv. com. on anti-drug program Robert Wood Johnson Found., 1989-2002; mem. nat. adv. com. on internat. narcotic policy UN Assn. of U.S.A., 1991; mem. adv. com. causes drug abuse Office Tech. Assessment, Congress U.S., 1992-94; commr. Conn. Alcohol and Drug Abuse Commn., 1992-93; bd. dirs. Coll. on Problems of Drug Dependence, 1990-94; trustee Assocs. of Cushing-Whitney Med. Libr., 1994—. With USPHS, 1967-69. Fellow: Coll. Problems of Drug Dependence, Am. Psychiat. Assn. (disting.); mem.: Soc. of Cin. in the State of Conn. (pres. 1998—2001), English-Speaking Union (pres. New Haven br. 1995—98), Am. Assn. History of Medicine (William Osler medal 1961), Am. Hist. Assn., Am. Inst. History of Pharmacy (Kraemers award 1974), New Haven County Med. Assn. (chmn. bicentennial com. 1983), Century Assn., Athenaeum Club (London), Cosmos Club. Office: Yale U PO Box 207900 New Haven CT 06520-7900 Office Phone: 203-785-4258. E-mail: david.musto@yale.edu.

**MUSTOE, THOMAS ANTHONY,** physician, plastic surgeon; b. Columbia, Mo., June 29, 1951; s. Robert Moore and Carolyn (Swett) M.; m. Kathryn Claire Stallcup, Aug. 13, 1977; children: Anthony, Lisa. BA cum laude in biology, Harvard Coll., 1973, MD cum laude, 1978. Diplomate Am. Bd. Otolaryngology, Am. Bd. Plastic Surgery; licensed Miss. 1985, Ill. 1991. Rsch. assoc. dept. microbiology Harvard Med. Sch., Cambridge, Mass., 1976-77; intern in medicine Mass. Gen. Hosp., Boston, 1978-79; resident in surgery Peter Bent Brigham Hosp., Boston, 1979-80; resident in otolaryngology Mass. Eye and Ear Infirmary, Boston, 1980-82, chief resident, 1982-83; resident in plastic surgery Brigham and Women's Hosp., Children's Hosp., Boston, 1983-84, chief resident, 1984-85; asst. prof. in surgery Wash. U. Sch. Medicine, St. Louis, 1985-89, assoc. prof., 1989-91; prof., chief divsn. plastic surgery Northwestern U. Med. Sch., Chgo., 1991—; plastic surgeon Northwestern Meml. Hosp., 1991—, Evanston Hosp., 1991—, Children's Meml. Hosp., 1992—, Shriner's Hosp. Chgo., 1994—. Co-chmn. Gorden Rsch. Conf., 1995; spl. cons. FDA, 1994—98; mem. sci. adv. panel Biologies, 1997, NCI, 1998; lectr. seminars, 2001. Editl. bd. Archives of Surgery, 1992-2004, Plastic and Reconstructive Surgery, 1993-2001, Wound Repair and Regeneration, 1992—, Jour. Surg. Rsch., 1997-2006; contbr. articles to profl. jours., more than 200 publs., book chpts.; book reviewer. Harvard Nat. scholar, 1969-73; Rhodes scholar candidate, Harvard Coll., 1973. Fellow: ACS (adv. coun. plastic surgery 1999—2002, surg. forum com. 1999—2002, editl. bd. jour. 2003—, surg. biology club III); mem.: AMA, Am. Soc. Plastic Surgery (sci. program chair 2005—), Am. Bd. Plastic Surgery, Coun. Plastic Surger Org., Double Boarded Soc. (pres. 1995—98), Chgo. Surg. Soc., Chgo. Plastic

Surg. Soc. (sec. 1996—97), Wound Healing Soc. (program com. 1990, audit com. 1992, program com. 1992, bd. dir. 1993—96, program com. 1994, fin. com. 1994—96, program com. 1997, pres. 1997—99), Assn. Acad. Chmn. Plastic Surgery (matching program and ctrl. application svc. com. 1994), Soc. U. Surgeons, Soc. Head and Neck Surgeons (membership com. 1993—95), Plastic Surgery Rsch. Coun. (rep. coun. acad. surgeons 1991—94, com. indsl. rels. 1992, program com. 1992—94, 1995, Judge Snyder & Crikelair awards 1991), Midwest Assn. Plastic Surgeons, Lipoplasty Soc. N.Am. (lipoplasty ednl. rsch. found. 1998—2000), Am. Assn. Plastic Surgery (rsch. and edn. com. 1994—96, chmn. 1996, mem. com. 1998—, co-chmn. ASPRS-ASAPS task force on emerging trends 1999—2000, chmn. instl. coun. com. 1999—), Am. Soc. Plastic and Reconstructive Surgery (rsch. fund proposal com. 1987—92, plastic surgery device com. 1989—93, resource book for plastic surgery residents com. 1991—93, socioecon. 1992—94, sci. program com. 1993—95, chmn. device and tecyhnique assessment com. 1994—96, co-chmn. gen. reconstruction subcom. 1995, ultrasonic lipectomy task force 1995—96, task force for outcomes and guidelines 1995—98, devices and tech. com. 1995—98, chmn. instrnl. com. 1999—2002, chmn. edn. com. 1999—, chmn. resource book com.), Aesculapian Club, Sigma Xi. Avocations: reading, golf, gardening, sports. Home: 144 Greenwood St Evanston IL 60201-4712

**MUTALIPASSI, LOUIS RICHARD,** psychologist, educator; b. Kansas City, Kans., Jan. 23, 1937; s. Louie R. Mutalipassi and Cleda E. (Miller) Wolverton; m. Edalee Kenworthy, July 14, 1962 (div. 1970); 1 child, Annemarie; m. Laura Ruth Posner, July 17, 1976; 2 children: Michael and Anthony. BA in Psychology, U. Calif., Santa Barbara, 1962; MA in Psychology, UCLA, 1965, PhD in Psychology, 1969. Lic. psychologist, Calif. Staff psychologist VA Med. Ctr., LA, 1969—76, chief psychology svc. Albany, NY, 1976—80; clin. assoc. prof. psychology UCLA and U. So. Calif., LA, 1980—; chief psychology svc. VA Med. Ctr., Long Beach, 1980—97; ret., 1997; clin. psychologist in pvt. practice Cypress, Calif., 1982—. Oral commr. State Bd. Med. Examiners, Calif., 1996—. Contbr. articles to profl. jour.; presenter in field. With USAF, 1954-58. With USAF, 1954—58. Mem.: APA. Avocations: golf, photography. Office Phone: 714-507-8099. Personal E-mail: loum@adelphia.net.

**MUTH, ERIC PETER,** optician, consultant; b. Munich, July 25, 1940; came to U.S., 1948, naturalized 1955; s. Erich Walter and Anna Lisa (Pentenrieder) M.; m. Rachel Hubbard, Apr. 4, 1971; children: Karl George, Ellen Anna. BS, Charter Oak Coll., 1978; degree (hon.), Anoka-Hennipen Tech. Coll., 1995. Sr. rsch. fellow Internat. Soc. for Philosophical Inquiry, 1991—96, pers. cons., 1996; cons. Nat. Acad. Opthamology Found. Mus., San Francisco, 1982—88, Nat. Mus. Hist. Smithsonian Inst., 1983—94, Gesell Inst. Human Devel., 1984—89; mem. adv. com. South. Cen. Cmty. Coll., Seattle, 1984—89; mem. adv. bd. internat. Scientific Inst., PR, 1989; adv. bd. Middlesex C.C. (vice chmn.), 1989; vol. VA, West Haven, Conn., 2001—. Mem. editl. bd. Dispensing Opticians, Butterworths Heinmann, 1998, co-author 2nd edit., 1998; contbr. the Social History of Eyeglasses in Japan, 1991, die Brille, Leipzig, 1989, Thinking on the Edge Agamennon, 1993; contbr. over 250 articles to profl. jours.; contbg. editor Optical Mgmt., 1979-80, OpticScan Canada, 1981-82, Indian Optician, 1982, Prism Mag., Can., 1988, 92; tech. editor Optical Index, 1980-82; book reviewer in field. Presdl. appointment U.S. Selective Svc. Sys., 1991-92; scoutmaster Boy Scouts Am., 1960-62; bd. dirs. ARC Conn. chpt., 1988; advisor Tri Hi-Y YMCA, 1964; founder, chmn. Korea-Vietnam Meml. com., Milford, 1985-86; organizer WWII Monument Com. 1991; trustee Conn. Visual Health Ctr., 1982-84; commr. Nat. Commn. on Opticianry Edn., 1989-93; life mem. Soc. 3d. U.S. Inf. Div., 1987; hon. Capt. 25th Bn. Royal Fusiliers, 1999; trooper Ct. State Militia, 2d co. gov.'s horse guard, 2002-04. Served with U.S. Army, 1957-59. Selected Reserves, 1965-69; Conn. Army N.G., 1960-64. Decorated Roman Cath. Knight Malta, Equestrian Knight of The Order of the Holy Sepulchre, Knight Comdr., Army Commendation medal; recipient Eng. Nelson/Wingate prize, 1983, Service Above Self award, Rotary, 1986, Optician of the Yr., Guild of Prescription Opticians Am., 1993, Senate Citation, State of Conn., 1993, German-Am. Friendship award, Germany, 1995, State of Conn. Justice of the Peace, 1995, cert. of appreciation, Nat. Libr. Medicine, Bethesda, Md., 1995, Med. Scis. Divsn. Nat. Mus. History, 1995, Mayoral Proclamation, Milford, Conn., 1998, Bronze medal of merit, Austrian Albert Schweitzer Soc., 1998, Chemical Corps Regimental Assn. Order of the Dragon, 1999, Oeuvre Humanitaire Croix d'Honneur, 1999, medal of merit, El Salvador Red Cross, 1999, Award of Merit, Army and Navy Union of USA, 2000, Vol. award, VA, 2003. Fellow: Conn. Opticians Assn. (pres. 1974, amb., chmn. membership and ethics coms., Optician of Yr. 1975), Opticians Assn. Am. (historian citation 1993, advancing opticianry award 1994, diploma in refractometry 1995, disting. svc. award 2000, honored fellow), Nat. Acad. Opticianry (regional membership chmn., faculty speakers bur., citation 1988), Internat. Acad. Opticianry; mem.: Nat. Contact Lens Examiners (cert.), Guild Prescription Opticians Am. (councilor 2001—02), Royal Lifesaving Soc. Can. (hon. assoc. 1998), Soc. Am. Mil. Engrs., Calif. Soc. Dispensing Opticians (hon.), Ari. Soc. Dispensing Opticians (hon.), Am. Bd. of Opticianry (master of ophthalmic optics 1972), Internat. Platform Assn., Contact Lens Soc. Am., Contact Lens Soc. Conn., Internat. Found. in Ophthalmics Optics, Conn. Guild Dispensing Opticians (pres. 1980, Optician of Yr. 1981), Charter Oak Coll. Alumni Assn. (bd. dirs. 1987, alumni citation 1995), Milford C. of C. (chmn. law and safety com. 1975, Cmty. Svc. award 1986), Disabled Am. Vets. (life DAV-NSF commendation 2004), Am. Legion Post 196 (life; parade marshal 1998, citation 1986). Avocations: skydiving, parasailing, ballooning, motorcycling, Tae Kwon Do. Home: 25 Parkland Pl Milford CT 06460-7723 Personal E-mail: eepmuth@nyc.com.

**MUTH, RICHARD FERRIS,** economics professor; b. Chgo., May 14, 1927; s. Merlin Arthur and Margaret Ferris Muth; m. Helene Louise Martin, Dec. 23, 1955; children: Lisa Helene, Laurianne Martin Love. Student, USCG Acad., 1945-47; AB, Washington U., St. Louis, 1949, MA, 1950; PhD, U. Chgo., 1958; M of Theol. Studies, Emory U., 1995. Lectr. polit. economy Johns Hopkins U., Balt., 1955-56; economist Resources for Future, Washington, 1956-58; assoc. prof. urban econs. U. Chgo., 1959-64; economist Inst. Def. Analyses, Arlington, Va., 1964-66, cons., 1966-69; prof. econs. Washington U., St. Louis, 1966-70, Stanford U., Calif., 1970-83; Callaway prof. econs. Emory U., Atlanta, 1983—2001, chmn. dept., 1983-90, prof. emeritus, 2001—. Vis. assoc. prof. econs. Vanderbilt U., 1958—59; vis. sr. fellow Urban Inst., Washington, 1976—77; vis. prof. Sch. Bus. U. Calif., Berkeley, 1991. Author (with others): Regions, Resources and Economic Growth, 1960, Cities and Housing, 1969, Public Housing, 1974, Urban Economic Problems, 1975; co-author (with Allen C. Goodman): The Economics of Housing Markets, 1989. Mem. Presdl. Task Force on Urban Renewal, 1969, Presdl. Task Forces on Urban Affairs and Housing, 1980—81, Presdl. Commn. on Housing, 1981—82. With USCG, 1951—52. Libertarian. Methodist. Office: Emory U Dept Econs Atlanta GA 30322-2240 Business E-Mail: rmuth@emory.edu.

**MUTH, SHARON A.,** language educator; d. Richard and Antonietta Losee; m. Michael G. Muth, Nov. 2, 1968; children: Michaela, Marissa 1 stepchild, Cassandra. B in Elem. Edn., Coll. St. Rose, Albany, NY, 1988, M in Reading, 1994. Spanish tchr. St. Pius X Sch., Loudonville, NY, 1988—90, Ravena (N.Y.) Coeymans Selkirk H.S., 1990—. Office: Ravena Coeymans Selkirk High Sch 2025 Rt 9 W Ravena NY 12143

**MUTOMBO, DIKEMBE (DIKEMBE MUTOMBO MPOLONDO MUKAMBA JEAN JACQUE WAMUTOMBO),** professional basketball player; b. Kinshasa, Zaire, June 25, 1966; m. Rose Mutombo; children: Carrie Biamba Wamutombo, Jean Jacques Dikembe Mutumbo Mplombo Jr. BA in Linguistics and Diplomacy, Georgetown U., 1991. Ctr. Denver Nuggets, 1991—96, Atlanta Hawks, 1996—2001, Phila. 76ers, 2001—02, New Jersey Nets, 2002—03, New York Knicks, 2003—04, Chicago Bulls, 2004, Houston Rockets, 2004—. Founder Dikembe Mutombo Found. Named NBA Defensive Player of Yr., 1995, 1997, 1998, 2001; named to 8 NBA All-star teams, NBA All-Rookie team, 1992; recipient President's Svc. award, Points of

Light Found., 1999, Henry P. Iba Citizen Athlete award, 1999. Fluent in English, French, Spanish, Poruguese, and five African dialects. Office: c/o Houston Rockets 1510 Polk St Houston TX 77002

**MUTTER, JOHN J., JR.,** writer, researcher; s. John J. Mutter, Sr. and Burnette V. Mutter; m. Karen L. Boerst, Aug. 21, 1982. Grad., Shawano Sr. H.S., Wis., 1961. Power plant operator State of Wis., Madison, Winnebago, Green Bay, Wis., 1982—2001, ret., 2001. Author: To Slay a Giant, 2000, Out in the Country, 2005; ghostwriter: I Will Sing My Songs Again, the biography of Ronnie Fuller, 2004; co-editor Shawano County Sesquicentennial 1853-2003. With USN, 1961—64, with U.S. Mcht. Marine, 1969—70, with U.S. Mcht. Marine, 1973—77, West Coast. Decorated The Vietnam Svc. Bar; recipient Outdoor Writing award, Coun. for Wis. Writers, 1990, Buzzard Buster award, Wolf Watershed Ednl. Project, 2000, 50th Bo Carter Meml. award, Waukesha Writers Group, 2002, 2d Pl. award, Al P. Nelson Feature Writing Contest, 2004. Mem.: Coun. for Wis. Writers, Wis. Regional Writers Assoc., Shawno County Hist. Soc. (life), Shawano Area Writers (pres. 2002). Avocations: writing, fishing, hunting, reading, managing woods for nature. Office: Burstone LLC N2787 McDonald Rd Shawano WI 54166-6956 Office Phone: 715-526-9277.

**MUTTERPERL, WILLIAM CHARLES,** lawyer, corporate financial executive; b. NYC, July 15, 1946; s. Martin and Muriel (Wurtzel) M.; m. Nancy Fay Borson, July 2, 1968; children: Matthew, Adam. BA, Dartmouth Coll., 1968; JD, Columbia U. N.Y.C., 1971. Bar: N.Y. 1972, R.I. 1978, U.S. Dist. Ct. (so. and ea. dists.) N.Y. 1973, U.S. Dist. Ct. R.I. 1979. Assoc. atty. Cleary, Gottlieb, Steen and Hamilton, N.Y.C., 1971-77; asst. gen. counsel Fleet Nat. Bank, Providence, 1977-79, gen. counsel, 1979-85; v.p., gen. counsel, sec. Fleet Fin. Group, Inc. (now Fleet Boston Fin Inc.), Providence, 1985-89, sr. v.p., gen. counsel, sec., 1989—2001; exec. dir. ind. oversight bd. Arthur Andersen LLP, 2002; ptnr. bus. law divsn. Brown, Rudnick, Berlack, Israels, LLP, 2002; vice chmn. PNC Fin. Svcs. Group, Pitts., 2002—. Bd. mem. Black Rock, Inc., NY, Beth Israel Deaconess Hosp., Boston; former pres. Boston Bar Found. Mem. Phi Beta Kappa. Democrat. Jewish. Office: PNC Fin Svcs Group One PNC Plaza 249 Fifth Ave Pittsburgh PA 15222-2707

**MUTTI, ALBERT FREDERICK,** retired minister; b. Hopkins, Mo., Feb. 13, 1938; s. Albert Frederick and Phyllis Margaret (Turner) M.; m. Etta Mae McClurg, June 7, 1959; children: Timothy Allen, John Frederick, Martin Kent. AB, Cen. Meth. Coll., 1960; MDiv., Garrett-Evang. Theol. Sem., 1963; DMin., St. Paul Sch. Theology, 1975; DD, Baker U., 1993, Ctrl. Meth. Coll., 2000. Pastor Union Star Charge, Mo., 1963-65; sr. pastor Crossroads Parish, Savannah, Mo., 1965-74; assoc. pastor. dir. Mo. West Conf. UMC, Kansas City, 1974-80, coun. dir., 1980-82; sr. pastor First United Meth. Ch., Blue Springs, Mo., 1982-87; dist. supt. Cen. Dist. UMC, Mo., 1987-89; dist. supr. Kansas City N. Dist., 1989-92; bishop Kans. Area United Meth. Ch., Topeka, 1992—2004; bishop in residence Saint Paul Sch. Theology, 2004. Author: Breath of New Life, Dancing In a Wheelchair. Chair Savannah Cmty. Betterment, 1971; bd. mem. St. Mary's Hosp., Blue Springs, 1986; dir. ARC, Savannah, 1968; bd. Discipleship, Nashville, bd. Global Ministries, NY; pres. Mo. Coun. Chs., Jefferson City, Gen. Commn. on Christian Unity, Dean Mo. Area Ministers Sch., Curator, Ctrl. Meth. Coll.; trustee St. Paul Sch. Theology; organizer Rural, Religion and labor Coun. Kans; coordinating coun. Chs. Uniting in Christ, 2004—; fund coord. Global AIDS, 2004-. Named Disting. Alumni Ctrl. Meth. Coll.; recipient Grad. award St. Paul Sch. Theology. Methodist.

**MUTTON, HOLLY BETH,** psychiatrist; b. Kenmore, N.Y., Jan. 6, 1966; d. David Kenneth and Susan Kathleen Mutton; life ptnr. Gregory F. Smith. BFA in Applied Media Arts, Edinboro U., Pa., 1988; postgrad., Canisius Coll., 1996; DO, NY Coll. Osteo. Medicine, 2002. Freelance graphic artist HB Graphics, East Amherst, NY, 1982—; resident asst. Edinboro U., 1984—88; salesperson The Ltd. Stores, Inc., Buffalo, 1988—91; art dir., account exec. RQC Ltd., Williamsville, NY, 1990—92; sales rep. Azerty Inc., Orchard Park, NY, 1992—97; nat. account mgr. McGregor Supplies Divsn., Elma, NY, 1997—98; resident pediats. U. Buffalo Med. Sch. Hosp. Consortiums, 2002—03, resident psychiatry, 2003—05, fellow child psychiatry, 2005—. Anatomy and embryology artist, tchg. asst., student amb. N.Y. Coll. Osteo. Medicine, Old Westbury, 1999—2000; vol. Sisters Hosp. Emergency Rm., Buffalo, 1993—95. Named Hon. Letter Carrier/cert. of appreciation, U.S. Postal Svc., 1990, winner Marilyn Monroe Lookalike Contest, Bon Ton Dept. Store and Warners, 1997; recipient Humanism and Excellence in Tchg. award, Arnold P. Gold Found., 2004. Mem.: Am. Acad. Pediat. (life), Western N.Y. Osteo. Med. Soc. (life), Am. Psychiatry Assn. (life), Am. Acad. Child and Adolescent Psychiatry (life). Office: Univ at Buffalo Med Sch Hosps Buffalo NY Office Phone: 716-887-5800.

**MUTUNAYAGAM, N. BRITO,** architecture educator; b. Quilon, Kerala, India; came to U.S., 1976; BSc in Engring., Kerala U., Trivandrum, India, 1963; D.T.C.P., Sch. Planning, New Delhi, 1967; M Engring., Asian Inst. Tech., Bangkok, 1974; D.E.D.P., Va. Tech., Blacksburg, 1981. Jr. engr. Kerala Govt., 1963-64, town planner, 1964-77; instr. Va. Tech., Blacksburg, 1977-81; assoc. prof. Coll. Architecture, U. Nebr., Lincoln, 1981-90, prof., 1990—, assoc. dean, 1994—99, 2000—02, interim dean, 2000. Cons. several archtl. firms, Nebr., Iowa, Tex., Mass., Mo., Ariz., Wash., Calif., 1984—2000; rural cmty. devel. projects throughout Nebr., 2000—; mem. Speakers Bur., U. Nebr., Lincoln, 1996, 2002, 03. Co-author: Cartography and Site Analysis, 1985, Designing With Solid Models Study Guide, 1995, Dimensions Reference Guide, 1995, Command Reference Manual, 1995. Fellow Ctr. for Great Plains Studies, 1985—; appt. fellow U. Nebr., 1988—. Mem. Am. Planning Assn., Nat. Geog. Soc. Avocations: computer graphics, music, television, video recording, model ships. Office: U Nebr 307 Architecture Hall Lincoln NE 68588-0105

**MUTZ, GREGORY THOMAS,** insurance company executive; b. Indpls., Dec. 19, 1945; BA, DePauw U., 1967; JD, U. Mich., 1973. Chmn. bd. dir. AMLI Realty Co. subs. UICI, Chgo., 1980—; chmn. bd. trustees AMLI Residential Properties Trust, Chgo.; pres., CEO UICI, Dallas, 1999—. Bd. dirs. Nat. Multifamiy Housing Coun., Chgo., 1995—, Alleghany/Chgo. Trust, 1996—. Lt. U.S. Army, 1968-69, Vietnam.

**MUTZ, JOHN MASSIE,** foundation administrator, former state official, former energy executive; b. Indpls., Nov. 5, 1935; s. John Loughery and Mary Helen (Massie) M.; m. Carolyn Hawthorne, June 21, 1958; children: Mark, Diana. BS in Advt. and Bus. Mgmt, Northwestern U., 1957, MS, 1958. Copy editor Indpls. News, summer 1953, 54; dir. public relations for residential bldg. products Aluminum Co. Am., Pitts., 1958-60; dir. advt. and public relations, sec., asst. to pres. Perine Devel. Corp., Indpls., 1960-61; instr. dept. public and environ. affairs Ind. U., 1976-79; v.p. Circle Fin. Corp., Indpls., 1962-79, Circle Leasing Corp., Indpls., 1962-79, Fast Food Mgmt. Corp., 1978-79; mem. Ind. Ho. of Reps., 1967—70, chmn. interim sch. fin. com., 1962-69, chmn. taxation subcom. of ways and means com., 1969-70; Republican candidate state treas., Ind., 1970; mem. Ind. State Senate, 1971—80, chmn. state budget com., 1977—78; lt. gov. State of Ind., 1981-89; pres. Lilly Endowment, Inc., 1989—93, PSI Energy, 1993—99; chmn. dept. of waterworks City of Indianapolis, 2002; bd. chmn. Lumina Found., 2002—. Spkr. in field. Columnist: Indpls. Bus. Jour.; author: Fundraising for Dummies. Mem. Sch. Property Tax Control Bd. Indpls., 1975-76; bd. govs. United Way Indpls., 1978-79; mem. bd. missions United Meth. Ch., Indpls., 1976-78; bd. dirs. Suemma Coleman Agy., 1975-79, Community Services Council Indpls., 1976-77; trustee Christian Theol. Sem., 1976-79. Mem. Nat. Restaurant Assn. (dir. 1978-79), Ind. Restaurant Assn. (dir. 1977-79), Marion County Mental Health Assn.. Northwestern U. Alumni Assn., Pi Alpha Mu, Deru (1955-57), Beta Theta Pi (v.p. 1956-57) Office: Lumina Found PO Box 1806 Indianapolis IN 46206-1806 Office Phone: 317-841-9793. Personal E-mail: j8128m@aol.com.

**MUTZ, OSCAR ULYSSES,** manufacturing and distribution executive; b. Edinburg, Ind., Feb. 12, 1928; s. Harold Winterberg and Laura Belle (Sawin) M.; m. Jean Greiling, Aug. 22, 1948; children: Marcia, H. William. BS, Ind. U., 1949. Vice pres. Peerless Corp., Indpls., 1954-63; v.p.: gen. mgr. Space Conditioning, Inc., Harrisonburg, Va., 1964-66; v.p., treas. Cosco, Inc., Columbus, Ind., 1966-67; exec. v.p., 1967-69; pres., 1969-71; chmn. bd. Court Manor Corp., Columbus, 1971-73; pres. Jenn Air Corp., Indpls., 1973-75; pres., CEO Mutz Corp., 1975-81; pres., dir. Haag Drug Co., 1977-78; pres. Forum Group, Inc. (merger Mutz Corp. and Excepticon, Inc.), Indpls., 1981-91; chmn., CEO, bd. dirs. Capital Industries, Inc., Indpls., 1991-96; chmn. Lakeland Auto Mall. 1996—. Pres. Ct. Manor Corp., co-chmn. bd. dirs. Sargent & Greenleaf, Safemasters; pres. Security Group, Inc., 1991-2004, also bd. dirs. Nat. trustee Fellowship Christian Athletes, 1985-91, chmn. nat. conf. ctr., 1994-96; mem. pres. coun. and dean's adv. coun. Ind. U. Mem. Ind. Mfrs. Assn. (chmn. 1980), Acad. Alumnae Fellows Ind. U. Sch. Bus., Lakeland Yacht Club, Grasslands Country Club, Lone Palm Country Club. Republican. Presbyterian. Office: Mutz Corporation 5119 Lake in the Woods Blvd Lakeland FL 33813-2942

**MUUSS, ROLF EDUARD,** retired psychologist, author; b. Tating, Germany, Sept. 26, 1924; came to U.S., 1953, naturalized, 1992. s. Rudolf A. and Else M.; m. Gertrude Louise Kremser, Dec. 22, 1953 (dec. April 1999); children: Michael John (dec.), Gretchen Elise. Diploma, Tchr. Coll., Flensburg, Germany, 1951; student. U. Hamburg, Germany, 1951, Ctrl. Mo. State Coll., 1951—52, Columbia Tchrs. Coll., 1952; MEd, Western Md. Coll. 1954; PhD, U. Ill., 1957; Masters Degree (hon.). U. Ambrosiana, Milan, 2004. Tchr. pub. sch., Germany, 1945-46, 51, 52-53; substitute prin., 1952-53; tchr. trainee U.S. Office Edn., 1951-52; houseparent Child Study Ctr., Balt., 1953; grad. asst. U. Ill., 1954-57; rsch. assoc. prof. Iowa Child Welfare Rsch. Sta., State U. Iowa, 1957-59; rsch. cons., 1960, 61; mem. faculty Goucher Coll., 1959-95, prof. edn., 1964-95, chmn. dept., 1972-75, dir. spl. edn., 1977-92, Elizabeth C. Todd disting. prof., 1980-85, chmn. dept. sociology and anthropology, 1983-85, prof. emeritus, 1995—. Rsch. assoc. edn. Johns Hopkins, 1962-63; part-time or summer tchr. U. B.C., 1962, Johns Hopkins U., 1962, 65, U. Del., 1965, Towson U., 1967, U. Ill., 1967; tchg. assoc. Sheppard and Enoch Pratt Hosp., 1969-80; guest lectr. Tchrs. Coll., Kiel, Fed. Republic Germany, 1977-78; hearing officer spl. edn. cases State of Md., 1980-96. Author: First-Aid for Classroom Discipline Problems, 1962, Theories of Adolescence, 1962, 5th edit., 1988, 6th edit., 1996, Grundlagen der Jugendpsychologie, 1982; also numerous articles; editor: Adolescent Behavior and Society: A Book of Readings, 1971, 4th edit., 1990, 5th edit., 1998. Served with German Air Force, 1942-45. Recipient award for disting. scholarship Goucher Coll., 1979; grantee Andrew W. Mellon Found., 1976-77. Fellow Am. Psychol. Soc., Am. Psychol. Assn., Md. Psychol. Assn. (treas. 1971-73); mem. Balt. Psychol. Assn. (chmn. membership com. 1966, v.p. 1970-71), Soc. Rsch. Child Devel., Soc. Rsch. on Adolescence, Kappa Delta Pi (v.p. Alpha chpt. 1956-57), Phi Delta Kappa. Home: 1540 Pickett Rd Lutherville Timonium MD 21093-5822 Personal E-mail: rolfmuuss@yahoo.com.

**MUY-RIVERA, MARTIN,** biochemist, researcher; b. Mexico. Jan. 30, 1963; s. Raul Muy and Blanca Rivera; m. Irina Pavlova, Jan. 21, 2001. PhD, 1989. Rsch. scientist InBios, Seattle, 2001—02, Swedish Med. Ctr. Seattle, 2002—. Cons. in field. Contbr. articles to profl. jours. Recipient Dr. Jorge Rosenkranz Med. Rsch. award, 1989. Mem.: AAAS, AAMI. Home: 1014 E Terrace St Apt C Seattle WA-98122 Office Phone: 206-405-2776. Personal E-mail: martinmuy@earthlink.net.

**MUZYKA, POLA MARIE,** film producer, artist; b. Wilkes-Barre, Pa., Apr. 26, 1948; d. Peter Joseph and Dorothy May Muzyka; m. Giancarlo Giuseppi Lui, July 3, 1970 (div. Apr. 18, 1986); children: Gianpaul Robert Lui, Joshua Chinko. Degree in theatre & fine arts, UCLA, 1967—88. Cert. effective speaking & human rels. Dale Carnegie & Assocs., 1981, corp. scriptwriting Internat. Film & TV Workshop, Maine, 1997. Prodr., actress, artist MEG-COMM Prodns., Wilkes-Barre, 1982—92; prodr., artist CMNProdns., Waleska, Ga., 1992—. Founder, dir. Christian Media News Alliance, Waleska, 1997—. Actor: (films, commercials, documentaries). Recipient Best Short Prodn. award, NY State Theater Festival Assn., 1980, NEPA Advertising award, Pola Muzyka, 1999, Addy award, 1998. Mem. 9. Office: CMNProdns PO Box 324 Waleska GA 30183 Business E-mail: pola@christianmediaalliance.com

**MUZYKA-McGUIRE, AMY,** marketing professional, nutritionist, consultant; b. Chgo., Sept. 24, 1953; d. Basil Bohdan and Amelia (Rand) Muzyka; m. Patrick J. McGuire, June 3, 1977; children: Jonathan, Elizabeth. BS, Iowa State U., 1975, postgrad., 1978—; registered dietitian, St. Louis U., 1980. Cert. dietitian. Home economist Nat. Livestock and Meat Bd., Chgo., 1975-77; dietary cons. various hosps. and nursing homes, Iowa, 1978-79; supr. foodsvc. Am. Egg Bd., Park Ridge, Ill., 1980-83; assoc. dir., mgr. foodsvc. Cole & Weber Advt., Seattle, 1984-85; prin., owner Food and Nutrition Comms., Federal Way, Wash., 1986—. Co-author: Turkey Foodservice Manual, 1987; editor: (newsletter) Home Economists in Business, 1975-77, Dietitians in Business and Industry, 1982-85; Food Net on Internet, 1995, Food and Culinary Profls. Newsletter, 1999-2001; contbr. articles to profl. jours. Named Outstanding Dietitian of Yr. North Suburban Dietetic Assn., 1983, Tastemaker of the Month, 2001, 02, 03. Mem. Am. Dietetic Assn., Internat. Foodsvc. Editl. Coun., Cons. Nutritionists, Internat. Assn. Culinary Profls. (CCP) (chair nutritional food scis. group 2003-05). Avocations: gardening, travel, music, food and beverage tastings. Home: 5340 SW 315th St Federal Way WA 98023-2034

**MWENDA, KENNETH KAOMA,** legal association administrator, consultant; LLB, U. Zambia, 1990; Gr.Dip, LCCI, U.K. 1991; DMS, IoC, U.K. 1992; BCL, U. Oxford, U.K., 1994; MBA, U. Hull, Eng., 1995; DBA, Pacific Western U., LA, 1996, PhD in Publs., 1999; PhD, U. Warwick, U.K., 2000. Cert. Bar, Zambia, 1991; cert. cumpolsory edn., devels. in comml. securities, intellectual property law. With trust funds and co-financing dept. Vice-Presidency of World Bank, Washington, 1998—99, with poverty reduction, mgmt. and pub. sector reform unit, 1999; counsel legal dept. World Bank, Washington, 1999—2000, projects officer, 2000—03, sr. projects officer, 2003—04, sr. counsel, 2004—. Vis. prof. U. Miskolc Sch. Law, Hungary, 1996; lectr. U. Zambia Law Sch., 1991—95, vis. prof., 2001; lectr. Warwick U. Law Sch., 1995—98; spkr. and presenter in field. Author: Legal Aspects of Corporate Capital and Finance, 1999, Contemporary Issues In Corporate Finance and Investment Law, 2000, Banking Supervision and Systemic Bank Restructuring, 2000, Zambia's Stock Exchange and Privatization Programme, 2001, The Dynamics of Market Integration: African Stock Exchange's in the New Millennium, 2000, Banking Supervision and Microfinance Regulation: Lessons from Zambia, 2002, Principles of Arbitration Law, 2003, Frontiers of Legal Knowledge: Business and Economic Law in Context, 2003, Anti-Money Laundering Law and Practice, 2005, Legal Aspects of Financial Services Regulation and the Concept of a Unified Regulator, 2006, The Legal Administration of Financial Services in Common Law Jurisdicitions: with special attention to the dual regulation system in Zambia, 2006, Combating Financial Crime: Legal, Regulatory and Institutional Frameworks, 2006, Contemporary Issues in International Economic Law, 2006, Economic Integration and Development in Africa, 2006. Tutor U. Zambia Law Sch., 1991—95. Staff Devel. fellow in law U. Zambia, 1991, U. Yale Law Faculty fellow, 1998; Rhodes scholar U. Zambia, 1992, U. Oxford, 1992-94, U. Hull, 1994-95. Fellow Royal Soc. Arts. of England, Inst. Commerce of England; mem. Internat. Bar Assn., Law Assn. of Zambia, Brit. Assn. Lawyers for Def. of Unborn. Office: The World Bank 1818 H St NW Washington DC 20433-0001 Personal E-mail: kmwenda@yahoo.com.

**MYAING, U. LINN,** ambassador; b. Oct. 15. 1947; married; 2 children. BS, Def. Svcs. Acad. With Myanmar fgn. svc., 1993—; Myanmar amb. to France (with non-resident accreditation to Belgium, the Netherlands. UNESCO and the EU), 1999—2001, to the U.S., 2001—. Officer Myanmar Navy, 1967—93. Office: Embassy of Myanmar (Burma) 2300 S St NW Washington DC 20008

**MYATT, WILLIAM HOWARD,** theater educator, director, actor; b. Maquoketa, Iowa, Mar. 1, 1961; s. Robert Bruce and Adabelle Marie Myatt; m. Christina Marie Schnock, Aug. 10, 2002; children: Anna Marie, Alexander Ashton, Zachary Leonard. BA, U. No. Iowa, Cedar Falls, 1979—84, MA, 1985—90. Cert. 7 - 12 Libr./Media Specialist Dept. of Edn., Iowa, 2001, k - 12 Talented and Gifted Educator Dept. of Edn., Iowa, 1995. Dir., actor Meml. Union Summer Resident Theatre, Ames, Iowa, 1982—83; drama dir., tchr. Burlington HS, Wis., 1984—85, No. U. HS, Cedar Falls, Iowa, 1985—87, Clinton HS, Iowa, 1987—90, Pleasant Valley Cmty. HS, Pleasant Valley, Iowa, 1990—. Workshop presenter Tenn. Thespian Conf., Nashville, 1991, Va. Thespian Conf., 1991—94, Ednl. Theatre Assn., Regional Conf., Minneapolis, Minn., 1991, Kans. Thespian Conf., 1992; workshop presenter, adjudicator Fla. Thespian Conf., Tampa Bay, 1992; workshop presenter Iowa HS Speech Assn., Des Moines, 1997—; mainstage adjudicator Ednl. Theatre Assn., Cincinnati, Ohio, 1994—, trustee, 1996—99. Contbr. articles. Aids quilt display com. Scholar Hazel B. Strayer award, U. No. Iowa Theatre Dept., 1982. Mem.: Iowa Ednl. Theatre Assn. (Hall of Fame 2005), Ednl. Theatre Assn. (pres., v.p. 2001—05, bd. dirs. local chpt. 2005, Hall of Fame 2005). Avocations: theater, reading, science fiction. Office: Pleasant Valley Comm HS PO Box 332 Pleasant Valley IA 52767-0332 Office Phone: 563-332-5151. Business E-mail: myattw@pleasval.k12.ia.us.

**MYCIELSKI, JAN,** retired mathematics professor; b. Wisniowa, Poland, Feb. 7, 1932; s. Jan and Helena (Bal) M.; m. Emilia Przezdziecka, Apr. 25, 1959. MS, U. Wroclaw, Poland, 1955, PhD, 1957. With Inst. Math., Polish Acad. Scis., Wroclaw, 1956-68; prof. math. U. Colo., Boulder, 1969—2002, prof. emeritus, 2002—. Vis. prof. Case Western Res. U., Cleve., 1967, U. Colo., 1967, Inst. des Hautes Etudes Scientifiques, Bures-sur-Yvette, 1978-79, dept. math. U. Hawaii, 1987; attache de recherche Centre National de la Recherche Scientifique, Paris, 1957-58; asst. prof. U. Calif., Berkeley, 1961-62, 70; long-term vis. staff mem. Los Alamos Nat. Lab., 1989-90. Author over 150 rsch. papers. Recipient Stefan Banach prize, 1965, Alfred Jurzykowski award, 1977, Waclaw Sierpinski medal, 1990. Mem. Am. Math. Soc., Math. Assn. Am., Polish Math. Soc., Assn. for Symbolic Logic. Office: U Colo Dept Math Boulder CO 80309-0395 Business E-mail: jmyciel@euclid.colorado.edu.

**MYER, DONALD BEEKMAN,** architect; b. Cleve., Aug. 25, 1937; s. Beekman Walter and Jennie Helen (Gimpel) M.; m. Ellen Jane Schwartz, June 10, 1970; 1 child. Jamie Beekman. BArch, U. Ill., 1961, MArch, 1962. Registered architect Va., D.C. Supervisory architect Nat. Park Svc., Phila., Washington, Cape, Mass., 1962-65; asst. sec. Commn. Fine Arts, Washington, 1965-97; adminstrn., budget and grants cons. Keyes, Lethbridge & Condon, Architects, Washington, 1968-70; clk. of works Washington Nat. Cathedral, 1998-2001; curator bldg. and grounds Tudor Place, Georgetown, 2001—02 strategic counsel cons., 2002—. Cons. Preservation Galveston (Tex.) History Found., 1968-69, Joint Com. on Landmarks, Washington, 1969; faculty cons. Sch. of Architecture, Cath. U. Am., 1990—2005; mem. bldgs. and grounds com. Protestant Episcopal Cathedral, 2003—; mem. U.S. Capital Vis. Ctr. Arts Panel, 2004-05; bd., dirs., chair design adv. com. Adams Meml. Found., 2006—. Author: Bridges and the City of Washington, 1974, Building Potomac Aqueduct, 1975; editor: Centennial History of Washington AIA, 1987. Mem. faculty Smithsonian Resident Assocs., Washington, 1973-81; pres. Washington Archtl. Found., 1998-2000; trustee Com. of 100 on the Fed. City, 1997-2000; mem. bldgs. and grounds com., Protestant Episc. Cathedral, 2003—. Named Arch. of Yr., D.C. Coun. Engring. and Archtl. Socs., 2005; named one of 77 People to Watch award, Washingtonian Mag., 1987; grantee Europa-Nostra Seminar Smithsonian Fgn. Currency Program, Poland, 1974. Fellow AIA (chair hist. resources 1976, v.p. found. 1980, chpt. pres. 1987, fellows selection jury 1998-2000, awarded Centennial Medal, Washington chpt. 2004); mem. Woodley Park Men's Club (pres. 1979-82), Lambda Alpha (hon.). Republican. Avocations: bridge history, travel, photography, furniture and clock restoration. E-mail: aspire2@earthlink.net.

**MYER, MARY ELIZABETH,** researcher; d. Margaret Mary Myer. BA, Regis Coll., Weston. Mass., 1993; MS, Boston Coll., Chestnut Hill, Mass., 2005. Assoc. analyst, quantitative rsch. AMR Rsch., Boston, 1998—2002; mgr. data adminstrn. Boston Coll., Chestnut Hill, Mass., 2002—. Mem.: Boston Young Profls. Assn., Assn. for Instl. Rsch., Am. Mgmt. Assn., Soc. of Competitive Intelligence Profls. Avocations: exercise, movies.

**MYERBERG, MARCIA,** investment banker; b. Boston, Mar. 25, 1945; d. George and Evelyn (Lewis) Katz; m. Jonathan Gene Myerberg, June 4, 1967 (div. Mar. 1994); 1 child, Gillian Michelle. BS, U. Wis., 1966. Corp. trust adminstr. Chase Manhattan Bank, N.Y.C., 1966-67; asst. cashier Glore Forgan, Wm. R. Staats, Phoenix, 1967-68; bond portfolio analyst Trust Co. of Ga., Atlanta, 1969-72; asst. v.p. 1st Union Nat. Bank, Charlotte, N.C., 1973-78; dir. cash mgmt. Carolina Power & Light Co., Raleigh, N.C., 1978-79; sr. v.p., treas. Fed Home Loan Mortgage Corp., Washington, 1979-85; dir. Salomon Bros. Inc., N.Y.C., 1985-89; sr. mng. dir. Bear, Stearns & Co. Inc., N.Y.C., 1989-93; mng. dir. Bear, Stearns Home Loans, London, 1989-93; chief exec. Myerberg & Co., L.P., N.Y.C., 1994—. Home: 37 W 12th St Apt 6K New York NY 10011-3205 Office: 780 3rd Ave New York NY 10017-2024

**MYERNICK, GLENN,** professional soccer coach; b. Dec. 29, 1954; Student, Hartwick Coll. Professional soccer player Dallas Tornado, 1977-79, Portland, 1980-82, Tampa Bay, Fla., 1983-84; asst. coach U. Tampa, 1985-86, Hartwick Coll., 1986-89; nat. coaching coord. US Soccer Team, 1989-96; asst. coach US Olympic Team, 1996; head coach Colo. Rapids, Denver, 1997—2000; asst. coach US Men's Nat. Team, 2002; head coach US Nat. Under-23 Men's Team, 2004—. Capt. U.S. Pan Am. Team, 1975, U.S. Olympic Team, 1976. Recipient Hermann Trophy as College Player of the Yr., 1976; named U.S. Soccer Fedn. Coach of the Yr. by U.S. Olympic Com., 1998. Office: US Soccer Federation 1801 S Prairie Ave Chicago IL 60616

**MYEROWITZ, P(AUL) DAVID,** cardiac surgeon, educator, writer; b. Balt., Jan. 18, 1947; s. Joseph Robert and Merry (Brown) M.; m. Susan Karen Macks, June 28, 1967 (div.); children: Morris Brown, Elissa Suzanne, Ian Matthew; m. Kathleen Mary Murphy, Aug. 10, 2001. BS, U. Md., 1966; MD, 1970; MS, U. Minn., 1977. Intern in surgery U. Minn., Mpls., 1970-71, resident in surgery, 1971-72, 74-77; resident in cardiothoracic surgery U. Chgo., 1977-79; practice medicine specializing in cardiovascular surgery Madison, Wis., 1979—; asst. prof. thoracic and cardiovascular surgery U. Wis., Madison, 1979-85; assoc. prof., 1985; chief sect. cardiac transplantation, 1984-85; Karl P. Klassen prof., 1985-97; chief thoracic and cardiovascular surgery Ohio State U. and Hosps., Columbus, 1985-97. Author: (book) Heart Transplantation, 1987, Heartland for Profit, 2004; contbr. articles to profl. jours. Served with USPHS, 1972-74. Mem.: ACS, Am. Assn. Thoracic Surgeons, Am. Coll. Cardiology. Jewish. E-mail: hrttx1@aol.com.

**MYERS, A. MAURICE,** waste management executive; b. Long Beach, Calif., May 20, 1940; s. Walter Ray and H. Priscilla (Larsen) M.; m. Elizabeth Jean Ashburn, July 16, 1960; children: Michele, Tracy, Leanne. BA, Calif. State U., Fullerton, 1964; MBA. Calif. State U., Long Beach, 1972. Fin. mgr. Ford Motor Co., Newport Beach, Calif., 1964-72; fin. cons. Merrill Lynch, Newport Beach, 1972-75; mktg. dir. Continental Airlines, L.A., 1975-82; v.p. ops. On TV, L.A., 1982-83; pres., CEO Aloha Airgroup, Honolulu, 1983-93; pres. Am. West Airlines, Phoenix, 1993-95; chmn., pres., CEO, bd. dirs. Yellow Corp., Overland Park, Kans., 1996-99; pres., CEO Waste Mgmt., Inc., Houston, 1999—2004; chmn. Waste Mgmt. Inc., Houston, 1999—. Bd. dirs. Hawaiian Elec. Industries, Honolulu, Tesoro Petroleum Inc., San Antonio, Pleasant Holidays, West Lake Village, Calif. Bd. dirs. Greater Houston Partnership, Keep Am. Beautiful. Mem. Nat. Assn. Mfrs., Waialae Country Club (Honolulu). Avocations: reading, golf, travel. Office: Waste Management 1001 Fannin St Ste 4000 Houston TX 77002-6711

**MYERS, ALBERT F.,** aerospace executive; b. New Orleans, La., Jan. 11, 1946; BS in Mech. Engring., U. Idaho, 1969, MS in Mech. Engring., 1971; MS in Indl. Mgmt., MIT, 1992. Active duty U.S. Army, 1972-75; various positions Dryden Flight Rsch. Ctr., 1975-81; mgr. flight controls engring. Northrop Grumman, 1981, corp. v.p., Bus. Stategy, 1992-94, corp. v.p., treas., 1994—2003, corp. v.p., Strategy and Technology, 2003—. Mem.: NAE. Office: Northrop Grumman Corp 1840 Century Park E Los Angeles CA 90067-2101*

**MYERS, ALLEN RICHARD,** rheumatologist; b. Balt., Jan. 14, 1935; s. Ellis Benjamin and Rosina (Blumberg) M.; m. Ellen Patz, Nov. 26, 1960; children: David Joseph, Robert Todd, Scott Patz. BA, U. Pa., 1956; MD, U. Md., 1960. Diplomate Am. Bd. Internal Medicine, Am. Bd. Rheumatology. Intern Univ. Hosp., Balt., 1960-61, resident in medicine Ann Arbor, Mich., 1961-64; fellow in rheumatology Mass. Gen. Hosp. and Harvard Med. Sch., Boston, 1966-69; dir. clin. tng. rheumatology U. Pa. Sch. Medicine, Phila., 1969-72, chief rheumatology sect., 1972-78; dep. chair medicine Temple U. Sch. Medicine, Phila., 1978-84, acting chmn. medicine, 1984-86, dean, 1991-95, prof. medicine, 1978—, assoc. v.p. Health Scis. Ctr., 1988-95. Vis. prof. Cardiothoracic Inst., U. London, 1988; mem. med. adv. bd. Scleroderma Rsch. Found., Santa Barbara, Calif., 1986. Mem. editl. bd. Arthritis & Rheumatism, 1985—90, Brit. Jour. Rheumatology, 1989—94; editor: Systemic Sclerosis, 1985, Medicine, 1986, 1993, 1996, 2000, 2004. Pres. Phila. Health Care Congress, 1994—; adv. com. Pa. Lupus Found., 1976—; bd. dirs. Phila. Conv. and Visitors Bur., 1994—. With USPHS, 1964-66. Recipient Margaret Whitaker prize U. Md. Sch. Medicine, 1960, Lindback Found. award Temple, 1981; named Physician of Yr. Temple U. Hosp., 1986. Master: Am. Coll. Rheumatology; fellow: ACP, Phila. Coll. Physicians (pres. 2000); mem.: Am. Fedn. Clin. Rsch. Avocations: walking, classical music, reading. Office Phone: 215-707-5127.

**MYERS, ANGELA MICHELLE,** music educator, department chairman; b. Kokomo, Ind., Nov. 29, 1978; d. Ronald Wayne Myers and Sandra Jane Myers Gaiser. BS in Instrumental Music Edn., Ball State U., Muncie, Ind., 2001. Band dir. Prince William County Sch., Stonewall Jackson HS, Manassas, Va., 2002; band dir., dept. chair Prince William County Sch., Bull Run Mid. Sch., Gainesville, Va., 2004—. Fine arts rep. Bull Run Mid. Sch. Adv. Council, Gainesville, Va., 2004—; curriculum cons. Prince William County Sch., Manassas, Va., 2004—, camp dir., instr., 2004—; presenter in field. Band pres. Ball State U., Sch. of Music, Muncie, Ind., 2000—01, 2000—01. Recipient Richard L. Dunham Band award, Ball State U. Marching Band, 2000, John R. Emens Leadership award, Ball State U. Sch. Music. Mem.: Sigma Alpha Iota, Va. Music Educators Assn., Music Educators Nat. Conf. Achievements include founding staff mem. Bull Run Mid. Sch., 2002.

**MYERS, C. DAVID,** manufacturing executive; BS, Pa. State U. CPA. Sr. mgr. KPMG L.L.P.; dir. fin. Airside Products Group, 1994-95; corp. cont. York (Pa.) Internat. Corp., 1995-98, v.p., fin. engineered systems group, 1998-2000, v.p., CFO, 2000—03, pres., 2003—05, CEO, 2004—05, also bd. dirs.; v.p., corp. officer, pres., bldg. efficiency bus. Johnson Controls Inc., Milw., 2005—. Office: Johnson Controls 5757 N Green Bay Ave Milwaukee WI 53209*

**MYERS, CONNIE LANINE,** elementary school educator; d. Eldon B. and Doris Gilbert White; m. Charles Lynn Myers, June 27, 1971; 1 child, Ashley Lanine. BS in Elem. Edn., Ft. Hays State U., 1971; MS in Adminstrn., Newman U., Wichita, Kans., 2001. Cert. elem. edn. K-8 Kans., ESL Kans., bldg. adminstrn. Kans. Tchr. 6th grade Unified Sch. Dist. 374, Sublette, Kans., 1971—77, tchr. 2d grade tchr., 1977—87, tchr. 1st grade, 1987—. North Ctrl. Assn. dir. Unified Sch. Dist. 374, Sublette, 2000—, curriculum dir., 2005—. Ednl. dir. Sublette Christian Ch., 1990. Mem.: ASCD, NEA, Sublette Edn. Assn., Delta Kappa Gamma. Office: Sublette Elem 301 S Inman Sublette KS 67877 Office Phone: 620-675-2286. Business E-mail: cmyers@usd374.org.

**MYERS, DANIEL WILLIAM, II,** lawyer; b. Camden, N.J., Mar. 21, 1931; s. Charles Rudolph II and Myrtle Henrietta (Kress) M.; m. Eileen Ethel Kohn, Nov. 22, 1959; children: Susan Leigh, Meredith Ann Myers Winner, Kathryn Kress. BS in Commerce, U. Va., 1952, LLB, 1957. Bar: Va. 1957, N.J. 1958, U.S. Dist. Ct. N.J. 1958, U.S. Supreme Ct. 1980. Assoc. Lewis & Hutchinson, Camden, 1958-60; ptnr. Myers, Matteo, Rabii, Norcross & Landgraf and predecessors, Camden, Cherry Hill, NJ, 1960-89, Montgomery, McCracken, Walker & Rhoads, 1989-94, of counsel, 1994-98, Steven J. Jozwiak, Cherry Hill, NJ, 1998—. 1st lt. U.S. Army, 1952-54. Mem. N.J. Bar Assn., Va. Bar Assn., Camden County Bar Assn., Am. Arbitration Assn., Exch. Club (pres. Cherry Hill chpt. 1969). Republican. Lutheran. Home: 1 E Atlantic Ave Harvey Cedars NJ 08008 Office: 532 Hollywood Ave at Rte 38 Cherry Hill NJ 08002 Office Phone: 856-661-1822.

**MYERS, DARYL RONALD,** engineer; b. Denver, July 12, 1948; s. James Elmer Myers and Betty Mae (Gannon) Welborn; m. Donna Lee Olsen, Oct. 3, 1990 (dec. Oct. 1995); m. Barbara Jane Bowker, Sept. 5, 1997. BS in Applied Math., U. Colo., 1970, postgrad., 1974-75. Staff physicist Smithsonian Radiation Biology Lab., Rockville, Md., 1974-78; metrology engr. Solar Energy Rsch. Inst. (now Nat. Renewable Energy Lab.), Golden, Colo., 1978-93; sr. scientist, task leader Solar Radiometric Metrology, 1993—. Project leader Joint U.S.-Saudi Arabian Solar Radiation Resource Assessment, 1997-2000, Joint Saudi Arabian/NASA Remote Sensing Validation Project, 1998-2001. Editor Optical Radiation News; contbr. articles to profl. jours. including Solar Energy, Solar Cells, ASME Jour. Solar Energy Engring. Russian and German interpreter, Cultural Diversity Com., Arvada, Colo., 1992. With U.S. Army, 1970-74. Recipient Outstanding Mentor award, Dept. of Energy, 2004, Outstanding Performance Staff award, 2005, Outstanding Team Staff award, 2006. Mem. ASTM, Precision Measurement Assn. (John Quincy Adams award 1979-80), Am. Solar Energy Soc., Coun. Optical Radiation Measurement (v.p. 2004—), Math. Assn. Am Democrat. Achievements include rsch. in algorithms for interpolation and corrections to measured precipitable water, aerosol optical depth, and radiometric data used in developing national solar radiation data base and international projects to establish global climate change trends via ground and satellite based instrumentation; development of revised terrestrial spectral solar radiation reference and improved solar radiometric instrument calibration concensus standards. Office: Nat Renewable Energy Lab 1617 Cole Blvd Golden CO 80401-3305 Office Phone: 303-384-6768. Business E-mail: daryl_myers@nrel.gov.

**MYERS, DAVID ALAN,** middle school music educator; b. Burlington, Vt., Apr. 24, 1956; s. Alan R. and Joanne F. (Beauchemin) M.; m. Shelle O'Lena, July 10, 1982; children: Lauren R., Carly E. BS in Music Edn., U. Vt., Burlington, 1978, MEd. 1992. Cert. tchr. music K-12, Vt. Counselor, instr. U. Vt. Summer Music Session, Burlington, 1975-81; music instr. band, chorus, gen. music Hazen Union Sch. Jr.-Sr. H.S., Hardwick, Vt., 1978-82; instr., condr., counselor Friends of Music Day Camp, Burlington, 1984-92; dir. instrumental music Shelburne (Vt.) Cmty. Sch., 1982—; bandmaster, condr., percussionist, arranger 40th Army Band, Colchester, Vt., 1981—. Guest condr. music festivals, New Eng., 1989—. Composer: (band music) Windridge, 1988, La Menagerie des Jouets, 1991, Spartacus, 1995, For Praise and Honor, 1995, A Seafaring Rhapsody, 1995, Green Mountain Tapestry, 1995, Prelude and March Humoresque, 1996, When the Stars Begin to Fall, 1997, Changing of the Guard, 1997, With Silent Eyes, They Look to the Sea, 1998, Danza Barbarica, 1999, Satin and Brass, 1999, A Pastoral Suite, 2000, Battered Brass Blues, 2000, Snow Country, 2001, Regalia, 2001, Variations on a Boboobo Song, 2002, Bagatelle for Flutes, 2003, Saxcapade, 2003, Mansfield Fantasy, 2003, The Damsel and the Dragon, 2004, Of Kings and Castles, 2004, An Irish Tale, 2005, All Brass and Blue, 2005, A Greater Courage, 2005, Fury, 2006; contbr. chpt. to books, article to profl. jours.; freelance composer and arranger, 1984—. Founder, dir. Shelburne (Vt.) Cmty. Band, 1990-93; coach Georgia (Vt.) Youth Soccer, 1992-95; choir dir. Ascension Ch., Georgia, Vt., 1994-99. Decorated Meritorious Svc. medal (2), Army Commendation medal, Army Achievement medal (4); recipient Gov.'s commendation for excellence in arts and cmty. svc. State of Vt., 1991; named

Tchr. of Yr. Shelburne PTO, 1985-86. Mem. ASCAP, U.S. Army Warrant Officer Assn., Am. Legion, Assn. for Concert Bands. Avocations: gardening, carpentry, bowling, running, music performance. Office: Shelburne Cmty Sch Harbor Rd Shelburne VT 05482 Office Phone: 802-985-3331. Business E-Mail: Dmyers@cssu.org.

**MYERS, DONALD JAMES,** museum director, art historian, educator; b. Marshalltown, Iowa, June 23, 1961; s. Wendell Duane and Nadine Carol (Paul) Myers; m. Joni Diane Anderson, June 29, 1985; children: Iris Justine, Dalton Grant. BA, Gustavus Adolphus Coll., St. Peter, Minn., 1983; MA, U. So. Calif., L.A., 1988; postgrad., U. Md., College Park. Staff auditor East Adrian Helgeson and Co., CPAs, Mpls., 1983—84; gallery asst. Vincent Price Gallery, East LA C.C., East Monterey Park, Calif., 1986—86; curatorial asst./rsch. asst. dept. sculpture and decorative arts Nat. Gallery of Art, Washington, 1986—90, Mellon asst. curator dept. sculpture and decorative arts, 1990—96; lectr. dept. art Cath. U. of Am., Washington, 1996—97; instr. art history Gustavus Adolphus Coll., Saint Peter, Minn., 1998—99; U. Md. Mus. fellowship dept. sculpture and decorative arts and dept. Italian Renaissance paintings Nat. Gallery of Art, Washington, 1999—99; dir. Hillstrom Mus. of Art, instr. art history Gustavus Adolphus Coll., Saint Peter, Minn., 2000—. Treas. bd. dirs. Arts Ctr. of Saint Peter, Minn., 2000—04, gallery com., 2000—04, treas. bd. dirs., 2006—. Author: (exhbn. brochure) Paul Granlund: A Retrospective Exhbn.; editor: (mus. collection summary catalogue) Sculpture: An Illustrate Catalogue, Nat. Gallery of Art, Washington; contbr.: mus. catalogue Systematic Catalogue of Portrait Medals, Nat.Gallery of Art, exhbn. catalogue The Colour of Sculpture, 1810-1940, Van Gogh Mus., Amsterdam, Obras Maestras de la Nat. Gallery of Art, Museo Nacional de Antropologia, Cordoba, Mex., The Currency of Fame: Portrait Medals of the Renaissance, Art for the Nation: Gifts in Honor of the 50th Anniversary of Nat. Gallery of Art, Encyclopedia of Italian Renaissance and Mannerist Art, The Dictionary of Art. Robert H. Smith fellowship and Travel grant, Smith Found., 1991. Mem.: Am. Assn. of Museums. Avocations: music (mem. folk trio Folky Dokey and swing band The Echos), athletic competition. Office: Hillstrom Mus of Art Gustavus Adolphus 800 W College Ave Saint Peter MN 56082 Office Phone: 507-933-7171. Business E-Mail: dmyers@gustavus.edu.

**MYERS, DOROTHY ROATZ,** artist; b. Detroit, Mar. 24, 1921; d. Harry Agustus and Lola May (Kelly) Roats; children: Bruce, Leslie Ann, Douglas. Student, Antioch Coll., 1941, Corcoran Gallery Art Sch., 1943, Art Students League, 1965—. Asst. to design dir. Harper & Row Pub., N.Y.C., 1981-87. Lectr. and writer on art-related affairs. Contbr. revs. to profl. publs.; exhibited in numerous shows including N.Y. ArtExpo, 1992, Art Miami, 1992, Cornell Med. Libr. Ann., 1992, Hellenic Art Inst. Exhbn., 1991, Vt. Inst. Natural Sci., 1983, Montserrat Gallery Internat. Exhbn. (hon. mention 1993); represented in permanent collection Ward-Nasse Gallery, N.Y.C. Recipient 1st place award for drawing Brookdale Coll., 1994, 2d place award for sculpture, 1993, Bronze medal for animal art, 1986, 20th Century award for Achievement Internat. Biog. Ctr.; apptd. Acad. Ofcl. Knighted Acad. Internazionale Dept. Arts, Italy. Mem.: Academia del Verbano, Italy, N.Y. Artists Equity, Garrison Art Ctr., Hellenic Art Inst., League Sci. et Edn. Sociale, Arts, Scis., Lettres: Soc. Academique de Edn. et Encouragement, Art Students League (life), Acad. Am. Poets.

**MYERS, DOUGLAS GEORGE,** zoological society administrator; b. LA, Aug. 30, 1949; s. George Walter and Daydeen (Schroeder) Myers; m. Barbara Firestone Myers, Nov. 30, 1980; children: Amy, Andrew. BA, Christopher Newport Coll., 1981. Tour and show supr. Annheuser-Busch (Bird Sanctuary), Van Nuys, Calif., 1970-74, mgr. zool. ops., 1974-75, asst. mgr. ops., 1975-77, mgr. ops., 1977-78; gen. services mgr. Annheuser-Busch (Old Country), Williamsburg, Va., 1978-80, park ops. dir., 1980-81; gen. mgr. San Diego Wild Animal Park, 1981-83, dep. dir. ops., 1983-85; CEO, Zool. Soc. San Diego, 1985—. Mem. Balboa Park Cultural Partnership; mem. steering com. conservation breeding specialists group Ctrl. Balboa Park Assn.; cons. in field. Mem. adv. com. of pres.' assn. Am. Mgmt. Assn. Mem.: Calif. Assn. Zoos and Aquariums, World Assn. Zoos and Aquariums, Am. Zoo and Aquarium Assn., Am. Assn. Museums, Rotary Club San Diego. Office: Zool Soc San Diego PO Box 120551 San Diego CA 92112-0551

**MYERS, EDDIE EARL,** psychologist; b. Ardmore, Okla., Nov. 24, 1937; s. Finis Weldon and Fern Durrell (Johnson) M.; m. Ineta June Moore, July 2, 1955 (div. Mar. 1988); children: Richard Weldon, Ronald Leland, Marilyn June, Rebecca Jean; m. Ann Clymer Taylor, July 15, 1988 (div. May 1996); Clark Clymer Taylor, Katy Ann Taylor; m. Katherine Call Emch, Dec. 28, 1996. BSEd, Tex. Christian U., 1958; MEd, U. N. Tex., 1967, EdD. 1969. Lic. psychologist Ohio, Nat. Drug Edn. Leadership Tng. Adelphi U., 1970. Machinist Chance Vaught Aircraft, Grand Prairie, Tex., 1957-58; 5th grade tchr., jr. high coach Ft. Worth Christian Schs., 1958-59; 6th grade tchr., jr. high coach Corpus Christi (Tex.) Ind. Sch. Dist., 1959-60; youth, music, ednl. min. Norton St. Ch. Christ, Corpus Christi, 1960-61, Procter St. Ch. Christ, Port Arthur, Tex., 1963-65; min. Cameron (Tex.) Ch. Christ, 1961-63; high sch. English tchr. Christian Schs., Inc., Dallas, 1965-66; psychology instr. Tex. Women's U., Denton, 1968-69; sr. rsch. assoc., dir. psychology dept. Ednl. Rsch. Coun. Am., Cleve., 1969-78; clin. psychologist pvt. practice Cleve., 1978—. Faculty dept. guidance and counseling U. Oreg. Workshop, Frankfurt, German, 1972; Ea. U.S. drug abuse task force Am. Soc. Health Assn., N.Y.C., 1971-73; chmn. drug abuse and alcoholism task force Fedn. Cmty. Planning, Cleve., 1970-71; adv. bd. Freedom House Rehab. Ctr., Cleve., 1993—; adj. assoc. prof. ednl. specialists Cleve. State U., 1970-74; mem. med. staff St. John Westshore Hosp., West Lake, Ohio, Fairview Hosp., Cleve. Author: Social Isolation and Personality, 1973, Handy Asks the Psychologist, 1974, (tchr. manual) Human Persons and Use of Psychoactive Agents, 1974; co-author: (tchr. manual) New Model Me: Operator's Guide to Coping with Aggression, 1974; contbr. articles to profl. jours. R & D grantee NIMH, Washington, 1974-78, Nat. Def. Edn. Rsch. Tng. grantee U.S. Dept Edn. Washington, 1965 69. Mem. APA, Cleve. Psychol. Assn. (bd. trustees 1981-85), Cleve. Acad. Consulting Psychologists (pres. 1984-86), Ohio Psychol. Assn. (bd. trustees 1978—), Phi Delta Kappa. Avocations: computers, golf, jet boating. Office: 3865 Rocky River Dr Ste 2 Cleveland OH 44111-4114 Office Phone: 216-251-5161. Personal E-mail: emyersbvoh@aol.com.

**MYERS, ELISSA MATULIS,** publishing executive, professional society administrator; b. Munich, Aug. 4, 1950; (parents Am. citizens); d. Raymond George and Anne Constance (Moley) Matulis; m. John Wake Myers, Sept. 13, 1967 (div. 1972); 1 child, Jennifer Anne Myers Bick. BA in English Lit., George Mason U., 1972, MA in English Lit., 1982. Dir. rsch. and info. Am. Soc. Assn. Execs., Washington, 1972-80, dir. mem. svcs., 1980-88, v.p., pub. Assn. Mgmt. mag., 1988-97; pres., CEO Nat. Informercial Mktg. Assn., Washington, 1997—2004, Electronic Retailing Assn., Washington, 1998—2003; chmn. Internet Radio Network. Chmn. Assn. Internet Radio Network, 2004; host weekly radio show Assn. Nation, Assn. Power and Politics. Pub. Principles of Association Management, 1976, 3d edit., 1996; columnist Forechoices, 1988-97. Bd. dirs. Ethics Resource Ctr., Washington, 1982-86; mem. Universal Postal Union Adv. Group 2000+; mem. Fed. Adv. Commn. on e-commerce; appointee DofC 1fac-4 Ecommerce, 2001-. Mem. Am. Soc. Assn. Execs. (cert.), Assn. Conv. Mktg. Execs., Greater Washington Soc. Assn. Execs. (bd. dirs. 2000—), Nat. Assn. Hispanic Mktg. Profls. (adv. bd.), Soc. Nat. Assn. Publs., Com. of 100 U.S. C. of C. Soc. Scholarly Pubs. Roman Catholic. Avocations: running, scuba diving. Home: 5315 Moultrie Rd Springfield VA 22151-1915 Office: AIR 5673 Ravnel Ln Springfield VA 22151 Office Phone: 703-626-9087. E-Mail: elissa@elissamyers.com.

**MYERS, ELLEN HOWELL,** historian, educator; b. Bryan, Tex., Feb. 16, 1941; d. Douglas Wister and Ann Olive (Emory) Howell; m. William Allen Myers, Dec. 23, 1967; 1 child, William Webb. Student, Mt. Vernon Jr. Coll., 1959—61, U. Madrid, 1961—62; BA, Sophie Newcomb Coll. of Tulane U., 1963; MA, U. Va., 1965, PhD, 1970. Lectr. U. Houston, 1966—67; instr. Okla. State U., Stillwater, 1967—70; asst. prof. San Antonio Coll., 1970—73, assoc. prof., 1973—77, prof. history, 1977—. Author: (student's rev. manuals

instrs. manuals) The American Nation, 1975, 1977, 1979, 1983, 1987, Test Bank for the West Transformed, 2000; contbr. articles to profl. jours. Mem. S.W. Conf. Commn. on Higher Edn. and Campus Ministry Meth. Ch., 1978—81; bd. dirs. Family Svc. Assn., 1978—85, pres., 1983—84; bd. dirs. San Antonio Area Red Cross, 1979—85, Laurel Heights Weekday Sch., 1980—83, chmn., 1982—83. Mem.: AAUP (exec. com. San Antonio Coll. 1973—74), Conf. on L.Am. History, S.W. Conf. on L.Am. Studies (exec. com. 1974—75), Tex. C.C. Tchrs. Assn., Tues. Musical Club, Jr. League of San Antonio (bd. dirs. 1977—79), Kappa Alpha Theta, Phi Alpha Theta. Democrat. Methodist. Home: 307 Arcadia Pl San Antonio TX 78209-5950 Office: 1300 San Pedro Ave San Antonio TX 78212-4201

**MYERS, ELMER,** psychiatric social worker; b. Blackwell, Ark., Nov. 12, 1926; s. Chester Elmer Myers and Irene Lewis; widowed; children: Elmer Jr., Keith, Kevin. BA, U. Kans., 1951, MA, 1962; student, U. Calif., Santa Barbara, 1977-78. Lic. clin. social worker; C.C. counselor credentials. Psychiat. social worker Hastings (Nebr.) State Hosp., 1960-62, State of Calif. Bur. Social Tng. Com., Sacramento, 1962-75; supr. psychiat. social worker State of Calif., Sacramento, 1975-80, Alta Calif. Regional Ctr., Sacramento, 1980-85. Exec. dir. Tri-County Family Svcs., Yuba City, Calif., 1966-69; cons. to four convalescent Hosps., Marysville and Willows, Calif., 1969-71; lectr. Yuba Coll., Marysville, 1971-76; assoc. prof. Calif. State U., Chico, 1972-73; cons. in field, Marysville, 1985—; group and individual therapist Depot Homeless Shelter, 1996—, facilitator HIV support group, 1993-2002, counselor, 1995—; cons., therapist New Millennium Group Home, 2000. Bd. dirs. Habitat for Humanity, 1993; juror Yuba County Grand Jury, Marysville, 1965, 1987—88; sec. Y's Men's Club, Yuba City, 1964—65; chmn. Tri-County Home Health Agy., Yuba City, 1974—76; vice-chmn. Gateway Projects, Inc., Yuba City, 1974—75; bd. dirs. Yuba County Truancy Bd., Marysville, 1964—67; asst. dir. Marysville Adult Activity Ctr., 1990—; active Yuba-Sutter United Way, 1971—73, 1991—92; active, sec. Tri-County Ethnic Forum, 1991—93; steering com. Yuba County Sr. Ctr. Assn., 1992, 1995—; chmn. Yuba County Cmty. Svcs. Commn., 1997—99; bd. dirs. Yuba-Sutter Gleaners, 1997—2004, fin. sec., 2006; chmn. Yuba-Sutter Commn. on Aging, 1996, bd. dirs., 1998, 2001; chmn. H.E.L.P. Working Group, HIV Prevention, 2000; bd. dirs. Christian Assistance Network, 1993, Golden Empire Health Sys. Agy., Sacramento, 1972—76, Youth Svcs. Bur., Yuba City, 1967, Bi-County Mental Retardation Planning Bd., Yuba City, 1972, Yuba County Juvenile Justice Commn., Marysville, 1982—90, Am. Cancer Soc., Marysville, 1985—92, Yuba County Rep. Ctrl. Com., 1983—90, Salvation Army, 1990—96, facilitator care proj., 1992—2002. Recipient Cert. Spl. Recognition, Calif. Rehab. Planning Project, 1969, Cert. Spl. Recognition, State of Calif., 1967, Cert. Spl. Recognition, Alta Calif. Regional Ctrs., 1985; named Vol. of Week, Appeal Dem. newspaper, 1999. Mem. Nat. Assn. Social Workers (cert.), Kern County Mental Health Assn. (chmn. 1978-79). Lodges: Rotary (bd. dirs. Marysville club 1975-76). Avocations: gardening, reading, computers. Home and Office: 3920 State Hwy 20 Marysville CA 95901-9003 E-mail: elm@syix.com.

**MYERS, EUGENE NICHOLAS,** otolaryngologist, educator; b. Phila., Nov. 27, 1933; s. David and Rosalind (Nicholas) Myers; m. Barbara Labov, June 10, 1956; children: Marjorie Rose, Jeffrey N. BS in Econs., U. Pa., 1954; MD, Temple U., 1960. Diplomate Am. Bd. Otolaryngology. Intern Mt. Sinai Hosp., NYC, 1960—61; resident Mass. Eye and Ear Infirmary, Boston, 1963—65; asst. prof. clin. otolaryngology U. Pa., 1968—72; prof. clin. oncology dept. oral pathology U. Pitts. Sch. Dental Medicine, 1975—82, prof. diagnostic svcs., 1982—2000, prof. dept. oral and maxillofacial surgery, 2000—; prof., chmn., chief dept. otolaryngology U. Pitts. Med. Ctr., 1972—2005, disting. prof. otolaryngology, 2006—. Cons. VA Med. Ctr., Pitts., 1972—, Children's Hosp., Pitts., 1972—. Editor: Cancer of the Head and Neck, 1981, 4th edit., 2003, Tracheotomy, 1985, 2d edit., 1998; mem. editl. bd. Laryngoscope, 1973—95, exec. editl. bd., 1995—2004, mem. editl. bd. Head and Neck Surgery, 1978—92, 1998—, AMA Archives of Otolaryngology, 1981—, Annals of Otology Rhinology and Laryngology, 1984—2005, Oncology, 1986—, European Archives of Oto-Rhino-Laryngology, 1990—97, Auris Nasus Larynx, 1996—, editor-in-chief (book) Advances in Orolaryngology, 1985—2001; co-editor: Butterworth's Intern Med. Revs., 1981—82; internat. editor Otolaryngology-Head and Neck Surgery, 1996—2005. Mem. adv. bd. Pa. Lion Hearing Rsch. Found., Pitts., 1983—99. Capt. M.C. U.S. Army, 1965—67. Recipient Cert. of Merit Com. Rsch., Am. Acad. Otolaryngology-Salicylate Otoxicity, 1965, Award of Merit, Am. Acad. Otolaryngology-Head and Neck Surgery Inc., 1978, Robert E. Shoemaker Rsch. award, Pa. Acad. Ophthalmology and Otolaryngology, 1979, Disting. Svc. award, Am. Acad. Oto-HNS, 2001. Fellow: Am. Acad. Otolaryngology (internat. com. on head and neck surgery 1981—83; bd. dirs. 1985—88, 1990—2003, pres. 1994—95; internat. coord. 1996—2003), Am. Laryngol. Assn. (sec. 1982—88, pres. 1989—90, mem. coun. 1990—93, James Newcomb award 1993, DeRoaldes award 2001, ALA award 2001), ACS (bd. govs. 1981—87, mem. adv. coun. 1985—87); mem.: Triological Soc. (mem. coun. 1989—92, v.p. Ea. sect. 1994—95), Am. Soc. Head and Neck Surgery (mem. coun. 1977—93, pres. 1988—90), Nat. Cancer Inst. (chmn. upper aerodigestive tract working group 1986—89), Am. Acad. Depts. Otolaryngology (mem. coun. 1978—80), Am. Bd. Otolaryngology (bd. dirs. 1981—99, pres.-elect 1994—96, pres. 1996—98), Pitts. Athletic Assn. Republican. Jewish. Office: U Pitts Sch Med Eye and Ear Inst Ste 500 200 Lothrop St Pittsburgh PA 15213-2546 Office Phone: 412-647-2111. Business E-Mail: myersen@upmc.edu.

**MYERS, GERALD E.,** humanities educator; b. Central City, Nebr., June 19, 1923; s. Harold W. and Mary (Ferguson) M.; m. Martha Coleman, Aug. 7, 1948; 1 son, Curt. BA, Haverford Coll., 1947; MA, Brown U., 1949, PhD, 1954. Instr. Smith Coll., 1950-52; asst. prof. Williams Coll., 1952 61; assc. prof. Kenyon Coll., 1961-65; prof. C.W. Post Coll., L.I. U., 1965-67, Queens Coll. and Grad. Center, City U. N.Y., 1967—; also dep. exec. officer Ph.D program Queens Coll. and Grad. Center, City U. N.Y. (Grad. Center); dir. intro. philosophy into N.Y.C. High Schs. project.; emeritus CUNY. Dir. humanities-and-dance projects, philosopher-in-residence Am. Dance Festival, Durham, N.C., 1979; project dir. African-Am. Perspectives in Am. Modern Dance, Am. Dance Festival/NEH. Author: Self, Religion and Metaphysics, 1961, Self: An Introduction to Philosophical Psychology, 1969, The Spirit of American Philosophy, 1970, William James: His Life and Thought, 1986; editor: The Black Tradition in American Modern Dance, 1988, African American Genius in Modern Dance, 1992; co-editor: Emotion Philos. Studies, 1983, Echoes from the Holocaust, 1998; cons. Free to Danced PBS documentary, 2001; contbr. articles to profl. jours. NEH fellow, 1981-82. Mem. Am. Philos. Assn. (past sec.-treas. Western div.), Metaphys. Soc. Am., Soc. Phenomenology and Existential Philosophy, Phi Beta Kappa. Home: 36 Gardner Ave New London CT 06320-4313 Office: 33 W 42nd St New York NY 10036-8003

**MYERS, HARDY,** state attorney general; b. Electric Mills, Miss., Oct. 25, 1939; m. Mary Ann Thalhofer, 1962; children: Hardy III, Christopher, Jonathan. AB with distinction, U. Miss., 1961; LLB, U. Oreg., 1964. Bar: Oreg., U.S. Ct. of Appeals (9th cir.), U.S. Dist. Ct. (Dist. of Oreg.). Law clerk U.S. Dist. Judge William G. East, 1964—65; pvt. practice Stoel Rives LLP and predecessor firms, 1965—96; atty. gen. State of Oreg., 1997—. Mem. Oreg. Ho. of Reps., 1975—85, spkr. of the ho., 1979—83; chair Com. on Judiciary, 1977—78, 1983—84; councilor Metropolitan Svc. Dist. (now Metro), 1985—86. Bd. directors Oregon Law Review. Pres. Portland City Planning Commn., 1973—74; chair Oreg. Jail Project, 1984—86, Citizens' Task Force on Mass Transit Policy, 1985—86, Oreg. Criminal Justice Coun., 1987—91, Portland Future Focus, 1990—91, Metro Charter com., 1991—92, task force on state employee benefits, 1994; co-chair gov. task force on state employee compensation, 1995; mem. Commn. on Judicial Branch, 1983—85. Mem.: Multnomah County Bar Assn., Oreg. State Bar, Omicron Delta Kappa, Phi Kappa Phi, Phi Eta Sigma. Democrat. Office: Office of Atty General Justice Dept 1162 Court St NE Salem OR 97310-1320 Office Phone: 503-378-4732.*

**MYERS, HARRY J., JR.,** retired publisher; b. Denver, Aug. 7, 1931; s. Harry J. and Edith M. (Reed) M.; m. Mary Kay Racine, June 21, 1958; children: Harry J., Hans R. (dec.), Peter C. BA, Colo. U., 1957; postgrad., U. Mo., 1959-60. Pub. or pub. dir. Meredith Corp., 1962-82, Geo, Archtl. Digest, Bon Appetit, Home, Sci. Am., Cowles Mag, 1982-95. Served with USMC, 1953-56. Mem. Kappa Tau Alpha, Phi Gamma Delta. Home: 46 W Ranch Trl Morrison CO 80465-9504

**MYERS, IRA LEE,** physician; b. Monrovia, Ala., Feb. 9, 1924; s. Ira W. and Azelea Juanita (Cobbs) Myers; m. Dorothy Will Foust, Sept. 4, 1943 (dec. June 6, 2003); children: Martha Crystal(dec.), Ira Grady, Stephen Allen, Joanna Lynn; m. Woodard H. Luker, Dec. 7, 2003. BS, Howard Coll., Birmingham, Ala., 1945; MD, U. Ala., Birmingham, 1949; postgrad., Harvard U. Sch. Public Health, Cambridge, Mass., 1953. Diplomate: Am. Bd. Preventive Medicine. Commd. officer USPHS, 1949-55; intern USPHS Marine Hosp., Seattle, 1949-50; epidemic intelligence officer Charleston, W.Va., 1950-52, Erie County Health Dept., Buffalo, 1952, Center Communicable Disease, Atlanta, 1952-55; resigned, 1955; adminstrv. health officer Ala. Dept. Health, Montgomery, 1955-63, state health officer, 1963-86. Sec. Ala. Bd. Med. Examiners, 1962-73; chmn. Ala. Bd. Registration Sanitarians, 1964-81, Ala. Air Pollution Control Commn., 1969-82; v.p. Ala. Pollution Control Fin. Authority, 1971-81; assoc. clin. prof. preventive medicine and pub. health U. Ala. Med. Sch.; mem. Ala. vol. med. adv. com. SSS, 1968-86; chmn. Ala. Health Care Hall of Fame, 1998—. Pres. Ala. div. Am. Cancer Soc., 1991-93; chmn. bd. dirs. Dalraida Health Ctr., 1992-98; chmn. Ala. Sr. Citizens Hall of Fame, 1997—. Recipient Ala. Sr. Citizens Hall of Fame Golden Eagle award, 1986, St. George medal Nat. Divisional award Am. Cancer Soc., 1989, 1st Ann. Vol. award Montgomery Bapt. Assn., 1993. Mem. AMA, Med. Assn. Ala. (William Henry Saunders award 1968, 1st annual Ira L. Myers Service award, 1986), Montgomery County Med. Soc., Ala. Pub. Health Assn. (D.G. Gill award 1967, established Ira L. Myers Scholarship Endowment), Am. Assn. Pub. Health Physicians, Assn. State and Territorial Health Officers (Arthur N. McCormick award 1976), Ala. Hosp. Assn. (hon.), State. Ala. Acad. Honor, Tuberculosis Assn. (Heacock Gold medal 1986), Montgomery Coun. of Aging (Srs. of Achievement award 1998, Gov.'s Lifetime Achievement award 1998). Lodges: Montgomery Kiwanis. Republican. Baptist. Achievements include initiating state narcotic control program, 1967, state hosp. service for indigent, 1958. Home and Office: 925 Green Forest Dr Montgomery AL 36109-1515

**MYERS, JACK FREDRICK,** artist, educator, writer; b. Lima, Ohio, Feb. 17, 1927; s. Harold Frank and Lesta Arvilla (Ross) M.; m. Frances Dydek, Apr. 30, 1949; children: Steven Ross, David Gene, Kevin Douglas. Student, Cleve. Inst. Art, 1947-49; MFA, Kent State U., 1980. Staff artist Bill Ripley & Assocs., Cleve., 1951-57; art dir. Premier Indsl. Corp., Cleve., 1957-70; instr. Cooper Sch. Art, Cleve., 1970-80; assoc. prof. art U. Dayton, Ohio, 1982-87; ret., 1992. Author: The Language of Visual Art, 1989, Windy Side of Care, 2002, The Greatest Gift, 2002. With USNR, 1945-46, PTO. Recipient First prize in art Newsweek/Paillard S.A., 1969. Home and Office: 22269 Country Meadows Ln Strongsville OH 44149-2000 Personal E-mail: jackms@adelphia.net. E-mail: jackms@wowway.com.

**MYERS, JAMES CLARK,** advertising executive, public relations executive; b. Chgo., Aug. 26, 1941; s. Herbert George Myers and Lenore (Goldberg) Levi; m. Judy Anne Schnitzer, Feb. 9, 1964; children: Jeffrey Stephan, Jeremy H. BA, Washington U. St. Louis, 1964. Acct. exec. Nahas, Blumberg, Zelikow, Houston, 1967-69; mgr. spl. events Houston Post, 1969-73; pres., creative dir. Motivators, Inc., Houston, 1973—2006. Vice-chmn. Internat. Sci. and Engring. Fair Coun., Washington, 1972-73; bd. dirs. Sci. Engring. Fair of Houston, 1973-79; spl. corrs. Navy Times Newspaper; pres. S.W. Houston 2000, Inc., 1999-06. Contbr. articles to newspapers. Chmn. Houston chpt. Boy Scouts Am.; mem. City of Houston Bldgs. and Stds. Commn., 2004—; dir. cmty. svcs. Brays Oaks Mgmt. Dist., Houston. Served to capt. USNR, 1964-96. Recipient Wood Badge award, Boy Scouts Am., 1979, Shofar award, 1981; named Fondren SW Citizen of Yr., 2002. Mem. Pub. Relations Soc. Am. (accredited, Silver Anvil award 1983, 87, Excalibur 2001), Bus. Adv. Fedn. (cert.) Jewish. Avocations: model railroading, square dancing, photography. Home: 8006 Duffield Ln Houston TX 77071-2017 Office Phone: 713-784-5560, 713-541-0447. Personal E-mail: motivators.inc@juno.com, braysoaksmd@hhcllp.com.

**MYERS, JAMES M.,** pet products executive; BS in Acctg., John Carroll Univ. CPA. Various positions to sr. audit mgr. KPMG LLP, 1980—90; v.p. fin. to v.p., controller PETCO, San Diego, 1990—96, sr. v.p., fin., 1996—98, exec. v.p., CFO, 1998—2004, CEO, 2004—. Office: PETCO 9125 Rehco Rd San Diego CA 92121 Office Phone: 858-453-7845.*

**MYERS, JEFFREY DANIEL,** concert pianist, music educator; b. Erie, Pa., June 7, 1970; s. Neal Anthony and Beryl Diane Myers; m. Molly R. Knapp, July 3, 2004. MusB, Mercyhurst Coll., Erie, Pa., 1993; MusM, Manhattan Sch. Music, N.Y.C., 1999; student, Chautauqua Sch. Performing Arts. Dir. Erie Piano Acad., Erie, Pa., 1999—; chmn. Neal A. Myers Found. Music Edn., 2004; mem. faculty Veritas Prep. Acad., Phoenix, 2006—. Soloist: piano recital Hubbard Hall, 1999, Cancer Benefit St. Andrews Roman Cath. Ch., 2006, piano soloist: Erie Chamber Orch., 2000, debut piano and violin concert: Classical Concert Series, Kent State U., 2002; Classical Concert Series, Kent State U., Ashtabula, Ohio, 2003. Avocations: painting, art history, travel, world history. Business E-Mail: jeff@myers-usa.com.

**MYERS, JESSE JEROME,** lawyer; b. Anthony, Kans., Sept. 30, 1940; s. Claud Lewis and Lucille S. (Robertson) M.; m. Claire H. Conni, Nov., 1966; children: Timothy Todd, Jessica Joy. BS, McPherson Coll., 1961, JD, Washburn U., 1970. Bar: Kans., 1970, Mo. 1996, U.S. Dist. Ct. Kans. 1970. Law clk. U.S. Dist. Ct. Judge Frank Theis, Wichita, Kans., 1970—72; individual practice law Wichita, Kans., 1972—74, 1995—; lawyer Cessna Aircraft Co., Wichita, Kans., 1974—75; v.p., dir., gen. counsel Martin K. Eby Constrn. Co., Wichita, Kans., 1975—95. Served with USN, 1963-67. Mem. Am. Bar Assn., Kans. Bar Assn.

**MYERS, JOHN JOSEPH,** archbishop; b. Ottawa, Ill., July 26, 1941; s. M.W. and Margaret Louise (Donahue) M. BA maxima cum laude, Loras Coll., 1963; Licentiate in Sacred Theology, Gregorian U., Rome, 1967; Doctor of Canon Law, Cath. U. Am., 1977; DD (hon.), Apostolic See, Vatican City, 1987. Ordained priest Roman Cath. Ch., 1966, bishop, 1987. Asst. pastor Holy Family Parish, Peoria, Ill., 1967-70; asst. dept. internat. affairs US Cath. Conf., Washington, 1970-71; assoc. pastor St. Matthew Parish, Champaign, Ill., 1971-74; adminstr. St. Mary's Cathedral, Diocese Peoria, 1977—78, 1984; vice chancellor Cath. Diocese Peoria, 1977-78, vocation dir., 1977-87, chancellor, 1978-87, vicar gen., 1982-90, mem. Prebyteral Coun., 1968—70, 1984—90, bd. Consultors, 1978—90; co-adjutor bishop, 1987-90; bishop of Peoria, Ill., 1990—2001; appointed Superior of Turks and Caicos Antilles, 2001; Archbishop of Newark, NJ, 2001—. Bd. govs. Canon Law Soc. Am., Washington, 1985-87; bd. dirs. Nat. Cath. Bio Ethics Ctr., Boston, 1999—; bd. gov.; mem. sem. com. Mt. St. Mary's Sem., Md.; 1989-94; bd. trustees Cath. U. Am., Washington, 1999-, Papal Found.; seminary com., fin. com. Archdiocese of N.J.; Ad Hoc Com. for By-Laws., Cat. U. Am., Washington; seminary bd. Kenrick-Glennon of the Archdiocese of St. Louis. Author: (commentary) Book V of the Code of Canon Law, 1983; contbr. numerous articles to religious publs. Mem. Canon Law Soc. Am., Nat. Conf. Cath. Bishops. (Canonical Affairs Com., 1988-2002, Com. on Shrines and Pilgrimages, 1990-, Com. on Vocations, 1995-1998, Ad Hoc Com. on Sexual Abuse, 2002, Com. on Hispanic Affairs, 2002-, and Com. on Aid to Eastern Europe, 1999-) Roman Catholic. Office: Archdiocese of Newark 171 Clifton Ave Newark NJ 07104-0500

**MYERS, JOHN T.,** physical therapist, educator; s. Robert and Helen Myers. BS in Sci. summa cum laude, Cleve. State U., Ohio, 1984; MBA, Heriot-Watt U., Edinburgh, Scotland, 1998. Lic. phys. therapist Ohio OTPTAT Bd., 1984. From staff phys. therapist to sr. phys. therapist, supr.

phys. therapy Cleve. Clinic Found., 1984—97; program dir., assoc. prof. Lorain County C.C., Elyria, Ohio, 1997—. Team leader. on-site reviewer for phys. therapist asst. programs Commn. on Accreditation in Phys. Therapy Edn., Dept. of Accreditation, Am. Phys. Therapy Assn., Alexandria, Va., 2005—; spkr. continuing med. edn., Cleve., 1984—; cons. to musicians and orchestras regarding injury prevention and treatment, Cleve., 1988—. Author: (chpt.) Treatment Approaches in the Performer with Cervico-brachial Pain, 1992; co-reviewer (textbook) Measurement of Joint Motion: A Guide to Goniometry; contbr. articles to profl. jours. Mem. Lorain County Tech. Prep. Consortium, Ohio, 1999—2003; chair Loraine County C.C. PTA Program Cmty. Adv. Cmty., Elyria, Ohio, 1997—2006; mem. Coll. Found. Adv. Bd., Lorain, Ohio, 2000—03. Recipient Outstanding Faculty award, Lorain County C.C., 1998-1999, Faculty Excellence award, Lorain County C.C. Found., 2001; Gait and Motion Analysis Sys. for Tchg. grant, 2001. Mem. Ohio Phys. Therapy Assn. (faculty liaison com.), Am. Phys. Therapy Assn. Achievements include design and development of structure and curriculum for the Physical Therapist Assistant Program at Lorain County Community College. Office: Lorain County CC 1005 Abbe Rd N HS 223 Elyria OH 44035 Office Phone: 440-366-7881.

**MYERS, JOHN WESCOTT,** air transportation executive; b. LA, June 13, 1911; s. Louis Wescott and Blanche (Brown) M.; m. Lucia Raymond, Mar. 21, 1941 (dec. Mar. 1999); children: Louis W. (dec.), Lucia R. AB, Stanford U., 1933; JD, Harvard U., 1936. Bar: Calif. 1936. Ptnr. law firm O'Melveny & Myers, L.A., 1936-42; from test pilot to sr. v.p., dir. Northrop Corp., 1942-54, 1954-79; chmn. bd. Pacific Airmotive Corp., 1954-79, Airflite, Long Beach, Calif., 1970-89, Flying M Assocs., Long Beach, 1989—. Owner Flying M Ranches, Merced, Calif., 1959—. Dir. Smithsonian Nat. Air and Space Dulles Ctr. Project. Fellow Soc. Exptl. Test Pilots; mem. Calif. Bar Assn., Los Angeles Bar Assn., Inst. Aerospace Scis., Order of Daedalians (hon.). Clubs: Bohemian, California, Los Angeles Country, Los Angeles Yacht, Sunset, Aviation Country, Conquistadores del Cielo. Republican. Home: 718 N Rodeo Dr Beverly Hills CA 90210-3210 Office: 3200 Airflite Way Long Beach CA 90807-5312

**MYERS, JOHNNIE DUMAS,** law educator; b. Macon, Ga., Dec. 18, 1948; d. Ella Pearl Bryant and Johnny Dumas; children: Badru, Akii. BA, Clark Atlanta U., 1970, PhD, 1995; MS, Ga. State U., 1976; cert., Hers Women Higher Edn. Adminstrn., 1997. Parole supr. Ga. Pardons and Paroles, Atlanta, 1973—76; instr. Kennesaw (Ga.) State U., 1977—83; asst. prof. criminal justice Albany (Ga.) State U., 1983—88; chairperson criminal justice dept. Morris Brown Coll., Atlanta, 1988—. Advisor to Beta Chi chpt. Alpha Phi Sigma Morris Brown Coll., Atlanta, 1993—, faculty athletics rep. to NCAA, 1992—, former pres. faculty coun., 1997—98; presenter United Negro Coll. Fund PEJER Project, Augusta, Ga.; panelist substance abuse edn. in instns. higher learning Lonnie Mitchell Conf. Substance Abuse, Balt., 2002. Mem. personnel com. Rainbow Pk. Bapt. Ch., Decatur, Ga., 1999—2001, mem. nomination com., 2000—02; exec. bd. Nat. Historically Black Colls. and Univs. Substance Abuse Consortium, Atlanta, 1999—2002; governance coun. CORK Inst., Morehouse Sch. Medicine, Atlanta, 1989—2002; participant selection com. Ga. Police Corps, Forsyth, 2002. Recipient Outstand Svc. and Dedication to Orgn., National HBCU Substance Abuse Consortium, 2001; fellow Particia Robert Harris, U. S. Dept. Edn. through Clark Atlanta U., 1990-1993. Mem.: Nat. Assn. Blacks in Criminal Justice, Acad. Criminal Justice Scis., Am. Correctional Assn., Nat. Conf. Black Polit. Scientist (2002 conv. local arrangements com. 2001—02), Delta Sigma Theta (life; chairperson career day com. 1995—97). Baptist. Avocations: reading, bowling, travel. Home: 4925 Thames Ct Lithonia GA 30038 Office: Morris Brown Coll 643 Martin Luther King Jr Dr Atlanta GA 30314 Personal E-mail: jdmyers6@juno.com. Business E-mail: johnnie.myers@morrisbrown.edu.

**MYERS, JULIE L.,** federal agency administrator; b. Shawnee, KS, 1969; m. John Wood, 2005. BA, Baylor U.; JD, Cornell U., 1994. Law clk. to Hon. C. Arlen Beam US Ct. Appeals (8th cir.); assoc. Mayer, Brown & Platt, Chgo., 1993—97; assoc. ind. counsel Office of Ind. Counsel Kenneth Starr, Washington, 1998—99; asst. U.S. atty. (ea. dist.) N.Y. US Dept. Justice, Bklyn., 1999—2001, chief of staff to asst. atty. gen. criminal divsn. Washington, 2003; dept. asst. sec. for money laundering and fin. crimes US Dept. Treasury, Washington, 2001—03; asst. sec. for export enforcement, Bur. Industry & Security US Dept. Commerce, Washington, 2003—05; spl. asst. to the Pres. for presdl. personnel The White House, Washington, 2005—06; asst. sec. US Immigration & Customs Enforcement US Dept. Homeland Security, Washington, 2006—. Office: US Dept Homeland Security US Immigration & Customs Enforcement 425 Eye St NW Rm 7100 Washington DC 20528*

**MYERS, KENNETH RAYMOND,** lawyer; b. NYC, Apr. 14, 1939; s. Cyril Burleigh and Dorothy (Podolyn) M.; m. Susan Kay Plotnick, Sept. 9, 1962; children: Lisa R., Jonathan S., Andrew C. SB, MIT, 1960; JD, Harvard U., 1963. Bar: Ill. 1963. Pa. 1968. Assoc. Ross, Hardies & O'Keefe, Chgo., 1963-68, Morgan, Lewis & Bockius, Phila., 1968-71, ptnr., 1972-2000; of counsel High, Swartz, Roberts & Seidel LLP, Norristown, Pa., 2000—. Mem. rules com. Environ. Hearing Bd., Harrisburg, Pa., 1984-89. Editor: Environmental Spill Reporting Handbook, 1992-2004; contbg. author: Environmental Law Practice Guide, 1992-2000; contbr. articles to profl. jours. Dir., past chair Water Resources Assn. Del. River Basin, Valley Forge, Pa.; dir. Albert Einstein Healthcare Network, 1997-2002, Germantown Hosp., 1998-99, Belmont Hosp., 1999-2001; pres. Am. Jewish Congress, Phila., 1996-99, mem. nat. commn., N.Y.C., 1984-99; treas. Jewish Social Policy Action Network, 2004—. Mem. ABA (rep. to U.S. Office Personnel Mgmt. 1975—), Pa. Bar Assn., Montgomery Bar Assn., Eta Kappa Nu. Home: 355 River Birch Cir Elkins Park PA 19027-1338 Office Phone: 610-275-0700. Personal E-mail: kmyers@highswartz.com, krmyers@alum.mit.edu.

**MYERS, LONN WILLIAM,** lawyer; b. Rockford, Ill., Nov. 14, 1946; s. William H. and Leona V. (Janvrin) M.; m. Janet L. Forbes, May 14, 1968; children: Andrew, Hillary, Corwin. BA, Mich. State U., 1968; MBA, Ind. U., 1973; JD, Harvard U., 1976. Bar: Ill. 1976, U.S.Ct. of Fed. Claims 1977, U.S. Tax Ct. 1977, U.S. Ct. Appeals (7th cir.) 1977. Ptnr. McDermott Will & Emery LLP, Chgo., 1976—2005, counsel, 2006—. Served to maj. USAR, 1968—80. Mem. ABA (capital recovery and leasing com. tax sect., tax exempt fin. com. tax sect.). Episcopalian. Office: McDermott Will & Emery LLP 227 W Monroe St Chicago IL 60606-5096 Home: 1623 Glenview Rd Unit 316 Glenview IL 60025-2982 Office Phone: 312-984-7537. E-mail: lmyers@mwe.com.

**MYERS, MARGARET JANE (DEE DEE MYERS),** television personality, editor; b. Quonset Pt., R.I., Sept. 1, 1961; d. Stephen George and Judith Ann (Burleigh) M. BS, U. Santa Clara, 1983. Press asst. Mondale for Pres., L.A., 1984; deputy Senator Art Torres, L.A., 1985; dep. press sec. to press sec. Mayor Tom Bradley, L.A., 1985-87; deputy press sec. Tom Bradley For Gov., L.A., 1986; Calif. press sec. Dukakis for Pres., L.A., 1988; press sec. Feinstein for Gov., L.A. and San Francisco, 1989-90; campaign dir. Jordan for Mayor, San Francisco, 1991; comm. cons. DeeDee Myers Assocs., Valencia, Calif., 1991—; press sec. Clinton for Pres., Little Rock, 1991-92, White House, Washington, 1993-94; co-host Equal Time, CNBC, Washington, 1995-97; contbg. editor Vanity Fair, Washington, 1995—. Mem. bd. of trustees, Calif. State U.,1999— Recipient Robert F. Kennedy award Emerson Coll., Boston, 1993. Democrat. Roman Catholic. Avocations: running, bicycling, music, major league baseball.

**MYERS, MARILYN GLADYS,** pediatric hematologist, oncologist; b. Lyons, Nebr., July 17, 1930; d. Leonard Clarence and Marian N. (Manning) M.; m. Paul Frederick Motzkus, July 24, 1957 (dec. Aug. 1982). BA cum laude, U. Omaha, 1954; MD, U. Nebr., 1959. Diplomate Am. Bd. Pediat. Intern Orange County Gen. Hosp., Orange, Calif., 1959-60, resident, 1960-62; fellow in hematology/oncology Orange County Gen. Hosp./Children's Hosp. L.A., 1962-64; assoc. in rsch., chief dept. hematology/oncology Children's Hosp., Orange, Calif., 1964-80, dir. outpatient dept., 1964-73, assoc. dir. leukapheresis unit, 1971-80; clin. practice hematology, oncology, rheumatology Orange, 1964-80; instr. Coll. Medicine U. Calif., Irvine, 1968-71, asst.

---

clin. prof. pediatrics, 1971—; pvt. practice hematology, oncology, rheumatology Santa Ana, Calif., 1980—. Clin. rschr. exptl. drugs. Contbr. articles to med. jours. Med. adv. com. Orange County Blood Bank Hemophiliac Found. Grantee Am. Leukemia Soc., 1963, Am. Heart Assn., 1964. Fellow Am. Acad. Pediat.; mem. AMA, Calif. Med. Assn., LA County Med. Assn., Orange County Med. Assn., Orange County Pediat. Soc., Southwestern Pediat. Soc., LA Pediat. Soc., Internat. Coll. Pediat., Orange County Oncologic Soc., Am. Heart Assn. (Cardiopulmonary Coun.). Republican. Methodist. Avocation: reading. Office: 2220 E Fruit St Ste 217 Santa Ana CA 92701-4459 Office Phone: 714-541-3393.

**MYERS, MARK D.,** federal agency administrator, geologist; b. Monroe, Wis., Apr. 24, 1955; s. Rhea Bowman and Ardelle Ione (Van Matre) M.; m. Alice Reding Myers, April 30, 1983; children: Justine Alice, Nathan Mark. BS in Geology and Geophysics with honors, U. Wis., 1977, MS in Geology, 1981; PhD in Geology, U. Alaska, 1994. Petroleum geologist ARCO Oil & Gas, Lafayette, La., 1981-83, ARCO Alaska, Inc., Anchorage, 1983-87; geologist, dir. Divsn. Oil & Gas, State of Alaska, Anchorage, 1988—2005; dir., US Geological Survey US Dept. Interior, Reston, Va., 2006—. Contbr. articles to scientific jours. Lt. USAF Reserve, 1977-2003 Mem. Am. Assn. Petroleum Geologists (del. 1992—), Alaska Geological Soc. (v.p. 1993, mem. bd. dirs. 1993-95), Soc. Sedimentary Geology, Eagle River Presbyn. Ch. (pres. bd. trustees 1993—). Avocations: commercial multiengine instrument pilot ratings, skiing, fishing, sailing. Office: US Geological Survey 12201 Sunrise Valley Dr Mail Stop 100 Reston VA 20192*

**MYERS, MARY KATHLEEN,** publishing executive; b. Cedar Rapids, Iowa, Aug. 19, 1945; d. Joseph Bernard and Marjorie Helen (Huntsman) Weaver; m. David F. Myers, Dec. 30, 1967; children: Mindy, James. BA in English and Psychology, U. Iowa, 1967. Tchr. Lincoln HS, Des Moines, 1967-80; editor Perfection Learning Corp., Des Moines, 1980-87, v.p., editor-in-chief, 1987-93; pres., founding ptnr. orgn. to promote Edward de Bono Advanced Practical Thinking Tng., Des Moines, 1992—; founder Myers House LLC, 2002. Pres. Innova Tng. & Cons., Inc., 2000-05. Editor: Six Thinking Hats, 1991, Lateral Thinking, 1993, Direct Attention Thinking Tools, 1997, Total Creativity, 1997 Focus on Facilitation, 2004, Simplicity, 2005; pub. A Disgrace to the Profession, 2002. Adv. bd. Sch. Bus., Econs. and Acctg., Simpson Coll., 1998—. Mem. ASTD, Am. Creativity Assn. (bd. dirs. 1997-2000, pres. 1999), Instrnl. Systems Assn. (mem. bd. dirs. 2002-04). Home: 813 56th St West Des Moines IA 50266-6314 Office: de Bono Thinking Systems 2570 106th St # A Des Moines IA 50322-3771 Office Phone: 515-334-2687. Business E-mail: kmyers@debonosystems.com.

**MYERS, MICHELE TOLELA,** academic administrator; b. Rabat, Morocco, Sept. 25, 1941; arrived in U.S., 1964; d. Albert and Lillie (Abecassis) Tolela; m. Pierre Vajda, Sept. 12, 1962 (div. Jan. 1965); m. Gail E. Myers, Dec. 20, 1968 (div. Oct. 2003); children: Erika, David. Diploma, Inst. Polit. Studies, U. Paris, 1962; MA, U. Denver, 1966, PhD, 1967; MA, Trinity U., 1977; LHD, Whittenberg U., 1994, Denison U., 1998, U. Denver, 1999. Asst. prof. speech Manchester Coll., North Manchester, Ind., 1967—68; asst. prof. speech and sociology Monticello Coll., Godfrey, Ill., 1968—71; asst. prof. communication Trinity U., San Antonio, 1975—80, assoc. prof., 1980—86, asst. v.p. for acad. affairs, 1982—85, assoc. v.p., 1985—86; assoc. prof. sociology, dean Undergrad. Coll. Bryn Mawr Coll., Pa., 1986—89; pres. Denison U., Granville, Ohio, 1989—98, Sarah Lawrence Coll., Bronxville, NY, 1998—. Comm. analyst Psychology and Commn., San Antonio, 1974—83; bd. dirs. Sherman Fairchild Found., 1992—; mem. Fed. Res. Bank Cleve., 1995—98; pres.'s commn. Nat. Collegiate Athletic Assn., 1993—97, JSTOR, 1999—, ARTSTOR, 2003—. Co-author (with Gail Myers): The Dynamics of Human Communication, 1973, The Dynamics of Human Communication, 6th and internat. edits., 1992, The Dynamics of Human Communication, French transl., 1984, Communicating When We Speak, 1975, Communicating When We Speak, 2d edit., 1978, Communication for the Urban Professional, 1977, Managing by Communicaton: An Organizational Approach, 1982, Managing by Communicaton: An Organizational Approach, Spanish transl., 1983, Managing by Communicaton: An Organizational Approach, internat. edit., 1982. Trustee Phila. Child Guidance Clinic, 1988—89; trustee assoc. The Bryn Mawr Sch., Balt., 1987—89; v.p., bd. dirs. San Antonio Cmty. Guidance Ctr., 1979—83, Bank One, Columbus, 1990—94. Fellow in acad. adminstrn., Am. Coun. Edn., 1981—82. Mem.: Am. Coun. Edn. (commn. on women in higher edn. 1990—92, bd. dirs. 1993—99, chmn. 1997—98). Home: 272 W 107th St #6B New York NY 10025 Office: Sarah Lawrence Coll One Mead Way Bronxville NY 10708 Office Phone: 914-395-2201. Business E-mail: mmyers@sarahlawrence.edu.

**MYERS, MIKE,** actor, scriptwriter, film producer; b. Toronto, Ont., Can., May 25, 1963; s. Eric and Bunny (Hind) M.; m. Robin Ruzan, 1993 (separated). Stage appearances: The Second City, Toronto, 1986-88, Chgo., 1988-89; actor, writer: Mullarkey & Myers, Can., 1984-86, (TV show) Saturday Night Live, 1989-94 (Emmy award for outstanding writing in a comedy or variety series 1989); (film) Wayne's World, 1992, So I Married an Axe Murderer, 1993, Wayne's World II (also screenwriter, prodr.), 1993, Austin Powers: International Man Of Mystery (also screenwriter, prodr.), 1997, Pete's Meteor, 1998, It's a Dog's Life, 1998, 54, 1998, Austin Powers: The Spy Who Shagged Me (also screenwriter, prodr.), 1999, Austin Powers: The Animated Series, 1999, Shrek (voice), 2001, Austin Powers Goldmember (also writer, prodr.), 2002, View from the Top, 2003, Shrek 4-D (voice), 2003, The Cat in the Hat, 2003, Shrek 2 (voice), 2004; actor: (TV movie) John and Yoko, 1985, Elvis Stories, 1989, Saturday Night Live: The Best of Phil Hartman, 1998, Saturday Night Live: The Best of Mike Myers, 1998, Saturday Night Live: 25th Anniversary, 1999, Madonna: The Video Collection 93,99, 1999; screenwriter: (tv movie) Murderers Among Us: The Simon Wiesenthal Story, 1989, Saturday Night Live: The Best of Mike Myers, 1998; TV appearances The Littlest Hobo, 1979, Russell Gilbert Show, 1998; dir. (film) The Bacchae, 1999. Recipient Can. comedy award, 2000.

**MYERS, MILES ALVIN,** educational association administrator, educator; b. Newton, Kans., Feb. 4, 1931; s. Alvin F. and Katheryn P. (Miles) M.; m. Celeste Myers; children: Royce, Brant, Roslyn. BA in Rhetoric, U. Calif., Berkeley, 1953, MAT in English, 1979, MA in English, 1982, PhD in Lang. and Literacy, 1982. Cert. secondary tchr. English. Tchr. English Washington Union High Sch., Fremont, Calif., 1957-59, Oakland (Calif.) High Sch., 1959-67, 69-74, Concord High Sch., Mt. Diablo, Calif., 1967-69; chmn. bd. dirs. Alpha Plus Corp. Preschs., Piedmont, Calif., 1968—2002; dir. All City High, 1973-74; tchr. English Castlemont High Sch., Oakland, 1974-75; mem. faculty U. Calif., Berkeley, 1975-85, adminstrv. dir. Bay Area writing project Sch. Edn., 1976-85, adminstrv. dir. nat. writing project Sch. Edn., 1979-85; pres., CEO Calif. Fedn. Tchrs., 1985-90; exec. dir. Nat. Coun. Tchrs. of English, Urbana, Ill., 1990-97, Edschool.com of Edvantage/Riverdeep, 1999—2001, Calif. Subject Matter Projects, U. Calif., 1997—98; dir. Inst. Rsch. on Learning and Tchg., Berkeley, Calif., 1998—; bd. dirs. Bay Area Sch. Reform Collabortive, 2000—; sr. rschr. ICA, UT LA, 2000—. Co-dir. Nat. Standards Project for English Language Arts, 1992-96; adj. prof. English U. Ill., Champaign-Urbana, 1991-94; vis. lectr. at numerous colleges and Univs.; rschr. in field. Author: The Meaning of Literature, 1973; co-author: Writing: Unit Lessons in Composition, Book III, 1965, The English Book-Composition Skills, 1980; author: A Procedure for Holistic Scoring, 1980, Changing our Minds, 1996; co-author: Exemplars of Standards for English Language Arts, 3 vols., 1997, Asilomar Testing Report, 2001, CSC Professional Code for English/ELA Teachers, 2005; editor Calif. Tchr., 1966-81; contbr. articles to profl. jours.; pub. monographs. Sgt. U.S. Army, 1953—55. Recipient cert. of Merit, Ctrl. Calif. Coun. Tchrs. of English, 1969, Commendation award Oakland Fedn. Tchrs., 1970, First Place award Internat. Labor Assn., 1971, Disting. Svc. award Calif. Coun. Classified Employees, 1991, Svc. award Nat. Writing Project, 1996. Fellow Nat. Conf. Rsch. in English; mem. Nat. Coun. Tchrs. of English, Nat. Conf. on Rsch. in English, Am. Fedn. of Tchrs. (legis. dir. Calif. Fedn. of Tchrs. 1971-72, Union Tchr. Press awards 1969-75, 86-89, 91, Ben Rust award Calif. Fedn. of Tchrs. 1994), Am. Edn. Rsch. Assn., Calif. Assn. Tchrs. of English (Disting. Svc. award 86), U.

---

Calif./Berkeley Alumni Assn. Home: 5823 Scarborough Dr Oakland CA 94611-2721 Office: Dir Inst Rsch on Learning & Tchg Berkeley CA 94704 Office Phone: 510-531-0409. Home Fax: 510-531-0409. Personal E-mail: milesmye@pacbell.net.

**MYERS, PHILLIP FENTON,** corporate financial executive, information technology executive; b. Cleve., June 24, 1935; s. Max I. and Rebecca (Rosenblum) M.; m. Hope Gail Strum, Aug. 13, 1961 B in Indsl. Engring., Ohio State U., 1958, MBA, 1960; D in Bus. Adminstrn., Harvard U., 1966. Staff indsl. engr. Procter & Gamble Co., Cin., 1958; sr. cons. Cresap, McCormack & Paget, N.Y.C., 1960—61; staff assoc. Mitre Corp., Bedford, Mass., 1961; cons. Sys. Devel. Corp., Santa Monica, Calif., 1963—64; dir. long range planning Electronic Splty. Co., L.A., 1966—68; chmn. Atek Industries, 1968—72; pres. Myers Fin. Corp., 1973—82; chmn. Amvid Comm. Svcs., Inc., 1975—79, Omni Resources Devel. Corp., 1979—83; chmn., pres. Am. Internat. Mining Co., Inc., 1979—83; pres. Advent Internat. Mgmt. Co., Inc., 1982—; chmn. Global Bond Mktg. Svcs., Inc., 1987—90; pres., CEO Whitehall Container Mfg. Corp., 1988—91; pres. Whitehall Motors Co., 1989—97, Allied Metamatter Tech. Corp., 1994—96; chmn. U.S. Water Resources, Inc., 1994—96; pres. Am. Tech. Venture Fund Mgmt., Inc., Advent Internat. Realty Corp., 1996—98, First Internat. Capital Corp., 1996—2000. Pres. Turbogen, Inc., 1995-98, Blue Star Material Techs. Inc., 1997-2000, founding dir. Warner Ctr. Bank, 1980-83; bd. dirs., pres. Cyber Security Systems, Inc., 2000—; lectr. bus. adminstrn. U. So. Calif., L.A., 1967-74; prof. Grad. Sch. Bus. Adminstrn. Pepperdine U., 1974-81. Trustee, treas. Chamber Symphony Soc. Calif., 1971-78; mem. campaign issues com. Reagan for Pres., 1976, 80; pub. safety commr. City of Hidden Hills, Calif., 1983-86; mem. Mayor's Blue Ribbon Fin. Com., 1981-82; mem. dean's select adv. com. Coll. Engring., Ohio State U., 1984-94; mem. state exec. com. Calif. Libertarian Party, 1988—region 61, 1989-90, chmn. strategic planning com.; dep. chmn. Los Angeles County Libertarian Party, 1991-92; chairperson campaign issues com. Marrou for Pres., 1991-92; chmn. bd. trustees WWII Hist. Soc., 1992—; first v.p. Armed Forces Cmty. Rels. Coun. Ctrl. Ohio, 2001-04. Capt. USAF, 1958-60. Ford Found. fellow, 1961-64 Mem. Soc. Automotive Engrs., Harvard Bus. Sch. Assn., Ohio State Alumni Assn., Harvard Bus. Club Columbus (bd. dirs. 1998—, pres. 1996-98), Ohio State Alumni Club (pres. 1998-99), Harvard Club Ctrl. Ohio (bd. dirs.). Personal E-mail: philmyers@wowway.com. *Personal philosophy: All out all the time. I stand for the creation of a new system of global governance which stresses individual liberty, freedom and responsibility, and which leads to a world that works for everyone with no one left out. In business, I stand for exceptional vision, creativity, innovation, and contribution.*

**MYERS, PHILLIP SAMUEL,** mechanical engineering educator; b. Webber, Kans., May 8, 1916; s. Earl Rufus and Sarah Katharine (Breon) M.; m. Jean Frances Alford, May 26, 1941; children: Katharine Myers Muirhead, Elizabeth Myers Baird, Phyllis Myers Rathbone, John, Mark. BS in Math. and Commerce, McPherson Coll., 1940; BSME, Kans. State Coll., 1942; PhDME, U. Wis., 1947. Registered profl. engr., Wis. Instr. mech. engring. Ind. Tech. Coll., Ft. Wayne, summer 1942; instr. U. Wis., Madison, 1942-47, asst. prof., 1947-50, assoc. prof., 1950-55, prof., 1955-86, emeritus prof., 1986—, chmn. dept. mech. engring., 1979-83. Cons. Diesel Engine Mfrs. Assn., U.S. Army, various oil and ins. cos. Contbr. articles to profl. jours. Chmn. Pine Lake com. We. Wis. Conf. Meth. Ch., 1955-60; Mem. Village Bd., Shorewood Hills, 1962-67. Recipient B.S. Reynolds Teaching award, 1964, McPherson Coll. Alumni citation of merit, 1971; Dugald Clerk award, 1971 Fellow ASME (Diesel Gas Power award 1971, Soichiro Honda award 1983), Soc. Automotive Engrs. (Colwell award 1966, 79, Horning award 1968, nat. pres. 1969, hon. mem.), AAAS; mem. NAE, Am. Soc. for Engring. Edn., Blue Key, Sigma Xi, Phi Kappa Phi, Sigma Tau, Pi Tau Sigma (Gold medal 1949), Tau Beta Pi (Ragnar Onstad Svc. to Soc. award 1978). Mem. Brethren Ch. Achievements include patents in field.

**MYERS, PHILLIP WARD,** otolaryngologist; b. Evanston, Ill., Nov. 11, 1939; s. R. Maurice and Vivian (Ward) M.; m. Lynetta Sargent, Dec. 22, 1963; children: Andrea, Ward, Alycia, Amanda, Andrew. BS, Western Ill. U., 1961; MD, U. Ill., 1965. Diplomate: Am. Bd. Otolaryngology. Intern St. Paul-Ramsey Hosp., 1965-66; resident in otolaryngology U. Louisville, 1966-68; resident Northwestern U., 1968-70, fellow, 1970-71; practice medicine specializing in otolaryngology Springfield, Ill., 1973—; clin. prof. otolaryngology So. Ill. U., Springfield, 1973—. Served to maj. M.C. AUS, 1971-73. Fellow Am. Soc. for Head and Neck Surgery, Am. Acad. Facial Plastic and Reconstructive Surgery; ACS, Am. Acad. Otolaryngology-Head and Neck Surgery. Achievements include research in perilymphatic fistulas. Home: 3423 N Oak Hill Rd Rochester IL 62563-9273 Office: So Ill Sch Medicine PO Box 19662 Springfield IL 62794-9662

**MYERS, R. DAVID,** library director, dean; b. Hutchinson, Kans., Mar. 27, 1949; s. William Raymond and Elizabeth (Haas) M.; m. Barbara Jean Burridge, Sept. 15, 1973; 1 child, John David. BA, U. No. Colo., 1972, MA, 1974; ABD, U. Mich., 1976; MA, U. Denver, 1979. Manuscript curator Western History Collection, Denver, 1976-79; rsch. assoc. Colo. Legis. Coun., Denver, 1979-81; reference specialist Libr. of Congress, Washington, 1981-84, reference supr., 1984-88; libr. dir. State Hist. Soc. of Wis., Madison, 1988-94; assoc. dean univ. libr. N.Mex. State U., Las Cruces, 1994-2001; dir. librs., prof. history Coll. Santa Fe, 2001—. Editor Am. history Macmillan Pub., N.Y.C. 1991-94; cons. history of medicine dept. U. Wis., Madison, 1993-94. Author bibliographies for Libr. of Congress, 1987, 88. Mem. ALA, Am. Hist. Assn., Orgn. Am. Historians, Labor and Working Class History Assn. (bd. dirs.). Avocations: research, writing, baseball, mysteries. Office: Fogelson Libr Coll Santa Fe 1600 St Michaels Dr Santa Fe NM 87505 Office Phone: 505-473-6576. Business E-mail: myers@csf.edu.

**MYERS, R(ALPH) CHANDLER,** lawyer; b. LA, Jan. 9, 1933; s. Ralph Cather and Winifred (Chandler) M.; m. Rebecca Blythe Borkgren, Jan. 11, 1963. BA, Stanford U., 1954, JD, 1958; LLD (hon.), Whittier Coll., 1968. Bar: Calif. 1959, U.S. Dist. Ct. (ctrl. dist.) Calif. 1959, U.S. Supreme Ct. 1971. Law clk., then assoc. Parker, Stanbury, Reese & McGee, L.A., 1958-63; assoc. Nicholas, Kolliner & Van Tassel, L.A., 1963-65; ptnr. Myers & D'Angelo and predecessors, L.A. and Pasadena, Calif., 1965—. Nat. panelist Am. Arbitration Assn., LA, 1964-2000; del. visitors Stanford U. Law Sch., Calif., 1970-73; judge pro tem panel LA Mcpl. Ct., 1971-81; mem. LA County Dist. Atty.'s Adv. Coun., 1976-83. Nat. vice chmn. Keystone Gifts, Stanford Centennial Campaign, 1987—92; trustee Whittier Coll., Calif., 1973—2001, chmn. bd. trustees Calif., 1981—87, trustee emeritus Calif., 2001—; trustee Flintridge Prep. Sch., LaCanada-Flintridge, Calif., 1981—88, chmn. bd. trustees, 1985—88; co-founder Whittier Law Sch., 1975, trustee, 1975—2001, chmn. bd. trustees, 1981—87, trustee emeritus, 2001—; bd. dirs. Opera Guild So. Calif., L.A., 1971—83, pres. 1980—82; bd. dirs. Guild Opera Co. L.A., 1974—83, pres., 1975—77; bd. dirs. Western Justice Ctr. Found., 1993—, pres., 2003—05; bd. dirs. L.A. Child Guidance Clinic, 1972—83, pres., 1977—79; bd. dirs. Opera Assocs. of the Music Ctr., L.A. 1976—78. Recipient Stanford Assocs. award, 1984, Centennial Medallion award, 1991, Gold Spike award Stanford U., 1989, Disting. Svc. award Whittier Law Sch., 1993, Outstanding Achievement award Stanford Assocs.; 1998; named R. Chandler Myers Dean's Suite in his honor Whittier Law Sch., 1997; Master's Cir. honoree Flintridge Prep. Sch., 1989. Mem. Wilshire Bar Assn. (bd. govs. 1972-81, pres. 1979-80), LA County Bar Assn. (trustee 1979-81), Stanford Law Soc. So. Calif. (bd. dirs. 1967-72, pres. 1970-71), Stanford Assocs. (bd. govs. 1992-97, treas. 1995-97), Jonathan Club, Univ. Club (Pasadena), Stanford Club LA (dir. 1963-70, pres. 1968-69). Home: La Canada 5623 Burning Tree Dr La Canada Flintridge CA 91011-2861 Office: Myers & D'Angelo 301 N Lake Ave Ste 800 Pasadena CA 91101-4108 Office Phone: 626-792-0007.

**MYERS, REX CHARLES,** historian, educator, retired dean; b. Cleve., July 1, 1945; s. Charles F. and Merial W. (Jones) M.; m. Susan L. Richards, Jan. 10, 1987; children: Gary W., Laura M. BA, Western State Coll., 1967; MA, U. Mont., 1970, PhD, 1972; postgrad., U. Wash., 1983, Harvard U., 1990.

Instr. Palo Verde Coll., Blythe, Calif., 1972-75; reference librarian Mont. Hist. Soc., Helena, 1975-78; prof., divsn. chmn., dean Western Mont. Coll., Dillon, 1979-86; dean S.D. State U., Brookings, 1986-91; acad. dean Lyndon State Coll., Lyndonville, Vt., 1991-95; lectr. Western State Coll., Gunnison, Colo., 1995-98, Mesa State Coll., 1998-99, Lawrence U., 1999—2005, Northwest Coll., Powell, Wyo., 2005—. Author: Montana Symbols, 1976, Montana Trolleys, 1970, Lizzie, 1989; co-author: Marble Colorado, 1970, Montana: Our Land and People, 1978, Montana and the West, 1984; contbr. articles to profl. jours. Bd. dirs. Ctr. for Western Studies, Sioux Falls, SD, 1990—, Gunnison Arts Ctr., Gunnison County Libr., Fox Valley Arts Alliance, Meml. Park Arboretum and Gardens. Summer stipend NEH, 1973; fellow James J. Hill Library, 1985. Mem.: AAUW, Mont. Oral History Assn. (chmn. 1980—83), Am. Conf. Acad. Deans, Western History Assn. (chmn. membership com. 1980—83), N.E. Kingdom C. of C. (bd. dirs.), Masons (master 1984), Kiwanis (pres. Dillon 1983, lt. gov. 1984, 1997, 2003), Phi Alpha Theta, Phi Kappa Phi. Unitarian Universalist. Office: Nortwest Coll 231 W Sixth St Powell WY 82435 Home: PO Box 503 Powell WY 82435 Office Phone: 307-754-6172.

**MYERS, RICHARD BOWMAN,** former Chairman of the Joint Chiefs of Staff; b. Kansas City, Mo., Mar. 1, 1942; m. Mary Jo Rupp; 3 children. BSME, Kans. State U., 1965; MBA, Auburn U., 1977; Diploma, Air Command/Staff Coll., Maxwell AFB, Ala., 1977, U.S. Army War Coll., 1981; postgrad., Harvard U., 1991. Commd. 2d lt. USAF, 1965, advanced through ranks to gen., 1997, ret., 2005, dir. tactical weapons & command & control acquisition programs, 1991—93, comdr. U.S. Forces Japan & 5th Air Force Yokota AFB, Japan, 1993-96; asst. to the chmn. of the Joint Chiefs of Staff US Dept. Def., Washington, 1996-97; comdr. Pacific Air Forces, Hickam AFB, Hawaii, 1997-98; comdr.-in-chief N.Am. Aerospace Def. Comm./U.S. Space Command, Peterson AFB, Colo., 1998—2000; vice chmn. Joint Chiefs of Staff, US Dept. Def., Washington, 2000—01, chmn., 2001—05; found. prof. mil. history & leadership Kans. State. U., 2006—. Bd. dirs. Northrop Grumman Corp., 2006—, Deere & Co., 2006—, United Technologies Corp., 2006—. Decorated Def. Disting. Svc. medal with three bronze oak leaf cluster, Disting. Svc. medal, Legion of Merit, Disting. Flying Cross with oak leaf cluster Air Force, Army, Navy, Coast Guard, Meritorious Svc. medal with three oak leaf clusters, Air medal with 18 oak leaf clusters, Air Force Commendation medal, others; recipient Presdl. Medal of Freedom, The White House, 2005. Office: Kans State U Dept History 208 Eisenhower Hall Manhattan KS 66506*

**MYERS, RICHARD HEPWORTH,** medical geneticist, educator; b. Austin, Nov. 1, 1947; s. Clark E. and Cora Henley (Hepworth) M.; m. Carol Anne Smith, Sept. 3, 1978; children: Margaret Anne, Madelyn Claire. BA, U. Kans., 1969; MEd, Ga. State U., 1973, MA, 1976, PhD, 1979. Diplomate Am. Bd. Med. Genetics; lic. psychologist. Asst. prof. in psychiatry Emory U., Atlanta, 1979-80; asst. prof. neurology Boston U. Sch. Medicine, 1980-87, assoc. prof. neurology, 1987—94, prof. neurology, 1994—; lectr. in neurology Harvard U. Med. Sch., Boston, 1980—; assoc. in neurology Mass. Gen. Hosp., Boston, 1980—; psychologist Univ. Hosp., Boston, 1980—. Vis. prof. MIT, Cambridge, Mass., 1993—. Contbr. articles to profl. jours. Fellow Am. Coll. Med. Genetics (founding); mem. APA, AAAS, Am. Soc. Human Genetics (mem. com. ethics of genome project 1992-94), Internat. Genetic Epidemiology Soc. Avocations: blues guitar, skiing. Office: Boston U Med Sch Dept Neurology 715 Albany St Boston MA 02118-2526

**MYERS, ROBERT DAVID,** judge; b. Springfield, Mass., Nov. 20, 1937; s. William and Pearl (Weiss) M.; m. Judith G. Dickenman, July 1, 1962; children—Mandy Susan, Jay Brandt, Seth William. AB, U. Mass., 1959; JD, Boston U., 1962. Bar: Ariz. 1963. Practice in Phoenix, 1963-89; presiding judge civil dept. Superior Ct. of Arizona in Maricopa County, 1991-92; presiding judge probate and mental health dept. Superior Ct. of Ariz., Maricopa County, Ariz., 1992-95, presiding judge, 1995-2000; pro tem judge Ariz. Ct. Appeals; judge Ariz. Superior Ct., 1989—2002; chief dep. Ariz. Atty. Gen., 2003—04; gen. counsel Ariz. Dept. Corrections, Phoenix, 2004—. Adj. prof. Ariz. State U. Sch. Law, 1997—; chmn. com. on exams and admissions Ariz. Supreme Ct., 1974-75, chmn. com. on character and fitness, 1975-76, mem. multi-state bar exam. com., 1976-85; bd. dirs. Nat. Conf. Met. Judges, 1997—, pres., 1998-99. Pres. Valley of Sun chpt. City of Hope, 1965-66, Cmty. Orgn. for Drug Abuse Control, 1972-73, Valley Big Bros., 1975; chmn. Mayors Ad Hoc Com. on Drug Abuse, 1974-75; bd. dirs. Maricopa County Legal Aid Soc., 1978. Recipient award for outstanding svc. and dedication to improving the legal profession and professionalism of the bar and bench Maricopa County Bar Assn., 1999, Superior Svc. award Ariz. chpt. ASPA, 2000, Justice Tom C. Clark award Nat. Conf. Metro. Cts., 2000. Mem. ATLA (nat. chmn. gov.), Ariz. Bar Assn. (gov., com. chmn., sect. pres.), Maricopa County Bar Assn. (dir., pres. 1979-80,Judge of yr., 1999, Henry S. Steven award 2000), Ariz. Trial Lawyers Assn. (pres., dir., co-editor newsletter), Phoenix Trial Lawyers Assn. (pres., dir.), Western Trial Lawyers Assn. (pres. 1977), Am. Judicature Soc. (spl. merit citation outstanding svc. improvement of adminstrn. justice 1986), Am. Bd. Trial Advocates (Phoenix chpt. Judicial Officer of Yr. award 2001), Sandra Day O'Connor Inn of Ct. (pres. 1991-92). Office: Ariz Dept Corrections 1601 W Jefferson Phoenix AZ 85007-2205 Office Phone: 602-542-1532.

**MYERS, ROBERT EUGENE,** writer, educator; b. L.A., Jan. 15, 1924; s. Harold Eugene and Margaret (Anawalt) M.; m. Joyce E. Daily, 1946 (div. 1949); 1 child, Kathleen; m. Patricia A. Tazer, Aug. 17, 1956; children: Edward E., Margaret A., Hal R., Karen I. AB, U. Calif., Berkeley, 1955; MA (Crown-Zellerbach fellow), Reed Coll., 1960; EdD, U. Ga., 1968. Employed in phonograph record bus., 1946-54; tchr. elem. sch. Calif., Oreg., Minn., 1954-61; rsch. asst. U. Minn., 1961-62; asst. prof. Augsburg Coll., 1962-63, U. Oreg., 1963-66; elem. tchr. Eugene, Oreg., 1966-67; assoc. prof. U. Victoria, 1968-70; assoc. rsch. prof. Oreg. System of Higher Edn., 1970-73; film maker, producer ednl. filmstrips, books, recs., 1973-77; learning resources specialist Oreg. Dept. Edn., Salem, 1977-81; with Linn-Benton Edn. Svc. Dist., Albany, Oreg., 1982-87; ret., 1987. Author: (with E. Paul Torrance) Creative Learning and Teaching (Pi Lambda Theta award 1971), 1970, La Ensenanza Creativa, 1970, Can You Imagine?, 1965, Invitations to Thinking and Doing, 1964, Invitations to Speaking and Writing Creatively, 1965, Plots, Puzzles, and Ploys, 1966, For Those Who Wonder, 1966, Timberwood Tales, Vol. II, 1977, Wondering, 1984, Imagining, 1985, What Next?, 1994, Facing the Issues, 1995, Cognitive Connections, 1996, Mind Sparklers, 1997, Multiple Ways of Thinking with Social Studies, 1997, Character Matters, 1999, It's Your Attitude That Counts, 2000, Mind Stretchers, 2001, Stories That Build Character, 2001, Think and Write, 2002, Now What, 2002, Spurs to Creative Thinking, 2002, Word Play, 2002, Developing Creative Thinking Skills, 2003, Learning from Nature, 2005, Exploring Character, 2005, Respect Matters, 2005, Language FUNdamentals Books 1 and 2, 2005, Lively Language 1 and 2, 2005, Motivational Writing Lessons, 2005, Lessons in Writing, 2006, Writing a Persuasive Essay, 2006, Time to Write, 2006; films: Feather (CINE Golden Eagle award), 1972, The Magic Net, 1972, Elephants, 1973 Exec. bd. Nat. Assn. Gifted Children, 1974-77. With U.S. Mcht. Marine, 1944-45. Recipient CINE Golden Eagle award Coun. Internat. Non-theatrical Events, 1973. Mem. Internat. Reading Assn. Democrat. Home: 1357 Meadow Ct Healdsburg CA 95448-3347

**MYERS, ROBERT JAY,** retired air transportation executive; b. Bklyn., Oct. 15, 1934; s. John J. and Clara S. (Martinsen) M.; m. Carolyn Erland, Aug. 10, 1963; children: Susan, Kenneth. BCE, NYU, 1955, postgrad., 1957-65; P.MD, Harvard U., 1972. With Grumman Corp., Bethpage, NY, 1964-94, v.p. resources, 1980-83, sr. v.p. bus. and resource mgmt., 1983-85, sr. v.p. corp. svcs., 1985-86; pres. Grumman Data Systems Corp., Bethpage, 1986-90; pres., chief operating officer, bd. dirs. Grumman Corp., 1991-94; ret., 1994. Sci. adv. coun. Ala. Space and Rocket Ctr., 1986-91. Adv. panel on recon. devel. N.Y. State Project 2000, 1985-86; mem. L.I. Project 2000; adv. bd. L.I. Youth Guidance, 1996-91; bd. dirs. Poly. U., 1991-98, North Shore Health System, 1994—, L.I. Mus. of Sci. and Tech., 1994-96; chmn. Huntington Hosp., 1996—2000. 1st lt. U.S. Army, 1955-57. Fellow Poly. U., 1987, Disting. Alumni award, 1989. Mem. Am. Def. Preparedness Assn. (dir.

1992-94), Navy League, Industry Exec. Bd., Nat. Space Club (bd. govs. 1986-89), Huntington Country Club (N.Y.), Audubon Country Club (Naples, Fla.). Presbyterian. Home: 200 Cheshire Way Naples FL 34110 Personal E-mail: rjm34@aol.com.

**MYERS, ROBERT K., III,** director, musician, composer; b. Fredericksburg, Va., Aug. 20, 1941; s. Robert K. Jr. and Ruby King Myers; m. Barbara Jo Bishop, May 18, 1977; children: Stephanie Conway, Amy Grammer. MusB, Eastman Sch. of Music, Rochester, NY, 1963; MusM, Eastman Sch. of Music, 1964; MusD, Northwestern U., 1985. Chmn. music dept. Saginaw Valley State Coll., University Center, Mich., 1967—74; head music program Grant MacEwan Coll. Edmonton, Alta., Canada, 1974—83; assoc. v.p. instl. assessment Berklee Coll. Music, Boston, 1985—. Composer-in-residence Midland (Mich.) Pub. Schs., 1967—69; vis. composer Northwestern U., Evanston, Ill., 1986; accreditation visitor/evaluator New Eng. Assn. Schs. and Colls., Bedford, Mass., 1987—2003. Composer: Enigma Virginia (1st prize Percussive Arts Soc., 1985). Fulbright Study grantee, US Govt./French Govt., 1965—67, Composer-in-Residence grantee, Ford Found., 1967—69. Mem.: Internat. Assn. Jazz Educators (nat. curriculum facilitator), New Eng. Ednl. Assessment Network (v.p. 2000—04). Office: Berklee Coll Music 1140 Boylston St MS-899 OP Boston MA 02215 Office Phone: 617-747-2226.

**MYERS, ROBERT MANSON,** language educator, writer; b. Charlottesville, Va., May 29, 1921; s. Horwood Prettyman and Matilda Manson (Wynn) M. BA summa cum laude, Vanderbilt U., 1941; MA, Columbia, 1942. Harvard, 1943; PhD, Columbia, 1948. Instr. English Yale, 1945-47; asst. prof. Coll. William and Mary, 1947-48, Tulane U., 1948-54; tchr. English Brearley Sch., N.Y.C., 1954-56; chmn. dept. English Osbourn High Sch., Manassas, Va., 1956-59; mem. faculty U. Md., College Park, 1959—, prof. English, 1968-86, prof. emeritus, 1986—. Author: Handel's Messiah, 1948, From Beowulf to Virginia Woolf, 1952, rev., 1984, Handel, Dryden, and Milton, 1956, Restoration Comedy, 1961, The Children of Pride, 1972, abridged edit., 1984 (Carey-Thomas award 1972, Nat. Book award 1973), A Georgian at Princeton, 1976, Quintet: Five Plays, 1991, Sixes and Sevens: Three Plays, 2004, The Bostonians: A Play, 2005, Poynton Park: A Play, 2005. Mem. bd. visitors Winthrop U. Fulbright Postdoctoral Research fellow U. London, 1953-54; Fulbright lectr. Rotterdam, Netherlands, 1958-59. Mem. Modern Lang. Assn., Am. Am. Soc. 18th Century Studies, Jane Austen Soc. N.Am., Phi Beta Kappa. Home: 3804 Deckford Pl Charlotte NC 28211-3408

**MYERS, ROBERTA,** editor-in-chief; b. 1960; 1 child. B, Colo. State Univ., 1982. Editl. asst. Rolling Stone Mag., 1982; mng. editor Seventeen; sr. editor In Style; editor-in-chief Tell, 1993—95; sr. articles editor Elle mag. Hachette Filipacchi Mags., 1995—97, editor-in-chief Mirabella mag. NYC, 1997—2000, editor-in-chief Elle mag., 2000—. Office: Hachette-Filipacchi Mags Inc Elle Mag 1633 Broadway 44th Fl New York NY 10019*

**MYERS, RODMAN NATHANIEL,** lawyer; b. Detroit, Oct. 27, 1920; s. Isaac Rodman and Fredericka (Hirschman) Myers; m. Jeanette Polisei, Mar. 19, 1957 (dec. 1996); children: Jennifer Myers Grabenstein, Rodman Jay. BA, Wayne State U., 1941; LLB, U. Mich., 1943. Bar: Mich. 1943, U.S. Supreme Ct. 1962. Agt. IRS, Detroit, 1943; from assoc. to ptnr. Butzel, Keidan, Simon, Myers & Graham, Detroit, 1943-90; of counsel Honigman Miller Schwartz and Cohn, Detroit, 1991—. Mem. blue ribbon task force Mich. Dept. Edn., 1988—90; founding mem., trustee Mich. chpt. Leukemia and Lymphoma Soc., founding pres., 1984—86, nat. trustee, 1984—; founding mem., trustee Detroit Sci. Ctr.; commr. Detroit Mcpl. Parking Authority, 1963—71; pres., trustee Bloomfield Twp. Pub. Libr.; trustee Temple Beth El, Bloomfield Hills, Mich.; bd. dirs. United Cmty. Svcs. of Met. Detroit, 1978—85, v.p., 1981—85, chmn. social svcs. divsn., 1982—85; bd. dirs. Children's Ctr. of Wayne County, Mich., 1963—88, pres., 1969—72. Mem. ABA, State Bar Mich. (chmn. atty. discipline panel, past vice chmn. unauthorized practice of law com., past mem. character and fitness com.). Home: 3833 Lakeland Ln Bloomfield Hills MI 48302-1328 Office: 2290 1st National Bldg Detroit MI 48226 Office Phone: 313-465-7490.

**MYERS, ROLLAND GRAHAM,** investment counselor; Diploma, St. Louis Country Day Sch., 1963; AB cum laude in History and Lit., Harvard U., 1966; postgrad. Faculties of Social Scis. and Law, U. Edinburgh, Scotland, 1966-67; postgrad. Fondation Nationale des Sciences Politiques and Faculte de Lettres et des Sciences Humaines, U. Paris, 1967-68. Trainee global credit dept. The Chase Manhattan Bank, N.A., N.Y.C., 1968-69, mem. 32nd spl. devel. program, 1969, strategic planner internat. dept., 1969-70, securities analyst, mktg. rep., fiduciary investment dept., 1970; assoc. Smith, Barney & Co., Inc., N.Y.C., 1971, account exec. N.Y. sales dept., 1971-72, instl. account exec. N.Y. internat. sales dept., 1972-74, 2nd v.p., stockholder, 1975-76; v.p., stockholder Smith Barney, Harris Upham & Co., Inc. (subs. SBHU Holdings, Inc.), N.Y.C., 1976-78; prin. W.H. Graham & Sons, family investment office, 1977-82, investment counsel, 1982—. Ltd. ptnr. Croke Patterson Campbell, Ltd., Denver, 1975—; joint founder, gen. ptnr. Mansion Disbursements, Denver, 1979—; pres., chmn. exec. com., bd. dirs. Fifty-Five Residents Corp., N.Y.C., 1980-84; bd. dirs. Fifty-Six Danbury Rd. Assn., Inc., New Milford, Conn. Trustee, mem. corp. Bishop Rhinelander Found. (Episcopal Chaplaincy at Harvard and Radcliffe Colls.), Cambridge, 1973-75; v.p., treas., bd. dirs. The Whitehill Graham Found., St. Louis, 1976—; bd. dirs., fin. com., bylaws com., mem. corp. Eliot Pratt Edn. Inc., Inc. (The Pratt Ctr.: Your Connection with the Natural World), New Milford, 1987-94; mem. corp. Kent (Conn.) Land Trust, Inc., 1989—, treas., 1989-93, bd. dirs., 1989-2003, adv. bd., 2003—; project financier Restoration of 1851 Samuel Curtiss Hosford House, Nat. Register Historic Dist., Falls Village, Conn., 1984-86; commr. Housatonic River Commn., Warren, Conn., 1985-93, vice chmn., 1986-87, chmn., 1988-92; commr. Conservation, Inland Wetlands and Watercourses Commn., Kent, 1988-93, vice chmn., 1988-92; mem. schs. and scholarships com., Office of Admissions and Fin. Aid, Harvard and Radcliffe Colls., 1991— Mem. Cum Laude Soc., Mary Inst. and St. Louis Country Day Sch. Alumni Assn., Harvard Alumni Assn., Capitol Hill Club (Washington), Harvard Club (N.Y.C.), Hasty Pudding-Inst. of 1770 (Cambridge), Wyo. Bus. Alliance, Wyo. Heritage Found., St. Andrew's Soc., New Eng. Soc. in City N.Y., St. George's Soc. N.Y. Republican. Episcopalian. Office: W H Graham & Sons Investment Counsel 1818 Evans Ave Ste 207 Cheyenne WY 82001-4664

**MYERS, SHARON DIANE,** auditor; b. Lawrence, Kans., Sept. 18, 1955; d. Richard Paul and Helen Carol (Overbey) M. AA, Mt. San Antonio Coll., Walnut, Calif., 1981; BSBA, Calif. State U., Pomona, 1983, MBA, 1986. Cert. fraud examiner; cert. govt. fin. mgr. Revenue agt. IRS, Glendale, Calif., 1984-85; auditor Def. Contract Audit Agy., L.A., 1985-92; auditor Office Inspector Gen. FDIC, Newport Beach, 1992—2002; auditor officer Inspector Gen., USPS, Portland, Oreg., 2002—. Instr. Azusa (Calif.) Pacific U., 1987, 88, West Coast U., San Diego, 1992. Musician, Sunday sch. supt. Covina (Calif.) Bapt. Temple, 1975-95, Liberty Bapt. Ch., Irvine, Calif., 1995-2002, Landmark Bapt. Ch., Olympia, Wash., 2002—. Mem. Assn. Govt. Accts. Republican. Avocations: piano, travel. Home: 2702 44th Ave NW Olympia WA 98502-3692

**MYERS, SOPHIA M.,** writer, researcher, artist, cartographer, translator; b. Coffeyville, Kans., Oct. 25, 1928; d. Anastasios M. and Georgia A. Mardikes; m. Ralph E. Myers, Dec. 24, 1980 (dec. Oct. 5, 2006); children: George A. Vedros, Nicholas M. Vedros. Degree, Mt. St. Scholastica, 1948. Cert. tchg. Avila Coll., 1949. Tchr. elem art several Grade Schs., 1949—54; advt. mgr., artist, writer Cavanaugh Cattle Co., 1955—59, Weldwheels, 1960—64; advt. mgr. Oppenheimer Industries, 1965—71; advt. mgr., ops. mgr. The Nat. Secrs. Assn., Internat. Kansas City, Mo., 1972—80; pvt. practice, 1980—. Red Herring, Potpourri; poems featured Sunday Kansas City Star; contbr. poetry, short stories, essays and articles publ. in numerous mags., anthologies and newspapers. Named to Women's Found. Greater Kansas City, 2005; recipient 1st Pl. free verse award, Springfield Writers Guild, 2002, The Vicki Millikin Bright award best poem, 2003, 2004, Winner two nat. contests. Mem.: Ptnrs. in Crime, Sisters in Crime, Okla. Writers' Fedn., Inc., The Writers' Cir. Warrensburg Writers Cir., Kans. City Press Club, Soc. Profl. Journalists, Kans. City Writers' Group, Okla. Writer's Federation, Inc., Mo. Poetry Soc.,

Mo. Writers Guild (1st Pl. free verse, 1st Pl. Best Lit. Poem award), Nat. League Am. Pen Women: Arts and Letters (pres. Kansas City br., 1st Pl. best poem Best Free Verse award). Avocations: painting, sculpting. Personal E-mail: smyers@kc.rr.com.

**MYERS, STERLING,** choir director; BA, Angelo State U., San Angelo, Tex., 1977; MA, Tex. Women's U., Denton, 1979. Choir dir. Wayland Baptist U., Plainview, Tex., 1988—. Home: Box 135 Robert Lee TX 76945

**MYERS, SUE BARTLEY,** artist; b. Norfolk, Va., Aug. 22, 1930; d. Louis and Rena M. Bartley; m. Bertram J. Myers, Nov. 24, 1949; children: Beth R., Mark F., Alyson S. Student, Stephens Coll., Va. Wesleyan. V.p. Jamson Realty Inc., Myers Realty Inc. Ltd. ptnr. Downtown Plaza Shopping Ctr., Warwick Village Shopping Ctr., Suburban Park Assocs. Solo shows at Village Gallery, Newport News, 1988, Artist at Work Gallery, Virginia Beach, Va., 1991, Va. Wesleyan U., Virginia Beach, 1991, 92, Will Richardson Gallery, Norfolk, Va., 1993, 94, Ctrl. Fidelity Bank, Norfolk, Va., 1995. Pres. adv. coun. Va. Wesleyan U., 1982-94; mayor's del. Sister Cities, Norwich, Eng., 1984, Kidikushu, Japan, 1982, Edinburgh, Scotland, 1991, Toulon, France, 1992; mem. entertainment com. Azalea Festival Norfolk, 1984; founder art scholarship Va. Wesleyan; bd. dirs. corp. campaign Va. Zool. Soc., 1996; trustee Guardian Angels, Jackson Meml. Hosp., Miami. Mem. Tidewater Artists Assn., Art Odyssey, Harbor Club, Bayville Golf Club. Jewish. Avocations: travel, physical fitness, reading, golf.

**MYERS, VIRGINIA ANNE,** art educator; b. Greencastle, Ind., May 8, 1927; d. Everett Clark Myers and Hurst (McKann) Bessie. BA in Fine Arts, George Washington U., Corcoran Sch. Art, 1949; MFA in Drawing and Painting, Calif. Coll. of Arts & Crafts, Oakland, 1951; postgrad. in print making, U. Ill., 1953—55, U. Iowa, 1955—61; studied with Stanley William Hayter, Paris, 1961—62. Rsch. asst. Sch. Art and Art History U. Iowa, Iowa City, 1958-61; instr. arts and crafts, phys. edn. Tucson Indian Tng. Sch., 1949-50; teaching asst. dept. art and architecture U. Ill., Champaign-Urbana, 1954-55; instr. printmaking U. Iowa, Iowa City, 1962-69, asst. prof. printmaking, 1969-74, assoc. prof., 1974-82, prof., 1982—. Bd. dirs., treas. Elizabeth Found. for Fellowships in the Visual Arts, N.Y, 1994-2005; pres. Iowa Foil Printer Corp. Author: (hardbound) Foil Imaging...A New Art Form, 2001, (manual) Creating Original Prints with Hot-Stamped foil, 1993; A Time of Malfeasance (21 engravings and drypoints), 1976, The Views from Tenacre: The Seasons (66 paintings and drawings), 1979, Landscape in Iowa (36 paintings, prints and drawings), 1986, The Ghost Elm and Other Views from Tenacre, 2006; contbr. articles to profl. jours., 57 paintings, drawings, prints. Fulbright fellow, Paris, 1961-62; grantee U. Iowa, 1973, 78, 84, 89, 93, 98-99, Iowa Arts Coun., 1974-77, 80, 85, Stanley Found., 1984-88, Thorson Found., 1984, 86, Arts and Humanities Initiative, 2005; elected to Iowa Women's Archives, U. Iowa, 1999; The Virginia A. Myers Print Study Room at U. Iowa Mus. Art named in her honor, 2006. Mem. Foil Stamping and Embossing Assn. (charter), Nat. Mus. of Women in Arts (charter). Achievements include patents for Iowa Foil Printer, 1992; Underwriters Laboratories, 1997. Avocations: gardening, reading, swimming. Home: Tenacre Print 4244 210th St NE Solon IA 52333-9657 Office: Univ Iowa Sch Arts & Art History Iowa City IA 52242 Office Phone: 319-644-2763. Business E-Mail: virginia-myers@uiowa.edu.

**MYERS, WALTER DEAN,** young adult book author; b. Martinsburg, W.Va., Aug. 12, 1937; foster s. Herbert Dean and Florence Brown; children from previous marriage: Karen, Michael Dean; m. Constance Brendel, June 19, 1973; 1 child, Christopher. BA, Empire State Coll., 1984. Employment supr. N.Y. State Dept. Labor, Bklyn., 1966-69; sr. trade book editor Bobbs-Merrill Co., Inc., N.Y.C., 1970-77. Author: (for children) Where Does the Day Go?, 1969 (Coun. Interracial Books for Children award 1968), The Dragon Takes a Wife, 1972, The Dancers, 1972, Fly, Jiimy, Fly!, 1974, The World of Work: A Guide to Choosing a Career, 1975, Fast Sam, Cool Clyde, and Stuff, 1975 (Woodward Park Sch. Ann. Book award 1976), Social Welfare, 1976, Brainstorm, 1977, Mojo and the Russians, 1977, Victory for Jamie, 1977, It Ain't All for Nothin', 1978 (ALA Best Books for Young Adults citation 1978), The Young Landlords, 1979 (ALA Best Books for Young Adults citation 1979, Coretta Scott King award 1980), The Black Pearl and the Ghost; or, One Mystery After Another, 1980, The Golden Serpent, 1980, Hoops, 1981 (ALA Best Books for Young Adults citation 1982), The Legend of Tarik, 1981 (Notable Children's Trade Book in Social Studies citation 1982), Won't Know Till I Get There, 1982, The Nicholas Factor, 1983, Tales of a Dead King, 1983, Mr. Monkey and the Gotcha Bird, 1984, Motown and Didi: A Love Story, 1984 (Coretta Scott King award 1984), The Outside Shot, 1984, Adventure in Granada, 1985, The Hidden Shrine, 1985, Duel in the Desert, 1986, Ambush in the Amazon, 1986, Sweet Illusions, 1986, Crystal, 1987, Shadow of the Red Moon, Fallen Angels, 1988, Scorpions, 1988 (Newbery Honor Book 1989), Me, Mop and the Moondance Kid, 1988, The Mouse Rap, 1990, Now Is Your Time!: The African American Struggle for Freedom, 1991 (Coretta Scott King award 1991), Somewhere in the Darkness, 1992 (Newbery Honor book 1993), A Place Called Heartbreak: A Story of Vietnam, 1992, The Righteous Revenge of Artemis Bonner, 1992, Mop, Moondance and the Nagasaki Knights, 1992, Young Martin's Promise, 1992, Malcolm X: By Any Means Necessary, 1993, The Test, 1993, Intensive Care, 1993, Fashion by Tasha, 1993, Dangerous Games, 1993, Brown Angels: An Album of Pictures and Verse, 1993, The Glory Field, 1994, Darnell Rock Reporting, 1994, The Story of the Three Kingdoms, 1995, One More River to Cross, 1995, How Mr. Monkey Saw the Whole World, 1996, (poetry) Here in Harlem: Poems in Many Voices, 2004. Recipient Margaret A. Edwards award ALA's Young Adult Library Services Assn., 1994.

**MYERS, WARREN POWERS LAIRD,** internist, educator; b. Phila., May 2, 1921; s. John Dashiell and Mary Hall (Laird) M.; m. Katharine Van Vechten, July 1, 1944, children: Warren Powers Laird, Jr., Anne Van Vechten Myers Evans, Duncan McNeir, Sara Myers Gormley. Grad., Episcopal Acad., 1939; BS, Yale U., 1943; MD, Columbia U., 1945; MS in Medicine, U. Minn., 1952; postgrad. (Eleanor Roosevelt Found. fellow), U. Cambridge, Eng., 1962-63. Diplomate: Am. Bd. Internal Medicine. Rotating intern Phila. Gen. Hosp., 1945-46; intern medicine Maimonides Hosp., N.Y.C., 1948-49; resident fellow in medicine Mayo Clinic, Rochester, Minn., 1949-52; clin. asst. Meml. Hosp., N.Y.C., 1952-54, asst. attending physician, 1954-58, assoc. attending physician, 1959, attending physician, 1959-90; instr. Cornell U. Med. Coll., 1955-56, asst. prof., 1956-59, assoc. prof., 1959-68, prof. medicine, 1968-86, prof. emeritus, 1986—; assoc. dean, 1977-86; chmn. dept. medicine Meml. Sloan-Kettering Cancer Ctr., N.Y.C., 1967-77; v.p. for ednl. affairs Meml. Hosp., 1977-81, Eugene W. Kettering prof., 1979-86; attending physician N.Y. Hosp., N.Y.C., 1968-86; mem. Sloan-Kettering Inst. Cancer Rsch., N.Y.C., 1969-90; mem. emeritus Meml. Sloan-Kettering Cancer Ctr., N.Y.C., 1990—; cons. Rockefeller U. Hosp., N.Y.C., 1977-86. Mem. clin. cancer tng. com. Nat. Cancer Inst., 1970-73, chmn., 1971-73, chmn. clin. cancer edn. com., 1975-78; adj. prof. medicine Dartmouth Med. Sch., 1987-96, prof. medicine emeritus, 1996—; cons. staff Mary Hitchcock Meml. Hosp., Hanover, N.H., 1987-96. Contbr. articles on cancer, bone metabolism, internal medicine, and med. edn. to med. jours. Bd. dirs. Rye (N.Y.) United Fund, 1969-72, chmn. budget com., 1968-69; bd. dirs. Damon Runyon-Walter Winchell Cancer Fund, 1976-86, pres., 1985-86; trustee Hitchcock Clinic, Lebanon, N.H., 1983-96, Dartmouth-Hitchcock Med. Ctr., Lebanon, 1983-95, chmn. exec. com., 1992-95, tchr.'s coll. Columbia U., 1980-86; trustee Friends of Norris Cotton Cancer Ctr., Dartmouth-Hitchcock Med. Ctr., Lebanon, 1997-2000, v.p., 1999-2000—; elder 5th Ave. Presbyn. Ch., 1969-86, Norwich Congregational Ch., deacon, 1998-2002. With M.C., USNR, 1946-47. Recipient Alumni award for research Mayo Clinic, 1952, Margaret Hay Edwards Achievement medal Am. Assn. Cancer Edn., 1993. Fellow ACP, N.Y. Acad. Medicine (v.p. 1983-85); mem. Am. Clin. and Climatological Assn., Am. Assn. Cancer Research, Endocrine Soc., Harvey Soc., Am. Fedn. Clin. Research, Practioners' Soc. of N.Y., AMA, Am. Assn. Cancer Edn. (pres. 1984-85), Am. Soc. Clin. Oncology, Founders and Patriots Pa., Yale Club, Charaka Club, Century Assn. (N.Y.C.), Alpha Omega Alpha. Presbyterian (elder 1969-86). Clubs: Yale, Charaka, Century Assn. (N.Y.C.). Address: 436 Joshua Rd White River Junction VT 05001-9028

**MYERS, WILLIAM GERRY, III,** lawyer; b. Roanoke, Va., July 13, 1955; AB, Coll. of William and Mary, 1977; JD, U. Denver, 1981. Bar: Colo. 1981, Wyo. 1982, D.C. 1987, U.S. Supreme Ct. 1990, Idaho 1997. Assoc. Davis & Cannon, Sheridan, Wyo., 1981-85; legis. counsel U.S. Sen. Alan K. Simpson, Wyo., 1985-89; asst. to atty. gen. U.S. Dept. Justice, Washington, 1989-92; dep. gen. counsel for programs U.S. Dept. Energy, Washington, 1992-93; dir. fed. lands Nat. Cattlemen's Assn., 1993-97; exec. dir. Pub. Lands Coun., Washington, 1993-97; atty. Holland and Hart, Boise, Idaho, 1997–2001, 2003—; solicitor U.S. Dept. of Interior, 2001–03. Office: Holland and Hart 101 S Capitol Blvd Ste 1400 Boise ID 83702-7714 Office Phone: 208-342-5000. E-mail: wmyers@hollandhart.com.

**MYERS, WILLIAM OSGOOD,** thoracic and cardiovascular surgeon; b. Hastings, Nebr., Aug. 19, 1929; s. Joy Uberto and Lena C. (Osgood) M.; m. Lois Mae Payne, Dec. 26, 1952; children: Jessica, Wendell, Inez, John, Michael. BA, Hastings Coll., 1951; MD, Northwestern U., 1955. Diplomate Am. Bd. Surgery, Am. Bd. Thoracic Surgery. Intern City Detroit Receiving Hosp., 1955–56, resident in anesthesiology, 1956–57; gen. practice medicine Blue Hill, Nebr., 1959—62; surg. resident Sacred Heart Hosp., Yankton, SD, 1962—65; instr. anatomy U.S.D. Med. Sch., Vermillion, SD, 1963—65; resident in gen. surgery U. Kans. Med. Ctr., Kansas City, 1965—66, resident in thoracic and cardiovascular surgery, 1966—68; cardiovasc. surgeon Marshfield Clinic, Marshfield, Wis.; and St. Joseph's Hosp., Marshfield, 1968—2000, chmn. sect. thoracic and cardiovascular surgery, 1972—76, chmn. dept. surgery, 1974—79; clin. prof. surgery U. Wis., 1996—; chmn. instl. rev. bd. Marshfield Rsch. Found., 2000—. Prin. investigator Coronary Artery Surgery Study, Nat. Heart, Lung and Blood Inst., 1973—; bd. dirs. Marshfield Med. Found., 1978-84. Contbr. articles to profl. jours. Chmn. rsch. com. Marshfield Med. Found., 1985-94, mem. 1996-2000; coun. on Cardiovascular Surgery AHA. Served with USAF, 1957-59. Mem.: ACS (pres. Wis. chpt. 1986, credentials com. 1988—2000), AMA, Western Surg. Assn., Ctrl. Surg. Assn., Frederick A. Coller Surgery Soc. (pres. 1998—99), Soc. Thoracic Surgeons, Am. Assn. for Thoracic Surgery, Am. Thoracic Soc., Am. Coll. Cardiology, Wis. Heart Assn. (bd. dirs. 1988—94), Wis. Surg. Soc. (pres. 1993, mem. coun.), Wis., Wood County Med. Socs. E-mail: lmpm@tznet.com, myersw@mmrf.mfldclin.edu.

**MYERS, WOODROW AUGUSTUS, JR.,** physician, health care management director; b. Indpls., Feb. 14, 1954; s. Woodrow Augustus Sr. and Charlotte T. (Tyler) M.; m. Debra Jackson, June 23, 1973; children: Kimberly Leilani, Zachary Augustus. BS, Stanford U., Calif., 1973, MBA, 1982; MD, Harvard U., 1977. Intern in internal medicine Stanford U. Med. Ctr., 1977-78, resident in internal medicine, 1978-80, fellow, critical care medicine, 1980-81; asst. prof. critical care medicine San Francisco Gen. Hosp., 1982-84; physician health advisor com. on labor and human resources U.S. Senate, Washington, 1984; commr. Ind. Dept. of Health, Indpls., 1985-90; health commr. N.Y.C. Dept. of Health, 1990-91; corp. med. dir. Assoc. Group, Indpls., 1991-95; dir. health care mgmt. Ford Motor Co., Dearborn, Mich., 1996—. Asst. prof. medicine Cornell Med. Coll., N.Y.C., 1990-91; trustee Stanford U., 1987-92; assoc. prof. medicine Ind. U. Sch. Medicine, 1992-95; assoc. clin. prof. medicine Wayne State U., 1997—; adj. assoc. prof. internal medicine U. Mich., 1998—; bd. dirs. Somnus Med. Techs. Bd. dirs. Stanford Health Systems, 1994-97, U. Calif.-San Francisco/Stanford Health Care, 1997; bd. overseers Harvard U., 1996—; mem. Medicare Payment Adv. Commn., 1997—; vice-chmn. vis. com. Harvard Med. Sch., 1997—. Robert Wood Johnson clin. scholar, Stanford U., 1980-82. Fellow ACP; mem. AMA, Inst. Medicine of NAS, Nat. Med. Assn.

**MYERS BROWN, JOAN,** performing company executive; b. Phila., Dec. 25, 1931; d. Julius Thomas Myers and Nellie (Woods) Lewis Myers; m. Frederick Johnson, 1951 (div.); m. Max Brown, Nov. 18, 1967 (div.); children: Dannielle C. Brown, Marlisa J. Brown-Saint. D (hon.), U. Arts, 1994. Dancer various prodns. U.S, Can., Caribbean, 1950—61, Pearl Bailey Prodns., nat. tour, 1961—66; choreographer Harlem Prodns., Atlantic City, 1958—67; dir., choreographer, tchr. Phila. Sch. of Dance Arts, 1960—; founder, exec. dir. Phila. Dance Co., 1970—. Bd. dirs. Univ. City Coun., 2000—, Arts and Bus. Coun., 1999—; hon. chair, founder Internat. Assn. Blacks in Dance; cons. Nat. Endowment for Arts, 1970—84, panelist, 1970—82, Ohio State Arts Coun., 1981—84, Mich. State Arts Coun., 1981—84; dance panel Pa. State Arts Coun., 1987, Md. State Arts Coun., 1990, Arts Presenters, 1995, NJ/Del. State Coun. on The Arts, 1994, The Kennedy Ctr. AAEP, 1996; advisor Nat. Dance Project, 1999—2004; dir. Wade Comm., 1983—. Mem. Mayor's Cultural Adv. Coun., 1984—; bd. dirs. Greater Phila. Cultural Alliance, Dance/USA, Citizens for Arts in Pa., Coalition of African-Am. Culture Inst., Spruce Family Planning Clinic. Named one of 50 Most Influential Women award, 1995; recipient award, Nat. Council Negro Women, 1983, Award of Merit, West Phila. C. of C., 1983, Arts and Humanities Cultural award, Phila. chpt. Continentals Socs., 1979, Philadelphians for Pub. Awareness award, 1984, Womens Way award, 1986, Theodore L. Hazlett Meml. award for excellence in the arts in Pa., 1986, Kool Achiever award, 1989, Black United Fund Arts award, 1989, Phila. Arts and Cultural award, 1989, Stella Moore Dance award, 1990, Black Unite Fund award, 1990, UNCF award, 1990, YWCA-Pioneer award, 1990, Excellence in Arts award, 1995, Arts and Business Coun. award, 1996, Chisolm award NPCBW, 1996, Keeper of the Flame award, 2003, mayoral award, Phila. Black Profls., 2004, Theater Co. Interact, 2004, Frontiers Internat., 2004; Nat. Endowment Arts Choreographic fellow, 1979. Democrat. Office: Phila Dance Co 9 N Preston St Philadelphia PA 19104-2299 Office Phone: 215-387-8200. Business E-Mail: jmb@philadanco.org.

**MYERSON, ALAN,** television director, film director; b. Cleve., Aug. 8, 1936; s. Seymour and Vivien I. (Caplin) M.; m. Irene Ryan, June 2, 1962; 1 son, Lincoln; m. Leigh French, May 15, 1977; children: Sierra French-Myerson, Darcy French-Myerson. Student, Pepperdine Coll., 1956-57, UCLA, 1957. Mem. theater/cinema faculty U. Calif., Berkeley, 1966, San Francisco State U., 1967, Internat. Film and TV Workshops, 2002, U. So. Calif, 2005—. Dir. (Broadway, Off Broadway) including This Music Crept By Me Upon the Waters, The Committee; dir.: Second City, N.Y.C. and Chgo., 1961, 62; founder, prodr., dir. The Committee, San Francisco, L.A. and N.Y., 1963-74; dir.: (films) Steelyard Blues, 1972, Private Lessons, 1981, Police Academy 5, 1988, It's Showtime, 1976; numerous TV shows, 1975—, including Ally McBeal, Judging Amy, Joan of Arcadia, Larry Sanders Show, Friends, Frasier, Picket Fences, Miami Vice, Dynasty, Laverne and Shirley, Ed, Boston Public, Gilmore Girls, Lizzie McGuire; TV films The Love Boat, 1976, Hi, Honey, I'm Dead, 1991, Bad Attitudes, 1991, Holiday Affair, 1996. Active in civil rights, peace, anti-nuclear movements, 1957- Recipient Emmy nomination 1997, Cable ACE award nominations, 1995, 96, 97, TV Comedy award nomination Dirs. Guild, 1997. Mem. ASCAP, Acad. Motion Picture Arts and Scis., Acad. TV Arts and Scis., Dirs. Guild Am. Office Phone: 310-559-7756.

**MYERSON, JACOB MYER,** retired diplomat; b. Rock Hill, S.C., June 11, 1926; s. Solomon and Lena (Clein) Myerson; m. Nicole Neuray, June 10, 1965 (dec. Oct. 1968); 1 child, Sylvie Anne; m. Helen Hayashi, Mar. 9, 1974 (dec. Jan. 1995). Student, Pa. State Coll., 1944. BA with distinction, George Washington U., 1949, MA, 1950; grad., Fgn. Service Inst., 1953. Joined U.S. Fgn. Svc., 1950; 3d sec. Office U.S. High Commr. Germany, Berlin, 1950-52; 2d sec. U.S. Mission to NATO and European Regional Orgn., Paris, 1953-55; also mem. U.S. permanent del. to coordinating com. InterGovtl. Consultative Group on EastWest Trade; internat. economist, internat. rels. officer State Dept., 1956-60, spl. asst. to under sec. state, 1965-66; adviser U.S. del. GATT session, Geneva, 1958; ministerial session OEEC, Paris, 1958; 1st sec., chief polit. sect. U.S. Mission to European Communities, Brussels, 1960-65; officer-in-charge NATO Polit. Affairs, Dept. State, 1966-68; adviser U.S. delegation ministerial sessions North Atlantic Council, 1966-67; dep. polit. adviser, counselor U.S. Mission to NATO, Brussels, 1968-70; counselor econ. affairs U.S. Mission to European Communities, Brussels, 1970-74; minister counselor, from 1974; U.S. rep. to UN Econ. and Social Council with rank of ambassador, 1975-77; alt. U.S. del. UN Gen. Assembly, 1975—76; alt. U.S. rep. UN Conf. on Trade and Devel., 1976; minister-counselor econ. and

comml. affairs Am. Embassy, Paris, 1977-80; ret., 1980; dep. sec. gen. OECD, Paris, 1980-88. With U.S. Army, 1944—46, ETO. Decorated Bronze Star, Order of the Sacred treasure Gold and Silver medal Japan; recipient Meritorious Svc. award, State Dept., 1960. Mem.: Am. Fgn. Svc. Assn. (Rivkin award 1969), Artus, Phi Beta Kappa, Phi Eta Sigma, Pi Gamma Mu. Address: 2 rue Lucien Gaulard 75018 Paris France

**MYERSON, ROBERT J.,** radiologist, educator; b. Boston, May 12, 1947; s. Richard Louis and Rosemarie M.; m. Carla Wheatley, Aug. 8, 1970; 1 child, Jacob Wheatley. BA, Princeton U., 1969; PhD, U. Calif., Berkeley, 1974; MD, U. Miami, 1980. Diplomate Am. Bd. Radiology. Asst. prof. dept. physics Pa. State U., State Coll., 1974-76; fellow Inst. Advanced Studies, Princeton, NJ, 1976-78; resident U. Pa. Hosp., Phila., 1981-84; assoc. prof. radiology Washington U. Sch. Medicine, St. Louis, 1984-97; prof. radiation oncology Wash. U. Sch. Medicine, St. Louis, 1997—. Contbr. articles to profl. jours. Recipient Career Devel. award Am. Cancer Soc., 1985. Fellow Am. Coll. Radiology; mem. Am. Coll. Radiation, Am. Soc. Therapeutic Radiologists, Am. Phys. Soc. Democrat. Jewish. Avocation: bicycling. Office: Washington U Radiation Oncology Ctr Box 8224 4921 Parkview Pl Saint Louis MO 63110-1001

**MYERSON, ROGER BRUCE,** economist, educator; b. Boston, Mar. 29, 1951; s. Richard L. and Rosemarie (Farkas) M.; m. Regina M. Weber, Aug. 29, 1982; children: Daniel, Rebecca. AB summa cum laude, Harvard U., 1973, SM, 1973, PhD, 1976. Asst. prof. decision scis. Northwestern U., Evanston, Ill., 1976-78, assoc. prof., 1979-82, prof., 1982-2001, Harold Stuart prof. decision scis., 1986-2001, prof. econs., 1987-2001; W.C. Norby prof. econs. U. Chgo., 2001—. Guest researcher U. Bielefeld, Federal Republic of Germany, 1978-79; vis. prof. econs. U. Chgo., 1985-86, 2000-01. Author: Game Theory: Analysis of Conflict, 1991, Probability Models for Economic Decisions, 2005; mem. editorial bd. Internat. Jour. Game Theory, 1982-92, Games and Econ. Behavior, 1988-97; assoc. editor Jour. Econ. Theory, 1983-93; also articles. Guggenheim fellow, 1983-84; Sloan rsch. fellow, 1984-86. Fellow Econometric Soc., Am. Acad. Arts and Scis. (Midwest v.p. 1999-2002). Office: U Chgo Dept Econs 1126 E 59th St Chicago IL 60637 Business E-Mail: myerson@uchicago.edu.

**MYERSON, TOBY SALTER,** lawyer; b. Chgo., July 20, 1949; s. Raymond King and Natalie Anita (Salter) M. BA, Yale U., 1971; JD, Harvard U., 1975. Bar: N.Y. 1977, Calif. 1977. Assoc. Coudert Bros., N.Y.C., 1975-77, 81, San Francisco, 1977-81, Paul, Weiss, Rifkind, Wharton & Garrison, N.Y.C., 1981-83, prtnr., 1983-89; mng. dir. Wassersteín Perella & Co., Inc., N.Y.C., 1989-90; ptnr. Paul, Weiss, Rifkind, Wharton & Garrison, N.Y.C., 1990—, co-chair, Corp. Dept. Lectr. U. Calif. Berkeley, 1979-81, Harvard U., Cambridge, Mass., 1982-83; visiting lectr. Yale U., New Haven, 1983-84; bd. dirs. Myerson, Van Den Berg & Co., Santa Barbara, Calif. Contbg. editor: Doing Business in Japan, 1983, Council on Foreign Rels., 1993—, Foreign Policy Assn., 1995—. Sec. Japan Soc., Inc., N.Y.C., 1985-89; bd. dirs. 1056 Fifth Ave. Corp., N.Y.C., 1985-88; mem. univ. resources com. Harvard U., 1997—. Mem. ABA (subcom. internat. banking, corp. and bus. law sect.), Internat. Bar Assn., N.Y. State Bar Assn., Assn. Bar City N.Y. (com. on fgn. and comparative law, chmn. 1988-89), Calif. Bar Assn. Avocations: art, music, literature, tennis, golf. Home: 1056 5th Ave New York NY 10028-0112 Office: Paul Weiss Rifkind Wharton & Garrison 1285 Ave of the Americas New York NY 10019-6065 Fax: 212-373-2753. E-mail: tmyerson@paulweiss.com.

**MYHR, GAYLE E.,** consumer science educator; b. Alexandria, Minn., Aug. 24, 1949; d. Reuben B. and Millie C. Myhr. BS in Home Econ. Edn., ND State U., Fargo, 1971. Tchr. family and consumer sci. Tracy Pub. Sch., Minn., 1971—2005. Coord. early childhood family edn. Tracy Pub. Sch., 1989—2005, parent educator, early childhood family edn., 1989—2005, sch. readiness coord., 1998—2005. Mem. Tracy Cmty. Edn. Adv. Com., 1986—2002. Mem.: NEA, Edn. Minn. Office: Tracy Pub Sch 934 Pine St Tracy MN 56175 Home: PO Box 31 Brandon MN 56315-0031 Business E-Mail: gmyhr@tracy.k12.mn.us.

**MYHRE, BYRON ARNOLD,** pathologist, educator; b. Fargo, ND, Oct. 22, 1928; s. Ben Arnold and Amy Lillian (Gilbertson) M.; m. Eileen Marguerite Scherling, June 16, 1953; children: Patricia Ann, Bruce Allen. BS, U. Ill., Champaign/Urbana, 1950; MS, Northwestern U., Evanston, Ill., 1952; MD, Northwestern U., 1953; PhD, U. Wis., 1962. Intern Evanston (Ill.) Hosp., 1953-54; resident Children's Meml. Hosp., Chgo., 1956-57, U. Wis. Hosp., Madison, 1957-60; assoc. med. dir. Milw. Blood Ctr., 1962-66; sci. dir. L.A. Red Cross Blood Ctr., 1966-72; dir. Blood Bank Harbor-UCLA Med. Ctr., Torrance, Calif., 1972-85, chief clin. pathology, 1985-2000; prof. pathology UCLA, 1972-2000, prof. emeritus, 2000—. Author: Quality Control on Blood Banking, 1974; (with others) Textbook of Clinical Pathology, 1972, Paternity Testing, 1975; editor seminar procs.; contbr. articles to profl. jours., chpts. to books. Served with USAF, 1954-56. Mem.: AMA, Harbor-UCLA Faculty Soc. (past pres.), Wis. Blood Bank Assn. (past pres.), L.A. Acad. Medicine (past pres.), Calif. Blood Bank Sys. (past pres.), Calif. Med. Assn., Assn. Clin. Scientists (past pres.), Coll. Am. Pathologists (chmn. blood bank survey com.), Am. Assn. Blood Banks (pres. 1978—79), Am. Soc. Clin. Pathology (dep. commr. commn. on continuing edn.), Palos Verdes Breakfast Club (past pres.). Home: 4004 Via Larga Vista Palos Verdes Estates CA 90274-1122 Office: Harbor UCLA Med Ctr 1000 W Carson St Torrance CA 90502-2004 Personal E-mail: bamyhre@cox.net.

**MYHRE, JANET,** mathematician, educator; b. Tacoma, Wash., Sept. 24, 1932; d. Leif Christian Klippen, Thelma Gladys Klippen; m. Philip Cushman Myhre, June 12, 1954 (div. Dec. 1984); 1 child, Karin Elizabeth; m. Leon Hollerman, May 29, 1988; 1 child, Jeremy Hollerman. BA summa cum laude, Pacific Luth. U., 1954; MA, U. Wash., 1956; PhD in Math. Stats, U. Stockholm, 1968. Prof. math. Claremont McKenna Coll., Claremont, Calif., 1962—. Vis. prof. U. Stockholm, 1971—72, Swiss Fed. Inst. Tech., Zurich, 1971—72, Wash. State U. Pullman, 1978; prof. math. Claremont Grad. U., 1968—; founder, pres. Math. Analysis Rsch. Corp., Claremont, 1973—; dir. Reed Inst. for Decision Sci. Claremont McKenna Coll., Claremont, 1975—; cons. Strategic Sci. Programs USN, Washington, 1968—; cons. EPA, Washington, 1976—77. Contbr. chpts. in books, articles to profl. jours. Bd. trustees mem. The Webb Schs., Claremont, 1984—88; officer Padua Hills Homeowners Assn., Claremont, 1988—94; mem. numerous blue ribbon com. USN involving reliability, nuclear safety and risk assessment, 1972—. Recipient Austin Bonis award, Am. Soc. Quality Control, 1984; Rsch. grant, Office Naval Rsch. 1973—83. Fellow: Am. Statis. Assn. (assoc. editor Technometrics 1969—75, coun. rep. 2001—03, pres. So. Calif. chpt. 2003—05); mem.: Padua Hills Mus. Com., Phi Beta Kappa (pres. CMC chpt. 2004—). Achievements include development of models/statistical theory used since 1972 by USN Ballistic Missile Program for reliability assessments; software/theory used by Fleet Ballistic Missile Program since 1990 for safety and risk assessment. Avocations: gardening, cooking, hiking, weaving. Office: Claremont McKenna Coll Bauer Hall 9th St Claremont CA 91711 also: Math Analysis Rsch Corp 4239 Via Padova Claremont CA 91711 Office Phone: 909-621-8876, 909-624-5298.

**MYHREN, TRYGVE EDWARD,** communications company executive; b. Palmerton, Pa., Jan. 3, 1937; s. Arne Johannes and Anita (Blatz) M.; m. Carol Jane Enman, Aug. 8, 1964; children: Erik, Kirsten, Tor; m. 2d Victoria Hamilton, Nov. 14, 1981; 1 stepchild, Paige. BA in Philosophy and Polit. Sci., Dartmouth Coll., 1958, MBA, 1959. Sales mgr., unit mgr. Procter and Gamble, Cin., 1963-65; sr. cons. Glendinning Cos., Westport, Conn., 1965-69; press. Auberge Vintners, 1970-73; exec. v.p. Mktg. Continental, Westport, 1969-73; v.p., gen. mgr. CRM Inc., Del Mar, Calif., 1973-75; from v.p. mktg. to pres. Am. TV and Comm. Corp., Englewood, Colo., 1975-80, chmn. bd., CEO, 1981-88; pres. Myhren Media Inc., Denver, 1989—. V.p., then exec. v.p. Time Inc., N.Y.C., 1987-88; mem. exec. com. Times Mirror, vice chmn., then bd. dirs. Nat. Cable TV Assn., Washington, 1982-91; mem. adv. com. on HDTV, FCC, 1987-89, pres. Providence Jour. Co.; bd. dirs. Advanced Mktg. Svcs., Inc., La Jolla, Calif.; Dreyfus Founders Funds, Inc., J. D.

Edwards, Inc., Verio, Inc., Nat. Cable TV Ctr., Denver, Cable Labs, Inc., Boulder, Colo., Peapod, Inc., Skokie, Ill.; pres. Myhren Media, 1989—; pres., CEO King Broadcast Co., 1991-96. Mem. Colo. Forum, 1984—, chmn. higher edn. com., 1986; bd. dirs., co-founder Colo. Bus. Com. for the Arts, 1985-91; mem. exec. coun. Found. for Commemoration U.S. Constn., 1987-90; mem. Nat. GED Task Force, 1987-90, Colo. Baseball Commn. 1989-91, Colo. Film Commn., 1989-91; trustee Nat. Jewish Hosp., 1989— (Humanitarian award 1996), R.I. Hosp., 1991-95, Lifespan Health Sys., 1994-97, U.S. Ski and Snowboard Team Found., 1998—; chmn. Local Organizing Commn. 1995 NCAA Hockey Championship; trustee, exec. com., chmn. fin. com. U. Denver, 1997—. Lt. (j.g.) USNR, 1959-63. Recipient Disting. Leader award Nat. Cable TV Assn., 1988. Mem. Cable TV Adminstrn. and Mktg. Soc. (pres. 1978-79, Grand Tam award 1985, One of A Kind award 1994), Cable Adv. Bur. (co-founder 1978), Cable TV Pioneers. Episcopalian. Address: Myhren Media Inc 280 Detroit St # 200 Denver CO 80206-4807 E-mail: trygm@earthlink.net.

**MYHRVOLD, NATHAN P.,** technology executive; b. Seattle, Aug. 3, 1959; BS in Math., UCLA, 1979, MS in Geophysics and Space Physics, 1979; M in Math. Econs., Princeton U., 1981; D in Theoretical and Math. Physics, 1983. Fellow dept. applied math. and theoretical physics Cambridge U., 1981-83; founder, pres., CEO Dynamical Sys., 1984-86; dir. spl. projects Microsoft Corp., Redmond, Wash., 1986, v.p. applications and content; chief tech. officer Advanced Tech. and Rsch., Redmond, Wash., Microsoft Corp., Redmond, Wash., 1996—99; founder, mgr. Microsoft Rsch.; CEO Intellectual Ventures, Bellevue, Wash., 2000—. Bd. trustees Inst. Advanced Study, Princeton, N.J.; mem. Nat. Info. Infrastructure Adv. Coun.; adv. bd. Princeton U. dept. physics. Photographer America 24/7, Washington 24/7; contbr. scientific papers articles to Science, Nature, Paleobiology, Physical Review, Fortune, Time, National Geographic Traveler and online mag. Slate; provided forward Juice: The Creative Fuel that Drives World Class Inventors. Mem. United Way Million Dollar Roundtable; co-contbr. with Paul Allen SETI Found. for Allen Telescope Array, 2000. Recipient 1st and 2nd Place title, World Championship of Barbecue, Memphis, James Madison medal, Princeton U., 2005. Achievements include patents in field; patents pending in field. Avocations: mountain climbing, photography, French Cooking, Formula Car Racing. Office: Intellectual Ventures 1756 114th Ave SE Ste 110 Bellevue WA 98004

**MYINT, SOE WIN,** geographer, educator; s. Pe Than Tun and Khin Nu Nu; m. Susie Tin Maung Aye, Dec. 26, 1987; 1 child, Su Thinzar. BS in Forestry, Rangoon U., 1983; postgrad., Internat. Inst.Aerospace Survey and Earth Sciences, 1988—89; MS in Natural Resources, Asian Inst. Tech., 1994; PhD in Geography, La. State U., 2001. Asst. plantation officer Forest Dept., Rangoon, Rangoon Division, Burma, 1983—85; dep. mgr. Timber Corp., 1985—92; rsch. assoc. UNEP/Environment Assessment Program for Asia and the Pacific, Bangkok, 1994—96, rsch. specialist, 1996—98; asst. prof. dept. geography U. Okla., Norman, 2001—05, Ariz. State U., Tempe, 2005—. Geog. info. sci. cons. WHO, Geneva, 1999. Recipient Best Poster Presentation award, 18th Asian Conf. on Remote Sensing, 1998, Robert C. West Field Rsch. award, La. State U. Dept. Geography and Anthropology, 2000, US Geog. Sci. Scholar award, First Internat. Conf. GISci., 2000, Best Student Paper award, Am. Soc. for Photogrammetry and Remote Sensing-Mid-South Region Meeting, 2000, William G. Haag award, La. State U., 2001, Best Student Paper award, U. Consortium Geog. Info. Scis. Assembly, 2000, Remote Sensing Speciality Group, Assn. Am. Geographers, 2001, Otis Paul Starkey award, Assn. Am. Geographers, 2001, Intergraph Young Scholar award, U. Consortium Geog. Info. Sci., 2002, Runner-up Early Career award, Remote Sensing Specialty Group, Assn. Am. Geographers, 2004; fellow, Netherlands Govt., 1988—89; grantee, NASA EPSCoR, 2001, 2002, U. Okla., 2002, Inst. Advanced Edn. Geospatial Scis., NASA, 2003—04, U. Calif., Santa Barbara, 2003, NSF, 2004—; scholar, French Govt., 1993—94, La. State U., 1999—2001; CPGIS scholar, 2005, CSISS scholar, 2003. Office: Ariz State U Dept Geography PO Box 870104 Tempe AZ 85287-0104 Home: 4175 W Shannon St Chandler AZ 85226 Office Phone: 480-965-6514. Office Fax: 405-325-6090, 480-965-8313. Business E-Mail: soe.myint@asu.edu.

**MYKLEBY, KATHY,** newscaster, reporter; Degree, U. Iowa, 1976. With KRNA-FM Radio, Iowa City, 1976, WKY-Radio, Oklahoma City, 1976—80, WVTV-TV Channel 18, Milw., 1980; reporter, anchor WISN, Milw., 1980—. Active telethon Children's Miracle Network; co-chmn. Briggs and Stratton Run/Walk for Children's Hosp. of Wis. Recipient Regional award for best TV feature, UP Internat., 1984, Best Single Report Contbg. to Cmty. Welfare award, Milw. Press Club, 1987, Press Club award, 1992, Best Spot News award, Wis. Broadcasters Assn., 1997. Office: WISN PO Box 402 Milwaukee WI 53201-0402 Office Phone: 414-937-3331.

**MYLARI, BANAVARA L.,** retired chemist; b. Bangalore, India, Jan. 29, 1937; arrived in U.S., 1962; s. Lakshman S. and Kaveramma Mylari; m. Aparna Pandit Mylari, Sept. 10, 1967; 1 child, Ravi. BSc with honors, Central Coll., Bangalore, India, 1960, MSc in Organic Chemistry, 1961; PhD in Organic Chemistry, Ind. U., 1966. Project leader Pfizer Inc., Groton, Conn., 1974—78, mgr., 1989, rsch. advisor, 1989—97, sr. rsch. fellow, 1997—. Pvt. medicinal chemistry cons., East Lyme, Conn., 2001—; presenter in field. Contbr. articles to profl. jours. Exec. com. mem. Conn. Valley Hindu Temple, Middletown, Conn. Mem.: Am. Chem. Soc. (fundraiser heterocyclic chemistry 1986—96, fundraiser Extraordinary award 1992). Hindu. Achievements include patents for therapeutic agents for diabetic complications; research in diabetes aldose reductase inhibitors; patents in field. Avocations: travel, sanskrit literature, vedic literature, invited speaker on hindu religion. Home: Harvest Glen East Lyme CT 06333 Personal E-mail: blmylari@aol.com.

**MYLNECHUK, LARRY HERBERT,** financial executive; b. Littlefork, Minn., Mar. 9, 1948; s. William and Marjorie (Raco) M.; m. Sandy L. Henderson, Mar. 14, 1970; children: Kendra Elizabeth, Scott William. BA, Lewis & Clark Coll., Portland, 1970; JD, Lewis & Clark Coll., 1974. Legal specialist Oreg. Dept. Edn., Salem, 1976-82; sr. v.p., dir. Morley Capital Mgmt. Inc., Portland, 1982-89; founder, pres. Integra Assocs., Inc., Lake Oswego, Oreg., 1989—; exec. dir. The Stable Value Assn., Inc., Lake Oswego, 1990-96; co-founder, prin. Residential Capital Mgmt., LLC, 2000. Cons. Hueler Analytics, Inc., Mpls., 1989—; conf. chmn. GIC Nat. Forum Conf., Washington, 1993-95; arbitrator NASD, NY Stock Exch.; guest lectr. Portland State U., 1978, U. Oreg., 1980; bd. dirs. SAR Found. Contbr. articles to profl. jours. Founder Woodstock Neighborhood Assn., 1975; mem. Multnomah County (Oreg.) Charter Rev. Commn., 1978, Tualatin (Oreg.) City Coun., 1980—84, Portland Com. on Fgn. Rels., 1976—98, bd. dirs., 1993—96; mem. Gov.'s Commn. on Adminstrv. Hearings, State of Oreg., 1988—89, Tchrs. Standards and Practices Commn., State of Oreg., 2000—02; mem. vestry, lay eucharistic min., del. State Episcopal Conv., 1996; mem. Diocesan Coun., 1996—98; mem. vestry Christ Ch. Parish, 1995—2000, Christ Episcopal Ch., 1998—2000; founding mem. St. Margaret's Ch., 2000—03; trustee St. Francis of Assisi Endowment Fund, 1993; bd. dirs. Patriot Found., 2002—. Fellow NEH, 1979, ednl. policy fellow George Washington U., 1980. Mem. SAR (pres. Lewis and Clark chpt.,pres. Oreg. State Soc. 1997, nat. trustee, 1997-98, v.p. Gen.-Pacific dist. 1999-2001), Western Pension Conf., Assn. Soc. Execs., World Affairs Coun. Oreg., Citizen Amb. Program to Western Europe, Gen. Soc. The War of 1812, Soc. Colonial Wars, Sons and Daus. of Pilgrims, Oregon Soc. Sons of the Revolution (co-founder, treas. 1996), Internat. Bus. Forum (mem. adv. bd. 1996), Sons of the Bench and Bar (charter), N. Am. Soc. Securities Adminstrs. (profl. stds. com. 1998), Oreg. Assn. Adminstrv. Law Judges, Soc. Magna Charta Barons, Crown of Charlegmagne Soc., Soc. Charlemagne's Descendants, Col. George Middleton Hist. Soc. (bd. dirs.) Democrat. Episcopalian. Avocations: hiking, diving. Office: Residential Capital Mgt LLC PO Box 1594 Lake Oswego OR 97035-0013 Office Phone: 503-697-8697.

**MYLONAKIS, STAMATIOS GREGORY,** lawyer, consultant; b. Athens, Aug. 18, 1937; s. Gregory S. and Vassiliki (Charalambopoulos) Mylonakis; m. Pamela H. Morton, May 5, 1965 (dec. Mar. 1978); 1 child, Gregory (dec.). BS, Nat. U. of Athens, 1961; MS, Ill. Inst. of Tech., 1964; PhD, Mich. State

U., 1970. Rsch. assoc. Ill. Inst. of Tech., Chgo., 1964—65; rsch. scientist Brookhaven Nat. Lab., Upton, NY, 1965—68; instr. U. Calif., Berkeley, 1971—73; group leader Rohm and Haas Co., Springhouse, Pa., 1973—76; supr. DeSoto, Inc., Des Plaines, Ill., 1976—79; staff scientist Borg-Warner Corp., Des Plaines, 1979—82, mgr., 1982—87; dept. head Enichem Am., Monmouth Junction, NJ, 1988—94; tech. advisor, registered patent agt. law firm Oblon, Spivak, Arlington, Va., 1994—2000; cons., patent law practitioner, 2000—; sci. fellow Nuc. Rsch. Ctr. Democritos, Athens, 1960—62. Tech. adv. bd. Ctr. Applied Polymer Rsch. Case Western Res. U., Cleve.; adv. bd. NSF Ctr. Polymer Interfaces Lehigh U. Editor: Jour. Applied Polymer Sci.; contbr. articles to profl. jours. Lt. Greek Army. Fellow Sci. Nuc. Rsch. Ctr. Democritos, Athens, Greece, 1960—62, NSF, Mich. State U., 1968—70, U. Calif., 1971—73. Mem.: AAAS, Am. Chem. Soc., N.Y. Acad. Scis., Sigma Xi. Greek Orthodox. Achievements include patents in field of polymer sci. tech. Avocations: photography, painting, travel. Home and Office: 7009 Cashell Manor Ct Derwood MD 20855-1201 Personal E-mail: mylonakis@msn.com. E-mail: sgmylonakis@aol.com.

**MYLOTTE, JOHN ARNOLD,** writer, educator; b. Phila., Pa., Aug. 26, 1942; s. Thomas Joseph and Pauline Ellen (Arnold) Mylotte; m. Eva Benda, Sept. 20, 1997; 1 stepchild, Ilya; m. Florence Ellen Noonan, Aug. 14, 1977 (div. Nov. 1992). BA in english, Villanova U., 1964; MA in english, Lehigh U., 1967; JD, Suffolk U. Law Sch., 1980; post grad, MIT, 1981. Bar: Mass. 1981. Tech. editor Naval Air Engring. Ctr., Phila., 1967—68; sr. tech. editor Navy Clothing & Textile Rsch. Lab., 1968—72, dir. tech. publ., 1973—91, dir. pub. rels., 1974—91; pres. TechWrite Assoc., 1987—. Adj. prof.,sr. lectr. Northeastern U., Boston 1981—. Author: (book) Guide to Writing the Formal Technical Report, 1985, The Art of Technical Writing, 1987; contbr. articles to jours. Elected mem. Framingham Town Mtg., 1975—78; Relay for Life Vol. Am. Cancer Society, 1995—; bd. mem. Big Brother-Big Sister Assn. Framingham, Mass., 1975—78, bd. pres., 1977—78. Recipient Command Hist. award, U.S. Navy Hist., 1981, Outstanding Performance award, U.S. Navy Dept., 1980—85. Mem.: Worcester County Poetry Soc., Longfellow Soc. (treas. 2005—), Soc. for Tech. Commn. (5 competitive tech. writing awards 1984—86). Independent. Unitarian Universalist. Avocation: writing. Office: TechWrite Assoc 11 Clemmons St Southborough MA 01772

**MYMIT, CHUCK W.,** music educator, musician; b. NYC, Dec. 15, 1948; s. Jack Mymit, Gloria Epstein; BMus in Composition, Berklee Coll. of Music, Boston, 1971; MA in Composition, NYU, 1982; postgrad., Five Towne Coll., NY, 2004—. Asst. prof. Five Towns Coll., Seaford, NY, 1973—87, prof. jazz studies Dix Hills, NY, 1973—87, 2000—; tchr. music N.Y.C. Bd. Edn., 1987—97; coord. music Peninsula Counceling Ctr., L.I., NY, 1997—2000; house pianist Nordstroms Dept. Store, L.I., 1997—2000. Jazz comml. pianist AF of M, Local 802, N.Y.C., 1973—; freelance arranger/composer, N.Y.C., 1973—; editor FTC Press Five Towns Coll., 2000—; guest condr. NMEA All State Jazz Ensemble, NY, 2002. Author: (book) A Beginner's Approach to Jazz Improvisation, 1973, Contemporary Harmony I and Workbook, 1977, Contemporary Harmony II and Workbook, 1979, Arranging for Small Band, 1980, Club Date Pianist, 1981, Voicing Techniques for the Arranger, 1997, Contemporary Concepts in Jazz Harmony, 2001; composer, pianist, arranger: CD's Tú Eras Mi Corazon, 1995; composer (pianist, arranger): The Romantic Pianist, 1995 (X-Tisch Sch. of Arts award for film composition, 95), Reflections, 1998, Ambience, 2001, music score, music performed at Carnegie Hall and Tilles Ctr., (commd.) Deer Park Sch., 2005, Lincoln Ctr., 2005. Named Most Valuable Player, Nordstroms Dept. Store, N.Y., 1997. Mem.: ASCAP, Manhattan Assn. Cabaret Artists, Internat. Assn. Jazz Educators. Avocation: sports. Office: Five Towns College 305 N Service Rd Dix Hills NY 11746 Office Phone: 631-427-7000.

**MYNBAEV, DJAFAR K.,** engineering physics educator; b. Leningrad, Russia, Nov. 7, 1939; came to U.S., 1991; s. Karim M. and Militza V. (Starchenkova) M.; m. Larisa S. Bartshevskaya, July 7, 1959 (div. Nov. 1986); children: Karim D., Aia D.; m. Bronislava Y. Kaplan, May 27, 1987. MS in Elec. Engring., Leningrad Elec. Engring. Inst., 1963, PhD in Engring. Physics, 1969. Sys. engr. sci. and Tech. Navigation Co., Leningrad, 1963-65; asst. prof. Leningrad Elec. Engring. Inst., 1969-70, sr. scientist, 1970-72, assoc. prof., 1973-91; assoc. adj. prof. N.Y. Inst. Tech., N.Y.C., 1991—. Cons. Foremost Soviet Sci. and Tech. Cos., Leningrad, Moscow, Kiev, 1972-91; adj. prof. Fordham U., Bronx, 1994—; adj. lectr. New City Tech. Coll./CUNY, Bklyn., 1994—. Contbr. articles to profl. jours; author: Theory of Gyroscopes, 1989; editor: Theory of Dynamic Systems, 1990. Recipient Medal for Excellent Work, USSR State, 1986. Mem. Am. Soc. Engring. Edn., Inst. of Navigation. Achievements include 26 patents. Office: New York Inst Tech 1855 Broadway New York NY 10023-7602

**MYREN, ALLEN W(ILLIAM),** retired music educator; s. Rolland H. and Marie E.E. Myren; m. Kathleen P. Nicoline; children: Scott A., Trista N., Laura A.C. BS in Music Edn. (cum laude), U. Wis., LaCrosse, 1970, BS in Math Edn. (cum laude), 1970; MS in Music Edn. (cum laude), U. Ill., 1977. Choral dir. LaCrescent (Minn.) Pub. Schs., 1970—71, Warren Twp. H.S., Gurnee, Ill., 1971—2004, Coll. Lake County, Grayslake, Ill., 1983—90; ret., 2004. Golf coach Warren Twp. H.S., Gurnee, 1974—2004; choral dir. concert Disneyland, 1986, 2002, Knott's Berry Farm, 1986, Sea World Fla., 1988, 90, Disneyworld, 1988, 90, 96, 2004, Ravinia Winterfest, 1990—2000, Carnegie Hall, 1998; guest condr. Lake County Children's Choral Festival, 1991, Midwest Luth. Choral Festival, 1993, Lakes Summer Choir, 1996, Nat. Luth. Choral Festival, 1992; adj. asst. prof. Millikin U., 2004—. Bd. dirs. Lake County (Ill.) Arts Coun., 1987—90; musician, arranger St. Paul Luth. Ch., Round Lake Beach, Ill., 1985—. Mem.: NARAS (clinician 1996, 1997, 1999), Am. Choral Dirs. Assn. (clinician 1996, 1997), Music Educators Nat. Conf. (clinician); dist. chairperson 1983—88, clinician 1984, 2000). Independent. Lutheran. Achievements include choral dir. award winning choruses. Avocations: golf, travel. Home: 190 Southridge Dr Gurnee IL 60031 Personal E-mail: amyren@earthlink.net.

**MYREN, RICHARD ALBERT,** criminologist, consultant; b. Madison, Wis., Aug. 9, 1924; s. Andrew Olaus and Olyanna (Olson) M.; m. Patricia Ross Hubin, June 12, 1948; children: Nina Ross Schroepfer, Tania Ellis Myren Zobel, Kristina Albee Myren Sheldon, Andrew James. BS, U. Wis., 1948; LLB, Harvard U., 1952; LLD (hon.), U. New Haven, 1976. Bar: N.C. 1954. Rsch. chemist U.S. Dept. Agr., No. Regional Rsch. Lab., Peoria, Ill., 1948-49; asst. to assoc. rsch. prof. pub. law and govt. Inst. Govt., Chapel Hill, NC, 1952-56; asst. to assoc. prof. Ohio U., 1956-66; dean, prof. Sch. Criminal Justice, State U. N.Y., Albany, 1966-76, Sch. Justice, Am. U., Washington, 1976-86, prof. emeritus, 1986—; cons. Washington, 1987—. Vis. prof. Inst. Criminology, Cambridge (Eng.) U., 1973-74, East China Inst. for Politics and Law, Shanghai, People's Republic of China, 1988; cons. law enforcement programs for children and youth Children's Bur., HEW, Washington, 1960-62; cons. Pres.'s. Com. on Juvenile Delinquency and Youth Crime, 1962-64, Pres.'s Commn. on Law Enforcement and Adminstrn. Criminal Justice, 1966, U.S. Law Enforcement Assistance Adminstrn., 1968-82, N.Y. State Temp. Commn. on Constl. Conv., 1967, N.Y. State Dept. Edn., 1967, 69, Calif. Coordinating Coun. for Higher Edn., 1969-70, Nat. Adv. Commn. on Criminal Justice Standards and Goals, 1971-72, Tenn. Higher Edn. Commn., 1976, Ky. Dept. Justice, 1977-78, NSF, 1978—, U.S. Civil Rights Commn., 1978, others. Author: Coroners in North Carolina: A Discussion of Their Problems, 1953, Indiana Sheriffs' Manual of Law and Practice, rev. edit, 1959, Indiana Conservation Officers' Manual of Law and Practice, 1961; (with Lynn D. Swanson) Police Work With Children, 1962; (with Carroll L. Christenson) The Walsh-Healey Public Contracts Act: A Critical Review of Prevailing Minimum Wage Determinations, 1966, Education in Criminal Justice, 1970, Law and Justice: An Introduction, 1988, Investigation for Determination of Fact: A Primer on Proof, 1989; contbr. to: Bases for Justice Systems: Law and the Social Sciences (Gordon E. Misner), 1980, Five Year Outlook: Problems, Opportunities and Constraints in Science and Technology, 1980; assoc. editor: Jour. Criminal Justice; contbr. articles to profl. jours. Bd. dirs. Sex Info. and Edn. Coun. U.S., 1972-75. Served with inf. AUS,

1943-46, ETO; with USNR, 1954-68. Fulbright rsch. scholar to Argentina Cordoba, 1964-65 Mem. N.C. Bar Assn., Sociedad Argentina de Sociología Personal E-mail: rpmyren@peoplepc.com.

**MYRICK, BISMARCK,** diplomat; b. Portsmouth, Va., Dec. 23, 1940; m. Marie Pierre Mbaye; children: Bismarck Jr., Wesley Todd, Allison Elizabeth. BA, U. Tampa, 1972; MA, Syracuse U., 1973, postgrad., 1979-80; LHD (hon.), Spelman Coll., 2002. Enlisted U.S. Army, 1959; desk officer for Somalia, U.S. Dept. State, Washington, 1980-82; advanced through grades to maj., 1975; ret., 1979; polit. officer Am. Embassy, Monrovia, Liberia, 1982-84; action officer office strategic nuclear policy bur. politico-milit. affairs U.S. Dept. State, 1985-87, dep. dir. policy plans and coordination bur. inter-Am. affairs, 1987-89, Una Chapman Cox fellow US-African Policy, 1988-90; consul gen. Am. Consulate Gen., Durban, South Africa, 1990-93, Capetown, South Africa, 1993-95; amb. to Lesotho, Am. Embassy, Maseru, 1995-98; diplomat-in-residence Atlanta U. Ctr. at Spelman Coll., 1998-99; U.S. amb. to Liberia Dept. of State, Monrovia, Liberia, 1999—2002; univ. lectr. internat. affairs Old Dominion U., 2002—; sr. fellow Joint Forces Staff Coll., Norfolk, Va., 2002—. Author: Three Aspects of Crisis in Colonial Kenya, 1975. Decorated Silver Star, Purple Heart, 4 Bronze Stars; named to U.S. Army Hall of Fame, 1996; named Ambassador Bismarck Myrick Days, City of Portsmouth, Va., 2000, Bismarck Myrick St. and Bismarck Myrick Crescent St. named in his honor, 2002. Mem.: World Affairs Coun. Hampton Rds. (bd. dirs. 2004—). Address: 1200 Mill Run Chesapeake VA 23322

**MYRICK, SUE WILKINS,** congresswoman, former mayor; b. Tiffin, Ohio, Aug. 1, 1941; d. William Henry and Margaret Ellen (Roby) Wilkins; m. Jim Forest (div.); children: Greg, Dan; m. Wilbur Edward Myrick Jr., Sept. 11, 1977. Student, Heidelberg Coll., 1959-60, LLD (hon.), 1995 Exec. sec. to mayor and city mgr., Alliance, Ohio, 1962-63; dir. br. office Stark County Ct. of Juvenile and Domestic Rels., Alliance, Ohio, 1963-65; pres. Myrick Advt. and Pub. Rels., Charlotte, NC, 1971-95; at-large mem. City Coun., Charlotte, NC, 1983—85; mayor Charlotte, NC, 1987-91; pres. Myrick Enterprises, 1992—94; mem. US Congress from 9th NC Dist., 1995—. Candidate for US Senate, NC, 1992; mem. energy and commerce com. US Congress, dep. majority whip, 2003—, co-chair cancer caucus. Active Heart Fund, Multiple Sclerosis, March of Dimes, Arts and Scis. Fund Dr.; bd. dirs. NC Inst. Politics; v.p. Sister Cities Internat.; mem. Pres. Bush's Affordable Housing Commn.; founder, coord. Charlotte vol. tornado relief effort; lay leader, Sunday sch. tchr. 1st United Meth. Ch.; treas. Mecklenburg Ministries. Recipient Woman of Yr. award Harrisonburg, Va., 1968; named one of Outstanding Young Women of Am., 1968, Senator George L. Murphy award, 1998, Yr. of the Sr. award, 2000, Sr. Legis. Achievement award, 2000, Small Grain Leadership award, 2000, Pub. Leadership in Tech. award, 2002, Pub. Svc. Leadership award, 2002, Small Bus. Survival Com. award, 2004, Oncology Medal of Honor award, 2005. Mem. Women's Polit. Caucus, Beta Sigma Phi. Republican. Methodist. also: US House of Reps 230 Cannon Ho Office Bldg Washington DC 20515-0001 Home and Office: 8437 Olde Troon Dr Charlotte NC 28277 Office Phone: 202-225-1976. E-mail: myrick@mail.house.gov.

**MYRRDIN, TERRY A.,** state agency administrator; b. San Diego, Aug. 31, 1950; d. Bernard O. Wallen, Jr. and Mary Ann Snyder; children: Sherilyn Ann Pillsbury, Gina Marie Pillsbury. AA, Am. River Coll., Sacramento, CA, 1970. Cert. clinical hypnotherapist Am. Coun. Hypnotists Examiners. Asst. govtl. program analyst Dept. Indsl. Rels., Sacramento, 1994—2000; spl. asst. Gov. Gray Davis, Sacramento, 2000—03; exec. office mgr., exec. divsns. Sec. of State, Sacramento, 2003—. Owner, wedding cons. Social Graces, 1985—87. Avocations: feng shui, travel, gardening, reading. Office: Sec of State 1500 11th St 6th Fl Sacramento CA 95814 Office Phone: 916-653-7244.

**MYSAK, LAWRENCE ALEXANDER,** oceanographer, climatologist and mathematics educator; b. Saskatoon, Sask., Can., Jan. 1940; s. Stephen and Nettie Mysak; m. Diane Mary Eeles, Aug. 15, 1974; children: Paul Alexander, Claire Anastasia. BSc, U. Alta., Can., 1961; MSc, U. Adelaide, Australia, 1963; AM, Harvard U., 1964, PhD, 1967. Rsch. fellow Harvard U., 1966-67; mem. faculty U. B.C., Vancouver, 1967-86, prof. math. and oceanography, 1976-86; Atmospheric Environ. Svc./Natural Scis. Engring. Rsch. Coun.; sr. indsl. rsch. prof. climatology McGill U., Montreal, Que., Canada, 1986-96, dir. Climate Rsch Group, 1986-90. Can. Steamship Lines prof. meteorology, 1989—, founding dir. Ctr. for Climate and Global Change Rsch., 1990-96. Vis. rsch. assoc. Oreg. State U., summer 1968; sr. visitor Cambridge (Eng.) U., 1971-72; vis. scientist Inst. Ocean Sci., Sidney, B.C., fall 1976, Nat. Ctr. Atmospheric Rsch., Boulder, Colo., 1977; vis. prof. U.S. Naval Postgrad. Sch., Monterey, Calif., summer 1981, Swiss Fed. Inst., Tech., Zurich, 1982-83, 2000-2001; George's Lemaître vis. prof. Cath. U. Louvain, Belgium, 1995; invitation fellowship for rsch. in Japan, Japan Soc. for Promotion of Scis., 1997; supr. 70 grad. and postdoctoral students, 1967—; vis. prof. Italian Nat. Inst. Geophysics and Volcanology, Bologna, 2001; exch. lectr. Royal Soc. Can. Nat. Acad. Scis. of Ukraine, 2002. Co-author: Waves in the Ocean, 1978; also articles in profl. jours.; assoc. editor Jour. Phys. Oceanography, 1977-92, Atmospheric-Ocean, 1988-91, Climatol. Bull., 1992-93; contbg. editor Am. Geophys. Union books on coastal and esturaine studies, 1987-2000; mem. editl. bd. Geophys. and Astrophys. Fluid Dynamics, 1983-96; series editor: Springer Atmospheric and Oceanographic Scis. Libr., 2001-. Decorated Order of Can.; recipient Patterson Disting. Svc. medal Environ. Can. Atmospheric Environment Svc., 1997, prix Michel-Jurdant, ACFAS, 2005. Fellow Acad. of Sci. of Royal Soc. Can. (v.p. Acad. of Sci. 1991-93, pres. 1993-96), Am. Meteorol. Soc., Am. Geophys. Union; mem. Can. Meteorol. and Oceanog. Soc. (co-recipient Pres.'s prize 1980, J.P. Tully medal Oceanography 1997, inaugural fellow 1999), Royal Soc. Can. (life), European Geophys. Union (co-recipient Pres.'s Disting. Svc. award 1989), Academia Europaea (fgn.), Internat. Assn. for Phys. Scis. of Ocean (v.p. 2003—). Office: McGill U 805 Sherbrooke St W Montreal PQ Canada H3A 2K6 Office Phone: 514-398-3768. Business E-Mail: lawrence.mysak@mcgill.ca.

**MYSEL, RANDY HOWARD,** publishing company executive; b. Bronx, N.Y., July 26, 1954; s. Sam and Esther (Sinsheimer) M.; m. Rosemary Eileen Vaccari, July 25, 1987; children: Steven, Samantha, Sophie, Lillie. AA, Queensboro C.C., Queens, N.Y., 1975; BA in Acctg., Queens Coll., 1977; MBA, Adelphi U., 1986; grad., Warwick Sch. Bus., London. Mktg./acctg. profl. CBS, Inc., N.Y.C., 1981-86; mktg. analyst Reed Reference Pub., N.Y.C., 1986, bus. mgr., 1987, v.p., planning, in-house sales New Providence, NJ, 1988-97, v.p., pub. Marquis Who's Who, 1998—2002. Creator in-house sales dept. Reed Reference Pub., creator all advt. revenue 1997-2002, in-house sales Martindale-Hubbell.

**MYSKINA, ANASTASIA,** professional tennis player; b. Moscow, July 8, 1981; d. Andrey and Galina Myskina. Profl. tennis player WTA Tour, 1998—. Recipient Commitment to Cmty Award, Fla. Times-Union, 2005. Achievements include Winner 10 WTA Tour singles titles; Winner 1 WTA Tour doubles title; Winner 3 ITF Women's Circuit singles titles, Winner 3 ITF Women's Circuit doubles titles; Member Russian Olympic Team 2000, 2004. Office: c/o WTA Tour Corp Hdqs One Progress Plz Ste 1500 Saint Petersburg FL 33701

**MYSLINSKI, NORBERT RAYMOND,** medical educator; b. Buffalo, Apr. 14, 1947; s. Bernard and Amelia Joan (Lesniak) M.; m. Patricia Ann Byrne, June 19, 1970 (dec. 1980); m. René Carter, Nov. 21, 1993; children: Matthew Ryan, Kelly Lynn. BS in Biology, Canisius Coll., 1969; PhD in Pharmacology, U. Ill. Chgo., 1973. Rsch. assoc. Tufts U., Boston, 1973—75; asst. prof. U. Md., Balt., 1975—80, assoc. prof. physiology, 1980—, co-dir. Facial Pain Clinic, 1980—84, instr. nursing, 1982—84; rsch. fellow U. Bristol, England, 1984—85; adj. assoc. prof. U. Md. Sch. Nursing, 1997—. Instr. C.C. Balt., 1980—82; dir. grad. program dept. physiology U. Md., 1981—97, dir. HS biomedical rsch. program, 2000—, mem. faculty Marine-Estuarine Environ. Scis. grad. program, 1988—97; founder, dir. Patricia Byrne Nursing Scholarship Fund Trocaire Coll., Buffalo, 1985; dir. NIH Minority Rsch. Apprentice Program Balt. Coll. Dental Surgery, 1988—99; mem. grant rev. com. Nat. Inst. Nursing Rsch., 1993—94; grant reviewer Dept. Health and Human

Svcs., 1993—94; cons. in field; appeared on more than 20 live TV and radio programs; founder, dir. Internat. Brain Bee, 1999—; chmn. Neuroscience Edn. Workshop, Prague, Czech Republic, 2003—; mem. com. Md. Higher Edn. Commn., 2003—. Editor newsletters Med. Soc. Md. Rsch., 1977-82, Brain Storm, 1999—; author book chpts., revs. and numerous abstracts on pharmacology and neurosci.; inventor in field; reviewer 7 jours. Rep. task force on aging U. Md., 1979—84; instr. Am. Heart Assn., Balt., 1978, ARC, Balt., 1977—83; Internat. Co. Md. chpt. ARC, 2003—; com. mem. Md. Higher Edn. Commn., 2003—; mem. Pres. Bush's Sec. of Edn. Summit on Sci., Washington, 2004; eucharistic min., pastoral visitor Cath. Ch., 1983—93; bd. dirs. Md. Brain Awareness Week, Md., 1996—, Balt. Brains Rule!, 2002—, Md. Brain Lit. Competition, 2000—, Md. Brain Art Competition, 2000—. Capt. U.S. Army, 1969—77. Grantee NIH, various drug cos. and founds.: USPHS fellow, 1969-73; recipient Alumni of Yr. award St. Mary's HS, Lancaster, NY, 1996, Disting. Alumni award outstanding career Canisius Coll., Buffalo, 1997, Time to Care Cmty. Svc. award U. Md., 1998, Founders Day Pub. Svc. award U. Md., 2000. Mem.: HS Neuroscience (founder 2003), Am. Soc. Pharmacology Exptl. Therapeutics, Soc. Neuroscience (pres. Balt. chpt. 1990—92, editor newsletter 1990—97, neuroscience literacy com. 1997—2001), Am. Physiol. Soc., Internat. Assn. Dental Rsch. (adv. 1980—81), Md. Soc. Med. Rsch. (exec. com. 1978—86, bd. dir. 1978—86), Internat. Brain Rsch. Orgn., European Brain Behavior Soc. (hon.). Republican. Home: 9395 Carrie Way Ellicott City MD 21042-1701 Office: U Md Sch Dentistry Dept Biomed Scis 666 W Baltimore St Baltimore MD 21201-1510 Office Phone: 410-706-7258. Office Fax: 410-706-0193. Business E-Mail: nrm001@dental.umaryland.edu.

**MYSSIOREK, DAVID,** surgeon; b N.Y.C., N.Y., July 22, 1954, s. Leon and Sylvia Myssiorek; m. Ann Glogowsky, July 1, 1979; 2 children. BA, SUNY, 1976; MD, NYU, 1980. Diplomate Am. Bd. Med. Examiners. Staff surgeon Lahey Med. Ctr., Burlington, Mass., 1985-86; assoc. prof. otolaryngology Albert Einstein Coll. Medicine, Bronx, 1986-88, L.I. Jewish Med. Ctr., New Hyde Park, NY, 1988—, sect. head head and neck surgery. Mem. adv. bd. Support for People with Oral and Head and Neck Cancer, N.Y.C., 1992—, THYCA. Author: (with others) An Atlas of Head and Neck Surgery, 1985, Appleton and Lange's Review of Surgery, 1989, Biologic Basis of Facial Plastic Surgery, 1993, Women's Primary Health Care, 1995; guest editor Otolaryngologic Clinics of North Am., 2001, Otolaryngol. Clinics N.Am., 2004. Head and neck surgery fellow Montefiore Med. Ctr., Bronx, 1984-85. Fellow ACS, Am. Soc. Head and Neck Surgery, Soc. Univ. Otolaryngologists, Triologic Soc.; mem. Am. Acad. Otolaryngology (mem. com. 1988-093), Am. Head and Neck Soc., N.Y. Head and Neck Soc. (mem. adv. bd. exec. coun.). Avocations: tennis, photography, snorkeling, canoeing, fly fishing. Office: LI Jewish Med Ctr 27005 76th Ave New Hyde Park NY 11040-1433 Office Phone: 718-470-7552. Business E-Mail: myssiore@lij.edu.

**MYSTER, RANDALL WALTON,** education educator, researcher; b. Rochester, Minn., Jan. 20, 1955; s. Cletis Eugene and Dorothy Walton Myster; m. Olga Vladimirovna Mironova, Feb. 23, 2003. BS, U. Minn., 1977; MS, Purdue U., 1980, Rutgers U., 1987, PhD, 1990. Rsch. scientist U. PR, San Juan, 1990—95, asst. prof., 1995—2001, U. Ctrl. Okla., 2001—. Contbr. articles to profl. jours. Recipient fellowship, Fulbright Found., 2004, Scholar of Yr., Am. Assn. U. Profls., 2005; fellowship, Nat. Sci. Found., 1987. Mem.: Ecol. Assn. Am., Assn. for Tropical Biology. Democrat. Episc. Avocations: jazz, saxophone, diving, cross country skiing, backpacking. Office: U Ctrl Okla 100 N University Edmond OK 73034 Office Phone: 405-974-5909.

**MYTELKA, ARNOLD KRIEGER,** lawyer; b. Jersey City, July 24, 1937; s. Herman Donald and Jeannette (Krieger) M.; m. Rosalind Marcia Kaplan, Dec. 17, 1961; children: Andrew Charles, Daniel Sommer. AB, Princeton U., 1958; LLB cum laude, Harvard U., 1961; postgrad., London Sch. Econs., 1961—62. Bar: N.J. 1961, U.S. Dist. Ct. N.J. 1963, U.S. Supreme Ct. 1970, U.S. Ct. Appeals (3d cir.) 1978, U.S. Dist. Ct. (so. and ea. dist.) N.Y. 1983. Law sec. Chief Justice N.J. Supreme Ct., Newark, 1962-63; assoc. Clapp & Eisenberg, Newark, 1963-68, prin., 1968-94; prin. Kraemer, Burns, Mytelka, Lovell & Kulka, Springfield, N.J., 1994—. Lectr. Rutgers Law Sch., Newark, 1973; mem. Am. Law Inst., Phila., 1989—; mem. cons. group The Law Governing Lawyers, 1990-99, Restatement of Restitution and UN/USA Enrichments; founding trustee Newark Legal Svcs. Project, 1965-68; trustee Edn. Law Ctr., 1974-75; chmn. dist. V ethics com. Supreme Ct. N.J., 1983-84, mem. 1981-84; trustee Legal Svcs. Found. Essex County, 1982—, pres., 1990-92; lectr. in land use law. Mem. editorial bd. N.J. Law Jour., 1991—; contbr. legal articles to profl. jours. Chmn. bd. trustees Ramapo Coll. NJ, 1979-80; mediator chancery divsn. NJ Superior Ct., 1990—, trustee, 1998-00, 2003—, spl. fiscal agt., 1997, 2003, 2005, spl. master, 1999-00. Frank Knox Meml. fellow Harvard U., London Sch. Econs. and Polit. Sci., 1961-62. Mem.: ABA (mem. litigation sect.), N.J. State Bar Assn. (chmn. appellate practices study com. 1977-79, chmn. land use law sect. 1983-85). Home: 56 Hall Rd Chatham NJ 07928-1723 Office: Kraemer Burns Mytelka Lovell & Kulka 675 Morris Ave Springfield NJ 07081-1523 E-mail: amytelka@kraemerburns.com.

**NA, TSUNG SHUN (TERRY NA),** Chinese studies educator, writer; b. Beijing, Nov. 3, 1932; came to U.S., 1964; s. Chi-L and Hui (Hu) N.; m. Yen Yen Chao, 1964. BA, Taiwan Normal U., 1956; MA, U. B.C., 1970; PhD, U. Minn., 1978. Assoc. prof. Taipei Normal Coll., Taiwan, Republic of China, 1956-64; vis. lectr. Ind. U., Bloomington, 1964-66; asst. prof. U. Minn., Mpls., 1970-80; vis. prof. Sun Yat-sen U., Taiwan, 1981-84; prof. Am. Inst. Chinese Studies, Charles Town, W.Va., 1985—. Author: (English books) A Linguistic Study of P'i-pa Chi, 1969, Studies on Dream of the Red Chamber: A Selected and Classified Bibliography, 1979, Supplement, 1981, Taiwan Studies on Dream of the Red Chamber: A Selected and Classified Bibliography, 1983, Chinese Studies in English: A Selected Bibliography, 1991, (Chinese) Mandarin Pronunciation, 1966, Teaching Chinese in the U.S.A., 1983, Studies on Chinese Classical Novels, 1985, A Collection of Short Stories, 1987; contbr. numerous articles, short stories, and research essays to jours. and newspapers in U.S., Taiwan, ROC, and China. Mem. MLA, Assn. Asian Studies. Office: Am Inst Chinese Studies PO Box 453 Charles Town WV 25414-0453

**NABEL, ELIZABETH G.,** cardiologist, researcher; BA summa cum laude, St. Olaf Coll., Northfield, Minn., 1974; postgrad., Union Theol. Sem., 1974—75, Columbia U., N.Y.C., 1975—77; MD, Cornell U., Ithaca, N.Y., 1981; DHC (hon.), Katholik U. Leuven, 2001. Diplomate Am. Bd. Internal Medicine and cardiovascular diseases. Intern & resident in internal medicine Brigham and Women's Hosp.-Harvard Med. Sch., Boston, 1981—84, clin. and rsch. fellow cardiovasc. divsn., 1984-87; asst. prof. internal medicine U. Mich., Ann Arbor, 1987-91, assoc. prof. internal medicine, 1991-94, prof. internal medicine, 1994—99, dir. Cardiovasc. Rsch. Ctr., 1992—99, prof. physiology, 1995—, chief divsn. cardiology, 1997-99; sci. dir. clin. rsch. Nat. Heart, Lung, and Blood Inst. NIH, Bethesda, Md., 1999—2005, dir. Nat. Heart, Lung, and Blood Inst., 2005—. Mem. sci. adv. bd. Vical Inc., San Diego, 1992-96; mem. arteriosclerosis, hypertension, and lipid metabolism adv. com. NHLBI, NIH, 1991-93, parent program project grant rev. com., 1995—, mem. task force on human gene therapy, 1992, mem. cardiology adv. com., 1993-94, mem. spl. emphasis panel arterial thrombosis, 1996; chair sci. pub. com. Am. Heart Assn., 1996-98, bd. dir. 1996-98; chair Atherosclerosis Thrombosis and Vascular Biology Coun., 2002—, Gordon Conf. on Vascular Cell Biology, 1996; pres. N.Am. Vascular Biology Orgn., 1996-97; sci. adv.bd. Keystone Symposia, 1999—, bd. dir. 2001—; mem. com. on space medicine Inst. of Medicine, 1991-2001; councilor and sec.-treas. Am. Soc. of Clin. Investigation, 2001—; lectr. Mayo Clinic, 1996, Yale Univ., 1997, Univ. of Texas, 1997, Womens Hosp., 1997, 2001, Univ. of Hawaii, 1980, Temple Univ., 1999, John Hopkins, 1999, 2000, 2002, Am. Heart Assn., 1999, Univ. of Mich., 2001, Vanderbilt Univ., 2001, Univ. of Va., 2002, among many others. Assoc. editor Jour. of Clin. Investigation, 1997—2002, mem. editl. bd., 2002—05, mem. bd. reviewing editors Science, 1998—2005, mem. editl. bd. New Eng. Jour. Medicine, 2001—; editor: Trends in Cardiovascular Medicine, 2001; cons. editor Circulation, Circulation Rsch., Atherial Thrombosis and Vascular Biology, 2000—05. Fellow Am. Coll.

Cardiology, Am. Heart Assn. (basic sci. coun., clin. cardiology coun., circulation coun., atherosclerosis coun., bd. dirs. 1996-97, sci. adv. and coord. com. 1996-97, chair sci. pub. com. 1996-97, sci. pub. com. 1994-96, sci. sessions program com. 1994-95; rsch. fellowship com. Mich. chpt. 1993-95, rsch. grant-in-aid com. 1994-96, vice chair rsch. grant-in-aid com. 1995-96, rsch. exec. com. 1995-96, rsch. com. 1995-96, chair peer rev. rsch. com. 1996-97); mem. AAAS, ACP, Am. Soc. for Biochemistry and Molecular Biology (Amgen Sci. award 1996), Am. Fedn. Clin. Rsch., Am. Soc. Investigative Pathology, Am. Soc. Clin. Investigation, N.Y. Acad. Scis., Am. Soc. Gene Therapy (bd. dirs. 1996), Assn. Am. Physicians, N.Am. Vascular Biology Orgn. (councillor 1994-95, sec., treas. 1994-95, pres. 1996-97), Inst. of Medicine, Ctrl. Soc. Clin. Rsch., Phi Beta Kappa, Alpha Omega Alpha. Office: NIH/NHLBI 31 Center Dr Bldg 31 Rm 5A52 Bethesda MD 20892

**NABER, FAITH,** retired librarian, educator; b. Miltonvale, Kans., Sept. 27, 1920; d. Peter Gombert and Mary Orilla (Grise) N.; m. Frank E. Robinson, Sept. 5, 1943 (div. July 1976); children: Paul David, Mary Martha Howard, John Timothy, Faith Ann, Frank Eric. AA, Kendall Coll., 1942; AB, Otterbein Coll., 1944; postgrad., Hartford (Conn.) Sem. Found., 1949-50; MLS, Ball State U., 1970; postgrad., Chgo. State U., 1979-83. Cert. sch. librarian K-12, Ill. Edn. missionary Meth. Ch., Philippines, 1950-55; tchr. Mississiawna Valley Sch., Union City, Ohio, 1957-60; librarian numerous secondary schs., Ohio, 1962-70, Bluffton (Ohio) Pub. Library, 1970-71, H.H. Conrady Jr. High Sch., Hickory Hills, Ill., 1971-86. Cons. Chgo. State U., 1976-80, Orchard Hill Farm Sch., Tinley Park, Ill., 1976—. Author: Philippine Dialect Primers. Leader Buckeye Trails council Girl Scouts U.S. 1955-56, Wapahani council, 1957-62; mem. Commn. on Status and Role of Women, No. Ill. Conf. United Meth. Ch., 1978-94. Mem. AAUW (program chmn. 1987-94, legis. chair 1987-91), Coalition Labor Union Women. Avocations: flowers, storytelling, world travel, children photography. Home: 21697 McClung Ave Southfield MI 48075-7804

**NABERS, DRAYTON, JR.,** state supreme court chief justice, retired insurance company executive; b. Birmingham, Ala., Dec. 2, 1940; s. Drayton Sr. and Jane (Porter) N.; m. Fairfax Smathers, Dec. 31, 1965; children: Drayton III, Mary James, Fairfax Virginia. BA, Princeton U., 1962; LLB, Yale U., 1965. Law clk. to justice Hugo Black U.S. Supreme Ct., Washington, 1965-66; assoc. Cabaniss, Johnston, Gardner, Dumas & O'Neal, 1967-71, ptnr., 1971-79; sr. v.p. ops., gen. counsel Protective Life Ins. Co., 1979; pres. Empire Gen. Life Ins. Co., 1980-82; pres., COO Protective Life Corp./Protective Life Ins. Co., 1982-92; pres., CEO Protective Life Ins. Co, Birmingham, Ala., 1992-94, chmn., pres., CEO, 1994—2002; fin. dir. State of Alabama, 2002—04; chief justice Alabama Supreme Ct., 2004—. Bd. dirs. Protective Life Corp., Protective Life Ins. Co., Am. Found. Life Ins. Co., Energen, Inc., Nat. Bank of Commerce. Chmn. Leadership Birmingham, United Way Ctrl. Ala., Am. Council Life Insurers, Cornerstone Schools of Ala. Mem. Ala. Acad. Honor, Birmingham Bar Assn., Ala. Bar Assn. Office: Alabama Supreme Court 300 Dexter Ave Montgomery AL 36104*

**NABHOLZ, JOSEPH VINCENT,** biologist, ecologist; b. Memphis, Nov. 3, 1945; s. Martin Peter and Helen Kathleen (Garbacz) N.; m. Sue Ann Winterburn, Aug. 12, 1972; children: Karen Stacey, Pamela Michelle. BS, Christian Bros. U., Memphis, 1968; MS, La. State U., 1973, PhD, 1978. Sr. biologist EPA, Washington, 1979—. Reviewer NSF and profl. jours., 1973—, Standards Methods Com., Am. Water Works Assn., Denver 18th through 21st edits.; evaluator Office Exptl. Learning U. Md., College Park, Md., 1984-86. Author: Estimating Toxicity of Industrial Chemicals to Aquatic Organisms Using Structure Activity Relationships, 1988, 94, ECOSAR Computer Program to Predict Aquatic Toxicity of Chemicals, 2005; co-author: Methods of Ecological Toxicology, 1981, Testing for Effects of Chemicals on Ecosystems, 1981; contbr. articles to profl. jours. Bd. dirs. Comty. Assn. Rollingwood Village (4th sect.), Woodbridge, Va., 1981-90, v.p. 1981-82, pres. 1983-90, maintainence chmn. 1990—. Decorated Army Commendation medal with oak leaf cluster, U.S. Army, Vietnam, 1969, '70. Mem. AAAS, Am. Inst. Biol. Scis. (life), Assn. Southeastern Biologists (life), Internat. Assn. Ecology, Ecol. Soc. Am. (life), Soc. Environ. Toxicology and Chemistry, Phi Kappa Phi (life). Roman Catholic. Achievements include pragmatic application of theory of chemical structure activity relationships for routine risk assessment of industrial chemicals for environmental toxicity. Home: 13627 Bentley Cir Woodbridge VA 22192-4340 Office: EPA 7403 1200 Pennsylvania Ave NW Washington DC 20460-0001 Office Phone: 202-564-8909. Office Fax: 202-564-9063. Business E-Mail: nabholz.joe@epa.gov.

**NABI, STANLEY ANDREW,** brokerage house executive; b. Baghdad, Iraq, Sept. 17, 1930; arrived in U.S., 1947; s. Moshi S. and Victoria T. (Mukamal) N.; m. Bette E. Miller, Mar. 31, 1968; children: Deborah Susan, Lisa Meryl. BA, Columbia U., 1952; postgrad., NYU, 1954—58. Gen. ptnr. Schweickart & Co., N.Y.C., 1954-72; gen. ptnr., chief investment officer Lazard Freres & Co., N.Y.C., 1973-84; exec. v.p. Bessemer Trust Co., N.A., 1985-95; pres., CEO Bessemer Investors Svcs., 1985-95; vice chmn., chmn. investment policy com. Wood, Struthers & Winthrop, N.Y.C., 1995-2000; chief investment officer DLJ Asset Mgmt. Corp., N.Y.C., 1996-2000; mng. dir., sr. advisor Credit Suisse Asset Mgmt., 2000—03; vice chmn. Silvercrest Asset Mgmt. Group, 2004—. Lectr. New Sch. Social Rsch., N.Y.C., 1963-68; investment cons. U.S. Steel and Carnegie Pension Fund, N.Y.C., 1979—; dir. Bargain Town U.S.A., N.Y.C., 1962-69; mem. pres.'s coun. New Sch. U., N.Y.C., 1989—; adj. prof. fin. Grad. Sch. Bus., Fordham U., N.Y.C., 1992-97. Editor: weekly jour. The Analyst, 1957-72; assoc. editor: jour. The Fin. Analysts Jour., 1971-83. Trustee NABI Found., 1964—. Served with U.S. Army, 1952-54. Mem. N.Y. Soc. Security Analysts (pres. 1971-72), Inst. Chartered Fin. Analysts, Assn. for Investment Mgmt. and Rsch. Office: 1330 Ave of the Americas New York NY 10019 Home: 1 Kensington Gate (PH-1) Great Neck NY 11021-1202 Business E-Mail: snabi@silvercrestgroup.com.

**NABOKOV, PETER FRANCIS,** writer; b. 1940; Staff reporter New Mexican newspaper, Santa Fe, 1967-68; instr. Am. Indian studies Monterey (Calif.) Peninsula Coll., 1970-73, 77-78; rsch. assoc. Human Resources Rsch. Orgn., Carmel, Calif., 1972-75; instr. U. Calif., Berkeley, 1979, 82; prof. UCLA. Author: Two Leggins: The Making of a Crow Warrior, 1967, Tijerina and the Courthouse Raid, 1970, Indian Running, 1981, Architecture of Acoma Pueblo: The 1934 Histgoric American Buildings Survey Project, 1986, India Running: Native American History and Tradition, 1987, Where the Lightning Strikes: The Lives of American Indian Sacred Places, 2006, (with Robert Easton) Native American Architecture, 1988; (under name Peter Towne) George Washington Carver, 1975; editor: Native American Testimony: An Anthology of Indian and White Relations: First Encounter to Dispossession, 1978. Address: care Oxford Univ Press 200 Madison Ave New York NY 10016-3903 Mailing: c/o Vintag Pub 375 Hudson St New York NY 10014*

**NABORS, ROBERT L.,** military officer; b. Boston; married; children: Robert, Richard, Jonathan. BS in Systems Engring., U. Ariz.; MS in Systems Mgmt., U. So. Calif.; grad. Sr. Officials in Nat. Security, Harvard U.; grad., Armed Forces Staff Coll. Commd. 2d lt. U.S. Army, advanced through grades to maj. gen., with 67th Signal Battalion Ft. Riley, Kans., overseas tours in Vietnam and Worms, Germany, also active duty tours Ft. Dix, NJ, Aberdeen Proving Grounds, Md., aide-de-Camp for Comdg. Gen., VII Corps, 1979-81; with Office of Dir. of Plans, Programs and Policy U.S. Army Readiness Command, 1983; then comdr. 509th signal Battalion U.S. Army, Italy; spl. asst. to U.S. Army's Dir. of Info. Sys. for Command Control. Comm. and Computers; chief Integration div. Architecture Directorate U.S. Army, dep. comdr. White House Comm. Agy., comdr. 2d Signal Brigade, 1990, comdr. 5th Signal Command, 1995-98, comdr. Comm.-Electronics Command and comdr. Ft. Monmouth NJ, 1998-2001. Decorated DSM, DSM, Def. Superior Svc. medal, Legion of Merit with 4 oak leaf clusters, Bronze Star, Meritorious Svc. medal with 4 oak leaf clusters, others; recipient Roy Wilkins award of Reknown, NAACP, 2000, Fed. Asian-Pacific Am. Coun. award, 2000, others. Mem. Mensa.

**NACE, BARRY JOHN,** lawyer; b. York, Pa., Nov. 28, 1944; s. John Harrison and Mildred Louise (Orwig) Nace; m. Andrea Marcia Giardini, Apr. 28, 1973; children: Christopher Thomas, Jonathan Barry, Matthew Andrew. BS, Dickinson Coll., 1965, JD, 1969, LLD (hon.), 1994. Bar: Md. 1970, DC 1971, Pa. 1972, W.Va. 1997, U.S. Ct. Appeals (3d, 4th and DC cirs.), U.S. Supreme Ct. Ptnr. Davis & Nace, Washington, 1972-78, Paulson & Nace, Bethesda, Md., 1978—85, 1998—; sr. ptnr. Paulson, Nace & Norwind, Washington, 1986-97. Fellow: Roscoe Pound Found. (trustee); mem.: ATLA (gov. 1976—87, pres. 1993—94), Am. Bd. Profl. Liability Attys., Am. Law Inst., Internat. Acad. Trial Lawyers (bd. govs. 2003—), Trial Lawyers Pub. Justice (found. bd. govs. 2003—), Met. DC Trial Attys. (pres. 1977—78, 1987—88, Atty. of the Yr. 1976), Montgomery County Bar Assn., DC Bar Assn., Nat. Bd. Trial Advocacy Civil Litig. (bd. govs. 2001—, pres.-elect 2005), Am. Inns of Ct., Lambert Soc. Avocations: golf, tennis, reading, racquetball. Home: 6208 Garnett Dr Chevy Chase MD 20815-6618 Office: Paulson & Nace 1615 New Hampshire Ave NW Washington DC 20009-2520 Office Phone: 202-463-1999.

**NACE, MORTON OLIVER, JR.,** human services manager; b. Tampa, Fla., June 30, 1937; s. Morton Oliver and Penelope Adele (Holland) N.; m. Eleanor Hart Moslow, June 27, 1964; children: Morton Oliver III, Jennifer Ann. BS, Boston U., 1964; MS, Syracuse U., 1974. Cert. literacy tutor Laubach Literacy Internat., Syracuse, NY. Exec. dir. Episcopal Diocese Chgo., 1964-70; dir. comm. Laubach Literacy Internat., Syracuse, N.Y., 1970-80; tng. and devel. specialist Rochester (N.Y.) Inst. Tech., 1980-96; adminstrv. asst., cons. City of Rochester, 1997—. Cons. tng. and orgn. devel., Rochester, 1982-98; facilitator retreats/tng. for new parish model The Apostle, 1990—; designer/presenter formats on discernment and daily ministry, 2000; asst. prof. Rochester Inst. Tech., Henrietta, N.Y., 1994; sales and consulting staff Human Resource Svcs., Rochester, 1995-97. Facilitator planning retreat City Coun. of Rochester, 1993; regional planning cons. Mayor-elect City Coun., Rochester, 1997, performance cons. and trainer, 1998—. With USAF, 1957-61. Mem. ASTD (Genesee Valley chpt., conf. presenter 1981-96), Profl. and Orgn. Devel. in Higher Edn. (nat. presenter on faculty/staff devel. 1993-96). Episcopalian. Avocations: photography, piano, physical exercise, history, travel. Home and Office: 2271 Westfall Rd Rochester NY 14618-3126 E-mail: mnance@frontiernet.net.

**NACHMAN, GERALD WEIL,** columnist, critic, writer; b. Oakland, Calif., Jan. 13, 1938; s. Leonard Calvert and Isabel (Weil) N.; m. Mary Campbell McGeachy, Sept. 3, 1966 (div. 1979). Student, Merritt Coll., 1955-57; BA in Journalism, San Jose State U., 1960. TV and humor columnist San Jose (Calif.) Mercury, 1960-63; feature writer N.Y. Post, N.Y.C., 1963-66; drama critic Oakland (Calif.) Tribune, 1966-71; syndicated humor columnist N.Y. Daily News, 1973-79; critic and columnist San Francisco Chronicle, 1979-93. Juror Pulitzer Prize Com. to choose best play, 1991. Author: The Portable Nachman, 1960, Playing House, 1978, Out on a Whim, 1983, The Fragile Bachelor, 1989; contbr. to (book) Snooze, 1986, Raised on Radio, 1998, Seriously Funny: The Rebel Comedians of the 1950's and 1960's, 2003; contbr. articles to newspapers, mag.; author, co-lyricist (revues) Quirks, 1979, Aftershocks, 1992, New Wrinkles, 1999, 2005. Recipient Page One award N.Y. Newspaper Guild, 1965, Deems Taylor award ASCAP, 1989. E-mail: nachnach@comcast.net.

**NACHMAN, MICHAEL WILLIAM,** education educator; b. Riverside, Calif., Feb. 6, 1960; PhD, U. Mich., Ann Arbor, 1990. Rsch. assoc. Cornell U., Ithaca, NY, 1991—95; prof. U. Ariz., Tucson, 1996—. Contbr. articles to profl. jours. Achievements include research in population genetics. Office: U Ariz Dept of Ecology and Evolution Tucson AZ 85721 Office Phone: 520-626-4595.

**NACHMAN, RONALD JAMES,** chemist, researcher; b. Takoma Park, Md., Feb. 1, 1954; s. Joseph Frank and Rosemary (Anderson) N.; m. Lita Rose Wilson, Dec. 18, 1976 (div. 1997). Student, Merritt Coll., 1975; BA in Chemistry, U. Calif., San Diego, 1976; PhD in Organic Chemistry, Stanford U., 1981. Rsch. asst. Scripps Inst. Oceanography, La Jolla, Calif., 1974-76; chemist Western Regional Rsch. Ctr., USDA, Berkeley, Calif., 1981-89, Vet. Toxicology and Entomology Rsch. Lab., College Station, Tex., 1989—. Vis. scientist dept. molecular biology Salk Inst., La Jolla, 1985, Scripps Rsch. Inst., La Jolla, 1988-89. Mem. editl. bd. The Jour. Peptides, guest editor, 2001, 02, 03, 04; mem. organizing com. Ann. Invertebrate Neuropeptide Conf.; contbr. sci. articles to profl. jours. Recipient USDA Cert. of Merit, 1988, 1991, 1994—2001, Arthur S. Flemming award for sci. achievement, 1994. Fellow Internat. Neoropeptide Soc. (bd. dirs. 2000—); mem. AAAS, Internat. Neuropeptide Soc., Am. Chem. Soc., N.Y. Acad. Scis., Sigma Xi. Avocations: travel, photography, jogging, racquetball. Home: 14891 Pollux Dr Willis TX 77318-5079 Office: USDA Southern Plains Agrl Rsch Ctr 2881 F And B Rd College Station TX 77845-4988

**NACHTIGAL, PATRICIA,** lawyer; b. 1946; BA, Montclair State U.; JD, Rutgers U.; LLM, NYU. Corporate atty. Ingersoll-Rand Co., Ltd., Hamilton, Bermuda, 1979—83, dir. taxes and legal, 1983—88, sec., mng. atty. 1988—91, v.p., gen. counsel, 1991—2000, sr. v.p., gen. counsel, 2000—, bd. dirs., 2002—. Gov., trustee Rutgers, State U. N.J., 1996—, chair, 2004—04. Office: Ingersoll-Rand Co Ltd 155 Chestnut Ridge Rd Montvale NJ 07645 Office Phone: 201-573-0123.

**NACHWALTER, MICHAEL,** lawyer; b. N.Y.C., Aug. 31, 1940; s. Samuel J. Nachwalter; m. Irene, Aug. 15, 1965; children: Helynn, Robert. BS, Bucknell U., 1962; MS, L.I. U., 1967; JD cum laude, U. Miami, 1967; LLM, Yale U., 1968. Bar: Fla. 1967, D.C. 1979, U.S. Dist. Ct. (so. dist.) Fla. 1967, U.S. Dist. Ct. (mid. dist.) Fla. 1982, U.S. Ct. Appeals (5th and 11th cirs.) 1967, U.S. Supreme Ct. 1975. Law clk. to judge U.S. Dist. Ct. (so. dist.) Fla.; shareholder Kelly, Black, Black & Kenny; now shareholder Kenny Nachwalter, P.A., Miami. Lectr. Law Sch. U. Miami. Editor-in-chief U. Miami Law Rev., 1966-67. Fellow Am. Coll. Trial Lawyers; mem. ABA, FBA, Am. Bd. Trial Advs., Fla. Bar Assn. (bd. govs. 1982-90), Internat. Soc. Barristers (dir.), Dade County Bar Assn., Jud. Qualifications Commn. (vice chmn. 1995-2000), Iron Arrow, Soc. Wig and Robe, Omicron Delta Kappa, Phi Kappa Phi, Phi Delta Phi. Office: Kenny Nachwalter PA 201 S Biscayne Blvd Ste 1100 Miami FL 33131-4327

**NACKEL, JOHN GEORGE,** medical association administrator; b. Medford, Mass., Nov. 4, 1951; s. Michael and Josephine (Maria) N.; m. Gail Helen Becker, Oct. 30, 1976; children: Melissa Anne, Allison Elizabeth. BS, Tufts U., 1973; MS in Pub. Health and Indsl. Engring., U. Mo., 1975, PhD, 1977. Sr. mgr. Ernst & Young, Chgo., 1977—83; nat. dir. health care cons. Cleve., 1983—87; regional dir. health industry svcs., 1987—91; mng. dir. health care Ernst & Young, Cleve., 1991—93; mng. dir. Health Consulting, LA, 1993—99, New Ventures, 1999—2000; CEO, Sogeti USA, LLC, 2000—01; chmn., CEO, Sértan Corp., Santa Fe Springs, Calif., 2002—03; exec. v.p. US Tech., Beverly Hills, Calif., 2003—05; pres., COO Salick Cardiovascular Ctrs., 2006—. Author: Cost Management for Hospitals, 1987 (Am. Hosp. Assn. book award 1988); mem. editl bd. Jour. Med. Systems, 1983-; contbr. articles to profl. jours Grantee Dept. Health Edn. Welfare, Washington, 1973-76. Fellow Am. Coll. Healthcare Execs., Healthcare Info. and Mgmt. Systems Soc. (articles award); mem. Inst. Indsl. Engrs. (sr.), U. Mo. Health Svcs. Mgmt. Alumni Assn. (pres.), L.A. Country Club, Annandale Golf Club. Republican. Avocations: golf, tennis, squash, paddle, photography. Home: 660 Linda Vista Ave Pasadena CA 91105-1145 Office: 8900 Wilshire Blvd Beverly Hills CA 90211 Office Phone: 213-967-3320. E-mail: jnackel@salickcardiovascularcenters.com.

**NACLERIO, ROBERT MICHAEL,** otolaryngologist, educator; b. N.Y.C., Mar. 30, 1950; s. Albert Paul and Lee Ann (Rabinowitz) N.; m. Sharon Ann Silhan, Mar. 30, 1983; children: Jessica, Daniel. BA, Cornell U., 1972; MD with honors, Baylor U., 1976. Diplomate Am. Bd. Otolaryngology. Intern in surgery Johns Hopkins Hosp., Balt., 1976-77, resident in surgery, 1977-78; resident in otolaryngology Baylor Coll. Medicine, Houston, 1978-80, chief resident in otolaryngology, 1982-83; fellow in clin. immunology divsn. Johns Hopkins U. Sch. Medicine, Balt., 1980-82, asst. prof. medicine and otolaryngology, 1983-87, asst. prof. pediat., 1986-87; dir. divsn. pediat. otolaryngology, 1986-94, assoc. prof. otolargyngology, medicine and pediat., 1987-92, prof. otolaryngology, medicine and pediat., 1992-94; chief of otolaryngology, head and neck surgery U. Chgo., Chgo., 1994—. Cons. Richardson-Vicks Inc., 1986-89, 90, NIH, 1987, Proctor & Gamble, 1987, 94, Sandoz Rsch. Inst., 1988, Schering Rsch., 1988, Wallace Labs., 1989, Joint Rhinologic Conf., 1989, Internat. Congress Rhinology, 1991, Norwich-Eaton Pharm. Inc., 1991-92, Ciba-Geigy Corp., 1991-92, Mktg. Corp. Am., 1993—, Astra, others; mem. med. bd. Children's Ctr., 1991-94, other local comms.; reviewer Am. Jour. Rhinology, others; lectr. in field. Editor: Rhinoconjunctivitis: New Perspectives in Topical Treatment, 1988; asst. editor: Am. Jour. Rhinology, 1986—, Rhinology, 1988—; mem. editl. bd. Otolaryngology-Head and Neck Surgery, 1990-97, Laryngoscope, 1990—, Jour. Allergy and Clin. Immunology, 1992-97; contbr. numerous chpts. to books, papers and abstracts to profl. jours. and procs. Fellow ACS, Am. Acad. Otolaryngology-Head and Neck Surgery (mem. com. 1985-90, 90-92, subcom. 1987-92), Am. Laryngol., Rhinol. and Otol. Soc., Inc.; mem. Am. Acad. Allergy and Immunology (mem. com. 1983-88, 88-89, 88-95, chmn. com. 1990-91, 91—), Jerome Glazer Meml. lectureship), Am. Fedn. Clin. Rsch., Am. Soc. Pediat. Otolaryngology (mem. rsch. com. 1990-94, chmn. subcom. 1990), Soc. Univ. Otolaryngologists-Head and Neck Surgeons, Pan-Am. Assn. Otorhinolaryngology, Internat. Symposium on Infection and Allergy of the Nose (v.p.). Office: U Chgo Sect O-HNS 5841 S Maryland Ave # 1035 Chicago IL 60637-1463 E-mail: rnacleri@surgery.bsd.uchicago.edu.

**NACOL, MAE,** lawyer; b. Beaumont, Tex., June 15, 1944; d. William Samuel and Ethel (Bowman) N.; children: Shawn Alexander Nacol, Catherine Regina Nacol. BA, Rice U., Houston, 1965; postgrad., South Tex. Coll. Law, 1966. Bar: Tex. 1969, U.S. Dist. Ct. (so. dist.) Tex. 1969, U.S. Supreme Ct., U.S. Dist. Ct. (we. dist.) Tex. 1970, U.S. Ct. Appeals (5th cir.). Pvt. practice law, Houston, 1969—; escrow officer Land Am./Commonwealth Land Title Co., Houston; mem. bd. devel. Prosperity Bank, Houston. Author, editor edml. materials on multiple sclerosis, 1981-85. Nat. dir. A.R.M.S. of Am. Ltd., Houston, 1984-85. Recipient Mayor's Recognition award City of Houston, 1972. Mem. Fed. Bar Assn., Houston Bar Assn. (chmn. candidate com. 1970, membership com. 1971, chmn. lawyers referral com. 1972), Assn. Trial Lawyers Am., Tex. Trial Lawyers Assn., Am. Judicature Soc. (sustaining), Houston Fin. Coun. Women, Houston Trial Lawyers Assn. Presbyterian. Office: 600 Jefferson St Ste 750 Houston TX 77002 also: 2600 S Gessner Ste 120 Houston TX 77063 E-mail: wmnacol@sbcglobal.net.

**NADADUR, SRIKANTH S,** molecular biologist; s. Srinivasa Chari and Lakshmi S Nadadur; m. Anuradha Mudipalli, July 13, 1987; 1 child, Saikrishna Srikanth. PhD, S.V. U., Tirupathi, AP, India, 1985; MSc, S. V. U., 1980. Biologist Us Epa, Durham, NC, 2000—, vis. scientist, 1998—2000; cancer rsch. scientist 1 Roswell Pk. Cancer Inst., Buffalo, 1994—98, rsch. assoc., 1992—94. Mem.: Soc. of Toxicology. Achievements include patents for As lead molecular biologist involved in the isolation and partial characterization of a novel cytosolic protein that protects the cell lysis caused by TNF. A patent was issued for this work; research in Isolated a novel cDNA with putative growth suppressor function. Its role in cancer and angiogenesis is currently being investigated; Isolated 27 novel cDNA fragments from human and mouse cells and they are currently part of EST database in GenBank. E-mail: nadadur.srikanth@epa.gov.

**NADAS, JOHN ADALBERT,** psychiatrist, educator; b. Innsbruck, Austria, Mar. 14, 1949; arrived in U.S., 1950; s. Julius Zoltan and Ibolya Erzsebet (Szöllösy) Nadas; m. Gabriella Ilona Ormay, Apr. 11, 1981; children: János, Miklós, István. BA, Case W. Res. U., 1970; MD, Duke U., 1974. Resident in psychiatry U. Chgo., 1974—77; pvt. practice Munster, Ind., 1977—84, Canton, Ohio, 1984—; instr. psychiatry Northeastern Ohio U. Coll. Medicine, Rootstown, 1985—86, asst. prof., 1986; coord. psychiat. edn. Mercy Med. Ctr., Canton, 1985—87, clin. dir. psychiat. svcs., 1990-91, Cons. Crisis Ctr., Canton, 1985—92. Author: Philosophical Basis of Depth Psychotherapy, 1983, Journey Toward Energy, 1995, Transformation, 1999. Trustee Sisters of Charity Found., Canton, 1996—2003. Named NCAA nat. collegiate epee champion, 1970; named to All-Am. Fencing Team, 1969, 1970. Mem.: AMA, Am. Psychiat. Assn., Hungarian Assn. (pres. 2000—03). Roman Catholic. Avocations: basketball, computer programming. Office: 1330 Mercy Dr NW Ste 320 Canton OH 44708-2624 Office Phone: 330-489-1495.

**NADASKAY, RAYMOND,** architect; b. Newark, Aug. 26, 1938; s. Charles and Marie (Roncskevitz) Nadaskay; m. Nancy Searle, 1962; 1 child, Cathy. BArch, Washington U., St. Louis, 1962. Registered architect, NJ, NY, Conn., Vt., Mass., Ill., Ohio, SC, Vt., Del.; registered planner; cert. NCARB. Designer Rotwein and Blake, Architects, Union, N.J., 1962-63, I.M. Pei, N.Y.C., 1963-64; designer, assoc. McDowell Goldstein, Morristown, N.J., 1964-72; pres. Nadaskay Kopelson Architects, P.A., Morristown, 1972—. Chair Mendham (N.J.) Twp. Hist. Preservation Commn.; mem. Mendham Twp. Roadscape Commn., Mendham Twp. Facilities Com., Mendham Twp. Open Space Com., Morristown Streetscape Com.; mem. Blue Ribbon adv. com. Morris County Hist. Preservation Trust Fund; trustee Ralston Cider Mill. Recipient numerous spl. commendations, awards of merit for variety of works. Mem.: NJ Soc. Archs. (conv. chmn. 1985—86, past pres. Newark Suburban chpt. 1984, Herman Litwak award AIA Newark Suburban chpt. 2001), Porsche Club (No. NJ). Avocations: woodworking, sailing, auto rally events, swimming. Office: Nadaskay Kopelson Architects 95 Washington St Morristown NJ 07960-6816 E-mail: nadaskayr@nkarchitects.com.

**NADEAU, BERTIN FELIX,** holding company executive; b. May 26, 1940; s. J.-D. and Irene (Daigle) N.; m. Juliette Angell, July 24, 1971; children: Eric, Shahn, Stephanie. BA, Coll. St-Louis, 1961; grad., Ecole des Hautes Etudes Commerciales de Montreal, 1964; postgrad., Harvard U.; DBA, Ind. U., 1969; LLD (hon.), Queen's U.; D in Fin. (hon.), Moncton U.; DBA (hon.), Sainte-Anne U.; D in Civil Law (hon.), Bishop's U. Chmn., CEO Unigesco Inc., 1982-94, Provigo Inc., 1989-93; chmn., CEO, Gescolynx Inc., Montreal, 1994—. Bd. dirs. Sun Life Fin., Inc., Sun Life Assurance Co. Can., Lafarge N.Am. Inc. Bd. dirs. Montreal Gen. Hosp. Found. Office: GescoLynx Inc 606 Cathcart Ste 1035 Montreal PQ Canada H3B 1K9

**NADEAU, JOSEPH EUGENE,** health care management consultant, information systems consultant; s. Edwin Tustin and Beatrice Margaret (Spiller) N.; m. Mary Lou Prendible, Dec. 2, 1961; children: Laura, Keith, Michael. BS in Math., Boston Coll., 1960. Cert. computer profl. Dir. sys. devel. Mass. Hosp. Assn., Burlington, 1967-72; S.E. regional mgr. Automatic Data Processing, Miami, Fla., 1972-73; S.E. regional mktg. mgr. Space Age Computer Sys., Louisville, 1973-74; prin. COMPUTERx Cons., Miami, 1974—. Asst. scoutmaster South Fla. coun. Boy Scouts Am., 1972-81. 1st lt. U.S. Army, 1960-64, Germany. Mem. Am. Hosp. Assn., Soc. Computer Medicine, Data Processing Mgmt. Assn., Hosp. Mgmt. Sys. Soc., Am. Sys. Mgmt. (pres. 1971-72), Hosp. Fin. Mgmt. Assn. (chmn. data processing com. 1967-84), Am. Arbitration Assn. (arbitrator 1980—). Home: 10260 SW 144th St Miami FL 33176-7034 Office: COMPUTERx Consulting 9719 S Dixie Hwy Ste 1 Miami FL 33156-2834 Business E-Mail: jnadeau@computerx-consulting.com.

**NADEAU, JOSEPH P.,** retired state supreme court justice; b. N.H. AB, Dartmouth Coll.; LLB, Boston U., 1962. Pvt. practice trial atty., 1962—81; justice Durham Dist. Ct., 1968-81; judge NH Superior Ct., 1981-92, chief justice, 1992; assoc. justice NH Supreme Ct., 2000—06. Mem. Jud. Br. Adminstrv. Coun., Supreme Ct. Jud. Ednl. Svcs. Com., Supreme Ct. Accreditation Commn.; pres. Am. Acad. Jud. Edn., 1990-92; participant ct. study program former Soviet Union, facutly jud. edn. program, Latvia, study programs in Russia, Georgia, Armenia; involved in jud. edn. seminars and legis. activities in Albania, Bulgaria, Kazakhstan, Poland; former vice-chair Nat. Conference of State Trial Judges. Mem. Gov.'s Commn. on Domestic Violence. Mem.: ABA (former chair CEELI Com.), N.H. Bar Assn.*

**NADEAU, ROBERT BERTRAND, JR.,** lawyer; b. Miami Beach, Fla., July 15, 1950; s. Robert B. and Ernestine Inez (Nicholson) N. BBA magna cum laude, U. Notre Dame, 1972; JD with honors, U. Fla., 1975. Bar: Fla. 1975, U.S. Dist. Ct. (mid. dist.) Fla. 1976, U.S. Dist. Ct. (so. dist.) Fla. 1982, U.S. Ct. Appeals (11th cir.) 1982. Asst. to pres. The Fla. Bar, Tampa, 1975-76; ptnr. Akerman, Senterfitt & Eidson, P.A., Orlando, Fla., 1976—. Arbitrator Am. Arbitration Assn., Orlando, 1987—. Mem. ABA, The Fla. Bar (chmn. student edn. and admission to bar com., vice chmn. 9th cir. grievance com.), Notre Dame Club Greater Orlando (pres. 1978-80). Avocations: golf, running. Office: Akerman Senterfitt PO Box 231 Orlando FL 32802 Office Phone: 407-423-4000. Business E-Mail: robert.nadeau@akerman.com.

**NADEL, ELLIOTT,** investment company executive; b. N.Y.C., Nov. 23, 1945; s. Archie and Faye (Braverman) N.; children: Lindsey, Amanda. BBA, Baruch Coll., 1969. MBA, 1971. Portfolio mgr. SwissRe Advisors, N.Y.C., 1973-74; v.p., stockbroker E. F. Hutton, N.Y.C., 1975-84, Shearson Lehman Bros., N.Y.C., 1984-85, Oppenheimer & Co., N.Y.C., 1985, Rooney Pace Inc., N.Y.C., 1986-87, Philips Appel & Walden, N.Y.C., 1987-88; sr. v.p. investments Moore, Schley & Cameron, N.Y.C., 1988-90, Prudential-Securities, N.Y.C., 1990-94; sr. v.p. Gilford Securities, N.Y.C., 1994-96, SFY Investments, 1996—97, Westrock Advisor, 1997—99, Tarpon Scurry Investments, 1999—2000, Chgo. Investments Group, 2001, EN Investments, 2001—; prin. Hedge Fund. With U.S. Army, 1969-74. Jewish. Avocations: jogging, reading, cars, golf, travel. E-mail: mrch1123@aol.com.

**NADEL, MONROE STANLEY,** retired architect, landscape architect; b. The Bronx, N.Y., July 24, 1922; s. Joseph Paurice Nadel and Rae Ruth (Gross); m. Evelyn Feldman, Sept. 6, 1953; children: Jonathan Oren, Jeremy Adam. Journeyman shipfitter, N.Y. Naval Shipyard Sch., 1943; BS in Social Sci., CCNY, 1949; BArch, Columbia U., 1956, MArch, 1975. Registered architect, N.Y.; registered landscape architect, N.Y. Shipfitter, estimator N.Y. Naval Shipyard, Bklyn., 1940—46; estimator M.W. Kellogg Co. Oil Refinery Engrs., N.Y.C., 1946—49, Nat. Supply Export Corp., Oil Well Supplies, N.Y.C., 1949—51; draftsman Seelye, Stevenson, Value & Knecht, Engrs., N.Y.C., 1951—52, Coffin & Coffin, Architects, N.Y.C., 1953, Alfred Hopkins & Assocs., N.Y.C., 1953-55; designer, draftsman York & Sawyer Architects, N.Y.C., 1955-60; architect Associated Archs. & Engrs., N.Y.C., 1960; architect, site planner Viola, Bernhard and Philips, Architects and Engrs., N.Y.C., 1960-65; architect Divsn. of Sch. Bldgs./N.Y. Bd. Edn. Bur. of Design, Long Island City, N.Y.C., N.Y., 1965-69, chief archtl. design sect., sr. arch. to adminstrv. arch., 1969-76, chief archtl. sect., contracts sect., cons. rev. sect., 1976-92; ret., 1992. Mem. AIA (emeritus, corp. mem.), Am. Soc. Landscape Architects (emeritus). Avocations: genealogy, stamp collecting/philately, gardening, yoga exercises. Home (Winter): 25 Plaza St W Apt 2D Brooklyn NY 11217 Home (Summer): PO Box 2183 Bridgehampton NY 11932-2183

**NADEL, NORMAN ALLEN,** civil engineer; b. NYC, Apr. 10, 1927; s. Louis and Bertha (Julius) N.; m. Cynthia Esther Jereski, July 6, 1952; children: Nancy Sarah Frank, Lawrence Bruce. B.C.E., CCNY, 1949; postgrad., Columbia U., 1949-50. Registered profl. engr., N.Y., Conn. Engr. Arthur A. Johnson Corp., N.Y.C., 1950-53; engr. Slattery Contracting Corp., N.Y.C., 1953-56; mgr., estimator Hartsdale Constrn. Corp., Hartsdale, NY, 1956-59; engr. MacLean Grove & Co., Inc., Greenwich, Conn., 1959-63, project mgr., v.p., 1966-70, pres., 1970-94; chmn. Nadel Assocs., Inc., Brewster, NY, 1988—. Cons. tunnel and underground constrn.; mem. com. on tunneling Transp. Rsch. Bd., Washington, 1974-75; mem. U.S. Nat. Com. on Tunneling Tech., Washington, 1976-82, chmn., 1980-81; chmn. adv. com. Superconducting Super Collider Underground Tech., 1992-94. Trustee Tunnel Workers Welfare Fund, N.Y.C., 1976-88; mem. adv. bd. CCNY Engring. Sch., 1992—. With USNR, 1945-46 Named Heavy Constrn. Man of Yr., United Jewish Appeal, 1984; Benjamin Wright award Conn. Soc. Civil Engrs., 1984, Townsend Harris medal City Coll. of N.Y. Alumni Assn., 1987. Fellow ASCE (Constrn. Mgmt. award 1986); mem. NAE, Conn. Acad. Sci. and Engring., The Moles (pres. 1982-83, Outstanding Achievement in Constrn. award 1985), Am. Arbitration Assn., Tau Beta Pi, Chi Epsilon. Office: Nadel Assocs Inc 420 Clock Tower Commons Brewster NY 10509-4060 Office Phone: 845-279-5516.

**NADELLA, SATYA,** information technology executive; b. 1967; MS in Computer Sci., U. Wis.; MBA, U. Chgo. Software devel. engr. Sun Microsystems Inc.; from group product mgr. to leader bCentral mktg. & bus. devel. Microsoft, Redmond, Wash., leader bCentral mktg. & bus. devel., 1999—2002, corp. v.p. Microsoft Bus. Solutions, 2002—. Office: One Microsoft Way Redmond WA 98052-6399*

**NADELMAN, MARTIN HERSHEL,** college president; s. Edward and Frances Nadelman; m. Susan Lynn Cook, June 19, 1971. BS, Rensselaer Poly. Inst., 1971; MEd, U. Vt., 1972; EdD, U. Md., 1987. Dean of men Atlantic Christian Coll., Wilson, NC, 1972—76; dean of students Wor-Wic Tech CC, Salisbury, Md., 1976—91, acting pres., 1986—87; pres. Martin CC, Williamston, NC, 1991—99, Alamance CC, Graham, NC, 1999—. Mem. Cmty. Coun., Burlington, NC; pres. Martin County United Way, Williamston, 1996—98; mem. State Employees' Credit Union, Burlington, 2005—06, Women's Resource Ctr., Burlington, 2001—04; bd. dirs. United Way of Alamance County, Burlington, 2000—02, Alamance Partnership for Children, Burlington, 1999—. Named Nat. Adminstr. of the Yr., Nat. Assn. Devel. Educators, 2005. Mem.: NC Assn. Devel. Educators (exec. com. 2002—), State Adminstr. of Yr. 2004), NC Assn. C.C. Presidents (assoc.; exec com. 1998—99).

**NADELSON, CAROL COOPERMAN,** psychiatrist, educator; b. Bklyn., Oct. 13, 1936; m. Theodore Nadelson, July 16, 1965; children: Robert, Jennifer. BA magna cum laude, Bklyn. Coll., 1957; MD with honors, U. Rochester, N.Y., 1961, Dir. med student edn. Beth Israel Hosp., Boston, 1974-79, psychiatrist, 1977; assoc. prof. psychiatry Harvard U. Med. Sch., Boston, 1976-79; rsch. scholar Radcliffe Coll., Cambridge, Mass., 1979-80; prof. psychiatry Tufts Med. Sch., Boston, 1979-95; vice-chmn., dir. tng. and edn. dept. psychiatry Tufts-New Eng. Med. Ctr., Boston, 1979-93; clin. prof. psychiatry Harvard Med. Sch., Boston, 1995—; psychiatrist dept. medicine, divsn. psychiatry Brigham and Women's Hosp., Boston, 1998, dir., ptnr. office for women's careers, 1998. Cons. Peace Corps, 2000. Editor: The Woman Patient, Vols. 1, 2 and 3, 1978, 82; Treatment Interventions in Human Sexuality, 1983; Marriage and Divorce: A Contemporary Perspective, 1984, Women Physicians in Leadership Roles, 1986, Training Psychiatrists for the '90s, 1987, Treating Chronically Mentally Ill Women, 1988, Family Violence, 1988, Women and Men: New Perspectives on Gender Differences, 1990, International Review of Psychiatry Vols. 1 & 2, 1993, 96, Major Psychiatric Disorders, 1982, The Challenge of Change: Perspectives on Family, Work and Education, 1983; editor-in-chief Am. Psychiatric Press, Inc., 1986—, pres., CEO, 1995—; contbr. over 217 articles to profl. jours. Trustee Menninger Found., 1988—. Recipient Gold Medal award Mt. Airy Psychiat. Ctr., 1981, award Case Western Res. U., 1983, Elizabeth Blackwell award Am. Med. Women's Assn., 1985, Women in Medicine Leadership Devel. award Am. Assn. Med. Colls., 1999, Alexandra Symonds award 2002; Picker Found. grant, 1982-83. Fellow: Am. Psychiat. Assn. (pres. 1985—86, Seymour D. Vestermark award 1992, Disting. Svc. award 1995), Ctr. Advanced Study Behaivoal Scos.; mem.: AMA (impaired physicians com. 1984, Sidney Cohen award 1988), Group for Advancement of Psychiatry (bd. dirs. 1984), Am. Coll. Psychiatrists (bd. regents 1991—94, Disting. Svc. award 1989), Phi Beta Kappa, Alpha Omega Alpha. Avocation: travel. Office: Brigham and Women's Hosp 75 Francis St PB502 Boston MA 02119 Home: 50 Longwood Ave 1114 Brookline MA 02446 Business E-Mail: carol_nadelson@hms.harvard.edu.

**NADER, LAURA,** anthropologist, educator; b. Winsted, Conn., Sept. 30, 1930; m. Norman Milleron, Sept. 1, 1962; 3 children Ba, Wells Coll., 1952; PhD, Radcliffe Coll., 1961. Faculty mem. U. Calif., Berkeley, 1960—, prof. anthropology; vis. prof. Yale Law Sch., New Haven, fall 1971; Henry R. Luce prof. Sch. Law Harvard Wellesley Coll., Mass., 1983-84; Henry R. Luce prof.

Sch. Law Stanford U. Law Sch., 1987-89. Field work in Mex., Lebanon, Morocco and US; mem. adv. com. NSF, 1971-75; mem. cultural anthropology com. NIMH, 1968—, chmn. to 1971, chmn. social scis. rsch. tng. rev. com., 1976-78; mem. NAS-NRC assembly behavioral and social scis., 1969-71, 73-75, 75—; mem. com. Nuclear and Alternative Energy Forms, NAS, 1976-80. Editor: Law in Culture and Society, 1969, The Disputing Process, 1978, No Access to Law-Alternatives to the American Judicial System, 1980, Harmony Ideology, 1990, Naked Science, 1996, The Life of the Law, 2000; contbr. articles to profl. jours.; author ednl. films, mem. editl. com. Law and Soc. Rev., 1967—. Mem. Calif. Coun. for the Humanities, 1975—79, Carnegie Coun. on Children, 1972—77; active Coun. Librs. at Libr. of Congress, Washington, 1988—. Radcliffe Coll. grantee, 1954-59; Thaw fellow Harvard U., 1955-56, 58-59; Peabody Mus. grantee, 1954-59; Am. Philos. Assn. grantee, 1955; Mexican Govt. grantee, 1957-58; Milton Fund grantee, 1959-60, Wellness Found. grantee, 1993-96; fellow Ctr. Advanced Study in Behavioral Scis., Stanford, Calif., 1963-64; NSF grantee, 1966-68; Wenner Gren Found. grantee, 1964, 66, 73; Carnegie Corp. grantee, 1975; Woodrow Wilson fellow, 1979-80; Wells Coll. Alumnae award, 1980; Radcliffe Coll. Alumnae award, 1984. Mem.: AAAS, Soc. Women Geographers (Outstanding Achievement award 1990), Am. Acad. Arts and Scis., Ctr. for Study of Responsive Law (trustee 1968—), Law and Soc. Assn. (trustee 1967—72), Harry Kalven prize 1995), Social Sci. Rsch. Coun., Am. Anthrop. Assn. (planning and devel. com. 1968—71, 1975—76), Am. Acad. Arts and Scis. Office: U Calif Dept Anthropology 313 Kroeber Hl Berkeley CA 94720-0001 Office Phone: 510-643-1218.

**NADER, RALPH,** advocate, lawyer, writer; b. Winsted, Conn., Feb. 27, 1934; s. Nadra and Rose (Bouziane) N. AB magna cum laude, Princeton U., 1955; LLB with distinction, Harvard U., 1958. Bar. Conn. 1958, Mass. 1959, U.S. Supreme Ct. 1959. Practiced law in Hartford, Conn., 1959—; lectr. history & govt. U. Hartford, 1961-63; founder Essential Info., 1982. Founder, Ctr. for Responsive Law, Essential Info., The Multinational Monitor Mag., Pub. Interest Research Group, Ctr. for Auto Safety, Pub. Citizen, Clean Water Action Project, Disability Rights Ctr., Pension Rights Ctr., Project for Corporate Responsibility; co-founder Princeton Project 55, 1989; lectr. to colls. and univs.; lectr. Princeton U., 1967-68 Author: Unsafe at Any Speed, 1965, Working on the System: A Manual for Citizen's Access to Federal Agencies, 1972, Action for a Change, 1972, You and Your Pension, 1973, Taming the Giant Corporation, 1976, The Lemon Book, 1980, The Big Boys, 1986, Winning The Insurance Game, 1990, No Contest: Corporate Lawyers and the Perversion of Justice in America, 1996, The Ralph Nader Reader, 2000, Crashing the Party: Taking on the Corporate Government in an Age of Surrender, 2002, In Pursuit of Justice: Collected Writing, 2000-2003, 2004, The Good Fight: Declare Your Independence and Close the Democracy Gap, 2004, Civic Arousal, 2004; co-author:(with John Abbots) Menace of Atomic Energy, 1979, (with Wesley J. Smith) Collision Course:The Truth About Airline Safety, 1993; editor: Whistle Blowing: The Report on the Conference on Professional Responsibility, 1972, The Consumer and Corporate Accountability, 1973; co-editor: Corporate Power in America, 1973, Verdicts on Lawyers, 1976, Who's Poisoning America, 1981; contbg. editor: Ladies Home Jour., 1973—. Presdl. candidate, 1996, 2000, 2004; With U.S. Army, 1959. Recipient Nieman Fellows award, 1965-66; named One of 10 Outstanding Young Men of Year U.S. Jr. C. of C., 1967 Mem. ABA, AAAS, Phi Beta Kappa. Green Party. Address: Ctr for Study of Responsive Law PO Box 19367 Washington DC 20036-9367

**NADER, ROBERT ALEXANDER,** judge, lawyer; b. Warren, Ohio, Mar. 31, 1928; s. Nassef J. and Emily (Nader) N.; m. Nancy M. Veauthier. BA, Western Res. U., 1950, LL.B., 1953. Bar: Ohio 1953. Ptnr. Paul G. Nader, Warren, 1953-83. Pres. Warren City Police and Fire Pension Bds., 1960-66; trustee Office Econ. Opportunity, 1970-72; mem. Warren City Coun., 1960-66, pres. pro tem, 1964-66; mem. Ohio Ho. of Reps., 1971-83, chmn. reference com., 1977-81, chmn. judiciary com., 1981-83; presiding judge Trumbull County Ct. Common Pleas, 1983-91; judge Ohio 11th Dist. Ct. Appeals, 1991-2003; trustee Family Svc. Assn., 1959-65. With AUS, 1946-48. Recipient Outstanding Young Man of Yr. award, 1964, award Am. Arbitration Assn., 1965, Community Action award Warren Area Bd. Realtors, 1967, Outstanding Svc. award Kent State U., Trumbull campus. 1978, Outstanding Svc. award Children's Rehab. Ctr., 1980; named to Warren H.S. Disting. Alumni Hall of Fame, 1993, Sports Hall of Fame, 2003. Mem. Ohio State Bar Assn., Trumbull County Bar Assn. (past pres., Pres.'s award for disting. svc. 2003), Ct. Appeals Judges Assn. (chmn. legis. com. 1995-98), Trumbull County Law Libr. Assn. (trustee 1958-72), Trumbull New Theatre (past pres.), KC, Elks, Lambda Chi Alpha. Roman Catholic. Home: 798 Wildwood Dr NE Warren OH 44483-4458 Office: 11th Dist Ct # Appeals 111 High St NE Warren OH 44481 *My parents provided me with a strong moral background and the inspiration to improve. I will never feel that I have achieved success and thus may continue to improve.*

**NADIG, GERALD GEORGE,** retired manufacturing executive; b. Astoria, N.Y., May 9, 1945; s. Charles Edwin and Louise (Hahn) N.; m. Nancy Hanford Stewart, June 20, 1970; children: Sara Hanford, Jennifer Stewart. AB cum laude, Harvard Coll., 1967, MBA, 1974. Various manfacturing positions, 1974—85; dir. mfg. Toyoda Machinery USA, Arlington Heights, Ill., 1985-87, v.p., gen. mgr., 1987-88; v.p., gen. mgr. Littell div. Allied Products Corp., Chgo., 1988-89; exec. v.p. pre finish metals Material Scis. Corp., 1989-90; pres. Pre Finish Metals Materials Scis. Corp., 1990-91; pres., chief oper. officer Material Scis. Corp., Chgo., 1991-96, pres., CEO, 1997—2003, chmn. bd. dirs., 1998—2003; bd. dirs. Tokheim Corp., 2000—03; ret. Mem. adv. bd. Masters in Mgmt. Program Northwestern U. Trustee Village of Lake Barrington, 1989-91. With U.S. Army, 1966-70. Mem. Soc. Mfg. Engrs. (sr.), Nat. Assn. Corp. Dirs. (bd. dirs. Chgo. chpt. 2002—), Barrington Area Cmty. Found. (bd. dirs.) Avocations: golf, tennis, game theory. Home: 24354 N Grandview Dr Barrington IL 60010-6218 Office Phone: 847-381-3161. Personal E mail: gerrynadig@aol.com.

**NADIRI, M. ISHAQ,** economics professor, researcher, consultant; b. Kabul, Afghanistan, Oct. 16, 1936; s. M. Alam and Gul-Nasa N.; m. Tahira Homayun, Sept. 9, 1978; children: Youssof, Khalid. BS with highest distinction, U. Nebr., 1958; MA, U. Calif.-Berkeley, 1960, PhD, 1965; postgrad., Yale U., 1962-63. Asst. prof. Northwestern U., Evanston, Ill., 1964-66, U. Chgo. Bus. Sch., 1966-67; research fellow Nat. Bur. Econ. Research, N.Y.C., 1968-70, research assoc., 1969—; full prof. econs. NYU, 1970—, Jay Gould prof. econs., 1975—, chmn. dept. econs., 1972-78; Disting. vis. prof. Am. U. Cairo, 1993. Cons. in field; participant seminars NSF Ctr. Strategic Studies, UN Assn.; sr. econ. adviser to Afghanistan Interim Govt., Pres. Hamid Karzai and govt. Islamic Rep. Afghanistan; CEO, Global Partnership for Afghanistan; mem. Pvt. Sector Devel. Task Force for Afghanistan; mem. Aid Coord. Com. of Afghanistan, Afghanistan-Am. Found. Author: books, including A Disequilibrium Model of Demand for Factors of Production, 1974; research, numerous publs. in field; editor books including The Importance of Technology and the Permanence of Structure in Industrial Growth, 1978, Commodity Markets and Latin American Development: A Modeling Approach, 1980; editorial bd.: Annals of Econs. and Social Measurement. Mem. Com. to Upgrade Central Park, N.Y.C.; mem. Com. to Help Afghan Refugees in the U.N. Miller fellow, 1958-59; U. Calif. fellow, 1959-60; Earnhart fellow, 1962-63, 63-64; grantee NSF, Ford Found., IBM Corp., AT&T Mem. Am. Econs. Assn., Econometrica Soc., Univs.-Nat. Bur. Econ. Research, Internat. Assn. Research in Income and Wealth; mem. AAAS, Am. Statis. Assn., Council Fgn. Relations, Phi Beta Kappa, Pi Sigma Alpha, Beta Gamma Sigma Office: NYU Dept Econs 269 Mercer St Fl 7 New York NY 10003-6633 Office Phone: 212-998-8969. Business E-Mail: min1@nyu.edu.

**NADJI, TAOUFIK,** physics professor, mathematician; BS in Theoretical Physics, U. Houari Boumedien, Algiers, Algeria, 1982; MS, Ctrl. Mich. U., Mt. Pleasant, Mich., 1985. Secondary tchg. cert. endorsement in physics Cen. Mich. U. Tchg. asst. Cen. Mich. U., 1985—86, Mich. State U., 1986—88; adj. faculty Saginaw Valley State U., Mid Mich. C.C., 1988—92; instr. physics and math. Interlochen Arts Acad., Mich., 1992—. Instr. physics and math.

Northwestern Mich. Coll., Traverse City, Mich., 1994—. Mem.: Am. Assn. Physics Tchrs. Muslim. Avocations: soccer, swimming, chess. Office: Interlochen Arts Academy PO Box 199 Interlochen MI 49643

**NADKARNI, SUCHETA,** finance educator; d. Subhash and Mrudvla Nadkarni. PhD, U. of Kans., 2000. Asst. prof. U. Nebr., Lincoln, 2000—06, assoc. prof., 2006—. Mem., editl. bd. Jour. of Mgmt. Inquiry, Jour. of Leadership and Orgnl. Studies, 2005—; editor, managerial and orgnl. cognition newsletter Acad. of Mgmt. Recipient Best Reviewer award, Managerial and Orgnl. Cognition Divsn., Acad. of Mgmt., 2003. Mem.: Acad. of Internat. Bus., Strategic Mgmt. Soc., Acad. of Mgmt. Avocations: travel, theatre, music. Office: University of Nebraska-Lincoln 12 th st and R St Lincoln NE 68512-0491 Office Phone: 402-472-8399.

**NADKARNI, VINAY,** pediatrician, researcher; m. Ellen Sue Deutsch, Oct. 22, 1984; children: Lauren, Lindsay, Andrew. BS, Duke U., Durham, N.C., 1979; MS, Georgetown U., Washington, 1980; MD, U. Md., Balt., 1984. Cert. pediatrics Am. Bd. Pediat., 1988, pediat. critical care medicine Am. Bd. Pediat., 1990. Dir. pediatric critical care fellowships Children's Hosp. Phila., 2001—. Sci. adv. bd. Am. Heart Assn., Dallas, 1999—. Bd. dir. Operation Smile, Norfolk, Va., 1990—. Grantee, Can. Am. Resuscitation Consortium NIH and CIHR, 2002—06. Fellow: Am. Acad. Pediat. (assoc.) Achievements include development of first national registry of CPR. Office: Children's Hosp Phila 34th St and Civic Ctr Blvd Philadelphia PA 19104 Office Phone: 215-590-7430. Office Fax: 215-590-4327.

**NADLER, GERALD,** management consultant, educator; b. Cin., Mar. 12, 1924; s. Samuel and Minnie (Krumbein) N.; m. Elaine Muriel Dubin, June 22, 1947; children: Burton Alan, Janice Susan, Robert Daniel. Student, U. Cin., 1942-43; BSME, Purdue U., 1945, MS in Indsl. Engring, 1946, PhD, 1949. Instr. Purdue U., 1948-49; asst. prof. indsl. engring. Washington U., St. Louis, 1949-52, assoc. prof., 1952-55, prof., head dept. indsl. engring., 1955-64; prof. U. Wis., Madison, 1964-83, chmn. dept. indsl. engring., 1964-67, 71-75; prof., chmn. dept. indsl. and sys. engring. U. So. Calif., L.A., 1983-93, IBM chair engring. mgmt., 1986-93, IBM chair emeritus. prof. emeritus, 1993—; v.p. Artcraft Mfg. Co., St. Louis, 1956-57; dir. Intertherm Inc., St. Louis, 1969-85. Pres. Ctr. for Breakthrough Thinking Inc., L.A., 1989—; vis. prof. U. Birmingham, Eng., 1959, Waseda U., Tokyo, 1963-64, Ind. U., 1964, U. Louvain, Belgium, 1975, Technion-Israel Inst. Tech., Haifa, 1975-76; spkr. in field. Author: The Planning and Design Approach, 1981; (with S. Hibino) Breakthrough Thinking, 1990, 2d edit., 1994, Creative Solution Finding, 1995; (with G. Hoffherr, J. Moran) Breakthrough Thinking in Total Quality Management, 1994, (with W. Chandon) Ask the Right Questions, 2003, Smart Questions, 2004; contbr. articles to profl. jours.; reviewer books, papers, proposals. Mem. Ladue Bd. Edn., St. Louis County, 1960-63, L.A. County Regional Med. Program, 1966-69; bd. dirs. USC Credit Union, 1994—. Served with USN, 1943-45. Gilbreth medal Soc. Advancement Mgmt., 1961, Editl. award Hosp. Mgmt. Mag., 1966, Disting. Engring. Alumnus award Purdue U., 1975, Outstanding Indsl. Engr. award, 1997; Book of Yr. award Inst. Indsl. Engrs., 1983, Frank and Lillian Gilbreth award, 1992; Phi Kappa Phi Faculty Recognition award U. So. Calif., 1990, Engring. Disting. Svc. award U. Wis. Madison, 2000. Fellow AAAS, Inst. Indsl. Engrs. (pres. 1989-90), Inst. Operations Rsch. and Mgmt. Scis., Inst. for Advancement Engrs., Am. Soc. Engring. Edn.; mem. NAE, Japan Work Design Soc. (hon. adv. 1968—), World Future Soc., Acad. of Mgmt., Engring. Mgmt. Soc., Sigma Xi, Alpha Pi Mu (nat. officer), Pi Tau Sigma, Omega Rho, Tau Beta Pi. Office: Univ Park GER 240 Dept Of I&se Los Angeles CA 90089-0193 Office Phone: 213-740-6415. Personal E-mail: gnadler@breakthroughthinking.com Business E-Mail: nadler@usc.edu.

**NADLER, HENRY LOUIS,** pediatrician, educator, geneticist; b. NYC, Apr. 15, 1936; s. Herbert and Mary (Kartiganer) N.; m. Benita Weinhard, June 16, 1957; children: Karen, Gary, Debra, Amy. AB, Colgate U., 1957; MD, Northwestern U., 1961; MS, U. Wis., 1965. Diplomate Am. Bd. Pediatrics, Am. Bd. Med. Genetics. Intern NYU Med. Ctr., 1961-62, sr. resident pediatrics, 1962-63, chief resident, 1963-64; teaching asst. NYU Sch. Medicine, 1962-63, clin. instr., 1963-64, U. Wis. Sch. Medicine, 1964-65; practice medicine specializing in pediatrics Chgo., 1965—; fellow Children's Meml. Hosp. dept. pediatrics Northwestern U., 1964-65; assoc. in pediatrics Northwestern U. Med. Sch., 1965-66, asst. prof., 1967-68, assoc. prof., 1968-70, prof., 1970-81, chmn. dept. pediatrics, 1970-81; prof. Northwestern U. Med. Sch. (Grad. Sch.), 1971-80; mem. staff Children's Meml. Hosp., 1965-81, head div. genetics, 1969-81, chief of staff, 1970-81; dean, prof. pediatrics, ob-gyn Wayne State U. Med. Sch., Detroit, 1981-88; prof. U. Chgo., 1988-89, U. Ill., 1989—; pres. Michael Reese Hosp. and Med. Ctr., Chgo., 1988-91; market med. dir. Aetna Health Plans, Phoenix, 1993-94, mktg. v.p., CEO, 1994-95; v.p. managed care/physician integration, med. dir. Am. Healthcare Sys., San Diego, 1995. Mem. vis. staff, div. medicine Northwestern Meml. Hosp., 1972-81; staff Children's Hosp. of Mich., 1981-88. Mem. editl. bd. Comprehensive Therapy, 1973-84, Am. Jour. Human Genetics, 1979-83, Pediatrics in Rev., 1980-83, Am. Jour. Diseases of Children, 1983-91; contbr. articles to profl. jours. Recipient E. Mead Johnson award for pediatric rsch., 1973, Meyer O. Cantor award for Disting. Svc. Internat. Coll. Surgeons, 1987; Irene Heinz Given and John La Porte Given rsch. prof. pediatrics, 1970-81. Fellow Am. Acad. Pediatrics; mem. Am. Soc. for Clin. Investigation, Am. Soc. Human Genetics, Am. Pediatric Soc., Soc. for Pediatric Rsch., Midwest Soc. for Pediatric Rsch., Pan Am. Med. Assn., Alpha Omega Alpha. Home and Office: 17720 Camino de La Mitra PO Box 3665 Rancho Santa Fe CA 92067-3665 Personal E-mail: hlnadler@aol.com

**NADLER, JERROLD LEWIS,** congressman, lawyer; b. Bklyn., June 13, 1947; m. Joyce L. Miller, 1976; 1 child, Michael. AB in Govt., Columbia U., 1969, JD, Fordham U. Sch. Law, 1978. Mem. Cmty. Planning Bd. 7, Manhattan, 1967-71; Dem. leader 67th Assembly Dist. Part C, 1969-71; exec. dir. Cmty. Free Dem., 1972; Dem. dist. leader 69th Assembly Dist. Part A, 1973-77; law clk. Morgan, Finnegan, Pine, Foley and Lee, 1976; mem. NY State Assembly from 69th dist., 1977-82, NY State Assembly from 67th dist., 1983-92, US Congress from 17th NY dist., 1992, US Congress from 8th NY Dist., 1993—, mem. subcommittees on surface transp., water resources, environment, 1993—94, ranking minority mem. subcommittee on comml./adminstrv. law, 1997—2000, mem. subcommittee on constrn., 1997—, mem. judiciary com., mem. transp. com., asst. whip, 2003—. Chmn. Assembly Com. on Corps, Authorities and Commn., 1991-92, Assembly Consumer Affairs and Protection Com., 1987-90, Assembly Com. on Ethics and Guidance, 1985-86, Assembly Subcom. on Mass Transit and Rail Freight, 1979-86, mem. Assembly Com. on Judiciary, Gov. Ops., Legis. Tax Study Commn.; mem. Assembly Com. Ways and Means, Housing, Real Property Tax, Health, Election Law, Ins. Founder, chmn. West Side Peace Com. 1969-71; pres. Zionist Orgn. Am. dist. 7A; active Common Cause, Met. Coun. on Housing, West Side Tenants Union; mem. nat. governing coun. Am. Jewish Congress. Recipient hon. recognition award NY State Nurses Assn., 1982, Disting. Svc. award Coalition on Domestic Violence, 1989, Legislator of Yr. award Internat. Assn. Firefighters, 2003; Pulitzer scholar Columbia U. Mem. NOW (Assembly Mem. of Yr. from NY chpt, 1980), NAACP, NY Bar Assn., NY Civil Liberties Union (honor roll), Citizens Union, League Conservation Voters, New Dem. Coalition, Ams. for Dem. Action (bd. dirs., nat. v.p.). Democrat. Office: US Ho Reps 2334 Rayburn Ho Office Bldgb Washington DC 20515-3208 Office Phone: 202-225-5635.*

**NADLER, JUDITH,** school librarian; BA in English and Romance Studies, U. Jerusalem; MLS, Israel Grad. Sch. With U. Chgo. Libr., from cataloger to dir., dir., 2004—. Office: Joseph Regenstein Libr U Chgo 1100 E 57 St Chicago IL 60637 Office Phone: 773-702-8743. Office Fax: 773-702-6623. E-mail: judi@uchicago.edu.

**NADLER, NONA JEAN,** social worker; b. Greensboro, N.C., Feb. 13, 1945; d. Quincy and Beulah (Snipes) Campbell; m. David Henegan, Feb. 7, 1963 (div. Sept. 1992); children: Shrella Henegan, David Jr. Henegan, Sheila Henegan, Tyrone Henegan, Sherry Henegan; m. Jerold Nadler, Nov. 22, 1992.

AA, Boricua Coll., Bklyn., 1988; BS, Boricua Coll., 1990. Registered dental technician N.Y., 1996, cert. arrhythmia technologist N.Y., 1989. Legal dept. adminstrv. asst. N.Y. Property Underwriting Inc., N.Y.C., 1971—86; child life specialist Interfaith Hosp., Bklyn., 1990—92; nursery dir. Rose Kennedy Family Ctr., Bklyn., 1992—93; borough dir. MHRA, Bklyn., 1993—95; bd. adminstr. Good Samaritan Devel. Ctr., Bklyn., 1995—99; client svcs. adminstr. Toddlers & Infant Program, Spl. Edn., Inc., Bklyn., 1999—. Child care cons., Bklyn., 1995—; Reiki cons. Metamorphiss Healing Ctr., Bklyn., 1996—; infancy parenting cons. Bank St. Coll., N.Y.C., 1991. Mem. N.Y.C. Children's Coun., Bklyn., 1995—. Named Bronze Leader, DAV, 2002—03, Silver Leader, 2003. Mem.: Nat. Geog. Soc., N.Y. Acad. Scis. Avocations: sponge art painting, writing, new age crafts, collecting DVD movies. Office: Toddlers & Infants Program Ste 5 401 Bloomingdale Rd Staten Island NY 10309

**NADLER, SIGMOND HAROLD,** surgeon; b. Bklyn., May 16, 1932; s. Morris and Rose (Levine) N.; m. Beverly Melcher, June 20, 1954; children: Geoffrey, Shail, Tamara, Kimberly. BA, State U. Iowa, 1955, MD, 1957. Intern Menorah Med. Ctr., Kansas City, Mo., 1957-58, resident in surgery, 1958-61, Roswell Park Meml. Inst., 1961-63, mem. staff, 1962-68, clin. coord. Ea. region clin. drug evaluation program, 1966-68, project dir. nat. adj. studies, 1966-68, assoc. chief cancer rsch. surgery, 1966-68; assoc. prof. surgery Jefferson Med. Coll., Phila., 1968-70; also dir. clin. cancer tng., asst. clin. prof. surgery SUNY, Buffalo, 1970-94, prof. emeritus, 1994—. Mem. Am. Soc. Clin. Oncology. Achievements include research in human tumor immunochemistry.

**NADLER-HURVICH, HEDDA CAROL,** public relations executive; b. Bronx, N.Y., June 15, 1944; d. Julius Louis and Julia Cohen; m. David George Nadler, Oct. 3, 1965 (div. 1979); 1 child, Laura Lee Nadler; m. Burton Earl Hurvich, Dec. 8, 1984. BBA, Baruch Coll., 1965. V.p., sec. Irving L. Straus Assocs., Inc., N.Y.C., 1965-80; pres. Mount & Nadler Inc., N.Y.C., 1999—. Avocations: aerobics, yoga. Office: Mount & Nadler 425 Madison Ave New York NY 10017-1110 Office Phone: 212-759-4440. E-mail: Hedda615@aol.com.

**NADOLSKI, DORA J.,** social sciences educator, researcher; d. Harold V. and Dora H. Glidewell; m. Thomas P. Nadolski (div.); 1 child, Christopher A. MA in Social Sci., Antioch U., Yellow Springs, OH, 1965; PhD in polit. social sci., U. Mo., Kansas City, 2000. Assoc. prof. polit. sci. Northwest Nazarene Coll., Nampa, Idaho, 1966—68; lectr. Rockhurst U., Kansas City, 1995—97; prof., lectr. Park U., Kansas City, 1997—. Instr. Bedai U., Kanazawa, Japan, Kanazawa U., Peace Corps, Turkey. Co-author: Survey of U.S. Econometric Modeling Organizations; author: Special Curriculum Methods for Teaching Foreign Students; editor: Social Science Consortium Newsletter; author: The Etatist Turkish Republic and Its Political and SocioEconomic Performance from 1980-1999: A Developing State Impacted by International Organizations and Interdependence, Ottoman and Secular Civil Law International Journal of Middle East Studies, 1977. Chair Cub Scouts Am., Reston, Va., 1982—88; donor, supporter Disabled Am. Vets., Washington, 1995—. Fellow, NDEA, Soc. Sci. Rsch. Coun., U.Erfurt; grantee, NEH; scholar Fulbright, Sophia U.; Chancellor's Interdisciplinary Fellowship, U. Mo. Mem.: Am. Polit. Sci. Assn., Soc. Advancement Socio-Economics, Pi Sigma Alpha. Catholic. Avocations: cross country skiing, swimming, church choir. Personal E-mail: dora_nadolski@comcast.net.

**NAEGELE, PHILIPP OTTO,** musician, educator; b. Stuttgart, Fed. Republic Germany, Jan. 22, 1928; came to U.S., 1940; s. Reinhold and Alice (Nordlinger) N.; m. Susanne Russin (div. 1980); 1 child, Matthias Dominic; m. Barbara Wright, Mar. 1992; 1 adopted child, Olivia Kaihua. BA, Queens Coll., 1949; MFA, Princeton U., 1950, PhD, 1955. Violinist, violist Marlboro (Vt.) Music Festival, 1950—; violinist Cleve. Orch., 1956-64; from asst. prof. to William R. Kenan Jr. prof. Dept. Music Smith Coll., Northampton, Mass., 1964—2000, William R. Kenan Jr. prof. music emeritus Dept. Music, 2000—; violist Cantilena Piano Quartet, 1980-96; mem. Boccherini Ensemble, 1980-84; adj. prof. violin Amherst Coll., 2000—. Mem. resident string quartet Kent (Ohio) State U., 1960-64; mem. violin faculty Cleve. Inst. Music, 1961-64, Vegh String Quartet, 1977-79; rec. artist Columbia Mus. Heritage Soc., Pro Arte, Nonesuch Records, Bayer Records, Marlboro Rec. Soc., Arabesque Records, Da Camera, Spectrum Records, Bayer Records, Sony Classical, Philomusica, Qualitone Records. Author: Marlboro Music/German Vocal Texts in Translation, 2006; contbr: New Groves Dictionary of Music, An Anthology, 2005, articles to profl. jours. With U.S. Army, 1955-56. Fellow Am. Council Learned Socs., 1949-50, Proctor fellow, 1952-53, Fulbright fellow, 1953-54. Mem. Phi Beta Kappa. Home: 57 Prospect St Northampton MA 01060-2130 Business E-Mail: pnaegele@smith.edu.

**NAEGELE, TIMOTHY DUNCAN,** lawyer; b. Santa Monica, Calif., Feb. 5, 1941; s. Kenneth Conrad and Lillian Alice (Duncan) N.; m. Sydene Ann Wallace, Dec. 18, 1964 (div. 1977); children: Kurt Duncan, Kirsten Ann. AB, UCLA, 1963; LLB, U. Calif., Berkeley, 1966; LLM, Georgetown U., 1969. Bar: Calif. 1966, U.S. Ct. Appeals (9th cir.) 1967, U.S. Dist. Ct. (no. dist.) Calif. 1967, U.S. Supreme Ct. 1970, D.C. 1973, U.S. Dist. Ct. D.C. 1973, U.S. Ct. Appeals (D.C. cir.) 1980, U.S. Dist. Ct. (ctrl. dist.) Calif. 1980, U.S. Ct. Appeals (10th cir.) 1987, U.S. Ct. Appeals (11th cir.) 1992, U.S. Ct. Claims 1996, U.S. Dist. Ct. Nebr. 1992. Asst. counsel U.S. Senate Banking Com., Washington, 1969-71; adminstrv. asst. Sen. Edward W. Brooke, Washington, 1971-73; ptnr. Brownstein, Zeidman & Schomer, Washington, 1973-77; mng. ptnr. Timothy D. Naegele & Assocs., Washington, 1977—. Author: A Journey Home: A Legacy of Love, 1985; contbr. articles to profl. jours. Capt. U.S. Army, 1967-69. Recipient Joint Svc. Commendation medal Def. Intelligence Agy., 1969. Mem. Fed. Bar Assn. (chmn. banking law com. 1971-74, exec. coun 1975—, vice chmn. coun. on financing 1974-75, chmn. coun. on fin. institutions and economy 1975-76), D.C. Bar Assn., Calif. Bar Assn., Ocean Reef Club (Key Largo, Fla.), Phi Delta Phi. Mem. Unity Ch. Avocations: fishing, golf, tennis, boating, hiking. Address: PO Box 6408 Malibu CA 90264-6408 Office Phone: 805-488-6020. E-mail: tdnaegele.associates@gmail.com.

**NAEL, KAMBIZ,** radiologist, researcher; s. Parviz Nael and Maryam Izady. MD, Shiraz U. Med. Sch., Iran, 2000. Cert. ECFMG, 2003, continuation Calif. Med. Bd., 2003. Intern Shiraz Med. U., 1999—2001; rsch. assoc. Okla. Neuropsychiatry Ctr., Okla. City, 2002—03. Rsch. asst. radiology dept. UCLA, 2003—04, rsch. fellow diagnostic cardiovasc. sect., radiology dept., 2004—. Author: (rsch.) Pulmonary MR Angiography at High Magnetic Field (Jour. Radiology, 2005), (invited review paper) 3D Contrast Enhanced MRA of the Thoraco-Abdominal Vessels (MRI Clinic N.Am., 2005), (clin. rsch.) Carotid MR Angiography at High Magnetic Field (Jour. Radiology, 2005). Fellow: Internat. Soc. MRI in Medicine (assoc.); mem.: Soc. Cardiovasc. Magnetic Resonance (assoc.), Radiol. Soc. N.Am. (assoc.) Avocations: tennis, travel. Office: UCLA Radiology Dept 10945 Le Conte Ave Ste 3371 Los Angeles CA 90095-7206 Office Phone: 310-825-0958. Office Fax: 310-825-0880.

**NAESER, NANCY DEARIEN,** geologist, researcher; b. Morgantown, W.Va., Apr. 15, 1944; d. William Harold and Katherine Elizabeth (Dearien) Cozad; m. Charles Wilbur Naeser, Feb. 6, 1982. BS, U. Ariz., 1966; PhD, Victoria U., Wellington, New Zealand, 1982. Geol. field asst. U.S. Geol. Survey, Flagstaff, Ariz., 1966; sci. editor New Zealand Jour. Geology and Geophysics, New Zealand Dept. Sci. and Indsl. Rsch., Wellington, 1974-76; postdoctoral rsch. assoc. U. Toronto, 1976-79, U.S. Geol. Survey, Denver, 1979-81, geologist, 1981—2006, scientist emeritus, 2006—. Adj. prof. Dartmouth Coll., Hanover, NH, 1985—97, U. Wyo., Laramie, 1984—91. Editor: Thermal History of Sedimentary Basins--Methods and Case Histories, 1989, Debris-Flow Hazards - Mechanics, Prediction and Assessment, 2000; contbr. articles on fission-track analysis to profl. jours. Docent, Denver Zoo, 1991-99. Fulbright fellow, New Zealand, 1967-68. Fellow Geol. Soc. Am.;

mem. Geol. Soc. New Zealand, Mortar Board, Phi Kappa Phi. Methodist. Office: US Geol Survey Mail Stop 926 A 12201 Sunrise Valley Dr Reston VA 20192-0002 Office Phone: 703-648-5328. Business E-Mail: nnaeser@usgs.gov.

**NAEVE, CLIFFORD MIKE,** lawyer; b. Rapid City, S.D., May 25, 1947; BSME, U. Tex., 1970; MPA, U. Tex., Austin, Tex., 1972; JD, George Washington, 1984. Bar: US Ct. Appeals (6th, 8th, 10th and DC cirs.) 1986. With profl. staff Senate Com. on Environment/Pub. Works, Washington, 1977-78; legis. dir. Office of Senator Lloyd Bentsen, Washington, 1978-80; mgr. fed. pub. affairs Aminoil USA, Inc., Washington, 1980-82; v.p. Mid-Continent Oil & Gas Assn., Washington, 1982-84; commr. Fed. Energy Regulatory Commn., Washington, 1985-88; ptnr., energy group Skadden, Arps, Slate, Meagher & Flom, Washington, 1988—. Mem. electricity adv. bd. to the Sec. Energy, 2002—. Contbg. author natural resources jour. The Future of the Natural Gas Market: Regulation and Prices, 1987; contr. to publications. Mem. ABA (sect. on natual resources law, sect. on pub. utility law), Fed. energy Bar Assn., Order of Coif, Tau Beta Pi, Pi Tau Sigma. Office: Skadden Arps Slate Meagher & Flom 1440 New York Ave NW Ste 600 Washington DC 20005 Office Phone: 202-371-7070. Office Fax: 202-661-8229. Business E-Mail: mnaeve@skadden.com.

**NAEVE, MILO MERLE,** curator, director; b. nr. Arnold, Kans., Oct. 9, 1931; s. Bernhardt and Fern (Yasmer) N.; m. Nancy Jammer, July 18, 1954. BFA, U. Colo., 1953; MA, U. Del., 1955. Curatorial asst. Henry Francis duPont Winterthur Mus., 1957, asst. curator, 1958, sec. of mus., 1959-63, registrar, 1963-65; editor Winterthur Portfolio, 1965-66; asst. dir. dept. collections Colonial Williamsburg, Va., 1967-69, curator, dir. dept. collections Va., 1970; dir. Colorado Springs (Colo.) Fine Arts Ctr., 1971-74; curator Am. arts Art Inst. Chgo., 1975-91; ret. Am. Arts, Art Inst. Chgo., 1991. Curator emeritus Field McCormick. Author: The Classical Presence in American Art, 1978, Identifying American Furniture: A Pictorial Guide to Styles and Terms, Colonial to Contemporary, 1981, 3rd edit., 1998, John Lewis Krimmel: An Artist in Federal America, 1987, 150 Years of Philadelphia Painters and Painting: Selections from the Sewell C. Biggs Museum of American Art, 1999; mem. editl. bd. Am. Art Jour.; contbr. articles to profl. jours. Trustee Skowhegan Sch. Painting and Sculpture, 1991-2005, Libr. Co. Phila., Nat. Coun. the Fine Arts Mus. San Francisco, 1991-2005 Recipient Robert C. Smith award for most disting. article pub. in field in U.S., Decorative Arts Soc., 1996. Fellow Royal Soc. Arts; mem. Coll. Art Assn. Am., Nat. Trust Hist. Preservation, Am. Assn. Museums, Museums Assn. (Eng.), Ill. Acad. Fine Arts (Lifetime Achievement award 1991), Century Assn., Grolier Club.

**NAEYE, RICHARD L.,** pathologist, educator; b. Rochester, N.Y., Nov. 27, 1929; s. Peter John and Gertrude Ellen (Lookup) N.; m. Patricia Ann Dahl, June 4, 1955; children: Nancy Ellen, Susan Amy, Robert Peter. AB, Colgate U., 1951; MD, Columbia U., 1955. Diplomate: Am. Bd. Pathology. Intern N.Y. Hosp., N.Y.C., 1955-56; resident Columbia-Presbyn. Med. Ctr., 1956-58, Mary Fletcher Hosp., Burlington, Vt., 1958-60; practice medicine, specializing in pathology Burlington, 1960-67, Hershey, Pa., 1967—; asst. attending pathologist Mary Fletcher Hosp., 1960-63; assoc. prof. U. Vt., 1963-67, prof. pathology, 1967; prof. dept. pathology M.S. Hershey Med. Ctr., Pa. State U. Coll. Medicine, 1967—; chmn. dept. pathology, 1967-97. Mem. NIH study sect. USPHS, 1968-72. Mem. editl. bd. Human Pathology, 1982-96, Pediatric Pathology, 1983-96, Pediatric and Perinatal Epidemiology, 1987-94, Modern Pathology, 1993-96, Fetal and Pediatric Pathology, 2004—; contbr. articles to med. jours. Markle scholar in acad. medicine, 1960-65. Mem. Am. Soc. Exptl. Pathology, U.S. Can. Acad. Pathology, Am. Soc. Pathologists, Am. Soc. Clin. Pathologists, Coll. Am. Pathologists, Pediatric Pathology Soc., Pa. Soc. Clin. Pathologists, Investigative Pathology. Home: 50 Laurel Ridge Rd Hershey PA 17033-2513 Office: Pa State U Coll Medicine Dept Pathology 500 University Dr Hershey PA 17033 Office Phone: 717-531-8352. Personal E-mail: richardnaeye@aol.com.

**NAFACH, JALAL,** endocrinologist; b. Damascus, Syria, Aug. 6, 1972; s. Nafach and Kroubeh; m. Maria Obeid. Diplomate Am. Bd. Internal Medicine. Endocrinologist Endocrine Cons. Nebr., Lincoln, 2002. Mem.: Am. Assn. Clin. Endocrinologists (assoc.). Office: Endocrine Consultants Nebraska 2355 Superior St Ste 101 Lincoln NE 68516 Office Phone: 402-437-0660. Office Fax: 402-437-0661. Personal E-mail: jnafach@yahoo.com.

**NAFISI, AZAR,** humanities educator; b. 1950; arrived in US, 1997; d. Ahmad and Nezhat Nafisi; m. Bijan Naderi; children: Negar, Dara. PhD in English Lit., Okla. U. Prof. Tehran U., Allemeh Tabatabai U.; vis. fellow Oxford U.; prof. Johns Hopkins U., Sch. Advanced Internat. Studies, Washington. Author: Eye of the Storm: Women in Post-Revolutionary Iran, 1992, Anti-Terra: A Critical Study of Vladimir Nabakov's Novels, 1994, Muslim Women and Politics of Participation, 1997, Religious Fundamentalism and the Human Rights of Women, 1999, Reading Lolita in Tehran: A Memoir in Books, 2003; contbr. Home: 12026 Gatewater Dr Potomac MD 20854-2875 Office: c/o Random House 1745 Broadway New York NY 10019

**NAFTALI, TIMOTHY J.,** library director, historian, educator, writer; BA magna cum laude, Yale U., 1983; MA, Johns Hopkins U., 1987, Harvard U., 1993, PhD in History, 1993. Asst. prof. Dept. History U. Hawaii, 1993—97; assoc. prof. U. Va., 1998—2006; dir. Presdl. Recordings Program and Kremlin Decision-Making Project Miller Ctr. of Pub. Affairs, U. Va., 1999—2006; dir. Richard Nixon Presdl. Libr., Yorba Linda, Calif., 2006—. Vis. prof. Dept. History Yale U., 1996—98; hist. cons. Nazi War Crimes and Imperial Japanese Govt. Records Interagency Working Group, Nat. Archives, US Dept. Justice, 1999—; Nat. Commn. on Terrorist Attacks upon the US (9/11 Commn.), 2003—04; instr. Centre for Counterintelligence and Security Studies (CI Centre), 2003—. Co-author: US-Canadian Softwood Lumber: Trade Disputes Negotiations, 1998, One Hell of a Gamble: Khrushchev, Castro and Kennedy, 1958-1964, 1997, The Presidential Recordings: John F. Kennedy, 2001, US Intelligence and the Nazis, 2004, 2005, Blindspot: The Secret History of American Counterterrorism, 2005; gen. editor Presdl. Recordings Series, 2003—; contbr. articles to profl. jours. Co-recipient Akira Iriye Prize for Internat. Hist., 1997—98; named prin. investigator, Nat. Hist. Publs. and Records Commn., 2002—; grantee MacArthur Fellowship in Internat. Security, 1990—91, Rsch. Fellowship, Kennan Inst. for Advance Russian Studies, Woodrow Wilson Internat. Ctr. for Scholars, 1996, Olin Fellowship in Nat. Security, 1996—98. Office: Richard Nixon Presdl Libr 18001 Yorba Linda Blvd Yorba Linda CA 92886*

**NAFTALIS, GARY PHILIP,** lawyer, educator; b. Newark, Nov. 23, 1941; s. Gilbert and Bertha Beatrice Naftalis; m. Donna Arditi, June 30, 1974; children: Benjamin, Joshua, Daniel, Sarah. AB, Rutgers U., 1963; AM, Brown U., 1965; LLB, Columbia U., 1967. Bar: N.Y. 1967, U.S. Dist. Ct. (so. dist.) N.Y. 1969, U.S. Ct. Appeals (2d cir.) 1968, U.S. Ct. Appeals (3d cir.) 1973, U.S. Ct. Appeals (D.C. cir.) 1993, U.S. Supreme Ct. 1974. Law clk. to judge U.S. Dist. Ct. So. Dist. N.Y., 1967—68; asst. U.S. atty. So. Dist. N.Y., 1968—74, asst. chief criminal divsn., 1972—74; spl. asst. U.S. atty. for V.I., 1972—73; spl. counsel U.S. Senate Subcom. on Long Term Care, 1975, N.Y. State Temp. Commn. on Living Costs and Economy, 1975; ptnr. Orans, Elsen, Polstein & Naftalis, N.Y.C., 1974—81, Kramer, Levin, Naftalis & Frankel, N.Y.C., 1981—. Lectr. Law Sch. Columbia U., 1976-88; vis. lectr. Law Sch. Harvard U., 1979; mem. deptl. disciplinary com. Appellate div. 1st Dept., 1980-86. Author: (with Marvin E. Frankel) The Grand Jury: An Institution on Trial, 1977, Considerations in Representing Attorneys in Civil and Criminal Enforcement Proceedings, 1981, Sentencing: Helping Judges Do Their Jobs, 1986, SEC Actions Seeking to Bar Securities Professionals, 1995, SEC Cease and Desist Powers Limited, 1997, The Foreign Corrupt Practices Act, 1997, Prosecuting Lawyers Who Defend Clients in SEC Actions, 1998, Obtaining Reports from a Credit Bureau for Litigation May be a Crime, 1999, Encouraging Cooperation by Individual Respondents in SEC Enforcement Investigations, 2002, Navigating the Foreign Corrupt Practices Act, 2002, Fugitive Disentitlement in Civil Forfeiture Proceedings, 2002; editor: White Collar Crimes, 1980. Trustee Boys Brotherhood Rep., 1978—; Blueberry Treatment Ctr., 1981-91, Joseph Haggerty Children's Fund, 1991—; bd. dirs.

The Legal Aid Soc., 2000—. Fellow: Am. Coll. Trial Lawyers; mem.: ABA (white collar crime com. criminal justice sect. 1985—, coun. criminal justice sect. 2002—05), N.Y. Coun. Def. Lawyers (bd. dirs. 2000—01), Internat. Bar Assn. (bus. crimes com. 1988—), N.Y. Bar Assn. (com. state legis. 1974—76, exec. com. comml. and fed. litigation sect.), Fed. Bar. Coun. (com. cts. 2d cir. 1974—77), Assn. of Bar of City of N.Y. (com. criminal cts. 1980—83, com. judiciary 1984—87, coun. criminal justice 1985—88, com. on criminal law 1987—90, 1997—2001). Home: 1125 Park Ave Apt 7B New York NY 10128-1243 Office: Kramer Levin Naftalis & Frankel 1177 Ave of The Americas New York NY 10036 Office Phone: 212-715-9253. E-mail: gnaftalis@kramerlevin.com.

**NAFTOLIN, FREDERICK,** gynecologist, educator; b. Bronx, NY, Apr. 7, 1936; s. Nathan and Jean (Pesacov) N.; children: Michael Eugene, Joshua Joseph; m. Marcie Myerson, Nov. 1, 1987. AA, UCLA, 1957; BA with honors, U. Calif., Berkeley, 1958; MD with honors, U. Calif., San Francisco, 1961; DPhil, U. Oxford, 1970. Intern King County Hosp., Seattle, 1961-62; resident in ob-gyn UCLA, 1962-66; asst. chief gynecology, reproductive endocrine fellow USPHS, Seattle, 1966-68; NIH fellow Oxford U., England, 1968-70; asst. prof. ob-gyn U. Calif., San Diego Sch. Medicine, 1970-73; assoc. prof. ob-gyn Harvard Med. Sch., 1973-75; prof., chmn. ob-gyn dept. McGill Faculty Medicine, Montreal, 1975-78; prof., chmn. dept. ob-gyn Yale Med. Sch., New Haven, 1978-2000, prof. debt. ob-gyn, 1978—2005, prof. dept. biology, 1983—2005; dir. Yale U. Ctr. for Rsch. in Reproductive Biology, 1986—2005, head reproductive neurosci. unit, 2000—03; med. dir. Bartron Med. Imaging; prof. dept. ob-gyn. NYU, 2006—, dir. rsch. in reproductive biology, 2006—. Vis. prof. U. Geneva, 1982-83, Weizmann Inst., 1991-92; vis. prof. Complutense U., Spain, 1999, prof extraordinaire, 1999. Author: 15 books including: Subcellular Mechanisms in Reproductive Neuroendocrinology, 1976, Abnormal Fetal Growth, 1978, Clinical Neuroendocrinology, 1979, Dilation of the Uterine Cervix, 1980, 2-vol. series Basic Reproductive Medicine, Vol. I, Basis of Normal Reproduction, Vol. II, 1981, Male Reproduction, Vol. III, Metabolism of Steroids by Neuroendocrine Tissues, Follicle Stimulation and Ovulation Induction, 1986; mem. editl. bd.: Jour. Soc. Gynecologic Investigation, Menopause, Gynecol. Endocrinology, African Jour. Reproductive Medicine, sect. editor: Reproductive Biology, jour. Exptl. Zoology, 2002—; editor: Reproductive Divsn. Am. Jour. Zoology; contbr. more than 600 articles to med. jours. Named Fogarty Internat. fellow, 1982, John Simon Guggenheim fellow, 1983, Berlex Internat. scholar, 1991; recipient Arnaldo Bruno prize, Acad. Di Lincei, Italy, 2002; fellow ad enundem, Royal Coll. Ob-Gyn. Mem. Am. Gynecol. and Obstet. Soc., Soc. Gynecol. Investigation (pres. 1991-92, Disting. Scientist award 2003), Endocrine Soc., Internat. Soc. Neuroendocrinology, New Haven Ob-Gyn. Soc., Can. Fertility Soc., Soc. for Neurosci., N.Am. Menopause Soc. (pres. 1998-99), Internat. Menopause Soc. (exec. com. 2000—), Soc. Exptl. Biology and Medicine (coun. 2000—). Office: NYU Dept Ob-Gyn 550 1st Ave Tish 528 New York NY 10016 Office Phone: 203-298-9315. Business E-Mail: frederick.naptolin@med.nyu.edu.

**NAFZIGER, JAMES ALBERT RICHMOND,** law educator; b. Mpls., Sept. 24, 1940; s. Ralph Otto and Charlotte Monona (Hamilton) N. BA, U. Wis., 1962, MA, 1969; JD, Harvard U., 1967. Bar: Wis. 1967. Law clk. to chief judge U.S. Dist. Ct. (ea. dist.) Wis., 1967-69; fellow Am. Soc. Internat. Law, Washington, 1969-70; adminstrv. dir., 1970-74; exec. sec. Assn. Student Internat. Law Socs., 1969-70; lectr. Sch. Law Cath. U. Am., Washington, 1970-74; assoc. prof. Law Coll. Law Willamette U., Salem, Oreg., 1977-80, prof., 1980-95, Thomas B. Stoel prof., 1995—, assoc. dean, 1985-86, dir. internat. programs, 1984—. Scholar-in-residence Rockefeller Found. Ctr., Bellagio, Italy, 1985; vis. assoc. prof. Sch. Law, U. Oreg. 1974-77; vis. prof. Nat. Autonomous U. Mex., 1978; hon. prof. East China U. of Politics and Law, 1999—; lectr. tutor Inst. Pub. Internat. Law and Internat. Rels., Thessaloniki, Greece, 1982; cons. Adminstrv. Conf. U.S., 1988-90, Internat. Com. Migration, 1997—; mem. bd. advisors Denver Jour. Internat. Law and Policy, Am. Jour. Comparative Law (bd. dirs. 1985—). Author: Conflict of Laws: A Northwest Perspective, 1985, Internat. Sports Law, 1988, 2d edit., 2004; editor: Procs. of Am. Soc. Internat. Law, 1977; co-editor: Law and Justice in a Multistate World, 2002; contbr. articles to profl. jours. Dir. Rsch. Ctr., Hague Acad. Internat. Law, 2005; adv. com. on internat. law U.S. Dept. of State, 2001—; bd. dirs. N.W. Regional China Coun., 1987—89. 1st lt. U.S. Army, 1962—64. Recipient Burlington No. Faculty Achievement award, 1988, Willamette U. Pres.'s award for excellence in scholarship, 2000. Mem.: ACLU (pres. chpt. 1980—81, mem. state bd. 1982—88, sec. 1983—87), ABA (legal spl. ctrl. and east European law initiative 1992—), Am. Br. Human Rights (com. chmn. 1983—88, co dir. studies 1991—95, v.p 1994—2000, pres. 2000—04, chmn. 2004—), Internat. Law Assn. (rapporteur 1990—2001, chmn. cultural heritage law com. 2001—), Nat. Sports Law Inst. (bd. advisors 2002—), Internat. Sports Law Assn. (v.p. 1992, pres. 2004—), Oreg. Internat. Coun. (pres. 1990—92), Am. Law Inst., Assn. Am. Law Schs. (chmn. law and arts sect. 1981—83, chmn. internat. law sect. 1984—85, chmn. law and arts sect. 1989—91, chmn. immigration law sect. 1990—91, chmn. internat. law workshop 1995, com. on sects. and ann. meeting 1995—98, chmn. internat. exchs. sect. 1999—2000, chmn. conflict of laws sect. 2003—04, U.S. Dept. of State adv. com.), Am. Coun. Learned Socs. (exec. com. 2002—, conf. adminstrv. officers), Internat. Studies Assn. (exec. bd. 1974—77, internat. law sect.), Washington Fgn. Law Soc. (v.p. 1973—74), Internat. Acad. Comparative Law, Am. Soc. Comparative Law (bd. dirs. 1985—, treas. 1997—2005), Am. Soc. Internat. Law (exec. coun. 1983—86, chmn. ann. meeting 1988, chmn. nominating com. 1989, exec. coun. 1992—95, exec. com. 1994—95, chief adminstrv. officer 2005—), Phi Kappa Phi, Phi Beta Kappa. Home: 3775 Saxon Dr S Salem OR 97302-6041 Office: Willamette U Coll Law Salem OR 97301

**NAGANO, KENT GEORGE,** conductor, music director; b. Morro Bay, Calif., Nov. 22, 1951; BA in Sociology & Music (high honors), U of Calif., Santa Cruz, 1970—74; MA in Composition, San Francisco State U., 1974—76; studied with, Laszlo Varga. Former asst. Opera Co. Boston; former prin. guest condr. Ensemble InterContemporain & the Dutch Radio Orch.; mus. dir. & condr. Berkeley Symphony, 1978—; mus. dir. Opéra de Lyon, 1989—98; assoc. prin. & guest condr. LSO, London, 1990; mus. dir., prin. condr. designate Hallé Orch., England, 1991-94, mus. dir., prin. condr., 1994-2000, Deutsche Symphonie, Berlin, 2000—, LA Opera; mus. dir. Bavarian State Opera, Munich, 2006—, Montreal Symphony Orch., 2006—. Has performed with numerous orchestras around the world; recordings include: Songs of the Auvergne, Peter and the Wolf, Turandot and Arlecchino (Grammy nom.), La Boheme, Dialogues of the Carelites, The Death of Klinghoffer (Grammy nom.), Love for Three Oranges (Grammy nom.), Susannah (Grammy award), La damnation de Faust, The Rite of Spring, Rodrgue et chimene. Recipient Seaver/NEA Conducting award, 1985; Record of Yr. award Gramophone; named "officer" of France's Order of Arts and Letters, 1993. Office: Van Walsum Management Ltd 4 Addison Bridge Place London W14 8XP England*

**NAGARKATTI, JAI PRAKASH,** chemical company executive; b. Hyderabad, India, Feb. 18, 1947; came to U.S., 1970; s. Surendranath and Shakuntala (Bai) N.; m. Linda Susan Slaughter, Mar. 14, 1975; 1 child, Shanti. BS, Osmania U., 1966, MS, 1968, Texas A&M Univ., 1973, PhD, 1976. Group leader Aldrich Chem. Co. Inc., Milw., 1977-78, supr. prodn., 1978-79, mgr. prodn., 1979-84, dir. prodn., 1985, v.p., 1985-87, pres., 1987—99; pres. fine chemicals Sigma Aldrich Corp., St. Louis, 1999—2002, pres. sci. rsch., 2002—04, pres., COO, 2004—05, pres., CEO, 2005—07, bd. dir. 2005—. Lectr. chemistry V.V. Coll., Hyderabad, 1969-70. Contbr. articles to profl. jours. Robert A. Welch fellow East Tex. State U., Commerce, 1974-76. Fellow Indian Chem. Soc.; mem. Am. Chem. Soc. (chmn. membership Milw. Pk. sect. 1981). Avocations: stamp collecting/philately, tennis. Office: Sigma Aldrich Corp 3050 Spruce St Saint Louis MO 63103*

**NAGDA, DURGA SHANKER,** environmental engineer, researcher; b. Udaipur, India, Dec. 25, 1941; came to U.S., 1977; m. Amba Nagda, May 28, 1958; children: Yugal, Pushpa, Krish, Dimple. Grad., Instn. Engrs. India, 1966; MPhil, U. Leeds, Eng., 1973. Registered profl. engr., land surveyor, Ky.

Instr. U. Jodhpur, India, 1964-70, 74-75; rsch. asst. U. Leeds, 1972-73; mine engr. Hindustan Zinc Ltd., Udaipur, 1974; lectr. Indian Sch. Mines, Dhanbad, 1975-77; instr., advisor Belmont Tech. Coll., St. Clairsville, Ohio, 1978-79; asst. prof. Hazard (Ky.) C.C., 1980-86; cons. engr. Day Engring., Hazard, Ky., 1982-86; rsch. and design engr. Hellard & Whitaker Engring., Hazard, 1986-87; chief engr. Whitaker Coal Corp., Hazard, 1987-88; environ. engr. Ky. Dept. Environ. Protection, Frankfort, 1988—2002; project engr. Fla. Dept. Transp., 2002—03; stormwater profl. engr. Pub. Works, Lake Mary, Fla., 2003—. Mem. NSPE, Inst. Explosive Engrs. (assoc.), Soc. Mining Engrs., Am. Inst. Mining, Metall., and Petroleum Engrs. Avocations: tennis, spiritual and scriptural studies, yoga. Home: 474 Lakepark Trl Oviedo FL 32765-8274 Office: City of Lake Mary Pub Works 911 Wallace Ct Lake Mary FL 32746 E-mail: nagdads@yahoo.com.

**NAGDIMON, ELLEN TARA,** artist, educator; b. N.Y.C., Dec. 13, 1957; d. Jeoash Morris and Evelyn (Uretzky) Nagdimon; m. J. Martin Kahn, June 7, 1994. BA, CUNY, 1981; cert. legal asst., Adelphi U., 1982. Studio liaison N.Y. Feminist Art Inst., N.Y.C., 1985-88; gallery asst. Studio K Gallery, Long Island City, NY, 1986-88; instr., cons. Children's Art Carnival, N.Y.C., 1990-92; instr. Forest Hills (N.Y.) Adult Edn., 1988-95. Chair, treas. Arts Anon Tools, Forest Hills, 1993—94. Exhibitions include Ceres Gallery, N.Y.C., 1985—87, NYU, 1985, 1988, Emerging Collector, N.Y.C., 1986—, Uptown Mpls. Balhoun Sq., 2002. Support provider Common Link, St. Paul, 2002—; mem. visual arts focus group Twin Cities, Minn., 2003—. Recipient exhbn. support, Artists' Space, 1985, Minn. Work Force Ctr., 2002, assistanceships, DCA, 1985; fellow, Vt. Studio Ctr., 1991. Mem.: Minn. Artist Orgn., Art Initiatives, Orgn. Ind. Artists. Avocations: travel, photography, cooking. Home: 4861 Grenwich Way N Oakdale MN 55128-

**NAGEL, DAVID,** software developer company executive, BS in Engring., MS in Engring., U. Calif., LA, PhD in Exptl. Psychology. Various exec. positions Apple Computer, Inc. & subs., 1988—96, AT&T Corp. & subs., 1996—2001; CEO Platform Solutions Group at Palm, Inc., 2001; bd. dir. Palm, Inc.; pres., CEO, bd. dir. PalmSource, Inc., Sunnyvale, Calif., 2001—05, advisor, 2005—. Bd. dir. Liberate Technologies, Palm. Office: Palmsource Inc 1188 E Arques Ave Sunnyvale CA 94085-4602

**NAGEL, SIDNEY ROBERT,** physics professor; s. Ernest and Edith (Haggstrom) Nagel. BA, Columbia U., 1969; MA, Princeton U., 1972, PhD, 1974. Rsch. assoc. Brown U., Providence, 1974-76; asst. prof. physics U. Chgo., 1976-81, assoc. prof., 1981-84, prof., 1984—, assoc. dean divsn. phy. scis., 1997-2001, Louis Block prof., 1998-2000, assoc. dean divsn. phy. scis., 1997-2000, Stein-Freiler disting. svc. prof., 2001—. Contbr. articles to profl. jours. Recipient Quantrell award for Excellence in Undergrad. Tchg., 1996, Klopsteg Meml. Lecture award Am. Assn. Physics Tchrs., 1998, Oliver E. Buckley prize Am. Phys. Soc., 1999; Alfred Sloan Found. fellow, 1978-82. Fellow AAAS, Am. Acad. Arts and Scis.; mem. NAS. Home: 4913 S Kimbark Ave Chicago IL 60615-2954

**NAGEL, THOMAS,** philosopher, lawyer, educator; b. Belgrade, Yugoslavia, July 4, 1937; came to U.S., 1939, naturalized, 1944; s. Walter and Carolyn (Baer) N.; m. Doris Blum, June 18, 1958 (div. 1973); m. Anne Hollander, June 26, 1979. BA, Cornell U., 1958; B.Phil., Oxford U., Eng., 1960; PhD, Harvard, 1963. Asst. prof. philosophy U. Calif., Berkeley, 1963-66; asst. prof. Princeton U., 1966-69, assoc., 1969-72, prof., 1972-80, NYU, 1980—, prof. philosophy and law, 1986—, Fiorello LaGuardia prof. law, 2001—03, Univ. prof., 2002—, Vis. prof. Rockefeller U., 1973, U. Mex., 1977, U. Witwatersrand, 1982, UCLA, 1986, U. Calif., Berkeley, 2004. Author: The Possibility of Altruism, 1970, Mortal Questions, 1979, The View from Nowhere, 1986, What Does It All Mean?, 1987, Equality and Partiality, 1991, Other Minds, 1995, The Last Word, 1997; author: (with Liam Murphy) The Myth of Ownership, 2002; author: Concealment and Exposure, 2002; assoc. editor: Philosophy and Public Affairs, 1970—82. Guggenheim fellow, 1966, NSF fellow, 1967-69, NEH fellow, 1978, 84-85, vis. fellow All Souls Coll., Oxford, Eng., 1990. Mem. Am. Philos. Assn., Am. Acad. Arts and Scis., Brit. Acad.

**NAGEL, TREVOR W.,** lawyer; b. Adelaide, Australia, 1951; BA, U. Adelaide, 1973, Dip. Ed., 1974, LLB with honors, 1980; LLM, U. Chgo., 1981; SJD, Harvard U., 1984. Barrister, New South Wales, Australia 1985, Barrister, High Court of Australia 1985, bar: Mass. 1986, DC 1996. Ptnr. Shaw Pittman LLP, Washington, Alston & Bird LLP, Washington, 2006—. Prof. U. Sydney Law Sch., Elton Mayo Sch. Mgmt., U. South Australia. Contbr. articles to profl. jours. Mem.: ABA, Internat. Bar Assn. Office: Alston & Bird LLP The Atlantic Bldg 950 F St NW Washington DC 20004 E-mail: trevor.nagel@alston.com.*

**NAGEL, VERNON J.,** chemicals executive, electronics executive; BBA, U. Mich. V.p. fin., CFO, treas., sec Stericycle Inc.; exec. v.p., CFO, treas. Kuhlman Corp., 1993—99; prin. Jepson Assocs., Inc., 1999—2001; CFO Acuity Brands, Inc., Atlanta, 2001—04, vice chmn., 2004, chmn., pres., CEO, 2004—. Office: Acuity Brands Inc 1170 Peachtree St NE Atlanta GA 30309*

**NAGER, GLEN D.,** lawyer; b. 1958; BBA highest honors, Univ. of Tex., Austin, 1979; JD, Stanford Univ., 1982. Bar: DC 1985. Law clk. Justice Sandra Day O'Connor, US Supreme Ct., Washington, 1983, Judge J. Skelly Wright, US Ct. of Appeals, DC Cir., Washington, 1986—88; asst. to solicitor gen. US Dept. of Justice, Washington, 1986—88; ptnr., chair, issues & appeals practice Jones Day, Washington. Pres. Law Rev., 1982; appointed by House and Senate as chmn., bd. dir. Office of Compliance of US Congress., Washington, 1995—2000; adv. bd. Washington Legal Found. Editorial adv. council Employee Rels. Law Journ. Named One of Nation's Top 45 Lawyers Under Age 45, Am. Lawyer mag., 2003; named one of Top 12 Employment Lawyers in Washington, DC, Legal Times mag., 2004. Mem.: ABA, Edward Coke Appellate Am. Inn of Ct., Order of Coif. Office: Jones Day 51 Louisiana Ave NW Washington DC 20001-2113 Office Phone: 202-879-5464. Office Fax: 202-626-1700. Business E-Mail: gdnager@jonesday.com.

**NAGI, LILLIAN S.,** biology professor; d. Mostafa H. Nagi and Wiam Youssif. MS in Biol. Scis., Bowling Green State U., Ohio, 2002. Instr. and rsch. asst. Bowling Green State U., Ohio, 1999—2002; rsch. technician Med. Coll. Ohio, Toledo, 2002—03; prof. Owens C.C., 2002—. Guest lectr. Academic Investment in Math and Sci., Bowling Green, Ohio, 2002. Mem.: NOW. Avocations: travel, music, alternative medicine, computers. Home: PO Box 464 Bowling Green OH 43402

**NAGIN, LAWRENCE M.,** lawyer; b. 1941; married. BA, U. So. Calif., 1962; JD, U. Calif., Hastings, 1965. Dep. pub. defender Pub. Defender's Office, 1966-68; pvt. practice law Beverly Hills, Calif., 1968-74; spl. counsel aviation matters City Atty's. Officer, L.A., 1974-76; sr. asst. city atty. L.A. Dept. of Airports, 1976; formerly v.p. Flying Tiger Line, Inc., L.A., sr. v.p., gen. counsel adminstrn. from 1984; exec. v.p. corp. affairs, gen. counsel United Airlines, Inc. (UAL Corp.), Elk Grove Village, Ill., 1990-96, U.S. Airways Inc., Arlington, Va., 1996—. Office: US Airways Inc 2345 Crystal Dr Arlington VA 22227-0001

**NAGIN, MARY DEBORAH,** artist; b. Amityville, Dec. 28, 1953; d. William and Helen Marcia (Fraedin) N.; m. Jeffrey Ross Webb, Nov. 11, 1990 (separated July 1993). BA in Art, SUNY, Plattsburgh, 1975; studied painting with Jeff Webb, 1978—83; MA in Painting, Adelphi U., 1983. Art instr. Friendship House, Glen Cove, NY, 1977-81, Woodward Mental Health Ctr., Freeport, NY, 1978-81, Norwood Ave. Sch., East Northport, NY, 1983-85, St. Mary of the Angels Home, Syosset, NY, 1983-85, Art League of L.I., NY, 1983—. Art instr. continuing edn. dept. Manhasset (NY) Pub. Schs., 1988-2000; guest instr. Mill Neck Manor Sch. for Deaf, 1998; Art Inst. at Owl 57 Gallery, Hewlett, NY, 1999-2000, Art Inst. N Shore Montessori Sch., Stony Brook, NY, 2000-01; curator Firehouse Gallery, Nassau C.C., Garden City, 1990; adj. instr. in watercolor St. John's U., NY, 1991; artist in residence Patchogue (NY) Sch. Dist., 1983; exhbn. chmn. Nat. Drawing Assn.

1987-89; gallery dir. Little Studio, Ltd., Port Washington, NY, 1985-89, Pub. Illust.: The Everything Home Improv. Book, by Tom Philbin: Adams Media Corp.. Approx. 170 Interior Illust., 1997, Woman's Day Home Remodeling (Vol. VIII, #4) illustrated article: "8 Easy Home Repairs", 1998, The Irish 100 by Tom Philbin Andrews McMeel Pub., Kan. City, MO. Ten Portraits, 1999. One woman shows at Malette Gallery, Garden City, N.Y., 1983, Univ. Ctr. Gallery, Adelphi U., Garden City, 1983, Art League L.I., N.Y., 1990, Huntington Arts Coun., 1993, Pen & Brush, N.Y.C., 1996, East Meadow Libr., 1998; exhibited in group shows SUNY Plattsburg Coll. Gallery, 1975, Syosset-Woodbury Cmty. Ctr., Jericho Pub. Libr., Plainview Pub. Libr., 1978-79, Adelphi U., 1988, Wunsch Arts Ctr., Glen Cove, N.Y., 1989. Recipient 1st prize for drawing I.A. S., 1976, 78, East Meadow Ann. Art Exhibit, 1977, 1st prize Arts Coun. of Freeport, 1986, 3d prize Great Neck Art Show, 1987, Hon. Mention, H.T.A.L., 1989. Mem. Nat. Drawing Assn. (exhibit chmn. 1987-89), Pastel Soc. Am. (Beatrice Vare award 1990), Huntington Twp. Art League, Nat. Art League, Pen and Brush Club (chair pastel divsn. 1992-93, Phillip Isenberg award 1992 and 1995 Solo Show Award- Pen and Brush), Salmagundi Club. Home: 280 Lowndes Ave Apt 307 Huntington Station NY 11746-1273

**NAGIN, RAY (CLARENCE RAY NAGIN JR.),** mayor; b. New Orleans, June 11, 1956; m. Seletha Smith, 1982; children: Jeremy, Jarin, Tianna. BSc in Acctg., Tuskegee U., 1978; MBA, Tulane U., 1994. With GM, 1978—81, Associates Corp., Dallas, 1981—85; contr. Cox Comm. S.E. La. cable sys., 1985—89, v.p., gen. mgr., 1989—2002; mayor City of New Orleans, 2002—. Mem. bd. dirs. United Way, Convenant Ho.; chmn. United Negro Coll. Fund Walkathon fundraising campaign; pres. 100 Black Men Metro New Orleans. Recipient Excellent Customer Svc. award, Better Bus. Bur. 1993, Disting. Bus. Ptnr. award, La. State Bd. Edn., 1994, Diversity and Role Model award, Young Leadership Coun., 1995, New Orleanian of Yr. award, Gambit weekly, 1998, Nat. Telly award, 2001, Most Influential Black Americans, Ebony mag., 2006. Office: Office of the Mayor New Orleans City Hall 1300 Perdido St Rm 2E04 New Orleans LA 70112 Office Phone: 504-565-7793. Office Fax: 504-565-6423.*

**NAGIOFF, ROGER B.,** investment company executive; Grad., City Univ., London. With Wedd Durlacher Mordaunt & Co., London, 1985—89, NatWest Markets, London, 1989—97; head European equity trading Lehman Bros. Holdings, London, 1997—99, head European equity div., 1999—2000, co-head global equities, 2000—04, COO Europe, head equities div., 2004—. Office: Lehman Bros Holdings 5th Fl 25 Bank St London E14 5LE England*

**NAGLE, JAMES W.,** lawyer; BA magna cum laude, Georgetown Univ., 1974, JD magna cum laude, 1980; MPA, Am. Univ., 1976. Bar: Mass. 1980. Ptnr., chair, labor, employment practices group Goodwin Procter LLP, Boston. Editor: Georgetown Law Jour.; contributing editor Covenants Not to Compete: A State-by-State Survey, ABA. Mem.: ABA (individual rights, responsibilities com.), Boston Bar Assn. (chair, labor, employment law sect. 1992—94). Office: Goodwin Procter LLP Exchange Pl 53 State St Boston MA 02109 Office Phone: 617-570-1233. Office Fax: 617-523-1231. Business E-Mail: jnagle@goodwinprocter.com.

**NAGLE, JEAN SUSAN KARABACZ,** retired sociologist, psychologist; b. Detroit, 1936; d. Peter and Hedy (Grusczynski) Karabacz; m. Robert D. Nagle, Nov. 20, 1956; children: Carl A., Sonya L., Paula E. BS in Sociology, Wayne State U., 1956; postgrad., U. Chgo., 1953-55; MA, N.Mex. Highlands U., 1960; PhD, Union Grad. Sch., 1977; postgrad., Bryn Mawr. Inst., 1981. Diagnostic technician Vocat. Counseling Inst., Detroit, 1952; rsch. technician United Auto Workers-CIO, Detroit, 1958; clin. psychology intern N.Mex. State Hosp., Las Vegas, 1962-63; clin. psychology trainee VA Hosp., Omah and Lincoln, Nebr., 1963-64; instr. sociology N.W. Mo. State U., Maryville, 1965-70, prof. sociology and psychology, 1971-92, ret., 1992. Bd. dirs. Inst. Discourse. Grantee N.W. Mo. State U., 1981, 82. Mem. APA, Am. Sociol. Assn., Am. Psychol. Soc., Midwest Sociol. Soc., Psychology/Sociology Club, Mo. Psychol. Assn., World Federalists, Psi Chi, Pi Gamma Mu. also: 3106 E 80th St Kansas City MO 64132-3638

**NAGLE, JOHN E.,** accountant; b. Davenport, Iowa, May 7, 1921; s. Thomas Ambrose Nagle and Pearl Margaret Cook; m. Mary Modesta Monnig, Nov. 23, 1946; children: Mary Ann, Thomas, Stephen, Jerelyn, Brian, Mary Beth, Melita, Therese, Mathew, Joan. BS, St. Ambrose, Davenport, Iowa, 1942; JD, U. Iowa, 1945; DHL, Marycrest Coll., 1978. CPA Iowa. Assoc. lawyer Cook Blair & Balluff, Davenport, Iowa, 1945—50; ptnr. Cook Blair Balluf & Nagle, Davenport, Iowa, 1950—75, Nagle, Blair & Sohr, Davenport, Iowa, 1975—2000, Nagle, Harris & Cook, Davenport, Iowa, 2000—05, Nagle, Cook & Doughty, Davenport, Iowa, 2005. Pres. Davenport Cmty. Chest, Iowa; chmn. bd. trustees Marycrest Coll., Davenport, Iowa, 1975—81. Recipient Pius X award, Nat. Fedn. Cath. Coll. Students, 1961. Mem.: ABA, Iowa State Bar Assn. (pres. jr. assn.), Order of Coif. Democrat. Roman Catholic. Home: Apt 303 1360 Kimberly Ridge Rd Bettendorf IA 52722 Office: Nagle and Cook 1313 Harrison St Davenport IA 52803 E-mail: acfirm@msn.com.

**NAGLE, JOHN FREDERICK,** physicist; b. Easton, Pa., Sept. 29, 1939; s. Edgar Eugene and Julia Elizabeth (Meeder) N. BA, Yale U., 1960, MS, 1962, PhD, 1965. Asst. prof. physics Carnegie-Mellon U., 1967—72, assoc. prof. physics and biol. scis., 1972—78, prof., 1978—. NATO Fellow, 1965—66, Alfred P. Sloan fellow, 1969—71, Guggenheim fellow, 1979—80. Fellow Am. Phys. Soc. (chair divsn. biol. physics 1992-93); mem. AAUP, Biophys. Soc. (Avanti prize in lipids 2003), Phi Beta Kappa, Sigma Xi. Office: Physics Dept Carnegie-Mellon U Pittsburgh PA 15213 Office Phone: 412-268-2764. Business E-Mail: nagle@cmu.edu.

**NAGLE, LINDA MARIE,** elementary school educator; b. St. Louis, Mar. 31, 1947; d. Clarence Allen and Lorraine Emma Marie (Rosemeyer) Roche; m. John Thomas Nagle, Aug. 2, 1969; children: Kari Aldag, J Christopher, Katherine. BSc, Ctrl. Meth. Coll., 1969; MA in Edn., U. Mo., St. Louis, 1973. Cert. tchr. K-8 Mo. Tchr. Pattonville Sch. Dist., St. Louis, 1969—76, St. Charles Presbyn. Ednl. Develop. Ctr., St. Charles, 1986—90; spl. edn. cons. St. Charles Sch. Dist., 1990—91, tchr. asst., 1991—92, tchr., 1992—93, 1993—. Elem. rep. Environ. Devel. Adv. Com. for the St. Charles Parks Dept., 2000—; mentor St. Charles Sch. Dist., 1997—. Mem. Life Seekers, 1977—79; neighborhood chmn. Christmas Candle Lighting, 1975—2005; vol. Connections to Success, 2005; mem./mission outreach vol. Calvary Ch., 1975—. Recipient Tchr. of the Yr., Lincoln Elem. Sch., 2005, Journey to Excellence Recognition, 2005, Ring of Excellence award, St. Charles C. of C., 2005. Mem.: Internat. Reading Assn., St. Charles Ednl. Assn., Mo. Nat. Edn. Assn., Nat. Edn. Assn. Evangelical. Avocations: reading, exercise, gardening, crafts. Home: 8 Du Sable Ct Saint Charles MO 63301 Office: Lincoln Elem Sch 625 South Sixth St Saint Charles MO 63301

**NAGLE, ROBERT OWEN,** lawyer; b. Watertown, S.D., Feb. 10, 1929; s. John Raymond and Kathleen Margaret (McQuillen) N.; m. Louise Emerson H'Doubler, Mar. 14, 1954; children— Robert Owen Jr., Charles Francis, Margaret Louise. BS in Econs., U. Wis., 1951; LLB, U. Calif., 1957. Bar: Calif. 1957. Asso. firm Morrison, Foerster, Holloway, Clinton and Clark, San Francisco, 1957-62, ptnr., 1962-64; gen. atty. Spreckels Sugar div. Amstar Corp., San Francisco, 1964-66, v.p., 1966-68, exec. v.p., 1968-71, v.p. parent co. N.Y.C., 1971-76; exec. v.p. Am. Sugar div. Amstar Corp., N.Y.C., 1975-76; pres., chief exec. officer Calif. and Hawaiian Sugar Co., San Francisco, 1976-82, also dir.; ptnr. Brobeck, Phleger & Harrison, 1982-86; pvt. investor Piedmont, Calif., 1986—. Bd. dirs. Providence Hosp., Oakland, Calif. Mem. Law Rev. Bd. dirs. San Francisco Bay Area coun. Boy Scouts Am.; trustee U. Calif. Berkeley Found., Wis. Alumni Rsch. Found., Pacific Vascular Rsch. Found., San Francisco. Served lt. j.g. USN, 1951-54, Korea. Decorated Bronze Star with V, Air medal. Mem. ABA, State Bar Calif., Bar Assn. San Francisco, Order of Coif. Clubs: Claremont Country, Pacific Union.

**NAGLE, RONALD K.,** music educator; BME with distinction, Ind. U., 1980; MME, Vander Cook Coll. Music, 2006. Music tchr. Michigan City Area Schs., Ind., 1995—. Music tchr. pvt. lessons, Trail Creek, Ind. Entertainer Michigan City C. of C., Ind., Michigan City Lions Club; organist Elks Club 432, 2000—03. With U.S. Army, 1971—73. Recipient Spl. Performance Scholarship award, Ind. U., 1979, Excellence in Edn. award, T.H. Bell. Sec. of Edn., 1986. Avocations: sports, basketball, weightlifting. Home: 621 Pinetree Dr Trail Creek IN 46360

**NAGLE, RONALD T.,** lawyer; b. Fort Dix, N.J., Feb. 10, 1964; s. Ronald N. and Irene G. Nagle; m. Anne M. Nagle, Nov. 3, 1990; children: Kate Alison, Jack Robert. BA, Franklin & Marshall U., 1986; JD magna cum alude, Seton Hall U., 1989. Bar: N.J. 1989, U.S. Ct. Appeals (3d cir.) 1994, U.S. Ct. Appeals (9th cir.) 2003. Law clk. hon. Kenneth C. Mackenzie Chancery Divsn. Superior Ct. N.J., Morristown, NJ, 1989—90; lawyer Pitney Hardin, Florham Park, NJ, 1990—2002, Kirkpatrick & Lockhart, Newark, 2002—03; ptnr. Ronald T. Nagle, PC, Morristown, NJ, 2003—. Mem.: Fed. Bar Assn., Morris County Bar Assn. Office: Ronald T Nagle Pc 32 Maple Avenue Morristown NJ 07960 Office Phone: 973-267-6780. Office Fax: 973-267-6738. Business E-Mail: rnagle@naglepc.com.

**NAGLER, BARRY,** lawyer; b. NYC, Feb. 21, 1957; s. Charles and Toby (Freyman) N.; m. Laurie Beth Carter, Aug. 23, 1981; children: Daniel, Alyssa. BA magna cum laude, Franklin & Marshall Coll., 1978; JD cum laude, Harvard U., 1981. Bar: Mass. 1981. Assoc. Foley, Hoag & Eliot, Boston, 1981-87; v.p., asst. gen. coun. Reebok Internat., Stoughton, Mass, 1987-95, v.p., gen. counsel, 1995-98, sr. v.p., gen. counsel, 1998-99, Hasbro Inc., Pawtucket, RI, 2000—. Treas., mem. nat. bd. dirs. Assn. Corporate Counsel, dir. N.E. chpt., 1993—. Author: Reebok Rules for Litigation Management, 1997; contbr. articles to profl. jours. Office: Hasbro Inc 1011 Newport Ave Pawtucket RI 02862

**NAGLER, LEON GREGORY,** retired management consultant; b. Buenos Aires, Jan. 29, 1932; (parents Am. Citizens); s. Morris and Golden (Golden) N.; m. F. Elise Charness, Dec. 20, 1953; children: Jeri Lynn, Sandra Michelle. BS cum laude, Boston U., 1953, MBA, 1954; JD, Cleve. State U., 1961. Bar: Ohio 1961. Tchr. psychology Cameron State Agrl. Jr. Coll., Lawton, Okla., 1956-57; supr. employment and tng. Jones & Laughlin Steel Corp., Cleve., 1957-65; exec. dir. indsl. rels. Charles Corp., Cleve., 1965-67; dir. personnel ITT Svc. Industries Corp., Cleve., 1967-72; v.p. personnel Builder Svcs. Corp., Clearwater, Fla., 1972-73; v.p. adminstrn. Damon Corp., Needham Heights, Mass., 1973-77; pres. Nagler & Co., Inc., Wellesley Hills, Mass., 1977-95, Nagler, Robins & Poe, Inc., 1995—2005; ret. Mem. Mayfield Heights (Ohio) Planning and Zoning Commn., 1965-67; sec. Mayfield Heights Zoning Bd. Appeals, 1963-65; chmn. Combined Health Fund, Mayfield Heights, 1963; pres. N.E. Ohio region. mem. nat. gov. coun. Am. Jewish Congress, 1972-73; bd. dirs. New Eng. region Anti-Defamation League, 1977-80; trustee Jewish Cmty. Ctrs. Greater Boston, 1990—; bd. dirs. Jewish Vocat. Svc., Boston, 1977—, sec., 1980-83, v.p., 1983-88; bd. dirs. Am. Friends Wingate Inst., 1987-2004, v.p. fin., 1987—; trustee Temple Beth Avodah, Newton, 1978-2004, v.p., 1979-83, pres., 1983-85; trustee Combined Jewish Philanthropies, Boston, 1985-1992; bd. overseers Combined Jewish Philanthropies, 1992-2004. Served with AUS, 1955-57. Mem. Boston U. Alumni Assn. (pres. N.E. Ohio 1969-73, nat. coun. 1973—), Masons, Wycliffe Golf and Country Club (bd. govs. 1999-2005, v.p. 2001-02, pres. 2003-05). Democrat. Personal E-mail: lnagler@adelphia.net.

**NAGLER, STEWART GORDON,** retired insurance company executive; b. Bklyn., Jan. 30, 1943; s. Henry and Mary Nagler; m. Bonnie Lawrence, Aug. 9, 1964 (dec.); children: David, Ellen; m. Ronnie Hendler, Jan. 9, 2000. BS summa cum laude, Poly. U., 1963. With Met. Life Ins. Co., N.Y.C., 1963—2004, exec. v.p., 1983-85, sr. exec. v.p., 1985-93, sr. exec. v.p., CFO, 1993-98, vice chmn. bd., 1998—2004, CFO, 1998—2004. Fellow Soc. Actuaries, Acad. Actuaries. E-mail: stunagler@optonline.net.

**NAGORSKE, LYNN A.,** bank executive; b. Minn. B in Acctg., Minn. State U. CPA. Sr. mgr. Audit Dept. KPMG Peat Marwick; sr. v.p. and controller TCF Bank, 1985, treas., CFO, 1986, exec. v.p., 1988, pres., 1993, bd. dirs., 1995; pres. & CFO TFC Bank Minn., 1997—98; pres. & COO TCF Bank, CEO, 2006—. Office: TCF Financial Corp 200 Lake St E Wayzata MN 55391*

**NAGORSKI, ZYGMUNT,** political scientist, writer; b. Warsaw, Sept. 27, 1912; came to U.S. 1948, naturalized, 1953; s. Zygmunt Julian and Maria Nagorski; m. Marie Bogdaszewski, Nov. 22, 1938; children: Maria, Andrew, Teresa. MA, U. Cracow, 1935; postgrad., U. Geneva, 1937-38, Internat. Inst. Trade and Berne, Switzerland, 1937-38. Reporter Chamartinas Times, 1948; editor-in-chief Fgn. News Svc., Inc., N.Y.C., 1949-56; chief Internat. Br. Office Rsch. USIA, Washington, 1956-59; fgn. svc. officer Cairo, 1959-61, Seoul, 1961-64, Paris, 1964-66; spl. asst. to pres. Fgn. Policy Assn., Inc., N.Y.C., 1966-68; mem. profl. staff Hudson Inst., Inc., 1968-69; dir. members meetings program Coun. Fgn. Rels., N.Y.C., 1969-78; v.p. Lehrman Inst., 1978-80; spl. advisor Aspen Inst. Adj. asst. prof. polit. sci. dept. Queens Coll., 1974-75; v.p. Human Resource Svcs., Inc., 1980-81; guest lectr. Wilton Park, Sussex, Eng., Fgn. Svc. Inst., Ctr. Study Human Values, Tanglewood, N.C., Experiment in Internat. Living (Vt.), also nummerous univs.; v.p., dir. exec. seminars programs Aspen Inst. Humanistic Studies, 1981-85; pres. Ctr. Internat. Leadership, N.Y.C., 1986—. Author: Armed Unemployment, 1945, The Psychology of East-West Trade, 1975; co-author U.S.-Japan Economic Relations, 1979; contbr. articles to newspapers and mags. Pres. Am. Friends Wilton Park, 1967-70, 94-96, Mid-Atlantic Club N.Y., 1972-90; bd. dirs. Scarsdale Adult Sch., 1968-72, Internat. U. Found. Served with Polish Army, 1939-45, under French and Brit. command. Decorated Brit. War medal, officer's cross Order of Merit (W. Germany); comdr. Order of Leopold II (Belgium); recipient Meritorious Svc. award USIA, 1965, Outstanding Fgn. Born Am. award Internat. Ctr. N.Y., 1988. Mem. Coun. Fgn. Rels., Am. Polit. Sci. Assn., Internat. Studies Assn., Polish Inst. Arts and Scis., Am. Fgn. Svc. Assn., Fgn. Svc. club, Nat. Press Club (Washington). Democrat. Roman Catholic. Home: Ctr for Internat Leadership Inc 3050 Military Rd NW 624 Washington DC 20015 Fax: 202-686-3769. Office Phone: 202-686-3767. E-mail: znagorski@aol.com.

**NAGOURNEY, HERBERT,** publishing company executive; b. NYC, Jan. 30, 1926; s. Isidor and Tillie (Burstein) N.; children: Adam, Beth, Eric, Sam. BS, Columbia U., 1946, MS, 1947. Pres. Profl. and Tech. Programs, N.Y.C., 1951-65; v.p. Macmillan Co., N.Y.C., 1965-69; pres. Quadrangle/New York Times Book Co., N.Y.C., 1969-76, New York Times Book Co., N.Y.C., 1971-76, Quartet Books, Inc., N.Y.C. and London, 1976-81, Knowledge Tree Group Inc., 1979-89; v.p., dir. Sci. DataLink, 1981-88; pres. Sci. Datalink 1990—2000; v.p., dir. Comtex Sci., 1981-90; pres. Profl. and Tech. Pub. Inc., 1989—. Served with AUS, 1944. Home: 320 Joshuatown Rd Lyme CT 06371-3000 Office: 45 Christopher St New York NY 10014-3533 Office Phone: 212-206-9501. E-mail: hnagourney@rcn.com.

**NAGPAL, MADAN LAL,** biochemist, educator, researcher; b. Kurram, Pakistan, Dec. 15, 1939; m. Raman Verma, Oct. 14, 1943; 1 child, Manish. PhD, Panjab Agrl. U., 1968. Asst. prof. Panjab Agrl. U., Ludhiana, India, 1968-75; rsch. assoc. prof. U. S.C., Columbia, 1987—. Scientist, chemist Dorn Vets. Hosp., Columbia, 1990-95. Rsch. grant U. S.C., 1989-91. Fellow Linnean Soc. of London. Achievements include contributions to the effects of cytokines in Leydig cell function/steroidogenesis in the field of endocrinology and biochemistry. Avocations: golf, fishing, travel, photography, hiking. Home: 709 Skylane Dr Hopkins SC 29061 Office: U SC Sch Medicine Garner's Ferry Rd Columbia SC 29209 E-mail: madan@med.sc.edu.

**NAGRA, PARMINDER,** actress; b. Leicester, England, Oct. 5, 1975; Actor: (films) Bend It Like Beckham, 2002, Ella Enchanted, 2004; (TV series) Turning World, 1996, Always and Everyone, 1999, ER, 2003—; (TV films) King Girl, 1996, Donovan Quick, 1999, Twelfth Night, 2003, Second Generation, 2003.

**NAGRIN, DANIEL,** dancer, educator, choreographer, writer; b. N.Y.C., May 22, 1917; s. Harry Samuel and Clara (Wexler) N.; m. Helen Tamiris, 1946 (dec. 1966); m. Phyllis A. Steele, Jan. 24, 1992. BS in Edn., CCNY, 1940; DFA, SUNY, Brockport, 1991; DHL, Ariz. State U., 1992; studied dance with Martha Graham, Anna Sokolow, Helen Tamiris, Mme. Anderson-Ivantzova, Nenette Charisse and Edward Caton, 1936-56; studied acting with Miriam Goldina, Sanford Meisner and Stella Adler, 1936-56. Tchr. Silvermine Guild Art, New Canaan, Conn., 1957-66, SUNY, Brockport, 1967-71, U. Md., College Park, 1970, Davis Ctr. Performing Arts, CCNY, 1973-75, Nat. Theatre Inst., Eugene O'Neill Found., Waterford, Conn., 1974, Hartmann Theatre Conservatory, Stamford, Conn., 1975-77; long-term resident tchr., Nat. Endowment for Arts sponsorship U. Hawaii, 1978-80, tchr., 1981, Bill Evans Dance Workshop, Seattle, 1981; prof. dance dept. Ariz. State U., Tempe, 1982-92; tchr. grad. liberal studies program Wesleyan U., Middletown, Conn., 1984, Dance Workshop for Movement Rsch., N.Y.C., 1984, Improvisation Workshop, Seattle, 1985, Improvisation, Choreography and Acting Technique for Dancers, Seattle, 1985, Dance Workshop, Glenwood Springs, Colo., 1990; prof. emeritus dance Ariz. State U., 1992. Tchr. summer sessions Conn. Coll., New London, 1959, 74; Am. Dance Festival at Conn. Coll., 1960, 77, Duke U., Durham, N.C., 1978, 80, 82, 87, 88, 92, Balasaraswati/Joy Ann Dewey Beinecke Chair Dising. Tchg., 1992; summer dance program Conn. Coll., 1979, E. La Tour Dance Workshop, Sedgewick, 1982, 83; dance workshop U. Minn. at Mpls., 1984, Stanford U., 1990; co-dir. Tamiris-Nagrin Summer Dance Workshop, Sedgewick, 1960-61, (with Tamiris) summer dance session C. W. Post Coll., Greenville, N.Y., 1962-63; dir. summer dance workshop Johnson (Vt.) State Coll., 1972, 73, 75, 76. Dancer (featured dance soloist on Broadway) Annie Get Your Gun, Lend an Ear, Touch and Go, Plain and Fancy (Billboard Donaldson award, 1954), (appearance in film) Just for You, (adapted and performed one-man theater piece) The Fall, from novel by Albert Camus, 1977—79, choreographer (solo works) Spanish Dance, 1948, Man of Action, 1948, Strange Hero, 1948, Indeterminate Figure, 1957, With My Eye and With My Hand, 1968, Jazz: Three Ways, 1958, 1966, Path-Silence, 1965, Not Me, But Him, 1965, The Peloponesian War, 1967—68, Untitled, 1974, Ruminations, 1976, Getting Well, 1978, Poems Off the Wall, 1981, Apartment 18C, 1993, Crosscurrents, 1997, Lost and Never Found, 1998, Someone for Theater X, Tokyo, Japan, What Did You Say?, 2001, others, (for groups) Faces from Walt Whitman, 1950, An American Journey, 1962, asst. choreographer (original Broadway prodns.) Up in Central Park, Stovepipe Hat, Show Boat, Annie Get Your Gun, By the Beautiful Sea, others; dir.: (off-Broadway) Volpone, 1957, The Firebugs, 1960, The Umbrella, 1961, Emperor Jones (Boston, 1963, others; (film choreography) His Majesty O'Keefe; actor: (video) The Art of Memory, 1985; (plays) Three Stories High, others; extensive touring U.S., Europe, The Pacific and Japan, 1957—84, conceived and directed (videos) Steps, 1972, The Edge is Also a Circle, 1973, Nagrin Videotape Library of Dances, 1985; author: How to Dance Forever: Surviving Against the Odds, 1988, Dance and the Specific Image: Improvisation, 1993, The Six Questions: Acting Technique for Dance Performance, 1997, Choreography and the Specific Image: Nineteen Essays and a Workbook, 2001. With spl. svcs. Army Airforce, 1942-43. Grantee Rebekah Harkness Found., 1962, Logan Found., 1965, N.Y. State Coun. on Arts and Nat. Found. for Arts and Humanities, 1967-68, N.Y. State Coun. on Arts, 1971-72, 73-74, 75-76, 76-77, 78-79, 80-81, Anne S. Richardson Fund, 1971, 73, 74, 75, 76, 78, Nat. Endowment for Arts, 1975, 79, 81, 83, Ariz. State U., 1983, 84, 85, 86, 88; CAPS fellow N.Y. State Coun. on Arts, 1978; fellow NEA, 1977-78, 80, 82, 83, 90, 91, Minn. McKnight Nat. fellow, 1996-97; commd. ballet Rebekah Harkness Ballet Found., 1986. Mem. Actors' Equity, Phi Kappa Phi (hon.). Avocation: reading. Home and Office: 208 E 14th St Tempe AZ 85281-6707 E-mail: nagrin@imap2.asu.edu.

**NAGY, ANN M.,** art educator, music educator; b. Jasper, Ind., Oct. 24, 1954; d. Maurice and Lillian Roos Beckman; m. James P. Nagy, Nov. 14, 1992; children: Rebecca, Christina. BS in Music Edn., Ind. State U., 1976, postgrad., 1977—91; BS in Art Edn., Univ. So. Ind., 2002. Keyboard instr. Conservatory of Music, Terre Haute, Ind., 1975—77; studio instr. Providence Music Sch., Jasper, 1977—85; music tchr. Marian Heights Acad., Ferdinand, 1985—91; parish accompanist, music tchr. Holy Redeemer Sch., Evansville, 1991—2001; art educator Westside Consolidated Sch., 1996—, Reitz Meml. H.S., 2001—. Supr. early ed. field experiences U. So. Ind., Evansville, 1996—, art educator, 2000—; cons. art edn. internship program U. Evansville, 2004—05. Author: (poem) Community, 1991 (Editor's Choice award, 1991), Invisible, 2004 (Editor's Choice award, 2004). Vol. (inner city arts program) Patchwork Ctrl., 2006; organist, choir dir. St. Boniface Ch., Evansville, 2005—; vol. March of Dimes, Evansville, 1998—; advocate Evansville Psychiatric Children's Hosp., 2002. Named Tchr. of Yr., Cath. Diocese of Evansville, 2001. Mem.: Nat. Art Educators Assn., Internat. Soc. Poets, Kappa Delta Pi, Phi Lambda Theta. Avocations: poetry, graphic design, keyboards, composer. Office: Reitz Meml High Sch Art Dept 1500 Lincoln Ave Evansville IN 47714 Office Phone: 812-476-4973 x268. Business E-Mail: anagy@mhs.evansville.net.

**NAGY, DONNA M.,** dean, law educator; BA, Vassar Coll., 1986; JD cum laude, NYU Sch. Law, 1989. Assoc. Debevoise & Plimpton, Washington, DC, 1989—94; asst. prof. U. Cin. Sch. Law, 1994—98, assoc. prof., 1998—99, prof., 1999—2001, Charles Hartsock Prof. Law, 2001—, assoc. dean faculty devel., 2002—04, interim dean, 2004—. Vis. prof. law U. Ill. Coll. Law, Urbana-Champaign, 2001; vis. scholar U. Canterbury Sch. Law, New Zealand, 2002. Co-author: Ferrara on Insider Trading and the Wall, 1995, 2002, Securities Litigation and Enforcement: Cases and Materials, 2003; contbr. articles to law jours. Recipient Howard C. Schott Publ. Prize, 2002, 2003; Order of Coif. Mem.: ABA (mem. sec. Bus. Law), Am. Assn. Law Schs. (sec. Bus. Assns., Securities Regulation, and Women in Legal Edn.), Soc. Am. Law Tchrs., ACLU, Vassar Club of Cin. (Alumni Appointments Chair 1995—99). Office: U Cin Coll Law Clifton Ave & Calhoun St Cincinnati OH 45221-0040 Office Phone: 513-556-0113. E-mail: donna.nagy@law.uc.edu.

**NAGY, ELIZABETH GARVER,** artist; b. Martinsville, Ill., Jan. 14, 1928; d. Ralph Tibbs and Evelyn Fasig Garver; m. William Roger Achleman (dec.); children: Shelly Marth, Todd Jeffrey; m. Stephen Michael Nagy (dec.); children: Stephanie Nagy-Agren, Patricia Nagy Adelman. Degree in art, Studio Sch. Advt. Art, Cin., 1948. Illustrator Wolf & Dessauer, Ft. Wayne, Ind., 1949—51; freelance illustrator Ft. Wayne, 1951—; art instr. Springfield (Ohio) Art Ctr., 1968—77, Fine Line Creative Arts Ctr., St. Charles, Ill., 1986—92. Presenter in field. One-woman shows include Mountainlair Gallery, W.Va. U., Morgantown, W.Va., 1974, Clay N Caboodle Cadence, Geneva, Ill., 1993, 1993, Transylvania County Arts Ctr., Brevard, N.C., 1999, many others, numerous group shows including most recently, exhibited in group shows at Schumacher Gallery, Columbus, Ohio, 1975, Old State Capitol Galleries, Baton Rouge, La., 1976, 1978, 1979, Greenhill, Woodmere Gallery, 1976—90, Phila. Civic Ctr., 1976—90, Port History Mus., Phila., 1976—90, Tweed Mus., Duluth, Minn., 1978, Bahr-West Mus., Manitowoc, Wis., 1979, Davenport Art Mus., Iowa, 1983, Transylvania County Arts Coun. Gallery 7, Brevard, 1996, 1997, Transylvania County Arts Ctr., Brevard, 1999—2005, many others, Represented in permanent collections Time Temporary, Ft. Wayne, Kane County Jud. Ctr., Geneva, Bankers Club Worldwide (N.Y.), Taipei, Taiwan, Springfield (Ohio) Art Mus., many others. Sec., bd. dirs. Springfield Art Ctr., 1969—76; mem. visual arts com. Dellora A. Norris Cultural Arts Ctr., St. Charles, 1980—88. Recipient award of excellence, Midwest Watercolor Soc., 1973, 3d award, 41st Ann. Artists Guild of Chgo., 1983, award of merit, The Anderson (Ind.) Fine Arts Ctr., 1988. Mem.: Phila. Water Color Soc. (hon. life), Transparent Watercolor Soc. Am. (signature), Watercolor West (signature), Western Ohio Watercolor Soc. (founder, 1st pres.). Avocations: creating wearable art, knitting, weaving, sewing, embroidery.

**NAGY, LOUIS LEONARD,** engineering executive, researcher; b. Detroit, Jan. 15, 1942; s. Alex and Helen Nagy; m. Dianna M. Skarjune, Aug. 5, 1961; children: Tammy, Kimberly, Kristine, Amanda. BSEE, U. Mich., Dearborn, 1965; MSEE, U. Mich., Ann Arbor, 1969, PhDEE, 1974. Registered profl. engr. Rsch. engr. U. Mich., Ann Arbor, 1962-69; staff rsch. engr. GM R & D Ctr., Warren, Mich., 1969-98; sr. staff rsch. engr. Delphi Rsch. Labs., Warren, 1999—. Contbr. articles to profl. jours.; patentee in field. Bd. dirs. Convergence Ednl. Found., Birmingham, Mich., 1990-97, Convergence Transp. Electronics Assn., Birmingham, 1990-97. Recipient R&D 100 award R&D Mag., 1998. Fellow IEEE; mem. Convergence Fellowship (bd. dirs. 1988-96), Vehicular Tech. Soc. (Spl. Recognition award 1979, Avant Garde award 1986, Paper of Yr. 1975), Soc. Automotive Engrs., Tau Beta Pi, Eta Kappa Nu. Avocations: electronics, antennas, radar, automotive radar, microwaves. Office: Delphi Rsch Labs MC 483-478-105 51786 Shelby Pkwy Shelby Township MI 48315 Business E-Mail: Louis.L.Nagy@delphi.com.

**NAGY, REBECCA MARTIN,** museum director; b. Statesboro, Ga., Jan. 16, 1953; d. John Staten and Kate Purvis Martin; m. Paul Davis Nagy, Dec. 9, 1989. BA, Ga. So. U., 1975; PhD, U. NC, 1983. Instr. Cleve. Mus. Art, Dept. Art Hist. Edn., 1982—85; sr. program coord. NC Mus. Art, Raleigh, NC, 1985—94, curator African art, 1997—2002, assoc. dir. edn., 1994—2002; dir. Harn Mus. Art, U. Fla., Gainesville, 2002—. Pres., bd. dirs. Gallery Art and Design, NC So. U., Raleigh, NC, 1999—2000; bd. mem. Arts Coun. African Studies Assn., 2003—05, Art in Public Places Trust, Gainesville, Fla., 2004—; curator various exhibitions NC Mus. Art, 1996—2003. Editor (author): North Carolina Museum of Art Handbook of the Collections, 1998, Sepphoris in Galitees Crosscurrents of Culture, 1998; author: Textiles in Daily Life in The Middle Ages, 1988. Recipient Dist. Alumna award, Ga. So. U., 2004; fellow, Internat. Partnership Among Mus. Programs, Am. Assn. Mus., 1994, Fulbright-Hays grant, U.S. Dept. Edn., 2000. Mem.: S.E. Art Mus. Dirs. Consortium, Fla. Art Mus. Dirs. Assn., Assn. Art Mus. Dirs., Gainesville Women's Forum, Rotary Club Gainesville. Office: Samuel P Harn Mus Art PO Box 112700 Gainesville FL 32611

**NAGY, STEPHEN MEARS, JR.,** physician, allergist; b. Yonkers, NY, Apr. 1, 1939; s. Stephen Mears and Olga (Zahoruiko) N.; m. Brenda Yu Nagy, 1966; children: Catherine, Stephen III. BA, Princeton U., 1960; MD, Tufts U., 1964. Diplomate Am. Bd. Internal Medicine, Am. Bd. Allergy and Immunology. Pvt. practice, Sacramento, Calif., 1971-2000; prof. Sch. Medicine U. Calif., Davis, 1974—. Author, editor Evaluation & Management of Allergic and Asthmatic Diseases, 1981; mem. editl. bd. Clinical Reviews in Allergy; creator Famous Teachings in Modern Medicine-Allergy Series slide collection. Capt. U.S. Army, 1966-68, Vietnam. Fellow Am. Acad. Allergy, Am. Coll. Allergy; mem. CMA, Sacramento-El Dorado Med. Soc. (bd. dirs. 1971-95, 1989-95). Avocations: bicycling, book collecting, opera, fencing. Office: 4801 J St Ste A Sacramento CA 95819-3746 Office Phone: 916-456-4782.

**NAHAI, FOAD,** plastic surgeon, educator; b. Teheran, Iran, Sept. 23, 1943; came to U.S., 1970; m. Shahnaz Mossanen, Aug. 4, 1969; children: Farzad R., Fariba R. BSc with honors, U. Bristol, Eng., 1966, MB ChB, 1969. Diplomate Am. Bd. Surgery, Am. Bd. Plastic Surgery. Med. and surg. intern United Bristol Hosps., 1969-70; intern in surgery Balt. City Hosps., 1970-71; resident in surgery Johns Hopkins Hosp., Balt., 1971-72; resident in gen. surgery Emory U. Affiliated Hosps., Atlanta, 1972-74, chief resident, 1974-75, fellow in hand surgery and microsurgery, 1975-76, resident in plastic surgery, 1976-77; instr. in surgery Emory U., Atlanta, 1975-76, 78, from asst. to assoc. prof., 1978-91, prof., 1991-98; pvt. practice Paces Plastic Surgery, Atlanta, 1998—. Author: (with S.J. Mathes) Clinical Atlas of Muscle and Musculocutaneous Flaps, 1979, Clinical Applications for Muscle and Musculocutaneous Flaps, 1982, (with others) Microvascular Surgery in Reconstruction of the Head and Neck, 1989, Plastic and Reconstructive Breast Surgery, 1990, Grabb's Encyclopedia of Flaps, 1990, (with Bostwick Eaves) Endoscopic Plastic Surgery, 1994, (with S.J. Mathes) Reconstructive Surgery, 1996, others; mem. editl. bd. Annals Plastic Surgery, 1984, Outlook Plastic Surgery, 1988, The Art of Esthetic Surgery, 2005; contbr. articles to profl. jours.; co-prodr. (movies) Breast Reconstruction After a Radical Mastectomy with Latissimus Dorsi Musculocutaneous Flap, 1978, The Tensor Fascia Lata Free Flap, 1979; prodr. (videotapes) TFL Neurosensory Flap for Coverage of Greater Trochanteric and Ischium, Rectus Abdominis Flap for Sternal Coverage, Gastrocnemius Muscle Flap for Coverage of Tibia, others. Recipient Gold Medal Paper Presentation Southeastern Surg. Conf., 1976, Best Paper award Atlanta Clin. Soc., 1980, award Am. Med. Writers Assn., 1983. Fellow ACS (3d Ann. Residents Competition award Ga. chpt. 1977); mem. Am. Assn. Plastic Surgeons (James Barrett Brown award 1982), Am. Soc. Aesthetic Plastic Surgery, Am. Soc. Plastic and Reconstructive Surgeons (rsch. grantee ednl. found.), Ga. Soc. Plastic Surgeons, Med. Assn. Ga. Surg. Soc., Med. Assn. Atlanta, Southeastern Soc. Plastic and Reconstructive Surgeons (Outstanding Resident award 1977), Internat. Assn. Univ. Plastic Surgeons, Plastic Surgery Rsch. Coun. (program chmn. 1988, chmn. 1989), Brazilian Coll. Surgeons (corr.), Brazilian Soc. Plastic Surgeons, Italian Soc. Plastic, Reconstructive and Aesthetic Surgery, Soc. Residents and Ex Residents of Inst. Reconstructive Surgery (hon.), Sociedad Jaime Planas de Cirurgia Plastica, Internat. Soc. Aesthetic Plastic Surgery (sec. gen. 2000-2004, 2d v.p. 2004—), Am. Soc. Aestetic Plastic Surgery (sec. 2003—). Office: Paces Plastic Surgery 3200 Downwood Cir NW Ste 640 Atlanta GA 30327-1624 Office Phone: 404-351-0051. Business E-Mail: linda@pacesplasticsurgery.com. E-mail: pacesplasticsurgery@aol.com.

**NAHAT, DENNIS F.,** performing company executive, choreographer; b. Detroit, Feb. 20, 1946; s. Fred H. and Linda M. (Haddad) N. Hon. degree, Juilliard Sch. Music, 1965. Prin. dancer Joffrey Ballet, NYC, 1965-66; prin. dancer Am. Ballet Theatre, NYC, 1968-79; co-founder Cleve. Ballet, 1976, Sch. of Cleve. Ballet, 1972; founder, artistic dir. Sch. Cleve. San Jose Ballet, 1996; founder New Sch. of Cleve. San Jose Ballet, 1996—; founder, artistic dir. San Jose Cleve. Ballet (now Ballet San Jose Silicon Valley), 1985—. Co-chair Artists Round Table Dance USA, 1991; trustee Cecchetti Coun. Am., 1991; mem. adv. bd. Ohio Dance Regional Dance Am.; dir. dance USDAN Ctr. for the Creative Performing Arts, NY, 1999—. Prin. performer Broadway show Sweet Charity, 1966-67; choreographer Two Gentlemen of Verona (Tony award 1972), 1969-70; (ballet) Celebrations and Ode (resolution award 1985), 1985, Green Table, Three Virgins and a Devil (Isadora Duncan award 1985); conceived, directed, choreographed Blue Suede Shoes, PBS, 1997-98. Grantee Nat. Endowment Arts, 1978, Andrew Mellon Found., 1985; recipient Outstanding Achievement award Am. Dance Guild, 1995, 96, 2000—. Avocation: cooking. also: Ballet San Jose Silicon Valley PO Box 1666 San Jose CA 95109-1666 also: Ballet San Jose Silicon Valley 40 N 1st St San Jose CA 95113-1200 Office Phone: 408-288-2820 Ext.225. Business E-Mail: dnahat@balletsanjose.com.

**NAHAVANDI, AMIR NEZAMEDDIN,** retired engineering firm executive; b. Tehran, Iran, Apr. 6, 1924; arrived in U.S., 1956, naturalized, 1970; s. Ahmad and Fatima Razaghi Nahavandi. Electromech. Engring. degree, Tehran U., 1947; MS in Mech. Engring, Carnegie Inst. Tech., 1957, PhD, 1960. Registered profl. engr., Pa. Engr. Tehran U., 1948-50; head design group Nat. Iranian Oil Co., Tehran, 1950-56; adv. engr. Westinghouse Electric Corp., Pitts., 1957-66; prof., chmn. dept. mech. engring. U. Vt., 1967-68; rsch. prof. N.J. Inst. Tech., 1969-77; prof. engring. and applied Sci. Columbia U., N.Y.C., 1977-81; chief scientist Electronic Assocs., Inc., West Long Branch, NJ, 1981-82; prin. Mazen, Inc., Long Branch, NJ, 1982-92. Decorated Sci. medal Govt. Iran. Fellow ASME; mem. N.Y. Acad. Scis., Phi Kappa Phi, Sigma Xi, Tau Beta Pi. Achievements include development of analytical models for stock market forecasting; research and development in dynamics of steam generators and boiling systems; research in thermal pollution of lakes and rivers; vibration of reactor structures; dynamic and accident analysis of conventional and nuclear power plants; solid-fluid interaction. Home: 7635 Eads Ave Unit 202 La Jolla CA 92037-4832 Personal E-mail: anahav@aol.com.

**NAHIGIAN, ROBERT JOHN,** real estate company executive, consultant; b. Boston, Feb. 24, 1956; s. John Moses and Theresa (Zeytoundjian) N.; m. Donna P. Dewar, Oct. 23, 1993; children: Jessica Lee, Kimberly Patricia. BA cum laude, Lehigh U., 1978; MS in Urban Planning, Columbia U., 1980. Cert. real estate mediator Mass., FRICS Royal Inst. Chartered Surveyors, 2005. Property mgr. Auburndale (Mass.) Realty Co., 1972-77; jr. planner Bethlehem (Pa.) Redevel. Authority, 1978; planner, tech. analyst Perkins & Will Archtl. Firm, N.Y.C., 1978-80; city planner, econ. developer City of Bowie, Md., 1980-81; v.p. The Norwood Group, Inc., Burlington, Mass., 1981-88; v.p., dir. The Robbins Group, Cambridge, Mass., 1988-89; pres. Auburndale Realty Co., Newton, Mass., 1989—. Dir., lectr. real estate studies Northeastern U., Boston, 1982—93; instr. real estate Boston U., 1994—; lectr., spkr. at convs. in field; Boston U. lectr. U. of Hong Kong Polytech.; 1st SIOR spkr. at Latin America's First Real Estate Conf., Bogota, Colombia, 1998; invited lectr. Czech Republic, Poland; mem. Greater Boston Real Estate Bd. Comml. Broker Assn., Govt. and Agy. Law Task Force Affairs rep., bd. dirs., 2002—; mem. Comml. Overlay State Task Force; apptd. by Gov. Romney Mass. Hwy. Real Estate Rev. Bd., 2004; apptd. chmn. Mass. Realtors Comml. Investment Coun., 2005—. Co-author: Master Office Leasing, 1993, rev. edit., 2000; contbr. articles to profl. jours., Mass. real estate sales exam book. Mem. Wang Ctr. for the Performing Arts, Boston, 1985; mem. presdl. adv. com. on Housing in Mass. Mass. Assn. of Realtors. Recipient Cert. of Appreciation, Exch. Club, 1991, Alumni award Lehigh U., 1993, N.E. Constrn. Show, So. Calif. Constrn. Show, Mex. Nat. Bd. Realtors, 1997, Dising. Achievement in cml. leasing Greater Boston Real Estate Bd., 1999; First Mass. Comml. Broker as Cert. Instr., Banker and Tradesman Top 125 Bus. Leaders in Mass. for 1999, 1st Comml Broker as Cert. Mass. Real Estate Mediator, 2001, Appreciation gift, CornNet Harvard Univ., 2005 Fellow: Royal Inst. Chartered Surveyors; mem.: Greater Boston Assn. Realtors (edn. task force), Worcester Regional Assn. Realtors (edn. task force), Comml. Brokers Assn. (govt. affairs rep., agy. law task force to Mass. Assn. Realtors 2002—03, bd. dirs. 2002—, 2004—05, coml. overlay state task force study, Broker Achievement Bronze award 2000, Broker Achievement Gold award 2001, Comml. Leasing Achievement Gold award 2001, Indsl. Deal of Yr. award 2001, Adv. Assignment of Yr. 2003, 2004, Appreciation Gift 2005, Adv. Assignment of Yr. 2005, 2005), Nat. Assn. Indsl. and Office Parks (New Eng.) chpt. membership com. 1993—96, membership com. chmn. 1996, exec. com. 1996, cert. appreciation Mass. chpt.), Am. Soc. Real Estate (counselors of real estate 1996, nat. conv. spkr. 1997, com. mem. nat. edn. com., nat. presdl. task force 1998—2000, vice chmn. pub. rels. com. 1998—2000, nat. spl. task force 2001, nat. chmn. pub. rels. and comm. 2001—02, nat. bd. dirs. 2001—04, CRE sec. New Eng./N.Y. chpt. 2005), Soc. Indsl. and Office Realtors (nat. vice chmn. office courses 1993—94, edn. exec. com. 1993—94, nat. regional v.p. 1994—96, nat. exec. com. 1994—96, nat. bd. dir. 1994—96, nat. chmn. instrs. com. 1994—97, nat. chmn. edn. com. 1994—98, ex officio edn. fund 1995—97, nat. chmn. edn. exec. com. 1995—97, nat. nominating com. 1995—98, Presdl. edn. task force 1995—99, bd. dir. New Eng. chpt. 1995—, pres. New Eng. chpt. 1998—99, spl. adv. and immediate past pres. 2000—, nat. budget and fin. com. 2000—02, v.p. nat. com. programs, nat. convention co-chmn., nat. bd. dirs. 2001, nat. vice chmn. designation courses edn. com., nat. nominating com. 2002, nat. vice chmn faculty com. 2003—04, nat. vice chmn. faculty com. 2006, sr. instr., instrs. com. and office mktg. forum, task force indsl. office leasing handbook, property evaluation forum, expert roundtable com., Nat. Real Estate Instr. of Yr. 1994, medal of appreciation New Eng. chpt. 1998—99, Appreciation medal New Eng. chpt. 1998—99, Nat. Real Estate Instr. of Yr. 2002, 2002, 2003, 2004, cert. appreciation, cert. profl. edn. com., cert. appreciation as outgoing nat. ednl. chair, Nat. Real Estate Instr. of Yr. 2004), Mass. Assn. Realtors (com. mem. 2001—, agy. law task force 2003—04, comml. bd. overlay task force 2004, bd. dirs. comml. investment coun. 2005—, govt. affairs com. for CBA), Nat. Assn. Realtors (cert. of appreciation 1992, Mass. mediation officer award 2001), Algonquin Club, Lehigh Club (class '78 pres. 1993—98), Lambda Alpha (bd. dirs. Boston chptr.). Republican. Mem. Armenian Apostolic Ch. Home: 365 Highland St Weston MA 02493-2624 Office: Auburndale Realty Co PO Box 66125 335 Auburn St Newton MA 02466-1902 Office Phone: 617-332-6900. E-mail: rob@siorcre.com.

**NAHMAD, ALBERT H.,** manufacturing executive; b. Oct. 15, 1940; m. Jane Davis; 2 children. BS in Mech. Engring., U. N. Mex., 1962; MS in Indsl. Adminstrn., Purdue U., 1963. Mgmt. cons. Arthur Young, N.Y.C.; group v.p W.R. Grace & Co.; pres., CEO Watsco, Inc., Coconut Grove, Fla., 1973—. Bd. dirs. Am. Bankers Ins. Group, Mayor's Jewelers. Mem. Fla. Coun. 100; chmn. bd. of trustees Miami Children's Hosp.; past chmn. Fla. chpt Young Presidents' Org.; bd. dir. Cmty. Partnership for the Homeless Inc. Mem. Chief Executives Org., World Presidents' Org. Office: Watsco Inc 2665 S Bayshore Dr Ste 901 Miami FL 33133*

**NAHMAN, NORRIS STANLEY,** electrical engineer; b. San Francisco, Nov. 9, 1925; s. Hyman Cohen and Rae (Levin) N.; m. Shirley D. Maxwell, July 20, 1968; children: Norris Stanley, Vicki L., Vance W., Scott T. BS in Electronics Engring. Calif. Poly. State U., 1951; MSE.E., Stanford U., 1952; PhD in Elec. Engring., U. Kans., 1961. Registered profl. engr., Colo. Electronic scientist Nat. Security Agy., Washington, 1952-55; prof. elec. engring., dir. electronics rsch. lab. U. Kans., Lawrence, 1955-66; sci. cons., chief pulse and time domain sect. Nat. Bur. Standards, Boulder, Colo., 1966-73, chief time domain metrology, sr. scientist, 1975-83, group leader field characterization group, 1984-85; v.p. Picosecond Pulse Labs, Inc., Boulder, 1986-90, scientific advisor, co-chair tech. adv. bd., 1990—; cons. elec. engr., 1990—; prof., chmn. dept. elec. engring. U. Toledo, 1973-75; prof. elec. engring. U. Colo., Boulder, 1966—; affiliate staff Los Alamos (N.Mex.) Nat. Lab., 1990—. Disting. lectr., prin. prof. Ctr. Nat. d' Etude des Telecomm. Summer Sch., Lannion France, 1978; disting. lectr. Harbin Inst. Tech., Peoples Republic China, summer 1982; mem. faculty NATO Advanced Study Inst., Castelvecchio, Italy, 1983, Internat. Radio Sci. Union/NRC; chmn. Internat. Intercomm. Group Waveform Measurements, 1981-90, chmn. Commn. A, 1985-86. Contbr. rsch. articles profl. jours.; patentee in field. Asst. scoutmaster Longs Peak coun. Boy Scouts Am., 1970-73, 75-89. With U.S. Mcht. Marine, 1943-46, U.S. Army, 1952-55. Ford Found. faculty fellow MIT, 1962; Nat. Bur. Standards sr. staff fellow, 1978-79; recipient Disting. Alumnus award Calif. Poly. State U., 1972, Order of Arrow Boy Scouts Am., 1976. Fellow IEEE (life), Internat. Sci. Radio Union); mem. Instrumentation and Measurement Soc. of IEEE (admstrv. com. 1982-84; editorial bd. Trans., 1982-86, Andrew H. chi Best Tech. Paper award 1984, Tech. Leadership and Achievement award 1987), Electromagnetic Acad., Am. Assn. Engring. Edn. (life), U.S. Mcht. Marine Vets. World War II (life), Am. Mcht. Marine Vets. (v.p. Denver chpt.), Am. Legion, Calif. Poly. State U. Alumni Assn. (life), Stanford U. (life), U. Kans. (life), Am. Radio Relay League Club (life), Sigma Pi Sigma, Tau Beta Pi, Eta Kappa Nu, Sigma Tau, Sigma Xi. Personal E-mail: nsnahman@ieee.org.

**NAHMENS, ISABELINA C.,** industrial engineer, researcher; b. Sao Paulo, Brazil, Jan. 18, 1977; d. Rafael A. Nahmens and Morelia C. Castro de Nahmens. BE in Indsl. Engring., U. Ctrl. Fla., Orlando, 2001, MS in Quality Engring., 2003, ABD in Indsl. Engring. and Mgmt. Sys., 2006. Engr. intern, Fla. Bd. Profl. Engineers, 2001, Six Sigma Black Belt, Am. Soc. Quality, 2006, cert. energy gauge rater, Fla. Solar Energy Ctr., 2002; grad. tchg. asst. Faculty Ctr. Tchg. and Learning U. Ctrl. Fla., 2006. Grad. rsch. assoc. Housing Constructability Lab U. Ctrl. Fla., Orlando, 2000—01, grad. tchg. asst., 2005. Vol. Feed the Homeless Ministry, Orlando, Fla., 2003. Fellow, U. Ctrl. Fla., 2001—02. Mem.: Inst. Indsl. Engrs., Am. Soc. Quality (pres. U. Ctrl. Fla student br. 2005—06), Golden Key, Tau Beta Pi. Avocations: travel, gardening, cooking, arts and crafts, running. E-mail: inahmens@mail.ucf.edu.

**NAHMIAS, DAVID E.,** prosecutor; b. Atlanta, 1964; BA summa cum laude, Duke Univ.; JD magna cum laude, Harvard Univ. Bar: Ga. 1991. Law clerk to Hon. Laurence H. Silberman U.S. Ct. Appeals (D.C. cir.), 1991—92; law clerk to Justice Antonin Scalia U.S. Supreme Ct., 1992—93; assoc. Hogan & Hartson L.L.P., Washington, 1993—95; asst. U.S. atty. (No. dist.) GA US Dept. Justice, Atlanta, 1995—2001, counsel for the asst. atty. gen. criminal divsn. Washington, 2001—03, dep. asst. atty. gen. criminal divsn., 2003—04, US atty. (no. dist.) Ga., 2004—. Editor: Harvard Law Review. Office: US Attys Office 600 US Courthouse 75 Spring St SW Atlanta GA 30303-3309*

**NAHRWOLD, DAVID LANGE,** surgeon, educator; b. St. Louis, Dec. 21, 1935; s. Elmer William and Magdalena Louise (Lange) N.; m. Carolyn Louise Hoffman, June 14, 1958; children: Stephen Michael, Susan Alane, Thomas James, Anne Elizabeth. AB, Ind. U., 1957, MD, 1960. Diplomate Am. Bd. Surgery, Am. Bd. Thoracic Surgery. Intern, then resident in surgery Ind. U. Med. Ctr., Indpls., 1960-65; postdoctoral scholar in gastrointestinal physiology VA Ctr., UCLA, 1965; asst. prof. surgery Ind. U. Med. Sch., 1968-70; assoc. prof. Coll. Medicine Pa. State U., 1970-73; vice-chmn. dept. surgery Pa. State U., 1971-82, assoc. provost, dean health affairs, 1981-82, prof., chief divsn. gen. surgery, 1974-82; Loyal and Edith Davis prof., chmn. dept. surgery Northwestern U. Med. Sch., Chgo., 1982-97; surgeon-in-chief Northwestern Meml. Hosp., Chgo., 1982-97; pres., CEO Northwestern Med. Faculty Found., Inc., 1996-99; prof. surgery, exec. assoc. dean clin. affairs Northwestern U. Med. Sch., 1997-99, prof. emeritus, 1999—. Mem. Nat. Digestive Disease Adv. Bd., 1985—89; bd. dirs. Am. Bd. Surgery, vice chmn., 1994—95, chmn., 1995—96; bd. dirs. Northwestern Healthcare Network, Am. Bd. Med. Specialties, 1997—2005; mem. exec. com. Accreditation Coun. for Grad. Med. Edn., 1999—2000; bd. commrs. Joint Commn. Accreditation Healthcare Orgns., 2002—, vice chmn. bd. commrs., 2005—; bd. dirs. Joint Commn. Resources, vice chmn. bd. dirs., 2005—06; pres. Am. Bd. Med. Specialties, 2002—04. Editor emeritus Jour. Laparoendoscopic Surgery, 1997-2004; mem. editl. bd. Surgery, 1981-94, Archives of Surgery, 1983-93, Digestive Surgery, 1986-99, Am. Jour. Surgery, 1994-2000, Jour. Gastrointestinal Surgery, 1996-2000, Current Opinion in Gen. Surgery, Jour. Lithotripsy and Stone Disease, 1988-92; contbr. articles to profl. jours. With MC U.S. Army, 1966—68. Recipient John P. Hubbard award, Nat. Bd. Med. Examiners, 2003. Fellow: ACS (bd. govs. 1992—98, vice chmn. 1994—96, chmn. bd. govs. exec. com. 1996—98, interim dir. 1999—2000, 1st v.p. 2006—, bd. regents, 1st v.p. elect 2005—06, Disting. Svc. award 2001), Philippine Coll. Surgeons (hon.); mem.: AMA, Chgo. Surg. Soc. (pres. 1993—94), Chgo. Med. Soc., We. Surg. Assn., Soc. Univ. Surgeons, Soc. Surgery Alimentary Tract (pres. 1989—90, trustee), Soc. Clin. Surgery (sec. 1984—88), Internat. Biliary Assn., Ill. Surg. Soc., Ill. State Med. Soc., Internat. Fedn. Surg. Colls. (hon.; treas. 1999—2002), Gastroenterology Rsch. Group, Collegium Internat. Chirurgiae Digestive (pres. U.S. chpt. 1988—90), Ctrl. Surg. Assn. (sec. 1994—97, pres.-elect 1997—98, pres. 1998—99, pres. Found. 2002—03), Assn. Surg. Edn., Assn. Acad. Surgery, Am. Surg. Assn. (2d v.p. 1993—94), Am. Surg. Soc., Alpha Omega Alpha, Sigma Xi. Office: Dept Surgery Galter 10-105 251 E Huron St Chicago IL 60611-2908 Office Phone: 312-695-4908. Business E-Mail: dnahrwol@nmh.org.

**NAIDICH, THOMAS PAUL,** neuroradiologist, educator; b. Bklyn., Apr. 8, 1944; s. James and Rose (Bitko) N.; m. Rochele Miriam Pudlowksi, Feb. 2, 1975 (div. Nov. 1981); children: 1 child, Sandra Rebecca; m. Michele W. Levin, Dec. 29, 1990. BA, Cornell U., 1965; MD, NYU, NY, 1969. Diplomate in radiology and in neuroradiology Am. Bd. Radiology. Intern Bronx Mcpl. Hosp. Ctr., NY, 1969-70; resident in radiology Montefiore Hosp., Bronx, NY, 1970-73; fellow in neuroradiology NYU Sch. Medicine, NY, 1973-75; prof. radiology and neurosurgery Mt. Sinai Med. Ctr. NYU, NY, 1998—, dir. neuroradiology NY, 1998—, vice chmn. radiology for acad. affairs, 2001—; Irving and Dorothy Regenstreif Rsch. prof. of neurosci., 2002—; asst. prof. Albert Einstein Coll. Medicine, Bronx, NY, 1975-77; from asst. to assoc. prof. Mallinckrodt Inst. Radiology, St. Louis, 1978-80; from assoc. prof. to prof. Northwestern U. Sch. Medicine, Chgo., 1980-88; clin. prof. neuroradiology U. Miami Sch. Med., Fla., 1988-98; dir. neuroradiology Bapt. Hosp. Miami, Fla., 1988-98; dir Clin. Imaging Rsch. Core, Mt. Sinai Med. Ctr., Mt. Sinai, NY, 2001—05. Author: (with R. M. Quencer) Clinical Neurosonography, 1987; (with Valavanis, Schubiger) Clinical Imaging of the Cerebello-Pontine Angle, 1987; (with Daniels, Haughton) Cranial and Spinal Magnetic Ressonance Imaging, 1987, (with Duvernoy, Cattin, Fatterpeker, Raybud, Risold, Salvolini, Scarabino) The Human Hippocampus, Anatomy, Vascularization and Serial Sections with MRAI, 3d edit., 2005; editor-in-chief Neuroradiology, 1980-91, chmn. editl. bd., 1991-93; assoc. editor Surg. and Radiol. Anatomy, 1991-97; founding editor Internat. Jour. Neuroradiology, 1994-00; contbr. articles to profl. jours. Recipient John Caffey award Soc. Pediatric Radiology, 1983. Mem. Am. Soc. Neuroradiology (treas. 1991-93, Cornelius Dyke award 1975), Am. Soc. Pediatric Neuroradiology (pres. 1994-95), gold medal Sociedad Ibero-latino Americana de Neurorradiologia (SILAN), European Soc. Neuroradiology (hon.), Brit. Soc. Neuroradiologists (hon.), Swiss Soc. Neuroradiology (hon.). Avocation: antique furniture. Office: Mt Sinai Med Ctr Dept Radiology Box 1234 1 Gustave Levy Pl New York NY 10029 E-mail: thomas.naidich@mountsinai.org.

**NAIDORF, LOUIS MURRAY,** architect; b. LA, Aug. 15, 1928; s. Jack and Meriam (Abbott) N.; m. Dorise D. Roberts, June 1948 (div.); children: Victoria Beth Naidorf; m. Patricia Ann Shea, June 1, 1968 (div.); m. Patricia Ruth Allen, Dec. 6, 1992 (dec.); m. Sandra Chronis, Apr. 20, 2004. BA, U. Calif., Berkeley, 1949, MA, 1950; Doctorate (hon.), Woodbury U., 2000. Registered architect, Calif. Designer Welton Becket Assocs., L.A., 1950-51, Pereira and Luckman, L.A., 1951-52; project designer Welton Becket Assocs., L.A., 1952-55, sr. project designer, 1955-59, v.p. dir. design, 1959-70, sr. v.p., dir. rsch., 1970-73; sr. v.p., design prin. Ellerbe Becket Assocs., L.A., 1973-95; dean Sch. Architecture and Design Woodbury U., L.A., 1990-2000; prin. Allen/Naidorf Design Cons., 1995—. Mem. peer rev. panel Nat. Endowment Arts, 1995—; vis. lectr. Calif. Poly. Sch. Architecture, San Luis Obispo, 1975-82; instr. UCLA Sch. Architecture, 1985, UCLA Landscape Archtl. Program, 1980-85, Otis-Parsons, L.A., 1986-92. Prin. works include Capitol Records Bldg., Century City, Los Angeles, Hyatt Regency, Dallas, Restoration Calif. State Capitol Bldg. Bd. dir. Nat. Trust for Garden Studies, L.A., 1986—, APC, 2000; trustee Woodbury U., 2000. Recipient Honor award Nat. Trust for Hist. Preservation, 1985. Fellow AIA (bd. dir. L.A. chpt. 1977-79, Silver Medal 1950, Nat. Honor award 1985, Educator of Yr. 1997, Legacy award, 2005). Personal E-mail: naidorf@msn.com. *Leadership often requires decisions based on limited information. Course corrections can be made but only after action is taken because you can't steer a car that isn't moving.*

**NAIFEH, STEVEN WOODWARD,** writer; b. Tehran, Iran, June 19, 1952; s. George Amel and Marion (Lamphear) N.; m. AB, Princeton U., 1974; JD, Harvard U., 1977, MA, 1978. Staff lectr. Nat. Gallery Art, Washington, 1976; assoc. Milbank, Tweed, Hadley & McCloy, N.Y.C., 1976; v.p. Sabbagh, Naifeh and Assocs., Washington, 1980; co-founder & editor Woodward/White, Inc. (publishers of Best Lawyers in Am., Best Doctors in Am., Best Dentists in Am.), Aiken, SC, 1981. Author: Culture Making: Money, Success and the New York Art World, 1976; (with Gregory White Smith) Moving Up in Style, 1980, Gene Davis, 1981, How to Make Love to a Woman, 1982, What Every Client Needs to Know About Using a Lawyer, 1982, The Bargain Hunter's Guide to Art Collecting, 1982, Why Can't Men Open Up?: Overcoming Men's Fear of Intimacy, 1984, The Mormon Murders: A True Story of Greed, Forgery, Deceit, and Death, 1988, Jackson Pollack: An American Saga, 1989 (Nat. Book award nomination for nonfiction 1990, Pulitzer Prize for biography 1991), Final Justice: The True Story of the Richest Man Ever Tried for Murder, 1993, A Stranger in the Family: A True Story of Murder, Madness, and Unconditional Love, 1995, On a Street Called Easy, In a Cottage Called Joye, 1996, Making Miracles Happen, 1997; editor: (with Smith) The Best Lawyers in America series, The Best Doctors in America series, The Best Dentists in America series. Office: Woodward White Inc 129 First Ave SW Aiken SC 29801

**NAIK, SAMEER VIJAYKUMAR,** mechanical engineer, educator; arrived in U.S., 1998; s. Vijaykumar and Vijaya Naik. BSME, U. Bombay, India, 1997; MSME, Purdue U., West Lafayette, Ind., 2000; PhD, Purdue U., 2004. Grad. rsch. asst. Purdue U., West Lafayette, Ind., 1998—2004, vis. asst. prof., 2004—. Finalist Chorafas award, Dmitris A. Chorafas Found., 2004; recipient Top Grad. Gold medal, U. Bombay, 1997. Mem.: AIAA, ASME, Am. Phys. Soc., Am. Soc. Engring. Edn., Am. Chem. Soc., The Combustion Inst.,

Optical Soc. Am. Office: Purdue University Mechanical Engineering 585 Purdue Mall West Lafayette IN 47907-2088 Office Phone: 765-494-6552. Business E-Mail: naiks@ecn.purdue.edu.

**NAIL, KATHY SUE See CAPSHAW, KATE**

**NAILS, KENNETH H.,** lawyer; b. 1942; BA, Ill. Benedictine Coll., 1965; JD, John Marshall Law Sch., 1968. Bar: Ill. 1968. Sr. v.p., gen. counsel Alliance Am. Insurers, 1980—90; v.p., gen. counsel Amica Mutual Ins. Co., Providence, 1990—93, sr. v.p., gen. counsel, 1993—. Chmn. Rhode Island Insurers Insolvency Fund; lobbyist. Mem.: ABA. Office: Amica Mutual Life Ins Co PO Box 6008 Providence RI 02940-6008 Office Phone: 800-652-6422 4912. Office Fax: 401-333-4610. E-mail: knails@amica.com.

**NAIMARK, GEORGE MODELL,** marketing and management consultant; b. NYC, Feb. 5, 1925; s. Myron S. and Mary (Modell) N.; m. Helen Anne Wythes, June 24, 1946; children: Ann, Richard, Jane. BS, Bucknell U., 1947, MS, 1948; PhD, U. Del., 1951. Rsch. biochemist Brush Devel. Co., Cleve., 1951; dir. quality control Strong, Cobb & Co., Inc., Cleve., 1951-54; dir. sci. svcs. White Labs., Inc., Kenilworth, N.J., 1954-60; v.p. Burdick Assocs., Inc., N.Y.C., 1960-66; pres. Rajah Press, Summit, N.J., 1963—, Naimark and Barba, Inc., Florham Park, N.J., 1966—, Naimark & Assocs., Inc., Florham Park, N.J., 1994—; dir. Alteon, Inc., 2000—. Bd. dirs. Alteon Inc., Ramsey, N.J. Author: a Patent Manual for Scientists and Engineers, 1961, Communications on Communication, 1971, 3d edit., 1987, A Man Called Skeeter, 1996; patentee in field; contbr. articles in profl. jours. With USNR, 1944-46. Fellow AAAS, Am. Inst. Chemists; mem. Am. Chem. Soc., N.Y. Acad. Scis., Am. Mktg. Assn. Home: 87 Canoe Brook Pky Summit NJ 07901-1404 Office: Naimark & Barba Inc 248 Columbia Tpke Ste 1 Florham Park NJ 07932-1210

**NAIMOLI, VINCENT JOSEPH,** diversified financial services company executive; b. Paterson, N.J., Sept. 16, 1937; s. Ralph A. and Margaret R. (Calabrese) N.; children—Christine, Tory Ann, Alyson, Lindsey. BSM.E., U. Notre Dame, 1959; MSM.E., N.J. Inst. Tech., 1962; MBA, Fairleigh Dickinson U., 1964; grad. Advanced Mgmt. Program, Harvard Bus. Sch., 1974. With Continental Group, 1965-77, v.p., gen. mgr. ops., 1975-77; pres., chief oper. officer Allegheny Beverage Corp., Balt., 1977-78; sr. v.p., group exec. Jim Walter Corp., Tampa, Fla., 1978-81; group v.p. packaging Anchor Hocking Corp., Lancaster, Ohio, 1981-83; chmn. bd., pres., chief exec. officer Anchor Glass Container Corp., Lancaster, 1983-89; chmn., pres., CEO Anchor Industries Internat., Tampa, Fla., 1990—; chmn., chief exec. officer Electrolux Corp., Atlanta, 1990-91; chmn., CEO Doehler Jarvis Corp., Toledo, 1991-95; CEO Ladish, Inc., Milw., 1992-95; chmn., pres., CEO Harvard Industries, 1993-97; mng. gen. ptnr., CEO Tampa Bay Devil Rays, 1992—2005, chmn., 2006—. Bd. dirs. Strategic Materials, Inc. Roman Catholic. Office: Anchor Industries Internat 1 Tropicana Dr Saint Petersburg FL 33705-1703

**NAIR, BALA RADHAKRISHNAN,** engineer; b. Belgaum, Mysore, India, Feb. 14, 1936; came to U.S., 1967; s. Cherukatt Balakrishnan and Malamal Parvathy Nair; m. Indira Rajagopal Menon, Dec. 9, 1963; children: Nandita, Sarita. BS in Mech. Engring., U. Madras, 1959; MS in Indsl. Engring., Kansas State U., 1969. Jr. engr. Larsen & Toubro, Ltd., Bombay, 1959-60; trainee AEC, Bombay, 1960-61, scientific officer, 1961-64; asst. engr. Voltas Ltd., Bombay, 1964-67; sr. engr. Crane Co., Chgo., 1969-72; design engr. Rockwell Internat., Pitts., 1972-74; sr. prin. engr. Westinghouse Electric Corp., Pitts., 1978—85, engring. mgr., 1986—. Patentee in field; contbr. articles to profl. jours. Recipient grand prize Excellence in Design, Design News Mag., Chgo., 1988, R & D Mag. award, 1993. Mem. ASME, Am. Nuclear Soc., Laser Inst. Am., Titanium Devel. Assn. Republican. Hindu. Avocations: reading, travel. Home: 5556 Forbes Ave Pittsburgh PA 15217 Office: Curtiss Wright Electromechanical Corp Cheswick PA 15024

**NAIR, GANESH KUMAR VENUGOPALAN,** endocrinologist, internist, educator; arrived in U.S., 1995; s. Venugopalan and Sreekumari Nair; m. Usha Kartha, Jan. 21, 1996; 1 child, Nikhil. Student, U. Kerala, 1981—83, MBBS, 1989. Diplomate in internal medicine and in endocrinology, diabetes and metabolism Am. Bd. Internal Medicine, cert. in thyroid ultrasound and guided biopsy, clin. densitometrist, lic. Jamaican Med. Coun. Intern Kerala U., Trivandrum, Kerala State, India, 1990—91; sr. ho. surgeon Gastroenterology Med. Coll. Trivandrum, 1991, rsch. asst. Gastroenterology, 1991—92; intern Ministry Health, Kingston, Jamaica, 1992; jr. resident Kingston Pub. Hosp., 1993—95; resident internal medicine Conemaugh Valley Meml. Hosp. Program Temple U., Johnstown, Pa., 1995—98; chief resident, internal medicine Conemaugh Valley Meml. Hosp. Program, 1998—99; fellow endocrinology, diabetes and metabolism U. Ark., 1999—2001, asst. prof. medicine, 2002—05; staff physician Ctrl. Ark. Vets. Healthcare Sys., Little Rock, 2002—05; attending endocrinologist Little Rock Diagnostic Clinic, 2005—. Assoc. program dir. endocrinology, diabetes and metabolism fellowship program U. Ark., Little Rock, 2003—05. Contbr. articles to profl. jours. Recipient Cert. of Merit, Sahodara Samajam Nair Sanodara Samajam. Karayogam, 1981, 1983. Fellow: ACP, Am. Coll. Physicians, Am. Coll. Endocrinology; mem.: Internat. Soc. Clin. Densitometry, The Endocrine Soc., Am. Assn. Clin. Endocrinologists. Office Phone: 501-227-8000. Personal E-mail: gnair@lrdc.com.

**NAIR, MIRA,** film director, film producer; b. Bhubaneshwar, Orissa, India, Oct. 15, 1957; m. Mahmood Mamdani; 1 child, Zohran. Student, U. New Delhi, Harvard U. Dir., prodr. (films) Salaam Bombay, 1988 (Camera d'Or and Prix du Publique, Cannes Film Festival, Acad. Award nominee for Best Fgn. Lang. Film), Mississippi Masala, 1991 (three awards at Venice Film Festival), Kama Sutra: A Tale of Love, 1996, Monsoon Wedding, 2001 (Golden Lion Award, Venice Film Festival), dir. only (films) Jama Masjid Street Journal, 1979, So Far From India, 1982, The Perez Family, 1995, September 11, 2002, Vanity Fair, 2004; prodr. only (films) Still, the Children Are Here, 2002; dir. (TV movies) India Cabaret, 1985 (American Film Festival Award for Best Documentary of 1985), Children of a Desired Sex, 1987, My Own Country, 1998, The Laughing Club of India, 1999, Hysterical Blindness, 2002. Office: Mirabi Films Inc 5 E 16th St 12th Fl New York NY 10003

**NAIR, RAMACHANDRAN P.K.,** agroforestry educator, researcher; b. Trivandrum, Kerala, India, Mar. 12, 1942; came to U.S., 1987. s. Krishna Kittu Pillai and Parukutty Amma; m. Vimala Devi Pillai, Aug. 29, 1973; children: Bindu, Deepa, Rekha. BS in Agr., Kerala U., 1961, MS in Agr., 1968; PhD, Pantnagar U., India, 1971; DSc in Agr., U. Goettingen, W. Germany, 1978; DSc (hon.), Kyoto U., 2002, U. Sci. and Tech., Kumasi, Ghana, 2005, U. Guelph, Ont., Can., 2006. Research asst. Kerala Agrl. U., 1961-66, lectr. in agronomy, 1966; post-doctoral fellow Rothamsted Experimental Sta., Harpenden, Eng., 1971-72; agronomist ICAR (CPCRI), Kasaragod, Kerala, 1972-76; Humboldt fellow U. Goettingen, 1976-78; prin. sci. Internat. Centre for Rsch. in Agroforestry, Nairobi, Kenya, 1978-87; prof. agroforestry U. Fla., Gainesville, 1987-2001, Disting. prof., 2001—. rschr. numerous orgns. Author: Intensive Multiple Cropping with Coconuts in India, 1979, Agroforestry Species: A Crop Sheets Manual, 1980, Soil Productivity Aspects of Agroforestry, 1984, An Introduction to Agroforestry, 1993; co-editor: Agroforestry: A Decade of Developments, 1987, Directions in Tropical Agroforestry Research, 1998, New Vistas in Agroforestry, 2004, Tropical Homegardens, 2006; editor: Agroforestry Systems in the Tropics, 1989, Agroforestry Systems 1982—, chief editor, 1994. Recipient Internat. Soil Sci. award, 2001, Internat. Agronomy award, 2000, Internat. Crop Sci. award, 2004, Disting. Educator, U. Fla., 2004, Sci. Achievement award, Internat. Union of Forest Rsch. Orgns., 2005, Advisor/Mentoring award, U. Fla., 2006, Humboldt prize, Germany, 2006. Fellow AAAS, Am. Soc. Agronomy (chair divsn. A-6 internat. agronomy 1995-96), Nat. Acad. Agrl. Scis. India, Soil Sci. Soc. Am.; mem. Internat. Soil Sci. Soc., Internat. Soc. Tropical Foresters, Soc. Am. Foresters (Barington-Moore award, 2004). Office: U Fla 118 Newins Ziegler Hall Gainesville FL 32611-0410 E-mail: pknair@ufl.edu.

**NAIR, SANKAR,** chemical engineer, educator; b. New Delhi, Sept. 19, 1975; arrived in U.S., 1997; BTech in Chem. Engring., Indian Inst. Tech., New Delhi, 1997; MS in Physics, U. Mass., 2002, PhD in Chem. Engring., 2002. Postdoctoral fellow Nat. Inst. Stds. & Tech., Gaithersburg, Md., 2002—03; asst. prof. Ga. Inst. Tech., Atlanta, 2003—. Contbr. articles to profl. jours. Grantee, NSF, 2005—, ExxonMobil Corp., 2006—; Nanoscale Interdisciplinary Rsch. Team grantee, NSF, 2004—. Mem.: AIChE (organizer tech. session 1998—2006), Am. Phys. Soc., Am. Chem. Soc. (grantee 2006—). Achievements include patents in field. Office: Ga Inst Tech 311 Ferst Dr NW Atlanta GA 30332-0100 Office Phone: 404-894-4826.

**NAIR, VELAYUDHAN,** pharmacologist, educator, academic administrator; arrived in U.S., 1956, naturalized, 1963; m. Jo Ann Burke, Nov. 30, 1957; children: David, Larry, Sharon. PhD in Medicine, U. London, 1956, DSc, 1976, LHD (hon.) h.c., 2003. Rsch. assoc. U. Ill. Coll. Medicine, 1956-58; asst. prof. U. Chgo. Sch. Medicine, 1958-63; dir. lab. neuropharmacology and biochemistry Michael Reese Hosp. and Med. Ctr., Chgo., 1963-68, dir. therapeutic rsch., 1968-71; prof. pharmacology FUHS/Chgo. Med. Sch., 1971—, disting prof., 2001, vice chmn. dept. pharmacology and therapeutics, 1971—76, dean Sch. Grad. and Postdoctoral Studies, 1976—2003, v.p. rsch., 1999—2003, v.p. dean emeritus, 2003—, disting. prof., 2001. Vis. assoc. prof. pharmacology FUHS/Chgo. Med. Sch., 1963—68, vis. prof., 1968—71, Harvard U., 1994, Johns Hopkins Sch. Medicine, 1995. Contbr. articles to profl. jours. Recipient Morris Parker award, U. Health Scis./Chgo. Med. Sch., 1972. Fellow: AAAS, Am. Coll. Clin. Pharmacology, N.Y. Acad. Scis.; mem.: AAUP, Internat. Soc. Devel. Neurosci., Am. Coll. Toxicology, Internat. Soc. Chronobiology, Soc. Neurosci., Soc. Exptl. Biology & Medicine, Pan Am. Med. Assn. (coun. on toxicology), Royal Inst. Chemistry (London), Brit. Chem. Soc., Am. Chem. Soc., Soc. Toxicology, Radiation Rsch. Soc., Am. Soc. Clin. Pharmacology & Therapeutics, Am. Soc. Pharmacology & Exptl. Therapeutics, Internat. Soc. Biochem. Pharmacology, Internat. Brain Rsch. Orgn., Cosmos Club (Washington), Alpha Omega Alpha, Sigma Xi. Office: Rosalind Franklin Univ Medicine and Sci 3333 Green Bay Rd North Chicago IL 60064-3037 Personal E-mail: velnair@comcast.net. *Success like happiness is relative and can only be gauged by one's own standards and ideals. There is probably no universal formula for either of them, but I have been guided by the following tenets: Dedication and committment to one's responsibilities and in the conduct of everyday life, honesty and sincerity in personal relations. One must have tolerance for those in less fortunate situations. As one grows older, one recognizes that no one makes it alone. As for me, I have received help from many; some of whom I can never repay except by passing on the gift which I was privileged to share. Above all, a faith that looks beyond the immediate helps to bear the inevitable ups and downs in life.*

**NAIR, VELUPILLAI KRISHNAN,** cardiologist; b. Kerala, India, Dec. 30, 1941; came to U.S., 1973; s. Veupillai and Bharathy Nair; m. Sathy C. Nair, Apr. 22, 1971; children: Parvathy, Pradeep. BSc, Kerala U., Trivandrum, India, 1961, MB BS, 1965, MD, 1971. Diplomate Am. Bd. Internal Medicine, Am. Bd. Cardiology. Intern, resident, fellow in cardiology Bergen Pines County Hosp., Paramus, NJ; asst. prof. N.Y. Med. Coll. Lincoln Hosp., Bronx, 1979-80; cardiologist, dir. cardiology svc. Somerset (Pa.) Hosp., 1980—, chief of med. dental staff, 1990-93. V.p. bd. dirs. Somerset Hosp., 1997, Somerset Health Svcs., 2000—; clin. asst. prof. Drexel U. Coll. Medicine, 1996—; bd. dirs. Somerset Hosp., 1993—99, 2000—. Former pres. Somerset County divsn. Am. Heart Assn.; bd. dirs. Somerset Hosp. Fellow ACP, Am. Coll. Cardiology; mem. AMA, Pa. Med. Soc., Somerset County Med. Soc. (former pres.), Soc. Hypertension, Soc. Echocardiography, Cardiac Club (advisor). Avocations: reading, tennis, travel. Office: 223 S Pleasant Ave Somerset PA 15501-2188 Office Phone: 814-445-7101. E-mail: vknair@pol.net.

**NAIRN, RODERICK,** immunologist, educator, biochemist; b. Dumbarton, Scotland, Mar. 25, 1951; came to U.S., 1976; s. James Bell and Muriel Elizabeth (Hyde) N.; m. Morag Gilhooly, Dec. 29, 1971; 1 child, Carolyn Mhairi. BS, U. Strathclyde, Glasgow, Scotland, 1973; PhD, U. London, 1976. Postdoctoral fellow Albert Einstein Sch. Medicine, N.Y.C., 1976-81; asst. prof. U. Mich. Med. Sch., Ann Arbor, 1981-87, assoc. prof., 1987-95, dir. student biomed. rsch. programs, 1989-92, dir. med. scientist tng. program, 1992-95; prof., chair dept. med. microbiology and immunology Sch. Medicine, Creighton U., Omaha, 1995—, interim dean, 1997-98, sr. assoc. dean academic affairs, 1998—. Contbr. chpts. to books, articles to profl. jours. Grantee NIH, Am. Cancer Soc. Mem. AAAS, Am. Che. Soc., Soc. for Microbiology, Am. Assn. Immunologists. Presbyterian. Office: Creighton U Sch Medicine Dept Med Microbiology & Immu Omaha NE 68178-0001 E-mail: rnairn@creighton.edu.

**NAJARIAN, JOHN SARKIS,** surgeon, educator; b. Oakland, Calif., Dec. 22, 1927; s. Garabed L. and Siranoush T. (Demirjian) N.; m. Arlys Viola Mignette Anderson, Apr. 27, 1952; children: Jon, David, Paul, Peter. AB with honors, U. Calif., Berkeley, 1948; MD, U. Calif., San Francisco, 1952; LHD (hon.), U. Athens, 1980; DSc (hon.), Gustavus Adolphus Coll., 1981; LHD (hon.), Calif. Luth. Coll., 1983. Diplomate Am. Bd. Surgery. Surg. intern U. Calif., San Francisco, 1952-53, surg. resident, 1955-60, asst. prof. surgery, dir. surg. research labs., chief transplant service dept. surgery, 1963-66, prof., vice chmn., 1966-67; spl. research fellow in immunopathology U. Pitts. Med. Sch., 1960-61; NIH sr. fellow and assoc. in tissue transplantation immunology Scripps Clinic and Research Found., La Jolla, Calif., 1961-63; Markle scholar Acad. Medicine, 1964-69; prof., chmn. dept. surgery U. Minn. Hosp., Mpls., 1967-93; med. dir. Transplant Ctr., clin. chief surgery Univ. Hosp., 1967-94; chief hosp. staff U. Minn. Hosp., Mpls., 1970-71, Regents' prof., 1985-95, Jay Phillips Disting. Chair in Surgery, 1986-93, prof. emeritus, prof. surgery, 1995—. Spl. cons. USPHS, NIH Clin. Rsch. Tng. Com., Inst. Gen. Med. Scis., 1965-69; cons. U.S. Bur. Budget, 1966-68; mem. sci. adv. bd. Nat. Kidney Found., 1968; mem. surg. study sect. A div. rsch. grants NIH, 1970; chmn. renal transplant adv. group VA Hosps., 1971; mem. bd. sci. cons. Sloan-Kettering Inst. Cancer Rsch., 1971-78; mem. screening com. Dernham Postdoctoral Fellowships in Oncology, Calif. div. Am. Cancer Soc. Editor: (with Richard L. Simmons) Transplantation, 1972; co-editor: Manual of Vascular Access, Organ Donation, and Transplantation, 1984; mem. editorial bd. Jour. Surg. Rsch., 1968—, Minn. Medicine, 1968—, Jour. Surg. Oncology, 1968—, Am. Jour. Surgery, 1967—, assoc. editor, 1982—; mem. editorial bd. Year Book of Surgery, 1970-85, Transplantation, 1970—, Transplantation Procs, 1970—, Bd. Clin. Editors, 1981-84, Annals of Surgery, 1972—, World Jour. Surgery, 1976—, Hippocrates, 1986—, Jour. Transplant Coordination, 1990—; assoc. editor: Surgery, 1971; editor-in-chief: Clin. Transplantation, 1986—. Bd. dirs., v.p. Variety Club Heart Hosp., U. Minn.; trustee, v.p. Minn. Med. Found. Served with USAF, 1953-55. Hon. fellow Royal Coll. Surgeons of Eng., 1987; hon. prof. U. Madrid, 1990; named Alumnus of Yr., U. Calif. Med. Sch., San Francisco, 1977; recipient award Calif. Trudeau Soc., 1962, Ann. Brotherhood award NCCJ, 1978, Disting. Achievement award Modern Medicine, 1978, Internat. Gt. Am. award B'nai B'rith Found., 1982, Uncommon Citizen award, 1985, Sir James Carreras award Variety Clubs Internat., 1987, Silver medal IXth Centenary, U. Bologna, 1988, Humanitarian of Yr. award, U. Minn., 1992, Najarian Festschrift award Am. Jour. Surgery, 1993, Jubilee medal Swedish Soc. Medicine, 1994. Fellow ACS; mem. AAAS, AMA, Internat. Pediat. Transplantation Assn. (pres. 1998-2000), Soc. Univ. Surgeons, Soc. Exptl. Biology and Medicine, Am. Soc. Exptl. Pathology, Am. Surg. Assn. (pres. 1988-89), Am. Assn. Immunologists, Transplantation Soc. (v.p. western hemisphere 1984-86, pres. 1994-96, Medawar prize 2004, Ellis Island medal of Hon, 2005), Am. Soc. Nephrology, Internat. Soc. Nephrology, Am. Assn. Lab. Animal Sci., Assn. Acad. Surgery (pres. 1969), Internat. Soc. Surgery, Soc. Surg. Chairmen, Soc. Clin. Surgery, Ctrl. Surg. Assn., Minn. Med. Soc., Hennepin County Med. Soc., Minn. Surg. Soc., Mpls. Surg Soc, St. Paul Surg. Soc. Howard C. Nafziger Surg. Soc., Portland Surg Soc., Halsted Surg. Soc., Am. Heart Assn., Am. Soc. Transplant Surgeons (pres. 1977-78), Coun on Kidney in Cardiovasc. Disease, Hagfish Soc., Italian Rsch. Soc., Minn. Acad. Medicine, Minn. Med. Assn., Minn. Med. Found., Surg. Biology Club,

Sigma Xi, Alpha Omega Alpha, others. Office: U Minn Surgery Dept Mayo Mail Code 195 420 Delaware St SE Minneapolis MN 55455-0374 Office Phone: 612-625-8444. Business E-Mail: najar001@umn.edu.

**NAJEE, (JEROME NAJEE RASHEED),** musician; b. NYC, Nov. 4, 1957; m. Regina Jackson, May 27, 1989; 2 children. Musician: (albums) Najee's Theme, 1986 (Soul Train Music award for Best Jazz Album, 1988), Day by Day, 1988, Tokyo Blue, 1990 (Soul Train Music award for Best Jazz Album, 1990), Just an Illusion, 1992, Share My World, 1994, Songs from the Key of Life, 1995, Morning Tenderness, 1998, Embrace, 2003, My Point of View, 2005, performs with various artists including Freddie Jackson, Will Downing, Jeffrey Osborne, Marcus Miller, Paul Jackson Jr., George Duke, Prince, and others. Recipient Image award for Outstanding Jazz Artist, NAACP, 2006. Office: FAN Entertainment Ste 689 3940 Laurel Canyon Blvd Studio City CA 91604 also: Heads Up Internat 23309 Commerce Park Rd Cleveland OH 44122 E-mail: najee@najeeonline.com.*

**NAJIMY, KATHY,** actress; Actress theater The Kathy and Mo Show, 1985-89 (also writer)(Obie award, 1989), Afterbirth: Kathy and Mo's Greatest Hits, 2004; Broadway shows Dirty Blonde, 2001; films Topsy and Bunker, Other People's Money, 1991, The Hard Way, 1991, The Fisher King, 1991, Soapdish, 1991, This Is My Life, 1992, Sister Act, 1992, Hocus Pocus, 1993, Sister Act 2: Back in the Habit, 1993, It's Pat, 1994, Jeffrey, 1995, Cats Dont' Dance, 1997, Nevada, 1997, Woman Without Implants, 1997, Hope Floats, 1998, Zack and Reba, 1998, Bride of Chucky, 1998, Attention Shoppers, 2000, Leaving Peoria, 2000, The Wedding Planner, 2001, Rat Race, 2001; TV: King of the Hill (voice), 1997-, Veronica's Closet, 1997-2001; TV movies: If These Walls Could Talk II, 2000, The Scream Team, 2002. Office: Creative Arts Agy 9830 Wilshire Blvd Beverly Hills CA 90212-1804

**NAJITA, TETSUO,** history professor; b. Honokaa, Hawaii, Mar. 30, 1936; s. Niichi and Kikuno (Manpuku) N.; m. Elinor Moon, Aug. 2, 1958; children: Mie Kim, Kiyoshi Young. BA, Grinnell Coll., 1958; MA, Harvard U., 1960, PhD, 1965; LLD, Grinnell Coll., 1989. Asst. prof. Carleton Coll., Northfield, Minn., 1964-66, Washington U., St. Louis, 1966-68; assoc. prof. U. Wis., Madison, 1968-69; Robert S. Ingersoll disting. prof. history/Japanese studies U. Chgo., 1969—2002, prof. emeritus, 2002—, dir. Ctr. for East Asian Studies, 1974-80, assoc. dean, 1983-87, master collegiate div. social scis., 1983-87. John A. Burns disting. visiting chair U. Hawaii, Manoa, 1994; chair dept. history U. Chgo., 1994-97; Ena H. Thompson lectr. Pomona Coll., 1996; Catherine Gould Chism vis. prof. U. Puget Sound, Tacoma; Maruyame Masao lectr. U. Calif., Berkeley, 2000; bd. dirs. Pacific Basin Inst., 2004. Author: Hara Kei in the Politics of Compromise, 1969 (J.K. Fairbank prize Am. Hist. Assn.), Intellectual Foundations of Modern Japanese Politics, 1974, Visions of Virtue in Tokugawa Japan, 1987, Tokugawa Political Writings, 1998. Grantee NEH 1973-74, 1980-81; Fulbright fellow 1961-63, 68, Guggenheim fellow 1980-81, Mellon Emeritus fellow. 2004-; recipient Yamagata Banto prize Prefecture of Osaka, 1989 Fellow Am. Acad. Arts and Scis.; mem. Am. Hist. Assn., Assn. for Asian Studies (v.p., pres. 1991-93), Phi Beta Kappa. Office: U Chgo Dept History 1126 E 59th St Chicago IL 60637-1580

**NAJJAR, DIANA,** elementary school educator; d. Carl and Mary Snider; children: David, Mark. BS in Elem. Edn., Ball State U., 1970; MS in Edn. with concentration in Spl. Edn., Val. C.-Purdue U., Indpls., 1977; postgrad. in gifted edn., Purdue U., 1981—83. Cert. elem. edn. tchr. Ind. Dept. Edn. Tchr. Indpls. Pub. Schs., 1970—72, The Orchard Sch., Indpls., 1984—. Gov.'s sch. task group State Dept. of Ind., 1984—86; creator dance curriculum; dance instr., choreographer sch. musicals, plays, operettas; screenwriter, actress Factor Blocks math video, 1999. Author: (book and math. kit) Namagram, 1997; author, actress: video Factor Blocks, 2000. Catechism coach St. George Ch., Indpls., 1989—95, 2005—06. Mem.: Nat. Assn. for the Gifted (legis. team 2005—05, legis. chmn. 1979—88, Svc. award 1985). Achievements include discovery of 4 set Venn diagram; created test to measure conceptual understanding of mathematical concepts through constructions; copywright Namagram book and design. Office: The Orchard Sch 615 W 64th St Indianapolis IN 46260

**NAJMABADI, FARROKH,** engineering educator; b. Tehran, Iran, Mar. 28, 1955; s. Hossien and Farangis Najmabadi; m. Alisa Chin, Dec. 21, 1981; children: Shannon Cassidy, Melissa Sheridan. BS, Tehran U., 1976; MS in Engring., U. Calif., Berkeley, 1977, PhD in Engring., 1982. Prin. inst. scientist UCLA, 1982—94; prof. elec. & computer engring. U. Calif. San Diego, 1995—, dep. dir. Ctr. Energy Rsch., 2004—. Chmn. rev./adv. panels Dept. Energy, numerous nat. labs. Editor: sci. jours.; contbr. scientific papers to profl. jours. Named Outstanding Engring. Prof., U. Calif. San Diego, 2003; recipient David Rose award of Excellence in Fusion Engring., Fusion Power Assocs., 1995, Leadership in Fusion Engring., 2004, Outstanding Achievement award, Fusion Energy divsn. Am. Nuc. Soc., 2002. Mem.: ANS, APS, IEEE, Eta Kappa Nu, Tau Beta Pi. Achievements include research in fusion energy and applied plasma physics; laser-matter and laser-plasma interaction. Office: U Calif San Diego 457b Ebuii MC 0438 La Jolla CA 92093-0438 Office Phone: 858-534-7869. Business E-Mail: fnajmabadi@ucsd.edu.

**NAKA, YOSHIFUMI,** surgeon, researcher; b. Aug. 9, 1959; arrived in U.S. 1993; s. Yasushi and Eiko Naka; m. Kayoko Tomoda Naka, Dec. 24, 1988; 1 child, Ryoko. Completion of premed. course, Osaka (Japan) U., 1980; MD, Osaka U., 1984, PhD, 1988. Cert. Japanese Bd. Surgery, lic. physician N.Y., Japan. Resident Osaka U. Hosp., 1984—86; rsch. and clin. fellow Osaka U. Med. Sch., 1986—89; resident Osaka Police Hosp., 1989—93; postdoctoral rsch. fellow dept. physiology Columbia U., N.Y.C., 1993—96, instr. clin. dept. surgery, 1996—99, asst. prof. surgery 1999—. Dir. cardiac transplantation and mech. circulatory support program N.Y.-Presbyn. Hosp., N.Y.C., 2003—. Guest editor: Annals of Thoracic Surgery, 2001; author: Atherosclerosis and Coronary/Artery Disease, 1996; contbr. to profl. jours. including Jour. of Clin. Investment, Nat. Sci., Proc. Nat. Acad. Sci., 2003; author: Cardiac Surgery in the Adult, 2003. Named Herbert Irving asst. prof. surg. treatment of atrial fibrillation, Columbia U. Physicians and Surgeons, 2001—; recipient grant, Found. for Advanced of Cardiac Therapies, 2002—; grantee KO-8 grant, Vein Graft Preservation Thrombosis, and Neointimal Disease/NIH, 2001—05. Mem.: ASAIO, Soc. Univ. Surgeons, Internat. Soc. for Heart and Lung Transplantation, N.Y. Soc. Thoracic Surgeons. Am. Heart Assn. Avocations: tennis, downhill skiing, reading, cooking. Office: Milstein Hosp Bldg 7-435 177 Ft Washington Ave New York NY 10032

**NAKAGAWA, ALLEN DONALD,** radiologic technologist; b. N.Y.C., Mar. 14, 1955; s. Walter Tsunehiko and Alyce Tsuneko (Kinoshita) N. BS in Environ. Studies, St. John's U., Jamaica, N.Y., 1977; MS in Marine Biology, C.W. Post Coll., 1980. Cert. radiologic technologist, in fluoroscopy, Calif. Research asst. environ. studies St. John's U., 1976-78; lab. asst. Bur. Water Surveillance, Nassau Co. of Health Dept., Wantaugh, NY, 1978; clin. endocrinology asst. U. Calif. VA Hosp., San Francisco, 1981-83; student technologist St. Mary's Hosp., San Francisco, 1985-86; radiologic technologist Mt. Zion Hosp., San Francisco, 1986-88; sr. radiologic technologist U. Calif., San Francisco, 1989—, urosurg. radiologic technologist, 1988-89, sr. radiologic technologist, 1989—, sr. surg. radiologic technologist, 2003—. Attendee U. Calif. San Francisco Trauma and Emergency Radiology Conf., 1995, U. Calif. San Francisco Musculoskeletal MRI Conf., 1996, PACS for Hour Hosp., 1998, Breast Imaging for Technologists and Health Care Providers, U. Calif. Stanford Health Care, 1999, Clinical MRI 2000, U. Calif., San Francisco, 2000, Resident Rev. Diagnostic Imaging, U. Calif. San Francisco, 2001, Digital X-ray & PACs for An Ednl. Forum, 2002. Mem.: ACLU, Calif. Acad. Scis., Calif. Soc. Radiologic Technologists, Am. Soc. Radiologic Technologists, Am. Registry Radiologic Technologists (licentiate; cert.), Sigma Xi. Democrat. Methodist. Avocations: photography, music, environmentalist, volunteering, studying advanced technology. Personal E-mail: datarover@yahoo.com. *If you know, believe and have faith in yourself first, only then can you endeavor to assist someone else. Otherwise, you have wasted your efforts and may have even caused a loss of life.*

**NAKAGAWA, KOJI,** endocrinologist, educator; b. Sapporo, Hokkaido, Japan, June 5, 1932; s. Satosu and Michi (Yokoyama) N.; m. Keiko Hirato, Oct. 20, 1962; children: Shin, Tamao Yamaguchi. MD, Hokkaido U., 1957, PhD, 1962. Lic. endocrinologist, Japan. Staff scientist Worcester Found. for Exptl. Biology, Shrewsbury, Mass., 1964-65; rsch. staff Syntex Rsch. Ctr., Palo Alto, Calif., 1965; rsch. fellow U. Utah Med. Ctr., Salt Lake City, 1965-66; rsch. assoc. 2d dept. medicine Hokkaido U. Sch. Medicine, Sapporo, 1967-83, asst. prof., 1983-89; prof. Health Adminstrn. Ctr., Hokkaido U. Edn., Sapporo, 1989-96, dir. Health Adminstrn. Ctr., 1990-96; prof. dept. nutrition Tenshi Coll., Sapporo, 2000—04. Contbr. articles to profl. jours. Fellow Japan Endocrine Soc.; mem. Endocrine Soc., Japanese Soc. Internal Medicine, Japan Diabetes Soc. Home: 2-8 4-chome Yamanote 1-jo Nishi-ku Sapporo 063-0001 Japan

**NAKAJIMA, HIROSHI,** education educator; b. Hiroshima, Japan, June 12, 1923; s. Iwao and Tamae (Takenaka) N.; m. Sei Sakao, May 2, 1966; children: Akihiko, Takehiko. Student, Nishogakusha Coll., 1942-44; BA, Waseda U., 1950; MA, 1954, EdD (hon.), 1989. Asst. prof. Japan women's Coll. Econs., 1954-59; lectr. Waseda U., 1954-63; asst. prof., 1963-68; prof. comparative and internat. edn., 1968-94; prof. emeritus, 1994—. Vis. prof. U. Helsinki, 1962-63; advisor Japanese Inst. Social Studies on Sweden, 1989—; vicechmn. youth com. Higashikurumeshi, 1978-83; mem. bd. edn. Higashikurumeshi, 1983-91. Served with Japanese Army, 1943-46. Recipient Acad. Hon. Medal U. Helsinki, 1963; decorated Nat. 3rd Order, 2000. Mem.: Comparative and Internat. Edn. Soc. (mem. 1963), Finnish Acad. Sci. and Letters (fgn. 1984). Home: 1-4-37 Minamisawa Higashikurume-shi Tokyo 203-0023 Japan Office Phone: 81-3-5606-4311. Business E-Mail: nakajima@textbook-rc.or.jp.

**NAKAMURA, HIROSHI,** urology educator; b. Tokyo, Mar. 22, 1933; s. Yataroh and Hideko (Tanaka) N.; m. Miyoko Kodachi, Aug. 13, 1966. MD, Keio U., Tokyo, 1960; PhD, Grad. Sch. Medicine, Keio U., 1966. Med. diplomate. Asst. resident Mt. Sinai Hosp., N.Y.C., 1962—63; rsch. fellow Cornell U. Med. Coll., N.Y.C., 1966—68; asst. Sch. Medicine Keio U., Tokyo, 1968—70; chmn. urology dept. Tokyo Elec. Power Hosp., Tokyo, 1970—73; vis. asst. prof. surgery Cornell U. Med. Coll., N.Y.C., 1973; chmn. urology Kitasato Inst. Hosp., Tokyo, 1973—77; chmn. dept., prof. urology Nat. Def. Med. Coll., Tokorozawa, Saitama, Japan, 1977—98, dir. dept. acad. affairs, 1994—96, prof. emeritus, 1999—; emeritus dir. Tokorozawa Ishikawa Clinic, 1998—. Author: Bedside Urology, 1983, Modern Clinical Point-Urology, 1993; editor: Up-to-Date Urology, 1983, Caveats & Pitfalls in Clinical Urology, 1999, Medical Ethics Q&A, 2002. Recipient Tamura award, Keio U. Sch. Medicine, 1967, All-around Med. award, Igaku-Shoin, Ltd., Tokyo, 1967, The Order of the Sacred Treasure, Emperor of Japan, 2003. Buddhist. Avocations: jazz, audiophile, travel, fishing, baseball. Home: 11-1-1204 Higashicho Tokorozawa Saitama 359-1116 Japan Office: Tokorozawa Ishikawa Clin Iseki Bldg 4F 9-22 Hiyoshicho Tokorozawa 359-1123 Japan Office Phone: 04-2925-7355. Business E-Mail: hiroshin@xd5.so-net.ne.jp.

**NAKAMURA, RICHARD,** mental health services professional; BA Psychology, Earlham Coll.; MA Psychology, NYU; PhD Psychology, SUNY, Stony Brook. Postdoctoral fellow intramural lab. neuropsychology Nat. Inst. Mental Health, 1976, chief behavioral and integrative neurosci., 1990, dir. sci. policy and program planning, 1990, acting dir., 2001—02. Mem. info. tech. bd. dirs. NIH. Recipient Disting. Svc. award, Dept. Health and Human Svcs. Sec., 2000, 2004, Outstanding Achievement award, NIH Asian/Pacific Am. Orgn.'s, 2001, Pres. Meritorious Exec. award, 2002. Office: Rm 235 6001 Executive Blvd Bethesda MD 20892-9669

**NAKAMURA, ROBERT MOTOHARU,** pathologist; b. Montebello, Calif., June 10, 1927; s. Mosaburo and Haru (Suematsu) N.; m. Shigeyo Jane Hayashi, July 29, 1957; children: Mary, Nancy. AB, Whittier Coll., 1949; MD, Temple U., 1954. Cert. of spl. qualification in pathologic anatomy, clin pathology, immunopathology, Am. Bd. Pathology. Prof. pathology U. Calif., Irvine, 1971-74, adj. prof. pathology, 1974-75; chmn. dept. pathology Scripps Clinic and Rsch. Found., La Jolla, Calif., 1974-92; sr. cons., 1992—; pres. Scripps Clinic Med. Group, La Jolla, 1981-91; prof. dept. immunology and exptl. and molecular medicine Scripps Rsch. Inst., 1997—; chmn. pathology Scripps Clinic, 1998-99, chmn. emeritus pathology, 1999—. Adj. prof. pathology U. Calif., San Diego, 1975-93. Co-editor: Jr. Clin. Lab. Analysis, 1989—; contbr. articles to profl. jours. Fellow: Coll. Am. Pathologists, Am. Soc. Clin. Pathologists, Assn. Clin. Scientists, Am. Coll. Nutrition; mem. Internat. Acad. Pathology, Avocation: reading. Home: 8841 Nottingham Pl La Jolla CA 92037-2131 Office Phone: 858-554-8166. Personal E-mail: rnakamura@pol.net.

**NAKAMURA, SHUJI,** engineering educator; b. Seto, Japan, May 22, 1954; BEE, U. Tokushima, Japan, 1977; MEE, U. Tokushima, 1979, DEng, 1994. R&D staff Nichia Chem. Industry, Ltd., 1979—84, group head R&D 1st sect., 1985—88, group head R&D 2nd sect., 1989—93, sr. rschr. dept. R&D, 1993—99; prof. materials dept. U. Calif., Santa Barbara, 1999—, dir., Solid State Lighting & Display Ctr. Vis. rsch. assoc. electronic engring. U. Fla., 1988—89. Mem. editl. bd.: Applied Physics Soc., 1998—2000; published several papers. Named Cree Prof. in Solid State Light and Display Endowed chair, 2001; recipient Nikkei Bus. Publications Engring. award, 1994, 1996, Best Paper award, Japanese Applied Physics Soc., 1994, 1997, Sakurai award, 1995, Nishina Meml. award. 1996, IEEE Lasers and Electro-Optics Soc. Engring. Achievement award, 1996, Spl. Recognition award, Soc. for Info. Display, 1996, Okochi Meml. award, 1997, medal award, Materials Rsch. Soc., 1997, Innovation in Real Materials award, 1998, C&C award, Jack A. Morton award, IEEE, 1998, Brit. Rank prize, 1998, Julius-Springer prize for applied physics, 1999, Takayanagi award, 2000, Carl Zeiss Rsch. award, 2000, Honda award, 2000, Crystal Growth and Crystal Tech. award, 2000, Asahi award, 2001, OSA Nick Holonyak award, 2001, LEOS Disting. Lectr. award, 2001, Benjamin Franklin medal in engring., Franklin Inst., 2002, Millennium Tech. prize for his inventions in light and laser tech., Millennium Prize Found., 2006. Mem.: NAE. Achievements include development of first group-III nitride-based blue/green LEDs; design of first group-III nitride-based violet laser diodes; patents in field. Office: Materials Dept Univ Calif Santa Barbara CA 93106-5050 Office Phone: 805-893-5552. E-mail: shuji@engineering.ucsb.edu.*

**NAKAMURA, TORU,** research scientist, educator; PhD, U. Colo. Boulder, 1999. Rsch. assoc. The Scripps Rsch. Inst., La Jolla, Calif., 1999—2004.

**NAKANISHI, ALAN,** ophthalmologist, state representative; b. Sacramento, Calif., Mar. 21, 1940; BA in Chem., Pacific Union Coll., 1962; MD, Loma Linda U.; MS in Health Adminstrn., Va. Commonwealth U. 1991. Intern, L.A. Coutny Med. Ctr. L.A. County Med. Ctr. U. So. Calif., 1965-66; resident, L.A. County Med. Ctr. Delta Eye Med. Group, 1966-69, ophthalmologist Stockton Calif., 1969—; mem. Lodi City Council, 1998—2001; mayor Lodi, Calif., 2001; mem. Calif. Ho. of Reps., 2002—; com. on aging and long-term care, com. on health, com. on higher edu. & com. on public employees, retirement and social security Calif. Ho. of Reps. Maj. M.C., U.S. Army, 1969-71. Office: Delta Eye Med Group 1617 Saint Marks Plz Stockton CA 95207-6423 also: State Capital PO Box 942849 Sacramento CA 94249

**NAKANISHI, DON TOSHIAKI,** Asian American studies educator, writer; b. LA, Aug. 14, 1949; m. Marsha Hirano; 1 child, Thomas. BA in Polit Sci. cum laude, Yale U., 1971; PhD in Polit. Sci., Harvard U., 1978. Instr. dept. urban studies Yale U., 1971; lectr. Coun. on Ednl. Devel. UCLA, 1973; instr. Asian Am. Studies Ctr., 1974, acting asst. prof. dept. polit. sci., 1975-78; vis. scholar Sophia U., Inst. Internat. Relations, Tokyo, 1978-89; adj. asst. prof. dept. polit. sci. UCLA, 1979-82, asst. rschr. Asian Am. Studies Ctr., 1979-82, from asst. prof. to full prof. Grad. Sch. Edn., 1982—, assoc. dir. Asian Am. Studies Ctr., 1985-87, chair interdepartmental program Asian Am. studies, 1989—90, dir. Asian Am. Studies Ctr., 1990—. Co-founder and publr.

Amerasia Jour., 1970-75, edtl. bd., 1975—; researcher Social Sci. Rsch. Coun. of N.Y. and the Japan Soc. for the Promotion of Sci. of Tokyo Joint-Project on Am.-Japanese Mut. Images, 1971-73; mem. Asian Am. task force for social studies guideline evaluation, Calif. State Dept. Edn., 1973; guest spkr. Ctr. for the Study of Ednl. Policy, Grad. Sch. Edn., Harvard U., 1974, Metropathways, Ethni-City Sch. Desegregation Program, Boston, 1974; researcher, co-project chair Hispanic Urban Ctr., Project Sch. Desegregation, L.A., 1974; numerous coms. UCLA; numerous conf. chmns.; cons., rschr., speaker, presenter in field. Co-editor: (with Marsha J. Hirano-Nakanishi) The Education of Asian and Pacific Americans: Historical Perspectives and Prescriptions for the Future, 1983, (with Halford H. Fairchild, Luis Ortiz-Franco, Lenore A. Stiffarm) Discrimination and Prejudice: An Annotated Bibliography, 1991, (with Tina Yamano Nishida) The Asian Pacific American Educational Experience: A Sourcebook for Teachers and Students, 1995, (with James Lai) National Asian Pacific American Political Almanac, 1996, 98, 2000; contbr. numerous articles to profl. jours., monographs, book reviews and reports. Chair Yale U. Alumni Schs. Com. of So. Calif., 1978—; bd. dirs. Altamed and La Clinica Familiar Del Barrio of East L.A., 1982—; commr. Bd. Transp. Commrs., City of L.A., 1984-90; v.p. Friends of the Little Tokyo Pub. Libr., 1986-88; co-chair nat. scholars adv. com. Japanese Am. Nat. Mus., 1987—; mem., bd. govs. Assn. of Yale Alumni, 1988-91; mem. exec. coun. Mayor's LA's Best Aftersch. Program, City of Los Angeles, 1988-90. Rsch. fellow Japan Soc. for the Promotion of Sci., 1978; recipient Nat. Scholars awrd for Outstanding Rsch. Article on Asian Pacific Am. Edn., Nat. Assn. for Asian and Pacific Am. Edn., 1985, Civil Rights Impace award Asian Am. Legal Ctr. of So. Calif., 1989; grantee Chancellors' Challenge in the Arts and Humanities, 1991, Calif. Policy Seminar, 1992, U. Calif. Pacific Rim Studies, 1992; recepient numerous other research and conference grants. Mem. Nat. Assn. for Interdisciplinary Ethnic Studies (bd. dirs. 1976-79), Assn. Asian Am. Studies (nat. pres. 1983-85), Nat. Assn. for Asian and Pacific Am. Edn. (exec. bd. dirs., v.p. 1983—). Home: 4501 N Berkshire Ave Los Angeles CA 90032 Office: UCLA Asian Am Studies Ctr 3230 Campbell Ave Los Angeles CA 90024-1546 E-mail: dtn@ucla.edu.

**NAKANISHI, YUKO JULIE,** engineering educator, consultant; b. Westland, Mich. d. Ukyo Stanley and Tatsuko Ann Nakanishi. BA in English Lit., Harvard U., 1987; MBA, Columbia U., 1993; MSCE, CCNY, 1997; PhD in Civil Engring., Polytech U., 2004. Chair NY Area Data Coun., NYC, 1997-99; sr. tchg. assoc., cons. Rensselaer Poly. Inst., Troy, NY, 1999-2000; mgr. program Urban ITS Ctr. Poly. U., Bklyn., 2000—05; chair subcommittee on tng., ed., and tech. transfer, 2003—05; prin., owner Nakanishi Rsch. and Cons., Rego Pk., NY, 2005—. Chair Freight and Intermodal Transp. Data Com., NY, 1997-2000; asst. dir. Univ. Transp. Rsch. Ctr., NYC, 1996-99; info. svc. com. Transp. Rsch. Bd., 1998—, critical transp. infrastructure protection com., chair edn., tng. and tech. transfer subcom. Contbr. articles to profl. jours. Fellow Eisenhower fellow, 1997—2000, Eno fellow, 2001. Mem. IEEE, ASCE, Inst. Transp. Engr., Intelligent Transp. Soc. N.Y. (treas., sec., bd. dirs.), N.Y. Data Coun. Office: Nakanishi Rsch and Consulting 93-40 Queens Blvd 6A Rego Park NY 11374 Office Fax: 347-512-1959. Personal E-mail: ynakan@aol.com.

**NAKARAI, CHARLES FREDERICK TOYOZO,** music educator; b. Indpls., Apr. 25, 1936; s. Toyozo Wada and Frances Aileen N. BA cum laude, Butler U., 1958, Mus.M., 1967; postgrad., U. N.C., 1967-70. Organist, dir. choirs Northwood Christian Ch., Indpls., 1954-57; min. music Broad Ripple Christian Ch., Indpls., 1957-58; asst. prof. music Milligan Coll., Tenn., 1970-72; pvt. instr. organ, piano Durham, NC, 1972—. Mem. faculty piano camp U. N.C.-Greensboro, 1996, 97, 2000, 01; adjudicator N.C. Music Tchrs. Assn., N.C. Fedn. Music Clubs, Raleigh Music Tchrs. Assn., Charlotte Piano Tchrs. Forum, Chapel Hill Music Tchrs. Assn. Composer: Three Movements for Chorus, 1971, Bluesy, 1979. With USAF, 1958—64. Mem. Am. Musicol. Soc., Coll. Music Soc., Am. Guild Organists, Music Tchrs. Nat. Assn., Music Libr. Assn., N.C. Music Tchrs. Assn., Organ Hist. Soc., Durham Music Tchrs. Assn., Triangle Guitar Soc. Address: 2312 Anthony Drive Durham NC 27705

**NAKASHIMA, TADAYOSHI,** retired biochemist, researcher; b. Yokkaichi, Mie-ken, Japan, Dec. 1, 1922; s. Chunosuke and Hina Nakashima; m. Fukuko Kondo, Nov. 15, 1947; 1 child, Rieko. BP, Nagoya Pharm. Coll., Aichi-ken, 1941—43; BS, Taihoku Imperial U., Taihoku, 1943—46; PhD, Kyushu U., Fukuoka, 1960—61. Rsch. Scientist U. of Miami, 1964. Acting chief, rsch. lab. Sanyo Penicillin Co., Nagoya, 1946—50; assoc. prof. Kwassui Coll., Nagasaki, 1951—62; post doctoral U. of Hawaii, 1962—64; vis. rsch. scientist U. of Bonn, Germany, 1966—69; rsch. prof. Inst. for Molecular and Cellular Evolution, U. of Miami, 1964—89. Author: (molecular evolution) Journals, (protoribosomes) In Molecular Evolution and Protobiology, 1984, (genetic code) Proc. Nat. Acad. Sci., 1972, (amino acid sequence) J. Biol. Chem.1966. Mem.: Am. Chem. Soc. Home: 7400 SW 159th Ter Palmetto Bay FL 33157-2452

**NAKATA, AKINORI,** epidemiologist, researcher; b. Kawasaki, Kanagawa, Japan, Feb. 23, 1967; s. Kenzo and Yoshiko Nakata; m. Sonoko Shiibashi, May 26, 2004. PhD, U. Tokyo, 1997. Domestic rsch. fellow Japan Soc. for Promotion of Sci., Kawaguchi, 1997—2000; rsch. fellow Nat. Inst. Indsl. Health, Kawasaki, 2000—, Nat. Inst. Occup. Safety Health, Cin. 2004—. Guest editor Nat. Inst. Indsl. Health, Kawasaki, 2005—; vis. rschr. U. Tokyo, 1997—2005. Contbr. articles to med. jours. Avocations: tennis, fishing, baseball. Office: Nat Inst Occup Safety Health CDC 4676 Columbia Pky Cincinnati OH 45226 Office Fax: 513-533-8596. Personal E-mail: nakataa-tky@umin.ac.jp.

**NAKATA, GARY KENJI,** lawyer; b. Okinawa. Japan, Nov. 13. 1964; arrived in U.S., 1971; s. Hiroshi Nakata and Miwako Kim; m. Jo Ann Akiko Tengan, Aug. 22, 1998. BBA in Fin., U. Hawaii, 1988; JD with distinction, U. of the Pacific, 1995. Bar: Hawaii 1996, Calif. 1996, US Dist. Ct. Hawaii, 1996; cert. mgmt. acct.; cert. fin. mgr.; cert. grad. Am. Banker's Assn. Nat. Sch. Regulatory Compliance. Credit analyst Bank of Hawaii, Honolulu, 1988-90, sr. credit analyst, 1990-92; law clk. Hawaii Atty. Gen. Tax Divsn., Honolulu. 1994: sr. assoc. Kobayashi, Sugita & Goda, Honolulu, 1995—2003; dep. corp. counsel City and County of Honolulu, 2003—04; CFO Honolulu City & County Employees Fed. Credit Union, 2004—. Mem. new product devel. adv. bd. Warren Gorham & Lamont, NYC. 1997-98. Editor-in-chief: The Transnational Lawyer. 1994. 95. Pres., enlisted adv. coun. Hawaii Air Nat. Guard, Honolulu, 1986-92: mem. ex officio alumni coun.. mem. membership com., mem. membership benefits subcom. U. Hawaii Alumni Assn., Honolulu, 1990-91; mem. fin. com. and bylaws subcom. Soc. Coll. Bus. Alumni and Friends, U. Hawaii Coll. Bus. Adminstrn. Alumni Affairs, Honolulu, 1990-91, founding member, treas., 1990-91, mem. steering com. to form alumni orgn., 1997-98, pres., 1998-2000; at-large rep., treas., legis. liaison Neighborhood Bd., Kaneohe, Hawaii, 1991-92. Mem.: ABA (bus. law sect., comml. fin. svcs. com., consumer fin. svcs. com.), Hawaii Fin. Regulatory Compliance Assn. (bd. dirs. 1997—2003, chairperson fair credit reporting act regulatory update com. 1998—2003), Inst. Cert. Mgmt. Accts. (bd. dirs. 1998—2000, dir. mem. acquisition 1998—2000), Calif. State Bar Assn., Hawaii State Bar Assn. (mem. real property and fin. svcs. sect. 1997—), Hawaii Jaycees (legal counsel 2000—01, exec. v.p. 2002, pres. 2003), Hawaii Bus. Jaycees (charter pres. 1991—92, chmn. bd. 1992—93, charter mem.). Office: Honolulu City & County Employees Fed Credit Union 2200 Kamehameha Hwy Ste 208 Honolulu HI 96819-2356 E-mail: gary@kalanet.com.

**NAKAYAMA, GRANTA Y.,** federal agency administrator, lawyer; SB, SM, MIT, 1981; JD, George Mason U., 1994. Bar: Va. 1994, DC 1995, US Ct. Appeals (4th cir.). Chief engr. Nuclear Core Mfg., Naval Nuclear Propulsion Program, US Navy, chief quality control Welding and Nondestructive Testing Branch; ptnr. Environ. Law and Product Safety Kirkland & Ellis LLP, Washington, 1994—2005; asst. adminstr. for enforcement & compliance assurance EPA, Washington, 2005—. Writing instr. George Mason U. Sch.

Law, 1993—94, adj. prof., 1998—. Contbr. articles to profl. jours. Lt. USN, 1981—86. Mem.: Soc. Automotive Engrs., Am. Welding Soc. Office: EPA 1200 Pennsylvania Ave NW Rm 3204 Washington DC 20046

**NAKAYAMA, PAULA AIKO,** state supreme court justice; b. Honolulu, Oct. 19, 1953; m. Charles W. Totto; children: Elizabeth Murakami, Alexander Totto. BS, U. Calif., Davis, 1975; JD, U. Calif., 1979. Bar: Hawaii 1979. Dep. pros. atty. City and County of Honolulu, 1979-82; ptnr. Shim, Tam & Kirimitsu, Honolulu, 1982-92; judge 1st Cir. Ct. State of Hawaii, Oahu, 1992-93; assoc. justice Hawaii Supreme Ct., Honolulu, 1993—. Mem. Am. Judicature Soc., Hawaii Bar Assn., Sons and Daughters of 442. Office: Hawaii Supreme Ct Ali'iolani Hale 417 S King St Honolulu HI 96813-2902*

**NAKAYAMA, WATARU,** engineering educator, consultant; b. Kamakura, Kanagawa, Japan, Jan. 7, 1936; s. Shiroh and Haru N.; m. Michiko Aoyagi, Jan. 8, 1967. BS, Defense Acad., Yokosuka, Japan, 1958; MS, Tokyo Inst. Tech., 1963, DEng, 1966. Lectr. U Sherbrooke, Que., 1969-70; rschr. Hitachi, Ltd., Tokyo, 1970-71, chief rschr. Tsuchiura, Japan, 1971-78, sr. rschr., 1978-88, sr. chief rschr., 1988-91, hon. engr., 1991-92; Hitachi chair prof. Tokyo Inst. Tech., 1989-92, prof., 1992-96; vis. prof. U. Md., 1996-98; pres. ThermTech Internat., 1998—. Lectr. in field. Author: (with others) Heat Transfer in Electronic and Microelectronic Equipment, 1990, High Performance Computing in Japan, 1992, Computers and Computing in Heat Transfer Science and Engineering, 1993; contbr. articles to profl. jours. Recipient New Tech. Innovation award Ichimura Found., 1978, best paper award Gas Turbine Soc. of Japan, 1984. Fellow IEEE (Itherm Achievement award 2000, Thermi award 2004), ASME (K-16 com. 1981—, chmn. Japanese chpt. 1990-92, Best Paper award 1981, Heat Transfer Meml award 1992, Electronic Packaging award 1996, Achievement award 2001), Inter-Pack (Achievement award 2001); mem. Japanese Soc. Mech. Engrs. (vice chmn. thermal engring. divsn. 1989-90, chmn. 1991-92, Best Paper award 1965, 80, Tech. award 1978), Heat Transfer Soc. Japan (pres. 1994). Achievements include patents for industrial application of heat transfer enhancement techniques to heat exchangers, rotating machinery, cooling systems of computers. E-mail: watnakayama@aol.com.

**NAKELL, MARTIN R.,** literature educator, writer; b. Alpena, Mich., June 23, 1945; s. Jack W. and Bernice (Davis) Nakell; m. Rebecca Anne Goodman, Aug. 27, 2000. BA, Calif. State U., Northridge, 1974; MA in Creative Writing, Calif. State U., San Francisco, 1974; DA, SUNY, Albany, 1983. Lectr. SUNY, Albany, 1980—83; prof. Chapman U., Orange, Calif., 1983-. Artist-in-residence Calif. Arts Coun., Sacramento/L.A., 1976—79; vis. prof. creative writing U. Calif., San Diego, 1997, San Diego, 2001; judge panel in fictions Ams. Awards, 1998; mem. Cultural Affairs Commn. City of L.A., 1999; judge Nat. Poetry Series, 2001; reader Getty Mus. Libr., 2002—; judge Internat. Belle Lettres award Ednl. Arts Found., 2004, 05, 06; lectr. in field; dir. creative writing program Chapman U., Italy. Author: Sources, 1973, Ramon, 1989, The Library of Thomas Rivka, 1998, Two Fields that Face & Mirror Each Other, 2001 (Pulitzer Prize nominee, 2001), Goings, 2001, Form, 2005, Settlement, 2006; asst. editor: Unmuzzled Ox, 1973—75; co-editor: Shankpainter, 1974—91; assoc. editor: Calif. Quarterly, 1989—91, pub.: Jahbone Press, 1991—; contbr. articles to jours. and anthologies;. author poetry, fiction, essay. Mem., subscriber Givat Havivah, Israel, 2000—, So. Poverty Law Ctr., Montgomery, Ala., 2002—. Recipient Gertrude Stein award in poetry, 1996; Interarts grantee, Nat. Endowment for the Arts, 1988, Summer Rsch. grantee, Chapman U., 1989, 1990, fellow in poetry, Fine Arts Work Ctr., Provincetown, Mass., 1974—75, fellowship in fiction, Blue Mountain Arts Ctr., 1985, grad. fellow, SUNY, Albany, 1989—93, Gell Found. Writers fellow, 1993. Mem.: Ednl. Arts Found. (mem. adv. bd.), L.A. Exptl. Poets Soc. (founding mem.). Jewish. Avocations: cooking, art, films, travel, swimming. Office: Chapman Univ 1 University Dr Los Angeles CA 90069 Office Phone: 714-997-6750. Business E-Mail: nakell@chapman.edu.

**NAKONECZNY, MICHAEL MARTIN,** artist; b. Detroit, Oct. 30, 1952; s. Michael and Edithe (Pheil) N.; 1 child, Alysha. Student, Kent State U., 1972-74; BA, Cleve. State U., 1979; MFA, Univ. Cin., 1981. Artist in residence Pub. Sch. 1, Long Island City, NY, 1986; instr. Cuyahoga C.C., Cleve., 1987, Cleve. Inst. of Art, 1988; vis. artist Herron Sch. of Art Ind. U., Indpls., 1990, Kansas City (Mo.) Art Inst., 1991; artist in residence Bemis Found., Omaha, 1992; vis. artist Tamarind Inst., Albuquerque, 1995, Ill. State U., 1997; assoc. prof. U. Alaska, Fairbanks, 2002—. Vis. artist Mont. State U., 1998. One-man shows include south Bend Regional Mus. of Art, Grover Thurston Gallery, Seattle, Graham Modern Gallery, NYC, 1988, Cleve. Ctr. Contemporary Art, 1993, Zolla Lieberman Gallery, Chgo. 1991-93, 96-2003, Horwitch LewAllen Gallery, Santa Fe, 1995, Purdue U., West Lafayette, Ind., 1995, Clark Gallery, Boston, 1999, Anchorage Mus. of History and Art, South Bend Regional Mus. Art, 2003; exhibited in group shows at Corcoran Gallery Art, Washington, 1985, Alternative Mus., NY, 1986, LA County Mus. Art, 1987, Graham Modern Gallery, NYC, 1989, Machida City Mus. Graphic Arts, Tokyo, 1993, Galleria Art, Sao Paulo, Brazil, 1994, Weatherspoon Art Gallery, U. NC, 1995, Chgo. Ctr. Book & Paper Arts, Columbia Coll., 1996, Banco Ctrl., Cuenca, Ecuador, 1996, Calif. Mus. Art, Santa Rosa, 1997, U. Alaska Mus., Fairbanks. Fellow, U. Cin., 1979—81, Ohio Arts Coun., 1990, Arts Midwest NEA Regional fellow, 1994—95, Ill. Arts Coun., 1995, Visual Arts 7, 1987. Address: 660 Rebecca St Apt 16 Fairbanks AK 99709-3563 Office Phone: 907-474-6545. Business E-Mail: ffmmn@uaf.edu.

**NAKU, ROLF D.,** gas industry executive; BS, NYU, 1973; MBA, Rensselaer Poly., 1974. With human resources and telecom. AMF, Inc.; joined Ultramar, 1983; v.p. human resources Ultramar Corp.; dir. compensation, benefits and human resources sys. Sunoco, Inc., 1998—2000, v.p. uman resources and pub. affairs, 2000—03, sr. v.p. human resources and pub. affairs Phila., 2003—. Office: Sunoco Inc Ten Penn Ctr 1801 Market St Philadelphia PA 19103-1699

**NALBANDIAN, DAVID,** professional tennis player; b. Cordoba, Argentina, Jan. 1, 1982; s. Norbeto and Alda. Jr. champion Jrs.-US Open, 1998; finalist Wimbledon, 2002; semi-finalist US Open, 2003, French Open, 2004; mem. Argentina Davis Cup team, 2002—04; winner Estoril Open, 2006. Nominee, Laureus World Sports Awards, 2003; named World Newcomer Yr. Achievements include highest world ranking #4, 2004. Avocations: fishing, soccer. Office: c/o Assn Tennis Profl 201 ATP Blvd Ponte Vedra Beach FL 32082*

**NALBANDYAN, ASHOT,** engineer; b. Yerevan, Armenia, Aug. 16, 1947; s. Soghomon and Sona Nalbandyan; m. Anoush Entsanoush Ter-Pogosian, Apr. 14, 1972; children: Aram, Arsen. Diploma in ELECTRO-MECHANICAL Engring. AND LIGHT electro-mech. engring. and light sources, Moscow Inst. Energy, 1966—72. Design engr. Luys Factory Light Sources and Lighting Equipments, Yerevan, Armenia, 1972—75, mgr., lighting equipment design divsn., 1975—87; self employed Yerevan, Armenia, 1987—90; chief R&D engr. Tmi Co., Los Angeles, 1994—96; technician L.P. Assocs., Hollywood, Calif., 1997—98; chief R& D engr. Lightning Strikes, Inc., Hollywood, Calif., 1998—. Recipient Tech. Achievement award, Acad. Motion Picture Arts And Scis., 2000, Engring. Emmy award, Acad. TV Arts and Scis., 2002-2003. Mem.: Illumination Engring. Soc. N.Am. Achievements include 20 USSR patents in light sources and lighting equipments. Avocations: gardening, fishing, hiking. Home: 12031 Monogram Ave Granada Hills CA 91344 Office: Lightning Strikes Inc 6601 Santa Monica Blvd Hollywood CA 90038 Office Phone: 323-461-6361. Office Fax: 323-461-3067. Personal E-mail: xenonarc@aol.com.

**NALCIOGLU, ORHAN,** radiologist, educator; b. Istanbul, Turkey, Feb. 2, 1944; came to U.S., 1966, naturalized, 1974; s. Mustafa and Meliha Nalcioglu. BS, Robert Coll., Istanbul, 1966; MS, Case Western Res. U., 1968; PhD, U. Oreg., 1970. Postdoctoral fellow dept. physics U. Calif., Davis, 1970-71; rsch. assoc. dept. physics U. Rochester, NY, 1971-74, U. Wis., Madison, 1974-76; sr. physicist EMI Med. Inc., Northbrook, Ill., 1976-77; prof. depts. radiol. scis., elec. engring. medicine and physics U. Calif., Irvine, 1977—, head divsn. physics and engring., 1985—; dir. biomed. magnetic resonance rsch., 1987—2002, dir. Rsch. Imaging Ctr., 1992—, vice chair dept. radiology, 2000—. Cons. UN, 1980-86; gen. chmn. IEEE Nuclear Sci. Symposium and Med. Imaging Conf., 1996, 99. Editor several books; guest editor IEEE Nuclear Sci. Symposium and Med. Imaging Conf., 1997; contbr. articles to profl. jours. Mobil scholar, 1961-66; recipient Athalie Clarke award for rsch. excellence, 2001, Outstanding Achievement in the Arts and Scis. award ATAA, 2002, Outstanding Scientist award Assembly of Turkish-Am. Assns., Washington, 2002. Fellow IEEE (pres. Nuclear and Plasma Scis. Soc. 1993-94, Millennium medal 2000, NPSS Richard Shea award 2000), Am. Assn. Physicists in Medicine, Internat. Soc. Magnetic Resonance in Medicine; mem. Nuclear and Plasma Scis. Soc., Internat. Soc. Magnetic Resonance in Medicine, Am. Assn. for Cancer Rsch., Soc. Nuc. Medicine. Office: Univ Calif Rsch Imaging Ctr Irvine CA 92697-5020 Business E-Mail: nalci@uci.edu.

**NALEN, CRAIG ANTHONY,** federal agency administrator; b. Montclair, NJ, Apr. 17, 1930; s. Paul Anthony and Mildred A. (Tucker) N.; m. Katherine Andrews, Dec. 30, 1953; children: Katherine M., David A., Peter H. BA, Princeton U., 1952; MBA, Stanford U., 1957. Mktg. exec. Procter & Gamble, Cin., 1957-62, Foremost-McKesson, San Francisco, 1962-64; divisional gen. mgr., corp. v.p. Gen. Mills Inc., Mpls., 1964-72; pres., also bd. dirs. Am. Photograph Corp., Great Neck, NY, 1972-75; pres., chmn. bd. dirs. STP Corp., Ft. Lauderdale, Fla., 1975-80; pres., chief exec. officer Overseas Pvt. Investment Corp. (govt. agy.), Washington, 1981-89, also bd. dirs.; chmn. AES Transpower, Washington, 1989-92. Bd. dirs. Glendale Internat. Corp., Ont., Canada, Sonex Corp. Bd. dirs., founder Children's World, Denver. Lt. USNR, 1952-55. Mem. Chevy Chase (Md.) Club, Gulf Stream Golf Club (Fla.), Gulf Stream Bath & Tennis Club (Delray Beach, Fla.), Valley Golf Club (Sun Valley, Idaho). Republican. Home: 532 Banyan Rd Gulf Stream FL 33483-7404 also: 3101 New Mexico Ave NW Apt 844 Washington DC 20016-5917 also: PO Box 2439 Ketchum ID 83340-2439

**NALLEY, MICHAEL DOUGLAS,** real estate company executive; s. Sandra Phillips; m. Carol Gene Nalley; children: Christopher Michael, Casey Erin. BBA in Fin., U. Tulsa, 1985. Cert. property mgr. Inst. Real Estate Mgmt., real property adminstr. Bldg. Owners & Managers Assn., comml. investment mgr. Cert. Comml. Investment Mgr. Property mgr. Wiggin Properties, Tulsa, 1985—88; property mgr., retail leasing Trammell Crow Co., 1988—95; v.p. ops. Compass Mgmt. & Leasing, Dallas, 1995—98; mng. dir. Trammell Crow Co., 1998—. Bd. mem. Make A Wish Found. Okla., Tulsa, 1991—95. Sgt. U.S. Army, 1976—80. Conservative. Methodist. Avocation: golf. Home: 5120 E 88th St Tulsa OK 74137 Office: Trammell Crow Co 2001 Ross Ave Ste 3400 Dallas TX 75201 Office Phone: 214-863-3007. Office Fax: 214-863-4000. Personal E-mail: mnalley16@cox.net. E-mail: mnalley@trammellcrow.com

**NALLY, DENNIS MATHEW,** finance company executive; b. Washington, Oct. 11, 1952; s. Thomas J. and Margaret (Allen) N.; m. Karen L. Kidder, June 18, 1977; children: Brian, Lindsay, Kathryn, Lauren. BBA, Western Mich. U., 1974; completed, Columbia U. Exec. Program, Penn State U. Exec. Program. CPA, Mich., Ohio. Staff acct. Price Waterhouse, Detroit, 1974-77, audit sr., 1977-78, audit mgr., 1978-85, audit ptnr., 1985, NYC, 1985-88, ptnr.-in-charge Dayton, Ohio, 1988—92, nat. dir. strategic planning, 1992—95, vice chmn fin. and key client svc. support, 1995—97, also mem. US firm policy com., US mgmt. com., and gen. coun. worldwide orgn., 1995—97; (Price Waterhouse merged with Coopers Lybrand in 1998); assurance and bus. adv. services leader for Americas theatre Pricewaterhouse-Coopers, 1996—2000, mng. ptnr. US Firm, 2000—01, chmn., sr. ptnr., 2002—, also mem. US bd. partners and principals, mem. US mgmt. com. Bd. dirs. US C. of C., US-Japan Bus. Coun.; bd. trustees St. Michael's Coll., Colchester, VT, NY POPs; mem. fin. com. Diocese of Bridgeport, Conn. Mem. AICPA, NY State Soc. CPAs. Avocations: golf, sailing, jogging, computers. Office: PricewaterhouseCoopers 300 Madison Ave New York NY 10017-6204 Office Phone: 646-471-4000.*

**NALTY, KEISHA JANICE,** secondary school educator; b. Bklyn., Feb. 9, 1979; d. Alfred George and Merna Amelia Nalty. BA in Polit. Sci., U. Fla., Gainesville, Fla., 2000, MA in Edn., 2001; student in Social Founds. Edn., U. Ga., Athens, Ga., 2003—. Cert. tchr. Profl. Standards Commn. Ga. Tchr. Fulton County Pub. Schs., Duluth, Ga., 2001—, chmn. talented and gifted eligibility River Trail Mid. Sch., 2003—06; tchr. Ga. State U., Atlanta, 2003—05. Tchr. Kennesaw (Ga.) State U., 2004—05. Counselor Coll. Reach Out Program U. Fla., 1998—2000; mentor Delta Sigma Theta, Ga., 2003—06. Scholar, Japanese Govt., 2005. Mem.: Nat. Coun. Social Studies, Golden Key, Delta Sigma Theta, Pi Lambda Theta.

**NAM, BYUNG-HO,** statistician, educator; b. Seoul, Republic of Korea, Oct. 6, 1961; s. Kyu-Chul Nam and Jae-Sun Jung; m. Heejae Im, July 11, 1964; children: Henie, Jenie, Annie. BA, Seoul Nat. U., 1980—84; MBA, Ea. Mich. U., Ypsilanti, 1986—90; MS, U. Mich., Ann Arbor, 1990—93; PhD, Boston U., 1994—2000. Rsch. asst. prof. Boston U., 2000—; biostatistitian Framingham Heart Study, Mass., 1996—; tchg. fellow Boston U., 1996—99, rsch. fellow, 1995—2000. Author: (book) Goodness-of-fit Tests and Model Validity. Deacon, group study leader Evergreen Ch. of Boston, Brookline, 1997—2002. Mem.: Am. Statis. Assn. Achievements include research in Performance measures of mathematical prediction models. Office: Boston Univ 111 Cummington St Boston MA 02215 E-mail: byungho@bu.edu.

**NAM, CHARLES BENJAMIN,** demographer, sociologist, educator, writer; b. Lynbrook, NY, Mar. 25, 1926; s. Samuel and Yetta (Huff) N.; m. Marjorie Lee Tallant, Jan. 1, 1956; children: David Wallace, Rebecca Jane. BA, NYU, 1950; MA, U. N.C., 1957, PhD, 1959. Statistician U.S. Bur. Census, Washington, 1950-53, chief edit. and social stratification br., 1957-64; statistician USAF, Montgomery, Ala., 1953-54; rsch. asst. U. N.C., Chapel Hill, 1954-57; prof. sociology Fla. State U., Tallahassee, 1964—96, chmn. dept. sociology, 1968—71, disting. rsch. prof., 1994—96, disting. rsch. prof. emeritus, 1996—; rsch. assoc. Ctr. for Demography and Population Health, 1967—, dir., 1967—82; mem. population adv. com. U.S. Bur. Census, 1978-81. Cons. population divsn. Orgn. for Econ. Coop. and Devel., 1968-70, UNESCO, 1978-83, Indonesian Ministry of Population and Environment, Jakarta, 1988-90; Social Sci. Rsch. Coun., 1981-88. Author: (with John K. Folger) Education of the American Population, 1967, Population and Society, 1968, (with Susan Gustavus) Population: The Dynamics of Demographic Change, 1976, Nationality Groups and Social Stratification, 1981; (with Susan Philliber) Population: A Basic Orientation, 1983; (with Mary Powers) The Socioeconomic Approach to Status Measurement, 1983, Our Population: The Face of America, 1988, Understanding Population Change, 1994; (with Richard Rogers and Robert Hummer) Living and Dying in the USA, 2000; (with Janusz Balicki and Ewa Fratczak) Mechanisms of Population Changes and Population Policy (in Polish), 2003, The Golden Door, 2006; editor: Demography, 1972-75; co-editor: (with David Sly, William Serow) International Handbook of Internal Migration, 1990, Handbook of International Migration, 1990; mem. editl. bd. Population Research and Policy Review, 1993-94. Fellow AAAS (rep. sect. K 1999-2004); mem. Am. Sociol. Assn. (chmn. sect. on population 1976-78), Population Assn. Am. (pres. 1979), Internat. Union for Sci. Study Population, Am. Statis. Assn. (chmn. social statistics sect. 1974), So. Sociol. Soc. (pres. 1981-82), So. Demographic Assn. (vice chmn. 1974-75; fellow 2001), Soc. Study Social Biology (bd. dirs. 1996-2006, exec. com. 1998-99). Home: 820 Live Oak Plantation Rd Tallahassee FL 32312-2413 E-mail: charlesnam2@earthlink.net.

**NAM, HEEKYUNG BIYA,** rehabilitation therapist; b. Andong, Republic of Korea, Mar. 22, 1974; arrived in U.S., 2001; d. Dong Seung Nam and Jungsuk Kim. BA in Dance Edn., Hanyang U., Seoul, Republic of Korea, 1996; BA in Psychology, Korean Ednl. Devel. Inst., Seoul, 2001; MA in Dance Movement Therapy, Antioch New Eng. Grad. Sch., Keene, NH, 2003. Lic. creative arts therapist NY, registered dance therapist NY. Ballet tchr., choreographer Kwon Jongok Dance Instn., Seoul, 1994—96; asst. prof. Korean Jr. Art Assn., Seoul, 1995; dep. mgr. sales and svc. Etec, Applied Material Co., Bundgang,

Republic of Korea, 1997—99; dance/movement therapist Sung Dong Cmty. Ctr., Seoul, 1999—2000; group leader after sch. program Univ. Settlement Soc., NYC, 2003—04; psychiat. rehab. therapist North Gen. Hosp., NYC, 2004—. Internat. scholar, Internat. Rotary Club, Chgo., 2001—03. Mem.: Nat. Psychol. Assn. for Psychoanalysis, Am. Group Psychotherapy Assn., Am. Dance Therapy Assn. Avocations: rollerblading, hiking, meditation, yoga. Office: North Gen Hosp Dept Psychiatry 1879 Madison Ave New York NY 10035

**NAM, KI-BONG,** mathematics professor; b. Masan, Korea, 1955; arrived in US, 1983; s. Moon-Woo and Eul-Yeon (Koo) Nam; m. Young Hee Esther Joo, May 9, 1982; children: Grace Hye-Eun, Sam-Young. BS Math., Hanyang U., Seoul, 1981; MA Math., Hanyang U., 1983; MS Math., U. Wis., Madison, 1996; PhD. U. Wis., 1998. Tchg. asst. Hanyang U., Seoul, 1981—83, Iowa State U., Ames, 1983—84; lectr. U. Wis., Whitewater, 1999—2002, asst. prof., 2003—06, assoc. prof., 2006—. Organizer internat. math. conf. Chonbuk U., Jeonju City, Republic of Korea, 2004, Jeonin U., 2006. Editor: Jour. Computational Math. and Optimization, 2005—, Jour. Applied Algebra and Discrete Structures, 2005—; assoc. editor: Internat. Jour. Applied Math. and Stats., 2005—; contbr. articles to profl. jours. Mem.: Korean-Am. U. Prof. Assn., Am. Math. Soc. Avocations: Go, chess. Home: 468 Presidential Ln Madison WI 53711 Office: Univ Wis Dept Math 800 W Main St Whitewater WI 53190 Office Phone: 262-472-5164. Business E-Mail: namk@uww.edu.

**NAMA, GEORGE,** artist; b. Pitts., 1939; BFA, MFA, Carnegie Mellon Univ. Adj. prof. Pratt Inst. Exhibitions include Atelier 17, Paris, Phila. Mus., Tibor de Nagy Gallery, NYC, Biblioteque Nationale, Paris, Jack Rutberg Gallery, L.A., Shepherd & Derom Galleries, NYC. Mem.: NAD (academician). Office: Pratt Institute 144 W 14th St New York NY 10011

**NAMATH, JOSEPH WILLIAM,** entertainer, former professional football player; b. Beaver Falls, Pa., May 31, 1943; s. John Andrew and Rose (Juhasz) N.; m. Deborah Lynn Mays, 1984 (div. 1999); 2 children. Grad., U. Ala. Quarterback N.Y. Jets, 1965-77, LA Rams, 1977; co-owner Joe Namath Instructional Football Camp, Dudley, Mass. Appeared in (films) C.C. and Company, 1970, Avalanche Express, 1978, Chattanooga Choo Choo, 1984, Going Under, 1990, Green Visionary, 1992; (TV appearances) Here's Lucy, 1972, The Brady Bunch, 1973, The Love Boat, 1980, 1981, The Big Show, 1980, Fantasy Island, 1981, The A-Team, 1986, ALF, 1986, Kate and Allie, 1988, Married...With Children, 1993, The John Laroquette Show, 1993, The Simpsons (voice), 1997, 2002; (TV series) The Waverly Wonders, 1978; (TV films) Marriage is Alive Well, 1980, Our Voices Ourselves, 1982; (stage appearances) Picnic, 1979, Li'l Abner, 1980, The Caine Mutiny Court-Martial, 1983, Sugar, 1984; leading role in musical Damn Yankees, 1981; author (autobiography): Namath: A Matter of Style, I Can't Wait Until Tomorrow...'Cause I Get Better-Looking Every Day, 1969; (announcer) The NFL on NBC, 1960, ABC Monday Night Football, 1985-86. Past chmn. Leukemia Soc. Coin Campaign; hon. chmn. Am. Hungarian Soc.; established scholarship for women athletes U. Ala. Named Am. Football League Rookie of Yr., Sporting News, 1965, to Am. Football League All-Star team, 1968, 72, Most Valuable Player of Super Bowl III, 1969, Dodge Man of Yr., N.Y. Jets, to Ala. Sports Hall of Fame, 1981; recipient Hickock Belt for Profl. Athlete of Yr., George Halas Most Courageous Athlete award; named to Pro Football Hall of Fame, 1985. Achievements include being a member of Super Bowl III Champion New York Jets, 1969.

**NAMBU, YOICHIRO,** physics professor; b. Toyko, Jan. 18, 1921; arrived in U.S., 1952; m. Chieko Hida Nambu, Nov. 3, 1945; 1 child, Jun-ichi. BS, U. tokyo, 1942; DSc, U. Tokyo, 1952; DSc (hon.), Northwestern U., 1987; degree (hon.), Osaka U., 1996. Research asst. U. Tokyo, 1945—49; prof. physics Osaka City U., Japan, 1950—56; mem. Inst. Advanced Study, Princeton, 1952—54; research assoc. U. Chgo., 1954—56, mem. faculty, 1956—, prof. physics, 1958, Henry Pratt Judson disting. svc. prof., 1978—91; Henry Pratt Judson Disting. Svc. prof. emeritus, dept. physics U. Chgo., Enrico Fermi Inst., 1991—. Contbr. articles to profl. jours. Recipient Dannie Heineman prize for Math. Physics, 1970, J. Robert Oppenheimer prize, 1976, Order of Culture, Japan Govt., 1978, Max Planck medal, German Physical Soc., 1985, Dirac medal, Internat. Centre for Theoretical Physics, 1986, Wolf prize in physics, Wolf Found., Israel, 1994, Gian Carlo Wick Commemorative medal, World Fedn. Scientists, 1995, US Nat. Medal Sci., Bogoliubov prize, Joint Inst. for Nuclear Rsch., Benjamin Franklin medal in Physics, Franklin Inst., 2005. Mem.: NAS, Georgian Acad. Sciences (fgn. fellow 1996), Am. Phys. Soc. (J.J. Sakurai prize 1994), Am. Acad. Arts and Scis., Japanese Acad. (hon.). Office: Univ of Chicago Enrico Fermi Inst 5640 S Ellis Ave EFI Box 29 RI 267 Chicago IL 60637 Office Phone: 773-702-7286. Business E-Mail: nambu@theory.uchicago.edu

**NAMDARI, BAHRAM,** surgeon; b. Oct. 26, 1939; s. Rostam and Sarvar Namdari; m. Kathleen Wilmore, Jan. 5, 1976; children: Mondona, Mietra, Ariana. MD, 1966. Diplomate Am. Bd. Surgery. Resident in gen. surgery St. John's Mercy Med. Ctr., St. Louis, 1969-73; practice medicine specializing in gen. and vascular surgery Milw., 1976—. Mem. staff St. Mary's Hosp., Milw., St. Luke's Hosp., Milw., St. Michael Hosp., Milw.; founder, pres. Famous Mealwaukee Foods Enterprises. Contbr. articles to med. jours.; patentee med. instruments and other devices. Cardiovascular Surgery fellow with Michael DeBakey, Baylor Coll. Medicine, Houston, 1974-75. Fellow ACS, Internat. Surgeons; mem. AMA, Med. Soc. Milwaukee County, Milw. Acad. Surgery, Wis. Med. Soc., Wis. Surg. Soc., Royal Soc. Medicine Eng. (affiliate), Am. Soc. Bariatric Surgery, World Med. Assn., Internat. Acad. Bariatric Medicine (founding mem.), Am. Acad. Cosmetic Surgery, Michael DeBakey Internat. Cardiovascular Soc. Office: Great Lakes Med and Surg Ctr 6000 S 27th St Milwaukee WI 53221 1805

**NAMEROW, DAVID MARK,** pediatrician; b. NYC, Dec. 12, 1947; s. Nathan and Claire (Goldstein) N.; m. Pearila Brickner, June 14, 1981; children: Jordan Ilana, Evan Gabrielle, Zoe Alexandra. BS, CCNY, 1968; MD, U. Louisville, 1972. Pediatric intern Children's Hosp. Med. Ctr., Cin., 1972-73, resident in pediatrics, 1973-75; fellow in adolescent medicine U. Md. Hosps., Balt., 1975-77; pediatrician Plaza Med. Assocs., Flanders, NJ, 1977-79; dir. adolescent medicine St. Joseph's Hosp. Med. Ctr., Paterson, NJ, 1977-81; founder, pediatrician PediatriCare Assocs., Fair Lawn, NJ, 1979—. Attending pediatrician, assoc. dir. dept. pediatrics Valley Hosp., Ridgewood, N.J., 1979—; adj. asst. clin. prof. pediatrics N.Y. Hosp.-Cornell Med. Ctr., N.Y.C., 1979—; dir. dept. pediatrics Valley Hosp., 2001-05. Fellow Am. Acad. Pediatrics; mem. Soc. for Adolescent Medicine, Ambulatory Pediatric Assn. Office: PediatriCare Assocs 20-20 Fair Lawn Ave Fair Lawn NJ 07410-2319 also: 400 Franklin Tpke Mahwah NJ 07430-3516 also: 901 Rte 23 S Pompton Plains NJ 07444 Office Phone: 201-791-4545. Personal E-mail: dnamerow@optonline.net.

**NAMROW, ERIC S.,** lawyer; b. Washington, Aug. 16, 1967; BA cum laude, Bucknell Univ., 1989; MPhil, Oxford Univ., England, 1993; JD, Univ. Md., 1996. Bar: Md. 1996, DC 2000. Law clerk, Hon. Lawrence F. Rodowsky Ct. of Appeals, Md., 1996—97; ptnr., intellectual property litig. Venable LLP, Washington. Assoc. editor Univ. Md. The Bus. Lawyer. Mem.: ABA, Bar Assn. of DC, Md. Bar Assn., Am. Intellectual Property Law Assn. Office: Venable LLP 575 Seventh St NW Washington DC 20004 Office Phone: 202-344-4621. Office Fax: 202-344-8300. Business E-Mail: esnamrow@venable.com.

**NANAGAS, MARIA TERESITA CRUZ,** pediatrician, educator; b. Manila, Jan. 21, 1946; arrived in U.S., 1970; d. Ambrosio and Maria (Pasamonte) Cruz; m. Victor N. Nanagas, Jr.; children: Victor III, Valerie, Vinnie. BS, U. of the Philippines, 1965, MD, 1970. Diplomate Am. Bd. Pediat. Intern, resident St. Elizabeth's Hosp., Boston, 1971-74; fellow in ambulatory medicine Children's Med. Ctr., Dayton, Ohio, 1976—, head divsn. gen. pediat., 1988-90, 95-97, co-interim head ambulatory pediat., 1989-90, med. dir. ambulatory pediat., 1990—. Clin. asst. prof. pediat. Wright State U., Dayton,

1977-83, clin. assoc. prof. pediat., 1983—, selective dir., 1989—, assoc. prof. pediat., 2000—; clin. asst. prof. family practice Wright State U., Dayton, 1999—; dir., preceptor Wright State U. residents continuing clinic Children's Med. Ctr., 1989—, attending physician family practice programs, 1978—. Active Miami Valley Lead Poisoning Prevention Coalition, 1992G. Fellow Am. Acad. Pediat.; mem. Western Ohio Pediat. Soc., Ambulatory Pediat. Assn. Office: Children's Med Ctr Health Clinic 1 Childrens Plz Dayton OH 45404-1898 Office Phone: 937-641-3500.

NANCE, ALLAN TAYLOR, retired lawyer; b. Dallas, Jan. 31, 1933; s. A.Q. and Lois Rebecca (Taylor) N. BA, So. Meth. U., 1954, LLB, 1957; LLM, NYU, 1978. Bar: Tex. 1957, N.Y. 1961. With Simpson Thacher & Bartlett, N.Y.C., 1960-65; asst. counsel J.P. Stevens & Co., Inc., N.Y.C., 1965-70, sec., 1970-78, asst. gen. counsel, 1970-89; counsel J.P. Stevens & Co. Inc. and WestPoint-Pepperell Inc., 1989-93; asst. gen. counsel WestPoint Stevens Inc., N.Y.C., 1993-98, ret., 1998. With USNR, 1957-59. Woodrow Wilson fellow Columbia U., 1959-60. Mem. Phi Beta Kappa. Home: 201 E 66th St New York NY 10021-6451

NANCE, CYNTHIA ELEANOR, law educator; b. Chgo., Sept. 3, 1958; d. Eual Dean and Fern Elizabeth Nance. BS in Econs., Chgo. State U., 1986; JD with distinction, U. Iowa, 1990, MA in Fin., 1991, ABD in Indsl. Rels., 1993. Lic.: Iowa Supreme Ct. 1990. Law clk. Glasson, Grove, Sole & McMannus, Cedar Rapids, Iowa, 1989; program coord. U. Iowa Labor Ctr., 1989—91; tchg. asst. U. Iowa Coll. Bus., 1991—93; faculty fellow U. Iowa Coll. Law, 1993—94; asst. prof. law U. Ark. Sch. Law, Fayetteville, 1994—99, assoc. prof. law, 1999—, dean, 2006—. Bd. dirs. Sources for Ind. Living, Fayetteville, Ark., 1994—97; mem. audit com. Law Sch. Admissions Coun., Newtown, Pa., 1994—98, fin. and legal affairs com., Newton, Pa., 1998—, chair fin. and legal affairs com., Newtown, Pa., 2003—; women of the elca anti-racism trainer Evang. Luther Ch. in Am., Chgo., 1996—2002; mem., adv. com. on corp. social responsibility Evang. Luth. Ch. of Am., Chgo., 1999—; bd. dirs. ACLU, Little Rock, 1998—99; pres. Ozark Mountain Masters Swim Team, Springdale, Ark., 1999—2001; bd. mem. Nat. Interfaith Com. for Worker Justice, Chgo., 1999—; mem. sect. on minorities in the law Am. Assn. of Law Schools, Washington, 1994—; chair labor and employment law sect. Am. Assn. of Law Schs., Washington, 2000—01, chair employment discrimination sect., 2001—02; co-chair Greensboro Massacre Truth and Reconciliation Commn. Adv. Com., NC, 2001—; mem. ch. coun. Good Shepherd Luth. Ch., Fayetteville, Ark., 2002—03. Recipient Martin Luther King Jr. Individual Achievement award, 2004, Woman of Distinction award, Girl Scouts N.W. Ark., Internat. award for profl. achievement, NIA, 2006; fellow Grad. Opportunities for Advanced Level Studies Found., U. of Iowa Coll. of Bus., 1990—92; Tchg. Fellow, U. of Iowa, Coll. of Law, 1993—94. Mem.: ABA (co-chair labor and employmentlaw sect. ethics and professionalism com. 2001—), mem. pro bono com. labor and employment law sect. 2003—, Outstanding Lawyer), Indsl. Rels. Rsch. Assn., Ark. Bar Assn. (jurisprudence and law reform com. 1995—, lawyer assistance program com. 1999—, com. on diversity 2000—, labor law sect.), W. B. Putman Am. Inn of Ct., Nat. Bar Assn., Alpha Kappa Alpha (chpt. pres. 1999—2002), faculty advisor 2001—, Outstanding Svc. award 2000), Beta Gamma Sigma, Phi Delta Phi. Liberal. Evangelical Lutheran. Avocations: swimming, travel, cooking. Home: 1653 Applebury Dr Fayetteville AR 72701 Office: U of Ark Sch of Law 225 Waterman Hall Fayetteville AR 72701 Office Phone: 479-575-2403. Personal E-mail: cnance@uark.edu.

NANCE, JOHN JOSEPH, lawyer, writer, air traffic controller, announcer, consultant; b. Dallas, July 5, 1946; s. Joseph Turner and Margrette (Grubbs) N.; m. Benita Ann Priest, July 26, 1968; children: Dawn Michelle, Bridgitte Cathleen, Christopher Sean. BA, So. Meth. U., 1968, JD, 1969; grad., USAF Undergrad. Pilot Tng., Williams AFB, Ariz., 1971. Bar: Tex. 1970, U.S. Ct. Appeals (fed. cir.) 1994. News reporter, broadcaster, newsman various papers and stas, Honolulu and Dallas, 1957-66; news anchorman Sta. WFAA-AM, Dallas, 1966-70; newsman including on camera Sta. WFAA-TV, Dallas; pvt. practice Dallas, 1970—; news dir. Newscom Network, Dallas, 1970; airline pilot Braniff Internat. Airways, Dallas, 1975-82, Alaska Airlines, Inc., Seattle, 1985—; chmn., pres. Exec. Transport, Inc., Tacoma, 1979-85; chmn., CEO EMEX Corp., Kent, Wash., 1987—; mng. ptnr. Phoenix Ptnrs., Ltd., Tacoma, Wash., 1995—; project devel. assoc. Columbia Tristar TV, 1997—; with Nance & Carmichael, PLLC, Austin, Tex., 1997—. Spkr. Human Mgmt., 1984—, Teamwork and Comms. in the Med. Profession; airline safety, advocate Ind. Cons., earthquake preparedness spokesman Ind. Cons.; dir. steering com. Found. for Issues Resolution in Sci. Tech., Seattle, 1987-89; speaker Northwestern Transp. Ctr. Deregulation and Safety Conf., 1987; cons. NOVA Why Planes Crash, PBS, 1987, ABC World News Tonight Crash of US AIR 427, 1994; aviation analyst ABC-TV and radio, 1995—; aviation editor ABC Good Morning Am., 1995—; broadcast analyst, 1986—; spkr. in field. Author: Scorpion Strike, 1982, Splash of Colors, 1984, Blind Trust, 1986, On Shaky Ground, 1988, Final Approach, 1990, What Goes Up, 1991, Operating Handbook USAF Air Carrier Safety and Inspection, 1991, Phoenix Rising, 1994, Medusa's Child, 1997, The Last Hostage, 1998, Blackout, 2000, Headwind, 2001, Turbulence, 2002, Skyhook, 2003, Fireflight, 2003; contbr. Transportation Deregulation in the U.S., 1988; actor: appeared in Sheep on the Runway, 1975; (TV series) Pandora's Clock, 1996; tech. advisor (TV series) Pandora's Clock, 1996; actor: (TV series) Medusa's Child, 1997; prodr.: USAF SOC CRM Program, 1992; author: USAF SOC CRM Program, 1992, USF Video Prodns.: ANG Introduction to CRM, 1992, The Teamwork Connection, 1996; dir.: The Teamwork Connection, 1996. Pres. Fox Glen Homeowners Assn., Tacoma, 1974-77; cons. Congl. Office Tech. Assessment, Tacoma, 1987; witness air safety hearings U.S. Congress, Washington, 1986-88; bd. dirs. St. Charles Borromeo Sch., Tacoma, 1975-78, Nat. Patient Safety Found. of AMA, 1997—; mem. Mayor's Vets. Task Force, Tacoma, 1991; bd. advisors Jour. Air Law and Commerce So. Meth. Sch. Law, 1995—; exec. bd. Sch. of Law, 1998—; bd. advisors Pacific Northwest Writer's Conf., 1994—; adv. bd. supply and logistics mgmt. program Portland State U., 1997-98. Capt. USAFR, 1975-94; lt. col. Persian Gulf. Decorated Merit Svc. medal; named Airline Safety Man of Year Wash. State Div. of Aeronautics, 1987; recipient Disting. Alumni award So. Meth. U., 2002. Fellow Chartered Inst. Transport (Canberra, Australia); mem. ABA, SAG, Tex. Bar Assn., Author's Guild Am., Res. Officers Assn. (life), Aircraft Owners' and Pilots' Assn., Phi Alpha Delta, Delta Chi. Home and Office: John Nance Prodns 4512 87th Ave W Tacoma WA 98466-1920 Office: Phoenix Ptnrs Ltd PO Box 24465 Federal Way WA 98093-1465

NANCE, LIBBA L., elementary school educator; m. Dwain Nance; children: Angie N. Cannell, Bryan S., Justin M. BS in Edn., U. of Memphis, 1971. Lic. elem. edn. tchr. Tenn., 1971. Tchr. St. Louis Sch., Memphis, 1971—73, Our Lady of Sorrows Sch., Memphis, 1992—94, St. Dominic Sch., Memphis, 1994—. Sch. coord. St. Dominic Sch. Nat. Geography Bee, City Spelling Bee, Reader's Digest Word Challenge; sch. coord. St. Agnes Acad.-St. Dominic Sch. Accelerated Reader, Family Math and Sci. Night. Mem. Dominican Assoc., Memphis; Make-A-Wish chmn. SAA-SDS Sch., Memphis. Mem.: Internat. Reading Assn., NCTM. Office: St Dominic School 30 Avon Rd Memphis TN 38117 E-mail: lnance@saa-sds.org.

NANCE, MARY JOE, retired secondary school educator; b. Carthage, Tex., Aug. 7, 1921; d. F.F. and Mary Elizabeth (Knight) Born; m. Earl C. Nance, July 12, 1946; 1 child, David Earl. BBA, North Tex. State U., 1953; postgrad., Northwestern State U. La., 1974; ME, Antioch U., Seattle, 1978. Cert. bus. educator. Tchr. Port Isabel (Tex.) Ind. Sch. Dist., 1953-79; tchr. English Tex. 1965, Splendora (Tex.) H.S., 1979-80, McLeod, Tex., 1980-81, Brownwood, Tex., 1981-84; ret., 1985. Vol. tchr. for Indian students, 1964—65; vol. tutor, tchr. ESL; active WAAC, 1942—43, WAC, 1945. Recipient Image Maker award Carthage C. of C., 1984; named on Meml. for Women, Washington. Mem. NEA, Tex. Tchrs. Assn., Tex. Bus. Tchrs. Assn. (Cert. of Appreciation). Nat. Women's Army Corps Vets. Assn., Air Force Assn. (life), Gwinnett Hist. Soc., Hist. Soc. Panola County, Panola County Hist. & Geneal. Assn., Nat. Hist. Soc. Baptist.

NANCE, RICHARD DAMIAN, geologist, consultant; b. St. Ives, U.K., Oct. 25, 1951; s. Richard William Morton and Edith Eleanor (Leach) N.; m. Rita Felice Carpenter, Aug. 28, 1982; children: André Bernard Carpenter, Sarah Marie Eleanor, Christopher Louis Morton. BS in Geology with honors, Leicester (U.K.) U., 1972; PhD in Geology, Cambridge (U.K.) U., 1978. Asst. prof. St. Francis Xavier U., Antigonish, Nova Scotia, 1976-80, Ohio U., Athens, 1980-82; sr. rsch. geologist Exxon Prodn. Rsch. Co., Houston, 1982-83; assoc. prof. Ohio U., Athens, 1983-90, prof. chmn., 1995—2000, prof., 1991—. Rsch. cons. Inst. for Environ. Studies, La. State U., Baton Rouge, 1977-81, Cominco Am. Inc., Spokane, Wash., 1984-85, Argonne Nat. Labs., Chgo., 1984-88. Author/editor 30 chpts. in books; contbr. over 100 articles to profl. jours. Grantee Geol. Survey Can., 1987-88, NSF, 90-94, 2003-06, Earthwatch, 1991-94, Nat. Geographic, 1993-95, Ohio U., 1981-92, 2001-06, U.S. Dept. Edn., 1996-2000, Unesco, 2004-. Fellow Geol. Assn. Can.; mem. Geol. Soc. Am., Am. Geophys. Union, Am. Assn. Petroleum Geologists, Royal Geol. Soc. Cornwall, Ussher Soc., Trevithick Soc., Soc. for Indsl. Archeology, Sigma Xi. Avocations: cornish mining history, stationary steam engines, jogging. Home: 3 Julian Dr Athens OH 45701-3661 Office: Ohio Univ Dept Geol Scis 316 Clippinger Labs Athens OH 45701 Office Phone: 740-543-1107. Business E-Mail: nance@ohio.edu.

NANCE, ROBERT LEWIS, oil industry executive; b. Dallas, July 10, 1936; s. Melvin Renfro Nance and Ruth Natlie (Seibert) Nowlin; m. Penni Jane Warfel; children: Robert Scott, Amy Louise, Catherine Leslie. BS, So. Meth. U., 1959; LLD (hon.), Rocky Mountain Coll., 1989. V.p. geology Oliver & West Cons., Dallas, 1960-66; prinr. Nance & Larue Cons., Dallas, 1966-69; pres., CEO Nance Petroleum Corp., Billings, Mont., 1969—. Bd. dirs. First Interstate Bank, Mont., MDU Resources, Rocky Mountain Coll., Billings, chmn., 1986—91; mem. Nat. Petroleum Coun., 1992—94; chmn. Petroleum Tech. Transfer Coun., 1996—99. Coun. pres. Am. Luth. Ch., Billings, 1980; trustee, chmn. Deaconess Med. Ctr., Billings; chmn. Deaconess Billings Clinic Healty Sys. Recipient Hall of Fame award Rocky Mountain Coll. Alumni, 1987, Disting. Svc. Trusteeship, Assn. Governing Bds. Univs. Colls., 1988. Mem. Am. Assn. Petroleum Geologists, Ind. Petroleum Assn. Am. (exec. com., nat. bd. govs., Roughneck of Yr. 2002), Ind. Petroleum Assn. Mountain States (v.p. Mont. 1977-79, Wildcatter of Yr. 1999), Mont. Petroleum Assn., Hilands Golf Club, Billings Petroleum Club. Avocations: fly fishing, scuba diving, skiing. Office: Nance Petroleum Corp PO Box 7168 550 N 31st St Billings MT 59103 Office Phone: 406-245-6248. Business E-Mail: bnance@nancepetro.com.

NANCE, WILLIAM R., JR., finance educator; s. William R. Sr. and Emily C. Nance; m. Vivian P. Nance, May 28, 1976; children: Rachel children: Cathleen. BS, Regis U., 1996; MBA, Union U., 1999; DBA, Nova Southeastern U., 2005. Gen. mgr. Capro, Inc., Selmer, Tenn., 1998—2000; asst. prof. mgmt. Union U., Jackson, Tenn., 2001—. Bd. dirs. Leaders Credit Union, Jackson. Sgt. U.S. Army, 1975—81. Sam M. Walton fellow in free enterprise, Walton Found., 2001—. Mem.: Acad. Mgmt., Exch. Club Jackson. Office: Union U 1050 Union University Dr Jackson TN 38305

NAND, SUCHA, medical educator; b. Thiriewal, Punjab, India, Feb. 3, 1948; d. Narsingh Dass and Swaran Devi; m. Surinder S. Nand, June 15, 1973; children: Ranveer, Rahul. Pre-med. student, Dayanand Ayur Vedic Coll., Amritsar, India, 1966; MB, BS, Med. Coll., Amritsar, India, 1971. Diplomate Am. Bd. Internal Medicine, Am. Bd. Hemotology, Am. Bd. Med. Oncology. Asst. prof. Stritch Sch. Medicine Loyola U., Maywood, Ill., 1981-88, assoc. prof. Stritch Sch. Medicine, 1989-95; prof. medicine, 1996—. Editor Jour. of Med. Coll., 1969-71; contbr. articles to profl. jours. Clin. fellow Am. Cancer Soc., 1981; Brilliant Student scholarships, 1962-71. Mem. Am. Soc. Hematology, Am. Soc. Clin. Oncology, S.W. Oncology Group; mem. leukemia com. 1988—). Avocations: chess, reading, running. Office: Loyola Univ Med Ctr 2160 S 1st Ave Maywood IL 60153-3304 Office Phone: 708-327-3182.

NANDA, AJAYA KUMAR, chemist, educator; b. Orissa, India, May 8, 1972; arrived in U.S., 2000; s. Udayanath and Bichitrabala Nanda; m. Sagarika Nanda. BS in Chemistry, India, 1993; MS in Organic Chemistry, Utkal U., Orissa, India, 1995; PhD, Indian Inst. Sci., Bangalore, 2000. Rsch. scholar Indian Inst. Sci., Karnataka, 1995—2000; postdoctoral rsch. scientist U. Mass., Amherst, 2000—01, Carnegie Mellon U., Pitts., 2003—03; vis. rsch. sci. U. So. Miss., Polymer Sci. Dept., 2004—. Leader Indian Inst. Sci., Karnataka, India. Recipient Best ACS Chemist award, 2004, Chemist of Yr. award, Am. Chem. Soc., 2004;, Coun. Sci. and Indsl. Rsch. scholar, 1995—2000. Mem.: Am. Chem. Soc. (hon.). Achievements include research in Bio-mimetic, Thermal responsive and Controlled architecture; anaerobic adhesives; energitic polymeric materials, polyperoxides; thermal labile polymers; atom transfer radical polymerization; bio-degradable polymers; mini emulsion polymerization; hybrid materials; polyurethane nano composities; good barrier plastics. Office: U So Miss PO Box 10076 118 Coll Dr Hattiesburg MS 39406 Office Phone: 601-266-6884. Personal E-mail: ajayananda@yahoo.com. Business E-Mail: ajaya.nanda@usm.edu.

NANDA, VED PRAKASH, law educator, director, academic administrator; b. Gujranwala, India, Nov. 20, 1934; arrived in U.S., 1960; s. Jagan Nath and Attar (Kaur) N.; m. Katharine Kunz, Dec. 18, 1982; 1 child, Anjali. MA, Punjab U., 1952; LLB, U. Delhi, 1955, LLM, 1958, Northwestern U., 1962; postgrad., Yale U., 1962-65; LLD, Soka U., Tokyo, 1997, Bundelkhand U., Jhansi, India, 2000. Asst. prof. law U. Denver, 1965—68, assoc. prof. law, 1968—70, prof. law, dir. Internat. Legal Studies Program, 1970—, Thompson G. Marsh prof. law, 1987—, Evans U. prof., 1992—, asst. provost, 1993—94, vice provost, 1994—. Vis. prof. Coll. Law U. Iowa, Iowa City, 1974—75; vis. prof. Fla. State U., 1973, U. San Diego, 1979, U. Colo., 1992; disting. vis. prof. internat. law Kent Coll. Law, 1981, Calif. We. Sch. Law, San Diego, 1983—84; disting. vis. scholar Sch. Law U. Hawaii, Honolulu, 1986—87; cons. Solar Energy Rsch. Inst., 1978—81, Dept. Energy, 1980—81. Co-author (with David Pansius): Litigation of International Disputes in U.S. Courts, 1987; editor: Law in the War Against International Terrorism, 2005; co-editor (with M. Cherif Bassiouni): A Treatise on International Criminal Law, 1973, Water Needs for the Future, 1977; co-editor: (with George Shepherd) Human Rights and Third World Development, 1985; co-editor: (with others) Global Human Rights, 1981, The Law of Transnational Business Transactions, 1981, World Climate Change, 1983, Breach and Adaption of International Contracts, 1992, World Debt and Human Conditions, 1993, Europe Community Law After 1992, 1993, International Environmental Law and Policy, 1995, European Union Law After Maastricht, 1996; co-editor: (with William M. Evan) Nuclear Proliferation and the Legality of Nuclear Weapons, 1995; co-editor: (with S.P. Sinha) Hindu Law and Legal Theory, 1996; co-editor: (with D. Krieger) Nuclear Weapons and the World Court, 1998; co-editor: (with George Pring) International Environmental Law and Policy for the 21st Century, 2003; editor, contbr. Refugee Law and Policy, 1989, mem. editl. bd. Jour. Am. Comparative Law, Indian Jour. Internat. Law, Transnational Pubs. O-chmn. Colo. Pub. Broadcasting Fedn., 1977—78; mem. Gov.'s Commn. on Pub. Telecomm., 1980—82. Mem. World Jurist Assn. (v.p. 1991—, pres. 1998-2000, hon. pres. 2000—), World Assn. Law Profs. (pres. 1987-93), UN Assn. (v.p. Colo. divsn. 1973-76, pres. 1986-88, 93-96, nat. coun. UNA-USA 1990—, mem. governing bd. UNA-USA 1995-2005), World Fedn. UN Assns. (vice-chmn. 1995-2001), Am. Assn. Comparative Study Law (bd. dirs.), Am. Soc. Internat. Law (v.p. 1987-88, exec. coun. 1969-72, 81-84, bd. rev. and devel. 1988-91, hon. v.p. 1995-96, counselor 2000—), Assn. Am. Law Schs., U.S. Inst. Human Rights, Internat. Law Assn. (exec. com. 1986—, hon. pres. 2001—), Colo. Coun. Internat. Orgns. (pres. 1989-90), Assn. U.S. Mem. Internat. Inst. Space Law (bd. dirs., exec. com. 1980-88), Internat. Acad. Comparative Law (assoc.), Acad. Internat. Commercial and Consumer Law, Order St. Ives (pres.), Rotary, Cactus Club), Univ. Club, Colo. Athletic Club. Office Phone: 303-871-6276. E-mail: vnanda@law.du.edu.

NANDA, VIVEK (VIC NANDA), software quality executive; b. New Delhi, Feb. 25, 1972; arrived in U.S., 2000; s. Hari Om and Versha Nanda; m. Dipti Dhir, Oct. 5, 1998; children: Ellora children: Hersh Rahul. BEng in Computer Engring., U. Pune, India, 1994; MS in Computer Sci., McGill U., Montreal,

Can., 1996. Cert. Info. Tech. Infrastructure Libr. Found.; software quality engr., Am. Soc. Quality, mgr. of quality organizational excellence, Am. Soc. Quality, quality auditor, Am. Soc. Quality, ISO 9000 lead auditor, Quality Mgmt. Inst. (RAB Accredited). Ops. developer Ericsson Rsch. Can., Montreal, 1996—97; sr. software quality specialist Architel Systems Corp. subs. Nortel Networks Co., Toronto, 1997—2000; sr. software quality assurance engr. Ulticom Inc., Mt. Laurel, NJ, 2000—06; quality mgr. Motorola Corp., Horsham, Pa., 2006—. Author: ISO 9001:2000 - Achieving Compliance and Continuous Improvement in Software Development Companies, 2003 (selected transl. by Spanish Assn. Standardisation and Cert., 2005), Quality Management System Handbook for Product Development Companies, 2005; spkr. and presenter (confs.) (Second Best Paper award Nat Technical Paper Conf. India, 1992), subject (interviews in profl. jours.) (contbr. scientific papers, articles to profl. jours. Events coord. Assn. South Asian Profls. N.J., Pennington, 2001—02. Mem.: IEEE (mem. rev. panel of Software Tech. mag. 2003), Am. Soc. Quality (mem. rev. panel Software Quality profl. jour. 2000, mem. std. rev. bd. Quality Press 2002). Avocations: travel, camping, hiking. Home: 325 Woodlake Dr Marlton NJ 08053 Office: Motorola Corp 101 Tournament Dr Horsham PA 19044 Office Phone: 856-787-2752, 215-323-2587. E-mail: vic.nanda@motorola.com.

NANDEDKAR, SANJEEV DATTATRAYA, medical researcher, educator; b. Pune, India, Dec. 28, 1955; s. Dattatraya Yadav and Madhumalti Dattatraya Nandedkar; m. Anjali Sanjeev Dadhe, Dec. 27, 1978; children: Desh Sanjeev, Vishesh Sanjeev. PhD, U. of Va., 1977—83. Med. rsch. asst. prof. Duke U. Med. Ctr., 1986—90; clin. applications mgr. Oxford Instruments Med. Systems, Hawthorne, NY, 1990—. Editor: emg on cd CASA Engring., Hopewell Junction, NY, 1997—. Author (editor): (multi-media text books) EMG on CD: Volumes I - III; author: (researcher) (sci. articles) Engring. and Med. Journals; author: (section editor) (rev. chapters) Textbooks on Clin. Neurophysiology. Recipient Disting. Svc., Am. Assn. of Electrodiagnostic Medicine, 2002, Excellence in Rsch. Writing, Assn. of Academic Physiatrists, 1997. Achievements include development of The Synergy Electromyograph; Multi Motor unit analysis and Median averaging; research in Computer simulations in Electromyography. Office: Oxford Instruments 12 Skyline Dr Hawthorne NY 10532 Personal E-mail: sanjeev@nandedkar.com.

NANGLE, JOHN FRANCIS, federal judge; b. St. Louis, June 8, 1922; s. Sylvester Austin and Thelma (Bank) N.; m. Jane Adams, June 7, 1986; 1 child, John Francis Jr. AA, Harris Tchrs. Coll., 1941; BS, U. Mo., 1943; JD, Washington U., St. Louis, 1948. Bar: Mo. 1948. Pvt. practice law, Clayton, 1948-73; judge U.S. Dist. Ct. Ea. Dist. Mo., 1973—, chief judge St. Louis, 1983-90; sr. judge U.S. Dist. Ct. So. Dist. Ga., 1990—, Ga., 1991—. Mem. 8th Cir. Jud. Coun.; mem. exec. com. Jud. Conf. U.S.; chmn. Jud. Panel on Multidist. Litigation. mem. working group on mass torts, mem. jud. resources working group. Mem. Ad Hoc Comm. on Asbestos, mem. jud. duty station, So. Dist. Ga. Mem. Mo. Rep. Com., 1958-73; mem. St. Louis County Rep. Cen. Com., 1958-73, chmn., 1960-61; pres. Mo. Assn. Reps., 1961, Reps. Vets. League, 1960; mem. Rep. Nat. Com., 1972-73; Grand Orator and bd. dirs. Masonic Home Mo. First Sgt. USAR, with AUS, 1943—46. Named Mo. Republican of Year John Marshall Club, 1970, Mo. Republican of Year Mo. Assn. Reps., 1971; recipient Most Disting. Alumnus award Harris-Stowe Coll., Most Disting. Alumnus award Washington U. Sch. Law, 1986. Mem. ABA, Legion of Honor DeMolay, Mo. Bar Assn., St. Louis Bar Assn., St. Louis County Bar Assn. (mem. com.). Office Phone: 912-650-4014.

NANIAN, MARJORIE KAY, lawyer, photographer, educator; b. Jackson, Mich., Oct. 16, 1953; d. Martin John and Anna (Manasian) Nanian; children: Maryann Y. Mugerian, George Nanian Mugerian. AA, Jackson CC, 1973; student, Harvard U., 1974; BS, Ctrl. Mich. U., 1975; JD, T. M. Cooley Law Sch., 1982. Bar: Mich. 1983, Tex. 1988. Pvt. practice, Mich. Adj. prof. polit. sci. Schoolcraft Coll., 2001—. Contbr. articles to profl. jours. Fellow: Mich. State Bar Found.; mem.: Tex. Bar Assn., Novi Bd. of Rev., Atty. Grievance Commn., Armenian Am. Bar Assn. (founder, pres. 1985—88), Mich. Bar Assn. Avocations: reading, freelance writing. Home and Office: 40562 Mill Rd Ct E Novi MI 48375 Office Phone: 248-231-7167. E-mail: mnanian@schoolcraft.edu.

NANKO, RAYMOND S., physician; b. Inglewood, Calif., Feb. 13, 1962; s. John and Veronica Marie (Thunder) N. DC, Cleve. Chiropractic Coll., 1985; MD, Ross U., 1994. Diplomate Am. Bd. Disability Analysts, Am. Bd. Family Practice, Am. Bd. Chiropractic Orthopedics, Am. Bd. Pain Mgmt. With ActiveCare Med. Spine & Pain Ctr., Muncie, Ind. Fellow Am. Back Soc.; mem. AMA, Ind. State Med. Assn., Ind. State Chiropractic Assn., Am. Chiropractic Assn., Am. Acad. Orthop. Medicine, Nat. Headache Found., Ind. State Med. Assn., Ind. State Chiropractic Assn., Coun. Orthop., Acad. Chiropractic Orthopedics, Arthritis Found., Internat. Spinal Injection Soc., Am. Assn. Orthopedic Medicine. Office: Active Care Med Spine & Pain Ctr 919 W Jackson St Muncie IN 47305-1554

NANNA, MICHAEL EDWARD, chemist, researcher; b. Santa Cruz, Calif., Oct. 2, 1956; s. Herman Nanna and Patricia Strong; m. Tania N. Niedzwiecki, May 13, 1989. BS in Indsl. Tech., Calif. Poly. State U., 1988, MS in Chemistry, 1993; PhD in Polymer Sci., ND State U., 2004. R&D chemist Behr Process Corp., Santa Ana, Calif., Morton Electronics Materials, Tustin, Calif., ETI, Fields Landing, Calif., Willamette Valley Co., Pineville, La. Mem.: Fedn. Socs. for Coatings Tech. (Leo Roon award 2003). Avocations: bicycling, jogging, fishing. Office: Willamette Valley Co 100 Dixie Mae Dr Pineville LA 71361

NANNE, LOUIS VINCENT, professional hockey team executive; b. Sault Ste. Marie, Ont., Can., June 2, 1941; s. Michael and Evelyn N.; m. Francine Yvette Potvin, Aug. 27, 1962; children: Michelle, Michael, Marty. BS in Mktg., U. Minn., 1963. Mem. Minn. North Stars hockey club, 1967-78, v.p., gen. mgr., 1978-88, pres., 1988-91; sr. v.p. Piper Capital Mgmt., Mpls., 1991-95; exec. v.p. Voyageur Asset Mgmt., Mpls., 1995—. Bd. govs. Nat. Hockey League, 1981-91; mem. internat. com. USA Hockey. Bd. dirs. Mpls. C.C. Found., 1986-90, Children's Home Soc., 1998—. Recipient Lester Patrick award NHL, 1989; named among Top 50 Coll. Players in 50 Yrs.; inducted into U. Minn. Hall of Fame, U.S. Hockey Heritage Hall of Fame award, Sault St. Marie Hall of Fame, U.S. Hockey Hall of Fame, Internat. Ice Hockey Hall of Fame. Mem. Interlachen Country Club (bd. dirs. 1992-95), Spring Hill Golf Club (bd. dirs. 1996-2004). Roman Catholic. Office: Voyageur Asset Management 100 S 5th St Ste 2300 Minneapolis MN 55402-1230

NANNEY, DAVID LEDBETTER, geneticist, educator; b. Abingdon, Va., Oct. 10, 1925; s. Thomas Grady and Pearl (Ledbetter) Nanney; m. Jean Kelley, June 15, 1951; children: Douglas Paul, Ruth Elizabeth Beshears. AB, Okla. Bapt. U., 1946; PhD, Ind. U., 1951; Laurea honoris causa, U. Pisa, Italy, 1994. asst. prof. zoology U. Mich., Ann Arbor, 1951-56, assoc. prof., 1956-58; prof. U. Ill., Urbana-Champaign, 1959-76, prof. genetics and devel., 1976-86, prof. ecology, ethology and evolution, 1987-91, prof. emeritus, 1991—. NIH sr. postdoctoral fellow Ind. U., 1949—51. Author (with Herbert Stern): The Biology of Cells, 1965, Experimental Ciliatology, 1980. Named Disting. Lectr., Sch. Life Scis., U. Ill., 1981; recipient Disting. Alumnus award, Okla. Bapt. U., 1972, Preisträger, Alexander von Humboldt Stiftung, Germany, 1984. Fellow: AAAS, Am. Acad. Arts and Scis.; mem.: Soc. Protozoologists, Am. Genetic Assn. (pres. 1982), Genetics Soc. Am. Home: 703 W Indiana Ave Urbana IL 61801-4835 Office: U Ill Dept Animal Biology 505 S Gregory St Urbana IL 61801 Business E-Mail: d-nanney@life.uiuc.edu.

NANOS, GEORGE PETER, JR., science administrator, military officer, physicist; b. Torrington, Conn., Apr. 11, 1945; s. George N.; m. Joanne Louise Knowles, July 5, 1969; 1 child, George. Grad., U.S. Naval Acad., 1967; PhD in Physics, Princeton U., 1974; attended, U.S. Naval Destroyer Sch., Newport, R.I., 1974, Def. Sys. Mgmt. Coll., Ft. Belvoir, Va., 1991. Joined U.S. Navy, 1967; commd. ensign USN; advanced through grades to vice admiral; antisub warfare gunnery officer USS Glennon (DD-840), 1967-69; engr. officer USS Forrest Sherman (DD-931), 1974-76; material officer mem. staff destroyer squadron 10, 1976-78; mgr. tech. devel. high energy laser program offie (NAVSEA PMS-405), 1978-82; engring. duty officer, 1980; combat sys. officer Norfolk Naval Shipyard, 1982-84; engr. officer USS America (CV-66); dep. dir. warfare sys. engring. space and naval warfare sys. cmd., 1984-86; head navigation br., 1988-90; head missile br. devel., prodn., operational missile subsys., 1990-92; dir. tech. divsn. strategic syss. program, 1992-94; dir. strategic sys. program, 1994-98; commr. naval sea sys. command, 1998—2002, retired, 2002; prin. dep. assoc. dir. Threat Reduction Directorate Los Alamos Nat. Lab., N.Mex., 2002—03, interim dir. N.Mex., 2003, dir. N.Mex., 2003—05. Decorated Legion of Merit, Disting. Svc. medal, Meritorious Svc. medal, Navy Achievement medal. Office Phone: 505-667-5101. Office Fax: 505-665-2679. E-mail: nanos@lanl.gov.*

**NANTON, NICHOLAS DAVID,** lawyer; b. Geoffrey B. and Helen M. Nanton; m. Kristina Lee Brock, July 27, 2002; 1 child, Brock. BS in Fin., U. Fla., Gainesville, 1998—2001, JD, 2001—04. CEO Loud Entertainment, LLC, Altamonte Springs, Fla., 2001—, Cinemark Music Group, LLC, Altamonte Springs, 2002—05; ptnr. Dicks & Nanton, P.A., Altamonte Springs, 2006—; dir. bus. devel., fin. svcs. and software PremiereTrade, LLC, Altamonte Springs. Contbr. articles. Mission team mem. Flames of Fire Ministry, Guatemala, 2000—04. Recipient Telly award, The Creative Group, 2006. Mem.: The Fla. Bar, Nat. Acad. Rec. Arts & Scis., Entertainment Arts & Sports Law Sect., Fla. Bar, Fla. Bar, Nat. Soc. Collegiate Scholars, Golden Key Nat. Honor Soc., Fla. Blue Key. Office: PremiereTrade LLC 220 E Central Pky Ste 1020 Altamonte Springs FL 32701 Business E-Mail: nanton@premieretrade.com.

**NANTZ, JAMES WILLIAM (JIM NANTZ),** television sports announcer; b. Charlotte, N.C., May 17, 1959; s. James William Jr. and Doris (Trull) N.; m. Ann-Lorraine Carlsen, Apr. 16, 1983; 1 child, Caroline Mackenzie. BA in Radio and TV, U. Houston, 1981. Radio announcer Sta. KTRH, Houston; sports announcer Sta. KHOU-TV, Houston; sports announcer, anchor Sta. KSL-TV, Salt Lake City; announcer CBS Sports, N.Y.C., 1985—. Actor: (film) Tin Cup, 1996. Achievements include CBS announcer for major Sporting events including NCAA Men's Basketball Final Four, PGA Master's Tournament. Office: CBS Sports 51 W 52nd St New York NY 10019-6119*

**NANULA, RICHARD,** health products executive; b. Los Angeles, 1960; married; 3 children. BA in economics, U. Calif., Santa Barbara; MBA, Harvard Bus. Sch. Joined Walt Disney Co., 1986, exec. v.p., CFO, 1991—94, pres. Disney Stores, 1994—96, CFO, 1996—98; pres., CEO Starwood Hotels and Resorts, NYC, 1998—99; chmn. and CEO Broadband Sports, 1999—2001; exec. v.p., CFO Amgen Inc., 2001—, exec. com. mem. Bd. dirs. Boeing Co., 2005—; bd. trustees Healthcare Leadership Coun. Avocations: basketball, tennis. Office: Amgen One Amgen Ctr Dr Thousand Oaks CA 91320-1799*

**NAOR, DANIEL,** food products executive; b. Paris, July 1, 1960; s. Shlomo and Sarah (Puderbeutel) N.; 1 child, Nathalie. BS in Élec. Engring., MIT, 1981, MS in Elec. Engring. and Computer Sci., 1981; MBA, INSEAD, 1990. Cert. engr. Project mgr. ELOP, Rehovot, Israel, 1985-87, mktg. mgr., 1988—89; assoc. McKinsey & Co., Paris, 1990—95, prin., 1995—98, Dallas, 1998—2002; v.p. strategy, planning and bus. devel. Frito Lay N.Am., Plano, 2002—05, group v.p. bus. integration, chief strategist, 2005—, s.r. v.p. transformation and strategy. Contbr. articles to profl. jours. Mem. bd. dirs. Dallas Theater Ctr. Bd., 1999-2002, Variety, 1997—. Capt. Israeli Air Force, 1981-85. Mem. IEEE, Tau Beta Pi, Sigma Xi (assoc.). Avocations: films, theater, ballroom and Latin dancing. Office: Frito Lay N Am 7701 Legacy Dr 3A-254 Plano TX 75024 Business E-Mail: Daniel.Naor@FritoLay.com.

**NAOUMOV, VIATCHESLAV I.,** mechanical engineer, educator; b. Kazon, Russia, Mar. 2, 1953; s. Igor P. Naoumov and Ludmila I. Naoumova; m. Irina Y. Guskova; 1 child, Anton V. Faculty mech. and aerospace engring. U. Tenn., Knoxville. Office: University of Tennessee 214 Perkins Hall 1506 Middle Dr Knoxville TN 37996

**NAOUMOVA, IRINA YEVGENIEVNA,** business educator, consultant; b. Omsk, Russia, Aug. 5, 1960; d. Yevgeny A. Guskov and Lydia N. Guskova; m. Viatcheslav I. Naoumov, Dec. 3, 1983; 1 child, Anton V. Naoumov. Grad., Kazan State U., Russia, 1982, PhD in Econs. and Mgmt., 1989. Asst. prof. Kazan State Tech. U., 1982—93, assoc. prof., 1993—95; assoc. prof., head Kazan State U., 1995—2002; vis. prof. U. Tenn., Knoxville, 2001—. Cons. Tatarstan C. of C., Kazan, 2000—05. Mem. Alliance of Universities for the Democracy, 2000. Grantee, Jr. Fellowship Devel. Program, 1996—97, Fulbright Assn., 2000—05. Mem.: Am. Acad. Mgmt., Internat. Acad. Edn. (corr.). Office: Univ Tenn Knoxville TN 37996 Office Phone: 865-974-1740.

**NAPACK, BRIAN,** publishing executive; b. 1962; Grad., Middlebury Coll.; MBA, Columbia U. Mgmt. cons. A.T. Kearney, Inc.; v.p. Paramount/Simon & Schuster; co-founder Disney Interactive Walt Disney Co., v.p., founder Disney Ednl. Publishing; CEO, founder ThinkBox; ptnr. LEK Consulting; pres. Holtzbrinck Publishers, 2006—. Office: Holtzbrinck Publishers LLC 175 5th Ave New York NY 10010-7703 Office Phone: 212-674-5151. Office Fax: 212-420-9314.*

**NAPADENSKY, HYLA SARANE,** engineering consultant; b. Chgo. Nov. 12, 1929; d. Morris and Minnie (Litz) Siegel; m. Arnaldo I. Napadensky; children: Lita, Yafa. BS in Math., MS in Math., U. Chgo. Design analysis engineer Internat. Harvester Co., Chgo., 1952-57; dir. rsch. Ill. Inst. Tech. Rsch. Inst. Chgo. 1957-88; v.p. Napadensky Energetics Inc., Evanston, Ill., 1988-94; engring. cons., Lutsen, Minn., 1994-98. Contbr. numerous articles to profl. jours. Bd. overseers Armour Coll. Engring. Ill. Inst. Tech., 1988-93. Mem. NAE, Sigma Xi. Home and Office: 3284 W Highway 61 Grand Marais MN 55604-7537

**NAPIER, CAMERON MAYSON FREEMAN,** historic preservationist; b. Shanghai, Dec. 5, 1931; d. Hamner Garland and Cameron Middleton (Brame) Freeman; m. John Hawkins Napier III, Sept. 11, 1964. Student, L'Ecole des Artes Municipale, Paris, 1950-51, Westhampton Coll./U. Richmond, 1951—53; BA, U. Ala., 1955. Photographer's asst. Scott, Demott & Perry, Montgomery, Ala., 1951; art dir. WCOV-TV, Montgomery, 1955; self-employed graphic designer Dallas, 1956-64; self-employed designer Alexandria, Va., 1965-71; restoration chmn. White House Assn. Ala., Montgomery, 1973-76, 1st vice regent, 1976-80, regent, 1980—. Co-founder Friends of Stratford Hall for No. Va., Alexandria, late 1960s; docent chmn. Lee's Boyhood Home, late 1960s; bd. dirs. Landmarks Found., Montgomery, 1971-75; advisor Conde Charlotte House, Mobile, Ala., 1994-95. Author, designer booklet: The First White House of the Confederacy, 1978 (nat. printers award 1979), The Struggle to Preserve the First White House of the Confederacy, 1982; contbr. to Ency. of So. Culture, Ency. of Ala.-online, 2006. Bd. dirs. English Speaking Union, Montgomery, 1980-83. Named Hon. First Lady, by the Gov.'s wife, Montgomery, Ala., 1985; recipient Awards of Excellence, Ala. Artist's Assn., Dallas, 1960, 1961, 1962, disting. svc. award, Ala. Hist. Commn., Montgomery, 1977, Cert. of Commendation, Gov. Ala., 1986, So. Patriot award, 1997, Lifetime Achievement award, Ala. Preservation Alliance, 2001, Jefferson Davis award, 1984, Winnie Davis award, United Dau. of Confederacy, 1985. Mem.: Antiquarian Soc. (pres. 1981—82), Sojourners Lit. Club (pres.), Order of the Crown in Am., Soc. Descs. of Colonial Clergy, Am. Soc. Most Venerable Order of the Hosp. St. John of Jerusalem (Am. Soc. officer sister 1995, named Comdr. Sister 2002), Nat. Soc. Colonial Dames in Am. (hist. properties com. 1994—95, state bd. mgrs. 1998—2000, ctr. vice chmn. 1998—2000), Daus. of Barons Runnymede, Militi Templi Scotia, Kappa Delta. Episcopalian. Avocations: jumbles, cryptoquotes, crossword puzzles, afternoon tea. Office: First White House Confed 644 Washington St Montgomery AL 36130-3057 Office Phone: 334-242-1861.

**NAPIER, JOHN HAWKINS, III,** historian; b. Berkeley, Calif., Feb. 6, 1925; s. John Hawkins and Lena Mae (Tate) Napier; m. Harriet Elizabeth McGehee, Aug. 30, 1950 (dec.); m. Cameron Mayson Freeman, Sept. 11, 1964. BA, U. Miss., 1949; MA, Auburn U., 1967; postgrad., Georgetown U., 1971; D (hon.), Napier U., Edinburgh, 2000. Journalist, tchr. Picayune (Miss.) H.S., 1946; commd. 2d lt. U.S. Air Force, 1949, advanced through grades to lt. col., 1966; ret., 1977. Staff dir. Congressional Com. on S.E. Asia, 1970; faculty Air War Coll., 1971-74; Air U. Command historian, 1974-77; asst. to exec. dir. Ala. Commn. on Higher Edn., Montgomery, 1977-78; adj. history faculty Auburn U., Montgomery, 1980-85; columnist Montgomery Advertiser, 1980-87; lectr. in field. Author: Lower Pearl River's Piney Woods: Its Land and People, 1985; The Air Force Officers Guide, 30th edit., 1995, Dr. Patrick Napier: His Ancestors and Some Descendants, 1991; contbr. articles to profl. jours. With USMC, 1943-46, col. Ala. State Defense Force, 1991-97, brig. gen., dep. comdr., 1997-99. Decorated Legion of Merit; Order of St. John of Jerusalem, Milit. and Hospitaller Order of St. Lazarus of Jerusalem, Sovereign Mil. Order of Temple of Jerusalem; recipient award of merit Ala. Hist. Commn., 1976, Ala. Disting. Svc. medal, 1999, merit award English-Speaking Union U.S., 1983; Taylor medal and grad. fellow U. Miss., 1949; Storrs scholar Pomona Coll., 1942-43. Fellow: Soc. Antiquaries Scotland; mem.: S.R. SAR (pres. 1974—75), Sons of Confederate Vets. (vice comdr. Ala. 1979—80), Ala. Hist. Assn. (pres. 1979—80), Royal Order Scotland, English-Speaking Union (pres. 1978—87, nat. dir. 1980—86, 1987—90, 1991—94), Scabbard and Blade, Royal Scots (Edinburgh), Mil. Order Carabao, Soc. Colonial Wars, Soc. War of 1812 (pres. Ala. 1980—82), St. Andrews Soc., Clan Napier in N.Am. (lt. to chief 1985—), Order 1st Families Va., Jamestowne Soc., Soc. Cincinnati, Ala. Assn. (pres. 1998—2001), Aztec 1847, Soc. Pioneers Montgomery (pres. 1979 80), Montgomery Country Club, Masons (32d degree), Pi Sigma Alpha, Phi Alpha Theta, Omicron Delta Kappa, Phi Kappa Phi, Sigma Chi. Democrat. Episcopalian. Home: Kilmahew 158 Mt Zion Rd Ramer AL 36069-6505

**NAPIER, WILLIAM JAMES, JR.,** marine oil and gas construction engineering consultant; b. Dallas, July 19, 1952; s. William James and Frankie (Hanchey) N.; m. Christine Ann Douget, June 18, 1977; children: Jay, Stephanie, George, Catherine. BS in Marine Biology, U. So. Miss., 1974; BS in Civil Engring., La. Tech. U., 1976. Project engr., field engr. inland svcs. divsn. McDermott Internat. Inc., Harvey, La., 1976-80, project coord. New Orleans and Houston, 1982-86, sr. project coord., project coord. worldwide bus. devel. New Orleans, 1986-89; project engr. McDermott Nigeria, Ltd., Warri, 1980-82; mgr. marine sales/dir. marine sales, nat. accounts mgr. Bailey Controls Co., New Orleans, 1989-92; pres. COO Balehi Marine, Inc., Lacombe, La., 1992-94; pres., owner Fairwinds Internat. Inc., Covington, La., 1994—. Elder Lakeview Christian Ctr., New Orleans, 1985-92. Mem. Soc. Naval Architects and Marine Engrs., Franco's Athletic Club. Republican. Baptist. Avocations: weightlifting, racquetball, bicycling. Office: Ste 350 11111 Richmond Houston TX 77082 Home and Office: 11111 Richmond Ste 350 Houston TX 77082 E-mail: bnapier@fairwindsintl.com.

**NAPLES, CAESAR JOSEPH,** lawyer, educator; b. Buffalo, Sept. 4, 1938; s. Caesar M. and Fannie A. (Occhipinti) N.; children: Jennifer, Caesar; m. Sandra L. Harrison, July 16, 1983. AB, Yale U., 1960; JD, SUNY, 1963. Bar: N.Y. 1963, Fla. 1977, Calif. 1988, U.S. Supreme Ct. 1965. With Moot & Sprague, Buffalo, 1965-69; asst. dir., employee rels. N.Y. Gov. Office, Albany, 1969-71; asst. v. chancellor SUNY, Albany, 1971-75; vice chancellor and gen. counsel Fla. State U. System, 1975-82; vice chancellor Calif. State U. System, 1983-92, vice chancellor emeritus, 1992—, prof. law and fin. emeritus Long Beach, 1983—; bd. dirs., gen. counsel, corp. sec. Open U., Denver and Wilmington, Del., 1999—2003; gen. counsel Walden U., 1989—2003. Cons. Govt. of Australia, U. Nev. Sys., Assn. Can. Colls. and Univs., Que., also other univs. and colls. Contbr. articles to profl. jours.; co-editor: Romanov Succession, 1989 with J. Victor Baldridge. Mem. Metlife Resources Adv. Bd., 1986-2002, chmn., 1992-2002; mem. Meml. Heart Inst. Long Beach Meml. Hosp., 1993—, bd. dirs., chmn. 1998—, found. bd., 1996—; bd. dirs. Calif. Acad. Math. and Scis., 1995—; mem. adv. bd. Incline Village Cmty. Hosp., 2004—. Capt. U.S. Army, 1963-65. Mem. Acad Pers. Adminstrn. (founder), Nat. Ctr. for Study Collective Bargaining Higher Edn. (bd. dirs.). Avocations: opera, tennis. Fax: 310-798-0065. Business E-Mail: cjnaples@csulb.edu.

**NAPLES, RONALD JAMES,** manufacturing executive; b. Passaic, NJ, Sept. 10, 1945; s. James V. and Lea A. Naples; m. Suzanne Lorraine Shoudy, June 17, 1967; children: Regen Jeffrey, Marcus Jamison, Tiffany Marie. BS, U.S. Mil. Acad., 1967; MA, Fletcher Sch. Law, 1972; MBA with distinction, Harvard U., 1974. Assoc. in corp. fin. Loeb Rhoades Co., 1973; fellow, spl. asst. to counselor to Pres. The White House, 1974; spl. asst. to adminstr. Fed. Energy Adminstrn., 1975; exec. dir. Presdl. Task Force on Energy, Washington, 1975-76; v.p. internat. Hunt Mfg. Co., Phila., 1976, exec. v.p., 1980-81, vice chmn., pres., CEO, 1981-86, chmn., CEO, 1987-95; also dir.; pres. Hunt Internat. Co., 1977-82; pres., CEO Quaker Chem. Corp., 1995-97, chmn., pres., CEO, 1997—. Bd. dirs. Glatfelter Paper Co.; chmn. Fed. Res. Bank, Phila., U. of Arts. Bd. dirs. Rock Sch. Pa. Ballet, ARC, Fgn. Policy Rsch. Inst., Phila., Phila. Mus. Art, Franklin Inst. With U.S. Army, 1967—71. Decorated Bronze star with oak leaf cluster, Army Commindation medal with oak leaf cluster, Air medal, Cross of Gallantry Vietnam; named Outstanding Young Man Am., U.S. Jaycees, 1977, CEO of Decade Bus. Equipment, Fin. World Mag., 1989; recipient Mil. Order Wars medal, U.S. Mil. Acad., 1967. Phila. Inc. Cmty. Leadership award, 1990, Human Rels. Civic Achievement award, Am. Jewish Coun., 1989, Semper Fidelis award, Marine Corps Scholarship Fedn., 1991, Stephen Girard award, Phila. Fin. Assn., 1992, Touching a Life award, Boys and Girls Club Am., 1994, Torch of Liberty award, Anti-Defamation League, 2002; Walter Heller fellow, Harvard U., 1974, White Ho. fellow, 1974—75. Mem.: Assn. Grad. U.S. Mil. Acad., Chief Execs. Orgn., World Pres.' Orgn., White Ho. Fellows Assn., Harvard Bus. Sch. Alumni Assn., Phila. Country Club, Harvard Bus. Sch. Club Phila., Pyramid Club, Racquet Club. Office: Quaker Chem Corp One Quaker Park 901 Hector St Conshohocken PA 19428

**NAPOLI, JOSEPH LEONARD,** biochemist; b. Poughkeepsie, N.Y., Aug. 13, 1948; s. Joseph L. Sr. and Lucy Ann (Cioffi) N.; 1 child, Matthew. BS, Siena Coll., 1970; MS, U. Mich., 1972, PhD, 1975; postgrad., U. Wis., 1975-79. Asst. prof. Southwestern Med. Ctr., Dallas, 1979-85; assoc. prof. biochemistry SUNY Sch. Medicine, Buffalo, 1985-91, prof., 1991—, assoc. chmn. dept. biochemistry, 1995—99; prof. nutrition, toxicology U. Calif. Berkeley, 1999—, chmn. dept. nutrition, toxicology, 2005—. Contbr. articles to profl. jours.; patentee in field. Rsch. grantee NIH, 1980—. Avocations: gardening, travel. Office Phone: 510-642-5202.

**NAPOLI, JOSPEH STEPHEN,** horticulturist, conductor; b. Kansas City, Mo., Jan. 28, 1944; s. Christopher and Mary Conte Napoli; m. Margaret Jean Wright, Aug. 28, 1980. BMEd, Fla. State U., 1966; MusM in Choral Conducting, U. South Fla., 1972. Singer Metro. Opera Nat. Co., NYC, 0195—1966; tchr. Adams Jr. H.S., Tampa, 1964—80; nurseryman Napoli's Nursery, 1980—84, Athens Wholesale Nursery, Ga., 1984—; condr. Athens Master Chorale, 1989—. Chmn. Ga. Green Ind. assn., 2004. Bd. Classic Ctr. Auth., Athens, 2004—. Recipient Disting. Prof. Yr., Ga. Green Ind. Assn., 2004. Mem.: So. Nursery Assn. Republican. Episcopalian.

**NAPOLITANO, ANDREW P.,** legal analyst, lawyer, judge; b. Newark, June 6, 1950; s. Andrew A. and Rita (Caruso) N. AB, Princeton U., 1972; JD, U. Notre Dame, 1975. Bar: NJ 1975, U.S. Supreme Ct. 1985, U.S. Ct. Appeals (3rd cir.) 1997, U.S. Dist. Ct. NY (So. Dist.) 2000, U.S. Dist. Ct. NY (Ea. Dist.) 2001, U.S. Ct. Appeals (2nd Cir.) 2001. Atty. Riker, Danzig, Scherer & Debevoise, Newark, Winne, Banta & Rizzi, Hackensack, NJ, 1975—87; judge Superior Ct. NJ, 1987-95; news analyst Fox News Channel, NYC, 1998-2000, judge, Power of Atty., 2000—01, sr. jud. analyst 2001—. V.p., gen. counsel Hackensack U. Med. Ctr., 1986-1987; asst. prof. law, constl. law, criminal law and procedure, and profl. ethics, Del. Law Sch. of Widener U., Wilmington, Del., 1980-81; adj. prof. law, basic and advanced constl. law, Seton Hall U., Newark, 1989-2001; faculty mem., NJ Civil Practice and Procedure, NJ Jud. Coll., Teaneck, NJ, 1989-97; lectr., NJ Civil Practice and Procedure, Constl. Law, Profl. Responsibility, Inst. for Continuing Legal Edn., New Brunswick, NJ, 1996, NJ Law Jour. Lecture Series, Newark, NJ, 1995-; legal/polit. commentator, Courtroom TV Network, NYC, 1996-97, MSNBC, Secaucus, NJ, 1997-98, Fox News Channel, NYC, 1998-2000; at-large trustee Am. Inns of Ct. Fedn.; founding pres., master, Justice Morris Pashman Am. Inn Ct., Hackensack, NJ, 1989-98; mem. NJ Supreme Ct. Com. on Civil Practice, 1982-85, 1989-94, 1996-98. Author: Constitutional Chaos: What Happens When the Government Breaks Its Own Laws, 2004; contbr. articles to profl. jours. Bd. governor Hackensack U. Med. Ctr., 1994—2002. With USAR, 1971—72. Fellow: Am. Bar Found.; mem.: Assn. Criminal Defense Lawyers NJ, Trial Attys. NJ, Assn. Trial Lawyers Am., NJ State Bar Assn., Essex County Bar Assn., Bergen County Bar Assn. Office: Fischbein Badillo Wagner Harding 909 Third Ave New York NY 10022 Address: Fox News Network LLC 1211 Avenue of the Americas New York NY 10036 Business E-Mail: anapolitano@fbwhlaw.com.

**NAPOLITANO, GRACE F.,** congresswoman; b. Brownsville, Tex., Dec. 4, 1936; d. Miguel and Maria Alicia Ledezma Flores; m. Frank Napolitano, 1982; 1 child, Yolando M., Fred Musquiz Jr., Edward M., Michael M., Cynthia M. Student, Cerritos Coll., L.A. Trade Tech, Tec Southwest Coll. Mem. Calif. Assembly, 1993-98, U.S. Congress from 38th Calif. dist., Washington, 1999—; mem. resources com., sml. bus. com. U.S. Ho. Reps.; mem. Ho. Com. on Internat. Relations. Councilwoman City of Norwalk, Calif., 1986-92, mayor, 1989-90; active Cmty. Family Guidance. Mem. Cerritos Coll. Found., Dischrist. Democrat. Roman Catholic. Office: US Ho Reps 1609 Longworth Ho Office Bldg Washington DC 20515-0538

**NAPOLITANO, JANET ANN,** governor; b. NYC, Nov. 29, 1957; d. Leonard Michael and Jane Marie (Winer) Napolitano. BS summa cum laude, U. Santa Clara, Calif., 1979; JD, U. Va., 1983. Bar: Ariz. 1984, U.S. Dist. Ct. Ariz. 1984, U.S. Ct. Appeals (9th cir.) 1984, U.S. Ct. Appeals (10th cir.) 1988, U.S. Ct. Appeals (5th cir.), U.S. Ct. Appeals (7th cir.), U.S. Ct. Appeals (8th cir.). Law clk. to Hon. Mary Schroeder U.S Ct. Appeals 9th Cir., 1983—84; assoc. Lewis & Roca, Phoenix, 1984—89, ptnr., 1989—93; U.S. atty. Dist. Ariz., Phoenix, 1993—97; atty. Lewis and Roca, Phoenix, 1997—98; atty. gen. State of Ariz., Phoenix, 1999—2002, gov., 2003—. Mem. Atty. Gen.'s Adv. Com., 1983—, chair, 1995—96; chair victims rights subcom. Ariz. Criminal Justice Commn.; chair Ariz. High Intensity Drug Traficking Area; mem. Ariz. Peace Officer Stds. and Tng. Bd., Ariz. Pros. Attys.' Adv. Coun.; past com. to study civil litigation abuse, cost and delay Ariz. Supreme Ct.; past pres. Ariz. Cmty. Legal Svcs. Corp.; past judge pro tem Ariz. Ct. Appeals. Contbr. articles to profl. jours. Chmn. Nucleus, 1989—91; active Phoenix Design Stds. Rev. Com., 1989—91, Ariz. Women's Forum, Charter 100; hon. chmn. Camp Fire Boys and Girls, 1999; 1st vice-chmn. Ariz. Dem. Com., 1990—92; active Dem. Nat. Com., 1992—92; chmn. Ariz. del. Dem. Nat. Conv., 1992, chmn., 2000; active Ariz. Bd. Tech. Registration, 1989—92; bd. dirs. Ariz. Fire Fighters and Emergency Paramedics Meml., Phoenix Children's Hosp., Actors' Lab Ariz., Inc., Ariz. Peace Officers Meml.; bd. regents Santa Clara U., 1992—. Named Ariz. Dem. of Yr., 1989; recipient Leader of Distinction award, Anti-Defamation League, Human Betterment award, Roots and Wings, Golden Apple award, West Valley NOW, Nat. Network To End Domestic Violence award, Woman of Distinction award, Crohns and Colitis Disease Found., Women Making History award, Nat. Mus. Women's History, Tribute to Women award, YWCA; fellow Dillard fellow; scholar, Truman Scholarship Found, 1977. Fellow: Ariz. Bar Found.; mem.: ABA, Raven Soc., Sandra Day O'Connor Inn of Ct. (barrister), Ariz. Women Lawyers Assn., Ariz. State Bar (chmn. civil practice and procedure com. 1991—92), Am. Judicature Soc., Maricopa County Bar Assn. (past long range planning com.), Ariz. Bar Assn. (past com. on minorities in law, past chmn. civil practice and procedure com.), Nat. Assn. Attys. Gen. (exec. com., tobacco bankruptcy working group, health care fraud group, co-chmn. civil rights com., stop underage smoking com.; exec. working group on prosecutorial rels.), Am. Law Inst., Alpha Sigma Nu, Phi Beta Kappa. Democrat. Avocations: hiking, walking, travel, reading, films. Office: Office of Gov 1700 W Washington Phoenix AZ 85007 Office Phone: 602-542-4331. Office Fax: 602-542-7601.*

**NAPOLITANO, STEVEN V.,** lawyer; b. NYC, June 30, 1959; BA, U. Notre Dame; attended, London Sch. Econs.; JD, Boston U., 1985. Bar: Ill. 1985. Ptnr., co-chair Private Equity practice group, mem. bd. dirs. Katten Muchin Zavis Rosenman, Chgo., NYC. Mem.: ABA, Ill. State Bar Assn., Assn. for Corp. Growth. Office: Katten Muchin Zavis Rosenman 525 W Monroe St Chicago IL 60661 also: 575 Madison Ave New York NY 10022 Office Phone: 312-902-5615. Office Fax: 312-577-8749. E-mail: steven.napolitano@kmzr.com.

**NAPP, GUDRUN F.,** artist; b. Kiel, Germany, Aug. 14, 1929; arrived in U.S., 1986; d. Walter Alexander and Erika Elisabeth (Burchard) Rode; m. Edmund Carl Napp, Dec. 29, 1951 (dec. Dec. 2000); children: Helenita F., Johann Christian, Anneke J., Florian D. Student, Art Sch., Kiel, 1949, Escuela Artes Plastias, Caracas, Venezuela, 1950, Toronto Coll. Art, Can., 1950—51. Assoc. dir. One Ear Soc., 1999—2001. Exhibited in group shows at Miami Beach Conv. Ctr., 1997, Art Expo LA, 1997, 98, Art Expo NY, 1998, Art Expo Fla., 2000, FIA Caracas Internat. Art Fair, 2003; one-woman shows include Art Am., 1997. Recipient cert. of excellence Art Horizon, NYC, 1988, hon. mention Royal Poinciana Fiesta, Miami, 1993, The Fla. Mus. of Hispanic and L.Am. Art, Miami, 1994, Miami Watercolor Soc. exhibit, 1999, One Ear Soc. exhibit. Mem. Am. Soc. Interior Design (industry ptnr. 2005), Nat. Collage Soc., Internat. Soc. Exptl. Artists (signature mem.), Miami Watercolor Soc. (signature mem., pres. 1995-96, trustee 1997, publicity chair 1998-99, 3rd place 1990), Art Expo Fla. Lutheran. Avocation: painting. Home and Studio: Studio Gallery Napp Inc An ASID Industry Ptnr 1034 Waterside Cir Weston FL 33327 2022 Office Phone: 954-217-1722. Personal E-mail: art1100@aol.com.

**NAPPI, JAMES FRANCIS,** hand surgeon, educator; b. Ashtabula, Ohio, June 3, 1971; s. Samuel and Caroline Rose Nappi; children: Justin, Veronica, Celia, Samuel. BS cum laude, John Carroll U., 1973; MD, Ohio State U., 1976. Diplomate Am. Bd. Plastic Surgery C.A.Q. Hand Surgery. Instr. surgery Ohio State U., Columbus, 1980-82, asst. prof. surgery, 1983-86, clin. asst. prof. surgery, 1987—; mem. provisional staff Curtis Hand Ctr., Balt., 1982-83; founder Hand and Microsurgery Assocs., Columbus, 1987—; instr. Agee Endoscopic Carpal Tunnel Release Sys., 1993—. Sect. head plastic surgery Grant/Riverside Hosps., Columbus, 1994-98, sect. head hand surgery Grant/Riverside Meth. Hosps., 1999—. Contbr. chpts. to books, articles to profl. jours. Active Animal Rsch. vs. Animal Rights, Ohio State U., 1990—. Recipient Edwin Ellison award Dept. Surgery Ohio State U., 1982. Mem.: Am. Soc. Peripheral Nerve, Assn. Acad. Surgery, Plastic Surgery Rsch. Coun., Am. Soc. Reconstructive Microsurgery (edn. com. 1994—96), Am. Soc. Surgery of the Hand (self assessment exam com. 1991—, vice chair 2000), Sigma Xi. Avocations: golf, sailing, woodworking, children. Office: Hand & Microsurgery Assocs 3400 Olentangy River Rd Columbus OH 43202-1576

**NAPPIER, DENISE L.,** state official; BA, Va. State U., 1973; MA in Cmty. Planning, U. Cin., 1975. Analyst Office Hartford (Conn.) City Mgr.; cons. Conn. Office of Policy and Mgmt.; dir. instnl. rels. U. Conn. Health Ctr.; city treas. City of Hartford, 1989—98; treas. State of Conn., Hartford, 1999—. Exec. dir. Riverfront Recapture, Inc. Office: Office of State Treas 55 Elm St Hartford CT 06106-1746

**NARAHASHI, TOSHIO,** pharmacology educator; b. Fukuoka, Japan, Jan. 30, 1927; arrived in U.S., 1961; s. Asahachi and Itoko (Yamasaki) Ishii; m. Kyoko Narahashi, Apr. 21, 1956; children: Keiko, Taro. BS, U. Tokyo, 1948, PhD, 1960. Instr. U. Tokyo, 1951-65; research assoc. U. Chgo., 1961, asst. prof., 1962, Duke U., Durham, NC, 1962-63, 65-67, assoc. prof., 1967-69, prof., 1969-77, head pharmacology dir., 1970-73, vice chmn. dept. physiology and pharmacology, 1973-75; prof., chmn. dept. pharmacology Northwestern U. Med. Sch., Chgo., 1977-94; Alfred Newton Richards prof. Med. Sch. Northwestern U., Chgo., 1983—, John Evans prof. Evanston, Ill.,

1986—. Mem. pharmacology study sect. NIH, 1976-80; mem. rsch. rev. com. Chgo. Heart Assn., 1977-82, vice chmn. rsch. coun., 1986-87, chmn., 1988-90; mem. Nat. Environ. Health Scis. Coun., 1982-86; rev. com. Nat. Inst. Environ. Health Scis., 1991-95. Editor: Cellular Pharmacology of Insecticides and Pheromones, 1979, Cellular and Molecular Neurotoxicology, 1984, Insecticide Action: From Molecule to Organism, 1989, Ion Channels, 1988—; specific field editor Jour. Pharmacology and Exptl. Therapeutics, 1972-97; assoc. editor Neurotoxicology, 1994—; contbr. articles to profl. jours. Recipient Javits Neurosci. Investigator award, NIH, 1986. Fellow AAAS; mem. Am. Soc. for Pharmacology and Exptl. Therapeutics (Otto Krayer award 2000), Am. Physiol. Soc., Soc. for Neurosci., Biophys. Soc. (Cole award 1981), Soc. Toxicology (DuBois award 1988, Merit award 1991, 1st Ann. Disting. Investigator Lifetime Achievement award 2001), Agrochem. Divsn. Am. Chem. Soc. (Burdick L. Jackson Internat. award 1989). Home: 175 E Delaware Pl Apt 7911 Chicago IL 60611-7745 Office: Northwestern U Med Sch Dept Mol Pharmaco Biol Chem 303 E Chicago Ave Chicago IL 60611-3008 Office Phone: 312-503-8284. Business E-mail: narahashi@northwestern.edu.

**NARAIN, AMITABH,** aerospace and mechanical engineering educator; b. India, July 30, 1955; came to U.S., 1978; s. Surendra and Suniti (Dayal) N.; m. Rooma Narain, July 12, 1985; children: Hursh, Jaya. BTech in Aerospace Engring., Indian Inst. Tech., Kharagpur, 1978; MS in Mechanics, U. Minn., 1980, PhD in Mechanics, 1983. Asst. prof. Mich. Technol. U., Houghton, 1983-89, assoc. prof. mech. engring., 1990—2006, prof., 2006—. Contbr. articles to profl. jours. Grantee, GM, 1997—2000, NSF, 2000—03, NASA, 2003—06. Mem. ASME (chmn. applied mechanics divsn. com. on fluid mechanics 2000-2003, fluids engring. divsn. com. on multi-phase flows), Am. Phys. Soc. Avocations: swimming, chess. Home: 1520 Brookside Dr Houghton MI 49931-2713 Office: Mich Technol U ME-EM 1400 Townsend Dr Houghton MI 49931-1200

**NARAIN, PREM,** agricultural scientist, educator, researcher; b. Lucknow, India, Jan. 3, 1934; s. Govind Narain Verma and Lalli Devi; m. Krishna Srivastava, June 14, 1955; 1 child, Dhirendra Verma. BSc (hons.), Lucknow U., 1953, MSc, 1954; PhD, Edinburgh (Scotland) U., 1969, DSc, 1984. Stats. investigator Ministry of Transport, New Delhi, 1955-58; asst. rsch. officer Indian Vet. Rsch. Inst., Izatnagar, 1958-61; asst. prof. Indian Agrl. Rsch. Stats., New Delhi, 1961-70, from prof. to sr. prof., 1970-78; joint dir. Indian Agrl. Stats. Rsch. Inst., New Delhi, 1978-81, dir., 1981-92; prin. scientist Indian Agrl. Rsch. Inst., New Delhi, 1992-93, dean, 1993-94, prof. emeritus, 1994—99. Author: Statistical Genetics, 1990; editor, chair Indian Soc. Agrl. Stats. Jour., 1983, Impact Of P.V. Sukhatme On Agricultural Statistics And Nutrition, 1984. Recipient Rafi Ahmad Kidwai prize Indian Coun. Agrl. Rsch., 1977, Sankhyiki Bhushan award Indian Soc. Agrl. Stats., 1991, O.P. Bhasin Found. award, 1992, Disting. Svc. award Math. Assn. India, 1993, Dr. M.S. Randhawa Meml. medal, Nat. Acad. Agrl. Sci., 1999, Nat. award Govt. of India, 2003. Fellow Indian Nat. Sci. Acad. (G.P. Chatterji Meml. prize 1987), Indian Acad. Sci.; mem. Nat. Acad. Agrl. Sci. (founding). Internat. Statis. Inst. (mem. 1989-93), Internat. Biometric Soc. (mem. coun. 1988-91). Home: B-3/27 A Lawrence Rd Keshav Puram New Delhi 110035 India E-mail: narainprem@hotmail.com.

**NARAIN, RALPH B.,** biologist; b. Wakenaam, Guyana, Feb. 22, 1968; s. Aaron and Rosie Narain. AS, Suffolk County CC, Riverhead, NY, 2001; BS, SUNY, Oneonta, 2003; postgrad. in entomology, U. Nebr., Lincoln, 2006—. Lab. tech. Aroaima Mining Co., Berbice, Guyana, 1992—96; machine operator NY Twist Drills, Bohemia, NY, 1997—2000; biologist Suffolk County Dept. Health Services, Arthropod-Borne Diseases Lab., Yaphank, 2003—. Vol. Shiv Uma Ganesh Temple, Central Islip, NY, 2000—06. Scholar, Proctor & Gamble, 2002—03; John J. New scholar, SUNY Coll., Oneonta, 2002—03. Mem.: Phi Theta Kappa. Home: 111 Lincoln Ave Holbrook NY 11741 Office: SCDHS Arthropod-Borne Disease Laboratory 335 Yaphank Ave Yaphank NY 11980 Office Phone: 631-852-5271. Personal E-mail: usralphn@aol.com. Business E-Mail: RNarain@suffolkcountyny.gov.

**NARASAKI, KAREN KEIKO,** advocate, lawyer; b. Seattle, Apr. 4, 1958; d. Richard and Dorothy Narasaki. BA magna cum laude, Yale U., 1980; JD, UCLA, 1985. Bar: Calif. 1985, Wash. 1986, admitted to practice: US Supreme Ct., US Ct. Appeals (9th Cir.). Law clk. to Judge Harry Pregerson US Ct. Appeals (9th Cir.), LA, 1985-86; sr. assoc. Perkins Coie, Seattle, 1986-92; Washington Rep. Japanese Am. Citizens League, 1992-94; pres. and exec. dir. Nat. Asian Pacific Am. Legal Consortium, Washington. Chairperson Nat. Council of Asian Pacific Americans, Asian Pacific Am. Media Coalition, Nat. Network Against Anti-Asian Violence, Washington, 1993—; chairperson, compliance/enforcement com. Leadership Conf. on Civil Rights, Washington, 1995—. Named one of 100 Most Powerful Women, Washingtonian Mag., 2001; recipient Community Award, Asian Pacific Am. Labor Alliance, 1999, Citizen Vol. Svc. Award, US Dept. Justice, 2000, Ruth Standish Baldwin Award, Greater Sacramento Urban League, 2004, We the People Award, Internat. Channel, 2004, Spirit of Excellence Award, ABA, 2005. Mem.: Nat. Assn. Pacific Am. Women's Forum, Nat. Asian Pacific Am. Bar Assn. (founding mem., bd. dir., Trailblazers Award 1994). Office: Nat Asian Pacific Am Legal Consortium 1140 Connecticut Ave NW Washington DC 20036-4001

**NARASIMHAN, PADMA MANDYAM,** physician; b. Bangalore, India; came to U.S., 1976; d. Alasingracher Mandyam and Alamela Mandyam Narasimhan; 1 child, Ravi. MD, Maulana Azad Med. Coll., New Delhi, 1970. Diplomate Am. Bd. Internal Medicine. Intern in internal medicine Flushing Hosp., N.Y.C., 1976-77; resident in internal medicine Luth. Med. Ctr., N.Y.C., 1977-79; fellow hematology, oncology Beth-Israel Med. Ctr., N.Y.C., 1979-81; asst. prof. King Drew Med. Ctr., L.A., 1983-87, Harbor UCLA, Torrance, 1987—2000, USC, 2003—. Mem. editorial bd. Jour. Internal Medicine, 1986—. Mem. ACP, AAPI, Am. Soc. Clin. Oncology, So. Calif. Acad. Clin. Oncology. Hindu. Avocations: travel, reading, meeting people, music, walking. Home: 6604 Madeline Cove Dr Palos Verdes Peninsula CA 90275-4608 Office Phone: 310-377-9555. Personal E-mail: padmanarasim@yahoo.com.

**NARAYAN, ASH,** lawyer; b. 1965; BS in acctg., Valparaiso U.; JD, Loyola Law Sch. Mng. prtnr. RGT Capital Mgmt., Irvine, Calif. Editor: Loyola Law Sch. Law Review. Mem.: Sports Lawyers Assn. (bd. dirs.), Inst. Cert. Fin. Planners, several State Bar Assn. and CPA Soc. Office: RGI Capital Mgmt 1 Park Plz #970 Irvine CA 92614 Office Phone: 949-955-5525. Business E-Mail: anaryan@rgtnet.com.

**NARAYAN, RAMESH,** astronomy educator; b. Bombay, Sept. 25, 1950; came to U.S., 1979; s. G.N. and Rajalakshmi (Sankaran) Ramachandran; m. G.V. Vani, June 6, 1977. BS in Physics, Madras U., 1971; MS in Physics, Bangalore U., 1973, PhD in Physics, 1979. Rsch. scientist Raman Rsch. Inst., Bangalore, India, 1978-83; postdoctoral fellow Calif. Inst. Tech., 1983-84, sr. rsch. fellow, 1984-85; assoc. prof. astronomy U. Ariz., Tucson, 1985-90, prof., 1990-91; prof. astronomy Harvard U., Cambridge, Mass., 1991—2003, chmn. dept., 1997-2001, Thomas Dudley Cabot prof. natural scis., 2003—. Sr. astronomer Harvard-Smithsonian Ctr. for Astrophysics, 1991—, assoc. dir., 1996-97; adv. bd. Inst. Theoretical Physics U. Calif., Santa Barbara, 1994-98, chmn., 1996-97; com. gravitational physics NRC, 1997-99; chmn. adv. bd. Ctr. for Gravitational Wave Physics, Pa. State U., 2001—; mem. adv. bd. Max Planck Inst. for Astrophysics, 2002-05, chmn., 2003-05. Contbr. articles to profl. jours. Named NSF Presdl. Young Investigator, 1989, George Darwin lectr. Royal Astron. Soc., 2002. Fellow: Royal Soc. London; mem.: AAAS, Internat. Astron. Union (mem. U.S. nat. com. 2000—03), Am. Astron. Soc. (mem. exec. com. High Energy Astrophys. Divsn. 2002—04). Achievements include research in the general area of theoretical astrophysics, specializing in accretion disks, black holes, gravitational lenses, gamma-ray bursts, radio pulsars, image processing and scintillation. Office: Harvard-Smithsonian Ctr Astrophysics 60 Garden St # 51 Cambridge MA 02138-1516

**NARAYANAMURTI, VENKATESH,** health science association administrator; b. Bangalore, Karnataka, India, Sept. 9, 1939; came to U.S., 1961; s. Duraiswami and Janaki (Subramaniam) N.; m. Jayalakshmi Krishnayya, Aug. 23, 1961; children: Arjun, Ranjini, Krishna. BSc, MSc, St. Stephen's Coll., Delhi, India, 1958; PhD, Cornell U., 1965. Instr., rsch. assoc. Cornell U., Ithaca, NY, 1965-68; mem. tech. staff AT&T Bell Labs., Murray Hill, NJ, 1968-76, dept.head, 1976-81, dir., 1981-87; v.p. rsch. Sandia Nat. Labs., Albuquerque, 1987-92; dean engring. U. Calif., Santa Barbara, 1992-98; dean engring. and applied scis. Harvard U., Cambridge, Mass., 1998—. Chmn. condensed matter and materials phys. panel NRC, 1996-99; mem. U. Calif. Pres.' Coun. for Nat. Labs., 1995-98; mem. NAE Pub. Info. Adv. Bd., 1993-94, NSF Dir.'s Strategic Planning Bd., 1994-98; mem. adv. bd. Miller Inst. for Basic Sci., U. Calif. Berkeley, 1999—. Author more than 180 publs.; patentee in field. Fellow IEEE, AAAS, Am. Phys. Soc., Indian Acad. Scis.; mem. NAE, Royal Swedish Acad. Engring. Scis. (fgn.). Avocations: long distance running, squash. Office: Harvard Univ DEAS Pierce Hall 217 29 Oxford St Cambridge MA 02138-2901

**NARAYEN, SHANTANU,** computer software company executive; BS in Elec. Engring., Osmania Univ., India; MS in Computer Sci., Bowling Green Univ.; MBA, Haas Sch. Bus. Sr. mgr. Apple Computer, Inc.; dir. desktop and collaboration products Silicon Graphics, Inc.; co-founder Pictra, Inc.; with Adobe Sys., Inc., San Jose, Calif., 1998—2001, v.p., gen. mgr. engring. group, 2001—05, pres., COO, 2005—. Office: Adobe Sys Inc 345 Park Ave San Jose CA 95110-2704 Office Phone: 408-536-6000.*

**NARBON, LILIAN,** writer; b. Marroco, Nov. 9, 1957; children: Roi, Reut, Anat, Kineret. Author: Avodat Habirurim-The Vital Connection Between Psychology and Spirituality, 2002, (children's book) Lily Pily, 2005, (fairy tale) Lily, the Princess of Kingdom Pily, 2005; composer: (songs) The Face of America; lyricist:, 2005; author: Agama, the Fairy Godmother, 2006, (children's book) The Agama Sisters. Jewish. Achievements include patents for safe ear clean button and protection with attachment device. Personal E-mail: Liliannarboni@aol.com.

**NARDELL, EDWARD ANTHONY,** pulmonologist, researcher; s. Carl Edward and Frances Elizabeth Nardell; m. Madeline Sylvia Crivello, Sept. 23, 1978; children: Maria Francesca, Anthony Joseph. MD, Hahnemann U., Phila., 1975. Chief pulmonary medicine Cambridge Hosp., Mass., 1981—2005; pulmonologist, rschr. Brigham & Women's Hosp., Boston, 2005—. Recipient Chadwick medal, Mass. Thoracic Soc., 2006. Fellow: Am. Coll. Chest Physicians. Office Phone: 617-732-7841.

**NARDELLI, ROBERT L.,** consumer home products company executive; b. Old Forge, Pa., May 17, 1948; m. Sue Nardelli; 4 children. BS in Bus., Western Ill. U., 1971; MBA, U. Louisville, 1975. With GE, 1971-88; exec. v.p., gen. mgr. worldwide parts and components Case Corp., Racine, Wis., 1988-91; pres., CEO Can. Appliance Mfg. Co. subs. GE, Toronto, Ont., Canada, 1991-92, GE Transp. Sys., Erie, Pa., 1992-95, GE Power Sys., 1995-2000, The Home Depot, Atlanta, 2000—, chmn., 2002—. Bd. dirs. The Coca-Cola Co, 2002—. Recipient Disting. Pennsylvanian Award, Gannon U., 1995, Disting. Alumni Award, Western Ill. U., 1998, Alumnus of the Year, U. Louisville, 2001. Mem.: President's Coun. on Service and Civic Participation, 2003. Office: The Home Depot 2455 Paces Ferry Rd Atlanta GA 30339*

**NARDI, GLEN,** publishing executive; Grad., US Naval Acad.; M in Personnel Mgmt., George Wash. U. Joined Knight Ridder, 1980; production mgr. Miami Herald, 1980—84; with Philadelphia newspapers Knight Ridder, 1984—87; various positions to v.p. ops. The State, Columbia, SC, 1987—2004; sr. v.p. ops., IT and circulation San Jose Mercury News, San Jose, 2004—. Office: San Jose Mercury News 750 Ridder Park Drive San Jose CA 95190

**NARDI RIDDLE, CLARINE,** chief of staff; b. Clinton, Ind., Apr. 23, 1949; d. Frank Jr. and Alice (Mattioda) Nardi; children: Carl Nardi, Julia Nardi. AB in Math with honors, Ind. U., 1971, JD, LHD (hon.), St. Joseph Coll. 1991. Bar: Ind. 1974, U.S. Dist. Ct. (so. dist.) Ind. 1974, Conn. 1979, Fed. Dist. Ct. Conn. 1980, U.S. Supreme Ct. 1980, U.S. Ct. Appeals (2d cir.) 1986, U.S. Ct. Appeals (D.C. cir.) 1994. Staff atty. Ind. Legis. Svc. Agy., Indpls., 1974-78, legal counsel, 1978-79; dep. corp. counsel City of New Haven, 1980-83; counsel to atty. gen. State of Conn., Hartford, 1983-86, dep. atty. gen., 1986-89, acting atty. gen., 1989, atty. gen., 1989-91, judge Superior Ct., 1991-93; assn. exec., sr. v.p., gen. counsel Nat. Multi-Housing Coun., Nat. Apartment Assn., 1995—2003; chief of staff Senator Joseph I. Lieberman, Washington, 2003—. Asst. counsel state majority Conn. Gen. Assembly, Hartford, 1979, legal rsch. asst. to prof. Yale U., New Haven, 1979; legal counsel com. on law revision Indpls. State Bar Assn., 1979; mem. Chief Justice's Task Force on Gender Bias, Hartford, 1988-90; mem. ethics and values com. Ind. Sector, Washington, 1988-90; co-organizer Ind. Continuing Legal Edn. Forum Inst. Legal Drafting Legislature and Pvt. Practice; Internat. Women's Yr. panelist Credit Laws and Their Enforcement; mem. Atty. Gen.'s Blue Ribbon Commn., Chief Justice's Com. Study Publs. Policy Conn. Law Jour., Law Revision Commn. Adminstrv. Law Study, Chief Justice's Task Force Gender, Justice and Cts., Gov.'s Task Force Fed. Revenue Enhancements; mem. exec. com. Jud. Dept.; mem. panel arbitrators Am. Arbitration Assn., 1994; gen. counsel Nat. Multi Housing Coun.; lectr. in field. Author: (with F.R. Rembusch) Drafting Manual for the Indiana General Assembly, 1976; sr. editor Ind. U. Law Sch. Interdisciplinary Law Jour.; contbr. articles to profl. jours. Bd. visitors Ind. U., Bloomington, 1974-92; mem. Gov.'s Missing Children Com., Hartford, Conn. Child Support Guidelines Com., Gov.'s Task Force on Justice for Abused Children, Hartford, 1988-90; mem. Mayor's City of New Haven Task Force Reorganization Corp. Counsel's Office, Gov.'s Child Support Commn., Mayor of New Haven's Blue Ribbon Commn.; former bd. dirs. New Haven Neighborhood Music Sch.; bd. dirs. mem. youth adv. com. Gov.'s Partnership Prevent Substance Abuse Workforce-Drugs Don't Work. Recipient Women in Leadership Recognition award Hartford Region YWCA, 1986, Award of Merit, Women & Law Sect. Conn. Bar Assn., 1989, Fellowship award South End Ladies Dem. Club, 1989, Woman of Yr. award Greater Hartford Fedn. of Bus. & Profl. Women's Clubs, 1990, Conn. Original award Somers-Mabelle B. Avery Sch., 1990, Cert. of Recognition, Consortium Law-Related Edn., 1990, Citizen award Conn. Task Force Children's Constl. Rights, 1991, Ann. award Hartford Assn. Women Attys., 1993; named Conn. History Maker, U.S. Dept. Labor, Women's Bur. & Permanent Commn. Status Women, 1989, Impact Player, The Conn. Law Tribune, 1992; inductee Ind. U. Sch. Law Alumni Acad. Fellow, 1999. Mem. ABA, Conn. Bar Assn. (chair com. on gender bias, Citation of Merit women and law sect. 1989), Nat. Assn. Attys. Gen. (chair charitable trusts and solicitation 1988-90), New Haven Neighborhood Music Sch. (bd. dirs.), Am. Arbitration Assn. (arbitration panel 1994), Ind. Bar Assn., Conn. Bar Assn. (chair com. gender bias legal profession), Indpls. Bar Assn., Ind. Civil Liberties Union (bd. dirs., mem. exec. com., chair long range planning com., mem. women's rights project, membership v.p., Disting. Svc. award), Conn. Consortium Law and Citizenship Edn., Inc. (bd. dirs.), Conn. Judges Assn. (mem. legislation com.), Ind. U. Law Sch. Alumni Assn. (bd. dirs.), Enomene Hon. Soc., Pleiades Hon. Soc., Mortar Bd. (nat. fellow), Alpha Lambda Delta. Democrat. Presbyterian. Office: Nat Multi Housing Coun 1850 M St NW Ste 450 Washington DC 20036-5803 Office Phone: 202-224-4041. Business E-Mail: clarine_nardi_riddle@lieberman.senate.gov.

**NARDONE, VINCENT JOSEPH,** artist, educator; b. South Orange, N.J., Oct. 19, 1937; s. Giuseppe Vincenzo Nardone and Michelina Marianne Magliaro. BA, Montclair State U., 1961; MFA, U. Calif., L.A., 1965; cert., Paris Am. Acad. Sch. Beaux Arts, 1978, Rosary Coll., Florence, 1981. Art specialist South Orange Sch. Dist., NJ, 1961—89, Maplewood Sch. Dist., NJ, 1961—89; freelance art instr. NJ 1990—2005. Cultural affairs advisor N.J. Music and Arts Mag., Chatham, NJ, 1964—75; painting instr. South Orange and Maplewood Adult Sch., NJ, 1966—70; adj. instr. art Seton Hall U., NJ, 1968—74. Exhibitions include Ctr. for Internat. Art/Culture Invitational, N.Y.C., 2005, Taiwan Ctr., N.Y. Annual Pastels Juried Open, 2005, Audubon Artists Annual, N.Y., 2005, Allied Artists of Am. Annual, 2005,

Represented in permanent collections Nat. Mus. Fine Arts, Budapest, Hungary, The Noyes Mus. Fine Arts, Oceanville, N.J., Bristol Myers-Squibb Co. Gallery, Princeton, N.J. Recipient Queen Fiabiola/Prix Rubens medal in painting, Belgium, LeSalon Painting award, Grand Palais, Paris, Silver medal, Seoul Internat. Arts in Graphics, Korea, Atlantic City Nat. award in graphics. Mem.: Allied Artists Am. (exec. bd.), Audubon Artists (v.p.). Roman Catholic. Avocation: art. Home: 1218 Minnehaha Tr Manasquan NJ 08736

**NARDOZZI, PETER MICHAEL,** pharmacist, clinical educator, lecturer, entrepreneur; b. Brockton, Mass., Nov. 6, 1937; s. Michael John Nardozzi and Doris M. (MacLea) Worthington; m. Sandra Scott Boyatsis (div. 1975); 1 child, Mark; m. Sandra Scafani, Dec. 31, 1984; 1 child, Cody Abernathy. BS in Pharmacy, Northeastern U., 1960; MS in Nutrition, Hawaii Inst. for Health, Diet and Nutrition, 1982; PharmD, Southeastern Coll. Pharm. Scis., Miami, Fla., 1992. Registered pharmacist, Fla., Maine, Mass.; lic. cons. pharmacist, Fla. Exec. v.p. Nardozzi Rexall Drug and other forms, Fla., 1960-77, Mass., 1960—77; propr. Bonnie & Clyde's Tavern, Brockton, Mass., 1974—76; treas. Columbian Enterprises Importing/Emeralds, Caribbean Salvage Diving Co., Boston, 1975-77; ptnr., v.p., pharmacist Oceanside Drug, Pompano Beach, Fla., 1965-87; pharmacist mgr. Grand Union Pharmacy Dept., Hialeah, Fla., 1977-78; chief pharmacist Shoppers Drug Mart, Ft. Lauderdale, Fla., 1978-80; pres. Carribean Salvage, Inc., Pompano Beach; dir. pharm. services Bodee Med. Facilities, Pompano Beach, 1981; founder, exec. v.p. Hawaii Diet Plan, Honolulu, 1982-84; founder, pres. Innovative Bus. Devel. Group, Albuquerque, 1984-85; pharmacist, mgr. Cunningham Drug, Singer Island, Fla., 1986-87, Popular Pharmacy, Miami, 1987—89, Pharmor Drug, Miami, 1989—93; pharmacist, clin. educator Rite Aid Corp., Bath, Maine, 1994—. mem. Rite Aid Adv. Coun. Region 66, 2004; assoc. Achievement Rsch. & Verification Systems, Albuquerque, 1984-85; bd. dirs. Alliance Enterprises, Albuquerque, Zyne Design, Taos, N.Mex.; founder, pres. ITOCAM-Alternative Medicine Cons. Co.; mem. Pharmacy in the Amazon Rainforest, Pharmacy on the Belize Reef, Internat. Expdns., Nat. Pharmacist Response Team divsn. FEMA, 2004-05; comty. medicine advocate for Maine Medicare Edn. Partnership, 2005-06; lectr. and trainer Rite Aid Medicare Part D Outreach, 2005; steering com. Franklin County Health Acess Rx Consortium, 2006—; part-time traveling pharmacist, 2006—; founder Alternative Pharm. Care; lectr. in field Author weight loss booklet, 1985; editor Nat. Nutrition Newsletter, 1982-84; health columnist; co-patentee nutritional diet supplement. Youth counselor Hawaii Supreme Ct., Honolulu, 1982; lectr. drug abuse Nat. Assn. Retail Druggists. Fellow Am. Soc. Cons. Pharmacists; mem. Am. Pharm. Assn., Am. Mktg. Assn., Nat. Small Bus. Assoc., Maine Pharmacy Assn., Fla. Pharm. Assn., Hawaii Soc. Corp. Planners, Ctr. for Entrpreneurial Mgmt., Soc. Integrative Medicine, Soc. Natural Pharmacy, Venture Founders, Mortar and Pestle Soc. E-mail: docn@gwi.net.

**NARENDRA, KUMPATI SUBRAHMANYA,** electrical engineer, educator; b. Madras, India, Apr. 14, 1933; came to U.S., 1954, naturalized, 1974; s. Subrahmanya and Sarada (Alladi) Kumpati; m. Barbara Lamb, Nov. 3, 1961. BEE with honors, U. Madras, 1954; MS, Harvard U., 1955, PhD, 1959; MA (hon.), Yale U., 1968; DSc (hon.), Anna U., Madras, 1995. Lectr., postdoctoral asst. Harvard U., Cambridge, Mass., 1959-61, asst. prof., 1961-65; assoc. prof. Yale U., New Haven, 1965-68; prof. elec. engring., 1968—, Harold W. Cheel prof. elec. engring., 2003—, chmn. dept. elec. engring., 1984-87, dir. Neuroengring. and Neurosci. Ctr., 1995-96. Cons. to comml. firms, 1961—; dir. Ctr. for Systems Sci., 1981—; disting. lectr. Tex. A&M Coll., 1997; disting. vis. scientist Jet Propulsion Lab., 1994—95; hon. vis. prof. Anna U., Madras, India, 1993—; mem. adv. bd. Inst. Advanced Engring., Republic of Korea; disting. lectr. U. N.Mex., 1999, U. Va., 2001; plenary spkr. Am. Control Conf., 2000; keynote spkr. Conf. on Intelligent Control, U. Va., 2001, Internat. Conf. of Soc. of Indsl. and Control Engring., Osaka, Japan, 2002; Hamilton lectr. Hamilton Inst., Ireland, 2003. Author: Frequency Domain Criteria for Absolute Stability, 1973, Stable Adaptive Systems, 1989, Learning Automata-An Introduction, 1989; editor: Applications of Adaptive Control, 1980, Adaptive and Learning Systems: Theory and Applications, 1987, Advances in Adaptive Control, 1991; editor issue on learning automata Jour. Cybernetics and Info. Sci., vol. I, 1977. Recipient John R. Ragazzini Edn. award Am. Automatic Control Coun., 1990, Leadership award Neural Network Soc., 1994, Hendrik W. Bode prize/Lectr. award Control Sys. Soc., 1995, Richard E. Bellman Control Heritage award 2003. Fellow AAAS, IEEE (life, Franklin V. Taylor award 1973, George S. Axelby award 1988, Outstanding Paper of neural network coun. 1991), Inst. Elec. Engrs. (U.K.); mem. Conn. Acad. Sci. and Engring., Sigma Xi. Home: 35 Old Mill Rd Woodbridge CT 06525-1523 Office: Yale U Ctr Systems Sci PO Box 2157 New Haven CT 06520-2157 Business E-Mail: kumpati.narendra@yale.edu.

**NARESH, ANUBHAV,** dentist, educator; s. Rekha Naresh. BS in Dental Surgery, U. Haryana. Oranising sec. Virasat, Panchkula, India, 2000—03; gen. sec. Urdu Parishad, Chandigarh, India, 2003—04; dentist Provider, Panchkula Haryana, India, 2004—, dir. Author: A Guide to Personality Development, 2005 (named Best Guide, 2005). Home: 169 Sector 17 Haryana Panchkula 134109 India Office: Provider SCO 32 First floor sector - 11 Haryana Panchkula 134109 India Office: 0172-5011381. Personal E-mail: anubhavnaresh@gmail.com. Business E-Mail: provider.pkl@hotmail.com.

**NARIN, STEPHEN B.,** lawyer; b. Phila., Nov. 23, 1929; s. Bernard E. and Anne (Lipsius) N.; m. Sandra C. Goldberg, Sept. 29, 1963; children: Howard Glen, Brenda Teri. BS, Temple U., 1951, LL.B., 1953; LL.M. in Taxation, NYU, 1960. Bar: Pa. 1954, U.S. Supreme Ct. 1958; CPA, Pa. Dep. atty. gen. Commonwealth of Pa., Harrisburg, 1955-57; instr. acctg. Temple U., Phila., 1954-55; lectr. in law grad. legal studies div. Temple U. Sch. Law, Phila., 1976-85; lectr. Practicing Law Inst., 1967-69; ptnr. Narin & Chait, Phila., 1970-89, Predecessor Ptnrships., Phila., 1955-70; v.p., gen. counsel Travelco Assocs., Phila., 1989-90; of counsel Krekstein, Wolfson & Krekstein, Phila., 1989-92; v.p., gen. counsel Eagle Nat. Bank, 1990-91; counsel Schachtel, Gerstley, Levine & Koplin, Phila., 1993-98; pvt. practice Rosemont, Pa., 1998—. Mem. Phila. County Bd. Law Examiners, 1961-65. Nat. governing coun. Am. Jewish Congress, 1963-84, nat. exec. com., 1978-84, pres. Greater Phila. council, 1965-67; active Nat. Commn. on Law and Social Action, 1964-84. Mem. Phila. Bar Assn., Phi Alpha Delta. Home and Office: 1459 County Line Rd Bryn Mawr PA 19010-1604 Office Phone: 610-527-0665. Personal E-mail: stenar6@verizon.net.

**NARITA, HIRO,** cinematographer; b. Seoul, Republic of Korea, June 26, 1941; arrived in Japan, 1945, arrived in U.S., 1957; s. Masao and Masako (Kojima) Morikawa; m. Barbara Parker, Sept. 8, 1971. BFA in Design, San Francisco Art Inst., 1964. Lectr. Mill Valley Film Festival, 1984, Hawaii Internat. Film Festival, 1984, San Jose State U., 2006. Dir. photography: (films) Farewell to Manzanar, 1976 (Emmy nomination, 1976); Never Cry Wolf, 1983 (Best Cinematography award Nat. Soc. Film Critics, 1983); Solomon Northrup's Odyssey, 1984; Go Tell It on the Mountain, 1985; Amerika, 1987; Honey, I Shrunk the Kids, 1989; The Rocketeer, 1991; Star Trek VI, 1992; Hocus Pocus, 1993; White Fang II, 1994; James & The Giant Peach, 1995; The Arrival, 1995; Stones & Paper, 1997; Conceiving Ada, 1998; Shadrach, 1998; I'll Be Home for Christmas, 1998; Dirty Pictures, 1999 (Emmy nomination, 2000); Half Past Autumn, 2001 (Emmy nomination, 2001); Technolust, 2002; The Darwin Awards, 2005; The Valley of the Heats' Delight, 2006. With U.S. Army, 1964—66. Mem.: Acad. Motion Picture Arts and Scis., Am. Soc. Cinematographers, Internat. Photographers Guild. Office Phone: 707-763-5358. Personal E-mail: phnarita@comcast.net.

**NARKIEWICZ-LAINE, CHRISTIAN K.,** museum director, painter, poet; Student, U. de Strasbourg, France, 1970—72, Athens, Greece, 1972—73; grad., Lake Forest Coll., Ill., 1975. Arch. critic Chgo. Sun-Times, 1978—81; editor Inland Arch., 1979—81; pub. Met. Press Ltd., 1983; dir., pres. Chgo. Athenaeum, 1988—. Arch. cons.; lectr. arch. history and aesthetics III. Inst. Tech. Author: Helmut John, 1984, Landmark Springfield, 1985; author: (anthology of poetry) Distant Fires, 1997; author: Inspiration: Nature and the

Poet (The Collected Poems of the Chicago architect, Louis H. Sullivan), 1999, Baltic Hours, 1999, Greenland, 2002, American Poets Against the War, 2006. Office: Mus of Architecture and Design 122 S Bench St Galena IL 61036

**NAROFSKY, REBECCA,** music educator; b. Hoffman Estates, Ill., Feb. 4, 1981; d. Wayne and Virginia Strong; m. James Narofsky, July 23, 2005. MusB in Edn., Ill. Wesleyan U., Bloomington, 2003. Tchr. music Prairie Ctrl. Sch. Dist., Forrest, Ill., 2003—. Mem.: Sigma Alpha Iota (pres. 2005—06, mem. Bloomington-Normal Alumnae chpt. 2005—06).

**NARRON, JERRY,** professional baseball manager; b. Goldboro, N.C., Jan. 15, 1956; Catcher St. Louis Cardinals, 1935, 1942, 1943, N.Y. Yankees, 1979; with Angels, 1981; mgr. Orioles' sys., 1989—92; mgr. minior league Double-A Hagerstown, 1990—91; mgr. minor league Triple-A Rochester, 1992; 3d base coach Tex. Rangers, 1994, interim mgr., 2001, mgr., 2001—02, Cin. Reds, 2005—. Office: Cin Reds Great Am Ballpark 100 Main St Cincinnati OH 45202*

**NARUSIS, REGINA GYTÉ FIRANT,** lawyer; b. Kaunas, Lithuania, Oct. 12, 1936; came to U.S., 1949, naturalized, 1955; d. Victor and Eugenia S. (Cesnavicius) Firant; m. Bernard V. Narusis, June 19, 1959; children: Victor John, Ellen Marie, Susan Marie. BA, U. Ill., 1957, JD, 1959. Bar: Ill. 1960. Ptnr. Narusis & Narusis, Cary, Ill., 1961—. Atty. City of McHenry (Ill.), 1973-93; village atty. Fox River Grove, Ill., 1967-73; asst. state's atty., McHenry County, Ill., 1968-75, head juvenile divsn., 1968-75. Mem. McHenry County Bd. Health, Woodstock, Ill., 1964-75, McHenry County Welfare Svcs. Com., 1968-75; mem., pres. Dist. 46 Sch. Bd., McHenry County, 1964-79; mem. administv. coun., mem. exec. bd. Marian Ctrl. Cath. H.S., 1981-91; bd. dirs. Cath. Found. for People of Diocese of Rockford, Ill., 1988-2002, chmn., 1991-2002; mem. fin. coun. Diocese of Rockford, 1997—; chpt. pres. Lithuanian Am. Cmty., Inc., 1989-91, exec. v.p., 1991-94, mem. Nat. Exec. Com., 1990-91, pub. rels. coun., 1990, pres., 1994-2000, pres. nat. bd. dirs., 2000—; mem. exec. com. United Faith Com. Rockford Diocese, 2002—. Mem. Ill. Bar Assn., Lithuanian-Am. Bar Assn., Inc. (v.p. 1990, pres. 1997), McHenry County Bar Assn., Kappa Beta Pi. Address: 213 W Lake Shore Dr Cary IL 60013-1023

**NASCA, THOMAS JOSEPH,** dean; b. Bklyn., June 1, 1949; m. Jean S. Styslinger; children: Patrick T., Brian J. children: Thomas J. Andrew J. BS, U. of Notre Dame, Ind., 1971; MD, Jefferson Med. Coll., Phila., 1975. Diplomate Am. Bd. Internal Medicine 1978, Am. Bd. Nephrology 1982. Intern Mercy Hosp. of Pitts., 1975—76, resident in internal medicine, 1976—79; fellow in nephrology RI Hosp.-Brown U., Providence, 1979—81; coord. of clin. services, dept. of medicine Mercy Hosp. of Pitts., 1981—85, chmn. and residency program dir., dept. of medicine, 1985—92; vice chmn., dept. of medicine Jefferson Med. Coll., Phila., 1992—91, assoc. dean for edn. and rsch., 1997—2000, acting dean, 2000—01, dean, 2001—; sr. v.p. Thomas Jefferson U., Phila., 2001—; pres. Jefferson U. Physicians, Phila., 2001—. Chmn. Residency Rev. Com. for Internal Medicine, Chgo., 2001—. Contbr. over 40 articles to profl. jours. Named White Plains H.S. Citizen of the Yr., Nat. Exch. Club, 1967; recipient Caduceus Award for Exemplary Leadership, Mercy Hosp. of Pitts., 1984, W.W.G. Mclauchlan Award for Exemplary Contbns. in Edn., 1993, The Christian R. and Mary F. Lindback Award for Disting. Tchg., Jefferson Med. Coll., 1994, Presentation of Award to Thomas Jefferson U., Class of 2000, Jefferson Med. Coll., 2000, Sister M. Ferdinand Clark Outstanding Alumnus Achievement Award, Mercy Hosp. of Pitts., 2001. Fellow: ACP, Coll. of Physicians of Phila.; mem.: Myasthena Gravis Assn. Western Pa. (bd. dirs. 1990—92), Assn. of Program Dirs. in Internal Medicine (mem. coun. 1990—2001, sec.-treas. 1995—99, pres. 2000—01), Chester Valley Golf Club, Pyramid Club, Alpha Omega Alpha. Avocations: golf, photography, basketball, marine aquarist, rugby. Office: Jefferson Med Coll 1025 Walnut St Philadelphia PA 19107 E-mail: thomas.nasca@jefferson.edu.*

**NASER, SALEH A.,** medical researcher, educator; PhD, N.Mex State U., 1993. Prof. U. Ctrl. Fla., Orlando, 1995—. Achievements include research in Crohn's disease etiology. Office: U Ctrl Fla 4000 Central Florida Blvd Orlando FL 32816

**NASGAARD, ROALD,** museum curator; b. Denmark, Oct. 14, 1941; s. Jens Larsen and Petra (Guldbaek) N. BA, U. B.C., 1965, MA, 1967; PhD, Inst. Fine Arts, N.Y. U., 1973. Lectr., asst. prof. U. Guelph, 1971-75; curator contemporary art Art Gallery of Ont., Toronto, 1975-78, chief curator, 1978-89, deputy dir., chief curator, 1989-93, sr. curator rsch., 1993; chair dept. art Fla. State U., Tallahassee, 1995—; co-dir. programming Inst. of Modern and Contemporary Art, Calgary, Alta., Canada. Vis. lectr. U. Guelph, York U.; vis. lectr., adj. prof. U. Toronto; rsch. fellow Nat. Gallery Phila. Libr. and Archives (summer), 2002. Author, curator: Ron Martin: World Paintings, 1976, Structures for Behavior, 1977, Garry Neill Kennedy: Recent Work, 1978, Ten Canadian Artists in the 1970's, 1980, Yves Gaucher: A Fifteen Year Perspective, 1978, The Mystic North: Symbolist Landscape Painting in Northern Europe and North America, 1890-1940, 1984, Gerhard Richter: Paintings, 1988, Individualities: 14 Contemporary Artists from France, 1991, Free Worlds: Metaphors and Realities in Contemporary Hungarian Art, 1991, Concealing/Revealing: Voices from the Canadian Foothills, 1997, Pleasures of Sight and States of Being: Radical Abstract Painting, 2001, co-organizer: The European Iceberg: Creativity in Germany and Italy Today, 1985. Mem. Toronto Pub. Art Commn., Gershon Iskowitz Found. Can. Council fellow, 1967-68, 70-71 Mem. Coll. Art Assn., Univ. Art Assn. Can., Assn. Can. Studies in U.S. Office: Office Phone: 850-644-8254. Business E-Mail: rnasgaar@mailer.fsu.edu.

**NASH, ALICIA,** application developer, physicist; b. San Salvador, Jan. 1, 1933; came to U.S., 1944; d. Carlos Roberto and Alicia (Lopez-Harrison) Larde; m. John Forbes Nash, Jr., Feb. 16, 1957; children: John Charles Martin Nash. BS in Physics, MIT, 1955, postgrad., 1959. Physicist Nuclear Devel. Corp. of Am., White Plains, N.Y., 1956-57, Tech. Ops., Burlington, Mass., 1957-58; rsch. assoc. MIT Computation Ctr., Cambridge, Mass., 1958-59; physicist, aerospace engr. R.C.A. Astro Divsn., Hightstown, N.J., 1960-66; programmer, analyst Mgmt. Data Processing, N.Y.C., 1972-74, Con Edison, N.Y.C., 1974-80, Blue Cross Blue Shield of N.Y., N.Y.C., 1980-82; systems/analyst programmer specialist N.J. Transit, Newark, 1983—. Mem. AAUW, MIT Club of Princeton (past pres., bd. dirs.), Soc. of Women Engring. Achievements include being the subject for the role of Alicia Nash in the movie "A Beautiful Mind." Home: 932 Alexander Rd Princeton Junction NJ 08550-1002 Office: NJ Transit One Penn Plaza East Newark NJ 07105 E-mail: alroad932@hotmail.com.

**NASH, CHARLES PRESLEY,** chemistry professor; b. Sacramento, Calif., Mar. 15, 1932; s. Clarence and Mildred Vida (Johnson) N.; m. Lois Olive Brown, May 29, 1955 (dec. May 1999); children: Nancy Caroline, Sandra Lee, James Roy, m. D.Clinton Congdon, June 3, 2002. BS, U. Calif., Berkeley, 1953; PhD, UCLA, 1958. Instr. chemistry UCLA, 1956-57; from instr. to assoc. prof. U. Calif., Davis, 1957-70, prof., 1970-93, prof. emeritus, 1993—, chmn. acad. senate, 1987-90, chmn. faculty assn., 1993-97; v.p. external rels. Coun. U. Calif. Faculty Assns., 1997—. Vis. sr. lectr. Imperial Coll., London, 1968-69; disting. vis. prof. USAF Acad., Colorado Springs, 1979-80. Contbr. articles to profl. jours. Bd. pres. Explorit Sci. Ctr., 1995-97. Recipient Disting. Teaching award U. Calif. Alumni, 1989; named Disting. Alumnus of Yr. Sacramento City Coll., 2000. Mem. Sigma Xi, Phi Lambda Upsilon. Office: U Calif at Davis Dept Chemistry Davis CA 95616 Business E-Mail: nash@chem.ucdavis.edu.

**NASH, CYNTHIA JEANNE,** journalist; b. Detroit, Dec. 24, 1947; d. Frederick Copp and Carolyn (Coffin) N.; child. Lydia Anne Maza; m. Richard Zahler, July 22, 1994. BA, U. Mich., 1969. Reporter Detroit News, 1970-75, sports columnist, 1975-77, Life Style columnist 1977-79, Life Style editor, 1979-82; news features editor Seattle Times, 1983; asst. mng. editor Sunday Seattle Times, 1983-86, assoc. mng. editor, 1986-97, dir. content devel., 1986-2000, dir., brand and content devel., 2000—. Mem. Harbor Sq. Club. Office: Seattle Times PO Box 70 Fairview Ave N & John St Seattle WA 98111-0070 E-mail: cnash@seattletimes.com.

**NASH, DAVID BRET,** physician; b. N.Y.C., Nov. 15, 1955; s. Albert J. and Charlotte Nash; m. Esther Jean Nash; children: Rachel and Leah (twins), Jacob. BA, Vassar Coll., 1977; MD, U. Rochester, 1981; MBA, U. Pa., 1986. Internship The Graduate Hosp., U. Pa., 1981-82, residency, 1982-84; med. dir. Health Evaluation Ctr., Hosp. U. Pa., Phila., 1988-90; chair, dept. health policy Jefferson Med. Coll., Phila., 1990—. Editor: Future Practice Alternatives, 1987, Providing Quality Care, 1989. Fellow ACP; mem. Phi Beta Kappa. Office: Thomas Jefferson U 115 Curtis Bldg 1015 Walnut St Philadelphia PA 19107-5005 Office Phone: 215-955-6969.

**NASH, DONALD GENE,** federal investigator, economist; b. Paris, Ill., July 20, 1945; s. Lelan and Mildred (Washburn) N.; m. Jo Ann Bellew, Aug. 29, 1964; children— Stacey Alan, Ryan Christopher, Shaun Christian BS, So. Ill. U., 1967, MS, 1969; postgrad., DePaul U., 1970-71. Farm mgr., test farms So. Ill. U., Carbondale, 1968-69; economist Commodity Futures Trading Commn., Chgo., 1969-77; v.p.-ops. Mid. Am. Commodity Exch., Chgo., 1977-86; sr. futures trading investigator Commodity Futures Trading Commn., Chgo., 1986—. Bd. trustees, treas. Friends of Danada, Wheaton, Ill., 2001—. With N.G. U.S. Army, 1968—74. Recipient Outstanding Mktg. award Wall St. Jour., 1966, award of merit Am. Farm Econ. Assn., 1967, cert. of merit Commodity Exch. Authority, merit award Naperville Art League, 1994, Honorable Mention award Danada Nature Show, 1995, 2002. Methodist. Avocations: photography, woodworking, sketching. Home: 923 Bainbridge Dr Naperville IL 60563-2002 Office: Commodity Futures Trading Commn 525 W Monroe St Ste 1100 Chicago IL 60661 Business E-Mail: dnash@cftc.gov.

**NASH, EDWARD L.,** advertising executive; b. N.Y.C., Nov. 8, 1936; s. Irving and Mina (Koppel) N.; m. Diana R. Kithcart, June 2, 1968; 1 child, Amelia. BA, CCNY, 1953. Dir. advt. Crowell, Collier, Macmillan, Inc., N.Y.C., 1961-62; v.p. mktg. LaSalle Extension U., Chgo., 1962-64; pres. Capitol Record Club, Inc., Los Angeles, 1964-69; founder, pres. Nash Pub., Los Angeles, 1969-74; exec. v.p. Rapp & Collins, N.Y.C., 1975-82; pres., chief exec. officer BBDO Direct, N.Y.C., 1982-86; owner, pres. Nash Direct Inc., N.Y.C., 1986-91; chmn. Nash, Wakeman & de Forrest, Inc., 1991-92; exec. v.p. Bozell, Jacobs, Kenyon & Eckhardt, N.Y.C., 1992-95; CEO, mng. ptnr. Team Nash, Inc., N.Y.C., 1996—. Lectr. in field; chmn. Direct Mktg. Day, N.Y.C., 1985, Internat. Direct Mktg. Conf., 1996; instr. NYU, 1998—, Va. Commonwealth U., 1998—. Author: Direct Marketing: Strategy/Planning/Execution, 1982, 2d edit., 1986, 3d edit., 1995, 4th edit., 2000; editor: The Direct Marketing Handbook, 1984, 2d edit., 1991, Database Marketing, 1993. Mem. Direct Mktg. Assn. (chmn. mktg. coun. 1980-82), NY Direct Mktg. Club (Silver Apple award 1999). Office: Team Nash Inc 245 E 58th St #21E New York NY 10022-1356 Office Phone: 646-497-0297. Business E-Mail: ednash@teamnash.com.

**NASH, HENRY WARREN,** marketing educator; b. Tampa, Fla., Sept. 19, 1927; s. Leslie Dikeman and Mildred (Johnson) N.; m. Frances Lora Venters, Aug. 20, 1950; children: Warren Leslie, Richard Dale. BS in Bus. Adminstrn, U. Fla., 1950, MBA, 1951; postgrad., Ind. U., 1951-53; PhD, U. Ala., 1965. Student asst. U. Fla., 1948-50, grad. asst., 1950-51, Ind. U., 1951-53; salesman Field Enterprises, Inc., Chgo., 1953; assoc. prof. bus. and econs. Miss. Coll., 1953-57; assoc. prof. marketing Miss. State U., 1957-66, prof., head dept., 1966-96; emeritus prof. mktg.; emeritus head dept. mktg., quantitative analysis, bus. law; dir. Coll. Bus. and Industry Acad. Advising Ctr., 1995-2000; prior. Southland Cons. Assoc., 1968-84; bd. dirs. Govt. Employees Credit Union, 1969-92, v.p., 1969-73, pres., 1973-78; ret., 2000. Author: (with others) Principles of Marketing, 1961 Served with USNR, 1945-46. Loveman's Merchandising fellow U. Ala., 1961-62 Mem. Am. Mktg. Assn., Am. Acad. Advt., Acad. Internat. Bus., So. Econ. Assn., So. Mktg. Assn. (sec. 1974-75, pres. 1976-77), Sales and Mktg. Execs. (internat. chmn. educators com. 1967-70), Miss. Retail Mchts. Assn. (bd. dirs.), Pi Sigma Epsilon (Nat. educator award 1966-77, head prof. 1967-69, nat. pres. 1967-71), Kiwanis (treas. Starkville club 1969-70, v.p. 1973-74, pres. 1974-75, lt. gov. 1977-78, gov. 1982-83), Blue Key, Beta Gamma Sigma, Omicron Delta Kappa, Mu Kappa Tau (nat. v.p. 1977-79, 86-88, pres. 1979-81, 88-90), Alpha Kappa Psi, Phi Kappa Phi (v.p. Miss. State U. 1990-91, pres. 1991-92). Baptist (tchr., deacon). Home: 2800 W Main St Cottage 302B Tupelo MS 38801-3027

**NASH, HORACE LYONS,** lawyer; b. San Jose, Calif., Dec. 19, 1955; BA with honors, U. Chgo., 1975; PhD, Stanford U., 1982; JD cum laude, Harvard U., 1985. Bar: Calif. 1985. Ptnr. Fenwick & West LLP, Mountain View, Calif., chair securities group. Named a Dealmaker of the Yr., Am. Lawyer mag., 2006. Mem.: State Bar Calif. Office: Fenwick & West LLP Silcon Valley Ctr 801 California St Mountain View CA 94041 Office Phone: 650-988-8500, 650-335-7934. Office Fax: 650-938-5200. E-mail: hnash@fenwick.com.*

**NASH, HOWARD ALLEN,** geneticist, researcher; b. NYC, Nov. 5, 1937; s. Harvey and Harriet (Ratner) N.; m. Dominie Maria Shortino, Aug. 31, 1963; children: Janet Elisabeth, Emily Julia. BS, Tufts U., 1957; MD, U. Chgo., 1961, PhD, 1963. Intern U. Chgo. Clinics, 1963-64; rsch. assoc. NIMH, Bethesda, Md., 1964-68, med. officer (res), 1968-84, chief, sec. molecular genetics, 1984—. Chmn. Gordon Conf. on Nucleic Acids, 1988; vice-chair FASEB Conf. on Genetic Recombination, 1993, chair, 1995. Assoc. editor Cell Jour., 1985-91; editl. bd. Current Biology Jour., 1993—2005, Genes to Cells, 1996—, Jour. Neurogenetics, 1998—. Lt. comdr. USPHS, 1964-68. Recipient Superior Svc. award USPHS, 1985, Disting. Svc. award HHS 1990, Alumni award for Disting. Rsch. U. Chgo., 1992. Fellow AAAS Am. Acad. Arts and Sci.; mem. NAS. Office: Lab Molecular Biology NIMH 35 Convent Dr Bethesda MD 20892-3736 Business E-Mail: howardnash@mail.nih.gov.

**NASH, JAMES LEE,** poet, security official; b. Lynchburg, Va., Oct. 1, 1957; s. James Belvy and Marjorie Lea Glden (Campbell) N. Grad., Brookville H.S., Lynchburg, 1977. VIP info. aide de camp Greater Ft. Lauderdale Broward County Conv. Ctr. Author: (poetry) Casus Belli, 1993, Enduring Significance, 1996; contbg. author: T.P.O.A., 1994, Treasure the Moment, 1996, A Shadow in the Light, 1999, Love and Other Observations, 1999, Melodies and Madness, 1999, Explanations, 2000, Other Planets are Places Too, 2000, The Erotic Adventures of a White Trash Southern Boy, 2002, Faces and Places on Capitol Hill, 2004. Mem. at large Dem. Exec. Com., Broward County, Fla., 1997-2000; mem. Croissant Park Civic Assn., Ft. Lauderdale, Fla., 1997-2000. Mem. Titanic Hist. Soc., Mu Am. Magicians. Avocations: playing piano, juggling. Home: 1114 F St NE #402 Washington DC 20002 Office: Mr Henrys 601 Pennsylvania Ave SE Washington DC 20003 E-mail: chg4600@aol.com.

**NASH, JESSIE MADELEINE,** journalist, science writer; b. Elizabeth City, N.C., Sept. 11, 1943; d. John W. and Jessie B.; m. E. Thomas Nash, June 9, 1970. AB in History magna cum laude, Bryn Mawr Coll., 1965. Clip girl to sec. Time Mag., N.Y.C., 1965-66, reporter rscher., 1966-70, stringer Bonn, Germany and Chgo., 1970-74, staff corr. Chgo., 1974-87, sr. sci. corr., 1987—. Mem. adv. com. on pub. infor. Am. Inst. of Physics, 1993-95. Contbr. articles to mags. Recipient Page One award Newspaper Guild of N.Y., 1981, award Leukemia Soc. Am., 1994, Popular Sci. Writing award, Am. Astronomical Soc., 1997. Mem. AAAS (Westinghouse award 1987, 90, Sci. Journalism award 1987, 91, 96,), Nat. Assn. Sci. Writers, Author's Guild, Sigma Xi (non mem.). Avocation: travel. Office: Time Mag 303 E Ohio St Chicago IL 60611-3373*

**NASH, JOHN DAVIDSON, JR.,** economist; b. Houston, Apr. 12, 1953; s. John Davidson and Virginia (Bryant) Nash; m. Sarah Hendrickson, June 26, 1962; children: Scott, Rachel. BS, Tex. A&M U., College Station, 1975; MA, U. Chgo., 1978, PhD, 1982. Asst. prof. econ. Tex. A&M U., College Station, 1980—83; economist Bur. Econ. FTC, Washington, 1982—83; dep. asst. dir. consumer protection FTC, 1983—84, asst. dir. trade regulation rules, 1984—86, advisor to chmn., 1986; agrl. sector economist L.Am. and Caribbean agrl. products divsn. The World Bank, 1986—, economist trade policy divsn., 1987—96, prin. economist to lead economist environmentally and socially sustainable devel. dept. Europe and Ctrl. Asia, 1996—2001, advisor commodities and trade, 2001—. Author (with others): Strategic Minerals for Defense Needs, 1979, Colombia: External Sector and Agriculture Policies for Adjustment and Growth, 1985, Best Practices in Trade Policy Reform, 1991, Trade Policy and Exchange Rate Reform in Sub-Saharan Africa, 1997, Trade Policy Reform: Lessons and Implications, 1998, Food and Agricultural Policy in Russia: Progress to Date and The Road Forward, 2002, Agriculture and the WTO: Creating a Trading System for Development, Liberalizing Agricultural Trade: Issues and Options for Sub-Saharan Africa in the WTO, 2003, Agricutura, Comercio y Desarcello: Multilateralism vs Proteccionism, 2005; contbr. articles to profl. jours. Mem.: So. Econ. Assn., We. Econ. Assn., Am. Econ. Assn., Omicron Delta Epsilon, Phi Kappa Phi, Phi Eta Sigma. Libertarian. Avocations: scuba diving, tennis, running. Home: 3307 Brandy Ct Falls Church VA 22042-3705 Office: The World Bank 18th And H Sts NW Washington DC 20433-0001 E-mail: jnash1@worldbank.org.

**NASH, JOHN FORBES, JR.,** mathematician, researcher; b. Bluefield, W.Va., 1928; BS in Math., MS in Math., Carnegie-Mellon U., 1948, ScD (hon.), 1999; PhD, Princeton U., 1950; PhD (hon.), U. Athens, 2000, U. Naples, 2003, U. Charleston, W.va., 2003. Rsch. asst., instr. Princeton (N.J.) U., 1950—51; Moore instr. MIT, 1951—53, asst. prof., 1953—57, assoc. prof., 1957—59; sr. rsch. mathematician Princeton U. Cons. RAND Corp., 1950, 52, 54; vis. mem. Inst. Advanced Study Princeton U., 1956—57, 1961—62, 1963—64; rsch. assoc. math. MIT, 1966—67. Co-recipient Nobel Prize in Econ. Scis., 1994, Bus. Week award, Erasmus i, Rotterdam, 1998, Leroy P. Steele prize in math., 1999; recipient von Neumann Theory prize, Ops. Rsch. Soc. Am., Pres.'s award, Nat. Alliance for the Mentally Ill, 1999; Sloan fellow, NSF fellow, Westinghouse scholar. Fellow: Am. Acad. Arts and Scis., Econometric Soc.; mem.: NAS. Office: Princeton U Fine Hall Math Dept Princeton NJ 08544-0001

**NASH, JOHN N.,** former professional basketball team executive; b. Phila., Nov. 28, 1946; s. John N. and Rosemary K. (Noon) N.; m. Anne Kelly (div.); children: Andrea, Carolyn; m. Ann Raley, Oct. 27, 1978 (div.); children: Brian, Barbara. BS, St. Joseph's U., 1968. Dir. group sales Phila. 76ers, 1969-71, asst. gen. mgr., 1981-86, gen. mgr., 1986-90; ticket mgr. athletic dept. U. Pa., Phila., 1971-72, Phila. Blazers, 1972-73, Phila. Flyers, 1973-75; exec. sec. Big 5 Basketball, 1975-81; v.p., gen. mgr. Washington Bullets, 1990-96; gen. mgr. N.J. Nets, 1996—2003, Portland Trailblazers, 2003—06.*

**NASH, LEONARD KOLLENDER,** retired chemistry professor; b. N.Y.C., Oct. 27, 1918; s. Adolph and Carol (Kollender) N.; m. Ava Byer, Mar. 3, 1945; children— Vivian C., David B. BS, Harvard, 1939, MA, 1941, PhD, 1944. Rsch. asst. Harvard U., Cambridge, Mass., 1943-44, instr., 1946-48, asst. prof., 1948-53, assoc. prof., 1953-59, prof. chemistry, 1959-86, chmn. dept., 1971-74; rsch. assoc. Columbia, 1944-45; instr. U. Ill., 1945-46; ret. Staff Manhattan Project, 1944-45 Author: Elements of Chemical Thermodynamics, 1962, The Nature of the Natural Sciences, 1963, Stoichiometry, 1966, Elements of Statistical Thermodynamics, 1968, ChemThermo, 1972. Recipient Mfg. Chemists' award, 1966; James Flack Norris award, 1975 Home: 1443 Beacon St Apt 614 Brookline MA 02446-4712

**NASH, MELVIN SAMUEL,** lawyer; b. Atlanta, Aug. 26, 1949; s. Ralph Samuel and Mary Pauline (Quarles) N.; m. Cynthia Joanna Hamrick, Aug. 21, 1980 (dec.); m. Kristine Marie Clark, Nov. 22, 1997. A.B., Ga. State U., 1974; J.D., U. Fla., 1976. Bar: Ga. 1977, U.S. Ct. Claims 1983, U.S. Ct. Internat. Trade 1983, U.S. Tax Ct. 1982, U.S. Ct. Appeals (5th cir.) 1978, U.S. Ct. Appeals (11th cir.) 1981, U.S. Supreme Ct. 1985. Asst. solicitor State Ct., Cobb County, Marietta, Ga., 1977-78; assoc. Milam & Smith, Austell, Ga., 1978; ptnr. Milam, Smith & Nash, Austell, 1978-79; sole practice, Marietta, 1979—; spl. master Cobb Superior Ct., 1982—; dir. Nash Trucking Co., Inc., Marietta, Security Fiedelity Mortgage, Marietta, Nash Properties, Marietta. Magistrate Prohac Vice State Ct. Cobb County, Marietta, 1980-82; candidate state rep. State of Ga. Dist. 21, Marietta, 1982. Served with USAF, 1967-71. Mem. ABA, Acad. Fla. Trial Lawyers, Assn. Trial Lawyers Am., Nat. Assn. Criminal Def. Lawyers, Ga. Assn. Criminal Def. Lawyers, Cobb County Bar Assn. (com. 1983-84), Cobb Criminal Def. Bar Assn. (sec., Seminar award 1984), State Bar Ga. (fee arbitrator 1982—), Atlanta Ski Club, Atlanta Track (Marathon finisher), Atlanta Lawyers Club. Democrat. Presbyterian. Office Phone: 770-422-0878. E-mail: melvinsnash@msn.com.

**NASH, NICHOLAS DAVID,** retail executive; b. Mpls., June 11, 1939; s. Edgar Vanderhoef and Nancy (Van Slyke) N. AB, Harvard U., 1962; MEd, Bowling Green State U., 1970; M. U. Minn., 1975. Head lower sch. Maumee Valley (Ohio) Country Day Sch., 1965-71; assoc. dir. Univ. Council for Edn. Adminstrn.; adj. asst. prof. Ohio State U., 1975-78; v.p. programming Minn. Public Radio, St. Paul, 1978-82, Am. Pub. Radio, St. Paul, 1982-85; pres. The Nash Co., 1985—. Bd. dirs. Artspace Projects, Inc. Contbr. articles to profl. jours. Bd. dirs. Nash Found., 1975-04, Humane Soc. Companion Animals, 2002—. Mem. Univ. Club St. Paul. Episcopalian. Home: 1340 N Birch Lake Blvd Saint Paul MN 55110-6716 Office: 2179 4th St Ste 2H Saint Paul MN 55110-3041 Business E-Mail: nicholasnash@post.harvard.edu.

**NASH, PAUL LENOIR,** lawyer; b. Poughkeepsie, NY, Jan. 29, 1931; s. George Matthew and Winifred (LeNoir) Nash; m. Nancy Allyn Thouron, Dec. 30, 1961; children: Andrew Gray, Laurie LeNoir, Daphne Thouron BA, Yale U., 1953; LLB, Harvard U., 1958. Bar: N.Y. 1959. Assoc. Dewey Ballantine, N.Y.C., 1958-66, ptnr., 1966—. Bd. trustees Peck Sch., Morristown, N.J., 1978-82. Served to capt. USMC, 1953-55. Mem. Assn. of Bar of City of N.Y. Republican. Home: 4 Westminster Pl Morristown NJ 07960-5810 Office: Dewey Ballantine LLP 1301 Avenue Of The Americas New York NY 10019-6022 Office Phone: 212-259-7100. Business E-Mail: pnash@deweyballantine.com. E-mail: pnash65131@aol.com.

**NASH, RICHARD EDIN,** publishing executive; b. Limerick, Republic of Ireland, June 30, 1970; came to U.S., 1988; s. Richard Oliver and Katherine Victoria (Sheehan) N. BA, Harvard U., 1992. Adv. Soft Skull Press, Manhattan, 1999—2001, pub. Bklyn, 2001—. Asst. dir. Yeats Drama Found., Dublin, Atlanta, 1991. Author, director, actor plays: Hair of the Dogma, 1990, The Frenzy of Sweeney, 1991, The Visit of the Old Lady, 1992. Recipient Gold medal for letter writing UNESCO, 1986, Young Writers award Dublin Sunday Tribune, 1991; Miriam Bass award for Creativity in Independent Pub. Assn. Am. Pub., 2006 Avocations: rugby, skiing. Office: Soft Skull Press 55 Washington St Brooklyn NY 11201 Office Phone: 718-643-1599. Office Fax: 866-881-4997.*

**NASH, SEYMOUR CY,** surgeon, urologist; b. N.Y.C., Nov. 18, 1931; s. Annette (Gersten) Cook; m. Sally Anne Kugler, Aug. 6, 1958; children: Allison, Elizabeth, Gregory. BS, U. Fla., 1952; MD, Washington U., St. Louis, 1956. Diplomate Am. Bd. Urology. Surg. intern Yale Med. Ctr., New Haven, Conn., 1956-57, surg. resident, 1957-59; clin. assoc. Nat. Cancer Inst., Bethesda, Md., 1959-61; urology resident Georgetown U. Hosp., Washington, 1961-64; pvt. practice in urology Miami Beach, Fla., 1964—; assoc. clin. prof. U. Miami Med. Sch., 1964-94; clin. dept. urology Mt. Sinai Hosp., Miami Beach. Co-author: Prostate Cancer Making Survival Decisions, 1994. Capt. USPHS, 1959-61. Fellow Am. Coll. Surgeons; mem. AMA, Am. Assn. Clin. Urologists, Fla. Med. Assn., Dade County Med. Assn. Republican. Jewish. Avocation: tennis. Office: 4302 Alton Rd Ste 670 Miami Beach FL 33140-2877 Office Phone: 305-531-7671.

**NASH, STEVE,** professional basketball player; b. Feb. 7, 1974; Degree, Santa Clara Coll., 1996. Player Phoenix Suns, 1996, Dallas Mavericks, 1998—2004, Phoenix Suns, 2004—. Named a Man of the Year, GQ mag., 2005; named MVP, NBA, 2005—06; named one of 100 Most Influential

People, Time Mag., 2006; named to NBA All-Star Game, 2002, 2003, 2005, All-NBA Third Team, 2003, 2002, All-NBA First Team, 2005, 2006; recipient Best NBA Player, ESPY awards, 2005. Office: c/o Phoenix Suns 201 E Jefferson St Phoenix AZ 85004*

**NASH, SYLVIA DOTSETH,** management consultant; b. Montevedio, Minn., Apr. 25, 1945; d. Owen Donald and Selma A. (Tollefson) Dotseth; married; 1 child, Lindsland Louise. Grad., Calif. Luth. Bible Sch., 1965; doctorate (hon.), Pilgrims Theol. Seminary, 1994. Office mgr. First Congl. Ch., Pasadena, Calif., 1968-75; pastoral asst. Pasadena Presbyn. Ch., 1975-78; dir. adminstrv. svcs. Fuller Theol. Sem., Pasadena, 1978-81; CEO Christian Mgmt. Assn., Diamond Bar, Calif., 1981-94; pres. Christian Healthcare Network, La Mirada, Calif., 1994-95; sr. cons. Lillestrand and Assocs., Chino Hills, Calif., 1996—. Cons. various orgns., 1985—. Author: Inspirational Management, 1992 (Your Church Mag. award 1992); editor: The Clarion, 1975-78, The Christian Mgmt. Report, 1981-94; mem. editl./adv. bd. Your Church Mag.; mem. editl. bd. Jour. Ministry Mktg. and Mtmg.; contbr. articles to profl. jours. Bd. dirs. Nat. Network of Youth Ministries, The Mustard Seed, Inc., Nat. Assn. of Ch. Bus. Adminstrn., Found. for His Ministry, Lamb's Players, Gospel Lit. Internat., Evang. Coun. for Fin. Accountability, Campus Crusade for Christ Internat. Sch. Theology. Mem. NAFE, Nat. Assn. Ch. Adminstrs. (sec. 1979-81), Am. Soc. Assn. Execs., So. Calif. Soc. Assn. Execs. Office: Lillestrand & Assocs 2729 Brookside Drive Chino Hills CA 91709

**NASH, WARREN LESLIE,** minister; b. Jackson, Miss., Aug. 26, 1955; s. Henry Warren and Frances Lora (Venters) N.; m. Valerie Ann Roberts, Nov. 22, 1980; children: John Wilson, Warren Graham, William Dixon. Student, U.S. Naval Acad., 1973-75; BS in Banking and Fin., Miss. State U., Starkville, 1980; MBA, U. Ala., Birmingham, 1982; profl. cert., Stonier Grad. Sch. Banking, Newark, Del., 1987; M of Theol. Studies, Emory U., 1995. Asst. br. mgr. 1st Nat. Bank of Birmingham, Ala., 1978-80, br. officer Ala., 1980-81, asst. v.p. Ala., 1981-84; v.p. AmSouth Bank, N.A., Birmingham, 1984-86, v.p., regional retail banking mgr. Montgomery, Ala., 1986-89; sr. v.p. AmSouth Bank, Montgomery, 1989-91; sr. v.p. consumer banking AmSouth Bank, N.A., Birmingham, 1991-93; v.p. productivity AmSouth Bank, Birmingham, 1993-94, sr. v.p. tech., 1994-95, sr. v.p. retail delivery, 1995-98; pres. Retail BancAssocs., LLC, Birmingham, 1998—2001; exec. dir. Canterbury United Meth. Ch., 2001—. Instr. fin. Samford U., Birmingham, 1982-84; v.p., Ala. Automated Clearing house, 1983-84. Counselor Jr. Achievement, Birmingham, 1980-82; loaned exec. United Way, Birmingham, 1980; com. chmn. Birmingham Festival Arts, 1985-86. Named one of Outstanding Young Men of Am., 1984, 85, 86. Mem. Am. Mktg. Assn. (bd. dirs. 1983-84), Am. Inst. Banking, Birmingham C. of C. (dept. coord. 1985), Newcomen Soc., Young Montgomerians Bus. Club, Summit Club, Kiwanis (local pres. 1985-86), Alpha Kappa Psi, Beta Gamma Sigma. Independent. Methodist. Office: Canterbury United Meth Ch 350 Overbrook Rd Birmingham AL 35213 Home: 3824 Spring Valley Rd Birmingham AL 35223-1568 Office Phone: 205-874-1555.

**NASH, WILLIAM ARTHUR,** civil engineer, educator; b. Chgo., Sept. 15, 1922; s. William A. and Rose (Keck) N.; m. Verna Lucile Baer, Aug. 8, 1953; children: Rebecca Ann, Phillip Arthur. BSCE, Ill. Inst. Tech., 1944, MS, 1946; PhD, U. Mich., 1949. Rsch. engr. David W. Taylor Model Basin, Navy Dept., Washington, 1949-54; mem. faculty U. Fla., Gainesville, 1954-67, head dept. engring. mechanics, 1964-67; prof. civil engring. U. Mass., Amherst, 1967—. Cons. to govt. and industry; hon. prof. Shanghai Inst. Tech., 1985; pres. Cons. Engring., Amherst, 1992—. Author: Theory and Outline of Strength of Materials, 4th edit., 1998 (translated into 10 langs.), Statics and Mechanics of Materials, 1991, Hydrostatically Loaded Structures, 1995; contbr. over 100 articles to profl. jours.; editor Internat. Jour. Nonlinear Mechanics. Recipient Humboldt US Sr. Scientist award, Fed. Republic Germany, 1986. Fellow ASME; mem. Internat. Assn. Shell and Spatial Structures, Am. Soc. Engring. Edn. (Curtis W. McGraw Rsch. award 1961), AIAA, Earthquake Engring. Rsch. Inst. Congregationalist. Office: 235 Marston Hall U Mass Amherst MA 01003 Office Phone: 413-534-4510.

**NASHAT, GUITY,** historian, education educator, researcher; b. Bagdad, Iraq, July 28, 1937; arrived in U.S., 1956; d. Muhammad Sadegh Nashat-Mirdamad and Qamar Afshar; m. Gary S. Becker, Oct. 31, 1979; children: Michael, Cryus Claffey stepchildren: Judy, Catherine. BA, Barnard Coll., N.Y., 1958; MS journalism, Columbia Univ., N.Y., 1959; PhD hist., Univ. Chgo., Chgo., 1974. Vis. asst. prof. Loyola Univ., Chgo., 1974—75; asst. prof. Univ. Ill., Chgo., 1975—83, assoc. prof., 1983—2006. Rsch. fellow Hoover Inst., Stanford Univ., 1995—. Author: The Origins of Modern Reform in Iran 1870-1880, 1982, Middle Eastern History Selected Reading Lists and Course Outlines from American Colleges and Universities, 1988; editor: Women and Revolution in Iran, 1984; co-author: Women in the Middle East and North Africa, 1999; co-editor: The Economics of Life, 1996, Women in Iran From the Rise of Islam to 1800, 2003, Women in Iran from 1800 to the Islamic Republic, 2003. Grantee Ford Found. Grant, Univ. Chgo., 1968—69, Soc. Sci. Rsch. Coun. summer grant, 1978, Soc. Sci. Rsch. Coun. grant, 1976—77; Ford Found. fellowship, Columbia Sch. of Journalism, 1958—59. Mem.: Mont Pelerin Soc., Qajar Studies Assn., Iranian Studies (exec. bd. mem. 1986—89), Middle Eastern Studies Assn. Office: Univ Ill at Chgo 601 S Morgan St Chicago IL 60607-7109 Office Phone: 312-996-3144. E-mail: gnashat@uic.edu.

**NASHED, M. ZUHAIR,** mathematics professor, editor; b. Aleppo, Syria, May 14, 1936; s. Zaki Nashed and Nabiha Mosalati; m. Ragda Yagan, Dec. 23, 1959; children: Ziad, Zaki, Zane, Nadia. SB in Elec. Engring., MIT, 1957, SM in Elec. Engring., 1958; MS in Math., PhD in Math., U. Mich., 1963. Asst. prof. Ga. Inst. Tech., Atlanta, 1963—65, assoc. prof., 1965—69, prof., 1969—76; prof. math. and elec. engring. U. Del.; prof., chair U. Ctrl. Fla., Orlando, 2002—. Assoc. prof. Am. U. Beirut, Lebanon, 1967—69; vis. prof. U. Mich., U. Wis., European and Middle Eastern univs. Editor: Jour. Numerical Functional Analysis & Optimization, 1979—, Jour. Integral Equations, 1987—; mem. editl. bd.: 15 jours., exec. editor: 2 book series; author: over 120 papers in math. and engring. jours.; editor: 7 books; editor: numerous books. Recipient Sigma Xi Rsch. award, Ga. Tech., 1966, 1974, Lester Ford award, Math. Assn. Am., 1969; grantee rsch. and conf. grants, U.S. Army Rsch. Office and USAF Rsch. Office. Mem. Am. Math. Soc. (chair, VLP program 2000—), Soc. Indsl. & Applied Math. (education com. 2000—). Office: Univ Central Florida 209 MAP Bldg Orlando FL 32816 Business E-Mail: znashed@mail.ucf.edu.

**NASHER, RAYMOND D.,** real estate developer, art collector; b. Boston, Oct. 26, 1921; BA, Duke Univ., 1943; MA, Boston Univ., 1950; LLD (hon.), So. Methodist Univ., 1973. Chmn. Comerica Bank, Tex., Nasher Co., Dallas. Chmn. Nat. Commn. Urban Develp., 1964—65; mem. U.S. Commn. to UNESCO, 1962—65; U.S. delegate to UN Gen. Assembly, 1967—68; mem. Pres. Com. on Arts & Humanities, Pres. Commn. on Urban Housing (Kaiser Commn.), 1967—68, U.S.-German Cooperative Delegation, 1967. Mem. Nat. Council UN Assn. for USA, 1996, bd. dirs., 1994—99; trustee V.P.'s Residence Found.; mem. bd. regents Am. Architects Found.; trustee The Am. Assembly; ambassador of cultural affairs City of Dallas, 1988—93; bd. mem. World Affairs Council of Greater Dallas, 1996; mem. Dallas Bus. Com. for the Arts; mem. nat. council Fine Art Mus. San Francisco; mem. internat. council Tate Gallery, London. Named one of Top 200 Collectors, ARTnews Mag., 2004, 2006; recipient Design of the Decade - 1960s, Am. Inst. Architects, Distinguished Svc. to Visual Arts award, No. Tex. Univ., Flora award, 1994. Mem.: Council for Fgn. Rels., Phi Beta Kappa. Avocation: collector of Oceanic, pre-Columbian, modern & contemporary art, especially sculpture. Mailing: 4701 Miron Dr Dallas TX 75220*

**NASHIF, TAYSIR N.,** researcher, writer; b. Tayyiba, near Jerusalem, Mar. 22, 1940; came to U.S., 1969; s. Najm A. and Aisha A. Nashif; m. Mayyada I. Nashif, Apr. 15, 1968; children: Fawz, Fayruz, Hanin. BA in Polit.

Sci./Arabic Lang. & Lit., Hebrew U., Jerusalem, 1964, MA in Internat. Rels., 1968; MA in Islamic Studies, U. Toronto, 1969; PhD in Polit. Sci., SUNY, Binghamton, 1974. Prof. U. Oran, Algeria, 1974—76, UN, N.Y.C., 1976—77, polit. affairs officer, 1980—81, reviser, editor, 1982—96; prof. Essex County Coll., Newark, 1985—93; chief Arabic verbatim reporting sect. UN, N.Y.C., 1996—2002. Author: The Palestine Arab and Jewish Political Leaderships, 1979, Nuclear Warfare in the Middle East, 1984, Nuclear Weapons in Israel, 1996, The Arabs and the World in the Next Century, 1999, Authority, Intellectual Freedom and Society, Palestinian Thinkers in the Twentieth Century, Authority, Thought and Social Change, Intellectual Activity and Social Change, Government, the Intellectual and Society in the Third World; contbr. articles on strategic, polit., and cultural issues to profl. jours. Grantee SUNY, 1971-73. Mem.: Third World Studies Assn., Am. Translators Assn., Mid. East Studies Assn., Am. Polit. Sci. Assn. Avocations: sea cruising, fishing, mountain climbing. E-mail: tnnashif@aol.com.

**NASKY, H. GREGORY (HAROLD GREGORY NASKY),** lawyer; b. Titusville, Pa., June 9, 1942; s. Harold G. and Majella Marie (Beck) N.; m. Rosanne Guson, July 22, 1967. AB, St. Bonaventure U., 1964; JD, U. Notre Dame, 1967. Bar: Pa. 1967, Nev. 1972, Hawaii, 2003. Assoc. Eaton & Hill, Warren, Pa., 1967-68, Vargas, Bartlett & Dixon, Reno, 1972-73; ptnr. Vargas & Bartlett, Las Vegas, Nev., 1974-94, mng. ptnr., 1981-91; of counsel Kummer, Kaempfer, Bonner & Renshaw, 1994—2006; prin. Resort Devel. Cons., 1998—2006; ptnr. Goodsill Anderson, Quinn & Stifel, Honolulu, 2006—. Corp. sec. Showboat, Inc. (NYSE-SBO), Las Vegas, 1978-98, bd. dirs., 1983-98, exec. v.p., 1995-98; bd. dirs. U. Notre Dame Law Assn., 1990-2000; mem. adv. bd. U. Nev. Sch. Medicine.; chmn. 1993, bd. dirs. Author: Inter Alia Jour. of State Bar of Nevada, A Glimpse of China, 1986; Nev. contbg. author: Real Property, Probate & Trust Law Jour., Disposition of Rents, 1981. Legal advisor Nev. Dance Theatre, Las Vegas, 1977-94, bd. dirs. 1988-2000; legal com. Nev. Resort Assn., Las Vegas, gaming regulations com. 1990-93; bd. dirs. Boulder Dam coun. Boy Scouts Am., Las Vegas, 1986-93; del. People to People Citizen Ambassador Program, People's Republic China, 1985, New Zealand/Australia, 1987, Hungary, Czechoslovakia and Poland, 1990, Russia and Estonia, 1992. Served to capt. JAGC, U.S. Army, 1968-72, Vietnam. Decorated Bronze Star, 1970. Mem. ABA (bus. sect. task force conflicts interest com. 1993-95), State Bar Nev. (chmn. fee dispute com. 1983-89, exec. com. mem. Gaming Law Sect. 1985-93), Am. Soc. Corp. Secs., Internat. Assn. Gaming Attys., Notre Dame Club Las Vegas (past pres. 1978-79), U. Nev. Las Vegas Found. (president's assocs. 1993, chmn.). also: Resort Devel Cons PMB A14 Ste 105 9101 W Sahara Ave Las Vegas NV 89117 Office: Goodsill Anderson Quinn and Stifel 1099 Alakea St Ste 1800 Honolulu HI 96813 Home: 4340 Pahoa Ave 8A Honolulu HI 96816 Office Phone: 702-792-7000, 808-547-5600. Business E-Mail: gnasky@kkbr.com, gnasky@goodsill.com

**NASLUND, ERIC CHRISTOPHER,** architectural firm executive; b. Madrid, May 28, 1960; B in Architecture, Calif. Polytechnic State U. Lic. Calif., N.Mex. Prin., ptnr. Studio E Archs., 1986—. Adj. faculty mem. Woodbury U., San Diego. Fellow: Am. Inst. of Architecture. Office: Studio E Architects 2411 Second Ave San Diego CA 92101 Office Phone: 619-235-9262. Business E-Mail: eric@studioearchitects.com.

**NASLUND, HOWARD RICHARD,** geological science educator; b. Green Hills, Ohio, Nov. 25, 1950; married, 1979; 5 children. BS, U. Ill., 1972; MS, U. Oreg., 1977, PhD, 1980. Leader East Greenland Expeditions, 1985, 1986, 1988, 1989; igneous petrologist Ocean Drilling Program, 1991, 97; asst. prof. Dartmouth Coll., 1979-87; assoc. prof. dept. geol. scis. and environ. studies SUNY, Binghamton, 1987-95, assoc. chmn. geol. scis. and environ. studies 1987-88, dir. grad. studies geol. scis., 1988-92, prof. dept. geol. scis. and environ. studies, 1995—, chmn. geol. scis. and environ. studies, 1992-95,97-2000. Vis. prof. Departamento de Geologia, U. Chile, 1995-96, vis. prof. Departamento de Ingeniería en Minas, U. de Santiago, Chile, 2001-02; outside rev. com. dept. geology SUNY, New Paltz, 1995, sponsored programs adv. coun., 1994-97, grad. coun., 1994-97, chair adv. com. on scholarship and rsch., 1994-97, material rsch. inst., 1991—, faculty senate, 1988-90, 96-98, 2005—; trustee Glenn G. Bartle Meml. Fund, 1988-90, 96-98, 2004-06; exec. com. of faculty Dartmouth Coll., 1982-85, com. on stds., 1981-86. Contbr. articles to profl. jours. J. William Fulbright scholar, 1995-96; rsch. grant USSAC, 1991, 92, 97, 98, 2005, NSF, 1982, 88, 90, 99, 2004, equipment grant NSF, 1990, 91. Mem. Geol. Soc. of Am. (Penrose Rsch. award 1974, 76), Mineralogical Soc. Am., Am. Geophys. Union, Sociedad Geologica de Chile, NY State Geol. Assn. (pres. 1997-98), Internat. Assn. Volcanology Chemistry Earth Interior. Office: Geol Scis SUNY Binghamton NY 13902-6000 Office Phone: 607-777-4313. Business E-Mail: Naslund@Binghamton.edu.

**NASO, VALERIE JOAN,** automobile dealership executive, travel company operator, artist, photographer, writer; b. Stockton, Calif., Aug. 19, 1941; d. Alan Robert and Natalie Grace (Gardner) McKittrick Naso; m. Peter Joralemon, May 31, 1971 (div.). Student pub. schs., Piedmont, Calif. Cert. graphoanalyst. Pres., Naso Motor Co. (formerly Broadway Cadillacs, Oakland, Calif.) Bishop, Calif., 1964—; freelance artist, 1965—; owner, operator Wooden Horse Antiques, Bishop, 1970-82; editor, writer, photographer Sierra Life Mag., Bishop, 1980-83; freelance writer, photographer, 1972—; owner, operator Boredom Tours, Bishop, 1981—; owner, sole photographer, Renaissance Photography, N.Y.C. and Bishop, Calif., 1982—, Keyboard Colors, 1986; cons. graphoanalyst, 1976—. Fiction, non-fiction work pub. in Horse and Horseman, Am. Horseman, Horse & Rider Mag., Cameo Mag., Desert Mag., Sierra Life Mag. Mem. Nat. Assn. Female Execs., Authors Guild, Inc., Authors League Am., Am. Film Inst., Archives of Am. Art, Lalique Soc. Am., Musical Box Soc. Internat., Alliance Francaise (N.Y. chpt.), Bishop C. of C., Victorian Soc. Am., Nat. Trust for Hist. Preservation, Am. Craft Coun., Nat. Rifle Assn. (life class: Cadillac LaSalle (nat. and so. calif. chpts.); Wagner Soc. (N.Y.C.). Office: 783 N Main St Bishop CA 93514-2427 also: PO Box 1625 Bishop CA 93515-1625

**NASON, BARRY MARK,** systems engineer, mathematician, educator; b. Newton, Mass., Jan. 24, 1948; s. Louis and Muriel Rose Nason; m. Diane Elizabeth Bowman, Aug. 26, 1974; 1 child, Elizabeth Anne. BS in Sys. Engring., U. Fla., 1973; MS in Stats., Wright State U., 1994; MS in Math., Tenn. State U., 2000. Cert. quality engr., Am. Soc. for Quality, 1993, reliability engr., Am. Soc. for Quality, 1994; CPIM Am. Prodn. and Inventory Control Soc., 1994. Systems analyst Combustion Engring., Chattanooga, 1973—76, performance analyst Windsor, Conn., 1976—78; sys. analyst divsn. Ingersoll Rand Torrington (Conn.) Co., 1978—82; project leader Colt Firearms, Hartford, Conn., 1982—88; mgr. devel. Garden Way, Inc., Troy, NY, 1988—90; sr. sys. designer Grumman Data Sys., Dayton, Ohio, 1990—94; sr. sys. engr. EDS-Mil. Sys., Dayton, 1994—96, EDS-TennCare, Nashville, 1996—2002; sys. arch. EDS-Kans. XIX, Topeka, 2002—. Contbr. articles to profl. jours. With U.S. Army, 1971—72. Mem. Am. Math. Soc. (assoc.), Math. Assn. Am. (assoc.), Am. Statis. Assn. (assoc.), Phi Kappa Phi (assoc.), Beta Theta Pi (life). Avocations: reading, mathematics. Home: 821 Justin St Lawrence KS 66049 Office: EDS Ste 204 3600 South Topeka Blvd Topeka KS 66611

**NASON, CHARLES TUCKEY,** retired diversified financial services company executive; b. Apr. 22, 1946; s. Raymond W. and Helen (Tuckey) Nason; m. Elizabeth Lucille Rabun, May 1, 1999; children: Rebecca Ann, Jill Nicole. BA, Washington and Jefferson Coll., 1968; MBA, U. Pitts., 1969. Cert. fin. planner, chartered fin. cons. Dist. sales mgr. Met. Life Ins. Co., Pitts., 1971-77; mng. dir. Acacia Grp. Cos., Pitts., 1977-88; founder, pres. Coordinated Capital Ltd., Pitts., 1982-85; pres., CEO Acacia Life Ins. Co., Washington, 1988—2003, chmn., 1988—2005, Acacia Fed. Savings Bank, Calvert Grp., Ltd. Chmn. devel. coun. exec. com. Washington and Jefferson Coll., 1982—85, trustee, 1988—, chmn. Nat. Am. Giving Fund, 1994—96; trustee Washington Fed. City Coun., 1988—; bd. dirs. Greater Washington Bd. Trade, chmn.-elect, 1993, chmn. Trust; bd. dirs. Washington Real Estate Investment Trust, Medstar Inc., Blue Cross Blue Shield Washington, 1991—93, Greater Washington Boys and Girls clubs, Am. Coun. Life Ins.,

1993—2000, Medlantic Healthcare Group, 1997—98. Lt. USAF, 1970—71. Mem.: Ins. Marketplace Stds. Assn. (bd. dirs. 1999—, chmn.-elect 2001, chmn. 2002), Inst. Cert. Fin. Planners (bd. dirs.), Nat. Assn. Securities Dealers, Estate Planning Coun. (bd. dirs.), Am. Soc. CLUS (pres. 1981—82), Gen. Agts. and Mgrs. Assn. (pres. 1984—85), Fiddlesticks Golf and Country Club, Talbout Country Club, Congl. Country Club, Burning Tree Club. Republican. Roman Catholic. Mailing: c/o Acacia Fed Savings Bank PO Box 6430 Falls Church VA 22040-9825*

**NASON, DOLORES IRENE,** computer company executive, social welfare administrator, minister; b. Seattle; d. William Joseph and Ruby Irene Lockinger; m. George Malcolm Nason, Jr.; children: George Malcolm III, Scott James, Lance William, Natalie Joan. Student, Long Beach (Calif.) City Coll.; cert. in Religious Edn. for elem tchrs., Immaculate Heart Coll., cert. teaching, cert. secondary teaching; attended, Salesian Sem. Buyer J. C. Penney Co., Barstow, Calif.; prin. St. Cyprian Confraternity of Christian Doctrine Elem. Sch., Long Beach; prin. summer sch. St. Cyprian Confraternity of Christian Doctrine Elem. Sch., Long Beach; pres. St. Cyprian Confraternity Orgn., Long Beach; dist. co-chmn. L.A. Diocese; v.p. Nason & Assocs., Inc., Long Beach, 1978—; pres. L.A. County Commn. on Obscenity & Pornography, 1984—; eucharistic minister St. Cyprian Ch., Long Beach, 1985—; bd. dirs. L.A. County Children's Svcs., 1988—; assoc. dir. social svcs. Disabled Resources Ctr., Inc., Long Beach, 1992—. Mem. scholarship com. Long Beach City Coll., 1984—90, Calif. State U., Long Beach, 1984—90; bd. dirs. County Access Svc. Inc., 2004—. Active Long Beach Civic Light Opera, 1973—96, Assitance League Long Beach, 1976—; vol. Meml. Children's Hosp., Long Beach, 1977—; pres. St. Cyprian's Parish Coun., 1962—. Mem.: KC (Family of Month award 1988), U. Pacific Club. Roman Catholic. Avocations: physical fitness, theater, choir, travel.

**NASON, NICOLE R.,** federal agency administrator; married; children: Alexandra, Abigail. Grad., Am. U., Washington, 1992; JD, Case Western Res. U., Cleve., 1995. Counsel House Judiciary Subcom. on Crime, Washington; govt. affairs counsel Met. Life Ins. Co., 1999—2000; comm. dir., counsel to US Rep. Porter J. Goss US Congress, 2000—02; asst. commr. Office of Congl. Affairs, U.S. Customs Svc., Washington, 2002—03; asst. sec. for govtl. affairs US Dept. Transp., Washington, 2003—06, adminstr., Nat. Hwy. Traffic Safety Adminstrn., 2006—. Office: Nat Hwy Traffic Safety Adminstrn US Dept Transp 400 7th St Washington DC 20590

**NASON, ROCHELLE,** conservation organization administrator; b. Oakland, Calif., May 21, 1959; d. Milton and Ann Frances (Reed) Nason. BA, U. Calif., Berkeley, 1984; JD, U. Calif., San Francisco, 1987. Bar: Calif. 1987. Law clk. to chief Justice Malcolm Lucas Supreme Ct. of Calif., San Francisco, 1987-88; litigation assoc. Morrison & Foerster, San Francisco, 1988-92; staff lawyer League to Save Lake Tahoe, South Lake Tahoe, Calif., 1992-93, exec. dir., 1993—. Adj. instr. Sierra Nev. Coll., Incline Village, 1992—94, Lake Tahoe C.C., 1992—96. Editor: The Traynor Reader, 1987; sr. rev. editor: Hastings Law Jour., 1986—87; editor: (jour.) Keep Tahoe Blue, 1992—; columnist: newspaper Tahoe Daily Tribune; contbr. articles to profl. jours. Mem. leadership coun. Tahoe-Truckee Regional Econ. Coalition, Stateline, Nev., 1992—94; v.p., bd. dirs. Jewish Cmty. South Lake Tahoe/Temple Bat Yam, 1992—99; bd. dirs. Tahoe Ctr. Sustainable Future, Glenbrook, Nev., 1995—98, Earthshare Calif., 2002—. Mem.: Thurston Soc., Order of Coif. Jewish. Avocations: backpacking, skiing. Office: League to Save Lake Tahoe 955 Emerald Bay Rd South Lake Tahoe CA 96150-6410

**NASR, NADIA,** librarian; b. Houston, Apr. 2, 1977; d. Ghazi Said Nasr and Patricia Maureen Moye. Grad., U. So. Miss., 2005. Cert. publ. libr. Md. Digitization specialist McCain Libr. and Archives, Hattiesburg, Miss., 2002—05; libr., digitization supr., digital cultural heritage coord. Enoch Pratt Free Libr., Balt., 2005—. Mem.: ALA, Miss. Libr. Assn., Md. Libr. Assn., Soc. Am. Archivists, Spl. Librs. Assn. Office: Enoch Pratt Free Libr 400 Cathedral St Baltimore MD 21201 Office Phone: 410-545-6342. Business E-Mail: nnasr@epfl.net.

**NASR, SAMIH H.,** pathologist, educator; MD, Damascus U., Syria, 1996. Lic. Am. Bd. Anatomic Pathology. Asst. prof. of pathology McGill U., Montreal, Que., Canada, 2003—05, Columbia U. Coll. of Physicians and Surgeons, N.Y.C., 2005—. Mem.: Renal Pathology Soc. Office Phone: 212-305-9669.

**NASRAOUI, OLFA,** computer scientist, educator, electrical engineer; b. Tunis, Tunisia, July 6, 1968; d. Ezzeddine Zidane Nasraoui and Fatma Braiek; m. Hichem Frigui, Apr. 3, 1993; children: Yasmine Frigui, Sara Frigui. BS in Computer Engring. with honors, U. Mo., Columbia, 1990, BSEE with honors, 1990, MSEE, 1992, PhD in Computer Engring. and Computer Sci., 1999. Asst. prof. elec. and computer engring. U. Memphis, 2000—04; endowed chmn. e-commerce dept. computer sci. and computer engring. U. Louisville, 2004—, founder, dir. Knowledge Discovery and Web Mining Rsch. Lab., 2004—. Panel organizer internat. confs., outreach/sci. fair activities; reviewer rsch. proposals NASA; mem. program com., organizing com. various internat. confs.; reviewer internat. jours. in field. Editor conf. procs. Faculty advisor local chpt. Soc. Women Engrs., Memphis, 2000—04. Recipient Best Paper award for Theoretical Developments in Computational Intelligence, Procs. Artificial Neural Networks in Engring., 2001, Career award, NSF, 2002, grantee, 2002—, So. Consortium for Elec. Engring. Edn., 2002—03, NASA, 2004—), Innovative Productivity Inc., 2006. Mem.: IEEE, IEEE Women in Engring., Internal Adv. Bd. Logistics and Distbn. Inst., MentorNet, Assn. Computing Machinery. Office: U Louisville Sch Engring CECS Dept Speed Louisville KY 40292 Office Phone: 502-852-0191.

**NASS, MERYL J.,** physician, writer, research scientist; b. Rockville Ctr., N.Y., Apr. 6, 1951; d. Leonard Ira and Irene Shirley Nass; m. John Duncan Abernethy, Aug. 13, 1977 (div. 1987); children: Abraham David Abernethy, Jacob Duncan Abernethy. BS in Biology, MIT, 1974; MD, Univ. Miss., 1980. Diplomate Am. Bd. of Internal Medicine, 1986. Physician hosp. and health care ctrs., 1985—98; self-employed, 1999—. mem. adv. bd. Alliance for Human Rsch. Protection, N.Y., 2001—, Nat. Vaccine Info. Ctr., Vienna, 2000—, Inst. for Molecular Medicine, Huntington Beach, Calif., 2000—; cons. Interamerican Devel. Bank, Washington, 2001—; presenter testimony on anthrax vaccine reaction NAS Inst. Medicine, U.S. Congress, major mass media, 1998—. Contbr. scientific papers to profl. jour., articles over 30 to profl. jour. Achievements include development of assessment and treatment strategies for fibromyalgia, Gulf War syndrome, chronic fatigue sydrome; discovery of first use of biological weapons in modern times; high rate of severe reactions to anthrax vaccine; research in establishing long-term safety and efficacy for vaccines and drugs before licensure and widespread use; improving criteria to distinguish between naturally occurring and deliberate outbreaks of disease; development of comprehensive epidemiologic surveillance to identify questionable disease outbreaks; research in mitigation of bioterrorism events. Office: Mount Desert Island Hosp 10 Wayman Lane Bar Harbor ME 04609 Office Phone: 207-288-5081 x220. Personal E-mail: mnass@gwi.net. Business E-Mail: mnass@anthraxvaccine.org

**NASS, RUTH,** pediatric neurologist; b. N.Y.C., Apr. 14, 1947; d. Samuel and Edna (Kadin) N.; m. Theodore Gross, Aug. 28, 1977; 1 child, Nora Gross. BA, Brandeis U., 1969; postgrad., MIT, 1969-70, Brandeis U., 1970-72; MD, Einstein Coll. Medicine, 1975. Diplomate Nat. Bd. Med. Examiners, Am. Bd. Pediatrics, Am. Bd. Psychiatry and Neurology with spl. competence in child neurology; lic. physician, N.Y. Resident pediatrics N.Y. Hosp., N.Y.C., 1975-77; resident neurology Columbia Presbyn. Hosp., N.Y.C., 1977-80; clin. rsch. fellow in neurology/neuropsychology Cornell U. Med. Coll., N.Y.C., 1980-82, instr. pediatrics, 1981-82, asst. prof., 1982-88, asst. prof. neurology, 1982-89; asst. attending pediatrics and neurology N.Y. Hosp., N.Y.C., 1982-89; divsn. chief pediatric neurology N.Y. Hosp., Cornell Med. Ctr., N.Y.C., 1986-89, assoc. attending pediatrician 1988-91; assoc. prof. clin. pediatrics Cornell Med. Coll., N.Y.C., 1988-89, assoc. prof. neurology and pediatrics, 1989-91; assoc. attending neurologist N.Y. Hosp., N.Y.C., 1989-

91; assoc. prof. neurology and pediatrics NYU Med. Ctr., N.Y.C., 1991—; assoc. attending pediatrician, neurologist Tisch Hosp., Bellevue Hosp., N.Y. U. Med. Ctr., 1991—; dir. learning diagnostics program NYU Med. Ctr., 1991—. Neurologic cons. N.Y. Foundling Hosp., N.Y.C., 1980-83; dir. Learning Disability Ctr. N.Y. Hosp.-Cornell Med. Ctr., 1983-91; neurologic cons. St. Mary's Hosp., Bklyn., 1984-86, Englewood (N.J.) Hosp., 1986, Hosp. for Spl. Surgery, N.Y.C., 1987-91; acting chief divsn. pediatric neurology N.Y. Hosp.-Cornell Med. Ctr., 1985-86; chief neurology Blythedale Children's Hosp., 1989-91; adj. assoc. prof. pediatrics N.Y. Hosp.-Cornell U. Med. Ctr., 1991—; NIH ad hoc site com. Nosology of Learning Disabilities, Washington, Isabelle Rapin, P.I., 1987, N.Y.C., 1988; external rev. panel Child Neurology Soc. Nosology Project in Presch. Child, 1989; ad hoc NIH site com. at Boston Children's Hosp. Program Project on Learning in At Risk Groups, 1990, ad hoc NIH site com. for Ctr. and Program Project on Neurobiology of Dyslexia, 1992; mem. written bds. com. Am. Acad. Psychiatry and Neurology, 1992-93; mem. NIH Consensus Com. on Early Identificaiton of Hearing Impairment, 1993; lectr. univs., hosps, orgns., workshops and symposiums. Ad hoc reviewer Neurology, Annals of Neurology, Cognitive Neurosci., Psychol. Bull., Pediatrics, Psychoneuroendocrinology, Jour. Neuro-oncology, Epilepsia; contbr. articles to profl. jours., chpts. to books. Mary Putnam Jacobie fellow, 1981; grantee NIH Nat. Rsch. Svc., 1980-83, NIH Biomed. Rsch., Cornell U. Med. Coll., 1983-84, March of Dimes, 1984-95, United Cerebral Palsy, 1984-87, Rita G. Rudel Found., 1986-88, NIH Ctr., 1991—; recipient Rockefeller Bros. Clin. Scholarship N.Y. Hosp.-Cornell Med. Coll., 1983-84. Mem. Am. Neurol. Assn., Am. Acad. Neurology, Am. Acad. Pediatrics (develop. disabilities com. 1992-93), Assn. for Rsch. in Nervous and Mental Diseases, Child Neurology Soc. (sci. selection com. 1988-89, 91-93, clin. practice com. 1991-93, award com. 1990-92), Internat. Child Neurology Soc., Am. Epilepsy Soc., Am. Acad. Cerebral Palsy, N.Y. Acad. Sci., Orton Dyslexia Soc., Soc. for Children with Attention Deficit Disorder. Office: NYU Med Ctr Rusk Rsch 212 550 1st Ave New York NY 10016-6402

**NASSAR, RAJA**, statistics educator, researcher, consultant; b. Lebanon, 1936; came to U.S., 1958; naturalized, 1971; m. Ita G. Schaeffer, 1965; 1 child, Mark BS. Am. U., Beirut, Lebanon, 1958; MS, U. Idaho, 1960; PhD, U. Calif., Davis, 1963. Rsch. fellow U. Idaho, Moscow, 1958—60; rsch. asst. U. Calif., Davis, 1960—63, rsch. assoc., 1963—64; mem. vis. faculty U. Minn., St. Paul, 1964—66; asst. prof. Kans. State U., Manhattan, 1966—68, assoc. prof., 1967—74, prof. stats., 1974—. Maxfield prof. math. and stats. Kans. State U., 1995—; vis. prof. Govt. Research Inst., Hamburg, Germany, 1969-70, Nat. Research Inst., Toulouse, France, 1974-75, U. Kiel, Germany, 1982-83, U. Giessen, Germany, 1992-93 Contbr. numerous artilces to sci. jours Alexander von Humboldt fellow, 1969, 82, French Govt. fellow, 1974; rsch. grantee Greek Orthodox. Avocations: tennis, travel, piano, reading. Office: La Tech U Math and Stats 305 Wisteria St Ruston LA 71270-4235 E-mail: nassar@coes.latech.edu.

**NASSAU, MICHAEL JAY**, lawyer; b. N.Y.C., June 3, 1935; s. Benjamin and Belle (Nassau) N.; m. Roberta Bluma Herzlich, June 26, 1971; children: Stephanie Ellen, William Michael. BA summa cum laude, Yale U., 1956, LLB cum laude, 1960. Bar: NY 1960, US Ct. Appeals (2d cir.) 1963, US Tax Ct. 1963, US Supreme Ct. 1965, US Dist. Ct. (so. dist.) NY 1978. Asst. instr. in constl. law Yale U., 1959-60; law clk. judge US Ct. Appeals 2d Cir., 1960-61; assoc. tax dept. Paul, Weiss, Rifkind, Wharton & Garrison, NYC, 1961-73; ptnr. Kramer Levin Naftails & Frankel LLP, and predecessor, NYC, 1974—. Mem. adv. bd. Matthew Bender Fed. Pension Law Service, 1975-76; mem. adv. com. NYU Ann. Inst. Employee Plans Exec. Compensation, 1976-79; mem. steering com. Am. Pension Conf., 1981-83; lectr. field; chair PLI Seminars, Deferred Compensation after Treasury Guidance, 2005; panelist various seminars employee benefits; panelist Pension Video Seminar, 1983; mem. N.E. region pension liaison group IRS. Mem. editl. bd. Bank Corp. Governance Law Reporter, 1989—; contbr. chpts. to books and articles to profl. jours. Recipient Excellence in Benefits award lifetime achievement benefits svc., Worldwide Employee Benefits Network, 2003. Charter fellow Am. Coll. Employee Benefits Counsel; mem. ABA (sect. taxation, employee benefits com. 1993—), NY State Bar Assn. (co-chmn. employee benefits sect. taxation 1976-78, mem. exec. com. sect. taxation 1976-79), Assn. Bar City NY (chmn. subcom. pension legis. of com. taxation 1975-76, employee benefits com. 1987-92), WEB (NY chpt. bd. dirs. 1990—, pres. 1993-94), Phi Beta Kappa. Office: Kramer Levin Naftalis & Frankel LLP 1177 Ave of the Americas New York NY 10036 Office Phone: 212-715-9416. Business E-Mail: mnassau@kramerlevin.com.

**NASSER, JACQUES**, banker, former automotive company executive; b. Beirut, Dec. 12, 1947; Degree in Bus. studies, Royal Melbourne Inst. Tech. With Ford of Australia, 1968-73; mem. fin. staff N.Am. truck ops. Ford Motor Co., 1973, mgr. profit analysis, product programming, 1973-75, with Asia-Pacific and Latin-Am. ops., 1977—80, dir., v.p. fin. and adminstrn., Auto-latina joint venture, 1987-90, chmn. Ford Europe, 1993—99, pres. Ford automotive ops., exec. v.p., 1996—99, v.p., 1993-96, pres., CEO Dearborn, Mich., 1999—2001, Ford of Australia, 1990-93; sr. ptnr. One Equity Partners LLC, NYC, 2002—; non-exec. chmn. Polaroid Corp., Waltham, Mass., 2002—. Office: One Equity Partners LLC 320 Park Ave 18th Fl New York NY 10022*

**NASSER, JOSEPH YOUSEF**, public safety administrator, consultant; b. Welch, W.Va., Mar. 19, 1943; s. Joseph H. and Betty Anne (Caldwell) N.; m. Janis Halligan Nasser; children: Robert, Eric, Melanie, Matthew, Michelle. BS, Pacific Western U., 1989, PhD, 1991. Patrolman, firefighter, emergency med. technician Mich. Dept. Pub. Safety, Oak Park, 1962-75; patrolman Daytona Beach (Fla.) Police Dept., 1975-76; lt., capt., dir. Volusia County (Fla.) Sheriff's Dept., 1976-90; pres., founder, owner Ctr. for Pub. Safety Studies, Ormond Beach, Fla., 1990—97; sr. v.p, RCC Cons Inc, 1997 Pres Associated Pub Safety Comm. Officer, Inc., 1987-88, Land Mobile Comm. Coun., Washington, 1988-89; chmn. Nat. Pub. Safety Planning Com./F.C.C., 1987-88; life mem. APCO, Inc. Past chmn. Fla. State Standards and Telecommunicator Cert. Com., Fla. State Emergency Mgmt. 9-1-1 Com.; past mem. exec. coun. Volusia County Emergency Med. Found.; past chmn. Volusia County Emergency Med. Svcs. Trust Fund Adv. Bd. Recipient Dayton Beach Cooper-Taylor Pub. Safety Achievement award, 1985, Nat. Achievement award Pub. Safety Comm. Coun., 1987, FCC Recognition award, 1987, APCO Life Mem. award, 1988, Emergency Mgmt. Recognition award State of Fla., 1989, Appreciation award Emergency Med. Found., 1990, Disting. Svc. award Volusia County Sheriff's Dept., 1990. Fellow Radio Club of Am.; mem. Associated Pub. Safety Comms. Ofcls. Internat. (life, Outstanding Achievement in Pub. Safety, 2001), Internat. Mcpl. Signal Assn. (sustaining, Journalistic Excellence award 1991). Republican. Methodist. Avocations: fishing, bowling, jogging, horseback riding. Home: 4507 Rangewood Dr Tallahassee FL 32309-8965 Office Phone: 850-224-4451. Personal E-mail: jynasser@comcast.net.

**NASSERIPOUR, MOHAMMAD MICHEL**, artist, architect; b. Teheran, Iran, Sept. 9, 1942; arrived in U.S., 1982; s. Moussa and Zari Nasseripour; m. Nooshazar Mary Sanei, Nov. 7, 1974; children: Melanie, Pearl. M in Art and Arch., Teheran U., 1971. Exhibitions include France, Paris, 1981, Art Gallery, NYC, 1988, Am. U., Washington, 1988, George Washington U., 1988, Beaux Art Mus., Teheran, 1996, Silk Road Festival, Smithsonian Instn., 2002, Opening Minds, Washington, 2003, NY Art Expo, 2006; author: The Life and Work of Behzad, 1999; co-author: Splendors of Iran: Lacquer Work Section, 2002, Guide to Iran: Persian Miniatures and Artists, 2003. Recipient Agha Khan award, Agha Khan Foun., 2001, Silk Road Festival award, Smithsonian Inst., 2002, Opening Mind award, Iranian Am. Tech. Coun., 2003. Mem.: Internat. Coun. Mus., Am. Inst. for Conservation. Office Phone: 202-489-4050.

**NASSETTA, CHRISTOPHER J.**, hotel facility executive; Various positions Oliver Carr Co., 1984-91, chief devel. officer; pres. Bailey Realty Corp., 1991-95; exec. v.p. Host Marriott Corp., 1995-97, COO, 1997-2000, pres.,

CEO Bethesda, Md., 2000—. Dir. CoStar Group Inc.; trustee Prime Group Realty Trust. Adv. bd. McIntire Sch. Commerce, U. Va. Office: Host Marriott Corp Ste 1500 6903 Rockledge Dr Bethesda MD 20817-1118*

**NASSTROM, ROY RICHARD**, educational consultant; b. Oakland, Calif., Oct. 28, 1930; s. Roy Richard and Edith Dolores (Spilman) N.; m. Sally Louise Shaw, Aug. 29, 1964; children: Karen, Eric. AA, U. Calif., Berkeley, 1955, BA, 1956, MA, 1964, PhD, 1971. Asst. to supt. Ravenswood Sch. Dist., East Palo Alto, Calif., 1964-65; acting instr. edn. U. Calif., Berkeley, 1965-68; asst. prof. ednl. adminstrn. U. Ky., Lexington, 1969-70; asst. prof. edn. Purdue U., West Lafayette, Ind., 1971-76; mediator, fact finder Ind. Edn. Employment Rels. Bd., 1974-76; asst. grad. dean Winona (Minn.) State U., 1976-77, chmn. ednl. adminstrn. dept., 1976-88, prof., 1976-01, prof. emeritus, 2001—, chmn. ednl. leadership dept., 1998-01; ednl. polit. cons. R. Nasstrom, 2002—. Cons., spkr. various orgns. and schs., 1969—; mem. bd. abstractors Ednl. Adminstrn. Abstracts, 1976-83; dir. post-masters studies Winona State U., 1992-99. Editor Ravenswood Report, 1964-65, U. Calif.-Berkeley Sch. Edn. Newsletter, 1965-68; bd of editors AASA Prof., 1979-82; manuscript reviewer various jours. and pubs, 1983-87; contbr. articles and revs. to profl. jours., chpts. to books. List mgr. Winona On-line Democracy, 2005—, mem. steering com., 2003—. With U.S. Army, 1952—54. Recipient numerous grants, 1969-98. Mem.Am. Ednl. Rsch. Assn. (paper reviewer 1983-2000), Calif. Alumni Assn., Am. Assn. Colls. for Tchr. Edn. (instnl. rep., paper reviewer), Nat. Assn. Scholars, Learning Club, Pi Sigma Alpha Avocation: photography. Home: 1702 Edgewood Rd Winona MN 55987-2149 Personal E-mail: rrn@hbci.com. Business E-Mail: nasstrom@cal.berkeley.edu.

**NAST, DIANNE MARTHA**, lawyer; b. Mount Holly, N.J., Jan. 30, 1948; d. Henry Daniel and Anastasia (Lovenduski) N.; m. Joseph Francis Roda, Aug. 23, 1980; children: Michael, Joseph, Joshua, Anastasia. BA, Pa. State U.; JD, Rutgers U., 1976. Bar: Pa. 1976, U.S. Dist. Ct. Pa. 1976, N.J. 1976, U.S. Dist. Ct. N.J 1976, U.S. Ct. Appeals (3d, 5th, 6th, 7th, 8th and 11th cirs.) 1976, U.S. Supreme Ct. 1982, U.S. Dist. Ct. Ariz. 1985. Dir., v.p. Kohn, Nast & Graf, P.C., Phila., 1976-95, Roda & Nast, P.C., Lancaster, Pa., 1995—. Mem. lawyers adv. com. U.S. Ct. Appeals (3d cir.), 1982-84, chmn., 1983-84, mem. com. on revision jud. conf. conduct rules, 1982-84; mem. Third Cir. Task Force on Selection of Class Clunsel, 2001-02mem. U.S. Ct. Appeals for the 3d Cir. Jud. Conf. Permanent Planning Com., 1983-90; bd. dirs. 3d Cir. Hist. Soc., Phila. Pub. Def., 1980-89, Fed. Jud. Ctr. Found., 1992-2002, chmn. 1997-2002; chmn. lawyers adv. com. U.S. Dist. Ct. (ea. dist.) Pa., 1982-90. Pres. Hist. Soc., 1988-91. Fellow ABA (coun. litigation sect. 1986-89, co-chmn. anti-trust com. litigation sect. 1984-86, div. dir. 1990-91, practical litigation editl. bd. 1989—, ho. of dels. 1992-94, mem. task force state justice initiatives, mem. task force of justice system, 1993, mem. task force long range planning com. 1994), Am. Law Inst. (chair internat. professionalism com. 1991-94, civil justice task force 1993-95), Am. Arbitration Assn. (bd. dirs., mem. alt. dispute resolution and mass torts task force), Am. Judicature Soc., Pa. Bar Assn. (bd. of dels. 1983-95), N.J. Bar Assn., Pa. Trial Lawyers Assn., Phila. Bar Assn. (bd. govs. 1985-87, chmn., bicentennial com. 1986-87, chmn. bench bar conf. 1988-89), Lancaster Bar Assn. (co-chair civil litigation and rules com. trial law sect.), Rutgers Law Sch. Alumni Assn. Home: 1059 Sylvan Rd Lancaster PA 17601-1923 Office: Roda & Nast PC 801 Estelle Dr Lancaster PA 17601-2130 Office Phone: 717-892-3000. E-mail: dnast@rodanast.com.

**NAST, EDWARD PAUL**, cardiac surgeon; b. Balt., Dec. 13, 1958; s. Richard Cecil and Lenora (Heilig) N.; m. Lauren Jean Nast; children: Bennett Ross, Jaclyn Rose. BS, Emory U., 1979; MD, U. Md., 1984. Diplomate Am. Bd. Thoracic Surgery, Am. Bd. Surgery. Intern Georgetown U. Med. Ctr., Washington, 1984-85, resident in gen. surgery, 1985-86, 88-91; fellow in cardiac surgery NIH, Bethesda, Md., 1986-88; resident in thoracic and cardiovascular surgery U. Md. Med. Sys., Balt., 1991-93; attending cardio-thoracic surgeon St. Joseph's Hosp. Health Ctr., Syracuse, NY, 1993—2002; cardiothoracic surgeon Arnot Ogden Med. Ctr., Elmira, NY, 2001—, chief, med. dir. cardiothoracic and vascular surgery, 2006—. Asst. attending cardiothoracic surgeon NY Presbyn. Hosp., Columbia U. Med. Ctr. NYC, 2002—; asst. clin. prof. cardiothoracic surgery Columbia U., NYC, 2002—. Contbr. articles to profl. jours. Named one of Outstanding Young Men of Am., 1996, 98. Fellow ACS, Am. Coll. Cardiology, Am. Coll. Chest Physicians; mem. Soc. Thoracic Surgeons, Phi Beta Kappa. Office: 600 Ivy St Ste 201 Elmira NY 14905 Home: 14 Prospect Ridge Horseheads NY 14845 Office Phone: 607-737-7780. Personal E-mail: enast@stny.rr.com. Business E-Mail: enast@aomc.org.

**NASTAL, DAVID THOMAS**, secondary school educator; s. Matthew John Nastal and Dorothy Mae McClain-Nastal. MusB in Music Edn., Westminster Coll., New Wilmington, Pa., 1976; M.Lit. Music, Cath. U. of Am., Washington, 1983. Lic. tchr. Va., 1987. Dir. of liturgy and music Star of the Sea Cath. Ch., Virginia Beach, Va., 1978—83, Roman Cath. Diocese of Dallas, Dallas, 1983—87; prof. of liturgy and music U. of Dallas, 1983—87; liturgical cons. and author Argus Comm., Dallas, 1985—87; prof. of liturgy and music Borromeo Coll., Cleve., 1987—88; dir. of music and liturgy St. Paschal Baylon Ch., 1988—98; music and liturgy dir. Our Lady of Mt. Carmel Ch., Newport News, Va., 1998—2002; dir. of performing arts Georgetown Visitation Prep Sch, Washington, 2002—. Contbg author Oreg. Cath. Press, Portland, Oreg., 1992—2005. Author: (teaching) Children's Choir Basics. Mem.: Am. Guild of Organists (dean - norfolk chpt. 1979—82), Am. Choral Dirs. Assn., Nat. Pastoral Musician (committee head - children's choirs 1998—2000), Music Educators Assn., Music Educators Nat. Conf. Avocations: swimming, running, travel. Office: Georgetown Visitation Preparatory School 1524 35th St NW Washington DC 20007 Office Phone: 202-337-3350. Business E-Mail: dnastal@visi.org.

**NASTASI, ALDO A.**, judge; b. NYC, Sept. 18, 1932; s. Anthony and Santina N.; m. Marie A. Nastasi, Dec. 26, 1954; children: Aldo, Robert, Marc, Anthony, David. B in Social Sci., Fordham U., 1954, LLD, 1959. Bar: N.Y. 1960, U.S. Supreme Ct. 1974. City ct. judge, Yonkers, N.Y., 1975-79; judge Westchester County Ct., N.Y., 1980-83, N.Y. State Supreme Ct., 1984-97, 98—. Councilman City of Yonkers, 1972-75, selected coun. majority leader. 1st lt. USMC, 1954-56. Mem. N.Y. State Lawyers Trial Assn., Westchester County Bar Assn., Columbia Lawyers Assn. (bd. dirs. 1992-98), Forham Law Alumni Assn. (Gov. Malcolm Wilson Disting. Alumnu award 2004) Republican. Roman Catholic. Avocations: golf, reading. Office: 9th Jud Dist Ct NY Westchester County Ct House 111 MLK Jr Blvd White Plains NY 10601 Office Phone: 914-824-5427.

**NATALE, BARBARA GUSTAFSON**, retired librarian; b. Hartford, Conn., Jan. 12, 1938; d. Carl William and Gertrude Fallon Gustafson; m. John Charles Natale, Sept. 12, 1959; children: Linda Skehan, John A., Mary Ellen. BA, U. Conn., 1959; MLS, So. Conn. State U., 1977. Libr. media specialist Windsor (Conn.) Pub. Schs., 1976—82; pub. svcs. libr. Manchester (Conn.) C.C., 1982—90, dir. libr. svcs., 1990—98, ret., 1998. Vice chmn. campus master planning com. Manchester (Conn.) C.C., 1992—98; mem. coun. librs. Conn. C.C.s, Hartford, Conn., 1992—95, chmn. coun. librs., 1993—95; evaluator New Eng. Assn. Schs. and Colls., Bedford, Mass., 1994—95; bd. dirs. Sea Call Supporters, Inc., sec., 2003—. Vol. Snow Libr., Orleans, Mass., 2003—05; sec. Friends of N.W. Park, 1981—87, vice chair, 1988—89; Windsor mayor's rep. Riverfront Recapture, Hartford, 1992—96; dist. capt., campaign coord. Windsor (Conn.) Dem. Com., 1978—92. Recipient Ednl. Excellence and Disting. Svc. award, Conn. C.C., 1994, Leadership Women award, Women's Caucus, Manchester (Conn.) C.C., 1994. Fellow: LWV, Wellfleet Garden Club; mem.: Conn. Libr. Assn. (bd. coll. and univ. sect. 1984—86, mem. ref. and adult svcs. com. 1986—90, chmn. 1989—90). Democrat. Avocations: travel, reading, gardening, bicycling, photography. Home: PO Box 1467 11 Pleasant View Dr East Orleans MA 02643

**NATALE, PATRICK J**, professional society administrator; m. Sheila Natale; 2 children. BS in Civil Engring., Newark Coll.of Engring.; MS in Engring. Mgmt., NJ Inst. of Tech.; grad., exec. mgmt. program, Yale U. Lic. profl.

engr., NJ; cert. Assn. Exec. (CAE). Various mgmt. positions PSE&G, NJ; v.p., northeast region Nat. Soc. Profl. Engr., exec dir., 1999—2002; exec. dir., chief staff officer, sec. Am. Soc. Civil Engr., Reston, Va., 2002—. Pres. Am. Soc. Civil Engr. Found., 2003—. Chmn. Goodwill Ind. of Nat. Capital Area of C., Am. Red Cross; asst. dist. commr. Boy Scouts of Am. Office: Exec Dir Am Soc Civil Engr 1801 Alexander Bell Dr Reston VA 20191-4400*

**NATALICIO, DIANA SIEDHOFF**, academic administrator; b. St. Louis, Aug. 25, 1939; d. William and Eleanor J. (Biermann) Siedhoff. BS in Spanish summa cum laude, St. Louis U., 1961; MA in Portuguese lang., U. Tex., 1964, PhD in Linguistics, 1969. Chmn. dept. modern langs. U. Tex., El Paso, 1973-77, assoc. dean liberal arts, 1977-79, acting dean liberal arts, 1979-80, dean Coll. Liberal Arts, 1980-84, v.p. acad. affairs, 1984-88, pres., 1988—. Bd. dirs. El Paso for Health Res. Bd. Dallas, chmn., 1989; mem. Presdl. Adv. Commn. on Ednl. Excellence for Hispanic Ams., 1991; bd. dirs. Sandia Corp., Trinity Industries; bd. dirs. Nat. Action Coun. for Minorities in Engring., 1993—; mem. Nat. Sci. Bd. 1994-2000; mem. NASA Adv. Coun., 1994-96; bd. mem. Fund for Improvement of Post-Secondary Edn., 1993-97; bd. dirs. Fogarty Internat. Ctr. of NIH, 1993-96; bd. chair Am. Assn. Higher Edn. 1995-96; bd. dirs. U.S.-Mexico Commn. for Ednl. and Cultural Exch., 1994—. Co-author: Sounds of Children, 1977; contbr. articles to profl. jours. Bd. dirs. United Way El Paso, 1990-93, chmn. needs survey com., 1990-91, chmn. edn. divsn., 1989; chmn. Quality Edn. for Minorities Network in Math. Sci. and Engring., 1991-92; chairperson Leadership El Paso, Class 12, 1989-90, mem. adv. coun., 1987-90, participant, 1980-81; mem. Historically Black Colls. and Univs./Minority Instns. Consortium on Environ. Tech. chairperson, 1991-93; trustee Rockefeller Found. Recipient Harold W. McGraw. Jr. prize in edn., 1997, Torch of Liberty award Anti-Defamation League B'nai B'rith, 1991, Conquistador award City of El Paso, 1990, Humanitarian award El Paso chpt. NCCJ, 1990; named to El Paso Women's Hall of Fame, 1990, Tex. Women's Hall of Fame, 1998. Mem. Philos. Soc. Tex. Avocations: hiking, bicycling, skiing, skating. Office: U Tex at El Paso Office of the Pres 500 W University Ave El Paso TX 79968-0001*

**NATANI, KIRMACH**, forensic psychologist; b. Milw., June 5, 1935; s. Whit Baer Naabane and Natasha Rucoss Nabona. BS in Clin. Psychology, Okla. U., 1970; PhD in Biopsychology, Okla. U. Health Sci. Ctr., 1977; postgrad., USAF Sch. Aerospace Medicine, San Antonio, 1977—79. Lic. clin. psychologist, health svc. provider, cert. forensic neuropsychologist, sr. disabiloty analyst, divorce mediator. Physics tech./profl. Lawrence Berkeley Lab., Berkeley, Calif., 1958—63; vol. Peace Corps, Thailand, 1963—65; clin. rschr. Okla. City VA Hosp., 1966—77; human factors engr. McDonnell-Douglas, St. Louis, 1980—92; postodoctoral resident/cons. St. Mary's Hosp., East St. Louis, Ill., 1992—97; pvt. practice clin. neuropsychologist, cons. Bi-State Neurometric Svcs., various cities, 1998—. Clin. mgr. Mo. Dept. Corrections, Farmington, Mo., 1999—2001; sr. care mgr. Magellan Behavior Health, St. Louis, 2001—02; ad hoc peer reviewer profl. psychology, rsch., practice, 2001—; mem. adv. com. NRC, 1978—83. Contbr. numerous articles to profl. jours., chpts. to books. With USAF, 1955—63. Recipient, Roche Labs. awards, 1973; grantee, Divsn. Polar Programs, NSF, 1966—75, Nature Publishing Group, 2006. Fellow: Am. Coll. Forensic Examiners; mem.: APA, Mo. Am. Psychol. Assn., Am. Bd. Disability Analysts, Am. Bd. Psychol. Specialities, Internat. Soc. Neurol. Regulation. Avocations: computer graphics, digital photographic restoration. Office Phone: 314-426-1875. Personal E-mail: knat3@juno.com.

**NATARAJAN, ANANTH**, medical products executive, biomedical engineer; BSE in biomedical and elec. engring., Duke U., 1990; MSE in biomedical engring., Johns Hopkins U., 1992; MD, U. Chicago., 1996. Co-founder, CEO Infinite Biomedical Tech., LLC, 1997—. Named one of Top 100 Young Innovators, MIT Tech. Review, 2004. Office: Infinite Biomedical Tech 3600 Clipper Mill Rd Ste 410 Baltimore MD 21211

**NATARAJAN, SATHIMA**, pathologist; arrived in U.S., 1991; d. Varadharajan and Vidina Rajan; m. Raj Natarajan, Sept. 14, 1988; children: Natasha, Sean Vijay. MB, BChir, Madras Med. Coll., Chennai, India, 1989; MD, Cedars-Sinai Med. Ctr., L.A., 1998, U. So. Calif., 1999. Asst. clin. prof. UCLA Med. Ctr., 1999—, chief gynecologic pathology divsn., 1999—, dir. cytopathology fellowship program, 2001—. Gynecologic oncology group faculty UCLA, 1999—, gynecologic pathology cons. outreach program, 1999—. Recipient Outstanding Tchg. award, UCLA Dept. Pathology, 1999—2000. Mem.: L.A. Soc. Pathologists (bd. mem. 2001—). Office: UCLA David Geffen Med Ctr 10833 Le Conte Ave Los Angeles CA 90095

**NATARELLI, LARISSA IVANOVNA**, language educator, researcher; b. Simpheropole, Crimea, Ukraine, July 21, 1952; arrived in U.S., 1994, naturalized, 2005; d. Ivan I. and Angelina S. Sklar; 1 child, Angelina M. Alrawas. BA in French and English, Kiev State Linguistic U., 1981; postgrad., Capella U., Mpls., 2001—. Cert. methods of fgn. lang. intensive tchg. Moscow State U., Russia, 1985. Rschr., instr. Kiev State Linguistic U., 1983—89; pres., instr. Fgn. Lang. Intensive Tchg. Ctr. Vesna, Kiev, 1988—90; exec. dir., instr. Internat. Joint Venture Coprikey, Kiev, 1990—92; dir., instr. Russian Ballet Acad. at Smith Opera Ho., Geneva, NY, 1996—97, Internat. Ctr. for Multicultural Edn., Dunedin, Fla., 1998—2000. Co-author: Methodology of Foreign Language Intensive Teaching, 1988. Mem.: Linguistic Soc. Am., Fla. Assn. Tchr. Educators. Achievements include research in quantum linguistics. Home: 8501 N 50th St Apt 1108 Tampa FL 33617-6122 Personal E-mail: larnat21@yahoo.com.

**NATARUS, BURTON F.**, municipal legislator, lawyer; b. Wausau, Wis., Nov. 7, 1933; BS in Polit. Sci., U. Wis., 1956, JD, 1960, postgrad., John F. Kennedy Sch. Govt., 1993. Chair appellate arbitrator: Cir. Ct. Cook County, Ill. Pvt. practice law, Chgo.; elected alderman 42d Ward, Chgo., 1971, elected democratic committeeman, 2004; chmn. Chgo. City Coun. Com. Traffic Control and Safety, 1997—; mem. Chgo. Plan Com. State St. Com., 1997—; elected NE Ill. Regional Transportation Task Force, 2004. Mem. Mayor's Zoning Reform Commn.; mem. Ctrl. Area Planning Task Force, Ill. Regional Transp. Task Force, State Street Coun. Mem. 2000 Yr. Chgo. Trade Del. to China. Capt. USAR, ret. Fellow Am. Acad. Polit. Sci.; mem. Internat. Soc. Poets, City Club, Greater North Michigan Ave. Assn., Streeterville C. of C., River North Assn., North Dearborn Assn., North State Astor, Lake Shore Dr. Assn., Streeterville Orgn. Active Residents, Ctrl. Mich. Ave. Assn. Address: 30 N La Salle St Ste 2900 Chicago IL 60602-2584 Office: City Hall Rm 306 121 N Lasalle St Chicago IL 60602-1202

**NATCHER, STEPHEN DARLINGTON**, retired lawyer, electronics executive; b. San Francisco, Nov. 19, 1940; m. Carolyn Anne Bowman, Aug. 23, 1969; children: Tanya Michelle, Stephanie Elizabeth. AB in Polit. Sci., Stanford U., 1962; JD, U. Calif., San Francisco 1965. Bar: Calif. 1966. Assoc. firm Pillsbury, Madison & Sutro, San Francisco, 1966-68; counsel Douglas Aircraft div. McDonnell Douglas Corp., Long Beach, Calif., 1968-70; v.p., sec. Security Pacific Nat. Bank, 1971-79; asst. gen. counsel Security Pacific Corp., 1979-80; v.p., sec., gen. counsel Lear Siegler, Inc., Santa Monica, Calif., 1980-87; v.p., gen. counsel Computer Sci. Corp., El Segundo, Calif., 1987-88; exec. v.p., gen. counsel, sec. CalFed Inc., 1989-90; sr. v.p. adminstrn., gen. counsel, sec. Wyle Electronics, Irvine, Calif., 1991-98; gen. counsel VEBA Electronics LLC, Santa Clara, Calif., 1998—2002, ret., 2002. With USCG, 1965-71. Mem.: St. Francis Yacht Club (San Francisco). Republican. E-mail: snatcher@starstream.net.

**NATH, JOGINDER**, genetics and biology educator, researcher; b. Joginder Nagar, Panjab, India, May 12, 1932; arrived in U.S., 1957; s. Moti Ram and Vira Wali (Khorana) N.; m. Charlotte Lynn Reese, Apr. 5, 1969; children—Pravene, Brian BS with honors, Panjab U, Amritsar, India, 1953, MS with honors, 1955; PhD, U. Wis., 1960. Research assoc. Am. Inst. Biol. Research, Madison, Wis. 1960-63; asst. prof. So. Ill. U., Carbondale, Ill., 1964-66; from asst. to assoc. prof. W.Va. U., Morgantown, 1966-72, prof., chmn. dept. genetics and devel. biology, 1972—. Contbr. articles on cytogenetics, mutagenesis, biochem genetics and cryobiology to profl. jours. Chmn. bd. Morgantown Day Sch., 1977—79. Recipient Alexander Hollaender award, Environ. Mutagen Soc., 1997, Edn. and Student Mems. Com. award, 2000, Mehra Meml. award, Panjab U., 2000; grantee, NSF, 1967—68, DOE, 1992—95, Nat. Inst. Occupl. Safety and Health, 1985—95, NIH, 2002—. Mem. Soc. Cryobiology, Environ. Mutagen Soc., Sigma Xi. Office: WVa U Coll Agr Dept Genetics & Devel Biology Morgantown WV 26506 Office Phone: 304-293-6256.

**NATHAN, ANDREW JAMES,** political science educator; b. NYC, Apr. 3, 1943; s. Paul S. and Dorothy (Goldeen) N.; children: Chloe Armann Nathan, Oliver Paul Bauer-Nathan, Isabel Rae Bauer-Nathan; 1 stepchild Alexandra Witke. BA summa cum laude, Harvard U., 1963, MA in East Asian Regional Studies, 1965, PhD in Polit. Sci., 1971. Lectr. U. Mich., Ann Arbor, 1971; research assoc. Ctr. for Chinese Studies, 1970; asst. prof. polit. sci. Columbia U., N.Y.C., 1971-75, assoc. prof., 1975-82, prof., 1982—2001; dir. East Asian Inst. Columbia U., N.Y.C., 1991-95, prof. political sci. 2001—; prof. polit. sci. Class of 1919, 2001—. Mem. steering com. China Internat. Bus. Project, 1978—; mem. nat. com. on U.S.-China rels., 1987—; chair adv. com. Human Rights Watch/Asia, 1995-2000; cons. Ambrica Prodns., Nat. Endowment for Democracy, others; lectr. in field. Author: A History of the China International Famine Relief Commission, 1965, Modern China, 1840-1972, An Introduction to Sources and Research Aids, 1973, Peking Politics, 1918-1923: Factionalism and the Failure of Constitutionalism, 1976, Chinese Democracy, 1985 (Levenson prize 1987), (with others) Human Rights in Contemporary China, 1986, China's Crisis, 1990; co-editor Popular Culture in Late Imperial China (with Robert S. Ross), 1985, The Great Wall & the Empty Fortress: China's Search for Security, 1997, China's Transition, 1997; co-editor: The Tiananmen Papers, 2001; contbr. book revs. to publs.; manuscript reviewer U. Calif. Press, Columbia U. Press, Harvard U. Press, others; coord. The Tienanment Papers, 2001; contbr. numerous articles to profl. jours. and current popular publs. Guggenheim fellow, 1973-74; fellow Am. Coun. Learned Soc.- Social Sci. Rsch. Coun., 1977-78, NEH fellow 1986-87, 1992-93; grantee Luce Found., 1979-82, 91-93, 92-95, Chiang Ching-Kuo Found., 1992, 1995-96, 1995-97, NSF, 1993-96 and others. Mem. Am. Polit. Sci. Assn., Assn. for Asian Studies, Coun. Fgn. Rels. Office: Polic Sci Dept Columbia U 420 W 118th St New York NY 10027-7213 E-mail: ajn1@columbia.edu.

**NATHAN, ARTHUR M.,** lawyer; b. Houston, July 20, 1951; s. Herman Nathan and Doris (Samuelson) Abramson; m. Arlene Kissner, May 29, 1988; children: Robert Michael Kissner, Jeffrey David Kissner, M. Douglas Kissner. BA magna cum laude, U. Tex., 1972, JD cum laude, 1975. Bar: Tex. 1975, admitted to practice: US Tax Ct. 1976, US Claims Ct. 1976, US Dist. Ct. (So. Dist.) Tex. 1976, US Ct. Appeals (5th Cir.). Assoc. Foreman, Dyess, Prewett, Rosenberg & Henderson, Houston, 1975-80; ptnr. Foreman & Dyess, Houston, 1980-81, Porter & Clements, Houston, 1981-90; ptnr., bus. and tax planning, mergers and acquisitions Haynes and Boone, LLP, Houston, 1990—, bd. dir. Author (seminar books): Advanced Tax Law Course, 1991, Building Blocks of A Business Law Practice, 1992; co-author (seminar book): Corporate, Partnership and Business Law, 1994, 95. Mem. Tax Law Exam Commn., 1999—2005. Fellow: Tex. Bar Found. (bd. dir.); mem.: ABA (corp. taxation com., taxation sect. 1987—, negotiated acquisitions com., bus. law sect. 1995—), State Bar Tex. (chmn. corp. tax problems com., tax sect. 1981—83, chmn. bus. tax. com. 1983—85, mem. coun. tax sect. 1985—87, venture capital com., bus. law sect. 1991—), Phi Eta Sigma, Phi Kappa Phi, Phi Beta Kappa, Order of Coif. Jewish. Office: Haynes and Boone LLP 1 Houston Ctr 1221 Mc Kinney Ste 2100 Houston TX 77010 Office Phone: 713-547-2009. Office Fax: 713-236-5551. Business E-Mail: arthur.nathan@haynesboone.com.

**NATHAN, DAVID GORDON,** pediatrician, educator; b. Boston, May 25, 1929; s. E. Geoffrey and Ruth (Gordon) Nathan; m. Jean Louise Friedman, Sept. 1, 1951; children: Deborah, Linda, Geoffrey. BA, Harvard U., 1951; MD, Harvard Med. Sch., 1955. Diplomate Am. Bd. Internal Medicine. Am. Bd. Pediat. Intern dept. medicine Peter Bent Brigham Hosp., Boston, 1955—56, sr. resident, 1958—59; jr. assoc. in medicine Brigham and Women's Hosp., Boston, 1961—67, sr. assoc. in medicine, 1967—; assoc. in medicine, hematology Childrens Hosp., Boston, 1963—68, chief, divsn. hematology, 1968—73, chief divsn. hematology and oncology, 1974—84; pediatrician-in-chief Dana Farber Cancer Inst., Boston, 1974—85; Robert A. Stranahan prof. pediat. Harvard Med. Sch., Boston, 1977—95; physician-in-chief Childrens Hosp., Boston, 1985—95; pres. Dana-Farber Cancer Inst., Boston, 1995—2000; Richard and Susan Smith prof. medicine Harvard Med. Sch., Boston, 1996—2000, prof. pediat., 1996—2000, Robert A. Stranahan Disting. prof. pediat., 2001—. Chair NIH Panel on Clin. Rsch., 1995—98; pres. emeritus Dana Farber Cancer Inst., 2001—. Author: Genes, Blood and Courage, 1994; editor: Hematology in Infancy and Childhood, 1993, 1997. With USMC, 1948—49. Recipient Nat. medal Sci., NSF, 1990. Fellow: AAAS; mem.: Am. Philos. Soc., Am. Soc. Hematology (pres. 1986), Am. Soc. Clin. Investigators, Assn. Am. Physicians, Soc. Pediatric Rsch., Am. Pediatric Soc., Am. Acad. Arts and Scis., Inst. Medicine NAS, Phi Beta Kappa (hon.). Avocations: tennis, hiking, sailing. Office: Dana-Farber Cancer Inst 44 Binney St Boston MA 02115-6084 E-mail: david_nathan@dfci.harvard.edu.

**NATHAN, FREDERIC SOLIS,** lawyer; b. NYC, June 24, 1922; s. Edgar Joshua and Mabel (Unterberg) N.; m. Frances E., Oct. 28, 1956; children: Jean E., Frederic S. Jr., William E.BA, Williams Coll., Williamstown, Mass., 1943; LLD, Yale U., 1948. Bar: N.Y. 1948, US Dist. Ct. (so. and ea. dists) N.Y. 1948, U.S. Ct. Appeals (2d cir.) 1953, U.S. Supreme Ct. 1968. Instr. Williams Coll., Williamstown, 1948; assoc. Rathbone Perry Kelley & Drye, N.Y.C., 1948-53; asst. U.S. atty. U.S. Attys.' Office (so. dist.) N.Y., N.Y.C., 1953-56; assoc. Greenbaum, Wolff & Ernst, N.Y.C., 1956-58, ptnr., 1959-65, 70-82; 1st asst. corp. counsel N.Y.C. Law Dept., N.Y.C., 1966-69; ptnr. Kelley, Drye & Warren, N.Y.C., 1982—. Mem. N.Y. Rep. County Com., N.Y.C., 1948-65; trustee Mt. Sinai Hosp., N.Y.C., 1970—; chmn. bd. FOJP Svc. Corp., N.Y.C., 1977-85, bd. dirs., 1979—; bd. dirs., v.p. Am. Jewish Soc. for Svc., N.Y.C., 1950—; bd. dirs. Everybody Wins Found., Inc., 1992—. With U.S. Army, 1943-45, ETO. Fellow Am. Coll. Trial Lawyers; mem. ABA, Assn. of Bar of City of N.Y. (exec. com. 1979-81), Fed. Bar Council (pres. 1975-76), Clubs: Century Assn., Yale of N.Y.C.; Sunningdale Country. Republican. Jewish. Home: 180 East End Ave New York NY 10128-7763 Office: Kelley Drye & Warren 101 Park Ave New York NY 10178-0062 Office Phone: 212-808-7840. Business E-Mail: fnathan@kelleydrye.com.

**NATHAN, GERALD DALE,** retired psychologist, researcher, writer; b. Norfolk, Nebr., Oct. 1, 1938; s. Raymond John and Esther Marie (Neuwerk) N.; m. Jo Anne Williams, Aug. 19, 1993; 1 child, Jeanid John; stepchildren: Rodney Wade, Erica Wren. Student, Wayne State Coll., Nebr., 1956—57, Yale U., 1959—60; BA, U. Nebr., 1966, MA, 1968, PhD (NDEA fellow), 1970. Diplomate Am. Bd. Sexology; lic. marriage counselor, Calif., lic. marital therapist, Oreg.; cert. sex educator, sex therapist; lic. psychologist, Oreg. Cons. psychologist Calavaras County Edn. Dept., San Andreas, Calif., 1970—72; pvt. practice sex and marital therapy, lifestyle stress mgmt. Salem, Oreg., 1972—2000; ret., 2000. Cons. psychologist Cmty. Counseling Center, Salem, 1972-73, William Temple House, Portland, Oreg., 1974-77; sex educator Oreg. Dept. Continuing Edn., Salem, 1972-74; vis. prof. Willamette U., Salem, 1981; bd. dirs. Morrison Charter H.S., Dallas, Oreg.; adj. instr. Chemeketa C.C., Salem, 2001-04 Active Salem Cmty. Chorus, 1978-84, pres., 1980-81; active Festival Chorale Oreg., 1986, 96, 2001-05; adv. bd. Friends Oreg. Areas 1997-98. With USAF, 1959-63 Fellow Am. Bd. Sexology; mem. APA, Am. Assn. Marriage and Family Therapy, Am. Assn. Sex Educators, Counselors and Therapists, Oreg. Assn. Marriage and Family Therapists (dir. 1976-77), Soc. Sci. Study Sex, Salem Psychol. Soc. (co-chmn. 1981-82), Nature Conservancy, Union Concerned Scientists, Am. Farmland Trust, Am. Minor Breeds Conservancy, World Wildlife Fund Office: 18075 Oakdale Rd Dallas OR 97338-9108 Personal E-mail: j_nathan1977@hotmail.com.

**NATHAN, NORMAN,** retired literature and language professor; b. Bklyn., Nov. 19, 1915; s. Michael and Fannie Nathan; m. Frieda Agin Nathan, July 21, 1940; children: Linda Kuzmack, Michele, Lois Anne. BA in English, NYU, 1936, MA in English, 1938, PhD in English, 1947. Machinist Bethlehem Shipyards, Hoboken, NJ, 1940—42; time study engr. Western Electric, Jersey City, 1943—45; tchr. CCNY, N.Y.C., 1946—48; prof. English Syracuse U., Utica, NY, 1949—68, Fla. Atlantic U., Boca Raton, Fla., 1968—93, prof. emeritus, 1994. Author: Judging Poetry, 1960, The Right Word, 1961, Prince William B., 1973, over 30 short stories; contbr. over 500 poems to various publs. Mem.: MLA, Phi Kappa Phi. Avocations: writing fiction, chess, theater. Home and Office: 900 N Taylor Apt 1405 Arlington VA 22203 Office Phone: 703-276-2776.

**NATHAN, PAUL S.,** retired editor, writer; b. Oakland, Calif., Apr. 2, 1913; s. Alfred Jacobs and Frances (Strause) N.; m. Dorothy Goldeen, July 14, 1935 (dec. Dec. 1966); children: Andrew J., Carl F., Janet D. Souza; m. Ruth Wilk Notkins, May 26, 1972 (dec. 2005). BA, U. Calif., Berkeley, 1934. Reporter Oakland Post-Enquirer, 1929-36; asst. play editor Paramount Pictures, NYC, 1937-48; Hosp. pub. rels. Will, Folsom & Smith, NYC, 1948-61; sci. editor Nat. Cystic Fibrosis Rsch. Found., NYC and Atlanta, 1963—73; columnist Rights and Permissions (subsequently Rights) Pubs. Weekly, NYC, 1946-98. US liaison Jerusalem Internat. Book Fair, 1976-77 Author: (play) Ricochet, 1980 (Edgar Allan Poe award of Mystery Writers Am. for best play of 1980), Texas Collects: Fine Arts, Furniture, Windmills & Whimseys, 1988; co-editor: (anthology) View: Parade of the Avant-Garde, 1991; author: (novels) Protocol for Murder, 1994, No Good Deed, 1995, Count Your Enemies, 1997; columnist Pub. News, London, 1998-2003; contbr. fiction and articles to Story, NY Times mag., Saturday Evening Post, Saturday Rev., others. Mem.: PEN, Mystery Writers Am., Authors League, Authors Guild, Dramatists Guild, Phi Beta Kappa. Home and Office: 141 E 33rd St New York NY 10016-4606 Personal E-mail: paulnathanny@aol.com.

**NATHAN, PETER E.,** psychologist, educator; b. St. Louis, Apr. 18, 1935; s. Emil and Kathryn (Kline) N.; m. Florence I. Baker, Nov. 26, 1959; children: David Edward, Anne Miller, Laura Carol, Mark Andrew. AB, Harvard U., 1957; PhD, Washington U., 1962. Research fellow psychology Harvard U., 1962-64, research asso., 1964-68, asst. prof. psychology, 1968-69; research psychologist Boston City Hosp., 1964-68, dir. alcohol study unit, 1967-70; prof. Rutgers U., New Brunswick, NJ, 1969-89, dir. clin. psychology tng., 1969-87, dir. Alcohol Behavior Research Lab., 1970-87, chmn. dept. clin. psychology, 1976-87, dir. Ctr. Alcohol Studies, 1983-89, Henry and Anna Starr prof. psychology, 1983-89; sr. program officer, health program MacArthur Found., 1987-89; v.p. acad. affairs, found. disting. prof. psychology U. Iowa, 1990—, dean faculties, 1990-93, provost, 1993-95, acting pres., 1995. Mem. advisory council VA, 1972-76; chmn. alcoholism com. Nat. Inst. on Alcohol Abuse and Alcoholism, 1973-76, co-chmn. spl. rev. com., 1985, mem. nat. adv. coun., 1990-94; mem. psychol. scis. fellowship rev. com. NIMH, 1977-79; chmn. N.J. State Community Mental Health Bd., 1981-84; mem. working group substance use disorders, DSM-IV. Author: Cues, Decisions, and Diagnoses, 1967, Psychopathology and Society, 1975, 2d edit., 1980, Experimental and Behavioral Approaches to Alcoholism, 1978, Alcoholism: New Directions in Behavioral Treatment and Research, 1978, Clinical Case Studies in the Behavioral Treatment of Alcoholism, 1982, Professionals in Distress, 1987, Neuropsychological Deficits in Alcoholism, 1987, Introduction to Psychology, 1987, 2d edit., 1990, Abnormal Psychology, 1992, 2d edit., 1996, A Guide to Treatments that Work, 1998, 2d edit., 2002; exec. editor: Jour. Studies Alcohol, 1983—90; assoc. editor Am. Psychologist, 1977—85, Contemporary Psychology, 1991—97, Prevention and Treatment, 1998—2001, Psychol. Bull., 2002—; mem. editl. bd. Jour. Clin. Psychology, 1969—95, Jour. Cons. Clin. Psychology, 1973—95, Profl. Psychology, 1976—89. Fellow Am. Psychol. Assn. (chmn. sect. 3 div. 12 1976-77, rep. to council 1976-79, 82-85, pres. div. 12 1984-85; Disting. Contbns. to Knowledge award 1999). Democrat. Jewish. Home: 248 Black Springs Cir Iowa City IA 52246-3800 Office: Univ Iowa E119 Seashore Hall Iowa City IA 52242-1316 Business E-mail: peter-nathan@uiowa.edu.

**NATHAN, RICHARD P(ERLE),** political science professor; b. Schenectady, N.Y., Nov. 24, 1935; s. Sidney Robert and Betty (Green) N.; m. Mary McNamara, June 5, 1957; children: Robert Joseph, Carol Hewit. AB, Brown U., 1957; M in Pub. Administrn. Harvard U., 1959, PhD, 1966. Legis. asst. U.S. Senator Kenneth B. Keating, Washington, 1959-62; dir. domestic policy rsch. Nelson A. Rockefeller, 1963-64; rsch. assoc. The Brookings Instn., Washington, 1966-69, sr. fellow, project dir. monitoring studies gen. revenue sharing, community devel. block grant and pub. svc. employment programs, 1972-79; associated staff The Brookings Inst., Washington, 1980-85; asst. dir. U.S. Office of Mgmt. and Budget, Washington, 1969-71; dep. undersec. U.S Dept. Health, Edn. and Welfare, Washington, 1971-72; prof. pub. and internat. affairs Woodrow Wilson Sch. Pub. and Internat. Affairs Princeton (N.J.) U., 1979-89, also dir. Princeton Urban and Regional Rsch. Ctr., 1979-89; Disting. prof. polit. sci. and pub. policy SUNY, Albany, 1989-97; provost Rockefeller Coll. Pub. Affairs and Policy, Albany, 1989-98. Co-dir. Rockefeller Inst., 1989—; assoc. dir. Nat. Adv. Commn. on Civil Disorders, 1967-68; vis. prof. govt. and fgn. affairs U. Va., 1972-77; chmn. Nixon Adminstrn. Transition Task Forces on Poverty and Intergovtl. Fiscal Rels., 1968, Domestic Coun. Com. on Welfare Reform Planning, 1969-70; mem. Commn. on Orgn. Govt. of D.C., 1970-72; bd. overseers New Sch. for Social Rsch., 1982-88; mem. working seminar on family and welfare Marquette U., 1986-87; selection com. Rockefeller Pub. Svc. Awards Program, 1976-78; income maintenance task force Nat. Urban Coalition, 1975-78; treas. Manpower Demonstration Rsch. Corp., 1974-81, chmn., 1981-98; mem. coun. scholars U.S. Libr. of Congress, 1989—; mem. N.Y. State Temp. Commn. Constl. Revision, 1993-94; mem. U.S. Adv. Commn. on Intergovtl. Rels., 1995-96; vis. fellow GAO, 1998-2000; cons. U.S. Gen. Acctg. Office, 1994-96. Author: Jobs and Civil Rights, The Role of the Federal Government in Promoting Equal Opportunity in Employment and Training, 1969, The Plot That Failed: Nixon and the Administrative Presidency, 1975, Monitoring Revenue Sharing, 1975, Revenue Sharing, The Second Round., 1977, Monitoring the Public Service Employment Program, 1978, America's Government: A Fact Book of Census Data on the Organization, Finances, and Employment of Federal, State, and Local Governments, 1979, Public Service Employment: A Field Evaluation, 1981, The Administrative Presidency, 1983, Reagan and the States, 1987, Social Science in Government Uses and Abuses, 1988, A New Agenda for Cities, 1992, Turning Promises into Performance: The Management Challenge of Implementing Workfare, 1993; co-author: (with Thomas L. Gais) Implementing the Personal Responsibility Act: A First Look, 1999, Social Science in Government, 2000; (with Gerald Benjamin) Regionalism and Realism, A Study of Governments in the New York Metropolitan Area, 2001; contbr. chpts. to books; editor: (with Harvey S. Perloff) Revenue Sharing and the City, 1968; (with John D. DiJulio, Jr.) The View From the States, Making Health Reform Work, Brookings Instn., 1994; mem. editl. bd. Urban Affairs Quar., 1978-85. Eisenhower fellow European Econ. Commn., 1977. Mem. ASPA (Intergovtl. Mgmt. award 1985), Nat. Acad. Social Inst., Nat. Acad. Pub. Adminstrn. (James E. Webb award 1988), Am. Pub. Human Svcs. Assn. (bd. dirs. 2000-02), Am. Polit. Sci. Assn. (Charles E. Merriam award 1987), Assn. for Pub. Policy Analysis and Mgmt. Assn for Pub. Policy Analysis and Mgmt. (pres.-elect 2000—, pres. 2003-04), Ft. Orange Club, Phi Beta Kappa, Theta Delta Chi. Republican. Jewish. Avocations: reading, travel, movies. Office: SUNY Rockefeller Inst Office of Co-Dir 411 State St Albany NY 12203-1003 E-mail: nathanr@rockinst.org.

**NATHANSON, HARVEY CHARLES,** electrical engineer; b. Pitts., Oct. 22, 1936; s. David Benjamin and Ella (Sachs) N.; m. Esther Janet Mishelevich, Oct. 13, 1963; children: Marc Elliot, Elinor Sharon. BSEE, Carnegie Inst. Tech., 1958, MSEE, 1959, PhD, 1962. Sr. engr. Junction Device Physics, Westinghouse, Research/Devel. Center, Pitts., 1962-67, fellow engr., 1968-72, mgr. silicon junction physics, 1972-77, mgr. microelectronics dept., 1978-90, chief scientist electronic div., 1990-95; chief scientist Northrop Grumman Sci. Tech. Ctr., 1996—2001; cons. Northrop Grumman, 2002—. Instr. Carnegie Inst. Tech., Pitts., 1959-60; chmn. Westinghouse Sat. Sci.

Honors Inst. for High Sch. Students, 1970-76; mem. adv. group on electron devices U.S. Dept. Def., 1976-86; adviser to Nat. Materials Bd., 1986-87. Contbr. articles to profl. jours.; mem. editorial bd. Solid State Electronics, 1985—; patentee in field. Bd. dirs. Temple Sinai, 1981-83, 95-97; pres. Brotherhood, 1993-95. Recipient IR100 award, 1965, hon. mention Outstanding Young Engr. award Eta Kappa Nu, 1967, Best Display Paper award Soc. Info. Display, 1972, Carnegie-Mellon Alumni award, 1982, Westinghouse Top Corp. Patent award, 1990; named to Westinghouse Order of Merit, Westinghouse Electric Corp., 1987. Fellow IEEE (editl. bd. Spectrum mag. 1989-91, 3e Millennium medal 2000, Pitts. Inventor of Yr. 2002); mem. IEEE Electron Device Soc. (pres. 1978-80), Fedn. Materials Socs. (bd. dirs. 1987-90), Sigma Xi, Eta Kappa Nu. Democrat. Jewish. Home: 5635 Marlborough Rd Pittsburgh PA 15217-1404 Office: Northrop Grumman Sci-Tech Ctr Advanced Tech Lab PO Box 1521-MS 3B10 Baltimore MD 21203 Business E-Mail: harvey.c.nathanson@ngc.com.

**NATHANSON, LARRY,** medical educator; b. Boston, Dec. 23, 1928; s. Robert Bernard and Leah (Rabin) N.; m. Anna Bloch, May 27, 1962; children: Andrew, Aran, Nicholas. AB, Harvard Coll., 1950; MD, U. Chgo., 1955. Diplomate Am. Bd. Internal Medicine, Am. Bd. Med. Oncology. Instr. medicine Harvard Med. Sch., Boston, 1966-68; from asst. to prof. Tufts U. Sch. Medicine, Boston, 1968-76; prof. medicine SUNY Stony Brook Sch. of Medicine, 1980-96, prof. emeritus, 1996—. Pres., CEO Oncology Cons. Cambridge, Mass., 1996—; cons. John Wayne Cancer Inst., Santa Monica, Calif., 1996—; councilor Cambridge Hist. Soc.; bd. dirs. Mass. Soc. for Med. Rsch. Editl. bd. Cancer, 1977—, Jour. Clin. Oncology, 1995-98, Seminars in Oncology, 1979-83, Med. & Pediat. Oncology, 1977-96, Jour. Cancer Edn. 1986-92; editor 6 books; contbr. 283 articles to profl. jours. Trustee Cold Spring Harbor Lab., 1990-94, Soc. Preservation L.I. Antiquities, Setauket, N.Y., 1982-92, Cambridge Sch. of Weston, 1997—, Mass. Soc. Med. Rsch., 2002—; active Herreshoff Marine Mus., Bristol, R.I., 2000—, Reliance Soc. Capt. U.S. Army Med. Corps., 1956-58. Recipient Disting Svc. award Cancer Rsch., Vet. Affairs Rev. Bd., 1974—78, Disting Svc. award, Winthrop U. Hosp., 1993, Disting Alumni award, Cambridge Sch. Weston, 2006; grantee, Nat. Cancer Inst., 1964—66. Fellow ACP; mem. Mass. Soc. Med. Rsch. (trustee 2002—), Harvard Club (Boston, N.Y.), Seawanhaka Corinthian Yacht Club (race com. 1990-96), Harvard Faculty Club, Sigma Xi. Avocations: sailing, squash, tennis, history. Office: Oncology Cons 3 Gray Gdns E Cambridge MA 02138-1401 Office Fax: 617-441-0043. Personal E-mail: larrymd@ix.netcom.com.

**NATHANSON, LINDA SUE,** publishing executive, writer; b. Washington, Aug. 11, 1946; d. Nat and Edith (Weinstein) N.; m. James F. Barrett. BS, U. Md., 1969; MA, UCLA, 1970, PhD, 1975. Tng. dir. Rockland Rsch. Inst., Orangeburg, NY, 1975—77; asst. prof. psychology SUNY, 1978—79; pres. Cabri Prodns., Inc., Ft. Lee, NJ, 1979—81; rsch. supr. Darcy, McManus & Masius, St. Louis, 1981—83; mgr. software tng., documentation On-Line Software Internat., Ft. Lee, 1983—85; pvt. practice Ft. Lee, 1985—87; founder, exec. dir. Edin. Group, Inc., Gillette, NJ, 1987—98; founder, pres. Edin Books, Inc., Gillette, 1994—. Author: (with others) Psychological Testing: An Introduction to Tests and Measurements, 1988; (with S.J. Thayer) Interview with an Angel, 1997, The Heart of Interview with an Angel, 1998; publ. A Funny Thing Happened at the Interview (G.F. Farrell), 1996, Angel Talk (R. Crystal), 1996; (audiobook with W. Barnes) I Built the Titanic: Past-Life Memories of a Master Shipbuilder, 1999, Thomas Andrews, Voyage into History, 2000; (audio book on CD with W. Barnes and F. Baranowski) My Life and Death: A Past-Life Interview with Titanic's Designer, 2005. Recipient Rsch. Svc. award 1978; Rsch. fellow Albert Einstein Coll. Medicine, 1978-79. Jewish. Home and Office: 102 Sunrise Dr Gillette NJ 07933-1944 Business E-mail: edinbooks@patmedia.net.

**NATHANSON, MELVYN BERNARD,** academic administrator, mathematician, educator; b. Phila., Oct. 10, 1944; s. Israel and Sophia (Manstein) N.; m. Marjorie Jane Frankel, Jan. 29, 1978; children: Alexander Philip, Rebecca Anne. BA, U. Pa., 1965; postgrad., Harvard U., 1965-66; MA, U. Rochester, 1968, PhD, 1972. Prof. So. Ill. U., Carbondale, 1971-81; dean Rutgers U., Newark, 1981-86; provost, v.p. acad. affairs Lehman Coll. CUNY, Bronx, 1986-91, prof. math. Grad. Sch., 1986—; pres. Short Hills Math. Vis. prof. Moscow State U. USSR, 1972-73, Inst. for Advanced Study, Princeton U., N.J., 1974-75, 76, 90-91, 99-2000, Harvard U., Cambridge, Mass., 1977-78, Rockefeller U., 1982-85, Rutgers U., 1991-93, Tel Aviv U. 2001. Author, editor fifteen books; contbr. articles to profl. jours. Fellow N.Y. Acad. Sci.; mem. AAAS, Am. Math. Soc., Math. Assn. Am., Assn. Mems. Inst. for Advanced Study (pres.). Office: CUNY Lehman Coll Dept Math Bronx NY 10468 Office Phone: 973-921-9615. Personal E-mail: melnathanson@hotmail.com. Business E-Mail: melvyn.nathanson@lehman.cuny.edu.

**NATHANSON, NEAL,** virologist, epidemiologist, educator; b. Boston, Sept. 1, 1927; s. Robert B. and Leah (Rabinowitch) N.; m. Constance Allen, June 8, 1954; children: Katherine L., John A., Daniel R.; m. Phoebe Starfield, Oct. 7, 1984. BA, Harvard U., 1949, MD, 1953. Chief polio surveillance unit USPHS, 1955-57; rsch. assoc., asst. prof. anatomy Johns Hopkins U., Balt., 1957-63, assoc. prof. epidemiology, 1963-68, prof., 1968-79; chmn. dept. microbiology U. Pa., Phila., 1979-93, vice dean rsch., 1993-95, dir. Office of AIDS Rsch., 1998-2000, vice provost rsch., 2000—03; assoc. dean Global Health Programs, 2003—. Editor-in-chief: Am. Jour. Epidemiology, 1964-79, Microbial Pathogenesis, 1985-88. Achievements include research in pathogenesis, immunology, and epidemiology of viral infections. Home: 1600 Hagys Ford Rd Apt 9W Narberth PA 19072-1049 Office Phone: 215-898-0848. E-mail: nathanson@mail.med.upenn.edu.

**NATHANSON, PAUL S.,** lawyer, educator; b. 1943; BA, Tulane Univ., 1964; JD, Duke Univ., 1967; MCL, Univ. Chgo., 1969. Bar: Calif., N. Mex. Assoc. O'Melveny & Myers, Los Angeles; founding dir. Nat. Sr. Citizens Law Ctr., Los Angeles, 1972—80; rsch. prof. Univ. N.Mex Sch. Law, 1980—; dir. Inst. Public Law, Univ. N.Mex., 1983—. Mem. bd. dir. Nat. Sr. Citizens Law Ctr., Internat. Ctr. for Not-For-Profit Law, Nat. Com. Preserve Social Security & Medicare, 1998—, vice chmn., 2001—03, chmn., 2003—; chmn. bd. KNME PBS TV, N.Mex.; mem. bd. dir. N.Mex Legal Aid Found. Mem.: ABA (founding mem., Commn. on Elderly), Am. Soc. Aging (past pres.), Gray Panthers (past nat. sec.). Office: UNM School of Law MSC11 6070 1 University of New Mexico Albuquerque NM 87131-0001

**NATHANSON, SAUL DAVID,** oncologist, surgeon, educator; b. Johannesburg, Dec. 12, 1943; came to U.S., 1975; s. Hymie Barnett and Freda Charlotte (Weinberg) N.; m. Maxine Elaine Zacks, Nov. 29, 1966 (div. Sept. 1978); children: Laurence Cecil, Joshua Russel; m. Jerrilyn Marie Burke, Feb. 18, 1979; children: Abigail Mary, Alison Megan. MD, U. Witwatersrand, Johannesburg, 1966. Diplomate Am. Bd. Surgery. Resident in surgery U. Witwatersrand, 1967-74; fellow in immunology UCLA, 1975-77, fellow in surg. oncology, 1977-80; chief resident in surgery U. Calif.-Davis, Sacramento, 1980-82; surg. oncologist Henry Ford Health Sys., Detroit, 1982—, dir. breast cancer ctr., 1991—; prof. surgery Case Western Res. U., Cleve., 1993—2005. Assoc. clin. prof. surgery U. Mich., Ann Arbor, 1985—2000; adj. assoc. prof. med. physics Oakland U., Rochester, Mich., 1993—; cancer liaison physician, Commn. on Cancer; prin. investigator for HFHS, ACS Oncology Group; endowed chair Breast Cancer Rsch., 2001. Contbr. over 200 articles and abstracts to sci. jours. Recipient Outstanding Tchr. awards U. Mich., 1982—2000; NIH grantee Nat. Cancer Inst., 1989. Fellow ACS, Soc. Surg. Oncology, Royal Coll. Surgeons; mem. Am. Soc. Clin. Oncology, Western Surg. Assn., Am. Assn. Cancer Rsch., Wayne County Med. Soc. (alt. del. 1994—96). Office: Henry Ford Health Sys 2799 W Grand Blvd Detroit MI 48202-2608 Office Phone: 313-916-2917. Business E-Mail: dnathan1@hfhs.org.

**NATHAN, JOHN B.,** career military officer; b. San Antonio; m. Sue Wooddell; children: Amy, Ryan. Grad. U.S. Naval Acad., 1970; MS in Aero Engring., 1972; Grad., USAF Test Pilot Sch., 1976. Enlisted USN, 1972, advanced through grades to adm., 2004; various assignments Fighter Squadron 213; topgun tng. officer Navy Fighter Weapons Sch.; pilot Fighter Squadron 51, 1980; sr. naval test pilot 4477 Test & Evaluation Squadron Nellis AFB, Nev., 1982—84; comdr. Strike Fighter Squadron 132; stationed on USS LaSalle, 1987; comdr. USS Nimitz, 1992—94; various assignments Allied Forces So. Europe; dep. comdr. Joint Task Force-Southwest Asia; comdr. UN Special Commn., Iraq; dir. air warfare Chief Naval Ops., 1998—2000; comdr. Naval Air Force US Pacific Fleet, 2000—01; comdr., Naval Air Forces USN, 2001—02, dep. chief naval ops. (warfare requirements & programs) Washington, 2002—04, vice chief naval ops., 2004—05; comdr. US Fleet Forces Command & US Atlantic Fleet, Norfolk, Va., 2005—. Decorated Disting. Svc. medal, Def. Superior Svc. medal, Def. Meritorious Svc. medal, Meritorious Svc. medal, Navy Commendation medal (Combat V), Legion of Merit, Bronze Star (Combat V), Air Force Achievement medal. Office: US Fleet Forces Command Fleet Pub Affairs (N02P) 1562 Mitscher Ave Ste 250 Norfolk VA 23551

**NATHWANI, BHARAT N.,** pathologist, educator; b. Bombay, Jan. 20, 1945; came to US, 1972; MBBS, Grant Med. Coll., Bombay, 1969, MD in Pathology, 1972. Intern Grant Med. Coll., Bombay U., 1968-69; asst. prof. pathology Grant Med. Coll., 1972; fellow in hematology Cook County Hosp., Chgo., 1972-73; resident in pathology Rush U., Chgo., 1973-74; fellow in hematopathology City of Hope Med. Ctr., Duarte, Calif., 1975-76, pathologist, 1977-84; prof. pathology, chief hematopathology U. So. Calif., L.A., 1984—. Contbr. 135 articles to profl. jours. Recipient Grant awards Nat. Libr. Medicine, Bethesda, Md., Nat. Cancer Inst., 1991. Mem. Internat. Acad. Pathology, Am. Soc. Clin. Pathology, Am. Soc. Hematology, Am. Soc. Oncology. Office: Hmr 209 2011 Zonal Ave Los Angeles CA 90033 Office Phone: 323-226-7064. Business E-mail: nathwani@usc.edu.

**NATION, DAVID ANTHONY,** retired computer scientist, sculptor; b. Waterloo, Iowa, Aug. 23, 1947; s. Harold Stanley and Martha Elizabeth (Loonan) N.; m. Jean Lea Bielefeldt, Aug. 9, 1969 (div. May 1979); 1 child, Justin David; m. Rebecca L. Johnson, Oct. 27, 1979. BS in Computer Sci., Iowa State U., 1970; MS, Johns Hopkins U., 1979. Computer scientist U.S. Govt., Washington, 1975—2001; ret., 2001. Author mapping software, pattern classication software, Web software, information visualization software; sculptor;solo shows: Dave Nation's Art Gallery, 1995—; Bay Country Art Guild Member Show, 2000, Treas., Emmanuel United Meth. Ch., Dorsey, md., 1987-2006. Sgt. USAF, 1970-73. Mem. SAG, Assn. for Computing Machinery. Democrat. Unitarian Universalist. Achievements include 3 patents in field. Avocations: sculpture, bird watching, genealogy, volkssport, photography. E-mail: dave@davenation.com.

**NATION, EARL F.,** retired urologist, educator; b. Zephyr, Tex., Jan. 16, 1910; s. Joseph Madison and Alma Emily (Johnson) N.; m. Evelyn Stapp Poynter, Aug. 11, 1936; children: William Earl, Robert Joseph. BA, San Diego State U., 1931; MD, Western Res. U., 1935. Lic. urologist, Calif.; diplomate Am. Bd. Urology. Internship, resident in urology Los Angeles County Gen. Hosp., 1935-39; pvt. practice Pasadena, Calif., 1941-90; ret., 1990. Instr., assoc. prof. urology U. So. Calif., L.A., 1941-55; sr. attending staff Huntington Meml. Hosp., Pasadena, 1941—, St. Luke Hosp., Pasadena, 1941—, also past pres.; pres. Pasadena Dispensary, 1946; lectr. Coll. Med. Evangelists (now Loma Linda U.), 1941-48. Mem. editorial bd. Jour. of Urology, 1958-66, Calif. Medicine, 1965-69, Forum on Medicine; contbr. articles to profl. jours., contbg. author to numerous books. Sec.-treas. Pasadena Breakfast Forum, 1970-73, pres. 1974-75. Crile rsch. scholar Western Res. U., 1931; recipient Monty award San Diego (Calif.) State U., 2005, Zeilstra award Huntington Hosp., 2005; honoree Am. Osler Soc. Mem. ACS, AMA, Am. Urol. Assn. (past pres.), Ramon Guiteras award 2002), Am. Osler Soc. (past pres.), L.A. County Med. Assn., Calif. Med. Assn., Pasadena Hist. Soc., So. Calif. Hist. Soc., Am. Soc. Clin. Urologists, Pasadena U. Club, Zamorano Club (v.p. L.A. chpt. 1991), Twilight Club, Alpha Omega Alpha. Republican. Avocations: book collecting, reading, writing, gardening, fishing. Home: # E 311 E Sierra Madre Blvd Apt E Sierra Madre CA 91024-2669 Personal E-mail: enoitan@gte.net.

**NATIONS, HOWARD LYNN,** lawyer; b. Dalton, Ga., Jan. 9, 1938; s. Howard Lynn and Eva Earline (Armstrong) Lamb; m. Ella Lois Johnson, June 4, 1960 (div. Nov. 1976); children: Cynthia Lynn Nations Garcia, Angela Jean Gordon Hernandez. BA, Fla. State U., 1963, JD, 1966. Bar: Tex. 1966; cert. trial atty. Tex. Bd. Legal Specialization. Assoc. Butler, Rice Cook & Knapp, Houston, 1966-71; pres. Nations & Cross, Houston, 1971—; v.p., dir., co-founder Ins. Corp. Am., Houston, 1972—; pres. Caplinger & Nations Galleries, Houston, 1973—, Nations Investment Corp., Houston, 1975—, NCM Trade Corp., Houston, 1975; v.p. Delher Am. Inc., Houston, 1975—; pres. Howard L. Nations, PC, Houston, 1971—, Trial Focus, Inc., 1995—. Founder Nations Found.; adj. prof. So. Tex. Coll. Law, Houston, 1967—; speaker in field. Author: Structuring Settlements, 1987; co-author: Texas Workers' Compensation, 1988, (with others) The Anatomy of a Personal Injury Lawsuit, 3rd rev. edit. 1991; editor: Maximizing Damages in Wrongful Death and Personal Injury Litigation, 1985; contbr. articles to profl. jours. Chmn., trustee Nat. Coll. Advocacy, Washington, 1985-92. With M.I. Corps, U.S. Army, 1957-60. Recipient Gene Cavin Excellence award State Bar Tex., 2000. Fellow Tex. Bar Found., Houston Bar Found. (life); mem. ATLA (exec. com. 1991-95), Nat. Bd. Trial Advocacy (diplomate civil trial advocacy), So. Trial Lawyers Assn. (pres. 1994-95), Tex. Trial Lawyers Assn. (pres. 1992-93). Office: The Sterling Mansion 4515 Yoakum Blvd Houston TX 77006-5821 Office Phone: 713-807-8400.

**NATIVIDAD, IRENE,** women's rights advocate; b. Manila, Philippines, Sept. 14, 1948; m. Andrea Cortese; 1 child, Carlo Natividad Cortese. Graduate, Long Island Univ.; 1971; LHD (hon.), Marymount Coll., 1994, Long Island Univ. Pres. Globe Women, Inc., Washington, Nat. Women's Political Caucus, 1985—89; chmn. Nat. Commn. on Working Women. Dep. vice chair Dem. Party Asian Caucus, 1982—84; pres. Global Summit of Women; co-chair Corp. Women's Dir. Internat., exec. dir. Philippine Am. Found.; bd. dir. Nat. Mus. Women in Arts, Nat. Assoc. Corp. Dir., Sallie Mae; adv. bd. Cigna, Wyndham Internat. Exec. editor Asian American Almanac, 1995, frequent commentator, panelist on TV news shows; contbr. columns in newspapers. Named one of 100 Most Power Women in Am., Ladies Home Jour., 1988, 74 Women Changing Am. Politics, Campaigns & Elections Mag., 1993, 25 Most Influential Working Mothers, Working Mother Mag., 1997, 21 Leaders for the 21st Century, Women's eNews, 2004, Top 25 Influential Asian Americans, A. Mag.; recipient Women Making History award, Women's Congl. Caucus, 1985, Magnificent 7 award, Bus. & Profl. Women/USA, 1995, Women of Genius award, Trinity Coll., Washington, DC, 2001. Office: Natividad Assn 504 1211 Connecticut Ave NW Washington DC 20036 Business E-mail: president@globewomen.com.

**NATOLI, JOSEPH,** language educator; b. Bklyn., Aug. 24, 1943; m. Elaine Tuminelli, June 6, 1970; children: Amelia, Brenda. BA, Bklyn. Coll., 1965, MA, 1968; PhD, SUNY, Albany, 1973. Asst. prof. English New Eng. Coll., Henniker, NH, 1971-73, 1973-75; acting dir. libr., adj. lectr. English Bluefield State Coll., W.Va., 1975-77; head reference and bibliography libr. Wake Forest U., Winston Salem, NC, 1977-81; bibliographer, adj. lectr. humanities U. Calif., Irvine, 1981-83, Mich. State U., East Lansing, 1983—, dir. study abroad program Europe, 1996—. Series editor SUNY Press Postmodern Culture, Albany, 1990—. Author: Mots D'Ordre, 1992, Hauntings, 1994, Primer to Postmodernity, 1997, Speeding to the Millenium, 1998, Postmodern Journeys, 2000, Memory's Orbit, 2003; editor: Twentieth Century Blake Criticism, 1982, Psychological Perspectives on Literature, 1984, Psychocriticism, 1984, Tracing Literary Theory, 1987, Literary Theory's Future(s), 1989, A Postmodern Reader, 1993, Postmodernism: The Key Figures, 2002. Mem. MLA. Office: Mich State Univ Writing Rhetoric Am Cultur Dept 241 Bessey Hall East Lansing MI 48824 Business E-Mail: natoli@msu.edu.

**NATOLI, JOSEPH T.,** financial administrator, former publishing executive; b. NYC; m. Jennifer Natoli; children: Danielle, Joey. Grad., U. South Fla.; MBA, Nova U. Joined Knight Ridder as staff acct., 1976; v.p. ops. Miami Herald Pub. Co., gen. mgr. 1993—94, pres. 1994—2001; pres., pub. San

Jose Mercury News, 2001—03; pub., chmn. Phila. Inquirer, 2004—06, Phila. Daily News, 2004—06; CFO, sr. v.p. bus. & fin. U. Miami, 2006—. Bd. mem. CEO Coun. for Growth. Bd. mem. Franklin Inst., Greater Phila. C. of C., United Way of Southeastern Pa., campaign chair, 2005; mem. cmty. adv. bd. Knight Found. Office: U Miami Miami FL 33124*

**NATORI, JOSIE CRUZ (JOSEFINA ALMEDA CRUZ NATORI),** apparel executive; b. Manila, Philippines, May 9, 1947; arrived in NYC, 1964; d. Felipe F. and Angelita A. (Almeda) Cruz; m. Kenneth R. Natori, May 20, 1972; 1 child, Kenneth E.F. BA in Econs., Manhattanville Coll., 1968; Degree (hon.), Acad. Art Coll., San Francisco, 2003. With Bache Securities, N.Y.C.; joined Merrill-Lynch Co. as an investment banker, 1971; v.p., 1976—77; owner, CEO The Natori Co., N.Y.C., 1977—. Bd. dirs. The Alltel Corp., 1995—. Bd. dirs. Philippine Am. Found., Jr. Achievement, Inc., 1992, Ednl. Found. for Fashion Industries; trustee Manhattanville Coll., Asian Cultural Coun.; commr. White House Conf. on Small Bus., 1995. Recipient Human Relations award Am. Jewish Com., N.Y.C., 1986, Harriet Alger award Working Woman, N.Y., 1987, Castle award Manhattanville Coll., Purchase, 1988, Galleon award Pres. Philippines, 1988, N.Y.C. Asian-Am. award, Friendship award Philippine-Am. Found., Hall of Fame award Mega Mags., Salute to Am. Fashion Designers award Dept. of Commerce, Ellis Island medal of Honor, 1994, Presdl. Awards for Filipino Individuals and Orgns. Overseas, Pamana ng Pilipino award Philippine Consulate Gen., 2002; named Bus. Woman of Yr. N.Y.C. Partnership and C. of C., 1998. Mem. CFDA, Young Pres.'s Orgn., Fashion Group, Com. of 200. Avocations: pianist, tennis player. Home: 45 E 62nd St New York NY 10021-8025 Office: The Natori Company 180 Madison Ave # 19 New York NY 10016-5267

**NATSIOS, ANDREW STEPHEN,** diplomat, former federal agency administrator; b. Holliston, Mass., Sept. 22, 1949; s. Basil Andrew and Eta (Lappas) Natsios; m. Elizabeth E. Macdonald; children: Emily, Alexander, Phillip. BA, Georgetown U., 1971; MPA, Harvard U., 1979. Mem. Mass. Ho. Reps., 1975—87; exec. dir. Northeast Pub. Power Assn., Milford, Mass., 1987—89; dir. Office of Fgn. Disaster Assistance USAID, 1989—91, asst. administr. Bur. Food and Humanitarian Assistance, 1991—93, administr. Washington, 2001—05; v.p. World Vision US, 1993—98; sec. adminstrn. and fin. Commonwealth Mass., 1999—2000; chmn. Mass. Turnpike Authority, 2000—01; Disting. Prof in the Practice of Diplomacy and Advisor on Internat. Devel. Georgetown U., 2006—. Spl. coord. Internat. Disaster Assistance and Spl. Humanitarian Coord. for Sudan The White House, 2004, spl. envoy to pursue ending the violence in the Darfur region of Sudan, 2006—. Author: U.S. Foreign Policy and the Four Horsemen of the Apocalypse, 1997, The Great North Korean Famine, 2001. USAR, 1972—95. Named Legislator of Yr., Mass. Mcpls. Assn., 1978; fellow U.S. Inst. Peace, 1998—99. Office: Edmund A Walsh Sch Fgn Svc 301 Intercultural Ctr 37th & O St NW Washington DC 20057 E-mail: asn8@georgetown.edu.

**NATTEL, STANLEY,** cardiologist, research scientist; b. Haifa, Israel, Jan. 28, 1951; arrived in Can., 1952; s. William and Julie (Zwirek) N.; m. Celia Anne Reich, Sept. 25, 1973; children: Jonathan, Ilana, Daniel, Sarah. BSc magna cum laude, McGill U., 1972, MD, 1974. Diplomate Am. Bd. Internal Medicine, Am. Bd. Cardiology. Intern in medicine Royal Victoria Hosp., 1974-75, resident in internal medicine, 1975-76; resident in clin. pharmacology Montreal Gen. Hosp., Que., Canada, 1976-78, cardiologist, clin. pharmacologist, 1981-87, dir. coronary care unit, 1983-87; fellow in cardiology Ind. U., 1978-80; fellow in physiology U. Pa., 1980-81; asst. prof. pharmacology, medicine McGill U., Montreal, 1981-87, assoc. prof., 1987—; cardiologist Montreal Heart Inst., 1987—, dir. rsch. ctr., 1990—2004; prof. dept. medicine U. Montreal, 1995—, Paul-David chair in cardiovasc. electrophysiology, 2003—. External reviewer Med. Rsch. Coun., 1981—, Ont. Health Ministry, 1983-84, NSF, 1992, others; chmn. libr. com. dept. pharmacology McGill U., 1982-86, mem. grad. com., 1984-89, chmn. grad. tng. com., 1986-89, departmental rep. grad. faculty coun., 1989-91, coord. grad. tchg. pharmacology, 1989-91; mem. oper. grants com. Can. Heart Found., 1983-86; chmn. clin. trials com. Montreal Gen. Hosp., 1983-87, chmn. pharmacy and therapeutics com., 1984-87, sec. clin. chemistry rev. com., 1984, course dir. drug therapy, 1984-87, acting dir. divsn. clin. pharmacology, 1984-85, mem. various coms., 1985-87; mem. fellowship awards com. FRSQ, 1988-90, mem. ctr. grants pharmacology/pharmacy com., 1989-90; chmn. pharmacology coun. Montreal Heart Inst., 1988-90, mem. search com. pharmacist-in-chief, 1989-90, mem. ethics com., 1991-2004, chmn. internal rsch. com., 1991-2004, mem. consultative com. exec. dir., 1991-2004, chmn. consultative com. rsch. ctr., 1991-2004; cons. coun. pharmacology Province of Quebec, 1989-90; mem. safety monitoring com. CAMIAT Study, 1990-95; assoc. prof. medicine U. Montreal, 1991-95, prof. 1995—, chmn. search com. dir. rsch. Sacré-Coeur Hosp., 1991, mem. rsch. com. Cormes faculty medicine, 1991—2002, mem. rsch. dept. medicine, 1991-2004; chmn. search com., dir. rsch. Maisonneuve Rosemont Hosp., 1996; mem. site visit team program project grant NIH, 1991, cons. program project grant, 1993, spl. reviewer cardiovascular study sect., 1993, 95, 97, 98; mem. oper. grants com. Med. Rsch. Coun. Can., 1988-93, chmn., 2002-05; mem. sr. pers. awards com. Can. Heart Found., 1994-96; lectr. in field. Assoc. editor Can. Jour. Physiology and Pharmacology, 1990-95, Br. Jour. Pharmacology, 2000—; mem. editl. bd. Jour. Cardiovasc. Electrophysiology, 1991—, Drugs, 1993—, Cardiovasc. Drugs and Therapy, 1993-2001, Circulation Rsch. 1995—, JACC, 1995-2000, Cardiovascular Rsch., 1999-2002, others; manuscript reviewer Am. Jour. Cardiology, Nature, Nature Medicine, Nature Genetics, New Eng. Jour. Medicine, PNAS, Science, others; contbr. chpts. to books and articles to profl. jours. Chmn. edn. com. Hebrew Acad. Sch., Montreal, 1991-92. Grantee Que. Heart Found., 1981—, Nordic Pharms., 1985-87, Knoll Pharms., 1991-93, others; fellow Med. Rsch. Coun. Can., 1979-81; McGill U. scholar, 1967-74 Sir Edward Beatty scholar McGill U., 1967-70, Rsch. scholar Med. Rsch. Coun., 1982-87, Sr. Rsch. scholar Fonds de la Recherche en Santé du Quebec, 1990-93; recipient Career Rsch. Achievement award Can. Cardiovasc. Soc., 2001. Fellow Am. Coll. Cardiology, Royal Coll. Physicians Can. (cert. medicine, cardiology), Am. Heart Assn. Royal Soc. Can.; mem. Am. Heart Assn. (coun. basic sci., leadership com. 2003-05), Royal Soc. Can., Am. Soc. Pharmacology and Exptl. Therapeutics, Can. Cardiovasc. Soc. (councilor 1992-95), Can. Soc. Clin. Pharmacology (Kenneth M. Piafsky Young Investigator award 1985), Pharm. Soc. Can. Biophys. Soc., Am. Heart Assn. (leadership com.). Avocations: studying jewish religious works, sports. Home: 5609 Alpine Ave Côte Saint Luc PQ Canada H4V 2X6 Office: Montreal Heart Inst 5000 Belanger St E Montreal PQ Canada H1T 1C8 Office Phone: 514-376-3330. Personal E-mail: stanleynattel@aol.com. Business E-Mail: stanley.nattel@icm-mhi.org.

**NAU, RICHARD WILLIAM,** mathematics professor, consultant, computer scientist, educator; s. Walter Herman and Bernice Ellen Nau; m. Sharol Anne Miller, July 27, 1963; children: Jennifer, William. BS, S.D. Sch. Mines and Tech., 1963, MS, 1965; PhD, U. Va., 1970. Prof. math and computer sci. Carleton Coll., Northfield, Minn., 1970—2006, Dow Corning, Midland, Mich., 1992—2002; vis. prof. U. Va. Charlestonville, 1970, U. Ill., Urbana, 1974, U. Minn., Mpls., 1983—84, Mpls., 2002, Mich. State U., East Lansing, 1992—93; Fulbright prof. U. Pt. Harcourt, Nigeria, 1980—81; software designer. Fellow, NDEA, 1968—69; grantee, NSF, 1987, 1988, 1989. Mem.: Math. Assn. Am., Soc. Indsl. and Applied Math., Assn. Computing Machinery. Avocations: travel, reading, scuba diving, bicycling, geocaching. Office: Carleton Coll 1 N College St Northfield MN 55057 Office Phone: 507-646-4361. Personal E-mail: rnau@carleton.edu.

**NAUGHTON, BLAKE ALAN,** finance educator, education educator; b. Ill., 1975; s. Aldace Naughton and Donna Lee Keller; m. Meredith Renee Boyt. BS, Stanford U., 1997; MEd, Harvard U., 1998; PhD, Stanford U., 2004. Hall dir. Truman State U., 1998—99; rsch. assoc. Mo. Dept. Higher Edn., 1999—2001; policy analyst Nat. Ctr. Pub. Policy and Higher Edn., 2001—03; rsch. asst. Stanford U., 2001—04; asst. prof. mgmt., edn. NW Mo. State U., Maryville, 2004—.

**NAUGHTON, BRUCE JAMES,** geriatrician, consultant; MD, SUNY, Buffalo, 1979. Lic. physician N.Y., 1994. Chief divsn. geriatric medicine Northwestern U. Sch. Medicine, Chgo., 1988—94, SUNY Buffalo Sch. Medicine, 2001—. Cons. quality of care, Buffalo, 1994—. Mem. Vis. Nurse Assn., Buffalo, 2004. Achievements include design of interdisciplinary training to improve care of hospitalized older adults. Office: Kaleida Health 3 Gates Circle Buffalo NY 14209 Office Phone: 716-887-4021. Office Fax: 716-887-4437.

**NAUGHTON, GAIL K.,** biomedical researcher, academic administrator; 3 children. BS, St. Francis Coll., NYC, 1976; MS, NYU, 1978, PhD med. sci., 1981, postdoctoral, dept. dermatology, 1982; MBA, UCLA, 2001. Asst. rsch. prof. NYU Med. Ctr., 1983—85; asst. prof. biology Queensborough Cmty. Coll., NYC, 1985—87; co-founder, dir. Advanced Tissue Sciences, 1987—2002, prin. scientist, 1987—89, sr. v.p., chief sci. officer, 1989—91, exec. v.p., COO, 1991—95, pres., COO, 1995—2000, vice chmn., 2000—02; dean, Coll. Bus. Adminstrn. San Diego State U., 2002—. Bd. dir. Calif. Health Inst., San Diego World Trade Ctr., San Diego Corp. Governance Inst.; mem. sci. adv. bd. Johns Hopkins Univ., Calif. Inst. Tech., Univ. Calif. San Diego, Univ. Wash., MIT. Mem. San Diego Sci. & Tech. Council, UCSD Connect Leadership Council. Named Inventor of the Yr., Intellectual Property Owners Assn., 2000. Mem.: Rotary Internat. Achievements include holding over 75 U.S. & fgn. patents in tissue engrning. Office: Coll Bus Adminstrn San Diego State Univ 5500 Campanile Dr San Diego CA 92182-8230*

**NAUGHTON, JAMES,** actor; b. Middletown, Conn., Dec. 6, 1945; s. James Joseph and Rosemary (Walsh) N.; m. Pamela Parsons, Oct. 1968; children: Gregory J., Keira P. BA, Brown U., 1967; MFA, Yale U., 1970. Broadway appearances include Edmund in Long Day's Journey Into Night, 1971 (Theatre World award, N.Y. Drama Critics award, Vernon Rice award 1971), Stone in City of Angels (Tony award 1990, Drama Desk award), I Love My Wife, 1977, Whose Life Is It Anyway, 1980, Chicago, 1996 (Tony award, 1997). Feature films include Paper Chase, 1972, Second Wind, 1975, A Stranger is Watching, 1981, Cat's Eye, 1982, The Glass Menagerie, 1987, The Good Mother, 1988, First Kid, 1996, The First Wives Club, 1996, The Proprietor, 1996, Oxygen, 1999, Labor Pains, 2000, Fascination, 2004, The Devil Wears Prada, 2006; TV appearances include: (series) Faraday and Company, 1973-74, Planet of the Apes, 1974, Making the Grade, 1982, Trauma Center, 1983, The Cosby Mysteries, 1994; (movies) F. Scott Fitzgerald and "The Last of the Belles", 1974, The Last 36 Hours of Dr. Durant, 1975, The Bunker, 1981, My Body, My Child, 1982, Parole, 1982, The Last of the Great Survivors, 1984, Between Darkness and the Dawn, 1985, Sin of Innocence, 1986, Necessity, 1988, Blown Away, 1990, The Birds II: Land's End, 1994, Couples, 1994, Cagney & Lacey: The Return, 1994, Cagney & Lacey: Together Again, 1995, Mixed Blessings, 1995, The Truth About Jane, 2000. Recipient Tony award Leading Actor in a Musical, 1997.*

**NAUGHTON, JAMES LEE,** internist; b. 1946; AB, Dartmouth Coll., 1968; MD, Harvard U., 1972. Intern U. Calif. Moffitt Hosp., San Francisco, 1972-73; resident in medicine U. Calif. Affiliated Hosps., San Francisco, 1973-75, San Francisco Gen. Hosp., 1975-76; fellow in nephrology U. Calif., San Francisco, 1976-77, assoc. clin. prof. medicine, 1982—; pvt. practice internal medicine, ptnr. Alliance Med. Group, Pinole, Calif., 1982—. Mem. Am. Bd. Internal Medicine (bd. dirs. 1995-2002, exec. com. 1997-2002, trustee found. 2000—). Office: Alliance Med Group 2160 Appian Way Ste 200 Pinole CA 94564-2524

**NAUGHTON, JAMES MARTIN,** journalist; b. Pitts., Aug. 13, 1938; s. Francis Patrick and Martha Ann (Clear) N.; m. Diana Marie Thomas, Sept. 5, 1964; children: Jenifer Mary Naughton Genovesi, Lara Marie, Michael Thomas, Kerry Marie. BA cum laude, U. Notre Dame, 1960. Reporter, photographer Painesville (Ohio) Telegraph, summer, 1955-60; reporter Cleve. Plain Dealer, 1962-69; Washington corr. N.Y. Times, 1969-77; nat. editor Phila. Inquirer, 1977-79, met. editor, 1979-83, assoc. mng. editor, 1980-86, dep. mng. editor, 1986-90, mng. editor, 1990-91, exec. editor, 1991-96; pres. The Poynter Inst. for Media Studies, St. Petersburg, Fla., 1996—2003, pres. emeritus, 2003—. Marsh prof. U. Mich., 1977 Served with USMC, 1960-62. Recipient Disting. Svc. award Sigma Delta Chi, 1973, Pulitzer prize juror, 1998-99, Heinz award juror, 2005. Roman Catholic. Home: 2500 Coffee Pot Blvd NE Saint Petersburg FL 33704-3466 E-mail: swamijim@mac.com.

**NAUGHTON, JOHN PATRICK,** cardiologist, educator; b. West Nanticoke, Pa., May 20, 1933; s. John Patrick and Anne Frances (McCormick) N.; children: Bruce, Marcia, Lisa, George, Michael, Thomas. AA, Cameron State U., Lawton, Okla., 1952; BS, St. Louis U., 1954; MD, Okla. U., 1958; MD (hon.), Kosin U., 1995. Intern George Washington U. Hosp., Washington, 1958-59; resident U. Okla. Med. Center, 1959-64; asst. prof. medicine U. Okla., 1966-68; assoc. prof. medicine U. Ill., 1968-70; prof. medicine George Washington U., 1970-75, dean acad. affairs, 1973-75; dean Sch. Medicine and Regional Rehab. Research and Tng. Center, 1970-75; dean Sch. Medicine SUNY, Buffalo, 1975-96, prof. medicine, physiology, social, preventive and rehab. medicine Sch. Medicine, 1975—, acting v.p. for health scis., 1983-84, v.p. clin. affairs, 1984-96, interim chmn. medicine, 2003—. Dir. Nat. Exercise and Heart Disease Project, 1972-83; chmn. policy adv. bd. Beta-blocker Heart Attack Trial Nat. Heart, Lung and Blood Inst., 1977-82; pres. Western N.Y. chpt. Am. Heart Assn., 1983-85, v.p. N.Y. State affiliate, 1985, pres. N.Y. State affiliate, 1988-90; chmn. clin. applications and preventions adv. com. Nat. Heart, Lung and Blood Inst., 1984; mem. Fed. COGME working group on consortia, 1996-97, N.Y. Gov.'s Commn. on Grad. Med. Edn., 1985, N.Y. State Coun. on Grad. Med. Edn., 1988-90, chmn. 1996—; pres. Assoc. Med. Schs. N.Y., 1982-84, mem. adminstrv. com. Coun. of Deans, 1983-89; mem. N.Y. State Dept. of Health Adv. Com. on Physician Recredentialing; mem. exec. com. Nat. Inst. on Disability and Rehab. Rsch. 1991-92; v.p. James H. Cummings Found. Author: Exercise Testing and Exercise Training in Coronary Heart Disease, 1973, Exercise Testing: Physiological, Biomechanical, and Clinical Principles, 1988 Career devel. awardee Nat. Heart Inst., 1966-71; recipient Brotherhood-Sisterhood award in medicine NCCJ, N.E. Minority Educators award, 1990, Acad. Alumnus of Yr. award Okla. U., 1990, award for svc. to minorities in med. edn., 1991, Frank Sindelar award N.Y. State Am. Heart Assn., 1995, James Platt White Soc. award, 1995, Outstanding Contbns. in the field of Health Care award Sheehan Meml. Hosp., 1995, Chancellor Charles P. Norton medal, SUNY, Buffalo, 1997, AMS Disting. Svc. award, 2001. Fellow ACP, Am. Coll. Cardiology, Am. Coll. Sports Medicine (pres. 1970-71, Citation award 2000), Am. Coll. Chest Physicians; Am. Coll. Preventive Medicine, Am. Heart Assn. (epidemiology coun. 2000—, coun. on nutrition, phys. activity and metabolism), Acad. Health Profls. Ins. Assn. (hon.). Office: SUNY Buffalo 128 Farber Hall 3435 Main St Buffalo NY 14214-3099 Business E-Mail: jpn@buffalo.edu.

**NAUGLE, LOUIS A.,** lawyer; b. Plainfield, NJ, Aug. 6, 1950; BA in polit. sci./history, Williams Coll., 1972; JD, Georgetown U., 1975. Bar: Pa. 1975, NY 1985, US Ct. Appeals 3rd Cir., US Supreme Ct., US Dist. Ct. We. Dist. Pa., US Dist. Ct. Mid. Dist. Pa., US Dist. Ct. Ea. Dist. Pa., US Dist. Ct. We. Dist. NY. Asst. atty. gen./asst. counsel Bur. Litig. Pa. Dept. Environ. Resources, 1975—84; asst. atty. gen. Environ. Protection Bur. NY Dept. Law, 1984—86; ptnr. Hodgson, Russ, Andrews, Woods & Goodyear, 1986—88; joined Reed Smith LLP, Pitts., 1988, ptnr., 1990—, also practice group leader environ. group. Vice chair Allegheny County Air Pollution Adv. Com.; adv. com. mem. Cert. Program in Environ. Law, Sci. & Policy U. Pitts. Law Sch. Mem.: ABA, Allegheny County Bar Assn., Pa. Bar Assn. Office: Reed Smith LLP 435 Sixth Ave Pittsburgh PA 15219 Office Phone: 412-288-8586. Office Fax: 412-288-3063. Business E-Mail: lnaugle@reedsmith.com.

**NAULT, WILLIAM HENRY,** publishing executive; b. Ishpeming, Mich., June 9, 1926; s. Henry J. and Eva (Perrault) N.; m. Helen E. Matthews, Nov. 28, 1946; children: William Henry, Rebecca Nault Marks, Ronald, George, Peter, Julia Nault Doyle, Robert, David. AB, No. Mich. U., 1948, LittD (hon.), 1988; MA, U. Mich., 1949; EdD, Columbia U., 1953, LHD (hon.), 1980, LLD (hon.), 1986, LittD (hon.), 1988. Dir. adult edn., Battle Creek, Mich., 1948—49; guidance counselor, 1949-50; prin. W.K. Kellogg High

Sch., Battle Creek, 1950-53; research assoc. Columbia U., 1953-54; asst. supt. Ridgewood, NJ, 1954-55; adj. prof. William Patterson U. N.J., 1954—55; dir. research World Book, Inc. (formerly Field Enterprises Edn. Corp.), Chgo., 1955-63, v.p., 1963-66, sr. v.p., editorial dir., 1966-68, exec. v.p. and editorial dir., 1968-83; pres., pub., chief operating officer World Book, Inc., 1983-84, gen. chmn. editorial adv. bds., 1968-99, pub., 1983-95, pub. emeritus, 1995—. Past vice chmn. Govt. Adv. Com. on Internat. Library and Book Programs, U.S. Dept. State; past mem. nat. adv. bd. Ctr. on Ednl. Media and Materials for Handicapped; past mem. exec. bd. Commn. Instns. Higher Edn., North Central Assn. Colls. and Secondary Schs.; mem. dean's adv. council Coll. Bus. and Pub. Adminstrn., U. Mo., Columbia; mem. nat. council Inst. Internat. Edn. Author material on courses of study. Mem. alumni com. Columbia Tchrs. Coll. Capital Campaign; mem. White House Conf. on Youth, White House Conf. on Librs., White House Conf. on Edn.; pres. Oak Park (Ill.) Bd. Edn., 1960-63; v.p. LaGrange (Ill.) Libr. Bd.; bd. regents Lincoln Acad., Ill.; past trustee Adler Planetarium, De Paul U., Chgo. Geol. Soc.; bd. dirs. H.V. Phalin Found. Grad. Study, World Book, Inc., A.J. Nystrom Co., Field Edn. Co., Libr. Movens, Inc.; mem. adv. bd. Rosary Coll.; mem. liberal arts and scis. adv. council De Paul U. Served with F.A., AUS, 1944-45. Recipient Columbia U. Tchrs. Coll. medal for disting. svc. in edn.; named Disting. Alumnus No. Mich. U., U. Mich., Columbia U. Fellow AAAS; mem. ALA, Chgo. Adminstrs. Assn. (trustee), Chgo. Geog. Soc. (dir.), Am. Acad. Polit. and Social Sci., Am. Edn. Rsch. Assn., Am. Assn. Sch. Adminstrs., ASCD, Chgo. Pubs. Assn. (past pres.), Ill. Assn. Sch. Adminstrs., Ill. Acad. Sci., NSTA, Nat. Council Tchrs. English, Assn. Am. Geographers, Assn. Childhood Edn. Internat., NAESP, Nat. Assn. Secondary Sch. Prins., Council for Advancement Sci. Writing, Internat. Platform Assn., Nat. Council Social Studies, Nat. Soc. Study Edn. Clubs: Mid-Am, Mchts. and Mfrs. Roman Catholic. Office: World Book Inc 525 W Monroe St Chicago IL 60661-3629 Personal E-mail: naultwh@aol.com, naultwh@comcast.net.

**NAULTY, SUSAN LOUISE,** archivist; b. Abington, Pa., May 28, 1944; d. Charles J. and Ruth E. (Schick) N. BA, Whittier Coll., 1967; MA, Loyola U., L.A., 1972. Tchr. history and English, Whittier (Calif.) H.S., 1968-70; from libr. asst. to asst. curator Huntington Libr., San Marino, Calif., 1972-91; archivist Richard Nixon Libr. and Birthplace, Yorba Linda, Calif., 1991—.

**NAUMAN, BRUCE,** artist; b. Ft. Wayne, Ind., Dec. 6, 1941; m. Judy Nauman, 1964 (div.); 2 children; m. Susan Rothenberg, 1989. BFA, U. Wis.-Madison, 1964; MFA, U. Calif., Davis, 1966; studied with Italo Scango, William Wiley, Robert Arneson, Frank Owen, Stephen Kaltenbach.; DFA (hon.), San Francisco Art Inst., 1989; ArtsD (hon.), Calif. Inst. Arts, 2000. Tchr. asst. to Wayne Thiebaud, 1964; instr. San Francisco Art Inst., 1966-68; instr. sculpture U. Calif., Irvine, 1970 Author: Pictures of Sculptures in a Room, 1966, Clear Sky, 1968, Burning Small Fires, 1968; one man shows include Nicholas Wilder Gallery, L.A., Sacramento State Coll., 1968, Galerie Konrad Fischer Dusseldorff, 1968, Los Angeles County Mus. Art (retrospective), 1972, U. Calif., Irvine, 1973, Stadtische Kunsthalle (retrospective), Dusseldorf, W. Ger., Art/Voir, Centre Beaubourg, Paris, 1974, Sculpture Am. Directions 1945-1975, Nat. Collection of Fine Arts, Smithsonian Inst., 1975, Body Works, Mus. Contemporary Art, Chgo., 1975, Drawing Now, Mus. Modern Art, N.Y.C., 1975, 200 Years Am. Sculpture, Whitney Mus., N.Y.C., 1976, The Artist and the Photograph, Israel Mus., 1976, Sculpture, Munster, W. Ger., 1977, A View of a Decade, Mus. Contemporary Art, Chgo., 1977, Made by Sculptors, Stedelijk Mus., Amsterdam, 1978, Words Words, Mus. Bochum, W. Ger., 1979, The Broadening of the Concept of Reality in the Art of the 60s and 70s, Mus. Haus Lange Krefeld, W. Ger., 1979, Albright-Knox Art Gallery, Buffalo, 1975, U. Nev., 1976, Mpls. Inst. Arts, 1978, Portland Center for Visual Arts, 1979, Leo Castelli Gallery, N.Y.C., 1982, Sperone Westwater Fischer, N.Y.C., 1982, Sperone Westwater, N.Y.C., 1990, 96, 2001, 02, Dia Ctr. for Arts, N.Y.C., 2002, DIA Ctr. Arts, N.Y.C., 2002, Corcoran Gallery Art, Washington, 2002-03, Ludwig Mus. Cologne, Germany, 2003, Deutsche Guggenheim, Berlin, 2003-04, Tate Modern, London, 2004-05, others; group exhbns. include Fischbach Gallery, William Geis, Bruce Nauman, San Francisco Art Inst., 1966, Am. Sculpture of the Sixties, Los Angeles County Mus. Art, 1967, Documenta IV, Kassel, W. Ger., 1968, When Attitudes Become Form, Kunsthalle, Berne, Switzerland, toured, Europe, 1969, Kompass IV, Van Abbermuseum, Eindohoven, Netherlands, 1969, Corcoran Gallery Art, Washington, 1969, Anti-Illusion: Procedures-Materials, Whitney Mus. Art, N.Y.C., 1969, Soloman R. Guggenheim Mus., N.Y.C., 1969, Holograms and Lasers, Mus. Contemporary Art, Chgo., 1970, Conceptual Art and Conceptual Aspects, N.Y. Cultural Center, 1970, Am. Art Since 1960, Princeton U., 1970, Info, Mus. Modern Art, N.Y.C., 1971, Diagrams and Drawing, Rijksmuseum Kroller-Mueller, 1972, USA West Coast, Kunstverein, Hamburg, W. Ger., 1972, Documenta V, Kassel, W. Ger., 1972, Gilder, Objedte, Filme, Konzepte, Stadische Galerie, Munich, 1973, Art and Image in Recent Art, Art Inst., Chgo., 1974, Carol Taylor Art, Dallas, 1983, Kunsthalle, Basel, Switzerland, 1986, Carnegie Mus. Art, 1991-92, La. Mus. Art, 1997-98, Henry Art Gallery, Seattle, 2000, Art Gallery NSW, 2001, Donald Young Gallery, Chgo., 2002, Austin Mus. Art, Austin, Tex., 2003, others; group show 64th Whitney Biennial, 1987; represented in permanent collections: Whitney Mus. Am. Art, Los Angeles County Mus. Art; prodr. numerous video works. Nat. Endowment Arts grantee, 1968; Aspen Inst. Humanistic Studies, grantee, 1970; recipient Wolf Prize in arts (xculpture) Wolf Found., Israel, 1993, Praemium Imperiale award, Japan, 2004; named Best Internat. Artist, Beaux-Arts Mag., Paris, 2004. Fellow: Am. Acad. Arts and Scis.; mem.: Am. Acad. Arts and Letters. Avocation: horseback riding. Office: Sperone Westwater 415 W 13 St New York NY 10014*

**NAUMANN, JOSEPH F.,** archbishop; b. St. Louis, June 4, 1949; BA, Cardinal Glennon Coll., St. Louis, 1971; degree in theology, Kenrick Sem., St. Louis, 1975. Ordained priest, St. Louis, 1975; transitional deacon St. Christopher's Parish, Florissant, Mo., 1974-75; assoc. pastor St. Dominic Savio Parish, Affton, Mo., 1975-79, Our Lady of Sorrows Parish, St. Louis, 1979-84; part-time assoc. pastor Most Blessed Sacrament Parish, St. Louis, 1984-89; pastor Ascension Parish, Normandy, Mo., 1989-94; vicar gen., 1994—97; auxiliary bishop, 1997—2004; titular bishop Caput Cilla, 1997—; coadjutor archbishop Archdiocese of Kansas City, Kans., 2004, archbishop Kans., 2005—. Office: Archdiocese of Kansas City 12615 Parallel Pkwy Kansas City KS 66109

**NAUMANN, WILLIAM CARL,** consumer products company executive; b. Peoria, Ill., Mar. 25, 1938; s. William Louis and Emma (Bottin) N.; m. Polly Roby, May 20, 1962 (div. 1980); children: Jeff, Heather, Derek; m. Patricia Gallagher, Sept. 9, 1993 BSCE, Purdue U., 1960; MBA, U. Chgo., 1975. With Inland Steel Products Co., Chgo. 1960—68, N.Y. dist. mgr., 1968—70, divsn. gen. mgr., 1971—74; group v.p., bd. dirs. Inryco, Melrose Park, Ill., 1974—81; asst. chief engr. Inland Steel Co., Chgo., 1981—82, asst. gen. mgr. corp. planning, 1982—83, asst. gen. mgr. sales, 1983—85, gen. mgr. sales and mktg., 1985—87; exec. v.p. sales and mktg., 1987; pres. Hussmann Food Svc. Co., Bridgeton, 1987—89; corp. v.p., chief quality officer Whitman Corp., Chgo., 1990—91; CEO Ranger Industries, 1992; sr. v.p., COO Pexco Holdings, Inc., Tulsa, 1993—96; chmn. bd. dirs., CEO Sports Holdings Corp., Montreal, Canada, 1996—97; pres., CEO Hatteras Yachts, Inc., New Bern, NC, 1997—2005, Hatteras Collection, 2005—. Past chmn., bd. dir. New Bern C of C.; bd. dirs. Craven C.C. Found., Craven County Airport Authority, Craven County Cmty. Found., Swiss Bear, New Bern Mil. Alliance. Mem. N.C. Mfrs. Assn. (bd. dirs.), Nat. Assn. Boat Mfrs. (bd. dir.), U. Chgo. Exec. Program Club (past pres.), U. Chgo. Alumni Assn. (past pres., bd. govs. 1986-95), Ea. Carolina Yacht Club, Ocean Reef Club, New Bern Golf and Country Club, Beta Gamma Sigma Avocations: boating, travel, cooking. Home: 41 Gables Rd New Bern NC 28562-7079 Office: Hatteras Yachts Inc 110 N Glenburnie Rd New Bern NC 28560-2703 Office Phone: 252-634-4828. Personal E-mail: wcnaumann@earthlink.net.

**NAUMER, CAROLA,** art historian, educator; d. Helmuth and Tomee Naumer. BA, Kansas State U., 1983, MA, 1987; PhD, Fla. State U., 1998. Instr. Fla. A&M U., Tallahassee, 1989—95, Bainbridge Coll., Ga., 1995—96, Tallahassee C.C., 1995—98; grad. tchg. asst. Fla. State U.,

Tallahassee, 1998—98; prof. Truckee Meadows C.C., Reno, 1999—. Participant NEH Summer Seminar, Naples, Italy, 2000. Contbr. articles to profl. jours. Mem.: Coll. Art Assn., Archaeol. Inst. Am. Office Phone: 775-673-8269. Office Fax: 775-674-4853. Business E-Mail: cnaumer@tmcc.edu.

**NAUMOV, IVAN I.,** physicist, educator; b. Tobolsk, Tyumen Region, Russia, Sept. 3, 1952; s. Ivan E. Naumov and Zoya D. Naumova; m. Svetlana A. Marchenko, July 28, 1953; 1 child, Nina I. Naumova. MS, Tomsk State U., Russia, 1974, DS, 1994, PhD, 1980. Rsch. scientist V.D. Kuznetsov Siberian Phys.-Tech.Inst., Tomsk, Russia, 1974—78; sr. rsch. scientist Inst. of Physics of Strength and Materials Sci. of USSR, Tomsk, 1980—88; vis. scientist I.E. Tamm Theoretical Physics Dept., P.N. Lebedev Phys. Inst., Moscow, 1988—89; leading rsch. scientist Inst. of Physics of Strength and Materials Sci. of Russian Acad. of Scis., Siberian Br., Tomsk, Russia, 1989—2001; postdoctoral rsch. assoc. Rutgers U., Piscataway, NJ, 2001—03; rsch. prof. U. Ark., Fayetteville, 2001—06. Mem. of dissertation coun. Inst. of Physics of Strength and Materials Sci. of USSR, Tomsk, Russia, 1994—2001. Recipient Young Scientists Competition award, 1984; grantee, Internat. Sci. Found., 1994, 1995. Achievements include patents for multi-stable vortex states inferroelectric nanostructures. Home: Apt 32 2100 N Leverett Ave Fayetteville AR 72703 Office: Rm 102A 870 W Dickson St Fayetteville AR 72703 Office Phone: 479-575-3365. Office Fax: 479-575-4580. Business E-Mail: inaumov@uark.edu.

**NAUMOVSKA, BILJANA,** control assurance consultant; permanent resident, US, 2005; d. Naum Naumovski and Snezanka Naumovska; m. Spase Petrovski, Dec. 8, 2004. BA in MIS, U. Mich., Dearborn, 2002; postgrad. in Bus. Adminstrn., Wayne State U., Detroit, 2003—. Data analyst co-op Fed. Mogul Co., Southfield, Mich., 2003—04; recruiter Infotree, Canton, Mich., 2004; control assurance cons. Deloitte & Touche LLP, Detroit, 2004—. Data analyst coop. Fed. Mogul Co, Southfield, Mich., 2003—04. Mem. Macedonian Cultural Ctr., Farmighton Hills, Mich., 2004. Wilfred Kean Meml. scholarship, Wayne State U., 2006. Mem.: ISACA (assoc.). East Orthodox. Avocations: piano, skiing, ballroom dancing, reading, volleyball. Personal E-mail: bnaumovska@deloitte.com.

**NAURATH, DAVID ALLISON,** engineering psychologist, researcher; b. Houston, Mar. 11, 1927; s. Walter Arthur and Joy Frances (Bradbury) N.; m. Barbara Ellen Coverdell; children: Kathleen Ann, David Allen, Cynthia Ellyn, Randall Austin. BA, Simpson Coll., Indianola, Iowa, 1948; MA, Southern Meth. U., 1949; postgrad., U. Denver, 1955-57. Job analyst U.S. Air Force, San Antonio and Denver, 1951-55, rsch. psychologist Lowry AFB, Colo., 1955-60, Navy, Life Scis. & Systems div., Point Mugu, Calif., 1960-76; engring. psychologist Navy Systems Engring., Point Mugu, 1976-83; ret. Presenter at profl. socs. and orgns. in field. Contbr. articles to Jour. Engring. Psychology, jour. Soc. for Info. Display, jour. Soc. Photo-optical Instrument Engrs. With USAAF, 1944-46. Mem. AAAS (life), IEEE (sr.), Am. Psychol. Assn., N.Y. Acad. Sci. (emeritus), Human Factors Soc. (panel mem. Certification of Human Factors Engrs. 1976), Soc. Engring. Psychologists, Soc. for Info. Display (life). Methodist. Home: 5633 Pembroke St Ventura CA 93003-2200

**NAVA, CARMEN P.,** communications executive; Degree in Bus. Adminstrn., U. So. Calif. 1984. Joined gen. mgmt. devel. program Pacific Bell, 1984., v.p., gen. mgr. Diverse Markets Group; regional pres. L.A. SBC Comm., L.A., 1997—99, pres. SBC Ctr. for Learning, 1999, pres. SBC West Consumer Markets San Antonio, 1999—. Bd. govs. U. So. Calif. Alumni Assn. Office: SBC Comm Inc 175 E Houston San Antonio TX 78205-2233

**NAVAB, APHRODITE DESIREE,** artist, educator, writer; b. Esfahan, Iran, Oct. 31, 1971; arrived in U.S., 1980; d. Ali and Katina Navab; m. Richard C. Foltz, Aug. 21, 1994; children: Shahrzad Foltz-Navab, Bijan Foltz-Navab. BA magna cum laude, Harvard U., 1993; MA, EdM, Columbia U., 2000, EdD, 2004. Asst. prof. U. Fla., Gainesville, 2004—. Adj. asst. prof. U. Fla., 2000—02, grad. faculty supr., 2000—, faculty minority mentor, 2001—02, vis. asst. prof., 2002—04, faculty advisor undergrad. photography, 2002—, chair photography Sch. Arts & Art History, 2003—04. Contbr. articles to profl. jours.; one-woman shows include Bernice Steinbaum Gallery, Miami, Brown Gallery, Duke U., Durham, N.C., Charles Culpeper Photography Gallery, NYC. Recipient David McCord prize Outstanding Visual Artist, Harvard U., Cambridge, Mass., 1993. Mem.: Soc. Internat. Studies, Nat. Art Edn. Assn., Coll. Art Assn. Avocations: travel, languages, literature. Office: U Fla Coll Fine Arts PO Box 115801 Gainesville FL 32611 E-mail: dnavab@ufl.edu.

**NAVANEETHAN, SANKAR DASS,** physician; s. Navaneethan Rangasamy and Jayamani Natarajan; m. Sangeetha Radhakrishnan. MBBS, Madras Med. Coll., India, 2000; MPH, U. SC, 2002; MD, Unity Health Sys., Rochester, NY, 2005. Diplomate Am. Bd. Internal Medicine. Internal medicine resident Unity Health Sys., Rochester, 2002—05, chief med. resident, 2005—. Recipient Primary Care award, Rochester Acad. Medicine, 2006, Best Poster award, U. Rochester, 2006, rsch. grant, Nat. Kidney Found., 2006; fellow, 2006; travel grantee, Unity Health Sys., 2004, 2006. Mem.: ACP (assoc.), So. Med. Assn. (assoc.), Cochrane Renal Group (assoc. travel grantee 2006) Achievements include systematic review of statins in kidney disease patients; systematic review of role of phosphate binders in kidney disease patients; systematic review of barriers on access to renal transplantation for African Americans in US; systematic review on the reasons for delayed referral to nephrologists for chronic kidney disease; systematic review on role of darbepoetin for chronic kidney disease. Office Phone: 585-723-2043. E-mail: sankardass@hotmail.cm.

**NAVAR, LUIS GABRIEL,** physiology educator, researcher, director; b. El Paso, Tex., Mar. 24, 1941; s. Luis and Concepcion (Najera) N.; m. Randa Ann Bumgarner, Oct. 15, 1965; children: Tonia, Tess, Gabriel, Daniel. BS, Tex. A&M U., 1962; PhD, U. Miss., 1966, postdoctoral study, 1966-69. Instr. dept. physiology/biophysics U. Miss., Jackson, 1966-67, asst. prof., 1967-71, assoc. prof., 1971-74, U. Ala., Birmingham, 1974-76, prof., 1976-88, assoc. prof. Nephrology Rsch. and Tng. Ctr., 1979-83, prof., 1983-88; prof., chmn. dept. physiology Tulane U. Med. Sch., New Orleans, 1988—, co-dir. Hypertension and Renal Ctr. of Excellence, 2001—. Vis. scientist Duke U. Med. Ctr., Durham, N.C., 1972-73; adv. bd. NIH Ctr. Sci. Rev., 1998-99; bd. dirs. Fedn. Am. Socs. Exptl. Biology, 1997-01. Assoc. editor News in Physiol Scis., 1994-2000, Am. Jour. Physiology, 1983-89, mem. editl. bd., 1982-83, 97—; mem. editl. bd. Kidney Internat., 1976-87, Kidney, 1992—, Clin. Sci., 1994-99, Jour. Am. Soc. Nephrology, 1996-2001, Jour. Am. Soc. Nephrology, 1996-2001, Am. Jour. Kidney Disease, 1997-2001, Jour. Am. Jour. Hypertension, 1999—, Hypertension, 1980-83, 2002-04, assoc. editor, 1993-2000, cons. editor, 2006—; contbr. chpts. to books, articles to profl. jours. Chmn. cardiorenal rsch. study com. Am. Heart Assn., 1994—95, nat. rsch. com., 1994—99, vice chair leadership com. coun. high blood pressure rsch.; cardiovascular and renal study sects. NIH, 1998—2000, chmn., 2000—02; bd. dirs. Consortium for Southeastern Hypertension Control, 1998—2000; vice chair leadership com. High Blood Pressure Rsch. Am. Heart Assn. Recipient Rsch. Career Devel. award, Nat. Heart, Lung and Blood Inst., 1974—79, Merit award, 1988—97, Bodil M. Schmidt Nielson Disting. Mentor and Scientist award, 2006, Lifetime Achievement award, COSEHC, 2006; vis. scholar Pfizer/ACCF, 2002. Fellow: AAAS; mem.: Assn. of Am. Med. Coll. (administrv. bd. of coun. of academic soc. 2004—), Assn. Chmn. Depts. Physiology (councillor 1993—95, pres.-elect 1995—96, pres. 1996—97, Disting. Svc. award 2003), Interam. Soc. Hypertension (chair awards com. 2003—), Am. Soc. Hypertension (coun. 1992—94, chmn. basic. sci. com. 1997, treas. 1997—2001, Richard Bright award 2001), Internat. Soc. Nephrology, Am. Soc. Nephrology, Am. Heart Assn. (Lewis K. Dahl Lectr. 1997, profl. and pub. edn. com. 1999—, kidney, high blood pressure couns., vice chmn. leadership com. high blood pressure rsch., Sci. Coun. Disting. Achievement award 1999, Corcoran Lectr. award 2001), Am. Physiol. Soc. (coun. 1991—94, Gottschalk Disting. Lectr. Renal Physiology 1997, pres.-elect 1997—98, pres. 1998—99, Bodil M. Schmidt-Nielson Disting. Mentor and Sci. award 2006). Democrat. Roman Catholic. Home:

10020 Hyde Pl New Orleans LA 70123-1522 Office: Tulane U Med Sch Dept Physiology 1430 Tulane Ave New Orleans LA 70112-2699 Office Phone: 504-988-5251. Business E-Mail: navar@tulane.edu.

**NAVARRA, TOVA,** writer; b. Newark, July 10, 1948; d. Joe and Rose Leslie Treihart; m. John G. Navarra Jr., Aug. 26, 1967 (div. 1998); children: Yolanda, John G. III; m. Robert B. Kern, July 10, 2004. BA magna cum laude, Seton Hall Univ., 1974; AAS, Brookdale C.C., Lincroft, NJ, 1984; postgrad., Fairleigh Dickinson U. Elem. sch. tchr., Jersey City, 1967-69; corr. Village Times, Long Island, NY, 1974-75; tchr. music, humanities, German, art, art history Seton Hall Prep. Sch., South Orange, NJ, 1975-78; entertainment, feature writer, press corr. Asbury Park Press, Neptune, NJ, 1978-85, feature writer, art critic, family writer, 1985-92; feature writer, art columnist Two River Times, Red Bank, NJ, 1993-94. Psychiatric charge nurse, 1985; supr. grant rsch. Vis. Nurse Assn. Ctrl. Jersey, Red Bank, N.J., 1993-94; art coord. Monmouth Players, Navesink, N.J.; lectr. at writing confs.; mem. Bayshore fitness and Wellness Ctr., Hazlet, N.J., 2005. Author: The New Jersey Shore: A Vanishing Splendor, 1985, Jim Gary: His Life and Art, 1987, Your Body: Highlights of Human Anatomy, 1990, Playing It Smart: What to Do When You're on Your Own, 1989, also, pub. On My Own: Helping Kids Help Themselves, (translated into Italian, Portuguese and Hebrew) 1994, 2d edit., 2003, An Insider's Guide to Home Health Care: An Interdisciplinary Approach (with Margaret Lundrigan), 1995, Wisdom for Caregivers, 1995; (staged readings) Through the Kunai Grass with Dad, 1988, Don't Cry, Pandora, 1989; (with Myron A. Lipkowitz and John G. Navarra) Therapeutic Communication: A Guide to Effective Interpersonal Skills for Health Care Professionals, 1990, Encyclopedia of Vitamins, Minerals, and Supplements, 1995, 2d edit., 2004; (with Lipkowitz), Allergies A-Z, 1994; Images of America: Howell and Farmingdale 1996; (with Lundrigan) Image of America: Levittown: The First Fifty Years, 1997, Staten Island, 1997, Staten Island II, 1998, Levittown II, 1998; Toward Painless Writing, 1998; The American Century: Staten Island (with Lundrigan), 1999; Seton Hall University: A Photographic History, 1999, Monmouth University, 2001, Encyclopedia of Asthma and Respiratory Disorders, 2003, Young People/Tough Problems, 2003, Encyclopedia of Allergies 2d edit., 2004, Encyclopedia of Complementary and Alternative Medicine, 2004; illustrator Drugs and Man, 1973; editor in chief Shore Affinity, 1979-81; contbg. editor Am. Jour. Nursing, 1990-94; staff writer, illustrator, photographer N.J. Music and Arts, 1978-81; editor Associated Univ. Presses, 1981-82; copywriter, photographer Jersey Shore Med. Ctr., 1985; feature writer, columnist Copley News Svc., 1988-93; health trend columnist Personal Fitness, 1989-90; assoc. editor The Courier, Middletown, N.J., May-Dec. 1998; lifestyle editor The Two River Times, Red Bank, N.G. May 1999-2000; contr. to Nursing Spectrum Magazine; photography exhbns. in N.Y., N.J., Pa. Mid-Atlantic Riviera Magazine, 2005; guest various radio and TV programs; contbr. photographs to books, articles and photogs. to mags., newspapers; solo exhibits include Atlantic City Art Ctr., 1982, O.K. Harris Works of Art, N.Y.C., 1990, Gallery Axiom, Phila., 1991, Monmouth U., 1991, M. Thomson Kravetz Gallery, Bay Head, N.J., Oceanic Pub. Libr., 2000, Navesink Libr. Theater, 2004, 05; group shows at Art Forms, Red Bank, 1991, Moravian Coll., Bethlehem, Pa., 1992. Mem. Gov.'s Coun. on Alcoholism and Drug Abuse Prevention, co-chair Later Childhood subcom., 1992 Mem. N.J. Playwrights Workshop (charter), N.J. State Nurses Assn. Avocations: singing, guitar, piano, dance, crafts. Office: Sanford J Greenburger Assocs care Faith H Hamlin 55 5th Ave New York NY 10003-4301

**NAVARRETE, JORGE EDUARDO,** ambassador; b. Mexico City, Apr. 29, 1940; s. Gabriel and Lucrecia (Lopez) N.; m. Marie Bolaños, 1965 (dec. Sept. 1985); 1 child, Federico Navarrete Linares; m. Angeles Salceda, July 31, 1986. BA in Econs., U. Mexico, 1970. Head econ. studies Nat. Fgn. Trade Bank, Mexico City, 1967-72; Mexican ambassador to Venezuela, 1972-75, Austria, 1976, Yugoslavia, 1977-78, UN, 1979; undersec. econ. affairs Ministry Fgn. Affairs, Mexico City, 1979-85; ambassador to Eng. London, 1986—. Author: Latin American External Debt, 1987. Avocation: chess.

**NAVARRO, BRUCE CHARLES,** lawyer; b. West Lafayette, Ind., Oct. 30, 1954; s. Joseph Anthony and Dorothy Gloria (Gnazzo) N.; children: Philip Joseph, Joanna Christina; m. Andrea Fox; children: Christi Renee, Karina Michelle. BA, Duke U., 1976; JD, Ind. U., 1980. Bar: D.C. 1980. Asst. counsel U.S. Senate Labor Subcom., Washington, 1981; acting dep. undersec. for legis. affairs Dept. Labor, Washington, 1984—85; atty. advisor EEOC, Washington, 1985—86; dir. Office of Congl. Rels. Office of Pers. Mgmt., Washington, 1986—89; prin. dep. asst. atty. gen. for legis. U.S. Dept. of Justice, Washington, 1989—91; spl. asst. to gen. counsel U.S. Dept. HHS, Washington, 1991; expert cons. U.S. Dept. Def., Washington, 1992; counsel to the vice chmn. U.S. Consumer Product Safety Commn., Bethesda, Md., 1992—95; prin. Navarro Regulatory and Legis. Affairs, Washington, 1995—; Fabiani & Co., Washington, 2005—. Mem. Arlington County (Va.) Rep. Com., 1983; bd. dirs. Prince William Cmty. Safe Kids Coalition, 1997-99, 2005—. Mem. D.C. Bar Assn. Roman Catholic. Avocations: music, golf. Home: 12631 Magic Springs Way Bristow VA 20136 Office: Ste 800 2121 K St NW Washington DC 20037 also: Fabiani and Co 1101 Pennsylvania Ave NW Ste 700 Washington DC 20004 Office Phone: 202-955-6006, 202-756-4583. Business E-Mail: nlra@verizon.net.

**NAVARRO, DAVE (DAVID MICHAEL NAVARRO),** musician, recording artist; b. Santa Monica, Calif., June 7, 1967; s. James Raul 'Mike' and Constance Colleen (Hopkins) Navarro; m. Carmen Electra, Nov. 22, 2003 (separated July 2006). Mem. band Jane's Addiction, 1986-91, 1997, Red Hot Chili Peppers, 1993—97, Spread; working with the band The Panic Channel. Recordings include (with Jane's Addiction) Jane's Addiction, 1987, Nothing's Shocking, 1988, Ritual de lo Habitual, 1990, (with Red Hot Chili Peppers) One Hot Minute, 1995, (solo album) Trust No One. 2001; composer (Films) Ugly Meets the People, 1995, Twister, 1996, Private Parts, 1997, Bringing Out the Dead, 1999, Ordinary Decent Criminal, 2000, Anger Management, 2003, S.W.A.T., 2003, Torque, 2004, (video) Soul Kiss, 1989 (also actor), Gift, 1993 (also actor), (video game) Grand Theft Auto: San Andreas, 2004; prodr., exec. prodr. Three Days, 1999; actor (TV mini series) House of Style, 1996-, I Love the 80s Strikes Back, 2003, Til' Death Do Us Part: Carmen & Dave, 2004, I Love the 90s, 2004, I Love the 90s Part Deux, 2005, (TV) Set in Skin, 2002, Carmen & Dave: An MTV Love Story, 2002, The Osbourne Family Christmas Special, 2003, (film) Sexual Intent, 1994, Floundering, 1994, Uptown Girls, 2003; co-host, Rock Stars 2005-; performer Camp Freddy, Lollapalozza, 2003-04; appeared in music video for Moby, "We Are All Made of Stars"; guest appearances include: Martial Law, 1999, Charmed, 2001, Punk'd, 2004, Celebrity Poker Showdown, 2004,Celebrity Blackjack, 2004 and MADtv, 2004 and several others; author Dont' Try This At Home, 2004. Office: care Warner Bros Records 3300 Warner Blvd Burbank CA 91505-4632

**NAVARRO, JOSE F., JR.,** retail executive; s. Jose Navarro Sr.; children: Gabriel, Marcel, Patricia Pico. Pres. Navarro Discount Pharmacies, Inc., Miami. Office: Navarro Discount Pharmacies Inc 5959 NW 37th Ave Miami FL 33142*

**NAVARRO, JOSEPH ANTHONY,** retired statistician, consultant; b. New Britain, Conn., July 6, 1927; s. Charles C. and Josephine V. (Bianco) N.; m. Dorothy G. Gnazzo; children: Kenneth M., Bruce C., Joseph S. BS, Cen. Conn. State U., 1950; MS, Purdue U., 1952, PhD, 1955. Rsch. staff, cons. GE, 1955-59; rsch. staff, mgmt. IBM, 1962-64; sr. staff mem., asst. dir. Inst. Def. Analyses, Alexandria, Va., 1964-72; pres., chief oper. officer System Planning Corp., Arlington, Va., 1972-86; dep. undersec. test and evaluation Dept. Defense, Washington, 1987-88; now pvt. practice cons., 1987—2005; pres. Wackenhut Applied Technologies Ctr., Fairfax, Va., 1989-90; ret., 2005. Contbr. articles to profl. jours. Mem. Bd. Trade, Washington, 1983-85. Mem. Internat. Test and Evaluation Assn. Clubs: COSMOS (Washington). Republican. Roman Catholic. Home: 8010 Grand Teton Dr Potomac MD 20854-4074 Personal E-mail: jadgnav@comcast.net.

**NAVARRO, MAX,** supply chain management company executive; b. San Antonio, Oct. 18, 1943; s. Jasper and Isabel Navarro; m. Irene Elizabeth Navarro; children: Scott, Elizabeth. BA, St. Mary's U., San Antonio, 1977, MS, 1980. Sr. mgr. Control Data Corp., San Antonio, 1980-85; founder Operational Technologies Corp., San Antonio, 1986—, chmn.; chmn., CEO Vutex Inc., 2004—. Chmn. bd. Performance Metrics Inc., San Antonio, 1986—. Pres. League United Latin Am. Citizens, San Antonio, 1970-72, Anti-Poverty Program, San Antonio, 1977. Recipient hon. citation Bexar County Commrs., 1978, City of San Antonio, 1980, award Cultural Arts Orgn., 1981, recognition award SBA, 1990. Mem. Def. Contractors Assn. (v.p. 1989-90), Am. Def. Preparedness Assn. (v.p. San Antonio chpt. 1989-90). Office: Operational Technologies Corp Ste 230 4100 NW Loop 410 San Antonio TX 78229 Office Phone: 210-731-0000. Office Fax: 210-731-0008.*

**NAVASKY, VICTOR SAUL,** publisher; b. NYC, July 5, 1932; s. Macy and Esther Blanche (Goldberg) N.; m. Anne Landey Strongin, Mar. 27, 1966; children: Bruno, Miri, Jenny. AB, Swarthmore Coll., 1954; LL.B., Yale U., 1959. Spl. asst. to Gov. G. Mennen Williams, Mich., 1959-60; editor, pub. Monocle Mag., 1961-65; editor NY Times mag., 1970-72, The Nation mag., NYC, 1978-94, pub., gen. ptnr., 1995—2005, pub. emeritus, 2005—; Delacorte prof. of mag. journalism Columbia U., NYC, 1999—; and chmn. Columbia Journalism Rev. Vis. scholarRussell Sage Found., 1975—76; Ferris prof. journalism Princeton U., 1976—77. Author: Kennedy Justice, 1971 (Nat. Book Award nominee), Naming Names, 1980 (Nat. Book award 1981), rev. edit., 1991, 2003, A Matter of Opinion, 2005 (recipient George S. Polk book award, 2006); editor: (with C. Cerf) The Experts Speak, 1984; playwright: (with Richard R. Lingeman) Starr's Last Tape, 1999. Mem. bd. mgrs. Swarthmore Coll., 1991-94; bd. trustees The New Sch. Served with U.S. Army, 1954-56. Guggenheim fellow, 1974-75; fellow Inst. of Politics, Harvard U., 1999; Sr. fellow Freedom Forum, 1994. Mem. Author's Guild (coun.), Com. To Protect Journalists (exec. com.), Phi Beta Kappa; fellow Am. Acad. Arts & Sciences Democrat. Jewish. Office Phone: 212-209-5411. Business E-Mail: vic@thenation.com.*

**NAVE, J. L.,** performing company executive; b. Nashville, May 4, 1972; BA Conducting, Belmont U., 1994; MA Arts Adminstrn., U. Cin., 1997, MBA, 1997. Orch. mgr. Northeastern Pa. Philharm.; orch. mgmt. fellow Am. Symphony Orch. League; pres., CEO Baton Rouge Symphony Orch., 2000—. Ops. chair First Night Scranton; grant recipient Pa. Coun. on Arts. Office: Baton Rouge Symphony Orch PO Box 14209 Baton Rouge LA 70898 Office Phone: 225-383-0500. E-mail: jlnave@brso.org.

**NAVIN-O'MEARA, CYNTHIA L.,** school psychologist; d. John Francis and Anita Louise Navin; m. Christopher Joseph O'Meara, Sept. 14, 1996; children: Maximilian Joseph O'Meara, Lauren Navin O'Meara. BS, U. Wis., LaCrosse, 1983, MS in Edn., 1985. Sch. psychologist Mississippi Bend Area Edn. Agy., Bettendorf, Iowa, 1985—96, Naperville Cmty. Unit Sch. Dist., Ill., 1996—. Parent edn. coord. PTA, El Sierra Sch., Ill., 2004—; vol. pub. assistance delivering shelter St. Mary of Goystn Ch., Downers Grove, Ill., 1997—. Mem.: NASP, Western Suburbs Sch. Psychologists. Avocations: swimming, hiking, spending time with family, travel. Office: Naperville Cmty Unit Sch Dist 203 W Hillside Rd Naperville IL 60540 Office Phone: 630-420-8699. Office Fax: 630-637-7348. E-mail: cnavinomeara@naperville203.org.

**NAVON, IONEL MICHAEL,** mathematics professor; b. Bucharest, Romania, Apr. 28, 1940; s. David and Sarah (Schwartzman) N.; m. Lily Marcu, May 11, 1967; children: Daria, Livia. BSc in Math., Hebrew U. Jerusalem, 1967, MSc in Atmospheric Scis., 1971; PhD in Applied Math., U. Witwatersrand, Johannesburg, South Africa, 1979. Sr. rsch. meteorologist Israel Meteorol. Office, Tel Aviv, 1973-74; head applied math sect. Tamam/Israel Aircraft Industry, Tel Aviv, 1974-76; sr. rsch. officer Counc. Sci. and Indsl. Rsch., Pretoria, South Africa, 1976-78, chief rsch. officer, 1979-80, sr. chief rsch. officer, 1981-83; vis. sr. scientist NASA/Goddard Space Flight Ctr., Greenbelt, Md., 1983-84; cons. NASA/Goddard Space Flight Ctr., Greenbelt, Md., 1984-85; sr. specialist researcher Coun. Sci. and Indsl. Rsch., Pretoria, 1984-85; assoc. rsch. scientist Supercomputer Rsch. Inst., Tallahassee, Fla., 1985-87; assoc. prof. math. Fla. State U., Tallahassee, 1987-1990, prof., 1991—, program dir. optimization and optimal control, 1993—, hon. prof. dept. meteorology Supercomputer Rsch. Inst., 1987—, faculty assoc. Supercomputer Computation Rsch. Inst., 1988—, faculty assoc. Geophys. Fluid Dynamics Inst., 1989—, dir. applied math dept. math, 1998—. Dir. applied math. Fla. State U., 1998—; cons. Ctr. Analysis Prediction of Storms, Norman, Okla., 1989, French Navy, 1995; leader Argonne Nat. Lab.; co-organizer Internat. Conf. Element Methods in Geophysics, Tallahassee, 1991; summer lecture series scientist NASA, 1991—; mem. panel nat. experts to rev. and conduct site visiting Okla. Sci. and Tech. Ctr.; keynote spkr. Internat. Conf. on Finite Element Methods, South Africa, 1992, Internat. Conf. on Optimization Techniques and Applications, Singapore, 1992, Assimilation of Meteorological and Oceanographic Observations, France, 1993. Editor spl. issues Computer and Math. with Applications; editor Monthly Weather Rev., 1991-94; assoc. editor Monthly Weather Rev., 2001, Jour. for Numerical Linear Algebra with Applications, 1991, Computational Fluid Dynamics Jour., 1992; chief editor spl. issue Dynamics of Atmospheres and Oceans, 1998; spl. editor Internat. Jour. on Computational Fluid Dynamics, 2003; contbr. over 95 refereed articles to sci. jours. Lt. Israel Civil Def., 1960-63. Grantee NSF, 1988, 91, 94—, 98-2001, 2002, 2003-06, NASA, 1991, 94, 97-99, 2006—; rsch. grantee Air Force Office Sci., 1989, 91, 94. Fellow Am. Meteorol. Soc.; Nat. Rsch. Coun. NASA/GSFC Delta Assimilation Office, 2000 (sr.); mem. Am. Math. Soc., Am. Geophys. Union, Soc. Indsl. and Applied Math. (organizer symposiums 2004-05), Israel Assn. Profl. Engrs., Am. Computing Machinery Assn. Avocations: ping-pong, photography, books. Home: 3138 Ferns Glen Dr Tallahassee FL 32309-2304 Office: Fla State U Dim. of Applied Math Bldg Itm 403 Tallahassee FL 32306 Office Phone: 850-644-6560. Business E-Mail: navon@ses.fsu.edu.

**NAVON, ROBERT,** real estate investor, retired publisher; b. N.Y.C., May 18, 1954; s. Jack and Estelle N. AB, CUNY, Bronx, 1975; MLS, SUNY, Geneseo, 1978; MA, PhD, U. Kans., 1987; postgrad., U. N.Mex., 1991-93. Coll. libr. N.Y. Inst. Tech., N.Y.C., 1978-79; tchr. history and English N.Y.C. Schs., 1983-86; pub. Selene Books, N.Y.C., 1984-86, Lawrence, Kans., 1986-88, El Paso, Tex., 1988-93, Marianna, Fla., 1996-99; tchr. ESL, Evergreen Inst., Korea, 1993-94; real estate investor, Panama City, Fla., 1995—. Author: Patterns of the Universe, 1977, Autumn Songs, 1983, The Harmony of the Spheres, 1991, Cosmic Patterns, 1993, Tales of the Future, 1999. Mem. Internat. Soc. for Comparative Study of Civilizations, Phi Beta Kappa. Avocations: chess, international travel, collecting movies. Home: PO Box 634 Panama City FL 32402

**NAVRATILOVA, MARTINA,** professional tennis player; b. Prague, Czech Republic, Oct. 18, 1956; came to US, 1975, naturalized, 1981. s. Miroslav Navratil and Jana Navratilova. Student, schs. in Czechoslovakia; Hon. doctorate, George Washington U., 1996. Tennis commentator/broadcaster HBO Sports, 1995-99; Profl. tennis player, 1973-94, 2003—. Player Czech Fed. Cup Team, 1975, U.S. Fed Cup Team, 1982, 86, 89, 95, 2003; mem. World Team Tennis, 2004—. Author: (with George Vecsey) Martina, 1985; (with Liz Nickles) The Total Zone, 1995, The Breaking Point, 1996, Killer Instinct, 1997, The Shape of Your Life, 2006; columnist. Co-founder Rainbow Card. Winner Czechoslovak Nat. singles, 1972-74, U.S. Open singles, 1983, 84, 86, 87, U.S. Open doubles, 1977, 78, 80, 83, 84, 87, 90, U.S. Open mixed doubles, 1987, 2006, Va. Slims Championsips, 1978, 83, 84, 85, 86, Va. Slims Championships, 1991, Wimbledon singles, 1978, 79, 82, 83, 84, 85, 86, 87, 90, Wimbledon women's doubles, 1976, 79, 81, 82, 83, 84, 86, Wimbledon mixed doubles, 1985, 93, 95, 2003, French Open singles, 1982, 84, Australian Open singles, 1981, 83, 85, Australian Doubles (with Betsy Nagelsen) 1980, (with Pam Shriver), 1982, 84, 85, 87, 88, 89, Australian Mixed Doubles, 2003, Roland Garros (with Pam Shriver) 1985, 87, 89, Italian Open doubles (with Gabriela Sabatini), 1987, (with Pam Shriver) COREL WTA Tour doubles team of yr., 1981-89, triple Crown at U.S. Open, 1987; recipient

Women's Sports Found. Flo Hyman award, 1987, BBC Lifetime Achievement Award, 2003; named Female Athlete of the Decade (1980s) The Nat. Sports Review, UPI, and AP, WTA Player of Yr., 1978-79, 82-86, Women's Sports Found. Sportswoman of Yr., 1982-84, Hon. Citizen of Dallas, AP Female Athlete of Yr., 1983; named to Internat. Tennis Hall of Fame, 2000; Martina Navratilova Day proclaimed in Chgo., 1992 Mem. Women's Tennis Assn. (dir., exec. com., pres.), Women's Tennis Assn. Tour Player's Assn. (pres. 1979-80, 83-84, 94-95). Achievements include being the holder of 167 singles titles and 173 doubles titles; holder of record of singles-match wins (1,309), 1991; holds record for 109 consecutive doubles matches won (with Pam Shriver).*

**NAWROCKI, DAVID NORMAN,** finance educator; b. East Chicago, Ind., Jan. 9, 1950; s. Arnold Norman and Jean (Kettring) N.; m. D. Christine Thomas, June 7, 1975; children: Jodi Lynmarie, Bryan Christopher. BS in Fin., Pa. State U., 1970, MBA, 1972, PhD, 1976. Econ. analyst Girard Bank, Phila., 1972-73; cons. Morgan Guaranty Trust, N.Y.C., 1974-75; instr. Pa. State U., University Park, 1971-75; asst. prof. fin. Drexel U., Phila., 1975-81; prof. fin. Villanova U., Pa., 1981—; Katherine M. and Richard J. Salisbury Jr. prof. fin. Villanova U., Pa., 2004—. Dir. Inst. for Rsch. in Advanced Fin. Tech., 2004—; pres. Computer Handholders, Arcola, Pa., 1982—, The Q Insight Group, San Diego, 1994—; bd. dirs. Aexpert, Inc., Lancaster, Pa., 1992-96; vis. prof. San Diego State U., 1991-92. Contbr. articles to fin. jours., 1973—; author (software) Portfolio Mgmt., 1983, CAPBUD, 1985; assoc. editor Fin. Rev., 1992-98, Internat Rev. of Fin. Analysis, 1992—; mem editl. adv. bd. Jour. of Fin. Planning, 1997—. Den leader Cub Scout Pack 119, Evansburg, Pa., 1990-95; adult leader Boy Scout Troop, 119, Evansburg, 1995-97, assoc. leader Explorer Post 119, 1997-99 Recipient Order of the Four Chaplains, Chapel of the Four Chaplains, Phila., 1981; Ben Franklin grantee State of Pa., Harrisburg, 1991. Mem. Am. Econ. Assn., Am. Fin. Assn., Ea. Fin. Assn., Beta Gamma Sigma, Phi Kappa Phi. Avocations: piano, flying, computers, travel. Office: Villanova U Fin Dept 800 Lancaster Ave Villanova PA 19085-1603 Mailing: Computer Handholder %D Nawrocki 96 Fenwick Cir Collegeville PA 19426-3414 E-mail: David.Nawrocki@villanova.edu.

**NAYAK, SUBHADARSHI,** research scientist; b. Cuttack, Orissa, India, Apr. 2, 1972; arrived in U.S.A., 2000; s. Gangadhar and Satyabhama Nayak; m. Jyoti Agrawal, Aug. 15, 2003. B in tech with honours, Indian Inst. Tech., Kharagpur, India, 1991—95; PhD, U. Tenn., Knoxville, 2000—03. Rsch. asst. Indian Inst. Tech., Kharagpur, West Bengal, 1995—95; engr., metallurgist Tractor Engrs. Ltd., Bombay, Maharastra, 1995—2000; sys. analyst, quality Infosys Techs. Ltd., Bangalore, Karnataka, 2000; grad. rsch. asst. U. Tenn., Knoxville, 2000—; summer intern Ford Motor Co., Dearborn, Mich., 2001. Contbr. articles, columns in newspapers, articles, scientific papers, (Second Prize, Outstanding Student Paper, Minerals, Metals, and Materials Soc., 2002). Sponsor and vol. Save the Children Fund, Cuttack, Orissa, India, 1990—2004. Recipient Materials Quiz, Nat. Level, Indian Inst. Tech., 1995, Citation Extraordinary Profl. Premise in Rsch., U. Tenn., 2002; fellow Merit Scholarship, Indian Inst. Tech., 1991-92, Grad. Fellowship, Tenn. Advanced Materials Lab., 2003; grantee High Temperature Materials Lab. User Program Grant, Oak Ridge Nat. Lab., 2000, 2001, Shared Rsch. Equipment User Program Grant, 2002. Mem.: Am. Ceramics Soc., Materials Rsch. Soc., Am. Physics Soc., ASM Internat. (membership coord. 1999—2000), Minerals, Metals, and Materials Soc. Office: Dept Materials Sci & Enrng Dougherty Enrng UT Knoxville TN 37996 Office Phone: 865-974-5160. Business E-Mail: snayak@utk.edu.

**NAYAR, BALDEV RAJ,** political science professor; b. Gujrat Dist., India, Oct. 26, 1931; arrived in Canada, 1964; s. Jamna Das and Durga Devi (Marwah) N.; m. Nancy Ann Skinner, Aug. 27, 1961; children – Sheila Jane, Kamala Elizabeth, Sunita Maria. BA, Punjab U., 1953; MA, 1956, U. Chgo., 1959, PhD, 1963. Asst. prof. Calif. State Coll., Hayward, 1963-64; mem. faculty dept. polit. sci. McGill U., 1964-94, assoc. prof., 1966-71, prof., 1971-94, prof. emeritus, 1996—, assoc. chmn., 1990-93. Rsch. assoc. Internat. Devel. Rsch. Centre, 1978 Author: Minority Politics in the Punjab, 1966, National Communication and Language Policy, 1969, The Modernization Imperative and Indian Planning, 1972, American Geopolitics and India, 1976, India's Quest for Technological Independence, 1983, India's Mixed Economy, 1989, The Political Economy of India's Public Sector, 1990, Superpower Dominance and Military Aid, 1991, The State and International Aviation in India, 1994, The State and Market in India's Shipping, 1996, Globalization and Nationalism, 2001, India and the Major Powers After Pokhran II, 2001; co-author: India in the World Order, 2003, The Geopolitics of Globalization, 2005. Bd. dirs. Shastri Indo-Canadian Inst., 1970-72, sr. fellow, 1978, 86. Recipient Watumull prize Am. Hist. Assn., 1966; Charles E. Merriam fellow, 1957; Carnegie Study New Nations fellow, 1962; Can. Council sr. fellow, 1967, 74; SSHRC leave fellow, 1982 Mem. Can. Asian Studies Assn. Office: McGill Univ Dept Polit Sci Montreal PQ Canada H3A 2T7 E-mail: baldev.nayar@mcgill.ca.

**NAYDAN, MICHAEL M.,** foreign language educator; b. Trenton, N.J., Oct. 20, 1952; s. William and Anna (Yaremko) N.; m. Roxanne Robak; 1 child Liliana Marika. BA magna cum laude, The American U., Washington, 1973, MA, 1975; MPh, Columbia U., 1980, PhD, 1984. Asst. prof. Yale U., New Haven, Conn., 1982-86; vis. assoc. prof. Rutgers U., New Brunswick, N.J., 1986-88; asst. prof. Pa. State U., Univ. Park, 1988-90, assoc. prof., 1990—. Gen. asst. Columbia U. Bakhmeteff Archive of Russian and East European History and Culture, 1979-81; adj. instr. Russian Rutgers U., Newark, 1982; preceptor and instr. Russian, Columbia Univ., 1980-82; acting instr. Russian Yale U., 1982-84; head of instruction Yale Russian and Slavic Summer Lang. Inst., 1984-86; panelist, lectr. on Russian and Slavic poets at convs. and meetings of nat. and internat. orgns. Translator: (books) The Poetry of Lina Kostenko: Wanderings of the Heart, 1990, Marina Tsvetaeva's After Russia, 1992, From Three Worlds: New Writing from Ukraine, 1996, Yuri Vynnyohuk's The Windows of Time Frozen and other Stories, 2000, Parlo Tychyna's The Complete Early Poetry Collections of Paulo Tychyna, 2000, A Hundred Years of Youth: A Bilingual Anthology of Ukranian Poetry, 2000, Landscapes of Memory: Selected Later Poetry of Lina Kostenko, 2002, Olga Sedakova's Poems and Elogies, 2003, Igor Klekh's A Country the Size of Binoculars, 2003, Yuri Andrukhovych's Perversion, 2003; contbr. articles and reviews to profl. jours. and encyclopedias, translations in book chpts., journals and periodicals; contbr. poetry to Monmouth Review, 1975, Poet Lore, 1977, Bitterroot, 1979; editor-in-chief Slavic and East European Journal, 1993-98; assoc. editor Comparative Literature Studies, 1990—; assoc. editor and co-founder Ulbandus Review: A Jour. of Slavic Langs. and Lits., 1977-84. Recipient Pushkin prize, 1975, 76, 81, Columbia U., Eugene Kayden Meritorious Achievement award in translation, U. Colo., 1993, Mihaly-Mogilat fellowship, Columbia U., 1979; grantee Schevchenko Scholarly Soc., 1980, Moore Fund, 1983-84, N.J. Dept Higher Edn., 1987-88 (2), Woskob Fellow in Humanities, Nat. Endowment for the Humanities, 1991-92, 95. Mem. Am. Assn. for Advancement of Slavic Studies, Am. Assn. Tchrs. of Slavic and East European Langs., Am. Assn. Ukranian Studies (v.p.), Phi Kappa Phi. Ukranian Catholic. Avocations: tennis, squash. Office: Pa State Univ Germanic andSlavic Studies Dept 311 Burrowes Bldg University Park PA 16802-5201

**NAYFEH, HASAN MUNIR,** research scientist; b. Munir Hasan Nayfeh and Hutaf Mahmoud Abu-Hantash-Nayfeh; m. Majd Fahim Jauhary, Aug. 2, 1998; children: Munir Hasan, Jana Hasan. PhD, MIT, Cambridge, Mass., 2003. Rsch. scientist, engr. IBM, Hopewell Junction, NY, 2000—. Contbr. articles to profl. jours. Recipient John Bardeen Scholarship award, Dept. of Def. fellowship. Achievements include patents pending for. Office: IBM Corp MS 42J 2070 Rte 52 Hopewell Junction NY 12533 Office Phone: 845-892-2376. Business E-Mail: nayfeh@us.ibm.com.

**NAYLON, MICHAEL EDWARD,** retired army officer; b. Rochester, N.Y., Jan. 15, 1943; s. Edward M. and Patricia (Brennan) N.; m. Beverly Marzano, Mar. 27, 1965; children: Michelle A. Faber, Colleen M. Burgos. BA, John Carroll U., 1965; MBA, Marymount U., 1986; grad., U.S. Army War Coll.,

1989. Indsl. rels. specialist Gen. Ry. Signal Co., Rochester, Farrell Co., Rochester; manpower adminstr. City of Rochester; employment mgr. U. Rochester; pers. dir. Interstate Brands Corp., Rochester; office mgr., dir. adminstrn., regional tng. coord. Nat. Machine Tool Builders Assn., McLean, Va.; chief US Army Res. Hdqs. Dept. of Army, Washington; staff officer Joint Chiefs of Staff, col., sr. res. advisor Dept. Def., Washington; with U.S. So. Command, Panama City, Panama; col. U.S. Army, ret. Dir. ops. Nat. Assn. Ret. Fed. Employees; nat. exec. dir. AMVETS; exec. dir. Presdl. Spl. Oversight Bd., Dept. Def. investigations of Gulf War chem. and biol. incidents; chief of staff Nat. Com. Employer Support of Guard and Res., Arlington, Va.; dep. dir. Office of Asst. Sec. of Def. for Res. Affairs, Pentagon, Washington. Mem. VFW, AMVETS, U.S. Army War Coll. Alumni Assn., John Carroll U. Alumni Assn., Res. Officers Assn. USA, Ret. Officers Assn., Am. Legion, Vietnam Vets. Home: 1434 Aldenham Ln Reston VA 20190-3901 E-mail: naylonmike@juno.com.

**NAYLOR, CRAIG G.,** engineering company executive; b. Media, Pa., Nov. 24, 1948; m. Sharon Jamison (dec.); 2 children. BE in Chem. Engring., Stevens Inst. Tech. Various chem. engring. positions Dupont, 1970—74, area supt. Teflon, 1977—79, project mgr. Teflon Wilmington, Del., 1979—81, product mgr. Teflon, 1981—83, customer svc. mgr. Polymer Products dept., 1983—84, devel. mgr. engring. polymer, 1984—85, devel. mgr. engring. polymers automotive Detroit, 1985—87, Asia Pacific regional dir. Tokyo, 1987—91, products dir. engring. polymers Wilmington, Del., 1991—92, Nylon resins bus. dir. Geneva, 1992—96, v.p., gen. mgr. engring. polymers, 1996—2000, group v.p., gen. mgr. engring. polymers, fluoroporucts and packagaing and indsl. polymers, 2000—02, group v.p. Performance Materials Wilmington, Del., 2002—. Office: DuPont DuPont Bldg 1007 Market St Wilmington DE 19898

**NAYLOR, JAMES CHARLES,** psychologist, educator; b. Chgo., Feb. 8, 1932; s. Joseph Sewell and Berniece (Berg) N.; m. Georgia Lou Mason, Feb. 14, 1953; children— Mary Denise, Diana Darice, Shari Dalice. BS, Purdue U., 1957, MS, 1958, PhD, 1960. Asst. prof. Ohio State U., 1960-63, asso. prof., 1963-67, prof. vice chmn. dept. psychology, 1967-68; prof. Purdue U., Lafayette, Ind., 1968-86, head dept. psychol. scis., 1968-79; prof., chmn. dept. psychology Ohio State U., Columbus, 1986-98, prof. emeritus, 1999—. Fulbright rsch. scholar, Umea, Sweden, 1976; Distng. scholar, vis. scientist Flinders U., South Australia, 1982-83, UNESCO ednl. cons. to Hangzhou U., Peoples Republic of China, 1984; chmn. Coun. Grad. Depts. Psychology, 1993-94; lead reviewer Psychology Program Rev. State U. Sys. Fla., 1996. Author: Industrial Psychology, 1968, A Theory of Behavior in Organizations, 1980; founder, editor: Organizational Behavior and Human Decision Processes; mem. editorial bd.: Prof. Psychology; Contbr. articles to profl. jours. Served with USN, 1950-54. Fellow AAAS, Am. Psychol. Soc., Am. Psychol. Assn.; mem. Psychonomic Soc., Psychmetric Soc., Internat. Assn. Applied Psychology, Soc. Organizational Behavior (founder), Midwestern Psychol. Assn. (coun. 1994-97), Phi Beta Kappa, Sigma Xi. Home: 176 Tucker Dr Columbus OH 43085-3064 Office: Ohio State U Dept Psychology Columbus OH 43210 E-mail: naylor.2@osu.edu.

**NAYLOR, JEFFREY GORDON,** retail executive; b. Montreal, Que., Can., Nov. 15, 1958; s. Gordon Charles and Patricia Grace (Pryde) N.; m. Shawn Elizabeth Baker, Oct. 6, 1984; 1 child, Madeleine Baker Naylor. BA in econs., Northwestern U., 1980, MBA, 1982. CPA, Ill. Pub. acct. Deloitte, Haskins & Sells, Chgo., 1982-86; assoc. N.Am. Venture Capital, Chgo., 1986-88; mgr. mergers and acquisitions A.C. Nielsen, Northbrook, Ill., 1988-90, dir. fin. analysis, 1990-91; dir. finance Kraft Foods Sales, Northfield, Ill., 1991-93, Kraft Foods Corp., Northfield, 1993-95; v.p. credit divsn. Sears Roebuck & Co., Hoffman Estates, Ill., 1995—; v.p. contr The LimitedInc; CFO, sen. v.p. fin. Dade Behring, Dearfield, Ill., 2000—01; sr. v.p., CFO Big Lots Inc., 2001—04; sr. exec. v.p., CFO TJX Cos. Inc., Framingham, Mass., 2004—. Prof. acctg. Keller Grad. Sch. Mgmt., Chgo., 1987-91. Treas. Episcopal Ch. of Northwestern U., Evanston, 1996—; mem. Brookfield Zoo, 1995—, Northwestern U. "N" Club, 1980—. Mem. AICPA, Ill. CPA Soc. Episcopalian. Avocations: swimming, gourmet cooking, reading, ice skating. Office: TJX Cos 770 Cochituate Rd Framingham MA 01701*

**NAYLOR, MAGDALENA RACZKOWSKA,** psychiatrist, educator; b. Warsaw, Aug. 4, 1950; arrived in U.S., 1981; d. Wlodzimierz Raczkowski and Urszula Raczkowska-Cieslik; m. Thomas Herbert Naylor, Dec. 14, 1985; 1 child, Alexander Watkins. MD, Warsaw Med. U., Poland, 1976, PhD, 1987. Diplomate psychiatry and neurology Nat. Bd. Certification in Psychiatry and Neurology, 1994. Asst. prof. Warsaw Med. U., 1977—83; rsch. assoc. Med. Coll. Va., Richmond, 1981—82; resident psychiatry Duke U., Durham, NC, 1984—88; pvt. practice psychiatry Richmond, Va., 1988—93; attending physician psychiatry Fletcher Allen Health Care, Burlington, Vt., 1993—; asst. prof. U. Vt., Burlington, 1993—99, assoc. prof., 1999—. Rsch. assoc. Med. Coll. Va., Richmond, Va., 1981—82; med. dir. women's program Psychiat. Inst. Richmond, Va., 1991—92; med. dir. partial hospitalization program Charter Westbrook Hosp., 1992—93; med. dir. psychiat. unit Fletcher Allen Health Care, Burlington, Vt., 1994—97; dir. mindbody medicine clinic U. Vt. Med./Flecher Allen Health Care, 1998—; assoc. dir. clin. neuroscience rsch. unit U. Vt. Med.; spkr. on search for meaning and integration of mind, body and spirit into med. practice. Author (with Thomas Naylor and William Willimon): The Search for Meaning, 1994, The Search for Meaning Workbook, 1994; contbr. articles to profl. jours. Com. mem. Vt. Pain & Symptom Mgmt. Com.; mem. Gailer Sch., Shelburn, Vt., 2001—03. Recipient Best Tchr. of Yr. Dept. of Psychiatry, U. Vt. Med. Sch., 1996, 1998; grantee, NIH, 2002, 2004, 2005, U. Vt. Med. Sch., 2004. Mem.: Am. Pain Soc., U. Vt. Med. Assn. Achievements include research in coping skills training for patients in chronic pain, obesity and chemical dependence. Home: 202 Stockbridge Rd Charlotte VT 05445 Office: U Vt UHC 1 S Prospect St Burlington VT 05401 Office Phone: 802-847-2673. Business E-Mail: magdalena.naylor@vtmednet.org.

**NAYLOR, MARY D.,** medical professor, director; BSN, Villanova U.; PhD, MSN, U. Penn. Assoc. dean, dir. undergrad. studies U. Penn. Sch. Nursing, Philadelphia, 1986—98, founder, dir. Living Independently for Elders (LIFE) program, 1998—; Marian S. Ware prof. gerontology; dir. RAND/Hartford Ctr. Inderdisciplinary Geriatric Health Care Rsch. U. Penn., Philadelphia. Named to Nat. Honor Soc. Nursing; recipient Lenore Williams award, U. Penn., Outstanding Alumni award, U. Penn. Sch. Nursing., Claire Fagin Disting. Rsch. award, U. Penn. Sch. Nursing, 2003, Disting. Lectr. award, Sigma Theta Tau, Pa. Nurses Assn. Nursing Rsch. award, Nightingale Award of Pa., McCann Scholar award, Joy McCann Found., 2004; Nat. Leadership Fellowship, W.K. Kellogg Found. Fellow: Leonard Davis Inst. Health Economics, Am. Heart Assn.; mem.: Inst. Medicine. Office: UPenn Sch Nursing Rm 364 NEB 420 Guardian Dr Philadelphia PA 19104-6069 Office Phone: 215-898-6088. E-mail: naylor@nursing.upenn.edu.*

**NAYLOR, PAUL DONALD,** retired lawyer; b. St. Bernard, Ohio, May 28, 1925; s. David Frederick and Erna Helen (Miller) N.; m. Geraldine L. Lacy, Jan. 20, 1945; children: Linda S., Paul Scott, Todd L. JD, U. Cin., 1948. Bar: Ohio 1948. Ptnr. Pulse & Naylor, Cin., 1949-65; pvt. practice Cin., 1965—2004; ret., 2004. Mem. Nat. Rep. Com. Lt. (j.g.) USN, 1943-46. Recipient Svc. to Mankind award Sertoma Internat. Mem. Cin. Bar Assn. (real property com. 1966-86), Ohio Bar Assn., Cin. Lawyers Club (pres. 1955), Order of the Coif. Home: 304 Amherst Ave Terrace Park OH 45174-1104

**NAYLOR, PHYLLIS REYNOLDS,** writer; b. Anderson, Ind., Jan. 4, 1933; d. Eugene Spencer and Lura Mae (Schield) Reynolds; m. Thomas A. Tedesco, Jr., Sept. 9, 1951 (div. 1960); m. Rex V. Naylor, May 26, 1960; children: Jeffrey, Michael. Diploma, Joliet Jr. Coll., 1953; BA, Am. U., 1963. Author more than 125 books including Crazy Love: An Autobiographical Account of Marriage and Madness, 1977, Revelations, 1979, A String of Chances, 1982 (ALA notable book), The Agony of Alice, 1985 (ALA notable book), The Keeper, 1986 (ALA notable book), Unexpected Pleasures, 1986, Send No Blessings, 1990 (YASD best book for young adults), Shiloh, 1991 (ALA notable book, John Newbery medal 1992), The Fear of Place, 1994, Sang Spell, 1998, Walker's Crossing, 1999, Blizzard's Wake, 2002, After, 2003. Recipient Golden Kite award Soc. Children's Book Writers Am., 1985, Child Study award Bank St. Coll., 1983, Edgar Allan Poe award Mystery Writers Am., 1985, 2004, Internat. book award Soc. Sch. Librs., 1988, Christopher award, 1989, Newbery award ALA, 1992, Nat. Endowment of Arts Creative Writing fellow, 1987. Mem.: PEN, Authors Guild, Soc. Children's Book Writers, Children's Book Guild of Washington (pres. 1974—75, 1983—84), Amnesty Internat., Physicians for Social Responsibility, Coun. for a Livable World. Unitarian Universalist. Avocations: theater, swimming. Home and Office: 9910 Holmhurst Rd Bethesda MD 20817-1618 Office Phone: 301-530-2340.

**NAYLOR, THOMAS HERBERT,** economist, educator, consultant; b. Jackson, Miss., May 30, 1936; s. Thomas Hector and Martha (Watkins) N.; m. Magdalena Raczkowska, Dec. 14, 1985; children: Susanne, Alexander. BS in Math., Millsaps Coll., 1958; BS in Indsl. Engring., Columbia U., 1959; MBA in Quantitative Bus. Analysis, Ind. U., 1961; PhD in Econs., Tulane U., 1964. Instr. Sch. Bus. Adminstrn. Tulane U., 1961-63; asst. prof. econs. Duke U., 1964-66, assoc. prof. econs., 1966-68, prof. econs., 1968-93, prof. emeritus econs., 1994—. Vis. prof. U. Wis., 1969-70, Middlebury Coll., 1993-94, U. Vt., 1994-96; pres. Social Systems, Inc., 1971-80; mng. dir. Naylor Group, 1980; cons., lectr. in over 30 countries. Co-author: (with Eugene Byrne) Linear Programming, 1963, (with Joseph L. Balintfy, Donald S. Burdick and Kong Chu) Computer Simulation Techniques, 1966, translated into Japanese, Portuguese and Spanish, (with John Vernon) Microeconomics and Decision Models of the Firm, 1969, translated into Spanish, (with James Clotfelter) Strategies for Change in the South, 1975, (with John M. Vernon and Kenneth Wertz) Managerial Economics: Corporate Economics and Strategy, 1983, (with William H. Willimon) The Abandoned Generation: Rethinking Higher Education, 1995, Downsizing the U.S.A., 1997, (with Rolf Österberg and William H. Willimon) The Search for Meaning in the Workplace, 1996, others; author or co-author of 30 books including: Computer Simulation Experiments with Models of Economic Systems, 1971, translated into Spanish, Polish, and Russian, Corporate Planning Models, 1979, Strategic Planning Management, 1980, The Corporate Strategy Matrix, 1986, translated into Hungarian, The Gorbachev Strategy, 1988, The Cold War Legacy, 1991, (with William H. Willimon and Magdalena R. Naylor), The Search for Meaning, 1994; editor: The Impact of the Computer on Society, 1967, The Design of Computer Simulation Experiments, 1969, The Politics of Corporate Planning and Modeling, 1978, Simulation Models in Corporate Planning, 1979, Simulation in Business Planning and Decision Making, 1981, others; co-editor: (with H. Brandt Ayers) You Can't Eat Magnolias, 1972, (with Michele H. Mann) Portfolio Planning and Corporate Strategy, 1983, (with Celia Thomas) Optimization Models for Strategic Planning, 1984, (with John DeGraff and David Wann) Affluenza, 2001, translated into French, German, Japanese and other langs., The Vermont Manifesto, 2003, others; contbr. numerous articles to profl. publs.; mem. editl. bd. jours. Exec. dir., founder L.Q.C. Lamar Soc., Washington, 1969-73; founder Second Vt. Republic, 2003. Named to Lambda Chi Alpha Alumni Hall of Fame, 1996. Mem.: Beta Gamma Sigma, Omicron Delta Kappa. Home: 202 Stockbridge Rd Charlotte VT 05445-9358 Office Phone: 802-425-4133. E-mail: info@vermontrepublic.org.

**NAZAIRE, MICHEL HARRY,** physician; b. Jérémie, Haiti, Sept. 29, 1939; s. Joseph and Hermance Nazaire; m. Nicole Lamarque, Dec. 28, 1968; children: Hannick, Carline. BS, DOE, Port-Au-Prince, Haiti, 1959; MD Faculty of Medicine and Pharmacology, State U. Haiti, 1966. Intern State U. Hosp., Port-Au-Prince, Haiti, 1965-66; resident physician Sanitarium, Port-Au-Prince, Haiti, 1966-68; physician pneumology, 1966-68; physician pneumo-phtisiology Port-Au-Prince, 1966—; fellow Klinik Havelhohe and Heckeshorn, Berlin, 1970-70, 89-91; attending physician Sanitarium, Port-Au-Prince, 1976-91. Dep. mem. Internat. Parliament for Safety and Peace, envoy-at-large Internat. State Parliament, mem. global environ. technol. network WHO. Contbr. articles to profl. jours. Recipient Physician's Recognition award, Am. Med. Assn., 2002, AMA, 2002, 2005. Fellow Internat. Soc. for Respiratory Protection, Am. Coll. Chest Physicians (assoc.); mem. AMA (Physician's Recognition award 2002), APHA, Am. Conf. Govtl. Indsl. Hygienists, Internat. Union Against Tb, Internat. Platform Assn., Physicians for Social Responsibility, European Respiratory Soc. Address: 12 B St NE Apt 103 Auburn WA 98002 Home Fax: 253-333-6520. E-mail: michharnazamed@earthlink.net.

**NAZARETH, ANNETTE LAPORTE,** commissioner, lawyer; b. Providence, Jan. 27, 1956; d. George Robert and Dolores (LaPorte) Nazareth; m. Roger Walton Fergunson, May 3, 1986; 2 children. AB magna cum laude, Brown U., 1978; JD, Columbia U., 1981. Assoc. Davis Polk & Wardwell, NYC, 1981-86; gen. ptnr., gen. counsel Mabon, Nugent & Co., NYC, 1986-91; mng. dir., gen. counsel Mabon Securities Corp., NYC, 1991—94; sr. v.p. Lehman Brothers, Inc., NYC, 1994—97; mng. dir., dep. head Salomon Smith Barney, NYC, 1997—98; sr. counsel to chmn. SEC, Washington, 1998—99, acting dir., Divsn. Investment Mgmt., dir., Divsn. Mkt. Regulation, 1999—2005, commr., 2005—. Mem.: Securities Industry Assn., Phi Beta Kappa. Office: SEC 100 F St NE Washington DC 20549 Office Phone: 202-551-6551.

**NAZARIAN, LAWRENCE FRED,** pediatrician; b. N.Y.C., May 17, 1940; s. Samuel George and Winifred Lucia (Zotian) N.; m. Sharon Louise Carlson, June 22, 1963; children: Douglas, Stephen, Sarah. BA, Yale U., 1960; MD, U. Rochester, 1964. Cert. Am. Bd. Pediatrics 1970. Pediatrician Panorama Pediatric Group, Rochester, NY, 1969—2004; clin. prof. pediatrics U. Rochester Sch. Medicine and Dentistry, 1969—. Bd. dirs. James P. Wilmot Found., Rochester. Assoc. editor Pediatrics in Rev. Jour., 1990-2004, editor-in-chief, 2005-; contbr. articles to profl. jours. Mem. troop com. Boy Scouts Am., Penfield, N.Y., 1978-88; mem. coun. com. Luth. Ch. of Reformation, Rochester, 1999—. Maj. USAR, 1967-69. Recipient Nat. Pediatric Tchg. award, Ambulatory Pediatric Assn., 2002. Fellow Am. Acad. Pediatrics; mem. Med. Soc. State of N.Y., Ctrl. N.Y. Pediatric Club, Monroe County Med. Soc., Rochester Acad. Medicine, Rochester Pediatric Soc. Avocations: hiking, camping, canoeing, gardening, cross country skiing. Office: U Rochester Med Ctr 601 Elmwood Ave Box 777 Rochester NY 14642 Office Phone: 585-275-0225.

**NAZARYAN, HOVAKIM,** mathematician, researcher; arrived in U.S., 2000; s. Roland and Eli Nazaryan. M in Math., Yerevan State U., 1994; PhD in Math., Yerevan State U., Byurakan Astrophysy. Obs., 1998. Postdoctoral position U. of Padua, Italy, 1999—2001; postdoctoral rsch. fellow Hampton (Va.) U., 2003—. Contbr. articles to profl. jours. Mem.: Am. Geophys. Union. Office: Hampton U 23 Tyler St Hampton VA 23668 Office Phone: 757-728-6368.

**NAZEM, FARZAD,** information technology executive; BS in Computer sci., Calif. Polytechnic State. Various tech. positions Sydis, Inc., Rolm Corp.; v.p., media and web server divsn. Oracle Corp., Redwood Shores, Calif.; exec. v.p. engring. and surfing Yahoo! Inc., Sunnyvale, Calif., 1996, chief tech. officer, 1997—. Office: Yahoo! Inc 701 First Ave Sunnyvale CA 94089 Office Phone: 408-349-3300. Office Fax: 408-349-3301.*

**NAZEM, FEREYDOUN F.,** venture capitalist, entrepreneur; b. Tehran, Iran, Dec. 29, 1940; came to US, 1960; naturalized, 1976; s. Hassan and Afsar N.; m. Susie Gharib, Jan. 20, 1973; children: Alexander, Taraneh. BS, Ohio State U., 1964; MSc, U. Cin., 1967; MBA, Columbia U., 1971. Sr. rsch. chemist Matheson Coleman & Bell, Norwood, Ohio, 1967-68; asst. v.p. investment analyst Irving Trust Co., NYC, 1969-74; v.p., venture capital officer Charter NY, NYC, 1974-75; mng. dir. Collier Enterprises, NYC, 1976-81; mng. ptnr. Nazem & Co. I, II, III and IV, NYC, 1981—; Explorer Fund, NYC, 1997—; Transatlantic Venture Fund, 1998—, Hedgeworth, L.L.C., NYC, 2003—; founder, chmn., CEO Flagship Healthcare Mgmt., NYC, 2004—. Bd. dirs. ETRIALS, Carey, NC, Netfabric Corp., New Milford, Conn. Author: The Chemical Industry and Energy Shortage, Hedgeworth Market Letter. Office:

---

Nazem & Co 645 Madison Ave New York NY 10022-1010 Office Phone: 212-340-9110. Business E-Mail: ffn@nazem.com. *You can have success and serenity at the same time. Become a possibilitarian- spend time solving problems, not worrying about them.*

**NAZEMETZ, PATRICIA,** human resources specialist; BA, MA, Fordham U. Benefits analyst W.R. Grace and Co.; various positions in human resources including benefits ops. mgr. Xerox Corp., Stamford, Conn., 1979—99, v.p. human resources, 1999—. Bd. dirs., chair human resources com. Nat. Bus. Group Health and Human Svcs., Long Island; trustee, vice-chmn. bd. Fordham U. Office: Xerox Corp 800 Long Ridge Rd Stamford CT 06904 Office Phone: 203-968-3000. Office Fax: 203-968-3218.

**NAZETTE, RICHARD FOLLETT,** lawyer; b. Eldora, Iowa, July 27, 1919; s. Hilmer H. and Genevieve A. (Follett) N.; m. Joan Chekak, June 20, 1942; children— Ronald D., Randall A. BA, U. Iowa, 1942, JD with distinction, 1946. Bar: Iowa bar 1946. Practiced in, Cedar Rapids, 1946—; partner firm Nazette, Marner, Wendt, Knoll & Usher, 1968—; asst. atty. Linn County, Iowa, 1951-56; county atty., 1957-63. Dir. United States Bank, Cedar Rapids, 1968-91, State Surety Co., Des Moines, 1966-78 Bd. dirs. Linn County Health Center, 1968-73, chmn., 1968-69; mem. Iowa Bd. Parole, 1981-84. Served with AUS, 1942-44. Fellow Am. Bar Found., Iowa Bar Assn. (bd. govs. 1972-76), Iowa State Bar Found.; mem. Linn County Bar Assn. (pres. 1963), Iowa County Attys. Assn. (pres. 1959), Iowa Acad. Trial Lawyers (pres. 1964), Masons (33rd degree Scottish Rite), Shriners, Jesters, Elks, Optimists (internat. v.p. 1955), Sigma Phi Epsilon. Republican. Presbyterian. Office: 100 1st St SW Cedar Rapids IA 52404-5701 Office Phone: 319-364-0124. Business E-Mail: rfnazette@nazmar.com.

**NEAL, A. MICHAEL,** utilities executive; BS, Ga. Inst. Tech., 1975. V.p., gen. mgr. Vendor Fin. Svcs. G.E. Capital, 1987—90, gen. mgr., Comml. Equip. Financing, 1990—94; sr. v.p. G.E. Co., 1993—; exec. v.p. G.E. Captial, 1994—2000; pres., COO G.E. Capital, 2000—02; pres., CEO G.E. Comml. Fin., 2002—. Mem. adv. bd. European Inst. Bus. Adminstrn. Bd. trustees Fairfield U.; trustee Ga. Tech. Found.; chmn. GE Capital United Way campaign. Office: GE Commercial Fin 260 Long Ridge Rd Stamford CT 06927

**NEAL, CAROLE ELKINS,** music educator; b. San Angelo, Tex., May 7, 1941; d. Wilson Homer and Dorothy (Blackburn) Elkins; children: Jay Garrison, Heather Neal Weitzel. BS, U. Md., 1963. Tchr. Prince Georges Co., Hyattsville, Md., 1963—64, Balt. Co., Towson, Md., 1964—65, McDonogh Sch., Balt., 1965—66; piano tchr. self employed, U. Pk., Md., 1973—2003; svc. mgr. Scan Furniture, Georgetown, DC, 1980—82; asst. to asst. athletic dir. U. Md., Coll. Pk., Md., 1984—86, asst. music summer programs, 1994—97. ESL tchr. Luth. Ch., Rehoboth, Del., 2004—; piano judge Am. Coll. of Musicians, 1995—. Vol. tchr. Concordia Luth. Sch., Hyattsville, Md., 1974—80; pres. Greater Laurel Music Tchrs. Assn. Mem.: Md. State Music Tchrs., Am. Assn. of Piano Tchrs., Paint Branch Garden Club. Avocations: gardening, tennis, golf, kayaking, horseback riding. Home: 2 Margate Ct Lewes DE 19958 E-mail: caroleneal@aol.com.

**NEAL, DARWINA LEE,** federal agency administrator; b. Mansfield, Pa., Mar. 31, 1942; d. Darwin Leonard and Ina Belle (Cooke) N. BS, Pa. State U., 1965; postgrad., Cath. U, 1968-70. Registered landscape architect. Landscape architect nat. capital region Nat. Pk. Svc., 1965-69, office of White House liaison, 1969-71, office of profl. services, 1971-74, div. design svcs., 1974-89, chief design svcs., 1989-95, chief landscape arch. office of stewardship and partnership Washington, 1996-98, chief cultural resource preservation svcs. nat. capital reg., 1998—. Judge numerous award juries. Contbr. articles to profl. jours.; co-author sects. of profl. bull., mag.; author introduction to book Women, Design and the Cambridge School; columnist: Land monthly, 1975-79. Recipient Merit award Landscape Contractors Met. Washington; recipient hon. mention Les Floralies Internat. Montreal, 1980 Alumni Achievement award Pa. State U. Arts and Architecture Alumni Soc., 1981 Fellow Am. Soc. Landscape Architects (v.p. 1979-81, pres. elect 1982-83, pres. 1983-84, trustee 1976-77, nat. treas. 1977-79, legis. coord. 1975-79, sec. Coun. Fellows 1988-90, del. to Internat. Fedn. Landscape Architects 1989-92, 00-03, ex-officio rep. to U.S./internat. coun. on monuments and sites 1985-98, liaison to historically black coll. and univ. program Dept. Interior, chair internat. task force 1999-00, Pres.' medal 1987), U.S. Internat. Coun. on Monuments and Sites (treas. 1998-04, trustee 2004—), Internat. Fed. Landscape Architects (sec. West Region, 2003-06, v.p. 2006—); mem. Landscape Archtl. Accreditation Bd. (roster vis. evaluators), Nat. Recreation and Parks Assn., Nat. Soc. Park Resources (bd. dirs. 1978-80), Nat. Trust Hist. Preservation, Pa. State U. Alumni Assn. (Washington met. chpt. trustee 1972-74), Am. Arbitration Assn. (nat. panel arbitrators), Com. 100 for the Fed. City, Preservation Action, Nat. Assn. Olmsted Parks, Beekman Pl. Condominium Assn. (bd. dirs. 1985-91, archtl. control com. 1977-00, landscape com. 2000-02), Alliance for Historic Preservation, Garden Conservancy, Scenic Am., Preservation Action, Preservation Roundtable, Hist. Soc. Washington Office: Nat Park Svc/Nat Capital Region Off Lands Resources & Plan 1100 Ohio Dr SW Washington DC 20242-0001

**NEAL, DENNIS MELTON,** elementary school educator; b. Lakeland, Fla., Feb. 7, 1966; s. M. H. and Alice Marie (Twiddy) N.; m. Christine Anne Rufo, Oct. 21, 1989; children: Lauren Elizabeth, Waverly Rose, Emma Katherine. AA, Polk C.C., Winter Haven, Fla., 1987; BS, Fla. So. Coll., 1991; MEd, Stetson U., 1995. Cert. elem. tchr., ednl. leader, prin., Fla. Guest svcs. Cypress gardens, Winter Haven, 1985-86; entertainer Boardwalk and Baseball, Baseball City, Fla., 1986-88; guest svcs. Hilton Walt Disney World, Orlando, Fla., 1988-91; tchr. Deltona (Fla.) Middle Sch., 1991-95, asst. prin., 1995-99, Heritage Middle Sch., Deltona, Fla., 1999-2000; prin. intern Pine Ridge H.S., 2000—. Chair correlate com., team leader Deltona Middle Sch., sch. adv. coun. Tchr. Lith. Ch. of Providence, Orange City, Fla., 1992-93; active Parent, Tchr., Student Assn. Named One of Top 100 Beginning Tchrs. in Nation, Sallie Mae Student Loan Assn., 1992. Avocations: soccer, racquetball, drawing, painting.

**NEAL, ELAINE ZIRLI,** health products executive; Cert. Coun. Certification IRB Profls., 2000; film N.Y.U., 1994. Sec. dept. physiology and biophysics Weill Med. Coll., Cornell U., N.Y.C., 1982—88; asst. to pres., CEO Bio-Technology Gen. Corp. (Savient Pharmaceuticals, Inc.), 1988—93; spl. projects coord., grants adminstrn. & rsch. svcs. N.Y.U. Sch. Medicine, 1994—95; asst. instl. rev. bd. North Shore-Long Island Health Sys., Manhasset, 1996—99, mgr. instl. rev. bd., 1999—2000, asst. dir. instl. rev. bd. Lake Success, 2001—. Awards steering com. Health Improvement Inst./U.S. HHS Office Human Rsch. Protections Award Excellence Human Rsch. Protection Program, Bethesda, 2003—, award panel judge, best practice, 2002—03, award criteria reviewer, 2002—03; moderator U.S. DHHS Office Rsch. Protections/U.S. FDA/Dept. VA/North Shore-LIJ Health Sys. Nat. Workshop Protecting Human Subjects: Whose Responsibility is it, Anyway?, Garden City, NY, 2002. Contbr. chapters to books. Bd. mem. Cmty. Bd. No. 11, Coun. of City of NY, 1996—98; mem. Little Neck/Douglaston Meml. Day Parade Com., 1995—96; mentor ARENA, 2005—; Andreas Zahler scholar Advanced Filmmaking Intensive, N.Y.U., 1994. Mem.: AAAS, Soc Rsch. Adminstrs., Applied Rsch. Ethics Nat. Assn., Pub. Responsibility Medicine and Rsch., Am. Soc. Bioethics and Humanities, Soc. Clin. Rsch. Assocs., Assn. Clin. Rsch. Profls., Am. Soc. Law, Medicine and Ethics, N.Y. Acad. Scis. Conservative. Achievements include research in NIH Natl. Ctr. for Research Resources Grant Awards for Improvements in Human Research Protections: IRB Oversight and Educational Enhancement Program (2002), Human Subjects Enhancement Program (2003). Office: North Shore-LIJ Health Sys 5 Dakota Dr Ste 307 New Hyde Park NY 11042 E-mail: elaine@nshs.edu.

**NEAL, GAIL FALLON,** physical therapist, educator; b. New Haven, May 6, 1938; d. Edward Francis and Ruth Alexina (Hutchinson) Fallon; m. Marcus Pinson Neal Jr.; children: Sandra Neal Dawson, Marcus Pinson III, Ruth-

---

Catherine Neal Perkins. Student, Mary Washington Coll., 1955-57; BS in Phys. Therapy, Med. Coll. Va., 1959. Lic. phys. therapist. Staff phys. therpist Univ. Hosps., U. Wis., Madison, 1959-61; chief phys. therapy Stoughton (Wis.) Cmty. Hosp., 1961-63; vol. phys. therapy Cerebral Palsy Ctr., Richmond, Va., 1963-64; pvt. practice Richmond, 1965—68; interim dir. Stuart Cir. Hosp., Richmond, 1968-69; phys. therpist on call St. Mary's Hosp., Richmond, 1968-74; pres., owner Capital Phys. Therapy Assocs., Richmond, 1989—. Phys. therapist St. Mary's Hosp., Richmond 1975-88; lectr. Med. Coll. Va., Richmond, 1992-93, John Tyler C.C., Richmond, 1992-94; adv. bd. phys. therapy Va. State Bd. Medicine, 1990-96, vice chmn., 1992-93, chmn. 1995-96. Adv. bd. Va. Opera, 1979—; bd. visitors Mary Washington Coll., Fredericksburg, Va., 1980-82, rector bd. visitors, 1982-84; pres. Richmond Symphony Orch. League, 1986-88. Named Clubwoman of Yr., Richmond Newsleader, 1972. Mem. Am. Phys. Therapy Assn., Richmond Acad. Medicine Aux. (pres. 1967-68), Med. Soc. Va. Alliance (pres. 1980-81), Med. Coll. Va. Hosps. Aux. (pres. 1973-75), Va. Cultural Laureate Soc. Avocations: reading, music, skiing, indian folklore. Home: Pony Bluffs 7301 Riverside Dr Richmond VA 23225-1066 Office: Capital Phys Therapy Assocs Stratford Hills Pony Bluffs Richmond VA 23225 Personal E-mail: gfncpta@hotmail.com.

**NEAL, HOMER ALFRED,** physics professor, researcher, academic administrator; b. Franklin, Ky., June 13, 1942; s. Homer and Margaret Elizabeth (Holland) Neal; m. Donna Jean Daniels, June 16, 1962; children: Sharon Denise, Homer Alfred Jr. BS in Physics with honors, Ind. U., 1961; MS in Physics (John Hay Whitney fellow), U. Mich., 1963, PhD in Physics, 1966. Asst. prof. physics Ind. U., 1967—70, assoc. prof., 1970—72, prof., 1972—81, dean research and grad. devel., 1976—81; prof. physics SUNY, Stony Brook, 1981—87, provost, 1981—86; prof. physics, chmn. U. Mich., Ann Arbor, 1987—93, v.p. rsch., 1993—97, interim pres., 1996—97, prof. of physics, 1987—2000, Samuel A. Goudsmit disting. prof. physics, 2000—, dir. of atlas project, 1997—. Bd. dirs. Ford Motor Co.; mem. Nat. Sci. Bd. 1980—86; mem. adv. coun. Oak Ridge Nat. Lab., 1993—99; mem. external adv. coun. Nat. Computational Sci. Alliance, 1997—; mem. applications strategy coun. Univ. Corp. for Advanced Internet Devel., 2000—; chmn. Argonne Zero Gradient Synchrotron Users Group, 1970—72; trustee Argonne Univs. Assn., 1971—74, 1977—80; physics adv. panel NSF, 1976—79, chmn. physics adv. panel, 1987—89; high energy physics adv. panel U.S. Dept. Energy, 1977—81. Contbr. articles to profl. jours. Mem. bd. regents Smithsonian Instn., 1989—2001; trustee Ctr. for Strategic and Internat. Studies, 1990—2000, Oak Ridge Nat. Lab., Tenn., 1993—99; mem. Smithsonian Coun. on the Nat. Mus. African Am. History and Culture, 2004—; mem. bd. overseers Superconducting Super Collider, 1989—93; trustee Environ. Rsch. Inst. of Mich., 1994—96, Lounsbery Found., 2005—, NY Sea Grant Inst., 1982—86. Recipient Stony Brook medal, 1986, Ind. U. Disting. Alumni award, 1994; fellow NSF, 1966—67, Sloan, 1968, Guggenheim, 1980—81. Fellow: AAAS, Am. Acad. Arts and Scis., Am. Phys. Soc.; mem.: Univs. Rsch. Assn. (trustee), Sigma Xi. Office: Dept Physics Rm 2477 Randall Lab 450 Church St Ann Arbor MI 48109-1040

**NEAL, IRENE COLLINS,** artist, educator; b. Greensburg, Pa., May 14, 1936; d. Oliver Shupe and Betsey Cowap (Mann) Collins; m. Paul Whitaker Neal, Nov. 24, 1960; children: Paul Collins Gordon, Betsey Whitaker. BA, Wilson Coll., Chambersburg, Pa., 1958; student, Sch. Visual Arts, Rio de Janeiro, 1976-77, Memphis Sate U., Tenn., 1979-80, U. Bridgeport, Conn., 1982-83; participant, Triangle Art Workshop, Pine Plains, N.Y., 1985. Guest spkr. Coll. Santa Fe, Albuquerque, 1994. One-woman shows include Allied Chem. Corp., Morristown, NJ, 1975, Planetarium Rio de Janeiro, 1977, Pat Ackerman Gallery, Memphis, 1980, Westmoreland Mus. Art, Greensburg, 1986, Wilson Coll., 1993, Cooper Classics Collections, NYC, 2001-02, Trans-Lux Cocteau Corp., Irene Neal Recent Paintings, Santa Fe, N.M., 2003; group exhbns. include Jersey City Mus., 1975, NJ State Mus., 1975, Somerset (NJ) Tri-State Mus., 1975, Nat. Arts Club, NYC, 1975, Garden State Watercolor Soc., 1975, Salao de Marinhas, Rio de Janeiro, 1977, Stamford Mus., 1984-85, 89, Branchville Soho Gallery, Ridgefield, Conn., 1984, Silvermine Guild, New Canaan, Conn., 1984, Stamford Libr., 1985, Shippee Gallery, NYC, 1986, 110 Greene St., NYC, 1986, Wilton (Conn.) Libr., 1986, Aldrich Mus. Contemporary Art, Ridgefield, 1987, Visual Arts Festival, Edmonton, Alta., Can., 1989, Mus. Art., Ft. Lauderdale, Fla., 1991-92, Salander-O'Reilly Galleries, Inc., NY, 1994, Vanderleelie Gallery, Edmonton, 1996, Galerie Piltzer, Paris, 1996, Fine Art 2000 Gallery, Stamford, 1996-97, York Coll., Queens, NY, 1997, Ctr. for Performing Arts, Stamford, 1997, Mus. Contemporary Art, Palm Beach, Fla., 1997, Griffis Art Ctr., New London, 1997, Vero Beach (Fla.) Mus., 1998, Flint (Mich.) Inst. Art, 1999, Mus. Contemporary Art, Denver, 1999, Gelabert Studios Gallery, NYC, 2000, Hotel de Ville, Brussels, 2000, 69th Regiment Armory, NYC, New New Painters, Real Avant Garde, 2000, Nat. Gallery, Prague, The Czech Repub., 2001-02 Galerie Anne-Lettrie, Paris, 2001, Durst Orgn., NYC, 2002-03, Musee du Bas-Saint Laurant Riviere de Lupe, Que., Can., 2002-03, Scope NY Stevenson Fine Art, Dylan Hotel, NYC, 2003, Mus. au Bus, St. Laurant, Que., 2003, Elfsar Collection, Ltd., Vancouver, BC, 2003, Juten Gallery, Toronto, 2003, Anew Found., Ft. Lauderdale, Fla., 2004, Westport (Conn.) Arts Ctr, 2004, Realtra, Cork, Ireland, 2005, Lurie Gallery, Miami, 2005, Pthalo Gallery, Miami, 2005, Diane Birdsall Gallery, Old Lyme, Conn., 2005, Troy Gallery, Stamford, Conn., 2005-06, A.N.E.W Found;., Ft. Lauderdale, Lurie Gallery, Miami, Pthalo Gallery, Miami, Diane Birdsall Gllery, Lyme, Conn., Troy Gallery, Stamford, Lurie Gallery, L.A., Miami, 2006, Diane Birdsall Gallery, 2006, A New Found. for the Arts, 2006; represented in permanent collections Planetarium Rio de Janeiro, Internat. Paper, NYC, Westmoreland Mus. Art, Greensburg, Pa., Pepperdine U., Malibu, Calif., Newport Harbor Art Mus., Newport Beach, Calif., Hoover Instn. Stanford U., St. Matthew's Episcopal Ch., Wilton, Columbia U., Ctr. Arts, Vero Beach, Fla., Mus. Art, Ft. Lauderdale, Alamo Rent A Car, Ft. Lauderdale, Denver Ctr. Performing Arts, Flint (Mich.) Inst. Art, Nat. Gallery, Prague, The Czech Rep., Wilson Coll., Chambersburg, Pa., The Appleton Mus. Art, Ocala, Fla., Nat. Mus. of Women in the Arts; pub., contbr. art to book New New Painting, 1996, catalog, 2000, Cooper Classics Collection, 2001-02; painting illustrated in Vicky Perry's book: Concepts and Techniques. Recipient Tift award, Wilson Coll., Chambersburg, Pa., 2003. Republican. Episcopalian. Avocations: ocean diving, tennis, golf, gardening. Home: 98 Maple Ave Old Saybrook CT 06475 Office Phone: 860-388-9291. Personal E-mail: icneal@aol.com.

**NEAL, JAMES G.,** librarian; BA in Russian Studies, Rutgers U., 1969; MS in Libr. Sci., Columbia U., 1972, MA in History, 1973, cert. in Advanced Librarianship. Social sciences libr. Queensborough Cmty. Coll., CUNY, 1973—76; head collection develop. dept. U. Notre Dame, 1977—79, head collection mgmt. dept., 1979—82, asst. dir. pub. services, 1982—83; asst. dean & head reference Pa. State U. Libraries, 1983—89; dean univ. libraries Ind. U., 1989—95; Sheridan Dir. Milton S. Eisenhower Libr. Johns Hopkins U., 1995—2001, dean libraries, 1999—2001; v.p. info. services & univ. libr. Columbia U., NYC, 2001—. Bd. dirs. Nat. Info. Standards Orgn.; chair bd. dirs. Rsch. Libraries Group; chair steering com. Scholarly Pub. and Academic Resources Coalition. Named Academic/Rsch. Libr. of Year, Assn. Coll. and Rsch. Libraries, ALA, 1997. Office: Columbia U 517 Butler Libr 535 W 114th St New York NY 10027 Office Phone: 212-854-2247. Business E-Mail: jneal@columbia.edu.*

**NEAL, JAMES PRESTON,** state senator, project engineer; b. Cin., July 1, 1935; s. James Preston and Desha Frank (Thompson) N.; m. Nancy Joan Tyner, June 11, 1961; children: Leslie Neal Driscoll, Karen Desha, James P. BSME, U. Ill., 1960. Registered profl. engr., Del. Project engr. DuPont Co., 1960-92; dir. Tetra Tech Inc., Christiana, Del., 1992-95; pres. Tech. Mgmt., 1994—2001. Mem. Del. Ho. of Reps., 1978-80; mem. Del. Senate, 1980-94, trustee U. Del., 2002—. Patentee in field. Councilman City of Newark, 1973-78; elder Presbyn. Ch.; bd. dirs. Christina Conservancy, 2004—; mem. Gov.'s Task Force on Sch. Librs., 2003—. With U.S. Army, 1954-56. Recipient Disting. Svc. award Forum to Advance Minorities in Engring., 1989, Disting. Svc. citation Del. Libr. Assn., 1994, Appreciation award Del. Autistic Program, 1999. Mem. Am. Legis. Exch. Coun. (sr. fellow, nat. officer 1991-94, Outstanding Leader 1989, Outstanding Legis. mem. 1994), Del.

Engring. Soc. (Engr. of Yr. 1989), Del. Acad. Scis. (bd. dirs. 1996—) Republican. Presbyterian. Avocations: photography, reading. Home and Office: 50 Bridlebrook Ln Newark DE 19711-2061

**NEAL, JOAN BURKES,** librarian; b. Phenix City, Ala., Feb. 27, 1928; d. George Ashby and Maybelle Ethel (Barnes) Burkes; m. Charles A. Land, May 25, 1944 (dec. Sept. 1947); 1 child, Jo Sandra Land; m. Ray Verlin Neal, Dec. 25, 1952 (dec. May 8, 1996); children: Jo Griffeth, J. Kim, Roger Verlin, Kathy Brown. BS in Edn., U. Ga., 1951, postgrad., 1966. Dir. kindergarten Fayetteville (Ga.) First Bapt. Ch., 1958-63; tchr. 3d grade Fayetteville Elem. Sch., 1964-67, libr., 1967—91. Bd. dirs. Atlanta PTA, 1977-80; spkr. Silver Haired Legis. Mem. Ga. State Dem. Party, Atlanta, 1977—; sec. ARC, Fayetteville, 1979-83; pres. Band and Athletic Boosters, Fayetteville, 1968-70. Mem. Fayette County Assn. Educators (pres., v.p., sec. 1963—), Ga. Assn. Educators (governing bd. Atlanta chpt. 1976-79, legis. chair 1981, 83), Fayette County Bus. and Profl. Women (pres. 1976-78, treas., sec.), Kappa Kappa Iota (pres. Fayetteville chpt. 1970-72). Avocations: reading, golf, politics, walking. Home: 432 Forrest Ave Fayetteville GA 30214-1327 E-mail: joann2271@bellsouth.net.

**NEAL, LEORA LOUISE HASKETT,** social services administrator; b. N.Y.C., Feb. 23, 1943; d. Melvin Elias and Miriam Emily (Johnson) Haskett; m. Robert A. Neal, Apr. 23, 1966; children: Marla Patrice, Johnathan Robert. BA in Psychology and Sociology, City Coll. N.Y., 1965; MS in Social Work, Columbia U., 1970, cert. adoption specialist, 1977; IBM cert. community exec. tng. program, N.Y., 1982. Cert. master social worker N.Y., lic. clin. social worker, lic. master social worker, N.Y.; cert. social worker, N.Y. Caseworker N.Y.C. Dept. Social Service, 1965-67, Windham Child Care, N.Y.C., 1967-73; exec. dir., founder Assn. Black Social Workers Child Adoption Counseling and Referral Service, N.Y.C., 1975-96; adoption tng. specialist cert. for Devel. Human Svcs., SUNY-N.Y. State Office Children and Family Svcs., Yonkers, 1996—. Cons. in field; founder Haskett-Neal Publs., Bronx, N.Y., 1993. Co-author: Transracial Adoptive Parenting: A Black/White Community Issue, 1993; contbr. articles to profl. jours. Pres. bd. dirs. Fountain Ave. Cmty. Devel. Corp. Child Welfare League Am. fellow, 1976; recipient cert. No Time to Lose cert. N.Y. State Dept. Social Svcs., 1989, Pyramid award NY Assn Black Social Workers, 2005. Mem. NAFE, Nat. Assn. Black Social Workers (Pyramid Outstanding Cmty. Svc. award), Columbia U. Alumni Assn., CCNY Alumni Assn., Missionary Com. Revival Team (outreach chair 1982-88). Democrat. Avocations: writing, religious studies, travel, cultural activities, history. Office: NY State Office of Children and Family Svcs SUNY 525 Nepperhan Ave Yonkers NY 10703-2857 Office Phone: 914-377-2079.

**NEAL, MICHAEL A.,** corporate financial executive; BS, Ga. Inst. Tech., 1975. With General Electric Co., 1979—; v.p. & gen. mgr., vendor fin. svcs. GE Capital, 1987—90, gen. mgr., comml. equip. financing, 1990—94, exec. v.p., 1994—99, pres., COO, 2000—02; pres. & CEO GE Comml. Fin., 2002—; vice chmn. General Electric Co., 2005—. Trustee Fairfield Univ., Ga. Tech. Found.; bd. mem. Soundwaters, Stamford, Conn.; mem. U.S. adv. bd. European Inst. Bus. Adminstrn. Mailing: General Electric Co 3135 Easton Tpke Fairfield CT 06828

**NEAL, PHIL HUDSON, JR.,** retired manufacturing executive; b. Birmingham, Ala., Nov. 17, 1926; s. Phil Hudson and Amy (Gross) N.; m. Sarah Swift Britton, Sept. 19, 1959; children: Amy Neal Ager, Phil Hudson, III, Samuel Abney Britton. AB, Duke U., 1950; MBA, Harvard U., 1952. Investment analyst First Nat. Bank, Birmingham, 1952-55; procedures analyst Gen. Electric Co., Hendersonville, NC, 1955-58; with Ala. By-Products Corp., Birmingham, 1958-79, asst. treas., 1964-68, treas., 1968-79; dir., v.p. Utility Tool Co., Birmingham, 1979-86; dir., pres. Nutec Metal Finishing Inc., Birmingham, 1986-92, chmn., 1992—2005; ret., 2005. Trustee Advent Episcopal Sch., 1967—, pres., 1968-89, trustee charitable endowment trust, 1981—; treas. Cathedral Ch. of Advent, 1981-82, mem. chpt., 1983-85, 86-89; bd. dirs. Greater Birmingham Ministries, 1975-77, Advent Episcopal Assn. for Edn., 1968-89, Jefferson County chpt. Ala. Soc. Crippled Children and Adults, 1977-79; trustee Ala. Found. for Hearing and Speech, 1967-74, v.p., 1968-69, pres., 1969-71. Served with USNR, 1945-46. Mem. Newcomen Soc. N.Am., Birmingham Country Club, The Club, The Summit Club, Phi Beta Kappa, Sigma Nu, Phi Eta Sigma. Episcopalian (vestryman, sr. warden). Home: 3336 Hermitage Rd Birmingham AL 35223-2004 also: 81 Old Duck Hole Rd East Orleans MA 02643

**NEAL, RICHARD EDMUND,** congressman, former mayor; b. Worcester, Mass., Feb. 14, 1949; s. Edmund J. and Mary H. (Garvey) N.; m. Maureen Conway, Dec. 20, 1975; children: Rory, Brendan, Maura, Sean BS, Am. Internat. Coll., Springfield, Mass., 1972; M.P.A., U. Hartford, Conn., 1976; postgrad., U. Mass., Amherst, 1982. Adminstrv. aide to Mayor City of Springfield, Mass., 1973-78; mem. city council Mass., 1978-83, mayor Mass., 1984-88; mem. U.S. Congress from 2nd. Mass. dist., 1989—; mem. ways & means com., budget com., social security subcommittee. Lectr. history and politics Springfield Tech. Community Coll., Mass., 1973-83; lectr. bus. and govt. Western New Eng. Coll., Springfield, 1979-82; project dir. Springfield Tech. Community Coll., 1979-82 Trustee ARC, YMCA, Springfield Named to Outstanding Young Men in Am., U.S. Jr. C. of C., Springfield; recipient John F. Kennedy award & Amb.'s award, Holyoke, Mass. St. Patrick's Day Com., Internat. Leadership award, Am. Ireland Fund, 2002. Mem. Am. Internat. Coll. Alumni Assn. (pres. 1980, Alumni Achievement award 1985). Springfield Library and Mus. Assn. (trustee) Clubs: Valley Press. John Boyle O'Reilly (Springfield). Democrat. Roman Catholic. Office: US Ho Reps 2266 Rayburn Ho Office Bldg Washington DC 20515-2102*

**NEAL, STEPHEN CASSIDY,** lawyer; b. San Francisco, Mar. 26, 1949; AB, Harvard U., 1970; JD, Stanford U., 1973. Bar: Ill. 1973, Calif. 1993. Ptnr. Kirkland & Ellis, Chgo., ptnr., bus. litigation Cooley Godward Kronish LLP (formerly Cooley Godward LLP), Palo Alto, Calif., 1995—, chmn., CEO. Fellow: Am. Coll. Trial Lawyers. Office: Cooley Godward LLP 5 Palo Alto Square #400 3000 El Camino Real Palo Alto CA 94306-2155 Office Phone: 650-843-5182. Office Fax: 650-857-0063. Business E-Mail: nealsc@cooley.com.

**NEAL, STU M.,** finance educator, writer; b. Portland, Maine, Aug. 18, 1952; s. Paul Millard and Barbara Neal; m. Pamela Acker, Dec. 1, 1983 (div. June 28, 2003); children: Nerissa Rene, Mineka Acker. Student, So. Maine Vocat. Tech. Inst., 1970—72. Prin., owner Neal-Godsoe Corp., Windham, Maine, 1978—93, Nealco Inc., Windham, 1989—92; regional sales mgr. Accu Industries, Inc., Ashland, Va., 1993—95; dist. bus. mgr. Matco Tools, Inc., Stow, Ohio, 1995—97; prin., owner SMN Group, Mechanicsville, Va., 1997—2003; dir. Ctr. Entrepreneurial Devel. C.C. Workforce Alliance, Richmond, Va., 1999—; pres. Fliprack, Mechanicsville, Va., 2003—. Co-chmn. Bus. Edn. Adv. Com. Maine Dept. Edn., Augusta, Maine, 1988—90; mem. econ. coun. Key Bank Maine, 1992. Author: Disc, 2002; contbr. columns in newspapers. Vice chmn. Windham (Maine) Town Coun., 1989—93; town rep. Greater Portland (Maine) coun., 1989—93; del. White House Conf. Small Bus., Washington, 1986; bd. dir. Windham (Maine) C. of C., 1978—92; adv. bd. Retail U. Career Ctr., Richmond, Va., 2004, Asian Am. Bus. Assistance Ctr., Ashland, Va., 2004. Mem.: Nat. Spkrs. Assn., Bull and Bear Club, Rotary (Paul Harris fellow 1988). Republican. Avocations: writing, fly fishing, scuba diving, camping, antique toys. Home: 10137 Spring Ivy Ln Mechanicsville VA 23116 Office: Ctr Entrepreneurial Devel Cmty Coll Workforce Alliance 501 E Franklin St Richmond VA 23219 Office Phone: 804-521-4320.

**NEALE, ERNEST RICHARD WARD,** retired university official, consultant; b. Montreal, Que., Can., July 3, 1923; s. Ernest John and Mabel Elizabeth (McNamee) N.; m. Roxie Eveline Anderson, June 3, 1950; children: Richard Ward, Owen Curtis. B.Sc., McGill U., Montreal, 1949; MS, Yale U., 1950, PhD, 1952; LL.D. (hon.), Calgary U., Alta., Can., 1977; DSc (hon.), Meml. U., Nfld., Can., 1989. Asst. prof. geology U. Rochester, N.Y., 1952-54; lectr.

---

chief Geol. Survey Can., Ottawa, Ont., 1954-63, div. chief, 1965-68, Calgary, 1976-81; commonwealth geol. liaison officer London, 1963-65; prof., head geology Meml. U., St. John's, Nfld., Can., 1968-76, v.p. acad., 1982-87; cons., Calgary, Alta., Can., 1987—. Chmn. nat. adv. bd. on sci. publs. NRC-Natural Scis. and Engring. Rsch. Coun., Ottawa, 1982-88. Author: Geology and Geophysics in Canadian Universities, 1980. Editor: Some Guides to Mineral Exploration, 1967, Geology of the Atlantic Region, 1968, The Geosciences in Canada, 1980; editor: Can. Jour. Earth Sci., 1974-79. Bd. dirs. Unitarian Ch. Calgary, 1993—, pres., 1995-96. Petty officer Royal Can. Navy, 1943-45. Decorated officer Order of Can.; recipient Queen's Jubilee medal, Govt. Can., 1977, 125 medal Can., 1992, Golden Jubilee medal Can. 2002, Integrity award, Calgary Rotary, 2003, William Irvine award, Unitarian Ch. Calgary, 2004, Alta. Centennial medal, 2005. Fellow Royal Soc. Can. (coun. 1972-75, chmn. com. pub. awareness of sci. 1987-91, Bancroft medal 1975), Geol. Assn. Can. (pres. 1973-74, Ambrose medal 1986, 1st E.R. Ward Neale medal 1995), Can. Geosci. Coun. (pres. 1975-76, R.T. Bell medal Can. Mining Jour. 1977), Geol. Soc. Am.; mem. Assn. Earth Sci. Editors, Nat. Def. (chmn. biol. and chem. def. rev. com. 1990-93), Univ. Club Calgary, Chancellor's Club, Crows Nest Club, Calgary Sci. Network (pres. 1989), Sigma Xi (nat. lectr. New Haven 1976, chmn. Avalon chpt. 1986). Avocations: golf, cross country skiing, hiking, canoeing. Home and Office: 5108 Carney Rd NW Calgary AB Canada T2L 1G2

**NEALE, GARY LEE,** utilities executive; b. Lead, S.D., Mar. 3, 1940; s. Vearl J. and Gladys M. (Trenkle) N.; m. Sandra C. Lovell, June 16, 1962; children: David G., Julie C. BA in Econs., U. Wash., 1962, MBA, 1965. Loan examiner Wells Fargo, 1966-69; sr. fin. analyst Kaiser Industries, 1969-70; chmn., pres., chief exec. officer Planmetrics, Chgo., 1970-89; pres., chief oper. officer No. Ind. Pub. Svc. Co., Hammond, 1989-93; chmn., pres., CEO NiSource Inc. (formerly No. Ind. Pub. Svc. Co.), Hammond, Ind., 1993—2005, chmn., 2005—. Bd. dirs. Modine Mfg., Racine, Wis., Am. Gas Assn., Arlington, Va., Ind. Gas Assn./Ind. Electric Assn., Indpls., Nipsco Industries Inc., Hammond. Bd. dirs. N.W. Ind. Symphony, 1990; mem. Ind. Energy Policy Forum, 1991. Lt. (j.g.) USN, 1962-64. Mem. Econ. Club Chgo., Chgo. Univ. Club, NYU Club. Office: NiSource Inc 801 E 86th Ave Merrillville IN 46410-6272*

**NEALON, WILLIAM JOSEPH, JR.,** federal judge; b. Scranton, Pa., July 31, 1923; s. William Joseph and Ann Cannon (McNally) N.; m. Jean Sullivan, Nov. 15, 1947; children: Ann, Robert, William, John, Jean, Patricia, Kathleen, Terrence, Thomas, Timothy. Student, U. Miami, Fla., 1942-43; BS in Econs., Villanova U., 1947; LL.B., Cath. U. Am., 1950; LL.D. (hon.), U. Scranton, 1975. Bar: Pa. 1951. With firm Kennedy, O'Brien & O'Brien (and predecessor), Scranton, 1951-60; mem. Lackawanna County Ct. Common Pleas, 1960-62; U.S. dist. judge Middle Dist. Pa., 1962—, chief judge, 1976-88, sr. judge, 1989—. Mem. com. on adminstrn. of criminal law Jud. Conf. U.S., 1979—; lectr. bus. law and labor law U. Scranton, 1951-59; mem. jud. council 3d Cir. Ct. Appeals, 1984—; dist. judge rep. from 3d Cir. Jud. Conf. of U.S., 1987—. Mem. Scranton Registration Commn., 1953-55; hearing examiner Pa. Liquor Control Bd., 1955-59; campaign dir. Lackawanna County chpt. Nat. Found., 1961-63; mem. Scranton-Lackawanna Health and Welfare Authority, 1963—; assoc. bd. Marywood Coll., Scranton; pres. bd. dirs. Cath. Youth Center; pres. Father's Club Scranton Prep. Sch., 1966; chmn. bd. dirs. Mercy Hosp., 1991-95; chmn. bd. trustees U. Scranton; vice chmn. bd. trustees Lackawanna Jr. Coll., Scranton; bd. dirs. St. Joseph's Children's and Maternity Hosp., 1963-64, Lackawanna County unit Am. Cancer Soc., Lackawanna County Heart Assn., Lackawanna County chpt. Pa. Assn. Retarded Children, Scranton chpt. ARC, Lackawanna United Fund, Mercy Hosp., Scranton, 1975—; trustee St. Michael's Sch. Boys, Hoban Heights; adv. com. Hosp. Service Assn. Northeastern Pa. Served to 1st lt. USMCR, 1942-45. Recipient Americanism award Amos Lodge B'nai B'rith, 1975; Cyrano award U. Scranton Grad. Sch., 1977; Disting. Service award Pa. Trial Lawyers Assn., 1979; named one of 50 Disting. Pennsylvanians Greater Phila. C. of C., 1980, Outstanding Fed. Trial Judge Assn. Trial Lawyers Am., 1983 Mem. Pa. Bar Assn., Lackawanna County Bar Assn. (Chief Justice Michael J. Eagen award 1987), Friendly Sons St. Patrick (pres. Lackawanna County 1963-64), Pi Sigma Alpha. Clubs: Scranton Country (Clarks Summit, Pa.) (bd. dirs.). Lodges: K.C. Office: US Courthouse PO Box 1146 Scranton PA 18501-1146

**NEAMAN, MARK ROBERT,** hospital administrator; b. Buffalo, Oct. 22, 1950; married. B, Ohio State U., 1972, MHA, 1974. Adminstrv. asst. Evanston (Ill.) Hosp., 1974-76, asst. to v.p. 1976-78, asst. v.p., 1978-80, v.p., 1980-84, sr. v.p., 1984-85, pres., exec. v.p., 1985-90, pres., 1990-92, pres., CEO, 1992—. Chmn. Am. College of Healthcare Execs., 2002—; bd. trustees Healthcare Leadership Coun. Fellow Am. Coll. Healthcare Execs. (chmn., RS Hudgens award 1988). Office: Evanston Northwestern Healthcare 1301 Central St Evanston IL 60201-1781*

**NEAR, TIMOTHY,** theater director; Grad., San Francisco State U., Acad. Music and Dramatic Art, London. Artistic dir. San Jose Repertory Theatre, 1987—. Past actress, dir. with numerous prestigious theaters including The Guthrie Theatre, Berkeley (Calif.) Repertory Theater, La Jolla (Calif.) Playhouse, The Alliance Theatre, Atlanta, The Mark Taper Forum, L.A., Ford's Theatre, Washington, Repertory Theatre of St. Louis, N.Y. Shakespeare Festival, Stage West, Mass., A.C.T., Seattle. Dir. Ghosts on Fire, La Jolla Playhouse (Drama League award), Singer in the Storm, Mark Taper Forum (Drama League award), Thunder Knocking on the Door (Drama League award). Recipient 1997 Woman of Achievement in the Arts, San Jose Mercury News and The Woman's Fund. Office: San Jose Repertory Theatre 101 Paseo De San Antonio San Jose CA 95113-2603

**NEARINE, ROBERT JAMES,** educational psychologist; b. Fitchburg, Mass., May 15, 1930; s. Raymond Johns and Beatrice Ailleen (Bulokland) N.; children: Luke, Martha, Amy. BS, Fitchburg State Coll., 1951; EdM, Tufts Coll., 1952; MA, U. Conn., 1965, profl. diploma, 1996; EdD, Boston U., 1973. Cert. advanced grad. specialization Boston U. Tchr. pub. schs., Holbrook, Mass., 1952-54, Groton, Mass., 1954-55, Winchester, Mass., 1955-59, supr. Inverness, Mont., 1959-60, guidance counselor Manchester, Conn., 1961-66, supr. of evaluation, 1966-73, adminstr. for funding and evaluation, 1973-76; spl. asst. for funding Hartford, Conn., 1976-78; spl. asst. for evaluation rsch. and testing Bd. Edn., Hartford, 1978-93; ednl. cons. Glastonbury, Conn., 1993—. Mem. requirements adv. com., 1991-92. Contbr. articles to profl. jours. Col. ret. U.S. Army. NDEA fellow Boston U., 1960-61, GE fellow Syracuse U., 1971, Ednl. Policy Inst. fellow George Washington U., 1979-80. Mem. APA, Nat. Assn. Test Dirs., Am. Ednl. Rsch. Assn., Nat. Coun. on Measurement in Edn., Res. Officers Assn. (nat. councilman 1994—), Amvets, Civitan (pres. 1998-99), Conn. state com. employee support of Guard and Res.), Am. Legion, Army and Navy Club, Victory Svcs. Club U.K., Assn. of U.S. Army, NG Assn. U.S., Gov.'s Foot Guard, Phi Delta Kappa. Avocations: military history, travel. E-mail: rjnear@sbcglobal.net.

**NEARING, VIVIENNE W.,** lawyer; b. NYC; d. Abraham M. and Edith Eunice (Webster) N. BA, Queens Coll.; MA, JD, Columbia U. Bar: N.Y., D.C., U.S. Dist. Ct. (so. and ea. dists.) N.Y., U.S. Ct. Appeals (2d cir.), U.S. Claims Ct. Ptnr. Stroock & Stroock & Lavan, N.Y.C. Gen. counsel Plays for Living, 1998—2002, gen. co-counsel, 2002—. Mem. editorial bd. Communications and the Law, 1978-82, adv. bd. 1982—; mem. editorial bd. U.S. Trademark Reporter, 1982-86. Bd. dirs. Light Opera of Manhattan, 1981-82, Lyric Opera N.Y., 1984-90, Concert Artists Guild, 1989-91, Plays for Living, 1998—. Mem. ABA, Fed. Bar Coun., N.Y. State Bar Assn., U.S. Trademark Assn., Copyright Soc. U.S.A., N.Y. Lawyers for Pub. Interest (bd. dirs. 1983-87), Am. Arbitration Assn., Common for Law and Social Justice, Carnegie Coun., Women's City Club, Respect for Law Alliance. Office: Stroock Stroock & Lavan 180 Maiden Ln New York NY 10038-4982 Business E-Mail: vnearing@stroock.com.

**NEARY, DANIEL P.,** insurance company executive; b. Carroll, Iowa, 1952; m. Shirley Neary; 4 children. Degree, U. Iowa, 1974. With Mut. of Omaha, 1975—, exec. v.p. group benefit svcs., 1999—2003; pres., bd. dirs. Mut. of

---

Omaha and United of Omaha, 2003—05, CEO, chmn., 2005—. Bd. dir. Comml. Fed. Bank, Comml. Fed. Corp., America's Health Ins. Plans, Creighton U. Bd. dirs. United Way, Midlands and Am. Red Cross; mem. Boy Scouts Am. Mid-Am. Coun.; chmn. Walk to Cure Diabetes Juvenile Diabetes Rsch. Found., 2004; bd. trustees Strategic Air & Space Mus. Mem.: Soc. Actuaries. Office: Mut of Omaha Mutual of Omaha Plz Omaha NE 68175*

**NEARY, PATRICIA ELINOR,** ballet director; b. Miami, Fla. d. James Elliott and Elinor (Mitsitz) N. Corps de ballet Nat. Ballet of Can., Toronto, Ont., 1957-60; prin. dancer N.Y. City Ballet, 1960-68; ballerina Geneva Ballet, Switzerland, 1968-70, ballet dir., 1973-78; guest artist Stuttgart Ballet, Germany, 1968-70; asst. ballet dir., ballerina West Berlin Ballet, 1970-73; ballet dir. Zurich Ballet, Switzerland, 1978-86, La Scala di Milano ballet co., Italy, 1986-88; tchr. Balanchine ballets, Balanchine Trust, 1987—.

**NEAS, JOHN THEODORE,** investment company executive; b. Tulsa, May 1, 1940; s. George and Lillian J. (Kaspar) N.; m. Sally Jane McPherson, June 10, 1966; children: Stephen, Gregory, Matthew. BS, Okla. State U., 1967, MS, 1968. With acctg. dept. Rockwell Internat., 1965; with contr.'s dept. Amoco Prodn. Co., 1966—67; audit and tax staff Deloitte, Haskins & Sells, 1968—75; pres. Nat. Petroleum Sales, Inc., Tulsa, 1975—; prin. Neas Investments Ltd. Partnership, 1997—, Sebring Investments Ltd. Partnership, 1997—. Stockholder N-H Dealership Investments, Inc., 1996—; mem. Coun. Oak Bldg. Mgmt., LLC, 1997—; mem. Brad Noe Autoplex, LLC, 1997—. Vet. Properties, LLC, 1994—; asst. instr. U. Tulsa, 1974; bd. dirs. Summit Bank. Mem. AICPA, Inst. Mgmt. Accts., Okla. Soc. CPAs, McClellan-Kerr Arkansas River Nav. Sys. Hist. Soc., Okla. Heritage Assn., Okla. State U. Pres.'s Club, Okla. State U. Coll. Bus. Adminstrn. Assocs. (v.p. memberships 1989-91, Hall of Fame 1991), Okla. Reg5tr. Dept. Hall of Fame 1993), Southern Hills Country Club, Gol Club Okla. Republican. Lutheran. Office: Nat Petroleum Sales 5401 S Harvard Ave Ste 200 Tulsa OK 74135-3861

**NEASE, JUDITH ALLGOOD,** marriage and family therapist; b. Arlington, Mass., Nov. 15, 1930; d. Dwight Maurice Allgood and Sophie Wolf Allgood Morris; m. Theron Stanford Nease, Sept. 1, 1962; children: Susan Elizabeth, Alison Allgood. Student, Rockford Coll., 1949-50; BA, NYU, 1953, MA, 1954; MS, Columbia U. Sch. Social Work, 1956. Lic. clin. social worker, marriage and family therapist. Psychiat. social worker Bellevue Psychiat. Hosp., N.Y.C., 1956-59, St. Luke's Hosp., N.Y.C., 1959-62; asst. psychiat. social work supr. N.J. Neuropsychiat. Inst., Princeton, 1962-64; group co-leader Ctr. for Advancement of Personal and Social Growth, Atlanta, 1973-76; asst. dir. social work supr., group co-leader Druid Hills Counseling Ctr., Columbia Theol. Sem., 1973-82; marriage and family therapist Cath. Social Svcs., Atlanta, 1978-87; chief Cmty. Mental Health Svc., Ft. McPherson, Atlanta, 1987-92; master's level clinician Ctr. for Psychiatry, Smyrna, Ga., 1990-92; pvt. practice Grayson, Ga., 1992—. Mem.: Am. Psychotherapy Assn. (diplomate). Democrat. Episcopalian. Home and Office: 3030 Hollywood Dr Decatur GA 30033-5126 Office Phone: 770-982-9590. E-mail: judynease@yahoo.com.

**NEAVEL, CELIA BETH,** medical association administrator; b. Blommington, Ind., Aug. 30, 1959; d. Richard Charles and Nancy Trager Neavel; m. Jose Carlos Cortez; children: Elizabeth, Elena, Geordi. BA with honors in liberal arts, U. Tex., 1981; MD, Baylor Coll. of Medicine, 1985. Diplomate Am. Bd. of Family Medicine, cert. Added Qualification, Adolescent Medicine. Asst. prof. Dept. of Family Medicine, Cin., 1989—91; contract physician Austin Regional Clin., Austin, Tex., 1991—91; clin. asst., prof. of Pediat. Scott and White, Temple, Tex., 1991—95; physician adv. Easter Seals Ctrl. Tex., Austin, Tex., 1995—; faculty Austin Med. Edn. Program, Austin, Tex., 1995—; dir., adolescent medicine Ctr. for Adolescent Health at People's Cmty Clin., Austin, Tex., 1994—. Med. dir. Phoenix Acad. Off-Site Clin., Austin, Tex., 2003—, Lifeworks St. Outreach Clin., Austin, Tex., 1996—, RGK Downtown Ctr. for Health Clin., Austin, Tex., 1996—; dir. Devel. Behavioral Primary Care Program, People's Cmty. Clin., Austin, Tex., 2004—. Co-author: (monograph) Integrating Child and Adolescent Mental Health Into Primary Care, 2002. Vol. lectrs. and physician Camp Disabled Children, Center Point, Tex., 1990—. Named Tex. Super Doctor, Tex. Monthly Mag., 2004; grant, Healthy Tomorrows from HRSA, 2005. Mem.: AMA, Physicians for Social Responsibility, Soc. of Adolescent Medicine, Tex. Med. Assn., Travis County Managed Care Regional Adv. Com. Office: Ctr for Adolescent Health Peoples Cmty Clin 2909 NIH 35 Austin TX 78722 Office Phone: 512-478-4939. Office Fax: 512-320-0702. E-mail: ibappmd@aol.com.

**NEAVES, WILLIAM BARLOW,** cell biologist, educator; b. Spur, Tex., Dec. 25, 1943; s. William Fred and Revvie Lee (Hefner) N.; m. Priscilla Wood, Jan. 28, 1965; children: William Barlow, Clarissa D'laine. AB magna cum laude, Harvard U., 1966; postgrad., Med. Sch., 1966-67, PhD, 1969. Lectr. vet. anatomy U. Nairobi, 1970-71, vis. prof., 1978; lectr. anatomy Harvard U., 1972; asst. prof. cell biology U. Tex. Health Sci. Ctr., Dallas, 1972-74, assoc. prof., 1974-77, prof., 1977—; Doris and Brian Wildenthal Prof. of Biomed. Sci., 1993—, dean Grad. Sch. Biomed. Scis., 1980-88, interim dean Southwestern Med. Sch., 1986-88, dean Southwestern Med. Sch., 1989-98, exec. v.p. acad. affairs, 1998—2000; prof. medicine U. Mo., Kans. City, 1998—2000; pres., CEO, bd. dirs. Stowers Inst. Med. Rsch., Kans. City, 2000—. Dir. Cerner Corp., Midwest Rsch. Inst., Kans. City Area Life Scis. Inst.; trustee Wash. U.; mem. nat. coun. Wash. U. Sch. Medicine; rsch. assoc. herpetology Los Angeles County Mus., 1970-73; vis. lectr. U. Chgo., 1976-77. Assoc. editor Anat. Record, 1975-87; mem. editl. bd. Biology of Reprodn., 1983-86, Jour. Andrology, 1987-89; contbr. chpts. to books, articles to profl. jours. Bd. dirs. Dallas Zool. Soc., 1989-94, Dallas Mus. Natural History, 1993-95, Damon Runyan-Walter Winchell Cancer Fund, 1986-97, v.p. 1990-92, Sigmund Endowment, 1998—. Rockefeller Found. fellow, 1970-71; Milton Fund grantee, 1970-71; Population Council grantee, 1973-75; NIH grantee, 1973-89; Ford. Found. grantee, 1976-78. Fellow AAAS; mem. Am. Assn. Anatomists, Am. Soc. Andrology (Young Andrologist award 1983), Dallas Assembly, N.Y. Acad. Scis., Soc. Study of Reprodn., Liaison Com. on Med. Edn. (joint com. of AMA and Assn. Am. Med. Colls.), Sigma Xi, Alpha Omega Alpha. Methodist. Office: Stowers Inst Med Rsch 1000 East 50th St Kansas City MO 64110 Office Phone: 816-926-4040. Business E-Mail: wbn@stowers-institute.org.*

**NEAVOLL, GEORGE FRANKLIN,** writer; b. Lebanon, Oreg., Aug. 20, 1938; s. Jesse Hunter and Mazie Maude (Meyer) N.; m. Laney Lila Hunter Hough, June 21, 1969 (dec. Nov. 2000); m. Joanne Darlen MacRoberts, May 4, 2002. BS, U. Oreg. 1965. Reporter, photographer Lebanon (Oreg.) Express, 1969-70; state editor Idaho State Jour., Pocatello, 1970-72; editorial writer The Jour.-Gazette, Ft. Wayne, Ind., 1972-75, Detroit Free Press, 1975-78; editorial page editor The Wichita (Kans.) Eagle, 1978-91, Portland (Maine) Press Herald, Maine Sunday Telegram, 1991-99. Vol. Peace Corps, India, 1967-69; bd. councilors Save-the-Redwoods League, 1980—; bd. dirs. Population Inst., 2002—. Recipient Edward J. Meeman award Scripps-Howard Found., 1973, Honor Roll award Izaak Walton League Am., 1974, Jamaica Daily Gleaner award Inter Am. Press Assn., 1985, Disting. Citizen award Bethany Coll., 1985, Servant Leadership award Southwestern Coll., 1987, Global Media award Population Inst., 1996, Henri A. Benoit award Greater Portland (Maine) C. of C., 1999, Restoration Leadership award Restore the North Woods, 2005; named Hon. Park Ranger, Nat. Park Svc., 1988 Mem.: NAACP, Nat. Press Club, Portland C. of C. Home: 151 North St No 204 Portland ME 04101-2794 Office Phone: 207-761-7043. Personal E-mail: gneavoll@maine.rr.com.

**NEBENZAHL, KENNETH,** rare book and map dealer, author; b. Far Rockaway, NY, Sept. 16, 1927; s. Meyer and Ethel (Levin) N.; m. Jocelyn Hart Spitz, Feb. 7, 1953; children: Kenneth (dec.), Patricia Suzanne Nebenzahl Frish, Margaret Spitz Nebenzahl Quintong, Suzanne Spitz Nebenzahl Nichol. Student, Columbia U. 1947-48; L.H.D. (hon.), Coll. William and Mary, 1983. Solicitor new bus. United Factors Corp., N.Y.C., 1947-50; sales rep. Fromm & Sichel, N.Y.C., 1950-52; v.p. Cricketeer, Inc., Chgo., 1953-58; pres. Kenneth Nebenzahl, Inc., Chgo., 1957—. Bd. dirs. Imago

Mundi, Ltd., London; cons. Rand McNally and Co., 1966-97. Author: Atlas of the American Revolution, 1974, Bibliography of Printed Battle Plans of the American Revolution, 1975, Maps of the Holy Land, 1986 (German edit. 1995), Atlas of Columbus and the Great Discoveries, 1990, also edits. in Spanish, German, Italian, Portugese and French langs.; Mapping Asia: The Silk Road and Beyond, 2,000 Years of Exploring the East, 2004, also edits. in French and Japanese langs.; contbr. articles to profl. jours. Trustee Glencoe Pub. Libr., 1963-69, pres., 1966-69; bd. dirs. North Suburban Libr. System, 1966-69, Beverly Farm Found., Godfrey, Ill., 1961-67, Nature Conservancy of Ill., 1980-88; trustee Adler Planetarium, 1969—, chmn., 1977-81; mem. exec. com. Northwestern U. Libr. Coun., 1973-75; sponsor Kenneth Nebenzahl Jr. lectures history cartography Newberry Libr., Chgo., 1965—; trustee John Crear Libr., Chgo., 1976-84; trustee U. Chgo., 1982—, mem. vis. com. to libr., 1978-96, chmn., 1987-95; co-chair Phillips Soc.-Libr. of Congress, Washington, 1995-98; bd. dirs. Evanston Hosp. Corp., 1978-85, Am. Himalayan Found., 1994—; mem. U.S. nat. adv. coun. World Wildlife Fund, 1993—; founding pres. Ill. Ctr. for Book, 1986-88. With USMCR, 1945-46. Recipient IMCoS-Tooley award (London), 1984. Fellow Royal Geog. Soc., Royal Soc. for Asian Affairs; mem. Manuscript Soc. (dir. 1965-71), Am. Library Trustees Assn. (nat. chmn. com. intellectual freedom 1967-68), Bibliog. Soc. Am., Newberry Library Assocs. (bd. govs. 1965-78, chmn. 1976-78), Newberry Library (trustee 1978-2003, vice chmn. 1994-2003, life trustee 2003—), Antiquarian Booksellers Assn. Am. (bd. govs. 1965-67, v.p. 1975-77), Am. Antiquarian Soc. (gov. 1981-85), Soc. History Discoveries (dir. 1974-76), Chgo. Map Soc. (dir. 1976-86), Caxton Club (Chgo.) (bd. govs. 1961-68, 74-80, pres. 1964-66), Wayfarers Club (Chgo.) (pres. 1979-80), Lake Shore Country Club, Century Club (NYC), Grolier Club (NYC) (bd. govs. 1998-99). Office: PO Box 370 Glencoe IL 60022-0370

**NEBERT, DANIEL WALTER,** molecular geneticist, research administrator; b. Portland, Oreg., Sept. 26, 1938; s. Walter Francis Nebert and Marie Sophie (Schick) Kirk; m. Myrna Siska, Mar. 12, 1960 (div. 1975); children: Douglas Daniel, Dietrich Andrew; m. Kathleen Dixon, Aug. 15, 1981 (div. 1997); children: Rosemarie Dixon, Rebecca Frances, David Porter, Lucas Daniel; m. Lucia Jorge Fung, Mar. 6, 2000. BA, Wesleyan U., 1959; BS and MS in Biochemistry, U. Oreg., 1964, MD, 1964. Lic. physician, Ohio; bd. qualified in pediats. and human genetics; Am. Bd. Pediat. and Human Genetics. Pediat. intern UCLA Hosps., 1964—65, resident pediat., 1965—66; postdoctoral fellow Nat. Cancer Inst., NIH, Bethesda, Md., 1966—68; sr. investigator Nat. Inst. Child Health and Human Devel., Bethesda, 1968—71, sect. head, 1971—74, lab. chief, 1974—89; prof. dept. environ. health U. Cin. Med. Ctr., 1989—, prof. dept. pediat. and molecular devel. biology, 1991—. Mem. faculty bd. cert. in human genetics NIH, 1981-89; coord. med. genetics program U.S.-China Coop. Med. Health Protocol, 1982-89; Pfizer lectr. U. Vt., Burlington, 1978, Stanford U., 1979; Wellcome vis. prof. biochemistry and molecular biology U. S.D., Vermillion, 1991; assoc. dir. physician scientist trng. program MD/PhD, U. Cin. Med. Ctr., 1994-98; mem. nat. adv. Environ. Health Scis. Coun., 2000-04; mem. expert sci. coun. protein info. resource Nat. Biomed. Rsch. Found. Georgetown U., Wash., 2000-; mem. external adv. bd. Howard U. Cancer Ctr., Wash., 1998-, U. Lisbon, 1998-, Inst. DNA and Human Genomics U. Panama, 1999-2004; dir. Ctr. Environ. Genetics, 1992-97 Mem. editl. bd. Molecular Pharmacology, 1972-1984, Biochem. Pharmacology, 1972-, Archives of Biochemistry and Biophysics, 1973-76, Archivees Internationales de Pharmacodynamie et de Therapie, 1975-81, Jour. Environ. Scis. and Health, 1976-81, Chemico-Biol. Interactions, 1977-83, Teratogenesis, Carcinogenesis and Mutagenesis, Devel. Pharmacology and Therapeutics, 1979-1987, 1980-86, Anticancer Rsch., 1981-83, DNA and Cell Biology, 1986—2003, Jour. Exptl. Pathology, 1986-1994, Molecular Endocrinology, 1988-1992, Endocrinology, 1989-2002, Molecular Toxicology, 1990-92, Pharmacogenetics Genomics, 1991—, Mutation Rsch., 1996-2001, Environ. Health Prospectives, 1997-, European Jour. Pharmacology, 2002-, Human Genomics, 2003—; assoc. editor DNA and Cell Biology, 1987-2003, Biochem. Pharmacology (N.Am.), 1994-2001, Mut. Rsch., 1996—, Environ. Health Perspectives, 1997—; commn. edit. Human Mutation, 2005-; contbr. more than 560 articles to profl. jours. Capt. USPHS, 1966-89 Recipient Meritorious Svc. medal USPHS, 1978, Frank Ayrey fellow award in clin. pharmacology, U.K., 1984, Bernard B. Brodie award, 1986, Ernst A. Sommer Meml. award, 1988; GM scholar, 1956-59, Lawrence Selling scholar, 1961, 63, Disting. Rsch. Professorship award, U. Cin., 1998, George Rieveschl Jr. award for disting. sci. rsch., U. Cin., 1999 Fellow AAAS; mem. Am. Soc. Human Genetics, Am. Soc. Pharmacology and Exptl. Therapeutics, Am. Soc. Biochemistry and Molecular Biology, Am. Soc. Clin. Investigation (emeritus 1984-), Soc. Toxicology (Disting. Lifetime Toxicology Scholar award, 2005), Human Genome Variation Soc. (founder), Sigma Xi Republican. Episcopalian. Avocations: gardening, golf, piano, art. Home: 20 Oliver Rd Cincinnati OH 45215-2631 Office: U Cin Med Ctr Dept Environ Health PO Box 670056 Cincinnati OH 45267-0001 Office Phone: 513-558-4239.

**NEBLETT, CAROL,** soprano; b. Modesto, Calif., Feb. 1, 1946; m. Philip R. Akre; 3 children. Studies with, William Vennard, Roger Wagner, Esther Andreas, Ernest St. John Metz, Lotte Lehmann, Pierre Bernac, Rosa Ponselle, George London, Jascha Heifetz, Norman Treigle, Sol Hurak, Dorothy Kirsten, Maestros Julius Rudel, Claudio Abbado, Daniel Barenboin, Erich Leinsdorf, James Levine, others. Soloist with Roger Wagner Chorale; performed in U.S. and abroad with various symphonies; debut with Carnegie Hall, 1966, N.Y.C. Opera, 1969, Met. Opera, 1979; sung with maj. opera cos. including Met. Opera, N.Y.C., Lyric Opera Chgo., Balt. Opera, Pitts. Opera, Houston Grand Opera, San Francisco Opera, Boston Opera Co., Milw. Florentine Opera, Washington Opera Soc., Covent Garden, Cologne Opera, Vienna (Austria) Staatsoper, Paris Opera, Teatro Regio, Turin, Italy, Teatro San Carlo, Naples, Italy, Teatro Massimo, Palermo, Italy, Gran Teatro del Liceo, Barcelona, Spain, Kirov Opera Theatre, Leningrad, USSR, Dubrovnik (Yugoslavia) Summer Festival, Salzberg Festival, others; rec. artist RCA, DGG, EMI; appearances with symphony orchs., also solo recitals, (film) La Clemenza di Tito; filmed and recorded live performance with Placido Domingo, La Fancuilla del West; numerous TV appearances.

**NECCO, EDNA JOANNE,** school psychologist; b. Klamath Falls, Oreg., June 23, 1941; d. Joseph Rogers and Lillian Laura (Owings) Painter; m. Jon F. Puryear, Aug. 25, 1963 (div. Oct. 1987); children: Laura L., Douglas F.; m. A. David Necco, July 1, 1989. BS, Ctrl. State U., 1978, MEd, 1985; PhD in Applied Behavioral Studies, Okla. State U., 1993. Med.-surg. asst. Oklahoma City Clinic, 1961-68; spl. edn. tchr. Oklahoma City Pub. Schs., 1978-79, Edmond (Okla.) Pub. Schs., 1979-83; co-founder, owner Learning Devel. Clinic, Edmond, 1983-93; asst. prof. profl. tchr. edn. U. Ctrl. Okla., Edmond, 1993-97, assoc. prof., 1998—2001, prof. profl. tchr. edn., 2002—. Adj. instr. Ctrl. State U., Edmond, 1989-93, Oklahoma City U., 1991-93; rsch. group Okla. State U., Stillwater, 1991-93; faculty senator U. Ctrl. Okla., 1998-2000; tri-coord. Am. Democracy project, 2003-05, campus exec. dir. U. Ctrl. Okla., 2005—; Coll. Edn. rep. AAUP, 2000-01; presenter in field Contbr. articles to profl. jours. Com. mem. Boy Scouts Am., SCUBA Post 604, Oklahoma City, 1981-86; mem. Edmond Task Force for Youth, 1983-87, Edmond C. of C., 1984-87; evaluator for Even Start Literacy Program, 1994-96, reviewer Okla. Even Start applicants, 1997 Named to State of Okla. Outstanding Profs.' Acad., 2003; recipient Provost award, 2004. Mem. AAUP, ASCD, PEO, Am. Psychol. Soc., Nat. Assn. for Sch. Psychologists, Am. Bus Women's Assn., Coun. for Exceptional Children, Learning Disabilities Assn., Am. Assn. for Gifted Underachieving Students, Am. Tchr. Educators, Okla. Learning Disabilities Assn., Okla. Neurosci., Okla. Assn. for Counseling and Devel., Okla. Psychol. Soc., U. Ctrl. Okla. Golden Key Nat. Honor Soc., Internat. Soc. for Study of Subjectivity, Am. Coun. on Rural Spl. Edn., Ctrl. State U. (Okla., life), Phi Delta Kappa. Republican. Avocations: scuba diving, underwater photography, water-skiing, travel, golf. Home: 3624 Equestrian Ct Edmond OK 73034-5871 Office: U Ctrl Okla Coll Edn 100 N University Dr Edmond OK 73034-5207 Business E-Mail: jnecco@ucok.edu.

**NECHEMIAS, STEPHEN MURRAY,** lawyer; b. St. Louis, July 27, 1944; s. Herbert Bernard and Toby Helen (Wax) N.; m. Marcia Rosenstein, June 19, 1966 (div. Dec. 1981); children: Daniel Jay, Scott Michael; m. Linda Adams,

Aug. 20, 1983. BS, Ohio State U., 1966; JD, U. Cin., 1969. Bar: Ohio 1969. Ptnr. Taft, Stettinius & Hollister, Cin., 1969—. Adj. prof. law No. Ky. U., Chase Coll. Law. Tax comment author: Couse's Ohio Form Book, 6th edit., 1984. Mem. Ohio State Bar Assn. (chmn. taxation com.), Cin. Bar Assn. (chmn. taxation sect. 1985), Legal Aid Soc. Cin. (pres., trustee). Democrat. Jewish. Home: 2490 Royalview Ct Cincinnati OH 45244 Office: 1800 US Bank Tower 425 Walnut St Cincinnati OH 45202-3923 Office Phone: 513-357-9392.

**NECHIN, HERBERT BENJAMIN,** lawyer; b. Chgo., Oct. 25, 1935; s. Abraham and Zelda (Benjamin) Nechin; m. Susan Zimmerman (div.); 1 child, Jill Rebecca; m. Roberta Fishman, Oct. 24, 1976; 1 child, Stefan. BA with distinction and with honors in history, Northwestern U., 1956; JD, Harvard U. Law Sch., 1959. Bar: Ill. 1960. From assoc. to ptnr. Brown Fox & Blumberg, Chgo., 1960-75; ptnr. Taussig Wexler & Shaw, Chgo., 1975-79, Fink Coff Stern, Chgo., 1979-81, Holleb & Coff, Chgo., 1981-2000; of counsel Levin & Schreder, Ltd., Chgo., 2000—04; assoc. dir. planned giving Northwestern U., Evanston, Ill., 2004—. Contbr. articles to profl. jours. Pres. Emanuel Congregation, Chgo., 1994—97. Staff sgt. USAR, 1960—66. Mem.: ABA, Am. Coll. Trust and Estate Counsel, Chgo. Bar Assn. (chmn. trust law com. 1990—91), Ill. Bar Assn., Cliff Dwellers Club, Union League Club, Phi Beta Kappa. Office: Northwestern U Office Alumini Rels and Devel 2020 Ridge Ave 3rd Fl Evanston IL 60208-4307 Office Phone: 847-491-7394. Business E-Mail: h-nechin@northwestern.edu.

**NEDAL, ARAR HAMDI,** research scientist; d. Abdquader and Beburs; m. Mazen Arar, Sept. 3, 1988; children: Rawan Arar, Yousef Arar. PhD (hon.), So. Meth. U., Dallas, 1996. U. Tex. Health Sci. Ctr. Asst. prof., cons. U. Tex. Health Sci. Ctr., San Antonio, 2000–06, rschr., 1998—. Health scientist VA, San Antonio, 2000—. Contbr. articles to profl. jours. Recipient rsch. grant, NIH. Mem.: Genetic Alliance (assoc.). Achievements include research in Health Service. Avocations: swimming, reading, travel. Home: 2422 Mill Creek San Antonio TX 78231 Office: U Tex Health Sci Ctr 7703 Floyd Curl San Antonio TX 78229 Office Phone: 210-567-0075. Home Fax: 210-567-4712; Office Fax: 210-567-4712. E-mail: ararn@uthscsa.edu.

**NEDELMAN, ADAM,** entrepreneur; b. Los Angeles, Calif., Dec. 6, 1966; s. Naomi and Charles Irving Nedelman. BA, San Francisco State U., 1990—94. Founder, chmn. of the bd. Psychology Online, Inc. Contbr. software. Ednl. Achievement, Vista Del Mar, 1996—99. Office: Psychology Online Inc 65 Hallam St San Francisco CA 94103 Home Fax: 475-252-8458. Personal E-mail: admin@psyline.com.

**NEDERLANDER, JAMES LAURENCE,** theater producer; b. Detroit, Jan. 23, 1960; s. James Morton and Barbara (Smith) N. Student, Cranbrook Prep, Boston U. Asst. mgr. Pineknob, Clarkston, Mich., producer N.Y.C.; v.p. Nederlander, N.Y.C., now pres. Trustee Comprehensive Cancer Ctr. Wake Forest U.; bd. dirs. Comprehensive Cancer Ctr. Wake Forest U. Bapt. Med. Ctr. Assoc. prodr.: (plays) The Tragedy of Carmen, 1984 (Tony award, 1984); Starlight Express, 1989; Cafe Crown, 1989; Private Lives, 2002 (Tony award); Who's Afraid of Virginia Woolf?, 2005; (musicals) On Your Toes, 1987; (shows) Barry Manilow, 1989; prodr.: (Shows) Mort Sahl, 1988, (shows) Kenny Loggins, 1988, (with Fred Molina) (musicals) Fiddler on the Roof, 2004, Billy Joel and Twyla Tharp's Movin Out, 2002 (Touring Broadway award, Best New Musical, Leaunge Am. Theaters & Prodn., 2005), Thoroughly Modern Millie, 2002 (Tony award), La Cage Aux Folles, 2004; co-prodr.: (shows) Billy Joel, 1990; Pink Floyd, 1994; 42; Mary Connick Jr., 1990; Yanni, 1993; Basia, 1994; Shari Lewis and Lambchop, 1994; Laurie Anderson, 1995; Ray Davies-20th Century Man, 1996; (plays) A Mid Summer Night's Dream, 1996; The Capeman, 1997. Mem. Com. Am. Candlelite Vigil, 1990; bd. trustees Intrepid Museum, 1990, Fizher Ctr. for Alzheimer's Rsch. Found.; bd. dirs. Midtown Mgmt. Group, 1996; exec. com. N.Y.C. Vis. Bur.; bd. dirs. ASPCA. Mem. Exec. League N.Y. Theatres.

**NEDERLANDER, JAMES MORTON,** theater executive; b. Detroit, Mar. 31, 1922; s. David T. and Sarah L. (Applebaum) N.; m. Charlene Saunders, Feb. 12, 1969; children: James Laurence, Sharon, Kristina. Student, Detroit Inst. Tech. Chmn. Nederlander Orgn., Inc. (formerly Nederlander Producing Co. Am., Inc.), N.Y.C., 1966—. Owner and operator of numerous theaters including Palace Theatre, Lunt-Fontanne Theatre, Nederlander Theatre, Brooks Atkinson Theatre, Gershwin Theatre, Neil Simon Theatre, Marquis Theatre, Minskoff Theatre, Richard Rodgers Theatre, N.Y.C., Greek Theatre, Pantages Theatre, Henry Fonda Theatre, L.A., Shubert Theatre, Chgo., Fisher Theatre, Masonic Temple, Detroit, Aldwych Theatre, Adelphi Theatre, Dominion Theatre, London; producer numerous shows for Broadway including She Loves Me, Will Rogers Follies, Me and My Girl, Orpheus Descending, Les Liaisons Dangereuses, Nicholas Nickleby, Annie, La Cage aux Folles, Nine, Applause, Not Now Darling, See Saw, Oliver, Abelard and Heloise, Sherlock Holmes, Treemonisha, Habeus Corpus, Otherwise Engaged, Whose Life is it Anyway?, Betrayal, Woman of the Year, Lena Horne: The Lady and Her Music, The Dresser, Noises Off, Merlin, Night and Day, My Fat Friend, Shirley MacLaine on Broadway, Sweet Charity, Benefactors, Breaking the Code; numerous road show prodns.; revivals: Peter Pan, She Loves Me, Hello Dolly, Hello Dolly Bees, The Music Man, I Do! I Do!, Oklahoma, On a Clear Day You Can See Forever, Fiddler on the Roof. Office: Nederlander Orgn Inc 1450 Broadway Fl 6 New York NY 10018-2201

**NEDERLANDER, ROBERT E.,** entertainment and television executive, lawyer; b. Detroit, Apr. 10, 1933; s. David T. and Sarah (Applebaum) N.; m. Caren Berman (div.); children: Robert E. Jr., Eric; Gladys Rackmil, Jan. 1, 1988. BA in Econs., U. Mich., 1955, JD, 1958, LLD (hon.), 1990. Ptnr. Nederlander, Dodge & Rollins, Detroit, 1960-90; pres. Nederlander Co. LLC (formerly Nederlander Orgn. Inc.), N.Y.C., 1981—, Nederlander TV & Film Prodns., N.Y.C., 1985—. Mng. gen. ptnr. N.Y. Yankees, 1990-91. Regent U. Mich., Ann Arbor, 1969-84; trustee Am. Health Found., 1989—; chmn. Gateway Am., 1991—. Recipient Disting. Alumni Svc. award U. Mich., 1985; named Man of Yr. by Gov.'s Com. on Scholastic Achievement, N.Y.C., 1991. Fellow ABA, Mich. Bar Assn. Avocations: tennis, baseball. Office: Nederlander Co LLC 1450 Broadway Ste 2000 New York NY 10018

**NEDOM, H. ARTHUR,** petroleum consultant; b. Lincoln, Nebr., Aug. 19, 1925; s. Henry Arthur and Pearle Bertrick (Swan) N.; m. Patricia Margaret Rankin, July 4, 1974; children: Richard A., Robert L., Nicole C. BS, U. Tulsa, 1949, MS, 1950; postgrad. in bus. adminstrn., Northwestern U., Evanston, Ill., 1968. Chief engr. Amerada Petroleum Corp., Tulsa, 1961-65, v.p., 1965-70, Natomas Co., San Francisco, 1971-74; also dir.; pres. Norwegian Oil Co., Houston, 1974-75; pres., mng. dir. Weeks Petroleum Ltd., Westport, Conn., 1975-82; cons., 1982—; chmn. bd. arbitration Prudhoe Bay Unit, 1983-85. Chmn. Offshore Tech. Conf., 1971; bd. dirs. Engrs. Joint Council, 1978 Contbr. articles to profl. jours. Served with inf. U.S. Army, 1943-45, ETO. Decorated Bronze Star; named Disting. Alumnus U. Tulsa, 1972 Mem. Soc. Petroleum Engrs. (dir. 1965-68, pres. 1967, Disting. Lectr. 1973, Disting. Svc. award 1978, DeGolyer Disting. Svc. medal 1981, Disting. mem. 1983, Disting. lectr. emeritus 1989, Legion of Honor 1998, v.p. SPE Found. 1988-89), AIME (dir. 1966-69, 76-79, pres. 1977, hon. mem. 1982, Disting. Svc. award 1993), Am. Assn. Engring. Soc. (dir. 1980-82, chmn. 1981, Spl. award 1979, Engring. Svc. award 1980). Home: 9924 S Sandusky Ave Tulsa OK 74137-5311 Personal E-mail: artnedom@aol.com.

**NEDZBALA, MICHAEL,** lawyer; b. Washington, Feb. 2, 1962; BA in Econ., Govt., Univ. Va., 1984; JD, UNC, 1987. Ptnr. Hunton & Williams LLP, Charlotte, NC, 1995—, co-head, asset securitization group, mem. global capital mkts. team. Mem.: Va. State Bar Assn., NC State Bar Assn., Mecklenburg Co. Bar Assn., UNC Banking Inst. (bd. adv.). Office: Hunton & Williams LLP Bank of Am Plz Ste 3500 101 S Tryon St Charlotte NC 28280 Office Phone: 704-378-4703. Office Fax: 704-378-4890. Business E-Mail: mnedzbala@hunton.com.

**NEECE, OLIVIA HELENE ERNST,** investment company executive, consultant; b. LA, Jan. 3, 1948; d. Robert and Beatrice Pearl Ernst; m. Huntley Lee Bluestein, 1967 (div. 1974); children: Melissa Dawn, Brendon Wade; m. Anthony Ray Neece, Mar. 20, 1976. Cert. interior design, UCLA, 1975, MBA, 1993; BSBA, U. So. Calif., 1990; postgrad., Claremont U., 1998—. Cert. interior designer Calif. Coun. for Interior Design; lic. gen. contractor, real estate broker, Calif. Staff designer Frances Lux Designs, LA, 1974; project designer Yates Silverman Inc., LA, 1974-77; owner Olivia Neece Planning & Design, Tarzana, Calif., 1977-86; v.p. project devel. Design Svc. /Aircoa, Englewood, Colo., 1986-87; v.p. project adminstrn. Hirsch-Bedner Assoc., Santa Monica, Calif., 1987—; treas.-sec. EON Corp., LA, 1980—87; owner Olivia Neece Planning & Design, Tarzana, 1980—88; dir. ops. The Ernst Group, LA, 1988—2005; pres. Neece Assocs., 2003—. Instr. ext. program UCLA, 1981—83; part-time prof. Calif. State U., Northridge, 1994—99; acad. rschr. Jet Propulsion Lab., 2000—02; spkr. in field. Co-author: A Step by Step Approach to Hotel Devel., 1988; contbr. chapters to books, articles to profl. jours. Co-chair LA Master Chorale Gala; mem. Hollywood Bowl Soc.; charter mem. L.A. County Mus. Art; vol. restoration of San Diego R.R. Mus., 1985—92; patron LA Philharm., LA Opera Soc.; Found. of Music Ctr. of Los Angels; fellow circle Ctr. Theatre Group; Patron and charter mem. of LA Country Mus. of Art; bd. dir..historian Master Choral Assoc. Recipient Holiday Inn Devel. award, Foster City, Calif., 1986, Warwick, R.I., 1988, 1st and 2d pl. awards, Lodging Hospitality Designers Cir., 1987, Gold Key award, Russell St. Inn, 1986, Best Paper award, Am. Conf. on Info. Systems, 2002. Mem. Am. Soc. Interior Designers (1st pl. portfolio competition 1974), Acad. of Mgmt. (Best Paper award 2002), Fin. Mgmt. Assn., Internat. Inst. Designers & Arch. (profl., v.p., bd. dir.), We. Acad. Mgmt., Assn. Info. Sys., Inst. Ops. Rsch. and Mgmt. Sci, Beta Gamma Sigma. Office: Neece Assoc 18200 Rosita St Tarzana CA 91356-4622

**NEEDELL, BENJAMIN F.,** lawyer; b. Rahway, N.J., 1941; BA, Rutgers U., 1963; LLB, St. John's U., 1966. Bar: NY 1967. Ptnr. real estate Skadden, Arps, Slate, Meagher & Flom LLP, NYC. Bd. dir. Rock and Roll Hall of Fame, 1986—, mem., 1990—, Wenner Media, inc., 1978—. Mem. St. John's Law Rev. Chmn. Stratton Mountain Sch., 1988—93, mem., 1980—; mem., chmn. NY Restoration Project, 2002—; mem. Westchester Land Trust, 2001—. Office: Skadden Arps Slate Meagher & Flom LLP 4 Times Sq New York NY 10036

**NEEDHAM, GEORGE AUSTIN,** investment banker; b. Beverly, Mass., Jan. 27, 1943; s. Everett Austin and Edith Strode (Walton) N.; m. Ellen Ann Levin, July 9, 1978; children: Michael Austin, Sarah Elisabeth, Paul Everett. BS in Bus. Adminstrn., Bucknell U., 1965; MBA, Stanford U., 1971. Portfolio mgr. Bankers Trust Co., N.Y.C., 1967-69; mng. dir. First Boston Corp., N.Y.C., 1971-84; chmn., CEO Needham & Co. Inc., N.Y.C., 1985—. Trustee Stanford Bus. Sch. Trust, Palo Alto, Calif., 1983-89. Served to 1st lt. U.S. Army, 1965-67. Mem. Fin. Analysts Fedn., Bond Club N.Y., The Links, Univ. Club, Sleepy Hollow Country Club, Coral Beach Club. Republican. Home: 79 E 79th St New York NY 10021-0202 Office: Needham & Co Inc 445 Park Ave New York NY 10022-2606 Office Phone: 212-705-0307. Business E-Mail: gneedham@needhamco.com.

**NEEDHAM, GEORGE MICHAEL,** association executive; b. Buffalo, July 3, 1955; s. Paul James and Dolores Ann (Duffy) N.; m. Joyce Elaine Leahy, Nov. 28, 1992; 1 stepchild, Katherine Callison. BA in English, SUNY, Buffalo, 1976, MLS, 1977. Various profl. positions Charleston (S.C.) County Libr., 1977-84; dir. Fairfield County Dist. Libr., Lancaster, Ohio, 1984-89; mem. svcs. dir. Ohio Libr. Assn., Columbus, 1990-92; exec. dir. Pub. Libr. Assn., Chgo., 1993-96; state librarian State of Mich., Lansing, 1996-99; v.p. mem. svcs. OCLC Online Computer libr. Ctr., Dublin, Ohio, 1999—. Trustee Learning Point Assocs, 2004—. Co-author: A Director's Checklist for Connecting Public Libraries to the Internet, 1995; author (book revs.) Booklist, 1994-2002 (video revs.), Libr. Jour., 1979-94. Bd. dirs. Fairfield County chpt. ARC, Lancaster, 1984-88, Mt. Prospect Theatre Soc., Mt. Prospect, Ill., 1993-96, Lib. Media Project, 1997—. Mem. ALA, Pub. Libr. Assn., Ohio Libr. Assn. Achievements include 2 time Jeopardy champion. Avocations: acting, traditional folk music, writing. Office: OCLC Online Computer Libr Ctr 6565 Frantz Rd Dublin OH 43017-3395 Office Phone: 614-761-5173. E-mail: needhamg@oclc.org.

**NEEDHAM, GLEN RAY,** entomology and acarology educator, researcher; b. Lamar, Colo., Dec. 25, 1951; s. Robert Lee and Evor Elaine (Kern) N.; m. Karla Marie Lohr, May 28, 1983; children: Kathleen Marie, John Harrison, Elizabeth Anne. BS, S.W. Okla. State U., 1973; MS, Okla. State U., 1975, PhD, 1978. Grad. rsch. asst. Okla. State U., Stillwater, 1974-78; asst. prof. Ohio State U., Columbus, 1978-84, assoc. prof., 1984—, co-organizer and coord. acarology summer program. Co-editor: Africanized Honey Bees and Bee Mites, 1988, Acarology IX: Proceedings and Symposia. Donor ARC, Columbus. Recipient Dist. Alumnus award Okla. State U., 1992. Mem. Acarology Soc. Am. (pres. 1994), Ohio Acad. Sci., Ohio Asthma Coalition, Ctrl. Ohio Asthma Coalition, Lions Club, Gamma Sigma Delta. Methodist. Achievements include research in tick and dust mite biology and control. Office: Ohio State U 318 W 12th Ave Columbus OH 43210 Office Phone: 614-688-3026. Business E-Mail: needham.1@osu.edu.

**NEEDHAM, KEITH ALAN,** language educator; b. Bay City, Tex., Jan. 5, 1967; s. Douglas Earl and Melba Louise Needham. BA, Tex. State U., 1991, MA, 1993. Cert. secondary English Tex. State U., 1991. Tchg. asst. Tex. State U., San Marcos, 1991—93; tchr. Austin Ind. Sch. Dist., Tex., 1993—94; instr. English Lamar U., Beaumont, Tex., 1994—., Dir. TALHent On Wheels, Beaumont, Tex., 2001—04, Adopt-A-Grandchild, Beaumont, 2004—. Recipient Julie and Ben Rogers Outstanding Cmty. Svc. award, 2004. Office: Lamar Univ PO Box 10023 Beaumont TX 77710 E-mail: KNForest34@aol.com.

**NEEDHAM, RICHARD LEE,** magazine editor; b. Cleve., Jan. 16, 1939; s. Lester Hayes and Helen (Bender) N.; m. Irene Juechter, Aug. 7, 1965; children: Margaret, Richard, Trevor. BA, Denison U., 1961; MA, U. Mo., 1967. Copy editor Sat. Rev., N.Y.C., 1967-68; editor-in-chief Preview Internat., N.Y.C., 1968-69; financial and N.Y. editor Instns. mag.; also editor Service World Internat., N.Y.C., 1969-70; copy dir. American Home mag., N.Y.C., 1970-71; exec. editor Ski Mag., N.Y.C., 1971-74, editor, 1974-92, editor-in-chief, 1992-94; sr. contbg. editor, 1994—; contbg. editor Yachting Mag., N.Y.C., 1996; editor Ency. of Skiing, 1978, Ski Fever, 1995; editl. dir. Times Mirror Mags. Conservation Coun., 1994-96; editor-in-chief Inside Tracks, 1996—2002; automotive writer Gannett Suburban Newspapers, 1995—; editor Arthritis Advisor, 2002—, Skiing Heritage, 2002—. Broadcaster: Ski Spot, CBS Radio, N.Y.C., 1978-83, On the Slopes, Audio Features Syndicate, 1984-87; author: Ski-50 Years in North America, 1992, Ski Fever!, 1995. Served to lt. USNR, 1961-65. Recipient Lowell Thomas award, 1985 Mem. N.Am. Ski Journalists Assn., Ea. Ski Writers Assn., Internat. Assn. Ski Journalists, Internat. Skiing History Assn. (Lifetime Achievement award). Home and Office: 481 Sandy Point Ave Portsmouth RI 02871-3515

**NEEDLEMAN, ALAN,** mechanical engineering educator; b. Phila., Sept. 2, 1944; s. Herman and Hannah (Goodman) N.; m. Wanda Sapolsky, Apr. 12, 1970; children: Deborah, Daniel BS, U. Pa., 1966; MS, Harvard U., 1967, PhD, 1970. Instr. applied math. MIT, Cambridge, 1970-72, asst. prof., 1972-75; asst. prof. engring. Brown U., Providence, 1975-78, assoc. prof., 1978-81, prof., 1981—, dean engring., 1988-91, Florence Pirce Grant Univ. prof. Vis. asst. prof. Tech. U. Denmark, Lyngby, 1973; vis. fellow Clare Hall, U. Cambridge, Eng., 1978; vis. prof. MIT, Cambridge, 1991. Contbr. articles to profl. jours. Guggenheim fellow, 1977. Fellow ASME, Am. Acad. Mechanics, Danish Ctr. for Applied Math. and Mechanics (fgn.), Groupe Francais de Mecanique des Matèriaux (hon.); mem. NAE. Home: 24 Elton St Providence RI 02906-4106 Office: Brown U Div Engring Providence RI 02912-0001 E-mail: Alan_Needleman@brown.edu.

**NEEDLEMAN, HERBERT LEROY,** psychiatrist, pediatrician; b. Phila., Dec. 13, 1927; s. J. Joseph and Sonia Rita (Shupak) Needleman; m. Shirley Weinstein, Sept. 12, 1948 (div. 1957); 1 child, Samuel; m. Roberta Pizor, June 2, 1963; children: Joshua, Sara. BS, Muhlenberg Coll., Allentown, Pa., 1948; MD, U. Pa., 1952. Intern Phila. Gen. Hosp., 1952—54; resident in pediat. Children's Hosp. of Phila., 1957—58, chief resident in pediat., 1958—59; resident in psychiatry Temple U. Med. Ctr., Phila., 1962—65, asst. prof. psychiatry, 1967—71; spl. fellow in psychiatry NIMH, Bethesda, Md., 1965—67; assoc. prof. psychiatry Harvard Med. Sch., Boston, 1971—81; prof. psychiatry and pediat. U. Pitts. Sch. Medicine, 1981—. Cons. air lead criteria document EPA, Washington, 1977; editor Ctrs. for Disease Control, Atlanta, 1978; mem. adv. com. on childhood lead poisoning prevention, 90; chmn. devel. toxicology subpanel NAS, 1986. Editor: Low Level Lead Exposure: The Clinical Implications of Current Research, 1980; contbr. articles to profl. jours. Chmn. Alliance to End Childhood Lead Poisoning, Washington, 1991—92, Com. of Responsibility, Boston, 1966—75; bd. dirs. Mass. Advocacy Ctr., Boston, 1972—80. Capt. U.S. Army, 1955—57. Recipient Sarah L. Poiley Meml. award, N.Y. Acad. Scis., 1985, The Charles A. Dana award, 1989, NAS IOM, 1990, H. John Heinz award, 1995, Edward Barsky award, Physicians' Forum, 1997, Disting. Grad. award, U. Pa. Sch. Medicine, 1999, Prince Mahidol award in pub. health, Bangkok, 2003, Vernon Houk award, Soc. Occupl. Environ. Health. Fellow: Am. Acad. Pediat.; mem.: Am. Acad. Pediat. Com. on Environ. Hazards, Am. Acad. Child and Adolescent Psychiatry, Am. Pediat. Soc., Soc. of Toxicology, Sigma Xi, Phi Beta Kappa. Democrat. Jewish. Avocations: trout fishing, carpentry. Office: Univ Pitts Sch Medicine 3520 5th Ave Pittsburgh PA 15213-3320 Office Phone: 412-383-3128. Business E-Mail: hlnlead@pitt.edu.

**NEEDLEMAN, JACK,** education educator, researcher; b. N.Y.C., May 12, 1948; s. Charles and Bella Needleman; m. Barbara Berney, May 30, 1981; children: Rachel Berney Needleman, David Berney Needleman. BS, CCNY, 1969; MA, Maxwell Sch., Syracuse U., N.Y., 1973; PhD, Harvard U., Cambridge, Mass., 1995. V.p. Lewin/ICF, Washington, 1973—90; asst. prof. Harvard U. Sch. Pub. Health, Boston, 1995—2003; assoc. prof. UCLA Sch. Pub. Health, 2003—. Mem. JCAHO Nursing Adv. Coun., Oakbrook Terrace, Ill., 2003—. Recipient Health Svcs. Rsch. Impact award, Acad. Health, 2006; grantee numerous grants, NIH, U.S. Agy. Healthcare, Rsch. and Quality, and Robert Wood Johnson Found. Mem.: Phi Beta Kappa. Jewish. Achievements include conducted widely-cited landmark studies on the association of hospital nurse staffing and quality of care. Office: Univ Calif PO Box 951772 Los Angeles CA 90095-1772 Office Phone: 310-267-2706. Business E-Mail: needlema@ucla.edu.

**NEEDLEMAN, JACOB,** philosophy educator, writer; b. Phila., Oct. 6, 1934; s. Benjamin and Ida (Seltzer) Needleman; m. Carla Satzman, Aug. 30, 1959 (div. 1989); children: Raphael, Eve; m. Gail Anderson, Dec. 1989. BA, Harvard U., 1956; grad., U. Freiburg, 1957-58; PhD, Yale U., 1961. Clin. psychology trainee West Haven (Conn.) Veterans Hosp. Adminstrn., 1960-61; rsch. assoc. Rockefeller Inst., NY, 1961-62; from asst. prof. to assoc. prof. philosophy San Francisco State U., 1962-66, prof. philosophy, 1967—, chair dept. philosophy, 1968-69. Vis. scholar Union Theol. Seminary, 1967-68; dir. Ctr. Study New Religions, 1977-83; lectr. psychiatry cons. med. ethics U. Calif., 1981-84. Author: Being-in-the-World, 1963, The New Religions, 1970, Religion for a New Generation, 1973, A Sense of the Cosmos, 1975, On the Way to Self-Knowledge: Sacred Tradition and Psychotherapy, 1976, Lost Christianity, 1980, Consciousness and Tradition, 1982, The Heart of Philosophy, 1982, Sorcerers, 1986, Sin and Scientism, 1986, Lost Christianity: A Journey of Rediscovery to the Centre of Christian Experience, 1990, Money and the Meaning of Life, 1991, Modern Esoteric Spirituality, 1992, The Way of the Physician, 1993, The Indestructible Question, 1994, A Little Book on Love, 1996, Time and the Soul, 1998; The American Soul, 2002, The Wisdom of Love, 2005; (trans.) The Primary World of Senses, 1963, Essays on Ego Psychology, 1964; editor Care of Patients with Fatal Illness, 1969, The Sword of Gnosis, 1973, Sacred Tradition and Present Need, 1974, Understanding the New Religions, 1978, Speaking of My Life: The Art of Living in the Cultural Revolution, 1979, Real Philosophy: An Anthology of the Universal Search for Meaning, 1991, The American Soul, 2002; contbr. Death and Bereavement, 1969, To Live Within, 1971, My Life with a Brahmin Family, 1972, The New Man, 1972, The Universal Meaning of the Kabbalah, 1973, The Phenomenon of Death. Grantee Religion in Higher Edn., Marsden Found., 1967—68, Ella Lymna Cabot Trust, 1969, Far West Inst., 1975. Office: San Francisco State U Dept Philosophy 1600 Holloway Ave San Francisco CA 94132-1722 Office Phone: 415-338-2216. Business E-Mail: jneedle@sfsu.edu.

**NEEDLEMAN, PHILIP,** cardiologist, pharmacologist; b. Bklyn., Feb. 10, 1939; m. Sima Needleman. BS in Pharmacology, Phila. Coll. Pharm. & Sci., 1960, MS in Pharmacology, 1962; PhD in Pharmacology, U. Md. Med. Sch., 1964. Fellow Sch. Medicine Washington U., St. Louis, 1965—67, from asst. prof. to prof. Sch. Medicine, 1967—75, prof. Sch. Medicine, 1975—89, adj. prof., 1976—89, chmn., dept. pharmacology, 1989, chief scientist, 1991, assoc. dean, spl. projects, 2004; sr. v.p., chief scientist Monsanto, 1989—93; pres. Searle Pharma. Co., 1993—2000; sr. exec. v.p., chief scientist, chmn. R&D Pharmacia (fomerly Monsanto/Searle), 2000—03; ptnr. Prospect Ventures Ptnrs., 2003—. Served on com. NIH study sects.; adv. com. FDA, NIH, Nat. Coun. Washington Univ. Med. Sch. Contbr. numerous articles to profl. jours. Bd. trustee Washington U.; bd. dir. Barnes-Jewish Hosp., St. Louis Plant and Biotechnology consortium, St. Louis Sci. Ctr.; sci. advisor to pres. for R&D Ben Gurion U., 2002—; bd. trustee; mem. adv. com. for the creation of Nat. Inst. for Biotechnology in the Negev; bd. trustee Donald Danforth Plant Sci. Ctr. Recipient John Jacob Abel award, Am. Pharmacology Soc., 1974, Rsch. Career Devel. award, NIH, 1974, 1976, Wellcome Creesy award in clin. pharmacology, 1977, 1978, 1980, 1987, Cochems Thrombosis Rsch. prize, 1980, Rsch. Achievement award, Am. Heart Assn., 1988, Second Century award, 1994, C. Chester Stock award Lectureship Meml. Sloan Kettering Cancer Ctr., 2001, Indsl. Rsch. Inst. medal, 2001, Am. Soc. Exptl. Therapeutics award, Dart/NYU Biotechnology Achievement awards, Biotechnology Study Ctr. NYU Sch. Medicine, 2005. Mem.: IOM, NAS (chair phamacology-physiology sect. 2001—04, bd. trustee NAS Coun. 2004, award for Indsl. Application of Sci. 2005). Achievements include pioneering studies on the role of Cox 1 and Cox 2 enzymes in inflammation, cardiovascular and renal disease, and in tumor progression; developing the first angiotensin receptor antagonist, the first thromboxane synthetase inhibitor; discovering atriopeptin, the atrial natriuretic factor, a novel endocrine peptide that allows the heart to communicate with the kidneys and blood vessels. Office: Prospect Venture Ptnrs 435 Tasso St Ste 200 Palo Alto CA 94301 Office Phone: 650-327-8800. Office Fax: 650-324-8838.*

**NEEL, HARRY BRYAN, III,** surgeon, scientist, educator; b. Rochester, Minn., Oct. 28, 1939; s. Harry Bryan and May Birgitta (Bjornsson) N.; m. Ingrid Helene Vaga, Aug. 29, 1964; children: Carlton Bryan, Harry Bryan IV, Roger Clifton. BS, Cornell U., 1962; MD, SUNY-Bklyn., 1966; PhD, U. Minn., 1976. Otolaryngologist. Intern Kings County Hosp., Bklyn., 1966-67; resident in surg. surgery U. Minn. Hosps., Mpls., 1967-68; clin. assoc. NCI/NIH, 1968—70; resident in otolaryngology Mayo Grad. Sch. Medicine Mayo Clinic, Rochester, Minn., 1970-74, cons. in otorhinolaryngology, 1974—2005, cons. in cell biology, 1981—2005, assoc. prof. otolaryngology and microbiology Med. Sch., 1979-84, prof., 1984—, also chmn. dept. otolaryngology. Mem. sci. adv. com. Pitts. Eye and Ear Found.; lifetime vis. prof. Hunan U., China, 2003—. Author: Cryosurgery for Cancer, 1976; contbr. chpts. to books, articles to profl. jours. V.p. bd. dirs. Minn. Orch. in Rochester, Inc., 1982, pres., chmn., 1983—84; mem. devel. com. Minn. Orchestral Assn., 1983, Mayo Found., 1983—86; bd. dirs. Mayo Health Plan, 1986—92, chmn., 1990—92; mem. bd. Mayo Mgmt. Svcs., Inc., 1992—94; mem. bd. regents U. Minn., 1991—2003, chair faculty staff, student affairs com., 1993—95, 1999, vice chmn. bd., 1995—97, chmn. fin. and ops. com., 1999, mem. audit com., 1995—2000, chair litigation review com., 2001—03, chair facilities com., 2001—03; bd. dirs. Greater Rochester Area Univ. Ctr., 1993—2003; trustee U. Minn. Found., 1996—2005, mem. fin. com., 1999—2005; chmn. U. Minn. Investment Adv. Com., 1999—2005; mem. State Commn. on U. Minn. Excellence, 2002; founder U. Minn.-

Rochester Neel Scholarship Endowment Fund Health Scis., 2003. With USPHS, 1968—70. Recipient travel award Soc. Acad. Chmn. Otolaryngology, 1974, Ira J. Tresley rsch. award Am. Acad. Facial and Reconstructive Surgery, 1982, Master Tchr. award in surgery Alumni Assn. Coll. Medicine, SUNY, Health Sci. Ctr., Bklyn., 1991, Notable award Nat. Assn. Collegiate Women Athletic Adminstrs., 1992, The Best Doctors in Am. award Woodward/White, 1992-. Mem. AMA (com. adminstrn. and fin. Minn. chpt. 2003—05), ACS (bd. govs. 1985-90, devel. bd. 1988—, treas. 1990-98, sec.-treas. Minn. chpt. 1983-85, pres. 1988-89), Am. Acad. Otolaryngology-Head and Neck Surgery (prize for basic rsch. in otolaryngology 1972, bd. dirs. 1988-91, established Neel Disting. Rsch. Lectureship Endowment Fund 1994, audit com. 1998-2000, chair investment adv. com. 1995—, chmn. audit com. 1999-2000), Minn. Med. Assn. (com. on adminstrn. and fin. 2003—, Pub. Svc. Achievement award 2003), Zumbro Valley Med. Soc., Am. Broncho-Esophagological Assn. (pres. 1989-90), Am. Laryngological, Rhinological and Oto. Sco. (Mosher award 1980, pres.-elect 1995-96, centennial pres. 1996-97, investment com. 1994—, historian, 2001—), Am. Laryngological Assn. (Casselberry award 1985, sec. 1988-93, v.p. 1994, pres. 1994—, Newcomb award 1996, Baker lectr. 1998), Assn. for Rsch. in Otolaryngology, Assn. Acad. Depts. in Otolaryngology (sec.-treas. 1984-86, pres.-elect 1986, pres. 1988-9), Alumni Assn. Cornell U. (Outstanding Alumni award 1985), Collegium ORL Amicitiae Sacrum (bd. dirs. 2000—), Am. Bd. Otolaryngology (bd. dirs. 1986-2005, treas. 1998-2004), Am Laryngol. Voice Rsch. and Edn. Found. (charter bd. dirs. 1996—), Rochester Golf and Country Club. Republican. Presbyterian. Home: 828 8th St SW Rochester MN 55902-6310 Office: Mayo Clinic 200 1st St SW Rochester MN 55905-0002

**NEEL, JOHN DODD,** cemetery executive; b. McKeesport, Pa., Aug. 7, 1923; s. Harry Campbell and Anna (Dodd) N.; m. Jean Wyatt, Feb. 11, 1948; children: Harry C., John Dodd II W. Wyatt (dec.), Jeffrey J BA, Pa. State U., 1946. From salesman to pres. Jefferson Meml. Park, Pitts., 1946-88, chmn. bd. dirs., 1988—; chmn. Jefferson Meml. Funeral Home. Former mem., and chmn now alt. Zoning Hearing Bd., Pleasant Hills, Pa., 1970—. Mem. adv. bd. Pa. State U., McKeesport; former mem. Pa. State Real Estate Commn. 1st lt. USAAF, 1943-45 Decorated Air medal with 4 clusters, D.F.C.; recipient George Washington cert. Freedom Found., 1974 Mem. Pa. Cemetery Fun. Assn. (pres. 1963-65), Internat. Cemetery and Funeral Assn. (pres. 1973-74), West Jefferson Hills C. of C. (pres. 1984), VFW, Am. Legion 57th Bomb Wing Assn., South Hills Country Club, Indian Lake Golf Club, Aero Club, OX-5CLUB, Kiwanis (pres. 1959), Masons, Shriners, Tau Kappa Epsilon, Delta Sigma Pi Presbyterian. Office: 401 Curry Hollow Rd Pittsburgh PA 15236-4636 Office Phone: 412-655-4500.

**NEEL, JUDY MURPHY,** management consultant; b. Rhome, Tex. d. James W. and Linna B. (Sease) Neel; m. Ellis F. Murphy, Jr., Dec. 30, 1975; children from previous marriage: Mary B. Schmidt, Janet E. Hollingsworth, Susan E. Salinas. BS, Northwestern U., 1977; MBA, Roosevelt U., 1983. V.p. Murphy, Tashjian & Assocs., Chgo., 1960-73; exec. dir. Automotive Affiliated Rep. Assn., Chgo., 1973-78; mgr. Automotive Svc. Ind. Assn., Chgo., 1978-80; exec. dir. Am. Soc. Safety Engrs., Des Plaines, Ill., 1980-98, Am. Assn. Diabetes Educators, 1999—2003; mgmt. cons., 2003—. Recipient Assn. Leadership Award Bus. Women's Network/Assn. Trends Mag., 1998. Mem. Chgo. Soc. Assn. Execs. (bd. dirs. 1979—, pres. 1985—, Shapiro award 1991), Am. Soc. Assn. Execs. (sec.-treas. 1994, found. dir. 1986-90, bd. dirs. 1990-95, Key award 1986). Republican. E-mail: jneelcae@aol.com.

**NEEL, RICHARD EUGENE,** economist, educator; b. Bluefield, Va., Jan. 7, 1932; s. Charles Richard and Zell LaVerne (Bowling) Neel; m. Binnie Jo LeFever, June 10, 1961; children: Jeffrey Richard, Cynthia Jo. BS, U. Tenn., 1954, MS, 1955; PhD, Ohio State U., 1960. Instr. econs. Ohio State U., 1958-60; asst. prof. econs. Coll. William and Mary, 1960-61; asst. prof. U. South Fla., 1961-63, assoc. prof., 1963-66, chmn. econs. and fin. programs, 1964-66, acting chmn. grad. program Coll. Bus Adminstrn., 1965-66; dir. instl. planning Fla. Tech. U., 1966-68, chmn. dept. econs., prof. econs., 1968-69; assoc. dean Sch. Bus. Adminstrn. Ga. State U., 1969-77, dean grad. studies Sch. Bus. Adminstrn., 1973-77, prof. econs. Sch. Bus. Adminstrn., 1969-78; dean Coll. Bus. Adminstrn. U. N.C., Charlotte, 1978-93, prof. econs., 1978-97, dean emeritus Belk Coll. Bus. Adminstrn., 1997—, prof. econs. emeritus, 1994—. Author (contbg auth): (book) The Case Study of Off-Campus Postsecondary Education on Military Bases, 1980; contbr. articles, monographs to profl pubs; editor: (book) Readings in Price Theory, 1973. Bd dirs Charlotte Foreign Trade Zone. Mem.: Beta Gamma Sigma, Phi Kappa Phi. Presbyterian. Office: U NC at Charlotte Dept Economics Charlotte NC 28223 Office Phone: 704-687-4122. Business E-Mail: reneel@email.uncc.edu.

**NEEL, SANDRA LAUREEN,** voice educator, vocalist; b. Derby, Conn., Nov. 23, 1941; d. John Wilson and Donna Elaine McKearin; m. Imre Zoltan Niamesny (div.); children: Laureen Elizabeth, Imre John; m. Eddie Dean Neel, Mar. 18, 1981. MusB, Lawrence U., 1963; postgrad., Akademie der Musik Darstellende Kunst, Vienna, Austria, 1966. Founder Bel Canto Studio, Westport, Conn., 1973—81, Bozeman, Mont., 1981—85, Albuquerque, 1985—. Sec. De Profundis Men's Choir, Albuquerque, 1998—2000; workshop presenter in field. Spkr., singer, adv. Very Spl. Arts, Albuquerque, 1995—. Named winner Young Artist's Competition, Green Bay Symphony, 1963, artist-in-residence, N.Mex. State, 1990—92. Mem.: Nat. Assn. Tchrs. Singing (N.Mex. program chair 1991—93, N.Mex. v.p. 1993—95, N.Mex. state pres. 1995—97). Republican. Christian Scientist. Avocations: writing, reading, acting, travel. Home and Studio: 3709 Frbbe St NE Albuquerque NM 87111 Office Phone: 505-822-0949.

**NEELAMEGHAM, SRIRAM,** chemical engineer, educator, researcher; PhD, Rice U., Houston, 1996. Assoc. prof. chem. and biol. engring. SUNY, Buffalo, 1997—2003, asst. prof. chem. engring., 2003—. Office: SUNY 906 Furnas Hall Buffalo NY 14260 Office Phone: 716-645-2911. Office Fax: 716-645-3822.

**NEELEMAN, DAVID,** air transportation executive; b. 1959; m. Vicki Neeleman; 9 children. Student, U. Utah. With Southwest Airlines; exec. v.p. Morris Air Corp., 1984—88, pres., 1988—94; CEO Open Skies, 1995—98; co-founder, bd. dir. WestJet, 1996—99; CEO, bd. dir. JetBlue Airways Corp., Forest Hills, NY, 1998—. Named Transport Industry Innovator, Time mag., 2000; named one of Top Ten Entrepreneurs of 2000, Bus. Week Mag.; Most Influential Bus. Travel Execs., Bus. Travel News, 2000; recipient NY Ten awards, Exec. Coun., 2004. Office: JetBlue Airways Corp 118-29 Queens Blvd Forest Hills NY 11415*

**NEELEY, BEVERLY EVON,** sociologist, consultant; b. Oakland, Calif., June 14, 1947; d. Chester Arthur Neeley Jr. and Thalia Evon Neeley-Littlefield; m. Niles Bruce, Sept. 13, 1970 (div. Aug. 1977); 1 child, Autumn Yvonne Curd BA, U. Calif., Berkeley, 1970, MPH, 1972; PhD, U. Calif., San Diego, 1983. Eligibility supr. W. Oakland Health Ctr., 1970-72; health edn. supr. San Diego County Drug Edn., 1972-74; proposal writer, cons. Cmty. Crisis Ctr., San Diego, 1974-77; sociologist, dir., sec., treas. Image Mind, Inc., Oakland, 1993—. Instr. Calif. State U., San Diego, 1976; health planner Health Sys. Agy., San Diego, 1978; mem. adv. bd. Help Other People Evole Inst., Oakland, 2000—; sr. acad. cons. Hercules NAACP Saturday Sch., 2002; tchrs., rschr. Adult Pub. Schs., 1983—. Author: The Ethiopian Grail: On the Origin of Cultural Excellence, 1994, Ancient Ethiopian Egyptian Cultural Excellence, 2003. Founder S.E. Drug Coalition, San Diego, 1974, Nu-Way Youth Svc. Ctr., San Diego, 1976. Mem. NAACP, Sojourner Truth Tenants Assn., Nat. Assn. Negro Bus. and Profl. Women's Clubs Inc. Avocations: reading, walking, cooking. Home and Office: 5915 Martin Luther King Jr Way B10 Oakland CA 94609 Office Phone: 510-653-7561. E-mail: drbneeley3@hotmail.com.

**NEELEY, SHIRLEY,** school system administrator; 1 child, Brandy. BA, U. Houston, EdD in Curriculum and Instrn.; MA, Prairie View A&M U. Supt. Galena Park Independent Sch. Dist., Tex., 1995—2004; commr. Tex. Edn. Agency, 2004—. Former pres. Tex. Assn. of Suburban and Mid-Urban Schs.; mem. So. Regional Edn. Bd., 2003; supt. Tex. Assn. of Sch. Bd.'s, 2003. Bd. mem. Harris County Youth Program, Tex. Academic Decathlon; bd. dirs. North Channel Area C. of C. Mem.: Houston Livestock Show (life; com. mem.), Rotary Club. Office: Tex Edn Agency 1701 N Congress Ave Austin TX 78701-1494 Office Phone: 512-463-8985. E-mail: commissioner@tea.state.tx.us.

**NEELY, CAMERON MICHAEL,** former professional hockey player; b. Comox, B.C., Can., June 6, 1965; Hockey player Vancouver Canucks, 1983-86, Boston Bruins, 1986-96. Player NHL All-Star Game, 1988-91. Recipient Bill Masterton Meml. trophy, 1993-94; named to Sporting News All-Star Team, 1987-88, 93-94; elected to the Hockey Hall of Fame, 2005 Office: Cam Neely Found Neely House 30 Winter St Ste 2D Boston MA 02108-4720

**NEELY, CHARLES B., JR.,** lawyer; b. Raleigh, N.C., Dec. 11, 1943; BA with honors, U. N.C., 1965; JD, Duke U., 1970. Bar: N.C. 1970. Lawyer Maupin Taylor P.A., Raleigh. Mem. 4th Cir. Jud. Conf. Mem. N.C. Ho. of Reps., 1995-99. Capt. USNR, JAGC, 1965-89. Fellow Am. Bar Found.; mem. ABA (taxation sect.), N.C. Bar Assn. (chmn. law office mgmt. sect. 1986-88, bd. govs. 1995-98), Inst. for Profls. in Taxation. Address: Maupin Taylor PA PO Drawer 19764 Ste 500 3200 Beechleaf Ct Raleigh NC 27619 E-mail: cneely@maupintaylor.com.

**NEELY, ELLEN J.,** lawyer; b. 1964; BA in Govt. and History, U. Tex.; JD, U. Chgo. Assoc. Wildman, Harrold, Allen & Dixon; asst. gen. counsel Chgo. Mercantile Exchange, 1995—99; v.p., gen. counsel Chgo. Stock Exchange, 1999—2001, sr. v.p. legal and market regulation, gen. counsel, corp. sec., 2001—05, pres. & gen. counsel, 2005—. Office: Chgo Stock Exchange One Financial Pl 440 S LaSalle St Chicago IL 60605

**NEELY, JOHN GAIL,** otolaryngologist; b. Oklahoma City, Dec. 10, 1939; MD, U. Okla., 1965. Intern U. Oreg. Med. Ctr., Portland, 1965-66; resident in surgery Baylor Hosp., Houston, 1968-69, resident in otolaryngology, 1969-72; fellow Otologic Med. Group, L.A., 1972-73; staff Barnes Hosp., St. Louis, 1992—, Jewish Hosp., St. Louis, 1992—; prof., dir. rsch. Washington U., St. Louis, 1992—. Mem. ACS, Am. Neurotology Soc., Am. Otol. Soc., Am. Acad. Otolaryngology, Head and Neck Surgery, Am. Univ. Otolaryngologists, Triologic Soc. Office: Washington U Sch Medicine Dept Oto Head-Neck Surgrey 660 S Euclid Ave Box 8115 Saint Louis MO 63110-1010 Office Phone: 314-362-7344. Business E-Mail: neelyg@ent.wustl.edu.

**NEELY, MARK EDWARD, JR.,** writer; b. Amarillo, Tex., Nov. 10, 1944; s. Mark Edward and Lottie (Wright) N.; m. Sylvia Eakes, June 15, 1966. BA, Yale U., 1966, PhD, 1973; LHD (hon.), Lincoln Coll., 1981. Visiting instr. Iowa State U., 1971—72; dir. Louis A. Warren Lincoln Library and Museum, Ft. Wayne, Ind., 1972—92; John Francis Bannon Prof. History and Am. Studies Saint Louis U., 1992—98; McCabe-Greer Prof. Civil War History Pa. State U., University Park, 1998—. Vis. instr. Iowa State U., Ames, 1971-72; editor Lincoln Lore, 1973—; mem. adv. bd. Ind. Historical Bureau, 1980—; mem. editorial adv. com. Ind. Mag. of History, 1981—; mem. editorial bd. Ulysses S. Grant Assn., 1981—. Author: The Abraham Lincoln Encyclopedia, 1981, The Lincoln Family Album: Photographs From The Personal Collection of a Historic American Family, 1990, The Fate of Liberty: Abraham Lincoln and Civil Liberties, 1991 (Pulitzer Prize for history 1992), The Last Best Hope on Earth: Abraham Lincoln and the Promise of America, 1993, Southern Rights: Political Prisoners and the Myth of Confederate Constitutionalism, 1999, The Union Divided: Party Conflict in the Civil War North, 2002, The Boundaries of American Political Culture in the Civil War Era, 2005; (with Harold Holzer and Gabor S. Boritt) The Lincoln Image: Abraham Lincoln and the Popular Print, 1984, The Confederate Image: Prints of the Last Cause, 1987; (with R. Gerald McMurty) The Insanity File: The Case of Mary Todd Lincoln, 1986; (with Holzer) Mine Eyes Have Seen the Glory: The Civil War in american Art, 1993. Mem. Abraham Lincoln Assn., Soc. Ind. Archivists (pres. 1980-81), Ind. Assn. of Historians (pres. 1987-88).*

**NEELY, RICHARD,** lawyer; b. Aug. 2, 1941; s. John Champ and Elinore (Forlani) N.; m. Carolyn Elaine Elmore, 1979; children: John Champ, Charles Whittaker. AB, Dartmouth Coll., 1964; LLB, Yale U., 1967. Bar: W.Va. 1967. Practiced in, Fairmont, W.Va., 1969-73; chmn. Marion County Bd. Pub. Health, 1971-72; mem. of W.Va. Ho. of Dels., 1971-73; justice, chief justice W.Va. Supreme Ct. of Appeals, Charleston, 1973-95; ptnr. Neely & Hunter, Charleston, 1995—. Chmn. bd. Kane & Keyser Co., Belington, W.Va., 1970-88. Author: How Courts Govern America, 1980, Why Courts Don't Work, 1983, The Divorce Decision, 1984, Judicial Jeopardy: When Business Collides with the Courts, 1986, The Product Liability Mess: How Business Can Be Rescued from State Court Politics, 1988, Take Back Your Neighborhood: A Case for Modern-Day Vigilantism, 1990, Tragedies of our Own Making: How Private Choices have Created Public Bankruptcy, 1994; contbr. articles to nat. mags. Mem. bd. advisors BNA Class Action Litigation Report. Capt. U.S. Army, 1967-69. Decorated Bronze Star, Vietnam Honor medal 1st Class. Mem.: Am. Legion, VFW, Internat. Brotherhood Elec. Workers, W.Va. Bar Assn., Fourth Cir. Jud. Conf. (life), Moose, Phi Sigma Kappa, Phi Delta Phi. Episcopalian. Office: Neely & Hunter 159 Summers St Charleston WV 25301-2134 Office Phone: 304-343-6500. Business E-Mail: rneely@neelyhunter.com.

**NEELY, SALLY SCHULTZ,** lawyer; b. LA, Mar. 2, 1948; BA, Stanford U., 1970, JD, 1971. Bar: Ariz. 1972, Calif. 1977. Law clk. to judge U.S. Ct. Appeals (9th cir.), Phoenix, 1971-72; assoc. Lewis and Roca, Phoenix, 1972-75; asst. prof. Law Sch. Harvard U., Cambridge, Mass., 1975-77; assoc. Shutan & Trost, P.C., LA, 1977-79; ptnr., sr. counsel Sidley Austin LLP, LA, 1980—. Co-chair Am. Law Inst.-ABA Chpt. 11 Bus. Reorgns., 1989-95, 97—, Banking and Comml. Lending Law, 1997-99, Nat. Conf. Bankruptcy Judges, 1988, 90, 95, 96, 97, 99, 02, 06, Fed. Jud. Ctr., 1989, 90, 94-95, Southeast Bankruptcy Law Inst., 2002, 06, Workshop Bankruptcy and Bus. Reorgn. NYU, 1992—; rep. 9th cir. jud. conf., 1989-91; mem. Nat. Bankruptcy Conf., 1993—, co-chair com. on legis., 2001—, mem. exec. com. Chair Stanford U. Law Sch. Reunion Giving, 1996; bd. vis. Stanford U. Law Sch., 1990-92. Mem.: ABA, Calif. Bar Assn., Am. Coll. Bankruptcy (mem. bd. regents 1998—2003, chair ednl. programs com. 2003—, bd. dirs. 2003—05, v.p. 2005—). Office: Sidley Austin LLP 555 W 5th St Ste 4000 Los Angeles CA 90013-3000 Office Phone: 213-896-6024. Business E-Mail: sneely@sidley.com.

**NEELY, WILLIAM CHARLES,** chemistry professor, consultant, research scientist; b. Cave City, Ark., Nov. 22, 1931; s. Kenneth Andrew and Sara Virginia Neely; m. Betty Jean Tibi, Dec. 7, 1956; children: Virginia Stringfellow, William(dec.). PhD, La. State U., 1962. Rsch. chemist Chemstrand Rsch. Ctr. Inc., Research Triangle Park, NC, 1962—66; prof. Auburn (Ala.) U., 1962—. Cons. Auburn Chem. Co. Inc., 1986—, Sci. Applications Internat., San Diego, 1995—. Contbr. articles to profl. jours.; inventor in field. Chmn. Bd. Zoning Adjustment, Auburn, 1986—96. With U.S. Army, 1954—56. Germany. Mem.: Sigma Xi (life). Home: 415 Hare Ave Auburn AL 36830 Office: Auburn U Dept Chemistry 257 Chemistry Bldg Auburn AL 36849 Office Phone: 334-844-4043. Business E-Mail: neelywc@auburn.edu.

**NEENAN, PETER ANTHONY,** state agency administrator; b. Sioux City, Iowa, Dec. 12, 1946; s. Edward W. and Margaret B. Neenan; m. Linda J. Fisher, Feb. 5, 1947. BA, Creighton U., 1969; MA, U. Iowa, 1972; PhD, U. Wis., 1982. Asst. prof. Simmons Coll., Boston, 1978—82, U. of NC, Chapel Hill, 1982—86, sr. rsch. assoc., 1987—2000; sr. rsch. scientist Rsch. Triangle Inst., Research Triangle Park, NC, 2000—01; dir. labor market info. Employment Security Commn. of NC, Raleigh, 2002—. Contbr. articles to profl. jours. Precinct chair Dem. Party of NC, 1985—86. Mem.: ALA, Nat. Assn. State

Workforce Agys., Nat. Assn. Welfare Rsch. and Stats., Am. Assn. Pub. Opinion Rsch., Am. Evaluation Assn. (co-chair human services tig 2001—02). Democrat. Roman Catholic. Avocations: travel, history, stamp collecting/philately. Office: Employment Security Commission of North 700 Wade Ave Raleigh NC 27611

**NEER, CHARLES SUMNER, II,** orthopedic surgeon, educator; b. Vinita, Okla., Nov. 10, 1917; s. Charles Sumner and Pearl Victoria (Brooke) N.; m. Eileen Meyer, June 12, 1990; children: Charlotte Marguerite, Sydney Victoria, Charles Henry. BA, Dartmouth Coll., 1939; MD, U. Pa., 1942. Diplomate Am. Bd. Orthopaedic Surgery (bd. dirs. 1970-75). Intern U. Pa. Hosp., Phila., 1942-43; asso. in surgery N.Y. Orthopedic-Columbia-Presbyn. Med. Center, N.Y.C., 1943-44; instr. in surgery Coll. Physicians and Surgeons, Columbia U., N.Y.C., 1946-47, instr. orthopaedic surgery, 1947-57, asst. prof. clin. orthopaedic surgery, 1957-64, asso. prof., 1964-68, prof. clin. orthopaedic surgery, 1968-90, prof. clin. orthopaedic surgery emeritus, spl. lectr. orthopaedic surgery, 1990—. Attending orthopaedic surgeon Columbia-Presbyn. Med. Ctr., N.Y.C.; chief adult reconstructive svc. N.Y. Orthopaedic Hosp.; chief shoulder and elbow clinic Presbyn. Hosp.; cons. orthopaedic surgeon emeritus N.Y. Orthopaedic-Columbia-Presbyn. Med. Ctr., 1991—; chmn. 4th Internat. Congress Shoulder Surgeons; chmn. Internat. Bd. Shoulder Surgery, 1992—. Founder, chmn. bd. trustees Jour. Shoulder and Elbow Surgery, 1990—; contbr. articles to books, tech. films, sound slides. Served with U.S. Army, 1944-46. Recipient Disting. Svc. award Am. Bd. Orthopaedic Surgeons 1975. Fellow ACS (sr. mem. nat. com. on trauma); Am. Acad. Orthop. Surgeons (com. on upper extremity, shoulder com.); mem. AMA, ACS (mem. com. trauma), Am. Bd. Orthop. Surgeons (bd. dirs. 1970-75, Disting. Svc. award 1975), Am. Shoulder and Elbow Surgeons (inaugural pres.), Am. Assn. Surgery Trauma, Am. Orthop. Assn., Mid-Am. Orthop. Assn. (hon.), N.Y. Acad. Medicine, Allen O. Whipple Surg. Soc., N.Y. State Med. Soc., N.Y. County Med. Soc., Pan Am. Med. Assn., Am. Trauma Soc., Soc. Latino Am. Orthop. y Traumatology, Internat. Soc. Orthop. Surgery and Traumatology, Va. Orthop. Soc. (hon.), Carolina Orthop. Alumni Assn. (hon.), Conn. Orthop. Club (hon.), Houston Orthop. Assn. (hon.), Soc. Française de Chirurgie Orthop. et Traumatology (hon.), Soc. Italiana Orthop. Etravmatologia e Traumatologia; patron, Shoulder and Elbow Soc. Australia, South African Shoulder Svc., Giraffe Club, Internat. Bd. Shoulder Surgery (chmn. 1992—), Alpha Omega Alpha, Phi Chi. Home and Office: 231 S Miller St Vinita OK 74301-3625 Office Phone: 918-256-6673. E-mail: elmcreekacres@junct.com. *Forever grateful I could be a doctor and especially to work in the exciting area of shoulder surgery.*

**NEESON, LIAM,** actor; b. Ballymena, No. Ireland, June 7, 1952; s. Barney and Kitty N.; m. Natasha Richardson, July 3, 1994; children: Michael Richard Antonio, Daniel Jack. Theatrical appearances include (Broadway) The Judas Kiss, 1998, Anna Christie, 1993 (Theatre World award, 1993); films include Excalibur, 1981, Krull, 1983, The Bounty, 1984, The Innocent, 1984, Lamb, 1986, Duet for One, 1986, The Mission, 1986, A Prayer for the Dying, 1987, Suspect, 1987, Satisfaction, 1988, The Good Mother, 1988, Next of Kin, 1989, Darkman, 1990, Crossing the Line, 1990, Ruby Cairo, 1991, Shining Through, 1992, Under Suspicion, 1992, Husbands and Wives, 1992, Leap of Faith, 1992, Ethan Fromme, 1992, Schindler's List, 1993 (Best Actor Acad. award nominee 1994), Nell, 1994, Rob Roy, 1995, Before and After, 1996, Michael Collins, 1996, Les Miserables, 1998, Star Wars: Episode I-The Phantom Menace, 1999, The Haunting, 1999, Gun Shy, 2000, K-19: The Widowmaker, 2002, Gangs of New York, 2002, Love Actually, 2003, Kinsey, 2004 (Best Actor, Los Angeles Film Critics Assn. award, 2004), Kingdom of Heaven, 2005, Batman Begins, 2005, Breakfast on Pluto, 2005, (voice) The Chronicles of Narnia: The Lion, the Witch, and the Wardrobe, 2005. Officer of the Order of the British Empire, 1999.*

**NEFF, AMY HANCOCK,** elementary school educator; b. Phila., Dec. 1, 1961; d. Vance and Doris (Kroesser) Hancock; m. Ernest William Neff, July 18, 1987; 1 child, Kaylee. BS in Edn., Bloomsburg U., 1983; MEd, Beaver Coll., 1990. Elem. tchr. Archdiocese of Phila., 1983-85; contract specialist GSA, 1985-86; elem. tchr. Neshaminy Sch. Dist., Langhorne, Pa., 1987—. Bldg. sci. rep. K-12 Sci. Adv. Com., Langhorne, 1987-99, 2001-2002; mem. Sci. Textbook Selection Com. Langhorne, 1991; sch. sci. fair coord., 1992-94; participant NASA Ednl. Workshop for Elem. Sch. Tchrs., Kennedy Space Ctr., Fla., 1990, Johnson Space Ctr., Houston, 1991; Project LABS participant Rohm and Haas Corp., summer, 1994, presenter Delaware Valley Sci. Week; presenter dist.-wide space and physics workshops, 1990-94; participant Sci. Lesson Study, 2004-2005; mem. Grade 4 Curriculum Devel. Com. for Social Studies, sci. program pilot tchr., 2006-. Rider Am. Cancer Soc., Bike-a-Thons, 1989-92, MS 150 Bike Tour, 1992; vol. Action Team, Langhorne, 1991. Mem. Am. Fedn. Tchrs., Nat. Sci. Tchrs. Assn. (dist. rep. nat. conv. 1991-93), Bucks County Sci. Tchrs. Assn., Phila. Area Elem. Sci. Tchrs. Assn., Kappa Delta Pi (v.p. 1981-82). Avocations: guitar, bicycling, singing, aerobics, yoga. Home: 12 Amaryllis Ln Newtown PA 18940-1246 Office: Oliver Heckman Elem Sch Cherry St Langhorne PA 19047

**NEFF, BONITA DOSTAL,** communication development facilitator; b. Grinnell, Iowa, Aug. 16, 1942; d. Lester Ernest and Mary Margaret (Hudnut) Dostal; m. Gregory Pall Neff, Apr. 27, 1974; 1 child, Kristiana. BA, U. N. Iowa, 1964, MA, 1966; PhD, U. Mich., 1973; AA cum laude, Lansing C.C., Mich., 1980. Cert. cycling instr. Edn. leadership fellow George Washington U., Washington, 1976-77; specialist Mich. State U., East Lansing, 1977-80, co-investigator family and child inst. energy rsch. team, 1980-82; asst. prof. comm. Purdue U., Hammond, Ind., 1982-87; pres. Pub. Comm. Assocs., Munster, Ind., 1986—; assoc. prof. comm. Valparaiso (Ind.) U., 1991—; tchr. scholar Nat. Comm. Assn., Inst. for Faculty Devel., 2006. Co-organizer European Comm. Conf., Dubrovnik, Croatia, 2002—; vis. prof. grad. comm. program U. Kadar, Croatia, 2003, Sogang U., Seoul, Republic of Korea, 2005; co-founding mem. Internat. Interdisciplinary and Intercultural Annual Conf. in Pub. Rels., Sogang; adv. bd. Australian Ctr. Pub. Comm.; presenter, cons. in field. Mem. adv. bd., reviewer Jour. Applied Comm. Rsch.; mem. editrl. bd. Jour. Promotional Mgmt., Jour. Pub. Rels. Rsch., Pub. Rels. Rev., on-line jour. multicultural comm. from Cyprus; reviewer Mgmt. Comm. Quar.: An Internat. Jour.; editor procs. on accreditation for nat. conf.; contbr. chpts. in books, profl. articles and poetry to jours. Mem. Nat. Steering Commn. for Revision of Pub. Rels. Curriculum, 1996—; chair nat. benchmark study on pub. rels. edn.; mem. Nat. Task Force Pub. Rels. Conf. 1998; mem. Lake County (Ind.) Cmty. Devel. Bd., 1984—; bd. dirs. Big Bros. and Big Sisters N.W. Ind., 1984, 87; pres., chmn. bd. dirs. N.W. Ind. Youth Chorus, 1985—; bd. dirs., mktg. com. N.W. Ind. Symphony, bd. dirs. PBS56-Ind.; sec. exec. com., 2000—; pub. rep. Nat. PBS Adv. Bd. Faculty Rsch. grant U. Mich., 1971, Consumer Product Safety Comn. grant, 1976-77, Ind. Arts Commn./Nat. Endowment for Arts grant, 1990-92, Valparaiso U. Diversity grant, 1996 Mem.: Nat. Commn. on Undergrad. and Grad. Pub. Rels. Curriculum (nat. task force for conf. 1998), Pub. Rels. Soc. Am. (advisor 2001, sec. internat. divsn. 2005—, established student chpt., chair 2006—), Internat. Acad. Bus. Disciplines (co-chair pub. rels. divsn.), World Comm. Assn., Assn. Educators in Journalism Mass Comm. (chair internat. com. 1994—96, scholarly liaison com. 1995—, chair elect rels. divsn.), Ctrl. States Comm. Assn. (founder and chmn. 1988—89, pub. rels. officer 1989—92), Nat. Comm. Assn. (founder and twice chair of pub. rels. divsn. 1988, chmn. nat. Pub. Rels. Rsch. awards com. PRIDE 1988, nat. legis. coun. rep. 1993—96, seminar leader 2006, nat. com. on convs. allied orgns., task force on nat. policy), Internat. Pub. Rels. Assn., Internat. Comm. Assn. (chmn. task force on accreditation 1988, newsletter editor 1997, chair planning pub. rels. divsn. internat. conf. South Korea, chair dissertation thesis award com. pub. rels. divsn.), Assn. Women in Comm. (assoc.; pres. Calumet chpt. 1985—90, advisor Valparaiso Student AWC, Inc. 1994—, advisor PRSSA student chpt. and PR agy.), Outstanding Communicator 1990, Nat. Outstanding chpt. advisor 1999). Democrat. Roman Catholic. Avocations: ballet, tap, piano, reading, professional clown. Home: 8320 Greenwood Ave Munster IN 46321-1813 Office: Pub Comm Assocs 8320 Greenwood Ave Munster IN 46321-1813 Office Phone: 219-464-6827. Business E-Mail: bonita.neff@valpo.edu.

**NEFF, DANIEL A.,** lawyer; b. Phila., Jan. 7, 1953; AB magna cum laude, Brown U., 1974; JD, Columbia U., 1977. Bar: N.Y. 1978, D.C. 1980. Ptnr., corp. dept. Wachtell, Lipton, Rosen & Katz, N.Y.C., mng. ptnr. of firm. Notes and comments editor: Columbia Law Rev., 1976-77. Named in Dealmaker of the Year article, Am. Lawyer mag., 2001. Mem. ABA, Phi Beta Kappa. Office: Wachtell Lipton Rosen & Katz c/o Gail Edelman 51 W 52nd St Fl 29 New York NY 10019-6150 Office Phone: 212-403-1218. Office Fax: 212-403-2218. Business E-Mail: daneff@wlrk.com.

**NEFF, DAVID M.,** lawyer; b. Allentown, Pa., Nov. 18, 1960; BSJ, Northwestern Univ., 1982; JD, DePaul Univ., 1985. Bar: Ill. 1985, US Dist. Ct. (no. Ill., ea. & we. Wis., we. Mich. dist.). Law clk. Judge Robert E. Ginsberg, US Bankruptcy Ct., no. dist. Ill., 1985—86; ptnr., co-chmn. Lodging & Timeshare practice group DLA Piper Rudnick Gray Cary, Chgo. Contbr. articles to profl. jours. Mem.: Internat. Soc. Hospitality Consultants (chmn.), ABA (co-chmn. publications, Bankruptcy & Insolvency subcommittee.), Am. Bankruptcy Inst., 7th Cir. Bar Assn. (Ill. bankruptcy liason), Chgo. Bar Assn. (chmn. bankruptcy & reorganization com. 1998—99). Office: DLA Piper Rudnick Gray Cary Suite 1900 203 N LaSalle St Chicago IL 60601-1293 Office Phone: 312-368-4042. Office Fax: 312-630-2758. Business E-Mail: david.neff@dlapiper.com.

**NEFF, DONALD LLOYD,** news correspondent, writer; b. York, Pa., Oct. 15, 1930; s. Harry William and Gertrude Marie N.; m. Abigail Trafford; 1 son, Gregory Harry. Student, Trinity Coll., San Antonio, 1949, York Coll. 1950-52, N.Y. U., 1953. Reporter York Dispatch, 1954-56, L.A. Mirror-News, 1956-57, UPI, L.A., 1957-61; with L.A. Times, 1961-64, bur. chief Tokyo, 1964; with Time mag., 1965-81, corr. Vietnam, 1965-66, writer N.Y.C., 1966-68, bur. chief Houston, 1968-70, L.A., 1970-73, Jerusalem, 1975-78, N.Y.C., 1978-79, sr. editor, 1973-75; news svcs. editor Washington Star, 1979-80. Author: Warriors at Suez: Eisenhower Takes America into the Middle East, 1981, Warriors for Jerusalem, The Six Days That Changed the Middle East, 1984; Warriors Against Israel, 1988, Fallen Pillars; U.S. Policy Toward Palestine and Israel since 1945, 1995, 2d edit., 2002, Fifty Years of Israel, 1998. Served with AUS, 1948-50. Recipient Theta Sigma Phi Matrix award, 1962, Calif.-Nev. AP Writing Contest best met. spot news story award, 1962, Overseas Press Club award for best fgn. article in a mag., 1979; finalist Am. Book Award History category, 1982. Mem. Fgn. Press Assn. (Israel pres. 1977, v.p. 1978)

**NEFF, FRED LEONARD,** lawyer; b. St. Paul, Nov. 1, 1948; s. Elliott Ira and Mollie (Poboisk) N.; m. Christa Ruth Powell, Sept. 10, 1989; 1 child, Lena. BS with high distinction, U. Minn., 1970; JD, William Mitchell Coll. Law, 1976. Bar: Minn. 1976, ND 1994, US Dist. Ct. Minn. 1977, US Ct. Appeals (8th cir.) 1985, US Supreme Ct. 1985, Wis. 1986, US Dist. Ct. (ea. and we. dists.) Wis. 1992. Tchr. Hopkins Pub. Schs., Minn., 1970-72; instr. U. Minn., Mpls., 1974-76; pvt. practice Mpls., 1976-79; asst. county atty. Sibley County, Gaylord, Minn., 1979-80; mng. atty. Hyatt Legal Svcs., St. Paul, 1981-83, regional ptnr., 1983-85, profl. devel. ptnr., 1985-86; pres. Neff Law Firm, Pa., Mpls., 1986—; CEO Profl. Devel. Inst. Inc., Edina, Minn., 1994—, also bd. dirs. Instr. Inver Hills Coll., 1973-77; counsel Am. Tool Supply Co., St. Paul, 1976-78; cons. Nat. Detective Agy., Inc., St. Paul, 1980-83; CEO A Basic Legal Svc., Bloomington, 1990—; CEO, bd. dirs. Profl. Devel. Inst. Inc., Edina, Minn., 1994—; lectr., guest instr. U. Wis., River Falls, 1976-77; spl. instr. Hamline U., St. Paul, 1977; vis. lectr. Coll. St. Scholastica, Duluth, Minn., 1977; program. faculty, cons. Employment Law Seminar for Colo. Fla., La., Oreg., Employment and Labor Law Seminar for Ala., Alaska, Calif., Conn., Ind., NC, Ohio, Va., NC Safety and Health at the Workplace, SC Labor Law, Ohio Safety at the Workplace; bd. dirs. Acceptance Ins. Holdings, Inc., Omaha; active Internat. Confederation Jurists, 1993; mem. faculty sem. Ariz. Safety at Workplace, Hawaii Employment & Labor, Miss. Employment & Labor Law, Del. Employment & Labor, Alaska Employment and Labor Law, Ga. Employment & Labor Law, NJ Employment & Labor, Wash. Employment Law, Mass. Employment & Labor Law, 1995—, Ark. Employment and Labor Law, Mo. Employment and Labor Law, Iowa Employment and Labor Law, Utah Employment and Labor Law; pres. Martial Arts Bookstore Internat., Inc., 1998; pres. Endless Fist Soc., Inc. 1998. Author: Fred Neff's Self-Defense Library, 1976, Everybody's Self-Defense Book, 1978, Karate Is for Me, 1980, Running Is for Me, 1980, Lessons from the Samurai, 1986, Lessons from the Art of Kempo, 1986, Lessons from the Western Warriors, 1986, Lessons from the Fighting Commandos, 1990, Lessons from the Ancient Japanese Masters of Self-Defense, 1990, Lessons from the Eastern Warriors, 1990, Mysterious Persons of the Past, 1991, Great Mysteries of Crime, 1991; host TV series Great Puzzles In History; co-host TV series Great Unsolved Crimes, Minn.; asst. editor: Hennepic County Lawyer, 1992—; Advisor to bd. Sibley County Commrs., 1979-80; speaker civic groups, 1976-82; mem. Hennepin County Juvenile Justice Panel, 1980-82, Hennepin County (Minn.) Pub. Def. Conflict Panel, 1980-82, 86—; Hennepin County Bar Assn. Advice Panel Law Day, 1987, mem. dist. ethics com., 1990-2004; mem. Panel Union Privilege Legal Svcs. div. AFL-CIO, 1986—, Signature Legal Svcs., 2003—; Montgomery Wards Legal Svcs. Panel, 1986—, Edina Hist. Soc., Decathlon Athletic Club; charter mem. Commn. for the Battle of Normandy Mus.; founding sponsor Civil Justice Found., 1986—; mem. com. for publ. Hennepin County Lawyer, 1992; pres. Endless Fist Soc., Inc., 1998—. Recipient Outstanding Tchr. award Inver Hills Coll. Student Body, 1973, St. Paul Citizen of Month award Citizens Group, 1975, Kempo Club award U. Minn., 1975, U. Minn. Student Appreciation award Kempo Club, 1978, Sibley County Atty. Commendation award, 1980, Good Neighbor award WCCO Radio, 1985, Lamp of Knowledge award Twin Cities Lawyers Guild, 1986, NW Cmty. TV Commendation award, 1989-91, Presdl. Merit medal Pres. George Bush, 1990, NW Cmty. TV award, 1991, HLS Leadership award, 1984, Mng. Attys. Guidance award, 1985, Creative Thinker award Regional Staff, 1986, HLS Justice award, 1986, Honors cert. for Authors, Childrens Reading Round Table of Chgo., 1988, Wisdom Soc. Wisdom award, 1998; numerous martial arts awards. Fellow Roscoe Pound Found., Nat. Dist. Attys. Assn.; mem. ABA, ATLA, Minn. Bar Assn. (com. on ethics 1994-2004, com. on alternative dispute resolution 1994—), Minn. Trial Lawyers Assn., Hennepin County Bar Assn. (dist. ethics com. 1990—2004, Wis. Bar Assn., Ramsey County Bar Assn., Am. Judicature Soc., Internat. Platform Assn., Am. Arbitration Assn. (panel of arbitrators 1992), Minn. Martial Arts Assn. (pres. 1974-78, Outstanding Instr. award 1973), Nippon Kobudo Rengokai (bd. dirs. North Ctrl. States 1972-76, regional dir. 1972-76), Endless Fist Soc. (pres. 1998), Internat. Confedn. Jurists, Edina C. of C., Southview Country Club, Masons, Kiwanis, Scottish Rite, Sigma Alpha Mu. Avocations: reading, far eastern and oriental studies, civic activities, physical conditioning. also: 1711 County Road B W Ste 340N Roseville MN 55113-4077 Office: 7400 Metro Blvd Ste 390 Edina MN 55439 Home: 4908 Poppy Ln Minneapolis MN 55435-4013 Office Phone: 952-831-6555.

**NEFF, JEANNE HENRY,** academic administrator; b. Fairmont, W. Va., Oct. 5, 1942; d. Percy Byron Henry and Rebecca Jacqueline Ridgely; m. Richard E. Kammer, Aug. 6, 1966 (div. July 1978); 1 child, Brian S. Kammer; m. Edward W.S. Neff II, Dec. 19, 1982; stepchildren: Larrie A., Edward W.S. III. BA, Wheeling Coll., 1964; MA, Rice U., 1966; ArtsD, Carnegie-Mellon U., 1976; postdoct., Harvard U., 1984. Instr. English Carlow Coll., Pitts., 1966-69; from asst. prof. to assoc. prof. English Wheeling (W. Va.) Coll., 1970-77, from assoc. dean to dean, 1977-80, academic v.p., 1980-86; v.p. academic affairs Susquehanna U., Selingsgrove, Pa., 1995—; pres. The Sage Colls., Troy and Albany, N.Y., 1995—. Bd. dirs. Capital Bank & Trust Co., Albany. Trustee Albany Acad., 1996—; mem. Waterfront Commn., Troy, N.Y., 1996—; dir., v.p. Troy Redevel. Found., 1996—. Mem. Am. Coun. Edn. (fellow 1978-79, mem. commn. leadership devel. 1995—), Assn. New Am. Colls. (mem. pres.'s coun. 1997—), Assn. Am. Colls. and Univs. (dir. 1984-88, chair Am. Conf. Academic Deans, 1987), Univ. Heights Assn. (dir. v.p. 1996—). Home: 46 1st St Troy NY 12180-3811 Office: The Sage Colls 45 Ferry St Troy NY 12180-4115

**NEFF, JOHN ADAM,** artist; b. Lebanon, Pa., May 5, 1926; s. John Adam Neff and Nellie Rebecca Botz; m. Marie Elizabeth Hekeler, Sept. 15, 1951. Sr. graphic designer Muirson Label Co., North Haven, Conn., 1950—72; owner

Crossmark Assocs., Wallingford, 1972—87; artist, 2005—. Exhibitions include Mystic Maritime Internat., Conn., DeCordova Mus., Mass., Watercolor USA, Springfield, Mo., Allied Artists Am., NYC, Represented in permanent collections New Britain Mus. Am. Art, Conn., Mus. Fine Arts, Springfield, Mass., Mus. Art, Sci. & Industry, Bridgeport, Conn., Ctrl. Conn. State U., New Britain, Westfield State Coll., Mass., New Haven Paint & Clay Club, Conn., Arts & Crafts Assn., Meriden, Conn., Town of Wallingford, City of Meriden, Wallingford Pub. Libr., Bristol Area Libr., Maine, State of Conn., AM. Consulate, Hong Kong, numerous others. Sgt. USAF, 1944—46. Mem.: Allied Artists Am., Hudson Valley ARt Assn., Arts & Crafts Assn., Meriden, Am. Soc. Maine Artists, Conn. Watercolor Soc. (bd. dirs.), Am. Soc. Marine Artists, Whiskey Painters Am., New Haven Paint & Clay Club. Episcopalian. Avocations: golf, skiing, photography. Home: 17 Parkview Rd Wallingford CT 06492-3051

**NEFF, JOHN BROWN,** financial portfolio manager; b. Wauseon, Ohio, Sept. 19, 1931; s. John Franklin Neff and Barbara (Brown) Hutton; m. Lillian Elizabeth Tulak, Oct. 4, 1935; children: Lisa, Stephen. BBA summa cum laude, U. Toledo, 1955; MBA, Case Western Reserve U., 1958; MA (hon.), U. Pa., 1984. Chartered fin. analyst. Asst. v.p. security analysis Nat. City Bank of Cleve., 1955-63; mng. ptnr., sr. v.p., portfolio mgr. Wellington Mgmt. Co., Valley Forge, Pa., 1963—95. Bd. dirs. Gen. Accident Ins., Crown Holdings, Inc., Amkor Tech., Inc., Chrysler Corp., Assn. Investment Mgmt. and Rsch. Author (with S.L. Mintz): John Neff on Investing. Chartered trustee U. Pa., Phila.; trustee Case Western U. Served with USN, 1951-53. Recipient Giving Forward award, Phil. Edn. Fund, 1995. Mem. Chartered Fin. Analysts Fedn. Fin. Analysts of Phila. Avocations: tennis, golf, travel, history.

**NEFF, MARIE TAYLOR,** museum director, artist; d. James Arthur Taylor and Pearl Jackson; m. Edward Lewis Neff, June 24, 1946 (dec. July 1, 1994); children: James Edward, Charles Lewis(dec.). Degree in art and photography, Western Tex. Coll., 1985. Studio artist, Post, 1943—; art instr. Neff Art Sch., Post, 1963—78; co-owner retail bus. Post, 1963—88; art instr. Post Art Guild, Kids n Art, Post, 1975—85; dir. OS Ranch Found. Mus., Post, 1991—. Represented in permanent collections, pvt. collections. Pres., bd. dirs. Post Commerce and Tourism Bur., 1994—2002; dir., coord. Tex. Plains Trail Region, 2002—04, treas., 2004—. Named Queen Panhandle South Plains, Mrs. Tex. Sr. Pageant, 1999. Mem.: North Tex. Mus. Assn. (pres. 2001—04), Tex. Assn. Mus. (planning bd. state conv. 1997—2001, trustee-sec. 2000—05), Post C. of C. (designer commemorative coin 1976, Woman of Yr. 1972), Post Art Guild (pres., founding mem. 1974—2003), Rotary. Avocations: archaeology, photography, reading, travel. Office: OS Ranch Found Mus Ste 3 201 E Main St Post TX 79356 E-mail: mtneff@caprock-spur.com.

**NEFF, MARY ELLEN ANDRE,** retired elementary school educator; b. Indiana, Pa., July 6, 1943; d. Frank Vincent and Marie Isabel (Elrick) Andre; children: Gary V. Jr., Traci Dawn. BS, Indiana U. Pa., 1965, MEd, 1971. Elem. sch. tchr. Blairsville (Pa.)-Saltsburg Sch. Dist., Derry (Pa.) Area Sch. Dist.; ret., 2002. Zone chmn. Lions Dist. 14E; bd. mem. Ind. County Tourist Bur. Mem.: PTA, NEA, Pa. State Edn. Assn., Derry Area Hist. Soc. (bd. dirs.), Saltsburg Hist. Soc. (pres.), Nat. Soc. DAR (vice regent), Westmoreland County Hist. Soc. (bd. dirs., sec.), Latrobe Lions Club (pres.), Delta Kappa Gamma (pres. 1986—90, treas. 1992—2000). Home: 17 Carriage Rd Greensburg PA 15601-9014 E-mail: meneff@infionline.net.

**NEFF, P(AUL) SHERRILL,** venture capitalist; b. Balt., Dec. 18, 1951; s. Paul Heston and Mary (Poulnot) N.; m. Sarah B. Barrett, June 20, 1976 (div. 1985); 1 child, Jacob Colin; m. Alicia Phyll Felton, May 26, 1988; children: Michael Felton, Jonathan Felton. BA, Wesleyan U., 1974; JD magna cum laude, U. Mich., 1980. Bar: Pa. 1980. Atty. Morgan Lewis & Bockius, Phila., 1980—84; investment banker Alex Brown & Sons, Inc., Balt., 1984—93, mng. dir., 1992—93; sr. v.p. corp. devel. U.S. Healthcare, Blue Bell, Pa., 1993—94; pres., CFO Neose Techs., Inc., Horsham, 1994—2000, pres., COO, 2000—02; mng. ptnr. Quaker Bio Ventures, Phila., 2002—. Bd. dirs Amicus Therapeutics, Biolex, Inc., Resource Capital Corp., Medmark, Inc., BioRexis Pharms., Inc., Regado Bioscis., Inc., WXPN-FM, Biotech. Inst.; bd. dirs., past chmn. Greater Phila. Venture Group. Mem. Pa. Biotech. Assn. (bd. dirs. 1996-2002, pres. 1998-99). Democrat. Jewish. Home: 619 Revere Rd Merion Station PA 19066-1007 Office: Quaker Bio Ventures 1811 Chestnut St Philadelphia PA 19103

**NEFF, RICHARD B. (RICHIE NEFF),** consumer products company executive; b. 1948; BS, Fairleigh Dickinson U., 1970. CPA. With Arthur Andersen & Co., 1970-73; various exec. positions including exec. v.p., CFO and dir. Transco Group, Inc., 1973-86; mng. ptnr. Greenwood Meadows Devel. Co., 1988—; exec. v.p., CFO, dir. Di Giorgio Corp., 1990—; pres. Las Plumas Lumber, 1991—; officer White Rose Foods, Inc., 1992—, CEO, co-chmn, 2000—. Office: Di Giorgio Corp 380 Middlesex Ave Carteret NJ 07008-3446*

**NEFF, ROBERT MATTHEW,** lawyer, finance company executive; b. Huntington, Ind., Mar. 26, 1955; s. Robert Eugene and Ann (Bash) N.; m. Lee Ann Loving, Aug. 23, 1980; children: Alexandra, Graydon, Philip. BA in English, DePauw U., 1977; JD, Ind. U. Indpls., 1980. Bar: Ind. 1980, U.S. Dist. Ct. (so. dist.) Ind. 1980, U.S. Supreme Ct. 1993. Assoc. Krieg, DeVault, Alexander & Capehart, Indpls., 1980-85, ptnr., 1986-88; ptnr. Baker & Daniels, Indpls., 1988-92; of counsel, 1993-96; dept. to chmn. Fed. Housing Fin. Bd., Washington, 1992-93; pres., CEO Circle Investors, Inc., Indpls., 1993-97, also bd. dirs.; chmn., CEO Senex Fin. Corp., Indpls., 1998—. Mem. faculty Grad. Sch. of Banking of South, 1988—90; chmn. Liberty Bankers Life Ins. Co., 1995—98, Am. Founders Life Ins. Co., Laurel Life Ins. Co., Aztek Life Assurance Co., 1996—97; bd. dirs. Quanta Surplus Lines Ins. Co., CH Assurance Ltd., Unified Fin. Svcs., Inc.; trustee 40/86 Mut. Funds. Exec. editor Ind. Law Rev., 1979-80. Participant Lacy Exec. Leadership Conf., Indpls., 1985-86; trustee DePauw U., 1977-80; bd. govs. Riley Children's Found., 1999-; del. White House Conf. on Aging, 2005. Mem. ABA (chmn. bus. law com. young lawyers divsn. 1988-90, banking law com. 1990-92), Ind. Bar Assn. (chmn. corps. banking and bus. law sect. 1987-88), DePauw Alumni Assn. (bd. dirs. 1982-88), Phi Kappa Psi, Phi Beta Kappa. Avocations: golf, fishing. Home: 7202 Merriam Rd Indianapolis IN 46240 Office: Senex Fin Corp 3500 DePauw Blvd # 3050 Indianapolis IN 46268 Office Phone: 317-613-3000. Business E-Mail: neffrm@senexco.com.

**NEFF, ROBERT WILBUR,** academic administrator, educator, minister; b. Lancaster, Pa., June 16, 1936; s. Wilbur Hildebr and Hazel Margaret (Martin) N.; m. Dorothy Rosewarne, Aug. 16, 1959; children: Charles Scott, Heather Lynn. BS, Pa. State U., 1958; BD, Yale Div. Sch., 1961, MA, 1963, PhD, 1969; DD, Juniata Coll., 1978, Manchester Coll., 1979; DHL, Bridgewater Coll., 1979. Asst. prof. Bridgewater Coll., 1964-65; mem. faculty dept. Bibl. studies Bethany Theol. Sem., 1965-77, prof., 1973-77; gen. sec. Ch. of the Brethren, Elgin, Ill., 1978-86; pres. Juniata Coll., 1986-98, pres. emeritus, 1998—. Vis. prof. Pa. State U., 1998-2003; assoc. for resource devel. The Village at Morrison's Cove, 1999-; mem. faculty North Park Sem., No. Bapt. Sem., Theol. Coll. No. Nigeria; bd. dirs. Mellon Bank (Ctrl.) Nat. Assn., exec. com., 1989, chair exec. com., 1993, chair CRA com., 1994-2001; mem. pres.'s com. NCAA, 1996-99; bd. dirs. Susquehanna Valley Ministry Ctr., 2002-, chair, 2004-; adj. faculty Bethany Theol. Sem., 1999—; cons. Archdiocese (Altoona/Johnstown), 2003—; lectr. Young Ctr. at Elizabethtown Coll., 2002; mem. USDA Del. to Baltic States, 2000. Mem. governing bd. Nat. Coun. Chs. of Christ, 1976-86, mem. exec. com., 1979-86; mem. Mid-East panel, 1980, 2d v.p., 1985-86; mem. ctrl. com. World Coun. Chs., 1983-92; rep. Assembly of World Coun. Chs., 1983, mem. exec. com. on interch. rels., 1980-84; mem. del. to China, 1981, chmn. presdl. panel, 1982-84; bd. dirs. Bethany Theol. Sem., 1978-86, So. Alleghenies chpt. ARC, 2004—; campaign chmn. United Way, Huntington County, 1989; chair higher edn. com. Ch. of Brethren, 1993-98. Danforth fellow, 1958-69. Mem. Soc. Bibl. Lit., Soc. Old Testament Study, Chgo. Soc. Bibl. Rsch., Soc. Values in Higher Edn., Coun. Ind. Colls. (nat. bd. dirs. 1991-94, mem. 1995-98), Pa. Coun. Ind. Colls. and Univs. (exec. com. 1988-90, 92-96, chair ann. conf. nominating com. 1993-94), Mid Atlantic Athletic Conf. (sec., mem. exec.

com. 1994-97). Democrat. Home: 7889 River Hill Ln Alexandria PA 16611 Office: Village at Morrisons Cove 429 Market St Martinsburg PA 16662 Office Phone: 814-793-5207. E-mail: rneff@pennswoods.net.

**NEFF, SEVERINE,** music educator; b. Waterbury, Conn., Dec. 17, 1949; d. Victor and Evangeline Josephine Neff; m. Joel Stanley Feigin, June 7, 1986. AB, Barnard Coll., 1971; MA, Yale U., 1972; MFA, Princeton U., NJ, PhD, 1979. Asst. prof. Bates Coll., Lewiston, Maine, 1979—80, U. Hawaii, Honolulu, 1980—81; fellow Cornell U., Ithaca, NY, 1981—83; asst. prof. Barnard Coll., N.Y., NY, 1983—91; assoc. prof. Cin. (Ohio) Coll.-Conservatory, 1991—92, prof. 1993—95; prof. music U. N.C., Chapel Hill, NC, 1995—2003, Eugene Falk disting. prof., 2004—. Author: Coherence, Counterpoint, Instrumentation, Instruction in Form, 1994, The Musical Idea, 1995, 2d edit., 2006, Norton Critical Score, 2006, Second String Quartet, Op. 10 by Arnold Schoenberg, 2006; editor: Theory and Practice, 1991—93, Music Theory Spectrum, 1999—2002. Fellow, Mellon Found., 1981; grantee, NEH, 1993, Arnold Schoenberg Ctr., 2004; scholar, Fulbright Found., 1998—99; Tchg. fellow, Mannes Inst., 2004—. Mem.: Soc. Music Theory (sec. 1991—94, revs. editor 2000—02, bd. dirs.), Coll. Music Soc. (theory rep. 2001—04, bd. dirs.). Achievements include discovery of unknown work of Arnold Schoenberg. Avocation: antiques. Office: Univ NC CB 3320 Chapel Hill NC 27599

**NEFF, THOMAS JOSEPH,** search firm executive; b. Easton, Pa., Oct. 2, 1937; s. John Wallace and Elizabeth Ann (Dougherty) N.; m. Susan Culver Paull, Nov. 26, 1971 (dec.); children: David Andrew, Mark Gregory, Scott Dougherty; m. Sarah Brown Hallingby, Jan. 20, 1989; stepchildren: Brooke, Bailey BS in Indsl. Engring., Lafayette Coll., 1959; MBA, Lehigh U., 1961. Assoc. McKinsey & Co., Inc., NYC and Australia, 1963-66; dir. mktg. planning Trans-World Airlines, NYC, 1966-69; pres. Hosp. Data Scis., Inc., NYC, 1969-74; prin. Booz, Allen & Hamilton, Inc., NYC, 1974-76; regional ptnr. Spencer Stuart, Inc., NYC, 1976-79; bd. dirs. Spencer Stuart & Assocs., NYC, 1976-79, pres., 1979-96, also bd. dirs., chmn. U.S., 1996—. Bd. dirs. Lord Abbett Mut. Funds, Ace Ltd., Hewitt Assocs., Inc.; chmn. Brunswick Sch., 1991-95. Co-author: Lessons From the Top, 1999, You're in Charge--Now What: The 8-Point Plan, 2005. Trustee, emeritus Lafayette Coll., 2004—. 1st lt. US Army, 1961-63. Mem. Links Club, Blind Brook Club, Quogue (NY) Beach Club, Quogue Field Club, Round Hill Club, Coral Beach Club, Quantuck Beach Club, Nat. Golf Links, Lost Tree Club, McArthur Golf Club. Republican. Roman Catholic. Office: Spencer Stuart & Assocs 277 Park Ave 29th Fl New York NY 10172-2998 Business E-Mail: tneff@spencerstuart.com.

**NEFF-ENCINAS, JULIE GAY,** bilingual education specialist, consultant; b. Chgo., June 21, 1957; d. Wesley Miles and Betty Ann (Pitts) Neff; m. Ernesto Valenzuela Encinas, July 5, 1980; children: Ariella, Gerard, Martin. BA, Hanover Coll., 1978; MEd, U. Ariz., 1979. Cert. secondary tchr. with bilingual edn. endorsement. Mid. sch. tchr. Cath. Diocese of Tucson, 1979-80; mem. adj. faculty No. Ariz. U., Flagstaff, 1993-96; tchr. bilingual edn. Tucson Unified Sch. Dist., 1980-89, bilingual edn. curriculum specialist, 1989-96, compliance project specialist, 1996—2000, improvement facilitator; bilingual edn. tchr. Tuscon Unified Sch. Dist., 1999—2003, bilingual edn. specialist, 0200—. Cons. S.W. Regional Lab., Los Alamitos, Calif., 1993-96; grant reviewer U.S. Dept. Edn., 1992—. Co-author Tucson Unified Sch. Dist. Compliance Procedures Manual for Bilingual Edn., 1993, Tucson Unified Sch. Dist. Comprehensive Plan for Bilingual Edn., 1993. Title VII Short Term Tng. grantee U.S. Dept. Edn., 1991-94, Title VII Systemwide Improvement grantee U.S. Dept. Edn., 1995-00. Avocation: birdwatching. Office: Tucson Unified Sch Dist Magee Middle Sch 1010 E 10th St Tucson AZ 85719-5813 Home: 7949 E Beverly St Tucson AZ 85710 Business E-Mail: julie.neff-encinas@tusd1.org. E-mail: jneffencinas@cox.net.

**NEFSKE, DONALD JOSEPH,** engineer; b. Detroit, Dec. 18, 1938; s. Frank J. and Esther M. N.; m. Susan Sung, Dec. 10, 1983. BS magna cum laude, U. Detroit, 1962; MS, U. Mich., 1964, PhD, 1969. Engr. Ford Motor Co., Dearborn, Mich., 1960—61; rsch. engr. GM, Warren, Mich., 1969—70, sr. rsch. engr., 1970—85, sr. staff engr., 1985—93, prin. engr., 1993—2003, tech. fellow, 2003—05; dir. Engring. Mechanics Group, Troy, Mich., 2005—. Contbr. articles profl. jour., chapters to books. Fellow ASME; mem. AIAA, Acoustical Soc. Am., Soc. Automotive Engr., Sigma Xi. Roman Catholic. Achievements include research in CAE methods for automotive vehicle noise and vibration, airbag safety systems. Office: Engring Mechanics Group 4178 Drexel Dr Troy MI 48098

**NEFTCI, SALIH NUR,** educator, writer; b. Kerkuk, Iraq, July 14, 1947; s. Nazim and Nermin Neftci; m. Gul Neftci; children: Merve, Emre. PhD, U. Minn., Mpls., 1974. Prof. CUNY, NYC, 1984—; head cert. fame Swiss Fin. Inst., Lausanne, 1998—; prof. New Sch., NYC, 1998—. Vis. prof. Hong Kong U. Sci. and Tech., 2005—. Author: Principles of Financial Engineering, Introduction to the Mathmatics of Financial Derivatives, China's Financial Market. Office Phone: 212-229-5717 3046. Personal E-mail: sneftci@wwc.com. E-mail: neftcis@newschool.edu.

**NEGELE, JOHN WILLIAM,** physics professor, consultant; b. Cleve., Apr. 18, 1944; s. Charles Frederick and Virgil Lea (Wettich) N.; m. Rose Anne Meeks, June 18, 1967; Janette Andrea, Julia Elizabeth. BS, Purdue U., 1965; PhD, Cornell U., 1969. Research fellow Niels Bohr Inst., Copenhagen, 1969-70; vis. assist. prof. MIT, Cambridge, 1970-71, faculty mem., 1971—, prof. physics 1979—, William A. Coolidge prof., 1991—, head nuclear and particle theory divsn., 1988-89, dir. Ctr. for Theoretical Physics, 1989-98. Cons. Los Alamos Sci. Lab., Brookhaven Nat. Lab., Lawrence Livermore Nat. Lab., Oak Ridge Nat. Lab.; mem. physics div. rev. com. Argonne Nat. Lab., (Ill.), 1977-83; mem. nuclear sci. div. rev. com. Lawrence Berkeley Lab., (Calif.), 1987—: mem. adv. bd., advising com. Inst. for Theoretical Physics, U. Calif.-Santa Barbara, 1982-86; mem. adv. bd. inst. for Nuclear Theory U. Washington, 1990—, chair 1992-94; program adv. com. Tandem Van de Graaff Accelerator, Brookhaven Nat. Lab., 1977-78, Bates Linear Accelerator, 1977-80, Los Alamos Meson Prodn. Facility, 1986-89, Brookhaven Alternating Gradient Synchraton, 1987-90. Author: Quantum Many Particle Systems, 1987; contbr. articles to profl. jours.; editor: Advances in Nuclear Physics, 1977—. Grantee NSF, 1965-69; grantee Danforth Found., 1965-69, Woodrow Wilson Found., 1965, Alfred P. Sloan Found., 1979, Japan Soc. for Promotion Sci., 1981, John Simon Guggenheim Found., 1982; Alexander von Humboldt Found. fellow, 1998. Fellow Am. Phys. Soc. (exec. com. 1982-84, program com. 1980-82, editorial bd. Phys. Rev. 1980-82, exec. com. topical group on computational physics 1992-93, chair divsn. of computational physics 1992-93, exec. com. 1992-94, Bonner prize com. 1984-85), AAAS (nominating com. 1987-91, mem. physics sect. com. 1991—), Fedn. Am. Scientists. Home: 70 Buckman Dr Lexington MA 02421-6000 Office: MIT Dept Physics 6-315 77 Massachusetts Ave Dept 6-308 Cambridge MA 02139-4307

**NEGER, PETER C.,** lawyer; b. NYC, Dec. 23, 1955; s. Edward B. Neger and Charlene M. (Oltarsh) Stahl; m. Melinda Beck, Sept. 12, 1982; children: Emily, Hillary. BA, Yale U., 1977; JD, Fordham U., 1981. Bar: N.Y. 1982, U.S. Dist. Ct. (so. and ea. dists.) N.Y. 1982, U.S. Ct. Appeals (2d cir.) 1982, U.S. Supreme Ct. 1986, U.S. Ct. Appeals (7th cir.) 1996. Assoc. Shea & Gould, N.Y.C., 1981-89; prin. 1990-94, Richards & O'Neil, LLP, N.Y.C., 1994—; Bingham McCutchen LLP, N.Y.C., co-chmn. product liability practice group. Mem.: Fed. Bar Coun., N.Y. State Bar Assn., Assn. Bar City N.Y., ABA (product liability com.), Food & Drug Law Inst., Defense Research Inst. (product liability com., drug & med. devices com.). Office: Bingham McCutchen LLP 399 Park Avenue New York NY 10022-4689 Office Phone: 212-705-7226. Office Fax: 212-752-5378. Business E-Mail: peter.neger@bingham.com.

**NEGI, DEVENDRA S.,** communications services company administrator; b. Varanasi, Uttar Pradesh, India, Aug. 8, 1953; s. Vidya Wati and (Deceased) Balwant S Negi. B of Mech. Engring., Indian Inst. Tech., 1974; MS in Indsl.

Engring, Kans. State U., 1981, PhD in Indsl. Engring, 1989. Engr. trainee Bharat Heavy Electricals Ltd., Hardwar, Uttar Pradesh, India, 1975—76, engr., 1976—79; grad. rsch. asst. Kans. State U., Manhattan, 1980, 1986—89; systems analyst Patso Co., Inc, Houston, 1981—82; indsl. engr. Millar Instruments, Inc., 1882—1984; ops. rsch. analyst Phillips Petroleum Co., Bartlesville, Okla., 1990—97; sr. tech. staff mem. AT&T, Florham Park and Murray Hill, NJ, 1997—2001, dist. mgr. Florham Park, 2001—04, group mgr. Middletown and Florham Park, 2004—. Vis. asst. prof. Ohio U., Athens, 1989—90. Mem.: Inst. Ops. Rsch. and Mgmt. Scis., Inst. Indsl. Engrs. Avocations: travel, movies, tennis. Home: 1428-1432 South Ave Apt 1-H Plainfield NJ 07062 Office: AT&T 180 Park Ave Florham Park NJ 07932 Office Phone: 732-420-0370. Personal E-mail: dsnegi@att.net, negids@gmail.com. Business E-Mail: dsnegi@homer.att.com.

**NEGISHI, EI-ICHI,** chemistry professor; arrived in U.S., 1960; BS in Organic Chemistry, U. Tokyo, 1958; PhD in Organic Chemistry, U. Pa., 1963. Rsch. chemist Teijin Ltd., 1958-65; postdoctoral assoc. Purdue U., 1966-68, asst. to H.C. Brown, 1968-72; asst. prof. Syracuse (N.Y.) U., 1972-76, assoc. prof., 1976-79; prof. Purdue U., West Lafayette, Ind., 1979-99, Herbert C. Brown disting. prof., 1999—. Lectr. in field. Recipient A. von Humboldt Rschr. award 1998—; Fulbright scholar, 1960-63. Mem.: Royal Soc. Chemistry (Sir E. Frankland Prize lectureship 2000), Japan Chem. Soc. (award 1997), Am. Chem. Soc. (Organometallic Chemistry award 1998), Sigma Xi, Phi Lambda Epsilon. Office: Purdue U Chem Dept 560 Oval Dr West Lafayette IN 47907-2084 Office Phone: 765-494-5301. Business E-Mail: negishi@purdue.edu.

**NEGRETE, GEORGE RAYMOND,** chemistry professor, researcher; b. Compton, Calif., Jan. 26, 1954; s. Guilibaldo Rivera and Irene M. Negrete; m. Josephine Lopez, Dec. 26, 1978; children: Robert Lopez, Jorge Andres. PhD, U. Calif., Santa Cruz, 1990. Fellow U. Calif., San Francisco, 1990—94; assoc. prof. U. Tex., San Antonio, 1994—; Nigms rev. subpanel NIH, Bethesda, Md., 2003—. Recipient Disting. Faculty Tchg. award, U. Tex. San Antonio Alumni Assn., 1997; fellow NIH Postdoctoral fellow, Nat. Cancer Inst., 1992—93. Mem.: Union of Concern Scientists, Am. Chem. Soc., Soc. for the Advancement of Chicanos/Latinos and Native Americans in Sci. (life; bd. dirs. 2004—06). Achievements include patents for novel fatty acid preparations. Office: Univ Tex Dept Chemistry 6900 N Loop 1604 W San Antonio TX 78249-0698 Office Phone: 210-458-5448. Office Fax: 210-458-7428. E-mail: george.negrete@utsa.edu.

**NEGRI, ROCCO ANTONIO,** artist, illustrator; b. Italy, June 26, 1932; came to U.S., 1959; s. Salvatore and Adele (Plattaroti) N.; m. Joan Becky Stewart, May 25, 1958; children: Ronald Edgar, Gene Darius. Student, Art Students League, N.Y.C., 1959-60, Sch. Visual Arts, 1960-64, Pratt Graphic Ctr., 1974-75. Illustrator children's books including Renfroe's Christmas, 1968, Journey Outside, 1969, Trouble River, 1969, Casa Means Home, 1970, Tales from Count Lucanor, 1970, Heracles The Strong, 1970, Bantu Tales, 1970, The Legs of the Moon, 1971, Charlie Dick, 1972, Coplas, 1972, The Great Fire, 1973, The Son of the Leopard, 1974, Pampalche of the Silver Teeth, 1976. Home: PO Box 1395 Blakeslee PA 18610

**NEGRON, JESUS (BUBU),** artist; b. Arecibo, Puerto Rico, 1975; Resident M&M Proyectos, San Juan, PR. Exhibitions include Primero Auxillios, ARCO, 2002, M&M Proyectos, Viego San Juan, 2002, Art Basel Miami Beach, 2002, We Surrender, Venice, Italy, 2003, 24/7, NY, 2003, Colectivo La Rlexible, Biennial Caribe, Santo Domingo, 2003, Stray Show, Chgo., 2004, Galeria Comerical, San Juan, 2004, Whitney Biennial: Day for Night, Whitney Mus. Am. Art, 2006.*

**NEGRON-GARCIA, ANTONIO S.,** law educator, former territory supreme court justice; b. Rio Piedras, P.R., Dec. 31, 1940; s. Luis Negron-Fernandez and Rosa M. Garcia-Saldana; m. Gloria Villardefrancos-Vergara, May 26, 1962; 1 son, Antonio Rogelio. BA, U. P.R., 1962, LL.B., 1964. Bar: P.R. bar 1964. Law aide and lawyer legal div. Water Resources Authority, 1962-64; judge Dist. Ct., 1964-69, Superior Ct., 1969-74; justice P.R. Supreme Ct., San Juan, 1974—2001; administrating judge, 1969-71; exec. officer Constl. Bd. for Revision Senatorial and Rep. Dists., 1971-72; mem. Jud. Conf., 1974—2000; first exec. sec. Council for Reform of System of Justice in P.R., 1973-74; prof. InterAmerican U. Puerto Rico, 2001—. Chmn. Gov.'s Advisory Com. for Jud. Appointments, 1973-74; lectr. U.P.R. Law Sch., 1973-74; columnist El Nuevo Dia newspaper, 2000. Mem. P.R. Bar Assn., Am. Judicature Soc. Roman Catholic. Office: Univ InterAmericana de Puerto Rico Apartado 70351 San Juan PR 00936-8351

**NEGROPONTE, JOHN DIMITRI,** Director of National Intelligence, former ambassador; b. London, July 21, 1939; s. Dimitri John and Catherine (Coumantaros) Negroponte; m. Diana Mary Villiers, Dec. 14, 1976; children: Marina, Alexandra, John, George, Sophia. BA, Yale U., 1960. Commd. fgn. svc. officer U.S. Dept. State, 1960; vice consul Hong Kong, 1961—63; 2nd sec. Saigon, 1964—68; mem. U.S. Del. to Paris Peace Talks on Vietnam, 1968—69; mem. staff NSC, 1970—73; polit. counselor Quito, Ecuador, 1973—75; consul gen. Thessaloniki, Greece, 1975—77; dep. asst. sec. of state for oceans & fisheries affairs US Dept. State, Washington, 1977—79, dep. asst. sec. for East Asian and Pacific affairs, 1980—81, U.S. amb. to Honduras Tegucigalpa, 1981—85, asst. sec. for oceans and internat. environ. and sci. affairs Washington, 1985—87; dep. asst. to Pres. for nat. security affairs NSC, Washington, 1987—89; U.S. amb. to Mex. US Dept. State, 1989—93; U.S. amb. to The Philippines Manilla, 1993—96, spl. coord. for post-1999 U.S. presence in Panama, 1996—97; exec. v.p. global markets McGraw-Hill Cos., N.Y.C., 1997—2001; permanent U.S. rep. UN, N.Y.C., 2001—04; U.S. amb. to Iraq US Dept. State, Baghdad, 2004—05; dir. Office Nat. Intelligence, Washington, 2001— Co-pres. U.S./Mex. Commn. for Ednl. and Cultural Exch., 1997—2001; chmn. The French-Am. Found., 1998—2001; mem. exec. com. U.S. Coun. for Internat. Bus., 1998—2001. Mem.: Fgn. Policy Assn., Am. Acad. Diplomacy, Coun. on Fgn. Rels., Am. Fgn. Svc. Assn. Greek Orthodox. Office: Office of Dir Nat Intelligence NEOB 725 17th St Washington DC 20500

**NEGROPONTE, NICHOLAS,** media specialist, educator; m. Elaine Negroponte. Founding chairman, dir. MIT Media Lab., Cambridge, Mass., 1986—; faculty MIT, Cambridge, Mass., 1966-86, Wiesner prof., media tech. Founder, Architecture Machine Group, MIT; bd. dirs. Motorola; spl. gen. ptnr. in a venture capital firm; founder, sr. columnist WiReD mag.; angel investor for over 40 start-ups, including three in China. Author: Being Digital, 1995 (NY Times Bestseller, translated into over 40 languages) Helped establish, chmn. 2BI Found., 1996-; chmn., One Laptop per Child (OLPC), 2005-. First to announce at the World Economic Forum at Davos, Switzerland in January 2005, the MIT Media Lab's research initiative to develop the world's first working $100 laptop for a non-profit program, One Laptop Per Child (OLPC). The computer allows hundreds of millions of underprivileged students worldwide to gain access to knowledge and modern forms of education. Office: MIT Media Lab Bldg E15 77 Massachusetts Ave Cambridge MA 02139-4307 also: MIT Media Lab Wiesner Building, E15 20 Ames St Cambridge MA 02139-4307 Office Phone: 617-253-5960. Office Fax: 617-258-6264. Business E-Mail: nicholas@media.mit.edu.*

**NEHAL, KISHWER SULTANA,** dermatologist; BA, Boston U., 1988, MD, 1992. Diplomate Am. Bd. of Dermatology, 1996, lic. NY, 1995. Dir., mohs micrographic and dermatologic laser surgery Meml. Sloan-Kettering Cancer Ctr., NYC, 1998—; assoc. prof. of dermatology Cornell U., Weill Med. Coll., 2005—; assoc. attending physician Meml. Sloan-Kettering Cancer Ctr., 2005—. Bd. dirs. Assn. Acad. Dermatologic Surgeons, 2006—; bd. trustees Sulzberger Inst. Dermatologic Edn., 2005—; non-melanoma skin cancer panel Nat. Comprehensive Cancer Network, 1999—; jour. reviewer Jour. of Am. Acad. Dermatology, 1999—, Jour. Dermatologic Surgery, 1999—; faculty mem. Procedural Dermatology Fellow, NYC, 2006—. Recipient Emma Willard Sch. Alumnae Assn. Outstanding Young Alumna Award, Emma Willard Sch., 2006. Fellow: Skin Cancer Found., Am. Soc. for Laser

Medicine and Surgery, Am. Soc. for Dermatologic Surgery, Am. Acad. Dermatology, Am. Coll. Mohs Micrographic Surgery and Cutaneous Oncology; mem.: Women's Dermatologic Soc. Achievements include research in real time noninvasive imaging of skin with confocal reflectance microscopy to map tumor margins in Mohs surgery; clinical application of real time dynamic telepathology in Mohs surgery. Office: Meml Sloan-Kettering Cancer Ctr 160 East 53rd St 2nd Fl New York NY 10022 Office Phone: 212-610-0782.

**NEHAMAS, ALEXANDER,** philosophy educator; b. Athens, Greece, Mar. 22, 1946; came to U.S., 1964; s. Albert and Christine (Yannuli) N.; m. Susan Glimcher, June 22, 1983; 1 child, Nicholas Albert Glimcher. BA, Swarthmore Coll., 1967; PhD, Princeton U., 1971; D in Philosophy (hon.), Athens, 1993. Asst. then assoc. prof. philosophy U. Pitts., 1971-81, prof., 1981-86; prof. philosophy U. Pa., 1986-90; vis. prof. Princeton (N.J.) U., 1978-79, 89, Edmund Carpenter prof. humanities, 1990—, prof. philosophy and comparative lit., 1990—, chair humanities coun., 1994—2002, chmn. program in Hellenic studies, 1994—2002. Dir. Princeton Soc. Fellow in Liberal Arts, 1999-2002; Mills vis. prof. U. Calif., Berkeley, 1983; Sather vis. prof., 1993; vis. prof. U. Calif., Santa Cruz, 1988; bd. dirs. Princeton U. Press; trustee Nat. Humanities Ctr., 1996-99, Athens Coll., 1996—. Author: Nietzsche: Life as Literature, 1985, The Art of Living: Socratic Reflectionsfrom Plato to Foucault, 1998, Virtues of Authenticity: Essays on Plato and Socrates, 1999, Only a Promise of Happiness, 2004; translator Plato's Symposium, 1989, Plato's Phaedrus, 1995; co-editor: Aristotle's Rhetoric: Philosophical Essays, 1994; contbr. articles to profl. jours.; mem. editl. bd. Am. Philos. Quar., 1981-86, History of Philosophy Quar., 1983-88, Ancient Philosophy, 1984—, Jour. Modern Greek Studies, 1986—, Arion, 1989—, Philosophy and Lit., 1989—, Philosophy and Phenomenological Rsch., 1990—. Recipient Lindback Found. Tchg. award, U. Pa., 1989, Behrman award in humanities, Princeton U., 1999, Ann. prize in Hellenic Studies Acad., Athens, 2000, Internat. Nietzsche prize, 2001, Mellon Disting. Achievement award, 2001; grantee Guggenheim fellow, 1983, NEH, 1978. Mem.: MLA, N.Am. Nietzsche Soc. (exec. com. 1988—91), Am. Soc. Aesthetics, Modern Greek Studies Assn. (exec. com. 1983—89), Am. Philos. Assn. (chmn. program 1982—83, exec. com. 1990—92, v.p. 2002, pres. 2003), Phi Beta Kappa (vis. prof. 1989, vis. scholar 1995). Office: Princeton U Dept Philosophy Princeton NJ 08544-0001

**NEHLS, RICHARD CHARLES,** lawyer; b. Detroit, Oct. 26, 1951; s. Edward J. and Helen (Hecker) N.; m. Sharon Kay Scudder, Mar. 29, 1975; children: Christopher, Jeffrey. BA, Miami U., Oxford, Ohio, 1973; JD, U. Chgo., 1976. Bar: Colo. 1976. Ptnr. Lirtzman & Nehls, Boulder, Colo., 1976—. Trustee Legal Aid Found., 1995-2003. Mem. Colo. Bar Assn. (trustee 1996-2002), Boulder County Bar Assn. (trustee 1990-95, pres. 1994-95). Democrat. Avocations: skiing, bicycling. Home: 385 Overlook Dr Boulder CO 80305-5258 Office: Lirtzman & Nehls 190 Arapahoe Ave Boulder CO 80302-5895 Office Phone: 303-444-5141. Business E-Mail: RNehls@LNHlaw.com.

**NEHRA, GERALD PETER,** lawyer; b. Detroit, Mar. 25, 1940; s. Joseph P. and Jeanette M. (Bauer) N.; m. children: Teresa, Patricia; m. Peggy Jensen, Sept. 12, 1987. B.I.E., Gen. Motors Inst., Flint, Mich., 1962; JD, Detroit Coll. Law. 1970. Bar: Mich. 1970, N.Y. 1972, Colo. 1992, U.S. Dist. Ct. (ea. dist.) Mich. 1970, U.S. Ct. (so. dist.) N.Y. 1972, U.S. Dist. Ct. (no. dist.) N.Y. 1976, U.S. Ct. Appeals (6th cir.) 1978. Successively engr., supr., gen. supr. Gen. Motors Corp., 1958-67; mktg. rep. to regional counsel IBM Corp., 1967-79; v.p. gen. counsel Church & Dwight Co., Inc., 1979-82; dep. chief atty. Amway Corp., 1982-83; dep. gen. counsel, 1983-92; dir. legal div., 1989-91; sec., dir. corp. law, 1991-92; v.p. gen. cousnel Fuller Brush, Boulder, Colo., 1991-92; pvt. practice, 1992—. Adj. instr. Dale Carnegie Courses, 1983-91. Recipient Outstanding Contbn. award Am. Cancer Soc., 1976. Mem. ABA, Mich. Bar Assn., Colo. Bar Assn., N.Y. State Bar Assn. Home and Office: 1710 Beach St Muskegon MI 49441-1008 Office Phone: 231-755-3800. Business E-Mail: gnehra@mlmatty.com.

**NEHRBASS, SETH MARTIN,** lawyer; b. Lafayette, La., Nov. 10, 1960; s. Neil Martin and Janet (Himbert) N.; m. Mary Elizabeth Dennis, Aug. 12, 2000; children: Gabriel, Fabian. Student, U. Catholique de l'Ouest, Angers, France, 1980, U. Paul Valéry, Montpellier, France, 1981; BS in Physics summa cum laude, U. Southwestern La., 1982; JD cum laude, Loyola U., 1990. Bar: U.S. Patent & Trademark Office 1984, La. 1990, U.S. Dist. Ct. (ea., mid., and we. dists.) La. 1990, U.S. Ct. Appeals (5th and fed. cirs.) 1990, U.S. Supreme Ct. 2006; cert. notary public, La. Patent examiner U.S. Patent & Trademark Office, 1982-84; patent agt. with law firm New Orleans, 1986-87; assoc. Pravel, Hewitt, Kimball & Krieger, New Orleans, 1987-97, shareholder, 1997-98, Garvey, Smith, Nehrbass & North, L.L.C., Metairie, La., 1998—. Adj. law faculty Tulane Law Sch., 1997—; judge practice round moot ct. teams Loyola Law Sch., 1992—; preparer questions patent bar exam PTO Q & A Bd., 1992-93; presenter in field. Contbr. articles to profl. jours. Den leader 2d grade Cub Scouts, Boy Scouts Am., Lusher Sch., Audubon Dist., 1991-92, 3d grade, 1994-95, asst. den leader 3d grade, 1992-93, 4th grade, 1993-94; soccer coach Carrollton Booster Club, New Orleans, 1993-95, Lakeview Soccer Club, New Orleans, 1995-96; adv. mem. La. Ctr. for Law and Civic Edn., 1996-98; mem. Coun. Internat. Vis. Greater New Orleans, 2000—. Recipient Hornbook award West Pub. Co., 1986-87, 87-88, Corpus Juris Secundum award, 1986-87, Am. Jurisprudence awards (2), 1986; scholar La. State U. Alumni Fedn., 1978, Coun. Devel. French La./French Govt., 1980-81, Loyola Law Sch., 1986. Mem. ABA (sect. law, sci., tech. 1988-91, law student divsn. liaison patent trademark and copyright law 1988-90, intellectual property law sect. 1988—, chmn. law student com. 1996-98, chmn. spl. com. drug crisis 1990-93, co-chmn. ann. meeting arrangements com. 1993 94, intel nat uvuation and laws com. 1994—, co-chmn. young lawyers com. 1998-99), Am. Intellectual Property Law Assn. (ADR com., internat. and fgn. law com., patent law com. 1994-2000), La. Bar Assn. (internat. law sect. 1992—, intellectual property law sect. 1996—, vice chmn. 1997-98, chair-elect 1998-99, chair 1999-2000), New Orleans Bar Assn. (interim chmn. ad hoc com. drug crisis 1991-92, chmn. intellectual property law com. 1991-95, chmn. law related edn. com. 1993-95), Round Table Club, Plimsoll Club, Loyola Law Sch. Moot Ct. Alumni Assn., Sigma Pi Sigma, Pi Delta Phi, Alpha Sigma Nu. Democrat. Roman Catholic. Avocations: gardening, photography, travel, hunting, fishing. Home: 453 Audubon Blvd New Orleans LA 70125-3503 Office: 3838 N Causeway Blvd Ste 3290 Metairie LA 70002 Office Phone: 504-835-2000. Business E-Mail: nehrbass@gsnn.us. E-mail: Nehrbass@aol.com.

**NEHRING, FLETCHER ALDRICH,** pharmacist; b. Northampton, Mass., June 28, 1979; s. Marcia Doza Sullivan and Craig Atwood Nehring. PharmD, U. RI, 2003. Registered Pharmacist Mass., 2004, Conn., 2003. Pharmacy practice resident St. Francis Hosp. and Med. Ctr., Hartford, Conn., 2003—04; pharmacist Cooley Dickinson Hosp., Northampton, Mass., 2004—06. Mem.: Kappa Psi Pharm. Frat., Inc., Freemasonry. Home: 12B Florence Rd Easthampton MA 01027-1008 Office: Cooley Dickinson Hosp 30 Locust St Northampton MA 01062 Office Phone: 413-582-2116. Personal E-mail: fneh9059@charer.net.

**NEHRING, RONALD E.,** state supreme court justice; b. Wisconsin, 1947; BA in History, Cornell U., 1976; JD, U. Utah, 1978. Bar: Utah 1978. Atty. Utah Legal Svcs.; shareholder Prince, Yeates and Geldzahler, Salt Lake City, 1982—94; judge U.S. Dist. Ct. (3d dist.) Utah, 1995—2003, Utah Supreme Ct., Salt Lake City, 2003—. Chmn. Bd. Dist. Ct. Judges; mem. adv. com. rules profl. conduct Utah Supreme Ct. Fellow: ABA. Office: Utah Supreme Ct PO Box 140210 Salt Lake City UT 84114-0210*

**NEHRIR, M. HASHEM,** electrical engineer, educator; b. Shiraz, Fars, Iran, Aug. 16, 1946; s. Mohammad Hossein Nehrir; m. Maryam Nehrir, Oct. 15, 1970; children: Ali Reza, Sara, Amin Reza. BSEE, Oreg. State U., 1969, MSEE, 1971, PhD, 1978. Instr. Shiraz U., 1971—75, asst./assoc. prof., 1978—86; vis. scholar Univ. Idaho, 1986—87; asst./assoc. prof. Mont. State U., Bozeman, 1987—96, prof., 1996—. Author: Basic Electric Circuits, 1981,

Hybrid Simulation of Engineering Systems, 1986 (Mont. State U. Alumini Assn. and Bozeman Area C. of C. award of excellence, 2001); contbr. articles to profl. jours. Rsch. grantee, NSF, 1992—95, 1997—2006, US Dept. Energy, 1994—2000, 2002—. Mont. State U., 1997, 2000, Rsch. fellow, Kumamoto U., Japan, 1998, Curtin U. Tech., Australia, 2001, 2004. Mem.: IEEE (sr.; vice-chair Mont. sect. 1997, chair 1998). Avocations: travel, hiking. Office: Mont State U Elec and Computer Engring Dept Bozeman MT 59717 Business E-Mail: hnehrir@ece.montana.edu.

**NEHS, WILLIAM SCOTT (SCOTT NEHS),** lawyer; b. Janesville, Wis., Mar. 7, 1966; m. Jacqueline Nehs. BA, Northwestern U., 1988; JD, U. Wis., Madison, 1991. Bar: Ill. 1991, Wis. 1991, US Dist. Ct. No. Dist. Ill. 1991, US Dist. Ct. We. Dist. Wis. 1991, US Dist. Ct. Ea. Dist. Wis. 1993. Assoc. Wildman, Harrold, Allen & Dixon, Chgo., 1991—99; dep. gen. counsel Pepsi-Cola Gen. Bottlers Inc., Rolling Meadows, Ill., 2000—01; asst. gen. counsel PepsiAmericas Inc. (formerly Whitman Corp.), Rolling Meadows, Ill., 2000—01, v.p. legal, 2001—, chief compliance officer. Pro bono work Legal Clinic for the Disabled, 1992—, Les Turner ALS Found., 1995—. Named one of The Top 40 Lawyers Under 40 in Ill., Chgo. Daily Law Bulletin, 2004. Mem.: Assn. of Corp. Counsel, Wis. State Bar, Chgo. Bar Assn. Office: Pepsiamericas Caribbean Inc 1475 E Woodfield Rd Ste 1300 Schaumburg IL 60173-5482

**NEIBERGER, RICHARD EUGENE,** pediatrician, nephrologist, educator; b. Onaga, Kans., Nov. 16, 1947; s. Earl Edward and Margaret Bell (Grim) N.; m. Mary June Chamberlain, Oct. 31, 1971; children: Ami, Eric, Chris, Robert. BS in Physics, U. Ctrl. Fla., 1971; PhD, U. Louisville, 1979, MD, 1982. Diplomate Am. Bd. Pediat., Nat. Bd. Med. Examiners. Intern, then resident in pediat. Albert Einstein Coll. Med., Bronx, N.Y., 1982-85, fellow in pediat. nephrology, 1985-88; asst. prof. U. Fla. Coll. Med., Gainesville, 1988-93, assoc. prof., 1993—; med. dir. pediatrics Renal Stone Disease Clinic, 1996—. Assoc. med. dir. Children's Kidney Ctr., Gainesville, 1989—; co-investigator on 6 rsch. studies, dir. Pediatric Rsch. Stone Disease Clin. U. Fla., rsch. peer rev. com. Am. Heart Assn., 1997-99; physician advisor Fla. Med. Quality Assurance, Tampa, 1994-2002. Contbr. articles to profl. jours. Active Children's Home Soc., Gainesville, 1994—2002, Ronald McDonald House, 1996—. Named one of Best Drs. in Am., Best Drs. in Fla., Best Pediatricians in Am.; grantee, CoInvest, Bethesda, Md., 1995—. Mem. AMA, Fla. Med. Assn., So. Med. Assn., Am. Soc. Nephrology, Internat. Pediat. Nephrology Assn., Am. Soc. Pediat. Nephrology, Fla. Soc. Pediat. Nephrology (pres. 1998). Republican. Methodist. Avocations: camping, skiing, travel. Office Phone: 352-392-4434. Business E-Mail: neiberger@peds.ufl.edu.

**NEIDELL, MARTIN H.,** lawyer; b. Bklyn., Apr. 5, 1946; s. Sidney B. and Sophie (Goldstein) N.; m. Suzan C. Rucker, June 23, 1968; children: Michael, Sari. BA magna cum laude, Lehigh U., 1968; JD cum laude, NYU, 1971. Bar: N.Y. 1972, U.S. Dist. Ct. (ea. and so. dists.) N.Y. 1973, U.S. Ct. Appeals (2d cir.) 1973. Law clk. to presiding justice U.S. Dist. Ct. (ea. dist.) N.Y., Bklyn., 1971-73; assoc. Stroock & Stroock & Lavan LLP, N.Y.C., 1973-79, ptnr., corp., securities law, 1980—, mem., operating exec. com. Editor NYU Law Rev., 1971. Trustee North Shore Synagogue, Syosset, N.Y., 1984-90. Office: Stroock & Stroock & Lavan LLP 180 Maiden Ln New York NY 10038-4925 Office Phone: 212-806-5836. Office Fax: 212-806-7836. Business E-Mail: mneidell@stroock.com.

**NEIDHARDT, FREDERICK CARL,** microbiologist, educator; b. Phila., May 12, 1931; s. Adam Fred and Carrie (Fry) N.; m. Elizabeth Robinson, June 9, 1956 (div. Sept. 1977); children: Richard Frederick, Jane Elizabeth; m. Germaine Chipault, Dec. 3, 1977; 1 son, Marc Frederick. BA, Kenyon Coll., 1952, DSc (hon.), 1976; PhD, Harvard U., 1956; DSc (hon.), Purdue U., 1988, Umea U., 1994. Research fellow Pasteur Inst., Paris, 1956-57; H.C. Ernst research fellow Harvard Med. Sch., 1957-58, instr., then assoc., 1958-61; mem. faculty Purdue U., 1961-70, assoc. prof, then prof., assoc. head dept. biol. scis., 1965-70; mem. faculty U. Mich., Ann Arbor, 1970—, chmn. dept. microbiology and immunology, 1970-82, F.G. Novy disting. univ. prof., 1989-99, F.G. Novy disting. univ. prof. emeritus, 2000—, assoc. dean faculty affairs, 1990-93, assoc. v.p. for rsch., 1993-96, acting v.p. for rsch., 1996-97, interim v.p. for rsch., 1997, v.p. for rsch., 1998. Cons. Dept. Agr., 1964-65; mem. grant study panel NIH, 1965-69, 1985-92; mem. commn. scholars Ill. Bd. Higher Edn., 1973-79; mem. test com. for microbiology Nat. Bd. Med. Examiners, 1975-79, chmn., 1979-83; mem. sci. adv. com. Neogen Corp., 1982-92; mem. basic energy scis. adv. com. U.S. Dept. Energy, 1994-98; Wellcome vis. prof. in microbiology U. Ky., 1986. Author books and papers in field; mem. editorial bd. profl. jours. Recipient award bacteriology and immunology Eli Lilly and Co., 1966; Alexander von Humboldt Found. award for U.S. sr. scientist, 1979; NSF sr. fellow U. Copenhagen, 1968-69 Mem. Am. Soc. Microbiology (pres. 1981-82), Am. Acad. Arts and Scis., Am. Soc. Biochemistry and Molecular Biology, Am. Inst. Biol. Scis., Genetics Soc. Am., Bavarian Acad. Sci., Soc. Gen. Physiology, Waksman Found. for Microbiology (bd. dirs., 1996—, pres. 2001—), Phi Beta Kappa, Sigma Xi. Office: U Mich Med Sch Dept Microbiology and Immunology Ann Arbor MI 48109-0620 Office Phone: 734-763-1209. E-mail: fcneid@umich.edu.

**NEIDHART, JAMES ALLEN,** oncologist, educator; b. Steubenville, Ohio, Aug. 30, 1940; s. James Leonard and Mary Jane (Daniels) N.; m. Patricia Irene Harpkamp, Aug. 16, 1966 (div. Apr. 1985); children— James, Jeffrey, Jennifer; m. Mary Eagan, Feb. 1986; children: Andrew, Rae Ann. BS, Union Coll., Alliance, Ohio, 1962; MD, Ohio State U., 1966. Diplomate Am. Bd. Internal Medicine, Am. Bd. Hematology and Oncology. Intern Bronson Hosp., Kalamazoo, Mich., 1966-67; resident Ohio State U., Columbus, Ohio, 1969-71; postdoctoral fellow Coll. Medicine, Ohio State U., Columbus, 1972-74, asst. prof. medicine, 1974-78, assoc. prof., 1978-84, dir. interdisciplinary oncology unit Comprehensive Cancer Ctr., 1975-80, dep. dir. Comprehensive Cancer Ctr., 1980-84; prof. medicine U. Tex.-Houston-M.D. Anderson Hosp. and Tumor Inst., 1984-86, Hubert L. and Olive Stringer prof. oncology, 1984-86, dep. head div. medicine, 1984-86, chmn. dept. med. oncology, 1984-86; dir. Cancer Rsch. and Treatment Ctr., U. N.Mex., Albuquerque, 1986-96, chief hematology and oncology, 1986-91; dir. Cancer Rsch. and Treatment Ctr. San Juan Regional Cancer Ctr., 1996—. Contbr. chpts. to Recent Advances in Clinical Therapeutics, Clinical Immunotherapy Former mem. bd. dirs. Am. Cancer Soc., Columbus; former v.p. Ohio Cancer Research Assocs. Served to lt. USN, 1967-69, Vietnam Mem. Am. Soc. Hematology, Am. Soc. Clin. Oncology, Am. Assn. Cancer Research, ACP, S.W. Oncology Group, Wilderness Soc., Sierra Club Home: 66 Road 2577 Aztec NM 87410-1020 Office: San Juan Regional Cancer Ctr Farmington NM 87401

**NEIDICH, BROOKE GARBER,** foundation administrator, art patron; m. Daniel Neidich. BA, NYU. Founder, chmn. NYU Child Study Ctr. Trustee Chapin Sch., Mt. Sinai - NYU Health Care Sys., NYU Med. Sch. Found.; bd. dir. Lincoln Ctr. Theater, Lubovitch Dance Co.; adv. coun. Children's Defense Fund - NY; vice chmn. Whitney Mus. Am. Art. Recipient Health Care Leadership Award achievement cmty. svc., United Hosp. Fund., 1999. Mailing: c/o Whitney Mus Am Art 945 Madison Ave New York NY 10021

**NEIDICH, GEORGE ARTHUR,** lawyer; b. NYC, Feb. 22, 1950; s. Hyman and Rosalyn N.; m. Alene Wendrow, Jan. 10, 1982; 1 child, Hannah Lauren. BA, SUNY, Binghamton, 1971; JD magna cum laude, SUNY, Buffalo, 1974; MLT, Georgetown U., 1981. Bar: N.Y. 1975, D.C. 1979, Va. 1996, Conn. 1990. Assoc. Runfola & Birzon, Buffalo, 1973-75, Duke, Holzman, Yaeger & Radlin, Buffalo, 1975-77; gen. counsel subcom. on capital, investments and bus. opportunity, com. on small bus. U.S. Ho. of Reps., Washington, 1977-79, subcom. on gen. oversight, 1979-80; sr. legal advisor Task Force Product Liability and Accident Compensation Office of Gen. Counsel, Dept. Commerce, Washington, 1980-81; assoc. Steptoe & Johnson, Washington, 1981-86, of counsel, 1986-89; gen. counsel, sr. v.p. Preferred Health Care, Ltd., Wilton, Conn., 1989-93; COO Value Behavioral Health, Inc., Falls Church,

Va., 1993-95; counsellor at law, 1995—; gen. counsel CareAdvantage, Inc., Iselin, NJ, 1999—. Adj. prof. Georgetown U. Law Ctr., 1985—87. Office: 9301 Morison Ln Great Falls VA 22066-4153 Office Phone: 703-757-2820. Personal E-mail: gneidich@aol.com.

**NEIDICH, PATRICK C.,** music educator, director; b. Oil City, Pa., May 1, 1977; s. Charles A. and Jean R. Neidich; m. Tara R. Baun, June 30, 2001; 1 child, Alana R. BS in Music Edn., Duquesne U., 1999; MusM in Trumpet Performance, U. Mich., 2001. Lic. tchg. VA, 2001. Music tchr. Fairfax County Sch., Springfield, Va., 2001—02; dir. bands Liberty H.S., Bealeton, Va., 2002—. Mem.: MENC. Office: Liberty High Sch 6300 Independence Ave Bealeton VA 22712 Office Phone: 540-439-6300. E-mail: pneidich@fcps1.org.

**NEIDITCH, H. MICHAEL,** historian; b. N.Y.C., May 17, 1946; BA, U. Pa., 1968; PhD, Cambridge U., 1978. Supr. history Cambridge U., 1969—71; lectr. U. Pa., 1972—80, asst. to the provost, 1972—80; legis. dir. on fgn. policy Congressman Benjamin S. Rosenthal (Dem.-N.Y.), 1980—83; dir. programs B'nai B'rith Internat., 1984—94; pub. B'nai B'rith Books, 1986—94; pres. Jerusalem Found. Inc. U.S., 1994—98; dir. devel. and endowment U.S. Holocaust Meml. Mus., 1998—2001; v.p. for leadership giving Am. Com. for the Weizmann Inst. Sci., Israel, 2001—; prin. cons. Nat. Slavery Mus., Fredericksburg, Va., 2000—02; chmn. bd. B'nai B'rith Klutznick Nat. Jewish Mus., Washington, 2002—04; series editor Jewish History, Life and Culture U. Tex. Press, 2004—. Adj. prof. history Am. U. Sch. Internat. Svc., Washington, 1988—2000. Trustee Wolgin Prizes, Israel. Recipient Sara Norton prize, 1971; U. Pa. Thouron scholar, St. John's Coll., Cambridge, 1968—71. Office: Am Com for the Weizmann Inst Sci #409 1730 Rhode Island Ave NW Washington DC 20036

**NEIDORFF, MICHAEL F.,** health care executive; b. Phila., Nov. 19, 1942; s. A. Harvey and Shirley R. (Rubin) N.; m. Noemi Karpati. BS, Trinity U., 1965; MA, St. Francis Coll., 1966. Mgr. Miles Labs., Ltd., 1969-75, dir., 1967-85; pres., CEO Physician Health Plan, 1985-95, Group Health Plan, Inc., St. Louis, 1995—96; treas. Centene Corp., St. Louis, 1996—2001, pres., CEO, 1996—2004, chmn., CEO, 2004—. Bd. dirs. Mark Twain Bank, St. Louis. Bd. trustees St. Louis Symphony Orch., St. Louis; bd. dirs. St. Louis Area coun. Boy Scouts Am., Grand Ctr., St. Louis. Mem. Mo. Managed Healthcare Assn. Office: Centene Corp 7711 Carondelet Ave Saint Louis MO 63105*

**NEIKIRK, WILLIAM ROBERT,** journalist; b. Irvine, Ky., Jan. 6, 1938; s. Lewis Byron and Nancy Elizabeth (Green) N.; m. Ruth Ann Clary, Sept. 19, 1960; children: Paul Gregory, John Stuart, Christa Lynn. BA in Journalism, U. Ky., 1960. Reporter Lexington (Ky.) Herald, 1959-60; state capital corr. AP, Frankfort, Ky., 1961-66, Baton Rouge, 1966-69; econ. corr. AP (Washington Bur.), 1970-74; nat. econ. writer Chgo. Tribune, Washington, 1974-83, White House corr., 1977, 94-98—, econ. columnist, 1980—, news editor Washington bur., 1983, fin. editor, 1988-91, sr. writer, 1991—, chief Washington corr., 1998—. Author: The Work Revolution, 1983, Volcker: The Money Man, 1987. Recipient Beck award Chgo. Tribune, 1975, Bus. Writing award U. Mo., 1978, 80, Bus. Writing award Amos Tuck Grad. Sch. Bus., Dartmouth Coll., 1980, John Hancock Bus. Writing award Wharton Sch. Fin., U. Pa., 1979, finalist, 1990, 91, John Hancock Bus. Writing award U. Houston, 1980, Loeb Bus. Writing award UCLA Grad. Sch. Mgmt., 1979, Chgo. Headliner Club award, 1979, 84, Raymond Clapper Meml. award, 1981, Barnet Nover award, 1994, Merriman Smith award, 1995, White House Correspondents Assn.; named to Ky. Journalism Hall of Fame, 1998, One of Top 100 Bus. News Luminaries of the Century, TJFR mag., 2000; co-recipient Pulitzer Prize, 2001. Mem. Gridiron Club (v.p.). Mem. United Ch. of Christ Mem. Christian Ch. (Disciples Of Christ). Home: 5121 38th St N Arlington VA 22207-1827 Office Phone: 202-824-2014. Business E-Mail: wneikirk@tribune.com.

**NEIL, DANIEL,** journalist; b. Jan. 12, 1960; married; 1 child. BA in creative writing, E. Carolina U., 1982; MA in English lit., N. Carolina U., 1986. Lectr. NC Wesleyan Coll., 1986—87; copy editor, arts columnist Spectator Mag., 1987—89; copy editor, arts reporter News & Observer, Raleigh, NC, 1989—91, automotive section editor, 1991—96; sr. contbg. editor Autoweek mag., 1994—97; automotive reviewer NY Times, 1995—2003; contbg. editor Attache Mag., 1997—99, Car & Driver mag., 1997—2003; sr. travel editor Expedia Travels Mag., 1993—2003; contbg. editor Worth Mag., 2001—03; automotive columnist LA Times, 2003—. Freelance columnist Conde Nast Traveler, Travel and Leisure, Baltimore Sun mag., Atlanta Jour.-Constn., Art Forum, Robb Report, numerous other newspapers and mag. Named to Houghton Mifilin's Best Am. Sports Writing, 2002; recipient Golden Wheel award, Detroit Free Press Club Found., 1992, Ken Purdy award, Internat. Motor Press Assn., 2001, Pulitzer Prize for criticism, 2004. Home: LA Times 202 W First St Los Angeles CA 90012

**NEIL, J. MEREDITH,** historian; b. Boise, Idaho, June 2, 1937; s. Carl Hurst and Ellen Addie (Hurt) N.; m. Virginia Mary Bivens, Aug. 16, 1958 (div. July 1992); children: John-Marcus Moore. AB, Yale U., 1959; MS, U. Wis., 1963; PhD, Wash. State U., 1966. Asst. prof. history Sam Houston State Coll., Huntsville, Tex., 1966-67; assoc. prof. Am. studies U. Hawaii, Honolulu, 1967-72; exec. dir. Idaho Bicentennial Commn., Boise, 1972-76; guest lectr. art history U. Victoria, B.C., 1976-77; city conservator Seattle, 1978-81; dir. Nicolaysen Art Mus., Casper, Wyo., 1983-89; realtor White-Riedel & Co., Boise, Idaho, 1992—2000. Author: Paradise Improved, 1972, Toward a National Taste, 1975, Saints and Odd Fellows, 1976, To the White Clouds, 2005; editor (with M. Fishwick): Popular Architecture, 1974; editor: Will James: The Spirit of the Cowboy, 1985. Bd. dirs. KTWO Cmty. Adv. Bd., Casper, 1984-85, Boise Allied Arts Coun., 1975-76, Idaho Historic Sites Rev. Bd., 1974-79; mem. Wyo. Coun. Arts, 1985-89; mem. Boise City Historic Preservation Commn., 1997—2002. Mem. Morey's Club (New Haven). Democrat. Methodist. Home: 300 S Straughan Ave Apt 402 Boise ID 83712-7854

**NEIL, KATHARINE CURRIE,** soprano, director; b. Carthage, N.C., June 16, 1931; d. Wilbur Hoke and Elizabeth Woltz Currie; m. Harry Irvine Tuggle (dec.); children: Lynn Tuggle Gilliland, Margaret Tuggle, Katharine Tuggle Echavarri; m. Bobby Joe Neil. BA, Agnes Scott, Decatur, Ga., 1952; MusM, Westminster Choir Coll., 1954. Min. music First Meth. Ch., Martinsville, Va., 1955—59, First Presbyn. Ch., Martinsville, 1969—73, adult music dir., 1989—95; min. music First Bapt. Ch., Danville, Va., 1974—76, First Meth. Ch., Martinsville, 1976—78; asst. prof. music Bridgewater (Va.) Coll., 1954—55; instr. music Patrick Henry CC, Martinsville, Va., 1971—73. Dir. Ridgerest (N.C.) Bapt. WMU Conf., 1974. Singer: Lost Colony Theater, 1954—55. Profl. soprano soloist Martinsville Civic Chorus, 1955—95; dir., founder Martinsville Singing Men, 1968—77; interim dir. music Black Mountain (N.C.) Presbyn., 1997—98. Mem.: Am. Choral Dirs. Assn. Avocations: singing, travel, bridge, dance, cooking.

**NEIL, ROBERT F.,** broadcast executive; Program dir. WYYY-FM, WSYR-AM, 1983, ops. mgr., 1983—84, WYAY-FM, Gainesville, Ga., 1984—86; station mgr. WSB-AM/FM, 1986—88, v.p. & gen. mgr., 1989—92; joined Cox Broadcasting, 1986, v.p. east, 1989—92, exec. v.p. radio, 1992—96; pres. CEO Cox Radio, 1996—. Named Radio Exec. of Yr., Radio Ink, 2003. Office: Cox Radio Inc 6205 Peachtree Dunwoody Rd Atlanta GA 30328

**NEIL, SANDRA EILEEN SILVERBERG,** psychologist; b. N.Y.C., Sept. 30, 1945; d. Marcus and Pearl (Bloom) Glickfeld; m. Robert Silverberg; children: Gerard David, Simonee Elizabeth, Julien Richard, Shari Beth Silverberg. BA, LaTrobe U., Melbourne, Australia, 1974, BEd in Counseling, 1976; MA in Clin. Psychology, U. Melbourne, 1986, PhD in Medicine, 1993. Registered clin. and forensic psychologist 1979, cert. family therapist Avanta Virginia Satir Network, 1981. Rsch. asst. dept. ednl. psychology U. Melbourne, 1965—68; clin. psychologist Janefield Hosp., Melbourne, 1975—77; clin. psychologist Prince Henry Hosp., Melbourne, 1977—79, Cairnmillar Inst., Melbourne,

1979—83; pvt. practice Melbourne, 1983—; clin. psychologist St. Vincent's Hosp., Melbourne, 1986—93; clin. psychologist and family therapist, founding dir. Satir Centre Australia, Armadale, Victoria, Australia, 1993—. Forensic psychologist Supreme Ct. Melbourne, 1976—87; media psychologist, 1977—; sworn marriage counsellor Atty. Gen's Dept., Melbourne, 1978—. Author: The Persistence of Obesity, 1986, The Psychodynamics of Obesity, 1993, The Family Chessboard, 1995; editor: A Matter Of Life: Psychological Theory, Research And Practice, 1999; author: A Journey Through Three Continents And Four Generations: A Family Reconstruction, 2001. Active Opera Australia. Fellow: Australian Psychol. Soc. (chmn. pub. and media rels. Victorian br. 1983—2004); mem.: APA, Internat. Coun. Psychologists (pres. 1997—2000, chair internat. rels. and human rights interest group 1990—, named World Area Chair 2000—), Internat. Acad. Family Psychology (Australian nat. rep. 1997—), Patron Opera Australia, Avanta, The Virginia Satir Internat. Network. Office: Satir Centre of Australia Suite 2 1051-A/B High St Armadale VIC 3143 Australia Office Phone: +613 9824 7755. Office Fax: +61 (0)3 98247865. E-mail: icp@netspace.net.au.

**NEIL, STUART,** management consultant, real estate broker; s. Judith Gottlieb; m. Christine Anne Kessler; children: Jaime Cameran, Glenn Skyler. BA, Marist Coll., Poughkeepsie, N.Y., 1971—73; MA, Fairfield U., Conn., 1974—76. Cert. Secondary English Tchr. N.Y. Bd. Edn., 1975, Bus. Edn. The U. of State of N.Y., 1975, School Counselor The U. of State of N.Y., 1982, Human Resource Profl. Soc. Human Resource Mgmt., 1993. Sr. ptnr. Interact Human Resources, Fort Collins, Colo., 1989—; broker/owner Stuart Neil Ltd., Fort Collins, 1993. Safety cons. SunBlest Mgmt., Fort Lupton, 2001—; safety & human resource cons. Colorstar Growers of Colo., Fort Lupton; safety & human resource mgmt. cons. SunValley Farms, Loveland, 2004—. With U.S. Army, 1963—66. Decorated Parachutist badge US Army, Purple Heart, Combat Infantrymans badge. Mem.: Soc. Human Resource Mgmt., Colo. Assn. Realtors, Disabled Vets., Mil. Order of Purple Heart, Am. Legion. Office: Interact Human Resources PO Box 270226 Fort Collins CO 80527 Office Phone: 303-753-5855. Personal E-mail: iamus@juno.com. Business E-Mail: interact@consultant.com.

**NEILAN, AIDAN JOSEPH,** radiologist; b. Galway, Ireland, Sept. 30, 1923; arrived in U.S., 1950; s. John and Honoria Killeen Neilan; m. Nuala Mary McCarthy, June 1, 1959; children: Katherine Rosemary, Rosemary Collette, David Aidan. MD, Nat. U. Ireland, 1948. Diplomate Am. Bd. Radiology. Intern New Rochelle Gen. Hosp., 1950—51; resident Wadsworth VA Hosp., 1970—74; chief orthop. radiology Wadsworth Hosp., L.A.; prof. radiology UCLA, L.A., 1979, prof. emeritus. Pres., CEO AJNCO, Inc., L.A., 1958. Capt. U.S. Army, 1953—55, France. Mem.: AMA, Irish Med. Assn., Brit. Med. Assn. Republican. Roman Cath. Avocations: piano, swimming, reading. Home: 30639 Rue Langlois Rancho Palos Verdes CA 90275 Office Phone: 310-377-1190. E-mail: neilan@cox.net.

**NEILL, DENIS MICHAEL,** management consultant; b. Grand Rapids, Mich., Apr. 27, 1943; s. Thomas Patrick and Agnes Josephine (Weber) N.; m. Mary Kathleen Golden, June 11, 1966; children: Mark, Erin. AB cum laude, St. Louis U., 1964, JD cum laude, 1967. Bar: Mo. 1967, D.C. 1969. Gen. atty. Office of Asst. Regional Counsel IRS, Newark, 1967-68; assoc. Arent, Fox, Kintner, Plotkin & Kahn, Washington, 1969-71, Morgan, Lewis & Bockius, Washington, 1971-72; atty. advisor office gen. counsel AID, Washington, 1972-73, asst. gen. counsel legis. and policy coordination, 1973-75, asst. adminstr. legis. affairs, 1975-77; sr. v.p. gen. counsel Aeromaritime Internat. Corp., Washington, 1977-80; counsel Surrey & Morse, Washington, 1980-81; sr. ptnr. Neill & Shaw, Washington, 1981-92; sr. law ptnr. Dalley, Neill, Assevero, Carroll & Nealer, Washington, 1992-93; pres. Neill & Co., Inc., Washington, 1981—; counsel Fin. Markets Internat., Inc., 1998—. Bd. dirs. Barker Found., 1981-86, Fed. City Nat. Bank, Washington, 1987. Lt. USCG, 1968-71. Recipient Superior Unit Citation AID, 1976, Disting. Honor award, 1977. Mem. ABA, FBA, D.C. Bar Assn., Mo. Bar Assn., Nat. Security Indsl. Assn. (bd. dirs. 1982-90), Capitol Hill Club, Columbia Country Club (Chevy Chase, Md.), Jefferson Islands Club. Democrat. Home: 5945 Searl Ter Bethesda MD 20816-2022 Office: Neill & Co 5945 Searl Ter Bethesda MD 20816-2022 E-mail: denisneill@aol.com.

**NEILL, RICHARD ROBERT,** retired publishing executive; b. N.Y.C., June 20, 1925; s. Robert Irving and Mildred Mary (Hall) N.; m. Patricia Mae Robinson, Dec. 27, 1952; 1 son, Robert Kenneth. AB summa cum laude, Princeton U., 1948; MA, N.Y. U., 1953. With Prentice-Hall, Inc., N.Y.C. and Englewood Cliffs, NJ, 1948-85, advt. mgr., 1953-58, v.p. advt., 1958-62; pres. Executive Reports Corporation, 1962-85, ret., 1985. Regional chmn. Princeton Alumni Giving, Yonkers, N.Y., 1960-63, Tarrytown-Irvington, N.Y., 1977-80 Pres. Tarrytown (N.Y.) Jr. High Sch. PTA, 1971-72; bd. dirs. Martling Owners, Tarrytown, 1980-84, 89-93. Lt. (j.g.) USNR, 1943-46, PTO. Mem. USN Meml. Found., Princeton Terrace Club (bd. govs. 1986-92), Phi Beta Kappa. Republican. Mem. Reform Ch. Home: 3306 Kendal Way Sleepy Hollow NY 10591 A thought acquired from one of my first bosses: "Everything happens for the best - or can be made to do so." This has been a lifelong help.

**NEILL, ROLFE,** retired newspaper executive; b. Mount Airy, N.C., Dec. 4, 1932; s. Kenneth A. and Carmen (Goforth) N.; m. Rosemary Clifford Boney, July 20, 1952 (div.); children: Clifford Randolph, Sabrina Ashley, Dana Catlin, Jessica Rosemary Ingrid, Quentin Roark Robinson; m. Ann Marshall Snider, Sept. 24, 1988. AB in History, U.N.C., 1954. Reporter Franklin (N.C.) Press, 1956-57; reporter Charlotte (N.C.) Observer, 1957-58, bus. editor, 1958-61; editor, pub. Coral Gables (Fla.) Times and The Guide, 1961-63, Miami Beach (Fla.) Daily Sun, 1963-65; asst. to pub. N.Y. Daily News, 1965-67, suburban editor, 1967-68, asst. mng. editor, 1968-70; editor Phila. Daily News, 1970-75; v.p., int. Phila. Newspapers Inc., 1970-75; chmn., pub. Charlotte (N.C.) Observer, 1975-98. Served with AUS, 1954-56.*

**NEILL, SAM,** actor; b. Northern Ireland, Sept. 14, 1947; m. Noriko Watanabe, 1989; 3 children. Student, U. Canterbury, Eng. Former film dir., editor, scriptwriter New Zealand Nat. Film Unit. Appearances include (film) Ashes, 1975, Land Fall, 1976, Sleeping Dogs, 1977, The Journalist, 1979, Just Out of Reach, 1979, Lucinda Brayford, 1980, My Brilliant Career, 1980, Attack Force Z, 1981, The Final Conflict, 1981, Possession, 1981, Enigma, 1983, The Country Girls, 1983, Robbery Under Arms, 1984, Plenty, 1985, For Love Alone, 1986, The Good Wife, 1987, A Cry in the Dark, 1988 (Australian Film Inst. award), Dead Calm, 1989, La Révolution Française, 1989, The Hunt for Red October, 1990, Death in Brunswick, 1990, Shadow of China, 1990, Until the End of the World, 1991, Memoirs of An Invisible Man, 1992, Rainbow Warrior, 1992, Hostage, 1992, The Piano, 1993, Jurassic Park, 1993, Country Life, 1993, Rudyard Kipling's Jungle Book, 1994, Restoration, 1994, Sirens, 1994, In the Mouth of Madness, 1995, Country Life, 1995, Victory, 1995, Cinema of Unease: A Personal Journey by Sam Neill, 1995 (also writer, dir.), Children of the Revolution, 1996, Snow White in the Black Forest, 1996, Revengers' Comedies, 1996, Event Horizon, 1997, Forgotten Silver, 1998, The Horse Whisperer, 1998, My Mother Frank, 1999, Bicentennial Man, 1999, The Story of Father Damien, 1999, The Dish, 1999, Monticello, 1999, Jurassic Park III, 2001, Dirty Deeds, 2002, Hyperspace Vol. 1: Life, 2002, Framed, 2003, Perfect Strangers, 2003, Wimbledon, 2004; (TV series) The Sullivans, 1976; (TV miniseries) Kane and Abel, 1985, Reilly Ace of Spies, 1986 (Best Actor award Brit. TV), Amerika, 1987, Zhivago, 2002; (TV movies) From a Far Country: Pope John Paul II, 1981, Ivanhoe, 1982, The Blood of Others, 1984, Arthur Hailey's Strong Medicine, 1986, Leap of Faith, 1988, Fever, 1991, One Against the Wind, 1991, The Sinking of the Rainbow Warrior, 1991, Family Pictures, 1993, In Cold Blood, 1996, Merlin, 1998, Sally Hemings: An American Scandal, 2000, Submerged, 2001, Space, 2001, Zookeeper, 2001, SuperCroc, 2001, Framed, 2001; writer, dir., editor: Telephone Etiquette, 1974; writer, editor: Four Shorts on Architecture, 1975. Recipient O.B.E. award, 1991. Office: Internat Creative Mgmt 8942 Wilshire Blvd Beverly Hills CA 90211-1934

**NEILL, VE,** make-up artist; b. Riverside, Calif., May 13, 1951; d. Charles and Eileen Anne (Bernasco) Flores. Grad., Louisville H.S., Woodland Hills, Calif. Credits include (TV movies) Cry for Help, 1978, The London Affair, 1978, Sultan and the Rock Star, 1979, Muppets Go to the Movies, 1981, First Lady of the World, 1982, Money on the Side, 1982, Jane Doe, 1986; (TV Spls.) Sold Out-Lily Tomlin, 1981, Lily for President, 1982, Comedy Store 15th Yr. Reunion, 1984; (TV pilots) One Night Band, 1981, T.J. Hooker, 1981, Madeline (Madeline Kahn), 1982, Girls Life, 1982, A-Team, 1982, Rock & Roll Mom, 1987, Kowalski Loves, 1987, Stephen King's The Shining, 1996 (Emmy award Best Make Up), From the Earth to the Moon, 1997 (Emmy award nomination); (TV show) Pee Wee's Playhouse (Emmy award 1988, Emmy award nominee 1989); (feature films) Star Trek: The Motion Picture (Saturn award 1981), The Incredible Shrinking Woman, 9 to 5, Monty Python at the Hollywood Bowl, Sword and the Sorcerer, The Last Star Fighter, All of Me, The Lost Boys, 1986 (Saturn award 1987), Beetlejuice, 1987 (Acad. award 1987, Saturn award 1988, Brit. Acad. award nominee 1988), Cocoon II, 1988, Big Top Pee Wee, 1988, Dick Tracy, 1989, Flatliners, 1989, Edward Scissorhands, 1990 (Acad. award nominee 1989, Brit. Acad. award nominee 1990), Curly Sue, 1990, Hook, 1991, Batman Returns, 1991 (Saturn award 1992, Acad. award nominee 1992, Brit. Acad. award nominee 1992), Hoffa, 1992 (Acad. award nominee 1992), Rising Sun, 1992, Mrs. Doubtfire, 1993 (Acad. award 1993), Ed Wood, 1993 (Acad. award 1994), Cobb, 1994, Junior, 1994, Batman Forever, 1995, Matilda, 1995, Evening Star, 1996, Mars Attack, 1996, Gattaca, 1996, Batman and Robin, 1996, Amistad, 1997, Stigmata, 1998, Man on the Moon, 1998, Galaxy Quest, 1999, How the Grinch Stole Christmas, 1999, Blow, 2000, A.I., 2000, Death to Smochy, 2001, Duplex, 2002, Blackout, 2002, Pirates of the Caribbean, 2002, (commercial) Sony Mini Disc, 1997, (mag.) Vanity Fair Hollywood Issue, 1998. Mem.: Brit. Acad. Film and TV, Acad. Motion Picture Arts and Scis. Avocations: antiques, hiking, travel. Office: IATSE Local 706 828 N Hollywood Way Burbank CA 91505

**NEILL, WILLIAM HAROLD, JR.,** fisheries science professor, researcher; b. Wynne, Ark., Oct. 21, 1943; s. William H., Sr. and Shirley A. (Ellis) N.; m. Charlotte A. Jackson, 1964; 1 child, Amanda K. BS in Zoology, U. Ark., 1965, MS in Zoology, 1967; PhD in Zoology/Statis., U. Wis., 1971. Rsch. fishery biologist Southwest Fisheries Ctr. Nat. Marine Fisheries Svc., Honolulu, 1971-74; assoc. prof. Agrl. Expt. Sta. Tex. A&M U., College Station, Tex., 1975—83; prof. Agrl. Expt. Sta. Tex. A&M U., 1993—; interim head Dept. Wildlife and Fisheries Sci. Tex. A&M U., 1992—93, interim assoc.head grad. programs and rsch., 2006—. Mem. organizing com. Advanced Rsch. Inst. on Mechanisms Fish Migration, NATO, 1980-82; mem. tech. com. So. Regional Aquaculture Ctr., USDA, 1987-89; mem. sci.-tech. adv. com. Corpus Christi Bay Nat. Estuary Program, 1994-97; mem. Tex. Sea Grant adv. bd., 1998-2005. Editor Tex. Jour. Sci., 1983-85; mem. editl. adv. bd. Critical Revs. in Aquatic Sci., 1986-90; assoc. editor Transactions of the Am. Fisheries Soc., 1995-97; contbr. numerous articles to sci. jours. and books. Grantee numerous orgns., 1975—. Fellow Tex. Acad. Sci.; mem. Am. Fisheries Soc. (life, Award of Excellence com. 1987, 89, chair Publ. Awards com. 1993, editl. bd. 1995), Am. Inst. Fishery Rsch. Biologists, Phi Beta Kappa, Sigma Xi, Phi Sigma, Gamma Sigma Delta. Office: Texas A&M U Dept Wildlife & Fisheries Sci 2258 TAMUS College Station TX 77843-2258 Office Phone: 979-845-5759. Business E-Mail: w-neill@tamu.edu.

**NEILON, PATRICK DANIEL,** special education educator; s. John Joseph and Brenda May Neilon; m. Hsin-Yen Sunny Kuo, July 26, 1997; children: John, Brenda. BA, San Francisco State U., 1985. Tchr. L.A. United Sch. Dist., 1996, tchr. spl. edn., 1997—99, San Bernardino City Unified Sch. Dist., 1999—. Pub. Pat and Sunny Press, Fontana, Calif., 2002—. Author (illustrator): The Day My Brain Ran Away, 2002, Super Duper Baby, 2003, I Want to Play, 2003. Founder Nat. Campaign Tolerance. Named to Wall of Tolerance Monument, 2005. Mem.: NEA (nat. conv. del. 2000, natino conv. del. 2003), San Bernardino Tchrs. Assn. (union rep. 2003—). Republican. Avocations: songwriting, skiing.

**NEILSEN, CRAIG H.,** hotel executive; b. 1942; MBA, JD, U. Utah. Pres. Cactus Pete, Inc., Jackpot, Nev., 1984—, Ameristar Casino Vicksburg, Miss., 1993—. Pres. & chmn. bd. dir Cactus Pete's Inc. Named best performing CEO, Am. Gaming Assn., 2002. Office: Ameristar Casinos Inc 3773 Howard Hughes Pkwy Las Vegas NV 89109

**NEILSON, ERIC GRANT,** physician, educator, health facility administrator; b. Bklyn., Sept. 14, 1949; s. Jack Drew and Lynette Elsie (Lundquist) N.; m. Linda Rae Apolzon, May 27, 1972; children: Tinsley, Sigrid. BS magna cum laude, Denison U., 1971; MD magna cum laude, U. Ala., 1975; MD (hon.), U. Pa., 1987. Asst. prof. U. Pa., Phila., 1980-87, assoc. prof., 1987-91, prof., 1991-98, C. Mahlon Kline prof., 1993-98, chief renal-electrolyte & hypertension divsn. dept. medicine, 1988-98; Hugh Jackson Morgan prof., chmn. dept. medicine Vanderbilt U. Med. Ctr., Nashville, 1998—. Attending physician Hosp. of U. Pa., 1980-98; physician-in-chief Vanderbilt U. Hosp., 1998—; cons. in field. Med. editl. bds. on sci. jours.; assoc. editor Kidney Internat., 1997—; contbr. numerous articles to profl. jours. Chmn. med. adv. bd. Lupus Found. of Phila., 1985-95; chmn. pathology A study sect. NIH, Bethesda, Md., 1990-92; chmn. grant rev. com. Nat. Kidney Found. of Delaware Valley; mem. adv. coun. NIDDK, NIH; mem. bd. sci. advisors Polycystic Kidney Found., 1997-2000; mem. postdoctoral fellowship com. Howard Hughes Med. Inst., 1997-2000. Recipient Clin. Scientist award Am. Heart Assn., 1980, Young Investigator award Am. Soc. Nephrology/Am. Heart Assn., 1985, Established Investigator award Am. Heart Assn., 1985-90, President's medal Am. Soc. Nephrology, 1994, AN Richard Disting. Achievement award, 1998, John P. Peters award, Am. Soc. Nephrology, 2005; named Disting. Alumnus, U. Ala., Birmingham, 2006. Fellow: ACP; mem.: Internat. Soc. Nephrology (treas. 2003—), Assn. Prof. Medicine (chmn. rsch. com. 2000—), Assn Subspilty. Profn. (trrasn—96, Disting. Prof. award 2003), Am. Assn. Immunologists, Am. Clin. Climatol. Assn., Am. Soc. Nephrology (John P. Peters award 2005), Assn. Am. Physicians, Am. Soc. Clin. investigation. Mem. Soc. Of Friends. Office: Vanderbilt U Med Ctr Dept Medicine D3100 Med Ctr N Nashville TN 37232-0001 Office Phone: 615-322-3146. Business E-Mail: eric.neilson@vanderbilt.edu.

**NEILSON, WINTHROP CUNNINGHAM, III,** communications executive, financial consultant, photographer; b. N.Y.C., Jan. 7, 1934; s. Winthrop Cunningham, Jr. and Frances Fullerton (Jones) N.; m. Ilse Rossenbeck, Jan. 4, 1957; children: Luise R., Victoria F.; m. Demaris King Hetrick, July 5, 1985; 1 child, Whitney C. C.; stepchildren: Norman P. Hetrick Jr., D. Page Hetrick. BA, Harvard U., 1956; grad. in security analysis, N.Y. Inst. Finance, 1963. Asst. prodr., asst. dir. Rangley Lakes Theater, 1955; gen. assignment reporter Albany (N.Y.) Times-Union, 1956-60; pub. info. writer, spkr. Consol. Edison, 1960—61; asst. dir. pub. rels. Union Svc. Corp., 1962; with Georgeson & Co., N.Y.C., 1962—81, prin., 1969—81; sr. v.p. D.F. King & Co. Inc., N.Y.C., 1982—86; founder, mng. dir. Krone Comm., Harrisburg, Pa., 1986—87; pres. Krone Group Inc., Harrisburg, 1987—89; mng. dir. Neilson/Hetrick Group, Montclair, NJ, 1990—93, Harrisburg, Pa., 1993—97, chmn. Chambersburg, Pa., 1987—; guest lectr. NYU, 1991; profl. nature photographer, 2001—. Author: series Aunt Jane, 1971, 73, The Reluctant Marriage, 1978, Investorism, 1981, Annual Reports, The Agony and the Ecstasy, 1985, Individual Investors, a Counterbalance to Institutional Investors, 1986; writer, assoc. editor: Trends, 1965-81; contbr. articles to profl. jours. Mem. Mountain Lakes (N.J.) Econ. Devel. Council, 1974-79, chmn., 1977-79; pres. Robert A. Taft Republican Club, Queens, N.Y., 1964-65, chmn., 1966-67; treas. 23d Assembly Dist. Rep. Party, 1966-67; county committeeman, 1964-67; del. N.Y. State Nominating Conv., 1966; campaign mgr. for 2 assemblymen and state senator; mem. exec. com. Chambersburg Cmty. Theater, Inc., 2002-03. Served with AUS, 1956-59. Recipient Investor Edn. Disting. Service award Nat. Assn. Investors Clubs, 1986. Mem. Nat. Investor Rels. Inst. (dir. 1980-84, v.p. manpower 1980-81, v.p. long-range planning 1981-84), Pub. Rels. Soc. Am. (charter, exec. com. investor rels. 1982-90, chmn. 1987, Pres. award 1987, charter inductee into Hall of Fame for Investor Rels.), Corp. Rels. Soc. Ctrl. Pa. (v.p. 1986-89, pres. 1994-95), Ctrl. Pa. Entrepreneurial Assn. (bd. dirs. 1988-89, adv. bd. tech. coun. Ctrl.

Pa. 1994-96), Chambersburg Country Club, DU Club, Hasty Pudding Club, Ausable Club. Lutheran. Home and Office: 3333 Carnoustie Dr Chambersburg PA 17201-8116 Home (Summer): Ausable Club 14 Neilson Way Saint Huberts NY 12943

**NEIMAN, JOSEPH BRUCE,** dermatologist; b. N.Y.C., July 28, 1947; s. Nathan and Sarah N.; BA, N.Y. U., 1968; M.D., U. Tenn., 1972; m. Karen Marcia Simon, Aug. 31, 1975. Intern, Brown U., Providence, 1973-74; resident SUNY, Buffalo, 1974-75, 76-78, chief resident, 1977; dir. adult health services, head community health screening Erie County Health Dept., Buffalo, N.Y., 1975-76; practice medicine specializing in dermatology and dermatologic surgery Boston, 1978-79, Williamsville, N.Y., 1980—; mem. staffs Buffalo Gen. Hosp., Millard Fillmore Hosp., Buffalo, Sisters of Charity Hosp., Buffalo; clin. asst. prof. dermatology SUNY, Buffalo, 1980—; cons. USPHS, Buffalo, 1979-81. Fellow Am. Acad. Dermatology; mem. AMA, Internat. Soc. Dermatologic Surgery, Am. Soc. Dermatologic Surgery, N.AM. Soc. Phlebology, N.Y. State Soc. Dermatology, Buffalo-Rochester Dermatol. Soc., Erie County Med. Soc., N.Y. State Med. Soc. Home: 48 Brandywine Dr Buffalo NY 14221-1804 Office: 1140 Youngs Rd Williamsville NY 14221-3625

**NEIMAN, KENNETH PAUL,** judge; b. NYC, July 4, 1945; s. Julius and Gertrude (Fox) N.; m. Jan Dumond, May 24, 1987; children: Jennifer Gottlieb, Anna L. Neiman, J. Matthew Gowdy, Kerri Escudero. BA, Tufts U., 1967; JD, Harvard Law Sch., 1971. Bar: N.Y. 1972, Mass. 1974, U.S. Dist. Ct. Mass. 1974, U.S. Ct. Appeals (1st cir.) 1981, U.S. Supreme Ct. 1978. Staff atty. Mental Health Info. Svcs., N.Y.C., 1971, Ctr. Social Welfare, Policy & Law, N.Y.C., 1971-73, rsch. fellow Legal Svcs. Corp. Rsch. Inst., Washington, 1978; mng. atty. Western Mass. Legal Svcs., Holyoke, 1973-81; prtnr. Fierst & Neiman, Northampton, Mass., 1981-94; U.S. magistrate judge Dist. Mass., Springfield, 1995—. Mem. ABA, Mass. Bar Assn., Mass. Bar Found., Hampshire County Bar Assn. Office: US Dist Ct 1550 Main St Springfield MA 01103-1422

**NEIMAN, LEROY,** artist; b. St. Paul, June 8, 1927; s. Charles and Lydia (Serline) Runquist; m. Janet Byrne, June 22, 1957. Student, Sch. Art Inst., Chgo., 1946-50, U. Ill., 1951, DePaul U., 1951; LittD (hon.), Franklin Pierce Coll., 1976; D (hon.), St. John's U., 1980, Iona Coll., 1985, Hofstra U., 1997, St. Francis Coll., 1998, St. Bonaventure U., 1999, Sch. of the Art Inst. of Chgo., 2006. Instr. Sch. Art Inst. Chgo., 1950-60, Saugatuck (Mich.) Summer Sch. Painting, 1957-58, 63, Sch. Arts and Crafts, Winston-Salem, NC, 1963; instr. painting Atlanta Youth Council, 1968-69; printmaker-graphics, 1971—; artist Olympics, ABC-TV, Munich, 1972, ofcl. artist Montreal, 1976, U.S. Olympics, 1980, 84; computer artist CBS-TV (Superbowl), New Orleans, 1978; ofcl. artist Goodwill Games CNN-TV, Moscow, 1986; 1st ofcl. artist Ky. Derby, Louisville, 1997; ofcl. artist Mardi Gras, New Orleans, 2002; LeRoy Neiman master classes Sch. of Art Inst. Chgo., 2006. Mem. adv. com. LeRoy Neiman Ctr. for Print Studies Sch. of Arts Columbia U., 1995; mem. adv. com. for N.Y.C. Commn. for Cultural Affairs, 1995, UCLA LeRoy Neiman Ctr. for Study of Am. Soc. and Culture, 1998; established LeRoy Neiman Art Ctr. for Youth, San Francisco, 2000, 05, Watsonville, Calif., 2002. One-man shows include Oehlschlaeger Gallery, Chgo., 1959, 61, O'Hana Gallery, London, Gallerie O. Bosc, Paris, 1962, Hammer Gallery, N.Y.C., 1963, 65, 67, 70, 72, 76, 78-79, 81-83, 85-87, 89, 92, 94, 97, 2000, 03, Huntington Hartford Gallery Modern Art, N.Y.C., 1967, Heath Gallery, Atlanta, 1969, Abbey Theatre, Dublin, Ireland, 1970, Museo de Bellas Artes, Caracas, Indpls. Inst. Arts, 1972, Hermitage Mus., Leningrad, Tobu Gallery, Tokyo, 1974, Springfield (Mass.) Mus. Fine Arts, 1974, 84, Knoedler Gallery, London, 1976, Casa gratica, Helsinki, 1977, Renée Victor, Stockholm, 1977, Okla. Art Ctr., Oklahoma City, 1981, Harrod's, London, 1982; retrospective show, Minn. Mus. Art, St. Paul, 1975, Meredith Long Galleries, Houston, 1978, Hanae Mori Gallery, Tokyo, 1988, New State Tretyakov Mus., 1988, Butler Inst., Youngstown, Ohio, 1990, Galerie Marcel Bernheim, Paris, 1993, Ky. Derby Mus., Louisville, 1995, 1997, Marlborough Gallery, NYC, 2000, The Fairfield, Sturgeon Bay, Wis., 2001, Nat. Art Mus. Sport, Ind. U.-Purdue U., 2001, Wildlife Experience, Parker, Colo., 2003; two-man show, Neiman-Warhol, Los Angeles Inst. Contemporary Art, 1981; exhibited in group shows at Art Inst. Chgo., 1954-60, Carnegie Internat., 1956, Corcoran Gallery Am., Washington, Walker Art Center, Mpls., 1957, Ringling Mus., Sarasota, Fla., 1959, Salon d'Art Mus., Paris, 1961, Nat. Gallery Portraiture, Smithsonian Instn., Washington, Minn. Mus. Art, 1969, Rotunda Della Basana, Milan, Italy, 1971, Royal Coll. Art, London, 1971, Minn. Mus. Art Nat. Tour, 1976-77, Whitney Mus., 1985; Master Prints of 19th and 20th Centuries, Hammer Gallery, N.Y., 1987, Salon d'Automne, Paris, 1992-93, Newport Art Mus., 2004; represented in permanent collections Mpls. Inst. Arts, Ill. State Mus., Springfield, Joslyn Mus., Omaha, Wodham Coll., Oxford, Eng., Nat. Art Mus. Sport, NYC, Museo De Ballas Artes Caracas, Hermitage Mus., Indpls. Inst. Arts, U. Ill., Balt. Mus. Fine Art, The Armand Hammer Collection, LA, Edwin & Ruth Kennedy Mus. Am. Art at Ohio U., Midwest Mus. Am. Art, Elkhart, Ind., Nat. Art Mus. Sport, Indpls.; executed murals at Merc. Nat. Bank, Hammond, Ind., Continental Hotel, Chgo., Swedish Lloyd Ship S.S. Patricia, Stockholm, ceramic tile mural, Sportsmans Park, Chgo., The Muhammad Ali Ctr., Louisville, 2005, Polo Mural, Southampton, N.Y., 2005; author: LeRoy Neiman—Art and Life Style, 1974, Horses, 1979, LeRoy Neiman: Posters, 1980, LeRoy Neiman: Catalogue Raisonné, 1980, Carnaval, 1981, LeRoy Neiman: Winners, 1983, Japanese translation, 1985, LeRoy Neiman, Monte Carlo Chase, 1988, The Prints of LeRoy Neiman, 1980-90, Big Time Golf, 1992, LeRoy Neiman, An American in Paris, 1994, LeRoy Neiman on Safari, 1997, The Prints of LeRoy Neiman 1991-2000, LeRoy Neiman, Five Decades, 2003, deluxe ltd. edit. The LeRoy Neiman Sketchbook, 2004; illustrator: 12 paintings deluxe edit. Moby Dick, 1975, 35 charcoal drawings deluxe edit. Casey at the Bat, 2000, trade edit., 2002. Served with AUS, 1942-46. Recipient 1st prize Twin City Show, 1953, 2d prize Minn. State Show, 1954, Clark Meml. prize Chgo. Show, 1957, Hamilton-Graham prize Ball State Coll., 1958, Municipal prize Chgo. Show, 1958, Purchase prize Miss. Valley Show, 1959, Gold medal Salon d'Art Modern Paris, 1961; award of merit as nation's outstanding sports artist AAU, 1976; Olympic Artist of Century award, 1979, Gold Medal award St. John's U., 1985. Address: 1 W 67th St New York NY 10023-6200

**NEIMARK, CORT ALAN,** lawyer; b. Perth Amboy, N.J., May 29, 1954; s. Harold and Norma (Schreibman) N.; m. Phyllis Hochberg, Aug. 24, 1991. BA, Emory U., 1976; MBA, Rutgers U., 1977; JD, U. Miami, Coral Gables, Fla., 1981. Bar: Fla. 1981, U.S. Dist. Ct. (so. dist.) Fla. 1981, N.Y. 1989, D.C. 1991. Staff atty. Travelers Ins. Co., West Palm Beach, Fla., 1981-83; assoc. Watterson & Dickenson, P.A., West Palm Beach, 1983-84, Miller, Shapiro & Miller, P.A., Boca Raton, Fla., 1984-85, Neimark & Neimark, P.A., Ft. Lauderdale, Fla., 1985-95, Neimark, Greene & Nadel P.A., 1995-97, Neimark & Nadel P.A., 1997—2005, Fowler White Burnett, PA, Ft. Lauderdale, 2006—. Bd. dirs. Leadership Broward Alumni, Am. Cancer Soc., Ft. Lauderdale C. of C., Stranahan House, Greater Fort Lauderdale C. of C.; planned giving coun. Nova Southeast Univ., Broward Lawyers Care Program; econ. devel. adv. bd. City Fort Lauderdale; chair Uptown Devel. and Improvement Group Mem. ABA, Attys. Title Ins. Fund, Fla. State Bar, N.Y. Bar, Washington Bar, Broward County Estate Planning Coun. Office: Fowler White Burnett PA 100 SE Third Ave Ste 1100 Fort Lauderdale FL 33394 Office Phone: 954-493-8000, 954-377-8100. Business E-Mail: cneimark@fowler-white.com. E-mail: cneimark@nnflalaw.com.

**NEIMS, ALLEN HOWARD,** pediatrician, educator, dean, researcher; b. Chgo., Oct. 24, 1938; s. Irving Morris and Ruth (Geller) N.; m. Myrna Gay Robins, June 18, 1961; children: Daniel Mark, Susan Roberta, Nancy Elizabeth. BA, BS, U. Chgo., 1957; MD, Johns Hopkins U., 1961, PhD, 1966. Intern, resident in pediatrics Johns Hopkins Hosp., 1961-62, 66-68; research asso. Lab. Neurochemistry, NIH, 1968-70; asst. prof. Physiol. chemistry and pediatrics Johns Hopkins Med. Sch., 70-72; assoc. prof. McGill U., 1972-77, prof. pharmacology and pediatrics, 1977-78; dir. Roche developmental pharmacology unit, 1972-78; prof., chmn. dept. pharmacology and therapeutics, prof. pediatrics U. Fla., Gainesville, 1978-89, dean Coll. Medicine, 1989-96, prof. pharmcology, pediat., 1996—; dir. Ctr. for Spirituality and

Health, 2002—. Dir. Ctr. Spirituality and Health; Fulton Bequest prof. U. Melbourne, Australia, 1994; mem. human embryology and devel. study sect. NIH, 1979-83; sci. cons. Can. Found. for Study of Sudden Infant Death, 1974-77, Nat. Soft Drink Assn., 1976-78, Internat. Life Scis. Inst., 1978-89; bd. sci. counsellors Nat. Inst. Child Health and Human Devel., 1984-89. Contbr. chpts. to books, articles to med. jours. Served to comdr. USPHS, 1968-70. NIH, Can. Med. Research Council grantee. Mem. Can. Assn. Research in Toxicology (pres. 1976-78), Am. Soc. Pharmacology and Exptl. Therapeutics (past mem. exec. cons. clin. pharmacology and drug metabolism), Am. Pediatric Soc., Am. Acad. Pediatrs. Democrat. Jewish. Office: U Fla Coll Medicine PO Box 100267 Gainesville FL 32610-0267 Office Phone: 352-392-0687. Business E-Mail: ahneims@ufl.edu.

**NEINAS, CHARLES MERRILL,** sports association executive, consultant; b. Marshfield, Wis., Jan. 18, 1932; s. Arthur Oscar and Blanche Amelia (Reeder) N.; children: Andrew, Toby. BS, U. Wis., 1957. Asst. exec. dir. Nat. Collegiate Athletic Assn., Kansas City, Mo., 1961-71; commr. Big Eight Conf., Kansas City, 1971-81; exec. dir. Coll. Football Assn., 1981—97; Dr. Patricia L. Pacey prof. econs. U. Colo., Boulder, 1981—85; with Pacey Ecometrics Group, Inc., 1985—. Adviser Am. Football Coaches Assn., 1997—; cons. NCAA Football, 1997—. Served with USNR, 1952-54. Office: Neinas Sports Svcs 6630 Gunpark Dr Boulder CO 80301-3372 Home: 5344 Westridge DR Boulder CO 80301-6501

**NEIS, ARNOLD HAYWARD,** pharmaceutical company executive; b. NYC, Feb. 13, 1938; s. Harry H. and Mary Ruth (Bishop) N.; children: Nancy R., Robert C. BS cum laude, Columbia U., 1959; MBA, NYU, 1967. With Scott Chem. Co., 1959-64; v.p. mktg., then v.p. Odell, Inc., N.Y.C., 1964-71, pres. Thayer Knomark div., 1969-71; pres., chief exec. officer E.T. Browne Drug Co., Inc., Englewood Cliffs, NJ, 1971—, chmn., 2000—. Dir. Esquire A.B. Stockholm, Knomark Can. Ltd., E.T. Browne Internat. Fellow Royal Soc. Chemists, Royal Geog. Soc., Am. Inst. Chemists, NY Acad. Scis.; mem. AAAS, Am. Chem. Soc., Am. Pharm. Assn., New Eng. Soc. (pres., bd. dirs.), Explorers Club (v.p., bd. dirs., Sweeney medal 1987), Chemists Club, Lotos Club, Soldiers, Sailors and Airmans Club (bd. dirs.), St. Georges Soc. (bd. dirs.), Ch. Club (bd. dirs.), Pilgrims of the U.S., Order St. John Episcopalian. Home: 898 Park Ave New York NY 10021-0234 Office: PO Box 1613 440 Sylvan Ave Englewood Cliffs NJ 07632-2700

**NEIS, ARTHUR VERAL,** healthcare and development company executive; b. Lawrence, Kans., May 30, 1940; s. Veral Herbert and Louise (Schlegel) N.; m. Fleeta Weigel, Apr. 12, 1969 (dec. 1999); children: Frederick Arthur, Benjamin Jason, Sarah Louise. BS in Bus., U. Kans., 1962, MS in Acctg., 1963. CPA, Kans., Iowa. Mgmt. cons. Arthur Andersen & Co., Kansas City, Mo. and Mpls., 1963-74; chief corp. acctg. Carlson Co., Mpls., 1974-76; contr. The Fullerton Cos., Mpls., 1976-78; asst. treas. Fru-Con Corp., St Louis, 1978-80, asst. contr., 1981, contr., 1982-86; corp. contr. LCS Holdings, Inc. (Weitz Corp. and Subsidars), Des Moines, 1986-87, v.p., treas., CFO, 1987—; treas., CFO Weitz Co., Des Moines, 1987-93, Life Care Services LLC, Des Moines, 1987—; v.p., treas., CFO, mem. exec. com. LCS Holdings and Subs., Inc., 1995—, also bd. dirs., trustee retirement plan. Adv. group Nat. Assn. Ins. Com., 1990—93; treas., exec. com. bd. Villa de Maria Montessori Sch., St. Louis, 1984—86; trustee Fin. Execs. Rsch. Found., 1994—2000, chair audit com., 1997—98, vice chair rsch., 1998—2000, chmn., 2000—01; mem. Internat. Acctg. Standards Bd.; trustee Plymouth Congl. Ch., 1997—97, found. trustee, 1998—2001, chair, 2000—01; active Des Moines Poetry Festival, 2000—04, treas. bd. dirs., 2003—04; bd. dirs. Inst. Humane Studies, George Mason U., Fairfax, Va., 1971—2006, exec. com., 1975—83, chmn., 1978—83; bd. dirs. Lake Country Sch., Mpls., 1973—78, Alliance for Arts and Understanding, co-chair, 1993—96, bd. trustees, 1993—2002, chair, 1996—2002. Mem. AICPA (v.p. co. fin. pvt. task force 2004, mem. task force pvt. co. reporting generally accepted acctg. practices 2004, mem. nominating com. 2000—), Kans. Soc. CPAs, Iowa Soc. CPAs, Fin. Execs. Inst. (bd. dirs. Iowa chpt. 1986, 88-94, sec. 1988-90, v.p. 1990-91, pres. 1991-92, com. on pvt. cos. stds. subcom. 2005—). Avocations: history, Asian art. Office: 1575 NW 106th St Clive IA 50325

**NEIS, JAMES MICHAEL,** lawyer; b. Chgo., Mar. 3, 1946; BA, DePaul U., 1969, JD, 1973. Bar: Ill. 1973, U.S. Tax Ct. 1974. Ptnr. Winston & Strawn LLP, Chgo., 1969—, mng. ptnr., 1993—2006. Adj. prof. law DePaul U., 1979-86; dir. Attys.' Liability Assurance Soc. Ltd., Bermuda, 2001-. Mem. ABA, Ill. State Bar Assn., Chgo. Bar Assn. Office: Winston & Strawn LLP 35 W Wacker Dr Ste 4200 Chicago IL 60601-1695 Office Phone: 312-558-5636. Business E-Mail: jneis@winston.com.

**NEISER, BRENT ALLEN,** foundation executive, public information educator, finance executive; b. Cin., 1954; s. Rodger and Hazel Neiser; m. Marion, Apr. 1, 1978; children: Christy Jean, Steven José, April Reneé. BA in Pub. Affairs, George Washington U., 1976; MA in Urban Studies, Occidental Coll., 1978; MBA, U. Louisville, 1979; M in Global Studies Internat. Security, U. Denver, 2005. Cert. fin. planner, 1985; cert. assn. exec., 1994; cert. sr. advisor, 2004; cert. in Homeland Security U. Denver, 2005; cert. in exec. edn. performance measurement Harvard Bus. Sch., 2006; chartered mut. fund counselor, 1996; accredited asset mgmt. specialist, 1998. Project mgr., analyst Legis. Research Com., Frankfort, Ky., 1978-84; pres. Moneyminder, Denver and Frankfort, 1983-91; dir. edn., govt. affairs Inst. Cert. Fin. Planners, Denver, 1985-91, exec. dir., 1991-94; pub. affairs, govt. rels. bus. strategies cons. The Brent Neiser Co., Englewood, Colo., 1994—; dir. collaborative programs Nat. Endowment for Fin. Edn., 1995—. Mng. dir. Fin. Products Stds. Bd., Denver, 1985-91; co-creator Personal Econ. Summit '93, Washington. Author: EPCOT/World Showcase External Directions, Walt Disney Imagineering, 1977, Personal Management, 1996, 2000, 03, Ignoring the Obvious! Public Diplomacy U.S. Foreign and Defense Policy, 2005. Vol., v.p. Big Bros./Big Sisters, Frankfort, 1982; del. Colo. Model Constn. Conv., 1987; mem. citizens budget rev. com. Greenwood Village; mem. long range planning com. Adoption Exch., Denver, 1992-93, bd. dirs., 1993-99; polit. action dir. Frankfort NAACP, 1983, legis. chmn. state conf., 1984; troop com. mem., asst. scoutmaster Boy Scouts Am., Englewood, 1993-99; bd. dirs. Young Ams. Bank Edn. Found., 1993-99, chair edn. coun.; mem. Leadership Denver, 1994; vol. host com. Denver Summit of the Eight, 1997; nat. spokesperson Protect our Children Campaign, 1996; active Annie E. Casey Found.: Nat. Foster Care Awareness Project, 1999-02; citizen's panelist News Hour with Jim Lehrer (PBS), 1998—; founding ptnr. Social Venture Ptnrs., Denver, 2000-04, Colo. Coun. of Advisors on Consumer Credit, 2000—, chmn., 2005-; mem. CFP bd. Consumer Adv. Coun. on Fin. Planning, 2001-03, 05-; bd. advisors Coll. Visual and Performing Arts, Winthrop U., 2002-05; mem. cmty. rels. bd. Daniels Coll. Bus., 2006-, U. Denver Lt. (j.g.) USNR, 1985-92. Recipient award of Excellence, Assn. Advance Am., 1996, 98, Summit award, Am. Soc. Assn. Exec., 2004; Pub. Affairs fellow Coro Found., 1976-77; fellow Ctr. for Social Innovation Stanford U., 2003, exec. seminar Aspen Inst., 2006. Mem. Denver World Affairs Coun., Denver Coun. on Fgn. Rels., Investors Edn. Assn. Colo. (bd. dirs. 1995-01), Nat. Assns. in Colo., Denver C. of C. (pub. affairs coun.), N.Am. Securities Adminstrs. Assn. (investment adviser and fin. planner adv. com.), Nat. Soc. Compliance Profls. (bd. dirs. 1987-89), Am. Film Inst. (writers workshop), Am. Polit. Items Collectors, Fin. Planning Assn. (Foresight Group, chair awards task force), Alliance for Investor Edn., Nat. Eagle Scout Assn., Snowboard Outreach Soc. developer incl. co-inventor Trivia Express Game, Denver, 1986; developer over 100 projects for disaster victims, low income families and children. Avocations: snowboarding, drums (jazz) and latin percussion music, golf, swimming, modern design. Office: 5860 Big Canyon Dr Englewood CO 80111-3516 Office Phone: 303-224-3501. E-mail: ban@nefe.org.

**NEISSER, HORST,** library director; b. Nuernberg, Germany, July 30, 1943; s. Heinrich and Eleonore (Mergner) Neisser. Student, U. Frankfurt, Germany, 1965-68; DPhil, U. Tuebingen, Germany, 1973. Subject specialist EKZ, Reutlingen, Germany, 1973-76; dir. City Libr. Saarbrücken, Germany, 1976-86, City Libr. Cologne, Germany, 1986—. Lectr Fochhochschule für Sozialwesen, Esslingen, Germany, 1973—76, Fachhochschule für Bibliotheken,

Cologne, Germany, 1987—; adv. in field. Author: (book) Die Jugendzeitschrift, 1975, Diskotheken in Deutschland, 1979, Traumzeiten, 1984, Der Gott der Ameise, 1993, Centratur, 1996, Centratur II, 1997. Mem.: Verband Deutscher Schriftsteller. Avocations: painting, music. Office: City Libr Cologne Josef-Haubrich-Hof 1 50676 Cologne Germany E-mail: neisser@centratur.de.

**NEISSER, ULRIC,** psychology professor; b. Kiel, Germany, Dec. 8, 1928; came to U.S., 1933; s. Hans Philip N. BA, Harvard U., 1950, PhD, 1956; MA, Swarthmore Coll., 1952; Laurea Honoris Causa, U. Rome, 1988, U. Aarhus, Denmark, 1993, U. Cluj, Romania, 1994. Instr. Swarthmore (Pa.) Coll., 1953-54, Harvard U., Cambridge, Mass., 1956-57; from asst. to assoc. prof. Brandeis U., Waltham, Mass., 1957-66; prof. psychology Cornell U., Ithaca, NY, 1967-80, Susan Linn Sage prof. psychology, 1980-83; Robert W. Woodruff prof. psychology Emory U., Atlanta, 1983-96; prof. psychology Cornell U., Ithaca, NY, 1996—2005. Author: Cognitive Psychology, 1967, Cognition and Reality, 1976; editor: Memory Observed, 1982, The School Achievement of Minority Children, 1987, Concepts and Conceptual Development, 1987, Remembering Reconsidered, 1988, The Perceived Self, 1993, The Rising Curve, 1998. Ctr. for Advanced Study in Behavior Scis. fellow, 1973-74, Guggenheim fellow, 1987-88. Fellow APA; mem. NAS, Am. Acad. Arts and Scis., Cognitive Sci. Soc., Internat. Soc. Ecol. Psychology, Psychonomic Soc. Office: Cornell U Dept Psychology Ithaca NY 14853

**NEITER, GERALD IRVING,** lawyer; b. LA, Nov. 11, 1933; s. Harry and Ida Florence (Alperin) N.; m. Margaret P. Rowe, Mar. 5, 1961; children: David, Karen, Michael. BSL, JD, U. So. Calif., 1957. Bar: Calif. 1958. Judge pro tem Mcpl. Cts., L.A. and Beverly Hills, 1970-94. Calif. Superior Ct., L.A. County, 1974-94, family law mediator, 1976—; prin. Gerald I. Neiter, P.C., L.A., 1981—. Lectr. State Bar of Calif., 1968, 76, 79, 81; former referee State Bar Ct.; arbitrator Am. Arbitration Assn.; mediator L.A. Superior Ct. Mem. ABA, Los Angeles County Bar Assn. (arbitrator), Beverly Hills Bar Assn., State Bar Calif. Office: 1925 Century Park E Ste 2000 Los Angeles CA 90067-2701 Office Phone: 310-277-2236. E-mail: Neitlaw@aol.com.

**NEITHERCUT, DAVID J.,** real estate company officer; BA, St. Lawrence U.; MBA, Columbia U. With real estate dept. Continental Bank; with comml. mortgage banking div. Draper & Kramer, Inc.; sr. v.p. fin. Equity Group Investments; joined Equity Residential, 1993, CFO, 1995—2004, exec. v.p. corp. strategy, 2004—05, pres., 2005—, CEO, 2006—. Office: Equity Residential Properties Trust 2 N Riverside Plz Ste 450 Chicago IL 60606-2600*

**NEITHERCUT, MARK EDWARD,** foundation consultant; b. Flint, Mich., June 26, 1951; s. Edward John and Elizabeth Koegel Neithercut; m. Helen Patrick Lownie, Oct. 6, 1990. BA with high honors in history, U. Mich., 1974; MA, Mich. State U., 1977; PhD, U. B.C., Vancouver, Can., 1984. From instr. to asst. prof. U. Ala., Tuscaloosa, 1982-85; dir. Mich. Met. Info. Ctr. Wayne State U., Detroit, 1985-93, assoc. prof. rsch., 1993; program officer Kresge Found., Troy, Mich., 1993-95; v.p. program Cmty. Found. for Southeastern Mich., Detroit, 1995—2005; prin. Neithercut Advs. LLC, Detroit, 2005—. Adj. prof. urban planning Wayne State U., Detroit, 1990—95; chmn. Mich. Nonprofit Rsch. Program, Aspen Inst., Washington, 2003—; membership com. Coun. on Founds., Washington, 1999—; bd. dirs. Detroit Local Initiatives Support Corp., Cyber Mich., Anna Paulina Found., 2005—. Bd. dirs. Mich. Housing Trust Fund, Lansing, 1994-98, Detroit Inst. Arts, 1993-2005, Detroit Artists Market, 1993-95; pres. Founders Jr. Coun., Detroit Inst. Arts, 1993-94; chmn. Detroit Area Grantmakers, 2001-2003; mem. cmty. found. leadership team Coun. of Found., 2001-2004; mem. adv. com. John S. and James L. Knight Found., Detroit, 2002-06; mem. bd. govs. Cranbrook Schs., 2003—. Named NSFRE Vol. of Yr., Detroit Inst. Arts, 1994; grantee Kresge Found., 1998—2004; James B. Angell scholar, U. Mich., 1974, Internat. Schoolboy fellow, English Spkg. Union, 1969—70, doctoral fellow, U. B.C., 1978—80. Mem. Grosse Pointe Club, Flint Rainbow Club, Detroit Athletic Club, Phi Beta Kappa. Avocations: steelhead fly fishing, tennis. Office: 300 River Pl Ste 5000 Detroit MI 48207 Office Phone: 313-568-9000. Business E-Mail: mark@mneithercut.com.

**NEITZKE, ERIC KARL,** lawyer; b. Mobile, Ala., Dec. 10, 1955; s. Howard and Otti S. Neitzke; m. Kathryn Sloan; children: Kyle, Blake, Blaire. BA, U. Fla., 1979, JD, 1982. Bar: Fla. 1982, U.S. Dist. Ct. (mid. dist.) Fla. 1987. Asst. state atty. 7th Jud. Cir., State Atty., Daytona Beach, Fla., 1982; assoc. Dunn, Smith & Withers, Daytona Beach, 1982—88, Monaco, Smith, Hood and Perkins, Daytona Beach, 1988—2003; sole practice Daytona Beach, 2003—. Adj. faculty family law and criminal law Daytona C.C.; chmn. adv. com. Juvenile Detention Ctr. Contbr. articles to profl. jours. Mem. ATLA, Fla. Acad. Trial Lawyers, Volusia Bar Assn., Fla. Assn. Criminal Def. Lawyers, Phi Beta Kappa. Avocations: water sports, shooting, travel. Home: 19 Lost Creek Ln Ormond Beach FL 32174-4840 Office: Eric K Neitzke PA 412 N Wild Olive Ave Daytona Beach FL 32118 Office Phone: 386-672-9283. Personal E-Mail: knightmas@aol.com.

**NEJELSKI, PAUL ARTHUR,** retired judge, freelance writer; b. Chgo., Feb. 24, 1938; s. Leo Lawrence and Rena Grace (Martin) N.; m. Marilyn Ray Mills, Oct. 2, 1965; children: Nicole Rena, Stephen Downing. BA magna cum laude, Yale U., 1959, LLB, 1962; MPA, Am. U., 1969; cert. of theol. studies, Georgetown U., 1989. Bar: N.J. 1963. Law clk. appellate div. N.J. Superior Ct., 1962-63; sr. atty. U.S. Dist. Ct. N.J., 1964-65; atty., asst. chief immigration unit Dept. Justice, Washington, 1965-69; chief cts. desk Nat. Inst. Justice, Washington, 1969-70; asst. dir. Criminal Justice Ctr., Harvard U., 1970-71; dir. planning phase Inst. Jud. Adminstrn.-ABA Juvenile Justice Standards Project, N.Y.C., 1971-73; dir. Inst. Jud. Adminstrn., NYU, 1973-76; dep. ct. adminstrn. Conn. Jud. Dept., Hartford, 1976-77; dep. asst. atty. gen. Office for Improvements in Adminstrn. Justice, Dept. Justice, Washington, 1977-79; dir. Action Commn. to Reduce Ct. Costs and Delay, ABA, Washington, 1979-81; cir. exec. 3rd Cir., Phila., 1981-84; ct. adminstr. U.S. Tax Ct., 1984-89; immigration judge Dept. Justice, Arlington, Va., 1989-98. Mem. faculty law NYU, 1972-74, U. Conn., 1976-77, U. Md., 1981-82; cons. Author: (with C.O. Philip) Where Do Judges Come From?, 1976; editor: Social Research in Conflict With Law and Ethics, 1976; contbr. articles to profl. and popular jours. With U.S. Army, 1963—65, with USN, 1965—68. Home: 4628 Western Ave Bethesda MD 20816-2749

**NELIGAN, PETER C.,** plastic surgeon; b. July 20, 1952; married; 2 children. BA, U. Dublin, Trinity Coll., 1973, MBBCh, 1975. Cert. Ont., 1985. Clin. fellow, plastic surgery The Hosp. for Sick Children, Toronto, Canada, 1983—84, rsch. fellow, plastic surgery, 1984—85, assoc. staff surgeon, 1995—, rsch. project dir., rsch. inst., 1995—; clin. fellow, microvascular surgery Toronto Gen. Hosp., Canada, 1985; clin. burn fellow The Ross Tilley Burn Ctr., Wellesley Hosp., Toronto, Canada, 1986; dir. The Ross Tilley Burn Ctr., The Wellesley Hosp., Toronto, Canada, 1992—93; attending plastic surgeon Laurentian Hosp., Sudbury, Canada, 1987—91, Sudbury Gen. Hosp., Canada, 1987—91, Sudbury Meml. Hosp., Canada, 1987—91, The Wellesley Hosp., Toronto, Canada, 1991—93, assoc. staff, 1993—2000; asst. prof., dept. surgery U. Toronto, Canada, 1991—97, chair, divsn. plastic surgery, 1996—, assoc. prof., dept. surgery, 1997—2002, prof., dept. surgery, 2002—; attending plastic surgeon The Toronto Hosp., Canada, 1993—, dep. head, divsn. plastic surgery, 1994—96, head, divsn. plastic surgery, 1996—; assoc. staff surgeon Mt. Sinai Hosp., Toronto, Canada, 1993—; cons., dept. surg. oncology Princess Margaret Hosp., Toronto, Canada, 1995—, Wharton chair in reconstructive plastic surgery, 1999—. Mem. editl. bd. Can. Jour. of Plastic Surgery, 1996—, Annals of Plastic Surgery, 2002—, Jour. of Reconstructive Microsurgery, 2002—, Brit. Jour. of Plastic Surgery, 2003—. Fellow: Royal Coll. Physicians and Surgeons of Can., Am. Coll. Surgeons (mem., adv. com. on plastic and maxillofacial surgery 2000—03), Royal Coll. Surgeons Ireland; mem.: Plastic Surgery Ednl. Found. (nominating com. 2002—), joint outcomes com. mem. 2002—), Ontario Soc. Plastic Surgery, Am. Burn Assn., Can. Med. Protective Assn., Irish Assn. Plastic Surgeons, Internat. Soc. for Burn Injuries, Can. Med. Assn., World Soc. Reconstructive Microsurgery (adv. coun. mem. 2001—), Plastic Surgery Rsch. Coun. (Snyder Award 1998,

Hardesty Award 2000), Internat. Confederation for Plastic Reconstructive and Aesthetic Surgery, Internat. Microsurg. Soc., Ontario Med. Assn., N.Am. Skull Base Soc. (program com. mem. 2003—), Can. Soc. Plastic Surgeons, Am. Soc. Plastic and Reconstructive Surgeons (mktg. com. mem. 1999—2002, scientific program com. mem. 1999—, bd. dirs. 2001—, ethics com. mem. 2003—, Certificate of Merit, Investigator award 1984), Am. Soc. for Reconstructive Microsurgery (membership com. mem. 1999—, nominating com. mem. 1999—2001, program com. mem. 2001—), Am. Assn. Plastic Surgeons (comm. com. mem. 1999—), Inst. Med. Sci. Office: Toronto Gen Hosp Eaton North 7-229 200 Elizabeth St Toronto ON M5G 2C4 Canada

**NELIPOVICH, SANDRA GRASSI,** artist; b. Oak Park, Ill., Nov. 22, 1939; d. Alessandro and Lena Mary (Ascareggi) Grassi; m. John Nelipovich Jr., Aug. 19, 1973. BFA in Art Edn., U. Ill., Champaign/Urbana, 1961; postgrad., Northwestern U., Evanston, Ill., 1963, Gonzaga U., Florence, Italy, 1966, Art Inst. Chgo., 1968; diploma (hon.), Accademia Universale Alessandro Magno, Prato, Italy, 1983. Tchr. art Edgewood Jr. High Sch., Highland Park, Ill., 1961-62, Emerson Sch. Jr. High Sch., Oak Park, 1962-77; batik artist Calif., 1977—; illustrator Jolly Robin Publ. Co., Anaheim, Calif., 1988—2001, Assistance League of Anaheim, Calif., 2000—. Supr. student tchrs., Oak Park, 1970-75; adult edn. tchr. ESL, ceramics, Medinah, Ill., 1974; mem. curriculum action group on human dignity, EEO workshop demonstration, Oak Park, 1975-76; guest lectr. Muckenthaler Ctr., Fullerton, Calif., 1980, 92, Niguel Art Group, Dana Point, Calif., 1989, Carlsbad A.A., 1990, ARt League, Oceanside Art Group, 1992; 2d v.p. Anaheim Hills Women's Club, 1990-91, rec. sec. 1991-92; fabric designer for fashion designer Barbara Jax, 1987; illustrator Assistance League Anaheim (Calif.), 2000—; muralist Lincoln Sch. Ill., 2002-2003. One-Woman shows include Lawry's Calif. Ctr., L.A., 1981-83, Whittier (Calif.] Mus., 1985-86, Anaheim Cultural Ctr., 1986-88, Ill. Inst. Tech., Chgo., 1989, Muckenthaler Cultural Ctr., Fullerton, 1990; also gallery exhibits in Oak Brook, 1982, La Habra, Calif., 1983, Millard Sheets Gallery, Pomona, Calif., 1996; represented in permanent collections McDonald's Corp., Oak Brook, Glenkirk Sch., Deerfield, Ill., Emerson Sch., Oak Park, Calif.; poster designer Saratoga Fine Arts. Active Assistance League, Anaheim, Calif., 1992—, 2d v.p. ways and means com., 1995—96, 1997—98, 2d v.p. ways and means, 2004—05, 2005—, historian, 2002—03, Anaheim Arts Coun., 2002—, 2004—06; chairwoman Toscanini Guild Orange County Performing Arts Ctr., 2006—. Recipient numerous awards, purchase prizes, 1979—; featured in Calif. Art Rev., Artists of So. Calif., Vol. II, Nat. Artists' Network, 1992, Batik for Artists and Quilters, 2001. Mem. AAUW (hospitality chmn. 1984-85), Soc. Children's Book Writers and Illustrators, Assistance League Anaheim, Orange Art Assn. (jury chmn. 1980). Roman Catholic. Avocations: cooking, gardening, travel. Home and Office: 5922 E Calle Cedro Anaheim CA 92807-3207 Personal E-mail: sgneli@adelphia.net.

**NELKIN, BARRY DAVID,** oncology researcher and educator; b. New Orleans, Dec. 12, 1951; s. Joseph William and Bertha (Washastrom) N.; m. Deborah Ann Medetsky, June 4, 1975; children: Moshe, Aryeh, Yehuda, Esther, Yisroel, Rivka, Bina, Yaakov, Miriam, Shira. BS, Johns Hopkins U., 1972; PhD, George Washington U., 1979. Postdoctoral fellow Johns Hopkins U. Sch. Medicine, Balt., 1979—82, instr. oncology, 1982—84, asst. prof., 1984—90, assoc. prof., 1990—2004, prof., 2004—. Mem. ad hoc study sect. U.S. Nat. Cancer Inst., Bethesda, 1989-; grant reviewer Dutch Cancer Soc., 1990, VA, 1990. Author: (with others) Tumor Cell Heterogeneity, vol. 4, 1982, Progress in Nonhistone Protein Research, 1985; editor: Genetic Mechanisms in Multiple Endocrine Neoplasia Type 2, 1996; mem. editl. bd. oncology reps., 1997-98; contbr. articles to profl. jours. Nat. Cancer Inst. grantee, 1988-. Mem. Am. Assn. Cancer Rsch., Am. Soc. Microbiology. Achievements include the cloning of human calcitonin gene; demonstration of oncogene mediated differentiation of medullary thyroid carcinoma cells; isolation of ras oncogene responsive transcriptional element in human calcitonin gene; cloning of human BARX2 and RREB transcription factor genes. Home: 3831 Labyrinth Rd Baltimore MD 21215-1505 Office: Johns Hopkins Sch Medicine 1650 Orleans St Baltimore MD 21231 Office Phone: 410-955-8506. E-mail: bnelkin@jhmi.edu.

**NELL, HERMAN,** consumer products company executive; Dir. info. tech. Motorola, Inc.; joined Fiskars Brands Inc., Madison, Wis., 2002, sr. v.p., chief info. officer. Named one of Premier 100 IT Leaders, Computerworld, 2005. Office: Fiskars Brands Inc 2537 Daniels St Madison WI 53718 Office Phone: 608-259-1649.*

**NELLA, JOHN,** aerospace engineer; b. Bklyn., July 10, 1947; s. John and Elena Nella; m. Madeline C. Helper, July 9, 1972; children: John Christopher, Emily Lauren. BSEE, Polytechnic Inst. Bklyn., 1968, PhD in Electrophysics, 1972; MSEE, Calif. Inst. Tech., Pasadena, Calif., 1969. Lic. contractor, Calif. Laser physicist Hughes Aircraft, Culver City, Calif., 1977—96; project mgr. TRW, Redondo Beach, Calif., 1977—96, Northrop Grumman Space Tech., Redondo Beach, 1996—. Contbr. articles to profl. jours., chapters to books. Mem.: IEEE, Amateur Radio Relay League. Achievements include invention of hyperspectral missile seeker. Avocations: woodworking, amateur radio, genealogy. Home: 7916 W 79 St Playa Del Rey CA 90293 Office: Northrop Grumman Space Tech 1 Space Pk Redondo Beach CA 90278

**NELLETT, GAILE H.,** adult education educator; b. Ottawa, Ill., Nov. 5, 1941; d. Edwin Edward and Mabel Delia (Higgins) Hausaman; m. Henry H. Nellett. BSN, Governors State U., University Park, Ill., 1993; MS in Nursing Adminstrn., Loyola U., Chgo., 1995, PhD, 1998. RN, Ill. ELNEC (End of Life Nursing Edn. Consortium) certified, 2001. Staff nurse med.-surg. and psychiat. units Cmty. Hosp. Ottawa, 1974-75, asst. head nurse, 1975-77, head nurse psychiat. unit, 1977-79, head nurse psychiat. and chem. dependency units, 1979-84, nursing mgr. psychiat. and chem. dependency units, 1984-92, program mgr. psychiat. and chem. dependency units, 1987-92, part-time home health nurse, 1992-94; rsch. asst. Loyola U., 1993-96; asst. prof. U. St. Francis, 1997—2005, sr. chmn. Conah, 2000—04, assoc. prof., 2005—, co-project dir. RRF grant, 2003—. Bd. dirs. Ottawa area United Way, 1976-92, v.p., 1985, sec., 1984, 86. Nursing Adminstrn. fellow Edward Hines Jr. VA, Hines, Ill., 1994, tuition fellow Loyola U., 1993-96. Mem. ANA, Ill. Nurses Assn. (bd. dirs. dist. 4 1974-80), Nat. Gerontologic Nurses Assn., Peer Assistance Network for Nurses (regional support person dist. 2 1988-), Midwest Nursing Rsch. Soc., Sigma Theta Tau, Rogerian Scholars Roman Catholic. Avocations: archery, hunting, handcrafts, reading. Home: 2768 E 2551st Rd Marseilles IL 61341 Office Phone: 815-740-3668. E-mail: gnellett@stfrancis.edu.

**NELLIGAN, ANNETTE FRANCES,** social worker; b. Bangor, Maine, Sept. 20, 1954; d. Paul James and Laura Jenny (Sumner) N.; m. Peter Jamie Smith, June 22, 1985 (dec. June, 1997); children: Angelica Grace Nelligan-Smith, Acatia Faith Nelligan-Smith. AA, U. Maine, Bangor, 1974; BS, U. Maine, 1977, MEd, 1978, EdD, 1995. Lic. clin. profl. counselor; lic. marriage and family counselor; lic. social worker; cert. secondary sch. tchr., Maine, sch. counselor, Maine. Tchr. Bangor H.S., 1978, Etna (Maine)-Dixmont Sch., 1979-80; residential advisor Penobscot Job Corps, Bangor, 1980-84; group life worker St. Andre's Home, Bangor, 1984; caseworker, supr. Maine Dept. Human Svcs., Bangor, 1984-96; clin. coord. Old Town Regional Program, Bangor, 1996—. Mem. Homeless Edn. Adv. Bd., Bangor, 1992-95; instr. counselor edn. U. Maine, 1996—. Mem. ACA, Assn. for Specialists in Group Work. Roman Catholic. Avocations: doll collecting, camping, skiing, sailing. Home: 24 Albert Ln Glenburn ME 04401-5505 Office: Jefferson St Old Town ME 04468 E-mail: annettenelligan@unit.maine.edu.

**NELLIGAN, WILLIAM DAVID, III,** professional association executive; b. Halstead, Kans., Aug. 10, 1926; s. William D. and Katherine (Roberts) N.; m. Dorothy Meyer, Aug. 17, 1952; children: Richard Arthur, Mark. Student, U. Wichita, 1944-46; BS, U. Kans., 1949. Display advt. salesman Kansas City Star and Times, Mo., 1949-51; mgr. SW Kans. Extension Ctr. U. Kans., Garden City, 1951-55, exec. dir. dept. postgrad. med. edn. Sch. Medicine Kansas City, Kans., 1955-64; asst. to pres. Med. Coll. Ga., Augusta, 1964-65; exec. v.p. Am. Coll. Cardiology, Bethesda, Md., 1965-92; v.p. Marion Merrell

DOW, Inc., Kansas City, Mo., 1992-94; exec. dir. Am. Soc. Nuc. Cardiology Bethesda, 1994-2001, Cert. Bd. Nuclear Cardiology, Damascus, Md., 1996—2004, Soc. Cardiovasc. CT, Damascus, Md., 2005—06, Soc. Atherosclerosis Imaging and Prevention, Damascus, Md., 2005—. Mem. Nat. Commn. Diabetes, 1975-76, adv. council Nat. Diabetes and Digestive and Kidney Diseases, 1987-88; bd. dir. Arthur E. Hertzler Research Found., Halstead, Kans., 1961—. Recipient Man with a Heart award N.Y. Cardiol. Soc., 1970, Presdl. citation Am. Coll. Cardiology, 1975, Disting. Service award Am. Coll. Cardiology, 1986, CLC Hall of Leaders award, 1986. Fellow Am. Coll. Cardiology; mem. AMA (citation of layman for disting. svc. 1993), Profl. Conv. Mgmt. Assn. (pres. 1974-75, Disting. Svc. award 1990), Am. Med. Writers Assn. (dir., exec. com., treas. 1970-78, Harold Swanberg Disting. Svc. award), Am. Soc. Assn. Execs. (cert., dir. 1975-78, sec.-treas. 1987-88, Key award 1984), Am. Assn. Med. Execs. (pres. 1986-87), Brit. Cardiac Soc. (hon.), Alliance for Continuing Med. Edn. (Pres.'s award 1994), Masons. Office: 9929 C Main St Damascus MD 20872-2068

**NELLY, (CORNELL HAYNES JR.),** rap artist; b. Austin, Tex., Nov. 2, 1974; s. Cornell Haynes and Rhonda Mack; children: Chanel, Cornell III. Formed St. Lunatics, 1993; co-owner, co-founder, spokesperson Vokal Clothing Co., St. Louis, 1997—; co-owner, founder Apple Bottoms, 2003—; co-owner Billy Ballew Motersports, NASCAR racing team, 2003—; CEO Derrty Entertainment, 2003—; co-owner Charlotte Bobcats, 2004—. Performer: (albums) Country Grammar, 2000 (Album of Yr., Source Hip-Hop Music awards, 2001), (with St. Lunatics) Free City, 2001, Nellyville, 2002 (Grammy award for best make rap solo performance, 2002, Grammy award best rap/sung collaboration for "Dilemma," featuring Kelly Rowland, 2002), Da Derrty Versions: The Reinvention, 2003, Iz U, 2004, Sweat, 2004, Suit, 2004, (singles) E.I., 2001, Ride With Me, 2001, (songs) Shake Ya Tailfeather (with P. Diddy and Murphy Lee), Bad Boys II soundtrack, 2003 (Grammy award best rap performance by a duo or group, 2003); actor: (films) Snipes, 2001, The Longest Yard, 2005. Founder 4sho4kids. Recipient New Artist of Yr., Source Hip-Hop Music awards, 2001, Best New Artist, BET awards, 2001, Best R&B/Soul or Rap New Artist, Soul Train Music Awards, 2001, Favorite Artist-Rap/Hip-Hop, Am. Music Awards, 2002, Source Found. Image Award, Source Hip-Hop Music Awards, 2003, Artist of Yr., 2003, Sammy Davis Jr. Entertainer of Yr., Soul Train Music Awards. Office: Uptown/Universal Records 1755 Broadway New York NY 10019 also: The 4Sho4Kids Found Inc 9648 Olive Blvd Ste 230 Saint Louis MO 63132 also: Vokal Clothing 1835 Belt Way Dr Saint Louis MO 63114-5815 Office Phone: 314-531-3346.

**NELMS, SHARON DEE,** music educator; d. Winford Elbert and Mary Elizabeth Hendricks; m. Steven Lawayne Nelms, Nov. 27, 1982; 1 child, Bethany. AA, Tyler Jr. Coll., Tex., 1979—81; MusB, Tarleton State U., Stephenville, Tex., 1981—83; MusM in Edn., San Angelo State U., Tex., 1985—87. Choral dir., k-12 Westbrook Ind. Sch. Dist., Tex., 1984—85; choral dir. Lincoln Mid. Sch., 1985—90, Moore Mid. Sch., 1990—98, Thompson Interm Sch., 1998—2000, Johnson Mid. Sch., 2000—05, Wylie HS, 2005—. Adjudicator Tex. Music Adjudicator Assn., 1994—; guest clinician Region 4, 8th grade Treble Choir, 2004. Choreographer The Life of Christ, Rose Heights Ch. of God, 1991—97. Worship team mem. Grace Cmty. Ch., Clear Lake, 1999—2000, McKinney Fellowship Bible Ch., 2000—05. Recipient Tchr. of Month, Johnson Mid. Sch., Tyler, 1994. Mem.: Tex. Adjudicator's Assn., Tex. Choral Dir.'s Assn., Tex. Music Educator's Assn. Mem. Christian Ch. Avocations: cooking, composing.

**NELON, ROBERT DALE,** lawyer; b. Shawnee, Okla., Aug. 8, 1946; s. Cecil Eugene and Neata Madelyn (Fox) N.; m. Freddie Anne Tipton, Aug. 2, 1975; children: Lindsay Anne, Gregory Tipton. BA, Northwestern U., 1968; JD, U. Okla., 1971. Bar: Okla. 1971, U.S. Dist. Ct. (we., no. and ea. dists) Okla. 1971, U.S. Ct. Appeals (10th cir.) 1971, (8th cir.) 1992, (2d cir.) 1993, U.S. Ct. Appeals for the Armed Forces 1972, U.S. Supreme Ct. 1989. Law clk. Okla. Atty. Gen., Oklahoma City, 1966-70; mem. Andrews, Davis, Legg, Bixler, Milsten & Price, Oklahoma City, 1971-95, Hall Estill Hardwick Gable Golden & Nelson, Oklahoma City, 1995—. Served to capt. USMCR, 1972-74. Mem. ABA, Okla. Bar Assn., Am. Judicature Soc. Democrat. Methodist. Office: Hall Estill Hardwick Gable Golden & Nelson Chase Tower Suite 2900 100 N Broadway Ave Oklahoma City OK 73102-8865 Office Phone: 405-553-2828. Business E-Mail: bnelon@hallestill.com.

**NELP, WIL B.,** physician, medical educator; s. Wil B. and Olive E. (Edwards) Nelp; m. Barbara M. Monroe; children: Todd, Nancy, Paige, Blaine. BA cum laude, Franklin Coll.of Ind.; 1951; MD, Johns Hopkins U., 1955; DSc (hon.), Franklin Coll., Ind., 1967. Lic. MD, 1955, Wash., 1962, cert. Am. Bd. Nuc. Medicine, 1972, Am. Bd. Internal Medicine. Intern asst. resident Johns Hopkins Hosp., Osler Med. Svc., Md., 1955—60; rsch. fellow Johns Hopkins Hosp., Dept. Medicine and Radiology, Divsn. Nuc. Med., Md., 1960—62; instr. Johns Hopkins U., Medicine and Radiology Dept., Md., 1961—62; asst. prof., assoc. prof., and prof. U. Wash., Dept. Medicine and Radiology, 1962—95; head dept. U. Wash., Nuc. Medicine, 1962—95; co-dir. U. Hosp., Thyroid Clin., Wash., 1978—83; attending physician Endocrine Thyroid Clin., Wash., 1983—; prof. emeritus U. Wash., Dept. Medicine and Radiology, 1996; assoc. staff Veterans Adminstrn. Hosp., Wash., Harborview Med., Seattle; cons. in nuc. medicine Group Health Coop. of Puget Sound, Providence Hosp., Northwest Hosp., Children's Orthopedic Hosp., Seattle, Madigan Army Hosp., Tacoma. Cons. Nat. Heart and Lung Inst., 1968—74; cons. to commr. FDA Radiopharmaceuticals, 1970—74; usp adv. panel, 1970—80; adv. to Romanian govt. UN Nuc. Medicine, IAEA, 1971—72; diagnostic rsch. adv. group Nat. Cancer Inst., 1977—81; usp adv. panel Radiopharmaceuticals, 1982—86; sec. coun. for nuc. medicine AMA, 1982—88; mem. adv. com. Elecro-magnetic Isotope Enrichment Facility, Oak Ridge Nat. Lab., Oak Ridge, 1986. Nuc. Regulatory Commn., Med. Uses of Isotopes, 1993—99. Dir. U. Wash. residency Nuc. Medicine Tng. Program, 1964—96; chrmn., organizer U. Wash. Med. Ethics, Human Use, Review Sys. in Exptl. Rsch., 1967—71; mem. Med. Staff Exec. Com., 1973—80; com. mem. Los Alamos Sci. Lab., N.Mex., 1976—80; coun. mem. AMA, Nuc. Med. Sect., 1976—79; affiliate mem. Assn. of Governing Bd. of U. and Coll., 1996—. Capt., acting chief med. svc. Offutt AFB USAF, 1957—59, Nebr. Named Outstanding Young Man of the Award, 1964; recipient NIH rsch. fellow, 1960—62, Disting. Scientist Award, Soc. of Nuc. Medicine, Western Region, 1980, Creative Devel. Award, NASA, 1980, Korean Soc. of Nuc. Medicine Honoree, 1990. Fellow: ACP, Am. Coll. Nuc. Physicians; mem.: Seattle Acad. Internal Med., Soc. Nuc. Med. (v.p. 1970—71, nat. pres. 1973—74), Am. Bd. of Nuc. Medicine (life; dir. 1984, treas. 1986, vice chmn. 1987), Johns Hopkins Med. Surg. Assn.

**NELSEN, HART MICHAEL,** sociologist, educator; b. Pipestone, Minn., 1938; s. Noah I. and Nova Nelsen; m. Anne Kusener, June 13, 1964; 1 dau., Jennifer. BA, U. No. Iowa, 1959, MA, 1963; M.Div., Princeton Theol. Sem., 1963; PhD (NSF faculty fellow), Vanderbilt U., 1972. Asst. prof. sociology Western Ky. U., Bowling Green, 1965-70, assoc. prof., 1970-73, Catholic U. Am., 1973-74, 1974-81, chmn. dept. sociology, 1974-77, mem. Boys Town Ctr. for Study Youth Devel., 1974-81; prof. sociology La. State U., Baton Rouge, 1981-84, chmn. dept. sociology, head dept. rural sociology, 1981-84, coordinator rural sociology research, 1981-84; dean Coll. Liberal Arts Pa. State U., 1984-90, prof. sociology, 1984—2004, prof. emeritus, 2004—. Author: (with Anne K. Nelsen) Black Church in the Sixties, 1975; co-author: The Religion of Children, 1977, Religion and American Youth, 1976; editor: (with others) The Black Church in America, 1971; adv. editor: Sociol. Quar, 1976-82; assoc. editor: Sociol. Analysis, 1977-80, Rev. Religious Research, 1977-80, 84—, editor, 1980-84; mem. editorial bd.: Social Forces, 1983-86. Co-rec. assoc. Capitol Hill Restoration Soc., 1979-80, v.p., 1980-81; mem. exec. bd. Lafitte Hills Assn., 1983-84; pres. Midtown Sq. Condo. Assn., 1996-99, pres., 1999-2001. Presbyterian Ch. grantee, 1966-69; NIMH co-grantee, 1969-72; Russell Sage Found. co-grantee, 1972-73; La. Gov.'s Commn. on Alcoholism and Drug Abuse grantee, 1982 Mem. Assn. Sociology Religion (exec. coun. 1974-76, 78-82, v.p. 1978-79, pres. 1980-81), Religious Rsch. Assn. (dir. 1977-80, pres.-elect 1985-86, pres. 1987-88), Soc. Sci. Study Religion (coun. 1981-83, exec. sec. 1984-87), Am.

Sociol. Assn., So. Sociol. Soc. (chmn. membership com. 1983-85), AAAS (rep. 1984-2000). Mem. United Ch. Of Christ. Home: Residence 1121 Market Sq Residences 801 Pennsylvania Ave NW Washington DC 20004-2615 E-mail: hmnelsen@mindspring.com.

**NELSEN, WILLIAM CAMERON,** educational consultant; b. Omaha, Oct. 18, 1941; s. William Peter and Ellen Lucella (Cameron) N.; m. Margaret Leone Rossow, May 30, 1981; children by previous marriage: William Norris, Shawna Lynn; 1 adopted dau., Sarah Ruth. BA, Midland Luth. Coll., Fremont, Nebr., 1963; MA, Columbia U., 1966; PhD, U. Pa., 1971; Fulbright scholar, U. Erlangen, W. Ger., 1964; D (hon.), Midland Luth. Coll., 1995. Program exec. Danforth Found., St. Louis, 1970-73; asst. dean, then v.p., dean coll. St. Olaf Coll., Northfield, Minn., 1973-80; dir. Project on Faculty Devel. Assn. of Am. Colls., 1979; pres. Augustana Coll., Sioux Falls, SD, 1980-86, Scholarship Am., St. Peter, Minn., 1986—2004; v.p. develop. NC Wesleyan Coll., Rocky Mount, NC, 2004—. Bd. dirs. 1st Nat. Bank and Bancommunity Svc. Corp., St. Peter, Minn., Learning Cmtys. Coalition, USA Funds. Author: Effective Approaches to Faculty Development, 1980, Renewal of the Teacher Scholar, 1981, also articles. Bd. dirs. S.D. Symphony, 1980-85, Sioux Falls YMCA, 1980-86, Luth. Ednl. Conf. N.Am., 1982-86, Sioux Falls United Way, 1983-86; nat. bd. advisors Coun. Aid to Edn.; mem. nat. coun. Connect Am., Points of Light Found., 1998-2003; chmn. bd. U.S. Dream Acad., 1999-2004; mem. exec. bd. Nat. Assembly, 2001-2004; bd. dirs. Nat. Scholarship Providers Assn., 1999-2004, chmn. bd., 2003-04; dir. Learning Comtys. Coalition; mem. Registry of Coll. and Univ. Pres.; interim v.p. devel. N.C. Wesleyan Coll.; bd trustees Midland Luth. Coll. Recipient McKee award Nat. Assn. Ptnrs. in Edn., 1999, award Freedoms Found., 2003; Danforth Grad. fellow, 1963, Woodrow Wilson fellow, 1963. Mem. Assn. Am. Colls. (bd. dirs. 1984-86), Shoreland Country Club (pres. 1996-99), Consortium for Advancement of Pvt. Higher Edn., Coun. of Ind. Colls., Nat. Dollars for Scholars, Rotary Club. Republican. Lutheran. Office: NC Wesleyan Coll 3400 N Wesleyan Blvd Rocky Mount NC 27804-8630

**NELSON, ALICE CARLSTEDT,** retired nursing educator; b. Strandquist, Minn., May 25, 1921; d. Peter Gustaf and Florence Olivia (Berg) Carlstedt; m. Armour Halstead Nelson June 5, 1954 (dec. Dec. 1993). RN, Bethesda Hosp., St. Paul, 1944; BS, Augustana Coll., 1948; MA, U. Chgo., 1954. RN, Minn., Ill., N.D., Iowa, Calif.; cert. lactation educator, cert. lifetime cmty. coll. tchr. Ob nurse Moline Luth. Hosp., Ill., 1943—44; asst. night supr. Bethesda Hosp., St. Paul, 1944—45; with Army Nurse Corps, 1945—46; ob nurse Miller Hosp., St. Paul, 1947; nurse intermediate grade Wadsworth VA Hosp., L.A., 1947—48; head nurse Crippled Children's Sch., Jamestown, ND, 1948—50; head nurse Sch. Handicapped Children U. Iowa, Iowa City, 1950—51; clin. instr. Chgo. Lying-In Hosp., 1951—54, St. Luke's Hosp., Fargo, ND, 1954—60; tchr., supr. lab. pre-sch. N.D. State U., Fargo, 1962—64; coll. health svc. Calif. Luth. U., Thousand Oaks, 1968—74, faculty dept. nursing, 1982—85; pvt. duty nurse Thousand Oaks, 1976—81; ret., 1990. State sec. League for Nursing, N.D., 1956-64; team mem. preparation Nat. Achievement Test in Nursing of Children, N.Y., 1959 Author: Post-War Europe Through The Eyes of Youth, 2002; editor: The Conquest of Chicago, 2004; contbr. articles to profl. jours. Various offices including Ch. Coun. Holy Trinity Luth. Ch., Thousand Oaks, 1964-90; founding bd. dirs. Honey Tree Pre-Sch., Thousand Oaks, 1972; mem. task force on aging S.W. Pacific Luth. Synod Office, L.A., 1979; parent-aide, hotline, etc. Child Abuse & Neglect, Ventura County, Calif., 1979-82; bd. dirs. La Serena Retirement Ctr., Thousand Oaks, 1985-88; mem. ch. choir Salemsborg Luth. Ch., Smolan, Kans., 1990-2000, mem. ch. coun., 1996-2000, tchr. adult classes, 1996-99 Recipient award writing contests Am. Jour. Nursing, 1969, Calif. Nurse, 1987, Outstanding Vol. award Ventura County Child Abuse & Neglect, 1982. Mem. Bethany Bibliophiles Book Club, Writer's Cramp Group Democrat. Avocations: travel, reading, writing.

**NELSON, ALLEN F.,** proxy solicitation company executive; b. Portland, Oreg., Oct. 17, 1943; s. Roy August and Mildred Mary (Jensen) N.; m. Johanna Molenaar, Dec. 8, 1973. BS, U. Iowa, 1965, MA, 1968. V.p. Shareholder Comm. Corp., N.Y.C., 1970-72; v.p. Trafalgar Capital Corp., N.Y.C., 1973; pres. Nelson, Lasky & Co., Inc., N.Y.C., 1974-76; account exec. Corp. Comm., Inc., Seattle, 1976-77; pres. Allen Nelson & Co. Inc., Seattle, 1977—. Mem. Fin. Analysts Fedn., Nat. Investor Rels. Inst., Nat. Security Traders Assn., Practicing Law Inst. (U.S. Presdl. rank rev. bd.), Pub. Rels. Soc. Am., Am. Soc. Corp. Secs., Can. Corp. Secs., Rainier Club, Montana Club, Vancouver Club. Home: 4400 Beach Dr SW Seattle WA 98116-3937 Office: Allen Nelson & Co Inc PO Box 16157 Seattle WA 98116-0157 Office Phone: 206-938-5783. E-mail: anelson@worldproxy.com.

**NELSON, ALLYSON LYN,** lawyer; b. Honolulu, June 16, 1976; d. Craig E. and Pamela K. Nelson. BA in Polit. Sci. and Russian, U. Ala., 1998; JD, U. Miss. Sch. Law, 2002. Bar: U.S. Appeals (5th cir.) La. 2002, U.S. Dist. Ct. (no. dist.) Miss. 2002, U.S. Dist. Ct. (so. dist.) Miss. 2002, Miss. Supreme Ct. 2002. Legislative intern U.S. Senator Richard Shelby, Washington, 1996—96; law clk. U.S. Dept. of Justice, Hon. Charles E. Pazar, Memphis, 2001—01; atty. and com. counsel Miss. Ho. of Representatives, Jackson, Miss., 2002—03; assoc. atty. Rushing & Guice, PLLC, Biloxi, Miss., 2003—04; asst. dist. atty. Office of the Hinds County Dist. Atty., Jackson, 2004—. Mem. Sexual Assault Response Team, Jackson, Miss., 2004—, Hinds County Multi-Disciplinary Child Abuse Rev. Team, Jackson, Miss., 2004—. Recipient Outstanding Student award, Oil and Gas Law, 2001, Energy Law, 2001; scholar Heidelberg & Woodliff Excellence award, 2001, Study in Prague, Czech Republic scholar, The Fund for Am. Studies, 1997, Scholarship for study in Russia, U.S. Dept. of State, 1999, Jeffery P. Reynolds, P.A. Environ. Law scholar, 2001, IOLTA scholar, Miss. Bar Found., 2000; Strong scholarship for Outstanding Freshman in Russian, 1995. Mem.: ABA, Jour. of Nat. Security Law, Miss. Bar Assn., Hinds County Bar Assn., Miss. Prosecutors Assns., Nat. Dist. Attorneys Assn., Dobro Slovo, Phi Delta Phi, Gamma Beta Phi. Avocations: travel, politics, history, government, foreign languages. Office Phone: 601-968-6568. Personal E-mail: allyson_76@hotmail.com. E-mail: allysonnelson@co.hinds.ms.us.

**NELSON, ANNE,** playwright, former reporter; married; 2 children. BA, Yale U. War corr. LA Times, NY Times, El Salvador, 1980—83, Guatemala, 1980—83; prof. journalism Columbia U., NYC, dir. Internat. Programs, Grad. Sch. Journalism, adj. assoc. prof. Sch. Internat. and Pub. Affairs. Author: (screenplays) The Guys, 2002, (plays) The Anglo-American Alliance, 2005, Savages, 2006. Guggenheim fellow, 2005—06, New Harmony Dramatists fellow. Mailing: c/o Internat Creative Mgmt 40 West 57th St New York NY 10019 Office: Sch Internat and Public Affairs Internat Affairs Bldg 13th Floor 420 West 118th St Mailcode 3323 New York NY 10027 Office Phone: 212-854-3239. E-mail: an115@columbia.edu.*

**NELSON, ARLEEN BRUCE,** social worker; b. Loma Linda, Calif., Oct. 25, 1926; d. Delbert Francis and Sarah Enns Bruce; m. A. Gordon Nelson, Oct. 29, 1948 (div. Sept. 1976); children: Gregory Bruce, Mark Andrew, Heidi, Scott Bradford. BA, UCLA, 1948; MSW, U. Wash., 1975. Cert. ACSW 1979, BCSW 1987, MSW Wash., 1989, LCSW Wash., 2001. Case worker L.A. County DPSS, L.A., 1949—50, 1958—61, child protective Svc. Supr., 1966—69; dir. Manson Migrant Daycare Ctr., Manson, Wash., 1970—72; I and A coord. Sr. Svc., Seattle, 1975—78; co-dir., psychotherapist Soc. Workers N. W., Seattle, 1979—95; coord., HIV-AIDS Seattle Counseling Svc. for Sexual Minorities, 1986—94, psychotherapist, supr., 1994—2000, intern supr., 1993—96; aux. faculty U. Wash., 1995—2001; clin. cons. Seattle Counseling Svcs., 2000—; intern supr. Seattle Counseling Svc. for Sexual Minorities, 2002—. Edn. com. Wash. Soc. of Clin. Social Work, Seattle, 1986. Co-founder Nat. Parents and Friends of Gays and Lesbians; dir. PNU / Mountain Region Nat. PFLAG, multi states, 1981—83, v.p., 1983—89; gay and lesbian advocate multiple T.V. appearances, 1978—85; task force for gays and lesbians Ch. Coun. of Greater Seattle, 1977—80; bd. mem. The Dorian Group, Seattle, 1980; co-founder Seattle Chap. Parents and Friends of Lesbians and Gays, Seattle, 1975; pres. Seattle Chap. PFLAG, 1993—94; Bd. Ch. and soc. PNW Conf. United Meth. Ch., Wash., 1970—82, commn. of race and religion Wash., 1982—88. Recipient The Dorian Award, Dorian Group,

1982, 1998 Cmty. Leadership Award, Greater Seattle Bus. Assn., 1999, Founders Award, Seattle PFLAG, 1989, Nat. PFLAG, 1991, Award for Dedication and Svc., Seattle Gay Clinic, 1994, Award of Merit for long Svc. to the Trans - gendered Cmty., The Trans-gendered Group, 2000. Mem.: Nat Assn. of Soc. Workers, Wash. Chap. NASW. Democrat. Methodist. Avocations: travel, reading. Office: Seattle Counseling Svc 1216 Pine St Seattle WA 98101 Office Phone: 206-323-1768.

**NELSON, ARTHUR HUNT,** real estate company executive; b. Kansas City, Mo., May 21, 1923; s. Carl Ferdinand and Hearty (Brown) N.; m. Eleanor Thomas, Dec. 27, 1954; children: Carl F. Frances, Pamela. AB, U. Kans., 1943; JD, Harvard U., 1949. Bar: Mass. 1949. Staff radiation lab. MIT, 1943-44; sr. engr., cons. Raytheon Mfg. Co., Boston, 1948-52; pvt. practice Boston, 1949; v.p., treas., dir. Gen. Electronic Labs., Inc., Cambridge, Mass., 1951-64, chmn. bd., 1959-63; treas., dir. Sci. Electronics, Inc., Cambridge, 1955-64, assocs. for Internat. Rsch., Inc., Cambridge, 1954—, pres., 1968—; treas., dir. Victor Realty Devel., Inc., Cambridge, 1959-76, pres., 1972-76, gen. ptnr., 1976—; Prospect Hill Exec. Office Park, Waltham, Mass., 1977—; chmn. Nelson Cos., 1990—, Cambridge Devel. Lab., Cambridge, 1994—2001. Bd. dirs. Internat. Data Group, Inc., Sterling Bank. Pres., trustee Tech. Edn. Rsch. Ctrs., Inc., 1965—; trustee Winsor Sch., Boston, 1978-88, treas., 1978-82; bd. dirs. Charles River Mus. Industry, Waltham, 1986—, pres. 1994—, pres., dir. 128 Bus. Coun. Inc., 1987—, Hist. Waltham Inc., 1996—, Am. Computer Fedn. Inc., 1996—, Charles River Pub. Internet Ctr. Inc., 1996—. Ensign USNR, 1944-46. Recipient Ernst & Young New Eng. Master Entrepreneur of Yr. award, 1999. Mem. ABA, Mass. Bar Assn., Boston Bar Assn., Boston Computer Soc. (bd. dirs. 1985-97, chmn 1994-97), Greater Boston C. of C., Harvard Club Boston, Beta Theta Pi, Phi Beta Kappa, Sigma Xi. Home: 75 Robin Rd Weston MA 02493-2436 Office: 75 3rd Ave Waltham MA 02451-7528

**NELSON, AUDREY MAY,** physician; b. Austin, Minn., Apr. 1, 1940; d. Glen Stanley and Clara May (Torgerson) N BA, U. Minn., 1962, BS, 1963, MD, 1965. Diplomate in internal medicine and rheumatology Am. Bd. Internal Medicine. Assoc. cons. Mayo Clinic, Rochester, Minn., 1972, cons. in internal medicine and rheumatology, 1972—2002; instr. medicine Mayo Med. Sch., Rochester 1973—76, from asst. prof. to assoc. prof. medicine, 1976—2000, prof., 2000—02, prof. emeritus, 2002—, chair pediat. rheumatology, 1993—2001; cons. staff Shriners Hosp. for Children, Mpls. 1985—2006. Bd. govs. Mayo Clinic, 1982-89; trustee Mayo Found., 1982-93, v.p., 1989-92 Trustee Christ United Meth. Ch., Rochester, 1995—2002, vice chair, 1999—2001, chair, 2001—02. Recipient Woman of Achievement award YWCA, Alumni Recognition award U. Minn. Alumni Med. Soc., 2002; named Woman Physician of Yr., Alpha Epsilon Iota Fellow: ACP, Am. Coll. Pediat., Am. Coll. Rheumatology (bd. dirs. 1995—99, Disting. Svc. award 2002); mem.: AMA (del. 1984—2002), Am. Group Practice Assn. (trustee 1991—96, v.p. 1995, pres.-elect 1996), Am. Med. Group Assn. (chair elect 1996—97, bd. dirs. 1996—99, chair bd. dirs. 1997—98), Minn. Med. Assn. (trustee 1985—2002, Disting. Svc. award 1999), Phi Beta Kappa, Alpha Omega Alpha. Avocation: sailing. Home (Summer): 2105 Valkyrie Dr NW Rochester MN 55901-8117 Office: Mayo Clinic 200 1st St SW Rochester MN 55905-0002

**NELSON, BARBARA KASZTAN,** marketing professional; d. Eugeniusz and Danuta Kasztan; m. Kelley Nelson, June 26, 2004. B in Mktg., Seton Hall U., 1998, MBA magna cum laude, 2004. Mktg. rsch. assoc. Schering Plough Pharms., Kenilworth, NJ, 1997—99, analyst, mktg. rsch., 1999—2001; sr. analyst, mktg. rsch. Novartis Pharms., East Hanover, NJ, 2001—03, mgr., mktg. rsch., 2003—05; assoc. dir. mktg. rsch., 2005—. Participant Habitat For Humanity, NJ, 2003—05. Mem.: Healthcare Businesswomens Assn., Am. Mktg. Assn., Beta Gamma Sigma, Panhellenic Coun. (pres. 1996—97), Alpha Sigma Tau. Office: Novartis Pharms One Health Pl East Hanover NJ 07936 E-mail: barbara.nelson@novartis.com.

**NELSON, BEN (EARL BENJAMIN NELSON),** senator, former governor, lawyer; b. McCook, Nebr., May 17, 1941; s. Benjamin Earl and Birdella Ruby (Henderson) N.; m. Diane C. Gleason, Feb. 22, 1980; children from a previous marriage: Sarah Jane, Patrick James; stepchildren: Kevin Michael Gleason, Christine Marie Gleason. BA in Philosophy, U. Nebr., 1963, MA in Philosophy, 1966, JD, 1970; LLD (hon.), Creighton U., 1992, Peru State Coll., 1993. Bar: Nebr. 1970. Instr. dept. philosophy U. Nebr., Lincoln, 1963-65; supr. Dept. Ins. State of Nebr., Lincoln, 1965-72; dir. ins., 1975-76; asst. gen. counsel, gen. counsel, sec., v.p. The Ctrl. Nat. Ins. Group Omaha, 1972-75, exec. v.p., 1976-77, pres., 1978-81, CEO, 1980-81; of counsel Kennedy, Holland, DeLacy & Svoboda, Omaha, 1985-90, Lumson, Dugan and Murray, Omaha, 1999—2001; gov. State of Nebr., Lincoln, 1991—99; US Senator from Nebr., 2000—. Com. rules and adminstrn. US Senate, com. commerce, sci. and transp., com. armed services, com. agr., nutrition and forestry. Co-chmn. Carter/Mondale re-election campaign, Nebr., 1980; chair Nat. Edn. Goals Panel, 1992-94; co-founder Gov.'s Ethanol Coalition, chair, 1991, 94; pres. Coun. of State Govs., 1994; bd. trustee Wesley House Found., Omaha, 1970-76. Recipient Friends of Nebr. Broadcasters award Nebr. Broadcasters Assn., 1993, Disting. Eagle award Nat. Eagle Scout Assn., 1994; named Amb. Plenipotentiary, 1993. Mem. ABA, Nat. Assn. Independent Insurers, Nat. Assn. Ins. Commrs. (exec. v.p. 1982-85), Nebr. Bar Assn., Consumer Credit Ins. Assn., Midwestern Govs. Assn. (chair 1994), Western Govs. Assn. (vice chair 1994, chair 1995), Happy Hollow Club, Omaha Club, Hillcrest Country Club. Democrat. Methodist. Avocations: reading, hunting, fishing. Office: US Senate 720 Hart Office Bldg Washington DC 20510 also: District Office Ste 205 7602n Pacific St Omaha NE 68114 Office Phone: 202-224-6551, 402-391-3411. Office Fax: 202-224-0012, 402-391-4725.*

**NELSON, BETTE STURR,** secondary school educator; b. Bethesda, Md., Nov. 19, 1947; d. Henry Dixon and Mildred Rogers Sturr; children: Sarah Elizabeth Turner, Elissa Marie Noble. BA in History and English, U. Calif., Santa Barbara, 1969; MA in Counseling, Ohio State U., Columbus, 1973. Cert. tchr. Edn. Dept., Calif., 1970. Tchr., counselor Kalamazoo Juvenile Home, 1972—75; tchr. Thomas Jefferson H.S., Fairfax, Va., 1976—84; reading tchr. Bloomfield Schs., NJ 1987—88; tchr. Mt. Diablo Unified Schs., Concord, Calif., 1989—. Gate chmn. Mt. Diablo Schs., 2004—. Mem. vestry Episc. Ch., Martinez, Calif., 2005—. Recipient Nat. Honor Roll Outstanding Educator award, Nat. Coun. Tchrs. English, 2006. Mem.: NEA (assoc.), East Bay Jr. League, Calif. Tchrs. Assn. (corr.), NCTE (life; v.p. 1980—81, named Tchr. of Yr. 1984), Kappa Delta Pi (life). Democrat. Episc. Avocations: travel, swimming, acting, theater. Office: Sequoia Middle School 265 Boyd Road Pleasant Hill CA 94523 Office Phone: 925-934-8174. Office Fax: 925-946-9063. Personal E-mail: bettnel@aol.com. Business E-Mail: nelsonb@mdusd.k-12.ca.us.

**NELSON, BILL (CLARENCE WILLIAM NELSON),** senator, former state treasurer; b. Miami, Fla., Sept. 29, 1942; s. C.W. and Nannie (Merle) N.; m. Grace H. Cavert, Feb. 19, 1972; children: C. William, Nan Ellen. BA, Yale U., 1965; JD, U. Va., 1968. Bar: Fla. 1968. Atty. Nelson, Normile and Dettmer, Melbourne, Fla., 1970-79, Maguire, Vorrhis and Wells, Pa., 1991—94; mem. Fla. Ho. of Reps. 1972-78, US Congress, 1979-91; payload specialist 1 Space Shuttle Columbia seventh orbital mission, 1986; treas. State of Fla., Tallahassee, 1991—2000; US Senator from Fla., 2001—; vice chmn. Dem. Senatorial Campaign com., 2000—. Mem. com. armed services US Senate, com. budget, com. commerce, sci., transp., com. fgn. relations, spl. com. aging Author: Mission: An American Congressman's Voyage to Space, 1988. Bd. dirs. Am. Astronautical Soc.; mem. Fla. Space Bus. Roundtable. Served to capt. USAR, 1965—75, reserved with U.S. Army, 1968—70. Recipient Public Svc. award, Nat. Crystallography Assn., 1988, Debus award, Nat. Space Club, Fla. Com., 1993, President's award, Fla. State Conf. NAACP, 2001. Mem.: Fla. Bar Assn., Brevard County Bar Assn., Assn. Space Explorers. Democrat. Episcopalian. Office: US Senate 716 Hart Sen Office Bldg Rm 716 Washington DC 20510 Address: Landmark Ctr Two Ste 410 225 E Robinson St Orlando FL 32801 Office Phone: 202-224-5274, 407-872-7161. Office Fax: 202-228-2183, 407-872-7165.*

**NELSON, BRUCE (MURRAY BRUCE NELSON),** former consumer products company executive; m. LaVaun Nelson; children: Suzanne, Connor. Grad., ID State U., 1968. Sr. mgmt. positions Boise Cascade, 1968-90; pres., CEO BT Office Products USA, 1991-94, Viking, 1995—98; pres. Office Depot Inc., Delray Beach, Fla., 1998—2000, CEO, 2000—04, chmn., 2001—04.

**NELSON, CALEB EDWARD,** law educator; b. Cleve., Sept. 20, 1966; s. David Aldrich and Mary Dickson Nelson; m. Elizabeth Kristol, Aug. 11, 1991; children: Maxwell David, Katherine Ellen. AB, Harvard U., 1988; JD, Yale U., 1993. Bar: Ohio 1993. Mng. editor and other editl. positions The Pub. Interest, Washington, 1988—90; law clk. to judge Stephen F. Williams U.S. Ct. of Appeals for the D.C. Circuit, Washington, 1993—94; law clk. to justice Clarence Thomas U.S. Supreme Ct., Washington, 1994—95; assoc. litig. dept. Taft, Stettinius & Hollister, Cin., 1995—98; prof. U. Va. Sch. Law, Charlottesville, 1998—. Vis. prof. Harvard Law Sch., 2006. Contbr. articles to profl. jours. Named Winner Scholarly Papers Competition, Assn. Am. Law Schs., 2000; recipient Paul M. Bator award, Federalist Soc., 2006. Mem.: Phi Beta Kappa. Office: Univ Virginia School Law 580 Massie Rd Charlottesville VA 22903-1789 Office Phone: 434-924-7372.

**NELSON, CARL,** journalist; Assoc. sports editor The New York Times. Mem.: Assoc. Press Sports Editors (ASPE) (assoc.). Office: NY Times Sports Desk 229 W 43rd St New York NY 10036 Office Phone: 212-556-7371.*

**NELSON, CARL ALFRED,** writer, international business educator; b. Pitts., Oct. 11, 1930; s. Alfred Helge Nelson and Isabel Alice (Younger) Newbauer; m. Barbara Long, June 2, 1956 (dec.); children: Jennifer, Allison, Monica. BS, U.S. Naval Acad., 1956; MS, U.S. Naval Post Grad., 1967; student, US Naval War Coll., 1970; D of Bus. Adminstrn., U. Internat. U., 1984. Enlisted USN, 1949, advanced through grades to capt., 1956-82; comdg. officer USS Worden CG-18, 4 others; v.p., dir. AMMEX Cons., Chula Vista, Calif., 1985-86; pres. Global Bus. & Trade, San Diego, 1982—. Prof. Calif. Sch. Internat. Mgmt.; lectr. in field. Author: Your Own Import-Export Business: Winning the Trade Game, 1988, Import-Export: How to Get Started in International Trade, 3d edit., 2000, Global Success, 1990, Managing Globally; A Complete Guide to Competing Worldwide, 1993, Protocol for Profit, 1998, International Business, 1998, Exporting, 1999, The Advisor, 1999, Secret Players, 2003; contbr. articles to profl. jours.; contbr. short stories to popular mags. Pres. Chula Vista Boys Club, 1988; exec. bd. dirs. Calif. Dem. Party, 1992-97, pres. S.D. Writers/Editors Guild, 1998, 2002; dir. Vietnam Vets.; active Econ. Devel. Commr., Chula Vista; founder, pres., CEO San Diego Internat. Book and Authors Festival, 2005. Decorated Legion of Merit, Bronze Star, Air medals, combat commendations; named Outstanding Alumni of Yr., U.S. Internat. U., 1989, Disting. Grad. Carriol HS, Pltts., 2006; recipient Disting. Global Educator award Calif. Sch. Internat. Mgmt., 2003. Mem. Assn. Global Bus., Acad. Internat. Bus., San Diego World Trade Assn., Authors's Guild of Am., Chula Vista C. of C. (dir. 1984-90, Internat. Focus award 1988), Optimist Club, 50 Yr. Mason (32 deg.). Home: 1385 Don Carlos Ct Chula Vista CA 91910-7130 Office Phone: 619-421-5923. E-mail: canelson56@cox.net.

**NELSON, CARL ROGER,** retired lawyer; b. Gowrie, Iowa, Dec. 26, 1915; s. Carl Helge and Inez Olivia (West) N.; m. Elizabeth Boswell Campbell, Apr. 27, 1946; children: Thomas C., Nancy L. AB, Grinnell Coll., 1937; MA, Columbia, 1938, LLB, 1941. Bar: N.Y. 1941. D.C. 1947, U.S. Supreme Ct. 1947. Law clk. to Chief Justice Stone, 1941-42; Washington asso. firm Root, Ballantine, Harlan, Bushby & Palmer, 1946-51; mem. firm Purcell & Nelson, Washington, 1951-80, Reavis & McGrath, 1980-83, Nelson Thurston Jones & Blouch, 1984-86. Mem. Administv. Conf. U.S., 1967—73. Served to capt. AUS, 1942-46. Fellow Am. Bar Found.; mem. ABA (mem. bd. dels. 1964-66, mem. coun. 1960-66, chmn. sect. adminstrv. law 1963-64), Chevy Chase (Md.) Club, Lawyers Club (Washington), Met. Club (Washington), Phi Beta Kappa. Mem. United Ch. of Christ. E-mail: nelsoncrv@comcast.net.

**NELSON, CAROL EVELYN,** retired pre-school educator; b. Grand Meadow, Minn., May 25, 1939; d. Charles Henry and Evelyn Hazel Lockwood; m. Loren Dean Nelson, Feb. 6, 1960; children: Sonia Jayne, Barrett Christopher, Bryce Phillip. BS, U. Minn., 1962. Cert. tchr., Minn. Substitute tchr. mil. schs. Camp Darby, Livorno, Italy, 1960—61; tchr. St. Paul Pub. Schs., 1962-63, Caledonia (Minn.) Pub. Schs., 1963-64, Rochester (Minn.) Pub. Schs., 1964-67, 83-87; early childhood educator Kids' Tree House, Rochester, 1987—2004; owner, mgr. CEN, Inc., Kids' Tree House, Rochester, 1989—99; ret., 2004. Mentor entrepreneurial tng. pilot program Minn. Women's Network, 1990-99. Canvasser, Rochester United Way, 1978-84; mem. climate control com., Elton Hills PTA, Rochester, 1983-85; leader Northwest Notables 4-H Club, Rochester, 1977-86. Mem. AAUW (Rochester, Minn. br. pres. 2002-04, chair Upper Midwest Regional Conf. Biannual Conf. 2004), Women Ind. Bus. Owners, Rochester Edn. Assn., S.E. Minn. Assn. for Edn. of Young Children, Rochester Civic Music Guild, Stock Club. Republican. Lutheran. Avocations: singing, reading. Personal E-mail: cenelson60@msn.com.

**NELSON, CAROL KOBUKE,** bank executive; m. Ken Nelson; 2 children. BA in fin. magna cum laude, Seattle U., Wash., 1978, MBA, 1984; attended grad. sch. Credit & Fin. Mgmt., Santa Clara U., Calif. With SeaFirst Bank (now Bank of Am.); sr. v.p., No. regional consumer exec. Bank of Am.; pres., COO Cascade Fin. Corp., Everett, Wash., 2001—02, pres., CEO, 2002—, Cascade Bank, Everett, Wash., 2001—. Exec. adv. bd. Albers Sch. Bus. and Economics Seattle U. Chair bd. dirs. United Way, Snohomish County; bd. dirs. Boys and Girls Club, Snohomish County, Econ. Devel. Coun., Snohomish County; adv. bd. Leadership Snohomish County; pub. facilities dir. Washington State Baseball Stadium. Named One of 25 Women to Watch, U.S. Banker Mag., 2003; named one of The 25 Most Powerful Women in Banking, 2004, 2005. Mem.: Wash. Bankers Assn. (bd. dirs.), Wash. Fin. League (bd. dirs.). Office: Cascade Financial Corp 2828 Colby Ave Everett WA 98201

**NELSON, CAROLYN,** state legislator; b. Madison, Wis., Oct. 8, 1937; m. Gilbert W. Nelson; children: Paul, John, Karla. BS, N.D. State U., 1959, MS, 1960. Sr. lectr. emeritus N.D. State U., 1968—; mem. N.D. Ho. of Reps., 1986-88, 92-94, N.D. Senate from 21st dist., 1994—; mem. judiciary com., vet. affairs com. N.D. Senate, minority caucus leader, 2000—. Mem. N.D. State Investment Bd., 1989-92. Mem. Bd. Edn., Fargo, N.D., 1985-91, pres., 1989-90; trustee N.D. Tchrs. Fund for Retirement, 1985-92, pres., 1990-92; mem. N.D. PTA, pres., 1978-81, N.D. Women's and Children's Caucus. Recipient Merit Svc. award Gamma Phi Beta, 1978, 90, Legis. Voices award Children's Caucus, 1995; named Legislator of Yr., N.D. Bar Assn., 2000, N.D. Student Assn., 2001. Mem. LWV, Am. Guild English Handbell Ringers (area chmn. 1982-84, nat. bd. dirs. 1982-90), Nat. Fedn. Music Clubs (Bd. dirs., legis. chair 2004—), N.D. Fedn. Music Clubs (life, pres. 1997-2001, nat. bd. mem., legis. chair, Rose Fay Thomas fellow 2001), Gamma Phi Beta, Phi Kappa Phi, Sigma Alpha Iota. Office: ND Senate State Capitol Bismarck ND 58505 Address: One 2d St S 5 402 Fargo ND 58103-1959 Business E-Mail: cnelson@state.nd.us.

**NELSON, CARY ROBERT,** language educator; b. Phila., May 15, 1946; s. Aaron and Sophie (Cohen) N. BA, Antioch Coll., 1967; PhD in English, U. Rochester, 1970. Asst. prof. English U. Ill., 1970-75, assoc. prof. English 1975-82, prof. English and Criticism and Interpretive Theory, 1982—, prof. Ctr. for Writing, 1991—, Jubilee prof. liberal arts and scis., 1991—. Project dir. Nat. Endowment for the Humanities grants U. Ill., 1983-85, founding dir. unit for criticism and interpretive theory, 1981-85, 96, coord. faculty criticism seminar 1977-82, 96; governing bd., exec. com. Abraham Lincoln Brigade Archives, 1994—, vice chair 1995—; cons. in field. Author: The Incarnate Word: Literature as Verbal Space, 1973, Our Last First Poets: Vision and History in Contemporary American Poetry, 1981, Repression and Recovery: Modern American Poetry and THe Politics of Cultural Memory 1910-1945, 1989, Shouts from the Wall: Posters and Photographs Brought Back from the Spanish Civil War by American Volunteers, 1996, Manifesto of a Tenured

Radical, 1997, Academic Keywords: A Devil's Dictionary for Higher Education, 1999; editor: Theory in the Classroom, 1986, W.S. Merwin: Essays on the Poetry, 1987, Regions of Memory: Uncollected Prose, 1949-82, 1987, Marxism and the Interpretation of Culture, 1988, Edwin Rolfe: A Biographical Essay and Guide to the Rolfe Archive at the University of Illinois at Urbana-Champaign, 1990, Cutural Studies, 1992, The Collected Poems of Edwin Rolfe, 1993, Higher Education Under Fire: Politics, Economics, and the Crisis of the Humanities, 1994, Trees Became Torches: Selected Poems of Edwin Rolfe, 1995, Trees Became Torches: Selected Poems of Edwin Rolfe, 1995, Madrid 1937: Letters of the Abraham Lincoln Brigade from the Spanish Civil War, 1996, Disciplinarity and Dissent in Cultural Studies, 1996, Will Teach for Food: Academic Labor in Crisis, 1997, The Aura of the Cause: A Photo Album for North American Volunteers in the Spanish Civil War, 1997, An Anthology of Modern American Poetry, 1999; editl. adv. bd. Literature and Psychology, 1985—; Academe: Bull. of the AAUP, 1996—, Jour. of Midwest MLA, 1996—; editl. bd. Coll. Lit., 1990—, Works and Days, 1995—; contbr. numerous articles to profl. jours. Fellowships U. of Ill. Ctr. for Advanced Study, 1978, 85-86, U. Ill. coll. of Liberal Arts and Scis. Faculty Study in a Second Discipline, 1987-88, Program for the Study of Cultural Values and Ethics, 1993-94, Program for Rsch. in Humanities, 1999—; grantee NSF, 1996. Mem. MLA (exec. coun. 1999—, 2d v.p. 1996-97, pres. 1996-97), Midwest MLA (pres. 1998), AAUP (nat. coun. 1995—, 2nd v.p. 2005-06, pres. 2006-), Tchrs. for a Dem. Culture, Kenneth Burke Soc., Ernest Hemingway Soc., Nat. Coun. of Tchrs. of English. Home: 808 S Lynn St Champaign IL 61820-6313 Office: English Dept U of Ill 608 S Wright St Urbana IL 61801-3668 E-mail: crnelson@uiuc.edu.*

**NELSON, CHARLOTTE BOWERS**, public administrator; b. Bristol, Va., June 28, 1931; d. Thaddeus Ray and Ruth Nelson (Moore) Bowers; m. Gustav Carl Nelson, June 1, 1957; children: Ruth Elizabeth, David Carl, Thomas Gustav. BA summa cum laude, Duke U., 1954; MA, Columbia U., 1961; MPA, Drake U., 1983. Instr. Beaver Coll., 1957-58, Drake U., Des Moines, 1975-82; office mgr. LWV of Iowa, Des Moines, 1975-82; exec. asst. Iowa Dept. Human Svcs., Des Moines, 1983-85; exec. dir. Iowa Commn. on Status of Women Dept. Human Rights, Des Moines, 1985; pub. adminstr. State of Iowa, 2006—. Bd. dirs., pres. LWV, Beloit, Wis., 1960-74; bd. dirs. LWV, Des Moines, 1974-82, Westminster House, Des Moines, 1988-97, pres. 1996-97. Recipient Gov.'s Golden Dome award as Leader of the Yr., 2002; named Visionary Woman, Young Women's Resource Ctr., 1994. Mem. Am. Soc. Pub. Adminstrn. (mem. exec. coun. 1984-92, 98-99, past pres., Mem. of Yr. 1993), Phi Beta Kappa, Pi Alpha Alpha. Home: 1141 Cummins Cir Des Moines IA 50311-2113 Office: Human Rights Dept Lucas State Office Bldg Des Moines IA 50319-0001 Office Phone: 515-281-4467. E-mail: charlotte.nelson@iowa.gov, nelson514@aol.com.

**NELSON, CHRIS A.**, state official; b. Mitchell, SD, Aug. 18, 1964; married; 1 child. BS, SD State Univ., 1987. Farmer/rancher self-employed, 1981—; UCC supr. State of SD, 1987—89, state election supr., 1989—2002, sec. of state, 2003—. Republican. Christian. Office: Office Sec of State 500 E Capitol Ave Ste 204 Pierre SD 57501 Office Phone: 605-773-3537. Fax: 605-773-6580.*

**NELSON, CHRIS B.**, physics professor; s. Bobby Joe and Roxanna Pauline Nelson; m. Diane Doucette Nelson (div.); children: Mathew, Christopher. BS in Physics, Idaho State U., Pocatello, 1983, MS in Physics, 1988; PhD in Physics, U. Utah, Salt Lake City, 2003. Postdoctoral staff Idaho Accelrator, Pocatello, 2003—04; vis. asst. prof. Idaho State U., Pocatello, 2004—05, Lamar U., Beaumont, Tex., 2005—. Avocations: pottery, hot rods, metaphysics. Office: Lamar Univ PO Box 10022 Beaumont TX 77710

**NELSON, CHRISTOPHER GRANT**, dermatologist; b. Peoria, Ill., Feb. 11, 1946; s. Grant Leonard and Shirlee Ann (Brunnenmeyer) N.; m. Mary Jo Donnelly, June 30, 1972; children: Christopher Jr., Andrew Anthony. BS, U. Iowa, 1968, MD, 1971. Diplomate Am. Bd. Dermatology; cert. clin. trial investigator. Intern Ball Meml. Hosp., Muncie, Ind., 1971-72; resident in dermatology U. Tex. Med. Br., Galveston, 1974-77; staff Bayfront Med. Ctr., St. Petersburg, 1977—, St. Anthony's Hosp., St. Petersburg, 1977—; tchr. Bayfront Med. Ctr., 1977—; affiliate assoc. prof. U. South Fla. Coll. Medicine, 1977—; staff Tampa Gen. Hosp., 2001—. Contbr. articles to profl. jours. Vol. Am. Cancer Soc. Mem. ACP, So. Med. Assn., Fla. Med. Assn., Am. Acad. Dermatology, Am. Soc. Dermatologic Surgery, Soc. Investigative Dermatology, Pinellas County Med. Soc., Fla. West Coast Soc. Dermatology (sec.-treas. 1982-84, pres. 1984-87), Fla. Soc. Dermatologic Surgery, St. Petersburg Yacht Club (bd. dirs. 1989-95, entertainment chmn. 1989-92, house and grounds com. 1987-95), Dragon Club, Masons, Royal Order of Jesters. Presbyterian. Avocations: sailing, scuba diving, photography, amateur ham radio. Office Phone: 727-895-8131.

**NELSON, COURTNEY ANN**, small business owner; b. Downers Grove, Ill., Aug. 19, 1978; d. Brian and Debbie Nelson. BS in Bus. Adminstrn. and Mktg., U. So. Calif., LA, 2000. Account mgr. Xerox - Q Document Solutions, Long Beach, Calif., 2000—01; dist. mgr. ADP, 2003—04; key accounts mgr. Fire On Ice, Inc, 2001—03; ptnr. Image-ination, 2002—. Mem. Newport Beach Jr. C. of C., Calif., 2002—04; social events coord., pres. USC Alumni Club of Newport Beach, Irvine, 2002—06; mem. Jr. League of Orange County, Irvine, 2003—05. Recipient Widney Alumni award, USC Alumni Assn., 2004; Bus. scholar, USC Marshall Sch. Bus., 1996—2000, Town and Gown scholar, USC Town and Gown Soc., 1996—2000. Mem.; USC Alumni Assn. of Newport and Irvine. Christian. Avocations: golf, travel, water sports. Office: Image-ination 20 Goldenrod Irvine CA 92614 Office Phone: 949-733-0300. Personal E-mail: cnelson@mylogostuff.com.

**NELSON, CRAIG ALAN**, management consultant; b. San Rafael, Calif., July 11, 1961; s. Kenneth Alfred and Anne Catherine (Laurie) N. BS in Fin., San Diego State U., 1984. Loan assoc. Union Bank, San Diego, 1984-85, comml. loan officer, 1985-86, corp. banking officer, 1986-87, asst. v.p., 1987-89, v.p. corp. banking, 1989-93; v.p. Alexander & Alexander, San Diego, 1993-95; sr. assoc. Goreham-Moore & Assoc., San Diego, 1995-98; v.p. Sedgwick Tech. Group Sedgwick of Calif., Inc., San Diego, 1998; v.p., dir. tech. Marsh Inc., La Jolla, Calif., 1998—; regional v.p. Comerica Tech. Banking Group, San Diego; regional v.p., sr. mgr. Bank of the West, San Diego, 2002—05; exec. v.p. First Nat. Bank. V.p. Sedgwick Tech. Group, 1997; pres. MIT Enterprise Forum, San Diego. Community group chair San Diego chpt. Am. Cancer Soc., 1989; mem. com. Juvenile Diabetes Assn.; bd. dirs. San Diego State Found., 1989—; pres. Am. Lung Assn., San Diego and Imperial counties, San Diego State U. Athletic Found., 2004—. Mem. San Diego State U. Young Alumni Assn. (pres. 1988-89, bd. dirs. emeritus 1989). Home: 429 Santa Dominga Solana Beach CA 92075 Office: First Nat Bank 401 W A St Ste 200 San Diego CA 92101 Office Phone: 619-235-1205. Personal E-mail: cnelson_madison@hotmail.com. Business E-mail: cnelson@banksandiego.com.

**NELSON, CRAIG T.**, actor; b. Spokane, Wash., Apr. 4, 1944; Appeared in (feature films) And Justice-for All, 1979, The Formula, 1980, Where the Buffalo Roam, 1980, Private Benjamin, 1980, Stir Crazy, 1981, Poltergeist, 1982, Man, Woman, and Child, 1983, The Osterman Weekend, 1983, All the Right Moves, 1983, The Killing Fields, 1984, Silkwood, 1984, Poltergeist II: The Other Side, 1986, Red Riding Hood, 1987, Action Jackson, 1988, Me and Him, 1988, Troop Beverly Hills, 1989, Rachel River, 1989, Turner & Hooch, 1989, I'm Not Rappaport, 1996, Ghosts of Mississippi, 1996, Devil's Advocate, 1997, Wag the Dog, 1997, The Skulls, 2000, All Over Again, 2001, The Incredibles (voice), 2004, The Family Stone, 2005; (stage prodns.) Friends, 1983-84, Ah, Wilderness!, 1998, (TV movies) How the West Was Won, 1978, Diary of a Teenage Hitchiker, 1979, Rage, 1980, Inmates: A Love Story, 1981, Murder in Texas, 1981, Paper Dolls, 1983, Alex: The Life of a Child, 1986, The Ted Kennedy, Jr. Story, 1986, Murderers Among Us: The Simon Wiesenthal Story, 1989, Extreme Close-Up, 1990, Drug Wars: The Camarena Story, 1990, The Josephine Baker Story, 1991, The Fire Next Time, 1993, Probable Cause, 1994, Top of the World, 1997, The Fifty, 1998, Creature, 1998, To Serve and Protect, 1999, Family Shield, 1999; (TV series)

Heroes: Made in the U.S.A. (host), 1986, Coach, 1989-97 (Emmy award, Leading actor in a comedy series, 1992), The District, 2000—04; producer (film documentaries) American Still; screenwriter (TV shows) The Lohman and Barkley Show, The Tim Conway Show, The Alan King Special, (miniseries) Creature, 1998, To Serve and Protect, 1999; prodr., writer (TV) Ride With the Wind, 1994; TV appearances include WKRP in Cincinnati, 1978, The Mary Tyler Moore Show, 1970, The White Shadow, 1978.*

**NELSON, DARRELL WAYNE**, academic administrator, research scientist; b. Aledo, Ill., Nov. 28, 1939; s. Wayne Edward and Olive Elvina (Peterson) N.; m. Nancyann Hyer, Aug. 27, 1961; children: Christina Lynne, Craig Douglas. BS in Agriculture, U. Ill., 1961, MS in Agronomy, 1963; PhD in Agronomy, Iowa State U., 1967. Cert. profl. soil scientist. Div. chief U.S. Army Chem. Corps., Denver, 1967-68; asst. prof. Purdue U., West Lafayette, Ind., 1968-73, assoc. prof., 1973-77, prof. agronomy, 1977-84; dept. head U. Nebr., Lincoln, 1984-88, dean for agr. rsch. and dir. Nebr. Agr. Experiment Sta., 1988—. Cons. U.S. EPA, Washington, 1977-79, Ind. Bd. of Health, Indpls., 1977-83, Eli Lilly Co., Indpls., 1976. Editor: Chemical Mobility and Reactivity in Soils, 1983. Served to capt. U.S. Army, 1967-68. Fellow AAAS, Am. Soc. Agronomy (bd. dirs., pres.-elect, pres. 2001, past pres. 2002, CIBA-Geigy award 1975, Agronomic Achievement award 1983, Environ. Quality Rsch. award 1985), Soil Sci. Soc. Am. (bd. dirs., pres. elect 1992, pres. 1993, past pres. 1994); mem. Internat. Soil Sci. Soc., Lions Lodge (treas. 1980-83, Lafayette, Ind. chpt.). Presbyterian. Avocations: fishing, skiing, jogging. Office: Univ of Nebr Agrl Rsch Divsn Lincoln NE 68583-0704 Office Phone: 402-472-2045. Business E-Mail: dnelson1@unl.edu.

**NELSON, DAVID ALDRICH**, judge; b. Watertown, NY, 1932; s. Carlton Low and Irene Demetria (Aldrich) Nelson; m. Mary Dickson, 1956; 3 children. AB, Hamilton Coll., 1954; postgrad., Cambridge U., Eng., 1954—55; LLB, Harvard U., 1958. Bar: Ohio 1958, N.Y. 1982. Atty.-advisor Office of the Gen. Counsel, Dept. of the Air Force, 1959—62; assoc. Squire, Sanders & Dempsey, Cleve., 1958—67, ptnr., 1967—69, 1972—85; judge U.S. Ct. Appeals (6th cir.), Cin., 1985—99, sr. judge, 1999—. Gen. counsel U.S. Post Office Dept., Washington, 1969—71; sr. asst. postmaster gen., gen. counsel U.S. Postal Svc., Washington, 1971; nat. coun. Ohio State U. Coll. Law, 1988—98. Trustee Hamilton Coll., 1984—88. Served to maj. USAFR, 1959—73. Recipient Benjamin Franklin award, U.S. Post Office Dept., 1969; Fulbright scholar, 1954—55. Fellow: Am. Coll. Trial Lawyers; mem.: Ohio Bar Assn., Fed. Bar Assn., Emerson Lit. Soc., Ct. of Nisi Prius (sgt. emeritus), Phi Beta Kappa.*

**NELSON, DAVID LEONARD**, data processing executive; b. Omaha, May 8, 1930; s. Leonard A. and Cecelia (Steinert) N.; m. Jacqueline J. Zerbe, Dec. 26, 1952; 1 child, Nancy Jo. BS, Iowa State U., 1952. Mktg. adminstr. Ingersoll Rand, Chgo., 1954-56; with Accuray Corp., Columbus, Ohio, 1956-87, exec. v.p., gen. mgr., 1967, pres., 1967-87, chief exec. officer, 1970-87; pres. process automation bus. unit Combustion Engring., Inc., Columbus, 1987-90; pres. bus. area process automation Asea Brown Boveri, Stamford, Conn., 1990-91, v.p. customer satisfaction Ams. region, 1991-93, v.p. customer support Ams. region, 1994-95; chmn. bd. dirs. Herman Miller Inc., Zeeland, Mich., 1995-2000, counsel, 2000—04. Patentee in field. Served to capt. USMCR, 1952-54. Mem. IEEE, Instrument Soc. Am., Newcomen Soc. N.Am., Tau Beta Pi, Phi Kappa Phi, Phi Eta Sigma, Delta Upsilon. Home: 1113 Roundhouse Ln Alexandria VA 22314-5935 Office Phone: 703-299-4588. Business E-Mail: david_nelson@hermanmiller.com.

**NELSON, DAVID LOREN**, geneticist, educator; b. Washington, June 25, 1956; s. Erling Walter and Marlys Joan (Jorgenson) N.; m. Claudia Jane Hackbarth, July 31, 1982; children: Jorgen William, Erik Alexander. BA, U. Va., 1978; PhD, MIT, 1984. Staff fellow NIH, Bethesda, Md., 1985-86; sr. assoc. Baylor Coll. Medicine, Houston, 1986-89, instr., 1989-90, asst. prof., 1990-94, assoc. prof., 1994-99, prof., 1999—. Dir. Human Genome Ctr., 1995-96. Editor: Genome Data Base, 1992-2000; assoc. editor Genomics, 1994-2002. Achievements include development of Alu PCR; discovery of fragile X syndrome gene (FMR-1), new form of genetic mutation (simple repeat expansion); identification of gene defects in Lowe Syndrome and Incontinentia Pigmenti. Office: Baylor Coll Dept Medicine Molecular & Human Genetics 1 Baylor Plz Houston TX 77030-3411 E-mail: nelson@bcm.tmc.edu.

**NELSON, DEAN B.**, media company executive; Process ctrl. engr. Shell Oil Co., 1981—83; with Boston Consulting Group, 1985—98, sr. v.p., 1998—2000; founder Capstone Consulting LLC, 2000, CEO, 2000—; chmn. PRIMEDIA Inc., NYC, 2003—, pres., CEO, 2005—. Bd. dirs. PRIMEDIA Inc., 2003—. Office: PRIMEDIA Inc 745 Fifth Ave New York NY 10151 Office Phone: 212-745-0100. Office Fax: 212-745-0121.*

**NELSON, DEBORAH JANE**, family and consumer science educator; d. Roy Irvin and Jane Maurine Nelson. BS in Vocat. Home Economics Edn., Colo. State U., Fort Collins, 1983; MA in Ednl. Psychology, U. Colo. at Denver, 1991. CFCS Am. Assn. of Family & Consumer Sciences, 1986. Tchr. home econ. Cripple Creek-Victor Sch., Colo., 1983—84; tchr. family and consumer scis. Jefferson H.S., Edgewater, 1984—2000, Alameda H.S., Lakewood, 2000—. Mem. career devel. focus team Jefferson County Pub. Schs., Golden, Colo., 2000—; mem. state stds. rev. team family and consumer scis. Colo. Cmty. Colleges Sys., Denver, 2002—04; state star event chair and evaluator Family, Career & Cmty. Leaders Am., 1983—. Contbr. articles to profl. jours. Walkamerica vol. Mar. of Dimes, Denver, 1974—; clarinetist Denver Concert Band, 1986—; supporter 4-H Clubs, El Paso County, 1991—; judge Job's Daughters, Denver, 1995. Named Colo. FACS Profl. of Yr., Colo. Assn. Family and Consumer Scis., 1995; named an Outstanding Tchr., Colo. Tchr. Awards, 1996. Mem.: NEA, Internat. Fedn. Home Econ., Assn. Career and Tech. Edn. (sec. Colo. divsn. 1999—2001, CATFACS Outstanding Tchr. 2003), Am. Assn. Family and Consumer Scis. (v.p. svcs. 2003—05). Avocations: swimming, scrapbooks, travel, clarinet, piano. Office: Alameda HS 1255 S Wadsworth Blvd Lakewood CO 80232-5406

**NELSON, DENNIS LEE**, finance educator; b. Randall, Minn., Nov. 4, 1929; s. George Otto and Emma Ida (Schwanke) N.; m. Joyce Marie Prozinski, Aug. 25, 1956; children: Constance, Kristin, Norma Joan. BS, St. Cloud State U., 1954; MA, U. Minn., 1964, PhD in Econs., 1970. Prof. econs. U. Minn., Duluth, 1964—, dir. ctr. for econ. edn., 1967-71, grad. faculty, 1970—, head dept. econs., 1971-77, assoc. chancellor, 1977-88, vice chancellor fin. ops., 1987-88. Mem. faculty Westhill Coll., U. Birmingham, Eng., 1996-97; instnl. rep. for adminstrs. on Nat. Collegiate Athletic Assn., 1978-87; adminstr., vis. faculty Oxford U., Eng., 1997, Yonsei U., Seoul, 1988, Moscow U., 1978, 84. Recipient Disting. Alumnus award U. Minn. Mem. Duluth Blueline Club, Duluth Quarterback Club, UMD Rasmussen Fund, UMD Hoop Club, Pres. Club U. Minn. Lutheran. Avocations: gardening, writing, reading, woodworking, bridge. Office: U Minn 10 University Dr Duluth MN 55812-2403

**NELSON, DENNIS STEPHEN**, protective services official; s. Johnny Ferrell and Barbara Jean Nelson; m. Dawn Glynn, Apr. 22, 1989; children: Stephen James, Jonathan Glynn. Student, Columbus State U., Ga.; grad. So. Police Inst., U. Louisville, 2004. Capt., divsn. dir. Gwinnett County Sheriff's Dept., Lawrenceville, Ga., 1997—2001; lt. col., dep. chief Forsyth County Sheriff's Office, Cumming, Ga., 2001. Law enforcement del. to Israel GILEE/Georgia State U., 2003. Contbr. State Certification Model Policy Manual. Com. mem. Fulton County Courthouse Security Commn., Atlanta, 2005; com. mem., assessor State of Ga. Certification Com., Duluth, 1995. Named Police Officer of Yr., City of Roswell Police Dept., 1995; recipient Outstanding Achievement award for state cert., Gwinnett County Sheriff's Dept., 1997. Mem.: Ga. Sheriffs' Assn., State of Ga. Law Enforcement Certification Com. (assoc.; founding mem. 1995), Commn. on Accreditation for Law Enforcement Agys. (assoc.; assessor 1995—, Accreditation Mgr. award 1995), Am. Dep. Sheriffs' Assn. (assoc.), Peace Officers Assn. of Ga. (assoc.), Nat. Sheriffs' Assn. (assoc.), Ga. Police Accreditation Coalition (assoc.; chmn., vice chmn., bd. dirs. 1991—2004), Ga. Assn. Chiefs of Police

(assoc. cert. of appreciation 1997), Internat. Assn. Chiefs of Police (assoc.). Republican. Methodist. Achievements include development of A.D.-V.A.N.C.E. countywide child safety education program. Home: 645 Melanie Ct Canton GA 30115 Office: Forsyth County Sheriff's Office 202 Veterans Memorial Blvd Cumming GA 30040 Office Phone: 770-205-4673. Office Fax: 770-205-4570. E-mail: dsnelson@forsythco.com.

**NELSON, DIANE W.**, broadcast executive; BS in Comm., Syracuse U. Dir. nat. promotions Walt Disney Records; dir. worldwide corp. promotions Warner Brothers Pictures, 1996—98, v.p. worldwide corp. promotions, 1998—2001, sr. v.p. family entertainment, 2001—02, exec. v.p. domestic mktg., 2002—04, exec. v.p. global brand mgmt., 2004—. Mailing: Warner Bros Pictures 4000 Warner Blvd Burbank CA 91522 Office Phone: 818-954-6000.*

**NELSON, DONALD ARVID (NELLIE NELSON)**, former professional basketball coach; b. Muskegon, Mich., May 15, 1940; Student, U. Iowa. Player Chgo. Zephyrs, 1962-63, LA Lakers, 1963-65, Boston Celtics, 1965-76; mem. Nat. Basketball championship teams, 1966, 68, 69, 74, 76; from asst. to head coach Milw. Bucks, 1976-87, also dir. player pers.; exec. v.p., part owner Golden State Warriors, Oakland, Calif., 1987-95, head coach, 1988-95, 2006—, NY Knicks, 1995-96; coach Dream Team II, 1994; coach, gen. mgr. Dallas Mavericks, 1996—2005. Named Coach of Yr. NBA, 1983, 85, 92. Mailing: Golden State Warriors 1011 Broadway Oakland CA 94607*

**NELSON, DONNA GAYLE**, state representative; b. Paducah, Tex., June 13, 1943; d. Jack Harold Williams and Hazel Louise (Cooper Moss) Stephens; m. Douglas Caldwell Nelson, June 24, 1966 (div. 1976); children: Kellye Lou Fetters, Robert Kreg Nelson, J. Gregory. AB, South Plains Coll., Levelland, Tex., 1963; BBA, West Tex. A&M U., Canyon, 1965, MBA, 1967. Founder Evergreen Mut., McMinnville, Oreg., 1975; co-founder Evergreen Life Line, McMinnville, 1978—; founder, corp. dir. AAA Profl. Promotions, McMinnville, 1977—; pres. Evergreen Bus. Mgmt. Co., McMinnville, 1978—; sr. v.p. Evergreen Helicopters, Inc., McMinnville, 1978—, Evergreen Internat. Aviation, Inc., McMinnville, 1978—; mem. Oreg. State Ho. of Reps., 2000—, chair veterans comm., mem. vice chair govt. bus. com., vice chair govt. com., vice chair agr. com. Bd. dirs. Evergreen Air Ctr., Inc., Marana, Ariz., Evergreen Aircraft Sales & Leasing Co., Evergreen Aviation Ground Logistics Enterprises, Inc.; sr. v.p., bd. dirs. Evergreen Internat. Aviation, Inc., McMinnville; speaker Nat. Speakers' Assn., Phoenix, 1986—; mem. adv. bd. Chemeketa Community Coll., McMinnville, 1984-85; owner 3N & Assocs. Inc., Donna G. Nelson Auctions, LLC; founder Yamhill Co. Market; teacher Tex., Calif., and Oregon; author, journalist. Poet World's Most Beloved Poetry, 1985 (Silver poet); writer Aviation/Space Writers' Assn., 1989-90; columnist It Takes Grit. Mem. Team 100 Rep. party, Washington, 1989; co-founder Poyama Land Treatment Ctr. Independence, Oreg., 1973; den mother, sustained membership chmn. Boy Scouts Am., McMinnville, 1977-79; dr. mem. March of Dimes, Heart Fund, McMinnville, 1973-75; sr. transportation com., Yamhill Co. Budget Parks, Elks Lions, Red Cross, NRA, N11B Farm Bur.; founder Newcomers Club, Fund for Hope, Free Enterprise Fund for Kids; bd. dirs. Humane Soc., Linfield Chamber Orch., Salvation Army. Named Woman of Excellence, Portland, Oreg., 1985. Mem. DAR, C. of C., McMinnville Duplicate Bridge Assn. (founder), Soroptimists Club, Elks, Lions, Beta Sigma Phi (pres. 1974-75, Woman of Yr. 1990). Republican. Baptist. Avocations: music, sports, bridge, writing, fishing, speaking, travel, fishing, computers, charity auctioneer. Home and Office: 2150 St Andrews Dr # 1252 Mcminnville OR 97128-2436 Office Phone: 503-472-8015. Business E-Mail: donnanelson@state.or.us.

**NELSON, DONNA JEAN**, chemistry educator, researcher; b. Eufaula, Okla., Aug. 29, 1952; d. John Howard Jr. and Dorotha (Eckelkamp) Baker; 1 child, Christopher Brammer. BS in Chemistry, U. Okla., 1974; PhD, U. Tex., 1979. Robert A. Welch pre-doctoral fellow, 1977, 78, 79; Robert A. Welch postdoctoral fellow, 1980; asst. prof. U. Okla., Norman, 1983-89, assoc. prof., faculty adminstrv. fellow Provost's Office, 1989—. Jr. faculty rsch. fellow Okla. U., 1984, assocs. disting. lectr., 1985-86; vis. prof. MIT, 2003. Asst. editor: Progress Mag., 2002—, assoc editor: AWIS Mag., 2002—03. Recipient Sooner Spotlight award U. Okla., 1986, Sequoyah medal Am. Indians in Sci. and Engring. Soc., 2003, Nat. Woman of Courage award NOW, 2004, Nat. Woman of Courage award, Nat. Orgn. for Women, 2004, Okla. Outstanding Prof., 2005; named Woman of Achievement, USBE and Info. Tech. Mag., 2003, Okla. Outstanding Prof., 2005; Robert A. Welch grantee, 1979; A.P. Sloan Found. travel awardee, 2003; Ford Found. fellow, 2003-04; Guggenheim awardee, 2003-04. Mem. Am. Chem. Soc. (women chemists com. 1988—, James Flack award com. 1987-90), Phi Lambda Upsilon, Alpha Chi Sigma, Iota Sigma Pi, Sigma Xi (nat. diversity com. 2001—). Home: 1700 Winding Ridge Rd Norman OK 73072-3149 Office: U Okla Dept of Chemistry Norman OK 73072 Office Phone: 405-325-2288. Business E-Mail: djnelson@ou.edu.

**NELSON, DORENE**, retired secondary school educator; b. Aberdeen, S.D., Jan. 29, 1945; d. Joe W. and Hazel M. (Dunker) Sager; m. Gordon C. Nelson, June 29, 1963; children: Carmel, Corey. BS, No. State Coll., 1967, MS, 1970. Cert. secondary English and social studies. English tchr. various schs., Mellette, SD, 1967—69, Groton, SD, 1969—2004; ret., 2004. Asst. debate coach. Mem.: S.D. Forensic Coaches Assn., Speech Communication Assn. S.D., Nat. Forensic League, Nat. Coun. Tchrs. English, S.D. Edn. Assn. Home: PO Box 675 Groton SD 57445-0675 Personal E-mail: gnelson@nvc.net.

**NELSON, DOROTHY WRIGHT (MRS. JAMES F. NELSON)**, federal judge; b. San Pedro, Calif., Sept. 30, 1928; d. Harry Earl and Lorna Amy Wright; m. James Frank Nelson, Dec. 27, 1950; children: Franklin Wright, Lorna Jean. BA, UCLA, 1950, JD, 1953; LLM, U. So. Calif., 1956; LLD (hon.), Western State U. Coll. Law, 1980, U. So. Calif., 1983, Georgetown U., 1988, Whittier U., 1989, U. Santa Clara, 1990, U. San Diego, 1997, Pepperdine U. Sch. of Law, 2003. Bar: Calif. 1954. Rsch. assoc. fellow U. So. Calif., 1953—56, instr., 1957, asst. prof., 1958—61, assoc. prof., 1961—67, prof., 1967—, assoc. dean, 1967—80; judge U.S. Ct. Appeals 9th Cir., 1979—95, sr. judge, 1995—. Com. to consider stds. for admission to practice in fed. cts. Jud. Conf. U.S., 1976—79; cons. project STAR Law Enforcement Assistance Adminstrn.; select com. on internal procedures Calif. Supreme Ct., 1987—; co-chair Sino-Am. Seminar on Mediation and Arbitration, Beijing, 1992. Contbr. articles to profl. jours.; author: Judicial Adminstration and The Administration of Justice, 1973; author: (with Christopher Goelz and Meredith Watts) Federal Ninth Circuit Civil Appellate Practice, 1995. Co-chair Confronting Myths in Edn. for Pres. Nixon's White House Conf. on Children, Pres. Carter's Commn. for Pension Policy, 1974—80; pres. Reagon's Madison Trust; mem. Nat. Spiritual Assembly of Bahais of U.S., 1967—; bd. dirs. Dialogue on Transition to a Global Soc., Weinacht, Switzerland, 1992; bd. vis. U.S. Air Force Acad., 1978; bd. dirs. Coun. on Legal Edn. for Profl. Responsibility, 1971—80, Constl. Right Found., Am. Nat. Inst. for Social Advancement; adv. bd. Nat. Ctr. for State Cts., 1971—76; adv. com. to promote equality for woman and men in cts. Nat. Jud. Edn. Program; bd. dirs. Pacific Oaks Coll., Childrens Sch. & Rsch. Ctr., 1996—98; adv. bd. World Law Inst., 1997—, Tahirih Justice Inst., Washington, 1998—; chmn. bd. Western Justice Ctr., 1986—; chair 9th Cir. Standing Com. on Alternative Dispute Resolution, 1998—. Named Law Alumnus of Yr., UCLA, 1967, Woman of Yr., Times, 1968, Disting. Jurist, Ind. U. Law, 1994; recipient Profl. Achievement award, 1969, AWARE Internat. award, 1970, Ernestine Stalhut Outstanding Woman Lawyer award, 1972, Humanitarian award, U. Judaism, 1973, Pax Orbis ex Jure medal, World Peace thru Law Ctr., 1975, Pub. Svc. award, Coro Found., 1978, Hollzer Human Rights award, Jewish Fedn. Coun., 1988, Medal of Honor, UCLA, 1993, Emil Gumpert Jud. ADR Recognition award, L.A. County Bar Assn., 1996, Julia Morgan award, YWCA, 1997, Samuel E. Gates Litigation award, Am. Coll. Trial Lawyers, 1999, Bernard E. Witkin award, State Bar Assn. Calif., 2000, Judge of the Year award, Pasadena Bar Assn., 2002, Thurgood Marshall Career Achievement award, 2005, Harry Sheldon award, Pasadena Human Relations Comm., 2006; fellow, Davenport Coll.; Lustman fellow, Yale U., 1977. Fellow: Davenport Coll.; Am. Bar Found.; mem.: ABA (sect. on jud. adminstrn., chmn. com. on edn. in jud. adminstrn. 1973—89, D'Alemberte/Raven award 2000), Assn. Am. Law Schs. (chmn. com. edn. in jud. adminstrn.), Am. Judicature Soc. (bd. dirs., Justice award 1985), Bar Calif. (bd. dirs. continuing edn. bar commn. 1967—74), Order of Coif (nat. v.p. 1974—76), Phi Beta Kappa. Office: US Ct Appeals Cir 125 S Grand Ave Ste 303 Pasadena CA 91105-1621 Office Phone: 626-229-7400. Business E-Mail: dorothy-nelson@ca9.uscourt.gov.*

**NELSON, DOUGLAS W.,** foundation administrator; b. 1946; BA, U. Ill., 1968; MA in History, U. Wyoming. Asst. secy. health and social svcs. State of Wis., Madison, 1967-85; dep. dir. Ctr. for Study Policy, Washington, 1985-90; with The Annie E. Casey Found., Greenwith, Conn., 1990—97, now exec. dir., pres., 1997—. Vice chair, bd. of trustees Foundation Ctr., NYC; co-chair, of trustees Jim Casey Youth Opportunities Initiative; trustee Balt. Campaign for Children and Youth, Balt. Community Found., Wis. Child Abuse and Neglect Trust Fund; bd. mem. E. Balt. Develop., Inc., Nat. Acad. on Aging; bd. mem., former chair Living Cities; chair NYC Special Adv. Panel on Child Welfare; prog. adv. Edna McConnell Clark Found. Recipient Jane Addams Disting. Leadership award. Office: The Annie E Casey Found 701 Saint Paul St Baltimore MD 21202-2311*

**NELSON, EDITH ELLEN,** dietician; b. Vicksburg, Mich., Sept. 26, 1940; d. Edward Kenneth and Anna (McManus) Rolffs; m. Douglas Keith Nelson; children: Daniel Lee, Jennifer Lynn. BS, Mich. State U., 1962; MEd in Applied Nutrition, U. Cin., 1979. Lic. dietitian, Fla. Clin. dietitian Macon (Ga.) Gen. Hosp., Blodgett Meml. Hosp., Grand Rapids, Mich.; grad. teaching asst. U. Cin., 1978-79; dir. nutrition svcs. Dialysis Clinic, Inc., Cin., 1979-88; cons. dietitian Panama City Devel. Ctr., Ft. Walton Beach Devel. Ctr., Fla., 1988-94; renal dietitian Dialysis Svcs. Fla., Ft. Walton Beach, 1989-92; cons. dietitian N.W. Fla. Community Hosp., Chipley, Fla., 1993-94; Beverly Enterprises, Panama City Beach, 1994-96, pvt. practice, Panama City, Fla., 1996—. Mich. Edn. Assn. scholar, 1958; Nat. Kidney Found. grantee, 1986. Mem. Am. Dietetic Assn., Fla. Dietetic Assn., Panhandle Dist. Dietetic Assn., Nat. Kidney Found. (coun. on renal nutrition, Fla. coun. on renal nutrition), Omicron Nu. Home and Office: 3522 Fox Run Blvd Panama City Beach FL 32408-7151 Personal E-mail: ediepcb@aol.com.

**NELSON, EDWARD GAGE,** brokerage house executive, bank executive, consultant; b. Nashville, May 17, 1931; s. Charles and Polly (Prentiss) N.; m. Carole Olivia Frances Minton, Sept. 17, 1960; children: Carole Gervais, Emily Minton, Ellen Prentiss BA in Polit. Sci., U. of South, Sewanee, Tenn., 1952. Exec. v.p. Clark, Landstreet & Kirkpatrick, Inc., Nashville, 1955-64, Commerce Union Bank, Nashville, 1968-72, pres., 1972-82, cons., 1985—, chmn., CEO, 1982-84; chmn., pres. Nelson Capital Corp., Nashville, 1985—. Hon. consul gen. Japan; bd. dirs. Werthan Packaging, Consumers Ins., Franklin Industries, Trans Arabian Investment Bank, Ctrl. Parking Sys., Ohio Star Forge, Bucyrus Internat., Inc.; mem. 1st adv. coun. Japan/Tenn. Soc. Trustee Vanderbilt U., Nashville, 1979—, chmn. med. ctr. bd., 1984-2003. Spl. agt. U.S. Army, 1955, Japan. Mem. Belle Meade Country Club, River Club (N.Y.C.). Republican. Episcopalian. Home: 1305 Chickering Rd Nashville TN 37215-4521 Office: Nelson Capital Corp 3401 W End Ave Ste 300 Nashville TN 37203-1085

**NELSON, EDWARD HUMPHREY,** architect; b. Winchester, Mass., Sept. 2, 1918; s. Richard MacDonald and Evelyn Miller (Humphrey) N.; m. Lois Whitaker Renouf, Sept. 24, 1948 (dec.); children: Susan, David, Sarah; m. Miriam P. Ketcham, Jan. 2, 1988. Grad., Lenox Sch., 1936; B.Arch., Yale, 1950. Pvt. archtl. practice, Tucson, 1953-61; sr. v.p. CNWC Architects, Tucson, 1961-88, pres., 1989-94; ret., 1994. Mem. adv. com. U. Ariz. Coll. Architecture, 1984-93. Works include: design for Tucson Community Ctr. Pres. Tucson Cmty. Coun., 1969-71, Tucson Art Ctr., 1960; bd. dirs. Tucson Housing Found., 1969-06, Estes Gardens Low Rent Sr. Housing, 2004-05, Tucson Symphony, 1977-84, Tucson United Way, 1980, NBA Tucson Housing, 2002-05, Tucson Art Mus., 1960-74, Tucson Trade Bur., 1976-91, pres., 1984; trustee Green Fields Sch., 1960-74; vestry St. Philips Episc. Ch., 1967-69, sr. warden, 1987-90, parish warden, 1993-94; convenor Episcopal Interparish Coun., 1990-92; mem. Episcopal Diocese of Ariz., S.W. Regional Parish; 1st Phila. City Troop, 1940—, horse cavalry, 1940-42. Served to capt. AUS, 1940-41, WWII, ETO. Decorated Bronze Star with oak leaf cluster, Purple Heart; recipient Disting. Citizen award U. Ariz., 1981, St. Philips medal St. Philips Episc. Ch., 2000. Fellow: AIA (pres. So. Ariz. chpt. 1962, emeritus 1994, chmn. Ariz. Fellows 1986—94); mem.: Ariz. Soc. Archs. (pres. 1963), U. Ariz. Press.'s Club, Yale Club (pres. Tucson chpt. 1962, 1983, dir. 1990—). Home: 2020 E 4th St Tucson AZ 85719-5114 E-mail: miriamned@cox.net.

**NELSON, EDWARD R.,** pianist, composer, educator, consultant; b. Newark, June 14, 1947; s. Sydney L. and Belle K. Nelson. MusB, Manhattan Sch. Music, NYC, 1969, M in Music Edn., 1971, M in Music Performance Piano, 1971. Cert. tchg. NJ, 1970, supervisor NJ, 1974. Music tchr. Bd. Edn., Elizabeth, NJ, 1969—87, chmn. HS music dept., 1982—87, supervisor fine and performing arts, Elizabeth Pub. Sch. Dist., 1987—2000; pvt. tchr., cons., composer NJ, 2000—05. Lectr. in field. Composer: (songs) Music for Band Saxophone, 1988, Pieces for Piano, 1996. Pres. Elizabeth Administrv. and Supervisory Coun., NJ, 1996—2000. Mem.: AARP, Music Educator's Nat. Conf. Achievements include performance or original music Carnegie Hall. Home: 22 Pebble Beach Dr Egg Harbor Township NJ 08234

**NELSON, EDWARD SHEFFIELD,** lawyer, retired utilities executive; b. Keevil, Ark., Feb. 23, 1941; s. Robert Ford and Thelma Jo (Mayberry) N.; m. Mary Lynn McCastlain, Oct. 12, 1962; children: Cynthia, Lynn (dec.), Laura. BS, U. Cen. Ark., 1963; LLB, Ark. Law Sch., 1968; JD, U. Ark., 1969. Mgmt. trainee Ark. La. Gas Co., Little Rock, 1963-64, sales engr., 1964-67, sales coordinator, 1967-69, gen. sales mgr., 1969-71, v.p., gen. sales mgr., 1971-73, pres., dir., 1973-79, pres., chmn., chief exec. officer, 1979-85; ptnr., chmn. bd., chief exec. officer House, Wallace, Nelson & Jewel, Little Rock, 1985-86; pvt. practice law Little Rock, 1986—; of counsel Jack, Lyon & Jones, P.A., 1991—. Bd. dirs. Fed. Res. Mem. N.G., 1957-63, Fellowship Bible Ch.; bd. dirs. U. Ark., Little Rock, vice chmn. bd. visitors, 1981; bd. dirs. Philander Smith Coll., 1981; chmn. Ark. Indsl. Devel. Commn., 1987, 88; past chmn. Little Rock br. Fed. Res. Bd. St. Louis; chmn. Econ. Expansion Study Commn., 1987—; bd. dirs. Ark. Ednl. TV Found., Ark. Game and Fish Commn. Found.; founder, 1st pres. Jr. Achievement Ark., 1987-88; Rep. nominee for Gov. of Ark., 1990, 94; co-state chmn. Ark. Reps., 1991-92, nat. committeeman Ark. GOP, 1993-2000; mem. Ark. Higher Edn. Coord. Bd., 1997-99; apptd. commr. Ark. Game and Fish Commn., 2000—. Named Ark.'s Outstanding Young Man Ark. J. C. of C., 1973; One of Am.'s Ten Outstanding Young Men U.S. Jr. C. of C., 1974; Citizen of Yr. Ark. chpt. March of Dimes, 1983; Humanitarian of Yr. NCCJ, 1983; Best Chief Exec. Officer in Natural Gas Industry Wall Street Transcript, 1983; recipient 1st Disting. Alumnus award U. Cen. Ark., 1987. Mem. Am. Ark., Pulaski County Bar Assns., Ark. C. of C. (dir.), Little Rock C. of C. (dir., pres. 1981), Sales and Mktg. Execs. Assn. (pres. 1975, Top Mgmt. award 1977), U. Ark. Law Sch. Alumni Assn. (pres. 1980), Sigma Tau Gamma (Ben T. Laney Leadership award for leadership and achievement 2000), Ark. Wildlife Fedn. (Conservationist of Yr. 2002), Am. Lung Assn. (Philanthropist of Yr. 2003). Fellowship Bible Ch. Office: 6th and Broadway 3400 TCBY Bldg Little Rock AR 72201 Office Phone: 501-375-1122. Personal E-mail: esn@jlj.com.

**NELSON, ELAINE EDWARDS,** lawyer; b. Waco, Tex., Sept. 16, 1947; d. Bedford Duncan and Joyce (Harlan) Edwards; m. David A. Nelson, Apr. 12, 1969; children: Carol Christine, Harlan Claire. BA, Baylor U., 1969, JD, 1978. Bar: Tex. 1978. Gen. counsel Austin Industries, Inc., Dallas, 1978—. Office: Austin Industries Inc 3535 Travis St Ste 300 Dallas TX 75204-1466 also: PO Box 2879 Dallas TX 75221-2879

**NELSON, ELIZABETH HAWKINS,** not-for-profit association administrator; b. Rockville Centre, NY, Jan. 27, 1931; arrived in Eng., 1951; d. Harry Dadmun and Gretchen (Hawkins) N.; m. Ivan Piercy, Dec. 7, 1960 (div. 1972); children: Catherine, Christopher, Nicholas; m. Claude Jacob Esterson, July 26, 1975 (div. 1998). BA, Middlebury Coll., 1951; PhD, U. London, 1953; DSc (hon.), City London U., 1993; PhD (hon.), Open U., 2003. Rsch. psychologist Mars Ltd., London, 1953-55; dir., mng. dir. rsch. unit Benton & Bowles, London, 1955-64; dir. Mass Observation Ltd., London, 1964-65; founder dir., chmn. Taylor Nelson/Sofres plc, London, 1965-92; chief exec. The Princess Royal Trust for Carers, London, 1992-95; chair coun. U. Roehampton, 1995—2001; chmn. South West London Cmty. NHS Trust, 1997—2002. Non-exec. dir. Royal Bank Scotland, Edinburgh, 1988—97; chmn. bd. UK Ecolabelling, 1992—98; pres. World Assn. Pub. Opinion Rsch., 1990—92; mem. City & Guilds, 1998—; mem. adv. com. on degree awarding powers Quality Assurance Agy., 1998—; chmn. Stargate Capital Investment Group Ltd., 2004—; CEO, Chronic Granulomatous Disorder Rsch. Trust, 2004—; dir. Bright Talk Ltd., 2004—. Vice chair coun. Open U., Milton Keynes, England, 1991—2001; dir. U.S. Open U., 1998—2001; non exec. dir. Bright Talk Ltd.; trustee Jeans for Genes, 2006, Immigration Adv. Svcs, 2005; mem. Doctors and Dentists Pay Rev. Bd., London, 1992—97. Decorated Order Brit. Empire; hon. fellow City & Guilds, 1994, U. Surrey, Roehampton, 2003. Fellow: Royal Soc. Arts, Market Rsch. Soc. (hon.); mem.: Freedom City of London, Internat. Women's Forum (bd. mem. 2001—05), First Forum U.K. Avocations: choral singing, opera, bridge. Home: 57 Home Park Rd London SW19 7HS England Office: 62 Trafalgar Sw London WC2N 5DY England Office Phone: 44 0 208 946 2317. Personal E-mail: liznlson53@aol.com.

**NELSON, ELMER KINGSHOLM, JR., (KIM NELSON),** political scientist, educator, writer, mediator, consultant; b. Laramie, Wyo., Sept. 14, 1922; s. Elmer Kingsholm and Alice (Downey) N.; m. Jane Beckwith Oliver, Aug. 4, 1945; 1 son, Elmer Kingsholm III (Kirk). BA, U. Wyo., 1943, JD, 1948, MA, 1949; Dr. Pub. Adminstrn., U. So. Calif., 1959. Instr. psychology U. Wyo., 1947-49; psychologist, staff psychologist dept. probation Contra Costa County, Calif., 1949-51; sr. psychologist Cal. State Dept. Corrections, San Quentin and Chino Prisons, 1951-52; asst. prof. criminology U. B.C., Can., 1952-54, assoc. prof., 1954-56, head criminology div., 1953-56; warden Haney Correctional Instn., B.C., 1956-58; assoc. dir. Youth Studies Ctr. U. So. Calif., 1958-59, dir. Youth Studies Ctr., 1959-64, assoc. prof. pub. adminstrn., 1958-61, prof., 1961—, dean Sch. Pub. Adminstrn., 1971-76, prof., co-dir. Sacramento Pub. Affairs Ctr.; head Bay Area Research Center, Berkeley, 1979—; prof. emeritus U. So. Calif. Dep. adminstr. Youth and Adult Corrections Agy., State of Calif., Sacramento, 1964-65; interim exec. dir. Office Criminal Justice Planning, spring 1975; dir. Nat. Study Probation and Parole, 1976-77; chmn. task force on corrections, asso. dir. Pres.'s Commn. on Law Enforcement and Adminstrn. of Justice, Washington, 1966-67; dir. nat. study of correctional adminstrn. U. So. Calif. for Joint Commn. on Correctional Manpower and Tng., 1967-69 Co-author: Corrections in America, 1975; contbr. articles, monographs, research reports to profl. jours. Advisor on mgmt. Boys Republic, Chino, Calif., 1967—; bd. dirs., v.p. Am. Justice Inst., Sacramento; bd. dirs. Human Interaction Rsch. Inst., L.A. Recipient Disting. Alumnus award U. Wyo., 1975, Exemplary Alumni award U. Wyo. Coll. Arts and Scis., 1994; Ford Found. Travel Study grantee, 1970-71; E. Kim Nelson endowed doctoral fellowship established at U. So. Calif., 1987. Sr. fellow Nat. Acad. Pub. Adminstrn.; mem. Wyo. Bar Assn., Alpha Tau Omega, Phi Beta Kappa, Phi Kappa Phi, Psi Chi. Home: 355 St Augustine Ct Benicia CA 94510-2866 Personal E-mail: eknscarq@aol.com.

**NELSON, FLORENCE ELY,** civic leader; b. N.Y.C., June 3, 1931; d. Albert H. and Constance (Jennings) Ely; m. Jerry Nelson, Nov. 21, 1964; children: Nicolas Jennings, Thomas Burr, James Pollock. DHL (hon.), Ariz. State U., 1995. Stage, screen technician various theaters, 1949-64. Design cons. Oaxaca Rest/Le Relais, Scottsdale, Ariz., 1986, Corp. Bldg. of Pinnacle Paradise Inc., 1986, pvt. residences, Scottsdale, 1986. Bd. dirs. Ariz. Mus. Sci. and Tech., Phoenix, 1984—, Ballet Ariz., Phoenix, 1985—, Scottsdale Prevention Inst., 1987—; coord. Boy Scouts Am., Ariz., 1977—; mem. Ariz. Opera, 1985; learning leader Paradise Valley Sch. Dist., Ariz., 1987—; mem. Ariz. Astronomy Bd. Recipient Disting. Achievement award Ariz. State U., 1990; mamed Woman of Achievement Jr. League of Ariz., 1987; named to Scottsdale's History Hall of Fame, 2000. Mem. Charter 100 (program chair 1985-86, membership com. 1986-87, v.p. 1987-88), Scottsdale Chairwomen (co-founder), Phoenix Com. Fgn. Relations (founder), Ariz. Assn. Gifted and Talented (hon. bd. dirs. 1986, pres. 1987—), Nat. Space Soc. (bd. dirs. 1984—). Clubs: Troon Golf and Country (Scottsdale), Skyline Golf and Country (Tucson), Pinnacle Peak Golf and Country (Scottsdale). Democrat. Episcopalian. Avocations: scuba diving, bicycling, cross country skiing, cooking.

**NELSON, FREDA NELL HEIN,** librarian; b. Trenton, Mo., Dec. 16, 1929; d. Fred Albert and Mable Carman (Doan) Hein; m. Robert John Nelson, Nov. 1, 1957 (div. Apr. 1984); children: Thor, Hope. Nursing diploma, Trinity Luth. Hosp., Kansas City, Mo., 1950; B. Philosophy, Northwestern U., 1961; MS in Info. and Libr. Sci., U. Ill., 1986. RN. Operating rm. nurse Trinity Luth. Hosp., Kansas City, Mo., 1950-52, Johns Hopkins Hosp., Balt., 1952, Wesley Meml. Hosp., Chgo., 1952-58, Tacoma Gen. Hosp., 1958-59, Chgo. Wesley Hosp., 1959-61; libr. asst. Maple Woods Campus Met. Community Colls., Kansas City, 1987-89, libr., libr. mgr. Blue Springs Campus, 1989-96; ret., 1996. Co-founder Coll. for Kids, Knox Coll., Galesburg, Ill., 1982. Nurses scholar Edgar Bergen Found., 1947; recipient Award of Merit, Chgo. Bd. Health, 1952. Avocations: swimming, walking, cross-word puzzles. Home: 5708 N Polk Dr Kansas City MO 64151

**NELSON, FREDERICK DICKSON,** judge; b. Chgo., Oct. 19, 1931; s. David Aldrich and Mary Ellen (Dickson) N. AB, Hamilton Coll., 1980; JD, Harvard U., 1983. Bar: Ohio 1984. Majority counsel subcom. on criminal law U.S. Senate Judiciary Com., Washington, 1983-85; spl. asst. to asst. atty. gen., Office of Legal Policy U.S. Dept. Justice, Washington, 1985-86, dep. asst. atty. gen., Office of Legal Policy, 1986-87; assoc. Taft, Stettinius & Hollister, Cin., 1988-89; of counsel, 1991-93; assoc. counsel to Pres. of U.S. The White House, Washington, 1989-90. Advisor to govts. of Ukraine and Russia, ABA Ctrl. and East European Law Initiative, 1992-93; adj. prof. constl. law Salmon P. Chase Coll. Law, U. No. Ky., 1994; chief of staff, legal coun. U.S. Rep. Steve Chabot, 1995-97; cons. Constnl. Comm. Albania, per Internat. Rep. Inst., 1998; pres. Civic Solutions, LLC, Cin., 1998-2002; co-creator, panelist Hotseat, Sta. WCPO-TV, (Cin. Channel 9), 2000-02; judge Hamilton County Ct. of Common Pleas, 2003—. Exec. editor Harvard Jour. of Law and Pub. Policy, 1982-83. Mem. Hamilton County Rep. Policy and Appts. Coms., 1999-2002; cons. Chabot for Congress Campaign, Cin., 1994, 98; mem. Ohio Bd. Uniform State Laws, Nat. Conf. Commrs. on Uniform State Laws, 2001—. Harry S. Truman Found. scholar, 1978-81. Mem. NATAS (Ohio Valley chpt.), Federalist Soc., Harvard Club of Cin. (bd. dirs. 1989, 2001-2005), Phi Beta Kappa. Republican. E-mail: fnelson1@cinci.rr.com.

**NELSON, GARY MICHAEL,** lawyer; b. Mpls., July 12, 1951; s. Emery Marshal and Henrietta Margaret (Flategraff) Nelson; m. Deb Snyder; 1 child, Courtney Snyder; children: Rachel Mary, Amy Margaret. BA, Gustavus Adolphus Coll., St. Peter, Minn., 1973; JD, Harvard U., 1976. Bar: Minn. 1976, U.S. Dist. Ct. Minn. 1976. With Oppenheimer Wolff & Donnelly, Mpls., 1976—97, mng. ptnr., 1987—89; mem. policy com., 1989—95, dep. chmn., 1991—93, chair, CEO, 1993—95; exec. v.p., gen. counsel, corp. sec. Ceridian Corp., Mpls., 1997—. Chair corp. practice inst. Minn. Inst. Legal Edn., Mpls., 1978-93. Recipient Significant Contbns. award Am. Girls' Clubs Am., 1982. Mem. ABA, Minn. State Bar Assn., Hennepin County Bar Assn. Corp. Legal Officers Group Lutheran. Avocations: fishing, hunting, hiking, reading. Home: 2685 Maplewood Rd Wayzata MN 55391 Office: Ceridian Corp 3311 E Old Shakopee Rd Minneapolis MN 55425-1640

**NELSON, GENEVIEVE MURPHY,** secondary school educator; b. Phila., May 2, 1963; d. John Joseph and Alice Joan (HcHale) Murphy; m. Robert R. Nelson, Oct. 19, 1985. BA, Cornell U., 1985; MS in Edn., U. Pa., 1989. Cert.

secondary school tchr., Pa. Rsch. technician Sch. of Dental Medicine U. Pa., Phila., 1985-89; tchr. biology Germantown Friends Sch., Phila., 1989—, head sci. dept., 1994—. Commonwealth Partnership Teaching fellow, 1991-94, Woodrow Nat. fellow, 1992; Presdl. award for excellence in math. and sci. tchg., 2001, Radioshack Nat. Tchr. award, 2002. Mem. Nat. Sci. Tchrs. Assn., Nat. Assn. Biology Tchrs. (Outstanding Biology Tchr. award 2006), Cornell Club of Greater Phila. (biotech. edn. com., bd. dirs. 1992). Avocations: cooking, reading. Office: Germantown Friends Sch 31 W Coulter St Philadelphia PA 19144-2898 Office Phone: 215-951-2300. Business E-Mail: genn@gfsnet.org.

**NELSON, GEORGE DRIVER,** astronomer, educator, former astronaut; b. Charles City, Iowa, July 13, 1950; s. George Vernon and Evelyn Elenor (Driver) N.; m. Susan Lynn Howard, June 19, 1971; children: Aimee Tess, Marti Ann. BS, Harvey Mudd Coll., 1972; MS, U. Wash., 1974, PhD, 1978; DSc (hon.), U. Colo., 2000; LHD (hon.), Towson U., 2001. Astronaut NASA, Houston, 1978-89; mission specialist Space Shuttle flight, 1984, 86, 88; assoc. vice provost for rsch., assoc. prof. astronomy U. Wash., Seattle, 1989-96; dir. project 2061 AAAS, Washington, 1996—2000; dir. sci., math., and tech. edn. Western Wash. U., Bellingham, 2002—. Adj. assoc. prof. edn. U. Wash., 1989-96. Recipient Haley Space Flight award AIAA, 1989. Unitarian Universalist. Avocations: reading, athletics, guitar. Office: SMATE Western Wash Univ 516 High St Bellingham WA 98225-9155 Office Phone: 360-650-3637. Business E-Mail: george.nelson@wwu.edu.

**NELSON, GLEN DAVID,** health products executive, physician; b. Mpls., Mar. 28, 1937; s. Andrew and Beatrice S. Nelson; m. Marilyn Carlson, June 30, 1961; children: Diana, Curtis, Wendy. AB, Harvard U., 1959; MD, U. Minn. 1963. Diplomate Am. Bd. Surgery, also sub-bd. bariatric and peripheral vascular surgery; cert. Am. Bd. Surgery, 1970. Intern Hennepin County Gen. Hosp., Mpls., 1963—64, resident in gen. surgery, 1964—69; staff surgeon Park Nicollet Med. Ctr. (formerly St. Louis Park Med. Ctr.), Mpls.; practiced surgery, 1969—86; chmn., pres. and CEO Park Nicollet Med. Ctr., 1975—86; chmn. and CEO Am. MedCenters, Inc., 1982—86; vice chmn. Medtronic, Inc., 1982—2002; chmn., prin. owner GDN Holdings, LLC, Minnetonka, Minn., 2002—. Current bd. dirs. Advanced BioSurfaces, Inc., Cardiovascular Systems, Inc., Carlson Holdings, Inc., Carlson Sch. Mgmt., DexCom, Inc., Harvard Univ. Dean's Coun., Itamar, Inc., Jackson Hole Group, Johns Hopkins Medicine Bd. of Visitors, LifeLinkMD, Minn. Public Radio, MinuteClinic (QuickMedx); dir. & chmn. The Perth Corp., Regent Aviation, Stanford Radiology Med. Imaging Adv. Bd., The St. Paul Co., Inc., Transneuronix, Inc., Univ.; Emeritus clinical prof. surgery, U. Minn.

**NELSON, GORDON LEIGH,** chemist, educator; b. Palo Alto, Calif., May 27, 1943; s. Nels Feike and Alice Virginia (Fredrickson) N. BS in Chemistry, U. Nev., 1965; MS, Yale U., 1967, PhD, 1970; DSc (hon.), William Carey Coll., 1988. Staff research chemist corp. research and devel. Gen. Electric Co., Schenectady, NY, 1970-74, mgr. combustibility tech. plastics div. Pittsfield, Mass., 1974-79, mgr. environ. protection plastics div., 1979-82; v.p. materials sci. and tech. Springborn Labs. Inc., Enfield, Conn., 1982-83; prof. chmn. dept. polymer sci. U. So. Miss., Hattiesburg, 1983-89; dean Coll. Sci. and Liberal Arts, prof. chemistry Fla. Inst. Tech., Melbourne, 1989—, mem. coun. sci., soc. pres., sec., 1989-90, chair-elect, 1991, chair, 1992. Cons. in field. Author: Carbon-13 Nuclear Magnetic Resonance for Organic Chemists, 1972, Carbon-13 Nuclear Magnetic Resonance for Organic Chemists, 2d edit., 1980; co-author: Polymeric Materials-Chemistry for the Future, 1989, Carbon Monoxide and Human Lethality, 1993; editor: Fire and Polymers-Materials and Tests for Hazard Prevention, 1990, 1995; co-editor: Fire and Polymers-Materials and Solutions for Hazard Prevention, 2001, Fire and Polymer IVs-Materials and Solutions for Hazard Prevention, 2005, editor books on coating sci. tech.; contbr. articles to profl. jours. Mem.: ASTM (E5 cert. of appreciation 1985, D1 1997), Soc. Advancement of Scandinavian Study, Coun. Colls Arts and Scis., Soc. Plastics Industry (structural plastics divsn., Man of Yr. 1979), Internat. Electrotech. Commn. (U.S. tech. adv. group on info. processing equipment), Soc. Soc. for Coatings Tech., Ctr. Sci. Tech. and the Media (bd. dir. 1991—94), Info. Tech. Industry Coun. (chmn. plastics task group), Am. Chem. Soc. (bd. dirs. 1977—85, 1987—89, pres. 1988, bd. dirs. 1992—94, 1st Nelson award Orlando sect. 1996, Charles Holmes Herty medal Ga. sect. 1998), Am. Inst. Chemists, Nev. Hist. Soc., Yale Chemists Assn. (pres. 1981—), Sigma Xi. Republican. Presbyterian. Avocations: travel, western U.S. history. Office: Fla Inst Tech Coll Sci & Liberal Arts 150 W University Blvd Melbourne FL 32901-6975 Office Phone: 321-674-7260.

**NELSON, GRANT STEEL,** law educator; b. Mitchell, SD, Apr. 18, 1939; s. Howard Steel and Clara Marie (Winandy) N.; m. Judith Ann Haugen, Sept. 22, 1962; children: Mary Elizabeth, Rebekah Anne, John Adam. BA magna cum laude, U. Minn., 1960; JD cum laude, 1963. Bar: Minn. 1963, Mo. 1971. Assoc. Faegre & Benson, Mpls., 1963-67; mem. law faculty U. Mo., Columbia, 1967-91, assoc. prof., 1970-72, prof., 1972-91, Enoch H. Crowder prof. law, 1974-91; prof. UCLA, 1991—. Bd. legal advisors St. Plains Legal Found., 1978-85; vis. asst. prof. U. Mich., Ann Arbor, 1969-70, Brigham Young U., Provo, Utah, 1976; vis. prof. U. Minn., Mpls., 1981-82, UCLA, 1989-90; disting. vis. prof. Pepperdine U., 1987-88, 2006; vis. endowed Campbell prof. U. Mo., Columbia, 1996-98; commr. Nat. Conf. Commrs. Uniform State Laws, 1983-91; adv. bd. West Pub. Law Sch Author: (with Van Hecke and Leavell) Cases and Materials on Equitable Remedies and Restitution, 1973; (with Whitman) Cases and Materials on Real Estate Finance and Development, 1976, Cases and Materials on Real Estate Transfer, Finance and Development, 1981, (with Osborne and Whitman) Real Estate Finance Law, 1979, (with Leavell and Love) Cases and Materials on Equitable Remedies and Restitution, 1980; (with Whitman) Land Transactions and Finance, 1983, 4th edit., 2004, Real Estate Finance Law, 1985, 4th edit., 2001, Cases and Materials on Real Estate Transfer, Finance and Development, 1987, 7th edit., 2006; (with Leavell, Love and Kovacic-Fleischer) Cases and Materials on Equitable Remedies, Restitution and Damages, 1986, 7th edit., 2005; (with Browder, Cunningham, Stoebuck and Whitman) Basic Property Law, 1989; (with Stoebuck and Whitman) Contemporary Property, 1996, rev. edit., 2002; co-reporter ALI Restatement of Property-Mortgages; contbr. articles to profl. jours. 1st It. AUS, 1964-65. Recipient award for meritorious service and achievement U. Mo. Law Sch. Found., 1974, Disting. Faculty Svc. award U. Mo.-Columbia Alumni Assn., 1978, Disting. Faculty award 1986, Disting. Non-Alumnus award, 1991, Rutter award UCLA Law Sch., 2000, Disting. Tchg. award UCLA Alumni Assn., 2002. Mem. Am. Law Inst., Assn. Am. Law Schs. (sect. chmn. 1976-77), Am. Coll. Real Estate Lawyers, Am. Coll. Mortgage Attys., Mo. Bar Assn. (vice chmn. property law coun. 1974-75, chmn. 1975-77), Order of Coif, Phi Beta Kappa, Phi Delta Phi. Office: UCLA Sch Law Hilgard Ave PO Box 951476 Los Angeles CA 90095-1476 Office Phone: 310-206-3154. Business E-Mail: nelson@law.ucla.edu.

**NELSON, H. WAYNE,** gerontologist, advocate; s. Hubert Wayne Nelson and Sandra Lynn Scott; m. Ela A. Alivio, Aug. 8, 2005; children: Cameron W., Sarah E. MA in History, Portland State U., 1980; MA in Humanities, Calif. State U., Dominguez Hills, 1982; MBA, City Coll., Bellevue, Wash., 1984; PhD, Oreg. State U., 1993. asst. to Gov. Victor Atiyeh Gov.'s Office, Salem, Oreg., 1983—85; dep. state long-term care ombudsman Oreg. Office Long-Term Care Ombudsman, Salem, 1985—87, acting state ombudsman, 1987—89; dep. dir., 1987—98; assoc. prof. health sci. Towson (Md.) U., 1998—. Cons. Nat. Citizen's Coalition Nursing Home Reform, Nat. Long-Term Care Ombudsman Resource Ctr., Washington, 1998—; cons., annual report author Natonal Assn. State Ombudsman Programs, Washington, 2002—; cons., trainer numerous state aging programs; spkr. in field. Author: (book) Elder Advocacy: Essential Practice and Skills Across Settings; contbr. entries to encys., articles to profl. jours. Dep. comdr. 10th med. regiment Mil. Dept. Md., Pikesville Military Reservation, 2001—06; founder Balt. County Med. Emergency Volunteers, 2003—06. Decorated Oreg. N.G. Commendation medal Gov., Oreg. N.G. Meritorious Svc. medal, Oreg. N.G. Exceptional Svc. medal, Wash. Army N.G. Commendation medal Mil. Dept. Md., Wash. State Active Duty medal Mil. Dept. Md., Md. N.G. Meritoriious Svc. medal with Oak Leaf Cluster Gov.; recipient Iris award, Ky. Cabinet Human Resources; fellow, Nat. Inst. Aging, 1996. Fellow: Gerontol. Soc. Am. (life; chair elect fellowship com., social rsch. and pub. policy sect. 2002—06). Avocation: emergency public health service. Office: Towson U 8000 York Rd Towson MD 21252 Office Phone: 410-704-4845. Personal E-mail: wnelson@towson.edu.

**NELSON, HAROLD BERNHARD,** museum director; b. Providence, May 14, 1947; s. Harold B. and Eleanor (Lavina) N. BA, Bowdoin Coll., 1969; MA, U. Del., 1972. Rsch. fellow NMAA Smithsonian Inst., Washington, 1976-77; curator Am. art Mus. Art & Archeol., U. Mo., Columbia, 1977-79; registrar Solomon R. Guggenheim Mus., N.Y.C., 1979-83; exhibition program dir. Am. Fedn. Arts, N.Y.C., 1983-89; dir. Long Beach (Calif.) Mus. of Art, 1989—. Juror Mus. Art, Sci. & Industry, Bridgeport, Conn., 1988, Clark County Dist. Libr., Las Vegas, Nev., 1984; speaker Am. Assn. Mus. Annual Conf., Detroit, 1985, Western Mus. Conf., Portland, Oreg., 1987, Grantmakers in Art Symposium, N.Y.C., 1986, Western Mus. Conf., Salt Lake City, 1985; adv. com. APA, Assn. Sci. and Tech. Ctrs.; panelist Aid to Spl. Exhibitions, NEA, Washington, 1986; participant Am. Legal Assn., ABA Conf., San Francisco, 1986; observer, respondent Mus. Symposium, NEA, Dallas, 1985. Author: Sounding the Depths: 150 Years of American Seascape, 1989, New Visions: Selina Trieff, 1997, Bountiful Harvest: American Decorative Arts from the Gail-Oxford Collection, 1997, For a New Nation: American Decorative Arts from the Gail-Oxford Collection, 1998, In Ye Grandest Manner and After Ye Newest Fashion, 2000, Conjunction: The Melba and Al Langman Collection, 2000, Tulips, Pomegranates and Kings: Delftware from the Collection of Benjamin F. Edwards III, 2000, Imps on a Bridge: Wedgwood Fairyland and Other Lustres, 2001, The Enamels of Annemarie Davidson, 2004, For the People: American Folk Art From the Collection of Thomas H. Oxford and Victor Gail, 2004, Engaging Nature: Contemporary Baskets From the Collection of Lloyd and Margit Cotsen, 2005, Crossing Boundries: The Ceramic Sculpture of Mineo Mizuno, 2005, Greene & Greene in Long Beach, 2005, Painting with Fire: Masters of Enameling in America 1930-1980, 2005. Office: Long Beach Mus Art 2300 E Ocean Blvd Long Beach CA 90803-2442 Office Phone: 562-439-2119.

**NELSON, HERBERT LEROY,** psychiatrist; b. Eddyville, Iowa, June 15, 1922; s. Albert and Bessie Mae (Durham) Nelson; m. Carol Lorayne Hofert, Dec. 23, 1943; children: Richard Kent, Vicki Lurae, Thadeus Leroy, Cylda Vermae. BA, U. Iowa, 1943, MD, 1946. Diplomate Am Bd Psychiatry and Neurology. Intern Univ Hosps. of U. Iowa, Iowa City, 1946-47; resident Brooke Army Med. Ctr, Fort Sam Houston, Tex., 1947-49, U.S. VA Hosp., Knoxville, Iowa, 1949-51, Oreg. State Hosp., Salem, 1951-52, clin. dir., 1952-63; asst. prof. psychiatry U. Iowa, Iowa City, 1963-66, assoc. prof., 1966-73, prof., 1973-84, prof. emeritus, 1984—; dir. Iowa Mental Health Authority, Iowa City, 1968-82; med. dir. Mideast Iowa Community Mental Health Ctr., Iowa City, 1969-84. Adj prof Tulane Univ, New Orleans, 1974—77. Co-author: 4 monographs; contbr. articles to profl jours. Served as capt MC U.S. Army, 1947—49. Fellow: Am Psychiat Asn; mem.: AMA, Am Col Mental Health Adminrs, Am Assn Psychiat Adminrs, Johnson County Med Soc, Iowa Psychiat Soc (pres 1970—71, chmn subcom psychiat care 1973—77). Republican. Methodist. Avocations: gardening, fishing, woodworking, painting, travel. Home and Office: Melrose Meadows #1009 350 Dublin Dr Iowa City IA 52246 E-mail: hlnelson@mchsi.com.

**NELSON, HOWARD JOSEPH,** geographer, educator; b. Gowrie, Iowa, Jan. 12, 1919; s. Joseph A. and Hannah (Swanson) N.; m. Betty Marie Garlick, June 18, 1944; children: Linda Ann, James Allan. BA with high honors, Iowa State Tchrs. Coll., 1942; MA, U. Chgo., 1947, PhD, 1949. Mem. faculty UCLA, 1949—, prof. geography, 1963-86, prof. emeritus, 1986—, chmn. dept., 1966-71. Author: (with W.A.V. Clark) Los Angeles, The Metropolitan Experience, 1976, The Los Angeles Metropolis, 1983. Served with AUS, 1943-46. Mem. Assn. Am. Geographers (regional councillor 1968-71), Sigma Xi. Home: 3939 Walnut Ave #162 Carmichael CA 95608 Office: Univ Calif Dept Geography Los Angeles CA 90024

**NELSON, IVORY VANCE,** academic administrator; b. Curtis, La., June 11, 1934; s. Elijah H. and Mattie (White) N.; m. Patricia Robbins, Dec. 27, 1985; children: Cherlyn, Karyn, Eric Beatty, Kim Beatty. BS with distinction, Grambling (La.) State U., 1959; PhD with distinction, U. Kans., 1963. Assoc. prof. chemistry So. U., Baton Rouge, 1963-67, head div. sci., 1966-68; prof. chemistry Prairie View (Tex.) A&M U., 1968-83, asst. acad. dean, 1968-72, v.p. rsch., 1972-82, acting pres., 1982-83; exec. asst. Tex. A&M U. System, College Station, 1983-86; chancellor Alamo C.C. Dist., San Antonio, 1986-92; pres. Cen. Wash. U., Ellensburg, 1992-99, Lincoln U., Pa., 1999—. DuPont teaching fellow U. Kans., 1959; rsch. chemist Am. Oil Co., 1962; sr. rsch. chemist Union Carbide Co., 1969; vis. prof. U. Autonomous Guadalajara, Mex., 1966, Loyola U., 1967; Fulbright lectr., 1966; cons. evaluation coms. Oak Ridge (Tenn.) Assoc. Univs., NSF, Nat. Coun. for Accreditation Tchr. Edn., So. Assn. Colls. and Schs.; mem. regional policy coms. on minorities Western Interstate Com. on Higher Edn., 1986-88; mem. exec. com. Nat. Assn. State Univs. and Land Grant Colls., 1980-82. Contbr. articles to profl. jours. Bd. dirs. Target 90, Goals San Antonio, 1987-89, coun. of pres.NAIDA,(1993-96) Commn. on Student Learning, Wash., 1992—, United Way San Antonio, 1987-89, Alamo Area coun. Boy Scouts Am., 1987-89, San Antonio Symphony Soc., 1987-91, Key Bank of Wash.; mem. bd. dirs. assn. Western U., (1995—) mem. com. for jud. reform State of Tex., 1991; mem. edn. adv. bd. Tex. Rsch. Park, 1987-89; bd. givs. Am. Inst. for character Edn., Inc., 1988-91; mem. adv. com. Tex. Ho. of Reps., 1978; chmn. United Way Campaign Tex. A&M U. System, 1984, others. Staff sgt. USAF, 1951-55, Korea. T.H. Harris scholar Grambling State U., 1959; fellow Nat. Urban League, 1969; finalist Pulitzer for general non-fiction, 1992. Mem. AAAS, Am. Chem. Soc. Tex. Acad. Sci., NAACP, Phi Beta Kappa, Sigma Xi, Phi Lambda Upsilon, Beta Kappa Chi, Alpha Mu Gamma, Kappa Delta Pi, Sigma Pi Sigma, Omega Psi Phi, Sigma Pi Phi, Phi Kappa Phi. Avocations: fishing, photography, sports. Office: Lincoln U Office of Pres PO Box 179 Lincoln University PA 19352-0999 Business E-mail: inelson@lincoln.edu.

**NELSON, JACK LEE,** education educator; b. Cheyenne, Wyo., Nov. 2, 1932; s. Myron Alfred and Mary Elizabeth (Baker) N.; m. Gwen Margret Names, Mar. 13, 1953; children: Jean Nelson Vollmer, Steven Lee. BA, U. Denver, 1954; MA, Calif. State U.-Los Angeles, 1958; Ed.D., U. So. Calif., 1961. Tchr. pub. schs., Riverside, Calif., 1956-58; instr. Calif. State U., Los Angeles, 1958-63; asst. prof., 1959-63; instr. Citrus Community Coll., Glendora, Calif., 1959-63; assoc. prof. SUNY, Buffalo, 1963-68, chmn. dept., 1966-68; prof. edn. Rutgers U., New Brunswick, NJ, 1968—, Disting. prof., 1975; dean, prof. Sch. Edn. San Jose (Calif.) State U., 1986-87. Chmn. dept. sci. and humanities edn. Rutgers U., 1972-75; vis. prof. Cambridge U., Eng., 1974, 75, 79, 80, 83, 84, 85; vis. scholar U. Calif., Berkeley, 1975-76, Stanford U., 1982-83, Western Australia Inst. Tech., 1985, U. Colo., 1989, U. Wash., 1993, U. Sydney, Australia, 1994-95, 2003, Edith Cowan U., Australia, 1997; cons. editor Random House Inc., McGraw-Hill Inc., Primis Pubs.; cons. author Scott, Foresman Publs.; mem. adv. coun. New World Dictionary; mem. San Diego County Supt. Com. on Tchr. Quality, 2000—. Author: (with J. Michaelis) Secondary Social Studies, 1980, (with V. Green) International Human Rights, 1980, (with Frank Besag) Foundations of Education, 1984, (with S. Palonsky and M. McCarthy) Critical Issues in Education, 1990, 5th edit., 2004; contbr. numerous articles to profl. jours.; editor: Social Sci. Rsch., 1964-68, Theory and Rsch. in Social Edn., 1982-85. Mem. exec. bd. ACLU, Middlesex County, N.J., 1968-83; mem. Erie County Dem. Com., 1967-68, N.J. Gov.'s Task Force on Edn. for Prisoners, 1970-74; mem. Highland Park Bd. Edn., N.J., 1972-75, pres., 1974-75; mem. Highland Park Hist. Commn., 1980-86; mem. nat. panel Project Censored, 1976—; mem. N.J. Rural Adv. Commn., 1992—, Carlsbad Sister Cities Commn., 2002-05, Carlsbad Sr. Citizen Commn., 2005—. Robert Taft Found. grantee Inst. in Govt., 1970, 86; Inst. for World Order grantee Rutgers U., 1973; Rutgers U. grantee; SUNY-Buffalo grantee, 1967-68; ACLU of N.J. grantee, 1972-73; US. Office Edn. grantee, 1967-68; N.J. Dept. Higher Edn. grantee, 1985-86 Mem. Am. Acad. Polit. and Social Sci., AAUP (editorial bd. 1977-80, rep. nat. council 1982-85, com. on acad. freedom and tenure 1983-86, com. on legis.

affairs 1992-95, 96-99, exec. bd., state confs. 1996-98), Am. Ednl. Research Assn., Internat. Studies Assn., Nat. Council for Social Studies, Social Sci. Edn. Consortium (bd. dirs. 1983-85), Phi Delta Kappa Home: 1360 Las Flores Dr Carlsbad CA 92008-1031 Office: Rutgers U Grad Sch Edn Rutgers U Grad Sch Edn New Brunswick NJ 08903 Business E-Mail: junelson@rci.rutgers.edu.

**NELSON, JAMES ALONZO,** radiologist, educator; b. Cherokee, Iowa, Oct. 20, 1938; s. Joe George and Ruth Geraldine (Jones) N.; m. Katherine Metcalf, July 16, 1966; children: John Metcalf, Julie Heaps. AB, Harvard U., 1961, MD, 1965. Asst. prof. radiology U. Calif., San Francisco, 1972-74; assoc. prof. U. Utah, Salt Lake City, 1974-79, prof., 1979-86, U. Wash., Seattle, 1986-2000, prof. emeritus, 2000—04; ptnr. Integra Ventures, Seattle, 2004. Dir. radiol. rsch. U. Calif./Ft. Miley VA Hosp., 1973—74, U. Utah, 1974—85, U. Wash., 1986—98; mem. bd. sci. advisors NeoVision, 1995—96, Oreg. Life Scis., 1995—; co-founder Circulation, Inc., 1996; mem. adv. panel on non-radioactive diagnostic agts. USP, 1984—96; mem. NIH RSN study sect., 1996—; RSN study sect., 1984—2004. Contbr. chpts. to books, articles to Am. Jour. Roentgenology, Radiology, Investigative Radiology, others. Capt. USAF, 1967-69. John Harvard scholar, 1957-61, James Picker Found. scholar, 1973-77; recipient Mallinkrodt prize Soc. Body Computerized Tomography, 1990, Roscoe Miller award Soc. Gastrointestinal Radiology, 1991. Fellow Am. Coll. Radiology (diplomate); mem. Radiol. Soc. N.Am., Assn. Univ. Radiology. Achievements include patents (with others) for Non-Surgical Peritoneal Lavage, Recursive Band-Pass Filter for Digital Angiography, for Unsharp Masking for Chest Films, Oral Hepatobiliary MRI Contrast Agent, non-surgical myocardial revascularization, magnetic gut motility monitor. Office: Integra Ventures 300 E Pine Seattle WA 98122 Office Phone: 206-832-1995. Business E-Mail: jalonzonel@comcast.net, nelson@integraventures.net.

**NELSON, JAMES C,** state supreme court justice; b. Moscow, Idaho, Feb. 20, 1944; m. Chari Werner; 2 children. BS, U. Idaho, 1966; JD cum laude, George Washington U., 1974. Fin. analyst SEC, Washington, 1970—73; pvt. practice Werner, Nelson and Epstein, Cut Bank, Mont., 1974—93; county atty. Glacier County, 1980—93; assoc. justice Mont. Supreme Ct., 1993—. Former mem. State Bd. Oil and Gas Conservation, also chmn.; former mem. State Gaming Adv. Counsel, Gov. Adv. Coun. on Corrections and Criminal Justice Policy; liaison to Commn. of Cts. of Ltd. Jurisdiction, mem. adv. com. Ct. Assessment Program. Former mem. Cut Bank Chamber of Commerce. First lieutenant U.S. Army, 1966—69. Office: Supreme Ct PO Box 203004 Helena MT 59620*

**NELSON, JAMES CARMER, JR.,** writer, editor, advertising executive; b. Denver, Nov. 10, 1921; s. James Carmer and Helen (McClelland) N.; m. Mary-Armour Ransom, Sept. 9, 1950; children: James Carmer III, Marie-Louise Nelson Graves, Jeffrey Armour, Sophia McClelland (dec.), Rebecca McClelland Nelson Sulla. AB, Yale, 1943. Mktg. editor Bus. Week mag., N.Y.C., 1946-48, illustration editor, 1948-52; freelance author Sonoma, Calif., 1952-57; copy chief Hoefer, Dieterich & Brown, Inc., San Francisco, 1957-59, v.p., creative dir., 1959-66, exec. v.p., 1966-76, pres., 1976-79, vice chmn., 1979-80; ptnr. John H. Hoefer & Assocs., 1972—82; vice chmn. Chiat/Day/Hoefer, 1980; pvt. advt. cons., 1980—87. Bd. dir. McKinney, Inc., Phila.; instr. Golden Gate Coll., San Francisco, 1958-59, Nat. Advt. Rev. Bd., 1971-75. Author: The Trouble With Gumballs, 1957, Great Cheap Wines: A Poorperson's Guide, 1977, Great Wines Under $5, 1983, Killing Dave Henderson, etc., 2006; contbr. articles and fiction to popular mags. Mem. Harold Brunn Soc. Med. Rsch., Mt. Zion Hosp., San Francisco; bd. assocs. Linus Pauling Inst. Sci. and Medicine, Palo Alto, Calif.; mem. Colony Found., New Haven; trustee Coro Found., 1965-75, Marin Art Complex; bd. mgrs. Marin County YMCA. Served with USNR, 1942-46. Mem. ASCAP. Clubs: Villa Taverna (San Francisco). Home: 649 Idylberry Rd San Rafael CA 94903-1231

**NELSON, JAMES HAROLD,** health sciences administrator; b. Gosnell, Ark., Apr. 26, 1936; s. J.D. and Louise (Gann) N.; m. Betty Sue Leonard, Sept. 21, 1974; children: Amelia Rebecca, Rachel Louise. BS, Ark. State U., 1961, MS, 1969; PhD, Okla. State U., 1972. Br. chief U.S Army Environ. Hygiene Agy., Edgewood, Md., 1972-76; from rsch. area mgr. to div. chief U.S. Army Biomed. R & D Lab., Fort Detrick, Md., 1976-92; project mgr. applied med. systems U.S Army Med. Materiel Devel. Activity, Fort Detrick, Md., 1992-96, dir., 1996-2000; chief liaison office U.S. Army Med. Rsch. & Materiel Command, U.S. Army Med. Dept. Ctr. and Sch., Fort Sam Houston, Tex., 2000—. Mem. Fed. Work Group Pest Mgmt., Washington, 1977-81; chmn. equipment com. Armed Forces Pest Mgmt. Bd., Washington, 1979-83; cons. dir. engrs. Ft. Detrick, 1976-2000; guest lectr. Acad. Health Scis., U.S. Army, Ft. Sam Houston, Tex., 1986-88. Contbr. articles to profl. jours.; assoc. editor: Jour. Am. Mosquito Control Assn., 1982-88; chmn. editorial bd.: Equipment & Insecticides-Mosquito Control, 1989. With USN, 1954-58. Recipient numerous commendations U.S. Army, Ft. Detrick, 1981-2000, R&D Achievement award Asst. Sec. of the Army, 1988, Order of Mil. Med. Merit, 1992. Mem. AAAS, AMVETS, Am. Pub. Health Assn., Assn. Mil. Surgeons U.S., Am. Legion, N.Y. Acad. Scis., Sigma Xi (pres. 1987-88). Presbyterian. Achievements include patent for far-forward surgical table. Home: 1315 Brook Bluff San Antonio TX 78248-2632 Office: US Army Med Res & Materiel Command US Army Med Dept Ctr & Sch 1400 E Grayson St Ste 303E Fort Sam Houston TX 78234-6100 Office Phone: 210-221-9498. E-mail: james.nelson@amedd.army.mil, nelsonjh@sbcglobal.net.

**NELSON, JENNIFER,** elementary school educator; BA in Elem. Edn., Catawba Coll., Salisbury, NC, 1995. Tchr. kindergarten Rowan Salisbury Sch. Sys., Woodleaf, NC, 1996—. Mem.: NCAE (ar 2004—06). Office: Woodleaf Elem Sch 9055 School St Woodleaf NC 27054 Office Phone: 704-278-2203. Office Fax: 704-278-2204. E-mail: nelsonjl@rss.k12.nc.

**NELSON, JOANN,** secondary school educator, educational consultant; b. Little Rock, Arkansas, July 11, 1943; d. Lucinda Nelson. BA cum laude (hon.), Philander Smith Coll., Little Rock, 1962—66; EdM, Cleveland State U., 1977—79. Cert. tchg. Ark., 1966; Ohio, 1966, 1987. English tchr. Cleve. Pub. Sch., 1966—78, dept. chmn., English, reading and language arts, 1978—96. Cons., Cleve., 1996—. Rec. sec. Neighborhood St. Club, Cleve., 1978—96. Mem.: Greater Cleve. Roundtable, Metro Cleve. Alliance of Black Sch. Educators, Nat. Coun. of Negro Women, Nat. Coun. of Teachers of English. Democrat. Baptist. Achievements include city wide lesson plans, Cleve. Pub. Sch. 1982; students' performance and reading tests, Cleve. Pub. Sch., 1986; proficiency test coord.,Cleve. Pub. Sch., 1994. Avocations: reading, theater, photography, travel, collecting brass and crystal. E-mail: njoann1@aol.com.

**NELSON, JOHN C.,** obstetrician, gynecologist; b. 1944; m. Linda Nelson; 8 children. MPH, U. Utah, 1993, MD. Diplomate Am. Bd. Ob-Gyn. Intern Providence Hosp., Portland, Oreg.; resident U. Utah Sch. of Medicine. Charter mem. Prospective Payment Assessment Commn.; dep. dir. Utah's Dept. of Health; leader govs. task force on child abuse and neglect, teenage pregnancy prevention. Com. mem. Utah Domestic Violence adv. com.; former mem. Salt Lake City Boys and Girls Club. Served in U.S. Army. Recipient Light of Learning award Utah State Office of Edn. Fellow Am. Coll. of Ob-Gyn.; mem. AMA (bd. trustees 1994-, sec-treas. 2002-04, pres-elect 2004, pres. 2004-05, immediate past pres. 2005-), Utah Med. Assn. (former pres.), Salt Lake County Med. Soc. (past pres.), Motion Picture Assn. Am. TV Parental Guidelines Monitoring Bd. Office: 370 9th Ave Ste 101 Salt Lake City UT 84103-3186 also: AMA 515 N State St Chicago IL 60610-4325*

**NELSON, JOHN HARRISON,** mathematics educator; b. Lubbock, Tex., Apr. 3, 1954; s. Orval Earl and Nancy Ann Nelson. BS, U. Montevallo, Ala., 1983—85. Cert. tchr. Tex. State Bd., 1999. Chemistry tchr. Russellville HS, Ala., 1985—87; math./sci. tchr. Brandon Hall Sch., Atlanta, 1987—93; math./sci. tchr. Iola HS, Tex., 1994—. Sgt. U.S. Army, 1972—75, Neu-Ulm, Germany. Recipient Sr. Elite, U. Montevallo, 1985. Avocations: tennis, coin

collecting/numismatics, puzzles. Home: 502 Southwest Pky #902 College Station TX 77840 Office: Iola HS 7237 Fort Worth St Iola TX 77861 Personal E-mail: jnelson3454@hotmail.com. Business E-Mail: jnelson@iolaisd.net.

**NELSON, JOHN HOWARD (JACK HOWARD NELSON),** journalist; b. Talladega, Ala., Oct. 11, 1929; s. Howard Alonzo and Barbara Lena (O'Donnell) N.; m. Virginia Dare Dickinson, Aug. 4, 1951 (div. Nov. 1974); children: Karen Dare, John Michael, Steven Howard; m. Barbara Joan Matusow, Dec. 7, 1974. Student, Ga. State Coll., 1953—57. Reporter Biloxi (Miss.) Daily Herald, 1947-51, Atlanta Constitution, 1952-65; so. bur. chief L.A. Times, Atlanta, 1965-70, with Washington bur., 1970—, Washington bur. chief, 1975-96, chief Washington corr., 1996—2002. Author: (with Gene Roberts, Jr.) The Censors and the Schools, 1963, (with Jack Bass) The Orangeburg Massacre, 1970, (with R.J. Ostrow) The FBI and the Berrigans, 1972, Captive Voices, Shocken Books, 1974, Terror in the Night, 1993. With AUS, 1951-52. Recipient Pulitzer prize for local reporting under deadline pressure, 1960; Drew Pearson award for gen. excellence in investigative reporting, 1974; Nieman fellow Harvard U., 1961-62, Shorenstein fellow Harvard U., 2002. Mem. The Gridiron Club. Home: 4 Wynkoop Ct Bethesda MD 20817-5936

**NELSON, JOHN KEITH,** electrical engineer, educator; b. Oldham, Lancashire, Eng., July 3, 1943; s. John Collins and Joyce Palfrey (Simmons) N.; m. Christine Anne Baker, Feb. 10, 1968; children: David John, Peter Mark. BS in Engring., U. London, 1965, PhD, 1969. Chartered profl. engr., Inst. Elec. Engrs. (U.K.). Rsch. fellow U. London, 1966-69; lectr., 1969-78, reader, 1978-79; rsch. mgr. GE, Schenectady, NY, 1979-82; prof. elec. power engring. Rensselaer Poly. Inst., Troy, NY, 1982—, Philip Sporn prof., 2001—, head dept., 1987—2001. Examiner U. Sri Lanka, 1970—85; cons. in field. Contbr. articles to profl. jours.; patentee in field. Recipient Snell premium, IEE, London, 1972, J.R. Beard award, 1976, Rsch. award, Brit. Coun., 1974, 76, Travel award, Royal Soc., London, 1976, Power Engring. Educator award Edison Elec. Inst., 1994, Fellowship award Am. Soc. Nondestructive Testing, 1997. Fellow: IEEE (tech. v.p. Dielectrics and Elec. Insulation Soc. 1991—92, Whitehead Meml. lectr. 1993, adminstrv. v.p. 1993—94, pres. 1995—96, tech. activities bd. 1995—96, membership devel. com. 1997—, Hans Tropper meml. lectr. 2002, Forster Disting. Svc. award 1998, Millennium medal 2000), Inst. Elec. Engrs. (U.K.). Episcopalian. Avocations: squash, sailing, scuba diving, flying. Office: Rensselaer Poly Inst Dept Elec Comp and Sys Engring Troy NY 12180-3590 Office Phone: 518-276-6329. Business E-Mail: k.nelson@ieee.org.

**NELSON, JOHN MARSHALL,** medical information services company executive; b. Madison, Wis., Oct. 28, 1941; s. Russell Arthur and Dorothea (Smith) N.; m. Linda Taylor, Oct. 13, 1962 (div. June 1968); children: Ann, David; m. Katherine Dianne Hoagland, Sept. 24, 1972; children: James, George AB, Harvard Coll., 1963; MD, Case Western Reserve U., 1967; MBA, U. Chgo., 1983. Diplomate Am. Bd. Internal Medicine. Staff assoc. NIH, Bethesda, Md., 1968-71; rsch. assoc., asst. prof. medicine Promis Lab. Med. Sch. U. Vt., 1973-76; med. dir. Madison Gen. Hosp., 1976-84; assoc. clin. prof. Med. Sch. U. Wis., 1976-84; v.p. corp. med. affairs Gen. Health Mgmt. Co., Madison, 1984-86; dir. med. and ednl. affairs Washington Hosp. Ctr., 1986-87; founder, pres. Nelson Info. Systems, Bethesda, Md., 1987—; co-founder, pres. JournalDoc, Bethesda, 2002—. Cons. Med. Sch. U. Utah, Salt Lake City, 1985-86; med. reviewer FDA, 1990-91. Contbr. articles to profl. jour. Coach youth soccer, 1984-85; merit badge counselor Boy Scouts Am., 1987; mem. Harvard Schs. Com., Md., 1988-91; vestry St. John's Episcopal Ch., Bethesda, 1988-91. Harvard Hon. Nat. Scholar, 1959-62; recipient Steuer Meml. award Case Western Reserve U., Cleve., 1967; grantee Nat. Inst. Medicine, NIH, 1992-97. Fellow ACP, Am. Coll. Physician Execs.; mem. AMA, Alpha Omega Alpha. Republican. Episcopalian. Avocations: swimming, reading, bicycling. Home: 6616 Millwood Rd Bethesda MD 20817-6058 Office: 4740 Chevy Chase Dr Chevy Chase MD 20815-6461

**NELSON, JOHN WOOLARD,** neurology educator, physician; b. Hagerstown, Ind., Mar. 9, 1928; s. John Hans and Marvel May (Woolard) N.; m. Nancy Louise Elam, July 21, 1966; 1 son, John Hancock. AB, Earlham Coll., 1950; MD, Ind. U., 1953. Diplomate Am. Bd. Psychiatry and Neurology. Instr. neurology U. Tenn. Coll. Medicine, 1959-61; asst. prof. neurology W. Va. U. Sch. Medicine, 1961-63; assoc. prof. neurology U. Tenn., 1963-66; assoc. prof. to prof. Med. Coll. Wis., Milw., 1966-72; clin. prof. neurology U. Minn., Duluth, 1972-73; prof., head dept. neurology U. Okla. Coll. of Medicine, Oklahoma City, 1973-88, prof. emeritus neurology, 1989—. Served with M.C. U.S. Army, 1955-56. Mem. Okla. County Med. Soc., Okla. Med. Soc., AMA, Am. Acad. Neurology, Am. Electroencephalographic Soc., Am. Med. Electroencephalographic Soc.

**NELSON, K. BONITA,** literary agent; b. Austin, Minn., July 5, 1945; d. Wallace Arthur and Opal Merdice (Lastine) N. BA, Hunter Coll., 1969; B in laws, LaSalle U., 1982. Lit. agt. Am. Play Co., Inc., N.Y.C., 1970-75; legal sec., reviewer Eastman & DaSilva, Esqs., N.Y.C., 1975-79; founder, pres. BK Nelson Literary Agy., N.Y.C., 1983—, BK Nelson Lect. Bureau, N.Y.C., 1994—; pres., publ. Internat. Media Comm., Inc., 1998. Bd. dirs. Dynaray, N.Y.; founder BK Nelson, Inc., 1995; founder Literacy Inst. for Edn. (Life) Inc., 1996. Collaborator: Looking for Canterbury, 1994; author: My Literary Agent, 1998; co-prodr. (movies) Dancing Dan's Christmas, 2006, (musical) Packed Full of Miracles, 2006, Mem. Authors Guild (assoc.), NAFE (assoc.), Nat. Assn. Campus Activities (assoc.), AAUW, (assoc.), Dramatists Guild (assoc.), Minority and Woman Owned Businesses. Avocations: yoga, stamp collecting/philately, automobiles. Home and Office: 1565 Paseo Vida Palm Springs CA 92264 Office: Bk Nelson Lecture Bureau 1565 Paseo Vida Palm Springs CA 92264-9508 Office Phone: 760-778-8800. Office Fax: 704-278-2204. E-mail: bknelson4@cs.com.

**NELSON, KADIR,** illustrator, artist; Grad., Pratt Inst., Bklyn. Prin. works include Life of Marvin Gaye, Swizz Beatz: Ghetto Stories, Angel, Represented in permanent collections Debbie Allen, Denzel Washington, Will and Jada Pinckett Smith, Spike Lee, others, exhibitions include Simon Weisenthal Ctr., Acad. Motion Pictures and Sciences, LA, Mus. African Am. History, Detroit, Smithsonian Anacostia Mus., Washington, Soc. of Illustrators and Studio Mus., Harlem, Bristol Mus., Eng., Citizens Gallery, Yokohama, Japan, Ctr. for Culture, Tijuana, Mex., commissions, Dreamworks Studio, Sports Illustrated, Coca-Cola, NY Times, Major League Baseball, children's picture books, Brothers of the Knight, 1999, Big Jabe, 2000, Dancing in the Wings, 2000, Salt in His Shoes, 2000, The Two of Us, 2001 (NAACP Image Award), children's books, Thunder Rose, 2003, Ellington Was Not a Street, 2004 (Coretta Scott King Illustrator award, 2005). Recipient Silver Medal, Soc. of Illustrators. Achievements include being conceptual artist for feature film "Amistad," and animated feature "Spirit: Stallion of the Cimarron.". Office: Ste 124 6977 Navaho Rd San Diego CA 92119 Office Phone: 888-310-3222.

**NELSON, KATHY,** broadcast executive; Sr. v.p., gen. mgr. MCA Records Inc.; pres. film music The Walt Disney Motion Picture Group, 1996—2001, Universal Music Group & Universal Pictures, 2001—. Bd. dir. Women in Film. Office: Universal Music Group 1755 Broadway New York NY 10019*

**NELSON, KEITH A.,** federal agency administrator; BA, U. Tex.; MA, U. Calif. Berkeley; MBA, U. Calif. LA. Sports journalist Dallas Morning News, Tyler Morning Telegraph; sr. mgr. bus. devel. Dow Jones & Co.; with US Dept. Labor, Washington, 2000—05, acting dep. chief info. officer, 2003—04, assoc. dep. sec. mgmt., 2004—05, assoc. asst. adminstrn. US Dept. Housing & Urban Devel., 2005—. Office: HUD 451 7th St SW Washington DC 20410 Office Phone: 202-710-1112.

**NELSON, KIMBERLY TERESE,** computer software company executive, former federal agency administrator; b. Phila., July 15, 1956; B, Shippensburg U.; M, U. Pa. Spl. asst. to sec., spl. asst. to deputy sec. adminstrn., spl. asst. deputy sec. field ops. Pa. Dept. Environ. Resources, 1987—95; dir. program integration and effectiveness then chief info. officer Pa. Dept. Environ. Protection, 1999—2001; asst. adminstr. for environ. info. EPA, Washington, 2001—05; exec. dir. e-govt. Microsoft Corp., Redmond, Wash., 2006—.*

**NELSON, LARRY A.**, statistics educator, consultant; b. Omaha, Oct. 28, 1932; s. Rudolph Lawrence and Elizabeth Coleman (Lewis) N. BS in Agronomy, Iowa State U., 1954; MS in Soil Sci., Tex. A&M U., 1958; PhD in Soil Sci.-Stats., N.C. State U., 1961. Soil scientist Iowa Agrl. Exptl. Sta., Ames, 1954-55; soils instr. Tex. A&I Coll., Kingsville, 1955; rsch. soil scientist Tex. A&M Rsch. Found., College Station, 1956; soils lab. instr. Tex. A&M U., College Station, 1956-58; rsch. asst. N.C. State U., Raleigh, 1959-61; asst. specialist in land classification Land Study Bur., U. Hawaii, Honolulu, 1961-64; asst. prof. exptl. stats. N.C. State U., Raleigh, 1964-66, assoc. prof. exptl. stats., 1966-71; prof. stats., 1971-89; prof. emeritus stats., 1989—, coord. Concade Project (Bolivia), 1999—2003, interim coord. internat. programs Coll. Agr. and Life Scis., 2002—03, asst. dean for internat. programs Coll. Agr. and Life Scis., 2003—. Lectr., tchr., cons. in field; spl. advisor head dep. stats. Kasetsart U., Bangkok, Thailand, 1973; evaluator quantitative skills IADS, Bangladesh, 1984; mem. rev. team Ctr. for Agrl. Econs. and Ctr. for Data Processing, Winrock Internat., Indonesia, 1985; statis. cons. PROCAFE, El Salvador, 1993-96, ICRAF, Nairobi, Kenya, 1991—; cons. Potash and Phosphate Inst. Can., China and India, 1990, 94, 96; ptnr. Statis. Rsch. Assocs., Honolulu, 1962-63. Assoc. editor Geoderma, 1976-84, Agronomy Jour., 1981-87; contbr. numerous articles to profl. publs. NATO fellow Data Analysis Lab., Lyngby, Denmark, 1978. Fellow AAAS, Am. Statis. Assn. (mem. biometrics sect. com. 1989-90, mem. com. on internat. rels. in stats. 1996-98), Am. Soc. Agronomy, Soil Sci. Soc. Am.; mem. Statis. Assn. Thailand (life), Internat. Biometric Soc. (bus. mgr. and treas. 1969 79, awards com. 1987-94, chmn. 1990-93, com. on edn. 1997-99), Internat. Statis. Inst., Sigma Xi, Gamma Sigma Delta (internat. pres. 1984-86, award of merit 1973-74, rep. to AAAS 1978-86), Phi Kappa Phi, Sigma Iota Rho. Baptist. Avocations: music, genealogy, diving, bicycling, travel. Home: 2816 Wycliff Rd Raleigh NC 27607-3035 Office: NC State U Coll of Agrl and Life Sci Office Internat Programs PO Box 7608 Raleigh NC 27695-7608 Office Phone: 919-515-2665. Personal E-mail: lnelson460@worldnet.att.net. Business E-Mail: larry_nelson@ncsu.edu.

**NELSON, LARRY DEAN**, telecommunications and computer systems company executive, consultant; b. Newton, Kans., Aug. 5, 1937; s. Carl Aaron and Leta V. (Van Eaton) N.; m. Linda Hawkins, June 2, 1972. BA, Phillips U., 1959; MS, Kans. State U., 1962; PhD, Ohio State U., 1965. From rsch. asst. to rsch. assoc. Rsch. Found., Ohio State U., Columbus, 1962—65; mathematician II Batelle Meml. Inst., Columbus, 1962—65; from mem. tech. staff to supr. math. dept., data sys. devel. Bellcomm, Inc., Washington, 1965—72; supr. mgmt. info. sys. dept. Bell Telephone Labs., Murray Hill, NJ, 1972—77; supr. rate and tariff planning divsn. AT&T, N.Y.C., 1977—79; dep. adminstr. rsch. and spl. programs adminstrn. U.S. Dept. Transp., Washington, 1979—81; pres. MCS, Inc., Washington, 1981—; supr. govt. comm. ctr. AT&T Bell Labs., 1985—89; mgr. govt. mktg. AT&T Network Sys., 1989—90, supr. secure info. sys. engring., 1990—94, disting. mem. tech. staff, secure sys. engring., 1995—96; tech. cons. AT&T Labs, Info. Security Ctr., AT&T, 1996—98; prin. network security engr., cons. mem. tech. staff Lucent Tech. Integrated Solutions Inc., 2003—, v.p. sys. engring. and integration, 2004—. Cons. Contel Info. Sys., Denver, 1982-85, Martin Marietta Corp., Denver, 1982-85; mem. info. assurance task force, info infrastructure group, intrusion detection task force, cybercrime subgroup Nat. Security Telecomms. Adv. Com. Contbr. articles to profl. jours. Organizer, sponsor Odd Jobs Club, Washington, 1967-72; pres. Mountain County Condominiums Assn., Dillon, Colo., 1975-83, 85—; treas. Chris' Landing Condominium Assn., 1986-90; del. or rep. to numerous confs. Mem. ABA (assoc., info. security com. 1991-99), Am. Nat. Stds. Inst. (info. tech. security tech. stds. com. 1997-2001, internat. rep. tech. com. on info. tech. security mgmt.), IEEE (sec. D.C. sect. 1982, cert. appreciation 1968), Sys., Man and Cybernetics Soc. (sec. 1981, v.p. 1982-83), Math. Programming Soc, Am. Math Soc., N.Y. Acad. Scis., Assn. Computing Machinery, Sigma Xi, Phi Kappa Phi, Pi Mu Epsilon Democrat. Mem. Disciples of Christ. Current work: information assurance, networks and network management, digital signature, public key infrastructure, and electronic commerce technology. Subspecialties: secure information technology systems and networks; systems engineering. Office: 5220 Pacific Concourse Dr Ste 200 Los Angeles CA 90045 Office Phone: 310-297-5436. Business E-Mail: ldnelson1@cox.net.

**NELSON, LAWRENCE EVAN**, manufacturing executive, consultant; b. Chgo., Dec. 3, 1932; s. Evan Thomas and Elizabeth Marie (Stettka) N.; m. Jean H. Clayton, July 11, 1953; children: Lori Jean, Lawrence Evan. BS with honors, So. Ill. U., 1959; MBA, U. Chgo., 1969. CPA, Ill. Sr. acct. Price Waterhouse & Co., CPA's, Chgo., 1959-65; sec.-treas. Bradner Cen. Co., Chgo., 1965-73; pres. Protectoseal Co., Bensenville, Ill., 1973-84, Plan Ahead Inc., Palos Park, Ill., 1984—. Author: (book) Personal Financial Planning, 1985. Treas. City of Palos Heights, Ill., 1964-68, alderman, 1970-71; trustee Palos Heights FPD, 1977-1995. Served with USNR, 1952-56. Mem. Am. Inst. CPA's, Ill. Soc. CPA's. Office: Plan Ahead Inc PO Box 164 Palos Park IL 60464-0164 Office Phone: 708-448-8569.

**NELSON, LINDA J.**, state legislator; b. Plentywood, Mont., June 12, 1942; m. Roger Nelson. Grad., Medicine Lake H.S. Farmer, rancher; mem. Mont. Ho. of Reps., 1989-94, Mont. Senate, Dist. 49, Helena, 1994—2004; mem. ethics com., mem. rules com., mem. fin. and claims com.; mem. agr., livestock and irrigation com.; mem. jt. appropriations subcom. natural resources/commerce; minority whip Mont. Senate, 1999—2002, dean of senate, 2003—04. Mem. Medicine Lake (Mont.) Sch. Bd., 1981-88, chair, 1984-88; active Mont. Dem. Party; dir. Nemont Tel. Coop.; bd. mem., chair Mont. Oil and Gas Conservation; mem. ELCA Synod Coun. Mem. N.E. Mont. Land and Mineral Owners Assn., Sheridan County Dem. Women. Democrat. Lutheran. Home: 469 Griffin Medicine Lake MT 59247-9708

**NELSON, LIONEL M.**, otolaryngologist; BA Physics, CUNY Queens, 1965; MD, Yale U., 1969. Diplomate Am. Bd. Otolaryngology, 1974. Pvt. practice, otolaryngology-head and neck surgery Lionel M. Nelson, MD, San Jose, Calif., 1974—; clin. faculty Stanford U. Sch. Medicine, Calif., 1986—2004; co-founder and med. dir. Apneon, Inc., Cupertino, Calif. 2003—; med. advisor Gyrus ENT, Bartlett, Tenn., 2001—05; med. dir. Somnus Med. Technologies, Inc, Sunnyvale, Calif., 1998—2001. Guest lectr. Sleep apnea treatments. Contbr. articles to profl. jours. Col. USAR, 1984—2001. Recipient Outstanding Tchr. Recognition Award, Am. Acad. Family Practice, 1987—91; Jonas Salk Med. Rsch. Scholar, City of NY, 1965. Fellow: ACS, Am. Acad. Otolaryngology-Head and Neck Surgery; mem.: Soc. U.S. Flight Surgeons, Am. Acad. Sleep Medicine, Alpha Omega Alpha, Phi Beta Kappa. Achievements include patents for Airway Implants for Sleep Apnea Treatment; Radiofrequency surgical instrumentation; invention of Airway implants for sleep apnea; development of Surgical and radiofrequency devices. Office: 2505 Samaritan Dr Ste 510 San Jose CA 95124 Office Phone: 408-358-6163. Business E-Mail: lnelson580@aol.com.

**NELSON, MARILYN CARLSON**, hotel executive, travel company executive; b. Mpls. m. Glen Nelson; children: Diana, Curtis C., Wendy. Student, U. Sorbonne, Paris, Inst. Hautes Etudes Econ., Geneve in internat. econs. with honors, Smith Coll., 1961; DBA (hon.), Johnson & Wales U.; DHL (hon.), Coll. St. Catherine, Gustavus Adolphus Coll. Securities analyst Paine Webber, Mpls.; pres., COO Carlson Cos., Inc., Mpls., 1998—2003, CEO, chmn., 1998—, also bd. dirs. Co-chair Carlson Holdings, Inc., 2000—; co-chair Carlson Wagonlit Travel, 1994-2003; disting. vis. prof. Johnson & Wales U.; bd. dirs. Exxonmobil Corp., Mayo Clinic Found., Com. to Encourage Corp. Philanthropy; chmn. Nat. Women's Bus. Coun., 2002-05; vice chair U.S. Travel and Tourism Adv. Bd.; bd. mem. Singapore Tourism Bur. Pres. United Way Mpls., campaign chair, 1984; bd. dir. United Way Am., 1984-90, U.S. Nat. Tourism Orgn., 1996-98, Ctr. for Internat. Leadership, 1989-2003; mem. disting. adv. coun. Coll. of St. Catherine, 1991-94; hon. bd. dirs. Svenska Inst., Stockholm, 1993—; mem. adv. bd. Hubert H. Humphrey Inst. Pub. Affairs, 1992-96; co-founder Minn. Women's Econ.

Roundtable, 1974—; chair Minn. Super Bowl Task Force, 1984-92; chair, founder Midsummer Internat. Festival of Music, 1992; co-chair New Sweden '88; past bd. dirs. Guthrie Theatre, Greater Mpls. Girl Scout Coun., Jr. Achievement, Jr. League Mpls., KTCA Pub. TV, Minn. Econ. Assn., Minn. Congl. Award, Minn. Opera Co., Women's' Assn. Minn. Symphony Orch.; trustee Smith Coll., Northampton, Mass., 1980-85, Macalester Coll., St. Paul, 1974-80; mem. adv. bd. Minn. Women's Yearbook; trustee Curtis L. Carlson Family Found. Named Sales Exec. of Yr., Sales and Mktg. Exec. of Mpls., Outstanding Individual in Tourism, Minn. Office of Tourism, 1992, Woman of Yr., Roundtable for Women in Foodsvc., 1995, Woman of Yr., Minn. Exec. Women in Tourism, 1991—92, Swedish Am. of Yr., King and Queen of Sweden, 2003, Minnesotan of Yr., Minn. Monthly mag., 2003, Businesswoman of Yr., U.S. Commerce Dept. Small Bus. Adminstrn., 2005; named one of The Top 25 Execs. Yr., Bus. Week, 1999, Exec. Yr. Corp. Report Minn., 1999, 100 Most Powerful Women, Forbes mag., 2004—06, 25 Most Influential People in Mktg. Industry, Meeting News mag., 2005, Forbes Richest Americans, 2006; named to Sales and Mktg. Execs. Hall of Fame, 2003; recipient Minn. Congl. award for initiative and svc. to cmty., cert. of commendation State of Minn., Cmty. Svc. award, YWCA, Independence award, Vinland Nat. Ctr., Cmty. Svc. award, Park-Nicollet Med. Ctr., Outstanding Mktg. Exec. of Yr. award, Minn. Distributive Edn. Club Am., Career Achievement award, Sales and Mktg. Execs. Mpls., Outstanding Achievement award, United Way Mpls., Extraordinary Leadership award, Greater Mpls. C. of C., Disting. Svc. award, United Way of Am., 1984—90, Nat. Caring award, Caring Inst., 1995, Outstanding Bus. Leader award, Northwood U., 1995, The 50 Most Powerful Women award in Am. Bus., Fortune, 1998—2003, United Way Minn. Disting. Svc. award, United Way's highest vol. honor, 1998, Good Neighbor award, WCCO Radio, 1999, Caring Heart award charitable contbns. by Larry King Cardiac Found., 1999, Am.'s 100 Most Important Women award, Ladies' Home Jr., 1999, The Most Powerful Women in Travel #1, Travel Agent Mag., 1997—2003, Svc. Above Self award, The Rotary Club Downtown, Minn., 1999, The Top 500 Women-Owned Bus.'s award, Working Woman, 1999—2001, The 25 Most Influential Executives award, Leisure Travel News, 2000, Northwest Airlines Disting. World Traveler award, Hospitality Sales and Mktg. Assn. Internat., 2000, Responsible Capitalism award, FIRST mag., 2001, Businesswoman of World, Bus. Women's Network, 2001, Glass Ceiling award, Minn. Women's Consortium, 2001, Great Swedish Heritage award, Swedish Coun. Am., 2002, Lifetime Achievement award, Internat. Investment Forum, 2002, Athena award, Athena Found., 2004, Lifetime Achievement award, Hospitality Sales and Mktg. Assn. Internat., 2004, 18th Ann. Lucia Travel award, 2005, many others. Mem. World Econ. Forum, World Travel and Tourism Coun., Travel Industry Assn. Am. (bd. dirs.), Hennepin County Med. Soc. Aux., Bus. Roundtable, Smith Coll. Alumni Assn., Smith Club Mpls., Woodhill Country Club, Mpls. Club, N.W. Tennis Club, Nat. Ctr. Social Entrepreneurs, Com. of 200, Hospitality Sales and Mktg. Assn. Internat. (Lifetime Achievement award 2004), Minn. Orchestral Assn., Orphei Dranger, Alpha Kappa Psi. Office: Carlson Cos Inc 701 Carlson Pkwy Minnetonka MN 55305 Office Phone: 763-212-5000.*

**NELSON, MARK D.**, music educator, arts education administrator; b. N.Y.C., June 4, 1954; s. Harry D. and Sylvia Allen Nelson. BA, Yale U., 1976; MusM, U. Ill., 1980; PhD, Princeton U., 1995. Asst. prof. music Lake Forest (Ill.) Coll., 1986—93; asst. prof., chmn. music dept. Wabash Coll., Crawfordsville, Ind., 1993—95; performing arts chmn., tchr. music, cultural history Hawken Upper Sch., Gates Mills, Ohio, 1998—2001, Ross Sch., East Hampton, NY, 2004—06, Webb Sch., Claremont, Calif., 2006—. Composer: Arboreal, 1985 (NJ Arts Coun. grant, 1985), Song Lines, 1998. Recipient William L. Dunn award for Outstanding Tchg. and Scholarly Promise., Lake Forest Coll., 1990. Mem.: Phi Kappa Phi, Soc. for Ethnomusicology, Coll. Music Soc., Phi Beta Kappa. Independent. Avocations: backpacking, photography, music of India and Java. Office: Ross Sch 18 Goodfriend Dr East Hampton NY 11937 Home: 1175 W Baseline Rd Claremont CA 91711 Office Phone: 631-907-5428. Personal E-mail: mdnelson@wesleyan.edu. E-mail: mnelson@webb.org.

**NELSON, MARTHA JANE**, magazine editor; b. Pierre, SD, Aug. 13, 1952; d. Bernard Anton and Pauline Isabel (Noren) Nelson. BA, Barnard Coll., 1976. Mng. editor Signs: Jour. of Women in Culture, NYC, 1976—80; staff editor Ms. Mag., NYC, 1980—85; editor-in-chief Women's Sports and Fitness Mag., San Francisco, 1985—87; exec. editor Savvy, NYC, 1988—89, editor-in-chief, 1989—91; asst. mng. editor People, 1993; founding editor In Style Mag., NYC, 1993—2002, exec. prodr. TV program Celebrity Weddings, 1997—2002, exec. prodr. TV programs Celebrity Homes, Celebrity Homes, 2001; mng. editor People Mag., NYC, 2002—06; editor, People group Time Inc., NYC, 2006—. Editor: Women in the American City, 1980; editor: (cons. editor) Who Weekly, 1992; contbr. articles to profl. jours. Bd. dirs. Painting Space 122, NYC, 1982—85, 1995—96, Urban Athletic Assn., 1986, ACRIA, Comm. Rsch. Inst. on AIDS, Am. Soc. Mag. Editors, Accessories Coun., 1999—2001, Athletic and Swim Club, 2000—; adv. bd. NYU Grad. Sch., 2000—03. Named One of the Top 25 Most Influential People in Media, Brill's Content, 1999; named one of 100 Most Powerful Women, Forbes Mag., 2004—06; recipient Child Victimization in the News award, Nat. Ctr. for Missing and Exploited Children, 2003, Achiever award, Cosmetic Exec. Women, 2000, Inspiration award, Women's Step Up Network, 2004, Matrix award, NY Women in Comm., Inc., 2004. Mem.: NY Women in Comm., Women in Film, Am. Soc. Mag. Editors.*

**NELSON, MARVIN DALE, JR.**, radiologist, educator; b. Hastings, Nebr., June 16, 1954; s. Marvin Dale Sr. and Patricia J. (Pingenot) N.; m. Mary C. Baron, Sep. 30, 1990; children: Kevin James, Andrew John. BS, MD, Loma Linda U., 1978; MBA, U. So. Calif., 1999. Diplomate Am. Bd. Radiology, Am. Bd, Diagnostic Radiology, Am. Bd. Pediat. Radiology, Am. Bd. Neuroradiology. Intern, resident in radiology Loma Linda U. Med. Ctr., 1978-82; fellow in neuroradiology Nat. Hosp. for Nervous Disease, London, 1985-86, Rothschild Founds., Paris, 1986; fellow in pediat. neuroradiology Children's Mem. Hosp., Chgo., 1986-87; asst. prof. radiology Children's Hosp.-USC Sch. Med., 1987-93, assoc. prof., 1993-2001; chmn. dept. radiology Children' Hosp., L.A., 1998—, prof., 2001—, John L. Gwinn prof. pediat. radiology, 2002—. Maj. USAF, 1982-85 Recipient Cornelius Dyke award for original rsch. Am. Soc. Radiology, 1990, Gabriel Wilson award for best paper Western Neuroradiol. Soc., 1997 Fellow Am. Coll. Radiology; mem. Am. Soc. Neurol. Radiology, Am. Soc. Pediat. Neuroradiology (pres. 2004-05), Western Neuroradiog. Soc. (pres. 2001). Office: Children's Hosp 4650 W Sunset Blvd Los Angeles CA 90027-6062 Office Phone: 323-669-4572. E-mail: mdnelson@chla.usc.edu.

**NELSON, MARVIN RAY**, retired life insurance company executive; b. Thornton, Iowa, Aug. 29, 1926; s. Clarence Anton and Rose Bessie (Nicolet) N.; m. Juanita Mae Brown, May 26, 1951; children: Nancy, Kenneth. BS, Drake U, 1951. Actuary Security Mut. Life Ins. Co., Lincoln, Nebr., 1951-58; assoc. actuary Life Ins. Co. N.Am., Phila., 1958-59; group actuary Bankers Life of Nebr., Lincoln, 1959-66; actuary Mut. Service Life Ins. Co., St. Paul, 1966-68; sr. v.p. Horace Mann Educators Corp., Springfield, Ill., 1968-77, Security Life of Denver, 1977-83, exec. v.p., 1988-91; pres., chief oper. officer, dir., mem. investment com. Midwestern United Life Ins. Co., Ft. Wayne, Ind., 1983-89; ret., 1991. Bd. dirs., treas. Ft. Wayne Urban League, 1983-87; bd. dirs. Taxpayers Research Assn., Ft. Wayne, 1984-88; pres. Shalom Pk. Men's Group, 2006. Mem. U.S. Army, 1946—47. Fellow Soc. Actuaries; mem. Am. Acad. Actuaries, Pi Kappa Phi. Home: 5224 S Shalom Pk Cir Aurora CO 80015-2263

**NELSON, MARY CARROLL**, artist, writer; b. Bryan, Tex., Apr. 24, 1929; d. James Vincent and Mary Elizabeth (Langton) Carroll; m. Edwin Blakeley Nelson, June 27, 1950; children: Patricia Ann, Edwin Blakely. BA in Fine Arts, Barnard Coll., 1950; MA, U. N.Mex., 1963. Juror Am. Artist Golden Anniversary Competition, 1987. Guest instr. continuing edn. U. N.Mex., 1991; com. co-organizer Affirming Wholeness, The Art and Healing Experience, San Antonio, 1992, Artists of the Spirit Symposium, 1994. Group shows include N.Mex. Mus., 1987, Art is for Healing, The Universal Link, San

Antonio, 1992, Fuller Lodge Art Ctr. Los Alamos, N.Mex., 1993, Layering, Albuquerque, 1993, Crossings, Bradford, Mass., 1994, The Layered Perspective, Fayetteville, Ark., 1994, Tree of Life, San Miguel de Allende, Mex., 1996, (honoree Magnifico, Albuquerque, 1997, Bravos award Excellence in Arts 2004, Achievement award Masterworks, 2005), Guardian Spirits, Marlborough, Eng., 1997, Memories in Multi-Media, Columbus, Ohio, 1998, Agora Gallery, NYC, 1998, Celtic Connections, Mass., 1998, Bridging Time and Space, Calif., 1999, Musings on the Millennium, Ohio, 2000, Layerists in Multi-Media/Affirming Wholeness, Albuquerque, 2000, The Birth of Wisdom, N.M.and Gordes, France, 2000, Tides of Change, Tex., 2001, Earth-Spirit, Ohio, 2001, Shadow & Light, Albuquerque, 2001, Landscape and Memory, Sedona, Ariz., 2002, dsg Gallery, Albuquerque, 2002, Albuquerque Mus., 2003, Fire in the Heart, Ashland, Oreg., 2003, Layered Images, Albuquerque, 2003, Masterworks Miniatures, 2004 (1st award Mixed Media, Juror Masterworks award 2005), Get the Lead Out, Los Alamos U., 2005, Weynich Gallery, Alburquerque, 2006, N.Mex. State U., Las Cruces, 2006, Soul Shrines, Las Cruces, 2006, Mus. Fine Arts, Las Cruces, 2006, Rock, Paper, Scissors, Los Alamos, N.Mex., 2006, Masterwork Miniatures, Albuquerque, 2006, Connections: We Are All One, Lexington, Ky., 2006, Art of Space, Las Cruces, 2006; represented in pvt. collections in U.S., Germany, Eng. and Australia; author: American Indian Biography Series, 1971-76, (with Robert E. Wood) Watercolor Workshop, 1974; (with Ramon Kelley) Ramon Kelley Paints Portraits and Figures, 1977, The Legendary Artists of Taos, 1980, (catalog) American Art in Peking, 1981, Masters of Western Art, 1982, Connecting, The Art of Beth Ames Swartz, 1984, Artists of the Spirit, 1994, Doris Steider, A Vision of Silence, 1997, Beyond Fear, A Toltec's Guide to Freedom and Joy, 1997, Layering, An Art of Time and Space, 1985, (catalog) Layering/Connecting, 1987; contbg. editor Am. Artist, 1976-91, Southwest Art, 1987-91; editor (video) Layering, 1990; arts corr. Albuquerque Jour. 1991-93; contbr. One Source Sacred Journeys, 1997, Lightstream, 2003; co-author: Bridging Time and Space, Essays on Layered Art, 1998, Toltec Prophecies of Don Miguel Ruiz, 2003; co-editor The Art of Layering: Making Connections, 2004 Mem. Albuquerque Arts Bd., 1984—88. Mem. Soc. Layerists in Multi-Media (founder 1982). Home: 1408 Georgia St NE Albuquerque NM 87110-6861 Personal E-mail: mcn50@comcast.net.

**NELSON, MARY KATHRYN**, bilingual counselor, small business owner, real estate agent, artist, singer; b. Chgo., May 28, 1954; d. James C. Nelson and Leila R. Cooke. BS in Social Work, So. Ill. U., 1978; MS in Rehab. Counseling, U. Ariz., 1982. Cert. rehab. counselor, substance abuse counselor, profl. counselor, Ariz.; nat. cert. counselor; lic. real estate agt., Ariz., lic. ins. agent Allstate, Ariz., 2006. Bilingual counselor III. Migrant Council, 1975-76; social worker Child Protective Svcs., 1980-85; bilingual clinician pvt. nonprofit agys., 1985-96; bilingual counselor contractor, counselor Suprme Ct. Ariz., Phoenix, 1995—; owner, mgr. Bilingual Svcs., LLC, Phoenix, 1985—, owner Peoria, Ariz., 1994—; real estate agt. Liberty Properties, Inc., 2003—05, Ken Meade Realty, Sun City, Ariz., 2005—06; bilingual agent Am. Farmer's Ins., Peoria, Ariz., 2006—, Weinstein-Fehris Realty, Scottsdale, Ariz., 2006—. Exhibited in group shows at Franciscan Renewal Ctr., Scottsdale, 2001, exhibitions include Artareas.com, 2001—; performer: Talent Show at Crossroads, 1999—2001; singer: Franciscan Renewal Ctr., 2000—01; exhibitions include Fountain Hills Ariz. Art Exhibit, 1995, Channel 22 Phoenix Cable Amateur Hr., Spanish Songs, 1996, Iberoamericana Internat. Art Exhibit, Miami, Fla., 1997, Phoenix K Lite Radio TV Commn., 1997, Peoria Sportscomplex Art Fair, Ariz., 1998, Franciscan Renewal Ctr. Art Fair, Scottsdale, Ariz., 1999, 2001, ArtAreas.com. Vol. Big Bros.-Big Sisters, Tucson, 1999; family advocate Cesar Chavez Farmworkers Union Labor Movement; art donor Ariz. Foster Care Assn., Paradise Valley, Ariz., 2001, donor original oil painting with World Trade Ctr. motif, 2001; founder Morris Dee's Ctr. for Justice/Civil Rights Mtml. Ctr.; mem. So. Poverty Law Ctr.; vol. campaign worker Jon Kyle for Senator, Phoenix, 1996—2006; fundraiser John Shadeg for Congressman, Ariz., 2002, Women Reps. for Ky., 1996—2006; choir mem. Franciscan Renewal Ctr., Paradise Valley, Ariz., 1999—2002. Recipient humanitarian award Inst. Arts Plastiques, 1997; named to Martin Luther King Meml. Wall of Tolerance, 2003. Mem. Drama Beat Acting Club. Republican. Avocations: singing, comedy, acting. Home: 12667 W Maya Way Peoria AZ 85383-2829 E-mail: marynelsonsc@aol.com.

**NELSON, MAURICE SANDY, JR.**, metal products company executive; BS in Indsl. Engring., Ga. Inst. Tech.; MS in Indsl. Engring., U. Tenn.; D (hon.), Marycrest Coll. Pres. aerospace and comml. div. Aluminum Co. of Am., 1987—92; pres., CEO, COO Inland Steel Co., 1992—96, Earle M. Jorgensen Co., Brea, Calif., 1997—. Chmn. adv. bd. Ga. Tech.; chmn. The Steel Svc. Ctr. Inst. Named Exec. of Yr., Metals Svc. Ctr. mag., 2001. Office: Earle M Jorgensen Co 10650 Alameda St Lynwood CA 90262-1754

**NELSON, MERLIN EDWARD**, retired management consultant, lawyer; b. Fargo, N.D., Jan. 30, 1922; s. Theodore G. and Eva C. (Hultgren) Nelson; m. Nancy Ellen Craig, 1952 (div. June 1962); children: Craig Edward, Brian Anthony; m. Janet April Pope, Aug. 30, 1963; children: Claudia Jane, Rolf Merlin. BS in Polit. Sci., U. Oreg., 1943; postgrad., Fordham U., 1943-44; JD, Yale U., 1948. Bar: Oreg. 1948, N.Y. 1954, U.S. Dist. Ct. DC 1954. Atty. Office Gen. Counsel, ECA, Washington, Paris, 1949-52; assoc. Davis, Polk, Wardwell, Sunderland & Kiendl, 1952-59; exec. asst. to v.p. AMF, Inc. N.Y.C., 1960-62; chmn., mng. dir. AMF Internat., Ltd., London, 1962-63; v.p., group exec. AMF, Inc., 1963-70, exec. v.p., vice chmn., dir., 1970-84; ret., 1984. Cons. AMF, Inc., 1984—; bd. dirs. Mitsui Found., Mizuho Found.; chmn. Tuckernuck Land Trust. Mem. Coun. Fgn. Rels.; mem. Phi Beta Kappa. Home and Office: 16 W 77th St Apt 12F New York NY 10024 5126 Office Phone: 212-579-0064. Personal E-mail: nelsonmj@earthlink.net.

**NELSON, MICHAEL ALLAN**, lawyer; b. Chgo., Apr. 25, 1947; m. Lucretia Susan Nelson, Sept. 13, 1951; children: Scott, Megan Elizabeth. AB, Hamilton Coll., 1969; MA in Tchg., Harvard U., 1970; JD, George Washington U., 1975. Bar: Va. 1975, D.C. 1976, Maine 1980. Jud. law clk. U.S. Dist. Ct. D.C., Washington, 1975—76; trial atty. US SEC, Washington, 1978—80; ptnr. Jensen Baird Gardner & Henry, Portland, Maine, 1980—. Chair advisory com. on rules profl. responsibility Maine Supreme Jud. Ct., Portland, 1996—. Bd. dirs., chair Cmty. Counseling Ctr., Portland, 1982—2006. Avocations: golf, travel, history. Office: Jensen Baird Gardner & Henry 10 Free St Portland ME 04102 Office Phone: 207-775-7271. Office Fax: 207-775-7935. Business E-Mail: mnelson@jbgh.com.

**NELSON, MICHAEL UNDERHILL**, educational association administrator; b. Balt., May 5, 1932; s. Cyril Arthur and Elise (Macy) N.; m. Barbara Gail Hutchins, June 25, 1960; children: Kevin Underhill, Bronwyn Hastings, Gayle Hutchins, Corey Williams. AB, Rutgers U., 1957, EdM, 1968. Salesman J & N Distbg. Co., New Brunswick, NJ, 1957-59; extension assoc. Univ. Coll., Rutgers U., New Brunswick, 1959-61; asst. dir. summer session Rutgers U., 1961-68; asst. dean sch. continuing edn., dir. summer sch. Washington U., St. Louis, 1969-81, dir. div. of profl. and community programs sch. continuing edn., 1975-78; exec. sec. N.Am. Summer Sessions, 1979—; account exec. Trio Printing Co., 1982-84; sr. procedures analyst McDonnell Douglas Corp, St. Louis, 1984-96. Bd. dirs. Adult Edn. Council of Greater St. Louis, 1975-78. Served with USMC, 1951-54. Mem. North Ctrl. Conf. Summer Schs. (pres. 1974-75), Am. Assn. Univ. Adminstrs., Assn. Univ. Summer Sessions, Am. Summer Sessions Senate, N.Am. Summer Sessions (pres. 1978), Alpha Sigma Lambda, Phi Delta Kappa. Episcopalian. Home and Office: 43 Belanger Dr Dover NH 03820-4602 Office Phone: 603-740-9880. Personal E-mail: NAASS@aol.com.

**NELSON, NANCY ELEANOR**, pediatrician, educator; b. El Paso, Apr. 4, 1933; d. Harry Hamilton and Helen Maude (Murphy) N. BA magna cum laude, U. Colo., 1955, MD, 1959. Intern, Case Western Res. U. Hosp., 1959-60, resident, 1963-65; pvt. practice medicine specializing in pediats., Denver, 1963-70; clin. prof. U. Colo. Sch. Medicine, Denver, 1988-2002, assoc. dean student affairs U. Colo. Sch. Medicine, 1988—. Mem. Am. Acad.

Pediats., AMA (sect. med. schs. governing coun. 1994-96), Denver Med. Soc. (pres. 1983-84), Colo. Med. Soc. (bd. dirs. 1985-88, mem. jud. coun. 1992—, mem. liason com. med. edn. 1995—).

**NELSON, NORMAN DANIEL,** government official; b. Dec. 30, 1968; married; 1 child. BSBA, U. Fla., 1991; MBA, U. Miami, 1997; MA, Georgetown U., 2000. Intern corp. fin. divsn. mergers and acquisitions Commerzbank AG, Frankfurt, 1992; intern corp. fin. divsn. internat. leasing and new stock issues Deutsche Bank AG, Frankfurt, 1992; commd. 2d lt. disting. mil. grad. USAR, 1991; advanced through grades to maj. USAR, C.E. and Civil Affairs, 2002; econ. plans and program officer U.S. Dept. of State, 1997—2001; pres., CEO Nelson Systems Internat. Corp., 1998—2000; fgn. svc. officer U.S. Dept. State, 2001—. Decorated Army Commendation medal (3); recipient Meritorious Honor award U.S. Dept. State, 2003; Fed. Chancellor scholar Alexander-von-Humboldt Found., 1991-92. Mem. Sigma Chi. E-mail: nelsonnd@state.gov.

**NELSON, PAMELA HUDSON,** artist, educator; b. Oklahoma City, Mar. 25, 1947; d. Charles Howard and Maurine Lanell (Curtis) Hudson; m. William Nelson, Feb. 18, 1968; children: Keith, Charles. BFA, So. Meth. U., Dallas, 1974. Artist, 1979—. Instr. Artlington Mus. Art, 1991; juror DART Garland (Tex.) Bus Transit Ctr., 1992, Site Sculpture Competition, Mcpl. Ctr., Plano, Tex., 1993; created, produced award for Leadership Tex., 1993, Girls Club Am., Dallas, 1987, 89; guest lectr. Dallas Mus. Art, 1993; supr. studio assts. in mentor program, 1988-91; pvt. art tutor, 1987-93; co-curator Theatre Gallery, Dallas, 1985; workshops Dallas Mus. Art, 1982, 85. One-woman shows include Toni Jones Gallery, Houston, 1980, 500 Exposition Gallery, Dallas, 1981, Clifford Gallery, Dallas, 1983, 85, Peregrine Gallery at the Crescent, Dallas, 1987, 91, Studio Gallery, Brookhaven Coll., Dallas, 1992, Artisana Gallery, Dallas, 1993; two and three person shows include Clifford Gallery, Dallas, 1979, Forum Gallery, Brookhaven Coll., 1988, Galveston Art Ctr., Galveston, Tex., 1992, Nat. Arts Club, N.Y.C., 2002; exhibited in group show at U. Houston, 1979, Toni Jones Gallery, Houston, 1979, Clifford Gallery, Dallas, 1984, DW Gallery, Dallas, 1984, Mus. of Art of the Am. West, Houston, 1985, Adolphus Hotel, Dallas, 1985, Tex. Christian U., Ft. Worth, 1986, Frito-Lay Corp., Plano, Tex., 1986, Caroline Lee Gallery, 1986, Cullen Ctr., Houston, 1987, LTV Ctr., Dallas, 1987, Laguna Gloria Art Mus., Austin, Tex., 1987, Dallas Pub. Libr., 1987, Tex. Commerce Tower, Dallas, 1988, Amarillo (Tex.) Art Ctr., 1988, Belo Mansion, Dallas, 1988, Nat. Mus. Women in the Arts, Washington, 1988, Ctr. Rsch. Contemporary Art, U. Tex., Arlington, 1988, The Gallery, So. Meth. U., Dallas, 1989, Dallas Mus. of Art, 1989, Hall-Barnett Gallery, New Orleans, 1989, X Art Gallery, New Orleans, 1990, Peregrine Gallery at the Crescent, Dallas, 1990, Ark. Arts Ctr., Little Rock, 1990, Very Spl. Arts Gallery, Washington, 1991, Cullen Ctr., Houston, 1991, Lubbock (Tex.) Arts Ctr., 1991, Arlington (Tex.) Art Mus., 1992, Collin County C.C., Plano, 1992, Ida Green Gallery, Austin Coll., Sherman, Tex., 1992; represented in permanent collections Corp. Hdqrs. Steak and Ale Corp., Dallas, M-TV Collection, N.Y.C.; prin. works include sculptures at Mississippi County Ct. House, Blytheville, Ark., 1986, Dallas Zoo, 1988, DFW Airport, 2002. Presdl. appointee U.S. Commn. Fine Arts, Washington, 2001—, vice chair, 2005—; bd. dirs. Tex. Sculpture Assn., 1987-89, Dallas Artists Rsch. and Exbn., 1989-91; mem. adv. coun. Dallas Arts Resource System, 1991; mem. steering com. Emergency Artists Support League, Dallas, 1992; exhbn. cons. SPCA and Dallas Zoo, 1993; participant, Dallas City Ctr. TIF Streetscape Project (recipient City of Dallas Urban Design award); dir. Open Art Project, Stewpot Shelter, Dallas; mem. Pub. Art Com., City of Dallas. Recipient award Laguna Art Mus., 1982, Merit award Tex. Christian U., 1984, Crystal award Dallas Cable System, 1985, Merit award Crescent Gallery, 1986, Merit award Alexandria Mus., 1987, Patrick Media Billboard award, 1988, Excellence '88 award Plz. of Ams., 1988, Hon. Mention award Longview Mus. and Arts Ctr., 1990, Legend award, Dallas Visual Art Ctr., Merit award, AIA; named Artist-in-Residence, Connemara Conservancy, 1993. Home: 312 S Harwood St Dallas TX 75201-5602 E-mail: pamelaandbill@hotmail.com.

**NELSON, PATRICIA L.,** lawyer; d. Charles Patrick McGerald and Inez Gallagher; m. Bruce Neil Nelson, May 29, 1980; 1 child, Adam. BA in Political Sci., U. Vt., 1980; JD magna cum laude, Suffolk U., 1999, cert. of distinction in intellectual property law. Bar: Mass. 1999. Rights mgr. Addison-Wesley Pub. Co., Reading, Mass., 1990—99; atty. Palmer & Dodge LLP, Boston, 1999—2001, Hill & Barlow, Boston, 2001—03, Fish & Richardson PC, Boston, 2003—. Trustee Arts/Boston, 2003—; vol. Lawyers for the Arts, Boston, 2002—. Named Super Lawyer Rising Star, Law & Politics/Boston Mag., 2005, 2006. Mem.: Licensing Execs. Soc., Copyright Soc. USA. Avocations: skiing, horseback riding. Office: Fish & Richardson PC 225 Franklin St Boston MA 02210-2809

**NELSON, PAUL D.,** retired religious organization administrator; m. Elaine Nelson. Grad., Adelphi Coll. Joined Focus on the Family, 1985, exec. v.p., COO; pres. Evang. Coun. for Fin. Accountability, 1994—2006. Mem. Nat. Panel on Nonprofit Sector, 2004. Named Exec. of Year, NonProfit Times, 1996. Office: Evang Coun for Fin Accountability Ste 130 440 W Jubal Early Dr Winchester VA 22601*

**NELSON, PAULA MORRISON BRONSON,** reading specialist; b. Memphis, Mar. 26, 1944; d. Fred Ford and Julia (Morrison) Bronson; m. Jack Marvin Nelson, July 13, 1968; children: Eric Allen, Kelly Susan BS, U. N.Mex., 1967; MA, U. Colo., Denver, 1985. Tchr. phys. edn. Grant Union Sch. Dist., Sacramento, 1967—68, Denver Pub. Schs., 1968—74, with program for pupil assistance, 1974—80; tchr. ESL Douglas County Pub. Schs., Parker, Colo., 1982—83; Chpt. 1 reading specialist Denver Pub. Schs., 1983—96, computer/reading specialist, 1996—98, reading specialist, tchr. gifted and talented, 1998—99, lead tchr. in charge instrn., 1999—2001, edn. cons., 2001—02. Demonstration tchr. Colo. Edn. Assn., 1970-72; mem. curriculum com. Denver Pub. Schs., 1970-72; mem. Douglas County Accountability Com., Castle Rock, Colo., 1986-92; mem. educators rev. panel Edn. for Freedom; computer trainer Denver Pub. Schs. Tech. Team, 1992-02; bd. dirs. Obie Harrington-Howes Found., 2005-. Co-author: Gymnastics Teacher's Guide Elementary Physical Education, 1973, Applauding Our Constitution, 1989; editl. reviewer G is for Geography, Children's Literature and the Five Themes, 1993; prodr. slide shows Brotherhood, 1986, We the People...Our Dream Lives On, 1987, Celebration of Cultures, 1988 Named Pub. Edn. Coalition grantee, Denver, 1987, 88, 89, 90, grantee Rocky Mountain Global Edn. Project, 1987, Wake Forest Law Sch., Winston-Salem, N.C., 1988, 89, 90, 92, Read to Achieve grantee Colo. State Dept. Edn., 2000, Chpt. II grant, 1991, Tech. grant, 1993, Title VI Reading grant, 1999, 2000; recipient Three R's of Freedom award State Dept. Edn., 1987, Nat. Recognition award Commn. on Bicentennial of Constn., 1987, Disting. Tchr. award City of Denver, 1994 Mem.: Denver Fedn. Tchrs., Am. Fedn. Tchrs., Tech. in Edn. Republican. Methodist. Avocations: snow and water skiing, tennis, sailing. Home: 18 Covewood Dr Norwalk CT 06853

**NELSON, PHILIP EDWIN,** food scientist, educator; b. Shelbyville, Ind., Nov. 12, 1934; s. Brainard R. and Alta E. (Pitts) N.; m. Sue Bayless, Dec. 27, 1955; children: Jennifer, Andrew, Bradley. BS, Purdue U., 1956, PhD, 1976. Plant mgr. Blue River Packing Co., Morristown, Ind., 1956-60; instr. Purdue U., West Lafayette, Ind., 1961-76, head dept. food sci., 1983—2003, Scholle chair prof., 2004—. Cons. PEN Cons., West Lafayette, 1974; chair Food Processors Inst., Washington, 1990-93; mem. adv. bd. USDA, 2002—. Editor: Fruit Vegetable Juice Technology, 1980, Principles of Aseptic Processing and Packaging, 1992. Recipient Pers. Achievement award USDA, 1997. Fellow Inst. Food Techs. (pres. 2001-02, Indsl. Achievement award 1976, Nicholas Appert award 1995, 49'er Svc. award 1995, Tanner Lectr. 1999), Internat. Acad. Food Sci. and Tech., 2003 (USDA specialty crops com., 2005-); mem. AAAS, Sigma Xi, Phi Tau Sigma (pres. 1976-77). Achievements include 11 U.S. and foreign patents. Office: Purdue U Dept Food Sci 745 Ag Mall Drive West Lafayette IN 47907-2009 E-mail: pen@purdue.edu.

**NELSON, PHILIP FRANCIS,** musicologist, consultant, conductor; b. Waseca, Minn., Feb. 17, 1928; s. Elmer Philip and Frances (Bretzke) Nelson; m. Georgia Ann Yelland, June 5, 1950; children: Curtis Ann, Philip Francis Jr. AB, Grinnell Coll., 1950; AM, U. N.C., 1956, PhD, 1958; Diplome (Fulbright scholar), U. Paris, 1957; student, Conservatoire Nat. de Paris, 1956-57; MA (hon.), Yale U., 1971; LHD (hon.), Grinnell Coll., 1981. Asst. prof. Ariz. State U., 1958-62, assoc. prof., 1962-63; prof., chmn. dept. music SUNY, Binghamton, 1963-70; prof., dean Sch. Music, Yale U., 1970-81; prof., provost, dean U. Calif., Santa Cruz, 1981-83; chmn. trustee com. Curtis Inst., 1982-83; sr. v.p. AED, N.Y.C., 1984-87; v.p. Aspen Inst. Humanistic Studies, 1987-89; interim chancellor Sch. Arts U. N.C., 1989-90, interim vice chancellor Chapel Hill, 1991, chmn. grad. sch. adv. coun., 1993-96, cons. arts and humanities, 1996—; assoc. fellow Nat. Humanities Ctr., 1990-91; cons. edn., arts, 1992-93; interim dir. N.C. Sch. Sci. and Math., 1999-2000; sr. cons. U. N.C. and Nat. Humanities Ctr., 2000—; cons. Park Found., 2003—; trustee N.C. Sch. Arts, 2005—. Music critic Phoenix Gazette, 1959—62; music cons. Tallesin West, 1959—63; chmn. Nat. Screening Com. Fulbright Awards in Musicology, 1965—68; cons. Nat. Endowment Arts, 1984—90; vis. lectr. Duke U., 1992—. Contbg. editor: College and Adult Reading List, 1962, Nicolas Bernier, Principles of Composition, 1964, Recherches sur la musique Française classique, 1979, 1980; co-author: Groves Dictionary of Music, 6th edit.; editor: Aspen Inst. Humanities, 1987—89. Bd. dirs. various symphonies, chamber music socs., arts groups; trustee Curtis Inst. Music, Phila., 1980—83; bd. dirs. Conn. Hospice, 1983—87, Nat. Soc. Prevent Blindness, 1987—93, bd. dirs., v.p., 1987—93; mem. Chapel Hill Arts Ctr., 1992—; Triangle J. Coun. Govt., 1992—95; trustee N.C. Sch. Arts, 2005; mem. exec. com. Conn. State Golf Assn., 1975—81; founder Seven Springs Soc., 1975. Lt. comdr. USCGR, 1952—72. Found. grantee. Mem.: Soc. Ethnomusicology, Société Française de Musicologie, Coll. Music Soc. (nat. coun., editor jour. 1966—69), Internat. Musicol. Soc., Am. Musicol. Soc., U.S. Srs. Golf Assn., Chapel Hill Country Club, Finley Golf Club, Yale Golf Club, Carolina Club, Elizabethan Grads. Club, Yale Club (N.Y.C.), Mory's Club (New Haven). Home: 621 Greenwood Rd Chapel Hill NC 27514-5921 Office Phone: 919-968-6486. *Keep casting bread on the waters-it may come back as French toast.*

**NELSON, PRINCE ROGERS See PRINCE**

**NELSON, RALPH ALFRED,** physician; b. Mpls., June 19, 1927; s. Alfred W. and Lydia (Johnson) N.; m. Rosemary Pokela, Aug. 7, 1954; children—Edward Ancher, Audrey Anne, Elizabeth Marie, Andrew William, Evan Robert. BA, U. Minn., 1949, MD, 1953, PhD, 1961. Diplomate Am. Bd. Internal Medicine. Intern Cook County (Ill.) Hosp., 1953-54; resident U. Minn. Hosps., Mpls., 1954-55, U. Minn. Mpls., 1955-56; fellow in physiology Mayo Grad. Sch., Rochester, Minn., 1957-60, resident in internal medicine, 1976-78; practice medicine specializing in internal medicine and clin. nutrition Sioux Falls, SD, 1978-79, Urbana, Ill., 1979—. Bd. dirs. Scott Research Lab., Fairview Park Hosp., Cleve., 1962-67; assoc. in physiology Western Res. U., Cleve., 1962-67; asst. prof. physiology Mayo Grad. Sch., 1967-73, Mayo Med. Sch., 1973, assoc. prof. nutrition, 1974; cons. in nutrition Mayo Clinic, 1967-76; assoc. prof. medicine U.S.D. Sch. Medicine, Sioux Falls, 1978-79; prof. nutrition U. Ill. Coll. Medicine, Urbana-Champaign, 1986—2002, chmn. dept. medicine prof. nutritional sci., physiology, biophysics dept. food sci. Sch. Agr., 1979-2002, also prof. medicine, exec. head dept. internal medicine, 1989-2002, exec. head four sites of Coll. Medicine, 2002, emeritus prof. internal medicine, emeritus prof. nutritional scis.; dir. med.research Carle Found. Hosp., Urbana, 1979—; cons. nutritional support service Danville (Ill.) VA Hosp., 1980—. Co-author: The Mayo Clinic Renal Diet Cookbook, 1974; contbr. articles on nutrition, physiology, and hibernation to sci. jours.; editor: Geriatrics, 1980—2002, The Physician and Sportsmedicine, 1980-88, Am. Jour. Clin. Nutrition, 1980-83. Cons. in nutrition Nat. Cancer Inst., 1976; cons. in nutrition HEW, 1976, 79, 89, Nat. Heart and Lung Inst., 1976. Served with USAF, 1945-47. Fulbright scholar, Morocco, 1988. Fellow ACP; mem. Am. Physiol. Soc., Am. Inst. Nutrition, Am. Soc. Clin. Nutrition, Central Soc. Clin. Research, Am. Gastroent. Assn. Lutheran. Home: 2 Illini Cir Urbana IL 61801-5813 Office: Carle Found Hosp Dir Med Rsch 611 W Park St Urbana IL 61801-2529 Office Phone: 217-383-3036. Personal E-mail: ralph.nelson@carle.com.

**NELSON, RALPH STANLEY,** lawyer; b. Mpls., Mar. 15, 1943; s. Stanley L. and Louise M. Nelson; m. Judy E. Nelson, July 8, 1867; children: Sara C., Amy E., David A. BS in Bus. Adminstrn., U. Minn., 1966; JD with honors, Drake U., 1972. Bar: Minn. 1973, Wash. 1982, Tex. 1985. Assoc. Wiese and Cox, Ltd., Mpls., 1973-76; atty. Burlington No. R.R., St. Paul, 1976-81; sr. corp. counsel Burlington No. Inc., Seattle, 1981-85; v.p. law and adminstrn. Burlington Motor Carriers Inc., Ft. Worth, 1985-88, exec. v.p. and gen. counsel, 1988-93, sr. v.p., gen. counsel Daleville (Indpls.), Ind., 1993-96, Trism Inc., Kennesaw, Ga., 1996-2001, exec. v.p., gen. counsel, 2001—, pres., CEO, 2001—03; sr. v.p., gen. counsel Tango Transport Inc., Shreveport, La., 2003—. Mem. law rev. Drake U. Mem. Order of the Coif. Office: 6009 Financial Plz Shreveport LA 71129-2615 Office Phone: 318-683-6605. Personal E-mail: ralphnelso@yahoo.com.

**NELSON, RAYMOND JOHN,** language educator, dean; b. Waterbury, Conn., Sept. 5, 1938; s. Raymond John and Eileen (McGrath) N.; m. Claudine Eva Ligot, Aug. 20, 1972; children: Sylvie, Christopher. BA, U. Conn., 1965; MA, Stanford U., 1967, PhD, 1969. Prof. English U. Va., Charlottesville, 1969—, dean faculty arts and scis., 1989-97. Author: Van Wyck Brooks: A Writer's Life, 1981, Kenneth Patchen and American Mysticism, 1984 (Melville Cane award Poetry Soc. Am. 1984); also articles. With USCG, 1958-62. Woodrow Wilson fellow, 1965-66, fellow NEH, 1971-72. Mem. Colonnade Club (U. Va.), Phi Beta Kappa. Avocation: photography. Office: U Va Dept English 219 Bryan Hall Charlottesville VA 22903

**NELSON, RICHARD ARTHUR,** lawyer; b. Fosston, Minn., Apr. 8, 1947; BS in Math., U. Minn., 1969, JD, 1974. Bar: Minn. 1974, U.S. Ct. Appeals (D.C. cir.) 1975, U.S. Dist. Ct. Minn. 1975. Law clk. U.S. Ct. Appeals (D.C. cir.), Washington, 1974-75; ptnr. Faegre and Benson, Mpls., 1975—, group head employee benefits group, 2002—. Seminar lectr. in employee benefits and labor laws, 1983—. Note and articles editor Minn. Law Rev., 1973-74. Active Dem.-Farmer-Labor Party Com., Mpls., Minn., 1976—, del. dist. and local coms. and convs., 1970—, state exec. com., 1990—; student rep. bd. regents U. Minn., Mpls., 1973-74; mem. IRS employee plans adv. couns., Mid-States Key Dist., 1996-2000, Ctrl. Mountains Region, 2001-05, Great Lakes Region, 2006-; chair Mpls. Pension Coun., 1999-00. Served with U.S. Army, 1970-72. Mem. ABA, Minn. Bar Assn. (chair employee benefits sect. 1997-98), Order of Coif, Tau Beta Pi. Lutheran. Office: Faegre and Benson 90 S 7th St Ste 2200 Minneapolis MN 55402-3901 Office Phone: 612-766-7321. Personal E-mail: rnelson@faegre.com.

**NELSON, RICHARD DAVID,** lawyer; b. Chgo., Jan. 29, 1940; s. Irving E. and Dorothy (Apolsky) N.; m. Davida Distenfield, Dec. 17, 1960; children: Cheryl, Laurel. BS in Acctg., U. Ill., 1961, LLB, 1964. Bar: Ill. 1964. Ptnr. Defrees & Fiske Law Offices, Chgo., 1964-81; ptnr., counsel, chief adminstrv. officer Heidrick & Struggles, Inc., 1981—2001; pres. Galrk Sheridan, Inc., Highland Park, Ill., 2001—. Bd. dirs., exec. com. Heidrick & Struggles, Inc., Chgo., 1991-99. Pres. Jewish Cmty. Ctrs. of Chgo., 1987-89; chmn. Sign Graphics Task Force, Highland Park, Ill., 1986-88; mem. bus. and econ. devel. commn., Highland Park, 1993-96, chmn. 2004-06, Ft. Sheridan Joint Plan Commn., 1997-2000. Mem. Ill. State Bar Assn., Chgo. Bar Assn., Standard Club, Northmoor Country Club. Office: Galrk Sheridan Inc 1896 Sheridan Rd Ste 200 Highland Park IL 60035-4635

**NELSON, RICHARD JOHN,** playwright, film director, screenwriter; b. Chgo., Oct. 17, 1950; s. Richard Finis and Viola (Gabriel) Nelson; m. Cynthia Blair Bacon; 2 children. BA, Hamilton Coll., 1972. Literary mgr. BAM Theatre Co., Bklyn., 1979-81; assoc. dir. Goodman Theatre, Chgo., 1980-83; dramaturg Guthrie Theatre, Mpls., 1981-82. Author: (plays and screenplays) The Killing of Yablonski: Scenes of Involvement in a Current Event, 1975, Conjuring an Event, 1976, Scooping, 1977, The Vienna Notes, 1978 (OBIE

award playwriting 1978-79), Jungle Coup, 1978, Bal, 1980, Rip Van Winkle, 1981, Chess, 1988, Principia Scriptoriae, 1987 (ABC-TV Playwriting award, London Theatre award, 1987), Roots in Water, 1988, Some Americans Abroad, 1989, The End of a Sentence, 1991, Two Shakespearean Actors, 1991 (Tony nomination, 1992, Antoinette Perry award nomination best play, 1992), Columbus and the Discovery of Japan, 1992, Life Sentences, 1993, Ethan Frome, 1993, Misha's Party, 1993, New England, 1994, The General From America, 1996; dir.: (plays and screenplays) The General From America, 2001; author: (plays and screenplays) Goodnight Children Everywhere, 1997; dir.: (plays and screenplays) Goodnight Children Everywhere, 2001 (Laurence Olivier award best new play, 2000, BBC award best new play, 2000); author, co-dir.: Between East and West, 1984; author, dir. Franny's Way, 2001; author: (adaptations) Moliere's Don Juan, 1979, Erdman's The Suicide, 1980, Brecht's Jungle of Cities, 1981, Goldoni's Il Campiello, 1981, de Beaumarchais's The Marriage of Figaro, 1982, The Return of Pinocchio, 1983, Chekhov's The Three Sisters, 1984, Fo's The Accidental Death of an Anarchist, 1984, Jitterbugging, 1989, Sensibility and Sense, 1990, and staging, The Three Sisters, 1995, Moliere's The Imaginary Cuckold and The School for Husbands, 1995, Strindberg's The Father, 1996, Pirandello's Enrico IV, 2001; author, dir.: (adaptations) James Joyce's The Dead, 1999 (N.Y. Drama Critics Circle award 1999-2000, Tony nominations book adaptation and lyrics, 1999, Tony award best book for a musical, 2000, Lucille Lortel award best new musical, 2000, Outer Critics Circle award nomination outstanding musical dir., 2000, FANY award nomination outstanding book of a musical and outstanding dir. of a musical, 2000); Isherwood's Madame Melville, 2000—01; author: (radio plays) Languages Spoken Here, 1987 (Giles Cooper award best radio play, 1988), Eating Words, 1989, Roots in Water, 1989, Advice to Eastern Europe, 1989, The American Wife, 1994, The Fall of Agnew, Hank Aaron's 715th, The Unrequited Lovers' Manual, Watergate: An Audio Memory; translator: The Wedding as The Marriage Dance: An Evening of Farce, 1980. Named hon. assoc. artist, Royal Shakespeare Co.; recipient OBIE citation innovative programming, BAM Theatre Co., 1979—80, Playwrights USA award, 1986, Lila Wallace Writers award, 1991—93, Lannan Literary award, 1995; fellow, Nat. Endowment for the Arts, 1979, 1986, 1987; grantee, Office for Advanced Drama Rsch., 1976, Rockefellor Found., 1979, 1988; Thomas J. Watson Travel fellow, 1972, Guggenheim fellow, 1983.

**NELSON, RICHARD LAWRENCE, JR.,** surgeon, educator; b. Evanston, Ill., Oct. 11, 1946; s. Richard Lawrence and Mary Jane Nelson; m. Susan Jane Berryman, June 17, 1972; children: Cicely Adams, Jospeh Lawrence, Moira Louise, Eric James, Patrick Matthew. BA, Stanford U., 1968; MD, U. Chgo., 1972. Diplomate Am. Bd. Surgery, Am. Bd. Colon and Rectal Surgery. Prof. surgery U. Ill., Chgo., 1980—; asst. prof., epidemiology and biometry U. Ill. Sch. Pub. Health, Chgo., 1987—. Cons. NIH, Bethesda, Md., 1991—2004; cons. consultation on incontinence WHO, 2001, 04; invited lectr. NAS, 1999. Author: Surgery of the Samll Intestine, 1998, 2d edit., 2000; musician: (albums) Championship Brass, 1998, Shaken Not Stirred, 2000; mem.: Champion Brass Band (Champions, NABBA, 1996, 1997, 1998, 2000, 2001, 2002). Past pres. Am. Bd. Colon & Rectal Surgery, past chair residency rev. com.; colorectal cancer collaborative rev. group mem. Cochrane Collaboration. Named one of Top 25 Cancer Rschrs. in U.S., Am. Cancer Soc., 1996; recipient Order of Brass Band World - New Years Honors List, Brass Band World, 2000. Fellow: ACS, Am. Soc. Colon and Rectal Surgery (pres. 2001—02). Roman Catholic. Achievements include patents for intestinal tubes. Avocations: music, bicycling, skiing, hiking, brass banding. Home: 2224 Lincolnwood Dr Evanston IL 60201-2020 Home Fax: 1 312 996 2704. Personal E-mail: rick.nelson@sth.nhs.uk.

**NELSON, ROBERT ARTHUR,** civil engineer; b. Davis, SD, Sept. 9, 1939; s. Kermit George and Georgia Alice Nelson; m. Mary Jean Ellsworth, Aug. 5, 1960 (dec. 2003); children: David, Michael, Karen, Chris. BSCE, S.D. Sch. Mines, 1961; cert. bus. mgmt., U. Calif. Riverside, 1971; MPA, U. So. Calif. LA, 1974. Project engr. S.D. Highway Dept., Vermillion, 1961-62; from jr. engr. to assoc. engr. Riverside (Calif.) County Flood Control Dist., 1965-67; sr. engr. Pub. Utilities City of Riverside, 1967—69; planning engr. Riverside County Flood Control Dist., 1969-77, asst. chief flood control engr., 1977-88; gen. mgr., chief engr. Riverside County Waste Mgmt. Dept., 1988—2002; ret., 2002; cons. engr., 2003—. Bd. trustees First United Meth. Ch. of Riverside, chmn. 2000-01. 1st lt. U.S. Army, 1962-65. Mem. ASCE (Young Engr. of Yr. 1974), Solid Waste Assn. N.Am., So. Calif. Waste Mgmt. Forum (pres. 1998-99), Riverside County/San Bernardino City Engrs. (pres. 1992), Kiwanis (pres. Uptown Riverside chpt. 1980-81, Golden Rule award 1979). Office Phone: 951-683-3496. Personal E-mail: rnelson01@earthlink.net.

**NELSON, ROBERT EDDINGER,** retired management consultant; b. Mentone, Ind., Mar. 2, 1928; s. Arthur Irven and Tural Cecile (Eddinger) N.; m. Carol J., Nov. 24, 1951; children: Janet K., Eric P. BA, Northwestern U., 1949; LHD, Iowa Wesleyan Coll., 1969, North Ctrl. Coll., 1987. Asst. dir. alumni rels. Northwestern U., Evanston, Ill., 1950-51; v.p., dir. pub. rels. Iowa Wesleyan Coll., Mt. Pleasant, 1955-58; vice chancellor for devel. U. Kansas City, 1959—61; v.p. instl. devel. Ill. Inst. Tech., Chgo., 1961-68; pres. Robert Johnston Corp., Oak Brook, Ill., 1968-69, Robert E. Nelson Assocs., Inc., Oak Brook, 1969—2004; ret. 2004. Bd. dirs. Chautauqua Workshop in Fund Raising and Instl. Relations, Continental Bank of Oak Brook Terr., The Sun Cos.; nat. conf. chmn. and program dir. Am. Coll. Pub. Relations Assn., 1961; trustee, Iowa Wesleyan Coll., 1962-68; faculty mem. Ind. U. Workshops on Coll. and Univ. Devel., 1963-65, Lorretto Heights Summer Inst. for Fund Raising and Pub. Relations, 1964-68; mem. Pub. Review Panel for Grants Programs, Lilly Endowment, Inc., 1975. Contbr. chpt. to Handbook of College and University Administration, 1970. With U.S. Army, 1951-54. Mem.: Chgo. Soc. Fundraising Execs., Nat. Small Bus. Assn., Nat. Soc. Fundraisers, Pub. Rels. Soc. Am., Coun. Fin. Aid to Edn. (bd. dirs. 1957—63), Union League, Internat. Club (Chgo.), Blue Key, Execs. Club, Club Internat., DuPage Club, Econ. Club, Masons, Delta Tau Delta. Methodist. Home: 5 Oakbrook Club Dr N101 Oak Brook IL 60523-1348

**NELSON, ROBERT LOUIS,** lawyer; b. Dover, NH, Aug. 10, 1931; s. Albert Louis and Alice (Rogers) N.; m. Rita Jean Hutchins, June 11, 1955; children: Karen, Robin Andrea. BA, Bates Coll., Lewiston, Maine, 1956; LLB, Georgetown U., 1959. Bar: D.C. 1960. With U.S. Commn. Civil Rights, 1958-63, AID, 1963-66; program sec. U.S. Mission to Brazil, 1965-66; exec. dir. Lawyers Com. Civil Rights Under Law, 1966-70; dep. campaign mgr. Muskie for Pres., 1970-72; v.p. Perpetual Corp., Houston, 1972-74; sr. v.p., gen. counsel Washington Star, 1974-76; pres. broadcast div. Washington Star Communications, Inc., 1976-77; asst. sec. of army U.S. Dept. Def., 1977-79; spl. advisor to chief N.G. Bur., Dept. Def., 1980-85; prin. Mid-Md. Communications Corp., 1981-85; ptnr. Verner, Liipfert, Bernhard, McPherson and Hand, 1979-87; gen. counsel Paralyzed Vets. Am., 1988-99, sr. counsel, 2000—04; prin. Non-Profit Advisors, 2005—. Vice chmn. D.C. Redevel. Land Agy., 1976-77; bd. dirs. Friends of Nat. Zoo, 1975—89, pres., 1982-84; bd. dirs. Downtown Progress, 1976-77, Fed. City Coun., 1976-77, 83-87, Pennsylvania Ave. Devel. Corp., 1976-77, Cmty. Found. Greater Washington, 1977-78, Pep Direct, 2003-04; trustee Wolfe's Neck Farm Found., 2001—. Served with AUS, 1953-54. Mem. D.C. Bar Assn., Army Navy Club (Washington). Democrat. Episcopalian. Home (Summer): Robins Nest Orrs Island ME 04066 Home (Winter): 11 Zeitler Farm Rd Brunswick ME 04011 Office Fax: 207-725-8482. E-mail: nonprofitadvisors@msn.com.

**NELSON, ROBERT LOUIS,** education educator, consultant; b. Manitowoc, Wis., Sept. 14, 1927; s. Louis Robert and Germaine Emily (Moser) N.; m. Catherine Mary Wojtanowska, Oct. 2, 1948; children: Karen Marie, Christine Mary, Robert Stephen. B of Edn., U. Wis., Whitewater, 1959; MS, U. Wis., Madison, 1968; MA, Ohio State U., 1969; PhD, Mich. State U., 1974. Tchr., prin., adminstr. Bark River Elem. Sch., Nashotah, Wis., 1952-68; tchr. Ctrl. High Sch., West Allis, Wis., 1969-71, Hale High Sch., West Allis, Wis., 1972-77; lectr. Cardinal Stritch Coll., Milw., 1975-77, Milw. Area Tech. Coll., 1972-74; lectr., counselor U. Wis., LaCrosse, 1977-89; freelance speaker, cons. Manitowoc, Wis., 1990—. Cons., lectr. Luth. Hosp., LaCrosse, 1987-89. Author: Downhill to Uphill, 1980, Teaching Vocabulary in Sensible Ways,

1984; contbr. articles to profl. jours. Vol. guide Pinecrest Hist. Village, Manitowoc, 1990—; libr. asst. Manitowoc Pub. Libr., 1990—. With U.S. Army, 1945-46. Mich. State U. scholar, 1966, Calif. State U. scholar, 1967; Ohio State U. fellow, 1968-69. Mem. Internat. Reading Assn., Nat. Coun. Tchrs. English, Wis. Hist. Soc., Manitowoc County Hist. Soc., Retired Tchrs. Assn., Phi Delta Kappa. Avocations: travel, photography, model trains, walking, biking. Home: 1129 S 12th St Manitowoc WI 54220-5221

**NELSON, ROGER HUGH,** finance educator, corporate financial executive, consultant; b. Spring City, Utah, Mar. 7, 1931; s. Hugh Devere and Maudella Sarah (Larsen) N.; m. DeEtte Munk, Aug. 26, 1955 (dec. Sept. 1998); children— Steven R., Deanne, Mark L. BS, U. Utah, 53, MS, 1953; Ed.D., Columbia U., 1958. Mem. faculty U. Utah Coll. Bus., 1953-97; mem. faculty Utah Mgmt. Inst., 1968-75; asst. dean U. Utah Coll. Bus., 1969-74, prof. mgmt., 1970-97, admin. mgmt. dept., 1976-82, dir. programs in emerging bus., 1989-97, dir. MBA integrative field studies, 1993-96, prof. emeritus, 1997—; v.p. Computer Logic Corp., 1970-73; pres. Oil Resources, Inc., 1980-88, Puma Energy Corp., 1981-88, The Ultimate Choice Catalog Co., 1986—, David Eccles Sch. of Bus. Faculty, 1995-96; chmn. bd. Am. Leisure & Sports Investment Corp., 1996—, Clubco.com, LLC, 2006—. Fin. and mgmt. cons., 1965—; founder Utah Small Bus. Devel. Ctr., U. Utah, 1979; trustee Utah Tech. Fin. Corp., 1998-2003; chmn. club website, 2006—. Author: Personal Money Management, 1973, The Utah Entrepreneur's Guide, 1995, also articles, reports, manuals. Active local Am. Heart Assn., Am. Cancer Soc. campaigns; mem. exec. bd. Utah Opera Co., 1981-85, gen. bd., 1985-89. Danforth Teaching fellow, 1957 Mem. Acad. Mgmt., Adminstrv. Mgmt. Soc., NEA, AAUP, Phi Kappa Phi, Beta Gamma Sigma, Phi Delta Kappa, Delta Phi Epsilon. Inventor comml. color separation camera and related dye-transfer processes. Home: 2662 Skyline Dr Salt Lake City UT 84108-2855

**NELSON, RON,** composer, educator, conductor; b. Joliet, Ill., Dec. 14, 1929; s. Walter E. and Lois (Fulton) N.; m. Helen Mitchell, 1954 (dec. 1967); children: Marc W., Kristen R.; m. Michele Miller, 2004. Mus.B., Eastman Sch. Music, 1952, Mus.M., 1953, Mus.D., 1956; postgrad., L'École Normale, Normale, Paris, 1954-55; MA, Brown U., 1959. Prof. Brown U., Providence, chmn. dept. music, 1963-73, Acuff chair of excellence in creative arts, 1991, prof. emeritus, 1993—. Film composer: HEW, Eastman Kodak, ARC, Columbia Pictures, commns. from, Cin. Symphony, Lima Symphony, Rochester Philharm., R.I. Philharm., Am. Bapt. Soc., U. Minn., Dartmouth Coll., Brown U., New Music Ensemble, LaSalle Coll., Western Mich. U., Classic Chorale, U.S. Air Force Band, Nat. Symphony Orch.; composer (for orch.) Savannah River Holiday, 1954, Sarabande: For Katherine in April, 1954, (opera) The Birthday of the Infanta, 1956; (cantata) The Christmas Story, 1958: (for orch.) Tocatta for Orchestra, 1963; (oratorio) What is Man?, 1964; (orch./wind ensemble) Rocky Point Holiday, 1968-69; This is the Orchestra; (orch. and tape trilogy) Trilogy: JFK-MLK-RFK, 1969; (choral) Prayer of Emperor of China, 1973; (choral) Thy Truth is Great, 1973; (choral) Psalm 95, 1974; (orch.) Five Pieces for Orchestra after Paintings by Andrew Wyeth, 1975; (choral) Prayer of St. Francis of Assisi, 1976; (orch.) Meditation and Dance for Orch., 1976; (choral) Six Pieces for Chamber Ensemble, 1977, Four Choral Pieces After the Seasons, 1978, Three Autumnal Sketches, 1979, Here We Come As in The Beginning, 1979, Mass in Honor of St. LaSalle, 1981, Three Nocturnal Pieces, 1982, Three Seasonal Reflections, 1982; composer: Fanfare for a Celebration, 1982; (choral) On Christmas Night, 1982; Medieval Suite, 1983; (choral) Dreams, 1982; (band) Fanfare for a Celebration, 1983; (cello-piano) And the Moon Rose Golden, 1983; (band) Medieval Suite, 1983; composer: Aspen Jubilee, 1984; (organ-brass) Pebble Beach Sojourn, 1984; (chorus-band) Te Deum Laudamus, 1985; (choral) Lost and Found, 1985, Light Years, 1985, Three Settings of the Moon, 1985, (strings-trumpet) Elegy, 1986, (brass) Brevard Fanfare, 1986, (chorus/band) Prime: The Hour of Sunrise, 1987, (choral) White, 1987, (choral) Another Spring, 1987, (choral) Miniatures from a Bestiary Parts I and II, 1988, (saxophone-band) Danza Capriccio, 1988, (choral) Three Pieces after Tennyson (1988) (choral) Three Mountain Ballads, 1989, (brass-winds-percussion) Fanfare for the Hour of Sunrise, 1989, (band) Morning Alleluias for the Winter Solstice, 1989, (band) Resonances, 1990; (chorus) And This Shall Be for Music, 1990, Invoking the Powers, 1991, Songs of Praise and Reconciliation, 1991, (band) Lauds: Praise High Day, 1992, To the Airborne, 1991, Passacaglia (Homage on B-A-C-H), 1992, Chaconne (In Memoriam), 1994, Sonoran Desert Holiday, 1994, (band), Epiphanies (Fanfares and Chorales bands), 1995, Courtly Airs and Dances, 1995, (orch.) Resonances II, 1996, (orch., band) Resonances III, 1996,(orch.) Panels (Epiphanies II), 1996, The Music of Ron Nelson, 1996, (euphonium and winds) Night Song, 1998, (band) Fanfare for the New Millennium, 1999, Proclaim This Day for Music, 2002, (choral) Let Us Find a Meadow, 2006, (band) Pastorale: Autumn Rune, 2006. Recipient ASCAP awards, 1962-2004?, Found. award for World tour, 1965-66, Nat. Band Assn. award, 1992, John Philip Sousa medal of merit, 1994; Fulbright fellow, 1954; Ford Found. commn., 1962, NEA grantee, 1973, 76, 79; awarded Acuff Chair of Excellence on the Creative Arts, 1991; winner Am. Bandmasters Assn. Ostwald Contest, 1993, Am. Band Assn. contest, 1992, Sudler Internat. Wind Band Competition, 1993.

**NELSON, RONALD L.,** travel services company executive, former film company executive; MBA, U. Calif., LA; B, U. Calif., Berkeley. Exec. v.p., CFO Paramount Comm. Inc. (formerly Gulf & Western Inc.), 1987-94, bd. dirs., 1992; CFO, founding mem. DreamWorks SKG, Univeral City, Calif., 1994—2003; sr. exec. v.p. fin. Cendant Corp., NYC, 2003, CFO, 2003—, pres., 2004—, also bd. dir. Bd. dir. Advanced Tissue Scis., Inc., 1997, PHH Corp. Office: Cendant Corp 9 W 57th St New York NY 10019*

**NELSON, ROY JAY,** retired French educator; b. Pitts., July 27, 1929; s. Roy J. and Ruth Brown (Bainbridge) N.; m. Anita Lee Chandler, Aug. 16, 1954; children: Wendy Nelson Wilson, Barbara Nelson Videira. BA, U. Pitts., 1951; MA, Middlebury Coll., 1952; PhD, U. Utah, 1958. Instr. French, U. Mich., Ann Arbor, 1957-60, asst prof , 1960 65, assn. prof , 1965 72, prof., 1972-94, prof. emeritus, 1994—. Author: Péguy poète du sacré, 1960, Causality and Narrative in French Fiction from Zola to Robbe-Grillet, 1989; editor: 20e siècle: La Problématique du discours, 1986; contbr. articles to French Rev. Recipient Ruth Sinclair counseling award U. Mich., 1982, cert. for outstanding tchg., 1986; faculty tchg. award Amoco Found., 1992. Mem. MLA, Am. Assn. Tchrs. French Avocation: writing fiction. Office: U Mich Dept Romance Langs and Lits Ann Arbor MI 48109-1275 Personal E-mail: rnelson01@comcast.net.

**NELSON, RUSSELL MARION,** surgeon, educator; b. Salt Lake City, Sept. 9, 1924; s. Marion C. and Edna (Anderson) N.; m. Dantzel White, Aug. 31, 1945 (dec.); children: Marsha Nelson McKellar, Wendy Nelson Maxfield, Gloria Nelson Irion, Brenda Nelson Miles, Sylvia Nelson Webster, Emily Nelson Wittwer (dec.), Laurie Nelson Marsh, Rosalie Nelson Ringwood, Marjorie Nelson Helsten, Russell Marion Jr.; m. Wendy Lee Watson, April 6, 2006. BA, U. Utah, 1945, MD, 1947; PhD in Surgery, U. Minn., 1954; ScD (hon.), Brigham Young U., 1970; DMS (hon.), Utah State U., 1989; LHD (hon.), Snow Coll., 1994. Diplomate: Am. Bd. Surgery, Am. Bd. Thoracic Surgery (dir. 1972-78). Intern U. Minn. Hosps., Mpls., 1947, asst. resident surgery, 1948-51; first asst. resident surgery Mass. Gen. Hosp., Boston, 1953-54; sr. resident surgery U. Minn. Hosps., Mpls., 1954-55; practice medicine (specializing in cardiovascular and thoracic surgery), Salt Lake City, 1959-84; staff surgeon LDS Hosp., Salt Lake City, 1959-84, dir. surg. research lab., 1959-72, chief cardiovascular-thoracic surg. div., 1967-72, also bd. govs., 1959-90, vice chmn., 1979-89; staff surgeon Primary Children's Hosp., Salt Lake City, 1960; attending in surgery VA Hosp., Salt Lake City, 1955-84, Univ. Hosp., Salt Lake City, 1955-84; asst. prof. surgery Med. Sch. U. Utah, Salt Lake City, 1955-59, asst. clin. prof. surgery 1959-66, asso. clin. prof. surgery, clin. prof., 1966-69, research prof. surgery, 1970-84, clin. prof. emeritus, 1984—; staff services Utah Biomed. Test Lab., 1970-84. Dir. tng. program cardiovascular and thoracic surgery at Univ. Utah affiliated hosps., 1967-84; mem. policyholders adv. com. New Eng. Mut. Life Ins. Co., Boston, 1976-80 Contbr. articles to profl. jours. Mem. White House Conf. on Youth and Children, 1960; bd. dirs. Internat. Cardiol. Found.; bd. govs. LDS Hosp., 1970-90, Deseret Gymnasium, 1971-75, Promised Valley Playhouse, 1970-

79; mem. adv. com. U.S. Sec. of State on Religious Freedom Abroad, 1996-99. lst lt. to capt. M.C., AUS, 1951-53. Markle scholar in med. scis., 1957-59; Fellowship of Medici Publici U. Utah Coll., 1967; Gold Medal of Merit, Argentina, 1974; named Hon. Prof. Shandong Med. U., Jinan, People's Republic of China, 1985; Old People's U., Jinan, 1986; Xi-an (People's Republic of China) Med. Coll., 1986, Legacy of Life award, 1993. Fellow A.C.S. (chmn. adv. council on thoracic surgery 1973-75), Am. Coll. Cardiology, Am. Coll. Chest Physicians; mem. Am. Assn. Thoracic Surgery, Am. Soc. Artificial Internal Organs, AMA, Dirs. Thoracic Residencies (pres. 1971-72), Utah Med. Assn. (pres. 1970-71), Salt Lake County Med. Soc., Am. Heart Assn. (exec. com. cardiovascular surgery 1972, dir. 1976-78, chmn. council cardiovascular surgery 1976-78). Utah Heart Assn. (pres. 1964-65), Soc. Thoracic Surgeons, Soc. Vascular Surgery (sec. 1968-72, pres. 1974), Utah Thoracic Soc., Salt Lake Surg. Soc., Samson Thoracic Surg. Soc., Western Soc. for Clin. Research, Soc. U. Surgeons, Am., Western, Pan-Pacific surg. assns., Inter. Am. Soc. Cardiology (bd. mgrs.), Phi Beta Kappa, Sigma Xi, Alpha Omega Alpha, Phi Kappa Phi, Sigma Chi. Mem. Ch. of Jesus Christ of Latter-day Saints (pres. Bonneville Stake 1964-71, gen. pres. Sunday sch. 1971-79, regional rep. 1979-84, Quorum of the Twelve Apostles 1984—). Office: 47 E South Temple Salt Lake City UT 84150-1200

**NELSON, SANDRA E.,** information technology executive; d. Samual Aaron and Nelia Mary Aronson; children: Ryan Dagen, Kyle Degn. Mgmt. of Tech., Kennedy Western U., Thousand Oaks, CA, 2000—02. Career & Tech. Edn. Wash., 2005. Curriculum devel. asst. SW Regional Sch. Dist., Dillingham, Alaska, 1985—89; media specialist Sumner Sch. Dist., Wash., 1989—95; dir. of its Fed. Way Pub. Schs., Federal Way, Wash., 1995—. Cons. in field, 1999—2005; prin., cons. Leadership upward, Tacoma, 1999 2005, trainer Aha Process, Baytown, Tex., 2000—05. Master: Assn. Computer Profls. in Edn. (pres. 2002—03); fellow: Wash. Assn. Sch. Administrs. (presenter 2002—05); mem.: Advancing Leadership (presenter 2003—05), Fed. Way C of C. Office Phone: 253-945-2111. E-mail: snelson@fwps.org.

**NELSON, SARA,** editor; With Bookreporter.com, Oxygen TV network, BP Report, Self Mag.; founding books editor Inside.com; sr. contbg. editor Glamour Mag.; pub. columnist NY Observer; pub. columnist, books editor NY Post; editor-in-chief Publisher's Weekly Mag., 2005—. Author: So Many Books, So Little Time: A Year of Passionate Reading, 2003. Office: Publishers Weekly 360 Park Ave S New York NY 10010 Office Phone: 646-746-6758. Office Fax: 646-746-6631.

**NELSON, SARAH MILLEDGE,** archaeology educator; b. Miami, Fla., Nov. 29, 1931; d. Stanley and Sarah Woodman (Franklin) M.; m. Harold Stanley Nelson, July 25, 1953; children: Erik Harold, Mark Milledge, Stanley Franklin. BA, Wellesley Coll., 1953; MA, U. Mich., 1969, PhD, 1973. Instr. archaeology U. Md. extension, Seoul, Republic Korea, 1970-71; asst. prof. U. Denver, 1974-79, assoc. prof., 1979-85, prof. archaeology, 1985—2004, rsch. prof., 2004—, chair dept. anthropology, 1985-95, dir. women's studies program, 1985-87, John Evans prof., dir. Asian studies, 1996, vice provost for rsch., 1998—2002, interim vice provost grad. studies and rsch., 2001—02. Vis. asst. prof. U. Colo., Boulder, 1974; resident Rockefeller Ctr. in Bellagio, Italy, 1996. Author: Archaeology of Korea, 1993, Gender in Archaeology: Analyzing Power and Prestige, 1997, 2d revised edit., 2004, (novel) Spirit Bird Journey, 1999, Ancient Queens: Archaeological Perspectives, 2003, Jade Dragon, 2004, co-author: Denver: An Archaeological History, 2001; editor: The Archaeology of Northeast China, 1995, Ancestors for the Pigs: Pigs in Prehistory, 1998, Handbook of Gender in Archeology, 2006; co-editor: Powers of Observation, 1990, Equity Issues for Women in Archaeology, 1994, Archaeology of the Russian Far East, 2005, In Pursuit of Gender: Worldwide Archaeological Perspectives, 2001, Korean Social Archaeology, 2005, Archarology of the Russian Far East, 2006. Active Earthwatch, 1989. Recipient Outstanding Scholar award U. Denver, 1989; grantee S.W. Inst. Rsch. on Women, 1981, Acad. Korean Studies, Seoul, 1983, Internat. Cultural Soc. Korea, 1986, Colo. Hist. Fund, 1995-97, Rockefeller Found. Residency, Bellagio, Italy, Wenner-Gren Found., 2000-02, Nat. Geographic Soc., 2000—. Fellow Am. Anthrop. Assn.; mem. Soc. Am. Archaeology, Asian Studies, Royal Asiatic Soc., Sigma Xi (sec.-treas. 1978-79), Phi Beta Kappa. Democrat. Avocations: travel, gardening. Home: 5878 S Dry Creek Ct Littleton CO 80121-1709 Office: U Denver Dept Anthropology Denver CO 80208-0001 Office Phone: 303-871-2682. Business E-Mail: snelson@du.edu.

**NELSON, SHIRLEY W.,** bank executive; From jr. teller to v.p., sr. mgr. Ctrl. Bank Med. Ctr. branch, Oakland, Calif., 1966—82; founder, chmn., CEO, pres. Summit Bank, Oakland, Calif., 1982—90, chmn., CEO, 1982—; Summit Bancshares Inc. Chmn. bd. Summit Bank Found., 1998—, No. Calif. Women's Leadership Forum. Co-chmn. No. Calif. Women's League Coun.; bd. dirs. Cal State Hayward Ednl. Found. Named One of 25 Most Powerful Women in Banking, U.S. Banker Mag., 2003. Office: Summit Bancshares Inc 2969 Broadway Oakland CA 94611-5710

**NELSON, STEVEN CRAIG,** lawyer; b. Oakland, Calif., May 11, 1944; s. Eskil Manfred and Florence Lucille (Boatman) N.; m. Kathryn Cassel Stoltz, Nov. 30, 1974 (div. Apr. 1997); children: Carleton Philip, Whitney Cassel. BA in Econs. with exceptional distinction, Yale U., 1966, LLB, 1969. Bar: DC 1969, Minn. Supreme Ct. 1975, U.S. Supreme Ct. 1973, Hong Kong 2000. From atty. adviser to asst. legal adviser U.S. Dept. State, Washington, 1969-74; from assoc. to ptnr. Oppenheimer, Wolff, Foster, Shepard & Donnelly, St. Paul and Mpls., 1975-85; ptnr., internat. practice group Dorsey & Whitney LLP, Mpls., 1985—, co-chmn., Asia practice Hong Kong & Mpls. Mem. bd. appeals NATO, Brussels. 197702993; adj. prof. law U. Minn. 1980-86; spkr. in field. Contbr. articles to profl. jours. Mem. ABA (chmn. internat. law and practice 1988-89), Minn. Bar Assn., Am. Fgn. Law Assn., Am. Soc. Internat. Law, Internat. Bar Assn (mem. coun. 1996 2000) Union Internat. des Avocats (1st v.p. 1991-94), Minkahda Club. Avocations: golf, tennis, skiing, sailing. Office: Dorsey & Whitney 3008 One Pacific Pl 88 Queensway Hong Kong SAR China Office Phone: 852-2105 0211. Office Fax: 852-2524-3000. Business E-Mail: nelson.steve@dorsey.com.

**NELSON, STEVEN D.,** art history professor; BA in studio art, Yale U.; MA, Harvard U.; PhD in the history of art and architecture, 1998. Mem. faculty Tufts U., Wellesley Coll.; asst. prof. African and African Am. art history UCLA, 1998—. Magalen O. Bryant Internat. Fellow, Radcliffe Inst. for Advanced Study, Harvard U., 2004—05. Office: Dept Art History UCLA 351 Dodd Hall Box 951417 Los Angeles CA 90095-1417

**NELSON, STEVEN DWAYNE,** lawyer; b. Austin, Minn. m. Vicky L. Staab, July 6, 1990. BA in English, SUNY, Buffalo, 1972; JD, U. Mont., 1978. Bar: Mont. 1978, U.S. Dist. Ct. Mont. 1978. Sole practice, Bozeman, Mont., 1978—; city prosecutor City of Bozeman, 1979-82; city atty. City of Ennis (Mont.), 1980-82; prof. U. Great Falls, Mont., 1990—, mediator Mont., 1998—. Mem. Mont. State Bar Assn., Phi Delta Phi. Avocations: fishing, skiing, hiking. Home and Office: 4590 Maiden Rock Rd Bozeman MT 59715-7769 Business E-Mail: snelson@ugf.edu.

**NELSON, STEVEN W.,** geologist, educator; b. Salt Lake City, Utah, Sept. 17, 1945; m. Noël Bridges, Sept. 10, 1966; children: Matthew, Aimee. BA in Geology, San Jose State Coll., Calif., 1969; MS, U. Nev., Reno, 1975. Rsch. geologist U.S. Geol. Survey, Anchorage, Alaska, 1975—95; prof. geology U. Alaska, Anchorage, 1996—2006. Cons. Top Notch Edn. Svcs., Anchorage, 1995—2006. V.p. Alaska Geology Inc., Anchorage, 1994—2006. Lt. USN, 1966—72. Mem.: GSA. Avocations: sailing, hunting. Home and Office: 2515 Cottonwood St Anchorage AK 99508

**NELSON, STUART OWEN,** agricultural engineer, researcher, educator; b. Pilger, Nebr., Jan. 23, 1927; s. Irvin Andrew and Agnes Emilie (Nissen) N.; m. Evelyn Joyce Fricke, Dec. 27, 1953 (dec. Nov. 1975); children: Richard Lynn, Jana Sue; m. Martha Ellen White Fuller, Apr. 8, 1979. BS in Agrl. Engring., U. Nebr., 1950; MS in Agrl. Engring., 1952; MA in Physics, U. Nebr., 1954; PhD in Engring., Iowa State U., 1972; DSc (hon.), U. Nebr.,

1989. Grad. asst. U. Nebr., Lincoln, 1952-54, rsch. assoc., 1954-60, assoc. prof., 1960-72, prof., 1972-76. Project leader Farm Electrification Rsch., Agrl. Rsch. Svc., USDA, Lincoln, 1954-59, rsch. investigations leader, 1959-72, rsch. leader 1972-76, rsch. agrl. engr. Russell Rsch. Ctr., Athens, Ga., 1976—; adj. prof. U. Ga., 1976—; sci. adv. coun. Am. Seed Rsch. Found.; mem. CAST Task Force on Irradiation for Food Preservation and Pest Control; adv. com. grain moisture measurement Nat. Coun. Weights and Measures; mem. sci. bd. 4th Internat. Conf. on Phys. Properties Agrl. Materials, Prague, 1985. Assoc. editor Jour. Microwave Power 1975-76, 95-2000; contbr. more than 500 articles to sci. and tech. jours. With USN, 1946-48. Recipient HM Crops and Soils award Am. Soc. Agronomy, 1966, Founders Gold medal Fed. Engr. of Yr. NSPE, 1985, Superior Svc. award USDA, 1986, Profl. Achievement Citation Engring. award Iowa State U., 1987, Ga. Engring. Found. medal of honor, 1999; named to U. Nebr. Biol. Systems Engring. Hall of Fame, 1999, USDA-ARS Sci. Hall of Fame, 2002. Fellow IEEE, Am. Soc. Agrl. Engrs. (Tech. Paper award 1965, 94, Engr. of Yr. award Ga. sect. 1988, chmn. Ga. sect. 1988-89, Cyrus Hall McCormick-Jerome Increase Case Gold Medal award 2000), Internat. Microwave Power Inst. (Decade award 1981), AAAS; mem. The Electromagnetics Acad., Internat. Soc. Agromaterials Sci. and Engring., Internat. Dielectrics Soc., Ga. Soc. Profl. Engrs. (Engr. of Yr. in Govt. award 1991, Engr. of Yr. 1998), Nat. Acad. Engring., Nat. Soc. Profl. Engrs., Orgn. Profl. Employees of Dept. of Agrl. (pres. Athens area chpt. 1984-86, nat. coun. rep. 1988-95, Profl. of Yr. award 1987), Athens Optimist (pres. 1980-81, 2000-2001, lt. gov. Ga. dist. 1983-84, Optimist of Yr. award 1982, disting. and outstanding lt. gov. Ga. dist. 1985), Assn. for Microwave Power in Europe for Rsch. and Edn., Sigma Xi, Sigma Tau, Gamma Sigma Delta, Tau Beta Pi. Methodist. Home: 270 Idylwood Dr Athens GA 30605-4635 Office: USDA Agrl Rsch Svc Russell Rsch Ctr PO Box 5677 Athens GA 30604-5677

**NELSON, SUE GRODSKY,** humanities educator, consultant; b. Bklyn., Apr. 1, 1943; d. Juliette Dorfman and Louis Grodsky; m. Michael R. Nelson, Nov. 23, 1968; children: Andrew Robert, John Samuel. BA, Allegheny Coll., Meadville, Pa., 1964; EdM, John Carroll U., University Heights, Ohio, 1995. Cert. tchr. Ohio, 1988. Asst. prodn. mgr. CBS, NYC, 1964—65; tchr./dept. chair of English, honors English, reading, journalism, French Cleve. Bd. of Edn., 1965—71; group home foster parent Jewish Children's Bur., Shaker Heights, Ohio, 1971—75; tchr. of English, inclusion English/learning cmty., career edn., journalism East Cleve. Bd. of Edn., 1972—98; adj. instr., reading cons. Cuyahoga CC, Cleve. Mem. tchr. rev. panel McDougal, Littell & Co., Evanston, Ill., 1990—92; presenter Cons. - Multiple Intelligences Workshops, Ohio, 1994—99; mem. adv. coun. John Carroll U., University Heights, Ohio, 1995—97; mem. Newbury Bd. of Edn., Ohio, 2000—04, past pres. Author: (instruction manual) Getting Elected to Public Office; contbr. anthology Humanities Programs Today; co-author/editor (instruction manual) Multiple Intelligences at Work!; editor: (inspirational lessons) Zen Shin Talks. Chairperson Social Action Coun., 2005—, People for Polensek, Cleve., 1977—90; vice chairperson and sec. Cuyahoga County Dem. Party, Cuyahoga County, Ohio, 1982—89; vol. coord. Boyle for Senate, Cleveland, Ohio, 1997—98; trustee Suburban Temple-Kol Ami, 2005—. Recipient Ashland Achievement award, Ashland Oil, Inc., 1992; Coach of State Champion - Oratorical Interpretation, Ohio H.S. Speech League, 1986. Mem.: NEA (life), East Cleve. Edn. Assn. (pres. 1982—83), Ohio Sch. Bd. Assn., Ohio Edn. Assn. (life; chairperson svc. coun. 1980—81). Democrat. Jewish. Avocations: reading, exercising, interior decorating, political activism, travel. Home: 10450 Bell St Newbury OH 44065 Office: Cuyahoga CC 2900 Community College Avenue Cleveland OH 44114 E-mail: m.s.nelson@juno.com.

**NELSON, SUSAN RHODES,** media specialist, educator; b. Birmingham, Ala., June 27, 1948; d. Horace and Evelyn Vines Rhodes; m. Roger Hudson Nelson, Dec. 19, 1970; children: Jay Matthew, Jon Bradley. BS, Auburn U., 1970; MA, U. Ala., Birmingham, 1973, EdS, 1985; MLIS, U. Ala., Tuscaloosa, 1997, EdD, 2001. Cert. tchr. Ala. Tchr. Jefferson County Bd. of Edn., Birmingham, 1970—94, media specialist, 1994—; adj. prof. U. Ala., Tuscaloosa, 2001—. Adv. bd. Jefferson County Librarians, Birmingham, 2001—; chmn. Jefferson County Elem. Librarians, Birmingham, 2003—; mem. bldg. leadership team Hueytown (Ala.) Elem. Sch., 1994—, tech. coord., 1994—; cons., rschr. Learning Through Sports, Birmingham, 2003—; leader People to People Ambassador Program, Birmingham, 2004—; online facilitator Ala. State Dept. Edn. Bd. dirs. Daycare, Bessemer, Ala., 2000—05. Named Leader of the Yr., Jefferson County 4-H, 1975, Tchr. of Yr., Hueytown Elem. Sch., 2003; recipient Exemplary Libr. Program award, Libr. and Media Professionals, 1999, 2003, Most Exemplary Elem. Libr. award, Jefferson County Libr. Links for Success, 2004. Mem.: ALA (assoc.), NEA (assoc.), Ala. Libr. Assn. (assoc.), Alpha Delta Kappa (treas. 2002—), Kappa Delta Pi (assoc.), Kappa Delta Epsilon (assoc.). Republican. Avocations: travel, music, reading, sports. Home: 11227 Apple Valley Rd Mc Calla AL 35111-2448 Office: Hueytown Elem Sch 112 Forest Rd Hueytown AL 35023 Office Phone: 205-379-4123. Personal E-mail: nelsonsr2@bellsouth.net. E-mail: snelson@jefcoed.com.

**NELSON, TAMI SUE,** music educator; b. Williamsport, Pa., Oct. 2, 1975; d. Christopher Michael and Gloria Jean Bower; m. Carl Thomas Nelson, June 20, 1998; 1 child, Adrianna Marie. B in Music Edn., Grove City Coll., Pa., 1997; M in Music Edn., U. Kans., Lawrence, 1999. Choir dir. Lee Mid. Sch. Wyoming, Mich., 1999—2003; band dir. Holy Name of Jesus Sch., 2000—05; tchr. music Godfrey- Lee Early Childhood Ctr., 1999—, Lee Mid. Sch., 2003—. Mem.: Music Educators Nat. Conf., Am. Orff- Schulwerk Assn., West Mich. Orff. Avocations: music, reading, cross stitch. Office: Godfrey Lee Pub Schs 961 Jooster St SW Wyoming MI 49509-1449 Home: 4475 Sutton Pl SW Grandville MI 49418 Office Phone: 616-452-8703 1110

**NELSON, TANNIS FLYNN,** parliamentarian, retired music educator; b. Wilmington, NC, July 8, 1952; d. Floyd W. and Ila (Blake) Flynn; m. R. Michael Nelson, Aug. 4, 1973; children: Laura Bethany, Steven Michael. Student, U. N.C., 1970-74. Piano instr., Wilmington, NC, 1968—99. Cons. in field. Active bd. mgrs. N.C. Congress of Parents and Tchrs., Raleigh, 1989—, pres., 1999-2003; pres. New Hanover County Coun. PTAs, Wilmington, 1992—; trustee Bapt. Children's Homes N.C. Recipient Vol. Svc. award Gov. of N.C., 1990, 91, 92, 2000, 2003, Ann. Vol. Action award President Bush, 1992; named Most Outstanding Sch. Vol., Nat. Assn. Vols. and Ptnrs. in Edn., 1993. Mem. Nat. Assn. Parliamentarians (registered), Wilmington C. of C. (edn. coun. 1993—). Baptist. Avocations: music, volunteering, tutoring, reading. Home: 211 Gregory Rd Wilmington NC 28405-3959 Personal E-mail: tfnelson@ec.rr.com.

**NELSON, THOMAS ADAMS,** electrical engineer, consultant; b. Berkeley, Calif., Aug. 26, 1921; s. Thomas Fleming and Mabel Margaretta (Adams) N.; m. Mary Anne Mares, July 12, 1958. AA, LA City Coll., 1942; BS, U. So. Calif., 1949, MS, 1953; postgrad. cert. bus. mgmt., UCLA, 1970. Registered profl. engr., Calif. Design engr. LA Dept. Water and Power, 1950—53, quality assurance engr., resident engr. factories in U.S., Europe and Japan, 1953—65, asst. chief quality assurance engr., 1965—68, chief quality assurance engr., 1968—72, sr. engr. in charge oper. engring., 1972—77, prin. engr., mgr. comm., transmission lines, sta. maintenance and distbn. trouble, 1977—80, rail transp. cons. on coal delivery to elec. generating stas. Ariz. and Nev., 1973-79, rep. to Calif. Power Pool 1975-77; cons. engr., transp. cons. LA, 1980—. Reviewer rail transit plans So. Calif. Rapid Transit Dist., LA County Transp. Commn., LA County Met. Transp. Authority, Orange County Transit Dist., Caltrans, San Diego Met. Transit Devel. Bd., 1977—. Editor, maj. author Railroad Chronology Compendium, 1976, 50 Years of Railroading in Southern California, 2001; editor Jour. Pacific R.R. Soc., 1980-84, 87-94, cons. editor, 1994-2005; contbr. articles to profl. jours., academic publs. and newspapers, 1991—. mem. Citizens Adv. Commn. for Met. Rail, Hollywood, Calif., 1982-84, Met. Rail CORE Forum, 1987; advisor Beijing ofcl. regarding rail transit, 2002, Spokane Transit Authority, 2003, 2006. Served to capt. USAAF, 1942-45, ETO. Mem. IEEE (sr.), Vehicular Tech. Soc., Pacific R.R. Soc. (bd. dirs. 1977-80, 82-85, v.p. 1986, pres. 1987-89, publs. mgr. 1981-94), Eta Kappa Nu, Tau Beta Pi, Phi Kappa Phi.

**NELSON, THOMAS C.,** manufacturing executive; BS in Indsl. Engring., Stanford U.; MBA, Harvard U. Investment banker Morgan Stanley & Co.; spl. asst. to Sec. of Def. Richard B. Cheney U.S. Dept. Defense, Washington, 1992; gen. ptnr. Wakefield Group, 1988; CEO, pres. Nat. Gypsum, Charlotte, 1999—, chmn, 2005—. Vice-chmn, policy advisory bd. Harvard U. Joint Ctr. for Housing Studies, 2003—. Office: Nat Gypsum Co 2001 Rexford Rd Charlotte NC 28211*

**NELSON, THOMAS G.,** federal judge; b. Idaho Falls, Idaho, 1936; Student, U. Idaho, 1955—59, LLB, 1962. Ptnr. Parry, Robertson, and Daly, Twin Falls, Idaho, 1965—79, Nelson, Rosholt, Robertson, Tolman and Tucker, Twin Falls, 1979; judge U.S. Ct. Appeals (9th cir.), Boise, Idaho, 1990—2003, sr. judge, 2003—. With Idaho Air N.G., 1962—65, with USAR, 1965—68. Mem.: ABA, Idaho Law Found., Am. Bd. Trial Advocates (pres. Idaho chpt.), Idaho Assn. Def. Counsel, Idaho State Bar (pres., bd. commrs.), Am. Coll. Trial Lawyers, Am. Bar Found., Phi Alpha Delta. Office: US Ct Appeals 9th Circuit 304 N Eighth St Boise ID 83702*

**NELSON, THOMAS JOHN,** music educator, musician; b. Ft. Monmouth, NJ, Mar. 17, 1970; s. John David and Barbara Stephanie Nelson; m. Lori Ann Roupp, June 18, 1994; children: Taylor Foster, Jaclyn Claire. BS in Music Edn., West Chester U., 1992; MusM, Mansfield U., 1998. Gen. music tchr. St. Joe's Cath. Sch., North Plainfield, NJ, 1992—93; asst. band dir. Allentown HS, NJ, 1992—93; 4-12 band dir. Williamson HS, Tioga, Pa., 1993—2000, Liberty Schs., Pa., 2000—. Pvt. percussion tchr. Robert M. Sides Music Ctr., Williamsport, Pa., 1993—2000, Liberty, 2000—; co-owner TC Prodns. Rec., Liberty, 1996—; tchr. Vic Firth Corp., Boston, 2003—. Author: (website) tomnelsondrums.com, 2003—; nat. rec. artist tomnelsondrums.com; composer: tomnelsondrums.com. Nominee Disney Hands Tchr. of Yr., 2004, Tchr. of Yr., So. Tioga Sch. Dist., 2004. Mem.: Music Educators Nat. Conf., Nat. Educators Assn., Arnot Sportsmen Club. Republican. Roman Catholic. Avocations: hunting, fishing, skiing, composing, reading. Home: 896 Decoursey Rd Liberty PA 16930 Office: Liberty HS PO Box 135 Liberty PA 16930

**NELSON, VITA JOY,** editor, publisher; b. N.Y.C., Dec. 9, 1937; d. Leon Abraham and Bertha (Sher) Reiner; m. Lester Nelson, Aug. 27, 1961; children: Lee Reiner, Clifford Samuel, Cara Ritchie. BA, Boston U., 1959. Promotion copywriter Street & Smith, N.Y.C., 1959-60; asst. to mng. editor Mademoiselle Mag., N.Y.C., 1959-60; mcpl. bond trader Granger & Co., N.Y.C., 1960-63; founder, editor, pub. Westchester Mag., Mamaroneck, NY, 1968-80, L.I. Mag., 1973-78; founder, editor, pub., pres. Moneypaper, 1981—. Pub. The Guide to Dividend Reinvestment Plans, Direct Investing; founder MP63 Fund; pres. Moneypaper Advisor Inc., 1999—. Author: (with Donald Korn) Create and Manage Your Own Mutual Fund, 1994. Bd. dirs. United Way of Westchester/Putnam County, 1998—2002; bd. govs., v.p. Am. Jewish Com., Westchester, 1979—89. Recipient citation Coun. Arts, 1972, Media award Pub. Rels. Soc. Am., 1974. Mem. Women in Comms. (Outstanding Communicator award 1983). Democrat. Home: Pleasant Ridge Rd Harrison NY 10528-1004 Office: The Moneypaper Inc 555 Theodore Frend Ave Rye NY 10580 Office Phone: 914-925-0022. E-mail: vitajoy@aol.com.

**NELSON, WALLACE JAY,** lawyer; b. Patrick County, Va., Aug. 1, 1926; s. Willie Everitt and Mollie Jane (Tudor) N.; m. Helen Nixon Blount Nelson, Oct. 27, 1951; children: Jane Elizabeth Shuart, Wallace J. Nelson Jr. BS, Va. Tech., Blacksburg, 1951; JD, The Am. U., Washington, 1960. Patent atty., U.S. Patent Office, Va. State Bar. Chem. lab. tech., analytical chemist Dept. U.S. Army, Radford, Va., 1951-55; patent examiner U.S. Patent Office, Washington, 1955-61; patent atty. Nat. Aeronautics and Space Adminstrn., Hampton, Va., 1961-86, pvt. practice, Hampton, Va., 1986—2002. Inventor Slosh Alleviator, 1969. Mem. AF&AM #306 Masonic Lodge (past master), Scottish Rite of Freemasonry USA. Va. State bar. Methodist. Avocations: spectator sports, reading, golf, fishing. Home: 34 Salt Pond Rd Hampton VA 23664-1736 E-mail: walheln@aol.com.

**NELSON, WALTER HENRY,** communications consultant, author; b. Munich, Mar. 23, 1928; parents Am. citizens; m. Rose Marie Carson, Mar. 4, 1950; children: Roger Stuart, Gregory Eugene, Victoria Eugenie; 2d marriage to Rita L. Christoffersen, June 30, 1962; 1 child, Samantha Christine. Student, NYU, 1944, Norwich U., 1944-46, Columbia U., 1949-50. News editor, info. analyst Radio Free Europe, N.Y.C., Munich, 1950-53; dir. mag. info. Am. Heritage Found., N.Y.C., 1953-55; mag. pub. dir., editor quar. Am. Petroleum Inst., 1955-57; dir. pub. rels. Reach, McClinton & Co., Inc., N.Y.C., 1957-59; v.p., gen. mgr. Candygram, Inc., Chgo., 1959-60; asst. to pres. Stevens Candy Kitchens, Inc., Chgo., 1960-61; assoc. in pub. rels. Fred Rosen Assocs., Inc., 1961-62; ptnr. Prittie and Nelson Internat. Pub. Rels., London, 1975-81; chmn. Nelson Assocs. Ltd., London, 1981-93; freelance author and comms. cons., 1993—. Pub. rels. dir. William H. Rentschler for U.S. Senator, 1959-60. Author: Small Wonder: The Amazing Story of the Volkswagen Beetle, 1965, rev., 1998, German edit., 1966, Br. edit., 1967, rev., 1971, Dutch edit., 1968, Spanish edit., 1974, revised edit., 1998, The Great Discount Delusion, 1965, The Berliners: Their City and Their Saga, 1969, Br. edit., 1969, The Soldier Kings: The House of Hohenzollern, 1970, Br. and Italian edits., 1971, German edit., 1972, 98, Ernest Hemingway, 1971, Germany Rearmed, 1972, The Londoners: Life in A Civilized City, 1974, Br. edit., 1975, Japanese edit., 1976, 77, (with Terence Prittie) Economic War Against the Jews, 1977, Br. Edit., 1978, the Siege of Buckingham Palace, 1980, The Minstrel Code, 1979, Spanish edit., 1982, Gautama Buddha: His life and his Teaching, U.K. edit., 1998, Buddha: Life & Teaching, U.S. edit., 2000; contbr. articles to popular mags., newspapers. Served in U.S. Army, 1946-49. Address: 23 Clifford Ave London SW14 7BT England E-mail: walter.nelson@blueyonder.co.uk.

**NELSON, WILLIAM EDWARD,** law educator; b. 1940. BA, Hamilton Coll., 1962; LLB, NYU, 1965; PhD, Harvard U., 1971. Bar: NY 1966. Law clk. to Judge Edward Weinfeld, 1965-66; law clk. to assoc. justice Byron R. White, US Supreme Ct., Washington, 1970-71; asst. prof. U. Pa., Phila., 1971-74, assoc. prof., 1974-75; Yale U., New Haven, 1975-80; prof. NYU Sch. Law, 1980—; past Joel S. and Anne B. Ehrenkranz prof. law, now Judge Edward Weinfeld prof. law. Mem. Order of Coif. Author: Americanization of the Common Law: The Impact of Legal Change on Massachusetts Society, 1760-1830, 1975; The Roots of American Bureaucracy, 1830-1900, 1982, The Fourteenth Amendment: From Political Principle to Judicial Doctrine, 1988. Office: NYU Sch Law Vanderbilt Hall Rm 430A 40 Washington Sq S New York NY 10012-1099

**NELSON, WILLIAM EUGENE,** lawyer; b. Roland, Iowa, Sept. 23, 1927; s. Sam J. and Katherine A. (Coffey) N.; m. Sherlee M. Stanford, July 11, 1959; children: Anne, Kristin, William. BA, U. Iowa, 1950; JD, Drake U. 1957. Bar: Iowa 1957, D.C. 1965, Md. 1976, W.Va. 2004. Trial atty. civil divsn. U.S. Dept. Justice, 1957—65, asst. chief tort sect., 1966—70, chief r.r. reorgn. unit, 1970—71; gen. counsel Cost of Living Coun. Phase I, 1971, chief econ. stblzn. sect., 1971—74; ptnr. Nelson and Nelson, LLP, Washington, Bethesda, Md., 1975—. Gen. counsel the Communicators, Inc., Myersville, Md. Assoc. editor Drake Law Rev., 1955-57. With USN, 1945—46. Recipient Atty. Gen.'s Disting. Svc. award, 1972. Mem.: Omicron Delta Kappa, Order of Coif. Home: 511 Colston Dr Falling Waters WV 25419 Office: Nelson & Nelson LLP 3 Bethesda Metro Ctr Ste 700 Bethesda MD 20814-6300 Office Phone: 301-961-1958. Personal E-mail: sswen@aol.com.

**NELSON, WILLIE HUGH,** musician, lyricist; b. Abbott, Tex., Apr. 30, 1933; children: Jacob, Lukas, Paula Carlene, Amy, Lana, Susie, Billy. Student, Baylor U. Salesman; announcer; host country music shows local Tex. stas.; bass player Ray Price's band; formed own band; personal appearances at Grand Ole Opry, Nashville, throughout U.S., 1964—; rec. artist Atlantic, Columbia and RCA records. Co-founder Willie Nelson's Biodiesel. Musician: (albums) Love & Pain, 1961, And Then I Wrote, 1962, Here's Willie Nelson, 1963, Country Willie: His Own Songs, 1965, Country Favorites: Willie Nelson Style, 1966, Live Country Music Concert, 1966, Make Way for Willie

Nelson, 1967, Texas in My Soul, 1968, Good Times, 1968, My Own Peculiar Way, 1969, Both Sides Now, 1970, Laying My Burdens Down, Yesterday's Wine, 1971, Willie Nelson & Family, 1971, The Willie Way, 1972, The Words Don't Fit the Picture, 1972, Shotgun Willie, 1973, Phases and Stages, 1974, Red Headed Stranger, 1975 (Grammy award Best Country Vocal Performance for song "Blue Eyes Crying In The Rain", 1975), Willie Nelson Live, 1976, The Sound in Your Mind, 1976, The Troublemaker, 1976, To Lefty from Willie, 1977, Stardust, 1978 (Grammy award Best Country Vocal Performance for song "Georgia on My Mind", 1978), Waylon & Willie, 1978 (Grammy award Best Country Vocal Performance By A Duo Or Group for song "Mammas Don't Let Your Babies Grow Up to Be Cowboys", 1978), Willie and Family Live, 1978, The Electric Horseman, 1979, Sings Kris Kristofferson, 1979, One for the Road, 1979, Pretty Paper, 1979, San Antonio Rose, 1980, Honeysuckle Rose, 1980 (Grammy award Best Country Song for "On The Road Again", 1980), Blue Skies, 1981, Somewhere over the Rainbow, 1981, Pancho & Lefty, 1983 (Vocal Duo Yr. (with Merle Haggard) Country Music Assn. Awards, 1983), Old Friends, 1982, Always on My Mind, 1982 (Grammy award Best Country Vocal Performance for song "Always On My Mind", 1982, Country Music Assn. awards: Album Yr., 1982, Single Yr. for "Always On My Mind", 1982), Tougher Than Leather, 1983, Without a Song, 1983, Take It to the Limit, 1983, Music from Songwriter, 1984, Portrait in Music, 1984, Angel Eyes, 1984, City of New Orleans, 1984, Me and Paul, 1985, Half Nelson, 1985 (Vocal Duo Yr. (with Julio Iglesias) Country Music Assn. Awards, 1984), Brand on My Heart, 1985, Funny How Time Slips Away, 1985, Partners, 1986, The Promiseland, 1986, Island in the Sea, 1987, Seashores of Old Mexico, 1987, What a Wonderful World, 1988, Horse Called Music, 1989, Born for Trouble, 1990, The IRS Tapes: Who'll Buy My Memories?, Willie Nelson, 1993, Across the Borderline, 1993, Moonlight Becomes You, 1994, Healing Hands of Time, 1994, Pancho, Lefty and Rudolph, 1995, Six Hours at Pedernales, 1995, Just One Love, 1996, Spirit, 1996, How Great Thou Art, 1996, Christmas with Willie Nelson, 1997, Hill Country Christmas, 1997, Teatro, 1998, Life's Railway to Heaven, 1998, Back to Back: Willie Nelson and Patsy Cline, 1998, Night and Day, 1999, Clean Shirt, 2000, Outlaws, 2000, Memories of Hank Williams, Sr., 2000, Me and the Drummer, 2000, Milk Cow Blues, 2000, Good Ol' Country Singin', 2000, Rainbow Connection, 2001, Tales Out of Luck, 2001, The Great Divide, 2002, Home is Where You're Happy, 2002, All of Me Live...in Concert, 2002, Stars & Guitars, 2002 (Grammy award (with Lee Ann Womack) Best Country Collaboration With Vocals for song "Mendocino County Line", 2002), Night Life, 2002, Country Willie, 2002, Is There Something on Your Mind, 2002, On the Road Again, 2002, Honky Tonk Heroes, 2003, Broken Promises, 2003, Reunion - Can't get the Hell Out of Texas, 2003, Willie Nelson and Friends: Live and Kickin', 2003, Standard Time, 2003, Keepsake, 2003, Run That By Me One More Time, 2003, I Just Don't Understand, 2003, Live in Amsterdam, 2004, Music Legends: The Best of Willie Live, 2004, Live at Billy Bob's Texas, 2004, It Always Will Be, 2004, Songs for Tsunami Relief, 2005, Countryman, 2005, You Don't Know Me, 2006, Just a Couple of Outlaws, 2006, All American Country, 2006; appeared on (album by Waylon Jennings) Good Hearted Woman, 1972 (Single Yr. (with Waylon Jennings) Country Music Assn. Awards, 1976), appeared with various artists (albums) Wanted: The Outlaws, 1976 (Vocal Duo Yr. (with Waylon Jennings) Country Music Assn. (CMA) Awards, 1976, Album Yr. (with Waylon Jennings, Tompall Glaser, Jessi Colter) Country Music Assn. Awards, 1976); actor: (films) The Electric Horseman, 1979, Honeysuckle Rose, 1980, Thief, 1981, Barbarosa, 1982, Songwriter, 1984, Red-Headed Stranger, 1986, Starlight, 1996, Gone Fishin', 1997, Wag the Dog, 1997, Stardust, 2000, The Journeyman, 2001, The Big Bounce, 2004, The Dukes of Hazzard, 2005; (film appearances include) Anthem, 1997, Dill Scallion, 1999, Austin Powers: The Spy Who Shagged Me, 1999; actor, co-writer musical score: (TV films) Stagecoach, 1986; performer: (theme song for film) Welcome Home, 1989, (songs) Cowboys Are Frequently, Secretly (Fond of Each Other), 2006, (movie soundtrack, Brokeback Mountain) He Was a Friend of Mine, 2005; (TV films appearances include) Where the Hell's That Gold, 1988, Once Upon a Texas Train, 1989, A Pair of Aces, 1990, Born for Trouble, 1990, Another Pair of Aces: Three of a Kind, 1991, Big Country, 1994, Big Dreams and Broken Hearts: The Dottie West Story, 1995, The Beach Boys: Nashville Sounds, 1996, Starlight, 1996, Farm Aid '96, 1996, Outlaw Justice, 1998; author: (autobiography) I Didn't Come Here (and I Ain't Leavin'), 1988; co-author (with Turk Pipkin): (memoir) The Tao of Willie, 2006. Served in USAF. Named Entertainer Yr., Country Music Assn. (CMA), 1979; named to, Nashville Songwriters Assn. Hall Fame, 1973, Country Music Hall Fame, 1993; recipient citation for Top Album Artist, Billboard mag., 1976, Special Humanitarian award, Nat. Farmers Orgn., 1986, Grammy Lifetime Achievement award, 1989. Achievements include performing Cowboys Are Frequently, Secretly (Fond of Each Other), which may be the first gay cowboy song by a major recording artist. Office: care Mark Rothbaum & Assocs Inc PO Box 2689 Danbury CT 06813-2689 Address: William Morris Agency 150 El Camino Beverly Hills CA 90212 Home: Austin TX*

**NELSONWILLIAMS, CECELIA ELAINE,** dietician, nutritionist; d. Henry Austin Williams and Geraldine Jackson; m. Reverend John Alexander Nelson, Aug. 26, 1995. MS, CUNY, 1982. Registered dietitian-nutritionist SUNY Edn. Dept., 1996. Food svc. dir., clin. nutritionist Sheepshead Nursing Home, Bklyn., 1987—93; nutrition cons. Met. Jewish Hospice Greater NY, 1994—; correctional health care nutricionist, 2002—. Adj. lectr. NYU Sch. Continuning Edn., NYC, 1992—96. Trustee N.Y. ann. conf. United Meth. Ch., White Plains, 1999—. Recipient Devoted and Loyal Svc. award, John Wesley United Meth. Ch., 1994, Vol. Am. Heart Assn. Recognition award, 1997. Mem.: Am. Dietetic Assn. (assoc.). Democrat. Methodist. Avocations: swimming, tennis, antique buyer, reading, travel. Home: PO Box 415 Mount Vernon NY 10552 Office: Health Edn Inst 100 Stevens Ave Mount Vernon NY 10550 Office Fax: 914-664-4797. Personal E-mail: ceceliard@aol.com.

**NEMANI, RAMAKRISHNA RAO,** research scientist; b. Amuzuru, Andhra Pradesh, India, June 1, 1957; s. Venkataratnam and Sarvalaxmi Nemani; m. Cristina Milesi, June 15, 1971; children: Maya Beatrice Memani children: Angelica Sesha. PhD, U. Mont., 1987. Rsch. prof. U. Mont., Missoula, 1988—2002; rsch. scientist NASA, Moffett Field, Calif., 2003—. Fellow Sr. Rsch. Fellow, NRC, 1997. Mem.: Am. Geophys. Union. Home: 1121 W Knickerbocker Drive Sunnyvale CA 94087 Office: NASA/Ames Rsch Ctr Ms 242-4 Moffett Field CA 94035 Office Phone: 650-604-6185. Office Fax: 650-604-4680. Business E-mail: rama.nemani@nasa.gov. E-mail: nemani911@gmail.com.

**NEMAT-NASSER, SIA,** engineering educator, researcher; b. Tehran, Apr. 14, 1936; married. BS, Calif. State U., Sacramento, 1960; MSCE, U. Calif., Berkeley, 1961, PhD in Structural Mechanics, 1964. Asst. prof. civil engring. Calif. State U., Sacramento, 1961—62; postdoctoral fellow Northwestern U., Evanston, Ill., 1964—65, prof. civil engring. and applied math., 1970—85; tchg. fellow U. Calif., Berkeley, 1963—64, asst. prof. applied mechanics San Diego, 1966—69, assoc. prof. applied mechanics, 1969—70, prof. applied mechanics and engring. scis., 1985—99, prof. mech. and aerospace engring. dept., 1999—, disting. prof. mechanics and materials—. Dir. U. Calif. Ctr. Excellence Advanced Materials, San Diego, 1986—; founding dir. materials sci. and engring. grad. program U. Calif., San Diego, 1989—94, dir. Inst. Mechanics and Materials, 1998—2000; cons. Jet Propulsion Lab., Pasadena, Calif., 1967—67, Systems Exploration, San Diego, 1967—67, Gulf-General Atomic, San Diego, 1969—69, BDM Corp., McLean, Va., 1983—83, S-Cubed, La Jolla, Calif., 1985—89, ANatech Research Corp, La Jolla, Calif., 1989—95; ccons. TRW, Redondo Beach, Calif., 1990—91; cons. Engring. Sci. Software Inc, Smithfield, RI, 1992—92, Trans-Science Corp., La Jolla, Calif., 1987—98, Sandia Nat. Laboratories, Albuquerque, 1993—98, Alpha Star Corp., West Los Angeles, Calif., 1995—97, Gen. Atomics, San Diego, 1995—97, BP Exploration, Houston, 1998—99, Logi-con, Albuquerque, 1998—2000; vis. prof. Tech. U. Denmark, Lyngby, 1972—73. Author: (book) On Elastic Stability Under Nonconservative Loads, 1972; editor: Mechanics Today, Vol. 1, 1974, Mechanics Today, Vol. 2, 1975, Mechanics Today, Vol. 3, 1976, Mechanics Today, Vol. 4, 1978, Mechanics Today, Vol. 5, 1980, Mechanics Today, Vol. 6, 1981, (seven book series)

Mechanics of Elastic and Inelastic Solids, 1980, (book) Three Dimensional Constitutive Relations and Ductile Fracture, 1981, Hydraulic Fracturing and Geothermal Energy, 1983, Theoretical Foundation for Large-Scale Computations of Nonlinear Material BehaviorDordrecht, 1984, Large Deformations of Solids: Physical Basis and Mathematical Modeling, 1986; author: Micromechanics: Overall Properties of Heterogeneous Materials, 1993, Micromechanics: Overall Properties of Heterogeneous Materials, 2d edit., 1999, Plasticity: A Treatise on Finite Deformation of Heterogeneous In Elastic Materials, 2004. Named John Dove Isaacs Chair in Natural Philosophy, U. of Calif. San Diego, 1995—2000; recipient Alburz Ednl. Found. prize, Iran, 1975, Gold medal, Tech. U. of Crete, Greece, 1997, Willard F. Rockwell medal, Internat. Tech. Inst., 2003, Faculty Rsch. Lectr. award, U. Calif., San Diego, 2005; fellow Arthur Gould Tasheira fellow, 1962—63, Forth Found., 1963—64, Tech. U. of Denmark, 1972—73, Danish Ctr. for Applied Math. and Mechanics, 1987. Fellow: ASME (chair-materials divsn. 1997—98, Lifetime Membership Certification and Life Fellow Designation 2001, Nadai medal 2002, Adaptive Structures and Materials Sys. Best Paper award 2003, Robert Henry Thurston Lecture award 2006, Hon. mem. award 2005), Soc. Engring. Sci. (dir. 1976—82, v.p. 1978—79, pres. 1979—80, William Prager medal in Solid Mechanics 2002, Am. Acad. Mechanics (sec. 1988—94, pres. 1996—97); mem.: NAE, ASCE, Internat. Soc. for Optical Engring., Minerals, Metals and Materials Soc., World Innovation Found. Office: U Calif San Diego 9500 Gilman Dr La Jolla CA 92093-0416 Business E-Mail: sia@ucsd.edu.

**NEMBHARD, DAVID A.,** engineering educator, researcher; b. Cleve., Oct. 20, 1964; s. Horace O. Nembhard, Carren S. Nembhard; m. Harriet Black, Dec. 7, 1967; children: Charlotte, Olivia, Naomi. BS in Sys. and Control Engring., Case Western Res. U., 1987, MS in Sys. Engring., 1990; PhD in Indsl. and Ops. Engring., U. Mich., 1994. Asst. prof. ops. mgmt. Auburn U., Auburn, Ala., 1994—98; asst. prof. indsl. engring. U. Wis., Madison, 1998—2003, assoc. prof. indsl. engring., 2003—. Contbr. articles to profl. jours. Fellow Rackham Merit, U. Mich., 1991—94; grantee, NSF and Decision Risk and Mgmt. Sci. Program, 2000—, Space and Naval Warfare Sys. Command and Dept. Def., 2000; scholar, Great Lakes Ctr. Truck and Transit Rsch., 1994, Nat. Achievement, Case Western Res. U. 1983—87. Mem.: IEEE, Am. Soc. Quality, Inst. Indsl. Engrs., Inst. Ops. Rsch. and Mgmt. Sci., Soc. Mfg. Engrs. (trea. chpt. 75 2001). Avocation: piano, racquetball, cycling. Office Phone: 608-265-9777.

**NEMEC, CHRISTOPHER E.,** music educator; b. Park Ridge, Ill., July 31, 1962; s. Emil F. Nemec and Barbara A. Hamilton. MusB in Edn., U. Memphis, 1985, postgrad., 1998. Organist-music adminstr., dir. children's and youth music Lindenwood Christian Ch., Memphis, 1983—. With Lindenwood Concerts, Memphis, 1982—; accompanist, assoc. condr. Gary Beard Chorale, Memphis, 1987—; intern Am. Boychoir, Princeton, NJ, 1996; singer Carnegie Hall, N.Y.C., 1997—2004; music dir. Gold Strike Casino, Tunica, Miss., 2003—04. Composer: (choral-orchestsal composition) Be Strong; prodr.: (musical productions) Producer of Lindenwood Concerts. Deliver meals Memphis Interfaith Assn., Memphis, 2003—05; tutor Hollywood Elem. Sch., Memphis, 2003—04. Mem.: Chorus USA, Am. Choral Dirs. Assn., Choristers Guild, Am. Guild Organists. Avocations: travel, yoga. Home: 196 Lenox Pl Memphis TN 38104 Office: Lindenwood Christian Ch 2400 Union Ave Memphis TN 38112 Office Phone: 901-458-1652. Home Fax: 901-458-0145; Office Fax: 901-458-0145. Personal E-mail: chrisnemec@bellsouth.net. E-mail: chris.nemec@lroom.org.

**NEMEC, EILEEN CARLA,** elementary school educator, consultant; d. Orville C. and Edith Clark; m. Eric E. Nemec, Aug. 10, 1968; 1 child, Paul Alan. BS in Elem. Edn., U. Wis., LaCrosse, 1972; M in Curriculum and Instrn., U. Wis., Madison, 1984. Clerk Felix Dept. Store, Viroqua, 1965—68; tchr. grades 5-6 Iowa Grant Sch. Dist., Linden, Wis., 1967—68; tchr. grade 6 Mt. Horeb Area Schs., Wis., 1968—; tchr. grades 3 and 4 Wis., 1978—. LTE sci. facilitator Dept. Pub. Instrn., Madison 1989—94; mem. adv. bd. John Muir Acad., Madison, 1993—; bd. dirs. Wis. Elem. Sci. Tchrs., Madison; sci. facilitator Cray Cad., SW Acad., various locations. Author: numerous plays and stories; news articles on ednl. events. Mem. planning com. Wis. Elem. Sci. Tchrs., 1994, 1998; mem. sci. standard setting panel CTB/McGraw-Hill, Green Lake and Madison, 1997; mem. Wis. Outstanding Sci. Educators Panel, Pigeon Lake Field Sta., 1999. Named Tchr. of Yr., Mt. Horeb Sch. Dist., 1983—84, 1993—94; recipient regional award, Wis. Soc. Sci. Tchrs., 1995, 30 yr. svc. award, Dept. Pub. Instrn., 1998, 35 yr. svc. award, 2002, Kohl Fellowship award, 1990. Mem.; Wis. Elem. Sci. Tchrs., Wis. Soc. Sci. Tchrs., Mt. Horeb Edn. Assn., Southwest Edn. Assn., Wis. Edn. Assn., NEA. Avocations: reading, writing, tennis, golf, travel. Office: Mt Horeb Sch Dist 200 Hanneman Mount Horeb WI 53572 E-mail: nemac3@mailbag.com.

**NEMEC, JOSEF,** retired organic chemist, researcher; b. Ostresany, Czechoslovakia, Sept. 7, 1929; came to U.S., 1969; s. Josef Nemec and Marie (Joskova) Nemcova; m. Anna Pastush, Aug. 29, 1975; 1 child, Marketa. MS, Inst. Chem. Tech., Prague, Czechoslovakia, 1954; PhD, Czechoslovak Acad. Scis., Prague, 1958. Organic chemist Inst. Chem. Tech., Prague, 1954-61; rsch. chemist Czechoslovak Acad. Scis., Prague, 1961-69; rsch. fellow in organic chemistry Wayne State U., Detroit, 1969-70; sr. rsch. scientist Squibb Inst. Med. Rsch., New Brunswick, NJ, 1970-75; staff mem. St. Jude Children's Rsch. Hosp., Memphis, 1975-84; sr. scientist Nat. Cancer Inst.-Program Resources, Inc. Cancer R&D Ctr., Frederick, Md., 1984-95; ret., 1995. Adj. prof. med. chemistry U. Tenn., Memphis, 1979-91; external examiner U. Zimbabwe, Harare, 1994—; cons. in field. Contbr. articles to scholarly and profl. jours. Grantee Nat. Cancer Inst., 1975-85. Mem. AAAS, Am. Chem. Soc., Royal Soc. Chemistry, Czechoslovak Soc. Arts and Scis. Achievements include patents in fields of anticancer agents, organic chemicals, semimicroequipment in organic chemistry; research in natural products, synthetic anticancer agents, monosaccharides, experimental semimicrotechniques in organic chemistry.

**NEMECEK, ALBERT DUNCAN, JR.,** retail executive, investment banker, management consultant; b. Helena, Mont., Mar. 10, 1936; s. Albert Duncan and Geneva (Reindle) N.; m. Marilyn Ann Shaughnessy, Sept. 7, 1963 (div.); children: Maureen Ann, Steven Mathew; m. Judith Eileen Swift, Sept. 18, 1981 (div.); 1 child, Jennifer Eileen. BS, U. Md., 1960, postgrad. in econs., 1961. Agt. IRS, Washington, 1961-65; tax dir. Macke Co., Washington, 1965-69; tax dir., then sec. Garfinckle, Brooks Bros., Miller & Rhoads, Inc., Washington, 1969-76, treas., 1976—, v.p., 1979—; mng. ptnr. Nemecek & Falleroni, 1987, Nemecek & Jacknis, investment bankers, mgmt. cons., Falls Church, Va., 1989; founder Nemecek & Co., Inc., Falls Church, 1990. Founder Entreprenurial Growth Fund, Falls Church. 1990. Founder The Leadership Group, 1996. Home: PO Box 21 Occoquan VA 22125-0021 Personal E-mail: fixit00001@aol.com. A man's success is measured by the respect he has gained from his peers, his understanding and compassion, respect for the feelings of others, appreciation of the world's beauty, and his attempts to leave the world better than he found it.

**NEMECEK, GEORGINA MARIE,** molecular pharmacologist; b. Mineola, N.Y., Aug. 27, 1946; d. George and Frances Valerie (Masaryk) N. AB, Mt. Holyoke Coll., 1968; PhD, U. Pa., 1972; Master's cert. in Project Mgmt., George Washington U., 2000. Cert. project mgmt. profl. Project Mgmt. Inst., 2005. Rsch. assoc. dept. biochemistry U. Mass. Med. Sch., Worcester, 1972-73, postdoctoral fellow of Am. Heart Assn., dept. biochemistry, 1974, asst. prof., 1974-80, assoc. prof., 1981-83; sr. scientist platelet dept. Sandoz Pharm. Corp., East Hanover, NJ, 1983-85, mem. sr. sci. staff, platelet dept., 1986, fellow, sect. head molecular biology 1987-91, fellow diabetes, 1991-93, study dir. regulatory toxicology, 1993-96; team rep. internat. project preclin. safety Novartis Pharm. Corp., East Hanover, 1997, assoc. dir. project mgmt., 1997-2000, dir. project mgmt., 2000—02, dir. integrative compound and product profiling, 2002—03, dir. project review, biomarker devel., 2003—04, dir. neurosci. project mgmt., biomarker devel., 2004—. Vis. scientist dept. molecular biology Princeton (N.J.) U., 1987, Sea Pharm. Inc., 1985, NATO, U. Libre, Brussels, 1979, biotechnology dept. Sandoz AG, Basel, Switzerland, 1988. Contbr. articles to profl. jours. Named Nat. Heart,

Lung, and Blood Inst. Young Investigator, NIH, 1977-81. Mem. Am. Soc. Pharmacol. Exptl. Therapeutics, N.Y. Acad. Scis. (chmn. biochem. sect. 1992-94), Project Mgmt. Inst., Sigma Xi. Avocations: boating, gardening, riding, needlecrafts. Office: Novartis Pharm Corp 1 Health Plz East Hanover NJ 07936-1005 Office Phone: 862-778-2342. Business E-Mail: georgina.nemecek@novatis.com.

**NEMEROFF, CHARLES BARNET,** neurobiology and psychiatry educator; b. Bronx, NY, Sept. 7, 1949; s. Philip Peace and Sarah (Greenberg) N.; m. Melissa Ann Pilkington, May 24, 1980 (div.); children: Matthew P. (dec. 1997), Amanda P., Sarah-Frances P.; m. Gayle Applegate, June 11, 2001. BS, CCNY, 1970; MS, Northeastern U., 1973; PhD, U. N.C., 1976, MD, 1981. Diplomate Am. Bd. Psychiatry and Neurology; lic. physician, N.C., Ga. Rsch. asst. ichthyology Am. Mus. Natural History, NYC, 1968-71; neurochemistry lab. McLean Hosp., Belmont, Mass., 1971-72; rsch. assoc. surgery Beth Israel Hosp., Boston, 1972-73; tchg. asst. biology Northeastern U., 1972-73; postdoctoral fellow Biol. Scis. Rsch. Ctr., U. N.C., Chapell Hill, 1976-77, rsch. fellow, 1977-83, clin. instr. psychiatry, 1983; resident psychiatry N.C. Meml. Hosp., Chapel Hill, 1981-83; asst. prof. dept. psychiatry and pharmacology Duke U., Durham, NC, 1983-85, assoc. prof. psychiatry, 1985-89, assoc. prof. pharmacology, 1986-89, prof. depts. psychiatry and pharmacology, 1989-91, chief divsn. biol. psychiatry, 1988-91; prof., chmn. dept. psychiatry and behavioral scis. Emory U. Sch. Medicine, Atlanta, 1991—, Reunette W. Harris prof. psychiatry and behavioral scis., 1994—. Vis. prof. physiology Cath. U., Santiago, Chile, 1978; sci. coun. Nat. Alliance for Rsch. Schizophrenia and Depression, 1997—; mem. coun. NIMH, 1999-2002; mem. biomed. rsch. counl NASA, 2000-03; bd. dirs. George West Mental Health Found., 1999—, Cypress Bioscis, Inc., 2001. Editor: (with A.J. Prange Jr.) Neurotensin, a Brain and Gastrointestinal Peptide, 1982, (with A.J. Dunn) Peptides, Hormones and Behavior, 1984, (with P.T. Loosen) Handbook of Clinical Psychoneuroendocrinology, Neuropeptides in Psychiatric and Neurological Disorders, 1987, Neuropeptides in Psychiatric Disorders, 1991, Neuroendocrinology, 1992, (with P. Kitabgi) The Neurobiology of Neurotensin, 1992, (with A.F. Schatzberg) Textbook of Psychopharmacology, 1995, 3d edit., 2004, (with A. F. Schatzberg) Recognition and Treatment of Psychiatric Disorders, 1999, (with Dennis S. Charney) The Peace of Mind Prescription, 2004 (Ken award Nat. Alliance of The Mentally Ill); editor-in-chief: Depression, 1993-00, Psychopharmacology Bull., 2001-02, Neuropsychopharmacology, 2001-; co-editor-in-chief: Critical Revs. in Neurobiology, 1992-01; contbr. chpts. to books and articles and abstracts to profl. jours. Recipient Michiko Kuno award U. N.C., 1978, 79, Merck award for acad. excellence, 1981, Merck award for young investigators Am. Geriatrics Soc., 1985, 2nd prize Anna Monica Found. for Rsch. in Endogenous Depression, 1987, Merit award NIMH, 1987, rsch. prize World Fedn. Socs. Biol. Psychiatry, 1991, Edward J. Sachar award Columbia U., 1993, Edward A. Strecker prize Instnl. Pa. Hosp., 1993, Outstanding Alumni award in health scis. Northeastern U., 1995, Disting. Alumni award U. NC Sch. Medicine, 1999, George Ham Alumni award dept. psychiatry U. NC, 2000, Charles Burlingame prize Inst. Living, 2002, Alumni award U. NC, 2006; grantee Nat. Inst. Aging, 1982-83, NIMH, 1983—, NIDA, 1996-98; predoctoral fellow Schizophrenia Rsch. Found., Soc. Scottish Rite, Lexington, Mass., 1975-76, postdoctoral fellow Nat. Inst. Neurol., Communicative Disorders and Stroke, 1977, Nanaline Duke fellow Duke U. Med. Ctr., 1985-87. Fellow Am. Coll. Neuropsychopharmacology (Mead Johnson Travel award 1982, Efron award 1987, coun. mem. 1993—, pres. 1997), Am. Coll. Psychiatrists (chmn. contbns. com. 1993-95, 95—, elec. mem. 1993-96, 96—, bd. regents 1994-97, first v.p. 1999, pres.-elect 2000, pres. 2001, Mood Disorders Rsch. award 1998, Bowis award 1999), Dean award, 2004; mem. AAAS, AMA, Soc. Neurosci. (program com. 1993-95), Internat. Soc. Psychoneuroendocrinology (pres. 1993-96, Curt P. Richter award 1985), Internat. Soc. Neuroendocrinology, Internat. Soc. Neurochemistry, Am. Soc. Neurochemistry (Jordi-Folch-Pi award 1987), Endocrine Soc., Soc. Neuroendocrinology, Soc. Biol. Psychiatry (A.E. Bennett award 1979, Gold medal award 1996), Am. Fedn. Clin. Rsch., Am. Pain Soc., Am. Psychiat. Assn. (coun. rsch. 1993-98, 02-04, chmn. 1994-95, bd. dirs. rsch. 1999—, chair coun. rsch. subcom. on psychiat. treatments 1999-03, Kempf award 1989, Samuel Hibbs award 1991, Rsch. prize 1996, Rsch. Mentoring award 2006, Disting. Psychiatrist lectr. Am. Meeting 1999, 03), Am. Coll. Physicians (William C. Menninger award 2000), Argentine Assn. Psychoneuroendocrinology (sci. coun.), Nat. Depressive and Manic Depressive Disorders Assn. (vice chair 1996-98, bd. dirs. 1999—, chair 1999-00, Gerald L. Klerman Lifetime Achievement award 1997), Anxiety Disorder Assn. Am. (chmn. sci. adv. bd. 2001-03), N.Y. Acad. Scis., Am. Found. for Suicide Prevention (sci. adv. bd. 1997—, bd. dirs. 1998—, v.p. 2006-, Rsch. prize 2001), Inst. Medicine, Sigma Xi, Alpha Omega Alpha. Democrat. Jewish. Office: Emory U Sch Medicine Dept Psychiatry 101 Woodroff Circle Atlanta GA 30322-0001 Office Phone: 404-727-8382. Business E-Mail: cnemero@emory.edu.

**NEMEROFF, MICHAEL ALAN,** lawyer; b. Feb. 16, 1946; s. Bernard Gregor and Frances (Gotleib) N.; m. Sharon Lynn Leininger, Sept. 22, 1974; children: Theodore, Patrick, James. BA, U. Chgo., 1968; JD, Columbia U., 1971. Asst. counsel Subcom. on Juvenile Delinquency of Senate Jud. Com., Washington, 1971-73; assoc. Sidley Austin LLP, Washington, 1973-78, ptnr., 1978—. Treas. Friends of Jim Sasser, 1978-96, Andy Ireland Campaign Com., 1984-92. Office: Sidley Austin LLP 1501 K St NW Washington DC 20005 Office Phone: 202-736-8000.

**NEMEROWICZ, GLORIA,** academic administrator; 2 children. BA, MA, Rutgers U., PhD in Sociology. Assoc. prof. sociology Monmouth Coll., NJ, provost NJ; exec. dir. Women's Leadership Inst. Wells Coll., Aurora, NY, 1993—96; pres. Pine Manor Coll., Chestnut Hill, Mass., 1996—. Author: (books) Children's Perceptions of Gender and Work Roles; co-author (with Eugene Rosi): Professionalism in Unpaid Work; contbr. op-ed pieces to newspapers. Office: Pine Manor Coll 400 Health St Chestnut Hill MA 02467

**NEMES, ATTILA,** soil scientist, researcher; b. Miskolc, Hungary, Nov. 14, 1970; s. Zoltán Nemes and Hedvig Sárossy; m. Anikó Ildikó Kádár, Aug. 31, 2002. MSc, Agri. U. of Gödöllő, Hungary, 1994; PhD, Wageningen U. and Rsch. Ctr., Netherlands, 2003. Rsch. assoc. Rsch. inst. for Soil Sci. and Agrl. Chemistry of the Hungarian Acad. Scis., Budapest, 1994—97; vis. scientist Purdue U., West Lafayette, Ind., 1996; rsch. assoc. The Winand Staring Ctr., Wageningen, 1997—98; vis. scientist U. Calif., Riverside, 1999, postdoctoral scientist, 2005—; rsch. assoc. ALTERRA Green World Rsch. Inst., Wageningen, 1999—2003; vis. scientist Hydrology and Remote Sensing Lab., US Dept. Agr., Beltsville, Md., 2003—. Contbr. articles to profl. jours., chapters to books. Mem. regional co-chair, nat. bd. mem. Assn. Student Housing Orgn., Budapest, 1991—93; mem., regional chair Assn. Agrl. and Rural Youth and 4H Clubs, Budapest, 1991—94. TEMPUS European Union fellow, European Union, 1993, 1996, Eötvös fellow, Hungarian Nat. Fellowship Bd., 1997, Internat. Agrl. Ctr. fellow, Ministry of Agr. Nature Mgmt. and Fisheries, The Netherlands, 1998, 2000, 2001, Huygens fellow, Netherlands Orgn. for Internat. Cooperation in Higher Edn., 1999. Mem.: Am. Geophys. Union, Soil Sci. Soc. Am. (assoc. editor, mem. editl. bd. jour., Editor's citation 2004), Crop Sci. Soc. Am., Agronomy Soc. Am., Toastmasters Internat. Avocations: travel, hiking, swimming, basketball, curling. Office: Hydrology and Remote Sensing Lab 10300 Baltimore Ave Bldg 007 Beltsville MD 20705 Office Phone: 301-504-5707. E-mail: anemes@hydrolab.arsusda.gov.

**NEMETZ, PETER NEWMAN,** economist, researcher, policy analysis educator; b. Vancouver, B.C., Can., Feb. 19, 1944; s. Nathan Theodore and Bel Nemetz; m. Roma E.S. Kellock, July 16, 1994; 1 stepchild, Fiona Susan. BA in Econs. and Polit. Sci., U. B.C., 1966; AM in Econs., Harvard U., 1969, PhD in Econs., 1973. Tchg. fellow, tutor Harvard U., Cambridge, Mass., 1971-73; lectr. Sch. Planning U. B.C., Vancouver, 1973-75, asst. prof. to assoc. prof. policy analysis, 1975-96, prof., 1996—, chmn., 1984-90. Non-resident faculty Green Coll., 1993-94, 95-97, St. John's Coll., 1997-2002; vis. scientist, rschr., collaborator Dept. Health Scis. Rsch. Mayo Clinic, 1986—; cons. consumer and corp. affairs, Can., 1977-80, B.C. Hydro, 2000-02; program chmn. The Vancouver Inst., 1987—; mem. bd. advisors evidence-based practice ctr. rsch. project U. Calif., San Francisco, 2000-01; mem. sr.

faculty Ctr. Health Svcs. and Policy Rsch., U. B.C., 1990-, dept. resource mgmt. and environ. studies, 1979—, Ctr. Japanese Studies, 1992—; mem. Inst. for Resources and Environment, U. B.C., 1997—, selection com. Rhodes Scholarship, 1991-99, mem. senate, 1998-2002, mgmt. com. Ctr. Southeast Asia Rsch., 1992-99, assoc. mem. Faculty Medicine dept. health care and epidemiology faculty medicine, 1995—; bd. dirs. U. B.C. Press, 1993-2002; assoc. Ctr. Pacific Basin Monetary and Econ. Studies, Econ. Rsch. Dept., Fed. Reserve Bank of San Francisco, 1991—. Editor Jour. Bus. Adminstrn., 1978-2004; mem. editl. bd. Jour. Internat. Bus. Edn., 2001—; contbr. articles to sci. jours. Life mem. BC-Yukon divsn. Can Nat. Inst. for Blind. Postdoctoral fellow Westwater Rsch. Ctr., Vancouver, 1973-75; grantee Natural Scis. and Engring. Rsch. Coun. of Can., 1976-92, Consumer and Corp. Affairs Can., 1978-80, Econ. Coun. of Can., 1979-80, Max Bell Found., 1982-84. Mem. Am. Econ. Assn., Internat. Epidemiol. Assn., Harvard Club of B.C. (pres. 1986-94), Vancouver Club. Jewish. Avocations: swimming, photography. Office: Sauder Sch Bus Univ BC Faculty Commerce Vancouver BC Canada V6T 1Z2 Office Phone: 604-822-8443. Business E-Mail: peter.nemetz@sauder.ubc.ca.

**NEMFAKOS, CHARLES PANAGIOTIS,** defense industry executive, strategic consultant; b. Athens, Greece, Oct. 21, 1942; s. Panagiotis Soterios and Mirka (Kyriakakis) N.; children: Mirka Leigh, Charles Jr.; m. Pamela Durrant; 1 child, Alexandra. BA, Pan Am. U., 1964; MA, Georgetown U., 1982. Cert. in nat. security. Health advisor USPHS, Washington, 1965-66; fed. mgmt. intern Dept. Navy, Washington, 1966-67; budget analyst Naval Ordnance Systems Command, Washington, 1967-71; supervisory budget analyst Naval Ship Systems Command, Washington, 1971-73; sr. budget analyst Office of Sec. of Def., Washington, 1973-75; divsn. dir. Office Budget and Reports Dept. Navy, Washington, 1975-76, assoc. dir., 1976-93, dep. asst. sec., 1994-95, dep. undersec., 1995—2001, sr. civilian ofcl. for fin. mgmt., comptr., 1998—2001; dir. internal programs devel. Lockheed Martin Corp., Manassas, Va., 2001—03; organizing mem. Nemfakos Ptnrs., LLC, Arlington, Va., 2003—. Bd. dirs. First Command Ednl. Found., Am. Automar and Atlantic Marine; mem. adv. bd. Advanced Tech. Inst., Global Maritek; adj. Rand Corp., Logistics Mgmt. Inst.; lectr. Naval Postgrad. Sch., Monterey, Calif., 1984—, Georgetown U., Washington, 1987—, Ind. U. Grad. Sch., 1996—, Def. Acquisition U., 2001—; mem. base structure com. Dept. Navy, Washington, 1990-91, mem. sr. advisors group, 1991-92, vice-chmn. base structure com., 1992-95; gen. administr. Mel McLean Youth, Inc., 1980-84; registrar Va. Youth Soccer Assn., 1984-86. Recipient Dept. Navy Superior Civilian Svc. award Asst. Sec. of Navy, 1980, Dept. Navy Disting. Civilian Svc. award Sec. of Navy, 1985, 87, 93, 2000, 01, Dept. Def. Disting. Civilian Svc. award Sec. of Def., 1990, 2000, 01, Dept. Navy Disting. Pub. Svc. award Sec. of Navy, 1995, Roger W. Jones award exec. leadership Am. U., 2000; named to Rank of Disting. Exec. Pres. of U.S., 1986, 95, to Rank of Meritorious Exec., Pres. of U.S., 1981, 91; named Career Civilian Exemplar Sec. of Def., 2004. Mem. Am. Assn. Budget and Program Analysis (dir.-at-large 1980-83), Am. Soc. Mil. Comptrs. (v.p. 1988-90), Fed. Execs. Inst. Alumni Assn., Tau Kappa Epsilon (chpt. pres. 1964-65). Greek Orthodox. Avocations: golf, tennis, soccer. Office Phone: 703-362-6391. Business E-Mail: charles@nemfakospartners.com.

**NEMIR, DONALD PHILIP,** lawyer; b. Oakland, Calif., Oct. 31, 1931; s. Philip F. and Mary (Shavor) N. AB, U. Calif., Berkeley, 1957, JD, 1960. Bar: Calif. 1961, U.S. Dist. Ct. (no. dist.) Calif. 1961, U.S. Ct. Appeals (9th cir.) 1961, U.S. Dist. Ct. (ctrl. dist.) Calif. 1975, U.S. Supreme Ct. 1980. Pvt. practice, San Francisco, 1961—. Home: PO Box 1089 Mill Valley CA 94942-1089 Office Phone: 415-421-0400. Personal E-mail: nemir@mindspring.com.

**NEMIRO, BEVERLY MIRIUM ANDERSON,** author, educator; b. St. Paul, May 29, 1925; d. Martin and Anna Mae Anderson; m. Jerome Morton Nemiro, Feb. 10, 1951-75; children: Guy Samuel, Lee Anna, Dee Martin. Student, Reed Coll., 1943-44; BA, U. Colo., 1947; postgrad., U. Denver. Tchr. Seattle Pub. Sch., 1945-46; fashion coord., dir. Denver Dry Goods Co., 1948-51; fashion dir. Denver Market Week Assn., 1952-53; free-lance writer Denver, 1958—. Moderator TV program Your French. Child, Denver, 1955-56; instr. writing and comm. U. Colo. Denver Ctr., 1970—, U. Calif., San Diego, 1976-78, Met. State Coll., 1985; dir. pub. rels. Fairmont Hotel, Denver, 1979-80; freelance fashion and TV model. Author, co-author: The Complete Book of High Altitude Baking, 1961, Colorado a la Carte, 1963, Colorado a la Carte, Series II, 1966, (with Donna Hamilton) The High Altitude Cookbook, 1969, The Busy People's Cookbook, 1971 (Better Homes and Gardens Book Club selection 1971), Where to Eat in Colorado, 1967, Lunch Box Cookbook, 1965, Complete Book of High Altitude Baking, 1961, (under name Beverly Anderson) Single After 50, 1978, The New High Altitude Cookbook, 1980. Co-founder, pres. Jr. Symphony Guild, Denver, 1959-60; active Friends of Denver Libr., Opera Colo.; mem. Friends of Painting and Sculpture, Denver Art Mus. Recipient Top Hand award Colo. Authors' League, 1969, 72, 79-82, 100 Best Books of Yr. award NY Times, 1969, 71; named one of Colo. Women of Yr., Denver Post, 1964. Mem. Am. Soc. Journalists and Authors, Colo. Authors League (dir. 1969-79), Authors Guild, Friends Denver Libr., Denver Women's Press Club, Kappa Alpha Theta. Address: Park Towers 1299 Gilpin St Apt 15W Denver CO 80218-2556

**NEMIROFF, MAXINE CELIA,** small business owner, art historian; b. Chgo., Feb. 11, 1935; d. Oscar Bernard and Martha (Mann) Kessler; m. Paul Rubenstein, June 26, 1955 (div. 1974); children: Daniel, Peter, Anthony; m. Allan Nemiroff, Dec. 21, 1979. BA U.So. Calif., 1955; MA, UCLA, 1974. Sr. instr. UCLA, 1974-92; dir., curator art gallery Doolittle Theater, Los Angeles, 1985-86; owner Nemiroff Deutsch Fine Art, Santa Monica, Calif. Leader of worldwide art tours; cons. L'Ermitage Hotel Group, Beverly Hills, Calif., 1982—, Broadway Dept. Stores, So. Calif., 1979—, Security Pacific Bank, Calif., 1978—, Am. Airlines, Calif. Pizza Kitchen Restaurants; art chmn. UCLA Thieves Market, Century City, 1960—, L.A. Music Ctr. Mercado, 1982—; lectr. in field. Apptd. bd. dirs. Dublin (Calif.) Fine Arts Found., 1989; mem. Calif. Govs. Adv. Coun. for Women, 1992; mem. art selection com. Calif. State Office Bldgs., 1997—. Named Woman of Yr. UCLA Panhellenic Council, 1982, Instr. of Yr. UCLA Dept. Arts, 1984; recipient Woman of Achievement award Friends of Sheba Med. Ctr., 2003; elected to Fashion Circle of the Costume Coun., L.A. County Mus. Art, 1997—; honoree L.A. Art Core 15th Ann. Awards Benefit, 2003. Mem. L.A. County Mus. Art Coun., UCLA Art Coun., UCLA Art Coun. Docents, Alpha Epsilon Phi (alumnus of yr. 1983). Avocations: tennis, horseback riding, skiing, piano and guitar. Personal E-mail: mumseyart@aol.com.

**NEMIROW, ARNOLD MYLES,** paper company executive; b. Hartford, Conn., Mar. 25, 1943; s. Benjamin and Elsie (Nozik) N.; m. Barbro Sandberg, Dec. 22, 1967 (dec. Aug. 1983); children: Matthew, Adam; m. Sharon Green, April 23, 1988; children: Kathryn, Robert. AB cum laude, Harvard U., 1966; JD, U. Mich., 1969. Bar: N.Y. Atty. Carter, Ledyard & Milburn, N.Y.C., 1969-73; asst. gen. counsel Celco Industries Inc., Hartford, 1973-74; atty., asst. gen. counsel Gt. No. Nekoosa Corp., Stamford, Conn., 1974-80, dir. indsl. rels., 1981-83, v.p., 1984-90; pres. Gt. Southern Paper Co., Cedar Springs, Ga., 1984-87, Nekoosa Papers Inc., Port Edwards, Wis., 1988-90; pres., CEO Wausau Papers, Wausau, Wis., 1990-94, Bowater Inc., Greenville, SC, 1995-2006, chmn., 1996—2006, now chmn. Office: Bowater Inc 55 E Camperdown Way Greenville SC 29601-3511

**NEMMERS, JOSEPH M., JR.,** pharmaceutical executive; b. Dec. 22, 1954; B in History, Ariz. State U. Numerous positions in comml. ops., mfg. and materials mgmt. Abbott Labs., Abbott Park, Ill., 1980—99, v.p., exec. dir. Clara Abbott Found., 1999—2000, divisional v.p. Acquisition Integration Mgmt., 2001—02, corp. v.p., 2001—02, v.p. hosp. products bus. sector, 2002, v.p. global comml. ops., 2002—03, sr. v.p. diagnostic ops., 2003—. Mem. supervisory bd. Abbott Mgmt. GmbH and Abbott Holding GmbH. Chmn. bd.

dirs. United Way Lake County, Carmel H.S.; bd. dirs. Ct. Appointed Spl. Advs., Boys and Girls Club Waukegan, both with USAR. Office: Abbott Labs 100 Abbott Park Rd Abbott Park IL 60064-6400

**NEMSER, EARL HAROLD,** lawyer; b. NYC, Jan. 17, 1947; s. Harold Summers and Eleanor Patricia (Beckerman) N.; m. Randy Lynn Lehrer, June 17, 1974 (div.); children: Eliza Sarah, Maggie Lehrer. BA, NYU, 1967; JD magna cum laude, Boston U., 1970. Bar: N.Y. 1970, U.S. Supreme Ct. 1975, U.S. Claims Ct. 1979, U.S. Tax Ct. 1985. Law clk. Hon. Collins J. Seitz chief judge U.S. Ct. Appeals 3rd Cir., 1970-71; ptnr. Cadwalader, Wickersham & Taft, NYC, 1971-95, Swidler Berlin Shereff Friedman, LLP, NYC, 1996—2001, sr. of counsel, 2002—04; pres. Park and 76th Street Co., Inc., NYC, 1998—; spl. counsel Dechert LLC, NYC, 2005—. Vice chmn. Interactive Brokers Group, LLC, Greenwich, Conn., 1995—; dir. Timber Hill, LLC, Greenwich, Caribbean Cellular Telephone Ltd., Tortola, BVI, 1997-02; solicitor gen. H.C., Guana Island, BVI. Spl. town atty. Town of Southampton, NY, 2002—; mem. bd. advisors Lenox Hill Hosp., Greenwich Land Trust. Mem. Assn. Bar City NY; dir. The Quiogue Assn., Greenwich Riding Trails Assn. (dir. 2005-). Office: Dechert LLC 30 Rockefeller Plaza New York NY 10112-2200 E-mail: earl.nemser@dechert.com.

**NEMUNAITIS, JOHN J.,** oncologist, medical association administrator; BA, Case Western Res. U., Cleve., 1978, MD, 1982. Bd. cert. internal medicine 1987. Asst. prof. medicine U. Wash., Seattle, 1991—92; dir. hematopoiesis program Western Pa. Hosp., Pitts., 1992—93; dir. clin. rsch. Tex. Oncology, P A, Dallas, 1993—2001; exec. med. dir. Mary Crowley Med. Rsch. Ctr., Dallas, 1995—. Bd. mem. instl. biosafety com. WIRB, 2001—. Contbr. articles to profl. jours. Mem.: Internat. Soc. for Cell and Gene Therapy (mem. cancer coun. 2005—). Office: Mary Crowley Medical Research Center 1717 Main St 60th Fl Dallas TX 75201 Office Phone: 214-658-1964.

**NEMYIER, MARGARET GERTRUDE,** sales executive; b. Herkimer, NY, Dec. 23, 1930; d. Franklin Clark and Reba Louise (Jones) Culver; m. Charles Henry Nemyier, July 22, 1978. BS, SUNY Oneonta, 1953; MS in Edn., SUNY Geneseo, 1973. Cert. tchr. N.Y. Elem. tchr. Richfield Springs Ctrl. Sch., NY, 1953—54, Ilion Ctrl. Sch., NY, 1954—57, Webster Ctrl. Sch., NY, 1957—76; sales rep. Equitable Ins. Co., Perfield, NY, 1976—77; sales clk. Fuelihan's Dress Store, East Rochester, NY, 1977—79; with Projansky Furier & Dress Shop, Victor, NY, 1979—81; sales rep. Avon Products, 1977—. Sec.-treas. Webster Plank North PTA, 1959; vol. cemetery tours Mt. Hope Cemetery Orgn., Rochester, NY, 1978—83; vol. fundraiser at various PBA's, 1977—79; reach for recovery vol. Am. Cancer Soc., Rochester, 1981—86; vol. Gen. Herkimer's Homesite, Ilion Little Theatre Club, 2004; mem. planning com. Chester Gilette-Grace Brown Ann., 2005—06; cert. disaster team vol. ARC, 2005—06; election insp. Monroe & Herkimer Counties, NY, 1990—; coord. Ilion HS Mega Reunion Com., 2002. Recipient Cert. of Appreciation, Dept. of Recreation and Parks, Rochester, 1980. Mem.: NEA (life), Red Hat Soc. Democrat. Methodist. Avocations: latch hook rugs, embroidery, traveling to historic places, collectibles, Scherenschnitte (German scissor cuttings). Home: 236 E Main St Ilion NY 13357

**NENNEMAN, RICHARD ARTHUR,** retired publishing executive; b. Chgo., Oct. 13, 1929; s. William T. and Fannie (Peterson) N.; m. Katherine Ann LaBrunerie, June 29, 1954; children: Ann Walker, Mary Lisa, Katherine Conley. AB magna cum laude, Harvard U., 1951, MA in Internat. Affairs, 1953. With No. Trust Co., Chgo., 1957-58; v.p., treas., dir. First Fed. Savs. & Loan Assn., St. Joseph, Mo., 1958-60; with Valley Nat. Bank. Phoenix, 1960-65; asst. v.p., 1963-65; bus. and fin. editor Christian Sci. Monitor, Boston, 1965-74; v.p., dir. investment rsch. Girard Bank, Phila., 1974-77, sr. v.p., chmn. trust investment policy com., 1977-82; mng. editor Christian Sci. Monitor, Boston, 1983-86; editor, exec. prodr., TV broadcasting Christian Sci. Pub. Soc., Boston, 1987; editor-in-chief Christian Sci. Monitor, 1988-93; ret., 1993. Mem. investment com. Gen. Accident Ins. Group., until 1982; dir. DLB Fund Group, 1994—. Contbr. to Understanding Our Century, 1984; editor: (with Earl Foell) How Peace Came to the World, 1986, The New Birth of Christianity, 1992, Persistent Pilgrim: The Life of Mary Baker Eddy, 1997. Trustee Barnes Found., until 1982; selectman Town of Weston, Mass., 1973-74. Served with AUS, 1954-57. Mem.: Coun. on Fgn. Rels. Home: PO Box 64 Lincoln MA 01773

**NENOV, IVO P.,** mathematical and software researcher; b. Nikolaevo, Bulgaria, May 5, 1964; arrived in U.S., 1995; s. Panayot Nenov Ivanov and Maria Todorova Ivanova; m. Albena Dragomirova Stoilova-Nenova, Aug. 16, 1987 (div. Apr. 7, 1994); 1 child. Lubomir Ivov. MS, Tech. U. Sofia, Bulgaria, 1990, PhD (hon.), 2003; cert. in internat. bus. mgmt., U. Del., 1992. Rschr. Microprocessor Control Lab., Sofia, Bulgaria, 1986—86; rschr., developer CAD R&D Ctr. Ltd., Sofia, 1990—92; developer, technologist DataMap-Europe Ltd., Sofia, 1993—94; self-employed rschr., developer, cons. Calif., 1995—. Participated, set up European br. Frontline Sys., Inc., Incline Village, Nev., 2003; presenter in field. Contbr. articles to profl. jours. Capt. arty. Bulgarian armed forces, 1982—84. Recipient prize, Nat. Olympiad of Math., 1985, prize for tech., Nat. Competition for Tech., Sofia, 1989, award for extraordinaty ability in sci., INS, 2000. Mem.: Am. Owners and Pilots Assn., Soc. Indsl. and Applied Math. Bulgarian Orthodox. Avocation: flying. Home and Office: 337 Saxonville Way Antelope CA 95843 Office Phone: 916-334-3465. E-mail: inenov@sbcglobal.net.

**NENOVA, TATIANA,** economist; BA/BS. Am. U., Paris, 1995; PhD, Harvard U., Boston, 2001. Rsch. asst. Nat. Bur. Econs. Rsch., Boston, 1996—2000; economist World Bank, Washington, 2001—04; economist corp. governance Rose program, 2004—06, sr. economist South Asia, 2006—. Contbr. articles to profl. jours. Recipient Outstanding Scholastic Achievement Trustee award for best academic performance in the class of 1995, Am. U., Paris, 1995; Franklin scholar, Benjamin Franklin Soc., Am. U., Paris, 1991—95. Mem.: Internat. Corp. Governance Network, Internat. Bar Assn., Am. Econ. Assn., Omicron Delta Epsilon (Alpha chpt.).

**NENSTIEL, SUSAN KISTHART,** fundraising professional; b. Hazleton, Pa., Aug. 21, 1951; d. Frank W. and Mary A. (Price) Kisthart. BS, Pa. State U., 1973; MBA, Wilkes Coll., Pa., 1982. Cert. fund raising exec. Control mgr. Barrett, Haentjens & Co., Hazleton, 1973-79, export mgr., 1979-86; exec. dir. Leadership Hazleton, 1986-87; devel. officer Planned Parenthood of NE Pa., Wilkes-Barre, 1986-87; ins. broker, office mgr. Nenstiel & Nenstiel, West Hazleton, Pa., 1988-96; assoc. dir. devel. Hospice St. John, 1996-97; devel. assoc. Luth. Svcs. N.E., 1997-98, reg. dir. devel., 1998-2000; exec. dir. LWV of Pa., 2000-01; sr. v.p. devel. Easter Seals Ea. Pa., 2001—03; dir. major gifts Albright Coll., 2003—05; devel. dir. Kutztown U., 2005—. Pres. YWCA, Hazleton, 1983-85, Women's Coalition of Greater Hazleton, 1987-91; sec. Govt. Study Commn., Hazleton, 1986; trustee Hazleton Area Pub. Libr., sec., 1987-89, v.p., 1990-91, pres., 1991-93; chmn. Luzerne County Commn. for Women, 1988-91; mem., chmn. Hazleton City Zoning Bd., 1988-92; treas. Pa. Women's Campaign Fund, 1987-91, pres., 1991-92; mem. Leadership Hazleton Adv. Coun., 1988-92; mem. Pa. Pub. Libr. Project, 1992-94; bd. dirs. Hazleton Health Care Found., 1992-2000, chairperson, 1994-99, Cmty. Banks, Inc., 1996-2001; mem. Greater Hazleton Health Alliance Bd., 1995-2000, sec., 2000; mem. Luzerne County Regional Bd. Cmty. Banks, N.A., 1993-2000, YWCA adv. coun., 1998-2000. Named one of Outstanding Women Penns Woods Coun. Girl Scouts USA, 1977, Outstanding Young Women in Am., 1985, Woman of Yr. Soroptimist Internat., 1984, Greater Hazleton Jaycee Disting. Svc. award, 1990; recipient Luzerne County Pathfinder's award, 1990, Hon. P.E.A.R.L. award YWCA, 1996; named to Pa. Honor Roll of Women, 1996. Mem. AAUW (br. pres. 1977-79, 97-2000, state sec. 1981-83, state treas. 1983-85, state pres. 1992-96, state bd. dirs. 2005, Br. Outstanding Woman of Yr. 1980, assn. program com. 1995-97, ednl. found. bd. dirs. 1999—2003, ednl. found. devel. v.p. 2001-03, mem. state bd., 2005—), Assn. Fund Raising Profls. (chpt. v.p. 2003-05, pres.-elect 2006—), Greater Hazleton C. of C. (bd. dirs. 1995-2000, treas. 1998-2000). Home: 362 Race St Macungie PA 18062-1036

**NENTWICH, MICHAEL ANDREAS ERHART,** director; b. Prague, Czech Republic, Sept. 6, 1941; came to U.S., 1994; s. Walter Joseph and Charlotte Rosina (Hawle) N. Student, schs. in Linz, Schörfling, Austria, Wellingborough, Eng., Karlsruhe, Germany, Nuremberg (Germany) U., Heidelberg (Germany) U., 1960-64, 65-69, PhD, 1973. German tchr. St. Olave's and St. Saviour's Grammar Sch., London, 1964-65; English lectr. Mannheim (Germany) U., 1969-75; vis. lectr. in German, Chinese U. Hong Kong, 1975-80; rsch. scholar in English Tech. U. Berlin, 1980-81; educator, cons. Goethe-Inst., Bremen, Germany, 1982, Madrid, 1983-85, Düsseldorf, Germany, 1985-88, São Paulo, 1988-92, Munich, 1992-94, N.Y.C., 1994-2000, exec. dir. Atlanta, 2000—06. Author: Der schottische Shaw, 1973, Werbemagie Advocacy Binder for Teachers of German in the USA, 1999; editor Modern Germany Update, Goethe News; contbr. articles to profl. jours. Recipient Sophie Bernsthen scholarship U. Heidelberg, 1968, Friendship award Fed. Rep. Germany, 2006; named Lexus Leader of Arts Pub. Broadcasting Atlanta, 2006. Avocations: music, painting, travel, theater. Office: Goethe-Inst Atlanta Colony Sq Plaza Level 1197 Peachtree St NE Atlanta GA 30361-3502 Office Phone: 404-892-2388. Business E-Mail: director@atlanta.goethe.org.

**NEPALES, RUBEN VIADO,** journalist; b. Calasiao, Pangasinan, Philippines, June 6, 1957; s. Pedro Parajas and Socorro Viado Nepales; m. Janet Susan Rodriguez Nepales, Aug. 2, 1985; children: Bianca Nicole Rodriguez, Rafaella Angelica Rodriguez. BA in Comm. Arts, U. Santo Tomas, Manila, Philippines, 1977. Contbg. writer Manila Bull., Philippine Daily Express and Times Jour., 1977—85; exec. editor Manila Extra Mag., L.A., 1996—97; L.A. corr., columnist Philippine Daily Inquirer, Makati, 1997—. Contbr. essays and articles to profl. jours. Named Outstanding Pangasinan Artist, Provincial Govt. of Pangasinan, 1984, Outstanding Profl. in the field of journalism, Celebrity Chronicle mag., 2004. Mem.: Hollywood Fgn. Press Assn. Roman Catholic. Avocation: travel. Home and Office: 11011 Whitegate Ave Sunland CA 91040 Office Phone: 818-352-6608. Personal E-mail: rvnepales@yahoo.com. Business E-Mail: rnepales@hfpa.org.

**NEPHEW, EDMUND A.,** physicist, retired mayor; b. Kinsman, Ohio, Apr. 26, 1928; s. Seward Ralph Nephew and Carrie Alice Bascom; m. Maria Theresia Goebhardt, Sept. 1, 1956; children: Thomas, Robert. BS, Youngstown State U., Ohio; MS, Ohio State U.; grad. studies, U. Gottingen, Germany, U. Tenn. With Oak Ridge (Tenn.) Nat. Lab., 1959—89, City of Oak Ridge (Tenn.), 1984—89. Physicist Oak Ridge (Tenn.) Nat. Lab., 1959—89; councilman Oak Ridge (Tenn.) City Council, 1989—97, mayor, 1991—95. Mem., officer Sister Cities Orgn., Oak Ridge, Tenn., 1990—; chmn. ACLU (local chpt.), Oak Ridge, Tenn., 1998; commr. Oak Ridge (Tenn.) Regional Planning Assn., Oak Ridge, Tenn., 1984—88. Pvt. U.S. Army, 1950—52. Democrat. Unitarian Universalist. Avocations: gardening, travel, reading, languages. Home: 119 Netherlands Rd Oak Ridge TN 37830

**NEPHEW, JULIA ANNE,** language educator; d. Albert Henry and Elizabeth Anne Nephew; m. Eric W. Bergman; 1 stepchild, Emily. BA in French, Gustanis Adolphus Coll.; MA in French, U. Mich., Ann Harbor, 1990; PhD in French Lit., U. Wis.-Madison, 1998. Instr. French Gustarus Adolphus Coll., 1994—96; prof. French Rockford Coll., 1998—2003; adj. prof. French Dominican U., 2003—. Co-founder and dir. Jane Addams Tenant Resource Ctr., Rockford, Ill., 2001—03. Recipient Phi Sigma Iota Fgn. Lang. Honor Soc., Phi Sigma Iota, 1999, Pi Delta Phi French Honor Soc., Pi Delta Phi, 1988; scholar Grad., U. Mich. 1988, Whiteside Scholarship Fund, 1984—88; Cmty. Engagement grant, Ill. Campus Compact, 2001—02, Partners in Action grant, 2002—03, Summer Rsch. grant, Rockford Coll., 2001, Summer Travel grant, 1999. Mem.: Betsy-Tacy Soc. (hon. bd. mem.), Medieval Assn. of Midwest, Sixteenth Century Studies, Christine de Pizan Soc. (treas. 2003—). Avocations: travel, cross country skiing, reading, bicycling. Personal E-mail: nephewja@yahoo.com.

**NEPOMUCENO, CECIL SANTOS,** physician; b. The Philippines, Feb. 1, 1936; came to U.S. 1967; s. Dominador and Augustina (Santos) N.; m. Edna Manacsa, Dec. 4, 1963; children: Joy, Regina, Celeste. MD, U. Santo Tomas, Manila, The Philippines, 1962. Diplomate Am. Bd. Phys. Medicine and Rehab. Intern St. Francis Hosp., Wichita, Kans., 1963; resident Baylor U. Med. Ctr., Dallas, 1967-70; staff physician HealthSouth Lakeshore Rehab. Hosp., Birmingham, Ala., 1994-99; prof. dept. rehab. medicine U. Ala., Birmingham, to 1994. Former cons. Social Security Adminstrn.; oral bd. examiner Am. Acad. Phys. Medicine and Rehab. Lt. col. USAMR, 1982-94, ret. Mem. Ala. Soc. Phys. Medicine and Rehab.(past pres.), So. Soc. Phys. Medicine and Rehab. (past pres.). Roman Catholic.

**NEPPL, WALTER JOSEPH,** retired retail executive; b. Halbur, Iowa, June 15, 1922; s. Frank and Anna (Halbur) N.; m. Marian Maher, Oct. 15, 1945; children: Eugenie Neppl Kauffman, Marilee Neppl Cumming, Deborah Neppl Johnson, John, Thomas (dec.), Christina Neppl Totino, Nancy Neppl Tripucka. With J.C. Penney Co., Inc., 1940—, mgr. store Albuquerque, 1954-55, dist. mgr. Pitts., 1955-61, store coordination mgr. N.Y.C., 1961-64, asst. to dir. dist. mgmt. mgr., 1964-65, gen. mdse. mgr. hard lines, 1965-67, v.p., 1967-68, gen. sales and mdse. mgr., 1968-71, dir. merchandising, 1971-72, exec. v.p., 1972-76, pres., chief operating officer, 1976-81, vice-chmn. bd., 1981-82, ret., 1982, dir., 1968-85. Bd. dirs. emeritus J.C. Penney Co. Inc. Trustee emeritus Geraldine R. Dodge Found. Served to capt. USAAF, 1943-45. Decorated D.F.C. Roman Catholic. Home: The Enclave 5345 Annabel Ln Plano TX 75093-3428

**NEPPLE, JAMES ANTHONY,** lawyer; b. Carroll, Iowa, Jan. 5, 1945; s. Herbert J. and Cecilia T. (Irlmeier) N.; m. Jeannine Ann Jennings, Sept. 9, 1967; children: Jeffrey B., Scott G., Carin J., Andrew J. BA, Creighton U., 1967; JD, U. Iowa, 1970; postgrad. in bus., Tex. Christian U., 1971; LLM in Taxation, NYU, 1982. Bar: Iowa 1970, Ill. 1973, U.S. Dist. Ct. (so. dist.) Iowa 1972, U.S. Dist. Ct. (cen. dist.) Ill. 1972, U.S. Dist. Ct.(no. dist.) Iowa 1975, U.S. Ct. Appeals (7th and 8th cirs.) 1975, U.S. Supreme Ct. 1975, U.S. Tax Ct. Claims 1976, U.S. Tax Ct. 1976. Tax acct. Arthur Young & Co., Chgo., 1970; v.p., treas., bd. dirs. Stanley, Rehling, Lande & VanDerKamp, Muscatine, Iowa, 1972-92; pres. Nepple, VanDerKamp & Flynn, P.C., Rock Island, Ill., 1992-98, Nepple Law P.L.C., 1999—. Scoutmaster Boy Scouts Am., Muscatine, 1982—85, dist. chmn., 2005—; trustee State His. Soc. Iowa, 1986—92, vice-chmn., 1991—93; bd. dirs. Iowa Hist. Found., 1988—95, pres., 1991—93; trustee Musser Pub. Libr., 2000—04; pres. Muscatine Hist. Preservation Commn., 2001—, chmn., 2001—04. Recipient Gov.'s Vol. award State of Iowa, 1988, 90, Jr. Achievement of the Quad Cities Bronze award, 1996, Silver award, 2000. Fellow: Ill. Bar Found., Iowa Bar Found., Am. Bar Found. (Am. Coll. Trust and Estate Counsel; mem.: ABA (tax sect. 1972—, chair bus. coop. & agrl. tax com. 2001—03), Iowa Bar Assn. (mem. tax sect. 1978—91, chmn. tax sect. 1988—91), Quad City Estate Planning Coun. (pres. 1987), Iowa Assn. Bus. and Industry (tax com. 1978—, chmn. 1986—88), Rock Island County Bar Assn., Scott County Bar Assn., Muscatine Bar Assn. (pres. 1982—83), Ill. Bar Assn. (fed. tax. sect. coun. 1993—99, chair 1997—98), Fed Bar Assn., Muscatine C. of C. (pres. 1985), Geneva Golf and Country Club (pres. 1990—91), Elks, Kiwanis (pres. Muscatine chpt. 1978). Republican. Roman Catholic. Home: 2704 Mulberry Ave Muscatine IA 52761-2746 Office Phone: 563-264-6840. Office Fax: 563-264-6844. Personal E-mail: nepple@machlink.com. Business E-Mail: jim@nepplelaw.com.

**NEPSTAD, DANIEL C.,** ecologist, educator; BA in Biology, Kalamazoo Coll., Mich., 1979; MS in Plant Ecology & Botany, Mich. State U., 1983; PhD in Forest Ecology, Yale U., 1989. Asst. scientist Woods Hole Rsch. Ctr., Mass., 1990—93, assoc. scientist, 1993—99, sr. scientist, 1999—; scientist, founding pres. Amazon Inst. Environ. Rsch. Belém, Brazil, 1995—; vis. prof. Fed. U. Pará, Belém, Brazil, 1995—; lectr. Yale U. Sch. Forestry & Environ. Studies, 2000—. Contbr. articles to profl. jours. Grantee Pew Scholars fellowship, Conservation and Environment, 1994—97. Office: Woods Hole Rsch Ctr PO Box 296 Woods Hole MA 02543 E-mail: dnepstad@whrc.org.*

**NEREM, ROBERT MICHAEL,** engineering educator, consultant; b. Chgo., July 20, 1937; s. Robert and Borghild Guneva (Bakken) Nerem; m. Jill Ann Thomson, Dec. 21, 1958 (div. 1977); children: Robert Steven, Nancy Ann Nerem Chambers; m. Marilyn Reed, Oct. 7, 1978; stepchildren: Christina Lynn Maser, Carol Marie Maser. BS, U. Okla., 1959; MS, Ohio State U., 1961, PhD, 1964; D (hon.), U. Paris, 1990. Asst. prof. Ohio State U., Columbus, 1964-68, assoc. prof., 1968-72, prof., 1972-79, assoc. dean Grad. Sch., 1975-79; prof. mech. engrng., chmn. dept. U. Houston, 1979-86; Parker H. Petit prof. Ga. Inst. Tech., Atlanta, 1987—; dir. Inst. for Bioengring. and Biosci., 1995—; dir. Ga. Tech/Emory Ctr. for the Engring. of Living Tissues NSF Engring. Rsch. Ctr., Atlanta, 1998—. Mem. Ga. Gov.'s Adv. Coun. on Sci. and Tech. Devel., Atlanta, 1992—95; Alza disting. lectr. Biomed. Engring. Soc., 1991; ASME Thurston lectr., 94; mem. sci. bd. FDA, 2000—03; sr. adv. for bioengring. Nat. Inst. Biomed. Imaging and Bioengring., 2003—06. Contbr. articles to profl. jours. Fellow: AAAS, ASME, Am. Inst. Med. and Biol. Engring. (founding pres. 1992—94), Instn. Mech. Engrs., U.K. (hon.); mem.: NAE, Polish Acad. Scis., U.S. Nat. Com. on Biomechanics (chmn. 1988—91), Internat. Fedn. for Med. and Biol. Engring. (pres. 1988—91), Japanese Soc. for Med. & Biol. Engring. (hon.), Internat. Union for Phys. and Engring. Scis. in Medicine (pres. 1991—94), Inst. Medicine, Biomed. Engring. Soc., Am. Acad. Arts and Scis. Home: 2950 Waverly Ct SE Atlanta GA 30339-4200 Office Phone: 404-894-2768. Business E-Mail: robert.nerem@ibb.gatech.edu.

**NERENG, LINDA RAE,** elementary school educator; b. Eau Claire, Wis., Feb. 21, 1957; d. Lloyd Eugene and Bernice Ruth (Peterson) Nicolet; m. Kenneth R. Nereng, June 23, 1947; children: TJ, Ashley. Bachelor's degree, U. Wis., Eau Claire, 1978, MEd, 1983. Tchr. St. Charles (Minn.) Pub. Sch., 1978—79, Blair-Taylor Sch. Dist., Blair, 1979—; summer recreation dir. City of Blair, 2002—. Chmn. kiddie parade Blaire Cheese Fest, 1986—; v.p. ch. coun. 1st Luth. Ch., Blair, 1996—2000. Recipient John and Ellie Ellison scholarship, U. Wis.-LaCrosse, 1999, Civic award, Blair Cheese Fest, 2003. Mem.: Blair-Taylor United Educators Assn. (negotiator for tchrs. union 2001—). Avocations: sewing, quilting.

**NERHOOD, ROBERT CLARKE,** obstetrician, gynecologist; b. Altoona, Pa., Aug. 27, 1944; s. Albert and Jeanne (VanOrmer) N.; m. Carolyn Haught, Aug. 27, 1965; children: Robert, Timothy; m. Deborah Brooks, Nov. 30, 1984. Student, W.Va. U., 1962-65, MD, 1969. Diplomate Am. Bd. Ob-Gyn. Intern Polyclinic Hosp., Harrisburg, Pa., 1969-70; resident in ob-gyn. W.Va. Hosp., Morgantown, 1970-73, Kessler Air Force Med. Ctr., 1973-75; clin. assoc. prof. Sch. Medicine Marshall U., Huntington, 1977-87; dir. resident edn. Allegheny Gen. Hosp./Med. Coll. Pa.; assoc. prof. ob-gyn. Med. Coll. Pa., 1989-92; chief ob-gyn. Berkshire Health Sys.; assoc. prof. Med. Sch. U. Mass.; with Mass. Bd. Perinatal Medicine; chmn. bd. Cabell Huntington Hosp., 2002—; prof. chmn. ob-gyn. divsn. Sch. Medicine Marshall U., Huntington, W.Va., 1992—. Mem. W.Va. Bd. Perinatal Medicine, 1977-87. Ob-gyn. editor Postgraduate Medicine, 1997—. Maj. USAF, 1973-75. Mem. Am. Coll. Ob-Gyn. (vice chair W.Va. sect. 1995-97, chair W.Va. sect. 1995-98, 2001-, mem. adv. coun. dist. IV 1992-98, 2001-). Office: Marshall U Sch Medicine Ob-Gyn 1600 Medical Center Dr Huntington WV 25701-3655 Office Phone: 304-691-1400. Office Fax: 304-691-1453.

**NERI, MANUEL,** sculptor, educator; b. Sanger, Calif., Apr. 12, 1930; s. Manuel and Guadalupe (Penilla) N.; children: Raoul Garth, LaTicia Elizabeth, Noel Elmer, Maximilian Anthony, Ruby Rose Victoria, Julia Marjorie, Gustavo Manuel Student, San Francisco City Coll., 1949-50, U. Calif. Berkeley, 1951-52, Calif. Sch. Arts and Crafts, 1952-57, Calif. Sch. Fine Arts, 1957-59; D (hon.), San Francisco Art Inst., 1990, Calif. Coll. Arts and Crafts, 1992, Corcoran Sch. Art., Washinton, 1995. Mem. faculty art Calif. Sch. Fine Arts, San Francisco, 1959-65; prof. art U. Calif., Berkeley, 1963—64, Davis, 1965—90. One-man shows of sculpture, from 1957, recent exhbns. include, Oakland Mus. Art, Oakland, Calif., 1976, Western Assn. Art Mus. Travelling Exhbn., 1980-83, Seattle Art Mus., 1981, Charles Cowles Gallery, N.Y.C., 1981, 82, 86, 89, 93, 95, 97, 2002, 2003, Middendorf Gallery, Washington, 1983, 84, Gimpel-Hanover & Andre Emmerich Galerien, Zurich, Switzerland, 1984, San Francisco Mus. Modern Art, 1989, Dia Ctr. for the Arts, Bridgehampton, N.Y., 1993, 1997, Corcoran Gallery Art, Washington, D.C., 1997, Palm Springs (Calif.) Desert Mus., 1998, Riva Yares Gallery, Scottsdale, Ariz., 2002, 05, Hackett Freedman Gallery, San Francisco, 2001, 2003, 05, Fresno (Calif.) Art Mus., 2005; numerous group shows, from 1955, including San Francisco Mus. Modern Art, 1980, 83, 84, 85, 86, Am. Acad. Arts and Letters, N.Y.C., 1981, 82, 84, Oakland Mus. (Calif.), 1982, 84, 85, Seattle Art Mus., 1983, 84, Inst. Contemporary Art, Richmond, Va., 1983, Hirshhorn Mus., 1984, Contemporary Arts Ctr., Cin., 1985, Mus. Fine Arts, Houston, 1987, Bronx Mus. Arts, 1988, Whitney Mus., N.Y., 1992, 95, The White Ho., Washington, D.C., 1994, 99, Mus. Moderner Kunst, Vienna, 1997, Isetan Mus., Japan, 1999; represented in permanent collections: Oakland Mus., Seattle Art Mus., San Francisco Mus. Modern Art, Honolulu Acad. Arts, Des Moines Arts Ctr., also numerous pvt. collections including Verlaine Found., New Orleans, Bank Am. Corp., San Francisco, Lannan Found., L.A. Portland (Oreg.) Art Mus., Fine Arts Mus. San Francisco, Calif., San Jose (Calif.) Mus. Art, others Recipient 1st Award in Sculpture Oakland Art Mus., 1953, Nat. Art Found. award, 1965, award San Francisco Art Inst., 1963, award in art Am. Acad. and Inst. Arts and Letters, 1982, award of merit in sculpture San Francisco Arts Commn., 1985; Guggenheim fellow, 1979; Nat. Endowment for the Arts grantee, 1980 Roman Catholic.*

**NERIA, YUVAL Y.,** psychologist, educator; b. Tel Aviv, July 9, 1952; s. Jacob and Zipora Neria; m. Mariana Judith Nahmisas, Feb. 5, 1985; children: Michal, Oren, Maya. PhD in Psychology, Haifa U., Israel, 1994. Mem. faculty Tel Aviv U., 1994—2002; assoc. clin. prof. Columbia U., NYC, 2002—, co-dir. ctr.; assoc. dir. trauma studies and svcs. NY State Psychiat. Inst. Lt. col. Israel armed forces, 1970—84. Decorated Medal of Valor Israeli Def. Forces. Office: Columbia U 1051 Riverside Dr Unit 69 New York NY 10032 Office Phone: 212-543-6061. Business E-Mail: ny126@columbia.edu.

**NERLOVE, MARC LEON,** economics professor; b. Chgo., Oct. 12, 1933; s. Samuel Henry and Evelyn (Andelman) N.; children: Susan, Miriam. BA, U. Chgo., 1952; MA, Johns Hopkins U., 1955, PhD, 1956. Analytical statistician USDA, Washington, 1956-57; assoc. prof. U. Minn., Mpls., 1959-60; prof. Stanford (Calif.) U., 1960-65, Yale U., 1965-69; prof. econs. U. Chgo., 1969-74; F.W. Taussig rsch. prof. Harvard Coll., Cambridge, Mass., 1967-68; vis. Cook prof. Northwestern U., Evanston, Ill., 1973-74, Cook prof., 1974-82; prof. econs. U. Pa., Phila., 1982-86, Univ. prof., 1986-93; prof. agr. and resource econs. U. Md., College Park, 1993—. Author: Dynamics of Supply, 1958, Distributed Lags and Demand Analysis, 1958, Estimation and Identification of Cobb-Douglas Production Functions, 1965, Analysis of Economic Time Series: A Synthesis, 1979, Household and Economy: Welfare Economics of Endogenous Fertility, 1987, Essays on Panel Data Econometrics, 2002; contbr. numerous articles to profl. jours. 1st lt. AUS, 1957-59. Recipient award Am. Farm Econ. Assn., 1956, 58, 61, 79, P.S. Mahalanobis medal Indian Econ. Soc., 1975. Fellow Am. Statis. Assn., Econometric Soc. (v.p. 1980, pres. 1981), Am. Acad. Arts and Scis., Am. Agrl. Econ. Assn.; mem. NAS, Am. Econ. Assn. (mem. exec. com. 1977-79, John Bates Clark medal 1969), Royal Econ. Soc., Phi Beta Kappa, others. Achievements include research on economics of agriculture with particular reference to developing countries, population and economic growth; analysis of categorical data, particularly business and household surveys. Office: U Md Dept Agr and Resource Econs College Park MD 20742-0001 E-mail: mnerlove@arec.umd.edu.

**NERN, CHRISTOPHER CARL,** lawyer; b. N.Y.C., Sept. 30, 1944; s. William Francis and Jule Anne (Allison) N.; m. Kathleen Jean Brogan, Aug. 24, 1974 (div. Nov. 1985). BA, Mich. State U., 1967; JD, Wayne State U., 1972. Bar: Mich. 1973, U.S. Dist. Ct. (ea. and we.) Mich. 1973, U.S. Ct. Appeals (6th cir.) 1974, U.S. Supreme Ct. 1979. Asst. atty. gen. State of Mich., Lansing, 1972-73; staff atty. corp. affairs div. Detroit Edison Co., 1973-74, sr.atty. rates and regulatory div., 1975-78, gen. atty. regulatory affairs div., 1978-82, assoc. gen. counsel, mgr., 1982-89, asst. v.p., asst. gen.

counsel, 1989-93, v.p., gen. counsel, 1993-2000, DTE Energy, 1993-2000; adj. prof. St. Mary's Coll., 2002—. Adj. prof. Lawrence Tech. U., 2002—. Mem. allocation com. United Found., Detroit, 1983, 86-87; bd. dirs. Oakland Parks Found., Oakland County, Mich., 1985, Mich. Opera Theatre, 1996—; trustee Music Hall Ctr. for the Performing Arts, 1987-93. Served with USAF, 1967-69. Mem. ABA (bd. trustees), Detroit Met. Bar Assn. (trustee found.), Am. Corp. Counsel Assn. (pres. Mich chpt. 1986-88), Econs. Club (Detroit), Detroit Golf Club, Detroit Athletic Club. Roman Catholic. Home: 1052 Stratford Ln Bloomfield Hills MI 48304-2930 E-mail: nernchris@aol.com.

**NERODE, ANIL,** mathematician, educator; b. L.A., June 4, 1932; s. Nirad Ranjan and Agnes (Spencer) N.; m. Sondra Raines, Feb. 12, 1955 (div. 1968); children: Christopher Curtis, Gregory Daniel; m. Sally Riedel Sievers, May 16, 1970; 1 child, Nathanael Caldwell. BA, U. Chgo., 1949, BS, 1952, MS, 1953, PhD, 1956. Group leader automata and weapons systems Lab. Applied Sci., U. Chgo., 1954-57; mem. Inst. for Advanced Study, Princeton, 1957-58, 62-63; vis. asst. prof. math. U. Calif. at Berkeley, 1958-59; mem. faculty Cornell U., 1959—, prof. math., 1965—, Goldwin Smith prof. math., 1990—, chmn. dept. math., 1982-87, dir. Math. Sci. Inst., 1986-97; acting dir. Center for Applied Math., 1965-66; vis. prof. Monash U., Melbourne, Australia, 1970, 74, 78, 79, U. Chgo., 1976, M.I.T., 1980, U. Calif., San Diego, 1981; disting. vis. scientist EPA, 1985-87; dir. Ctr. for Found. of Intelligent Sys. Cornell U., 1997—2001. Prin. investigator numerous grants; mem. sci. adv. bd. EPA, 1988-93, chair tech. adv. panel Global Change, 1990-92; mem. sci. adv. bd. Ctr. for Intelligent Control, Harvard-MIT-Brown U., 1988-94; cons. to govt. and industry; co-founder Clearsight Corp., 1995. Author: (with John Crossley) Combinatorial Functors, 1974, (with Richard Shore) Logic for Applications, 2d edit., 1996, (with G.A. Metakides) Principles of Logic and Logic Programming, 1996, (with B. Khoussainov) Automata Theory and its Applications, 2001; editor Advances in Mathematics, 1967-70, Jour. Symbolic Logic, 1967-82, Annals of Pure and Applied Logic, 1983-96, Future Generation Computing Systems, 1983-97, Jour. Pure & Applied Algebra, 1988-2005, Annals of Math. and Artificial Intelligence, 1989—, Logical Methods in Computer Sci., 1991-94, Computer Modelling and Simulation, 1991—, Constraints, 1995-2001, Grammers, 1997-2001, (with J. Remmel, S. Goncharov, Y. Ershov) Handbook of Recursive Algebra, 1998. Mem. AIII, IEEE, Assn. Computing Machinery, Am. Math. Soc. (assoc. editor procs. 1962-65, v.p. 1991-94), Soc. Indsl. and Applied Math., Math. Assn. Am., Assn. Symbolic Logic, European Assn. for Theoretical Computer Sci. Home: 406 Cayuga Heights Rd Ithaca NY 14850-1402 Office: Cornell U 545 Mallott Hall Dept Math Ithaca NY 14853-4201 E-mail: anil@cornell.edu.

**NÉRON, MARTIN,** musician; s. Raymond Néron and Louise Chiricota. B Music, U. Montreal, 1990; MusM, Westminster Choir Coll., Princeton, N.J., 1996; D in Musical Arts, Manhattan Sch. Music, N.Y.C., 2001. Collaborative pianist Westminster Choir Coll., Princeton, 1997—. Musician (pianist): (compact disk) Greek Songs for Romantics and Realists, L'Heure Exquise. Recipient 1st prize, Can. Music Competition, 1989; grantee, Fonds les Amis de l'Arts Awards, 1992—92, Canadian-Italian Profl. and Businessmen Assn. 1991—93, Conseil des Arts du Québec, 1992, 1994, 1996; scholar, Manhattan Sch. Music, 1996—98. Mem.: Nat. Assn. Tchrs. Singing. Personal E-mail: mneron@msn.com.

**NES, MARGARET ISABEL,** artist; b. Paris, Sept. 17, 1950; d. David Guilick and Elizabeth (Houghton) N.; m. Robert Earl Alderisio, Oct. 2, 1942. Art tchr. San Felipe Children's Home, San Cristobal, N.Mex., 1982-83. One-woman shows include White Crane Gallery, Taos, N.Mex., 1980, Gallery Sigala, Taos, 1980-83, Variant Gallery, Taos, 1985, Kyle Belding Gallery, Denver, 1987-88, E.S. Lawrence Gallery, Taos, 1988-91, Edith Lambert Gallery, Santa Fe, N.Mex., 1996-99, 97, Collins Pettit Gallery, Taos, 1995, many others; exhibited in group shows at Harwood Found., Taos, 1980, C. Grimaldis Gallery, Balt., 1981, Highland U., Las Vegas, N.Mex., 1982-84, Stables Art Ctr., Taos, 1982-89, 90, FACET Gallery, Taos, 1984, Sweeny Ctr., Santa Fe, 1985, Taos Spring Arts Celebration, 1985-95, Denver ARt Mus., 1986, Taos Arts Festival, 1986-94, E.S. Lawrence Gallery, Taos, 1986, El Taller Gallery, Austin, Tex., 1986, Santa Fe Arts, 1988, Md. Pastel Soc., Balt., 1989, Lancaster (Ohio) Arts Festival, Ctr. Arts of S.W., Santa Fe, Rotunda, Russell Senate Office Bldg., Washington, 1991, Opening Scene Gallery, Taos, 1993, 94, Taos Art Assn., 1994, Eiteljorg Mus., Indpls., 1994, Hahn Ross Gallery, Santa Fe, N.Mex., 1997-2005; represented in permanent collections at Mt. Sinai Med. Ctr., N.Y.C., U. Tex. Law Sch., Austin, Mountain Bell Telephone Co., Denver, Mary Cabot Enterprises, Taos Recipient Best in Traditional award Taos Today Show, 1985, Best in Show award Taos Spring Arts Celebration, 1985, Grumbacher award Taos Today Show, 1985, Best Pastel award Taos Today Show, 1989, Best in Contemporary award Taos Today Show, 1989, Rembrandt Pastel award Md. Pastel Soc. Exhibit, Balt., 1989, Best of Show, Taos Invites Taos, 1993, 1st pl. award Taos Art Assn. Mems. Show, 1994. Office: PO Box 424 El Prado NM 87529-0424

**NESBIT, LYNN,** literary agent; BA in Speech, Northwestern U. Asst. to agent Sterling Lord; head literary dept. Internat. Creative Mgmt.; ptnr. Janklow & Nesbit Assocs., N.Y.C., 1989—. Achievements include representing leading authors, among others, Tom Wolfe, Toni Morrison. John LeCarre, Jimmy and Rosalynn Carter, Anne Rice, Nora Ephron, Michael Crichton and Gail Sheehy.

**NESBIT, SANDI MICHELLE,** corporate financial executive; b. Marietta, Ga., Aug. 30, 1963; d. Walter DeForest (Stepfather) and Linda S. Van Fleet, William E. Ray; m. Eric James E Nesbit, Oct. 11, 1998; 1 child, Cora Helene. Title Insurance Agent Tenn., 2002; Notary Public at Large Tenn., 2000. Ceo/founder NNBS, Inc., Anytime Services.com, Rockford, Tenn., 1999—; mgr. Nationwide Homes, Alcoa, Tenn., 1998—2000. Author: (educational workbook) The Title Searchers Handbook. Hon. chmn. Nat. Rep. Congl. Com., 2003. Pentacostal. Avocations: travel, reading, music, animals. Office: NNBS Inc 3532 Calvert St Rockford TN 37853-3926 Office Phone: 865-977-8808.

**NESBIT, WILLIAM TERRY,** small business owner, consultant; b. Pitts., Jan. 30, 1945; s. William Frank and Glenna (Cleeton) N.; divorced. Owner, CEO Narrow Gauge Car Shop, Evergreen Outdoor Ctr., Shiremanstown, Pa., 1972—; mem. faculty Millersville (Pa.) U., 1976-81, Temple U., Phila., 1979, Nat. Aquatic and Small Craft Sch., Bemis Point, NY, 1980, Harrisburg (Pa.) Area C. C., 1981-82, 91, Dickinson Coll., Carlisle, Pa., 1982-83. Judge 32d Capital Area Sci., Engring. Fair, Dickinson Coll., Carlisle, Pa., 1989; mem. tech. briefs reader adv. panel NASA, 2000—. Co-developer ARC basic and whitewater canoeing programs for instrn., 1977-79; inventor, developer The Z Drag for Boat Rescues, 1980; developer, mfr. first HOn3 ready-to-run plastic rolling stock having NMRA warrant; contbg. author: The Brown Book, 2d edit., 1982. Vol. ARC, 1961—; contbr. A.C. Kalmbach Meml. Libr., Chattanooga; benefactor Carlyton Sch. Dist. Libr., Carnegie, Pa. Recipient award for Humanity ARC, 1967, award for 30 Yrs. Vol. Svc., 1991; named Class I Radiol. Protection Officer, U.S. Dept. Def. and NRC, 1993. Mem. Math. Assn. Am., Nat. Assn. Canoe Liveries and Outfitters (founding), Nat. Model Railroad Assn. (life, mid-eastern region bd. dirs. 1997-2001, supt. Susquehanna divsn. 1996-2000, edn. chair 2002-), Conewago Canoe Club (canoe ing. officer 1999—) Episcopalian. Avocation: ferroequinology. Office: Evergreen Outdoor Ctr PO Box 3081 Shiremanstown PA 17011-3081 Business E-Mail: william.nesbit@dla.mil.

**NESBITT, CHARLES RUDOLPH,** lawyer, energy executive, consultant; b. Miami, Okla., Aug. 30, 1921; s. Charles Rudolph and Irma Louise (Wilhelmi) N.; m. Margot Dorothy Lord, June 6, 1948; children: Nancy Margot Nesbitt Nagle, Douglas Charles, Carolyn Jane Nesbitt Gresham-Fiegel. BA, U. Okla., 1942; JD, Yale U., 1947. Bar: Okla. 1947, U.S. Supreme Ct. 1957. Pvt. practice, Oklahoma City, 1948-62, 67-69, 75-91, 95—; atty. gen. Okla., 1963-67; mem. Okla. Corp. Commn., 1968-75, chmn., 1969-75; sec. of energy State of Okla., 1991-95; pvt. practice Oklahoma City, 1995—. Okla. rep., v.p. Interstate Oil and Gas Compact. Trustee endowment fund St. Gregory's Coll.; pres. Hist. Preservation, Inc.; pres. bd. trustees Okla. Mus. Art; v.p., bd. dirs. Western History Collections Assocs., U. Okla. Librs.; mem.

panel arbitrators Am. Arbitration Assn., NASD, NYSE. With AUS, 1942-46. Mem. ABA, Okla. Bar Assn., Oklahoma City C. of C., Phi Beta Kappa, Phi Delta Phi. Episcopalian. Home: 1703 N Hudson Ave Oklahoma City OK 73103-3428 Office: 125 NW 6th St Oklahoma City OK 73102-6014 Office Phone: 405-235-5333.

**NESBITT, JOHN ARTHUR,** recreational therapist, writer, educator, researcher; b. Detroit, Mar. 29, 1933; s. John Jackson and Anna Maye (Hartley) N.; children: John Arthur, and Victoria Bowen. Attended, Howe Mil. Sch., 1945-51, Olivet Coll., 1952-53; BA, Mich. State U., 1955; MA, Columbia Univ., 1961, EdD, 1968. Registered hosp. recreation dir.; cert. therapeutic recreation splty. Program dir. Jaycees Internat., Miami, Fla., 1957-60; therapeutic recreation specialist Rusk Inst. Rehab. Medicine, N.Y.U., Bellevue Med. Ctr., 1960-61; dir. World Commn. on Vocat. Rehab., Rehab. Internat., N.Y.C., 1963-65; dep. dir. gen. World Leisure and Recreation Assn., N.Y.C., 1964-66; asst. sec. gen. Rehab. Internat., N.Y.C., 1966-68; assoc. prof., coord. rehab. svc., leisure studies San Jose State U., Calif., 1968-72; prof., chmn. recreation edn. program U. Iowa, Iowa City, 1972-76, prof. therapeutic recreation, 1977-91, prof. emeritus, 1991—. Pres., CEO Spl. Recreation disABLED Internat., Inc., 1979—; dir., vice chair People to People Com. Disability, 1964-2000; chmn. sub com. recreation and leisure U.S. President's Com. on Employment of Handicapped, 1972-81; dir. Internat. Ctr. on Spl. Recreation, 1978—. Author, editor books in field; editor Alert Mag., 1956; Jaycees Internat. World, 1957-60; Internat. Rehab. of Disabled Rev., 1965-68; Therapeutic Recreation Jour., 1968-70; Jour. Iowa Parks and Recreation, 1974-76; Play, Recreation, and Leisure for People Who Are Disabled, 1977; Fed. Funding for Spl. Recreation, 1978; New Concepts and New Processes in Spl. Recreation, 1978; New Horizons in Profl. Tng. in Recreation Svc. for Handicapped Children and Youth, 1983; Nisbet, Nesbitt Family Surname Assn. Newsletter, 1983-86; Spl. Recreation for DisABLED Digest, 1988-89; U.S.A. Ban Fireworks and Fireworks Safety Campaign Bull., 1988—; UNAGRAM, 1997-99; sr. editor Recreation and Leisure Svc. for Disadvantaged, 1969 (Nat. Recreation Lit. award); editor, compiler Spl. Recreation Compendium of 1,500 Resources for Disabled People, 3d edit., 1989; Special Recreation for Disabled Press, University Heights, Iowa, 1989; webmaster Global Vision Rehab. and Recreation for People with Disabilities American Stop Fireworks Victimization Campaign, Eric Collection. Bd. dirs. United Cerebral Palsy Assn., San Mateo and Santa Clara County, 1970-72; bd. dirs. Harold Russell Found., 1971-73; Goodwill Industries Santa Clara County, 1969-72; rehab. counselor, master therapeutic recreation specialist; bd. dir. Hawkeye Area Poverty Cmty. Action Program, Iowa; Iowa Pk. and Recreation Assn., Am. Leisure and Recreation Assn., Washington, others; bd. dirs., state v.p. Iowa Aging Coalition, Iowa; bd. dirs., founding pres. Santa Clara County Assn. on Recreation Handicapped, Iowa; bd. dirs., tech. adv. Disability Internat. Found., 1997—. Served in USAFR, 1955-57; maj. Ret. Recreation Svc. Ill. and handicapped fellow; recipient numerous awards and citations for work with handicapped, including Torch of Gold Award, Nat. Boy Scouts Am.; Appreciation Award Philippines Found. Mem. Nat. Therapeutic Recreation Soc. (pres. 1970-71, Disting. Svc. Award), Nat. Rehab. Assn.; Am. Assn. Leisure and Recreation (bd. dir. 1977-80, Tommy Wilson svc. Handicapped Youth award); Nat. Consortium on Phys. Edn. and Recreation for Handicapped (pres. 1976-77, Nat. Scholarship award); Nat. Forum Comml. Recreation and Handicapped (chmn. 1979); Iowa Parks and Recreation Assn. (bd.dir. 1973-75, 89-90); Nat. Rehab. Counseling Assn.; Council Exceptional Children; Pi Sigma Epsilon. Presbyterian. Avocations: art, travel, genealogy, cmty. svc. Office: Spl Recreation disABLED Internat 701 Oaknoll Dr Iowa City IA 52246-5168 Office Phone: 319-466-3192. Business E-Mail: john-nesbitt@uiowa.edu.

**NESBITT, LA FONTE,** lawyer; b. Spartanburg, SC, Nov. 16, 1958; BS cum laude, James Madison U., 1980; JD, U. Va., 1988. Bar: Va. 1988, DC 1991, US Dist. Ct. (ea. Dist. Va.). Exec. ptnr. Holland & Knight LLP, Washington, mem. dir. com.; exec. ptnr. Holland & Knight LLP (No. Va. and Md.). Spkr. in the field. Mem.: ABA (mem. real property, probate and trust law, forum on affordable housing and cmty. develop. law), DC Bar (mem. real estate, housing and land use sect.), Va. State Bar, Omicron Delta Kappa, Leadership Washington, Pi Gamma Mu. Office: Holland & Knight LLP 2099 Pennsylvania Ave NW Ste 100 Washington DC 20006 Office Phone: 202-457-7047.

**NESBITT, MITZI EVALEE,** voice educator, director; d. Sylvan Julian and Mildred Evelyn (Moe) Nylander; divorced; 1 child, Travis Orlo. AA in Music, N.W. Coll., Kirkland, Wash., 1970; BA in Music, Calif State U. - Hayward, 1975; MA in Music, Dance, Drama, Calif State U., Fullerton, 1994. Cert. tchr. Calif. Music tchr. Christian Ctr. Sch., Dublin, Calif., 1972-76; vocal music tchr. Phoenix Elem. Schs., 1976-79; Placentia (Calif.) Unified Sch. Dist., 1979-85, Corona/Norco (Calif.) Unified Sch. Dist., 1988-92, 1997—, 4th grade tchr., 1992-97. Pvt. practice, Norco, Calif., 1985—; adv. bd. Nat. Orff Schulwerk, Redlands, Calif., 1994. Author, composer: Oh California, 1994, Lion, Witch, and the Wardrobe, 1994. Music dir. Children's Theatre Experience, Chatsworth, Calif., 1996—; pianist Calvary Christian Ctr., Corona, 1987-97. Named Tchr. of Yr., Stallings Elem. Sch., 2004, Bravo award finalist, 1995; recipient Mentor Tchr. award, Corona Norco Unified Sch. Dist., 1994-96. Mem.: Am Orff Schulwerk (sec. 1993—2006). Avocations: jogging, photography, sewing, yoga, tennis.

**NESBITT, PAUL EDWARD,** historian, author, educator; b. Balt., Dec. 25, 1943; s. William Ervin and Margaret Caroline (Shaw) N.; m. Donna Jean Coppock, Aug. 15 1966 (dec. 1972); children: Erik-Paul A., Janelle M.; m. Pamela Jean Lichty, May 25, 1974 (div. 1983); m. Anita Louise Wood, Dec. 8, 1984 (div. 1989); m. Paula Jane Sawyer, May 7, 1994. AB, U. Wash., 1965; MA, Wash. State U., 1968, PhD (hon.), 1970; PhD, U. Calgary, Alta., Can., 1972. Reader anthropology U. Wash., 1965; grad. rschr.-tchr. Wash. State U., 1966-68; instr. Tacoma C.C., Wash., 1968-69; grad. rschr.-tchr. U. Calgary, 1969-71; exec. Hudson's Bay Co., Calgary, 1971; prof. Western Oreg. U. Monmouth, 1971-74, state librarian State of Calif., Sacramento, 1974-97; ret., 1997. Dir. Am. Sch. of Interior Design, San Francisco, 1974, HBC Bow Fort Rsch., Morley, Atla., 1970-71; instr. Am. River Coll., Sacramento, 1980-86. Contbr. articles to profl. jours. Exec. mgr. Calif. State Govt. United Way Campaign, 1986, 87, also bd. dirs., mem. fiscal and comml. coms., El Dorado County and Sacramento chpts., 1988—; designer, cultural rsch. cons. pvt. contracts western states, 1960—; exec. dir. Heritage Areas Assn., 1993—, pres. bd. dirs., 1994—. Fellow Am. Anthropol. Assn.; mem. Calif. Hist. Soc., Am. Inst. Interior Designers (profl. 1974-77, bd. dirs. energy planning and devel. cos. 1986-88), AIA (Ctrl. Valley chpt. 1975-77), Rotary. Home: 3177 Clark St Placerville CA 95667-6405 E-mail: heritage@innercite.com.

**NESBITT, RICHARD,** stock exchange executive; BA in bus. administrn., Univ. Western Ontario, Can.; MBA, Univ. Toronto, 1985; MSc in acctg. and fin., London Sch. Economics. Position at Mobil Oil Can. Ltd., CIBC Wood Gundy; pres. and CEO HSBC Securities Can.; pres. and COO BayStreetDirect Inc.; gov. Toronto Stock Exch., 1996—99, pres. TSX Markets, 2001—04, CEO TSX Group Inc., 2004—. Former lectr. Univ. Western Ontario Sch. Bus. Office: TSX Group Inc PO Box 450 130 King St W 3rd Fl Toronto ON Canada Office Phone: 416-947-4670. Office Fax: 416-947-4662.

**NESBITT, WANDA L.,** ambassador; b. Phila., Dec. 1956; married. BA in Internat. Rels. and French, U. Pa., 1978; postgrad., Nat. War Coll., 1996—97. Vice-consul State, Port-au-Prince, Haiti, 1982—83, Paris, 1983—85, with Bur. L.Am., 1986—88, regional consular officer Kinshasa, Zaire, 1990—92, with consular affairs Kinshasa, Zaire, 1992—93, with legis. affairs, 1995—96, dep. chief of mission Kigali, Rwanda, 1997—99, Dar es Salaam, Tanzania, 1999—2001, U.S. amb. to Madagascar 2002—. Office: DOS Amb 607 Braxton Pl Alexandria VA 22301 E-mail: nesbittwl@state.gov.

**NESHAT, SHIRIN,** artist; b. Qazvin, Iran, 1957; MFA, U. Calif. Berkeley, 1979—82. Hon. prof. Berlin Inst. Arts, 2004. One-woman shows include Woman of Allah, 1993—97, Tate Gallery, London, 1998, Whitney Mus. Am. Art, Phillip Morris Branch, NY, 1998, Maison Europeene des Photographie, Paris, 1998, Tensta Konsthall, Spanga, Sweden, 1999, Henie Onstad Artsentre, Oslo, Norway, 1999, Galerie Jerome de Noirmont, Paris, 1999, D'Amelio

Terras, NY, 1999, Patrick Painter Gallery, LA, 1999, Art Inst. Chgo., 1999, Wexner Ctr., Columbus, Ohio, 2000, Matrix, Berkeley Art Mus., Calif., 2000, Dallas Mus. Art, 2000, Lia Rumma, Milan, 2000, Kunsthalle Wien, Vienna, 2000, Pitti Discovery, Florence, 2000, Serpentine Gallery, London, 2000, Barbara Gladstone Gallery, NY, 2001, Kanazawa Contemporary Art Mus. Kanazawa, Japan, 2001, Patrick Painter, Santa Monica, 2001, Irish Mus. Modern Art, Dublin, 2001, Musee d'Art Contemporain de Montreal, Passage, Regina Gouger Miller Gallery, Carnegie Mellon U., 2002, Banco di Brasil, Rio de Janeiro, 2002, Castello di rivoli, Turin, 2002, Walker Art Ctr., Mpls., 2002, Contemporary Arts Mus., Houston, 2003, Museo de Arte Moderno, Mexico City, 2003, Lumen Travo Gallery, Amsterdam, 2003, Galeria Filomena Soares, Lisbon, 2003, Miami Art Mus., 2003, Tooba, Asia Soc. Mus., NY, 2003, Auckland Art Gallery, New Zealand, 2004, Hiroshima City Mus. Contemporary Art, 2005, Museo de Arte Contemporaneo, Leon, Spain, 2005, Hamburger Bahnhof, Mus. Fur Gengewart, Berlin, 2005, exhibited in group shows at Documenta XI, Venice Biennale, 1999 (Golden Lion award), Whitney Biennale, 2000; prodr.: (films) Turbulent, 1998, Rapture, 1999, Fervor, 2000, Zarin, 2005. Recipient Infinity award, Internat. Ctr. Photography, 2002, Hiroshima Freedom prize, 2005. Office: Storefront for Art and Architecture 97 Kenmara St New York NY 10012 Office Phone: 212-431-5795. Office Fax: 212-431-5755.

**NESHEIM, ROBERT OLAF,** retired food products executive; b. Monroe Center, Ill., Sept. 13, 1921; s. Olaf M. and Sena M. (Willms) Nesheim; m. Emogene P. Sullivan, July 13, 1946 (div.); children: Barbara Mowry, Susan Yost(dec.), Sandra Rankin; m. Doris Howes Calloway, July 4, 1981 (dec.). BS, U. Ill., 1943, MS, 1950, PhD, 1951; postgrad. in advanced mgmt. program, Harvard U., 1971. Farm Mgr. Halderman Farm Mgmt. Svc., Wabash, Ind., 1946-48; instr. U. Ill., 1951; mgr. feed rsch. The Quaker Oats Co., Barrington, Ill., 1952-64; prof., head of dept. animal sci. U. Ill., 1964-67; dir. nutrition rsch. The Quaker Oats Co., Barrington, Ill., 1967-69, v.p. R & D, 1969-78, v.p. sci. & tech. Chgo., 1978-83; sr. v.p. sci. & tech. Avadyne, Inc., Monterey, Calif., 1983-85; pres. Advanced Healthcare, Monterey, 1985-91; ret., 1991. Food and nutrition bd. NAS, 1972—78, chmn. com. in mil. nutrition rsch. FNB, 1982—97; chmn. Bioscis. Info. Svcs., 1982—84. Capt. U.S. Army, 1943-46, South Pacific. Fellow Am. Inst. Nutrition (treas. 1983-86), AAAS; mem. Inst. Food Technologists, Fed. Socs. Exptl. Biologists (treas. 1973-79), APHA, Corral de Tierra Club (Salinas, Calif.). Avocations: gardening, golf. Home: Apt 407 200 Glenwood Cir Monterey CA 93940

**NESIN, JEFFREY DAVID,** academic administrator; b. NYC; m. Diane Garvey, 1968; children: Kate Dillon, Sarah Grace. BA in Eng. Lit., Hobart Coll., 1966; MA in Eng. Lit., SUNY, Buffalo, 1971, MA in Am. Studies, 1973. Faculty dept. humanities & scis. Sch. Visual Arts, NYC, 1974-91; pres. Memphis Coll. Art, 1991—. Asst. to pres. Sch. Visual Arts, 1982-91; cons. Smithsonian Instn., IBM, 1st Tenn. Bank; panelist, speaker in field. Contbg. editor: High Fidelity, Creem; contbr. reviews, interviews, essays to mags.; adv. editor Jour. Popular Music and Society. Recipient Thomas W. Briggs Found. Cmty. Svc. award, 1998. Mem. Am. Studies Assn., Met. Am. Studies Assn. (past pres.), Assn. Ind. Colls. Art & Design (bd. dirs. 1991—), Nat. Assn. Schs. Art & Design (chair commn. on accreditation, exec. com. and bd. 1999—), Ctr. for So. Folklore (bd. and exec. com. 2000—), Memphis Rotary. Avocations: mystery novels, baseball, music. Office: Memphis Coll Art Office of President 1930 Poplar Ave Memphis TN 38104-2756 Office Phone: 901-272-5101.

**NESLAGE, JOHN EDWARD,** lawyer; b. Pampa, Tex., Aug. 13, 1946; AA cum laude, N.Mex. Milit. Inst., 1966; BBA magna cum laude, Tex. Tech. U., 1969; JD cum laude, U. Houston, 1972. Bar: Tex. 1972. Mem. Baker Botts L.L.P., Houston. Mem. ABA, State Bar Tex., Houston Bar Assn., Phi Kappa Phi, Phi Alpha Delta, Order of the Barons. Office: Baker Botts LLP One Shell Plz 910 Louisiana Houston TX 77002-4995 Office Phone: 713-229-1342.

**NESMITH, RICHARD A.,** education educator, consultant; b. Lakeland, Fla., Jan. 13, 1959; s. Wendell B. and Patricia A. NeSmith; m. Melissa M. NeSmith; children: Ricky A., Wendell C. BS, Hyles-Anderson Coll., 1983, MRE, 1984; D in Ministry, Bethany Theol. Sem., 1986; BS, USC, 1991, MEd, 1993; specialists in edn., Augusta State U., 1997; PhD, Curtin U. Tech. 2003. Tchg. cert. biology SC State Dept. Edn., 1991, educator cert. biology, ednl. leadership, mid. grade Ga. State Dept. Edn., 1995, curriculum validator Western Australia Curriculum Coun., 2000, cert. prin., supt. Ill. Dept. Edn., 1981. Secondary sci. tchr. SC Dept. Edn., Lexingington, 1992—93; sch. prin. Winfield Heights Christian Sch., Whiteville, SC, 1994—95; secondary sci. tchr. Ga. Pub. Schs., Ga., 1995—98; head sci. and math dept. Maranatha Christian Coll., Perth, Australia, 1999—2001; asst. prof. edn. Ea. Ill. U., Charleston, 2003—; asst. prof. of edn. Lake Erie Coll., Painesville, Ohio, 2002—03. Bd. examiners Ohio State Dept. Edn., Columbus, 2002—03. Sci. author, cons.: BioSci. Edn., 1996—, mid-level editor: Ill. Sci. Tchrs. Assn. Jour. (Spectrum). Mem.: Assn. Childhood Edn. Internat. (assoc.; v.p. Ill. chpt.), Am. Rsch. Ednl. Assn. (assoc.), NSTA (assoc.), Nat. Mid. Sch. Assn. (assoc.), Phi Delta Kappa (assoc.). Conservative. Baptist. Achievements include research in middle school students perception of effective teaching and learning; various approaches to improving the curriculum and teaching of science in secondary school; professional development using multimedia DVD technology. Avocations: hiking, travel, computers, writing. Office: Ea Ill Univ 600 Lincoln Avenue Charleston IL 61920 Office Phone: 217-581-9882. Business E-Mail: bioscience_ed@yahoo.com.

**NESPOLI, PAOLO ANGELO,** astronaut; b. Milan, Apr. 6, 1957; s. Luigi and Maria Nespoli. BS in Aerospace Engring., Poly. U, N.Y., 1988, MS in Aeronautics and Astronautics, 1989; laurea in ingegneria meccanica, U. degli Studi di Firenze, Italy, 1990. Registered profl. engr.; lic. pvt. pilot, advanced scuba diver, NitrOx diver, master parachutist, cert. parachutist instr.; jump master, demolition expert. Non-commd. officer, parachute instr. Scuola Militare de Paracudutismo, Pisa, Italy, 1977—80; spl. forces operator 9° Btg d'Assalto "Col Moschin", Livorno, Italy; mem. multinat. peacekeeping force Italian Army, Beirut, 1982—84, ret., 1987; design engr. Proel Tecnologie, Florence, Italy, 1989—91; mem. astronaut tng. divsn., European Astronaut Ctr. European Space Agy., Cologne, Germany, 1991—98; mem. EUROMIR project European Space Tech. Ctr., Noordwijk, Netherlands, 1995—96; mem. spaceflight tng. divsn. NASA, Johnson Space Ctr., Houston, 1996—98; astronaut Italian Space Agy., 1998; joined European Space Agy. European astronaut corps European Astronaut Ctr., Cologne, Germany, 1998; astronaut, mission specialist candidate NASA, Johnson Space Ctr., Houston, 1998—. Temporary assignment Gagarin Cosmonaut Tng. Ctr., Star City, Russia, 2004; mission specialist STS-120 to Internat. Space Station, 2006. Avocations: scuba diving, aircraft piloting, assembling computer hardware and electronic equipment, computer software. Office: Astronaut Office NASA Johnson Space Ctr Houston TX 77058 Address: European Space Agy 8-10 rue Mario Nikis 75738 Paris France*

**NESS, ANDREW DAVID,** lawyer; b. San Francisco, Oct. 29, 1951; s. Orville Arne and Muriel M. (Trendt) N.; m. Rita M. Kobylenski, May 25, 1980; children: Katherine, Austin, Emily. BS, Stanford U., 1974; JD, Harvard U., 1977. Bar: Calif. 1977, DC 1979, Va. 1986, U.S. Dist. Ct. (No. Dist.) Calif. 1977, U.S. Dist. Ct. D.C. 1983, U.S. Dist. Ct. (Ea. Dist.) Va. 1988, U.S. Ct. Appeals (4th Cir.) 1989. Law clk. U.S. Dist. Ct., San Francisco, 1977-78; assoc. Lewis, Mitchell & Moore, Vienna, Va., 1979-82, ptnr., 1982-87, Morgan, Lewis & Bockius LLP, Washington, 1987-2000, Thelen Reid & Priest LLP, Washington, 2000—, mng. ptnr. D.C. office, 2001—, mem. partnership coun. and exec. com., 2003—. Instr. U. Md., College Park, 1987-90; mem. faculty constrn. exec. program Stanford (Calif.) U., 1984-87. Co-editor Fed. Govt. Construction Contracts, 2003; contbr. chpts. to books, articles to profl. jours. Mem. ABA (forum on constrn. industry, pub. contract law sect.). Avocations: hiking, bicycling. Office: Thelen Reid & Priest LLP 701 Eighth St NW Washington DC 20001 Office Phone: 202-508-4368. Business E-Mail: adness@thelenreid.com.

**NESS, BERNICE HAGIE,** retired music educator; b. Mpls., Sept. 4, 1926; d. John Leonard and Mathilda Caroline Hagie; m. Elmo Vernon Ness, Aug. 3, 1974. BS, U. Minn., Mpls., 1948, MEd, 1950. Elmo. music supr. Lake Co. Schs., Two Harbors, Minn., 1950—51, Mounds View Dist. #621, New Brighton, Minn., 1951—54; tchr., choral music & music theory Mounds View H.S., New Brighton, Minn., 1954—81, tchr., choral music & French, 1981—83; ret., 1983. Mem. adv. bd. U. Minn. Alumni Band, Mpls., 1949—51, coun. mem., 1996—98; dir., arranger Mounds View Choral, New Brighton, Minn., 1996—2006. Chair, music com. Abiding Savior Ch., Mounds View, Minn., 1985—94; mem., music com. Christ the King Ch., New Brighton, Minn., 1995—97. Recipient Pillar award, Mounds View H.S., 2005.

**NESS, NORMAN FREDERICK,** astrophysicist, educator, academic administrator; b. Springfield, Mass., Apr. 15, 1933; s. Herman Hugo and Eva (Carlson) N.; children: Elizabeth Ann, Stephen Andrew. BS, Mass. Inst. Tech., 1955, PhD, 1959. Space physicist, asst. prof. geophysics UCLA, 1959-61; NAS-NRC postdoctoral rsch. assoc. NASA, 1960-61; rsch. physicist in space scis. Goddard Space Flight Center, Greenbelt, Md., 1961-86, head extraterrestrial physics br., 1968-69, chief Lab. for Extraterrestrial Physics, 1969-86; pres. Bartol Rsch. Inst. U. Del., 1987-2000, prof. Bartol Rsch. Inst., Newark, 1987—2005; dir. NASA Space Grant Coll. Consortium, Del., 1991—2005. Lectr. math. U. Md., 1962-64, assoc. research prof., 1965-67 Contbr. articles profl. jours. Recipient Exceptional Sci. Achievement award NASA, 1966, 81, 86, Arthur S. Flemming award, 1968, Space Sci. award AIAA, 1971, Disting. Svc. medal NASA, 1986, Nat. Space Club Sci. award, 1993, Emil Wiechert medal German Geophys. Soc., 1993, Space Sci. award COSPAR, 1996. Fellow Am. Geophys. Union (John Adam Fleming award 1965); mem NAS, Acad. Nat. dei Lincei Achievements include research in interplanetary and planetary magnetic fields by satellites and space probes. Home: 9 Wilkinson Dr Landenberg PA 19350-9359 Personal E-Mail: nfnudel@yahoo.com.

**NESS, PAMELA MILLER,** elementary school educator; b. Boston, May 5, 1951; d. Edwin Haviland and Rosalind S. Miller; m. Paul Marc Ness. BA in Art History, Swarthmore Coll., Pa., 1972; MA, Harvard U., Cambridge, Mass., 1973; MLS, Simmons Coll., Boston, 1987. Registrar The Bostonian Soc., Mass., 1973—75; chief designer, tchr. of needlepoint, embroidery & design, asst. mgr. needlework dept. Women's Ednl. & Indsl. Union, Boston, 1975—86; asst. libr. Mass. Hort. Soc., Boston, 1986—87; libr. dir., English and social studies tchr. grades 4 & 6, adv. grades 6 & 9 The Fenn Sch., Concord, 1987—92; 4th grade tchr., house adv. The Dalton Sch., NYC, 1992—94, 7th grade English tchr., house adv., grade level coord., 1994—98, mid. sch. learning specialist, 6th grade English tchr., house adv., 1998—. Presenter in field. Contbr. articles and papers to profl. jours. and pubs. Recipient 1st Place award, Haiku Poets No. Calif. San Francisco Internat. Tanka contest, 2001. Mem.: Pen & Brush (artist mem., pen sect., poetry divsn. 2004—05), Haiku N. Am. (mem. exec. com. 2002—05, chair planning com. biannual conf., NYC 2003), Tanka Soc. Am. (newsletter editor 2000—03, 1st Pl. Internat. Tanka Contest 2004), Haiku Soc. Am. (reg. coord. NE metro region 1998—2000, chair edn. com. 1998—2004, 1st v.p. 2001—03, newsletter editor 2003—04, pres. 2006—), Phi Beta Kappa. Avocations: knitting, flower arranging, reading, walking. Home: 33 Riverside Dr #4G New York NY 10023 Office: The Dalton Sch 108 E 89th St New York NY 10128 Office Phone: 212-423-5333.

**NESS, ROBERTA,** medical educator, researcher, dean; b. San Bernardino, Calif., July 28, 1958; m. David Ness; children: Joel, Sara. MD, Cornell U., 1984; MPH, Columbia U., 1989. Lic. physician. Clin. assoc. U. of Pa., Phila., 1988—93, asst. prof., U. of Pitts., 1993—98, assoc. prof., 1998—2002, prof., 2002—, chmn. Dept. Epidemiology, 2003—, interim dean Grad. Sch. Pub. Health, 2005—. Dir. epidemiology of women's health program U. of Pitts., 1995—; dir. cancer epidemiology program U. of Pitts. Cancer Inst., 1997—. Contbr. over 100 articles to profl. jours. Mem. sci. adv. panel HJ Heinz, Internat., Pitts., 2001; core mem. early markers of adult disease workgroup and study assembly NICHD/EPA/CDC, Washington, 2001; rep. rsch. am. Coalition of Scientists/Politicians, Washington, 2002; advisor RDA on self-testing for STDs Ctrs. for Disease Control and Prevention, Washington, 2002. Named one of Top 25 Women Drs., Pitts. Post-Gazette, 1998; recipient Sklar award for Outstanding Rsch., U. of Md., 1980, Pa. Leadership award for Outstanding Contbns. to Reproductive Rsch., Family Health Coun., 1996, Rsch. Paper award, Soc. for Epidemiol. Rsch., 1999; fellow Tng. Grant fellow, NIH, 1988. Office: U Pitts A528 Crabtree Hall 130 DeSoto St Pittsburgh PA 15261 Office Phone: 412-624-3056. Business E-Mail: repro@pitt.edu.

**NESS, SUSAN,** federal official; married; 2 children. BA, Rutgers U., 1970; JD cum laude, Boston Coll.; MBA, U. Pa. Asst. counsel com. banking, currency and housing U.S. House of Reps.; founder, dir. jud. appointments project Nat. Women's Polit. Caucus; commr. FCC, Washington, 1994—2001. Chair Charter Rev. Commn., Montgomery County, Md.; vice chair Montgomery County Task Force on Cmty. Access TV; pres. Montgomery County Commn. for Women. Named one of 12 to Watch, Electronic Media, 1997. Mem. Nat. Assn. Regulatory Utility Commrs. (com. comm.), Leadership Washington, Fed. Comm. Bar Assn.

**NESSMITH, H(ERBERT) ALVA,** dentist; b. Miami, Fla., Nov. 27, 1935; s. William Boyd and Florence Editha (Lowe) N.; m. Paula Ann Fox, Oct. 1, 1960 (div. 1984); children: Amy Susan, Lynn Margaret, Mark Alva. Student, U. Miami, Fla., 1953-56; DDS, Northwestern U., 1960. Gen. practice dentistry, Tequesta, Fla., 1963—; dental cons. Palm Beach-Martin County Med. Ctr., Jupiter, Fla., 1970—; rsch. assoc. Colgate Palmolive Co., 1997—. Calibrated caries examiner, cons. Colgate Dental Rsch., 1997—. Mem. advmnstry. bd. United Meth. Ch. Tequesta, Jupiter, 1970—, chmn. 1988 001, pres. Meth Men, 1984; chmn. Coun. on Ministries, 1992-94, mem. staff parish rels. com. 1999—; pres. Jupiter Elem. PTO; clarinetist Symphonic Band of Palm Beaches, Fla. Concert Band; pianist and clarinetist United Meth. Ch.; active Village of Tequesta Hist. Commn., 1992-96, Jupiter (Fla.) Cmty. Resource Ctr., 1994—; mem. admnstrv. bd., v.p. Christian Dental Soc., 1994—, v.p., 1995—, Andean Rural Health Care, 1999—. Mem. ADA, North Palm Beach County Dental Soc., Fla. Dental Assn., Jupiter-Tequesta-Juno Beach C. of C. Lodges: Kiwanis (pres. Jupiter/Tequesta chpt. 1980-81). Democrat. Avocations: mission dentistry, latin american studies, gardening, music, travel. Home: 196 River Dr Tequesta FL 33469-1934 Office: Inlet Profl Bldg 175 Tequesta Dr Jupiter FL 33469-2733

**NESSON, CHARLES R.,** lawyer, educator; b. Feb. 11, 1939. AB, Harvard U., 1960, LLB, 1963. Bar: DC 1964, Mass. 1971. Law clk. to Assoc. Justice John Marshall Harlan, US Supreme Ct., Washington, 1964-65; spl. asst. civil rights divsn. US Dept. Justice, 1965-66; asst. prof. law Harvard Law Sch., Cambridge, Mass., 1966-69, prof., 1969—, Weld prof. law, 1993-, assoc. dean, 1979-82, faculty co-dir. Berkman Ctr. Internet and Soc., 1997-. Co-author: Problems, Cases and Materials on Evidence, 3rd edit., 2001. Office: Harvard Law Sch 1563 Massachusetts Ave Cambridge MA 02138 Office Phone: 617-495-4609. Office Fax: 617-496-4947. Business E-Mail: nesson@law.harvard.edu.

**NESTER, WILLIAM RAYMOND, JR.,** retired academic administrator; b. Cin., Feb. 19, 1928; s. William Raymond and Evelyn (Blettner) N.; m. Mary Jane (dec.); children: William Raymond, Mark Patrick, Brian Philip, Stephen Christopher. BS, U. Cin., 1950, EdM, 1953, EdD, 1965, DHL (hon.), 2005, No. Ky. U., 2001, U. Nebr., 2002. Dir. student union U. Cin., 1952-53, asst. dean of men, 1953-60, dean of men, 1960-67, assoc. prof. edn., 1965-70, dean of students, 1967-69, vice provost student and univ. affairs, 1969-76, prof. edn., 1970-78, assoc. sr. v.p., assoc. provost, 1976-78; v.p. student svcs. Ohio State U., Columbus, 1978-83, prof. edn. 1978-83; pres. Kearney State Coll., 1983-93, prof. emeritus, chancellor emeritus, 1993—; v.p. univ. rels. devel. No. Ky. U., 1996-99. Pres. emeritus Mus. Nebr. Art, 1991—; cons. on higher edn., 1993—. Pres. Metro-Six Athletic Conf., 1975-76. Mem. Am. State Colls. and Univs. (bd. dirs.), Ctrl. States Intercollegiate Conf. (pres. 1986-89), Nat. Assn. Student Pers. Admnstrs. (past regional v.p., mem. exec. com.).

Am. Assn. Higher Edn., Ohio Assn. Student Pers. Adminstrs. (past pres.), Nat. Intrafrat. Conf. (pres. 1991-92), Frat. Scholarship Officers Assn. (past pres.), Mortar Bd., Pi Kappa Alpha (nat. pres. 1978-80, pres. nat. interfrat. conf. 1988-89, past pres. Pi Kappa Alpha Ednl. Found.), Omicron Delta Kappa, Phi Delta Kappa, Phi Alpha Theta, Phi Eta Sigma, Sigma Sigma. Episcopalian. Home: 7674 Coldstream Dr Cincinnati OH 45255-3932 E-mail: wrnchanem@cs.com.

**NESTEROVIC, RASHO,** professional basketball player; b. May 30, 1976; Center Minnesota Timberwolves, Minn., 1998—2003, San Antonio Spurs, Tex., 2003—. Home: San Antonio Spurs One SBC Ctr San Antonio TX 78219

**NESTLER, ERIC J.,** psychiatrist, researcher; b. NYC, July 7, 1954; s. Herbert A. and Mildred D. Nestler; m. Susan DeRenzo; children: David I, Matthew E., Jane D. MD, PhD, Yale U., 1983, BA, 1976. Diplomate Am. Bd. Psychiatry and Neurology. Prof. Yale U. Sch. Medicine, New Haven, 1987—2000; disting. prof., chmn. U. Tex. Southwestern Med. Ctr., Dallas, 2000—. Fellow: AAAS; mem.: Inst. of Medicine. Achievements include discovery of how drugs of abuse change nerve cells in the brain to cause addiction. Office: Univ Tex Southwestern Med Ctr 5323 Harry Hines Blvd Dallas TX 75390-9070 Office Phone: 214-648-1111. Office Fax: 214-648-4947. Business E-Mail: eric.nestler@utsouthwestern.edu.

**NESTLER, JOHN EDWIN,** endocrinology educator; b. Passaic, N.J., Sept. 24, 1952; m. Michelle Dumont, Dec. 29, 1990. BA in Chemistry (with honors) and German, Haverford Coll., 1975; MD, U. Pa., 1979. Diplomate Am. Bd. Internal Medicine, Am. Bd. Endocrinology and Metabolism; cert. Nat. Bd. Med. Examiners. Intern Med. Coll. Va., Richmond, 1979-80, resident, 1980-82, chief med. resident, instr. in medicine, 1982-83, fellow in endocrinology, 1985-86, asst. prof. medicine, 1986-91, assoc. prof. medicine, 1991—, dir. med. affairs, BioClin, 1991-95, prof. medicine, 1995—, chmn. divsn. endocrinology and metabolism, 1997—, vice chmn. dept. internal medicine, 2003—; fellow in endocrinology U. Pa., Phila., 1983-85. Reviewer various profl. jours.; vis. prof. Dalhousie U., Halifax, N.S., 1991; invited speaker several major confs. including NIH/NICHD Conf. on Polycystic Ovary Syndrome, Bethesda, Md., 1990. Author numerous original publs., book chpts., abstracts. Recipient Sandra Tate Russell Meml. Rsch. award Am. Diabetes Assn. Va. affiliate, 1986, Clin. Assoc. Physician award NIH, 1985-87, rsch. trainee awards Phila. Endocrine Soc., 1984, 85. Fellow Am. Coll. Physicians; mem. AAAS, Internat. Diabetes Found., European Assn. for Study of Diabetes, Cen Va. Assn. Diabetes Educators, Am. Assn. Diabetes Educators, Am. Diabetes Assn. (pres. 1990—), Am. Fedn. Clin. Rsch., Internat. Soc. for Androgenic Disorders, The Endocrine Soc., So. Soc. for Clin. Investigation. Achievements include research on diabetes, steroids, and insulin. Home: 5800 Three Chopt Rd Richmond VA 23226-2337 Office: Med Coll Va Div Endocrinology PO Box 980111 Richmond VA 23298-0111

**NESTOR CASTELLANO, BRENDA DIANA,** real estate company executive; b. Palm Beach, Fla., Nov. 10, 1948; d. John Joseph and Marion O'Connor Nestor; m. Robert Castellano. Student, U. Miami, Fla., 1978. Lic. real estate broker, Fla. Salesman Oscar E Dooley, Inc., Miami, Fla., 1978-80; prin. Brenda Nestor Assocs., Miami Beach, Fla., 1980—. Exec. v.p., bd. dirs. D.W.G. Corp., 1988-94, N.V.F. Corp., Salem Corp., 1988-97, Southeastern Pub. Svc., Graniteville Co., 1988-94, Essex Ins., Chesapeake Ins.; exec. v.p., dir. Security Mgmt. Bd. dirs. Vizcayan Mus.; dir. Miami's Jackson Meml. Found. Named Ms. Charity, City of Miami, 1985, Lady Comdr., State of Fla. Mem. Miami Beach Bd. Realtors (bd. dirs. 1984—), Real Estate Securities and Exch. Com., Knights of Malta, Doubles Club (N.Y.C.), La Gorce Country Club, Fisher Island Club, Surf Club, Ocean Reef Club, Carnegie Abbey (R.I.) Espicopalian. Avocations: golf, tennis, boating. Home and Office: 39 Palm Ave Miami FL 33139-3263 E-mail: ladybnestor@aol.com.

**NETA, BENY,** mathematics educator, researcher; b. Tripoli, Libya, Nov. 2, 1945; s. Shalom and Ahuva (Vittori) N.; m. Tamar Czerklevitz, Aug. 15, 1971; children: Itay, Leeor, Maital. BSc, Tel Aviv U., 1967, MSc, 1971; PhD, Carnegie-Mellon U., 1977. Asst. prof. math. No. Ill. U., De Kalb, 1977-80; asst. prof. numerical analysis Tex. Tech U., Lubbock, 1980-84; assoc. prof. Naval Postgrad. Sch., Monterey, Calif., 1985-92, prof., 1992—. Rsch. adv. Nat. Rsch. Coun. Nat. Academics. Guest editor Geophys. and Astrophys. Fluid Dynamics, Computers and Math. with Applications, Mathematical and Computer Modelling; contbr. articles to profl. jours. Pres. Lubbock chpt. PTA, 1983-84. Grantee Nat. Acad. Scis., 1984-85. Mem. AIAA, Internat. Assn. for Math. and Computers in Simulation, N.Y. Acad. Scis.; fellow Am. Inst. Aeronautics and Astronautics (assoc.). Home: 1410 Augusta Pl Monterey CA 93940-6403 Office: Naval Postgrad Sch Dept Math Code MA/Nd Monterey CA 93943 Office Phone: 831-656-2235. Business E-Mail: bneta@nps.edu.

**NETESSINE, SERGUEI,** finance educator; PhD, MS, U. Rochester, N.Y., 1997—2001; MS, BS, Moscow Inst. Electronic Tech., Russia, 1989—95. Asst. prof., ops. & info. mgmt. The Wharton Sch., U. Pa., Phila., 2001—. Office: The Wharton Sch 3730 Walnut St Ste 500 Philadelphia PA 19104 Office Phone: 215-573-3571. Business E-Mail: serguei@netessine.com.

**NETHERCUTT, GEORGE RECTOR, JR.,** lawyer, consultant, former congressman; b. Spokane, Wash., Oct. 7, 1944; s. George Rector and Nancy N.; m. Mary Beth Socha Nethercutt, Apr. 2, 1977; children: Meredith, Elliott. BA in English, Wash. State U., 1967; JD, Gonzaga U., 1971. Bar: D.C. 1972. Law clk. to Hon. Raymond Plummer U.S. Dist. Ct. Alaska, Anchorage, 1971; staff counsel to U.S. Senator Ted Stevens Washington, 1972; chief of staff to U.S. Senator Ted Stevens, 1972-76; pvt. practice Spokane, Wash., 1977-94; mem. 104th-108th Congresses from 5th Wash. dist., Washington, 1995—2005; ptnr. Lundquist, Nethercutt & Griles, LLC, Washington, 2005—. Mem. house appropriations and sci. coms.; mem. bd. Heola Mining Co., ISR Arcadis Co., Washington Policy Ctr., Juvenile Diabetes Rsch. Found. Internat., 2005—; chmn. U.S. sect. Permanent Joint Bd. Def., U.S., Can., 2005—. Chmn. Spokane County Rep. Party, 1990-94, co-founder Vanessa Behan Crisis Nursery, pres. Spokane Juvenile Diabetes Found., 1993-94. Mem. Masons (lodge #34), Lions Club (Spokane Ctrl.), Sigma Nu. Republican. Presbyterian. Avocations: running, handball, squash. Office: Lundquist Nethercutt & Griles LLC 400 N Capital St Ste 475 Washington DC 20001 Office Phone: 202-589-0015. Business E-Mail: gnethercutt@lngassociates.com.

**NETHERLAND, JOSEPH H.,** manufacturing executive; BS in Indsl. Engring., Ga. Inst. Tech.; MBA, U. Pa. Bus. planner machinery group FMC Technologies, 1973-78, ops. mgr. ordnance divsn., 1978-83, mgr. fluid control divsn., 1983-84, mgr. wellhead divsn., 1984-85, gen mgr. wellhead divsn., 1985-89, gen. mgr. specialized machinery group, 1989-99, pres., 1999—2006, chmn., CEO, 2001—. Bd. dirs. Am. Petroleum Inst. Mem. adv. bd. Dept. Engring. Tex. A&M Univ.; mem. Pres. Council Ga. Inst. Tech. Recipient Don E. Waggener Butch Griffin award, Spindletop Internat., 2002. Office: FMC Technologies 1803 Gears Rd Houston TX 77067*

**NETHERY, JOHN JAY,** government official, military officer; b. Mpls., June 4, 1941; s. Ronald Jay and Mary Vesta (McVeety) N.; m. Sonya Elisabeth Magin, July 27, 1968; children: William Jay, Mary Elisabeth (dec.), Sarah Ann. BA, U. Denver, 1963, MPA, 1968. Mgmt. intern USAF Logistics Command, San Antonio, 1969-71, budget analyst Dayton, Ohio, 1971-72; chief, fiscal analysis USAF Hdqrs., Washington, 1973-80, chief, investment div., 1980-81, chief budget mgmt., 1981-85; dep. asst. sec. programs and budget Dept. of USAF, Washington, 1986-88, asst. to undersecretary, 1988-89; dep. asst. sec. fin. ops., 1989—. Mem. Air Force Sci. bd. for the correction of mil. records, Washington, 1990—. Recipient Gov.'s Scholastic award Gov. of Colo., 1968, Presdl. Rank award, 1988. Mem. Sr. Execs. Assn., Air Force Assn. Presbyterian. Avocations: history, military minatures. Office: Dept USAF SAF/FM The Pentagon Washington DC 20330-1130 E-mail: Jnethery@aol.com.

**NETRAVALI, ARUN N.,** communications executive; b. Bombay, May 26, 1946; m. Chitra Netravali; 2 children. BS in Tech. with honors, Indian Inst. Tech., Bombay, 1967; MS, Rice U., 1969, PhD, 1970; PhD (hon.), Ecole Polytechnique Federale, Lausanne, Switzerland, 1994. With NASA, Orlando, Fla., 1970-72; mem. tech. staff AT&T Bell Labs., Holmdel, NJ, 1972-78, head visual comm. rsch. dept. Murray Hill, NJ, 1978-83, dir. computing systems rsch., 1983-92, exec. dir. rsch., comm. scis. divsn., 1992-94; pres. Bell Labs., Murray Hill, NJ, 1999—2001; chief scientist Lucent Tech. (formerly Bell Labs.), Murray Hill, NJ, 2001—04; mng. ptnr. Omni Capital, LLC, NJ, 2004—. Former adj. prof. media lab. MIT, Cambridge, Mass; lectr. City Coll. N.Y., Columbia U., MIT, Rutgers U.; advisor Ctr. for Telecomm. Rsch. of Columbia U., 1987—, EPFL Swiss Fed. Inst. Tech., Lausanne, 1986—, Beckman Inst. of U. Ill. Co-author: Digital Pictures: Representation and Compression, 1987, Visual Communication Systems, 1989, Digital Video: An Introduction to MPEG-2, 1996; contbr. 100 tech. papers to sci. jours.; patentee for 64 inventions. Mem. N.J. Govs. Com. on Schs. Program. Recipient Journal award Soc. of Motion Pictures and TV Engrs., 1982, Ann. Asian Am. Corp. Employees award Orgn. Chinese Ams., 1991, Engr. of Yr. award Assn. Engrs. of India, 1992, Nat. Medal of Tech. Laureate, 2001, Padma Bhushan award Govt. of India, 2001. Fellow IEEE (editor Communications 1984—, mem. editorial bd. Proceedings of IEEE 1980-84, Fink prize 1980, L.G. Abraham prize 1985, 91, Alexander Graham Bell medal 1991, mem. digitals TV com.), AAAS; mem. NAE, Tau Beta Pi, Sigma Xi. Avocation: tennis. Office: Lucent Techs 600 Mountain Ave Rm 6A412 New Providence NJ 07974-2008 E-mail: arunnetravali@att.com.

**NETSIRI, CHAIYAPOJ,** applications engineer; b. Bangkok, Thailand, May 29, 1964; s. Chote and Patcharin Netsiri. BSEE, King Mongkut's Inst. Tech., Bangkok, 1986; MS in Computer Sci., Chiba U., Japan, 1996; PhD in Elec. Engring., U. Tokyo, 1999. Prodn. engr. Kang Yang Electric MFG Co., Ltd., Samutprakarn, Thailand, 1987—89; elec. engr. Tom Tech Co., Ltd., Bangkok, 1990—92; R&D engr. Yamada Kikai Kogyo Co., Ltd., Chiba, Japan, 1992—94; rsch. assoc. U. Cambridge, England, 1999—2001, Albert Einstein Coll. Medicine, Bronx, NY, 2001—03; sr. staff assoc. Columbia U., N.Y.C., 2003—04; rsch. scientist Rice U., Houston, 2004; sr. applications engr. MicroMRI, Inc., Phila., 2005—. Fellow, U. Cambridge, 1999—2001; grantee Royal Soc., 2000—01; scholar, Nagai Found., 1994—95, Japanese Govt., 1995—99. Mem.: Soc. Neurosci. (assoc.), IEEE (assoc.).

**NETTELBECK, FRED ARTHUR,** poet; b. Chgo., Nov. 9, 1950; s. Manfred Emil Nettelbeck and Thelma Anderson; m. Billy Joe Nettelbeck, July 17, 1999; children: James, Danny, Amandla. Student, El Camino Coll., 1969—71. Author: The Quick and The Dead, 1970, Spectator, 1977, Large Talk, 1983, Americruiser, 1983, The Kiss Off, 1984, Hands on a Mirror, 1987, Albert Ayler Disappeared, 1989, Ecosystems Collapsing, 1992, Hurting Music, 1998, All Fell Down, 2003, Everything Written Exists, 2004, (with John M. Bennett) Lap Gun Cut, 2006, others; editor: This is Important mag., 1980—. Democrat. Avocations: fishing, enthogenic plants. Home and Office: PO Box 69 Beatty OR 97621 Office Phone: 541-533-2486. Personal E-mail: fanettelbeck@fanettelbeck.com.

**NETTELHORST, ROBIN PAUL,** academic administrator, writer; b. Ohio, Mar. 14, 1957; s. Paul Merrit and Naomi Jean (Saylor) N.; m. Ruth Williamson, June 25, 1983; children: Vanessa Rachel, Nichole Antoinette, Sarah Brittany. BA, L.A. Bapt. Coll., 1979; MA, UCLA, 1983. Lectr. Christian Heritage Coll., El Cagon, Calif., 1984; lectr. old testament and bibl. langs. L.A. Bapt. Coll., 1984—87; novelist, 1987—; v.p. Quartz Hill Sch. Theology, Calif., 1992—. Webmaster Quartz Hill Sch. Theology, 1996—. Editor Quartz Hill Jour. Theology, 1994—; author short stories; contbr. articles to mags.; host (internet and FM Radio broadcast) Beyond the Box, 1999-2004; writer weekly column Ridge Rider News; author: What Dreamers Be These Rocks: Tableland, Book I, 2000, Dreams of Nothingness: Tableland, Book II, 2000, Awakens the Dreamer: Tableland, Book III, 2000, The Wrong Side of Morning, 2000, With a Rod of Iron, 2000, Antediluvian, 2000, Somewhere Obscurely, 2000, The Complaint of Jacob, 2005, Does God Have a Long Nose? 2006, Somewhen Obscurely, 2006, Fades the Flower, 2006. Ordained deacon Quartz Hill Cmty. Ch., 1989—. Mem. Am. Acad. Religion, Soc. Bibl. Lit. Baptist. Avocations: camping, reading, stamp collecting/philately, coin collecting/numismatics. Office: Quartz Hill Sch Theology 43543 51st St W Quartz Hill CA 93536-5608 Office Phone: 661-722-0891. Business E-Mail: robin@theology.edu. To hold the hand of God, to listen to his heart, to feel his pain, to taste his joys, to long for his happiness—that is to love God.

**NETTELS, ELSA,** English language educator; b. Madison, Wis., May 25, 1931; d. Curtis Putnam and Elsie (Patterson) Nettels. BA, Cornell U., 1953; MA, U. Wis., 1955, PhD, 1960. From instr. to asst. prof. English Mt. Holyoke Coll., South Hadley, Mass., 1959-67; from asst. prof. to prof. English Coll. William and Mary, Williamsburg, Va., 1967-97, prof. emeritus, 1997—. Author: James and Conrad, 1977 (South Atlantic MLA award, 1975), Language, Race and Social Class in Howells' America, 1988, Language and Gender in American Fiction: Howells, James, Wharton, and Cather, 1997; contbr. articles to profl. jours. Fellow, NEH, 1984-85. Mem.: MLA, South Atlantic MLA (mem. editl. bdl. 1977—83), Henry James Soc. (mem. editl. bd. 1983—). Office: Coll William and Mary Dept English Williamsburg VA 23187 Office Phone: 221-3905. Business E-Mail: exnett@wm.edu.

**NETTELS, GEORGE EDWARD, JR.,** retired mining executive; b. Pittsburg, Kans., Oct. 20, 1927; s. George Edward and Mathilde A. (Wulke) N.; m. Mary Joanne Myers, July 19, 1952; children: Christopher Bryan, Margaret Anne, Katherine Anne, Rebecca Jane. BSCE, U. Kans., Lawrence, 1950. With Black & Veatch Engrs., Kansas City, Mo., 1950-51, Spencer Chem. Co., Kansas City, Mo., 1951-55, Freeto Constrn. Co., Pittsburg, 1955-57; pres. Midwest Minerals, Inc., Pittsburg, 1957—; chmn. bd. McNally Pittsburg Mfg. Corp., 1970-76, pres., CEO, 1976-87, ret., 1987. Past chmn. bd. Nat. Limestone Inst.; bd. dirs. Pitts. Indsl. Devel. Com. Mem. bd. advisors U. Kans. Endowment Assn.; mem. Kans. U. Chancellor's Club, Kans., Inc.; past pres. Bd. Edn. 250, Pittsburg; past chmn. bd. trustees Mt. Carmel Hosp.; past mem. Kans. Commn. Civil Rights; chmn. Kans. Republican Com., 1966-68; Kans. del. Rep. Nat. Conv., 1968, Kans. Bus. and Industry Com. for Re-election of Pres., 1972. With AUS, 1946-47. Recipient Disting. Svc. citation U. Kans., 1980, Disting. Engring. citation U. Kans., 1985; named Kansan of Yr. Natives Sons and Daus. Kans., 1986. Mem. ASCE, NAM (past dir.), Kans. C. of C. and Industry (dir., chmn. 1983-84), Kans. Right to Work (dir.), Pittsburg C. of C. (past dir.), Kans. U. Alumni Assn. (pres. 1977), Kans. Leadership Com., Crestwood Country Club, Wolf Creek Golf Club (Olathe), Tau Beta Pi, Omicron Delta Kappa, Beta Theta Pi. Office: Midwest Minerals Inc 509 W Quincy St Pittsburg KS 66762-5689 Business E-Mail: george@midwestminerals.com.

**NETTESHEIM, TIMOTHY ALAN,** lawyer; b. Milw., Nov. 27, 1956; s. Joseph Harold and Marilyn Jo (Groeling) N.; m. Jeanne M. Martin (div. Feb. 17, 1986); 1 child, Morgan Leigh; m. Susanne Story Desmond, May 17, 1986; children: Margaret Story, Michael Timothy, Sara Susanne. BA in Econs., U. Wis., Milw., 1978; JD, U. Pacific, Sacramento, Calif., 1981, LLM in Tax, 1982. Bar: Calif. 1981, Wis. 1982, U.S. Dist. Ct. (we. dist.) Wis. 1982, U.S. Tax Ct. 1983, U.S. Ct. Appeals (7th cir.) 1986, U.S. Dist. Ct. (ea. dist.) Wis. 1988, U.S. Ct. Claims 1991. Ptnr. Murphy & Desmond S.C., Madison, Wis., 1982-88; assoc. Whyte & Hirschboeck S.C., Milw., 1988-89; ptnr. Reinhart, Boerner, VanDeuren, Norris & Rieselbach S.C., Milw., 1989—, mng. shareholder. Adj. prof. adj. tax program U. Wis.-Milw. Sch., 1989-93; adj. prof. gen. practice Wis. Law Sch., Madison, 1992-93, 97. Contbr. articles to profl. jours. Panel mem. allocations com. United Way, Madison, 1986, 87, mem. fundraising subcom., Milw., 1993. Named Outstanding Instr., Wis. Inst. CPAs, Milw., 1990-94. Mem. Calif. State Bar, Wis. State Bar (mem. LLC subcom. 1993, bd. dirs. tax sect.), Milw. Bar Tax (bus. and bankruptcy sects.), Wis. State and Local Tax Club. Met. Milw. C. of C. (mem. tax policy com.). Office: Reinhart Boerner VanDeuren SC PO Box 2265 W233 N2080 Ridgeview Pkwy Waukesha WI 53188 Office Phone: 262-951-4524. E-mail: tnet@reinhartlaw.com.

**NETTL, BRUNO,** anthropologist, musicologist, educator; b. Prague, Czechoslovakia, Mar. 14, 1930; s. Paul and Gertrud (Hutter) N.; m. Wanda Maria White, Sept. 15, 1952; children: Rebecca, Gloria. AB, Ind. U., 1950, PhD, 1953; MA in L.S, U. Mich., 1960; LHD (hon.), U. Chgo., 1993; LHD (hon.), U. Ill., 1996, Carleton Coll., 2000, Kenyon Coll., 2002. Mem. faculty Wayne State U., Detroit, 1953-64, asst. prof., 1954-64, music librarian, 1958-64; mem. faculty U. Ill., Urbana, 1964—, prof. music and anthropology, 1967—, chmn. div. musicology, 1967-72, 75-77, 82-85. Vis. lectr., Fulbright grantee U. Kiel, Fed. Republic of Germany, 1956-58; cons. Ency. Brit., 1969—; cons. on ethnomusicology to various univs.; vis. prof. Williams Coll., 1971, Washington U., 1978, U. Louisville, 1983, U. Wash., 1985, 88, 89, 93, 95, 98, 2000, Fla. State U., 1988, Harvard U., 1989, U. Alta., 1991, Colo. Coll., 1992, Northwestern U., 1993, U. Minn., 1994, U. Chgo., 1996, 2006, Carleton Coll., 1996, U. So. Calif., 2002, U. Denver, 2005. Author: Theory and Method in Ethnomusicology, 1964, Music in Primitive Culture, 1956, Folk and Traditional Music of the Western Continents, 1965, 2nd edit., 1973, Eight Urban Musical Cultures, 1978, The Study of Ethnomusicology, 1983, new edit., 2005, The Western Impact on World Music, 1985, The Radif of Persian Music, 1987, rev. edit., 1992, Blackfoot Musical Thought, 1989, Comparative Musicology and Anthropology of Music, 1991, Heartland Excursions, 1995, In the course of Performance, 1998, Encounters in Ethnomusicology, a Memoir, 2002; co-author Excursions in World Music, 1992, 3rd edit., 2000, 4th edit., 2003; editor Ethnomusicology, 1961-65, 98-2002, Yearbook of the International Folk Music Council, 1975-77; sr. adv. editor Garland Ency. of World Music; contbr. articles to profl. jours. Recipient Koizumi prize in ethnomusicology, Tokyo, 1994. Fellow Am. Acad. of Arts and Scis.; mem. Soc. Ethnomusicology (pres. 1969-71), Am., Internat. musicol. socs., Internat. Coun. for Traditional Music, Coll. Music Soc., Am. Musicological Soc. (hon.), Soc. for Ethnomusicology (hon.) Home: 1423 Cambridge Dr Champaign IL 61821-4958 Office: U Ill Sch Music Urbana IL 61801 Office Phone: 217-333-9613. Business E-Mail: b-nettl@uiuc.edu.

**NETTLES, BARRIE L.,** music educator; b. Oct. 2, 1942; s. Edgar and Arletta (Keller) Nettles; m. Patsy Silagy, Oct. 19, 1974. Studies, Navy Sch. Music, 1960, Berklee Coll. Music, 1967. Arranger, performer Army Band of the Pacific, Honolulu, 1961—63; music therapist Pennhurst State Sch., Pa., 1964—67; asst. to exec. v.p. Frank Music Corp., Music Theatre Internat., N.Y.C., NY, 1967—72; prof., dept. chair Berklee Coll. Music, 1972—; writer Down Beat Mag., 1968. Author (editor): Harmonies, Supplement to Harmonies - 1,2,3,4, 1984—89, The Chord Scale Theory and Jazz Harmony, Advance Music, 1991, Recordings; Numberous Children, Holiday Recordings, 1967—89, Saxes, 1989; arranger, composer, performer: Freelance performer: Woodwind and Brass, 1967—; performer (musician): (songs) (with) Herb Pomeroy, Charlie Mariano, Jimmy Moser, Smokey Robinson, 3 Degrees, Stylistics, Phil Wilson, John LaPorta, Richy Cole, Earl Grant, —; arranger: Danny Thomas, Steve Lawrence, Woody Herman, Buddy Rich, Dave Stahl, Steve Rochinski, —. Avocations: literature, model building, woodworking. Home: 27 Brush Hill Rd Sherborn MA 01770 Address: 82 Mattachee Rd South Yarmouth MA 02664 also: Big Tancook Island B0J3G0 Canada Office: Berklee Coll Music 1140 Boylston St fac box 422 Boston MA 02215 E-mail: pbnettles@netzero.com.

**NETTLES, JENNIFER,** singer; b. Atlanta, Ga., Sept. 12, 1974; BA, Agnes Scott Coll., Decatur, Ga. Lead singer Soul Miner's Daughter, 1996, Jennifer Nettles band, Sugarland, 2002—. Signed to Mercury Records. Singer: (albums) (solo albums) Story of Your Bones, 2000, (with Sugarland) Twice the Speed of Life, 2004. Recipient Ind. Musician of Yr. award, 2001, New Duo/Group award, Acad. Country Music, 2006. Office: Gail Gellman Mgmt 23852 PCH 920 Malibu CA 90265 Office Phone: 310-456-2620. Office Fax: 310-456-1415. E-mail: gellmanmgmt@aol.com, sugarlandall@aol.com.*

**NETTLES, JOHN BARNWELL,** obstetrics and gynecology educator; b. Dover, N.C., May 19, 1922; s. Stephen A. and Estelle (Hendrix) N.; m. Eunice Anita Saugstad, Apr. 28, 1960; children: Eric, Robert, John Barnwell; m. 2d, Sandra Williams, Sept. 14, 1991; stepchildren: Steven Williams, Clayton Williams. BS, U. S.C., 1941; MD, Med. Coll. S.C., 1944. Diplomate: Am. Bd. Obstetrics and Gynecology. Intern Garfield Meml. Hosp., Washington, 1944-45; research fellow in pathology Med. Coll. Ga., Augusta, 1946-47; resident in ob-gyn. U. Ill. Rsch. and Ednl. Hosps., Chgo., 1947-51; instr. to asst. prof. ob-gyn. U. Ill. Coll. Medicine, Chgo., 1951-57; asst. prof., assoc. prof., prof. ob-gyn. U. Ark. Med. Ctr., Little Rock, 1957-69; dir. grad. edn. Hillcrest Med. Ctr., Tulsa, 1969-73; prof. ob-gyn Coll. Medicine U. Okla., Oklahoma City, 1969-78; chmn. dept. ob-gyn. U. Okla.-Tulsa Med. Coll., 1975-80, prof., 1980—, mem. coun. on residency edn. in ob-gyn., 1974-79. Dir. Tulsa Obstet. and Gynecol. Edn. Found., 1969-80; Coordinator med. edn. Nat. Def., Ark., 1961-69; mem. S.W. regional med. adv. com. Planned Parenthood Fedn. Am., 1974-78; mem. adv. com. Health Policy Agenda Am. People, 1982-85, rev. com. Accrediation Coun. for Continuing Med. Edn., 1987-92. Contbr. articles on uterine malignancy, kidney biopsy in pregnancy, perinatal morbidity and mortality, human sexuality sch. age pregnancy to profl. jours. Served as lt. (j.g.) M.C. USNR, 1945-46; as lt. 1953-54. Recipient Nat. Faculty award. Fellow Am. Coll. Ob-Gyn. (dist. sec.-treas. 1964-70, dist. chmn. exec. bd. 1970-73, v.p. 1977-78, Disting. Svc. award 1998, Dist. VII Outstanding Clin. Prof. award 1989, Nat. Tchr. award 1992), ACS (bd. govs. 1969-71, program com. 1970-71, Surg. forum 1977-84, adv. com. gyn/ob 1985-92), Royal Soc. Health, Royal Soc. Medicine; mem. Ark. Obstet. and Gynecol. Soc. (exec. sec. 1959-69), Ctrl. Assn. Obstetrics and Gynecology (exec. com. 1966-69, pres. 1978-79), Internat. Soc. Advancement Humanistic Studies in Gynecology, Assn. Mil. Surgeons U.S., AMA (sect. coun. on obstetrics and gynecology 1975-96, chmn. 1982-96, del. from Am. Coll. Obstetricians and Gynecologists 1987-96, governing coun. sr. physicians group 2003—, Young at Heart award Young Physicians sect. 1994), Nurses Assn. So. Med. Assn. (chmn. obstetrics 1973-74), Okla. Med. Soc. (Ed L. Calhoun Leadership in Organized Medicine award, 2004), Tulsa County Med. Soc., Chgo. Med. Soc., Am. Assn. for Maternal and Infant Health, Assn. Am. Med. Colls., APHA, Am. Assn. Sex Edn. Counselors and Therapists (S.W. regional bd. 1976-79), Soc. for Gynecol. Investigation, AAAS, Am. Soc. for Study Fertility and Sterility, Internat. Soc. Gen. Semantics, So. Gynecol. and Obstet. Soc. (pres. 1981-82), Am. Cancer Soc. (pres. Okla. div. 1979-83, St. George's medal 1991), Comm. on In-Tng. Exam. in Ob-Gyn, Am. Coll. Nurse Midwives (governing bd. examiners 1979-83), Sigma Xi (pres. Tulsa chpt. 1992-93), Phi Rho Sigma. Lutheran. Office: U Okla Health Sci Ctr 1145 S Utica Ave Ste 600 Tulsa OK 74104-4070 Office Phone: 918-582-0955. Business E-Mail: John-Nettles@ouhsc.edu. To live fully, with faith and trust in God and his people, working with others to make our world a little better, and willing to fill the gaps wherever they are.

**NETTLES, SAUNDRA R. MURRAY,** psychologist, writer, educator; b. Atlanta, Ga., Jan. 6, 1947; d. Edna Lewis and George Halbert Rose; m. Donald Gaines Murray, Mar. 14, 1972 (div.); m. Reginald Nettles (div.); children: Alana Denise Murray, Kali Nicole Murray. BA, Howard U., 1963—67; MS, U. of Ill. Grad. Sch. of Libr. and Info. Sci., 1967—68, Howard U., 1972—74, PhD, 1972—76. Prof. of human devel. U. of Md., 1994—2003; prin. rsch. scientist Johns Hopkins U. Ctr. for Social Orgn. of Schools, Balt., 1988—99; dir. office of field services United Planning Orgn., Washington, 1983—87; sr. rsch. scientist Am. Inst. for Rsch., Washington, 1978—82. Contbr. articles to profl. jours. Mem. Jack and Jill of Am., Columbia, Md., 1989—92; rsch. scholars panel Pathways to Coll. Network, Boston, 2001—04. Mem.: APA, APA Sect. on the Psychology of Black Women (pres. 1986—87), Environ. Design Rsch. Assn., Am. Ednl. Rsch. Assn. Office: Georgia Southern Univ Po B 8144 Statesboro GA 30460-8144 Office Phone: 912-681-0672. Office Fax: 912-681-5091. E-mail: snettles@georgiasouthern.edu.

**NETTO, AMBA CECILE,** military officer; b. Lafayette, La., Aug. 3, 1980; d. Michael R. Netto and DeciAmba C. Morgan; m. Terry J. Meadows, June 25, 2003 (div.); children: Kailly M. Paulson, Kayne M. Paulson. Commd. In USAF, 1999, advanced through grades to staff sgt., 2003, security forces Albuquerque, 1999—2004, info. mgr. Columbus, Miss., 2004—06. Tng.

assessor police reform directorate USAF, Kabul, Afghanistan, 2005—. Named Non-Commisioned Officer of Qua., 14th Comm. Squadron Comdr., USAF, 2005. Office Phone: 662-434-7096.

**NETTO, PAUL V.,** critical care nurse; b. Santa Cruz, Calif., Oct. 1, 1951; s. Joseph and Mary C. Netto; m. Patricia L. Jaynes-Netto (dec.); children: Paul V. Jr., Joseph P.; Matthew R.; m. Cathy J. Montgomery-Netto, Aug. 12, 1984. ASN, Sierra Coll., Rocklin, Calif., 1985, AA in Art, 1993; BA in Studio Art cum laude, Calif. State U., 2000. RN Calif., critical care RN. RN supr. Carmichael (Calif.) Convalescent, 1986—87; supr., dir. Mt. Olivette Care Ctr., Carmichael, 1988—89; RN, clin. mgr. Roseville (Calif.) Cmty. Hosp., 1989—95; asst. dir. Hilltop Manor, Auburn, Calif., 1993—95; RNII CICU/MSICU Sutter Roseville Med. Ctr., 1995—. Nurse rep. Calif. Nurses Assn., Sacramento, 1998—. Author: Brothers and Friends, 2001; author: (illustrator) The Birds In The Hand, 2005; composer, performer (audio album) Pearls and Swine, 1991. Mem.: NRA (life), Jews for Preservation of Firearms Ownership, Golden Key Nat. Honor Soc. Libertarian. Avocations: travel, scuba diving, fishing, target shooting, writing. Home: PO Box 756 Meadow Vista CA 95722 Office: Sutter Roseville Med Ctr 1 Medical Ctr Plz Roseville CA 95561 Office Phone: 916-781-1522.

**NETZEL, PAUL ARTHUR,** fundraising management executive, consultant; b. Tacoma, Sept. 11, 1941; s. Marden Arthur and Audrey Rose (Jones) Netzel; m. Diane Vaszul, Mar. 21, 1963; children: Paul M., Shari Ann. BS in Group Work Edn., George Williams Coll., 1963. Program dir. S. Pasadena-San Marino (Calif.) YMCA, 1963—66; exec. dir. camp and youth programs Wenatchee (Wash.) YMCA, 1966—67; exec. dir. Culver-Palms Family YMCA, Culver City, Calif., 1967—73; v.p. met. fin. devel. YMCA Met. Los Angeles, 1978—78, exec. v.p. devel., 1979—85; pres. bd. dirs. YMCA Employees Credit Union, 1977—80; chmn N. Am. Fellowship of YMCA Devel. Officers, 1980—83; chmn., CEO Netzel Assocs., Inc., 1985—; pvt. practice cons., fund raiser. Adj. faculty U. So. Calif. Coll. Continuing Edn., 1983—86, Loyola Marymount U., 1986—90, Calif. State U., 1991—92, UCLA Extension, 1991—2002. Bd. mgrs. Culver-Palms YMCA, Culver City, 1985—2002, chmn., 1989—91, 1991—93; mem. Culver City Bd. Edn., 1975—79, pres., 1977—78; mem. Culver City Edn. Found., 1982—91, Culver City Redevel. Agy., 1980—88, chmn., 1983—84, 1987—88, vice chmn., 1985—86; chmn. bd. dirs. Calif. Youth Model Legislature, 1987—92; mem. World Affairs Coun., 1989—92; mem. adv. bd. Automobile Club So. Calif., 1996—2002; mem. Culver City City Coun., 1980—88, vice mayor, 1982, 1984—85, mayor, 1983, 1986—87; bd. dirs. L.A. Psychiat. Svc., 1971—74, Goodwill Industries of So. Calif., 1993—97, L.A. County Sanitation Dists., 83, 1985—87, Western United Way, 1986—93, vice chmn., 1991—92. Recipient Man of Yr. award, Culver City C. of C., 1972. Mem.: Nat. Soc. Fund Raising Execs. (v.p. bd. dirs. Greater L.A. chpt. 1986—88, pres. bd. dirs. 1989—90, nat. bd. dirs. 1989—91, vice chmn. 1994, Profl. of Yr. 1983), Mountain Gate Country Club, Rotary Internat. (L.A. # 5 pres. 1992—93, treas. L.A. found. 1995—96, gov. dist. 5280 1997—98, chmn. L.A. conv., founding chmn. internat. convention 2008 host orgn. com., named to Dist. 5280 Hall Fame 2005), Calif. Club. Address: Netzel Assocs Inc 9696 Culver Blvd Ste 105 Culver City CA 90232-2753 Home: 12336 Ridge Cir Los Angeles CA 90049-1151 E-mail: pretzel@earthlink.net.

**NETZER, DICK,** economics professor; b. NYC, May 14, 1928; s. Solomon and Sue (Dick) Netzer; m. Carol Risika, Dec. 30, 1945; children: Jenny, Katherine. BA, U. Wis., 1946; MA, M.P.A., Harvard U., 1948, PhD, 1952. Successively economist, sr. economist, asst. v.p. Fed. Res. Bank Chgo., 1948-60; econ. cons. Regional Plan Assn., N.Y.C., 1960-80; assoc. prof. N.Y. U., 1961-64, prof. econs., 1964—, dean Grad. Sch. Pub. Adminstrn., 1969-82, dir. Urban Research Center, 1981-86. Cons. in field, 1960—. Author: Economics of the Property Tax, 1966, The Economics of Public Finance, 1974, The Subsidized Muse, 1978, Urban Politics New York Style, 1990; editor: N.Y. Affairs, 1973—88. Mem. Mayor N.Y.C. Fiscal Adv. Com., 1969—73; treas. Colony-South Bklyn. Houses, 1968—73; mem. Mcpl. Securities Rulemaking Bd., 1978—81, vice chmn., 1980—81; bd. dirs. Mcpl. Assistance Corp., N.Y.C., 1975—97, Citizens Union Found.; bd. dirs., treas. Adolph and Esther Gottlieb Found., 1975—, v.p., 1979—88, pres., 1989—. Fellow: Am. Inst. Cert. Planners; mem.: Nat. Tax Assn., Regional Sci. Assn., Am. Econs. Assn., Assn. Cultural Econs. Internat. (pres. 1993—94). Home: 41 Huckleberry Ln East Hampton NY 11937-2830 Office: 295 Lafayette St New York NY 10012 Office Phone: 212-998-7510. Business E-mail: dick.netzer@nyu.edu.

**NETZER, NANCY,** museum director, art historian, educator; b. Pitts., July 25, 1951; m. Robert A.S. Silberman, Nov. 10, 1974. MA, Harvard U., 1978, PhD, 1986; LittD (hon.), U. Ulster, No. Ireland, 2000. Asst. curator Mus. Fine Arts, Boston, 1982-90; prof. art history Boston Coll., 1990—; dir. McMullen Mus. Art, 1990—. Bd. advs. Internat. Ctr. Medieval Art., N.Y.C., 1990-94; dir. Internat. Ctr. Medieval Art, 1995-2000 Author: Medieval Objects in the Museum of Fine Arts, 1986, vol. II, 1991, Cultural Interplay in the Eighth Century, 1994, Memory and the Middle Ages, 1995, Fragmented Devotion, 2000, Secular Sacred, 2006. Bd. advisors Woodrow Wilson Nat. Fellowship Found.; gov. appointee bd. dirs. Mass. Found. Humanities; bd. dirs. ICMA, 1995. Fellow: Soc. Antiquaries. Office: McMullen Mus Devlin Hall #423 140 Commonwealth Ave Chestnut Hill MA 02467-3800 Business E-mail: netzer@bc.edu.

**NETZER, NIKOLAUS C.,** physician, medical researcher, publishing executive; b. Augsburg, Bavaria, Germany, Oct. 3, 1961; arrived in US, 1999; s. Norbert H. and Waltraud E. Netzer; m. Cordula M. Peterle, Apr. 4, 1997; 1 child, Anika. BS, Wilhelm-Hausenstein Coll., Munich, 1981; MD, Ludwig Maximilian U., Munich, 1988, PhD, 1989. Fellow dept. pediatric genetics Univ. Hosp., Munich, 1988—90; fellow pulmonary dept. Univ. Hosp., Freiburg, Germany, 1992—96, assoc. prof. dept. sports medicine Ulm, Germany, 1996—2001, asst. prof. pulmonary dept. Univ. Hosp., Case Western Res. U., Cleve., 1996—99; rsch. physician Walter Reed Army Med. Ctr., Washington, 2000—01; dir. Sleep Disorders Clinic, Bayerisch, Germany, 2001—; prof. medicine U. Ulm, Germany, 2004—. Mem. adv. bd. Med. Pub./ Nat. Libr. Medicine, Washington, 2000—01. Editor: Sleep Medicine, 1992, Free Breathing, 1991, Sleep Apnea Screening, 1990. Grantee, Friedrich Ebert Found., 1984—86, Brendan Schmitt Mann Found., 1987—88. Mem.: Acad. Mountain Sports and Health, Soc. of Applied Sleep Med. Chmn., Am. Thoracic Soc. Program. Democrat. Roman Catholic. Achievements include patents for integrated humidification for CPAP and BiLevel CPAP Devices. Avocations: history, golf, skiing, mountain climbing, politics. Home: 3293 Bradford Rd Cleveland Heights OH 44118 Office Phone: 216-402-3953. E-mail: nikinetzer@yahoo.com.

**NETZLY, DWIGHT H.,** lawyer; b. Navarre, Ohio, May 7, 1919; s. Harry E. Netzly and Lillian N. Ramsey; m. Martha L. Emerick, Jan. 29, 1949; children: Duane, Dwight K., Doyle, Derek. BSBA, Kent State U., 1948; LLB, William McKinley Law Sch., 1952. Bar: Ohio 1952. Acct. H.C. Schwitzgebul, Canton, Ohio, 1948-52; pvt. practice law and acctg. Massillon, Ohio, 1952—. Sgt. U.S. Army, 1941-45. Mem. Am. Assn. Atty. CPAs, Ohio State Bar Assn., Ohio Soc. CPAs, Am. Legion (state treas. 1993-94). Republican. Home: 6179 Pigeon Run Rd SW Navarre OH 44662-8738 Office: 1237 Lincoln Way E Massillon OH 44646-6954 E-mail: dhnetz@aol.com.

**NEU, CARL HERBERT, JR.,** management consultant; b. Miami Beach, Fla., Sept. 4, 1937; s. Carl Herbert and Catherine Mary (Miller) N.; BS, MIT, 1959; MBA, Harvard U., 1961; m. Carmen Mercedes Smith, Feb. 8, 1964; children— Carl Bartley, David Conrad. Cert. profl. mgmt. cons. Indsl. liaison officer MIT, Cambridge, 1967-69; coord. forward planning Gates Rubber Co., Denver, 1969-71; pres., co-founder Dyna-Com Resources, Lakewood, Colo., 1971-77; pres., founder Neu & Co., Lakewood, 1977—; mng. dir. Pro-Med Mgmt. Systems, Lakewood, 1981—; lectr. Grad. Sch. Pub. Affairs, U. Colo. Denver, 1982-84. Mem. exec. coun. Episcopal Diocese Colo., 1974; mem. Lakewood City Coun., 1975-80, pres., 1976; chmn. Lakewood City Charter Commn., 1982, Lakewood Civic Found., Inc., 1986-91; pres. Lakewood

Parade, 1978, bd. dirs., 1978-80; pres. Classic Chorale, Denver, 1979, bd. dirs., 1978-83; pres. Lakewood Pub. Bldg. Authority, 1983—; bd. dirs. Metro State Coll. of Denver Found., 1990—, treas., 1994-97; bd. dirs Kaiser Permanente Health Adv. Com., 1990—, chair, 1997. With U.S. Army, 1961-67. Decorated Bronze Star medal, Army Commendation medal; recipient Arthur Page award AT&T, 1979; Kettering Found. grantee, 1979-80. Mem. Internat. City Mgrs. Assn., Lakewood-So. Jefferson County C. of C. (bd. dirs. 1983-89, chmn. 1988, chmn. 1987-88), Jefferson County C. of C. (chmn. 1988). Republican. Episcopalian. Contbr. articles to profl. jours. Home: 8169 W Baker Ave Denver CO 80227-3129

**NEU, CHARLES ERIC,** historian, educator; b. Carroll, Iowa, Apr. 10, 1936; s. Arthur Nicholas and Martha Margaret (Frandsen) N.; m. Deborah Dunning, Sept. 2, 1961 (div. 1978); children: Hilary Adams, Douglas Bancroft.; m. Sabina deWerth Tuck, Mar. 27, 1999. BA, Northwestern U., 1958; PhD, Harvard U., 1964. Instr. history Rice U., 1963-64, asst. prof., 1964-67, asso. prof., 1968-70; asso. prof. history Brown U., Providence, 1970-76, prof., 1976—2003, prof. emeritus, 2003—, chmn. dept. history, 1995—98, 1999—2002. Dir. summer seminar NEH, 1979, 1986—87, 1989, 92, 2005; adj. prof. history U. Miami, 2004—. Author: An Uncertain Friendship: Theodore Roosevelt and Japan, 1906-1909, 1967, The Troubled Encounter: The United States and Japan, 1975, America's Lost War: Vietnam, 1945-1975, 2005; co-editor: The Wilson Era: Essays in Honor of Arthur S. Link, 1991, Artists of Power: Theodore Roosevelt, Woodrow Wilson, and Their Enduring Impact on U.S. Foreign Policy, 2006; editor: After Vietnam: Legacies of a Lost War, 2000. Adv. coun. Vietnam Ctr. Tex. Tech. U. Recipient, Woodrow Wilson Found. fellowship, 1958—59, Am. Coun. Learned Socs. fellowship, 1975—76, Charles Warren Ctr. fellowship, 1971—72, Howard Found. fellowship, 1976—77, Guggenheim fellowship, 1981—82, Barrett Hazeltine citation for disting. undergrad. tchg., 1998; fellow, NEH, 1968—69; guest scholar, Woodrow Wilson Ctr., 1988. Mem. Am. Hist. Assn., Orgn. Am. Historians, Soc. Historians of Am. Fgn. Policy, Phi Beta Kappa. Democrat. Home: 4929 SW 71st Place Miami FL 33155 Personal E-mail: cneu@bellsouth.net.

**NEU, IRENE DOROTHY,** historian, educator; b. Cin. d. Frederick Francis and Mary Clara (Holterman) Neu; m. Robert Leslie Jones, Nov. 25, 1976. BA, Marietta Coll., 1944; MA, Cornell U., 1945, PhD, 1950. Fellow, Rsch. Ctr. Entrepreneurial History Harvard U., Cambridge, Mass., 1950—51; instr. Rockford (Ill.) Coll., 1951—52, Conn. Coll., New London, 1953—54; assoc. prof. history S.E. Mo. State Coll., Cape Girardeau, 1956—62, prof. history, 1962—64; assoc. prof. history Ind. U., Bloomington, 1964—70, prof. history, 1970—86, prof. emeritus history, 1986—. Author: Erastus Corning, Merchant and Financier, 1794-1872, 1960; co-author: The American Railroad Network, 1861-1890, 1956; contbr. articles to profl. jours. Fulbright fellow, Italy, 1954—55, Social Sci. Rsch. Coun. faculty fellow, 1960—61, Eleutherian Mills Hist. Libr. sr. fellow, 1970. Mem.: AAUW, Nat. Soc. Arts and Letters, Ind. Hist. Soc., Orgn. Am. Historians, Phi Beta Kappa. Home: 206 Brentwood St Marietta OH 45750-1509

**NEU, RICHARD W.,** credit agency executive; B of Acctg., Ea. Mich. U., 1977. Sr. audit mgr. KMPG Peat Marwick; sr. v.p., chief fin. officer FirstFed Mich. Corp., 1985—89, chief fin. officer, 1989—95; exec. v.p., chief fin. officer Charter One Fin., Inc., 1995—. Past chmn. Thrift Industry Acctg. Com. Office: Charter One Fin Inc 1215 Superior Ave Cleveland OH 44114

**NEUBAUER, JOHN M.,** music educator, consultant; b. Normal, Ill., Jan. 16, 1968; s. Martin E. and Catherine A. Neubauer. B in Music Edn., Millikin U., Decatur, Ill., 1990. Cert. tchr. Ill. Choral dir. Manual H.S., Peoria, Ill., 1992—95, Crete Monee H.S., Ill., 1993—2001, Burbank H.S., 2001—02, Mundelein H.S., Ill., 2002—. Dir. nat. champion chair Keynote Arts, Orlando, Fla., 2000, Orlando, 01; choreographer Mantena H.S., Ill., 2003—05, Watseka H.S., Ill., 2004—05.

**NEUBAUER, JOSEPH,** food services company executive; b. Oct. 19, 1941; s. Max and Herta (Kahn) Neubauer; children: Lawrence, Melissa. BS in Chem. Engring. Tufts U., 1963; MBA in Fin, U. Chgo., 1965. Asst. treas. Chase Manhattan Bank, 1965—68, asst. v.p., 1968—70, v.p., 1970—71, asst. treas. Pepsico Inc., Purchase, NY, 1971—72, treas., 1972—73, v.p., 1973—76; v.p. fin. and control Wilson Sporting Goods Co., River Grove, Ill., 1976—77, sr. v.p., gen. mgr. team sports divsn., 1977—79; exec. v.p. fin. and devel., CFO, dir. ARA Svcs., Inc., Phila., 1979—81; pres., COO, dir. ARA Services, Inc., Phila., 1981—83, pres., CEO, 1983—84; chmn., CEO ARA Svcs., Inc. (in 1994, name changed to Aramark Corp.), Phila., 1984—. Bd. dirs. Wachovia Corp., Verizon Corp., Federated Dept. Stores; trustee Penn Mut. Life Ins. Co. Chmn., CEO Phila. Orch. Assn., Mann Music Ctr., Inroads/Phila., Inc.; trustee Hahnemann U., Tufts U., Mus. Am. Jewish History, Greater Phila. First Corp., Com. Econ. Devel., U. Chgo.; bd. govs. Joseph H. Lauder Inst. Mgmt. and Internat. Studies, U. Pa.; dir. The Barnes Found. Mem.: Bus. Roundtable, Bus. Coun., Phila. C. of C., Locust Club, Union League Club. Office: ARAMARK Corp 1101 Market St Philadelphia PA 19107*

**NEUBAUER, PETER BELA,** psychoanalyst; b. Krems, Austria, July 5, 1913; came to US, 1941, naturalized, 1946; s. Samuel and Rose (Blau) N.; m. Susan Rachlin, Nov. 25, 1953 (dec.); children: Joshua Rachlin, Alexander Lewis. MD, U. Berne, 1938. Intern Lawrence Meml. Hosp., New London, Conn., 1941, Beth-El Hosp., Bklyn., 1942; resident in psychiatry Bellevue Hosp., NYC, 1943-45; dir. Child Devel. Ctr. Jewish Bd. Family Children's Svcs., NYC, 1951-83; clin. prof. psychiatry Psychoanalytic Inst., NYU, 1979—. Lectr. child psychoanalysis Psychoanalytic Inst. Tng. Research Columbia U., 1973 Author: Children in Collectives: Child Rearing Aims and Practices in Kibbutzim, 1965. Early Child Day Care, 1974, Process of Child Development, 1976, (with Alexander Neubauer) Nature's Thumbprint, 1990; contbg. author: Fathers and Their Families, 1989; mem. editorial bd. Psychoanalytic Study of the Child, 1978. Recipient Hulse award NY Council Child Psychiatry, 1975, Heinz Hartmann award NY Psychoanalytic Soc., 1981, Mary S. Sigourney award, 1994. Mem. Am. Psychoanalytic Assn., Am. Acad. Child Psychiatry, Assn. Child Psychoanalysis, Internat. Assn. Child and Adolescent Psychiatry, Assn. Child Psychoanalysis (pres. 1974-76). Office: 33 E 70th St New York NY 10021-4941 Office Phone: 212-288-2348.

**NEUBAUER, RICHARD A.,** library science educator, consultant; b. Meadville, Pa., Oct. 9, 1933; s. Carl Gustave and Velma Winston (Watson) N.; m. Janice Ernest; children: David, Lynda, Karl, Jennifer; m. Carol Barton. BS, Clarion U., 1955; MLS, SUNY, Geneseo, 1966; attended, Kent St. U. 1966-68, Simmons Coll., 1970-72. Cert. profl. libr., sch. libr., tchr. Tchr. geography Franklin (Pa.) Sch. Dept., 1957-58, N. Bedford County Schs., Woodbury, Mass., 1958-60; tchr. history Hornell (N.Y.) Jr. High Sch., 1960-62, sch. libr., 1962-65; prof. libr. sci. Edinboro (Pa.) U., 1965-68, assoc. libr. Hamilton Univ., 1965-68; dir. sch. librs. Duxbury (Mass.) Sch. Dept., 1968-69; dir., cons. Pub. Libr., Lincoln, Mass., 1969-70; prof. libr. sci. Bridgewater (Mass.) State Coll., 1969-78, chair dept. libr. sci., 1978-80, prof. libr. sci., 1980-91, coord. libr. media program, 1991-95; prof. emeritus libr. sci., 1996—. Adj. prof. libr. sci. U. R.I., Kingston, 1975-88; cons. Tabor Acad., Marion, Mass., 1970-71, Abington (Mass.) Pub. Libr. Trustees, 1973-76, Duxbury Free Libr., 1968-72. Author: Planning the Elementary School Library, 1968; author, editor Exploring the U.S.-Northeast, 1994. Chmn. Mass. Dept. Edn. Cert., Quincy, 1989-90; resource cons. Project Contemporary Competitiveness, Bridgewater, Mass., 1973-83. 1st lt. USMC, 1955-57. Inst. grantee HEA of 1965 Edinboro U., 1968. Mem. NEA, Am. Libr. Assn., Intellectual Freedom Found., Mass. Assn. of Edn. Media, Mass. Sch. Libr. Media Assn., Mass. Tchrs. Assn. Democrat. Avocations: gardening, woodworking, reading. Home: 22 Pleasant St Carver MA 02330-1013

**NEUBERG, HANS W.,** internist, educator; b. Hannover, Germany, Mar. 26, 1921; came to U.S., 1937, naturalized, 1943. s. Georg and Gertrud (Dux) N.; m. Birgit Aron, Apr. 8, 1949; children: Peter G., Gerald W. BS, Wagner Coll. 1941; MD, Columbia U., 1950. Diplomate Am. Bd. Internal Medicine. Intern

Presbyn. Hosp., N.Y.C., 1950-53, asst. resident, NRC fellow in medicine, 1953-54, asst. attending physician, 1966-80, assoc. attending physician, 1980-91, attending physician, 1992—; pvt. practice, 1954-83. Instr. medicine Columbia U. Coll. Phys. and Surg., N.Y.C., 1954-63, assoc. in medicine, 1963-67, asst. prof. clin. medicine, 1967-80, assoc. clin. prof. medicine, 1980-91, clin. prof. medicine, 1992—, mem. Instnl. Rev. Bd. With AUS, 1943-46. Fellow ACP; mem. Alpha Omega Alpha. Mem. Am. Diabetes Assn. Home: 3213 Kendal Way Sleepy Hollow NY 10591 Office: 620 W 168th St New York NY 10032-3702 Personal E-mail: Neubergh@aol.com.

**NEUBORNE, BURT,** law educator; b. 1941; AB, Cornell U., 1961; LLB, Harvard U., 1964. Bar: NY 1965. Assoc. Casey, Lane & Mittendorf, NYC, 1964-67; staff counsel NY Civil Liberties Union, NYC, 1967-72; asst. legal dir. ACLU, NYC, 1972-74, legal dir., 1983—86; assoc. prof. NYU Sch. Law, 1974-76, prof., 1976—, John Norton Pomeroy prof. of law, 1991—, dir. Brennan Ctr. for Justice, 1994—. Spl. counsel NOW Legal Def. and Edn. Fund, 1991-; comnr. NYC Commn. Human Rights, 1988-93. Co-author: Political and Civil Rights in the United States, Vol. I, 1976, Vol. II, 1979. Master: Am. Acad. Arts & Sciences. Office: NYU Sch Law Vanderbilt Hall Rm 307 40 Washington Sq S New York NY 10012-1099 Office Phone: 212-998-6172. E-mail: burt.neuborne@nyu.edu.

**NEUENSCHWANDER, PIERRE FERNAND,** medical educator; BS in Chemistry, 1985; PhD in Biochemistry & Molecular Biology, SUNY, Stony Brook, 1990. Lab. tchg. asst. SUNY, Stony Brook, 1985-86, lecture tchg. asst. in biochemistry, 1986, 87; assoc. rsch. scientist Cardiovascular Biology Rsch. Program Okla. Med. Rsch. Found., Oklahoma City, 1990-93, sr. rsch. scientist, 1993-94, found. rsch. scientist, 1994-95, asst. mem., 1995-2001; assoc. prof. biochemistry U. Tex. Health Ctr., Tyler, 2001—. Co-editor Trigger newsletter; rev. Jour. Biol. Chemistry; contbr. articles to profl. jours. Recipient Am. Heart Assn. Travel stipend, 1994, Internat. Soc. Haematology Travel award, 1992, Am. Soc. Hematology Travel award, 1989, 90. Mem. Am. Heart Assn. (coun. on thrombosis), Am. Chem Soc. (divsn. biol. chemistry), Internat. Soc. Thrombosis and Haemostasis, Sigma Xi, Alpha Chi Sigma. Office: Univ Tex Health Ctr Biomed Rsch Lab C8 11937 US Hwy 271 Tyler TX 75708 Office Phone: 903-877-7678. E-mail: Pierre.Neuenschwander@uthct.edu.

**NEUER, PHILIP DAVID,** lawyer, real estate consultant; b. Bklyn., May 31, 1946; s. Murray and Adele (Jacobs) Neuer; m. Rena Donna Levine, July 30, 1972 (div. 1987); children: Jeremy Evan, Linzy Michelle, Sari Faith. BBA, CCNY, 1968; postgrad., Boston U., 1968-69; JD, Seton Hall U., 1976. Bar: N.J. 1976, U.S. Dist. Ct. N.J. 1977, U.S. Supreme Ct. 1980. Asst. town atty. Town of West Orange, NJ, 1976-77; assoc. Margolis and Bergstein, Verona, 1979-80; ptnr. Slavitt and Slavitt, West Orange, 1980-81; assoc. Mandelbaum and Targan, West Orange, 1981-83; ptnr. Margolis Neuer, Verona, 1984-91; of counsel Slavitt Simon & Neuer, Parsippany, 1991-2000; exec. v.p., gen. counsel Safer Textiles Group, Safer Devel. and Mgmt. Co., Newark, 1993—; of counsel Lum, Danzis, Drasco, Positan & Kleinberg, LLC, Roseland, 2000—02. Faculty mem. NYU Grad. Sch. Real Estate, N.Y.C., 2004—. Mem. editl. bd. Internat. Jour. Corp. Real Estate, 1998—2004. With USN, 1969—73. Named to, Inst. Corp. Real Estate Hall of Fame, 2002. Mem.: ABA, Urban Land Inst., Inst. Corp. Real Estate (bd. dirs., pres. 1998—2002), Internat. Assn. Corp. Real Estate Execs. (pres., bd. dirs., gen. counsel NJ chpt., internat. bd. dirs. 1993—2002), Assoc. Mem. of Yr. 1993), N.J. Corp. Real Exec. of the Yr. 1993), Essex County Bar Assn., N.J. State Bar Assn., Mensa. Office: 1875 McCarter Hwy Newark NJ 07104-4211 Office Phone: 973-482-0840. E-mail: pdn@neuerlaw.com, pdneuer@aol.com.

**NEUFELD, ELIZABETH FONDAL,** biochemist, educator; b. Paris, Sept. 27, 1928; married, 1951. PhD, U. Calif., Berkeley, 1956; DHc (hon.), U. Rene Descartes, Paris, 1978; DSc (hon.), Russell Sage Coll., Troy, N.Y., 1981; DSc (hon.), Hahnemann U. Sch. Medicine, 1984; DSc (hon.), Queens Coll., 1996. Asst. rsch. biochemist U. Calif., Berkeley, 1957—63; with Nat. Inst. Arthritis, Metabolism and Digestive Diseases, Bethesda, Md., 1963—84, research biochemist, 1963—73, chief sect. human biochem. genetics, 1973—79, chief genetics and biochem. br., 1979—84; prof. Dept. Biol. Chemistry Sch. Medicine U. Calif., 1984—, chmn. Dept. Biol. Chemistry Sch. Medicine, 1984—2004. Named Passano Found. sr. laureate, 1982, Calif. Scientist of Yr., 1990; recipient Dickson prize, U. Pitts., 1974, Hillenbrand award, 1975, Gairdner Found. award, 1981, Albert Lasker Clin. Med. Rsch. award, 1982, William Allan award, 1982, Elliott Cresson medal, 1984, Wolf Found. prize, 1988, Christopher Columbus Discovery award for biomed. rsch., 1992, Nat. Medal of Sci., 1994. Fellow: Fellow AAAS; mem.: NAS, Am. Soc. Gene Therapy, Am. Soc. Clin. Investigation, Am. Soc. Cell Biology, Am. Soc. Biochemistry and Molecular Biology (pres. 1992—93), Am. Chem. Soc., Am. Soc. Human Genetics, Am. Philos. Soc., Am. Acad. Arts and Scis, Inst. Medicine of NAS. Office: UCLA David Geffen Sch Medicine Dept Biol Chemistry 33-257 CHS 33-355 CH Box 951737 Los Angeles CA 90095-1737 Business E-Mail: eneufeld@mednet.ucla.edu.

**NEUFELD, ELLIS JACOB,** pediatrician, hematologist, researcher; b. Oakland, Calif., Feb. 27, 1958; BA, Wesleyan U., Middletown, Conn., 1979; MD, Wash. U., St. Louis, Mo., PhD, 1985. Asst. prof. pediat. Harvard Med. Sch., Boston, 1993—99, assoc. prof. pediat., 1999—; assoc. chief hematology/oncology Children's Hosp. Boston, 2003—. Office: Children's Hospital Boston 300 Longwood Ave Boston MA 02115 Office Phone: 617-919-2139. E-mail: ellis.neufeld@chboston.org.

**NEUFELD, MICHAEL JOHN,** curator, historian; b. Edmonton, Alta., Can., July 7 1951; s. Henry John and Isabel Grace (Mitchell) N.; m. Sheila Faith Weiss, May 29, 1983 (div. Dec. 1992); m. Karen Lee Levenback, June 14, 1994. BA with 1st class honors, U. Calgary, Alta., 1974; MA, U. B.C., Vancouver, Can., 1976, Johns Hopkins U., 2001; PhD in History, 1984. Hist. rschr. Dept. Supply and Svcs., Ottawa, Ont., Canada, summer 1973, 74; teaching asst. Johns Hopkins U., Balt., 1979-80; instr. Clarkson U., Potsdam, NY, 1983-84, from part-time instr. to part-time asst. prof., 1983-85; vis. asst. prof. SUNY, Oswego, 1985-86, Colgate U., Hamilton, NY, 1986-88; Verville fellow Nat. Air and Space Mus., Washington, 1988-89, Smithsonian postdoctoral fellow, 1989-90, curator aeronautics, 1990-99, curator space history, 1999—. Curator Air Power in WWII series, 1991-94; sr. lectr. Johns Hopkins U., 2001. Author: The Skilled Metalworkers of Nuremberg, 1989, The Rocket and the Reich, 1995; editor: Planet Dora, 1997; co-editor: The Bombing of Auschwitz, 2000; contbr. articles and book revs. to profl. jours. Recipient History Manuscript award AIAA, 1995, Dexter Prize SHOT, 1997, NSF Scholar's award History of Sci. and Tech. Program, 1989-90. Mem. German Studies Assn., Soc. Mil. History, Soc. for History Tech., History of Sci. Soc., Amnesty Internat. Avocation: amateur astronomy. Office: Nat Air & Space Mus Divsn Space History MRC 311 Smithsonian Instn PO Box 37012 Washington DC 20013-7012 Office Phone: 202-633-2434. E-mail: neufeldm@si.edu.

**NEUFELD, PETER,** lawyer; b. Bklyn. BA, U. Wis.; degree (hon.), Northeastern U. Sch. Law; LLD (hon.), Gonzaga U. Ptnr. Cochran, Neufeld & Scheck LLP, N.Y.C. Co-founder, dir. The Innocence Project, Benjamin Cardoza Sch. Law, Yeshiva U., N.Y.C., 1992—; mem. N.Y. State's Commn. Forensic Sci. Co-author (with Barry Scheck and Jim Dwyer): Actual Innocence: Five Days to Execution and Other Dispatches from the Wrongly Convicted, 2000. Named one of the Top 100 Influential Lawyers in Am., Nat. Law Jour., 2000. Office: Cochran Neufeld & Scheck LLP 99 Hudson St 8th fl New York NY 10013 Address: Benjamin N Cardozo Sch Law Yeshiva Univ Brookdale Ctr 55 Fifth Ave (at 12th St) New York NY 10003

**NEUGEBAUER, CYNTHIA A.,** lawyer; b. Queens, NY, Apr. 26, 1964; SUNY, Buffalo, 1986; MA, SUNY, Stony Brook, 1987; JD, Touro Coll., 1994. Bar: NJ 1995, NY 1996, US Dist. Ct. Ea. Dist. NY, US Dist. Ct. No. Dist. NY, US Dist. Ct. So. Dist. NY. Ptnr. Wilson, Elser, Moskowitz, Edelman & Dicker LLP, NYC. Mem. appellate courts com. State of NY. Mem.: ABA. Office:

Wilson Elser Moskowitz Edelman & Dicker LLP 23rd Fl 150 E 42nd St New York NY 10017-5639 Office Phone: 212-490-3000 ext. 2496. Office Fax: 212-490-3038. Business E-Mail: neugebauerc@wemed.com.

**NEUGEBAUER, MARCIA,** physicist, researcher; b. NYC, Sept. 27, 1932; d. Howard Graeme MacDonald and Frances (Townsend) Marshall; m. Gerry Neugebauer, Aug. 25, 1956; children: Carol, Lee. BS, Cornell U., 1954; MS, U. Ill., 1956; D of Physics (hon.), U. New Hampshire, 1998. Grad. asst. U. Ill., Urbana, 1954-56; vis. fellow Clare Hall Coll., Cambridge, Eng., 1975; sr. research scientist Jet Propulsion Lab. Calif. Inst. Tech., Pasadena, 1956-96, disting. vis. scientist, 1996—2003; vis. prof. planetary sci. Calif. Inst. Tech., Pasadena, 1986-87. Mem. com. NASA, Washington, 1960-96, NAS, Washington, 1981-94; Regents lectr. UCLA, 1990-91; adj. sr. rsch. sci. Lunar & Planetary Lab., U. Ariz., 2002-; bd. dirs. Acad. Svcs. Corp., Ariz. St Acad., pres., 2004—. Contbr. numerous articles on physics to profl. jours. Named Calif. Woman Scientist of Yr. Calif., Mus. Sci. and Industry, 1967, to Women in Tech. Internat. Hall of Fame, 1997; recipient Exceptional Sci. Achievement medal NASA, 1970, Outstanding Leadership medal NASA, 1993, Disting. Svc. medal NASA, 1997, COSPAR award for space sci., 1998. Fellow Am. Geophys. Union (sec., pres. solar planetary relationships sect. 1979-84, editor-in-chief Rev. Geophysics 1988-92, pres.-elect 1992-94, pres. 1994-96) mem. governing bd. Amer. Inst. Physics, 1995-97. Democrat. Home: 7519 S Eliot Ln Tucson AZ 85747-9627 Office: U Ariz Lunar & Planetary Lab 1629 E Univ Blvd Tucson AZ 85721 Business E-Mail: nmeugeb@lpl.Arizona.edu.

**NEUGEBAUER, RANDY (ROBERT R. NEUGEBAUER),** congressman; b. St. Louis, Dec. 24, 1949; m. Dana Collins; 2 children. BBA in Acctg., Tex. Tech U., Lubbock, 1972. Mgr. Sentry Property Mgmt., Lubbock, Tex., 1972—75; instr. South Plains Coll., Lubbock, 1975—78; v.p. First Nat. Bank, Lubbock, 1975—82; pres. Prestige Homes, Lubbock, 1983—87; pres., CEO Lubbock Land Co., 1987—2003; mem. US Congress from 19th Tex. dist. 2003—, mem. agr. com., 2006—, mem. fin. svcs. com. Chair Ports-to-Plains Trade Coalition, 1996—2003. Mem. City Coun., 1992—98; mayor pro tempore, 1994—96. Mem.: West Tex. Home Builders Assn. (pres. 1990). Republican. Baptist. Office: US Ho Reps 429 Cannon Ho Office Bldg Washington DC 20515 Office Phone: 202-225-4005.*

**NEUGEBAUER, VOLKER EGDAR,** biomedical scientist, neuroscientist; b. Werneck, Bavaria, Germany, June 11, 1964; came to U.S., 1995; s. Erich Karl and Rosemarie (Gehring) N.; 1 child, Benjamin David. MD, U. Würzburg, Germany, 1991, PhD equivalent, 1992. Med. lic., Germany. Intern U. Würzburg, 1991-92, postdoctoral fellow, 1992-95; rsch. scientist U. Tex. Med. Br., Galveston, 1995-97, asst. prof. dept. anatomy and neuroscis., 1998—2002, clin. asst. prof. dept. anesthesiology, 1996-99, mem. Marine Biomed. Inst., 1999—, assoc. prof. neurosci. and cell biology, 2002—, assoc. dir. neurosci. grad. program, 2004—. Instr. Acad. Phys. Therapy, Schweinfurt, Germany, 1993-95; invited lectr. nationally and internationally. Contbr. chapters to books, articles to profl. jours. Recipient 1st award Lower Franconia Meml. Endowment for Sci., Würzburg, 1993, Rsch. Career Devel. award German Rsch. Coun., Bonn, 1995, Pain Rsch. award German Soc. for Study of Pain, Heidelberg, 1995. Mem. Internat. assn. for Study of Pain, German Neurosci. Assn., Soc. for Neurosci., Sigma Xi. Roman Catholic. Achievements include development of animal (rat) model for acute arthritis; discovery of antinociceptive and analgesic potencies of drugs acting on spinal neurotransmitter and neuropeptide receptors; discovery of antiepileptogenic potency of metabotropic glutamate receptor agonists (presynaptic) as novel anticonvulsants; definition of the role of neuropeptides and glutamate receptors in cocaine sensitization; discovery of metabotropic glutamate receptors and non-opioid neuropeptides as novel targets for pain relief; identification of the amygdala as a key player in the emotional component of pain; computerized analysis sys. to measure audible and ultrasonic vocalizations as higher integrated pain responses. Office: Marine Biomed Inst Dept Neurosci and Cell Biology U Tex Med Rsch Bldg 2 138 Galveston TX 77555-1069 Office Phone: 409-772-2124. Business E-Mail: voneugeb@utmb.edu.

**NEUHARTH, ALLEN HAROLD,** newspaper publisher; b. Eureka, S.D., Mar. 22, 1924; s. Daniel J. and Christina (Neuharth) N.; m. Loretta Fay Helgeland, June 16, 1946 (div. 1972), m. Lori Wilson, Dec. 31, 1973 (div. 1982), m. Rachel Fornes, March 21, 1993; children: Daniel J. II, Jan, Alexis Rae Fornes-Neuharth. BA cum laude, U. S.D., 1950. Reporter Rapid City Jour., SD, 1948; staff writer Mitchell Daily Republic, SD, 1949; staff writer AP, Sioux Falls, SD, 1950-52; editor, pub. SoDak Sports, Sioux Falls, 1952-54; from staff to asst. mng. editor Miami Herald, Fla., 1954-60, asst. mng. editor Fla., 1958-60; asst. exec. editor Detroit Free Press, 1960-63; gen. mgr. Times-Union and Democrat and Chronicle, Rochester, NY, 1963-66; exec. v.p. Gannett Co., Inc., Washington, 1966-70, pres., COO, 1970-73, pres., CEO, 1973-79, chmn., CEO, 1979-86; founder, chmn. USA Today, 1982; chmn. Gannett Co., Inc., Washington, 1986-89, Gannett Found., Arlington, Va., 1989-91; founder Freedom Forum, chmn., 1986—97, sr. adv. chmn. Author: Confessions of an S.O.B., 1989. Trustee, chmn. Gannett Found. Inf. AUS, 1943-46, ETO, PTO. Decorated Bronze Star; recipient Horatio Alger award, 1975; named Outstanding Chief Exec. of Yr. in Pub. and Printing Industry for 3 consecutive yrs; named to Advt. Hall of Fame, 2006. Mem. Am. Newspaper Pubs. Assn. (bd. dirs. 1968-82, chmn., pres. 1979-80), Jockey Club (Miami), Ocean Reef Club (Key Largo, Fla.), Sky Club, Sigma Delta Chi (past nat. region I dir.). Office: Freedom Forum 1101 Wilson Blvd Ste 2300 Arlington VA 22209-2265*

**NEUHAUS, GRAHAM FRANK,** psychology professor, researcher; d. Edwin Henry and Louise McGehee Frank; m. Edward Kessler Neuhaus, Mar. 12, 1977; children: Edward Jr., Laura Louise, William H., Eleanor Palmer. A. Mt. Vernon Coll., 1973; BFA in Art History, U. Tex., Austin, 1974; M in Psychology, Houston Bapt. U., 1990; D in Ednl. Psychology, U. Houston, 2000. Lic. sch. psychologist Tex., psychologist Tex. Ind. rschr. Riverside Pub., Houston, 1995—98; pres. Cognitive Concepts and Cons., Houston, 1998—2000; adj. prof. U. Houston, 2001—; adv. bd. Neuhaus Edn. Ctr., Houston, 2000—06. Presenter in field. Contbr. articles to profl. jours. Bd. dirs. Friends of DePelchin, 1992; Sunday sch. tchr. St. Martin's Episcopal Ch., 1980, 1999, 2002—; bd. dirs. Park People, Inc., 1991—97; campus adv. team Hunter's Creek Elem. Sch., 1992—93; bd. dirs. Internat. Dyslexia Assn., Houston, 2002—05. Mem.: Am. Edn. Rsch. Assn., Tex. Assn. Sch. Psychologists, Nat. Assn. Sch. Psychologists, Tex. Psychol. Assn., Am. Psychol. Assn., Psi Chi. Episcopalian. Achievements include patents for improved rapid automated naming apparatus; rapid automatized naming method and apparatus. Avocations: reading, travel, walking, tap dancing. Office: Univ Houston Downtown Social Sci Dept 1 Main St STe 625 Houston TX 77002

**NEUHAUS, JOSEPH EMANUEL,** lawyer; b. Glen Ridge, N.J., Aug. 17, 1957; s. Gottfried and Helen (Bull) N.; m. Cynthia Ann Loomis. BA, Dartmouth Coll., 1979; JD, Columbia U., 1982. Bar: N.Y. 1986, D.C. 1986, U.S. Dist. Ct. (so. and ea. dists.) N.Y. 1987. Law clk. to sr. judge U.S. Ct. Appeals, Washington, 1982-83; law clk. to Hon. Lewis F. Powell, Jr. U.S. Supreme Ct., Washington, 1983-84; legal asst. Iran-U.S. Claims Tribunal, The Hague, Netherlands, 1984-85; assoc. Covington & Burling, Washington, 1986-87, Sullivan & Cromwell, N.Y.C., 1987-91, ptnr., 1992—. Co-author: Guide to the UNCITRAL Model Law on International Commercial Arbitration, 1989. Mem. Assn. Bar City N.Y. (com. sec. 1989-92). E-mail: neuhausj@sullcrom.com.

**NEUHAUS, PHILIP ROSS,** investment banker; b. Houston, Dec. 25, 1919; s. Hugo Victor and Kate Padgitt (Rice) N.; m. Elizabeth Lacey Thompson, Oct. 31, 1942 (div. 1976); children: Philip Ross (dec.), Lacey Neuhaus Dorn, Elizabeth Neuhaus Armstrong, Joan Neuhaus Schaan; m. Barbara R. Haden, Aug. 14, 1968; 5 stepchildren. Grad., St. Mark's Sch., Southborough, Mass., 1938; BA, Yale, 1942. With Nat. City Bank of Cleve., 1946-47, McDonald & Co., Cleve., 1947; with Neuhaus & Co., 1947; chmn. Underwood, Neuhaus & Co., Inc., Houston, 1948-89; hon. chmn. Lovett Underwood Neuhaus & Webb, Houston, 1989-92; sr. v.p. Kemper Securities Inc., Houston, 1992-95, Everen Securities, Inc., Houston, 1995-99, Wachovia Securities Inc. (for-

merly First Union Securities, Inc.), Houston, 1999—. Chmn. bd. Voss-Woodway, Inc., 1994—. Mem. adv. bd. Tex. Children's Hosp., 1973-; assoc. Rice U.; advisory bd. Salvation Army, Houston, 1969-91. Served to capt., cav. AUS, 1942-45. Mem. Securities Industry Assn. Am. (bd. govs., chmn. Tex. dist. 1973, exec. com. 1975), Houston Soc. Financial Analysts (pres. 1959), Stock and Bond Club Houston (past pres.), Nat. Fedn. Financial Analysts (v.p. 1963, dir.) Clubs: Bayou, Houston Country, Houston, Eagle Lake Rod and Gun. Home: 407 Thamer Ln Houston TX 77024-6939 Office: Wachovia Securities Inc Ste 1100 909 Fannin Houston TX 77010-1001 Office Phone: 713-853-2221.

**NEUHAUSER, DUNCAN VONBRIESEN,** medical educator; b. Phila., June 20, 1939; s. Edward Blaine Duncan and Gernda (vonBriesen) Neuhauser; m. Elinor Toaz, Mar. 6, 1965; children: Steven, Ann. BA, Harvard U., 1961; MHA, U. Mich., 1963; MBA, U. Chgo., 1966, PhD, 1971. Rsch. assoc. U. Chgo., 1965—70; asst. prof. Sch. Pub. Health, Harvard U., Boston, 1970—74, assoc. prof., 1974—79; cons. in medicine Mass. Gen. Hosp., Boston, 1975—80; assoc. dir. Health Systems Mgmt. Ctr. Case Western Res. U., Cleve., 1979—85, prof. epidemiology, biostats., orgnl. behavior, 1979—, prof. medicine, 1981—, prof. family medicine, 1990—, Charles Elton Blanchard prof. health mgmt., 1995—, co-dir. Health Systems Mgmt. Ctr., 1985—. Mem. biomed. staff Metrohealth Med. Ctr., 1981—; adj. mem. med. staff Cleve. Clinic Found., 1984—99; vis. prof. Vanderbilt U. Sch. Nursing, 1998—, Karolinska Med. Sch., Stockholm, 2002—. Author: numerous books, sci. papers; editor (jours.): Health Matrix, 1982—90, Med. Care, 1983—97 Vice chmn. bd. dirs. Vis. Nurse Assn. Greater Cleve., 1983—84, chmn., 1984—85; bd. dirs. New Eng. Grenfell Assn., Boston, 1972—, Braintree (Mass.) Hosp., 1975—86; trustee Internat. Grenfell Assn., St. Anthony, Nfld., Canada, 1975—83, Blue Hill (Maine) Hosp., 1983—94, Hough Norwood Health Ctr., 1983—94, chmn., 1993—94; mem. vis. com. Columbia U. Sch. Nursing, 2000—; founding bd. dirs. Acad. for Healthcare Improvement, 2004—. Recipient E.F. Meyers Trustee award, Cleve. Hosp. Assn., 1987, Hope award, Nat. Multiple Sclerosis Soc., 1992, Neuhauser lectr., Soc. Pediatric Radiology, 1982, Freedlander lectr., Ohio Permanente Med. Group, 1986, Univ. medal, Tohoku Med. U., Sendi, Japan, 2001, Arthur Shapiro Best Book of Yr. Hypnosis award, 2003; scholar Keck Found., 1982—; Kellogg fellow, U. Chgo., 1963—65, Duncan Neuhauser Endowed chair in cmty. health improvement at Case Western Res. U. and MetroHealth Med. Ctr., 2003. Mem.: Soc. for Clin. Decision Making, Inst. Medicine NAS, Cleve. Skating Club, Kollegewidgwok Yacht Club (Blue Hill) (commodore 1991—93), St. Botolph Club (Boston), Beta Gamma Sigma. Home: 2655 N Park Blvd Cleveland Heights OH 44106-3622 Home (summer): PO Box 932 Blue Hill ME 04614-0932 Office: Case Western Reserve U Med Sch 10900 Euclid Ave Cleveland OH 44106-4945 Office Phone: 216-368-3726. Office Fax: 216-368-3970. Business E-Mail: duncan.neuhauser@case.edu, dvn@case.edu.

**NEUHAUSER, FRANK LOUIS,** retired lawyer; b. Louisville, Sept. 29, 1913; s. Frank Alexis and Ida May (Young) Neuhauser; m. Mary Virginia Clark, Feb. 3, 1945; children: Charles, Linda, Frank, Alan. BSEE, U. Louisville, 1934; JD, George Washington U., 1940; PhD (hon.), U. Louisville, 1979. Bar: DC 1940, Va. 1966. Electrolysis engr. Louisville Gas & Elec. Co., 1934—36; engr., lawyer GE Schenectady, NY, and Washington, 1936—78, patent counsel small appliance divsn. Fairfield, Conn., 1953—55, mgr. patent operation Washington, 1955—73; lawyer Bernard & Brown, Washington, 1979—88. Pres. Am. Patent Law Assn., Washington, 1969—70; past chmn. Nat. Coun. Patent Law Assns.; past chmn. patent sect. DC Bar, Bar Assn. DC. Past pres. pastoral coun. Our Lady of Mercy Ch., Potomac; past bd. dirs. Potomac (Md.) Citizens Assn., Shady Grove Pregnancy Ctr., Gaithersburg, Md., Self Help for Hard of Hearing People, Montgomery County, Md., Montgomery County Chamber. Lt. comdr. USN, 1942—46. Recipient 1s pl. 1st Nat. Spelling Bee, 1925. Mem.: ABA (past chmn. patent sect.), Am. Intellectual Property Assn. Roman Catholic. Avocations: gardening, golf, exercise, reading, volunteer work. Home: 3100 N Leisure World Blvd Apt 522 Silver Spring MD 20906 E-mail: mvfln@aol.com.

**NEUKOM, WILLIAM H.,** lawyer; b. Chgo., Nov. 7, 1941; s. John Goudey and Ruth (Horlick) N.; m. Diane McMakin, Dec. 28, 1963 (div. Jun. 1977); children: Josselyn, Samantha, Gillian, John. BA, Dartmouth Coll., 1964; LLB, Stanford U., 1967. Bar: Calif., Wash., U.S. Dist. Ct. (we. dist.) Wash., U.S. Dist. Ct. (no. dist.) Calif., U.S. Ct. Appeals (9th cir.) 1968, U.S. Supreme Court 1974. Atty. MacDonald, Hoague & Bayless, Seattle, 1968—77; ptnr. Preston, Gates & Lucas (formerly Shidler, McBroom, Gates & Lucas), Seattle, 1978—85; v.p., law corp. affairs Microsoft Corp., Redmond, Wash., 1985—93, exec. v.p. law & corp. affairs, sec., 1994—2002; ptnr. Bus. Practice Group Preston Gates & Ellis LLP, Seattle, 2002—, mem. exec. com., chair, 2004—. Wash. State Delegate House of Delegates, 1999—2005; chair Decennial Governance Commn. Trustee Seattle Art Mus., 1993-99; mem. Assn. Gen. Counsel, 1994—; bd. dirs. Greater Seattle C. of C., 1987—, exec. com. 1988—, YMCA Greater Seattle, 1988—, Corporate Coun. Arts, 1988—, exec. com. 1993—, Nature Conservance (Wash. chpt.), 1991-99, Oreg. Shakespeare Festival, 1993-99. Fellow: ABA (chmn. young lawyers divsn. 1977—78, ho. of dels. 1978—80, sec. 1983—87, ho. of dels. 1989—98, pres.-elect 2006—); mem.: Wash. State Trial Lawyers Assn., Wash. State Bar Assn., Seattle-King County Bar Assn. (chmn. young lawyers divsn. 1972—73). Avocations: fly fishing, skiing, running, golf, jazz. Office: Preston Gates & Ellis LLP 925 Fourth Ave Seattle WA 98104 Office Phone: 206-370-8120. Office Fax: 206-370-6165. E-mail: billn@prestongates.com.*

**NEUMAIER, GERHARD JOHN,** environmental services administrator, consultant; b. Covington, Ky., July 27, 1937; s. John Edward and Elli Anna (Raudies) N.; m. Ellen Elaine Klepper, Oct. 24, 1959; children: Kevin Scott, Kirsten Lynn. BME, Gen. Motors Inst., 1960; MA in Biophysics, U. Buffalo, 1963. Research ecologist, project mgr. Cornell Aero. Lab., Buffalo, 1963-70; pres., chief exec., chmn. bd. Ecology and Environment Inc., Buffalo, 1970—. Recipient Theodore Roosevelt Citizen of Yr. award City of Buffalo, 1990, Paul McClennan Environ. Citizen of Yr. award Erie County, 2000. Mem. APHA, Air Pollution Control Assn., Internat. Assn. Gt. Lakes Research, Inst. Environ. Scis., Ecol. Soc. Am., Am. Inst. Biol. Scis., Urban Land Inst., Arctic Inst. N.Am., Nat. Parks and Conservation Assn., Defenders of Wildlife, Nat. Wildlife Fedn., Wilderness Soc., Am. Hort. Soc., Smithsonian Assocs., Nat. Audubon Soc. Home: 284 Mill Rd East Aurora NY 14052-2805 Office: Ecology & Environment Inc 368 Pleasant View Dr Lancaster NY 14086-1316 Office Phone: 716-684-8060.

**NEUMAN, CHARLES P.,** electrical and computer engineering educator; b. Pitts., July 26, 1940; s. Daniel and Frances G. Neuman; m. Susan G. Neuman, Sept. 4, 1967 BS in Elec. Engring. with honors, Carnegie Inst. Tech., 1962; S.M., Harvard U., 1963, PhD in Applied Math., 1968. Tchg. fellow Harvard U., Cambridge, Mass., 1962-64, rsch. asst., 1964-67; mem. tech. staff Bell Telephone Labs., Whippany, NJ, 1967-69; asst. prof. elec. engring. Carnegie-Mellon U., Pitts., 1969-71, assoc. prof., 1971-78, prof. elec. engring., 1978-83, prof. elec. and computer engring., 1983—, undergrad. advisor, 1994—. Mem. editorial bd. Internat. Jour. Modelling and Simulation, Control and Computers; contbr. numerous articles to profl. jours. Mem. IEEE (sr., assoc. editor Trans. on Systems, Man and Cybernetics), Inst. Mgmt. Scis., AAAS, Instrument Soc. Am. (sr.), Soc. Harvard Engrs. and Scientists, Soc. Indsl. and Applied Math., Sigma Xi, Phi Kappa Phi, Tau Beta Pi, Eta Kappa Nu Office: Carnegie-Mellon U Dept Elec & Computer Engring Pittsburgh PA 15213 Office Phone: 412-268-2460. Business E-Mail: cpn@ece.cmu.edu.

**NEUMAN, CLIFFORD,** computer scientist, educator; s. Peter H-X. Neuman and Barbara Diane (Allen) Gordon; m. Grace Ruth (Kwok) Neuman. BS Computer Sci. and Engring., MIT, 1985; MS Computer Sci., U. Wash., 1988, PhD Computer Sci., 1992. With MIT Project Athena, Cambridge, 1985—86; sr. rsch. scientist U. So. Calif., Info. Scis. Inst., Marina del Rey, 1991—; rsch. assoc. prof. U. So. Calif., Dept. Computer Sci., L.A. 1992—; chief scientist CyberSafe Corp., Issaquah, 1992—2001; dir. U. So. Calif., Ctr. Computer Sys. Security, Marina del Rey, 2002—. Participant Internet Rsch. Task Force, 1991—, Internet Engring. Task Force, 1991— Co-designer Kerberos com-

puter security sys., designer Prospero distributed computer sys., NetCheque elec. payment sys.; contbr. articles to profl. jours Mem. King County (Wash.) Search and Rescue, 1987-91; bd. dirs. Beth Shir Sholom, 2006—, Ladera Heights Civic Assn., 2006—. Named Top Ten Tech. Innovators, InfoWorld Mag., 2002. Mem.: IEEE, Usenix Assn., Internet Soc., Assn. Computer Machinery. Achievements include development of Kerberos authentication sys; NetCheque electronic payment sys; Prospero Directory Svc. Avocations: flying, hiking, skiing, photography, cooking, amateur radio. Office: U So Calif Information Scis Inst 4676 Admiralty Way Marina Del Rey CA 90292 Office Phone: 310-822-1511. E-mail: ww07@clifford.neuman.name.

**NEUMAN, EDWARD GEORGE,** mathematician, educator; b. Rydultowy, Katowice, Poland, Sept. 19, 1943; arrived in U.S., 1984; s. Emanuel and Matylda Neuman; m. Barbara Warszawa, Sept. 21, 1974; children: Emanuel Karol, Magdalena Natalia. Undergrad., grad., U. Wroclaw, Poland, 1962—67, PhD in Math., 1972. Asst. prof. U. Wroclaw, 1976—84; assoc. prof. So. Ill. U., Carbondale, 1986—89, prof. math., 1989—. Chmn. numerical analysis dept. U. Wroclaw, 1981—84. Mem. editl. bd.: Internat. Jour. Mathematical Analysis and Applications, 2005—, Internat. Jour. Applied Math. and Statis., 2005—; contbr. articles to profl. jours. Fellow Summer Undergrad. Tchg. fellow, So. Ill. U., Carbondale, 1999; grantee, Polish Acad. Scis., 1974—84. Mem.: Polish Math. Soc. (assoc.), Rsch. Group in Math. Inequalities and Applications (assoc.), Soc. for Indsl. and Applied Math. (assoc.). Achievements include research in spline theory, special functions and mathematical inequalities. Office: So Ill Univ Carbondale Dept Math Neckers 373 Carbondale IL 62901-4408 Office Phone: 618-453-6501. Business E-Mail: edneuman@math.siu.edu.

**NEUMAN, GERALD L.,** law educator; AB, Harvard U., 1973, JD, 1980; PhD in Math., MIT, 1977. Law clk. to Hon. Abner J. Mikva DC Cir. Ct.; atty. Foley, Hoag & Eliot, 1981—84; faculty mem. U. Pa. Law Sch., 1984—92, Columbia Law Sch., NYC, 1992—; Herbert Wechsle prof. of fed. jurisprudence. Vis. prof. Johann Wolfgang Goethe-Universität, Frankfurt, 1989; vis. scholar Max Planck Inst. for Comparative Pub. Law and Internat. Law, Heidelberg, 1994, European U. Inst., Florence, 1998, Florence, 2001. Contbr. articles to law jours. Office: 435 W 116th St New York NY 10021 E-mail: gneuman@law.columbia.edu.

**NEUMAN, ISABEL,** mathematics educator; b. N.Y.C., Dec. 3, 1939; d. J. Morton and Irene Finke; m. David Wagner Neuman, June 18, 1960; children: Randi Levin, Leslie Spillman, Andrea Malkin. BS, Syracuse U., 1960; MA, Ariz. State U., 1978. Cert. Edn. Specialist Ariz. State U., 1980, in Elem. Edn. Ariz. Dept. Edn. Tchr. Westwood Sch., Park Forest, Ill., 1960—62, Little Friends, N.Y.C., 1968—70, Holiday Park, Phoenix, 1976—2002, math coach, tchr., 2002—. Pres. Hadassah, Phoenix, 1980—82. Named Tchr. of Yr., Walmart, Tempe, Ariz., 2002; recipient Vol. award, 4-H, 2003, Urban Forest award, Phoeniz Pk. and Recreation, 2003; grantee, Wells Fargo, 1999, 2001. Mem.: Nat. Coun. Tchrs. Math. Avocations: reading, music box collecting, travel, music. Home: 15806 W Acapulco Ln Surprise AZ 85379

**NEUMAN, LINDA KINNEY,** retired state supreme court justice, lawyer; b. Chgo., June 18, 1948; d. Harold S. and Mary E. Kinney; m. Henry G. Neuman; children: Emily, Lindsey. BA, U. Colo., 1970, JD, 1973; LLM, U. Va., 1998. Ptnr. Betty, Neuman, Hellstrom & Bittner, 1973-79; v.p., trust officer Bettendorf Bank & Trust Co., 1979-80; dist. ct. judge, 1982-86; supreme ct. justice State of Iowa, 1986—2003; ptnr. Betty Neuman & McMahon. L.L.P., Davenport, Iowa, 2003—05. Mem. adj. faculty U. Iowa Law Sch., 2003-; part-time jud. magistrate Scott County, 1980-82; mem. Supreme Ct. continuing legal edn. commn.; chair Iowa Supreme Ct. commn. planning 21st Century; mem. bd. counselors Drake Law Sch., time on appeal adv. com. Nat. Ctr. State Cts.; mem. Uniform State Laws Commn., 2004. Trustee St. Ambrose U. Recipient Regents scholarship, U. Colo. award for disting. svc. Fellow ABA (life; chair appellate judges conf., mem. appellate standards com., JAD exec. coun.); mem. Am. Judicature Soc., Iowa Bar Assn., Iowa Judges Assn., Scott County Bar Assn., Nat. Assn. Woman Judges (bd. dirs.), Dillon Am. Inn of Ct. (pres. 2003-04), U.S. Assn. Constl. Law, Am. Acad. ADR Attys, Nat. Uniform Laws Comm. (commnr., 2004). Office Phone: 563-289-3255. Business E-Mail: lkn@neumanadr.com.

**NEUMAN, MICHAEL A.,** former communications company executive; BA, Univ. We. Ont. Pres. Cerberus Canada, Worldlinx Telecommunications, Bell ExpressVu Satellite TV, Teleglobe Europe, 2001—02, Bell Mobility subs. of Bell Canada Enterprises, 2002—05; pres., COO EchoStar Comm. Corp., Englewood, Colo., 2005—06.*

**NEUMAN, NANCY ADAMS MOSSHAMMER,** civic leader; b. Greenwich, Conn., July 24, 1936; d. Alden Smith and Margaret (Mevis) Mosshammer; m. Mark Donald Neuman, Dec. 23, 1958; children: Deborah Adams, Jennifer Fuller, Jeffrey Abbott. BA, Pomona Coll., 1957; LLD, 1983; MA, U. Calif., Berkeley, 1961; LHD, Westminster Coll., 1987. Disting. lectr. Am. govt. Pomona Coll., 1990; disting. vis. prof. Washington and Jefferson Coll., 1991, 94, Bucknell U., 1992. Editor: A Voice of Our Own: Leading American Women Celebrate the Right to Vote, 1996, True to Ourselves: A Celebration of Women Making a Difference, 1998. Pres. Lewisburg (Pa.) LWV, 1967-70; bd. dirs. LWV Pa., 1970-77, pres., 1975-77; bd. dirs. LWV U.S., 1977-90, 2nd v.p., 1978-80, 1st v.p., 1982-84, pres., 1986-90; mem. Pa. Gov.'s Commn. on Mortgage and Interest Rates, 1973, Pa. Commonwealth Child Devel. com., 1974-75, Nat. Commn. on Pub. Svc., 1987-90; bd. dirs. Housing Assistance Coun., Inc., Washington, 1994—2003, pres., 1978-80; Nat. Coun. Agrl. Life and Labor, 1974-79, Nat. Rural Housing Coalition, 1975-95, Pa. Housing Fin. Agy., 1975-80, Jud. Inquiry and Rev. Bd. Pa., 1989-93; disciplinary bd. Supreme Ct. Pa., 1980-85; mem. Pa. Gov.'s Task Force on Voter Registration, 1975-76, Nat. Task Force for Implementation Equal Rights Amendment, 1975-77; mem. adv. com. Pa. Gov.'s Interdepartmental Coun. on Seasonal Farmworkers, 1975-77; mem. Appellate Ct. Nominating Commn. Pa., 1976-79; mem. Fed. Jud. Nominating Commn. Pa., 1977-85, chmn., 1978-81, 82-83; mem. Pa. Gov.'s Study Commn. on Pub. Employee rels., 1976-78; del. Internat. Women's Yr. Conf., 1977; bd. dirs. ERAmerica, Inc., 1977-79, 77-79, Nat. Low Income Housing Coalition, 1979-82; Rural Am., 1979-81, Fed. Home Loan Bank Pitts., 1979-82; mem. Nat. adv. com. Women, 1978-79; mem. nat. adv. com. Pa. Neighborhood Preservation Support Sys., 1976-77; bd. dirs. Pa. Women's Campaign fund, 1984-86, 92-2002, pres., 1992-96, 2001-02, Rural coalition, Washington, 1984-90. Com. on the Constitutional Sys., 1988-90, Am. Judicature Soc., 1989-93; exec. com. Leadership Conf. Civil Rights, 1986-90; bd. dirs. Pennsylvanians for Modern Cts., 1986—; trustee Citizen's Rsch. Found., 1989-99; mem. mid. dist. Pa. adv. com. judicial and U.S. atty. nominations, 1993-94; bd. dirs. Pathmakers, 1993-97, pres. 1993-95; bd. dirs. Capital Concerts, 1997—. Virginia Travis lectureship Bucknell U., 1982; Woodrow Wilson vis. fellow, 1993-2000; recipient Disting. Alumna Award MacDuffie Sch. Girls, 1979, Liberty Bell award Pa. Bar Assn., 1983, Barrows Alumni Award Pomona Coll., 1987, Disting. Daus. of Pa. award, 1987, Thomas P. O'Neill Jr. award for Exemplary Pub. Svc., 1989. Mem. ABA (com. election law and voter participation 1986-90, accreditation com. 1990-96, coun. sect. of legal edn. 1997-2003), Disting. Daughters Pa. (pres. 2005—), Cosmos Club Home: 190 Verna Rd Lewisburg PA 17837-8747 Business E-Mail: neuman@bucknell.edu.

**NEUMAN, ROBERT STERLING,** art educator, artist; b. Kellogg, Idaho, Sept. 9, 1926; s. Oscar C. and Katherine (Samuelson) N.; m. Helen Patricia Feddersen, Apr. 6, 1947 (div. 1971); children: Ingrid Alexandra, Elizabeth Catherine; m. Sunne Savage, June 3, 1979; 1 dau. Christina Mary. Student, U. Idaho, 1944-46; BAA., M.F.A., Calif. Coll. Arts and Crafts, 1947-51; student, San Francisco Sch. Fine Arts, 1950-51, Mills Coll., 1951. Assoc. prof. art Brown U., 1962-63; lectr. drawing Carpenter Center for Visual Arts, Harvard, 1963-72; prof. art. chmn. dept. Keene (N.H.) State Coll., 1972-90. Exhbns. include: Mus. Modern Art, Whitney Mus. Am. Art, Carnegie Internat., Fogg Mus. Art, Harvard U., San Francisco Mus. Art, Boston Mus. Fine Arts, Worcester (Mass.) Art Mus., Allan Stone Gallery, NYC, 1956—, also, Japan and Europe. Served with AUS and USAAF, 1945-46. Recipient

Howard Found. award for painting, 1967; Fulbright grantee, 1953-54; Guggenheim fellow, 1956-57; Bender grantee San Francisco Art Assn., 1952. Home: 135 Cambridge St Winchester MA 01890-2411

**NEUMAN, SHLOMO P.,** hydrologist, educator; b. Zilina, Czechoslovakia, Oct. 26, 1938; came to U.S., 1963, naturalized, 1970; s. Alexander Neumann and Klara (Pikler) Lesny; m. Yael B. Neuman, Jan. 30, 1965; children: Gil, Michal, Ariel. BSc in Geology, Hebrew U., Jerusalem, 1963; MS in Engring. Sci., U. Calif., Berkeley, 1966, PhD in Engring. Sci., 1968. Cert. prof. hydrogeologist. Acting asst. prof., asst. rsch. engr. dept. civil engring. U. Calif., Berkeley, 1968-70, vis. assoc. prof. dept. civil engring., 1974-75; sr. scientist, assoc. rsch. prof. Inst. Soil and Water Agrl. Rsch. Orgn., Bet-Dagan, Israel, 1970-74; prof. hydrology dept. hydrology and water resources U. Ariz., Tucson, 1975-88, Regents' prof. dept. hydrology and water resources, 1988—. Cons. to U.S., Can. and Swedish govts. on hydrologic issues concerning nuc. waste disposal; vis. scientist dept. isotope Weizmann Inst. Sci., Rehovot, Israel, 1976; maitre de rsch. Ctr. d'Informatique Geologique, Ecole Mines Paris, Fountainebleau, France, 1978, dir. rsch., 1981; vis. prof. dept. fluid mechanics and heat transfer Tel-Aviv U., 1981; hon. appointment concurrent prof. Nanjing U., China; disting. lectr. in hon. prof. Nanjing Hydraulic Rsch. Inst., China, 1998—. Mem. editl. bd. Jour. Hydrology, 1977—84, Water Sci. and Tech. Libr. (The Netherlands), 1983—86, Stochastic Environmental Research and Risk Assessment, 1992—, Water Resources Rsch. Jour., 2006—, Hydrogeology Jour., 1999—2004, guest editor spl. issue in memory of Eugene S. Simpson, 1997—98; contbr. more than 300 profl. publs. including papers, books and reports. Hebrew U. scholar, 1962-63, Edwin Letts Oliver scholar, 1965-66; Jane Lewis fellow, 1966-68; recipient Cert. of Appreciation award USDA, 1975, C.V. Theis award Am. Inst. Hydrology, 1990, Fellow Geol. Soc. Am. (O.E. Meinzer award 1976, Birdsal Disting. Lectr. 1987), Am. Geophys. Union (4th Walter B. Langbein lectr. hydrology 1996, Robert E. Horton award 1969, Robert E. Horton medal, 2003), mem. ISI highly cited rschrs. database, Soc. Petroleum Engrs. of AIME, NAE, Assn. Groundwater Scientists and Engrs. of Nat. Well Water Assn. (Sci. award 1989), Ariz. Hydrol. Soc., Internat. Assn. Hydrogeologists. Jewish. Office: U Ariz Dept Hydrology & Water Resou Tucson AZ 85721-0001 Business E-Mail: neuman@hwr.arizona.edu.

**NEUMANN, ANDREW,** artist; BS, Emerson Coll. Lectr. filmmaking Sch. of Mus. Fine Arts, Boston; artist-in-residence iEAR Studio, Rensalear Polytech Inst., Visual Studies Workshop. Exhibitions include FPAC Gallery, Boston, Gallery Bershad, ARCADE, DeCordova Mus., albums, No Fly Zone, Scramble: Lock: Combination. Fellow Guggenheim Meml. Found., 2004. Office: c/o Bitform Gallery 529 W 20th St New York NY 10011*

**NEUMANN, CHARLES HENRY,** mathematician, educator; b. Washington, Jan. 30, 1943; s. Bernhardt Walter and Emma (Habitz) Neumann; m. Cheryl Elaine Girard, June 18, 1965; children: Matthew Roy, Kristen Elizabeth. AS, Alpena (Mich.) CC, 1962; BS in Math., Mich. State U., 1964, MAT in Math. 1965. Sci. tchr. Alpena (Mich.) Pub. Schs., 1965-66; instr. math. Alpena CC, 1966-84, math. sci. dept. chair, 1969-84; prof. Oakland CC, Bloomfield Hills, Mich., 1984—. Scoutmaster troop 92 Boy Scouts Am., Alpena, 1981—84; bd. dirs. Luth. Social Svcs. Mich., 1996—2005, vice chair of bd., 1999—2003, chmn. bd., 2004—05; trustee Mich. Edn. Spl. Svcs., 1975—93, 2002—, pres., 1976—93, v.p., 2005—; mem. exec. com. Oakland County Dem. Com., Mich., 1995—96; bd. dirs. Mich. Vision Svc. Assn., 1985—89, Ohio Vision Svc. Assn., 1988—89, Blue Cross Blue Shield Mich., 1986—94. Mem.: NEA (del. 1974—80, mem. adv. com. membership 1993—96), Oakland CC Faculty Assn. (v.p. 1995—98, v.p. 1998—2001), Mich. Assn. Higher Edn. (v.p. two-yr. colls. 1970—96, 2002—04), Mich. Math. Assn. Two-Yr. Colls., Mich. Edn. Assn. (bd. dirs. 1974—80), Am. Math. Assn. Two-Yr. Colls., Math. Assn. Am., Phi Kappa Phi. Lutheran. Avocations: collecting antique books, racquetball, cross country skiing. Home: 5871 Warbler Clarkston MI 48346-2973 Office: Oakland CC 2900 Featherstone Rd Auburn Hills MI 48326-2817

**NEUMANN, ED,** human resource executive; BS in Acctg., West Chester U. CPA, Pa. Audit mgr. Ernst & Young LLP, Phila.; sr. mgr. corp. audit Crown, Cork & Seal Co., Inc., 1996-97; various positions HR Logic, Waltham, Mass., 1997-2000, CFO, 2000-2001, sr. v.p., CAO, 2001-. Office: HR Logic Inc 1050 Winter St Ste 1000 Waltham MA 02451-1402

**NEUMANN, EDWARD SCHREIBER,** transportation engineering educator; b. Harvey, Ill., Mar. 6, 1942; s. Arthur Edward Schreiber and Adeline Ruth (Spenks) N.; m. Carole Ann Dunkelberger, Apr. 19, 1969; children: Edward Schreiber, Jonathan David. BSCE, Mich. Technol. U., 1964; MS, Northwestern U., 1967, PhD, 1969, Cert. in Prosthetics, 2000. Registered profl. engr., W.Va., Nev.; cert. prosthetist Am. Bd. Certification. Mem. faculty W.Va. U., Morgantown, 1970-90, prof. transp. engring., 1980-90, interim dir. Harley O. Staggers Nat. Transp. Ctr., 1982-95, dir., 1985-90; prof. U. Nev., Las Vegas, 1991—, chmn. dept., 1991-99, dir. Transp. Rsch. Ctr., 1991-98, dir. Ctr. Disability and Applied Biomechanics, 2003—. Editor numerous conf. procs.; contbr. articles and rsch. reports to profl. lit. Bd. dirs. Mason Dixon Hist. Park Assn., 1978-90; chmn. new transp. systems and tech. com. transp. rsch. bd. mem. 1998-2004, emeritus, 2004. Capt., C.E., AUS, 1969-70. Resources for Future fellow, 1969. Fellow Inst. Transp. Engrs.; mem. ASCE (chmn. com. on automated people movers, chmn. exec. com. urban planning and devel. divsn., chmn. exec. com. urban transp. divsn., James Laurie prize 1996), Nat. Soc. Profl. Engrs., Am. Soc. Engring. Edn., OITAF-NACS, Advanced Transit Assn. (bd. dirs., pres. 1990-98), Sigma Xi, Tau Beta Pi, Phi Kappa Phi, Phi Eta Sigma, Chi Epsilon. Presbyterian. Home: 935 E Eldorado Ln Las Vegas NV 89123-0515 Office: UNLV Dept Civil Environ Engring Las Vegas NV 89154-4015 Office Phone: 702-895-1072. Business E-Mail: neumann@ce.unlv.edu.

**NEUMANN, FORREST KARL,** retired health facility administrator; b. St. Louis, Oct. 7, 1930; s. Metz Earl and Ruth (McGhee) N.; m. Erika Stefanie Turkl, Feb. 11, 1955; children: Tracey Neumann Liberson, Karen Neumann Kruger, Scott, Lisa. BS, Roosevelt U., 1953; MS in Hosp. Adminstrn., Northwestern U., 1955. Adminstrv. resident Louis A. Weiss Hosp., Chgo., 1954-55; mem. staff Sparrow Hosp., Lansing, Mich., 1957-90; CEO, pres., dir. Edward W. Sparrow Hosp., Lansing, 1962-90; pres., chief exec. officer, dir. Mason Gen. Hosp., Mich., 1973-85; chmn. bd. Caymich Ins. Co. Ltd., Cayman Islands, 1979-91, emeritus dir. Cayman Islands, 1991—; chmn. bd. Caymich Ins. Co. (Barbados) Ltd., 1986-91; pres., CEO, Mich. Hosp. Assoc. Ins. Co., 1990-96; dir. Mich. Hosp. Assocs. Ins. Co., 1976-98; pres., CEO Sparrow, Inc., 1984-90. Chmn. bd. Mich. Hosp. Assn. Ins. Co., 1979-90; dir. First of Am. Bank Corp., 1980-95, Auto Owners Ins. Co., 1980-90. Chmn. hosp. div. United Community Chest, 1965-68, chmn. budget steering com., 1970-71, bd. dirs., mem. exec. com., 1969-75; mem. adv. com. Capitol Area Comprehensive Health Planning Assn., 1969, bd. dirs., 1971-75, treas., 1974-75; mem., vice chmn. Mich. Arbitration Adv. Com., 1978 bd. mem. dirs. Grad. Med. Edn., Inc., 1971-80, pres., 1972-73, treas. 1973. 1st lt. Med. Svcs. Corps USAF, 1955—58. Fellow Am. Coll. Hosp. Adminstrs. (life); mem. Southwestern Mich. Hosp. Council (trustee 1968-73, pres. 1970-71), Am. Hosp. Assn. (del. 1979-87), Mich. Hosp. Assn. (1st v.p. 1972-73, bd. dirs., exec. com., treas. 1974-75 com. 1976-77, Meritorious Key award 1979), Rotary.

**NEUMANN, HERSCHEL,** retired physics professor; b. San Bernardino, Calif., Feb. 3, 1930; s. Arthur and Dorothy (Greenhood) N.; m. Julia Black, June 15, 1951; 1 child, Keith. BA, U. Calif., Berkeley, 1951; MS, U. Ore., 1959; PhD, U. Nebr., 1965. Theoretical physicist GE, Richland, Wash., 1951—57; instr. physics U. Nebr., Lincoln, 1964—65; asst. prof. physics U. Denver, 1965—71, assoc. prof. physics, 1971—85, prof. physics, 1985—2006; ret., 2006; chmn. physics and astronomy U. Denver, 1985—97, assoc. chmn. physics and astronomy, 2001—04, interim chmn. physics and astronomy, 2004—06, chmn. physics and astronomy, 2006. Contbr. over 20 articles to profl. jours. Dir. numerous pub. outreach programs in physics.

Mem. Am. Assn. Physics Tchrs. Home: 964 Salem Aurora CO 80011-6344 Office: U Denver Dept Physics Astronomy Denver CO 80208-2238 Office Phone: 303-871-3544. Business E-Mail: hneumann@du.edu.

**NEUMANN, JEFFREY JAY,** photographer, minister; b. Cleve., Aug. 6, 1948; s. Fred and LaVerne (Vavra) N.; m. Charlene Rose Sparrow, Apr. 21, 1968 (dec.); children: Stephan, Corene, Lara; m. Carolyn Hannah, Nov. 4, 1972; 1 son, Jeffrey. Ordained to ministry, 1962. Lithographer, camera operator Advertype, Inc., Cleve., 1972; lab. technician Vista Color Lab., Cleve., 1972-73; prodn. mgr. Mort Tucker Photography, Cleve., 1973-78; owner, photographer Photography by Jeffrey Neumann, Wadsworth, OH, 1978—. Lectr. in field. Author: Thirty Years as Jehovah's Slave, 1999, Forty Years as Jehovah's Willing Slave, 2002, 120 Years Preaching the Good News of the Kingdom, 2002, To Have and Remember the Perfect Wedding, 2003, I Found Atlantis, 2005. Mem. Sm. Bus. Mgmt. Adv. Com., 1980-83. Mem. Internat. Platform Assn., Profl. Photographers Am. (awards), Wedding and Portrait Photographers Internat. (awards), Profl. Photographers Ohio (awards). Jehovah'S Witness. Home and Office: 9960 Mount Eaton Rd Wadsworth OH 44281-9028 E-mail: jneumann@neo.rr.com.

**NEUMANN, LINDA KAY,** marketing professional; b. Wyandotte, Mich., Feb. 5, 1959; d. Michael and Raelene Fern (Bongart) Goldman; m. David Dewain Neumann, Mar. 31, 1980; children: Rachel Anne, Kyle Wayne. Student, Mesa CC, San Diego, 1976—86; grad. with honors, Bank Mktg. Sch., 1991. Mail clk., securities clk. Hawaiian Trust Co. Ltd., Honolulu, 1977-78, supr., 1979-81; securities vault clk., bank card clk. Union Bank Calif., San Diego, 1981-82, sales adminstrv. asst., 1983-86, mktg. adminstrv. asst., mktg. officer, 1986-88, from mktg. asst. v.p. to mktg. v.p. 1992-94, mktg. v.p., mgr., 1994-96, bus. and sales planning mgr., v.p., 1996—2002; pres. Brilliant Mktg. Ideas, Inc., San Diego, 2002—. Chmn. San Diego Retail Coun., Am. Banking Assn., Am. Inst. Banking, 1996—97. Pres. Rolling Hills Elem. PTA, 1995—96; parliamentarian Deer Canyon Elem. PTA; nat. del. San Diego Imperial Coun. Girl Scouts, 2002—05; mem. NC C. of C.; chmn. bd. dirs. San Diego Safety Coun., Pacific Safety Coun., 2000—05; bd. dir., pres. Westview Found., 2001—06; bd. dirs., sec. Difference Makers Internat., 2004. Mem.: Calif. Activity Dirs. Assn., San Diego Employers Assn., Nat. Soc. Fundraising Execs., Advt. Splty. Inst. Promotional Products Assns., Bank Mktg. Assn., San Diego Direct Mktg. Assn., Advt. Club San Diego, Direct Mktg. Assn., Am. Soc. Autism. Office: Brilliant Marketing Ideas PO Box 721419 San Diego CA 92172-1419 Business E-Mail: linda@brilliantmarketingideas.com. E-mail: ideas@adexec.com.

**NEUMANN, LISELOTTE,** professional golfer; b. Finspang, Sweden, May 20, 1966; With LPGA, 1987—. Mem. European Solheim Cup Team, 1990, 92, 94, 96, 98. Named Golf Digest Rolex Rookie of Year, 1988, Swedish Golfer of Year, 1994, GolfWorld's Most Improved Golfer, 1994. Achievements in LPGA victories include: U.S. Women's Open, 1988, Mazda Japan Classic, 1991, Minn. LPGA Classic, 1994, Weetabix Women's Brit. Open, 1994, GHP Heartland Classic, 1994, Chrysler-Plymouth Tournament of Champions, 1996, PING/Welch's Championship, 1996, First Bank-Edina Realty Classic, 1996, Welch's Championship, 1997, Toray Japan Queens Cup, 1997, Standard Register Ping, 1998, Chick-fil-A Charity Championship, 1998; other victories include: European Open, 1985, German Open, 1986-88, French Open, 1987, Solheim Cup, 1998. Office: LPGA 100 International Golf Dr Daytona Beach FL 32124-1092

**NEUMANN, MARK W.,** former congressman, real estate developer; b. Waukesha, Wis., Feb. 27, 1954; m. Sue; 3 children. BS, U. Wis., Whtiewater, 1975; MS, U. Wis., River Falls, 1977. Real estate developer Neumann Devels. (now Neumann Corp.), 1980—; mem. 104th and 105th Congresses from 1st Wis. dist., 1994-97; candidate Wis. State Senate, 2004. Mem. appropriations, nat. security, vets. affairs, HUD and ind. agys., budget coms. Address: W330 N6233 Hasslinger Dr Nashotah WI 53058-9432

**NEUMANN, NANCY RUTH,** private school educator; b. L.A., Feb. 1, 1948; d. Robert Thomas and Frances Andersen; m. Bernd Fritz Dietmar Neumann, June 26, 1971; children: Peter, Christina, Linda, Christoph, Karin. BA, U. Calif., Riverside, 1969; MA, Sorbonne U., Paris, 1971; credentials, Calif. State U., San Bernardino, 1985. Cert. community coll. tchr. various subjects, Calif., studio tchr. Calif. Missionary, reading instr., Maroua, Cameroon, Africa, 1971-73; instr. Pasadena (Calif.) City Coll., 1974-75; secondary tchr. Riverside (Calif.) Christian Sch., 1985-86; studio tchr. Vista Films, Culver City, 1986, Hollywood (Calif.) Studios, 1986-88, Paramount Studios, Hollywood, Calif., 1986—2006, MGM - Lorimar Prodns., Culver City, Calif., 1986-91, Universal Studios, Universal City, Calif., 1986-90, R.J. Louis Prodns., Burbank, Calif., 1987, Michael Landon Prodns., Culver City, 1987-88, Carsey-Werner Prodns., L.A., 1988; instr. Riverside Community Coll., 1988; studio tchr. Bob Booker Prodns., Hollywood, 1988-90, Walt Disney Prodns., Burbank, 1992—; exec. producer Am. Pictures, Riverside, 1989—; studio tchr. NBC Prodns., Burbank, 1990—2003, New Line Cinema, 1991—2006, 20th Century Fox, 1993—2004, Warner Bros., 1996—2004, CBS, 2005—06. Pvt. tutor, Riverside, L.A., 1987—; drama coach Grace Ch., Riverside, 1981-82, Magnolia Ave. Bapt. Ch. Riverside, 1986-89. Author: several plays, 1981-89; writer 80 songs, 1968—2004; pub. access TV prodr. Nancy Norway Presents: Windmills, L.A. and Riverside, 1994-2004; TV prodr., 1994-2006. Coach mock trial Riverside Christian H.S., 1985-86; choir dir. Riverside Christian Sch., 1985-86; Sunday Sch. tchr. Grace Bapt. Ch., Harvest Christian Fellowship, Riverside, Magnolia Ave. Bapt. Ch., 1968-92, Wheat, Oil and Wine Christian Fellowship, Riverside, Sunday sch. supt., 1992-93; children's choir dir. Grace Bapt. Ch., 1981-82; Christian edn. coord., Sunday sch. tchr., and vacation Bible sch. dir. First United Meth. Ch., Riverside, 2002-03. Recipient Golden Star Halo award, Star Sapphire Halo award, Jeanie Golden Halo award for acting and teaching So. Calif. Motion Picture Coun., 1994 Mem. Nat. Assn. Christian Educators, Internat. Alliance of Theatre and Stage Employees, Internat. Platform Assn., Greater L.A. World Trade Ctr. Assn., Sons of Norway (study scholar 1967), Delta Phi Alpha. Democrat. Avocations: photography, music, travel, production of films and videos. Office: Walt Disney Studios 500 S Buena Vista St Burbank CA 91521-0006 Home: 1244 SE Seaport Cir Corvallis OR 97333-3110 E-mail: nrneumann@yahoo.com.

**NEUMANN, PETER GABRIEL,** computer scientist; b. NYC, Sept. 21, 1932; s. J.B. and Elsa (Schmid) N.; m. Elizabeth Susan Neumann; 1 child, Helen K. AB, Harvard U., 1954, SM, 1955; Dr rerum naturarum, Technische Hochschule, Darmstadt, Fed. Republic Germany, 1960; PhD, Harvard U., 1961. Mem. tech. staff Bell Labs, Murray Hill, NJ, 1960-70; Mackay lectr. Stanford U., 1964, U. Calif., Berkeley, 1970-71; prin. scientist SRI Internat., Menlo Park, Calif., 1971—. Adj. prof. U. Md., 1999. Author: Computer-Related Risks, 1995. Recipient Nat. Computer Sys. Security award, 2002; Fulbright grantee, 1958—60. Fellow AAAS, IEEE, Assn. for Computing Machinery (editor jour. 1976-93, chmn. com. on computers and pub. policy 1985—). Avocations: music, tai chi. Office: SRI Internat EL-243 333 Ravenswood Ave Menlo Park CA 94025-3493 Business E-Mail: pneumann@acm.org.

**NEUMANN, RONALD DANIEL,** nuclear medicine physician, educator; b. Watertown, Wis., Oct. 10, 1947; BS summa cum laude, Carroll Coll., 1970; MD with highest honors, Yale U., 1974. Diplomate Nat. Bd. Med. Examiners, Am. Bd. Nuclear Medicine; lic. physician, Md., D.C. Resident in pathology Yale-New Haven Hosp., 1974-77, resident in nuclear medicine, 1977-79, chief resident in nuclear medicine, 1978-79, attending physician, 1979-85; asst. prof. diagnostic radiology Sch. Medicine Yale U., 1979-83, assoc. prof. diagnostic radiology and pathology, 1983-86; dep. chief dept. nuclear medicine NIH, Bethesda, Md., 1985-88, chief. dept. nuclear medicine, 1988—, dir. nuclear medicine residency tng. program, 1986-92; clin. prof. diagnostic radiology and nuclear medicine Sch. Medicine George Washington U., Washington, 1986—. Chmn. med. isotopes and radiation safety com. West Haven VA Med. Ctr., 1979-85; mem. clin. rsch. panel Nat. Inst. Diabetes and Digestive and Kidney Diseases, 1987-88; mem. radiation safety com. NIH and Nat. Ctr. for Health Stats., 1987-89. Patentee Antigen-specific composi-

tion and in-vivo methods for detecting and localizing an antigenic site and for radiotherapy; contbr. over 200 articles and abstracts to med. and sci. jours., 30 chpts. to books and conf. proceedings. Nat. Merit scholar; NASA summer fellow. Fellow Am. Coll. Chest Physicians; mem. AAAS, Am. Soc. for Investigative Pathology, Soc. Nuclear Medicine (co-chmn. C.M.E. program 1995-96, pres.-elect 1997, pres. Mid.-Atlantic chpt. 1998), Internat. Acad. Pathology (U.S. and Can. divsns.), European Assn. Nuclear Medicine, Sigma Xi., Delta Sigma Nu. Office: NIH-CC Dept Nuclear Medicine 10 Center Dr Ms 1180 Bethesda MD 20892-0001

**NEUMANN, RONALD ELDREDGE,** ambassador; b. Washington, Sept. 30, 1944; s. Robert G. N. and Marlen Eldredge; m. Margaret Elaine Grimm, Jan 23, 1966; children: Helen, Brian. BA, U. Calif., Riverside, 1966, MA, 1967; student, Nat. War Coll., 1990—91. Joined Fgn. Svc., 1970; vice-consul Am. Embassy, Tabriz, Iran, 1973-76; desk officer office of so. European affairs US Dept. State, Washington, 1976-77, aide to asst. sec. Near East and South Asian Affairs, 1977-78, desk officer Jordanian Affairs, 1978-81, dep. dir. Arabian Peninsula Affairs, 1983-86, dir. No. Gulf affairs, 1991-94; dep. chief mission Am. Embassy, Sana'a, North Yemen, 1981-83; with Arabic Lang. Tng., Washington, 1986-87; dep. chief mission Am. Embassy, Abu Dhabi, United Arab Emirates, 1987-90; US amb. to Algeria US Dept. State, Algiers, 1994-97, dep. asst. sec. for near ea. affairs Washington, 1997-2000, US amb. to Bahrain Manama, 2001—04, spl. negotiator with Spain, 2000—01; counselor for polit. mil. affairs Am. Embassy, Baghdad, Iraq, 2004—05; US amb. to Afghanistan US Dept. State, Kabul, 2005—. 1st. lt. US Army, 1969-70, Vietnam. Decorated Bronze Star, Combat Infantry Badge, Army Commendation medal, State Dept. Superior Honor medal, Presdl. Meritorious Svc. award. Mem. Am. Fgn. Svc. Assn., U. Calif. Riverside Alumni Assn., Officer Candidate Sch. Alumni Assn., Assn. of 5th Divsn. Nat. War Coll. Alumni, Phi Beta Kappa. Avocations: reading, backpacking, bicycling, hiking. Office: US Embassy Kabul APO AE 09316

**NEUMANN, ROY COVERT,** architect; b. Columbus, Nebr., Mar. 1, 1921; s. LeRoy Franklin and Clara Louise (Covert) N.; children: Tali, Scott; m. Donna Corwin, Oct. 11, 2003. Student, Midland Coll., 1939-40, U. Calif.-Berkeley Armed Forces Inst., overseas, 1942-43; AB, U. Nebr., 1948, BArch, 1949; MA, Harvard U., 1952; postgrad., U. Wis., Iowa State U. Registered profl. architect, Iowa, Nebr., Kans., Minn., S.D., N.Y., Mass., Ohio, Pa., Tenn., Ky., Va., W.Va., Ga., Mich., Mo., Ill., Wis., Tex., Colo. Ptnr., architect R. Neumann Assocs., Lincoln, Nebr., 1952-55; officer mgr. Sargent, Webster, Crenshaw & Folley, Schenectady, NY, 1955-59; dir. architecture, ptnr. A.M. Kinney Assocs., Cin., 1959-65; officer mgr. Hunter, Campbell & Rea, Johnstown, Pa., 1965-66; dir. architecture, ptnr. Stanley Cons., Muscatine, Iowa, 1966-76; pres., chmn. bd. Neumann Monson P.C., Iowa City, 1976—. Ptnr. Clinton St. Ptnrs., Iowa City, 1983—, Iris City Devel. Co. Mt. Pleasant, Iowa, 1986, Linn Mar Elem./Mid. Sch., Marion, Iowa. Prin. works include Harbour Facilities, Antigua, W.I., S.C. Johnson Office Bldg., Racine, Wis., Iowa City Transit Facility Bldg., addition to Davenport Ctrl. High Sch., V.A. Adminstrv. Office Bldg., Iowa City, Johnson County Office Bldg., Iowa City Mercer Park Aquatic Ctr., Iowa City, Coll. Bus. U. Iowa, Iowa City, renovation Lawrence County Courthouse, Deadwood, S.D., H.S. and Elem. Schs., Mt. Pleasant, Iowa, Riverview Ctr., Muscatine, Iowa, Muscatine County Adminstv. Bldg., Iowa. Mem. bd. edn. Muscatine Community Sch. Dist., 1974-76. Served with USN, 1942-46, PTO. Recipient Honor award Portland Cement Assn., 1949, Lorraine D. Wright award for outstanding constrn. Camanche (Iowa) H.S., 1998-99. Mem. AIA (Honor award 1975), Constrn. Specifications Inst. (pres. 1974-76, Honor award 1983, 84, 85, 86), Soc. Archtl. Historians, Archtl. Assn. London, U. Nebr. Alumni Assn., Harvard U. Alumni Assn., Iowa City C. of C., Phi Kappa Psi, Univ. Athletic Club (Iowa City), Masons, Ea. Star, Elks Republican. Presbyterian. Avocations: golf, fishing, medieval history, big band music. Home: 312 Locust St Muscatine IA 52761-3510 Office: Neumann Monson Architects 111 E College St Iowa City IA 52240-4012 Office Phone: 319-338-7878. E-mail: roy@neumannmonson.com.

**NEUMANN, SERINA ANN LOUISE,** psychologist, researcher; b. Fitchburg, Mass., Dec. 29, 1970; d. James Martin Neumann and Annette Marie Rooney; m. Mark Cardiff, Feb. 19, 1973. BS in Psychology and Bus. cum laude, U. Pitts., 1992; MA in Clin. Psychology and Behavioral Medicine, U. Md., Balt., 1999, PhD in Clin. Psychology and Behavioral Medicine, 2001. Lic. Psychologist Bur. Profl. Occupl. Affairs, Pa., 2003. Postdoctoral scholar, cardiovasc. behavioral medicine rsch. tng. program U. Pitts., 2001—04, rsch. asst. prof., 2004—05; ast. prof. psychiatry and behavioral scis. Eastern Va. Med. Sch., 2006—. Author articles and papers in field. Fellow Ruth L. Kirschstein Nat. Rsch. Svc. award, NIH, Nat. Heart, Lung, and Blood Inst., 2001-2004; Loan Repayment Program grant, NIH, 2002—, Grant (NIMH) Kiosk award, 2005—. Mem.: APA (mem. Health Psychology Divsn. 38), Internat. Soc. Behavioral Medicine, Soc. Behavioral Medicine, Am. Psychosomatic Soc. (program com. student mem. 2000—01, Citation award 2005), Phi Kappa Phi. Achievements include discovery of preliminary evidence of an association between genetic variation in the choline transporter gene and parasympathetic-cardiac function, depressive symptomatology; corticolimbic reactivity and subclinical measures of atherosclerosis. Office: Eastern Va Med Sch Dept Psychiatry 825 Fairfax Ave Norfolk VA 23501 Office Phone: 757-446-5888. Business E-Mail: neumansa@evms.edu.

**NEUMANN, THOMAS WILLIAM,** archaeologist; b. Cin., Aug. 30, 1951; s. William Henry and Virginia Marie Neumann; m. Mary Louise Spink, Sept. 3, 1988. BA in Anthropology, U. Ky., 1973; PhD in Anthropology, U. Minn., 1979. Instr. U. Minn., Mpls., 1977-79; asst. prof. Syracuse U., 1979-86, dir. archaeology field program, 1979-86; sr. ptnr. Neumann & Sanford Cultural Resource Assessments, Syracuse, 1983 87; dir. scientist R. Christopher Goodwin & Assocs., Inc., Frederick, Md., 1987-92. Rsch. assoc. Terrestrial Environ. Specialists, Phoenix, N.Y., 1980-83, SUNY Rsch. Found., Potsdam, 1985-87; external reviewer NSF, Washington, 1982-85; dir. Ctr. for Archaeol. Rsch. and Edn., Houston, Minn., 1982-84; vis. assoc. prof. Emory U., 1991-93, 96-2000, 2002-06, U. Ga., 1997; ind. cons., 1991—; mgr. Diachronics divsn. Pocket Park-Wentworth Analytical Facility, 1993—. Author, co-author more than 80 monographs including 2 winners of the Anne Arundell County Hist. Preservation award; asst. editor Anamensis, 1972-73; contbr. more than 40 articles to profl. jours. Nat. Trust Historic Preservation honor award. Recipient Oswald award U. Ky., 1973; co-recipient Vt. Gov.'s medal for Stonewalls and Cellarholes; grantee Am. Philos. Soc., 1981, Appleby-Mosher Found., 1983, Landmarks Assn. Ctrl. N.Y. 1984. Mem. AAAS, N.Y. Acad. Sci., Soc. for Am. Archaeology, Ea. States Archaeol. Fedn., Mid. Atlantic Archaeol. Conf., Ga. Coun. Profl. Archaeologists, Register of Profl. Archaeologists, Phi Beta Kappa. Roman Catholic. Achievements include development of use of vegetation successional stages for cultural resource assessments; identification of cause of passenger pigeon extinctions, microlithic compound tool industry in the eastern prehistoric U.S., contingency planning budget system for Archdiocese of Atlanta. Home and Office: Ind Archeol Cons 3859 Wentworth Ln SW Lilburn GA 30047-2260

**NEUMANN, WILLIAM ALLEN,** retired state supreme court justice; b. Minot, N.D., Feb. 11, 1944; s. Albert W. and Opal Olive (Whitlock) N.; m. Jaqueline Denise Buechler, Aug. 9, 1980; children: Andrew, Emily. BSBA, U. N.D., 1965; JD, Stanford U., 1968. Bar: N.D. 1969, U.S. Dist. Ct. N.D. 1969. Pvt. practice law, Williston, N.D., 1969-70, Bottineau, N.D. 1970-79; judge N.D. Judicial Dist. Ct., N.E. Judicial Dist., Rugby and Bottineau, 1979-92; justice N.D. Supreme Ct., Bismarck, 1993—2005; exec. dir. State Bar Assn., ND, 2005—. Chmn. elect N.D. Jud. Conf., 1985-87, chmn. 1987-89. Mem. ABA, State Bar Assn. N.D., Am. Judicature Soc. (bd. dirs. 1998-2004). Lutheran. Office: ND State Bar Assn 504 N Washington St Bismarck ND 58501 Office Phone: 701-255-1404.

**NEUMEIER, JOHN,** choreographer, ballet company director; b. Milw., Feb. 24, 1942; s. Albert and Lucille N. BA, Marquette U., 1961, DFA (hon.), 1987; student, Stone-Camryn Ballet Sch., Chgo., 1957-62, Royal Ballet Sch.,

London, 1962-63; student of Vera Volkova, Copenhagen, 1962-63. Dancer Sybil Shearer Co., Chgo., 1960-62, Stuttgart (Fed. Republic Germany) Ballet, 1963-69; artistic dir. Frankfurt (Fed. Republic Germany) Opera Ballet, 1969-73, Hamburg (Fed. Republic Germany) State Opera Ballet, 1973—; prof. City of Hamburg, 1987; dir. Hamburg Ballet, 1996, ballettintendant, 1997—. Found. ballet sch. Hamburg State Opera, 1978; found. ballet ctr. John Neumeier, ballet sch., Hamburg State Opera co. one roof, 1989. Guest choreographer for various cos. including Am. Ballet Theatre, Royal Ballet London, Royal Danish Ballet, Nat. Ballet Can., Royal Winnipeg Ballet, Stuttgart Ballet, Munich Opera, Vienna Opera, Ballet du XX siecle, Brussels, Opera de Paris, Opera of Stockholm, Mariinsky Theatre, St. Petersburg; guest opera dir. Otello, Munich Opera, Hamburg State Opera; ballet dir. (films) Rondo, 1971 (Prix Italia 1972), Third Symphony of Gustav Mahler (Golden Camera award 1978), Legend of Joseph, Wendungen (String Quintet in C major by Schubert), 1979, Scenes of Childhood, The Lady of the Camellias, 1986, Othello, 1987, Illusions - Like Swan Lake, 2002, Death in Venice, 2004, St. Matthew Passion and Sylvia, 2005; choreographer Romeo and Juliet, The Nutcracker, 1971, Daphnis and Chloé, 1972, Third Symphony of Gustav Mahler, 1975, Illusions-Like Swan Lake, 1976, A Midsummer Night's Dream, 1977, Sleeping Beauty, The Lady of the Camelias, 1978, Matthaeus-Passion, 1981, Giselle, 1983, Sixth Symphony of G. Mahler, 1984, Peer Gynt, 1989, Fifth Symphony of G. Mahler, 1989, Requiem, 1991, A Cinderella Story, 1992, Ódyssee, 1995, Vivaldi Or What You Will, 1996, Sylvia, 1997, Images from Bartók, 1998, Messias, 1999 (Danza Danza award 2001), Nijinsky, 2000, Giselle, 2000, Sounds of Empty Pages, The Seagull, 2002, Death in Venice, 2003, Preludes CV, 2003, The Little Mermaid, a homage to Hans Christian Andersen for his 200th birthday celebrations, 2005, Songs of the Night, 2005. Decorated knight's cross Danebrog Order (Denmark); recipient Dance mag. award, 1983, Fed. German Cross of Merit, 1987, German Dance prize, 1988; title of Prof. conferred by City of Hamburg, 1987, Deutscher Tanzpreis, Fed. Republic of Germany, 1988; recipient Prix Diaghilev award, France, 1988, Order Des Arts et des Lettres award French Minister Culture, 1991, Carina Ari award, Stockholm, 1994, Nijinsky medal Polish Minister Culture, 1996, Danebrog Order in Gold, Denmark, 2000, Bayerischer Theaterpres, 2001, First prize for best contemporary choreography, Vasva 2002, Wilhelm Hansen prize, 2002, Medal for Art and Science, 2003; named Hon. Mem. Semper Opera, 2002, Knight of the Region of Knox French President Jacques Chirac, 2003, Porselli prize, Italy, 2004, Hans Christian Andersen Embassador, 2004, 05; Saeculum prize for his lifework, Dresden, 2005, Steffen Kempe prize, 2005; Hamburg John Neumeier Found. named in his honor, 2006. Mem. Acad. der Kuenste Hamburg, Acad. der Kuenste Berlin, Golden Mask, 2002 (Medal for Sci, 2003). Roman Catholic. Office: Ballettzentrum Hamburg Caspar-Voght-Strasse 54 D-20535 Hamburg Germany E-mail: intendanz@hamburgballett.de, presse@hamburgballett.de.

NEUMEIER, MATTHEW MICHAEL, lawyer, educator; b. Racine, Wis., Sept. 13, 1954; s. Frank Edward and Ruth Irene (Effenberger) N.; m. Annmarie Prine, Jan. 31, 1987; children: Ruthann Marie, Emilie Irene, Matthew Charles. B in Gen. Studies with distinction, U. Mich., 1981; JD magna cum laude, Harvard U., 1984. Bar: NY 1987, Mich. 1988, Ill. 1991, US Dist. Ct. (ea. dist.) Mich. 1988, US Dist. Ct. (ea., no. dists. and trial bar) Ill. 1991, US Ct. Appeals (7th cir.) 1992, US Ct. Appeals (fed. cir.) 1998, US Supreme Ct. 1991. Sec.-treas. Ind. Roofing & Siding Co., Escanaba, Mich., 1973-78; mng. ptnr. Ind. Roofing Co., Menominee, Mich., 1977-78; law clk. to presiding justice US Ct. Appeals (9th cir.), San Diego, 1984-85; law clk. to chief justice Warren E. Burger US Supreme Ct., Washington, 1985-86; spl. asst. to chmn. US Constn. Bicentennial Commn., Washington, 1986; assoc. Cravath, Swaine & Moore, NYC, 1986-88; spl. counsel Burnham & Ritchie, Ann Arbor, Mich., 1988; assoc. Schlussel, Lifton, Simon, Rands, Galvin & Jackier, P.C., Ann Arbor, Mich., 1988-90, Skadden, Arps, Slate, Meagher & Flom, Chgo., 1990-96; ptnr. Jenner & Block, Chgo., 1996—. Adj. prof. computer law and high tech. litig. John Marshall Law Sch., Chgo., 1999—. Editor: Harvard Law Rev., 1982-84; Pres., bd. dirs. Univ. Cellar Inc., Ann Arbor, 1979-81; bd. dirs. Econ. Devel. Corp., Menominee, 1978-79, Midwestern divsn. Am. Suicide Found., sec., 1992-97, Commonwealth Plaza Condominium Assn., dir., 1999—, pres., 2000—; dir. Harvard Law Soc. Ill., 2003-, sec. 2005-; mem. vestry Ch. Our Savior, 1997-2000; bd. dirs. Chgo. Children's Mus., 1999-, sec., 2003-; chmn. Harvard Law Sch. 15 Yr. Reunion Gift Fund, 1999; vice chair Harvard Law Sch. 20 Yr. Reunion Gift Fund, 2003-04. Mem. ABA, State Bar Mich., Assn. of Bar of City of NY, Chgo. Bar Assn., Ill. State Bar Assn., Def. Rsch. Inst., The 410 Club, Econ. Club Chgo., City Club of Chgo. Republican. Avocations: classic automobiles, piano, choir. Office: Jenner & Block LLP Ste 4100 One IBM Plz Chicago IL 60611 Office Phone: 312-923-2749. E-mail: mneumeier@jenner.com.

NEUMEYER, JOHN LEOPOLD, chemistry professor; b. Munich, July 19, 1930; came to U.S., 1945, naturalized, 1950; s. Albert and Martha (Stern) N.; m. Evelyn Friedman, June 24, 1956; children: Ann Martha, David Alexander, Elizabeth Jean. BS, Columbia U., 1952; PhD, U. Wis., 1961. Rsch. chemist Ethicon Inc., New Brunswick, NJ, 1952-57, FMC Corp., Princeton, NJ, 1961-63; sr. staff chemist Arthur D. Little, Inc., Cambridge, Mass., 1963-69; prof. medicinal chemistry, chemistry Northeastern U., Boston, 1969-91, dir. grad. sch., 1978-85, univ. disting. prof., 1982—92, univ. disting. prof. emeritus, 1992—; chmn. bd., chief sci. officer, co-founder Rsch. Biochem. Internat., Natick, 1981-97; pres., co-founder Brain Rsch. Labs., Inc., 1999—2002. Mem. com. of revision U.S Pharmacopeia, 1970-85; lectr. in psychiatry dept. psychiatry Harvard Med. Sch., 1996—; Boudewijn Tieboel vis. prof., Groningen-Utrecht Inst. for Drug Exploration, Holland, 1997, dir. medicinal chemistry program Alcohol and Drug Abuse Rsch. Ctr. McLean Hosp., Belmont, Mass., 1996—; vis. prof. chemistry U. Konstanz, Germany, 1975-77cons. in field. Contbr. articles to profl. jours., chapters to books; patentee in field. Mem. Bd. Health, Wayland, Mass., 1968-75, Pesticide Bd., Mass., 1972-75; mem. panel to sec. HEW Commn. on Pesticides and their Relationship to Environ. Health, 1969; mem. Mass. Tech. Collaborative, 1996-2002. Served to cpl. U.S. Army, 1953-55. Recipient Lunsford Richardson award, 1961, Marie Curie award in Nuclear Medicine, 1992; sr. Hayes Fulbright fellow, 1975-76, Henry A. Hill award for Outstanding Svc. to the Northeastern Sect., Am. Chem. Soc., 1998. Fellow: AAAS (mem. at large 1983—87, chmn. pharm. sci. sec. 1992—93), Am. Assn. Pharm. Scis. (Rsch. Achievement award in medicinal chemistry 1982); mem.: Am. Chem. Soc. (bd. editors Jour. Medicinal Chemistry 1974—88, chmn. divsn. med. chem. 1982, councilor 1985—, trustee 1990—93, N.E. sect. chmn.-elect 2002, chmn. 2003), Am. Soc. Exptl. Pharm. and Exptl. Therapeutics, Am. Soc. Neurosci., Acad. Pharm. Scis. Office: Harvard Med Sch/McLean Hosp ADARC 115 Mill St Belmont MA 02478-1041 E-mail: jneumeyer@mclean.harvard.edu.

NEUNER, FRANK X., JR., lawyer; b. Baton Rouge, May 23, 1951; s. Frank X. and Mary Frances (Ellis) N.; m. Tracy Owens, May 27, 1972; children: Gretchen, Hearin, Trip, Mary Frances. BS in Mgmt., La. State U., 1972, JD, 1976. Bar: La. 1976, U.S. Dist. Ct. (ea. and we. dists.) La., U.S. Ct. Appeals (5th cir.). Assoc. Franklin, Moore & Walsh, Baton Rouge, 1976-77; ptnr. Onebane, Donohoe, et al, Lafayette, La., 1977-87, Laborde & Neuner, Lafayette, 1987—. La. State Bar, Lafayette, (ho. dels.1982—, pres.-elect 2004). Bd. dirs. United Way, Lafayette, chmn. leadership campaign, 1992; pres. Cathedral Carmel Found., Lafayette, 1987-91; bd. dirs. Nike La. Open, Lafayette, 1992-93. Republican. Roman Catholic. Mem. ABA, La. Assn. Def. Counsel, Lafayette Parish Bar Assn. (pres. 1988), Maritime Lawyers Assn., Def. Rsch. Inst., S.E. Admiralty Law. Office: Laborde & Neuner 1001 W Pinhook Rd PO Box 52828 Lafayette LA 70505-2828

NEUNZIG, CAROLYN MILLER, elementary, middle and high school educator; b. L.I., May 5, 1930; kd. Stanley and Grace (Walsh) Miller; m. Herbert Neunzig, May 28, 1955; children: Kurt Miller, Keith Weidler. BA, Beaver Coll., Glen Side, Pa., 1953; MSSc, Syracuse U., 1989; postgrad., Adelphi U.; Cert., N.C. State U., Raleigh. Cert. in language arts, reading and English, N.C., permanent cert. in secondary English, N.Y., leader, Great Books Found. Reading tchr. grades K-6 St. Timothy's Sch., Raleigh, N.C., 1971-83, 5th grade tchr., 1983-88, 5th grade lead tchr., 1986-88; tchr. English and geography 7th grade St. Timothy's Mid. Sch., Raleigh, 1991—; tchr Am

govt. 12th grade St. Timothy's Mid. Sch./Hale H.S., Raleigh, 1991-93. Instr. continuing edn. program history Meredith Coll., Raleigh, 1990-91, spl. high sch. registration commr., 1991-93, instr. presdl. classroom, 1998, 99; mem. Ctr. Study of Presidency, 1998-2005. Asst. election ofcl. Wake County, N.C., 200, 04. Mem. AAUW, Am. Acad. Polit. and Social Sci., Acad. Polit. Sci.

NEURAUTER, ELIZABETH STRAIN, secondary school educator; b. Indpls., Mar. 7, 1959; d. Edward Richard Strain and Elizabeth Meyer (Strain) Gunn; m. Ronald Otto Neurauter, July 7, 1984; children: Stacy Marie, Ronald Paul, Beatrice Grace, Clara Helen. BA, Elmhurst Coll., Ill., 1981; EdM, Nat. Louis U., Wheeling, Ill., 2004; cert. advanced studies ednl. leadership, Nat. Louis U., 2005. Cert. tchr. English, ESL and psychology Ill. Staff asst. for vol. affairs ESL/ABE dept. Coll. DuPage, Glen Ellyn, Ill., 1991—94, ESL tchr. H.S. summer credit program, 2002—; tutor English lang. learner, asst. dir. student activities Glenbard South H.S., Glen Ellyn, 1994—. Presenter in field. Legis. apptd. mem. Ill. Literacy Coun., 1998. Nominee Golden Apple award, 2000; named Person of Character, Glen Ellyn Character Counts Coalition, 2004. Mem.: ASCD, Nat. Assn. Realtors, Ill. Assn. Realtors, Ill. Assn. Tchrs. English, Nat. Coun. Tchrs. English, Archaeol. Conservancy. Republican. Avocations: archaeology, real estate. Home: 22W521 Burr Oak Dr Glen Ellyn IL 60137 Office: Glenbard South HS 23W200 Butterfield Rd Glen Ellyn IL 60137 Office Phone: 630-469-6500.

NEUREITER, NORMAN P., science association director; b. Jan. 24, 1932; m. Georgine Reid; 4 children. BS in Chemistry, U. Rochester, 1952; PhD in Organic Chemistry, Northwestern U., 1957. With Humble Oil & Refining Co., 1957—63, NSF Internat. Affairs Office, 1963—65; dep. sci. attache U.S. Dept. State, Bonn, 1965—67, sci. attache Warsaw, 1967—69; with White House Office Sci. and Tech. Policy, 1969—73, Tex. Instruments, 1973—96, v.p. corp. staff, 1980—89, dir. Japan, v.p. Asia, 1989—96; sci. and tech. adv. to U.S. Sec. of State, 2000—03; dir. ctr. sci., tech., and security policy AAAS, 2004—. Disting. presdl. fellow NAS Internat. Affairs, 2003—; space studies bd. NAS/Nat. Rsch. Coun., 2004—. Office: AAAS 1200 New York Ave NW Washington DC 20005 Office Phone: 202-326-6493. Business E-Mail: neureit@aas.org.

NEUROHR, SHIRLEY ANN, retired special education educator; b. Chgo., Nov. 18, 1936; d. Anton and Anna (Ludvik) Sedlak; m. Joseph Henry Neurohr, Apr. 7, 1956 (dec. 1995); children: Debora Neurohr-Wearne, Kathleen Neurohr Rodenhauser, Jacqueline Neurohr Rueden; m. James Brennan, 2001. AA in Edn., Morton Coll., 1955; BA Psychology/Sociology summa cum laude, Mundelein Coll., 1977; MS in Edn. Adminstrn. with dept. honors, Winona State U., 1983. Cert. elem. edn. tchr., learning disabilities edn., behavioral disorders edn., elem. adminstrn. Elem. tchr. St. Mary's Cath. Sch., Tomah, Wis., 1978-80, elem. prin., 1980-85; secondary tchr. behaviorally disordered Sparta (Wis.) Sr. H.S., 1985-86, 86—; elem. tchr. behaviorally disordered Tomah Area Sch. Dist., 1986-87, secondary tchr. behaviorally disordered, 1987-90, secondary tchr. learning disabled, 1990—2001; ret., 2001. Mem. Edn. for Employment Coun., Tomah, 1990-95, Spl. Edn. Transition Task Force, Tomah, 1988-93, Sch. to Work Task Force, Tomah, 1990-95. Troop leader, program cons., v.p. coun. Girl Scouts DuPage County Coun., DuPage, Ill., 1963-77; lay min. Diocese of LaCrosse, Wis., 1985; mem. St. Mary's Coun. Cath. Women, 1977—. Recipient Thanks Badge, DuPage County coun. Girl Scouts U.S., 1976; named Woman of Yr., St. Joseph's Coun. of Cath. Women, 1977. Mem. AAUW (Tomah br. 1977-95, v.p., past sec.-treas.), ASCD, Nat. Coun. Tchrs. English, Midwest Reading Coun., Tomah Edn. Assn. (bldg. rep. 1986, asst. v.p., pres. 2000), Sierra Club Nat. Wildlife Found., Crane Found., Monroe County Ret. Tchrs. Assn (pres. 2005), Delta Kappa Gamma (sec. Alpha Upsilon chpt., pres. 2006), Master Gardeners Assn. Democrat. Roman Catholic. Avocations: travel, gardening, birding. Home: 23584 Emblem Ave Tomah WI 54660-9731 Personal E-mail: shirlgym@charter.net.

NEUSEL, MARA DICLE, mathematician, educator; b. Stuttgart, Germany, May 14, 1964; d. Günter and Ayla Neusel. Diploma in math., U. Göttingen, Germany, 1988, Dr. rer. nat., 1992, Privatdozentin, 2001. Lectr. Yale U., New Haven, 1995—95, Otto von Guericke U., Magdeburg, Germany, 1995—97, Yale U., 1998—99; assoc. prof. Tex. Tech U., Lubbock, 2002—. Visitor Queens U., Kingston, Ont., Canada, 1997; vis. asst. prof. U. Minn., Mpls., 1998, U. Notre Dame, Ind. 1999—2002; reviewer in field. Mem.: Ctr. Rsch. Math., Text and Acad. Author, Assn. Women in Math., Math. Assn. Am., Am. Math. Soc. Achievements include research in inverse invariant theory and steenrod ops. Office Phone: 806-742-2566.

NEUTRA, DION, architect; b. LA, Oct. 8, 1926; s. Richard Joseph and Dione (Niedermann) N.; m. Lynn Smart; children: Gregory, Wendy, Haig, Nicholas. Student, Swiss Inst. Tech., 1947-48; B.Arch. cum laude, U. So. Calif., 1950. With Richard J. Neutra (architect), Los Angeles, 1942-55; assoc. Neutra & Alexander, Los Angeles, 1955-60; asso. Robert E. Alexander, Los Angeles, 1960-62; prin. Richard & Dion Neutra, Architects and Assos., Los Angeles, 1962—; pres. Richard J. Neutra, Inc., 1970—. Exec. cons. Neutra Inst. for Survival Through Design, L.A.; lectr. Calif. State U., L.A., Sacramento City Coll., Mira Costa State U., Cabrillo State U., Soka U., Tokyo, San Diego City Coll., Germany, Switzerland, England, Austria; vis. prof. Calif. State U., Pomona, 1970, 1985—86, Va. Commonwealth U. 1998; vis. lectr. U. Minn., 2000, Fullerton U., 2001, Nat. Bldg. Mus., 2002, SHPO Puerto Rico, 2003, U. So. Calif. Prin. works include various residential, ednl., religious and instnl. facilities including Am. Embassy Karachi, Pakistan, Gettysburg Cyclorama Ctr., Simpson Coll. Libr., Adelphi Univ. Libr., Libr. and Resource Ctr. for City of Huntington Beach, Calif., Treetops Townhouses, 1980; exhbns. View from Inside, 1984, 86, 92, 98, 99, travelling show, 2000, Visions & Exiles, Vienna, 1995, Am. Century Art and Culture, Whitney Mus., NYC, 1999. Mem. Silver Lake-Echo Park Dist. Plan Adv. Com., Master Plan City of LA, 1970-71; mem. Citizens to Save Silver Lake, 1973-76; dir. Child Care and Devel. Services, 1970-71, Preservation and Maintenance of Existing Neutra Projects. Served with USNR, 1944-46. Street named Neutra Place in firm's honor, Silverlake, 1992; Neutra Centennial, 2002, Firm's 80th Anniversary Celebration, 2006; fellow Neutra Inst. for Survival Through Design, 2004. Mem. AIA, Nat. Council Archtl. Registration Bds., Alpha Rho Chi. Studio: Richard & Dion Neutra 2440 Neutra Pl Los Angeles CA 90039-4400 Office Phone: 323-666-1806. E-mail: dion@neutra.org.

NEUWIRTH, ALAN JAMES, lawyer; b. NYC, July 4, 1943; s. Bernard and Audrey (Hattenbach) N.; m. Patricia E. Neuwirth, Sept. 4, 1966; children: John A., Daniel P. BA, Lehigh U., 1965; JD, NYU, 1969. Bar: N.Y. 1970, U.S. Dist. Ct. (so. and ea. dists.) N.Y. 1972, U.S. Ct. Appeals (2d cir.) 1972, U.S. Ct. Internat. Trade 1983, U.S. Ct. Appeals (Fed. cir.) 1984, U.S. Supreme Ct. 1988. Assoc. Miller & Summit, N.Y., 1970-72, Ratheim, Hoffman, Kassel & Silverman, N.Y.C., 1973-75; ptnr. Kassel, Neuwirth & Geiger, N.Y.C., 1976-86, Webster & Sheffield, N.Y.C., 1987-90; mng. ptnr. Tokyo Office Morgan, Lewis & Bockius LLP, sr. ptnr., bus. & fin. practice group, 1990—. With U.S. Army, 1969-74, USAR. Mem. ABA, Assn. of Bar of City of N.Y., Internat. Trade Commn., Trial Lawyers Assn. Office: Morgan Lewis & Bockius LLP 101 Park Ave New York NY 10178-0060 Office Fax: 212-309-6001. Business E-Mail: aneuwirth@morganlewis.com.

NEUWIRTH, BEBE (BEATRICE NEUWIRTH), dancer, actress; b. Newark, Dec. 31, 1958; d. Lee Paul and Sydney Anne Neuwirth; m. Paul Dorman, 1984 (div.); m. Michael Danek. Student, Juilliard Sch., 1976-77. Appeared: (on Broadway) A Chorus Line (as Sheila), 1975-90, Dancin', 1978-82, Little Me, 1982, Sweet Charity, 1986-87 (Tony award for best featured actress in a musical, 1986), Damn Yankees, 1994-95, Chicago, 1996 (Tony award for best actress in a musical, 1997, Outer Critics Circle award for best actress in a musical, 1997, Drama League Award for disting. performance, 1997, Drama Desk Award for outstanding actress in a musical, 1997, Astaire Award for best female dancer, 1997), Fosse, 1999-2001, Funny Girl, 2002, Here Lies Jenny, 2004; (off Broadway) include West Side Story, 1981, Upstairs at O'Neal's, 1982-83, The Road to Hollywood, 1984, Just So, 1985, Waiting in the Wings: The Night the Understudies Take the Stage, 1986, Showing Off, 1989, Kiss of the Spider Woman (London), 1993, Pal Joey, 1995, Here Lies Jenny, 2004.

Prin. dancer on Broadway Dancin', 1982; leading dance role Kicks, 1984. Actor: (TV series) The Edge of Night, 1981, Cheers, 1986-93 (Emmy award for Best Supporting Actress in a Comedy Series 1990, 91), (voice) Aladdin, 1993, (voice) All Dogs Go to Heaven: The Series, 1996, Deadline, 2000-01; (TV series guest appearances) Frasier, 1994-2003; (TV miniseries) Wild Palms, 1993; (TV films) Without Her Consent, 1990, Unspeakable Acts, 1990, Dash and Lilly, 1999, Cupid & Cate, 2000, Sounds From a Town I Love, 2001; (films) Say Anything, 1989, Green Card, 1990, Bugsy, 1991, The Paint Job, 1992, Malice, 1993, Jumanji, 1995, (voice) All Dogs Go to Heaven 2, 1996, The Adventures of Pinocchio, 1996, The Associate, 1996, Dear Diary, 1996, Celebrity, 1998, The Faculty, 1998, (voice) An All Dogs Christmas Carol, 1998, Summer of Sam, 1999, Liberty Heights, 1999, Getting to Know You, 1999, Tadpole, 2002, How to Lose a Guy in 10 Days, 2003, Le Divorce, 2003, The Big Bounce, 2004. Vol. performances for March of Dimes Telethon, 1986, Cystic Fibrosis Benefit Children's Ball, 1986, Ensemble Studio Theater Benefit, 1986, Circle Repertory Co. Benefit, 1986, all in N.Y.C. Democrat.

NEUWIRTH, ROBERT SAMUEL, obstetrician, gynecologist, educator; b. NYC, July 11, 1933; s. Abraham Alexander and Phyllis Neuwirth; children from previous marriage: Susan, Jessica, Laura, Michael, Alexander. BS, Yale U., 1955, MD, 1958. Intern Presbyn. Hosp., NYC, 1958-59, resident, 1959-64; asst. prof. ob-gyn. Columbia U., NYC, 1964-68, assoc. prof., 1968-71, prof., 1972-2001, Babcock prof., 1977-2001, Babcock prof. emeritus, 2001—. Dir. ob-gyn. Bronx Lebanon Hosp., NYC, 1967-72, Woman's Hosp., NYC, St. Luke's Hosp. Ctr., 1974—, St. Luke's Roosevelt Hosp., 1981-91; prof. Albert Einstein Coll. Medicine, 1971-72; cons. WHO, NIH, AID, FDA; interim dir. St. Luke's Roosevelt Hosp., 1998-2000. Author: Hysteroscopy, 1975; contbr. articles to profl. jours. Mem.: ACOG, Assn. Vol. Sterilization (chmn. biomed. com. 1971—), Am. Assn. Profs. Ob-Gyn., NY Obstet. Soc., Soc. Gynecol. Investigation, Am. Gynecol. and Obstet. Soc. Office: St Lukes Roosevelt Hosp 1000 10th Ave Dept Ob New York NY 10019-1147 Office Phone: 212-523-8368.

NEVAI, LUCIA, writer; b. Des Moines, Sept. 11, 1945; d. Darwin Thomas and Ruth Marcella (Courson) Lynner; m. Andrew Nevai, July 6, 1968 (div. Sept. 1984); children: Nandor, Matthew. BA, New Sch. Social Rsch., 1967. Author: (novels) Seriously, (short stories) Normal, Star Game (Winner of The Iowa Short Fiction Award 1987), (anthologies) New Stories from The South 2002, The Year's Best, Francis Ford Coppola's Zoetrope: All Story, Fault Lines: Stories of Divorce, The Algonkian, The Way We Write Now: Short Stories from the AIDS Crisis, Closing: An Anthology of American Short Fiction on The Art of Selling, American Fiction Award Anthology No. 4, The Iowa Award: The Best Stories from Twenty Years, Best of the South, 2005, Best of Tin House, 2006, (short stories) Glimmer Train, 2006, My Father Married Your Mother: Writers Talk About Stepparents, Stepchildren, and Everyone in Between, 2006; contbr. articles in numerous profl. jours. Recipient Iowa Award For Lit., Iowa Review, 2001, Winner PEN Syndicated Fiction Award, Chgo. Tribune Mag., Am. Fiction Award, American Fiction No. 4, Best Fiction, Newsday Mag., State Mag. Home and Office: 579 Totem Lodge Averill Park NY 12018

NEVANS, ROY NORMAN, food products executive, producer; b. N.Y.C., July 1, 1931; s. Al Nevans and Lillian (Schiff) Margolis; m. Virginia Place, Dec. 31, 1961; children: Lisa Ann, Laurel Sue, Judith Lynn. BS, U. Pa., 1953; MBA, Columbia U., 1957. Mgmt. trainee Henningsen Foods, Inc., N.Y.C., 1958-60, mgr. export sales div., 1960-65, mgr. nat. sales div., 1965-70, v.p. mktg. White Plains, NY, 1970-90; mng. dir. Henningsen Van Den Burg, Waalyk, Holland, 1979-90, Henningsen Nederland B.V., Waalyk, 1984-90, Henningsen Foods, Ltd., London, 1977-90; pres. Royco Internat. Inc., Stamford, Conn., 1991—. Pres Royal Productions, Ltd, New York, NY, 1966, New York, 73, Int TV Productions, Ltd, London, 1971—; exec producer NCM Entertainment, Inc, New York, NY, 1982—; bd dirs Global Educ Mgt, Wall St Inst, World Trade Club. Prodr.: (Broadway plays) Gandhi, 1969, Solitaire Double Solitaire, 1972; (TV series) Juke Box, 1978—79; exec. prodr.: (TV miniseries) Roots of Rock and Roll, 1981. Lt comdr USN, 1953—56. Mem.: NATAS, US Naval Order, US Naval War Col, Univ Pa Club, Jaguar Touring Club, River Club. Avocations: classic cars collector, boating, theater. Home: 74 Greenwich Hills Dr Greenwich CT 06831 also: 1945 Gulf of Mexico Dr #108 Longboat Key FL 34228 also: 302 W 12th St New York NY 10014 Office: Royco Internat Inc 1177 High Ridge Rd Stamford CT 06905-1203 E-mail: roycointl@att.net.

NEVARES, LANE GORDON, travel company executive, writer, photographer; s. Danion Nevares, Jr. and Rose Mary Nevares; m. Natalie Werner, Aug. 21, 1999; children: Joaquin Lysando children: Solana Rose. BA, U. Tex., 1989. Asst. assignments editor KDFW-TV, Dallas, 1995—96; mgr. luxury travel Absolute Travel, N.Y., 1996—. Vis. lectr. in field. Photographer The Citadel, NY Times, Sunday Travel Sect., 1998, BigNews Mag. Literacy tchr. Hartley Ho. Centro de Educacion de Trabajadores, N.Y., 1997—2002; vol. photographer Bowery Residents Com., NYC, 2005—, Taproot Found., 2006—. Grantee, U. Tex., 1985—89; scholar, State of Tex., 1985—89; Hispanic Leadership Opportunity Program fellow, Ford Found., 1988—89. Mem.: Am. Soc. Travel Agents (assoc.). Office Phone: 212-627-1950.

NEVELOFF, JAY A., lawyer; b. Bklyn., Oct. 11, 1950; m. Arlene Sillman, Aug. 26, 1972; children: David, Kevin. BA, Bklyn. Coll., 1971; JD, NYU, 1974. Bar: N.Y. 1975, D.C. 1992, U.S. Dist. Ct. (so. and ea. dists.) N.Y. 1975, U.S. Ct. Appeals (2d cir.) 1975, U.S. Supreme Ct. 1982. Assoc. Marshall, Bratter, Greene, Allison & Tucker, N.Y.C., 1974-82, Rosenman, Colin, Freund, Lewis & Cohen, N.Y.C., 1982-83, ptnr., 1983-88, Kramer, Levin, Naftalis, Nessen, Kamin & Frankel, N.Y.C., 1988—. Editor N.Y. Real Property Service. Mem. planning bd. Briarcliff Manor, 1995—. Mem. ABA (vice chmn. com. partnerships, joint ventures and other investment vehicles 1988-95), Am. Law Inst., Am. Coll. Real Estate Attys., N.Y. State Bar Assn. (financing com.), Endeavor Global Adv. Bd., Practising Law Inst. (lectr. 1988—, mem. adv. bd. 1991—), Assn. Bar City N.Y. (real property law com., lectr. 1984-88), Law Jours. Seminars (lectr. 1987—), Strategic Resources Inst. (lectr. 1994-98), Internat. Health Network Soc. (vice chmn. 1995-2000), Inst. Internat. Rsch. (lectr. 1994—). Home: 134 Alder Dr Briarcliff Manor NY 10510-2218 Office: Kramer Levin Naftalis & Frankel LLP 1177 Ave of the Americas New York NY 10036 Business E-Mail: jneveloff@kramerlevin.com.

NEVES, KERRY LANE, lawyer; b. San Angelo, Tex., Dec. 19, 1950; s. Herman Walter and Geraldine (Ball) N.; m. Sharon Lynn Briggs, July 28, 1973; 1 child, Erin Lesli. BBA, U. Tex., 1975, JD, 1978. Bar: Tex. 1978, U.S. Dist. Ct. (so. and ea. dists.) Tex. 1979, U.S. Ct. Appeals (5th cir.) 1979, U.S. Dist. Ct. (we. dist.) 1980; cert. personal injury trial law, Tex. Bd. Legal Specialization, 1994. Ptnr. Mills, Shirley, Eckel & Bassett, Galveston, Tex., 1978—93, Neves & Crowther, Galveston, Tex., 1993—2002; priv. practice Law Offices of Kerry L. Neves, Galveston, 2002—. Vice-chmn. Bldg. Stnds. Commn., Dickinson, Tex., 1991-98; mem. City Coun. Dickinson, Tex., 1998—; bd. dirs. Houston-Galveston Area Coun., 2002—. Sgt. USMC, 1969-72. Fellow Tex. Bar Found. (life); mem. ABA, State Bar Tex. (grievance com. 1989-92, disciplinary rules profl. conduct com. 1990-92, dir. dist. 5 1997-2000), Galveston County Bar Assn. (pres. 1989-90), U. Tex. Law Alumni Assn. (pres. 1991-92). Avocations: gardening, wine, reading. Home: RR 2 Box 95 Dickinson TX 77539-9204 Office: 1802 Broadway St Ste 206 Galveston TX 77550-4953 Office Phone: 409-765-7774. Personal E-mail: bkwds@aol.com.

NEVEU, JEAN, printing company executive; Contr., mgr. Quebecor, Inc., Montreal, 1969—79; in mag. pub. and distbn., 1979—88; chmn., CEO Quebecor Printing Inc., 1989—2002; pres., CEO Quebecor World Inc., 2003—; pres., CEO Quebecor Inc., 1999—, chmn., 1999—. Chmn. Groupe TVA Inc.; bd Quebecor Media Inc. Chmn. Fondation du centre Hospitalier PierreBoucher; active Mutins de Longueuil; bd. dirs. Internationaux du sport de Montréal. Office: Quebecor Inc 612 Saint Jacques St Montreal PQ Canada H3C 4M8

**NEVIASER, ROBERT JON,** orthopaedic surgeon, educator; b. Washington, Nov. 21, 1936; s. Julius Salem and Jane Frances (Gibbons) N.; m. Anne Maclean Shedden, Dec. 3, 1966; children: Jeanne Nicole, Robert Jon Jr., Ian Maclean, Andrew Shedden. Grad., Phillips Acad., Andover, Mass., 1954; AB, Princeton U., 1958; MD, Jefferson Med. Coll., 1962. Diplomate Am. Bd. Orthop. Surgery with cert. of added qualification in surgery of hand. Intern NY Hosp., Cornell Med. Ctr., NYC, 1962-63, asst. resident, 1963-64; asst. resident in orthopaedic surgery NY Orthop. Hosp., Columbia-Presbyn. Med. Ctr., NYC, 1964-66, jr. Annie C. Kane fellow, resident, 1966-67; fellow in surgery of the hand Orthop. Hosp., LA, 1969-70; asst. prof. divsn. orthop. and hand surgery, chmn. dept. U. Conn., Hartford, 1970-71; assoc. prof. orthop. surgery George Washington U., Washington, 1971-76, prof., 1976—; dir. orthop. edn., assoc. chmn. dept. orthop. surgery, 1984-87, chmn. dept. orthop. surgery, 1987—; chmn. governing bd. Med. Faculty Assocs. George Washington U. Med. Ctr., 1995-98, trustee, 2000—03, 2005—. Editor-in-chief Jour. of Shoulder and Elbow Surgery, 1997—; contbr. articles in field to profl. jours. Lt. comdr. USNR, 1967-69. Fellow Am. Soc. Surgery of the Hand, Am. Acad. Orthop. Surgeons, Ea. Orthop. Assn., Am. Shoulder and Elbow Surgeons, Am. Orthop. Assn., Princeton Club (NY), Manor Country Club, Cosmos Club, Alpha Kappa Kappa, Alpha Omega Alpha. Republican. Office: 2150 Pennsylvania Ave NW Washington DC 20037-3201 Office Phone: 202-741-3301. Business E-mail: rneviaser@mfa.gwu.edu.

**NEVILL, WILLIAM ALBERT,** chemistry professor; b. Indpls., Jan. 1, 1929; s. Irwin Lowell and Mary Marie (Barker) N.; m. Nancy Neiman (Roll), May 19, 1979; children: Paul David, John Michael, Steven Joseph, Anne Marie, Deborah Ruth. BS, Butler U., 1951; PhD, Calif. Inst. of Tech., 1954. Rsch. chemist Procter and Gamble, Cin., 1954; chemistry prof., chmn. dept. Grinnell Coll., 1956-67; prof. chemistry Ind. U., Purdue, Indpls., 1967-83, chmn. dept., 1967-72, dean sch. sci., 1972-79, dir. grad. studies, 1979-83; pres. B and N Cons. Co., 1972-93; vice chancellor acad. affairs La. State U., Shreveport, La., 1983-85, prof., 1983-94; pres. Catoctin Assoc., 1993—. Arbitrator, mediator, Ind. Employment Rels. Bd., 1975-83. Author: Gen. Chemistry, 1967, Expt. in Gen. Chemistry, 1968. Bd. dir. Indpls. Sci. and Engring. Found., 1972-75, 79-82, Westminster Found., Lafayette, Ind., 1972-74, Am. Chem. Soc., 1986-92. With U.S. Army, 1954-56; col., USAR, 1956-84. Grantee NSF, 1959-74; Grantee NIH, 1963-70; Grantee Office Naval Rsch., 1953 Mem. Ind. Acad. Sci., Am. Chem. Soc., chmn. sect. 1972, counselor 1973-92. Presbyterian.

**NEVILLE, AARON,** musician; b. New Orleans, La., Jan. 24, 1941; m. Joel; 1 d., Ernestine; 3 s., Aaron, Jr., Ivan, Jason. Singer (singles): Over You, 1959, Tell It Like It Is, 1966, 91; (albums): Greatest Hits, 1967, Orchid in the Storm, 1990, The Classic: My Greatest Gift, 1990, Tell It Like It Is, 1991, Warm Your Heart, 1991, The Grand Tour, 1993, Aaron Neville's Soulful Christmas, 1993, The Tatooed Heart, 1995, Can't Stop my Heart, 1995, Doing It Their Own Way, 1996, To Make Me Who I Am, 1997, Uptown Rulin'-Best of Neville, 1999, Valence Street, 1999, Very Best of Aaron Neville, 2000, Devotion, 2000, Aaron Neville: Ultimate Collection, 2001, Aaron Neville: The Best of the Millenium Collection, 2002, Gospel Roots, 2003, Love Songs, 2003, Believe, 2003, Nature Boy, 2003, Aaron Neville Christmas Prayer, 2005; singles (with Linda Ronstadt) Don't Know Much, 1990 (Grammy award, Best Pop Duo with Linda Ronstadt, 1989), All My Life, 1990(Grammy award, Best Pop Duo with Linda Ronstadt, 1990), featured on Midnight at St. Jude's; albums (with Neville Brothers) Wild Tchoupatoulas, 1976, The Neville Brothers, 1977, Fiyo On the Bayou, 1981, Nevillization, 1984, Treacherous: A History of the Neville Brothers (vol. 1), 1986, Uptown, 1987, Yellow Moon, 1989, Brother's Keeper, 1990, Treacherous vol. 2, 1992, Family Groove, 1992, Live on Planet Earth, 1994, Mitakuye Oyasin, 1996, The Very Best of the Neville Brothers, 1997, Valance Street, 1999, Uptown Rulin, 1999, Walkin' In the Shadow of Life, 2004; guest appearances Superbowl XXIV, New Orleans, 1990, Superbowl XL, New Orleans, 2006. Recipient Grammy award with Neville Brothers, Best Pop Instrumental Performance for Healing Chant, 1989, Down Beat Blues, Soul, R&B Group award, 1990, Grammy award, Best Country Collaboration with vocals with Trisha Yearwood for I Fall to Pieces, 1994; co-recipient with Neville Brother, Chairman's award, NAACP Image awards, 2006; named Best Male Singer, Rolling Stones critics poll (2 years in row) Address: c/o William Morris Agy 151 El Camino Drive Beverly Hills CA 90212 also: Elevation Group 360 17th St Ste 200 Oakland CA 94612*

**NEVILLE, BRUCE DAVID,** librarian; b. Painesville, Ohio, June 14, 1955; s. Wayne Foster and Barbara Lee (Naughton) N. BS, U. Miami, 1977; MLS, Fla. State U., 1992. Biologist Gen. Devel. Corp., Miami, 1977-83; assoc. scientist Environ. Sci. & Engring., Miami, 1983-86; environ. scientist Kimley-Horn & Assocs., West Palm Beach, Fla., 1986-87, Gaby & Gaby, Inc., South Miami, Fla., 1987-90; libr. Terra Inc., Tallahassee, Fla., 1990-92, U. Tex., El Paso, 1992-96, U. N.Mex., Albuquerque, 1996—. Co-author: The Wentletrap Book, 1999, New Mexico Bird Finding Guide, 3d edit., 2002, Science and Technology Research Writing Strategies for Students, 2002; contbr. articles to profl. jours. Elected bd. dirs. Tropical Audubon Soc., Miami, 1982-89. Mem. N.Mex. Ornithological Soc. (bd. dirs. 1998-2006), Fla. Ornithological Soc. (sec. 1985-93), Conchologists of Am., High Desert Shell Club (founder 1998—), Beta Phi Mu. Avocation: avid birder and conchologist. Office: Centennial Libr MSC05-3020 U Nmex Albuquerque NM 87131-0001 Business E-mail: bneville@unm.edu

**NEVILLE, ELIZABETH EGAN,** artist, educator; b. Albany, N.Y., May 16, 1937; d. Philip Sidney and Harriet Rust Egan; m. Robert Cummings Neville, June 8, 1963; children: Naomi Louise, Leonora Alice. BA, Smith Coll., 1959; MA in Tchg., Harvard U., 1961. Dir. Neville Art Enterprises, Milton, Mass., 1969—. Art instr. Town of Huntington, NY, 1982—88, Adelphi U., Garden City, NY, 1983—85; dir. Milton Art Mus., 1993—97 art instr., 1998—; lectr. in field. Art Cmte. Art N.Eng.; (Represented in permanent collections Heckscher Mus., Huntington, L.I., Fine Arts Mus. L.I., Hempstead, N.Y., Maritime Mus., State U. N.Y., Throgs Neck, Katonah Gallery, N.Y., Hudson-Athens Lighthouse Preservation Soc., Symbols of Jesus, 2001, Boston Confucianism, 2000, The God Who Beckons, 1999, The Cosmology of Freedom, 1995, Creativity and God, 1995, God the Creator, 1992, Eternity and Times Flow, 1993, A Theology Primer, 1991, Behind the Masks of God, 1991, Recovery of the Measure, 1989, The Butterfly as Companion, 1989, The Puritan Smile, 1987, solo exhbns., Neville Gallery, 2004, Boston U. Sch. Theology, 1998, Claremont Sch. Theology, Calif., 1997, 1995, 1991, Sturdy Meml. Hosp. Gallery, Attleboro, Mass., 1997, Weston Theol. Inst., Mass., 1995, U. Mass. Med. Ctr. Gallery, Worcester, 1994, Kaaterskill Gallery, Columbia-Greene C.C., Hudson, N.Y., 1992, Milton Art Mus., Mass., 1990, NoHo Gallery, NYC, 1981, 1983. Mem. Newport Mus., RI, 2006—, Capt. Robert Forbes Mus., Milton, 1989—; pres. bd. trustees Milton Art Mus., 2001, 2003. Grantee, Henry Luce Found., 1990, Milton Cultural Arts Coun., 1995, 1996, 1997, 2006. Mem.: Nat. Mus. Women in Art (charter mem.), Women's Caucus for Art, Harvard Mus. Boston (adv. bd. fine arts com. 1998—), Smith Coll. Club Boston, Milton Garden Club (chair Smithsonian garden history 2001—), Alpha Kappa XI. Democrat. Avocations: landscape architecture, photography, history, citrus horticulture.

**NEVILLE, JACK L. (DREW), JR.,** lawyer; b. Okla. City, Okla., July 29, 1947; BA, Univ. Okla., 1969, JD, 1972. Bar: Okla. 1972, Okla. Supreme Ct., US Dist. Ct. (we., no., ea. dist. Okla., so. dist. NY, so. dist. Fla., Colo., no., ea. dist. Tex.), US Ct. Appeals (5th, 7th, 10th, 11th cir.). Legis. asst. U.S. Senate, 1974—75; asst. U.S. atty. we. dist. Okla., 1975—76; atty. pvt. practice, 1976—2000; ptnr., litigation practice Hartzog Conger Cason & Neville, Okla. City, Okla., 2000—. Mem. adv. com. US Ct. Appeals (10th cir.). Master: Luther Bohanon Am. Inn of Ct.; fellow: Am. Coll. Trial Lawyers; mem.: ABA, Fed. Bar Assn. (past pres. Okla. City chpt.), Okla. Bar Assn., Okla. County Bar Assn. Office: Hartzog Conger Cason & Neville Ste 1600 201 Robert S Kerr Ave Oklahoma City OK 73102 Office Phone: 405-235-7000. Office Fax: 405-996-3403. Business E-mail: dneville@hartzoglaw.com.

**NEVILLE, JAMES MORTON,** retired lawyer, consumer products company executive; b. Mpls., May 28, 1939; s. Philip and Maurene (Morton) N.; m. Judie Martha Proctor, Sept. 9, 1961; children: Stephen Warren, Martha Maurene Hereford. BA, U. Minn., JD magna cum laude, 1964. Bar: Minn. 1964, Mo. 1984. Assoc. Neville, Johnson & Thompson, Mpls., 1964-69, ptnr., 1969-70; assoc. counsel Gen. Mills, Inc., Mpls., 1970-77, sr. assoc. counsel, 1977-83, corp. sec., 1976-83; v.p., sec., asst. gen. counsel Ralston Purina Co., St. Louis, 1983-84, v.p., gen. counsel, sec., 1984-96, v.p., gen. counsel, 1996-2000, v.p., sr. counsel, 2000-01; ret., 2001; chmn. The Thompson Ctr., 2002. Lectr. bus. law. U. Minn., 1967-71. Named Man of Yr., Edina Jaycees, 1967. Mem. ABA, Mo. Bar Assn., U.S. Supreme Ct. Bar Assn., St. Louis Bar Assn., U. Minn. Law Sch. Alumni Assn., Old Warson Country Club, Ladue Racquet Club, Order of Coif, Phi Delta Phi, Psi Upsilon. Episcopalian. Home: 9810 Log Cabin Ct Saint Louis MO 63124-1133 Personal E-mail: jnev57@aol.com.

**NEVILLE, PHOEBE,** choreographer, dancer, educator; b. Swarthmore, Pa., Sept. 28, 1941; d. Kenneth R. and Marion (Eberbach) Balsley; m. Philip E. Hipwell, June 21, 1969 (dissolved Sept. 1978); m. Philip Corner, Nov. 3, 1996. Student, Wilson Coll., 1959-61. Cert. practitioner body mind centering, registered somatic movement therapist. Instr. Bennington (Vt.) Coll., 1981-84, 87-88; vis. lectr. UCLA, 1984-86. Dancer, choreographer Judson Meml. Ch., N.Y.C., 1966—70, Dance Uptown Series, 1969, Cubiculo Theatre, 1972—75, Delacorte Dance Festival, 1976, Dance Umbrella Series, 1977, Riverside Dance Festival, 1976, 1978, N.Y. Seasons, 1979—, dancer, artistic dir. Phoebe Neville Dance Co., N.Y.C., 1975—, Jacob's Pillow Splash! Festival, 1988—, Dance Theater Workshop Winter Events, 1988—, Mersdith Wonk Benefit, 1994, performances with Philip Corner: Venice, Genoa, San Michele al' Adige, 1996—, BBB Festival, Thailand, Genoa, Salso Maggiore, Terme, 1997—, Seoul NY Max Festival, N.Y.C., 1998, Malpartida de Caseras, Spain, Caserano, Italy, 1998, Besancon, France, 1998, Paris, Lyon, 1999, Saluggia, Italy, 1999, Performance Festival, Odense, Denmark, 1999, 2001, Bassano del Grappa, Genoa, Italy, 2000, 2001, 2002, Novarra, Italy, 2002—; performances with, Ghent, Belgium, 2002—; performances with: Castelvetro di Modena, 2003; Argos Festival, 2003. Recipient Creative Artist Public Svc. award, 1975; Nat. Endowment for Arts fellow, 1975, 79, 80, 85-87, 92-94, Choreographic fellow N.Y. Found. for Arts, 1989. Mem.: Internat. Assn. Healthcare Practitioners, Internat. Somatic Movement Edn. and Therapy Assn. (registered), Body-Mind Centering Assn. (cert. practitioner and tchr.). Buddhist.

**NEVILLE, ROY GERALD,** research scientist, chemical executive, consultant; b. Bournemouth, Dorsetshire, Eng., Oct. 15, 1926; came to U.S., 1951, naturalized, 1957; s. Percy Herbert and Georgina Lallie (Jenkins) N.; m. Jeanne Frances Russ, July 26, 1952; children: Laura Jean, Janet Marilyn. BSc with honors, U. London, 1951; MSc, U. Oreg., 1952, PhD, 1954; FRIC, Royal Inst. Chemistry, London, 1963, DSc (hon.), 1973. Research chemist Monsanto Chem. co., Seattle, 1955-57; sr. chem. engr. Boeing Co., Seattle, 1957-58; sr. research scientist Lockheed Missiles & Space Co., Palo Alto, Calif., 1958-61; sr. staff scientist Rockwell Internat. Corp., Los Angeles, 1963-67; head dept. materials Scis. Lab., Boeing Sci. Research Labs. Boeing Co., Seattle, 1967-69; sr. environ. engring. specialist Bechtel Corp., San Francisco, 1969-73; pres. Engring. & Tech. Cons., Inc., Redwood City, Calif., 1973—. Contbr. numerous sci. articles on inorganic and organic synthesis, thermally stable polymers, pollution control processes to profl. jours. and books; many U.S. and fgn. patents in field; associateship Southampton U., England, 1951. Founder, dir. R.G. Neville Hist. Chem. Libr. The Chem. Heritage Found., Phila.; dir. Sequoia Hosp. Found., Redwood City, Calif. Fulbright scholar to U.S., 1951; USPHS fellowship, 1951-52, Research Corp. fellow, 1952-54; chartered chemist, London. Fellow AAAS, Royal Soc. Chemistry (London), Am. Inst. Chemists; mem. AIChE, Am. Chem. Soc., History Sci. Soc., Soc. Study Early Chemistry, Royal Instn. Great Britain, Rsch. Soc. Am., Soc. Mining Engrs. of AIME, Calif. Mining Assn., Sigma Xi. Office: ETC Inc 1552 Viscaino Rd Pebble Beach CA 93953-3303

**NEVILLE, THOMAS LEE,** food service company executive; b. Columbus, Ind., Jan. 1, 1947; s. Frank Thomas and Esquline Coons (Davis) N.; m. Shavona Rose Lagneau, Aug. 10, 1966; children: Timothy David, Sherry Lynn. AAS, Austin Peay State U., Clarksville, Tenn., 1994. Cert. exec. chef; cert. food exec. Enlisted U.S. Army, 1966, apptd. WO1, 1976, commd. CW3, 1986; food advisor Army Food Rsch., Devel. and Engring. Ctr., Natick, Mass.; ret. U.S. Army, 1990; gen. mgr. KCA Corp., Hopkinsville, Ky., 1990—. Mem. Warrant Officers Assn., 1976-90. Mem. Ret. Officers Assn., Am. Soc. Quality Control, Am. Culinary Fedn., Am. Mgmt. Assn., Internat. Food Svc. Execs. Assn., Masons. Home: 1728 Clara Ct Clarksville TN 37040-7823 Office: KCA Corp PO Box 641 Hopkinsville KY 42241-0641 Office Phone: 270-886-5551. Business E-mail: tneville@kcacorp.com.

**NEVIN, ANN IRENE,** education educator; b. Schenectady, N.Y., Nov. 6, 1937; d. George William Nevin and Helen Wilhelmina Wernecke; children: David Egner, Jonathan McLean, Ruth Beecher, Rose Amberson. BA magna cum laude, Westminster Coll., 1969; MS in Edn., U. Minn., 1977; MEd., U. Vt., 1970; PhD, U. Minn., 1977. Prof. U. Vt., Burlington, Vt., 1969—90, Ariz. State U. West, Phoenix, 1991—2002, Fla. Internat. U., Miami, Fla., 2003—. Co-author: Turning learning inside out., 1994, Models of curriculum based assessment 3rd edit., 1999, Collaborative consultation 3rd edit., 2000, A guide to co-teaching: Practical tips for facilitating student learning, 2004, Creativity and collaborative learning 2d edit., 2005. Recipient Outstanding Novice Debater award, U. Vt. Debate Club, 1958, Pres.'s Achievement medal, Ariz. State U., 2001; fellow, U. Vt., 1968—70, U. Minn., 1975—76; grantee, U. Vt., 1987—88, Ariz. State U. West, 1997—98; Henrietta Lee scholarship, Westminster Coll., 1959—60, Eichenaur scholar, 1959. Mem.: Assn. Tchr. Educators, Am. Ednl. Rsch Assn. Achievements include devel. developer of Vermont consulting teacher program. Office Phone: 954-483-3175. Home Fax: 954-885-7662. Personal E-mail: nevina@bellsouth.net.

**NEVIN, CROCKER,** investment banker; b. Tulsa, Mar. 14, 1923; s. Ethelbert Paul and Jennie Crocker (Fassett) N.; m. Mary Elizabeth Sherwin, Apr. 24, 1952 (div. 1984); children: Anne, Paul, Elizabeth, Crocker; m. Marilyn Elizabeth English, Nov. 3, 1984; 1 child, Jennie Fassett. Grad. with high honors, St. Paul's Sch., 1942; AB with high honors, Princeton U., 1946. With Vick Chem. Co., 1949-50, John Roberts Powers Cosmetic Co., 1950-52; with Marine Midland Grace Trust Co. of N.Y., 1952—, exec. v.p., 1964-66, pres., 1966-70, chmn. bd., chief exec. officer, 1968-73; also dir.; vice chmn. bd. Evans Products Co., N.Y.C., 1974-76, Drexel Burnam Lambert Co., investment bankers, N.Y.C., 1976-88; chmn. bd., chief exec. officer CF & I Steel Corp., Pueblo, Colo., 1985-93. Dir. Magnatck, Inc. Chmn. exec. com. ACCION Internat. Lt. (j.g.) AC USN, 1942-46. Mem. Riverside Yacht Club, N.Y. Yacht Club (v.p.), Blind Brook Club. Home: 20 Hope Farm Rd Greenwich CT 06830

**NEVIN, HUGH WILLIAMSON, JR.,** lawyer; b. Sewickley, Pa., Dec. 9, 1946; s. Hugh Williamson and Eleanore (George) N.; m. Eliza Scott Nevin, June 16, 1972; 1 child, John Irwin. BA, Harvard U., 1968, JD, 1974. Bar: Pa. 1975, U.S. Dist. Ct. (We. Dist.) Pa. 1975. Pres., CEO, chmn. internat. bus. group Cohen & Grigsby, Pitts., 1986—2001, Bonita Springs, Fla., 2001—, Naples, Fla., 2004—. With U.S. Army, 1968-70. Mem. Phi Beta Kappa. Presbyterian. Office: Cohen & Grigsby 27200 Riverview Center Blvd Bonita Springs FL 34134 Office Phone: 239-390-1900. Business E-mail: hnevin@cohenlaw.com.

**NEVIN, JOHN ROBERT,** business educator, consultant; b. Joliet, Ill., Jan. 27, 1943; s. Robert Charles and Rita Alice (Roder) N.; m. Jeanne M. Conroy, June 10, 1967; children: Erin, Michael. BS, So. Ill. U., 1965; MS, U. Ill., 1968, PhD, 1972. Asst. prof. bus. U. Wis., Madison, 1970—71, assoc. prof. bus., 1977—83, prof. bus., 1983—, Grainger Wis. disting. prof. bus., 1989—, exec. dir. Grainger Ctr. for Supply Chain Mgmt., 1992—, assoc. dean masters program, 1999—2002, exec. dir. The Ctr. Brand and Product Mgmt., 2003—. Mem. investment adv. com. Venture Investors of Wis., Inc., Madison,

1986-99. Author: International Marketing: An Annotated Bibliography, 1983; mem. editl. bd. Jour. of Mktg. Channels, The Haworth Press, Inc., 1991—; contbr. articles to profl. jours. Bd. dirs. Madison Civic Ctr., 1983—99. Mem. Am. Mktg. Assn. (bd. dirs. PhD consortium 1979 editorial bd. Jour. of Mktg. Chgo. chpt. 1983-97), Assn. for Consumer Rsch. Avocations: golf, skiing, running. Home: 7514 Red Fox Trl Madison WI 53717-1860 Office: U Wis Grainger Ctr Supply Chain Mgmt 975 University Ave Madison WI 53706-1324 Office Phone: 608-262-8912. E-mail: jnevin@bus.wisc.edu.

**NEVIN, PHILLIP,** professional baseball player; b. Fullerton, Calif., Jan. 19, 1971; First baseman San Diego Padres, 1999—2005, Anaheim Angles, 1998—99, Detroit Tigers, 1995—97, Houston Astros, 1995—95, Tex. Rangers, 2005—06, Chgo. Cubs, 2006, Minn. Twins, 2006—. Office: Minn Twins H Humphrey Metrodome 900 S Fifth St Minneapolis MN 55415*

**NEVIN, ROBERT CHARLES,** information systems executive; b. Dayton, Ohio, Nov. 4, 1940; s. Robert Steely and Virginia (Boehme) N.; m. Linda Sharon Fox, Apr. 16, 1966; children: Heather, Andrew. BA, Williams Coll., 1962; MBA, U. Pa., 1970. Fin. planning mgr. Huffy Corp., Dayton, Ohio, 1971-72, asst. treas., 1972-73, treas., 1973-75, v.p. fin., 1975-79, exec. v.p., 1982-85; pres., gen. mgr. Frabill Sporting Good, Milw., 1979-82; exec. v.p. Reynolds & Reynolds, Dayton, Ohio, 1985-88, pres. bus. forms divsn., 1988-97; pres. automotive group, 1997—. Bd. dirs. Reynolds & Reynolds, Olympic Title Ins. Co. Bd. dirs., pres. Camp Fire Girls, Dayton, 1975; bd. dirs. ARC, 1977; participant, then trustee Leadership Dayton, 1986-95; vice chmn. Med. Am. Corp.; trustee, treas. Victory Theater Assn., 1985-91, Dayton Mus. Natural History, 1982-96, trustee, chmn. Alliance for Edn., Dayton Art Inst. 1st lt. USN, 1962-70. Mem. Beta Gamma Sigma, Racquet (Dayton), Dayton Country, Country Club of the North. Republican. Episcopalian.

**NEVINS, JOHN J.,** bishop; b. New Rochelle, N.Y., Jan. 19, 1932; Student, Iona Coll., N.Y., Cath. U. Washington, Tulane U. Ordained priest Roman Cath. Ch., 1959. Ordained titular bishop of Rusticana and aux. bishop Diocese of Miami, 1979—84; first bishop Diocese of Venice, Fla., 1984—. Office: PO Box 2006 1000 Pinebrook Rd Venice FL 34292

**NEVINS, JOSEPH ROY,** geneticist, educator; b. June 21, 1947; BS, U. Okla., 1970, MS, 1972; PhD, Duke U., 1976. Asst. prof. molecular cell biology Rockefeller U., 1979-82, assoc. prof., 1982-87, investigator Howard Hughes Med. Inst., 1986-87; prof. microbiology Duke U. Med. Ctr., 1987-90, investigator Howard Hughes Med. Inst., 1987—, prof. genetics and head, sect. genetics, 1990-94, chmn. dept. genetics, 1994—. Lectr. in field. Dept. Microbiology and Immunology fellow Duke U. Med. Ctr., 1972-76, Postdoctoral fellow Rockefeller U., 1976-79; guest scholar Inst. Virus Rsch., Kyoto U., 1986. Fellow Am. Acad. Arts & Sciences. Mem. Am. Soc. Microbiology, Am. Soc. Virology, Am. Assn. Cancer Rsch. Office: Duke U Med Ctr Howard Hughes Med Inst Dept Genetics Box 3054 Durham NC 27710-0001

**NEVINS, LYN (CAROLYN A. NEVINS),** school disciplinarian; b. Chelsea, Mass., June 9, 1948; d. Samuel Joseph and Stella Theresa (Maronski) N.; m. John Edward Herbert, Jr., May 1, 1979; children: Chrissy, Johnny. BA in Sociology, Edn., U. Mass., 1970; MA in Women's Studies, George Washington U., 1975. Cert. tchr., trainer. Tchr. social studies Greenwich (Conn.) Pub. Schs., 1970-74; rschr. career/vocat. edn. Conn. State Dept. Edn., Hartford, 1975-76; rschr., career/vocat. edn. Area Coop. Edn. Svcs., Hamden, Conn., 1976-77; program mgr., trainer career edn. and gender equity Coop. Ednl. Svcs., Norwalk, Conn., 1977-83, trainer, mgr., devel., Beginning Educator Support and Tng. program Trumbull, Conn., 1987—; state coord. career edn. Conn. State Dept. Edn., Hartford, 1982-83; supr. Sacred Heart U., Fairfield, 1992—. Bias com. Conn. State Dept. Edn., Hartford, 1981—; vision com. Middlesex Mid. Sch., Darien, Conn., 1993-95; ednl. quality and diversity com. Town of Darien, 1993-95; cons., trainer career devel./pre-retirement planning Cohen and Assocs., Fairfield, 1981—, Farren Assocs., Annandale, Va., 1992—, Tracey Robert Assocs., Fairfield, 1994—; freelance cons., trainer, Darien, 1983-87; presenter Nat. Conf. GE, 1980, Career Edn., 1983, Am. Edn. Rsch. Assn., 1991, Nat. Conf. New Tchr. Induction, 2006; mem. statewide B.E.S.T. adv.com., 2006; lectr. in field. Tennis coach Spl. Olympics, 1993—, Darien (Conn.) Girls' Softball League, 1992-96, tennis coach. Spl. Olympics Summer Games, 1997—; tennis coach Unified Ptnr. Spl. Olympics Nat. Games, 2005-06; tennis coach, Conn. delegation Nat. Games for Spl. Olympics, 2005—06; bldg. com. Darien HS, 1999—. Mem. NOW (founder, state coord. edn. 1972-74), ASCD. Avocations: tennis, running, walking, golf, travel. Home: 4 Hollister Ln Darien CT 06820-5404 Office: Coop Ednl Svcs 40 Lindeman Drive Trumbull CT 06611-4723 Business E-mail: nevinsl@ces.k12.ct.us.

**NEVINS, PATRICK FREDRICK,** librarian; b. Oak Park, Ill., Jan. 21, 1950; s. George Howard and Mary Jane Nevins; m. Barbara Ann Borowski, July 30, 1977; children: Kimberly J., Timothy P. BA, U. Ill., Chgo., 1972; MA in Libr. Sci., Rosary Coll., Fremont, Calif., 1976. Libr. student asst. U. Ill., Chgo., 1969-72, math. libr. supr., 1972-76; libr. tech. asst. Northeastern Ill. U., Chgo., 1972; head libr. Markham Pub. Libr., Ill., 1976-78, Grande Prairie Pub. Libr., Hazel Crest, Ill., 1978-79, Richton Park Pub. Libr., Ill., 1980—. Adv. com. rep. Suburban Libr. Svcs., Burr Ridge, Ill., 1984-84, 97-99; bldg. cons. Homewood (Ill.) Pub. Libr., 1997; rep. Swan Coun., 2003—. Leisure svcs. com. mem. Homewood-Flossmoor (Ill.) Pk. Dist., 1989-92, 93-96, pk. commr., 1997—, v.p., 1999-2002, pres., 2002—; softball and baseball coach Homewood (Ill.) Baseball, 1990-97; vol. Cancer Support Ctr., Homewood, 1997—, bd. mem., 2001-2003. cmty. vol., 2003—. Recipient Cmty. Svc. award Ill. Assn. Pk. Dists. and Ill. Pk. and Recreation Assn., 1993, 2004, Thomas R. Jones Humanitarian award, 2005. Mem. ALA, Ill. Libr. Assn. Ill. Assn. Pk. Dists. Avocations: reading, basketball, storytelling. Home: 1343 18/th St Homewood IL 60430-3831 Office: Richton Pk Pub Libr Dist 4045 Sauk Trl Richton Park IL 60471-1239 Office Phone: 708-481-5333.

**NEVINS, SHEILA,** television producer; b. NYC; d. Benjamin and Stella Nevins; m. Sidney Koch, 1972; 1 child, David Andrew. BA, Barnard Coll.; MFA, Yale U. TV prodr. Great Am. Dream Machine, NET, 1971-73, The Reasoner Report, ABC, 1973, Feeling Good, Children's TV Workshop, 1975-76, Who's Who, CBS, 1977-78; dir. documentary and family programming HBO, N.Y.C., 1978-82; v.p. documentary programming Home Box Office, N.Y.C., 1986-95, sr. v.p. original programming 1998-99; exec. v.p. original programming HBO, N.Y.C., 1999—2003, pres. documentary and family, 2004—. Bd. dirs. Film Forum, Creative Capital, Ind. Feature Project. Bd. dirs. Women's Action Alliance. Named Woman of Achievement YMCA, 1991, Top 25 Women in TV, Emmy mag., 1996, Top 25 Smartest Women Am., Mirabella Mag., 1999; named one of Top 50 Women in TV, Hollywood Reporter Mag., 2005; named to Broadcasting and Cable Hall of Fame, 2000; recipient Peabody award, 1986, 1992, 1995, 1996, 1997, 1999, 2000, 2003, 2004, Glaad Media award, 1989, Acad. Award for Documentary, 1993, 1996, 1998, 1999, 2000, 2001, 2003, Emmy award, 1994, 1995, 1996, 1997, 1998, 1999, 2000, 2002, 2003, 2004, Media award Mental Health Assn. N.Y.C., 1996, Personal Peabody award, 1999, NATAS Silver Cir., 2000, Wellness Cmty. award, 2001, Humanitarian award, Nat. Bd. Rev., 2002, Lucy award, Women in Film, 2003, Three Arts award. Mem.: Internat. Documentary Assn. (Vision award 1998), N.Y. Women in Film (Muse award 1998), Writers Guild Am.*

**NEVINS, WILLIAM J.,** oil and gas brokerage executive, consultant; b. Yonkers, N.Y., Sept. 10, 1952; s. Francis Robert and Alice Frances (Stäger) N.; m. Joan Evelyn Leach, June 8, 1975 (div. June, 1980). BA in English Lit. and Fin., U. Miami, Coral Gables, Fla., 1974; postgrad. studies in Law, Western State U., Fullerton, Calif. 1974-75. CEO Nevins Enterprises Ltd., various cities, U.S., 1976—; CEO, pres. Century 21, Heritage Realty, Inc., North Miami, Fla., 1985-87; N&Z Heritage Realty, Inc. Miami, 1987-96; sr. assoc., registered rep. Texakoma Fin. Oil and Gas, 1996-98; oil and gas broker Western Am. Securities, Reef Exploration, Inc., 1998—2001, v.p., 1998-2001, sr. v.p., 2001—, Geo Cos. of N.A. Inc., 2002—; oil and gas broker, sr. v.p. GeoSecurities Inc., 2002—, Geo Natural Resources, Inc.,

2002—; sr. v.p. Geo Cos. of N.Am., Inc., 2002—03, Prolific Energy, LLC, 2003; exec. dir. Am. Landmark Securities, Inc./ Prodigy Oil & Gas, LLC, 2004—. V.p., bd. dirs. Pyramid Fin. Svcs., Inc., North Miami Beach, Fla., 1982; cons. Park West Overtown Devel. Com., Miami, 1984—85, Miami Beach Developers and Investors Conf., 1985—90; exec. dir. Plummer Securities, Inc., 2006—, Chatant Petroleum, Inc. 2006—. Author: Oil Patch and Oilmen, 2004. Vol. asst. mgr. John V. Lindsay Miami Dem. Primary Campaign, 1972; founder Universal Children's Found. Inc., 1995. Mem. Nat. Assn. Security Dealers (registered rep.), Security Investment Protection Corp. Orgn., Nu Beta Epsilon. Roman Catholic. Avocations: game fishing, antique autos, coin collecting/numismatics, travel, yachting. Office: Nevins Enterprises Ltd 13237 Montfort Dr Ste 438 Dallas TX 75240-1117 Office Phone: 305-453-9260. Personal E-mail: wjnevins@yahoo.com.

**NEVITT, GABRIELLE A.,** zoologist, educator, ecologist; d. Peter K. and Marjorie A. Nevitt. PhD in Zoology, U. Wash., Seattle, 1990. Prof. U. Calif., Davis, 1995—. Achievements include research in sensory ecology. Office Phone: 530-756-6355. E-mail: ganevitt@ucdavis.edu.

**NEVIUS, CYNTHIA NELL,** artist, educator; d. Gerald Marsily and Nellie Agnes Nevius; children: Kristen Jennifer Lum, Stacy Tiana Lum. BA, Calif. State U., San Jose, 1966; MFA, Colo. State U., 1983. Tchg. Credential U. Nev., Reno, 1970. Art instr. Santa Fe C.C., 1985—88, U. Calif. ext., San Diego, 1991—2004, Bishop's Sch., La Jolla, Calif., 1994—2005, Balboa City Sch., San Diego, 2005—. Scenic artist Santa Fe Opera, 1983; bd. dirs. Artist's Gallery, Santa Fe, 1989; dir. Athenaeum - Painting trip to France, La Jolla, 1998. Painting, Primary Recovery (Selected for publ. in The Davis Visuals, vol. on Light, 1991), Life and Love (art selected for publ. in Bo Tree Calendars, In Praise of Women Artists, 1989), Duality I (selected for the permanent mus. collection, Colo. State U., 1983), one-woman shows include Lyceum, San Diego, Gallery Above, Art Union, exhibited in group shows at Art Inst. Calif., San Diego Hospice, Small Works, Atheneaum. Vol. A Reason to Survive, San Diego, 2005; art instr. Elder Hostel, Durango, Colo., 1981; vol. Philippines U.S. Peace Corps, Washington, 1967—69. Recipient Best of Show, 18th Ann. Art Exhbn., 1978, Award Excellence, Ann. Juried Art Assn. Show, 1979. Mem.: San Diego Mus. Art, Young Audiences (bd. dirs., artists rep. 1990—92, artist-in-residence 1990), San Diego Art Inst., Nat. Mus. Women Artists. Mem. Self Realization Fellowship. Achievements include Chosen for interview in The Publication, San Diego Arts Magazine; Published in changing Women Magazine, winter, 1988. Avocations: horticulture, bicycling, theater, pottery, travel. Home: 3312 Vancouver Avenue San Diego CA 92104 Personal E-mail: thia3@cox.net.

**NEW, MARIA IANDOLO,** pediatrician, educator; b. N.Y.C. d. Loris J. and Esther B. (Giglio) Iandolo; m. Bertrand L. New, 1949 (dec. 1990); children: Erica, Daniel, Antonia. BA, Cornell U., 1950; MD, U. Pa., 1954; degree in medicine (hon.), U. degli Studi di Roma, Rome, 1999, U. di Parma, Italy, 2000. Diplomate Am. Bd. Pediat. Med. intern Bellevue Hosp., N.Y.C., 1954-55; resident in pediat. N.Y. Hosp., 1955-57; fellow NIH, 1957-58, 61-64; practice medicine specializing in pediat. N.Y.C., 1955—; mem. staff N.Y. Hosp., dir. Pediatric Endocrine and Metabolism Clinic, 1964—2004, attending pediatrician, 1971-80; pediatrician-in-chief N.Y.-Presbyn. Hosp., 1980—2002, dir. pediatric endocrinology, 1998—2002; prof. pediat. Mt. Sinai Sch. Medicine, N.Y.C. Asst. prof. dept. pediat. Joan and Sanford Weill Med. Coll. of Cornell U., N.Y.C., 1963-68, assoc. prof., 1968-71, prof., 1971-2004, Harold and Percy Uris prof. pediatric endocrinology, 1978-2004, prof., 1980-2004, chmn. dept. pediat., 1980-2002; program dir. Childrens Clin. Rsch. Ctr., 1996-2002; assoc. dir. Pediatric Clin. Rsch. Ctr., 1980-88; adj. faculty prof. Rockefeller U., 1981—; career scientist N.Y.C. Health Rsch. Coun., 1966-75; adj. attending pediatrician dept. pediat. Meml. Sloan-Kettering Cancer Ctr., 1979-93; cons. United Hosp., Port Chester, N.Y., 1977—, North Shore Univ. Hosp., 1982-97, dept. pediat. Cath. Med. Ctr. Bklyn. and Queens, N.Y., 1987—; vis. physician Rockefeller U. Hosp., N.Y.C., 1973-87; mem. endocrine study sect. NIH, 1977-80, Gen. Clin. Rsch. Ctrs. Adv. Com.; chmn. Divsn. Rsch. Resources Gen. Clin. Rsch. Ctrs. Com. NIH, 1987-88; bd. dirs. Robert Wood Johnson Clin. Scholars Program; mem. N.Y. State Gov.'s Task Force on Life and Law, 1985—; mem. NIH Reviewers Res.; mem. FDA endocrinology and metabolism drug adv. com., 1994—; panelist ACGME bd. appeals, 1994—; cons. Meml. Sloan-Kettering Cancer Ctr., 1993—, Meml. Hosp. for the Cancer and Allied Diseases, 1993—; hon. mem. pediat. dept. Blythedale Children's Hosp., Valhalla, N.Y., 1992—; mem. rsch. adv. com. Population Coun. Ctr. for Biomed. Rsch., 1991-97. Editor-in-chief Jour. Clin. Endocrinology and Metabolism, 1994-99; mem. editl. adv. coun. Jour. Endocrinological Investigation, 1995—; mem. editl. bd. Jour. Women's Health, 1993, Endotext; com. editor Jour. Steroid Biochemistry, 1985; mem. adv. bd. pediatric anns., assoc. editor Metabolism. Trustee Irma T. Hirschl Trust. Recipient Mary Jane Kugel award Juvenile Diabetes Found., 1977, Katharine D. McCormick Disting. Lectureship, 1981, Robert H. Williams Disting. Leadership award, 1988, Albion O. Bernstein award Med. Soc. State N.Y., 1988, medal N.Y. Acad. Medicine, 1991, Disting. Grad. award U. Pa. Sch. Medicine, 1991, Optimate Recognition award Assn. Student-Profl. Italian-Ams., 1991, Outstanding Woman Scientist award N.Y. chpt. Am. Women in Sci., 1986, Maurice R. Greenberg Disting. Svc. award, 1994, Humanitarian award Juvenile Diabetes Found., 1994, Rhône Poulenc Rorer Clin. Investigator Lecture award, 1994, Dale medal Brit. Endocrine Soc., 1996, MERIT award USPHS, NIHCHD, 1998, 11th Ann. award for excellence in clin. rsch. USPHS, NIH, 1998; grantee; named to Hall of Honor, NICHD, 2003. Fellow AAAS, Italian Soc. Endocrinology (hon.); mem. NAS (sr. mem. Inst. Medicine), AAAS, APHA, Am. Soc. Human Genetics, Am. Acad. Pediat., Soc. for Pediatric Rsch., Harvey Soc., Endocrine Soc. (mem. coun. 1981-84, pres. 1991-92, Fred Conrad Koch award 2003), Lawson Wilkins Pediatric Endocrine Soc. (pres. 1985-86), Am. Soc. Nephrology, Am. Soc. Pediatric Nephrology, Am. Fedn. Clin. Rsch., Am. Diabetes Assn., European Soc. Pediatric Endocrinology, Soc. for the Advancement of Women's Health Rsch. (basic sci. award 1996), Am. Coll. Clin. Pharmacology, Am. Clin. and Climatol. Assn., N.Y. Acad. Scis., Pan Am. Med. Assn., Assn. Am. Physicians, Am. Fertility Soc., U.S. Pharmacological Conv. (elected), Am. Acad. of Arts and Scis. (elected 1992), Alpha Omega Alpha. Office: Mt Sinai Sch Medicine Box 1198 1 Gustav L Levy Pl New York NY 10029 Office Phone: 212-241-7847. E-mail: maria.new@mssm.edu.

**NEW, ROSETTA HOLBROCK,** retired secondary school educator, retired department chairman, retired nutrition consultant; b. Aug. 26, 1921; d. Edward F. and Mabel (Kohler) Holbrock; m. John Lorton New, Sept. 3, 1943; 1 child, John Lorton Jr. BS, Miami U., Oxford, Ohio, 1943; MA, U. No. Colo., 1971; PhD, Ohio State U., 1974; student, Kantcentrum, Brugge, Belgium, 1992, Lesage Sch. Embroidery, Paris, 1995, Kent State U., 1998. Cert. tchr. Colo. Tchr. English and sci. Monahans (Tex.) H.S., 1943—44; emergency war food asst. USDA, College Station, Tex., 1945—46; dept. chmn. home econs., adult edn. Hamilton (Ohio) Pub. Schs., 1946—47; tchr., dept. chmn. home econs. East H.S., Denver, 1948—59, Thomas Jefferson H.S., Denver, 1959—83; ret., 1983. Exec. bd. Denver Pub. Schs.; lectr. in field; exec. dir. Ctr. Nutrition Info. U.S. Office Edn. Grantee, Ohio State U., 1971—73. Mem.: Internat. Platform Assn., Fairfield (Ohio) Hist. Soc., Ohio State Home Econs. Alumni Assn., Ohio State U. Assn., Hamilton Hist. Soc., Am. Vocat. Assn., Am. Home Econs. Assn., Nat. Trust for Hist. Preservation, Cin. Art Mus., Internat. Old Lacers, Embroiders Guild Am., Rep. Club Denver, Order White Shrine of Jerusalem, Daus. of the Nile, Masons, Order of Ea. Star, Phi Upsilon Omicron. Presbyterian. Office Phone: 513-863-2252.

**NEWBAUER, JOHN ARTHUR, JR.,** editor; b. Newport, R.I., Apr. 24, 1928; s. John Arthur and Theo Caroline (Trewhella) N.; m. Marilyn Mahler, Oct. 14, 1956; children: April, Dana, Miranda. BA, U. Calif., Berkeley, 1951. Sr. editor and writer sci. and engring., rocket devel. dept. U.S. Naval Ordnance Test Sta., China Lake, Calif., 1951-56; editor in chief Astronautics and Aeronautics jour., N.Y.C., 1963-83; adminstr. sci. publs. AIAA, 1983-91, cons. editor, 1991—; editor in chief Aerospace Am., 1983-87, aquisitions editor, 1987-89. Fellow AIAA (assoc.), Brit. Interplanetary Soc. Office Phone: 718-768-7697.

**NEWBERG, ESTHER,** literary agent; d. Marion Newberg. MA, Wheaton Coll., Norton, Mass., 1963, degree, 2003. Worked with Gov. Ella Grasso, Conn., Robert F. Kennedy, Bella Abzug, Morris Udall Presdl. Campaign, 1976; joined Internat. Creative Mgmt., N.Y.C., 1976, v.p., co-dir. lit. dept., 1988, sr. v.p.; co-dir. lit. dept. Recipient Matrix Award, N.Y. Women in Comm., 1997. Office: Internat Creative Mgmt 40 W 57th St New York NY 10019 E-mail: enewberg@icmtalent.com.*

**NEWBERN, WILLIAM DAVID,** retired state supreme court justice; b. Oklahoma City, May 28, 1937; s. Charles Banks and Mary Frances (Harding) N.; m. Barbara Lee Rigsby, Aug. 19, 1961 (div. 1968); 1 child, Laura Harding; m. Carolyn Lewis, July 30, 1970; 1 child, Alistair Elizabeth. BA, U. Ark., 1959, JD, 1961; LL.M., George Washington U., 1963; MA, Tufts U., 1967. Bar: Ark. 1961, U.S. Dist. Ct. (we. dist.) Ark. 1961, U.S. Supreme Ct. 1968, U.S. Ct. Appeals (8th cir.) 1983. Commd. 1st lt. advanced to maj. U.S. Army JAGC, 1961-70; Prof. law U. Ark., Fayetteville, 1970-84; adminstr. Ozark Folk Ctr., Mountain View, Ark., 1973; judge Ark. Ct. Appeals, Little Rock, 1979-80; assoc. justice Ark. Supreme Ct., Little Rock, 1985-99. Mem. faculty sr. appellate judges seminar NYU, 1987-91; panel chmn. com. on profl. conduct Ark. Supreme Ct., 2001—05. Editor Ark. Law Rev., 1961; author: Arkansas Civil Practice and Procedure, 1985, (with John J. Watkins) 4th edit., 200. Mem. Fayetteville Bd. Adjustment, 1972-79; bd. dirs. Decision Point, Inc., Springdale, Ark., 1980-85, Hot Springs Music Festival, 2000—03; bd. dirs. Little Rock Wind Symphony, 1993-2001, pres. 1993-95. Fellow Ark. Bar Found.; mem. Ark. Bar Assn., Am. Judicature Soc. (bd. dirs. 1985-89), Inst. Jud. Adminstrn., Ark. IOLTA Found. (bd. dirs. 1985-87). Democrat. Avocations: string band-guitar, mandolin, banjo and brass quintet-tuba. Personal E-mail: dnewbern@aristotle.net.

**NEWBERRY, CONRAD FLOYDE,** aerospace engineering educator; b. Neodesha, Kans., Nov. 10, 1931; s. Ragan McGregor and Audra Anitia (Newmaster) N.; m. Sarah Louise Thonn, Jan. 26, 1958; children: Conrad Floyde Jr., Thomas Edwin, Susan Louise. AA, Independence Jr. Coll., 1951; BEME with aero. sequence, U. So. Calif., 1957; MSME, Calif. State U., LA, 1971, MA in Edn., 1974; D.Environ. Sci. and Engring., UCLA, 1985. Registered profl. engr., Calif., Kans., NC, Tex.; chartered engr., UK. Mathematician LA divsn. N.Am. Aviation Inc., 1951-53, jr. engr., 1953-54, engr., 1954-57, sr. engr., 1957-64; asst. prof. aerospace engring. Calif. State Poly. U., Pomona, 1964-70, assoc. prof. aerospace engring., 1970-75, prof. aerospace engring., 1975-90, prof. emeritus, 1990—; staff engr. EPA, 1980-82; engring. specialist space transp. systems div. Rockwell. Internat. Corp., 1984-90; prof. aeronautics and astronautics Naval Postgrad. Sch., Monterey, Calif., 1990—2002, prof. emeritus, 2002—, acad. assoc. space systems engring., 1992-94. Recipient John Leland Atwood award as outstanding aerospace engring. educator AIAA/Am. Soc. Engring. Edn., 1986, Fred Merryfield Design award ASEE, 1997. Fellow: AIAA (dep. dir. edn. region VI 1976—79, dep. dir. career enhancement 1982—91, chmn. L.A. sect. 1989—90, chmn. Point Lobos sect. 1990—91, chmn. acad. affairs com. 1990—93, dir.tech. aircraft sys. 1990—93, chmn. Point Lobos sect. 1999—2001); mem.: IEEE, ASME, AAAS, NSPE, Am. Soc. Naval Engrs., Calif. Water Pollution Control Assn., Assn. Unmanned Vehicle Sys. Internat., Soc. Allied Weight Engrs., Soc. Automotive Engr., Water Environ. Fedn., Exptl. Aircraft Assn., Inst. Environ. Scis., Air and Waste Mgmt. Assn., Soc. Naval Architects and Marine Engrs., Am. Helicopter Soc., U.S. Naval Inst., Am. Meteorol. Soc., Am. Soc. Engring. Edn. (divsn. exec. com. 1976—80, chmn. aerospace divsn. 1979—80, exec. com. ocean, marine engring. divsn. 1982—85, exec. com. 1989—94, exec. com. ocean, marine engring. divsn. 1990—97, program chmn. 1991—93, chmn. 1993—95, chmn. Profl Interest Coun. 1995—97, bd. dirs. 1995—97, trustee 1999—2002), Am. Acad. Environ. Engrs. (cert. air pollution control engr.), Calif. Soc. Profl. Engrs., Royal Aero. Soc., Inst. Advancement Engring., Brit. Interplanetary Soc., Planetary Soc., SID, Kappa Delta Pi, Sigma Gamma Tau, Tau Beta Pi. Democrat. Achievements include research on aircraft, spacecraft, missiles, and engine design, waveriders, aircrew centered system design and related impacts on exergy, quality, concurrent engineering, cost and environmental controls. Home: 9463 Willow Oak Rd Salinas CA 93907-1037 Personal E-mail: cfnacmdesign@msn.com.

**NEWBERRY, DANIEL M.,** elementary school educator; b. Augusta, Ga., Dec. 23, 1958; m. Karen Kruck, June 25, 1988; 1 child, Jordan Alice. AA, Abraham Baldwin Coll., Tifton, Ga., 1978; BMEd, Troy State U., Ala., 1981; MMEd, Valdosta State Coll., Ga., 1988. Band dir. Washington-Wilkes Mid. Sch., Washington, 1982—85; grad. asst. dir. Valdosta State Coll., Ga., 1986—88; band dir. Charlie A. Gray Mid. Sch., Moultrie, Ga., 1988—. Mem.: Ga. Music Educators Assn., Music Educators Nat. Conf. Home: 1730 Gatewood Cir Moultrie GA 31768 Office: Charlie A Gray Mid Sch 812 11th Ave NW Moultrie GA 31768 Office Phone: 229-890-6189.

**NEWBERRY, EDWARD J.,** lawyer; b. Schenectady, NY, Sept. 25, 1962; BA, BS, George Mason Univ., 1984; JD, Georgetown Univ., 1989. Former staff mem. U.S. Rep. Frank Wolf, Washington, U.S. Ho. Rep. Appropriations Com., Washington, 1984—91; ptnr., Public Policy, Mcpl. Representation, mem. exec. com. Patton Boggs LLP, Washington, 1991—. Office: Patton Boggs LLP 2550 M St NW Washington DC 20037-1350 Office Phone: 202-457-5285. Office Fax: 202-457-6315. Business E-mail: enewberry@pattonboggs.com.

**NEWBERRY, STEPHEN G.,** semiconductor equipment company executive; BS, USNA, Annapolis, 1975; MBA, Harvard Univ. Mgmt. positions through group v.p. global ops. & planning Applied Materials Inc., 1980—97; exec. v.p., COO Lam Rsch. Corp., Fremont, Calif., 1997—98, pres., COO, 1998—2005, pres., CEO, 2005—. Bd. dir. Nextest Systems Corp., Semiconductor Equip. & Materials Internat. Office: Lam Rsch Corp 4650 Cushing Pkwy Fremont CA 94538*

**NEWBOLD, JOHN LOWE,** retired banker, financial consultant; b. Washington, Dec. 26, 1935; s. John Lowe and Katharine Emily (Wilkins) N.; m. Judith Allen Bourne, June 20, 1959; children: Jennifer Hathaway, Timothy Bourne, Michael Fleming. BS, Yale U., 1957; MBA, NYU, 1963; sr. execs. program cert., MIT, 1970. Asst. v.p., credit instr. Citibank, N.A., N.Y.C., 1968-69, v.p. retail trade unit, 1969-70, v.p. info. svcs. dept., 1970-72, v.p., corp. bank head Tokyo, 1972-73, v.p., country head Singapore, 1974-76, sr. v.p., shipping dept. head N.Y.C., 1976-85, divsn. exec., Global Shipping Divsn., 1985—97, divsn. exec., Global Transp. Divsn., 1989—93; ret., 1997; chmn., dir. Mchts. Fund, Inc., Bethesda, Md., 1981—2003. Bd. dirs. Castalia Ptnrs. Ltd. Trustee Reeves Reed Arboretum, Summit, N.J., 1999-2002, Summit Area Cmty. Coun., 1983-86, United Way, Summit, 1984-92; pres. PTA Presidents' Coun., Summit, 1981-83; pres., dir. One Fifth Ave. Apt. Corp., 2001-06, Friends of Chilmark Libr., Mass., 2003-06, vice-chmn., 2003—; mem. vestry Grace Ch., N.Y.C., 2006—; v.p. Abel's Hill Assn., Chilmark, Mass., 2006—. Served as lt. (j.g.) USNR, 1957-63. Mem. Yale Club of Ctrl. N.J. (trustee 1980-85), Abel's Hill Assn. (v.p. 2006—). Home: 1 Fifth Ave 11J New York NY 10003 Office Phone: 212-674-5881. Personal E-mail: jocknewb@aol.com.

**NEWBORG, GERALD GORDON,** state archives administrator; b. Ada, Minn., Dec. 13, 1942; s. George Harold and Olea (Halstad) N.; m. Jean Annette Gruhl, Aug. 14, 1964; children: Erica, Annette. BA, Concordia Coll., Moorhead, Minn., 1964; MA, U. N.D., 1969; MBA, Ohio State U., 1978. Cert. archivist. Tutor, preceptor Parsons Coll., Fairfield, Iowa, 1964-67; state archivist Ohio Hist. Soc., Columbus, 1968-76; v.p. Archival Systems Inc., Columbus, 1978-81; state archivist State Hist. Soc. of N.D., Bismarck, 1981—. Instr. Franklin U., Columbus, 1974; adj. prof. Bismarck State Coll., 1985-86. Co-author: North Dakota: A Pictorial History, 1988. Recipient Resolution of Commendation Ohio Ho. of Reps., Columbus, 1976. Mem. Soc. Am. Archivists, Nat. Assn. Govt. Archives & Records Adminstrs. (bd. dirs. 1984-86, sec. 1994-99), Midwest Archives Conf., N.D. Libr. Assn. (exec. bd. 1985-86). Home: 1327 N 18th St Bismarck ND 58501-2827 Office: State Hist Soc 612 E Boulevard Ave Bismarck ND 58505-0660

**NEWBORN, JUD,** anthropologist, writer, curator, educator, historian; b. NYC, Nov. 8, 1952; s. Solomon and Rita Newborn. BA magna cum laude in Anthropology and English, NYU, 1974; postgrad., Clare Hall, Cambridge U., 1974-75; MA in Anthropology, U. Chgo., 1977, PhD with distinction, 1994. Free-lance writer, N.Y.C., Munich, Chgo., 1974—; publicist Oxford U. Press, N.Y.C., 1975-76; founding historian, co-creator Mus. Jewish Heritage (N.Y. Holocaust Meml. Commn.), N.Y.C., 1986-92, 96-00. Spl. cons. Cinema Arts Ctr., 1986—2005; cons., spkr., lectr. in field; cons. Holocaust Resource Ctr. CUNY, Queensborough; dir. devel., spl. projects curator Cinema Arts Centre, LI, 2005—. Author: Shattering the German Night: The Story of the White Rose Anti-Nazi Resistance, 1986, Herder Verlag, 2002, Sophie Scholl and the White Rose, 2006; contbg. editor Diplomatic World Obs., UN, 1999-00; freelance writer, lyricist. Fulbright fellow, 1980-82; Newcombe fellow, 1984-85. Mem. ASCAP, Am. Anthrop. Assn., Am. Hist. Assn., Authors Guild, Assn. Holocaust Orgns., N.Y. Old Growth Forest Assn. (bd. mem.), Nat. Lesbian and Gay Journalists Assn., Nat. Writers Union, Phi Beta Kappa.

**NEWBRANDER, WILLIAM CARL,** health economist, management consultant; b. Irumagawa, Japan, Sept. 14, 1951; parents Am. citizens; s. Virgil Ray and Ella Jeannette (Rae) N.; m. Nancy Sharon Wilson, June 15, 1974; children: Sharon, Billy, Andrew, Jonathan, Daniel. BA, Wheaton Coll., 1973, M of Hosp. Adminstrn., 1975; M of Applied Econs., U. Mich., 1981, PhD, 1983. Tchg./rsch. asst. U. Mich., Ann Arbor, 1979—83; mgmt. specialist VA-HSR&D, Ann Arbor, 1980—83; hosp. adminstr. Whittaker Corp., Tabuk, Saudi Arabia, 1983—85; health economist WHO, Geneva, 1985—92; dir. health financing program Mgmt. Scis. for Health, Cambridge, Mass., 1992—. Author: Health Policy and Planning, 1988, 89, 90, 91, 94, Health Planning and Mgmt., 1988, 90, 91, 96, Decentralization in a Developing Country, 1991, Hospital Economics and Financing in Developing Countries, 1992, World Health Forum, 1994,Modelling in Health Care Finance: A Compendium of Quantitative Techniques for Health Care Financing, 1999, Private Health Sector Growth in Asia: Issues and Implications, 1997, Extending Access to Health Care Through Public-Private Partnerships: The PROSALUD Experience, 2000, Ensuring Equal Access to Health Services: User Fee Systems and the Poor, 2001. Eagle Scout advisor, scout troop com. chmn. Boy Scouts Am., Geneva and Hopkinton, Mass., 1990-2004; mgr. Little League baseball team, Geneva and Hopkinton, 1990-2000; elder First Congl. Ch., Hopkinton, 1995-99; chmn. bd. dirs. Pioneers, U.S., Orlando, Fla., 1997-2000. Capt. U.S. Army, 1975-79. VA Rsch. fellow, 1981-83. Fellow Am. Coll. Healthcare Execs. Home: 33 Valleywood Rd Hopkinton MA 01748-1634 Office Phone: 617-250-9500. E-mail: wnewbrander@yahoo.com.

**NEWBRUN, ERNEST,** oral biology and periodontology educator; b. Vienna, Dec. 1, 1932; came to U.S., 1955; s. Victor and Elizabeth (Reichl) N; m. Eva Miriam, June 17, 1956; children: Deborah Anne, Daniel Eric, Karen Ruth. BDS, U. Sydney (New South Wales), 1954; MS, U. Rochester, 1957; DMD, U. Ala., 1959; PhD, U. Calif., San Francisco, 1965; Odont. Dr. (hon.), U. Lund, Sweden, 1988; DDSc (hon.), U. Sydney, 1997. Cert. periodontology, 1983. Rsch. assoc. Eastman Dental Ctr., Rochester, NY, 1955-57, U. Ala. Med. Ctr., Birmingham, 1957-59; rsch. fellow Inst. Dental Rsch., Sydney, Australia, 1960-61; rsch. tchr. trainee U. Calif., San Francisco, 1961-63, postdoctoral fellow, 1963-65, assoc. prof., 1965-70, prof. oral biology, 1970-83, prof. oral biology and periodontology, 1983-94, prof. emeritus, 1994—. Cons. FDA, 1983—. Author: Cariology, 1989, Pharmacology and Therapeutic Dentistry, 1989, (with others) Pediatrics, 1991; editor: Fluorides and Dental Caries, 1986; mem. editl. bd. Jour. Periodontal Rsch., 1985-90, Jour. Periodontology, 1990-2005. Bd. dirs. Raoul Wallenberg Dem. Club, San Francisco, 1987-92. Fellow AAAS (chmn. dental section, 1988-89), Internat. Assn. Dental Rsch. (pres. 1989-90). Jewish. Avocations: gardening, hiking, skiing, opera, theater. Office Phone: 415-476-1004. Business E-Mail: ernest.newbrun@ucsf.edu.

**NEWBURGER, BETH WEINSTEIN,** communications executive; b. Schenectady, July 8, 1937; d. H. Edward and Shirley (Diamond) Weinstein; m. Alan C. Newburger, Jan. 23, 1963 (dec. Oct. 1980); children: Mark, Lori, Eric, Jill; m. Richard Schwartz, May 26, 1989. BA, Cornell U., 1959. Dir. advt. New Republic, Washington, 1974-77; mktg. mgr. Washington Post, 1977-84; pres. Owlcat/Digital Rsch., Inc., Monterey, Calif., 1984-86; pres., CEO Corabi Internat. Telemetrics, Inc., Alexandria, Va., 1986-95; assoc. adminstr. Gen. Svcs. Adminstrn., Washington, 1996—2001; dir. comm. Nat. Trust for Hist. Preservation, 2001—04; pres., CEO Epoch Comm. LLC, 2004—. Chmn. bd. Health Street, Inc., Bethesda, Md., 1985—95; mem. NASA adv. coun. Tech. Commercialization Adv. Com., 1995—98; co-chmn. President's Comm. on Celebration of Women in Am. History, 1998—2000; commr., exec. dir. Women's Progress Commemorative Commn., 2000—01; bd. dirs. Nat. Women's History Project, 2000—02; adv. bd. Eleanor Roosevelt Papers, 2000—; bd. dirs. Nat. Women's Hall of Fame, 2001—04; trustee Jewish Women's Archives, 2002—. Chmn. bd. Capital Children's Mus., Washington, 1994—98, trustee, 1984—2005; trustee, exec. com. Nat. Childrens Mus., 2005—; bd. dirs. Arena Stage, Washington, 1993—, BOAT/U.S., 1990—. Named Woman of Yr., Svc. Guild, Washington, 1972, 73. Mem. Women in Advt. and Mktg. (bd. dirs. 1986-89). Home: 1401 N Oak St Arlington VA 22209-3648 Office Phone: 703-351-5276. Business E-Mail: beth@epoch1.net.

**NEWBURGER, HOWARD MARTIN,** psychoanalyst; b. NYC, May 16, 1924; s. Bernhard and Bertha (Travers) N.; m. Doris Schekter, July 3, 1949; children: Amy, Barry, Cary. BA, NYU, 1948, MA, 1950, PhD, 1952; tng. in Jungian, Neo-Freudian and Horneyian psychoanalysis. Cert. in group psychotherapy and psychodrama. Rotating intern N.J. Dept. Instns. and Agys., 1948-49; chief psychologist N.J. State Instn., Annandale, 1949-52; dir. psychoanalysis Div. Social Def. UN, 1952; pvt. practice in psychoanalysis and group psychotherapy, 1952—; dir. rsch. HEW, 1958; rsch. assoc. Beth Israel Hosp., 1958-69. Staff mem. St. Agnes Hosp., White Plains, 1991-93; lectr., adj. assoc. prof. NYU, 1951-60, chmn. dept. exceptional child and youth, 1954-62; chmn. faculty and supr. treatment Inst. Applied Human Dynamics, 1960-99; prelect prof. psychology John Jay Coll. Criminal Justice, 1969-72; chmn. bd. dirs. Inst. Applied Human Dynamics, N.Y.C. and Westchester, N.Y., 1960-81, exec. v.p., 1983-85; dean faculty IAHD, 1999-2002; forensic examiner N.Y.S. Supreme Ct., 2005-; lectr., cons. in field. Co-author: Winners and Losers. Assoc. editor: Excerpta Medica, 1951-62. Contbr. articles and papers to tech. jours. Trustee Acad. Jewish Religion, 1991-96. Served with AUS, World War II, ETO; with AUS, MTO. Recipient Outstanding Service to Humanity award Inst. Applied Human Dynamics for Handicapped, 1970 Mem. Am. Psychol. Assn., Am. Soc. Group Psychotherapy and Psychodrama (sec.-treas. 1954-55). Office: 4 Timber Trl Rye NY 10580-1935 Office Phone: 914-967-4011. *Our country affords tremendous opportunity. Through the development of our inner resources, and their assertion, we can all have happy and effective lives.*

**NEWBURY, KIRSTEN RAE,** computer scientist, educator; b. Inglewood, Calif., July 20, 1946; d. Ray Selmer and Ella Louise (Carter) Newbury. BS, U. Wis., Oshkosh, 1971; MS, U. Colo., 1980; postgrad., Army War Coll., 1987; EdD in Adult and Higher Edn., Mont. State U., 1998, EdD, 1998. Cert. Java Instr., Cisco; flight instr. FAA, project mgmt. profl. 2005. Chief info. sys. Mont. State Dept. Labor and Industry, Helena; dir. personal property and bus. lic. div. County of Fairfax, Va.; analyst officer U.S. Army Pentagon, Washington; battalion commdr. U.S. Army, Frankfurt, Germany, assoc. prof. West Point, NY; adj. tchr. computer tech. Helena Coll. Tech., U. Mont., chmn. computer electronics tech. dept., 2002—03; computer cons. 2004—. Adj. prof. Western Mont. Coll., U. Mont.; del. People-to-People Women Computer Sci. Profls. program, China; coord. 1st statewide program for instrs. new to 2-yr. coll. sys.; faculty practitioner U. Phoenix; faculty fellow for svc. learning Mont. Campus Compact, 1999—2000, mentoring fellow, 2001—03. Del. to China Citizen's Amb. Program, 1993. Lt. col. U.S. Army, 1964—88. Mem.: Women in Mil. Svc. Am., Project Mgmt. Inst., Assn. Computing Machinery. Business E-Mail: krgraham@acm.org.

**NEWBY, EARL FERNANDO,** education educator; b. Louisville, Apr. 14, 1948; BS, Tenn. State U., 1970; MA, U. Louisville, 1972; EdD, Spalding U., 1998; MA, Vanderbilt U., 2002. Cons., tchr. edn. Ky. Dept. Edn., Frankfort, 1970; tchr., prin. Jefferson County Schs., Louisville, 1971-75, Greater Clark County Schs., Jeffersonville, Ind., 1975-98; cons., computer tech. Newby & Assocs., Louisville, 1996—; asst. prof. Morehead (Ky.) State U., 1998—. Adj. prof. Western Ky. U., Bowling Green, 1998; prof. Eastern Ky. U., 1999-2004; assoc. prof. Austin Peay State U., Clarksville, Tenn., 2004-2006; apptd. to serve on many scholastic audit sch. rev. teams, 2002—; presenter So. Regional Coun. Ednl. Adminstrs., 2004, Nat. Coun. Profs. of Ednl. Adminstrs., 2004, Internat. Conf. Profs. of Black Sch. Educators, 2004, Am. Assn. Sch. Adminstrs. Nat. Conf. (presentation and session convener), 2005. Author: Leadership Perspectives, 2004; contbr. articles to profl. publs. Named to Order Ky. Cols. Mem. Am. Assn. Sch. Adminstrs. (presenter cons.), NAESP (presenter ann. internat. conf. San Diego, Calif. 2001), So. Regional Coun. Ednl. Adminstrs., Nat. Coun. Profs. Ednl. Adminstrn. (presenter nat. conf. Houston 2001, Sedona, Ariz. 2003), Nat. Assn. Black Sch. Educators, Ky. Assn. Sch. Adminstrs., Ky. Assn. Black Sch. Educators, Lexington Assn. Black Sch. Educators, Kappa Alpha Psi, Phi Delta Kappa, Pi Lambda Theta (presenter profl. assn. in edn. ann. conf. Mpls. 2001), Sigma Rho Sigma. Democrat. Methodist. Avocations: tennis, basketball, reading, bowling, golf. Home: PO Box 211 Harrods Creek KY 40027-0211 Office: Austin Peay State U Educational Leadership Studies Coll Profl Programs and Social Scis Clarksville TN 37044 Fax: 859-622-1126.

**NEWBY, JOHN ROBERT,** metallurgical engineer; b. Kansas City, Mo., Nov. 17, 1923; s. Merritt Owen and Gladys Mary (McCleery) N.; m. Audry Marie Loniker, Sept. 21, 1963 (div. 1980); children: Deborah A., Walter J., William F., Matthew O., Robert J. BA, U. Mo., Kansas City, 1947; BS in Metall. Engring., Colo. Sch. Mines, 1949; MS, U. Cin., 1963. Cert. profl. engr. Chemist Bar Rusto Plating Corp., Kansas City, 1949; supr. United Chromium, Ferndale, Mich., 1949-52; prin. rsch. metallurgist Armco Inc., Middletown, Ohio, 1952-85; prin. John Newby Cons., Middletown, 1985—; mem. The Edison Materials Tech. Ctr., Dayton, Ohio, 2001—. Cons. Phoenix Cons., Inc., Cin., 1988—. Author, editor: Formability 2000, 1982, Metallic Materials, 1978, Sheet Metal Forming, 1976; editor: Mechanical Testing, Vol. 8, 9th edit., 1985. Scoutmaster Boy Scouts Am., Middletown, 1952-86, now asst. dist. commr.; chmn. Safety Coun., Middletown, 1978-80. Staff sgt. USAF, 1943-46, PTO. Fellow ASTM (chmn. 1963—, chmn. E-28 com. on mech. testing 1998-2002, Award of Merit 1984), ASM (sustaining mem., chpt. chmn. 1970, Award of Merit 1980); mem. SAE (sect. chmn. 1984). Democrat. Achievements include patent for high strength formable steel sheet; development of interstitial free steel, strain analysis process for metallic sheet formability. Home and Office: 100 Marymont Ct Middletown OH 45042-3735

**NEWBY, KELLI,** education educator; b. Toledo, Mar. 17, 1979; d. Ronald and Denise Newby; m. Christopher Lee Thomas. BA in English Comm., Mass. Coll. of Liberal Arts, North Adams, 2001; MA in Theatre Studies, Kent State U., Ohio, 2003; MFA in Fiction, Bennington Coll., Vt., 2005—. Instr. Mass. Coll. of Liberal Arts, North Adams, 2003—. Author: (short story) Mind's Eye. 2006. Office: Mass Coll of Liberal Arts 375 Church St North Adams MA 01247 Office Phone: 413-662-5199. Personal E-mail: kellinewby@yahoo.com. Business E-Mail: k.newby@mcla.edu.

**NEWBY, PAUL MARTIN,** state supreme court justice; b. Asheboro, NC, May 5, 1955; s. Samuel O. and Ruth (Parks) N.; m. Macon Tucker, Apr. 16, 1983. BA in Public Policy studies magna cum laude, Duke U., 1977; JD, U. NC, 1980. Bar: NC 1980, US Dist. Ct. (we. dist.) NC 1981, US Dist. Ct. (mid. dist.) NC 1983, US Dist. Ct. (ea. dist.) NC. 1985, US Ct. Appeals (4th cir.) 1986. Research & teacher asst. U. N.C. Sch. of Law, 1979—80; assoc. Van Winkle, Buck, Wall, Starnes & Davis, Asheville, NC, 1980-84; v.p., gen. counsel Cannon Mills Realty & Devel. Corp., Kannapolis, NC, 1984-85; asst. atty. (ea. dist.) N.C. US Dept. Justice, Raleigh, 1985—2004, chief fin. litigation (ea. dist.) N.C., 1994—99; assoc. justice NC Supreme Ct., 2004—. Chmn. bd. dirs. Pregnancy Life Care Ctr., Raleigh, 1986. Mem. NC Bar Assn., Christian Legal Soc. Avocation: tennis. Office: NC Supreme Ct PO Box 2170 Raleigh NC 27602*

**NEWBY, TIMOTHY JAMES,** education educator, researcher; b. Nampa, Idaho, Oct. 9, 1955; s. Neal Arthur and Margy Lou (Hooker) N.; m. Deedra Diane Hays, May 3, 1978; children: Timbre, Landon, Alexis, Brayden. BS, Brigham Young U., 1979, PhD, 1984. Prof. Purdue U., West Lafayette, Ind. Mem. Am. Edn. Rsch. Assn. Home: 216 Berwick Dr Lafayette IN 47909-6904 Office: Purdue U Curriculum and Instruction BRNG 3138 West Lafayette IN 47907*

**NEWCOM, JENNINGS JAY,** lawyer, director; b. St. Joseph, Mo., Oct. 18, 1941; s. Arden Henderson and Loyal Beatrice (Winans) N.; m. Cherry Ann Phelps, Apr. 4, 1964; children: Shandra Karine, J. Derek Arden. BA, Graceland U., Lamoni, Iowa, 1964; JD, Harvard U.. 1968; LLD (hon.), Graceland U., 1994. Bar: Ill. 1968, Calif. 1973, Mo. 1979, Kans. 1981, Colo. 1999. Atty. McDermott, Will & Emery, Chgo., 1968-73; ptnr. Rifkind, Sterling & Lockwood, Beverly Hills, Calif., 1973-79; Shook, Hardy & Bacon L.L.P., Kansas City, Mo., 1979-99, Davis, Graham & Stubbs, LLP, Denver, 1999—; gen. counsel Lovell Minnick Ptnrs. LLC, LA, 1999—; dir. Skillpath Seminars, Overland Park, Kans.; bd. dirs. Duff & Phelps Holdings LLC, Chgo., Atlantic Asset Mgmt. LLC, Stamford, Conn., Berkeley Capital Mgmt., LLC, San Francisco, ClariVest Asset Mgmt. LLC. Trustee Hubbard Found., Linde Found. Mem. Denver Bar Assn., State Bar Assn. Calif. Office: Davis Graham & Stubbs LLP 1550 17th St Ste 500 Denver CO 80202-1500 Office Phone: 303-892-7318. Business E-Mail: j.newcom@dgslaw.com.

**NEWCOMB, ELDON HENRY,** retired botany educator; b. Columbia, Mo., Jan. 19, 1919; s. Ernest Henry and Ruby Josephine (Anderson) N.; m. Joyce Bright Rieling, June 21, 1949; children— Norman Robert, Barbara Pauline, Cynthia Irma. Student, U. Kansas City, 1936-38; AB, U. Mo., 1940, A.M., 1942; PhD, U. Wis., 1949; DS honoris causa, U. Mo., Columbia, 1993. Asst. prof. botany U. Wis.-Madison, 1949-54, assoc. prof., 1954-58, prof., 1958-90, prof. emeritus, 1990—; dir. Inst. Plant Devel., 1979-88; chmn. dept. botany U. Wis.-Madison, 1982-88, Folke Skoog prof. botany, 1987—. Cons. Shell Devel. Co., 1954-59; mem. expdn. to Great Barrier Reef, 1973. Sr. author: Plants in Perspective, 1963; mng. editor Protoplasma, 1969-73; mem. editorial bd. Ann. Rev. Plant Physiology, 1965-69, Protoplasma, 1973-99, Planta, 1981-90; contbr. articles to profl. jours. Served with AUS, 1942-45. NRC predoctoral fellow U. Wis., 1946-49; Guggenheim Found. fellow U. Calif. at Berkeley, 1951-52; Sci. Faculty fellow Harvard, 1963-64; Fulbright Sr. Research scholar Australian Nat. U., Canberra, 1976 Mem. NAS, Am. Soc. Cell Biologists, Am. Acad. Arts and Scis., Bot. Soc. Am., Am. Soc. Plant Physiologists, Soc. Devel. Biology, Phi Beta Kappa (pres. Wis. Alpha chpt. 1978-79), Sigma Xi. Home: 52 Oak Creek Trl Madison WI 53717-1510 Office Phone: 608-262-1057. Business E-Mail: enewcomb@wisc.edu.

**NEWCOMB, MARTIN EUGENE, JR.,** chemistry professor; b. Mishauaha, Ind., Nov. 17, 1946; s. Martin Eugene and Yolanda Frances (Saliani) N.; 1 child, Jennifer Ruth. BA, Wabash Coll., 1969; PhD in Chemistry, U. Ill., 1973. Asst. prof. Tex. A&M U., College Station, 1973-81, assoc. prof., 1981-85, prof. chemistry, 1985-91, Wayne State U., Detroit, 1991-2001; prof. U. Ill., Chgo., 2001—. Contbr. articles to Accounts of Chem. Rsch., 1988, Jour. Am. Chem. Soc. 1989— Named Dreyfus Tchr.-Scholar, Camille and Henry Dreyfus Found., 1980-85. Mem. AAAS, Am. Chem. Soc.(Arthur C. Cope Scholar award, 1994, James Flack Norris award in Physical Organic Chemistry, 2000). Office: U Ill Chgo Dept Chemistry Chicago IL 60607

**NEWCOMB, ROBERT WAYNE,** electrical engineer educator; b. Glendale, Calif., June 27, 1933; s. Robert Dobson and Dorothy Opal (Bissinger) Newcomb; m. Sarah Eleanor Fritz, May 22, 1954; children: Gail E., Robert W. BSEE, Purdue U., 1955; MS, Stanford U., 1957; PhD, U. Calif., Berkeley, 1960. Registered profl. engr., Calif. Rsch. intern Stanford Rsch. Inst., Menlo

Park, Calif., 1957-60; tchg. assoc. U. Calif., Berkeley, 1957-60; asst. and tenured assoc. prof. Stanford U., 1960—70; prof. elec. engring. U. Md., College Park, 1970—. Bd. dirs. PARCOR Rsch. program, Universidad Politecnica de Madrid, Spain. Author: Linear Multisport Synthesis, 1966, Active Integrated Circuit Synthesis, 1968, Concepts of Linear Systems and Control, 1968, Network Theory, 1967; editor: Neurocomputing Letters, 2002—06. Recipient IEEE CAS Edn. award, 2001; Fulbright fellow, 1963; Fulbright-Hays fellow, 1976; Robert Wayne Newcomb Lab. opened at U. Politecnica Madrid, 1995. Fellow IEEE (life, golden jubilee medal 1999), Am. Inst. Med. and Biol. Engrs.; mem. Soc. Indsl. and Applied Math., Math. Assn. Am., Acad. Am. Poets. Avocations: films, literature, poetry, guitar. Home: 13120 Two Farm Dr Silver Spring MD 20904-3418 Office: U Md Microsystems Lab Elec/Computer Engring College Park MD 20742-0001 Office Phone: 301-405-3662. Business E-Mail: newcomb@eng.umd.edu.

**NEWCOMBE, NORA,** psychology professor; b. in Psychology, Anticoch Coll., Ohio, 1972; PhD in Psychology and Social Relations, Harvard U., 1976. Asst. prof. Dept. Psychology Pa. State U., 1976—81; assoc. prof. Dept. Psychology Temple U., 1981—87, prof., 1987—, dir. undergrad. studies, 1981—86, assoc. chair Dept. Psychology, 1986—89, dir. Cognitive Divsn., 1995—99, James H. Glackin Disting. faculty fellow, 2003—. Vis. scholar U. Pa., 1986—87, 1993—94, Princeton U., 1999—2000; vis. scholar Spatial Cognition Group Wissenschaftsckolleg, Berlin, 2003—04; editor Jour. Exptl. Psychology: Gen., 1996—2001; guest editor spl. issues on early memory Jour. Exptl. Child Psychology, 1993—94; assoc. editor Psychological Bull., 1990—94; cons. editor Child Develop., 1982—96, Developmental Psychology, 1981—87, Jour. Cognition and Develop., 2002—, Psychological Sci., 2004—; reviewer Behavioral and Brain Sciences, Jour. Exptl. Psychology: Learning, Memory, and Cognition, Psychological Rev., Psychonomic Bull. and Rev., Science. Co-editor (with L.S. Liben and A.H. Patterson): (book) Spatial representation and behavior across the life span, 1981; author: Child development: Change over time, 1996; co-author (with J. Huttenlocher): Making space: The development of spatial representation and reasoning, 2000; contbr. articles to profl. journals, chapters to books. Fellow Am. bd. Cornell Inst. Rsch. on Children, 2003—. Recipient Paul W. Eberman Faculty Rsch. award, Temple U., 2004; fellow James McKeen Cattell, 1999—2000. Fellow: Am. Psychological Soc., APA (chair early career award com. 1995, publications and comm. bd. 1998—2000, chair coun. elders 1999—2000, exec. com. divsn. 1 1999—2000, pres. divsn. 7 2001—02, com. scientific awards 2004—06, George A. Miller award 2004), AAAS (sec. sect. psychology 2002—06), Am. Acad. Arts and Sciences; mem.: Soc. Rsch. Child Develop. (program com. 1993—99, co-chair program com. 1995—97), Sigma Xi, Psychonomic Soc. (governing bd. 2002—06), Jean Piaget Soc., Internat. Soc. Study of Behavioral Develop., Internat. Soc. Infant Studies, Cognitive Neuroscience Soc., Cognitive Develop. Soc. (bd. dirs. 2003—). Office: Dept Psychology Temple Univ 1701 N 13th St Rm 565 Philadelphia PA 19122-6085 Office Phone: 215-204-6944. Office Fax: 215-204-8100. E-mail: newcombe@temple.edu.*

**NEWCOMER, JOHN WHITNEY,** psychiatrist, researcher, educator; b. Subic Bay Naval Base, Philippines; s. John L. and Barbara L. Newcomer; m. Barbara L. Freedman, Aug. 4, 2001; children: Leah Eliza, Adam Samuel. AB, Brown U., 1981; postgrad., U. Calif., San Francisco, 1984, Yale U., 1984; MD, Wayne State U., 1985. Diplomate Nat. Bd. Med. Examiners, Am. Bd. Psychiatry and Neurology with added qualification in Geriatric Psychiatry. Intern in internal medicine Sinai Hosp., Detroit, 1985—86; resident in psychiatry Stanford U. Sch. Medicine, Calif., 1986—89, rsch. fellow in psychiatry Dept. Vets. Affairs Med. Ctr. Palo Alto, Calif., 1988—90; instr. dept. psychiatry Washington U. Sch. Medicine, St. Louis, 1990—92, asst. prof. psychiatry, 1992—2000, adj. asst. prof. psychology, 1997—2001, assoc. prof. psychiatry, 2000—, med. dir. Ctr. for Clin. Studies; dir. assoc. med. psychology rsch. Malcolm Bliss Mental Health Ctr., St. Louis, 1990—95. Chmn. drug utilization rev. bd. Mo. Dept. Social Svcs., Divsn. Med. Svc., 1997—; mem. study sect., spl. emphasis panels, ad hoc mem. treatment assessment sect. NIMH, 1998—; rsch. med. safety officer Gen. Clin. Rsch. Ctr., 2001—04; lectr. in field.; rsch. psychiatrist Malcolm Bliss Mental Health Ctr., St. Louis, 1990—95; mem. med. staff Barnes Hosp., St. Louis, 1990—94, Jewish Hosp., St. Louis, 1990—94, Barnes/Jewish Hosps., St. Louis, 1994—; cons. in field. Contbr. numerous articles, abstracts to profl. publs. Recipient Scientist Devel. award, NIMH, 1992—97, Ind. Scientist award, 1997—2002. Mem.: AMA, AAAS, Am. Diabetes Assn., Am. Coll. Psychiatrists, Internat. Soc. Psychoneuroendocrinology, Soc. for Neurosci., Am. Pschopathol. Assn., Ea. Mo. Psychiatric Assn., Am. Psychiat. Assn., Am. Coll. Neuropsychopharmacology, Alpha Omega Alpha, Sigma Xi, Phi Beta Kappa. Office: Washington U Sch Medicine Dept Psychiatry 660 S Euclid Ave Campus Box 8134 Saint Louis MO 63110

**NEWELL, BARBARA ANN,** coatings company executive; b. Portland, Oreg., Mar. 20, 1945; d. John Wesley and Marion Josephine (Hill) Clausen; children: Shamaz, Hukam (dec.), Mardana. BA, Lindenwood Coll. for Women, 1968; MA, Portland State U., 1972; PhD, Summit U., 2000. Owner Shamaz Trading Co., Ukiah, Calif., 1974-77; mgr. small bus. dept. Ernst & Ernst, Portland, 1977-78; CFO All Heart Lumber Co., Ukiah, 1978-83; CFO, CEO Performance Coatings Inc., Ukiah, 1983—, chmn. bd. dirs., 1992—. Chmn. bd. dirs. Rural Visions Found.; treas. chmn. fin. com. Mendocino County Health Clinic, bd. dirs., 2001-03; CEO, chmn. bd. dirs. Dusky Rose & Assoc., Botanics of Calif.; founder Potter Valley Cafe, 2000; owner Hukam Maj Arabian Horse Ranch, 1998—. Founder, chair Penofin Jazz Festival; chmn. bd. dirs. Mendocino Ballet Co.; bd. dirs. Potter Valley Youth and Cmty. Ctr. Mem. Nat. Paint and Coatings Assn., Golden State Paint and Coatings Assn., Ukiah C. of C. (mem. econ. devel. com. 1993-94), Women in Coatings (Leadership award 1994), Leadership Mendocino. Avocations: showing Arabian horses, reading, children, organic gardening, dance. Office: Penofin-Performance Coatings Inc PO Box 1569 Ukiah CA 95482-1569 Office Phone: 707-462-3023. Business E-Mail: ceo@penofin.com.

**NEWELL, CHARLDEAN,** public administration educator; b. Ft. Worth, Oct. 14, 1939; d. Charles Thurlow and Mildred Dean (Looney) Newell. BA, U. North Tex., 1960, MA, 1962; PhD, U. Tex., 1968; cert., Harvard U., 1988. Instr. U. North Tex., Denton, 1965-68, asst. prof., 1968-72; assoc. prof., dir. Fedn. North Tex. Area Univs., Denton, Dallas, 1972-74; assoc. prof., assoc. v.p. acad. affairs U. North Tex., Denton, 1974-76, assoc. prof., chair dept. polit. sci., 1976-80, prof. polit. sci., 1980-92, assoc. v.p., spl. asst. to chancellor, 1982-92, regents prof. pub. adminstrn., 1992—2002, prof. emerita, 2002—. Cons. Miss. Bd. Trustees State Instns. Higher Learning, Jackson, 1983—84, Ednl. Testing Svc., Princeton, NJ, 1980, Princeton, 82, Princeton, 85, Spear Down & Judin, Dallas, 1994—95, North Tex. Inst. Edn. Visual Arts, Denton, 1993—94; bd. regents Internat. City/County Mgmt. Assn., Washington, 1994—98, vol. credentialing adv. bd.; 2002—; trainer Emergency Leaders Program, 2005—. Author (with others): City Executives: Leadership Roles, Work Characteristics and Time Management, 1989, The Effective Local Govt. Mgr., 2004, Essentials of Tex. Politics, 2004, Texas Politics, 2005; contbr. articles to profl. jours. Chmn. Denton Charter Rev. Com., 1978—79; mem. Denton CSC, 1989—97, chmn., 1992—97; active Denton Blue Ribbon Capital Improvements Com., 1995—96; mem. Denton Devel. Plan Com., 1996—97, Denton Pub. Utilities Bd., 1997—, chmn., 2002—; v.p. Denton Christian Pre-Sch. Bd., 2001—02, pres., 2002—05, mem., 2005—; City Coun. Ethics Com., 2004; v.p. Our Daily Bread, 2005—, vice-chair, 2005—; mem. exec. coun. Episcopal Diocese Dallas, 1985—88. Recipient Elmer Staats Career Pub. Svc. award, Nat. Assn. Sch. Pub. Affairs Adminstrn., 1993. Fellow: Nat. Acad. Pub. Adminstrn.; mem.: Am. Soc. for Pub. Adminstrn. (sect. chmn. 1982—83, mem. editl. bd. 1985—88, Donald C. Stone award 2004), Internat. City/County Mgmt. Assn. (hon.), Pi Alpha Alpha (exec. coun. 1995—99), Pi Sigma Alpha (exec. coun. 1988—92). Democrat. Avocations: spectator sports, reading. Home: 2008 Tremont Cir Denton TX 76205-7408 Business E-Mail: cn0003@unt.edu.

**NEWELL, ERIC JAMES,** financial planner, retired insurance company executive; b. Toronto, Ont., Can., Sept. 24, 1930; came to U.S., 1959, naturalized, 1970; s. James and Anne (Brown) N.; m. Essie Miskelly, Sept. 30,

1950; 1 son, Eric Wayne. Student, U. Toronto, 1951-53. Pub. acct. W.J. Wilcox & Co., Toronto, 1949-53; chief acct. Toronto Mut. Life Ins. Co., 1953-57; asst. sec. Holland Life Ins. Co., Toronto, 1957-59; with Penn Mut. Life Ins. Co., Phila., 1959-86, assoc. controller, 1965-70, 2d v.p., controller, 1970-84, v.p., controller, 1984-86, ret., 1986; fin., tax cons., 1986—; dir. Hotel Brunswick, Lancaster, Pa., 1982-85. Mem. Traffic and Transp. Bd., Cherry Hill, N.J., 1971-73, Zoning Bd., 1975-78; vice chmn. Cherry Hill Econ. Devel. Bd., 1973-75; pres. Greater Kingston Civic Assn., Cherry Hill, 1970-76; Democratic committeeman, Camden County, 1976-79; vice chmn. Dem. Party, Cherry Hill, 1976-79. Fellow Life Mgmt. Inst., Royal Commonwealth Soc.; mem. Fin. Execs. Inst., Am. Inst. Corp. Contrs., N.Y. Ins. Accts. Club (chmn. 1984), Nat. Soc. Tax Profls., Royal Black Knights of Ireland, Loyal Orange Assn. (past master), Scotch-Irish Soc. of U.S. (mem. coun., pres. 1999), Am. Legion, Masons. Presbyterian (deacon 1969-72). Home and Office: 20 Wordsworth Street Galloway NJ 08205

**NEWELL, JOYCE R.,** social studies educator; Pianist First Christian Ch., 1993—98; treas. Audubon Homeowners Assn., Tupelo, Miss., 1990—2000. Grantee, EXPECT Found., 1994—2005. Mem.: DAR (chair Am. history 1990—, Outstanding Am. History Tchr. award), Miss. Coun. Social Studies (treas. 1998—), Miss. Geographic Alliance (tchr. cons. 1992—, bd. dirs.), Carriage Hills Garden Club (v.p. 1979—80, pres. 1980—81), Delta Kappa Gamma (v.p. then pres. 1995—). Baptist. Avocations: music, reading. Home: 1209 Winwood Cove Tupelo MS 38801 Office: Saltillo HS 146 Tiger Dr Saltillo MS 38866 also: Itawamba CC Eason Blvd Tupelo MS 38804

**NEWELL, KATHERINE CLAIBORNE,** librarian; b. Columbia, Mo., Aug. 1, 1957; d. Jerry David and Anna Faye (Hooks) Claiborne; children: David, Danny. Student. U. Neuchâtel, Switzerland, 1977-78; BA in History and French, U. Del., 1979; MS in Libr. Sci. and Info. Studies, Drexel U., Phila., 1994. Mgmt. trainee, supr. C&P Telephone Co., Washington, 1979-80; office mgr. Bus. & Ins. Mgmt., Bethesda, Md., 1980-81, Gauge Corp., Wilmington, Del., 1981-82; exec. asst. Med. Soc. Del., Wilmington, 1982-89; spl. collections asst. Langston Hughes Meml. Libr., Lincoln University, Pa., 1989-92, interlibr. loan libr. Pa., 1992-95, spl. collections libr. Pa., 1995-98; rsch. libr. Hagley Mus. and Libr., Wilmington, Del., 1998—2002; dir. J. Lewis Crozer Libr., Chester, Pa., 2002—04, New Castle (Del.) Pub. Libr., 2004—. Mem. ALA, Del. Libr. Assn., New Castle Hist. Soc., Beta Phi Mu, Phi Alpha Theta, Pi Delta Phi. Office: New Castle Pub Libr 424 Delaware St New Castle DE 19720 Office Phone: 302-328-1995. Business E-Mail: knewell@nccde.org.

**NEWELL, MARK E.,** lawyer; m. Jo Ann Newell; 2 children. BA summa cum laude, Albion Coll., 1977; MPP, Kennedy Sch. of Govt., 1981; JD magna cum laude, Harvard Univ., 1981. Bar: DC 1983. Law clk. Judge Malcolm R. Wilkey, US Ct. of Appeals, DC Cir., 1981—82, Justice Lewis F Powell Jr., US Supreme Ct., 1982—83; joined Latham & Watkins, 1983—, mng. ptnr. Washington, 1993—2000, chief operating ptnr., 2000—. Editor and treas. Harvard Law Rev., 1981. Mem.: ABA, DC Bar, Phi Beta Kappa. Office: Latham & Watkins Ste 1000 555 Eleventh St NW Washington DC 20004-1304

**NEWELL, MICHAEL ALFRED,** electrical engineer; b. L.A., May 26, 1963; s. Paul Eugene and Clare Fritzsche Newell; m. Thuy Lam Newell. BSEE, Calif. Poly. State U., 1990. Electronics design engr. Space Payloads Group, Pasadena, Calif., 1983—86; software engr. Qualitel Svcs., Pomona, Calif., 1986—88; sr. mem. tech. staff Jet Propulsion Lab., Pasadena, 1988—. ASIC designer Cassini Spacecraft Jet Propulsion Lab., Pasadena, 1992—94, electronics lead APEX reconfigurable hardware Flight Experiment, Pasadena, 1994—97, Muses CN electronics cognizant engr., Pasadena, 1998—2001, Deep Impact avionics lead, 2001—; Gilgamesh Supercomputer electronics cognizant engr. Caltech, Pasadena, 2000—; task mgr. extreme electronics, Electronics Parts Program NASA, Pasadena, 2001—. Contbr. articles to profl. jours.; patentee in field. Exec. advisor JPL Explorer Post, Pasadena, 1993—2001. Mem.: IEEE. Avocations: bicycling, reading. Home: 3545 N Glenrose Ave Altadena CA 91001 Office: Jet Propulsion Lab 4800 Oak Grove Dr Pasadena CA 91109 Personal E-mail: mikenewell@earthlink.net. Business E-Mail: Michael.A.Newell@jpl.nasa.gov.

**NEWELL, MIKE,** film director; b. St. Albans, England, Mar. 28, 1942; m. Bernice Stegers; 3 children. Attended, Cambridge U. Films include: The Awakening, 1980, Bad Blood, 1983, Dance With a Stranger, 1985, The Good Father, 1986, Amazing Grace and Chuck, 1987, Soursweet, 1988, Enchanted April, 1991, Into the West, 1992, Four Weddings and a Funeral, 1994, An Awfully Big Adventure, 1995, Donnie Brasco, 1997, Pushing Tin, 1999, Mona Lisa Smile, 2003, Harry Potter and the Goblet of Fire, 2005; exec. prodr. (films) Photographing Fairies, 1997, 200 Cigarettes, 1999, Best Laid Plans, 1999, High Fidelity, 2000, Traffic, 2000; TV films include: Big Soft Nellie, Mrs. Mouse, Baa Baa Blacksheep, The Melancholy Hussar, Ready When You Are Mr. McGill, Destiny, The Man in the Iron Mask, 1977, The Gift of Friendship, Blood Feud, 1983, Common Ground, 1990; exec. prodr., dir. (TV series) The Branch, 2003, dir. (TV movie) Jo, 2002. Office: Dogstar UK 5 Sherwood St London W1V 7RA England Address: ICM Ste 219 8942 Wilshire Blvd Beverly Hills CA 90211*

**NEWELL, PAUL HAYNES, JR.,** engineering educator; b. Nashville, July 1, 1933; s. Paul Haynes Newell; m. Martha A. Newell; children: Paul Haynes III, Mike, Nan. B.M.E., U. Tenn., 1958, M.M.E., 1961; Mech.E., Mass. Inst. Tech., 1964, PhD, 1966. Registered profl. engr., Ala., Tenn., Tex., N.J. student aux. mech. engring. U. Tenn., 1957; instr. mech. engring., 1958-62; NSF sci. faculty fellow MIT, 1962-65; assoc. prof. U. Ala. Coll. Engring., 1966-69; prof. mech. Tex. A&M U., 1969-72, assoc. dean engring., 1972, prof., head indsl. engring. dept., 1972-74, prof., head combined programs of behavioral engring., bioengring., cybernetic engring., hygiene and safety engring., indsl. engring., 1972-74; prof. biomed. engring., dept. phys. medicine Baylor Coll. Medicine, 1969-74, prof. biomed. engring., dept. physiology, 1970-74, prof. biomed. engring., dept. community medicine, 1972-74, prof. biomed. engring., dept. rehab., 1972—, mem. grad. faculty, 1970-74, prof. Houston, from 1971; pres., prof. Newark Coll. Engring., NJ Inst. Tech., 1974-78; pres. Newell Engring., Greenbrier, Tenn., 1979—. Bd. dirs. NJ Bell Tel. Co., Mid Atlantic Nat. Bank, Thomas-Betts Corp. Contbr. articles to profl. jours., chapters to books. Mem. liaison com. NSF, Newark Transp. Coun., N.J. Safety Coun.; sec. exec. com. coun. Boy Scouts Am., Birmingham, Ala., 1966—68; bd. dirs. N.J. State Opera, United Hosps. Newark. With USMCR, Korea. NSF Sci. Faculty fellow. Mem.: NSPE, ASME, AAAS, N.J. Soc. Engrs., Am. Fluid Power Soc., Pres.'s Assn., Soc. Engring. Sci., Soc. Advanced Med. Sys., Internat. Soc. Prosthetics and Orthotics, Inst. Engring. Deans, Biomedical Engring. Soc., Am. Soc. Engring. Edn., Am. Soc. Artificial Internal Organs, Am. Inst. Indsl. Engrs., Am. Heart Assn., Am. Congress Rehab. Medicine, Ala. Acad. Scis., N.Y. Acad. Scis., Am. Soc. Tool and Mfg. Engrs., Rotary, Sigma Xi, Pi Tau Sigma, Phi Kappa Phi, Tau Beta Pi. Address: 1855 Lake Rd Greenbrier TN 37073-4619 Office: Newell Engring Greenbrier TN 37073-4619

**NEWELL, SHIRLEY ANN CECIL,** retired art dealer, artist; d. Francis M. and Ora A. Cherry, Sr.; m. Richard A. Cecil (div.); children: David B., Valerie A., Vicki E.; m. David B. Newell (div.). Student, U. Tenn., 1958—61, Calif. Luth. Coll., 1970, U. Calif., 1971, Ga. State U., 1977. Pvt. practice art instr., Atlanta, 1970; prin., owner Collectors Art, Atlanta, 1979—85, Cecil B. Day Investment Co., Ga., 1986—95, adminstrv. asst. Ga.; adminstr. Siemens Energy and Automation, 1998—2006; ret., 2006. Exhibitions include Oxnard Art Club Festival of Art, Hilton Head Art League, Garden Club of Ga., Habitat Atlanta. Mem. Nat. Mus. Women of the Arts, Washington, Roswell Cultural Arts; charter mem. High Mus. Art, Atlanta; mem. Americans for the Arts Action Fund, Washington; bd. dirs. DeKalb Coun. Arts, 2005—; bd. dirs. Peachtree Arts Atlanta (Ga.) High Mus. Art, 1998—99, sec. suburban art com., 1982—83; mem. individual arts com. coalition Olympics '96, Atlanta, 1996. Recipient award, WSB Radio. Civic Svc. award, Boys Club Am., 1971. Mem.: Roswell Cultured Arts, Nat. Women Arts. Methodist. Avocations: reading, dance, art.

**NEWHALL, DAVID, III,** retired federal official; b. Phila., Dec. 6, 1937; s. David Jr. and Jane Martyn (Dunn) N. AB in Politics, Princeton U., 1961. Mgr. Bell Tel. Co. of Pa., Norristown, 1961-63; adminstrv. asst. U.S. Rep. R.S. Schweiker, Washington, 1963-69; chief of staff U.S. Senator R.S. Schweiker, Washington, 1969-81, HHS, Washington, 1981-83; pres. Marmion Plantation Co., King George, Va., 1983—85; prin. dep. asst. sec. def.(health affairs) U.S. Dept. Def., Washington, 1985-90, acting asst. sec. def. (health affairs), 1989-90; gen. ptnr. Marmion Partnership Restorations, 1990—. Bd. dirs. We. Healthcare Alliance, Phoenix, 1995-97; chmn. compliance com. and lead dir. TrailBlazer Health Enterprises, LLC, Dallas, 1997—. Mem. Princeton Tower Club. Republican. Episcopalian. Home and Office: 7382M Marmion Ln King George VA 22485-7300

**NEWHALL, JOHN HARRISON,** retired business executive, management consultant; b. Phila., Sept. 29, 1933; s. Blackwell and Mary Large (Harrison) N.; m. Jane Carol Ward, July 15, 1961; children: Carol Newhall Neilson, Thomas Blackwell, Daniel Ward. BA, Williams Coll., 1955; MBA, Harvard U., 1960. Product mktg. mgr. Campbell Soup Co., Camden, NJ, 1960—67; product group mgr. Gen. Foods Corp. (now Kraft Corp.), White Plains, NY, 1967—70; dir. corp. planning, gen. mgr. Europe H.J. Heinz Co., Pitts., 1970—77; v.p. mktg. Sunoco Corp., Phila., 1977—81; chmn., CEO Aitkin-Kynett Co. (subs. Foote Cone & Belding), Phila., 1981—84; mng. dir., exec. v.p. Campbell-Ewald Co., N.Y.C., 1984—86; prin. mgmt. cons. SRI Internat., Menlo Park, Calif., 1987—90; mng. dir. Strategic Directions, Narberth, Pa., 1990—99; pres. Advanced Promotion Techs., Deerfield Beach, Fla., 1992—93; CEO The Newcomen Soc. of the U.S., Exton, Pa., 1999—2003; ret., 2003. Mem. devel. coun. Williams Coll., Williamstown, Mass., 1977-87, regional vice chmn. capital campaign, 1991-93; mem. Com. of 70, Phila., 1981-84; bd. dirs. Bryn Mawr (Pa.) Hosp., 1982-88, The Haverford (Pa.) Sch., 1980-86, mem. headmaster selection com., 1992, mem. strategic planning com., 1994; bd. dirs. World Affairs Coun., Phila., 1982-86, Found. for Vascular Hypertension Rsch., Phila., 1982-2001, chmn., 1987; bd. dirs. Jr. Achievement, Phila., 1977-81, vice chmn., 1981; bd. dirs. SE chpt. ARC, Phila., 1981-84; bd. dirs. Pa. Economy League, 1981-84; vestryman, lay reader Episcopal Ch., 1964-70, chmn. ann. campaign, 1992, vice chmn. capital campaign, 1994; mem. bd. overseers Hospitality Hall of Honor, 2000-2003; bd. dirs. M.D.I. Drug and Alcohol Abuse Found., 2005—. Lt. USN, 1955—58. Recipient Cert. of Merit Chapel of Four Chaplains, 1983, 85. Mem. Assn. Nat. Advertisers (exec. com. 1977-81), Harvard Bus. Sch. Club Phila. (pres. 1994-96, chmn. 1996-98), Merion Cricket Club (Haverford), Gulph Mills (Pa.) Golf Club, Harbor Club (Seal Harbor, Maine), Union League Club Phila. Republican. Episcopalian. Avocations: skiing, golf, gardening, sailing, swimming. Home: 414 Righters Mill Rd Penn Valley PA 19072-1423 Personal E-mail: jnewhall@verizon.net.

**NEWHART, BOB (GEORGE ROBERT NEWHART),** entertainer; b. Oak Park, Ill., Sept. 5, 1929; m. Virginia Quinn, Jan. 12, 1963; 4 children. BS, Loyola U., Chgo., 1952. Acct. U.S. Gypsum Co.; copywriter Fred Niles Film Co.; star TV variety show Bob Newhart Show, 1961; star TV series The Bob Newhart Show, 1972—78, Newhart, 1982-90, Bob, 1992, George & Leo, 1997. Rec. artist (album) The Button Down Mind of Bob Newhart, 1960, The Button Down Mind Strikes Back, 1961, Behind the Button Down Mind, 1961, The Button Down Mind on TV, 1962, Bob Newhart Faces Bob Newhart, 1964, Windmille Are Weakening, 1965, This Is it, 1967, The Best of Bob Newhart, 1971, Very Funny Bob Newhart, 1973; royal command performance, London, 1964; appeared in films Hell is for Heroes, 1962, Hot Millions, 1968, Catch 22, 1970, On a Clear Day You Can See Forever, 1970, Cold Turkey, 1971, First Family, 1980, Little Miss Marker, 1980, In and Out, 1997, Rudolph the Red-Nosed Reindeer: The Movie (voice), 1998, Legally Blonde 2: Red, White & Blonde, 2003, Elf, 2003; TV films include Thursday's Game, 1974, Marathon, 1980, The Librarian: Quest for the Spear, 2004; TV appearances (1960-) include The Ed Sullivan Show (a.k.a. Toast of the Town, (8 Times), Jack Parr Show, 1960, The Andy Williams Show, 1962, 1964, & 1966, The Dean Martin Show (24 Times), Rowan & Martin's Laugh-In, 1968 & 1969, The Tonight Show Starring Johnny Carson (also guest host), It's Garry Shandling's Show, 1990, Late Night with David Letterman, 1991, Murphy Brown, 1994, The Simpsons (voice), 1996, Mad TV, 2001, ER, 2003, Saturday Night Live (host 1980, 1995), Desperate Housewives, 2005, (PBS) Bob Newhart: Unbuttoned (Honored Am. Master 2005), 2005, and numerous others. Grand marshall Tournament Roses Parade, 1991. With U.S. Army, 1952-54. Recipient Emmy award, 1961, Peabody award, 1961, Sword of Loyola award, 1976, Legend to Legend award, 1993, three Grammy awards 1960, Kennedy Ctr. Mark Twain award, 2002, Icon award, TVLand, 2005; named to TV Acad. of Arts & Sci. Hall of Fame, 1993; honored as an American Master (Bob Newhart: Unbuttoned), PBS, 2005. Best Known Trademarks: Stammering delivery while talking; Telephone monologues as part of act; One-sided conversations. Office: c/o Capell Rudolph 11601 Wilshire Blvd Ste 1840 Los Angeles CA 90025-1759

**NEWHOUSE, ALAN RUSSELL,** retired federal official; b. N.Y.C., Feb. 27, 1938; s. Russell Conwell and Clara Lucille (Scovell) N.; m. Margo Stiles Hicks, Feb. 3, 1960; children: Daryl, Jeffrey, William. BEE, Cornell U., 1960. Engr. Bur. of Ships, Washington, 1964-66; nuc. power engr., chief West Milton field office AEC, Schenectady, NY, 1966-69; sr. exec. AEC, ERDA, U.S. Dept. Energy, Washington, 1969-92; dep. asst. sec. Space and Def. Power Systems Office Nuc. Energy, Washington, 1992-93; dir. Office Space and Def. Power Systems, 1993-95; dir. Project Prometheus Office of Exploration, NASA, 2003—04; ind. cons., 1995—2006. Composer numerous musical works. Mem. Cmty. Orchestra So. Md. in Concert. Lt. USN, 1960-64. Mem.: AIAA, IEEE, Am. Soc. Naval Engrs., Am. Nuc. Soc. Unitarian Universalist. Home and Office: 24670 Greenview Dr Hollywood MD 20636-4823 E-mail: consultant@arnewhouse.com.

**NEWHOUSE, DONALD E.,** newspaper publishing executive; b. 1930; s. Samuel Newhouse. Student, Syracuse U. With Advance Publs. Inc., Staten Island, NY, 1951—, pres., 1979—; chmn. The Associated Press, N.Y.C., 1997—2002. Treas. Herald Am., Syracuse, 1960—, The Post Standard, Syracuse, 1960—, The Syracuse Herald Jour., 1960—, The Herald Co. Inc., 1960—; co-founder Metro-Suburbia, Inc., N.Y.C., 1963; prin. The Trenton (N.J.) Times, Times of Trenton Pub. Corp.; pres. The Star Ledger, Newark. Named one of Forbes Richest Americans, 2006. Office: Advance Publications Inc 950 Fingerboard Rd Staten Island NY 10305-1453

**NEWHOUSE, JEFFREY H.,** radiologist, educator; b. N.Y., Dec. 10, 1942; s. Edward and Dorothy DeLay Newhouse; m. Nancy Hargadon, June 4, 1983; children: Amy Lee, Edward Walter. AB, Princeton U., N.J., 1963; MD, Harvard U., Boston, Mass., 1967. Diplomate Am. Bd. Radiology, 1972. Intern gen. surgery Roosevelt Hosp., N.Y., 1967—70; resident diagnostic radiology Mass. Gen. Hosp., Boston, 1970—74, instr. radiology, 1974—78, asst. prof. radiology, 1978—83; instr. radiology Med. Sch. Harvard U., Boston, 1974—78, asst. prof. radiology Med. Sch., 1978—83; assoc. prof. radiology Columbia-Presbyn. Med. Ctr. Columbia Coll. Physicians and Surgeons, N.Y., 1983—88, chief Divsn. Abdominal Radiology, 1983—; prof. of radiology and urology Columbia Coll. of Physicians and Surgeons and NY Presbyn. Hosp., New York, 1988—; vice chmn. Dept. Radiology N.Y. Presbyn. Hosp., 1998—. Disting. scientist Armed Forces Inst. Pathology, Washington, 1996. Co-author: Understanding MRI, Essentials of Uroradiology, Textbook of Uroradiology (2nd and 3rd eds.); editor: Urologic Radiology and General Abdomen, MRI of the Urinary Tract, Clinical MRI, Gamuts in Radiology; contbr. 172 scientific papers. Maj. med. corps. U.S. Army, 1972—74. Recipient Best Sci. Paper award, Soc. Uroradiology, 1981, online jour., 2002, Tchr. of Yr. award, Dept. Urology, Columbia U. Med. Ctr., 2000, Dept. Radiology, Columbia U. Med. Ctr., 2004; scholar, Gen. Motors, 1959—63, James Picker Found., 1969—72. Fellow: Am. Coll. Radiology (chmn. com. appropriateness criteria 2002—05); mem.: Bronxfield Field Club, Union Boat Club. Avocations: skiing, tennis, sailing, sculling. Home: 10 Hilltop Road Bronxville NY 10708 Office: Columbia University Medical Center 177 Fort Washington Avenue New York NY 10032 Office Phone: 212-305-7898. Business E-Mail: jhn2@columbia.edu.

**NEWHOUSE, JOSEPH PAUL,** economist, educator; b. Waterloo, Iowa, Feb. 24, 1942; s. Joseph Alexander and Ruth Linnea (Johnson) Newhouse; m. Margaret Louise Locke, June 22, 1968; children: Eric Joseph, David Locke. BA, Harvard U., 1963, PhD, 1969; postgrad (Fulbright scholar), Goethe U., Frankfort, Germany, 1963—64. Staff economist Rand Corp., Santa Monica, Calif., 1968—72, dep. program mgr., health and biosci. rsch., 1971—88, sr. staff economist, 1972—81, head econs. dept. 1981—85, sr. corp. fellow, 1985—2001; John D. MacArthur prof. health policy and mgmt., dir. div. Health Policy Rsch. and Edn., Harvard U., 1988—. Lectr. UCLA, 1970—83, adj. prof., 1983—88; mem. faculty Rand Grad. Sch., 1972—88; dir. Rand-UCLA Ctr. for Study Health Care Fin. Policy, 1984—88, co-dir., 1988—92; prin. investigator health ins. study grant HHS, 1971—86; chmn. health svcs. rsch. study sect. HHS-Agy. for Health Care Policy and Rsch., 1989—93; mem. Nat. Commn. Cost Med. Care, 1976—77; mem. health svcs. devel. grants study sect. HEW, 1978—82, Inst. Medicine of NAS, 1978—, mem. coun., 1991—97; mem. Physician Payment Rev. Commn., 1993—96; chmn. Prospective Payment Assessment Com., 1996—97; vice chair Medicare Payment Assessment Commn., 1997—2001, mem., 2001—; bd. regents Nat. Libr. Medicine, 1999—; bd. dirs. Aetna, ABT Assocs., Nat. Com. Quality Assurance. Author: The Economics of Medical Care, 1978, The Cost of Poor Health Habits, 1991, A Measure of Malpractice, 1993, Free for All?, 1993, Pricing the Priceless, 2002; editor: Jour. Health Econs., 1981—; assoc. editor: Jour. Econ. Perspectives, 1992—98, mem. editl. bd.: New Eng. Jour. Medicine, 2003—; contbr. articles to profl. jours. Recipient David Kershaw award and prize, Assn. Pub. Policy and Mgmt., 1983, Baxter Am. Found. prize, 1988, Adminstr.'s citation, Health Care Fin. Adminstrn., 1988, Hans Sigrist Found. prize, 1995, Elizur Wright award, 1995, Zvi Griliches award, 2000, Kenneth Arrow award, 2001, Paul A. Samuelson Excellence cert., TIAA CREF, 2003. Fellow: AAAS, Am. Acad. Arts and Scis.; mem.: Am. Soc. Health Economists (pres. 2005—), Internat. Health Econs. Assn. (pres. 1996—98, bd. dirs. 1996—2002), Econometric Soc., Royal Econ. Soc., Am. Econ. Assn., Assn. for Health Svcs. Rsch. (bd. dirs. 1991—, pres. 1993—94, Article of Yr. award 1989). Office: Harvard U Health Policy Rsch and Edn 180 Longwood Ave Boston MA 02115-5821

**NEWHOUSE, MARK WILLIAM,** publishing executive; b. N.Y.C., Oct. 14, 1948; s. Norman Nathan and Alice (Gross) Newhouse; m. Lorry A. Whitehead, June 1, 1974; children: Jesse Louis, Charlotte Ann. BA, Yale U., 1969. V.p., gen. mgr. The Star-Ledger, Newark, 1980—. Bd. dirs. Newspaper Assn. Am., 2005—. Bd. dirs. N.Y.C. Opera, 1992—, pres., 1993—; bd. dirs. Audit Bur. Circulations, 1995—2004, Glimmerglass Opera, 1997—, N.Y.C. Outward Bound Ctr., 2004—. Office: Newark Morning Star Ledger Co One Star Ledger Plz Newark NJ 07102-1200

**NEWHOUSE, SAMUEL IRVING, JR., (SI NEWHOUSE JR.),** publishing executive; b. 1928; m. Victoria Carrington Benedict de Ramel. Pub. Vogue mag., 1964; chmn. Condé Nast Publs. Inc., N.Y.C., 1975—; also chmn. bd. dirs., CEO Advance Publs. Inc., S.I., NY, 1979—. Named one of Top 200 Collectors, ARTnews Mag., 2004, 2006, Forbes Richest Americans, 2006; recipient Henry J. Fisher award, Mag. Pubs. Assn., 1985. Avocation: Collector of Modern and contemporary art. Address: Advance Pubs Inc 950 Fingerboard Rd Staten Island NY 10305-1453*

**NEWICK, CRAIG DAVID,** architect; b. Orange, N.J., Feb. 14, 1960; s. Russel Forester and Helen (Welch) N.; m. Linda Hammer Lindroth, June 6, 1987; 1 child, Zachary Eran. BA in Architecture, Lehigh U., 1982; MArch, Yale U., 1987. Registered architect, Conn. Designer, draftsman The Archtl. Studio, Easton, Pa., 1983-84; job capt., project designer Svigals & Assocs., New Haven, 1985; designer, draftsman Centerbrook (Conn.) Architects, 1986; job capt., project designer Allan Dehar Assocs., Architects & Planners, New Haven, 1988-90; ptnr. Lindroth & Newick, New Haven, 1991—; designer Cesar Pelli & Assocs., Inc., New Haven, 1992; project arch. Tai Soo Kim Ptnrs., Hartford, Conn., 1995—2001; prin. Newick Archs., New Haven, 2001—. Vis. faculty Vis. Critics Studio, Lehigh U., 1993; vis. critic Wesleyan U., 1990-2005, R.I. Sch. Design, 1988, Yale U., 2000-05; faculty Creative Arts Workshop, New Haven, 1991, 92; co-dir. Eyebeam Competition, N.Y.C. Exhibitions include Out Of Bounds; author: Simultaneous Space (first prize artists books, 1994). Recipient 1st place award Am. Visionary Set Design Competition, 1989, 3d place award Astronauts Meml. Design Competition, 1988, ID Mag. Am. Design Rev. award, 1990, 2d prize African Burial Ground Competition Mcpl. Arts Soc. N.Y., 1994, 1st place drawing award Conn. Soc. Architects, 1997, AIA Conn. honor award, 2000. AIA Conn. Design award, 2005, Nat. AIA Design award, 2006; grantee New Eng. Found. for arts, 1992, NEA Interarts grantee Rockefeller Found., 1989-90, Found. for Contemporary Performance art, 1989, 90, Humanities Coun. of Fairfield U., 1995, AIA Conn. Designer award, 2006; New Eng. Found. for Arts Regional fellow, 1993, Conn. Commn. on the Arts fellow, 1998, others. Mem. Architecture League N.Y. (young architects Forum 1991, emerging voices, 1996). Office: Newick Archs 85 Willow St New Haven CT 06511

**NEWILL, JAMES WAGNER,** accounting executive; b. Greensburg, Pa., Dec. 22, 1934; s. James Meyers and Ruth Elizabeth (Wagner) N.; m. Helene Margaret Dolibois, Feb. 18, 1957; 1 child, J. Eric. BBA, St. Vincent Coll., Latrobe, Pa., 1962. CPA, Pa., Ohio, Fla. Staff acct. George Conti & Co., CPA, Greensburg, 1962-65; internal auditor Duquesne Light Co., Pitts., 1965-67; supr. accounts payable and gen. ledger Kennametal, Inc., Latrobe, 1967-71; asst. controller Glosser Stores, Inc., Johnstown, Pa., 1971-73; controller, asst. treas. Meridian Plastics, Inc., Byesville, Ohio, 1973-76; regional controller Friendly Ice Cream Corp., Wilbraham, Mass., 1976-79; pres. J.W. Newill Co., Troy, Ohio, 1979-92; pvt. practice Fla., 1993—. Bd. dirs. 1st Commonwealth Fin. Corp., Indiana, Pa., 1999—. Elected town commr. Highland Beach, 2005—; v.p. bd. dirs. Troy-Hayner Cultural Ctr., Troy, Ohio, 1982—85, fin. adv. bd. Highland Beach, Fla., 2003—05. To staff sgt. USAF, 1954—58. Mem. AICPA, Pa. Inst. CPAs, Ohio Soc. CPAs, Fla. Inst. CPAs, Nat. Assn. Accts., Sea Ranch Club Boca (bd. dirs. 1999-2001), Masons, Shriners, Scottish Rite, Rotary (chmn. com., Paul Harris fellow), Elks. Republican. Presbyterian. Avocations: travel, tennis, theater. Office Phone: 561-395-0987.

**NEWKIRK, JOHN BURT,** retired metallurgical research administrator; b. Mpls., Mar. 24, 1920; s. Burt Leroy and Mary Louise (Leavenworth) N.; m. Carolyn Mae Jordan, Aug. 4, 1951; children: Jeffrey Burt (dec.), John Jordan, Victoria Louise Lierheimer, Christina Newkirk Seldomridge. B in Metall. Engring., Rensselaer Poly. Inst., 1941; MS, Carnegie Inst. Tech., 1947, ScD, 1950. Metall. investigator Bethlehem Steel Co., Pa., 1941-42; Fulbright postdoctoral fellow Cambridge (Eng.) U., 1950-51; research metallurgist research lab. Gen. Electric Co., Schenectady, 1951-59; prof. Cornell U., 1959-65; Phillipson prof. U. Denver, 1965-74, prof. phys. chemistry, 1975-84, Phillipson prof. emeritus, 1984—; pres. Denver Biomaterials, Inc., 1969-86, Colo. Biomed., Inc., 1987-2000; ret., 2000. Editor Revs. on High Temperature Materials, 1973-78; co-editor: 16 ann. volumes Advances in X-Ray Analysis; contbr. articles profl. jours. Lt. USNR, 1942-46. Fellow Am. Soc. Metals (life); mem. Sigma Xi, Tau Beta Pi, Phi Kappa Phi, Alpha Sigma Mu (internat. pres. 1950), Alpha Tau Omega. Republican. Baptist. Personal E-mail: jack@snowvalley.org.

**NEWLAND, CHESTER ALBERT,** public administration educator; b. Kansas City, Kans., June 18, 1930; s. Guy Wesley and Mary Virginia (Yoakum) N. BA, U. N. Tex., Denton, 1954; MA, U. Kans., 1955, PhD, 1958. Social Sci. Rsch. Coun. fellow U. Wis. and U.S. Supreme Ct., 1958-59; instr. polit. sci. Idaho State U., Pocatello, 1959-60; mem. faculty U. North Tex., Denton, 1960-66, prof. govt., 1963-66, dir. dept. govt., 1963-66; prof. polit. sci. U. Houston, 1967-68; dir. Lyndon Baines Johnson Libr., Austin, Tex., 1968-70; prof. pub. adminstrn. U. So. Calif., 1966-67, 68-71, 76-82, 84-92, Duggan disting. prof. pub. adminstrn., 1992—; prof. George Mason U., Fairfax, Va., 1982-84. Mem. faculty Fed. Exec. Inst., 1971-76, dir. 1973-76, 80-81; mgr. task force on fed. labor-mgmt. rels. U.S. Pers. Mgmt. Project, Pres.'s Reorgn., Washington, 1977-78. Editor in chief Pub. Adminstrn. Rev., 1984-90; contbr. articles to profl. jours. Chmn. Mcpl. Rsch. Coun., Denton, 1963-64; city councilman Denton, 1964-66; mem. Pub. Sector Commn. on Productivity and Work Quality, 1974-78; trustee Sacramento (Calif.) Mus. History, Sci. and Tech., 1993-95; mem. UN Devel. Program Kazakhstan, 1997-2000, strategy review program, 2002, Moldova, 1994, Kuwait, 1991, 95-96; cons. Poland, 1990-91, Hungary, 1991, Czech and Slovak Republics, 1992, Bank of Greece, 1999-2002, 04, Taiwan, 2001. Fellow Nat. Acad. Pub. Adminstrn., (trustee 1979-82, nominating com. 2006-); mem. Southwestern Social Sci. Assn. (chmn. govt. sect. 1964-65), Am. Soc. Pub. Adminstrn. (pres. Dallas-Ft. Worth chpt. 1964-65, nat. coun. 1976, 78-81, editl. bd. jour. 1972-76, chmn. publ. com. 1975-79, program chmn. 1977, nat. pres. 1981-82, Dimock award 1984, Van Riper award 2002), Am. Polit. Sci. Assn., Internat. Pers. Mgmt. Assn. (program chmn. 1978, Stockberger award 1979), Am. Acad. Polit. and Social Sci., Internat. City Mgmt. Assn. (hon.; mem. Calif. bd. 2003-05), Nat. Assn. Schs Pub. Affairs and Adminstrn. (Staats Pub. Svc. award 1989). Office: Univ Southern California 1800 I St Sacramento CA 95814-3004

**NEWLAND, RUTH LAURA,** small business owner; b. Ellensburg, Wash., June 4, 1949; d. George J. and Ruth Marjorie (Porter) N. BA, Cen. Wash. State Coll., 1970, MEd, 1972; EdS, Vanderbilt U., 1973; PhD, Columbia Pacific U., 1981. Tchr. Union Gap (Wash.) Sch., 1970-71; owner Newland Ranch Gravel Co., Yakima, Wash., 1998; ptnr. Arnold Artificial Limb, Yakima, 1981-86, owner, pres. Yakima and Richland, Wash., 1986—. Owner Newland Ranch, Yakima, 1969—. Contbg. mem. Nat. Dem. Com., Irish Nat. Caucus Found.; mem. Pub. Citizen, We The People, Nat. Humane Edn. Soc.; charter mem. Nat. Mus. Am. Indian. George Washington scholar Masons, Yakima, 1967. Mem. NAFE, NOW, Am. Orthotic and Prosthetic Assn. Internat. Platform Assn., Nat. Antivisection Soc. (life), Vanderbilt U. Alumni Assn., Peabody Coll. Alumni Assn., Columbia Pacific U. Alumni Assn., World Wildlife Fund, Nat. Audubon Soc., Greenpeace, Mus. Fine Arts, Humane Soc. U.S., Wilderness Soc., Nature Conservancy, People for Ethical Treatment of Animals, Amnesty Internat., The Windstar Found., Rodale Inst., Sierra Club (life), Emily's List. Democrat. Avocations: reading, gardening, sewing, handcrafts. Home: 2004 Riverside Rd Yakima WA 98901-8540 Office: Arnold Artificial Limb 9 S 12th Ave Yakima WA 98902-3106 *Personal philosophy: God first. Then be politically and socially conservative but liberal in your concern for others.*

**NEWLIN, LYMAN WILBUR,** bookseller, consultant; b. Buda, Ill., May 26, 1910; s. Fred Matheny and Maude Lillian (Potter) N.; m. Evy Ottonia Magnusson, 1966; children: Fred M. II, Erik B.M. Student, Coll. Emporia, Kans., 1928-30, U. Chgo., 1930-32. Buyer, bus. mgr. Follett Book Co., Chgo., 1934-44; mgr. Minn. Book Store and Macalester Coll. Book Store, Mpls. and St. Paul, 1944-48; co-owner Broadwater Lodge, Hackensack, Minn., 1948-65; founder, owner Broadwater Books, Lewiston, NY, 1948—; buyer, dept. mgr. Kroch's & Brentano's Book Store, Chgo., 1951-65; regional mgr. Richard Abel and Co., Portland, Oreg. and Zion, Ill., 1966-69, asst. to pres. 1969-75; founder, prin. counselor Lyman W. Newlin Book Trade Counsellors, Lewiston, NY, 1975—; mdse. mgr. Coutts Library Services, Inc., Lewiston, 1976-90; pub. rels. advisor The Charleston (Coll. Libr.) Conf., 1985—; pub. liaison Book News, Inc., Portland, 1989—; v.p. Zenaida Pub., Amherst, Mass., 2004—. Program coord. Acad. of Scholarly Pub. seminar Coll. of Charleston, 1995—; cons. Rutgers U. Press, New Brunswick, N.J., 1975-81; panelist and lectr. to acad. librs. and schs., booksellers. Pub. Rev. Index Quar. Guide to Profl. Revs., 1941-43; co-editor: Scholarly Publishing, Books, Journals, Publishers and Libraries in the Twentieth Century, 2002; pub. rels. advisor, contbr. Bi-Monthly Publ. Against the Grain, 1985—; contbr. articles to profl. jours. Founder, 1st pres. Boy River Chain of Lakes Improvement Assn., Cass County, Minn., 1961-65, Concerned Parents Orgn., Freehold, 1976-79; trustee, v.p., sec., chmn. new libr. bldg. com. Lewiston Pub. Libr., 1985-98, pres. bd. trustees, 1998-2002; committeeman Niagara County Dem. Party, 1987—, sec., 1988-90; mem. coun. Luth. Ch. Messiah, Lewiston, 1982-93, deacon, 1992-97; mem. Town of Lewiston Sr. Citizens Adv. Bd., 1992—; mem., com. person Zion Luth. Ch., Niagara Falls, N.Y., 1995—. Named Dem. of Yr., Town of Lewiston, 2003. Mem. ALA, Assn. Book Travelers (50 Yr. award 1984), Am. Booksellers Assn. (50 yr. bronze plaque 1998), Soc. Scholarly Pub. (program com. 1985), Am. Assn. Pubs. (emeritus), Pi Kappa Delta. Lutheran. Democrat. Avocations: amateur ornithology, American folk music, New Orleans jazz, collecting books. *If the Golden Rule is truly one's rule in living, no other rule is needed.*

**NEWLIN, STEPHEN DORE,** chemicals executive: b. Pierre, S.D., Feb. 8, 1953; s. Douglas M. and Mary Newlin; m. Terry Ochsner, Aug. 17, 1975; children: Grant, Scott. BSCE, S.D. Sch. Mines & Tech., 1975; Advanced Mgmt. Program, Harvard U., 1990. Dist. rep. Nalco Chem. Co., Naperville, Ill., 1976-80, sales rep., 1980-82, dist. mgr. Watergy group, 1982-84, sales mgr. Watergy group, 1984-87, gen. mgr. Watergy group, 1987-90, gen. mgr. Unisolv group, 1990-92, gen. mgr. pulp & paper group, 1992-93, v.p.-pres. Nalco Pacific, 1993-94, pres. Nalco Europe, 1994, pres. specialty divsn., 1996, pres., 1998, COO, vice chmn., 2000; chmn. Nalco Exxon Energy Chemicals, 2000—01; private investor and bus. advisor, 2001—03; pres. indsl. ctr. Ecolab Inc., 2003—06; chmn., pres., CEO PolyOne Corp., 2006—. Bd. dirs. Black Hills Corp., 2004—. With USPHS. Mem. Paper Industry Mgrs., Triangle Alumni Assn. Avocation: sports. Office: PolyOne Corp 33587 Walker Rd Avon Lake OH 44012*

**NEWLIN, WILLIAM RANKIN,** lawyer; b. Pitts., Dec. 1, 1940; s. Theodore F. Newlin and Elizabeth Crooks; m. Ann Kleinschmidt, Aug. 25, 1962; children: Steffler Ann, Shelley Kay, William Rankin II. AB, Princeton U., 1962; JD, U. Pitts., 1965; DBA (hon.), Robert Morris Coll., 1997. Bar: Pa. 1965. Assoc. Buchanan Ingersoll, Pitts., 1965-71, ptnr., 1971—, mng. dir., 1980—; mng. gen. ptnr. CEO Venture Fund, Pitts., 1985—; chmn. bd. Kennametal Inc., Latrobe, Pa., 1996—. Bd. dirs. bd. Nat. City Bank Pa., Pitts., Parker/Hunter, Pitts., Black Box Corp., Pitts., Pitts. Regional Alliance, (hon.) British Consul, Pitts. Editor in chief U. Pitts. Law Rev., 1963; contbr. articles to profl. jours. Chmn., Gov. Thornburgh's Corp. Adv. Com., 1980-82; bd. dirs. Mfr. Studies Bd. nat. Rsch. Coun., Washington, 1988-89, Pitts. High Tech. Coun., 1982—. Pa. Tech. Coun. Recipient Entrepreneur of Yr. award Ernst & Young, Inc. Mag./ Merrill Lynch, 1991. Fellow Am. Bar Found., Pa. Bar Found.; mem. ABA (corp. banking, bus. law sect.), Pa. Bar Assn. (mem. coun. corp. banking and bus. law sect. 1973-82, chmn. sect. 1979-81, Spl. Achievement award 1982), Allegheny County Bar Assn., Bar of City of N.Y., Am. Law Inst., Pa. S.W. Assn. (trustee), Greater Pitts. C. of C. (bd. dirs.), Duquesne Club (dir. 1982-85), Rivers Club (bd. dirs. 1983—), Laurel Valley Golf Club, Allegheny Country Club (bd. dirs. 1988—). Office: Buchanan Ingersoll One Oxford Centre 301 Grant St Fl 20 Pittsburgh PA 15219-1410 E-mail: newlinwr@bipc.com.

**NEWMAN, ANDREW EDISON,** restaurant manager; b. St. Louis, Aug. 14, 1944; s. Eric Pfeiffer and Evelyn Frances (Edison) N.; m. Peggy Gregory, Feb. 14, 1984; children: Daniel Mark, Anthony Edison. BA, Harvard U., 1966, MBA, 1968. With Office of Sec. Def., Washington, 1968-70; with Edison Bros. Stores, Inc., St. Louis, 1970-95, v.p. ops. and adminstrn., 1975-80, dir., 1978-96, exec. v.p., 1980-86, chmn., 1987-95; chmn., CEO Race Rock Internat., St. Louis, 1995—. Bd. dirs. Lee Enterprises, Davenport, Iowa. Trustee Washington U. Office: 8000 Maryland Ave Saint Louis MO 63105-3752

**NEWMAN, ANDY,** journalist; Bklyn. Bur. reporter New York Times. Author: (articles) Serving Days who Serve God, 2005 (Art Feature award, Association of Alternative Newsweeklies, 2003), Fire Dept. Chaplain Resigns After Remarks About 9/11, 2005. Mem.: Association of Alternative Newsweeklies (organization/bylaws chmn. 1999—2001, editl. chmn. 2001—03). Office: The New York Times 229 W 43rd St New York NY 10036*

**NEWMAN, BARBARA MILLER,** psychologist, educator; b. Chgo., Sept. 6, 1944; d. Irving George and Florence (Levy) Miller; m. Philip R. Newman, June 12, 1966; children: Samuel Asher, Abraham Levy, Rachel Florence. Student, Bryn Mawr Coll.; AB with honors in Psychology, U. Mich., 1966, PhD in Devel. Psychology, 1971. Undergrad. research asst. in psychology U. Mich., 1963-64, research asst. in psychology, 1964-69, teaching fellow, 1965-71, asst. project dir. Inst. for Social Research, 1971-72, univ. lectr. in psychology and research assoc., 1971-72; asst. prof. psychology Russell Sage Coll., 1972-76, assoc. prof., 1977-78; assoc. prof. and chair dept. family rels. and human devel. Ohio State U., 1978-83, prof. and chair, 1983-86, assoc. provost for faculty recruitment and devel., 1987-92, prof., 1992-2000; prof. and chair dept. human devel. and family studies U. R.I., 2000—. Author: Development Through Life, 1975, 9th edit., 2006; author: (with P. Newman) Living: The Process of Adjustment, 1981, Understanding Adulthood, 1983; author: Adolescent Development, 1986, When Kids Go to College, 1992, Childhood and Adolescence, 1997; author: (with P. Newman, L. Landry-Meyer and B. Lohman) Life Span Development: A Case Book, 2003; contr. articles to profl. jours. Mem.: AAAS, APA, Soc. Rsch. in Child Devel., Am. Psychol. Soc., Nat. Coun. Family Rels., Groves Conf. on Marriage and Family, Soc. for Rsch. on Adolescence. Office: U RI Human Devel and Family Studies 112 Transition Ctr Kingston RI 02881 Office Phone: 401-874-7135. Business E-Mail: bnewman@uri.edu.

**NEWMAN, BARRY INGALLS,** retired bank executive; b. N.Y.C., Mar. 19, 1932; s. M.A. and T.C. (Weitman) N.; m. Jean Short, Mar. 6, 1965; children: Suzanne, Cathy, David. BA, Alfred U., 1952; JD, NYU, 1955. Bar: N.Y. 1957, Ohio 1958, U.S. Supreme Ct. 1967, Calif. 1990; practice in N.Y.C., 1957. Assoc., then ptnr. firm Shapiro Persky Marken & Newman, Cleve., 1957-63; asst v.p. Meinhard & Co. (now Meinhard Comml.), N.Y.C. 1963-65; v.p. Amsterdam Overseas Corp., N.Y.C., 1966-68; pres. No. Fin. Corp., L.A., 1968-72; sr. v.p. Aetna Bus. Credit, Inc., Hartford, Conn., 1972-78; exec. v.p. Security Pacific Fin. Group, San Diego, 1978-81, chmn., pres., CEO, 1981-82; sr. exec. v.p. Gt. Am. Bank, 1982—88, ret., 1988. Chmn. bd. dirs. San Diego County Capital Asset Leasing Corp., 1984-2000. Chmn. San Diego County Treasury Oversight com., 1995—; bd. govs. San Diego Found.; pres. San Diego County Civil Svc. Commn.; mem. planning commn. City of Escondido; judge pro tem Superior Ct., 2001—; mem. pub. utilities adv. commn. City of San Diego; treas. The Episcopal Diocese of San Diego, 1993—2001, v.p. bd. dirs., 2006—. Recipient Disting. Svc. award Cleve. Jr. C. of C., 1961. Mem. ABA, N.Y. State Bar Assn., Ohio Bar Assn., Calif. Bar Assn., San Diego Bar Assn., San Diego County Taxpayers Assn. (past pres., past chmn., dep. foreman 1999-2000.), Univ. Club of San Diego (past pres.), Masons. Republican. Home: 3308 Avenida Sierra Escondido CA 92029-7937 Office Phone: 760-743-5005. Personal E-mail: BNewmanlaw@aol.com.

**NEWMAN, BARRY MARC,** pediatric surgeon; b. NYC, Dec. 13, 1951; s. Sheldon and Miriam Newman; m. Jane Post, July 2, 1989; 1 child, Alexander Ross. BA, U. Pa., 1973; MD, SUNY, Stony Brook, 1976. Diplomate Nat. Bd. Med. Examiners, Am. Bd. Surgery, Am. Bd. Pediatric Surgery. Resident in surgery N.Y. Med. Coll., N.Y.C., 1976-78; sr. resident in surgery SUNY, Stony Brook, 1978-81; chief resident pediatric surgery Childrens Hosp. of Buffalo, 1981-83, fellow pediatric surgery and gastroenterology, 1983-84; asst. prof. surgery U. Va., Charlottesville, 1984-88, U. Ill., Chgo., 1988-93; dir. pediatric surgery Luth. Gen. Children's Hosp., Park Ridge, Ill., 1991-96; clin. assoc. prof. surgery U. Chgo., 1993-95; dir. pediatric surg. svcs. Loyola U. Med. Ctr., Maywood, Ill., 1996—, co-dir. surg. laparoscopy lab., 1996-97, assoc. prof. surgery and pediatrics, 1996—2004, prof. surgery and pediatrics, 2004—. Instr. Adv. Trauma and Life Support, ACS, Chgo., 1984—. Contr. articles to profl. jours., chapters to books. Grantee, NIH, 1982—83, 1987—88. Fellow ACS, Am. Coll. Chest Physicians, Am. Acad. Pediatrics; mem. Am. Gastroenterol. Assn., Am. Pediatric Surg. Assn., Am. Coll. Physician Execs. Democrat. Jewish. Avocations: wine collecting, scuba diving, underwater photography, personal computing. Office: Loyola U Med Ctr Dept Surgery 2160 S 1st Ave Dept Surgery Maywood IL 60153-3304 Office Phone: 708-327-2782. Business E-Mail: bnewma1@lumc.edu.

**NEWMAN, BRUCE MURRAY,** retired art gallery owner; b. NYC, Jan. 27, 1930; s. Meyer and Evelyn (Kantor) Newman; m. Judith S Brandus, June 26, 1965; 1 child, Emily Rachel. BA, Pratt Inst., 1953, D (hon.), 1997, BFA (hon.), 1998, degree (hon.) in fine arts, 1997. Pres. Newel Art Galleries Inc., NYC, 1975—2001. Lectr mus and univs; mem regional adv bd Chase Manhattan Bank; mem regional adv bd J P Morgan Chase Bank. Author: Fantasy Furniture, 1989, Don't Come Back Until You Find It, 2006; featured numerous TV & radio programs, mags. and other publs, guest CBS Morning Show, 1988. Assoc mem Mt Sinia Med Ctr, 1988—; bd dirs New York City Ctr, 1988—90; trustee Pratt Inst, Brooklyn, NY, 1983—. Named Man of the Yr., Pratt Inst., 1993; recipient Designer Award, Art Dirs. Club, 1984. Mem.: Victorian Soc Am, Am Soc Interior Designers (bd dirs 1989—). Avocations: golf, reading, jogging, travel.

**NEWMAN, CAROL L.,** lawyer; b. Yonkers, NY, Aug. 7, 1949; d. Richard J. and Pauline Frances (Stoll) N. AB/MA summa cum laude, Brown U., 1971; postgrad., Harvard U. Law Sch., 1972-73; JD cum laude, George Washington U., 1977. Bar: D.C. 1977, Calif. 1979. With antitrust divsn. U.S. Dept. Justice, Washington and L.A., 1977-80; assoc. Alschuler, Grossman & Pines, L.A., 1980-82, Costello & Walcher, L.A., 1982-85, Rosen, Wachtell & Gilbert, L.A., 1985-88, ptnr., 1988-90; v.p. Kech, Mahin & Cate, L.A., 1990-94; pvt. practice L.A., 1994—. Adj. prof. Sch. Bus., Golden Gate U., spring 1982. Commr. L.A. Bd. Transp. Commrs., 1993—98, v.p., 1995—96; pres. Bd. Taxicab Commrs., 1999—2001; candidate for State Atty. Gen., 1986; bd. dirs. Women's Progress Alliance, 1996—98. Mem. ABA, State Bar Calif., L.A. County Bar Assn., Ventura County Bar Assn., L.A. Lawyers for Human Rights (co. pres. 1991-92.), Log Cabin (bd. dirs 1992-97, 2003), pres. 1996-97), Calif. Women Lawyers (bd. govs. 1991-94), Order of Coif, Phi Beta Kappa. Office Phone: 818-225-0056. E-mail: cnewman540@aol.com.

**NEWMAN, CHARLES ANDREW,** lawyer; b. LA, Mar. 18, 1949; s. Arthur and Gladys Newman; m. Elizabeth F.; children: Anne R., Elyse S. BA magna cum laude, U. Calif., 1970; JD, Washington U., 1973. Bar: Mo. 1973, US Dist. Ct. (ea. dist.) Mo. 1973, US Dist. Ct. (so. dist.) Ill. 2001, US Dist. Ct. (ea. dist.) Mich. 2002, US Ct. Appeals (8th cir.) 1975, US Supreme Ct. 1976, DC 1981, US Tax Ct. 1981, US Claims Ct. 1981, US Ct. Appeals (11th cir.) 1994, US Ct. Appeals (9th cir.) 1995, US Ct. Appeals (3d, 5th, 7th and 10th cirs.) 1996, US Ct. Appeals (6th cir.) 1997, Ill. 2001, US Dist. Ct. (so. dist.) Ill. 2001, Wis. 2003, US Dist. Ct. (ea. dist.) Wis. 2003, NY. 2006. From assoc. to ptnr. Thompson & Mitchell, St. Louis, 1973-96; ptnr. Thompson Coburn, St. Louis, 1996-97, Bryan Cave LLP, St. Louis, 1997—. Lectr. law Washington U. St. Louis, 1976-78. Bd. dirs. Hawthorn Found., 1997-2000; trustee Mo. Bar Found., 1990-96, mem. Mo. Bar Bd. Govs. 1980-84; bd. dirs. United Israel Appeal, N.Y.C., 1990-93, Coun. Jewish Fedns., N.Y.C., 1992-95, United Jewish Appeal Young Leadership Cabinet, N.Y.C., 1985-88, Ctr. for Study of Dispute Resolution, 1985-88, Legal Svcs. Ea. Mo., 1985-94, St. Louis Community Found., 1992-2001, vice-chmn. 1997-99, St. Louis chpt. Young Audiences 1993-95, Planned Parenthood St. Louis, 1986-89, Jewish Fedn., St. Louis, 1986-98, asst. treas., 1989-90, v.p. fin. planning, 1990-93, asst. sec., 1994-95; v.p. Repertory Theatre, St. Louis, 1986-89, sr. v.p., 1990-91; pres. St. Louis Opportunity Clearinghouse, 1974-78. Recipient Lon O. Hocker Meml. Trial award Mo. Bar Found., 1984, What's Right with the Region award, FOCUS St. Louis, 2005. Mem. Bar Assn. Met. St. Louis (Merit award 1976). Democrat. Avocations: golf, reading, music, sailing. Office: Bryan Cave LLP One Metropolitan Square Saint Louis MO 63102-2750 Office Phone: 314-259-2000. Business E-Mail: canewman@bryancave.com.

**NEWMAN, CHARLES MICHAEL,** mathematician, physicist, educator; b. Chgo., Mar. 1, 1946; s. Harry M. and Dorothy Thelma (Pollack) N.; m. Arlene Milgram, July 5, 1970; children: Jennifer, Serena. BS in Physics, BS in Math., MIT, 1966; MA, Princeton U., 1968, PhD in Physics, 1971. Asst. prof. NYU, 1971-73, prof., 1989—, dir. grad. studies, 1996—98, dept. chair, 1998—2001, dir. Courant Inst. Math., 2002—06; asst. prof. Ind. U., Bloomington, 1973-75, assoc. prof., 1975-79; prof. U. Ariz., Tucson, 1979-90, regents prof., 1990-91. Editor book series on probability and applications, 1988—; assoc. editor: Annals of Probability, 1985-90, Annals of Applied Probability, 2006; author: Random Matrices and Their Applications, 1986; contbr. articles to Nature, Comm. Math. Physics, Physical Rev. Letters and others. J.S. Guggenheim fellow, 1984-85, A.P. Sloan fellow, 1978-81, NATO fellow, 1975-76; NSF grantee, 1974—, U.S.-Israel Binational grantee, 1978-81. Fellow Inst. Math. Stats., Am. Acad. Arts & Scis.; mem. NAS, Internat. Assn. Math. Physicists, Am. Math. Soc. Achievements include co-invention of cascade model of community food web structure, of model for three dimensional wetting phase transition; mathematical demonstration of consistency of neo-Darwinian evolution with fossil record patterns of punctuated equilibria; research concerning discontinuity of certain phase transitions; nature of spin glass models; full scaling limit of two-dimensional percolation. Office: Dept Math Warren Weaver Hall 1117 251 Mercer St New York NY 10012 Business E-Mail: newman@cims.nyu.edu.

**NEWMAN, CONSTANCE BERRY,** federal agency administrator; b. Chgo., July 8, 1935; d. Joseph Alonzo and Ernestine (Siggers) B.; m. Theodore Roosevelt Newman, July 25, 1959 (div. 1980). AB, Bates Coll., 1956; BSL, U. Minn., 1959; JD (hon.), Bates Coll., 1972, Amherst Coll., 1980; LHD (hon.), Central State U., 1991. Dir. VISTA, Washington, 1971-73; commr. Consumer Product Safety Commn., Washington, 1973-76; asst. sec. U.S. HUD, Washington, 1976-77; pres. The Newman & Hermanson Co., Washington, 1977-82; cons. Govt. of Lesotho, 1987-88; dir. nat. voter coalition Bush-Quayle '88, Washington, 1988; dir. Office Pers. Mgmt., Washington, 1989-92; under sec. Smithsonian Instn., Washington, 1992-2000; vice chair D.C. Fin. Responsiblity and Mgmt. Assistance Authority, 1994—2000; ptnr. Upstart Ptnrs., 2000—01; asst. adminr. bur. for Africa USAID, Washington, 2001—04; asst. sec. for African affairs US Dept. State, 2004—. Mem. adj. faculty John F. Kennedy Sch. Govt., Harvard U., Cambridge, Mass., 1979-82. Contbr. articles to profl. jours. Mem. Administrn. Conf. U.S., Washington, 1973-76, 1989—; commr. M.L. King Fed. Holiday Commn., Washington, 1989; chmn. Def. Adv. Com. on Women in the Svcs., Washington, 1985-86; trustee Community Coll. Balt., 1985-88; adv. to chmn. 1988 Rep. Nat. Conv., New Orleans, 1988; bd. overseers Morehouse Coll. Sch. Medicine, Atlanta, 1976-77; bd. dirs. Brookings Instn., Aspen Inst., Coun. for Excellence in Govt. Recipient Pub. Svc. award Ohio State U., 1991. Mem. NAACP, Exec. Women in Govt. (founding mem.), Internat. Repub. Inst., 1998-2000. Republican. Avocation: photography. E-mail: newmancb@state.gov.

**NEWMAN, DAVA JEAN,** aerospace engineering educator, director; b. Helena, Mont., Aug. 11, 1964; d. Daniel L. Newman and Deanna A. (Mack) Elliott. BS in Aerospace Engring., U. Notre Dame, 1986; MS in Tech. and Policy, MIT, 1989, MS in Aeronautics and Astronautics, 1989, PhD in Aerospace Biomed. Engring., 1992. Engr. Boeing Co., Seattle, 1986; cons., lectr. Internat. Space U., Strasbourg, France, 1987—; rsch. fellow NASA Ames Rsch. Ctr., Mountain View, Calif., 1989-92; asst. prof. U. Houston, 1992-93; C.S. Draper asst. prof. aerospace engring. MIT, Cambridge, Mass., 1993-95, prof. aeronautics, astronautics and engring. sys., 1998—2004, full prof. aeronautics, astronautics and engring. sys., 2004—, dir. Tech. and Policy Program, 2003—. Bd. dirs. Aeronautics and Space Engring. Nat. Acad.; cons. NASA Hdqs., Washington, 1995-96, Trotti and Assocs., Inc., Boston, 1996—, Nascent Technologies, Inc., 1999; affiliate faculty Health, Scis. and Tech. Harvard/MIT. Author: Interactive Aerospace Engineering and Design, 2002; contbr. author: Fundamentals of Space Life Sciences, 1997; contbr. over 100 articles to profl. jours.; author, prodr. U.S./Russian Astronaut Training Video, 1996. Bd. dirs. OMNISport 2001, 1990-2004; advisor KEYS To Empowring Youth, Cambridge, 1995—. Named Prof. of Yr., U. Houston, Soc. Automotive Engrs., 1993; recipient Manned Space Flight award NASA, 1995, Nat. Aerospace Educator award Women in Aerospace, 2001; numerous rsch. grants NASA, 1993—. Fellow AIAA (assoc.); mem. Am. Soc. for Engring. Edn., Internat. Soc. Biomechanics, Union Concerned Scientists, NY Acad. Scis., Soc. Women Engrs. Democrat. Achievements include rsch. in astronaut biomechanics and energetics for space flight and on the moon and Mars; world record holder of women's human-powered hydrofoil speed record. Office: MIT Rm 33-307 77 Massachusetts Ave Cambridge MA 02139-4307 Business E-Mail: dnewman@mit.edu.

**NEWMAN, DEAN GORDON,** business consultant; b. North Branch, Iowa, Mar. 17, 1929; s. Floyd William and Hazel Jane (Covault) N.; m. Maggie Newman; children: Gary Dean, Craig William. BA, Simpson Coll., 1950; MBA, Stanford U., 1952. From trainee to mgr. GE, Syracuse, N.Y. and Chgo., 1952—62, mgr. employee and cmty. rels. DeKalb, 1963—69; v.p. employee and pub. rels. United Nuclear Corp., Elmsford, NY, 1969—71; v.p. employee rels. Apache Corp., Mpls., 1971-83, v.p. human resources and comm., 1983-87; v.p. mktg. Nelson Cons. Group, Mpls., 1989-92; chmn., CFO Linear Fitness Systems, Inc., Allenspark, Colo., 1998—2004. Pres. Apache Found., 1973—87; v.p. bd. dirs. Boys Clubs, Mpls., 1978—85; chmn. Boys and Girls Club Mpls., 1985—88, exec. com., 1988—89; v.p. fin., bd. Boys and Girls Club Larimer County, 1993—96; vice chmn. Bus. Econs. Edn. Found. 1986—88, chmn. fin. com., 1988—89; com. mem., treas. Allenspark Sr. Adv. Com., 1999—2003; treas. Allenspark Fire Protection Dist., 2000—05, bd. dirs., 2000—05. With USNR, 1952—55, Korea. Nat. Meth. scholar, 1946—50, Hicks fellow, 1952. Mem.: Nat. Assn. Mfrs. (dir. 1981—87), Allenspark Area Club (bd. dirs., treas. 2000—03, Founder's award 2002, Boulder County Honoring Our Elders award 2003), Pi Gamma Mu, Sigma Tau Delta, Epsilon Sigma, Alpha Tau Omega. Republican. Methodist. Home and office: 2930 Bryn Mawr Pl Longmont CO 80503 Office Phone: 303-747-2825. E-mail: mdnewman85@earthlink.net.

**NEWMAN, DIANA S.,** foundation administrator, consultant; b. Toledo, June 15, 1943; d. Fred Andrew and Thelma Elizabeth (Hewitt) Smith; m. Dennis Ryan Newman, Feb. 15, 1964; children: Barbara Lynn Newman LaBine, John Ryan, Elizabeth Anne. Student, Oberlin Coll., 1961-64. Asst. treas. Marble Cliff Quarries Co., 1964-68; cmty. vol., 1968-83; dir. Ohio Hist. Found., Columbus, 1983-90; v.p. advancement The Columbus (Ohio) Found., 1990-95; pres. Philanthropic Resource Group, Columbus, 1995—. Author: Opening Doors: Pathways to Diverse Donors, 2002 (AFP/Skystone Ryan prize for rsch., 2003), Nonprofit Essentials: Endowment Building, 2005. Bd. dirs. Leader Inst., Inc., 2001-04; mem. governing bd. First Cmty. Ch., 1983-88, chair, 1987-88; bd. dirs. LWV Ctrl. Ohio, 1968-72, Ohio Mus. Assn., 1985-90, Crittenton Family Svcs., Columbus, 1992-95; founder Franklin County Com. on Criminal Justice, Columbus, 1972; pres. Jr. League Columbus, 1980-81. Mem. Assn. Fundraising Profls. (bd. dirs. Ctrl. Ohio chpt. 1985-88, 2004-, nat. rsch. coun. 2003—, Outstanding Profl. Fundraiser 2004), Ctrl. Ohio Planned Giving Coun. (bd. dirs. 1990-2001, pres. 1998), Columbus Female Benevolent Soc. (bd. dirs. 1984—). Home: 1944 Chatfield Rd Columbus OH 43221-3702 Office: Philanthropic Resource Group 926 Augusta Glen Dr Columbus OH 43235 Office Phone: 614-486-4787. Business E-Mail: diana@diananewman.com.

**NEWMAN, DONALD LYNN,** psychologist, consultant; b. Jeffersonville, Ind., Jan. 5, 1951; s. Mason Lynn and Rita Scott Newman; m. Kathy Jean Hopkins, July 28, 1993; children: Higgens McPheaters, Isabella Catalina, Fannie Jean. BA in Sociology, U. Ariz., 1974; MSW, Ariz. State U., 1976; M in Sch. Psychology, No. Ariz. U., 1996. LCSW Ariz.; cert. sch. psychologist Ariz. Dept. Edn. Founder, CEO Family Preservationists: Counseling Assocs., Phoenix, 1991—94, AmeriPsych, Inc., Phoenix, 1994—2005; exec. dir. Gen. Health Corp. ResCare Inc. (formerly AmeriPsych, Inc.), Phoenix, 2005—. Author: PREP-R: Parenting and Resource Education Program-Revised. Exec. dir. Cmtys. in Need, Phoenix, 1991—2005; pres. Children with Challenges, Phoenix, 1995—2005. Grantee State of Ariz., 1995—2005. Mem.: Nat. Assn. Sch. Psychologists (life). Democrat. Buddhist. Avocations: running, travel, fly fishing, gardening, food preserving. Office: AmeriPsych Inc 3877 N 7th St Ste 220 Phoenix AZ 85014 Fax: 602-728-0632. Office Phone: 602-728-0630. Business E-Mail: dnewman@ameripsych.com.

**NEWMAN, EDWIN HAROLD,** news commentator; b. NYC, Jan. 25, 1919; s. Myron and Rose (Parker) N.; m. Rigel Grell, Aug. 14, 1944; 1 child, Nancy (Mrs. Henry Drucker). BA, U. Wis., 1940; postgrad. (fellow), La. State U., 1940. With Washington bur. Internat. News Svc., 1941, U.P., 1941-42, 45-46, N.Y. Daily PM, 1946-47; ind. Washington news bur., 1947; asst to Eric Sevareid at Washington bur. CBS, 1947-49; freelance writer, broadcaster London, 1949-52; with European Recovery Program, 1951-52, NBC, 1952—, chief news bur. London, 1956-57, Rome, 1957-58, Paris, 1958-61, news commentator NYC, 1961-83; columnist King Features Syndicate, 1984-89. Moderator 1st Ford-Carter Debate, 1976, 2d Reagan-Mondale debate, 1984; moderator ann. conf. former secs. of state, 1983—, former secs. of def., 1987—. Narrator: TV spls. including Japan: East is West, 1961, Orient Express, 1964, Who Shall Live?, 1965, Pensions-The Broken Promise, 1972, Violence in America, 1977, I Want It All Now, 1978, Spying for Uncle Sam, 1978, Oil and American Power, 1979, The Billionaire Hunts, 1981, Congress: We the People, 1983-84, On Television, 1985-86, Freud, 1987, The Borgias, 1988; host Saturday Night Live, 1984; drama critic WNB C-TV, 1965-71 (Emmy awards 1966, 68, 70, 72, 73, 74, 82, Peabody award 1966); author: Strictly Speaking: Will America Be The Death of English?, 1974, A Civil Tongue, 1976, Sunday Punch, 1979, I Must Say, 1988; contbr. articles and revs. to various periodicals, U.S., Can. and Eng.; chmn. usage panel Am. Heritage Dictionary, 1975-80. Served from ensign to lt. USNR, 1942-45. Decorated chevalier Legion of Honor France; recipient awards Overseas Press Club, 1961, awards U. Wis. Sch. Journalism, 1967, awards U. Mo. Sch. Journalism, 1975 Mem. AFTRA, Authors Guild, Screen Actors Guild. Address: care Richard Fulton Inc 66 Richfield St Plainview NY 11803-1441

**NEWMAN, EILEEN,** not-for-profit organization executive; 1 child. Exec. dir. Film/Video Arts, N.Y.C., 1998—. Program officer New Visions for Pub. Schs. Mem.: The N.Y. Film/Video Coun. (bd. dirs.), N.Y. Women in Film and TV (bd. dirs., past v.p.), Educators for Social Responsibility (v.p.). Office: Film/Video Arts 462 Broadway Ste 520 New York NY 10013

**NEWMAN, ERIC A.,** neuroscientist; b. NY, May 9, 1950; s. Arnold and Augusta Newman; m. Janice I. Gepner, June 1, 1975; children: Mark H., Sarah F. PhD, MIT, Cambridge, Mass., 1977. Prof. U. Minn., Mpls., 1999—. Achievements include discovery of functions of glial cells in the central nervous system. Office: University of Minnesota 321 Church St SE Minneapolis MN 55455 Office Phone: 612-625-2699.

**NEWMAN, FREDRIC SAMUEL,** lawyer, communications executive; b. York, Pa., June 22, 1945; s. Nat. Howard and Josephine (Farkas) N.; m. Mary E. Kiley, May 19, 1973; children: Lydia Ann, Anne Marie, Pauline. AB cum laude, Harvard U., 1967; JD, Columbia U., 1970; cert. the exec. program, U. Va., 1984. Bar: N.Y. 1971, U.S. Dist. Ct. (so. and ea. dists.) N.Y. 1972, U.S. Ct. Appeals (2d cir.) 1974, U.S. Ct. Claims 1993. Assoc. White & Case, N.Y.C., 1970-80; asst. gen. counsel Philip Morris Cos., N.Y.C., 1981-87; gen. counsel, v.p., sec. Philip Morris Cos., Inc., N.Y.C., 1987-90; chief exec. officer TeamTennis, Inc., 1991; prin. Law Office of Fredric S. Newman, N.Y.C., 1992-95; founding ptnr. Hoguet Newman & Regal, LLP, 1996—; pres., CEO, Pathe Comm. Corp., N.Y.C., 1993-97. Bd. dirs. Exel Ins. Co., Bermuda. Trustee Calhoun Sch., N.Y.C., 1985-88; bd. dirs. N.Y. Fire Safety Found., N.Y.C., 1985-88; treas. Clean Water/Clean Air Bond Act Com., 1996. Fellow Am. Bar Found.; mem. Columbia Law Sch. Assn. (bd. dirs. 1999-2001). Office: 10 E 40th St New York NY 10016-0200

**NEWMAN, GERALDINE ANNE,** advertising executive; b. Boston, Apr. 01; d. Joseph M. and Clara (Bistry) N. BS, UCLA; postgrad., Alliance Francaise, Paris, Los Angeles Sch. Fine Arts, NYU. Writer Tinker Dodge and Delano, N.Y.C., 1970-72, Ketchum Advt., N.Y.C., 1972-75, Advt. to Women, N.Y.C., 1975-78; v.p., creative supr. Young and Rubicam, N.Y.C., 1978-83; v.p., assoc. creative dir. Backer Spielvogel Bates Worldwide Internat. Div., N.Y.C., 1983-90; pres. Geraldine Newman Comm., Inc., N.Y.C., 1990—. County committeewoman Dem. Party, N.Y.C., 1972; advt. adviser Youth at Risk, Breakthrough Found., Food Bank, Food for All, Gifts that Give Back. Featured in Adweek Mag., 1986, Response Mag., 2004; winner Andy award 1975, 78, 82, 84, Clio award 1982, ERA award, 1998, 2004, Astrid award Mercomm Internat., 2002, numerous others. Mem.: Ad Club N.Y., Electronic Retailing Assn., Ad-net (bd. dirs. 1984—89, creative dir. 1986—89, Pres.'s award 1988), N.Y. Women in Film. Avocations: travel, painting. Home and Office: 315 E 72nd St New York NY 10021-4625 Office Phone: 212-988-3395. E-mail: advertisingmuse@aol.com.

**NEWMAN, HOWARD NEAL,** lawyer, educator; b. N.Y.C., June 11, 1935; s. Herman and Sarah (Steinsaltz) N.; m. Carol Redstone, Dec. 25, 1960; children: Leslie, Amy. AB, Dartmouth Coll., 1956, MBA, 1957; MS, Columbia U., 1959; JD, Temple U., 1970. Trainee to asst. v.p. Roosevelt Hosp., N.Y.C., 1957-65; assoc. adminstr. Pa. Hosp., Phila., 1965-70; commr. Med. Services Adminstrn., Washington, 1970-74; pres. Dartmouth-Hitchcock Med. Center, Hanover, N.H., 1974-80; adminstr. Health Care Financing Adminstr., Dept. Health and Human Services, Washington, 1980-81; ptnr. Memel, Jacobs, Pierno & Gersh, Washington, 1982-86, Powell, Goldstein, Frazer & Murphy, Washington, 1986-88; dean, prof. health policy and mgmt. NYU, 1988-94, prof. health policy and mgmt., 1994—. Served with USAR, 1959-65. White House fellow, 1967-68 Mem. Nat. Inst. for Dispute Resolution, D.C. Bar Assn. Jewish.

**NEWMAN, J. BONNIE,** academic administrator, former government official; b. Lawrence, Mass., June 2, 1945; d. William Michael and Louise Catherine (Casey) Newman BA, St. Joseph's Coll., Maine, 1967; MEdn, Pa. State U., 1969; LHD (hon.), Rivier Coll., Nashua, NH, 1993, LLD (hon.), Notre Dame Coll., Manchester, NH, 1984, Keene State Coll., NH, 1987; LHD (hon.), St. Joseph's Coll., Standish, Maine, 1990. Exec. dir. Forum on NH's Future, 1978-80; dir. 1980-82; dean of students, U NH, Durham, 1969—72, dean of students, 1972-78, interim dean Whittemore Sch. of Bus. and Econs., 1998—99; interim pres., 2006—; chief of staff Congressman Judd Gregg, 1981-82; assoc. dir. Office Presdl. Pers. The White House, Washington, 1982-84, asst. sec. commerce for econ. devel., 1984-85, asst. to the Pres. for Mgmt. and Adminstrn., 1989—91; exec. dean Kennedy Sch. Govt., Harvard U., 2000—05. Bd. dirs. NH Charitable Found., Citizens Advisors, Lumina Found., Markem Corp.; chmn. US Navy Acad. Bd. of Visitors. Bd. dirs. Gov.'s Econ. Devel. & Land Use Com., 1979-80. Named Alumni Fellow, Pa. State U.; recipient Granite State Award, Yankee Award, Pub. Rels. Soc., Lifetime Achievement Award, Bus. and Industry Assn. of NH, New England Coun.'s Leadership Award, Abigail Adams Award, Mass. Women's Polit. Caucus, 2005. Mem.: Bus. and Industry Assn. NH (pres. 1985—88), Econ. Club of NY. Republican. Roman Catholic. Office: Office of Pres / U NH Thompson Hall 105 Main St Durham NH 03824 Office Phone: 603-862-2450. Office Fax: 603-862-3060.*

**NEWMAN, JOAN MESKIEL,** lawyer; b. Youngstown, Ohio, Dec. 12, 1947; d. John F. and Rosemary (Scarmuzzi) Meskiel; children: Anne R., Elyse S. BA in Polit. Sci., Case-Western Reserve U., 1969; JD, Washington U., St. Louis, 1972, LLM in Taxation, 1973. Bar: Mo. 1972. Assoc. Lewis & Rice, St. Louis, 1973-80, ptnr., 1981-90, Thompson Coburn, St. Louis, 1990—. Adj. prof. law Washington U. Sch. Law, St. Louis, 1975-92; past pres. St. Louis chpt., mem. Midwest Pension Conf. Mem. nat. coun. Washington U. Sch. Law, 1988—91; chmn. bd. dir. Great St. Louis coun. Girl Scouts USA, 1975—92, officer, 1978—92; mem. cmty. wide youth svcs. panel United Way Greater St. Louis, 1992—96; fin. futures task force Kiwanis Camp Wyman, 1992—93; chmn. staff blue ribbon fin. com. Sch. Dist., Clayton, 1986—87; vol. Women's Self Help Ctr.; bd. dirs. Parents as Teachers, 2001—04; bd. dirs., exec. com. Girl Scouts USA, 1993—99, nat. treas., 1996—99; bd. dirs. Met. Employment and Rehab. Svcs., 1980—2001, chmn. bd. dir., 1994—96; bd. dirs. Jewish Ctr. Aged, 1990—92, bd. dirs., 2000—2001, Jewish Fedn. St. Louis, 1991—96, City Mus., 1998—2001, Parents as Tchrs., 2000—; chmn. bd. dir. Women of Achievement, 1993—96; bd. dir. United Way Greater St. Louis, 2000—, Oasis, 1999—2001; bd. dirs. MERS/Goodwill Industries, 2001—, Walker Scottish Rite Ctr., 2002—. Named Woman of Achievement

St. Louis, 1991. Mem. Mo. Bar Assn. (staff pension and benefits com. 1991—), Bar Met. St. Louis (past chmn. taxation sect.), St. Louis Forum, Order of Coif (hon.). Office Phone: 314-645-5001. Business E-Mail: joan@joannewmanassociates.com.

**NEWMAN, JOHN M., JR.,** lawyer; b. Youngstown, Ohio, Aug. 15, 1944; BA, Georgetown U., 1966; JD, Harvard U., 1969. BAr: Ill. 1970, Calif. 1972, Ohio 1976. Law clerk ctrl. dist. U.S. Dist. Ct., Calif., 1969-70, asst. U.S. Atty. ctrl. dist. Calif., 1970-75; ptnr. Jones, Day, Cleve. Fellow Am. Coll. Trial Lawyers; mem. Phi Beta Kappa. Office: Jones Day North Point 901 Lakeside Ave E Cleveland OH 44114-1190 Office Phone: 216-586-7207. Business E-Mail: jmnewman@jonesday.com.

**NEWMAN, JOHN MERLE,** lawyer; b. Cleve., June 25, 1934; s. Emanuel Robert and Theresa Esther (Dreissinger) N.; 1 child, Thomas Edward; m. Thelma Aitken, July 10, 1992; 1 child, Jennifer Ann Newman-Brazil. AB, Miami U., Oxford, Ohio, 1957; LLB, Cornell U., 1957. Bar: N.J. 1971, U.S. Ct. Appeals (3d cir.) 1961, U.S. Dist. Ct. N.J. 1983, U.S. Dist. Ct. (so. and ea. dists.) N.Y. 1983; cert. civil atty. Supreme Ct. of N.J. Assoc. Bertram Polow, Morristown, N.J., 1960-62; ptnr. Porzio Bromberg & Newman P.C., Morristown, 1962-76, 80—; presiding judge chancery/family divsn. Superior Ct. of N.J., Morristown, 1976-80. Trustee, officer Cmty. Med. Ctr., Randolph Libr., Morristown, 1970-74, Hist. Speedwell Mus., Morristown, 1991—, Family Svc., Morristown, 1988-91; trustee Occupational Tng. Ctr., Morristown, 1965-69. Recipient Cert. of Acad. Performance U. Edinburgh, Scotland, 1956, Trial Bar award N.J. Trial Lawyers Assn., 1997, various certs. for bar and cmty. svcs. Fellow Internat. Soc. Barristers; mem. ABA (litigation sect., environ. subcom., environ. law sect. corp. counsel subcom., class action various coms.), Am. Bd. Trial Advs., N.J. State Bar Assn., Morris County Bar Assn., Omicron Delta Kappa. Avocations: bicycling, tennis. Office: Porzio Bromberg & Newman 163 Madison Ave Ste 6 Morristown NJ 07960-7323

**NEWMAN, JOHN NICHOLAS,** naval architect educator; b. New Haven, Mar. 10, 1935; s. Richard and Daisy (Neumann) N.; m. Kathleen Smedley Kirk, June 16, 1956; children—James Bartram, Nancy Kirk, Carol Ann. BS Mass. Inst. Tech., 1956, MS, 1957, Sc.D., 1960; postgrad., Cambridge U., Eng., 1958-59; D Technicae honoris causa, U. Trondheim, Norway, 1992. Research naval architect David Taylor Model Basin, Navy Dept., Washington, 1959-67; assoc. prof. naval architecture MIT, Cambridge, 1967-70, prof., 1970—, prof. emeritus. Vis. prof. U. New South Wales, Australia, 1973, U. Adelaide, Australia, 1974, Tech. U. Norway, 1981-82; cons. Navy Dept., Dept. Justice, pvt. firms. Author: Marine Hydrodynamics, 1977; Contbr.: articles to profl. jours., including Sci. Am. Recipient prize Am. Bur. Shipping, 1956; Walter Atkinson prize Royal Instn. Naval Architects, 1973, also Bronze medal, 1976; Guggenheim fellow, 1973-74; research grantee Office Naval Research; NSF. Mem. AAAS, NAE, Soc. Naval Architects and Marine Engrs. (Davidson medal 1988), Norwegian Acad. Sci. Home: 1 Bowditch Rd Woods Hole MA 02543-1201 Business E-Mail: jnn@mit.edu.

**NEWMAN, JON O.,** federal judge; b. NYC, May 2, 1932; s. Harold W. Jr. and Estelle L. (Ormond) Newman; m. Martha G. Silberman, June 19, 1953 (dec. Feb. 2005); children: Leigh, Scott, David. Grad., Hotchkiss Sch., 1949; AB magna cum laude, Princeton U., 1953; LLB, Yale U., 1956; LLD (hon.), U. Hartford, 1975, U. Bridgeport, 1980, Bklyn. Law Sch., 1995, N.Y. Law Sch., 1996. Bar: Conn. 1956, D.C. 1956. Law clk. to Hon. George T. Washington U.S. Ct. Appeals, 1956—57; sr. law clk. to Hon. Earl Warren U.S. Supreme Ct., 1957—58; ptnr. Ritter, Satter & Newman, Hartford, Conn., 1958—60; counsel to majority Conn. Gen. Assembly, 1959; spl. counsel to gov. Conn., 1959—61; asst. to sec. HEW, 1961—62; adminstrv. asst. to U.S. senator, 1963—64; U.S. atty. Dist. of Conn., 1964—69, U.S. dist. judge, 1972—79; pvt. practice, 1969—71; U.S. cir. judge Hartford, 1979—93; chief judge U.S. Ct. of Appeals 2d Cir., Hartford, 1993—97, sr. judge, 1997—. Co-author: Politics: The American Way, 1964, A Genealogical Chart of Greek Mythology, 2003. With USAR, 1954—62. Recipient Learned Hand medal, Fed. Bar Coun., 1987. Fellow: Am. Bar Found.; mem.: ABA, Am. Judicature Soc., Conn. Bar Assn., Am. Law Inst. Democrat. Office: US Ct Appeals 2d Cir 450 Main St Hartford CT 06103-3022*

**NEWMAN, JOSEPH HERZL,** advertising executive, consultant; b. N.Y.C., Dec. 1, 1928; s. Max A. and Tillie C. (Weitzman) N.; m. Ruth Zita Marcus, Dec. 19, 1954 (div. Feb. 1987); children: Deborah Lynn, David Alan, Mark Jonathan; m. Nancy Kramer Deutschman, Aug. 19, 1990 (dec. Feb. 2005); stepchildren: Pamela Sue Deutschman, Douglas Hayes Deutschman, Cindi Elaine Deutschman-Ruiz. AB, Bethany Coll., W.Va., 1949; MS Grad. Sch. Bus., Columbia U., 1956. With 20th Century Fox Film Corp., NYC, 1949—53; media supr. Fred Wittner Advt. Agy., NYC, 1953—56; media dir. O.S. Tyson & Co., NYC, 1956—64; v.p., media dir. Marsteller Inc., NYC, 1965—85; v.p., assoc. media dir. HBM/Creamer, NYC, 1985—87; Della Femina, McNamee, Inc., NYC, 1987—89; pres. Newman And Assocs., Cleve., 1989—. Mem. faculty Advt. Age Media Workshop, 1972; past chmn. media mgrs. adv. com. Bus. Publs. Audit of Circulation Inc., N.Y.C.; condr. profl. media planning seminars, 1989-99. Contbr. articles to profl. jours. Past chmn. bus.-to-bus. media com. Am. Assn. Advt. Agys.; vice chmn. tax incentive rev. coun. City of Mayfield Heights, Ohio, 1994-97, chmn., 1997-2005, co-vice chmn., 2005-06; mem. master plan adv. com. City of Mayfield Heights, 2003-04; mem. mayor's cmty. coun., 2006—; rep. Mayfield Heights to Euclid Creek Watershed Coun., 2003-. With U.S. Army, 1950-52. Mem. Bus. Mktg. Assn. (past mem. media comparability coun., media data form com. and rsch. resource com., Agy. Exec. of Yr., N.Y. chpt. 1960, 66, 71, 73, cert. bus. communicator). Home and Office: 6338 Woodhawk Dr Mayfield Heights OH 44124-4153 Office Phone: 440-449-1804. E-Mail: nknewmansion@aol.com.

**NEWMAN, KENNETH E.,** lawyer; b. N.Y.C., Sept. 28, 1946; s. Stanley and Muriel (Orenstein) N.; m. Michele M. Jette; children: Douglas C., Jason B., Gregory R. BA, Queens Coll., N.Y.C., 1967; JD, St. John's U., N.Y.C., 1971. Bar: N.Y. 1972, U.S. Supreme Ct. 1976, U.S. Ct. Appeals (2nd cir.) 1974, U.S. Ct. Appeals (D.C. cir.) 1974, U.S. Ct. Appeals (3d cir.) 1980, U.S. Ct. Appeals (10th cir.) 1982, (4th cir.) 1988, U.S. Dist. Ct. (so. dist.) N.Y. 1974, (ea. dist.) N.Y. 1979. Trial atty. U.S. Dept. Justice, Washington, 1971-73, atty. gen. honors program appointee; assoc. Donovan Leisure Newton & Irvine, N.Y.C., 1973-80, ptnr., 1980-95; sr. v.p., ea. regional counsel Walt Disney Co., N.Y.C., 1995—. Trial faculty Practicing Law Inst., N.Y.C., 1983-94. Dir. Jr. Achievement NY. Mem. ABA, Fed. Bar Coun., Assn. Bar City of N.Y. Office: The Walt Disney Co 77 W 66th St New York NY 10023

**NEWMAN, LAWRENCE,** lawyer, educator; b. NYC, May 31, 1931; s. Herman and Sarah (Steinsaltz) N.; m. Helaine J. Glickstein, June 6, 1954; children: Debra, Daniel, Karen. AB, Dartmouth Coll., 1952; LL.B., Yale U., 1955; S.JD, N.Y. Law Sch., 1963. Bar: N.Y. 1956. Law clk. to Hon. Lawrence E. Walsh U.S. Dist. Ct., NYC, 1955-57. Adj. prof. U. Pa. Law Sch., Phila., 1969—, Yale U. Law Sch., 1983—85; Everett B. Birch adj. prof. wills and estate planning Columbia U. Law Sch., NYC, 1994—. Author: (with Albert Kalter) Postmortem Estate Planning, 1976, 2nd edit., 1994. Mem. exec. com. Am. Friends of Hebrew U., chmn. bd., 1994-98. Fellow Am. Bar Found., Am. Coll. Trust and Estate Coun.; mem. ABA (chmn. sect. legal edn. 1979-80, chmn. com. estate & gift taxation 1976-78), Estate Planning Council N.Y.C. (pres. 1978-79), N.Y. State Bar Assn. Office: NYU Sch Law 435 West 116th St New York NY 10027-7297 Office Phone: 212-854-2640. E-mail: lnewman@law.columbia.edu.

**NEWMAN, LAWRENCE WALKER,** lawyer; b. Boston, July 1, 1935; s. Leon Bettoney and Hazel W. (Walker) N.; children: Timothy D., Isabel B., Thomas H. AB, Harvard U., 1957, LL.B., 1960. Bar: D.C. 1961, N.Y. 1965. Atty. U.S. Dept. Justice, 1960-61, Spl. Study of Securities Markets and Office Spl. Counsel on Investment Co. Act Matters, U.S. SEC, 1961-64; asst. U.S. atty. So. Dist. N.Y., 1964-69; assoc. Baker & McKenzie, N.Y.C., 1969-71, ptnr., 1971—. Mem. internat. adv. coun. World Arbitration Inst., 1984-87; adv. com. Asia Pacific Ctr. for Resolution of Internat. Trade Disputes, 1987—;

adv. bd. Inst. for Transnat. Arbitration, 1988—; chmn. U.S. Iranian Claimants Com., 1982—; adv. bd. World Arbitration and Mediation Report, 1993-2002, co-chmn., 2002—; bd. adv. to Corporate Counsel's Internat. Adviser, 1995—. Co-author: The Practice of Internat. Litigation, 1992, 2d edit. 1998, Litigating Internat. Commercial Disputes, 1996; columnist N.Y. Law Jour., 1982—; bd. advisors Corp. Counsel's Internat. Adviser; contbr. articles to profl. jours., chpts. to books; editor: Enforcement of Money Judgments, Attachment of Assets, Internat. Arbitration Checklists; chmn. editl. bd. Juris Pub., Inc.; co-editor: Revolutionary Days: The Iran Hostage Crisis and the Hague Claims Tribunal, A Look Back, 1999, Take the Witness: The Experts Speak on Cross-examination, 2006. Mem. Internat. Bar Assn. (com. dispute resolution, com. constrn. litigation), Inter-Am. Bar Assn., Fed. Bar Coun., Am. Fgn. Law Assn., Maritime Law Assn. U.S., Assn. Bar City N.Y. (com. on arbitration and alternative dispute resolution 1991-94, com. internat. comml. dispute resolution, 2000—, chmn. 2003—), Am. Arbitration Assn. (corp. counsel com. 1987—, panel internat. arbitrators), U.S. Coun. Internat. Bus., Ct. Arbitration of Polish Chamber Fgn. Trade (panel of arbitrators), Brit. Col. Internat. Comml. Arbitration Ctr., Am. Law Inst., Bar Assn. City N.Y. (inaugural mem. com. on internat. comml. dispute resolution, chmn. 2003—). Office: Baker & McKenzie 805 3rd Ave New York NY 10022-7513 Office Phone: 212-891-3970. E-mail: lwn@bakernet.com.

**NEWMAN, LEONARD JAY,** retail jewel merchant, gemologist; b. Milw., Oct. 25, 1927; s. David and Pia Goldie (Smith) N.; m. Louise Shainberg, Jan. 14, 1951; children: Shelley, Marty, Alan, Heidi, Dee. BS, Purdue U.; postgrad., Washington U., St. Louis. Owner, mgr. Newman's Diamond Ctr., Jasper, Ind., 1951—; tchr. The Jasper Ctr., Ind., 1970-80. Bd. dirs. Sta. WFIU Pub. Radio, VUJC Found., State Bd. Health Systems Agy., sub area Health Systems Agy., Internat. Harp Competition, Bloomington United Way, Ind. U. Hillel Found.; consellor Sr. corps Re. Execs.; 1st v.p. Vincennes Univ. Found.; past pres. Jasper Community Arts Commn.; pres. Friends of Arts; commnr. Boy Scouts Am.; mem. Dubois County Mental Health Assn.; lay adv. bd. Convent Immaculate Conception Sisters of St. Benedict, Ferdinand, Ind,; adv. bd. Jasper Hist. Soc., German Club, Young Abe Lincoln Soc., WFIU pub. radio; bd. dirs. Dubois County Crippled Children's Soc., Bloomington (Ind.) Symphony, Patoka Valley Vocat. Coop., Patoka Valley Rehab., Beth Shalom, Monroe County Purdue Alumni, Camerata Orch., Ind. U. Friends of Music, Ind. Jewish Hist. Soc., Hillel Found.; pres. Jasper Edn. Fund; mem., chmn. nominee com. Raintree Coun. Girl Scouts U.S.A., bd. dirs.; Midwest bd. dirs. Anti-Defamation League. Recipient Outstanding Citizenship award Purdue U. Alumni Assn., 1980 Outstanding Alumni award Jasper High Sch., Ronald Reagan Medal, 1994, Outstanding Community Svc. award Bloomington, Ind. C. of C., 2000, 01, Gov.'s award Sagamore of the Wabash, 2001. Mem. Nat. Assn. Jewelry Appraisers (sr.), Ind. Jewelers Orgn. Am., Retail Jewelers Am., Jasper C. of C., Jaycees (Rooster, past pres., past nat. bd. dirs., Disting. Svc. award 1957), Monroe County Purdue Alumni Club (bd. dirs.), Nat. Soc. Arts and Letters (bd. mem.), Svc. Corp. Ret. Execs. (pres.), Purdue Agrl. Alumni Assn. (hon.), Skull and Crescent (hon.), Hadassah, Sigma Alpha Mu, Alpha Phi Omega, Lions, Masons, Shriners (past pres.), B'nai Brith, Temple Beth Shalom (pres.). Office: Newman's Diamond Ctr 3 D Pl Jasper IN 47546 Home: 3754 Villa Glen Ct Bloomington IN 47401 E-mail: newmangem@insightbb.com.

**NEWMAN, LESLÉA,** writer; b. Bklyn., Nov. 5, 1955; d. Edward and Florence Newman; m. Mary Vazquez. BS in Edn., U. Vt., 1977; cert. in poetics, Naropa Inst., Boulder, Colo., 1980. Author: A Letter to Harvey Milk, 1988, Heather Has Two Mommies, 1989, In Every Laugh a Tear, 1992, Fat Chance, 1994, Too Far Away to Touch, 1995, Remember That, 1996, Still Life with Buddy, 1997, Out of the Closet and Nothing to Wear, 1997, Matzo Ball Moon, 1998, Girls Will Be Girls, 2000, Signs of Love, 2001, Cats, Cats, Cats!, 2001, Dogs, Dogs, Dogs!, 2002, Runaway Dreidel, 2002;: She Loves Me, She Loves Me Not, 2002, Felicia's Favorite Story, 2002, Pigs, Pigs, Pigs!, 2003, Best Short Stories of Leslea Newman, 2003, The Best Cat in the World, 2004 (Muse Medallion Best Children's Book award Cat Writers Assn., awards), The Boy Who Cried Fabulous, 2004, A Fire Engine for Ruthie, 2004, Where is Bear?, 2004, Hachiko Waits, 2004 (Henry Bergh Children's Book Honor award), Jailbait, 2005, The Eight Nights of Chanukah, 2005. Recipient fiction award Highlights for Children, 1992; fellow Mass. Artists Fellowship, 1989, NEA, 1997. Mem. Author's Guild, Poets and Writers, Soc. Children's Book Writers and Illustrators, Pub. Triangle. Avocations: crossword puzzles, bowling, collage-making. Address: PO Box 815 Northampton MA 01061-0815

**NEWMAN, LIBBY,** painter, printmaker, curator; b. Rockland Me., Nov. 17, 1925; d. Hyman and Dora (Horowitz) Goldberg; children— Don, Andrea Newman Orsher. BFA U. Arts; postgrad. U. Pa., Villanova U. Mem. visual arts panel Pa. Council on Arts, 1971-76; artist-in-residence/curator exhbns. University City Sci. Ctr., Phila., 1975—; co-curator sculpture Gov.'s Mansion, Harrisburg, Pa., 1979—88; one-woman shows Phila. Art Alliance, 1971, 2003, Mangel Gallery, Phila., 1972, 75, 78, 84, 88, 92, 95, 99, 2004, 05, University City Sci. Ctr. Gallery, Phila., Tianjin Fine Arts Coll., China, 1988, 89; group shows include Mangel Gallery, 1972-2000, Pa. Acad. Fine Arts, Phila., Peale Galleries of Pa. Acad. Fine Arts, Woodmere Art Mus., Chestnut Hill, Pa., Moore Coll. Art, Phila., Fritz Miller Gallery, N.Y.C., William Penn State Mus., Harrisburg, Pa., Fountain Gallery, Portland, Oreg., Del. Art Mus., Wilmington, Phila. Mus. Art, Circle Gallery, N.Y.C., Chgo., So. Allegheries Mus. Art, Loretto, Pa., Pa. Mus. Phila. Civic Ctr., Moore Coll. Art, Phila., 1982, Sichuan Fine Arts Inst., Changging, People's Republic China, 1985, Tianjin Fine Arts Coll., People's Republic China, 1986, Art in City Hall, Phila., 1986, King St. Mus., Szekesherva, Hungary; represented in permanent collections Phila. Mus. Art, Nat. Mus. Belgrade (Yugoslavia), Mus. Modern Art, Buenos Aires, Argentina, U. Pa. Law Sch., Mus. Phila. Civic Ctr., Temple U. Law Sch., Phila., Glassboro State Coll. (N.J.), Free Library Phila., University City Sci. Ctr., Phila., St. Joseph's Coll., Phila., St. Charles Borromeo Sem., Overbrook, Pa., Temple U. Health and Sci. Ctr., Phila., Nationalities Service Ctr., Phila., Phila. Assn. Clin. Trials;, Mus. Andropologico, Guayagui, Equador, Indus Valley Sch. Arts and Architecture, Karachi, Pakistan, 2006, Biblioteca Alexandrina and International Biennale, 2006; Editor: R. Buckminster Fuller Sketchbook, 1981; A City Sketched: A Guide to the Art and History of Philadelphia, 1976. Mem. Mayor's Com. for Sci. and Tech., 1979-82. Recipient Fleischer Art Meml. award; Cheltenham Nat. Graphic award; Best Pictures of the Yr. award Phila. Art Alliance; Carl Zigrosser Nat. Meml. award Am. Color Print Exhbn., Disting. Daus. Pa. award, 1992; chosen for vis. artist project Brandywine Graphics, 1984; Nat. Endowment grantee, 1973; fellowship of the Pa. Acad. of Fine Arts, Perry Owens award, Mayor's citation City of Phila., 1995. Mem. Artists Equity Assn. (pres. Phila. chpt. 1969-71), Am. Color Print Assn., Phila. Art Alliance, Phila. Watercolor Club. Home: 2401 Pennsylvania Ave Apt 7b34 Philadelphia PA 19130-3029 Office Phone: 215-765-4555. Personal E-mail: libby2401@aol.com.

**NEWMAN, MARIE STEFANINI,** law librarian, educator; b. Boston, Aug. 30, 1951; d. Mario and Elizabeth (Just) S.; m. Gary Nathaniel Newman, Sept. 30, 1978; children: Alexander, Elizabeth. AB, Smith Coll., 1973; MS, Columbia U., 1981; JD, Rutgers U., 1983. Bar: N.Y. 1984. Jr. librarian Bayonne (N.J.) Pub. Library, 1974-75; editor Microfilming Corp. Am., Glen Rock, N.J., 1975-78; circulation librarian SUNY Downstate Med. Ctr. Bklyn., 1979-80; head reference svcs. N.Y. Law Sch., N.Y.C., 1984-90, adj. assoc. prof. law, 1985-90; assoc. dir. Pub. Svcs., lectr. U. Pa. Law Sch., 1991-93; dep. libr. dir. and adj. prof. law Pace U. Sch. Law, White Plains, N.Y., 1993-99, libr. dir., assoc. prof. law, 1999—. Database mgr. Internat. Comml. Law, 1994—. Mem. Am. Assn. Law Libraries. Office: Pace Law Libr 78 N Broadway White Plains NY 10603-3710 Business E-Mail: mnewman@law.pace.edu.

**NEWMAN, MICHAEL RODNEY,** lawyer; b. NYC, Oct. 2, 1945; s. Morris and Helen Gloria (Hendler) Newman; m. Cheryl Jeanne Anker, June 11, 0967; children: Hillary Abra, Nicole Brooke. Student NASA Inst. Space Physics, Columbia U., 1964; BA, U. Denver, 1967; JD, U. Chgo., 1970. Bar: Calif. 1971, U.S. Dist. Ct. (cen. dist.) Calif. 1972, U.S. Ct. Appeals (9th cir.) 1974, U.S. Dist. Ct. (no. dist.) Calif. 1975 U.S. Supreme Ct. 1978, U.S. Dist. Ct.

(so. dist.) Calif. 1979, U.S. Tax Ct. 1979, U.S. Dist. Ct. (ea. dist.) Calif. 1983. Assoc. David Daar, 1971-76; ptnr. Daar & Newman, 1976-78, Miller & Daar, 1978-88, Miller, Daar & Newman, 1988-89, Daar & Newman, 1989—; judge pro-tem L.A. Mcpl. Ct., 1982—, L.A. Superior Ct., 1988—. Vice chmn., bd. dirs. German-Am. C. of C.; bd. govs., fin. and phys. devel. com. U. Haifa, Israel; bd. dirs., chmn. bus. devel. group, chmn. bus. generation com. Consulegis EEIG; founder, facilitator 1st, 2d and 3d Ann. German-Am. Strategic Partnership Confs.; lectr. in field. Mem. LA Citizens Organizing Com. for Olympic Summer Games, 1984, mem. govtl. liaison adv. commn., 1984; mem. So. Calif. Com. for Olympic Summer Games, 1984; cert. ofcl. Athletics Congress of U.S., co-chmn. legal com. S.P.A.-T.A.C., chief finish judge; trustee Massada lodge B'nai Brith; bd. dirs. Ctr. for the Study of Emerging Markets, Calif. State U. Fullerton Grad. Sch. Bus. and Econs. Recipient Maths. award, USN Sci., 1963. Mem.: TAC (bd. dirs., Disting. Svc. award 1988), ABA (multi-dist. litigation subcom., com. on class actions), Lawyers Profl. Liability Bar Assn., German-Am. C. of C. (vice chmn.), So. Pacific Assn., Conf. Ins. Counsel, Los Angeles County Bar Assn. (chmn. attys. errors and omissions prevention com., mem. cts. com., mem. internat. law com., state cts. coord. com. litigation sect.), Rotary Club (internat. com.), City Club on Bunker Hill, Breakfast Club, Porter Valley Country Club. Office: Daar & Newman 865 S Figueroa St Ste 2300 Los Angeles CA 90017-2567 Office Phone: 213-892-0999. Business E-Mail: mnewman@daarnewman.com.

**NEWMAN, MURIEL KALLIS STEINBERG,** art collector; b. Chgo., Feb. 25, 1914; d. Maurice and Ida (Nudelman) Kallis; m. Albert H. Newman, May 14, 1955; 1 son by previous marriage, Glenn D. Steinberg. Student, Art Inst. Chgo., 1932-36, Ill. Inst. Tech., 1947-50, U. Chgo., 1958-65. Hon. life trustee, benefactor Met. Mus. Art, N.Y.C., vis. com. dept. 20th Century Art, acquisitions com., 1981—, decorative arts com., 1989, Costume Inst. Dir., 20th Century Painting and Sculpture Com., Art Inst. Chgo., 1955-80, governing mem. inst., 1955—; pioneer collector Am. abstract expressionist art, 1949—, major show of collection, Met. Mus. Art, N.Y.C., 1981, personal collection of costumes and jewelry, 1981. Bd. govs. Landmarks Preservation Council, Chgo., 1966-78; woman's bd. U. Chgo., 1960-81, Art Inst. Chgo., 1953—, 20th century com., Asian com.; trustee Mus. Contemporary Art, 1970, benefactor, 1970; trustee Chgo. Sch. of Architecture Found., 1971, Archives Am. Art, 1976; bd. dirs. Bright New City Urban Affairs Lecture Series, 1966—; trustee Art Inst. Chgo., mem. African and American art com. Recipient Scroll Recognition of Pub. Svc., U.S. Dept. State, 1958; named Disting. Benefactor, Art Inst. Chgo., 1998. Mem. Antiquarian Soc. of Art Inst. Chgo., Chgo. Hist. Soc. (mem. guild 1958—), Arts Club Chgo., Casino Club Chgo., Arts Club (Chgo.), Casino Club (Chgo.) *Searching for truth is a given for a life of value. For me visual art ontologically reveals the truth of the search. Striving for excellence is the spearhead with which to proceed.*

**NEWMAN, MURRAY ARTHUR,** aquarium administrator; b. Chgo., Mar. 6, 1924; emigrated to Can., 1953, naturalized, 1970; s. Paul Jones and Virginia (Murray) N.; m. Katherine Greene Rose, Aug. 8, 1952; 1 child, Susan. BSc, U. Chgo., 1949; postgrad., U. Hawaii, 1950; MA, U. Calif., Berkeley, 1951; PhD, U. B.C., Vancouver, Can., 1960. Curator fisheries UCLA, 1951-53; curator fisheries Ichthyology Mus. U. B.C., 1953-56; curator Vancouver Pub. Aquarium, 1956-66, dir., 1966-93; pres. Mana Aquarium Cons. Fgn. adv. Nat. Mus./Aquarium Project, Taiwan; past chmn. adv. com. Western Can. Univs. Marine Biol. Soc.; co-chmn. Enoshima (Japan) Internat. Aquarium Symposium, 1997; spl. advisor Enoshima Aquarium, 1998, Port of Nagoya Pub. Aquarium, 1999, 2000; hon. com. Fifth Internat. Congress, Monaco, 2000, Sixth Internat. Congress, Monterey, 2004, grand opening new Enoshima Aquarium, 2004. Author: Life in a Fishbowl: Confessions of an Aquarium Director, 1994. Served with USN, 1943-46. Decorated Order of Can.; recipient Man of Yr. award City of Vancouver, 1964; Centennial award Govt. Can., 1967, cert. of merit, 1988; Harold J. Merilees award Vancouver Visitors Bur., 1976, 75 Achievers award, 1987, Silver Bravery medal Royal Soc. Can., 1992, Can. 125 medal, 1992, Golden Jubilee medal, 2002. Mem. Am. Assn. Zool. Parks and Aquariums, Internat. Union Dirs. Zool. Gardens, Can. Assn. Zool. Parks and Aquariums (pres. 1978-79), Vancouver Club, Round Table Club. Office: Vancouver Pub Aquarium PO Box 3232 Vancouver BC Canada V6B 3X8

**NEWMAN, NORMAN RICHARD,** lawyer; b. Indpls., Dec. 10, 1934; s. Irving and Anne Newman; m. Pauline Nelson, Dec. 28, 1958; children: Anne Leslie Smeltzer, Mark Alan, Eric Daniel. AB, Ind. U., 1956, LLB, 1960. Bar: Ind. 1960. Ptnr. Dann, Pecar, Newman&Kleiman, P.C., Indpls., 1965—. Mem. Am. Coll. of Real Estate Lawyers, Washington, 1983—; spkr. in field; counsel to major nat. and regional real estate developers Projects Mall of Am. and Circle Ctr. Mall. Author: (legal commentary) Indiana Continuing Legal Education Forum, ALI/ABA - The Practical Lawyer. Recipient Listed in Best Lawyers in Am., 1983—; Named an Ind. Super Lawyer, 2004—. Avocation: golf. Office: Dann Pecar Newman&Kleiman PC One American Sq Ste 2300 Indianapolis IN 46282 Office Phone: 317-632-3232. E-mail: nnewman@dannpecar.com.

**NEWMAN, PAUL,** actor, food products executive, race car driver; b. Cleve., Jan. 26, 1925; s. Arthur S. and Theresa (Fetzer) N.; m. Jacqueline Witte, Dec. 1949 (div. 1958); children: Scott (dec. 1978), Susan, Stephanie; m. Joanne Woodward, Jan. 29, 1958; children: Elinor, Melissa, Clea. BA, Kenyon Coll., 1949; postgrad., Yale U. Sch. Drama, 1951; studied with Lee Strasberg, Actor's Studio; LHD (hon.), Yale U., 1988. Founder, pres. Newman's Own Found., Inc., Westport, Conn., 1982—; co-founder Double H Ranch, 1992—. Appeared on Broadway in: Picnic, 1953-54, Desperate Hours, 1955, Sweet Bird of Youth, 1959, Baby Want a Kiss, 1964; Actor (films) The Silver Chalice, 1954, Somebody Up There Likes Me, 1956, The Rack, 1956, The Helen Morgan Story, 1957, Until They Sail, 1957, The Long Hot Summer, 1958 (Best Actor award Cannes Internat. Film Festival, 1958), The Left Handed Gun, 1958, Cat on a Hot Tin Roof, 1958, Rally 'Round the Flag Boys!, 1958, The Young Philadelphians, 1959, From the Terrace, 1960, Exodus, 1960, The Hustler, 1961 (British Film Acad. award for best foreign actor, 1961), Paris Blues, 1961, Sweet Bird of Youth, 1962, Hemingway's Adventures of a Young Man, 1962, Hud, 1963, A New Kind of Love, 1963, The Outrage, 1964, The Prize, 1964, What a Way to Go!, 1964, Lady L, 1965, Harper, 1966, Torn Courtain, 1966, Hombre, 1967, Cool Hand Luke, 1967, The Secret War of Harry Frigg, 1968, Winning, 1969, Butch Cassidy and the Sundance Kid, 1969, WUSA, 1970, Pocket Money, 1972, The Life and Times of Judge Roy Bean, 1972, The MacIntosh Man, 1973, The Sting, 1973, The Towering Inferno, 1974, Drowning Pool, 1975, Buffalo Bill and the Indians or Sitting Bull's History Lesson, 1976, Slap Shot, 1977, Quintet, 1979, Fort Apache, The Bronx, 1980, When Time Ran Out, 1980, Absence of Malice, 1981, The Verdict, 1982, The Color of Money, 1986 (Acad. award for best actor, 1987, Nat. Bd. of Review award for best actor, 1987), Fat Man and Little Boy, 1989, Blaze, 1989, Mr. and Mrs. Bridge, 1989, The Hudsucker Proxy, 1994, Nobody's Fool, 1994 (NY Film Critics Circle award for best actor, Nat. Soc. of Film Critics award for best actor, 1994, Berlin Film Fest. Silver Bear for best actor, 1995), Super Speedway, 1997, Twilight, 1998, Message in a Bottle, 1999, Where the Money Is, 2000, Sweet Dreams, 2001, The Road to Perdition, 2002, (voice only) Cars, 2006; actor, dir., writer, Harry and Son, 1984; actor, dir. Sometimes A Great Notion, 1971; actor (TV movies) Come Along With Me, 1982, Our Town, 2003; (TV series) Tales of Tomorrow, 1951, The Aldrich Family, 1952-53; (TV mini-series) Empire Falls, 2005 (Emmy award for outstanding supporting actor in a miniseries or a movie, 2005, best performance by an actor in a supporting role in a series, miniseries or motion picture made for TV, Hollywood Fgn. Press Assn. (Golden Globe award), 2006, outstanding performance by a male actor in a TV movie or miniseries, Screen Actors Guild award, 2006); dir., prodr. (films) Rachel, Rachel, 1968 (Golden Globe Award for best dir., Prodrs. Guild of Am. Award for best motion picture prodr., NY Film Critics Circle award for best dir., 1968), The Effect of Gamma Rays on Man-in-the-Moon Marigolds, 1973, The Shadow Box, 1980, Glass Menagerie, 1987 Served with AC USNR, 1943-46. Recipient Theatre World Award, 1953, Man of Yr. award Hasty Pudding Theater, Harvard U., 1968, Cecil B. DeMille award, 1984, Acad. award for lifetime achievement, 1985, SAG lifetime achievement award, 1985, D.W. Griffith Best Actor award Nat Bd. Rev. Motion Pictures, 1986, Kennedy Center Honors lifetime achievement award, 1992, Jean Hersholt Humanitarian award Acad. Motion Pictures Arts and Scis., 1993; named World Film Favorite, Hollywood Foreign Press, 1963, 65, 67. Best Motion Picture Prodr. of Yr., Prodrs. Guild of Am., 1968. Address: Newman's Own Inc 246 Post Rd E Westport CT 06880-3615*

**NEWMAN, PAUL DOUGLAS,** history professor; b. Washington, May 28, 1968; s. F. Douglas Newman and Margaret L. Magruder; children: Forrest, Leo. BA in History, York Coll. Pa., 1990; MA in US History, U. Ky., 1992, PhD in US History, 1996. Assoc. prof. history U. Pitts., Johnstown, Pa., 1998—. Author: Fries's Rebellion: The Enduring Struggle for the American Revolution, 2004; editor: Pennsylvania History: A Journal of Mid-Atlantic Studies, 2005—. Business E-Mail: pnewman@pitt.edu.

**NEWMAN, PAULINE,** federal judge; b. NYC, June 20, 1927; d. Maxwell Henry and Rosella Newman. BA, Vassar Coll., 1947; MA, Columbia U., 1948; PhD, Yale U., 1952; LLB, NYU, 1958. Bar: N.Y. 1958, U.S. Supreme Ct. 1972, U.S. Ct. Customs and Patent Appeals 1978, Pa. 1979, U.S. Ct. Appeals (3d cir.) 1981, U.S. Ct. Appeals (fed. cir.) 1982. Research chemist Am. Cyanamid Co., Bound Brook, NJ, 1951—54; mem. patent staff FMC Corp., N.Y.C., 1954—75, Phila., 1975—84, dir. dept. patent and licensing, 1969—84; judge U.S. Ct. Appeals (fed. cir.), Washington, 1984—; Disting. prof. George Mason Law Sch., 1995—. Program specialist Dept. Natural Scis. UNESCO, Paris, 1961—62; mem. State Dept. Adv. Com. on Internat. Indsl. Property, 1974—84; lectr. in field. Contbr. articles to profl. jours. Trustee Phila. Coll. Pharmacy and Sci., 1983—84; bd. dirs. Med. Coll. Pa., 1975—84, Midgard Found., 1973—84. Mem. ABA (coun. sect. patent trademark and copyright 1983—84), Coun. Fgn. Rels., U.S. Trademark Assn. (bd. dirs. 1975—79, v.p. 1978—79), Pacific Indsl. Property Assn. (pres. 1979—80), Am. Inst. Chemists (bd. dirs. 1960—66, 1970—76), Am. Chem. Soc. (bd. dirs. 1972—81), Am. Patent Law Assn. (bd. dirs. 1981—84), Yale Club, Vassar Club, Cosmos Club. Office: US Ct Appeals Nat Cts Bldg 717 Madison Pl Washington DC 20439-0002*

**NEWMAN, PHILIP ROBERT,** psychologist; b. Dec. 17, 1942; s. Samuel M. and Sara Rose (Dumain) N.; m. Barbara Miller, June 12, 1966; children: Samuel Asher, Abraham Levy, Rachel Florence. AB with high distinction, U. Mich., 1964, PhD, 1971. Asst. prof. psychology U. Mich., Ann Arbor, 1971-72, Union Coll., Schenectady, NY, 1972-76; dir. human behavior curriculum project APA, Washington, 1977-81; pvt. practice psychology Columbus, Ohio, 1978-2000, South Kingston, RI, 2000—. Adj. prof., sr. rschr. young scholars program Ohio State U., 1990-98; adj. prof. human devel. and family studies U. R.I., 2000—; cons. Agy. Instrnl. TV, 1979. Author: (with B. Newman) Development through Life: A Psychosocial Approach, 1975, 9th edit., 2006; Infancy and Childhood Development and Its Context, 1978, An Introduction to the Psychology of Adolescence, 1979, Personality Development through the Life Span, 1980, Living: The Process of Adjustment, 1981, Understanding Adulthood, 1983, Principles of Psychology, 1983, Adolescent Development, 1986, When Kids Go to College: A Parents Guide to Changing Relationships, 1992, Childhood and Adolescence, 1997, (with B. Newman, L. Landry-Meyer, B. Lohman) Life Span Development: A Case Book, 2003; editor: (with B. Newman) Development Through Life: A Case Study Approach, 1976. Woodrow Wilson fellow U. Mich., 1964, Univ. fellow, 1964-66, Horace H. Rackham Rsch. scholar, 1969-71. Mem. APA, APHA, Internat. Assn. Applied Psychology, Internat. Sociol. Assn., Soc. Psychol. Study Social Issues, Am. Sociol. Assn., Nat. Coun. Family Rels., Groves Conf. Marriage and Family, Ea. Psychol. Assn., N.Y. Acad. Sci., Gerontol. Soc. Am., Am. Orthopsychiat. Assn., Am. Statis. Assn., Soc. for Rsch. on Child Devel., Soc. for Rsch. on Adolescence, Phi Beta Kappa, Sigma Xi, Phi Kappa Phi. Home and Office: 240 Broad Rock Rd Wakefield RI 02879 Office Phone: 401-559-1245. Personal E-Mail: prn10@yahoo.com.

**NEWMAN, R. DONALD,** paper company executive; V.p., resident mgr. Bowater, Inc., Calhoun, Tenn., 1987; v.p. Bowater, Inc., Canadian Newsprint Oper., 1998—2001; v.p., strategic planning Bowater, Inc., 2001—02, exec. v.p., COO Greenville, SC, 2002—. Office: Bowater Inc 55 E Camperdown Way Greenville SC 29602*

**NEWMAN, RACHEL,** editor; b. Malden, Mass., May 1, 1938; d. Maurice and Edythe Brenda (Tichell) Newman; m. Herbert Bleiweiss, Apr. 6, 1973 (div. Apr. 1989); m. Michael Lucas, Feb. 24, 2004. BA, Pa. State U., 1960; cert., N.Y. Sch. Interior Design, 1963. Accessories editor Women's Wear Daily, N.Y.C., 1964—65; designer, publicist Grandoe Glove Corp., N.Y.C., 1965—67; assoc. editor McCall's Sportswear and Dress Merchandiser mag., N.Y.C., 1967; mng. editor McCall's You-Do-It Home Decorating, 1968—70, Ladies Home Jour. Needle and Craft mag., N.Y.C., 1970—72; editor-in-chief Am. Home Crafts mag., N.Y.C., 1972—77; fashion dir. Good Housekeeping mag., N.Y.C., 1977—78, home bldg. and decorating dir., 1978—82; editor-in-chief Country Living mag., N.Y.C., 1978—98; founding editor Country Cooking mag., 1985—90, Dream Homes mag., 1989—2000, Country Kitchens mag., 1990—93, Country Living Gardener Mag., 1993—2000, Healthy Living mag., 1996—2000. Bd. dirs. Mothers and Others for a Livable Planet. Named Disting. Alumna, Pa. State U., 1988; recipient Cir. of Excellence award, Internat. Furnishings and Design Assn., 1992, YMCA Hall of Fame, 1992; Pa. State U. Alumni fellow, 1986. Mem.: Am. Soc. Mag. Editors, Am. Soc. Interior Designers, Nat. Home Fashions League, N.Y. Fashion Group. E-mail: Rachelsfree@earthlink.net.

**NEWMAN, RANDY,** singer, songwriter, musician; b. Los Angeles, Calif., Nov. 28, 1943; s. Irving and Adele N.; m. Gretchen Newman; children: Amos, Eric, John Patrick, Alice, Degree, II. Calif. Arranger, singer, songwriter, musician various record firms; singer-composer: (albums) including Randy Newman, 1968, Twelve Songs, 1969, Live, 1971, Sail Away, 1972, Good Old Boys, 1974, Little Criminals, 1977, Born Again, 1979, Trouble In Paradise, 1983, Land of Dreams, 1988, Bad Love, 1999; (with others) Randy Newman's Faust, 1995; appeared in film: Ragtime, 1981; also TV and concert engagements; music composer for films: Performance, 1970, Pursuit of Happiness, 1971, Cold Turkey, 1971, Ragtime, 1981, The Natural, 1984 (Grammy award for Best Instrumental Composition, 1984), Three Amigos (also co-wrote screenplay), 1986, Parenthood, 1989, Avalon, 1990, Awakenings, 1990, Toy Story, 1995 (Annie award for Individual Achievement in Music, 1995), Michael, 1996, James and the Giant Peach, 1996, Cats Don't Dance, 1997 (Annie award for Feature Video Prodn. Music, 1997), A Bug's Life, 1998 (Grammy award for Best Instrumental Composition for Motion Picture, 2000), Pleasantville, 1998, Toy Story 2, 1999 (Grammy award for Best Song Written for Motion Picture, 2001, Annie award for Outstanding Individual Achievement for Music in an Animated Feature Prodn., 2000), Meet the Parents, 2000, Monsters, Inc., 2001 (ASCAP award for Top Box Office Film, 2001, Acad award for Best Original Song, 2002, Grammy award for Best Song Written for Motion Picture, 2003), Mike's New Car, 2002, Seabiscuit, 2003 (ASCAP award for Top Box Office Film), Mr. 3000, 2004, Meet the Fockers, 2004 (ASCAP award for Top Box Office Film, 2005), Cars, 2006; composer for TV Series: Monk, 2002 (Emmy award for Outstanding Main Title Theme Music, 2004, ASCAP award for Top TV Series, 2005); recorded 30 Years of Randy Newman (4 CD set), 1998. Named to Songwriters' Hall of Fame, 2002. Office: care Cathy Kerr Mgmt 9079 Nemo St Los Angeles CA 90069-5511*

**NEWMAN, RICHARD G.,** engineering company executive; BSCE, Bucknell U.; MSCE, Columbia U.; grad. Assoc. Mgmt. Program, UCLA. Former CEO AECOM Tech. Corp., LA, 2002—, chmn. Bd. dirs. Southwest Water Co., 13 mutual funds under Capital Rsch. and Mgmt. Co., Sempra Energy, San Diego, 2002—, mem. audit and corp. governance coms. Fellow: Inst. for Advancement of Engring.; mem: NSPE, Am. Soc. Civil Engrs., Chief Executives Orgn. Office: AECOM Tech Corp 555 S Flower St Ste 3700 Los Angeles CA 90071-2300 Office Phone: 215-593-8000. Office Fax: 213-593-8729.*

**NEWMAN, RICHARD LANCASTER,** aviation consultant, educator; b. Oakland, Calif., Mar. 9, 1938; s. Richard Lancaster and Eleanor June (Wagstaff) N.; m. Marianne Mason Large, Mar. 21, 1964 (div. 1980); 1 child, James Lancaster; m. Linda Kelsey-Jones, Apr. 24, 1989. BS, Rensselaer Poly. Inst., 1960; postgrad. Pa. State U., 1960-62; MS, Purdue U., 1974; PhD, Kennedy-Western, 1993. Engr. Douglas Aircraft, Santa Monica, Calif., 1962-66; pilot Northwest Airlines, St. Paul, 1966; sr. engr. Allison div. Gen. Meotors, Indpls., 1967-74; prin. Crew Systems, Yellow Springs, Ohio, San Marcos, Tex., 1974—; adj. asst. prof. Ohio State U., Columbus, 1982-85; adj. instr. U. Dayton, Ohio, 1975-79; adviser Internat. Civil Aviation Orgn., UN, Sao Jose dos Campos, Brazil, 1984. Co-patentee vibration damping coatings. Author: Head-Up Displays: Designing the Way Ahead, also research articles. Adviser Vol. Adv. Corps, Indpls., 1970-73; mem. Sugar Creek Ski Patrol, Bellbrook, Ohio, 1983-85. Named Flight Instr. of Yr., Central region, FAA, 1978. Fellow AIAA (assoc., sect. chmn. 1966-85), Can. Aero. and Space Inst.; mem. Soc. Exptl. Test Pilots, System Safety Soc. (sr.), Human Factors Soc. Avocations: skiing, soaring.

**NEWMAN, ROBERT GABRIEL,** physician; b. The Netherlands, Oct. 26, 1937; came to U.S., 1939; s. Randolph H. and Eva E. (Feilchenfeld) N.; m. Seiko Kusuba, Oct. 26, 1968; children— Henry Seiji, Hana Marie. BA, NYU, 1958; MD with honors, U. Rochester, 1963; MPH, U. Calif.-Berkeley, 1969. Intern and resident in surgery Univ. Hosps., Cleve., 1963-65; dist. health officer N.Y.C. Health Dept., 1968; dir. Nat. Nutrition Survey of N.Y.C., 1969-70; asst. commr. N.Y.C. Health Dept., 1970-74; health cons., 1974-76; assoc. gen. dir. Beth Israel Med. Ctr., N.Y.C., 1976-78, CEO, pres., 1978-97; prof. dept. community medicine Mt. Sinai Sch. Medicine, N.Y.C., 1982-94; prof. depts. epidemiology and social medicine/psychiatry Albert Einstein Coll. of Medicine, 1994—; CEO, pres. Continuum Health Ptnrs. Inc. (formerly Greater Met. Health), N.Y.C., 1997—2000, pres. emeritus; dir. Baron Edmond de Rothschild Chem. Dependency Inst., N.Y.C., 2000—. Cons. addiction problems Govt. of Hong Kong, 1975-85 Author book in field of methadone treatment; contbr. articles to profl. jours. Trustee U. Rochester, NY, 1994—2002. With USAF, 1965—67. WHO fellow, 1972 Fellow N.Y. Acad. Medicine, Am. Coll. Preventive Medicine; mem. Public Health Assn. N.Y.C., Hosp. Assn. N.Y. State (past chmn. 1992), Greater N.Y. Hosp. Assn. (past chmn. bd.), Am. Public Health Assn. Office: Continuum Health Ptnrs Inc 555 W 57th St Fl 18 New York NY 10019-2925 E-mail: rnewmanm@icaat.org.

**NEWMAN, ROCHELLE JOYCE,** artist, educator, writer; b. Bklyn., May 11, 1939; d. Saul Rosenberg and Esther Deborah (Modlin) Sugerman; m. Richard Charles Newman; 1 child, Vanessa Alexandra. Student, Alfred U., 1956-58; BA, Hunter Coll., 1960; MFA in Sculpture, Cranbrook Acad. Art, 1962. Prof. creative arts dept. No. Essex C.C., Haverhill, Mass., 1967—95, prof. emerita, 1995. Sr. lectr. creative arts dept. Bradford (Mass.) Coll.; workshop condr.; scholar-in-residence Hambidge Ctr. for Creative Arts and Scis., Rabun, Ga.; artist-in-residence Roswell (N.Mex.) Mus. and Art Ctr.; adj. faculty fine arts dept. Merrimack Coll., North Andover, Mass., 2001—. Author: Malleable Matter/Stretchable Space, 2000; co-author: The Golden Relationship: Art, Math, Nature, Universal Patterns, 1983, The Surface Plane, 1992, Space, Structure and Form, 1996; exhibited Interart Gallery, N.Y.C., 1980, Art Complex Mus., Duxbury, Mass., 1981, Soc. Arts and Crafts, Boston, 1982, Thousand Island Crafts Mus., Framingham, Mass., 1984, Maison de Culture, Montreal, 1984, Newport Art Mus., 1985, Newton (Mass.) Arts Ctr., 1985, Bradford Coll., 1987, others. Mem. visual arts panel Mass. Coun. on Arts and Humanities, 1981 Mem. Mass. Assn. Craftsmen, Soc. Layerists in Multimedia, Am. Tapestry Alliance, Boston Seven. Home: PO Box 5162 Haverhill MA 01835-0162 Personal E-mail: pythpress@sprynet.com.

**NEWMAN, RYAN,** race car driver; b. South Bend, Ind. Degree in vehicle structure engring., Purdue U., 2001. Racecar driver Penske Racing So., 2001—. Named winner, All-Am. Midget Series, 1993, Rookie of the Yr., USAC Nat. Midget Series, 1995, USAC Silver Crown Series, 1996, Sprint Car, 1999, winner, USAC Coors Light Silver Bullet Series, 1999, Pepsi Automobile Racing Club Am. 200, 2000, Automobile Racing Club Am. Ky. Speedway, 2000, Automobile Racing Club Am. Lowe's Motor Speedway, 2000; recipient, Roger Penske 500, 2002, 2005, Sylvania 300, 2005; scholar Rich Vogler Meml. scholar, 2001. Office: c/o Penske Racing 136 Knob Hill Rd Mooresville NC 28117*

**NEWMAN, SAMUEL,** retired trust company executive; b. NYC, Mar. 12, 1938; s. Aaron and Rachel (Hershkowitz) Newman; m. Carolyn Gropper, Oct. 27, 1963; children: Marci Ann, Jodi Robin, Michael David. BBA, CUNY, 1971; grad. Advanced Mgmt. Program, Harvard U., 1982. Methods analyst Bankers Trust Co., NYC, 1960-67; project leader Clark O'Neill SVC Corp., Fairview, NJ, 1967-68; sr. v.p. Irving Trust Co., NYC, 1968-85; sr. v.p., gen. mgr. trade svcs. and GEOSERVE legal and regulatory support Mfrs. Hanover Trust (merger with Chem. Bank 1992), NYC, 1985-92; sr. v.p., gen. mgr. funds transfer and trade svcs. Chem. Bank, NYC, 1992-93; sr. v.p. and bus. head payment products First Fidelity Bank NA, Newark, 1993-95; head dept. project support Fleet Pa. Svcs. Inc., Scranton, Pa., 1995-98; dir. new bus. devel., mgr. customer svc., internat. fin. instns. Fleet Bank, NYC, 1998—2001; dir. float mgmt. Fleet Nat. Bank, Melville, NY, 2001—03. Past chmn. bd. dirs. SWIFT Terminal Svcs.; past chmn. NY Clearing House funds transfer com.; speaker industry confs. Contbr. articles to profl. jours. Advisor Nat. Conf. of Commrs. on Uniform State Laws; former mem. US coun. Internat. Banking Exec. Com., US del. to Uncitral Working Group on Internat. Payments; former chief US del. to tech. com. 168 Internat. Standards Orgn. Mem. Soc. Worldwide Fin. Telecom. (bd. dirs. 1978-92, dep. chmn 1989-92), Internat. Fin. Svcs. Assn. (bd. dirs. 2001—03). Avocation: foreign currency note collection. Office: 39 Wyandanch Ave Wyandanch NY 11798 Personal E mail: wallstbk@aol.com.

**NEWMAN, SANDRA SCHULTZ,** state supreme court justice; BS, Drexel U., 1959; MA, Temple U., 1969; JD, Villanova U., 1972; D (hon.), Gannon U., 1996, Widener U., 1996, Clarion U., 2000, Drexel U., 2001. Bar: Pa., U.S. Dist. Ct. (ea. dist.) Pa., U.S. Ct. Appeals (3d cir.), U.S. Supreme Ct. Asst. dist. atty. Montgomery County, Pa., 1972—74; pvt. practice, 1974—93; judge Commonwealth Ct. of Pa., 1993—95; justice Pa. Supreme Ct., 1995—. Past chair bd. consultors Villanova U. Law Sch.; mem. jud. coun. Supreme Ct. of Pa., liaison to the 3rd cir. task force on mgmt. of death penalty litigation, liaison to Pa. lawyers fund for client security bd., liaison to domestic rels. procedural rules com.; liaison Pa. Bar Inst.; jud. work group HHS; mem. adv. com. Nat. Ctr. for State Cts., Am. Law Inst.; mem. Drexel U. Coll. Bus. and Adminstrn.; lectr. and spkr. in field. Author: Alimony, Child Support and Counsel Fees, 1988; contbr. articles to profl. jours. Named named Disting. Daughter of Pa.; recipient Phila. award for Super Achiever, Pediatric Juvenile Colitis Found. Jefferson Med. Coll. and Hosp, 1979, award for Dedicated Leadership and Outstanding Contbns. to the Cmty. and Law Employment, Drexel 100 award, Police Chiefs Assn. of Southeastern Pa., 1993, Medallion of Achievement award, Villanova U., 1993, Susan B. Anthony award, Women's Bar Assn. Western Pa., 1996, award, Justinian Soc., 1996, Tau Epsilon Law Soc., 1996, Legion of Honor Gold Medallion award, Chapel of Four Chaplain, 1997, honored by, Women of Greater Phila., 1996, Person of Yr. award, Shomrim of Phila., 1998, Women of Distinction award, Greater Phila. Council of Jewish Women Internat., 2005, Person of Yr. award, Pa. State Constables Assoc., 2005. Fellow: Pa. Bar Found., Am. Bar Found.; mem.: Montgomery Bar Assn., Nat. Assn. Women Judges, Am. Law Inst. Office: Supreme Ct Pa Ste 400 100 Four Falls Corporate Ctr West Conshohocken PA 19428-2950*

**NEWMAN, SHERRYL HOBBS,** former district secretary; BA in Chemistry, Rutgers U., 1986, BA in Economics, 1986; MBA in Management, Lubin Graduate Sch. of Bus. Pace Univ., White Plains, NY, 1992. Exec. sec.-Tax Operation Bureau NYC-Dept. of Finance, 1986, special projects coordinator-Program Devel. Divsn., 1986—87, special property coordinator-Program Devel. Divsn., 1986—87, asst. to dir.-Taxpayer Assistance Divsn., 1987—89, unit mgr.-Taxpayer Corr., 1989—90, unit mgr.-Real Estate Tax Assistance,

1990—92, acting dep. dir.-Taxpayer Assistance Divsn., 1992—93, city collector-Property Bureau, 1993—96; dir. Customer Svc. Adminstrn.-Office of Tax and Revenue, Washington, 1997—99, Citywide Customer Svc. Adminstrn.-Office of the City Adminstr., Washington, 1999, Dept. of Motor Vehicles, Washington, 1999—2003; sec. dist. DC Govt., 2003—09; dep. CFO, Office Tax & Revenue, 2005—. Democrat. Office: John A Wilson Bldg 1350 Pennsylvania Ave NW Rm 419 Washington DC 20004 Business E-Mail: shnewman@dc.gov.*

**NEWMAN, SLATER EDMUND,** psychologist, educator; b. Boston, Sept. 8, 1924; s. Max and Gertrude (Raphael) N.; m. Corrine Lois Silfen, June 18, 1950 (div. 1968); children: Kurt Douglas, Jonathan Mark, Eric Bruce; m. Patricia Ellen Christopher Thomas, July 2, 1969; 1 stepchild, Arthur C. Thomas III. BS, U. Pa., 1947; MA, Boston U., 1948; PhD, Northwestern U., 1951. Research psychologist U.S. Air Force, 1951-57; prof. emeritus psychology N.C. State U., Raleigh, 1957—2003, prof. emeritus, 2003—. Vis. fgn. mem. Exptl. Psychology Soc. U.K., 1973-74, 82-83, 90. Contbr. chpts. to books, articles to profl. publs. Bd. dirs. ACLU, 1992—97, mem. biennial conf. com., 1994—97, mem. task force internat. human rights, 1994—2005, mem. spl. nominating com., 1996, mem. constn. com., 1996—97, mem. youth affairs com., 1997, mem. nat. adv. coun., 1998—; pres. NC Civil Liberties Union, 1991—97; chair Com. on Internat. Human Rights, 1988—; chair founding com. Wake County chpt. ACLU, 1969, pres., 1969—72, 1984—86, bd. dirs., 1969—73, 1976—82, 1984—90, 1991—97, life mem., 2002—; mem. Ann. Slater Newman, ACLU of Wake County, 2006; mem. steering com. ACLU-Affiliate Leadership Network, 1991—95; founding mem. North Carolinians Against the Death Penalty, 1967, bd. govs., 1967—73; mem. Mayor's Com. UN Week, Raleigh, 1986—95; active Amnesty Internat.; co-founder, coord. Com. to Reverse Arms Race, 1982—; co-founder, mem. steering co. North Carolinians Against Apartheid, 1985—87; mem. Wake County Com. Bicentennial US Constn., 1987—89; co-founder, co-chair NC Com. for Celebration of Human Rights, 1989—97; mem. Human Rights Week Com., NC State U., 1993—99, founder, 1993, chair, 1993—96; co-founder, co-chmn. Human Rights Coalition NC, 1997—; co-founder North Carolinians for Ratification, Com. on Elimination of All Forms of Discrimination Against Women, 1997, chmn., 1998—; mem. civil rights adv. bd. NC Mus. History, 2001—. Served with USAF, 1943—46, 2d lt. USAF, 1952—53. USPHS spl. rsch. fellow U. Calif.-Berkeley, 1965-66; U. London hon. rsch. fellow, 1973-74, 82-83, 90; recipient W.W. Finlator award ACLU of Wake County, 1997, Norman Smith award ACLU of N.C., 1998; recipient Frank Porter Graham Award, ACLU of N.C., 2004. Fellow: APA, AAAS, Assn. for Psychol. Sci.; mem.: AAUP (pres. N.C. State U. chpt. 1968—69), Carolinas Conf. for Undergrad. Rsch. in Psychology (co-founder 1976, co-advisor), Ea. Psychol. Assn., N.C. Cognition Group (founder 1972), Southea. Psychol. Assn. (exec. com. 2001—04, sec.-treas. 2004—), Southea. Workers in Memory (founder 1969), So. Soc. Philosophy and Psychology, Psychonomic Soc., UN Assn. (bd. dirs. Wake County chpt. 1991—95), Psi Chi (v.p. southea. region 1990—94, nat. coun. 1990—94, nat. pres.-elect 1996—97, nat. coun. 1996—99, nat. pres. 1997—98, nat. past pres. 1998—99), Sigma Xi. Home: 315 Shepherd St Raleigh NC 27607-4031 Office: NC State U Dept Psychology Raleigh NC 27695-7650 Office Phone: 919-515-1728. Business E-Mail: slater_newman@ncsu.edu. E-mail: slaterpat@mindspring.com.

**NEWMAN, STACEY CLARFIELD,** artist, curator; b. N.Y.C., July 21, 1956; d. Wallace J. Clarfield and Elinor (Kandel) Clarfield-Toberoff; m. Fredric Alan Newman, Nov. 27, 1983; children: Benjamin Clarfield, Marissa Paige, Alexandra Brooke Student, Franklin & Marshall, 1974—76; BS Labor Rels. and Mgmt., U. Bridgeport, 1978. Dir. ops. Nat. Rec. and Video Studios, N.Y.C., 1978—80; dir. tech. ops. VCA/Teletronics, N.Y.C., 1980—82, cons., client rep./MTV, 1981—83, exec. producer, 1982—85, dir. tech ops. prodr.; artist, art curator Stacey Clarfield Newman Studios, Scarsdale, NY, 1986—. Merchandise cons. Tahari Fashions, N.Y.C., 1985—86; artist mem., jury com. You Gotta Have Art program White Plains Hosp. Ctr., NY, 1990—92; art tchr. collage Scarsdale Adult Edn. Program, 1993—95; artist in residence Scarsdale Elem. Schs., 1995—97; art cons., curator Manhattan Transfer, Inc., N.Y.C., 1997—2000; mem. faculty Young at Art enrichment program Scarsdale, 2002—; juror Figure and Form Edward Hopper House Mus., N.Y.C., 2004. One-person shows include Quogue Gallery, N.Y., 1986, Piermont Fine Arts Gallery, N.Y., 1997-98, 2001, Manhattan Transfer, Inc., 1997, J&W Gallery, New Hope, Pa., 1999, Studio 4 West, 1999, 93 South Gallery, 2000, Adele Greenberg Salon, Cambridge, Mass., 2000, Amb. Galleries, Palm Beach, Fla., 2001, Viridian Gallery, N.Y.C., 2001, 02, 05, Viridian Gallery @ Chelsea, 2002, 04, 05; exhibited in juried group shows: Piermont Fine Art Gallery, 1995, 96, 98, 99, 2000, 01, Anaya Gallery, Scarsdale, 1986, Katonah Gallery, N.Y., 1986, Gallery at Jamaica, Stratton Mountain, Vt., 1987, CDS Contemporary Art, Albuquerque, 1989, Mari Galleries, Mamaroneck, N.Y., 1992, Manhattan Transfer, Inc., 1993, 98, 93 South Gallery, Nyack, N.Y., 1998-99, Bibro Fine Arts Gallery, Chelsea, N.Y., 1998, Weber Fine Art, Scarsdale, 1998, 2000, J&W Gallery, New Hope, 1998, 99, 2001, 02, Studio 4 West, Hewlett Mus., 2000, Amb. Gallery, Palm Beach, 2000, Viridian Gallery, N.Y.C., 2000-04, Adele Greenberg Salon, 2000, 01, A Pirate Space, Denver, 2001, Contemporary Art Oasis, Denver, 2001, Manhattanville Coll. Gallery, 2002, Nat. Assn. Women Artists, N.Y.C., 2003, Chgo. Fine Arts Bldg. Gallery, 2003, Inklings, Viridian Artists, Chelsea, 2005, 06, News Art, Viridian Artists, 2005, John Jay Coll. Pres.'s Gallery, 2005, Fountain St. Gallery, Cape Girardeau, Mo., 2006; commd. Am. Soc. Plastic and Reconstructive Surgeons, L.A. Conv. Ctr., 1988, White Plains Hosp. Ctr., 1989, 90, Cystic Fibrosis Found., N.Y.C., 1990, Joan Kroc Found., Calif., 1989-91 1st v.p. bd. dirs. Internat. Coll. Surgeons Aux., Chgo., 1988—90; mem. Gala com. Juvenile Diabetes Found., 2000; Regional v.p. Am. Cancer Soc., White Plains, 1986—88; bd. dirs. White Plains Hosp. Ctr. Aux.; fund raiser, event planner Holocaust Commn., NY, 1998; active Scarsdale Tremum Synagogue Gala, 2001, 2002; fund-raiser Alternative Arts and Music Events, Scarsdale Teen Ctr., 2003—; liaison Scarsdale H.S. PTA, Alternative Art and Music Events, Scarsdale Teen Ctr., 2003—05; bd. mem. com on spl. edn. Scarsdale Sch. Dist. Mem. Internat. Platform Assn., Nat. Mus. Women in Contemporary Arts, Nat. Assn. Women Artists, Inc., Katonah Mus., Nat. Mus. Women in Arts (artist), Nat. Arts Club Avocations: piano, photography, tennis, kayaking, skiing. Studio: 21 Wayside Ln Scarsdale NY 10583-2911 Personal E-mail: StaceySCN21@aol.com.

**NEWMAN, STEPHEN ALEXANDER,** chemical engineer; b. Auburn, NY, Apr. 12, 1938; s. Solomon and Anna (Reich) N.; m. Mary Ellen Lassoe, May 26, 1964; children: Sharon Rose, Lori Suzanne. BSChemE, Rensselaer Poly. Inst., 1960; MSChemE, MIT, 1962; PhD, Rutgers U., 1976. Registered profl. engr., N.J. Rsch. engr. M.W. Kellogg Co., Piscataway, N.J., 1962-67; tech. mgr. Foster Wheeler Energy Corp., Clinton, NJ, 1967—96; prin. engr. Kvaerner Process, Bridgewater, NJ, 1996—99, cons. engr., 1999—, clients have included ABB Lummus Global (Bloomfield, NJ) and Kvaerner Process (Bridgewater, NJ). Organizer, conf./symposium chmn. Nat. Thermodynamics Conf., 1978, World Congress Chem. Engring., Montreal, 1981, CODATA Congress, Jerusalem, 1984; panel NAS, 1980-82; cons. Nat. Bur. Standards, Washington, 1979; chmn. various project coms. U.S. Dept. Energy, 1977-84; spkr. in field. Editor: Thermodynamics of Aqueous Systems with Industrial Applications, 1980, Chemical Engineering Thermodynamics, 1983, Shale Oil Upgrading and Refining, 1983, Acid and Sour Gas Treating Processes, 1985; book and article reviewer Chem. Engring. mag., Gulf Publs., 1980—; contbr. numerous articles to profl. jours. Pres. Mens' Club Temple Israel, Union, N.J., 1980-81. AEC fellow, 1961-62; grantee NSF, 1978, 84. Fellow AIChE (chmn. nat. rsch. com 1984-85, co-founder Design Inst. Phys. Property Data 1977, vice chmn. 1979-85, award 1983); mem. Am. Petroleum Inst. (chair contractors com. on tech. data 1978-96), Gas Processors Assn. (project monitor 1976-85, tech. com., Am. Assn. Engring. Socs. Jewish. Home: 941 Douglas Ter Union NJ 07083-6523 Office Phone: 908-688-5167.

**NEWMAN, STEPHEN MICHAEL,** lawyer; b. Buffalo, Jan. 12, 1945; s. Howard A. and Mildred (Ballow) N.; m. Gayle Mallon, May 24, 1969; children: Holly, Deborah. AB, Princeton U., 1966; JD, U. Mich., 1969. Bar: N.Y. 1969, Fla. 1976. Assoc. Hodgson, Russ, Andrews, Woods & Goodyear, Buffalo, 1969-73; ptnr. Hodgson Russ, LLP (formerly Hodgson, Russ,

Andrews, Woods & Goodyear), Buffalo, 1973—2004, Nixon Peabody, LLP, Buffalo, 2005—. Lectr. in field. Bd. dirs. Leukemia Soc., United Jewish Fedn. Buffalo Inc., Jewish Ctr. Greater Buffalo Inc.; Temple Beth Zion; bd. dirs., chpt. chmn., exec. com. Am. Jewish Com., Buffalo chpt.; bd. advisors Am. Lung Assn., Southeast Fla. chpt. Fellow Am. Coll. Trusts and Estates Coun.; mem. ABA (personal svc. corps. com. tax sect.), N.Y. State Bar Assn. (chair trusts and estates law sect. 2001), Princeton Club of Fla. Office: Nixon Peabody LLP 4400 PGA Blvd Ste 900 Palm Beach Gardens FL 33410 Office Phone: 561-626-3011. Business E-Mail: snewman@nixonpeabody.com.

**NEWMAN, STEVEN DAVID,** psychologist, consultant; b. Oxford, Ohio, Sept. 5, 1961; s. David William Newman and JoAnne Marie Slighting; m. Mary Christine Schaefer, May 27, 1985; children: Anna, Hayley. BA, Miami U., 1983; PsyD, Hahnemann U., Phila., 1988. Diplomate Am. Bd. Profl. Psychology, 2000. Psychologist Pauline W. Lewis Ctr., Cin., 1988—91; clinical psychologist United Samaritus Med. Ctr., Danville, Ill., 1991—2002, Mountain Regional Svcs., Cheyenne, Wyo., 2003—. Cons. psychologist pvt. practice, Crawfordsville, Ind., 2000—03. Fellow: Acad. Clinical Psychology; mem.: APA. Office: Mountain Regional Svcs 115 Evelyn Dr Cheyenne WY 82003

**NEWMAN, STEVEN HARVEY,** insurance company executive, director; b. Bklyn., Apr. 26, 1943; s. Charlotte Newman Bart; m. Lenore Blaustein, June 14, 1964; children: Richard, Michael, Stephanie. BS, Bklyn. Coll., 1963. Actuarial asst. Royal Globe Ins. Co., N.Y.C., 1963-65; asst. sec. Ins. Rating Bd., N.Y.C., 1965-69; v.p. sr. casualty actuary Am. Internat. Group, N.Y.C., 1969-82; exec. v.p. Home Ins. Co., N.Y.C., 1982-85, pres., 1985-86, also bd. dirs.; chmn., CEO Underwriters Reinsurance Co., Woodland Hills, Calif., 1987—2001; now chmn. Platinum Underwriters Holdings, Ltd., Bermuda, 2002—. Chmn. GCR Holdings, 1993-97, Reins. Assn. Am., 1995-96. Fellow Casualty Actuarial Soc. (pres. 1981-82); mem. Am. Acad. Actuaries, Internat. Actuarial Assn.

**NEWMAN, STUART,** lawyer; b. Hackensack, N.J., June 7, 1947; s. Joseph and Rose (Wilenski) N.; m. Tina Gilson; children: Leslie, Dara, Mindy, Robert, Jessica. BA, SUNY, Cortland, 1971; JD cum laude, Albany Law Sch., 1974. Bar: N.Y. 1975, Ga. 1978. Assoc. Dewey, Ballantine LLP, N.Y., 1974-76; from assoc. to ptnr. Jackson, Lewis LLP, Atlanta, 1976—. Lectr. U. Ala., Tuscaloosa, 1980-84, Auburn U., 1986—. Dir. Ruth Mitchell Dance Co. of Atlanta, 1986-88; sec., bd. trustees N.Y. Mil. Acad., 2000-. Mem. ABA, Atlanta Bar Assn., Ga. Bar Assn., Lawyers Club Atlanta, Commerce Club, Shakerag Hounds, Inc., Bear Creek Hounds, Inc. Office: Jackson Lewis LLP 1900 Marquis One Tower 245 Peachtree Center Ave NE Atlanta GA 30303-1222

**NEWMAN, TERRY E.,** lawyer; b. Chgo., Jan. 15, 1947; BA, Loyola U., Ill., 1969; JD, DePaul U., 1977. Bar: Ill. 1977, U.S. Dist. Ct. (no. dist.) Ill. 1977, D.C. 1991. Asst. states atty. Cook County, 1977-78; ptnr. Katten Muchin Zavis Rosenman, Chgo. Sec. bd. trustees City Coll. Chgo., 1989. Mem. ABA, Ill. State Bar, D.C. Bar, Chgo. Bar Assn. (real estate tax sect.). Office: Katten Muchin Zavis Rosenman 525 W Monroe St Ste 1600 Chicago IL 60661-3649 Office Fax: 317-577-8781.

**NEWMAN, THOMAS DANIEL,** archaeologist, school system administrator, minister; b. London, May 12, 1922; s. Frederick and Margaret (O'Leary) N.; m. Louise Johannah Albertano, Apr. 1, 1963; 1 dau., Susan (Mrs. Alan J. Rennie). Student, Glasgow Sch. Accounting, 1946, Unity Sch. Christianity, 1962-66, Harvard Div. Sch., 1967—; DSc, Alma Coll., 1975. Ordained to ministry Ch. of Christ, 1966. Mng. dir. Thomas Newman (Printers) Ltd., 1945-49; mng. dir. H. & M.J. Pubs. Ltd., 1947-49, Forget-Me-Not Greeting Cards Ltd., 1949-61, Diplomat Greetings Ltd., 1957-61, Nevill's Ltd., 1955-57; pastor Christ's Ch., Springfield, Mo., 1966-67, Longwood, Brookline, Mass., 1967-99; adminstrv. dir. Am. Schs. Oriental Rsch., 1968, treas., 1970—, trustee, 1972—. Pastor Jefferson (N.H.) Cmty. Chapel, 2000—; founder Carthage Rsch. Inst., Khereddine, Tunisia, 1975, Cyprus Archaeol. Rsch. Inst., Nicosia, 1977; cons. Joint Archeol. Expdns. to, Ai, 1969-73, to; Tell-El-Hesi, 1970-73, to, Idalion, 1970-73; mem. Joint Archeol. Expdn. to, Caesarea Maritima, 1971, to; Carthage, 1975; dir. Logistics Survey Qu'Rayyah, Saudi Arabia, 1973; pub. cons. (Dead Sea Scrolls Com.), 1968-73; Trustee Allbright Inst. Archeol. Rsch., Jerusalem.; Am. Center Oriental Rsch., Amman, Jordan. Served with RAF, 1940-45. Mem. Archeol. Inst. Am., Soc. Bibl. Lit., Soc. O.T. Studies, Masons, Harvard Faculty Club, Univ. Club Boston. Home and Office: 359 Ivy Dahlonega GA 30533 Office Phone: 706-864-5853. Personal E-mail: revtomn@alltel.net.

**NEWMAN, URSULA IRENE,** music educator; b. Toledo, May 24, 1954; d. Lowell Cauffiel and Ursula Irene Zrinka; m. Bruce Lee Newman, Nov. 15, 1986; children: Joanna, Betsy; m. Larry Spieldenner (div.); 1 child, Larry Spieldenner. Attended, Mary Manse Coll., Toledo, Columbia U., N.Y. Lic. realtor. Owner Ursula Cauffiel Sch of Music, Toledo, 1980—90. Adv. Ursula Cauffiel Sch. of Music, Toledo, 1990—; music dir. Temple Beth Israel, Phoenix, 1999—2001. Founder PracticeMusic, 2004—. Mem.: Desert Valley Music Teachers Assn., Music Tchr. Nat. Assn. Avocations: swimming, acting. Home: 10201 N 109th Pl Scottsdale AZ 85259-4809 Personal E-mail: grandpiano2002@aol.com.

**NEWMAN, WILLIAM ARTHUR,** lawyer; b. Dupont, Pa., Oct. 10, 1947; s. Jerome Mager and Doris Evelyn (Ross) N.; m. Pamela Jane Schneider, May 19, 1974; children: Romy S., T. R. BA, Yale U., 1969; JD, U. Mich., Ann Arbor, 1973. Bar: NY 1973, US Dist. Ct. So. Dist. NY 1973. Assoc. Debevoise & Plimpton, NYC, 1973-77; Richards, O'Neil & Allegaert, NYC, 1977-79, ptnr., 1979—90; prin. Blumenthal & Lynne PC, 1990—98; shareholder Greenberg Traurig, NYC, 1998—99; now ptnr. McGuireWoods LLP, NYC, co-mng. ptnr. NYC office. Bd. dirs. On2.com Inc., 2000—. Office: McGuireWoods LLP 7th Fl 1345 Ave of the Americas New York NY 10105-0106 Office Phone: 212-548-2160. Office Fax: 212-548-2170. Business E-Mail: wnewman@mcguirewoods.com.

**NEWMAR, JULIE CHALANE,** actress, dancer, real estate businesswoman; b. Hollywood, Calif. d. Donald Charles and Helene (Jesmer) Newmeyer; m. J. Holt Smith, Aug. 5, 1977 (div. Apr. 1986); 1 child, John Jewl Smith. Student, UCLA. Actress TV series, plays, movies. Mem. Actors Studio, N.Y. and Los Angeles. Appeared on Broadway in Marriage Go Round (Tony award), Damn Yankees, Guys and Dolls, Irma La Douce, Stop the World, L'il Abner, Dames At Sea; films: Seven Brides for Seven Brothers, Marriage Go Round, Mackenna's Gold, The Maltese Bippy, Streetwalkin', 1985, Dance Academy, 1987, Ghosts Can't Do It, Oblivion I and II, To Wong Foo, Thanks for Everything, Julie Newmar; TV: Rhoda the Robot in My Living Doll, Catwoman on Batman, guest starred on Get Smart, The Monkees, Bewitched, Route 66, Hart to Hart, Love American Style, Star Trek, Twilight Zone, Beverly Hillbillies, Columbo, Fantasy Island, Melrose Place, Hope & Gloria, The Making of Seven Brides for Seven Brothers, 1997; prima ballerina with L.A. Opera Co.; video: Too Funky (George Michael); Thierry Mugler high fashion shows, Paris. Recipient Antoinette Perry award. Avocations: gardening, piano.

**NEWMARK, CRAIG ALEXANDER,** communications executive; b. Morristown, NJ, Dec. 6, 1952; s. Leon and Joyce Newmark. BS, Case Western Reserve U., 1975, MS in Computer Sci., 1977. Computer programmer IBM, NJ, 1979—93; systems security architect, gen. cons. Charles Schwab, Calif., 1993—95; ind. contractor, software sys. architect Bank of America, Calif., 1995—97, Intel, Calif., 1995—97, Sun Microsystems, Calif., 1995—97; founder, chmn., customer service rep. Craigslist, San Francisco, 1995—. Featured in AP, Wall Street Journal, NY Times, LA Times, USA Today, Business Week, Time Mag., and Esquire Mag. Auth. of bd. Climate Theatre, Haight-Ashbury Food Program; supporter of local writers through Grotto Nights. Named #1 Most Efficient US Job Site, Forrester Rsch. Report, Wall St. Jour., 2000, Best Cmty. Website - People's Voice, Webby Awards, 2001, The Elite of the Online Employment Industry, WEDDLE's User's Choice Awards, 2004, 50 online destinations for the quarterlifer, Hatch Mag., 2004, 50 Coolest Websites, Time mag., 2004, Person of the Year, Webby Awards, The Internat. Acad. Digital Arts and Sciences, 2005, Webby Person of Yr., 2005; named one of World's 100 Most Influential People, Time Mag., 2005, 26 Most Fascinating Entrepreneurs, Inc.com, 2005. Achievements include millions of people use Craigslist to research subjects such as: jobs, housing, goods & services, events, friendships, and advice; first commercial transmission of a website into space by Deep Space Communications Network, March 11, 2005. Office: Craigslist 1319 9th Ave San Francisco CA 94122-2308 Office Phone: 415-566-6394. Office Fax: 415-504-6394. Business E-Mail: craig@craigslist.org.*

**NEWMARK, EMANUEL,** ophthalmologist; b. Newark, May 25, 1936; s. Charles Meyer and Bella (Yoskowitz) Newmark; m. Tina Steinberg, Aug. 25, 1957; children: Karen Beth, Heidi Ellen, Stuart Jeffrey. BS in Pharmacy, Rutgers U., 1959; postgrad., U. Amsterdam, The Netherlands, 1960-63, Armed Forces Inst. Pathology, Washington, 1971; MD, Duke U., 1966; postgrad., Harvard U., 1967. Diplomate Am. Bd. Ophthalmology. Intern George Washington U. Hosp., Washington, 1966; trainee NIH rsch. U. Fla., Gainesville, 1967—70; resident ophthalmology U. Fla. Hosp., 1967—70; instr. dept. ophthalmology U. Fla., 1970; cons. ophthalmology Gainesville VA Hosp., 1970; clin. instr. ophthalmology U. Tex. Med. Sch., San Antonio, 1971—72; cons. ophthalmology Kerrville VA Hosp., Tex., 1971—72; asst. chief ophthalmology svc. Brooke Army Gen. Hosp., Fort Sam, Tex., 1971—72. Clin. asst. prof. ophthalmology Bexar County Hosp. and Clinics, San Antonio, 1971—72; tchg. faculty Joint Commn. Allied Health Pers. in Ophthalmology, commr., 2004—; sec., treas. Palm Beach Eye Assocs., Atlantis, Fla., 1973—98; pharm. adv. com. Agy. Health Care Adminstrn. Bd. Optometry, 1991—; mem. adv. bd. Fla. east coast chpt. Nat. Sjorgren's Syndrome; chief ophthalmology JFK Med. Ctr., 1984, chmn. CME and edn. com., 2004—; staff ophthalmologist West Palm Beach VA Hosp., 2005—, Regional Eye Inst., 1998—2006. Contbr. chapters to books, articles to profl. jours.; exec. editor Ophthalmic Medical Assisting: An Independent Study Course. Alumni assoc. Rutgers Coll. Pharmacy, 1990—, chmn. reunion, 1986, 2001, Duke U. Med. Alumni Assn., NC, 1967—; centurian Diamor Club-Duke U. Med. Sch., NC, 1982—; campaign chmn., nat. vice chmn. Israel Bonds, Palm Beach County, Fla., 1988—90; participant charitable organs.; v.p. Palm Beach Liturgical Culture Found., 1994—2000, pres., 2000—01. Decorated Lion of Judea State of Israel; recipient Gates of Jerusalem medal, 1991, Jerusalem medal, 1996, Recognition award, Joint Commn. Allied Health Personnel in Ophthalmology, 2001, U.S. Army Commendation medal. Fellow: ACS, Am. Acad. Ophthalmology (del. to coun. 1996—2001, allied health edn. com. 1997—2002, editor Refinements 1998—2000, rep. to joint com. allied health pers. in ophthalmology 2004—, Fla. state chmn. edn. trust, Achievement award 2001, Councillors award 2001, Secretariat award 2005); mem.: AMA, Fla. Soc. Ophthalmology (ethics chmn. 1985—90, pres. 1990—91, James W. Clower Jr. Cmty. Svc. award 1995), Palm Beach County Ophthal. Soc. (pres. 1984—85, Ophthalmologist of Yr. 2004), Palm Beach County Med. Soc. (chair ethics com. 1997—2000, vice chair ethics com. 2002, bd. dirs. 2003, bd. dirs. mem.-at-large 2003—, coun. on ethical and jud. affairs 2004—06, trustee 2005), Fla. Med. Assn. (bo. dels. 1993—95, 2001—05), Am. Orgn. for Rehab. Through Tng. Fedn. (nat. exec. com.-campaign cabinet 1987, pres. 1987—90, Palm Beach Men's Achievement award 1988, Pres. award 1989), Founder's Soc. Duke U. Jewish Avocation: travel. Home: 180 Palm Cir Atlantis FL 33462-6627 Office: West Palm Beach Vets Med Ctr 7305 Military Trail West Palm Beach FL 33410 Office Phone: 561-422-8690. Personal E-mail: mannynewmark@msn.com.

**NEWMARK, LEONARD DANIEL,** linguistics educator; b. Attica, Ind., Apr. 8, 1929; s. Max Jacob and Sophie (Glusker) N.; m. Ruth Broessler, Sept. 16, 1951; children: Katya. MA, U. Chgo., 1947; MA, Ind. U., 1951, PhD, 1955. Instr. English U. Ill., Urbana, 1951; vis. asst. prof. linguistics U. Mich., Ann Arbor, 1961; assoc. prof. English Ohio State U., 1954-62; assoc. prof. linguistics Ind. U., Bloomington, 1962-63; prof. linguistics U. Calif., San Diego, 1963-91, prof. emeritus, 1992—, chmn. dept., 1963-71, 79-85, head program in Am. lang. and culture, 1979-84, rsch. linguist Ctr. for Rsch. in Lang., 1992—. Author: Linguistic History of English, 1963, Spoken Albanian, 1997, Standard Albanian, 1982, Albanian-English Dictionary, 1998, Albanian Handbook, 1999; editor UCSD Emeriti Newsletter: Chronicles, 2001-2004; inventor memory aid device. Mem. Linguistics Soc. Am., Dictionary Soc. N.Am., Phi Beta Kappa. Business E-Mail: ldnewmark@ucsd.edu.

**NEWMARK, MARILYN,** sculptor; b. NYC, July 20, 1928; d. Edward Ellis and Mabel (Davies) Newmark; m. Leonard J. Meiselman, Mar. 15, 1952. Student, Adelphi Coll., 1945—47, Alfred U., N.Y., 1949. Sculpture specializing in horses, equestrian figures, dogs, foxes. *Marilyn Newmark drew her first horse at the age of four, began working with clay in high school, and started selling her work, in ceramic, when she was seventeen. In 1970 she began casting her sculptures in bronze. Miss Newmark's models are produced as unique, limited editions or by commission. She has done work for Franklin Mint, New York Racing Association, Thoroughbred Breeders Associations, Professional Horseman's Association, Thoroughbred Breeders of Kentucky, the Japan Racing Association, and others. She has won over 90 awards at national and international exhibitions. Miss Newmark has hunted, shown, driven, and hacked her own horses for most of her life.* Exhibited in group shows Derby Mus., Fleischer Mus., Scottsdale, Leigh Yawkey Woodson Art Mus., Wis., Bennington Ctr. for Arts, Vt., NAD, NYC, Nat. Arts Club, NYC, Smithsonian Instn., Washington, Mus. of Horse, Ky., Port of History Mus., Pa., Marietta/Cobb Mus. Art, Wildlife Experience, Denver, Nat. Geog. Soc., Washington, Allegheny Colls. Galleries, Butler Inst. Am. Art; represented in permanent collections Nat. Mus. Racing, Saratoga, N.Y., Internat. Mus. Horse, Ky. Horse Park, Brookgreen Gardens, S.C., also pvt. collections. Recipient Anna Hyatt Huntington award, 1970-72, 75, 78, 80-83, 86, 88, 90, 97, 2002, Gold medal, 1973, award Coun. Am. Artists Socs., 1972, 73, 79, 80, Hudson Valley John Newington award, 1973, 77, Gold medal, 1979, Elliot Liskin Meml. award, 1989, 96, Academician NAD Edin P. Speyer award, 1974, 93, 99, Artist Fund award, 1982, Michael Gressel award, 2006. Fellow Nat. Sculpture Soc. (coun. 1973-75, rec. sec. 1976, sec. 1977-79, coun. 1981-83, 92-97, 2006-; Bronze medal 1986, Mildred Victor Meml. award 1996, Leonard Meiselman Meml. award 2003), Audubon Artists (Elliott Liskin Meml. award 2000, 02), Am. Artists Profl. League (Gold medal 1974, 77, medal of hon. 1987), Allied Artists Am. (Gold medal 1981, 93, In Memoriam award 1994), Pen & Brush Club (Gold medal 1977, Salmagundi Club award 1982, 83, 91, C. Dunwiddie Meml. award 1999, 2004), Soc. Animal Artists (jury of admissions 1972-75, 90—, bd. dirs. 1991—, v.p. 1998—, Legacy award 2002), Am. Acad. Equine Art (founding mem., dir. sculpture 1980—), Nassau Suffolk Horsemans Assn. (dir. 1968-82), Catherine Lorillard Wolfe Art Club, Smithtown Hunt Club, Meadowbrook Hunt Club. Address: 22 Woodhollow Rd Roslyn Heights NY 11577-2217 Office Phone: 516-621-5914.

**NEWMARK, PHILLIP ALLAN,** biology professor; s. Martin Irving and Ravelle Lynne Newmark; m. Sonia Elaine Wolpow, Oct. 3, 1992; children: Elena Rachel, Carl Martin. BA, Boston U., 1987; PhD, U. Colo., Boulder, 1994. Rsch. assoc. II Dana-Farber Cancer Inst., Boston, 1987—88; postdoctoral fellow U. Barcelona, Catalonia, 1995—96, Carnegie Inst. Wash., Balt. 1997—2001; asst. prof. U. Ill., Urbana, 2001—. Post-doctoral fellow Damon Runyon Cancer Rsch. Found., 1995—97, NIH, 1997—2000. Contbr. articles to profl. jours. Recipient Career award, NSF, 2003—; grantee, NIH, 2003—; scholar, Damon Runyon Cancer Rsch. Found., 2003—05; U. Colo. fellow, Boettcher Found., 1991—92. Mem.: Soc. Exptl. Biology and Medicine (editl. bd. mem.), Soc. For Devel. Biology, Am. Soc. Cell Biology, Phi Beta Kappa. Achievements include research in developed freshwater planarian as model organism for studying regeneration in animals. Avocations: running, reading, trumpet, flugelhorn. Office: U Ill 601 S Goodwin Ave B107 CLSL Urbana IL 61801 Office Phone: 217-244-4674. Office Fax: 217-244-1648. E-mail: pnewmark@life.uiuc.edu.

**NEWMARK, RICHARD ALAN,** chemist; b. Urbana, Ill., Nov. 11, 1940; s. Nathan M. and Anne Mae (Cohen) N.; m. Joan Friedman, July 4, 1965; children: David, Merel. AB, Harvard Coll., 1961; PhD, U. Calif., Berkeley, 1964. Postgrad. fellow Mass. Inst. Tech., Cambridge, 1964-66; asst. prof. U. Colo., Boulder, 1966-69; rsch. chemist 3M, St. Paul, 1969-72, rsch. specialist, 1972-76, sr. rsch. specialist, 1976-81, staff scientist, 1981-92, corp. scientist, 1992—2001; cons., 2002—. Councilor Minn. section Am. Chem. Soc., Washington, 1992-94. Contbr. articles to profl. jours. Chair Dist. 1 Cmty. Coun., St. Paul, 1984-88; co-chair St. Paul Sch. Bd. Commn. of Gifted and Talented, 1986-88; treas. Neighborhood Energy Consortium 2004-05, treas. St. Paul Audubon Soc. 2004—. Recipient award 3M Carlton Soc., 1993, Minn. award Am. Chem. Soc., 2000. Mem.: Sigma Xi, Phi Beta Kappa. Jewish. Avocations: skiing, bicycling. Office: 3M 201-bs 05 Saint Paul MN 55144-0001 Office Phone: 651-270-9345. E-mail: neumarque@comcast.com.

**NEWMARK, WILLIAM D.,** conservation biologist; b. St. Louis, Mo., Feb. 22, 1952; s. Philip and Marjorie Newmark. BA with distinction, U. of Colo., 1974, BA with distinction, 1977; MS, U. of Mich., 1980, PhD, 1986. Tech. adviser Coll. of African Wildlife Mgmt., Mweka, Tanzania, 1987—91; vis. scholar U. of Calif., San Diego, 1991—92, U. of Utah, Salt Lake City, 1993—94; rsch. curator Utah Mus. of Natural History, Salt Lake City, 1994—. Team leader Usambara Forest Fragmentation Project, Tanzania, 1987—; tech. cons. Norwegian Internat. Devel. Agy., Dar es Salaam, 1993—94; vis. sr. lectr. global environment faculty U. of Dar es Salaam, Tanzania, 1996—97; tech. cons. World Bank, African Families, Washington, 2000—; stap expert UNEP -Global Environment Facility, N.Y.C., 2003—. Author: (book) The Conservation of Mount Kilimanjaro, 1991, Conserving Biodiversity in East African forests: A Study of the Eastern Arc Mountains, 2002. Recipient rsch. grant, NSF, MacArthur Found., Nat. Geog. Soc., Earthwatch Inst., Critical Ecosys. Partnership. Mem.: Soc. For Conservation Biology, Ecol. Soc. of Am., Am. Soc. for the Advancement of Sci. Achievements include research in Reserve And Corridor Design; Patterns Of Extinction And Movement Of Vertebrate Species; Conservation And Development. Office: Utah Mus of Natural History 1390 E Presidents Cir Salt Lake City UT 84112 Office Phone: 801-581-6927. E-mail: bnewmark@umnh.utah.edu.

**NEWMEYER, FREDERICK JARET,** linguist, educator; b. Phila., Jan. 30, 1944; s. Alvin S. and Fritzie B. (Nisenson) N.; m. Carolyn V. Platt, Apr. 28, 1968 (div. 1974); m. Marilyn M. Goebel, Dec. 25, 1993. BA, U. Rochester, 1965, MA, 1967; PhD, U. Ill. 1969. Asst. prof. linguistics U. Wash., Seattle, 1969-75, assoc. prof., 1975-81, prof., 1981—, chair, 1990-2000. Vis. prof. U. London, 1979, Cornell U., 1981, U. Md., 1982, UCLA, 1982-83, La Trobe U., Australia, 1987. Author: English Aspectual Verbs, 1975, Linguistic Theory in America, 1980, Grammatical Theory, 1983, Politics of Linguistics, 1986, Possible and Probable Languages, 2005; editor: Linguistics: The Cambridge Survey, 1988, Natural Language and Linguistic Theory, 1987-2003; assoc. editor: Language, 1980-85. NEH fellow, 1973-74. Fellow AAAS; mem. Linguistic Soc. Am. (sec.-treas. 1989-94, v.p. 2001, pres. 2002). Avocation: gardening. Home: 4621 NE 107th St Seattle WA 98125-6947 Office: U Wash Dept Linguistics Seattle WA 98195-4340 E-mail: fjn@u.washington.edu.

**NEWPORT, ELISSA L.,** psychology professor; b. St. Louis, July 3, 1947; d. Eugene and Anita Evelyn (Ginsberg) N.; m. Theodore Supalla, Oct. 12, 1980; children: Susanna, Zachary. Student, Wellesley Coll., 1965-67; BA, Barnard Coll., 1969; MA, U. Pa., 1974, PhD, 1975. Asst. prof. U. Calif. San Diego, La Jolla, 1974-79; assoc. prof., prof. U. Ill., Champaign, 1979-88; prof. U. Rochester, NY, 1988—. George Eastman prof. brain in cognitive sciences and linguistics NY, chair Dept. Brain and Cognitive Sciences NY. Mem. editorial bd. Cognitive Psychology, 1981—, Language Acquisition, 1989—. Editor: (book series) MIT Press, 1982—; contbr. articles to profl. jours. Alfred P. Sloan Found. fellow MIT, 1981, U. Pa., 1982; NIH rsch. grantee, 1980—; recipient Arnold O. Bediman Rsch. award U. Ill., 1982-83, William Bonsall Vis. Chair in Humanities Stanford U., 1984, Claude Pepper award of excellence, NIH. Fellow Am. Acad. Arts and Scis.; mem. AAAS, NAS, Am. Psychol. Assn., Soc. Rsch. in Child Devel., Linguistic Soc. Am., Cognitive Sci. Soc. Office: Univ Rochester Dept Psychology Meliora Hall 414 Rochester NY 14627-0268 Office Phone: 585-275-8689. E-mail: newport@bcs.rochester.edu.*

**NEWQUIST, JUDY LYNNE ROOS,** elementary school educator, education educator; d. John Peter and June Janette (Johnson) Roos; m. Russell Duane Newquist, Mar. 6, 1976; children: Nichole, Matthew, Jennifer. BS, Iowa State U., Ames, 1976; BA in Edn., Buena Vista U., Storm Lake, Iowa, 1998; MA in Edn., Morningside Coll., Sioux City, Iowa, 2005. Med. social worker Ottumwa Regional Health Ctr., Iowa, 1976—2000; tchr. Ottumwa Cmty. Schs., 1998—, mem. dist. adv. com., 1999—2000. Mem. parent adv. com. Cardinal Cmty. Schs., Eldon, Iowa, 1996—2005. Sunday sch. tchr. Agency (Iowa) Meth. Ch., 1981—2000, mem. adminstrv. bd., 1982—83. Mem.: Alpha Delta Kappa. Avocations: reading, travel, genealogy, quilting, gardening. Office: Evans Mld Sch 812 Chester Ave Ottumwa IA 52501 Business E-Mail: newquist@aea15.k12.ia.us.

**NEWSOM, CAROLYN CARDALL,** management consultant; b. South Weymouth, Mass., Feb. 27, 1941; d. Alfred James and Bertha Virginia (Roy) Cardall; m. John Harlan Newsom, Feb. 4, 1967; children: John Cardall, James Harlan. AB, Brown U., Providence, R.I., 1962; MBA, Wharton Sch., 1978; PhD, U. Pa., 1985. Systems engr. IBM, Seattle, 1964-70, Newsom S.E. Services, Seattle, 1970-76; instr. U. Pa. Wharton Sch., Phila., 1978-81; v.p., prin. sr. cons. PA Cons. Group, Princeton, NJ, 1981-88; pres. Newsom Assocs., Yardley, Pa., 1988; ptnr. Bus. Strategy Implementation, Princeton, NJ, 1989-90; pres. Strategy Implementation Solutions, Yardley, Pa., 1990—. Examiner N.J. Gov.'s Performance Excellence Award, 1993, sr. examiner, 1994—2002, judge, 2003—06; examiner Malcolm Baldrige Nat. Quality Award, 2003—05. Trustee St. Mary Hosp., Langhorne, Pa., 1986—94; sec. bd. dir. Gordonstown Am. Found., 1999—2005; bd. dir. Chandler Hall, 1980—87. Mem.: Quality N.J. (vice chair 1998—99), Am. Soc. for Quality, Am. Acad. Mgmt., Brown Alumni Assn. (pres.-elect 1993—95, pres. 1995—97). Office: Strategy Implementation Solutions 1588 Woodside Rd Yardley PA 19067-2611

**NEWSOM, DAVID DUNLOP,** ambassador, educator; b. Richmond, Calif., Jan. 6, 1918; s. Fred Stoddard and Ivy Elizabeth (Dunlop) N.; m. Jean Frances Craig, Nov. 17, 1942; children: John, Daniel, Nancy, David, Catherine. AB, U. Calif., 1938; MS, Columbia U., 1940; LLD, U. Pacific, 1979. Pulitzer traveling scholar, 1940-41; pub. Walnut Creek (Calif.) Courier-Jour., 1946-47; 3d sec. info. officer Am. embassy, Karachi, Pakistan, 1948-50; 2d sec. vice consul Oslo, 1950-51; pub. affairs officer Baghdad, Iraq, 1952-55; officer-in-charge Arabian peninsula affairs Dept. State, Washington, 1955-59; with Nat. War Coll., 1959-60; 1st sec. Am. embassy, London, 1960-62; dep. dir. Office. No. African Affairs, Dept. State, Washington, 1962-63, dir., 1963-65; U.S. ambassador Libya, 1965-69; asst. sec. state for African affairs, 1969-74; U.S. ambassador Indonesia, 1974-77, Philippines, 1977-78; undersec. state of polit. affairs Washington, 1978-81; dir. Inst. Study of Diplomacy, Sch. Fgn. Svc., Georgetown U., 1981-90, Marshall Coyne vis. prof. diplomacy, 1989-91; interim dean Sch. Fgn. Svc. Georgetown U., 1995-96; Cumming Meml. prof. internat. rels. U. Va., 1991-98; spl. adviser U.S. del. UN Gen. Assembly, 1972, 78, 79, 80. Sr. fellow The Miller Ctr., U. Va., 1999-2003; mem. com. on sci., tech. and health aspects of fgn. policy Nat. Rsch. Coun., 1999. Author: (book) Soviet Brigade in Cuba, Diplomacy and The American Democracy, The Public Dimension of Foreign Policy, The Imperial Mantle. Served to lt. USNR, 1942-46. Recipient Commendable Service award USIS, 1955; Dept. State Meritorious Service award, 1958; Nat. Civil Service League award, 1972; Rockefeller Pub. Service award, 1973; Lifetime award Am. Fgn. Svc. Assn., 2000. Mem. U.S. Fgn. Svc. Assn., Coun. Fgn. Rels., Cosmos Club. Presbyterian. Home: 500 Crestwood Dr 2504 Charlottesville VA 22903

**NEWSOM, GAVIN,** mayor; b. San Francisco, Oct. 10, 1967; s. William and Tessa Newsom; m. Kimberly Guilfoyle Newsom, Dec. 8, 2001. BA in Polit. Sci., Santa Clara U., 1989. Founder PlumpJack Wines Mgmt. Group, San Francisco, 1992—; pres. Pkg. and Traffic Commn., San Francisco, 1996—97; supr. Office of Bd. Suprs., San Francisco, 1997—2004; mayor City of San Francisco, 2003—. Office: City Hall Room 200 1 Dr Carlton B Goodlett Place San Francisco CA 94102*

**NEWSOM, GERALD HIGLEY,** astronomy educator; b. Albuquerque, Feb. 11, 1939; s. Carroll Vincent and Frances Jeanne (Higley) N.; m. Ann Catherine Bricker, June 17, 1972; children: Christine Ann, Elizabeth Ann. BA, U. Mich., 1961; MA, Harvard U., 1963, PhD, 1968. Research asst. McMath-Hulbert Obs., Pontiac, Mich., summers 1959, 61; research asst. astronomy dept. U. Mich., Ann Arbor, 1959-61; research asst. Shock Tube Lab. Harvard U., Cambridge, Mass., 1962, 64-68; research asst. dept. physics Imperial Coll., London, 1968-69; asst. prof. astronomy Ohio State U., Columbus, 1969-73, assoc. prof., 1973-82, prof., 1982—2004, acting chmn. dept. astronomy, 1991-93, vice chmn. dept. astronomy, 1993—2004, acting asst. dean, 1985-86; sr. post-doctoral research asst. Physikalisches Institut, Bonn, Fed. Republic of Germany, 1978. Author: Astronomy, 1976, Exploring the Universe, 1979; contbr. articles to profl. jours. Fellow Woodrow Wilson Found., 1961-62, NSF, 1961-63; grantee Noble Found., 1961-64. Mem.: Am. Astron. Soc., Internat. Astron. Union. Home: 46 W Weisheimer Rd Columbus OH 43214-2545 Office: Ohio State U Dept Astronomy 140 W 18th Ave Columbus OH 43210-1173 Office Phone: 614-292-2632. Business E-Mail: gnewsom@astronomy.ohio-state.edu.

**NEWSOM, JAMES THOMAS,** lawyer; b. Carrollton, Mo., Oct. 6, 1944; s. Thomas Edward and Hazel Love (Mitchell) N.; m. Sherry Elaine Retzloff, Aug. 9, 1986; stepchildren: Benjamin A. Bawden, Holly K. Bawden. AB, U. Mo., 1966, JD, 1968. Bar: Mo. 1968, U.S. Supreme Ct. 1971. Assoc. Shook, Hardy & Bacon, London and Kansas City, Mo., 1972, ptnr., 1976—. Mem. Mo. Law Rev., 1966-68. Lt. comdr. JAGC, USNR, 1968-72. Mem. ABA, Kansas City Met. Bar Assn., U. Mo. Law Sch. Law Soc., U. Mo. Jefferson Club, Order of Coif, Perry (Kans.) Yacht Club, Stone Horse Yacht Club (Harwich Port, Mass.). Avocations: skiing, sailing, auto racing. Office: Shook Hardy & Bacon 2555 Grand Blvd Kansas City MO 64108-2613 Office Phone: 816-474-6550. Business E-Mail: jnewsom@shb.com.

**NEWSOM, JOHN HARLAN,** physician; b. Worland, Wyo., May 6, 1940; s. John Cecil and Arlene Zelda (Finch) N.; m. Carolyn Cardall, Feb. 4, 1967; children: John Cardall, James Harlan. BS, U.S. Naval Acad., 1963; MD, U. Wash., 1971. Diplomate Am. Bd. Family Practice. Intern Doctors Hosp., Seattle, 1971-72; physician in pvt. practice, Newport, Oreg., 1972-73; physician Group Health, Seattle, 1973-74; pvt. practice Yardley, Pa., 1974—; mem. med. staff St. Mary Med. Ctr., 1974—, chmn. family practice dept., 1978-80, pres. med. staff, 1980-81, 2006, v.p. med. affairs, 1983—85, 1999—2004. Trustee St. Mary Hosp., Langhorne, Pa., 1981-83; bd. dirs. Pennswood Village, Newtown, Pa., 1987-81; clin. asst. prof. Temple U. Sch. Medicine, 1978-91; clin. instr. Pa. State Med. Sch., 2000-01. Contbr. articles to profl. jours. Pres. Parents at Lawrenceville, N.J., 1989-90. Lt. USN, 1963-67. Decorated Bronze Star; named a Top Doc, Phila. Mag., 2002. Fellow Am. Acad. Family Physicians; mem. U. Wash. Alumni Assn. (pres. Del. Valley chpt. 1989-90), Pa. Med. Soc. (del. 1985), Coll. Physicians Phila., Bucks County Med. Soc. (pres. 1985). Office: 1588 Woodside Rd Yardley PA 19067-2611

**NEWSOME, CHRISTA ANNE,** elementary school educator; b. Indpls., Nov. 9, 1967; d. Charles Lindbergh Sternecker and Carol Greb Sternecker-Lego; m. Travis Addison Newsome, Nov. 19, 1963; children: Anne Nicole, Julia Elizabeth. AS in Info. Systems Tech., C.C. of the Air Force, Offutt Air Force Base, 1995; BS in Edn. cum laude (honors.), U. Nebr., Omaha, 1998. Satellite comm. operator USAF, Mildenhall (RAF Mildenhall), Suffolk, England, 1986—88; mobile radio operator/instr. 55th WG/Det 1, Bellevue (Offutt AFB), Nebr., 1988—95; spl. edn. tchr. Lewis and Clark Mid. Sch., Omaha, 1998—99; title I math tchr. Oglethorpe County Mid. Sch., Lexington, Ga., 2000—05, 7th grade math and social studies tchr., 2005—. Teen worker Athens Ch. of Christ, Athens, Ga., 2005—06. Decorated Accomodation Medal USAF, Good Conduct Medal with 1 oak leaf cluster, Nat. Def. Svc. Medal, Non-Commissioned Officer Profl. Mil. Edn. Grad. award; grantee Eagle grantee, C.C. of the Air Force, 1995. Mem.: Ga. Edn. Assn. (assoc.), Kappa Phi Delta. Libertarian. Christian. Avocations: reading, interior decorating, travel, gardening, scrapbooks. Office: Oglethorpe County Board of Education 747 Athens Rd Lexington GA 30648 Office Phone: 706-743-8146.

**NEWSOME, FREDERICK V.,** medical educator; b. Charleston, W.Va., July 7, 1946; s. Moses and Ruth (Bass) N.; children: Akasemi, Imhotep, Nubia, Hatshepsut. BA in Chemistry, Harvard U., 1968; MD, W.Va. U., 1972; MSc in Tropical Medicine, London Sch. Hygiene & Tropical Medicine, 1981. Diplomate Am. Bd. Internal Medicine. Instr. in medicine Coll. of Physicians and Surgeons Columbia U., N.Y.C., 1975-78; instr. in medicine Albert Einstein Med. Sch., Bronx, 1979-80; sr. lectr. in medicine U. Jos, Nigeria, 1981-88; clin. prof., head dept. of medicine Coll. of Health Scis. Usmanu Danfodio U., Sokoto, Nigeria, 1988-90; chief ambulatory medicine The Meth. Hosp., Bklyn., 1991-92; asst. prof. medicine Columbia U. Coll. Physicians & Surgeons, N.Y.C., 1992—. Author: An African American Philosophy of Medicine, 2005; contbr. articles to profl. jours. Fellow ACP, West African Coll. Physicians, Royal Soc. Tropical Medicine and Hygiene; mem. Nat. Med. Assn., Assn. for Study Afro-Am. Life and History. Office: Harlem Hosp Dept Medicine Rm 14131 135th St & Malcolm X Ave New York NY 10037 Office Phone: 212-939-1411. E mail: fvn1@columbia.edu

**NEWSOME, HEBER H., JR.,** retired academic administrator; Dean Va. Commonwealth U. Med. Coll., 2000—05, clinical prof.; ret., 2005. Office: Deans Office PO Box 980565 Sanger Hall Richmond VA 23298 Office Phone: 804-828-9788. Business E-Mail: hhnewsom@vcu.edu.

**NEWSOME, JAMES E.,** mercantile exchange executive; m. Mei Mei Newsome; children: Molly, Riley. BS in Econ., U. Fla., 1982; MS in Agr., Miss. State U., 1985, PhD in Animal sci./Agri. Econs., 2001. Mem. U.S. Commodity Futures Trading Commn., Washington, 1998-01; chmn. Commodity Futures Trading Commn., Washington, 2001—04; pres. NY Mercantile Exch., Inc., NYC, 2004—, CEO, 2004—. Mem. Pres. Working Group on Fin. Markets; mem. U.S. Corp. Fraud Task Force; assoc. v.p. Miss. Cattlemen's Assn. and Beef Coun., chmn. Miss. Agribus. Coun., mem. Gov's. Task Force on Future Miss. Agri., pres. Fla. Future Farmers Am., pres. U. Fla. Agrl. Coun. Mem. Assn. Miss. Agri. Orgns. (pres.). Office: NYMEX World Fin Ctr One N End Ave New York NY 10282-1101*

**NEWSOME, JOHN DAVID, JR.,** music educator; b. Fitzgerald, Ga., Apr. 6, 1969; s. John David Newsome and Linda Hair Scurlock; m. Leanne Paige McMichen, Aug. 4, 2001; children: Sandra Elizabeth, Sarah Danielle; m. Melissa Diane Presley (div.). MusB, Troy State U., 1987—91. Band dir. Clinch County H.S., Homerville, Ga., 1991—94, Tattnall County H.S., Reidsville, Ga., 1994—97, Treutlen H.S., Soperton, Ga., 1997—2004, Fitzgerald H.S., 2004—. Composer: Atlantic Eagle Overture, 2002, Discata Mexicana, 2002. Recipient John Phillip Sousa award, Instrumentalist Mag., 1987. Mem.: Profl. Assn. Ga. Realtors, Ga. Music Educators Assn. Avocations: golf, web site design. Office: Fitzgerald HS Marching Canes 601 W Cypress St Fitzgerald GA 31750

**NEWSOME, LEE ANN,** anthropologist, educator; BA, U. of Fla., 1982, MA, 1986, PhD, 1993. Curator of collections So. Ill. U. Ctr. for Archaeological Investigations, Carbondale, 1993—2001; assoc. prof. Pa. State U., U. Pk., 2002—. Contbr. articles in Jour. of Ethnobiology, Am. Antiquity, Southeastern Geology. Office: Dept of Anthropology Pa State U 316 Carpenter Bldg University Park PA 16802-3404

**NEWSOME, MELINDA,** anthropologist; b. San Diego, Feb. 7, 1960; d. Elbert B. Whalley and Susan Osborn; children: William R. IV, Alexander Scott. BA in anthropology, U. Calif., San Diego, 1998. Dir. devel. San Diego Mus. of Mon, San Diego Archaeological Ctr. Project mgr. (book, exhibit) Footsteps Through Time: 4.4 my of Human Evolution, 2001. Pres. PTA, Turtleback Elem., 1996—97. Office: San Diego Arch Ctr 16666 San Pasqual Village Escondido CA 92027 Personal E-mail: melinda_new@yahoo.com.

**NEWSOME, OZZIE,** professional sports team executive; b. Muscle Shoals, Ala., Mar. 16, 1956; s. Ethel Newsome and Ozzie Newsome Sr.; m. Gloria Jenkins. BS, U. Ala. Tight end Cleveland Browns, 1978-90; v.p., player personnel Baltimore Ravens, 1996—99, sr. v.p., football ops., 1999—2002, gen. mgr., 2002—. Active Big Bros., Athletes in Action; bd. dirs. Police Athletic League. Named Ala. Amateur Athlete of Yr., Ala. Sportswriters Assn., 1977; named to AFC Pro-Squad, 1981, Outstanding Team Player, 1981, All Pro, Pro-Football Writers Assn. and Sporting News, 1979; Cleveland Browns All-Time Leading Receiver, MVP on Offense, Cleve. TD Club (three times); ranked among NFL's top 10 in receptions; became 14th player in NFL history to make over 500 receptions; all-time leading tight end in NFL history; leading receiver in AFC, 1984; inducted into Coll. Football Hall of Fame, 1994; Inductee Pro Football Hall of Fame, 1999, Canton Ohio. Mem. Fellowship of Christian Athletes. Office: 11001 Owings Mills Blvd Owings Mills MD 21117-2857

**NEWSOME, RANDALL JACKSON,** judge; b. Dayton, Ohio, July 13, 1950; s. Harold I. and Sultana S. (Stone) N. BA summa cum laude, Boston U., 1972, JD, U. Cin., 1975. Bar: Ohio 1975, U.S. Dist. Ct. (so. dist.) Ohio 1977, U.S. Ct. Appeals (6th cir.) 1979, U.S. Supreme Ct. 1981. Law clk. to chief judge U.S. Dist. Ct. (so. dist.) Ohio, 1975-77; assoc. Dinsmore & Shohl, Cin., 1978-82; judge U.S. Bankruptcy Ct. (so. dist.) Ohio, 1982-88, U.S. Bankruptcy Ct. (no. dist.) Calif., Oakland, 1988—2004, chief judge, 2004—. Faculty mem. Fed. Jud. Ctr., ALI-ABA, 1987—; mem. Nat. Conf. of Bankruptcy Judges, 1983—, mem. bd. govs., 1987-88, pres., 1998-99. Contbg. author: Chapter 11 Theory and Practice, 1994—, Collier on Bankruptcy, 1997—. Fellow Am. Coll. Bankruptcy; mem. Am. Law Inst., Phi Beta Kappa. Democrat. Office: US Bankruptcy Ct PO Box 2070 Oakland CA 94604-2070 Office Phone: 510-879-3530.

**NEWSTEAD, JENNIFER G.,** lawyer; AB, Harvard U.; JD, Yale Law Sch. Mng. editor Yale Law Jour.; editor Yale Jour. Internat. Law; law clerk Judge Laurence H. Silberman, US Court of Appeals, DC Circuit, Justice Stephen G. Breyer, US Supreme Ct.; assoc. Davis Polk & Wardwell, NY; former dep. asst. attorney gen. Office of Legal Policy US Dept. Justice, prin. dep. asst. attorney gen., Office of Legal Policy, 2002; assoc. gen. counsel Exec. Office of the President, Washington, gen. counsel, Office of Mgmt. and Budget. Adj. prof. law, national security law Georgetown U. Law Ctr., 2002. Office: Office of Mgmt and Budget EEOB 17th & Pennsylvania Ave NW Rm 254 Washington DC 20503-0001 Office Phone: 202-395-5044. Office Fax: 202-395-7289.

**NEWTON, ARTHUR RICHARD (RICHARD NEWTON, A. RICHARD NEWTON),** engineering educator; b. Melbourne, Australia; m. Petra Newton; children: Amrita, Neris. B in engring., U. Melbourne, Australia, 1973, M in engring. sci., 1975, LLD (hon.), 2003; PhD in elec. engring. and computer sci., U. Calif., Berkeley, 1978. Asst. prof. U. Calif., Berkeley, 1979—82, assoc. prof., 1982—85, prof., 1985—, vice chmn. dept. elec. engring. and computer sciences, 1985—88, chmn., 1999—2000, dean Coll. Engring., 2000—, Roy W. Carlson prof. engring.; co-founder SDA Systems (now Cadence Design Systems), PIE Design Systems, Simplex Solutions, Crossbow Tech., Synopsys Inc., Silicon Light Machines, acting pres. and CEO, 1994—95; venture ptnr. The Mayfield Fund, 1988—2002, Tallwood Venture Capital, 2003—. Hon. prof. integrated circuit design Nat. Chiao Tung U., Taiwan; cons. various companies including Hewlett-Packard, IBM Corp., GE, Motorola, Philips, RCA, Sony Corp., and many others, 1979; founding mem. steering com. Elec. Design Interchange Format, 1983—89, founding mem. tech. com., 1983—88; mem. tech. program com. ACM/IEEE Design Automation Conf., 1986—89, tech. program chair, 1988—89, vice chair, 1990, gen. chair, 1991, indsl. program chair, 1992—93; mem. tech. program com. Internat. Fedn. for Info. Processing Very Large Scale Integration Conf., Australia, 1987, 89, 91, European Design Automation Conf., 1991—95, ASIA-PACIFIC Conf. on Circuits & Systems, 1991—95; mem. WG 10.5 VLSI com. Internat. Fedn. for Info. Processing, 1991—98; mem. Info. Sci. & Tech. (ISAT) com. Def. Advanced Rsch. Projects Agcy., 1995—98; mem. steering com. Internat. Computer Initiative Sci. Ctr., Moscow, 1992—2001; mem. sci. adv. group Nat. Info. and Comm. Tech. (ICT), Australia, 2002—; mem. tech. adv. bd. CAD Framework Initiative, 1988—97, Sequent Computers Inc., Portland, Oreg., 1985—92, Cadence Design Systems, San Jose, Calif., 1989—93, chair tech. adv. bd., 1992—93; mem. tech. adv. bd. Synopsys Inc., San Jose, Calif., 1989—, IMEC, Leuven, Belgium, 1991—97, Objectivity Inc., Menlo Pk., Calif., 1988—94, QuickTurn Design Systesm, Mountain View. Calif., 1993—95, Interconnetix, Portland, Oreg., 1993—97, Simplex Solutions, Sunnyvale, Calif., 1995—2002, Sonics Inc., 1995—, Lightspeed Semiconductor, 1996—, Microsoft Rsch., 1997—, Airgo Networks, 1998—, Form Factor, 1998—, Pharmix Inc., 2002—; mem. tech. coun. Microelectronics Inc., 2000—. Bd. trustees Anita Borg Inst. for Women and Tech., 2001—. Recipient C. Holmes McDonald Disting. Tchg. Award, Eta Kappa Nu, 1986, Best Paper award, European Solid State Circuits Conf., 1983, ACM/IEEE Design Automation Conf., 1987, 1990, Phil Kaufman Award, Electronics Design Automation Consortium (EDAC), 2003. Fellow: IEEE (mem., session organizer Computer Aided Network Design (CANDE) com, 1978, assoc. editor Transactions on Computer Aided Design 1985—88, administv. com. Circuits and Systems Soc. 1986—89, tech. program com. internat. Solid-State Circuit Conf. 1988—89, tech. program com. Internat. Conf. on Computer Aided Design 1984—86, 1989—90, Internat. Conf. on Computer Design Best Paper Award 1988. Circuits and Systems Soc. Golden Jubilee Medal 2000), Am. Acad. Arts & Sciences; mem.: NAE, Assn. for Computing Machinery. Office: U Calif Coll Engring 320 McLaughlin Hall # 1700 Berkeley CA 94720-1700*

**NEWTON, CINDY LYNN,** elementary school educator; b. Frankfort, Ind., Nov. 1, 1954; d. William Max and Barbara Lois Cline; m. Robert Allen Newton, Dec. 28, 1974; 1 child, Amber Lynne Robinson. BSc, Ind. U., 1994; M in Edn., Ind. Wesleyan U., 1999. Reading Endorsement Ind. U., 1994, Academy of Leadership for Teachers Ind., 1999. Elem. tchr. Eastview Elem. Connersville, Ind., 1994—. Tech. bldg. go-to Eastview Elem., Connersville, Ind.; armstrong educator Ind. U., 2005—; supervising tchr. Ind. U. East, 1995—; state reading dist. rep. Ind. State Reading Assn., 1998—; staff devel. inservice provider Eastview Elem., Connersville, Ind., 1995—. Dir. for 40 days of purpose Pk. Pl. Ch. of God, Connersville, Ind., 2005, sunday sch. tchr., 1981—2006; tchr. yr. selection com. Fayette County Schools, Connersville, Ind., 2000—06; state officer rep. Ind. State Read Assn., 1998—2006. Recipient Ind. U. Armstrong Tchr. Educator award, Ind. U., 2005, Citizen's Adv. Achievement award, 3Rivers SWM Dist., 2005, Outstanding Svc. award, Ind. State Reading Assn., 2003, Chritel DeHann's Excellence in Edn. Project e, 2000. Outstanding Profl. award, Ind. Wesleyan U., 1999, Tchr. of Yr., Fayette County Sch. Corp., 1998, Three Rivers Solid Waste Mgmt. Environ. Citizen's award; fellow Gifted and Talented Action Rsch. grant, State of Ind., 2000. Master: Connersville Area Reading Coun. (assoc.); mem.: ASCD, Internat. Reading Assn. (assoc.), Ind. Computer Educators (assoc.), Ind. State Reading Assn. (assoc.; sec. 2001—02. Outstanding Svc. award 2003), Delta Kappa Gamma. Achievements include development of elementary computer clubs. Office: Eastview Elem 401 S Fountain St Connersville IN 47331 Office Phone: 765-825-5541. E-mail: cnewton@fayette.k12.in.us.

**NEWTON, DEAN,** state representative; m. Anita Newton. Grad., Kans. U.; degree in Law, NYU. Atty. Sonnenschein, Nath & Rosenthal; mem. Kans. Ho. of Reps., 2001—. Founder Kids for Brighter Future, 1998—; Project Smile, 1999—. Republican. Home: 8802 Cedar Dr Prairie Village KS 66207-2214

**NEWTON, DON ALLEN,** economic development consultant; b. Laurel, Miss., Oct. 19, 1934; s. Wilfred L. and Mary (McMullan) N.; m. Coleta Farrell, Oct. 11, 1958; children: Don Jr., Coleta Midge Rast. AA, Meridian CC, Miss., 1954; BA, U. Ala., 1956; postgrad. in Assn. Mgmt., U. NC; postgrad. in Econ. Devel., U. Okla. Asst. mgr. Meridian C. of C., 1956; mgr. Winston County C. of C., Louisville, Miss., 1960—61; asst. dir. Delta Coun. Indsl. and Cmty. Devel. Bd., Stoneville, Miss., 1961—62, dir., 1963—70; exec. v.p. Met. Devel. Bd., Birmingham, Ala., 1970—74; pres. Birmingham Regional C. of C., 1974—99; pub. Birmingham Mag., Birmingham Bus. Mag., 1974—99; pres. Birmingham Area C. of C. Found., Inc., 1988-99, Devel. Assocs. Econ. Devel., 1999. Contbr. articles to profl. jours., newspapers. Former appointee Ala. Export Coun.; bd. dirs. Birmingham Met. Devel. Bd., Ala. Sports Found. Lt. USNR, 1957-60. Named Ala. Mktg. Man of Yr., 1972. Mem.: Sigma Chi. Home: 4156 Glenbrook Dr Birmingham AL 35213 Office: Development Assocs PO Box 530093 Birmingham AL 35253-0093

**NEWTON, ELIZABETH PURCELL,** counselor, consultant, author; b. Madison, N.C., June 3, 1925; d. Charles Augustus and Anna Meta (Buchanan) P.; m. William Edward Newton, June 11, 1949; children: James Purcell, Betsy Newton Hein, Christina Newton Harwood. A.A., Peace Coll., 1944; B.A., U. N.C., 1946; M.Ed., Ga. State U., 1969; Ed.S., West Ga. Coll., 1981. Tchr., counselor S. Cobb High Sch., Austell, Ga., 1965-69; counselor, dept. head Wheeler High Sch., Marietta, Ga., 1969-76; counselor, div. head guidance services Walton High Sch., Marietta, Ga., 1976—90; ret., 1990; sch. rep. Coll. Bd., Princeton, N.J., 1981—90, panelist, presenter S.E. region, Atlanta, 1983-85; presenter Ga. Sch. Counselors Assn., Atlanta, 1980—90; cons. Panhandle Area Edn. Coop., Chipley, Fla., 1985. Author: Steps to College Admissions, 1978; Student's Guide to College Admissions, 1981; Student's Guide to Career Preparation, 1982. Sch. rep. Citizens Adv. Council, Marietta, 1981, 82, 85. Ga. Dept. Edn. grantee, 1981; named Outstanding Woman in Edn., Atlanta Jour., 1985. Mem. Cobb Counselor Assn. (organizer, chmn. nominations com. 1985), Ga. Sch. Counselors Assn. (Secondary Counselor of Yr. 1983), Am. Sch. Counselors Assn. (Nat. Secondary Counselor of Yr. 1984), Phi Delta Kappa. Presbyterian.

**NEWTON, ESTHER MARY,** anthropologist, educator; b. NYC, Nov. 28, 1940; d. Saul B. and Virginia Newton. BA, U. Mich., 1962; MA, U. Chgo., 1964, PhD, 1968. Asst. prof. CUNY, Queens, 1968-71; from asst. prof. to assoc. prof. anthropology SUNY, Purchase, 1971-92, prof. anthropology, 1992—, Kempner disting. professorship, 1999; adj. prof. Am. culture and women's studies U. Mich., Ann Arbor, 2004—. Coord. women's studies program SUNY, Purchase, 1984-86; vis. prof. Yale U., 1970, U. Amsterdam, 1993; affiliated scholar CUNY, 1992-93; scholar in residence U. Calif., Santa Cruz, 1993; curator exhbn. Gay and Lesbian Cmty. Svcs. Ctr., 1993. Author: Mother Camp: Female Impersonators in America, 1972, reprinted with new introduction, 1979, Cherry Grove, Fire Island: Sixty years in America's First Gay and Lesbian Town, 1993, Margaret Meade May Me May, 2000; co-author: (with Shirley Walton) Womanfriends, 1976; contbr. to anthologies including The Lesbian Issue: Essays from Signs, 1985, Hidden from History: Reclaiming the Gay and Lesbian Past, 1989, International Gay Studies: The Amsterdam Conference, 1994, History of Homosexuality in Europe and America, 1994, Writing Lesbian and Gay Culture, 1995; mem. editl. bd. The Cutting Edge: Lesbian Life and Literature Series, Between men, Between Women: Lesbian and Gay Studies Series, GLQ: Jour. of Queer Studies, Jour. of Homosexuality, Jour. Sexuality in History; contbr. to books including Amazon Expedition, 1973, Anthropology and American Life, 1974, Symbolic Anthropology: A Reader in the Study of Symbols and Meaning, 1977, Strategies des femmes, 1984, Pleasure and Danger: Exploring Female Sexuality, 1984, Homosexuality, Which Homosexuality? Vol. 2, 1987, The Lesbian and Gay Studies Reader, 1993; contbr. articles to mags. and jours. La Verne Noyes scholar U. Chgo., 1962-63; training grantee NIH, 1963-65, faculty support grantee SUNY, Purchase, 1987, 92; pre-doctoral fellow NIMH, 1965-67; recipient experienced faculty travel award SUNY, 1987, 91; Rockefeller Humanities fellow, 1999. Mem. Am. Anthrop. Assn. (cochair commn. lesbian and gay issues, 1994-96). Avocation: dog training. Office: Divsn Social Sci SUNY Purchase NY 10577

**NEWTON, FLOYD CHILDS, III,** lawyer; b. Griffin, Ga., Feb. 4, 1955; s. Floyd Childs Jr. and Jean (Hunt) N.; m. Katrina Dalton, Aug. 30, 1986; children: Stephanie, Amanda, Natalie. BA, Princeton (N.J.) U., 1977; JD, U. Ga., 1980. Bar: Ga. 1980, U.S. Dist. Ct. (no. dist.) Ga. 1980, U.S. Ct. Appeals (11th cir.) 1980. Ptnr. King & Spalding, Atlanta, 1980—. Mem. Nat. Assn. Bond Lawyers (pres. 1998-99). Office: King & Spalding 1180 Peachtree St Atlanta GA 30309 Office Phone: 404-572-4600. Business E-Mail: fnewton@kslaw.com.

**NEWTON, FREDERICK J., III,** utilities executive; married; 2 children. BBA in Human Resources, U. R.I.; MBA in Labor Rels. and Human Resources, San Diego State U. Mgr. human resource functions Pepsico, Tex., Kans. and Calif.; sr. dir. human resources Unilever, N.Y.C.; sr. v.p. human resources Venator Group, N.Y.C.; exec. v.p., chief adminstrv. officer Cinergy Corp., Cin., 2002—. Vis. lectr. prof. Bellarmine U. Bd. dirs. Kentuckiana Minority Supplier Devel. Coun., Greater Louisville Inc., Louisville Orch., Lincoln Heritage coun. Boy Scouts Am., Pritchard Com. Officer USN. Mem.: Soc. Human Resource Mgmt., Human Resource Planning Soc., Conf. Bd. Office: Cynergy Corp 139 E 4th St Cincinnati OH 45202

**NEWTON, HERBERT BRUCE,** oncologist; b. San Diego, Nov. 8, 1956; s. Jefferson Frederick and Leona Maxine (Reese) N.; m. Cheryl Lynn Donaldson, Jul. 6, 1991; children: Alexander James, Ashley Rene. BA, SUNY, 1979, MS, 1980, MD, 1984. Diplomate Am. Bd. Psych. & Neurology. Internship SUNY Buffalo Affiliated Hosp., Buffalo, 1984-85, residency U. Mich. Medical Ctr., Ann Arbor, Mich., 1985-88; fellowship neuro oncology Meml. Sloan-Kettering Cancer Ctr., N.Y., 1988-90; asst. prof. dir. neuro-oncology The Ohio State U., Columbus, 1990-96, assoc. prof. dir. neuro-oncology, 1996—2004, prof. neurology, dir. neuro-oncology, 2004—, co-dir. Dardinger Neuro-oncology Ctr., Esther Dardinger chair in neuro-oncology, 2004—, grad. faculty Neurosci. Grad. Studies program, 1991—; staff physician sec. neurology dept. pediatrics Children's Hosp., Columbus, 1991—. Adv. profl. edn. com., Am. Cancer Soc., Columbus, 1991—; cons. Cen. Ohio Brain Tumor Support group, Columbus, 1990—. Contbr. articles to profl. jours. Recipient rsch. grant for treatment of malignant glioma, Amgen, 1994. Fellow Am. Acad. Neurology, Royal Soc. Medicine; mem. European Soc. Med. Oncology, Am. Acad. Neurology, Internat. Soc. Analytical Cytology, Am. Assn. Cancer Rsch., Ctrl. Soc. Neurol. Rsch. Avocations: basketball, reading, music, art. Office: Ohio State U dept Neurology 1654 Upham Dr 456 Means Hall Columbus OH 43210 Office Phone: 614-293-8930. E-mail: newton.12@osu.edu.

**NEWTON, HUGH C.,** public relations executive; b. N.Y.C., Oct. 17, 1930; s. Avery Curtis and Ruth (Juster) N.; m. Charlotte Eloise Wallin, Nov. 3, 1956 (div. 1968); 1 child, Margaret Wren Newton Rossello; m. Joanne Elaine Harding, Dec. 27, 1969; children: Matthew Curtis, Christopher Stuart, Kimberly Kelly. BA, Washington & Lee U., 1952. Reporter Danville (Va.) Bee, 1955; mgr. news Carnegie Inst. Tech., Pitts., 1956-57; staff writer Westinghouse Elec., Pitts., 1957; acct. exec. Burson Marsteller Assn., Pitts., 1958-59; asst. dir. pub. rels. Rockwell Mfg., Pitts., 1959-61; mgr. spl. projects Reynolds Metals Co., Richmond, Va., 1961-64; dir. pub. rels. Nat. Right to Work Com., Washington, 1964-67, Air Transport Assn., Washington, 1967-68; pres. Hugh C. Newton & Assocs., Washington, 1968—. Mem. Interstate Commn. on Potomac River Basin, Washington, 1982-89. Contbr. to Lesly's Public Relations Handbook, 1991. Bd. dirs. Friends of the Torpedo Factory Art Ctr., Alexandria, Va., 1987-91. Recipient Silver Anvil award Pub. Rels. Soc. Am., 1966, 85. Mem. Nat. Press Club. Episcopalian. Avocation: stamp collecting/philately. Office: Hugh C Newton & Assocs 108 N Washington St Alexandria VA 22314

**NEWTON, JOHN MILTON,** academic administrator, psychologist, educator; b. Schenectady, Feb. 25, 1929; s. Harry Hazleton and Bertha A. (Lehmann) N.; m. Elizabeth Ann Slattery, Sept. 11, 1954; children: Patricia,

Peter, Christopher. BS, Union Coll., Schenectady, 1951; MA, Ohio State U., 1952, PhD, 1955. Lic. psychologist, Nebr. Rsch. psychologist Electric Boat divsn. Gen. Dynamics Corp., Groton, Conn., 1957-60; mem. faculty U. Nebr.-Omaha, 1960—, prof. psychology, 1966-99, chmn. dept., 1967-74, acting vice chancellor acad. affairs, 1994-95, prof. emeritus, 1999—, dean Coll. Arts and Scis., 1974-94, dean emeritus, 1999—. Cons. in field, 1960-72 Author research papers in field. Served to 1st lt. Med. Service Corps, AUS, 1955-57. Mem. Am. Psychol. Assn., Psychonomic Soc., Midwestern Psychol. Assn. Home: 5611 Jones St Omaha NE 68106-1232 Office: Univ of Nebr-Omaha Dept Psychology Omaha NE 68182-0274 Business E-Mail: jnewton@mail.unomaha.edu.

**NEWTON, KENNETH KURT,** physician, educator, administrator; b. Landsberg, Germany, May 18, 1927; came to U.S., 1946; s. Arthur Neuweg and Margaret Joan (Blume) Newton. BA, U. Buffalo, 1951; MD, Western Res. U., 1955; grad., US Army Command/Gen. Staff Coll., Ft. Leavenworth, Kans., 1972; flight surgeon tng., US Army Aviation Sch., Ft. Rucker, Ala., 1974. Med. lic. Ohio, Mich. Advanced through ranks to col. U. S. Army, 1946-97; intern Henry Ford Hosp., Detroit, 1955-56, resident in internal medicine, phys. medicine and rehab., 1956-60; preceptor, dept. family medicine Wayne State U., Mich. State U., U. Mich., 1960—; clin. assoc. prof. medicine Wayne State U., Detroit, 1995—; dir. med. edn. Holy Cross Hosp., Detroit, 1976-88, chief dept. medicine, 1977-79, 91, pres. of staff, 1982-83; departmental surgeon Reserve Officers Assn. of Mich., Detroit, 1988-98; pres. EKG Assocs., P.C., Detroit, 1990—. Med. officer 107th med. battalion, Mich. Army N.G., 1955-57, divsn. artillery surgeon, 46th inf. divsn., 1957-59, command surgeon, 1959-75, state surgeon, 1975-85, post surgeon Camp Atterbury Res. Forces Tng. Area, 1985-89, divsn. surgeon 70th divsn., Livonia, Mich., 1989-92, flight surgeon U.S. Army 1993; instr., course dir. ACLS, Am. Heart Assn., 1977—, Acad. Health Scis., U.S. Army, Ft. Sam Houston, Tex., 1992—; mem. governing bd. Holy Cross Hosp. 1988-92, pres. 1990; tchr. U. Buffalo, N.Y., 1950-51, preceptor U. Essen, Germany, 1980, U. Göttingen, Germany, 1993, U. München, Germany, 1993, Humboldt U., Berlin, 1993; med. advisor to Selective Svcs. Sys., Washington, 1968-76; mem. ad hoc med. panel to Res. Forces Policy Bd., Dept. Army, Washington, 1972; mem. adv. group for Aerospace R&D, NATO, 1978; mem. med. evaluation bds. State of Mich., Lansing, 1975-85. Decorated Legion of Merit, 1977, 97; recipient cert. of pub. svc. State of N.Y., 1958, Disting. Svc. medal State of Mich. 1985, Spl. tribute State of Mich. Senate, 1985, Invitation Governing Mayor of Berlin, 1990, Conspicuous Svc. order, State of N.Y., 1997. Mem. (life) Sr. Army Reserve Comdrs. Assn., (life) Reserve Officers Assn. (nat. surgeon 1993), (life) Nat. Guard Assn. (dir. 1979-82), Am. Heart Assn. (course dir. 1980—), Soc. of Med. Consultants to the Armed Forces, Confedn. Interalliée des Officiers de Reserve NATO (del. 1973—, vice chief del. 1986). Avocations: travel, photography, music and the arts, national security. Office: 15252 Gratiot Ave Detroit MI 48205-1327 E-mail: kennethknewtonmd@aol.com.

**NEWTON, LISA HAENLEIN,** philosopher, educator; b. Orange, N.J., Sept. 17, 1939; d. Wallen Joseph and Carol Bigelow (Cypiot) Haenlein; m. Victor Joseph Newton, June 3, 1972; children: Tracey, Kit, Cynthia Perkins, Daniel Perkins, Laura Perkins. Student, Swarthmore Coll., 1957-59; BS in Philosophy with honors, Columbia U., 1962, PhD, 1967. Asst. prof. philosophy Hofstra U., Hempstead, NY, 1967-69; from asst. prof. to assoc. prof. Fairfield (Conn.) U., 1969—78, prof., 1978—; dir. program applied ethics, 1983—, dir. program environ. studies, 1986—; lectr. in medicine Yale U., 1984—. Lectr., cons. in field. Author: Ethics and Sustainability, 2002, Ethics in Am., Study Guide, 2d edit., 2003, Ethics in Am. Source Reader, 2d edit., 2003, Business Ethics and the National Environment, 2004, Permission to Steal, 2006; co-author: Watersheds, 1994, 4th edit., 2005; author, 2004; co-author: Wake-Up Calls, 2d edit., 2003; co-editor: Taking Sides: Controversial Issues Bus. Ethics, 8th edit., 2004, Taking Sides: Controversial Issues Bus. Ethics, 9th edit., 2006; contbr. articles to profl. jours. Mem. exec. bd. Conn. Humanities Coun., 1979—83. Mem.: Internat. Soc. Environ. Ethics (mem. exec. bd.), Assn. Practical Prof. Ethics (exec. bd.), Soc. Bus. Ethics (past pres.), Am. Soc. Bioethics and Humanities, Soc. Ethics Across Curriculum, Am. Soc. Polit. and Legal Philosophy, Am. Philos. Assn., Am. Soc. Value Inquiry (past pres.), Phi Beta Kappa (local sec.). Home: 1870 Redding Rd Fairfield CT 06824 Office: Fairfield U Program Applied Ethics Fairfield CT 06824 Office Phone: 203-254-4128. Business E-Mail: lhnewton@mail.fairfield.edu.

**NEWTON, NELL JESSUP,** dean, law educator; b. St. Louis, Apr. 30, 1944; d. Robert Edward and Marcella (Boehm) Mier. BA, U. Calif., Berkeley, 1973; JD, U. Calif., Hastings, 1976. Bar: Calif., Washington, U.S. Ct. Appeals (9th crct.), U.S. Supreme Ct. Prof. Cath. U. Sch. Law, 1976-92; prof. Washington Coll. Law Am. U., Washington, 1992—98; dean U. Denver Law Sch. 1998—2000, U. Conn. Sch. Law, Hartford, 2000—06, U. Calif. Hastings Coll. Law, San Francisco, 2006—. Lectr. Internat. Law Inst., Washington, 1984-89; prof. Pre-Law Summer Inst. for Native Am. Students, U. N.Mex. Law Sch., Albuquerque, 1990, 91, 93; panelist, speaker NEH 1981; presenter S.W. Intertribal Ct. of Appeals, 1990; panelist Orgn. Am. Historians, 1991; vis. prof. Boston Coll. Law Sch., Hastings Law Sch. Co-author: American Indian Law, 3d edit., 1991; contbr. articles to profl. jours. NEH fellow Harvard Law Sch., 1980. Mem. Assn. Am. Law Schs. (Native Am. rights sect., mem. exec. com. 1987—, chair 1987-88, oral argument newsletter editor 1987—, mem. women in legal edn. sect. 1987—, chair profl. devel. workshop com. 1992, sec. 1993), Balt.-Washington-Va. Women Law Tchrs. Group (planning com. Symposium on Scholarship I 1985, II 1986), Thurston Soc., Order of Coif. Office: U Calif Hastings Coll Law 200 McAllister St San Francisco CA 94102 Office Phone: 415-565-4700. E-mail: newtonn@uchastings.edu.*

**NEWTON, PAUL GEORGE,** musician, retired librarian; b. Syracuse, N.Y., Dec. 1, 1930; s. Wayland LeRoy and Georgia Crumrine Newton; m. Dahlia Lorraine Brazell, Dec. 24, 1961; children: Jessica Suzanne, Roy Christopher. MusB cum laude, Syracuse U., 1952; MusM, Ind. U., 1954; PhD, U. North Tex., 1968; MLS, U. N.C., 1974. Instr. Augustana Coll., Sioux Falls, SD, 1954—56; prof. Wayland Bapt. Coll., Plainview, Tex., 1958-56, 1960—64; asst. prof. N.W. La. State Coll., Natchitoches, 1958—59, Stephen F. Austin State U., Nacogdoches, Tex., 1964—65, Ark. State U., Jonesboro, 1965—66; orch. dir. Forsyth County Schs., Winston-Salem, NC, 1968—69; music libr. Mars Hill (N.C.) Coll., 1969—83; libr. dir. Martin Meml. Coll., Pulaski, Tenn., 1983—93. Violist Asheville (N.C.) Symphony Orch., 1979—83; archivist Mars Hill Coll., 1979—83. Recipient Merit award, Kennedy-Douglass Mus., Florence, Ala., 1994. Mem.: So. Appalachian Mineral Soc., Am. Musicol. Soc., Ark. Archaeol. Soc. Avocations: travel, art, archaeology, geology, photography. Home: 114 S Sam Davis Ave Pulaski TN 38478 Office: 94 W Ridge Rd Mars Hill NC 28754 E-mail: dbnewton@usit.net.

**NEWTON, RHONWEN LEONARD,** writer, data processing executive, consultant; b. Lexington, N.C., Nov. 13, 1940; d. Jacob Calvin and Mary Louise (Moffitt) Leonard; children: Blair Armistead Newton Jones, Allison Page, William Brockenbrough III. AB, Duke U., Durham, N.C., 1962; MS in Edn., Old Dominion U., Norfolk, Va., 1968. French tchr. Hampton Pub. Schs., 1962-65, Va. Beach Pub. Schs., 1965-66; instr. foreign lang. various colls. and univs., 1967-75; foreign lang. cons. Portsmouth Pub. Schs., Va., 1973-75; dir. The Computer Inst., Inc., Columbia, S.C., 1983; pres., founder The Computer Experience, Inc., Columbia, 1983-88, RN Enterprises, Columbia, 1991—. Author: WordPerfect, 1988, All About Computers, 1989, Microsoft Excel for the Mac, 1989, Introduction to the Mac, 1989, Introduction to DOS, 1989, Introduction to Lotus 1-2-3, 1989, Advanced Lotus 1-2-3, 1989, Introduction to WordPerfect, 1989, Advanced WordPerfect, 1989, Introduction to Display/Write 4, 1989, WordPerfect for the Mac, 1989, Introduction to Microsoft Works for the Mac, 1990, Accountant, Inc for the Mac, 1992, Introduction to Filemaker Pro, 1992, Quicken for the MAC, 1993, Quicken for Windows, 1993, WordPerfect for Windows, 1993, Advanced WordPerfect for Windows, 1993, Lotus 1-2-3 for Windows, 1993, Introduction to Quick Books, 1994, Quick Book for Windows, 1994, Introduction to Word for Windows, 1995, Introduction to File Maker Pro 4.0, 1998,

Introduction to Microscoft Word, 1999, Introduction to Microsoft Excel, 1999, Introduction to AOL, 1999, Introduction to Excel, 1999, Using America OnLine, 1999. Mem. Columbia Planning Commn., 1980-87; bd. dirs. United Way Midlands, Columbia, 1983-86, Assn. Jr. Leagues, NYC, 1980-82, SC Wildlife Fedn., 1997-98; trustee Heathwood Hall Episcopal Sch., Columbia, 1979-85; active SC Episcopal Home Bd., 1999-2005, chmn., 2001-2003; vestry Trinity Cathedral, 1999-02; active SC Real Estate Appraisers Bd., 2000, sec., 2002—. Mem. Investment Club (pres. 1995-97, regional coun.), Nat. Assn. Investors Corp. (dir. S.C. Midlands regional coun. 1998-02). Republican. Episcopalian. Avocations: golf, walking. Home and Office: 1635 Kathwood Dr Columbia SC 29206-4509 Personal E-mail: rhonwenln@yahoo.com.

**NEWTON, TERRY FERNANDO,** health facility specialist, writer; b. Miami, Fla., Dec. 10, 1956; s. Julius Lee Newton and Frances Louise Cason; children: Torrence Levine, Patrick Fernando. Student, Fla. Montanari, 1976—78. Specialist child care Montanari Clin. Sch., Hialeah, Fla., 1976—79; technician mental health Miami Variety Children's Hosp., Coral Gables, Fla., 1979—80; psychiat. nurse technician Cedars of Lebanon Hosp., Miami, Fla., 1980—82; from office asst. dir. of safety to health info. specialist II Jackson Hosp., Miami, 1982—83, health info. specialist II, 1983—. Bd. dir. Body Mind & Soul Inc., Miami; 1st v.p. Lip Tongue & Ear Prodn., Miami, 1999—. Author: A Composition in Verse, 1996, A Cascade of Memories, 1998, America at the Millenium, 2000, Earthbeat, 2002, Theatre of the Mind, 2003. Active media rep. Concern & Committed Bros. Inc., Miami, 2002; bd. dir. BMS Movement, 2001—. Named African Am. Achiever, JM Family Enterprise, Inc., 1998—2003, Cmty. Achiever, Macedonia Ch., 1999; named to Internat. Poetry Hall of Fame, 1997, Miami Dade Office of Mayor, Bd. County Commrs.; recipient Accomplishment award, Gov. Lawton Chiles, 1997, Renaissance award, Macedonia Ch., 2006, Unsung Hero award, Coconut Grove Negro Women Club, 2006. Mem.: Fla. State Poetry Hosts Coalition (promotor 2003), Concern Bros. Inc. Poetry Club (dir. 2001, Mentor award 1997). Avocations: reading, performing, basketball, birdwatching. Home: 10762 SW 145th St Miami FL 33176 Office Phone: 786-222-2791. E-mail: renee@jazzandpoetry.net.

**NEWTON, VIRGINIA,** archivist, historian, librarian; d. John Walter and Reba Catherine Newton; m. Alvin E. Schmid, 2003. Student, Inst. Tecnológico y de Estudios Superiores de Monterrey, Nuevo Leon, Mex., 1957; AA in Bus. Adminstrn., Stephens Coll., 1958; BA in History, Okla. State U., 1960; M of Librarianship, U. Wash., 1963; cert. in libr. sci., U. Tex., 1968, MA in Latin Am. Studies, History, Archives and Libr. Sci., 1975, PhD in Latin Am. Studies, History, Archives and Libr. Sci., 1983. Libr. Inst. Pub. Affairs U. Tex., Austin, 1963-65, libr. Art Libr., 1965-67; coord. Sr. Cmty. Svcs. Program Econ. Opportunities Devel. Corp., San Antonio, 1968-69; archivist, spl. collections libr. Trinity U., San Antonio, 1969-73; spl. collections and reference libr. Pan Am. U., Edinburg, Tex., 1974-77; archivist, records analyst Alaska State Archives and Records Svc., 1983-84, dep. state archivist, 1984-87; state archivist Alaska State Archives & Records Mgmt. Svcs., 1988-93; dir. Columbus Meml. Libr. OAS, Washington, 1993—2001. Archives cons. Ford Found. for Brazilian Archivists Assn., 1976, Soc. for Ibero-Latin Thought, 1980, Project for a Notarial Archives Computerized Guide, 1980; chair Alaska State Hist. Records Adv. Bd., 1988-93, coords. steering com., 1991-93; cons. Puerto Rican Hist. Records Adv. Bd., 1997-99. Author: An Archivists' Guide to the Catholic Church in Mexico, 1979; contbr. articles to profl. publs. Founder jail libr. Bexar County Jail, San Antonio; hon. dep. sheriff Bexar County, 1972-75; mem. Dem. party; chair Dems. Abroad in Mex., 1979-81; mem. Dems. Abroad Del. The Dem. Nat. Conv., N.Y., 1980; vice- chair Bill Egan Forum Greater Juneau Dem. Precinct, 1986-88 Recipient Commendation award Gov. of Alaska William Sheffield, 1985, Disting. Alumnae award U. Tex. Sch. Libr. and Info. Sci., 1998; Masonic Scholarship for internat. rels. George Washington U., 1960-61; univ. fellow U. Tex.-Austin, 1982-83, post masters fellow U.S. Dept. Edn.-U. Tex., Austin, 1967-68; scholar Orgn. Am. States, 1980, 81, Fulbright-Hays scholar, 1979, 80, scholar Nat. Def. Fgn. Lang.-U. Tex., Austin, 1978-79, scholar Calif. State Libr., 1962-63. Mem. AAUW (bd. dirs. 1983-86, scholar 1983), Nat. Assn. Govt. Archives and Records Adminstrs. (bd. dirs. 1989-93, chair membership com. 1989-93), Alaska Hist. Soc. (bd. treas. 1988-94), Alaska Libr. Assn., Acad. Cert. Archivists (cert. 1989), Rotary, Phi Kappa Phi. Democrat. Unitarian Universalist. Avocations: skiing, dance, researching, reading, hiking. Office: 206 Laurel Heights Place San Antonio TX 78212

**NEWTON, WAYNE (CARSON WAYNE NEWTON),** entertainer, actor, recording industry executive; b. Norfolk, Va., Apr. 3, 1942; s. Patrick and Evelyn (Smith) N.; m. Elaine Okamura, 1968 (div.); 1 child, Erin; m. Kathleen McCrone, April 9, 1994; 1 child, Lauren Ashley. L.H.D. (hon.), U. Nev.-Las Vegas, 1981; Doctorate (hon.), William Woods U. Owner Tamiment Internat. Resort. Appearances include Sands, Caesar's Palace, Desert Inn, Flamingo and Frontier hotels, Las Vegas, Harrah's Club, Reno and Lake Tahoe, I Love N.Y. Concert, Americana Hotel, N.Y.C., Talk of the Town, London, London Paladium, Grand Ole Oprey House, Nashville, 4th of July, Washington, Astrodome, Houston, Hollywood (Calif.) Bowl, Melodyland, Anaheim, Calif., Circle Star, San Francisco, Sea World, Orlando, Fla., Sherman House, Chgo., Wis. State, Iowa State fairs, Valley Forge Music, Westbury Music fairs, Deauville and Eden Roc hotels, Miami Beach, Carlton Club, Bloomington, Minn., hotels Atlantic City, N.J., before U.S. troops, Vietnam, Beirut, & Persian Gulf; TV appearances include Red, White & Wow, A Christmas Card, (TV miniseries) North and South: Book II, 1986, TV spls. Opryland, 1973, Joys, 1976, Happy Birthday, Las Vegas, 1977, The Wayne Newton Special, 1982, The Real Las Vegas (TV series), 1996, Las Vegas on Ice, 1997, Feed the Children, 1997, Elvis Meets Nixon, 1997, VH1 Divas Las Vegas, 2002; film appearances in 80 Steps to Jonah, 1969 (also composer), Licence to Kill, 1989, The Adventures of Ford Fairlane, 1990, The Dark Backward, 1991, Best of the Best II, 1993, Night of the Running Man, 1994, Vegas Vacation, 1997; video appearances in Who's Your Daddy?, 2003; host, prodr. The Entertainer, 2005—; guest appearances include Jackie Gleason and His American Scene Magazine, 1962, 1964, The Mike Douglas Show, 1964, The Lucy Show, 1965, Bonanza, 1966, Here's Lucy, 1968, 1970, The Tonight Show Starring Johnny Carson, 1971, 1972, The Dean Martin Show, 1971, 1974, Switch, 1976, Vega$, 1979, 1981, The Highwayman, 1988, Full House, 1990, L.A. Law, 1991, Roseanne, 1991, Perfect Strangers, 1992, Renegade, 1994, 1995, Tales from the Crypt, 1994, The Fresh Prince of Bel-Air, 1995, Ellen, 1997, Ally McBeal, 1998, The Pretender, 2000, Las Vegas, 2003, 7th Heaven, 2004, The Tonight Show with Jay Leno, 2004, Larry King Live, CBS This Morning, E! Entertainment Television, Entertainment Tonight and others; albums include Danke Schoen, 1963, In Person!, 1964, Wayne Newton in Person!, 1964, Summer Wind, 1965, Red Roses for a Blue Lady, 1965, Now!, 1966, It's Only the Good Times, 1967, Old Rugged Cross, 1966, One More Time, 1968, Walking on New Grass, 1968, Can't You Hear the Song?, 1972, Change of Heart, 1978, Daddy Don't You Walk So Fast, 1972, Coming Home, 1989, God Is Alive, 1991, Showstoppers, 1992, Rock of Ages, 1992, A Merry Little Christmas, 1992, Moods & Moments, 1992, Christmas Song, 1995, Branson City Limits, 1998, Real Thing, 2004, Song of the Year: Wayne Newton Style, Tomorrow; author (with Dick Maurice): Once Before I Go, 1989. A supporter St. John's Indian Mission, Levene, Ariz.; chmn. USO Celebrity Circle. Recipient citation as distinguished recording artist and humanitarian, 1971; Freedom Lantern award Commonwealth of Mass., 1979, Entertainer of Yr. award Variety Clubs So. Nev., 1973, Gov.'s award Commonwealth of Mass., 1976, cert. of appreciation Gov. of Nev., 1978, Founders award St. Judes Childrens Hosp., Humanitarian award Am. Cancer Soc. Cancer Research Ctr., Lifetime Achievement award, First Am. in the Arts, 2000, Congl. medal, Honor Soc. Citizenship award, medal of honor, Dept. Def., US Legion of Valor's Citizen award, Jimmie L. Howard Meml. award, Medal of Honor, City Las Vegas, Ellis Island Medal of Honor, 1999, American Legend award, Washington, D.C., 1999, VFW Hall of Fame award, Am. Legion Exceptional Citizen award, star on the Hollywood Walk of Fame, award for Daddy Don't Walk So Fast ASCAP, platinum record for Danke Schoen, also gold album and gold records; named one of 10 Outstanding Young Men of Am. Nat. Jaycees, 1976; named Most Disting. Citizen of Yr. NCCJ, Outstanding Indian Entertainer of

Yr. Navajo Nation, 1980, Entertainer of Yr., Nev. Mag., Casino Player Mag., 1999, Top Three Entertainers of the Century in Nev. and Around the World, Reno Gazett Jour. Amb. Goodwill, State of Nev, Veteran Fgn. Wars of US Hon. Vietnam Veteran, Hon. Green Beret, 1999; knighted, 1998; renamed in his honor Las Vegas' McCarran Internat. Airport main thoroughfare Wayne Newton Blvd.; inducted Gaming Hall of Fame, Am. Gaming Assn.

**NEWTON, WILLIAM ALLEN, JR.,** pediatrician, pathologist; b. Traverse City, Mich., May 19, 1923; s. William Allen and Florence Emma (Brown) N.; m. Helen Patricia Goodrich, Apr. 21, 1945; children: Katherine Germaine, Elizabeth Gale, William Allen, Nancy Anne. BSc cum laude, Alma Coll., Mich., 1943; MD, U. Mich., 1946. Diplomate: Am. Bd. Pathology, Am. Bd. Pediatrics. Intern Wayne County Gen. Hosp., Detroit, 1947; resident in pediatric pathology/oncology/hematology Children's Hosp. Mich., Detroit, 1948-50; resident in pediat. Children's Hosp. Phila., 1950; dir. labs. Children's Hosp. Columbus, Ohio, 1952-88, rsch. pathologist Ohio, 1989—; mem. faculty Coll. Medicine, Ohio State U., 1952—, prof., 1965—, chief pediatric pathology, 1952-89, chief divsn. pediatric hematology, 1952—82, prof. emeritus, 1989—. Chmn. pathology com. Children's Cancer Study Group, 1965-91; chmn. Pathology Com. Intergroup Rhabdomyosarcoma Study Group; chmn. pathology com. Late Effects Study Group. Contbr. articles to med. jours. Trustee, mem. exec. com. Am. Cancer Soc., Ohio div., 1972-86; mem. adv. com. on childhood cancer Am. Cancer Soc.; chmn. exec. com. Consortium for Cancer Control of Ohio, 1982-86; mem. sci. adv. com. Armed Forces Inst. Pathology; pres. Internat. Consortium for Cure of Childhood Cancer in China, 2000—. Served to capt. M.C. U.S. Army, 1950-52, brig. gen. Res. ret. Mem. Ohio State Med. Assn. (com. on cancer), Midwest Soc. Pediatric Research (mem. council 1960-63, pres. 1964-65), Soc. Pediatric Research, Am. Pediatric Soc., Pediatric Pathology Club (pres. 1968-69), Am. Soc. Clin. Oncology, Internat. Soc. Pediatric Oncology, Sigma Xi, Phi Sigma Pi. Republican. Baptist. Home: 2500 Harrison Rd Johnstown OH 43031-9540 Office: PO Box 6957 Columbus OH 43205 Office Phone: 614-722-3269. Business E-Mail: wnewton@chi.osu.edu.

**NEWTON-JOHN, OLIVIA,** singer, actress; b. Cambridge, Eng., Sept. 26, 1948; arrived in Australia, 1954, arrived in England, 1964, arrived in Am., 1975; d. Brin and Irene (Born) Newton-John; m. Matt Lattanzi, Dec. 1984 (div. 1995); 1 child, Chloe Rose Lattanzi. Student pub. schs. Co-owner Koala Blue, 1982—. Singer, actress in Australia, Eng. and US, 1965—; actress: (films) Funny Things Happen Down Under, 1965, Tomorrow, 1970, Grease, 1978, Xanadu, 1980, Two of a Kind, 1983, It's My Party, 1996, Sordid Lives, 2000; (TV) Timeless Tales from Hallmark, 1990, A Mom for Christmas, 1990, A Christmas Romance, 1994, Snowden on Ice (voice), 1997, The Christmas Angel: A Story on Ice, 1998, The Wilde Girls, 2001; singer: (albums) If Not for You, 1971, Let me Be There, 1973, If You Love Me Let Me Know, 1974, Long Live Love, 1974, First Impressions, 1974, Have You Ever Been Mellow, 1975, Clearly Love, 1975, Come on Over, 1976, Don't Stop Believin', 1976, Making a Good Thing Better, 1977, Greatest Hits, 1977, Totally Hot, 1978, Grease, 1978, Xanadu, 1980, Physical, 1981, Greatest Hits, 1982, (with John Travolta) Two of a Kind, 1984, Soul Kiss, 1985, The Rumour, 1988, Warm And Tender, 1989, Back To Basics-The Essential Collection, 1992, Gaia, 1994, Heathcliff, 1995, Back With A Heart, 1998, The Main Event, 1998, Two, 2002, Indigo-Women of Song, 2004, Stronger Than Before, 2005; TV prodn. In Australia, 1988. Decorated as Officer, Order of Brit. Empire, 1979, Order of Australia, 2006; named one of 50 Most Beautiful People in the World, People mag., 1998, one of 100 Greatest Women of Rock N Roll, VH1.; recipient Acad. Country Music, 1973, Country Music Assn. U.K., 1974-75, Country Music Assn. award, 1974, Grammy award, 1973-74, AGVA award, 1974, Billboard Mag. award, 1974-75, People's Choice award 1974, 1976, 1979, Record World award, 1974-76, 1978, Nat. Assn. Retail Merchandisers/Cashbox, 1974-75, Am. Music award 1974-76, Nat. Juke Box award, 1980, Lifetime Achievement award, Australian Record Industry Assn., 2002. Address: PO Box 2710 Malibu CA 90265-7710 Office: MCA 70 Universal City Plz North Hollywood CA 91608-1011*

**NEWTOWN, THANDIE,** actress; b. Lusaka, Zambia, Nov. 6, 1972; m. Ol Parker, July 11, 1998; 1 child, Ripley. Actor: (films) Flirting, 1991, Pirate Prince, 1991, The Young Americans, 1993, Loaded, 1994, Interview with the Vampire: The Vampire Chronicles, 1994, Jefferson in Paris, 1995, The Journey of August King, 1995, The Leading Man, 1996, Gridlock'd, 1997, Beloved, 1998, Besieged, 1998, Mission: Impossible II, 2000, It Was an Accident, 2000, The Truth About Charlie, 2002, Shade, 2003, The Chronicles of Riddick, 2004, Crash, 2004 (recipient, Outstanding Performance by a Cast in a Motion Picture, SAG awards, 2006); (TV series) ER, 2004. Office: Lions Gate Entertainment 555 Brooksbank Ave Vancouver V7J 355 Canada*

**NEXSEN, JULIAN JACOBS,** lawyer; b. Kingstree, S.C., Apr. 14, 1924; s. William Ivey and Barbara (Jacobs) N.; m. Mary Elizabeth McIntosh, Jan. 28, 1948; children: Louise Ivey (Mrs. Heyward Harles Bouknight, Jr.), Julian Jacobs Jr. Student, The Citadel, 1941-43; BS magna cum laude, U. S.C., 1948, JD magna cum laude, 1950. Bar: S.C. 1950, U.S. Supreme Ct. 1960. Ptnr. firm Nexsen Pruet, LLC, Columbia, SC. Trustee Richland County Pub. Libr., chmn., 1976-77; trustee Providence Hosp., chmn., 1984-86; trustee Providence Found.; Providence Ministries, Sisters of Charity of St. Augustine Health Sys.; past bd. dirs. Columbia Music Festival Assn., ARC Richland-Lexington Counties, Ctrl. Carolina Cmty. Found.; mem. U.S.C. Law Sch. partnership bd.; elder Eastminster Presbyn. Ch., trustee Congaree Presbytery, 1967-87, Synod, S.C., 1976; mem. Trinity Presbytery Coun. Lt. inf. AUS, 1943-46, ETO, capt., 1950-51, Korea. Decorated Bronze Star with oak leaf cluster; recipient Compleat Lawyer award U.S.C. Sch. Law. Mem. ABA, S.C. Bar (treas., bd. govs. 1974-79, ho. of dels. 1980-92), Richland County Bar Assn. (pres. 1974-75, Disting. Svc. award 1987), Am. Bar Found., S.C. Bar Found. (pres. 1971-72), S.C. Law Inst. (coun., exec. com. 1986—), Am. Law Inst., Am. Coll. Trust and Estate Counsel (regent 1973-82), Am. Judicature Soc., Forest Lake Country Club, Palmetto Club, The Order of Coif, Kiwanis (bd. dirs. 1972-74, 77-79), Phi Beta Kappa. Home: 2840 Sheffield Rd Columbia SC 29204-2332 Office: Nexsen Pruet LLC Drawer 2426 1441 Main St Columbia SC 29202-2426 Office Phone: 803-253-8247. Business E-Mail: jnexsen@nexsenpruet.com.

**NEXSEN, JULIAN JACOBS, JR.,** lawyer; b. Columbia, S.C., Sept. 22, 1954; s. Julian J. and Mary Elizabeth (McIntosh) N.; m. Christine Spigner Johnston, Feb. 25, 1984; children: Elizabeth Kincaid, Julian J. III, Sarah Ivey. BA, Washington and Lee U., 1976; JD, U. S.C., 1979. Bar: S.C. 1979, U.S. Ct. Appeals (4th cir.) 1982. Assoc. Nexsen, Pruet, Jacobs & Pollard, Columbia, S.C., 1979-84; assoc. in house counsel, asst. sec. Greenwood (S.C.) Mills, Inc., 1984-95, exec. v.p., 1999—2001; exec. v.p., COO Greenwood Devel. Corp., 1995-99, pres., CEO, 1999—. Bd. dirs. CountyBank, Greenwood Devel. Corp., Ctrl. Trust Co., Partnership for a Greater Greenwood, Greenwood Genetic Ctr.; trustee Self Family Found. Self Regional Healthcare Ctr.; trustee First Presbyn. Ch. Bd. visitors Lander Coll., 1985-87; bd. dirs. Edn. Enrichment Found., 1986-89, Greenwood United Way, 1989-92, Greenwood Community Theatre, 1989-93, Greenwood Uptown Devel. Corp., 1991-93; bd. deacons 1st Presbyn. Ch., 1990-93, session, 1993-96; trustee Self Meml. Hosp., 1992-98; bd. dirs. Greenwood County Econ. Alliance, 1999-2001. Mem. ABA, Am. Corp. Counsel Assn., S.C. Bar Assn., Greater U. S.C. Alumni Assn. (bd. govs. 2004—), Forest Lake Club, Greenwood Country Club, S.C. C. of C. (bd. dirs. 1990-93). Presbyterian. Home: 512 E Henrietta Ave Greenwood SC 29649-3142 Office: Greenwood Devel Corp PO Box 1546 Greenwood SC 29648-1546 Business E-Mail: jnexsen@greenwooddevelopment.com.

**NEY, ALEXANDER,** artist, sculptor; b. Leningrad, Russia, Sept. 27, 1939; arrived in U.S., 1974; m. Liz Ney; children: Yana, Hannah, Joel. Student, Acad. Fine Art, Leningrad, 1954—57, Art Sch. Surikon Inst., Moscow, 1957—58, Repin Inst. Fine Arts, Leningrad 1960—69. Cert. artist France, Russia, U.S. One-man shows include Hansen Gallery, N.Y.C., 1974, Wingspread Gallery, Northeast Harbor, Maine, 1977, Eduard Nakhamkin Fine Arts, N.Y.C., 1979, 1979, 1980, Gallery Saireido, 1992, Chassidic Art Inst., Bklyn., 1996, Duke U. Mus. Art, 1998, sculpture, Scientist, 1986, Stargazer, 1988,

Thundering Saxophonist, 1998, Windows at Tiffany & Co., N.Y.C., 1978—94, Atlanta, 1982, Boston, 1991—94, Represented in permanent collections Zimmerli Art Mus., Rutgers U., New Brunswick, C.A.S.E. Mus. Jersey City, Yeshiva Univ. Mus., N.Y.C., Mus. Beeldan aan Zee, The Netherlands. Grantee, Robert Rauschenberg's Change, Inc., 1997, Adolph & Esther Gottlieb Found., 1997. Mem.: Union Artists (young artists divsn.). Office: c/o Bill Bowler Internat Creative Mgmt 40 W 57th St New York NY 10019

**NEY, BOB (ROBERT WILLIAM NEY),** congressman; b. Wheeling, W.Va., July 5, 1954; s. Robert Paul and Dorothy (McCloud) Ney; m. Elizabeth Mikropoulous; children from previous marriage, Robert William III, Kayla Marie. Student, Ohio U., 1972—74; BS in Edn., Ohio State U., 1976. Records mgr. Ohio Motor Vehicles Bur., 1976—77; Am. Embassy tchr., supr. affiliate Shiraz U., Iran, 1977—78; health and edn. prog. mgr. Ohio Office of Appalachia, 1978—79; safety dir. City of Bellaire, Ohio, 1980; mem. Ohio State Ho. Reps., 1980—82, Ohio State Senate, 1985—95, US Congress from 18th Ohio dist., 1995—, mem. fin. svcs. com., former chmn. housing subcommittee, mem. ho. adminstrn. com., mem. transp. and infrastructure com., chmn. congl. mailing standards commn., chmn. com. on the libr., vice chmn. joint com. on printing, dep. majority whip. Pleaded guilty to federal charges in the congl. investigation into corruption & bribery involving disgraced lobbyist Jack Abramoff., 2006. Bd. trustees Bethesda Hosp. Recipient Ky. Colonel award, 1984, Watchdog of the Treasury award, United Conservatives of Ohio, 1984—85, 1987, Conservation Legis. of Yr., League of Ohio Sportsmen, 1986, Person of Yr., Ohio Enterprise, 1987, Disting. Legis. Svc. award, Ohio Human Svcs. Dirs. Assn., 1989, Homeownership Hero award, Homeownership Alliance, 2004, Legis. Achievement award, Nat. Coun. State Housing Agencies, 2005. Mem. Kiwanis, Jaycees, Elks (Citizen of Yr. 1982), Lions, Sportsmen clubs, NRA Republican. Roman Catholic. Office: US Ho Reps 2438 Rayburn Ho Office Bldg Washington DC 20515-3518 Office Phone: 202-225-6265.*

**NEY, EDWARD N.,** ambassador, advertising executive, public relations executive; b. St. Paul, May 26, 1925; s. John Joseph and Marie (Noonan) N.; m. Suzanne Hayes, 1950 (div. 1974); children: Nicholas, Hilary, Michelle; m. Judith I. Lasky, May 24, 1974. BA (Lord Jeffrey Amherst scholar 1942), Amherst Coll., 1947. With Young & Rubicam, Inc., N.Y.C., 1951-86, chmn., pres. CEO, 1970-86; chmn. Paine Webber/Young & Rubicam Ventures, N.Y.C., 1987-89; vice-chmn. Paine Webber, Inc., N.Y.C., 1987-89; amb. to Can., Am. Embassy, Ottawa, Ont., 1989-92; chmn. bd. advisors Burson-Marsteller, N.Y.C., 1992-98; chmn. emeritus Young & Rubicam Advt., N.Y.C., 1999—. Mem. adv. bd. Coun. on Fgn. Rels., 1975—, Ctr. for Strategic and Internat. Studies (C.S.I.S.), 1986—; honorary chmn. Advt. Coun.; mem. Advt. Hall of Fame. Life Trustee Amherst Coll., 1979—; Trustee Bush Presidential Libr. Found., James A. Baker III Inst. for Public Policy, Rice U., Museum of TV/Radio (MTR), 1982—. Office: Young Rubicam Advt 285 Madison Ave New York NY 10017-6486 Business E-Mail: ed.ney@nyc.yr.com.

**NEY, PETER ERNEST,** mathematician, educator; b. Brno, Czech Republic, July 6, 1930; s. Paul E. and Katherine B. Ney; m. Irene Paulu Ney, July 28, 1993; children: Paul A., Christine E. BS, MIT, Cambridge, 1951; MA, Columbia U., N.Y.C., 1952, PhD, 1961. Instr. math. Cornell U., Ithaca, NY, 1958—60, asst. prof., opers. rsch., 1960—63, assoc. prof., opers. rsch., 1963—65; vis. asst. prof., stats. Stanford U., Calif., 1963—64; assoc. prof., math. U. Wis., Madison, 1965—67, prof., math., 1967—2000, chmn., dept. math., 1974—77, emeritus prof., math., 2000—. Author: Branching Processes, 1971; editor: Advances in Probability, 1971—84, Annals of Probability, 1988—90; contbr. articles to profl. jours. Fellow, Guggenheim Found., 1971—72, Fulbright Found., 1984, Humboldt Found., 1991, 1994. Fellow: Inst. Math. Stats. (coun. mem.); mem.: Internat. Math. Soc., Am. Math. Soc. Home: 104 Riverside Dr Unit C606 Cocoa FL 32922 Office: Dept Math Univ Wis 480 Lincoln Dr Madison WI 53706 Office Phone: 608-263-3054. Business E-Mail: ney@math.wisc.edu.

**NEYER, JEROME CHARLES,** consulting civil engineer; b. Cin., July 15, 1938; s. Urban Charles and Marie Helen (Hemsteger) N.; m. Judy Ann Drolet, June 17, 1961; children: Janet, Karen. BCE, U. Detroit, 1961; MCE, U. Wash., 1963. Registered profl. engr. 16 states. Facilities engr. Boeing Co., Seattle, 1961-62; found. engr. Metro Engrs., Seattle, 1962-65; project engr. Hugo N. Helpert Assocs., Detroit, 1965-70; pres. NTH Cons. Ltd., Farmington Hills, Mich., 1970—. Adj. prof. U. Detroit, 1973-79. Contbr. articles to profl. jours. Mem. mineral well adv. bd., Lansing, Mich., 1975, mem. constrn. safety stds. bd., 1982; chmn. bldg. appeals bd. City of Farmington Hills, 1983. Mem. ASTM, ASCE (br. pres. 1973-74), Engring. Soc. Detroit, Cons. Engrs. Mich. (pres. 1981), Mich. Soc. Profl. Engrs. (bd. dirs. 1980), Assn. Engring. Firms Practicing in the Geoscis. (pres. 1991). Roman Catholic. Avocations: golf, tennis. Home: 26478 Ballantrae Ct Farmington Hills MI 48331-3528 Office: NTH Consultants Ltd 38955 Hills Tech Dr Farmington MI 48331-3434 Office Phone: 248-553-6300. Business E-Mail: jneyer@nthconsultants.com, jneyer007@comcast.net.

**NG, DOMINIC,** bank executive; b. Hong Kong, Jan. 24, 1959; s. William N.; m. Ellen Wong. BBA in Acctg., U. Houston, 1980. CPA, Calif., Tex. Dir. Chinese bus. svcs. group, sr. mgr. audit group Deloitte & Touche, L.A., Houston, 1980-90; pres., CEO Seyin Investment, Inc., L.A., 1990-92, East-West Fed. Bank f.s.b., San Marino, Calif., 1992—. Dir. Kiang Su-Chiang Kiang Assn. So. Calif.; dir. adv. coun. Asian Pacific Family Ctr.; dir. Family Clinics; dir. adv. coun. San Gabriel chpt. Am. Red Cross; dir. Asian adv. coun. Loyola Marymount U.; active Jonathan Club. Mem. AICPA, Am. League Fin. Instns. (dir.), Nat. Assn. Chinese Am. Bankers (pres.), Com. 100. Office: East-West Fed Bank FSB 415 Huntington Dr San Marino CA 91108 J55B*

**NG, HON KEUNG TONY,** mathematics professor; b. Hong Kong, China, Mar. 25, 1975; BSc, Chinese U., Hong Kong, 1997, MPhil., 1999; MSc, McMaster U., Hamilton, Can., 2000; PhD, McMaster U., Hamilton, Canada, 2002. Asst. prof. statistics So. Meth. U., Dallas, 2002—. Author: Precedence-type Tests and Applications, 2006; contbr. articles to profl. jours. Office: So Meth U Dept Statis Sci 3225 Daniel Ave Dallas TX 75275-0332 Office Phone: 214-768-2465. Office Fax: 214-768-4035.

**NG, JOHN DANIEL,** ophthalmologist, educator; s. Andre Jose and Theresa Ng; m. Patti Adams Ng, June 21, 1986; children: Coral Janelle, Fisher Ward. BS in Neurosci., U. Rochester, 1983; MS in Physiology, Georgetown U., 1984; MD, George Washington U., 1988. Diplomate Am. Bd. Ophthalmology. Flight surgeon U.S. Army, Ft. Sheridan, Ill., 1989—91, comprehensive ophthalmologist Ft. Gordon, Ga., 1994—95, faculty oculoplastic surgeon Ft. Sam Houston, Tex., 1997—2000; assoc. prof. Casey Eye Inst., Portland, Oreg., 2000—. Contbr. articles to profl. jours.; reviewer Ophthalmology jour., 1995—. Recipient Meritorious Svc. award, U.S. Army. Fellow: Am. Acad. Ophthalmology (Achievement award); mem.: Health for Humanity, Elks. Baha'I. Avocations: bicycling, hiking, scuba diving, snow shoeing, tai chi. Office: Casey Eye Inst 3375 SW Terwilliger Blvd Portland OR 97239 Office Phone: 503-494-3010.

**NG, LAWRENCE MING-LOY,** pediatrician; b. Hong Kong, Mar. 21, 1940; arrived in U.S., 1967, naturalized, 1977; s. John Iu-cheung and Mary Wing (Wong) N.; m. Bella May Ha Kan, June 25, 1971; children: Jennifer Wing-mui, Jessica Wing-yee. MBBS in Medicine, U. Hong Kong, 1965. Diplomate Am. Bd. Pediat. House physician Queen Elizabeth Hosp., Hong Kong, 1965-66, med. officer, 1966-67; resident physician Children's Hosp. of Los Angeles, 1967-68, Children's Hosp. Med. Ctr., Oakland, Calif., 1968-70; fellow in pediatric cardiology, 1970-72; now mem. tchg. staff; practice medicine specializing in pediat. and pediatric cardiology, San Leandro, Calif., 1972—, Oakland, Calif., 1982—; mng. ptnr. Pediatric Med. Assocs. of East Bay, 1990—. Chief pediat. Oakland Hosp., 1974-77, Meml. Hosp., San Leandro, 1986-88; chief pediat. Vesper Meml. Hosp., 1977-79, sec. staff, 1984, v.p. staff, 1985; founder Pediatric Assocs. of East Bay, 1990. Active Republican Party. Recipient Small Bus. Leadership award, Oakland Chinatown C. of C., Comty. Svc. award, Ethnic Health Inst., Family Bridges Comty. Svc. award, Spl. Congl. Recognition cert., 2004. Fellow: Am. Acad. Pediatrics; mem.: AMA, Chancellor's Assocs. U. Calif. at Berkeley, Children's First Healthcare Network (bd. dirs. 1997—), Oakland Chinatown C. of C. (bd. dirs. 1986—91, 1986—91, adv. bd. 1992—, Cmty. Spirit award 2000), Ethnic Health Inst. (bd. dirs. 1998—, Frank Stagger Sr. Cmty. svc. award 2004), Fedn. Chinese Med. Socs. (dir. 1998—), Chinese-Am. Physicians Soc. (sec. 1980, pres. 1983, exec. dir. 1997—2001, bd. dirs. 2003—), Chinese-Am. POlit. Assn. (life), Orgn. Chinese Ams. (chpt. pres. 1984), Smithsonian Assocs., L.A. Pediat. Soc., Alameda County Assn. Primary Care Practitioners (membership chmn. 1993—97, sec.-treas. 1994—97), Am. Heart Assn., Calif. Med. Assn., Family Bridges Inc. (bd. dirs. 2002—, Kenneth Hoh award for cmty. svc. 2004), Stanford U. Alumni Assn. (life), Consumer's Union (life), Hong Kong U. Alumni Assn. (sec. No. Calif. chpt. 1992—96, pres. 1997—2000, chair 2001—), Friends of Hong Kong U. (bd. dirs. 2001—, treas. 2003—), Oakland Asian Cultural Ctr. (life 1996—99, treas. 1996—99), U.S. Golf Assn., San Leandro Golf Club, No. Calif. Golf Assn., Commonwealth Club, PGA Tour Ptnrs. Club (life). Republican. Buddhist. Avocations: golf, photography, web design. Office: 345 9th St Ste 204 Oakland CA 94607-4206 also: 101 Callan Ave Ste 401 San Leandro CA 94577-4523 Office Phone: 510-357-7077. E-mail: larryn@pedmed.com.

**NG, WING CHIU,** accountant, educator, application developer, lawyer, advocate; b. Hong Kong, Oct. 14, 1947; came to U.S., 1966; s. Bing Nuen and Oi Ying (Lee) Ng. BS, MS, Yale U., 1969; PhD, NYU, 1977; JD, U. Hawaii, 2000. Bar: Hawaii 2001; CPA, Hawaii. Rsch. assoc. SUNY, Stony Brook, 1972-74; asst. prof. U. Md., College Park, 1974-76; rsch. physicist U. Bonn, Fed. Republic of Germany, 1976-78; chartered acct. Richter, Usher & Vineberg, Montreal, Can., 1978-80; pvt. practice Honolulu, Hawaii, 1980—; pres. Bowen, Ng & Co., Honolulu, 1983-84. Asia-Am. Investment, Inc., Honolulu, 1983—, Mathematica Pacific, Inc., Honolulu, 1984—. Part-time prof. U. Hawaii, Honolulu, 1982—; ptnr. Advance Realty Investment, Honolulu, 1980—; dir. S & L Internat., Inc., Honolulu, 1987—. Creator: (computer software) Time Billing, 1984, Dbase General Ledger, 1987, Dbase Payroll, 1987, Dbase Accounts Receivable, 1989; co-author: Draft Constitution of the Federal Republic of China (http://frchina.blogspot.com), 1994. Dir. Orgn. of Chinese Ams., Honolulu, 1984-86, Fedn. for a Dem. China, Honolulu, 1990—, Hong Kong, 1991—; dir. Alliance Hong Kong Chinese in U.S., 1995—. Included in Prominent People of Hawaii, Delta Pub. Co., 1988. Mem. AICPA, Hong Kong Soc. Accts., Hawaiian Trail & Mountain Club (auditor 1987—). Democrat. Buddhist. Avocations: hiking, the internet. Office: 1149 Bethel St Ste 306 Honolulu HI 96813-2210

**NGANDU, PIUS NKASHAMA,** education educator; b. Mbujimayi, Kasai, Congo, Sept. 4, 1946; arrived in France, 1973; s. Prosper Kalonji and Marcelline Musuamba; m. Godelieve Ngandu-Kalenga, Sept. 28, 1968 Diploma, Lovanium-Kinshasa, 1970; LLD, U. Strasbourg, France, 1981; postgrad., Univ. Annaba-Constantine, Algeria, 1982-90, Univ. Aarhus, Denmark, 1988-90, U. Baton Rouge, 1995, Albuquerque, 1995, Portland, 1995, 96. Charge de cours Univ. Limoges, France, 1990—, maitre Confs. Invite, 1990-91; prof. Univ. Zaire, Lubumbashi, 1975—, Univ. Annaba-Constantine, 1982—, U. Paris III-Sorbonne Nouvelle, 1998—, La State U., 2000—; dir. Ctr. for French and Francophone Studies, La. State U., Baton Rouge; disting. prof. Bibliotheque: World Wide, BWW Soc./LAPGS. Dir. lit. Edits. L'Harmattan and Nouvelles du Sud, Paris, 1990—; pres. Groupe de Rsch. Interdisciplinaires about Afrique, Paris, 1992—; coord. Notre Libr., Paris, 1993-94. Author: Le pacte de sang, 1984, Ecritures et discours litteraires, 1989, (theatrical works) May Britt de Santa Cruz, 1993, Le doyen marri, 1994, Le fils du mercenaire, 1994, Un jour de grand soleil, 1994, Yakouta, 1995, Citadelle d'espoir, 1995, Bidi ntwilu, bidi mpelelu, 1995, Enseigner les litteratures africaines, 2000, Dictionaire Critique des Oeuvres Littéraires, 2002, En suivant le sentier, 2005, (theatrical works) L'empire des ombres vivantes, Bonjour monsieur le Ministre, 1983, others, Mulongeshi Wanyi, 2003. Recipient Fonlon-Nichols award excellence creative writing, African Lit. Assn., Bruxelles, 2004, Prix Tabalayi, Canada. Office: La State U Dept French Studies Baton Rouge LA 70810 Home: 977 Elysian Dr Baton Rouge LA 70810-2615 E-mail: nngandl@lsu.edu.

**NGO, CHIU Y.,** electrical engineer; s. Hor and Wai-Yau Ngo; m. Christy Lao; children: Vincent, Lawrence. BSEE (hon.), U. Hong Kong, 1984; M in Engring., Philips Internat. Inst., Eindhoven, The Netherlands, 1986; MSc, U. So. Calif., L.A., 1991, MSc in Applied Math., 1993, PhD in Elec. Engring., 1995; MSc in Mgmt., Poly. U., N.Y., 2001. Sr. mem. rsch. staff, project leader Philips Rsch., Briarcliff Manor, NY, 1995—2002; prin. engr. Samsung Electronics, San Jose, Calif., 2002—. Mem.: IEEE, IET (chartered engr.). Achievements include patents in field. Office: Samsung Electronics 75 W Plumeria Dr San Jose CA 95134

**NGO, KHIEM VIET,** research scientist; b. Saigon, Vietnam, Sept. 23, 1973; s. Ngoan Viet Ngo and Xuan (Maria) Thi Tran. BS in Math., Va. Poly. Inst. and State U., 1997, MS in Math., 1998; MSME, U. Ill., 1999; postgrad., Stanford U., 2003—. Summer intern NASA Goddard Space Flight Ctr., Greenbelt, Md., 1999—99; mech. engr. Naval Air Warfare Ctr., China Lake, Calif., 2000—00; rsch. scientist, dept. of elec. & computer engring. U. Va., Charlottesville, 2001—03. Adj. faculty math. No. Va. C.C., Annandale, 1999. Recipient Freshman prize, Va. Tech., Dept. Math., 1995, award, Golden Key Nat. Honor Soc., 1996, Achievement award, NASA Goddard Space Flight Ctr., 1999; scholar, Va. Tech., Dept. Math., 1995. Mem.: IEEE, Soc. Indsl. and Applied Math., Eta Kappa Nu, Pi Mu Epsilon. Achievements include research in the impact of variations on 1-D flow in gas turbine engines via Monte Carlo simulation; on development of a vehicle movement algorithm for a virtual Maglev-guideway signaling system for the discrete-event simulation of magnetically levitated trains; co-development of the failure mode scenarios for the Monte Carlo probabilistic simulation of trains; research in Analytical Derivation Related to Nonlinear Energy Pumping in Coupled Oscillators; Introduction to Eigenvalue Perturbation Theory; Eigenvalues of Infinite Mass-Spring Systems; Approximate and Exact Solutions of the Extended Timoshenko Beam Model; discovery of a formula for the area of a triangle in terms of its three medians. Home: 10501 Moonglow Ct Manassas VA 20112 Office: Dept Aeronautics and Astronautics Stanford Univ 496 Lomita Mall Durand Bldg Stanford CA 94305-4035 E-mail: khiem.ngo@stanford.edu.

**NGO, TUNG THANH,** writer, photographer; b. Soctrang, Vietnam, May 18, 1936; came to U.S., 1975; s. Lung The Ngo and Thui Thi Lam; m. Amy Vu, Jan. 12, 1962; children: Peter, Vincent, Mike, Vinh. B of Law, U. Saigon, Vietnam, 1964; M of Pub. Affairs, U. Pitts., 1970. Judge advocate, corps II South Vietnam Armed Forces, Pleiku, 1964—66; assemblyman, gen. sec. Nat. Constituent Assembly, Saigon, Vietnam, 1966—67; dean, prof. Hoa-Hao U., Long Xuyen, Vietnam, 1970—75; sr. tchr. Garden Grove (Calif.) Sch. Dist., 1978—86; computer operator Alta Bates Med. Ctr., Berkeley, 1987—2001; writer, photography instr. Vietnamese Photography Assn., Calif., 1981—. Author: (in Vietnamese) Visiting California, 1995, Entering Photography I, 1999, Entering Photography II, 2000; editor: Vietnam's Traditional Angling, 1977, Dr. Cung or Boat People, 1987, Selection of Photgraphs, 2001. Grantee The Ford Found., 1975; hon. fellowship The Hong Kong Photography Club of L.A., 2000, The Vietnamese Artists Photography Assn., 2000. The Vietnamese Artistic Photography Assn. (v.p. 1981—, hon. fellowship 2000), The Vietnamese Artistic Photography Assn. in No. Calif. (chpt. pres.). Home: 49 Killybegs Rd Alameda CA 94502

**NGO, VAN TAN (TAN VAN),** financial planner, poet; b. Dai Loc, Quang Nam, Vietnam, June 17, 1952; s. Hoa Ngo and Tai Ta Tran; m. Kim Phuong Thi Do-Phan, Apr. 2, 1987. Diploma in Fin. Planning, Quebec Inst. Fin. Planning, 1996. Cert. fin. planner IQPF, 1996. Translator, instr. USN, Saigon, Vietnam, 1972—75; fin. planner, fin. security advisor Sun Life-Clarica, Montreal, Que., Canada, 1978—; chartered adminstr. Order of Chartered Adminstrs., Que., 1994; profl. mgr. Can. Inst. Mgmt., 1995. Mem. Chamber of Fin. Sec. Que.; pres. conf. attendant representing Montreal city Clarica, 2005. Editor: Vietnam-Can. Newspaper, 1982—86, author poems worldwide in numerous lit. mags. and websites, cited in Vietnamese and English. Campaign organizer Tsunami, 2005; organizer NGO Humanitarian & Development projects in the third-world countries, Chanchu Typhoon Relief Campaign for Vietnam, 2006; founder Quang Da Assn.; project initiator for creation of Vietnamtown in Montreal. Recipient Citation award, US Naval Support Facility Comdr., Vietnam, 1972, Achievement award, Naval Advisory Group Comdr., Saigon, 1974, Macaulay Club award, Sun Life Ins. Co. Can., 1995, Five Star Club award, 1995, Nat. Quality award, Chamber Fin. Sec. Que., 1998, Outstanding Poetry award, Internat. Soc. Poets, 2004, Award of Excellence, Clarica, 2005, Order of Merit, 2006. Mem.: World Movement for Prosperity (pres., found. 1992—), Vietnam-Can. Found. (pres., found. 1982—), Montreal Fin. Security Chamber (Nat. Quality Award 1998). Achievements include development of poetry therapy initative for Duy Tan University; helped bring internat. co-operation to reorganization and consolidation of Univ. Danang, Vietnam. Office: Sun Life-Clarica 1001 Dorchester Sq Ste 600 Montreal PQ H3B 1N1 Canada Office Phone: 514 866 5811 ext.202. Office Fax: 514 731 9782. Personal E-mail: ngovantan@yahoo.com. Business E-mail: van.tan.ngo@clarica.com.

**NGOUAJIO, MATHIEU,** horticulturist, researcher; s. David Sokeng and Jeanne Tsague; m. Babette Rita Ndongmo, Aug. 20, 1986; children: Lynne Lionnelle, Amanda Laurette, Boris Duvalier, Erica Zanguim. BS, U. Dschang, 1986; MS, Va. Tech., 1990; PhD, Laval U., 1999. Asst. prof. U. Dschang, Cameroon, 1990—95; rsch. assoc. U. Calif., Riverside, 1999—2001; asst. prof. Mich. State U. (assoc.), Am. Ext. Specialist Asch. Mich. State U. (assoc.), Am. Soc.Plasticulture (assoc.), Am. Soc. Hort. Sci. (assoc.; chair 2001—04), Internat. Soc. Hort. Sci. (assoc.), Weed Sci. Soc. Am. (assoc.; chair 2003—04), North Ctrl. Weed Sci. Soc. (assoc.), European Weed Rsch. Soc. (assoc.), Internat. Weed Sci. Soc. (life), Gama Sigma Delta (assoc.). Office: Michigan State Univ 428 Plant and Soil Sciences Bldg East Lansing MI 48824 Office Phone: 517-355-5191 1410. Home Fax: 517-432-2242; Office Fax: 517-432-2242. Personal E-mail: ngouajiom@hotmail.com. E-mail: ngouajio@msu.edu.

**NGU, ANNE HEEHIONG,** education educator, researcher; PhD in Computer Sci., U. Western Australia, 1990. Rsch. assoc. Inst. of Sys. Sci., Singapore, 1990—92; assoc. prof. U. of NSW, Sydney, Australia, 1992—2000; rsch. scientist Telcordia Technologies, NJ, 2000—01; assoc. prof. Tex. State U., San Marcos, 2002—. Contbr. articles to profl. jours. U. Rsch. studentship, U. Western Australia, 1986, ITK fellowship, Tilburg U., 1991, Workflow Mgmt. grant, Australian Rsch. Coun., 1999. Mem.: ACM. Office Phone: 512-245-3409.

**N'GUEREKATA, GASTON MANDATA,** mathematician, department chairman; b. Paoua, Cntl. African Rep., May 20, 1953; arrived in U.S., 1995; s. Jean and Therese N'guerekata; m. Beatrice N'guerekata, July 1, 1992; children: Chimei, Manuella, Gaston Jr., Yona, Chelsea. MSc, U. Montreal, Can., 1976; PhD. U. Montreal, 1980. Sec. sci. and tech. Govt. Ctrl. African Rep., Bangui, Central African Republic, 1987—92, spokesman to head of state, 1992—93; rector U. Bangui, 1995—2001; chmn. Dept. Math. Morgan State U., Balt., 2001—. Author: Topics in Almost Automorphy, 2005, Almost Automorphic and Almost Periodic, 2001; editor: Internat. Jour. Evolution Equations, 2005—. Decorated French Legion Hon.; recipient Dean's Rsch. award, Morgan State U., 2001; grantee, NSF, 2005. Mem.: Nat. Assn. Mathematicians, Math. Assn. Am. Am. Math. Soc. Office: Morgan State Univ Dept Math 1700 East Cold Spring Lane Baltimore MD 21251

**NGUYEN, A. MINH THONG,** philosopher, educator; b. Nha Trang, Vietnam, July 3, 1967; s. Biet Van Nguyen and Lan Thi Hoang; m. Nhi Suong Huynh, Feb. 28, 1998; children: Cynthia Lily Chang, Vivian Minette Huynh. BA, MA, MPhil, PhD, Columbia U., N.Y. Vis. instr. philosophy Ga. State U., Atlanta, 2001—02; vis. asst. prof. philosophy U. Louisville, 2002—03; asst. prof. philosophy Ea. Ky. U., Richmond, Ky., 2003—. Mem.: Am. Philos. Assn. (Rockefeller Essay prize 2002). Office: Eastern Kentucky University Philosophy 268 Case Annex 521 Lancaster Avenue Richmond KY 40475 Office Phone: 859-622-8667. Office Fax: 859-622-2976. Business E-Mail: minh.nguyen@eku.edu.

**NGUYEN, CHARLES CUONG,** engineering educator, researcher, dean; b. Danang, Vietnam, Jan. 1, 1956; arrived in U.S., 1978, naturalized, 1978; s. Buoi and Tinh Thi Nguyen; m. Kim-Bang Pham, Aug. 5, 1989; children: Carissa Kim Thuy Duong, Olivia Quynh Duong, Dylan Nhat Khang, Parker Duy Khang. Diploma, Konstanz U., Fed. Rep. Germany, 1978; MS with distinction, George Washington U., 1980, DSc with superiour performance, 1982. Engr. Siemens Corp., Erlangen, Germany, 1977-78; lectr. George Washington U., Washington, 1978-82; asst. prof. engring. Cath. U. Am., Washington, 1982-85, assoc. prof. elec. engring., 1985-92, prof., 1992—, chmn. dept. elec. engring. and computer sci., 1997-2001, dean Sch. Engring., 2001—. Cons. Mitre Corp., Meridian Corp., Jet Propulsion Lab., others; dir. Ctr. Artificial Intelligence and Robotics, 1985—; mem. organizing coms. various robotics confs.; sr. rsch. assoc. NAS, 1990—; program vice chair IEE-Internat. Conf. Robotics 2d Automation, 1997, Internat. Symposium and Robotic Automation, 1997; chmn. organizing com. Robotics Internat., Internat. Symposium Robotics and Mfg. Founding editor, editor-in-chief: Jour. Intelligent Automation and Soft Computing; editor: (book) Robotics and Manufacturing, Vol. 5, 1994, Intelligent Automation and Soft Computing, Vol. 1, 1994, Intelligent Automation and Soft Computing, Vol. 2, 1994; mem. editl. bd.: Jour. Intelligent and Fuzzy Sys., Engring. Design and Automation, assoc. editor: Computers and Elec. Engring.: An Internat. Jour., 1992—, guest editor: Jour. Robotic Sys.; contbr. scientific papers to profl. jours. Apptd. by Pres. Bus to bd. dirs. Vietnam Edn. Found., 2004—07. Recipient Rsch. Initiation award, Engring. Found., 1985, Disting. Alumni Scholar award, George Wash. U., 2002, Lifetime Achievement award, World Automation Congress, 2004, Cmty. Svc. award in Edn., Asia Entertainment Inc., 2004; fellow, NASA-Am. Soc. Elec. Engring., 1985, 1986, NASA-Am. Soc. Elec. Engring. Summer, Goddard Space Flight Ctr., 1994. Mem.: IEEE (sr.; program v.p. Washington chpt.), Soc. Mfg. Engrs. (sr. Robotics Internat.), Internat. Soc. Mini-and Microcomputers, Tau Beta Pi (faculty advisor), Sigma Xi. Roman Catholic. Avocations: guitar, singing, tennis, skiing, ping pong/table tennis. Business E-Mail: nguyen@cua.edu.

**NGUYEN, CLIFFORD HAM-THIEM,** telecommunications engineer; b. Saigon, Vietnam, Nov. 7, 1962; came to U.S., 1982; s. Nghi Duc Nguyen and Lien Kim Hoang; m. Julie Thach Pham. BSEE, Poly. U., 1988, MSEE, 1989; MA in Stats., Columbia U., 1998. Electronics engr. DoD-ARDEC, Dover, N.J., 1989-91; switch engr. Bell Atlantic/NYNEX, N.Y.C., 1991-96, sr. engr. 1996-99, sr. specialist, 1999, Lucent, 1999-2000; ops. mgr. Bell Labs, 2000—, mem. tech. staff. Achievements include research in telecommunications infrastructures and their interdependencies with other critical infrastructures, especially during disruptive events; methodologies and tolls for wireline and wireless network planning, design, and deployment decisions; development of network performance analysis on data, voice, optical; planning, designing, engineering telecommunication networks with broad range of technologies and products. Business E-Mail: cliffnguyen@lucent.com.

**NGUYEN, DONG,** computer scientist, researcher, application developer, educator; s. Dao Nguyen and Khau Thi Le; m. Dung Xuan Phi, Dec. 30, 1976; children: Henry Huy, Huy Tuan. BS in Computer Sci. and Engring., Calif. State U., Long Beach, 1985, MS in Computer Sci., 1988; PhD in Computer Engring. and Applied Math., Claremont Grad. U., 2000, exec. MBA, 2002, MS in Math., 1997. Software engr. Info. Internat., Inc., Culver City, Calif., 1984—86; sr. software engr. CALCOMP, Anaheim, Calif., 1986—90; sr. programmer analyst Sys. Divsn. Ball Aerospace, Huntington Beach, Calif., 1985—87; sr. firmware engr. Micro Tech., Inc., Anaheim, Calif., 1990—92; sr. software engr., sys. engr. Beckman Instruments, Brea, 1990—97; sr. staff engr. B/E Aerospace, Irvine, Calif., 1997—2001; sr. adv. engr., rschr. Kofax

Image Products, Irvine, Calif., 2001—03; software engr. mgr. Celerity Group, Inc., Yorba Linda, 2003—. Lectr. Cal State Univ., Longweach, 1998—2000, in field. Prodr.(music concerts): Young Love, 1992—94. Achievements include research in reliability modeling and evaluation in real-time distributed multimedia systems; recovery blocks in real-time distributed systems; failure mode and effect analysis in software reliability; reliability modeling and evaluation in computer networks and distributed systems; development of rasterization algorithm which greatly improved the speed of converting the vector data to raster data in printers/plotters; dynamic camera calibration for the scanner's automatic camera calibration in real-time without manual operations from users. Personal E-mail: nguyendg@aol.com.

**NGUYEN, DUOC TAN,** small business owner; b. Tan Quoi, Cantho, Vietnam, Apr. 5, 1944; U.S., 1988; s. Hay Tan Nguyen and Kiev Thi Tran; m. Luu Thi Ha, Aug. 15, 1984; 1 child, Nguyen Nghia Hieu. Law cert., Law U., Cantho, 1974. Cert. acctg., tax, notary pub. Dir. criminal investigation Rokee Hdqs., South Vietnam, 1966—75; transl. Refugee Camp, Thailand and Philippines, 1988—89; pres. South Vietnam Police Forces Orgn., Calif., 1990—95; sec. Vietnamese Cmty. in So. Calif., 1996—2002; immn. Collective Com., 2002—. Advisor South Vietnam Police Orgn., 1998—2000; sec. Vietnamese Nat. Support Assn. Editor: South Vietnamese Police Forces Orgn. Mag., 1992—. Mem. ACLU, 1998—; sec. Hungviet Orgn., Calif., 1992—. Mem.: U.S. Fed. Police Orgn. Avocations: basketball, football, fishing, music, poetry. Home: #2 7091 Trask Ave #2 Westminster CA 92683 Office: Vietnamese Cmty Svcs # 208 15355 Brookhurst St Westminster CA 92683 Office Phone: 714-775-2964.

**NGUYEN, HAN VAN,** mechanical engineer; b. Danang, Vietnam, June 10, 1956; came to U.S., 1974; s. Tien Van Nguyen and Dieu Anh Khoa Nguyen; m. Thien-Tam Trang, Jan. 7, 1995; children: Brandon Huy, Bryan Minh. BSME with distinction, Iowa State U., 1979; MSME, Purdue U., 1981, PhD, 1986. Registered profl. engr., Calif., Wash. Grad. rsch. asst. Purdue U., West Lafayette, Ind., 1979—83; sr. engr. Westinghouse Electric Corp., Sunnyvale, Calif., 1983—87; assoc. tech. fellow Boeing Co., Downey and Huntington Beach, Calif., 1987—. Mem. adj. faculty Calif. State Poly. U., Pomona, 1995-97. Contbr. articles to profl. jours. (recipient Meritorious Invention awards, 1998, 2000). Bd. dirs. L.A. Coun. Engrs. and Scientists, 2000-01, Asian Am. Profl. Assn., 2002-04. Recipient Cert. Appreciation. Rockwell Internat. Corp., 1989, 94, Instant Compensation award, 1992, 94, Achievement award NASA Group, 1992; Iowa State U. scholar; Purdue U. fellow. Fellow: AIAA (assoc.; liquid propulsion tech. com. 2000—, conf. session chair 2002, 2003, 2005, 2006), Inst. Advancement Engring.; mem.: Sigma Xi, Golden Key, Phi Eta Sigma, Pi Mu Epsilon, Eta Kappa Nu, Pi Tau Sigma, Tau Beta Pi, Phi Kappa Phi. Achievements include development of numerous thermo-fluid models to evaluate the design and predict the performance of launch vehicle propulsion systems, and publications in space propulsion. Office: The Boeing Co MC H012-B201 5301 Bolsa Ave Huntington Beach CA 92647-2048 Business E-Mail: han.v.nguyen@boeing.com.

**NGUYEN, HOAN KIM HUYNH,** mathematician; b. Saigon, Vietnam, Nov. 2, 1978; s. Phu Trong Nguyen and Nhieu Thi Huynh. BS, Va. Tech, Blacksburg, 1999; MS, Va. Tech, 2000; PhD, Va. Poly. Inst. and State U., Blacksburg, 2004. Mathematician Naval Rsch. Lab., Washington, 2000—04; postdoctoral fellow Statis. and Applied Math. Scis. Inst., Research Triangle Park, NC, 2004—05. N.C. State U., Raleigh, NC, 2005—. Grad. tchg. asst. Va. Tech., 2001—03. Recipient Outstanding Presentation, SIAM-SEAS, 2004, Sr. Award, Math. Dept., Va. Tech. 2000; T.W. Hatcher Scholarship, Va. Tech, 1997—99, David. P. Roselle Scholarship, 1998—99. Mem.: SIAM, Am. Math. Soc. Achievements include research in Volterra Systems with Realizable Kernels. Avocations: travel, swimming, sudoku, reading. Home: 8015 Garlot Dr Annandale VA 22003 Office: North Carolina State Univ PO Box 8205 Raleigh NC 27695-8205 Office Phone: 919-513-0634. Office Fax: 919-515-8967. E-mail: hknguyen@ncsu.edu.

**NGUYEN, HUONG TRAN,** former elementary and secondary language educator, former district office administrator; b. Haiphong, Vietnam, Nov. 16, 1953; came to the U.S., 1971; d. Joe (Quang) Trong Tran and Therese (Nguyet-Anh) (Do) Dotran; m. Tony (Phu) The Nguyen; children: Long Tran Nguyen, Ty Tran Nguyen. B in Liberal Studies, San Diego State U., 1976, tchg. credential grades K-12, 1977; M in Curriculum Devel., Point Loma Coll., 1984; lang. devel. specialist cert., Calif. Commn. Credentialing, 1991; PhD in Edn., Curriculum & Instrn., U. Calif. Riverside, 2004. ESL tchr. San Diego (Calif.) Job Corps, 1978-80; resource tchr. grades K-12 San Diego (Calif.) Unified Sch. Dist., 1980-82; resource tchr. SEAL project grades K-12 Long Beach (Calif.) Unified Sch. Dist., 1982-83, ESL specialist. 1983-85, 85-92, English lang. devel. tchr., chair, 1992-95; adminstr., 1996-98: sr. fellow officer U.S. Dept. Edn., Office Bilingual & Minority Lang. Affairs, Washington, 1995-96; from disting. tchr.-in-residence to asst. prof. Calif. State U., Long Beach, 1998—2004, asst. prof., 2003—. Instr. curriculum PhD Program Calif. State U., 2004. Named Outstanding Tchr. of 1994, Disney Co. Am. Tchr. Awards, Washington, 1994, Outstanding Tchr. in Fgn. Lang./ESL, Disney Co. Am. Tchr. Awards, Washington, 1994. Mem.: Pacific Am. Edn., Calif. Assn. Asian Pacific Bilingual Edn., Calif. Coun. Tchr. Edn., Am. Ednl. Rsch. Assn., Nat. Coun. Tchrs. English. Avocations: reading, travel, gardening, meditation, yoga. Office: Calif State U Coll Edn Dept Tchr Edn 1250 N Bellflower Blvd Long Beach CA 90840-0001 Office Phone: 562-985-4536. Business E-Mail: hnguye10@csulb.edu.

**NGUYEN, KHANH GIA,** medical educator; b. Hanoi, Vietnam, Dec. 17, 1940; arrived in Can., 1972; s. Lien Bich and Lan Chi Nguyen; m. Nga Thi Ho, Dec. 30, 1940; children: Van Thanh Nguyen-Ho, Phong Nguyen-Ho. Cert. of physics, chemistry and biology, Saigon U., 1961, MD, 1969. Diplomate Am. Bd. Pathology, Am. Bd. Pathology in Cytopathology, cert. pathologist Royal Coll. Surgeons, Can. Asst. prof. pathology U. Sask., Saskatoon, Canada, 1978—82; pathologist Plains Health Ctr., Regina, Canada, 1978—80; pathologist, head provincial cytology lab. Pasqua Hosp., Regina, Canada, 1980—82; asst. prof. pathology U. Alta., Edmonton, Alberta, Canada, 1982—84, assoc. prof. pathology, 1984—92, prof. lab. medicine and pathology, 1992—2006; pathologist U. Alta. Hosp., Edmonton, Alberta, Canada, 1982—2006, pathologist and head of electron microscopy, 1987—2000, pathologist and head of cytology, 1997—2004; prof. emeritus lab. medicine and pathology U. Alta., 2006—; pathologist B.C. Cancer Agcy., Vancouver, Canada. 2006—. Cons. pathologist Can. Tumor Reference Ctr., Ottawa, Ontario. Canada. 1982—87. Author: Essentials of Aspiration Biopsy Cytology, 1991, Essentials of Exfoliative Cytology, 1992, Essentials of Cytology: An Atlas, 1993, Critical Issues in Cytopathology, 1996; mem. editl. bd.: Vietnamese Med. Jour., 2001—. Acta Cytologica Jour., 1985—2006; contbr. articles to profl. jours. Accreditation com. for Can. sch. cytotechnology Can. Med. Assn., Ottawa, Ont., Canada, 1992—2000. Recipient Med. Excellency award, Vietnamese Am. Rsch. Found., Westminster, CA, USA, 2004. Fellow: Internat. Acad. Cytology (assoc.; membership com. 1989—92, editl. com. 1992—95, exam. bd. 1995—2002); mem.: Royal Coll. Physicians and Surgeons of Can., Can. Soc. Cytology (hon.; chmn. 1984—85, sec.-treas. 1985—89), Papanicolaou Soc. of Cytopathology (assoc.; member-at-large 1991—99). Achievements include research in cytopathology, pathology, patient care. Personal E-mail: khanhnguyen1730@hotmail.com. Business E-Mail: kngwyen@cha.ab.ca.

**NGUYEN, LAN THI HOANG,** physician, educator; b. Hai-Duong, Vietnam, July 18, 1950; came to U.S., 1975; d. Thua Nang and Niem Thi (Do) N.; m. Khanh Vinh Quoc, Oct. 15, 1981. MD, U. Kans., 1983. Intern St. Mary Med. Ctr./UCLA, Long Beach, Calif., 1983-84; resident City of Faith Med. Rsch. Ctr.-Oral Roberts Sch. Medicine, Tulsa, 1986-88; fellow VA Med. Ctr.-Wadsworth-UCLA, 1988-90; physician Santa Ana (Calif.) Med. Ctr., Doctors Hosp. Santa Ana, Fountain Valley (Calif.) Regional Med. Ctr. Clin. assoc. prof. family medicine Keck Sch. Medicine U. So. Calif., L.A., 2002—. Contbr. articles to profl. jours. V.p. Vietnamese Am. Med. Rsch. Found. Kans. Med. scholar, 1979-81. Fellow: ACP, Am. Coll. Endocrinology, Am. Coll. Nutrition; mem.: Am. Assn. Clin. Endocrinologists (charter). Office: 14971 Brookhurst St Westminster CA 92683-5556 Office Phone: 714-839-5898.

**NGUYEN, RU,** entomologist; b. Nhatrang, Khanh Hoa, Vietnam, Dec. 12, 1944; s. Tam Nguyen and Van Thi Le; m. Kim-Dung Thi Nguyen, Jan. 28, 1981; 1 child, Kim-Anh. BS, Coll. Agr., Saigon, Vietnam, 1966; PhD, U. Fla., 1975. Asst. entomologist U. Fla., Gainesville, 1976—78; rsch. fellow Alexander von Humboldt-Stiftung/U. Bonn, Germany, 1978—79; rsch. entomologist, leader USDA-APHIS-PPQ, Ft. Lauderdale, Fla., 1980—82; rsch. entomologist divsn. plant industry Fla. Dept. Agr., Gainesville, 1982—. Mem. Caribbean fruit fly tech. com. Fla. Dept. Agr., 1983—; mem. citrus leafminer task force U. Fla., Gainesville, 1994—98; mem. nat. genetic resources adv. coun. USDA, Washington, 2000—. Contbr. articles to profl. jours.: author: (book) Catalog of Aleyrodidae on Citrus and Their Natural Enemies, 1993. Recipient Disting. Svc. to Agr. award, Gamma Sigma Delta Honor Soc. of Agr., 1995, Outstanding Achievement award in developing Fly Free Zone, Fla. Dept. Agr. and Consumer Svcs., 1984. Mem.: Fla. Entomol. Soc. (Team Rsch. award 1997, Achievement award for rsch. 2002), Internat. Orgn. for Biol. Control, Entomol. Soc. Am. Office: Divsn Plant Industry PO Box 147100 Gainesville FL 32614 Office Phone: 352-372-3505. Business E-Mail: nguyenr@doacs.state.fl.us.

**NGUYEN, SAN DUY,** psychiatrist, educator; b. Langson, Vietnam, Sept. 25, 1932; arrived in Can., 1971, naturalized, 1977; s. Nguyen Duy and Tran Tuyet, Quyen (Trang) San; m. Eddie Jean Cieslelski, Aug. 24, 1971; children: Thuan Le San, Megan Thuloan San, Muriel Mylinh San, Claire Kimlan San, Robin Xuanlan San, Baodan Edward San. MD, U. Saigon, 1960; postgrad, U. Mich., 1970. Intern Cho Ray Hosp., Saigon, 1957—58; resident Univ. Hosp., Ann Arbor, Mich., 1968—70, Lafayette Clinic, Detroit, 1970—71, Clarke Inst. Psychiatry, Toronto, Ont., Canada, 1971—72; chief of psychiatry S. Vietnamese Army, 1964—68; sr. psychiatrist Queen St. Mental Health Ctr., Toronto, 1972—74; unit dir. Homewood San., Guelph, 1974—80; cons. psychiatrist Guelph Gen. Hosp., Guelph, 1974—80, St. Joseph's Hosp., Guelph; practice medicine specializing in psychiatry Guelph, 1974—80; unit dir. inpatient svc. Royal Ottawa Hosp., Ont., Canada, 1980—84, dir. psychiat. rehab. program, 1985—87; asst. prof. psychiatry U. Ottawa Med. Sch., 1980—85; assoc. prof. psychiatry, 1985—87; bd. dir. Hong Fook Mental Health Svc., Toronto, 1987—; dir. East-West Mental Health Ctr., Toronto, 1987—; chmn., bd. dir. Access Alliance Multicultural Health Ctr., Toronto, 1988—; cons. UN High Commr. for Refugees, 1987—. Author: Etude du Tetanos au Vietnam, 1960, Psychosomatic Medicine: Theoretical, Clinical, and Transcultural Aspects, 1983, Uprooting, Loss and Adaptation, 1984—87, S.E. Asian Mental Health, 1985, Ten Years Later: Indochinese Communities in Can., 1988, Refugee Resettlement and Well-Being, 1989; co-author: The Psychology and Physiology of Stress, 1969. Served, 1953—68, Army Republic of Vietnam. Mem.: NY Acad. Sci., Internat. Soc. Hypnosis, Am. Soc. Clin. Hypnosis, Am. Psychiat. Assn., Can. Psychiat. Assn., Can. Med. Assn. Buddhist. Office: 2238 Dundas St W Ste 306 Toronto ON Canada M6R 3A9

**NGUYEN, VAN THUAN,** finance educator; s. Bich Van and Om Thi Nguyen. BA in Econ., Odense U., Denmark, 1995—99; MS in Econ., U. So. Denmark, Odense, 1999—2001; PhD in Fin., U. Miss., Oxford, 2001—05. Intern European Commn., European Union, Brussels, 1999—2000; rsch. & tchg. asst. U. Miss., 2001—05; asst. prof. fin. Fairleigh Dickinson U., Madison, NJ, 2005—. Author: (book series) Advances in Quantitative Analysis of Finance and Accounting; contbr. articles to profl. jours. Rsch. grant, European Commn., 1999, Standand & Poors, 2004, Travel grant, U. Miss., 2004. Mem.: Danish Lawyers and Economists (assoc.), Profl. Risk Mgrs. Internat. Assn. (assoc.), Fin. Mgmt. Assn. (assoc.), Am. Fin. Assn. (assoc.), Beta Gamma Sigma.

**NGUYEN, D.O. TUAN H.,** plastic surgeon; b. Saigon, Vietnam, Dec. 18, 1966; s. Chau H. Nguyen and Trang X. Vu; m. Thuy-Anh P. Nguyen, Mar. 14, 1994; children: Bao-Tam Nguyen, Viet-Tien Nguyen, Duc-Toan Nguyen, Maithy Nguyen. BS, Calif. State Poly. U., 1992; D in Osteopathy, U. Health Scis.-Coll. Osteo. Medicine, Kansas City, Mo., 1996. Cert. Am. Bd. Osteo. Gen. Surgery, 2002. Intern Ohio U. Coll. Osteo. Medicine-Grandview Hosp. & Med. Ctr., 1996—97; resident gen. surgery Wright State U. Sch. Medicine, Dayton, 1997—98, Weill Med. Coll. Cornell U. (Wyckoff), Bklyn., 1998—2002. V.p. Union Vietnamese Student Assns. So. Calif., 1990—92; pres. Vietnamese Student Assn., Pomona, Calif. 1988—89; commr. of student svcs. Cerritos CC, Norwalk, Calif., 1986—87. Mem.: Am. Coll. Osteo. Surgeons, Am. Osteo. Assn.

**NGUYEN-DINH, THANH,** internist, geriatrician, acupuncturist; b. Saigon, Vietnam; s. Bam and Chanh (Thi Duong) Nguyen-Dinh; m. Kim-Chi Nguyen-Dinh; children: Trung, Kim-Trang, Kim-Trinh, Trong. MD, Free U. Brussels, 1974; Tropical MD, Antwerp Tropical Med. Inst., 1975. Diplomate Am. Bd. Internal Medicine, Am. Bd. Geriat. Medicine, Am. Bd. Forensic Examiners, Am. Bd. Forensic Medicine, Am. Bd. Acupuncture and Neuromuscular Therapy, Am. Assn. Integrative Medicine. Asst. prof. medicine Howard Med. Svc., Washington, 1981—2004; physician dir. St. Elizabeth Unit, D.C. Gen. Hosp., Washington, 1983-94. Co-dir. Howard U. Md. Clinics, D.C. Gen. Hosp., 1990-96. Contbr. articles to profl. jours. Fellow ACP, Am. Assn. Integrative Medicine (diplomate). Avocations: chess, swimming. Office: 611 S Carlin Springs Rd Ste 211 Arlington VA 22204-1078 Personal E-mail: drtnd@yahoo.com.

**NGUYEN-OGHALAI, TRACY UYENTRANG,** medical educator, researcher; d. Thao Nguyen and Yem Thi Cao; m. John Steven Oghalai, Dec. 28, 1996; children: Kevin James Oghalai. Thomas Patrick Oghalai. MD. U. Tenn., Memphis, 1993. Asst. prof. U. Tex. Med. Br., Galveston, 2003—. Recipient Jr. Career Devel. award Geriatric Medicine, Assn. Subspecialty Profs., 2005—; BIRCWH scholar, U. Tex. Med. Br., Ctr. Interdisciplinary Rsch. Women's Health, 2006—. Office: U Tex Med Br ' 301 Univ Blvd Rte 1165 Galveston TX 77555 Office Phone: 409-772-7402.

**NIBLACK, TRACEY,** social studies educator; d. Tom and Katherine Neet; m. Jeff Niblack, June 20, 1998. BS in Edn., U. Mo., Columbia, 1998. Educator Claremore (Okla.) Pub. Schs., 2000—04, Ladue Pub. Schools, St. Louis, 2004—. Class sponsor Claremore H.S., 2000—04; club sponsor Ladue Horton Watkins H.S., St. Louis, 2004—, student coun. sponsor, 2005—. Recipient Stuart and Lorton award for Excellence in Tchg. Okla. History, Okla. Hist. Soc. 2003. Office: Ladue Public Schools 1201 S Warson Rd Saint Louis MO 63124 Office Phone: 314-983-5844.

**NIBLEY, ANDREW MATHEWS,** media specialist; b. Maxwell AFB, Ala., May 25, 1951; s. Owen Smoot and Frances Elizabeth (Browder) N.; children: Kevin Mathews, Carlyle Gower, Leath Michael; m. Kelly Jane Colbert, Aug. 16, 2004. Attended, Montgomery Coll, Rockville, Md., 1970-72, Univ. Md., 1973. Legis. corr. UPI, Hartford, Conn., 1975-78; bur. chief Concord, N.H., 1979, Treasury corr. Washington, 1980. Reuters N.Am., Washington, 1980-82, editor-in-charge, 1982, news editor, 1983-85, N.Y.C., 1985-87; news editor Europe Reuters Holdings, London, 1987-89; editor, America Reuters America Inc., N.Y.C., 1989-94, sr. v.p., news and TV, 1993-94; editor, exec. v.p., bd. dirs. Reuters New Media Inc., N.Y.C., 1994-97; pres. Digital and Media Publishing Reuters Group PLC, N.Y.C., 1998—99; exec. v.p. Reuters Am. Holdings Plc.; pres. Reuters TV Am., Inc., 1998-99; pres., CEO Get Music LLC, 1999—2001; chmn. Marsteller, N.Y.C., 2003—. Mem. Knight-Bagehot editl. panel Columbia U., 1999-99; bd. dirs. Sportsline USA, Inc., Kinecta Corp., Oddcast LLC, Nervestruck Media, Xlantic LLC; exec. mgmt. com. Reuters Am. Holdings, Inc., 1994-99; bd. dirs. New Directions for News, Overseas Press Club Found. Mem. Gov.'s Coun. on Alcoholism and Drug Abuse, mem. media subcom., 1991-92; trustee N.J. Ctr. for Family Studies; bd. advisors Grad. Sch. Journalism U. Calif., Berkeley, 1993-98; bd. dirs. NY chpt. Leukemia and LYmphoma Soc. Am. Recipient Meritorious Service award Nat. Press Club. Mem. Am. Soc. Newspaper Editors (editl. bd. 1992-93), Overseas Press Club (program vice chmn. 1990-93, bd. govs. 1993-96, treas. 1996-2000), Fgn. Press Assn., Internat. Platform Assn., N.Y. New Media Assn., Triathlon Fedn. Am., Montclair Golf Club (Verona, N.J.), Essex Running Club, The Athletic and Swim Club (N.Y.C.). Avocations: golf, tennis, jogging, racquetball, triathlons. Home: 53 W 94th St Apt 1G New York NY 10025-7131 Office: Marsteller 230 Park Ave South New York NY 10003 E-mail: amibley@hotmail.com.

**NIBLOCK, ROBERT A.,** consumer home products company executive; b. Fla., 1962; m. Melanie Niblock; 2 children. BA in Acctg., U. NC. Acct. Ernst & Young, 1986—93; dir. tax Lowe's Companies Inc., Mooresville, NC, sr. dir. tax Mooresville, NC, v.p., treas., 1997—99, sr. v.p. fin. Mooresville, NC, 1999—2000, sr. v.p., CFO, 2000—01, exec. v.p., CFO, 2001—03, pres., 2003—, CEO, chmn., 2005—. Bd. dirs. Lowe's Companies Inc., 2004—. Office: Lowe's Companies Inc 1000 Lowe's Blvd Mooresville NC 28117*

**NICA, NINEL,** physicist; s. Nicolae and Floarea Nica; m. Ioana Nica; 1 child, Emilian Marius. MS in Nuclear Reactos, U. Bucharest, 1986, PhD in Nuclear Physics, 1999. Rsch. assoc. Cath. U. Louvain, Belgium, 2000—02; rsch. scientist Tex. A&M U., College Station, 2002—. Rsch. scientist Nat. Inst. Physics and Nuc. Engring., Bucharest, 1989—2000. Fellow, Niels Bohr Inst., Roskilde, Denmark, 1991—92. Mem.: Am. Phys. Soc., Sigma Xi. Achievements include research in low energy nuclear physics spectroscopy, precision measurements, nuclear data evaluation. Office: Texas A&M University Cyclotron Institute Corner of Spence and University College Station TX 77843-3366 Office Phone: 979-845-1411.

**NICASTRI, ANN GILBERT,** science educator; b. N.Y.C., May 26, 1934; d. Ralph and Ruth Gilbert; m. Anthony D. Nicastri, July 2, 1960; children: RuthAnn, Christina, Catherine, Daniel. BA magna cum laude, Bklyn. Coll., 1954; MA, Columbia U., N.Y.C., 1956. Tchg. asst. Barnard Coll., N.Y.C., 1954—55; tchr. Balt. Jr. H.S., 1960—61, Balt. Jr. Coll., 1961—62, Julia Richman H.S., N.Y.C., 1962—63, Midwood H.S., Bklyn., 1955—60, tchr. biology, AP biology, rsch., 1986—2004; adj. faculty fellows program Bklyn. Coll., 2004—. Judge NYCSEF Sci. Contest, 2002—06; rsch. coord. student projects Midwood H.S., Bklyn., 2003—04. Recipient ISEF Mentor award, USAF, 2004; NSF fellow, Harvard U., Boston, 1957—58, Columbia U., 1959. Mem.: N.Y. Acad. Sci., Kappa Delta Pi, Phi Beta Kappa. Home: 164 Beach 143rd St Neponsit NY 11694 Personal E-mail: agnicastri@aol.com.

**NICCHI, VINCENT, JR.,** cardiologist; b. Bklyn., Nov. 16, 1955; s. Vincent Sr. and Rosalie (Martino) N.; m. Kathleen Mary Healy, May 26, 1985; children: Kristina Rose, Lisa Marie, Michelle Kathleen, Vincent Michael. BS in Chemistry, Bklyn. Coll., 1977; MD, U. Noreste, Tampico Tamps, Mex., 1981. Diplomate Am. Bd. Internal Medicine, Am. Bd. Cardiovasc. Diseases, Am. Bd. Nuc. Cardiology. Intern Maimonides Med. Ctr., Bklyn., 1982-83, resident, 1983-85; fellow in cardiology Deborah Heart Lung Ctr., Browns Mills, NJ, 1985-87; invasive/interventional cardiologist Ariz. Heart Inst., 1987-96; founder Cardiac Care Consultants, Sun City, Ariz., 1996—; mem. staff Boswell Hosp., Sun City. Past chmn. credential com. Del Webb Hosp., Sun City West, Ariz., past mem. med. exec. com. Fellow: Am. Coll. Cardiology; mem.: AMA. Roman Catholic. Office: Cardiac Care Consultants 13188 N 103d Dr Ste 201 Sun City AZ 85351

**NICCOLLS, WESLEY OLIVER, SR.,** retired electronics technician; b. Star, Idaho, Jan. 17, 1918; s. Herbert Oliver Niccolls and Hazel Katherine Gillaspy; m. Doris Louise Ball, June 1, 1946; children: James Leslie, Wesley Oliver, Douglas Eldon, Jeffry Herbert, Linda Jane, Barbara Louise, John William. Student, L.A. City Coll., 1938—39, Modesto Jr. Coll., Calif., 1940—42, U.S. Navy Electronics, Treasure Island, Calif., 1943. Radio tech. U.S. Navy Reserve, PTO, 1942—45; tech. advisor electronics supply office U.S. Navy, North Chgo., Ill., 1946—51; electronics engr. tech. Diamond Ordnance Fuze Lab., Washington, 1951—70. Achievements include design of production inspection instrumentation for Smart Bomb fuze; electronic circuit in TOW anti-tank missile; fluidics pitch-a-yaw sensing device; patents for the latest major class of direct current motors known as brushless DC motors first used in all space vehicles and the robotics industry; neon photoconductor ring oscillator circuit; photoelectric ring oscillator circuit with voltage doubler; low and high pressure steam whistle; patents pending in fields of desalization and nuclear waste disposal. Home: 508 S 25th St Arlington VA 22202 Fax: 703-418-1829.

**NICE, CARTER,** conductor; b. Jacksonville, Fla., Apr. 5, 1940; s. Clarence Carter and Elizabeth Jane (Hintermister) N.; m. Jennifer Charlotte Smith, Apr. 4, 1983; children: Danielle, Christian, Olivia. MusB, Eastman Sch. Music, 1962; MusM, Manhattan Sch. Music, 1964. Asst. condr., concert master New Orleans Philharm., 1967-79; condr., music dir. Sacramento Symphony, 1979-92; music dir., condr. Bear Valley Music Fest., 1985—; mus. dir., condr. Sacramento Met. Orch., 2005—. Office: 579 Hevington Ct Sacramento CA 95864 Office Phone: 916-973-1138. Personal E-mail: ccniii@aol.com.

**NICE, DON,** artist; b. Visalia, Calif., 1932; BFA, UCLA, 1954; MFA, Yale Univ., New Haven, 1964. Tchr. Mpls. Sch. of Art; tchr. to dean Sch. Visual Arts, NYC; artist-in-residence Dartmouth Coll., Hanover, NH, 1982—. One-man shows: Gallery Moos, Toronto, 1980, Hood Mus. of Art, Dartmouth Coll, 1982, Images Gallery, Toledo, Ohio, 1983, Lincoln Ctr. Art Gallery, NYC, 1983, Nancy Hoffman Gallery, NYC, 1984, Univ. Okla.-Norman, 1985, Fine Arts Mus. Long Island, NY, 1985, Pace Editions, NYC, 1986, John Berggruen Gallery, San Francisco, 1987, 89, Lake Placid Ctr. for Arts, NY, 1987, Elaine Horwitch Galleries, Palm Springs. Calif., 1987, Sun Valley Ctr. for Arts and Humanities, Idaho, 1990; group exhbns.: Mus. Modern Art, NYC, 1984, Chrysler Mus., Norfolk, Va., 1984, Stamford Mus., Conn., 1984, Paine Art Ctr. and Arboretum, Wis., 1985, Sordoni Art Gallery, Wilkes Barre, Pa., 1985, Vassar Coll., NY. 1986, Contemporary Arts Ctr., New Orleans, 1986, Mus. of Art, RI Sch. Design, 1987, Rutgers Barclay Gallery, Santa Fe, 1988, Barbara Fendrick Gallery, NYC, 1989; principal works: wall of murals at Nat. Fine Arts Commn., Lake Placid, Art in Arch. Project, Veterans Adminstrn., White River Junction, NY; represented in permanent collections: Whitney Mus. Am. Art, Penn. Acad. of Fine Arts, Nat. Mus. of Art, Canberra, Australia, Hedendaagse Kunst, Utrecht, Holland, Del. Art Mus., Chase Manhattan Bank. Recipient Ford Found. Purchase award, 1963. Mem.: NAD (academician). Office: Tandem Press-Univ Wisconsin 201 S Dickinson St Madison WI 53703 Office Phone: 608-263-3437.

**NICELY, OLZA M. (TONY),** insurance company executive; b. Va., 1943; BBA, Georgia Coll. Cert. gen. ins. Ins. Inst. Am. Endorsement clk GEICO, 1961—73, asst. v.p., 1973—80; v.p. GEICO Ins. Cos., 1980—85, sr. v.p., 1985—87, exec. v.p., 1987—89, pres., 1989—, CEO, 1991—, chmn. Washington, 1993—. Trustee Geo. Mason Univ. Found. Mem.: Ins. Inst. for Hwy Safety, Property Casualty Insurers Assn. Am. Office: GEICO One Geico Plaza Washington DC 20076-0001

**NICHOL, EUGENE R.,** academic administrator; m. Glenn George; children: Jesse, Jenny, Soren. BA, Okla. State U., 1973; JD, U. Tex., 1976. Prof. law U. Fla., 1984—85; J.G. Cutler prof., dir. Bill of Rights Law Coll. of William and Mary, Williamsburg, Va., 1985—88, pres., 2005—; dean, prof. law Sch. Law, U. Colo., Boulder, 1988—95, prof. law, 1996—99; dean Sch. Law, U. NC. Chapel Hill, 1999—2005. Contbr. articles to profl. jours. Fellow: ABA (Edward R. Finch Award 2003), Am. Law Inst. Office: Coll William and Mary PO Box 8795 Williamsburg VA 23187-8795 Office Phone: 757-221-1693. Office Fax: 757-221-1259.

**NICHOL, GENE RAY, JR.,** academic administrator, law educator; b. Dallas, May 11, 1951; s. Gene R. and Dolores (Dumas) N.; m. Janet Castle, Aug. 20, 1973 (div. 1978); m. Glenn George. Nov. 25, 1984. BA in Philosophy, Okla. State U., 1973; JD, U. Texas, 1976. Bar: Alaska 1978. Assoc. Ely, Guess and Rudd, Anchorage, 1976-78; asst. prof. W.Va. U., Morgantown, 1978-80, assoc. prof., 1980-82; prof. law U. Fla., Gainesville, 1983-84; Cutler prof. law, dir. Inst. of Bill of Rights Law Coll. William and Mary, Williamsburg, W.Va., 1984-88; dean U. Colo. Law Sch., 1988-95, dean, Burton Craige prof. law U. NC Sch. of Law, 1999—2005; pres. Coll. William & Mary, Williamsburg, Va., 2005—. Host Culture Wars, KBDI T.V.,

Denver, 1995-96. Author: (with M. Redish) Federal Courts; columnist: Rocky Mt. News, 1999-2000, Raleigh News and Observer, 2000-04; contbr. articles to profl. jours. Posten research grantee U. W.Va., 1980, 81, 82. Mem. Nat. Lawyers Guild (coms. 1978, vice chair Colo. reapportionment comm.), Am. Law Inst., ACLU (coms. 1978—), Am. Bar Found. Fellows, Order of Coif. Roman Catholic. Avocation: back packing. Office: Coll of William and Mary Office of Pres PO Box 8795 Williamsburg VA 23187-8795 E-mail: gnichol@wm.edu.*

**NICHOLAOU, MARY C(ONSTANTINE),** literature and language professor, publishing executive; b. Alexandria, Egypt, Oct. 4, 1935; d. Constantine Michael Nicholaou and Eudokia Theophilos Finikiotis-Nicholaou. MA in Secondary English, Bklyn. Coll., 1984, postgrad., 2000—; MEd in Tchg. of English, Columbia U., 2000. Lic. English tchr. NY. Tchr. English NY State Bd. Edn., 1984—95; prof. English composition St. John's U., S.I., 2001—02, L.I. U., 2002—04; pub. Eros Books, S.I., 2000—. Editor, pub. (newsletter) Psyche, 2000, (mag.) Desire, 2002, author, editor, pub., translator (novels) Cynthia, Cracks, Desire, The Scion, It Takes a People, also short stories. Mem.: Small Press Ind. Pubs. Avocations: creative dramatics, crafts, ceramics, embroidery, travel. Office: Eros Books Pub 463 Barlow Ave Staten Island NY 10308 Home: 463 Barlow Ave Staten Island NY 10308 Office Phone: 718-317-7484. E-mail: marynicholaou@aol.com.

**NICHOLAS, ARTHUR SOTERIOS,** manufacturing executive; b. Grand Rapids, Mich., Mar. 6, 1930; s. Soterios D. and Penelope A. (Kalapodes) N.; m. Bessie Zazanis, Aug. 25, 1957; children: Niki Stephanie, Arthur S., Thomas. BS in Chem. Engring, U. Mich., 1953; BA in Indsl. Mgmt, Wayne State U., 1957. Registered profl. engr., Mich. Project engr. B.F. Goodrich Co., 1953-54; plant mgr. Cadillac Plastics and Chem. Co., 1954-69; pres., chief exec. officer Leon Chem. and Plastics, Inc., Grand Rapids, 1960-69; with U.S. Industries, Inc., 1969-73, pres., chief operating officer, 1973; now pres. The Antech Group. Bd. dirs. ERO Industries, Inc. Patentee in field. Judge Jr. Achievement, Chgo. Served with USNR, 1948-49. Recipient Distinguished Alumni award Grand Rapids Jr. Coll., 1970 Mem. Young Pres. Orgn., Soc. Plastic Engrs., Mich. Acad. Sci., Arts and Letters, Chgo. Coun. on Fgn. Rels., Pres.' Assn. Mem. Greek Orthodox Ch. Clubs: Chgo. Athletic Assn. (Chgo.), Executives (Chgo.). Office: 2300 Barrington Rd # 411 Hoffman Estates IL 60195-2082 Home: 467 Park Barrington Barrington IL 60010 Personal E-mail: anicholas@aol.com.

**NICHOLAS, CAROLINE JEAN,** retired nurse, consultant; b. Lansing, Mich., Feb. 11, 1935; d. Homer Paul and Lucinda Rachel (McDonald) Anderson; m. William C. Nicholas (div.); children: Jan Marie, David Craig, Jill Elizabeth. BSN, Mich. State U., East Lansing, 1956, MA, 1969. RN Mich. Staff nurse Med. Hosp., East Lansing, 1956—57, clin. instr., 1957—62; nurse, 1962—86; nursing instr. Lansing CC, 1967—79; nurse cons. Mich. Dept. and Pub. Health, 1979—90, ret., 1990. Docent Women's Hist. Soc. and Hall of Fame, Lansing, 1980—; elder, deacon Presbyn. Ch. Mem.: Phi Kappa Phi, Sigma Theta Tau, Alpha Omicron Pi. Avocations: reading, sewing, cross stitch. Home: 2734 Trudy Ln Lansing MI 48910-3826

**NICHOLAS, DAVID ROBERT,** minister, college president; b. L.A., May 10, 1941; s. Robert Grant and Pearl Elizabeth (Pickard) N.; m. Donna Lynn Roberts, June 28, 1969; children: Joy Lynn, Faith Elizabeth. AB, Azusa Pacific U., 1963; MS, U. So. Calif., 1967; MDiv., L.A. Bapt. Theol. Sem., 1966; ThM, Talbot Theol. Sem., 1971; ThD, Grace Theol. Seminary, 1982. Ordained to ministry Gen. Assn. Regular Bapt. Chs., 1970. Dir. admissions, mem. faculty L.A. Bapt. Coll., Newhall, Calif., 1966-71; dean, pres. Van Nuys (Calif.) Christian Coll., 1972-76; pastor Tri-Lakes Bapt. Ch., Columbia City, Ind., 1977-78; acad. dean, assoc. prof. Southwestern Coll., Phoenix, 1978-80; sr. pastor, acad. supt. Grace Bapt. Ch., Yuba City, 1980-82; sr. pastor Placerita Bapt. Ch., Newhall, 1982-84; pres., prof. theology Shasta Bible Coll., Redding, Calif., 1985—. Chmn. Greater Redding Area Christian Edn. Conv., 1988—; mem. accreditation commn. Transnat. Assn. Christian Colls. and Schs., 1994—; trustee Regular Bapt. Conf. So. Calif., 1983-85, pres., 1963-65; dir. Bapt. Youth Assn., So. Calif., 1969-71. Author: Foundations of Biblical Inerrancy, 1978, What's A Woman to Do...In the Church?, 1979, Church Discipline: Option or Obligation, 1991, Biblical Judgments, Dictionary of Pre-Millenial Theology, 1996; contbr. articles to religious jours.; recordings include Trombone Testimonies, 1990; Bible tchr. broadcast program Truth for Today, 1988—, Bible Answer Man, 1978-80. Trustee Christian Heritage Coll., El Cajon, Calif., 1981-85, Northwest Bapt. Seminary, Tacoma, Wash., 1993—; mem. steering com. Calif. Activists Network, Los Altos, Calif., 1991; del. Conf. on the Preservation of the Family, 1991; gov. Am. Coalition for Trad. Values, Washington, 1984; chaplain Los Angeles County Bd. Suprs., 1984. Recipient Svc. award Am. Legion, 1955. Mem. Evang. Theol. Soc., Creation Rsch. Soc., Shasta County Evang. Ministerial Assn. (pres. 1992-95), Kappa Tau Epsilon. Republican. Home: 8264 Taylor Ln Redding CA 96001-9530 Office: Shasta Bible Coll 2951 Goodwater Ave Redding CA 96002-1544 Office Phone: 530-221-4275.

**NICHOLAS, FREDERICK M.,** lawyer; b. NYC, May 30, 1920; s. Benjamin L. and Rose F. (Nechols) N.; m. Eleanore Berman, Sept. 2, 1951 (div. 1980); children: Deborah, Jan, Tony; m. Joan Fields, Jan. 2, 1983. AB, U. So. Calif., 1947; postgrad., U. Chgo., 1949-50; JD, U. So. Calif., 1952. Bar: Calif. 1952, U.S. Dist. Ct. Calif. 1952, U.S. Ct. Appeals (9th cir.) 1952. Assoc. Loeb & Loeb, L.A., 1952-56; pvt. practice Beverly Hills, 1956-82; pres., atty. Hapsmith Co., Beverly Hills, 1980—. Bd. dirs. Malibu Grand Prix, L.A. 1982—90; gen. counsel Beverly Hills Realty Bd., 1971—79; founder, pres. Pub. Counsel, L.A., 1970—73. Author: Setting Up a Shopping Center, 1960, Commercial Real Property Lease Practice, 1976. Chmn. Mus. Contemporary Art, L.A., 1987—93, life trustee, 2002—; chmn. com. Walt Disney Concert Hall, L.A., 1987—95; trustee Music Ctr. Los Angeles County, 1987—95, L.A. Philharm. Assn. 1987 95, Mus. Flying, Santa Monica, Calif., 1991—2002, Frederick R. Weisman Art Found., 2003—, Frederick R. Weisman Philanthropic Found., 2003—, Pitzer Coll., 1992—95, Art Ctr. Coll. Design, 2003—; chmn. Calif. Pub. Broadcasting Commn., Sacramento, 1972—78; pres. Maple Ctr., 1977—79; co-developer Ronald Reagan Bldg., Washington, 1998; adminstr. Estate of Sam Francis, 1996—. Capt. U.S. Army, 1941—46. Named Citizen of Yr. Beverly Hills Bd. Realtors, 1978, Man of Yr. Maple Ctr., 1980, Outstanding Founder in Philanthropy, Nat. Philanthropy Day Com., 1990; recipient Pub. Svc. award Coro Found., 1988, Medici award LA C. of C., 1990, Founders award Pub. Counsel, 1990, Trustees award Calif. Inst. Arts, 1993, City of Angels award L.A. Ctrl. Bus. Assn., Disting. Svc. award U. So. Calif. Law Sch. Class of 1952, 2002, Parkinson Spirit of Urbanism award U. So. Calif. Archtl. Guild, 2004, Equal Justice Advocacy award ACLU Found., 2005, AIA L.A. Cmty. Svc. award, 2006. Mem. Beverly Hills Bar Assn. (bd. govs. 1970-76, Disting. Svc. award 1974, 81, Exceptional Svc. award 1986, 2004), Beverly Hills C. of C. (Man of Yr. 1983). Home: 1001 Maybrook Dr Beverly Hills CA 90210-2715 Office: Hapsmith Co 3844 Culver Center St Ste B Culver City CA 90232 Business E-Mail: fmnicholas@hapsmithco.com.

**NICHOLAS, HENRY THOMPSON, III,** former electronics company executive; b. 1959; BSEE, MSEE, UCLA, PhD in EE. With TRW; dir. microelectronics PairGain Techs.; co-founder, pres., CEO Broadcom Corp., Irvine, Calif., 1991—2003. Named one of Top 20 Entrepreneurs, 1997 Red Herring, 1997, World's Top Cyber Elite, 1997 Time Digital Mag., 1997; recipient Entrepreneur of the Yr. award, Ernst & Young, 1996, Forbes Richest Americans, 2006.*

**NICHOLAS, LAWRENCE BRUCE,** finance company executive; b. Dallas, Nov. 9, 1945; s. J.W. and William Elouise (Whiteacre) N.; m. Virginia Pearl Farmer, Aug. 5, 1967; children: Helen Brooke, John Lawrence, Alexis Bradlee. BBA, So. Meth. U., 1968. Mem. sales staff Nicholas Machinery Co., Dallas, 1963-69; sales mgr. Indsl. and Comml. Rsch. Corp., Dallas, 1969-74; v.p. Precision Concepts Corp., Dallas, 1974-76, gen. mgr., 1976-78, pres. Addison, Tex., 1978-86, INCOR Inc., Addison, 1974-91, dir.; pres. The Octagon Group Corp., 2006—. Pres., dir. Multiple Axis Machine Corp.,

1981-96, Investment Svcs. Corp., 1991-93; mem. adv. bd. Consultores Patrimoniales, Mex. City, 1992—; pres. Equity Capital Interests, Inc., San Antonio, Tex., 1993—; chmn. bd. dirs. Cross Securities Internat. Corp., San Antonio, 1993-94; pres. Worldwide Exec. Aviation, San Antonio, 1996—, Octagon Group Ltd., San Antonio, 2006—; bd. dirs. Sea Hawke Yachte Ltd., Can., 2003—. Served as officer Ordnance Corps, U.S. Army, 1968, N.G., 1968-74. Mem. NRA, Soc. Mfg. Engrs., Nat. Shooting Sports Found., Safari Club Internat.

**NICHOLAS, LYNN B.,** medical association administrator; b. Tenn. BS in med. tech., Tenn. Wesleyan Coll.; M in mgmt., Cent. Mich. U., 1983. Bd. cert. fellow Am. Coll. Healthcare Exec. (ACHE). Med. technologist to sr. v.p. clinical and ambulatory svc. Morristown Meml. Hosp., NJ; exec. v.p., COO NJ Hosp. Assn., 1995—2000; pres., CEO La. Hosp. Assn., 2000—04; CEO Am. Diabetes Assn., Alexandria, Va., 2004—. Mem. bd. gov. Am. Coll. Healthcare Exec.; chair La. Health Works Commn.; mem. La. Health Care Commn.; rep. La. hosp. Am. Hosp. Assn. Recipient Early Career Healthcare Exec. award (first recipient in NJ). Am. Coll. Healthcare Exec. Office: Am Diabetes Assn 1701 N Beauregard St Alexandria VA 22311 Office Phone: 703-549-1500, 800-342-2383. Office Fax: 703-739-9346.*

**NICHOLAS, LYNN HOLMAN,** historian, researcher, writer; b. New London, Conn., Nov. 11, 1939; d. William Grizzard Holman and Carol (Ackiss) Wakelin; m. Robert Carter Nicholas III, Dec. 20, 1965; children: William C., R. Carter, Philip H. Student, Radcliffe Coll., 1957-59; diploma, U. Madrid, 1960; BA, Oxford (Eng.) U., 1964. Mem. adv. panel Presdl. Commn. on Holocaust Assets in the U.S., 1999. Author: The Rape of Europa: The Fate of Europe's Treasures in the Third Reich and the Second World War, 1994 (Nat. Book Critics Circle award 1995), Cruel World: The Children of Europe in the Nazi Web, 2005. Decorated chevalier Légion d'Honneur (France); named Amicus Poloniae, Govt. of Poland, 2003. Personal E-mail: lynnick105@aol.com.

**NICHOLAS, NICHOLAS CONSTANTINE,** retired military officer; b. Balt., Apr. 20, 1929; s. Constantine and Helene (Kalymnny) Nicholas; m. Sammie Ruth Vick (div.); children: Carolyn H., Lois E. stepchildren: Deborah L., Jana D.; m. Linda Lee Elkins, Sept. 2, 1977. *Orphaned at the age of seven, Col. Nicholas went to Dorothy, West Virginia to live with his godparents, Agapios and Irene Kostas, who were his mother's aunt and uncle. He remained a member of their family for eight years. The Kostases were a positive influence on his character, instilling in him a work ethic for success and compassion for those in need. A lane in Dorothy is named for them. Daughter Lois is an emergency room nurse at the Baylor Medical Center in Texas. Daughter Jana and her husband, Carl DeNunzio, own the American Cutting and Drilling Company in Florida.* BA, U. Md., 1952; MA, U. Okla., 1973; attended, USAF Sch. Aviation Medicine, 1956, USAF Sch. Aerospace Medicine, 1975. Commissioned 2d lt. to col. USAF, Coll. Pk., Md., 1952—71; obervor B-36 and B-52 Aircraft Ramey AFB, PR, Carswell AFB, Tex., 1954; comdr. 4th Physiological Tng. Flight, Carswell AFB, Tex. 1956—63; chief physiological tng. unit Little Rock AFB, Ark., 1963—66; command coord. aerospace physiology Hdqs. Strategic Air Command, Omaha, 1966—70, Pacific Air Force and Command. 15th Physiological Training Unit Kadena AFB, 1970—72; chief dept. medicine USAF Sch. of Health Care Scis. Sheppard AFB, 1972—76; chief med. sys. div. Office of Se. of Def., Washington, 1976—78; chief Health Policy and Programs Divsn., 1978—84, Biomed. Sci. Corps., 1981—84. Cons. aerospace physiology Surgeons General USAF, Wash., DC, 1977—88, cons. med. edn. and tng., 1977—88; cons. MedTech Comm. Inc., N.Y.C. *Serving thirty-two years in the Air Force, Col. Nicholas made significant contributions to aerospace, clinical and environmental medicine, and to flying safety and disaster preparation. He also contributed to local, state, and national civilian medical projects. As chief of the Biomedical Sciences Corps, he served in a general officer position and was responsible for the career development and utilization of 2,460 officers and 6,300 enlisted personnel in 21 biomedical disciplines supporting aerospace, clinical and environmental medicine, as well as research and development programs for the Air Force and Department of Defense.* Author: Use of Modified Partial Pressure Suits to Aleviate Orthostatic Hypotension, 1962; co-author: Human Decompression Tests for B-58 Escape Capsule System, 1964, USAF/USN Physician Assistant Program: Military Medicine, 1977. Pres. Young Dem. Club, Coll. Pk, Md., 1950—52; delegate State Convention Young Dem. Club, Anapolis, Md., 1951, Nat. Convention Young Dem. Club, St. Louis, 1951; mem. inaugural Gala for Pres. Truman, Wash., DC, 1949. Col. USAF, 1952—84. Recipient Men's League award Outstanding Achievement and Svc. to U., U. Md., 1950. Mem.: Arnold Air Soc., Scabbard and Blade, Aerospace Physiologist Soc., Air Force Assn., Assn. Mil. Surgeons of US, Mil. Officers Assn. (life), Aerospace Medicine Assn. (life), Phi Alpha Theta, Omicron Delta Kappa, Phi Kappa Tau. Epsc. Avocations: stamp collecting/philately, walking, reading. Home: 8724 Racquet Club Dr Fort Worth TX 76120 Personal E-mail: lindlinicholas@aol.com.

**NICHOLAS, PETER M.,** medical products executive; married; 3 children. BS, Duke U.; MS, U. Pa. Former corp. dir. mktg., gen. mgr. med. products divsn. Millipore Corp.; various sales, mktg., and gen. mgmt. positions Eli Lily and Co.; co-chmn. bd. Boston Sci., Natick, Mass., 1979—95, CEO, 1979—99, chmn. bd., 1995—. Chmn. bd. trustees, mem. bd. exec. com. Duke U.; mem. Mass. Bus. Roundtable, Mass. Bus. High Tech. Coun., CEOs for Fundamental Change in Edn., Boys and Girls Club Boston. Named one of World's Richest People, Forbes Mag., 2001—04. Fellow: Nat. Acad. Arts and Scis. (trustee); mem.: Boys and Girls Club, Boston, CEOs Fundamental Change Edn., Mass. Bus. High Tech. Coun., Mass. Bus. Roundtable. Office: Boston Sci 1 Boston Sci Pl Natick MA 01760-1537*

**NICHOLAS, RALPH WALLACE W.,** anthropologist, educator; b. Dallas, Nov. 28, 1934; s. Ralph Wendell and Ruth Elizabeth (Oury) N.; m. Marta Ruth Weinstock, June 13, 1963. BA, Wayne U., 1957; MA, U. Chgo., 1958, PhD, 1962. From asst. prof. to prof. Mich. State U., East Lansing, 1964-71; prof. anthropology U. Chgo., 1971—, chmn. dept., 1981-82, dep. provost, 1982-87, dean of coll., 1987-92; dir. Ctr. Internat. Studies, 1984-95, William Rainey Harper prof. anthropology and social scis., 1992-2000, William Rainey Harper prof. emeritus, 2000—; pres. Internat. House of Chgo., 1993-2000. Cons. Ford Found., Dhaka, Bangladesh, 1973 Author: (with others) Kinship Bengali Culture, 1977, The Fruits of Worship, 2003; editor: Jour. Asian Studies, 1975-78. Sec. Coun. Am. Overseas Rsch. Ctrs., 2005—; v.p. Am. Inst. Indian Studies, 1974—76, treas., 1993—2001, pres.-elect, 2001—02, pres., 2002—; trustee Bangladesh Found., 1972—2005; dir. Indo-Am. Ctr., Chgo. Ford Found. fgn. area tng. fellow, India, 1960-61; Sch. Oriental and African Studies research fellow, London, 1962-63; sr. Fulbright fellow, West Bengal, India, 1968-69 Fellow AAAS, Am. Anthrop. Assn., Royal Anthrop. Inst. (Eng.); mem. Asian Studies, India League of Am. Found. (trustee). Office: U Chgo Dept Anthropology 1126 E 59th St Chicago IL 60637-1580 also: Am Inst Indian Studies 1130 E 59th St Chicago IL 60637

**NICHOLAS, ROBERT A.,** lawyer; BA magna cum laude, Amherst Coll., 1976; JD, Columbia U., 1980. Bar: NY 1981, Pa. 1985. Asst. dist. atty. Manhattan Dist. Atty.'s Office, 1980—85; with Reed Smith LLP, 1985—, former head Del. Valley Region litig. group, mng. ptnr. Phila. and Wilmington offices, 2000—, mem. exec. com. Bd. mem. World Affairs Coun. of Phila. Office: Reed Smith LLP 2500 One Liberty Pl 1650 Market St Philadelphia PA 19103-7301 Office Phone: 215-851-8252. Office Fax: 215-851-1420. Business E-mail: rnicholas@reedsmith.com.

**NICHOLAS, RONALD WAYDE,** business consultant; b. Dallas, July 29, 1938; s. J.W. Nicholas and Helen Eloise Whiteacre Duniven; m. Wanda Elaine Hagen, Aug. 27, 1960; children: Charles Wayde, Laurence Eliot. BBA, U. Tex., 1960. Dir. instnl. sales Anderson Clayton Foods, Dallas and Sherman, Tex., 1962-84; comml. dir. Anderson, Clayton S.A. de C.V., Mexico City, 1984-86; ptnr., operator 2 retail businesses, Pittsburg, Tex., 1986-87; assoc. gen. dir. Filippo's Pride, S.A. de C.V., Mexico City, 1987-97; bus. cons. Ray & Berndtson, Mexico City, 1997—. Cmty. advisor Jr. League of Mexico City, 1996—. Co-founder, bd. dirs. Am. Charities, A.C., Mexico City,

1996—; co-founder, chair Am. Charities Golf and Tennis Classic, 1996—; bd. mem. Tex./Mexico Bus. Coun., 2000—. Capt. U.S. Army, 1960-62. Mem. Am. C. of C. (bd. dirs. 1993-94, procedures auditor 1995-96), U.S./Mex. C. of C. (chair agr. com., bi-nat. bd., Mexico City bd. 1992—), VFW, Am. Soc. of Mex. (bd. dirs., pres.), Am. Benevolent Soc. (sec., bd. dirs., pres.), U. Tex. Ex Students Assn. (bd. dirs., v.p.), Phi Sigma Kappa (treas., pres.). Avocations: golf, stamp collecting/philately, cooking. Office: Ray & Berndtson Palo Santo 6 Col Lomas Alta Mexico City Mexico 11950 E-mail: ronwan@aol.com.

**NICHOLAS, STEPHEN J.,** orthopedic surgeon, sports medicine physician; BA in Biology, Harvard U., Cambridge, Mass., 1982; MD, NY Med. Coll., Valhalla, NY, 1986. Dir. Nicholas Inst. Sports Medicine and Athletic Trama, Lenox Hill Hosp., NYC, 2001—; chief, bioskills lab. Lenox Hill Hosp., NYC. Mem. adv. bd., Med. Leadership Coun. Lenox Hill Hosp.; worked extensively with profl. and collegiate athletes; orthopaedist NY Jets, NY Islanders, Hofstra U., & NJ Galdiators. Mem. NYC Sports Commn.; mem. alumni adv. bd. NY Med. Coll. Mem.: AMA, Am. Orthopaedic Assn., Quigley Orthopedic Soc., Med. Soc. State NY, Greater Met. Sports Medicine Soc., Am. Orthopedic Soc. for Sports Medicine (mem. publs. com.), Am. Coll. Sports Medicine, Am. Acad. Orthopedic Surgeons, The Forum Club. Office: 130 E 77th St New York NY 10021 Office Phone: 212-737-3301.

**NICHOLAS, THOMAS ANDREW,** artist; b. Middletown, Conn., Sept. 26, 1934; s. Michael and Lena (Sequenzia) N.; m. Gloria R. Spencer, Oct. 11, 1958; 1 child, Thomas Michael. Student of Ernst Lohrmann, 1949-53; scholarship student, Sch. Visual Arts, NYC, 1953-55 Instr. Famous Artists Schs., Inc., Westport, Conn., 1958-60; instr. painting, Rockport, Mass., 1963-66. Commd. by Franklin Mint Gallery Am. Art to produce lithographs of Am. coastline, 1977; one-man shows include Grand Cen. Galleries, NYC, 1962, 64, 66, 68, 70, 78, I.F.A. Galleries, Washington, 1964-92, A. Huney Gallery, San Diego, 1980. 82;, Carolyn Hill Gallery, Soho, NYC, 1988-89, 2 person show, 1992; represented in permanent collections Butler Inst. Am. Art, Youngstown, Ohio, Ga. Mus., Athens, New Britain Art Mus., Conn., U. Utah, Adelphi U., Greenshields Mus., Montreal, Can., Farnsworth Mus., Rockland, Maine, Springfield Art Mus., Mo., Ranger Collection at NAD (2 works), Peabody Mus., Salem, Mass., Hispanic Soc. Am., Peter A. Juley and Son Collection, Nat. Mus. Am. Art, Smithsonian Inst., Washington, NYC (3 works); recipient numerous awards 1957—, including, Emile Lowe award for watercolor Am. Watercolor Soc. 1961, watercolor prize 1964, Gold medal honor 1969, Clare Stout award 1971, Mary S. Litt award 1972, medal honor for watercolor Knickerbacker Artists 1962, Purchase award watercolor Butler Inst. Am. Art 1962, Henry Ward Ranger Fund purchase watercolor NAD 1962, 71, Obrig prize watercolor 1964, 66, 79, 87, gold medal honor watercolor Allied Artists Am. 1962, Grumbacher prize 1978, Today Mag. Art medal 1970, 74, gold medal honor watercolor Am. Artists Profl. League 1964, best landscape award 1974, gold medal 1978, Edwin S. Webster award honor watercolor Boston Soc. Watercolor 1964, gold medal honor watercolor Hudson Valley Art Assn. 1964, DuMond Meml. award 1971, Isabel Stinschneider Meml. award 1972, Herman Wick Meml. award Salmagundi Club, NYC, 1966, 2d prize 1966, June Justin J. Impasto award 1972, Arthur T. Hill prize 1973, Arthur T. Hill Meml. prize 1975, Louis Z. Seley prize 1978, Gwynne Lennon prize 1979, Gold medal honor oil Rockport Art Assn. 1966, 1969, 1976, 1985, 1996, 1997, 1999, 2002, 2003, cash award Wichita Centennial Watercolor 1970, Providence Art Club prize 1972, gold medal Franklin Mint Competition 1974, Gold medal Honor Acad. Assn. 1976, others. Elizabeth Greenshields grantee, 1961, 62; recipient Gold medal of Honor New Eng. Watercolor Soc., Boston, 1985, Acad. Artists Assn., 1985; named Knickerbocker Honoree Artist of Yr., 1989; recipient Grumbacher award watercolor, Acad. Artists Assn., 1990, Grumbacher Gold medal Gouache New Eng. Watercolor Soc., 1992, Gouache Transparent Watercolor, 1995. Mem. NAD (assoc. 1963-70, academician, 1970-, cert. merit watercolor 1992), Am. Watercolor Soc. (ea. v.p. 1994—, Dolphin fellow), Boston Watercolor Soc., Conn. Watercolor Socs., Allied Artists Am., Knickerbocker Artists (dir.'s prize 1971, Gold medal 1989), Boston Guild Artists (Grumbacher Gold medallion award watercolor 1988, No. Shore Arts Assn. award oil 1991), Rockport Art Assn. (Silver medal 1988, 94, Darrand award oil 1992, Cirino award 1st prize Gouache 1992, Clark Polupar award Gouache 1992, Cooley award graphics 1995, Clark Popular award Gouache 1995, Cirino award Gouache 1995, Davis Meml. award watercolor 1996, Mills Meml. award Gouache 1996), Hudson Valley Artists (Gold medal 1974, 85, 94, Huntington Meml. award oil 1995, Bohnert Meml. award oil 1996), Hudson Valley Art Assn. (honoree 2000). Office: Tom Nicholas Gallery 65 Main St Rockport MA 01966-1512 Office Phone: 978-546-9647. Personal E-mail: tangallery@aol.com. *I have been fortunate to have been encouraged by my family at an early age and have a number of people to thank for their support, especially my wife. I feel artists must never compromise their ideals and principles, no matter how high their standards. Originality and professional ethics with one's work make goals achieved meaningful. On the one hand, an artist should inwardly feel that there is little he can't accomplish, and yet he must learn to work within his realized limitations.*

**NICHOLAS, WILLIAM RICHARD,** lawyer; b. Pontiac, Mich., June 19, 1934; s. Reginald and Edna Irene (Bartlett) N.; m. Diana Lee Johnson, Aug. 20, 1960; children: Susan Lee, William Richard Jr. BS in Bus., U. Idaho, 1956; JD, U. Mich., 1962. Bar: 1963. Of counsel Latham & Watkins, Los Angeles, 1962-96. Contbr. numerous articles on taxation. Lt. (j.g.) USN, 1956-59. Mem. Calif. Bar Assn., Los Angeles County Bar Assn., Am. Coll. Tax Counsel. Home: 1808 Old Ranch Rd Los Angeles CA 90049-2207 Office: Latham & Watkins 633 W 5th St Ste 4000 Los Angeles CA 90071-2005 Office Phone: 310-485-1234.

**NICHOLAS, (RICHARD G. SMISKO),** bishop, b. Perth Amboy, N.J., Feb. 25, 1936; s. Andrew and Anna (Totin) S. Grad., Christ the Saviour Sem., Johnstown, Pa., 1959; student, Patriarchal Theol. Acad., Istanbul, Turkey; BA, U. Youngstown, 1961; BTh, U. Pitts. Ordained priest Am. Carpatho-Russian Orthodox Greek Diocese, 1959. Pastor Sts. Peter and Paul Ch., Windber, 1959-62; prefect of discipline. tchr. Christ the Saviour Sem., Johnstown, 1963-65; pastor Sts. Peter and Paul Ch., Homer City, 1965-71, St. Michael's Ch., Clymer, 1971-72, St. Nicholas Ch., N.Y.C. 1972-78; elevated to archimandrite Am. Carpatho-Russian Orthodox Greek Cath. Diocese, 1976; abbot Monastery of Annunciation, Tuxedo Park, N.Y., 1978-82; elected titular bishop of Amissos, aux. bishop Ukrainian Orthodox Diocese of Ecumenical Patriarchate, 1983; consecrated bishop Am. Carpatho-Russian Orthodox Greek Cath. Diocese, 1985, bishop, 1985—. Asst. Christ the Saviour Cathedral, 1963-65; chmn. XIV Diocesan Coun., New Brunswick, N.J., 1985, XV Diocesan Coun., Pitts., 1991, elevated to Met., 1998. Russian Orthodox. Office: 312 Garfield St Johnstown PA 15906-2122

**NICHOLL, JEFFREY SCOTT,** neurologist, educator; b. Stamford, Conn., Aug. 13, 1949; s. Robert George and Helen Holmes (Wilson) N.; m. Katherine Maris Mattes, Mar. 2, 1996; 1 child, Colleen Marie. BA, U. Pa., 1970; MD, Georgetown U., 1974. Diplomate in psychiatry, neurology, and clin. neurophysiology Am. Bd. Psychiatry and Neurology, Am. Bd. Emergency Medicine, Am. Bd. Clin. Neurophysiology. Intern Hosp. of the Good Samaritan, L.A., 1974—75; resident in psychiatry UCLA, 1975—77, 1978—79, fellow in epilepsy, 1998—2000; fellow in consultation-liaison psychiatry U. Calif., Irvine, 1979—80; emergency physician various instns, Calif., 1979—87, Kaiser-Permanente, San Diego, 1987—95; resident in neurology Tulane U., New Orleans, 1995—98, assoc. prof. clin. neurology and psychiatry, 2000—; clin. instr. neurology UCLA, 1998—2000. Avocations: sailing, swimming. Office: Tulane Univ Sch Medicine TB 52 1440 Canal St New Orleans LA 70112 Office Phone: 504-588-5231.

**NICHOLLS, BRUCE GILBERT,** lawyer; b. Lancaster, Pa., Sept. 26, 1955; s. Gilbert Lee and Joyce King (Bieber) N.; m. Elizabeth Sherrill Maul, Aug. 25, 1986. AB, Dartmouth U., 1977; CAS, Harvard U., 1983; MCF, Princeton U., 1985; JD, Suffolk U., 1988. Bar: Conn. 1987, Mass. 1988, U.S. Ct. Appeals (1st cir.) 1988, D.C. 1990, U.S. Supreme Ct. 1991. Atty. Day, Berry & Howard, Boston, 1987-94; ptnr. Nicholls & Maul, Boston, 1994—. Mem.

ABA, Boston Bar Assn., Mass. Bar Assn., Boston Athenaeum, Peabody Mus. Salem, Eastern Point Yacht Club. Avocation: sailing. Office: 12 Eastern Point Blvd Gloucester MA 01930-4231 Business E-Mail: bnicholls@juno.com.

**NICHOLLS, PETER J.,** academic administrator; BS in Math., London U., 1967; PhD in Math., Cambridge U., Eng., 1970. Prof. math. scis. No. Ill. U., 1971—91, acting dean Coll. Liberal Arts and Scis., 1988—89, assoc. dean Coll. Liberal Arts and Scis., 1987—88, 1989—91; dean Coll. Arts and Scis. Kans. State U., 1991—2002, prof. math., 1991—2002; provost, acad. v.p. Colo. State U., Ft. Collins, 2002—05; provost, exec. v.p. U. Conn., Storrs, 2005—. Office: Office of the Provost U Conn 352 Mansfield Rd Unit 2086 Storrs Mansfield CT 06269-2086 Office Phone: 860-486-4037.

**NICHOLLS, RICHARD AURELIUS,** retired obstetrician, gynecologist; b. Norfolk, Va., Aug. 12, 1941; s. Richard Beddoe and Aurelia (Gill) Nicholls; m. Geri Bowden, Feb. 24, 1986. BS in Biology, Stetson U., Deland, Fla., 1963; MD, Med. Coll. Va., 1967. Diplomate Am. Bd. Ob-Gyn. Ret., 1998; intern Charity Hosp. Tulane divsn., New Orleans, 1967—68, resident in ob-gyn., 1968—71; asst. prof. ob-gyn. Tulane Med. Sch., New Orleans, 1973—74, clin. asst. prof., 1974—83; pvt. practice specializing in ob-gyn. Pascagoula, Miss., 1974—89, Ocean Springs, Miss., 1989—98; ret. Mem. staff Singing River Hosp., chmn. surg. and ob-gyn. depts., 1979—80, chmn. ob-gyn. dept., 1984; mem. staff Ocean Springs Hosp., laser com., pharmacy com. and therapeutics com., chmn. ob -gyn. dept., mem. exec. bd., 1990—91, sec., treas. staff, 1991—92, exec. bd., 1991—92, chief staff, 1993—94. Contbr. articles to profl. jours. Bd. dirs. Miss Racing Assn. Maj. U.S. Army, 1971—73. Fellow: ACS, ACOG; mem.: Am. Cancer Soc. (bd. dirs. Jackson County br.), Am. Veneral Disease Soc., Conrald Collins Ob-Gyn Soc., Gulf Coast Ob-Gyn. Soc., New Orleans Ob-Gyn Soc., New Orleans Grad. Me4d. Assembly, So. Med. Soc., AMA, Am. Assn. Gynecol. Laparoscopists, Am. Fertility Soc., Singing River Med. Soc., Miss. State Med. Soc.

**NICHOLS, ALBERT L.,** economic consultant; b. Poughkeepsie, N.Y., Feb. 13, 1951; s. Albert and Margaret (Schaefer) N.; m. Eve Kaufman, June 16, 1973; children: Matthew, Elizabeth. AB, Stanford U., 1973; M of Pub. Policy, Harvard U., 1975, PhD, 1981. Assoc. prof. Harvard U., Cambridge, Mass., 1977-83, 85-88, dir. adminstrv. planning, 1988-89; dir. econ. analysis EPA, Washington, 1983-85; v.p. Nat. Econ. Rsch. Assocs., Cambridge, 1989—2004; dir. LECG, LLC, Cambridge, 2004—. Author: Targeting Economic Incentives for Environmental Protection, 1984; contbr. numerous articles to profl. jours. Nat. Merit scholar, 1969. Mem. ABA, AAAS, Am. Econ. Assn., Phi Beta Kappa. Avocation: woodworking. Home: 14 Baskin Rd Lexington MA 02421-6929 Office Phone: 617-761-0152. E-mail: anichols@lecg.com.

**NICHOLS, ALBERT MYRON,** retired minister; b. Creston, Iowa, Oct. 17, 1914; s. Albert Maurice and Lou (Myers) N.; m. Phyllis Cochran, June 28, 1939; children: Byron Albert, Phillip Garrett. AB, UCLA, 1936; BS, San Francisco Theol. Sem., 1940; DD, Occidental Coll., 1952. Ordained to ministry United Presbyn. Ch. in U.S.A., 1940. Pastor chs., North Hollywood, Calif., 1940-43; assoc. pastor Pasadena (Calif.) Presbyn. Ch., 1943-57; pastor 1st Presbyn. Ch., Pendleton, Oreg., 1957-82, ret., 1982. Chmn. gen. assembly com. on responsible marriage and parenthood United Presbyn. Ch. in U.S.A., 1959-62, mem. Bd. Christian Edn., 1966-72; mem. 1st coun. Synod of Pacific; moderator Oreg. Synod, 1968, 69; stated clk. Ea. Oreg. Presbytery, 1975-99. Pres. Pasadena Child Guidance Clinic, 1955-57, Glen Eddy Residents Assn., 2004; trustee San Francisco Theol. Sem., 1963-84; life trustee Lewis and Clark Coll., Portland, Oreg.; active Pendleton City Recreation Commn., 1965-2001; founding bd. dirs. Presbyn. Intercommunity Hosp., Whittier, Calif.; mem. State of Oreg. Health Coun., 1985-88, State Trauma Adv. Bd., 1987-91; chmn. City of Pendleton Capital Improvements Commn., 1983-2001. Named 1st Citizen of Pendleton, 1984. Home: 114 Glen Eddy Dr Niskayuna NY 12309 Personal E-mail: nicholsm@gleneddy.com.

**NICHOLS, C. WALTER, III,** retired trust company executive; b. NYC, Aug. 25, 1937; s. Charles Walter and Marjorie (Jones) N.; m. Anne Sharp, Aug. 8, 1959 (dec. Nov. 1996); children: Blair, Sandra, Walter, Hope; m. Helga Faulenbach, Aug. 24, 2002. V.p. Citibank, N.Y.C., 1962-78, J.P. Morgan & Co., N.Y.C., 1979-93; 1st v.p. Republic Nat. Bank N.Y., N.Y.C., 1994. Bd. dirs. Nichols Found., Inc., 1959—, Greenwich House, 1969-94, Westport River Watershed Alliance, 2004—; trustee Choate Rosemary Hall, 1972-77, 82-89, Westover Sch., 1979-81, ea. N.Y. chpt. Nature Conservancy, 1978-87; Caramoor Music Festival, 1980-90, John Jay Homestead, 1980-2000, Nat. Audubon Soc., 1983-87; mem. adv. bd. Wildlife Conservation Soc. (Bronx Zoo), 1987-94; trustee Guillain-Barré Syndrome Found. Internat., 2004—. Served to 1st lt. U.S. Army, 1960-62. Decorated Army Commendation medal. Mem. Naturist Soc., Nat. Assn. Railroad Passengers (bd. dirs. 1996-98), Am. Assn. for Nude Recreation, Yale (N.Y.C.) Club. Home: 1 Bent Oak Run Westport MA 02790-5179

**NICHOLS, CARL WHEELER,** retired advertising agency executive; b. Ottawa, Kans., Oct. 9, 1923; s. Carl Wheeler and Cora Merle (Hanks) N.; children: Christine, Carl Wheeler, Nancy, Matthew; m. Anna Norris, Apr. 18, 1992. Student, Baker U., 1940-41, U. Mo., 1941-43; BA, U. Mich., 1944. Research analyst Cunningham & Walsh, Inc. (advt. agy.), N.Y.C., 1946-49, copywriter, 1949-58, co-creative dir., v.p., 1958-59, dir. account mgmt., 1959-61, pres., 1961-69, chmn., chief exec. officer, 1969-85, chmn. emeritus, 1986. Trustee Vero Beach Mus. Art, 1996, chmn. bd. trustees, 2002—03. Capt. USMCR, 1943-46, 50-52, Korea. Named to Advt. Hall of Fame, 1986. Mem. N.Y. Advt. Coun. (bd. dirs. 1974-85), Am. Advt. Fedn. (dir. 1972—, chmn. 1975-76), Advt. Ednl. Found. (bd. dirs., sec., treas. 1983-91), Birch-wood Farms Golf Club, John's Island Club, Sigma Xi. Presbyterian (elder). Home: 241 Island Creek Dr Vero Beach FL 32963-3304

**NICHOLS, CLYDE RICHARD,** minister, consumer products company executive; b. N.Y.C., Apr. 15, 1945; s. William and Novella Nichols; m. Marsha A. Wade, Oct. 11, 1986; children: Forest, Marvin, Anthony, Gerald. BS, Met. State Coll., Denver, 1985; ThD, Berean Bible Coll., Dallas, 1994. Ordained pastor and bishop Fellowship of Deliverance Chs., Inc. Correction officer City and County Denver, 1981-92; sr. pastor, founder Redeeming Love Ch., Denver; sr. dir. M&C Enterprises, Inc., Denver; exec. dir. Josie M. Bedford Found. Dir. membership Greater Metro Denver Ministers Alliance Orgn., Denver, 1997-99. Bd. dirs. Denver Opportunities for Outreach and Reflection 2000—. Recipient award for outstanding cmty. work Cheyenne (Wyo.) br. NAACP, 1982, award for outstanding cmty. activities 24th Syl Morgan Acad. Arts, Denver, 1992, Juanita Gray award. Avocations: travel, reading, computers. Home and office: PO Box 31092 Aurora CO 80041-0092 Business E-Mail: mcenterpr31092@aol.com. E-mail: rev98crn@aol.com.

**NICHOLS, DANA,** language educator; d. Don and Jean Nichols. AA in English & Fgn. Langs., Gainesville State Coll., GA, 1995; BA in English & Spanish, Mercer U., Macon, Ga., 1997; MA in English, Ga. State U., Atlanta, 1998. Instrml. lab asst. Gainesville State Coll., Ga., 1997—2002, asst. prof. English, Spanish, 2002—. Scholar, Phi Theta Kappa, 1995—97. Mem.: Popular Culture Assn., Am. Soc. Study So. Lit. Avocations: travel, horseback riding. Office: Gainesville State Coll PO Box 1358 Gainesville GA 30503 Office Phone: 770-531-6071. Home Fax: 770-531-6067. Business E-Mail: dnichols@gsc.edu.

**NICHOLS, DAVID GREGORY,** anesthesiologist, pediatrician, educator; b. Hampton, Va., Oct. 1, 1951; MD, Mt. Sinai Sch. Medicine, 1977. Diplomate Am. Bd. Anesthesiology, Am. Bd. Pediatrics, Am. Bd. Critical Care Medicine. Intern Children's Hosp., Phila., 1977-78, resident in pediatrics, 1978-80; resident in anesthesiology U. Pa. Hosp., Phila., 1981-83; fellow in anesthesiology Critical Care Children's Hosp., Phila., 1983; assoc. prof. anesthesiology, critical care & pediatric medicine Johns Hopkins U. Sch. Medicine, Balt., 1991—98, prof. anesthesiology, critical care & pediatric medicine, 1998—, vice dean edn., 2000—. Dir. Pediat. ICU, Johns Hopkins U. Hosp., Balt., 1991-97, Pediat. Anesthesiology and Critical Care Medicine, 1997—.

Mem. Am. Soc. Anesthesiology, Soc. for Pediat. Rsch., Soc. Critical Care Medicine, Am. Thoracic Soc. Office: John Hopkins Sch Medicine 733 N Broadway Ste 115 Baltimore MD 21205

**NICHOLS, DEBRA,** bank executive; Sr. v.p. and dir. women's fin. adv. svcs. Wachovia Bank, Charlotte, NC, 1997—. Office: Wachovia Corp 301 South College St Charlotte NC 28288-0570

**NICHOLS, DONALD ARTHUR,** economist, educator; b. Madison, Conn., Dec. 20, 1940; s. Edward Charles and Ruth (Nilson) Nichols; m. Linda Powley, Aug. 19, 1962 (dec. Oct. 1982); children: Charles Spencer, Elizabeth Clarke; m. Barbara Jakubowski Noel, May 22, 1983 (dec. Dec. 26, 2000); m. Jane Bartels, Sept. 26, 2001. BA, Yale U., 1962, MA, 1963, PhD, 1968. Mem. faculty dept. econs. U. Wis., Madison, 1966—2006, prof., 1977—2006, chmn. dept. econs., 1983-86, 88-90, mem. exec. com. faculty senate, 1987-90, chmn., 1989-90, dir. Robert M. LaFollette Sch. Pub. Affairs, 2002—06, Wis. Idea fellow, 2004—06, emeritus prof., 2006—; lectr. Yale U., 1970—71; sr. economist Senate Budget Com., Washington, 1975—76; dep. asst. sec. for econ. policy and rsch. Dept. Labor, Washington, 1977-79; dir. Ctr. for Rsch. on Wis. Economy. Econ. advisor to gov. State of Wis., 1983—86; exec. sec. Gov.'s Coun. Econ. Advisors, 1983—86; mem. Gov.'s Export Strategy Commn., 1994—95, Gov.'s Econ. Growth Coun., 2003—; mem. acad. adv. coun. Fed. Res. Bank of Chgo., 2004—; bd. dirs. Thompson, Plumb Funds, 1987—, Sustainable Woods Co-operative, 2001—03; dir. Ctr. for World Affairs and Global Economy, 1995—2000; affiliate Christensen Assocs., Madison, 1999—; cons. in field. Author: (with Clark Reynolds) Principles of Economics, 1970, Dollars and Sense, 1994; contbr. articles to profl. jours. Trustee U. Wis. Bookstore, 1990-95; bd. advisors Am. Players Theatre, Spring Green, Wis., 1993-2001, Taliesin Coun., 2001-04. NSF fellow, 1963-66, 70-72; Nat. Commn. Employment Policy rsch. grantee, 1980-82; recipient William H. Kiekhofer Meml. Teaching prize U. Wis., 1973 Mem. Am. Econ. Assn., Royal Econ. Soc. Office: Univ Wis 1180 Observatory Dr Madison WI 53706

**NICHOLS, DONNA MARDELL,** nurse anesthetist; b. Mpls., Mar. 24, 1936; d. Donald Burma and Lucille Elvera Nichols. Diploma, Northwestern Hosp. Sch. Nursing, Mpls., 1957, Mpls. Sch. Anesthesia, 1959; BS in Nurse Anesthesia, U. Minn., 1977. RN Minn., 1957. Nurse anesthetist Hennepin County Med. Ctr., Mpls., 1959—60, Eden Twp. Hosp., Castro Valley, Calif., 1960—63, Bethesda Hosp., St. Paul, 1963—64, Meml. Bapt. Hosp., Houston, 1964—67, St. Joseph's Hosp., St. Paul, 1967—95; ret., 1995. Mem.: Minn. Assn. Nurse Anesthetists (bd. dirs. 1975—77), Am. Assn. Nurse Anesthetists (emeritus, cert. anesthetists). Avocations: golf, gardening, antiques. Home: 10427 Upton Ave S Bloomington MN 55431

**NICHOLS, EDIE DIANE,** real estate broker; b. Grahamstown, Eastern Cape Province, Republic of South Africa, Mar. 28, 1939; arrived in U.S., 1963; d. Cyril Doughtry and Dorothy Ethel (Nottingham) Tyson; m. John F. Nichols, Dec. 16, 1962 (div. Dec. 1978); 1 child, Ian Tyson. Adminstrv. asst. Am. Acad. Medicine, N.Y.C., 1963-64, Jack Lenor Larsen, Inc., N.Y.C., 1964-70; v.p. John Scott Tones, Inc., N.Y.C., 1971-76, Howard J. Rubenstein Assocs. Inc., N.Y.C., 1976-80; dir. comm. Carl Byoir & Assocs., N.Y.C., 1981-83; account supr. Hill and Knowlton, N.Y.C., 1983-85; broker Cross & Brown Co., N.Y.C., 1986-88; v.p. Marc Nichols Assocs., Inc., N.Y.C., 1989-95; mng. ptnr. Nichols Brown Internat., N.Y.C., 1995—2004; real estate broker Citi-Habitats, N.Y.C., 2005—. Trustee Ctrl. Pk. Hist. Soc., N.Y.C., 1978-80. Mem. NOW, Internat. Assn. Corp. and Profl. Recruitment, N.Y. Women in Comm. (pub. rels. chair 1980-81, v.p., programs bd. dirs. 1985-87), Fin. Women's Assn. of N.Y. (bd. dirs. 1997-98), City Club of N.Y. (trustee, v.p., fin. and devel. 1987-89). Democrat. Episcopalian. Office: Citi-Habitats 118 Perry St New York NY 10014 Home: 16 Stuyvesant Oval Apt 10F New York NY 10009 Office Phone: 212-561-0690. E-mail: ednny@aol.com.

**NICHOLS, EDWARD EDSON,** artist; b. Chgo., Nov. 6, 1929; s. Byron Davis and Dorothy Edson Nichols; m. Maxine Clara McClendon, Mar. 28, 1967; children: Patricia, Joan, Christopher, Jennifer. BFA, U. Kans., 1957, MFA, 1959. Asst. prof. art Miss. Women's U., Columbus, 1959—65; from asst. prof. to prof. U. Tex. Pan Am., Edinburg, 1966—99. Curator exhibits U. Tex. Pan Am., Edinburg, 1970—94. Watercolor, Ram Island, 1963, Rio Grande Regatta, 1991, Heart Strings, 2002, 13 mus. exhibits; 20 one-man shows; prin. works in 65 pub. and pvt. collections. With USN, 1952—56. Fellowship, Huntington Hartford Found., 1960, 1964, Rsch. grant, U. Tex. Pan Am., 1975. Mem.: Tex. Watercolor Soc. (Purple Sage Brush award 1998). Home: 2018 Shary Rd Mission TX 78572

**NICHOLS, ELIZABETH GRACE,** nursing educator, dean; b. Tehran, Iran, Feb. 1, 1943; d. Terence and Eleanor Denny (Payne) Quilliam; m. Gerald Ray Nichols, Nov. 20, 1965; children: Tina Lynn, Jeffrey David. BSN, San Francisco State U., 1969; MS, U. Calif., San Francisco, 1970, D of Nursing Sci., 1974; MA, Idaho State U., Pocatello, 1989. Staff nurse Peninsula Hosp., Burlingame, Calif., 1966-72; asst. prof. U. Calif.-San Francisco Sch. Nursing, 1974-82; chmn. dept. nursing Idaho State U., Pocatello, 1985-87; assoc. dean Coll. Health Scis. Sch. Nursing U. Wyo., Laramie, 1985-91, asst. to pres. for program revs., 1991-95; dean Coll. Nursing U. N.D., 1995—2004, Mont. State U., Bozeman, 2004—. Cons. U. Rochester, NY, 1979, Carroll Coll., Mont., 1980, divsn. Nursing Dept. HHS, Washington, U. Maine, Ft. Kent, 1992, Stanford Hosp. Nursing Svc., Calif., 1981—82, Ea. N.Mex. U., 1988, Met. State U., Minn., 1998, U. Nev-Reno, 2003; cons. evaluator Higher Learning Commn., 1993—2004; site visitor CCNE, 1998—; mem. accreditation review com. The Higher Learning Commn., 2001—04, budget com. Contbr. articles to profl. jours. Mem. adv. bd. U. Calif. Home Care Svc., San Francisco, 1975—82, Ombudsman Svc. of Contra Costa Calif., 1979—82, Free Clin. of Pocatello, 1984; mem. bd. of rev. coun. baccalaureate & higher degree programs, 1990—92; mem bd. dirs. United Way of Grand Forks/East Grand Forks, 2000—04. Recipient Jo Eleanor Elliott award, 1994; fellow ACE, U. Maine Sys., 1990—91. Fellow: Am. Acad. Nursing, Gerontol. Soc. Am. (chmn. clin. medicine sect. 1987, sec. 1990—93); mem.: ANA, Western Inst. Nursing (chmn. 1990—92, bd. govs., bd. dir. mid-west alliance), Idaho Nurses Assn. (dist. 51 adv. bd. dir. 1982—84), ND Nurses Assn. (pres. 2003—04), Oakland Ski Club. (1st v.p. 1981—82), Sigma Theta Tau. Democrat. Office Phone: 406-994-3784. Business E-Mail: egnichols@montana.edu.

**NICHOLS, EUGENE DOUGLAS,** mathematics professor; b. Rovno, Poland, Feb. 6, 1923; came to U.S., 1946, naturalized, 1954; s. Alex and Anna (Radchuk) Nichiporuk; m. Alice Bissell, Mar. 31, 1951. BS, U. Chgo., 1949, postgrad., 1949-51; MEd, U. Ill., 1953, MA, 1954, PhD, 1956. Instr. math. Roberts Wesleyan Coll., North Chili, N.Y., 1950-51, U. Ill., 1951-56; assoc. prof. math. edn. Fla. State U., 1956-61, prof., head dept., 1961-73; dir. Project for Mathematical Devel. of Children, 1973-77; dir. math program NSF, 1958-61; dir. Math. Inst. Elem. Tchrs., 1961-70; pres. Nichols Psychol. Svc., 1992—; prof. math. edn. Fla. State U., 1974-90. Chmn. U. Ill. Com. on Sch. Math., 1954-55; cons. editor math McGraw-Hill Book Co., 1956 Co-author: Modern Elementary Algebra, 1961, Introduction to Sets, 1962, Arithmetic of Directed Numbers, 1962, Introduction to Equations and Inequalities, 1963, Introduction to Coordinate Geometry, 1963, Introduction to Exponents, 1964, Understanding Arithmetic, 1965, Elementary Mathematics Patterns and Structure, 1966, Algebra, 1966, Modern Geometry, 1968, Modern Trigonometry, 1968, Modern Intermediate Algebra, 1969, Analytic Geometry, 1973, Holt Algebra 1, 1974, 78, 82, 86, 92, Holt Algebra 2, 1974, 78, 82, 86, 92, Holt Geometry, 1974, 78, 82, 86, Holt School Mathematics, 1974, 78, 81, Holt Pre-Algebra, 1980, 86, Holt Mathematics, 1981, 85, Elementary School Mathematics and How to Teach It, 1982, Geometry, 1991, Holt Pre-Algebra, 1992, Mathematics Dictionary and Handbook, 1993, 95, 98, 99; author: Pre-Algebra Mathematics, 1970, Introductory Algebra for College Students, 1971, Mathematics for the Elementary School Teacher, 1971, College Mathematics, 1975, College Mathematics for General Education, rev. edit., 1975. Named Fla. State U. Disting. Prof., 1968-69; recipient Disting. Alumni award U. Ill. Coll. Edn., 1970. Mem. Am. Math. Soc., Math. Assn. Am., Sch. Sci. and Math. Assn., Nat. Coun. Tchrs. Math., Coun. Basic

Edn., Text and Acad. Authors Assn., Pi Mu Epsilon, Phi Delta Kappa. Home: 3386 W Lakeshore Dr Tallahassee FL 32312-1305 Office Phone: 570-253-9362. Personal E-mail: eunichols@aol.com. *Do not look for a career-look for opportunities to do kind things for others. Be honest with yourself and with those around you.*

**NICHOLS, GUY WARREN,** retired institute executive, retired utilities executive; b. Colchester, Vt., Oct. 27, 1925; s. Guy W. and Gladys (Tomlinson) N.; m. Shirley Hibbard, June 21, 1947; children: Pamela, Gail, Sally. BSCE, U. Vt., 1947; postgrad., Worcester Poly. Inst. Sch. Indsl. Mgmt., 1953-56; MS in Bus. Adminstrn., MIT, 1961. With New. Eng. Electric System, Westborough, Mass., 1947-84, exec. v.p., 1968-70, pres., 1970-84, chief exec. officer, 1972-84, chmn. bd., 1978-84. Bd. dirs. Amoresco Inc. Chmn., trustee Woods Hole Oceanographic Instn., 1985-95. Sloan fellow, MIT, 1961. Fellow Am. Acad. Arts and Scis. Office: 25 Research Dr Westborough MA 01582-0001 Personal E-mail: looncall99@comcast.net.

**NICHOLS, HENRY ELIOT,** lawyer, director, savings and loan association executive; b. NYC; m. Frances Griffin Morrison, Aug. 12, 1950 (dec. July 1978); children: Clyde Whitney, Diane Spencer; m. Mary ann Wall, May 31, 1987. BA, Yale U., 1946; JD, U. Va., 1948. Bar: D.C. 1950, U.S. Dist. Ct. 1950, U.S. Ct. Appeals 1952, U.S. Supreme Ct. 1969. Assoc. Frederick W. Berens, Washington, 1950-52; sole practice Washington, 1952—. Real estate columnist Washington Star, 1966-81; pres., gen. counsel Hamilton Fed. Savs. & Loan Assn., 1971-74; vice chmn. bd. Columbia 1st Bank (formerly Columbia 1st Fed. Savs. & Loan Assn.), Washington, 1974-90, bd. dirs.; pres. Century Fin. Corp., 1971-90; regional v.p. Preview, Inc., 1972-78; bd. dirs., exec. com. Columbia Real Estate Title Ins. Co., Washington, 1968-78. Contbr. articles to profl. jours. Nat. adv. bd. Harker Prep. Sch., 1975-80; exec. com. Father Walter E. Schmitz Meml. Fund, Cath. U., 1982-83; bd. dirs. Vincent T. Lombardi Cancer Rsch. Ctr., 1979-84; del. Pres. Johnson's Conf. LAw and Poverty, 1967; vice chmn. Mayor's Ad Hoc Com. Housing Code Problems, Washington, 1968-71; mem. Commn. Landlord-Tenant Affairs Washington City Coun., 1970-71; vice chmn. Washington Area Realtors Coun., 1970; exec. com., dir. Downtown Progress, 1970; bd. dirs. Washington Mental Health Assn., 1973, Washington Med. Ctr., 1975. Capt. USAAF, 1942-46. Mem. Am. Land Devel. Assn., Nat. Assn. Real Estate Editors, Washington Bd. Realtors (pres. 1970, Realtor of Yr. 1970, Martin Isen award 1981), Greater Met. Washington Bs. Trade (bd. dirs. 1974-80), U.S. League Savs. Assns. (attys. com. 1971-80), Washington Savs. and Loan League, ABA, D.C. Bar Assn., Internat. Real Estate Fedn., Yale Club, Cosmos Club, Rolls Royce Club, Antique Auto Club, St. Elmo Club, Omega Tau Rho. Episcopalian. Achievements include patents in field. Home: Apt 905 4550 N Park Ave Chevy Chase MD 20815 Office Phone: 301-718-7888.

**NICHOLS, HENRY LOUIS,** lawyer; b. Collin County, Tex., Nov. 7, 1916; s. Jesse Cleveland and Leva (Stiff) N.; m. Elaine Guentherman, May 17, 1949; children: David Michael, Martha Marie. LL.B., So. Meth. U., 1940. Bar: Tex. 1939. Asst. city atty., Dallas, 1946-50; pvt. practice, 1951—. Mem. adv. bd. Ctr. for Legal Mcpl. Studies. Served to lt. col. AUS, 1941-46; col. USAR ret. Rsch. fellow Southwestern Legal Found., 1964. Fellow Am. Bar Found.; mem. ABA, Dallas Bar Assn. (pres. 1963), State Bar Tex., Tex. Bar Found. (charter), Park City Club. Home: 3131 Maple Ave Apt 13H Dallas TX 75201-1206 Office: 1800 Lincoln Plz Dallas TX 75201 Office Phone: 214-965-9900. Business E-Mail: hnichols@njdhs.com. *As a night-school graduate (Law School), I believe the opportunities in America are unlimited for anyone willing to work. Nowhere in the world are such opportunities available. We who live in the U.S.A. are blessed and the most fortunate of all people. We should strive to maintain that which our fathers preserved for us.*

**NICHOLS, IRIS JEAN,** retired illustrator; b. Yakima, Wash., Aug. 2, 1938; d. Charles Frederick and Velma Irene (Hacker) Beisner; (June 1963); children: Reid William, Amy Jo; m. David Gary Nichols, Sept. 21, 1966. BFA in art, U. Wash., 1978. Freelance illustrator, graphic designer, Seattle, 1966—2004; med. illustrator, head dept. illustration Swedish Hosp. Med. Ctr., Seattle, 1981-86; owner, med. and sci. illustrator Art for Medicine, Seattle, 1986—2003; ret. 2003. Med. illustrator U. Wash., Seattle, 1966-67; part-time med. illustrator, graphic coord. dept. art The Mason Clinic, 1968-78; instr. advanced illustration Cornish Coll. Arts, Seattle, 1988-90; organized, coordinated and gifted the artwork of Prof. Glen E. Alps of U. Wash. after his death in 1996 Illustrator various books including Bryophytes of Pacific Northwest, 1966, Microbiology, 1973, 78, 82, 94, 98, Introduction to Human Physiology, 1980, Understanding Human Anatomy and Physiology, 1983, Human Anatomy, 1984 Regional Anesthesia, 1990, many other med. and sci. books, and children's books on various subjects; exhibited in group shows at Seattle Pacific Sci. Ctr., summer 1979, 82, Am. Coll. Surgeons (1st prize 1974), N.W. Urology Conf. (1st prize 1974, 76, 2d prize 1975); pub. illustrations Constellation Pk. and Marine Res., City Seattle Pk., 1999, Whale Tail Park, Seattle. Pres. ArtsWest (formerly West Seattle Arts Coun.), 1983; chmn. West Seattle (Wash.) H.S. Art Acquisition Com., 2003—. Named to West Seattle H.S. Alumni Hall of Fame, 1986, Matrix Table, 1986-96. Mem. Assn. Med. Illustrators (Murial McLatchie Fine Arts award 1981), Nat. Mus. Women in the Arts (Wash. state com., bd. dirs. 1987-95, pres. 1993-94), Women Painters of Wash. (pres. 1987-89), U. Wash. Alumni Assn., Lambda Rho (pres. alumni assn. 1995-98, treas. 2002-04) Avocations: artwork, printmaking, small books.

**NICHOLS, J. LARRY,** energy executive, lawyer; b. Oklahoma City, July 6, 1942; s. John Whiteman and Mary (Davis) N.; m. Polly Puckett, Oct. 16, 1971; children: Tyler, Sally. BA in Geology, Princeton U., 1964; JD, U. Mich., 1967. Bar: Okla. 1967. Law clk. to chief justice U.S. Supreme Ct., Washington, 1967-68; spl. asst. to asst. atty. gen. U.S. Dept. Justice, Washington, 1968-70; dir. Devon Energy Corp., Oklahoma City, 1971—, pres., 1976—2003, CEO, 1980—, chmn., 2000—. Dir. Am. Stock Exch. Commr. Urban Renewal Authority Bd., Oklahoma City, 1989; pres. domestic petroleum coun. Okla. Nature Conservancy. Mem. Okla. Bar Assn. (bd. dirs., v.p.), Ind. Petroleum Assn. Am. (bd. dirs.), NAM (bd. dirs.), Oklahoma City C. of C., Econ. Club (pres. 1988-89). Office: Devon Energy Corp 20 N Broadway Ave Ste 1500 Oklahoma City OK 73102-8260*

**NICHOLS, JAMES RICHARD,** civil engineer, consultant; b. Amarillo, Tex., June 29, 1923; s. Marvin Curtis and Ethel (Nichols) N.; m. Billie Louise Smith, Dec. 24, 1944; children: Judith Ann, James Richard Jr., John M. BS in Civil Engring., Tex. A&M U., 1949, MS in Civil Engring., 1950; DHum (hon.), Tex. Wesleyan U., 1990. Registered profl. engr., Tex., Okla., N.Mex. Ptnr. Freese & Nichols, Inc., Cons. Engrs., Fort Worth, 1950-76, pres., 1977-88, chmn., 1988—. Chmn. Tex. Bd. Profl. Engrs. Former chmn. Ft. Worth Conv. and Visitors Bur.; bd. dirs. Pub. Comm. Found. North Tex., Tex. A&M Rsch. Found., Tex. Wesleyan U.; co-chmn. Metroplex Mission with Billy Graham. With U.S. Army, 1943—46. Fellow: Am. Soc. Engrs. Coun.; mem.: NSPE, ASCE (hon.), Tex. Water Conservation Assn., Ft. Worth C. of C. (bd. dirs., adv. coun.), Rotary, Ft. Worth Club, Exch. Club. Methodist. Home: 4821 Overton Woods Dr Fort Worth TX 76109-2429 Office: Freese & Nichols Inc 4055 Internat Plz Ste 200 Fort Worth TX 76109-4895 Office Phone: 817-735-7300. Personal E-mail: jrn@freese.com.

**NICHOLS, JAMES WALKER,** retired music educator; b. Sheboygan, Wis., Jan. 23, 1929; s. Verne Walker and Myrtle Olle Nichols; m. Eileen Elizabeth Costa, Aug. 15, 1959; children: Barbara Pettijohn, Ruth Paredes, James, David, Mark. B in Music Edn., Northwestern U., 1952, MusM, 1956. Music tchr. Earlville (Ill.) H.S., 1952—56, Torrance (Calif.) H.S., 1956—59, Grossmont H.S., La Mesa, Calif., 1959—88, Traner Sch., Reno, 1991; entertainment dir. San Diego Chargers, 1969—90; band dir. Southwest H.S., San Diego, 1994—2004; ret., 2004. Dir. Jimmy Nichols Jazz Band, Milw., 1944—50. Named Oustanding Music Tchr., Calif. Music Educators Assn., 1999; recipient Tchr. of Yr. award, 1998, Music Excellence award, San Diego Youth Symphony, 2001, Music Sweepstakes, 32 Sch. Dists., 1956. Mem.: NEA, ASCAP, Calif. Tchrs. Assn., So. Calif. Sch. Band and Orch. Assn. (adjudicator, Gold award 2004). Personal E-mail: jwnichols2005@hotmail.com.

**NICHOLS, JANET HILDRETH,** elementary school educator, childbirth and parenting educator; b. Glenwood Springs, Colo., July 1, 1948; d. Pershing Loveland and Myrna Jean Nichols; children: Carrie Christine Schultz, Taylor James Pruss. BA, U. N.Colo., 1971, MA, 1973. Lic. childbirth educator Lamaze Internat., 1982, cert. prenatal parenting instr. Prenatal Parenting, 2003. Spl. edn. tchr., kindergarten tchr. Ouray Pub. Schs., Colo., 1971—72; spl. edn. tchr. Jefferson County Schs., Lakewood, Colo., 1973—74; child find evaluator St. Vrain Pub. Schs., Longmont, Colo., 1979—80, tchr. physically handicapped, 1985—87; lead tchr. Mountain View Presch., Boulder, Colo., 1983—84; pre-acad. tchr. Boulder Valley Schs., 1987—92; kindergarten tchr. Douglass Elem. Sch., 1992—2006; tchr. Rocky Mt. Sch. for Gifted and Creative, 2006—. Childbirth & parenting instr. Boulder Cmty. Hosp., 1990—. Contbr. Head Start, Boulder, 1988—89. Grantee Math Edn. grant, Found. Boulder Valley Schs., 1995, Reading Comprehension grant, 2002, Map Making grant, 2003. Mem.: Lamaze Internat. (assoc.). Home: 1775 Holeman Dr Erie CO 80516 Business E-Mail: jan.nichols@bvsd.org. E-mail: jannichols548@yahoo.com.

**NICHOLS, JOHN ALDEN,** retired history professor; b. Westerly, R.I., Feb. 28, 1919; s. Thomas Pitman and Jennie Althea (Howland) N.; m. Barbara Searles Tuttle, June 8, 1946 (dec. Dec., 1975); children: Catherine Tyler Nichols Thompson, David Alden, Margaret Foster. BA with high honors, high distinction, Wesleyan U., Middletown, Conn., 1941; MA, Columbia U., 1948, PhD, 1951. History instr. Wesleyan U., Middletown, Conn., 1948-50, asst. prof. history, 1959-61, Skidmore Coll., Saratoga Springs, N.Y., 1950-51; fellowship Ford Found., 1951-52; editor Ginn & Co., Boston, 1952-59; assoc. prof. history U. Ill., Champaign-Urbana, 1961-67, prof. history, 1967-89; ret., 1989. Author: (books) Germany After Bismarck, 1958, The Year of the Three Kaisers, 1987; mng. editor Daedalus, 1959-61. Schiff fellow, Columbia U., N.Y.C., 1947, sr. rsch. fellow, Fulbright Program, West Germany, 1963. Mem. AAUP, Am. Hist. Assn., Philosophy Club (U. Ill.). Democrat. Avocations: piano, electronic organ. Home: 505 W Pennsylvania Ave Urbana IL 61801-4922 Home (Summer): 1741 Upper Hollow Rd Dorset VT 05251-9610

**NICHOLS, JOHN DOANE,** diversified manufacturing corporation executive; b. Shanghai, 1930; m. Alexandra M. Curran, Dec. 4, 1971; children: Kendra E., John D. III. BA, Harvard U., 1953, MBA, 1955. Various operating positions Ford Motor Corp., 1958-68; dir. fin. controls ITT Corp., 1968-69; exec. v.p., COO Aerojet-Gen. Corp., 1969-79, Ill. Tool Works Inc., Chgo., 1980-81, CEO, dir., 1982-95, chmn., 1986-96; pres., CEO Marmon Group Inc., Chgo., 2002—. Bd. dirs. Household Internat., Philip Morris Cos., Inc., Rockwell Internat.; overseer Harvard U., 1994-99, vis. com. Sch. Edn., com. athletics, com. univ. resources. Trustee U. Chgo., 1987-93, Lyric Opera Chgo., Mus. Sci. and Industry, Jr. Achievement Chgo., Chgo. Commerce Club Civic Com.; life trustee Chgo. Symphony Orch.; bd. dirs. Art Inst. Chgo., past chmn.; mem. bd. govs. Argonne (Ill.) Nat. Lab., 1988-93; vice chmn. exec. com. Chgo. Cmty. Trust, 1997—. Mem. Harvard Club (NY, Chgo.), Indian Hill Club (Winnetka, Ill.), Chgo. Club, Comml. Club, Econ. Club Chgo. Office: Marmon Group Inc 225 W Washington St Chicago IL 60606*

**NICHOLS, KATIE,** investment company executive; b. Des Moines, May 19, 1940; d. Gardner (Mike) and Lois (Thornburg) Cowles; m. Julian Strauss, June 11, 1960 (div. 1971); children: Elizabeth Lois Strauss Grossi, Gwen Beatrix Strauss Jenkins, Kate Anne Strauss Long; m. Roger Marvin Nichols, Sept. 1, 1973 (div. 1981); m. H.E. Rummel, Mar. 27, 1983 (div. 1994). Student, Cornell U., 1957—61. Prin., v.p. The Rummel Group, Inc., St. Petersburg, Fla., 1985—2003, chmn., 2003—, pres., 2003—, CEO, 2003—. Trustee Cowles Charitable Trust, NYC, 1985—. Vol. Hosp. Albert Schweitzer, Deschapelles, Haiti, 1961-63; vice chmn. Fla. Human Rels. Commn., Tallahassee, 1974-75; Dem. candidate Fla. Pub. Svc. Commn., 1976; commr. Fla. Pub. Svc. Commn., 1981-89, chmn., 1987-89; vice chmn. Fla. Corrections Commn., 1994-98; bd. dirs. Nat. Coun. on Crime and Delinquency, San Francisco, 1990—, chmn. 1997-98; bd. dirs. HAS2001 Campaign for Hosp. Albert Schweitzer, Haiti; trustee Cowles Charitable Trust, 1985—. Recipient Honor award, Fla. Human Rels. Commn., 1985. Mem. NOW, Emily's List, League of Women Voters of Fla. Democrat. Episcopalian. Avocations: reading, needlepoint. Home: 1682 Oceanview Dr Tierra Verde FL 33715-2500 Office: The Rummel Group Inc 1641 1st Ave N Saint Petersburg FL 33713-8935

**NICHOLS, LAURIE I.,** nurse; d. Halsey T. Jr. and Jean Lois Nichols; 1 child, Andrew. AAS in Nursing, Ocean County Coll., 1979; BA in Applied Arts and Scis., Georgian Ct. U., 2006. RN NJ. Nurse ICN St. Peters U. Hosp., New Brunswick, NJ.

**NICHOLS, MARGARET IRBY,** librarian, educator, library and information scientist; b. Maud, Tex., July 9, 1924; d. James Rainwater and Winnie (Pride) Irby; m. Irby Coghill Nichols Jr., Apr. 18, 1953 (div. Jan. 1992); children: Nina Nichols Austin, Irby C. Nichols III. BA, U. North Tex., 1945; MLS, U. Tex., 1957. Libr. Mercedes (Tex.) H.S., 1945-46; cataloger Bethany (W.Va.) Coll., 1946; chief reference libr. Tex. Tech U., Lubbock, 1946-48; ref. libr. El Paso Pl., 1949-51; chief reference libr. N.Mex. Mil. Inst., Roswell 1951-53; sch. libr. South Jr. H.S., Roswell, 1954-55; acad. dean Selwyn Sch., Denton, Tex., 1965-67; prof. Sch. Libr. and Info. Scis. U. North Tex., Denton, 1968-91, assoc. dean Sch. Libr. and Info. Scis., 1989-91, emeritus prof., 1996. Cons. in field, 1991—; exec. bd. North Tex. Regional Libr. Sys., 1996—, chair, 1997-99; chmn. exec. bd. Libr. Ptnrs., 2003— Author: Core Reference Collections, 1986, 2d edit., 1993, Guide to Reference Sources, 4th edit., 1992, Reference Sources for Small and Medium Libraries, 1988, 2d edit., 1994, Texas Information Sources, 1996, Building And Using A Core Reference Collection, 4th edit., 2004; contbr. articles to profl. jours. Named one of 100 Libr. Champions of 20th Century, Tex. Libr. Assn., 2001; recipient Margaret Irby Nichols award (named in her honor), North Tex. Regional Libr. Sys., 2004; Margaret Irby Nichols scholar, U. North Tex., 1992. Mem AI A (mm, com 1988 92), Tex I ibr. Assn. (exec. bd. 1983-86, 88-92, pres. 1984-85, Disting. Svc. award 1990, Lois Bebout Outstanding Svc. award Ref. Roundtable 1995, Tex. Libr. Champion 2001, recipient Elizabeth Crabb Disting. Svc. award 2003). Home: 2514 Royal Ln Denton TX 76209-2244 E-mail: nichols2514@charter.net.

**NICHOLS, MARK A.,** music educator; b. Ga., 1973; s. Glenn and Rita Nichols. MusB in Edn., Troy U., Ala., 1996; MusM in Edn., U. So. Miss., Hattiesburg, 2000. Band dir. Daleville H.S. Leader Boy Scouts Am., Montgomery, Ala., 1992—, Ala. Hiking Trails Soc., 2001—. Recipient Wallace Leadership scholarship, Troy U., 1992. Mem.: Ala. Bandmasters Assn., Ala. Jazz and Blues Fedn., MENC, Omicron Delta Kappa, Phi Mu Alpha. Avocations: backpacking, music-making, travel. Office: Daleville Band 626 N Daleville Ave Daleville AL 36322 Office Phone: 334-598-4462.

**NICHOLS, MICHAEL COOPER,** food products executive, lawyer; b. Birmingham, Ala., Feb. 4, 1952; s. F.W. and Jeannett (Cooper) N.; m. Marcia Couch, Sept. 23, 1976; children: Joshua, Jessica, Zachary, Anna. BA with honors, Brown U., 1974; JD, Emory U., 1977. Bar: Ga. 1977, Tex. 1981. Mem. Ga. Ho. of Reps., Atlanta, 1977-81; chief adminstrv. officer Appletree Mktg., Houston, 1988-91; gen. counsel SYSCO Corp., Houston, 1981-88, v.p., 1991—98, v.p., sec., gen. counsel, 1998—. Pres. Houston Food Bank, Houston, 1990—92; trustee Houston Police Officer Pension Fund; vice chmn. Houston Civil Svc. Commn., co-chmn.; bd. dir. Congregation Beth Israel, 1986. Home: 12155 Maple Rock Houston TX 77077 Office Phone: 281-584-1471. E-mail: nichols.mike@corp.sysco.com.

**NICHOLS, MIKE,** stage and film director; b. Berlin, Nov. 6, 1931; s. Nicholaievitch and Brigitte (Landauer) Peschowsky; m. Patricia Scott, 1957 (div.); m. Margot Callas, 1974 (div.); 1 child; m. Annabel Davis-Goff (div.); 2 children; m. Diane Sawyer, Apr. 29, 1988. Student, U. Chgo., 1950-53; student acting, Lee Strasberg. Ptnr. with Elaine May in comedy act; first appeared at Playwrights Theatre Club, Compass Theatre, Chgo.; N.Y. debut An Evening with Mike Nichols and Elaine May, 1960; acted in A Matter of Position, Phila., 1962; dir. (plays) Barefoot in the Park, 1963 (Tony award best dir.), The Knack, 1964, Luv, 1964 (Tony award best dir.), The Odd Couple, 1965 (Tony award best dir.), The Apple Tree, 1966, The Little Foxes, 1967, Plaza Suite, 1968 (Tony award best dir.), The Prisoner of 2d Avenue, 1971 (Tony award best dir.), Uncle Vanya (co-adapted), 1973, Streamers, 1976, Comedians, 1976, The Gin Game, 1977, (L.A. Drama Critics award) Drink Before Dinner, 1978, Lunch Hour, 1980, Fools, 1981, The Real Thing, 1984 (Tony award 1984,), Hurlyburly, 1984, Social Security, 1984, Elliot Loves, 1990, Death and the Maiden, 1992, Monty Python's Spamalot, 2005 (Outer Critic Cir., outstanding direction of a musical, 2005, Julia Hansen award for excellence in directing, Drama League, 2005, Tony award for best direction of a musical, 2005), (Julia Hansen Award excellence in directing, The Drama League, 2005); (films) Who's Afraid of Virginia Woolf?, 1966, (Academy award nomination best director 1966), The Graduate, 1967 (Academy award best director 1967), Catch-22, 1970, Carnal Knowledge, 1971, The Day of the Dolphin, 1973, The Fortune, 1975, Heartburn, 1986, Biloxi Blues, 1987, Working Girl, 1988 (Academy award nomination best director 1988), Wolf, 1994; dir., prodr.: Silkwood, 1983 (Academy award nomination best director 1983), Postcards From the Edge, 1990, Regarding Henry, 1991, The Birdcage, 1996, Primary Colors, 1998, What Planet Are You From?, 2000, Closer, 2004; prodr. All the Pretty Horses, 2000; prodr.: (musical) Annie, 1977; (TV movie) dir., exec. prodr. Wit, 2001, (miniseries) dir. Angels in America, 2003 (Emmy award Outstanding Directing for a Miniseries, Movie or Dramatic Special, 2004); performed at N.Y. musical Pres. Johnson's Inaugural Gala, 1965.

**NICHOLS, MIKE THOMAS,** writer; b. Fort Worth, Mar. 2, 1949; s. Samuel Delone and Margaret Ophelia (Greer) N. BA in Journalism, U. North Tex., 1971. Reporter Fort Worth Star Telegram, 1969-72, copy editor news, 1972-82, copy editor features, 1982-85, humor columnist, travel writer, 1985; freelance writer, editor Fort Worth. Author: Life and Other Ways to Kill Time, 1988, Balaam Gimble's Gumption, 2004 (Joe Bob Briggs Humor award for Funniest Tex. Book, Tex. Inst. Letters, 2005).

**NICHOLS, NANCY DIANE,** music educator; b. Akron, Ohio, Nov. 23, 1969; d. Philip Michael and Janis Leona Noles; m. Richard Alan Nichols, Feb. 12, 1994; children: Richard Clifton, Preston Michael, Natalie Elizabeth. MusB in Piano Pedagogy, Bob Jones U., 1991, MusM in Music Edn., 1997. Pvt. piano instr. Keyboard Artistry, Simpsonville, SC, 1993—94, Encore Music Studios, Columbus, Ohio, 1994—95, Fairfax (Va.) Christian Sch., 1995—97; pvt. piano and flute instr. Tampa, Fla., 1997—; Kindermusik instr., 1998—2000; adj. piano instr. Clearwater (Fla.) Christian Coll., 2005—. Mem.: Am. Coll. Musicians. Home: 4303 Woodside Manor Dr Tampa FL 33624 Personal E-Mail: nancynic1@netzero.net.

**NICHOLS, RALPH ARTHUR,** lawyer; b. Clinton, N.Y., Jan. 27, 1919; s. Arthur Britcher and Carrie Lena (Pitcher) N.; m. Pamela Crow Bermingham, May 3, 1947 (dec. Feb. 1980); children: Jeremy Nichols Pierce, Ralph A. Jr., Melinda Nichols Mayer; m. Victoria Requa Lalli, Sept. 5, 1981. AB, Hamilton Coll., 1940; LLB, Yale U., 1947. Bar: Conn. 1949, N.Y. 1947, U.S. Dist. Ct. (so. dist.) N.Y. 1949, U.S. Dist. Ct. Conn. 1950, U.S. Supreme Ct. 1959. Assoc. Burke & Burke, N.Y.C., 1947-49, Maguire, Walker & Middleton, Stamford, Conn., 1949-54; assoc., then ptnr. Cummings & Lockwood, Stamford, 1954—. Founder, former bd. dirs. Stamford Land Conservation Trust; former bd. dirs. Conservationists Stamford, Inc., Stamford YMCA; former bd. dirs., sec. Stamford Area Commerce and Industry; trustee Stamford YMCA. Lt. USNR, 1942-46, ETO, PTO. Fellow: Am. Coll. Trust and Estate Counsel; mem.: ABA, Yale Club (N.Y.C.), Woodway Country Club (Darien, Conn.), Phi Delta Phi. Republican. Episcopalian. Office: Cummings & Lockwood 6 Landmark Sq Stamford CT 06901 Home: 32 Bank St New Canaan CT 06840-6238 E-mail: rnichols@cl-law.com.

**NICHOLS, ROB (ROBERT STANLEY NICHOLS),** think-tank executive, former federal agency administrator; b. Seattle; m. Rebecca Nichols; 1 child Henry Alexander BS in Polit. Sci., George Washington U. Press advance rep. Office of Presdl. Advance The White House, Washington, staff asst. to Chief of Staff John Sununu; personal aide to sec. US Dept. Transport., Washington; mgr. campaign US Rep. Jennifer Dunn, 1994; polit. dir. Wash. State Rep. party, 1995; press sec. U.S. Rep. Jennifer Dunn, 1996-97; comms. dir. US Senator Slade Gordon, Electronic Industries Alliance; dep. asst. for pub. affairs US Dept. Treasury, Washington, asst. sec. for pub. affairs, 2003—05; pres., COO Fin. Services Forum, Washington, 2005—. Office: Fin Services Forum 601 Thirteenth St NW Ste 750 S Washington DC 20005 Fax: (202-224-9393.*

**NICHOLS, ROBERT HASTINGS,** lawyer; b. Mpls., Aug. 22, 1941; s. James Hastings and Judith (Beach) Nichols; m. Jean Christy, Nov. 30, 1968; children: Marc O., Seth J., Ethan D., Rebecca J. AB, Yale U., 1963; JD, U. Chgo., 1967. Bar: Ill. 1967, U.S Dist. Ct. (no. dist.) Ill. 1967, U.S. Ct. Appeals (7th cir.) 1972, U.S Dist. Ct. (ea. dist.) Wis. 1975, U.S. Ct. Appeals (DC cir.) 1976, U.S. Supreme Ct. 1986, U.S. Ct. Appeals (8th cir.) 1975; cert. in Pub. Affairs Coro Found., 1964. Ptnr. Cotton, Watt, Jones and King, Chgo., 1967—95; sr. atty. and coord. United Airlines Master Exec. Coun., Air Line Pilots Assn., Internat. AFL-CIO, 1995—. Cons. Govt. of New Zealand, Auckland, 1980; mem. lawyers coord. com. AFL-CIO. Contbr. articles to legal pubs. Mem.: Columbia Yacht Club. Democrat. Presbyterian. Home: 1030 E 49th St Chicago IL 60615-1814 Office: 9550 W Higgins Rd Ste 1000 Rosemont IL 60018 Office Phone: 847-292-1700. Business E-Mail: nicholsr@alpa.org.

**NICHOLS, ROBERT LEIGHTON,** civil engineer; b. Amarillo, Tex., June 24, 1926; s. Marvin Curtis and Ethel Nichols; m. Frances Hardison, June 8, 1948; children: Eileen, William C., Michael T. BSCE, Tex. A&M U., 1947, M3CE, 1948. Grad. asst., instr. Tex. A&M U., 1947-48; assoc. Freese & Nichols (and predecessors), Ft Worth, 1948-50, prin., 1950-77, v.p., 1977-88, pres., 1988-91, vice chmn., 1991-92, pres. emeritus, 1992—. Mem. Bldg. Stds. Commn., 1956—62; pres. Tri-State Water Resource Coalition, 2003—. Chmn. Horn Frog dist. Boy Scouts Am., pres. Longhorn coun., 1990—93, Ozark Trails coun., 1998—99; mem. City Coun., Webb City, Mo., 2004—; pres. Environ. Task Force Jasper and Newton Counties, Mo., 2004—. Mem.: NSPE (pres. 1977—78, pres. Ednl. Found.), ASCE, Environ. Task Force Jasper and Newton Counties (pres. 2003—), Tri-state Water Resource Coalition (pres. 2002—), Nat. Inst. Engring. Ethics (pres. 1995—97), Tex. Pub. Works Assn., Tex. Water Utilities Assn., Am. Pub. Works Assn., Water Environ. Assn. Tex. (pres. 1962—63), Water Environ. Fedn., Tex. Water Conservation Assn., Am. Water Works Assn., Tex. Soc. Profl. Engrs. (pres. 1965—66), C. of C. Webb City, Mo. (exec. dir. 1997—2001), Masons, Chi Epsilon, Tau Beta Pi. Methodist. Office Phone: 417-673-7151. E-mail: rln@freese.com.

**NICHOLS, ROBERT LYMAN,** retired foreign service officer, lecturer; b. Milw. s. Malcolm Strong and Ruth Mary (Lyman) N.; m. Virginia Lee Straghan, Sept. 7, 1947 (dec. 1989); children: Robert Gibbs (dec.), Nancy Lee, Peter Lyman. Student, Swarthmore Coll., 1942-43; BA, Tufts U., 1949; MA, Fletcher Sch. Law & Diplomacy, Medford, Mass., 1950; diploma, U.S. Army War Coll., Carlisle, Pa., 1969. Fgn. svc. officer US Dept. State, The Philippines, 1951-53, USIA, Italy, 1954—56, Holland, 1956—58, Taiwan, 1959—61, 1969—71, Hong Kong, 1961—65, Singapore, 1971—74; dir. Chinese divsn. Voice of America, 1966-69; dep. dir. East Asia Cultural Afairs U.S. Dept. State, Washington, 1974-76; dep. dir. East Asia USIA, Washington, 1977-79; ret., 1979; part-time faculty Cape Cod C.C., Barnstable, Mass., 1981—2004; tchr. of Chinese Light House Charter Sch., Orleans, Mass., 1997. China tour leader Chinese Ednl. Travel, Nat. Com. US-China Rels. and Smithsonian, 1980—95, 1999; tchr. Chinese Cape Cod Assn. Contbr. articles various newspapers Bd. dirs. Cape Cod Human Svcs., Hyannis, Mass., 1987-2004, chmn., 1990-91. Quartermaster 1st class, USN, 1943-46, Pacific. Episcopalian. Avocations: boating, fishing, theater acting, yoga. Home: 248 Kates Path Yarmouth Port MA 02675-1451 Personal E-mail: rlnichols@comcast.net.

**NICHOLS, RONALD LEE,** surgeon, educator; b. Chgo., June 25, 1941; s. Peter Raymond and Jane Eleanor (Johnson) N.; m. Elsa Elaine Johnson, Dec. 4, 1964; children: Kimberly Jane, Matthew Bennett. MD, U. Ill., 1966, MS, 1970. Diplomate Am. Bd. Surgery (assoc. cert. examiner, New Orleans, 1991), Nat. Bd. Med. Examiners. Intern U. Ill. Hosp., Chgo., 1966-67, resident in surgery, 1967-72, instr. surgery, 1970-72, asst. prof. surgery, 1972-74; assoc. prof. surgery U. Health Scis. Chgo. Med. Sch., 1975-77, dir. surg. edn., 1975-77; William Henderson prof. surgery Tulane U. Sch. Medicine, New Orleans, 1977—2002, vice chmn. dept. surgery, 1982-91, staff surgeon, 1977—2002, prof. microbiology, immunology, 1979—; William Henderson prof. surgery emeritus, 2003—; sr. vis. surgeon Med. Ctr. La., New Orleans, 1988—. Cons. surgeon VA Hosp., Alexandria, La., 1978-93, Huey P. Long Hosp., Pineville, La., 1978-2002, Lallie Kemp Charity Hosp., Independence, La., 1977-85, Touro Infirmary, New Orleans, Monmouth Med. Ctr., Long Branch, NJ, 1979-88; sr. vis. surgeon Med. Ctr. La., New Orleans, 1988—; mem. VA Coop. Study Rev. Bd., 1978-81, VA Merit Rev. Bd. in Surgery, 1979-82; sci. program com. 3d Internat. Conf. Nosocomial Infections, Ctr. Disease Control, sci. program and fundraising com. 4th Internat. Conf.; bd. dirs. Nat. Found. Infectious Diseases, 1989-2003, v.p., 1994-97, pres.-elect., 1997-99, pres., 1999-2001, trustee, 2003—; hon. fellow faculty Kasr El Aini Cairo U. Sch. Medicine, 1989; adv. com. on infection control Ctrs. for Disease Control, 1991-97; disting. guest, vis. prof. Royal Coll. Surgeons Thailand, 1989, 1992; infectious diseases adv. bd. Roche Labs., 1988-95, Abbott Labs., 1990-92, Kimberly Clark Corp., 1990-99, SmithKline Beecham Labs., 1990-95, Fujisawa Pharm., chmn., 1990-99, Bayer Pharm., 1994-2001, Merck Sharpe Dohme, 1996, Depotech, 1996, Zeneca Pharm., 1997-2000, Rhone-Poulenc Rorer, 1997-99, Wyeth-Ayrest Labs., 1998—, Pfizer Pharm., 1999, Searle Pharm., 1999-2001, GlaxoWellcome, 1999, Aventis, 1999-2000, Cubist Pharm., 2000—, Regent Med., 2003—, others; study group Prophylaxis Antibiotic Project La. Health Care Rev., Inc., 1995-2000, Nat. Com. Study Blood Borne Disease Transmission make Nat. Policy, Rockefeller Brothers Fund, 2001-03; apptd. by gov. La. commn. HIV and AIDS, 1999-; lectr. Royal Coll. Physicians and Surgeons, Can., 1998, Internat. Infectious Disease Soc. Ob-gyn., 1998, 2000 NY State Surg. Symposium, 1998, Dept. Surgery, U. Ark., 1998; nat. policy com. study innovative surgery reg. Greenwall Found., 2003—; lectr. in field. Author: (with Gorbach, Bartlett and Nichols) Manual of Surgical Infection, 1984; author, guest editor: (with Nichols, Hyslop Jr. and Bartlett) Decision Mking in Surgical Sepsis, 1991; guest editor, author: Surgical Sepsis and Beyond, 1993; mem. editl. bd. Current Surgery, 1977—, Hosp. Physician, 1980—, Infection Control, 1980-86, Guidelines to Antibiotic Therapy, 1976-81, Am. Jour. Infection Control, 1981-99, Internat. Medicine, 1983—, Confronting Infection, 1983-86, Current Concepts in Clin. Surgery, 1984—, Fact Line, 1984-91, Host/Pathogen News, 1984—, Infectious Diseases in Clin. Practice, 1991—, surg. sect. editor, 1992—, Surg. Infections: Index and Revs., 1991—, So. Med. Jour., 1992-97, ANAEROBE, 1994—, Surg. Infections, 1998—, Clin. Infectious Diseases, 1999—; editl. adv. bd. MD Consult Infectious Diseases, 2002-04; mem. adv. bd. Physician News Network, 1991-95; patentee (with S.G. schoenberger and W.R. Rank) Helical-Tipped Lesion Localization Needle Device; patentee in field. Elected faculty sponsor graduating class Tulane Med. Sch., 1979-80, 83, 85, 87, 88, 91-92; apptd. La. Commn. HIV and AIDS, 1999—. Maj. USAR, 1972-75. Recipient House Staff tchg. award U. Ill. Coll. Medicine, 1973, rsch. award bd. trustees U. Health Scis., Chgo. Med. Ctr., 1977, Clin. Prof. of Year U. Health Sci., 1977, Tchg. award Owl Club, 1980-86, 90, Douglas Stubbs Lectr. award Nat. Med. Assn. Surg. Sect., 1987, Prix d'Elegance award Men of Fashion, New Orleans, 1993; named Prof. of Yr. U. Health Sci., Chgo. Med. Sch., 1977, Clin. Prof. of Yr. Tulane U. Sch. Medicine, 1979, Brit. Jour. Surgery Lectr., 1997, 1st Ann. Warren Cole Lectr., 2001; elected to Wall of Fame, Lakeview H.S., Chgo., 2006. Fellow Infectious Disease Soc. Am. (mem. FDA subcom. to develop guidelines in surg. prophylaxis 1989-93, co-recipient Joseph Susman Meml. award 1990), Am. Acad. Microbiology, Internat. Soc. Univ. Colon and Rectal Surgeons, ACS (mem. oper. rm. environ. com. 1978-80, vice chair oper. rm. environ. com. 1980-81, chmn. oper. rm. environ. com. 1981-83, sr. mem. oper. rm. environ. com. 1983-87, mem. internat. rels. com. 1987-93, sr. mem. internat. rels. com. 1993-97); mem. AMA, Nat. Found. for Infectious Diseases (bd. dirs.), Joint Commn. on Accreditation of Health Care Orgn. (Infection Control adv. group. 1998-98, sci. program com. 3d internat. conf. nosocomial infections CDC/Nat. Found. Infectious Diseases 1990, FDA Subcom. to Develop Guidelines in Surg. Prophylaxis, 1989-93; prophylactic antibiotic study group La. Health Care Rev. Inc. 1996-2000, clin. advisor, mem., 2001—, AIDS commr. State of La. 1992-94, mem. 1999-), 5th Nat. Forum on AIDS (sci. program com.), U.S. Pharmacopeial Convention Inc. (adv. panel surg. drugs and devices 1995-2000, nominating com. The Heinz Awards 1995-96), Assn. Practitioners in Infection Control (physician adv. coun. 1991-98), Internat. Soc. Anaerobic Bacteria, So. Med. Assn. (vice chmn. sect. surgery 1980-81, chmn. 1982-83), Assn. Acad. Surgery, NY Acad. Sci., Warren H. Cole Soc. (pres.-elect 1988, pres. 1989-90), Assn. VA Surgeons, Soc. Surgery Alimentary Tract, Inst. Medicine Chgo., Midwest Surg. Assn., Ctrl. Surg. Assn., Ill. Surg. Soc., European Soc. Surg. Rsch., Collegium Internationale Chirugiae Digestivae, Chgo. Surg. Soc. (hon.), New Orleans Surg. Soc. (bd. dirs. 1983-87), Soc. Univ. Surgeons, Surg. Soc. La., Southeastern Surg. Soc., Phoenix Surg. Soc. (hon.), Hellenic Surg. Soc. (hon.), Ctrl. NY Surg. Soc. (hon.), Tulane Surg. Soc., Alton Ochsner Surg. Soc., Am. Soc. Microbiology, Soc. Internat. de Chirugie, Surg. Infection Soc. (sci. study com. 1982-83, fellowship com. 1985-87, ad hoc sci. liaison com. 1986-89, program com. 1986-87, chmn. ad hoc com. rels. with industry 1990-93, mem. sci. liaison com. 1995-96), Soc. for Intestinal Microbial Ecology and Disease, Soc. Critical Care Medicine, Am. Surg. Assn., Kansas City Surg. Soc., Bay Surg. Soc. (hon.), Cuban Surg. Soc. (hon.), Panhellenic Surg. Soc. (hon.), Tacoma Surg. Club (hon.), Sigma Xi, Alpha Omega Alpha. Episcopalian. Home: 1521 7th St New Orleans LA 70115-3322 Office: 1430 Tulane Ave New Orleans LA 70112-2699 Office Phone: 504-988-5168. Personal E-mail: rlnmd@yahoo.com. Business E-Mail: ronald.nichols@tulane.edu.

**NICHOLS, SHARON LOUISE,** educator, researcher; b. Williamsport, Pa., June 12, 1969; d. William Nichols and Patricia Ann Thompson. BA, Bucknell U., 1991; MA, U. Ariz., 1997, PhD. 2003. Postdoctoral rsch. fellow Ariz. State U., Phoenix, 2003—04; asst. prof. ednl. psychology U. Tex., San Antonio, 2004—. Co-author (with Tom Good): America's Teenagers Myths and Realities: Media Images, Schooling, and the Social Costs of Indifference. Mem.: APA, Am. Ednl. Rsch. Assn. (chair adolescence spl. interest group 2005—). Office: U Tex at San Antonio 501 W Durango Blvd Ste DB 4342 San Antonio TX 78207 Office Phone: 210-458-2035. Business E-Mail: sharon.nichols@utsa.edu.

**NICHOLS, STEPHEN GEORGE,** Romance languages educator; b. Cambridge, Mass., Oct. 24, 1936; s. Stephen George and Marjorie (Whitney) N.; m. Mary Winn Jordan, June 22, 1957 (div. 1972); children: Stephen Frost (dec.), Sarah Winn; m. Edith Karetzky, 1972; stepchildren: Laura Natalie Karetzky, Sarah Karetzky Rothman. AB cum laude, Dartmouth Coll., 1958; PhD, Yale U., 1963; LittD (hon.), U. Genève, 1992. Asst. prof. French UCLA, 1963-65; assoc. prof. comparative lit. U. Wis.-Madison, 1965-68, chmn. dept., 1967-68; prof. Romance langs. and comparative lit. Dartmouth Coll., 1968-84, chmn. dept. comparative lit., 1969-72, 74, 79-82, chmn. dept. romance langs., 1974-77, Edward Tuck prof. French, 1984-85, chmn. dept. French and Italian, 1983-77, liaison officer Sch. Criticism and Theory, 1983-85; faculty Dartmouth Inst., 1983-85, faculty dir., 1984-85; prof. romance langs. U. Pa., 1985-86, Edmund J. Kahn Disting. prof. humanities, 1986-92; James M. Beall prof. French and humanities Johns Hopkins U., Balt., 1992—; grad. group chmn. French and Italian U. Pa. 1986-88, chmn. dept. romance langs., 1987-88, assoc. dean for humanities, 1988-91; acting chair French, 1993-94; dir. grad. studies dept. French The Johns Hopkins U., Balt., 1992-94; R. Champlin and Debbie Sheridan interim dir. Eisenhower Libr., Johns Hopkins U., 1994-95, chmn. dept. French, 1995—. Dir. sch. Criticism and Theory, 1995-2000; vis. prof. U. Tel Aviv, 1977, NYU, 1979-81, Exeter (Eng.) U., 1980, Amz.State U., 1982, U. Calif., Irvine, 1985, Sch. Criticism and Theory, 1989, 95, Humanities Rsch. Inst. U. Calif., 1990, Ecole Pratique des Hautes Etudes, Paris, 1995, U. Pa., 1995, Dartmouth Coll. 1995-96, Cornell U., 1996—, Ecole Normale Superieure, Paris, 1996, 98,

2000, 02, U. Paris, 1997; rev. panelist NEH, 1979-81, 84, 91, Guggenheim fellow, 1987-88; ACLS sr. fellow, 2001-02; Phi Beta Kappa vis. scholar, 1983-84; Lauder fellow Aspen Inst. for Humanistic Study, 1988; adv. bd. Inst. d'Etudes Francaises d'Avignon, Bryn Mawr Coll., 1965—; dir. seminar NEH, 1975-79, Mellon summer seminar in humanities Johns Hopkins U., 1993, 94; exec. com. Ea. Comparative Lit. Conf.; mem. adv. coun. dept. comparative lit. Princeton U., 1982-88, chmn., 1984-88; co-dir. Ctr. Cultural Study, U. Pa., 1986-92; co-dir. Louis Marin Ctr. for French Studies, 1992—; advisor Waverly Consort, 1987-95; adv. bd. Soc. Humanities Cornell U., 1993—; reviewer Guggenheim Fellowship applications, medieval sect., 1995—; French, 1996—; chair task force on artifact in libr. collections Coun. on Libr. Info. Resources, 1999-2001. Author: Formulaic Diction and Thematic Composition in the Chanson de Roland, 1961, The Songs of Bernard de Ventadorn, 1962, 2d edit., 1968. Le Roman de la Rose, 1967, 72, Comparists at Work, 1968, The Meaning of Mannerism, 1972, Mimesis: From Mirror to Method, Augustine to Descartes, 1982, Medieval and Renaissance Theories of Representation, 1984, Romanesque Signs: Early Medieval Narrative and Iconography, 1983, 85, Images of Power: History/Text/Discourse, 1986, The Legitimacy of the Middle Ages, 1988, The New Philology, 1990, Boundaries and Transgressions, 1991, The New Medievalism, 1991, Commentary as Cultural Artifact, 1992, Medievalism and the Modernist Temper: On the Discipline of Medieval, 1996, The Whole Book: Miscellany and Order in the Medieval Manuscript, 1996, The Evidence in Hand: The Artifact in Library Collections, 2001, L'Altérité du Moyen Age, 2003; editor: (book series) Parallax: Revisions of Culture and Society, 1987—; asst. editor French Rev., 1968-88; mem. editl. bd. Olifant, 1974-94, Medievalia et Humanistica, 1974-95, Medievalia, 1975—, Comparative Lit. Studies, 1986, Publ. of the MLA, 1988-89, Recentiores, 1991—, Modern Lang. Notes, 1992; adv. bd. Colleagues Press, 1986-96, Exemplaria: A Jour. Medieval Theory, 1987—; adv. com. PMLA, 1980-84; adv. editor Romanic Rev., 1986—, Storia della Storiographia, 1992—. Rotary Found. fellow U. d'Aix Marseilles, France, 1958-59; fellow Inst. for Rsch. in Humanities, 1966-67, NEH fellow, 1978-79, sr. fellow Sch. of Criticism and Theory, 1988—. Fellow Medieval Acad. Am.; mem. Acad. Lit. Studies (nominating com. 1974-78, sec.-treas. 1978-87), Dante Soc., Internat. Comparative Lit. Assn., New Eng. Medieval Assn. (adv. com. 1981-85), MLA (chmn. com. on careers 1985-86, James Russell Lowell prize com. 1986-88, com. on proff. ethics 1987-88, del. assembly 1994-97), Medieval Acad. Am., Soc. Rencevals (sec.-treas. Am. sect. 1964-69). Home: 5 Saint Martins Rd Baltimore MD 21218-1815 Office: Johns Hopkins Univ Romance Languages and Lit 3400 N Charles St Baltimore MD 21218 Office Phone: 410-516-4736. E-mail: stephen.nichols@jhu.edu.

**NICHOLS, STEVEN,** apparel executive; b. 1942; With Nichols Foot Form Corp., 1962-79; pres. Stride Rite Retail Corp., 1979-82, Stride Rite Footwear, 1982-86, dir., v.p. merchandise, 1980-86; pres., chmn. bd. K-Swiss, Inc., Westlake Village, Calif., 1987—. Recipient INC 500 award, INC Mag., 2001. Office: K-Swiss Inc 31248 Oak Crest Dr Westlake Village CA 91361-4643 Fax: (818) 706-5390.

**NICHOLS, STEVEN PARKS,** mechanical engineer, educator, lawyer, academic administrator; b. Cody, Wyo., July 1, 1950; s. Rufus Parks Nichols and Gwen Sena (Frank) Keyes; m. Mary Ruth Barrow, Aug. 5, 1990; 1 child, Nicholas Barrow Nichols. PhD, U. Tex., Austin, 1975, JD, 1983. Assoc. dir. Tex. Space Grant Consortium, Austin, 1989-91, dir. Design Projects Program, 1989—2002; dep. dir. Ctr. for Energy Studies, U. Tex., Austin, 1988-91, dir. of Ctr., 1991-99, acting dir. Ctr. for Electromechanics, 1994-99, assoc. prof. mech. engring., 1996—2000, prof. mech. engring., 2004—, assoc. chair dept. mech. engring., 1999—2001, dir. Ctr. for Energy and Environ. Resources, 1998—99, fellow Ctr. for Nano and Molecular Scis., 1998—99, dir. Chair of Free Enterprise, 2001—, fellow 2001—, assoc. v.p. rsch., 2002—. Bd. dirs. Assn. Mfg. Excellence; chmn. Nat. Coun. Space Grant Dirs., NASA, 1989-92; bd. dirs. So. Coalition for Advanced Transp., 1994-99, chair elect 1998-99, chair 1998-00; bd. dirs. Nat. Inst. for Engring. Ethics, 1996-01; chmn. mgmt. divsn. ASME Internat., 1999-01, exec. com. engring. and tech. mgmt., 1999-; rsch. integrity officer, 2004-. Patentee (with others) pulsed welding techniques, railgun igniter, inert burner, rail thruster, other patents pending. Recipient Olympus Innovation award, 2005. Fellow ASME (Disting. Lectr. award 2004-05), IC2 Inst. (sr.), Ctr. Nano and Biotech.; mem. NSPE, ABA, Am. Soc. Engring. Edn. (Fred Merryfield Design award 2001), Nat. Inst. Engring. Ethics (bd. govs. 1997-93, 96-01), NY Acad. Scis. Home: 1400 Lorrain St Austin TX 78703-4023 Office: U Tex Dept Mech Engring Austin TX 78712

**NICHOLS, TERRY JEAN,** elementary school educator, music educator; b. Marion, Ind., Feb. 22, 1950; d. Gordon Clayton and Dorothy Lee (Mendell) Hoyt; m. Gary Wilbur Nichols, May 26, 1973; children: Gary Allen, Terry Jason, Jerry Ryan, Kerry Andrew. BS, U. Indpls., 1972; M Comms., W.Va. U., 2003. Vocal music tchr. Decatur (Ind.) County Schs., 1972-73; gen. and vocal music tchr. Wood County Schs., Parkersburg, W.Va., 1973—80; tchr. gen. and vocal music Edison Jr. HS, Parkersburg, W.Va., 1973—80; gen. and vocal music tchr. Jackson Jr. HS, 1980—93, Jefferson Elem. Ctr. Parkersburg, 1993—, Organist Christ United Meth. Ch., 1974—2004; handbell dir. Christ United Meth., 1976—2004; accompanist Wood Co. Elem. Music Festival, 1993—, Wood Co. Elem. Honors Choir, 1995—; adj. faculty W.Va. U., 2005—. Mem. NRA, Am. Choral Dirs. Assn., Wood Co. Reading Coun., Am. Federation Tchrs. (tchr cert. of commendation award, 1992-93), Am. Assn. Ret. Persons, Music Educators Nat. Conf., W.Va. Music Educators Nat. Conf., Ind. Music Educators Nat. Conf., U. Ind. Alumni Assn., Mu Phi Epsilon. Republican. Meth. Avocations: walking, piano, reading, crocheting. Home: 3508 6th Ave Parkersburg WV 26101-6313 Office: Jefferson Elem Ctr 1103 Plum St Parkersburg WV 26101-4936 Office Phone: 304-420-9554. Personal E-mail: terryjean3508@hotmail.com. Business E-mail: tjnichol@accewss.k12.wv.us.

**NICHOLS, TIM,** song writer, publisher; m. Patsy Nichols; children: Tyler, Landon. Writer: songs Heads Carolina, Tails California (Jo Dee Messina), I'll Think of a Reason Later, Girls Lie Too (Terri Clark), This Ain't No Thinkin' Thing, writer (with Craig Wiseman): songs Live Like You Were Dying (Tim McGraw) (Song of Yr. Country Music Assn., 2004). Office: Big Loud Shirt Industries LLC 1105 17th Ave S Nashville TN 37215

**NICHOLS, VICKI ANNE,** financial consultant, librarian; b. Denver, June 10, 1949; d. Glenn Warner and Loretta Irene (Chalender) Adams; m. Robert H. Nichols. Oct. 28, 1972 (div.); children: Christopher Travis, Lindsay Meredith. BA, Colo. Coll., 1972; postgrad., U. Denver, 1976-77. Treas., controller, dir. Polaris Resources, Inc., Denver, 1972-86; controller InterCap Devel. Corp., 1986-87; treas., controller, dir. Transnat. Cons., Ltd., 1986-91; web coord. Jefferson County (Colo.) Pub. Libr., 1996—. Dir., owner Nichols Bus. Services. Home: 4305 Brentwood St Wheat Ridge CO 80033-4412 Office: 10200 W 20th Ave Lakewood CO 80215 Business E-Mail: vnichols@jefferson.lib.co.us.

**NICHOLS, WAUNELL B.,** elementary school educator; d. Thomas Olem and Audrey Bennett; m. William Garvie Nichols, Sept. 26, 1970; children: William Garvie Jr., Johnny Carl, Alicia Lynn. BA in sci., Abraham Baldwin Agrl. Coll., 1986—87; BS in edn., Valdosta State U., 1988—89; MS in edn., Ga. Southwestern U., 1999—2001. Early Childhood Education, K-4 GA, 1989, Middle Grades Education, 4-8 GA, 1991, Teacher Support Specialist GA, 1999, ESOL Endorsement GA, 2002, Masters Middle Grades Education GA, 2001. Tchr. Berrien Co. Bd. of Edn., Nashville, Ga., 1989—91, Tift Co. Bd. of Edn., Tifton, Ga., 1992—. Student advisor Omega Co-Ed Y-Club, Ga., 1997—; reader of the yr., head chmn. Internat. Reading Assoc., Tifton, Ga., 1992—2006. Recipient Omega Tchr. of the Yr., Omega Elem. Sch., 1997—98. Mem.: Nat. Coun. for History Edn., Internat. Reading Assoc. (corr.). Office Phone: 229-528-4293.

**NICHOLS, WILLIAM CURTIS,** psychologist, educator, marriage and family therapist, consultant; b. Fayette, Ala., Apr. 16, 1929; s. William Curtis and Eva (Hargett) N.; m. Alice Louise Mancill, May 29, 1954 (dec. 1990); children: Alice Camille, William Mancill, David Paul; m. Mary Anne Pace,

Feb. 29, 1992. AB, U. Ala., 1953; EdD, Columbia U., 1960. Diplomate Am. Bd. Profl. Psychology. Asst. prof. sociology U. Ala., Birmingham, 1960-63; postdoctoral fellow Merrill-Palmer Inst., 1963-64, mem. psychotherapy faculty, 1965-69; prof. sociology Samford U., Birmingham, Ala., 1963-65; pvt. practice clin. psychology and marital and family therapy Grosse Pointe, Mich., 1969-73, 76-87; pvt. practice psychology, marital and family therapy Birmingham, Mich., 1976-87; prof. home and family life, dir. marriage and family counseling Fla. State U., 1973-76; exec. dir. Gov.'s Constituency Children, Fla., 1987-89; pvt. practice marital and family therapy S.E. Family Inst., 1989-90; pres. William Nichols Assocs., Organizational Cons., 1990-91; cons., marital and family therapist Atlanta, 1992—97; cons. in field, 1997-98; with The Nichols Group, Inc., 1998. Adj. prof. clin. psychology U. Detroit, 1976-83; adj. prof. family therapy Fla. State U., 1990-91; adj. prof., grad. faculty child and family devel. dept. U. Ga., 1992-05, founder, chair adv. com. Family Therapy Archives, 1993—, The Nichols Group, Inc., 1998-99. Author: Treating People in Families: An Integrative Framework, 1996, Marital Therapy: An Integrative Approach, 1988, Treating Adult Survivors of Childhood Sexual Abuse, 1992, The AAMFT: Fifty Years of Marital and Family Therapy, 1992, Family Therapy Around the World: A Festschrif to Florence Kaslow, 2004; co-author: Systematic Family Therapy, 1986; editor: (with others) Handbook of Family Development and Intervention, 2000; editor The Family Coord., 1970-75, Jour. Marriage and Family Counseling, 1974-76, Contemporary Family Therapy: An Internat. Jour., 1986-2006, Family Therapy News, 1986-91, The Internat. Connection, 1996-99; mem. editl. bd. Internat. Jour. Family Therapy, 1977-85, Jour. Divorce and Remarriage, 1976-83, 85—, Sage Family Studies Abstracts, 1977-99, Family Systems Medicine, 1982-96, Jour. Marital and Family Therapy, 1984—, Jour. Family Psychotherapy, 1990—, Jour. Family Psychology, 1986-90. Mem. mental health and health coms. Detroit Mayor's Commn. on Children and Youth, 1966-69; bd. dir. Family and Children's Svc., Oakland, Mich., 1977-87, chmn., 1984-86, dir. emeritus, 1987—. With C.E. U.S. Army, 1948-49. Recipient Svc. award Ala. Assn. for Mental Health, 1962, Spl. award for Outstanding Contbns. Fla. Assn. Marriage and Family Therapy, 1977, 82, 90; NSF fellow U. Colo., 1963, Disting. Svc. to families award Southeastern Coun. on Family Rels., 1996. Fellow: APA, Am. Assn. Marriage and Family Therapy (dir. 1969—72, founding editor Jour. Marital and Family Therapy 1974—76, chmn. accreditation com. 1976—77, pres.-elect 1979—80, dir. 1979—83, pres. 1981—82, Spl. awards 1976, 1978, Disting. Leadership awards 1982, 1983, Disting. Leadership award 1991, Orgnl. Contbns. award 1992), Am. Psychol. Soc.; mem.: Am. Family Therapy Acad. (charter), Internat. Family Therapy Assn. (bd. dirs. ex-officio 1996—98, charter, editor Internat. Connections 1996—99, pres.-elect 1998—99, pres. 2000—01), Ga. Assn. for Marriage and Family Therapy (pres.-elect 1994—95, pres. 1996), Mich. Bd. Marriage Counselors (chmn. 1980—87), Nat. Coun. on Family Rels. (bd. dir., exec. com. 1969—78, pres. 1976—77), Mich. Assn. Marriage Counselors (pres. 1969—71, chmn. profl. liaison com. 1972—73), Mich. Inter-Profl. Assn. on Marriage, Divorce and Family (com. chmn. 1968—71, 1974—86, trustee 1977—80, Orgnl. Contbn. award 1992), Assn. Marital and Family therapy Regulation Bds. (MFT examination adv. bd. 1989—92), Am. Assn. Marriage and Family Therapy Edn. and Rsch. Found. (trustee 1992—94). Home: 755 W Lake Dr Athens GA 30606 E-mail: nicholsw@aol.com.

**NICHOLS, WILLIAM FORD, JR.,** foundation administrator, educator, health science association administrator; b. Palo Alto, Calif., July 4, 1934; s. William Ford and Elizabeth (Woodyatt) N.; m. Rosemary Peterson, 1988; children: Deborah, John, Andrew. AB, Stanford U., 1956, MBA, 1958. CPA, Calif. With Price Waterhouse, San Francisco, 1958-69, Price Waterhouse & Co., Sydney, Australia, 1966; asst. contr. Saga Corp., Menlo Park, Calif., 1969-72, contr., 1972—, asst. treas., 1981-83; assoc. prof. San Jose State U. 1983-88; treas. William and Flora Hewlett Found., Menlo Park, 1985-2000. Trustee Investment Fund for Founds., 1991-2001. Bd. dirs. Lucile Packard Found. for Children's Health, Palo Alto, Calif., 1999—2006; trustee Oreg. Shakespeare Festival Endowment Fund, 2005-. Mem. AICPA, Calif. Soc. CPA's, Inst. Mgmt. Accts. (nat. v.p. 1974-75, bd. dirs.), Fin. Execs. Inst. (pres. Santa Clara Valley chpt. 1979-80), Palo Alto Club, Alpha Omega Alpha (asst. treas. 1985—). Home: 620 Sand Hill Rd Apt 220-D Palo Alto CA 94304-2098

**NICHOLS, WILLIAM OWEN,** conservationist; b. Appleton, Wis., Mar. 11, 1939; s. Freeman Alfred and Lila (Arvidson) N.; m. Susan Karen Babbitt, Oct. 20, 1962; children: Sarah Kay, John Freeman. BS in Biology, U. Wis. 1961. Park ranger Yellowstone Nat. Park, 1960-61, Shenandoah Nat. Park, 1964-70; supr. park ranger Mammoth Cave Nat. Park, 1970-73; chief park ranger Cumberland Gap Nat. Park, 1973-82; supt. Abraham Lincoln Birthplace, 1982-85, Vicksburg (Miss.) Nat. Mil. Park, 1985—. Pres. United Way of West Ctrl. Miss., Vicksburg, 1990-91; bd. dirs. Miss. Children's Home Soc., Jackson, 1986—; trustee Vicksburg-Warren County Libr., 1992—. Mem. Rotary (pres. Vicksburg club 1989-90). Presbyterian. Avocations: gardening, bird watching, walking, reading. Office: Vicksburg Nat Mil Park 3201 Clay St Vicksburg MS 39183-3469 Address: Nichols 1004 Windy Lake Dr Vicksburg MS 39183-8751

**NICHOLSON, BRUCE J.,** insurance company executive; BS, St. Olaf Coll., Northfield, Minn., 1968. With Ministers Life Ins. Co., Mpls., 1975-1984, Towers Perrin Co, Mpls., 1984-1990; exec. v.p., CFO Lutheran Brotherhood, Mpls., 1990—97, exec. v.p., COO, 1997—99, pres., COO, 1999—2000, pres., CEO, 2000—02, Thrivent Fin. for Lutherans, Mpls., 2002—. Mem. bd. regents St. Olaf Coll.; bd. mem. Luther Sem., Minn. Orchestral Assn., Minn. Bus. Partnership, Fox Cities C. of C. Fellow: Soc. of Actuaries; mem.: Am. Acad. of Actuaries. Office: Thrivent Financial for Lutherans 625 4th Ave S Minneapolis MN 55415*

**NICHOLSON, CIE (CYNTHIA NICHOLSON),** marketing executive, beverage company executive; b. Chgo. With R.J. Reynolds; dir. innovation Pepsi Cola N. Am., 1997; dir. Mountain Dew, 2000; v.p. Mountain Dew Pepsi Cola N. Am., v.p. flavors, 2002, v.p. carbonated soft drink flavors, v.p. non-carbonated beverages, 2004—05, chief mktg. officer, exec. v.p., 2005—. Named a Marketer of the Year, Brandweek, 2002. Avocation: golf. Office: Pepsi North America 700 Anderson Hill Rd Purchase NY 10577*

**NICHOLSON, COY LEE,** English educator, writer; b. Hanford, Calif., Sept. 15, 1936; s. Coy Hargrove and Retha Alice Nicholson. AA, Little Rock Jr. Coll., 1955; BA, Millsaps Coll., 1957; MA, U. Miss., 1959. General Secondary Certificate in Teaching State of Calif., 1960. Tchr. Turlock HS, 1959—64; instr. Modesto Jr. Coll., 1964—96. Author: (book) Common Ground, 2000; author: (and illustrator) Speakeasy, 2005. Mem. Democratic Nat. Com.; founder of Retha Alice Medley Nicholson prize Yellville-Summit H.S., Ark., 2001. Recipient Cert. of Recognition for Achievement in Lit. Arts, Stanislaus County Arts Coun., Calif., 2001; Wallstreet Jour. fellow, Fresno State U., 1961, scholar, Nat. Endowment for the Humanities, 1964, 1978. Mem.: Acad. Am. Poets (assoc.). Avocation: calligraphy. Home: 1605 June Dr Modesto CA 95350

**NICHOLSON, DIANE M.,** special education educator; BS in Psychology, Ga. Coll., 1977; MEd in Behavior Disorders, West Ga. Coll., 1989, EDs in behavior disorders, 1993. Cert. K-12 in behavior disorders, learning disabilities, mental retardation and inter-related TSS, early childhood edn. 2005. Behavior disorder/learning disability resource room instr. Whitesburg Elem. Sch., Carroll County Bd. Edn., 1980—87, 1988—91; academic therapist Burwell Psychoeducational Ctr., Carrollton, Ga., 1987—88; behavior disordered program instr. Ctrl. Mid. Sch. Carroll County Bd. Edn., 1991—92; grad. asst., tchg. asst. spl. edn. dept. West Ga. Coll., Carrollton, 1992—93, tchng. asst. for seminar for pre-tchrs., 1993, adj. instr., 1993—95, instr., 1994, adj. instr., 1995; resource tchr. for emotional and behavior disorders/learning disabled/mildly mentally handicapped Carroll County Bd. Edn., Ga., 1993—. Consultant, team mem. (book) Language Movement Strategies, 1983. Mem.: Phi Delta Kappa. Avocations: reading, computers. Home: 25 Agean Way Whitesburg GA 30185

**NICHOLSON, DOUGLAS ROBERT,** accountant; b. Avon, N.Y., Dec. 4, 1921; s. Robert William and Ruth (Neff) N.; m. Gertrude Jane Scott, Apr. 24, 1944; children— Laurie, Scott, Susan, Steven. AB, U. Rochester, 1942, MS, 1948. Baseball player St. Louis Cardinal Farm Teams, 1942, 46; staff acct. Oliver & Clapp, 1948-49; sr. acct. Charles L. Clapp & Co., 1949-51; tchr. income taxes U. Rochester, 1950-61; office mgr. Williams, Clapp & Co., 1951-53, ptnr., 1953-56; prin. Haskins & Sells, CPA's, Rochester, N.Y., 1956-59, ptnr., 1959-67, ptnr.-in-charge Rochester office, 1967-82. Author: After Reagan-Bush is it Too Late, 2002. Pres. Estate Planning Coun. Rochester; team capt. YMCA capital fund dr., 1961, Rochester Inst. Tech. new campus fund dr., 1964; chmn. spl. gifts com. U. Rochester, 1965, group leader 38 million capital fund campaign, 1966; mem. acctg. adv. bd. Syracuse U., 1968; adv. com. M.S. program Rochester Inst. Tech. Bd. Dirs.; treas. Highland Hosp., Rochester; bd. dirs. Hosp. Computer Ctr. Rochester, Rochester Regional Rsch. Libr. Coun.; mem. deferred giving adv. coun. Rochester Inst. Tech.; mem. N.Y. State Bd. Pub. Accountancy, 1977-82. Lt. USN, 1942-45, WWII. Decorated two battle stars; recipient Gannett Newspapers awards, 1956, SUNY Empire State medal for philanthropy, 1999. Mem. AICPA, N.Y. State Soc. CPAs (past pres. Rochester), Nat. Assn. Accts., Am. Acctg. Assn., Am. Mgmt. Assn., Rochester C. of C., Beta Alpha Psi. Democrat. Unitarian (trustee). Clubs: Oak Hill Country, University, Genesee Valley. Home and Office: 663 Lake Rd Webster NY 14580-1552

**NICHOLSON, ELLEN ELLIS,** clinical social worker; b. Boston, Apr. 1, 1940; d. George Letham and Mary Stirling (Money) McIver; divorced; 1 child, Matthew Norman Ellis. Dental Hygienist, Forsyth Coll., 1959; BS, Northeastern U., 1973, MEd in Counseling, 1974; MSW, Boston U., 1984. Registered dental hygienist, Mass. Dental hygienist, 1959—66; clin. coord., pvt. dental practice Forsyth Dental Ctr., Boston, 1966—70; dir. vol. counseling Solomon Mental Health Ctr., Lowell, Mass., 1974—75; social worker East Boston Social Ctrs., Inc., 1976—77; dir. youth family counseling, 1977—79; supr. family svc. Boston Housing Authority, 1979—81; social worker Mass. Soc. Prevention Cruelty to Children, Hyannis, 1984—86, supr., 1986—93, clinic dir., 1993—95; dir. profl. svcs. Child and Family Svc. of Cape Cod, Hyannis, 1995—98, dir., 1998—2005, dir. Abuse Prevention Svcs., 1995—96, cons., therapist Child & Family Svcs. Cape Cod, 2005—. Psychotherapist Riverview Sch., Sandwich, Mass., 1989-93. Advisor youth group Christ Episcopal Ch., Needham, Mass., 1960-64, St. Paul's Ch., Newburyport, Mass., 1964-65; vol. counselor Solomon Mental Health Ctr., Lowell, 1972-74; chair Barnstable County Children's Task Force, 1994-96; intern. adv. com. Barnstable County Sexual Abuse Intervention Network, 1994-96; mem. task force Barnstable County Juvenile Firesetters, 1995-96, mem. steering com., 1996—; mem. adv. bd. Cape and Islands Child Advocacy Ctr.; mem. Cape & Islands Domestic Violence Coun. Bd., 1998—. Mem. NASW, Am. Profl. Soc. on Abuse of Children, Assn. for Treatment of Sexual Abusers, Sigma Phi Alpha, Sigma Epsilon Rho, Kappa Delta Pi. Avocations: travel, ballroom dancing, skiing. Office: Child and Family Svc Cape Cod 1019 Rt 132 Hyannis MA 02601-1839

**NICHOLSON, HENRY HALE, JR.,** surgeon; b. Statesville, NC, June 22, 1922; s. Henry Hale and Martha Haseltine (Miller) N.; m. Freda Hyams, Sept. 24, 1956; children: Henry Hale III, Thomas Dalton Miller, John Christie, Michael Witherspoon, Freda Amanda, W. Stuart Cooper. BA in Chemistry, Duke U., 1944, MD, 1947; grad., USAF Sch. Aviation Medicine, 1952. Diplomate Am. Bd. Gen. Surgery, Am. Bd. Colon and Rectal Surgery. Rotating intern U. Wis. Gen. Hosp., Madison, 1947-48; resident in gen. surgery Med. Coll. Va., Richmond, 1948-49, Alton Ochsner Hosp. and Clinic, New Orleans, 1949-51, 53-55; inaugeral resident in colon and rectal surgery, 1955-56; resident in gen. surgery Tulane U., La. Charity Hosp., New Orleans, 1949-51, 53-55; pvt. practice gen., colon and rectal surgery, aerospace medicine Charlotte, NC, 1956—; sr. surg. staff mem. Carolinas Med. Ctr. and Mercy Hosp., Charlotte. Sr. active staff Presbyn. Hosp., Charlotte; sr. active teaching staff Carolinas Med. Ctr., 1956-85, cons. staff, 1985—; surg. cons. Surgeon Gen. USAF, 1971-82. Mem. Airport Authority Charlotte/Douglas Internat. Airport, 1992—; mem. Mayor's Com. of 100 to study regional transp. and make appropriate recommendations, 1993-94; sr. examiner FAA, 1952—; mem. athletic-med. bd. N.C. Shrine Bowl, 1980-2003. With U.S. Army, 1943-46. Maj. flight surgeon USAF, 1951-53, Korea; col. USAFR, 1961-82. Decorated Legion of Merit; recipient Disting. Svc. medal N.C.; decorated command flight surgeon award U.S. Air NG, 1981, 1st alternate flight surgeon award USAF, 1982. Fellow ACS, Am. Soc. Colon and Rectal Surgeons; mem. Mecklenburg County Med. Soc. (pres. 1972), Charlotte Surg. Soc. (pres. 1987), Shriners (Scottish Rite), Masons (32 degree), Jesters, Alton Ochsner Surg. Soc., Hazel Creek Trout Club, Robert Burns Soc., St. Andrews Soc. of Carolina, Air Force Assn., Hound Ears Club (Blowing Rock, N.C.), Charlotte Country Club, Alpha Tau Omega, Phi Chi, Omicron Delta Kappa. Methodist. Avocations: golf, skiing, fly fishing, travel, painting.

**NICHOLSON, HOWARD LEE,** history professor; b. Hagerstown, Ind., Jan. 1, 1950; s. Floyd and Grace Trilby Nicholson; 1 child, Erik Lee. PhD, Miami U., Oxford, Ohio, 1992. Lic. tchr. Ind., 1973. Prof. No. Mich. U., Marquette, 2000—06; prof. history, soc. studies edn. Benefactor student tchg. scholar No. Mich. U., 2005—06. Mem.: Nat. Coun. Social Studies, Nat. Hist. Soc. (assoc.). Home: 912-20 Cleveland Ave Marquette MI 49855 Office: Northern Michigan University 1401 Presque Isle Ave Marquette MI 49855 Office Phone: 906-227-2586. Home Fax: 906-227-2229; Office Fax: 906-227-2229. Business E-Mail: hnichols@nmu.edu.

**NICHOLSON, JACK,** actor; b. Neptune, NJ, Apr. 22, 1937; raised by John and Ethel May N.; m. Sandra Knight, June 17, 1962 (div. Aug. 8, 1968); children: Jennifer, Lorraine Broussard. Acting debut: (Hollywood stage prodn.) Tea an Sympathy; actor: (films) Cry-Baby Killer, 1958, Studs Lonigen, 1960, Little Shop of Horrors, 1960, Ensign Pulver, 1964, The Trip, 1967, Easy Rider, 1969 (Acad. award nomination best supporting actor), Five Easy Pieces, 1970, Carnal Knowledge, 1971, A Safe Place, 1971, The Last Detail, 1974 (Cannes Film Festival prize, BAFTA award best actor, Acad. award nomination best actor), Chinatown, 1974 (BAFTA award best actor, Acad. award nomination, NY Film Critics Circle award, Golden Globe award best actor), Tommy, The Passenger, 1975, The Fortune, 1975, One Flew Over the Cuckoo's Nest, 1975 (Golden Globe award best actor, Acad. award best actor, NY Film Critics Circle award, BAFTA award best actor), The Missouri Breaks, 1976, The Last Tycoon, 1976, The Shining, 1980, The Postman Always Rings Twice, 1981, Reds, 1981 (BAFTA award best supporting actor, Acad. award nomination best supporting actor), The Border, 1982, Terms of Endearment, 1983 (Acad. award best supporting actor, Golden Globe award best actor), Prizzi's Honor, 1985, Heartburn, 1986, The Witches of Eastwick, 1987, Broadcast News, 1987, Ironweed, 1987 (Acad. award nomination best actor), Batman, 1989, Man Trouble, 1991, A Few Good Men, 1992, Hoffa, 1992, Wolf, 1994, The Crossing Guard, 1995, Mars Attacks!, 1996, The Evening Star, 1996, Blood and Wine, 1996, As Good As It Gets, 1997 (Acad. award best actor, Golden Globe award best actor, SAG award best actor), The Pledge, 2001, About Schmidt, 2002 (Acad. award nomination best actor, Golden Globe award best actor), Anger Management, 2003, Something's Gotta Give, 2003, The Departed, 2006; prodr.: Head, 1968, Ride the Whirlwind, The Shooting; dir.: Drive, He Said, 1971; dir., actor: (films) Goin' South, 1978, The Two Jakes, 1990. Co-recipient (with Bobby McFerrin) Grammy award for best recording for children, 1987; recipient Life Achievement award, Am. Film Inst., 1994, Cecil B. DeMille award, 1999. Office: Bresler Kelly & Assocs 11500 W Olympic Blvd Ste 510 Los Angeles CA 90064-1578*

**NICHOLSON, JIM (ROBERT JAMES NICHOLSON),** secretary of veterans affairs, former ambassador; b. Struble, IA, Feb. 4, 1938; s. Don and Helen Nicholson; m. Suzanne Nicholson; children: Nick, Katie, R.J. BA, U.S. Mil. Acad., West Point, 1961; MA in Pub. Policy, Columbia U., 1969; JD, U. Denver, 1972; PhD in Pub. Soc. (hon.), Regis U., 2001; PhD (hon.), John Cabot U., 2002. Atty., Denver, 1973-78; founder Nicholson Enterprises, Inc., 1978, Renaissance Homes, Denver, 1987; committeeman from Colo. Rep. Nat. Com., 1986—2000, vice chmn, 1993—97, chmn., 1997—2001; US amb. to The Holy See US Dept. State, Rome, 2001—04; sec. US Dept. Veterans

Affairs, Washington, 2005—. Chmn. task force presdl. primaries and caucuses Rep. Nat. Com., 1996, chmn. rules com., 1993-97, mem. budget com. Author: (non-fiction) The United States and the Holy See-The Long Road, 2002. Bd. dirs. Daniels Fund. With U.S. Army, 1961—69, with USAR, 1969—91. Decorated Bronze Star, Combat Infantry badge, Meritorious Svc. medal with oak leaf cluster, Vietnamese Cross for Gallantry, 2 Air medals, Horatio Alger award, 2000, Pres. medal, Georgetown U., 2003; inducted as a Knight in the Sovereign Mil. Order of Malta, 1999, named a Knight of the Grand Cross of the Order of Pius IX, 2003. Office: US Dept Veterans Affairs 810 Vermont Ave Washington DC 20420*

**NICHOLSON, JOSEPH BRUCE,** real estate developer; b. San Jose, Calif., Jan. 21, 1940; s. Wilmot Joseph and Ruth (Russell) N.; m. Susan Knight, Nov. 1963 (div. 1972); children: Kelsey Erin, Craig Wilmot; m. Linda Mirassou, Aug. 1992. BArch, U. Oreg., 1963. Exec. v.p. Nicholson-Brown Inc., Santa Clara, Calif., 1967-80; prin. Nicholson Assocs., Aptos, Calif., 1977—; v.p., gen. mgr. Nicholson-Wilson Co., Santa Clara, 1980-83; prin. The Nicholson Co., Campbell, Calif., 1984—; v.p. Pacific Property Ventures Inc., Campbell, 1988—; pres. Nicholson Constrn. Inc., Campbell, 1989—; v.p. Nicholson Property Mgmt. Inc., Campbell, 1989—; pres. The Nicholson Family Found., 1996—. Bd. dirs. Transmetrics Inc., San Jose. Bd. dirs. Triton Mus., Santa Clara, 1979, Hope Rehab. Svc., San Jose, 1979, United Way Ctrl. Area, San Jose, 1991. Devel. Engring. Rsch. Inst., Carmel, Calif., 1999—, Tannery Art Ctr., Santa Cruz, 2003—; mem. adv. bd. de Saisset Mus., Santa Clara U., 1991; trustee Mus. of Art and History, Santa Cruz, 1993; pres. Cabrillo Festival of Contemporary Music, Santa Cruz, Calif., 2000—. Lt. USN, 1963—67. Mem. Rotary, Commonwealth Club (San Francisco), World Trade Club (San Francisco), Santa Cruz Yacht Club, Tennis Club Rio Del Mar. Republican. Avocations: travel, reading, art, painting, tennis. Home: 218 Shoreview Dr Aptos CA 95003-4621 Business E-Mail: brucenicholson@thenicholsonco.com

**NICHOLSON, LELAND ROSS,** retired utilities executive, energy consultant; b. Carrington, ND, Feb. 21, 1924; s. Malcom and Lena May (Kerlin) N.; m. Virginia E. Blair, Mar. 16, 1946; children: Heather Le Nicholson Studebaker, Leland B., Holly Kay. Student, Northwestern U., 1940-41; BSEE, U.N.D., 1949; postgrad. in utility mgmt., U. Minn., 1952. Planning and mktg. engr. Minkota Power Coop., Grand Forks, ND, 1949-54; dir. new bus. Kans. Power & Light Co., Topeka, 1954-64, v.p. mktg., 1964-76, sr. v.p., 1976-80, exec. v.p., 1980-83, also bd. dirs.; pres. Kans. Power & Light Gas Service, Topeka, 1985-88, ret., 1988; pres., chief operating officer The Gas Service Co., Kansas City, Mo., 1983-85. Pres. Indsl. Devel. Corp., Topeka; chmn. Kans. Coun. on Electricity and Environment; exec. com. Kansas City Labor Mgmt. Coun., 1986-89; mem. Mktg. Execs. Conf.; bd. dirs. Gas Service Energy Corp., Kansas City, Merchants Nat. Bank, Topeka. Idea innovator heat pump water heater, photo cell controlled yard light, hydrogen fuel cell, electric grill. Bd. dirs., area relations com. Kansas City (Mo.) Area Econ. Devel. Council, 1983-89; bd. dirs. Kansas City Pvt. Industry Coun., 1986-89, Kansas City Downtown Council; trustee U. Mo., Kansas City, 1984-91; mktg. chmn. Kansas City Full Employment Council; past chmn., mem. Topeka-Shawnee County Planning Commn.; adult adv. com. Sea Scouts. Master sgt. USMC, 1942-46. Mem. Am. Gas Assn., Midwest Gas Assn. (bd. dirs. 1985-89), Mo. Valley Electric Assn. (chmn. 1979-81), Edison Electric Inst. (mktg. chmn. 1978-80), Assoc. Industries of Mo., Kans. Assn. Commerce and Industry, Greater Kansas City (Mo.) C. of C. (bd. dirs. 1979-82), Shawnee Yacht Club (Topeka) (commodore 1972-74), Lake Gaston Assn. (pres. 1993-97), Kansas City Club, Rotary. Republican. Congregationalist. Avocations: sailing, canoeing, fishing, reading, electronics.

**NICHOLSON, MARILYN LEE,** arts administrator; b. San Jose, Calif., Feb. 7, 1949; d. John Hart Nicholson and Betty Ann (Price) Shepardson; m. Neal Luit Evenhuis. BA in English and History, U. Ariz., 1972; BFA in Studio, U. Hawaii-Manoa, Honolulu, 1977, MA in English, 1977, AS, 1984. Edn. coord., dir. Bishop Mus. Arts and Crafts Sch., Honolulu, 1977-79; owner Fiber Arts Store, Kailua, Hawaii, 1978-82; field coord. Hawaii State Found. on Culture and Arts, Honolulu, 1981-85; exec. dir. Sedona (Ariz.) Arts Ctr., 1986-92, Volcano (Hawaii) Art Ctr., 1992—. Mem. bd. artist selection com. Ariz. Indian Living Treasures, 1988-92; bd. dirs., treas Sedona Cultural Arts Ctr., 1987-92; conf. speaker Nat. Assembly Arts Agys., 1988. Founding Chmn. Sedona Gallery Assn., 1990-92; mem. com. Sedona Acad., 1986-92; mem. steering com. community plan City of Sedona, 1989-91; commr. Arts & Cultural Ctr., Sedona, 1989-91; mem. exec. com. planning Volcano Community Assn., 1993-96. Recipient Mayor's award for Disting. Svc., Sedona City Coun., 1992. Mem. Hawaii Mus. Assn. (bd. dirs. 1995-00), Cooper Ctr. Coun. (bd. dirs. 1992—), Aloha Festivals-Hawaii Island (bd. dirs. 1992-99). Office: Volcano Art Ctr PO Box 129 Volcano HI 96785

**NICHOLSON, R. STEPHEN,** former cultural organization administrator; b. Radford, Va., Mar. 4, 1926; s. Roy S. and Ethel Dovie (Macy) Nicholson; m. Carol Peterson; 1 child, Suzanne Carpenter. AB, Duke U., 1950; MA, Syracuse U., 1956; PhD, Mich. State U., 1971. Pres. Daley Coll., Chgo., 1969-71; prof. Lansing C.C., Lansing, Mich., 1963-66, acad. dean, 1967-76; pres. Clark County C.C. (now So. Nev. C.C.), 1971—76, Mt. Hood C.C., 1976—85; chancellor Oakland C.C., 1985-90; vice chancellor Higher Colls. of Tech., United Arab Emirates, 1990-92; CEO Internat. Christian Leadership, 1992-93, Mercy Corps Internat., 1994—95, chmn. bd. dirs., 1997—2004. Pres. Creative Futures; bd. dirs. MCI, Green Plains Renewable Energy Corp., 2004—. Sr. fellow for higher edn. M.J. Murdock Trust, 1993—95, 1996—99; chair bd. dir. N.W. Autism Found., 2000—02; bd. dir. Green Plains Reusable Energy, Inc., 2004—. Mem.: World Affairs Coun., Am. Acad. Polit. and Social Scis., Am. Sociology Assn., Am. Sch. Administrs. Assn., N.W. Assn. Cmty. and Jr. Coll.s (pres. 1976), Am. Assn. Cmty. and Jr. Colls. (pres. Pres.'s Acad. 1982, bd. dirs. 1985—87), Am. Futurist Soc., Japan-Am. Soc., Gresham C. of C. (dir. 1977—79), Rotary Club (pres, 1983, Paul Harris fellow 1996), Phi Delta Kappa. Home and Office: 9685 Irvine Bay Ct Las Vegas NV 89147-8365 E-mail: stevenicholson@cox.net.

**NICHOLSON, RALPH LESTER,** botanist, educator; b. Lynn, Mass., Aug. 25, 1942; s. Nathan Aaron and Muriel Spinney (Buxton) N. BA, U. Vt., 1964; MS, U. Maine, 1967; PhD, Purdue U., 1972. Prof. botany and plant pathology Purdue U., West Lafayette, Ind., 1972—. Contbr. chpts. to books, more than 100 articles to profl. jours. Active Big Bros./Big Sisters, Lafayette, Ind., 1974—. Fellow Am. Phytopathol. Soc. Office: Purdue U Botany and Plant Pathology Lafayette IN 47907 E-mail: nicholson@btny.purdue.edu.

**NICHOLSON, RICHARD SELINDH,** educational association administrator; b. Des Moines, Apr. 5, 1938; s. George Eugene and Margaret (Selindh) N.; m. Mary Lou Weisbrod, Aug. 1, 1958 (div. 1971) 1 child, Jeffrey Richard; m. Lois Ann Karls, Aug. 15, 1976; 1 child, Gregory Michael. BS, Iowa State U., 1960; PhD, U. Wis., 1964; LHD (hon.), CUNY, 1994, CUNY-Mt. Sinai Med. Ctr., 1994. Rsch. assoc. U. Wis., Madison, 1963-64; asst. prof. Mich. State U., East Lansing, 1964-67, assoc. prof., 1967-70; program dir. NSF, Washington, 1970-77, div. dir., 1977-82, chief of staff, 1983-85, asst. dir., 1985-89; exec. dir. Nat. Sci. Bd. Commn., Washington, 1982-83; exec. officer, pub. Science AAAS, Washington, 1989—. Cons. on sci. affairs Pres. of U.S., Washington, 1978-79; exec. sec. Pres.' Com. on Nat. Medal Sci., Washington, 1976-84; mem. Pres.' Nat. Commn. on Superconductivity, 1989; vice chair Commn. on Phys. Scis., Math and Resources NRC, 1989—, Edn. Coordinating Coun., 1991—, com. on environ. rsch., 1991-92, co-chair coun. on competitiveness, 1993—; mem. statutory vis. com. Nat. Inst. of Stds. and Tech., 1990-93; vis. com. chemistry dept. Harvard U., 1989—; bd. dirs. Quality Edn. for Minorities Network, 1989—; trustee Gordon Rsch. Conf., 1989—; sci. policy adv. com. space, sci. and tech. U.S. Ho. Reps., 1992—; co-chair Coun. on Competitiveness, 1993—, Dept. of Energy Panel on Basic Rsch., 1995—; chmn. edn. adv. com. Genetech, 1993—. Mem. editorial bd. Analytical Chemistry, 1980-82, Chem. and Engring. News, 1985-88; contbr. articles to profl. jours. and chpts. to books. Served as seaman USN, 1956-63. Recipient Presdl. Disitng. Ranking, Pres. Reagan, 1982, Alumni Citation Merit award Iowa State U., 1983. Fellow AAAS; mem. Am. Chem. Soc. (chmn. Mich. State U. sect. 1968-70), Chem. Soc. Washington

(nominations com. 1977), Cosmos Club, Nat. Press Club. Avocations: sports, tennis, reading. Office: AAAS 1200 New York Ave NW Ste 100 Washington DC 20005-3941 Home: 6009 Villa Roma Bonsall CA 92003-6220*

**NICHOLSON, ROBERT ARTHUR,** college president; b. Pepin, Wis., Oct. 13, 1923; s. Arthur W. and Ethel (Weeden) N.; m. Dorothy Nelis, June 17, 1944; children: Paul, Gary. BS, Anderson U., Ind., 1944; MA, NYU, 1946, PhD, 1953. With Anderson U., 1945-90, successively instr., asst. prof., assoc. prof. music, chmn. dept., asst. to dean, 1945-58, dean, 1958-83, v.p., 1964-83, pres., 1983-90, pres. emeritus, 1990—. Author: Handbook to the Hymnal of the Church of God, 1953, So I Said Yes! A Personal Memoir, 2006; editor: Hymnal of the Church of God, 1953, 71. Interim CEO Ch. of God Ministries, Inc., 1998, cons.; 1997-99; interim exec. pastor, Park Place Ch. of God, 1995; interim min. of music, 1999-2002; mem. pub. bd. Ch. of God, 1955-80, chmn. commn. higher edn., 1963-70, 83-86, vice chmn., 1970-83, cons., 1990-96; cons. Warner Pacific Coll., Oreg., 1990-98, N.Ind. United Meth. Found., Inc., 1992-95, Anderson Pub. Libr., 1994-95, United Faith Housing Corp., 1994, Hopewell Ctr., 1996, Alexandria Cmty. Ctr., Inc., 1997, Family Network Agy., Inc., 1997-2000, Wilson Boys and Girls Club, 1997, Cmty. Found. Grant County, 1998, United Way Anderson and Madison County, Ind., 1998, 2000, Anderson Area C. of C., 1998, 2001, Christian Ctr., 2001; bd. dirs. Anderson Symphony Orch., 1974-87, 93-94, United Way Madison County, 1985-89, 91-94, Minnetrista Cultural Found., 1988-2002; bd. dirs., v.p. Anderson Internat., 1990-93; bd. dirs. Cmty. Hosp. Madison County, 1986-95, vice chmn., 1988-94, interim pres., CEO, 1991; mem. Madison County Comty. Found., Inc., 1991-2003, pres., 1991-98. Mem. Associated Colls. of Ind., Ind. Colls. and Univs. of Ind. (chmn. 1988-89), Anderson Area C. of C. (bd. dirs. 1985-90, vice chmn. and chmn. elect 1988, chmn. 1989). Home: 2727 Crown Pointe Cir Apt 127 Anderson IN 46012-3265

**NICHOLSON, SCOTT RICHARD,** library scientist, researcher, educator; b. Fergus Falls, Minn., Mar. 27, 1971; s. R W and Connie Nicholson; life ptnr. Kenneth Lavender. BS in math with computer sci., U. of Okla., 1988—92, M of libr. and info studies, 1995—96; PhD in info sci., U. of North Tex., 1997—2000. Computer cons. U. Okla., 1992—95; reference & electronic services libr. Tex. Christian U., Fort Worth, 1996—97; statisticalmodeler Citigroup, 2000—01; asst. prof. Syracuse U., 2001—. Rsch. cons. Info. Inst. of Syracuse, 2001—. Author: (web publication) AskScott - Your Guide to Finding It on the Internet; contbr. articles to profl. jours. Recipient Prof. of the Yr., Syracuse U. Sch. of Info. Studies, 2004, Emerging Leader, ALA, 1996; Doctoral fellowship, U. of North Tex., 1997—2000. Mem.: Assn. for Libr. and Info. Sci. Edn., Am. Soc. for Info. Sci. and Tech., Founder of Syracuse U. ALA Student Group (hon.; founder and advisor 2001), ALA (life), Phi Kappa Phi, Beta Phi Mu, Phi Beta Kappa. Unitarian Universalist. Achievements include first to use the term Bibliomining, which is the combination of data warehousing, data mining, and bibliometrics for library evaluation, and was instrumental in the development of the field. Avocations: board games, pottery, kayaking, saxophone. Office: Syracuse Univ Sch of Info Studies Syracuse NY 13244 Office Phone: 315-443-1640. Office Fax: 315-443-5806. Personal E-mail: scott@scottnicholson.com.

**NICHOLSON, SEAN,** science educator; s. Stanley and Colleen Nicholson; m. Claire Rehnberg, Aug. 19, 1989; children: Caitlin, Kevin, Ryan. PhD, U. Wis., Madison, Wis., 1997. Asst. prof. U. Pa., Phila., 1997—2004; assoc. prof. Cornell U., Ithaca, NY, 2004—. Office: Cornell University 133 MVR Hall Ithaca NY 14853 Office Phone: 607-254-6498. Office Fax: 607-255-4071. Business E-mail: sn243@cornell.edu.

**NICHOLSON, WILL FAUST, JR.,** bank executive; b. Colorado Springs, Colo., Feb. 8, 1929; s. Will Faust and Gladys Olivia (Burns) N.; m. Shirley Ann Baker, Nov. 26, 1955; children: Ann Louise Nicholson Naughton, Will Faust III. S.B., M.I.T., 1950; MBA, U. Denver, 1956. V.p. Van Schaack & Co., Denver, 1954-66; pntr. N. G. Petry Constrn. Co., Denver, 1966-70; sr. v.p. Colo. Nat. Bankshares, Inc., Denver, 1970-75, pres., 1975-95, chmn. bd., chief exec. officer, 1985-95; chmn. Rocky Mountain Bankcard Sys., Denver, 1995—2001. Bd. dirs. Boys and Girls Clubs of Metro Denver; active Downtown Denver, Inc., Colo. Assn. of Commerce and Industry, chmn. 1990-91, Denver Urban Renewal Authority, 1958-59, Denver Bd. Water Commrs., 1959-65, pres. 1964, 65; Nat. Western Stock Show. With USAF, 1950-53. Mem. Assn. Bank Holding Cos. (bd. dirs. 1979-87, 89-91, exec. com. 1980-85, vice chmn. 1981-82, chmn. 1983-84), US C. of C. (bd. dirs. 1990-2005, chmn. 1999-2000), US Golf Assn. (exec. com. 1974-82, v.p. 1978, 79, pres. 1980, 81), Denver Country Club, Univ. Club Colo., Univ. Club NY, Castle Pines Golf Club, Royal and Ancient Golf Club (St. Andrews, Scotland), Augusta (Ga.) Nat. Golf Club. Republican. Episcopalian. Home: 37 Polo Club Cir Denver CO 80209-3307 Office: Rocky Mountain BankCard Sys Inc PO Box 5168 Denver CO 80217-5168

**NICHOLSON, WILLIAM JOSEPH,** energy and environmental consultant; b. Tacoma, Aug. 24, 1938; s. Ferris Frank and Athyleen Myrtle (Fesenmaier) Nicholson; m. Carland Elaine Crook, Oct. 10, 1964; children: Courtney, Brian, Kay, Benjamin. SB in ChemE, MIT, Cambridge, Mass., 1960, SM in ChemE Practice, 1961; PhD in ChemE, Cornell U., Ithaca, NY, 1965; MBA, Pacific Luth. U., Tacoma, Wash., 1969. Registered profl. chem. engr., Wash. Sr. devel. engr. Hooker Chem. Co., Tacoma, 1964—69, Battelle N.W., Richland, Wash., 1969—70; planning assoc. Potlatch Corp., San Francisco 1970—75, mgr. corp. energy svc., 1976—94, dir. corp. energy and environ. svcs., 1994—2002, ind. energy and environ. cons., 2002—; chair energy coun. Am. Forest and Paper Assn., Washington, 1990—2002. U.S. expert environ. labeling Internat. Stds. Orgn., 1994—2000; adv. bd. Forest Products lab. U. Calif., Richmond, 1992—2003, chmn. adv. bd., 1993—95, 2003, adv. bd. Coll. Natural Resources, 1993–931 adv. com.; fed. Biomass, 2000—05; project peer reviewer USDOE, 2004—. Mem.: AAAS, AIChE (assoc.), Am. Chem. Soc., Commonwealth Club (San Francisco), Sigma Xi. Republican. Avocations: history, genealogy. Home and Office: PO Box 1114 Ross CA 94957-1114 Office Phone: 415-457-2425. Personal E-mail: nicholsonhome@aol.com.

**NICHOLSON, WILLIAM NOEL,** clinical neuropsychologist; b. Detroit, Dec. 24, 1936; s. James Eardly and Hazel A. (Wagner) N.; m. Nancy Ann Marshall, June 15, 1957; children: Anne Marie, Kristin, Scott. AB, Wittenberg U., 1959; MDiv, Luth. Theol. Sem., Phila., 1962; PhD, Mich. State U., 1972. Diplomate Am. Bd. Forensic Examiners, Am. Bd. Med. Psychotherapists; lic. clin. psychologist, Mich.; ordained to ministry Luth. Ch., 1962; cert. Nat. Register Health Care Providers in Psychology, Assn. of State and Provincial Psychology Bds. Parish pastor Our Saviour Luth. Ch., Saginaw, Mich., 1962-69; intern in psychology Ingham Mental Health Bd., 1971-72; resident in psychology Bay-Arenac Mental Health Bd., 1972-74; dir., psychologist Riverside Ctr., Bay City, Mich., 1974-75; pastor, psychologist Psych Studies and Clergy Consultation of Mich., 1989—2003. Pres. Bay Psychol. Assocs., P.C., Bay City, 1975—2002; cons. Gov.'s Office of Drug Abuse, 1972-74. Author: A Guttman Facet Analysis of Attitude-Behaviors Toward Drug Users by Heroin Addicts and Mental Health Therapists, 1972, An Episcopalian Guide to the Augsburg Confession, 1997; contbr. articles to profl. jours. Mem. APA, Mich. Psychol. Assn. Office: 820 Arlington Ave Ste 2 Petoskey MI 49770 Office Phone: 231-347-4700. Personal E-mail: fatherbill36@hotmail.com.

**NICHTER, RHODA SAMUELS,** writer, educator; b. Bklyn., June 22, 1926; d. Joseph and Celia Samuels; m. Murray Nichter, June 26, 1948; children: Shelli Binder, Judith Morris. Student, Bklyn. Coll., 1943-47. Cert. smoking cessation specialist. Smoking cessation specialist St. Francis Hosp., Roslyn, NY, 1975—. Dept. of Drug and Alcohol Addiction, Hempstead, NY, 1978—; nonsmokers rights coord. Am. Lung Assn., Hauppauge, NY, 1978—81. Author: Yes, I Do Mind if You Smoke, 1978, How to Stop Smoking Once and For All, 1980; prodr., host Smoking and Your Health, WHPC-FM-Radio, 1980—. Pres., founder, activist Group Against Smoking Pollution of NY, Plainview, 1971—; past pres. Women's Am. Orgn. for Rehab. through Tng.;

pres. YJCC In Between Couples Club. Recipient Nonsmokers' Rights award Am. Lung Assn., 1980. Avocations: lap swimming, painting, art and antique collecting, bridge. Home: 7 Maxine Ave Plainview NY 11803-3606 Office Phone: 516-938-0080.

**NICITA, RICK,** agent; m. Paula Wagner, 1984. Agent Creative Artists Agy., co-chmn. Beverly Hills, Calif., 1995—. Chmn. Am. Cinematheque; former vice-chmn. Am. Film Inst. Named one of most influential people in Hollywood, Entertainment Weekly mag., Premiere mag. Office: Creative Artists Agy 9830 Wilshire Blvd Beverly Hills CA 90212-1825

**NICK, GEORGE,** painter; b. 1927; Student, Cleve. Inst. Art, Bklyn. Mus. Art Sch., Art Students League; BFA, MFA, Yale Univ. Faculty Hollins Univ., Va., Mass. Coll. of Art, 1969—94; now faculty NY Studio Sch. One-man exhbns.: Schoelkolpf Gallery, Tibor de Nagy Gallery, Fischbach Gallery; group exhbns.: Corcoran Gallery, Mus. Balt., Pa. Acad. Fine Arts, Butler Inst. Am. Art, Flint Inst., Boston Mus. Fine Arts, NAD; represented in permanent collections: Boston Mus. Fine Arts, Met. Mus. Art, Folks Mus., Essen, Germany, Nat. Mus., Johannesburg, So. Africa, Hirshorn Mus and Sculpture Garden, Washington, John Updike, Bob Dylan, Gov. Michael Dukakis. Grantee Nat. Endowment for Arts, Dept. of Interior Bicentennial grant. Mem.: NAD (academician). Mailing: c/o Concord Art Assn 37 Lexington Rd Concord MA 01742 Office: NY Studio Sch 8 W 8th St New York NY 10011

**NICK, LLOYD,** museum director, art educator; b. Rochester, N.Y. BFA, Hunter Coll.; MFA, U. Pa. Chair art dept. Methodist Coll., Fayetteville, NC, Am. Coll., Monaco, dean of students; prof. art, dir. art progs. Oglethorpe U Atlanta, 1984—; founder, dir. Oglethorpe U. Mus., Atlanta. Recipient NEH grant. Office: Oglethorpe U Mus 4484 Peachtree Rd NE Atlanta GA 30319

**NICKEL, ALBERT GEORGE,** advertising agency executive; b. Pitts., July 12, 1943; s. Frank George and Dorothy (Wiefling) N.; m. Dana Cooper; children: Mark, Grace, Olivia. AB, Washington and Jefferson Coll., 1965; MBA, Ind. U., 1967. Mktg. rsch. analyst Pfizer, Inc., N.Y.C., 1967, prod. svc. rep., 1967-68, mktg. rsch. mgr., 1968-69, product mgr., 1969-70, USV Internat., Tuckahoe, NY, 1970-71; account supr. Sudler & Hennessey, N.Y.C., 1973-77; sr. v.p. mgmt. group supr. Young and Rubicam, N.Y.C., 1977-79; chmn., pres., COO Dorritie Lyons & Nickel, Inc., N.Y.C.; chmn., pres., CEO HMC Group Omnicom, Inc., 1999—; pres., chmn., CEO Lyons, Lavey, Nickel, Swift, Inc., 2000—. Trustee Wilton YMCA, Five Town Found.; bd. dirs., exec. com. Wilton LaCrosse Assn.; bd. trustees Dominican Coll., Healthcare Businesswoman's Assn., Wilton H.S. Long Range Planning Team, Am. Coun. on Sci. and Health; co-chmn. TBWA WorldHealth. Capt. USAF, 1969. Recipient Ellis Island medal of honor and honor soc., 2002. Mem. Pharm. Rsch. and Mfrs. Assn. (bd. dirs.), Healthcare Mktg. and Comm. Coun. (bd. dirs.), Vis. Nurses Assn. (mem. found. bd.), Midwest Healthcare Mktg. Assn., Wilton Riding Club (pres.), Shore and Country Club, Silver Spring Country Club. Home: 65 Keelers Ridge Rd Wilton CT 06897-1608 E-mail: anickel@llns.com.

**NICKEL, HENRY V.,** lawyer; b. Chgo., Aug. 8, 1943; AB, U. Va., 1965; JD, George Washington U., 1968. Bar: D.C. 1968. Mem. Hunton & Williams LLP, Washington, ptnr., resources, regulatory, environ. law, 1976, head adminstrv. law group, 1994. Rsch. editor: George Washington Law Rev., 1967-68. Mem. Order of Coif. Office: Hunton & Williams LLP 1900 K St NW Washington DC 20006-1109 Office Phone: 202-955-1561. E-mail: hnickel@hunton.com.

**NICKEL, JANET MARLENE MILTON,** retired geriatrics nurse; b. Manitowoc, Wis., June 9, 1940; d. Ashley and Pearl Milton; m. Curtis A. Nickel, July 29, 1961; children: Cassie, Debra, Susan. Diploma, Milw. Inst.; ADN, N.D. State U., 1988. Nurse Milw. VA, Wood, Wis., 1961-62; supervising nurse Park Lawn Convalescent Hosp., Manitowoc, 1964-65; newsletter editor Fargo (N.D.) Model Cities Program, 1970-73; supervising night nurse Rosewood on Broadway, Luth. Hosps. and Homes, Fargo, 1973-92; assoc. dir. nursing Elim Care Ctr., Fargo, 1992-94, night nurse, 1994—2005; ret., 2005. Mem. Phi Eta Sigma.

**NICKEL, KAREN JUNE,** secondary school educator; b. Clinton, Mo., Dec. 21, 1945; m. Flint None Nickel. BS in Edn., SW Bapt. U., 1988, MS in Edn., 1999. Elem., English, mid. sch. and HS tchr. Mo. Fifth grade tchr. Wheatland (Mo.) R-II Sch., 1988—94; HS social studies tchr. Wheatland R-II Sch., 1997—; mid. sch. comm. arts and social studies tchr. Wheatland (Mo.) R-II Sch., 1995—97; curriculum coord. Wheatland R-II Sch., 1995—. Contbr. poetry to lit. pub. Mem.: Wheatland Edn. Assn. (pres. 1990—), APA Tchrs. Psychology, Mo. Coun. Social Studies, Nat. Coun. Social Studies. Avocations: crocheting, reading, gardening, rockhound, piano. Home: 6740 SE 1401 Rd Weaubleau MO 65774 Office: Wheatland R-II Sch P O Box 68 Hwy 83 South Wheatland MO 65779 Personal E-mail: teacher5cents@yahoo.com.

**NICKEL, FRANK (NICK) T.,** diversified financial services company executive; m. Carol Nickell. BS in Bus. Adminstrn. and Acctg., U. N.C. CPA AICPA. With A.M. Pullen & Co., 1971—77; from mem. staff to pres., CEO Kelso & Co., L.P., N.Y., 1977—98, pres., 1998—, CEO, 1998—. Bd. dir. BlackRock Inc., Bear Stearns Cos., Earle M. Jorgensen Co. Bd. visitors U. N.C.; trustee NYU Hosps. Ctr. Avocations: bridge, golf. Office: Kelso & Co 320 Park Ave Fl 24 New York NY 10022

**NICKELL, JOE,** paranormal expert; b. Lexington, Ky., Dec. 1, 1944; s. James Wendell and Ella Kathleen (Turner) Nickell; m. Diana Harris, 2006; 1 child, Cherette. BA, U. Ky., 1967, MA, 1982, PhD, 1987. Profl. stage magician, Toronto Ont. Canada, 1968-71; pvt. investigation, 1973-731 mus. exhibit designer Dawson City (Yukon) Mus., 1975-76; freelance investigative writer, 1976—; tchg. asst. U. Ky., Lexington, 1980-87, instr., 1987-95; sr. rsch. fellow Com. for Sci. Investigation of Claims of Paranormal, Amherst, NY, 1995—. Author: Inquest on the Shroud of Turin, 1983, Secrets of the Supernatural, 1988, The Magic Detectives, 1989, Pen, Ink and Evidence, 1990, Wonder Workers!, 1991, Ambrose Bierce is Missing, 1992; co-author (with Robert A. Baker): Missing Pieces, 1992; author: Mysterious Realms, 1992, Looking for a Miracle, 1993; editor: Psychic Sleuths, 1994; author: Camera Clues, 1994, Entities, 1995, Detecting Forgery, 1996; editor: The Outer Edge, 1996; co-editor: The UFO Invasion, 1997; co-author (with John F. Fischer): Crime Science, 1999; author: Real Life X-Files, 2001, The Mystery Chronicles, 2004, Unsolved History, 2005, Secrets of the Sideshows, 2005; co-author (with Benjamin Redford): Lake Monster Mysteries, 2006. Office: Ctr for Inquiry 3965 Rensch Rd Amherst NY 14228-2743 Office Phone: 716-636-1425 310.

**NICKELS, GREG,** mayor; b. Chgo., Aug. 7, 1955; s. Bob and Kathie Nickels; m. Sharon Nickels; children: Jacob, Carey. Legis. asst. to Council member Norm Rice City of Seattle, 1979—87; mem. King County Coun., 1987—2002; mayor City of Seattle, 2002—. Chair Seattle/King County Bd. Health, 1996—2001; mem. exec. com. bd. dirs. of Sound Transit. Office: City Hall PO Box 94749 Seattle WA 98124-4749*

**NICKELS, JOHN L.,** retired state supreme court justice; m. Merita Nickels; 7 children. Bachelor's degree, No. Ill. U.; law degree, DePaul U. Pvt. practice, 20 yrs; judge Appellate Ct.; cir. judge 16th Jud. Cir.; supreme ct. justice State of Ill., 1992-98; ret., 1998. Bd. dirs. Kane County Bank & Trust Co.; bd. trustees Waubonsee Coll.; mem. Kane County Planning Commn., Zoning Bd. Appeals; mem. St. Gall's Parish, Elburn. Home: 17901 Owens Rd Maple Park IL 60151

**NICKENS, HARRY CARL,** medical association administrator; b. Monterey, Tenn., June 25, 1944; s. Van B. and Martha (Winningham) N.; m. Alicia Beck, Aug. 26, 1967; children: Kimberly, Cassidee, Brad. BS, Tenn. Tech. U., 1966, MS, 1968; EdD, U. Tenn., 1972. Counselor Va. Western C.C., Roanoke, 1972-76, dir. student devel., 1977-78, dean students, 1979-84, exec. dir. community devel. and tng., 1985-89; pres. Coll. Health Scis., Roanoke,

1989—2001; v.p. cmty. rels. and devel. Ephraim McDowell Health, Danville, Ky., 2003—06, dir. cmty. rels., 2006. Chair Roanoke Valley Chamber's Sch., originator Grad, Ctr.; pres. Ephraim McDowell Health Care Found., 2003-06. Pres. Roanoke Valley Career Edn.; bd. dirs. Va. Cares, Adult Care Ctr., Am. Heart Assn., Va. Amateur Sports, Salvation Army; bd. suprs. Roanoke County; trustee St. Catherine Coll. Mem. Kiwanis (pres. Roanoke chpt. 1990, pres. Danville chpt. 2006, vice chmn. cmty. devel. coun.). Baptist. Avocation: gardening. Home: 107 Patrick Henry Ct Danville KY 40422 Office: Ephraim McDowell Health 217 South 3rd St Danville KY 40422 Office Phone: 859-239-2632. Business E-Mail: hnickeus@emhealth.org.

**NICKERSON, DON C.,** lawyer, retired prosecutor, judge; married; 3 children. JD, Drake U., 1977. Bar: Iowa 1977, admitted to practice: US Ct. Appeals (8th Cir.) 1977, US Dist. Ct. (So. Dist.) Iowa 1977. US atty. US Dist. Ct. (So. Dist.), Iowa, 1993—2001; assoc. gen. counsel Wellmark Blue Cross & Blue Shield, Iowa, 2001—03; judge Dist. Ct. (5th Dist.), Iowa, 2003—. Bd. mem. Urban Dreams, United Way of Central Iowa, Cmty. Focus, Inc., Des Moines Enterprise Cmty. Recipient Medal of Honor, Drake U., Cmty. Svc. award, Iowa State Bar Assn. Mem.: Commn. on Planning for the 21st Century, Polk County Bar Assn., Iowa Nat. Bar Assn., Iowa State Bar Assn. Office: State of Iowa Dist Ct 5C Polk County Courthouse 500 Mulberry Rm 212 Des Moines IA 50309 Office Phone: 515-245-4500, 515-286-3391. Office Fax: 515-286-3858.

**NICKERSON, GARY LEE,** educational consultant; b. Cleve., Nov. 7, 1942; s. Alto Lee and Louisa Evelyn (Watson) Nickerson; m. Barbara Marie Butler, Aug. 17, 1968; 1 child, L'Oreal. BS, Ohio U., Athens, 1966; MA, Atlanta U., 1971. Cert. secondary tchr. Ohio. With Cleve. Pub. Schs., 1966-98; sci. dept. chmn. John F. Kennedy High Sch., Cleve., 1985-98; youth edn. coord. Cleve. Bot. Garden, 1999—2002; sci. mgr. Cleve. Mcpl. Schs., 2002—04; ednl. cons. Ohio Dept. Edn., 2004—. Sci. instr. Std. Oil Elem. Tchg. Retraining Program, 1986, Cleve. Ednl. Found. Elem. Tchg. Retraining Program, 1990—, Baldwin Wallace U. Upward Bound Program, 1992; physics instr. Case Western Res. U., Cleve., 1988, engring. project instr. MEIOP Summer Program, 91; mem. adv. panel Ednl. Devel. Ctr., Inc., Newton, Mass., 1989—98; tchr. trainer Kent State U. Trivet Program, 1991—98; sci. tchr. Gov.'s Inst. Gifted and Talented Cleve. State U., 1992—98. Co-author: curriculum guides. Trustee N.E. Ohio Sci. and Engring. Fair, 2001—04. Recipient cert. of Excellence in Tchg., Rotary, 1990. Mem.: NAACP, Sci. Edn. Coun. Ohio, Nat. Sci. Tchrs. Assn., Cleve. Regional Coun. Sci. Tchrs. (bd. dirs. 1986—87, pres. 2002—), Metrocabse Assn., Urban League, Kappa Alpha Psi. Democrat. Baptist. Avocations: ice skating, tennis, swimming, singing, weightlifting. Home: 5871 White Pine Dr Cleveland OH 44146-3075 Personal E-mail: ganickers@aol.com.

**NICKERSON, GREG,** public relations executive; b. Iowa, Nov. 3, 1958; BS in Agrl. Journalism, Iowa State U., 981. Mkt. analyst, exec. editor Brock Assocs., Brookfield, Wis., 1981-85; with pub. rels. dept. Bader Rutter & Assocs., Brookfield, 1985-88, acctg. group supr., 1988-90, v.p., group supr., 1990-92, v.p., dir. pub. rels. group, 1992-98, exec. v.p., 1998—. Office: Bader Rutter & Associates 13845 Bishops Dr Brookfield WI 53005-6604

**NICKERSON, GUY ROBERT,** lumber company executive; b. Salt Lake City, May 20, 1956; s. Charles Augustus and Florence May (Fogel) N.; m. Maggie Rose McDonnell, May 30, 1992; children: Melissa Marie, Rebecca Rose. B Acctg., U. Utah, 1977, M Profl. Accountancy, 1978. CPA, Utah. Sr. mgr. Deloitte Haskins & Sells, Salt Lake City and N.Y.C., 1978-87; v.p. fin. Anderson Lumber Co., Ogden, Utah, 1987-96, v.p. ops., 1996—2001; pvt. investor Salt Lake City, 2001—.

**NICKERSON, JAMES FINDLEY,** retired education educator; b. Gretna, Nebr., Dec. 16, 1910; s. Elmer Samuel and Lulu Perkins (Patterson) Nickerson; m. Juanita M. Bolin, Mar. 3, 1934; children: Ann Rogers Nickerson Lueck, Maria De Miranda. BS, Nebr. Wesleyan U., 1932; MA, Columbia Tchrs. Coll., 1940; PhD, U. Minn., 1948; ScD (hon.), Yankton (S.D.) Coll., 1971. Tchr. pub. schs., Giltner, Nebr., 1932-35; sch. music supr. Gordon, Nebr., 1936-38, Bayshore, LI, 1939-41, Grand Island, Nebr., 1941-42; instr. Coll. Edn., music supr. HS U. Minn., 1942-46, vis. prof. Coll. Edn., 1948; asst. prof. music edn. U. Kans., 1946-48, assoc. prof., 1948-53; prof. psychology, dean edn., dir. summer caur. Mont. State U., 1954—64, head dept. psychology, 1954—56; rsch. assoc. Electronics Rsch. Lab., 1958—64; v.p. acad. affairs N.D. State U., Fargo, 1964—66; pres. Minn. State U., Mankato, 1966—73, disting. svc. prof., pres. emeritus, 1973—76. Mem. vis. com. Schola Cantorum, N.Y.C., 1938—39, Choral Arts Soc., Washington, 1969—71, Harvard Grad. Sch. Edn., 1970—76; rsch. assoc. dept. psychology U. So. Calif.; with human factors divsn. USN Electronics Lab., San Diego, 1953—54; bd. dirs. Svc. Mems. Opportunity Colls.; mem. steering com. Pacific N.W. Coun. Higher Edn., 1962; cons. pub. edn. Office Gov. Wash., 1964; exec. sec., study dir. interim com. edn. Wash. Legislature, 1959—60; chmn. regional conf. womanpower Nat. Manpower Coun. and Mont. State Coll., 1957; mem. adv. com. sci. edn. NSF, 1968—71, chmn., 1970—71. Stringbass Mont. State Coll. Symphonette, 1959—63, Mankato Symphony Orch., 1967—73, 1983—93, bd. dirs., 1987—90. Named Nickerson Conf. Rm. in his honor, Student Union, Minn. State U., 2003; named to Internat. Adult and Continuing Edn. Hall of Fame, 1999; recipient Alumni award, Nebr. Wesleyan U., 1968, Sec. Def. medal for Outstanding Pub. Svc., 1981, citation, Am. Coun. Edn., 1981, James F. Nickerson medal of Merit for Outstanding Svc. to Mil. Edn., Am. Assn. Sr. Colls. and Univs., 1981; Danforth Found. Adminstrn. grantee, 1969. Mem.: Edn. Commn. States (commr. 1967—73, mem. task force coord., governance and structure postsecondary edn. 1973), Assn. Minn. Colls. (pres. 1972), Am. Assn. Higher Edn. (chmn. resolutions com. 1974), Am. Assn. Colls. Tchr. Edn. (bd. dirs. 1969—71), Am. Assn. State Colls. and State Univs. (bd. dirs. 1966—71), Nat. Assn. Student Univs. and Land Grant Colls. (senate, chmn. divsn. tchr. edn. 1962—65, sec. coun. acad. officers 1965), Sigma Xi, Phi Mu Alpha Sinfonia. Home and Office: 77 Stadium Rd Apt 23 Mankato MN 56001-1022

**NICKERSON, JERRY EDGAR ALAN,** business executive; b. North Sydney, N.S., Can., Apr. 28, 1936; s. Jeremiah Beldon and Jean Frances (Innes) N.; m. Jean Frances Ritcey, Sept. 20, 1958; children: Mark Alan, Jerry Ross. B.Commerce, Dalhousie U., 1958. Chmn. bd. H.B. Nickerson & Son, Ltd., North Sydney. Bd. dirs. Gt. West Life & Annuity, Gt. West Life Assurance Co., Seaside Cable TV Ltd., Great-West Lifeco Inc., London Ins. Group, London Life Ins., Power Fin., Inc., Power Corp. Can., Can. Life Fin. Corp., Can. Life Assurance Co., Can. Life Capital Corp Mem. Chief Execs. Orgn., Zeta Psi. Office: HB Nickerson & Sons Ltd PO Box 130 North Sydney NS Canada B2A 3M2 Personal E-mail: jeanickerson@aol.com.

**NICKERSON, JOHN MITCHELL,** political science professor; b. Lewiston, Maine, July 1, 1937; s. Elmer Winfield and Marion Gertrude (Howard) N. BA, U. Maine, 1959; MA, Wash. State U., 1966; PhD, U. Idaho, 1971. Commd. 2d lt. US Army, 1959, advanced through grades to capt., resigned, 1967; rsch. assoc. Bur. Pub. Adminstrn. U. Maine, Orono, 1967—68, mem. grad. faculty, 1970—88, asst. prof., assoc. prof. polit. sci. Augusta, 1970—81, prof., 1981—; developer 10 baccalaureate degrees pub. adminstrn.; dir. New Eng. Govtl. Rsch. Inst., Inc., Waterville, Maine, 1971. Lectr. Colby Coll., Waterville, Maine, 1979, Maine State Dedimus Justice; cons. in field. Author: The Control of Civil Disturbances, 1968; Municipal Police in Maine - A Study of Selected Personnel Practices with Emphasis on Recruit Selection and Training, 1969; (with others) A Study of Policy-Making: The Dynamics and Adaptability of the United States Federal System, 1971; editor, author foreward: Is the Municipality Liable for Insufficiently Trained Police? (James P. Murphy), 1968; contbr. articles to profl. jours. Mem. Maine State Police Planning Adv. Group, 1984-87, Maine State Bd. Assessment Rev., 1981-84, Maine Hwy. Safety Com., 1984-87; vice chmn. adv. bd. Salvation Army, Augusta, 1980-85; trustee, treas. Lithgow Library, 1980-85; incorporator Kennebec Valley Med. Ctr., Augusta, 1980-97. Dept. Justice grantee, 1967. Mem. Am. Polit. Sci. Assn., New Eng. Polit. Sci. Assn., Northeastern Polit. Sci. Assn., Acad. Polit. Sci. (life), Am. Acad. Polit. and Social Sci. (life), Am. Soc. for Pub. Adminstrn., ACLU (life), Kennebec Hist.

Soc. (life), Kennebec Valley Humane Soc. (life), Maine Civil Liberties Union (life, legis. com.), Pi Sigma Alpha, Pi Alpha Alpha. Home: 190 Capitol St Apt 216 Augusta ME 04330-6237 Office: U Maine at Augusta 46 University Dr Augusta ME 04330 Office Phone: 207-621-3287. Business E-Mail: john.nickerson@maine.edu.

**NICKERSON, ROSEMARY GRZESIK,** humanities educator; b. Bklyn., Nov. 10, 1959; d. Stanley Grzesik and Maria Rose Laria; m. Michael LeRoy Nickerson, Oct. 2, 1988; children: Hannah, Andrea. BA, Rutgers U., New Brunswick, N.J., 1987; PhD, Stony Brook U., N.Y., 1988. Assoc. prof. Hagerstown C.C., Md., 1988—. Democrat. Office: Hagerstown Cmty Coll 11400Robinwood Dr Hagerstown MD 21742

**NICKLAUS, JACK WILLIAM,** professional golfer; b. Columbus, Ohio, Jan. 21, 1940; s. Louis Charles, Jr. and Helen (Schoener) N.; m. Barbara Bash, July 23, 1960; children: Jack William II, Steven Charles, Nancy Jean, Gary Thomas, Michael Scott. Student, Ohio State U., 1957-62, D of Athletic Arts (hon.), 1972; LLD (hon.), U. St. Andrews, 1984. Chmn., chief exec. officer Golden Bear Internat., Inc. Player U.S. Ryder Cup Team, 1969, 71, 73, 75, 77, 81, 83, 87. Author: My 55 Ways to Lower Your Golf Score, 1964, Take a Tip From Me, 1968, The Greatest Game of All, 1969, Jack Nicklaus' Lesson Tee, 1972, Golf My Way, 1974, Jack Nicklaus' Playing Lessons, 1976, On and Off the Fairway, 1978, Play Better Golf, Vols. 1-3, 1980, 81, 83, The Full Swing, 1982, My Most Memorable Shots in the Majors, 1988. Chmn. Ohio div. Am. Cancer Soc., 1967; chmn. sports div. Nat. Easter Seal Soc., 1967. Named PGA Player of Year, 1967, 72, 73, 75, 76, Dunlop Profl. Athlete of Yr., 1972, Golfer of Year Profl. Golfers Assn., 1973, Byron Nelson award, 1964, 65, 72, 73, Bob Jones award, 1975; named Sportsman of Year, Sports Illus. mag., 1978; named to World Golf Hall of Fame; named Athlete of the Decade for 1970-79, 1979, Golfer of the '70s, 1979, Golfer of the Century, 1988; recipient Presdl. Medal of Freedom, The White House, 2005. Mem. President's Club Ohio State U., Phi Gamma Delta. Achievements include playing on over 105 golf courses on 5 continents, 12 ranked in U.S. Top 100; hosted 185 profl. tournaments 1973—; won 73 official tournaments; maj. tournaments won include Tournament of Champions, 1963, 64, 71, 73, 77, U.S. Amateur, 1959, 61, U.S. Open, 1962, 67, 72, 80, U.S. Masters, 1963, 65, 66, 72, 75, 86, Brit. Open, 1966, 70, 78, PGA Championship, 1963, 71, 73, 75, 80, Internat. Pro-Amateur, 1973,Tournament Players Championship, 1974, 76, 78, Australian Open, 1964, 68, 71, 75, 76, 78, World Series of Golf, 1962, 63, 67, 70, 76, PGA Seniors Championship, 1991, U.S. Senior Open, 1991, 93. Office: Golden Bear Realty Inc 11684 US Hwy #1 North Palm Beach FL 33408*

**NICKLE, DENNIS EDWIN,** electronics engineer, consultant, deacon; b. Sioux City, Iowa, Jan. 30, 1936; s. Harold Bateman and Helen Cecilia (Killackey) H. BS in Math., Fla. State U., 1961. Ordained deacon Roman Cath. Ch., 1979. Reliability mathematician Pratt & Whitney Aircraft Co., West Palm Beach, Fla., 1961-63; br. supr. Melpar Inc., Falls Church, Va., 1963-66; prin. mem. tech. staff Xerox Data Sys., Rockville, Md., 1966-70; sr. tech. officer WHO, Washington, 1970-76; software tech. mgr. Melpar divsn. E-Sys., Inc., Falls Church, 1976-95; software process improvement mgr. Bell Atlantic, Arlington, Va., 1996-97; sr. software mgr. Litton Denro, Gaithersburg, Md., 1997—2001; cons., 2001—. Lectr. in field; coord. D.C. Software Process Improvement Network, 1995—2001, chair, 1997—2002. Author: Stress in Adolescents, 1986; co-author: Handbook for Handling Non-Productive Stress in Adolescence, Standard for Software Life Cycle Processes, IMPEESA Junior Leader Training Guide, Standard for Software Quality Assurance, 1984-91, Standard for Developing Software Life Cycle Processes, Configuration Management Procedures, Software Quality Assurance Procedures, Software Development Procedures; editor: Mama's Good Italian Cookbook, 2004; contbr. to profl. jours. Chief judge for computers Fairfax County Regional Sci. Fair, 1964-88; scoutmaster, commr. Boy Scouts Am., 1957-92; youth custodian Fairfax County Juvenile Ct., 1973-87; chaplain No. Va. Regional Juvenile Detention Home, 1978-88; moderator Nocturnal Adoration Soc.; parochial St. Michael's Ch., Annandale, Va., 1979-89, Christ the Redeemer, Sterling, Va., 1990-93. With U.S. Army, 1958-60. Recipient Eagle award, Silver award, Silver Beaver award, other awards Boy Scouts Am.; Ad Altare Dei, St. George Emblem, Diocese of Richmond. Mem. Assn. Computing Machinery, Computer Soc., Am. Soc. for Quality Control, CODSIA (chmn. working groups), ORLANDO II (Govt./industry working group), Old Crows Assn., Rolm Mil-Spec Computer Users Group (internat. pres.), San Antonio I (select industry coord. group), Nat. Security Indsl. Assn. (conv. com. 1985-96, software quality assurance subcom., regional membership chmn. 1981-89, nat. exec. vice-chmn. 1989-94, chmn. 1994-96), Am. Security Coun., IEEE (sr., stds. working group in computers 1983—, Outstanding Vol. award 1993, Golden Core 1996), Def. Software Devel. Stds. Adv. Bd. (chmn. 1991-96), Soc. Software Quality, Hewlett-Packard Users Group, Smithsonian Assn., Internat. Platform Assn., NRA (endowment), Nat. Eagle Scout Assn. (life), KC (4 deg.), Alpha Phi Omega (life), Sigma Phi Epsilon. Home: 43245 Preston Ct Ashburn VA 20147-5307 Office Phone: 703-729-2653.

**NICKLES, DON (DONALD LEE NICKLES),** former senator; b. Ponca City, Okla., Dec. 6, 1948; s. Robert C. and Coeweene (Bryan) N.; m. Linda L. Morrison, Sept. 5, 1968; children— Donald Lee II, Jennifer Lynn, Kim Elizabeth, Robyn Leigh. BA in Bus. Adminstrn., Okla. State U., 1971. Owner, operator Don Nickles Profl. Cleaning Svc., Stillwater, Okla., 1968-71; v.p., gen. mgr. Nickles Machine Co., Ponca City, 1972—80; mem. Okla. Senate, 1979-80, U.S. Senate from Okla., 1981—2005; founder, prin. The Nickles Group lobbying, 2005—. Asst. majority whip, 1996-2003; chmn. Senate Rep. policy com., mem. com. on energy and natural resources, com. on rules and adminstrn., com. on budget fin., budget com., mem. arms control observer group, rural health caucus, world climate conv. observer group, Rep. task force on nat. security and regulatory reform, senate budget com., 2003-05; passed legislation to provide for econ. and employment impact statement for all new laws and regulations; mem., bd. dirs. Valero Energy Corp., 2005- Chmn. platform com. Rep. Nat. Conv., 1992; bd. dirs. Ponca City United Way; bd. advisors Close Up Found.; mem. Kay Coun. for Retarded Children, Ponca City, St. Mary's Roman Cath. Parish Coun.; mem. adv. bd. Salvation Army, Ponca City. With USNG, 1970-76. Named one of Outstanding Young Men of Am., U.S. Jaycees, 1983. Mem. Fellowship Christian Athletes, Ponca City C. of C. Clubs: Rotary. Republican. Office: The Nickles Group Ste 530 607 14th St NW Washington DC 20005

**NICKLES, SHELLEY KAPLAN,** curator, educator; b. Kingston, N.Y., Apr. 3, 1964; d. Jerome Allen and Leah (Maskowsky) Kaplan; m. John Peter Nickles, Sept. 3, 1995; 1 child, Kealani Rose. BA in History, Cornell U., 1986; MA in Early Am. Culture, U. Del., 1990; PhD in history, U. Va., 1999. Instr. Parsons Sch. Design, N.Y.C., Washington, 1996—2002; mus. curator Nat. Mus. Am. History Smithsonian Instn., Washington, 1999—2006. Adj. asst. prof. George Washington U., 2002—04. Editor: (exhibit rev.) Home Cultures Jour., 2003—04; contbr. articles to profl. jours. Fellow, Winterthur and Hagley Mus., Wilmington, 1993, Wolfsonian Mus., Miami Beach, 1994, Smithsonian Instn., 1995—97; Lois F. McNeil fellow, Winterthur Mus., Wilmington, 1988—90. Mem.: Am. Studies Assn., Soc. Winterthur Fellows, Orgn. Am. Historians.

**NICKLIN, EMILY,** lawyer; b. Cooperstown, N.Y., June 24, 1953; d. George Leslie Jr. and Katherine Mildred (Aronson) N.; m. Jay Schleusener, Dec. 28, 1974; children: Max, Lucas, Anna. BA, U. Chgo., 1975, JD, 1977. Bar: Ill. 1977, U.S. Dist. Ct. (no. dist.) Ill. 1979, U.S. Ct. Appeals (7th cir.) 1979. Law clk. to judge U.S. Dist. Ct. (no. dist.) Ill., Chgo., 1977-79; assoc. Kirkland & Ellis, Chgo., 1979-83, ptnr.; mem. firm mgmt. com., 1995—. Tchr. Ill. Continuing Legal Edn. Bar Program, Chgo., 1983—; fellow Salzburg Seminar, Austria, 1983; dep. corp. counsel City of Chgo., 1989-91; mem. bd. trustees, Univ. Chgo.; lectr. law, Univ. Chgo., 2001. Named one of Am. Top 50 Women Litigators, Nat. Law. Jour., 2001, 30 Tough Lawyers, Chgo. Mag. Mem. Nat. Inst. Trial Advocacy (tchr., team leader 1982—), Order of Coif,

Phi Beta Kappa. Office: Kirkland & Ellis LLP 200 E Randolph St Fl 54 Chicago IL 60601-6636 Office Phone: 312-861-2387. Office Fax: 312-861-2200. Business E-Mail: enicklin@kirkland.com.

**NICKLIN, GEORGE LESLIE, JR.,** psychoanalyst, educator, physician, writer; b. Franklin, Pa., July 25, 1925; s. George Leslie and Emma (Reed) N.; m. Katherine Mildred Aronson, Sept. 30, 1950 BA, Haverford Coll., 1949; MD, Columbia U., 1951; cert. in psychoanalysis, William A. White Inst., NYC, 1962. Diplomate Am. Bd. Psychiatry and Neurology. Resident, then chief resident Bellevue Psychiat. Hosp., NYC, 1953-56; pvt. practice specializing in psychoanalytic psychiatry, 1956—; staff Bellevue Hosp., 1956—; assoc. clin. prof. psychiatry NYU Med. Sch., 1970—; dir. LI Inst. Psychoanalysis, 1978-88, dir. emeritus, 1988—, dir. emeritus. Mem. Com. to Award Martin Luther King Peace Prize. Author: Doctors In Peril, 2000, War Stories, 2005. Mem. Corp. Haverford Coll., 1957-2003; founder, trustee Westbury Friends Sch., 1957-2006; founder Friends World Coll., 1958. With AUS, 1943-46, ETO. Decorated Purple Heart (3) with oak leaf cluster (3), Bronze Star with oak leaf cluster and three battle stars. Fellow Am. Acad. Psychoanalysis, Am. Psychiat. Assn. (disting. life fellow, 2003); mem. AAAS, NAACP, Soc. Med. Psychoanalysts (pres. 1986-87), White Psychoanalytic Soc., Assn. for World Edn. (charter trustee, treas. 1970-78), 9th Inf. Divsn. Assn., Vets. of the Bulge, Mil. Order of the Purple Heart. Clubs: Gardiner's Bay Country (Shelter Island, NY). Mem. Soc. Of Friends. Home (Summer): PO Box 88 Shelter Island NY 11964-0088 Home (Winter): The Medford L Way Medford NJ 08055 *Education is essential to the future evolution of human society. But education alone is not enough. Integrity, creative thinking and informed action open the path to the future.*

**NICKLIN, SHAWN DOUGLAS,** history educator; b. Pa, Mar. 14, 1971; s. George Dewitt Nicklin and Donna Lee Garman; m. Debra Michelle Bateman, July 14, 1991; children: Taylor Jennings, Alexandria Nicole. A in edn., Frostburg State U., 1991, B in edn., 1994, M in edn., 2002. History tchr. Lockerman Mid. Sch., Denton, Md., 1995—99; social studies tchr. No. HS, 1999—. Presenter in field. Mem., presenter W.Va. Reading Coun., 2002—04, Garrett Reading Coun., 2003—04, rep. young authors. Mem.: NEA, Md. State Tchrs. Assn., Phi Theta Kappa. Avocations: writing, running, chess. Home: 108 Colonial Dr Accident MD 21520 E-mail: sdnicklin@hotmail.com.

**NICKOLETT, CHIP,** information technology executive, consultant; s. Kay and Ronald D. Nickolett; m. Jacqueline Marie Sharak, May 7, 1988; children: Heather Marie, Jacob Matthew, Paige Marie. AS in Bus. Data Processing, Waukesha County Tech. Coll., 1984. Sys. analyst DCI Mktg., Milw., 1986—91; mgr. tech. svcs. Catalyst USA, Brown Deer, Wis., 1991—93; sr. cons. Ingres Products Divsn., ASK Group, Alameda, Calif., 1993—94; regional project mgr. Computer Assoc., Islandia, NY, 1994—97; dist. mgr. Caribou Lake Software, Mpls., 1997—99; pres. Comprehensive Solutions, Brookfield, Wis., 1999—. Mem., ingres product adv. coun. Computer Assoc., Islandia, NY, 2003—. Contbr. articles to profl. jours. Mem. Children's Cir. of Care, Milw.; mem., pres.'s coun. Children's Hosp. Wis., Milw., 2000, mem. Emelie Vogel Nunnemacher Soc.; mem. bus. adv. coun. Nat. Rep. Congl. Com., Washington, 2000. Recipient Congl. Medal of Distinction, Nat. Rep. Congl. Com., 2001. Mem.: NRA, Nat. Ctr. Employee Ownership, Project Mgmt. Inst., North Am. Ingres Users Assn. (pres. 2000—01). R-Consevative. Achievements include registered trademarks. Avocations: working with children, donating to charitable causes. Office: Comprehensive Solutions 250 N Sunny Slope Rd Ste 300 Brookfield WI 53005 Office Phone: 262-785-8101. E-mail: chipn@comp-soln.com.

**NICKOLOFF, EDWARD LEE,** radiology physicist; m. Diane Zambetti; children: Andrea Lee, Edward Jr Lee. BS, Lebanon Valley Coll., Annville, Pa., 1965; MS, U. of N.H., 1968; DSc, Johns Hopkins U., 1977. Lic. nuclear medicine physics and diagnostic radiology physics Am. Bd. Radiology, cert. health physicist Am. Bd. Health Physics, lic. diagnostic imaging physics Am. Bd. Med. Physics. Asst. prof. of radiology, acting dir. of physics and engring. dept. radiology Johns Hopkins Med. Instns., Balt., 1977—81; prof. of clin. radiology, chief hosp. physicist dept. radiology Columbia U. Physicians and Surgeons, N.Y.C., 1982—. Contbr., tchr., adviser Columbia U.; presenter in field. Contbr. articles and abstracts to profl. jours., chpts. to books. Fellow: Am. Coll. Radiologists (life), Am. Coll. Med. Physics (chmn.), Am. Assn. Physicists Medicine. Independent. Achievements include research in image quality and radiation dosimetry. Avocations: hiking, gardening, reading, theater. Office: Columbia U Physicians and Surgeons 177 Fort Washington Ave New York NY 10032-3784 Business E-Mail: eln1@columbia.edu.

**NICKON, ALEX,** chemist, educator; b. Poland, Oct. 6, 1927; came to U.S., 1955, naturalized, 1961; s. Steve and Maria (Nickon); m. Beulah Monica Godby, Aug. 22, 1950; children— Dale Beverly, Linda Cheryl, Leanne Marie. B.Sc., U. Alta., 1949; MA, Harvard U., 1951, PhD, 1953. Vis. lectr. Bryn Mawr Coll., 1953; postdoctoral fellow Birkbeck Coll., U. London, England, 1953-54, NRC, Ottawa, Canada, 1954-55; NSF sr. fellow; Imperial Coll., London, 1963-64; U. Munich, Germany, 1971-72; mem. faculty Johns Hopkins, 1955—, prof. chemistry, 1964-94, Vernon K. Krieble prof. chemistry, 1975-94, prof. emeritus, 1994—. Vis. assoc. dean Sch. on Profl. Tng., 1975-95; mem. medicinal chem. panel NIH, 1966-70; postdoctoral panel NRC, 1968-69. Sr. editor Jour. Organic Chemistry, 1965-71; Am. assoc. editor: Tetrahedron Reports, 1978-96. Recipient Md. Chemist award, 1990; Sloan Found. fellow, 1957-61 Fellow N.Y. Acad. Scis.; mem. Am. Chem. Soc. (nat. awards com. 1974-76), Brit. Chem. Soc. Home: 770 Knoll Rd Copper Canyon TX 75077 Personal E-mail: nickontx@yahoo.com.

**NICKSON, GRAHAM,** artist; b. Knowle Green, Lancashire, Eng., 1946; arrived in NYC, 1976; Student, Sch. of Art, Harris Coll., Preston, Eng., 1963, Camberwell Sch. Arts, Crafts, London, 1965, Painting Sch., Royal Coll. Art, 1969; Harkness fellow, Sch. Art, Yale Univ., 1976. Head, first-year diploma studies Byam Shaw Sch. Art, London, 1974; painting faculty Rome Scholarships, British Sch., Rome, 1975; lectr., drawing Phila. Sch. Art, 1980; faculty NY Studio Sch., 1977—1981—88, dean, 1988—. One-man shows include Salander O'Reilly Galleries, NYC, 1997, 1998, Adelaide Ctrl. Gallery, Australia, 1995, Camino Real Gallery, Boca Raton, Fla., 1996, Glenn Horowitz Gallery, E. Hampton, NY, 1996, exhibitions include Terry Dintfass Gallery, NY, 1996, Lizan-Tops Gallery, E. Hampton, NY, 1996, NAD, NYC, 1996, Art Mus., Fla. Internat., 1996, Ark. Art Ctr., Little Rock, 1997, Represented in permanent collections Albright Knox Art Gallery, NY, Met. Mus. Art, NYC, Neuberger Mus., NY, La Jolla mus. Contemporary Art, Calif., Israel Mus. Recipient Prix de Rome, British Sch. at Rome, 1972; grantee Guggenheim Fellowship in Painting, 1989, Ingram Merill Fellow in Painting, 1993; Howard Found. Fellow in Fine Art, 1980. Office: Dean NY Studio Sch 8 W 8th St New York NY 10011 Office Phone: 212-673-6466. Office Fax: 212-777-0996.

**NICOARA, ANDREEA CARINA,** mathematics professor; d. Ioan Lucian Nicoara and Ana Eugenia Bursan. BS in Math. (hon.), Stanford U., Calif. 1997; MA in Math., PhD in Math., Princeton U., NJ, 2002. Benjamin Peirce asst. prof. math. Harvard U., Cambridge, Mass., 2002—. Contbr. articles to profl. jours. Recipient Boothe prize for Excellence in Writing, Stanford U., 1994, Firestone medal for Excellence in Rsch., 1997, Robert M. Golden medal for Excellence in the Humanities, 1997; Luce fellow, Princeton U., 1997—99, Postdoctoral fellow, NSF, 2003—06. Mem.: Am. Math. Soc. (Waldemar J. Trjitzinsky Meml. Fund award 1996), Kokikai Aikido (instr. 2004, black belt 2004), Phi Beta Kappa. Democrat. Roman Catholic. Avocations: art history, comparative religion, Aikido, fencing, travel. Office Phone: 617-495-2482.

**NICODEMUS, KAREN A.,** college president; d. Elwin Edison Williams and Elsie Marie Saathoff; m. George Nicodemus, May 26, 1973. BA in History, John F. Kennedy Coll., Wahoo, Nebr., 1974; M in Phys. Edn. and Sports Adminstrn., U. Nebr., 1979, PhD in Ednl. Adminstrn., 1990. Instr. sociology, health and phys. edn., coach Cochise Coll., Douglas, Ariz., 1986—93, divsn. chair health and phys. edn./SMASS, 1990—93, dir. planning and assessment,

1993–96, acting dean of instrn. Sierra Vista, Ariz., 1995–96, v.p. instrn. Douglas, 1996–97, acting pres., 1997–98, pres., 1998–. Cons., evaluator North Ctrl. Assn., 1998–; sec., chair Ariz. C.C. Pres.'s Coun., Phoenix, 2000–04; women's basketball coach Cochise Coll., 1986–94, women's volleyball coach, 1987–90, coord. NCA self-study report, 1994–96. Mem. Ariz. Mex. Commn., Phoenix, 2003–, Cochise Cmty. Found., Sierra Vista, 2002–, Sierra Vista Regional Health Ctr., 2002–, Ariz. Town Hall, Phoenix, 2000; gov.'s appointee Ariz. State Bd. Edn., 2005. mem. Cochise County Workforce Investment Bd., 1999–2002. Recipient Master Tchr. award, U. Nebr. Alumni, 2004. Mem.: Am. Assn. C.C.s, Ariz. C.C. Assn. (chair 2002–03), Rural Policy Roundtable. Avocations: horseback riding, softball. Office: Cochise Coll 4190 W Hwy 80 Douglas AZ 85607

**NICOGOSSIAN, ANRAULD E.T.**, education educator; b. Dnieprepetrovsk, Ukraine; naturalized U.S. citizen, 1972; m. Barbara Ann Gallagher; 4 children. Student, Coll. St. Louis, Teheran, Iran, 1953; B in Biology, Lycee Franco-Iranian Razi, Teheran, 1956; MD, Teheran U., 1964; MS in Aerospace Medicine, Ohio State U., 1972. Diplomate Am. Bd. Preventive Medicine. Resident in medicine Pahlavi U. Hosp., Teheran U., 1963-65; intern Sydenham City Hosp., N.Y.C., 1965-66; resident in medicine Mt. Sinai Hosp. Svcs., Elmhurst, NY, 1966-68, chief med. resident, 1968-69, fellow pulmonary medicine, 1969-70; resident in aerospace and preventive medicine Ohio State U., Columbus, 1970-72; med. rsch. officer cardiovascular br. NASA Johnson Space Ctr., Houston, 1971-76, Apollo-Soyuz test project crew surgeon, 1974-75, chief med. ops. life scis. divsn. Washington, 1976-78, mgr. operational medicine office life scis. divsn., 1978-83, chief space medicine br. life scis. divsn., 1983–, chief med. officer office space flight, 1992–; pvt. practice Fairfax (Va.) Immediate Care Ctr., 1984-91; dir Office Internat. Med. Policy, Distinag. rsch. prof. George Mason U., Fairfax, Va., 2005–. Chmn. med. policy bd. NASA, 1979-2001, mem. rev. team for human presence in space, space sta. redesign and space sta. transition, 1992-93, mem. hdqrs. contingency action team, 1992-2001, dep. assoc. adminstr. for ops. and space flight for life and microgravity scis. and applications, 1993-2000, assoc. adminstr. for life and microgravity scis. and applications, 2000-2001, chief health and med. officer, 2001, sr. advisor for health to NASA adminstr.; staff physician Barnett Gen. Hosp., Patterson, N.J., 1967-68, LaGuardia Hosp., Queens, N.Y., 1968-70; vis. physician student health ctr. Ohio State U., Columbus, 1970-72, clin. instr. dept. internal medicine, 1971-72; assoc. clin. prof. dept. cmty. medicine Wright State U., Dayton, Ohio, 1978-84; affiliate faculty ACLS and ATLS tng. ctr. Georgetown U. Hosp., Washington, 1980-84; asst. prof. dept. preventive medicine Uniformed Svcs., U. Health Scis., Washington, 1977–; vis. faculty; lectr. in physiology and medicine Moscow State U., 1995. Co-author: Space Physiology and Medicine, 1983, 3d edit., 1994, Life Sciences Considerations for Long Duration Missions, 1994; contbr. articles to profl. jours., chpts. to books; mem. editl. bd. Aviation, Space and Environ. Medicine Jour., 1978-93, 96. Scholar Nat. TB and Respiratory Disease Assn., 1970, Link Found., 1970-71; recipient Meritorious Svc. medallion Am. Heart Assn., 1980, 82, Jeffries Med. Rsch. award AIAA, 1982, Past Pres. award No. Va. chpt. Am. Heart Assn., 1983, Strughold award Aerospace Med. Assn., 1984, Tech. Publs. award Aerospace Med. Assn., 1985., Yuri Gagarin medal USSR Fedn. Cosmonautics, 1987, Disting. Svc. award Am. Soc. Gravitational and space biology, 1989, Allan D. Emil Meml. award Internat. Aero. Fedn., 1990, Life Scis. award internat. Acad. Astronautics, 1990, Cert. Appreciation Coun. Mins., Armenia, 1990, Commemorative award and medal Yuri Gagarin Cosmonaut Tng. Ctr., 1990, Presdl. Letter of Commendation for Cmty. Svcs., 1990, Letter of Appreciation U.S. Surgeon Gen., 1990, S.P. Korolev medal Russian Fedn. Cosmonautics, 1993, Internat. Cooperation award AIAA, 1993, Cert. of Appreciation Russian Space Agy., 1994, Achievement award 1995, numerous others. Fellow ACP, Am. Coll. Preventive Medicine, Am. Astron. Soc. (chmn. awards com. 1990-93, bd. dirs. 1988–, Melbourne W. Boyton award 1984, W. Randolph Lovelace II award 1993), Aerospace Med. Assn., Am. Astronautical Soc.; mem. AAAS, Nat. Assn. Residents and Interns, Am. Thoracic Soc., Tex. Thoracic Soc., Internat. Acad. Astronautics (Tech. Publs. award 1985, chair life scis. sect. 1995), Internat. Union Physiol. Socs., Korean Aeromed. Soc. (hon.), Acad. Scis. of Armenian Republic (fgn. mem.). Office: Sch Pub Policy George Mason Univ 4400 Univ Dr Fairfax VA 22030 Office Phone: 703-728-7277. E-mail: anicogoss@gmu.edu.

**NICOL, DOMINIK**, writer, photographer; b. northern Oltenia, Romania, Sept. 25, 1930; came to U.S., 1969, naturalized, 1976; s. Dumitru and Valentina (Sandulescu) Nicolaescu-Stroe. Diploma in Chemistry and Tech. of Antibiotics, The Tech. Sch., Bucharest, Romania, 1954. Photo-reporter Agerpress, Bucharest, 1950-51; med. photographer Cantacuzino Hosp., Bucharest, 1955-68; ret., 1995. Author, editor: Self Encounter, 1979, Ten Oneiric Sketches, 1980, Rendes-Vous sau Intalnire cu mine insumi, 1987; (play) Vacuum (Colocviu de albis), 1979, Vacuum-Void, 1988, Pe portativul vietii, 1992. Home: 334 W 49th St Apt 4FE New York NY 10019-7308

**NICOLADIS, MICHAEL F.**, engineering company executive; b. New Orleans, Aug. 15, 1960; s. Frank and Peggy (Yemelos). N. B in Engring. magna cum laude, Vanderbilt U., 1982; MBA, Duke U., 1984. Assoc. N-Y Assocs., Inc., Metairie, La., 1984-85, v.p., 1985-97, COO, sr. v.p., 1997–. Mem. Holy Trinity Greek Orthodox Cathedral, New Orleans. Fuqua scholar, Conoco scholar Duke U. Mem.: ASCE, Am. Pub. Works Assn., Am. Coun. Engring. Cos., Soc. Am. Mil. Engrs., Chi Epsilon, Tau Beta Pi. Avocations: tennis, reading, travel. Office: N Y Assocs Inc 2750 Lake Villa Dr Metairie LA 70002-6786 Office Phone: 504-885-0500. Business E-Mail: mnicoladis@n-yassociates.com.

**NICOLAI, PAUL PETER**, lawyer; b. Trenton, N.J., Jan. 22, 1953; s. Ernest and Preziosa E. (Cattani) N.; m. Anne Marie Elizabeth LaRochelle, May 14, 1976; children. Caroline Emma, Peter Ernest, Margaret Elizabeth, Alexandra Marie, Elizabeth Anne. BA, Am. Internat. Coll., 1975; JD, Western New Eng. Coll., 1979. Bar: Mass. 1979, U.S. Dist. Ct. Mass. 1980, U.S. Ct. Appeals (1st cir.) 1983, U.S. Supreme Ct. 1984, N.Y. 1987, Washington DC 1987, U.S. Ct. Appeals (Fed. cir.) 1990, U.S. Tax Ct. 1991, Conn. 2003. Legal asst. Friendly Ice Cream Corp., Wilbraham, Mass., 1976-79, staff counsel, 1979-81, co. counsel, 1981-88; pres. Nicolai Law Group, P.C., Springfield, Mass., 1990—. Pes., dir., chair bus. plan rev. com. WMV Forums, Inc., 2000–02. editl. bd.: ABA/BNA Lawyers Manual on Profl. Conduct. Bd. dirs. Citizens for Ltd. Taxation, Mass., 1981-84, chmn., 1984-97; mem. We. Mass. exec. com. NCCJ, mem. We. Mass. and Conn. devel. com. 1995-99, nat. trustee, 1991-99; corporator Springfield Day Nursery, Inc., 1995—, mem. mktg. com., 1995-96, Springfield Libr. Mus. Assn., Inc., 1985-2003; bd. dirs. Pioneer Valley Montessori Soc., Inc., Springfield, 1985-93, v.p., 1988-92, pres., 1992-93; bd. dirs., chmn. Citizens Econs. Rsch. Found., Inc., Boston, 1984-97; mem. adv. bd. Springfield Enterprise Ctr., 1998—2003. Mem. ABA (bd. editors lawyer's manual on profl. conduct 2005–), Am. Arbitration Assn. (arbitration panel 1992–), Mass. Bar Assn. (fee arbitration bd. 2000–, chmn. 2003-2004, 2005–, fee arbitration panel 1997–, arbitration and mediation panel 1999-2002, law practice mgmt. sect. coun. 2002-05, Ho. of Dels., regional dels., 2004-05), Hampden County Bar Assn. (arbitration and mediation panel 1998-2002), Assn. Bar City N.Y., D.C. Bar Assn., Fed. Cir. Ct. Appeals Bar Assn., Am. Internat. Coll. Corp. (reunion com., 2000, nat. bd. dirs., v.p. 1989-90, pres. 1990-91, corporator 2000–), Soc. Everett Barney Inc. (treas., chs. 1992-99, dir. 1995-2002, sec. 1996-99), We. Mass. Tech. Bus. Coun. (bd. dirs. 2002-2003), We. Mass. Econ. Devel. Coun. (bd. dirs. 2004-), We. Mass. Software Assn. (bd. dirs. 1998-2001, treas. 2000-01), We. Mass. Venture Forums, Inc. (2000-02), Springfield Underride Com. (chmn. and treas. 2005). Roman Catholic. Avocation: reading. Home: 24 Venture Dr Springfield MA 01119-2727 Office: Nicolai Law Group PC 146 Chestnut St Ste 501 Springfield MA 01103-1539 Office Phone: 413-272-2000. Business E-Mail: paul.nicolai@niclawgrp.com.

**NICOLAIDES, MARY**, lawyer; b. N.Y.C., June 7, 1927; d. George and Dorothy Nicolaides. BCE, CUNY, 1947; MBA with distinction, DePaul U., 1975, JD, 1981. Bar: Ill. 1982, U.S. Dist. Ct. (no. dist.) Ill. 1982, U.S. Patent Office 1983. Sr. design engr. cement subs. U.S. Steel Corp., N.Y.C., then Pitts., 1948-71; sole practice Chgo., 1982–. Republican. Greek Orthodox. Address: 233 E Erie St Apt 1804 Chicago IL 60611-2903

**NICOLAIDES, STEVE**, film producer; Prodr. (with Jeffrey Stott) The Princess Bride, 1987, It Takes Two, 1988, When Harry Met Sally..., 1989, Misery, 1990, Boyz N the Hood, 1991, A Few Good Men, 1992, (with John Singleton) Poetic Justice, 1993, Little Big League, 1994, A Boy Called Hate, 1995, Buddy, 1997, The Deep End of the Ocean, 1999; exec. prodr. Shaft, 2000, Marci X, 2003, School of Rock, 2003, The Forgotten, 2004, Annapolis, 2006, Nacho Libre, 2006.*

**NICOLAOU, ANDREAS I.**, finance educator, consultant; BSc, Athens U. Economics and Bus.; PhD, So. Ill. U. CPA Ohio. IT audit mgr. Delloite & Touche, Lemesos, Cyprus; prof. Bowling Green (Ohio) State U., 2000—. Mgmt. cons., Athens, Greece, 1999—2000. Contbr. articles to profl. jours. Mem.: Assn. Info. Systems, Am. Acctg. Assn. (nat. com. chair 2005—06). Achievements include research in behavioral effects of IS adoption/use. Office: Bowling Green State University Dept Accounting & MIS BA 332 Bowling Green OH 43403 Office Phone: 419-372-2932. Office Fax: 419-372-2875. Business E-Mail: anicol@cba.bgsu.edu.

**NICOLAOU, K. C.**, chemistry professor; b. Karavas, Kyrenia, Cyprus, July 5, 1946; came to U.S., 1972; s. Costa and Helen (Yettimi) N.; m. Georgette Karayianni, July 15, 1973; children: Colette, Alexis, Christopher, Paul. BSc, Bedford Coll., London, 1969; PhD, U. Coll., London, 1972; DSc, U. London, 1994; PhD (hon.), U. Athens, 1995. Rsch. assoc. Columbia U., N.Y.C., 1972-73, Harvard U., Cambridge, Mass., 1973-76; from asst. prof. to Rhodes-Thompson prof. chemistry U. Pa., Phila., 1976-89; prof. chemistry U. Calif. at San Diego, La Jolla, 1989—; Darlene Shiley prof. chemistry, chmn. dept. The Scripps Rsch. Inst., La Jolla, Calif., 1989—; Aline W. & L.S. Skaggs prof. Skaggs Inst. for Chemical Biology, Scripps Rsch. Inst., 1996—. Vis. prof. U. Paris, 1986; mem. exec. com. Diann. Cyprus Conf. on Drug Design; mem. med. study sect. D, NIH, 1988-90; mem. internat. adv. bd. Angewandte Chemie, 1994—. Author: (with N. A. Petasis) Selenium in Natural Products Synthesis, 1984, (with E. J. Sorensen) Classics in Total Synthesis, 1996; co-editor: Synthesis, Germany, 1984-90, Chemistry and Biology, 1994; editl. bd. Prostaglandins, Leukotrienes and Medicine, 1978-88, Synthesis, 1990—, Accounts of Chem. Rsch., 1992—, Carbohydrate Letters, 1993—, Chemistry-A European Jour., 1994—, Perspectives in Drug, Discovery and Design, 1994—, Indian Jour. of Chemistry, Sect. B, 1995—; mem. bd. consulting editors Tetrahedron Publs., 1992—; mem. adv. bd. Contemporary Organic Synthesis, 1993—; mem. regional adv. bd. J. C. S. Chem. Comm., 189—, J. C. S. Perkin I, 1991—; contbr. articles to profl. jours.; patentee in field. Recipient Japan Soc. for Promotion Sci. award 1987-88, U.S. Sr. Scientist award Alexander von Humboldt Found., 1987-88, Alan R. Day award Phila. Organic Chemists Club, 1993, Pfizer Rsch. award, 1993-94, Paul Janssen Prize, 1994, Alexander the Great Award Hellenic Cultural Soc. of San Diego, 1994, Rhone-Poulenc medal Royal Soc. of Chemistry, 1995, Chem. Pioneer Am. Inst. of Chemists, 1996, Inhoffen Medal of Gesellscaft fur Biotechnologische Forschung mbH (GBF) Tech. U. of Braunschweig, 1996, Linus Pauling award, 1996, Schering prize, Aspirin prize, Max Tischler Lecture prize, Yamada prize, Nagoya medal, Centenary medal, Royal Soc., Paul Karrer medal, Esselen award, Nobel Laureate Signature award, Petrahedron prize; fellow A.P. Sloan Found., 1979-83, J. S. Guggenhiem Found., 1984; Camille and Henry Dreyfus scholar, 1980-84, Arthur C. Cope scholar, 1987. Fellow N.Y. Acad. Scis., AAAS; mem. Nat. Acad. Scis., Am. Chem. Soc. (Creative Work in Synthetic Organic Chemistry award 1993, William H. Nichols medal N.Y. sect. 1996, Ernest Guenther award in chemistry of natural products 1996), Chem. Soc. London, German Chem. Soc., Japanese Chem. Soc. Office: Scripps Rsch Inst Dept Chemistry 10550 N Torrey Pines Rd La Jolla CA 92037-1000*

**NICOLAS, KENNETH LEE**, import/export company executive; b. San Francisco, Feb. 7, 1944; s. Norman L. and Bernice L. (Hameister) N.; m. Anne Vanderwielen, July 5, 1992 (dec.); children: Juliana M., Camille G. BA in Polit. Sci., Calif. State U., Fullerton, 1968; MA in Legis. Affairs/Econs., George Washington U., 1975. Exec. asst. Congressman Richard T. Hanna, Washington, 1970-72; sr. staff officer Nat. Assn. Ednl. Broadcasters, Washington, 1972-74; founder, pres. Nicolas Assocs. Internat., Inc., 1972—80; exec. dir. Am. Coll. Nuc. Physicians, Washington, 1974-77; aide to the Pres. White House, Washington, 1977-80; v.p. McSweeney & Co. Consulting, Newport Beach, Calif., 1980-83, L.E. Peterson & Co. Investment Banking, Costa Mesa, Calif., 1983-85; founder, pres. Fin. Strategies Group, Inc., Newport Beach, 1985—; CEO Tradex Internat., Inc., Newport Beach, 1988-94; founder, CEO Trade Access Group, Inc., 1994—. Adj. prof. Orange Coast Coll., Costa Mesa, 1983-97, internat. MBA program U. So. Calif., 1989-90, Thunderbird Sch. Internat. Bus., Orange County, 1990-92, U. Calif., Riverside and Irvine, 1996-98; adj. prof. internat. bus. MBA program Webster U., 1998—. Author: (article series) Business to Business Mag., 1984-87 (Excellence award 1984-87). Bd. dirs., v.p. Leukemia Soc. Am., Orange County, Calif., 1982-88; chmn. Holiday Project, 1992-94; mem. bd. mgrs., chmn. capital devel. com. Orange County YMCA, 2001—, gen. campaign chmn., fedn. chief parent/child program, 2002–; nation chief Orange Blossom Nation, Indian Princess Program. With U.S. Army, 1968-70, Vietnam. Recipient Outstanding Svc. award Nat. Holiday Project, 1993, Nat. Svc. Appreciation award Pres. Jimmy Carter, 1980, Excellence award Leukemia Soc. Am., 1988. Mem. Japan Am. Soc. (Orange County chpt. chmn. bd. dirs. 1997—), Japan Am. Soc. So. Calif. (exec. bd. 1996-98). Avocations: Karate, sailing, travel, chess, swimming. E-mail: finadvisor@cox.net.

**NICOLATUS, STEPHEN JON**, financial consultant; b. Salt Lake City, June 6, 1950; s. George Stephen and Viola (Renikas) N. BS in Polit. Sci., U. Utah, 1975; MS in Agril. Econ., U. Ariz., 1977. Rsch. assoc. U. Ariz., Tucson, 1975-77; rsch. lab. asst. Utah Cooperative Assn., CENEX, Salt Lake City, 1977; rsch. assoc. Frank K. Stuart & Assocs., Salt Lake City, 1977-81, v.p., 1981-89; prin. Stuart, Nicolatus & Peterson, Salt Lake City, 1989-90; prin. Houlihan, Dorton, Jones, Nicolatus & Stuart, OTRA Securites, Salt Lake City, 1990-95; pres. We. Econ. and Valuation Cons., 1995—. Econs. faculty U. Phoenix, Salt Lake City, 1985—, area chair econs., 1987-95. With USAFR, 1968-74. Mem. Am. Soc. Appraisers (cert. sr. appraiser, bus. valuation), Wasatch Front Econ. Forum, SLC Chpt. of ASA (pres. 1998-99). Greek Orthodox. Avocations: golf, stock market, snorkeling, skiing. Home: 1021 Cutter Ln Park City UT 84098-7553 Office: 675 E 2100 S Ste 260 Salt Lake City UT 84106 also: 2441 Tech Ctr Ct Ste 111 Las Vegas NV 89128

**NICOLAU, SIOBHAN**, cultural organization administrator; Grad., Goucher Coll., Latin Am. Inst. Former sr. program officer Ford Found.; pres., founder Hispanic Policy Develop. Project, 1981—; mem. Nat. Film Archive of Philanthropy. Trustee Ewing Marion Kauffman Found., 1993—2002, 2003—; bd. mem. Public/Private Ventures, Enterprise Found. Office: Hispanic Policy Develop Project 122 E 42nd St New York NY 10168*

**NICOLETTI, PAUL LEE**, retired veterinarian, educator; b. Goodman, Mo., Oct. 26, 1932; s. Felix and Clarice N.; m. Earlene Blackburn, June 6, 1954; children: Diana, Julie, Nancy. BS in Agr., U. Mo., 1956, DVM, 1956; MS, U. Wis., 1962. Diplomate Am. Coll. Vet. Preventive Medicine. Veterinarian USDA, Mo., Wis., N.Y., 1956-68, UN FAO, Tehran, Iran, 1968-72, USDA, Jackson, Miss., 1972-75, Gainesville, Fla., 1973-78; prof. vet. medicine U. Fla., Gainesville, 1978—2003, prof. emeritus, 2003—. Recipient awards from Fla. Cattleman's Assn., 1978, Dairy Farmers, Inc., 1978, Borden award, 1979, Gold Star award Fla. Veterinary Medicine Assoc., 1981, 86, U. Austral, Chile, 1981, P.R. Dairy Assn., 1978, faculty alumni award U. Mo., 1987; named Basic Scis. Tchr. of Yr. Nat. Student Am. Vet. Med. Assn., 1994, Alumnus of Yr. award, U. Fla. Disting. Svc. award, 2003. U. Fla. Disting. Svc. award 1999, Lifetime Achievement award 2004), Am. Coll. Vet. Preventive Medicine (pres. 1997-98), Phi Zeta (nat. pres. 1997-99). Home: 2552 SW 14th Dr Gainesville FL 32608-2042 Office: Univ of Fla Coll Vet Medicine PO Box 110880 Gainesville FL 32611-0880 Office Phone: 352-392-4700 x5860. Business E-Mail: nicolettip@mail.vetmed.ufl.edu.

**NICOLL, EDWARD J.**, internet financial company executive; JD, Yale U. Co-founder, pres. Waterhouse Investor Svcs., Inc. (sold to Toronto-Dominion Bank and became TD Waterhouse), 1979—96; chmn., CEO Datek Online Holdings, Corp., Iselin, NJ, 1999—2002; CEO Instinet Group, Inc., 2002—. Trustee New Cmty. Found. Fellow Yale U. Achievements include first to to attend Yale Law without a college degree.

**NICOLL, JANE ELLEN**, archivist, librarian; b. Rockford, Ill., May 24, 1954; d. William Alexander and Mary Louise (Howard) Nicoll; m. Carl Peter Stover, May 14, 1983; children: Benjamin Alexander Stover, Andrew Jacob Stover, Michael David Stover. BFA, U. Ill., Urbana, 1976, MLS, 1978. Cert. archivist Acad. of Cert. Archivists, 1990. Reference libr. and archivist local history collection Pk. Forest Pub. Libr., Ill., 1979–2005; exec. dir. Ridge Hist. Soc., Chgo., 2005—. Bd. dir. Pk. Forest Hist. Soc., Ill., co-founder and archivist, 1985—; curator and co-creator 50th Anniversary Ho. Mus., 1998—; mem. adv. bd. Matteson Hist. Mus., 2003. Contbr. articles to profl. jours. Second in command 50th Anniversary Com., Park Forest, Ill., 1996—2000; vol. Pk. Forest Hall of Fame, 1994—. Educate and Automate Digital grantee, Ill. State Libr. 1998–99. Mem.: Ill. Assn. of Museums (assoc.), Chgo. Area Archivists (assoc.), Soc. of Am. Archivists (assoc.), Midwest Archives Conf. (assoc.), South Suburban Heritage Assn. (assoc.), Ill. Heritage Assn. (assoc.). Methodist. Achievements include development of digital website, Park Forest: An Illinois Planned Community. Avocations: antiques, cooking, swimming. Office: Ridge Hist Soc 10621 S Seeley Ave Chicago IL 60643 Office Phone: 773-881-1675. Business E-Mail: parkforesthistory1@yahoo.com.

**NICOLS, ANGELA C.**, software engineer, consultant; b. Jamaica, N.Y., Apr. 15, 1940; d. Henry Ralph and Josephine Sadie (Zarcone) Grieco; m. Otto John Nicols, May 21, 1960; children: Annemarie Nicols-Grinenko, Elizabeth Marie Crevani, John Joseph, William Joseph, Richard Joseph. BS in Math., Hofstra U., 1979; MS in Math. and Computer Sci., Adelphi U., 1985. Supr. programs/project leader Book Clubs Info. Sys. Doubleday and Co. Inc., Garden City, N.Y. 1979-87; mgr. software engring. Martin Marietta Info. Sys., Orlando, Fla., 1987-94; with Apopka Hist. Soc., 1994—, pres., 2005—; computer cons. and trainer, owner Nicols Cons., Apopka, 1995—. Vol. Apopka H.S. Adv. Coun., 1994-97; sec. Bd. Edn.: Bishop Moore H.S., Orlando, 1995-98. Mem. St. Francis Disabilities Com., 1995—; mem. pastoral coun. St. Francis of Assisi Ch., mem. social action commn., 2000-03; chair helping hands Errol Estates Property Owners Assn., 2005—. Mem. AAUW, IEEE Computer Soc., Assn. for Computing Machinery, Math. Assn. Am., Nat. Assn. Women in Computing, Am. Math. Soc., Coun. Cath. Women, Gray Panthers, Foliage Garden Club of Apopka (2d v.p. 1996-2001, 2005—), Errol Estates Country Club (comms. com. 1998-2000), Henry Nehrling Soc. (bd. dirs. 2006—), Golfside Village Homeowners Assn. (exec. v.p. 1999—), Kappa Mu Epsilon. Office Phone: 407-886-2057. E-mail: angenic@cfl.rr.com.

**NICOLS, HOWARD J.C.**, lawyer; b. Woodhaven, NY, 1956; BA summa cum laude, SUNY, Albany, 1978; JD cum laude, Cornell U., 1981. Bar: Ohio 1981, NY 2000, US Ct. Appeals, 2nd, 6th, 9th, 10th Circuits 2003, US Dist. Ct. 2003, Northern Dist. Ohio 2003. Ptnr., litigation Squire, Sanders & Dempsey, LLP, Cleve., mem. mgmt. com. Master bencher Judge Anthony J. Celebrezze Am. Inn Ct.; chancellor Cornell Moot Ct. Bd.; presenter in field. Bd. editor Cornell Internat. Law Jour.; co-author: Taxes on Profits of Multinational Companies and Implications for Russia, 2004. Mem.: Cleve. Bar Assn. Office: Squire Sanders & Dempsey LLP 4900 Key Tower 122 Public Sq Cleveland OH 44114-1304 Office Phone: 216-479-8743. Office Fax: 216-479-8780. Business E-Mail: hnicols@ssd.com.

**NICOLSON, DAN HENRY**, plant taxonomist; b. Kansas City, Mo., Sept. 5, 1933; s. John Whitley and LeOna Johanna (Teget) N.; m. Alice Black Crawford, Aug. 22, 1959; children: John Crawford, Sarah Whitley, David Teget. AB, Grinnell Coll., 1955; MBA, Stanford U., 1957; MSc, Cornell U., 1959, PhD, 1964. Asst. curator Smithsonian Instn., Washington, 1964-65, assoc. curator, 1965-74, curator, 1974—. Author: Flora of Dominica, 1991; co-author: An Interpretation Van Rheede's Hortus Malabaricus, 1988, The Forsters and the Botany of the Second Cook Expedition (1772-1775), 2004; co-editor: Flora of the Hassan District, 1976. Mem. Internat. Assn. Plant Taxonomy (v.p. 1987-93, pres. 1993-99, past pres. 1999-2005), Washington Biologists Field Club (treas. 1981-97), Washington Bot. Soc. (pres. 1989-90, treas. 1997-2006). Office: Dept Botany MRC-166 Nat Mus Natural History Smithsonian Instn Washington DC 20013-7012 Business E-Mail: nicolson@si.edu.

**NICYPER, DEAN R.**, lawyer; s. Raymond Seymour and Geraldine G. Nicyper; m. Louise L. Meryman, Aug. 12, 1979; children: Hope, Ky. BA, Marlboro Coll., 1976; JD, Am. U., 1985. Bar: N.Y. 1986. Musician Widespread Depression Orch., N.Y.C., 1976—81; assoc. Cahill Gordon & Rendel, N.Y.C., 1985—94; of counsel Flemming, Zulack & Williamson LLP, N.Y.C., 1994—96, ptnr., 1996—. Bd. dirs Am. Horse Trials Found., Centerville, Md.; vice chmn., bd. trustees Marlboro (Vt.) Coll., 1999—; guest commentator Countdown TV, N.Y.C., 1996, N.Y.C., 98; cross-country contr.; dir. Millbrook (N.Y.) Horse Trials, 2000—. Composer: (mus. composition) All That Rhythm, 1980, musician 4 recs. with Widespread Depression Orch. Mem.: ABA, Copyright Soc., Assn. of Bar of City of N.Y. Avocations: oil painting, equestrian competitions. Office: Flemming Williamson Zanders LLP 1 Liberty Plz New York NY 10006

**NIDECKER, ANDREAS CORNELIS**, radiologist, educator; b. Tiel, The Netherlands, Oct. 1, 1947; s. Hans Jakob and Rosemarie (Hoggenberg) Nidecker; children from previous marriage: Florian, Maja, Eva. MD, Med. Sch. U. Basel, Switzerland, 1973. Diplomate Am. Bd. Radiology. Internship Lawrence Gen. Hosp., Toronto, Canada, 1973—74, 1976—79; asst. prof. radiology U. Basel, 1985-99, prof., 1999—; pvt. practice Basel, 1982—. Mem. Arbeitsgruppe Knochentumoren, Deutsches Krebforschungsfentrur; co-owner IMAMED Radiologie Nordwest, Basel. Mem. exec. com., past pres. Internat. Physicians Prevention Nuc. War, 1982—; mem. constl. coun. Basel Canton. Mem.: Swiss Soc. Radiology, Radiol. Soc. N.Am., Internat. Soc. Skeletal Radiology. Avocations: hiking, skiing, travel, music. Office: IMAMED Radiologie Nordwest Untere Rebgasse 18 4058 Basel Switzerland E-mail: anidecker@bluewin.ch, andreas.nidecker@imamed.ch.

**NIDES, THOMAS RICHARD**, diversified financial services company executive; s. Mr. and Mrs. Arnold R. Nides BA, U. Minn. Campaign staffer, midwest region polit. and fin. div. Mondale-Ferraro presdl. campaign, 1984; polit. action com. dir. Dem. Congressional Campaign Com., 1985—86; spl. asst. Tony Coelho, House Majority, 1986—89; exec. asst. to spkr. Ho. of Reps. Thomas Foley, 1989—93; chief of staff Michael Kantor, US Trade Rep., 1993—94; v.p. housing impact Fannie Mae, 1995—96, sr. v.p. human resources, 1997—2001; prin., head of corp. affairs Morgan Stanley, NYC, 1996—97; campaign mgr., vice-presidential campaign Joe Lieberman, 2000; global chief adminstrv. officer Credit Suisse First Boston LLC, NYC, 2001—04, mem., oper. com.; pres., CEO Burson-Marsteller, NYC, 2004—05; chief adminstrv. officer Morgan Stanley, NYC, 2005—. Office: Morgan Stanley 1585 Broadway New York NY 10036

**NIDETZ, MYRON PHILIP**, health care delivery systems consultant; b. Chgo., Dec. 29, 1935; s. David J. and Rose Y. (Yudell) N.; m. Linda Freeman, Dec. 18, 1960; children: Julia, Allison. BS, U. Ill., 1958; M in Bus. and Commerce, Hamilton Inst., Phila., 1972; MPA, Roosevelt U., 1981. Diplomate Am. Acad. Med. Adminstrs. Dir. Union Coop. Eye Care Ctr., Chgo., 1961-65; dir. med. adminstrv. svcs. Michael Reese Hosp. and Med. Ctr., Chgo., 1965-75; assoc. dir. program to imrpove med. care and health svcs. AMA, Chgo., 1975-79; exec. dir. North Ctrl. Dialysis Ctrs., Chgo., 1979-92; pres.

Myron P. Nidetz & Assocs., Inc., Chgo., 1992—. Disting. vis. lectr. health care adminstrn. Roosevelt U., Chgo., bd. govs., 1992—2005, pres. pub. adminstrn. coun., 1993—2005, mem. curriculum rev. com. pub. adminstrn., 1992—97, chair admissions com., 1992—2005, chair coun. and chpt. leadership com., 1998—; vis. lectr. Ind. U. N.W., 2003—, arts cons., 2005—; Nat. Inst. Corrections tech. cons. U.S. Dept. Justice, 1978—90; adj. prof. program chair Calumet Coll., St. Joseph U., Whiting, Ind., 1997—99. Mem. adv. bd. Inst. of Medicine, 1979—2000; active Health Planning Facilities Bd., Ill., 1979—93, Ill. Dept. Pub. Aid, 1992—99, Ill. Dept. Aging 1992—99; mem. adv. bd. Am. Kidney Fund, chmn. Midwest core group, 1979—92; mem. adv. bd. Nat. Kidney Found., West. area satellite group, state legis. com., 1992—99; cmty. coord. AARP, 1992—98; pres. bd. dirs. Suburban Area Agy. on Aging, 1997—99, sr. adv. cons., 1999—2004; mem. Munster Area Rotary Club, Humane Soc. of the Calumet Area, Friends of Theatre at the Ctr., Munster Hist. Soc., Lake County Devel. Com.; bd. dirs., mem. ethics com. Hospice of Calumet Area; counselor Svc. Core of Ret. Execs., 1992—2002; bd. dirs. Active Srs. Found., 1999—2003, chair bd. devel. com.; regional rev. panelist Ind. Arts Commn., 2002; bd. dirs. Lake County Pub. Libr. Found., Friends of Emerson Sch. for Visual and Performing Arts., 2005—. With U.S. Army, 1959—60. Fellow: APHA, Am. Acad. Med. Adminstrs., Royal Soc. Health; mem.: AMA, Humane Soc. of Calumet Area, 21st Century Fund (trustee), Lake County Libr. Found. (bd. dirs.), Humane Soc. of the Calumet Area, Hospice of the Calumet Area, Ind. Pub. Health Assn., Ill. Pub. Health Assn., Am. Mgmt. Assn., Assn. U. Programs Health Adminstrn., Gerontol. Soc., Inst. Soc. Ethics and Life Scis., Am. Mgmt. Assn., Am. Hosp. Assn., Am. Geriatrics Soc., Am. Acad. Polit. and Social Sci., Nat. Renal Adminstrs. Assn. (govt. affairs com.), Am. Assn. Kidney Patients, Nat. Dialysis Assn. (sec.), Assn. Hosp. Med. Edn., Munster Hist. Soc., Friends of the Theatre, Ind. Regional Arts Commn. (commr.), Munster Rotary Club, Ind. U. Northwest Ctr. for Cultural Discovery & Learning Group, Ind. U. Northwest Theatre Patron, Ind. U. Northwest (curatorate), Books, Brushes & Bands (bd. dir.), Munster Ednl. Found. (bd. dir.), Hammond Cmty. Concerts Assn. Soc., Hammond Cmty. Concerts Assn., No. Ind. Arts Assn. (bd. dir., devel. com.), Lyric Opera Chpt., Auditorium Bldg. Soc., NW Ind. Excellence in Theatre Found. (bd. dir.), Ill. Theatre Ctr. Guild (chmn. 1990—91), Ill. Theatre Ctr., Northwest Ind. Symphony Soc. (bd. dirs.), No. Ind. Arts Assn. (bd.dir.).

NIEBRUEGGE, MICHAEL E., lawyer; b. Alton, Ill., Mar. 21, 1952; BA, Harvard U., 1974; JD, Cornell U., 1977. Bar: Ill. 1977, U.S. Dist. Ct. (no. dist.) Ill. 1977, Tex. 1982, U.S. Dist. Ct. (so dist.) Tex. 1988. Lectr. bus. law Northwestern Univ., Chg., Ill., 1979—80; v.p., gen. counsel Gulf Coast Royalty Co., Houston, 1981—82; atty. Mayer, Brown, Rowe & Maw LLP, Chgo., 1977—81, Houston, 1982—84, ptnr., 1984—, ptnr.-in-charge, 1995—. Lectr. Northwestern U., Chgo., 1979-80. Mem. State Bar Tex., Tex. Assn. Bank Counsel. Office: Mayer Brown Rowe & Maw LLP Ste 3600 700 Louisiana St Houston TX 77002-2730 Office Phone: 713-546-0507. Office Fax: 713-632-1800. Business E-Mail: mniebruegge@mayerbrownrowe.com.

NIEBUHR, PAUL DAVID, music educator; b. Cedar Rapids, Iowa, Nov. 7, 1963; s. Edwin Henry and Vera Louise (Cordes) Niebuhr; m. Lisa Ann Grubb-Niebuhr, June 3, 1989; children: Elias John, Elisabeth Louise, Evan Wayne. MusB in Edn., Morningside Coll., 1987; student, We. Iowa Tech. U. Lic. Tchr. Iowa Dept. Edn., 1987. Educator Sutherland Sch., Iowa, 1987—90, Benton Cmty. Sch., Van Horne, Iowa, 1990—93, Battle Creek-Ida Grove, Iowa, 1993—94, Gehlen Cath. Sch., Le Mars, Iowa, 1996—98, 2000—; ins. salesman Sioux City, Iowa, 1994—96; devel. assoc. United Way, Sioux City, 1999—2000. Fireman Sutherland Fire Dept., 1989—90, Kingsley Fire Dept., 1993—, tng. officer, 2005—; mem. edn. com. Kingsley United Meth. Ch., 2003—05. Named Alumni Tchr. of Yr., Morningside Coll., Sioux City, 2004. Mem.: Iowa Band Dir.'s Assn. (mem. jazz band com. 1990—91). Methodist. Avocations: hunting, camping, fishing, cars. Home: 114 Dover Box 626 Kingsley IA 51028 Office: Gehlen Catholic Sch 709 Plymouth St NE Le Mars IA 51031 Office Phone: 712-546-4181.

NIEBYL, JENNIFER ROBINSON, obstetrician, gynecologist, educator; BSc, McGill U., Montreal, 1963; MD, Yale U., 1967. Diplomate Am. Bd. Ob-Gyn., Am. Bd. Maternal and Fetal Medicine. Intern in Internal Medicine N.Y. Hosp.-Cornell Med. Ctr., 1967-68, resident in ob-gyn., 1968-70, Johns Hopkins Hosp., Balt., 1970-73, fellow in maternal and fetal medicine, 1976-78, mem. staff, 1973—88, U. Iowa Hosps. and Clinics, Iowa City, 1988—; prof., head ob-gyn. dept. U. Iowa Sch. Medicine, Iowa City, 1988—. Mem. ACOG, Am. Gynecol. and Obstetrical Soc., Soc. Gynecol. Investigation, Soc. Maternal Fetal Medicine, Inst. Medicine of NAS. Office: U Iowa Hosps & Clinics 200 Hawkins Dr Iowa City IA 52242 Office Phone: 319-356-1976.

NIED, THOMAS HERMAN, retired media specialist; b. Queens, NY, May 4, 1942; s. Herman Joseph and Margaret (Jos) N.; m. Carol J. Thomas, June 6, 1964; children: Stacey, Allison. BA, Rutgers U., 1964, LLB, 1967; LLM in Taxation, NYU, 1972. CPA, N.J., Ga. Tax mgr. Ernst & Young, N.Y.C., Atlanta, Newark and Trenton, N.J., 1968-77; v.p. taxation N.Y. Times Co., N.Y.C., 1977-97; v.p. fed. tax Universal Music Group (formerly Polygram Holding Inc.), N.Y.C., 1997—2004, ret., 2004. Founder Media Tax Group, 1979, mem., 1979-99. Mem. ABA, AICPA, Tax Execs. Inst. (bd. dirs. 1986-2004, pres. N.Y. chpt. 1991-92, exec. com. 1992-93), Newspaper Assn. of Am. (chmn. tax com. 1995-97, chmn. ind. contractor task force 1995-97, mem. pub. policy com. 1995-97). Avocations: travel, reading, stamp collecting/philately, birding. Home: 31 Vreeland Ct Princeton NJ 08540-6760 Personal E-Mail: tomnied@aol.com.

NIEDERAUER, GEORGE H., bishop; b. LA, June 14, 1936; s. George and Elaine N. BA Philosophy, St. John's Seminary, Camarillo, CA, 1959; BA Sacred Theology, Catholic U., Washington, DC, 1962; MA English Lit., Loyola U., L.A., 1962; PhD English Lit., USC, 1966. Ordained priest 1962, named prelate of honor (monsignor) 1984, named bishop Diocese of Salt Lake City, 1994. Asst. pastor Our Lady of the Assumption Parish, Claremont, Calif., 1962—63; priest in residence Holy Name of Jesus Parish, Los Angeles, 1963—65; instr. English Lit. St. John's Seminary Coll., Camarillo, Calif., 1965—79; instr. of English Lit. Mt. St. Mary's Coll., Los Angeles, 1967—74; English Dept. chmn. St. John's Seminary Coll., Camarillo, 1968—77, spiritual dir., 1972—79; part-time instr. Spiritual Theology St. John's Seminary Theologate, 1976—79, full-time instr. of Spiritual Theology, 1979—87; part-time instr. of English Lit. St. John's Seminary Coll., 1979—92; rector St. John's Seminary, 1987—92, spiritual dir., 1979—95; co-dir. Cardinal Manning House of Prayer for Priests, Los Angeles, 1992—95; bishop Salt Lake City, 1995—. Mem. Nat. Fedn. of Spiritual Dirs., pres., 1975—77; mem. bd. of the Comm. of Priests' Retreat Archdiocese L.A.; mem. select comm. for revision of U.S. Cath. Conf. "Program for Priestly Formation" 3rd edit.; mem. Vatican Visitation Team for Theologaters; spkr. World Vision Internat., Fuller Theol. Sem., Calif. Lutheran Coll. Mem.: Camarillo Ministerial Assn., Western Assn. of Spiritual Dirs. (pres. 1973—75), Alpha Sigma Nu (Jesuit Honor Soc. - LMU chpt.). Avocations: classical music, stamp collecting/philately, reading, film appreciation. Office: Chancery Office 27 C St Salt Lake City UT 84103-2302

NIEDERBERGER, JANE, information technology executive; m. Mark Niederberger; children: Amy, Sarah. BS in nutrition, Simmons Coll., 1982; MBA in health care adminstrn., Northeastern U. Various mgmt. positions Harvard Pilgrim Health Care, Boston, 1983—96; with IT divsn. Anthem, Inc., Indpls., 1997, acting chief info. officer, 1998—99, sr. v.p., chief info. officer, 1999—. Bd. dir. Managed Care Exec. Group. Bd. mem. Jr. Achievement, Indpls. Recipient Women and Hi Tech Leading Light award, 2002. Office: Anthem Inc 120 Monument Cir Indianapolis IN 46204

NIEDERDEPPE, JEFFREY DANIEL, researcher; b. Phoenix, July 7, 1977; s. David Lee and Cynthia Rose Niederdeppe; m. Lee Megan Humphreys, Sept. 23, 1977. BA in Comm., U. Ariz., Tucson, 1999; MA in Comm., U. Pa., Phila., 2001. Rsch. assoc. RTI Internat., Research Triangle Park, NC,

2001—03; rsch. fellow U. Pa., Phila., 2003—. Mem.: APHA, Internat. Comm. Assn., Golden Key Nat. Honor Soc., Phi Beta Kappa. Office: U Pa 3620 Walnut St Philadelphia PA 19146 Office Phone: 215-573-5824.

NIEDERHUBER, JOHN EDWARD, federal agency administrator, oncologist, surgeon, immunologist; b. Steubenville, Ohio, June 21, 1938; s. William Henry and Helen (Smittle) N.; m. Tracey J. Williamson (dec. Dec. 2001); children: Elizabeth Ann, Matthew John. BS, Bethany Coll., 1960; MD, Ohio State U., 1964. Diplomate Am. Bd. Surgery. Internship, surgery Ohio State U. Hosp., Columbus, 1964-65; from resident surgery to prof. U. Mich. Med. Ctr., Ann Arbor, 1967—80, prof. surgery, prof. microbiology and immunology, 1980-87, chief divsn. surg. oncology sect. gen. surgery, 1983—86, assoc. dean rsch., 1982—85, sr. assoc. dean med. sch., 1983—85; cons. Wayne County Gen. Hosp., Mich., 1973-84; cons. surgery Ann Arbor VA Hosp., 1973-87; prof. surgery, oncology, molecular biology and genetics The Johns Hopkins U. Sch. Med., Balt., 1987-91; Emile Holman prof. surgery, chair, dept. surgery, head sect. surgical scis. Stanford (Calif.) U. Sch. Medicine., 1991-95, prof. microbiology and immunology, 1991-97; chief of surgery Stanford (Calif.) U. Hosp., 1991-95; dir. planning Comp. Cancer Ctr. Stanford (Calif.) Med. Ctr., 1991-95; prof. surgery and oncology Stanford U. Sch. Medicine U. Wis., Madison, 1997—2005, asst. dean oncology, dir. Comprehensive Cancer Ctr., 1997—2002; dep. dir. for translational & clin. sciences, COO Nat. Cancer. Inst., NIH, Bethesda, Md., 2005—, acting dir., 2006—. Vis. prof. Howard Hughes Med. Inst. dept. molecular biology and genetics Howard Hughes Med. Inst., The Johns Hopkins U. Sch. Medicine, Balt., 1986-87; cons. in field. Author books on cancer and surgery; mem. editl. bd. Jour. Immunology, 1981-85, Jour. Surg. Res., 1989-95, Current Opinion in Oncology, 1989—95, Cure, 2002-04, Annals of Surgery, 1991—97, Surg. Oncology, 1991—, Jour. Clin. Oncology, 1993, Annals of Surg. Oncology, 1993—, Jour. ACS, 1994—, The Oncologist, 1995—, Surgery, 1999—2000; contbr. articles to profl. jours. Active bd. sci. councilors NCI divsn. Cancer Treatment, 1986-91, chmn., 1987-91, Gen. Motors Cancer Rsch. Found. Awards Assembly, 1988-92, 98-2003; chmn. nat. cancer adv. bd. NCI, 2002—05; mem. C-Change, 2001—, mem. planning and budget com., vice-chair cancer ctrs. constituency com., vice-chair rsch. com., 2005-, mem. CEO Roundtable, 2003—. Served to capt. U.S. Army, 1965-67 Recipient USPHS Rsch. Career Devel. award Nat. Inst. Allergy and Infectious Disease, 1974-79, Disting. Faculty Svc. award U. Mich., 1978, Alumni Achievement award Ohio State U. Coll. Medicine, 1989, Alumni Achievement award in Medicine Bethany Coll., 1995; vis. rsch. fellow divsn. immunobiology Karolinska Inst., Stockholm, 1970-71, Am. Cancer Soc. Jr. Faculty Clin. fellow, 1977-79. Fellow ACS; mem. Am. Soc. Transplant Surgeons, Transplantation Soc., Am. Surg. Assn., Am. Assn. Immunologists, Am. Assn. Cancer Insts. (v.p. 1999-2001, pres. 2001-03), Coller Surg. Soc., Soc. Univ. Surgeons, Assn. Acad. Surgeons, Soc. Surg. Oncology (v.p. 1999-2001, pres. 2001-02), Clin. Surg. Soc., Am. Assn. Cancer Rsch., Am. Soc. Clin. Oncology, Soc. Clin. Surgery, Biology Club II, Robert M. Zollinger-Ohio State U. Surg. Soc., Pacific Coast Surg. Assn., Soc. Surgery of the Alimentary Tract. Avocations: golf, gardening. Office: Nat Cancer Inst NIH Bldg 31 Room 11A03 31 Center Dr MSC 2590 Bethesda MD 20892-2590 Office Phone: 301-496-6511. Business E-Mail: niederhj@mail.nih.gov.

NIEDERMAN, JAMES CORSON, retired internist, educator; b. Hamilton, Ohio, Nov. 27, 1924; s. Clifford Frederick and Henrietta (Corson) N.; m. Miriam Camp, Dec. 12, 1951; children— Timothy Porter, Derrick Corson, Eliza Orton, Caroline Noble. Student, Kenyon Coll., 1942—45, DSc (hon.), 1981; MD, Johns Hopkins U., 1949. Intern Osler Svc. Johns Hopkins Hosp., Balt., 1949-50; asst. resident in medicine Yale-New Haven Med. Center, 1950-51, assoc. resident, 1953-55; med. ctr. practice specializing in internal medicine, infectious disease and clin. epidemiology New Haven, 1955-97; instr. Yale U., 1955-58, asst. prof., 1958-66, assoc. prof., 1966-76, clin. prof. medicine and epidemiology, 1976-97, emeritus clin. prof. medicine and epidemiology, 1997—, clin. prof. emeritus epidemiology and pub. health, 1998; mem. Nat. Coun. for Johns Hopkins Medicine. Trustee Kenyon Coll., 1974-97, trustee emeritus, 1997—; bd. counselors Smith Coll., 1970-77. Served to 1st lt. M.C. U.S. Army, 1951-53. Fellow Silliman Coll., Yale U. Fellow Am. Coll. Epidemiology; mem. Infectious Diseases Soc. Am., Am. Epidemiol. Soc., Johns Hopkins Med. and Surg. Assn.; mem. The Kenyon Rev. Bd. Trustees, Conn. Soc. Arts and Scis. Clubs: Yale (N.Y.C.), New Haven Lawn. Democrat. Episcopalian. Achievements include research in clin. epidemiology of Epstein Barr virus infections and demonstration of its causal relationship of infectious mononucleosis. Home: 429 Sperry Rd Bethany CT 06524-3544 Home Fax: 203-393-1902. E-mail: jcniederman@sbcglobal.net.

NIEDERMAN, MICHAEL STEVEN, physician, educator; b. NYC, Mar. 30, 1953; s. L. Louis and Betty Doris (Kornblau) N.; m. Ronna Diane Kay, Aug. 15, 1976; children: Alex, Eric. AB, Boston U., 1974, MD, 1977. Intern Northwestern U. Med. Sch., Chgo., 1977-78, resident, 1978-80; pulmonary medicine fellow Yale U. Sch. Med., New Haven, 1980-83; dir. Med. ICU Winthrop U. Hosp., Mineola, N.Y., 1983-97, chief pulmonary and critical care medicine, 1997—; assoc. prof., then prof. medicine SUNY, Stony Brook, 1990—. Dir. Microbiology Assembly, Am. Thoracic Soc., N.Y.C., 1990-91. Editor: Respiratory Infections (textbook), 1994; editor-in-chief Clin. Pulmonary Medicine, 1994—; mem. editl. bd. Am. Jour. Respiratory and Cridical Care Medicine, 1994—, Chest, 1994—; contbr. numerous articles to profl. jours. Fellow ACP, Am. Coll. Chest Physicians (credentials com. 1991—), Coll. Critical Care Medicine; mem. Phi Beta Kappa, Alpha Omega Alpha. Avocations: skiing, tennis, golf, jazz music. Office: Winthrop Univ Hosp 222 Station Plz N Ste 400 Mineola NY 11501-3893 Office Phone: 516-663-2381. E-mail: mniederman@winthrop.org.

NIEDERMAYER, SCOTT, professional hockey player; b. Edmonton, Alta., Can., Aug. 31, 1973; Defenseman NJ Devils, 1991—2005, Anaheim Ducks (formerly Mighty Ducks of Anaheim), 2005—. Mem. Team Can., Olympic Games, Nagano, Japan, 1998, Salt Lake City, 2002, Team Can., World Cup of Hockey, 1996, 2004; player NHL All-Star Game, 1998, 2001, 04. Named to All-Rookie Team, NHL, 1993, Second All-Star Team, 1998, First All-Star Team, 2004, 2006; recipient James Norris Meml. Trophy, 2004. Achievements include being a member of Stanley Cup Champion New Jersey Devils, 1995, 2000, 2003; being a member of gold medal winning Canadian Hockey Team, Salt Lake City Olympic games, 2002; being a member of World Cup Champion Team Canada, 2004. Office: c/o Anaheim Ducks 5695 E Katella Ave Anaheim CA 92806*

NIEH, JASON, educator; BS, MIT; MS, PhD, Stanford U. Prof. Columbia U., NYC, 1999—; tech. advisor Microsoft Consent Decree, NYC, 2003—. Recipient SUR award, IBM, 2000, 2004, Faculty Early Career Devel. award, US NSF, 2001, Faculty award, IBM, 2004, 2006, Early Career Prin. Investigator award, US Dept. Energy, 2003, Young Investigator award, Sigma Xi, 2004, Disting. Faculty Tchg. award, Columbia U., 2004. Office Phone: 212-939-7160.

NIEHAUS, MARY C., lawyer; b. 1961; BA with honors, Grinnell Coll., 1985; JD cum laude, Northwestern U., 1988. Bar: Ill. 1988, U.S. Dist. Ct. (no. dist.) Ill. 1988, U.S. Tax Ct. 1989. With Sidley & Austin, Chgo., 1988—, ptnr., 1996—. Mem. editl. staff Northwestern U. Law Rev., 1987-88. Mem. Order of Coif, Phi Beta Kappa. Office: Sidley & Austin Bank One Plz 10 S Dearborn St Chicago IL 60603 Fax: 312-83-7036. E-mail: mniehaus@sidley.com.

NIEHAUS, SHERRY M., social welfare administrator; b. Heber Springs, Ark., Dec. 12, 1946; d. Ewing W. and Fay D. Mays; m. Joseph T. Niehaus, May 27, 1972 (div.); children: Vincent E., Jessica F.; m. Stephen P. Mers, Apr. 30, 1992. Tabulating clk. Dover Elevator, Cin., 1968-71; data machine operator Little Rock Water Works, 1971-76; acctg. clk. Mays Mission for the Handicapped, Heber Springs, 1978-85, exec. dir., 1985-95, pres., 1995—. Sec. Ark. State Rehab. Coun., Little Rock, 1999—2005, chair, 2003—04. Vol. Tax Income Assistance, Heber Springs, 1978; bd. sec. Cmty. Sch. Cleburne County, Heber Springs, 1987—. Mem.: Rotary (bull. editor Cleburne County Club 1995—, sec. 2000—01, 2003—04). Avocations: horses, reading, gene-

alogy, computers, martial arts. Home: 2208 Misty Ln Heber Springs AR 72543 Office: Mays Mission for the Handicapped 604 Colonial Dr Heber Springs AR 72543 Business E-Mail: sniehaus@maysmission.org.

NIEHOFF, KARL RICHARD BESUDEN, brokerage house executive; b. Cin., May 11, 1943; s. Karl George and Jean (Besuden) N.; children: K. Richard B. Jr., Kelly B. BA, U. Cin., 1967. Corp. trust ops. officer 5th-3d Union Trust, Cin., 1968-74; v.p., gen. mgr. Sabina (Ohio) Water Co., 1974-76; v.p., sec. Weil, Roth and Irving, Inc., 1974-76; co-mgr., mcpl. fin. dept. Thomson McKinnon Securities, Cin. and N.Y.C., 1976—78; chmn. Cin. Stock Exch., Inc., Cin., 1975, pres., 1976—89; exch. rep., founding mem. Consol. Quote, Consol. Tape Oper. Coms., 1979-90, alt., 1991-92; pres. Fin. Instruments Svcs. Corp., Cin., Chgo., London, 1985-90; sr. v.p. Trading Svcs. NASDAQ, Inc., 1990—92; v.p. D.E. Shaw & Co., NYC, 1992-94; pres. D.E. Shaw Securities, LLC, NYC, 1992—94; pres., mng. ptnr. Niehoff and Assocs., NYC, 1994-99; mng. dir., chief of party OTC Capital Mkt. Devel. Project, Ceto, Warsaw, 1994—96; dep. advisor Ministry Mass Privatization, Republic of Poland, Warsaw, 1994-96; v.p., dir. Third Market Trading Corp., Chicago, 1994-98; pres., dir. SBX Inc., Cin., Princeton, NJ, 1997-2000; mng. dir. trading and tech. Unified Mgmt. Corp., Indpls., 1999—2000; pres. VSX Techs. Inc., NYC, Indpls., 1999—2000, Mark Securities, Inc., Pelham Manor, NY, 2002—; pres., CEO Webix, Inc., NYC, 2000—02; chmn. The X-Change Corp., NYC, 2002, pres., 2002; co-founder, mng. ptnr. U.S. OTC Markets, LLC, NYC, 2005—; pres., sec. Schuyler Pk. Manor Coop., Pelham Manor, NY, 2000—. Witness U.S. Ho. Reps. Consumers Protection and Fin. Com., 1977, other gen. oversight, GAO com. panels and inquiries, 1987—94; v.p. Wit Capital Corp., N.Y.C., 1998—99; pres. DSM-Wit, 1998—99; mem. Cin. Stock Exch., 1974—89, trustee, 1974—90, chmn. bd. trustees, 1975; voting mem. Inter-Market Trading Com., 1980—90, Stock Exch. Chief Execs. Com., 1988—90; mem. P.B.W. Stock Exch., Phila., 1975—77, GLOBEX Task Force Com., 1988—89, Easdaq, Brussels, 1995—96; associate mem. NY Stock Exch., 1996; vis. lectr. U. Cin. Coll. Bus. Adminstrn., Xavier U. Bus. Adminstrn. Coll., Cin.; long-term planning com. Chgo. Bd. Options Exch., 1987—88; pres. Digital Stock Market, N.Y.C., 1998—99; vis. com. U.S. Info. Agy., N.Y.C., 1992—95; mng. dir. trading and tech. Unified Mgmt. Corp., Inc., Indpls. and N.Y.C., 1999—2000; pres. WEBIX, Inc., 1999—2002; bd. dirs., audit com. Equity Analysts, L.L.C., Cin.; instl. trading com. Boston Stock Exch., instl. adv. com., 2004. Trustee, sec. Contemporary Arts Ctr., Cin., 1975-83; mem. Young Mens Mercantile Libr. Assn., NYC-40, adv. com., 1974-77; mem. devel. com. Tangeman Gallery of Art, 1981-82; pres., dir. Bermuda Condominium High Assn., Delray Beach, Fla., 1999-06. Mem.: Boston Securities Traders Assn., Internat. Ops. Divsn., Securities Traders Assn. N.Y. (chmn. listed trading com. 1993, OTC Bull. Bd. 2002—04, com. chmn. STA trading subcom. 2002—04), India House, Keeneland Assn., Queen City Mcpl. Bond Club (trustee 1974—80), NYAC Yacht Club (Pelham Manor), N.Y. Athletic Club, Cin. Stock and Bond Club (trustee and 1st v.p. 1974—90), Nat. Arts Club, Phi Alpha Theta.

NIEHUSS, JOHN MARVIN, lawyer; b. Ann Arbor, Mich., Mar. 7, 1937; s. Marvin Lemmon Niehuss and Lois Celicia Markham; m. Rosemary Juliette Neaher, June 30, 1973 (div. Mar. 1991); children: Juliette, John. BA, Amherst Coll., 1958; JD, U. Mich., 1962. Assoc. atty. Sullivan & Cromwell, N.Y.C., 1966-69; legal advisor Govt. of Zambia, Lusaka, 1969-71; loan officer, dir. World Bank, Washington, 1971-73, 90-91; dep. asst. sec. U.S. Treasury Dept., Washington, 1974-77, 89-90; v.p. Merrill Lynch, N.Y.C., 1977-89; gen. counsel Inter-Am. Devel. Bank, Washington, 1992-99, Export-Import Bank U.S., Washington, 1999—2001; dir. Pvt. Fin. of Infrastructure Ctr., Internat. Law Inst., Washington, 2005—. Mem. adv. bd. Internat. Law Inst., Washington, 1977—. Mem. Coun. Fgn. Rels., Met. Club. Avocations: golf, hiking, fly fishing. Home: 3019 45th St NW Washington DC 20016-3523 Office Phone: 202-362-1164. Personal E-Mail: niehuss@gmail.com.

NIELD, MARGARET, nursing researcher; d. Wallace Hicks Davidson and Elsie Hyde. BS, Macalester Coll., St. Paul, 1966; MS, U. Ariz., Tucson, 1971; PhD, U. Ill., Chgo., 1989. Cert. clin. nurse specialist, Tex., 1999. Nurse rschr. Sharp Meml. Hosp., San Diego, 1990—94; asst. prof. U. Tex., Austin, 1994—97; career devel. fellow VA Greater LA Healthcare Sys., 1999—2005; assoc. prof. U. Hawaii, Honolulu. Chair nursing sect. Am. Thoracic Soc., NYC, 1992—94, Calif. Thoracic Soc., 1999—2001. Contbr. articles to profl. jours. Grantee Career Devel. award, Dept. Veterans Affairs, 1999—2005; postdoctoral fellow, UCLA, 1997—99. Mem.: Sigma Theta Tau. Avocation: travel. Home: 901 10th St Santa Monica CA 90403 Office: VA Greater Los Angeles Healthcare System 11301 Wilshire Blvd 111Q Los Angeles CA 90073 Office Phone: 310-268-4593. Personal E-Mail: mnield@earthlink.net. Business E-Mail: margaret.nield@med.va.gov.

NIELSEN, FORREST HAROLD, research nutritionist; b. Dancy, Wis., Oct. 26, 1941; s. George Adolph and Sylvia Viola (Blood) N.; m. Emily Joanne Currie, June 13, 1964; children: Forrest Erik, Kistin Emily. BS, U. Wis., 1963, MS, 1966, PhD, 1967. NIH grad. fellow, dept. biochemistry U. Wis., Madison, 1963-67; rsch. chemist, Human Nutrition Rsch. Inst. USDA, Beltsville, Md., 1969-70, rsch. chemist Human Nutrition Rsch. Ctr. Grand Forks, ND, 1970-86, ctr. dir. and rsch. nutritionist, 1986-2001, rsch. nutritionist, 2001—. Adj. prof. dept. biochemistry and molecular biology, U. N.D., Grand Forks, 1971—, speaker in field. Assoc. editor Magnesium and Trace Elements Jour., 1990-93; mem. editl. bd. Jour. Trace Elements in Exptl. Medicine, 1988—2004, Biol. Trace Element Rsch. Jour., 1979—, Jour. Nutrition, 1984-88, Biofactors, 1997—; contbr. articles to profl. jours. Capt. U.S. Army, 1967-69. Recipient Klaus Schwarz Commemorative Medal and award Internat. Assn. of Bioinorganic Scientists; named Scientist of Yr. U.S. Dept. Agrl., 1993. Mem. Internat. Soc. Trace Element Rsch. in Humans (gov. bd. 1989—, pres. 1992-95), Soc. for Exptl. Biology and Medicine, Am. Soc. Nutrition, N.D. Acad. Sci. (pres. 1988-89), Internat. Bone and Mineral Soc., Sigma Xi (pres. U. N.D. chpt. 1976-77). Lutheran. Achievements include patent for use of Boron Supplements to Increase in Vivo Production of Hydroxylated Steroids; discovery of the nutritional essentiality of the trace elements boron and nickel. Office: USDA ARS GFHNRC 2420 2 Ave N Stop 9034 Grand Forks ND 58202-9034 Office Phone: 701-795-8455. Business E-Mail: fnielsen@gfhnrc.ars.usda.gov.

NIELSEN, GEORGE LEE, architect; b. Ames, Iowa, Dec. 12, 1937; s. Verner Henry and Verba Lucile (Smith) N.; m. Karen Wall, Feb. 28, 1959; children: David Stuart, Kristina, Melissa. B.Arch., Iowa State U., 1961; M.Arch., M.I.T., 1962. Registered arch., Mass., Ohio, N.Y., Ill., Ind., Ky., Miss., Kans., Colo., Mich., Nat. Coun. Archtl. Registration Bds. Designer Perry, Shaw, Hepburn & Dean, Boston, 1961-64, F.A. Stahl & Assos., Cambridge, Mass., 1964-65; project architect Peirce & Pierce, Boston, 1965-70; project mgr. A.M. Kinney Assos., Cin., 1970—, partner, 1978—; sec. A.M. Kinney Assocs., Inc., Ill., 1993—, also dir. Cin.; v.p. A.M. Kinney Inc., Cin., 1992-94, pres., 1994-99, also dir.; sr. prin. A.M. Kinney Inc. Assocs., 1999—. Architect prin. works include Avco Rsch. Lab., Cin. (Ohio) Children's Hosp. Med. Ctr., Square D. Corp., Nalco Chem. Co., Olin Corp., Mead Johnson/Bristol Myers Squib, Cin. (Ohio) Gas and Elec. Co., Novartis Pharm. Corp., Hoechst Celanese, Hoechst Marion Roussel, Martek Bioscis., Witco Corp., Sotheby's, Shell Chem. Co., Bayer Corp., U. Ky. Biomed./Biol. Scis. Rsch. Bldg., U. Ky. Chandler Med. Ctr. Patient Care Facility, Wright Patterson and Edwards AFB Sci. Rsch. Bldg. With U.S. Army, 1962—64. Mem.: AIA (design awards 1970—71, 1974, 1978, 1981, 1991, 1994, 1995, 2001, 2002). Episcopalian. Home: 5680 Windridge View Cincinnati OH 45243-2518 Office: A M Kinney Inc 150 E 4th St Fl 6 Cincinnati OH 45202-4131 Office Phone: 513-421-2265.

NIELSEN, GREG ROSS, lawyer; b. Provo, Utah, Sept. 24, 1947; s. Ross T. and Carma (Peterson) N.; m. Jo Rita Beer, Sept. 3, 1971; children: Jennifer, Jerilyn, Eric Michael, Brittany Anne. BA in Polit. Sci. magna cum laude, Brigham Young U., 1971; JD cum laude, Harvard U., 1975. Bar: Ariz. 1975, U.S. Dist. Ct. Ariz. 1975, U.S. Ct. Appeals (9th cir.) 1977, Utah 1990, Nev. 2003. Assoc. Snell & Wilmer, Phoenix, 1975-80, ptnr., 1981—2004, mng. ptnr. Salt Lake City, 1991—2002, adminstrv. coord. real estate practice group Phoenix, 1988-90; gen. counsel franchise fin. GE Comml. Fin., Scottsdale,

Ariz., 2004—. Mem. dist. com. Theodore Roosevelt coun. Boy Scouts Am., 1988-90; trustee Utah Heritage Found., 1998-2000, Swaner Nature Preserve, 2002-04. Hinckley scholar Brigham Young U., 1970; fellow Ford Found., 1970. Mem. ABA. Republican. Mem. Lds Ch. Office: GE Comml Fin Franchise Fin 17207 N Perimeter Dr Scottsdale AZ 85255 Office Phone: 480-585-2234. Business E-Mail: greg.nielsen@ge.com.

**NIELSEN, GWYN ENGLISH,** writer, illustrator, publishing executive, language educator; b. Plainfield, N.J., Dec. 12, 1958; d. Richard English and Valerie Victoria Youtkus; m. Christian Anthony Nielsen, June 22, 1986 (div. Nov. 1996); 1 child, Saxony Annin. BA in English/Comm. cum laude, Bucknell U., 1981. Cert. English tchr. N.J.J. Dept. Edn. State Bd. Examiners. Adminstrv. coord. Group W Satellite Comm., N.Y.C., 1981—83; dir. drama Ctrl. Bucks H.S. East, Buckingham, Pa., 1983—84; English tchr. Rahway (N.J.) H.S., 1984—85; English and drama tchr. Mother Seton Regional H.S., Clark, NJ, 1985—89; English tchr. Connackamack Sch., Piscataway, NJ, 1989—90; pres. Video Sta. CGS Inc./Overlook Video, Summit, NJ, 1990—2002, CGS Press, Scotch Plains, NJ, 1997—. English tutor Mentor Learning Group, Summit, 1989; substitute tchr. Bd. Edn., Scotch Plains, Westfield, 2000—; playwright, dir. Performing Arts Studio, Scotch Plains, 2001; tchr. Summit Cmty. Ctr., Summit, NJ, 2002—03; English tchr., playwright, dramatist Scotch Plains-Fanwood Pub. Sch., NJ. Author, illustrator: children's book Torey the Turkey Goes Skiing, 1998, author, pub.: poetry Teaching Love Life, 2000, children's book Serendipity and the Dream Catcher, 2003; vocalist Music for All Seasons, Scotch Plains, NJ. HEART grantee, Union County Arts Coun. bd. freeholders, 2002. Mem.: Soc. Children's Book Writers and Illustrators, Acad. Am. Poets, Publishers Mktg. Assn., Bucknell Univ. Assn. of the Arts, Alpha Lambda Delta. Presbyterian. Avocations: singing, acting. Office: CGS Press PO Box 1394 Mountainside NJ 07092

**NIELSEN, HARALD CHRISTIAN,** retired chemist, researcher; b. Chgo., Apr. 18, 1930; s. Svend Aage and Seena (Hansen) N.; m. Eloise Wilma Soule, Dec. 19, 1953; children: Brenda Mae, Paul Erick, Gloria Lynn, Judy Ann (dec.). BA, St. Olaf Coll., 1952; PhD, Mich. State U., 1957. Cereal grain protein chemist Nat. Ctr. for Agrl. Utilization Rsch. (formerly No. Regional Rsch. Ctr.), Agrl. Rsch. Svc., USDA, Peoria, Ill., 1957—87; ret., 1987. Contbr. articles to profl. jours. Mem. Peoria Area Combined Fed. Campaign Coord. Com., 1980—87; pres. local 3247 Am. Fedn. Govt. Employees, AFL-CIO, 1977—86; active Peoria Prostrate Cancer Support Group, 1996—2005, editor newsletter, 2000—05. Mem.: Nat. Assn. Ret. Fed. Employees (officer chpt. 268 1989—92, pres. chpt. 268 1991, editor chpt. newsletter 1999—2004), Am. Assn. Cereal Chemists. Democrat. Lutheran. Home: 2318 N Gale Ave Peoria IL 61604-3229 *What useful thing have I accomplished this day? What did I learn today? These two questions I ask myself at the end of each day.*

**NIELSEN, JAKOB,** computer interface engineer; b. Copenhagen, Oct. 5, 1957; arrived in U.S., 1990, naturalized, 2001; s. Gerhard and Helle (Hofner); m. Hannah Kain, Feb. 18, 1984. MS in Computer Sci., Aarhus (Denmark) U., 1983; PhD in Computer Sci., T.U. of Denmark, 1988. Rsch. fellow Aarhus U., 1983-84; vis. scientist IBM User Interface Inst., Yorktown Heights, NY, 1985; adj. asst. prof. T.U. Denmark, Lyngby, 1986-90; mem. rsch. staff Bell Comm. Rsch., Morristown, NJ, 1990-94; disting. engr. Sun Microsystems, Mountain View, Calif., 1994-98; principal Nielsen Norman Group, Mountain View, Calif., 1998—. Author: Hypertext and Hypermedia, 1990, Usability Engineering, 1993, Multimedia and Hypertext: The Internet and Beyond, 1995, Designing Web Usability: The Practice of Simplicity, 2000, Homepage Usability: 50 Websites Deconstructed, 2001, Prioritizing Web Usability, 2006; editor: Coordinating User Interfaces for Consistency, 1989, Designing User Interfaces for International Use, 1990, Usability Inspection Methods, 1994, International User Interfaces, 1996; mem. editl. bd.: Behavior and Info. Tech., 1989—, Hypermedia Jour., 1989—95, Interacting with Computers, 1989—, Internat. Jour. Human-Computer Interaction, 1989—, Internat. Jour. Man-Machine Studies, 1991—94, ACM Networker, 1997—2000, Personal Technologies, 1997—2004; contbr. articles to profl. jours. Mem.: Assn. for Computing Machinery (papers co-chair internat. conf. 1993, editl. bd. Networker 1997—2000, spl. interest group on computer human interaction). Achievements include holder 79 patents in field; founding of discount usability engineering approach; invention (with R. Molich) of heuristic evaluation method for cost-effective improvement of user interfaces; demonstration (with T.K. Landauer) that user testing and heuristic evaluation both follow same mathematical model; definition of the parallel design method for rapidly exploring user interface alternatives; patents for.

**NIELSEN, JENNIFER LEE,** molecular ecologist, researcher; b. Balt., Mar. 21, 1946; d. Leo Jay and Mary Marriott (Mules) N.; divorced; children: Nadja Wilson, Allisha Ochs MFA, Ecole des beaux Arts, Paris, 1968; BS, Evergreen State Coll., 1987; MS, U. Calif., Berkeley, 1990, PhD, 1994. Artist, Seattle, 1969-78; fish biologist Weyerhaeuser Co., Tacoma, 1978-89; resource cons. Berkeley, 1989-90; rsch. biologist USDA-Forest Svc., Albany, Calif., 1990-99; vis. scientist Stanford U., Pacific Grove, Calif., 1994-99; supr. fisheries Alaska Sci. Ctr., Anchorage, 1999—. Rsch. assoc. Calif. State U. Mossland-ing Marie Sta., 1995-99; adj. prof. integrated biology U. Calif., Berkeley, 1998; adj. prof. U. Alaska, Fairbanks, 1999—, U. Alaska Anchorage, 2001-; supervisory rsch. fishery biologist U.S. Geol. Svc., Alaska Sci. Ctr., Anchorage, 1999—. Editor-in-chief: Reviews in Fish Biology and Fisheries, 1999—; editor: Evolution and the Aquatic Ecosystem, 1995, Advisory Editor Environment Biology of Fishes, 1998—; contbr. over 100 articles to profl. jours.; paintings exhibited at Metro. Mus. Modern Art, 1966; represented in numerous pvt. collections, U.S. and Europe. Mem. Am. Fisheries Soc. (pres. chpt. 1993-94, genetics sect. pres. 1999-2001, pres.-elect of society 2005, pres. 2006-), Molecular Marine Biology and Biotech. (regional editor 1995), Animal Behaviour Soc. (policy com. 1993-94). Avocations: painting, cooking, gardening, skijoring. Office: USGS Alaska Sci Ctr 1011 E Tudor Rd Anchorage AK 99503-6119 Office Phone: 907-786-3670. E-mail: jennifer_nielsen@usgs.gov.

**NIELSEN, LESLIE,** actor; b. Regina, Sask., Can., Feb. 11, 1926; s. Ingvard and Maybelle Nielsen; m. Monica Bayar, 1950 (div. 1955); m. Sandy Ullman, 1958 (div.); children: Thea, Maura; m. Brooks Nielsen, 1981 (div. 1983). Student, Neighborhood Playhouse, N.Y.C. Former announcer, disk jockey, Can. radio; feature films include The Vagabond King, 1956, Forbidden Planet, 1956, Ransom!, 1956, The Opposite Sex, 1956, Hot Summer Night, 1957, Tammy and the Bachelor, 1957, Night Train to Paris, 1964, Harlow, 1965, Dark Intruder, 1965, Beau Geste, 1965, Gunfight in Abilene, 1967, The Reluctant Astronaut, 1967, Rosie, 1967, Counterpoint, 1967, Dayton's Devils, 1969, How to Commit Marriage, 1969, Change of Mind, 1969, The Resurrection of Zachary Wheeler, 1971, The Poseidon Adventure, 1972, Viva, Knievel, 1977, City of Fire, 1979, Airplane!, 1980, Wrong is Right, 1982, Creepshow, 1983, Spaceship, 1983, Soul Man, 1986, The Patriot, 1986, Nuts, 1987, Nightstick, 1987, Home Is Where the Hart Is, 1987, The Naked Gun, 1988, Dangerous Curves, The Repossessed, The Naked Gun 2 1/2: The Smell of Fear, 1991, All I Want for Christmas, 1991, Surf Ninjas, 1993, The Naked Gun 33 1/3: The Final Insult, 1994, Rent-a-Kid, 1995, Dracula: Dead and Loving It, 1995, Spy Hard, 1996, Family Plan, 1997, Mr. Magoo, 1997, Wrongfully Accused, 1998, 2001: A Space Travesty, 1999, Camouflage, 2001, Kevin of the North, 2001, Men with Brooms, 2002, Scary Movie 3, 2003, Scary Movie 4, 2006; TV films include Crime Syndicated, 1952, Man Behind The Badge, 1954, See How They Run, 1964, Shadow Over Elveron, 1968, Hawaii Five-O, 1968, Companions in Nightmare, 1968, Trial Run, 1969, Deadlock, 1969, Night Slaves, 1970, The Aquarians, 1970, Hauser's Memory, 1970, Monty Nash, 1971, They Call It Murder, 1971, Incident in San Francisco, 1972, Snatched, 1973, The Letters, 1973, Can Ellen Be Saved?, 1974, Brinks! The Great Robbery, 1976, Little Mo, 1978, miniseries Back Stairs At the White House, 1979, Institute For Revenge, 1979, Ohms, 1980, The Night The Bridge Fell Down, 1980, Murder Among Friends, 1982, Cave-In, 1983, Blade in Hong Kong, 1985, The Loner, Fatal Confession: A Father Dowling Mystery, Chance of a Lifetime, 1991, Harvey, 1996, Mr. Willowby's Christmas Tree, 1995, Safety Patrol, 1998, Santa Who?, 2000,

Noël Noël, 2003; numerous other TV appearances including dramatic series Studio One, Armstrong Circle Theater, Goodyear Playhouse; TV series include The New Breed, 1961, The Bold Ones, 1963-67, Peyton Place, 1965, Bracken's World, 1969-70, Shaping Up, 1984, Police Squad, 1982, The Golden Girls, 1992, (voice) Pumper Pups, 2000, Liography, 2001, Zeroman, 2004; toured country in one man show Darrow, 1979; co-author: The Naked Truth, 1993. With Can. Air Force, WWII.*

**NIELSEN, LINDA MILLER,** councilman; b. Cedar Falls, Iowa, Apr. 13, 1948; d. Donald Hugh and Mary I. (Hansen) Miller; m. Kenneth Andrew Nielsen, Aug. 22, 1970; children: Annette Marie, Kirsten Viola. BS in Home Econs., Iowa State U., 1970, MS in Food Sci., 1972. Rsch. asst. Iowa State U., Ames, 1970-72, rsch. assoc., 1972-74, instr., 1975-76; city councilwoman City of Charleston, W.Va., 1988—; minority leader Charleston City Coun., 2003—; asst. dir. continuing edn. and cmty. svc. W.Va. State Cmty. and Tech. Coll., 1998—. Leader Girl Scouts U.S.A., 1978-96; chair environ. and recycling com. of Charleston, 1991-2003, realignment com. of Charleston, 1992-94, 2002, mcpl. planning com., 1988—, fin. com., 1995—, storm water com., 1997-99, 2003—, parks and recreation com., 1988-95; classroom vol. Kanawha County Schs., Charleston, 1978-90; mem., officer Forest Hills Comm. Assn., Charleston, 1983-87. Contbr. articles to profl. publs. Mem. NICS (bd. dirs. 1994—), Sigma Xi, Iota Sigma Pi, Omicron Nu. Republican. Avocations: hiking, camping, reading, sewing, cooking. Personal E-mail: nielsen413@charter.net.

**NIELSEN, MORTEN ØRREGAARD,** economics professor; b. Herning, Denmark, Nov. 14, 1976; arrived in U.S., 2003; s. Jens Ørregaard and Inga Irene Skytte Nielsen. BS in Econs., U. Aarhus, Denmark, 1998, MSc in Econs., 2001, PhD in Econs., 2003; MSc in Econometrics and Math. Econs., London Sch. Econs. and Polit. Sci., 1999. Postdoctoral rsch. fellow Dept. Econ. U. Aarhus, Denmark, 2003—03; asst. prof. econ. Dept. Econ. Cornell U., Ithaca, NY, 2003—. Contbr. articles to profl. jours. Mem.: Inst. Math. Stats., Am. Econ. Assn., Econometric Soc. Office Phone: 607-255-6338.

**NIELSEN, NANCY H.,** health organization executive; m. Don Nielsen; 5 children. BA, W.Va. U., 1964; MS in Microbiology, Cath. U., 1967, PhD in Microbiology, 1969; MD, SUNY, Buffalo, 1967. Past chief med. officer N.Y. State Dept. Health Western Region; former pres. med. staff Buffalo Gen. Hosp.; asst. dean med. edn., clin. prof. medicine U. Buffalo Sch. Medicine and Biomed. Sci., Buffalo; sec. US Dept. Health and Human Svcs. Adv. Com. on Regulatory Reform, 2002; assoc. med. dir. for quality, interim chief med. officer Independent Health Assn., NY. Bd. dirs. Med. Liability Mut. Ins. Co.; assoc. med. dir. for quality Ind. Health Assn. N.Y. Bd. dirs. Nat. Patient Safety Found. Recipient Samuel P. Capen award, U. Buffalo Alumni Assn., 1996. Fellow: ACP; mem.: AMA (vice speaker Ho. of Dels. 2000—03, speaker Ho. of Dels. 2003—, bd. trustees, Coun. on Sci. Affairs), Med. Soc. State of N.Y. (spkr. ho. dels. 1995—2000), Erie County Med. Soc. (former pres.). Office: Independant Health Assn 511 Farber Lakes Dr Buffalo NY 14221 also: AMA 515 N State St Chicago IL 60610 Business E-Mail: nielse@buffalo.edu.*

**NIELSEN, NIELS CHRISTIAN, JR.,** theology studies educator; b. Long Beach, Calif., June 2, 1921; s. Niels Hansen and Frances (Nofziger) N.; m. Erika Kreuth, May 10, 1958; children—Camilla Regina, Niels Albrecht. BA, George Pepperdine Coll., L.A., 1942; BD, Yale U., 1946, PhD, 1951. Ordained to ministry Meth. Ch., 1946. Pastor Woodbury (Conn.) Meth. Ch., 1944-46; instr. religion Yale U., New Haven, 1948-51; faculty Rice U., Houston, 1951—, J. Newton Rayzor prof. religious studies., prof. emeritus, 1991—; Amax presdl. prof. humanities Colo. Sch. Mines, Golden, 1982-83. Author: Philosophy and Religion in Contemporary Japan, 1957, Geistige Landerkunde USA, 1960, A Layman Looks at World Religions, 1962, God in Education, 1966, Solzhenitsyn's Religion, 1975, The Religion of Jimmy Carter, 1977, The Crisis of Human Rights, 1978, Religions of the World, 1982, Revolutions in Eastern Europe: The Religious Roots, 1991, Fundamentalism, Mythos and World Religions, 1993; editor: Religion After Communism in Russia, 1994; contbr. articles to profl. jours. Mem. Am. Acad. Religion, Am. Philos. Soc., Am. Soc. Study Religion (sec. 1977-89), Soc. European Culture, Soc. for Values in Higher Edn. Democrat. Home: 2424 Swift Blvd Houston TX 77030-1806 Office Phone: 713-667-0783. Personal E-mail: niels@ruf.rice.edu.

**NIELSEN, PAUL DOUGLAS,** engineering executive, retired military officer; s. Jack Alton and Shirley Mae (Gillette) N.; m. Dorothy Webb Spragins, May 3, 1975. BS in Physics and Math., USAF Acad., 1972; MS in Applied Sci., U. Calif., Davis, 1973, PhD in Plasma Physics, 1981; MBA, U. N.Mex., 1977; postgrad., Nat. War Coll., 1988-89. Physicist Nat. Security Agency Ft. George G. Meade, Md., 1973—75; space sys. procurement officer nuc. techs. Air Force Weapons Lab., Kirtland AFB, N.Mex., 1975—77; sys. programs mgmt. officer nuc. techs. Air Force Sys. Command, Andrews AFB, Md., 1977—78, aide to comdr., 1977—78; space sys. procurement mgmt. officer Hdqrs. AFSC, Andrews AFB, Md., 1978; mil. rsch. assoc. Dept. Energy Lawrence Livermore Nat. Libr., 1978—81; asst. chief advanced sys., chief Satellite Attitude Control br., Satellite Engring. divsn., sec. Air Force Office Spl. Projects, L.A. Air Force Sta., Calif., 1981—84; sys. program dir. electronics sys. divsn. Command Ctr. Processing and Display Sys. Replacement Program, Hanscom AFB, Mass., 1984—85; sys. program dir. Space Def. Ops Ctr., 1985—87; chief engr. Strat. Sys. Deputate, ESD, Hanscom AFB, Mass., 1987—88; mil. asst., col. Office of Asst. Sec. Def., Washington, 1989-92; comdr. Rome Lab., Griffiss AFB, 1992-95; command dir. Cheyenne Mountain Ops. Ctr., Cheyenne Mountain Air Sta, Colo., 1995—96, chief ops., 1996-97; brig. gen., dir. plans N.Am. Aerospace Def. Command, Peterson AFB, Colo., 1997—99, vice comdr. Aero. Systems Ctr., AFMC, Wright-Patterson AFB, Ohio, 1999-2000; comdr. Air Force Rsch. Lab., Wright-Patterson AFB, 2000—04; CEO, dir. Software Engring Inst. Carnegie Mellon U., Pitts., 2004—. With USAF, 1972, ret. USAF, 2004, 2d lt., 1972, 1st lt., 1974, capt., 1976, major, 1981, lt. col., 1986, col., 1989, brigadier gen., 1997, major gen., 2001. Decorated Def. Superior Svc. medal with oak leaf cluster, Meritorious Svc. medal with two oak leaf clusters, Disting. Svc. medal, Legion of Merit, Def. Meritorious Svc. medal; fellow Hertz Found., Livermore, Calif., 1972-73, 78-81. Fellow AIAA (Hap Arnold award 2002), IEEE, Armed Forces Comm. and Electronics Assn., Air Force Assn. Office: Software Eng Inst Carnegie Mellon Univ 4500 Fifth Ave Pittsburgh PA 15213-3890 Home: 30 Wedgewood Ln Pittsburgh PA 15215-1560 Office Phone: 412-268-7740. Business E-Mail: nielsen@sei.cmu.edu.

**NIELSEN, PHILIP EDWARD,** physicist, research manager; b. Chgo., July 18, 1944; s. John Edward and Doris Anne (Roessler) N.; m. Mary Jane Hill, Aug. 21, 1971; children: Aaron P., June E., David C. BS in Physics, Ill. Inst. Tech., 1966; MS in Physics, Case Western Reserve U., 1968, PhD, 1970. Commd. 2d lt. USAF, 1970, advanced through ranks to col., 1988; ret., 1996; chief, interaction physics group AF Weapons Lab., Kirtland AFB, N.Mex., 1970-74; assoc. professor physics AF Inst. Tech., Wright-Patterson AFB, Ohio, 1974-79; dep. dir. Directorate of Aerospace Studies, Kirtland AFB, 1980-84; dep. chief, missile divsn. AF Studies and Analyses, Pentagon, Washington, 1984-86, chief, force analyses divsn., 1986-87; dir. tech. Fgn. Tech. Divsn., Wright-Patterson AFB, 1988-92; chief, tech. requirements HQ AF Materiel Command, Wright-Patterson AFB, 1992-96; dir. tech. ctr. MacAulay-Brown, Inc., Dayton, Ohio, 1996—. Author: Effects of Directed Energy Weapons, 2000. Pres. Shadowbrook Homeowners Assn., Mt. Vernon, Va., 1986-87. Recipient USAF R & D award, 1975, Supr. Rsch. award Air Command and Staff Coll., Montgomery, Ala., 1980, Disting. Govt. Svc. award Albuquerque-Santa Fe Fed. Exec. Bd., 1983, Devel. Planning cert. of merit AF Systems Command, Washington, 1983. Mem. AAAS, Am. Phys. Soc., Inst. Ops. Rsch. and Mgmt. Sci., Mil. Ops. Rsch. Soc. Achievements include co-discovery (with P.L. Taylor) of an effect in the low-temperature thermoelectric power of metals and alloys now known as the "Nielsen-Taylor" or "N-T" effect; resolution of many puzzling results in the laser-induced breakdown thresholds of clean and aerosol-laden atmospheres; analysis of solid response to laser

radiation which provided insights needed to extrapolate small scale experiments to large scale applications. Home: 9138 Payne Farm Ln Dayton OH 45458-9388 Office: MacAulay-Brown Inc 4021 Executive Dr Dayton OH 45430-1062

**NIELSEN, TOD,** information technology executive; BS, Cent. Wash. U. Various mgmt. positions Microsoft Corp., 1988—2000; CEO CrossGain (acquired by BEA Systems, Inc.), 2000—01; sr. v.p. developer programs BEA Systems, Inc., San Jose, Calif., 2001, exec. v.p. engring., chief mktg. officer, 2001—05; sr. v.p., global sales support Oracle Corp., Redwood Shores, Calif., 2005; pres., CEO Borland Software Corp., Cupertino, Calif., 2005—. Office: Borland Software Corp 20450 Stevens Creek Blvd Ste 800 Cupertino CA 95014 Office Phone: 800-817-4BEA, 408-570-8000, 408-863-2800. Office Fax: 408-570-8901.*

**NIELSEN, WENDY CHRISTINE,** literature educator; d. William C. and Margaret A. Nielsen; m. Gabriel G. Farrell. BA, U. Calif., La Jolla, Calif., 1994; degree, Georg Aug. U., Göttingen, Germany, 1996; PhD, U. Calif., Davis, Calif., 2001. Lectr. writing program U. Calif., Santa Barbara, Calif., 2001—03; prof. Montclair (N.J.) State U., 2003—. Co-author: Compendium of Twentieth Century Novelists and Novels, (bibliography) Comparative Literature and Comparative Cultural Studies; contbr. articles to profl. jours. Mem.: MLA, Women in German (Dissertation prize 2002), N.Am. Soc.Study of Romanticism, Am. Comparative Lit. Assn., Phi Beta Kappa. Office: Montclair State University English Dept Montclair State University Montclair NJ 07043 Office Phone: 973-655-7960.

**NIELSEN-JONES, IAN RICHARD,** lottery and gaming executive, consultant; b. Winchester, Eng., Jan. 24, 1950; arrived in Can., 1950, arrived in US, 1995; s. Richard and Jean-Marie (Edwards) Nielsen-J.; m. Linda Ann George, June 10, 1972; children: Christopher James, Alison Leigh, Eric Philip. BA in Econs., Loyola Coll., 1971; MA in Econs., McMaster U., 1972. From investigator to dep. dir. investigation & rsch. Competition Bur., Ottawa, Ont., Canada, 1972-89; pres. Ont. Lottery Corp., Toronto, Sault Ste. Marie, Canada, 1989-93; mng. dir. nat. lottery Rank Orgn. Plc, London, 1993-94; pres. gaming and recreation Rank Canada Ltd., Toronto, 1994-95; COO CUE Network Corp., Irvine, Calif., 1995-97; pres., CEO Online Internat. Corp., Smithtown, NY, 1997-99, Gaming Mgmt. Corp., Del., 1999-2000, Entertainment Mgmt. Group Ltd., British Virgin Islands, 2001—. Bd. dirs. Lotto4U.com, Calif., Computer Radio Network, Ltd., Toronto, Granada Empresarial, S.A., Dominican Republic, LotCo Plc, London. Hon. bd. dirs. Bushplane Mus., Sault Ste. Marie, Ont.; bd. dirs. Econ. Devel. Corp., Sault Ste. Marie, 1992-93, United Way, 1990-93, Plummer Hosp., 1991-93, Algoma Univ. Coll., 1991-93. Named newsmaker of yr., Gaming and Wagering Mag., 1992. Avocations: writing, music, running, coin collecting/numismatics, travel. Home: 8 Zinfandel Ct RR5 Niagara-on-the-Lake ON Canada L0S 1J0 Office Phone: 416-954-2612. Personal E-mail: iannielsenjones@sympatico.ca.

**NIEMANN, CHESTER S., JR.,** retired band director, customer service administrator; b. Belleville, Ill., Apr. 27, 1941; s. Chester S. and Louise J. Niemann; m. Judith Ann Horton, Mar. 16, 1980; children: Laura L., Daniel E., C. Scott, Sheryl L., Austin G., Shaun P., Joshua M. B in Music Edn., U. Ga., 1964; M in Arts Edn., Murray State U., 1984. Cert. tchr. Fla. From lt. to capt. US Army, 1964—69; band dir. Wilbersham County Schs., Clarksville, Ga., 1969—71, Caldwell County Schs., Princeton, Ky., 1971—73, Morgan County Schs., Sturgis, Ky., 1974—75, Brevard County Schs., Titusville, Fla., 1975—79, St. Lucie County Schs., Ft. Pierce, Fla., 1979—86, Volusia County Schs., Deland, Fla., 1986—89; quality control mem. GIS Mktg., Deland, 1989—92; band dir. Calvary Christian Acad., Fla., 1992—94, Trinity Christian Acad., Deltona, Fla., 1994—2004. Composer: Lord of the Dance, 1994, Folk Song Ste. Organizer, founder Theater Craft Symphony Orch., 1984. Named Tchr. of Yr., Trinity Christian Acad., 2000. Avocations: model trains, gardening. Home: 3120 Hickory Tree Ln Deland FL 32724

**NIEMEIER, CHARLES D.,** accountant; b. 1956; BBA, Baylor U.; JD, Georgetown U. Bar: 1995. Ptnr. Williams & Connolly LLP, Washington, 1988—99; chief acct. enforcement divsn., co-chair fin. fraud task force SEC, 1999—2002; bd. dirs. Pub. Acctg. Oversight Bd., 2002—, acting chmn., 2003. Office: Pub Co Acctg Oversight Bd 1666 K St NW Washington DC 20006-2803 Office Phone: 202-207-9100. Office Fax: 202-862-8430.*

**NIEMETH, CHARLES FREDERICK,** lawyer; b. Lorain, Ohio, Nov. 25, 1939; s. Charles Ambrose and Christine Cameron (Mollison) N.; m. Anne Marie Meckes, Oct. 12, 1968. BA, Harvard U., 1962; JD, U. Mich., 1965. Bar: Calif. 1966, N.Y. 1984. Assoc. O'Melveny & Myers, Los Angeles, 1965-72, ptnr., 1973—2005, Baker & McKenzie, N.Y.C., 2005—. Mem. leadership com. Corp. Fund of Lincoln Ctr. Mem. nat. com. Mich. Law Sch. Fund; trustee Challengers Boys and Girls Club, 1968-83; mem. bus. adv. coun. UCLA, 1979-83; mem. exec. com. Internat. Student Ctr., 1979-83; bd. dirs. Olympic Tower Condominium, 1986-92, N.Y. Philharm.; bd. visitors Mich. Law Sch., mem. Tri-Bar Opinion Com. Mem. Riviera Tennis Club, Regency Club, N.Y. Athletic Club, Field Club (Greenwich, Conn.), Harvard Club (NYC). Democrat. Roman Catholic. Home: 70 Oneida Dr Greenwich CT 06830-7131 Office: Baker & McKenzie 1114 Avenue of the Americas New York NY 10036 Office Phone: 212-891-3568. E-mail: charles.f.niemeth@bakernet.com.

**NIEMEYER, PAUL VICTOR,** federal judge; b. Princeton, NJ, Apr. 5, 1941; s. Gerhart and Lucie (Lenzer) Niemeyer; m. Susan Kinley, Aug. 24, 1963; children: Jonathan K., Peter E., Christopher J. AB, Kenyon Coll., 1962; student, U. Munich, Federal Republic of Germany, 1962—63; JD, U. Notre Dame, 1966. Bar: Md. 1966, U.S. Dist. Ct. Md. 1967, U.S. Ct. Appeals (4th cir.) 1968, U.S. Supreme Ct. 1970, U.S. Dist. Ct. (so. dist.) Tex. 1977, U.S. Ct. Appeals (5th cir.) 1978, U.S. Ct. Appeals (3d cir.) 1980. Assoc. Piper & Marbury, Balt., 1966—74, ptnr., 1974—88; U.S. dist. judge U.S. Dist. Ct. Md., Balt., 1988—90; circuit judge U.S. Ct. Appeals (4th cir.), Balt., 1990—. Lectr. advanced bus. law Johns Hopkins U., Balt., 1971—75; lectr. Md. Jud. Conf., Md. Ct. Clks. Assn.; sr. lecturing fellow in appellate advocacy Duke U. Sch. of Law, 1994—; mem. standing com. on rules of practice and procedure cts. appeals, 1973—88; atty. grievance com.-hearing panel, 1978—81; select com.-profl. conduct, 1983—85; adv. com. on Fed. Rules of Civil Procedure, 1993—2000; chmn., 1996—2000. Co-author: Maryland Rules Commentary, 1984, Maryland Rules Commentary supplement, 1988, Maryland Rules Commentary, 3d. edit., 2003; contbr. articles to profl. jours. Recipient Spl. Merit citation, Am. Judicature Soc., 1987. Fellow: Am. Law Inst., Md. Bar Assn. (Disting. Svc. award litigation sect. 1981), Md. Bar Found., Am. Bar Found., Am. Coll. Trial Lawyers; mem.: Lawyers' Round Table, Wednesday Law Club. Republican. Episcopalian. Office: US Cir Ct Md US Courthouse 101 W Lombard St Ste 910 Baltimore MD 21201-2611*

**NIEMEYER, PETER EDUARD,** history educator; b. Balt., Apr. 4, 1972; s. Paul V. and Susan K. Niemeyer; m. Kathryn A. Foley, Oct. 18, 1997; children: Walker, Maya. AB magna cum laude, Kenyon Coll., Gambier, Ohio, 1994; MDiv, Harvard U., Cambridge, Mass., 1998. Cert. tchr. secondary sch. history and social studies Mass. Tchr. Watson Ho. Group Home, Cambridge, Mass., 1997—99, coord. edn., 1998—99; tchr. social studies Mt. Greylock Regional H.S., Williamstown, Mass., 1999—. Firefighter Williamstown Fire Dept., Mass., 2002—. Grantee, Carnegie Harvard Children's Studies, 1997. Mem.: Nat. Coun. Social Studies, Gale Hose Co. (2d asst. foreman 2002—). Office: Mount Greylock Regional High Sch 1781 Cold Spring Rd Williamstown MA 01267

**NIEMI, JANICE,** retired lawyer, retired state legislator; b. Flint, Mich., Sept. 18, 1928; d. Forrest Jesse and Norma (Bell) Bailey; m. Preston Niemi, Feb. 4, 1953 (div. 1987); children: Ries, Patricia. BA, U. Wash., 1950, LLB, 1967; postgrad., U. Mich., 1950-52; cert., Hague Acad. Internat. Law, The Netherlands, 1954. Bar: Wash. 1968. Assoc. firm Powell, Livengood, Dunlap & Silverdale, Kirkland, Wash., 1968; staff atty. Legal Svc. Ctr., Seattle, 1968-70;

judge Seattle Dist. Ct., 1971-72, King County Superior Ct., Seattle, 1973-78; acting gen. counsel, dep. gen. counsel SBA, Washington, 1979-81; mem. Wash. State Ho. of Reps., Olympia, 1983-87, chmn. com. on state govt., 1984; mem. Wash. State Senate, 1987-95; sole practice Seattle, 1981-94; superior ct. judge King County, 1995-2000; chief criminal judge, 1997-2000; ret., 2000; mem. Wash. State Gambling Commn., 2002—. Mem. White Ho. Fellows Regional Selection Panel, Seattle, 1974—77, chmn., 1976, 77; incorporator Sound Savs. & Loan, Seattle, 1975; bd. dirs. Artists Trust; mem. panel Am. Arbitration Assn., 2003—. Bd. visitors dept. psychology U. Wash., Seattle, 1983—87, bd. visitors dept. sociology, 1988—98; mem. adv. bd. Tacoma Art Mus., 1987—; mem. Wash. State Gender and Justice Commn., 1987—89; Bd. dirs. Allied Arts, Seattle, 1971—78, Ctr. Contemporary Art, Seattle, 1981—83, Women's Network, Seattle, 1981—84, Pub. Defender Assn., Seattle, 1982—84, Artist's Trust, 2002—. Named Woman of Yr. in Law, Past Pres.'s Assn., Seattle, 1971, Woman of Yr., Matrix Table, Seattle, 1973, Capitol Hill Bus. and Profl. Women, 1975. Mem. Wash. State Bar Assn., Wash. Women Lawyers, Am. Arbitration Assn. (panel 2003—). Democrat. Home: PO Box 20516 Seattle WA 98102-1516 Personal E-mail: janicen@aol.com.

**NIEMI, RICHARD GENE,** political science educator; b. Green Bay, Wis., Jan. 10, 1941; s. Eugene H. and Dorothy M. (Stevens) N.; m. Shirley A. Gill, Aug. 4, 1962; children: Nancy, Patricia, Jennifer, Julie. BA, Lawrence Coll., 1962; PhD, U. Mich., 1967. Asst. prof. polit. sci. U. Rochester, NY, 1967-71, assoc. prof. NY, 1971-75, prof., 1975—99, disting. grad. tchg. prof. NY, 1983-86, chmn. dept. polit. sci. NY, 1979-83, assoc. dean NY, 1986-89, sr. assoc. dean NY, 1989-91, Watson prof. NY, 1999—, now assoc. dept. chair and dir. undergraduate studies NY. Vis. prof. U. Lund, Sweden, 1974, 81, U. Iowa, 1985; vis. rschr. Kobe U., Japan, 1991. Co-author (with M. Kent Jennings): (poliical science book) The Political Character of Adolescence, 1974; author: Generations and Politics, 1981, How Generations Perceive Each Other, 1974; co-author (with others): Minority Representation and the Quest for Voting Equality, 1992; co-author: (with Jane Junn) (Education Book) Civic Education: What Makes Students Learn, 1998; co-author (with others) (Political Science Book) Term Limits in the States, 1999; co-editor (with Harold Stanley): (Polit. Sci. Book) Vital Statistics on American Politics, 2003, 9th edit.; co-editor: (with Herbert Weisberg) (Politic. Sci. Book) Controversies in Voting Behavior, 2001; co-editor: (Polit. Sci. Book) Comparing Democracies, 1996, 2d edit, 2002; co-editor: Trends in Public Opinion. Fellow, Guggenheim Found., 1983—84, Ctr. for Advanced Study in Behavioral Sci., 1989; grantee, NIMH, 1969—70, Ford Found., 1972—73, NSF, 1974—77, 1980—86, 1994—. Am. Ednl. Rsch. Assn., 1997—98, U.S. Dept. Edn., 1997—99, 2001—02. Mem. Am. Polit. Sci. Assn., Phi Beta Kappa. Lutheran. Home: 45 Boniface Dr Rochester NY 14620-3333 Office: U Rochester Dept Polit Sci Rochester NY 14627-0146 E-mail: niemi@rochester.edu.*

**NIEMIEC, DAVID WALLACE,** investment company executive; b. Midland, Mich., Dec. 17, 1949; s. George E. and Eleanor (Yack) N.; m. Melanie Taveau Mason, Oct. 4, 1975; children: Elizabeth Street, Margaret Johnson AB, Harvard U., 1972, MBA, 1974. Assoc. Dillon, Read & Co., Inc., N.Y.C., 1974-78, v.p., 1979-81, sr. v.p., chief adminstrv. officer, 1982-83, mng. dir., chief adminstrv. officer, 1984-97, vice chmn., 1991-97; mng. dir. Saratoga Ptnrs., N.Y.C., 1998—2001, adv., 2001—. Bd. dirs. Emeritus Corp., Seattle; bd. dirs., trustee Templeton Funds, Ft. Lauderdale. Trustee Nightingale-Bamford Sch., N.Y.C., 1993-2004; bd. govs. The Mannes Coll. of Music, N.Y.C., 1996—. Mem. Union Club N.Y.C. Republican. Unitarian Universalist. Office: Saratoga Ptnrs 535 Madison Ave New York NY 10022-4212 Office Phone: 212-906-7044.

**NIEMIEC, EDWARD WALTER,** retired professional association executive; b. Detroit, Nov. 1, 1936; s. Walter A. and Mary N.; m. Nancy M. Bennett, Aug. 25, 1962; children: Lisa, Julie, Brenda. BS, U. Detroit, 1959, MBA, 1961. With Paine Webber Jackson & Curtis, N.Y.C., 1959-80, exec. v.p., dir. adminstrv. divsn., to 1980; v.p., bd. dirs. Moseley, Hallgarten, Estabrook, Weeden, Inc., 1980-82; also bd. dirs. Moseley, Hallgarten, Estabrook & Weeden Holding Corp.; pres., CEO, dir., mem. exec. com. Securities Settlement Corp. (subs. The Travelers 1982), N.Y.C., 1980-87; pres., dir. Inc. Trading Co, subs. Instinet Corp., 1988-89; COO Instinet Corp. subs. Reuters Holdings Plc., 1988-89; group v.p. AICPA, N.Y.C., 1989—2001. Served with U.S. Army. Roman Catholic.

**NIEMIEC, MARGARET G.,** elementary school educator; d. Thomas Liddell Gustenhoven and M. Phyllis Kennedy; m. Michael J. Niemiec, Apr. 15, 1978; children: Katherine, Ellen, Anne. BA, Mt. Holyoke Coll., 1974, MA, Seton Hall U., 1993; EdD, Rutgers U., 2004. Mgr. Equitable LIfe Assurance Soc., NYC, 1974—80; tchr. Hillsborough (NJ) Twp. Schs., 1994—. Part-time faculty mem. Walden U., Mpls., 2005—06. Mem.: ASCD, Internat. Reading Assn. Avocations: reading, knitting.

**NIENHUIS, ARTHUR WESLEY,** physician, researcher; b. Hudsonville, Mich., Aug. 9, 1941; s. Willard M. and Grace (Prince) Nienhuis; children: Carol Elizabeth, Craig Wesley, Kevin Robert, Heather Grace. Student, Cornell Coll., 1959-61; MD, UCLA, 1963-68. Am. Bd. Internal Medicine, Am. Bd. Hematology. Intern Mass. Gen. Hosp., Boston, 1968-69, asst. resident, 1969-70; clin. assoc. NHLBI, NIH, Bethesda, Md., 1970-72; clin. fellow hematology Children's Hosp., Boston, 1972-73; chief clin. & svc. Molecular Hematology NIH, Bethesda, Md., 1973-77; dept. clin. dir. NHLBI, NIH, Bethesda, Md., 1976-93, chief clin. Hematology Branch, 1976-93; dir. St. Jude Children's Rsch. Hosp., Memphis, 1993—2004. Editor BLOOD-J Am. Soc. Hematology, Bethesda, Md., 1988-92; chmn. Hematology Bd. Am. Bd. Internal Med., Phila., 1988-92. Editor: Molecular Basis of Blood Diseases, 1986, 93. Mem. Am. Soc. Hematology (pres. 1994), Am. Soc. Clin. Investigation, Am. Physicians, Nat. Cancer Adv. Bd. Office: St Jude Children's Rsch Hosp 332 N Lauderdale St Memphis TN 38105-2729 E-mail: Arthur.Nienhuis@stjude.org.

**NIENOW, BETH MARIE,** librarian; b. Rochester, Minn., Jan. 22, 1961; d. Duane Reuben and Elaine Nienow. BA, Hamline U., St. Paul, 1983; MLS, U. Wis., 1984; MA, Mankato (Minn.) State U., 1998. Libr. U. N.D., Grand Forks, 1984-89; U. Tenn., Chattanooga, 1989-91; grad. asst. Mankato State U., 1991—93; libr. Rochester Pub. Libr., 1994—. Lutheran. Home: 2303 Fisher Ct NW Rochester MN 55901-8084 Office: Rochester Pub Libr 101 2d St SE Rochester MN 55904

**NIEPORENT, DREW,** restaurant group executive; Owner Montrachet, NYC, 1985—; co-owner Tribeca Grill, NYC, 1990—; pres., owner Myriad Restaurant Group, NYC, 1993—; Nobu, NYC, Next Door Nobu, NYC, Nobu 57, NYC, Centrico, NYC, Crush Wine and Spirits, NYC, Pulse, NYC, The Coach House, NYC. Guest lectr. Cornell U., NYU, NYC, Syracuse (N.Y.) U., New Eng. Culinary Inst., N.Y.Restaurant Assn., New Sch., NYC. Hon. co-chairperson, master ceremonies Starfish Found., 1995; co-chair Share Our Strength's Taste Nation, N.Y.C., 1997—99; guest honor Tourette Syndrome Assn. Dinner, 1997; culinary chair Momentum Project. Named Man of the Yr., Food Beverage Assn., 1993, Humanitarian of the Yr., James Beard Found., 2000, Restaurateur of the Yr., Bon Appetit Mag., 2000; recipient Gates Jerusalem medal, Israel Bonds, 1994, Oustanding Svc. award, James Beard Awards, 1995. Mem.: Am. Inst. Wine and Food (bd. dirs.). Office: Myriad Restaurant Group 375 Greenwich St New York NY 10013*

**NIERENBERG, NICO,** software developer company executive; Attended and studied econ. and computer scis., U. Calif., LA, U. Calif., San Diego. Sys. programmer, applications developer SAIC; sys. software chief Rogers, Kirkham and Associates; co-founder Unify Corp.; founder Actuate Corp., South San Francisco, Calif., 1993—, CEO, 1993—2000, chmn. bd., chief architect, 2000—. Venture cons. Accel Ptnrs.; serves on bd. dirs. to software companies. Office: Actuate Corp 701 Gateway Blvd South San Francisco CA 94080-7084 Office Phone: 650-837-2000. Office Fax: 650-827-1560.

**NIESE, HENRY ERNST,** artist, educator; b. Jersey City, Oct. 11, 1924; s. Bene Emil and Ruth (Halsted) N.; m. Paula Gerson, May 1, 1964; children: Mary Roberts, William Cody. Cert., The Cooper Union, N.Y.C., 1949, Acad. Grande Chaumiere, Paris, 1949; BFA, Columbia U., 1955. Instr. Bklyn. Mus., 1951-55, Newark Mus., 1952-55; with St. Bernards Sch., Gladstone, NJ, 1960—66, Horace Mann Sch., N.Y.C., 1964—65; univ. art dept. Ohio State U., Lima, 1966-69; prof. art dept. U. Md., Coll. Park, 1969-96, Univ. Honors prof., 1982-94; vis. artist Coll. Creative Studies U. Calif., Santa Barbara, 1975; guest fellow Yale U., New Haven, 1979; founder, dir. Eagle Voice Ctr., Glenelg, Md., 1979—. Cons. Nat. Inst. Health, Bethesda, Md., 1992—; lectr. Nat. Forest Svc., Portland, Oregon, 1993—; guest lectr. Va. Tech., Goucher Coll., Md. Inst. Coll. of Art, 2003-06, USCG Hdqrs., Washington, USDA, Washington, U.S. Commodities Futures Trading Commn., Mustardseed Found., Va.; presenter HUD office Native Am. programs, 2002-03. Artist 27 one man shows in N.Y.C., Dallas, Washington, New Haven, other cities; group shows include Mus. Modern Art, Whitney Mus., Boston, Newark, Toledo, Ogunquit Mus., Mus. City, St. Louis, N.Y. World's Fair; works in permanent collections at Corcoran Gallery, Washington, Whitney Mus., N.Y.C., Newark Mus., Nat. Mus. Am. Art, Washington, N.J. State Mus., Trenton, others; dancer 16 Sundances Rosebud Sioux Reservation, S.D.; dance leader Eagle Voice Ctr., 1981-98; author The Man Who Knew The Medicine; Bill Eagle Feather's Teaching, 2002. Pulitzer fellow, 1954; recipient W.A. Clark prize Corcoran Gallery, 1955, Emily Lowe award Joe and Emily Lowe Found., 1955; named Diniktiyi, 1983, Asgayakanunawu by Chief, Etowah/Cherokee Nation, 1984. Mem. Ctr. for Respect of Life and Environment (bd. advisors 1989-94). Native American. Home: PO Box 44 Glenelg MD 21737-0044

**NIESEN, JAMES LOUIS,** theater director; b. St. Louis, Feb. 15, 1946; s. James Louis and Emily Elise (Brennecke) N. BFA, Ill. Wesleyan U., 1968; MFA, Ohio U., 1974. Actor Stage South, Columbia, S.C., 1974-75, Long Wharf Theatre, New Haven, 1977-78, Geva Theater, Rochester, N.Y., 1978-79; freelance dir., 1980-83; stage mgr. Roundabout Theater, N.Y., 1982-83; artistic dir. Irondale Ensemble Project, N.Y., 1983—. Panelist N.Y. Found. on the Arts, N.Y., 1988-89. Author: (book) Game Guide, 1988; contbr. articles to profl. jours.; dir. (play) St. Joan of the Stockyards, 1993, Danton's Death, 1994, You Can't Win, 1994, Andrew Carnegie Presands the Jew of Malta, 1996, The Mother, 1997, Degenerate Art, 1998, The Murals of Rockefeller Center, 2002, The Pope and the Witch, 2000, Brecht on Brecht, 2000, Jungle of Cities, 2001, Peter Pan, 2001, Seuss Centennial Tour, 2004, Outside the Law, 2004. Mem. Actors Equity Assn. Avocations: folk music, country music, tennis. Home: 419 Pacific St Brooklyn NY 11217-2204 Office: Irondale Ensemble Project PO Box 150604 Brooklyn NY 11215-0604 Office Phone: 718-488-9233. E-mail: jim@irondale.org.

**NIETERS, GERARD ANTHONY,** lawyer; b. St. Louis, Mar. 23, 1961; s. Richard Francis and Joan Ellen (Setchfield) N.; m. Mary Christine Gierer, June 1, 1985; children: Whitney Christine, Stephen Gerard, Chloe Elizabeth, Bethany Marie. BSBA, U. Mo., St. Louis, 1983; JD and MBA, St. Louis U., 1987. Bar: Mo. 1987, Ill. 1990. Assoc. atty. Kramer & Frank, P.C., 1987-90; assoc. legal counsel Mercantile Bank, St. Louis, 1990-95; staff atty. Am. Gen. Fin., Inc., O'Fallon, Mo., 1995—. Mem.: Nat. Lawyers Assn., Mo. Bar Assn. Roman Catholic. Avocations: softball, soccer. Office: 19 Osperey Way O Fallon MO 63366-8039 Office: 113 Triad Ctr W O Fallon MO 63366-7542

**NIETO, JUAN MANUEL,** emergency medicine physician; b. Alpine, Tex., Sept. 24, 1949; s. Edmundo Miguel and Socorro (Herrera) N.; children: Ana Raquel, Cristina Marie. BS, U. Notre Dame, 1970; MD, U. Colo., 1974. Intern LA County, U. So. Calif. Med. Ctr., 1974-75; physician Cmty. Health Found., LA, 1975-77; physician emergency dept. Physicians Med. Group, Marina Del Ray, Calif., 1977-78; resident in emergency medicine Denver Gen.-St. Anthony Hosp. Sys., 1978-80; mem. staff North Colo. Med. Ctr., Greeley, 1980-83; emergency physician, med. dir. emergency dept. Brackenridge Hosp., Austin, Tex., 1984-85; practice medicine Austin, 1983—. Emergency physician Emergency Physicians Affiliates, 1986-89; assoc. prof. U. Tex. Health Sci. Ctr., San Antonio, 1994—; mem. planning com. Starflight Helicopter Air Transport, 1985; instr. advanced cardiac life support, 1977; bd. dirs. Nat. Chicano Health Orgn., 1971-74; advisor East Los Angeles Hypertension Screening Program, 1978; med. advisor Weld County Ambulance Service, 1980-83; med. dir. Air Life, 1980-83; med. dir. Alamo Heights Emergency Med. Svc., 1988-90, med. dir. AMR Ambulance, 1991-98; amb. Nat. Health Svc. Corps, 2003—. Del. Colo. Med. Soc., 1983. Fellow: Nat. Hispanic Med. Assn., Am. Acad. Emergency Medicine, Am. Coll. Emergency Physicians, NYU Wagner Sch. (leadership fellow 2001); mem.: APHA, Nat. Hispanic Medicine Assn., Soc. Academic Emergency Medicine, Physicians for a Nat. Healthcare Program, Nat. Hispanic Med. Assn., Travis County Med. Soc., Tex. Med. Assn., Nat. Hispanic Med. Assn. (leadership fellow, advisor, board mem. 2001—, mem. adv. bd. 2003—, Leadership award 2006), Amnesty Internat. Office: Phone: 210-358-2078. E-mail: jmnietomd@sbcglobal.net, juan-nieto@msn.com.

**NIETO, MARIO,** civil engineer; b. Cuba; BS in Civil Engring., Univ. Miami, 1984. Registered Prof. Engr., Fla. Various positions to area mgr. and v.p. Parsons Corp.; engring. ops., mgmt. svcs. area mgr. Washington Group Internat., Deerfield Beach, Fla., 2005—. Named one of 50 Most Important Hispanics in Tech., Bus., Hispanic Engineer and Info. Tech. mag., 2005. Office: Washington Group Internat 800 Fairway Dr Deerfield Beach FL 33441 Office Phone: 954-421-8080.*

**NIEUWSMA, MILTON JOHN,** writer, journalist; b. Sept. 5, 1941; s. John and Jean (Potter); m. Marilee Gordon, Feb. 1, 1964; children: Jonathan, Gregory, Elizabeth. BA, Hope Coll., Holland, Mich., 1963; postgrad., Wayne State U., 1963—65; MA, U. Ill., 1978. Pres. Trans. Am. Syndicate, Inc., Chgo., 1988—97; vis. prof. Rutgers U., New Brunswick, NJ, 1990—95, St. Xavier U. Chgo., 1996—97. Author: Kinderlager, 1998, Surviving Auschwitz, 2005; writer, cons.: Children of The Shoah, PBS, 2005 (2 Emmy awards, 2006); contbg. editor: Chgo. Tribune, L.A. Times, others. Home: 2421 Central-Idlewood Beach Holland MI 49424-2277 Personal E-mail: mnieuwsma@macatawa.com.

**NIEVA, CONSTANTINO S.,** priest, researcher; b. Boac, Mariduque, Philippines, July 9, 1929; U.S. s. Juan Morente Nieva and Elvira Sarmiento Nieves. LLB, U. Philippines, Manila, 1953; BA, San Jose Sem., Manila, 1960; STD, Pontifical Gregorian U., Rome, 1970. Bar: Phillipines. Author: (book) This Trans— God, 1971; contbr. articles to religious jours. Mem.: Modern Lang. Assn. Am., Medieval Acad. Am. Independent. Avocation: piano.

**NIEVIEDGAL, CAROL BELMARCE,** elementary school educator; b. New Bedford, Mass., Sept. 4, 1948; d. Palmira Ferreira Belmarce and Baldomar Chaves Ferreira; m. John Theodore Nieviedgal, May 24, 2003; children: Derek Carl Araujo, John T. IV. BS Elem. Edn., Bridgewater State Coll., Bridgewater, Mass., 1970; MA in Counseling Psychology, Lesley U., Cambridge, Mass., 2005. Cert. Elem. Tchr. Mass. Bd. of Edn., 1970, Prin./Asst. Prin. K-8 Mass. Bd. of Edn., 1982. Second grade tchr. Cushman Sch., Dartmouth, Mass., 1970—82, acting prin., 1973—83, kindergarten tchr., 1982—83, DeMello Sch., Dartmouth, Mass., 1983—. Sec Bristol County Educators Assn., Raynham, Mass., 2001—03; first v.p. Delta Kappa Gamma Psi Chpt., New Bedford, Mass., 2001—03, second v.p., 1999—2001. Ch. lector St. Bernard's Ch., Assonet, Mass., 1985—2001. Mem.: AAUW (assoc.), Dartmouth Educators Assn. (assoc.), Mass. Tchrs. Assn. (assoc.), Nat. Educators Assn. (assoc.), Bridgewater State Coll. Alumni Assn. (assoc.), Coll. Club of New Bedford (assoc.; corr. sec. 1996—98), Nat. Kindergarten Alliance (assoc.), Mass. Sch. Counselors Assn. (assoc.), Harvard-Radcliffe Club (assoc.). Independent. Non-Denom. Achievements include Bristol County Educators Assn. Disting. Svc. Award; Bristol County Educators Assn. Human Rels.Award. Avocations: travel, dance, music, cooking, reading.

Home: 11 Joaquin Ave Assonet MA 02702-1568 Office: DeMello Sch 654 Dartmouth St Dartmouth MA 02748 Office Phone: 508-996-6759. Office Fax: 508-990-2519. Personal E-mail: carolbelmarce@aol.com. Business E-mail: cbelmarce@dartmouthps.org.

**NIEWALD, WILBUR,** artist; b. Kans. City, Mo., 1925; married. Vis. artist Vt. Studio Ctr.; instr. to chmn., sr. prof., painting Kans. City Art Inst., 1949—92, prof. emeritus, 1992—. Represented in permanent collections Met. Mus. Art, NYC, Moffett Family Collection, Heartland Spine & Specialty Hosp., Kans. City, exhibitions include (selected) Wright State Univ. Art Galleries, 1996, Rider Univ., 2004, Albrecht-Kemper Mus. Art, 2004, Marianna Kistler Beach Mus. Art, 2004. Recipient Disting. Teaching of Art award, Coll. Art Assn., 1988, Charlotte Street Lifetime Achievement award, 1999. Mem.: NAD (academician 1994—). Mailing: Albrecht-Kemper Mus Art 2818 Frederick Ave Saint Joseph MO 64506

**NIEWIAROSKI, TRUDI OSMERS (GERTRUDE NIEWIAROSKI),** social studies educator; b. Jersey City, Apr. 30, 1935; d. Albert John and Margaret (Niemeyer) Osmers; m. Donald H. Niewiaroski, June 8, 1957; children: Donald H., Donna, Margaret Anne, Nancy Noel. AB in History and German, Upsala Coll., East Orange, N.J., 1957, MEd, Montgomery County Pub. Schs., Rockville, Md., 1992. Cert. tchr. Md. Tchr. geography Colego Americano, Quito, Ecuador, 1964-66; bd. dirs. Cotopaxi Acad., Quito, 1964-65; tchr. speed reading Escuela Lincoln, Buenos Aires, Argentina, 1966-67; substitute tchr. Montgomery County Pub. Schs., Rockville, 1978-83, tchr. social studies, 1984—. Del. Eisenhower People to People Educators' Del. Vietnam, 1993; pres. Fulbright Meml. Fund Program, 1997; resident tchg. fellow Russia-Ukraine Excellence in Tchg. Program, 1997; resident scholar in Korea, The Korea Soc., 1999. Author curricula; contbr. chpts. to books, articles to profl. jours.; lectr. at workshops. Bd. dirs. Cotopaxi Acad., Quito, 1964-65; pres. Citizens Assn., Potomac, Md., 1977-81; leader Girl Scouts U.S., 1975-76; adv. coun. Milken Found.; pres. Fulbright Meml. Fund Program Japan Alumni, 1999—. Recipient Md. Tchr. of Yr. award State of Md. Edn. Dept., 1993, finalist nat. Tchr. of Yr., 1993, Disting. Alumni award Upsala Coll., 1993, Nat. Educator award Milken Found., 1994, Summer Fellowship Korean Studies Program, 1999, Joseph Malone fellowship Sultanate of Oman, 2003, Goethe Inst. fellowship, Germany, 2003; Fulbright fellow, India, 1985, China, 1990, Japan Keizai Koho Ctr. fellow, 1992, Fulbright Meml. Fund Tchr. Program fellow, Japan, 1997, Fulbright fellow, South Africa, 2001, Malone fellow, Oman, 2003, U. Tex. Mideast Inst. fellow, 2005; UMBC-U. Mex. Art and Culture scholar, 1995; mem. Cuba Study Tour, 2004, Dar Al Islam Study Tour, Iran, 2004; fellow U. Pitts. and Freeman Found., China, 2004; Fulbright fellow, China, 2004; Egypt fellow U. Tex. Middle East Inst., 2005. Mem. AAUW, ASCD, Nat. Coun. Social Studies, Md. Coun. for Social Studies, Asia Soc., Smithsonian Instn., Montgomery County Hist. Soc., Spl. Interest Groups-China, Japan and Korea, Md. Bus. Roundtable for Edn., Nat. Social Studies Suprs. Assn., Kappa Delta Pi. Avocations: cake and cookie decorating, travel. Office: R Montgomery High Sch Rockville MD 20852 Office Phone: 301-279-8442. Personal E-mail: niewiaroski.dandt@aol.com. Business E-mail: trudi_niewiaroski@fc.mcps.k12.md.us.

**NIFFENEGGER, AUDREY ANNE,** artist, writer; b. June 13, 1963; BFA, Sch. of the Art Inst. of Chgo., 1985; MFA, Northwestern U., Evanston, Ill., 1991. Asst. prof., art, printmaking Columbia Coll. Chgo. Ctr. for Book and Paper Arts, 1995—; on sabbatical, 2004—05. Author: (novels) The Time Traveler's Wife, 2003 (Publishers Weekly paperback bestseller, NY Times bestseller), The Three Incestuous Sisters: An Illustrated Novel, 2005. E-mail: aniffenegger@popmail.colum.edu.

**NIFONG, MICHAEL B.,** prosecutor; b. Wilmington, NC, Sept. 14, 1950; m. Cy Gurney; children: Bryan Gabriel, Sarah Katherine. AB in Polit. Sci., U. NC, Chapel Hill, 1971; JD, U. NC, 1978. Bar: NC 1978. Math. tchr., boys phys. ed. tchr., Southport, NC, 1971—72; social worker New Hanover County Dept. Social Services, Wilmington, NC, 1972—75; atty. Durham County Dist. Atty. Office, NC, 1978—79, asst. dist. atty. NC, 1979—2005, dist. atty. NC, 2005—. District Atty 14 Prosecutorial Dist Durham County Judicial Bldg 201 East Main St Durham NC 27701 Office Phone: 919-564-7100. Office Fax: 919-560-3220.

**NIGAM, HEMANSHU,** lawyer, Internet company executive; BA in Polit. Theory, Wesleyan U., Conn., 1987; JD, Boston U. Sch. Law, 1990. Dep. district atty. LA County Dist. Atty. Office, 1990—97; trial atty., criminal divsn. US Dept. Justice, Washington, 1997—2000; v.p., dir. worldwide internet enforcement Motion Picture Assn./Motion Picture Assn. Am., 2000—02; corp. atty., criminal compliance, security & law enforcement affairs, digital integrity group, Microsoft law and corp. affairs Microsoft Corp., Redmond, Wash., 2002—06; dir., consumer security outreach and child safe computing; chief security officer, MySpace.com News Corp., NYC, 2006—. Spkr. in field. Mem.: Washington State Bar Assn., Calif. State Bar Assn. Achievements include being a proven leader in online safety and security; served as a federal prosecutor against Internet child exploitation for the US Department of Justice; an advisor to a Congressional commission on online child safety; an advisor to the White House on cyber stalking. Office: News Corp 1211 Avenue of Americas 8th Fl New York NY 10036*

**NIGBOR, DONALD E.,** electronics executive; BS engineering, MS engineering, Rensselaer Polytechnic Institute; MBA, Amos Tuck School of Business, Dartmouth College. Manufacturing analyst Intermedics, 1980—84; gen. mgr. Benchmark Electronics Inc., 1984—90, bd. dir., 1986—, pres., 1986—2001, CEO, 2001—05, chmn., 2001—. Office: c/o Benchmark Electronics 3000 Technology Dr Angleton TX 77515

**NIGHSWONGER, DAVID GLENN,** music educator; b. Glendale, Calif., Apr. 26, 1954; s. William E. Nighswonger and Carolyn Marie Greer; m. Sharon Kay Deibert, Aug. 29, 1981; children: Dana Amalia, Samantha Jo. BA in Edn., Ctrl. Wash. U., 1977, MusM, 1985. Cert. in contg. edn. Wash., 1977. Tchr. music North Mason Sch. Dist., Belfair, Wash., 1977—79, Rosalia (Wash.) Sch. Dist., 1981—94, Onalaska (Wash.) Sch. Dist., 1994—2001, Harrington (Wash.) Sch. Dist., 2001—. Mem. scholarship com. Davenport (Wash.) First Presbyn. Ch., 2005—06. Mem.: Wash. Music Edn. Assn. (conf. presenter 1998—), Bi-County Music Dirs. (v.p. 2005—), South West Wash. Music Edn. Assn. (chmn. honor massed band festival 1998—2000), Lions Club. Democrat. Presbyn. Avocations: fly fishing, baseball, woodworking. Home: 410 W Willis Harrington WA 99134 Office: Harrington School District 204 100 S Sherlock Harrington WA 99134 Office Phone: 509-253-4331. Office Fax: 509-456-6306. Personal E-mail: nighswonger@centurytel.net. Business E-mail: dnighswonger@harrsd.k12.wa.us.

**NIGHTINGALE, DEBORAH SEIFERT,** systems engineer, consultant; b. Dayton, Ohio, Sept. 10, 1949; m. Tom Seifert, 1971; children: Jessica, Danielle, Jordan. BS, U. Dayton, 1970; MS, Ohio State U., 1975, PhD, 1979. Programmer U. Dayton Rsch. Inst., 1968-71; sr. engring. scientist Wright Patterson AFB, 1971-79; project leader Allied Signal Engines, 1979-80; mgr. facility planning, factory modernization, Corp CIM Com., 1980-84, mfg. sys. engr., indsl. engr., ops. support, chmn., 1984-87, sr. project mgr. mktg. svc., dir. strategic planning, 1987-96; cons. Paradise Valley, Ariz., 1996—; prof., focus lead, Lean Enterprise Team & Lean Aerospace Initiative Dept. of Aerospace & Aeronautics, MIT, Cambridge, Mass., 1997—. Contbr. articles to profl. jour. Mem. NAE (4th decade com. 1993—), Inst. Indsl. Engr. (pres. elect 1994—), Soc. Mfg. Engr. Computer and Automated Sys. Assn. Home: 43 Canterbury St Andover MA 01810-2850 Office: Dept Aerospace & Aeronautics MIT Rm 33-312 77 Mass Ave Cambridge MA 02139

**NIGHTINGALE, EDMUND JOSEPH,** clinical psychologist, educator, consultant; b. St. Paul, Jan. 10, 1941; s. Edmund Anthony and Lauretta Alexandria (Horejs) N.; m. Marie Arcara, Apr. 9, 1978 (dec. April 1992); 1 child, Edmund Bernard. Student, Nazareth Hall Prep. Sem., 1959—61; AB, St. Paul Sem., 1963; AB magna cum laude, Cath. U. Louvain, Belgium, 1965,

MA, 1967; STB cum laude, Cath. U. Louvain, 1967; postgrad., U. Minn. 1971; MA, Loyola U., Chgo., 1973, PhD Clin. Psychology, 1975. Lic. clin. psychologist, Ill., Minn., cert. Nat. Registry Health Svc. Providers in Psychology; diplomate clin. psychology Am. Bd. Profl. Psychology. With Cath. Archdiocese St. Paul and Mpls., 1967—73; intern clin. psychology Michael Reese Hosp. and Med. Ctr., Chgo., 1973—74; with West Side VA Hosp., Chgo., 1974—75; staff psychologist Student Counseling Ctr., Loyola U., Chgo., 1975; staff psychologist, clin. coord. inpatient unit Drug Dependency Treatment Ctr., 1975—80; chief psychology VA Med. Ctr., Danville, Ill., 1980—86, VA Med. Ctr. Mpls., 1986—2006; ret., 2006; cons., 2006—. Mem. pers. bd. Archdiocese St. Paul and Mpls., 1968-70; lectr. psychology, Loyola U., Chgo., 1975; asst. professorial lectr. psychology, St. Paul Xavier Coll., Chgo., 1975-78; adj. asst. prof. psychology in psychology, Abraham Lincoln Sch. Medicine, Med. Ctr. U. Ill., Chgo., 1977-82; adj. prof. psychology Purdue U., 1981-87; asst. prof. psychology Med. Sch., U. Minn., 1987—, clin. assoc. prof. psychology Coll. Liberal Arts, 1986-90; adj. asst. prof., 1990—; clin. asst. prof. U. Ill. Sch. Medicine, Urbana/Champaign, 1982-87; mem. grad. faculty counseling psychology Ind. State U., Terre Haute, 1983-86 Founding editor: Louvain Studies, 1966; editor: VA Dir. Psychology Staffing and Svcs., 1982, 83, 84, 85, 87 Bd. dirs. Inst. Postgrad. Studies, Ill. Psychol. Assn Fellow APA (clin. psychology, psychotherapy, pub. svc., psychol. hypnosis, sec. treas. pub. svc. 1990-91, coun. reps. 1999-2004, Karl F. Heiser Presdl. award for Adv. 2002, divsn. Psychologists Pub. Svc. Disting. Contbns. award 2002); mem. AAAS, Am. Psychol. Soc., Assn. for Advancement Psychology, Ill. Psychol. Assn. (clin. psychology and acad. sects., sec. 1982-83, pres.-elect 1983-84, pres. 1984-85), Am. Group Psychotherapy Assn., Am. Soc. Clin. Hypnosis, Minn. Psychol. Assn. (pub. svc.-pres. 1997-99), Eagle Scout Assn., Assn. VA Chief Psychologists (sec., treas 1987-90, pres.-elect 1990-91, pres. 1991-92, past pres. 1992-93, Outstanding Leadership award 1992), Minn. Soc. Clin. Hypnosis (bd. dirs. 1999-2001), Nat. MS Soc. (trustee Minn. chpt. 2005—). Office: VA Med Ctr Minneapolis MN 55417 Home: 28 W Marie Ave West Saint Paul MN 55118

**NIGHTINGALE, ELENA OTTOLENGHI,** pediatric geneticist, academic administrator, educator; b. Livorno, Italy, Nov. 1, 1932; arrived in U.S., 1939, naturalized; d. Mario Lazzaro and Elisa Vittoria (Levi) Ottolenghi; m. Suart L. Nightingale, July 1, 1965; children: Elizabeth, Marisa. AB summa cum laude, Barnard Coll., 1954; PhD, Rockefeller U., 1961; MD, NYU, 1964. Asst. prof. Cornell U. Med. Coll., N.Y.C., 1965—70, Johns Hopkins U., Balt., 1970—73; fellow in clin. genetics and pediat. Georgetown U. Hosp., Washington, 1973—74; sr. staff officer NAS, Washington, 1975—79, sr. program officer Inst. Medicine, 1979—82, sr. scholar-in-residence, 1982—83; spl. advisor to pres. Carnegie Corp. N.Y., N.Y.C., 1983—94; sr. program officer, 1989—94; scholar-in-residence Inst. of Medicine, NAS, Washington, 1995—. Vis. assoc. prof. Harvard Med. Sch., Boston, 1980—84, vis. lectr., 1984—95; adj. prof. pediat. Georgetown U. Med. Ctr., 1984—, George Washington U. Med. Ctr., 1994—; mem. recombinant DNA adv. com. NIH, Bethesda, Md., 1979—83. Editor: The Breaking of Bodies and Minds: Torture, Psychiatric Abuses and the Health Professions, 1985, Prenatal Screening, Policies and Values: The Example of Neural Tube Defects, 1987, Promoting the Health of Adolescents: New Directions for the 21st Century, 1993, Adolescent Risk and Vulnerability: Concepts and Measurement, 2001; co-author: Before Birth: Prenatal Screening for Genetic Disease, 1990; contbr. numerous sci. articles to profl. publs. Bd. dirs. Amnesty Internat., U.S.A., Washington, 1989—91, Ctr. for Youth Svcs., Washington, 1980—84, Sci. Svc., Inc., Washington, 1985—96. Fellow: AAAS (chmn. com. on sci. freedom and responsibility 1985—88), N.Y. Acad. Scis.; mem.: Inst. Medicine of NAS (chmn. com. on health and human rights 1987—90), Genetics Soc. Am., Am. Soc. Human Genetics (social issues com. 1982—85), Am. Soc. Microbiology, Sigma Xi, Phi Beta Kappa. Office: NAS 500 5th St NW Washington DC 20001 Business E-Mail: enightin@nas.edu.

**NIGHTINGALE, STUART LESTER,** public health service officer; b. NYC, Jan. 26, 1938; s. Lester M. Nightingale and Beatrice L. N. (Leibowitz) Helpern; m. Elena Ottolenghi, July 1, 1965; children: Elizabeth S., Marisa O. BA, Yale U., 1959; MD, NYU, 1964. Diplomate Am. Bd. Internal Medicine. Intern in medicine and surgery Montefiore Hosp. and Med. Ctr., Bronx, 1964—65, resident in internal medicine, fellow in adolescent medicine, 1965—66, resident internal medicine, fellow adolescent medicine, 1967—69, asst. attending physician, 1969—70; resident in anatomical pathology NYU Sch. Medicine, 1966—67; med. dir. drug abuse adminstrn. Dept. Health and Mental Hygiene State of Md., 1971—72; chief treatment and rehab. office of programs, spl. action office for drug abuse prevention Exec. Office of Pres., Washington, 1972—74, chief office treatment and rehab., spl. action office for drug abuse prevention, 1974—75; dir. divsn. resource devel. Nat. Inst. on Drug Abuse, Rockville, Md., 1974—76; asst. to dir. Bur. Drugs, FDA, Rockville, 1976—79; dep. assoc. commr. for health affairs FDA, Rockville, 1979—82, acting assoc. commr. for health affairs, 1979—82, assoc. commr. for health affairs, 1982—2000; sr. med. adv. to dir. global health affairs and chief med. officer Office of the Asst. Sec. for Planning and Evaluation Dept. HHS, Washington, 2000—04, chief med. officer Office Pub. Health Emergency Preparedness, 2004—, dep. asst. sec. Office Pub. Health Emergency Preparedness, 2005—. Vis. physician Balt. City Hosps., 1970-72; clin. instr. dept. medicine Coll. Medicine SUNY, Bklyn., 1970; asst. physician outpatient dept., instr. dept. medicine Johns Hopkins U. Sch. Medicine, Balt., 1970-72, med. dir. drug abuse ctr., 1970-71, instr. dept. med. care and hosps. Sch. Hygiene and Pub. Health, 1971-74, rsch. program mgr. health svcs. rsch. and devel. ctr., 1970-71; chmn. rsch. involving human subjects com. FDA, 1979-84; liaison mem. Commn. on Fed. Drug Approval Process, U.S. Congress, 1980-81; mem.-at-large U.S. Pharmacopeial Conv., Inc., 1985-95; bd. trustees The Milton Helpern Libr. of Legal Medicine, N.Y.C., 1982-2000; bd. dirs. Nat. Coun. on Patient Info. and Edn., Washington; mem. forum on drug devel. and regulation Inst. Medicine, NAS, Washington, 1986-2000. Contbr. author Jour. AMA, 1985-99, Am. Family Physician, 1980-99, Capt. M.C., USAR, 1966-72; with USPHS. Recipient Disting. Svc. Spl. Action Office for Drug Abuse Prevention award Exec. Office of Pres., 1975, Pub. Health Superior Svc. award, 1983, Disting. Contbn. award Nat. Coun. Patient Info. and Edn., 1987, Achievement award Am. Assn. Physicians for Human Rights, 1990, Presdl. Meritorious Exec. Rank award, 1990, 2005, Pub. Health Svc. Spl. Recognition award, 1993, Sec.'s Recognition award Dept. HHS, 1999. Fellow ACP; mem. AMA, Sr. Execs. assn., Cosmos Club. Office: Dept Health and Human Svcs 200 Independence Ave SW Washington DC 20201-0004 Office Phone: 202-205-2882. Business E-Mail: stuart.nightingale@hhs.gov.

**NIGHTINGALE, SUZANNE M.,** management consultant; d. Stanley Wren and Ann Mary Nightingale; m. Kathleen P. Clementson, May 20, 2004. BA in Econ., U. San Francisco, 1985. Cert. sys. engr. Microsoft Corp., Redmond WA, 2000; spiritual healer Okla. City, Okla., 1985; lic. pvt. pilot, single engine land FAA, 1989. Project mgr. Lockheed Missiles and Space Co., Sunnyvale, Calif., 1982—89. Constrn. project mgr. Nightingale Assoc., The Sea Ranch, Calif., 1983—89, prin., Cape Coral, Calif., 1989—; data base analyst Lockheed Missiles and Space, Sunnyvale, Calif., 1987—89; corr. Door County Adv., Sturgeon Bay, Wis., 1991—94. Dir. Interfaith Events to Promote Cmty. Unity, Fort Myers, 1997—2002, Quality Life Acad., Fort Myers, 2004—05; founder Wash. Island Aviation Libr., Washington Island, Wis., 1990—94. Achievements include invention of purifier for diesel fuel using magnetic technology; design of major contribution to data base dictionary of first national security project employing artificial intelligence for intelligence analysis. Avocations: writer, artist, pilot. Home and Office: Nightingale Assocs 309 Cape Coral Pky W #206 Cape Coral FL 33914-5973 Office Phone: 239-945-2579.

**NIGHTINGALE, WILLIAM JOSLYN,** management consultant; b. Mpls., Sept. 16, 1929; s. William Isaac and Gladys (Joslyn) N.; children: Paul, Sara, William Joslyn, Jr., Margaret. BA, Bowdoin Coll., 1951; MBA, Harvard U., 1953. Mktg. mgr. Gen. Mills. Inc., Mpls., 1955-66; sr. assoc. Booz, Allen & Hamilton Inc., N.Y.C., 1966-68; v.p. fin. Hanes Corp., Winston-Salem, NC, 1969; pres. Bali Co. Inc., N.Y.C., 1970—95; founder, pres., chmn., sr. adviser Nightingale & Assocs. LLC, Stamford, Conn., 1975—2000. Bd. dirs. Ring's

End Inc.; trustee Naragansett Tax Free Bond Fund, Churchill Tax Free Bd. Fund. Active numerous charitable orgns.; vestryman St. Luke's Episcopal Ch., 1975-78, sr. warden, 1989-91; mem. Darien Representative Town Meeting, 1971-74. Lt. (j.g.) USNR, 1953-57. Mem. Wee Burn Country Club, Noroton, Conn., Yacht Club, Harvard Club, NYC. Republican. Home: 195 Rowayton Ave Norwalk CT 06853-1237

**NIGO,** fashion designer; b. Japan; Stylist, editor Popeye Mag.; founder, owner Nowhere Ltd., Tokyo, 1993—, Bathing Ape brand, Tokyo, 1993—, BAPE CUTS hair salon, BAPE cafe and gallery, APE SOUNDS, 2000—, BAPE TV; co-owner Billionaire Boys Club clothing line. BAPE/Pepsi camouflaged can, Pepsi Co.; featured in DUB Mag. Recipient Asia's Heroes award, Time Asia. Achievements include owner of many clothing stores across Tokyo, Kyoto, Osaka, London, NYC. Avocation: art and Hollywood memorabilia collecting. Office: Bathing Ape 91 Greene St New York NY 10013*

**NIGRIN, DANIEL J.,** hospital administrator, endocrinologist, medical educator; BA in biophysics, Johns Hopkins U., 1987, MD, 1991; MS in med. informatics, Mass. Inst. Tech., 1999. Pediatric internship Johns Hopkins U., 1992—94, pediatric residency, 1994—96; fellowships in pediatric endocrinology and informatics Children's Hosp. Boston, 1996—98, now chief info. officer, 2001—, also asst. in endocrinology; asst. prof. pediatrics Harvard Med. Sch. Named one of Premier 100 IT Leaders, Computerworld, 2005. Office: Children's Hosp Boston Wolbach Bldg Rm 115 300 Longwood Ave Boston MA 02115 Office Phone: 617-355-5067. Office Fax: 617-730-0019. E-mail: daniel.nigrin@childrens.harvard.edu.*

**NIGRO, KENNETH MICHAEL,** music educator, musician; b. Waterbury, Conn., Nov. 27, 1954; s. Ugo Mario and Antoinette Rose Nigro; m. Karen Lynn Milo, July 17, 1976; 1 child, Kyle Michael. BS in Music Edn., Ctrl. Conn. State U., 1976; MusM in Applied Music, U. Miami, 1980; degree in Adminstrn., Sacred Heart U., 2000. Cert. educator Conn., administrator Conn. Freelance musician, 1979—; tchr. music Wilby H.S., Waterbury, Conn., 1997—; lectr. saxophone, improv and combo, dir. saxophone ensemble U. Conn., Storrs, 1987—2004. Lectr. Ctrl. Conn. State U., New Britain, Conn., 1982—87, Naugatuck Valley C.C., Waterbury, Conn., 2004—; clinician, musician Yamaha Corp. Am., Indpls., 1998—. Author: The Complete Saxophone; composer: (songs) Big Schleps, 2001, 84 Again, 2004, The Complete Saxophone, 2005; musician: White Nights Jazz Festival, 1995, Fifty-third Presdl. Inaugural, 1997, (albums) New Millenium Jazz Ensemble CD, 1998; contbr. articles to profl. jours. Recipient Saxophone Svc. Performance award, Saxophone Jour., 1977; scholar, U. Miami, 1979—80. Mem.: Nat. Assn. Coll. Wind & Percussion Instrs, Pi Kappa Lambda, Phi Beta Mu. Avocations: bicycling, swimming, running. Personal E-mail: kyamasax@aol.com.

**NIGRO, R. LISA,** artist, foundation administrator, director; b. Milford, Conn., Nov. 6, 1962; d. John (Giovanni) Horace (Orazio) and Pauline Pearl Nigro; life ptnr. Flynn Gibbons Mauthe; 1 child, Tymberline Elise Mauthe. Assoc. - Liberal Arts, Cape Cod C.C., Barnstable, Mass., 1982; BFA - Painting, U. Mass., Amherst, 1985; MFA, U. Tex., Austin, 1994. Graphic designer, San Francisco, 1995—97; instr. - desktop pub./graphic design Artists TV Access, San Francisco, 1998; graphic designer Boston, 1985—92; founder Sisterhood of Burnin'Bush - Coalition for Women in the Arts, Gerlach, Nev., 2004—; founder/exec. dir. Draka Arts, Gerlach, 2003—. Founder/organizer Burnin'Bush Fire & Metal Arts Festival, Gerlach, 2003—; author/artist MIT Press - Leonardo Jour., Boston, 2003; faculty dept. art Tex. State U., San Marcos, 2006—. Mobile installation (art car), Draka the Dragon (Orange Show Ctr. for Visionary Art Grant 2004-06, Houston Art Car Mus. grant, 2004), (Burning Man Art Installation Grant, 2000), sculpture/installation, Dahud-Ahes the Mermaid (Burning Man Art Installation Grant, 2001), installation & performance, Diana of Ephesus: Fertility Goddess as Sundial (Burning Man Art Installation Grant, 1999), drawing, Disjointed Fantasy (Basil H. Alkazzi Award, 1988), painting, Twisted Into (Mass. Arts Lottery Grant, 1989). Mem.: seriouswheels.com, steelgirl.com, Fund for Women Artists, Houston Art Car Klub (assoc.). Avocations: camping, hiking, travel, reading. Office: Draka Arts Found 1617 W Magnolia Ave San Antonio TX 78201-5443 Office Phone: 210-885-2956. Personal E-mail: lisa@lisanigro.com. E-mail: lisa@drakaarts.org.

**NIGRO, RUSSELL M.,** former state supreme court justice; b. Phila., Mar. 23, 1946; BA, Temple U.; JD, Rutgers U., 1973. Atty. priv. practice, Phila., 1974—87; judge Phila. Ct. of Common Pleas, 1987; justice Pa. Supreme Ct., Phila., 1996—2006. Former chmn. staffing com. Phila. Ct. of Common Pleas, established Arbitration Appeals Program; lecturer civil law Pa. Bar Inst.; lecturer Temple U. James E. Beasley Sch. of Law; chair Pa. Supreme Ct. Capital Case Standards Com.; mem. Pa. Futures Commn. on Justice in 21st Century. Mem.: Pa. Bar Assn. (William J. Brennan Jr. Disting. Jurist award 2002).*

**NIGUIDULA, FAUSTINO NAZARIO,** surgeon, educator; b. June 27, 1926; came to U.S., 1953, naturalized, 1970; s. Aquilino Uriarte and Encarnacion (Nazario) N.; children: David, Diane, Susan, John, Stephan, Daniel, Nancy, Kathy; m. Barbara Ann Brooks, Dec. 17, 1977; children: Andrew, Nicole. Intern Arnot-Ogden Meml. Hosp., Elmira, N.Y., 1953-54; resident in surgery Strong Meml. Hosp., Rochester, N.Y., 1954-59; instr. surgery U. Rochester, 1958-59; resident in thoracic surgery Buffalo Gen. Hosp., 1959-61; fellow in pediatric cardiothoracic surgery Children's Hosp., Buffalo, 1961-62, Hosp. Sick Children, Toronto, Ont., 1963-64; clin. instr. U. Buffalo, 1965-66; asst. prof. Temple U., Phila., 1967-70; assoc. prof. surgery, pediat., 1970-75; clin. assoc. prof. Rutgers U., 1979-83; prof. surgery, prof. pediat. N.Y. Med. Coll., 1983—. Chief pediatric cardiothoracic surgery St. Christopher's Hosp. Children, Phila., 1967-75, Westchester Med. Ctr., Valhalla, N.Y., 1983—; dir. pediatric cardio-thoracic surgery Deborah Heart and Lung Ctr., Browns Mills, N.J., 1975-83. Mem. ACS, AAAS, Soc. Thoracic Surgeons, Am. Heart Assn., Assn. Thoracic and Cardiovasc. Surgeons Asia, Soc. Philippine Surgeons Am., Cardiology Soc. Poland (hon., 7th commemorative medal 1982), N.Y. State Med. Soc., N.Y. Acad. Scis., Westchester County Med. Soc., Westchester Acad. Medicine. Presbyterian. Office: Westchester Med Ctr 95 Grasslands Rd Valhalla NY 10595 Home: 48 Roma Orchard RD Peekskill NY 10566-4870

**NIGUIDULA, KATHLEEN ANN,** music educator, musician; b. Upper Darby, Pa., Apr. 5, 1972; d. Faustino Nazario Niguidula and Brenda Marie Maybury; m. Christopher Jordan O'Neill, Aug. 30, 2004; 1 child, Luke O'Neill. B in Music Edn., Eastman Sch. Music, 1994; MusM in Piano Performance, Boston Conservatory, 1998. Cert. K-12 music tchr. N.Y., Tex., Mass. Music tchr., choir dir. grades 6-8 Aldine Ind. Sch. Dist., Houston, 1994—95; music tchr., choir dir. grades 7-8 Norwood Pub. Schs., Mass., 1998—99; music tchr. K-8 Music On The Move, Chelsea, Mass., 1999—2001; piano tchr. Timeline Music, Wakefield, Mass., 1998—2001; music tchr. Wolf Sch., Providence, 2001—05; piano tchr. Music Sch. R.I. Philharm., Providence, 2001—; registrar, 2005—. Freelance accompanist, Boston, 1996—; choir dir. K-5 after-school programs Wolf Sch., Providence, 2001—05; coord. early childhood music Music Sch. R.I. Philharmonic, 2002—04. Music dir., organist Islington Cmty. Ch., Westwood, Mass., 1999—2004. Finalist piano, Florida Concerto Competition, 1989; recipient Excellence in Music award, Sarasota Visual and Performing Arts, 1990, 1st prize Composition, Women's Soc. Sarasota, 1990, 1st prize Music Performance, Shriner's Club, 1990; scholar, Eastman Sch. Music, 1990—94. Mem.: Orff-Schuwerk Assn., Music Educators Nat. Conf., Music Tchrs. Nat. Assn., New Eng. Piano Tchrs. Assn., Chopin Club. Personal E-mail: kathleen-o@cox.net.

**NII, SHIRO,** director, virologist, educator; b. Naruto, Tokushima, Japan, Jan. 12, 1932; parents Atsushi and Toyo (Toyota) N.; m. Etsuko Tada, Mar. 29, 1960; children: Satoshi, Keiko Maeda, Yoshiko Fujita, MD, Osaka U., 1956, PhD, 1961. Lic. physician. Rsch. assoc. Rsch. Inst. for Microbial Diseases

Osaka U., Japan, 1961—66, assoc. prof. Rsch. Inst. for Microbial Diseases, 1966—78; prof. Okayama U. Med. Sch., Japan, 1978—97, dean, 1993—95; prof. emeritus Okayama U., 1997—; prof. Kawasaki Coll. Allied Health Professions, Kurashiki, Japan, 1997—98; pres. Niimi Coll., Japan, 1998—2002; academic adminstr. CAC Rehab. Coll., Hiroshima, 2002—03, dir., 2003—06, dir. emeritus, 2006—. Councilor Okayama U., 1990-92; hon. prof. Jiangxi (China) Med. Coll., 1993; guest prof. Dalian (China) Med. Coll., 1994; expert adviser Sci. and Tech. Com., 1994; pres. Univ. and Coll. Assn. Okayama Prefecture, 1995, 43d Ann. Meeting of Japanese Virologists, 1995. Co-author: (book) Virology, 1997; editor, co-author: (book) Essentials of Microbiology, 1993, 98; contbr. articles to sci. jours. Mem.: Japanese Assn. Infectious Diseases (auditor 1995—98), Japanese Soc. Virology (hon.). Avocations: reading, baseball, walking. Home: 372-1-206 Hama Okayama 703-8256 Japan Office: 372 1 206 Hama Okayama 703 8256 Japan

**NII, YUKO,** artist; b. Tokyo, Toshima-ku, Japan, Oct. 22, 1942; arrived in US, 1963; d. Satoshi and Chieko Nii. BFA, Macalester Coll., St. Paul, Minn., 1965; MFA, Pratt Inst., Bklyn., 1969. Residency Yaddo, Saratoga Springs, NY, 1980, 1982; artist (painter); founder, dir. Williamsburg Art and Hist. Ctr., Bklyn., 1996—. Costume and stage set designer Chiang Ching Dance Company, N.Y.C., 1977—78, Zignal I at La-Mama, 1978—79; contbr. N.Y. Jour., Japan, 1982—83, NY Arts Mag., 2002, 11211 mag., 2004, Friends and Mentors Art Show catalog, 2001. One-woman shows include Elaine Benson Gallery, L.I., 1977, 1986, 1994, Fairleigh Dickenson U., N.J., 1978, Berkshire Mus., Mass., 1979, Monique Lnowlton Gallery, N.Y.C., 1979, Vered Internat. Gallery, L.I., 1979, Haber Theodore Gallery, N.Y.C., 1980, Internat. Monetary Fund, Washington, 1980. Recipient Woman of Yr., Office of Bklyn Borough Pres. Howard Golden, 1998, Office of Gov. of N.Y. State George Pataki, 2001, Office of Bklyn Borough Pres. Marty Markowitz, 2003, Outstanding Citizen award, N.Y.C. Coun., 2003; fellow, Pratt Inst., Bklyn., 1966—69; scholar, Macalester Coll., St. Paul, Minn., 1963—65. Home: 385 Clinton Ave Brooklyn NY 11238 Office: Williamsburg Art & Hist Ctr 135 Broadway Brooklyn NY 11211 Office Phone: 718-486-7372. Home Fax: 718-486-6012. Personal E-mail: wahcenter@earthlink.net.

**NIJENSOHN, DANIEL EDGARDO,** neurosurgeon; b. Mendoza, Argentina, Nov. 8, 1946; s. Leon and Mary Bekerman N.; m. Goldie L., June 25, 1972; children; Zev D., Samuel E. BA, Nat. Coll. Mendoza, Argentina, 1962; MD summa cum laude, Nat. U. Cuyo Med. Sch., Argentina, 1970; MS in Neurosurgery, U. Minn., 1976; PhD in Neuroanatomy, Nat. U. Cuyo, 1976. Rsch. asst. dept. physiology U. Cuyo, 1964-66; intern U. Buenos Aires, 1969-70, Baylor Coll. Medicine Affiliated Hosps., Tex. Med. Ctr., Houston, 1970-71; resident Mayo Clinic, U. Minn. Sch. Medicine, 1971-76; staff mem. Gamma Knife Ctr. Yale-New Haven (Conn.) Health; courtesy staff Griffin Hosp., Derby, Conn.; sr. attending staff Bridgeport (Conn.) Hosp.; chief divsn. neurosurgery St. Vincent's Med. Ctr., Bridgeport; assoc. clin. prof. neurol. surgery Yale U. Sch. Medicine. Presenter in field. Contbr. articles to profl. jours. Recipient Myrtle Wreath award Conn. Region Hadassah, 1981; Med. Sch. scholar. Fellow Am. Coll. Surgeons, Am. Coll. Neurosurgeons, Am. Heart Assn., Argentine Coll. Neurosurgeons; mem. AMA, Am. Assn. Neurol. Surgeons, L.Am. Neurol. Fedn. (founding), New England Neurol. Soc. (trustee), Conn. Med. Soc., Conn. Soc. Neurol. Surgeons (pres. 1997-99), Fairfield County Med. Assn., Greater Bridgeport Med. Soc., Congress Neurol. Surgeons, Interam. Coll. Physicians & Surgeons, Mayo Alumni Assn., Mayo Alumni Neurol. Soc. Office: Neurol Surgeons 340 Capitol Ave Bridgeport CT 06606-5445 Fax: 203-336-5802. E-mail: nijensohn@aol.com.

**NIJINSKY, TAMARA,** actress, puppeteer, author, librarian, educator; b. Vienna; arrived in U.S., 1961; d. Waslaw and Romola (de Pulszky) Nijinsky; widowed; 1 child, Kinga Maria Szakats-Gaspers. Student, Europe; postgrad. studies in U.S. Mem., actress Nat. Theater of Budapest; owner, tchr. Tamara Nijinsky Performing Art Studio, Montreal; tchr. speech/drama, French and German, libr. Cath. H.S., Phoenix; established non-profit internat. orgn. The Waslaw and Romola Nijinsky Found., Inc., 1991, exec. dir., 1991—. Lectr. in field. Author: Nijinsky and Romola, 1991. Decorated chevalier de l'Ordre des Arts et des Lettres, officier de l'Ordre des Arts et des Lettres (France); recipient Nijinsky medal, Pagart, Poland, Polish Order of Arts and Letters, 1997, La Medaille Vermeil de Paris, 2000. Roman Catholic. Avocations: reading, computer, swimming. Office: Nijinsky Foundation Inc PO Box # 15981 Phoenix AZ 85060-5981 Fax: 602-840-9605.

**NIJMAN, JAN,** geographer, educator; b. Heemskerk, The Netherlands, Oct. 15, 1957; arrived in U.S., 1987; BA in Human Geography, U. Amsterdam, 1980, MA in Human Geography, 1985; PhD in Geography, U. Colo., 1990. Freelance journalist, Netherlands, 1981—87; cons., rschr. Regioplan, Amsterdam, 1985, U. Amsterdam Sch. Environ. Scis., 1986; tchg. asst. dept. geography U. Ill., Champaign-Urbana, 1987—88; instr. dept. geography U. Colo., Boulder, 1988—90; asst. prof. geography U. Miami, Fla., 1990—94, assoc. prof. geography Fla., 1994—98, prof. dept. geography and regional studies Fla., 1998—, dir. internat. studies program Coll. Arts and Scis. Fla., 1993—98. Cons. internat. dvisn. Moran, Stahl & Boyer, Boulder, 1989—90; disting. vis. rsch. prof. Amsterdam Study for the Met. Environment U. Amsterdam, 1996; mem. sr. panel geography and regional sci. program NSF, Washington, 1998—2000; mem. com. for rsch. and exploration Nat. Geog. Soc., Washington, 2001—; presenter in field. Author: The Geopolitics of Power and Conflict: Superpowers in the International System, 1993, The Global Moment in Urban Evolution, 1996; editor (with R. Grant): The Global Crisis in Foreign Aid, 1998, 2000. Grantee, U. Miami, 1990—92, 1993, 1996, 1997, 2000, 2002, 2002, Assn. Am. Geographers, 1997, Nat. Geog. Soc. 1998—2000, NSF, 1998, 2001, 1999, 2002—, 2003—, Knight Jr. fellow, U. Miami, 1990—92, John Simon Guggenheim Meml. Found., 2003. Mem.: Koninklijk Nederlands Aardrijkskundig Genootschap, Internat. Studies Assn., Assn. Am. Geographers (Warren Nystrom award 1991). Office: Univ Miami Dept Geography and Regional Studies PO Box 8067 Coral Gables FL 33124-2221

**NIJMAN, JENNIFER T.,** lawyer; b. Aug. 27, 1962; BA, U. Ill., 1984; JD, U. Chgo., 1987. Bar: Ill. 1987, U.S. Dist. Ct. Ill. (no. dist.) 1987, Wis. 1991. Assoc. to ptnr. Winston & Strawn LLP, Chgo., 1994—, co-chmn. environ. dept. Bd. dirs. Inst. Interest Law Initiative; pres. bd. dirs. Ctr. Conflict Resolution; chair Ill. Legal Needs Study, Ill. Coalition for Equal Justice. Contbr. articles to profl. jours. Mem.: ABA (mem. environ. litigation com.), Economic Club Chgo., Ill. State Bar Assn., Chgo. Bar Assn. (pres. 2002—03). Office: Winston & Strawn LLP 35 W Wacker Dr Chicago IL 60601-9703 Office Phone: 312-558-5771. Office Fax: 312-558-5700. E-mail: jnijman@winston.com.

**NIK, NINFA,** literature and language professor; m. Sam Nik; children: Shervin Andrew, Jason Arshan. MA in French, U. Tex., Arlington, MA in Spanish; PhD in Humanities, U. Tex., Dallas. Lang. tchr. Iran-Am Soc., Tehran; assoc. prof. Tex. Woman's U., Denton. Author plays, musicals. Mem.: Alpha Chi, Phi Sigma Iota, Sigma Delta Pi. Avocations: classical music, travel, reading. Office: Tex Woman's Univ Language Dept PO Box 425829 Denton TX 76204 E-mail: nnikt@twu.edu.

**NIKAIDO, HIROSHI,** microbiologist; b. Tokyo, Mar. 26, 1932; arrived in U.S., 1962; s. Tatsuya and Ryo Nikaido; m. Kishiko Jokura, Mar. 11, 1963; children: Michio, George. MD, Keio U., Tokyo, 1955, D in Med. Sci., 1961. Assoc. bacteriology Harvard Med. Sch., Boston, 1963-64, asst. prof., 1965-69; assoc. prof. U. Calif., Berkeley, 1969-71, prof., 1971—. Sci. adv. Essential Therapeutics, Mountain View, Calif., 1992—2002. Co-author: Microbial Biotechnology, 1995; contbr. articles to profl. jours. Recipient Paul Ehrlich award, Paul Ehrlich Found., 1969, Freedom to Discover Achievement award, Bristol-Myers Squibb, 2004. Fellow: Am. Acad. Microbiology; mem.: Am. Acad. Arts and Scis., Am. Soc. Biochemistry and Molecular Biology, Am. Soc. Microbiology (editor Jour. Bacteriology 1998—2002, Hoechst-Roussel award 1984).

**NIKAIDOH, HISASHI,** pediatric cardiac surgeon, professor; b. Tokyo, Sept. 21, 1934; s. Tatsuya and Ryo Nikaidoh; m. Lynn Ann Zuttermeister, Oct. 21, 1952; children: Kimi Lynn, Ken Paul. MD, U. Tokyo, 1959. Cert. bd. surgery Am. Bd. Surgery, 1967, bd. thoracic surgery Am. Bd. Thoracic Surgery, 1995. Prof. cardiothoracic surgery U. Tex. Southwestern Med. Ctr., Dallas, 2002—. Recipient Distingwished Svc. award in Medicine, Children's Med. Ctr. Dallas, 2000; Fullbright Travel Grant, Fullbright Commn., 1960. Fellow: ACS (mem. Leadership Soc. 2005), Am. Acad. Pediatrics; mem.: Ctrl. Surg. Assn., Am. Pediatric Surgery Assn., Soc. Thoracic Surgeons. Christian. Office: Univ Tex Southwestern Med Ctr Dallas 1935 Motor St Dallas TX 75235 Office Phone: 214-456-5000. Office Fax: 214-456-5015. Business E-Mail: hisashi.nikaidoh@utsouthwestern.edu.

**NIKAS, RICHARD JOHN,** lawyer; b. Long Beach, Calif., Sept. 9, 1968; s. John Nikolas and Dorothy (Bernardo) N. BA in Internat. Rels., U. So. Calif., 1991, JD, 1995. Bar: Calif. Spl. projects coord. Vessel Assist Assn. Am., Newport Beach, Calif., 1989-94; ptnr. Herrick Nikas, LLP, Costa Mesa, Calif., 2003—. Guest lectr. maritime law U. So. Calif., L.A., 1998—; lectr. admiralty and maritime law Calif. Maritime Acad., Vallejo; chmn. USCG Working Group on Nat. Maritime Incident Reporting Sys., Washington, 1997—, designated proctor in admiralty, The Maritime Law Assn. of the U.S.A. Author: Benedict on Admiralty, 1998, Moore's Federal Practice, 1998, The Last Yankee, 1999, Recreational Boating Law, 2000, Admiralty Practice and Procedure, 2000. Head football coach Ocean View H.S., Huntington Beach, 1995; mentor Huntington Beach Unified Sch. Dist., 1997—; pitcher Greek Olympic Baseball Team, Atlantic City Surf Profl. Baseball Club; mng. gen. ptnr. Old Reliable Baseball, LLC; bd. govs. The Am. Mariner, Loyola U., 1999. Recipient Best Oralist award Spong Nat. Invitational Moot Ct., Williamsburg, Va., 1995, Meritorious Pub. Svc. medal USCG. Mem. Calif. State Bar Assn., Maritime Law Assn., Soc. Naval Architects and Marine Engrs. (chmn. panel 0-38), Assn. Profl. Ball Players Am. Avocation: baseball. Address: 17652 Wrightwood Ln Huntington Beach CA 92649-4969 Office Phone: 714-546-1400. E-mail: rnikas@herricknikas.com.

**NIKIAS, CHRYSOSTOMOS L. (MAX NIKIAS),** engineering educator; b. Cyprus, Greece; arrived in US, 1979; m. Niki Nikias. Diploma in elec. and mech. engring., Nat. Tech. U., Athens, Greece, 1977; MS in elec. engring., SUNY, Buffalo, 1980, PhD in elec. engring., 1982; PhD (hon.), U. Cyprus, 2000. Prof. elec. and computer engring. U. Conn., Northeastern U.; prof. elec. engring.-systems U. So. Calif., 1991—, assoc. dean engring., 1992—2001, founding dir. Integrated Media Systems Ctr., 1996—2001, dean Andrew and Erna Viterbi Sch. Engring., 2001—05, Zohrab A. Kaprielian Chair in Engring., provost, sch. engring., sr. v.p. academic affairs, 2005—. Bd. dirs. Lord Found., Calif., Alfred Mann Inst. Biomedical Engring. Bd. trustees Chadwick Sch., Palos Verde Peninsula, Calif. Recipient Outstanding Tchr. Award, Nat. Technol. U., 1993. Fellow: Calif. Coun. on Sci. and Tech., IEEE (Signal Processing Best Paper Award 1988, Fred W. Ellersick Award of Outstanding Unclassified Paper at Mil. Comm. 1992, AH Reeves Premium Award 2002); mem.: Russian Acad. Nat. Sci. (fgn. mem.), Phi Kappa Phi. Office: U So Calif Sch Engring Office of the Dean Los Angeles CA 90089-1450

**NIKIRK, SILVA SUSAN,** minister, writer, dancer; b. NYC, Mar. 13, 1947; d. Victor and Lina Silva; m. Gerald Eugene Nikirk, Jan. 29, 1988. English, City Coll. of N.Y., N.Y., 1966; fashion mktg., Fashion Inst. Tech., N.Y., 1967; Biblical studies, Heart to Heart Internat., Norwich, Conn., 1993. Rev. Ordination Kingsway Fellowship Internat., Iowa, 1992; cert. Dance Tchg. Nat. Dance Tchrs. of Am., 1985. Profl. dancer Broadway, Off Broadway Theatre & TV, N.Y., 1964—72; dir. fashion merchandising sch. Barbizon Sch. of Queens, Rego Pk., Queens, NY, 1973—75; mgmt. cons. RTW Mgmt., N.Y., 1975—77; profl. ballroom tchr. Fred Astaire, Arthur Murray, various ind. dance studios, 1977—89; profl. ballroom dancer, 1977—86, theatrical, exhbn., Am. smooth ballroom dance champion, 1982—85; night club act Hamilton & Silva, 1980—85; profl. ballroom adjudicator Nat. Dance Coun. of Am., Arthur Murray Internat., Nat. Dance Tchrs. Assn., N.Am. Dance Tchrs. Assn., 1986—; profl. ballroom adjudictor Nat. Dance Coun. of Am., Arthur Murray Internat., 2006—; choreographer Ind. Dance Teams, 1977—89; author & mktg. cons. Arthur Murray Internat., Coral Gables, Fla., 1985—89; cosmetic cons. Estee Lauder, Inc., Conn., 1989—91; co-founder, ordained min., v.p. bd. dirs. Nikirk Ministries, Colchester, Conn., 1992—. Ordained min., nat. & internat. speaker inter Denom. chs. and confs., USA, Holland, Belgium, Switerland, Germany, Iceland, 1992—; pastor VINE Tng. and Worship Ctr., 1997—2005; dir. founder Watchmen Sch. of Prayer, Colchester, Conn., 1998—. Co-host (TV series) Voice In New Eng. T.V. Broadcast, 1996—; dancer (discotheque) Beatles Tour, 1965; author: (tchg. video, manual) Arthur Murray Bronze Theatrical Ballroom Syllabus, 1986—88, (tchg. video) Watchmen Sch. of Prayer, 2002; contbr. articles pub. to profl. jour. Mem.: Nat. Dance Tchrs. Coun. Am., N.Am. Dance Tchrs. Assn. (adjudicator 2006—), Nat. Dance Tchrs. Assn. (master tchr. and adjudicator 2006—), Assn. Jewish and Christian Believers, Kingsway Fellowship Internat. Messianic Jew. Avocation: gardening. Office: Nikirk Ministries PO Box 211 Colchester CT 06415 Office Phone: 860-537-5881. Business E-Mail: snikirk@nikirkvoice.org.

**NIKITIN, ALEXANDER YU.,** pathologist; b. St. Petersburg, Russia, Sept. 28, 1960; s. Yurii V. Nikitin and Valentina D. Nikitina; m. Andrea Fleken-Nikitin, Feb. 24, 1995; children: Dmitri Yu., Maria Yu. Nikitina. MD (hon.), Acad. Pavlov First Med. Inst., St. Petersburg, Russia, 1983; PhD, Prof. Petrov Rsch. Inst. Oncology, St. Petersburg, Russia, 1988. Asst. prof. rsch. dept. molecular medicine Univ. Tex. Health Sci. Ctr., San Antonio, 1999—2000; asst. prof. pathology Cornell U., Ithaca, NY, 2000—. Contbr. articles to profl. jours. Vice chair pathology and lab. medicine standing com. Mouse Models of Human Cancers Consortium, Bethesda, Md., 1999—2004; organizer Ann. Practical Workshop on Pathology of Mouse Models for Human Disease, Bar Harbor, Maine, 2002—. Recipient Midcareer award in Mouse Pathobiology, NIH, 2002—; grantee, 2002—; Dept. of Def., 2001—04, 2000—03. Mem.: AAAS, Soc. Toxicologic Pathology, Am. Assn. Cancer Rsch. Achievements include first to develop a novel genetic model of human ovarian cancer; development of new classification of mouse proliferative pulmonary lesions; discovery of syndrome of multiple endocrine neoplasia in Rb +/- mice. Office: Cornell Univ T2014AVRT Ithaca NY 14850

**NIKITIN, ALEXEY G.,** biology professor, researcher; s. Gennadi A. Nikitin. PhD, Bowling Green (Ohio) State U., 1997. Asst. prof. Grand Valley State U., Allendale, Mich., 2001—. Office: Grand Valley State U 1 Campus Dr Allendale MI 49401 Office Phone: 616-331-1281.

**NIKODINOV, ANGELA,** professional figure skater, Olympic athlete; b. Spartanburg, S.C., May 9, 1980; Competitive history includes 2nd place Pacific Coast Jr., 1994, 3rd place Southwest Pacific Jr., 1994, 5th place U.S. Championships Jr., 1994, 2nd place Pacific Coast Jr., 1995, 3rd place Southwest Pacific Jr., 1995, 5th place U.S. Championships Jr., 1995, 6th place World Jr. Selections Competition, 1996, 2d place Pacific Coast Sr., 1996, 5th place U.S. Olympic Festival, 1995, 1st place Southwest Pacific Sr., 1996, 3rd place O. Nepela Meml., 1996, 1st place Pacific Coast Sr., 1997, 3rd place World Jr. Selection Competition, 1997, 2nd place Pokal Der Blauen Scwerter, 1996, 4th place U.S. Championships, 1997, 4th place Skate America, 1997, 5th place U.S. Championships, 1998, 11th place World Jr. Championships, 1998, 4th place Goodwill Games, 1998, 2nd place Keri Lotion Figure Skating Classic, 1998, 3rd place Four Continents Championships, 1999, 3rd place Skate America, 1998, 3d place U.S. Championships, 1999, 12th place World Championships, 1999, 7th place Skate America, 1999, 5th place Keri Lotion Figure Skating Classic, 1999, 4th place Cup of Russia, 1999, 4th place U.S. Championships, 2000, 1st place Four Continents, 2000, 9th place World Championships, 2000, 3d place Cup of Russia, 2001, 3rd place Nations Cup, 2001, 3rd place, U.S. Championships 2001, 2nd place, Great American Figure Skating Challenge, 2001, 5th place Workd Championships, 2001, 4th

place, U.S. Championships, 2002, 1st place, Pacific Coast Sectionals, 2004, 5th place, U.S. Championships, 2004. Avocations: water-skiing, skiing, rollerblading, jet skiing. Office: USFSA 20 1st St Colorado Springs CO 80906-3624

**NIKOLAI, LOREN ALFRED,** accounting educator; b. Northfield, Minn., Dec. 14, 1943; s. Roman Peter and Loyola (Gertrude) N.; m. Anita Carol Baker, Jan. 15, 1966; children: Trishia, Jay. BA, St. Cloud State U., 1966, MBA, 1967; PhD, U. Minn., 1973. CPA, Mo. Asst. prof. U. N.C., Chapel Hill, 1973-76; assoc. prof. U. Mo., Columbia, 1976-80, prof., 1980-82, Ernst & Young Disting. prof. Sch. Accountancy, 1982—, dir. masters programs, 2002—. Author: Financial Accounting: Concepts and Uses, 1988, 3d edit., 1995, Intermediate Accounting, 1980, Accounting Information for Business Decisions, 2000, 2d edit., 2004. Recipient Editors Choice award in Student-Faculty award Fedn. Schs. of Accountancy, 1989, Disting. Alumni award St. Cloud U., 1990, Coll. of Bus. Faculty Mem. of Yr. award, 1991, Mo. Outstanding Acctg. Educators award, 1993; Kemper fellow U. Mo., 1992, Alumni award MU Faculty, 1996, UM Presdl. awd. for Outstanding Teaching, 1999; Coll. of Bus. Teacher of the Yr., 1999. Mem. AICPA, Am. Acctg. Assn., Mo. Soc. CPAs, Fedn. Schs. of Acctg. (pres. 1994). Office: U Mo Sch Accountancy 303 Cornell Hall Columbia MO 65211-0001 Business E-Mail: nikolai@missouri.edu

**NIKOUI, HOSSEIN REZA,** quality assurance professional; b. Tehran, Iran, Feb. 4, 1949; came to U.S., 1977; s. Gholam Reza and Monireh (Jahanshahi) Nikoui; m. Niki Forouzi, Nov. 3, 1983; children: Neda Lili, Amir Reza. BSChemE, Arya-Mehr Univ., Tehran, 1971; MEng in Ops. Rsch., U. Toronto, 1981; cert. in quality assurance, Ryerson Univ., Toronto, 1983; cert. sys. approach/quality improvement, Madonna U., Livonia, Mich., 1996; MSBA in Quality and Ops. Mgmt., Madonna U., 1998; cert. in lean mfg., U. Mich., 2001. Registered profl. engr.; cert. quality engr., quality auditor, quality systems lead auditor, quality mgr. Quality engr. Gen. Motors, Tehran, 1971-72, supt. supplier quality assurance, 1973-74, mgr. quality assurance, 1975-78, resident materials mgr. Oshawa, Ont., Can., 1978-79; mgr. quality control G.S. Woolley, Toronto, 1979-82, mgr. quality assurance, 1982-85; dir. corp. quality assurance The Progressive/Woolley Group, Toronto, 1985-88, Manchester Plastics, Troy, Mich., 1988-97; dir. quality assurance Collins & Aikman Plastics, Manchester, Mich., 1997-99; dir. corp. quality assurance Oakwood Group, Dearborn, Mich., 1999-2000, dir. sys., 2000-01; lean mfg. coach Ford Motor Co., 2001—02, paint area mfg. super., 2002—03, quality oper. system leader, 2003—04, lead assessor quality operating sys., 2005—06, supplier tech. assistance, 2006—. Instr. Centenial Coll., Toronto, 1984-88; cons. Can. Post Corp., Toronto, 1985-86. Contbr. articles to profl. jours. Fellow Am. Soc. for Quality; mem. ASTM, Soc. Plastic Engrs., Am. Inst. Indsl. Engrs., Soc. Automotive Engrs., Engring. Soc. Detroit, Inst. of Quality Assurance. Avocations: collecting stamps and coins, tennis, reading, classical music. Home: 5539 Pinecrest Estates Dr Ann Arbor MI 48105-9351 Personal E-mail: hrnikoui@aol.com.

**NILES, DEBORAH OLIVE,** benefits compensation analyst; b. Port of Spain, Trinidad & Tobago, Sept. 13, 1967; d. Timothy Nathaniel and Joan Elaine Niles; children: Aundre Maurice Eugene, Jorden Kayleigh Niles-Foster. BS, Westfield State Coll., 1999. Police officer Westfield State Coll., Mass., 1994—2002; res. police officer Westfield Police Dept., 1999—2002; adminstrv. specialist Westfield State Coll., 2002—. Rape investigator Westfield State Coll., 1998—2002, domestic violence investigator, 1998—2002. Author: (poetry) Works by D.Niles. Specialist U.S. Army, 1986—89, Weisbaden, Germany, staff sgt. Nat. Guard, 2000—. Decorated Army Achievement Medal U.S. Army; recipient Editors Choice awards for Outstanding Achievemnet in Poetry. Home: 26 St Paul Street Westfield MA 01085 Office: Westfield State College 577 Western Ave Westfield MA 01086 Personal E-mail: spoken_word03@yahoo.com. E-mail: dfailey@wsc.ma.edu.

**NILES, JOHN GILBERT,** lawyer; b. Dallas, Oct. 5, 1943; s. Paul Dickerman and Nedra Mary (Arendts) N.; m. Marian Higginbotham, Nov. 21, 1970; children: Paul Breckenridge, Matthew Higginbotham. BA in History, Stanford U., 1965; LLB, U. Tex., 1968. Bar: Tex. 1968, Calif. 1969, U.S. Dist. Ct. (cen. dist.) Calif. 1973, U.S. Ct. Appeals (9th cir.) 1973, U.S. Dist. Ct. (so. dist.) Calif. 1977, U.S. Supreme Ct. 1979, U.S. Dist. Ct. (no. dist.) Calif. 1983. Assoc. O'Melveny & Myers, Los Angeles, 1973-77, ptnr. 1978-99; of counsel, 1999—. Judge pro tem mcpl. ct. L.A.; spkr., panel mem. Practicing Law Inst., Calif. C.E.B. Served to lt. comdr. USNR, 1968-72, Vietnam. Mem. ABA, Los Angeles County Bar Assn., Am. Judicature Soc. Clubs: Bel-Air Bay (Pacific Palisades, Calif.); Calif. (Los Angeles). Avocation: sailing. Home: 1257 Villa Woods Dr Pacific Palisades CA 90272-3953 Office: O'Melveny & Myers 400 S Hope St Los Angeles CA 90071-2899 Office Phone: 213-430-6050.

**NILES, THOMAS MICHAEL TOLLIVER,** former business association executive; b. Lexington, Sept. 22, 1939; s. John Jacob and Rena (Lipetz) N.; m. Carroll C. Ehringhaus, July 22, 1967; children: John Thomas, Mary Chapman. BA, Harvard U., 1960; MA, U. Ky., 1962. Commd. fgn. service officer US Dept. State, Washington, 1962, U.S. ambassador to Can., Ottawa, 1985-1989; then permanent rep. EEC, Brussels; asst. sec. Europe and Can. US Dept. State, Washington, 1991-93, amb. to Greece Athens, 1993-97; v.p. Nat. Def. U., 1997-98; pres. U.S. Coun. Internat. Bus., 1999—2005. Recipient Superior Honor award Dept. State, 1982, 85, Presdl. award, 1988, 89, 94. Mem. Phi Beta Kappa

**NILLES, JOHN MICHAEL,** lawyer; b. Langdon, N.D., Aug. 20, 1930; s. John Joseph and Isabel Mary (O'Neil) N.; m. Barbara Ann Cook, June 22, 1957; children: Terese M., Daniel J., Marcia L., Thomas M., Margaret J. BA cum laude, St. Johns U., 1955; JD cum laude with distinction, U. N.D., 1958. Bar: N.D. 1958, U.S. Dist. Ct. N.D. 1958, U.S. Ct. Appeals (8th cir.) 1958, Minn. 1991. Shareholder, dir., pres. Nilles, Hansen and Davies, Ltd., Fargo, ND, 1958-90, of counsel, 1990-95; exec. v.p., gen. counsel Met. Fin. Corp., Mpls., 1990-95, First Bank F.S.B., Mpls., 1995; ret. 1996. Pres., bd. dirs. Legal Aid Soc. N.D., Fargo, 1970-76, Red River Estate Planning Coun., 1980-87; vice-chmn. disciplinary bd. Supreme Ct. N.D., 1984-90. Bd. editors N.D. Law Rev., 1957-58. Mem. exec. bd. Red. River Valley coun. Boy Scouts Am., 1959-70; bd. regents U. Mary, Bismarck, N.D., 1967-77; pres., dirs. Cath. Charities, Fargo, 1959-65, Southeast Mental Health Ctr., Fargo, 1972-80. Staff sgt. USAF, 1951-54. Fellow Am. Coll. Trust and Estate Counsel (state dir. 1979-90); mem. ABA, State Bar Assn. N.D., Minn. Bar Assn., Order of Coif. Republican. Roman Catholic. Avocations: tennis, downhill skiing, cross country skiing, hunting, gun collecting. Home: 10412 Fawns Way Eden Prairie MN 55347-5117

**NILSEN, ARTHUR CHRISTIAN,** lawyer; b. Rockville Centre, N.Y., Dec. 30, 1946; s. Arthur and Lillian Alfheld (Christiansen) N.; m. Linda Marie Rom Oleschlager, July 27, 1966 (div. Jan. 1987); children: Christopher James, Karla Lynn; m. Donna Jean Holmes, Apr. 22, 1978; children: Arthur Christian, Arthur Jorgen, Johanna Blanche. BS, Cornell U., 1969; MBA in Fin., JD, Samford U., 1986. Bar: Ala., Ga. Dir. of ops. M.D. Anderson Tumor Inst., Houston, 1976-78; dir. exec. svcs./ops. PFM, Inc., St. Louis, 1978-83; atty. Roe & Rowell, Birmingham, Ala., 1983-86; regional ptnr. Hyatt Legal Svcs., Atlanta, 1986-88; atty. Law Offices of Frederick Hanna, Atlanta, 1988-89; mng. atty. Siler & Jonap, Atlanta, 1989-92; mng. ptnr. Jonap & Assocs., Atlanta, 1992-94; mng. ptnr., cons. A.C. Nilsen & Assocs., Atlanta, 1994—; mng. atty. Law Offices of Kenneth S. Nugent, P.C., Atlanta, 1995—96; CEO, CFO Thomas W. Malone, P.C., Atlanta, 2001—02; mng. atty. Attys. Kaufman & Assocs., P.A., Atlanta, 2004—06, Law Offices of Jeffery C. Dover, P.C., Atlanta, 2006—. Bd. dirs. Law Offices Richardson, Phoenix, Ariz. Active nat. and local Rep. coms., 1975; mem. Roswell United Meth. Choir, 1978, Bd. Stewards. Mem. ABA, ATLA, Ga. Trial Lawyer's Assn., Masons, Men's Club. Republican. Methodist. Avocations: golf, swimming, fishing, reading, writing. Office: A C Nilsen & Assocs PO Box 243 Roswell GA 30077-0243 Home: 190 Riding Trail Ct Roswell GA 30075-1758 Office Phone: 770-518-1133. E-mail: artn@doverlawfirm.com.

**NILSSON, ANDERS ROBERT,** science educator, researcher; b. Stockholm, May 3, 1956; s. Karl Olof and Sylvi Nilsson. Doctoral degree, Uppsala U., Sweden, 1989. Chem. engring., Royal Inst. of Tech. Prof. Uppsala U., 1999—2000; assoc. prof. Stanford U., Calif., 2000—. Guest prof. Stockholm U., 2001—. Recipient Shirley award, Lawrence Berkeley Lab., 1998, Lindbomska award, Royal Swedish Acad. of Scis., 1991; fellow, Inst. of Physics, 2004. Mem.: Am. Phys. Soc. Office: Stanford Synchrotron Radiation Lab MS 69 2575 Sand Hill Rd Menlo Park CA 94025 Office Phone: 650-926-2233. Office Fax: 650-926-4100. Business E-Mail: nilsson@slac.stanford.edu.

**NIMETZ, MATTHEW,** lawyer, investment company executive; b. Bklyn, June 17, 1939; s. Joseph L. and Elsie (Botwinik) N.; m. Gloria S. Lorch, June 24, 1975; children: Alexandra Elise, Lloyd. BA, Williams Coll., 1960, LL.D. (hon.), 1979; BA (Rhodes scholar), Balliol Coll., Oxford U., Eng., 1962, MA, 1966; LL.B., Harvard U., 1965. Bar: NY 1966, DC 1968. Law clk. to Justice John M. Harlan, US Supreme Ct., 1965-67; staff asst. to Pres. Johnson, 1967-69; assoc. firm Simpson Thacher & Bartlett, NYC, 1969-74, ptnr., 1974-77; counselor Dept. of State, Washington, 1977-80, acting coord. refugee affairs, 1979-80, under sec. of state for security assistance, sci. and tech., 1980; ptnr. firm Paul, Weiss, Rifkind, Wharton & Garrison, NYC, 1981-2000; mng. dir. Gen. Atlantic LLC, Greenwich, Conn., 2000—. Commr. Port Authority NY and NJ, 1975-77; dir. World Resources Inst., chmn., 1982-94; mem. NY State Adv. Coun. on State Productivity, 1990-92; presdl. envoy Greece-Macedonian Negotiations, 1994-95, spl. rep. UN Sec. Gen., 1999—. Trustee William Coll., 1981-96; chmn. UN Devel. Corp., 1986-94; bd. dir. Charles H. Revson Found., 1997-98, NY State Nature Conservancy, 1997—; chmn. Carnegie Forum in US, Greece and Turkey, 1996-98; chmn. Ctr. for Democracy and Reconciliation in S.E. Europe, 1998—; chair internat. adv. com. Ctrl. European U., Budapest, Hungary, 2001-05. Mem. Assn. of Bar of City of NY, Coun. on Fgn. Rels. Clubs: Harvard (NYC). Office: Gen Atlantic LLC 3 Pickwick Plz Greenwich CT 06830-5538 E-mail: mnimetz@generalatlantic.com

**NIMKARN, SAROJ,** endocrinologist, researcher; MD (hon.), Mahidol U., Bangkok, 1991. Lic. Am. Bd. of Pediats. and Subboard Pediat. Endocrinology. Clin. instr. pediats. dept. pediats. Siriraj Hosp., Mahidol U., Bangkok, 2001—03, asst. prof. pediats. dept. pediats. faculty medicine, 2003—04; asst. prof. pediats. Med. Coll. of Wis., Milw., 2004—05, Mt. Sinai Sch. of Medicine of NYU, N.Y.C., 2005—. Recipient Recognition Winning Poster award, Nat. Coop. Growth Study, 1999, Fellowship Rsch. Tng. grant, Lilly Rsch. Labs., Divsn. of Eli Lilly & Co., 1999, Endocrine Soc. Endocrinology award, Endocrine Soc. of Thailand, 2003, Investigator award, 11th Asian Congress of Pediat. and 1st Asian Congress of Pediat. Nursing, 2003, Free Paper award, 44th Siriraj Sci. Ann. Meeting, Faculty of Medicine, Siriraj Hosp., 2004, grant for rsch. devel., Faculty of Medicine, Siriraj Hosp., 2001. Mem.: Pediat. Endocrine Soc. of Thailand, Asia Pacific Pediat. Endocrine Soc., Lawson Wilkins Pediat. Endocrine Soc., Med. Coun. of Thailand, The Endocrine Soc. Office: Mt Sinai Sch Medicine Box 1198 1 Gustave LLevy Pl New York NY 10029 Office Phone: 212-241-8210. Office Fax: 212-241-5405. Business E-Mail: saroj.nimkarn@mssm.edu.

**NIMNI, MARCEL EPHRAIM,** biochemistry educator; b. Buenos Aires, Feb. 1, 1931; came to U.S., 1955; s. Sam and Sarah Dora (Freedman) N.; children: Elizabeth, Brian Sam; m. Fabiola Cordoba, Dec. 21, 1996. BS in Pharmacy, U. Buenos Aires, 1954, PhD, 1960; MS, U. So. Calif., 1957; MD honoris causae (hon.), Maimonides U., 2002. Cert. nutrition specialist. Rsch. fellow U. So. Calif., L.A., 1960-61, asst. prof. biochemistry, 1963-66, assoc. prof., 1966-72, prof., 1972—, prof. surgery, 1990—, prof. orthop., 1980—; dir. biology Don Baxter Labs., Glendale, Calif., 1962. Cons. Hancock Labs., Glendale, Calif., 1962; cons. Hancock Labs., Anaheim, Calif., 1970-78, pathobiochemistry study sect. NIH, 1980-85, orthopaedics and biomechanics study sect., 1987-90; mem. NASA Tissue Engring. Rev. Bd., 2002—; dir. biochemistry rsch. Orthopaedic Hosp., L.A., 1980-91; cons. Tillots Pharma Labs., Basle, Switzerland, 1986-94; dir. surg. rsch. Children's Hosp. of L.A., 1991-98, dir. Tissue Engring. Lab., 1998—; mem. adv. bd. Maimonides U., Buenos Aires. Editor: Collagen: Biochemistry, Biotechnology and Molecular Biology, Vols. I-V,1987-91; editor Matrix, 1980-93, Connective Tissue Rsch., 1973-91, Jour. Orthopaedic Rsch., 1989-94; patentee collagen tech., transderman drug delivery. Recipient Merit award NIH, 1987; rsch. grantee NIH Arthritis Inst., 1966-94, NIH Aging Inst., 1982-2000. Fellow AAAS, Am. Coll. Nutrition, Soc. Biomaterials (Founders award 1986); mem. Am. Inst. Nutrition, Am. Assn. Biochem. and Molecular Biology. Office: Univ So Calif EDM-191 Keck Sch Medicine Los Angeles CA 90033 Office Phone: 323-224-5067. Personal E-mail: nimni007@aol.com.

**NIMOITYN, PHILIP,** cardiologist; b. Phila., Pa., Mar. 6, 1951; s. Benjamin Solomon and Edith (Ornstein) N.; m. Hillary Rachel Saul, June 11, 1989. BS in Biology with distinction, Phila. Coll. Pharmacy and Sci., 1972; MD, Thomas Jefferson U., 1976. Cert. Nat. Bd. Med. Examiners, Am. Bd. Internal Medicine, Am. Bd. Cardiovascular Disease. Intern Hahnemann U. Hosp., Phila., 1976-77; resident in internal medicine Thomas Jefferson U. Hosp., Phila., 1977-79, cardiovascular disease fellow, 1979-81, instr. medicine, 1981-90, clin. asst. prof., 1990—; attending physician Pa. Hosp., Phila., 1995—; cons. physician Wills Eye Hosp., Phila., 1981—; attending physician Penn. Hosp., Phila., 1995—. Author: (with others) Artificial Cardiac Pacing, 1984, Quick Reference to Cardiovascular Disease, 1987, Cardiac Emergency Care, 1991; contbr. articles to profl. jours. Recipient Cert. of Merit for Sci. Exhibits AMA, 1974, 2d prize for sci. exhibits Ind. State Med. Assn., 1974. Fellow Am. Coll. Cardiology; mem. AMA, Pa. Med. Soc., Phila. County Med. Soc. Office: 1128 Walnut St Ste 401 Philadelphia PA 19107-5568 Office Phone: 215-629-1158. Business E-Mail: philip.nimoityn@mail.tju.edu.

**NING, TAK HUNG,** physicist, microelectronic technologist; b. Canton, China, Nov. 14, 1943; came to U.S., 1964; s. Hong and Kwai-Chan (Lee) N.; m. Yin Ngao Fan; children: Adrienne, Brenda. BA in Physics, Reed Coll., 1967; MS in Physics, U. Ill., 1968, PhD in Physics, 1971. IBM Rsch. Div., Yorktown Heights, N.Y., 1973-78, mgr. bipolar devices and cirs., 1978-82, mgr. Advanced Silicon Technology Lab., 1982-83, mgr. silicon devices and technology, 1983-90, mgr. VLSI design and tech., 1990-91; IBM fellow, 1991—. Patentee in field. Fellow IEEE (assoc. editor Trans. on Electron Devices 1988-90, J.J. Ebers award 1989, Jack a. Morton award 1991), Am. Phys. Soc.; mem. NAE (Pan Wen-Yuan award 1998). Home: 3085 Weston Ln Yorktown Heights NY 10598-1962 Office: IBM T J Watson Research Ct Yorktown Heights NY 10598*

**NING, XUE-HAN (HSUEH-HAN NING),** physiologist, researcher; b. Peng-Lai, Shandong, People's Republic of China, Apr. 15, 1936; came to U.S., 1984; s. Yi-Xing and Liu Ning; m. Jian-Xin Fan, May 28, 1967; 1 child, Di Fan. *Grandfather Xi-Quan was a doctor of traditional Chinese medicine and master of Si-Nai-Tang (the meaning is "seek truth from facts") Chinese Pharmacy. Father was the general manager of Li-Hua Textile Mill, Tsingdao, China. Wife, MD Shanghai First Medical College, 1960 an emeritus doctor and associate research professor in Shanghai Research Institute of Sports Science. She was a medical and physiological researcher in the Research and Training Group of high jumper Zhu Jian-Hua, who broke the world record 3 times.* MD, Shanghai 1st Med. Coll., People's Republic of China, 1960; post grad., Chinese Traditional Medicine Coll. for Advanced Study, 1960—61; postgrad. in Physiology, U. Mich., 1984—87. Rsch. fellow, rsch. assoc., assoc. prof., leader cardiovasc. group, head cardiovasc. rsch. unit Shanghai Inst. Physiology, Acad. Sinica, 1960—87; prof. and chair hypoxia dept. Shanghai Inst. Physiology, 1988-90, vice chairperson academic com., 1988-90; NIH internat. rsch. fellow U. Mich., Ann Arbor, 1984-87; prof. and dir. Hypoxia Physiology Lab. Academia Sinica, Shanghai, 1989-90. Acting leader, High Altitude Physiology Group, Chinese mountaineering and sci. expdn. team to Mt. Everest, 1975; leader High Altitude Physiology Group, Dept. Metall. Industry of China and Ry. Engring. Corps, 1979; vis. prof. dept. physiology Mich. State U., East Lansing, U. Mich., U. Wash. Med. Sch., 1989-97; affiliate prof. U. Wash., 1997—; rsch. scientist Children's Hosp. and Regional Med. Ctr., Seattle, 1997—. Author: High Altitude Physiology and Medicine, 1981, Reports on Scientific Expedition to Mt. Qomolungma, High Altitude Physiology, 1980, Environment and Ecology of Qinghai-Xizang (Tibet) Plateau, 1982, Self-Health Care at High Altitude, 2006; mem. editl. bd. Chinese Jour. Applied Physiology, 1984-1992, Acta Physiologica, 1988-91, Chinese Jour. Physiology (Taiwan) 2004-; contbr. articles to profl. jours. Recipient Merit award Shanghai Sci. Congress, 1977, All-China Sci. Congress, Beijing, 1978, Super Class award Academia Sinica, Beijing, 1986, 1st Class award Nat. Natural Scis., Beijing, 1987, 2d Class award Acad. Sinica Sci. and Technol. Achievements, 1992, # 1 Best Article award Tzu-Chi Med. Jour., Taiwan, 1995. Mem. Am. Physiol. Soc., Am. Heart Assn. Internat. Soc. Heart Rsch., Internat. Soc. for Mountain Medicine, Royal Soc. Medicine, Shanghai Assn. Physiol. (bd. dirs. 1988-91), Chinese Assn. Physiol. (com. applied physiology 1984-93, com. blood, cardiovascular, respiratory and renal physiology 1988-93), Chinese Soc. Medicine, Chinese Soc. Biomed. Engring. Achievements include first to electrocardiography record at summit of Mt. Everest; research in predictive evaluation of mountaineering performance; characteristics for high altitude adaptation and acclimatization; effect of medicinal herbs on cardiac performance; cardiovascular adaptation and resistance to hypoxia and ischemia; injury threshold of short-cycle-intermittent hypoxia and gene expression in heat; the critical temperature 30 degrees celsius "temperature protective threshold" for modulating myocardial energy, metabolic pathways, and gene expression to resist ischemia and hypoxia; stress pathways and inactivates apoptosis to maintain myocardial stability and improve functional recovery during reperfusion and reoxygenation. Home: 7033 43rd Ave NE Seattle WA 98115-6015 Office: U Wash Dept Pediatrics Box 356320 1959 NE Pacific St Seattle WA 98195-0001 Business E-Mail: xh@u.washington.edu.

**NINIVAGGI, DANIEL A.,** lawyer; b NYC, June 27, 1964; m. Katie Ninivaggi; children: Caleb, Matthew, Jane, Jack. BA, Columbia U., 1986; MBA, U. Chgo., 1988; JD, Stanford U., 1991. Bar: Ill. 1991, NY 1995, Mich. 2003. Assoc. Skadden, Arps, Slate, Meagher & Flum, Winston & Strawn LLP, NYC, 1992—98, ptnr., 1998—2003; v.p., sr. gen. counsel Lear Corp., Southfield, Mich., 2003—04, sr. v.p., gen. counsel, 2004—. Office: Lear Corp 21557 Telgraph Rd PO Box 5008 Southfield MI 48086-5008 Office Phone: 248-447-1500. Business E-Mail: dninivaggi@lear.com.

**NIÑO, DEANNA HOLLYE,** lawyer; d. Alfredo and Hollye Niño. BA, U. Vt., 1991; JD, U. Denver, 1995. Atty., pension investigator U.S. Dept. Labor, Boston, 1996—99; atty. Marcia Wagner and Assocs., Boston, 1999—2000, Greenberg Traurig, LLP, N.Y., 2000—. Instr. Internat. Found. Employee Benefit Plans, Brookfield, Wis., 2000—; spkr. in field; presenter in field. Contbr. articles to profl. jours. Recipient Good Job award, U.S. Dept. Labor, 1998. Mem.: ABA, N.Y. Bar Assn. Office: Greenberg Traurig LLP Attorneys At Law 200 Park Avenue New York New York NY 10166 Office Phone: 212-801-9243. Home Fax: 212-805-9243; Office Fax: 212-805-9243. Business E-Mail: ninod@gtlaw.com.

**NIPP, TOM,** mayor, protective services official, artist; With Henry County Hosp., New Castle, Ind., 1963—64; fire fighter, chief New Castle Fire Dept., 1969—2004; dep. state fire marshal Ind. Fire Marshal's Office State of Ind., 1994; mayor New Castle, 2004—. Prin. works include murals in sch., race cars, 1972—85; composer; musician: (songs) group. Councilman City New Castle, 1996—2004; vol. mission work Ch. of God, Navajo Reservation, 1964. Recipient Exec. Fire Officer, Nat/ Fire Acad. State award Sagamore of the Walbash, 2004. Avocations: music, ping pong/table tennis, softball, fishing. Office: City New Castle 227 N Main St New Castle IN 47362

**NIRENBERG, DARRYL D.,** lawyer; b. Middletown, N.Y., Sept. 23, 1959; s. Alex Jack and Sandra (Levine) N. BA cum laude, Colgate U., 1981; JD, George Washington U., 1987. Legis. asst. Senator S.I. Hayakawa, Washington, 1981-82; profl. staff Agr. Com. U.S. Senate, 1983-86, assoc. Rep. counsel Fgn. Rels. Com. U.S. Senate, 1987-89; Rep. dep. staff dir. Fgn. Rels. Com. U.S. Senate, 1990-91; chief of staff Senator Jesse Helms, Washington, 1991-95; ptnr., Public Policy, Def. & Nat. Security practices, & hiring ptnr. Patton Boggs LLP, Washington; vice chmn. N.Y. State Coll. Reps., 1979-80, Fairfax County Young Rep., Va., 1982-83, campaign aide Sen. Jacob K. Javits, 1980; counsel Rep. Platform Com. 2000, Presd. Inauguration Com. 2001; mem. Moot Ct. Team George Washington U. Mem. Phi Alpha Theta. Jewish. Office: US Senate Com on Fgn Relations 452 Dirksen Bldg Washington DC 20510-0001 also: Patton Boggs LLP 2550 M St Nw Washington DC 20037-1350 Office Phone: 202-457-6022. Office Fax: 202-457-6315. Business E-Mail: dnirenberg@pattonboggs.com.

**NIRENBERG, LOUIS,** mathematician, educator; b. Hamilton, Ont., Can., Feb. 28, 1925; arrived in U.S., 1945, naturalized, 1954; s. Zuzie and Bina (Katz) Nirenberg; m. Susan Blank, Jan. 25, 1948; children: Marc, Lisa. BSc, McGill U., Montreal, 1945, DSc (hon.) 1986; MS, NYU, 1947, PhD, 1949; DSc (hon.), U. Pisa, Italy, 1990, U. Paris Dauphine, 1990, McMaster U., Can. 2000. Mem. faculty NYU, 1949—, prof. math., 1957—, dir. Courant Inst. 1970—72. Visitor Inst. Advanced Study, 1958; hon. prof. Nannkai U., Zhejiang U. Author rsch. articles. Recipient Crafoord prize, Royal Swedish Acad., 1982, Nat. medal of Sci., 1995; fellow NRC, 1951—52, Sloan Found., 1958—60, Guggenheim Found., 1966—67, 1975—76, Fulbright, 1965. Mem.: NAS, Ukrainian Acad. Sci. (fgn.), Accademia di Scienze e Lettere (fgn.), Istituto Lombardo, Accademia dei Lincei (fgn.), French Acad. Scis. (fgn.), Am. Philos. Soc., Am. Math. Soc. (v.p. 1976—78, M. Bocher prize 1959, L.P. Steele prize 1994), Am. Acad. Arts and Scis., European Acad. Scis. (hon.). Home: 221 W 82nd St New York New York NY 10024-5406 Office: Courant Inst 251 Mercer St New York NY 10012-1185 Business E-Mail: nirenl@cims.nyu.edu.

**NIRENBERG, MARSHALL WARREN,** biochemist; b. NYC, Apr. 10, 1927; s Harry Edward and Minerva (Dykewsky) Nirenberg; m. Perola Zaltzman, July 14, 1961. BS in Zoology, U. Fla., 1948, MS, 1952; PhD in Biochemistry, U. Mich., 1957. Postdoctoral fellow Am. Cancer Soc. at NIH, 1957—59; postdoctoral fellow USPHS at NIH, 1959—60; mem. staff NIH, 1960—; rsch. biochemist, chief lab. biochem. genetics Nat. Heart, Lung and Blood Inst., NIH, Bethesda, Md., 1962—. Co-recipient Louisa Gross Horowitz prize Columbia, 1968, Nobel prize in physiology or medicine, 1968; recipient Molecular Biology award, NAS, 1962, award in biol. scis., Washington Acad. Scis., 1962, medal, HEW, 1964, Modern Medicine award, 1963, Harrison Howe award, Am. Chem. Soc., 1964, Nat. Medal Sci., Pres. Johnson, 1965, Hildebrand award, Am. Chem. Soc., 1966, Research Corp. award, 1966, A.C.P. award, 1967, award merit, Gairdner Found., Can, 1967, Prix Charles Leopold Meyer, French Acad. Scis., 1967, Franklin medal, Franklin Inst., 1968, Albert Lasker Med. Research award, 1968, Priestly award, 1968. Fellow: AAAS, Nat. Acad. Scis.; mem.: NAS, Pontifical Acad. Scis., Leopoldina Deutsche Akademie der Naturforscher, Soc. Devel. Biology, Soc. for Study Devel. and Growth, Washington Acad. Scis., Harvey Soc. (hon.), Biophys. Soc., Am. Acad. Arts and Scis., Am. Chem. Soc. (Paul Lewis award enzyme chemistry 1964), Am. Soc. Biol. Chemists. Achievements include research in mechanism protein synthesis, genetic code, nucleic acids, regulatory mechanisms in synthesis macromolecules, and neurobiology.*

**NIRO, CHERYL,** lawyer; b. Feb. 19, 1950; d. Samuel James and Nancy (Canezaro) Ippolito; m. William Luciano Niro, July 1, 1979; children: Christopher William, Melissa Leigh. BS with highest honors, U. Ill., 1972; JD, No. Ill. U., 1980. Bar: Ill. 1981, U.S. Dist. Ct. (no. dist.) Ill. 1981, U.S. Ct. Appeals (7th cir.) 1990, U.S. Supreme Ct. 1999, cert.: negotiator, mediator, facilitator, arbitrator. Ptnr. Quinlan & Carroll, Chgo.; pres. Judicial Dispute Resolution, Inc., Chgo.; exec. dir. commn. on professionalism. Ill. Supreme Ct. Spl. counsel to Atty. Gen., 1996—99; tchg. asst. program instrn. lawyers mediation and negotiation workshops and guest lectr. Harvard Law Sch. Program of Instrn. for Lawyers Harvard U.; mem. adapt. panel U.S. Ct. Appeals (7th cir.); found. dir. Nat. Ctr. for Conflict Resolution Edn.; mem. copyright arbitration royalty panel U.S. Libr. of Congress, 2000—05; mem. London Ct. of Internat. Arbitration. Named 100 Women Making A Difference, 2001; named one of Ten Most Influential Women Lawyers in Ill, Am Lawyer Media, 2000; named to Today's Chgo. Woman Mag. Hall of Fame, 2002.

Mem.: ATLA, ABA (comn multijurisdictional practice, standing comt bar servs, dispute resolution sect coun, house delegs), Nat. Caucus State Bar Assns. (pres.-elect), Internat. Ctr. for Healing the Law (mem. bd. adv.), Internat. Bar Assn., Ill. State Bar Assn. (mem assembly 1993, bd govs 1994—97, treas 1995—96, 2d vpres 1997—98, pres 1999—2000, standing comt legal-related educ pub), Ill Trial Lawyers Asn. Home: 633 N East Ave Oak Park IL 60302-1715 Office: Quinlan & Carroll 30 N Lasalle St Ste 2900 Chicago IL 60602-2590 Office Phone: 312-917-8839. Business E-Mail: cherylniro@qclaw.com.

**NIRSCHL, ROBERT PHILLIP,** orthopedic surgeon; b. South Milwaukee, Wis., Aug. 28, 1933; s. Boyd A. and Helen (Wozny) N.; m. Mary Ann Oleniczak, June 21, 1958; children: Suzanne, Robert C., Julie. Student, Coll. Holy Cross, 1951-53, Marquette U., 1953-54; MD, Med. Coll. Wis./Marquette U., 1958; MS, U. Minn., 1965. Diplomate Am. Bd. Orthop. Surgery. Intern St. Mary's Hosp., Duluth, Minn., 1958-59; resident in orthop. Mayo Clinic, Rochester, Minn., 1959-63; lt. comdr. USN, Washington, 1963-65; pvt. practice Arlington, Va., 1965—. Attending orthop. surgeon Va. Hosp. Ctr., Arlington, v.p. med. staff, 1980—83, dir. Hand Surgery Svc., 1975—85, mem. hosp. med. exec. com., 2006—; chief orthop. surgery No. Va. Cmty. Hosp., 1971—82; founding dir. Nirschl Orthop. Ctr. for Sports Medicine and Joint Reconstrn., 1974—, Nirschl Orthop. Sport Med. Ctr. Orthop. Sports Medicine Fellowship Program Va. Hosp. Ctr., Arlington, 1987—; mem. clin. faculty Georgetown U. Med. Ctr., 1965—; orthop. cons. Pres.'s Coun. Phys. Fitness, Washington, 1981—87; mem. sports sci. com. USTA, NYC, 1987—94; course dir. numerous symposia in field. Author: Arm Care, 1981, rev. edit., 1996, Isoflex Exercise System, 1983; chief med. editor Orthop. Today, 1983-93; mem. editl. bd. The Physician and Sportsmedicine, 1992—, The Med. Sentinel, 1996-02, Orthopedics Today, 2003-; creator 9 video programs; contbr. chpts. to books and over 125 articles to profl. publs.; patentee in field. Chmn. Jeffersonian Health Policy Found., Williamsburg, Va., 1994—97; mem. Va. Bd. Medicine, 2000—04; trustee Marymount U., Arlington, 2005—. Grantee Pfizer Inc., 1992-93, Sano Corp, 1993-94, Iomed Corp., 1999-2000. Mem.: AMA, Am. Orthop. Assn., VA Orthop. Soc. (Lifetime Career award 2005), Arlington County Med. Soc. (pres. 1977, chmn. legis. com. 1987—2004, Welburn award 1995), Med. Soc. Va. (chmn. sports medicine com. 1973—84, trustee polit. action com. 1990—2002, legis. com. 1995, liability com. 2005—, trustee polit. action com. 2006—), Va. Orthop. Soc. (pres. 1998—99, career award 2005), Washington Orthop. Soc., Ea. Orthop. Assn., Soc. Tennis Medicine and Sci. (exec. com.), Am. Orthop. Soc. Sports Medicine (ethics com 1992—97, bd. dels. 2002—), Am. Acad. Orthop. Surgery (health fin. com. 1994—2000, comm. and state soc. coms. bd. of counselors 2000—03, bd. counselors 2000—06), Washington Golf and Country Club. Republican. Roman Catholic. Avocation: fitness activities. Office: Nirschl Orthop Ctr Sports Medicine & Joint Reconstrn 1715 N George Mason Dr Ste 504 Arlington VA 22205-3670 Office Phone: 703-525-2200. Personal E-mail: nirschlorthopaedics@comcast.net.

**NISBET, TOMA A.,** nursing administrator; Diploma with honors, St. Mark's Hosp. Sch. Nursing, 1967; BSN with honors, No. Ill. U., 1969, MSN with honors, 1973. Internship Winnebago County Dept. Pub. Health-Health Adminstrn. & Family Planning; night staff nurse Sycamore Municipal Hosp., Ill., 1967-68; evening relief supr., charge nurse DeKalb County Nursing Home, Ill., 1969; pub. health nurse DeKalb County Health Dept., Ill., 1969-71; divsn. dir. nursing svcs. Winnebago County Dept. Pub. Health, Rockford, Ill., 1974-84; pub. dir. nursing svcs. divsn. of health & med. svcs. State of Wyo., Cheyenne, 1985-87, policy devel. & spl. projects state program mgr. divsn. of health & med. svcs., 1987-88, state bd. nursing exec., 1988—. Spokesperson for NLX D-A-Y Pub. Rels. for Burroughs Wellcome, N.Y.C., 1987; project coord. for health svcs. No. Ill. U. Sch. Nursing, DeKalb, 1973-74, instr. 1979-84. Author of numerous articles. Awarded numerous rsch. grants. Mem. ANA, Nat. Coun. State Bds. of Nursing (bd. 1988-95, AEC com. mem. 1990-94, mem. nomination com. 1991-92, enhl. program task force 1994-95, alternate examination com. 1994-95), Wyo. Commn. on Nursing & Nursing Edn., Wyo. Orgn. Nurse Execs., Wyo. State Bd. of Nursing Home Adminstrs. (sec. 1988-89, vice-chmn. 1990-95), Wyo. Advanced Practitioner of Nursing Orgn.

**NISENHOLTZ, MARTIN ABRAM,** telecommunications executive, educator; b. Phila., Apr. 1, 1955; s. Louis William and Rhoda Greta (Koenig) N.; m. Anne Ermine Stockler, July 26, 1981; children: Johanna, Marjorie. BA, U. Pa., 1977, MA, 1979. Research scientist NYU, N.Y.C., 1979-83; mgr. Ogilvy & Mather, N.Y.C., 1983-84, v.p., 1984-89, sr. v.p., 1989-94; dir. content strategy Ameritech Corp., Chgo., 1994-95; pres. N.Y. Times Electronic Media Co., 1995-99; CEO N.Y. Times Digital, 1999—2005; sr. v.p. digital ops. The N.Y. Times Co., 2005—. Mem. ops. Ogilvy & Mather Direct, 1992—94; adj. assoc. prof. NYU, 1983—; bd. dirs. internet advtsg. bur. Ctr. for Comm., 1999. Mem. Annenberg Sch. Alumni Bd., 1996—; bd. dirs. N.Y. Leukemia and Lumphoma Soc., 2005—. Recipient Merrill Panott Citizenship award, 1997, Ten award, 2003; grantee Nat. Endowment Arts, 1981. Mem.: Online Pubs. Assn. (founding chmn. 2001—04), Interactive Svcs. Assn. (dir. 1985—94, chmn. 1991, Disting. Svc. award 1994). Office: NY Times Digital 500 7th Ave New York NY 10018 Business E-Mail: martin@nytimes.com.

**NISH, WAYNE PAUL,** chef, restaurant owner; b. NYC, July 23, 1951; s. John and Dorothy (Bugelli) N.; children: Caitlin Nicola, Alexandra Jane. Student, Long Island U., 1969-70, Cornell U., 1972-73, CCNY, 1973-74; diploma, N.Y. Restaurant Sch., 1983. Assoc. chef The Quilted Giraffe, N.Y.C., 1984-87; prt. owner Aurora, N.Y.C., 1987-88; exec. chef La Colombe d'Or, N.Y.C., 1988-89; chef, co-owner March Restaurant, N.Y.C., 1990—. Adv. bd. mem. N.Y. Restaurant Sch., 1991—. Fund raiser Women's Campaign Fund, 1992, 93, 94. Recipient Three Stars award N.Y. Times, 1988, 92, 95, Forbes Mag., 1989, Four Stars award Forbes Mag., 1993, 94; named Am.'s top Restaurant Zagat Survey, 1993, 94, 95. Mem. Am Inst. Wine and Food, James Beard Found. Democrat. Roman Catholic. Avocations: cooking, photography, driving. Office: March Restaurant 405 E 58th St New York NY 10022-2302 Home: 405 E 58th St New York NY 10022-2302*

**NISHIMURA, JOSEPH YO,** retired retail executive, accountant; b. Berkeley, Calif., Nov. 4, 1933; s. Masamoto and Kimiko (Ishihara) N.; m. Joyce Toshiye Mori, Sept. 1, 1956; children: Brenda Joyce, Stephen Lloyd. AB cum laude, Princeton U., 1956; MBA, Stanford U., 1961. CPA, Calif., N.Y.; cert. Employee Benefit Specialist. Audit supr. Touche Ross & Co., San Francisco 1961-66; contr. Scott Co. of Calif., Oakland, 1966-67, Purity Stores, Inc., Burlingame, Calif., 1967-69; pres. Cubit Sys. Corp., Burlingame, 1969-72; sr. v.p. Golden West Fin. Corp., Oakland, 1972-73; exec. v.p. Victory Mkts., Inc., Norwich, N.Y., 1973-90; gen. ptnr. Mori Enterprises, 1994—2005. Dir. Carl's Drug Co., Rome, N.Y., 1988-90, mem. site devel. com., Wakefern Food Corp., Edison, N.J., 1996—. V.p., bd. dirs. Chenango Meml. Hosp., Norwich,

1981-87; bd. dirs. United Fund, Norwich, 1984-90, N.Y. State Food Mchts. Assn., 1988-90, Binghamton (N.Y.) Philharmonic, 1988-98, treas., 1990-93; cons. Mori Charitable Unitrust, 2005-. Served to lt. (j.g.) USN, 1956-59; Japan. Mem. AICPA, Calif. Soc. CPAs, Marbella Country Club, Princeton (N.Y.C.) Club. Democrat. Presbyterian.

**NISHIMURA, PETE HIDEO,** oral surgeon; b. Hilo, Hawaii, Aug. 7, 1922; s. Hideichi and Satsuki N.; m. Tomoe Nishimura, June, 1949; children: Dennis Dean, Grant Neil, Dawn Naomi. Student, U. Hawaii, 1940-44; D.D.S., U. Mo., 1947; MSD., Northwestern U., 1949. Practice dentistry specializing in oral surgery, Honolulu, 1952—; pres. Oral Surgery Group, 1978—. Mem. coun. Nat. Bd. Dental Examination; dir. Hawaii Dental Svc., 1962-85, pres., 1970-72, 76-78; pres. State Bd. Dental Examiners, Delta Sigma Delta, Fedn. Dentaire Internat. Served with U.S. Army, 1952-54. Named Disting. Alumni, U. Mo. Hawaii, 2004; recipient Citation for outstanding pub. svc. toward the devel. of state plan for emergency mgmt. resources, Dir. Emergency Planning, Exec. Office of Pres. of U.S., 1968, Lifetime Achievement award, Hawaii Dental Assn. Fellow Am. Coll. Dentists, Internat. Coll. Dentists; mem. ADA, Hawaii Dental Assn. (past pres., Lifetime Achievement award 2006), Delta Dental Plans Assn. (dir.), Honolulu County Dental Soc., Hawaii Soc. Oral Surgeons, Am. Assn. Oral and Maxillofacial Surgeons, Western Soc. Oral and Maxillofacial Surgeons, Am. Assn. Dental Examiners, Pierre Fauchard Acad. (citation for oustanding contbn. to arts and sci. of dentistry 1987). Democrat. Home: Apt 606 4389 Malia St Honolulu HI 96821 Office: 848 S Beretania St Honolulu HI 96813-2551 E-mail: hilopete@aol.com.

**NISHIYAMA, CHIAKI,** economist, educator; b. Fukuoka-ken, Japan, Aug. 9, 1924, s. Michiki and Teruko (Tsuji) N.; m. Shigeko Okabe, June 9, 1957; children: Keita, Mikiko. BA in Econs., Rikkyo U., Tokyo, 1950; MA in Polit. Sci., U. Chgo., 1952, PhD in Social Thought, 1960, postgrad. in econs., 1959-60. Lectr. U. Chgo., 1957-61; assoc. prof. Rikkyo U., 1962-64, prof. econs., 1964-90, prof. emeritus, 1990—. Sr. rsch. fellow Hoover Instn., Stanford U., 1977—; prof. econs. Grad. Sch. Internat. Mgmt., U. Japan, 1994-97; lectr. Tng. Inst., Min. Trade and Industry, Japanese Govt., 1964-66, Gakushuin U., 1970-71, Waseda U., 1972-74; exec. dir. Assembly on U.S.-Japan Econ. Policy, 1972-76; prime minister's spl. envoy to White House, 1971, 75; specialist counselor Japan Employers' Assn., 1975-85; del. European Assembly, Strasbourg, France, 1982; world travel for Japanese Min. Fgn. Affairs, Japan External Trade Orgn., 1968-82; lectr. various univs., U.S. and Europe, 1976-94; mem. Am. Citizen to Citizen Econ. and Fin. Mgmt. Del. to the USSR, 1991; spl. envoy of Japan to Germany, Czechoslovakia, Hungary, Bulgaria, Ukraine, Russia, 1991. Author numerous books including: Lecture on Modern Economics, 1964, Free Economy, Its Policies and Principles, 1974, The Price for Prosperity, 1974, A Monetary History and Analysis of the Japanese Economy, 1968-70, 74, Reflection on Japanese Economy, 1976, Monetarism, 1976, The Last Chance for Creativity, Liberty and Prosperity, 1981, Human Capitalism, 1982, The Fourth Philosophy, Vol. I, 1982, Vol. II, 1983, No Limits to Growth, 1984, The Essence of Hayek, 1984, The Japanese Economy, 1987, Paradigm Shift, 1987, Japanese Economy and Life Tomorrow, 1988, A New Economics Under a New Paradigm, 1991, The End of Recession, 1994, Depression or New Prosperity, 1998, Market Economy: New Way, 1999, Chicago Boys, 2003, Japan in the New Century and Blackship, 2005, Reason and Its Limits from Asian Paradigm, 2005; editl. bd. Jour. Internat. Money and Fin., 1981—. Hon. fellow Inst. Econ. Affairs, London, 1976—; mem. adv. bd. Econ. Inst. Paris, 1984-86, Carl Menger Inst., Wien, 1984; councilor The Daiwa Securities Welfare Found., 1994—. Recipient Japan Econ. Lit. award Japan Econ. Jour., 1974; Eahart fellow, 1960-61, E.C. Nef fellow, 1958-59, Woodrow Wilson Internat. Ctr. for Scholars fellow, 1976-77; grantee Relm, 1962-64, Ford, 1965-66, Lilly, 1966-67, Bank of Japan, Bankers Assn. Japan, other fin. orgns., 1978-83. Mem. Am. Enterprise Inst. (adj. scholar), Am. Econ. Assn., Econometric Soc., Japan Econs. Assn., Econ. Assn., Statis. Soc., Mont Pelerin Soc. (pres. 1980-82, sr. v.p. 1982-85, hon. v.p. 1986-88), Japan Econ. Rsch. Ctr. (spl. member. 1964). Episcopalian. Office: Nishiyama-Kenkyushitsu 5-15-18 Kamiuma Setagaya-ku 154-0011 Tokyo Japan

**NISKANEN, WILLIAM ARTHUR, JR.,** economist, think-tank executive; b. Bend, Oreg., Mar. 13, 1933; s. William Arthur and Nina Elizabeth (McCord) Niskanen; m. Kathryn Washburn; children: Lia, Pamela, Jaime. BA, Harvard U., 1954; MA, U. Chgo., 1955, PhD, 1962. Staff economist RAND Corp., Santa Monica, Calif., 1957—62; staff dir. U.S. Dept. Def., Washington, 1962—64; divsn. dir. Inst. Def. Analyses, Washington, 1964—70; asst. dir. Office of Mgmt. and Budget, Washington, 1970—72; prof. U. Calif., Berkeley, 1972—75; chief economist Ford Motor Co., Dearborn, Mich., 1975—80; prof. UCLA, 1980—81; mem. Coun. Econ. Advisers, Washington, 1981—85; chmn. CATO Inst., Washington, 1985—. Author: Bureaucracy and Representative Goverment, 1971, Reaganomics, 1988, Policy Analysis and Public Choice, 1998, Going Digital, 1998, Autocratic, Democratic and Optimal Government, 2004, After Enron: Lessons for Public Policy, 2005; editor: Regulation mag., 1990—96. Founder Nat. Tax Limitation Com. Mem.: Atlantic Econ. Assn. (past pres.), Pub. Choice Soc. (past pres.), Am. Econ. Assn. Republican. Office: Cato Inst 1000 Massachusetts Ave NW Washington DC 20001-5400 Office Phone: 202-789-5236. Business E-Mail: wniskan@cato.org.

**NISSEN, DAVID R.,** utilities executive; B, Northwestern U., 1975; MBA, U. Chgo. Staff strategic planning and bus. devel. G.E. Captial, 1981—83; mktg. G.E. Card Svcs., 1983—87, gen. mgr., 1987—90, G.E. U.S. Consumer Fin. Svcs., 1990—93; officer G.E., 1996—2001, sr. v.p., 2001—; pres., CEO G.E. Consumer Fin., 2002—. Named one of Ten Retail Banking Heros, Retail Banker Internat., 2003. Avocations: golf, jet skiing, tennis. Office: GE Global Consumer Fin 1600 Summer St Stamford CT 06927

**NISSENBLATT, MICHAEL JEFFREY,** medical oncologist; b. Bronx, NY, June 4, 1948; m. Marlene Nissenblatt; 1 child, Doree; 1 child, Paulina. MD, Columbia P&S, 1973. Diplomate Am. Bd. Internal Medicine. Intern Johns Hopkins, Balt., 1973-74, resident, 1974-75, 75-76, fellow, 1976-78; assoc. dir. med. oncology RW Johnson U. Hosp., New Brunswick, 1996—; staff St. Peter's Med. Ctr., New Brunswick; clin. prof. medicine RW Johnson U. Sch. Medicine, 1996—. Dir. Ctrl. NJ Oncology Ctr., 1981—2004. Recipient Chamber of Commerce award, 2003, Partners in Caring award, Am. Cancer Soc., 2004. Fellow ACP; mem. AMA, AAAS, Am. Radiol. Assn., Am. Soc. Clin. Oncology, Cancer Chemotherapy Found., Johns Hopkins Med. Surgeons Soc., Maimonides Soc., Middlesex County Med. Soc., N.J. Breast Cancer Coalition, others. Jewish. Avocations: running, astronomy, anthropology, motivational speaking. Office: Ctrl Jersey Oncology Ctr PA 205 Easton Ave New Brunswick NJ 08901-1722 Office Phone: 732-828-9570. Personal E-mail: mjnmotor@aol.com.

**NISSENSON, ALLEN RICHARD,** physician, educator; b. Chgo., Dec. 10, 1946; s. Harry and Sylvia Lillian (Chapnitsky) N.; m. Charna H. Karp, May 28, 1978; 1 child, Ariel Rose. BS in Medicine, Northwestern U., 1967, MD, 1971. Diplomate Am. Bd. Internal Medicine, bd. cert. internal medicine and nephrology. Intern in medicine Michael Reese Hosp. and Med. Ctr., Chgo., 1971-72, resident in internal medicine, 1972-74; fellowship in nephrology Northwestern U., Chgo., 1974-76; assoc. medicine Northwestern U. Med. Sch., Chgo., 1976-77; asst. medicine UCLA Sch. Medicine, 1977-82, assoc. prof. medicine, 1982-88, prof. medicine, 1988—; dir. dialysis program UCLA Ctr. for the Health Scis., 1977—, med. dir. renal mgmt. strategies, assoc. dean David Geffen Sch. Medicine, 2006—. Adj. attending physician Northwestern Meml. Hosp., Chgo., 1976-77; asst. attending physician UCLA Ctr. for Health Scis., 1977-82, assoc. attending physician, 1988—; attending physician nephrology Wadsworth VA Hosp., 1978—; cons. on peritoneal dialysis Baxter-Travenol Labs., 1981—; mem. nephrology adv. com. Nephrology Nursing Edn. Grant, Calif. State U., 1983-90; vice chmn. Forum of End Stage Renal Disease Networks, 1988-91; mem. sci. adv. bd. Nat. Kidney Found., 1989-91, chmn. coun. on clin. nephrology, dialysis and transplantation, 1989-91; cons. on End Stage Renal Disease reimbursement Rand Corp., 1990—, others. Editor-in-chief Advances in Renal Replacement Therapy, 1993—, Hemodialysis Internat., 2004—; mem. editl. bd. Dialysis and

Transplantation, 1978—, UCLA Health Insights, 1981-89, Perspectives in Peritoneal Dialysis, 1983—, Internat. Jour. Artificial Organs, 1984—, Seminars in Dialysis, 1987—, Am. Jour. Nephrology, 1989—, Am. Jour. Kidney Diseases, 1989—, Geriat. Nephrology and Urology Jour., 1989—; mem. editl. adv. bd. Contemporary Dialysis, 1983—, Nephrology Practice Today, 1989—, Hematopoietic Therapy Index and Revs., 1993—, Primary Care Reports, 1994—; editl. cons. Am. Jour. Nephrology, 1981-88; contbr. chpts. to books, abstracts and articles to profl. publs. Recipient Nat. Kidney Found. So. Calif. Cmty. Svc. award, 1981; Robert Wood Johnson policy fellow Office of Sen. Paul Wellstone, 1994-95. Fellow ACP; mem. Am. Soc. for Artifical Internal Organs, Am. Fedn. for Clin. Rsch., Am. Soc. Nephrology, Internat. Soc. Nephrology, Internat. Soc. Artificial Organs, Western Soc. for Clin. Investigation, European Dialysis and Transplant Assn., N.Am. Soc. for Dialysis and Transplantation, Renal Physicians' Assn. (bd. dirs. 1993—, sec. bd. dirs. 1994—, pres. 1999-2001), Calif. Renal Physicians (bd. dirs. 1987—). Office: UCLA Med Ctr Dialysis Ctr Ste 565-59 200 Medical Plaza Los Angeles CA 90024-6945 E-mail: anissenson@mednet.ucla.edu.

**NISSIM, SHAI,** special education educator, consultant; s. Oved Aicha and Nadia Aicha-Ora. MEd (hon.), Bkyn. Coll., 1995; EdD, Columbia U., 2003. Lic. N.Y. State Edn. Dept., 1995, cert. Bilingual (Hebrew/English)tchr. N.Y. State Edn. Dept., 1996. Spl. edn. tchr. United Cerebral Palsy, N.Y.C., 1991—; ESL/CLD instr. Interagency Coun. Mental Retardation, N.Y.C., 1996—; ednl. evaluator N.Y. Devel., N.Y.C., 1999—2002. Sgt Isreali Defense Forces, 1980—83. Mem.: Tchrs. English to Spkr. of other Languages (assoc.), Am. Assn. Mental Retardation (assoc.). Democrat. Jewish. Avocations: travel, swimming, camping. Office: PO Box 7069 New York NY 10116 Personal E-mail: snissim1@aol.com.

**NISSINEN, MIKKO PEKKA,** dancer, performing arts company executive, artistic director; b. Helsinki, Finland; arrived in U.S. 1987; Grad., Finnish Nat. Ballet Sch., 1977; postgrad., Leningrad Acad. Ballet Sch., 1979-80. Mem. corps de ballet Finnish Nat. Ballet, Helsinki, 1977-79, soloist, 1980-82; grand sujete Dutch Nat. Ballet, Amsterdam, The Netherlands, 1982-84; soloist Basel (Switzerland) Ballet, 1984-87, San Francisco Ballet, 1987-88, prin. dancer, 1988-96; artistic dir. Marin Ballet, 1996-97, Alberta Ballet, Calgary, Canada, 1998—2002, Boston Ballet, 2001—. Guest artist La Bayadere Nat. Ballet Can., 1989; guest artist Oberlin Dance Collective, 1993; bd. dirs. Le Don Des Etoiles; guest tchr. Royal Acad. Danciang, 1993, Kennedy Ctr. Ednl. Program, 1994, Nat. Ballet Sch., Toronto, 1994; lectr. on dance history and state of dance today Stanford U., Lethbridge U.; St. Mary's Coll., Christensen Soc.; artistic com. N.Y. Choreographic Inst.; juror Prix de Lausanne, Benois de la Danse, Helsinki Internat. Ballet Competition. Dancer Sleeping Beauty, San Francisco Ballet, Swan Lake, Bizet Pas de Deux, Handel-a Celebration, Haffner Symphony, Variations de Ballet, Rodin, Rodeo, Con Brio, Ballet d'Isoline, Giuliani: Variations on a Theme, Tchaikovsky Pas de Deux, Symphony in C, Theme and Variations, Ballo della Regina, The Nutcracker, Airs de Ballet, Maelstrom, Dark Elegies, Harvest Moon, Napoli, Job, The Wanderer Fantasy. In the middle, somewhat elevated, Calcium Light Night, Le Corsaire Pas de Deux, Dreams of Harmony, Pulcinella, The Dream, Don Quixote, Giselle, A Midsummer Night's Dream, Les Biches, Sleeping Beauty, Pyrrich Dances, Masse, Le Tombeau de Couperin, Symphony in C, The Four Temperaments, The Prodigal Son, Rodin, Pierrot Lunaire, La Fille mal gardée, Swan Lake, Henze, Five Tangos, In and Out, Bits and Pieces, Jeu de Cartes, Gala Des Etoiles, Can. Internat. Ballet Gala, 1989, 1990, 1991, 1992, 1993, 1994, 1995, Reykjavik Arts Festival, 1990, Internat. Ballet Gala, Kuopio, Finland, 1992, Vail, Colo., 1993, Night of Stars Ballet Gala, Helsinki, 1993; profiled in nat. and internat. radio and TV programs CNN Worldwide Report, 1992, featured on cover Dance Mag., 1992; choreographer Full Evening Nutcracker, Marin Ballet, 1996, Alta. Ballet, 2000, Nutcracker, 2003—04, Swan Lake, 2004. Recipient 1st prize Nat. Dance Competition, Kuopio, Finland, 1978; fellowship exec. program for non-profit leaders, Stanford Univ. Mem.: Artistic Com. NY Coreographic Inst. Office: Boston Ballet 19 Clarendon St Boston MA 02116-6100*

**NISSL, COLLEEN KAYE,** lawyer; b. McMinnville, Oreg., June 3, 1950; d. Anton Arthur and Luella Elaine (Kerr) N.; m. Roger Philip Sugarman; children: Jordan Elizabeth, Zachary Max. BA, Ohio Wesleyan U., 1972; JD, U. Toledo, 1975. Bar: Ohio 1975, U.S. Dist. Ct. (so. dist.) Ohio 1977, U.S. Supreme Ct. 1980. Litigation sect. chief Atty. Gen. Ohio, Columbus, 1976-82; sr. counsel Battelle Meml. Inst., Columbus, 1982-84; v.p., asst. gen. counsel Borden Chemical, Inc., Columbus, 1984—. Mem. ABA, Ohio Bar Assn., Columbus Bar Assn. (chmn. alt. dispute resolution com.). Democrat. Roman Catholic. Avocations: skiing, bicycling, antiques. Office: Borden Inc 180 E Broad St 27th Fl Columbus OH 43215

**NISSLEY, M. JOHN,** dean, educator; b. Morgantown, Pa., Mar. 30, 1949; s. Ira and Ruth S. (Stoltzfus) N.; m. Lois C. Musselman, Oct. 24, 1970; children: Monica Dawn, Lara Nicole. BS, Pa. State U., 1974; MRE, Grand Rapids Bapt. Sem., 1983; DMin, Bethel Theol. Sem., 2000. Ordained to ministry Mennonite Ch., 1986. House parent Clayton Coll. for Boys, Denver, 1968-70; youth counselor Millersville (Pa.) Youth Village, 1975; camp dir. Tel-Hai Camp, Honey Brook, Pa., 1975-81; pastor Masonville Mennonite Ch., Washington Boro, Pa., 1984-90; assoc. dir. for evangelism Ea. Mennonite Bd. Missions, Salaunga, Pa., 1989—93; sr. pastor Ephreta (Pa.) Mennonite Ch., 1993—2000; prof. spiritual formation and pastoral theology Winebrenner Theol. Sem., Findlay, Ohio, 2000—. Long range planning com. Locust Grove Mennonite Sch., Smoketown, Pa., 1988; campus pastor Millersville Christian Fellowship, 1986-88. V.p. Millersville Internat. House, 1987-95; pastor of descipleship Stonebridge Ch. of God, Findlay, 2000-02 Office: Winebrenner Theol Sem 950 N Main St Findlay OH 45840 Office Phone: 419-434-4247. Business E-Mail: jnissley@winebrenner.edu.

**NISSLY, KENNETH L.,** lawyer; b. Mesa, Ariz., Oct. 25, 1952; m. Marjorie J. Nissly, Aug. 17, 1974; children: Jennifer, Paul Bar, San Diego State U., 1974; JD, U. Calif., San Francisco, 1977. Bar: Calif. 1977, US Dist. Ct. (No. Dist.) Calif., US Dist. Ct. (Ea. Dist.) Calif., US Ct. Appeals (9th Cir.), US Dist. Ct. (Ea. Dist.) Tex., US Dist. Ct. (Ea. Dist.) Va., US Dist. Ct. (Dist. Del.), US Ct. Appeals (Fed. Cir.). Assoc. Thelen, Marrin, Johnson & Bridges, San Jose, Calif., 1977-85, ptnr., 1985—98; ptnr., litig. dept Thelen Reid & Priest LLP, 1998—, mng. ptnr. Silicon Valley office. Mem.: Calif. State Bar Assn., Santa Clara County Bar Assn. (judge pro tem neighborhood small claims ct. program 1985—), ABA, Order of Coif, Phi Beta Kappa. Avocation: flying. Office: Thelen Reid & Priest LLP 225 W Santa Clara St Ste 1200 San Jose CA 95113-1723 Office Phone: 408-292-5800. Office Fax: 408-287-8040. Business E-Mail: kennissly@thelenreid.com.

**NISSMAN, DAVID M.,** lawyer, former prosecutor; b. 1953; m. Carolina Zapata Nissman; 3 children. BA magna cum laude, Emory U., 1975; JD, U. Oreg., 1978. Dep. dist. atty., Eugene, Oreg.; adj. law prof. U. Oreg.; U.S. atty. St. Croix. V.I.; pub. Office of Legal Edn., Dept. of Justice; former U.S. atty. Dist. of Virgin Islands. CEO Bridge Capital, Corpus Juris Pub. Co. Author: Proving Federal Crimes, 2001. Recipient Chief Inspector's Award, USPS, 1991, NRC Award, 1994, Environmental Div. Award, U.S. Dept. Justice, 2000, Dir. Awards, Exec. Office U.S. Attys.

**NITECKI, JOSEPH ZBIGNIEW,** librarian; b. Dabrowa Górnicza, Poland, Jan. 31, 1922; came to U.S., 1951, naturalized, 1956; s. Henryk W. and Antonina S. N.; m. Sophie V. Zboinski, June 17, 1945; children: Zbigniew H., Danuta B. BA in Philosophy, Wayne State U., 1955; MA, Roosevelt U., 1959; MA in L.S., U. Chgo., 1963. Various profl. and adminstrv. positions in libraries U. Chgo., 1961-63, Chgo. City Coll., 1963-66, U. Wis., Milw., 1967-70, Temple U., Phila., 1970-78; prof., exec. dir. libraries U. Wis., Oshkosh, 1978-80; dir. libraries SUNY, Albany, 1980-88, vis. prof. Sch. Info Sci. and Policy, 1988-90, prof. emeritus, 1990—. Cons. library issues. Author, editor compiler and reviewer in field; ranch. and manuscript reader. Served with Polish Armed Forces under Brit. command, 1939-48. Recipient 1st. prize Polish Émigré Poetry Contest, 2001. Mem. ALA, Beta Phi Mu. Home: 430 Coburg Village Way Rexford NY 12148-1461 E-mail: jzniteckisr@aol.com.

**NITIKMAN, FRANKLIN W.,** lawyer; b. Davenport, Iowa, Oct. 26, 1940; s. David A. and Janette (Gordon) N.; m. Adrienne C. Drell, Nov. 28, 1972. BA, Northwestern U., 1963; LLB, Yale U., 1966. Bar: Ill. 1966, U.S. Dist. Ct. (no. dist.) Ill. 1967, U.S. Tax Ct. 1972, Fla. 1977, D.C. 1981. Assoc. McDermott, Will & Emery, Chgo., 1966-72, ptnr., 1973—. Co-author: Drafting Wills and Trust Agreements, 1990. Bd. dirs. Owen Coon Found., Glenview, Ill., 1985—, Jewish Fedn. Met. Chgo., Jewish United Fund, 1994—2003, Spertus Inst. Jewish Studies, Chgo., 1991—, chmn. bd., 1999—2002. Fellow Am. Coll. Trust and Estate Coun., Am. Bar Found.; mem. Standard Club, Arts Club (Chgo.). Home: 365 Lakeside Pl Highland Park IL 60035-5371 Office: McDermott Will & Emery LLP 227 W Monroe St Ste 4700 Chicago IL 60606-5096 Office Phone: 312-984-7614. Business E-Mail: fnitikman@mwe.com.

**NITOWSKY, HAROLD MARTIN,** physician, educator; b. Bklyn., Feb. 12, 1925; s. Max and Fannie (Gershowitz) N.; m. Myra Heller, Nov. 28, 1954; children— Fran Ellen, Daniel Howard. AB, N.Y. U., 1944, MD, 1947; MS, U. Colo., 1952. Intern Mt. Sinai Hosp., N.Y.C., 1947-48; resident pediats. U. Colo. Med. Center, 1948-50; USPHS postdoctoral fellow U. Colo., 1950-51; staff Sinai Hosp., Balt., 1953-67, dir. pediat. rsch., 1960-67; faculty Johns Hopkins Sch. Medicine, 1953-67, assoc. prof. ob-gyn., pediats., molecular genetics, 1962-67; prof. pediats. and genetics Albert Einstein Coll. Medicine, 1967—. Cons. Nat. Inst. Child Health and Human Devel., 1966—; Sr. surgeon USPHS, 1951-53 Contbr. articles on nutrition, metabolism, genetics to profl. jours. Mem. Am. Pediat. Soc., Soc. Pediat. Rsch., Am. Soc. Human Genetics. Home: 25 Devonshire Rd New Rochelle NY 10804-3925 Office: Albert Einstein Coll Med Dept Ob-Gyn Divsn Reproductive Genetics 1695 Eastchester Rd Bronx NY 10461-2374 Personal E-Mail: nidoc@aol.com.

**NITSCHKE-SHAW, DEBRA ANN,** education educator, dean; d. Edward John and Mary Elizabeth Nitschke; m. Edward Houghton Shaw II, Aug. 9, 1975; children: Nathaniel Houghton Shaw, Lindsay Ludlow Shaw. BA, New England Coll., Henniker, NH, 1975; MEd, Keene State Coll., Keene, NH, 1977; PhD, Fielding Univ., Santa Barbara, Calif., 1997. Special edn. tchr. Dame Sch., Concord, NH, 1975—81, kindergarten tchr., 1981—98, Henniker Cmty. Sch., 1983—85; dir. tchr. edn. New Eng. Coll., 1985—. Tchr. cons. Campus Compact NH, 1996—; adv. bd. mental health Henniker Br. Concord NH; sch. bd. mem., chair Henniker Sch. Bd., 1987—93. Author: The Partnership Development Tool Kit, 1998; contbr. chapters to books. Sch. bd. mem. Henniker Sch. Dist., 1987—93, sch. bd. chair, 1991—93. Recipient Tchr. of the Yr., New Eng. Coll., 1999, Henniker Sch. Dist., 1984. Mem.: CEC, ASCD. Office: New Eng Coll Box 22 Ctr Ednl Henniker NH 03242

**NITTOLY, PAUL GERARD,** lawyer; b. Bklyn., July 13, 1948; s. Edward Joseph and Philomena (Lorenzo) Nittoly; m. Maryann Racioppi, May 31, 1970; children: Melissa Beth, Matthew Edward. AB, Rutgers U., 1970; JD, NYLS, 1973. Bar: N.J., U.S. Dist. Ct. NJ 1973, U.S. Supreme Ct. 1979, U.S. Ct. Appeals (3d cir.) 1990, U.S. Dist. Ct. (so. and ea. dist.) NY 1998, cert.: NJ Supreme Ct. (trial atty. civil and criminal law). Asst. prosecutor, sr. trial atty. Essex County Prosecutor's Office, Newark, 1974-79; ptnr. Shanley & Fisher, P.C., Morristown, NJ, 1979-99, Drinker Biddle & Shanley LLP, Florham Park, NJ, 1999—2003, Drinker Biddle & Reath, LLP, Florham Park, 2003—. Moot trial ct. judge Seton Hall Law Sch., Newark, 1982—; lectr. symposium perinatal malpractice ACOG and Rutgers U. Med. Sch., Morristown, NJ, 1984; mem. practitioner's adv. group U.S. Sentencing Commn., 1992—2002. Author: Readings in White Collar Crime, 1991; mem. editl. adv. bd. Corporate Criminal Liability Reporter; contbr. chapters to books. Pres. C. Willard Heckel Am. Inn. of Ct., 1995—97, master; del. adv. Am. Bd. Trial Advs.; v.p. Legal Svcs. Found. Essex County. Capt. U.S. Army, 1972. Mem.: ABA, Assn. Fed. Bar State N.J. (trustee 2000—), Trial Attys. N.J. (pres. 2005—06), Assn. Criminal Def. Attys. N.J., Nat. Assn. Criminal Def. Lawyers, Morris County Bar Assn., Essex County Bar Assn. (pres. 1998—99, Samuel S. Saiber Profl. Achievement award 2005), N.J. Bar Assn., Park Ave. Club (Morristown), Delta Upsilon. Roman Catholic. Home: 275 Meetinghouse Ln Mountainside NJ 07092-1305 Office: Drinker Biddle & Reath LLP 500 Campus Dr Fl 4 Florham Park NJ 07932-1047 Office Phone: 973-549-7180. Business E-Mail: paul.nittoly@dbr.com.

**NITZARIM, YOEL DAVID,** language educator; b. Chgo., Aug. 29, 1949; s. Maurice and Elaine Pearl Smith; m. Esther Marsha Nitzarim; children: Rachel Sarah, Gavriella Leebah. BA, Northeastern Ill. U., Chgo., 1974; MEd, Northeastern Ill. U., 1983. Cert. secondary edn. in English Ill. ESL tchr. Kibbutz Newe Eitan Regional HS, Israel, 1976—77, Kibbutz Maoz Haim Elem. Sch., Israel, 1976—77, Morton Jr. Coll., Cicero, Ill., 1988; ESL tchr. Soviet refugees Human Coll./ The Jewish Vocat. Svc. Temple Menorah, Chgo., 1989, 1991—92; ESL instr. Rogosin HS, Migdal Ha'Emeq, Israel, 1978—79, ORT Israel Vocat. HS, Osefia, Israel, 1978—79; adult English seminar tchr. Cultural Ctr. Kfar Tabor, Israel, 1978—79; prep. seminar course biology Oranim Coll., Tivon, Israel, 1979; Hebrew and Jewish social studies tchr. Jewish Reconstructionist Congregation, Evanston, Ill., 1982—83; Jewish social studies tchr. B'nai Tikvah, Deerfield, Ill., 1982—83; English tchr. Aquinas Cath. HS, Chgo., 1980—82, St. Benedict HS, Chgo., 1984—86, Austin Career Edn. Ctr., Chgo., 1989—92; writing tchr. Columbia Coll., Chgo., 1988; asst. prof. English East-West U., Chgo., 1999—2002; instr. English Benedictine U., Lisle, Ill., 2002—03; instr. English composition Coll. Lake County, Grayslake, Ill., 2005—, instr. English, 2005—. Author: (essays, poetry, photography, short stories) Affair of the Mind; contbr. articles to profl. jours. Founding mem. Nat. Campaign for Tolerance, a project of the So. Poverty Law Ctr., 2005—. Mem.: English Teachers Assn. of Israel. Jewish. Avocations: reading, writing, music, travel, dogs. Personal E-mail: Ynitzari1@aol.com.

**NITZE, WILLIAM ALBERT,** government official, lawyer, not-for-profit developer, energy executive; b. NYC, Sept. 27, 1942; s. Paul Henry and Phyllis (Pratt) N.; m. Ann Kendall Richards, June 5, 1971; children: Paul Kendall, Charles Richards. BA, Harvard U., 1964, JD, 1969; BA, Oxford U., 1966. Bar: N.Y. 1970, U.S. Supreme Ct. 1987. Assoc. Sullivan and Cromwell, N.Y.C., 1970-72; v.p. London Arts, Inc., N.Y.C., 1972-73; counsel Mobil South Inc., N.Y.C., 1974-76; gen. counsel Mobil Oil Japan, Tokyo, 1976-80; asst. gen. counsel exploration and producing divsn. Mobil Oil Corp., N.Y.C., 1980-87; dep asst. sec. for environment, health and natural resources U.S. Dept. State, Washington, 1987-90; pres. Alliance to Save Energy, Washington, 1990-94, Gemstar Group, Washington, 2001—05; asst. adminstr. for internat. activities U.S. EPA, Washington, 1994-2001; chmn. GridPoint, Inc., Washington, 2003—; with HiEnergy Techs., Irvine, Calif., 2006—, Oceana Energy Co., Washington, 2006—. Chmn. Hi Energy Tech., Inc., Irvine, Calif., 2006—, Oceana Energy Co., Washington, 2006—; mem. adv. com. Sch. Advanced Internat. Studies, Washington, 1982-95, professorial lectr., 1993-94, 2001—; vis. scholar Environ. Law Inst., Washington, 1990; bd. dirs. Charles A. Lindbergh Fund, Mpls., 1990-94, Nat. Symphony Orch. Assn., Washington, 1990-2002, Atlantic Coun. U.S., Washington, 2002—; bd. dirs. Charles Darwin Found., Inc., 2001—, Falls Church, Va., vice chmn. 2002-03, chmn. 2003-; bd. dirs. Climate Inst., Washington, 2001-, vice chmn., 2001-02, chmn. 2003-; Trustee Aspen Inst., Queenstown, Md., 1988—, Krasnow Inst., Fairfax, Va., 1996-2001. Mem.: Coun. on Fgn. Relns., Aspen Bar City NY, Links Club, Cosmos Club, Met. Club. Republican. Episcopalian. Avocations: running, piano, collecting art. Home: 1537 28th St NW Washington DC 20007-3059 Office: Ste 100 1785 Mass Ave NW Washington DC 20036 Office Phone: 202-331-2485. Business E-Mail: wnitze@gridpoint.com.

**NITZKI-GEORGE, DIANE M.,** pharmacist, medical writer; d. Rosemary F. and Edward H. Nitzki; m. Gerald J. George, May 22, 1982; 1 child. Michael L. George. B in Chemistry, No. Ill. U., 1976; B in Pharmacy, Creighton U., 1980; MBA, Keller Grad. Sch., 1992. Registered pharmacist Nebr., 1980, Ill., 1982. Staff pharmacist Bishop Clarkson Meml. Hosp., Omaha 1980—82, Luth. Gen. Hosp.; Park Ridge, Ill., 1982—87; inpatient pharmacy mgr. U.S. Naval Hosp., Great Lakes, Ill., 1987—89; pharmacy mgr. Parkside Luth. Hosp., Park Ridge, Ill., 1989; clin. info. mgr. Baxter Healthcare Corp., Deerfield, Ill., 1990—2002; med. writer DNG Consulting, Deerfield, Ill., 2002—; clin. pharmacist Evanston Hosp.

Home Infusion Svc., Evanston, Ill., 2003—. Author: Generic Alternatives to Prescription Drugs, Extended Stability for Parenteral Drugs, 3d edit. Vol. webmaster Holy Cross Sch. & Ch., Deerfield, Ill., 1999—; vol. middle sch. sci. fair judge, 1999—2003, 2005—; active Highland Park Music Club, 2003—. Recipient Achievement award, Baxter Healthcare Corp., 1991—97, Svc. award, Rho Chi Honor Soc., 1980, Pres.'s award for Sci. Achievement, Arnar-Stone Labs., 1978, others. Mem.: Am. Soc. Health-Sys. Pharmacist, Am. Med. Writers Assn. Achievements include worked closely with FDA to import an injectable multivitamin drug to the U.S. during a period of national shortage in which patients were at risk of injury (1997). Avocation: singing. Office: DNG Consulting 401 Locust Place Deerfield IL 60015 E-mail: dngconsulting@comcast.net.

**NIVARTHI, RAJU NAGA,** anesthesiology educator; b. Nandyal, India, June 16, 1964; came to U.S., 1993; s. Kameswara Sarma and Suseelamma Nivarthi; m. Aparna Nagaraju Nivarthi; children: Nidhi, Aditya. BSc with Chemistry, Zoology and Botany, Sri Venkateswara U., Tirupati, India, 1984; MSc in Biochemistry, Sri Kirshnadevaraya U., Anantapur, India, 1986; PhD, U. Hyderabad, 1996. Fellow Sch. Life Scis., U. Hyderabad, India, 1987-93; rsch. asst. prof. dept. anesthesiology NYU Med. Ctr., NYC, 1996, scientist, 1996-99, Wyeth-Ayerst Rsch., Pearl River, NY, 1999-2001; sr. scientist, mgr. analytical biochemistry Bristol-Myers Squibb, Syracuse, NY, 2001—05, mgr. immunology and molecular biology, biologics quality control, 2005—. Contbr. articles to profl. jours. Jr. Rsch. fellow Coun. Sci. and Indsl. Rsch., India, 1987, Sr. Rsch. fellow Coun. Sci. and Indsl. Rsch., 1990, Postdoctoral fellow NIH, 1998; recipient cert. of merit Pharmacia & Biotech Prize for Young Scientists, 1997, named 2000 Outstanding Scientist of 20th Century, 1998, Internat. Biographical Ctr. Mem. AAAS, Acad. Med. Cmty., Am. Chem. Soc., Am. Soc. Anesthesiologists, Am. Soc. Biochemistry and Molecular Biology, Internat. Anesthesia Rsch. Soc., Internat. Soc. for Study of Xenobiotics, Nat. Geographic Soc., N.Y. Acad. Scis. Office: Bristol-Myer Squibb 6000 Thompson Rd East Syracuse NY 13057-5050 Home: 161 North Way Camillus NY 13031-1253 Office Phone: 315-432-9612. Personal E-mail: rnivarthi@yahoo.com.

**NIVEN, JAMES GRAHAM,** auctioneer, art appreciator, philanthropist; b. Hollywood, Calif., 1945; s. David and Primula (Rollo) Niven; m. Fernanda Wetherill (div. 1995); children: Eugenie, Fernanda; m. Lee Auchincloss, Oct. 22, 2005. BA, Harvard Coll. Gen. ptnr. Pioneer Associates Co., 1982—98; chmn. bd. Global Natural Resources, 1989—94; auctioneer Sotheby's (North & South Am.) Holdings, Inc., NYC, 1997—, sr. v.p., dir. bus. devel., 1997—2000, vice chmn, 2000—. Trustee MoMA, NYC, 1988—, chmn. trustee com. on film and media; trustee Ralph Lauren Ctr. Cancer Care & Prevention, NYC, Nat. Ctr. for Learning Disabilities, Inc.; founding mem., spl. projects com. Meml. Sloan-Kettering Cancer Ctr., NYC, overseer & mgr., 1978—; bd. dir. Lynton Group, Inc., co-chmn. bd. dirs., 1994—97; bd. dir. Noel Group, Inc., Prospect Group, Inc., Lincoln Snacks Co., Tatham Offshore, Inc., HealthPlan Services, CBT Bancshares, Inc.; adv. dir. Houston Nat. Bank. Luncheon co-chmn. United Hosp. Fund Honors, 2006. Recipient Award for Excellence in Philanthropy, Soc. Meml. Sloan-Kettering Cancer Ctr., 2005. Office: Sothebys 1334 York Ave New York NY 10021 also: Mus Modern Art 11 W 53rd St New York NY 10019 Office Phone: 541-312-5682. Office Fax: 541-312-5684.*

**NIVISON, DAVID SHEPHERD,** language educator, philosopher; b. Farmingdale, Maine, Jan. 17, 1923; s. William and Ruth (Robinson) N.; m. Cornelia Green, Sept. 11, 1944; children— Louise, Helen Thom, David Gregory, James Nicholas. AB summa cum laude, Harvard U., 1946, MA, 1948, PhD, 1953. Instr. Chinese Stanford U., 1948-52, Ford Found. faculty fellow, 1952-53, instr. Chinese and philosophy, 1953-54; Fulbright research scholar Kyoto, Japan, 1954-55; lectr. philosophy Stanford U., 1955-58, asst. prof. Chinese and philosophy, 1958-59, assoc. prof., 1959-66, prof., 1966-88, Walter Y. Evans-Wentz prof. Oriental Philosophies, Religions and Ethics, 1983-88, chmn. dept. philosophy, 1969-72, 75-76, acting chmn. dept. Asian langs., 1985-86, emeritus, 1988—. Author: The Life and Thought of Chang Hsüeh-ch'eng, 1738-1801, 1966, The Ways of Confucianism: Investigations in Chinese Philosophy, 1996; co-author: Chinese Language, Thought and Culture: Nivison and His Critics, 1996; editor, co-compiler: Stanford Chinese Concordance Series, 1979; co-editor: Confucianism in Action, 1959, Studies on the Modern Text of the Bamboo Annals (in Chinese), 2002; contbr. articles to profl. jours. and encys. Served with AUS, 1943-46. Recipient Prix Stanislas-Julien Inst. de France, 1967; Am. Council Learned Socs. fellow, 1973; John Simon Guggenheim fellow, 1973-74 Mem. Assn. Asian Studies, Am. Philos. Assn. (v.p. Pacific div. 1978-79, pres. 1979-80), Am. Oriental Soc. (Western br. v.p. 1964-65, sec. 1965-70, pres. 1971-72), AAUP (pres. No. Calif. Conf. 1964-66), Internat. Acad. Chinese Culture (Beijing, Peoples Republic of China), Phi Beta Kappa. Home: 1169 Russell Ave Los Altos CA 94024-5066 Business E-Mail: dnivison@stanford.edu.

**NIX, EDMUND ALFRED,** lawyer; b. Eau Claire, Wis., May 24, 1929; s. Sebastian and Kathryn (Keirnan) N.; m. Mary Kathryn Nagle Daley, Apr. 27, 1968; children: Kim, Mary Kay, Norbert, Edmund Alfred, Michael. BS, Wis. State U., 1951; LL.B., U. Wis., 1954, postgrad. in speech, 1956-57. Bar: Wis. 1954. Practice in, Eau Claire, 1954-65; dist. atty. Eau Claire County, 1958-64; U.S. atty. Western Dist. Wis., Eau Claire, 1965-69, U.S. magistrate, 1969-70; dist. atty. La Crosse County, Wis., 1975-77; mcpl. judge City of La Crosse, 1992—. Co-chmn. United Fund, Eau Claire, 1958; Pres. Young Democrats Wis., 1951-53; mem. adminstrv. bd. Wis. Dem. party, 1953-54; chmn. 10th Congl. dist., 1965; sec. Kennedy for Pres. Club Wis., 1959-60. Served with AUS, 1954-56. Mem. Fed. Bar Assn., Wis. Bar Assn. (state chmn. crime prevention and control com.), La Crosse County Bar Assn. (pres.), Nat. Dist. Attys. Assn., KC. Roman Catholic. Office: 123 4th St N La Crosse WI 54601-3235 E-mail: nixe@ffax.net.

**NIX, JAMES RAYFORD,** nuclear physicist, consultant; b. Natchitoches, La., Feb. 18, 1938; s. Joe Ebbin and Edna (Guin) N.; m. Sally Ann Wood, Aug. 19, 1961; children: Patricia Lynne, David Allen. BS in Physics, Carnegie Inst. Tech., 1960; PhD in Physics, U. Calif., Berkeley, 1964. Summer physicist Lawrence Livermore (Calif.) Nat. Lab., 1961; rsch. asst. Lawrence Berkeley Lab., 1961-64, postdoctoral physicist, 1966-68; NATO postdoctoral fellow Niels Bohr Inst., Copenhagen, 1964-65; mem. staff Los Alamos (N.Mex.) Nat. Lab., 1968-77, 89-94, group leader, 1977-89, fellow, 1994-98, sci. cons., 1998—. Vis. prof. Centro Brasileiro de Pesquisas Fisicas, Rio de Janeiro, 1974; cons. Calif. Inst. Tech., Pasadena, 1976, 79; chmn. Gordon Research Conf. Nuclear Chemistry, New London, NH, 1976; chmn. physics divsn. adv. com. Oak Ridge (Tenn.) Nat. Lab., 1976, 97; chmn. nuc. sci. divsn. vis. com. Lawrence Berkeley Lab., 1980-82. Contbr. articles to numerous publs. Recipient Alexander von Humboldt Sr. U.S. Scientist award, Univ. Munich and Max-Planck Inst. for Nuc. Physics, 1980—81; fellow, Phi Kappa Phi, Berkeley, 1960—61; scholar, Alfred P. Sloan Found., Pitts., 1956—60. Fellow: Am. Phys. Soc. (exec. com. 1973—75); mem.: AAAS, Phi Kappa Phi, Sigma Xi. Democrat. Home and Office: 12 Los Pueblos Los Alamos NM 87544-2659 Personal E-mail: j_r_nix@hotmail.com.

**NIX, KEMIE RICHARDS,** educational association administrator, editor; b. Atlanta, Dec. 10, 1938; d. James McDowell and Evelyn Knight Richards; m. John Arthur Nix, July 22, 1961; children: Mary Evelyn Nix Hollowell, John Arthur Jr. EdB, Emory U., 1960, EdM, 1970. Tchr. Westminster Schs., Atlanta, 1961—87; founder, dir. Children's Lit. for Children, Atlanta, 1986—2002, Reader-to-Reader, Atlanta, 1986—2002; co-founder, co-dir. Reader-to-Patient, Atlanta, 1990—2000; co-founder Biblioteca Juvenil de Mayaguez, PR, 1991—2001; dir. Reader-to-Reader:Africa, Atlanta, 1990—2006. Children's book editor Atlanta Jour./Constn., 1976—91, Parents' Choice, 1995—2006. Bd. dirs. United Bd. of Books for Young People, Wilmington, Del., 1996—98, Children's Lit for Children, Atlanta, 1996—2006, Mt. Kenya Acad., Nyeri, Kenya, 2002—06. Named to Coca-Cola Centennial Olympic Wall, Atlanta, 1996, Kemie Nix Libr. named in her honor, Primary Sch., Nyeri, 1992, Mt. Kenya Acad., Nyeri, 2001. Mem.: ALA (Newbery com. 1994, Notable Books com. 1998—99, Newbery com. 2002, Caldecott com. 2006), Internat. Reading Assn. Democrat. Presbyterian. Avocations: birdwatching, animals, reading. Home and Office: Reader-to-Reader: Africa 104 Madison Ave Peachtree City GA 30269 Office Phone: 770-487-4420. Fax: 770-487-4154.

**NIX, LINDA ANNE BEAN,** public relations executive; b. Sept. 20, 1943; d. Norman Arthur and Gladys Mae (Charlton) Bean, Jr.; m. Henry Taylor Betts, Jr., Sept. 5, 1964 (div. 1970); m. John Asa Nix, Nov. 24, 1971 (div. 1990). Student, Syracuse U., 1961-64; BA, Scarritt Coll., 1965; postgrad., Middle Tenn. State U., 9171-73. Mobile coord. Children's Mus., Nashville, 1966-67; promotion dir. Sta. WDCN-TV/8, Nashville, 1969-82; dir. pub. info. Sta. WYES-TV/12, New Orleans, 1982—; mktg. dir. Sta. KOFY-TV Radio San Francisco, 1989-91, Sta. KUSI-TV, San Diego, 1992-93; self-employed in pub. rels., 1992—. Mem. pub. info. adv. com. Pub. Broadcasting Service, Washington, 1977-80, chmn. 1979-80, mem. festival task force, 1979-80. Author, editor: (tchr. workbook) Yellow Submarine, 1968; contbr. Great Chefs, 2001—; contbr. articles to profl. jours. Bd. dirs. Nashville League for Hearing Impaired, 1973-76, Tennessee Williams/New Orleans Literacy Festival, 1995--; chmn. membership com. Coun. Cmty. Svcs., Nashville, 1978-80; mem. allocation panel United Way Greater Nashville, 1979-81, United Way Greater New Orleans, 1982-86. Mem. Pub. Rels. Soc. Am. (chmn. accreditation com. 1985, pres. New Orleans chpt. 1988), Broadcast Promotion and Mktg. Execs., Inc. (Promax) (bd. dirs. 1982-91, pres. 1989-90). Avocations: flying, sewing. Home and Office: PO Box 7068 Metairie LA 70010-7068 Office Phone: 504-581-5000. E-mail: lagator@mindspring.com.

**NIX, PATRICIA,** artist; d. Nobe Astin Briggs and Lela Mae (Lucas) Rockstrom; m. (dec.); children: Pandora Nix Shaw, William Riley Jr., John Houston. BA, NYU, 1982. One-woman shows include Tower Gallery, Southampton, N.Y., 1978—82, 1985, NYU, 1980, Sutton Gallery, N.Y.C., 1982—83, Baumgartner Gallery, Washington, 1984, S.I. (N.Y.) Mus., 1986, Andre Zarre Gallery, N.Y.C., 1987, S.I. (N.Y.) Mus., 1988, Nerlino Gallery, N.Y.C., 1988, Andre Zarre Gallery, 1991, U. Windsor (Ont., Can.) Mus., Griffin McGear Modern Gallery, N.Y.C., 1989, San Angelo (Tex.) Mus. of Art, 1991, Hurlbutt Gallery, Greenwich, Conn., 1990, Galerie Donguy, Paris, 1994, Dillon Gallery, N.Y.C., 1994—98, numerous group shows including most recently, exhibited in group shows at Merill Chase Galleries, Chgo., 1999, Am. Embassy, Rome, Italy, 1999, Hilligoss Galleries, 2000—03, Tex. Tech. Mus., Lubbock, 2000; represented in numerous permanent collections, designer sets and costumes (ballets) Petrushka, Pulcinella, Jeu de Cartes, 2002, Totem Altar, Saint Peters Ch., N.Y.C., 2004, Gallerie Mary Claude Goinnard, Paris, France, 2005, Totem Altar, St. John the Devine Cathedral., N.Y.C., 2005, Mary Claude Goinnard, Paris, France, 2005. Office Phone: 212-686-3512.

**NIXON, ARLIE JAMES,** gas and oil company executive; b. Ralston, Okla., May 22, 1914; s. James Gordon and Wella May (Platt) N.; m. Wylie Elizabeth Jones, Apr. 21, 1939 (div May 1950); children: Cole Jay, Kathleen (Mrs. S. Brent Joyce); m. Lisa Marie Grant, Dec. 7, 1981 (div. June 1989). BS, Okla. State U., 1935. Airline capt. Trans World Airlines, N.Y.C., 1939-74; pres. Crystal Gas Co., Jennings, Okla., 1960—, Blackburn Gas Co., Jennings, 1964—, Blackberry Oil Co., Jennings, 1969—. Represented U.S. in several ofcl. dels. to internat. aviation tech. meetings, also represented Internat. Fedn. Air Line Pilots Assns. at internat. confs. Lt. (j.g.) USNR, 1935-63. Mem. Internat. Fedn. Air Line Pilots Assn. (congress v.p 1972), Internat. Platform Assn., Wings Club. Democrat. Office: PO Box 68 Jennings OK 74038-0068 Office Phone: 918-454-2241.

**NIXON, CHARLES WILLIAM,** acoustician; b. Wellsburg, W.Va., Aug. 15, 1929; s. William E. and Lenora S. (Treiber) Nixon; m. Barbara Irene Hunter, May 19, 1956; children: Timothy C., Tracy Scott. BS, Ohio State U., 1952, MS, 1953, PhD, 1960. Tchr. spl. edn. Ohio and W.Va. Pub. Schs., Wheeling, 1954—56; rsch. audiologist Aeromed Lab., Wright Patterson AFB, Ohio, 1956—67; supervisory rsch. audiologist Armstrong Lab., Wright Patterson AFB, 1967—96, Veridian, Dayton, 1996—2004. Chair W4 Am. Nat. Stds. Inst., N.Y.C., 1968—96; U.S. rep. hearing protection Internat. Stds. Orgn., Geneva, 1968—96; USAF rep. NRC-NAS Hearing Com., Washington, 1976—94; chair robotics panel Joint Dirs. Labs., Washington, 1987—88. Author: reports and book chpts. Cpl. U.S. Army, 1953—55. Recipient Meritorious Svc. medal, U.S. Dept. Def., Dayton, Ohio, 1986, Outstanding Civilian Svc. award, 1996. Fellow: Acoustical Soc. Am.; mem.: Rsch. Soc. Am. Achievements include research in noise exposure, voice communications, hearing protection, sonic boom, active noise reduction, 3-D audio displays, others. Home: 4316 Sillman Pl Dayton OH 45440-1141 E-mail: cwnixon@woh.rr.com.

**NIXON, CYNTHIA,** actress; b. NYC, Apr. 9, 1966; d. Walter and Anne Nixon; children: Samantha Mozes, Charles Ezekiel Mozes. BA in English, Barnard Coll., 1988. Founding member The Drama Dept., 1996. Actor: (plays) The Philadelphia Story, 1980 (Theatre World Award, 1981), Indiscretions, 1996 (Tony Award nom., 1996, Tony award, best performance by leading actress in a play, 2006), Rabbit Hole, 2006, The Prime of Miss Jean Brodie, 2006; (films) Little Darlings, 1980, Prince of the City, 1981, Tattoo, 1981, I Am the Cheese, 1983, Amadeus, 1984, The Manhattan Project, 1986, O.C. and Stiggs, 1987, Let It Ride, 1989, Through an Open Window, 1992, The Pelican Brief, 1993, Addams Family Values, 1993, Baby's Day Out, 1994, The Cottonwood, 1996, 'M' Word, 1996, Marvin's Room, 1996, Advice From a Caterpillar, 1999, The Out-of-Towners, 1999, Igby Goes Down, 2002, The Paper Mache Chase, 2003; (TV series) Sex and the City, 1998—2004 (Emmy nom. for Outstanding Supporting Actress in a comedy series, 2002, Emmy award Outstanding Supporting Actress in a Comedy Series, 2004); (TV miniseries) Tanner '88, 1988; (TV films) The Seven Wishes of a Rich Kid, 1979, The Private History of a Campaign That Failed, 1981, Rascals and Robbers, The Secret Adventures of Tom Sawyer and Huck Finn, 1982, My Body, My Child, 1982, Fifth of July, 1982, The Murder of Mary Phagan, 1988, Women & Wallace, 1990, Love She Sought, The, 1990, Face of a Stranger, 1991, Love, Lies and Murder, 1991, Kiss-Kiss, Dahlings!, 1992, Sex and the Matrix, 2000, Papa's Angels, 2000, Stage on Screen: The Women, 2002, Tanner on Tanner, 2004, Warm Springs, 2005. Office: William Morris Agency One William Morris Place Beverly Hills CA 90212*

**NIXON, DANIEL WALKER,** oncologist, researcher; b. Brunswick, Ga., Sept. 8, 1943; s. Marvin Elesberry and Mildred Anita (Whitehead) N.; m. Sandra Gayle Brakefield, July 18, 1970; children: William B., Marvin A. BS, U. Ga., 1965, MD, 1969. Diplomate Am. Bd. Internal Medicine, Am. Bd. Med. Oncology; lic. physician S.C., N.Y. Asst. prof. Med. Coll. Ga., Augusta, 1973-75; from assoc. prof. to prof. Emory U., Atlanta, 1975-87; assoc. dir. divsn. cancer prevention and control, Nat. Cancer Inst. NIH, Bethesda, Md., 1987-89; v.p., prof. edn. Am. Cancer Soc., Atlanta, 1989-94; Folk prof., assoc. dir. prevention and control Hollings Cancer Ctr., Med. U. S.C., Charleston, 1994—99; pres. Inst. Cancer Prevention, N.Y.C., 1999—2004. Mem. sci. bd. Cancer Treatment Rsch. Found. Author: Cancer Recovery Eating Plan, 1994; editor: Cancer Chemoprevention, 1994; editor-in-chief Preventive Medicine, 1999—2004; contbr. more than 100 articles to med. jours. Capt. USNR. Recipient several found. awards; grantee NIH, 1975–2004. Mem. Nutrition Oncology Adjuvant Therapy Soc. (pres. 1996), Army and Navy Club, Druid Hills Country Club. Achievements include research in cancer prevention and nutrition; chemoprevention and cancer metabolism. Office Phone: 843-577-6957. Personal E-mail: dnixonan@aol.com.

**NIXON, DAVID,** dancer; b. Windsor, Ont., Can. Student, The Nat. Ballet Sch. Dancer Nat. Ballet Can., 1978—82, 1st soloist, 1982—84; prin. dancer Deutsche Opera Ballet, Berlin, 1985—90, Komische OperaBallet, Berlin, 1991—93; artistic dir. Ballet met., Columbus, Ohio, 1995—2001, No. Ballet Theatre, England, 2001—. Various guest appearance including Munich Ballet, 1990-91, Staatsoper, Berlin, 1990, Birmingham Royal Ballet, 1990-93. Dancer Bayernhaus Staatsoper Munich, 1990—91, Alexander Godunov and Stars, 1982, Milw. Ballet, 1984, Sydney Ballet Australia, 1984, World Ballet Festival Tokyo, 1985, 1988, Hamburg Ballet, 1988, 1989, Staatsoper Berlin, 1988—91, Bayerisches Staatsballet, 1988—90, Komische

Opera Berlin, 1990—93; prodr.: David Nixon's Dance Theatre, Hebbel Theatre Berlin, 1990, 1991; choreographer Butterfly, 1983, La Follia, 1984, Dangerous Liaisons, 1990, 1996, African Fantasy, 1990, Celebrate Mozart, 1991, Sudden Impulse, 1994, A Summer's Nights Reflections, 1995, Full-Length Nutcracker, 1995, Butterfly, 1996, Beauty and the Beast, 1997, Carmen, 1997, Romeo and Juliet, 1998, Swan Lake, 1998, Dracula, 1999, A Midsummer Nights Dream, 2000—03, A Celebration of Dance with Music by Gershwin, 2001, Wuthering Heights, 2002, Peter Pan, 2004, Undine, 2006. Recipient Ollivier award, 2005. Office: Northern Ballet Theatre West Park Centre Spen Ln Leeds LS16 5BE England

**NIXON, EUGENE RAY,** chemist, educator; b. Mt. Pleasant, Mich., Apr. 14, 1919; s. William S. and Grace (Brookens) N.; m. Phyllis R. Jones, June 10, 1945; children — Cynthia L., Emily E. Sc.B. summa cum laude, Alma Coll., 1941; PhD, Brown U., 1947. Research chemist Manhattan Project, 1942-46; instr. chemistry Brown U., 1947-49; mem. faculty U. Pa., Phila., 1949-85, prof. chemistry, 1965-85, vice dean grad. sch., 1958-62, acting chmn. dept. chemistry, 1965-66, dir. materials research lab., 1969-72, prof. emeritus, 1985—. Vis. prof. U. London, 1963-64; vis. lectr. Bryn Mawr Coll., 1957-58 Mem. Am. Chem. Soc., Am. Phys. Soc., Soc. Applied Spectroscopy (Jour. award 1965, Spectroscopist of Yr. award Del. Valley sect. 1988), Coblentz Soc. (bd. mgrs.), Sigma Xi. Research, publs. on phys. chemistry, molecular structure and molecular spectroscopy, properties of crystals, intermolecular interactions, laser spectroscopy and laser chemistry. Home: 35 Julio Dr Apt 106 Shrewsbury MA 01545-3049

**NIXON, JEREMIAH W. (JAY NIXON),** state attorney general; b. DeSoto, Mo., Feb. 13, 1956; s. Jeremiah and Betty (Lea) Nixon; m. Georganne Nixon; children: Jeremiah, Will. BS in Polit. Sci., U. Mo., 1978, JD, 1981. Ptnr. Nixon, Nixon, Breeze & Roberts, Jefferson County, Mo., 1981—86; mem. Mo. State Senate from Dist 22, 1986—93; atty. gen. State of Mo., 1993—. Chmn. select com. ins. reform; creator video internat. devel. and edn. opportunity program. Named Outstanding Young Missourian, Jaycees, 1994, Outstanding Young Lawyer, Barrister's Mag., 1993; recipient Conservation Fedn. Mo award, 1992. Mem.: Mo. Assn. Trial Attys., Midwest Assn. Attys. Gen., Nat. Assn. Attys. Gen. Democrat. Methodist. Office: Office of Atty General Supreme Ct Bldg 207 W High St Jefferson City MO 65101*

**NIXON, JUDITH MAY,** librarian; b. Gary, Ind., June 14, 1945; d. Louis Robert Sr. and Mable Sophia (Reiner) Vician; m. Cleon Robert Nixon III, Aug. 20, 1967; 1 child, Elizabeth Marie. BS in Edn., Valparaiso U., 1967; MA in LS, U. Iowa, 1971. Tchr. U.S. Peace Corps, Tonga, 1968—69; popular books libr. Lincoln Libr., Springfield, Ill., 1971—73; ref. libr. Cedar Rapids (Iowa) Pub. Libr., 1974—76; ref.coord. U. Wis., Platteville, 1976—82; bus. libr. U. Ariz., Tucson, 1982—84; consumer and family sci. libr. Purdue U., West Lafayette, La., 1984—93, Krannert mgmt. and econs. libr., 1993—2005, humanities, social sci. and edn. head libr., 2005—. Editor: Industry and Company Information, 1991, Organization Charts, 1992, 2d edit., 1996, Hotel and Restaurant Industries, 1993; editor quar. serial Lodging and Restaurant Index, 1985-93. Leader Girl Scouts U.S., Lafayette, 1985—. Recipient John H. Moriarty award Purdue U. Librs., 1989. Mem. ALA (chairperson bus. reference and svcs. sect. 1995-96, GALE Rsch. award for excellence in bus. librarianship 1994). Home: 2375 N 23rd St Lafayette IN 47904-1242 Office: Purdue U Libraries Humanities Social Sci Edn Libr 504 W State St West Lafayette IN 47907-2058 Office Phone: 765-494-2927. Business E-Mail: jnixon@purdue.edu.

**NIXON, MARNI,** singer; b. Altadena, Calif., Feb. 22, 1930; d. Charles and Margaret (Wittke) McEathron; m. Ernest Gold, May 22, 1950 (div. 1969); m. Lajos Frederick Fenster, July 23, 1971 (div July 1975); m. Albert David Block, Apr. 11, 1983. Student, L.A. City Coll., UCLA, U. So. Calif., Tanglewood, Mass. Dir. vocal faculty Calif. Inst. Arts, Valencia, 1970-72; pvt. tchr., vocal coach, condr. master classes, 1970—; pvt. voice tchr., coach, condr. master classes, 1970—; head apprentice divsn. Santa Barbara Music Acad. of West, 1980; formerly dir. opera workshop Cornish Inst. Arts, Seattle. Tchr. in field; judge Met. Opera Internat. Am. Music Awards, Nat. Inst. Music Theatre, 1984—87; dialect dir., opera recs. Actor: (musicals) Pasadena (Calif.) Playhouse, 1940—45; (films) Sound of Music, 1964, I Think I Do, 1996; (TV series) Boomerang, 1975; (plays) My Fair Lady, 1994, Taking My Turn, 1983, Opal, 1992—94, Cabaret, 1998, Ballymore, 1999, Follies, 2000—01, James Joyce's The Dead, 1999—2001, Nine, 2003; singer (soloist): Roger Wagner chorale, 1947—53; singer: (Operas) New Eng. Opera Co., LA Opera Co., Ford Found. TV Opera, 1948—63, San Francisco Spring Opera, 1966, Seattle Opera, 1971—73, classical recitals and appearances with symphony orchs. throughout U.S., Can., Eng., Israel, Ireland; voice dub: (films) My Fair Lady; The King and I; An Affair to Remember; West Side Story; Disney's Mulan; others; singer: (albums) Columbia, Mus. Heritage Records, Capital, RCA Victor, Ednl. Records, Reference Recs., Varese-Sarabande, Nonesuch; author: I Could Have Sung All Night: My Story. Nominee Drama Desk award, 2 Grammy award, NARAS; recipient 4 Emmy awards for best actress, 2 Action for Childrens TV awards, 1977, Chgo. Film Festival award, 1977, 2 Gold Records for Songs from Mary Poppins and Mulan. Mem.: Nat. Assn. Tchrs. Singing (pres. N.Y. chpt. 1994—97, panelist new music).

**NIXON, PATRICIA SAUNDERS,** music educator, actress; b. Norfolk, Va., Nov. 22, 1955; d. John Edward Saunders and Marie Ewing; m. Jimmie Larry Nixon, July 7, 1979; children: Jimmie Larry Jr.(dec.), Annette Marie. BS in Music Edn., Norfolk State U., 1978, MusM in Vocal Performance, 1988; postgrad. in Vocal Performance, Shenandoah U. Conservatory, 2002—. Music instr. VA Sch. for Deaf, Blind and Multi-Disabled, Hampton, Va., 1978—2000; choral dir. Norview Mid. Sch. Norfolk Pub. Schs., 2000—01; choral dir. Wilson H S Portsmouth (Va.) Pub. Schs. 2001—02; vis al insti Norfolk State U., 2002—; dir. jazz vocal ensemble, 2003—. Choir dir., pianist intermediate choir Ebenezer Bapt. Ch., Portsmouth, 1991—. Photography, D-Day (pub., 2002), Whose in the Drivers Seat Now?, 2003; actor: Porgy and Bess; musician: Va. Symphony Pops, I. Sherman Green Chorale, others; singer: Let My People Go. Mem. Brighton/Prentice Pk. Civic League, Portsmouth, 1998—, Va. and Nat. Minority Caucus, 1990—2002. Recipient Apple for the Tchr. award, Alpha Chi chpt. Iota Phi Lambda Sorority, Inc., 1993, Christian Svc. award, Ebenezer Bapt. Ch. Vacational Bible Sch., 2000—01, 2001 Team Ptnr. Recognition award, U. S. Olympic Com., 2001, We Teach the Children Whole Village award, Va. Edn. Assn., 2001, Outstanding Performance in A Tribute to African Am. Sacred Music award, Parkview United Meth. Ch., 2001, Black Educators' award, Delicados, Inc. Portsmouth Chpt., 1997, A Salute to Black Achievers in the Tidewater Area award, Martin Luther King, Jr. Meml. Ch. Choir, 1996, A Tribute to Excellence award in classical voice category, Area II NAACP ACT-SO Coalition, 2005; grantee VTAG, Shenandoah U., 2002. Mem.: AAUP, NEA (del. 1999—2000), NAACP (A Tribute to Excellence award), Nat. Assn. Teachers and Singing, Am. Choral Directors Assn., Intercolligiate Music Assn., Va. Choral Dirs. Assn., Hampton Edn. Assn. (pres. 1998—2000), Va. Edn. Assn., Portsmouth Edn. Assn. (assoc.), Norfolk Edn. Assn. (assoc.; del. 2000), The Am. Choral Directors Assn. (assoc.), Nat. Assn. of Negro Musicians Tidewater Area Musicians Chpt. (assoc.), Music Educators Nat. Conf. (assoc.), VA Sch. at Hampton Edn. Assn. (assoc.; pres. 1998—2000, del. 1999—2000), Chancel Choir of Ebenezer Bapt. Ch. (assoc.), Va. Opera Guild (assoc.), Alpha Kappa Alpha (co-chmn. music 49th Mid-Atlantic Regional Conf. 2002, Leadership Excel award 2000), Gamma Delta Omega Chpt. of Alpha Kappa Alpha Sorority, Inc. (assoc.; publicity chmn. 1998—99, Cert. of Appreciation 1999). Democrat. Avocations: performing, crafts, photography, computer technology, travel. Home: 1019 Centre Ave Portsmouth VA 23704-7005 Office: Norfolk State U 700 Park Ave Norfolk VA 23504 Personal E-mail: psnixon@aol.com. Business E-Mail: psnixon@nsu.edu.

**NIXON, RALPH ANGUS,** psychiatrist, educator, research neuroscientist; b. Somerville, Mass., Jan. 29, 1947; s. Ralph Angus and Eleanor Nixon; m. Katharine Sangree Faulkner, Aug. 20, 1974; children: Abigail, Rebecca. AB, Brandeis U., 1968; PhD in Cell and Biology, Harvard U., 1974; MD,

U. Vt., 1976. Intern Mass. Gen. Hosp., 1976, Salem Hosp., 1977; resident in psychiatry Mass. Gen. Hosp., 1977-79, McLean Hosp., 1979-80; clin. assoc. in psychiatry Mass. Gen. Hosp., Boston, 1980-97; assoc. in neurosci. Children's Hosp Med. Ctr., Boston, 1982-88; staff physician Rehab. Ctr. for Aged, Boston, 1984-90; asst. prof. psychiatry Harvard Med. Sch., Boston, 1982-86, assoc. prof., 1986-96; assoc. neuropathologist McLean Hosp., Belmont, Mass., 1982-90, assoc. psychiatrist, 1988-93, neuropathologist, 1991; psychiatrist, 1993-97; prof. psychiatry and cell biology NYU Med. Sch., N.Y.C., 1997—, vice chmn. dept. psychiatry, 2001—; dir. rsch. Nathan Kline Inst.-NYU Med. Ctr., Orangeburg, dir. ctr. dementia rsch., 1997—. Mem. sci. rev. com. Am. Fedn. for Aging Rsch., 1990-92; mem. neurosci., behavior and sociology of aging rev. com., subcom. A, Nat. Inst. on Aging, NIH, 1991-95, chmn., 1994-95; dir. labs. for molecular neurosci. McLean Hosp., 1992; mem. adv. bd. Internat. Congress Alzheimer's Disease, 1993—. Mem. editl. bd. Jour. Neurochemistry, 1986-96, Neurochem. Rsch., 1988—, Harvard Rev. Psychiatry, 1992—, Neurobiology of Aging, 1994—, Alzheimer's Disease Rev., 1997—; contbr. over 200 biol. articles to Sci. Jour. Cell Biology, Jour. Biol. Chem., Annals N.Y. Acad. Sci., Proc. NAS, chpts. to books; Proteases and Protease Inhibitors Banner C Nixon R.A. eds. Annals Acad. Sci. vol. 67, 1992. Hon. bd. dirs. Ch. League for Civic Concerns, Boston, 1987-89. Recipient Merit award NIH, 1990, Leadership and Excellence in Alzheimer Disease award, Nat. Inst. Aging, 1992, Temple Discovery award Alzheimers Assn., 1999, N.Y. State OMH Rsch. award, 1999, Career Leadership award, Nat. Inst. on Aging, 1999, Zenith award, Alzheimer's Assn., 2003; Ethel DuPont Warren fellow, 1979-80, rsch. fellow Med. Found., 1980-82, Alfred P. Sloan Found., 1981-83, Scottish Rite Schizophrenia Rsch. Program, 1983-85. Mem. AAAS, Soc. for Neurosci., Fedn Am. Scientists, Am. Soc. for Biochemistry, Internat. Soc. for Neurochemistry, Am. Psychiat. Assn., Am. Soc. for Cell Biology, Am. Assn. for Geriatric Psychiatry, Gerontol. Soc. Am., Am. Assn. Neuropathologists, N.Y. Acad. Sci. Achievements include 5 patents (with others) on diagnosis and treatment of Alzheimer's disease. Office: Nathan Kline Inst NYU Med Ctr 140 Old Orangeburg Rd Orangeburg NY 10962-1157

**NIXON, SANDRA L.,** retired registrar; b. Kansas City, Mo., Feb. 23, 1944; d. C. Harold and Anna Pearl Scott-Mann; m. Hiram Luttmers Jr., Mar. 6, 1965 (div. Aug. 1973); children: Hiram Charles, Gerald Lee; m. Douglas L. Nixon, July 16, 1976; children: Karen, Katherine, Raymond. Student, Cen. Mo. State U., 1962-63, Nat. Coll., 1991-93. Credit clk. Harzfeld's, Kansas City, Mo., 1963-65; typist/receptionist Powers Regulator Co., Overland Park, Kans., 1965-69; ins. typist Comml. Union Ins. Co., Kansas City, Mo., 1969-73; typist Social Security admin. Kansas City, Mo., 1973-78; dir. of Mothers Day Out Birchwood Bapt. Ch., Independence, Mo., 1978-80; accompanist K.C. Mo. Sch. Dist., Kansas City, Mo., 1979-81; registrar Northeast Mid. Sch., Kansas City, Mo., 1981-2000; ind. fashion coord., team leader Weekenders aka Sandi's Butterfly Boutique, 2001—. Mem. ABWA (pres. 1990-91, Woman of Yr. 1992-93), VFW Aux. Post 4242 (sr. v.p. 2000-2001, pres. 2001-2004, sr. v.p. 2004-2005). Baptist. Avocations: piano, square dancing, precious moments. Office Phone: 816-260-4538. E-mail: sandy.nixon@fellowship.net.

**NIXON, SCOTT WEST,** oceanography science educator; b. Phila., Aug. 24, 1943; s. Robert Scott West and Elizabeth (Wright) West Nixon; m. Pendleton Hall, (div.); children: Carter Hall, Elizabeth Pendleton; m. Virginia Lee. BA, U. Del., 1965; PhD, U. N.C. 1970. Prof. oceanography U. R.I., Kingston, 1970—, dir. sea grant coll. program, 1983-2000. Mem. ocean studies bd. NRC, 1999-2004. Author: (with others) A Coastal Marine Ecosystem, 1978, The New England High Salt Marshes, 1982; co-editor-in-chief Estuaries, 1988—2006; also articles. Recipient Ketchum award Woods Hole Oceanographic Inst., 1992, Achievement award New Eng. Estuarine Rsch. Soc., 2000, Achievement award Nat. Sea Grant Assn., 2001, Lifetime appointment Nat. Assn. of Nat. Academies, 2002; grantee NSF, NOAA, EPA, Office Water Resources Rsch., State of R.I. Mem. Am. Soc. Limnology and Oceanography (governing bd. 1984-87), Estuarine Rsch. Fedn. (Odum award 2003) Office: U RI Bay Campus Dept Of Oceanography Narragansett RI 02882 Office Phone: 401-874-6803. Business E-Mail: swn@gso.uri.edu.

**NIXON, TIMOTHY FRANCIS,** lawyer; b. Two Rivers, Wis., Mar. 15, 1958; AS in Maritime Sci. with high honors, Northwestern Mich. Coll., 1979; BS in Pub. and Environ. Adminstrn. cum laude, U. Wis., Green Bay, 1987; MA in Pub. Policy and Adminstrn., JD with honors, U. Wis., Madison, 1990. Bar: Wis., US Dist. Ct. (ea. and we. dists.) Wis., US Dist. Ct. (we. dist.) Mich., US Dist. Ct. (no. dist.) Ill., US Ct. Appeals (7th cir.), US Supreme Ct. Cadet sailor Cleve. Cliffs Iron Co., 1977, US Steel Corp., 1978, 1979, Am. Steamship Co., 1978, US Mcht. Marine Officer, lic. 1st class pilot and Gt. Lakes mate Buffalo, 1979—85, Bethlehem Steel Corp., Seven Hills, Ohio, 1986, 1987; law clk. Office of Adminstrv. Legal Svcs., U. Wis., Madison, 1989—90; law clk. Godfrey & Kahn, S.C. (formerly LaFollette Sinykin, LLP), Green Bay, Wis., 1990, assoc. atty., 1991—96, shareholder, ptnr., 1997—. Intern Exec. Office of Pres., Office Mgmt. and Budget, Washington, 1988; lead atty. bus. fin. and restructuring team Godfrey & Kahn, S.C., 2002—; mem. adjl. faculty U. Wis., Green Bay, 2001—, instr. outreach and ext., 2002—; instr. Criminal Justice Dept. Exec. Devel. Inst., Fox Valley Tech. Coll., 2001—04; police mgmt. assessor, criminal justice dept., 2000—; spkr. in field. Co-author: No Small Change: The Bankruptcy Abuse Prevention and Consumer Protection Act of 2005; contbr. articles to profl. jours.; asst. editor Voyageur Mag., 2004—. Pres. Village of Waunakee, Wis., 1997—2001, chair planning commn., econ. devel. com., mem. growth task force, EMS dist. bd., pres. Cmty. Devel. Authority, 1998—2001, village trustee, 1995—97, Waunakee Tax Increment Dist. Nos. 2 and 3 Bd. Rev., 2000, rep. Am. Pub. Power Assn. Legis. Rally Washington, 2000—01, village trustee, 1995—97, chair pers. com., police com., indsl. devel. com., planning commn., stormwater mgmt. com., boundary agreement com., utility commn., mem. citizen adv. com., 1993—95, v.p. police com., mem. zoning appeals bd., mem. utility commn.; bd. dirs. Green Bay Area C. of C., 2004—; mem. water commn. City of Green Bay, 2003—, v.p., 2003—04, pres., 2004—, lead negotiator suburban water sales agreements; trustee Wis. Maritime Mus., 2004—05, chair audit com., mem. collections com., co-chair dir. search com.; bd. edn. Notre Dame Acad., Green Bay, 2003—, chair fin. com., 2004—; mem. DOT Roadway Grant Adv. Com. League of Wis. Municipalities, 2000, mem. legis. com., 2000—01; vice chair Dane County North Mendota Pky. Planning Com., 2000—01; gov.'s appointee South Ctrl. Wis. Regional Planning Commn. Study Com., 2000—01; account exec. Dane County United Way, 1998, 2000, cabinet mem., cmtys. divn. chair, 1999; asst. den leader, merit badge coord., mem. troop com. Boy Scouts Am., 1998—2003; alt. gov.'s appointee Wis. Patients Compensation Panel, 1983—85; mem. parish coun., maintenance com., facilities com., pub. rels. com., catechist, AC cantor St. John the Bapt. Parish, Waunakee, 1999—2001. Named Wis. Super Lawyer, Milw. Mag., 2005; named one of 50 People You Should Know in Green Bay, Bay Bus. Jour., 2005; recipient George B. Rector Cmty. Svc. award, Gt. Lakes Maritime Acad. Alumni Assn., 2000. Mem.: KC, ABA, Turnaround Mgmt. Assn., St. Thomas More Lawyers Soc. of Wis., Comml. Law League of Am., Hon. Robert J. Parins Inn of Ct., Am. Soc. Pub. Adminstrn., Am. Bankruptcy Inst., Western Dist. Wis. Bar Assn., Ea. Dist. of Wis. Bar Assn., 7th Cir. Ct. Appeals Bar Assn., Milw. County Bar Assn., Dane County Bar Assn., Brown County Bar Assn., Western Dist. Bankruptcy Bar (v.p. 1997—98, pres. 1998—99), State Bar Wis. (bd. dirs. bankruptcy, insolvency and creditors rights sect. 2004—, legis. and exemptions com., chair creditor edn. com.), INSOL Internat., U. Wis. Green Bay Law Alumni Assn. (founder), Order of Coif. Roman Catholic. Avocations: Great Lakes history, genealogy, travel. Office: Godfrey & Kahn SC 333 Main St Ste 600 Green Bay WI 54301 Office Phone: 920-436-7693. Fax: 920-436-7988. E-mail: tnixon@gklaw.com.

**NIZNIK, CAROL ANN,** electrical engineer, educator, consultant; b. Saratoga Springs, NY, Nov. 10, 1942; d. John Arthur Niznik and Rosalia Sopko; m. Donald H. Watster, Jan. 11, 1964. AAS in Engring. Sci., Alfred (NY) State Coll., 1962; BSEE, U. Rochester, NY, 1969, MSEE, 1972; PhD in Elec. Engring., SUNY, Buffalo, 1978. Technician Taylor Instrument Corp., Rochester, 1962-64; sr. technician IBM Corp., Poughkeepsie, NY, 1964-68; rsch.

scientist Eastman Kodak Corp., Rochester, 1969-70; sr. engr. Xerox Corp., Webster, NY, 1971-74; rsch. ast. prof. SUNY, Buffalo, 1979-80; assoc. prof. elec. engring. U. Pitts., Pitts., 1980-83; pres., cons. NW Sys. Function: Software Theoretical Protocol Devel. and Performance Evaluation, Rochester, 1975—. Adj. prof. math. Rochester Inst. Tech., 1993-94; faculty fellow Battelle/Rit/White Sands Missile Range, 1994-97; vis. assoc. prof. Ctr. Brain Rsch., Sch. Medicine. U. Rochester, dept. math., 1983-84 Author tech. monograph on cerebellum prosthesis component, monograph missile def. to homeland def. and security software R & D; contbr. some 80 articles to profl. confs. and jours., 32 conf. publs. presentations; patentee in field. Recipient fellowships, grants and 16 US govt. contracts, Irmgard Flugge-Lotz award outstanding tchg. and academic achievement, 1983, Engr. of Yr. award SUNY Buffalo Engring. Alumni Assn., 2004, Star Wars Strat. Def. Initiative Orgn. (SDIO) Phase I SDIO/SBIR Contract Def. Nuc. Agy., 1986, Congestion Controlled Sequential Contention Resolution Protocol award Rockwell Internat. Corp. Thousand Oaks Patriot Missile Software. Mem. IEEE (sr.), Sigma Xi, Eta Kappa Nu, Tau Beta Pi. Roman Catholic. Avocations: doll collecting, gardening. Office: NW Sys PO Box 18133 Rochester NY 14618-0133 Personal E-mail: dr_carol_niznik@yahoo.com.

**NJIE, VERONICA P.S.**, clinical nurse, educator; d. Edward G. Njie and Grace B.S. Daniels-Njie. BSN, Howard U., Washington, 1992; MSN, The Cath. U. Am., Washington, 1996. RN Washington, clin. specialist in med.-surg. nursing. Tchr. Dept. Edn., Banjul, Gambia, The Gambia, 1980—82; state registered nurse (SRN) Royal Victoria Hosp., Banjul, 1985—86; rsch./field asst. Med. Rsch. Coun., Fajara, 1986—87; nurse technician Howard U. Hosp., Washington, 1988—90, clin. nurse II, 1990—96; clin. nurse N.W. Health Care Ctr. Beverly Enterprise, 1990—98; clin. instr. Montgomery Coll., Tacoma Park, Md., 1996; asst. prof. nursing Balt. City C. C., Balt., 1997. Contbr. articles to profl. jours. Recipient Intramural Rsch. Tng. award, NIH, 2000. Mem.: Md. Assn. Higher Edn., ANA, Nat. League Nursing, Sigma Theta Tau. Democrat. Roman Catholic. Avocations: reading, travel, theater, dance, movies. Office: Johns Hopkins U Sch Nursing 525 N Wolfe St Baltimore MD 21205 Office Phone: 410-502-2606. Personal E-mail: vpnjie@aol.com. Business E-Mail: vnjiel@son.jhmi.edu.

**NJOKU, SCHOLASTICA IBARI**, retired college librarian, writer; d. David Mgbahuruike Njoku and Elizabeth Ekeoma Ukaegbu; divorced; children: Anthony, Emelia, Martina, Iheanyi, Chinedu, Onyekachi. BA cum laude in English, Wiley Coll., 1963; MLS, U. Oreg., 1965, MS in Edn., 1967, PhD in Edn., 1969; diploma in writing for children and teenagers. Inst. Children's Lit., Conn., 1996. Ref. libr. Knapp Libr. Project, Portland, Oreg., 1965—66; asst. edn. libr. Portland State U., 1969—70; assoc. prof. edn. Miss. Valley State Coll., Itta Bena, 1970—72; ref. coun. Oreg. State Libr., Salem, 1974—81, on-line cataloger, 1981—86; ref. libr. Portland C.C. 1986—2003; ret., 2003. Multicultural mentoring com. Portland C.C., 1996—2003, edinl. adv. coun. com., 1999—2003, women history planning com., 1999—2003. Author: The Miracle of A Christmas Doll, 1986, Dog What?, 1989; contbr. poems to poetry anthologies. Recipient 3d prize Poetry award, Ann. Reader's Digest, United Negro Coll. Fund, 1963. Mem.: ALA, The Willamette Writers, Pacific NW Libr. Assn., Oreg. State Poetry Assn., Am. Assn. Higher Edn., Oreg. Libr. Assn., Delta Sigma Theta (Sisterhood award 2006). Democrat. Roman Catholic. Avocations: gardening, story telling, reading, writing. Home: 307 NE Holland St Portland OR 97211

**NNAEMEKA, OBIOMA GRACE**, French language and women's studies educator, consultant, researcher; b. Agulu, Anambra, Nigeria; came to U.S., 1974; d. Christopher Egbunike and Jessie Ifemelue (Ogbuefi) Obidiegwu; children: Ike, Uchenna. BA with honors, U. Nigeria, Nsukka, 1972; MA, U. Minn., 1977, PhD with distinction, 1989. Rsch. fellow U. Nigeria, 1972-74, lectr., 1982-87; asst. prof. Concordia Coll., Minn., 1988-89, Coll. Wooster, Ohio, 1989-91; assoc. prof. Ind. U., Indpls., 1991—2000, prof., 2000—. Cons. Govt. Senegal, Dakar, 1990-92; commentator Internat. Svc. Radio Netherlands, Hilversum, 1990—; Edith Kreeger Wolf Disting. prof. Northwestern U., 1992. Author: Agrippa d'Aubigné: The Poetics of Power and Change, 1998; editor: The Politics of Mothering, 1996, Sisterhood, Feminisms, & Power, 1997; contbr. articles to profl. jours. Founder, pres. Assn. African Women's Scholars, 1995; convener, organizer First Internat. Conf. Women in Africa & African Diaspora, 1992. Named Achiever of Yr. Leadership Nigeria Network, 1994; grantee from McArthur Found., Rockefeller Found., Swedish Internat. Devel. Agy., Swedish Agy. for Rsch. Cooperation with Developing Countries, 1991-92. Mem. Am. Assn. Tchrs. French, Ind. Fgn. Lang. Tchrs. Assn., Modern Langs. Assn., African Studies Assn., African Lit. Assn. Avocations: reading, travel. Office: Ind U Dept Fgn Langs Cultrs 425 University Blvd Indianapolis IN 46202-5148 E-mail: waad@iupui.edu.

**NOAH, JULIA JEANINE**, retired librarian; b. Craig, Mo., July 14, 1932; d. Hiram Curtis and Eloise Julia (Puckett) True; m. Raymond Laverne Noah, Sept. 5, 1964; children: David Scott, Danny Ray, Deborah Jill, Douglas True. BS, U. Ill., 1953; MA in Library Sci., U. South Fla., 1983. Asst. rsch. librarian Parke, Davis & Co., Detroit, 1953-55; cataloging librarian U. Mo., Columbia, 1955-57; sch. librarian High Point Elem. Sch., Clearwater, Fla., 1968; library aide Clearwater High Sch., 1973-78; reference asst. Dunedin (Fla.) Pub. Library, 1978-84, dir. info. svcs., 1984-88, library dir., 1988-94; ret. Mem. DAR, Fla. Libr. Assn., Pinellas Genealogy Soc., Nat. Soc. Colonial Dames XVII Century, Daus. of Union Vets. of the Civil War 1861-1865, Nat. Soc. Magna Charta Dames, Nat. Soc. Women Descendants of the Ancient and Hon. Artillery Co., Nat. Soc. Daus. of Founders and Patriots of Am., Phi Kappa Phi, Beta Phi Mu Republican. Presbyterian. Avocations: antiques, genealogy.

**NOAM, ELI MICHAEL**, telecommunications industry executive, educator; b. Jerusalem, Aug. 22, 1946; came to U.S., 1963; s. Ernst and Lotte (Dahn) N.; m. Nadine Strossen, 1980. AB, Harvard U., 1970, AM, 1972, PhD in Econs., 1975, JD, 1975. Bar: N.Y. 1996, D.C. 1997. Asst. prof. Princeton (N.J.) U., 1975-76, Columbia Bus. Sch., N.Y.C., 1981-84, prof. finance and econ., 1984—; commr. N.Y. State Pub. Svc. Commn., N.Y.C., 1987-90. Dir. Columbia Inst. for Tele-Info., N.Y.C., 1983-87, 1990—; contbr. articles, Financial Times Online, 2003-; appointed to White House IT advisory com., 2003-. Author or editor: Telecommunications Regulation: Today and Tomorrow, 1982, Video Media Competition, 1985, Law of International Telecommunications in the United States, 1988, The Cost of Libel, 1989, Television in Europe, 1991, Telecommunications in Europe, 1991, Telecommunications in Western Asia, 1997. Telecommunications in Latin America, 1998. Telecommunications in Africa, 1998. Bd. dirs. IRS Computer Modernization, Washington, D.C., 1988-89, Fed. Telecom System FTS-2000 Selection. Washington, 1990—. With Israel Air Force, 1967, 73. Grantee NSF, 1982, 85, 86; fellow German Marshall Fund U.S., 1983-84. 1966-68, Mideast Wars; Fellow Freedom Forum Media Center, 1996. Mem. Coun. on Fgn. RELs., Phi Beta Kappa. Jewish. Avocations: flying, skiing, diving. Office: Columbia U Inst Tele-Info 809 Uris Hall New York NY 10027*

**NOBACK, RICHARDSON KILBOURNE**, medical educator; b. Richmond, Va., Nov. 7, 1923; s. Gustav Joseph and Hazel (Kilborn) N.; m. Nan Jean Gates, Apr. 5, 1947; children: Carl R., Robert K., Catherine E. MD, Cornell U., 1947; BA, Columbia U., 1943. Diplomate Am. Bd. Internal Medicine. Intern N.Y. Hosp., 1947-48; asst. resident Cornell Med. div Bellevue Hosp., N.Y.C., 1948-50, chief resident, 1950-52; instr. medicine Cornell U., N.Y.C., 1950-53; asst. prof. medicine SUNY Upstate Med. Ctr., Syracuse, 1955-56; assoc. prof. medicine U. Ky. Med. Ctr. Lexington, 1956-64; exec. dir. Kansas City (Mo.) Gen. Hosp. and Med. Ctr., 1964-69; assoc. dean, prof. medicine U. Mo. Sch. Medicine, Columbia, 1964-69; founding dean Kansas City, 1969-78, prof. medicine, 1969-90, prof. and dean emeritus, 1990—. Cons. U. Tenn., U. Mich., U. Del., Northeastern Ohio Group, U. Mo., Eastern Va. Med. Sch., Tex. Tech. U. Contbr. numerous articles to profl. jours. Bd. dirs. Kansas City Gen. Hosp., Truman Med. Ctr. Wayne Miner Health Ctr., Jackson County Med. Soc., The Shepherd's Ctr., Am. Fedn. Aging Rsch., Mo. Gerontol. Inst., The Shepherd's Ctrs. of Am.; dir. Mo. Geriatric Edn. Ctr., 1985-88. Capt. USAF Med. Svcs. 1953-55. Recipient medal of honor Avila Coll., Kansas City, 1968, merit award Met.

---

Med. Soc., 1991, recognition award Mo. Soc. Internal Medicine, 1993. Mem. AMA, Mo. Med. Assn. (former mem. ho. of dels., v.p. 1992), Am. Geriatric Soc., Alpha Omega Alpha, Phi Kappa Phi. Avocations: photography, writing, travel. Home: 2912 Abercorn Dr Las Vegas NV 89134-7440 Personal E-mail: nanori@earthlink.net.

**NOBE, KEN**, chemical engineering professor; b. Berkeley, Calif., Aug. 26, 1925; s. Sidney and Kiyo (Uyeyama) N.; m. Mary Tagami, Aug. 31, 1957; children: Steven Andrew, Keven Gibbs, Brian Kelvin. BS, U. Calif., Berkeley, 1951; PhD, UCLA, 1956. Jr. chem. engr. Air Reduction Co., Murray Hill, NJ, 1951-52; asst. prof. chem. engring. UCLA, 1957-62, assoc. prof., 1962-68, prof., 1968—, chmn. dept. chem., nuclear and thermal engring., 1978-83, founding chmn. chem. engring., 1983-84. Mem. tech. staff Ramo-Wooldridge Corp., El Segundo, Calif., 1958-59 Div. editor: Jour. Electrochem. Soc, 1967-91, Electrochimica Acta, 1977-85 With U.S. Army, 1944—46. Recipient Disting. Tchg. award, UCLA, 1962. Mem. Electrochem. Soc. (Henry B. Linford award 1992), Am. Chem. Soc., Internat. Soc. Electrochemistry, Am. Electroplaters Surfacing Fin. Soc. (Abner Brenner Gold medal 2000), Sigma Xi. Office: UCLA Dept Chemical Engring Los Angeles CA 90095-1592 Business E-Mail: nobe@seas.ucla.edu.

**NOBEL, JOEL J.**, biomedical researcher; b. Phila., Dec. 8, 1934; s. Bernard D. and Golda R. (Nobel) Judovich; m. Bonnie Sue Goldberg, June 19, 1960 (div.); children: Erika, Joshua; m. Loretta Schwartz, Oct. 28, 1979 (div.); 1 child, Adam. AB, Haverford Coll., 1956; MA, U. Pa., 1958; MD, Thomas Jefferson Med. Coll., Phila., 1963. Intern Presbyn. Hosp., Phila., 1963-64; resident in surgery Pa. Hosp., Phila., 1964-65; resident in neurosurgery U. Pa. Hosp., 1965-66; practice medicine specializing in biomed. engring. rsch. and healthcare tech. assessment, hosp. planning and mgmt., Phila., 1968—; dir. research Emergency Care Research Inst., Plymouth Meeting, Pa., 1968-71, dir., pres., 1971—2001; pres. Plymouth Inst., 1979—2002; founder and pres. emeritus ECRI, 2001—; founder, pres. ECRI Bhd, Malaysia, 2001—; CEO The Nobel Group, 2002—, chmn. Arab Health award, 2004—05. Chmn. tech. policy com., exec. bd., chmn. strategic planning com. Consumers Union; cons. in field. Publisher Health Devices, 1971-2001, Health Devices Alerts, 1977-2001; contbr. articles to profl. jours. With USNR, 1966—68. Smith, Kline & French fgn. fellow, 1962; grantee HEW, 1968-72; grantee Am. Heart Assn., 1965-66 Mem. AMA, APHA, Assn. Advancement Med. Instrumentation, Critical Care Med. Soc., Pa. Med. Assn., Navy League, US Naval Inst., Brit. Officers Club Phila. Home: 1434 Monk Rd Gladwyne PA 19035-1315 Office: ECRI 5200 Butler Pike Plymouth Meeting PA 19462-1298 Business E-Mail: jjnobel@ecri.org.

**NOBIL, JAMES HOWARD, JR.**, real estate investor, developer, broker, consultant; b. Columbus, Ohio, Mar. 21, 1955; s. James Howard Nobil and Carol Mae (Wiesenberger) Greenbaum; m. Elizabeth Ann Corro, Apr. 16, 1983 (div. 1998); children: Jonathan James Michael, Jennifer Carrie Lee. BA in Polit. Sci., Tufts U., Medford, Mass., 1975; postgrad., George Washington U., 1978—80. Lic. real estate broker Md., Va., D.C., Fla.; cert. leasing specialist ICSC. Account exec. Riviere Securities Corp., Washington, 1977-78; v.p. ops. Fed. Realty Investment Trust, Bethesda, Md., 1978-83; mng. gen. ptnr. NRW Devel. Co., Vienna, Va., 1983-84; v.p. acquisitions Oxford Nut. Properties Corp., Bethesda, 1984-85; 1st v.p. Washington Real Estate Investment Trust, Bethesda, 1985-86; pres. Washington Comml. Properties, Inc., McLean, Va., 1986—; Rent Verification Svcs. (subs. of Washington Comml. Properties, Inc.), McLean, 1986—. Mem. Internat. Coun. Shopping Ctrs., Nat. Assn. Realtors, D.C. Area Comml. Brokers Coun. Avocations: running, boating, skiing, tennis. Office: Washington Comml Properties Inc 1420 Beverly Rd Mc Lean VA 22101

**NOBLE, ALICE L.**, writer, researcher; b. Rome, Ga., Apr. 20, 1934; d. Bruce Gary Landers and Lucille Mae Pyle-Landers; m. Donald Eugene Noble, May 28, 1998. Student, Anthony's Real Estate Sch., Fresno, Calif., 1967—69, Calif. Chrsitian Coll., 1970—73, Internat. Assn. Assessing Officers, Chgo., 1980—81, Writers Digest Sch., L.A., 1999—2001. Real estate agt., Fresno, Calif., 1965—73; owner White Fang Pub., Delta Junction, Ark., 2003—. Author: (novels) Elusive Autumn, 2003, On the Kenai, 2003. Mem.: Creative Writers Anchorage. Republican. Presbyterian. Avocations: hiking, stamp and coin collecting, writing. Home: 2508 Healy St Delta Junction AK 99737 Mailing: PO Box 100 Delta Junction AK 99737 Office: White Fang Pub 2508 Healy St Delta Junction AK 99737 Office Phone: 907-895-4454. Business E-Mail: dnoble@wildak.net.

**NOBLE, DOUGLAS**, architecture educator; BS in Architecture, Calif. State Poly. U., 1981, BArch, 1982; MArch, U. Calif., Berkeley, 1983, PhD in Architecture, 1991. Registered Calif., 1985. With Cashion-Horie-Cocke-Gonzalez Architects, 1978—84; tchg. asst. U. Calif., Berkeley, 1983—88, lectr., 1988—91, rsch. asst., 1988—89; prof. U. So. Calif., 1991—; with Kenneth S. Wing and Assocs., 1985—86. Co-editor: Software for Architects; A Guide to Software for the Architectural Profession, (conf. procs.) Mission, Method, Madness; Computer Supported Design in Architecture, 1992. Fellow: AIA; mem.: Assn. for Computer Aided Design in Architecture (pres. 1998), Phi Kappa Phi. Office: 204 Watt Hall U So Calif Sch Architecture Los Angeles CA 90089-0291 Business E-Mail: dnoble@usc.edu.

**NOBLE, ERNEST PASCAL**, pharmacologist, biochemist, educator; b. Baghdad, Iraq, Apr. 2, 1929; came to U.S., 1946; s. Noble Babik and Barkev Grace (Kasparian) Babikian; m. Inga Birgitta Kilstromer, May 19, 1956; children—Lorna, Katharine, Erik BS in Chemistry, U. Calif.-Berkeley, 1951; PhD in Biochemistry, Oreg. State U., 1955; MD. Case Western Res. U., 1962. Diplomate Nat. Bd. Med. Examiners. Sr. instr. biochemistry Western Res. U., Cleve., 1957-62; intern Stanford Med. Ctr., Calif., 1962-63, resident in psychiatry Calif., 1963-66, research assoc., asst. prof. Calif. 1965-69; assoc. prof. psychiatry, psychobiology and pharmacology U. Calif.-Irvine, 1969-71. prof., chief neurochemistry, 1971-76, 79-81; dir. Nat. Inst. Alcohol Abuse and Alcoholism HEW. 1976-78, assoc. adminstr. sci., alcohol, drug abuse and mental health, 1978-79; Pike prof. alcohol studies. dir. Alcohol Research Ctr. UCLA Sch. of Medicine, 1981—. Mem. various med./sci. jour. editorial bds.; contbr. numerous articles to profl. jours., chpts. to books V.p. Nat. Coun. on Alcoholism 1981-84; pres. Internat. Commn. for the Prevention of Alcoholism and Drug Dependency, 1988. Fulbright scholar, 1955-56; Guggenheim fellow, 1974-75; Sr. Fulbright scholar, 1984-85; recipient Career Devel. award NIMH. HEW, 1966-69 Fellow Am. Coll. Neuropsychopharmacology; mem. Internat. Soc. Neurochemistry, Am. Soc. Pharmacology and Expti. Therapeutics, Research Soc. on Alcoholism. Office: UCLA 760 Westwood Plz Los Angeles CA 90095-8353

**NOBLE, HELEN BONNER**, artist; b. Northville, Mich., Mar. 27, 1922; d. George Coburn and Helen Josephine (McCambridge) Harper; m. Morton Noble, Jr., June 27, 1943; children: Martha, Kathryn, Elizabeth, John. Student, Wayne State U., Case Western REs. U., 1939-43, Santa Barbar Art Inst. One-woman shows include Gallery 932, Ventura, Calif., 1983, The Oaks Gallery, Ojai, Calif., 1988; group shows include Bradley Galleries, Santa Barbara, Calif., 1978, 79, Meredith Niles Gallery, Santa Barbara, 1980-83, Merida-Rapp Graphics, Louisville, 1986; other exhibits include 3rd Women in Art Exhbn., Springfield, Ill. 1983, 2nd Ann. Nat. Print Exhbn. of Springfield Art Assn., 1982, 24th Ann. Nat. Exhbn. of Prints and Drawings, Oklahoma City, 1982, 40th Ann Nat. Juried Print Exhbn., Clinton, N.J., 1996, others; represented in collections; curator small work exhbn., StoneMetal Press, San Antonio, 2005-06. Office Phone: 805-965-3121. Personal E-mail: mnoble56@aol.com.

**NOBLE, JAMES WILKES**, actor; b. Dallas, Mar. 5, 1922; s. Ralph Byrne and Lois Frances (Wilkes) N.; m. Carolyn Owen Coates, May 19, 1956; 1 child: Jessica Katherine. Student, North Tex. Coll., Arlington, 1939-41, So. Methodist U., Dallas, 1941-43, 1946-47. Lectr. acting and mime Am. Acad. Dramatic Art, 1956-59. Mem. Lydia Tanower Modern Dance Co., 1937-39; title role in 1st TV drama, The Egoist on Dumont TV, 1943; 1st N.Y. Stage appearance Helena's Room, 1947; 1st Broadway appearance: The Big Knife,

---

1949; others include: The Velvet Glove, 1949; Medea, 1951; Come of Age, 1952; A Far Country, 1961; Strange Interlude, 1963; 1776, 1971; The Runner Stumbles, 1976; mem. Am. Mime Theatre, 1952-59; appeared in numerous TV dramas and soap operas; appeared in more than 200 plays in theatres throughout the world most recent: Stratford Characters in Stratford-Upon-Avon, England, T.S. Eliot in The Poet's Theatre, Cambridge, Mass., 1996, Out of Order, Calgary, Alta., Can., 1997, Moon Over Buffalo, Edmonton, Alta., 1998; TV appearances include the role of the Governor on Benson, ABC-TV, 1979-86, series First Impressions, CBS-TV, 1987, series Archies, NBC-TV, 1990, Law and Order, 1991; movies include: Dragonfly, 1965; The Sporting Club, 1967; 1776, 1972; Promises in the Dark, 1978; Ten, 1979; Being There, 1979; Airplane II, 1983; You Talkin' To Me?, 1986; Tiger's Tale, 1987, Chances Are, 1988, Absent Minded Professor, 1989, Law and Order, 1991, All My Children, 1992; numerous other appearances. Author jour. article on Am. mime. Active Lee Strasberg Theater, Theatre Artists Workshop. Served as lt. USNR, 1943-46, P.T.O. Named Hon. Gov., N.J., N.Y., 1982; appreciation award Am. Heart Assn., 1983. Mem. Actors Studio (life), Actors Equity, SAG, AFTRA. Democrat. Roman Catholic. Avocation: photography. Office: Paradigm Agy 10100 Santa Monica Blvd Los Angeles CA 90067-4003

**NOBLE, JOHN HENRY, JR.**, education educator, researcher; s. John Henry and Florence Veronica Noble; m. Mary Anne Lavelle; children: Craig John, Sean Stephen, Tracy Anne. BA, Manhattan Sem., Ill., 1958; MSW, Cath. U. of Am., Washington, DC, 1961; MA, Boston Coll., Chestnut Hill, 1961; PhD, Brandeis U., Mass., 1966. Cert. ACSW NASW/N.D., 1963. Project dir. Med. Found., Boston, 1968—70; dir. program evaluation Rehab. Svcs. Adminstrn., U.S. Dept. of Health, Edn., and Welfare, Washington, 1970—72. Dir., policy rsch. and analysis for social svcs. and human devel. Office of Asst. Sec. for Planning and Evaluation, U.S. Dept. of Health, Edn., and Welfare, Washington, 1973—80; budget analyst Office of Dep. Asst. Sec., Planning, Budget, and Evaluation, U.S. Dept. of Edn., Washington, 1980—83; assoc. commr., policy rsch. and analysis Va. Dept. of Mental Health, Mental Retardation, and Substance Abuse, Richmond, 1983—86; prof. SUNY at Buffalo, 1986—93; endowed prof. for social justice Cath. U. of Am., Washington, 1993—2005. Author over 100 articles and book chpts. Bd. mem. Human Svcs. Rsch. Inst., Cambridge, 1980—2006, Alliance for Human Rsch. Protection, N.Y.C. 2000—06. Recipient Endowed Prof., Cath. U. of Am., 1993—2005. Liberal. Roman Catholic. Avocations: bicycling, hunting, fishing, gardening, classical and modern languages. Personal E-mail: jhnoble@verizon.net.

**NOBLE, JOSEPH VEACH**, retired museum director; b. Phila., Apr. 3, 1920; s. Joseph Haderman and Helen Elizabeth (Veach) N.; m. Olive Ashley Mooney, June 21, 1941 (dec. Sept. 1978); children: Josette, Ashley, Laurence; m. Lois Cook Cartwright, Oct. 27, 1979. Student, U. Pa., 1942. Cameraman dir. DeFrenes and Co. Studios, Phila., 1939-41; studio mgr. WPTZ, Philco TV Sta., Phila., 1941-42, DeFrenes and Co. Studios, 1946-49; gen. mgr. Murphy-Lillis Prodns., N.Y.C. 1949-50; exec. v.p. Film Counselors, Inc., N.Y.C. 1950-56, dir., 1950-82; operating adminstr. Met. Mus. Art, 1956-67, vice dir. adminstrn., 1967-70; dir. Mus. City N.Y., 1970-85; exec. dir. Soc. Medalists, 1985-95. Photog. salon exhibitor, from 1936; lectr. CCNY, 1949-51 Author: The Techniques of Painted Attic Pottery, 1965, The Historical Murals of Maplewood, 1961, Forgery of the Etruscan Terracotta Warriors, 1961; Contbr.: Ency. Brit. 1970. Trustee Corning Mus. of Glass, 1970—; mem. Morrow Meth. Ch., pres. trustees, 1972-77; chmn. N.Y. State Bd. Hist. Preservation 1972-76; co-chmn. Save Venice, Inc., 1972; trustee Brookgreen Gardens, 1971—, pres., 1976-90, chmn., 1990-95, chmn. emeritus, 1995—. With AUS, 1942-46. Recipient Venice Film Festival medal for photography in sci., 1948, Sigma Xi award 1963, Maple Leaf award Maplewood, N.J., 1966, 87, Gold medal for The Big Apple N.Y. Film Festival, 1979, Disting. Svc. award Maplewood C. of C., 1987. Fellow Soc. Antiquaries London, Am. Numismatic Soc.; mem. N.Y. State Assn. Museums (pres. 1970-72), NAD (medal 1976), Nat. Sculpture Soc. (medal 1978, 91), Artists' Fellowship (medal 1978), Archeol. Inst. Am. (treas. 1963-70), Museums Council N.Y.C. (chmn. 1965-67), Am. Assn. Museums (pres. 1975-78, Disting. Svc. Awd., 1991), Cultural Instns. Group N.Y.C. (chmn. 1984-85), Soc. Promotion Hellenic Studies; Am. Watercolor Soc. (medal 1982). Clubs: Maplewood Country; Explorers (N.Y.C.), Century Assn. (N.Y.C.). Office: Brookgreen Gardens PO Box 3368 Pawleys Island SC 29585-3368 Home: 7226 Williams Dr S Saint Petersburg FL 33705-6158 As a classical archaeologist I always have been guided by the ancient saying, "Let the light of the past illumine a pathway to the future.".

**NOBLE, MILDRED M.**, retired social worker; b. Ont., Can., July 13, 1925; d. Edward Paibomasai and Mary Baids; 1 child, Carol Mills. BA, Boston Coll., 1984; MS. MIT, 1988. Cert. in alcohol counseling Boston Med. Ctr. Lectr. Harvard U., Cambridge, Mass., Radcliffe Coll., U. Mass., Amherts, Boston Coll., Wheelock Coll., Wellesley (Mass.) Coll., 1997—, R.I. Mus., Providence, 1997. Author: Sweet Grass, 1998; prodr., dir. video Clan Women in the 90s, 1990 (Thanks Be to Grandmother Winifred Found. grantee). Advocate Native Am. Cmtys. in New Eng. Region, Boston Indian Coun., 1972—; cultural coord. Children's Mus., Boston, 1978; bd. dirs. Native Am. Ctr. of Boston, 1972—, Boston Writer's Room, 1997. Recipient Cert. of Recognition, Mass. Ctr. for Native Am. Awareness, Inc., 1994. Home: 255 Massachusetts Ave Boston MA 02115-3505

**NOBLE, RALPH C.**, animal scientist, department chairman; s. Willie G. Noble: m. Debra Tazewell; 1 child, Rachel C. BS, Tuskegee U., Ala., 1973, MS, 1975; PhD. U. Ill.-Champaign-Urbana. 1981. Cert. artificial insemination technician Ala., forage mgmt. Coop. Ext., Ala., beef quality assurance Coop. Ext. Ala. Instr. Tuskegee U., 1975—77, from asst. to assoc. prof., 1982—2005, acting coord. George Washington Carver agrl. expt. sta., 1985—86, coord. of CSREES animal sci. rsch. program, 1986—97, coord. animal, poultry and vet. scis. program, 2002—05; rsch./tchg. asst. U. Ill. Champaign-Urbana, 1978—81; chmn. dept. animal scis. NC A&T State U. Greensboro, 2005—. Cons. Heifer Internat., Gainsville, Fla. 1990—2005; dir. strategic alliance for the Ala. goat industry Tuskegee U. 2001—05; advisor Ala. Farmers Fedn. Meat Goat and Sheep subcom., Montgomery, 2002—05; bd. dirs. NRCS-AL Grassland Res. com., Auburn, Ala., 2003—05; mem. adv. com. U.S. Poultry & Egg Assn., Atlanta, 2002—03; advisor Nat. Pre-Vet. Medicine Assn., Stillwater, Okla., 2002—04; chair livestock com. Macon County Farmers Orgn., Inc., Tuskegee, 1988—2005; mem. planning com. farmers conf. Tuskegee U. Coop. Ext. Program, 1982—2005; contbg. editor Am. Assn. Animal Sci., Urbana, 1985—86. Vol. eyeglass collection Lions Club, Tuskegee, 1986—90; sec. Sigma Xi, Tuskegee; pres., sec. Gamma Sigma Delta, Tuskegee; mem. Humane Soc. of the Piedmont, Greensboro, 2006—; mem. adv. com. to the bishop ELCA SE Luth. Ch., Atlanta, 1986—88; bd. dirs. St. Luke Luth. Ch., Tuskegee, 1988—98. Recipient Outstanding Faculty Performance award for tchg., Tuskegee U. 1987, 1997, Outstanding Faculty Performance award for svc., 2002, Outstanding Recognition award for tech. assistance to small farmers in the Southea. US, Heifer Project Internat., 2002, Alumni Merit Honor, Tuskegee U. Vet. Alumni Assn., 2005. Mem.: Phi Kappa Phi (licentiate). Office: NC A&T State U Webb Hall Ste 101 1601 E Market St Greensboro NC 27411 Office Phone: 336-334-7547. Office Fax: 336-334-7288. E-mail: rcnoble@ncat.edu.

**NOBLE, RONALD KENNETH**, Secretary General of Interpol; b. Ft. Dix, NJ, Sept. 24, 1956; BA cum laude, U. NH, 1979; JD, Stanford U., 1982. Bar: Pa. 1983, NJ, 1983. Sr. law clk. to Hon. A. Leon Higginbotham Jr. US Ct. Appeals 3rd Cir., Phila., 1982-84; asst. US atty. ea. dist. Pa. Office Atty. Gen., Phila., 1984-88; spl. counsel & chief of staff criminal divsn. US Dept. Justice, Washington, 1988-89, dep. asst. atty. gen., 1989; asst. prof. law NYU Sch. Law, 1990—92, assoc. prof., 1992—99, prof., 1999—; asst. sec. for enforcement US Dept. Treasury, Washington, 1993-94, under sec. for enforcement, 1994-96; sec. gen INTERPOL, Lyon, France, 2000—. Pres. Fin. Action Task Force, 1994—; mem. exec. com. INTERPOL, 1994—; mem. Root-Tilden Scholar Selection Bd., 1990—; chmn. Customs Ops. Adv. Com., 1993—; chmn. Bank Secrecy Act Adv. Com., 1993—. Articles editor Stanford Law

Rev., 1981-82. Mem. Am. Law Inst. Office: NYU Sch of Law Vanderbilt Hall 40 Washington Sq S Rm 420 New York NY 10012-1099 also: INTERPOL Gen Secretariat 200 quai Charles de Gaulle 69006 Lyons France

**NOBLES, LAURENCE HEWIT,** retired geology educator; b. Spokane, Wash., Sept. 28, 1927; s. Harry and Florence (Giffin) N.; m. Barbara Joanne Smith, Aug. 28, 1948; children: Heather C., Laurence F. BS, MS, Calif. Inst. Tech., 1949; PhD, Harvard, 1952. Instr. geology Northwestern U., 1952-55, asst. prof., 1955-61, assoc. prof., 1961-67, prof., 1967-90, prof. emeritus, 1990—, also asst. dean Coll. Arts and Scis., 1966-67, asso. dean, 1968-70; acting dean Northwestern U. (Coll. Arts and Scis.), 1970-72, dean adminstrn., 1972-81, v.p. adminstrn. and fin. planning, 1981-86. Trustee Adler Planetarium, 1980-86; faculty rep. Big Ten Conf., 1976-81; trustee Chgo. Acad. Scis., 1967-87, pres., 1973-78, hon. trustee, 1987—. Mem. Am. Geophys. Union, Geol. Soc. Am. E-mail: lnobles@cablespeed.com.

**NOBLIN, ELIZABETH,** elementary school educator; b. Searcy, Ark., Mar. 31, 1979; d. Terry and Carolyn Noblin. BS in Elem. Edn., Harding U., 2001; MS in Libr. Media and Info. Tech., U. Ctrl. Ark., 2004. 3rd grade tchr. Cabot Pub. Schs., Ark., 2001—. Mem.: Internat. Reading Assn.

**NOBLITT, HARDING COOLIDGE,** political scientist, educator; b. Marion, N.C., Oct. 31, 1920; s. Walter Tate and Nellie Mae (Horton) N.; m. Louise Hope Lester, July 3, 1943; 1 son, Walter Thomas. BA, Berea Coll., 1942; MA, U. Chgo., 1947, PhD, 1955. Mem. faculty Concordia Coll., Moorhead, Minn., 1950-90, prof. polit. sci., 1956-90, Wije Disting. prof., 1979-82, chmn. dept., 1964-72, prof. emeritus, 1990. Mem. editorial bd.: Discourse: A Review of the Liberal Arts, 1957-67, acting editor, 1959-60. Democratic candidate Congress, 1962; del. Dem. Nat. Conv., 1964; chmn. Profs. for Johnson-Humphrey, Minn. 1964; chmn. platform com. Dem. State Conv., 1968; mem. Gov's Citizens Council on Aging, 1963-68; mem. City Charter Commn., Moorhead, 1985—; mem. Minn. Higher Edn. Coordinating Bd., 1971-81, sec., 1974-75, pres., 1979-80. Served with AUS, 1943-46, ETO. Recipient 1st ann. Great Tchr. award Concordia Coll., 1960; recipient Flaat Disting. Service award Concordia Coll., 1982 Mem. Am. Polit. Sci. Assn., Am. Legion, Phi Kappa Phi, Pi Gamma Mu, Tau Kappa Alpha, Pi Kappa Delta Presbyterian (elder). Home: 2014 4th St S Moorhead MN 56560-4131 Office: Concordia Coll Dept Polit Sci Moorhead MN 56560

**NOBLITT, NANCY ANNE,** aerospace engineer; b. Roanoke, Va., Aug. 14, 1959; d. Jerry Spencer and Mary Louise (Jerrell) N. BA, Mills Coll., Oakland, Calif., 1982; MS in Indsl. Engring., Northeastern U., 1990; JD, Coll. William and Mary, 2003. Data red specialist Universal Energy Sys., Beaver Creek, Ohio, 1981; aerospace engr. turbine engine divsn. components br. turbine group aero-propulsion lab. Wright-Patterson AFB, Ohio, 1982-84, engine assessment br. spl. engines group, 1984-87; lead analyst cycle methods computer aided engr. GE, Lynn, Mass., 1987-90, Lynn PACES project coord., 1990-91; software sys. analyst Sci. Applications Internat. Corp., with artificial intelligence McLean, Va., 1991-92, software engring. mgr. intelligence applications integration Hampton, Va., 1992-93, mgr. test engring. and sys. support, 1993-94, mgr. configuration mgmt., 1994, mgmt. asst. to TBMCS program mgr., 1994-95; sr. simulation engr. Chem Demil, 1995-98; supervisory engr. Analytical Mechanics Assocs., Hampton, 1998-99; sr. project engr. Newport News (Va.) Shipbuilding Inc., 1999-00; quality assurance mgr. Sci. Applications Internat. Corp., 2005—. Tutor math. and sci. Centerville Sch. Bd., Ohio, 1982-86; tutor math. and physics Marblehead Sch. Bd., Mass., 1988-90; tutor math., chemistry and physics Poquoson Sch. Bd., Va., 1994—; rep. alumnae admissions Boston area Mills Coll., 1987-91, trustee, bd. govs., 1995-98; mem. Citizens for Hilton Area Revitalization, 1994—. Math. and sci. tutor Centerville Sch. Bd., Ohio, 1982-86, math. and physics tutor Marblehead (Mass.) Sch. Bd., 1988-90; tutor math., chemistry and physics Poquoson Sch. Bd., Va., 1994—; rep. alumnae admissions Mills Coll., Boston area, 1987-91, trustee/bd. govs., 1995-98; mem. Citizens for Hilton Area Revitalization, 1994—. Recipient Notable Achievement award USAF, 1984, Spl. award Fed. Lab. Consortium, 1987. Mem. Soc. Mfg. Engrs., Sports and Entertainment Law Soc., Phi Alpha Delta. Avocation: book collecting. Home: 58 Hopkins St Newport News VA 23601-4034 Office: SAIC Suffolk VA 23535 Office Phone: 757-686-9815.

**NOBLITT, NILES L.,** medical products executive; s. William S. and Genevieve Noblitt. Grad., Rose Hulman Inst. Tech., Terre Haute, Ind., 1974. Co-founder, chmn. Biomet, Inc., Warsaw, Ind., 1977—; CEO Biomet-Merck, joint venture, Darmstadt, Germany, 1997—. Bd. dir. Advanced Medical Tech. Assn., Washington. Trustee Rose Hulman Inst. Tech. Office: Biomet Inc 56 E Bell Dr Warsaw IN 46582 Office Phone: 574-267-6639. Office Fax: 574-267-8137.

**NOBUMOTO, KAREN S.,** prosecutor; BA, U. Hartford, 1973; JD Southwestern U., 1989. Dep. dist. atty. County of L.A. Named Unsung Hero, KFWB Radio, 1997, Prosecutor of Yr., Century City Bar Assn., 1998, Person of Yr., Met. News-Enterprise, 2001, Lawyer of Yr., Calif. Lawyer Mag., 2003, Alumna of Yr., Southwestern U., 2003, Super Lawyer, L.A. mag., 2004. Mem.: L.A. County Bar Assn., Calif. Assn. Black Lawyers, Assn. Dep. Dist. Attys., Black Women Lawyers L.A., Women Lawyers Assn. L.A., John M. Langston Bar Assn. (pres. 1997), State Bar Calif. (pres. 2000—), Coalition 100 Black Women, Breakfast Club, Chancery Club. Office: LA Dist Attys Office 210 W Temple St Ste 18000 Los Angeles CA 90012-3210 Office Phone: 310-288-1216. E-mail: karennobu@aol.com.

**NOCE, DAVID D.,** federal judge; b. 1944; AB, St. Louis U., 1966; JD, Mo., 1969. Bar: Mo. Law clk. to Hon. H. Kenneth Wangelin US Dist. Ct. (ea. and we. dists.) Mo., 1972-73; law clk. to Hon. John F. Nangle US Dist. Ct. (ea. dist.) Mo., 1973-75; asst. US atty. (ea. dist.) Mo US Dept. Justice, St. Louis, 1975-76; magistrate judge US Dist. Ct. (ea. dist.) Mo., St. Louis, 1976—. Adj. prof. law St. Louis U. Sch. Law, Washington U. Sch. Law, St. Louis U. Author: Jury Instructions Drafting Workbook Ment, 1999. Served with U.S. Army, 1970-74. Mem. ABA, Mo. Bar, Bar Assn. Met. St. Louis, Fed. Magistrate Judges Assn. Office: US Courthouse 17th Flr N 111 S 10th St Saint Louis MO 63102 Office Phone: 314-244-7630.

**NOCE, DONNA,** retail executive; With Petrie Stores, Lerner NY; merchandising v.p. separates, dresses and suits Ann Taylor Stores, 1996—2000; v.p. merchandising and planning AnnTaylor.com, 2000—02; v.p. Ann Taylor Factory Stores, 2002, sr. v.p.; exec. v.p. merchandising and design Ann Taylor LOFT, 2006—. Office: Ann Taylor Stores Corp 7 Times Square 15th Fl New York NY 10036*

**NOCENTELLI, CARMEN,** literature educator; d. A. Nocentelli; m. S. J. Truett, Dec. 4, 1993. PhD, Stanford U., Calif., 2004. Asst. prof. english and comparative lit. U. N.Mex, Albuquerque, 2004—. Translator: Spostare il centro del mondo (Nonino Internat. prize, 2001); contbr. articles to profl. jours. Recipient Susan Geiger Faculty award, U.N.Mex. Feminist Rsch. Inst. Bd., 2005; fellow, Stanford U., 1997—98; grantee, Andrew W. Mellon Found., 1997, U. N.Mex, 2005; scholar, Fulbright Found., 1990—92; Mrs. Giles Whiting Dissertation fellowship, Stanford (Calif.) U., 1998—99, Mayers fellowship, The Huntington Libr., 2006, Lumsden-Kouvel fellowship, The Newberry Libr., 2006, Hall of Nations scholarship, Am. U., 1990-92, J. Douglas Canfield scholar, Jour. for Early Modern Cultural Studies Bd., 2003. Mem.: MLA, Group Early Modern Cultural Studies. Office: Department of English 1 University of New Mexico Albuquerque NM 87131-0001 Office Phone: 505-277-6347.

**NOCERA, JOSEPH,** editor, writer; b. May 1952; married; 3 children. BS in Journalism, Boston U. Contbg. editor Newsweek; exec. editor New England Monthly, Fortune Mag.; editorial dir.; editor Wash. Monthly; columnist The Profit Motive column, GQ, Esquire, 1988—90; sr. editor Tex. Monthly Mag.; editor-at-large Fortune Mag.; columnist Money Mag., 1998; fin. columnist NY Times, 2005—. Anchor PBS Frontline Documentary, Betting on the Market, 1997; master's project adv., grad. sch. journalism Columbia Univ.

Contbr. articles to Wall Street Journal, Newsweek, Wash. Monthly; author: Bidness: The Booms and Busts of the Texas Economy, 1986, A Piece of the Action: How the Middle Class Joined the Money Class, 1994 (NY Pub.Li-br.Helen Bernstein award for best non-fiction book of yr., 1995). Named one of 100 Business News Luminaries of the Century, The Journalist and Financial Reporting, 2000; recipient John Hancock award, 1983, 1984, 1991, Gerald Loeb award, 1993, 1996. Office: Columnist NY Times 229 W 43rd St New York NY 10036*

**NOCHIMSON, DAVID,** lawyer; b. Paterson, NJ, June 19, 1943; s. Samuel S. and Mildred (Singer) N.; m. Roberta Maizel, June 5, 1966 (div. 1972); m. Gail Burgess, May 26, 1978. BA, Yale U., 1965; LLB, Columbia U., 1968; LLM, Australian Nat. U., Canberra, 1969. Bar: N.Y. 1970, Calif. 1977. Assoc. Paul, Weiss, Rifkind, Wharton and Garrison, N.Y.C., 1970-72; sr. v.p. Comprop Equities Corp., N.Y.C., 1972-76; assoc. Mitchell, Silberberg and Knupp, L.A., 1977-80, ptnr., 1980-83, Ziffren, Brittenham, Branca, Fischer, Gilbert-Lurie & Stiffelman, L.A., 1983—. Adv. com. UCLA Entertainment Symposium, 1979-99, co-chmn., 1981-82. Contbr. articles to Encyclopedia of Investments, 1982, profl. jours. Pres. Friends of the L.A. Free Clinic, 1994-96; trustee Santa Monica (Calif.) Mus. of Art, 1995—. Fulbright scholar, Australia, 1968-69. Mem. ABA (forum com. on entertainment and sports industries 1982—, editor The Entertainment and Sports Lawyer 1982-89, chmn. 1989-92), Internat. Bar Assn. (Vice chmn. entertainment com. 1986-90), Am. Bar Found., Beverly Hills Bar Assn. Democrat. Jewish. Avocations: tennis, racquetball, yoga, playing piano, hiking. Office: Ziffren Brittenham Branca Fischer Gilbert-Lurie and Stiffelman 1801 Century Park W Los Angeles CA 90067-6406 Office Phone: 310-552-3388.

**NOCHLIN, LINDA,** art history educator; b. NYC, Jan. 30, 1931; d. Jules and Elka (Heller) Weinberg; m. Philip Nochlin (dec. 1960); 1 child, Jessica; m. Richard Pommer, June 3, 1968; 1 child, Daisy. BA in philosophy, Vassar Coll., 1951; MA in English, Columbia U., 1952; PhD in art history, NYU Inst. Fine Arts, 1963; doctorate (hon.), Mass. Coll. Art, Parsons Sch. Design, Colgate U., 1987; LittD (hon.), Harvard U., 2003. Instr. Vassar Coll. Poughkeepsie, NY, 1952-63, asst. prof., 1963-66, assoc. prof., 1966-69, prof., 1969-71, Mary Conover Mellon Prof. Art History, 1971-79; disting. prof. art history CUNY, 1980—90; prof. art history and humanities Yale U., 1990—92, Robert Lehman Prof. Art History; Lila Acheson Wallace Prof. Modern Art NYU Inst. Fine Arts, NYC, 1993—. Vis. prof. Columbia U., NYC, 1967-68, 75-76, Hunter Coll., NYC, 1970, Stanford U., 1971, CUNY Grad. Ctr., NYC, 1975-76; mem. editl. bd. Yale Jour. Criticism, Vassar Quarterly. Author: (essay) Why Have There Been No Great Women Artists?, 1971, (books) Realism and Tradition in Art, 1948-1900, 1966, Realism, 1971, 1993, Women as Sex Object: Studies in Erotic Art, 1730-1970, 1972, Women, Art and Power and Other Essays, 1988, The Politics of Vision: Essays on Nineteenth-Century Art and Society, 1989, The Body in Pieces: The Fragment as Metaphor of Modernity, 1994, Representing Women, 1999; co-editor: The Jew in Text: Modernity and Construction of Identity, 1995; Co-curator/co-author (with Anne Sutherland Harris) (exhibition and catalogue) Women Artists: 1550-1950, LA County Mus. Art, 1976. Named Scholar of Yr., NY State Coun. for Humanities, 1997; recipient Harbison Award for gifted teaching, Danforth Found., 1972, Woman of Yr. Award, Mademoiselle Mag., 1977, Disting. Svc. to the Visual Arts Award, ArtTable, 2003; Fulbright Fellowship, 1958—59, Fels Fellowship, 1962—63, Am. Coun. Learned Societies Fellowship, 1972—73, NEH Fellowship, 1977—78, Guggenheim Fellowship, 1984—85, Inst. Advanced Studies Fellowship, 1985, Resident Fellowship Bellagio Study and Conf. Ctr., Rockefeller Found., 1999, Self and History: A Symposium in Honor of Linda Nochlin presented at NYU, 1999. Fellow: Am. Philos. Soc., Am. Acad. Arts and Sciences; mem.: Am. Assn. Univ. Professors, Coll. Art Assn. (Arthur Kingsley Porter Prize for article Gustave Courbet's Meeting: A Portrait as a Wandering Jew 1968, Frank Jewett Mather Prize 1978, Ann. Recognition Award, Com. on Women and the Arts 1998), NOW, Phi Beta Kappa. Office: NYU Inst Fine Arts James B Duke House 1 E 78th St New York NY 10021

**NOCHMAN, LOIS WOOD KIVI (MRS. MARVIN NOCHMAN),** retired literature educator; b. Detroit, Nov. 5, 1924; d. Peter K. and Annetta Lois (Wood) Kivi; m. Harold I. Pitchford, Sept. 6, 1944 (div. May 1949); children: Jean Wood Pitchford Scott, Joyce Lynn Pitchford Undiano; m. Marvin A. Nochman, Aug. 15, 1953; 1 child, Joseph Asa. AB, U. Mich., 1946, AM, 1949. Tchr. adult edn., Honolulu, 1947, Ypsilanti (Mich.) H.S., 1951—52; spl. instr. English Wayne State U., Detroit, 1953—54; tchr. Highland Park (Mich.) Coll., 1950—51. instr. English, 1954—83; ret., 1983. Mem. exec. bd. Highland Park Fedn. Tchrs., 1963—66, 1973, del. to nat. conv., 64, 1971—74; rep. higher edn. Mich. Fedn. Tchrs. Exec. Com., 1972—76; mem. faculty adv. com. Gov's Commn. Higher Edn., 1973—. Contbr. articles to profl. jours. Tchr. Baha'i Schs., Davison, Mich., 1954—55, 1958—59, 1963—66, Beaulac, Quebec, Canada, 1960, Greenacre, Maine, 1965; sec. local spiritual assembly Baha'is, Ann Arbor, Mich., 1953, sec. Detroit, 1954, chmn., 1955; mem. nat. com. Baha'is U.S., 1955—58; sec. com. and coun. Baha'i Schs., Davison, Mich., 1956, 1958, 1963—68; Baha'i lectr. subject of local TV show Senior Focus, 1992. Recipient Women's Movement plaque, Women Lawyers Assn. Mich., 1975. Mem.: MLA, NOW, Nat. Soc. Lit. and Arts, Am. Fedn. Tchrs., Mich. Coll. English Assn., Nat. Coun. Tchrs. English, Women's Equity and Action League (sec. Mich. chpt. 1975—79), Alpha Gamma Delta, Alpha Lambda Delta. Avocation: U.S. Swimming Master Champion.

**NODDINGS, NEL,** education educator, writer; b. Irvington, N.J., Jan. 19, 1929; d. Edward A. Rieth and Nellie A. (Connors) Walter; m. James A. Noddings, Aug. 20, 1949; children: Chris, Howard, Laurie, James, Nancy, William, Sharon, Edward, Vicky, Timothy. BA in Math., Montclair State Coll., 1949; MA in Math., Rutgers U., 1964; PhD in Edn., Stanford U., 1973; PhD (hon.), Columbia Coll., 1993, Queen B.U., Can., 2006, Montclair State U., 2006. Cert. tchr. Calif., NJ. Tchr. Woodbury (N.J.) Pub. Schs., 1949-52; tchr. math. dept. Matawan (N.J.) High Sch., 1958-62, chair, asst. prin., 1964-69; curriculum supr. Montgomery Twp. Pub. Schs., Skillman, NJ, 1970-72; dir. precollegiate edn. U. Chgo., 1975-76; asst. prof. Pa. State U., State College, 1973; from asst. prof. to assoc. prof. Stanford (Calif.) U., 1977-86, prof., 1986—, assoc. dean, 1990-92, acting dean, 1992-94, Lee L. Jacks prof. child edn., 1992-98, prof. emeritus, 1998—; prof. philosophy and edn. Columbia U., N.Y.C., 1998—. Bd. dirs. Ctr. for Human Caring Sch. Nursing, Denver, 1986-92; cons. NIE, NSF and various other sch. dists. Author: Caring: A Feminine Approach to Ethics and Moral Education, 1984, Women and Evil, 1989; author: (with W. Paul Shore) Awakening the Inner Eye: Intuition in Education, 1984; author: (with Carol Witherell) Stories Lives Tell, 1991; author: The Challenge to Care in Schools, 1992, Educating for Intelligent Belief or Unbelief, 1993, Philosophy of Education, 1995, Starting at Home: Caring and Social Policy, 2002, Educating Moral People, 2002, Happiness and Education, 2003; editor (with Suzanne Gordon and Patricia Benner): Caregiving, 1996; editor: (with Michael Katz and Kenneth Strike) Justice and Caring, 1999; editor: Educating Citizens for Global Awareness, 2005, Critical Lessons: What Our Schools Should Teach, 2006. Mem. disting. women's adv. bd. Coll. St. Catherine. Recipient Anne Roe award for Contbns. to Profl. Devel. of Women, Harvard Grad. Sch. Edn., 1993, medal for disting. svc. Tchrs. Coll. Columbia, 1994, Willystine Goodsell award, 1997, Laureate chpt. Kappa Delta Pi, Pi Lambda Theta award, 1999, award for disting. leadership in edn. Rutgers U., 2004; Spencer Mentor grantee, Spencer Found., 1995-97. Fellow Philosophy of Edn. Soc. (pres. 1991-92); mem. Am. Ednl. Rsch. Assn. (Div B, 2000, Lifetime achievment award), Am. Philos. Assn., Nat. Acad. Edn. (pres. 2001—), John Dewey Soc. (pres. 1994-96), Phi Beta Kappa (vis. scholar). Avocation: gardening. Office Phone: 732-988-9695. Business E-Mail: noddings@stanford.edu.

**NODDINGS, SARAH ELLEN,** lawyer; b. Matawan, NJ; d. William Clayton and Sarah Stephenson (Cox) Noddings; children: Christopher, Aaron. BA in Math., Rutgers U., New Brunswick, N.J., 1965, MSW, 1968; JD cum laude, Seton Hall U., Newark, 1975; postgrad., UCLA, 1979. Bar: Calif. 1976, Nev. 1976, N.J. 1975, U.S. Dist. Ct. (ctrl. dist.) Calif. 1976, U.S. Dist. Ct. N.J.

1975. Social worker Carteret (N.J.) Bd. Edn., 1970-75; law clk. Hon. Howard W. Babcock, 8th Jud. Dist. Ct., Las Vegas, Nev., 1975-76; assoc. O'Melveny & Myers, L.A., 1976-78; atty. Internat. Creative Mgmt., Beverly Hills, Calif., 1978-81, Russell & Glickman, Century City, Calif., 1981-83; from atty to v.p. Lorimar Prodns., Culver City and Burbank, Calif., 1983—93; atty., v.p. Warner Bros. TV, Burbank, Calif., 1993—2001, sr. atty., 1999-2001; pvt. practice, 2001—. Dir. county youth program, rsch. analyst Sonoma County People for Econ. Opportunity, Santa Rosa, Calif., 1968-69; VISTA vol. Kings County Cmty. Action Orgn., Hanford, Calif., 1965-66; officer, PTA bd. West H.S., Casimir Mid. Sch. and Arlington Elem. Sch. Mem.: USTA (capt.), Media Dist. Intellectual Property Bar Assn. (bd. dir. 1999—2001), L.A. County Bar Assn. (intellectual property sect.), Women Entertainment Lawyers, Acad. TV Arts and Scis. (nat. awards com. 1994—96), L.A. Copyright Soc. (trustee 1990—91), Women in Film, South Bay Marine League (B-2 rep.). Avocations: travel, tennis, skiing, bicycling, swimming.

**NODDLE, JEFFREY,** retail and food distribution executive; BA, U. Iowa. Various positions, including pres. 2 food divsns. Supervalu Inc., Eden Prairie, Minn., 1976-92, exec. v.p. mktg., 1992-95, exec. v.p. mktg.; pres., COO wholesale food cos., 1995-99, COO, 2000-01, pres., CEO, 2001—, Chmn., 2002—. Bd. mem. Ind. Grocers Alliance Inc., Food Industry Ctr., U. Minn., Acad. Food Mktg., St. Joseph's U., Pa.; corp. bd. Donaldson Co. Inc.; chmn. bd. Food Mktg. Inst. Bd. dir. Greater Twin Cities United Way; bd. overseers U. Minn. Carlson Sch. Mgmt.; exec. com. Minn. Bus. Partnership. Office: Supervalu Inc 11840 Valley View Rd Eden Prairie MN 55344-3691*

**NODEEN, JANEY PRICE,** information technology executive; b. Scotland Neck, NC, Nov. 7, 1959; d. Wade Hampton and Joyce Ann (Councill) P.; m. Thomas Nodeen. BS in Info. Sci., Christopher Newport Coll., 1987; grad., Def. Sys. Mgmt. Coll., 1994; grad. advanced mgmt. program, Nat. Def. U., 1995. Engring. analyst Newport News (Va.) Shipbldg., 1978-86; mgr. submarine info. resources and computer ops. Dept. of the Navy, Washington, 1986-93, mem. exec. devel. program, 1993-96, sr. staff Navy Acquisition Reform Exec., 1995, dep. program exec. officer Submarines for Acquisition, 1996-97; prin. Burke Consortium, Inc., Springfield, Va., 1997—. Mil. legis. fellow for Congressman Sam Gejdenson, 1994; sr. exec. fellow John F. Kennedy Sch. Govt. Harvard U., class officer, 1994. Home: 6915 Ashbury Dr Springfield VA 22152-3221 Office: Burke Consortium Inc Ste 510 5500 Cherokee Ave Alexandria VA 22312

**NOE, ADRIANNE,** museum administrator; PhD in History, U. Del. Assoc. dir. Armed Forces Inst. Pathology; dir. Nat. Mus. Health and Medicine, Washington. Adj. prof. computational biosciences George Mason U., Fairfax County, Va.; v.p. bd. dirs. Nat. Health Sci. Consortium. Fellow, Guggenheim Found.; History fellow, USAF. Mem.: Med. Mus. Assn. (past pres.), Washington Soc. for the History of Medicine (pres.), Acad. Medicine. Office: Nat Mus Health and Medicine Bldg 54 6825 16th St NW Washington DC 20306-6000

**NOE, ELIZABETH HARDY,** lawyer; b. Albertville, Ala., Sept. 24, 1964; d. John William and Nancy Jo (Luther) Hardy; m. George McRae Noe, Nov. 6, 1993. BA, Agnes Scott Coll., 1986; JD, U. Va., 1989. Bar: La. 1989, Ga. 1996. Assoc. Jones, Walker, Waechter, Poitevent, Carrere & Denegre, New Orleans, 1989-94; of counsel Paul, Hastings, Janofsky & Walker, Atlanta, 1995—, mem. policy com., co-chmn. atty. devel., ptnr., 2001—. Mem. ABA, La. Bar Assn., Ga. Bar Assn. Office: Paul Hastings Janofsky & Walker 600 Peachtree St NE Ste 2400 Atlanta GA 30308-2265 Office Phone: 404-815-2287. Business E-Mail: elizabethnoe@paulhastings.com.

**NOE, ELNORA (ELLIE NOE),** retired chemicals executive; b. Evansville, Ind., Aug. 23, 1928; d. Thomas Noe and Evelyn (West) Dieter. Student, Ind. U.-Purdue U., Indpls. Sec. Pitman Moore Co., Indpls., 1946—60; with Dow Chem. Co., Indpls., 1960-90, pub. rels. asst. then mgr. employee comm., 1970-87, mgr. cmty. rels., 1987-90, DowBrands, Inc., Indpls., 1986-90, vice chmn. Indpls. C. of C. corp. affairs discussion group, 1988—89, chmn., 1989-90; mem. steering com. Learn About Bus. Recipient 2d pl. award as Businesswoman of Yr., Indpls. Bus. and Profl. Women's Assn., 1980, Indpls. Profl. Woman of Yr. award Zonta, Altrusa, Soroptomist & Pilot Svc. Clubs, 1985. DowBrands Great Things Cmty. Svc. award, 1991. Mem. Am. Bus. Women Assn. (Woman of Yr. award 1965, past pres.), Ind. Assn. Bus. Communicators (hon., Communicator of Yr. 1977), Assn. Women in Comm. (Louise Eleanor Kleinhenz award 1984), Zonta (dist. pub. rels. chmn. 1978-80, area dir. 1980-82, pres. Indpls. club 1977-79, bd. dirs. 1993-95, 2000-02, 04-06, v.p. 2006—), Dow Indpls. Retiree Group (pres. 1995—). Personal E-mail: elenoe@aol.com.

**NOE, GUY,** retired social services administrator; b. Brussels, Jan. 28, 1934; came to U.S., 1955, naturalized, 1961; s. Marinus Cornelis and Johana Dorothea (Beijne) N.; 1 child, Jeanette Sue. BS, Regional Agrl. Sch., Loiret, France, 1954. Social worker State of Wyo., Casper, 1962-66; dir. Natrona County (Wyo.) Dept. Public Assistance, Casper, 1966-79, Wyo. Div. Mental Health, Cheyenne, 1979-82, asst. adminstr. Divsn. of Youth Svcs., 1992-95; former mgr. Platte County Office Pub. Assistance and Social Svcs., Wheatland, Wyo., dir. low income energy assistance programs, 1994-95. Lectr. in field. V.p. Wyo. chpt. Big Bros., 1976-77; chmn. adv. coun. social svcs. State of Wyo., 1969-79; bd. dirs. Casper United Way, 1970—, Casper Salvation Army, 1970—, Casper chpt. ARC, 1977—; mem. Gov's Drug Abuse Adv. Bd., 1992—; pres. State Employees Assn. Named Outstanding Adminstr. State of Wyo., 1976; recipient Youth Svcs. award Wyo. Human Resources Confedn., 1988; named to Wyo. Dept. Family Svcs. Hall of Fame, 2005. Mem. ASPA, Am. Public Welfare Assn. (Wyo. membership chmn.), Wyo. State Employees Assn. (pres. 1996-97), Toastmasters. Democrat. Home: 2731 Deming Blvd Cheyenne WY 82001-5709

**NOE, JAMES ALVA,** retired judge; b. Billings, Mont., May 25, 1932; s. James Alva Sr. and Laura Madlen (Parmenter) N.; m. Patricia Arlene Caudill, Aug. 4, 1956; children: Kendra Sue, Jeffrey James, Bradley John, Kirkwood Merle. BA in Polit. Sci., U. Wash., 1954, LLB, 1957; LittD hon., Christian Theol. Sem., 1986. Bar: Wash. 1958, U.S. Dist. Ct. (we. dist.) Wash. 1958, U.S. Ct. Appeals (9th cir.) 1959. Dep. prosecuting atty. King County, Seattle, 1958-61; trial lawyer Williams, Kastner & Gibbs, Seattle, 1961-67; judge Seattle Mcpl. Ct., 1967-71, King County Superior Ct., 1971-96; ret., 1996. Moderator Christian Ch. (Disciples of Christ) in the U.S. and Can., 1977-79. Fellow: Am. Bar Found. (life); mem.: Hall-o. of dels. 1976-78, 1982—87, 1991—96, 2003—, bd. govs. 1991—94, chmn. jud. divsn. 1988—89, chmn. nat. conf. state trial judges 1981—82, sr. lawyers divsn. coun. 2001—), Nat. Jud. Coll. (trustee 1988—91, 1995—2001, chair 1999—2001), Wash. State Superior Ct. Judges Assn. (pres. 1984—85, Wash. State Jurist of Yr. award 1991). Home: 8250 SE 61st St Mercer Island WA 98040-4902

**NOEL, AMY SUE,** elementary school educator; b. Latrobe, Pa., May 18, 1977; d. Stanley Paul and Gail Susan (Rubis) Klejka; m. Michael Steven Noel, Aug. 4, 1969. BS in Edn., Calif. U., Pa., 2001; M in Literacy, Ind. U. Pa., 2006. Elem. sch. tchr. GLSD, Latrobe, Pa., 2001—. Personal E-mail: aklejkanoel@yahoo.com.

**NOEL, BARBARA HUGHES MCMURTRY,** retired music educator; b. Mt. Vernon, Wash., Feb. 27, 1929; d. Lowell Robinson and Mary Evelyn (Hayton) Hughes; children: Sarah Kathleen, Martha Elizabeth. BM, U. Ky., 1951, MM, 1952; PhD, U. Ill., 1972; student, Oberlin Conservatory, 1947-49. Instr. music Union Coll., Barbourville, Ky., 1952-54; instr. music and fine arts Annie Wright Sem., Tacoma, 1957-63; organist, choirmaster Episc. churches, Calif., Wash., 1954-66; chmn. music dept. U. Richmond (Va.), 1971-76, Mankato (Minn.) State U., 1976-78; dean coll. humanities and fine arts Tex. Woman's U., Denton, 1978-81; dean coll. visual and performing arts U. Mass. Dartmouth, North Dartmouth, 1981-89; prof. music U. Mass., Dartmouth 1990—96, ret. 1996. Cons. for various music orgns. and univs., 1976—; textbook pubs., 1980—; reviewer Nat. Endowment for the Humanities. Book reviewer Providence Sunday Jour., 1984—; contbr. articles to music jours.

contbr. New Grove Dictionary of Music, 1974. Bd. dirs. Community Symphony Orchs., Mankato, 1976-78, New Bedford, Mass., 1981-87. Grad. fellow Danforth Found., U. Ill., 1966-71. Mem. Coll. Music Soc. (treas. 1983-87, v.p. 1979-83, coun. mem.), Nat. Assn. Schs. Music (undergrad. commr. 1978-81). Episcopalian. Avocations: reading, travel, hiking. Home: 301 Linden Ponds Way BC 521 Hingham MA 02043

**NOEL, DON OBERT, JR.,** retired editor, columnist; b. Elizabeth, NJ, Nov. 27, 1931; s. Don O. and Catherine (Pyle) N.; m. Elizabeth Bradford Foulds, Aug. 29, 1953; 1 child, Emily Rebecca. BA in Am. Studies, Cornell U., 1954. Reporter Hartford (Conn.) Times, 1958-68, asst. mng. editor, 1968-69, editorial page editor, 1969-74, editor in chief, 1974-75; sr. corr. WFSB-TV, host Face the State Post-Newsweek Stas., 1975-84; polit. columnist op-ed page Hartford Courant, 1984-97, ret., 1997. Author: Jamaica memoir, Near a Far Sea, 2006. Bd. sec. Blue Hills Civic Assn., Hartford, 1988-05; bd. dirs. ACLU of Conn., 1998-, chair, 2005-. Served alt. mil. duty Am. Friends Svc. Com., Tokyo, 1954-56. Recipient Sevellon Brown Meml. award New England AP, 1964, Nat. Journalism award AMA, 1972, Nat. Journalism award Am. Soc. Planning Officials, 1972, 74; fellow Alicia Patterson Found., 1966-67; finalist Pulitzer Prize for non-deadline reporting, 1964. Mem. Soc. Of Friends. Avocations: gardening, birdwatching, language study. Home: 141 Ridgefield St Hartford CT 06112-1837 Office Phone: 860-247-2080. Personal E-mail: dononoel@yahoo.com.

**NOEL, EDWIN LAWRENCE,** lawyer; b. St. Louis, July 11, 1946; s. Thomas Currie and Christine (Jones) N.; m. Nancy Carter Simpson, Feb. 7, 1970; children: Caroline, Edwin C. BA, Brown U., 1968; JD cum laude, St. Louis U., 1974. Bar: Mo. 1974, U.S. Dist. Ct. (ea. dist.) Mo. 1974, U.S. Ct. Appeals (8th cir.) 1974, U.S. Ct. Appeals (6th cir.) 1978, U.S. Ct. Appeals (7th cir.) 1994, U.S. Supreme Ct. 1986. Ptnr. Armstrong, Teasdale, LLP, St. Louis, 1974—, mng. ptnr., 1993-97. Bd. dirs. Corley Printing Co., St. Louis, Home Fed. Savs. Bank of Mo., 1988—93. Bd. dirs. Edgewood Children's Ctr., St. Louis, 1982-92, St. Louis Assn. for Retarded Citizens, 1984-87, Churchill Sch., 1988-94, Whitfield Sch., 1991-95; chmn. Mo. Clean Water Com., Jefferson City, 1982-88. Mem. Mo. Bar Assn., Bar Assn. Met. St. Louis, Attys. Liability Assurance Soc. (bd. dirs. 1995—). Republican. Episcopalian. Home: 301 S Mcknight Rd Saint Louis MO 63124-1884 Office: Armstrong Teasdale LLP 1 Metropolitan Sq Ste 2600 Saint Louis MO 63102-2740 Office Phone: 314-621-5070. Business E-mail: enoel@armstrongteasdale.com.

**NOEL, FRANKLIN LINWOOD,** judge; b. NYC, Dec. 7, 1951; s. Charles Alexander and Mayme (Loth) N.; m. Ellen Barbara Perl, Sept. 15, 1979; children: Kate Alexandra, Charles David. BA, SUNY, Binghamton, 1974; JD, Georgetown U., 1977. Bar: D.C. 1977, U. S. Dist. Ct. D.C. 1978, U.S. Ct. Appeals (D.C. cir.) 1978, Pa. 1979, Minn. 1983, U.S. Ct. Appeals (8th cir.) 1983, U.S. Dist. Ct. Minn. 1984. Assoc. Arnold & Porter, Washington, 1977-79; asst. dist. atty. Phila. Dist. Attys. Office, 1979-83; asst. U.S. atty. U.S. Attys. Office, Mpls., 1983-89; U.S. magistrate judge U.S. Dist. Ct., Mpls., 1989—. Legal writing instr. U. Minn., Mpls., 1989-92, adj. prof. Law Sch., 1996—. Mem. League of Am. Wheelman, Phi Beta Kappa. Episcopalian. Avocation: bicycling. Office: US Dist Ct 300 S 4th St Minneapolis MN 55415-1320

**NOEL, JEANNE KAY,** biotechnology company executive; b. Grosse Pointe, Mich., June 26, 1946; d. Wade Stephen and Katharine Adair (Jahimiak) Fuller. BS, U. Mich., 1967; PhD, 1970. NIH rsch. fellow UCLA, 1971-74; dir. R & D, sci. products div. Abbott Labs., L.A., 1974-78; dir. mktg. Alpha Therapeutic Corp., L.A., 1978-81; mgr. healthcare devel. Cetus Corp., Emeryville, Calif., 1981-83, dir. diagnostics bus., 1983-86; pres., cons. J. Kay Noel & Assocs., Inc., El Cerrito, Calif., 1986—; v.p. planning and bus. devel. Axion Pharms., Inc., South San Francisco, Calif., 1992-93. Mem. AAAS, Am. Assn. Clin. Chemistry, Sigma Xi. Office Phone: 510-525-4250. E-mail: kay@jknoel.net.

**NOEL, JODY LYNN See MAYER, JODY**

**NOEL, MARY MARGARET,** nutritionist, educator; b. Tacoma, July 13, 1948; d. Webster Young and Katharine Adair; m. George W. Noel, June 30, 1973; children: Katherine Mary, Joseph William. BS in Dietetics, Mich. State U., 1969; MPH, U. Mich., 1973; PhD in Family Ecology, Mich. State U., 1988. Registered dietitian. Intern in dietetics Barnes Med. Ctr., St. Louis, 1970; nutrition cons. Vis. Nurse Assn., St. Louis, 1970-72; clin. nutritionist U. Mich., Ann Arbor, 1973-76; instr. dietetics Mich. State U., East Lansing, 1975-76; cons. in nutrition East Lansing, 1976-86; exec. dir. Dairy Coun. of Mich., Okemos, 1986-88; asst. prof. family practice, Coll. Human Medicine Mich. State U., East Lansing, 1988-93, assoc. prof., 1993—2000, prof., 2000—, assoc. chair dept., 1997—. Mem. Neighborhood Assn., East Lansing, 1983-97; bd. dirs., treas. Downtown Devel. Authority, East Lansing, 1986-96; vol. East Lansing Pub. Schs., 1982-98. Grantee, NIH, 1997—2001. Mem. Am. Dietetic Assn. (sect. sec. 1970—), Mich. Dietetic Assn. (parliamentarian 1972—, nominating com., Recognized Young Dietitian 1977), Soc. for Tchrs. of Family Medicine, Vis. Nurses of Lansing (vice chair, then chair 1987-91) Office: Mich State U Dept Family Practice Coll Human Medicin B101 Clin Ctr East Lansing MI 48824 Business E-mail: noel@msu.edu.

**NOEL, RANDALL DEANE,** lawyer; b. Memphis, Oct. 19, 1953; s. D.A. and Patricia G. Noel; m. Lissa Johns, May 28, 1977; children: Lauren Elizabeth, Randall Walker. BBA with honors, U. Miss., 1975, JD, 1978. Bar: Miss. 1978, U.S. Dist. Ct. (no. and so. dists.) Miss. 1978, Tenn. 1979, U.S. Dist. Ct. (we., mid. and ea. dists.) Tenn. 1979, U.S. Ct. Appeals (5th and 6th cirs.) 1984, U.S. Supreme Ct. 1986. Assoc. Armstrong/Allen, PLLC, Memphis, 1978-85, ptnr., 1985—, mgr. litig. practice group, 1990-94; mgmt. com. Armstrong, Allen, Prewitt, Gentry, Johnston & Holmes, Memphis, 1994—97; chief mem. Armstrong/Allen, PLLC, Memphis, 2002—04; ptnr. Butler, Snow, O'Mara, Stevens & Cannada, 2004—. Fin. com. Memphis in May Internat. Festival, 1980-81; pres. Carnival Memphis, 1996; bd. dirs. Christ United Meth. Ch., Memphis, 1984-87, 89-91, chmn. bd. trustees, 1995; mem. Leadership Memphis, 1994-95. Fellow Am. Bar Found., Tenn. Bar Found., Memphis Bar Found.; mem. ABA (young lawyers divsn., fellow dir. 1988-90, editor The Affiliate newsletter 1987-88, dir. Affiliate Outreach project 1988—, vice-chmn. Award of Achievement com. 1986, ALI-ABA bd. 1992-97, div. dir. litig. sect., 2002, coun. litig. sect., mem. House of Dels., standing com. fed. judiciary), Am. Counsel Assn. (pres. 1997), Tenn. Bar Assn. (pres. young lawyers divsn. 1990, pres. litig. sect. 1988, bd. govs. 1989—, pres. 1999, Pres.'s Disting. Svc. award 1988-89), So. Conf. Bar Pres. (pres. 2000), Memphis and Shelby Bar Assn. (mem. jud. recommendations, law week nominations and membership coms.), Miss. Bar Assn. (South Rsch. Inst., Tenn. Def. Lawyers Assn., Am. Judicature Soc. (bd. dirs. 1992-96), Tenn. Legal Cmty. Found. (pres. 1999-2001), Tenn. Supreme Ct. Hist. Soc. (bd. dirs. 2005). Home: 2938 Tishomingo Ln Memphis TN 38111-2627 Office: Butler Snow O'Mara Stevens & Cannada PLLC Ste 500 Crescent Ctr 6075 Poplar Ave Memphis TN 38119 Business E-mail: randy.noel@butlersnow.com.

**NOËLDECHEN, JOAN MARGUERITE,** writer; b. West Islip, NY, May 20, 1963; d. Warren G. Noëldechen and Joan Marguerite Walter. BA in English and Drama, Flagler Coll., St. Augustine, Fla., 1985. Author: (novel) Dreamers Out of Step, 1995, 00, (poetry) Ashes and Embers, 1996, (poetry) Ashes & Embers: Complete Poems, 2000, (poetry) Following Angels and Wolves, 1997, (novella) Eve's Journey, 1999, 00, (anthologies) Bedside Prayers, 1997, Bless the Day, 1998, Trinity Poems, 1999, (screenplays) Takoma Blue, 2003, (screenplays) Borrowed Starling, 2004, (poetry) House Blessings, 2004, (poetry) Everyday Blessings, 2005, 06, (poetry) Beyond Katrina, 2005, (poetry) Pocket Prayers, 2006, (poetry) Forever in Love, 2006; co-author (with Silvi M. Richardson): And the Angels Sing, 1995, Shadowdance, 1996, Pasaquan Daze, 1996, (play) And the Angels Sing, 1996. Mem. Thomas Wolfe Soc. Avocations: reading, cooking, gardening, hiking, photography.

**NOER, RICHARD J.,** physics professor, researcher; b. Madison, Wis., July 3, 1937; s. Rudolf J. and Anita M. (Showerman) N.; m. Raymonde Tasset, Aug. 17, 1967; children— Geoffrey, Catherine BA, Amherst Coll., 1958; PhD, U. Calif., Berkeley, 1963. Physicist Atomic Energy Research, Harwell, Eng., 1963-64; asst. prof. physics Amherst Coll., Mass., 1964-66; from asst. prof. physics to prof. Carleton Coll., Northfield, Minn., 1966—98, Laurence McKinley Gould prof. natural scis., 1998—2004, emeritus, 2004—, chmn. dept. physics, 1974—77, 1989—92, 2001—02. Vis. prof. Cornell U., 2004; physicist Ames Lab., Iowa, summers 1977-80, 82-84; rsch. physicist U. Geneva, 1980-81, 84-85; vis. scientist U. Paris, Orsay, France, 1972-73, Cornell U., summers 1986, 88-91, Centre d'Etudes Nucléaires, Saclay, France, 1992-93, KEK High Energy Accelera, Tsukuba, Japan, 2000-01. Co-author: Revolutions in Physics, 1972; contbr. articles to profl. jours. Mem.: AAAS, Am. Assn. Physics Tchrs., Am. Phys. Soc., Sigma Xi, Phi Beta Kappa. Home: 101 Winona St Northfield MN 55057-2232 Office: Carleton Coll Dept Physics Northfield MN 55057 Business E-Mail: rnoer@carleton.edu.

**NOETH, CAROLYN FRANCES,** speech and language pathologist; b. Cleve., July 21, 1924; d. Sam Falco and Barbara Serafina (Loparo) Armaro; m. Lawrence Andrew Noeth Sr., June 29, 1946; children: Lawrence Andrew Jr. (dec.), Barbara Marie. AB magna cum laude, Case Western Res. U., 1963; MEd, U. Ill., 1972; postgrad., Nat. Coll. Edn., 1975—. Lic. speech and lang. pathologist, Ill. Speech therapist Chgo. Pub. Schs., 1965; speech, lang. and hearing clinician J. Sterling Morton High Schs., Cicero and Berwyn, Ill., 1965-82, tchr. learning disabilities/behavior disorders, 1982, dist. ednl. diagnostician, 1982-84, Title I Project tchr., summers 1966-67, lang. disabilities cons., summers 1968-69, in-svc. tng. cons., summer 1970, dir. Title I Project, summers 1973-74; learning disabilities tchr. West Campus of Morton, 1971-75; chmn. Educable-Mentally Handicapped Opportunities Tchrs. Com., 1967-68; spl. edn. area and in-sch. tchrs. workshops, 1967—. Chmn. in compiling and publishing Student Handbook, Cleve. Coll., 1962; contbr. lyric parodies and music programs J. Sterling Morton H.S. West Retirement Teas, 1972-83. Precinct elections judge, 1953-55; block capt. Mothers March of Dimes and Heart Fund, 1949-60; St. Agatha's rep. Nat. Cath. Women's League, 1952-53; collector various charities, 1967, 93-94, 98, 99, 2000, 2001, 2002; mem. exec. bd. Morton Scholarship League, 1981-84, corr. sec., 1981-83; vol. Am. Cancer Soc., 1985—; vol. judge Ill. Acad. Decathlon, 1988—. First recipient Virda L. Stewart award for Speech, Western Res. U., 1963, Outstanding Sr. award, 1963. Mem. Am. Speech, Lang. and Hearing Assn. (life, cert.), Ill. Speech, Lang. and Hearing Assn. (life), Coun. Exceptional Children (divsn. for learning disabilities, pioneers divsn., chpt. spl. projects chmn., exec. bd. 1976-81, chpt. pres. 1979-80), Coun. for Learning Disabilities, Profls. in Learning Disabilities, Kappa Delta Pi, Delta Kappa Gamma (chmn., co-chmn. chpt. music com. 1979—, state program com. 1981-83, chpt. music rep. to state 1982—, chmn. chpt. promotion com. 1993-94, 96—), St. Norbert's Women's Club (Northbrook, Ill.), Case-Western Res. U., U. Ill. Alumni Assns., Lions (vol. Northbrook 1966-93). Roman Catholic. Home and Office: 1849 Walnut Cir Northbrook IL 60062-1245 Personal philosophy: "This above all: to thine own self be true; and it must follow as the night the day; Thou canst not then be false to any man." (Shakespeare's Hamlet).

**NOFFKE, FRANK EDWARD,** educational planner, writer, educator; s. Harry John and Elsie Strack Noffke; m. Ruth Ann Thompson, July 23, 1943 (dec. June 20, 1978); children: James T., Cody. BA, Ind. U., Bloomington, 1938; EdM, Wash. State, Pullman, 1957. Math. instr. U.S. Mil. Acad., West Point, NY, 1945—46; asst. dean student union and activities Case Inst. of Tech., Cleve., 1946—49; planning dir. Compton student union and activities Wash. State, Pullman, 1949—59; v.p. Coll. Planning Assoc., Kalamazoo, 1959—61; planning dir. Coll. union, student activities and values rsch. Baldwin-Wallace Coll., Berea, Ohio, 1961—64; planning dir. student union (designated father of the union) Calif. State U., Long Beach, 1964—80; pres. Frank Noffke Assoc., Pentwater, Mich., 1950—; instr. grad. sch. edn. Calif. State U. at Long Beach, 1972—75. Cons. coll. union and long range planning for universities Frank Noffke Assoc., 1950—; counselor/dir. emeritus veterans affairs dept. Calif. State U., Long Beach, 1972—80; counselor Peace Edn. on campuses World U., Ojai, Calif., 1983—83; chair inter-assn. com. Assn. of Coll. Unions; chair Coun. of Nat. Student Pers. Assns.; mem. Calif. State Post-Secondary Evaluation Team for New Universities, 1984—86, 1995; cons. in field. Author: Planning for a Coll. Union, 1965, 2d edit., 1996; contbr. articles to profl. jours. Mem. UN Non-Governmental Com. on Disarmament, 1995—2000, 2003—; chair and peace adv. OPEN Peace Edn. Network of West Mich., Pentwater, Mich., 1988—; liaison rep. to Rep. Kucinich OPEN Peace Network of West Mich., Washington, 2001—. Maj. Signal Corps U.S. Army, 1941—46. Recipient cert. of appreciation, U.S. Dept. Health, Edn. and Welfare, 1979, Hon. Citizen of Tucson, Ariz., Edn. Com. Excellence award, Nat. Assn. of Veterans Program Adminstrs. Mem.: Pentwater Svc. Club, Phi Kappa Phi (life). Independent. Congregational U.C.C. Achievements include first to organize peace enclave in W. Mich; invention of regional Peacekeeper O.P.E.N. award. Avocations: tennis, reading, writing. Home: 5631 Vaughn Street Pentwater MI 49449

**NOFFSINGER, NANCY LEIGH,** special education educator; b. Princeton, Ky., Oct. 20, 1948; d. Charlie H. and Margaree (Oates) N. BS, Murray (Ky.) State U., 1980, masters equivalent, 1982, postgrad., 1987. LPN, 1974. Sch. nurse, then spl. edn. tchr. Dawson Springs (Ky.) Bd. Edn., 1980-83; spl. edn. substitute tchr. various counties, Ky., 1983-85; spl. edn. tchr. Critten County Bd. Edn., Marion, Ky., 1985—98, Christian County Bd. Edn., Hopkinsville, Ky., 1998—2003; ret., 2003; sub. tchr., 2004—. Mem. NEA, ACLU, Ky. Edn. Assn. (1st dist. pres. 1996-97, human and civil rights state com. 1994—, chair 1997-98), Crittenden County Edn. Assn. (pres. 1992-95, 97-98, chair KePAC legis. chair 1995-97), Christian County Edn. Assn. (bldg. rep. 1998-2003), Nature Conservancy, World Wildlife Fund, Sierra Club, Nat. Wildlife Fedn. Democrat. Office Phone: 270-619-1117. Personal E-mail: nancy@noffsinger.net.

**NOFFZE, JENNIFER NOEL,** museum administrator; b. Anderson, Ind., Dec. 23, 1976; d. Barry Lynn Noffze and Carolyn Marie Carr. BA, Ball State U., 2000. Rsch. analyst Aspen Sys. Corp., Indpls., 2000—01; asst. collections dept. Children's Mus. Indpls., 2001—02, registrar, archist, 2002—. Vol. Meals on Wheels, Indpls., 2002—; campaign vol. Rep. Party, Anderson, 1998. Mem.: Soc. Ind. Archivists, Midwest Registrars Com., Assn. Midwest Mus. Lutheran. Avocations: boating, travel, reading, knitting, hiking. Home: Apt 43 3055 N Meridian Indianapolis IN 46208

**NOGALES, LUIS GUERRERO,** investment company executive; b. Madera, Calif., Oct. 17, 1943; s. Alejandro Cano and Florence (Guerrero) N.; children: Alicia Fipp, Maria Cristina. BA in Polit. Sci., San Diego State U., 1966; JD, Stanford U., 1969. Asst. to pres. Stanford U., Calif., 1969-72; White House fellow, asst. to sec. U.S. Dept. Interior, Washington, 1972-73; exec. v.p., dir. Golden West Broadcasters, L.A., 1973-80; pres. Nogales, Bermudex, Chase and Tamayo, L.A., 1981-82; chmn., chief exec. officer UPI, Washington, 1983-86; pres. ECO Internat. News Svc., 1987, Univision, 1987-88; gen. ptnr. Nogales Castro Ptnrs., 1989-90; mng. ptnr. Nogales Investors Mgmt. LLC, LA, 1990—. Bd. mem. Edison Internat., KB Home, Arbitron Inc. Bd. dirs. State of Calif. Bd. Higher Edn., Sacramento, 1973-79, LA Redevelopment Agy., 1973-76, United Way Am., Alexandria, Va., 1984-88; trustee Claremont U. Ctr. and Grad. Sch., 1987; chmn. MALDEF, 1980-82; bd. trustees J. Paul Getty Trust, LA, 2000-. Mayo Clinic, Rochester, Minn., 2003-. Office: Nogales Investors Mgmt LLC Ste 900 9229 W Sunset Blvd Los Angeles CA 90069 Office Phone: 310-276-7439. Office Fax: 310-276-7405.*

**NOGAY, ARLIE R.,** lawyer; m. Mary J. Hackett; children: Walter, Robert. AB in anthropology, Brown U., 1981; JD magna cum laude, U. Pitts., 1987. Bar: Pa. 1987. Assoc. Reed Smith LLP, Pitts., 1987—96, ptnr., 1996—, practice group leader corp. & securities group, 2002—. Mem.: Allegheny

County Bar Assn., Pa. Bar Assn., ABA. Office: Reed Smith LLP 435 Sixth Ave Pittsburgh PA 15219 Office Phone: 412-288-4594. Office Fax: 412-288-3063. Business E-Mail: anogay@reedsmith.com.

**NOGINA, ELENA Y.,** mathematics professor, researcher; d. Yuri M. Malinsky and Olga V. Nogina; m. Sergei N. Artemov, Dec. 15, 1984; children: Dmitry Nogin, Aleksey Nogin. M in Math. & Edn., Moscow U., PhD in Math. Vis. prof. U. Montpellier, III, 1992; vis. rschr. U. Amsterdam, 1994; rschr. Acad. Sci., Moscow; assoc. prof. Moscow U., CUNY, NYC, 2001—. Math. logic & computability theory dept. chair Moscow U., 1983—97, dir. math. & computer sci. program for liberal arts/linguistics, 1993—97. Contbr. scientific papers. Recipient Svc. in Edn. medal, USSR Parliament, 1987, Sci. Achievements medal, USSR Nat. Exhbn.; Rsch. grant, Internat. Sci. Found., 1993—95, Nat. Grant Program Univs. Russia, 1994—97, Russian Found. Basic Rsch., 1994—97, CCRI, 2004—05, PCS-CUNY, 2005—06. Mem.: NY Acad. Sci., Moscow Matematical Soc., Assn. Symbolic Logic, Am. Math. Soc. Home: 21 S End Ave Penthouse 2V New York NY 10280-1071

**NOGINOV, MIKHAIL A.,** physicist, researcher, educator; b. Dolgoprudnyi, Russia, May 28, 1962; arrived in U.S., 1991; s. Anatolii M. and Lidia V. (Platonova) N.; m. Natalia Noginova (Chernova), July 3, 1982; children: Maxim M., Julia M. MSEE, Moscow Inst. Physics and Tech., 1985; PhD in Physics and Math., USSR Acad. Scis., Moscow, 1990. Engr., from jr. staff rschr. to staff rschr. Gen. Physics Inst. of USSR Acad. Scis., 1985—91; rsch. assoc. MIT, Cambridge, 1991-93; from asst. to assoc. rsch. prof. dept. physics Ala. Agrl. Mech. U., Huntsville, 1993-97; assoc. rsch. prof. Ctr. for Materials Rsch., Norfolk (Va.) State U., 1997—99, from asst. to assoc. prof. dept. physics, 1999—. Adj. assoc. prof. Va. Poly. Inst., Va. Tech., Blacksburg, 1999-2003; grant proposal reviewer NSF, CRDF; panel reviewer NSF; jour reviewer sci. jours. including Optical Soc., Am. Phys. Soc., others; mem., chmn. various conf. coms. Author: Solid-State Randm Lasers, 2005; contbr. articles to profl. jours., chapters to books. Mem.: IEEE, Am. Phys. Soc., Optical Soc. Am. (faculty adv. student chpt. Norfolk State U. 2003—), Sigma Xi. Achievements include research in spectroscopic characterization and study of energy transfer processes in laser and nonlinear optical materials; energy transfer upconversion in laser materials, optimization of solid-state laser materials, nonlinear optics, holographic recording; photorefraction mechanisms and holographic currents in dielectric and semiconductor crystals; intrinsic optical bistability in broad variety of materials with different mechanisms and nonlinearity; stimulated emission in ensembles of micro-size, nano-size particles with optical gain, potential miniature light sources for integrated optics; optoelectronics and nanoscale devices (random lasers). Avocations: travel, windsurfing. Office: Norfolk State U Ctr for Materials Rsch 700 Park Ave Norfolk VA 23504-3993 Personal E-mail: mnoginov@hotmail.com. Business E-Mail: mnoginov@nsu.edu.

**NOGLOWS, WILLIAM P.,** electronics executive; BS in Chem. Engring., Ga. Inst. Tech. From various mgmt. positions to exec. v.p. Cabot Corp., Aurora, Ill., 1984—98, exec. v.p., 1998—2003; chmn. Cabot Microelectronics Corp., Aurora, 2003—, pres., 2003—, CEO, 2003—. Office: Cabot Microelectronics Corp 870 N Commons Dr Aurora IL 60504*

**NOGUCHI, HIDEO,** insurance company executive; b. Kyoto, Jan. 17, 1945; s. Tasao and Ishiko (Tsujii) Noguchi; m. Eleanor Kazuko Horii, May 7, 1970; children: Mark H.Y., Mitchell H.Y. BBA, U. Hawaii, 1969. Buyer RCA Purchasing Co., Tokyo, 1969—73; ins. specialist Continental Ins. Agy., Honolulu, 1973—82; CEO Noguchi & Assocs., Inc., Honolulu, 1983—. Cons. in field. Named to Coll. Bus. Adminstrn. Alumni Hall of Honor, U. Hawaii, 2004; recipient Nat. New Agt. Leadership award, CNA Corp., 1974, Key Club award, CNA Co., 1975, 1979—81, Nat. New Agt. Leader II, Continental Assurance Co., Can Co., 1975, Aloha Club award, 1983, VIP Club award, Pacific Guardian Life, 1984—86, Persistency Leader of Region award, 1984. Mem.: Hawaii Ind. Ins. Agents Assn., Urasenke Hawaii Assn. Profl. Ins. Agents, Rotary (bd. dirs. 1980). Office: 1314 S King St Ste 560 Honolulu HI 96814-1978 Office Phone: 808-596-2700.

**NOGUCHI, SOICHI,** astronaut; b. Yokohama, Japan, Apr. 15, 1965; married; 3 children. Bachelor in Aero. Engring., U. Tokyo, 1989, M in Aero. Engring., 1991. Flight instructor cert. as CFII and MEI. Mem. mfg. dept. Ishikawajima-Harima Heavy Industries Co., Ltd., Japan, 1991—96; astronaut Nat. Space Devel. Agy. Japan (merged with Inst. of Space & Astronautic Sci. and Nat. Aerospace Lab. of Japan and renamed Japan Aerospace Exploration Agy. in 2003), 1996—; tech. specialist Astronaut Office Space Sta. Br. Johnson Space Ctr., Houston, 1996, qualified mission specialist, 1998—; participated in the basic tng. course for Russian manned space systems Gagarin Cosmonaut Tng. Ctr., 1998; assigned tech. duties to support Japanese Experiment Module (Kibo) develop. tests Johnson Space Ctr., Houston, mission specialist, STS-114/ULF-1(Utilization and Logistics Flight), 2001—. Mem.: Japan Soc. Aero. and Space Scis. Will serve as MS-1 (mission specialist) and EV-1 on the Return To Flight Mission of STS-114 (Discovery), during which the crew will test and evaluate new procedures for flight safety and shuttle inspection and repair techniques in July, 2005; second Japanese astronaut ever to walk the void of three spacewalks. Office: NASA Johnson Space Ctr Astronaut Office/CB Houston TX 77058

**NOGUCHI, THOMAS TSUNETOMI,** writer, pathologist; b. Fukuoka, Japan, Jan. 4, 1927; arrived in U.S., 1952; s. Wataru and Tomika Narahashi Noguchi. Doctorate of Medicine, Nippon Med. Sch., Tokyo, 1951; DSc (hon.), Worcester State Coll., 1985. Dep. med. examiner Los Angeles County Dept. Chief Med. Examiner, L.A., 1961-67, coroner, 1967-82; prof. forensic pathology U. So. Calif. Med. Sch., L.A., 1982-99, prof. emeritus forensic pathology, 1999—. Author: Coroner, 1983 (N.Y. Times Bestseller, 1984), Coroner at Large, 1985, Unnatural Causes, 1988, Physical Evidence, 1990. Recipient Imperial medal Order Sacred Treasure, His Majesty the Emperor of Japan, 1999. Fellow: Am. Acad. Forensic Sci. (chmn. sect. 1966); mem.: AMA, AAAS, World Assn. Med. Law (treas.), Calif. Assn. Criminalists, Calif. State Coroners Assn. (pres. 1974—75), Nat. Assn. Med. Examiners (pres. 1983), Internat. Acad. Legal and Social Medicine, Am. Soc. Law, Medicine and Ethics, Am. Coll. Legal Medicine. Republican. Avocations: fine arts, gourmet oriental cooking, painting stills and abstracts. Office: U So Calif Med Ctr 1200 N State St Rm 2520 Los Angeles CA 90033-1029 Business E-Mail: noguchi@hse.usc.edu.

**NOGUERAS, JUAN JOSE,** surgeon; b. Rio Piedras, P.R., Apr. 23, 1956; s. Juan Jose and Agustina (Soroeta) N.; m. Michele LeMoal, Sept. 22, 1984; children: Nicole, John, Robert. AB in Biochemistry, Princeton U., 1978; MD, Jefferson Med. Coll., 1982. Diplomate Am. Bd. Surgery, Am. Bd. Colon and Rectal Surgery, Nat. Bd. Med. Examiners. Instr. surgery Wilford Hall Air Force Med. Ctr., San Antonio, 1987-90; staff dept. colorectal surgery Cleveland Clin. Fla., Weston, 1991—, chmn. divsn. surgery, 2000—. Presenter in field. Contbg. author: Current Controversies in Breast Cancer, 1984, Pre-test Self Assessment and Review, 1987, Textbook and Atlas of Laparoscopic Colorectal Surgery, Intestinal Stomas, 1993; reviewer: Surgical Endoscopy, 1993—, So. Med. Jour., 1993—; contbr. articles to profl. jours. Maj. M.C., U.S. Army, 1987-90. Recipient A.W. Martin Marino Sr. M.D. award Soc. Colon and Rectal Surgeons, 1991; Fellow U. Minn., 1990-91. Fellow ACS, Am. Soc. Colon and Rectal Surgeons, Soc. Am. Gastrointestinal Endoscopic Surgeons, Crohn's and Colitis Found. Am. (chmn. med. adv. com. 1992-96), Dominican Coll. Surgeons (hon.), Midwest Soc. Colon and Rectal Surgeons (pres. 1993-94). Home: 2505 Poinciana Dr Weston FL 33327-1415 Business E-Mail: noguerj@ccf.org.

**NOGUERE, SUZANNE,** trade association administrator, poet; b. Bklyn., Dec. 1, 1947; d. Eugene R. and Virginia Helene (Braun) N.; m. Henry Grinberg, June 5, 1983. BA in Philosophy magna cum laude with honors, Columbia U., N.Y.C., 1969. Classified asst. mgr. Printing News, Melville, NY, 1973–2006, sr. acct. exec., 1999—2006. Ins. mem. svcs. Nat. Assn. for Printing Leadership, Paramus, NJ, 2006—. Author: (children's books) Little Koala, 1979, Little Raccoon, 1981, (poetry collection) Whirling Round the

Sun, 1996; poet (with artist Miriam Adams): (exhibitions) Leaf Lines, 1998, poet (with artist Lesley Nishigawara): (exhibitions) Left Out, 2003; co-author (with James V. Hatch): The Stone House, A Blues Legend, 2000; co-author: (plays) Klub Ka, The Blues Legend, U. Iowa, 2002, La MaMa E.T.C., 2004, U. Md., 2006. Recipient Discovery award The 92nd St. Y Unterberg Poetry Ctr. and The Nation mag., 1996. Mem. Acad. Am. Poets, Poetry Soc. Am. (Gertrude B. Claytor Meml. award 1989), Poets House, Dramatists Guild Am., Authors Guild. Home: 27 W 96th St Apt 12B New York NY 10025-6614 Office: Nat Assn for Printing Leadership 75 W Century Rd Paramus NJ 07652 Office Phone: 800-308-6397 326, 800-642-6275 ext. 6304. E-mail: snoguere@napl.org.

**NOH, HONGSEOK,** engineering educator; b. Seoul, Korea, Nov. 27, 1970; arrived in U.S., 1999; s. Jaeyong Rho and Younghee Hwang; m. Sunhee Noh, Oct. 8, 1999; children: David, Grace, Abraham. BS, Korea U., Seoul, 1994, MS, 1996; PhD, Ga. Inst. Tech., Atlanta, 2004. Grad. rsch. asst. Ga. Inst. Tech., Atlanta, 2000—04; asst. prof. Drexel U., Phila., 2004—. Contbr. articles to profl. jours. Dir. U. Bible Fellowship of Atlanta, 2001—04, U. Bible Fellowship of Phila., 2004—. Mem.: IEEE, ASME, Soc. Mfg. Engrs. (Drexel chpt. advisor 2004—). Avocations: soccer, reading. Office: Drexel Univ Rm 2-115 3141 Chestnut St Philadelphia PA 19104 Office Phone: 215-895-2273. Office Fax: 215-895-1478. E-mail: mosesnoh@coe.drexel.edu.

**NOH, JUN-YONG,** computer scientist, researcher; b. Seoul, Republic of Korea, 1970; s. Jae-Young Noh and Yoo-im Bang. Bachelor magna cum laude, U. So. Calif., 1994, Master, 1996, PhD, 2002. Rschr. on brain-like computer Info. Scis. Inst., Marina del Rey, Calif., 1997; rschr. facial animation U. So. Calif., L.A., 1998—. CEO Digital Clone Lab., L.A. 2002—. Pvt., 1999, Seoul. Achievements include patent for expression cloning. Avocations: scuba diving, travel. Home: 13173 Pacific Promenade #101 Playa Vista CA 90094-2147

**NOHR, BARBARA J.,** secondary school educator; b. Chgo., May 1, 1946; d. Ray E. and Harriet S. Allen; 1 child, Natalie. BS, Loyola U., Chgo., 1968; MGS, Roosevelt U., Chgo., 1981. Tchr. St. Mary's Sch., Buffalo Grove, Ill., 1970—77; h.s. tchr. Sacred Heart of Mary, Rolling Meadows, Ill., 1977—81; tchr. Warren Twp. H.S., Gurnee, Ill., 0198.

**NOHRNBERG, JAMES CARSON,** language educator; b. Berkeley, Calif., Mar. 19, 1941; s. Carson and Geneva Gertrude (Gibbs) N.; m. Stephanie Payson Lamport, June 14, 1964; children: Gabrielle L., Peter Carson L. Student, Kenyon Coll., 1958-60; BA, Harvard Coll., 1962, postgrad., 1965-68; PhD, U. Toronto, 1970. Tchg. fellow dept. English U. Coll., U. Toronto, 1963-64; jr. fellow Soc. of Fellows Harvard U., 1965-68; acting instr. dept. English Yale U., New Haven, 1968-69, lectr., 1969-70, asst. prof., 1970-75, assoc. prof., 1975; prof. English U. Va., Charlottesville, 1975—. Adj. instr. English Harvard U., Cambridge, 1967; Gauss Seminars in Criticism lectr. Princeton U., 1987; lectr. various univs., 1974—. Author: The Analogy of The Faerie Queene, 1976, 80, Like Unto Moses: The Constituting of an Interruption, 1995; mem. editl. bd. Spenser Ency., 1977-90, Spenser Studies, 1977—; contbr. articles to profl. jours. and poems to mags.; editor vols. on allegory, Bible, Homer, Dante, Boiardo, Spenser, Milton, Thomas Pynchon, Northrop Frye, among others. Recipient Am. Acad. Poets prize Harvard U., 1962; Woodrow Wilson fellow, 1962, jr. fellow Harvard U., 1965-68, Morse fellow Yale U., 1974-75, U. Va. Ctr. for Advanced Studies fellow, 1975-78, Guggenheim fellow, 1981-82, Ind. U. Inst. for Advanced Studies fellow, 1991, U. Va. Sesquicentennial fellow, 2003-2004. Mem.: MLA, Am. Comparative Lit. Assn., Milton Soc., Spenser Soc., Phi Beta Kappa. Presbyterian. Avocations: poetry, collecting books and records. Home: 1874 Wayside Pl Charlottesville VA 22903-1631 Office: U Va Dept English Bryan Hall Charlottesville VA 22903 Office Phone: 434-924-6629. Business E-Mail: jcn@virginia.edu.

**NOJI, ERIC K.,** epidemiologist; MD, U. Rochester; MPH, Johns Hopkins Bloomberg Sch. Pub. Health, 1987. Prof. Johns Hopkins U. Sch. Med., Baltimore, Md.; attending emergency physician Johns Hopkins Hosp., Baltimore, Md.; with CDC, Atlanta, 1989—, asst. branch chief emergency response, 1989, chief disaster assessment & epidemiology, 1990—95, assoc. dir. bioterrorism preparedness & response, 2001—; chief of Emergency Health Intelligence Unit, WHO Health Information Network for Advanced Planning (HINAP), Geneva, 1996—2000; med. expert White House Office of Homeland Security, Washington, 2001—; dep. chief Med. & Pub. Health Unit, US Humanitarian Assistance Mission for Operation Iraqi Freedom, Washington, 2003—; prof. internat. health Tulane U. Sch. Pub. Health & Tropical Medicine. Sr. fellow Homeland Security Policy Inst., George Washington U.; sr. policy advisor CDC, Washington, Dept. Homeland Security (FEMA), Washington, Pentagon's Chemical & Biological Def. Program, Washington. Author: over 200 scientific articles & publications, The Public Health Consequences of Disasters, 1997. Pres. Soc. Alumni Johns Hopkins Bloomberg Sch. Pub. Health. Recipient Woodrow Wilson award for Disting. Govt. Svc., 2005. Mem.: Inst. Medicine.*

**NOKES, JEFFERY D.,** history professor; b. Murray, Utah, Sept. 2, 1966; s. Vernon Doyle and Tava Lee Nokes; m. Gina Park, Dec. 21, 1990; children: Carly J., Mandy T., Kelsey G., Caleb Jeffery, Joseph Jeffery, Isaac Thomas. BA, Brigham Young U., Provo, Utah, 1991; MEd, Utah State U., Logan, 1996; PhD, U. Utah, Salt Lake City, 2005. Cert. Tchr. Utah State Office Edn., 1991. History tchr. Bingham HS, South Jordan, Utah, 2001—05; instr. Brigham Young U., 2005—. Adult hs tchr. Southpointe HS, Sandy, Utah, 1997—. Missionary LDS Ch., Stockholm, 1985—87, various leadership roles in local congregations Riverton, Utah, 1990—2006. Named HS History Tchr. of Yr., Utah Coun. for the Social Studies, 2005. Mem.: NEA. R-Liberal. Mem. Lds Ch. Achievements include research in effective methods of teaching. Avocations: camping, fishing, reading. Office: Brigham Young Univ 201 MCKB Provo UT 84062

**NOLAN, ALAN TUCKER,** lawyer, writer, arbitrator; b. Evansville, Ind., Jan. 19, 1923; s. Val and Jeannette (Covert) N.; m. Elizabeth Clare Titsworth, Aug. 26, 1947 (dec. Nov. 1967); children: Patrick A., Thomas C., Mary F., Elizabeth T., John V.; m. Jane Ransel DeVoe, Feb. 7, 1970; adopted children: John C. DeVoe, Ellen R. DeVoe, Thomas R. DeVoe. AB in Govt., Ind. U., 1944, LHD with honors, 1993; LLB, Harvard U., Cambridge, Mass., 1947. Bar: Ind. 1947. Law clk. U.S. Ct. Appeals (7th Cir.), Chgo., 1947-48; assoc. Ice, Miller, Donadio & Ryan, Indpls., 1948-58, ptnr., 1958-93, ret., 1993—. Chmn. Disciplinary Commn. Supreme Ct. Ind., Indpls., 1966-73. Author: The Iron Brigade, 1961, As Sounding Brass, 1964, Lee Considered, 1991; editor (with S. Vipond) Giants in Tall Black Hats, 1998, (with Gary Gallagher) The Myth of the Lost Cause and Civil War History, 2000, Rally Once Again, 2000; contbg. editor The Civil War, 1985-89; contbr. numerous articles to profl. jours. Life mem. NAACP Indpls., v.p., 1950-54; bd. dirs., founder Ind. Civil Liberties Union, Indpls., 1953-60; bd. dirs. Indpls. Art League, 1981-87; chmn., bd. trustees Ind. Hist. Soc., Indpls., 1986-93; trustee Eiteljorg Mus., Indpls., 1987-93. Fellow Co. Mil. Historians, Am. Bar Found., State Hist. Soc. Wis.; mem. ABA, Ind. Bar Assn., Indpls. Bar Assn. (bd. mgrs. 1958-60, chmn. Grievance Com. 1960-64), Indpls. Civil War Round Table, Ensemble Music Soc. (bd. dirs. 1999—). Democrat. Roman Catholic. Avocations: travel, gardening, reading. Home and Office: 3307 Bay Road North Drive Indianapolis IN 46240 Office Phone: 317-585-1988. Personal E-mail: indynolan@sbcglobal.net.

**NOLAN, J. MICHAEL, JR.,** retired lawyer; b. Newark, June 19, 1949; BA with honors, St. Vincent Coll., 1971; JD, Villanova U., 1975. Bar: N.J. 1975. Law clk. Hon. Samuel Alcorn, Jr. appellate divsn. Superior Ct. N.J., 1975-76; asst. prosecutor Essex County, N.J., 1976-77; spl. coun. N.J. Supreme Ct., 1984-85; ptnr. Pitney, Hardin, Kipp & Szuch, Morristown, NJ, 1977—. Fellow Am. Bar Found.; mem. N.J. State Bar Assn. (chmn. casino law sect. 1987-88). Office: Pitney Hardin Kipp & Szuch PO Box 1945 Park Ave at Morris County Morristown NJ 07962-1945

---

**NOLAN, JAMES P.,** lawyer; BA, St. Bonaventure Univ., 1970; JD with honors, Univ. Balt. Sch. of Law, 1974. Ptnr. Council, Baradel, Kosmerl & Nolan PA, 1982—, mng. dir. Bd. trustees Historic Annapolis Found., 2003—; mem. exec. coun. Nat. Conf. of Bar Presidents, 2003—. Mem. Annapolis and Anne Arundel County C. of C., Annapolis Inner West St. Devel. Adv. Com., Annapolis Comprehensive Planning Econ. Liaison Group, City of Annapolis Teen Adv. Bd. Recipient Maryland Leadership in Law award, Daily Record, 2002. Fellow: ABA; mem.: Md. Inst. for Continuing Profl. Edn. of Lawyers (trustee), Pro Bono Resource Ctr. of Md. (bd. dir.), Anne Arundel County Bar Assn. (pres.), Maryland State Bar Assn. (pres. 2002—03). Office: Council Baradel Kosmerl & Nolan PA 4th Fl 125 West St PO Box 2289 Annapolis MD 21404-2289

**NOLAN, JANIECE SIMMONS,** health facility administrator; b. Ft. Worth; d. James Coleman and Berenice Johnson Simmons; m. Robert L. Nolan; children: Douglas, Patricia, Nancy, Margaret, Sheffield, Gemini Janiece. BA, U. Tex., 1961, MA, 1963; PhD, Tulane U., 1968; MPH, U. Calif., Berkeley, 1975. Diplomate Am. Coll. Healthcare Execs. Rsch. scientist Tex. Nuc. (Nuc. Chgo.), Austin, 1963-65; head cell biology Gulf South Rsch. Inst., New Orleans, 1968-70; postdoctoral fellow dept. physiology/anatomy U. Calif., Berkeley, 1970-72; rsch. physiologist, acting assoc. chief of staff for rsch. VA Hosp., Martinez, Calif., 1970-75; COO, v.p. adminstrn. John Muir Med. Ctr., Walnut Creek, Calif., 1977-97; pres., CEO John Muir Physician Network, Walnut Creek, 1997—. Commr. State Commn. Emergency Svcs., Sacramento, 1997; mem. corp. adv. bd. for grad. program in health mgmt. rsch. U. Calif., Berkeley, 2003; mem. industry adv. bd. Ctr. for Health Mgmt. Rsch., 2004—. Capt. USNR, (ret.) Woodrow Wilson fellow, 1960; named Woman of Yr., Women Health Care Execs., San Francisco, 1989; recipient Navy Commendation medals (3), Humanitarian Svc. medal, 2 Armed Forces Res. medals (2) Mem.: Ind. Physician Assn., Med. Group Mgmt. Assn., Am. Mil. Surgeons of the U.S., Assn. Integrated Health Delivery Systems, Rotary (Paul Harris fellow), Phi Beta Kappa (No. Calif. Assn. bd. dirs. 2005—). Avocations: international travel, genealogy. Office: John Muir Physician Network 1340 Treat Blvd Ste 450 Walnut Creek CA 94597 Office Phone: 925-952-2880. Business E-Mail: Janiece.Nolan@johnmuirhealth.com.

**NOLAN, JOAN PARMETER,** librarian; b. Olean, N.Y., Sept. 16, 1934; d. Howard and Doris (Root) Parmeter; m. Kevin J. Nolan, Feb. 11, 1961; children: Sharon, Bruce, Gary, Laurie. BS in Edn., Clarion U., 1956; MS in Libr. Sci., Case Western Res. U., 1959; EdD, Temple U., 1988. Libr. Linesville Sch. Dist., Pa., 1956-59, Cameron County Sch. Dist., Emporium, Pa., 1959-61, Wissahickon Sch. Dist., Ambler, Pa., 1961-65; dir. libr. media svcs. North Penn Sch. Dist., Lansdale, 1968—96; reference libr. Gwynedd Mercy Coll., Gwynedd Valley, Pa., 1997—. Instr. Drexel Inst. Tech., Phila., 1965-69, Villanova U., 1988, Montgomery Community Coll., 1982-84. Mem. ALA, NEA, Pa. Sch. Librs. Assn., Chester-Montgomery Sch. Librs. Assn. (sec. 1968—), Pa. Edn. Assn., Pa. Learning Resources Assn., Beta Phi Mu, Pi Gamma Mu, Phi Gamma Delta. Office: 843 Lombardy Dr Lansdale PA 19446

**NOLAN, JOHN BLANCHARD,** lawyer; b. Providence, Aug. 30, 1943; s. John O'Leary and Elizabeth Rita (Blanchard) Nolan; m. Marguerite Ruth Hartley, Mar. 1, 1969 (dec. Aug. 1988); children: Suzanne, Caroline, Danielle; m. Lillian B. Prestley, 1989. AB, Brown U., 1965; JD, Georgetown U., 1968. Bar: Conn. 1968, U.S. Dist. Ct. Conn. 1969, U.S. Ct. Appeals (2d cir.) 1969, U.S. Dist. Ct. (so. dist.) N.Y. 1973, N.Y. 1974, U.S. Cat. Appeals (1st cir.) 1991, U.S. Dist. Ct. Ariz. 1994, U.S. Supreme Ct. 1995. Assoc. Day, Berry & Howard, Hartford, Conn., 1969-76, ptnr., 1976—. Bd. dirs. Spiritus Wines, Inc.; chmn. local rules practice adv. com. U.S. Bankruptcy Ct., 1981—. Corporator St. Francis Hosp. Med. Ctr., Hartford, 1982—; bd. dirs. Greater Hartford Arts Coun., Inc., 1993—, v.p., mem. exec. com.; mem. parish coun. Ch. St. Timothy; trustee St. Mary Home Found., 1983—, U. Hartford Art Sch., 1988—94. Fellow: Conn. Bar Found.; mem.: ABA, Insolvency Internat., Hartford County Bar Assn., Conn. Bar Assn., Am. Bankruptcy Inst., Loomis Chaffee Sch. Alumni Assn. (bd. dirs. 1996—98), Hartford Golf Club (bd. dirs. 2000—03, v.p. 2004—). Democrat. Roman Catholic. Avocations: golf, skiing, travel, wines. Home: 34 Northmoor Rd West Hartford CT 06117-1709 Office: Day Berry & Howard 185 City Place Hartford CT 06103-3499 Office Phone: 860-275-0100. Business E-Mail: jbnolan@dbh.com.

**NOLAN, JOHN EDWARD,** lawyer; b. Mpls., July 11, 1927; s. John E. and Teresa (Franey) Nolan; m. Joan Dobbins, June 3, 1950; children: Carol N. Klatt, John Edward III(dec.), Kelly N. Spencer, Richard Clark, Patricia N. McNeill. BS, U.S. Naval Acad., 1950; JD, Georgetown U., 1955. Bar: DC 1955, U.S. Supreme Ct. 1959. Md. 1961. Law clk. to Justice Clark U.S. Supreme Ct., 1955-56; adminstrv. asst. to Atty. Gen. Robert F. Kennedy, 1963-64; assoc. Steptoe & Johnson, Washington, 1956-62, ptnr., 1962-63, 1965—. Assoc. counsel Cuban families com. Cuban Prisoners Exch., Havana, 1962—63; spl. counsel refugee subcom. Senate Jud. Com., Vietnam, 1967—68; mem. CPR Panel Disting. neutrals, Washington; mediator U.S. Ct. Appeals DC cir.; mem. exec. com. Lawyers Com. Civil Rights Under Law; vis. fellow Wolfson Coll., Cambridge (Eng.) U., 1987, 92; bd. dirs. Iomega, Inc. Trustee Robert F. Kennedy Meml., 1969—; moderator Aspen Inst., 1980—; gen. counsel, bd. dirs. U.S. Naval Acad. Found., 1997—; bd. dirs. Fund Dem. Majority. Served from 2d lt. to capt. USMC, 1950—54, Korea. Decorated Silver Star, Bronze Star with combat V, Purple Heart. Mem.: ABA, Am. Law Inst., DC Bar Assn., U.S. Naval Acad. Alumni Assn. (bd. counsel, trustee 1997—), Univ. Club (N.Y.C.), Congl. Club, Met. Club (Washington). Democrat. Roman Catholic. Office: 1330 Connecticut Ave NW Washington DC 20036-1704 Personal E-Mail: jnolan@steptoe.com.

**NOLAN, JOHN MICHAEL,** lawyer; b. Conway, Ark., June 21, 1948; s. Paul Thomas and Peggy (Hime) N. BA, U. Tex., 1970, JD, 1973; LLM in Taxation, George Washington U., 1976. Bar: Tex. 1973, D.C. 1975, U.S. Ct. Mil. Appeals 1973, U.S. Ct. Appeals (D.C. cir.) 1975, U.S. Tax Ct. 1975, U.S. Supreme Ct. 1975. Chief counsel to chief judge U.S. Ct. Mil. Appeals, Washington, 1976-77; assoc. Winstead, McGuire, Sechrest & Minick PC, Dallas, 1977-81; shareholder Winstead Sechrest & Minick PC, Dallas, 1981—. Editor in Chief The Advocate, 1973-76. Capt. JAGC, U.S. Army, 1973-76. Named one of Outstanding Young Men in Am., US Jaycees, 1976; Keeton fellow Chancellor Coun.; named Best Lawyers in Am., Tex. Super Lawyer Fellow Dallas Bar Found.; Tex. Bar Found.; mem. ABA (real property, probate and trust sect., real property com., partnerships, joint ventures, and other investment vehicles), Tex. Bar Assn. (real property, probate and trust sect.), DC Bar Assn., Dallas Bar Assn. (real estate group), Tex. Coll. Real Estate Lawyers, Am. Coll. Real Estate Lawyers, Coll. State Bar Tex., Real Estate Coun. Club. Presbyterian. Home: 6681 Crest Way Ct Dallas TX 75230-2868 Office: Winstead Sechrest & Minick 5400 Renaissance Tower 1201 Elm St Ste 5400 Dallas TX 75270-2199 Office Phone: 214-745-5251. Business E-Mail: jnolan@winstead.com.

**NOLAN, JOHN THOMAS, JR.,** retired oil industry administrator; b. Boston, Apr. 15, 1930; s. John T. Sr. and Margaret M. (Craig) N.; m. Mary Sharkey, May 7, 1955; children: Anne, Margaret, John T. III, Stephen, Michael. AB, Cath. U. Am., 1951; PhD, MIT, 1955. Chemist Texaco, Inc., Beacon, NY, 1955—59, group leader, 1959—69, supr., 1969—79, asst. mgr., 1979—82, dir. strategic rsch., 1987—92, assoc. dir., 1987—82; ret., 1992. Contbr. over 5 articles to profl. jours. Bd. dirs. Cmty. Coll. Found., 1987—, chmn. 1989-92, chmn. planning com. 1992—. Mem. Am. Chem. Soc., Sigma Xi, Phi Beta Kappa. Achievements include patents in field. Home: 18 Relyea Ter Wappingers Falls NY 12590-5824

**NOLAN, JOSEPH THOMAS,** journalism educator, communications consultant; b. Waterbury, Conn., Apr. 11, 1920; s. Thomas Francis and Mary Margaret (Gaffney) N.; m. Virginia Theodate Tappin, May 6, 1943; children— Carol Nolan Rigolot, David J. AB, Holy Cross Coll., 1942; MA in English Lit., Boston U., 1945; PhD in Econs, NYU, 1973. Washington corr. UPI, 1943-49; writer, copy editor N.Y. Times, N.Y.C., 1949-55; mgr. editorial and press services RCA Corp., N.Y.C., 1955-62; sr. v.p. corporate communi-

---

cations Chase Manhattan Bank, N.Y.C., 1962-74; prof. journalism and pub. affairs U. S.C., Columbia, 1974-76; v.p. pub. affairs Monsanto Co., St. Louis, 1976-85; Gannett vis. prof. communications U. Fla., 1985-86; prof. communications U. North Fla., Jacksonville, 1986-92; adj. prof. bus. and comm. Flagler Coll., St. Augustine, Fla., 1985—95. Contbr. articles to various mags. Fellow Pub. Rels. Soc. Am. Roman Catholic. Home: 30 Park Terrace Dr Saint Augustine FL 32080-5334

**NOLAN, MIKE,** professional football player; b. Balt., Md., Mar. 7, 1959; Attended, Univ. Oregon. Asst. coach Univ. Oregon, 1981—82, Satnford Univ., 1982—83, Rice Univ., 1984—85; coach LSU, 1986; linebackers coach, spl. teams asst. Denver Broncos, 1987; def. coord. NY Giants, 1993—96, Wash. Redskins, 1997—99, NY Jets, 2000; wide receivers coach Balt. Ravens, 2001, def. coord., 2002—04; head coach San Francisco 49ers, 2005—. Office: San Francisco 49ers Marie P DeBartolo Sports Ctr 4949 Cetennial Blvd Santa Clara CA 95054*

**NOLAN, OWEN,** professional hockey player; b. Belfast, Northern Ireland, Feb. 12, 1972; m. Diana Nolan; 1 child, Jordan. Right wing Cornwall Royals, 1988—90, Halifax Citadels, 1990—91, Que. Nordiques, 1990—95, Colo. Avalanche, 1995, San Jose Sharks, 1995—2003, Toronto Maple Leafs, 2003—04, Phoenix Coyotes, 2006—. Player NHL All-Star Game, 1992, 96, 97, 2000, 02; mem. Team Can., Olympic Games, Salt Lake City, 2002. Recipient Emms Family Award, OHL, 1989, Jim Mahon Meml. Trophy, 1990. Achievements include being the first overall draft pick in NHL entry draft, 1990; being a member of gold medal Canadian Hockey team, Salt Lake City Olympic Games, 2002. Office: Phoenix Coyotes Hockey Club 5800 W Glenn Dr, Ste 350 Glendale AZ 85301*

**NOLAN, RICHARD THOMAS,** clergyman, educator; b. Waltham, Mass., May 30, 1937; s. Thomas Michael and Elizabeth Louise (Leishman) N.; life ptnr. Robert C. Pingpank, Sept. 14, 1955. BA, Trinity Coll., 1960; Diploma in Theol. Studies, Berkeley Div. Sch., 1960; MDiv. in Theol. Studies, Hartford Sem. Found., 1963; postgrad. in Religious Edn., Union Theol. Sem., 1963; MA in Religion, Yale U., 1967; PhD in Philosophy of Religion, NYU, 1973; postgrad. in Career Assessment, Ctr. Career Devel. and Ministry, 1987; postgrad. in Biomed. Ethics, Harvard U., 1991. Ordained deacon Episcopal Ch., 1963, priest, 1965; cert. in clinical pastoral edn. Conn. Valley Hosp., 1962, in death, dying and bereavement Waterbury Hosp. Health Ctr., Conn., 1977. Instr. Latin and English Watkinson Sch., Conn., 1961-62; instr. math. Choir Sch. of Cathedral of St. John the Divine, NYC, 1962-64; instr. math. and religion, assoc. chaplain Cheshire Acad., Conn., 1965-67; instr. Hartford Sem. Found., Conn., 1967-68, asst. acad. dean, lectr. philosophy and edn., 1968-70; instr. Mattatuck C.C., Waterbury, Conn., 1969-70, asst. prof. philosophy and history, 1970-74, prof., 1974-78, prof. philosophy and social sci., 1978-92, prof. emeritus, 1992—; vicar St. Paul's Parish, Bantam, Conn., 1974-88, pastor emeritus, 1988—; pres. Litchfield Inst., Conn. and Fla., 1984-96; adj. lectr. in philosophy Palm Beach C. C., Fla., 2000—02. Ethics com. Waterbury Hosp. Health Ctr., 1984—88; vis. and adj. prof. philosophy, theology and religious studies Trinity Coll., Conn., L.I. U., U. Miami, St, Joseph Coll., Conn., Pace U., Teikyo Post U., U. Conn., Hartford Grad. Ctr., Ctrl. Conn. State U., 1964—95, Broward C.C., Fla.; lectr. philosophy and theology Barry U., Fla., 1973, 1989—92, 1997—98; adj. assoc. in continuing edn. Berkeley Div. Sch. Yale U., 1987—89; Rabbi Harry Halpern Meml. lect., Southbury, Conn., 1987; adj. prof. philosophy Fla. Atlantic U., 1998—99; adj. prof. The Union Inst., Fla., 1999; faculty of cons. examiners Charter Oak State Coll., Conn., 1990—93; assoc. for edn. Christ Ch. Cathedral, Conn., 1988—94, hon. canon, 1991—; cons. Dept. Def. Activity Non-Traditional Ednl. Support, Ednl. Testing Svc., Princeton, NJ, 1990; vis. scholar Coll. Preachers, Washington Nat. Cathedral, 1994; supply priest Episcopal Diocese of S.E. Fla., 1994—2002; ret. priest-in-residence St. Andrew's Ch., Lake Worth, Fla., 2002—; soc. regents Cathedral Ch. St. John the Divine, 2002—. Author (with H. Titus and M. Smith): Living Issues in Philosophy, 7th edit., 1979, Indonesian edit., 1984, 8th edit., 1986, 9th edit., 1995; author: (with F. Kirkpatrick) Living Issues in Ethics, 1982, 2d edit., 2000, Chinese edit., 1988 (Honored Author for Books Exceeding 100,000 Copies award Wadsworth Pub. Co., 1986); editor, contbr. Diaconate Now, 1968, host Conversations With..., 1987—89; author (with Robert C. Pingpank): Soul Mates: More Than Partners (online), 2004. Notary pub., Fla. Recipient Founder's Day award, NYU, 1973; Rsch. fellow Med. Ethics, Yale, 1978, Bus. Ethics, 1987. Mem. Am. Acad. Religion, Am. Philos. Assn., Authors Guild, End of Life Choices, Fla. (adv. bd. 1998—). Interfaith Alliance, Integrity, Boston Latin Sch. Alumni Assn., Tabor Acad. Alumni Assn., McCook Fellows Soc. Trinity Coll., Cavalier King Charles Spaniel Club, Yale Legacy Partners, Harwood Soc. Cheshire Acad., Society of The Torch of NYU, Founders Soc. of the Wash. Nat. Cathedral, Lambda Legal, Compass West Palm Beach, Phi Delta Kappa. Independent. Episcopalian. Home: 2527 Egret Lake Dr West Palm Beach FL 33413-2161 Personal E-mail: canon@rtnolan.com. *Who am I? By baptism I am a resurrected child of God born to love and be loved; my pilgrimage among others is lived within this baptismal identity, more enduring than any achievement.*

**NOLAN, SHARON THERESA,** nurse, educator; b. Hackensack, N.J., Jan. 22, 1953; d. Louis and Doris Marzitelli; m. Kevin Nolan, Sr., Sept. 4, 1982; 1 child, Kevin Jr. AA in Edn., Bergen CC, Paramus, NJ, 1972; RN, Felician Coll., Lodi, NJ, 1976; BS in Health Edn., Fairleigh Dickinson U., Rutherford, NJ, 1980. RN NJ, 1977, NY, 1982. Staff nurse Hackensack U. Med. Ctr., 1975—79, children's diabetic health educator, 1979—81; staff nurse Tri Cities Nursing, Albany, NY, 1982—84; sch. nurse, tchr. Clifton Pub. Schs., NJ, 1981—96, Middlesex Pub. Schs., NJ, 1998—2001; tchr. health occupations Old Bridge HS, Matawan, NJ, 2004—. Recipient Hon. Commn., Congl. Youth Leadership Coun., DC, 2006. Mem.: SSNA Middlesex County Run. Assn., N J Edn. Assn. Catholic. Office: Old Bridge HS 4207 Rt 516 Matawan NJ 07747

**NOLAN, STANTON PEELLE,** surgeon, educator; b. Washington, May 29, 1933; s. James Parker and Ellen Dubose (Peelle) N.; m. Marion Faro, June 16, 1955; children: Stanton Peelle Jr., Tiphanie Ravenel Clarke. BA, Princeton U., 1955; MD, U. Va., 1959, MS, 1962. Diplomate Am. Bd. Surgery, Am. Bd. Thoracic Surgery. Intern U. Va. Med. Ctr., Charlottesville, 1959-60, asst. resident gen. surgery, 1960-61, research fellow surgery, 1961-62, asst. resident gen. surgery, 1962-64, chief resident gen surgery, 1964-65, chief resident thoracic cardiovascular surgery, 1965-66; rsch. assoc. Clinic of Surgery Nat. Heart Inst., NIH, Bethesda, Md., 1966-68; asst. prof. surgery U. Va. Med. Ctr., Charlottesville, 1968-70, assoc. prof. surgery, 1970-74, surgeon in charge div. thoracic cardiovascular surgery, 1970-93, prof. surgery, 1974-81, Claude A. Jessup prof. surgery, 1981-98, clin. prof. surgery, 1998—2004, prof. surgery, 2004—, med. dir. Thoracic Cardiovascular post-operative unit, 1989-93. Established investigator Am. Heart Assn., 1969-74; mem. surgery A study sect. NIH, Washington, 1972-76, surgery and bioengring. study sect. 1984-87, chmn. 1985-87; cons. thoracic cardiovascular surgery VA Hosp., Salem, Va., 1968-98, Am. Bd. Surgery cons. to qualifying examination com., 1988-91; surg. cons. Bur. Crippled Children, Charlottesville, 1968-93; vis. cons. cardiothoracic surgery Aga Khan U., Karachi, Pakistan, 1995, vis cons. World. Health Svcs., Madras, India, 1997, cons. So. Petrochem. Industries Corp. SPIC, Chennai, India 2000; vis. prof. U. Hanover (Germany) 1990; vis. prof. Cardiac Surgerey, U. Wis. 1992. Mem. editl. bd. Jour. Surg. Rsch., 1973-79, Annals of Thoracic Surgery, 1979-88; mem. sci. adv. bd. Jour. for Heart Valve Disease, 1993—2006; mem. editl. adv. bd. ECRI Operating Rm. Risk Mgmt., 1992—; co-editor: Comprehensive Thoracic Surgery Curriculum, TSDA, 1995; contbr. articles to profl. jours., chpts. to books. Bd. mgrs. Ctrl. Va. Health Network, 2000—05; mem. Westminster Canterbury Blue Ridge, chmn. Residents' Assn., 2004—06; bd. dirs. Piedmont Liability Trust, 1989—2005, chmn. Claims Com., 1989—2006, chmn. bd., 1991—2004. Recipient John Horsley Meml. prize U. Va. Med. Sch., 1962, Merit award Rsch. Forum of Am. Coll. Chest Physicians, 1968, Clyde Watson Disting. Svc. award Pastoral Care and Edn., 2006, Stanton P. Nolan Professorship Thoracic and Cardiovascular Surgery, U. Va. Bd. Visitors, 2006; rsch. fellow Va. Heart Assn., 1961-62, Am. Cancer Soc., 1963-64; grantee NIH, 1968-84, Am. Heart Assn., 1970-73, Medtronic

Corp., 1975-81. Fellow ACS (com. allied health pers. 1996—2004, exec. com. 1997-2000, vice chair); Am. Coll. Cardiology, Am. Surg. Assn.; mem. Am. Assn. Thoracic Surgery, Am. Heart Assn. (coun. on cardiovasc. surgery 1969-99, anesthesiology, radiology and surgery study com. 1991-94), Andrew G. Morrow Soc., Assn. Acad. Surgery, Assn. Advancement of Med. Instrumentation (chair 1998-2000, chair-elect 1996, co-chmn. cardiac valve com. 1974-2005, mem. internat. stds. strategy com. 1989—2005, bd. dirs. 1990-2000, stds. bd. 1991—2005, edn. com. 1992-93, nominating com. 1996-2000, chair 1998-2000, govt. rels. com. 1996-2000), Internat. Stds. Orgn. (chmn. subcom. on cardiovascular surg. implants 1982-2001), Assn. Clin. Cardiac Surgeons, Halsted Soc. (exec. com. 1985-89), Coord. Com. on Perfusion Affairs (chmn. 1990-2000), Internat. Assn. Cardiac Biol. Implants (sci. com. 1994), Am. Assn. for Vascular Surgery, Muller Surg. Soc. (pres. 1979), Soc. Internat. de Cirurgie, Soc. Vascular Surgery, Soc. Thoracic Surgeons (ad hoc com. on industry rels. 1992-97, stds. and ethics com. 1993-95, 98-2001, edn. and resources com. 1996-97), Soc. Univ. Surgeons, Southeastern Surg. Congress, So. Surg. Assn. (2d v.p. 1982), Thoracic Surgery Found. Rsch. and Edn. (chair New Century Soc. com. 1997-2000), Va. Surg. Soc. (v.p. 1980-83, pres. 1984), Va. Vascular Soc. (exec. coun. 1985-86), Soc. Critical Care Medicine, Raven Soc., Assn. Am. Med. Colls. (rep. coun. acad. socs. 1992-01), Chevy Chase Club, Alpha Omega Alpha, Omicron Delta Kappa. Home: #5204 250 Pantops Mountain Rd Charlottesville VA 22911-8702 Office: U Va TCV Surgery PO Box 800679 Charlottesville VA 22908-0679 E-mail: snolan@virginia.edu.

**NOLAN, TED (THEODORE JOHN NOLAN),** professional hockey coach; b. Sault Ste. Marie, Ont., Can., Apr. 7, 1958; m. Sandra Nolan; children: Brandon, Jordan. LLD (hon.), Laurentian U., 2002. Player Detroit Red Wings, 1981—84, Pitts. Penguins, 1985—86; head coach Sault Ste. Marie Greyhounds, 1988—94; asst. coach Hartford Whalers, 1994-95; head coach Buffalo Sabres, 1995—97; head coach, dir. hockey ops. Moncton Wildcats, 2005—06; head coach NY Islanders, 2006—. Pres., CEO Ted Nolan Found. Named Sault Ste. Marie Citizen of Yr., 1990—91; recipient Order of Ontario, 1993, National Aboriginal Achievement Award, 1994, Jack Adams Award, NHL, 1997. Office: NY Islanders Nassau Veterans Meml Coliseum 1255 Hempstead Turnpike Uniondale NY 11553*

**NOLAN, VAL, JR.,** retired biologist, lawyer; b. Evansville, Ind., Apr. 28, 1920; s. Val and Jeannette (Covert) N.; m. Susanne Howe, Dec. 23, 1946 (div. Aug. 29, 1980); children: Val, Ann Clare, William Alan; m. Ellen D. Ketterson, Oct. 17, 1980. AB, Ind. U., 1941, JD, 1949. Bar: Ind. 1949. Dep. U.S. marshal, 1941; agt. White House Detail, U.S. Secret Service, 1942; asst. prof. law Ind. U., 1949-52, assoc. prof., 1952-56, prof., 1956-85, prof. emeritus, 1985—, research scholar in zoology, 1957-68, prof. zoology, 1968-77, prof. biology, 1977-85; prof. emeritus, 1985—; acting dean Sch. Law, 1976, 80. Author: (with F.E. Horack, Jr.) Land Use Controls, 1955, Ecology and Behavior of the Prairie Warbler, 1978; editor Ind. Law Jour., 1945-46, Jour. Avian Biology, 1989—2005, Current Ornithology, 1994-2004. Served with USNR, 1942-46. Guggenheim fellow, 1957; recipient Ind. U. Disting. Alumni Svc. award, 1987; named to Acad. Law Alumni Fellows, Ind. U., 1988. Fellow AAAS, Am. Ornithologists Union (v.p. 1989-90, Brewster Meml award 1986), Animal Behavior Soc.; mem. Brit. Ornithologists Union, Cooper Ornithol. Soc., Wilson Ornithol. Soc. (co-recipient with Ellen D. Ketterson) Margaret M. Nice award 1998), Assn. Field Ornithologists, Ecol. Soc. Am., Am. Soc. Naturalists, Deutsche Ornithologen-Gesellschaft, Nederlandse Ornithologische Unie, Soc. Study of Reprodn., Phi Beta Kappa, Sigma Xi. Democrat. Home: 4675 E Heritage Woods Rd Bloomington IN 47401-9312 E-mail: vnolan@indiana.edu.

**NOLAN, VICTORIA,** theater director; b. Portland, Maine, June 15, 1952; d. Herbert Wallace and Diane Katharine (Kremm) N.; m. Clarkson Newell Crolius, Aug. 30, 1980; children: Covey Emmeline, Wilhelmina Adams. BA magna cum laude, U. Maine, 1976. Publicity asst. Loeb Drama Ctr. Harvard U., Cambridge, Mass., 1975; pub. rels. asst. to dir. Sch. Arts Boston U., 1975-76; mgmt. asst. TAG Found., N.Y.C., 1976-77; mng. dir. Ram Island Dance Co., Portland, 1977-78; dir. devel. Ctr. Stage, Balt., 1979-81, assoc. mng. dir., 1981-87; mng. dir. Ind. Repertory Theatre, Indpls., 1988-93; dep. dean, mng. dir. and prof. Yale Sch. Drama Yale Repertory Theatre, New Haven, 1993—. Program evaluator Nat. Endowment Arts, Washington, 1988—, panelist, 1991—; mem. Indpls. Cultural Consortium, v.p., 1991-93; bd. dir. Greater Indpls. Progress Com., Indpls. Urban League, Arts Coun. Indpls.; mem. nat. bd. Theatre Comm. Group, N.Y.C., treas., 1995-99; bd. dir. New Haven Arts Industry Coalition, co-chair, 1997-99, treas., 1999-2002. Mem. exec. com. League Resident Profl. Theatres, 2000-04. Nat. Performing Arts Mgmt. fellow Exxon, Doner Fedn. and NEA, 1978; Elizabeth L. Mahaffey arts adminstrn. fellow Conn. Commn. on the Arts, 2000; recipient SetonElm Ivy award Yale U. and City of New Haven, 2005. Home: 120 Rimmon Rd Woodbridge CT 06525-1915 Office: Yale Repertory Theater PO Box 208244 Yale Station 222 York St New Haven CT 06520-8244

**NOLAN, WILLIAM C., JR.,** energy executive; b. 1939; BA, Yale U., 1961, JD, 1964. Mem. law dept. Murphy Oil Corp., El Dorado, Ark., 1964—69, chmn. bd. dirs., 2002—; founding ptnr. Nolan and Alderson, Attys., El Dorado, 1969—; pres. Noalmark Broadcasting. Office: Murphy Oil Corp PO Box 7000 200 Peach St El Dorado AR 71731-7000 also: Nolan and Alderson Attys 202 W 19th St El Dorado AR 71730*

**NOLAN, WILLIAM JOSEPH, III,** banker; b. NYC, Apr. 6, 1947; s. William J. Jr. and Alice Nettleton (Edwards) N.; m. Wendy Collison French, Mar. 21, 1981; children: William J. IV, Anina Chrysler. Student, Hackley Sch., Tarrytown, N.Y., 1958-65; E.S.U. scholar, Eastbourne Coll., U.K., 1966; BA, Colgate U., 1970; MBA, Stanford U., 1973. V.p. Bankers Trust Co. N.Y.C., 1973-83; mng. dir. Becker-Paribas, N.Y.C., 1983-84; exec. v.p., treas. PaineWebber, N.Y.C., 1984-2001. Bd. trustees Adirondack Mus. (Blue Mountain), 1996—, (treas. 2000—). Mem. Pub. Securities Assn. (money market exec. com. 1985-89, chmn. 1987-88, dir. 1988-91, treas. 1990), Adirondack League, Piping Rock Club, Union Club of N.Y.C. Home: 1088 Park Ave New York NY 10128-1132

**NOLAND, CHRISTINE A.,** judge; b. 1945; BA, JD, La. State Univ. Law clk. to Hon. John V. Parker U.S. Dist. Ct. (La. mid. dist.), 5th circuit, magistrate judge Baton Rouge, 1987—. Mem. ABA, La. State Bar, La. trial Lawyers Assn., Baton Rouge Bar Assn., Dean Henry George McMahon Inn of Ct. (counselor 1995-97). Office: Russell B Long Fed Bldg & Courthouse 777 Florida St Rm 278 Baton Rouge LA 70801-1717 Office Phone: 225-389-3592.

**NOLAND, KENNETH CLIFTON,** artist; b. Asheville, N.C., Apr. 10, 1924; s. Harry C. and Bessie (Elkins) N.; m. Cornelia Langer (div.); children: Cady, William L., Lyndon; m. Stephanie Gordon, 1967 (div.); m. Peggy Schiffer; children: Samuel Jesse (div.); m. Paige Rense, 1994. Student, Ozzip Zadkine, Paris, 1948-49; studied, Black Mountain Coll., N.C., summers, 1950, 51. Tchr. Inst. Contemporary Arts, 1950-52, Cath. U., 1951-60. One man shows include Galerie Creuze, Paris, 1949, Tibor de Nagy Gallery, N.Y.C., 1957, 58, Jefferson Pl. Gallery, 1958, French & Co., N.Y.C., 1959, Bennington Coll., 1961, Andre Emmerich Gallery, N.Y.C., 15 shows from 1960-83, Andre Emmerich Gallery, Zurich, Switzerland, 1973, 76, 79, 82, David Mirvish Gallery, Toronto, Can., 1965, 67, 74, 76, Jewish Mus., 1965, Salander O'Reilly Galleries, N.Y.C., 1989, Leo Castelli Gallery, N.Y., 1995, Gana Art Gallery, Seoul, 1995-96, also other galleries in Milan, Italy, Paris, Zurich, Dusseldorf, Hamburg and Cologne, Fed. Republic Germany, London, Montreal and Toronto, Can.; retrospective show Guggenheim Mus., N.Y.C., 1977; group shows include Kootz Gallery, N.Y.C., 1954, Norman Mackenzie Art Gallery, Regina, Sask., Can., 1963, Corcoran Gallery, Washington, 1956, 59, 63, 64, 67, 70, 75, Corcoran Gallery Biennial in Italy, 1964, Fogg Art Mus., Cambridge, Mass., 1965, 72, Mus. Modern Art, N.Y.C., 1965, 68, Nat. Gallery, Washington, 1968, U.S. Pavilion Expo 67, Montreal, Art Inst. Chgo., 1962, 70, 72, 76, Balt. Mus., 1957, 70, 77, Jewish Mus., 1963, Tate Gallery, London, 1964, 74, Guggenheim Mus., 1961, 66, 70, 73-74, 76-77, L.A. County Mus., 1964, Inst. Contemporary Art, Boston, 1964, 65, 67, Whitney

Mus., N.Y.C., 1961-67, 69-73, 76, Met. Mus. N.Y.C., 1968, 70, Mus. Fine Arts, Boston, 1972, Albright-Knox Gallery, Buffalo, 1978, 80, Ameringer Howard Fine Art, NY, 99; Meredith Long Gall., Houston,Tex., 99; Andre Emmerich, CLosing Exhibition of Gall., NY, 99; CHAC-Mool Gall., CA, 99, Ameringer/Howard Gall., N.Y.C., 1999-2001, Farnsworth Mus. Art, Maine, 2002, Naples (Fla.) Mus., 2002; represented in permanent collections Salander O'Reily Galleries, N.Y.C., Mus. of Fine Arts, Houston, 1994, Ft. Lauderdale, 1994; Arte Metro Roma, Rome Colosseum Ctrl. Subway Mosaic Installed, 1995. Trustee Bennington (Vt.) Coll. Recipient 1st prize Premio Nacional Internat., Inst. Torcuato de Tella, Buenos Aires, 1964, Creative Arts award Brandeis U., 1965, 4th prize Corcoran Biennale, 1967; recipient The N.C. Award/medal of arts, 1995.

**NOLAND, MARCUS,** economist, educator; b. Greensboro, NC, Mar. 29, 1959; BA, Swarthmore Coll., 1981; PhD, Johns Hopkins U., 1985. Sr. fellow Inst. for Internat. Econs., Washington, 1985—; asst. prof. U. So. Calif., L.A., 1990-91; sr. economist Coun. Econ. Advisers, Washington, 1993-94. Vis. prof. Saitama U., Urawa, Japan, 1988—89; vis. scholar Korea Devel. Inst., Seoul, 1991; vis. assoc. prof. Johns Hopkins U., Balt., 1991—98; vis. prof. Tokyo U., 1996, U. Ghana, 1997; cons. Internat. Food Policy Rsch. Inst., 1999—; POSCO vis. fellow East-West Ctr., Honolulu, 2000. Author: Pacific Basin Developing Countries, 1991, Avoiding the Apocalypse: The Future of the Two Koreas, 2000, Korea After Kim Jong-il, 2004; editor: Economic Integration on the Korean Penninsula, 1998; co-author: Japan in the World Economy, 1988, Reconcilable Differences?, 1993, Global Effects of the Asian Currency Devaluations, 1998, No More Bashing: Building a New Japan-US Economic Relationships, 2001, Industrial Policy in an Era of Globalization, 2003; co-editor: Pacific Economic Dynamism, 1993. Recipient Ohira Meml. prize, 2002; Japan Soc. for Promotion of Sci. fellow, 1988, Internat. Affairs fellow Coun. on Fgn. Rels., 1993, Coun. for Internat. Rsch. of Scholars fellow, 1997. Mem. Coun. on Fgn. Rels. Office: Inst for Internat Econs 1750 Massachusetts Ave NW Washington DC 20036-1207 E-mail: mnoland@iie.com.

**NOLAND, MARIAM CHARL,** foundation executive; b. Parkersburg, W.Va., Mar. 29, 1947; d. Lloyd Henry and Ethel May (Beare) Noland; m. James Arthur Kelly, June 13, 1981. BS, Case Western Res. U., 1969; M in Edn., Harvard U., 1975. Asst. dir. admissions, fin. aid Baldwin-Wallace Coll., Berea, Ohio, 1969-72; asst. dir. admissions Davidson (N.C.) Coll., 1972-74; case writer Inst. Edn. Mgmt., Cambridge, Mass., 1975; sec., treas., program officer The Cleve. Found., 1975-81; v.p. The St. Paul Found., 1981-85; pres. Community Found. for S.E. Mich., 1985—. Trustee Coun. Mich. Founds., 1988-98, Coun. on Founds., 1994-99, Henry Ford Health System, 1994-2002, 2004— Alma Coll., 1994-2004, John S. and James L. Knight Found., 2002—, Detroit Riverfront Conservancy, 2003—; commr. Detroit 300, 2000-01. Office: Community Found SE Mich 333 W Fort St Ste 2010 Detroit MI 48226-3134 Office Phone: 313-961-6675. Business E-Mail: mnoland@cfsem.org.*

**NOLAND, ROBERT LEROY,** retired manufacturing company executive; b. Lawrence, Kans., Sept. 7, 1918; s. Harry L. and Angela (Scola) N.; m. Delpha Mae Mierndorf, June 16, 1962; children: Gary, Fabra Jeanine, Derice Elizabeth. BS in Mech. Engring, Calif. Inst. Tech., 1941. Design and devel. rocket propelled devices Calif. Inst. Tech., 1941-45; supr. propulsions Naval Ordnance Test Sta., China Lake, Calif., 1945-46; asst. chief engr. Aerojet Gen. Corp., 1946-52; cons. engr. plastic components, rockets and missiles, 1952-54; exec. v.p. Rienhold Engring. and Plastics Co., 1954-57, pres., 1957-59; exec. v.p. Haveg Industries, Wilmington, Del., 1959-66, Ametek, Inc., Paoli, Pa., 1966-68, pres., bd. dirs., 1968-88; pres., chief exec. officer, dir. Ketema Inc., Bensalem, Pa., 1988-92, ret., 1992; chmn. bd. Myricom, 1994—. Mem. Desert Rsch. Inst. Found. Bd. Home: 5555 East Lake Blvd Carson City NV 89704-9266

**NOLD, AURORA RAMIREZ,** finance company executive; b. Honolulu, Apr. 21, 1958; m. Allan Jeffrey Nold, Aug. 1, 1995. BSBA cum laude, St. Louis U., 1969, MS in Bus. Administrn. magna cum laude, 1975, PhD summa cum laude, 1986. Exch. prof., dept. chairperson mgmt. St. Louis U., Baguio City, Philippines, 1980-86, dean Coll. Bus., 1980—86; rsch. asst. East/West Ctr. for Am. Studies, Honolulu, 1986-87; dir. Am. studies USIS, Washington, 1987-89; fin. cons. Shadow Hill Samaritan, Long Beach, Calif., 1989-93; dir. A&A Edu Care Consultancy Programs, Inc., Las Vegas, Nev., 1993—; prin., owner Felocor Diversified Funding, Las Vegas, Nev., 2005—. Bd. advisors Am. Biog. Inst., Raleigh, N.C., 1995—, Internat. Biog. Ctr., Cambridge, Eng., 1995—; rschr. S.H.S. Inc., Las Vegas, 1995—; prof. econs., bus and mgmt. C.C. So. Nev.; prof. stats. U. Nev., Las Vegas; tutor C.C. So. Nev.; pres., founder Felocor Diversified Funding Co Author: Business Education in the Philippines, 1986; contbr. articles to profl. jours. Pres. Rep. Presdl. Task Force, Las Vegas, 1995—. Cultural Exch. grant Fulbright Am. Studies, 1987, scholarship grant St. Louis U., 1979-86; recipient Appreciation award Nat. Humane Edn. Soc., 1996, Nat. Park Trust, 1996, Nat. Law Enforcement Officers Meml. Fund, 1997, Oustanding Cmty. and Profl. Achievement Commemorative medal Am. Biog. Inst., 1997, internat. cultural diploma of honor, 2000. Mem. AAUW, NAFE, Asian Am. Studies Assn., U.S. Profl. Bookkeepers Assn., Am. Cash Flow Assn., Las Vegas C. of C., Nev. Faculty Alliance Republican. Mem. Lds Sch. Avocations: collecting rare coins, writing, reading, music and coin collecting. Office Phone: 702-242-6020. Personal E-mail: auroranold@aol.com.

**NOLD, CARL RICHARD,** museum administrator; b. Mineola, N.Y., Nov. 26, 1955; s. Carl Frederick and Joan Catherine (Heine) N.; m. Mary Beth Krivoruchka (div.). BA in History magna cum laude, St. John's U., Jamaica, N.Y., 1977; MA in History Mus. Studies, SUNY, Oneonta, 1982. Pres. Gregory Mus., Hicksville, N.Y., 1977; registrar N.Y. State Hist. Assn., Cooperstown, 1978-80; dir. curator Gadsby's Tavern Mus., Alexandria, Va., 1980-84; dir. State Mus. Pa., Harrisburg, 1984-91; exec. dir. Mackinac State Hist. Parks, Lansing, Mackinac Island, Mich., 1992—2003; pres., CEO Historic New Eng. (Soc. Preservation New England Antiquities), Boston, 2003—. Grant reviewer Inst. Mus. Svcs., Washington, 1982-90, 95—, mus. assessment prog. reviewer, 1985—, panelist, 1992-94; panelist mus. grant program Nat. Endowment for Humanities, 1990-93, panelist challenge grant program, 1997. Co-author: Gadsby's Tavern Mus. Interpretive Master Plan, 1984; contbr. articles to profl. jours. Mem. adv. bd. for Grad. History George Mason U., Fairfax, Va., 1982-84, Ctr. for Great Lakes Culture, Mich. State U., 2000-2002; adv. com. Susquehanna Mus. Art, Harrisburg, 1989-91; bd. dirs. Harrisburg-Hershey-Carlisle Tourism and Visitor Bur., 1987-91; bd. sec., 1990-91; mem. mayor's adv. bd. city of Mackinac Island, 1993-2003; mem. task force Mich. Cultural Tourism, 1999—; mem. Essex Nat. Heritage Commn., 2003-06. Mem. Assn. of Midwest Mus. (treas 1998-2000, pres. 2000-2002, Mich. Mus. Assn. (bd. dirs. 1995-98, bd. sec. 1999-2001, recipient Dist. Svc. award, 2002), Am. Assn. Mus. (vis. com. mus. accreditation 1989—, chmn. coun. of regions 2000-01, MAP adv. com. 2002-, bd. dirs. 2003—, chair fin. com.), Am. Assn. for State and Local History (elections chmn. 1990, mem. performance measurement program task force 2002-03), Cooperstown Grad. Assn. (bd. dirs. 1985-87), St. Botolph Club-(Boston). Home: 21 Grove St Winchester MA 01890-3837 Office: Hist New Eng 141 Cambridge St Boston MA 02114-2702

**NOLEN, CRYSTAL ME'KELLE,** poet, educator; b. Lexinton Park, Md., July 2, 1972; d. A. Jay, Jr. and Carolyn L. Nolen; children: Stanley, Garney. BA in English, Norfolk State U., 1999. Teacher's asst., sch. cmty. trainer Norfolk (Va.) Pub. Sch. Sys., 1993—. Coord. Million Woman Mar. Bus Trip, Norfolk, 1997. Actor: (plays) Summers in Suffolk, 2000. Home: PO Box 367 Portsmouth VA 23705 Personal E-mail: Cryswrites2000@aol.com.

**NOLEN, ROY LEMUEL,** retired lawyer; b. Montgomery, Ala., Nov. 29, 1937; s. Roy Lemuel Jr. and Elizabeth (Larkin) N.; m. Evelyn McNeill Thomas, Aug. 28, 1965; 1 child, Rives Rutledge. BArch, Rice U., 1961; LLB, Harvard U., 1967. Bar: Tex. 1968, U.S. Ct. Appeals (5th cir.) 1969. Law clk. to sr. judge U.S. Ct. Appeals (5th cir.), 1967-68; assoc. Baker Botts LLP, Houston, 1968-75, ptnr., 1976-2000; co-head Corp. Dept., 1985-90; mem.

exec. com., 1988-91; adminstrv. ptnr., 1997-2000; ret., 2001. Cmty. rep. instnl. animal care and use com. M.D. Anderson Cancer Ctr., 2001—06. Bd. dirs. Houston Ballet Found., 1980-92, Rice Design Alliance, 1995-96; exec. com. Contemporary Arts Mus., 1990-96, 97-2002; exec. com. Houston Symphony Soc., 1994-99, gen. counsel, 1994-98; trustee Menil Found. (Menil Collection), 1999—, sr. warden Christ Ch. Cathedral, 1991-92, chancellor, 2003—; chmn. Houston area devel. initiative Episcopal Diocese of Tex., 1997. 1st lt. USMC, 1961-64. Mem.: State Bar Tex., Briar Club, Paul Jones Dancing Club, Allegro, Coronado Club. Episcopalian. Office: Baker Botts LLP One Shell Plz 910 Louisiana St Houston TX 77002-4995

**NOLEN, SAMUEL AUGUSTUS,** lawyer; b. Circleville, Ohio, Nov. 18, 1954; s. Jake Thomas and Amelia Aerl (Maverick) N.; m. Gail Anne McCurdy, May 17, 1980; children: S. Maverick, Maury McCurdy. Student, U. Regensburg, 1974-75; BA cum laude, Vanderbilt U., 1976; JD, Washington and Lee U., 1979. Bar: Del. 1979, US Dist. Ct. Del. 1980, US Ct. Appeals (3d cir.) 1985, US Supreme Ct. 2004. Law clk. Del. Ct. Chancery, Wilmington, 1979-80; assoc. Richards, Layton & Finger, Wilmington, 1980-86, mem., 1986—. Bd. dirs. Lex Mundi Pro Bono Found., 2006—. Mem. ABA, Internat. Bar Assn. (sec. bus. orgns. com., sect. bus. law), Del. Bar Assn. (sect. corp. law), World Affairs Coun. Wilmington, Inc. (bd. dirs.), Lex Mundi Ltd. (bd. dirs. 2002—, coun. com. 2003—), Greenville Country Club. Republican. Episcopalian. Office: Richards Layton & Finger 1 Rodney Sq Wilmington DE 19801-3305 Office Phone: 302-651-7752.

**NOLEN, WILLIAM GILES,** lawyer, accountant; b. Fayetteville, Ark., Aug. 4, 1931; s. William Jefferson and Marie (Giles) N.; m. Carole Turner, Aug. 25, 1957; children: Kathy, Thomas (dec.). BSBA, U. Ark., 1960; JD, U. Houston, 1980. Bar: Tex. 1980; CPA, Tex. Auditor Arthur Andersen & Co., Houston, 1960-66; sec., treas. Brown & Root (U.K.) Ltd., London, 1966-69; v.p. Highlands Ins. Co., Houston, 1969-73, sr. v.p., 1973-80, dir., 1973-88; v.p. Halliburton Co., Dallas, 1980-82; sr. v.p. Brown & Root, Inc., Houston, 1982-86; exec. v.p. Highlands Ins. Co., Houston, 1986-88; of counsel Whitmore, Sheppard & Pollicoff, Houston, 1988-92, Pollicoff, Smith & Myres LLP, Houston, 1992-95, Policoff, Smith, Myres & Remels LLP, Houston, 1995-2000, Pollicoff, Smith & Remels, Houston, 2000—02. Maj. USAF, 1951-56. Mem. Am. Assn. Atty. CPAs (past pres., bd. dirs.), Tex. Soc. CPAs (Tex. CPA of Yr. 1961), Mensa. Presbyterian.

**NOLET, GUUST,** geophysicist; MSc cum laude in Geophysics, Utrecht U., Netherlands, 1972, PhD cum laude, 1976. Tchg. asst. dept. med. physics Utrecht U., Netherlands, 1967—68, tchg. assts. depts. physics and geophysics, 1969—72, mem. faculty earth sci. dept., 1976—85, prof., 1985—91; prof. dept. geosciences Princeton U., NJ, 1991—97, George J. Magee prof. geophysics and geol. engring., 1997—; rsch. assoc. Netherlands Orgn. for Advancement of Pure Rsch., 1972—75. Head dept. geophysics Utrecht U., 1985—87, assoc. dean faculty of earth scis., 1987—88; dir. Internat. Sch. Applied Geophysics, Erice, Italy, 1986—87; vis. prof. Inst. Geophysics and Planetary Physics U. Calif., San Diego, 1988—89; v.p. European Seismol. Commn., 1990—92; vis. prof. U. Nice, France, 1997—98, 2005; mem. com. seismology NRC, 2000—04; assoc. chair dept. geosciences Princeton U., 2001—; vis. prof. LGIT U. Joseph Fourier, Grenoble, France, 2004; mem. EarthScope Sci. and Edn. Com., 2005. Contbr. articles to profl. jours.; editor: Geophys. Jour. Royal Astron. Soc., 1982—86, Modern Approaches to Geophysics, 1988—2002, Jour. Seismology, 1998—2001; assoc. editor: Jour. Geophys. Rsch., 1993—95. Recipient Lagrange prize, Royal Acad. Scis., Humanities and Fine Arts Belgium, 1980, Vening Meinesz prijs, Netherlands Orgn. for Advancement of Pure Rsch., 1983, Beno Gutenberg medal, European Geophys. Soc., 2006, Bownocker medal, Ohio State U., 2006; grantee Cecil H. and Idan Green fellowship, 1988. Fellow: Am. Geophys. Union (pres. seismology sect. 1998—2000), Am. Acad. Arts & Scis.; mem.: Academia Europaea, Royal Netherlands Acad. Scis. (corr.; earth sci. coun. 1990—91). Office: Dept Geosciences Princeton U 320 Guyot Hall Princeton NJ 08544 E-mail: nolet@princeton.edu.*

**NOLF, DAVID M.,** financial consultant; b. Hartford, Conn., Nov. 25, 1942; s. Richard A. and Erreld I. (Manstan) N.; m. Linda J. Anderson, June 20, 1964; 1 child, Cristina E. BSchemE, Lafayette Coll., 1964; MBA, U. Conn., 1968. Prodn. engr. Am. Cyanamid, Wallingford, Conn., 1664-66; adminstrn. supr. Electric Boat Div. Gen. Dynamics, Groton, Conn., 1966-71; chief fin. and adminstrv. officer, corp. sec. Analysis and Tech. Inc., North Stonington, Conn., 1971—99; cons., 2001—. Bd. dirs. Reflextite Corp. Chmn. Ch. Fin. Com., Westerly, R.I., 2002—; trustee Westerly Hosp., 1993—, chmn. 2003—; bd. dirs. The Day Newspaper, 1997—. Mem.: Beta Gamma Sigma, Tau Beta Pi. Avocations: fishing, golf. Home: 347 Lantern Hill Rd Mystic CT 06355-3623

**NOLKER, DAVID BRETT,** music educator; s. James Leroy and Glenda Jeanne Nolker; m. Jill Brewer Puyear, July 13, 1985; children: Daniel Aaron, Allison Jeanne. B Music Edn., Ctrl. Meth. Coll., 1985; M Music Edn., Wichita State U., 1989; PhD, U. Mo., Columbia, 2001. Dir. music Bent County Schools, Las Animas, Colo., 1985—87, Westminster Coll., Fulton, Mo., 1994—96; dir. vocal music Gasconade County Schools, Hermann, Mo., 1988—93; dir. music edn. Augustana Coll., Rock Island, Ill., 1996—2002; asst. prof. music edn. U. NC, Greensboro, 2002—. Rschr Music Rsch. Inst., Greensboro, 2004—; dir. music Hermann United Meth. Ch., 1989—93, Trinity Episcopal Cathedral, Davenport, Iowa, 1999—2001. Contbr. articles to profl. publs. Named Hon. U. Marshal, U. NC, Greensboro, 2004; New Faculty Rsch. grantee, 2003. Mem.: NC Music Educators Assn. (chmn. tchr. edn. 2003—06), Nat. Assn. Music Edn. (chmn. spl. rsch. interest group social scis. 2002—04), Kappa Delta Pi, Omicron Delta Kappa, Pi Kappa Lambda, Phi Mu Alpha Sinfonia (province gov. 1999—2001), Sigma Alpha Iota (hon.). Avocation: equestrian trail riding. Office: U NC Greensboro 1000 Spring Garden St Greensboro NC 27402 Office Phone: 336-334-3642.

**NOLL, AMY,** secondary educator; b. Madison, Wis., Sept. 12, 1956; d. David John and Eva Joyce (Tappen) N. BA, Milton (Wis.) Coll., 1978; MA, L.I. U., 1990. Tchr. orch. Sun Prairie (Wis.) Pub. Schs., 1979-85; freelance violinist N.Y.C., 1985—; tchr. orch. Hicksville (N.Y.) Pub. Schs., 1987—. Violinist Akron (Ohio) Symphony Orch., 1979-80, Canton (Ohio) Symphony Orch., 1979-80, Madison (Wis.) Symphony Orch., 1980-85; conducting debut Lincoln Ctr., 1999; violinist Nepethe Ensemble, 1994—. Recipient Tchr. Excellence award, Hicksville Pub. Schs, 1989, PTSA Founders Day award, 1994—95, Paul Vetrano Tchr. of the Yr. award, 2000. Mem. Nat. Sch. Orch. Assn., Am. String Tchrs. Assn., Music Educators Nat. Conf., Nassau Music Educators Assn. Avocations: chamber music, jogging, travel, reading, printmaking. Office: Hicksville Pub Schs Division Ave Hicksville NY 11801 Home: 5 Dorchester St Huntington Station NY 11746-8407

**NOLL, JEANNE C.,** retired music educator; b. Reading, Pa., Aug. 12, 1935; d. Carl Foreman and Barbara Rebecca (Mengel) Winter; m. Clair W. Noll; children: Eric W., Douglas C. BS Music Edn., Lebanon Valley Coll., Annville, Pa., 1957; music student, West Chester U., Milligan U., Lehigh U., MIT. Cert. tchr. Pa. 1961. Tchr. elem. music North Coventry Elem. Sch., Chester County, Pa., Yokohama Army Sch., Japan, 1957—58; tchr. vocal jr. H.S. Reading Sch. Dist., Pa., 1959—61; organist, choir dir. St. Paul's United Ch. of Christ, Fleetwood, Pa., 1967—2001, organist/choir dir. emerita, 2002—; tchr. vocal music elem., jr. and sr. H.S. Kutztown Area Sch. Dist., Pa., 1981—94. Dir. show choir Kutztown Area Sch. Dist., 1981—94; accompanist Kutztown Cmty. Choir, 1999—2001, organist, mem., 2001—. Del. 17th congl. dist. Rep. Nat. Conv., NY, 2004, del. 6th congl. dist. Phila., 2000; com. woman Pa. Rep. state com. Harrisburg, 1998—; active Berks Area Muhlenberg Coun. Rep. Women, 1996, 2d v.p. 2005; vice chair Berk County Rep. Com., 2005—. Mem.: East Penn Valley Kiwanis Club (Dir., Key Club Advisor 1994—, Kiwanian of the Year 2000). Mem. United Ch. Of Christ. Avocations: travel, singing, reading, politics.

**NOLL, MARK A.,** historian; BA in English, Wheaton Coll.; MA, Trinity Evangelical Div. Sch., Ill.; PhD in History of Christianity, Vanderbilt Univ., 1975. Faculty Wheaton Coll., Ill., 1979—, now McManis prof. Christian Thought Dept. History, 2006—, co-founder and dir. Inst. Study Am. Evangs., 2006—. Vis. lectr. Harvard Div. Sch., Chgo. Div. Sch., Westminster Theol. Sem., Regent Coll., Vancouver, BC. Contbr. articles to religious journals. Fellow: Am. Acad. Arts & Sci. Office: Wheaton Coll Dept History 501 College Ave Wheaton IL 60187 Office Phone: 630-752-5865. Business E-Mail: mark.noll@wheaton.edu.

**NOLL, RICHARD A.,** apparel executive; BBA, Pa. State Univ.; MBA with distinction, Carnegie Mellon Univ. CEO U.S. sock bus. Sara Lee Corp., Chgo., 1992—2002, COO bakery group, 2002—03, CEO bakery group, 2003—05, sr. v.p., pres. & COO branded apparel, 2005—06, CEO branded apparel, 2006; CEO Hanesbrands Inc., Winston Salem, NC, 2006—. Office: Hanesbrands Inc 1000 E Hanes Mill Rd Winston Salem NC 27105*

**NOLL, RICHARD DEAN, JR.,** psychologist, educator, historian; b. Detroit, Oct. 27, 1959; s. Richard Dean and Betty Ann (Adamczak) Noll; m. Mary Beth McAndrews, Apr. 27, 1986 (div. 1993); m. Susan J. Naylor, May 13, 1994 (div. 2002); 1 child, Wolfgang; 1 child, Dylan James Patterson. BA, U. Ariz., 1979; MA, New Sch. for Social Rsch., 1982; PhD, New Sch. for Rsch., 1992. Lic. clin. psychologist, Pa. Staff clin. psychologist Ancora Psychiat. Hosp., Hammonton, NJ, 1985-88; clin. psychologist in pvt. practice Phila., 1988-92; instr. dept. psychology West Chester U., Pa., 1992-94; postdoctoral fellow Harvard U., Cambridge, Mass., 1994-96, Lectr. in History of Sci., 1997-98; resident fellow Dibner Inst. History of Sci. and Tech. MIT, 1995-96; assoc. prof. psychology De Sales U., 2000—. Invited lectr. Acad. Scis., Budapest, Hungary, 1991; Jagellonian U., Krakow, Poland, 1991, Chinese Acad. Scis., Beijing, 1994, Castello U., Sao Paulo, Brazil, 1996, Bauhaus U., Weimar, Germany, 2002, Inst. for Religion, Sugang U., Seoul, Korea, 2004, U. Cape Town, South Africa, 2005, others; vis. scholar MIT, 1995-96. Author: The Encyclopedia of Schizophrenia and the Psychotic Disorders, 1992, 3d rev. edit., 2006, Vampires, Werewolves and Demons: Twentieth Century Case Reports in the Psychiatric Literature, 1992, The Jung Cult, 1994 (Best Book in Psychology Assn. Am. Publishers 1994), The Aryan Christ, 1997; contbr. articles to profl. jours. Wenner-Gren Found. for Anthropol. Rsch. grantee, 1993. Office Phone: 610-282-1100 ext. 1268. E-mail: richard.noll@desales.edu.

**NOLL, ROGER GORDON,** economist, educator; b. Monterey Park, Calif., Mar. 13, 1940; s. Cecil Ray and Hjordis Alberta (Westover) Noll; m. Robyn Schreiber, Aug. 25, 1962 (dec. Jan. 2000); 1 child, Kimberlee Elizabeth; m. Ann Seminara, Dec. 2, 2001. BS, Calif. Inst. Tech., 1962; AM, Harvard U., 1965, PhD in Econs., 1967. Mem. social sci. faculty Calif. Inst. Tech., 1965-84, prof., 1973-82, inst. prof., 1982-84, chmn. div. humanities and social scis., 1978-82; prof. econs. Stanford U., 1984—2006, Morris M. Doyle centennial prof. of pub. policy, 1990—2002, dir. pub. policy program, 1986—2002, dir. Am. Studies Program, 2001—02, dir. Ctr. for Internat. Devel., 2002—06, prof. emeritus, 2006—; Jean Monnet prof. European U. Inst., 1991; vis. fellow Brookings Instn., 1995-96, non-resident sr. fellow, 1996—2000, vis. scholar, 2003. Sr. staff economist Coun. Econ. Advisors, Washington, 1967—69; sr. fellow Brookings Instn., Washington, 1970—73; mem. tech. adv. bd. Com. Econ. Devel., 1978—82; mem. adv. coun. NSF, 1978—89, NASA, 1978—81, SERI, 1982—90; mem. Pres.'s Commn. Nat. Agenda for Eighties, 1980; chmn. L.A. Sch. Monitoring Com., 1978—79; mem. Commn. Behavioral Social Scis. and Edn. NAS, 1984—90, mem. bd. sci., tech. and econ. policy, 2000—06; mem. energy rsch. adv. bd. Dept. Energy, 1986—89; mem. Sec. Energy Adv. Bd., 1990—94, Calif. Coun. Sci. and Tech., 1995—2000; mem. bd. on sci., tech. and econ. policy NRC, 2001—. Author: (book) Reforming Regulation, 1971, The Economics and Politics of Deregulation, 1991, The Economics and Politics of the Slowdown in Regulatory Reform, 1999; co-author: Economic Aspects of Television Regulation, 1973, The Political Economy of Deregulation, 1983, The Technology Pork Barrel, 1991; editor: Government and the Sports Business, 1974, Regulatory Policy and the Social Sciences, 1985, Challenges to Research Universities, 1998; co-editor: Constitutional Reform in California, 1995, Sports, Jobs and Taxes, 1997, A Communications Cornucopia, 1998; supervisory editor: Info. Econs. and Policy Jour., 1984—92. Recipient 1st ann. book award, Nat. Assn. Ednl. Broadcasters, 1974; fellow Guggenheim, 1983—84; grantee NSF, 1973—82. Mem.: Am. Econ. Assn. Democrat. Home: 4153 Hubbartt Dr Palo Alto CA 94306-3834 Office: Stanford U Dept Econs Stanford CA 94305 Office Phone: 650-723-2297. Business E-Mail: rnoll@stanford.edu.

**NOLLY, ROBERT J.,** pharmacist, health facility administrator, educator; b. Amsterdam, N.Y., Jan. 8, 1947; m. Diera R. Lehtonen, June 21, 1969; children: Shelby Alexandra, Kirby Alycia, Kendall Alexis. BS in Pharmacy with honor, Albany Coll. Pharmacy, 1970; MSc in Hosp. Pharmacy, Ohio State U., 1979. Pharmacy extern Matt Pharmacy, Canajoharie, N.Y., 1967-70; pharmacy intern Park Row Drugs, Canajoharie, 1970-71, asst. mgr., 1971-72; staff pharmacist Mary Imogene Bassett Hosp., Cooperstown, N.Y., 1972-74, 75-77; med. svc. rep. Dista Products Co., Eli Lilly and Co., Indpls., 1974-75; resident hosp. pharmacy Grant Hosp., Columbus, Ohio, 1977-79; asst. dir. pharmacy svcs. City of Memphis Hosp., 1979-81, U. Tenn. Bowld Hosp., Memphis, 1982, dir. pharmacy svcs. and materials mgmt., 1982-85, asst. administr. pharmacy svcs. and materials mgmt., 1985—90, administr., 1991—92, administr. svcs., 1992—98, exec. dir., 1999—2002. Asst. prof. Coll. Pharmacy U. Tenn., Memphis, 1979-92, assoc. prof.1992-; lectr. Columbus Tech. Inst., 1978-79; trustee Diversified Svcs., Inc., Tenn. Hosp. Assn., 1990-96, mem. pharmacy adv. com., 1990; bd. dirs. Ava Marie Nursing Home, chmn. nom. com., 1988, 89, mem. long-range planning com., 1989, 90, mem. constn. and by-laws com., 1990, mem. govtl. rels. com., 1991-93; presenter in field. Editor U. Tenn. Bowld Hosp. Pharmacy Newsletter, 1987-91; mem. editl. bd. Drug and Therapeutics Newsletter, U. Tenn. Coll. Pharmacy, 1989, 90. Usher Ch. of Holy Spirit, 1988-96; mem. Am. Cancer Soc. Recipient Order of Round award Am. Cancer Soc., 1992. Mem. Am. Soc. Hosp. Pharmacists, Tenn. Soc. Hosp. Pharmacists (mem. com. 1988, constn. and by-laws com. 1985, 88, 89, 90, mem. nominating com. 1989, orgn. and goals com. 1991, strategic planning com. 1992), Tenn. Pharmacists Assn. (pharmacy tech. task force 1988, 89, 90, ho. dels. 1988, 89, 90, 91, 92, 94, chmn. tech. curriculum com. 1991, tech. edn. accreditation com. 1991, 92, 94), Memphis Area Soc. Hosp. Pharmacists (pres.-elect 1984, pres. 1985, past pres. 1986, chmn. nominating com. 1991), Tenn. Hosp. Assn. (liaison Tenn. Med. Assn. com. 1991), Mid-South Healthcare Materials Mgmt. Assn., Kappa Psi, Rho Chi. Home: 2927 Mikeyair Dr Germantown TN 38138-7148 Office Phone: 901-448-1144. E-mail: rnolly@utmem.edu.

**NOLTE, LINDA MARIE,** language educator; AB in Recreation Adminstrn., San Diego State U., 1972, MA in Phys. Edn., 1973; MA, US Internat. U., 1991; PhD, Claremont Grad. U. Cert. Advanced Placement, English Lit. San Diego County Dept. Edn., 2002, Digital HS Trng. Calif., 2002, Ryan Single Subject Clear Calif. Commn. Tchr. Credentialing, 1973, Standard Secondary Calif. Commn. Tchr. Credentialing, Gifted and Talented Educator San Diego Unified Sch. Dist., CC Instr. in Pub. Svcs./Adminstrn. Calif. Commn. Tchr. Credentialing, CC Instr. in Basic Skills Calif. Commn. Tchr. Credentialing, CC Instr. in Phys. Edn. Calif. Commn. Tchr. Credentialing. English tchr., English lang. devel. tchr., ESL tchr., reading tchr. San Diego Unified Sch. Dist., 1995—2004; English tchr., English lang. devel. tchr. Fallbrook Union HS Dist., Calif., 2004; reading specialist Eagles Peak Charter Sch., Vista, Calif., 2006—. Adj. prof. Nat. U. La Jolla, Calif., 1996—; adv. African Am. Student Union Mission Bay HS, 1997—98, mem. senate bill 1882 com., 1998—2002, chair sch. site adv. com., 2000—02, facilitator, tchr. Camp MiniTown, advisor Gay-Straight Alliance Club; adj. instr. U. San Diego, 2002—; mem. U. San Diego We. Assn. Schs. & Colls., 2003—05; tesol adv. bd. U. San Diego, 2005—; mem. tech. com. Fallbrook HS, 2004—; journalist Nat. Med. Assn., 2004; English lang. devel. instr. Bethesda Christian U., Anaheim, Calif., 2004—06. Author: (children's book reviews) The San Diego Union Tribune, 1974; contbr. articles to profl. jours. Troop organizer Tierrasanta Girl Scouts Am., San Diego, 1986—87; girl scout leader Tierrasanta Girl Scouts, 1986—93; mem. adv. bd. The Sudanese English Project, San Diego, 1999—2000; mem. Tierrasanta Recreation Coun. Fellow Edn., Claremont Grad. U., Summer 1993. Mem.: Tierrasanta Jr. Women's Club (officer), San Diego Edn. Assn. (secondary 2002, site rep. 2002—03, bd. dirs. 2003—04, tchr. harassment com. 2003—05, biliteracy com. 2003—04), Tierrasanta Tennis Club (pres.). Office: Eagles Peak Charter Sch 981 Vale Terrace Dr Vista CA 92084 Business E-Mail: lnolte@eaglespeak.org.

**NOLTE, NICK,** actor; b. Omaha, Feb. 8, 1941; m. Sheila Page, 1966 (div. 1971), Sharon Haddad, May 10, 1978 (div. 1983); Rebecca Linger, Feb. 19, 1984 (div. 1995); 1 child, Brawley King. Student, Ariz. St. Univ., Eastern Ariz. Coll., Pasadena City Coll., Phoenix City Coll.; studies with, John Paul, Allen Dutton. Actor: (play) The Last Pad, 1973, (TV movies) Winter Kill, 1974, The California Kid, 1974, Death Sentence, 1974, (TV series) Adams of Eagle Lake, 1975, (TV movies) The Treasure Chest Murder, 1975, The Runaway Barge, 1975, (mini-series) Rich Man, Poor Man, 1976; (films) Return to Macon County, 1976, The Deep, 1977, Who'll Stop the Rain, 1978, North Dallas Forty, 1979, Heart Beat, 1980, Cannery Row, 1982, 48 Hours, 1982, Under Fire, 1983, The Ultimate Solution of Grace Quigley, 1984, Teachers, 1984, Down and Out in Beverly Hills, 1986, Weeds, 1987, Extreme Prejudice, 1987, Farewell to the King, 1988, Three Fugitives, 1988, New York Stories, 1989, Everybody Wins, 1989, Q & A, 1990, Another 48 Hours, 1990, Prince of Tides, 1991, Cape Fear, 1991, Lorenzo's Oil, 1992, The Player, 1992, Blue Chips, 1994, I'll Do Anything, 1994, I Love Trouble, 1994, Jefferson in Paris, 1995, Mulholland Falls, 1996, Mother Night, 1996, Nightwatch, 1997, Afterglow, 1997, U-Turn, 1997, Affliction (also exec. prod), 1998, Thin Red Line, 1998, The Best of Enemies, 1999, Simpatico, 1999, Breakfast of Champions, 1999, The Golden Bowl, 2000, Trixie, 2000, Investigating Sex (also prod.), 2001, The Good Thief, 2002, Northfork, 2003, The Hulk, 2003, (voice) Over the Hedge, 2006, Peaceful Warrior, 2006.*

**NÖLTING, BENGT,** physicist, researcher; b. May 1, 1962; BS in Physics, Humboldt U., Berlin, 1986, MS, 1987; PhD, Ruhr U., Bochum, Germany, 1991. Scientist U. Cambridge, England, 1994—97; dir. Prussian Pvt. Inst. Tech., Berlin, 1997—. Vis. prof. Vienna (Austria) U. Tech., 2001. Author: Protein Folding Kinetics--Biophysical Methods, 1999, 2d edit, 2005, Methods in Modern Biophysics, 2003, 2d edit., 2005. Achievements include studying structure of biological macromolecules; development of biophysical technologies and energy technologies. Office: Prussian Pvt Inst Tech Berlin Am Schlosspark 30 D-13187 Berlin Germany E-mail: nolting@pitb.de.

**NONAS, CONSTANTINE JAMES,** retired general surgeon; b. Jersey City, N.J., May 19, 1934; s. Demetrios P. and Ariadne (Marcopul) N.; m. Francis Tsistinas, Nov. 15, 1970; children: Stephanie Anne, Demetri K. BS in Biology, Coll. of Holy Cross, 1955; MD, Tufts U., 1959. Diplomate Am. Bd. Surgery. Intern Mountainside Gen. Hosp., Montclair, NJ, 1959-60; resident in gen. surgery, 1960-61, Letterman Gen. Hosp., San Fransisco, 1963-67; resident in gen. and perivascular surgery Bronxn Lebannon Hosp., NY, 1969-70; chief profl. svcs. Malcolm Grow Med. Ctr., Andrews AFB, 1980-82; chief gen. surgery dept. Kaiser-Permanento, Va., 1988—2006, ret., 2006. Col. USAFMC, 1974. Fellow ACS (Washington, D.C. and Va. chpts.); mem. Chesapeake Vascular Soc., Assn. of Mil. Surgeons, Air Force Assn. of Surgeons. Republican. Greek Orthodox. Avocations: golf, reading.

**NONIS, DAVID,** professional sports team executive; b. Burnaby, BC, Can., May 25, 1966; m. Susan Nonis; 1 child, Nicholas. BA, U. Maine, 1988, MBA, 1990. Asst. corp. contracts, computer scouting and team svcs. Vancouver Canucks, 1990—94, sr. v.p., dir. hockey ops., 1998—2004, gen. mgr., 2004—; mgr. hockey ops. NHL, 1994—98. Office: Vancouver Canucks 800 Griffiths Way Vancouver BC Canada V6B 6G1*

**NONNA, JOHN MICHAEL,** lawyer; b. N.Y.C., July 8, 1948; s. Angelo and Josephine (Visconti) N.; m. Jean Wanda (Cleary), June 9, 1973; children: Elizabeth, Caroline, Marianne, Timothy. BA, Princeton U., 1970; JD, NYU, 1975. Bar: N.Y. 1976, U.S. Dist. Ct. (so. dist.) N.Y., 1978, U.S. Ct. Appeals (2d cir.) 1978, U.S. Ct. Appeals (9th cir.) 1980, U.S. Ct. Appeals (5th cir.) 1997, U.S. Dist. Ct. Conn. 1988, U.S. Supreme Ct. 1998. Law asst. to Hon. D.L. Gabrielli N.Y. Ct. Appeals, Albany, 1975-77; assoc. Reid and Priest, N.Y.C., 1977-84; ptnr. Werner and Kennedy, N.Y.C., 1984-99, LeBoeuf, Lamb, Greene, and MacRae, N.Y.C., 1999—. Contbr. articles to profl. jours. Dep. mayor, trustee Pleasantville, N.Y., 1990-95; mayor, 1995-2003; acting justice, 1983-89. With USNR, 1970-75. Mem. U.S. Olympic Team, 1972, 1980; Paul Harris fellow Rotary Internat. Fellow Am. Bar Found. (life); mem. ABA (torts and ins. practice sect. com. chair 1986-87, 92-93), N.Y. State Bar Assn. (chair comml. and fed. litig. sect. 1998-99, co-editor in chief 2000, N.Y. ins. law practice), Assn. Bar City N.Y., N.Y. Fencers Club (pres. 1990-93). Avocations: fencing, running, piano. Office: LeBoeuf Lamb Greene & MacRae 125 W 55th St New York NY 10019-5369 Office Phone: 212-424-8311. Business E-Mail: jnonna@llgm.com.

**NOONAN, CHARLES THOMAS,** lawyer; b. Ashland, Ky., May 27, 1924; s. Arthur Kelly and Tina May (Beam) N.; m. Constance Charlotte Snelling, Nov. 10, 1945; children: Thomas, Susan, Karl, James, Todd. AB magna cum laude, Harvard Coll., 1945, JD, 1949. Bar: Pa., U.S. Supreme Ct. English and lit. tchr. Harwich (Mass.) H.S., 1945-46; pvt. practice Allentown, Pa., 1950-52; ptnr. Donecker & Noonan, Allentown, 1952-89, Noonan and Prokup, Allentown, 1989—. Dir., legal counsel Mchts. Bank Allentown, 1974-91; assoc. Cedar Crest Coll., 1986—, trustee, 1994—, chmn. bd., 1997—. Dir., treas., pres. East Pa. Union Sch. Dist., Emmaus, 1954-59; deacon Solomons Ch., Macungie, Pa., 1959-60; dir., pres. Allentown Jr. C. of C., 1950-60; chmn. Lehigh County Pub. Solicitations Bd., Allentown, 1955-57. Recipient Disting. Svc. award Allentown Jr. C. of C., 1958; named Col. Order of Ky. Cols., Louisville, 1966. Mem. ABA, Pa. Bar Assn. Lehigh County Bar Assn., Phi Beta Kappa, Republican. Avocations: skiing, tennis, water skiing, music, reading. Home: 3817 Larkspur Dr Allentown PA 18103-9740 Office: Noonan and Prokup 526 W Walnut St Allentown PA 18101-2322

**NOONAN, FRANK RUSSELL,** finance company executive; b. Boston, July 21, 1942; s. Russell F. and Barbara (Yutronich) N.; m. Patricia Bernadette Saulnier, Aug. 22, 1964; children: Kathleen, Kelly, Kristin. BA, U. N.H., 1964. Fin. mgmt. trainee GE, Lynn, Mass., 1966-69, corp. auditor Schenectady, N.Y., 1969-74, audit administr., 1974-76, fin. mgr. mechanical drive turbine dept. Fitchburg, Mass., 1976-78, fin. mgr. air conditioning divsn. Louisville, 1978-81; sr. v.p., chief fin. officer Union Mutual Ins. Co., Portland, Maine, 1981-86, UNUM Corp., Portland, 1986-89; sr. v.p., group The Dun & Bradstreet Corp., N.Y.C., 1989-90; chmn., CEO R.H. Donnelley Corp., Purchase, N.Y., 1991—. Bd. trustees U. N.H. Found.; dir. China Big.com. Chmn. N.Y. United Hosp. Med. Ctr., 1995—, Maine Coll. Art; trustee Found. Blood Rsch., Scarborough, Maine, 1982-89; vice chmn. bd. govs. Buick Classic, 1996—; bd. trustees Manhattanville Coll., 1998—. Mem. Yellow Pages Pubs. Assn. (bd. dirs. 1996-2000). Republican. Avocations: tennis, skiing, music, golf, model trains.

**NOONAN, JACK,** application developer; With field engring. and sys. devel. IBM Corp., 1967—77; from with software devel., mktg., customer svc. to v.p. corp. product support Amdahl Corp., Santa Clara, Calif., 1977—85; v.p. Product Group Candle Corp., 1985—90; pres., CEO Microrim Corp., 1990—91; pres. SPSS Inc., Chgo., 1992—, CEO, 1992—, bd. dir. Bd. dir. Morningstar, Inc., Repository Technologies, Inc., Fortel Inc.; adv. com. Geneva Tech. Ptnrs., Inc. Office: SPSS Inc 233 S Wacker Dr 11th Fl Chicago IL 60606

**NOONAN, JACQUELINE ANNE,** pediatrician, educator; b. Burlington, Vt., Oct. 28, 1928; BA, Albertus Magnus Coll., 1950; MD, U. Vt., 1954, DSc (hon.), 1980. Diplomate Am. Bd. Pediatrics, Am. Bd. Pediatric Cardiology. Intern N.C. Meml. Hosp., Chapel Hill, 1954-55; resident in pediatrics Children's Hosp., Cin., 1955-57; rsch. fellow Children's Med. Ctr., Boston, 1957-59; asst. prof. pediatrics State U. Iowa Sch. Medicine, 1959-61; asst. prof. pediatrics cardiology U. Ky. Coll. Medicine, Lexington, 1961-64, assoc. prof., 1964-69, prof., 1969-99, chmn. dept. pediatrics, 1974-92, emeritus prof., 1999—. Mem. embryology and human devel. study sect. NIH, 1973-78; mem. U.S.-USSR Symposium on Congenital Heart Disease, 1975; mem. sub. bd. pediatric cardiology Am. Bd. Pediatrics, 1977-82; examiner, mem. test. com. Nat. Bd. Med. Examiners, 1984-90, exec. com., 1991-95; participant various confs. in field; vis. prof. Vanderbilt U., Nashville, 1987; spkr. in field. Contbr. articles, revs. to med. publs.; mem. editl. bd. Am. Jour. Diseases Children, 1970-80, Am. Jour. Med. Edn., 1975-78, Pediatric Cardiology, 1978-90, Am. Heart Jour., 1994-96, Clin. Pediatrics, 1990-99. Fellow: Royal Coll. Irish Physicians (hon.); mem.: AMA, So. Soc. Pediat. Rsch. (pres. 1972), Soc. Pediat. Rsch., NIH Alumni Assn., Ky. State Med. Assn., Irish-Am. Pediat. Soc. (pres. 1990—2001), Fayette County Pediat. Soc., Am. Pediat. Soc., Assn. Med. Sch. Pediatrics (dept. chmn. exec. com. 1978—81), Am. Coll. Cardiology (gov. Ky. chpt. 1989—92), Am. Acad. Pediatrics (chmn. cardiol. sect. 1972—74). Office Phone: 859-257-4679.

**NOONAN, JOHN GERARD,** bishop; b. Limerick, Ireland, Feb. 26, 1951; BA, St. John Vianney Coll. Sem., Miami; MDiv, St. Vincent de Paul Regional Sem., Boynton Beach; MEd, Boston Coll. Ordained priest Archdiocese of Miami, 1983; pres./rector St. John Vianney Coll. Sem., 1996—2005; Aux. Bishop of Miami, 2005—. Office: Archdiocese of Miami 9401 Biscayne Blvd Miami FL 33138

**NOONAN, JOHN T., JR.,** federal judge, law educator; b. Boston, Oct. 24, 1926; s. John T. and Marie (Shea) Noonan; m. Mary Lee Bennett, Dec. 27, 1967; children: John Kenneth, Rebecca Lee, Susanna Bain. BA, Harvard U., 1946, LLB, 1954; student, Cambridge U., 1946—47; MA, Cath. U. Am., 1949, PhD, 1951, LHD, 1980. Holy Cross Coll., 1980, Loyola U., Chgo., 1999; LLD, U. Santa Clara, 1974, U. Notre Dame, 1976, Loyola U. South, 1978, St. Louis U., 1981, Duquesne U., 1995, Valparaiso U., 1996, U. San Diego, 1999, Gonzaga U., 1986, U. San Francisco, 1996. Bar: Mass. 1954, U.S. Supreme Ct. 1971. Mem. spl. staff Nat. Security Council, 1954-55; pvt. practice Herrick & Smith, Boston, 1955-60; prof. law U. Notre Dame, 1961-66, U. Calif., Berkeley, 1967-86, chmn. religious studies, 1970-73, chmn. medieval studies, 1978-79; judge U.S. Ct. Appeals (9th cir.), San Francisco, 1985-96, sr. judge, 1996—. Oliver Wendell Holmes, Jr. lectr. Harvard U. Law Sch., 1972; Pope John XXIII lectr. Cath. U. Law Sch., 1973; Cardinal Bellarmine lectr. St. Louis U. Div. Sch., 1973; Ernest Messenger lectr. Cornell U., 1982; John Dewey Meml. lectr. U. Minn., 1986; Baum lectr. U. Ill., 1988; Strassberger lectr. U. Tex., 1989; chmn. bd. Games Rsch., Inc., 1961—76; overseer Harvard U., 1991—97; Maguire chair in ethics Libr. of Congress, 2002; vis. prof. U. Catania, Sicily, Italy, 2002; vis. Disting. prof. kaw Emory U., 2000; Erasmus lectr. U. Notre Dame, 2003. Author: The Scholastic Analysis of Usury, 1957, Contraception: A History of Its Treatment by the Catholic Theologians and Canonists, 1965, Power to Dissolve, 1972, Persons and Masks of the Law, 1976, The Antelope, 1977, A Private Choice, 1979, Bribes, 1984, The Responsible Judge, 1993, Professional and Personal Responsibilities of the Lawyer, 1997, Canons and Canonists in Context, 1997, The Lustre of Our Country, 1998, Narrowing the Nation's Power, 2002, A Church That Can and Cannot Change, 2005; editor: Natural Law Forum, 1961—70, Am. Jour. Jurisprudence, 1970, The Morality of Abortion, 1970. Chmn. Brookline Redevel. Authority, Mass., 1958—62; cons. Papal Commn. on Family, 1965—66, Ford Found., Indonesian Legal Program, 1968, NIH, 1973, 1974; expert Presdl. Commn. on Population and Am. Future, 1971; pres. Thomas More-Jacques Maritain Inst., 1977—; trustee Population Coun., 1969—76, Phi Kappa Found., 1970—76, U. San Francisco, 1971—75; mem. com. theol. edn. Yale U., 1972—77; cons. U.S. Cath. Conf., 1979—86; sec., treas. Inst. for Rsch. in Medieval Canon Law, 1970—88; trustee Grad. Theol. Union, 1970—73; exec. com. Cath. Commn. Intellectual and Cultural Affairs, 1972—75; bd. dirs. Ctr. for Human Values in the Health Scis., 1969—71, S.W. Intergroup Rels. Coun., 1970—72, Inst. for Study Ethical Issues, 1971—73. Recipient St. Thomas More award, U. San Francisco, 1974, Christian Culture medal, 1975, Laetare medal, U. Notre Dame, 1984, Campion medal, Cath. Book Club, 1987, Alemany medal, Western Dominican Province, 1988; fellow Guggenheim fellow, 1965—66, 1979—80, Ctr. for Advanced Studies in Behavioral Scis. fellow, 1973—74, Wilson Ctr. fellow, 1979—80, Kluge chair in Am. law and govt., Libr. Congress Ctr. for Scholars, 2002. Fellow: Am. Acad. Arts and Scis., Am. Soc. Legal Historians (hon.); mem.: Am. Law Inst., Canon Law Soc. Am. (gov. 1970—72), Am. Soc. Polit. and Legal Philosophy (v.p. 1964), Phi Beta Kappa (senator United chpts. 1970—72, pres. Alpha of Calif: chpt. 1972—73). Office: US Ct Appeals 9th Cir 95 7th St San Francisco CA 94103-1526*

**NOONAN, JOSETTE MARIE,** music educator; b. Melrose Park, Ill., Mar. 6, 1955; d. Frank Eugene and Barbara Ann Noonan. ADN, Waubonsee Coll., Ill., 1984; MusB, DePaul U., 1990. Registered Profl. Nurse, Ill., 1984; cert. musikgarten educator 1999, dir. music ministries 2005. Music dir. St. Mary's Ch., West Chgo., Ill.; RN surg. resource team Children's Meml. Med. Ctr., Chgo., 1985—90; singer Grant Pk. Symphony Chorus, 1985—90; artist in residence Coll. of DuPage, Glen Ellyn, Ill., 1987—88; asst. dir. Light Opera Works, Evanston, Ill., 1990—91; RN rehab. Oak Pk. Hosp., Ill., 1992—97; soprano soloist and sect. leader First United Meth. Ch. at Chgo. Temple, Chgo., 1993—2004, children's choir dir., 1999—2003; voice tchr. No. Ill. U. Cmty. Sch. of Music, DeKalb, Ill., 1999—2002; music and movement tchr. No. Ill. U. Suzuki Sch., DeKalb, 1999—2002; tchr. voice and strings Countryside Music Sch., Elburn, Ill., 1999—; music tchr. Creative Beginning Presch., 2005—06. Violist Celebration String Quartet, Arlington Heights, Ill., 2000—04; dir. Countryside Players, Elburn, Ill., 2002—, Kindechor and Angeli Musicali Children's Choirs St. Mary's, West Chgo., Ill., 2005—06; founder and adminstr. Patrick Edgar Triplett Meml. Scholarship Program; rehabilitative music specialist Healing Harps, DeKalb, Ill., 2000—03, guest artist German Song Text Workshop, Vienna, 2004—, Assisi Music Festival, Italy, 2005—06, Mladi Fest, Medjugorje, Bosnia-Herzegovina, 2005, Accademia Voci d'Estate, Verona, Italy, 2006, Art Song Festival, 2006. Composer: (songs) Songs for Children's Worship; arranger (musical) From Mozart to Moulin Rouge; singer: (improvisatory music for dance troupe) The Death of the King, author of poems. Past pres. Ill. Collegiate Music Educators, Mokena, Ill., 2000—01; canvas voters to encourage passage of referendum for schs. Save our Schs., West Chgo., Ill., 1970; fed and clothed homeless people First United Meth. Ch. at Chgo., Chgo., 2000—02; care and concern ministry First United Meth. Ch. at Chgo. Temple, Chgo., 2002—04; mem. Pax Christi, 2005—06, Christian Peacemaker Team, 2005—06, Kairos Retreat Leadership Team, 2006. Recipient Invitation to sing for Martin Katz, DePaul U., 1987, Invited to sing for John Wustman, 1988, Invitation to sing Honors Recitals, 1985—88, Invited to sing and speak at a meml. concert honoring composer, Moses Hogan, Abyssinian Bapt. Ch. NY, 2002, First prize, Italian Cultural Soc. Voice Competition, 1988. Mem.: Nat. Assn. Pastoral Musicians, Nat. Guild Hypnotists (assoc.), Am. Choral Dirs. Assn. (assoc.; treas. local chpt. 1999—2001), Music Educator's Nat. Conf. (assoc.; pres. of ill. collegiate assn. 2000—01), Healing Harps (assoc.). Independent. Achievements include Specialist in German Lied interpretation; development of music program for autistic children at Northern Illinois University; Set up music and movement program for local preschool; Planned, executed and evaluated a weekend workshop for music education students in the state of Illinois entitled, What I didn't learn in music school. Avocations: backpacking, german language and culture, scuba diving, fiddling, hypnosis. Home: 324 Church St West Chicago IL 60185 Office: St Mary's Church 140 North Oakwood Avenue West Chicago IL 60185 Office Phone: 630-231-0013. Office Fax: 630-293-2671. E-mail: scotchdiva@aol.com.

**NOONAN, KENNETH J.,** pediatrician, surgeon, educator; m. Carrie A. Askew; children: Claudia A., Samuel O., Peter A. BA in Biology, Luther Coll., Decorah, Iowa, 1985, BA in Math., 1985; MD, U. Iowa, Iowa City, 1989. Cert. Am. Bd. Orthop. Surgery, 1996. Consulting physician St. Vincent's Children Splty. Hosp., Indpls., 1997—2001, St. Vincent's Children Hosp., Indpls., 1997—2001; co-dir. orthopaedic sect. Cerebral Palsy Clinic Riley Hosp., Indpls., 1997—2001; dir. Scoliosis Clinic Riley Children's Hosp., Indpls., 1999—2001; asst. prof. dept. orthopedics Ind. U. Sch. Medicine, Indpls., 1997—2001; assoc. prof. dept. orthopedics and rehab. U.

Wis. Hosp. and Clinics, Madison, 2001—, assoc. prof. dept. pediat., 2002—; dir. pediatric orthopedics Dean Health Systems, Madison, 2001—. Med. student advisor U. Wis., Madison, 2001—; clin. planning com. Am. Family Children's Hosp., Madison, 2003—; edn. com. Dept. Orthopedics and Rehab., Wis., 2005—. Recipient Kaye Wilkins Outstanding Clin. Paper award, Pediatric Orthop. Soc. N.Am., 2001, Okagaki Tchg. award, U. Wis. Hosp. and Clinics, Dept. Orthopedics and Rehab., 2003, Children Matter award, U. Wis. Hosp. and Clinics, 2004, Excellence in Innovation award, Allergan, 2005; 3M scholar, Luther Coll., 1982, 1983. Mem.: Pediat. Orthop. Assn. N.Am., Am. Acad. Orthopedic Surgery (mem. trauma evaluation com. 2003—, The Ponseti Method for Idiopathic Clubfoot Videotape 2000), Alpha Omega Alpha. Office: UW Hospital and Clinics 600 Highland Ave Rm K4/731 Madison WI 53792 Office Phone: 608-263-1344. Office Fax: 608-263-5631.

**NOONAN, PATRICK FRANCIS,** conservation executive; b. St. Petersburg, Fla., Dec. 2, 1942; s. Francis Patrick and Henrietta (Donovan) N.; m. Nancy Elizabeth Peck, Aug. 15, 1964; children: Karen Elizabeth (dec.), Dawn Wiley AB, Gettysburg Coll., 1961-65; M.City and Regional Planning, Catholic U. Am., 1967; MBA, Am. U., 1971. V.p., pres. The Nature Conservancy, 1968—80; founder, dir., chmn. Am. Farmland Trust, 1980—97; chmn., pres. The Conservation Fund, 1985—2003, chmn. emeritus, 2003—. Trustee Nat. Geog. Soc., 1990—; vice chmn. Nat. Geog. Edn. Found, 1995—; trustee Gettysburg Coll., 1978—91, Duke U. Sch. Environment, 1979—, Ind. Sector, 1984—91, Am. Conservation Assn., 1986—, Natural Resources Coun. Am., 1996—2002; dir. Ashland, 1991—, Internat. Paper, 1993—2004, Saul Ctrs., 1993—; mem. Pres.' Commn. on Am. Outdoors, 1985—87, Pres.' Commn. on Environ. Quality, 1991—93, Pres.' Commn. on White House Fellows, 2001—. MacArthur Found. fellow, 1985-90. Home: 3553 Hamlet Pl Chevy Chase MD 20815

**NOONAN, PATRICK SUTTON,** management educator; b. Springfield, Ill., July 11, 1955; s. Patrick Arthur and Julia Ann (Sutton) N.; m. M. Jo Howarth, Apr. 27, 1985; children: Paul Howarth, William Prindiville. BS in Engring. Sci., Yale U., 1977, MBA, 1984; MS in Engring. Sci., Harvard U., 1989, PhD in Decision Scis., 1992. Dir. and gen. mgr. East River Consort, Boston, 1978-80; pres. Greenpeace New Eng., Boston, 1980-82; assoc. McKinsey & Co., Inc., N.Y.C., 1984-88; cons. MicroMentor, Inc., Cambridge, Mass., 1984-89; prin. Planning Techs. Group, Inc., Lexington, Mass., 1989—98; assoc. prof. Emory U., 1993—; Fulbright sr. specialist, 2005. Prodr. record albums, including Laurasia, 1978, Undiscovered Country, 1988, Beat Noir, 1996, Scott's Red Star, 2000; prodr. film Journey to Georges Bank, 1982. Office Phone: 404-727-0549.

**NOONAN, PEGGY,** writer; b. Bklyn., Sept. 7, 1950; d. Jim and Mary Jane (Byrne) N.; m. Richard Kahn, Nov. 27, 1985 (div. 1990); 1 child, Will. BA in English Literature & Journalism, Fairleigh Dickinson U., Rutherford, N.J., 1974, PhD in Humane Letters (hon.), 1990. Premium adjuster Aetna Ins. Co., Newark, 1968-70; student Amateur Protester of Vietnam; temp. agency sec. N.Y.C., 1974; news staffer WEEI Radio (CBS station), Boston, 1974, editl. dir., 1975-77; writer, editor CBS News, N.Y.C., 1977-80, commentary for Walter Cronkite and Dan Rather, 1980-81, full time commentary writer for Dan Rather, 1981-84; White House speech writing tech. Ronald Reagan, Washington, 1984-86; White House speech writer George Bush, Washington, 1988-89; contbg. editor The Wall St. Jour., Time, Good Housekeeping. Bd. dir. The Manhattan Inst. Author: What I Saw at the Revolution: A Political Life in the Reagan Era, 1990, Life, Liberty, & the Pursuit of Happiness, 1995, Simply Speaking: How to Communicate Your Ideas With Style, Substance, and Clarity, 1998, The Case Against Hillary Clinton, 2000, When Character was King: A Story of Ronald Reagan, 2001, A Heart, a Cross and a Flag, 2003, John Paul the Great: Remembering a Spiritual Father, 2005; contbr. articles to Forbes, Mirabella, Newsweek, N.Y. Times, O Mag., Time, Wash. Post. Coll. Guest Editor Mademoiselle, 1990; Mother of Yr. award, 1990; Nat. Mother's Day Com., 1990. Mem. Judson Welliver Soc. Republican. Roman Catholic. also: ICM 40 W 57th St Fl 16 New York NY 10019-4001*

**NOONAN, ROBERT HARRY,** art and music educator; b. Mpls., Sept. 18, 1924; s. William Earl and Nellie Morene Noonan; BS in Chemistry, Northwestern State Coll., 1948; MusB in Music Edn., Centenary Coll., 1963. Cert. tchr. music, chemistry, sci., math., visually talented and musically talented La. Sr. chemist Ark. Fuel Oil Co., Shreveport, La., 1948-53; grad. asst. U. Wyo., Laramie, 1953-54; asst. chief chemist Atlas Processing Co., Shreveport, 1955-58; Frenh horn player Shreveport Symphony Orch., 1948-72; sch. sys. employee East Baton Rouge Sch. Sys., Baton Rouge, 1972-81; pub. sch. tchr. Ascension Parish Schs., Donaldsonville, La., 1981-95; tchr. visually talented St. James Parish Schs., Lutcher, La., 1997—2001. Composer, arranger: music One Step from the Edge, 1999—2000, I Am Your Child, 2000—01, Finding My Way, 2001—02; composer: symphony for Yalley Youth Orch., 2002, two string quartets, a piano trio, a sonata for clarinet and piano, music for voices and strings, theater, 2003; one-man shows include Jones Creek Libr., Baton Rouge, 1993, Donaldsonville HS, La., 1994, Galvez Libr., La., 1994, Westbank Libr., Harvey, La., 1995, Bruno Gallery, New Orleans, 1997, exhibited in group shows, Baton Rouge, Jackson, Plaquemine, Morgan City, numerous others, Represented in permanent collections, La., Tex., Miss., Ala., Okla., others. Chmn. La. Sch. Employees Coun.l, 1977—81; art gallery mgr. Blue Sage Ctr. for Arts, Paonia, Colo. With Air Corps U.S. Army, 1943—46. Grantee Goals 2000, State of La., 1995—96, Spl. Arts, 1997—99. Mem.: Jefferson Art Guild, St. Bernard Art Guild (pres. 1999—2001), New Orleans Art Assn. (v.p. 1998—2000, art gallery mgr. Blue Sage Ctr. for the Arts), Am. Chem. Soc. (sr. grade chemist 1948—58), La. Partnership for the Arts. Avocations: outdoor painting, writing article for newspapers. Home: 433 Delta Ave Paonia CO 81428-8413 Office Phone: 970-527-4090. Personal E-mail: robmusart@paonia.com.

**NOONAN, SUSAN ABERT,** public relations executive; b. Lancaster, Pa., May 10, 1960; d. James Goodear and Carole (Althouse) Abert; m. David Lindsay Noonan, July 28, 1986; children: Caroline du Pont, Elizabeth Augusta. BA, Mt. Holyoke Coll., 1982. Account exec. Merill Lynch, N.Y.C., 1982-83; sr. v.p. Cameron Assocs., N.Y.C., 1983-88; pres., founder Noonan/Russo Comm. (now Euro RSCG Life NRP), N.Y.C., 1988—. Mem. Nat. Investor Rels. Inst.

**NOONAN, TIMOTHY PAUL,** musicologist, educator; b. Milw., Apr. 30, 1960; s. James J. and Betty J. Noonan; m. Jill A. Ehn; children: Christopher, Paul. BA, U. Wis., Milw., 1982, MusM, 1984; PhD, U. Wis., Madison, 1996. Lectr. music U. Wis., Milw., 1996—. Spkr. at confs. in field. Mem.: Am. Beethoven Soc., Soc. Eighteenth-Century Music, Mozart Soc. Am., Am. Musicological Soc. Democrat. Roman Catholic. Office: U Wis Milw Music Dept 2600 E Kenwood Blvd Milwaukee WI 53212

**NOONAN, WILLIAM DONALD,** lawyer, physician; b. Kansas City, Mo., Oct. 18, 1955; s. Robert Owen and Patricia Ruth Noonan. AB, Princeton (N.J.) U., 1977; JD, U. Mo., Kansas City, 1980; postgrad., Tulane U., 1981-83; MD magna cum laude, Oreg. Health Scis. U., 1991. Bar: Mo. 1980, U.S. Ct. Appeals (5th cir.) 1982, U.S. Patent & Trademark Office 1982, U.S. Ct. Appeals (D.C. cir.) 1984, Oreg. 1985, U.S. Ct. Appeals (9th Cir.) 1985. Assoc. Shurgue, Mion, Zinn, Washington, 1983-84, Keaty & Keaty, New Orleans, 1984-85; ptnr. Klarquist, Sparkman LLP, Portland, Oreg., 1985—; intern in internal medicine Portland Providence Med. Ctr., 1993-94; resident in ophthalmology Casey Eye Inst., Portland, 1994-95. Adj. prof. patent law Tulane U., New Orleans, 1984-85, U. Oreg., 1992-93. Casenotes editor U. Mo. Law Rev., 1979. Nat. Merit scholar. Mem. ABA, AMA (Leadership award 1994), Alpha Omega Alpha (pres. Oreg. chpt. 1990-91). Independent. Avocations: raising horses, running, travel, genealogy. Office: 1600 World Trade Ctr 121 SW Salmon St Portland OR 97204-2901 Office Phone: 503-226-7391.

**NOONE, LAURA PALMER,** academic administrator, lawyer; BBA, U. Dubuque; MBA, JD, U. Iowa; PhD in higher edn. adminstrn., Union Inst. Atty gen. civil practice, Iowa, Ariz.; judge City of Chandler, Ariz.; faculty mem. U. Phoenix, 1987—91, dir. acad affairs, 1991—2001; provost, sr. v.p. acad. affairs, 1994—2000, pres., 2002—. Adj. faculty Grand Canyon Univ., Chandler-Gilbert Cmty. Coll.; mem. Ariz. State Bd. for pvt. postsecondary edn.; trustee Phoenix Internat. Sch. Law. Mem.: ABA, Ariz. State Bar Assn., Maricopa County Bar Assn. Office: University of Phoenix 4615 E Elwood St Phoenix AZ 85040

**NOONE, R. BARRETT,** plastic surgeon; b. Scranton, Pa., Oct. 30, 1939; s. Robert Patrick and Margaret Ann (Barrett) N.; m. Barbara Ellen Atkins, May 29, 1965; children: Robert B. Jr., Megan J., Genevieve C., Rebecca B., Theresa Ann. BS, U. Scranton, 1961; MD, U. Pa., 1965. Diplomate Am. Bd. Surgery, Am. Bd. Plastic Surgery. Rotating intern Hosp. of U. Pa., Phila., 1965-66, resident in surgery, 1966-71, resident in plastic surgery, 1971-73; asst. prof. surgery Sch. Medicine, U. Pa., Phila., 1974-83, clin. assoc. prof. surgery, 1983-89, clin. prof. surgery, 1989—; head sect. on plastic surgery Pa. Hosp., Phila., 1974-80; chief svc. plastic surgery Bryn Mawr (Pa.) Hosp., 1977—2005, chmn. dept. surgery, 1991—2001; chief svc. plastic surgery Lankenau Hosp., Phila., 1980-91; exec. dir. Am. Bd. Plastic Surgery, 1997—. Bd. dirs. Am. Bd. Plastic Surgery, 1987-94, vice chmn. 1993-94; bd. dirs. Plastic Surgery Ednl. Found., Chgo., 1981-91, pres. 1989-90. Contbr. articles to profl. jours. Bd. dirs., trustee Rosemont (Pa.) Sch. of the Holy Child, 1983-87, U. Scranton, 1998—2004. Capt. USAF, 1967-69. Recipient Frank J. O'Hara Disting. Alumnus award U. Scranton, 1986. Fellow ACS (bd. govs. 1994-98); mem. AMA (del. plastic surgery 1986-88), Am. Soc. Plastic and Reconstructive Surgery (bd. dirs. 1989-90, 92-95, chmn. bd. trustees 1994-95), Am. Assn. Plastic Surgeons (sec. 1995-98, v.p. 1998-99, pres.-elect 1999-2000, pres. 2000-01, disting. fellow 2006), Northeastern Soc. Plastic Surgeons (pres. 1985-86), Robert H. Ivy Soc. (pres. 1982-83), Merion Cricket Club, Phila. Country Club, Eagles Mere Country Club. Republican. Roman Catholic. Avocations: golf, tennis, photography, swimming, travel, reading. Home: 234 Cheswold Hill Rd Haverford PA 19041-1814 Office: Plastic & Reconstructive Surg Assocs 888 Glenbrook Ave Bryn Mawr PA 19010-2506 Office Phone: 610-527-4833. E-mail: RBNoone@aol.com.

**NOONKESTER, JAMES RALPH,** retired college president; b. Flatridge, Va., June 10, 1924; s. Reggie L. and Arcie (Parks) N.; m. Naomi Hopkins, June 10, 1947; children: Myron Craig, Lila. BA, U. Richmond, 1944, LLD, 1968; ThM, So. Bapt. Theol. Sem., 1947, PhD, 1949; LHD (hon.), Blue Mountain Coll., 1982; postgrad., Harvard U., 1980. Minister edn. 1st Bapt. Ch., Charlottesville, Va., 1950-52; prof., head div. religion and philosophy William Carey Coll., Hattiesburg, Miss., 1952-53, acad. dean, 1953-56, pres., 1956-89, pres. emeritus, 1989—. Pres. Miss. Found. Ind. Colls.; mem. Edn. commn. So. Bapt. Conv., chmn., 1983; bd. dirs. Miss. Sch. Bldg. Assn. Workers Compensation Trust, 1993-95, chmn., 1994. Chmn. bd. dirs. Am. Cancer Soc., Miss. divsn., 1966; campaign chmn. United Givers Fund, 1975-76, pres. 1976-77; coun. chmn. Boy Scouts Am., dir. Planned Giving Pine Burr area Boy Scouts Am., 1990-93; trustee Hattiesburg Pub. Schs., 1990-95, pres. bd. trustees, 1992-95 Named Outstanding Grad. English U. Richmond, 1944, Hattiesburg's Outstanding Young Man of 1956, Sales and Mktg. Execs. Man of Yr., 1983; recipient Silver Beaver award Boy Scouts Am., 1981, HUB award, 1983 Mem. NEA, Miss. Edn. Assn., Hattiesburg Concert Assn. (bd. dir.), So. Assn. Bapt. Colls. and Schs. (pres.), Miss. Assn. Colls. (pres.), Hattiesburg C. of C. (pres. 1966), Kiwanis, Phi Beta Kappa, Phi Delta Kappa, Chi Beta Phi, Omicron Delta Kappa. Home: 100 Lesley Ln Hattiesburg MS 39402-2922 Office Phone: 601-264-0268.

**NOOR, RONNY,** language educator, writer; MA, Tech. U., Berlin, 1986, Okla. State U., 1989, PhD, 1994. Lectr. Salisbury State U., Md., 1995—96; sr. lectr. U. Tex., Brownsville, 1996—98, asst. prof., 1999—2004, assoc. prof., 2004—. Contbr. essays, short stories, articles to profl. jours. Recipient Exceptional Merit award, 2001, Wall of Tolerance honoree, Civil Rights Meml. Ctr., Montgomery, Ala., 2005, Faculty Appreciation award, SSSP/ASPIRE, 2005, 2006. Mem.: Nat. Writers Assn., South Ctrl. MLA, Popular Culture Assn. Achievements include research in literature and linguistics. Avocations: piano, tennis. Office Phone: 956-882-8239. E-mail: noorronny@yahoo.com.

**NOORBAKHSH, MASOOD,** county official; b. Iran, 1951; BS in math., Fla. Inst. Tech., MS in ops. rsch. Cons. to Computer Sciences Corp.; Price Waterhouse, NASA, US Dept. Navy; dir. info. systems and ops. George Mason U., Fairfax, Va.; chief info. officer Prince William County, Woodbridge, Va., 1997—. Named one of Premier 100 IT Leaders, Computerworld, 2005. Office: Prince William County Govt 1 County Complex Ct Woodbridge VA 22192*

**NOORDERGRAAF, ABRAHAM,** biophysics educator; b. Utrecht, Netherlands, Aug. 7, 1929; s. Leendert and Johanna (Kool) N.; m. Geertruida Alida Van Nee, Sept. 6, 1956 (div. Jan. 2001); children: Annemiek (Mrs. James A. Young), Gerrit Jan, Jeske Inette, Alexander Abraham. B.Sc., U. Utrecht, 1953, MS, 1955, PhD, 1956; MA (hon.), U. Pa., 1971. Teaching asst. U. Utrecht, 1949-50, asst. dept. physics, 1951-53, research asst. dept. med. physics 1953-55, research fellow dept. med. physics, 1956-58, sr. research fellow dept. med. physics, 1959-65; tchr. math. and physics Vereniging Nijver-heidsonderwijs, Utrecht, 1951; research asst. U. Amsterdam, Netherlands, 1952; vis. fellow dept. therapeutic research U. Pa., Phila., 1957-58; assoc. prof. biomed. engring. Moore Sch. Elec. Engring., U. Pa., 1964-70, acting head electromed. div., 1968-69, prof. biomed. engring., 1970-97, assoc. dir. biomed. engring. tng. program, 1971-76, asso. dir. sch., 1972-74, chmn. grad. group in biomed. electronic engring., 1973-75, chmn. biomed. bioengring., 1973-76, chmn. grad. group bioengring., 1975-76, dir. systems and integrative biology tng. program, 1979-84; prof. physiology Sch. Vet. Medicine U. Pa., 1976-97, prof. Dutch culture Sch. Arts and Scis., 1983-97, prof. anesthesia Med. Sch., 1990-97, prof. emeritus, 1997—. Vis. prof. biomed. engring. U. Miami, 1970-79, Erasmus U. Med. Sch., Rotterdam, The Netherlands, 1970-71, Tech. U., Delft, 1970-71, Polish Acad. Scis., Warsaw, 1975; hon. vis. prof. physiology U. Ljubljana, 1994—; mem. cardiovasc. study sect. NIH, 1985-89, temp. mem., 1998—; cons. sci. affairs divsn. NATO, 1973—; participant numerous internat. confs. in field. Author: (with I. Starr) Ballis-tocardiography in Cardiovascular Research, 1967, Circulatory System Dynamics, 1978; contbg. author: Biological Engineering, 1969; Editor: (with G.N. Jager and N. Westerhof) Circulatory Analog Computers, 1963, (with G.H. Pollack) Ballistocardiography and Cardiac Performance, 1967, (with E. Kresch) The Venous System: Characteristics and Function, 1969, (with J. Baan and J. Raines) Cardiovascular System Dynamics, 1978, (with Reichenbach-Consten) Two Hundred Years of Netherlands-American Inter-action; sci. editor Biophysics and Bioengring. Series, 1976-94; contbr. numerous articles to profl. jours.; Referee: Biophys. Jour., 1968—, Physics in Medicine and Biology, 1969—, Bull. Math. Biophysics, 1972-84, Circulation Research, 1973—; mem. editorial adv. bd.: Jour. Biomechanics, 1969-84; assoc. editor: Bull. Math. Biology, 1973-84. V.p. Haverford Friends Sch. PTA, 1968—70. Recipient S. Reid Warren Jr. award U. Pa. Sch. Engring. and Applied Sci., 1986, Christian and Mary Lindback award U. Pa., 1988, Lifetime Achievement award, 2001, Internat. Order of Merit, 2003, Arthur C. Guyton award, 2003. Fellow IEEE (life, mem. adminstrv. com. engring. in medicine and biology group 1967-70, mem. edn. com. group biomed. engring. 1968-70, sec. Phila. chpt. 1974-75, mem. regional coun. profl. group engring. in medicine and biology 1974-77), AAAS, N.Y. Acad. Scis., Explorers Club, Intl. Soc. Electromed. (bd. dirs. 1987-94; bd. dirs. Epilepsy Explorers Club, Intl. Coll. Physicians Phila., Am. Coll. Cardiology, Royal Soc. Medicine London; mem. Nederlandse Natuurkundige Vereniging, Ballisto-cardiograph Research Soc. U.S.A. (sec.-treas. 1965-67, pres. 1968-70), Biophys. Soc. (charter), European Soc. for Noninvasive Cardiovascular Research (co-founder 1960, sec.-treas. 1960-61, mem. com. on nomenclature 1960-61, officer 1961-62, Herman C. Burger award 1978, Disting. Rsch. Award, 1993), Cardiovascular System Dynamics Soc. (co-founder 1976, pres. 1976-80, hon. life 1986), Franklin Inst., John Morgan Soc., Biomed. Engring. Soc. (founding mem., chmn. membership com. 1978-79, dir. 1972-75), Am. Heart Assn., Instrument Soc. Am. (sr. mem.), Soc. Math. Biology (charter

mem.), Am. Physiol. Soc., Microcirculatory Soc. Am. Assn. Med. Systems and Informatics, Pa. Acad. Sci., Sigma Xi, Phi Zeta. Presbyterian. Achievements include discovery (with Maximilian Moser) of impedance-defined flow, generalizing William Harvey's 1628 theory of blood circulation. Home: 620 Haydock Ln Haverford PA 19041-1208 Office: U Pa 101 Hayden Hall Philadelphia PA 19104-6392 Office Phone: 215-898-5881. Business E-Mail: anoor@seas.upenn.edu.

**NOORMETS, ASKO,** ecologist; PhD, Mich. Technol. U., Houghton, 2001. Rsch. asst. prof. U. Toledo, 2001—. Grantee, USDA Forest Svc., 2003, 2003, 2004, NASA, 2005; scholar, Sci. Environment for Ecol. Knowledge, NSF, 2005, Summer Inst., Duke U. Ctr. on Global Change, 2006. Mem.: Internat. Union Forestry Rsch. Orgns., Am. Geophys. Union, Ecol. Soc. Am. Achievements include research in age-dependent changes in forest carbon balance. Office: University Toledo Dept EEES 2801 W Bancroft St MS 604 Toledo OH 43606 Office Phone: 419-530-5498.

**NOOYI, INDRA K.,** food products executive; b. Madras, India, Oct. 28, 1955; m. Raj K. Nooyi; 2 children. BS, Madras Christian Coll., India, 1976; MBA, Indian Inst. Mgmt., Calcutta, 1978; M Pub. and Pvt. Mgmt., Yale U., 1980. Product mgr. Johnson & Johnson, India, Mettur Beardsell, Ltd., India; dir. internat. corp. strategy projects Boston Cons. Group, 1980—86; bus. devel. exec. Motorola, Inc., v.p., dir. corp. strategy and planning, 1986—90; sr. v.p. strategic planning PepsiCo, Inc., Purchase, NY, 1994-2000, sr. v.p., sr. v.p. strategic planning PepsiCo, Inc., Purchase, NY, 1994-2000, sr. v.p., CFO, 2000-01, pres., CFO, 2001—, pres., CEO, 2006—. Bd. dir. Phoenix Home Life Mut. Ins. Co. Bd. dir. PepsiCo Found.; trustee Convent of Sacred Heart Sch., Greenwich, Conn. Named one of Most Powerful Women, Forbes Mag., 2005, 50 Women to Watch, Wall St. Jour., 2005, 100 Most Powerful Women, Forbes Mag., 2006. Achievements include being the first women CEO for PepsiCo, Inc. Office: PepsiCo, Inc 700 Anderson Hill Rd Purchase NY 10577-1444*

**NOPAR, ALAN SCOTT,** lawyer; s. Myron E. and Evelyn M. Nopar; m. Angela P. Yancey, Aug. 26, 2000. BS, U. Ill., 1976; JD, Stanford U., 1979. Bar: Ariz. 1979, U.S. Dist. Ct. Ariz. 1980, U.S. Ct. Appeals (9th cir.) 1980, U.S. Supreme Ct. 1982, Calif. 1989; CPA, Ill. Assoc. O'Connor, Cavanagh, Anderson, Westover, Killingsworth & Beshears P.A., Phoenix, 1979-85, ptnr., 1985-87; of counsel Tower, Byrne & Beaugureau, Phoenix, 1987-88; ptnr. Minutillo & Gorman, San Jose, Calif., 1989-91, Bosco, Blau, Ward & Nopar, San Jose, 1991-96; exec. v.p., gen. counsel, dir. AmeriNet Fin. Systems, Inc., Ontario, Calif., 1996-97; sole practice law Palo Alto, Calif., 1998-99; ptnr. Bosco, Ward & Nopar, Palo Alto, 2000—04, Bosco & Nopar, Palo Alto, 2004—. Mem. Ariz. Rep. Caucus, Phoenix, 1984-88. Mem. AICPA, ABA (bus. law and law practice mgmt. sects., mem. forum com. on franchising), Ariz. Bar Assn. (bus. law sect.), Calif. State Bar Assn. (bus. law sect.). Avocations: golf, skiing, tennis, bicycling. Office: 425 Sherman Ave Ste 100 Palo Alto CA 94306-1849

**NORA, AUDREY HART,** physician; b. Picayune, Miss., Dec. 5, 1936; d. Allen Joshua and Vera Lee (Ballard) H.; m. James Jackson Nora, Apr. 9, 1966; children: James Jackson Jr., Elizabeth Hart. BS, U. Miss., 1958, MD, 1961; MPH, U. Calif., 1978. Diplomate Am. Bd. Pediat., Am. Bd. Hematology and Oncology. Resident in pediat. U. Wis. Hosp., Madison, 1961-64; fellow in hematology/oncology Baylor U., Tex. Childrens Hosp., Houston, 1964-66, asst. prof. pediat., 1966-70; assoc. clin. prof. pediat. U. Colo. Sch. Medicine, Denver, 1970—; dir. genetics Denver Childrens Hosp., 1970-78; commd. med. officer USPHS, 1978, advanced through grades to asst. surgeon gen., 1983, cons. maternal and child health Denver, 1978-83, asst. surgeon gen. regional health adminstr., 1983-92, dir. maternal & child health bur., health resources and svc. adminstrn., 1992-99. Mem. adv. com. NIH, Bethesda, 1975-77; mem. adv. bd. Metronet Health, Inc., Denver, 1986-92; mem. adv. bd. Colo. Assn. Commerce and Industry, Denver, 1985-92, WIC program USDA, 1989-99; mem. adv. coun. NICHD, 1992-99; bd. mem. RMC for Health Promotion and Edn., pres., 2004-05. Author: (with J.J. Nora) Genetics and Counseling in Cardiovascular Diseases, 1978, (with others) Blakiston's Medical Dictionary, 1980, Birth Defects Encyclopedia, 1990, (with J.J. Nora and K. Berg) Cardiovascular Diseases: Genetics, Epidemiology and Prevention, 1991; contbr. articles to profl. jours. Recipient Virginia Apgar award Nat. Found., 1976. Fellow Am. Acad. Pediat.; mem. Am. Pub. Health Assn. (governing coun. 1990-92, coun. maternal and child health 1990—), Commd. Officers Assn., Am. Soc. Human Genetics, Teratology Soc., Western Soc. Pediatric Rsch. Presbyterian. Avocations: cooking, hiking, quilting. Office: 1973 S Kenton Ct Aurora CO 80014-4709

**NORA, JAMES JACKSON,** physician, writer, educator; b. Chgo., Ill., June 26, 1928; s. Joseph James and Mae Henrietta (Jackson) N.; m. Barbara June Fluhrer, Sept. 7, 1949 (div. 1963); children: Wendy Alison, Penelope Welbon, Marianne Leslie; m. Audrey Faye Hart, Apr. 9, 1966; children: James Jackson Jr., Elizabeth Hart Nora. AB, Harvard U., 1950; MD, Yale U., 1954; MPH, U. Calif., Berkeley, 1978. Diplomate Am. Bd. Pediat., Am. Bd. Cardiology, Am. Bd. Med. Genetics. Intern Detroit Receiving Hosp., 1954-55; resident in pediat. U. Wis. Hosps., Madison, 1959-61, fellow in cardiology, 1962-64; fellow in genetics McGill U. Children's Hosp., Montreal, Canada, 1964-65; assoc. prof. pediat. Baylor Coll. Medicine, Houston, 1965-71; prof. genetics, preventive medicine and pediat. U. Colo. Med. Sch., Denver, 1971—, prof. emeritus, 1986. Dir. genetics Rose Med. Ctr., Denver, 1980—; dir. pediatric cardiology and cardiovasc. U. Colo. Sch. Medicine, 1971-78; mem. task force Nat. Heart and Lung Program, Bethesda, Md., 1973; cons. WHO, Geneva, 1983—; mem. U.S.-U.S.S.R. Exch. Program on Heart Disease, Moscow and Leningrad, 1975. Author: The Whole Heart Book, 1980, 2d rev. edit., 1989; author: (with F.C. Fraser) Medical Genetics, 4th Rev. edit., 1994; author: Genetics of Man, 2d rev. edit., 1986, Cardiovascular Diseases: Genetics, Epidemiology and Prevention, 1991, The Upstart Spring, 1989, The Psi Delegation, 1989, The Hemingway Sabbatical, 1996, Songs from a Brazen Bull, 2001, Panacea, 2002, What Every Senior Needs to Know About Health Care, 2004, Half-Open Windows, 2005, Progress Notes, 2005, The 9/11 Dialogues, 2006. Mem. com. March of Dimes, Am. Heart Assn., Boy Scouts Am. 2nd lt. USAAC, 1945—47. Grantee Nat. Heart, Lung and Blood Inst., Nat. Inst. Child Health and Human Devel., Am. Heart Assn., NIH; recipient Virginia Apgar Meml. award. Democrat. Presbyterian. Avocations: writing fiction, poetry.

**NORA, LOIS MARGARET,** neurologist, educator, academic administrator, dean; BS in Biology with honors, U. Ill., 1976; MD, Rush Med. Coll., Chgo., 1979; JD, U. Chgo., 1987; MBA, U. Ky., 2002. Fellow Am. Bd. Neurology, Am. Bd. Electrodiagnostic Medicine; bar: Ill. 1988, D.C. 1988. Intern in family medicine Cmty. Meml. Gen. Hosp., LaGrange, Ill., 1980; resident in neurology Rush-Presbyn.-St. Luke's Med. Ctr., Chgo., 1981-84, chief resident in neurology, 1983-84, fellow electromyography and neuromuscular disease, 1984-85; asst. prof. dept. neurology, asst. dean clin. curriculum Rush Med. Coll., Chgo., 1987-94, assoc. prof. dept. neurology, 1994-95; fellow Ctr. for Clin. Med. Ethics U. Chgo., 1993-95; assoc. dean acad. affairs, assoc. prof. dept. neurology U. Ky. Coll. Medicine, 1995—2002; prof. neurology U. Ky. Coll. Law, 1996—2002; pres. Northeastern Ohio Univ. Coll. of Med., 2002—, dean, 2002—. Spkr. in field. Contbr. articles to profl. jours., chpts. to books. Vice chair Epilepsy Found. of Greater Chgo., 1988-90, chair, 1991, chair strategic planning com. 1990-92, bd. dirs., 1987-94; bd. dirs. Epilepsy Found. of Am., 1992-95, co-chair quality standards com. 1992-94; mem. needs assessment com. United Way of Chgo., 1989-90; camp physician children's summer camp program Muscular Dystrophy Assn., 1984-86; vol. tchr. Christ the King Elem. Sch., 1996—2002. Mem. AMA (mem. dean's com. on family violence curriculum 1993, mem. report and resolutions subcom. for reference com. C 1997), Am. Acad. Neurology (mem. ethics com. 1997—2002), Am. Assn. Electrodiagnostic Medicine (author profl. practice com. 1991—97, sec., treas., 1999-2002, pres.-elect, 2002-03, pres. 2003-04), Soc. Clin. Neurologists. Office: Northeastern Ohio U Coll Med PO Box 95 4209 St Rt 44 Rootstown OH 44272

**NORA, WENDY ALISON,** lawyer; b. New Haven, Conn., Feb. 14, 1951; d. James Jackson Nora and Barbara June (Fluhrer) P.; m. Jay Robert Vercauteren, Aug. 21, 1973 (div. Nov. 1981); children: Lucas Jay, Eric Robert. BA, U. Wis., 1971, JD, 1975. Bar: Wis. 1975, U.S. Dist. Ct. (w. dist.) Wis. 1975, U.S. Dist. Ct. (e. dist.) Wis. 1991, U.S. Supreme Ct. 1986. Pvt. practice, Cross Plains, Wis., 1975-81, Madison, Wis., 1981-84, Mpls., 1986-90, Madison, Wis., 1991—; developer, incorporator, pres. Cmty. Investment Credit Corp., Madison, 1997—. Atty. State of Wis., 1977-81, asst. pub. defender, 1983-84. Fellow U. Minn. Mem. ABA (vice-chmn. adminstrv. law sect., criminal law and juvenile justice com. 1982—). Home: 6931 Old Sauk Rd Madison WI 53717-1122 Office: 8530 Greenway Blvd 209 Middleton WI 53562-4606

**NORBACK, CRAIG THOMAS,** writer; b. Pitts., Nov. 14, 1943; s. Howard George and Maybelle Veronica Montaigne (Cosse) Norback; m. Judith Carol Shaul, Oct. 12, 1976. BS, Washington U., St. Louis, 1967; postgrad., Drew U., 1986—. Author, co-author, compiler, producer over 150 books, including: The Misspeller's Dictionary, 1972, Everything You Can Get from the Government for Free or Almost for Free, 1975, The Dream Machine: The Golden Age of American Automobiles 1946-65, 1976, Great Songs of Madison Avenue, 1976, Great North American Indians, 1977, The Health Care Directory, 1977, The Older American's Handbook, 1977, The Educational Marketplace, 1978, Famous American Admirals, 1978, Newsweek Travel Guide to the U.S., 1978, The Dow Jones-Irwin Guide to Franchising, 1979, The Horseman's Catalog, 1979, The Must Words, 1979, The Practical Inventor's Handbook, 1979, ABC Complete Book of Sports Facts, 1980, ABC Monday Night Football, 1980-81, 1982, The Bible Almanac, 1980, Check Yourself Out, 1980, The Signet Book of World Winners, 1980, The TV Guide Almanac, 1980, The World's Great News Photos (1840-1980), 1980, The Allergy Encyclopedia, 1981, American Expressions, 1981, The Computer Invasion, 1981, The Consumer's Energy Handbook, 1981, 500 Questions New Parents Ask, 1987, Business Week Almanac, 1982, The International Yellow Pages, 1982, The Puzzle King's Bafflers, 1982, The Associated Press Sunday Crossword Puzzle Book, 1983, Chilton's Job Textbook Series: Advertising Management, 1983, Office Management, 1983, It's a Fact, 1983, National Education Association Parent and Child Success Library: Helping Your Child Read, 1983, How Letters Make Words, 1983, How to Prepare Your Child for School, 1983, Learning the Alphabet, 1983, Learning to Add, 1983, The Ultimate Toy Catalog, 1983, U.S. Publicity Directory, various years, Advertising and Promotion Management, 1983, America Wants to Know, 1983, Certified Professional Secretary modules I through VI, 1984, East Coast Publicity Directory, 1984, Human Resources Yearbook, 1987, 88, 89, 90, Princeton Area Job Finder, 1986-87, Career Encyclopedia, 1987, Travel Publicity Directory, 1987, 88, 89, 90, Arthur Young Guide to Venture Capital, 1987, Hazardous Chemicals on File, 1988, Joint Ventures, 1992. Home: 3112 Kaitlyn Ct Princeton Junction NJ 08550-5349

**NORBECK, GEORGE,** psychiatrist, consultant; b. Vermillion, S.D., Jan. 15, 1937; s. Kermit George and Winfree Virginia Norbeck; m. Joyce Erickson (div.); children: John, Kari, Kirsten, Tyra; m. Mary Jeanette Moore, June 5, 1977. BA, St. Olaf Coll., Northfield, Minn., 1959; BS, MD, U. Minn., Mpls., 1964; M Social Psychiatry, UCLA, 1971. Diplomate Am. Bd. Psychiatry and Neurology, 1976. Flight surgeon USAF, Beale AFB, Calif., 1965—67; resident psychiatry UCLA, 1970; staff psychiatrist St. John's Hosp., Santa Monica, Calif., 1970—71, Ulleraker Psychiat. Rsch. Hosp., Uppsala, Sweden, 1971—72, Karolinska Psychiat. Outpatient Clinic, Stockholm, 1972—73; chief inpatient psychiat. dept., outpatient psychiat. dept. Palo Alto VA Med. Ctr., Calif., 1973—95; med. cons. Social Security Disability, Oakland, Calif., 2000—. Treas. Santa Clara County Psychiat. Soc., 1976—78, pres., 1978; state air surgeon Calif. Air N.G., 1983—93. Col. USAF, 1975—93. Fellow: Am. Psychiat. Assn.; mem.: No. Calif. Psychiat. Soc. Avocations: horseback riding, singing, Broadway shows, trombone.

**NORBECK, JACK CARL,** library exhibitor; b. Greensburg, Pa., Dec. 8, 1940; Cert., Opticians Inst., 1971; Cert. U. Conn., Ratcliffe Hicks Sch. Agriculture, 1964. Founder, pres. Norbeck Rsch., Coplay, Pa., 1978—. Designer 71 mag. covers. Author: The Encyclopedia of American Steam Traction Engines; contbr. articles to profl. jours.; 70 mag. covers, more than 200 photo exhibits. Mem. YMCA. Named Internat. Man of the Yr., 2000—01; recipient 20th Century award, Am. Medal of Honor, 2001, Noble prize, 2001, Internat. Ambs. medal and Gold Record of Achievement, 2001. Mem.: USA Gymnastics, Am. Legion, Union Hist. Fire Soc., The Authors Guild, Am. Soc. Agrl. Engrs., Hist. Steam Assns. Lutheran. Achievements include design of 70 magazine covers. Home: 117 N Ruch St 8 Coplay PA 18037-1712

**NORBECK, JANE S.,** retired nursing educator; b. Redfield, SD, Feb. 20, 1942; d. Sterling M. and Helen L. (Williamson) N.; m. Paul J. Gorman, June 28, 1970. BA in Psychology, U. Minn., 1965, BSN, 1965; MS, U. Calif., San Francisco, 1971, DSN, 1975. Psychiat. nurse Colo. Psychiat. Hosp., Denver, 1965-66, Langley Porter Hosp., San Francisco, 1966-67; pub. health nurse San Francisco Health Dept., 1968-69; prof. U. Calif. Sch. of Nursing, San Francisco, 1975—2003, dean, 1989-99, dept. chair, 1984-89, prof. and dean emeritus, 2003. Chair study sect. Nat. Inst. of Nursing Rsch., 1990-93, mem. editl. bd. Archives of Psychiat. Nursing, 1985-95, Rsch. in Nursing and Health, 1987-2003. Co-editor: Annual Review of Nursing Research, 1996-97; contbr. articles to profl. jours. Mem. ANA, Am. Acad. Nursing, Inst. of Medicine, Sigma Theta Tau.

**NORBERG, ARTHUR LAWRENCE, JR.,** historian, physicist, educator; b. Providence, Apr. 13, 1938; s. Arthur Lawrence Sr. and Margaret Helen (Riley) N.; children: Catherine E. Norberg Morin, Patricia A. Norberg Fetta, Timothy E., Gregory T. BS in Physics, Providence Coll., 1959; MS in Physics, U. Vt., 1962; PhD in History of Sci., U. Wis., 1974. Asst. prof. physics St. Michael's Coll., Winooski, Vt., 1961-63, 64-68; assoc. scientist Westinghouse Electric Co., Pitts., 1963-64; instr. in physics U. Wis., Whitewater, 1968-71; rsch. historian U. Calif., Berkeley, 1973-79, program mgr. NSF, Washington, 1979-81, dir. Charles Babbage Inst. for History of Info. Processing U. Minn., Mpls., 1981—93, 1999—2006, prof. history of sci. and tech., 1995—2005, assoc. prof. computer sci., 1981-95, prof. computer sci., 1995—2005, prof. emeritus, 2005—. Del. Am. Coun. Learned Socs., N.Y.C., 1981-87; mem. adv. coun. NASA, Washington, 1988-93; endowed ERA Land Grant chair U. Minn., 1989-93, 99—2006. Editor: Annals of the History of Computing, 1982-93; adv. editor Tech. and Culture, 1985-92, (books) Transforming Computer Technology: Information Processing for the Pentagon, 1996, Computers and Commerce, 2005; contbr. articles to profl. jours. Founding pres. City Works-A Tech. Ctr., Mpls., 1987-90; exec. dir. Charles Babbage Found., 1984-94; trustee Charles Babbage Found., 1993-96. Fellow AAAS; mem. History of Sci. Soc. (treas. 1975-80), Brit. Soc. for History of Sci., Soc. for History of Tech., Sigma Xi. E-mail: norberg@cs.umn.edu.

**NORBERG, RICHARD EDWIN,** physicist, researcher; b. Newark, Dec. 28, 1922; s. Arthur Edwin and Melita (Roefer) N.; m. Patricia Ann Leach, Dec. 27, 1947 (dec. July 1977); children—Karen Elizabeth, Craig Alan, Peter Douglas; m. Jeanne C. O'Brien, Apr. 1, 1978. BA, DePauw U., 1943; MA, U. Ill., 1947, PhD, 1951. Research assoc., control sytems lab. U. Ill., 1951-53, asst. prof., 1953; vis. lectr. physics Washington U., St. Louis, 1954—, mem. faculty, 1955—, prof. physics, 1958—, chmn. dept., 1962-91. Mem. editl. bd. Magnetic Rsch. Rev. Served with USAAF, 1942-46. Co-recipient ISMAR prize, 2004. Fellow Am. Phys. Soc., Internat. Soc. Magnetic Research. Home: 7134 Princeton Ave Saint Louis MO 63130-2308 Office: Washington U Dept Physics PO Box 1105 Saint Louis MO 63188-1105 Business E-Mail: ren@wuphys.wustl.edu.

**NORCEL, JACQUELINE JOYCE CASALE,** educational association administrator; b. Nov. 19, 1940; d. Frederick and Josephine Jeanette (Bestafka) Casale; m. Edward John Norcel, Feb. 24, 1962. BS, Fordham U., 1961; MS, Bklyn. Coll., 1966; 6th yr. cert., So. Conn. State U., 1980; postgrad., Bridgeport U. Elem. tchr. NYC Pub. Schs., 1961-80; prin. Coventry (Conn.) Schs., 1980-84, Trumbull (Conn.) Schs., 1984—2003, Frenchtown Elem. Sch., 2003—. Guest lectr. So. Conn. State U., 1980; cons.

Monson (Mass.) Schs., 1984; mem. Conn. State Prin. Acad. Adv. Bd., 1986-88; mem. adj. faculty Sacred Heart U., Fairfield, Conn., 1985—, So. Conn. State U., summer 1991; fed. rels. coord. Nat. Assn. Elem. Sch. Prins., Conn., 1999-2002. Editor: Best of the Decade, 1980; mem. editl. adv. bd. Principal Matters; contbr. articles to profl. jours. Chmn. bldg. com. Trumbull Bd. Edn., 1978-80; chmn. Sch. Benefit Com., Trumbull, 1985-86; catechist Bridgeport Diocese, Roman Cath. Ch., Conn., 1975-85, youth min., 1979-84, coord., evaluator leadership tng. workshops for teens and adults, 1979-84; mem. St. Stephen's Parish Coun., 1993-97, trustee, 1997—, Eucharist min., 1999—, lector, 1990-; com. mem. New Sch. Bldg. Town of Trumbull, 2001-05. Recipient Town of Trumbull Svc. award, 1982, Nat. Disting. Prin. award, 1988, Joseph Formica Disting. Svc. award EMSPAC, 1994. Mem.: ASCD, Assoc. Tchrs. Math. in Conn., New Eng. Coalition Ednl. Leaders, Ea. Conn. Coun. Internat. Reading Assn., Conn. Assn. Elem. Sch. Prins., Trumbull Adminstrs. Assn. (pres.-elect 1989—91, pres. 1991—93, 2002—), Conn. Assn. Supervision and Curriculum Devel., Nat. Assn. Elem. Sch. Prins. (del. to gen. assemblies 1984—90, zone I dir. 1987—90, del. to gen. assemblies 1994—), Hartford Area Prins. and Suprs. Assn. (local pres. 1981—82), Conn. Assn. Schs. (bd. mem. 2000—05), Adminstrn. and Supervision Assn. (sec. 1980—81, pres. 1981—82, exec. bd. 1982—93), Elem. Mid. Sch. Prins. Assn. (pres. 1985—86, state elected rep. 1989—90, fed. rels. coord. 1990—94, dists. 1, 2 and 3 dir. 1995—98, commr. 1997—2000, fed. rels. coord. 1999—2002, Citizen of Yr. award 1991, Pres.'s award 1981—85), N.E. Regional Elem. Prins. Assn. (rep. 1984—86, sec. 1986—87), Delta Kappa Gamma (v.p. 1996—2000), Pi Lambda Theta, Phi Delta Kappa (v.p. rsch. and projects 1993—95, Disting. Fellow award 1992). Home: 5240 Madison Ave Trumbull CT 06611-1016 Office: Frenchtown Elem Sch 30 Frenchtown Rd Trumbull CT 06611 Office Phone: 203-452-4227. Personal E-mail: norcelJ98@yahoo.com.

**NORCIA, STEPHEN WILLIAM,** advertising executive; b. NYC, Jan. 21, 1941; s. William Matthew and Amelia (Marrone) N.; m. Martha Elizabeth Whelan, Apr. 22, 1978; children: Matthew F., Daniel P., Anne E. BA, U. Conn., 1962. Media planner and buyer SSC&B, N.Y.C., 1965-66; account exec. McCann-Erickson Co., Chgo., 1966-68, v.p., dep. mgr. Milw., 1971-72, v.p., mgmt. supr. N.Y.C., 1972-74, sr. v.p., gen. mgr. Atlanta, 1974-78, exec. v.p., gen. mgr. N.Y.C., 1978-81; exec. v.p., mem. exec. policy com., mem. mgmt. com. Lintas, N.Y.C., 1981-94, exec. v.p., 1989-91, world wide client dir., dir. bus. devel., 1991-94, also bd. dirs.; mng. ptnr. Earle Palmer Brown, N.Y.C., 1994-96; dir. global account DDB, N.Y.C., 1996-99, mng. dir., 1998-2000; v.p. bus. devel. Agency.com, 2000—; owner cons. co. Norcia Group, 2002—; founder, prin. Topsail Group, 2003. Account exec. Needham, Harper & Steers, Chgo., 1968-70; dir. mktg. product devel. workshop Interpub., N.Y.C., 1970-71; bd. dirs. Communication Counselors Network; adj. prof. Fordham U., Iona Coll. Bd. dirs. U. Ga. Master of Br. Mgmt. Program, 1985, 86, 87, Advt. Edn. Found., 1999—. 1st lt. U.S. Army, 1962-65. Recipient Robert E. Healy award Interpub. Group Cos., 1975, Effie award Am. Mktg. Assn., 1985, Grand Effie award Am. Mktg. Assn., 1984. Mem. Am. Assn. Advt. Agys., Advt. Club N.Y., Am. Yacht Club. Republican. Roman Catholic. Avocations: tennis, boating, skiing, bicycling. Home: 53 Otter Cove Dr Old Saybrook CT 06475 Office: Topsail Group PO Box 488 Old Saybrook CT 06475 Office Phone: 860-510-0450.

**NORCOTT, FLEMMING L., JR.,** state supreme court justice; b. New Haven, Oct. 11, 1943; BA, Columbia U., 1965, JD, 1968; LLD (hon.), U. New Haven, 1993, Albertus Magnus Coll., 2004. Bar: Conn. 1968. Peace corps vol. U. East Africa, Nairobi, Kenya; legal staff Bedford-Stuyvestant Restoration Corp.; asst. atty. gen. Office Atty. Gen., V.I.; judge Superior Ct., 1979-87, Appellate Ct., 1987-92; assoc. justice Conn. Supreme Ct., Hartford, 1992—. Hearing examiner Conn. Commn. Human Rights and Opportunities; co-founder, exec. dir. Ctr. Advocacy, Rsch. and Planning, Ind., New Haven; lectr. Yale U. Bd. govs. U. New Haven; bd. dirs. Dixwell Community House, Ea. Collegiate Football Officials. Assn., New Haven Football Officials Assn., Long Wharf Theatre; assoc. fellow Calhoun Coll., Yale U.; bd. trustees Yale-New Haven Hosp. Mem. Omega Psi Phi Office: Conn Supreme Ct 231 Capital Ave Hartford CT 06106*

**NORCROSS, ALVIN WATT,** retired personnel administrator, consultant; b. Buffalo, N.Y., Sept. 21, 1918; s. William Watt and Nettie Anne (Alexander) Norcross; m. Charlotte Anne Guptill, Oct. 23, 1948; children: David Lichty, Nancy Dayna. BA, Baldwin-Wallace Coll., 1940; MPA, Harvard U., 1948. Employment mgr. Nat. Screw & Mfg. Co., Cleve., 1941-43; spl. asst. to dir. civilian pers. Dept. of the Air Force, Washington, 1954-58; chief of employment Gen. Svcs. Adminstrn., Washington, 1959-61; asst. dir. pers. U.S. Treasury Dept., Washington, 1961-67; dep. dir. Bur. Pers. Mgmt. Evaluation U.S. Civil Svc. Commn., Washington, 1967-73; project mgr., pub. adminstrn. advisor UN, Kabul, Afghanistan, 1975-80, chief tech. advisor Male, Republic of Maldives, 1982-84; ret., 1984. Pers. expert, cons. Agy. for Internat. Devel., Washington, 1974-75; cons. on exec. pay Orgn. Resource Counselors, Inc., N.Y.C., 1975; prin. assoc., cons. Exec. Mgmt. Svcs., Inc., Arlington, Va., 1981. Author of pamphlets; Councilman Town of Vienna, Va., 1959-65; mem. Svc. Corps of Ret. Execs., New Bedford, Mass., 1984-87, Recycling/Solid Waste Com., Westport, Mass., 1986-94; mem. citizen advd. com. Mass. Dept. Mental Health, 1989-97. 1st lt. USAF, 1943-46; lt. col. USAFR, 1946-72, ret. Mem. ASPA, Old Dartmouth Hist. Soc., Westport Hist. Soc., Westport River Watershed Alliance (bd. dirs. 1989-98), Harvard Club Greater New Bedford (adv. bd. mem. 1997-98), YMCA Greater New Bedford. Avocations: travel, tennis, drama, walking. Home: 36 Shirley St Westport MA 02790-1333

**NORCROSS, MARVIN AUGUSTUS,** veterinarian, researcher, retired federal official; b. Tansboro, NJ, Feb. 8, 1931; s. Marvin A. and Katherine V. (McGuigan) N.; m. Diane L. Tuttle, Nov. 22, 1956 (div. 1991); children: James, Janet. Student, Rutgers U., 1954-55; VMD, U. Pa., 1959, PhD, 1966. Pathologist Merck Sharp & Dohme Rsch. Labs., Rahway, NJ, 1966-69, dir. clin. research, 1969-72, sr. dir. domestic vet. research, 1972-75; dir. div. vet. med. rsch. Ctr. Vet. Medicine, FDA, Rockville, Md., 1975-78, assoc. dir. for rsch., 1978-82, assoc. dir. for human food safety, 1982-84, assoc. dir. for new animal drug evaluation, 1984-87; asst. dep. adminstr., then dep. adminstr. Sci. and Tech., Food Safety and Inspection Svc. USDA, Washington, 1987-93, exec. asst. to the adminstr., 1993-94; U.S. coord. for Codex Alimentarius USDA, Washington, 1994-96, sr. sci. advisor to adminstr., 1996; cons. vet. medicine and food safety, 1996—. Adj. prof. Va.-Md. Regional Coll. Vet. Medicine, Blacksburg, 1980-85 Contbr. articles to profl. jours. Trustee Scotch Plains (NJ) Cmty. Fund, 1969-72. Lt. AUS, 1952-54; col. Res., 1954-83 (ret.) Recipient FDA Merit award, 1978, Meritorious Presdl. Rank award, 1989; named to Artillery OCS Hall of Fame, 2000. Mem. AAAS, Am. Assn. Avian Pathologists, Am. Vet. Med. Assn., Assn. Mil. Surgeons US, Civil Affairs Assn., Inst. Food Technologists, Nat. Assn. Fed. Veterinarians, NJ Acad. Sci., NY Acad. Scis., Res. Officers Assn., Soc. Toxicologic Pathology, Sigma Xi. Home and Office: 14304 Brickhowe Ct Germantown MD 20874-3431 Office Phone: 877-899-9426. Personal E-mail: mjnorcross@bww.com.

**NORD, HENRY J.,** transportation executive; b. Berlin, May 1, 1917; came to U.S., 1937, naturalized, 1943; s. Walter and Herta (Riess) N.; children: Stephen, Philip. Student, U. Oxford, Eng., 1934, Northwestern U., 1938-40, Ill. Inst. Tech., 1942; JD, De Paul U., 1949. CPA, Ill. Apprentice in export, Hamburg, Germany, 1935- 37; with GATX Corp., Chgo., 1938-85, comptroller, 1961-67, v.p., 1967-71, exec. v.p., 1971-78, vice chmn. v.p., 1978-80, v.p., 1980-82, cons., 1982-84, fin. cons., 1982—, dir., 1964-78. Dir. Planned Lighting, Inc. to 1988. Trustee DePaul U. Served to 1st lt. AUS, 1943—46. Mem. Internat. Law Assn. Clubs: Tavern (Chgo.). Home: 1000 N Lake Shore Pl Chicago IL 60611-1308 Office: 111 N Wabash Ave Chicago IL 60602-1936

**NORD, PAUL ELLIOTT,** lawyer, accountant; b. Mar. 22, 1936; s. Abe and Rose (Guss) N.; m. Marcia B. Gross, June 13, 1965; children: Howard, Aimee, Samuel. Student, U. Utah, 1952-56; JD, John F. Kennedy U., 2000. CPA, Calif.; bar: Calif., 2000, U.S. Tax Ct., U.S. Ct. Appeals (9th cir.). Staff acct. Robinson, Nowell & Co. (merged with Muncy McPherson & Co.), 1966-73, ptnr., 1973-81, mng. ptnr., 1981-87; ptnr. BDO Seidman, 1988-95,

sr. ptnr., 1995—2000; pvt. practice Walnut Creek, Calif., 2000—. Bd. dirs. Congregation Beth Sholom, San Francisco, 1969-87, pres. 1979-81; mem. budget and allocations com. Jewish Fedn., East Bay, 1981-84. With U.S. Army, 1957-58, 61-62. Ford Found. scholar. Mem. Am. Inst. CPAs (acctg. standards exec. com. 1979-81), Calif. Soc. CPAs (chmn. sub-com. acctg. principles 1981-83), Club Sport. Jewish. Home: 931 Walnut Ave Walnut Creek CA 94598-3738 Office: 3075 Citrus Cir Ste 155 Walnut Creek CA 94598 Office Phone: 925-906-9300. Personal E-mail: paulnord@ca.astound.net. Business E-Mail: paulnordlaw@gmail.com.

**NORD, ROBERT EAMOR,** lawyer; b. Ogden, Utah, Apr. 11, 1945; s. Eamor Carroll and Ella Carol (Winkler) N.; m. Sherryl Anne Smith, May 15, 1969; children: Kimberly, P. Ryan, Debra, Heather, Andrew, Elizabeth. BS, Brigham Young U., 1969; JD, U. Chgo., 1972. Bar: Ill. 1972, U.S. Dist. Ct. (no. dist.) Ill. 1972, U.S. Ct. Appeals (D.C. cir.) 1974, U.S. Dist. Ct. (mid. dist.) Fla. 1976, U.S. Ct. Appeals (7th cir.) 1977, U.S. Dist. Ct. (no. dist.) Ind. 1978, U.S. Dist. Ct. (no. dist.) Fla. 1979, U.S. Supreme Ct. 1981, U.S. Dist. Ct. (ea. dist.) Mich. 1984, U.S. Ct. Appeals (11th cir.) 1985, U.S. Ct. Appeals (3d cir.) 1996, U.S. Ct. Appeals (2d cir.) 2002. Assoc. Chadwell & Kayser, Chgo., 1972-75; from assoc. to ptnr. Hinshaw & Culbertson, Chgo., 1975—2002, of counsel, 2003—. Assoc. internat. legal counsel LDS Ch., Moscow. Republican. Mem. Lds Ch. Home: 481 Woodlawn Ave Glencoe IL 60022-2175 Office: Hinshaw & Culbertson 222 N La Salle St Ste 300 Chicago IL 60601-1081 also: Gen Counsel Portbstrasse 5-7 D-60435 Frankfurt am Main Germany E-mail: robert_nord@excite.com.

**NORD, WALTER ROBERT,** business administration educator, researcher, consultant; b. Mt. Kisco, N.Y., July 2, 1939; s. Arthur William and Elizabeth (Reimstedt) N.; m. Ann Feagan, June 10, 1967. BA in Econs., Williams Coll., 1961; MS in Organizational Behavior, Cornell U., 1963; PhD in Social Psychology, Washington U., St. Louis, 1967. Asst. prof. organizational psychology Washington U., 1967-70, assoc. prof., 1970-73, prof., 1973-89; prof. mgmt. U. South Fla., 1989—, Disting. Univ. prof., 2001; vis. prof. faculty commerce Northwestern U., 1981, U. B.C. (Can.), Vancouver, 1975-76. Author: (with S. Tucker) Implementing Routine and Radical Innovations, 1987; editor: Concepts and Controversy in Organizational Behavior, 1972, rev. edit, 1976; (with P. Frost and V. Mitchell) Organizational Reality, 1978, rev. edit., 1982, 86, 92; (with H. Meltzer) Making Organizations Humane and Productive, 1982; (with P. Frost and V. Mitchell) Managerial Reality, 1989, HRM Reality, 1992; (with A. Brief) Meanings of Occupational Work, 1990, (with S. Clegg and C. Hardy) Handbook of Organization Studies, 1996 (George Terry Book award 1997), 2d edit., 2006, (with P. Frost and L. Krefting) Managerial and Organization Reality, Stories of Life and Work, 2004. Fellow APA; mem. Acad. Mgmt. (named Disting. Educator 2002). Home: 6004 Pratt St Tampa FL 33647-1043 Office: U South Fla Sch Bus Tampa FL 33620-5500 Office Phone: 813-974-1787. E-mail: wnord@coba.usf.edu.

**NORDBERG, JOHN ALBERT,** federal judge; b. Evanston, Ill., June 18, 1926; s. Carl Albert and Judith Ranghild (Carlson) N.; m. Jane Spaulding, June 18, 1947; children: Carol, Mary, Janet, John. Student, Carleton Coll., 1943—44, student, 1946—47; JD, U. Mich., 1950. Bar: Ill. 1950, U.S. Dist. Ct. (no. dist.) Ill. 1957, U.S. Ct. Appeals (7th cir.) 1961. Assoc. Pope & Ballard, Chgo., 1950-57; ptnr. Pope, Ballard, Shepard & Fowle, Chgo., 1957-76; judge Cir. Ct. of Cook County, Ill., 1976-82, U.S. Dist. Ct. (no. dist.) Ill., Chgo., 1982-95, sr. judge, 1995—. Editor-in-chief, bd. editors Chgo. Bar Record, 1966-74 Magistrate of Cir. Ct. and justice of peace Ill., 1957-65. Served with USN, 1944-46; PTO Mem. ABA, Chgo. Bar Assn., Am. Judicature Soc., Law Club Chgo., Legal Club Chgo., Union League Club of Chgo., Order of Coif. Office: US Dist Ct #1886 219 S Dearborn St Chicago IL 60604-1706

**NORDBY, EUGENE JORGEN,** orthopedic surgeon; b. Abbotsford, Wis., Apr. 30, 1918; s. Herman Preus and Lucille Violet (Korsrud) N.; m. Olive Marie Jensen, June 21, 1941; 1 child, Jon Jorgen BA, Luther Coll., Decorah, Iowa, 1939; MD, U. Wis., 1943. Diplomate Am. Bd. Orthopaedic Surgery. Intern Madison Gen. Hosp., Wis., 1943-44, asst. in orthopedic surgery Wis., 1944-48; practice medicine specializing in orthopedic surgery Madison, Wis., 1948—. Pres. Bone and Joint Surgery Assocs., S.C., 1969—91; chief staff Madison Gen. Hosp., 1957—63; assoc. clin. prof. U. Wis. Med. Sch., 1961—; bd. dirs. Wis. Physicians Svcs., 1958—, chmn., 1979—; dir. Wis. Regional Med. Program, Chgo. Madison and No. R.R.; bd. govs. Wis. Health Care Liability Ins. Plan; chmn. trustees S.M.S. Realty Corp.; mem. bd. attys. Profl. Responsibility of Wis. Supreme Ct., 1992—. Mem. editl. bd. Clin. Orthopaedics and Related Research, 1944—, Spine, 1994-2000. Pres. Vesterheim Norwegian Am. Mus., Decorah, Iowa, 1968-97, pres. emeritus, 1997—. Served to capt. M.C., AUS, 1944-46 Decorated Knight 1st class Royal Norwegian Order St. Olav; named Notable Norwegian Dane County Norwegian-Am. Fest, 1995; recipient Disting. Svc. award Internat. Rotary,1 987, Den Hoyeste Aere award Vesterheim, 1993, Lyman Smith, MD and Eugene J. Nordby, M.D. award for minimally invasive spine surgery established N.Am. Spine Soc., 1998, The Nordby Bldg. designated Wis. Phys. Svc. Health Ins. Co., 1998, Internat. Therapy Soc. Lifetime Achievement award, 2006. Fellow Wisdom Hall of Fame; mem. Acad. Orthop. Surgeons (bd. dirs. 1972-73, 1st chmn. bd. councilors 1972), Clin. Orthop. Soc., Assn. Bone and Joint Surgeons (pres. 1973), Internat. Soc. Study Lumbar Spine, State Med. Soc. Wis. (chmn. 1968-76, treas. 1976-97, Coun. award 1976), Am. Orthop. Assn., N.Am. Spine Soc., Internat. Intradiscal Therapy Soc. (sec. 1987-99, exec. dir. 1996-2006, exec. dir. emeritus 2006—, Eugene J. Nordby Rsch. award established in his honor 1993, Lifetime Achievement award 2006), Wis. Orthop. Soc., Dane County Med. Soc. (pres. 1957), Nat. Exch. Club, Madison Torske Klubben (founder, pres. 1978-98, pres. emeritus 1998—), Norwegian Am. Orthop. Soc., Am. Acad. Orthop. Surgeons, Am. Orthop. Assn., Norwegian Am. Found., Phi Chi. Lutheran. Home: 7824 Courtyard Dr Madison WI 53719 Office: 304 S Whitney Way Madison WI 53705 Office Phone: 608-831-2356. Personal E-Mail: ejnor@charter.net. We must remember no matter how dedicated we are to the accumulation of knowledge, it isn't always what you know that matters but what you can think of in time.

**NORDELL, HANS RODERICK,** journalist, retired editor; b. Alexandria, Minn., June 26, 1925; s. Wilbur Eric and Amelia (Jasperson) N.; m. Joan Projansky, Apr. 30, 1955; children: Eric Peter, John Roderick, Elizabeth Sabin. AB magna cum laude, Harvard U., 1948; B Litt, U. Dublin, 1951. Exec. editor World Monitor: The Christian Science Monitor Monthly; with Christian Sci. Monitor, Boston, 1948-93, arts editor, 1968-73, asst. chief editorial writer, 1973-83, home forum editor, 1983-85, feature editor, 1985-87; exec. editor World Monitor: The Christian Science Monitor Monthly, Boston, 1988-93. Bd. dirs. Cmty. Music Ctr., Boston, 1970-94, corp. chair, 1994—; bd. dirs. Young Audiences, 1970-88; mem. Com. for Harvard Theatre Collection, 1977-91; trustee Berklee Coll. Music, 1970-97, trustee emeritus, 1997—. With USMCR, 1944-46. Fellowship Rotary Found., 1950-51. Mem.: Harvard Musical Assn., St. Botolph Club, Phi Beta Kappa. Christian Scientist. Home: 25 Meadow Way Cambridge MA 02138-4635

**NORDENBERG, MARK ALAN,** academic administrator, law educator; b. Duluth, Minn., July 12, 1948; s. John Clemens and Shirley Mae (Tappen) N.; m. Nikki Patricia Pirillo, Dec. 26, 1970; children: Erin, Carl, Michael. BA, Thiel Coll., 1970; JD, U. Wis., 1973. Bar: Wis. 1973, Minn. 1974, U.S. Supreme Ct. 1976, Pa. 1985. Atty. Gray, Plant, Mooty & Anderson, Mpls., 1973—75; prof. law Capital U. Law Ctr., Columbus, Ohio, 1975—77, U. Pitts., 1977—, acting dean Sch. Law, 1985—87, dean Sch. Law, 1987—93, interim sr. vice chancellor & provost, 1993—94, Disting. Svc. prof., 1994—, interim chancellor, 1995—96, chancellor, 1996—. Mem. U.S. Supreme Ct. Adv. Com. on Civil Rules, Washington, 1988-93, Pa. Supreme Ct. Civil Procedure Rules Com., Phila., 1986-92; reporter civil justice adv. group U.S. Dist. Ct., Pitts., 1991-96; bd. dirs. Mellon Fin. Corp. Author: Modern Pennsylvania Civil Practice, 1985, 2d edit., 1995. Bd. dirs. Allegheny Conf. on Cmty. Devel., Pitts., Pitts. Coun. on Higher Edn., Pa. Assn. Colls. and Univs., Assn. Am. Univs.; trustee Thiel Coll., Greenville, Pa., 1987—97; bd.

dirs. Pitts. Life Scis. Greenhouse, The Tech. Collaborative. Named Vectors Pitts. Person of Yr. in Edn., 1996, Person of Yr., 1997, Pitts. Mag. Person of Yr., 2001, Hon. Consul for Great Britain. Fellow Am. Bar Found.; mem. ABA, Pa. Bar Assn., Allegheny County Bar Assn., Pitts. Athletic Assn., Duquesne Club. Office: U Pitts Cathedral of Learning Pittsburgh PA 15260 Business E-Mail: norden@pitt.edu.

NORDGREN, RONALD PAUL, engineering educator, researcher; b. Munising, Mich., Apr. 3, 1936; s. Paul A. and Martha M. N.; m. Joan E. McAfee, Sept 12, 1959; children: Sonia, Paul. BS in Engring., U. Mich., 1957, MS in Engring., 1958; PhD, U. Calif., Berkeley, 1962. Rsch. asst. U. Calif., Berkeley, 1959-62; mathematician Shell Devel. Co., Houston, 1963-68, staff rsch. engr., 1968-74, sr. staff rsch. engr., 1974-80, rsch. assoc., 1980-90; Brown prof. civil and mech. engring. Rice U., Houston, 1989-2000, prof. emeritus, rsch. prof., 2001—. U.S. nat. com. on theoretical and applied mechanics NRC, 1984-86, U.S. nat. com. for rock mechanics, 1991-95. Contbr. articles to profl. jours.; assoc. editor Jour. Applied Mechanics, 1972-76, 81-85; patentee in field. Fellow: ASME; mem.: NAE, Sigma Xi. Home: 492 Utica Ave Boulder CO 80304-0754 Office Phone: 303-440-1047. Business E-Mail: nordgren@rice.edu.

NORDGREN, WILLIAM BENNETT, engineering executive; b. Salt Lake City, Mar. 5, 1960; s. Kent Widstoe and Eliza (Schmuhl) N.; m. Carolyn B. Erickson, June 26, 1981; children: William Tyson, Cameron Lynn, Cassy Erin. BS, Brigham Young U., 1986, MS, 1989. Engr. Boeing Airplanes Co., Seattle, 1986-88; pres. CIM Engring. Assocs., Orem, Utah, 1988-89; v.p. engring. Prodn. Modeling Corp., Orem, 1989-93; pres. F & H Simulations, Inc., Orem, 1993—2002; pres., CEO, Flexsim Software Products, Inc., 2002—. Developer, polar coordinant mill. Mem. Soc. Mfg. Engrs., Inst. Indsl. Engrs. Republican. Mem. Lds Ch. Avocations: fishing, camping, sports.

NORDHAUS, ROBERT RIGGS, lawyer; b. Albuquerque, Mar. 27, 1937; s. Robert J. and Virginia (Riggs) N.; m. Jean Friedberg, June 27, 1964; children: Ronald E., Hannah E. BA, Stanford U., 1960; LLB, Yale U., 1963. Bar: N.Mex. 1963, D.C. 1981, U.S. Supreme Ct. 1982. Asst. counsel U.S. House Reps., Washington, 1963-74, counsel interstate and fgn. commerce com., 1975-76; asst. adminstr. FEA, Washington, 1977; gen. counsel Fed. Energy Regulatory Commn., Washington, 1977-80; ptnr. Van Ness, Feldman & Curtis, Washington, 1981-93; gen. counsel Dept. of Energy, Washington, 1993-97; ptnr. Van Ness Feldman, Washington, 1997—. Professorial lectr. George Washington Law Sch., Washington, 2001—. 2d. lt. U.S. Army, 1960. Mem. Fed. Energy Bar Assn. (bd. dirs. 1989-92). Office: Van Ness Feldman Ste 700 1050 Thomas Jefferson St NW Washington DC 20007-3877 Office Phone: 202-298-1800.

NORDLAND, GERALD, museum administrator, historian, consultant; b. LA; AB, JD, U. So. Calif. Dean of faculty Chouinard Art Sch., L.A., 1960-64; dir. Washington Gallery of Modern Art, 1964-66, San Francisco Mus. Art, 1966-72, Frederick S. Wight Art Galleries, UCLA, 1973-77, Milw. Art Mus., 1977-85; ind. curator, author, editor Chgo., 1985—. Author: Paul Jenkins, 1972, Gaston Lachaise/The Man and His Work, 1974, Richard Diebenkorn, 1987, rev. edit., 2001, Frank Lloyd Wright: In the Realm of Ideas, 1988, Zhou Brothers, 1994, Ynez Johnston, 1996, Lev Syrkin, 1998, Twentieth Century American Drawings, 1998, Jon Schueler: To The North, 2002, In the Spirit of the Times, 2003, Emerson Woelffer: A Solo Flight, 2003. Gaston Lachaise Found. grantee, 1973-74; John Simon Guggenheim Found. fellow, 1985-86. Home and Office: 645 W Sheridan Rd Chicago IL 60613-3316 Office Phone: 773-348-5133.

NORDLEY, GERALD DAVID, investor, writer; b. Mpls., May 22, 1947; s. V. Gerald and Evelyn May (Whitesel) N.; (div. 1973); 1 child, Sharon; m. Gayle Ann Wiesner, May 9, 1976; children: Jeffrey Goldberg, Andrew Nordley. BA in Physics, Macalester Coll., 1969; MS in System Mgmt., U. So. Calif., L.A., 1980. Enlisted USAF, 1969, commd. 2nd lt., 1970, advanced through grades to maj., 1982; inter-range ops. officer Network Ops. Div., Sunnyvale AFB, Calif., 1973-76; chief orbital ops. br. Def. Satellite Communications Directorate, L.A. AFB, 1976-81; chief spacecraft engr. br. DSCS III Program Office, L.A. AFB, 1981-82; battle dir. Mangilsan Liason Annex, Mang Il San, South Korea, 1983; chief advanced propulsion br. A.F. Rocket Propulsion Lab., Edwards AFB, Calif., 1984-86; rsch. staff mgr. ARIES office Astronautics Lab., Edwards AFB, 1986-89; ret. USAF, 1989; writer, pvt. investor Sunnyvale, 1990—. Mem. dir. Macalester Coll. Rep. Club, St. Paul, 1967-68; pres. Park Knowles Estates Property Owners Assn., Boron, Calif., 1988; co-chair Silicon Valley Writers Workshop, Cupertino, Calif., 1992, 93; treas. CONTACT: Cultures of the Imagination, 1997—. Decorated Air Force Commendation medal with 4 oak leaf clusters, Meritorious Svc. medal with 1 oak leaf cluster; recipient Anlab award Analog Mag., 1992, 93, 2000. Fellow Brit. Interplanetary Soc.; mem. AIAA (sr.; elec. propulsion com. 1984-86), Air Force Assn., Sci. Fiction Writers Am., Whensday People Writers Group, Space Access Soc., Am. Legion. Unitarian Universalist. Avocation: amateur astronomy. E-mail: gdnordley@aol.com.

NORDLIE, MARGARET A., biology professor, director; b. Madison, Wis. D of Arts, U. N.D., 1991. Asst. prof. Medctr. One Coll. Nursing, Bismarck, 1991—95; assoc. prof. biology U. Mary, Bismarck, 1995—. Author: (study guide) Principles of Human Physiology. Mem.: Assn. Coll. and Univ. Biology Educators, Human Anatomy and Physiology Soc. Office: Univ Mary 7500 Univ Dr Bismarck ND 58504 Office Phone: 701-355-8148. Business E-Mail: mnordlie@umary.edu.

NORDLIE, ROBERT CONRAD, biochemistry educator; b. Willmar, Minn., June 11, 1930; s. Peder Conrad and Myrtle (Spindler) N.; m. Sally Ann Christianson, Aug. 23, 1959; children: Margaret, Melissa, John. BS St. Cloud State Coll., Minn., 1952; MS, U. N.D., 1957, PhD, 1960. Tchg., rsch. asst. biochemistry U. N.D. Med. Sch., Grand Forks, 1955-60, James J. Hill rsch. prof. biochemistry, 1962-74, Chester Fritz disting. prof. biochemistry, 1974—, Cornatzer prof., chmn. dept. biochemistry and molecular biology, 1983-2000, Chester Fritz disting. emeritus prof., 2000—. Hon. prof. San Marcos U., Lima, Peru, 1981, 82—; emeritus prof., 2000-; NIH fellow Inst. Enzyme Rsch., U. Wis., 1960-61; mem. biochemistry study sect. NIH; merit rev. com. VA, 1994—; cons. enzymology Oak Ridge, 1961—; vis. prof. Tokyo Biomed. Inst., 1984; mem. predoctoral fellowship rev. group Howard Hughes Inst., 1990-93. Mem. editorial bd.: Jour. Biol. Chemistry, Biochimca et Biophysica Acta. Research publs. on enzymology relating to metabolism of various carbohydrates in mammalian livers, regulation blood sugar levels. Served with AUS, 1953-55. Recipient Disting. Alumnus award St. Cloud State U., 1983; recipient Sigma Xi Rsch. award, 1969, Golden Apple award U. N.D., 1968, Edgar Dale award U. N.D., 1983, Burlington No. Faculty Scholar award, 1987, Thomas J. Clifford Faculty Achievement award for excellence in rsch. U. N.D. Found., 1993, Hippocratic Dignity award, 2005. Mem. AAAS, Am. Soc. Biol. Chemistry and Molecular Biology, Am. Chem. Soc., Internat. Union Biochemists, Soc. Exptl. Biology and Medicine, Am. Inst. Nutrition, Sigma Xi, Alpha Omega Alpha. Home: 162 Columbia Ct Grand Forks ND 58203-2947 Office Phone: 701-777-2751. Business E-Mail: rnordlie@medicine.nodak.edu.

NORDLINGER, GERSON, investor; b. Washington, Feb. 2, 1916; s. Gerson and Camille (Bensinger) N. BA, George Washington U., 1935; BCS, Benjamin Franklin U., 1939. Head Navy Dept. Bur. Aeros. Budget, 1946-50; trustee Washington Real Estate Investment Trust, 1961-98; pres. Nordlinger Investment Corp., Washington, 1955—. Chmn. D.C. Arts Commn., 1965-67; v.p. Nat. Symphony Assn., 1953—, Nat. Ballet, 1966-70, Alliance Francaise, 1980—; pres. Prevention of Blindness Soc., 1960-67; treas. Friendship House, 1951-69; vice chmn. D.C. Recreation Bd., 1960-67; trustee Washington Performing Arts Soc., Mt. Vernon Coll., Washington Opera, Cathedral Choral Soc., Phillips Collection; life trustee Nat. Symphony Orch., 1952—; state com. Republican Party, 1952-64. Lt. comdr. Supply Corps, USNR,

1941-46, PTO. Recipient Angel of Arts award, 2001. Mem. D.C. Inst. CPAs, Cosmos Club, Met. Club. Home: 2700 Calvert St NW # 515 Washington DC 20008-2621 also: 3900 Galt Ocean Dr Fort Lauderdale FL 33308-6631 Personal E-mail: gersonn@aol.com.

NORDLOH, DAVID JOSEPH, literature and language professor, dean; b. Cin., May 3, 1942; s. Joseph Westerman and Josephine (Fusz) N.; m. Barbara Jane Beddow, June 29, 1968; children: Geoffrey David, Jennifer Ellen Blum. AB in English, Coll. of Holy Cross, 1964; PhD in English, Ind. U., 1969. Asst. prof. English Ind. U., Bloomington, 1969—75, assoc. prof. English, 1975—81, prof. English, 1981—, assoc. dean faculties, 2003—. Vis. assoc. prof. U. Va., Charlottesville, 1978; dir. Am. Studies Program, Ind. U., 1987-94. Gen. editor: A Selected Edition of W.D. Howells, 1974—; editor: Twayne's United States Author's Series, 1978-90; co-editor: American Literary Scholarship, 1986—; mem. editl. bd. Walter Scott Edition, 1984—; adv. bd. The Writings of James Fenimore Cooper, 1995—. Pres. Bloomington Symphony Orch., 1986-88, 93-94. Fulbright scholar, 1982-83. Mem. Am. Lit. Assn. Home: 3123 E Diana Ct Bloomington IN 47401-4407 Office: Ind Univ English Dept 1020 E Kirkwood Ave Bloomington IN 47401-5048 Office Phone: 812-855-2809. Business E-Mail: nordloh@indiana.edu.

NORDLUND, DONALD CRAIG, lawyer; b. Chgo., May 23, 1949; s. Donald E. and Jane (Houston) N.; m. Sally Baum, Sept. 7, 1975; children: Courtney Elizabeth, Michael Andrew, Laurie Katherine. AB polit. sci. & journalaism, Stanford U., 1971; JD, Vanderbilt U., 1974. Assoc. Ware & Freidenrich, Palo Alto, Calif., 1974-77; atty. Hewlett-Packard Co., Palo Alto, 1977-87, assoc. gen. counsel, sec., dir., 1987-99; sr. v.p., gen. counsel, sec. Agilent Technologies, Inc., 1999—. Panelist ann. disclosure doc. seminar Practicing Law Inst., 1982—2005, co-chmn., 2002—04; bd. dirs Addison Ave. Fed. Credit Union, 1985—; sec., dir. Agilent Tech. Found. and various Agilent Tech. subsidiaries, 1999—; mem. corp. law com. ABA, 2005—. Chmn., bd. dirs. Santa Clara County chpt. Jr. Achievement, 1995-97. Mem.: Assn. Gen. Counsel (v.p. 2005—06), Assn. Corp. Counsel (bd. dirs. San Francisco chpt. 1984—2000, pres. 1989—90, nat. bd. dirs. 1995—2001, Founding dir. Bay Area Chapter), Soc. Corp. Sec. and Governance Profl. (pres. San Francisco region 1986—88, bd. dirs. 1987—90, mem. exec. com. 1988—89, chmn. securities law com. 1995—98, nat. chmn. 1999—2000), Foothills Tennis and Swimming Club. Avocations: tennis, skiing, sailing, golf. Office: Agilent Technologies Inc 395 Page Mill Rd Palo Alto CA 94306-2024

NORDMAN, CHRISTER ERIC, chemistry professor; b. Helsinki, Finland, Jan. 23, 1925; came to U.S., 1948, naturalized, 1960; s. Eric Johan and Gertrud (Nordgren) N.; m. Barbara Lorraine Neal, Nov. 28, 1952 (div. 1993); children: Christina, Aleta, Eric, Carl; m. Outi Marttila, Dec. 28, 1994. Dipl. Ing., Finnish Inst. Tech., Helsinki, 1949; PhD, U. Minn., 1953. Research asso. Inst. Cancer Research, Phila., 1953-55; mem. faculty U. Mich., Ann Arbor, 1955—, prof. chemistry, 1964-95; prof. emeritus, 1995—. Mem. U.S. Nat. Com. Crystallography, 1970-72. Served with Finnish Army, 1943-44. NIH spl. fellow, 1971-72; recipient A.L. Patterson award, 1997. Fellow AAAS; mem. Am. Chem. Soc., Am. Phys. Soc., Am. Crystallographic Assn., Finnish Soc. Scis. and Letters. Home: 27 Haverhill Ct Ann Arbor MI 48105-1406 Office: Univ Mich Dept Chemistry Ann Arbor MI 48109 E-mail: cnordman@umich.edu.

NORDMAN, KATIE, reading specialist; d. Paul William and Jane Mary Rhinhart; m. Dale James Nordman, Apr. 16, 2005. BS in Edn., Worcester State Coll., 1999, MEd in Reading, 2004. Cert. reading specialist and elem. tchr. Mass. Elem. tchr., Mass., 1999—2002; reading tchr. Southborough, Mass., 2002—. Tchr., Barquismeto, Venezuela, 2000—01. Mem.: Internat. Reading Assn., Mass. Tchr. Assn.

NORDQVIST, ERIK ASKBO, transportation executive; b. Copenhagen, Aug. 8, 1943; s. Joergen and Lissie (Moeller) Nordqvist; m. Kirsten Vibeke Kenholt, Sept. 17, 1970 (dec. June 28, 2002); children: Ken-Martin, Alexander. Student, Danish Comml. Coll. Commerce, London, 1963—64, U. SC, 1964—65. Vice pres. Import Center W.S., L.A., 1964-65; mgr. Denning Freight Forwarders Ltd., Toronto, Ont., Can., 1965-66; sales dir. overseas Samson Transp. Co., Copenhagen, 1967-68; mng. dir., pres. Seair AS, Copenhagen, 1969-71, Nordbird Group, Holbaek, Denmark, 1971—, Nordbird AS, 1971—; chmn. European Steamship Line, Vedbaek, 1995—, European Airline Sys., Vedbaek, 1995—; owner Rederiet Waterest I/S, 1998—, AidsKit, Copenhagen, 2003—; co-owner Pastamannen, Klampenborg, Denmark, 2003—; owner Ballerum Shipping, Denmark, A-rEst Co., Ballerum, 2006. Co-owner Nordbird Oil, Nordbird Fin., Copenhagen, Nordbird Internat. Financing Ltd., Toronto, Ont.; v.p. N. Sea Products Inc., High Point, N.C., 1980—; bd. dirs. Fino Travel, Odense, Denmark, Annex Furniture Galleries, European Broadcast Comm., Vedbaek, On Holding Ltd., Gibraltar, Olsen & Nordqvist Holding, Holbaek, Denmark, pres., 1986—, NQ-Byg Aps, Holbaek, Auto Dan-Am., Holbaek, Autotel Internat., Roskilde, On Holding APS, Vedbaek Dansk-Fransk Osters Aps, 3 Danish Open, U.S. Gt. Britain, Japan, Tins and Cans, Denmark; chmn. European Broadcast Comm., Charlottenlund, Denmark, London, European Aid Found., Vedbaek, Denmark, Lac, Albanien; cons. Frederikshavns. Skibsvaerf AS, Copenhagen Cmty. Chmn. European Broadcast Comm., Copenhagen and London, 1992—, European Aid Found., Copenhagen and N.Y.C.; del. Internat. Red Cross, Copenhagen, 1994—. Recipient Devel. honor for shipping City of Le Havre, France, 1971. Mem. Det Udenrigspolitiske Selskab, Funen Soc. (founder, past pres.). Lutheran. Office: EAS/ESL/RSD 312 Ballerumvej 7700 Thisted Denmark Office Phone: 45893994. E-mail: enq@sol.dk.

NORDSTRAND, NATHALIE ELIZABETH JOHNSON, artist; b. Woburn, Mass., Nov. 6, 1932; d. Edward N. and Ruth Peterson Johnson; m. Robert I. Nordstrand, Jan. 12, 1962. AA, Bradford Jr. Coll., 1952; BA, Columbia U., 1954; studied with Jay Connaway, Don Stone, Roger Curtis, Paul Grisiki. Rsch. assoc. Gerontology Age Ctr. of New Eng., Boston, 1955-64; clk. corp. dir. Johnson Bros. Greenhouses, Inc., Woburn, 1958-84; owner Nordstrand Gallery, Rockport, Mass. 1970-99. Exhibited at Nat. Acad. Galleries, NYC, Springfield Mus. Fine Arts, Hammond Mus., North Salem, NYC, Bhulabha Meml. Inst., Bombay, India, Copley Soc. at Boston Symphony Hall, Hermann Fine Arts Ctr., Marietta, Ohio, Am. C. of C., Hong Kong, 1975-76, Silvermine Guild, Conn., 1976, Wall of Fame, Balt. Watercolor Soc., 1976, Ann. Copley Masters Exhbn. Boston, 1970-92. Permanent one woman shows include Rockport (Mass.) Art Assn., 1969, Laura Knotts Art Gallery, Bradford Coll., 1982, Reading Pub. Libr. Found., 1997; paintings in Nat. Mus. Am. Art, Smithsonian Inst., 1994, Best of Watercolors, 1995, Best of Oil Painting, 1996, Landscape Inspirations, 1997, Gallery of Marine Art, 1998. Planning bd. North Suburban Art Festival, 1963—68; chair. planned giving Barnard Coll., NYC, 2003—04. Named Citizen of Yr., Reading chpt. Am. Cancer Soc., 1983; recipient Louis E. Seley award, Salmagundi Art Club, 1974, Excellence in Watercolor award, Rockport Art Assn., 1997, Philip Isenberg Meml. award, Salmagundi Club, 1997, more than 180 awards in nat. and regional competition, 1960—, Joseph Santoro Meml. award, Rockport Art Assn., 2005, Ogden Pleissner Meml. award, Salmagundi Art Club, 2006. Fellow Am. Artist Profl. League (Gold medal 1971, 75, award 1978-79); mem. Acad. Artists Assn. (Watercolor awards 1973-74, 76-77, New Eng. Heritage award 1993), Copley Soc. Boston (master artist), Hudson Valley, North Shore (bd. dirs. 1964-67, 86—), Rockport Art Assn. (Lifetime Dedication to Promotion of Art award 1999, Joseph Santoro Meml. award 2005), Affiliated Art Assn. Mass. (v.p. 1980), Am. Watercolor Soc. (charter, program chmn. 1960-86, Pres.'s awards 1973-80), Am. Watercolor Soc. (juror internat. exhbn. 1992), Allied Artists Am. (Watercolor award 1973-74), New Eng. Watercolor Soc. (2d v.p. 1984-90), Boston Watercolor Soc. (award 1975), Guild Boston Artists (bd. dirs. 1986-99, A Lassall Ripley award 1993), Reading Mus. Fine and Performing Arts (charter, bd. dirs. 1993), Nat. Mus. Women in Arts (charter mem.), Salmagundi Art Club (40 awards including MacGowin Tuttle Meml. award 1976, 78-79, Elliot Liskin Meml. award 1988, Steven Blackman award 1988, Joseph Hartley award 1989, 2001, 2002, Mortimer Freehof Meml. award 1991, Bruce Crane award 1994, Rita

Duis Meml. award 2001, Margery Saroka Meml. award 2003, Thomas Moran award 2004, Ogden Pleissner Meml. award 2006). Methodist. Address: 384 Franklin St Reading MA 01867-1036 Personal E-mail: nordstrands@aol.com.

NORDSTROM, BLAKE W., retail executive; b. 1960; With Nordstrom, Inc., Seattle, 1974—, v.p. & gen. mgr. Wash./Alaska region, 1991—95, co-pres. Seattle, 1995—2000, pres., 2000—, bd. dir., 2005—. Office: Nordstrom Inc 1617 Sixth Ave Seattle WA 98101-1742*

NORDSTROM, BRUCE A., department store executive; b. 1933; married. BA, U. Wash., 1956. With Nordstrom, Inc., Seattle, 1956—, v.p., 1964-70, pres., 1970-75, chmn., 1975-77, co-chmn., 1977—, dir. Office: Nordstrom Inc 1617 6th Ave Seattle WA 98101-1742*

NORDYKE, ELEANOR COLE, demographer, researcher, community health nurse; b. Los Angeles, June 15, 1927; d. Ralph G. and Louise Noble (Carter) Cole; m. Robert Allan Nordyke, June 18, 1950; children: Mary Ellen Nordyke-Grace, Carolyn Nordyke Cozzette, Thomas J., Susan Nordyke Bell., Gretchen Nordyke Worthington. BS, Stanford U., 1950; P.H.N. accreditation, U. Calif.-Berkeley, 1952; MPH, U. Hawaii, 1969. RN. Pub. health nurse San Francisco Dept. Health, 1950-52; nurse-tchr. Punahou Sch., Honolulu, 1966-67; clinic coordinator East-West Population Inst., East-West Ctr., Honolulu, 1969-75, population rschr., 1975-82, rsch. fellow, 1982-92. Cons. Hawaii Commn. on Population, Honolulu, 1970-83; mem. Hawaii Policy Action Group for Family Planning, Honolulu, 1971-89, chmn., 1976-77; nurse-cons. vol. Straub Clinic and Hosp., 2001--. Author: The Peopling of Hawaii, 1977, 2d rev. edit., 1989, A Profile of Hawaii's Elderly Population, 1984; author: (with Robert Gardner) The Demographic Situation in Hawaii, 1974; author: Pacific Images-Views from Captain Cook's Third Voyage, 1999; editor: I'm Third-An American Boy of Depression Years - Memoirs of Robert A. Nordyke, MD, 2003; mem. editl. bd. Hawaiian Jour. History, 1980—; contbr. articles to profl. jours. Bd. dirs. YMCA, Honolulu, 1970-85, YMCA Camp Erdman Br., 1985—, vice-chmn. 1978-79, chmn. YMCA Camp Erdman, 1989-92; bd. dirs. Hawaii Planned Parenthood, 1974-78, Friends of Libr. of Hawaii, 1985-87, 2002-2005; trustee Hawaiian Hist. Soc., 1978-82, Arcadia Retirement Residence, Honolulu, 1978-87; mem. liberal arts coun. Hawaii Pacific U., 1988—. Mem. Population Reference Bur., Hawaii Econ. Assn., Hawaiian Hist. Soc., Friends of East-West Ctr., Friends of Univ. Hawaii Sch. Medicine, Stanford Nurses Alumni Assn., Stanford Alumni Assn. (bd. dirs. Hawaii chpt.), U. Hawaii Sch. Pub. Health Alumni Assn. (life), Gen. Fed. Women's History Club, Adventure Club of Honolulu, Book Reading Clubs, Captain-Cook Soc., Outrigger Canoe Club, Morning Music Club, Caledonian Soc., Phi Beta Kappa. Democrat. Congregationalist. Avocations: music, art, swimming, Hawaii, travel. Home: 2013 Kakela Dr Honolulu HI 96822-2158 Personal E-mail: rnordyke@aol.com.

NORELL, MARK ALLEN, paleontologist, curator; b. St. Paul, July 26, 1957; s. Albert Donald Norell and Helen Louise Soltau; m. Vivian Pan, Nov. 1, 1991; 1 child, Inga Pan. BS, Long Beach State U., 1980; MS, San Diego State U., 1983; PhD, Yale U., 1988. Assoc. curator Am. Mus., N.Y.C., 1989—99, chmn. dept., 1996—99, divsn. chmn., curator, 1999—2005. Adj. assoc. prof. dept. biology Yale U., New Haven, 1991—; adj. prof. Columbia U., 1995—; lectr. in the field. Author: All You Need to Know About Dinosaurs, 1991, Discovering Dinosaurs, 1995, 2d edit., 2000 (recipient Young Readers Book of Yr. award, Scientific American), Searching for Velociraptor, 1996, A Dinosaur and Its Nest, 1999, Unearthing the Dragon, 2005, and several others; contbr. articles to profl. jours. Named Disting. Alumnus, Long Beach State U., 2000, NYC Leader of Yr., NY Times. Fellow: Explorer's Club, Willi Hennig Soc.; mem.: Soc. Vertebrate Paleontology (Romer prize 1987). Achievements include contributing to the investigation of unearthing the remains of a perfectly preserved 130 million-year-old new species of dinosaur in China, which provides a look at how prehistoric creatures slept. Office: Am Museum of Natural History 79th at Central Park W New York NY 10024-5192 Office Phone: 212-769-5804. Business E-Mail: norell@amnh.org.

NORELLI, TERIE THOMPSON, state legislator; b. Orange, N.J., July 7, 1952; d. George Russell and Iverna C. (Weber) Thompson; m. Allen M. Norelli, Dec. 31, 1973; children: Gina Marie, Daniel Thompson. BS in Math. summa cum laude, U. NH, 1985. Tchr. math. Winnacunnet H.S., Hampton, NH, 1985—95; mem. NH Ho. of Reps., Concord, 1996—, sci., tech. and energy com., 1996—2003, telecomm. oversight com., 1997—2003, ho. Dem. leadership, 1998—, asst. Dem. whip, 2002—04, asst. Dem. leader, 2005—, chair clean air subcom., 1998—2003, electric utility restructuring oversight com., 1998—2003, pub. works and hwys. com., 2003—05, rules com., 2003—05, co-chair reproductive rights caucus, 1996—, mem. legis. caucus for children, 1997—2002, mem. fin. com., 2005—. Participant in devel. series geometry insvc. workshops U. NH, 1986-89. Area team Nat. Abortion Rights Action League of NH, Portsmouth, 1990-94, bd. dirs., Concord, 1996-2000; chair Naral-Prochoice NH Pac, 2001-; bd. dirs. Sexual Assault Support Svcs., Portsmouth, 1992-96, pres. bd., 1993-95; del. to Joint US-China Conf. on Women's Issues, Beijing, 1995; organizing com. Bringing Back Beijing '95, Statewide Women's Conf., Concord, 1996, Beijing +5 Tri-State Preperation Conf., 1999; adv. bd. Feminist Health Ctr. Ports, Portsmouth, 1996-97; mem. Leadership Seacoast, 1995. Recipient NH Women's Lobby Meritorious Svc. award, 2002, Naral Pro-Choice N.H. Champion for Choice award, 2003, NASW-NH Legislator of Yr. award, 2004. Mem. Phi Beta Kappa, Phi Kappa Phi, Pi Mu Epsilon. Avocations: travel, arts and culture, running. Office: Rm 210 LOB State St Concord NH 03301 Office Phone: 603-271-2136.

NOREM, RICHARD FREDERICK, surgeon; b. Baton Rouge, Apr. 14, 1961; s. Richard Norem I and Norem Sally; m. Merrilyn Bush; 1 child, Erick F. MD, Tulane U., New Orleans, 1988. Gen. surgeon La. Laparoendoscopic Surg. Clinic, Alexandria, La., 1994—. Med. dir. Synergy Home Health, Alexandria, 2004—06. Office: Louisiana Laparoendoscopic Surgical Clin 301 Fourth Street Alexandria LA 71301 Office Phone: 318-448-1040. Office Fax: 318-448-0548.

NOREM, RICHARD FREDERICK, SR., musician, educator; b. Joliet, Ill., June 28, 1931; s. Oscar Lewis and Mabel Vera (Meyer) N.; m. Sally Lou Jarvis, July 24, 1954; 1 son, Richard Frederick II. Mus.B., U. Rochester, 1953, Mus.M., 1958; postgrad., Guildhall Sch., London, 1974. Instr. Joliet Musical Coll., Ill., 1951-53; tchr. Rochester Pub. Schs., NY, 1956-57; mem. faculty La. State U., Baton Rouge, 1957-95, prof., asst. dean music, 1969-84, prof. emeritus Baton Rouge, 1995. Dir., sec.-treas. Bank Commerce, 1983-97; bd. dirs., sec.-treas. NBC Fin. Corp., 1988-97; adv. bd. First Am. Tenn. Bank., 1997-99, AmSouth Bank, 1999-2003; ptnr. Am. Train Yard. Mem. Baton Rouge Symphony Orch., 1957—, Timm Woodwind Quintet, 1957-95; founder La. State U. Faculty Brass Quintet (now named Norem Brass Quintet of La. State U.), 1999. With USMC Band, 1953-56. Mem. Am. Legion (past post comdr.), Rolls-Royce Owners Club (sec.-treas. So. Delta region 1982-98, regional chmn. 1997-99), Norwegian Club Baton Rouge, La. State U. Faculty Club, Baton Rouge Model R.R. Club, Rotary (Paul Harris fellow). Republican. Episcopalian. Home: 4821 Sweetbriar St Baton Rouge LA 70808-8660 Office: La State U Sch Music Baton Rouge LA 70803-0001 Office Phone: 225-924-0711. Business E-Mail: richard@clamp.net. *I have been blessed by the divine creator with an artistic talent in music to which I have dedicated my life. Early during my performing career I knew I must share with others the knowledge I had obtained in music; consequently my goals have been to train and educate the hundreds of music students I have worked with during my teaching career. I have also continued to bring beauty to our world in my own way as an active performing musician in the Baton Rouge Symphony Orchestra.*

NOREN, JERRY JAY, medical educator; b. Willmar, Minn., Jan. 7, 1945; BS, BA, U. Minn., 1967, MD, 1970; MPH, Harvard U., 1976. Lic. preventive medicine Am. Bd. of Preventive Medicine, occupl. medicine Am. Bd. of Preventive Medicine. Prof. U. Wis., Madison, 1976—99, dir. and assoc. dir. adminstrv. medicine master's, 1976—83; Winston Churchill traveling fellow

English Speaking Union, London, 1978; congl. fellow U.S. Ho. Reps. Inst. of Medicine, Washington, 1981—82; assoc. prof. U. Wis., 1982—99, assoc. vice chancellor for acad. affairs and policy, 1984—85, vice chancellor for health scis., 1985—93; interim chancellor Minn. State Colls. and Univs., St. Paul, 1993—95; prof. George Bush Sch. Govt. and Pub. Svc. Tex. A&M U., College Station, 1999—2002; pres. health sci. ctr. Tex. A&M U. Sys., College Station, 1999—2000; prof. Tex. A&M U. Sys. Health Sci. Ctr., College Station, 1999—2002, U. of Nebr., Lincoln, 2002—, exec. v.p., provost, 2002—. Contbr. articles to profl. jours. Capt. U.S. Army, 1971—73. Recipient Jay Noren Day named in his honor City of Milw. Proclamation, Mayor of Milw., 1993, Upjohn award for leadership and svc., U. Minn., 1970, Recognition for Leadership of Minn. Health Workforce Redesign Project award, Nat. Inst. of Health Policy, 2002, Resolution of Appreciation for Svc. as Pres. of Tex. A&M Sys. Health Sci. Ctr. award, Tex. A&M U. Sys. Bd. of Regents, 2000, Resolution of Gratitude in Appreciation for Guiding Minn.'s Higher Edn. Merger from Concept to Reality award, Bd. of Trustees, Minn. State Colls. and Univs., 1995, Letter of Commendation for Contbn. to Higher Edn., Senate Majority Leader Minn. Legislature, 1995. Office: U Nebr 3835 Holdrege St Lincoln NE 68583-0743 Office Phone: 402-472-5242. Office Fax: 402-472-5240.

**NORFLEET, LEONTINE SANDRA,** retired biologist; d. James Edward and Dorothy Calloway Norfleet. BS, CUNY, NYC, 1957; MA in Biol. & Physiological Scis., Hunter Coll., NYC, 1964; MBA in Human Resources Mgmt., Adelphia Coll., Garden City, NY, 1994. Clin. microbiologist Bklyn. Jewish Hosp.; asst. bacteriologist NYC; med. rschr. LI Jewish Hosp., New Hyde Pk., NY; biochemistry assoc. Endo Labs./Dupont-Merck/Bristol Meyers Squibb, Garden City, quality assurance specialist, scientist, auditor, quality engr. Vol. NYC Ballet. Mem.: Orera Guild, ABT Guild, Guild. Democrat. Roman Catholic. Avocations: exercise, ballet, reading, movies. Home: 111-39 201 St Saint Albans NY 11412

**NORGAARD, RICHARD BRUCE,** economist, educator, consultant; b. Washington, Aug. 18, 1943; s. John Trout and Marva Dawn (Andersen) N.; m. Marida Jane Fowle, June 19, 1965 (div.); children: Kari Marie, Marc Anders; m. Nancy A. Rader, June 5, 1993; children: Addie Nelle, Mathiesen Rader. BA in Econs., U. Calif., Berkeley, 1965; MS in Agrl. Econs., Oreg. State U., 1967; PhD in Econs., U. Chgo., 1971. Instr. Oreg. Coll. Edn., 1967-68; asst. prof. agrl. and resource econs. U. Calif., Berkeley, 1970-76, assoc. prof., 1976-77, 80-87, assoc. prof. energy and resources, 1987-92, prof. energy and resources, 1992—. Project specialist Ford Found., Brazil, 1978-79; environ. cons. to internat. devel. agencies; sci. com. on problems of the environment U.S. Nat. Rsch. Coun.; founding chmn. bd. Redefining Progress, 1993-97; sci. adv. bd. US EPA, 2000-04; mem. ind. sci. bd. Calif. Bay-Delta Authority. Author: Development Betrayed: The End of Progress and a Coevolutionary Revisioning of the Future, 1994; chpt. rev. editor Millenium Ecosys. Assessment, 2004-05; mem. editl. bd. numerous academic jours.; contbr. articles to profl. jours. Active civil rights, environ., and peace orgns. Mem. AAAS, Am. Econs. Assn., Internat. Soc. Ecol. Econs. (pres. 1998-2001, past pres. 2002-2003), Fedn. Am. Scientists, Assn. Environ. and Resource Econs., Am. Inst. Biol. Scis. (bd. dirs. 2000-, treas. 2004—). Home: 1198 Keith Ave Berkeley CA 94708-1607 Office: U Calif Energy & Resources Program 310 Barrows Hall Berkeley CA 94720-3050 Business E-Mail: norgaard@berkeley.edu.

**NORGLE, CHARLES RONALD, SR.,** federal judge; b. Mar. 3, 1937; BBA, Northwestern U., Evanston, Ill., 1964; JD, John Marshall Law Sch., Chgo., 1969. Asst. state's atty. DuPage County, Ill., 1969-71, dep. pub. defender Ill., 1971-73, assoc. judge Ill., 1973-77, 78-81, cir. judge Ill., 1977-78, 81-84; judge U.S. Dist. Ct. (no. dist.) Ill., Chgo., 1984—. Mem. exec. com. No. Dist. Ill.; mem. 7th Cir. Jud. Coun., 7th Cir. Jud. Conf. planning com., subcom. grant requests Fed. Defender Orgn., Fed. Defender Svcs. Com.; adj. faculty Northwestern U. Sch. Law, John Marshall Law Sch., Chgo.; pres. Atticus Finch Inn Ct. Mem. ABA, Fed. Bar Assn., Fed. Circuit Bar Assn., Ill. Bar Assn., DuPage County (Ill.) Bar Assn., Nat. Attys. Assn., DuPage Assn. Women Attys., Chgo. Legal Club, Northwestern Club. Office: US Dist Ct 219 S Dearborn St Ste 2346 Chicago IL 60604-1802

**NORGREN, WILLIAM ANDREW,** retired religious denomination administrator; b. Frostburg, Md., May 5, 1927; s. William Andrew and Martha Elizabeth Leona (Richardson) N. BA, Coll. William and Mary, 1948; STB, now STM, Gen. Theol. Sem., NYC, 1953; LittB, Oxford U., Eng., 1959; DD (hon.), Gen. Theol. Sem., NYC, 1984, Berkeley Div. Sch. at Yale, 1995. Ordained to ministry Episcopal Ch., 1953. Chaplain Christ Ch. Cathedral, Oxford, 1955-59; exec. dir. Commn. on Faith and Order Nat. Coun. Chs. of Christ in U.S.A., NYC, 1959-71, mem. gen. bd., 1979-95; pastoral asst. Trinity Ch., NYC, 1972-74; assoc. ecumenical officer Episcopal Ch., NYC, 1975-79, ecumenical officer, 1979-94, theol. cons., 1995-2000. Observer 2d Vatican Coun., Roman Cath. Ch., Vatican City, 1963-65; mem. assemblies World Co. Chs., various cities, 1961, 68, 83, 91. Editor: Living Room Dialogues, 1965, Implications of the Gospel, 1988, Toward Full Communion and Concordat of Agreement, 1991; author: Commentary on Called to Common Mission, 1999. Fellow, Gen. Theol. Sem., 1953—55. Democrat. Episcopalian. Avocations: art, music, theater, walking.

**NORIEGA, ELIZABETH GOVEA,** elementary school educator; d. Fernando and Anita Govea; m. Gerardo Noriega, Jan. 22, 1971; children: Annelisa, Christina, Bianca, Mikaela. B in Liberal Arts, Our Lady of the Lake U., San Antonio, 1993. Cert. social studies Tex., 1993. Tchr. Davis Mid. Sch., San Antonio, 1993—2004, Longfellow Mid. Sch., San Antonio, 2004—. Home: 5218 Ebony Dr San Antonio TX 78228 Office: Longfellow Middle School 1130 E Sunshine St San Antonio TX 78228 Office Phone: 210-433-0311.

**NORINS, ARTHUR LEONARD,** dermatologist, educator; b. Chgo., Dec. 2, 1928; s. Russell Joseph and Elsie (Lindemann) N.; m. Mona Lisa Wetzer, Sept. 12, 1954; children: Catherine, Nan, Jane, Arthur. BS in Chem. Engring., Northwestern U., 1951, MS in Physiology, 1953, MD, 1955. Diplomate: Am. Bd. Dermatology; subcert. in dermatopathology. Intern U. Mich., Ann Arbor, 1955-56; resident in dermatology Northwestern U., Chgo., 1956-59; asst. prof. Stanford U., 1961-64; prof., chmn. dept. dermatology, prof. pathology Ind. U. Sch. Medicine, Indpls., 1964-93, prof. emeritus, 1993—. Mem. staff Riley Children's Hosp., Univ. Hosp., Wishard Hosp.; cons. VA Hosp. Contbr. articles to profl. jours. Capt. M.C. U.S. Army, 1959-61. Recipient Pres.' award Ind. U., 1979 Fellow ACP; mem. Am. Acad. Dermatology (bd. dirs.), Am. Dermatol. Assn., Soc. Pediatric Dermatology (founder, past pres.), Am. Soc. Dermatopathology, Am. Soc. Photobiology (founder), Soc. Investigative Dermatology. Home: 10100 Torre Ave Apt 211 Cupertino CA 95014-2168 Office: 550 University Blvd Ste 3240 Indianapolis IN 46202-5149 E-mail: norinssr@ix.netcom.com.

**NORKIN, CYNTHIA CLAIR,** retired physical therapist; b. Boston, May 6, 1932; d. Miles Nelson and Carolyn (Green) Clair; m. Stanislav A Norkin, Feb. 19, 1955 (dec. 1970); 1 child, Alexandra. BS in Edn., Tufts U., 1954; cert. phys. therapist, Bouve Boston Coll., 1954; MS, Boston U., 1973, EdD, 1984. Instr. Bouve Boston Coll., 1954—55; staff phys. therapist New Eng. Med. Ctr., Boston, 1954—55, Abington (Pa.) Meml. Hosp., 1965—70, Ea. Montgomery Country Vis. Nurse Assn., 1970—72; asst. prof. phys. therapy Sargent Coll./Boston U., 1973—84; assoc. prof. phys. therapy, dir., founder Ohio U. Sch. Phys. Therapy, Athens, 1984—95, ret. 1995. Consult Boston Ctr Independent Living, Cambridge Vis Nurse Asn, Mass Medicaid Cost Effectiveness Project, 1978; secy Health Planning Coun Greater Boston, 1976—78; book, manuscript reviewer F A Davis Co, 1986—; arthritis adv comt Ohio Dept Health. Author (with P Levangie and C Norkin): Joint Structure and Function: A Comprehensive Analysis, 1983, 4th edit., 2005; author: (with D J White) Joint Measurement: A Guide to Goniometry, 1985; author: 3d edit., 2003. Trustee Brimmer and May Sch, 1980. Mem.: APHA,

AAAS, Athens County Vis Nurse Asn (secy adv coun 1984—95), Mass Asn Mental health, Mass Physical Therapy Asn (chair quality assurance comt 1980—83), Am Physical Therapy Asn (on site evaluator comn on accreditation 1986—95). Episcopalian.

**NORLAND, DONALD RICHARD,** retired foreign service officer; b. Laurens, Iowa, June 14, 1924; s. Norman and Aletta (Brunsvold) N.; m. Patricia Bamman, Dec. 13, 1952; children: Richard Boyce, David, Patricia D. Student, Iowa State Tchrs. Coll., 1941-43, N.W. Mo. State Tchrs. Coll. 1943-44; BA, U. Minn., 1948, MS, 1950; postgrad., U. Mich., 1951-52, Grenoble U., France, 1948-49. Instr. history and polit. sci. U. No. Iowa, 1949-51; teaching fellow U. Mich., 1951-52; with Fgn. Svc., U.S. Dept. State, 1952-81; posts include Rabat, Morocco, 1952-56, Washington, 1956-58, Abidjan, Ivory Coast, 1958-60; mem. NATO del., Paris, 1961-63, NATO delegation, The Hague, The Netherlands, 1964-69; dep. chief mission Conakry, Guinea, 1970-72; U.S. Dept. State fellow Stanford (Calif.) U., 1969-70; dep. dir. Office Mil. Assistance and Sales, Bur. Politico-Mil. Affairs, Dept. State, Washington, 1972-73, chief polit. officers counseling br. Office Pers., 1973-75; dep. dir. Office Mgmt. Ops., 1975-76; amb. to Botswana, Lesotho and Swaziland, 1976-79; amb. to Chad, 1979-81; ret. Fgn. Svc., U.S. Dept. State, 1981; lectr. African affairs; internat. cons., specialist econ. devel. Chmn. African studies Fgn. Svc. Inst. of U.S. Dept. of State, Washington, 1987-89; program dir. Ctr. for Internat. Pvt. Enterprise affiliate U.S. C. of C., Washington, 1990-91; sr. cons. World Space, Inc., 1995, sr. policy advisor, 1996—. Bd. dirs. Calvert New Africa Fund, 1995. Lt. (j.g.) USNR, 1943-46. Mem. Am. Fgn. Svc. Assn. (v.p. for retirees 1993-95, sec. 1995-97, mem. editl. bd. Fgn. Svc. Jour. 1992-95), World Space Found. (pres. 1997-98). Home: 4000 Cathedral Ave NW Apt 636B Washington DC 20016 5286 Office Phone: 202-338-2026. E-mail: donnorland@aol.com.

**NORMAN, ALBERT GEORGE, JR.,** lawyer; b. Birmingham, Ala., May 29, 1929; s. Albert G. and Ila Mae (Carroll) N.; m. Catherine Marshall DeShazo, Sept. 3, 1955; children: Catherine Marshall, Albert George III. BA, Auburn U., 1953; LLB, Emory U., 1958; MA, U. NC, 1960. Bar: Ga. 1957. Assoc. Moise, Post & Gardner, Atlanta, 1958-60, ptnr., 1960-62, Hansell & Post, Atlanta, 1962-86, Long, Aldridge & Norman, Atlanta, 1986-2000. Dir. Atlanta Gas Light Co., 1976-2000. Served with USAF, 1946-49. Mem. ABA, Ga. Bar Assn., Atlanta Bar Assn., Lawyers Club Atlanta (pres. 1973-74), Am. Law Inst., Am. Judicature Soc. (dir. 1975-78), Old War Horse Lawyers Club, (pres. 1991-92), Cherokee Town and Country Club. Episcopalian. Office: 134 Peachtree St NW Atlanta GA 30303-1802 Personal E-mail: almarnorman@mindspring.com.

**NORMAN, ARNOLD MCCALLUM, JR.,** engineer; b. Little Rock, May 1, 1940; s. Arnold McCallum and Ann Carolyn (Gibson) N.; m. Sylvia Burton, July 1, 1962 (div. 1967); m. Marisha Irene Malin, June 7, 1969; children: Frank Lee, Paul James. BS in Physics, Ga. Inst. Tech., 1962. Test engr. Rocketdyne div. Rockwell Internat., Canoga Park, Calif., 1962-64, engr. in charge of various programs, 1964-75, engr. in charge, project engr. large chem. lasers, 1975-85, project engr. space sta. propulsion system, 1985-87, project engr. nat. launch system health mgmt. systems, 1987-92, project engr. kinetic energy weapons, 1993-94; project engr. advanced propulsion systems Rockwell Internat., Canoga Park, Calif., 1994-95, sr. engring. specialist, 1995-96; health mgmt. sys. team head, x-33 Aerospike rocket engine Boeing-N.Am. Rocketdyne Divsn., Canoga Park, Calif., 1996-97; cons. rocket propulsion sys., ops. and health mgmt., 1997—. Mem. ops. com. health mgmt. ctr. U. Cin., 1988-94; mem. program com. Am. Internat. Conf. on Engring. Applications of Artificial Intelligence, 1988-90; presenter in field. Mem. editorial bd. Jour. Applied Intelligence, 1990-94; author numerous papers in field. Bd. dirs. Sebastopol Ctr. for Arts, 2000—, treas., 2003—04, pres. 2005-. Fellow AIAA (assoc., sect. chair sr. adv. com. 1991-93, San Fernando Valley sect., chmn. 1989-90, sys. effectiveness & safety com. 1995-97), Instrument Advancement Engring; mem. Sonoma County Astronomical Soc., Tau Beta Pi. Avocations: astronomy, woodworking, photography. Home: 4053 Bones Rd Sebastopol CA 95472-9756

**NORMAN, BEN ERIC,** mathematician, educator; b. Bogota, Colombia, July 25, 1967; s. Ben Burge and Cathy Norman. BS in Math., U. Calif., Davis, 1991, MA in Math., 1993. Part-time instr. math. Sacramento City Coll., 1993—; computer resource specialist U. Calif., Davis, 1997—. Author: (anthology) Honesty Awakened, 2002 (Merit award, 2002). Mem.: Math. Assn. Am. Avocations: Bible study, poetry. Office: Sacramento City Coll 3835 Freeport Blvd Sacramento CA 95822

**NORMAN, BOBBY DON,** artist, writer, research scientist; b. Dallas, June 5, 1933; s. Reuben Ray Norman and Bessie Mae Norman-Gregory; m. Mae Pearl Delley (dec. July 8, 2001); 1 child, Parette Michelle. Cert. grad. (hon.), S.W. Sch. Bus. Adminstrn., 1959. Mgr. Mile High Club, Dallas, 1955—57; city distbn. clk. U.S. Post Office, Dallas, 1956—66; office mgr., co-dir. So. Christian Leadership Conf., Dallas, 1969—73; cmty. liaison dir. Planned Parenthood N.E. Tex., Dallas, 1974—76; exec. v.p., gen. mgr. Davis Norman & Zanders, Inc., Dallas, 1977—78; house mgr., supr. Fed. Bur. Prisons, Dallas, 1982—83; supr. Halfway House Tex. Dept. Corrections, Dallas, 1983—84; artist, writer, scientist, publ. speaker Dallas, 1955—. Founder, pres. Assn. Advancing Artists and Writers, Inc., Dallas, 1969—76; active Internat. Platform Assn. Pub. Spkrs., Dallas, 1977—78. Author: Artistic Theological Science, 1998, Biblical Geology, 1998, Time of Babel: Biblical Geology and Tectonics, 2004. Commr. Greater Dallas Cmty. Rels. Commn., 1970—72; mem. block partnership mem. Greater Dallas Coun. Chs., 1970—71; organizer, tactical negotiator Dallas-Ft. Worth Coalition for the Free Flow of Info., 1970—72. Cpl. USAF, 1951—55, Korea. Recipient Tng. award, So. Christian Leadership Conf., 1969, Svc. award, Greater Dallas Cmty. Rels. Commn., 1972, Art award, Black C. of C., 1973. Mem.: Dallas Black C. of C. Baptist. Achievements include research in in Biblical geology. Avocations: fishing, art. Office: Art Religious PO Box 191904 Dallas TX 75219-8509 Office Phone: 214-534-2584.

**NORMAN, CHARLENE WILSON,** secondary school educator; b. Ft. Campbell, Ky., Apr. 19, 1949; d. Charles B. and Mary (Powe) Wilson; m. John D. Norman, Mar. 21, 1971; children: David, Mary Katharine. AS, Mid. Ga. Coll., 1969; BS in Edn., Ga. So. U., 1971; MEd in Math., Ga. Coll., 1979. Cert. tchr., Ky., Ga. Tchr. Tabor Jr. H.S., Warner Robbins, Ga., 1971-72, Windsor Acad., Macon, Ga., 1972-78, North Cobb H.S., Acworth, Ga., 1978-79, Campbell H.S., Smyrna, Ga., 1979-81, U. Ky., Lexington, 1981—, Bryan Sta. H.S., Lexington, 1982—. Insvcs. presenter Fayette County Bd. Edn., Lexington, 1988—; presider Nat. Coun. Tchrs. Math., Paducah, Ky., 1993; state conf. presider Ky. Coun. Tchrs. Math., Lexington. Asst. Sunday sch. tchr. First United Meth. Ch., Paris, Ky., 1989-96. Named Outstanding Tchr., Tandy Corp., 1991-92, FAME Outstanding tTchr., Nat. City Bank and Fayette County Schs., 1994, 96, Star Tchr., 1978, Math. Edn. Svc. and Achievement award, 2004. Mem. Nat. Coun. Tchrs. Math., Ky. Coun. Tchrs. Math., Lexington Coun. Tchrs. Math. (pres. 1990). Avocations: reading, crafts. Home: 173 Northland Dr Paris KY 40361-9133 Office: Bryan Sta HS 1866 Edgeworth Dr Lexington KY 40505-2010 E-mail: cnorman@fayette.k12.ky.us.

**NORMAN, CHRISTINA,** broadcast executive; b. July 30, 1963; m. Charles Hunt; children: Zoe, Asha. BA, Boston U. Freelance prodn. coord MTV, 1986—91, prodn. mgr. 1991—93, supervising prodr., on-air promotions, 1993—94, dir., on-air promotions, 1994—95, v.p., on-air promotions, 1995—97, sr. v.p., on-air promotions 1997—99, sr. v.p., mktg. and on-air promotion, 1999—2002; exec. v.p. and gen. mgr. VH1, 2002—04, pres., 2004—05, MTV, 2005—. Named one of 10 Most Powerful Blacks in TV, Ebony mag., 2002; named to 100 Most Powerful Women in Hollywood list, Hollywood Reporter, 2003, 40 under 40 list, Crain's N.Y. Bus., 2003; recipient Nat. Pub. Svc. award, Television Acad. Emmy Awards, 2002, Namiq Qasar Vision award, 2003. Office: VH1 20th Fl 1515 Broadway New York NY 10036*

**NORMAN, COLIN ARTHUR,** astrophysics educator; b. Melbourne, Australia, May 3, 1948; came to U.S., 1984; s. Howard Arthur Norman and Jean Olice (Macgregor) Downing; m. Wen Shen, June 2, 1988; children: Alexandra Jean, Arthur Shen, Victoria Amelia. BE with honours, U. Melbourne, 1969; DPhil, Oxford U., 1973. Rsch. fellow Magdalen Coll., Oxford U., England, 1973—77, U. Calif., Berkeley, 1975—77; asst. prof. U. Leiden, Netherlands, 1977—84; prof. physics and astronomy Johns Hopkins U., Balt., 1984—; head acad. affairs divsn. Space Telescope Sci. Inst. Johns Hopkins U., 1987—91, head Hubble fellow program, 1991—94. Sr. rsch. fellow Inst. Astronomy, Cambridge, Eng., 1981-84, European So. Obs., Munich, 1983-84, 2000-03; vis. prof. U. Paris, 1983; Sackler lectr. Cambridge, 1995, Astor lectr. Oxford U., 2002; prof. fellow U. Melbourne, 2002—; prin. investigator Hubble Origins Project, 2004-05; Minnaert prof. U. Utrecht, Netherlands, 2005; Blaauw Prof. Groningen U., 2006. Editor: Stellar Populations, 1987, Quasar Absorption Lines, 1988, Massive Stars and Star Formations, 1991; contbr. articles to astrophysics jours. Rhodes scholar, 1970-73; recipient Perelberg prize Scotch Coll., Melbourne, 2002. Fellow Royal Astron. Soc.; mem. Am. Phys. Soc., Am. Astron. Soc., Amnesty Internat., Greenpeace, Johns Hopkins Club, Hamilton St. Club. Office: Johns Hopkins U Dept Physics and Astronomy Baltimore MD 21218 Office Phone: 410-516-7329. Business E-Mail: norman@stsci.edu.

**NORMAN, DONALD ARTHUR,** psychologist, educator; b. NYC, Dec. 25, 1935; s. Noah N. and Miriam F. N.; m. Martha Karpati (dec.); children: Cynthia, Michael; m. Julie Jacobsen; 1 child, Eric. BSEE, MIT, 1957; MSEE, U. Pa., 1959, PhD in Psychology, 1962; degree in psychology (hon.), U. Padua, Italy, 1995; PhD in Indsl. Design (hon.), Tech. U. Delft, The Netherlands, 2006. Lectr. Harvard U., 1962-66; prof. dept. psychology U. Calif.-San Diego, La Jolla, 1966-92, prof. emeritus, 1992—, prof., chair dept. cognitive sci., 1988-92, chair dept. psychology, 1974-78; Apple fellow Apple Computer Inc., Cupertino, Calif., 1993-97, v.p. advanced tech., 1995-97; exec. info. appliances Hewlett Packard, Palo Alto, Calif., 1997-98; cofounder, prin. Nielsen Norman Group, Fremont, Calif., 1998—; pres. learning sys. UNext, 1999—2001; prof. departments elec. engring., computer sci., psychology and cognitive sci. Northwestern U., 2001—. Cons. to industry on human centered product design. Author: Human Information Processing, 2d edit., 1977, Learning and Memory, 1982, User Centered System Design, 1986, The Psychology of Everyday Things, 1988, The Design of Everyday Things, 1989, 2002, Turn Signals Are the Facial Expressions of Automobiles, 1992, Things That Make Us Smart, 1993, The Invisible Computer, 1998, Emotional Design, 2004; mem. editl. bd. Ency. Brit. Recipient Excellence in Rsch. award, U. Calif., 1983, Benjamin Franklin medal in Computer and Cognitive Sci., Franklin Inst., 2006. Fellow: APA, Am. Psychol. Soc. (charter fellow, Franklin V. Taylor award 2005), Assn. Computing Machines (Lifetime Achievement award (Human-Computer Interaction Group)), Cognitive Sci. Soc. (chmn., founding mem.), Human Factors and Ergonomics Soc., Am. Acad. Arts and Scis.; mem.: Inst. Design, IIT Chicago (trustee), Sigma Xi. E-mail: norman@nngroup.com.

**NORMAN, E. GLADYS,** retired finance educator, management consultant; b. Oklahoma City, June 13, 1933; d. Joseph Eldon and Mildred Lou (Truitt) Biggs; m. Joseph R.R. Radeck, Mar. 1, 1953 (div. Aug. 1962); children: Jody Norman, Ray Norman, Warren Norman (dec. May 1993), Dana Norman; m. Leslie P. Norman, Aug. 26, 1963 (dec. Feb. 1994); 1 child, Elayne Pearce. Student, Fresno (Calif.) State Coll., 1951-52, UCLA, 1956-59, Linfield Coll., 1986-95. Lic. tax preparer Calif., 2005. Math. aid U.S. Naval Weapons Ctr., China Lake, Calif., 1952-56, computing systems specialist, 1957-68; systems programmer Oreg. Motor Vehicles Dept., Salem, 1968-69; instr. in data processing, dir. Computer Programming Ctr., Salem, 1969-72; instr. in data processing Merritt-Davis Bus. Coll., Salem, 1972-73; sr. programmer, analyst Teledyne Wah Chang, Albany, Oreg., 1973-79; sr. systems analyst Oreg. Dept. Vets. Affairs, Albany, 1979-80; instr. in bus. computers Linn-Benton C.C., Albany, 1980-95; ret., 1995. Computer cons. for LBCC Ret. Sr. Vol. Program, 1995-2002; presenter computer software seminars State of Oreg., 1991-93, Oreg. Credit Assoc. Conf., 1991, Oreg. Regional Users Group Conf., 1992; computer tchr. Linn-Benton C.C., 1999-2001; computer cons. Oremet-Wah Chang, 1996-2002, Oreg. State Yr. 2000 Project, 1997-98; adj. prof. Chemeketa C.C., 2000-02; computer cons. in field. Mem.: Assn. Info. Tech. Profls. (bd. dirs. 1977—84, assoc. v.p. 1988, bd. dirs. 1989—95, region sec. 1995—96, region treas. 1999, region sec. 2000—04, 2002—04, region treas. 2005, Diamond Individual Performance award 1985). Democrat. Avocations: drawing, painting, gardening.

**NORMAN, GREGORY JOHN,** professional golfer; b. Mt. Isa, Australia, Feb. 10, 1955; m. Laura Norman, July 1, 1981; children: Morgan-Leigh, Gregory. Profl. golfer, 1976—; chmn., CEO Gt. White Shark Enterprises Inc., Hobe Sound, Fla. Winner Brit. Open Championship, 1986, 93, 20 PGA Tour titles, 68 additional internat. titles; winner Vardon trophy, 1989, 90, 95; recipient Arnold Palmer award for leading money winner, 1995, Byron Nelson trophy for the lowest scoring average, 1995; ranked #1 in World Golf Ranking for 331 Weeks; named PGA Player of Yr., 1995, PGA Tour Player of Yr., 1995; named to World Golf Hall of Fame, 2001. Achievements include being the leading Money Winner PGA Tour 1986, 90. Office Phone: 561-743-8818.

**NORMAN, JESSYE,** soprano; b. Augusta, Ga., Sept. 15, 1945; d. Silas St. and Janie (King) N. B.M. cum laude, Howard U., 1967; postgrad., Peabody Conservatory, 1967; M.Mus., U. Mich., 1968; MusD (hon.), U. South, 1984, Boston Conservatory, 1984, U. Mich., 1987, U. Edinburgh, 1989, Cambridge U., 1989. Debut, Deutsche Oper, Berlin, 1969, Italy, 1970; appeared: in operas Die Walküre, Idomeneo, L'Africaine, Marriage of Figaro, Aida, Don Giovanni, Tannhauser, Gotterdammerung, Ariadne auf Naxos, Les Troyens, Dido and Aeneas, Oedipus Rex, Herodiade, Les Contes d'Hoffmann; debut in operas, La Scala, Milan, Italy, 1972, Salzburg Festival, 1977, U.S. debut, Hollywood Bowl, 1972, appeared with, Tanglewood Festival, Mass., also Edinburgh (Scotland) Festival, debut, Covent Garden, 1972; appeared in 1st Great Performers recital, Lincoln Center, N.Y.C., 1973—; other guest performances include, L.A. Philharm. Orch., Boston Symphony Orch., Am. Symphony Orch., Chgo. Symphony Orch., San Francisco Symphony Orch., Cleve. Orch., Detroit Symphony, N.Y. Philharm. Orch., London Symphony Orch., London Philharm. Orch., BBC Orch., Israel Philharm. Orch., Orchestre de Paris, Nat. Symphony Orch., English Chamber Orch., Royal Philharm., London Phila. Orch., Milw. Symphony Orch., Stockholm Philharm. Orch., Vienna Philharm. Orch., Berlin Philharm. Orch.; tours, Europe, S. Am., Australia, numerous recs., Columbia, EMI, Philips Records; PBS TV spcls. include Kathleen Battle and Jessye Norman Sing Spirituals, 1991, Concert at Avery Fisher Hall, 1994; recordings include Amazing Grace, Brava, Jessye!, Jessye Norman at Notre Dame (Cable Ace award), Lucky to Be Me, Sacred Songs, With a Song in My Heart, In The Spirit. Nat. spokesperson Partnership for the Homeless, Lupus Found.; bd. mem. Ms. Found., Nat. Music Found., City-Meals-on-Wheels, N.Y.C., N.Y. Bot. Garden, Paine Coll., Augusta, Ga. Recipient 1st prize Bavarian Radio Corp. Internat. Music Competition, 1968, Grand Prix du Disque, Acad. du Disque Francais, 1973, 76, 77, 82, 84, Deutsche Schallplatten, Preis, 1975, 81, Alumni award U. Mich., 1982, Outstanding Musician of Yr. award Musical Am., 1982, Grand Prix du Disque Academie Charles Cros, 1973, Commandeur de l'Ordre des Arts et des Lettres, France, 1984, Grammy awards, 1980, 82, 85, Legion d'Honneur, France, 1989, Radcliffe medal Radcliffe Coll. Alumnae Assn., 1997, numerous other awards; named hon. life mem. Girl Scouts U.S., 1987; inductee Am. Classical Music Hall of Fame, 2002. Mem. Royal Acad. Music (hon.), Alpha Kappa Alpha, Gamma Sigma Sigma, Sigma Alpha Iota, Pi Kappa Lambda. Clubs: Friday Morning Music (Washington). Office: L'Orchidee PO Box S Crugers NY 10521-0710

**NORMAN, JOHN BARSTOW, JR.,** graphics designer, educator; b. Paola, Kans., Feb. 5, 1940; s. John B. and Ruby Maxine (Johnson) N.; m. Roberta Jeanne Martin, June 6, 1967; children: John Barstow III, Elizabeth Jeanne. BFA, U. Kans., 1962, MFA, 1966. Designer and illustrator Advt. Design, Kansas City, Mo., 1962-64; asst. instr. U. Kans., Lawrence, 1964-66; art dir. Hallmark Cards, Inc., Kansas City, 1966-69; instr. dept. art U. Denver,

1969-73, asst. prof., 1973-78, assoc. prof., 1978-93, disting. prof., 1980-93, prof. emeritus, 1993—; sr. designer Mo. Coun. Arts & Humanities, 1966-67; cons. designer Rocky Mt. Bank Note Corp., Denver, 1971—. Cons. designer Signage identity System, U. Denver; bd. dirs. comm. U. Denver; tech. cons. Denver Art Mus., 1974—, designed exhbns, 1974-75; adv. cons. Jefferson County (Colo.) Sch. System, 1976—; chmn. Design and Sculpture Exhn., Colo. Celebration of the Arts, 1975-76. One-man shows include GalleryCortina, Aspen, Colo., 1983; commd. works include Jedda, Saudi Arabia, Synegistics Corp., Denver; represented in permanent collections Pasadena Ctr. for Arts, N.Y. Arts Dirs. Club, Calif. State U./Fiber Collection, Pasadena Ctr. Arts, N.Y. Art Dirs. Club, Midland Art Coun./Fiber Collection, Geologic Soc. Am.; represented in traveling exhbns. L.A. Art Dirs. Show and N.Y. Art Dirs. Show, U.S., Europe, Japan, 1985; featured in Denver Post, 1984, Post Electric City Mag., 1984, Rocky Mt. News, 1984, Douglas County Press, 1984, Mile High Cable Vision, 1985, Sta. KWGN-TV, 1985, Les Krantz's Am. Artists, 1988; illustrated Survey of Leading Contemporaries, 1988, U.S. Surface Design Jour., 1988; co-work represented in film collectin Mus. Modern Art, N.Y.C.; selected fashion show designs displayed Sister City dels., Denver, 1987. Recipient Silver medal award N.Y. Internat. Film and Video Competition, 1976, Design awards Coun. ADvancement and Support Edn., 1969, 71, 73, 76, Honor Mention award L.A. Art Dirs. Club, 1984, Honor Mention award N.Y. ARt Dirs. Club, 1984, Native Am. Wearable Art Competition, 1985, 5th pl. Nat. Wind Sail Am. Banners Competition, Midland, Mich., 1985, also awards for surface designs in Colo. Ctr. for Arts Wearable ARt Competition, 1984-85, Foothills Art Gallery Nat. Wearable Competition, 1984-85, Fashion Group Denver Competition, 1984-85. Mem. Art Dirs. Club Denver (Gold medals 1974-82, Best of Show Gold medal 1983, Honor Mention award 1984, 3 gold medals 1989), Univ. Dirs. Assn. Home: PO Box 507 Lake George CO 80827-0507 Office Phone: 719-339-1751. Personal E-mail: normanranch@earthlink.net.

**NORMAN, JOHN EDWARD**, petroleum landman; b. Denver, May 22, 1922; s. John Edward and Ella (Warren) Norman; m. Hope Sabin, Sept. 5, 1946; children: J. Thomas, Gerould W., Nancy E., Susan G., Douglas E. BSBA, U. Denver, 1949, MBA, 1972. Clk., bookkeeper Capitol Life Ins. Co., Denver, 1940—42, 1945—46; salesman Security Life and Accident Co., Denver, 1947; bookkeeper Ctrl. Bank and Trust Co., Denver, 1947—50; automobile salesman H.A. Hennies, Denver, 1950; petroleum landman Continental Oil Co. (name changed to Conoco Inc. 1979), Denver, 1950—85; ind. petroleum landman, 1985; ind. investor, 1985—. Lectr. pub. lands Colo. Sch. Mines, 1968—85; lectr. mineral titles and landmen's role in oil industry Casper Coll., 1969—71. Mem. Casper Mcpl. Band Commn., 1965—71, mem. band, 1961—71, mgr., 1968—71; former musician, bd. dirs. Casper Civic Symphony; former bd. dirs. Jefferson Symphony, performing mem., 1972—75; mem. choir, vestryman, past dir. acolytes Episc. Ch. Served U.S. Army, World War II. Mem.: Rocky Mountain Petroleum Pioneers, Rocky Mountain Oil and Gas Assn. (pub. lands com. 1981—85), Denver Assn. Petroleum Landmen, Wyo. Assn. Petroleum Landmen (pres.), Assn. Petroleum Landmen (dir. at large, chmn. publs. for regional dir.), Elks. Episcopalian. Home and Office: 2710 S Jay St Denver CO 80227-3856

**NORMAN, MARY MARSHALL**, academic administrator, alcohol/drug abuse services professional, educator; b. Auburn, NY, Jan. 10, 1937; d. Anthony John and Zita Norman. BS cum laude, LeMoyne Coll., 1958; MA, Marquette U., 1960; EdD, Pa. State U., 1971. Cert. alcoholism counselor. Tchr. St. Cecilia's Elem. Sch., Theinsville, Wis., 1959-60; vocat. counselor Marquette U., Milw., 1959-60; dir. testing and counseling U. Rochester (N.Y.), NY, 1960-62; dir. testing and counseling, dean women, assoc. dean coll. Corning (N.Y.) C.C., Corning (N.Y.) C.C., 1962-68, asst. dean students, dir. student activities, asst. prof. ps University Park, 1962-68; rsch. asst. Ctr. for Study Higher Edn. Pa. State U., University Park, Pa., 1969-71; dean faculty South Campus C.C. Allegheny County, West Mifflin, Pa., 1971-72, campus pres., coll. v.p., 1972-82; pres. Orange County C.C., 1982-86; alcohol counselor Sullivan County Alcohol Drug Abuse Svc., 1985-90; sr. counselor Horton Family Program, 1990-96, ednl. cons., writer, 1996—. Cons. Boricua Coll., N.Y.C., 1976-77; reader NSF, 1977-78; govtl. comm. Am. Assn. Cmty. and Jr. Colls., 1976-79, bd. dirs., 1982—; chmn. middle state accreditation teams; chmn. Ernest Boyer, pres. Carnegie Found., 1987. Contbr. articles to profl. jours. Active Econ. Devel. Seneca County, Seneca County Tourism Bd.; com. to redefine the Liberal Arts degree Carnegie Found., 1982; mem. planning bd. Town of Seneca Falls, 2006—; active St. Patrick's Ch.; bd. dirs. Orange County United Way, Orange County Alcoholism and Drug Abuse Coun., 1993—96, Seneca County Hist. Soc., 1997—, Guild and Altar Soc., 1999. Mem. Nat. Women's Hall of Fame. Mem.: Pa. Coun. on Higher Edn., Nat. Am. Coun. on Edn. (Pa. rep. identification women for adminstrn. 1978—82, pres. 1980—96, bd. dirs.), Pitts. Coun. Women Execs. (charter), Pa. Assn. Acad. Deans, Pa. Assn. Two-Yr. Colls., Am. Assn. Women in Cmty. and Jr. Colls. (charter, Woman of the Yr. 1981), Nat. Assn. Women Deans and Counselors, Am. Assn. Higher Edn., Seneca County S. of C. (bd. dirs., mem. tourism com.), Orange County C. of C. (bd. dirs.), Amnesty Internat. (charter mem. women's coun. 2000—), Concerned Citizens for Good Govt. (charter), Kiwanis (planning bd. Seneca Falls 2006), Gamma Pi Epsilon. Home: 9 S Park St Seneca Falls NY 13148-1423

**NORMAN, PHILIP SIDNEY**, physician; b. Pittsburg, Kans., Aug. 4, 1924; s. P. Sidney and Mildred A. (Lawyer) N.; m. Marion Birmingham, Apr. 15, 1955; children: Margaret Reynolds, Meredith Andrew, Helen Elizabeth. AB, Kans. State Coll., 1947; MD cum laude, Washington U., U. Kans., 1951. Intern Barnes Hosp., St. Louis, 1951-52; resident Vanderbilt U. Hosp., Nashville, 1952-54; fellow Rockefeller Inst., 1954-56; instr. medicine Johns Hopkins U. Sch. Medicine, Balt., 1956-59, asst. prof., 1959-64, assoc. prof., 1964-75, prof., 1975—, chief allergy and immunology div., 1971-91. Editor Jour. of Allergy and Clin. Immunology, 1993-98; contbr. chpt. to books, articles to profl. jours. Served with USAAF, 1943-46; Served with USPHS, 1954-56. Fellow Am. Acad. Allergy (pres. 1975); mem. Am. Fedn. Clin. Research, Am. Assn. Immunologists, Am. Soc. Clin. Investigation, Am. Assn. Physicians, N.Y. Acad. Scis., Soc. Exptl. Biology and Medicine, Am. Thoracic Soc., Am. Clin. and Climatol. Assn., Johns Hopkins Med. Soc., Alpha Omega Alpha. Episcopalian. Office: Johns Hopkins U Asthma and Allergy Ctr 5501 Hopkins Bayview Cir Baltimore MD 21224-6821 Office Phone: 410-550-2300. Business E-Mail: pnorman@jhmi.edu.

**NORMAN, PHYLLIS B.**, volunteer; b. Chgo., Oct. 25, 1924; d. Philip James and Rosemary Benzel Line; m. Lester Ralph Norman, Sept. 8, 1945 (dec. July 2005); children: Elizabeth Anne, Lester Ralph Jr., Mary Sue. With Electrical Rsch. Lab., Evanston, Ill.; film reader, electron microscopist, data analyst, radioactive chemistry technician Los Alamos Sci. Lab., Los Alamos. Cadet nurse in WWII, Hammond, Ind.; adv. bd. Palo Duro Sr. Ctr.; vol. Mem.: DAR (hon. state regent 1999—2001, state chaplain, pres. state officers club, regent Valle Grande chpt., state conservation chmn. 1993—95, state organizing sec. 1991—93, state 2d vice regent 1995—97, state vice regent 1997—99, state regent 1999—2001, nat. vice chmn. S.W. dist. for chpt. achievement awards 1998—99, treas. vice regents club 1998—99, mem. state regents club, fifty yr. club, heritage club, nat. officer club), Los Alamos Hist. Soc. (past pres.), Arlington Heights Hist. Soc. (life), Order of Eastern Star (grand rep.), Los Alamos Garden Club (past pres.). Republican. Methodist. Home: 5007 Kokopelli Dr NE Rio Rancho NM 87144-0549

**NORMAN, RALPH LOUIS**, retired physicist, consultant; b. Kingston, Tenn., Mar. 25, 1933; s. Walter Hugh and Helen Irene (Smith) N.; m. Agnes Irene Pickel, Sept. 5, 1964; children: Mark Alan, Max Alvin. BS, U. Tenn., 1959; LL.B., Blackstone Sch. Law, 1967, JD, 1971; certificate, Indsl. Coll. Armed Forces, 1969; MA in Pub. Adminstrn, U. Okla., 1971; D.Sci. (hon.), Apollo Research Inst., 1976. Engr. Chrysler Corp. Missile Div., Huntsville, Ala., 1959-60; physicist Army Rocket & Guided Missile Agy., Redstone Arsenal, Ala., 1960-61; asst. project mgr. Army Missile Command, Redstone Arsenal, 1961-62, project mgr., 1962-89, ret., 1989; cons. to several def. contractors, 1989—; faculty Athens (Ala.) Coll., 1970-71, Calhoun Jr. Coll., Decatur, Ala., 1971-74, 85-90, U. Montevallo, Ala., 1973-74, U. Ala. at Huntsville, 1976-77, Columbia (Mo.) Coll., 1977-79. Cons. firm Bishop and

Sexton, 1973—, Athens (Ala.) State Coll.; reviewer NSF, 1974-76; FAA examiner. Contbr. articles profl. jours. Served with USN, 1951-55. Recipient Dept. Def. commendations, 1961, 65, Dept. Army commendation, 1972 Mem. N.Y. Acad. Scis., Assn. U.S. Army. Home: 102 Nobleton Ln NW Huntsville AL 35806-4014 *I strive to make the knowledge gained through my research benefit all mankind.*

**NORMAN, ROBERT ANDREW**, dermatologist, educator; s. Laurence and Estelle Norman; m. Carol Norman; children: Daniel, Benjamin; 1 child, Fionna Lillian. DO, Midwestern U., Chgo.; MPH, U. South Fla., Tampa. Cert. Am. Bd. Family Practice, Am. Bd. Dermatology. Physician Dermatology and Skin Cancer Ctrs. Fla., Tampa, 1982—; assoc. prof. medicine Nova Southeastern U., Ft. Lauderdale, Fla. Pres. Dermatology Healthcare, Tampa, 1994—. Editor, author The Woman Who Lost Her Skin (And Other Dermatological Tales), Geriatric Dermatology, Clinical Geriatrics; author: (book of poetry) Dermatopoetics, Tennis: Volleys of the Mind, Images of America: Tampa, Mastero, Medical Detective, A Doctor's Little Instruction Book, A Dermatologist's Little Instruction Book, To Life! Stories and Quotes for a Healthy, Happy and Spiritual Life, I Can't Wait Until Tomorrow: Stories, Essays, and Poems on Medicine, Baby Farm, Shootoff!; editor: Where Wisdom Shines; author: Limericks of Florida, Take Two Aspirin and See Yourself in the Morning, Next, Gaspar Returns, Mother Nature, Father Time, over 200 articles to profl. jours.; musician, composer (CD) Florida Blues, Renaissance Man. Vol. Gift For Tchg., Tampa, Gt. Am. Teach-In, Tampa, Am. Cancer Soc., Tampa; pres. Hillsborough County Osteo. Med. Soc., Tampa, Fla., Maimonides Soc., Tampa, 1998—2006; state dir. SCTP, Fla. Recipient multiple nat. writing awards, 1st prize creative non-fiction, Fla. Freelance Writers Assn., 2003, 1st prize stories for children, 2003; fellow, Mass. Arts Lottery, 1992. Mem.: Am. Acad. Dermatology (assoc.), Optimist Club (founding mem.-). Office: 8002 Gunn Hwy Tampa FL 33626 Office Phone: 813-880-7546.

**NORMAN, STEPHEN PECKHAM**, finance executive; b. Norwich, Conn., May 20, 1942; BA, Yale U., 1964; JD, U. Pa., 1967. Bar: Conn. 1967, N.Y. 1972. Corp. sec. Am. Express Co., N.Y.C., 1982—2003, corp. sec., chief governance officer, 2003—. Mem. Am. Soc. Corp. Secs. (past chmn.). Clubs: Am. Yacht (Rye). Republican. Episcopalian. Home: 6 Highland Park Pl Rye NY 10580-1736 Office: Am Express Co 200 Vesey St New York NY 10285 Office Phone: 212-640-5583. E-mail: stephen.p.norman@aexp.com.

**NORMAN, WILLIAM STANLEY**, travel and tourism executive; b. Roper, N.C., Apr. 27, 1938; s. James Colbitt and Josephine Cleo (Woods) N.; m. Elizabeth Patricia Patterson, May 31, 1969; children: Lisa Renée, William Stanley II. BS, West Va. Wesleyan U., 1960; MA, Am. U., 1967; exec. program, Stanford U., 1976. Math. tchr. Washington High Sch., Norfolk, 1961; commd. USN, 1962; advanced through grades to capt., 1977; naval flight officer Airborne Early Warning Squadron Eleven, 1962-65; asst. combat info. ctr. officer U.S.S. Constellation, 1965; staff officer air weapons systems analysis Office Chief Naval Ops., Pentagon, Washington, 1965-66; history and fgn. affairs instr. U.S. Naval Acad., 1966-67; social aide The White House, 1967-69; carrier div. staff officer SE Asia, 1969-70; spl. asst. to Chief Naval Ops. for Minority Affairs, 1970-72; asst. to Chief Naval Ops. for Spl. Projects, 1972-73; dir. corp. action Cummins Engine Co. Inc., Columbus, Ind., 1973-74, exec. dir. corp. responsibility, 1974-76; exec. mktg. mgr., 1976-77; exec. dir. distbn. mktg. Cummins Engine Co. Inc., Columbus, Ind., 1977-78; v.p. eastern divsn., 1978-79; v.p. sales and mktg. Amtrak, Washington, 1979-81, group v.p., 1981-84, exec. v.p., 1984-94; pres., CEO Travel Industry Assn. of Am., Washington, 1994—2005. Bd. dirs. Corn Products Internat.; chmn. bd. Logistics Mgmt. Inst., McLean, Va., 1992—. Bd. dirs. USN Meml. Found., Washington, 1980—2003, Internat. Consortium on Health Effects of Radiation, 1993—2003, An-Bryce Found., 1993—; bd. overseers Hospitality Industry Hall of Honor and Archives, 1995—; trustee W.Va. Wesleyan Coll., Buckhannon, 1996—. Capt. USNR. Mem. Travel Industry Assn. Am. (bd. dirs. 1980—, chmn. bd. 1987-89, chmn. bd. dirs. of found. 1990-92), UN Assn. U.S. (bd. dirs. 1983—, bd. govs. 1985—), Coun. on Fgn. Rels., United Nations Assn. of U.S. (mem. nat. coun.). Democrat. Episcopalian. Avocations: golf, tennis, jogging, walking, bicycling. Home: 1308 Timberly Ln Mc Lean VA 22102-2504 also: 8244 Livorno Dr Orlando FL 32836-8756 Personal E-mail: wsnorman1@aol.com.

**NORMAN, WYATT THOMAS, III**, landman, consultant; b. Austin, Tex., Dec. 30, 1952; s. Wyatt Thomas Jr. and Frances Claire (Bliss) N. BS in Agronomy, Tex. A&M U., 1975. Cert. profl. landman, environ. site assessor. Mgr. farm and ranch Bennett Bros., Inc., Pearsall, Tex., 1975-78; landman Corpus Christi, Tex., 1978—; pres. Norman & Co. Inc., Corpus Christi, 2005—. Mem. Flour Bluff (Tex.) Vol. Fire Dept., 1984-90. Mem. Am. Assn. Profl. Landmen, Corpus Christi Assn. Profl. Landmen (v.p.), Assn. Former Students, Century Club, Padre Isles Property Owners Assn., Internat. Game Fish Assn., Corpus Christi Town Club, Single Action Shooting Soc., Coastal Conservation Assn., Tex. Riviera Pistoleros, Paloma de Arcabus Club (charter, treas.), Safari Club Internat. Republican. Presbyterian. Avocations: hunting, fishing, skiing. Home: 13946 Man O'War Ct Corpus Christi TX 78418-6340 Office: 615 Leopard St Ste 434 Corpus Christi TX 78476-2225 Personal E-mail: wtn111@aol.com.

**NORMAND, ROBERT**, retired lawyer; b. Montreal, Que., Can., Sept. 24, 1936; s. Lucien and Eva (Rochon) N.; m. Madeleine Scott, Sept. 16, 1961; children: Eric, Yves, Genevieve. BA, U. Montreal, 1956; LLL, U. Sherbrooke, Que., 1960; diploma, Inst. d'etudes politiques, Paris, 1962. Bar: Que. 1960. Legal advisor Nat. Assembly, Quebec City, 1962-67, law clk., 1967-71; asst. dep. min. justice Que. Govt., Quebec City, 1970-71, dep. min. justice, 1971-77, dep. min. intergovtl. affairs, 1977-82, dep. min., 1982-87; pres., pub. Le Soleil (Hollinger), Quebec City, 1987-93; v.p. corp. affairs UniMedia Inc., 1993-94, dep. min. internat. affairs, 1994-96; pres., dir. gen. Télé-Québec, 1996-99, ret., 1999. Que. Study Com. on Expropriation 1965-67; guest prof. legis. law faculty Laval U., Ottawa U., 1971; pres. Que. Police Inst., 1974; chmn. Com. Supervising Olympic Security, 1974-76; chmn. Uniform Law Conf. Can.; dir. Caisse de Dépot et Placement du Québec, 1982-87; v.p. Can. del. Diplomatic Conf. on travel contracts, Brussels, 1970; pres. Can. del. at convs. Internat. Inst. French Lang. law, 1974, 76. V.p. Hosp. du Saint-Sacrement, Quebec City, 1988-94; vice chmn. Inst. Rsch. on Pub. Policy, Montreal, 1988-94; pres. Que. Symphony Orch., Quebec City, 1989-92; consul gen. Sweden, Quebec City, 1989-94; co-pres. United Way Campaign Greater Quebec Region, 1989, hon. chmn. Telethon for Cerebral Palsy, 1990; mem. Citizens Forum, Spicer Commn., 1990-91; chmn. Ec. Nat. de l'Humour, 1997-99. Capt. Can. Army, 1954-60. Named Queen's Counsel, 1971, Comdr., Royal Order of the Polar Star, Sweden, Chevalier de la Legion d'honneur, France; recipient Pub. Adminstrn. award of excellence Nat. Sch. Pub. Adminstrn. Alumni, Quebec City, 1986. Mem. Investment Dealers Assn. Can. (dir. 1989-94), Que. Garrison Club (dir. 1991-96), Profl. Liability Ins. of Que. Bar (dir. 1991-94), Que. Bar (supervisory com. 1988-93), La Commanderie de Bordeaux. Roman Catholic. Avocations: fishing, hunting. Home: 2750 de L'Anse Sainte-Foy PQ Canada G1W 2G5 E-mail: robenorm@videotron.ca.

**NORMANDEAU, ANDRE GABRIEL**, criminologist, educator; b. Montreal, Que., Can., May 4, 1942; s. Gabriel E. and Laurette D. (Sauve) N.; m. Pierrette La Pointe, Aug. 14, 1965; children: Alain, Louis, Jean. MA in Criminology, U. Pa., Phila., 1965. PhD in Sociology, 1968. Asst. prof. criminology U. Montreal, 1968-71, assoc. prof., 1971-76, prof., 1976—, chmn. dept. criminology, 1970-80, dir. Internat. Ctr. Comparative Criminology, 1983-89, dir. Rsch. Inst. on Police, 1990—. Author: Public Attitudes and Crime, 1970, The Measurement of Crime, 1975, Patterns of Robbery, 1980, Crimes of Violence, 1985, A Vision of the Police, 1990, Crime Prevention, 1993, Justice and Minorities, 1995, Community Policing, 1998, Death Penalty, 2003, Terrorism, 2006. Woodrow Wilson fellow, 1964-68 Mem. Internat. Soc. Criminology, Am. Soc. Criminology, Am. Sociol. Assn., Can. Criminal Justice Assn. Roman Catholic. Home: 3150 Ave Kent Montreal PQ

Canada H3S 1N1 Office: Dept Criminology U Montreal Montreal PQ Canada H3C 3J7 Office Phone: 514-343-6111 ext 3999. Business E-Mail: andre.normandeau@umontreal.ca. *Happiness is achieved by working for it, not by waiting for it to come to you.*

**NORMANN, MARGARET ELLA**, deacon, educator; b. Providence, Jan. 13, 1931; d. Parker Edward and Margaret Millard (McDowell) Monroe; m. Conrad Neil Normann, July 17, 1953; children: Andrea Kristin Mudge, Margaret Ingrid Wierdsma, Conrad Neil, Parker Monroe. BA in Drama, Vassar Coll., 1952; MA in English, NYU, 1966; MS in Recreation and Leisure, So. Conn. State U., 1978. Ordained deacon Protestant Episcopal Ch. 1993. Human svc. officer, dir. recreation programs Town of Bedford, NY, 1975—83; cmty. edn. coord., writer Cmty. Residences Info. Svc. Program, White Plains, NY, 1983—91; initiator, exec. dir. Apropes Housing Opportunities and Mgmt. Enterprises, Inc., Bedford, 1985—93; deacon Ch. of the Holy Communion, Mahopac, NY, 1993—99; chaplain Four Winds Hosp., Cross River, NY, 1993—99. Writing instr., tutor, evaluator SUNY Empire State Coll., Hartsdale, NY, 1984—99. Recipient Disting. Svc. Alumnae award, Lincoln Sch., Providence, 1988, Cert. of Merit, State of N.Y., Albany, 1991, Mickey Leland Home for the Homeless award, 1991. Republican.

**NORMENT, ERIC STUART**, newspaper editor; b. Butler, Pa., July 26, 1956; s. Hillyer Gavin and Reva Lucille (Shepherd) N.; m. Ann Hobin, Aug. 22, 1987; children: Timothy Hobin, Peter John, Laura Mary, Daniel Hillyer. BA, U. Chgo., 1979; MS, Northwestern U., Evanston, Ill., 1980. Reporter Paddock Publs., Arlington Heights, Ill., 1980-83; asst. night editor Cape Cod Times, Hyannis, Mass., 1983; copy editor The Boston Herald, 1983-85, copy desk chief/news, 1985-87, features prodn. editor, 1987-88, asst. Sunday editor, 1988-94, Sunday editor, 1994—. Instr. journalism Northeastern U., Boston, 1984. Recipient Peter Lisagor Pub. Svc. award Chgo. Headline Club, 1981, Edn. Reporting award Ill. Press Assn., 1981. Office: 1 Herald St Boston MA 02118-2200 E-mail: enorment@bostonherald.com.

**NORQUIST, DAVID L.**, federal agency administrator; b. 1966; BA, MA, U. Mich., Georgetown U. Staff mem. appropriations com. US Ho. of Reps.; dep. under sec. for fin. mgmt., comptr. US Dept. Def., acting prin. under sec., comptr., dep. under sec. for budget and appropriations affairs, comptr.; CFO US Dept. Homeland Security, 2006—. Office: US Dept Homeland Security Seventh and D Streets SW Washington DC 20528 Office Phone: 202-401-4782. Office Fax: 202-772-9646.*

**NORQUIST, GROVER GLENN**, economist; b. Sharon, Pa., Oct. 19, 1956; s. Warren Elliott and Carol (Lutz) N. BA, Harvard Coll., 1978; MBA, Harvard U., 1981. Exec. dir. Nat. Taxpayers Union, Washington, 1978-79, Coll. Rep. Nat. Com., Washington, 1981-82, Ams. for Reagan Agenda, Washington, 1982-83; chief speechwriter U.S. C. of C., Washington, 1983-85; field dir. Citizens for Am., Washington, 1985; founder, pres. Ams. for Tax Reform, Washington, 1985—. Econs. advisor UNITA, Angola, 1985-88; mem. Small Bus. Survival Com., 1994. Author: Rock the House, 1995; polit. columnist Am. Spectator mag., 1992—. Speechwriter DuPont for Pres. Campaign, Washington, 1987; issues mgr. Bush for Pres. Campaign, Washington, 1988; lectr. Krieble Found., Albania, Romania, 1992; advisor Tory Party Scotland, 1989. Mem.: Am. Society Competitiveness (pres.), Am. Conservative Union (bd. dirs.), NRA (bd. dirs.). Office: Ams for Tax Reform Ste 200 1920 L St NW Washington DC 20036-5036*

**NORQUIST, JOHN OLAF**, former mayor; b. Princeton, N.J., Oct. 22, 1949; s. Ernest O. and Jeannette (Nelson) N.; m. Susan R. Mudd, Dec. 1986; children: Benjamin Edward, Katherine Elisabeth. Student, Augustana Coll., Rock Island, Ill., 1967-69; BS, U. Wis., 1971, MPA, 1988. Assemblyman Wis. State Assembly, Madison, 1974-82, co-chmn. state joint com. fin., 1980-81; mem. Wis. State Senate, 82-88, asst. majority leader, 1984-85, 87; mayor City of Milw., 1988—2004. Adj. assoc. prof. Sch. Arch. U. Wis., Marquette U. Author: The Wealth of Cities, 1998. Bd. dirs. Congress for the New Urbanism. Sgt. USAR, 1971-77. Mem. Wis. Alliance of Cities, Congress for New Urbanism (bd. dirs.). Democrat. Presbyterian. Avocation: map collecting.

**NORRBY, KLAS CARL VILHELM**, pathology educator; b. Shanghai, Jan. 8, 1937; s. Åke Vilhelm and Ingrid Maria (Wedblad) N.; m. Ulla Margareta Hjort, June 17, 1961; children: Katarina, Cecilia, Jacob. BSc, Uppsala (Sweden) U., 1957; MB, Göteborg (Sweden) U., 1959, MD, 1964, PhD, 1970. Asst. prof. pathology Göteborg U., 1967-71; sr. lectr. in pathology Linköping U., 1972-84, chmn. Inst. Med. Microbiology and Pathology, 1980-84; prof. pathology, regal chair Göteborg U., 1985—; vis. prof. in cell biology Harvard Med. Sch., Boston, 1989-90; chmn. Inst. Labor Medicine Sahlgrenska U. Hosp., Göteborg, 1997-2000. Author of over 200 articles to profl. jours. Sub.-lt. Royal Swedish Navy Med. Corps, 1972-86. Office: Sahlgrenska U Hosp Dept Pathology SE-41345 Göteborg Sweden

**NORRID, HENRY GAIL**, osteopathic physician and surgeon, researcher, educator, healthcare facility administrator; b. Amarillo, Tex., June 4, 1940; s. Henry Horatio and Johnnie Belle (Combs, Cummins) N.; m. Andreia Maybeth Hudson, Jan. 29, 1966 (dec. 1988); children: Joshua Andrew, Noah Adam; m. Cheryll Diane Payne, Mar. 19, 1989 (div. Aug. 2000); stepchildren: Kim Sheri Payne, Matthew Dominic Payne; m. Carolyn A. Layton, June 8, 2002; stepchildren: Crissey Ann Elizabeth Bruce, David Randall Marshall Bruce. AA, Amarillo Coll., 1963; BA, U. Tex., 1966; MS, W. Tex. State U., 1967; DO, Kirksville Coll., 1973. Diplomate Bd. Osteo. Physicians and Surgeons, Nat. Bd. Examiners Osteo. Physicians and Surgeons; cert. basic sci. tchr. Iowa, Tex., Colo. Intern Interboro Gen. Hosp., Bklyn., 1973-74; attending physician dept. gen. practice Osteo. Hosp. and Clinic N.Y., N.Y.C., 1974-77; gen. practice medicine specializing in osteo. Amarillo, Tex., 1978—; emergency care physician Amarillo Emergency Receiving Ctr. Amarillo Hosp. Dist., 1978-79, Ready Care Emergency Ctr., Arlington and Bedford, Tex., 1990-92, St. Anthony Hosp., Amarillo, 1992. Emeritus mem. consulting staff physician dept. family practice Northwest Tex. Hosp., Amarillo, 1995; emergency/trauma physician Tex. EM Care, 1995—; mem. mass casualty nat. disaster response team ARC, 1995; contract staff physician Tex. Tech. Univ. Sch. Medicine and Health Scis. Ctr., med. dept. and infirmary Tex. Dept. Corrections, Dir. Dept. Criminal Justice, 1992-94; med. cons. rehab. medicine vocat rehab. divsn. Tex. Rehab. Commn., Plano, 1992-94; cattleman, ranch owner, Van Zandt County, Tex.; lectr. osteo. prins. and practice, The Osteo. Hosp. and Clinic N.Y., 1974-77, mem. credentials com., 1975-76; mem. exec. com. Southwest Osteo. Hosp., Amarillo, 1983-84, chief of staff, 1984-85; mem. dept. family practice Northwest Tex. Hosp., Amarillo, 1981-82, mem. credentials com., 1984-85, joint practice com. dept. family practice, 1986-87; mem. orgnl. com. for devel. of dept. osteo. prins. and practices, chmn. N.Y.C. group N.Y. Coll. Osteo. Med., 1977; mem. founding com. N.Y. Coll. Osteo. Medicine, N.Y. Inst. Tech., Old Westbury L.I., 1976-77; mem. North Tex. Support Group, Dallas; instr. human anatomy and physiology dept. biol. scis. Amarillo Coll., 1998-2001, fall 2003. Contbr. articles to Tex. Jour. Sci., other publs. Scout physician Llano Estecado coun. Boy Scouts Am., Tex., 1978-85; vol. physician Hurricane Katrina, 2005; active Polk St. Meth. Ch., Amarillo. Served to E-4 U.S. Army, 1956-63. Recipient William M. Giltner Meml. Fund award 1972, Humanitarian award Am. Cath. Conf., 1979, Century award Boy Scouts Am., 1982, Pfizer Sr. Med. Student award, 1973; Maxwell D. Warmer Meml. scholar 1973; scholar Kirksville Coll. Osteo. Medicine, 1970; Tex. Legislature scholar, 1969-73; named to Eminent Soc. Border Legionaires, 11th Armored Cavalry Regiment, Germany, 1958. Mem. Am. Coll. Gen. Practitioners, Tex. Osteo. Med. Assn. (pres. dist. I, mem. ho. of dels. 1981-82, 95), Tex. C.C. Tchrs. Assn., SAR, The Sons of Republic of Tex., Am. Osteo. Assn., World Future Soc. (profl.), Gen. Soc. War of 1812, N.Y. Acad. Scis., Ex-Student's Assn. of The Univ. Tex. (life), 11th Armored Cavalry Regiment Assn., 36th (Tex.) Inf. Divsn. Assn. (life), Baron of the Magna Charta (Somerset chpt. Magna Charta Barrons 1994—), Masons, Am. Legion, Beta Beta Beta, Sigma Sigma Phi (pres. 1972), Alpha Phi Omega, Psi Sigma Alpha, Theta Psi, Theta Psi Clowns (1969-73). Avocations: astronomy, short wave listening, camping, fishing, anthropology.

**NORRIS, ALAN EUGENE,** federal judge; b. Columbus, Ohio, Aug. 15, 1935; s. J. Russell and Dorothy A. (Shrader) N.; m. Nancy Jean Myers, Apr. 15, 1962 (dec. Jan. 1986); children: Tom Edward Jackson, Tracy Elaine; m. Carol Lynn Spohn, Nov. 10, 1990. BA, Otterbein Coll., 1957, HLD (hon.), 1991; cert., U. Paris, 1956; LLB, NYU, 1960; LLM, U. Va., 1986; HLD (hon.), Capital U. Law Sch., 2001. Bar: Ohio 1960, U.S. Dist. Ct. (so. dist) Ohio 1962, U.S. Dist. Ct. (no. dist) Ohio 1964. Law clk. to judge Ohio Supreme Ct., Columbus, 1960-61; assoc. Vorys, Sater, Seymour & Pease, Columbus, 1961-62; ptnr. Metz, Bailey, Norris & Spicer, Westerville, Ohio, 1962-80; judge Ohio Ct. Appeals (10th dist.), Columbus, 1981-86, U.S. Ct. Appeals (6th cir.), Columbus, 1986—. Contbr. articles to profl. jours. Mem. Ohio Ho. of Reps., Columbus, 1967—80. Named Outstanding Young Man, Westerville Jaycees, 1971; recipient Legislator of Yr. award Ohio Acad. Trial Lawyers, Columbus, 1972. Mem. Ohio Bar Assn., Columbus Bar Assn. Lodges: Masons (master 1966-67). Republican. Methodist. Office: US Ct Appeals 328 US Courthouse 85 Marconi Blvd Columbus OH 43215-2823*

**NORRIS, ALBERT STANLEY,** psychiatrist, educator; b. Sudbury, Ont., Can., July 14, 1926; s. William and Mary (Zell) N.; m. Dorothy James, Sept. 2, 1950; children: Barbara Ellen, Robert Edward, Kimberly Ann. MD, U. Western Ont., 1951. Intern Ottawa (Ont.) Civic Hosp., 1951-52; resident in psychiatry U. Iowa, Psychopathic Hosp., Iowa City, 1953-55, Boston City Hosp., 1955-56; practice medicine Kingston, Ont., Canada, 1956-57; instr. Queen's U., Kingston, 1956-57; asst. prof. psychiatry U. Iowa, 1957-62, asso. prof., 1962-64, 1965-66, prof., 1966-72; asso. prof. U. Oreg., 1964-65; prof. So. Ill. U. Sch. Medicine, Springfield, 1972-84; chmn. dept. psychiatry, 1972-82; prof. emeritus, 1984—; practice medicine specializing in psychiatry Cedar Rapids, Iowa, 1984—. Vis. prof. U. Auckland, N.Z., U. Otago, New Zealand, U. Liverpool. Contbr. chpts. to books, articles to med. jours. Fellow Am. Psychiat. Soc. (life); mem. AMA, Am. Psychopath. Assn., Soc. Biol. Psychiatry, Can. Psychiat. Soc., Am. Soc. Psychoanalytic Ob-Gyn, Royal Soc. Medicine. Republican. Presbyterian. Home: 5 Penfro Dr Iowa City IA 52246-4927 Office: PO Box 1408 Cedar Rapids IA 52406-1408 Personal E-mail: asnorris@msn.com. *A life is only fulfilled by a quest, a vision of the future and a commitment to a greater value than one's self. A flickering candle is poor light, unless there is no other.*

**NORRIS, BLANCHE LEE,** business consultant, educator; b. Washington, Dec. 30, 1958; d. Arthur Norman and Helen (Calos) Lee; m. Barry L. Norris, June 8, 1991. BA magna cum laude, No. Ill. U., 1982; MEd, U. Ill., 2002. Behavior counselor Nutri/Systems, Aurora, Ill., 1983-84, ctr. mgr., 1984-87, area mgr., 1987-89; employment and tng. officer KDK Tng., Employment and Bus. Svc., Geneva, Ill., 1989-91; seminar leader Bus. and Profl. Inst. Coll. of DuPage, Glen Ellyn, Ill., 1989-97; seminar leader Joliet (Ill.) Jr. Coll., 1997—2000. Seminar leader, Waubonsee Cmty. Coll., Sugar Grove, Ill, 2000—. Sponsor Compassion, Colorado Springs, 1989—. Avocations: international travel, wellness, nutrition. Home: 44W-36 Hazelcrest Dr Sugar Grove IL 60554 Personal E-mail: blannorr@aol.com.

**NORRIS, CAROL BROOKS,** retired librarian; b. Porterdale, Ga., Dec. 22, 1943; d. James P. and Georgia E. (Queen) Brooks; m. Frederick W. Norris, Aug. 30, 1963; children: Lisa C., Mark F. Student, Milligan Coll., Tenn., 1961—63; BA, Phillips U., Enid, Okla., 1965; MLS, U. Md., College Park, 1982; postgrad., East Tenn. State U., Johnson City, 1978—80, postgrad., 1991, U. Tenn., Knoxville, 1988, postgrad., 1990. Caseworker Dept. Child Welfare, Enid, 1966-67; homebound tchr. New Haven (Conn.) Pub. Schs., 1967-70; English tchr. Putnam (Okla.) High Sch., 1965-66, U.S. Army, Boeblingen, Germany, 1975-77, Cen. Tex. State Coll., 1977; tchr. adult basic edn. Johnson City (Tenn.) Schs., 1977-79; systems analyst East Tenn. State U., Johnson City, 1980-82, libr., assoc. prof., 1982—2006; ret., 2006. Mem. tchr. edn. adv. coun. East Tenn. State U., 1989—92, mem. univ. coun., 1989—91, mem. faculty senate, 1985—88, sec. senate, 1986—87, mem. women's studies steering com., 1993—2001, writing com., rsch. devel. com., 1993—96, common. women, 2001—, chmn. commn. women, 2003—04, co-chair campus ALA/NCM exhibit, 2004—05. Author: (with others) Library Hi Tech Bibliography, 1987, 90, Read More About It, 1989, Notable Women in the Life Sciences, 1996, Tennessee Landscape, People and Places, 1996, Notable Women in the Physical Sciences, 1997; editorial advisor Nat. Forum jour., 1981-86; contbr. articles to profl. jours. Mem.: ALA (campus co-chmn. com. exhibit Changing the Face of Medicine 2004—05), Kappa Delta Pi, Phi Kappa Phi, Boone Tree Libr. Assn. (v.p. 1986—88), East Tenn. Online Users Group (v.p. 1983—84, pres. 1984—85), Tenn. Libr. Assn. (sec. 1982—83), Delta Kappa Gamma. Democrat. Mem. Christian Ch. Avocations: reading, writing, travel, photography. Office: East Tenn State U 70665 Johnson City TN 37614

**NORRIS, CHARLES DONALD,** chemistry professor; b. San Antonio, Aug. 20, 1966; m. Kara Marie Lehman, July 29, 2000. BS, U. S. Fla., Tampa, 1988, MS, 1991, PhD, 1995. CEE dept. sci. rsch. mgr U. Ctrl. Fla., Orlando, 2000—. Adj. prof. chemistry Valencia CC, Orlando, Fla., 2004—. Deacon, small groups dir. E. Orlando Bapt. Ch., Fla., 2004—06. Fellow, U. Ctrl. Fla., 1995—2000; scholar, U. Miami, 1984—85; Provost's scholar, U. S. Fla., 1988. Mem.: Am. Chem. Soc., Sigma Xi (assoc. Grant in Aid of Rsch. 1992-1993). R-Conservative. Baptist. Avocation: herpetology. Home: 12708 Reverend Hobson Ct Orlando FL 32828 Office: CEE Dept Univ Ctrl Fla 4000 Central Florida Blvd Orlando FL 32816 Office Phone: 407-823-5092. Office Fax: 407-823-3315. Business E-mail: cdnorris@mail.ucf.edu.

**NORRIS, CHARLES HEAD,** lawyer, manufacturing executive; b. Boston, Sept. 14, 1940; s. Charles Head and Martha Marie N.; m. Diana D. Strawbridge, July 27, 1974 (div. 1994); children: Margaret Dorrance, Cecilia Walker; m. Ceil T. Walker, Oct. 13, 2001. BA, U. Pa., 1963; JD, 1968; MA, U. Wash., 1965. Mem. Morgan, Lewis & Bockius, Phila., 1968-77; pres., chief exec. Artemis Corp., 1978-79; chmn. bd., chief exec., 1979-91; chmn. exec. com., vice-chmn. bd. Remington Rand Corp., 1979-81; ptnr. Artemis Energy Co., 1980-92; chmn., CEO Norris Investment Co., 1992—. Chmn. Norris Mfg. Co., 1994—. Garret Precision Products, 1996—; chmn., CEO AmTech Engring. Co., 1996—; trustee maj. stockholders' voting trust Campbell Soup Co., 1987-90; bd. dirs. SBSF Funds, Inc., 1988-91, Del. Trust, 1987-91. Mem. Harvard U. Overseas Com. to Visit Libr., 1989—; mem. Pa. Commn. to Crime and Delinquency, 1980-84; mem. Thouron Award Selection Com., 1985-90; mem. Pa. Electoral Coll., 1980; mem. West Pikeland Twp. Suprs., 1969-72; mem. bd. visitors Carnegie Mellon U. Sch. Urban and Pub. Affairs, 1988-90; corp. mem. Belmont Hill Sch., 1990—. Served with USAF, 1960. Mem. ABA, Pa. Bar Assn., Am. Econ. Assn., Phila., Knickerbocker, Vicmead Hunt, Everglades (bd. dirs. 1986-91), Bath and Tennis Club (treas., bd. dirs. 1985-91), Sunningdale Golf Club, The Brookline (Mass.) Country Club, Coral Beach and Tennis Club, Mid Ocean Club, Rolling Rock Club. Office: PO Box 772719 Memphis TN 38177-2719 Address: Clark Tower 5100 Poplar Ave Ste 2700 Memphis TN 38137 Office Phone: 973-808-4905. Business E-mail: bfoust@amtechengineering.com.

**NORRIS, CHARLES RICHARD, JR.,** physician, psychiatrist; b. Danville, Ill., Jan. 6, 1949; s. Charles Richard and Elenor Joy (Bailey) Norris; m. Francesca Emanuele Norris, May 18, 1979; children: Charles III, Jacqueline L. BS in Chemistry, Bates Coll., Lewiston, Maine; MD, U. Vt., Burlington. Internship Albany Med. Sch., NY, 1975—76; residency Inst. of Living, Hartford, Conn., 1976—79; dir. Horizon Hosp., Clearwater, Fla., 1981—82; dir. outpatient svcs. Inst. of Living, Hartford, Conn., 1983—85, dir. ambulatory svcs., 1985—86; dir. addiction treatment Fair Oaks Hosp., Delray Beach, Fla., 1986—91; dir. MetLife Health Care. Miami, Fla., 1991—95; pvt. practice Boca Raton, Fla., 1996—. Cons. in field. Author: Family Addiction and Surviving Drug Abuse, 1990; contbr. articles pub. to profl. jour., chapters to books. Fellow: APA; mem.: AMA, Fla. Psychiat. Assn. Avocation: skiing. Office: 7301a W Palmetto Pk Rd, Ste 106C Boca Raton FL 33433 Office Phone: 561-482-7850.

**NORRIS, CHUCK (CARLOS RAY),** actor; b. Ryan, Okla., Mar. 10, 1940; s. Ray and Wilma Norris; m. Dianne Holochek, Dec., 1958 (div. 1988); children: Mike, Dina, Eric; m. Gena O. Kelly, Nov. 28, 1998; children:

Dakota Alan, Danilee; stepchildren: Kelley, Tim. Film appearances include The Wrecking Crew, 1969, Return of the Dragon, 1972, The Student Teachers, 1973, Slaughter in San Francisco, 1974, Breaker!, Breaker!, 1977, Good Guys Wear Black, 1978, Force of One, 1979, The Octagon, 1980, An Eye for an Eye, 1981, Silent Rage, 1982, Forced Vengeance, 1982, Lone Wolf McQuade, 1983, Missing in Action, 1984, Missing in Action II:The Beginning, 1985, Code of Silence, 1985, Delta Force, 1986, Firewalker, 1986, Hero and the Terror, 1988, Delta Force 2: Operation Stranglehold, 1990, The Hitman, 1991, Hellbound, 1994, Top Dog, 1995, Forrest Warrior, 1996, Bells of Innocence, 2003, Dodgeball: A True Underdog Story, 2004 The Cutter, 2006; actor, co-screenwriter (films) Invasion, U.S.A., 1985, Braddock: Missing in Action III, 1987; actor, co-exec. prodr. (films) Sidekicks, 1993; actor (TV films) Wind in the Wire, 1993; actor, exec. prodr. (TV films) Logan's War: Bound by Honor, 1998, The President's Man, 2000, The President's Man: A Line in the Sand, 2002, Walker, Texas Ranger: trial By Fire, 2005; actor, (TV series) Walker, Texas Ranger, 1993-2001; actor, exec. prodr. (TV series) Walker, Texas Ranger, 1995-2001, Sons of Thunder, 1999; exec. prodr. (films) Birdie and Bogey, 2004; author: (with Joe Hyams) The Secret of Inner Strength: My Story, 1988, The Secret Power Within: Zen Solutions to Real Problems, 1996, (with K. Abraham) Against All Odds, 2004; host: The Ultimate Stuntman: A Tribute to Dar Robinson. Founder, pres. United Fighting Arts Fedn.; founder, chmn. Kick Start Found., Houston, 1992; founder, World Combat League, 2005. Profl. world middleweight karate champion, 1968-74; Named Fighter of the Yr., Black Belt mag., 1969, Veteran of the Yr., Am. Veteran awards, 2000 Mem.: NRA. Address: Kick Start Found Ste 403 427 W 20th St Houston TX 77008

**NORRIS, DARELL FOREST,** retired insurance company executive; b. Pontiac, Mich., Oct. 19, 1928; s. Forest Ellis and Mabel Marie (Smith) N.; m. Thordis Marie Johansen, Aug. 21, 1955; children: Dara Lee, Jennifer, Lisa, Nancy. BS, U. Kans., 1950. CLU; ChFC. Reporter, mem. sports staff Kansas City (Mo.) Star, 1950-51; pilot TWA, 1955-58; divsn. agy. mgr. Merced (Calif.) region Farmers Group, Inc., 1959-62, sales rep. Colorado Springs (Colo.) region, 1962-64, regional agy. mgr. Aurora, Ill., 1964-66, regional sales mgr. Santa Ana, Calif., 1966-69, mem. mgmt. tng. program staff, dir. agys. L.A., 1969—71, regional mgr. Austin, Tex., 1971-73, v.p. sales L.A., 1973-76, v.p. field ops. midwestern zone, 1976-79, v.p. field ops. western zone, 1979—. Pres. Farmers New World Mgmt. Co., 1977-81, v.p. staff ops., 1981-85, sr. v.p. life co. ops. and staff support svcs., 1985-90, farmers cons., 1990-93, gen. ins. cons., 1993—, vice chmn., 2. Vice chmn. bd. dirs. Northridge Hosp. Med. Found.; chmn. bd. deacons 1st Bapt. Ch., Granada Hills, Calif., 1977-89; sustaining mem. Rep. Nat. Com. Served with SAC, USAF, 1951-55; capt. Calif. Air N.G., 1958-82. Mem. Am. Soc. CLUs, ChFC, Ins. Edn. Assn. (trustee 1982-84). E-mail: DNorris88@aol.com.

**NORRIS, DOLORES JUNE,** elementary school educator; b. Belmore, N.Y., Feb. 10, 1938; d. Abe and Doris Cyril (Stahl) Wanser; m. William Dean Norris, June 11, 1960; children: William Dean II, Ronald Wayne, Darla Cyrille. BS in Elem. Edn., So. Nazarene U., 1959; MS in Computer Edn., Nova U., 1988, EdS in Computer Applications, 1990. Cert. elem. edn. and computer sci. tchr., Fla. Tchr. 4th and 5th grades Ruskin (Fla.) Elem. Sch. 1959-61; tchr. 5th grade Emerson Elem. Sch., Kansas City, Kans., 1961-63; tchr. 1st grade Hickman Mills, Mo., 1964-65; tchr. 3d and 4th grades Lake Mary Elem. Sch., Sanford, Fla., 1968-72; tchr. 1st grade St. Charles Cath. Sch., Port Charlotte, Fla., 1976-77; primary tchr. Meadow Park Elem. Sch., Port Charlotte, 1978-89; computer specialist Vineland Elem. Sch., Rotanda West, Fla., 1989-90, Myakka River Elem. Sch., Port Charlotte, 1990—, tech. trainer, 1995—. Reading coun. Charlotte County Schs., Port Charlotte, 1987—, rep., 1989-90, in-svc. com. 1990-93, 98; program planner Meadow Park Elem. Sch., 1988-89; program planner Myakka River Elem. Sch. 1991-93, 2004-05; tech. facilitator Myakka Tiver Elem. Sch., 1999—; instr. in edn. U. Phoenix, 2002—. Mem. Rotary, Punta Gorda, Fla., 1982-86; co-dir. teens Touring Puppet Group, Punta Gorda, 1982-86; puppet co-dir. NOW Teens, Punta Gorda, 1976-80. Mem. Internat. Tech. in Edn., Fla. Assn. Computers in Edn., pres. Southwest Florida Assn. Computers in Edn. Avocations: piano, swimming, travel. Home: 1171 Richter St Port Charlotte FL 33952-2870 Personal E-mail: norrisd@hotmail.com.

**NORRIS, FLOYD HAMILTON,** financial journalist; b. LA, Sept. 6, 1947; s. Floyd H. and Martha Leota (Buntin) N.; m. Mary Christine Bockelmann, Oct. 5, 1984; 1 child, John Buntin. Student, U. Calif., Irvine, 1965-68; MBA, Columbia U., 1982. Reporter Coll. Press Svc., Washington, 1969-70; reporter, editor Manchester (N.H.) Am., 1970-72; reporter Concord (N.H.) Monitor, 1972-74, UPI, 1974-77; press sec. Sen. Dick Durbin, Washington, 1977-78; bus. writer and editor AP, N.Y.C., 1978-81; columnist for The Trader column Barron's Nat. Bus. and Fin. Weekly, N.Y.C., 1982-88; fin. columnist N.Y. Times, N.Y.C., 1988-98, mem. editl. bd., 1998-99, chief fin. corr., 1999—. Compiled and edited with wife The New York Times Century of Business, 1999. Bd. advisor Knight Bagehot Fellowship Program, Columbia U. Named a Walter Bagehot Fellow in Econ. and Bus. Journalism, Columbia U.; Recipient lifetime achievement, Fin. Writers Assn., N.Y., 1998, Gerald Loeb award for fin. journalism commentary, UCLA Anderson Sch. Mgmt., 2001, lifetime achievement award, 2003. Mem.: Soc. Am. Bus. Editors and Writers (dir.). Office: Fin Columnist N Y Times 229 W 43rd St New York NY 10036-3959 E-mail: norris@nytimes.com.*

**NORRIS, FRANK B.,** historian; b. LA, June 17, 1950; s. Harold B. and Beryl Z. Norris; m. Candy Dyer, Apr. 2, 1988; 1 child, Alice M. PhD, U. Wash., 1994. Historian Westec Svcs., San Diego, 1977—83, Nat. Pk. Svc., Skagway, Alaska, 1983—88, Anchorage, 1990—. Author: (hist. book) Histories of NPS Units in Alaska; contbr. 20 articles in field With Alaska Hist. Soc., 1985; pres Alaska Assn. Hist. Preservation, 1990—99, Anchorage Hist. Properties, Inc., 2005. Recipient Beaver Log award, Alaska Hist. Soc., 1995. Office: National Park Service 240 W Fifth Ave Anchorage AK 99501 Business E-mail: frank_norris@nps.gov.

**NORRIS, GLENN L.,** lawyer; b. Clarinda, Iowa, Sept. 25, 1946; s. Harold E. and Darlene Louise (Crane) N.; m. Dale Bailey, Jan. 28, 1967 (div. June 1990); m. Tiffinny C. Sparks, Nov. 14, 1998; children: Christopher Steven, Catherine Beth, Glenn Leonard Jr., Janet Darlene. BA, Simpson Coll., 1968; JD with honors, U. Iowa, 1971. Bar: Iowa 1971, So. Dist. Iowa 1971, U.S. Dist. Ct., no. dist., Iowa, 8th circuit, 1972, U.S Supreme Ct., 1976. Law clerk U.S. Dist. Judge Hanson, Ft. Dodge, Iowa, 1971-73; assoc. Hawkins, Hedberg & Ward, Des Moines, Iowa, 1973-78; ptnr. Hawkins & Norris, P.C., Des Moines, Iowa, 1978—. Editor: Iowa Academy of Trial Lawyers Handbook, 3d edit., 1999. Mem. tech. com. Iowa Supreme Ct. Commn. for Planning for 21st Century, 1996-98, Iowa Supreme Ct. Budget Adv. Com., 1997—; dir. men's chorus Sacred Heart Knights of Columbus. Recipient St. George award for Disting. Svc. to Cath. Scouting, Boy Scouts Am., Eagle Scout. Fellow Iowa Acad. Trial Lawyers; master C. Edwin Moore Am. Inn of Ct. (pres. 1998-2000); mem. Am. Bd. Trial Advs. (cert. civil trial advocate 2000—), Iowa State Bar Assn. (mem. fed. practice com. 1999—), Iowa Assn. Trial Lawyers (bd. govs. 1987-98). Roman Catholic. Home: 6205 Oakwood Hills Dr Johnston IA 50131-1962 Office: Hawkins & Norris PC 2501 Grand Ave Ste C Des Moines IA 50312-5311 E-mail: gnorrislaw@hotmail.com.

**NORRIS, JAMES HAROLD,** lawyer; b. New Kensington, Pa., Sept. 18, 1953; s. J. Harold and Eleanore Rose (Arch) N.; m. Ann Marie Annase, Nov. 25, 1988; children: Ryan, Scott, Nicholas. BA, Washington Jefferson Coll., 1975; JD, Duquesne U., 1978. Bar: Pa. 1978, U.S. Dist. Ct. (we. dist.) Pa. 1978, U.S. Ct. Appeals (3d cir.) 1984, U.S. Ct. (no. dist.) W.Va. 1996, U.S. Supreme Ct., 2003. Assoc. Ruffin Hazlett Snyder Brown & Stabile, Pitts., 1979-83; ptnr. Eckert Seamans Cherin & Mellott, Pitts., 1983—; exec. v.p., gen. counsel Academy System. Adj. prof. U. Pitts. Sch. Law, 2000—04; chief counsel Allegheny Regional Asset Dist. Bd. dirs. Epilepsy Found. Western Pa., Western Pa. Growth Fedn., North Hills YMCA, 2002—06. Mem. Allegheny County Bar Assn., Pa. Bar Assn. (chmn. adminstrv. law sect.

1992-94, spl. achievement award 1993). Home: 3475 Palomino Dr Gibsonia PA 15044 Office: Eckert Seamans Cherin & Mellott 600 Grant St Pittsburgh PA 15219-2702 Office Phone: 412-566-6159. Business E-mail: jnorris@eckertseamans.com.

**NORRIS, JEANNIE,** headmaster; Head of sch. Miss Hall's Sch., Pittsfield, Mass., 1996—. Mem. bd. dirs. Secondary Sch. Admission Test Bd., 2004—05. Mem.: Nat. Assn. of Principals of Schs. for Girls. Office: Miss Hall's Sch PO Box 1166 492 Holmes Rd Pittsfield MA 01202-1166

**NORRIS, JO ANNE WAREHAM,** intervention specialist, consultant; b. Roaring Spring, Pa., Jan. 31, 1953; d. C. Roscoe and Wilma Irene (Allen) Wareham; m. Raymond H. Norris, June 16, 1973; children: Charles (dec.), Joanna. BSEd, West Chester (Pa.) U., 1981; MEd, U. Del., 1992. Cert. sch. counselor, Pa., Md.; nat. cert. sch. counselor, Nat. Bd. Cert. Counselors; lic. profl. counselor, Pa. Exec. sec. Keystone Auto Club, Phila., 1973-78; office mgr. Holy Family Ch., Newark, Del., 1985-88; staff asst., dean's office U. Del., Newark, 1988-93; child devel. counselor Cecil County Pub. Schs., Elkton, Md., 1993—2002; intervention specialist Lancaster Sch. Dist., Pa., 2002—06; sch. counselor Columbia Boro Sch. Dist., Pa., 2006—. Mem. NEA, ACA, ASCD, Am. Sch. Counselors Assn., Pa. Sch. Counselors Assn., Pa. State Edn. Assn., Lancaster Edn. Assn, Kappa Delta Pi (Outstanding Mem. of Yr. U. Del. chpt. 1993). Avocations: travel, computers, desktop publishing. Home: 1121 State Rd Lincoln University PA 19352-1005 Office Phone: 717-291-6161. E-mail: jnorris@columbia.k12.pa.us.

**NORRIS, JOHN ANTHONY,** health products executive, lawyer, educator; b. Buffalo, Dec. 27, 1946; s. Joseph D. and Maria L. (Suite) Norris; m. Kathleen E. Mullen, July 13, 1969; children: Patricia Marie, John Anthony II, Joseph Mullen, Mary Kathleen, Elizabeth Mary. BA, U. Rochester, 1968; JD, MBA with honors, Cornell U., 1973; cert., Harvard U., 1986. Bar: Mass. 1973. Assoc. Peabody, Brown, Boston, 1973-75; from assoc. to ptnr., exec. com., v.p., dir. Powers Hall, Boston, 1975-80; chmn. bd., pres., CEO, founder Norris & Norris, Boston, 1980-85; dep. commr., COO FDA, Washington, 1985-88, chmn. action planning and cap comms., 1985-88, chmn. reye syndrome com., 1985-87, chmn. trade legis. com., 1987-88; corp. officer, exec. v.p. Hill & Knowlton, Inc., N.Y.C., 1988-93; worldwide dir. Health Scis. Cons. Group, 1988-93; chmn. health scis. policy coun. Health Scis. Cons. Group, 1989-93; chmn. bd., pres., CEO, founder John A. Norris, Esq., PC, Boston, 1993—; pres., CEO Nat. Pharm. Coun., Reston, Va., 1995-96. Instr. Tufts Dental Sch., 1974—79, Boston Coll. Law Sch., 1976—80, Boston U. Law Sch., 1979—83, Harvard U. Pub. Health Sch., 1988—; mem. bd. editors FDA Drug Bull., FDA Consumer Report, 1985—88; bd. dirs. Summit Tech., Inc., Cytologics, Inc., Horus Therapeutics, Inc., Nat. Applied Scis., Med. Knowledge Processing, Inc.; trustee Caritas Christi Healthcare Sys. Editor-in-chief: Cornell Internat. Law Jour., 1971—73, founder, faculty editor-in-chief: Am. Jour. Law and Medicine, 1973—81, assoc. editor: Medicolegal News, 1973—75, reviewer: New Eng. Jour. Medicine Law-Medicine Notes, 1980—81. Mem. U.S. Pres. Chernobyl Task Force, 1986, vice-chmn. health affects sub-com.; mem. Fed. Pain Commn.; chmn. Mass. Stuatory Adv. Com. Regulation Clin. Labs., 1977—83; mem. Mass. Gov.'s blue ribbon task force hosp. determination of need DON, 1979—80; chmn. Mass. Clin. Lab. Regulatory Commn.; mem. U.S. Intra-Govtl. AIDS Task Force, 1987; chmn. bd. dirs. Boston Holiday Project, 1981—83; bd. dirs. Mass. 4-H Found., 1982—2002, vice-chmn. bd. dirs., 1996—2002; chmn. U.S. del. Japan, Austria, Saudi Arabia, 1987, Finland, Denmark, Italy, 1986; chmn. Boston alumni and scholarship com. U. Rochester, 1979—85, mem. trustees coun., 1979—85, chmn. reunions; mem. exec. com. Cornell Law Sch. Assn., 1982—85, class pres., chmn. reunions; trustee Jordan Hosp., 1978—80, mem. exec. com., 1979—80, chmn. CEO search com., 1980; chmn. Joseph D. Norris, Esq. Health Law and Pub. Policy Fund, 1979—; mem. IOM Drug Devel. Forum, 1986—88, co-chmn. end points sub-com., 1987—88. With U.S. Army, 1972—73. Named one of Ten Outstanding Young Leaders award, Jaycees, 1982; recipient Kansas City Hon. Key award, 1988, award Merit, FDA, 1987—88, PHS award, 1987, HHS Sec. award, 1988; Comprehensive Health Planning fellow, 1970—73. Mem.: ABA (vice-chmn. medicine and law com. 1977—80), Internat. Coun. Global Health Progress (bd. dirs. 1989—95), Soc. Computer Applications Med. Care Informatics (bd. dirs. 1984—85), Am. Soc. Law and Medicine (1st v.p. 1975—80, chmn. bd. dirs. 1981—84, life mem. award 1981), Nat. Health Lawyers, Am. Soc. Hosp. Attys., Mass. Bar Assn., Phi Kappa Phi. Home: 531 W Washington St Hanson MA 02341-1067 Office Phone: 781-447-3732. E-mail: John_Norris_Sr@NorrisCapital.com.

**NORRIS, JOHN HART,** lawyer, director; b. New Bedford, Mass., Aug. 4, 1942; s. Edwin Arter and Harriet Joan (Winter) Norris; m. Anne Kiley Monaghan, June 10, 1967; children: Kiley Anne, Amy O'Shea. BA, Ind. U., 1964; JD, U. Mich., 1967. Bar: Mich. 1968, U.S. Ct. Mil. Appeals 1969, U.S. Supreme Ct. 1974, U.S. Ct. Claims 1975, U.S. Tax Ct. 1979. From assoc. to ptnr. Monaghan, Campbell, LoPrete, McDonald and Norris, 1970-83; of counsel Dickinson, Wright, Moon, Van Dusen & Freeman, 1983-84, ptnr., 1985—; dep. asst. atty. gen. State of Mich., 1997—. Natural gas law counsel to claims mediator Columbia Gas Transmission Corp.; chpt. 11 bankruptcy procs. Wilmington (Del.) Bankruptcy Ct., 1992—; dep. asst. atty. gen. State of Mich., 1997—; bd. dirs. Prime Securities Corp., Ray M. Whyte Co., Ward-Williston Drilling Co., One Stop Capital Shop. Contbr. articles to profl. jours. Trustee Boys and Girls Clubs Southeastern Mich., 1979—, Mich. Wildlife Habitat Found.; trustee, bd. dirs. African Wildlife Found.; mem. Rep. State Fin. Com.; founder, co-chmn. Rep. Majority Club; trustee Mercy Coll. Detroit, Detroit Hist. Soc., 1984—; trustee, 1st vice chmn. bank inst. Fellow: Mich State Bar Found., mem.: ABA (litig. and natural resources sects.), Def. Orientation Conf. Assn., Fin. and Estate Planning Coun. Detroit, Am. Arbitration Assn., Detroit Bar Assn. (mem. pub. adv. com.), Oakland County Bar Assn., State Bar Mich. (chmn. environ. law sect. 1982—83, probate and trust law sect., mem. energy conservation task force, mem. oil and gas com.), Mich. Oil and Gas Assn. (mem. legal and legis. com.), Detroit Zool. Soc., Yondotega Club, Bloomfield Hills Country Club, Turtle Lake Club, Prismatic Club, Hundred Club, Thomas M. Cooley Club, Detroit Athletic Econ. Club (Detroit), Blue Key, Phi Delta Phi. Home: 1325 Buckingham Ave Birmingham MI 48009-5881 Office: Dickinson Wright 38525 Woodward Ave Ste 2000 Bloomfield Hills MI 48304-2971 Office Phone: 248-433-7227. Business E-mail: jnorris@dickinsonwright.com.

**NORRIS, JOHN STEVEN,** healthcare company executive; b. Chgo., Apr. 25, 1943; s. Norris Dale and Olive (Grissinger) N.; m. Susan Jean Armstrong, May 3, 1975; children: Lindsey Jean, Whitney Ann, John Scott. BA, U. Ariz., 1967; B in Fgn. Trade, Thunderbird, The Garvin Grad Sch. Internat. Mgmt., 1968; MPH, U. Ariz., 1995. Diplomate Am. Coll. Healthcare Exec.; lic. nursing home adminstr., gen. contractor, real estate broker. Inspection officer Citicorp, Brazil, Colombia, Mex., Peru, Venezuela, 1968—73, asst. cashier NYC, 1973—74; pres., gen. mgr. Phoenix Athletic Club, 1974-76; bus. mgr. Phoenix Pub. Inc., 1976-77; project mgr. Environ. Constn. Co., Phoenix, 1977-79; pres. AGN Devel. Corp., Phoenix, 1979—, Valley View Realty, Inc, Phoenix, 1981-87; exec. v.p., sec., pres. RGW Constrn. Co., Inc.; pres. Norris/Roberts Group, Inc., Phoenix, 1987-90; CEO Christian Care Co. Inc., Phoenix, 1990—. Chmn. Covenant Health Network, 2001—. Ex officio bd. dirs. Christian Care Found.; chmn. bd. dirs. Dove's Transitional Housing, Inc.; bd. dirs. Alliance Provider Network; bd. dirs., past chmn. region 1 Area Agy. Aging. Recipient award of honor Ariz. Assn. Homes and Svcs. for Aging, 1999, Time and Talent award Am. Assn. Homes and Svcs. for the Aging and U. North Tex., 2004. Fellow: Am. Assn. Home Svcs. Aging (retirement housing profl.), Am. Coll. Healthcare Adminstrs.; mem.: Rotary Internat. (treas., past pres. Phoenix club, Paul Harris fellow, Service Above Self award 2002), Phi Delta Theta. Republican. Avocations: skiing, racquetball, horsemanship. Home: 6912 East Paradise Dr Scottsdale AZ 85254 Office: Christian Care Cos 2002 W Sunnyside Dr Phoenix AZ 85029-3534 Office Phone: 602-443-5411. Business E-mail: john.norris@christiancare.org.

**NORRIS, LINDA BETH,** museum administrator; b. Suffern, NY, Oct. 6, 1955; d. James Aller and Doris Baird Norris; m. Drew Bancroft Harty, Jan. 1, 1986; 1 child, Anna Harty. AB, Cornell U., Ithaca, NY, 1977; MA, SUNY-Oneonta, Cooperstown, 1982. Dir. Del. County Hist. Assn., Delhi, NY, 1982—94, Upstate History Alliance, Oneonta, NY, 1994—2006; mng. ptnr., founder Riverhill, Treadwell, NY, 1994—. Adj. instr. Hartwick Coll., Oneonta, 2004—06; grant reviewer Inst. Mus and Libr. Svcs., NY State Coun. Arts, NY Coun. Humanities. Author: Good Times: Delaware County's Community Album, 1997; exhibit, Coming Up on the Season: Migrant Farmwork in the Northeast, 2001. Mem. mus. exch. Am. Assn. Museums-Internat. Coun. Museums, Miskolc, Hungary, 1992; mem. group study exch. Rotary, Mumbai, India, 1998. Linda B. Norris Gallery named in her honor, Delaware County Hist. Assn. Office: Riverhill PO Box 232 Treadwell NY 13846

**NORRIS, LONNIE HAROLD,** dean; b. Houston, Nov. 22, 1942; m. Donna M. Farmer, June 18, 1966; children: Marlaina M., Michael A. BA in Chemistry, Fisk U., 1964; DMD, Harvard U., 1976, MPH, 1977. Cert. diplomate Am. Bd. of Oral/Maxillofacial Surgeons. Asst. prof. oral & maxillofacial surgery Tufts U. Sch. Dental Medicine, Boston, 1981-88, assoc. prof., 1988-95, prof., 1995—, interim dean, 1995-96, dean, 1996—. Mem. com. dental accreditation; chmn. coun. deans Am. Dental Edn. Assn., 2005—. Mem. Gov.'s commn. Study Oral Health Staus and Accessibility Dental Care Svcs. Residents Commonwealth Mass. Named Disting. Practitioner, Nat. Acads. Practice, Dentist of the Yr., New Eng. chpt. Pierre Fauchard Acad. Fellow: Pierre Fauchard Acad., Internat. Coll. Dentists, Am. Bd. Oral/Maxillofacial Surgery, Am. Assn. Oral/Maxillofacial Surgeons, Am. Coll. Dentists, Am. Acad. Dental Sci., Phi Beta Kappa, Omicron Kappa Upsilon. Avocation: travel. Office: Tufts U Sch Dental Medicine 1 Kneeland St Boston MA 02111-1527 Office Phone: 617-636-6636. Business E-Mail: lonnie.norris@tufts.edu.

**NORRIS, MARK MARSTON,** historian, educator; b. Wheaton, Ill., July 4, 1963; s. Paul Clifton and Barbara Alice Norris; m. Marla Gay Stevens, Oct. 7, 1964; children: Mark Marston III children: Althea Grace, Cassandra Mable. BA in History and English summa cum laude, Spring Arbor Coll., 1995; MSc in Brit. History, U. Edinburgh, Scotland, 1988, PhD in Brit. History, 1996; postgrad., Grace Sem., 1999—. Coord. acad. records Spring Arbor Coll., 1985—87; adminstrv. asst. Nat. Libr. Scotland, Edinburgh, 1988—90; tutor Birkbeck Coll., U. London, 1991—92; rsch. asst. Oxford (Eng.) U., England, 1992—92; part-time lectr. London Guildhall U., 1992—93; adj. instr. York Coll. Pa., 1994—2001; adj. prof. Harrisburg (Pa.) Area C.C., 1995—98; adj. instr. Millersville U. Pa., 1995—99; lectr., adj. prof. Messiah Coll., Grantham, Pa., 1996—2004; chair dept. history and social studies Grace Coll., Winona Lake, Ind., 2004—, dir. Millennial Scholar Acad., 2006—. Dir. Millennial Scholars Acad., 2006. Asst. editor: Oxford Dictionary of National Biography, Chancery Decree Rolls: C78/86-130, vol. 254, The Religious Papers of John Winthrop; contbr. articles and revs. to publs. Pastor, ch. planter Cmty. Cornerstone Ch., York, Pa., 2000—04; ch. planting facilitator Grace Brethren Ch., York, Pa., 1998—99. Mem.: Am. Hist. Assn. (assoc.), Ind. Coun. Social Studies (assoc.), N.Am. Conf. on Brit. Studies (assoc.), Conf. on Faith and History (assoc.), London Goodenough Trust (assoc.). Avocations: travel, reading. Home: 1167 E Wellington Warsaw IN 46582 Office: Grace College 200 Seminary Dr Winona Lake IN 46590 Office Phone: 574-372-5100 6256. Personal E-mail: norrismm@grace.edu.

**NORRIS, MARTY TODD,** elementary school educator; b. Orlando, Fla., May 5, 1969; s. Charles E. and Patricia A. Norris. B in Elem. Edn., U. Ctrl. Fla., 1996, M in Sci., 2003, D in Edn., 2007. Cert. ESOL Endorsement Fla. Dept. Edn., 2000, Secondary Sci. Grades 5-9 Fla. Dept. Edn., 2000. Elem. tchr. Ventura Elem., Kissimmee, Fla., 1996—98; 6th grade sci. tchr. Neptune Mid. Sch., Kissimmee, 1998—2006; secondary edn. sci. resource specialist Osceola Dist. Schs., Kissimmee, Fla., 2006—. Academic team chair Neptune Mid. Sch., Kissimmee, 2001—03, sci. dept. chair, 2000—04, dean students, 2004—. Recipient Sallie Mae Tchr. of Yr., Ventura Elem./Osceola Schools, 1997. Mem.: ASCD, Am. Ednl. Rsch. Assn. Office: Osceola Dist Schs Secondary Edn 817 Bill Beck Blvd Kissimmee FL 34744 Office Phone: 407-870-4995. Personal E-mail: norrism@cfl.rr.com. Business E-Mail: norrism@osceola.k12.fl.us.

**NORRIS, MICHAEL BYRON,** museum staff member; b. Montgomery, Ala., Nov. 13, 1952; s. Crockett Jones and Beverly Agan Norris; m. Katherine Daly Egan, Aug. 29, 1992; 1 child, Connor Jones. MA in Classics, U. Calif., 1981, PhD in Art History, 1994. Life Instructor Credential for the Calif. CC's Calif., 1988. Assoc. mus. educator Met. Mus. of Art, NYC, 1999—; asst. mus. educator Cloisters, 1995—99. Contbr. articles to profl. jours. Commr. Teaneck Hist. Preservation Commn., Teaneck, NJ, 2002—05. Fellow Chester Dale fllow, Met. Mus. of Art, 1987-1988; grantee Vidda Found. Grant, The U. of Calif., Santa Barbara, 1988; scholar German Acad. Exch. Svc., German govt. (DAAD), 1984; Jacob Javits Program fellow, US Dept. Edn., 1988-1991, Nat. Grad. Program fellow, 1986-1987, Kress Grants-in-Aid, U. Calif., Santa Barbara, 1983, 1984, Kress fellow, 1985-1986. Mem.: Nat. Art Edn. Assn. (assoc.), Italian Art Soc. (assoc.), Internat. Ctr. for Medieval Art (assoc.), Friends of Vatican Libr. (assoc.), Coll. Art Assn. of Am. (assoc.), Am. Assn. of Mus.'s (assoc.). Independent. Roman Catholic. Home: 318 Morningside Terr Teaneck NJ 07666-4033 Office: The Met Mus of Art 1000 Fifth Avenue New York NY 10028 Office Phone: 212-396-5083. E-mail: mike.norris@metmuseum.org.

**NORRIS, PAUL J.,** chemicals executive; Grad., Mt. St. Mary's Coll.; MBA, U. Md. With mktg. and bus. devel. divsns. W.R. Grace, 1971—81; v.p., then pres. catalysts & chemicals Englehard Corp., 1981—89; pres. fluorine products Allied Signal Inc., 1989—94, pres. polymers, 1994—97, sr. v.p., pres. splty. chems. unit, chmn. UOP, 1997-98; pres. W.R. Grace, Columbia, Md., 1998—2003, CEO, 1998—2005, chmn., 1999—2005, non-exec. chmn., 2005—. Office: WR Grace 7500 Grace Dr Columbia MD 21044

**NORRIS, PHILIP JOHN,** medical educator, researcher; b. Carmichael, Calif., May 25, 1967; s. John Clark Norris and Ann Dorothy Benson; m. Alexandra Margot Burgess, June 24, 2000; children: Katherine Ann, Alexander Campbell children: Cleo Elisabeth. BA, BS, U. Calif., Berkeley, 1989; MD, Columbia U., 1995. Diplomate Internal Medicine Am. Bd. Internal Medicine, 1995, Infectious Diseases Am. Bd. Internal Medicine, 1991. Intern internal medicine The Presbyn. Hosp. in the City N.Y., 1995—96; resident internal medicine Duke U. Med. Ctr., Durham, NC, 1996—98; clin. and rsch. fellow in infectious diseases Mass. Gen. Hosp., Boston, 1998—2001, instr. medicine, 2002—03; dir. immunology and assoc. investigator Blood Systems Rsch. Inst., San Francisco, 2004—. Recipient award, Calif. Scholarship Fedn., 1985, Scholar's award, Bank Am. Corp., 1985, James B. Black award, Pacific Gas and Electric Co., 1985—89, Clin. Scientist Devel. award, Doris Duke Charitable Found., 2000—05; scholar, Chancellor U. Calif., 1985—89, U. Calif. Alumni Assn., 1985—89; Nat. Merit Scholar, Nat. Merit Scholarship Corp., 1985. Mem.: Infectious Diseases Soc. Am. Republican. Episcopalian. Office: Blood Sys Rsch Inst 270 Masonic Ave San Francisco CA 94118 E-mail: pnorris@bloodsystems.org.

**NORRIS, REBECCA SACHS,** religious studies educator; d. Robert Green and Jean Woolf Sachs, Carolyn Levin Sachs (Stepmother); m. Harry L. Norris, May 27, 1978; children: Jesse Alexander, Leah Elizabeth. BA, Clark U., Worcester, Mass., 1969—73; PhD, Boston U., 1992—99. Asst. prof. Merrimack Coll., North Andover, Mass., 2002—; lectr. Boston U. Sch. Medicine, 2002—. Contbr. articles to profl. jours. and pubs. Post-Doctoral fellow, Boston U., 2000—01. Mem.: AAUW, Am. Anthropology Assn., Am. Acad. Religion (organizer, co-chair anthropology group 2003—, mem. New Eng. maritimes regional bd.). Avocations: gourmet baking, weaving, bobbin lace. Office: Merrimack Coll 315 Turnpike St C-2 North Andover MA 01845 Office Phone: 978-837-5000 4521. Business E-Mail: norrisr@merrimack.edu.

**NORRIS, RICHARD ANTHONY,** accountant, waste management administrator; b. Birmingham, Eng., July 6, 1943; s. Albert Edward and Audrey (Rowley) N.; m. Geri M., Jan. 20, 1947; 1 child, Karen Louise. BA, U. Leeds, York, Eng., 1966. Chartered acct., Can. Auditor Price Waterhouse & Co., Bristol, Eng., 1966-70, mgr. Montreal, Que., Can., 1970-78; mgr. corp. acctg., controller Can. Pacific Enterprises, Montreal, Calgary, Alta., Can., 1978-85; v.p. fin. US Ops. Laidlaw Waste Systems Inc., North Richland Hills, Tex., 1986-96; v.p., CFO Nexcycle, Inc., Dallas, 1997-2000; sr. v.p., CFO Casella Waste Systems Inc., Rutland, Vt., 2000—. Home: 448 Curtis Brook Rd Rutland VT 05701 Office: Casella Waste Sys Inc 25 Greens Hill Ln Rutland VT 05701 Office Phone: 802-775-0325. E-mail: Richard.Norris@casella.com.

**NORRIS, THOMAS BRYANT,** lawyer; b. Knoxville, Tenn., Apr. 7, 1960; s. Thomas Bryant and Patricia Sampson Norris; m. Vickie Adcock, Dec. 12, 1987; 1 child, Katherine Ann. BS, Middle Tenn. State U., 1982; JD, Nashville Sch. of Law, 1996. Bar: Tenn 1996. V.p. Nutrionics, Inc., Parsons, Tenn., 1983—; lawyer Sole Practioner, Nashville, 1996—. Lectr. in field, Tenn., 2004—; judicial internship Judge A.A. Birch, 1983. Contbr. articles various profl. jours. Dir. Belle Pointe Homeowners Assn., Nashville, 2005—08; tutor proctor Tenn. Bd. Law Examiners, Nashville, 1997—. Mem.: Nashville Bar Assn., Tenn. Bar Assn., Am. Bar Assn., Harry Phillips Inn of Court. Avocations: cooking, martial arts, bibliophile. Office: 1808 W End Ave Ste 1400 Nashville TN 37203 Office Phone: 615-321-5594. Office Fax: 615-321-5594.

**NORRIS, TRACY HOPKINS,** retired public relations executive; b. Ainsworth, Iowa, Nov. 1, 1927; s. Lee E. and Ruth C. (Simpson) N.; m. Emilie Lathrop, Nov. 11, 1956; 1 child, Shawn Tracy. BA, Cornell Coll., 1952; MA, U. Iowa, 1957. Admissions counselor Cornell Coll., Mt. Vernon, Iowa, 1952—54; dir. news bur. Wittenberg U., Springfield, Ohio, 1956—70; exec. dir. rels. and comm. Ball State U., Muncie, Ind., 1970—88; ret., 1988. Active United Way Springfield, Ohio, Muncie, 1965—. Served with USN, 1945-48. Recipient Silver Anvil award, Pub. Rels. Soc. Am., 1967. Mem.: Coun. for Advancement and Support Edn., Exch. Club. Lutheran Avocations: golf, travel, gardening. Home: 3700 Allen Ct Muncie IN 47304 Personal E-mail: tnorris629@aol.com.

**NORRIS, VIRGINIA OAKLEY,** secondary school educator; b. L.A., Jan. 14, 1928; d. Earl James Taylor Oakley and Florence Marian (Ashley) Guthrie; m. Robert Matheson Norris, Jan. 5, 1952; children: Donald Oakley Norris, James Matheson Norris, Elizabeth Anne-Norris Dodson. AA, UCLA, 1946, BA, 1948. Cert. secondary tchr., Calif. Tchr., art dept. chmn. Anaheim Union H.S., Calif., 1949—51; engring. draftsman Hughes Aircraft, L.A., 1951; tchr. Santa Barbara City Schs. and H.S., Santa Barbara, 1963—79; tchr./spinning U. Calif. Santa Barbara Ext., 1973; instr./fiber arts adult edn. Santa Barbara City Coll., 1972—84; demonstrator various schs., mus., chs., confs. and fairs, Calif., 1972—. Workshop for fiberarts groups presenter, Calif., New Zealand, Norfolk Island and Faroe Islands, 1973—. Contbr. articles to profl. jours. Bd. dirs., pres. Arboleda Park Improvement Assn., Santa Barbara, 1960-81; mem. Santa Barbara County Libr. Adv. Com., 1964-72, Goleta Valley Gen. Plan Adv. Com., Santa Barbara, 1973-81. Recipient Best Handspun Wool award Nat. Handcrafted Wool Showcase, 1978. Mem. Wellington Handweavers and Spinners Guild, Santa Barbara Fiber Arts Guild (pres. 1977-79), New Zealand Spinners, Weavers and Woolcraft Soc., Tawa Spinners Guild, UCLA Alumni Assn., U. Calif. Santa Barbara Faculty Women's Club (pres. 1984-86), Chi Omega. Congregationalist. Home: 4424 Nueces Dr Santa Barbara CA 93110-2006

**NORRIS, WILLIAM ALBERT,** lawyer, mediator, retired judge; b. Turtle Creek, Pa., Aug. 30, 1927; s. George and Florence (Clive) Norris; m. Jane Jelenko, Feb. 17, 1991; children: Barbara, Donald, Kim, Alison, David Jelenko. Student, U. Wis., 1945; BA, Princeton U., 1951; JD, Stanford U., 1954. Bar: Calif. 1955, D.C. 1955. Assoc. Northcutt Ely, Washington, 1954—55; law clk. to Justice William O. Douglas US Supreme Ct., Washington, 1955—56; sr. mem. Tuttle & Taylor, Inc., LA, 1956—80; judge U.S. Ct. Appeals (9th cir.), LA, 1980—97; atty. Folger, Levin & Kahn, LA, 1997—2000, mediator, 1997—; sr. counsel Akin Gump Strauss Hauer & Feld, LLP, 2000—. Spl. counsel Pres.' Kennedy's Com. on Airlines Controversy, 1961; mem. Calif. State Bd. Edn., 1961—67; mem. bd. dir. L.A. Eye Inst., 2001—. Trustee Calif. State Colls., 1967—72, Craft and Folk Art Mus., 1979—87; pres. L.A. Bd. Police Commrs., 1973—74; founding pres., trustee Mus. Contemporary Art, L.A., Calif., 1980—97; Dem. nominee for atty. gen. State of Calif., 1974. With USN, 1945—47. Office: Akin Gump Strauss Hauer & Feld LLP Ste 2400 2029 Century Park E Los Angeles CA 90067 Office Phone: 310-229-1047. Business E-Mail: wnorris@akingump.com.

**NORRIS, WILLIAM ROBERT,** engineer, researcher; b. Ft. Kent, Maine, Dec. 28, 1963; m. Julie Marie Hansen, Sept. 18, 1998; children: Josh, Jeremy, Sean. BS, U. Ill., 1996, MS, 1997, PhD, 2001. Rsch. assoc. Constrn. Engring. Rsch. Lab., Champaign, Ill., 1995—2001, Nat. Ctr. Supercomputer Applications, Urbana, Ill., 1996—2001; staff engr. Deere and Co., Moline, Ill., 2001—. Contbr. articles to profl. jours. Staff sgt. U.S. Army, 1986—92. Decorated Meritorious Svc. medal US Army, Army Commendation (2 awards), Army Achievement (3 awards); named Rsch. Asst. of Yr., Corps Engrs., 2000; recipient William A. Chittenden award, Gen. Engring. Dept. Univ. Ill., Urbanna, Champaign, Ill., 1998, Best Paper award, Internat. Conf. Systemics, Cybernetics and Informatics, 2001, hon. mention, Internat. ASAE Conf., 2001, John Deere Innovation award, 2005. Mem.: VFW, ASME, IEEE, Am. Assn. for Artifical Intelligence, Am. Soc. of Agrl. Engr., Soc. of Automotive Engr., Autism Soc., Mensa, Am. Legion, Alpha Epsilon, Gamma Epsilon, Sigma Xi, Tau Beta Pi, Phi Kappa Phi. Achievements include development of a method for incorporating human operators in (virtual a reality based rapid prototyping) system design; discovery of new method for and type of fuzzy logic system for multi-objective autonomous vehicle control; method for reducing rule base sizes through for incorporating control strategies. Avocations: robotics, computers, travel, reading, weightlifting, artificial intelligence. Office: John Deere C & CE Divsn 14401 Carowind Blvd Charlotte NC 28273 Office Phone: 704-587-2909. Business E-Mail: norriswilliamr@johndeere.com.

**NORSTEN, TODD,** artist; Attended Norfolk Program, Yale U., 1989; BFA, Minn. Coll. Art and Design, 1990. One-man shows include Paintings and Drawings, Willmar Cmty. Coll., Minn., 1992, Vermillion Gallery, Minn., 1992, Montgomery Glasoe Fine Art, Minn., 1994, New Paintings, 1996, Paintings and Drawings, Jennifer Armetta Fine Art, Chgo., 1997, Sighting, Weinstein Gallery, Minn., 1998, TrueFalse, 2001, Paintings, Stwphen Wirtz Gallery, San Francisco, 1999, Recent Paintings, Finesilver, San Antonio, 1999, Allsomeone, High Point Ctr. Printmaking, Minn., 2003, Happy Happy Happy, Franklin ArtWorks, Minn., 2004, Treasures from the Upper Midwest, Cohan and Leslie, 2006, Safety Club, Midway Contemporary Art, Minn., 2006, exhibited in group shows at Marks and Lines, Montgomery Glasoe Fine Arts, 1993, Brown Whiskey Club, 1995, Composing a Collection, Walker Art Ctr., Minn., 1996, Visitor's Voices: Recomposing the Collection, 1996, Dialogues, 1997, 11/5/98, Elizabeth Dee Gallery, NY, 1998, Five McKnight Artists, MCAD Gallery, Minn., 1999, Summer Show, Margaret Thatcher Gallery, NY, 2000, Uncanny Visions, Plains Art Mus., Fargo, 2004, Abstract Painting in Minnesota, Minn. Mus. Am. Art, 2005, Young Americans, Ararío Mus., Seoul, 2006, Whitney Biennial: Day for Night, Whitney Mus. Am. Art, NY, 2006. Mailing: c/o Cohan and Leslie 138 Tenth Ave New York NY 10011*

**NORSTRAND, IRIS FLETCHER,** psychiatrist, neurologist, educator; b. Bklyn., Nov. 21, 1915; d. Matthew Emerson and Violet Marie (Anderson) Fletcher; m. Severin Anton Norstrand, May 20, 1941; children: Virginia Helene Norstrand Villano, Thomas Fletcher, Lucille Joyce. BA, Bklyn. Coll., 1937, MA in Biochemistry, 1965, PhD in Biochemistry, 1972; MD, L.I. Coll. Medicine, 1941. Diplomate Am. Bd. Psychiatry and Neurology, cert. geriat. psychiatry. Intern Montefiore Hosp., Bronx, NY, 1941-42; asst. resident in neurology N.Y. Neurol. Inst.-Columbia-Presbyn. Med. Ctr., N.Y.C., 1944-45;

pvt. practice Bklyn., 1947-52; resident in psychiatry Bklyn. VA Med. Ctr., 1952-54, resident in neurology, 1954-55, staff neurologist, 1955-81, asst. chief neurol. svc., 1981-91, staff psychiatrist, 1991-95. Neurol. cons. Indsl. Home for Blind, Bklyn., 1948-51; clin. prof. neurology SUNY Health Sci. Ctr., Bklyn., 1981—; attending neurologist Kings County Hosp., Bklyn., State U. Hosp., Bklyn.; cons. in field. Contbr. articles to profl. jours. Mem. Nat. Rep. Congl. Com., Rep. Senatorial Inner Circle. Recipient Spl. plaque Mil. Order Purple Heart, 1986, Spl. Achievement award PhD Alumni Assn. of CUNY, 1993, Lifetime Achievement award Bklyn. Coll., 1995, others. Fellow Am. Psychiat. Assn., Am. Acad. Neurology, Internat. Soc. Neurochemistry, Am. Assn. U. Profs. Neurology, Am. Med. EEG Soc. (pres. 1987-88), Nat. Assn. VA Physicians (pres. 1989-91, James O'Connor award 1987), N.Y. Acad. Scis., Sigma Xi. Republican. Presbyterian. Avocations: writing, piano, travel, reading. Home: 7624 10th Ave Brooklyn NY 11228-2309

**NORSWORTHY, LAMAR,** petroleum company executive; b. 1946; With Holly Corp., Dallas, 1967—, pres., 1971-75, treas., 1975—88, chmn., pres., CEO, 1988—2005, chmn., 2005—. Bd. dir. Cooper Cameron, Triton Energy Ltd. Bd. dir. Dallas Mus. Nat. History, Zale Lipshy Univ. Hosp.; mem. bd. vis. M.D. Anderson Cancer Ctr. Office: Holly Corp 100 Crescent Ct Ste 1600 Dallas TX 75201-6927*

**NORTH, A. FREDERICK,** physician; b. Milw., July 3, 1931; s. Alexander F. and Florence (Reineking) N.; m. Jane Whittlesey, Dec. 18, 1954; children: Lindsay Elizabeth, Robert Whittlesey, Wendy Katherine. Student, Yale Coll., 1953; MD, Yale U., 1956. Intern Strong Meml. Hosp., Rochester, N.Y., 1956-58, resident pediatrics, 1960-62; instr. pediatrics U. Rochester, 1962-66; sr. pediatrician Project Head Start, Washington, 1966-68; assoc. prof. pediatrics George Washington U., Washington, 1968-72; assoc. med. dir. Children's Hosp. of D.C., Washington, 1968-72; vis. prof. pediatrics, pub. health U. Pitts., 1972-79; physician for retarded persons Govt. of D.C., Washington, 1978-88; pvt. practice in pediat. Rockville, Md., 1988—. Cons. various locations, 1966-88. Author: Infant Care, 1980; contbr. articles to publs. Lt. USNR, 1958-60. Fellow Acad. of Pediatrics, Am. Pub. Health Assn.; mem. Am. Pediatric Soc., Ambulatory Pediatric Assn. (pres. 1966-67), Chevy Chase Club. Republican. Episcopalian. Home: 5703 Overlea Rd Bethesda MD 20816-1918 Office Phone: 301-229-2159. Personal E-mail: afnorth@msn.com.

**NORTH, ANN R.,** secondary school educator; d. Robert Warner and Gladys M. Riemer; m. Ronald R. North, Dec. 20, 1980; children: Brianna E., Derek R. BFA, U. R.I., 1973; BA, Salve Regina Coll., 1975; MA, Gov.'s State U., 2000. Cert. tchr. R.I., 1975, Ill., 1975. Tchr. Rich South H.S., Richton Park, Ill., 1976—85, Lincoln- Way H.S., New Lenox, Ill., 1995—. Tchr. Joliet (Ill.) Jr. Coll., 2004—. Office Phone: 815-462-6-3000. Personal E-mail: anorth@lw210.org.

**NORTH, DOUGLASS CECIL,** economist, educator; b. Cambridge, Mass., Nov. 5, 1920; s. Henry Emerson and Edith (Saitta) North; m. Elisabeth Willard Case, Sept. 28, 1972; children from previous marriage: Douglass Alan, Christopher, Malcolm Peter. BA, U. Calif., Berkeley, 1942, PhD, 1952; D in Natural Scis. (hon.), U. of Cologne, Federal Republic of Germany, 1988, U. Zurich, Switzerland, 1993, Stockholm Sch. of Econs., Sweden, 1994, Prague Sch. Econs., 1995. Asst. prof. econs. U. Wash., 1950—56, assoc. prof., 1957—60, prof., 1960—83, chmn. dept., 1967—79, prof. emeritus, 1983—; dir. Inst. Econ. Research, 1960—66, Nat. Bur. Econ. Research, 1967—87; Spencer T. Olin prof. in arts and scis. Washington U., St. Louis, 1983—. Pitt prof. Am. history and instns. Cambridge U., 1981—82; fellow Ctr. for Advanced Study on Behavioral Scis., 1987—88; co-founder Internat. Soc. for the New Institutional Econ., 1997. Author: The Economic Growth of the U.S. 1790-1860, 1961, Growth and Welfare in the American Past, 1966; author: (with L. Davis) Institutional Change and American Economic Growth, 1971; author: (with R. Miller) The Economics of Public Issues, 1971, 1974, 1976, 1978, 1980; author: (with R. Thomas) The Rise of the Western World, 1973; author: Structure and Change in Economic History, 1981, Institutions, Institutional Change and Economic Performance, 1990. Recipient Nobel Prize in Econ. Sci., Nobel Found., 1993; fellow Guggenheim Found., 1972—73; grantee, Social Sci. Rsch. Coun., 1962, Rockefeller Found., 1960—63, Ford Found., 1961, 1966, NSF, 1967—73, Bradley Found., 1986—. Fellow: Am. Acad. Arts and Scis.; mem.: Econ. History Assn., The Brit. Acad. (corr.), Am. Econ. Assn. Office: Dept Econ Washington Univ Rm 305 Elliot Hall Box 1208 Saint Louis MO 63130*

**NORTH, E(DWARD) LEE,** retired writer, former aerospace company professional; b. Englewood, N.J., June 2, 1924; s. Edward Louis North and Genevieve Jean (Smith) North Francais; m. Florence Kirkland Hennen, Aug. 29, 1945; children: Patrick Lee, Diane North Goncalves. BA, Washington and Jefferson Coll., 1946. Sports editor Washington Reporter, Pa., 1947-49; publicity dir. Washington and Jefferson Coll., 1949-51; writer, editor Grumman Aerospace Corp., Bethpage, NY, 1951-78, proposal mgr., 1978-89. Hon. consul Free Polish Govt., London, 1980-95. Author: For This One Hour, 1970, Redcoats, Redskins, and Red-Eyed Monsters: A human-interest history of West Virginia, 1979, Battling the Indians, Panthers, and Nittany Lions, 1991, The Fifty-Five West Virginias, 1998, Mark of the White Wolf, 2000, Snowflakes on the Don, 2002, Eyes that Haunt, 2005; co-author (with Jane Wyman): Chris, the Rhode Island Wonder Dog, 1993; co-author: (with Arthur Dromerhauser) The History of Bay Shore High School Athletics, 1994. Chmn. Good Govt. Party, Suffolk County, NY, 1956—57; bd. of policy Liberty Lobby, Washington, 1975—2001; chmn. Islip Town (NY) Conservative Party, 1970s; historian Brightwaters Village, 1990—. Recipient Gold Cross of Merit Free Poland Govt., 1985. Mem.: The Authors Guild, Football Writers of Am., Am. Edn. Assn. (bd. dirs. 1992—), Rep. Nat. Com., Assn. of Pub. Historians of N.Y. State, Phi Kappa Psi. Episcopalian. Avocations: tennis, golf, bridge, Scrabble, study of wolves. Home: 55 Woodland Dr Brightwaters NY 11718 Personal E-mail: north444@aol.com.

**NORTH, GARY L.,** career military officer; B in Polit. Sci., East Carolina U.; MPA, Golden Gate U., 1984, M in Human Resources Mgmt., 1986; M∙in Nat. Resource Strategy, Nat. Def. U., 1994. Advanced through grades to lt. gen. USAF, 2006; weapons sys. officer 35th tactical fighter squadron Kunsan AB, Republic of Korea, 1978—79; F-4G Wild Weasel elec. warfare officer 561st and 563rd tactical fighter squadrons George AFB, Calif., 1979—80; fighter lead-in training Holloman AFB, N.Mex., 1981—82, Hill AFB, Utah, 1981—82; squadron scheduler, squadron weapons officer19th tactical squadron Shaw AFB, SC, 1982—85, wings weapons officer, 363rd tactical fighter wing SC, 1985—86; F-16 weapons officer, fligt comdr. 526th tactical fighter squadron Ramstein AB, Germany, 1986—87, aide-de-camp, F-16 instr. pilot to Commander-in-Chief of USAF Europe, 1987—89; asst. ops. officer 19th tactical fighter squadron, wing chief standardization and evaluation Shaw AFB, SC, 1990—93, chief wing weapons and safety Operation Desert Storm, comdr. 33rd fighter squadron SC, 1990—93; comdr. 35th ops. group Misawa AB, Japan, 1994—96; comdr. 8th fighter wing Kunsan AB, Republic of Korea, 1999—2000; chief joint requirements divsn., dep. dir. joint matters USAF Hdqs., Washington, 1996—97, dep. dir. politico-military affairs for Asia-Pacific, joint staff, 2002—04; dir. ops. U.S. Pacific command Camp H.M. Smith, Hawaii, 2004—06; comdr. 9th Air Force, U.S. Ctrl. Command Air Forces Shaw AFB, SC, 2006—. Decorated Df. Superior Svc. Medal with two oak leaf clusters, Legion of Merit with oak leaf cluster, Disting. Flying Cross with "V" device and oak leaf cluster, Meritorious Svc. Medal with oak leaf cluster, Air Medal with four oak leaf clusters, Aerial Achievement Medal with wto oak leaf clusters, Air Force Commendation Medal with two oak leaf clusters, Combat Readiness Medal with four oak leaf clusters; recipient Lance P. Sijan USAF Leadership Award, 1993. Office: USAF Air Force Pentagon Washington DC 20330*

**NORTH, HELEN FLORENCE,** classicist, educator; b. Utica, NY; d. James H. and Catherine (Debbold) N. AB, Cornell U., 1942, MA, 1943, PhD, 1945; LLD (hon.), Rosary Coll., 1982; DLitt (hon.), Trinity Coll., Dublin, 1984, Fordham U., 1999; LHD (hon.), La Salle U., 1985, Yale U., 1986. Instr. classical lang. Rosary Coll., River Forest, Ill., 1946-48; faculty Swarthmore

Coll., 1948—91, prof. classics, 1961-91, chmn. dept., 1959-91, emerita, 1991—, Centennial prof. classics, 1966-73, 78-91, Kenan prof., 1973-78, sr. rsch. scholar, 2003—. Vis. asst. prof. Cornell U., 1952—; vis. assoc. prof. Barnard Coll., 1954—55; vis. prof. LaSalle Coll., Phila., 1965, Am. Sch. Classical Studies, Athens, 1975, Athens, 87; Blegen disting. vis. rsch. prof. Vassar Coll., 1979. Author: Sophrosyne: Self-Knowledge and Self-Restraint in Greek Literature, 1966, From Myth to Icon: Reflections of Greek Ethical Doctrine in Literature and Art, 1979, (with Mary C. North) The West of Ireland: A Megalithic Primer, 1999, Cork and the Rest of Ireland: A Megalithic Primer II, 2003; translator: John Milton's Second Defense of the English People, 1966; editor: Interpretations of Plato: A Swarthmore Symposium, 1977; co-editor: Of Eloquence, 1970; editor Jour. History of Ideas; mem. editl. bd. Catalogus Translationum et Commentariorum, 1979. Bd. dirs. Am. Coun. Learned Socs., 1977-85; trustee LaSalle U., 1972-2003, chmn. bd. trustees, 1991-93; trustee King's Coll., Am. Acad. in Rome; chmn. com. on Classical Sch. Recipient Harbison prize Danforth Found., 1969, Centennial medal Am. Acad. Rome, 1995; named Distinguished Daughter of Pa., 1989, del. of Am. Philological Assn. to Am. Coun. Learned Socs., 1991-95; grantee Am. Coun. Learned Socs., 1943-45, 73, fellow, 1971-72, 87-88; Mary Isabel Sibley fellow Phi Beta Kappa Found., 1945-46, Ford Fund Advancement Edn. fellow, Fulbright fellow Rome, 1953-54, Guggenheim fellow, 1958-59, 75-76, AAUW, 1963-64; grantee Danforth Found., 1962, Lindbach Found., 1966; Sr. fellow NEH, 1967-68; NEH Coll. Tchrs. fellow, 1983-84; Martin classical lectr. Oberlin Coll., 1972. Mem. Am. Philol. Assn. (dir. 1968—, pres. 1976—, Charles J. Goodwin award 1969, Disting. Svc. medal 1996), Classical Assn. Atlantic States, Catholic Commn. Intellectual and Cultural Affairs (chmn. 1968-69), Am. Acad. Arts and Scis., Am. Philos. Soc., Soc. Religion Higher Edn., Phi Beta Kappa (bd. vis. scholars 1975-76, senate 1991—2003), Phi Kappa Phi. Home: 604 Ogden Ave Swarthmore PA 19081-1131 Personal E-mail: hnorth1@swarthmore.edu.

**NORTH, JOHN ADNA, JR.,** accountant, real estate appraiser; b. Atlanta, Oct. 20, 1944; s. John Adna and Julia Osborn (Napier) N.; m. Alexa Ruth Bryans, Mar. 20, 1976; 1 child, William Bryans. BA in Econs., U. Ga., 1966; M of Profl. Accountancy, Ga. State U., 1977, M of Taxation, 1980; JD, Woodrow Wilson Coll. Law, Atlanta, 1980. CPA, Ga.; cert. real estate appraiser. Trust administr. Trust Co. Bank, Atlanta, 1968-71; fin. produce sales exec. Dean Witter Reynolds Inc., Atlanta, 1971-73; with acctg. firm and in pvt. practice Atlanta, 1973-80; multi-state tax, staff, gen. tax counsel Texaco Inc., White Plains, N.Y., 1980-87; mgr. multi-state tax Price Waterhouse, Atlanta, 1987-88; dir. various corps. MacMillan Bloedel (USA) Inc., Wilmington, Del., 1988-91; pres. Cobb Svc. Assocs. Inc., Marietta, Ga., 1991—. Chmn. supervisory com. Texaco Fed. Credit Union, Atlanta, 1980-88; bd. dirs., treas Atlanta Credit Union League, 1986-87; v.p. The Planning Forum, Atlanta, 1984-85. Alumni trustee The Lovett Sch., Atlanta, 1985-89. Capt. U.S. Army, 1966-68. Mem. Nat. Soc. Scabbard and Blade, Mil. Order of Stars and Bars, Beta Alpha Psi. Anglican. Avocations: personal computers, building custom fly fishing rods, genealogy.

**NORTH, JULIE A.,** lawyer; b. Canberra, Australia, Mar. 20, 1962; BA cum laude, Hamilton Coll., NY, 1984; JD magna cum laude, Syracuse Univ., 1989. Bar: NY 1990. Assoc. Cravath Swaine & Moore LLP, NYC, 1989—97, ptnr., litig., 1997—. Notes, comments editor Syracuse Law Rev. Bd. trustees Hamilton Coll., Clinton, NY; bd. visitors Syracuse Univ. Coll. of Law. Office: Cravath Swaine & Moore LLP Worldwide Plz 825 Eighth Ave New York NY 10019-7475 Office Phone: 212-474-1752. Office Fax: 212-474-3700. Business E-Mail: jnorth@cravath.com.

**NORTH, MARJORIE MARY,** columnist; b. Mt. Clemens, Mich., Oct. 21, 1945; d. Robert Haller and Hilla Beryl (Willard) Wright; m. William B. Hirons; children: Laura, Christina, Angela. Student, Wayne State U., 1963—66. Features editor Elizabeth City (N.C.) Daily Advance, 1966-69; news/mng. editor Brandon (Fla.) News, 1977-78; city editor Leesburg (Fla.) Comml., 1978-79; metro editor Sarasota (Fla.) Herald Tribune, 1979-80, Fla. West editor, 1980-85, daily columnist, 1985—. Host Weekly Interview Show, SNN-TV, 1997—. Author: Sarasota: A City For All Seasons, 1994, (plays) With the Best Intentions, 1994, Back in the Game, 1998. Recipient Layout, Creativity and Overall Publ. awards Fla. Press Assn., numerous comty. awards and citations; winner Fla. shorts competition Fla. Studio Theater New Play Festival, 1994, 98; Paul Harris fellow. Avocations: tennis, entertaining, theater. Office: Sarasota Herald-Tribune PO Box 1719 Sarasota FL 34230-1719 E-mail: mnorth10@comcast.net.

**NORTH, OLIVER LAURENCE (OLLIE NORTH),** syndicated columnist, retired military officer; b. San Antonio, Oct. 7, 1943; m. Betsy Stuart, 1967; children: Tait, Dornin, Sarah, Stuart. Student, SUNY, Brockport; B, US Naval Acad., Annapolis. Commd. lt. USMC, 1966, advanced through ranks to lt. col., ret., 1990; mem. NSC, 1981—83; counter-terrorism coord. The White House, 1983—86; host, War Stories Fox News Channel; founder Freedom Alliance, 1990. Lectr. Oxford, Cambridge, Trinity Colls. Syndicated columnist; author: Under Fire: An American Story, 1991, War Stories: Operation Iraqi Freedom, 2003; co-author (with Joe Musser): War Stories II: Heroism in the Pacific, 2004; co-author: (with Sara Horn) A Greater Freedom: Stories of Faith from Operation Iraqi Freedom, 2004; co-author: (with Joe Musser) (novels) Mission Compromised, 2002, Jericho Sanction, 2003, The Assassins, 2005. Decorated Silver Star, Bronze Star, Purple Hearts (2). Address: Creators Syndicate Ste 700 5777 W Century Blvd Los Angeles CA 90045*

**NORTH, RICHARD RALPH,** neurologist; b. Hamilton, Ont., Can., Aug. 8, 1934; came to U.S., 1960; s. Ralph Edward and Dorothea Bernice (Pilton) N.; m. Lois Joan Wessler, Aug. 27, 1955; children: Elizabeth Ann, Amy Jo, Julie Lynn, Kristin Lee. MD, Queen's U., Can., 1959. Diplomate Am. Bd. Psychiatry and Neurology, Am. Bd. Clin. Neurophysiology. Intern Hotel Dieu Hosp., Kingston, Ont., Can., 1959-60; neurology resident Baylor U., Houston, 1960-63, fellow in neurology, 1963-64, 1964-66, asst. prof., 1966-67, U. Tex., Dallas, 1967-69, assoc. prof., 1969-82, clin. prof., 1982—; pvt. practice Neurologic Clinic of Tex., Dallas 1984. Med. advisor Dallas Epilepsy Assn., Dallas area Parkinson's Soc., Tex. Neurofibromatsis Found. Recipient Prof.'s Prize in Ophthalmology award Queen's U., 1959. Fellow EEG Soc.; mem. Am. Acad. Neurology, Am. Epilepsy Soc., Soc. EEG Soc. Home: 7106 Highland Heather Ln Dallas TX 75248-7502 Office: Neurologic Clinic of Tex 7777 Forest Ln Ste 410 Dallas TX 75230-2505 E-mail: rrnorth@sbcglobal.net.

**NORTH, ROBERT L.,** computer software executive; b. Topeka, Sept. 19, 1935; BEE, Stanford U., 1953, MEE, 1958; postgrad., UCLA Grad. Bus. Sch., 1977; post grad. Stanford Grad. Bus. Sch., 1981. Tech. staff mem. Aerospace Corp., 1962-65; various positions TRW, 1965-81, v.p. gen. mgr., 1981-86; CEO HNC Software, Inc., San Diego, 1987-2000, chmn., 2000—. Mem. San Diego C. of C., 1983-84; bd. dir. San Diego Econ. Devel. Coun., 1983-84, United Way Pres. Coun., 1984 Office: Fair Isaac Corp 3661 Valley Centre Dr San Diego CA 92130-3317

**NORTH, SHERRI L.,** elementary school educator; b. McComb, Miss., Nov. 15, 1960; d. Joseph Paul and Bernice V. North. BA, Northeast La. U., 1983; MS, La. Tech. U., 2000. Tchr. Ctrl. Elem., Calhoun, La., 1984—2000, Calhoun Elem. Sch., 2000—. Sch. improvement team leader Calhoun Elem. Sch., 2004—. Chmn. bd. Christian edn. Cypress St. Ch. God, West Monroe, La., 2004—. Named Tchr. of Yr., Calhoun Elem., 2003—04. Home: 206 New Chapel Hill West Monroe LA 71291 E-mail: north@opsb.net.

**NORTH, WILLIAM HAVEN,** foreign service officer; b. Summit, NJ, Aug. 17, 1926; s. Eric M. and Gladys (Haven) N.; m. Jeanne Foote, Sept. 2, 1950; children: Jeannette Haven, William Ashby, Charles Eric. BA in History with honors, Wesleyan U., Middletown, Conn., 1949; MA in History, Columbia, 1951. Program officer ICA, Ethiopia, 1953-57; then dep. chief program officer ICA (African-European Regional Office), Washington, 1958—61; asst. dir. for program USAID Mission, Nigeria, until 1965; dir. Ctrl. and Western African affairs AID, Washington, 1966-70, U.S. AID mission to Ghana,

1970-76; dep. asst. adminstr. Africa Bur. AID, 1976-82, spl. asst. Office of the Adminstr., 1982-83, assoc. asst. adminstr. Ctr. Devel. Info. and Evaluation, 1983-89, ret.; pvt. cons. Internat. Devel. for World Bank, 1989—, UN Devel. Program USAID, 1989—; coord. Evaluation of Global Environ. Facility, 1993, Evaluation Spl. Porgram of Asst. to Africa, 1997-98, Evaluation DAC/OECD Eval. Group, 1998; evaluator UNDP Aid Coordination, 1998—. Evaluator UNDB Global Program for HIV/AIDS, 2000, African Governance Capacity Bldg, UNDP, Danida, Denmark, 2002-03; fellow Ctr. for Internat. Affairs, Harvard U., 1965-66; chmn. experts group on evaluation Devel. Assistance Commn., OECD, 1985-88; vice-chmn. editl. bd. Fgn. Svc. Jour., 1983-86; mem. adv. panel on evaluation Inter-Am. Devel. Bank, 1993-94; prin. evaluator Internat. Fin. Corp.; program dir. U.S. Fgn. Assistance Oral History Program, 1995—; cons. UN Devel. Coop. Policy Branch, 2000-02. Interviewer Iraq, Afghanistan, Sudan for US Inst. Peace and Assn. Diplomatic Studies and Tng., 2005—06. Mem. devel. com., Program Cmty. Ministry Montgomery Co., 2000—; evaluator USAID Program in Iraq, 2003-04. Served with AUS, 1944-46. Recipient Meritorious Svc. award for exemplary achievement in pub. adminstn., W.A. Jump Honor cert., Superior Honor award for Nigerian Relief Adminstn., Equal Employment Opportunity award, Disting. Honor award AID, Presdl. Meritorious Svc. medal, Adminstrs. Career Svc. award. Mem. Soc. for Internat. Devel., African Studies Assn., Assn. Diplomatic Studies and Tng., Am. Evaluation Assn., Applachian Mountain Club. Methodist. Home and Office: Internat Development 6748 Brigadoon Dr Bethesda MD 20817-5436 Personal E-mail: willnorth@aol.com.

**NORTHCUTT, CLARENCE DEWEY,** lawyer; b. Guin, Ala., July 7, 1916; s. Walter G. and Nancy E. (Homer) Northcutt; m. Ruth Eleanor Storms, May 25, 1941. AB, U. Okla., 1939, LL.B., 1938. Bar: Okla. 1938. Pvt. practice, Ponca City, 1938—. Mem. bd. visitors U. Okla. Served with AUS, 1941-46. Decorated Bronze Star, Air medal with oak leaf cluster, Order St. John of Jerusalem; named Outstanding Citizen of Ponca City, 1982; inducted to Okla. Hall of Fame, 2001. Fellow Am. Coll. Trial Lawyers, Am. Coll. Trust and Estate Attys., Am. Bar Found.; mem. Acad. Univ. Fellows, Internat. Soc. Barristers, Am. Bd. Advocacy, Internat. Acad. Trial Lawyers, Okla. Bar Assn. (pres. 1975, bd. govs.), Ponca City C. of C. (past pres.). Clubs: Mason, Kiwanian. Democrat. Baptist. Home: 132 Whitworth Ave Ponca City OK 74601-3438 Office: PO Box 1669 Ponca City OK 74602-1669 Office Phone: 580-762-1655. E-mail: cdnorth@northcuttlawfirm.com.

**NORTHCUTT, MARIE ROSE,** elementary school educator, special education educator; b. White Plains, N.Y., Feb. 2, 1950; d. Carlo and Marcelline Marie Rose DeMarco; m. Kenneth Walter Northcutt, Mar. 17, 1984; children: James Lee, Thomas Joseph. BA, Lynchburg Coll., 1972; MA, Columbia U. 1977. Cert. elem. and secondary tchr., N.Y. Tchr. Petersburg (Va.) Pub. Schs., 1972-74; asst. relocation mgr. Ticor Co., White Plains, 1974-75; 3rd grade tchr. Resurrection Sch., Rye, 1975-76; 6th grade tchr. Harrison (N.Y.) Cen. Sch. Dist., 1976-78, learning disabilities specialist, 1981—; tchr. of emotionally handicapped N.Y.C. Schs., 1978-80; learning evaluator Empire State Coll., White Plains, 1981-82. Ind. evaluation cons., White Plains, 1981—; chair Mid. States Sub-com. Active Harrison H.S. PTA. Mem. Assn. for Children with Learning Disabilities, Westchester County Assn. for Children with Learning Disabilities, Spl. Edn. Parents Tchrs. Assn., Orton Soc., Phi Delta Kappa. Roman Catholic. Avocations: reading, cooking. Home: 81 Griffin Pl White Plains NY 10603-3609 Office: Harrison Cen Sch Dist Union Ave Harrison NY 10528-2108 Office Phone: 914-835-3300.

**NORTHEN, CHARLES SWIFT, III,** retired bank executive; b. Birmingham, Ala., Jan. 25, 1937; s. Charles Swift and Jennie Hood (Hunt) N.; m. Margaret Carson Robinson, Dec. 27, 1959 (div. 1972); children: Margaret Allen, Charles Swift IV, Bryce Robinson; m. Betty Jean Taylor, Oct. 3, 1981. BA cum laude, Vanderbilt U., 1959. MA, 1961. Chartered fin. analyst. Mem. staff trust dept. Birmingham Trust Nat. Bank, 1960-64; with First Ala. Bank Birmingham, 1964-80, sr. v.ps., trust officer, 1975-80, Central Bank of South, Birmingham, 1981-85; exec. v.p. 1st Ala. Bankshares, 1985-95, corp. investment officer, 1993-95; mng. dir. Sterne, Agee & Leach, Inc., Birmingham, 1995-98, investment cons., 1998—2001; ret. Lectr. So. Trust Sch., Birmingham So. Coll.; pres. First Ala. Investments Inc.; dir. Hubbard Press, Findlay, Ohio. Bd. dirs. United Presbyn. Found., N.Y.C., 1977-86; mem. Birmingham Com. Fgn. Rels., 1970—. Mem. Ala. Security Dealers Assn. (pres.), Ala. Soc. Fin. Analysts (pres.), Inst. Chartered Fin. Analysts, Newcomen Soc., SAR, Kiwanis, Mountain Brook Club, The Club, Soc. Colonial Wars (Ala. gov. 2005-06). Presbyterian. Home: 3024 N Woodridge Rd Birmingham AL 35223-2748

**NORTHERN, RICHARD,** lawyer; b. Louisville, Dec. 17, 1948; s. James William and Mary Helen (Barry) Northern; m. Mary Lou Grundy, Aug. 28, 1971; children: James Barry, Nancy Hope, Mary Grace. BA in English, U. Louisville, 1970, JD, 1976; MPA, Harvard U., 1977. Bar: Ky. 1976, U.S. Dist. Ct. (we. and ea. dists.) Ky. 1977. Staff writer Courier-Jour., Louisville, 1970-72; dir. planning devel. Jefferson County Govt., Louisville, 1972-76; legis. dir. Office of U.S. Rep. Romano Mazzoli, Washington, 1977-78; spl. asst. U.S. Sec. of Interior, Washington, 1979-80; ptnr., mem. exec. com. Wyatt, Tarrant & Combs, Louisville, 1980—. Bd. dirs. Nugent Sand Co. Chmn. bd. dirs. Cath. Edn. Found., Inc., Louisville, 1998—; dir. Jewish Hosp. & St. Mary's Healthcare Found., 1981—; dir., mem. exec. com. Louisville Tech. Pk., 2005—; treas. Metro Louisville Devel. Authority, 2005—; chair athletic adv. bd. Spalding U., 2005—; chmn.-elect Jewish Hosp. Found., 2006—. White House fellow, 1979, U.S.-Japan Leadership fellow, Japan Soc., Inc., 1988. Democrat. Roman Catholic. Office: Wyatt Tarrant & Combs 2800 Citizens Plz Louisville KY 40202-2898 Office Phone: 502-562-7234. Business E-Mail: rnorthern@wyattfirm.com.

**NORTHEY, WILLIAM THOMAS,** microbiologist, educator; b. Duluth, Minn., Aug. 10, 1928; s. William Thomas Northey and Mary Ellen Riley; m. Margaret Esparra, July 1, 1972; m. Elizabeth L. Van Laeke, Aug. 12, 1950 (div. June 15, 1970); children: Kathleen, William Northey III, Bruce, Brian, Barry, Brett, Suzanne. BA, U. of Minn., 1950; MA, U. of Kans., 1957, PhD, 1959. Rsch. asst. Abbott Labs., Chgo., 1950—51, Naval Med Rsch. Unit #4, Gt. Lakes, Ill., 1951—55; tchg. and rsch. U. of Kans., Lawrence, Kans., 1955—59; from asst. prof. to prof. emeritus Ariz. State U., Tempe, Ariz., 1959—85, prof. emeritus, 1985—. Cons. Unidynamics Corp., Goodyear, Ariz., 1960—63, AiResearch Corp.. Phoenix, 1963—65; pres., dir. Iatric Corp., Tempe, 1960—92. Contbr. articles to profl. jours. Vol. United Fund, Phoenix; grant reviewer Ariz. Heart Assn., Phoenix; bd. dir. Ariz. Br. of Allergy Found. of Ariz., Phoenix. Seaman aboard USNR, 1946—51. Grantee, NIH, 1960—85, USAF, 1963—68. Fellow: Am. Acad. of Microbiology; mem.: Am. Soc. of Immunology, Am. Soc. of Microbiology (pres. Ariz. chpt. 1963). Achievements include development of scorpion anti-venom; research in aeroallergens in Arizona. Avocations: skiing, swimming, reading. Home: 4818 N 72nd Way Scottsdale AZ 85251-1302

**NORTHRIP, ROBERT EARL,** lawyer; b. Sleeper, Mo., May 8, 1939; s. Novel and Jessie (Burch) N.; m. Linda Kay Francis, June 15, 1968; children: Robert E. Jr., William F., Darryl F., David F. BA, Southwest Mo. State, 1960; MA, U. N.C., 1965; JD, U. Mo., 1968. Bar: Mo. 1968, U.S. Dist. Ct. (we. dist.) Mo. 1968, U.S. Ct. Appeals (10th cir.) 1976, U.S. Ct. Appeals (8th cir.) 1980, U.S. Ct. Appeals (9th cir.) 1983, U.S. Ct. Appeals (3d cir.) 1987, U.S. Supreme Ct. 1978. Ptnr. Shook, Hardy & Bacon, Kansas City, Mo., 1968—. Active Nelson Art Gallery, Soc. of Fellows, Kans. City, Mo. 1st lt. US Army, 1963-65. Mem. ABA, Mo. Bar Assn., Lawyers Assn. Kansas City, Mo. Orgn. Def. Lawyers, Kansas City Met. Bar Assn., U. Mo. Alumni Assn. (past pres. Kansas City chpt.), Nat. Soc. Arts and Letters. Republican. Avocations: baseball, football. Office: Shook Hardy & Bacon 2555 Grand Blvd Kansas City MO 64108-2613 Home: 6439 Wenonga Rd Mission Hills KS 66208 Office Phone: 816-474-6550. Business E-Mail: rnorthrip@shb.com.

**NORTHROP, MARY RUTH,** retired mental health nurse; b. Washington, June 5, 1919; d. William Arthur and Emma Aurelia (Kaech) N. Diploma in nursing, Georgetown U., 1951, BS in Nursing cum laude, 1952; MS, U. Md.,

1958; MA in Anthropology, U. Va., 1970. RN, Va. Asst. dir. nursing U. Md. Hosp., Balt., 1958-60; dir. nursing Georgetown U. Hosp., Washington, 1961; nursing rep. ARC, Pa., 1962, regional dir. nursing New Eng. and N.Y., 1963-68; pediatric nursing cons. Va. Dept. Health, Richmond, 1971-84; clin. nursing specialist Va. Dept. Mental Health and Mental Retardation, Petersburg, Va., 1988-99. Adj. asst./assoc. prof. U. Md. Sch. Nursing, Balt., 1958-60. Author: Matthew Ryan and Mary Schmitz of North Star Township, Brown County, Minnesota, 1998; editor Lively Experiment, 2001—. Nursing fellow rsch. HEW, U. Md., Bethesda, 1957-68, nursing fellow anthropology U. Va., 1968-70; recipient Recognition Georgetown U. Alumni Assn. Richmond, 1987. Mem. ANA, Va. Nursing Assn., DAR (chpt. regent 1983-86, dist. treas. 1992-95), Nat. Soc. Women Descendants Ancient and Hon. Arty. Co. (treas. Va. chpt. 1995—), Daus. of Founders and Patriots of Am. (registrar Va. 1997—), Order of First Families of R.I. and Providence Plantation (charter), Sons and Daus. of Colonial and Antebellum Bench and Bar (charter), Soc. First Families of Minn., Mensa, Sigma Theta Tau. Republican. Roman Catholic. Avocations: genealogy, reading, travel. Home: 300 W Franklin St Apt 401E Richmond VA 23220-4967

**NORTHRUP, CHRISTIANE,** obstetrician, gynecologist; b. Buffalo, Oct. 4, 1949; d. George Wilbur and Edna (Zwilling) N.; children: Ann Christiane, Kate Northrup. BA, Case Western Res., 1971; MD, Dartmouth Coll., 1975. Diplomate Am. Bd. Ob-Gyn. Intern Tufts New Eng. Med. Ctr. Affiliated Hosps., Boston, 1975; intern then resident Tufts New Eng. Med. Ctr., Boston, 1976-79; assoc. clin. prof. ob-gyn Tufts U. Sch. Medicine, Boston, 1979-80; clin. instr. ob-gyn U. Vt. Coll. Med., Portland, Maine, 1980—82, asst. clin prof. ob-gyn, 1982—2001; practice medicine specializing in ob-gyn Gynecol. Assocs., South Portland, 1979-85, Women's Health Care Orgn. Women to Women, Yarmouth, Maine, 1985—96; private practice ob-gyn, Yarmouth, Maine, 1979—. Mem. high risk perinatal group Maine Med. Ctr., Portland, 1981-83. Author: Mother-Daughter Wisdom, 2005, The Wisdom of Menopause, 2001, Women's Bodies, Women's Wisdom, 1998; contbr. various articles on women's health to profl. jours Fellow Am. Coll. Ob-Gyn; mem. Am. Holistic Med. Assn. (sec. 1986-88, pres. 1988-90), Am. Holistic Med. Found. (pres. 1986-88). Avocations: music, harpist, skiing, movies, yoga. Office: PO Box 199 Yarmouth ME 04096

**NORTHRUP, HERBERT ROOF,** economist; b. Irvington, N.J., Mar. 6, 1918; m. Eleanor Pearson, June 3, 1944; children: James Pearson, Nancy Warren, Jonathan Peter, David Oliver, Philip Wilson. AB, Duke U., 1939; A.M., Harvard U., 1941, PhD, 1942. Instr. econs. Cornell U., 1942-43; sr. hearing officer Nat. War Labor Bd., 1943-45; asst. prof. econs. Columbia U., 1945-49; labor economist Nat. Indsl. Conf. Bd., 1949-52; indsl. relations cons. Ebasco Services, 1952-55; v.p. indsl. relations Penn-Texas Corp., N.Y.C., 1955-58; employee relations mgr. Gen. Electric Co., 1958-61; prof. industry Wharton Sch., U. Pa., Phila., 1961-88, prof. emeritus, 1988—, chmn. dept. industry, 1964-69, dir. indsl. rsch. unit, 1964-88, chmn. Labor Rels. Coun., 1968-85. Cons. and expert witness on manpower, pers. and labor rels. problems for many cos.; arbitrator in labor rels. disputes. Author: Organized Labor and the Negro, 1944, Unionization of Professional Engineers and Chemists, 1946, Economics of Labor Relations, 1950, 9th edit., 1981, Government and Labor, 1963, Readings in Labor Economics, 1963, Boulwarism: Labor Policies of General Electric Company, 1964, Negro and Employment Opportunity, 1965, Hours of Labor, 1965, Compulsory Arbitration and Government Intervention in Labor Disputes, 1966, Restrictive Labor Practices in Supermarket Industry, 1967, Negro in the Automobile Industry, 1968, Negro in the Aerospace Industry, 1968, Negro in the Rubber Tire Industry, 1969, Negro in Paper Industry, 1969, Negro in the Tobacco Industry, 1970, Negro Employment in Basic Industry, 1970, Negro Employment in Southern Industry, 1970, Negro Employment in Land and Air Transport, 1971, Impact of Government Manpower Programs, 1975, Open Shop Construction, 1975, The Impact of OSHA, 1978, Objective Selection of Supervisors, 1978, Black and Other Minority Participation in the All-Volunteer Navy and Marine Corps, 1979, Manpower in the Retail Pharmacy Industry, 1979, The Impact of the ATT-EEO Consent Decree, 1979, Multinational Collective Bargaining Attempts, 1979, Multinational Union Organizations in the Manufacturing Industries, 1980, Employee Relations and Regulations in the 80s, 1982, Internat. Transport Workers' Federation and Flag of Convenience Shipping, 1983, Open Shop Construction Revisited, 1984, Personnel Policies for Engineers and Scientists, 1985, Doublebreasted Operations and Pre-Hire Agreements in Construction: The Facts and the Law, 1987, The Federal Government as Employer: The Federal Labor Relations Authority and the PATCO Challenge, 1988, The Changing Role of Women in Research and Development, 1988, Government Protection of Employees in Mergers and Acquisitions, 1989, The Railway Labor Act, 1990, Union Corporate Campaigns and Inside Games as a Strike Form, 1994, Union Violence: The Record and the Response by Courts, Legislatures, and the NLRB, rev. edit., 1999, Construction Union Tactics to Regain Jobs and Public Policy, 2006, The Impact of Union-Management Relations on Urban Industrial Employment, 2000, The Great Paper Strike and Its Aftermath: International Paper vs. the United Paperworkers, 2006, also over 300 articles in field. Mem. Am. Econ. Assn., Indsl. Relations Research Assn., Am. Arbitration Assn., Phi Beta Kappa. Clubs: Harvard (N.Y.C.); Harvard-Radcliffe (Phila.); University (Washington), Faculty (U. Pa.). Home and Office: 205 Avon Rd Haverford PA 19041-1612 Office Phone: 610-642-1293.

**NORTHUP, ANNE MEAGHER,** congresswoman; b. Louisville, Jan. 22, 1948; d. James L. and Floy Gates (Terstegge) Meagher; m. Robert Wood Northup, Apr. 12, 1969; children: David, Katherine, Joshua, Kevin, Erin, Mark. BA in Econs. and Bus., St. Mary's Coll. Notre Dame, South Bend, Ind., 1970. Mem. Ky. Ho. of Reps., Frankfort, 1987-96; U.S. Congress from 3d Ky. Dist., 1997—; mem. house appropriations com.; founder Home Reading Caucus, 1998; mem. speaker's drug free task force, 1998; chair speaker's task force on education, 1998; mem. World Trade Org. congl. advisory group, 1999, free trade working group, 2000, comm. on educational accountability, 1993—95, economic development task force, 1991—92, task force to study highway needs, 1990—91, state debt capacity task force. Mem. fin. adv. bd. EPA, 1989-93; mem. home econs. adv. bd. U. Ky. Coll. Agr., 1992— Appeared on Meet the Press, Fox News Sunday, Larry King Live, CNN & Co., Hardball with Chris Matthews. Mem. exec. com. Partnership Ky. Sch. Reform, 1990—; bd. dirs. Greater Louisville Pub. Radio, 1993—, Hospice Louisville, 1994—, Ky. Cancer Consortium, 1992—; mem. cmty. adv. bd. Jr. League Louisville, 1993—; active Holy Spirit Cath. Ch. Named Outstanding Woman of Achievement St. Matthews BPW, 1990; recipient Cath. Schs. Disting. Alumni award, 1991, U. Notre Dame award of the yr. Ky. Alumni Assn., 1991, Clearing the Air award Am. Lung Assn. of Ky., 1991, Svc. Above Self award St. Matthews Rotary Club, 1992, Pub. Svc. award Am. Heart Assn., 1992, Sacred Heart Acad. Alumna award, 1994, Nat. Fedn. of Ind. Bus./Guardian of Small Bus. award, 1996, 97, 98, Legislator of Yr. award Environ. Industry Assn., 1997, Outstanding Freshman Mem. of Congress award Nat. Industries for Blind, 1997, Spirit of Enterprise award U.S. C. of C., 1997, Bulldog award Watchdogs of Treasury, 1998, Jefferson award Citizens for Sound Economy, 1998, Outstanding Support award Am. Printing House for Blind, 1998, Legislator of Yr. award Assn. Equipment Distbrs., 1999, Cmty. Healthcare Champion award Nat. Assn. Cmty. Health Ctrs., Inc., 1999, Spirit of Enterprise award C. of C., 1999, Susan B. Anthony Congl. award, 1999, Pub. Policy Adv. of Yr. award Nat. Assn. Women Bus. Owners, 1999, Honor Roll of Legis. Achievement in Econ. Devel. award So. Econ. Devel. Coun., Inc., 1999. Mem. Nat. Order Women Legislators, Nat. Conf. State Legislators, Nat. Rep. Legis. Conf., Inst. Rep. Women, So. Legis. Conf. (alternate from Ky. to fiscal affairs and govtl. com.), Nat. Fedn. Ind. Bus. Republican. Roman Catholic. Office: US Ho Reps 2459 Rayburn Ho Office Bldg Washington DC 20515-1703 also: Dist Office 600 Martin Luther King Jr Pl #216 Louisville KY 40202

**NORTON, CHERYL J.,** academic administrator; m. Henry Norton; children: Joel, Aaron. B in Phys. Edn. and Recreation with honors, Denison U., 1971; EdM, Columbia U., M in Applied Physiology, EdD in Applied Physiology, 1980. From temp. faculty mem. to full prof. Met. State U.,

Denver, 1976, chair dept. human performance, sport and leisure studies, 1992—96, interim assoc. dean Sch. Profl. Studies, 1996—97, provost, v.p. for acad. affairs, 1997—2004; pres. So. Conn. State U., New Haven, 2004—. Pres. Colo. Assn. for Health, Phys. Edn., Recreation and Dance; pres. Ctrl. dist. Am. Alliance Health, Phys. Edn., Recreation and Dance. Author 2 books; contbr. articles to profl. jours. Fellow: Am. Coll. Sports Medicine (past pres. regional chpt.). Office: So Conn State Univ 501 Crescent St New Haven CT 06515

NORTON, DAVID K., publishing executive, human resources specialist; married; 5 children. BS, Mich. State U. Dir. human resources Quaker Oats Co., Chgo., PepsiCo, Inc., 1990—94, sr. v.p. food systems, 1994—95, sr. v.p. human resources Frito-Lay N.Am., 1996—2000; exec. v.p. human resources Starwood Hotels & Resorts Worldwide, Inc., White Plains, NY, 2000—06; sr. v.p. human resources NY Times Co., NYC, 2006—. Office: New York Times Co 229 W 43d St New York NY 10036

NORTON, DOUGLAS EVATT, mathematician, educator; b. Danville, Ill., Aug. 2, 1957; s. Luther Hooper and Lucy Evatt N.; m. Kathryn Ann Friggle, Sept. 15, 1979; children: Hannah, Jacob. BS, Wake Forest U., 1979; MA, U. Wis., 1984; PhD, U. Minn., 1989. Asst. prof. math. scis. Villanova (Pa.) U., 1989-96, assoc. prof. math. scis., 1996—, chair dept. math. scis., 2003—. Fulbright lectr., rsch. scholar U. Botswana, 1996-97. Contbr. articles to profl. jours. Co-pres. Haverford H.S. Parent-Tchr. Student Assn., Havertown, Pa., 1999-2000. Rotary fellow 1979-80. Mem. AAAS, AAUP, Am. Math. Soc., Math. Assn. Am., Soc. for Indsl. and Applied Math., Assn. for Women in Math., Nat. Coun. Tchrs. Math., Pa. Acad. Sci., Phi Beta Kappa, Omicron Delta Kappa, Phi Kappa Phi, Sigma Xi. Home: 12 Llandaff Rd Havertown PA 19083 Office: Villanova U Dept Math Scis 800 Lancaster Ave Villanova PA 19085 Fax: 610-519-6928. Office Phone: 610-519-4850. E-mail: douglas.norton@villanova.edu.

NORTON, DOUGLAS RAY, former auditor general; b. Portales, N.Mex., Mar. 23, 1933; s. Clayton G. and Lillian W. Norton; m. Wanda Jones, May 23, 1951 (div. July 1979); children: Debbie Norton Goodman, Vicki Norton Hulet, Denise Norton Jolley; m. Roberta J. Andersen, July 31, 1998. BS, U. Ariz., 1963. CPA, Ariz. Staff acct., audit supr. Ernst & Ernst, Tucson, Ariz., 1963-67; ptnr. Baker, Price & Norton, Prescott, Ariz., 1968-75, Lester Witte & Co., Prescott, Ariz., 1975-76; auditor gen. State of Ariz., Phoenix, 1976-99; ret., 1999. Former mem. Profl. Adv. Bd. Sch. Acctg. Ariz. State U., Tempe; former mem. acctg. bd. advisors U. Ariz. Pres. Prescott Bd. Edn., 1976. Served with U.S. Army, 1953-55. Mem. AICPA, Ariz. Soc. CPAs, Nat. Assn. State Auditors, Comptrollers and Treasurers (pres. 1993-94), Nat. State Auditors Assn. (pres. 1982-83), Lions (pres. Prescott chpt. 1973-74). Home: PO Box 3120 Chino Valley AZ 86323-2707

NORTON, DUNBAR SUTTON, economic developer; b. Hoquiam, Wash., Jan. 30, 1926; s. Percy Dunbar and Anna Fedelia (Sutton) N.; m. Kathleen Margaret Mullarky, Dec. 21, 1948 (dec. Apr. 1994); children: Priscilla K., Rebecca J., Jennifer A., Douglas S.; m. Mary Ethel Wolff, May 25, 1996. Student, U. Oreg., 1946—48; diploma, U.S. Army Command & Gen. Staff, 1964. Enlisted U.S. Army, 1944, commd. 2d lt., 1948, advanced through grades to lt. col., ret., 1974; dir. econ. devel. dept. Yuma County C. of C., Ariz., 1974—83; exec. v.p. Lakin Enterprises, Yuma, 1983—87; owner Norton Cons., Yuma, 1987—. Corp. mem. Greater Yuma Econ. Devel. Corp., 1984-96, vice chmn., 1993-95; dir. Lower Colo. River Rsch. Ctr. Ariz. West Coll./No. Ariz. U., 1996-2000 Mem. Yuma County Indsl. Devel. Authority, 1984-90, 92-2006, pres., 1992-2006; chmn. fundraising com. Yuma Cross Park Coun., 1984-88, sec., 1988-90, v.p., 1990-92, bd. dirs., 1982-96; bd. dirs. Yuma Leadership, 1984-93, Yuma Youth Leadership, 1993-96, Ariz. Partnership Air Transp., 1990-96, v.p., 1993-95; chmn. devel. com. Yuma County Airport Authority, 1985-92, v.p., 1992-2002, pres., 2003-04, chmn. mktg. com., 2004; vice chmn. Yuma Main St. Bd., 1988-90, Yuma County Geog. Info. Sys. Task Force, 1991-95, Yuma Kids Voting, 1990-91; bd. dirs. Yuma County Civic Trusteeship, 1993-95, Ariz. We. Coll. Found. Bd., 2000-02, chmn. scholar awards commn., 2000-02; chmn. The Southwest Inst., 1995-96, What's Best for Our Kids, 1995-96, Yuma Sch. Dist. No. 1 New Elem. Sch. Planning Com., 1996-97, co-chmn. maintain level budget override com., 1999-2001; trustee Yuma County Libr., 1996-02; chmn. Yuma County Complete Count com. U.S. Census, 1990, 95, 2000; mem. Yuma County Town Hall Com., 1999—. Decorated Legion of Merit with oak leaf cluster, Bronze Star, Meritorious Svc. and Army Commendation Medal with Oak Leaf Cluster Mem. Ariz. Assn. for Econ. Devel. (bd. dirs 1975-82, pres. 1982-83, legis. affairs com. 1987-2002, Developer of Yr. 1978, William W. Lampkin award 2001), Yuma Execs. Assn. (sec.-treas., exec. dir. 1987—) Republican. Roman Catholic. Avocations: golf, swimming, singing. Home and Office: 12267 E Del Norte Yuma AZ 85367-7356 Office Phone: 928-342-6217. Personal E-mail: yumexec@msn.com.

NORTON, EDWARD, actor; b. Boston, Aug. 18, 1969; s. Edward and Robin Norton. BA in History, Yale U., 1991. Motion picture and stage actor. Actor: (films) Everyone Says I Love You, 1996 (L.A. Film Critics Assn. award, 1996), Primal Fear, 1996 (nominee Best Supporting Actor Oscar, 1996, Chgo. Film Critics Assn. award, 1996, Golden Globe award, 1996, Nat. Bd. Rev. award, 1996), The People vs. Larry Flynt, 1996, Rounders, 1998, American History X, 1998 (nominee Best Actor Oscar, 1999, Chgo. Film Critics Assn. award, 1999, Golden Satellite award, 1999), Fight Club, 1999, The Score, 2001, Death to Smoochy, 2002, Red Dragon, 2002, Frida, 2002, The Italian Job, 2003, Kingdom of Heaven, 2005; actor, co-prodr. 25th Hour, 2002, dir., prodr. Keeping the Faith, 2000; exec. prodr.: (films) Dirty Work, 2004.

NORTON, EDWARD C., economist, educator; PhD, MIT, Boston, 1990. Asst. prof. Harvard Med. Sch., Boston, 1990—93; sr. economist RTI Internat., Research Triangle Park, NC, 1993—96; prof. U. N.C. Chapel Hill, 1996—. Recipient Phillip and Ruth Hettleman prize, U. N.C. Chapel Hill, 2003. Mem.: Am. Soc. Health Economists (bd. trustees 2004—06). Office: Dept Health Policy and Adminstrn Univ North Carolina Chapel Hill NC 27599

NORTON, ELEANOR HOLMES, congresswoman, lawyer, educator; b. Washington, June 13, 1937; d. Coleman and Vela (Lynch) Holmes; m. Edward W. Norton (div.); children: Katherine Felicia, John Holmes. BA, Antioch Coll., 1960; MA in Am. Studies, Yale U., 1963, LLB, 1964. Bar: Pa., 1965, U.S. Supreme Ct., 1968. Law clk. to Judge A. Leon Higginbotham Fed. Dist. Ct., 1964-65; asst. legal dir. ACLU, 1965-70; exec. asst. to mayor City of N.Y., 1971-74; chmn. N.Y.C. Commn. on Human Rights, 1970-77, EEOC, Washington, 1977-81; sr. fellow Urban Inst., Washington, 1981-82; prof. law Georgetown U., Washington, 1982—; del. (at large) US Congress from DC, 1990—; mem. coms. on govt. reform and transp./infrastructure. Named one of 100 Most Influential Black Americans, Ebony mag., 2006. Democrat. Office: US Ho of Reps 2136 RaybunHo Office Bldg Washington DC 20515-0001 Office Phone: 202-225-8050. Office Fax: 202-225-3002.*

NORTON, ELIZABETH WYCHGEL, lawyer; b. Cleve., Mar. 25, 1933; d. James Nicolas and Ruth Elizabeth (Cannell) Wychgel; m. Henry Wacks Norton Jr., July 16, 1954 (div. 1971); children: James, Henry, Peter, Fred; m. James Cory Ferguson, Dec. 14, 1985 (div. Apr. 1988). BA in Math., Wellesley Coll., 1954; JD cum laude, U. Minn., 1974. Bar: Minn. 1974. Summer intern Minn. Atty. Gen.'s Office, St. Paul, 1972; with U.S. Dept. Treasury, St. Paul, 1973; assoc. Gray, Plant, Mooty, Mooty & Bennett, P.A., Mpls., 1974-79, prin., 1980-94; of counsel, 1995-96. Mem. Minn. Lawyers Bd. Profl. Responsibility, 1984-89; mem. U. Minn. Law Sch. Bd. Visitors, 1987-92. Trustee YWCA, Mpls., 1979-84, 89-91, co-chmn. deferred giving com., 1980-81; chmn. by-laws com., bd. dirs., 1976-77, lectr.; treas. Minn. Women's Campaign Fund, 1985, guarantor, 1982-83; budget and fin. com. bd. dirs., 1984-87; trustee Ripley Meml. Found., 1980-84; treas. Jones-Harrison Home, 1967, bd. dirs., 1962-69, 2d v.p., chmn. fin., 1968-69; mem. Sen. David Durenberger's Women's Network, 1983-88. Durant scholar. Fellow Am. Bar Found.; mem. ABA (mediation task force family law sect. 1983-84),

Minn. Bar Assn. (human rights com. family law sect., task force uniform marital property act 1984-85), Minn. Bar Found. (dir. 1991-94), Hennepin County Bar Assn. (pres. 1987-88, chmn. task force on pub. edn. 1984, chmn., mem. exec. com. family law sect. 1979-94), Minn. Inst. Legal Edn., Minn. Women's Lawyers (exec. com.), Hemlock Soc. of S.W. Fla. (co-chmn. 1999-2001), U. Minn. Law Sch. Alumni Assn. (dir. 1975-81, exec. com. 1981-83), Wellesley Club (Naples, pres. 2002-04), Phi Beta Kappa. Home: 26 Water Oaks Way Naples FL 34105-7157 Personal E-mail: betsynorton@swfla.rr.com.

NORTON, FLOYD LIGON, IV, lawyer; b. Shreveport, La., Oct. 23, 1950; s. Floyd Ligon III and Grace Louise (Julian) N.; m. Kathleen Fair Patterson, Nov. 24, 1979; children: Caroline, Elizabeth. BA with honors, U. Va., 1972, JD, 1975. Bar: Va. 1975, D.C. 1975. Assoc. Reid & Priest, Washington, 1975-83, ptnr., 1983-95, Morgan Lewis & Bockius, 1995—. Mem. ABA, Fed. Energy Bar Assn. Episcopalian. Home: 4107 Bradley Ln Bethesda MD 20815-5236 Office: Morgan Lewis & Bockius 1111 Pennsylvania Ave NW Washington DC 20004-5802 E-mail: fnorton@morganlewis.com.

NORTON, FRAN, recreation director; b. July 5, 1950; m. Richard Spitz, Jr. BFA, Rochester Inst. Tech., 1972. Park technician Frederick Douglass NHS Nat. Parks-East, Washington, 1972-75; supr. park technician John F. Kennedy Ctr. Performing Arts, Washington, 1975-80; supr. park ranger Klingle Resource Ctr. Nat. Capital Region, Washington, 1980-81, regional vol., grants mgr., 1982-84, supr. park ranger Career Conservation Devel. Corp., 1990; self employed Annapolis, Md., 1984-90; site mgr. Arlington House, Robert E. Lee Meml. George Washington Meml. Pkwy., McLean, Va., 1993-94; unit mgr. cultural resources, site mgr. Arlington House Clara Barton NHS, Glen Echo Park, Women in Mil. Svc. Am., McLean, 1994-98; chief ranger, divsn. interpretation Ft. Sumter, Sullivan's Is., S.C., 1998—. Office: 1214 Middle St Sullivans Island SC 29482-9717 Fax: 843-883-3910.

NORTON, GALE ANN, former secretary of the interior; b. Wichita, Mar. 11, 1954; d. Dale Bentsen and Anna Jacqueline (Lansdowne) N.; m. John Goethe Hughes, Mar. 26, 1990. BA, U. Denver, 1975, JD, 1978. Bar: Colo. 1978, U.S. Supreme Ct. 1981. Jud. clk. Colo. Ct. of Appeals, Denver, 1978-79; sr. atty. Mountain States Legal Found., Denver, 1979-83; nat. fellow Hoover Instn. Stanford (Calif.) U., 1983-84; asst. to dep. sec. USDA, Washington, 1984-85; assoc. solicitor US Dept. Interior, Washington, 1985-87; pvt. practice law Denver, 1987-90; atty. gen. State of Colo., Denver, 1991—99; sr. counsel Brownstein, Hyatt & Farber, P.C., 1999—2000; sec. US Dept. Interior, Washington, 2001—06. Lectr. U. Denver Law Sch., 1989; transp. law program dir. U. Denver, 1978-79. Contbr. chpts. to books, articles to profl. jours. Past chair Nat. Assn. Attys. Gen. Environ. Com.; co-chair Nat. Policy Forum Environ. Coun.; candidate for 1996 election to U.S. Senate; chair environ. commn. Rep. Nat. Lawyers Assn. Named Young Career Woman Bus. and Profl. Women, 1981, Young Lawyer of Yr. 1991, Mary Lathrop Trailblazer award Colo. Women's Bar Assn., 1999. Mem. Federalist Soc., Colo. Women's Forum, Order of St. Ives. Republican. Methodist. Avocation: skiing.

NORTON, GLYN PETER, literature educator; b. Exeter, Devonshire, England, May 22, 1941; s. Trevor Thomas and Betty (Marshall) N.; m. Victoria Josefina Perez, Oct. 28, 1966; children: Alexandra, Leslie. AB, U. Mich., 1963, AM, 1965, PhD, 1968. Asst. prof. Dartmouth Coll., Hanover, NH, 1968-71; prof. French lit. Pa. State U., University Park, 1971-88; prof. French lit., chmn. dept. romance langs., dir. Ctr. Fgn. Langs., Lits. and Cultures, Williams Coll., Williamstown, Mass., 1988-93, Willcox B. and Harriet M. Adsit prof. internat. studies, 1993—. Author: Montaigne and the Introspective Mind, The Ideology and Language of Translation in Renaissance France, 1984, Improvisation and Inspiration in Quintilan, 2006; editor: The Cambridge History of Literary Criticism, vol. III, 1999; contbr. articles to ednl. jours. Recipient medal City of Melun, France, 1985; NEH fellow, 1973-74, Guggenheim fellow, 1986-87; Am. Coun. Learned Socs. grantee, 1980-81, 85. Fellow Camargo Found.; mem. MLA, Renaissance Soc. Am., Soc. Francaise des Seiziemistes. Avocations: music, gardening, travel. Office: Williams Coll Dept Romance Langs Weston Hall Williamstown MA 01267 Business E-Mail: glyn.p.norton@williams.edu.

NORTON, JANE E. (JANE BERGMAN), lieutenant governor; b. Grand Junction, Colo. d. Walter F. and Elinor (Pitman) Bergman; m. Mike Norton; children: Lacee, Tyler. BS in Health Sci., with distinction, Colo. State U., 1976; MS in Mgmt., Regis U. With Med. Group Mgmt. Assn., Englewood, Colo.; mem. Colo. Ho. Reps., 1986—87; regional dir. U.S. Dept. Health and Human Svcs.; exec. dir. Colo. Dept. Pub. Health Environment, 1999—2002; lt. gov. State of Colo., Denver, 2003—. Chair Colo. Commn. on Indian Affairs; del. Aerospace State Assn., Edn. Commn. of States; co-chair Colo. Space Coalition; Colo. spokesperson Go Red for Women Campaign Am. Heart Assn.; hon. chair Prematurity Campaign Colo. March of Dimes; hon. chair Colo. Freedom Meml. Bd. dirs. Internat. Found. Electronic Systems, Am. Coun. Young Polit. Leaders; nat. bd. adv. Inst. Sci. and Space Studies; adv. bd. women's health U. Colo.; bd. adv. Colo. History Day; co-chair Colo. Health Disparities Commn. Named Woman of Distinction, Girls Scouts, 2005, Public Servant of Yr., Rocky Mt. Family Coun.; recipient Disting. Veterans Advocate award, United Veterans Com. Colo., Legislator of Yr. award, Persons Living with HIV Action Network of Colo., David M. Clark, S.J. Innovative Leadership award, Regis U., Family Values award, State of Colo., Honor Alumna award, Colo. State U. Coll. Applied Human Sci., US Public Health Svc. award outstanding accomplishment increasing childhood immunization rates, Outstanding Svc. to Seniors award, US Adminstrn. on Aging. Mem.: Nat. Lt. Governors Assn. (chair-elect 2006), Omicron Kappa Upsilon (hon.). Republican. Avocations: hiking, skiing. Office: Office Lt Governor 130 State Capitol Denver CO 80203*

NORTON, KAREN ANN, accountant; b. Nov. 1, 1950; d. Dale Francis and Ruby Grace (Gehlhar) N. BA, U. Minn., 1972; postgrad., U. Md., 1978; MBA, Calif. State Poly. U., Pomona, 1989. CPA Md. Securities transactions analyst Bur. of Pub. Debt, Washington, 1972-79, internal auditor, 1979-81, IRS, Washington, 1981; sr. acct. World Vision Internat., Monrovia, Calif., 1981-83, acctg. supr., 1983-87; sr. sys. liaison coord. Home Savs. Am. (name changed to Washington Mut.), 1987-97, sys. auditor, 1997-2000; sect. mgr., 2000—02, group mgr., v.p., 2003—04, v.p., 2005—; project mgr. II Indy Mac Bank, 2004—05, v.p. to pres., 2005—. Author: (poetry) Ode to Joyce, 1985 (Golden Poet award 1985). 2d v.p. chpt. Nat. Treasury Employees Union, Washington, 1978, editor chpt. newsletter; mem. M-2 Prisoners Sponsorship Program, Chino, Calif., 1984-86. Recipient Spl. Achievement award Dept. Treasury, 1976, Superior Performance award Dept. Treasury, 1977-78; Charles and Ellora Alliss scholar, 1968. Mem. Angel Flight, Flying Samaritans, Habitat for Humanity. Avocations: flying, chess, tennis. E-mail: skypilot@pacbell.net.

NORTON, MARY BETH, history educator, writer; b. Ann Arbor, Mich., Mar. 25, 1943; d. Clark Frederic and Mary Elizabeth (Lunny) N. BA, U. Mich., 1964; MA, Harvard U., 1965, PhD, 1969; DHL (hon.), Siena Coll., 1983, Marymount Manhattan Coll., 1984, De Pauw U., 1989; DLitt (hon.), Ill. Wesleyan U., 1992. Asst. prof. history U. Conn., Storrs, 1969-71; from asst. prof. to prof. Cornell U., Ithaca, NY, 1971-87, Mary Donlon Alger prof. Am. history, 1987—. Pitt prof. Am. history and instn. U. Cambridge, 2005—06. Author: The British-Americans: The Loyalist Exiles in England, 1774-1789, 1972, Liberty's Daughters: The Revolutionary Experience of American Women, 1750-1800, 1980 (Berkshire prize for Best Book Woman Historian 1980), Founding Mothers and Fathers: Gendered Power and the Forming of American Society, 1996 (finalist Pulitzer prize in history 1997), In the Devil's Snare: The Salem Witchcraft Crisis of 1692, 2002 (Amb. Book award of English-Speaking Union 2003); co-author: A People and A Nation, 1982, 7th rev. edit., 2004; editor: AHA Guide to Hist. Literature, 3d rev. edit., 1995; co-editor: Women of America: A History, 1979, To Toil the Livelong Day: America's Women at Work, 1790-1980, 1987, Major Problems in American Women's History, 1989, 3d rev. edit., 2003; contbr. articles to profl. jours. Trustee Cornell U., 1973-75, 83-88; mem. Nat. Coun. Humanities, Washing-

ton, 1979-84. Woodrow Wilson Found. fellow, 1964-65, NEH fellow, 1974-75, Shelby Cullom Davis Ctr. fellow Princeton U., 1977-78, Rockefeller Found. fellow, 1986-87, Soc. for Humanities fellow Cornell U., 1989-90, John Simon Guggenheim Meml. Found. fellow, 1993-94, Starr Found. fellow Lady Margaret Hall, Oxford U., 2000, Mellon postdoctoral fellow Huntington Libr., 2001. Fellow Soc. Am. Hist. (exec. bd. 1974-87, 2003—, Allan Nevins prize 1970); mem. Am. Hist. Assn. (v.p. for rsch. 1985-87), Am. Acad. Arts and Sci., Orgn. Am. Hist. (exec. bd. 1983-86), Berkshire Conf. Women Hist. (pres. 1983-85) Democrat. Methodist. Office: Cornell U Dept History 325 Mcgraw Hall Ithaca NY 14853-4601 E-mail: mbn1@cornell.edu.

NORTON, MAX C., writer, educator; b. Rigby, Idaho, Feb. 20, 1920; s. Robert Leandor and Alice Ida Norton; m. Adrianna Mae Van Konynenburg; children: Maxwel V.K., Gale Dirk, Jenni Sahlman. AA, Modesto Jr. Coll., Calif.; studied. U. Pacific, Stockton, Calif.; BA, Stanford U., 1949, Denver U. Emeritus prof. Calif. State U., Turlock, 1985—. Mem. editl. bd. Inst. for Gen. Semantics, San Francisco, 1964. Author: The Alice Saga, 2000, The Alice Saga: 1933 The Forgotten Man Chronicles, vol. II, 2004. Mem.: Am. Speech Language Hearing Assn. (life). Home: 5766 Stoddard Rd Modesto CA 95356 Personal E-mail: maxnorton@sbcglobal.net.

NORTON, NATHANIEL GOODWIN, marketing executive; b. Chgo., Jan. 7, 1948; s. Wilbur H. and Eva (Geneen) N.; m. Ariel Taylor, Nov. 15, 1980 (div. July 1987). BA, U.N.C., 1969. Mktg. mgr. Canteen Corp., Chgo., 1971-74; sr. v.p. Mathieu, Gerfen & Bresner, N.Y.C., 1974-83; pres., ptnr. Rand Pub. Rels., N.Y.C., 1983-89; ind. marketing cons. North Hampton, N.H., 1989—.

NORTON, NORMAN JAMES, retired exploration geologist, educator; b. Du Quoin, Ill., Apr. 26, 1933; s. James Harlan Norton and Helen Jane (Riley) Norton Rosen; m. Bettie Jean Greer, July 7, 1955; children— Matthew James, Jane Alison BS, So. Ill. U., 1958; MS, U. Minn., 1960, PhD, 1963. From asst. to prof. biology Hope Coll., Holland, Mich., 1964-74; prof., chmn. dept. biology Ball State U., Munice, Ind., 1974-78, acting v.p. acad. affairs, 1978-79; acting dean Ball State U. Coll. Arts and Scis., 1979-81; provost, v.p. acad. affairs Ind. U. Pa., 1981-83; cons. geologist Gulf Oil Corp., Houston, 1970-83; sr. staff geologist Gulf Oil Exploration and Prodn. Co., Houston, 1983-85; biostratigrapher, stratigraphic services, exploration Chevron Overseas Petroleum Inc., San Ramon, Calif., 1985-91; supr. biostratigraphy sect. Chevron U.S.A., Inc., Houston, 1991-93; acting divsn. geologist Chevron U.S.A. Inc., Houston, 1993-95, divsn. geologist, 1995—, geol. cons., 1997-98, ret., 1998. Contbr. articles to profl. jours. Chmn. bd. trustees Kiawah Island Natural Habitat Conservancy, 2002—. With USAF, 1952—56. Recipient Outstanding Tchr. Educator award Sr. Class of Hope Coll., 1969, acad. citation for disting. achievement Mich. Acad. Scis., Art and Letters, 1969, Outstanding Achievement award Chevron Overseas Petroleum Inc., 1990. Mem. Am. Assn. Stratigraphic Palynologists (Disting. Svc. award 1978, chmn. bd. trustees found., archives com. 1970—, constrn. revision com.). Home: 514 Ruddy Turnstone Johns Island SC 29455 E-mail: njnorto@attglobal.net.

NORTON, PETER K., retired computer utilities programmer, writer; b. Aberdenne, Wash. Nov. 14, 1943; m. Eileen Harris Norton, 1983 (div. 2000). Programmer, Norton Utilities (sold bus. to Symantec). Co-author (with David Wild): Peter Norton's Computing Fundamentals, 1995; co-author: (with Arthur Griffith) Peter Norton's Complete Guide to Linux, 1999; co-author: (with Scott Clark) Peter Norton's New Inside the PC, 2002, and several others; contbr. articles to profl. jours. Trustee Mus. Modern Art, N.Y.C. Named one of Top 200 Collectors, Artnews Mag., 2004. Avocation: Collector of Contemporary Art.*

NORVELL, JOHN EDMONDSON, III, retired neuroscientist, educator; b. Charleston, W.Va., Nov. 18, 1929; s. John Edmondson Jr. and Mathilde (Wood) N.; m. Rosemary Justice, June 2, 1962; children: John Edmondson IV, Scott Justice. BS, U. Charleston, 1953; MS, W.Va. U., 1956; PhD, Ohio State U., 1966. From asst. to assoc. prof. Med. Coll. Va., Richmond, 1966-76; prof., chmn. Oral Biology U., Tulsa, 1976-87; prof., 1987-89; prof., chmn. Universidad Central del Caribe, Bayamon, P.R., 1990-91; prof. Oral Roberts U., Tulsa, 1992—98, prof. emeritus, 1998. Invited sci. editor New Eng. Jour. Medicine, 1970; chmn. Okla. State Anatomical Bd., Tulsa, 1978-89; vis. prof. Sch. Medicine U. Nairobi, Kenya, 1982, Sch. Med. Scis., U. Benin, Nigeria, 1989; seminar speaker Zhongshan Med. Coll., Guangzhou, People's Republic of China, 1983; gov.'s mini-cabinet on health and human resources, Okla., 1980-90. Author: Atlas of Neuroanatomy, 1976, Atlas of Cross Sections of Human Body, 1982. Mem. Am. Assn. Anatomists, Soc. Neurosci., Transplantation Soc. Sigma Xi. Achievements include research in degenerationa and regeneration of the intrinsic nerve fibers of hearts and kidneys after transplantation. Home: 7018 E 100th St Tulsa OK 74133-6235 Office: Oral Roberts U Dept Biology 7777 S Lewis Ave Tulsa OK 74171-0003 Business E-Mail: jnorvell9@cox.net

NORVILLE, CRAIG HUBERT, lawyer; b. N.Y.C., June 10, 1944; s. Hubert G. and Harriett (Johnson) N.; 1 child, Margaret Amelia. AB, Harvard U., 1966; LLB, U. Va., 1969. Bar: N.Y. 1971, Pa. 1979, Tenn. 1985, Nev. 2000. Instr. law U. Mich., 1969-70; assoc. Cravath, Swaine & Moore, N.Y.C., 1970-76; sr. atty. Bethlehem (Pa.) Steel Corp., 1976-80; v.p., assoc. gen. counsel Holiday Corp. (name changed to The Promus Cos. Inc.), Memphis, 1980-84, v.p., gen. counsel, 1984-86, sr. v.p., gen. counsel, 1986-93, spl. counsel, 1993-99; of counsel Jones Vargas, Las Vegas, 2000—01, ptnr., stockholder, 2001—. Gen. counsel Diocese of the West, Orthodox Ch. in Am., 2000—. Articles editor U. Va. Law Rev. Mem. Raven Soc., Hasty Pudding Inst. of 1770, Order of Coif, Harvard Varsity Club (Cambridge, Mass.). Avocations: golf, skiing, fishing, tennis, squash. Address: 3773 Howard Hughes Pky Las Vegas NV 89109 Office Phone: 702-862-3396. E-mail: chn@jonesvargas.com.

NORVILLE, DEBORAH ANNE, news correspondent; b. Aug. 8, 1958; d. Zachary S. and Merle Olson Norville; m. Karl G. Wellner Dec. 12, 1987; children: Karl Nikolai, Kyle Maximilian, Mikaela Katharina. ABJ summa cum laude, U. Ga., 1979. Reporter Sta. WAGA-TV, Atlanta, 1978-79, anchor, reporter, 1979-81, Sta. WMAQ-TV, Chgo., 1982-86; anchor NBC News, NYC, 1987-89; news anchor Today Show, NBC, NYC, 1989, co-anchor, 1990-92; corr. Street Stories, CBS, NYC, 1992-94; co-anchor America Tonight, CBS, NYC, 1994; anchor Inside Edition, King World Prodns., 1994—; contbg. editor McCall's, NYC; host Deborah Norville Tonight MSNBC, NYC, 2004—05. Author: Back on Track: How to Straighten Out Your Life When it Throws You a Curve, 1997, I Don't Want To Sleep Tonight, 1999, I Can Fly, 2001. Bd. dirs. Greater N.Y. coun. Girl Scouts U.S., 1989-; Broadcaster's Found.; mem. steering com. Rita Hayworth Gala Alzheimer's Assn; nat. celebrity spokesperson McCall's March of Dimes, 2001, 02. Recipient Outstanding Young Alumni award Sch. Journalism, U. Ga., Emmy award, 1985-86, 89, Gracie Award, Am. Women in Radio and TV; named Person of Yr., Chgo. Broadcast Advt. Club, 1989, 91, Anchor of Yr. 2000, Washington Journalism Rev., 1989. Mem. Soc. Profl. Journalists. Office: Inside Edition 555 W 57th St Ste 1300 New York NY 10019-2925

NORWITZ, TREVOR S., lawyer; b. Cape Town, South Africa, Oct. 21, 1964; came to the U.S., 1989; s. Rubin Gabriel and Marionne Joyce Norwitz; m. Shannon Lieberman, Jan. 19, 1992; children: Raphael Shai, Herschel Sam. B in Bus. Sci., U. Cape Town, 1986; BA in Juris, Oxford (Eng.) U., 1989, MA, 1993; LLM, Columbia U., 1990. Bar: N.Y. 1991. Assoc. Cravath, Swaine & Moore, N.Y.C., 1990-94, Wachtell, Lipton, Rosen & Katz, N.Y.C. 1994-98, ptnr., 1999—. Adj. lectr. Columbia Law Sch., 2004—. Contbr. articles to profl. jours. Chmn. U. Cape Town Fund, 2003—. Rhodes scholar 1987. Mem. ABA (bus. sect. com., com. corp. laws). Office: Wachtell Lipton Rosen & Katz 51 W 52nd St Fl 29 New York NY 10019-6150 Office Phone: 212-403-1000. E-mail: tsnorwitz@wlrk.com.

**NORWOOD, BERNARD,** economist; b. Boston, Nov. 21, 1922; s. Hyman and Rose (Fink) N.; m. Janet Lippe, June 25, 1943; children: Stephen Harlan, Peter Carlton. BA, Boston U., 1947; MA, Fletcher Sch. Law and Diplomacy, 1948, PhD, 1957. Internat. economist State Dept., 1949-58; joined U.S. Fgn. Svc., 1955; 1st. sec. U.S. mission to European Communities, Brussels, Belgium, 1958-62; asst. chief comml. policy and treaties divsn. Dept. State, 1962; chmn. trade staff com. Office Spl. Rep. for Trade Negotiations, Exec. Office Pres., 1963-67; assigned The Nat. War Coll., 1967-68; advisor divsn. internat. fin. bd. govs. Fed. Res. Sys., 1968-75; prin. assoc., sr. cons. Nathan Assocs., Inc., 1975-94. Mem. U.S. del. to negotiations and confs. GATT, Geneva, 1953-67. Served with AUS, 1943-46. Home and Office: 5610 Wisconsin Ave # 21D Chevy Chase MD 20815-4415

**NORWOOD, BRANDI AISHA,** middle school educator; b. Atlanta, Oct. 17, 1978; d. Sara Clements and David A. Norwood. BS, Tenn. State U., Nashville, 2000; MEd in Ednl. Leadership, Troy State U., Augusta, Ga., 2003; cert. in Ednl. Leadership, U. West Ga., Carrollton, 2004; EdS in Ednl. Leadership, Argosy U., Sarasota, Fla., 2006. 7th grade life sci. tchr. Henderson Mid. Sch., Jackson, Ga., 2001—05; 7th grade life sci. and social sci. tchr. Clements Mid. Sch., Covington, Ga., 2005—. Cheerleading coach Clements Mid. Sch., Covington, Ga., 2005—; asst. coach girls basketball Henderson Mid. Sch., Jackson, 2001—05, head coach girls track, 2001—05, cheerleading coach, 2001—05. Mem.: Ga. Assn. Educators (assoc.), Profl. Assn. Ga. Educators (assoc.), Pi Lambda Theta (assoc.). Democrat. Baptist. Avocations: reading, travel. Home: 9129 Carr Cir Covington GA 30014 Office Phone: 770-784-2934. Personal E-mail: norwoodbrandi@netscape.net.

**NORWOOD, BRANDY RAYANA (BRANDY),** singer, actress; b. McComb, Miss., Feb. 11, 1979; d. Willie and Sonia Norwood; m. Robert Smith, 2001 (div. 2003); 1 child, Sy'rai. Student, Pepperdine U. Singer: (albums) Brandy, 1994 (NAACP Image Award: Best New Artist, 1996), De Falda Cortina, 1995, Never S-A-Y Never, 1998, Full Moon, 2002, Afrodisiac, 2004; actor: (TV series) Thea, 1996, Moesha, 1995—2001 (NAACP Image Award: Best Youth Actor/Actress, 1997), Brandy: Special Delivery, 2002; (TV films) Cinderella, 1997; actor, exec. prodr.: (TV films) Double Platinum, 1999; actor: (films) I Still Know What You Did Last Summer, 1998; voice Osmosis Jones, 2001, judge (TV series) America's Got Talent, 2006—. Named Favorite New Artist, Am. Music Awards, 1996; recipient Grammy award (with Monica) Best R&B Performance By A Duo Or Group With Vocal for song "That Boy Is Mine", 1998. Office: 15030 Ventura Blvd 710 Sherman Oaks CA 91403

**NORWOOD, CHARLES WHITLOW, JR.,** congressman; b. Valdosta, Ga., July 27, 1941; m. Gloria Norwood; 2 children. BS, Ga. So. U., 1964; DDS, Georgetown U., 1967. Pvt. practice, Augusta, Ga., 1969-94; owner Norwood Tree Nursery, 1984—; mem. U.S. Congress from 9th Ga. dist. (formerly 10th), 1995—, mem. commerce com. and the workforce coms., vchmn. health subcom., chmn. workforce protection com.; pres. Georgia Dental Assoc., 1983. Capt. U.S. Army, 1967-69, Vietnam. Decorated Combat Medic badge, Bronze Star for Meritorious Svc., Bronze Star for Meritorious Achievement. Mem. Ga. Dental Assn. Republican. Methodist. Office: US Ho Reps 2452 Rayburn Ho Office Bldg Washington DC 20515-1010

**NORWOOD, COLVIN GAMBLE, JR.,** lawyer; b. New Orleans, Dec. 10, 1947; s. Colvin Gamble and Dorothy P. (Pecot) N.; m. Susan Clark, Dec. 29, 1971; children: Benjamin, Colvin Gamble III. BS in Physics, Tulane U., 1969, JD, 1972. Bar: La. 1972, Tex. 2004. Assoc. Deutsch, Kerrigan & Stiles, New Orleans, 1972-73, Schumacher, McGlinchey, Stafford & Mintz, New Orleans, 1974-75; ptnr., dir., mng. dir. McGlinchey Stafford, New Orleans, 1986—. Chmn. law firm solicitation United Fund of Greater New Orleans, 1983; chmn. Xavier U. of La.; bd. dirs., treas., New Orleans Pro Bono Project. Capt. US Army, 1971-73. Fellow Am. Coll. of Trial Lawyers, La. Bar Found.; mem. ABA, Internat. Assn. Def. Counsel, Product Liability Adv. Coun., World Trade Ctr., La. Supreme Ct. Hist. Soc., Sigma Pi Sigma, Omicron Delta Kappa, Sigma Alpha Epsilon. Avocations: photography, computer programming, office automation. Home: 6031 Perrier St New Orleans LA 70118-5940 Office: McGlinchey Stafford 643 Magazine St New Orleans LA 70130-3477

**NORWOOD, DEBORAH ANNE,** law librarian; b. Honolulu, Nov. 12, 1950; d. Alfred Freeman and Helen G. Norwood; 1 child, Nicholas Evans. BA, U. Wash., 1972, M in Law Librarianship, 1979; JD, Willamette U., 1974. Bar: Wash., U.S. Dist. Ct. (we. dist.) 1975, U.S. Ct. Appeals (9th cir.) 1980. Ptnr. Evans and Norwood, 1975-79; law libr. U.S. Courts Libr., Seattle, 1980-89; state law libr. Wash. State Law Libr., Olympia, 1989—2002, reporter of decisions, 1994-2001; asst. dir. pub. svcs. Jacob Burns Law Libr. George Washington U., Washington, 2002—. Mem. Freedom to Read Found. Mem. Am. Assn. Law Librs. (chmn. state, ct. and county spl. interest sect. 1995-96, chair legal info. svcs. to pub. spl. interest sect. 2001-02). Office: Jacob Burns Law Libr George Washington U 716-20th St NW Washington DC 20052 Office Phone: 202-994-7338. E-mail: dnorwood@law.gwu.edu.

**NORWOOD, E(DWARD) ANDREW,** lawyer; b. San Diego, Oct. 4, 1962; s. Robert George and Mabel Ruth (Turner) N.; m. Shannon Williams, May 30, 1987; 1 child, Robert Glenn. BA, U. Ala., 1984, JD, 1987. Bar: Ala. 1987, Tenn. 1989, U.S. Dist. Ct. (mid. dist.) Ala. 1988, U.S. Dist. Ct. (mid. dist.) Tenn. 1989. Staff atty. Supreme Ct. Ala., Montgomery, 1987-88; assoc. King & Ballow, Nashville, 1988—. Editor Jour. of Legal Profession, 1986-87. Office: King & Ballow 1200 Noel Pl 200 4th Ave Nashville TN 37219

**NORWOOD, JANET LIPPE,** economist; b. Newark, Dec. 11, 1923; d. M. Turner and Thelma (Levinson) Lippe; m. Bernard Norwood, June 25, 1943; children: Stephen Harlan, Peter Carlton. BA, Douglass Coll., 1945; MA, Tufts U., Medford, Mass., 1946; PhD, Fletcher Sch. Law and Diplomacy, 1949; LLD (hon.), Fla. Internat. U., 1979, Carnegie Mellon U., Phila., 1984, Harvard U., Cambridge, Mass., 1997, Rutgers U., 2003. Instr. Wellesley Coll. 1948-49; economist William L. Clayton Ctr., Tufts U., 1953-58, with Bur. Labor Stats. U.S. Dept. Labor, Washington, 1963-91; dep. commr., then acting commr. Bur. Labor Stats. Dept. Labor, Washington, 1975-79, commr. labor stats., 1979-92; sr. fellow The Urban Inst., Washington, 1992-99; counselor, sr. fellow N.Y. Conf. Bd., 2001—. Dir. Nat. Opinion Rsch. Ctr., chair adv. coun. unemployment compensation, 1993—96; pres. COSSA, 2001—02; mem. bd. sci. counselors Nat. Ctr. Health Stats.; chair panel on food insecurity NAS, 2004—05; mem. adv. bd. Bur. Transp. Stats., 2005; chair panel on offshoring Nat. Acad. Pub. Adminstrn., 2005—; chair panel to evaluate Title IV and Fulbright-Hayes programs NAS, 2006—. Author: Organizing to Count: Change in the Federal Statistical System, 1995; contbr. Named Hall Disting. Alumni, Rutgers U., 1987; recipient Disting. Achievement award, Dept. Labor, 1972, Spl. Commendation award, 1977, Philip Arnow award, 1979, Elmer Staats award, 1982, Pub. Svc. award, 1984, Presdl. Disting. Exec. Rank, 1988, Elizabeth Scott award, Com. Pres.'s Statis. Assns., 2002. Fellow: AAAS, Nat. Assn. Bus. Economists, Royal Statis. Soc., Am. Statis. Assn. (pres. 1989, Founder's award 1997); mem.: Nat. Inst. Statis. Sci. (bd. trustees 1991—2000), Nat. Acad. Sci. (assoc.), Nat. Acad. Pub. Adminstrn., Internat. Assn. Ofcls. Stats., Internat. Statis. Inst., Douglass Coll. Soc. Disting. Achievement, Cosmos Club (pres. 1995—96). Home: 5610 Wisconsin Ave Ph 21-d Chevy Chase MD 20815-4444 Personal E-mail: janetnor@aol.com.

**NOSAKHERE, AKILAH SHUKURA MONTSHO,** librarian, consultant, editor, writer; b. Money, Miss., July 7, 1956; d. David Westbrook and Beatrice Birt. BS, Ball State U., Muncie, Ind., 1980—83, MEd, 1983—84; MLS, Atlanta U., 1986—87. Info. mgr. Nuc. Assurance Corp., Norcross, Ga., 1987—89; libr., record analyst EPA, Atlanta, 1989—92; head, circulation dept. Perimeter Coll., Dunwoody, Ga., 1992—95; Africana studies and ednl. libr. Ga. State U. Libr., Atlanta, 1995—99, head, collection devel., 1999—2002; spl. collections libr. AUC Woodruff Libr., Atlanta, 2002—. Mng. editor Internat. Jour. of Africana Studies, Atlanta, 2003—. Contbr. articles to profl. jours. Co-chair Nat. Coalition of Blacks for Reparations in Am., Atlanta, 2001—; book donations Africa's Children's Fund, Atlanta,

1996—2003. Recipient Outstanding Cmty. Vol., Ga. State U. African Am. Students Services, 1998, Citation for Outstanding Contributions to Africa's Children's Fund, Inc., Ga. Sec. of State, 2003; grantee Whitney-Carnegie Grant, ALA, 1997. Mem.: ALA, Nat. Coun. for Black Studies (mem. editl. bd. 2003—), African Am. Studies Librs. (chair, membership com. 2003—), African Studies Assn. (assoc.; chair, book donations com. 2003—). Office: AUC Woodruff Libr Archives & Spl Coll 111 James P Brawley Dr SW Atlanta GA 30314-4207 Office Phone: 404-978-2057. Office Fax: 404-978-2108. Personal E-mail: akilah7@myway.com. E-mail: akilah@auctr.edu.

**NOSANOW, BARBARA SHISSLER,** museum program director, curator; b. Roanoke, Va. d. Willis Morton and Kathryn Sabin (Bradford) Johnson; m. John Lewis Shissler Jr., July 28, 1957 (dec. May 1972); children: John Lewis Shissler III, Ada Holland Shissler; m. Lewis Harold Nosanow, Oct. 15, 1973. AB, Smith Coll., 1957; MA, Case Western Res. U., 1958. Asst. mng. editor Jour. Aesthetics and Art Criticism, Cleve. Mus. Art, 1958-63; dir. publs. and rsch. Mpls. Inst. Arts, 1963-72; dir. U. Minn. Art Mus., Mpls., 1972-76; dir. exhbns. and edn. Nat. Archives, Washington, 1976-79; curator Smithsonian Instn., Washington, 1979-82; asst. dir. Nat. Mus. Am. Art, Smithsonian Instn., 1982-88; dir. Portland (Maine) Mus. Art, 1988-93, Art Spaces, 1993—; study leader, lecturer Smithsonian Study Tours of France and Russia, 1997—. Lectr. in field. Past mem. various rev. panels NEH, Washington. Bd. dirs. Md. Com. for Humanities, Balt., 1980-83. Mem. Internat. Women's Forum. Avocation: travel. Office: Art Spaces 3386 Piperfife Ct Keswick VA 22947-9142 Office Phone: 434-923-0019.

**NOSBUSCH, KEITH D.,** multi-industry high-technology company executive; BS in Elec. and Computer Engring., U. Wis., Milw., 1974, MBA, 1976. Joined Allen-Bradley (subs. Rockwell Internat.), Milw., 1974; mktg. devel. specialist, indsl. control div. Rockwell Internat., 1978, sr. market planner, corp. planning, 1980, mgr. bus. planning, motion ctrl. div., 1982, devel. engring. mgr., motion ctrl. div., 1983, dir. prod. planning and devel., motion ctrl. div., 1985, v.p., presence sensing, automation group, 1988, v.p. control logix, automation group, 1994, pres. Automation Control Sys., 1998—2004, pres., CEO Rockwell Automation, 2004—, chmn., 2005—. Bd. dirs. Manitowoc Co., 2003—, Met. Milw. Assn. of Commerce. Advisory coun. U. Wis., Milw. Sch. Bus.; bd. trustees Boys & Girls Club of Milw. Mem.: Nat. Assn. Mfrs. (bd. govs.), Mfrs.' Alliance (bd. trustees). Office: Rockwell Automation 1201 2d St Milwaukee WI 53204

**NOSCO, PETER ERLING,** humanities educator, consultant; b. NYC, Mar. 13, 1950; s. John and Beatrice Nosco; m. Margaret Joan Button, June 19, 1976; children: John Alexander, Jean Nosco Wright. BA, Columbia U., 1971; MA (hon.), Cambridge U., Eng., 1973; PhD, Columbia U., 1978. Prof. U. of So. Calif., Los Angeles, Calif., 1986—2003, U. Brit. Columbia, 2003—; asst. prof. St. John's U., Queens, NY, 1979—86. Project dir. Fulbright Group Projects Abroad; dir. NEH Summer Inst. for Coll. Tchrs.; pres. faculty and acad. senate U. So. Calif., 2001—02. Author: (book-length monograph) Remembering Paradise; editor: (scholarly book) Confucianism and Tokugawa Culture; translator: Some Final Words of Advice (Saikaku oritome) (Transl. Ctr. (Nat. Endowment for the Arts Columbia U.), 1980). Recipient Fulbright Sr. Rsch. fellowship, Dept. of Edn., 1986, grant to lead a Fulbright Group Projects Abroad field study of Japan, 1998; grantee grant to direct a summer inst. for coll. tchrs., NEH, 2002. Fellow: L.A. Inst. for the Humanities; mem.: Am. Acad. of Religion, Am. Hist. Assn., Assn. for Asian Studies. Office: UBC-Asian Studies 401-1871 W Mall Vancouver BC Canada V6T 1Z2 Office Phone: 604-822-2835. Personal E-mail: peter.nosco@ubc.ca.

**NOSÉ, YUKIHIKO,** surgeon, educator; b. Iwamisawa, Hokkaido, Japan, May 7, 1932; came to U.S., 1962; s. Minoru and Haru (Murakami) N.; m. Bonnie Jean MacDonald, Mar. 15, 1965 (div. 1987); children: Kimi Willhelmina, Ken Willem, Kevin Scott; m. Ako Funakoshi, May 5, 1990. MD, U. Hokkaido, Sapporo, Japan, 1957, PhD, 1962. Surgeon in charge sect. artificial organs U. Hokkaido Sch. Medicine, 1961-62; rsch. assoc. Maimonides Hosp., Bklyn., 1962-64; postgrad. fellow dept. artificial organs Cleve. Clinic Found., 1964-66; mem. staff dept. artificial organs Cleve. Clinic, 1966—89, chmn. dept. artificial organs, 1970—90, chmn. emeritus, 1990—; prof. surgery Baylor Coll. Medicine, Houston, 1991—. V.p. Internat. Ctr. Artificial Organs and Transplantation, Cleve., 1979—; adj. prof. surgery Tokyo Med. Coll., Tsukuba (Japan) U., Keio (Japan) U.; cons., mem. surgery and bioengring. study sect. NIH, 1981-87; assoc. dean Asian region Internat. Faculty Artificial Organs, 1992—; prof. Bologna (Italy) U. Sch. Medicine, 1994—. Author: Manual on Artificial Organs: Volume I-The Artificial Kidney, 1969, Volume II-The Oxygenator, 1973, Cardiac Engineering, 1970, Die Kunstliche Niere, 1974, Plasmapheresis, Historical Perspective, Therapeutic Applications and New Frontiers (with Kambic), 1983, Future Perspective for the Development of Artificial Organs (with Kolff), 1988; contbr. to numerous profl. publs. Fellow Am. Inst. Med. and Biol. Engring. N.Y. Acad. Sci.; mem. AMA, AAAS, Internat. Soc. Artificial Organs (trustee, past pres.), Am. Soc. Artificial Internal Organs (past pres., trustee), World Apheresis Assn. (congress pres. 1994), Am. Soc. Testing Materials (chair subcom. on cardiovascular prosthesis in med. and surg. materials and devices, Moses award 1979), Am. Heart Assn., Am. Soc. Apheresis, Am. Soc. Artificial Internal Organs (pres. 1992, congress pres. 1994), Am. Soc. Biomaterials, Assn. Advancement Med. Instrumentation. Achievements include development of various types of artificial organs including cardiac prosthesis, artificial kidney, hepatic assist, respiratory assist, plasmapheresis, biomaterials. Home: 1111 Hermann Dr Houston TX 77004-7142 Office: Baylor Coll Medicine One Baylor Plaza Dept Surgery Houston TX 77030 Office Phone: 713-798-4434. Business E-mail: ynose@bcm.tmc.edu.

**NOSKI, CHARLES H.,** telecommunications executive, Degree, Calif. State U., Northridge, 1973. Corp. v.p., controller Hughes Elec. Corp., 1990—92, senior v.p., CFO, 1992—99, vice chmn., 1996—99; with Haskins & Sells (known as Deloitte & Touche), 1973-83, ptnr., 1983-90; v.p., CFO AT&T Corp., N.Y.C., 1999—2002; vice chmn. of bd. AT&T Corp., 2002; corp. v.p., CFO Northrup Grumman, 2003—05. Sr. advisor Blackstone Group, 2003—; bd. dirs. Air Products and Chemicals Inc., Northrop Grumman Corp., Teledyne Technologies Inc., Microsoft Corp., 2003—. Office: AT&T Corp 32 Ave of the Americas New York NY 10013-2412

**NOSLER, PETER COLE,** construction company executive; b. Portland, Oreg., May 7, 1940; s. Lyle and Elizabeth (Lewis) Nosler; m. Kay Hanson, Apr. 25, 1971; 1 child, Alexander. BS in Physics and Math., Walla Walla Coll., 1962; postgrad., U. Wash., 1962-63, U. Calif., Berkeley, 1965-70. Physicist GE, Richland, Wash., 1963-65; pvt. practice Portland, 1970-72; project mgr. Stone Constrn., San Leandro, Calif., 1972-75; v.p. ops. Rudolph & Sletten, Foster City, Calif., 1975-90; founder, pres. DPR Constrn. Inc., Redwood City, Calif., 1990, CEO. Lectr. Stanford U., Palo Alto, Calif., 1988—. Recipient Young Constrn. Profl. of Yr. award, Jour. Bldg. Design and Constrn., 1978. Mem.: Soc. Model Exptl. Engring. Avocations: model engineering and construction, history. Office: DPR Constrn Inc 1450 Veterans Blvd Redwood City CA 94063-2612*

**NOSLER, ROBERT AMOS,** sports association executive; b. Ashland, Oreg., Apr. 21, 1946; s. John Amos and Louise (Booz) N.; m. Joan Kathleen Hilliard, July 15, 1967; children: Christie Lynn, Jill Ann, John Robert. Student, U. Oreg., 1965. V.p., gen. mgr. Nosler Bullets, Inc., Bend, Oreg., 1974-88, pres., chief exec. officer, 1988-90; pres., CEO Nosler, Inc., Bend, 1990—. Regional bd. dirs. US Bank. Editor: Nosler Reloading Manual #1, 1976. Bd. dirs. Bend C. of C., 1984-88, treas., 1988; chmn. Central Oreg. Welcome Ctr. Steering Com., 1988. With USN, 1966-70; trustee Ctrl. Oreg. Community Coll. Found., 1992-98; trustee Nat. Rifle Assn. Found., 1995—. Recipient Pres.' award Bend C. of C., 1984, 87, 88. Mem. Nat. Reloading Mfrs. Assn. (bd. dirs. 1982-86, 90-93, pres. 1984-86), Greater Bend Rotary (dir. 1989-91). Republican. Lutheran. Avocations: hunting, outdoors, sports. Office: Nosler Inc 107 SW Columbia St Bend OR 97702-1014

**NOSTWICH, THEODORE DANIEL,** literature educator, researcher; b. Akron, Ohio, Sept. 14, 1925; s. John and Amelia Rose Nostwich; m. Ann Elizabeth Baker, Mar. 21, 1953; children: Mark, Paul, Michael, Elisabeth, Sarah. BA, Ohio State U., 1948, MA, 1950; PhD, U. Tex., 1968. Asst. prof. Ferris State U., Big Rapids, Mich., 1955—58; Purdue U., West Lafayette, Ind., 1962—63; Del Mar Coll., Corpus Christi, Tex., 1963—68; asst. prof. to prof. Iowa State U., Ames, 1968—95; lectr. Am. Lit. U. Glasgow, Scotland, 1996; prof. Iowa State U., 1996—98; ret. 1998. Rschr. in Am. lit. Editor: Dreiser's Heard in Corridors, 1988, Dreiser's Journalism Volume 1, 1988, Dreiser's Newspaper Days, 1991, Dreiser's "Fulfillment and Other Tales", 1992, Dreiser's "Dawn", 1998. Grantee Travel grantee, NEH, 1987—89. Mem.: Nat. Assn. Scholars, Am. Studies Assn. Achievements include research in Theordore Dreiser's biography and writings. Avocations: classical music, art galleries, collecting postage stamps. Home: 707 Hodge Ave Ames IA 50010 Office: Iowa State Univ Dept English Ames IA 50012 Office Phone: 515-294-3367.

**NOTARO, ANTHONY,** application developer; b. Queens County, NY, Sept. 13, 1956; s. Ignatius and Ida Notaro. AA, Nassau C.C., Garden City, NY, 1976; BS in Computer Sci., Hofstra U., 1978. Data analyst Hofstra U., Hempstead, NY, 1978; programmer Sperry Corp., Great Neck, NY, 1978—80; sys. designer L.I. Lighting Co., Hicksville, NY, 1980—84; sr. sys. analyst Grumman Corp., Bethpage, NY, 1984—85; self-employed cons. West Hempstead, NY, 1985—90; engr. Keyspan Energy Corp., Hicksville, 1990—. Plant engr. Shoreham (NY) Nuclear Power Sta., 1990—94; elec. supervising svc. operator Hewlett (NY) Elec. Ops., 1994—97. Contbr. articles on martial arts to profl. publs. Vol. Fedn. United Martial Arts, NJ, 1986—89, Fedn. Practicing Ju Jitsus, NJ, 1982—. Recipient Ismael Quiles award, South Bronx Cmty., 1988. Mem.: IEEE, Assn. Computing Machinery, Amred Forces Comms. Electronics Assn., Am. JuJitsu Assn., U.S. Navy Seals Mus. Assn. (life). Republican. Roman Catholic. Avocation: martial arts. Home: 319 Garfield Ave Hempstead NY 11552 Office: Key Span Energy Corp 175 E Oco Country Rd Hicksville NY 11801

**NOTAROS, BRANISLAV M.,** electrical engineer, educator; b. Zrenjanin, Serbia-Monteneg (Yugoslavia), Jan. 2, 1965; s. Milivoj D and Smilja J Notaros; m. Olivera K Micic; children: Jelena, Milica. BSEE, U. Belgrade, 1988, MSEE, 1992, PhD in Elec. Engring., 1995. Tchg. and rsch. asst. Elec. Engring. Dept. U. Belgrade, Serbia, 1989—96, asst. prof. Elec. Engring. Dept., 1996—98; rsch. assoc. U. Colo., Boulder, 1998—99; asst. prof. U. Mass. Dartmouth, 1999—2004, assoc. prof., 2004—. Dir. of telecom. lab. Advanced Tech. and Mfg. Ctr., U. of Mass. Dartmouth, 2001—. Author: Collection of Examination Questions and Problems in Electromagnetics, 1998, Collection of Examination Problems in Fundamentals of Electrical Engineering with Solutions, 1997, Electromagnetic Theory, 2003; contbr. chapters to books, articles to profl. jours. Recipient Marconi Premium, Instn. Elec. Engrs., London, 1999, Young Scientist award, Internat. Union of Radio Sci., Toronto, Can., 1999, IEEE MTT-S Microwave prize, Microwave Theory and Techniques Soc., Inst. IEEE, 2005. Mem.: IEEE (sr. Microwave prize Microwave Theory and Techniques Soc. 2005). Christian Orthodox. Avocations: swimming, skiing, travel. Home: 1 Aster Ln South Dartmouth MA 02748 Office: U Mass Dartmouth ECE Dept 285 Old Westport Rd Dartmouth MA 02747-2300 Office Phone: 508-910-6464. Business E-Mail: bnotaros@umassd.edu.

**NOTEBAERT, RICHARD C.,** telecommunications industry executive; b. 1947; m. Peggy Notebaert; 2 children. B.A., U. Wis., 1969, MBA, 1983. With Wisconsin Bell, 1969-83; v.p. marketing and operations Ameritech, Chicago, 1983-86; pres. Ameritech Mobile Comm., 1986-89, Indiana Bell Telephone Co., 1989-92, Ameritech Services, 1992-93, pres., COO, 1993-94; chmn., pres., CEO Ameritech Corp., Chicago, 1994—99; pres., CEO Tellabs, 2000—02; chmn., CEO Qwest Commun. Internat., Denver, 2002—. Bd. dirs. AON Corp., Cardinal Health, Inc., Qwest Comms. Internat., Inc.; trustee, corp. leadership bd. dirs. U. Notre Dame, mem., bus. coun.; chmn., Reliability and Interoperability Coun. FCC, 2002—; apptd. mem. Nat. Security Telecom. Adv. Com., 2003—. Co-chmn. Alexis de Toqueville Soc. United Way; bd. dirs. Denver Ct. Performing Arts; vice chmn., civic com. The Commi. Club Chgo.; bd. dirs. The Executives Club, Chgo. Recipient Dist. Alumni award, U. Wis., 1999. Office: Qwest Commn Internat 1801 California St Denver CO 80202*

**NOTHAFT, FRANK EMILE,** economist; b. Jersey City, Apr. 10, 1956; s. Frank Emil and Rita Johanna (Laer) N.; m. Lisa Beth Greenfield, June 13, 1981; children: Frank Austin, Daniel Blake, John Paul. BA, N.Y.U., 1976; MA, Columbia U., 1977, MPhil, 1979, PhD, 1986. Economist Bd. Govs. Fed. Reserve System, Washington, 1983-86; sr. economist Freddie Mac, McLean, Va., 1986-88, dep. chief economist, 1988-90, dir., office of chief economist, 1990—2001, chief economist, 2001—, v.p., 2004—. Contbr. articles to profl. jours. Sec., bd. dirs. Falls Church Housing Corp., Va., 1988-91. Sloan Found. grantee, 1982; Columbia U. fellow, 1976-79; recipient Founders' Day award, N.Y.U., 1976. Mem. Am. Econ. Assn., Am. Real Estate Urban Econs. Assn. (bd. dirs. 1990-92, 2002-04, 06-), Fin. Mgmt. Assn. (bd. dirs. 2006-). Office: Freddie Mac 8200 Jones Branch Dr Mc Lean VA 22102-3110

**NOTKIN, LEONARD SHELDON,** architect; b. N.Y.C., Apr. 1, 1931; s. Murry and Evelyn (Mofshatz) N.; m. Ann Mathilda Stefanko, Nov. 24, 1956; children: Jennifer, Mead. BArch, U. Pa., 1954. Registered architect, N.Y., Mass., Ohio, Pa., Nat. Coun. Archtl. Registration Bds. Architect, Percival Goodman (Architect), N.Y.C., 1956-58; Architect Bloch and Hesse (Architects), N.Y.C., 1958-59; Resnick and Green (Architects), N.Y.C., 1959-60; architect, prin., v.p. The Architects Collaborative, Inc., Cambridge, Mass., 1960-95; chief design critic Boston Archtl. Center, 1964-69; mem. Lexington (Mass.) Design Adv. Com., 1970-73, chmn., 1972; profl. studio critic Harvard Grad. Sch. Design, 1974-76; pres. Boston Design Assocs., Inc., Waltham, Mass., 1995—. Major recent works include Intermediate Sch. 137, Bronx, N.Y., 1976, Visual Arts Instructional Facility SUNY, Purchase, 1976, Lahey Clinic Med. Ctr., Burlington, Mass., 1976—, W. Penn Hosp., Pitts., 1977, St. Francis/St. George Hosp., Cin., 1978, Blue Cross/Blue Shield of Conn. Hdqrs., North Haven, Temple U. Hosp., Phila., composite hosp. Loring AFB, Limestone, Maine, Med. Facilities, Fort Drum, N.Y., Health Care Internat. Ltd., Glasgow, Scotland, Intensive Care Hosp. and Hotel, U. Ky. Cancer Rsch. Ctr., Children's Hosp. Med. Ctr. Rsch. Lab., Cin., new main entrance, lobby and admissions facilities Hosp. of U. Pa., Phila., Childrens Hosp., Kuwait, 1996, Health Facilities, Algiers, Algeria, 1996, Nigeria, 2003, Office Building/Auburn, Mass., Greenfield Comty. Coll., Mass. Served with U.S. Army, 1954-56. Recipient Design award for IBM Hdqrs., Gaithersburg, Md. Progressive Architecture mag., 1964; 1st pl. award for Worcester (Mass.) Community Center AIA, 1966; Design award for Worcester Found. Exptl. Biology bldg. Mass. chpt. AIA, 1968; Design award NIH Research Lab., Bethesda, Md. GSA, 1972; Best Bldg. of Yr. award for Norwalk (Conn.) High Sch. Assn. for Better Community Design, 1972; Honor award (Conn.) Soc. Architects AIA 1974 Mem. AIA Mass. State Assn. Architects, Boston Soc. Architects (dir. 1976-79, spl. design citation 1993). Office: Boston Design Assocs Inc 393 Totten Pond Rd Waltham MA 02451-2003 Office Phone: 781-259-9190.

**NOTO, LUCIO A.,** gas and oil industry executive; b. Apr. 24, 1939; BS in Physics, U. Notre Dame; MBA, Cornell U.; Woodrow Wilson Fell., U. Notre Dame; Bache Fell., Cornell U. With Mobil Corp., 1962—2002; pres. Mobil Saudi Arabia, 1981—85, chmn., 1985—86; v.p. planning and econs. Mobil Corp./Mobil Oil Corp. (now Exxon Mobil Corp.), 1986—88, CFO, 1989—93, pres., 1993—2002, chmn., bd. dir. CEO, COO, 1994—99, vice chmn., 1999—2001; mng. ptnr. Midstream Partners LLC. Bd. dir. IBM, Altria Group, UAG Inc., Comml. Internat. Bank Egypt, Shinsei Bank, Stem Cell Innovations. Dir. Am. Petroleum Inst. Pub. Policy Com., The Bus. Coun., The Coun. on Fgn. Rels. and Bus. Roundtable.*

**NOTTERMAN, DANIEL A.,** pediatrician, educator; BA, Cornell U., 1973; MA in Philosophy, Tufts U., 1977; MD, NYU, 1978. Diplomate Am. Bd. Pediatrics. Intern, resident NYU Med. Ctr., N.Y.C., 1978—81, chief resident in pediat., 1981—82; rsch. fellow clin. pharmacology Cornell Med. Ctr., N.Y.C., 1983—84; dir. divsn. pediatric critical care medicine N.Y. Hosp. Cornell Med. Ctr., N.Y.C., 1985—97; postdoctoral rschr., prof. Princeton (N.J.) U., 1992—93; chief pediatric svcs. Bristol-Myers Squibb Children's Hosp. Robert Wood Johnson U. Hosp., 2002—; chair dept. pediat. U. Medicine and Dentistry N.J. - Robert Wood Johnson Med. Sch., 2002—. Office: Robert Wood Johnson Med Sch 1 Robert Wood Johnson Pl MEB 306 New Brunswick NJ 08903 Home: 7 Symmes Ct Cranbury NJ 08512 Office Phone: 732-235-7900. Business E-Mail: d.notterman@umdnj.edu.

**NOTTI, DONNA BETTS,** special education educator; b. Manassas, Va., Sept. 4, 1968; d. William Jackson and Christine Joan (Fant) B.; m. David L. Notti, Oct. 14, 1995. BS in Spl. Edn., Old Dominion U., Norfolk, Va., 1990. Tchr., counselor Southeastern Cooperative Ednl. Programs, Norfolk, Va., 1991—2004; vol. tutor Tonelson Teaching and Learning Ctr., Norfolk, Va., 1989; secondary spl. edn. tchr. Chesapeake City Schs., Va., 2004—. Chair child study com. Oscar Smith HS, Chesapeake, Va., 2006—. Mem. Coun. for Exceptional Children (v.p. 1989-90), Coun. for Children With Behavior Disorders, Coun. for Exceptional Children-Mental Retardation, Am. Re-ED Assn., Va. State Reading Assn., Chesapeake Reading Coun. Lutheran. Office: 1994 Tiger Dr Chesapeake VA 23320 Personal E-mail: dbnotti@yahoo.com.

**NOTTINGHAM, EDWARD WILLIS, JR.,** federal judge; b. Denver, Jan. 9, 1948; s. Edward Willis and Willie Newton (Gullett) N.; m. Cheryl Ann Card, June 6, 1970 (div. Feb. 1981); children: Amelia Charlene, Edward Willis III; m. Janis Ellen Chapman, Aug. 18, 1984 (div. Dec. 1998); 1 child, Spencer Chapman. AB, Cornell U., 1969; JD, U. Colo., 1972. Bar: Colo. 1972, U.S. Dist. Ct. Colo. 1972, U.S. Ct. Appeals (10th cir.) 1973. Law clk. to presiding judge U.S. Dist. Ct. Colo., Denver, 1972-73; assoc. Sherman & Howard, Denver, 1973-76, 78-80, ptnr., 1980-87, Beckner & Nottingham, Grand Junction, Colo., 1987-89; asst. U.S. atty. U.S. Dept. Justice, Denver, 1976-78; U.S. dist. judge Dist. of Colo., Denver, 1989—. Mem. Jud. Conf. of the U.S. Com. on Automation and Tech., 1994-2000, chmn., 1997-2000. Bd. dirs. Beaver Creek Met. Dist., Avon, Colo., 1980-88, Justice Info. Ctr., Denver, 1985-87, 21st Jud. Dist. Victim Compensation Fund, Grand Junction, Colo., 1987-89. Mem. ABA, Colo. Bar Assn. (chmn. criminal law sect. 1983-85, chmn. ethics com. 1988-89), Order of Coif, Denver Athletic Club, Delta Sigma Rho, Tau Kappa Alpha. Episcopalian. Office: US Dist Ct 901 19th St Denver CO 80294 Office Phone: 303-844-5018. E-mail: NottinghamChambers@cod.uscourts.gov.

**NOTTINGHAM, JUANITA C.,** medical/surgical nurse; b. Bozeman, Mont., Dec. 24, 1916; d. Lyman L. Crockett and Gussie Kienast; m. Armond L. Bean, Oct. 29, 1939 (dec. Apr. 1985); children: Linda Davis, Shirley Pomeroy, Timothy Bean; m. Charles E. Nottingham, Sept. 18, 1992. Diploma in nursing, Mont. Deaconess Hosp., Gt. Falls, 1939; BSN, Mont. State U., 1971, MSN, 1973. Lic. RN Mont., Ind., pub. health nurse Alaska. Head nurse St. John's Hosp., Linny, Mont., 1970—72; asst. prof. Anderson (Ind.) U., 1974—77; pub. health nurse State of Alaska, Fairbanks, Alaska, 1977—83; counselor North Slope Borough, Anaktuvk Pass, Alaska, 1984—85. Adv. bd. Patient Hostel-Tanana Chiefs, Fairbanks, 1974—77; counselor Crisis Counseling., Fairbanks, 1980, Rescue Mission, Fairbanks; vis. counselor Fairbanks Correctional Ctr., 1985—2001. Author: Tundra Tales, 2001; contbr. articles to profl. jours. Named a clinic after, North Slope Borough Adminstrn., Anakturuk Pass, 1980; recipient Social Svc. Worker of Yr., State of Alaska, 1984. Mem.; Alpha Beta Tau. Republican. Avocations: music, writing. Home: PO Box 80946 Fairbanks AK 99708

**NOTTINGHAM, ROBINSON KENDALL,** insurance company executive; b. Balt., Apr. 4, 1938; s. Robinson Jr. and Juliet (Moore) N.; m. Elizabeth LeViness, Aug. 26, 1960; children: Robinson Kendall Jr., Charles Denmead. BA in Polit. Sci., Johns Hopkins U., 1959; postgrad., Johns Hopkins U., Washington, l965. With Am. Internat. Group, Inc., Hong Kong and Bangkok, 1968-71; mng. dir. Hanover Ins. Co., Universal Ins. Co., Bangkok, 1971-73, Am. Internat. Ins. Co., Lagos, Nigeria, 1973-75; regional pres. African div. Am. Internat. Underwriters, N.Y.C., 1975-78, Middle Ea. div., 1978-83, European div., 1983-86; chief exec. officer for Japan and Korea Am. Internat. Group, Inc., Tokyo, 1986-89; chmn., bd. dirs., CEO Am. Life Ins. Co., Wilmington, Del., 1989—; exec. v.p., life ins. Am. Internat. Group, 1998—. Bd. dirs. AIG Overseas Fin. (Japan) Inc., Tokyo, Am. Home Assurance Co., N.Y.C., AIU Ins. Co., N.Y.C.; trustee John Hopkins U., 2005 Pres. USO Coun., Tokyo, 1987-89; mem. world bd. govs. USO, Washington, 1987-97; mem. adv. coun. Johns Hopkins U. Sch. Advanced Internat. Studies, Washington, 1984-96. Served to lt. comdr. USNR, 1960-68. Mem. Princeton Club (N.Y.C.), Short Hills Club (N.J.), Bay Head Yacht Club (N.J.), Baltusrol Club (Springfield, N.J.), Chevy Chase (Md.) Club, Met. Club (Washington), Univ. and Artist Club (Washington), Delta Phi. Republican. Episcopalian. Avocation: sailing. Office: Am Life Ins Co 1 Alico Plz Wilmington DE 19899 E-mail: ken.nottingham@aig.com.

**NOTTINGHAM, WILLIAM JESSE,** retired religious organization administrator, retired minister; b. Sharon, Pa., Nov. 22, 1927; s. Jess William and Alice May (Green) Nottingham; m. Patricia Clutts, Feb. 1, 1949; children: Theodore Jess, Deborah Joan Selke, Timothy Alice, Gregory Philip. BA, Bethany Coll., W.Va., 1949, DD (hon.), 1987; BD, Union Theol. Sem., N.Y.C., 1953; PhD, Columbia U., 1962; DD (hon.), Christian Theol. Sem., Indpls., 1984. Ordained to ministry Christian Ch. (Disciples of Christ), 1945, ministerial standing United Ch. of Christ. Machinist apprentice Westinghouse, 1943—45; pastor Ch. of Christ, Canoe Camp and Covington, Pa., 1949-50; field worker Ch. of the Master, N.Y.C., 1950-53; assoc. min. Nat. City Christian Ch., Washington, 1954-58; fraternal worker Coun. on Christian Unity, France, 1958-65; with CIMADE and Centre de Glay; with youth dept. World Coun. of Chs., Geneva, 1965-68; exec. sec. for Latin Am. and Caribbean Christian Ch. (Disciples of Christ) and United Ch. Christ, Indpls., 1968-76; exec. sec. East Asia and Pacific Divsn. Overseas Ministries, Christian Ch. (Disciples of Christ), 1976-83; pres., exec. sec. Europe Divsn. Overseas Ministries Christian Ch. (Disciples of Christ), Indpls., 1984-94, pres. emeritus, 2004; affiliate prof. mission Christian Theol. Sem., 1995—2005; ret., 2005. Author: Christian Faith and Secular Action: An Introduction to the Life and Thought of Jacques Maritain, 1968, The Practice and Preaching of Liberation, 1986, The Social Ethics of Martin Bucer 1491-1551, 1962; translator: God's Underground, 1970, Prayer at the Heart of Life, 1975, Materialist Approaches to the Bible, 1985, Madeleine Barot, 1991; contbr. articles to theol. jours. Mem. Ind. Faith and Labor Network, Com. To Free Lori Berenson. Chaplain USNR, 1954—65. Recipient Disting. Alumnus award, Union Theol. Sem., 1999, Martin Luther King, Jr. Drum Major for Justice award, 2003; Fulbright scholar, Strasbourg, France, 1953—54. Mem.; Disciples Justice Action Network, United Christian Missionary Soc., Assn. Disciples for Theol. Discussion, Indpls. Peace and Justice Ctr. (bd.). Democrat. Personal E-mail: nottingham50@sbcglobal.net. Business E-Mail: bnottingham@cts.edu.

**NOTZ, JOHN KRANZ, JR.,** arbitrator, mediator, retired lawyer; b. Chgo., Jan. 5, 1932; s. John Kranz and Elinor (Trostel) N.; m. Janis Wellin, Apr. 23, 1966; children: Jane Elinor Notz (Mrs. Ian H. Watson), John Wellin. BA, Williams Coll., Williamstown, Mass., 1953; JD, Northwestern U., Evanston, Ill., 1956. Bar: Ill. 1956, Fla. 1957, Wis. 1989, U.S. Supreme Ct. 1960. Assoc. 1st Nat. Bank Chgo., 1954, 1956; from assoc. to ptnr. Gardner, Carton & Douglas, Chgo., 1960-95, of counsel, 1990-95; ret., 1996. Arbitrator, mediator Am. Arbitration Assn., Chgo. Internat. Dispute Resolution Assn., The Practice and Dispute Resolution Inc., Nat. Futures Assn. N.Y. Stock Exch. Contbr. articles to profl. jours. Sec. State Corp. Acts Adv. Com., 1982-95, chmn., 1987-89; pres. Chgo. Lit. Club, 1996-97, Ill. Inst. Continuing Legal Edn., 1980-91, chmn., 1990-91; bd. dirs., former pres. Black Point Historic Preserve, Inc.; trustee Graceland Cemetery, bd. Am. Kerill. Historians (former treas.). 1st lt. USAF, 1957-60. Recipient Service award Northwestern U., 1978 Fellow Am. Bar Found. (life), Ill. Bar Found. (life), Chgo. Bar Found. (life); mem. Am. Law Inst., Ill. State Bar Assn., Chgo. Bar Assn., Wis. State Bar, Lawyers Club City Chgo., Racquet Club Chgo., Lake Geneva (Wis.) Country Club,

Mid-Day Club (Chgo.), Literary Club (Chgo.), Caxton Club (Chgo.), Cliff Dwellers (Chgo.), The Antiquarian Soc. (fin. com.). Office: care Gardner Carton & Douglas LLP 191 N Wacker Dr 3700 Chicago IL 60606-1698 Office Phone: 312-569-1088.

**NOUR, NAWAL M.,** obstetrician, gynecologist, health facility administrator; arrived in US, 1980; BA, Brown U., 1984; MD, Harvard U., 1994; MPH, Harvard U., 1999. Chief residency Brigham and Women's Hosp., Boston, 1998; instr. dept of Obstetrics, Gynecology and Reproductive Biology Harvard Sch. of Medicine; dir. obstetric resident practice Brigham and Women's Hosp., Boston; founder African Women's Health Practice, 1999—. Recipient Commonwealth Fund Harvard U., 1999; fellow H. Rchard Nesson Fellowship, Brigham and Women's Hosp., 1999, MacArthur Found., 2003. Office: Brigham and Women's Hosp 75 Francis St Boston MA 02115

**NOURBAKHSH, M. REZA,** medical educator; PhD in Phys. Therapy, U. Iowa, Iowa City, 1993. Lic. orthopaedic clin. specialist Am. Bd. of Phys. Therapy Specialists. Asst. prof. Des Moines U., Osteopathic Med. Sch., 1999—2001; assoc. prof. North Ga. Coll. and State U., Dahlonega, 2002—. Contbr. articles to profl. jours. Achievements include research in Alternative Medicine and Low Back Pain. Office: North Ga Coll and State U 155 Sunset Dr Dahlonega GA 30597 Office Phone: 706-864-1766. Office Fax: 706-864-1943. E-mail: mrnourbakhsh@ngcsu.edu.

**NOVA, CRAIG,** writer; b. Los Angeles, July 5, 1945; s. Karl and Elizabeth (Sinclair) N.; m. Christina Barnes, July 2, 1977; children: Abigail, Tate. BA, U. Calif.-Berkeley, 1967; M.F.A. Columbia U., 1969. Disting. prof. humanities U. N.C., Greensboro, 2005—. Author: Turkey Hash, 1972, The Geek, 1975, Incandescence, 1978, The Good Son, 1982, The Congressman's Daughter, 1986, Tornado Alley, 1989, Trombone, 1992, The Book of Dreams, 1994, The Universal Door, 1997, Brook Trout and the Writing life, 1999, Wetware, 2001, Cruisers, 2004. Recipient Harper-Saxton prize Harper and Row, Pubs., 1972; recipient award in lit. Am. Acad. and Inst. Arts and Letters; Guggenheim Found. fellow, 1977; fellow Nat. Endowment for Arts, 1973, Nat. Endowment for Arts, 1975, Creative Artists Pub. Service, 1976; NEA fellow, 1985; story included in Best Am. Short Stories, 1987. E-mail: nova@sover.net.

**NOVACEK, MICHAEL JOHN,** curator, museum director; b. Evanston, Ill., June 3, 1948; s. Albin John and June Shirley (White) N.; 1 child, Julie. BA in Zoology, UCLA, 1971; MA in Biology, San Diego State U., 1973; PhD in Paleontology with honors, U. Calif., Berkeley, 1978; PhD (hon.), Long Island U., 1996. Lectr. dept. zoology San Diego State U., 1976-77, asst. prof., 1977-79, assoc. prof., 1979-82; asst. curator dept. vertebrate paleontology Am. Mus. Natural History, N.Y.C., 1983-85, chmn., 1983-89, assoc. curator, 1985-89, curator, 1989—, v.p., dean sci., 1989—94, v.p., provost sci., 1994—. Adj. prof. San Diego State U., 1982—; panel mem. systematic biology program NSF, 1986-90, mem. bioadv. com., 1992—; adj. prof. dept. biology CUNY, 1987—; chmn. biospherics com. Yale U., New Haven, 1993—; expedition leader, Wyo., Mex., Chile, Mongolia; lectr. in field. Editor: Extinction and Phylogeny, 1992, Mammal Phylogeny, 1993; contbr. over 100 articles to profl. jours. Grantee Nat. Geog. Soc., 1985-86, 88-90, Eppley Found., 1986-88, NSF, 1989-95, Sloan Found., 1990, Internat. Rsch. and Exch. Bd.; Nat. Needs postdoctoral fellow NSF, 1979-80; recipient Roy Chapman Andrews Soc. Disting. Explorer's award, 2003. Fellow Explorers Club, Am. Acad. Arts and Scis. (bd. dirs. 1995-); mem.Sch. Study Evolution, Soc. Systematic Biologists (pres. 1992-93), Systematics Agenda 2000 (co-chair 1992—). Avocations: music, climbing, bicycling, skiing, art. Office: Am Mus Natural History Central Park West at 79th New York NY 10024

**NOVACK, ALVIN JOHN,** physician; b. Red Lodge, Mont., Mar. 11, 1925; s. John and Anna Geraldine (Maddio) N.; m. Betty P. Novack, Jan. 10, 1952; children— Vance, Deborah, Michelle, Mitchel, Craig, Brad, Mary Ellen, Garth. MD, U. Wash., 1952. Intern Harper Hosp., Detroit, 1952, resident in surgery, 1953; resident in otolaryngology Johns Hopkins U., 1954-57; resident in surgery Columbia-Presbyn. Med. Center, N.Y.C., 1957-60, fellow head and neck surgery, 1957-60; dir. head and neck surgery Swedish Hosp., Seattle, 1960-91; dir. otolaryngology Children's Orthopedic Hosp., Seattle, 1965-78; ret., 1991. Contbr. articles to med. jours. Served to lt. AUS, 1940-43. Nat. Cancer Inst. fellow, 1957-60 Fellow A.C.S.; mem. AMA, Am. Acad. Otolaryngology and Head and Neck Surgery, Soc. Head and Neck Surgeons, North Pacific Surg. Assn., Pacific Coast Surg. Assn., Seattle Surg. Soc.

**NOVACK, KENNETH JOSEPH,** lawyer; b. Boston, Aug. 25, 1941; s. Hyman and Dorothy Ruth N.; m. Marianne Margaret Lefebvre; children: Laura Ann, Sara Elizabeth, Emily Kate, Jeffrey Nicholas. BA (Rufus Choate scholar), Dartmouth Coll., 1963; LL.B., Harvard U., 1966. Bar: Mass. 1966, D.C. 1972. With Mintz, Levin, Cohn, Ferris, Glovsky and Popeo, P.C., Boston, 1996—98, 2004—, named ptnr., 1970, mem. exec. com., 1972—98, mng. ptnr Boston, 1972—78, pres., CEO, 1991-94, sr. counsel, 2004—; vice chmn. AOL Inc. (AOL and Time Warner merge, 2001), 1998—2001, Time Warner Inc. (formerly AOL Time Warner), 2001—04. Bd. dirs. Time Warner Inc., 2001—, Paratek Pharms., 2002—. Vice chmn. Mus. Sci., Boston, Tufts-New England Med. Ctr., Combined Jewish Philanthropies; pres. Teen Action Campaign Inc.; trustee Facing History and Ourselves, Novack Family Found. Mem. ABA, Internat. Bar Assn., Boston Bar Assn. (co-chmn. securities law com. 1970-85), D.C. Bar Assn., Am. Law Inst. Clubs: St. Botolph, Harvard Republican. Office: Mintz Levin Cohn Ferris Glovsky and Popeo PC 1 Financial Ctr Fl 39 Boston MA 02111*

**NOVACK, ROBERT,** lawyer; b. Jersey City, May 3, 1953; BA, Rutgers U., 1975; JD cum laude, U. Miami, 1978. Bar: N.J. 1978, U.S. Dist. Ct. N.J. 1978, N.Y. 1985, U.S. Ct. of Appeals (2nd and 3rd cirs.). Law clk. to Hon. Harry A. Margolis N.J. Superior Ct., Law Divsn., 1978-79; ptnr. Budd, Larner, Gross, Rosenbaum, Greenberg & Sade, P.C., Short Hills, NJ; ptnr. litig., office ptnr. in charge Edwards & Angell LLP, Short Hills, NJ, 1997—. Adj. prof. Rutgers U. Sch. of Law; mem. Lawyers Adv. Com., US Dist Ct. NJ; past chmn. Supreme Ct. NJ Dist. Ethics Com. Author: (with Harry A. Margolis) Tort Claims Against Public Entities, 1984, 1st rev. edit., 1986, 2nd rev. edit., 1988, 3rd rev. edit., 1990. Mem. ABA, Fed. Bar Assn., N.J. State Bar Assn., Trial Attys. of N.J., Essex County Bar Assn. Office: Edwards & Angell LLP 51 John F Kennedy Pkwy Short Hills NJ 07078 Office Phone: 973-921-5225. Office Fax: 973-376-3380. Business E-Mail: rnovack@edwardsangell.com.

**NOVAK, ALAN LEE,** retired pharmaceutical company executive; b. Chgo., Oct. 25, 1928; s. Samuel Adolph and Tina Lillian (Oris) N.; m. Delores Jane Tonkel, Dec. 17, 1950; children: Shaya Ray, G. Alexander, Cheryl Lynn. BS, Fla. So. Coll., 1951. Cert. purchasing mgr. Police officer Lakeland (Fla.) Police Dept., 1952-53; sales rep. Sinclair Refining Co., Tampa, Fla., 1954-58; prin. Novak's Texaco s/s and Fuel Co., Tampa, 1958-62; sales rep. Burroughs Wellcome Co., Columbus, Ohio, 1962-70, purchasing agt. Research Triangle Park, NC, 1970-74, dir. purchasing, 1974-94. Bd. dirs. Eastern N.C. Better Bus. Bur., 1989-96. Active N.C. Coun. on the Holocaust, 1996—2002; vol. Friends Helping Friends Vet. Dept., N.C. State U., 1994—; records dept. Raleigh Polic Dept., 1994—; area contact Am. Israel Polit. Affairs Coun. Raleigh, 1984—86; fin. sec. Temple Beth Or, Raleigh, 1975—77, treas., 1996—97; pres. Raleigh Chpt. B'nai B'rith, 1999—2000. With U.S. Army, 1946—47, Japan. Mem. Am. Legion Jewish War Vets. 1st Cav. Divsn. Assn. Drug, Chem., and Allied Trades Assn. (area rep. 1975-78, bd. dirs. 1978-84, treas. 1985, v.p. 1986, pres. 1987-88), Nat. Assn. Purchasing Mgmt., Purchasing Mgmt. Assn. Carolinas-Va., Triangle Purchasing Assn., Raleigh C. of C., Burroughs Wellcome Retirees Club (pres.), Tau Kappa Epsilon, Omicron Delta Kappa. Lodges: B'nai B'rith (Double Chai award 1985-87), AMRAN Shrine Temple (charter). Republican. Jewish. Avocations: hunting, fishing. Personal E-mail: zayden@bellsouth.net.

**NOVAK, BARBARA,** art history educator; b. NYC; d. Joseph and Sadie (Kaufman) N.; m. Brian O'Doherty, July 5, 1960. BA, Barnard Coll., 1951; MA, Radcliffe Coll., 1953, PhD, 1957. TV instr. Mus. Fine Arts, Boston, 1957-58; mem. faculty Barnard Coll., Columbia U., N.Y.C., 1958-98, prof. art history, 1970—, Helen G. Altschul prof., 1984-98, prof. emeritus, 1998—. Vis. Mellon prof. U. Pitts., 1971; mem. adv. coun. Archives of Am. Art, NAD Author: American Painting of the 19th Century, 1969, revised edit., 1979, Nature and Culture, 1980, rev. edit., 1995, Voyages of the Self, 2006, The Thyssen-Bornemisza Collection 19th Century American Painting, 1986, Alice's Neck, 1987, The Margaret-Ghost, 2003, (novels) The Ape and the Whale, 1995, (play) The Ape and the Whale: Darwin and Melville in Their Own Words, 1987 (performed at Symphony Space 1987), Dreams and Shadows: Thomas H. Hotchkiss in 19th Century Italy, 1993; co-editor: Next to Nature, 1980; mem. editorial bd. Am. Art Jour. Commr. Nat. Portrait Gallery. Recipient disting. tchg. award, Coll. Art Assn., 1997, Lawrence Fleishman award for outstanding scholarship, Archives Am. Art, 1999, medal of distinction, Barnard Coll., 2002; Fulbright fellow, Belgium, 1953—54, Guggenheim fellow, 1974, Nat. Book Critics nominee, 1980, L.A. Times Book Award nominee, 1980, Am. Book Award paperback nominee, 1981. Fellow Soc. Am. Historians, Phila. Atheneum; mem. Soc. Am. Historians, Am. Antiquarian Soc., Coll. Art Assn. (dir. 1974-77, Disting. Tchg. of Art History award 1997), PEN. Achievements include honored with Barbara Novak professorship in art history at Barnard Coll. and Columbia U., 2004; Barbara Novak Acquisition Fund at Nat. Portrait Gallery.

**NOVAK, DAVID,** theology studies educator, rabbi; b. Chgo., Aug. 19, 1941; s. Syd and Sylvia (Wien) N.; m. Melva Ziman, July 3, 1963; children: Marianne, Jacob George. AB in Classics and Ancient History, U. Chgo., 1961; M in Hebrew Lit., Jewish Theol. Sem. Am., 1964; PhD, Georgetown U., 1971. Ordained rabbi, 1966. Rabbi Shaare Tikvah Congregation, 1966—69; dir. Jewish chaplaincy St. Elizabeth's Hosp., 1966—69; rabbi Emanuel Synagogue, Oklahoma City, 1968—72, Beth Tfiloh Congregation, Balt., 1972—77, Congregation Beth El, Norfolk, Va., 1977—81, Congregation Darchay Noam, Far Rockaway, NY, 1981—89; Edgar M. Bronfman prof. modern Judaic studies U. Va., Charlottesville, 1989—97; J. Richard and Dorothy Shiff chair of Jewish studies U. Toronto, 1997—. Lectr. philosophy Oklahoma City U., 1969-72, New Sch. for Social Rsch., 1982-84; lectr. Jewish studies Balt. Hebrew Coll., 1972-77; adj. asst. prof. philosophy Old Dominion U., 1977-81; vis. assoc. prof. Talmud Jewish Theol. Sem. Am., 1986-88; adj. assoc. prof. Baruch Coll., CUNY, 1984-88, adj. prof., 1989; founder, v.p., coord. panel Halakhic Inquiry Union Traditional Judaism/Inst. Traditional Judaism; disting. vis. prof. religion and corp. ethics Drew U., 1995; Yarnton/Lancaster lectr. Oxford U., 1996; Charles E. Test, MD Disting. vis. scholar Princeton U., 2004, vis. prof. religion, 2006. Contbg. editor First Things. Sec.-treas. Inst. on Religion and Pub. Life. Essay winner Hyman G. Enelow prize Jewish Theol. Sem. Am., 1975; recipient Rabbi Jacob B. Augus award Jewish Theol. Sem. Am., 1984, Best Book Constructive Religious Thought award Am. Acad. of Religion, 2000; Woodrow Wilson Internat. Ctr. for Scholars fellow, 1992-93. Fellow Acad. for Jewish Philosophy, Am. Acad. for Jewish Rsch.; mem. Am. Theol. Soc., Assn. for Jewish Studies, Am. Acad. Religion. Office: Univ Coll 15 King's College Cir Toronto ON Canada M5S 3H7 Office Phone: 416-946-3229. Business E-Mail: david.novak@utoronto.ca.

**NOVAK, DAVID C.,** restaurant company executive; Sr. v.p., mktg. Pizza Hut, 1986—90; exec. v.p., mktg. and nat. sales Pepsi-Cola Co., 1990—92, COO, N. Am., 1992—94; pres., CEO N. Am. Kentucky Fried Chicken, 1994—97; group pres., CEO, Pizza Hut, KFC Tricon Global Restaurants, Inc., Louisville, 1996—97, vice-chmn., 1996—97, pres., 1997—, CEO, 2000—; chmn. Yum! Brands, Inc. (formerly Tricon Global Restaurants, Inc.), 2001—. Bd. dirs. J.P. Morgan Chase, Yum Brands, Inc., 1997—. Office: Yum Brands Inc 1441 Gardiner Ln Louisville KY 40213-1914*

**NOVAK, DENNIS E.,** physician; b. East Liverpool, Ohio, Jan. 5, 1946; BA, Bklyn. Coll., 1966; Lic. in Med. Sci., U. Brussels, 1972; MD, Rutgers U., 1974. Diplomate Am. Bd. Family Medicine, Nat. Bd. Med. Examiners. Resident in family practice Monmouth Med. Ctr., Long Branch, NJ, 1974-77; clin. asst. prof. UMDNJ-Robert Wood Johnson Med. Sch., 1977—; chmn. dept. family medicine Cmty. Med. Ctr., 1978—; pvt. practice, 2001—. Physician reviewer, quality assurance HealthSouth Rehab. Hosp. Mem. exec. adv. bd. Ocean County coun. Boy Scouts Am., asst. scoutmaster Ocean Coun., 1997-2002, com. chair Troop 165, 2000—; former trustee United Way Ocean County., Area VII Physician Rev. Org., 1983-86; bd. dir. Interfaith Hospitality Network Ocean County Homeless Program, 2002-04. Named one of Top Docs in NJ, Castle-Connolly NJ Monthly, 2001, 2002, 2003, 2004, 2005. Fellow Am. Acad. Family Medicine; mem. Ocean County Acad. Family Medicine (v.p. 1983), Ocean County Med. Soc. (bd. trustees 1983-87). Avocations: photography, scuba, guitar. Address: 1001 Lacey Rd PO Box 780 Forked River NJ 08731-0780 Office Phone: 609-693-8900. Personal E-mail: dennisnovakmd@expressfind.com.

**NOVAK, GORDON S., JR.,** computer scientist, educator; b. Colo., 1947; m. Susan Raye Strawn, May 7, 1977; children: Genevieve, Courtney. BSEE, U. Tex., 1969, MA in Computer Sci., 1971, PhD in Computer Sci., 1976. Mgr. sys. programming Tracor Inc., Austin, Tex., 1966-76; instr. U. Tex., Austin, 1976-77, asst. prof., 1978-81, 83-84, assoc. prof., 1984-98; prof., 1998—; dir. Artificial Intelligence Lab. U. Tex., Austin, 1984-99; computer sci. SRI Internat., Menlo Park, Calif., 1977-78. Vis. asst. prof. Stanford (Calif.) U., 1981-83. Contbr. articles to profl. jours. Office: U Tex Dept Computer Sci Austin TX 78712

**NOVAK, GREGORY,** marketing professional; b. Johnstown, Pa., Oct. 19, 1949; s. Eugene F. and Joan (Tross) N.; m. Naomi Sosia Wall; children: Rebecca, Jeffrey, Jacqueline. BA, U. Vt., 1971. Project dir. Dun & Bradstreet, N.Y.C., 1973-74; sr. analyst Colgate Palmolive, N.Y.C., 1974-76; mgr. brand rsch. R.J. Reynolds, Winston-Salem, NC, 1976-77, mgr. group new brand rsch., 1977-80, dir. new bus., 1980-81, dir. group mktg., 1981-84; nat. dir. mktg. Deloitte Haskins & Sells, N.Y.C., 1984-90; pres. Novak Mktg. Inc., 1990—. Office: Novak Mktg Inc 29 Brandon Dr Mount Kisco NY 10549-3720 Office Phone: 914-241-1900. Business E-Mail: greg@novakmarketing.com.

**NOVAK, JIRI,** professional tennis player; b. Zlin, Czech Republic, Mar. 22, 1975; m. Katerina Novak, June 4, 1999; children: Jakub, Jiri Jr., Katerina. Profl. tennis player ATP Tour, 1993—. Achievements include Winner singles titles: Auckland, 1996, Mexico City, 1998, Gstaad, 2001, Munich, 2001, Gstaad, 2003, Tokyo Outdoor, 2004; Winner doubles titles: Bogota, 1996, Santiago, 1995, Casablanca, 1996, Gstaad, 1996, Ostrava, 1997, San Marino, 1998, Mexico City, 1998, Indianapolis, 1998, Split, 1998, Stuttgart Outdoor, 2000; Stuttgart Indoor, 2000, Gstaad, 2000, Dubai, 2000, Montreal/Toronto TMS, 2001, Miami Ericsson Open, 2001, Stuttgart, 2004. Office: ATP Tour Internat Hdqrs 201 ATP Blvd Ponte Vedra Beach FL 32082

**NOVAK, JOE,** artist; b. Springfield, Mass., Oct. 15, 1930; s. Benjamin D. and Mae (Lavitt) N. BA, Dartmouth Coll., 1952; JD, Harvard U., 1955. One-man shows include Vered Gallery, East Hampton, NY, 1985, 87-88, Milari Ltd., N.Y.C., 1989, Light Emanations, Tesuque, N.Mex., 1992, Bank of Santa Fe, 1996, Davidson & Daughters, Portland, Maine, 1997, McKesson Plz., San Francisco, 1998, Sirius Art Gallery, Santa Fe, 2000, Circle Elephant Art, LA, 2001, 03, Evo Gallery, Santa Fe, 2001, 02, 04, Hood Mus. Art, Dartmouth Coll., 2002, Etherton Gallery, Tucson, 2004, Bert Green Fine Art, LA, 2005; exhibited in group shows at Parrish Art Mus., Southampton, N.Y., Guild Hall Mus., East Hampton, NY, Mus. Fine Arts, Santa Fe, Palm Springs Art Mus., Calif., Vered Gallery, Milari, Ltd., Olaf Clasen Gallery, Cologne, Germany, Jill George Gallery, London, Lewallen Gallery, Santa Fe, Circle Elephant Art, LA, Anderson Contemporary Art, Santa Fe, James Kelly Contemporary, Santa Fe, Evo Gallery, Santa Fe and others; works in pub. collections include Boston Mus. Fine Arts, Guild Hall Mus., U. Tex.-Pan Am., Mus. Fine Arts, Santa Fe, Mus. Art, Ft. Lauderdale, Fla., Hood Mus. Art, Dartmouth Coll., U. Calif.-Berkeley Art Mus., Frost Art Mus. Fla. Internat.

U., Miami, Cin. Art Mus., Mus. Fine Arts, Springfield, Mass., Tucson Mus. Art, Palm Springs Art Mus.; subject of articles. Lt. USN, 1955-58. Recipient awards for art. Home: PO Box 162 Rancho Mirage CA 92270-0162 E-mail: kiva@dc.rr.com.

**NOVAK, JOSEPH ANTHONY,** law librarian; b. Detroit; s. Thomas Paul and Mary Cecilia N. AA, Macomb C.C., Warren, Mich., 1984; BA, Oakland U., 1986; JD, Mich. State U., 1991; M Libr. and Info. Sci., Wayne State U., 1998. Intern Wayne County Pub. Defender's Office, Detroit, 1986; intern Office of Jud. Assistance 3d Jud. Ct. Mich., Detroit, 1993, law clk. to Hon. Diane M. Hathaway, intern, 1996; law libr. St. Louis Correctional Facility, 2000—01, Mid-Mich. Correctional Facility, 2001—03; asst. libr. Mound Correctional Facility, 2003—. Vol., Vol. Income Tax Assistance Program, Detroit, 1995–2001. Recipient Outstanding Vol. Volunteer Income Tax Assistance Program, 1995, 96, 98, 99, 2000, The Spirit of Am. Is In the Heart of Its Volunteers IRS, 1995, 96, 97, 99. Mem. Am. Assn. Law Librs., Am. Corrections Assn., Spl. Librs. Assn., Acctg. Aid Soc., County State Agy. Librs., Mich. Corrections Assn., Mich. Libr. Assn., KC. Democrat. Roman Catholic. Avocations: coin and stamp collecting, biking, walking, bowling. Home and Office: 3524 Hamlet Sterling Heights MI 48310-6905

**NOVAK, JOSEPH DONALD,** science educator; b. Mpls., Dec. 2, 1930; s. Joseph Daniel and Anna (Podany) N.; m. Joan Owen, July 18, 1953; children: Joseph Mark, William John BS, U. Minn., 1952, MA, 1954, PhD, 1958; Doctorate (hon.), U. Comanhue, Neuquen, Argentina, 1998, Pub. U. Navarra, 2002, U. Urbino, 2006. Teaching asst. U. Minn., Mpls., 1952-56, instr., 1956-57; asst. prof. Kans. State Tchrs. Coll., 1957-59, Purdue U., West Lafayette, Ind., 1959-62, assoc. prof., 1962-67; prof. Cornell U., Ithaca, NY, 1967-95, prof. emeritus, 1995—; pres. Joseph D. Novak Knowledge Consultants, Inc.; sr. rsch. scientist U. West Fla. Knowledge constrn. and orgn. cons. to Procter & Gamble and other cos.; cons. to over 400 schs and colls., 1975—; vis. fellow Harvard U., 1965-66, disting. vis. prof. U. N.C., Wilmington, 1980, U. West Fla., 1987-88; vis. prof. U. South Fla., 1995; sr. rsch. scientist U. West Fla., 1996—. Author: Learning How to Learn, 1984, in 10 langs., 1984—96, Educational Psychology: A Cognitive View, 1978, A Theory of Education, 1977, Aprendizaje Significativo: Techieas y Aplicaciones, 1997, Learning, Creating and Using Knowledge: Concept Maps as Facilitative Tools for Schools and Corporations, 1998, Teaching Science for Understanding, 1998, Assessing Science Understanding, 2004, Una aportacion a la mejora de la calidad de la docentia universitaria: Los mapas Conceptuales, 2000, Errores Conceptuales: Diagnosis, Tratamientoy Reflexiones, 2001, 15 others; contbr. over 40 chpts. to books, over 130 articles to profl. jours. Fellow Tozer Found., Lydia Anderson, 1955-56; research assoc. Harvard U., 1965-66; Fulbright-Hayes Sr. Scholar, Australia, 1980 Fellow: AAAS (sec. sect. Q); mem.: NSTA, Coun. Sci. Soc. Presidents (1st hon. award for rsch. in sci. edn. 1998), Am. Ednl. Rsch. Assn., Assn. for Edn. of Tchrs. of Sci., Nat. Assn. in Sci. Tchr. (pres. 1968, Outstanding Contbns. Sci. Tchg. Through Rsch. award 1990), Nat. Assn. Biology Tchrs. (hon.), Sigma Xi. Avocations: hiking, swimming, dance, music. Office: Cornell U Dept Edn Kennedy Hall Ithaca NY 14853 Home: 77 Alcott Cir Taunton MA 02780-1056 Personal E-mail: jnovak@ihmc.us. Business E-Mail: jdn2@cornell.edu.

**NOVAK, LARRY RAY,** secondary school educator, music educator, director; b. Mpls., Aug. 3, 1947; d. Raymond Joseph and Jenny Rose Novak; m. Zelda Rae Kurth, June 21, 1997; children: John, David. BS, Concordia Coll., 1969; MA, Mankato State Coll., 1980; postgrad., U. Wis., 1981—. Tchr. Luth. High West, Detroit, 1970—72, Concordia St. Paul HS, 1972—79, Shattuck Sch., Faribault, Minn., 1975—78, Round Lake (Minn.) Pub. Sch., 1978—79, Lakefield (Minn.) Pub. Sch., 1979—90, Redwood Falls (Minn.) Pub. Sch., 1990—94, Park Rapids (Minn.) Pub. Sch., 1994—. Judge Minn. State HS League, Mpls., 1979—; adv. bd. Park Rapids Pub. Sch., 1996—. Assoc. dir. Park Rapids Cmty. Band; coun. mem. Faith Bapt. Ch., Park Rapids, 2000—05. Named Tchr. of Yr., Lakefield Pub. Schs., 1989. Mem.: Minn. Band Dirs. Assn., Music Educators Nat. Conf., Edn. Minn., Lions Club. Baptist. Avocations: reading, camping, auto restoration, music. Home: 212 Henrietta Ave S Park Rapids MN 56470 Office: Park Rapids Pub Sch 401 Huntsinger Ave Park Rapids MN 56470 Office Phone: 218-237-6422. Personal E-mail: zrkn@unitek.com.

**NOVAK, LESLIE HOWARD,** lawyer; b. Chgo., May 10, 1944; s. Sidney and Sadie (Jensky) N.; m. Nancy Ruth Sherman, July 2, 1967; children: Heidi Ellen, Shani Beth. BS in Bus. with high distinction, U. Minn., 1966, JD cum laude, 1969. Bar: Minn. 1970, U.S. Dist. Ct. Minn. 1970, U.S. C. Appeals (8th cir.) 1974, U.S. Supreme Ct. 1995. Assoc. Robins, Kaplan, Miller & Ciresi, Mpls., 1969-77, ptnr., 1977-92, Mackall, Crounse & Moore, PLC., Mpls., 1992—, mng. ptnr., 1997-99. Bd. dirs. Am. Israel C. of C. and Industry of Minn., Mpls., 1981—, founding pres., 1981-91; founding sec., founding bd. dirs. Assn. N.Am.-Israel Chambers Commerce, Inc., 1993—; bd. dirs. United Jewish Fund and Coun., St. Paul, 1986—; founding dir. Illusion Theater and Sch.; past bd. dirs., past pres. Jewish Family Svc. of St. Paul; past bd. dirs. Mt. Zion Temple. Named Leading Am. Atty., Am.'s Registry Outstanding Profls. Mem. Hillcrest Country Club, Gopher Golf Boosters Club (sec., bd. dirs.), Phi Delta Phi, Beta Gamma Sigma. Avocations: biking, golf, tennis, skiing. Office: Mackall Crounse & Moore PLC 1400 AT&T Tower 901 Marquette Ave Minneapolis MN 55402-2859 Office Phone: 612-305-1460. Business E-Mail: lhn@mcmlaw.com.

**NOVAK, MARK,** lawyer; b. Buffalo, N.Y., Jan. 28, 1952; s. Eugene Francis and Joan (Tross) N.; m. Charlene Mary Ingoglia, Sept. 2, 1972; children: Jason Charles, Jennifer Rose. BA, U. Rochester, 1974; JD, Loyola U., Chgo., 1977. Bar: Ill. 1977, U.S. Dist. Ct. (no. dist.) Ill. 1977, U.S. Ct. Appeals (7th cir.) 1978. Assoc. Anesi, Ozmon & Lewin, Ltd., Chgo., 1977—83; ptnr. Anesi, Ozmon, Rodin, Novak & Kohen, Ltd., Chgo., 1983—, pres., 2006—. Fundraiser Christmas is for Kids Charity, Chgo., 1992—. Mem. ATLA (product liability sect. 1985—), ABA, Ill. Trial Lawyers Assn., Trial Lawyers for Pub. Justice, Chgo. Bar Assn. (jud. evaluation com 1993 ). Home: 1212 N Lake Shore Dr Chicago IL 60610-2371 Office: Anesi Ozmon Rodin Novak & Kohen Ltd 161 N Clark St Fl 21 Chicago IL 60601-3206 Office Phone: 312-372-3822.

**NOVAK, RANDI RUTH,** systems engineer, computer scientist; b. Chgo., July 10, 1954; d. Bernard Richard and Shirley Ann (Fiedorczyk) Novak; children: Rona Rachel Reich, Bonnie Shaina Reich. BS in Math., U. Calif., Santa Cruz, 1976, BA in Econs. with honors, 1976; postgrad., U. Rochester, 1976-78. Rsch. asst. U. Calif., Santa Cruz, 1974-76; Russian translator U. Chgo., 1977—78; intern economist Congl. Budget Office, Washington, 1977; engr. Lockheed MSC, Sunnyvale, Calif., 1978-82; software engr. contractor Silicon Valley Systems, Belmont, Calif., 1982, 83-84, Data Encore (subs. of Verbatim), Sunnyvale, 1982-83; systems programmer CompuPro/Viasyn Corp., Hayward, Calif., 1984-87; mem. tech. staff Network Equipment Techs., Redwood City, Calif., 1987-89; v.p. engring., founder Segue Setups, Burlingame, Calif., 1989-92, ptnr., 1992—; sr. tech. staff NEC Am., San Jose, Calif., 1992—94; sr. systems engr. Hitachi Computer Products, Santa Clara, Calif., 1994-96; prin. engr. Rapid-City Comms./Bay Networks/Nortel Networks, Santa Clara, Calif., 1996—2002, Trapeze Networks, Pleasanton, Calif., 2002—04; prin. engr. tech. staff Foundry Networks, San Jose, 2004—. Fellow Dept. Treasury, 1974-76, NSF, 1977-78, U. Rochester, Rush Rhees fellow. Mem. IEEE Computer Soc., Am. Math. Assn., Computer Profls. for Social Responsibility, Soc. for Computing and Info. Processing, Internat. Platform Assn., Calif. Scholarship Fedn. (life). Avocations: piano, oboe, music, photography, mathematics. Home: 4166 School St Pleasanton CA 94566-6218 Office Phone: 408-207-1528. Personal E-mail: rrnovak@comcast.net.

**NOVAK, RAYMOND FRANCIS,** environmental services administrator, pharmacology educator; s. Joseph Raymond and Margaret A. (Cerutti) N.; m. Frances C. Holy, Apr. 12, 1969; children: Jennifer, Jessica, Janelle, Joanna. BS in Chemistry, U. Mo., St. Louis, 1968; PhD in Phys. Chemistry, Case Western Res. U., 1973. Assoc. in pharmacology Northwestern U. Med. Sch.,

Chgo., 1976-77, asst. prof. pharmacology, 1977-81, assoc. prof., 1981-86, prof., 1986-88; prof. pharmacology Wayne State U. Sch. Medicine, Detroit, 1988—; dir. Inst. Environ. Health Scis. Wayne State U., Detroit, 1988—, dir. EHS Ctr. in Molecular and Cellular Toxicology with Human Application, 1994—, dir. interdisciplinary grad. program in Molecular and Cellular Toxicology, 1994—. Mem. toxicology study sect. NIH, Bethesda, Md., 1984-88, mem. and chair numerous grant review com.; adj. sci. Inhalation Toxicology Rsch. Inst., Lovelace Biomed. and Environ. Rsch. Inst., 1991-98; program leader Epidemiology and Environ. Carcinogenesis, Karmanos Cancer Inst. and Comprehensive Cancer Ctr., 1996-98. Assoc. editor Toxicol. Applied Pharmacology, 1992-96, Toxicol. Scis., 2004—; editor Drug Metabolism and Disposition, 1994-2000; mem. editorial bd. Jour. Toxicology and Environ. Health, 19 87-92, In Vivo, 1986—, Toxic Substances Jour., 1993-98; mem. bd. pub. trustees Am. Soc. Pharmacology and Experimental Therapeutics, 1994-2000; publr. over 125 sci. manuscripts, review articles and book chpt. in profl. jour. and books. Co. comdr., field grade officer (Major) USAR, 1968—99. Recipient Disting. Alumni award U. Mo., St. Louis, 1988; grantee Nat. Inst. Environ. Health Sci., 1979—, Gen. Medicine sect. NIH, 1979-82, 89-94. Mem. Am. Soc. for Biochem. and Molecular Biology, Soc. Toxicology (councilor 1996-98, chmn. cont. edn. com. 1995-96), Am. Assn. for Cancer Rsch., Am. Soc. for Pharmacology and Exptl. Therapeutics (bd. publ. trustees 1994-99), Am. Soc. Hematology, Internat. Soc. for Study Xenobiotics. Achievements include patents in field. Office: Wayne State U Inst Environ Health Scis 2727 2nd Ave Rm 4000 Detroit MI 48201-2671 Office Phone: 313-577-0100. Business E-Mail: R.Novak@wayne.edu.

**NOVAK, ROBERT DAVID SANDERS,** columnist, commentator; b. Joliet, Ill., Feb. 26, 1931; s. Maurice Pall and Jane Anne (Sanders) N.; m. Geraldine Williams, Nov. 10, 1962; children: Zelda, Alexander. AB, U. Ill., 1952; LLD (hon.), Kenyon Coll., 1987; LittD (hon.), U. Ill., 1998; DHL (hon.), U. St. Francis. Reporter Joliet (Ill.) Herald-News, 1947-51, Champaign-Urbana (Ill.) Courier, 1951-52, AP, Omaha, Lincoln, Nebr., Indpls. and Washington, 1954-58, Wall St. Jour., Washington, 1958-63; syndicated columnist N.Y. Herald-Tribune, Washington, 1963-66; commentator Corinthian Broadcasting, Washington, 1963-65, Metromedia, Washington, 1966-76, RKO-Features, Washington, 1976-78; syndicated columnist Chgo. Sun-Times, Washington, 1966—; commentator Cable News Network, Washington, 1980—2005, Am. Voice, 1993—2002, Fox News, 2006—. Pub. Evans-Novak Polit. Report, Washington, 1967—, Evans-Novak Tax Report, Washington, 1985-92, Evans-Novak Japan Report, Washington, 1989-92; contbg. editor Readers Digest, 1979—. Author: The Agony of the GOP, 1965, Lyndon B. Johnson: The Exercise of Power, 1967, Nixon In The White House, 1971, The Reagan Revolution, 1981, Completing the Revolution, 2000. Trustee Bullis Sch., Potomac, Md., 1987-98, Phillips Found., 1991—, Children Charities Found., 1994—, Youth Leadership Found., 2003—. 1st lt. U.S. Army, 1952-54. Recipient ACE award Cable Broadcasting Industry, 1990, Laureate Order of Lincoln, Lincoln Acad. Ill., 1999. Mem. Soc. Profl. Journalists, Washington Gridiron Club, Nat. Press Club (Fourth Estate award, 2001), Army and Navy Club. Office: Ste 1203 1750 Pennsylvania Ave NW Washington DC 20006-4501 Office Phone: 202-393-4340. Personal E-mail: evansnovak@aol.com.

**NOVAK, ROBERT DENNIS,** contractor, real estate developer; b. Poughkeepsie, N.Y., Jan. 12, 1954; s. William Henry and Terese Edna Novak; m. Barbara Jean Owen, Aug. 21, 1999; m. Deborah Ann Cross (div.); children: Jessica Ann, Jennifer Lee, Jonathan Charles. Grad high sch, N.Y. Pres. Wilro Constrn., Inc., Hopewell Junction, 1973—; v.p. Billings Plz. Corp., 1987—2001; pres. Lamp Light Assocs., 1987—2001. Mem.: Nat. Homebuilders Assn. Avocations: bicycling, scuba diving, camping, motorcycling. Office: Wilro Constrn Inc 25 Clove Hollow Rd Hopewell Junction NY 12533 Office Phone: 845-724-4697.

**NOVAK, ROBERT LOUIS,** civil engineer, pavement management consultant; b. Chgo., Feb. 29, 1928; s. Louis and Frances (Kucera) N.; m. Virginia Staas, Jan. 22, 1955 (div. 1962); children: Susan Grace, Nina Louise; m. Joyce Eloise Keen, May 7, 1966; stepchildren: Robert John Moore, William Keen Moore, Marilyn Joyce Moore, James Clifford Moore. BCE, Ga. Inst. Tech., 1948. With Am. Bridge Co., 1948-49; soils engr. Soil Testing Svc., Chgo., 1952-54; chief materials engr. Skidmore Ownings and Merrill USAF Acad., Colorado Springs, 1954, dir. field invest; asst. dir. engring. O'Hare field constrn. Naess & Murphy, Chgo., 1958-60; pres. Novak, Dempsey & Assocs., Palatine, Ill., 1960-85; ptnr. Infrastructure Mgmt. Svcs., Arlington Heights, Ill., 1985-89, cons., 1989—. Contbr. articles to profl. jours. With U.S. Army, 1950-52. Mem. ASTM, Am. Pub. Works Assn. (life; Meritorious Svc. award 1990), Transp. Rsch. Bd. Achievements include a pioneer in field of pavement mgmt. and development of one of the first pavement management computer software programs. Home: 1066 Truman St Nokomis FL 34275-4401

**NOVAK, TERRY LEE,** public information officer, educator, dean; b. Chamberlain, SD, Sept. 1, 1940; s. Warren F. and Elaine M. N.; m. Barbara Hosea, Aug. 29, 1981; 1 child, David. B.Sc., S.D. State U., 1962; postgrad. (Rotary fellow), U. Paris, 1962-63; M.P.A., Colo. U., 1965, PhD, 1970. Asst. city mgr. City of Anchorage, 1966-68; city mgr. City of Hopkins, Minn., 1968-74, City of Columbia, Mo., 1974-78, City of Spokane, Wash., 1978-91; v.p. bus. and fin. Ea. Wash. U., Cheney, 1991—94; prof. public adminstrn., 1992—, dir. grad. program pub. adminstrn., 1994-95; dir. Spokane Joint Ctr. for Higher Edn., 1995-98; bus. mgr. Riverpoint campus Wash. State U., 1998-99; prof pub. adminstrn. Eastern Wash. U., 1999—. Asst. adj. prof. U. Mo., Columbia, 1975, 77; adj. instr. Gonzaga U., Spokane, 1986-88; mem. nat. adv. coun. on environ. policy and tech. EPA. Author: Special Assessment Financing in American Cities, 1970; contbr. articles to profl. jours. Mem. ASPA, Internat. City Mgrs. Assn. (Acad. Profl. Devel.). Episcopalian. Office: 668 N Riverpoint Blvd Spokane WA 99202-1677 E-mail: tnovak@terrynovak.net.

**NOVAK, THEODORE J.,** lawyer; b. Dec. 8, 1940; BS, U. Ill., Urbana-Champaign, 1962; JD, Chgo.- Kent Coll. of Law, Ill. Inst. Tech., 1968. Bar: Ill. 1967, U.S. Dist. Ct. (no. dist.) Ill. 1967. Ptnr. Rudnick & Wolfe, Chgo.; ptnr., Real Estate, Land Use & Devel. practices, chmn. Land Use & Condemnation practice, mem. policy com. DLA Piper Rudnick Gray Cary, Chgo., 2005—. Adj. prof. Northwestern Univ. Sch. Law, 1998—; lectr. Univ. Chgo. Law Sch., 2000—. Co-author: Ill. Zoning, Eminent Domain & Land Use Manual, 1997; contbr. articles to profl. jours. Mem.: ABA, Am. Coll. Real Estate Lawyers, Ill. State Bar Assn., Chgo. Bar Assn., Lambda Alpha Internat., Ely chpt. Office: DLA Piper Rudnick Gray Cary Suite 1900 203 N La Salle St Chicago IL 60601-1293 Office Phone: 312-368-4037. Office Fax: 312-236-7516. Business E-Mail: theodore.novak@dlapiper.com.

**NOVAKOV, GEORGE JOHN, JR.,** gifted and talented educator, consultant, administrative assistant; b. New Orleans, Apr. 1, 1945; s. George John Novakov Sr. and Gloria (Edwards) Frost; m. Ann Marie Mariano, Dec. 27, 1969; children: Jay, Jaime. BA, New Orleans, 1967, MEd, 1970, postgrad., 1985, Tulane U., Loyola U. 1985. Tchr. New Orleans Pub. Schs., 1967—; adminstrv. asst., dir. admission Edna Karr Secondary Sch., 1994—; student data mgr. Edna Karr Secondary Sch., 1994—. Grant writer asst. Edna Karr Secondary Sch., New Orleans Pub. Libr. 1987-99. Author: (play) The Christmas Caper, 1980. Ind. Study Humanities fellow, 1991. Mem. La. Assn. of Computer Using Educators (assoc. editor newsletter, 1992), Greater New Orleans Coun. of Tchrs. of English, Presenter at Nat. Edn. Computer Conf., 1998, 2002. Democrat. Roman Catholic. Avocations: opera, science fiction, computers. Office: Edna Karr Secondary Sch 3332 Huntlee Dr New Orleans LA 70131-7046 Home: 70440 6th St Covington LA 70433 Office Phone: 504-398-7115. Business E-Mail: george_novakov@nops.k12.la.us.

**NOVAKOV, TIHOMIR NONE,** physicist, researcher; b. Apatin, Yugoslavia, Mar. 16, 1929; s. Milos and Nada Novakov; m. Marica Cvetkovic, May 16, 1953; 1 child, Anna. PhD in Physics, U. Belgrade, Belgrade Yugoslavia, 1958. Sr. scientist Lawrence Berkeley (Calif.) Nat. Lab., 1963—; asst. prof.

U. Of Belgrade, Belgrade, Yugoslavia (Serbia), 1958—63. Contbr. over 150 articles to profl. jours. Mem.: Acad. Scis. Belgrade, Am. Geopysical Union, Nat. Chemistry Inst. Slovenia (hon.), Austrian Soc. Microchemistry (hon.). Office: Lawrence Berkeley National Laboratory One Cyclotron Road Berkeley CA 94720 Office Phone: 510-486-6928. Office Fax: 510-486-7303. Business E-Mail: tnovakov@lbl.gov.

**NOVALES, RONALD RICHARDS,** zoologist, educator; b. San Francisco, Apr. 24, 1928; s. William Henry and Dorothy (Richards) N.; m. Barbara Jean Martin, Dec. 19, 1953; children: Nancy Ann, Mary Elizabeth. BA, U. Calif., Berkeley, 1950, MA, 1953, PhD, 1958; postgrad., UCLA, 1951-52. Asst. prof. biol. scis. Northwestern U., Evanston, Ill., 1958-64, assoc. prof., 1964-70, prof., 1970-80, prof. neurobiology and physiology, 1981-93, prof. biology 6 yr. med. program, 1993, emeritus prof. neurobiology and physiology, 1993—. Cons. A.J. Nystrom Co., 1969 Mem. editorial bd.: The American Zoologist, 1969-73; Contbr.: articles to profl. jours. Ency. Brit. Book of Year. Served with U.S. Army, 1953-55. NSF research grantee, 1959-73, 75-78 Fellow AAAS. Unitarian Universalist. Home: 2008 Mcdaniel Ave Evanston IL 60201-2125 *Remember not to "die on the barbed wire" of all the conflicting demands of your work. It is possible for you to cut through the individual strands and to make a successful rush for the enemy's trench.*

**NOVARRO, NEVA K.,** economics professor; b. Rochester, N.Y., July 3, 1974; d. Jack and Lynn Kerbeshian; m. Joseph A. Novarro, Nov. 3, 2001; 1 child, Carina. BA magna cum laude, Pomona Coll., Claremont, Calif., 1996; PhD, Stanford U., Calif., 2003. Rsch. asst. Fed. Res. Bd., Washington, 1996 –98, Stanford U., Palo Alto, Calif., 1999—2003; asst. prof. Coll. Holy Cross, Worcester, Mass., 2003—. Instr. Stanford U., Palo Alto, Calif., 2001—02. Contbr. articles to profl. jours. Recipient Morris B. Pendleton Econs. Meml. prize, Pomona Coll., 1996, Barbara Sanford Allen Music prize, 1996, Bertha Clendenen McCord Meml. Music prize, 1996, Tileston Physics I prize, 1996, Outstanding Tchg. Asst. award, Stanford U., 2000; fellow, 1998, Found. Tchg. Econs., 2002; Olin fellow, The Bradley Found., 2002. Mem.: Am. Econ. Assn., Phi Betta Kappa. Office: College of the Holy Cross 1 College Street Worcester MA 01610 Office Phone: 508-793-3835. Business E-Mail: nnovarro@holycross.edu.

**NOVELLI, WILLIAM DOMINIC,** retirement association executive; b. Pitts., May 21, 1941; s. Dominic M. and Celeste J. (DeFife) Novelli; m. Frances D. Bickell, Aug. 1, 1964; children: Peter M., Alexander G., Sarah J. BA, U. Pa., 1963, MA, 1964; postdoctoral studies, NYU, 1967—69. Mgr. mktg. Lever Bros. Co., NYC, 1964—69; supr. account Wells, Rich, Greene, NYC, 1969—70; dir. advt. and creative services Peace Corps and Action, Washington, 1970—72; pres., co-founder Porter Novelli, 1972—90; exec. v.p. CARE; pres. Campaign for Tobacco-Free Kids; assoc. exec. dir. AARP, Washington, 2000—01, CEO, 2001—. Instr. mktg. mgmt. U. Md., instr. health communication and mass media, Dept. Communication Arts and Theatre. Mem. editl. rev. bd. Jour. Health Care Mktg.; contbr. Mem. adv. coun. population communication services program Johns Hopkins U.; mem. adv. panel US AID; vol. cons. United Way Am.; vice chmn. task force on profl. communications Nat. Coun. on Patient Info. and Edn.; bd. dir. Ctr. for Consumer Health Edn., Reston, Va., Campaign for Tobacco-Free Kids. Named one of 100 Most Influential Pub. Relations Professionals fo 20th Century. Mem.: Am. Mktg. Assn. (chmn. attitude rsch. conf. 1985). Office: AARP 601 E St NW Washington DC 20049 Office Phone: 202-434-2300. Business E-Mail: wnovelli@aarp.org.

**NOVELLO, ANTONIA COELLO,** state health commissioner, pediatric nephrologist, former Surgeon General of the United States; b. Fajardo, P.R., Aug. 23, 1944; d. Antonio and Ana D. (Flores) Coello; m. Joseph R. Novello, May 30, 1970. BS, U. P.R., Rio Piedras, 1965; MD, U. P.R., San Juan, 1970; MPH, Johns Hopkins Sch. Hygiene, 1982; DrPh (hon.), Johns Hopkins U., 2000; DSc (hon.), Med. Coll. Ohio, 1990, U. Ctrl. Caribe, Cayey, P.R., 1990, Lehigh U., 1992, Hood Coll., 1992, U. Notre Dame, Ind., 1991, N.Y. Med. Coll., 1992, U. Mass., 1992, Fla. Internat. U., 1992, Cath. U., 1993, Washington Coll., 1993, St. Mary's Coll., 1993, Ea. Va. Med. Sch., 1993, Ctrl. Conn. State U., 1993, Georgetown U., 1993, U. Mich., 1994, Mt. Sinai Sch. Medicine, 1995; LHD (hon.), Alvernia Coll., 1996; HHD (hon.), Kings Coll., 1996; D in Health Sci. (hon.), Ponce Sch. of Medicine, 1996; D in Law (hon.), Gannon U., 1997; LHD (hon.), Loyola U., 1997; DSc (hon.), U. North Tex., Ft. Worth, 2002, Howard U., 2003, NYU, 2003, Pace U., 2003, others. Diplomate Am. Bd. Pediatrics. Intern in pediatrics U. Mich. Med. Ctr., Ann Arbor, 1970-71, resident in pediatrics, 1971-73, pediatric nephrology fellow, 1973-74, Georgetown U. Hosp., Washington, 1974-75; project officer Nat. Inst. Arthritis, Metabolism and Digestive Diseases NIH, Bethesda, Md., 1978-79, staff physician, 1979-80; exec. sec. gen. medicine B study sect., div. of rsch. grants NIH, Bethesda, 1981-86; dep. dir. Nat. Inst. Child Health & Human Devel., NIH, Bethesda, 1986-90; surgeon gen. US Dept. Health & Human Services, Washington, 1990-93; spl. rep. for health and nutrition UNICEF, NYC, 1993—96; vis. prof. health policy and mgmt. Johns Hopkins U. Sch. of Hygiene and Pub. Health, 1996—99; commr. of health State of NY, 1999—. Clin. prof. pediatrics Georgetown U. Hosp., Washington, 1986, 89, Uniformed Svcs. U. of Health Scis., 1989; adj. prof. pediatrics and communicable diseases U. Mich. Med. Sch., 1993; adj. prof. internat. health Sch. Hygiene and Pub. Health, Johns Hopkins U., Balt.; prof. dept. health policy mgmt. and behavior SUNY, 1999—; clin. prof. pediats. U. Rochester, N.Y., 1999—; mem. Georgetown Med. Ctr. Interdepartmental Rsch. Group; legis. fellow U.S. Senate Com. on Labor and Human Resources Washington, 1982-83; mem. Com. on Rsch in Pediatrics Nephrology, Washington; participant grant assoc. program seminars Nat. Inst. Arthritis, Diabetes and Digestive and Kidney Diseases, NIH, Bethesda, 1980-81; pediatric cons. Adolescent Medicine Svc., Psychiat. Inst., Washington, 1979-83; nephrology cons. Met. Washington Renal Dialysis Ctr. affiliate Georgetown U. Hosp., Washington, 1975-78; phys. diagnosis class instr. U. Mich. Med. Ctr., Ann Arbor, 1973-74; chair Sec.'s Work Group on Pediatric HIV Infection and Diseases, DHHS, 1988; cons. WHO, Geneva, 1989; mem. Johns Hopkins Soc. Scholars, 1991. Contbr. numerous articles to profl. jours. and chpts. to books in field; mem. editorial bd. Internat. Jour Artificial Organs, Jour. Mexican Nephrology. Served in USPHS, 1978-99. Recipient Intern of Yr. award U. Mich. Dept. Pediatrics, 1971, Woman of Yr. award Disting. Grads. Pub. Sch. Systems, San Juan, 1980, PHS Commendation medal HHS, 1983, PHS Citation award HHS, 1984, Cert. of Recognition, Disk Force Grants, NIH, 1985, PHS Outstanding Svc. medal HHS, 1988, PHS Unit Commendation, 1988, PHS Surgeon Gen.'s Exemplary Svc. medal, 1989, PHS Outstanding Unit citation, 1989, DHHS Asst. Sec. for Health Cert. of Commendation, 1989, Surgeon Gen. Medallion award, 1990, Alumni award U. Mich. Med. Ctr., 1991, Elizabeth Blackwell award, 1991, Woodrow Wilson award for disting. govt. svc., 1991, Congl. Hispanic Caucus medal, 1991, Order of Mil. Med. Merit, 1991, Washington Times Freedom award, 1992, Charles C. Shepard Sci. award, 1992, Golden Plate award, 1992, Elizabeth Ann Seton award, 1992, Ellis Island Congl. Medal of Honor, 1993, Legion of Merit medal, 1993, Athena award Alumnae Coun., 1993, Nat. Citation award Mortar Bd., 1993, Disting. Pub. Svc. award, 1993, Healthy Am. Fitness Leaders award, 1994, Pub. Leadership Edn. Network Mentor award, 1994, Disting. Svc. award Nat. Coun. Cath. Women, 1995, James E. Van Zandt Citizenship award, 1995, Ronald McDonald Children's Charities Excellence award, 1995, Hispanic Heritage Leadership award, 1998, Disting. Alumnus award Am. Assn. of State Colls. and Univs., 1997, Humanitarian award Am. Cancer Soc., 2001, James Smithson Bicentennial medal Smithsonian Inst., 2002; named Health Leader of Yr., COA, 1992; inductee Nat. Women's Hall of Fame, 1994, Internat. Pediatric Hall of Fame Miami Children's Hosp., 1996, Am. Med. Women Assn. Hall of Fame, 2002. Fellow Am. Acad. Pediatrics (Excellence Pub. Svc. award 1993); mem. AMA (Nathan Davis award 1993, Meritorious Svc. award 1993), Luther L. Terry award, 2000), Inst. Medicine, Internat. Soc. Nephrology, Am. Soc. Nephrology, Latin Am. Soc. Nephrology, Soc. for Pediatric Rsch., Am. Pediatric Soc., Assn. Mil. Surgeons U.S., Am. Soc. Pediatric Nephrology, Pan Am. Med. and Dental Soc.

(pres.-elect, sec. 1984), D.C. Med. Soc. (assoc.), Johns Hopkins U. Soc. Scholars, Alpha Omega Alpha. Avocation: collecting antique furniture. Office: NY State Health Commr Corning Tower Empire State Plz Albany NY 12237 Office Phone: 518-474-2011.*

**NOVELLY, PAUL ANTHONY,** petrochemical and refining company executive; b. St. Louis, 1943; m. Mary Katherine Novelly; 4 children. B in commerce, St. Louis U., 1965. With Shell Oil Co., St. Louis, 1962-68, Apex Oil Co., Inc., St. Louis, 1968—; pres. Apex Oil Co., Inc., St. Louis, 1980—; chmn., CEO Apex Oil Co., Inc., St. Louis. Dep. chmn. bd. dirs. Liquid Funding, Ltd., 2001—; vice chmn. bd. dirs. Clark Oil & Refining Co., St. Louis; bd. dirs. The Bear Stearns Companies, N.Y.C., 2002—. Recipient Horatio Alger award, 2000. Office: Apex Oil Corp 8235 Forsyth Blvd Ste 400 Clayton MO 63105*

**NOVICH, BRUCE ERIC,** chemicals executive; b. Phila., Mar. 15, 1957; s. Samuel David and Vivian Rose Novich; m. Susan S. Novich, Sept. 5, 1982; children: Scott, Spencer, Corey. BA, Colgate U., 1979; BSChemE, MIT, 1980, MS in Geology, 1982, MSCE, 1982, ScD in Materials Processing, 1984. V.p. R & D and engring. Ceramics Process System, Milford, Mass., 1984-95; global bus. dir. electronics-zebralink PPG Industries, Pitts., 1995-2000; global bus. dir. Fujifilm Electronic Materials, 2000—04, Fuji Film Electronic Materials, Inc., Kingstown, RI, 2004—. Contbr. articles to profle. jours. Recipient 2 R & D 100 awards. Achievements include 25 patents in ceramics, composites and electronic packaging. Office: Fuji Film Electronic Materials Inc 80 Circuit Dr N North Kingstown RI 02852 Office Phone: 401-247-2333. Business E-Mail: bruce_novich@fujifilm-ffem.com.

**NOVICH, NEIL S.,** metals distribution company executive; BA in Physics summa cum laude, Harvard U., 1974; MS in Nuclear Engring., MIT, 1979, MS in Mgmt., 1981. Former dir. Bain & Co.; COO Ryerson Inc., Chgo., 1994—99, chmn., pres., CEO, 1999—. Dir. W.W. Grainger, Inc. Trustee Field Mus. Natural History, Children's Home & Aid Soc. Ill.; mem. vis. com. Divsn. Phys. Scis., U. Chgo. Nat. Sci. Found. scholar, Ford scholar. Mem. Phi Beta Kappa. Office: Ryerson Inc 2621 W 15th Pl Chicago IL 60608*

**NOVICK, AILEEN MARY,** historic site director, educator; b. Worcester, Mass., Apr. 28, 1975; d. Francis Michael and Catherine Theresa Novick; m. Marc Lionel Carbonneau, Dec. 6, 2003. BA in History, Bates Coll., 1997; MA in Pub. History, Northwestern U., Boston, 2003. Asst. editor New Eng. Hist. Geneal. Soc., Boston, 1997—2000; editl. asst. Yale U. Press, New Haven, 2000—01; program dir. Historic Locust Grove, Louisville, 2004—. Recipient Charles A. Dana scholar, Bates Coll., 1994, Ernest P. Muller prize, 1997, Freer award, Northwestern U. History Dept., 2003. Mem.: New Eng. Mus. Assn., Am. Assn. State and Local History. Avocations: cello, camping, hiking. Office: Historic Locust Grove 561 Blankenbaker Ln Louisville KY 40207

**NOVICK, ANDREW CARL,** urologist; b. Montreal, Apr. 5, 1948; came to U.S., 1974; s. David and Rose (Ortenberg) N.; m. Thelma Silver, June 29, 1969 (div. Dec. 1983); 1 child, Lorne J.; m. Linda Friedman, May 24, 1992; children: Rachel H., Eric D. BSc, McGill U., 1968, MD, CM, 1972. Diplomate Am. Bd. Urology. Resident in surgery Royal Victoria Hosp., Montreal, 1972—74; resident in urology Cleve. Clinic Found., 1974—77, staff dept. urology, 1977—, head sect. renal transplant, 1977—, chmn. Urol. Inst., 1985—, chmn. Organ Transplant Ctr., 1985—92. Trustee Am. Bd. Urology, 1995—2001, Urology Residence Rev. Com., 1997—2002. Editor: Vascular Problems in Urology, 1982, Stewart's Operative Urology, 1989, Renal Vascular Disease, 1995, Innovations in Urologic Surgery, 1997, Campbell's Urology, 2002, Operative Urology at the Cleveland Clinic, 2006; contbr. more than 500 articles to profl. jours. Fellow ACS, Med. Coun. Can.; mem. Am. Urol. Assn., Am. Assn. Genito-Urinary Surgeons, Clin. Soc. Genito-Urinary Surgeons. Office: Cleve Clinic Found 9500 Euclid Ave A100 Cleveland OH 44195-0001 Home: 24875 Woodside Ln Beachwood OH 44122 Office Phone: 216-444-5584. E-mail: novicka@ccf.org.

**NOVICK, DAVID KANDEL,** science educator, department chairman; b. Media, Pa., Sept. 3, 1965; s. Harold and Gladys Novick; m. Joanna Victoria Kandel, Aug. 12, 1997; children: Zachary Kandel, Brandon Kandel, Rachel Kandel. BS, Union Coll., Schenectady, NY, 1988; PhD, Tufts U., Medford, Mass., 1997. Rsch. technician ii Dana Farber Cancer Inst., Reinherz Lab, Dept. Immunobiology, Brookline, Mass., 1988—90; lab instr. dept. biology Tufts U., Medford, Mass., 1990—97; postdoc. assoc. human med. genetics unit U. Vt. Med. Sch. Lab of Bertrand C. Liang, Burlington, Vt., 1998—99; sci. chair West Nottingham Acad., Colora, Md., 1999—2001, Darrow Sch., New Lebanon, 2001—05, Gann Acad., Waltham, Mass., 2005—; adj. faculty Berkshire CC, Pittsfield, Mass., 2004; online adj. faculty Colo. Tech. U. Online, Colo., 2005—. Presenter in field. Mem.: AAAS, Nat. Assn. Biology Tchrs., Nat. Sci. Tchr. Assn., Sigma Xi (assoc.). Jewish. Home: 31 Hampshire Ave Sharon MA 02067 Office: Gann Acad 333 Forest St Waltham MA 02452 Office Phone: 781-642-6800 301. Office Fax: 781-642-6805. Personal E-mail: dknovick@verizon.net. E-mail: dnovick@gannacademy.org.

**NOVICK, JULIUS LERNER,** theater critic, educator; b. N.Y.C., Jan. 31, 1939; s. Solomon Joseph and Ethel (Lerner) N.; m. Phyllis Belle Spaeth, May 27, 1983; 1 child, Ilana BA, Harvard U., 1960; D.F.A., Yale U., 1966. Theatre critic WNDT-TV, Channel 13, N.Y.C., 1968-70; asst. prof. English NYU, N.Y.C., 1969-72; assoc. prof. lit. SUNY-Purchase, 1972-80, prof., 1980—2001, emeritus, 2002—; theatre critic The Village Voice, N.Y.C., 1958-89, The N.Y. Observer, N.Y.C., 1987-91, Newsday, N.Y.C., 1992-94, Kempner Disting. prof., 1997-99. Vis. lectr. drama div. Juilliard Sch., N.Y.C., 1968-71; dramaturg The Acting Co., N.Y.C., 1971-73; vis. critic Dartmouth Summer Repertory Co., Hanover, N.H., 1976, 79, 80, 82, 83, 84; master critic Nat. Critics Inst., Waterford, Conn., 1971—Author: Beyond Broadway, 1968. Fulbright scholar, 1960-61; Woodrow Wilson fellow, 1961-62; Guggenheim fellow, 1977; recipient George Jean Nathan award for dramatic criticism, 1981-82 Mem.: Am. Theatre and Drama Soc., Assn. for Theatre in Higher Edn., Assn. for Jewish Studies, Am. Theatre Critics Assn., Am. Soc. for Theatre Rsch. Jewish. E-mail: Jluddite@aol.com.

**NOVICK, NELSON LEE,** dermatologist, internist, consultant, surgeon, writer; b. Bklyn., June 27, 1949; s. Benjamin and Vivian (Meltzer) N.; m. Meryl Sohnis, June 20, 1971; children: Yonatan, Yoel, Ariel, Daniel, Avraham, Shmuel, Yehudah. BA in Biology magna cum laude, Bklyn. Coll., 1971; MD, Mt. Sinai Sch. Medicine, 1975. Diplomate Am. Bd. Internal Medicine, Am. Bd. Dermatology, Am. Bd. Med. Examiners. Resident internal medicine Mt. Sinai Med. Ctr., N.Y.C., 1975—78, postgrad. preceptee, 1980—83, outpatient dept. clinic chief, dermatology svc., 1983—2003, attending, 2004—; resident Skin and Cancer Unit NYU Med. Ctr., N.Y.C., 1978—80; clin. prof. Mt. Sinai Sch. Medicine, N.Y.C., 2004—. Cons. Westwood-Squibb Skin Care Info. Ctr., Vaseline Intensive Care Rsch., Bausch & Lomb, Schering-Plough, Sandoz Internat., Procter & Gamble, Lever-2000, Novartis, Bradley Pharms., Merz Pharms., Inst. for Med. Info., Collagenesis Corp., PediFix, Biocell Tech., others. Author: Saving Face, Skin Care for Teens, Super Skin, Baby Skin, You Can Do Something About Your Allergies, You Can Look Younger at Any Age, Diseases of the Mucus Membranes, (novel) In the Path of the Wolf, (audiotape series) Keeping That Baby Skin Look, Healthier and Younger-Looking Skin, Lunchtime Beauty Fixes for a Prettier Face, Breathing Easier, Fido, Food and Fumes; co-author: The External Ear; reviewer Annals Internal Medicine, Jour. Am. Acad. Dermatology, Jour. Dermatol. Surgery, Internat. Jour. Dermatology; editl. advisor Skin & Aging Health Report, Snyder Comm., Your Baby Wallboard Program; former med. editor Current Podiatric Medicine, Jour. Am. Analgesia Soc. Contbr. articles to profl. jours. Regent's Coll. scholar, 1971, Max and Leah Strauss Fund scholar, 1971, Grand St. Found. scholar, 1971; recipient Dept. Dermatology award for contbg. to edn. of residents, 2000-01, Dept. Dermatology award for exceptional svc. in patient care, 2001-02; Dept. Dermatology award for two decades of outstanding svc., 2003. Fellow ACP (direct election), Am. Acad. Dermatology (Leadership Cir. 2006), Am. Soc. Dermatol. Surgery, Am. Acad. Cosmetic Surgery, Skin

Cancer Found. (hon.); mem. AMA, AAAS, Soc. Investigative Dermatology, Skin Phototrauma Found., Internat. Soc. for Androgenic Disorders, Skin Cancer Found. (charter), N.Y. Acad. Scis., N.Y. County Med. Soc., Am. Soc. Dermatologic Surgery, Am. Analgesia Soc. (past bd. dirs.), Am. Soc. Cosmetic Dermatology & Aesthetic Surgery (charter), Nature Conservancy, Audubon Soc., Nat. Geog. Found., N.Y. Zool. Soc., Am. Mus. Natural History, Smithsonian Instn., Nat. Wildlife Fedn., The Wilderness Soc., Author's Guild, Author's League Am., Phi Beta Kappa. Jewish. Office: 328 E 75th St New York NY 10021-3317 Office Phone: 212-772-9300. E-mail: nnovickmd@aol.com. *The true measure of a person's success in life is not how much he accomplished, but how much of his God-given potential he has used.*

**NOVICK, PETER J.,** cell biologist, educator; PhD, U. Calif., Berkeley, 1981. Prof. cell biology Yale U., New Haven. Contbr. articles to profl. jours. Fellow: Am. Acad. Arts & Scis. Office: Dept Cell Biology Yale U Sch Medicine 333 Cedar St PO Box 208002 New Haven CT 06520-8002 E-mail: Peter.Novick@yale.edu.*

**NOVICK, ROBERT T.,** lawyer; b. Oct. 6, 1958; BA, Bucknell Univ., 1980; JD cum laude, Am. Univ., 1983. Bar: DC 1984, US Ct. Internat. Trade. Assoc. Steptoe & Johnson LLP, Washington, 1983—90, ptnr., 1991—97; counselor Office of U.S. Trade Rep., Washington, 1997—99, gen. counsel, 1999—2001; ptnr., chmn. Trade dept. Wilmer Cutler Pickering Hale & Dorr, Washington, 2001—. Commr. Adv. Commn. on Electronic Commerce, U.S. Congress. Editor (exec.): Am. Univ. Law Rev. Office: Wilmer Cutler Pickering Hale & Dorr 1899 Pennsylvania Ave NW Washington DC 20006 Mailing: Wilmer Cutler Pickering Hale & Dorr 2445 M St NW Washington DC 20037 Office Phone: 202-663-6140. Office Fax: 202-663-6363. Business E-Mail: robert.novick@wilmerhale.com.

**NOVICK, STEPHEN ALAN,** cardiologist; b. Hackensack, NJ, July 25, 1938; m. Rita Lynn Schneider; children: David, Michael, Jonathan. BA in Chemistry magna cum laude, Bklyn. Coll., 1959; MD with honors, SUNY, 1963. Intern L.I. Coll. Hosp., Bklyn., 1963—64, resident, chief resident in internal medicine, 1965—67; fellow cardiology Mt. Sinai Med. Ctr., N.Y.C., 1967—69; dir. prenatal cardiology clinic Mt. Sinai Hosp., N.Y.C., 1969—. Dir. cardiac clinic Mt. Sinai Hosp., N.Y.C., 1970—2000; dir. cardiology, dir. ICU Yonkers (N.Y.) Profl. Hosp., 1972—79; cons. cardiologist St. John's Riverside Hosp., Yonkers, NY; cons., presenter in field. Contbr. articles to profl. jours. Founder, dir. Little TOR Homeowners Assn., New City, NY, 1973—75, Bklyn. Coll. Soc. for Free Discussion of Politics, 1955—59. Recipient cardiology fellowship, NIH, 1967—69. Fellow: N.Y. Cardiol. Soc.; mem.: Phi Beta Kappa. Avocations: history, violin, singing, writing. Office: 133 E 73rd St New York NY 10021 also: 984 N Broadway Yonkers NY 10701 Office Phone: 914-423-7267.

**NOVIKOV, SERGEI PETROVITCH,** mathematician; b. Gorky, Russia, Mar. 20, 1938; s. Peter Sergeevitch and Ludmila (Keldysh) N.; m. Eleonora Vikentievna Tsoi, Oct. 2, 1962; children: Irina, Maria, Peter. B.Math., Moscow State U., 1960; PhD in math., Steklov Math. Inst., Moscow, 1964; PhD (hon.), U. Athens, 1988, U. Tel Aviv, 2000. Rsch. prof. math. Steklov Math. Inst., Moscow, 1964-75; chmn. math. dept. Landau Inst. Theoretical Physics, Moscow, 1975-96; disting. prof. math U Maryland, Coll. Park, 1996—. Chmn. geometry and topology Steklov Math. Ins., 1983—, Moscow State U., 1983—. Contbr. articles to profl. jours. Recipient Moscow Math. Soc. Young Mathematicians prize, 1964, Lenin Prize, 1967, Fields medal Internat. Math. Union, 1970, Lobachevskii Internat. Prize, Acad. of Sci. of the USSR, 1981, Wolf prize in math. Wolf Found., Israel, 2005. Mem. Moscow Math. Soc. (pres. 1985-96), Internat. Assn. of Math. Physicists (v.p. 1986-90), London Math. Soc. (hon. mem.), Serbian Acad. of Sci. and Art (hon. mem.), Acad. of Sci of the USSR (corresponding mem. 1966-81, full mem. 1981—), elected foreign mem. of the Academia de Lincei, Italy, 1991, mem. Academia Europea, 1992, foreign mem. of the NAS, 1994, mem of the Pontifical Acad. of Sci. (Vatican), 1996. Office: Landau Inst Kosygin St 2 Moscow Russia also: Dept of Math Math Bldg U of Maryland College Park MD 20742-4015

**NOVIKOVA, IRINA,** science educator; b. Moscow, Nov. 16, 1975; d. Boris Konstantinovich and Larissa Ivanovna Novikova; m. Eugeniy Eugenievich Mikhailov, June 7, 2003; 1 child, Catherine Eugeny Mikhailova. PhD, Tex. A&M U., College Station, 2003. Postdoctoral fellow Harvard-Smithsonian Ctr. for Astrophysics, Cambridge, Mass., 2003—06; asst. prof. Coll. of William and Mary, Williamsburg, Va., 2006—. Recipient New Focus Student award, Optical Soc. Am., 2001. Office: Coll of William&Mary PO Box 8795 Williamsburg VA 23185

**NOVINA, CARL D.,** science educator; s. Philip and Ulla I. Novina; m. Alexandra Anglewicz, Sept. 15, 2001; 1 child, Elias Philip. MD, Columbia U., NY, 1991; PhD, Tufts U., Boston, 2000. Asst. prof. Dana-Farber Cancer Inst. Harvard Med. Sch., Boston, 2004—. Office: Dana-Farber Cancer Inst 44 Binney St D1420B Boston MA 02115 Office Phone: 617-582-7961. Business E-Mail: carl_novina@dfci.harvard.edu.

**NOVITCH, MARK,** physician, retired pharmaceutical executive; b. New London, Conn., Apr. 23, 1932; s. Charles Weinger and Mary (Margolick) N.; m. Katherine Louise Henderson, Oct. 9, 1971; 1 dau., Julia Drummond. AB, Yale U., 1954; MD, N.Y. Med. Coll., 1958. Intern, asst. resident in medicine Boston City Hosp., 1958-60; rsch. fellow Harvard Med. Sch., 1960-62, asst. in medicine, 1962-64, instr. medicine, 1964-67; mem. med. staff Peter Bent Brigham Hosp., Boston, 1962-67; asst. physician Univ. Health Svcs., Harvard U., 1961-67; asst. to dep. asst. sec. for health and sci. affairs HEW, Washington, 1967-71; dep. assoc. commr. for med. affairs FDA, Washington, 1971-78, assoc. commr. for health affairs, 1978-81; dep. commr. food and drugs HHS, 1981-85; corp. v.p. The Upjohn Co., Kalamazoo, 1985-86, sr. v.p. sci. adminstrn., 1986-88, exec. v.p., 1989-90, vice-chmn. bd. dirs., 1991-93; prof. health scis. George Washington U., Washington, 1994-97. Adj. prof. George Washington U., 1997—2001; bd. dirs. Kos Pharm., Inc., Nat. Acad. Soc. Ins., chmn. bd. dirs. Food and Drug Law Inst., 2001—02; pres. U.S. Pharmacopeial Conv. Inc., 1990—95, trustee, 1990—2000. Bd. dirs. Nat. Fund Med. Edn. USPHS fellow, 1960-62; Brookings Instn. fed. exec. fellow, 1970-71 Mem. Mass. Med. Soc. Home: 3558 Albemarle St NW Washington DC 20008-4214

**NOVITZ, CHARLES RICHARD,** broadcast executive, reporter; b. Chgo., Oct. 25, 1934; m. Eve Krzyzanowski, Feb. 11, 1988; 1 child, Alexandra Maris. BS in Journalism, U. Ill., Champaign-Urbana, 1956; MS, Columbia U., 1960; MPA, NYU, 1971. Reporter, writer, editor City News Bur., Chgo., 1956-57, UPI, Chgo., 1957-59; editor, writer, field producer NBC News, N.Y.C. and Chgo., 1959-60; with ABC News, 1960-79; mgr. ABC News (TV network syndication), 1973-79; mng. dir. TV News Assn. N.Y.C., 1979-81; producer, exec. NBC News, N.Y.C., 1982-85, 87; assoc. Rowan & Blewitt, Inc./Exec. TV Workshop, N.Y.C., 1985-95; pres. NovaNews Comm. Cons., N.Y.C., 1994—. On-air talent Money Call News, 1988; freelance TV producer, cable and pub. TV series, 1985—; adj. instr. LIU, 1967-69, NYU, 1969-70; asst. adj. prof. Lehman Coll., 1970-71; adj. prof., producer interactive televised course CUNY, 1972-75 Mem. Silurians, Broadcast Pioneers, Radio TV News Dirs. Assn., Alumni Assn. Columbia Grad. Sch. Journalism (pres. 1979), Deadline Club N.Y.C. (pres. 1969), Deadline Club Found. (pres. 1999—), Soc. Profl. Journalists-Sigma Delta Chi (pres. 1981-82). Office: 160 West End Ave Apt 29D New York NY 10023-5616 also: 392 Moonstone Beach Rd Wakefield RI 02879-5102 Office Phone: 212-787-6908. Personal E-mail: evevideo@earthlink.net.

**NOVOA, YANIRA,** diplomat; b. San Salvador, El Salvador, Mar. 5, 1956; arrived in U.S., 1977; d. Numa Pompilio and Donna Rodriguez Novoa. BA, Mount Marty Coll., Yankton, S.D., 1977—81. Coun. gen. Min. Fgn. Affairs,

El Salvador, 1990—98, min. counselor, 1998—2002, free trade agreement investment chpt. mem., 1997—2002. Recipient Mother Jerome scholarship, Mount Marty Coll. Mem.: Internat. Ct. Justice. Home: 247 W Irving St Lincoln NE 68521-3005

**NOVOGROD, NANCY GERSTEIN,** editor; b. NYC, Jan. 30, 1949; d. Max and Hilda (Kirschbaum) Gerstein; m. John Campner Novogrod, Nov. 7, 1976; children: James Campner, Caroline Anne. AB, Mt. Holyoke Coll., 1971. Sec. fiction dept. The New Yorker, NYC, 1971-73, reader, 1973-76; asst. editor Clarkson Potter/Pubs., NYC, 1977-78, assoc. editor, 1978-80, editor, 1980-83, sr. editor, 1984-86, exec. editor, 1987; sr. editor HG (House & Garden mag.), NYC, 1987-88, editor-in-chief, 1988-93, Travel + Leisure, NYC, 1993—; editl. dir. Am. Express Pub., NYC, 2000—. Bd. dirs. Am. Soc. Mag. Editors. Bd. dirs. NY Bot. Garden, 1991—; exec. com., bd. dirs. Mount Holyoke Coll., 1992—97; adv. bd. Breast Cancer Rsch. Found., 1993; bd. dirs. Children's Advocacy Ctr. Manhattan, 2003. Office: Travel + Leisure 1120 Avenue of the Americas New York NY 10036-6700 Personal E-mail: nancy.g.novogrod@aexp.com.

**NOVOTNEY, DONALD FRANCIS,** superintendent of schools; b. Streator, Ill., July 10, 1947; s. Andrew Stephen and Irene Marie (Lux) Novotney; m. Jane Francis Loeffelholz, June 3, 1972; children: Nicole, Tara, Thomas, Michael, Theresa. BA, Loras Coll., 1969; MS in Tchg., U. Wis., Platteville, 1973; MS, U. Dayton, 1985. Cert. tchr., Wis.; cert. tchr. and adminstr., Ohio. Prin. Holy Ghost Sch., Dickeyville, Wis., 1969-75, St. John Sch., Green Bay, Wis., 1975-76, Beaver Dam (Wis.) Cath. Schs., 1976-83; coord. Jordan Cath. Schs., Rock Island, Wis., 1983-85; supt. schs. Diocese of Fargo, ND, 1985—87, Diocese of La Crosse, Wis., 1987—2001, Diocese of Jefferson City, Mo., 2002—. Mem. Nat. Cath. Edn. Assn. (del. to nat. congress for Cath. schs.). Republican. Roman Catholic. Avocations: athletics, travel. Home: 4000 Terra Bella Jefferson City MO 65109 Office: Diocese of Jefferson City 402 N Clark Ave Jefferson City MO 65102 Personal E-mail: donnjanen@aol.com.

**NOVOTNY, DAVID JOSEPH,** lawyer; b. Melrose Park, Ill., Oct. 3, 1953; s. Joseph F. and Dorothy E. (Erickson) N.; m. Gladys Ruth Korynecky, May 1, 1982. BSc, DePaul U., 1975, JD, 1978. Bar: Ill. 1978, U.S. Dist. Ct. (no. dist.), Ill. 1978, U.S. Ct. Appeals (7th cir.) 1985, U.S. Dist. Ct. (no. dist.), Ind. 1995, U.S. Dist. Ct. (cen. dist.) Ill. 1999. Law clk. to justice Ill. Appellate Ct., Chgo., 1978-80; assoc. Rooks, Pitts & Poust, Chgo., 1980-83, Peterson, Ross, Schloerb & Seidel (now Peterson & Ross), Chgo., 1983-88, ptnr., 1988—. Arbitrator Am. Arbitration Assn., 1987—, Cir. Ct. Cook County Ct.-Annexed Arbitration, 1990—. Exec. editor DePaul Law Rev., 1978. Mem. ABA, Ill. State Bar Assn., 7th Cir. Bar Assn., Soc. Trial Lawyers, Asia-Pacific Lawyers Assn., Lawyer-Pilots Bar Assn., Legal Club Chgo., Def. Rsch. Inst. Office: Peterson Ross 200 E Randolph St Ste 7200 Chicago IL 60601-7719

**NOVOTNY, DONALD WAYNE,** electrical engineer, educator; b. Chgo., Ill., Dec. 15, 1934; s. Adolph and Margaret Novotny; m. Louise J. Eenigenburg, June 26, 1954; children: Donna Jo Kopp, Cynthia Mason. BEE, Ill. Inst. Tech., 1956, MS, 1957; PhD, U. Wis., 1961. Registered profl. engr., Wis. Instr. Ill. Inst. Tech., 1957-58; mem. faculty U. Wis., Madison, 1958—, prof. elec. engring., 1969-96, Grainger prof. power electronics, 1990—96, prof. emeritus, 1996—, chmn. dept. elec. and computer engring., 1976-80. Vis. prof. Mont. State U., 1966, Eindhoven (The Netherlands) Tech. U., 1974, Tech. U. Louvain, Belgium, 1986; Fulbright lectr. Tech. U. Ghent, Belgium, 1981; diw. Wis. Elec. Machines and Power Electronics Consortium, 1981—96; assoc. dir. Univ.-Industry Rsch. Program, 1982—93; chmn. elec. engring. program Nat. Technol. U., 1989—2003; cons. to industry. Author: Introductory Electromechanics, 1965, Vector Control and Dynamics of AC Drives, 1996; contbr. scientific papers to profl. jours.; assoc. editor: Electric Machines and Power Systems, 1976—99. Named Disting. Lectr., IEEE-IAS, 1995; recipient Outstanding Paper award, Engring. Inst. Can., 1966, Outstanding Achievement award, IEEE-IAS, 1998; fellow, GE, 1956, Ford Found., 1960; grantee, numours industries and govt. agys. Fellow: IEEE (prize paper award 1983, 1984, 1986, 1987, 1990, 1991, 1993, 1994, 3d Millennium medal 2000); mem.: Am. Soc. Engring. Edn., Rotary, Sigma Xi, Eta Kappa Nu, Tau Beta Pi. Congregationalist. Home: 1421 E Skyline Dr Madison WI 53705-1132 Office: U Wis Dept Elec and Computer Engring 1415 Engineering Dr Madison WI 53706-1607 Office Phone: 608-262-6926. Business E-Mail: novotny@engr.wisc.edu.

**NOVOTNY, VLADIMIR,** engineering educator, consultant; b. Olomouc, Czech Rep., Aug. 30, 1938; came to U.S., 1969, naturalized, 1983; s. Vladimir and Frantiska Novotny; m. Lynn Emily Braasch, June 14, 1975; children: Paul Martin, Eric Vladimir. Diploma in Engring., Tech. U., Brno, Czech Rep., 1963, degree in Sci., 1968; PhD, Vanderbilt U., 1971. Diplomate by eminence Am. Acad. Environ. Engring. Rsch. engr. Water Mgmt. Inst., Brno, Czech Rep., 1962-69; rsch. assoc. Vanderbilt U., Nashville, 1969-71; project engr. Aware, Inc., Nashville, 1970-73; pres. Aquanova Internat., Ltd., Mequon, Wis., 1989—2005; prof. Marquette U., Milw., 1973—2002, prof. emeritus, 2003—; CDM chair, prof. Northeastern U., Boston, 2003—; dir. Ctr. Urban Environ. Studies, Northeastern U., 2003—. Dir. Inst. Urban Environ. Risk Mgmt. Marquette U., Milw., 1998—2002; dir. workshop NATO, Vienna, 1994; expert pollution abatement Venezia Nuova, Venice, Italy, 1989—2001. Author: Handbook of Nonpoint Pollution, 1981, Water Quality, 1994; editor: Management of Degraded River Basins, 1995. Rsch. grantee, Water Environ. Rsch. Found., Alexandria, Va., 1992, 1995, U.S. EPA, Washington, 1993, 1997, 2003, Ill. EPA, 2000—03. Mem. Internat. Water Assn. (chmn. com. 1993-98, chair internat. conf., Chgo., 1993, Edinburgh, 1998, Milw. 2001), Internat. Water Resource Assn., Am. Water Resources Assn. (dir. 1985-89), Water Environ. Fedn., Internat. Water Acad., Norway, 2002- Office: Northeastern U 360 Huntington Ave Boston MA 02115 Home: 780 Centre St UnitC Newton MA 02458 E-mail: novotny@coe.neu.edu.

**NOVROCKI, MICHAEL W.,** secondary school educator; BA, U. Scranton, Scranton, Pa., 1993; MA, Millersville U., Pa., 1996. Cert. tchr. secondary edn. social studies Pa., 2001. Tchr. social studies Abington Heights H.S., Clarks Summit, Pa., 2001—03, Lake-Lehman (Pa.) H.S., 2003—. Coord. nat. history day Abington Heights H.S., Washington, 2001—03, Lake-Lehman H.S., Pa., 2003—. Mem.: Pa. Coun. Social Studies. Avocation: travel. Office: Lake-Lehman School District Old Route 115 Lehman PA 18627-0038

**NOWACK, JAMES ALBERT,** education educator; b. Buffalo, Minn., Jan. 31; s. Albert Leo and Arlene Bertha Nowack; m. Dorothy Joan Paschen, Mar. 31, 2000. B in Music, Augsburg Coll., 1985; M of Music, Kent State U., 1989; M, U. Minn., 1991; D of Musical Arts, U. Iowa, 1994. Music prof. Wis. Luth. Coll., 1994—. Mem.: Am. Choral Dir. Assn. Avocation: gardening. Office: Wis Luth Coll 8800 W Blue Mound Rd Milwaukee WI 53226 Business E-Mail: james.nowack@wcc.edu.

**NOWACKI, JAMES NELSON,** lawyer; b. Columbus, Ohio, Sept. 12, 1947; s. Louis James and Betty Jane (Nelson) N.; m. Catherine Ann Holden, Aug. 1, 1970; children: Carrie, Anastasia, Emma. AB, Princeton U., 1969; JD, Yale U., 1973. Bar: Ill. 1973, N.Y. 1982, U.S. dist. Ct. (no. dist.) Ill. 1973, U.S. Ct. Appeals (7th cir.) 1978, U.S. Ct. Appeals (6th cir.) 1987, U.S. Supreme Ct. 1992. Assoc. Isham, Lincoln & Beale, Chgo., 1973, Kirkland & Ellis, Chgo., 1980—. Mem. Winnetka Sch. Bd. Dist. 36, Ill. 1983-91, bd. pres. 1989-91; mem. New Trier Sch. Bd., 1997-99, bd. pres., 1997-98. Harlan Fiske Stone prize Yale U., 1972. Mem. ABA (forum com. on constrn. industry, litigation sect.), Mid-Am. Club, Skokie Country Club. Home: 708 Prospect Ave Winnetka IL 60093-2320 Office: Kirkland & Ellis LLP 200 E Randolph St Fl 60 Chicago IL 60601-6636 Business E-Mail: jnowacki@kirkland.com.

**NOWAK, ANDREW,** music educator; s. Joseph and Anne Nowak; m. Remona G Logan, Aug. 27, 1983; children: Andrew, Jason, Heather Marie. BS in Music Edn., Wayne State U., Detroit, 1971; MusM, Wayne State U., 1982. Dir. of bands Gibraltar Pub. Schs., Gibraltar, 1973—81; music theory instr. Wayne State U., Detroit, 1981—82; vocal music tchr. Taylor Cmty. Schs., Taylor, 1981—83; dir. of bands Bad Axe Pub. Schs., Bad Axe, 1983—87, dir. of choirs/gen. music, 1986—, chair dept. music, 1995—, dir. madrigals, 2000—. Adjudicator (choir and band), 1983—; profl. piano accompanist, 1969—; condr. choral workshop Mich. State U., 2004—; mem. honors choir Ctrl. Mich. U., 2003—. Arranger (band arrangement) McArthur's Park. Pres. Lake DeBay Assn., Sand Point, Mich., 2004; v.p. Caseville Sch. Bd., Caseville, Mich., 1999—2001; chmn. Tri-County Honors Band, Mich., 1984—89; historian Caseville Cmty. Arts Coun., Caseville, Mich., 1985—87. Named Educator of the Yr., Bad Axe Pub. Schs., 1991; recipient Barbara Lipinski Award of Merit, Mich. Soc. for Autistic Citizens, 1991; grantee Walmart Found. grantee, Walmart, 2001, 2003, Tech. grantee, EDS, 2003, Fed. Drug-Free Schools/Cmty. Grant for Anti-Drug Musical, Fed. Govt., 1993. Mem.: Bad Axe Edn. Assn. (v.p. 2004), Mich. Edn. Assn., Mich. Sch. Band and Orch. Assn. (assoc.), Gibralter United Tchrs. (assoc.), Mich. Competing Band Dir. Assn. (assoc.), Am. Choral Dir. Assn. (assoc.), Mich. Sch. Vocal Music Assn. (assoc.), Tri-County Bargaining Assn. (assoc.; vice-president/bldg. rep/negotiator 1983), NEA (assoc.), Phi Mu Alpha (assoc.; treas./historian 1970—73). Office Phone: 989-269-9593.

**NOWAK, JERRY (GERALD C. NOWAK),** music educator, musician, writer; b. Detroit, Mich., Apr. 16, 1936; s. John and Lucille Nowak; m. Judith C. Christian, Sept. 30, 1937; children: Amy Elizabeth DeGrgorio, Christopher Gerald. BS in Music Edn., Coll. of N.J., 1954—58, MA, 1968. Music tchr. Hunterdon Ctrl. Regional H.S., Flemington, NJ, 1958—69; prof. emeritus Bucks County C.C., Newtown, Pa., 1969—. Co-author: Conducting Music, Not the Musicians, 2002, The Art of Expressive Playing, 2004, musician (founding mem.) Phila. Saxophone Quartet, NJ Saxophone Quartet; musician: (composer, arranger) more than 800 pub. compositions and arrangements for instrumental and vocal ensembles; condr. rec. sessions in N.Y.C., Phila., Washington and London. Pres. Raritan Twp. Athletic Assn., Flemington, NJ, 1980—82. Mem.: ASCAP. Home: 42 Madison Ave Flemington NJ 08822 Office: Bucks County CC Swamp Rd Newtown PA 18940 Office Phone: 908-782-5128. Personal E-mail: jerrynowak@blast.net.

**NOWAK, JOHN E.,** law educator; b. Chgo., Jan. 2, 1947; s. George Edward and Evelyn (Bucci) N.; m. Judith Johnson, June 1, 1968; children: John Edwin, Jeffrey Edward. AB, Marquette U., 1968; JD, U. Ill., 1971. Law clk. Supreme Ct. of Ill., Chgo., 1971-72; asst. prof. U. Ill., Urbana, 1972-75, assoc. prof., 1975-87, law prof., 1978—, grad. coll. faculty, 1982—, Baum prof. Law, 1993—. Chmn. Constl. Law Sch. Sect.; faculty rep. Big Ten Intercollegiate Conf., Schaumburg, 1981—91; vis. prof. law U. Mich., Ann Arbor, 1985; Lee disting. vis. prof. Coll. William and Mary, 1993; Williams vis. prof. law U. Richmond, 2003. Co-author: Treatise on Constitutional Law, 1986, 3d edit., 1999, supplement, 2006, Story's Commentaries on the Constitution, 1987, Constitutional Law, 7th edit. 2004, Principles of Constitutional Law, 2004, 2d edit., 2006, Supplement to Treatise on Constitutional Law, 2005. Scholar-in-Residence, U. of Ariz., Tucson, 1985, 87. Mem. Assn. of Am. Law Schs. (chmn. constl. law sect., accreditation com. 1980-88), Nat. Collegiate Athletic Assn. (mem. infractions com. 1987—), Am. Law Inst., Am. Bar Assn., Ill. Bar Assn., Order of the Coif (Triennial Book award com.). Roman Catholic. Home: 1701 Mayfair Rd Champaign IL 61821-5522 Office: U Ill Coll Law 504 E Pennsylvania Ave Champaign IL 61820-6909 Office Phone: 217-333-6757. Business E-Mail: jnowak@law.uiuc.edu.

**NOWAK, JUDITH ANN,** psychiatrist; b. Albany, N.Y., Feb. 18, 1948; d. Jacob Frank and Anne Patricia Nowak. BA, Cornell U., 1970, MD, 1974. Diplomate in psychiatry Am. Bd. Psychiatry and Neurology. Resident U. Va. Hosp., Charlottesville, 1974-77; fellow in psychiatry Westchester divsn. Cornell U. Med. Coll. Westchester Div., White Plains, N.Y., 1977-78; clin. affiliate Cornell U. Med. Coll., White Plains, N.Y., 1978-79; staff psychiatrist Chestnut Lodge Hosp., Rockville, Md., 1979-81; med. officer in psychiatry St. Elizabeths Hosp., Washington, 1981—; pvt. practice Washington, 1981—. Clin. asst. prof. of psychiatry, George Washington U., Washington, 1981-89; clin. assoc. prof. psychiatry, George Washington U. 1989-94, clin. prof. psychiatry, 1994—. Mem. Am. Psychiat. Soc. (pub. affairs rep. 1995), Am. Psychoanalytic Soc., Washington Psychiat. Soc. (sec. 1989-90, 2001-2003, pres. 1991-92), D.C. Med. Soc. (speaker ho. of dels. 1996-98, chair coun. med. specialty socs. 1998-2000). Office Phone: 202-887-5495.

**NOWAK, LINDA ILENE,** education educator; BS, Calif. Poly. State U., San Luis Obispo, 1974; MBA, Mercer U., Atlanta, 1991; PhD in Bus. Adminstrn., St. Louis U., Mo., 1996. Prof. mktg. Sonoma State U. Rohnert Park, Calif., 1996—. Mktg. advisor Sonoma County AIDS Prevention Task Force, Santa Rosa, Calif., 1997—2006. FIPSE grant, Fed. Govt., 1997—98, Sr. fellow, Fullbright Found., 2005—. Mem.: Acad. Mktg. Sci. (assoc.; reviewer 1996—2006). Achievements include research in positive emotional experiences influences brand equity and repurchase intentions in hospitality industries as significantly as product quality and svc. quality. Office: Sonoma State Univ 1801 East Cotati Ave Rohnert Park CA 94928-3609 Office Phone: 707-664-3954.

**NOWAK (JAROSZ), LINDA THERESE,** special education educator, consultant; b. Buffalo, Nov. 25, 1954; d. Joseph John Sr. and Theresa E. Jarosz; m. Raymond John Nowak, June 18, 1982; 1 child, Raymond John Jr. BS in Edn., Buffalo State Coll., 1988, MEd, 1994, Niagara U., N.Y., 1998. Cert. sch. dist. adminstr. N.Y., sch. adminstr. and supervision N.Y., spl. edn. tchr. N.Y., elem. edn. tchr. N.Y. Spl. edn. cons. tchr. West St. Elem. Sch. Niagara Wheatfield Cen. Sch. Dist., Sanborn, NY, 1989—, prin. summer sch., 1999—2000, head tchr. summer sch., 2001—04. Adj. prof. edn. Niagara U., 2004—. Fundraiser, supporter United Spinal Assn., Milford, NH, 2003—05; vol. Am. Cancer Soc., Amherst, NY, 2001—03; bd. dirs., mem. devel. com. Niagara Frontier Ctr. for Ind. Living, Niagara Falls, 2002—05., Orleans/Niagara Tchr. Ctr. grantee, 2002—04. Mem.: ASCD (assoc.), Am. Fedn. Tchrs., NY State United Tchrs. Coun. for Exceptional Children, Delta Kappa Gamma (assoc.). Democrat. Roman Catholic. Avocation: collecting antiques. Home: 5761 Dunnigan Rd Lockport NY 14094 Office: West St Elem Sch 5700 West St Sanborn NY 14132 Office Phone: 716-215-3200. Personal E-mail: ltnowak82@adelphia.net. Business E-Mail: lnowak@nwcsd.org.

**NOWAK, LISA M.,** astronaut, military officer; b. Washington, D.C., May 10, 1963; d. Alfredo and Jane Caputo; m. Richard T. Nowak; 3 children. BS in Aerospace Engring., USN Acad., Annapolis, Md., 1985; MS in Aeronautical Engring., USN Postgrad. Sch., Monterey, Calif., 1992, degree in Aeronautical Engring., 1992. Commd. ensign U.S. Navy, Annapolis, 1985, advanced through grades to cmmdr.; Temporary duty NASA Johnson Space Ctr., Houston, 1985; student pilot USN Flight Sch., 1986; trainee Electronic Warfare Sch., Corry Sta., Fla., 1988; pilot Electronic Warfare Aggressor Squadron 34, Point Magu, Calif., 1989—90; grad. student USN Postgrad. Sch., Monterey, Calif., 1990—92; engr. Systems Engring. Test Directorate, Pauxent River, Md., 1993; student test pilot U.S. Navy Test Pilot Sch., Pauxent River, Md., 1993—94; aircraft systems project officer Strike Aircraft Test Squadron, Pauxent River, Md., 1994—95; acquistion project USN Air Systems Command, 1995—96; astronaut NASA Johnson Space Ctr., Houston, 1996—. Mission specialist STS-121 (Discovery), a return-to-flight test mission and assembly flight to the International Space Station, 2006. Recipient Navy Commendation medal, Navy Achievement medal. Mem.: AIAA, USN Acad. Alumni Assn., Tau Beta Pi. Achievements include Over 1,100 flight hours using 30 different aircraft. Avocations: bicycling, crossword puzzles, gourmet cooking, running, rubber stamps, skeet shooting, piano. Office: Astronaut Office/CB Johnson Space Ctr Houston TX 77058*

**NOWAK, ROBERT MICHAEL,** chemist; b. South Milwaukee, Wis., Oct. 28, 1930; s. Casimer M. and Anita Marie (Anderson) N.; m. Susan Lora Boyd, Oct. 12, 1957; children: Karen Sue Nowak Sapsford, Janet Lynn Nowak McMorris. Student U. Wis., Racine, 1949-51; BS U. Wis., Madison, 1953; PhD, U. Ill., 1956. Rsch. chemist Phys. Rsch. Lab., Dow Chem. Co., Midland, Mich., 1956-64, from group leader to asst. lab dir., 1964-72; dir. rsch. and devel. plastics dept. Dow Chem. Co., Midland, 1972-73, dir. rsch. and devel. Olefin and Styrene plastics depts., 1973-78, dir. rsch. and devel. plastics dept.,

1978-83, dir. cen. rsch., 1983-90, chief scientist, dir. cen. rsch. and devel., 1990-94; pres., CEO Mich. Molecular Inst., Midland, 1994—. Contbr. articles to profl. jours.; patentee organic reaction mechanisms and reinforced plastics. Mem. NAE, AIChE, Am. Chem. Soc. Office: MI Molecular Inst 1910 W Saint Andrews Rd Midland MI 48640-2657 E-mail: nowak@mmi.org.*

**NOWE, RONALD JOHN,** state legislator, small business owner; b. Gloucester, Mass., Feb. 7, 1946; children: Ronald Jr., Miguel. Student, Hesser Coll., 1976. Owner, mgr. Now Ins. Agy., Epping, N.H., agy. mgr.; propr., mgr. Kamper Kampania Kampground, 3d Street Grocery; mgr., propr. Oak Grove Golfing; mem. N.H. Ho. of Reps. Mem., chmn. wildlife and marine resources com., com. whip, legis. adminstrn. chmn., chmn. sheriff com., mem. long range planning com. Mem. Pub. Water Access Adv. Bd.; vice chair Epping Planning Bd. Mem. DAV (jr. vice. comdr. 1983-94), VFW, Am. Legion, Masons. Republican. Home: PO Box 327 Epping NH 03042 Office: Legis Office Bldg Rm 308 Concord NH 03301

**NOWELL, LIONEL L.,** food products executive; BS in Bus. Adminstrn., Ohio State U., 1976. CPA. Various fin. analysis positions Owens-Corning Fiberglas Corp., Packard Electric Divsn., GM, Inc.; various audit and control positions Pizza Hut divsn. PepsiCo., Inc., 1983-91; v.p., controller audit activities food and internat. retail Pillsbury Co., 1991, v.p., CFO Haagen-Dazs, v.p. fin. bakeries and foodservice unit; v.p. fin. Pillsbury N.Am., 1996-98; sr. v.p. strategy and bus. devel. RJR Nabisco Holdings Corp., NYC, 1998—99; controller PepsiCo, Inc, 1999—2000; sr. v.p., treasurer PepsiCo, Inc., 2001—; CFO Pepsi Bottling Co, Inc, 2000—01. Dir. Gifts in Kind Internat. Mem. AICPAs. Office: PepsiCo, Inc 700 Anderson Hill Rd Purchase NY 10577*

**NOWELL, PETER CAREY,** pathologist, educator; b. Phila., Feb. 8, 1928; s. Foster and Margaret (Matlack) Nowell; m. Helen Worst, Sept. 9, 1950; children: Sharon, Timothy, Karen, Kristin, Michael. BA, Wesleyan U., Middletown, Conn., 1948; MD, U. Pa., 1952. Intern Phila. Gen. Hosp., 1952—53; resident pathology Presbyn. Hosp., Phila., 1953—54; med.-teaching, research specializing in cancer Phila., 1956—; from instr. to prof. pathology Sch. Medicine U. Pa., 1956—, chmn. dept. pathology, 1967—73; dir. (Cancer Center) 1973—75. Lt. M.C. USNR, 1954—56. Recipient Rsch. Career award, USPHS, 1964—67, Parke-Davis award, 1965, Lindback Disting. Tchg. award, 1967, Passano award, 1984, Rous-Whipple award, Am. Assn. Pathology, 1986, de Villers award, Leukemia Soc. Am., 1987, Mott prize, GM Cancer Rsch. Found., 1989, AIME, Am. Phys., 1984, Lasker Found. award, 1998. Home: 345 Mount Alverno Rd Media PA 19063-5313 Office: U Pa Sch Medicine Dept Pathology & Lab Medicine Philadelphia PA 19104-6082 Office Phone: 215-898-8066. Business E-Mail: nowell@mail.med.upenn.edu.

**NOWICK, ARTHUR STANLEY,** metallurgy and materials science educator; b. NYC, Aug. 29, 1923; s. Hyman and Clara (Sperling) N.; m. Joan Franzblau, Oct. 30, 1949; children: Jonathan, Steven, Alan, James. AB, Bklyn. Coll., 1943; A.M., Columbia U., 1948, PhD, 1950. Physicist NACA, Cleve., 1944-46; instr. U. Chgo., 1949-51; asst. prof., then assoc. prof. metallurgy Yale U., 1951-57; mgr. metallurgy research IBM Corp Research Center, Yorktown Heights, NY, 1957-66; prof. metallurgy Columbia U., 1966-90, Henry Marion Howe prof. metallurgy and materials sci., 1990-95, prof. emeritus, 1996—. Adj. prof. chem. engring. and materials sci. dept. U. Calif., Irvine, 2001; Frank Golick lectr. U. Mo., 1970; vis. prof. Technion, Haifa, Israel, 1973; co-chmn. Internat. Conf. Internal Friction, 1961, 69; cons. in field. Author: Crystal Properties Via Group Theory, 1995; co-author: Anelastic Relaxation in Crystalline Solids, 1972; co-editor: Diffusion in Solids, 1975, Diffusion in Crystalline Solids, 1984; contbr. articles to profl. jours. Named David Turnbull lecturer Materials Rsch. Soc., 1994; gold medalist Internat. Conf. Internal Friction, 1989. Fellow AIME, Am. Phys. Soc.; mem. Materials Rsch. Soc. (Turnbull lectr. 1994), Sigma Xi (pres. Kappa chpt. 1983-85). Home: 24 Hillsdale Dr Newport Beach CA 92660-4234 Office: U Calif Irvine 916 Engineering Tower Irvine CA 92697-2575 Business E-Mail: anowick@uci.edu.

**NOWICKI, GEORGE LUCIAN,** retired chemical company executive; b. Rutherford, N.J., Dec. 4, 1926; s. Justin Nowicki; m. Mary Elisabeth Baker, Aug. 30, 1947; children: Barbara, Peter, Paul, James. BSChemE, CCNY, 1949; MSChemE, NYU, 1956. Registered profl. engr., N.Y., Pa. Chemist Ideal Toy Co., N.Y.C., 1949; chem. engr. Bklyn. Union Gas Co., 1949-50, Sonotone Corp., Elmsford, N.Y., 1950-52; dept. head Burroughs Wellcome Co., Tuckahoe, N.Y., 1952-70; v.p. mfg. Quaker Chem. Corp., Conshohocken, Pa., 1970-79, v.p. domestic ops., 1984-89, ret., 1989; pres. Selby Batersby Co., Phila., 1979-81; mng. dir. Quaker Chem. Holland BV, Uithoorn, The Netherlands, 1981-84. Chmn. bd. Overdale Corp., Alsip, Ill., 1987-89, Quaker Chem. Can. Ltd., Toronto, 1985-89. Pres. Ctrl. Sch. Dist. 7, Hartsdale, N.Y., 1960-69, Westchester County Sch. Bds. Assn., White Plains, N.Y., 1965; bd. dirs. Suburban Gen. Hosp., Norristown, Pa., 1986; mem. governing bd. Vt. Common Cause, 1993-2004; bd. dirs. Martha Canfield Libr., Arlington, Vt., 1994-2000; counselor Svc. Corps Ret. Execs., 1993-95. With USN, 1944—46, WWII. Mem. Am. Inst. Chem. Engrs., Mfrs. Assn. Del. Valley (bd. dirs. 1987-89). Avocations: swimming, skiing, video photography, stamps. Home: 1611 Cold Spring Rd Williamstown MA 21267-2784

**NOWIK, JOHN DAVID,** music educator, musician; b. Allentown, Pa., Aug. 26, 1960; s. Stanley John and Helen Mary Nowik; m. Martha Elizabeth Huddleston, Jan. 9, 1982; children: Clare Magdalena children: Elizabeth J., Anna M., Krystyna H. Sofia M., Katerina T. Lucia F., Johanna C., Alexander B., Monica R. MusB, Westminster Choir Coll., 1982; MusM, Emory U., 1996. Organist, choir dir. St. Joseph the Worker Ch., Fallsington, Pa., 1980—83; instr., organist St. Joseph's Prep. Sch., Princeton, NJ, 1981—85; cathedral organist, dir. music Cathedral St. Francis of Assisi, Metuchen, NJ, 1983—2001; univ. organist Seton Hall U., South Orange, NJ, 1996—; dir. music, organist Immaculate Conception Sem., South Orange, NJ, 1996—. Dir. concerts, arts Cathedral Concert Series, Metuchen, NJ, 1984—2001; assoc. condr. Brunswick Symphony Orch., New Brunswick, NJ, 1985—2001. Editor (contributor) hymnal. Recipient Excellence in Achievement award, Middlesex County Cultural and Heritage Commn., 1993; scholar, Emory U., 1995—96. Mem.: Conf. Roman Cath. Cathedral Musicians, Am. Guild Organists (dean 1993—95). Roman Catholic. Avocations: composing, music, bicycling, stamp collecting/philately. Office: Seton Hall U 400 South Orange Ave South Orange NJ 07079 Office Phone: 973-761-9069. Business E-Mail: nowikjoh@shu.edu.

**NOWINSKI, FRANK LAWRENCE,** lawyer; b. Chgo., June 5, 1955; s. Edward and Joan (Kawa) N.; m. Roxanne Thomson, Aug. 18, 1979; children: David, Joan, Steven. BA cum laude, Augustana Coll., 1977; JD, Loyola U., Chgo., 1980. Bar: Ill. 1980, U.S. Dist. Ct. (cen. dist.) Ill. 1982, Iowa 1986. Assoc. Marvin L. Schrager, P.C., Moline, Ill., 1980-83; ptnr. Huntoon, Nowinski & Swanson, Ltd., Moline, 1983-2000; ptnr. Katz, Huntoon and Fieweger, P.C., Moline, Ill., 2000—. Spl. asst. to Ill. Atty. Gen., 1982-83; instr. bus. law Person Wolinsky CPA Rev. Course, Davenport, Iowa, 1983-89. Bd. dirs. Rock Island County Am. Heart Assn., 1985-91, v.p., 1988-91; active Quad City Planning Coun., trustee Don E. and Charlotte Williams Charitable Found., 2003—; bd. dirs. Cmty. Found. Great River Bend, 2005—. Mem. Ill. Bar Assn. (coun. employee benefits sect. 1988-96, sec. 1992-93, vice chair 1993-94, chmn. 1994-95), Iowa Bar Assn., Rock Island County Bar Assn., Rock Island County Bd. Realtors (affiliate), Rock Island Jaycees (v.p. 1982, Outstanding Local Jaycee pres. 1987), Kiwanis (bd. dirs. Moline club 1984-86, v.p. 1992-93, pres. 1993-94), Ontario Can. Camps Farthest Out (chmn. 1995-98). Republican. Episcopalian. Avocations: basketball, golf, gardening. Office: Katz Huntoon and Fieweger PC 1000 36th Ave Moline IL 61265-7126 Office Phone: 309-797-3000. Business E-Mail: fnowinski@katzlawfirm.com.

**NOWITZKI, DIRK,** professional basketball player; b. Germany, June 19, 1978; s. Joerg and Helen N. Forward Dallas Mavericks, 1998—. With German Army, 1997-98. Named to All-NBA Second Team, 2002, NBA All-Star Team, 2002—06, All-NBA First Team, 2006. Achievements include winner All-Star 3-point Contest, 2006. Avocations: reading, playing saxaphone.*

**NOWLAN, CHARLES F.,** controller; married; 3 children. B, U. Ala., 1976. CPA 1979. Mem. audit staff Coopers & Lybrand, 1977—80; with acquisition, tax and pension areas McWane, 1980—91, v.p., controller, 1991—. Mem. pres.'s coun. Fla. Coll., Tampa; elder Cahaba Hts. Ch. of Christ. Mem.: AICPA, Birmingham C. of C. Office: McWane 2900 Hwy 280 Ste 300 Birmingham AL 35223

**NOWLAND, JAMES FERRELL,** lawyer; b. Talladega, Ala., Dec. 7, 1942; s. James Franklin and Wilma Delene (Dean) N.; m. Faye Roberts, Aug. 28, 1964; children: Angela Roschelle, James Ferrell II. BS, Jacksonville (Ala.) State U., 1967; BS in Med. Technology, U. Ark., 1972; grad., U. S. Army Med. Ctr., 1974; JD, Oglethorpe U., 1983. Bar: Ga. 1984, U.S. Dist. Ct. (no. dist.) Ga. 1984, U.S. Ct. Appeals (11th cir.) 1984, U.S. Supreme Ct. 1988. Chemist U.S. Army C.E., Marietta, Ga., 1972-97; pvt. practice Cobb County, Ga., 1984— 1967-72. Mem. ABA, Ga. Bar Assn., Cobb County Bar Assn. Home: 50 Mt Calvary Rd Marietta GA 30064-1918 Office: PO Box 1847 Marietta GA 30061-1847

**NOWLIN, CONNIE BLACKWELL,** artist; b. Jacksonville, Fla., Oct. 1, 1948, d. Joseph Earl Blackwell and Harryet Hazel Steward Blackwell; m. Phillip Neil Nowlin, Aug. 22, 1970; children: Stewart Andrew, Erin Blake. BS, East Tenn. State U., 1970; postgrad., Arrowmont Sch. Crafts, 1973—78; EdM, U. N.C., Charlotte, 1979. Art tchr. West Charlotte High, 1970—86, Myers Park H.S., Charlotte, 1986—2006. Mem. tchr. adv. bd. Mint Mus. Craft and Design, Charlotte, 1998—. Home: 100 Emory Pl Huntersville NC 28078

**NOWLIN, JAMES ROBERTSON,** federal judge; b. San Antonio, Nov. 21, 1937; s. William Forney and Jeannette (Robertson) N. BA, Trinity U., 1959, MA, 1962; JD, U. Tex., Austin, 1963. Bar: Tex. 1963, Colo. 1993, U.S. Dist. Ct. D.C. 1966, U.S. Ct. Claims 1969, U.S. Supreme Ct. 1969, U.S. Dist. Ct. (we. dist.) Tex. 1971. Assoc. Kelso, Locke, & King, San Antonio, 1963-65; assoc. Kelso, Locke & Lepick, San Antonio, 1966-69; legal counsel U.S. Senate, Washington, 1965-66; propr. Law Offices James R. Nowlin, San Antonio, 1969-81; mem. Tex. Ho. of Reps., Austin, 1967-71, 73-81; judge U.S. Dist. Ct. for Western Dist. Tex., Austin, 1981-99, chief judge, 2000—03, sr. judge, 2003—. Instr. Am. govt. and history San Antonio Coll., 1964-65, 71-73. Capt. U.S. Army, 1959-60, USAR, 1960-68. Fellow State Bar Found (life); mem. San Antonio Bar Assn., Colo. Bar Assn. Republican. Presbyterian. Avocations: pilot, skiing, hiking, jogging. Office: US Courthouse 200 W 8th St Austin TX 78701-2325 Office Phone: 512-916-5675. Business E-Mail: james_r_nowlin@trwd.uscourts.gov.

**NOWOCIN, DEBRA TERESE,** gifted and talented secondary education educator; b. Chicago Heights, Ill., Aug. 4, 1951; d. Anthony F. and Anita G. (Cioe) N. BS in Edn., Ea. Ill. U., 1973; gifted cert., Nat. Coll. Edn., 1978; MS in Edn., No. Ill. U., 1981. Cert. tchr., gifted tchr., gen. adminstrv. Tchr., grades 4-6 Sch. Dist. 170, Chicago Heights, 1973-76, tchr. title I summer sch., 1974-76, tchr. summer enrichment program, various yrs., sci. and gifted enrichment tchr., grade 7, 1976—. Tchr. Worlds of Wisdom and Wonder program for gifted and talented children Ctr. for Gifted, Nat.-Louis U., Evanston, Ill., 1990-97; coord. sci. fair Washington Jr. High Sch. (team sponsor); co-sponsor Spartan Explorers Social Studies Club; key leader Bldg. a Presence Sci., 2002-. Appeared in video Team Up With TV: Using Video in the Classroom, 1991. Active various dist. curriculum coms. Recipient Presdl. award for excellence in sci. teaching nominee, 1984, 96. Mem. NSTA, Ill. Coun. for Gifted, Ill. Sci. Tchrs. Assn., Ill. Jr. Acad. Sci. (sec., treas. region 9, asst. to state safety chmn.), South Suburban Sci. Coun., Kappa Delta Pi. Home: 121 E 24th St Chicago Heights IL 60411-4248 Office: Washington Jr High Sch 25 W 16th Pl Chicago Heights IL 60411-3475 Personal E-mail: dnowocin@sbcglobal.net.

**NOYES, HENRY PIERRE,** physicist; b. Paris, Dec. 10, 1923; s. William Albert and Katharine Haworth (Macy) N.; m. Mary Wilson, Dec. 20, 1947; children—David Brian, Alan Quinn, Katharine Hope. AB magna cum laude, Harvard U., 1943; PhD, U. Calif., Berkeley, 1950. Physicist MIT, 1943-44, U. Calif., Berkeley, 1949-50; Fulbright fellow U. Birmingham, England, 1950-51; asst. prof. U. Rochester, NY, 1951-55; group leader Lawrence Livermore Lab., 1955-62; Leverhulme lectr. U. Liverpool, England, 1957-58; adminstrv. head theory sect. Stanford Linear Accelerator Center, 1962-69; asso. prof. Stanford U., 1962-67, prof., 1967-2000, prof. emeritus, 2000—; prin. investigator Mereon, 2005—. Vis. scholar Center Advanced Study Behavioral Scis., Stanford, 1968—69; prin. investigator Mereon, 2005—; cons. in field. Author papers in field. Chmn. Com. for Direct Attack on Legality of Vietnam War, 1967; mem. steering com. Peace Political Action Group, Stanford U., 1970-72; mem. policy com. U.S. People's Com. on Iran, 1977-79. Served with USNR, 1944-46. Fellow NSF, 1962; Fellow Nat. Humanities Faculty, 1970; recipient Alexander von Humboldt U.S. Sr. Scientist award, 1979. Mem. Alternative Natural Philosophy Assn. (pres. 1979-87, 1st alternative natural philosopher award 1989), Am. Phys. Soc., AAAS, Sigma Xi. Achievements include research in bit-string physics. E-mail: noyes@slac.stanford.edu. What success I may have had has come because I have tried to bring together my physics and politics and family to serve the people. I aim to achieve a unified materialist philosophy that might help others to create a world than my own. I sum up this philosophy as "fixed past - uncertain future".

**NOYES, RICHARD HALL,** bookseller; b. Evanston, Ill., Feb. 12, 1930; s. George Frederick and Dorothy (Hall) N.; m. Judith Claire Mitchell, Oct. 10, 1953; children— Catherine, Stephanie, Matthew. BA, Wesleyan U., 1952. Tng. program, elementary-high sch. salesman Rand McNally & Co., Colo., Utah, Idaho, Wyo., 1955-59; founder, owner, mgr. The Chinook Bookshop, Colorado Springs, Colo., 1959—. Contbr. to A Manual on Bookselling, 1974, The Business of Book Publishing, 1984; contbr. articles to newspapers and trade jours. Co-chmn. Colo. Media Coalition, 1974—; bd. dirs. Colorado Springs Fine Arts Ctr., 1977-81, Citizens Goals for Colorado Springs, 1976-88; trustee Fountain Valley Sch., 1979-81; vice chmn. Colorado Springs Charter Rev. Commn., 1991-92; mem. adv. coun. U. Colo., Colorado Springs, 1997—, Downtown Partnership, 1998—. Served with AUS, 1952-54. Recipient Intellectual Freedom award Mountain Plains Librs. Assn., 1977, Disting. Svc. award U. Colo., 1980, Recognition award Pikes Peak Arts Coun., 1989, Charles S. Haslam award, 1990), Entrepreneur of Yr. award U. Colo., 1992, Gordon Saull award for outstanding bookseller Mountains and Plains Booksellers Assn., 1996. Mem. Am. Booksellers Assn. (pres., dir.) Home: 1601 Constellation Dr Colorado Springs CO 80906-1609

**NOYES, ROBERT EDWIN,** publisher, writer; b. N.Y.C., June 22, 1925; s. Clarence A. and Edith (LaDomus) N.; m. Janet Brown, Mar. 24, 1952 (div. June 1963); children— Keith, Steven, Mark, Geoffrey; m. Mariel Jones, July 24, 1964; children— Rebecca, Robert. BS in Chem. Engring. Northwestern U., 1945. Chem. engr. Am. Cyanamid Co., Pearl River, NY, 1947; sales exec. Titanium Pigment Corp., N.Y.C., 1948-55; market research mgr. U.S. Indsl. Chem. Co., N.Y.C., 1956-58; sales mgr. atomic energy Curtiss Wright Export, N.Y.C., 1958-60; founder, pres., chmn. bd. Noyes Data Corp., Westwood, NJ, 1960-99; pub. Noyes Press, Noyes Publs., Westwood, 1961-99, Noyes Strategic Pubs., Saddle River, NJ, 1999—. Served to lt. (j.g.) USNR, 1945-47. Mem.: AIAA, Am. Inst. Chem. Engrs., Am. Chem. Soc., N.Y. Yacht Club. Episcopalian. Home: 224 W Saddle River Rd Saddle River NJ 07458-2620

**NOZKOWSKI, THOMAS,** painter; b. Teaneck, NJ, 1944; BFA, Cooper Union, NYC, 1967. Assoc. prof. Mason Gross Sch. of the Arts, Rutgers U., NJ, 2000—. One-man shows include Max Protetch Gallery, NYC, 1990,

1991, 1993, 1995, 1997, 2000, 2001, 2003, exhibited in group shows at From Earth To Archetype, Ledisflam Gallery, NY, 1990, 10 Abstract Painters, Baumgartner Galleries, Washington, 1991, Shades of Difference, Sandra Gering Gallery, NYC, 1992, Return of the Cadavre Exquis, The Drawing Center, NYC, 1993, A Hundred Hearts, The Contemporary, NYC, 1994, Re-Picturing Abstraction, 1708 Gallery, Richmond, Va., 1995, New Narrative Abstraction, Bklyn. Coll., 1996, Purely Painting, Elizabeth Harris Gallery, NYC, 1997, Pertaining to Painting, Contemporary Arts Mus., Houston, 2002, 181st Ann.: An Invitational Exhbn. Contemporary Art, Nat. Acad. Mus., NYC, 2006, exhibitions include Michael Berger Gallery, Pitts., 2003, pub. collections, Whitney Mus., NYC, San Francisco Mus. Modern Art, Orlando Mus. Art, Fla., Mus. Modern Art, NYC, Met. Mus. Art, Hirshhorn Mus. and Sculpture Garden, Washington, High Mus. Art, Atlanta, Corcoran Gallery of Art, Washington, Bklyn. Mus. Art. Recipient Am. Acad. Arts and Letters Purchase prize, 1998, 1999, Am. Acad. Arts and Letters Award in Painting, 1999; grantee Nat. Endowment for the Arts Individual Artist Grant, 1984, NY State Creative Artists Pub. Svc. grant, 1985, NY State Found. for the Arts fellowship, 1989, John Simon Guggenheim Meml. Found. fellowship, 1993. Mailing: c/o Max Protetch Gallery 511 W 22nd St New York NY 10011*

**NRIAGU, JEROME OKON,** environmental geochemist; b. Ora-eri Town, Anambra, Nigeria, Oct. 24, 1942; arrived in U.S., 1993; s. Martin and Helena (Anaekwe) N.; children: Chinedu Delbert, Uzoma Vivian, Osita Jide. BSc with honors, U. Ibadan, Nigeria, 1965, DSc, 1987; MS, U. Wis., 1967; PhD, U. Toronto, Ont., 1970. Rsch. scientist Environment Can., Burlington, Ont., 1970-93; prof. environ. chem. sch. of pub. health U. Mich., Ann Arbor, 1993—; dir. environ. health scis. program, 1996-99; rsch. prof. Ctr. for Human Growth and Devel., U. Mich., 1997—. Adj. prof. U. Waterloo, Ont., 1985—96; vis. scientist NOAA, Ann Arbor, 1992; bd. dirs. Ecology Ctr. Mich., Alliance to End Childhood Lead Poisoning, Washington, 1998—. Author: Lead and Lead Poisoning in Antiquity, 1983; editor: (book series) Advances in Environmental Science and Technology, 1982—, Trace Metals in the Environment, 1996—, 29 books on various environ. topics, 1979—, Sci. of the Total Environment, 1983—; mem. editl. bds.: 9 jours.; contbr. articles to profl. jours. Recipient Rigler medal, Can. Soc. Limnologists, 1988; Fulbright sr. fellow, 2002. Fellow: Royal Soc. Can. (Romanowski medal 1999); mem.: AAAS, Am. Pub. Health Assn. Roman Catholic. Avocations: photography, reading (African authors), travel. Office: Univ Michigan Environ/Indsl Health 109 Observatory St Ann Arbor MI 48109-2029

**NSOFOR, LESLIE MONAGOLUM,** food scientist, researcher; b. Oguta, Nigeria, July 10, 1955; arrived in U.S.A., 1997; s. Francis Chukwudifu Nsofor and Florence Chinelo Anamaleze; m. Obianuju Nwamaka Ikpeze, Apr. 29, 1983; children: Leslie, Valentine, Stephanie. BS in microbiology, U. Nigeria, 1978; MS in food sci., Utah State U., 1983, PhD in food sci., 1984. Lectr. Kaduna (Nigeria) Poly., 1978—80; grad. rsch. asst. Utah State U. 1981—84, post doctoral rsch. fellow, 1984—85; assoc. prof., assoc. dean Fed. U. Tech., Owerri, Nigeria, 1986—97; adj. assoc. prof. Mich. State U. 1999—; rsch. dir., co-owner, dept. CEO Soy Ultima LLC, East Lansing, Mich., 2000—. Acting head of dept. Abia State U., Uturu, Nigeria, 1990—92; mem. senate Fed. U. Tech., Owerri, Nigeria, 1994—96; founder Lensof Konsult LLC, Lansing, 2006—. Co-author 27 jour. articles, Instrument for Measuring Milk Coagulation in Cheese Vat. Ch. harvest com. St. Joseph Cath. Chaplaincy, Imo State Univ., Owerri, Nigeria, 1996—97. Rsch. grant, Internat. Found. Sci., 1989. Roman Catholic. Achievements include patents for soy beverage mfg. method. Avocations: jogging, jazz, travel. Home: 4436 Wagon Wheel Ln Lansing MI 48917 Office Phone: 517-332-0771. E-mail: lensofor@aol.com.

**NTAIMO, LEWIS,** engineering educator, researcher; b. Kitwe, Zambia, May 21, 1973; s. Laso and Alice Bwalya Ntaimo; m. Chloe Agnes Balfour; children: Joseph Mulenga, Claire Mumba, Ceanah Bwalya. PhD in Systems and Indsl. Engring., U. Ariz., Tucson, 2004. Rsch. asst. dept. mining and geol. engring. U. Ariz., Tucson, 1999—2000, rsch. asst. dept. sys. and indsl. engring., 2001—04; asst. prof. dept. indsl. and sys. engring. Tex. A&M U., College Station, 2004—. Grantee, NSF, 2005—. Mem.: Inst. Indsl. Engrs. (assoc.; faculty advisor student chpt. 2005—06). Office: Tex A&M U 3131 Tamu College Station TX 77843 Office Phone: 979-862-4066. Office Fax: 979-847-9005. Business E-Mail: ntaimo@tamu.edu.

**NTZIACHRISTOS, VASILIS,** bioengineer; Diploma in elec. engring., Aristotle U., 1993; postgrad., U. Copenhagen Med. Sch., 1994—95; MS in Bioengring., U. Pa., 1998, PhD in Bioengring., 2000. Asst. prof. radiology Harvard U. Med. Sch.; head lab. for biooptics and molecular imaging Mass. Gen. Hosp. Named one of Top 100 Innovators, MIT Tech. Review, 2004. Office: Mass Gen Hosp Rm 5406 Radiology 149 13th St Charlestown MA 02129 Business E-Mail: vasilis@helix.mgh.harvard.edu.

**NUCCIARONE, A. PATRICK,** lawyer; b. Denville, N.J., Aug. 29, 1947; s. H. Joseph and Alice Marie (McGuirk) N. BA, U. So. Calif., 1969; JD, George Washington U., 1973. Bar: N.J. 1973, N.Y. 1981, Vt. 1984, U.S. Dist. Ct. N.J. 1973, U.S. Dist. Ct. (no. dist.) Ohio 1986, U.S. Ct. Appeals (3d cir.) 1976, U.S. Supreme Ct. 1995. Com. staff asst. U.S. House of Reps., Washington, 1971-72; staff asst. Exec. Office of Pres. of U.S., Washington, 1972-73; asst. U.S. Atty. Office of Atty. Gen., Newark, 1974-83, chief counsel, 1978-83; spl. asst. Atty. Gen. Office of Atty. Gen., Montpelier, Vt., 1984; ptnr. Hannoch Weisman, Roseland, NJ, 1984-91, Dechert, Price & Rhoads, Princeton, NJ, 1991-95; fed. monitor US Dist. Ct., NY, 2001—. Co-chmn. N.J. Hazardous Waste Force, Trenton, 1978-83; supr. Rutgers U. Environ. Law Clinic, Newark, 1978-83; mem. Environ. Expn. Adv. Bd., Trenton, 1985-90; chmn. ann. seminar on impacts of environ. law bus. trans. Practicing Law Inst., 1986-92, mem. adv. com. on environ. law, 1986—; mem. faculty NYU Summer Inst. on Environ. Law, 1991-94. Contbr. articles to profl. jours. Recipient Outstanding Service award U.S. Dept. Justice, Washington, 1980, Spl. Achievement awards U.S. Dept. Justice, 1978, 79, Presdl. Citation for Excellent Performance Exec. Office of Pres., Washington, 1975. Mem. ABA (vice chmn. sect. on natural resources, energy and environ. law 1987-93), N.J. State Bar Assn. (bd. dirs. environ. law sect. 1985-90). Office: 1540 Hwy 138 Ste 107 Wall NJ 07719-3766 Office Phone: 732-280-4800.

**NUCHI, LIOR O.,** lawyer; b. Tiberius, Israel, Aug. 8, 1960; BA, Columbia Univ., 1982; JD, NYU, 1987. Bar: Calif. St. bus. ptnr. Bingham McCutchen, East Palo Alto, Calif.; ptnr., chmn. Cross-Border Transactions group & Israel practice Pillsbury Winthrop Shaw Pittman, Palo Alto, Calif., 2004—. Mem.: Nat. Assn. of Corp. Directors, Silicon Ventures, Calif.-Israel C. of C. Office: Pillsbury Winthrop Shaw Pittman 2475 Hanover St Palo Alto CA 94304-1114 Office Phone: 650-233-4803. Office Fax: 650-233-4545. Business E-Mail: lior.nuchi@pillsburylaw.com.

**NUCKOLLS, JOHN HOPKINS,** physicist, researcher; b. Chgo., Nov. 17, 1930; s. Asa Hopkins and Helen (Gates) N.; m. Ruth Munsterman, Apr. 21, 1952 (div. 1983); children: Helen Marie, Robert David; m. Amelia Aphrodite Liaskas, July 29, 1985. BS, Wheaton Coll., 1953; MA, Columbia U., 1955; DSc (hon.), Fla. Inst. Tech., 1977. Physicist U. Calif., Lawrence Livermore Nat. Lab., 1955—, assoc. leader thermonuclear design divsn., 1965-80, assoc. leader laser fusion program, 1975-83, divsn. leader, 1980-83, assoc. dir. physics, 1983-88, dir., 1988-94, assoc. dir. at large, 1994-97, dir. emeritus, 1997—. Mem. emeritus U.S. Strategic Command Strategic adv. group; tech. adv. bd. Network Physics, Inc.; cons. def. sci. bd. Dept. Def.; mem. adv. coms. to dir. CIA, 1993-99. Recipient E.O. Lawrence award Pres. and AEC, 1969, Fusion Leadership award, 1983, Edward Teller medal Internat. Workshop Laser Interaction and Related Plasma Phenomena, 1991, Resolution of Appreciation, U. Calif. Regents, 1994, Sec. of Def. Outstanding Pub. Svc. medal, 1996, Disting. Assoc. award U.S. Dept. Energy, 1996, Career Achievement award Fusion Power Assocs., 1996. Fellow: AAAS (J.C. Maxwell prize 1994), Am. Phys. Soc.; mem.: NAE. Office: Lawrence Livermore Nat Lab PO Box 808 Livermore CA 94551-0808 Office Phone: 925-422-5435. Personal E-Mail: jhnuckcl@aol.com.

**NUCKOLS, FRANK JOSEPH,** psychiatrist; b. Akron, Ohio, Apr. 7, 1926; s. William Alexander Jr. and Jean (Harrison) N.; m. Jane Fleetwood McIntosh, June 16, 1948; children: Claud Alexander, John Andrew. BA, U. Louisville, 1946; MD, U. Ala., 1951. Diplomate Am. Bd. Psychiatry and Neurology, cert. med. profl. Nat. Assn. Disability Examiners, 2005. Intern Holy Name Jesus Hosp., Gadsden, Ala., 1951; ward physician Ala. State Hosp., Tuscaloosa, 1951-52; resident U. Louisville, USPHS Hosp., Lexington, Ky., 1953-56; mem. faculty dept. psychiatry U. Ala. Med. Ctr., Birmingham, 1958-68, dir. tng. psychiat. residents, 1964-68, head div. community psychiatry, 1964-68, head continuing psychiat. edn. for physicians, 1964-68; chief psychiat. staff in-patient svc. U. Hosp., Birmingham, 1966-68; dir. tng. Hill Crest Hosp., Birmingham, 1975-79; pvt. practice Birmingham, 1968-93; cons. Ala. Div. Disability Determinations, Birmingham, 1993—. Staff Med. Ctr. East Hosp., Birmingham, Bapt. Med. Ctr. Montclair, Birmingham; cons. staff St. Vincent's Hosp., Birmingham, Lloyd Noland Hosp., Birmingham, South Highland Hosp., Birmingham; vis. faculty, mem. interuniv. forum in cmty. psychiatry Harvard U., Boston, 1963-66; vis. faculty Baylor U. Med. Sch., Houston, 1967-71. Sr. surgeon USPHS, 1956—. Ensign USNR, 1943—45. Fellow Am. Psychiat. Assn. (disting., life), So. Psychiat. Assn.; mem. Med. Assn. Ala., So. Med. Assn., Jefferson County Mental Health Assn. (v.p. 1960), Jefferson County Med. Soc., Mental Health Assn. State Ala. (chmn. profl. adv. com. 1961), Nat. Assn. Disability Examiners (cert. med. profl. 2005, State Ala. Med. Cons. of Yr. 2005, Commr.'s Citation 2005), Phi Beta Pi, Tau Kappa Epsilon. Home and Office: 300 Royal Towers Dr Apt 720 Vestavia AL 35209 Office Phone: 205-870-7196.

**NUCKOLS, OTIS WILLS,** lawyer, educator; b. Cumberland, Va., Mar. 25, 1921; s. Marshall Waverly Nuckols and Annie Bowden Camden; m. Dorothy Brown Hale, May 24, 1946; children: Pamela, Patricia, Thomas. BA cum laude, Lincoln Meml. U., 1948; JD, U. Richmond, 1951; CLU, Am. Coll., 1964. Bar: Va. 1951. Legal claims staff Va. Farm Bur. Ins. Cos., Richmond, 1951—64, dir. mktg., 1964—70, exec. v.p., CEO, 1970—86; ptnr. Sinnott, Nuckols & Logan, P.C., Midlothian, Va., 1986—. Adj. prof. Va. Commonwealth U., Richmond, 1986—2002; instr. ins. seminars various ins. cos., Richmond, 1986—2002. Treas. Va. Coun. on Econ. Edn., Richmond, 1970—86; chair ethics bd. Richmond Assn. Life Underwriters, 1990—2002; elder Presbyn. Ch. Sgt. U.S. Army, 1942—46. Recipient Appreciation of Svc. award, Va. Poly. Inst., 1982. Mem.: ABA (life), Am. Legion (life), Willow Oaks Country Club, Commonwealth Club, Alpha Psi Omega, Tau Kappa Alpha. Republican. Avocation: reading. Home: 3119A Stony Point Rd Richmond VA 23235 Office: Sinnott Nuckols & Logan PC 13811 Village Mill Dr Midlothian VA 23114 Office Phone: 804-378-7600 ext. 3303.

**NUDING, DORIS LEONA,** law librarian, researcher; b. Chgo., Dec. 26, 1949; d. Donald Harold and Leona Elvira (Fremgen) Thompson; m. William E. Nuding Jr., July 13, 1949; children: Tracy, Kelly. Cert. legal asst., Roosevelt U., 1987. Lic. real estate broker. Clk./typist Continental Ill. Nat. Bank, Chgo., 1968-70; clk./typist Personal Trust Banking Attys. W. Clement & Jesse Stone Found., 1972-74; sec., asst. to dir. pub., dir. achievment motivation Nat. Com. for Prevention of Child Abuse, Chgo., 1974-83; sales coord. Arnstein & Lehr, Chgo., 1981-91; legal asst., sec. Querry & Harrow, Chgo., 1991—; real estate assoc. Barid & Warner, 2003—. Mem.: Am. Assn. Law Librs., Chgo. Assn. Law Librs., Solo Libr. Soc., Am. Legion Aux. (pres. 1995—98, sec. 1999—2004). Avocations: reading, computers, writing. Office: Baird & Warner 3236 Vollmer Olympia Fields IL 60461-2827 also: Querrey & Harrow Ltd 175 W Jackson Blvd Ste 1600 Chicago IL 60604 Office Phone: 708-283-5290. Personal E-Mail: dnuding1@juno.com. Business E-Mail: dnuding@querrey.com, doris.nuding@bairdwarner.com.

**NUECHTERLAIN, JAMES HOWARD,** music educator; b. Frankenmuth, Mich., Sept. 14, 1953; s. Howard and Erema Nuechterlain; m. Donna Sue Nuechterlain, June 23, 2001; children: Patrick, Joshua. MM Music Edn., Mich. State U., East Lansing, Michigan, 1988; BME, Grand Valley State U., Allendale, Michigan, 1980; BS Bus. Adminstrn., Ferris State U., Big Rapids, Michigan, 1975. Band and orch. dir. Monroe Pub. Schools, Monroe, Mich., 1988—; band dir. Marcellus Cmty. Schools, Marcellus, Mich., 1984—88, Vicksburg Cmty. Schools, Vicksburg, Mich., 1980—81; dept. head JC Penny Co., Battle Creek, Mich., 1975—76. Mem.: Mich. Sch. Band and Orch. Assn., Nat. Mus. Conf. Office: Monroe High School 901 Herr Road Monroe MI 48161 E-mail: nuechten@monroe.k12.mi.us.

**NUECHTERLEIN, KEITH H.,** psychology professor; b. Akron, Ohio, Sept. 23, 1948; s. Harold F. and Frieda D. L. Nuechterlein; m. Nancy Alexander Nuechterlein, Apr. 27, 1981. BA, U. Minn., 1970, PhD, 1978. Cert. psychologist Bd. of Psychology, Calif., 1980. Asst. prof. dept. psychiatry UCLA, 1978—85, assoc. prof. dept. psychiatry and psychology, 1985—89, prof., 1989—. Dir. UCLA Aftercare Rsch. Program, 1980—; co-chair MATRICS Neurocognition Com., L.A., 2002—; dir. UCLA Ctr. for Neurocognition and Emotion in Schizophrenia, 2003—. Contbr. articles to profl. jours. Recipient Joseph Zubin Meml. Fund award, N.Y. State Psychiat. Inst., 1995, Disting. Sci. Achievement in Psychology, Calif. Psychol. Assn., 1997; grantee Devel. Processes in Schizophrenic Disorders, NIMH, 1983—, Transmission of Vulnerability Factors in Schizophrenia, 1994—, Ctr. Neurocognition and Emotion in Schizophrenia, 2003—08. Fellow: Neuropsychopathological Assn., Am. Psychol. Soc.; mem.: AAAS, APA, Soc. for Psychophysiological Rsch., Soc. for Rsch. in Psychopathology (pres.-elect 2004—06). Achievements include research in MATRICS Consensus Cognitive Battery for Clinical Trials in Schizophrenia; development of Degraded-Stimulus Continuous Performance Test; 3-7 Continuous Performance Test; research in Cognitive Domains in Schizophrenia; Attentional Deficits in Schizophrenia. Office: UCLA Dept Psychiatry 300 UCLA Medical Plz Rm 2240 Los Angeles CA 90095-6968 Office Phone: 310-825-0036. Office Fax: 310-206-3651. Business E-Mail: keithn@ucla.edu.

**NUERNBERG, WILLIAM RICHARD,** lawyer; b. Pitts., July 7, 1946; s. William W. and Frances (Hubler) N. BA cum laude, Denison U., 1968; JD cum laude, U. Mich., 1971. Bar: Pa. 1971, U.S. Dist.Ct. (we. dist.) Pa. 1971, Fla. 1995. Mem. Eckert Seamans Cherin & Mellott LLC, 1981-98; ptnr. Duane Morris LLP, Miami, 1999—. Bd. govs. Big Bros. Greater Miami. Pitt fellow U. Pitts. Sch. Bus., 1987-88. Mem. ABA, Pa. Bar Assn., Fla. Bar Assn., Miami City Club. Office: Duane Morris LLP 200 S Biscayne Blvd Ste 3400 Miami FL 33131-2318

**NUESSLE, WILLIAM RAYMOND,** surgeon; b. Bismarck, N.D., Sept. 17, 1951; s. Robert Frederick and Margaret Elizabeth (Bergeson) N.; m. Anna Maria Marlow, June 26, 1982; children: Aaron, Alexa, Matthew. BS, U. N.D. 1973, BS Medicine, 1975; MD, U. Ala., 1977. Diplomate Am. Bd. Surgery and Colon and Rectal Surgery. Resident gen. surgery Ochsner Found., New Orleans, 1977-1982; resident colon and rectal surgery U. La., Shreveport, 1982-83; colon and rectal surgeon Quain and Ramstat Clinic, Bismarck, ND, 1983-90, Clinic for Colon & Rectal Surgery, Huntsville, Ala., 1990—, Huntsville (Ala.) Hosp., 1990—, Crestwood Hosp., Huntsville, 1990—. Fellow ACS, Am. Soc. Colon and Rectal Surgeons; mem. SAGES. Avocations: tennis, fishing, music. Office: Clinic for CRS 115 Manning Dr SW Ste D101 Huntsville AL 35801-4341 Office Phone: 256-533-6070. Personal E-mail: wrn@hiwaay.net.

**NUGENT, GARY W.,** lawyer; b. Shreveport, La. BBA in Fin., So. Methodist U., 1988; JD, Northwestern U., 1991. Bar: Calif. 1991, US Dist. Ct., Calif. (Ninth Circuit Ct. of Appeals). Assoc. Jones Day (formerly Jones, Day, Reavis & Pogue), Los Angeles, Calif. 1996—2002, ptnr., civil litigation, 2002—. Mem.: ABA, Calif. State Bar Assn., Los Angeles County Bar Assn. Office: Jones Day 555 S Flower St # 50 Los Angeles CA 90071-2300 Office Phone: 213-489-3939. Office Fax: 213-243-2539. Business E-Mail: gnugent@jonesday.com.

**NUGENT, HELEN JEAN,** history professor; b. Indpls., Oct. 14, 1934; d. John Isaac and Ruth Augusta (Mather) McClelland; m. Paul Thomas Nugent, Aug. 19, 1935; children: Paula Jean Nugent Barickman, Thomas J. Nugent II, Ruth E. B. Nugent Simard. BA, Franklin Coll., 1956; MA, U. Ill., 1965, Ind. U., 1971; PhD, Mich. State U., 1983. Lifetime cert. in secondary edn., Ind. Tchr. grades 9-12 Union City H.S., Ind., 1956—57, Seven Mile H.S., Ohio, 1957—58; tchr. history St. Rose Acad., Vincennes, Ind., 1962—64; instr. history Margaret Hall Sch., Versailles, Ky., 1964—66; lectr. history Ind.U./Purdue U., Columbus, 1976—82; vis. lectr. hist. U./Purdue U., Columbus, 2001; dir. Can. studies Franklin Coll. Ind., 1984—95, chair dept. history, 1996—99, prof. emerita history, dir. emerita Can. studies, 1999—. Contbr. numerous articles, papers to profl. jours., chpts. to books. Mem. Franklin Coll. Alumni Coun., 2002—05. Recipient Alumni award Franklin Coll., 1997. Mem. Mid West Assn. Can. Studies (v.p. 1990-92, exec. coun. 1992-94), Assn. Can. Studies U.S. (exec. bd. 1993-97), Ind. Hist. Soc., Phi Alpha Theta, Theta Alpha Phi, Delta Kappa Gamma, Phi Kappa Phi. Anglican Catholic.

**NUGENT, JOHN HILLIARD,** communications executive; b. Paterson, NJ, Aug. 20, 1944; s. James Joseph and Jacqueline Ann (Storms) N.; m. Mary Elizabeth Maher, June 3, 1967; 1 child, Jill Frances. BA, Columbia U., 1970; MSA, Southeastern U., 1978; DBA, Bus. Sch., Lausanne, Switzerland, 1989. CPA; cert. fraud examiner Nat. Assn. Cert. Fraud Examiners, Austin. Adminstr. Chase Manhattan Bank, N.Y.C., 1970-71; analyst U.S. Dept. of Army, Washington, 1971-72; chmn. Strategic Planning & Rsch. Corp., Dallas, 1977-95; pres. AT&T Aviation Tech. and Sys., Ltd., Arlington, Va., Hong Kong, Beijing, 1993; exec. CDX, Inc., Dallas, 1995; pres., bd. dirs. SA Telecomm., Inc., Richardson, Tex., 1996-97, also bd. dirs., pres., 1996; mng. dir. Cordoba Capital, Southport, Conn., 1998-99. V.p., fin. acct. AdCon Inc./Internat. Bank, Reston, Va., 1971-79; CFO HDS, Inc., Reston, 1979-82; pres. Group L Corp., Herndon, Va., 1983-85; pres., bd. dirs. AT&T/Datotek, Dallas, 1985-92; assoc. prof. telecomms. Grad. Sch. Mgmt. U. Dallas, 1999—. Author: Corporate Decline: Causes, Symptoms, and Prescriptions for a Turnaround, 1989, Plan to Win: Analytical and Operational Tools-Gaining Competitive Advantage, 2002, 2nd edit., 2003. Cpl. USMC, 1962—66. Mem. AICPAs, Greater Washington Soc. CPAs, Tex. Soc. CPAs, Nat. Assn. Accts., Dallas Com. on Fgn. Rels., Nat. Assn. Cert. Fraud Examiners, Columbia Club of N.Y. Republican. Avocation: reading. Office: Grad Sch Mgmt U Dallas Irving TX 75062-4736 Address: 2469 County Road 855 Mc Kinney TX 75071 Office Phone: 214-682-8025. Personal E-Mail: jnugent@texoma.net. Business E-Mail: jnugent@gsm.udallas.edu.

**NUGENT, NELLE,** theater, film and television producer; b. Jersey City, May 24, 1939; d. John Patrick and Evelyn Adelaide (Stern) N.; m. Donald G. Baker, June 6, 1960 (div. 1962); m. Benjamin Janney, June 22, 1969 (div. Apr., 1980); m. Jolyon Fox Stern, Apr. 7, 1982; 1 child, Alexandra Fox Stern. BS, Skidmore Coll., 1960, DHL (hon.), 1981. Chmn. bd. McCann & Nugent, Prodns. Inc., NYC, 1976-86; pres. Foxboro Prodns., Inc., NYC, 1985-94; pres., CEO Foxboro Entertainment, 1990-94; pres. The Foxboro Co., Inc.; co-prin. Golden Fox Films, Inc. Adj. faculty NYU, N.Y.C., 2003—. Stage mgr. various off-Broadway shows, 1960-64; stage mgr. Broadway plays Any Wednesday, 1963-64, Dylan, 1964, Ben Franklin in Paris, 1964-65; prodn. supr., then gen. mgr., 1969-76, assoc. mng. dir. Nederlander Corp.; operating theaters and producing plays in NYC and on tour, 1970-76; co-founder McCam & Nugent Prodns., Inc., 1976; prodr.: Dracula, 1977 (Tony award), The Gin Game (Tony nom.), The Elephant Man, 1978 (Tony award, Drama Critics award), Morning's at Seven, 1980 (Tony award), Home, 1980 (Tony nomination), Amadeus, 1981 (Tony award); also produced: Rose and Piaf, 1980, Otherwise Engaged, The Life and Adventures of Nicholas Nickleby, 1981 (Tony award, Drama Critics award), The Dresser (Tony award nominee), 1981, Mass Appeal, 1981; The Lady & The Clarinet, 1982; The Glass Menagerie (revival), 1983; Painting Churches (Obie award), 1983; Total Abandon, 1983; All's Well That End's Well, 1983 (Tony nominee); Pilobolus Dance Company, 1983; Pacific Overtures (revival), 1984; Much Ado about Nothing/Cyrano de Bergerac (repertory) (Tony award nominees), 1984; Leader of the Pack (Tony award nominee), 1985, The Life and Adventures of Nicholas Nickleby (revival) (Tony award nominee), 1986; prodr.: TV spls.; Morning's At Seven, Piaf; Pilobolus; prodr. A Fighting Choice, 1986-88, A Conspiracy of Love, 1987, The Final Verdict, 1990 (Cable Ace award nominee Best Picture); exec. prodr. (TV pilot) Morning Maggie, 1987, Dick Clark Prodns., 1988-90, (feature films) Student Body, 1993, Getting In, 1994, Jane Doe, 1996; (TV films) In the Presence of Mine Enemies, 1995-96 (Houston Festival Silver Star award), A Town Has Turned to Dust, 1997 (World Festival Silver medal 1998), After the Storm (Best Feature Film NY Internat. Independent Film & Video Festival, 2000), Angelciti Festival (Best Feature 2001), Houston Worldfest (Platinum award, Best Film Made for TV 2001), (Broadway prodn.) The Smell of the Kill, 2002, Sly Fox, 2004, A Mother, A Daughter and a Gun, 2005, And Then There Were None, London, West End, 2005. Mem.: Prodrs. Guild Am. East (exec. bd.), League Am. Theaters. Office: 222 E 44th St 4th Fl New York NY 10017

**NUGENT, ROBERT J., JR.,** fast food company executive; b. 1942; BBA, U. Cin., 1964. Loan officer Citizens Savs., 1964-67; asst. v.p. Gem City Savs., 1967-69; v.p. Ponderosa System Inc., 1969-78, Ky. Fried Chicken, 1978-79, Foodmaker Inc., San Diego from 1979, exec. v.p. ops., mktg., 1985-95, CEO, pres., 1995-99, Jack in the Box, Inc., San Diego, 1999—. Office: Jack in the Box Inc 9330 Balboa Ave San Diego CA 92123-1598

**NUGENT, S. GEORGIA,** academic administrator; m. Thomas J Scherer. B cum laude, Princeton U., 1973; PhD in classics, Cornell U. Instr. Swarthmore Coll.; assoc. prof. Brown U., 1985; asst. prof. Princeton U., 1979, dean, Harold McGraw Jr. Ctr. for tchg. and learning, asst. to pres., 1992—95; assoc. provost, 1995; pres. Kenyon Coll., 2003—. Author books. Recipient Wriston award for excellence in tchg. Office: President Ransom Hall Kenyon Coll Gambier OH 43022 Office Phone: 740-427-5111. Office Fax: 740-427-2335. Business E-Mail: nugent@kenyon.edu.*

**NUGENT, TED (THEODORE ANTHONY NUGENT),** musician; b. Detroit, Dec. 13, 1948; s. Warren Henry and Marion (Johnson) Nugent; m. Sandra Janowski, 1970 (div. 1976); children: Sasha Emma, Theodore Tobias, Starr; m. Shemane Deziel, Jan. 21, 1989; 1 child, Rocco. Student, Oakland Community Coll., Detroit. Profl. off-road racer, 1984—; Mich. County Sheriff dep., 1978—; host Ted Nugent Morning Show WWBR, Detroit. Pres. Ted Nugent United Sportsmen of Am. Guitarist, 1958—, mem. group, Amboy Dukes, 1965, solo artist, 1965—; Albums:(with Amboy Dukes) Ted Nugent and the Amboy Dukes, 1968, Migration, 1969, Journey to the Center of the Mind, 1969, Marriage on the Rocks, 1970, Call of the Wild, 1973, Survival of the Füittest, 1974, Tooth, Fang, and Claw, 1974, Dr. Slingshot, 1975; (solo albums) Ted Nugent, 1975, Free for All, 1976, Cat Scratch Fever, 1977, Double Live Gonzo, 1977, Weekend Warriors, 1978, State of Shock, 1979, Scream Dream, 1980, Great Gonzos/The Best of Ted Nugent, 1981, Intensities in Ten Cities, 1981, Nugent, 1982, Penetrator, 1984, Little Miss Dangerous, 1986, The Ultimate Collection, 1987, If You Can't Lick 'Em-...Lick 'Em, 1988, Call of the Wild, 1991, Out of Control, 1993, Spirit of the Wild, 1995, Motor City Madness, 1996, Live at Hammersmith '79, 1997, Super Hits, 1998, Over the Top, 1998, On the Edge, 1998, Loaded for Bear: The Best of Ted Nugent, 1999, Noble Savage, 2001, Full Blontal Nugity, 2001, Take No Prisoners, 2002, The Ultimate Ted Nugent, 2002, Take Two, 2002, Craveman, 2002; (with Damn Yankees) Damn Yankees, 1990, Don't Tread, 1992; author: Blood Trails: The Truth about Bowhunting, 1991, God, Guns and Rock 'n' Roll, 2000, Blood Trails II: The Truth about Bowhunting, 2004; co-author: (with Shemane Nugent) Kill It and Grill It: A Guide to Preparing and Cooking Wild Game and Fish, 2002; actor (TV series) Surviving Nugent, 2003-04; editor, publisher Ted Nugent Adventure Outdoors Mag.; creator, prodr. Ted Nugent Spirit of the Wild, PBS; contbr. articles to profl. jours. Sheriff dep. Mich. County, 1978—; founder Ted Nugent Kamp for Kids; appointee Mich. State Parks Found.; bd. dirs. Lyme Alliance. Named Man of Yr., 1999, Mich. Recreation and Parks Assn., Mich. Conservationist of Yr., 1999; named to The Native Am. Strongheart Soc.; recipient Nat. Arbor Day Conservation Award, 1999, ATV Image Award,

2004. Mem.: ASCAP, Safari Club Internat., Native Am. Strongheart Soc., Quality Deer Mgmt. Assn. of Mich. (dir.), Ducks Unlimited (life sponsor), Mich. Bowhunters (life), Nat. Trappers Assn. (life), Nat. Rifle Assn. (life; bd. dirs. 1995—). Office: Nugent USA 4008 W Michigan Ave Jackson MI 49202*

**NUGENT, TIMOTHY SCOTT,** alcohol/drug abuse services professional; b. Iowa City, Apr. 23, 1947; s. Stephen Francis and Ina Kammeyer Nugent; m. Katherine Werner, Nov. 26, 1970 (div. Nov. 10, 1986); children: Patrick Stephen, Lisa Kathleen; m. Susan Thorne, Apr. 3, 1992. BA, U. Fla., 1969, MEd, 1972. Cert. addictions profl. 2000. Field rep. Pa. Dept. Justice, Pitts., 1972—74; program dir. S. Fla. Regional Planning Coun., Miami, 1974—76; dir. regulatory Deltona Corp., Miami, 1977—81; exec. dir. Ybor Redevel. City of Tampa, Fla., 1981—85; dir. downtown redevel. City of Tallahassee, Tallahassee, 1991—93; govtl. and devel. cons., 1985—91; exec. dir. Lee County Fla. Redevel. Agy., 1994—96; therapist S.W. Fla. Addiction Svcs., Ft. Myers, 1996—. Oral exam evaluator, bd. dirs. Fla. Cert. Bd., Tallahassee, 2000—. Mem.: Ybor City C. of C. (pres. 1987). Home: 2373 Woodland Ter Fort Myers FL 33907-5818

**NUGENT, WALTER TERRY KING,** historian; b. Watertown, N.Y., Jan. 11, 1935; s. Clarence A. and Florence (King) Nugent; m. Suellen Hoy, 1986; children from previous marriage: Katherine, Rachel, David, Douglas, Terry, Mary. AB, St. Benedict's Coll., 1954, DLitt, 1968; MA, Georgetown U., 1956; PhD, U. Chgo., 1961. Instr. history Washburn U., 1957—58; asst. prof. Kans. State U., 1961—63, Ind. U., Bloomington, 1963—64, assoc. prof., 1964—68, prof., 1968—84, assoc. dean Coll. Arts and Scis., 1967—71, dir. overseas study, 1967—76, chmn. history dept., 1974—77; Andrew V. Tackes prof. history U. Notre Dame, 1984—2000, Andrew V. Tackes prof. emeritus, 2000—. Paley lectr., Fulbright vis. prof. Hebrew U., Jerusalem, 1978—79; summer seminar dir. NEH, 1979, 84, 86; vis. prof. U. Hamburg, U. Warsaw, 1982; Mary Bell Washington Fulbright prof. U. Coll., Dublin, 1991—92. Author: (book) The Tolerant Populists, 1963, Creative History, 1967, The Money Question During Reconstruction, 1967, Money and American Society 1865-1880, 1968, Modern America, 1973, From Centennial to World War: American Society 1876-1917, 1977, Structures of American Social History, 1981, Crossings: The Great Transatlantic Migrations 1870-1914, 1992; author: (with Martin Ridge) The American West: The Reader, 1999, Into the West: The Story of Its People, 1999 (Caughey award, 2000); author: Making Our Way: A Family History, 2003. Bd. dirs. U.S.-Israel Ednl. Found., 1985—89. Recipient medal of Merit, Warsaw U., 1992; Newberry Libr. fellow, 1962, Guggenheim fellow, 1964—65, Huntington Libr. fellow, 1979, 1985, Beinecke fellow, Yale U., 1990. Mem.: Soc. Historians the Gilded Age and Progressive Era (pres. 2000—02), Soc. Am. Historians, We. Hist. Assn. (pres. 2005—06, hon. life mem.). Democrat. E-mail: wnugent@nd.edu.

**NUGTEREN, CORNELIUS,** air force officer; b. Colton, S.D., Feb. 7, 1928; s. Adrian Joe and Marie Johanna N.; m. Liane Albrecht, Sept. 22, 1956; children: Cecile, Aneli. BA, Central Coll., Pella, Iowa, 1951. Commd. 2d lt. USAF, 1953, advanced through grades to maj. gen., 1980; advisor Vietnam Air Force, 1970-71; served in Germany, 1971-77; vice comdr. (Air Logistics Center), Utah, 1977-79; comdr. (Aerospace Rescue and Recovery Service), Scott AFB, Ill., 1979-81; chief (Joint U.S. Mil. Aid Group), Greece, 1981-82; comdr. Air Logistics Ctr., Robins AFB, Ga, 1983-88; ret.; cons. for def. industries Warner Robins, Ga., 1988-94; v.p. Chem. Tech. Internat., Warner Robins, Mercer U. Engring. Rsch. Ctr., Warner Robins, 1996—. Decorated D.S.M., Legion of Merit, Bronze Star, Superior Service medal; recipient USAF EEO award, 1979; named to Ga. Aviation Hall of Fame, 2004. Mem. Air Force Assn., Order Daedalians, Internat. Order Hansen, Order of the Sword. Office: 114 Holly Dr Warner Robins GA 31088-6615 Office Phone: 478-955-3909. E-mail: gennewt@aol.com. *Service to one's country is not just a job...it's a calling. Integrity to and within the institution to which you belong is an absolute necessity. Loyalty to peers and subordinates is equally important as loyalty to your superiors. Attitude toward life, humankind and profession is key determinant to success. Goals should be set high enough so as to be unattainable. Standard of conduct must always include duty, honor, country.*

**NULAND, ANTHONY C. J.,** lawyer; b. NYC, 1943; AB cum laude, Princeton U., 1965; JD, NYU, 1968. Bar: N.Y. 1969, D.C. 1977, Ga. 1978. Asst. dir. divsn. market regulation SEC, 1975-76, assoc. dir. divsn. market regulation, 1976-77; now ptnr. Seward & Kissel, N.Y.C., 1977—. Office: Seward & Kissel 1200 G St NW Ste 350 Washington DC 20005-3881 Office Phone: 202-737-8833.

**NULAND, SHERWIN,** surgeon, writer; b. N.Y.C., Dec. 8, 1930; s. Meyer and Violet (Lutsky) N.; m. Sarah Peterson, May 29, 1977; children: Victoria Jane, Andrew Meyer, William Peterson, Amelia Rose. BA, NYU, 1951; MD, Yale U., 1955. Surgeon Yale-New Haven Hosp. (Conn.), 1962—92; clin. prof. surgery Yale Sch. Medicine, New Haven, 1962—; mem. faculty Instn. for Social and Policy Studies, Yale U. Author: The Origins of Anesthesia, 1983, Doctors: The Biography of Medicine, 1988, Medicine: The Art of Healing, 1991, How We Die: Reflections on Life's Final Chapter, 1994 (Nat. Book award for non-fiction, 1994, Pulitzer prize finalist, 1995), The Wisdom of the Body: How We Live, 1997, The Mysteries Within: A Surgeon Reflects on Medical Myths, 2000, Leonardo da Vinci, 2000, Lost in America, 2003, The Doctors' Plague, 2003, Maimonides, 2005; contbg. editor The New Republic, mem. editl. bd. Perspectives in Biology and Medicine. V.p. Conn. Hospice, New Haven, 1978-80. Hastings Ctr. fellow. Fellow AAAS, ACS; mem. New Eng. Surg. Soc., Assocs. of Yale Med. Sch. Libr. (chmn. 1982-94), Yale-China Assn. (chmn. med. 1988-93), History of Medicine and Allied Scis. (chmn. bd. jour. 1979-2002). Democrat. Jewish. Avocation: tennis. Home: 29 Old Hartford Tpke Hamden CT 06517-3523 Office: PO Box 6356 Hamden CT 06517-0356 Office Phone: 203-776-5635. E-mail: snuland@comcast.net.

**NULAND, VICTORIA,** US permanent representative to NATO, m. Robert Kagan. BA, Brown U. Chief of staff to dep. sec. of state US Dept. State, 1993—96, dep. dir. former Societ Union affairs, 1997—99, US dep. perm. representative to NATO in Brussels, 2000—03, US perm. representative to NATO, 2005—; prin. dep. nat. security adv. to US v.p. Cheney Office of the Vice President, 2003—05. "Next Generation" fellow Coun. on Fgn. Relations, 1999—2000, state dept. fellow, 1996—97; speaks Russian, French and some Chinese. Recipient Disting. Civilian Svc. medal, US Sec. Defense. Office: US Mission NATO Blvd Leopold III 1110 Brussels Belgium*

**NULL, ELISABETH HIGGINS,** librarian, editor; b. Worcester, Mass., Dec. 1, 1942; d. Carter Chapin Higgins and Katharine Huntington (Bigelow) Doman; m. Henry Harrison Null IV, July 13, 1963 (div. 1970); children: John Higgins, Jacob Van Vechten. BA, Sarah Lawrence Coll., Bronxville, N.Y., 1983; MA, Yale U., 1985, MPhil in Am. History, 1989; MA in Folklore, U. Pa., 1987; M Libr. and Info. Sci., Cath. U. Am., 1995. V.p. Abington Pub. Co., Clark's Summit, Pa., 1966-70; CEO Green Linnet Records, Danbury, Conn., 1971-81; vis. lectr. Am. Musical Life, Georgetown U., 1991-98; libr. and conversion specialist nat. digital libr. program Libr. of Congress, Washington, 1996-98, expert cons., 1995; writer on edn. issues Rural Sch. and Cmty. Trust, 1999—2005; rsch. coord. congl. campaign Janine Selendy (Dem.) N.Y. Dist. 17, 2002, 2004; freelance editor, writer Null Editl. Svcs., 2005—; rsch. assoc. for Journalist John Dickerson, 2005—. Bd. dirs. Maine Folklife Ctr., Horizon Internat., New Haven; program co-chair Washington Folk Festival, 1999-2000; program chair Folklore Soc. Greater Washington, 1993-94; humanities scholar-in-residence Conn. Coun. for Humanities and Conn. Dept. for the Arts, Waterbury, Conn., 1986-87; fieldworker in folklore Waterbury Ethnic Music Project, 1986-87. Singer 2 recordings: The Feathered Maiden, 1977, American Primitive, 1981; performance career with guitarist Bill Shute included 6 appearances with Garrison Keillor's A Prairie Home Companion; major venues include Phila. Folk Festival, Bklyn. Mus., Mus. Natural History. Incorporator John Woodman Higgins Armory, Worcester, Mass., 1966—; sec. Stanton Park Neighborhood Assn., Washington, 1990; bd. dirs. John and Clara Higgins Found., 1999—. Folger Shakespeare Libr. Seminar fellow,

1989-91. Mem. ALA, Am. Folklore Soc. Democrat. Episcopalian. Avocations: folk music performer, song writer. Home and Office: 706 Bonifant St Silver Spring MD 20910-5534 Office Phone: 301-587-2286. Personal E-mail: enul@starpower.net.

**NULL, PAUL BRYAN,** minister; b. Oakland, Calif., May 7, 1944; s. Carleton Elliot and Dorothy Irene (Bryan) N.; m. Renee Yvonne Howell, Aug. 23, 1969; children: Bryan Joseph, Kara Renee. BS, Western Bapt. Coll., 1973; MDiv, Western Conservative Bapt. Sem., 1979; DMin, Trinity Theol. Sem., 1994. Ordained to ministry Bapt. Ch., 1982. Asst. pastor Bethel Bapt. Ch., Aumsville, Oreg., 1972-74, sr. pastor, 1974-87, The Calvary Congregation, Stockton, Calif., 1987-94; pastor Sierra Cmty. Ch., South Lake Tahoe, Calif., 1994—99; exec. pastor Dayspring Fellowship, Salem, Oreg., 1999—2004; gen. dir. Conservative Bapt. Assn. No. Calif. and Nev., 2004—. Trustee Conservative Bapt. Assn. of Oreg., 1982-85, mem. Ch. extension com., 1975-85. Radio show commentator Food for Thought, 1987. Panel mem. Presdl. Anti-Drug Campaign, 1984; bd. dirs. Western Bapt. Coll., Salem, 1998—. Served with U.S. Army, 1965-67. Named Outstanding Young Man Am., 1979. Mem. Conservative Bapt. Assn. of Am., No. Calif. Conservative Bapt. Assn. (pres. 1992-93), Delta Epsilon Chi. Avocations: weight training, aerobics, writing, hiking, cross country skiing. Home: 2922 Lonnie Beck Way Stockton CA 95209 Office: 1545 St Marks Plz Ste 1 Stockton CA 95207 Office Phone: 209-954-0499. Personal E-mail: nextgenpbn@sbcglobal.net. Business E-Mail: paul@nextgenchurches.com.

**NULL, WILLIAM SETH,** lawyer; b. N.Y.C., Apr. 15, 1954; s. Douglas P. Null and Barbara M. (Black) Schacker; m. Lauren E. Thaler, May 10, 1981; children: Danielle, Evan. BA, Hampshire Coll., 1977; JD, Yeshiva U., 1980. Bar: N.Y. 1981, U.S. Dist. Ct. (ea. and so. dists.) N.Y. 1981, U.S. Supreme Ct. 1987. With Null & Null, P.C., Garden City, N.Y., 1980-83, Kraver & Martin, N.Y.C., 1983-85, Cuddy & Feder LLP, White Plains, NY, 1985—, mng. ptnr., 1999—. Dir. The Housing Partnership, Elmsford, NY, 1995—2001, White Plains Bridge of Friendship Found., 1994—; dir. Westchester chpt. Juvenile Diabetes Rsch. Found. Internat., 1998—2003, 2006—, pres., 2004—06; dir. Gilda's Club Westchester, 2001—, The Briarcliff Manor Edn. Found., 2001—03, White Plains Hosp. Ctr., 2002—. Office: Cuddy & Feder LLP 90 Maple Ave White Plains NY 10601-5105 Office Phone: 914-761-1300. E-mail: wnull@cuddyfeder.com.

**NULTON, WILLIAM CLEMENTS,** retired lawyer; b. Pittsburg, Kans., Feb. 22, 1931; s. Perley Edgar and Mary Celia (Anderson) N.; m. Vicki Smith, Aug. 20, 1956; children: Carnie, Erica. BA, Kans. U., 1953, LLB with honors, 1958; postgrad., NYU, 1953-54. Bar: Kans. 1958, Mo. 1959. Sr. atty. Great Lakes Pipe Line Co., Kansas City, Mo., 1958-66, asst. sec., 1961-66; assoc. Blackwell, Sanders, Matheny, Weary & Lombardi, Kansas City, 1966-68, ptnr., 1968-81; assoc. Shughart Thomson & Kilroy, Kansas City, 1981-83, ptnr., 1983-94. Contbr. articles to profl. jours. Bd. dirs. Corinth Hills Home Assn., Shawnee Mission, 1974-76, Faith Friends, 1999-2004, Front Porch Alliance, 1999—2006, Ivanhoe neighborhood coun., 2003—, Kansas City Civil Rights Consortium, 1993—, Marillac Acad., 1994-99; pres. Beta Theta Pi Kansas City Alumni Assn., 1977 (Man of Yr. award 2002); mem., elder Village United Presbyn. Ch., Prairie Village, Kans., 1976—, trustee, 1992-94, endowment bd., 1997-2001; bd. dirs. Prairie Village Mcpl. Found., 1987—, v.p., 2000—05, pres., 2005—; Kans. adv. com. U.S. Civil Rights Commn., 1994—, acting chmn., 1998; Shawnee Mission Unified Bd. Edn., 1969-73, v.p., 1973; pres. Corinth Flem. Bd. Edn., Johnson County, Kans., 1969; chmn. Full Employment Task Group on Employment Disabled, Kansas City, 1987. Summerfield scholar, Kans. U., 1949—53, Root-Tilden scholar, NYU, 1953—54. Mem. ABA (mgmt. chmn. labor and employment law sect., com. on arbitration and collective bargaining 1989-92), Am. Acad. Hosp. Attys. (co-chmn. task group on bylaws for small rural hosps. 1992-93), Mo. Bar Assn. (chmn. labor law com. 1982), Nat. Health Lawyers Assn. (co-chmn. task group on alternative dispute resolution in health care field 1990-91), Phi Beta Kappa, Order of Coif. Republican. Home: 7908 El Monte St Shawnee Mission KS 66208-5047

**NUMANN, PATRICIA JOY,** surgeon, educator; b. Bronx, N.Y., Apr. 6, 1941; BA, U. Rochester, 1962; MD, SUNY Health Sci. Ctr., Syracuse, 1965. Intern, resident SUNY Health Sci. Ctr., Syracuse, 1970, from asst. prof. to assoc. prof. surgery, 1970-89, assoc. dean Coll. Medicine, 1978-84, assoc. dean Coll. Medicine Clin. Affairs, prof. surgery, 1989—, Lloyd S. Rogers prof. of surgery, med. dir., 1997—. Dir. breast care program SUNY Health Sci. Ctr., Syracuse, 1986—; presenter in field. Contbr. chpts. to books, articles to profl. jours. Found. bd. dirs. Vera House, Syracuse, 1993-94; hon. bd. dirs. F.A.C.T., Syracuse, 1994. Named one of Women of Distinction, N.Y. State Gov. Mario Cuomo, 1994, Disting. Tchg. Prof. SUNY, 1994, Disting. Svc. Prof.; recipient Disting. Surgeon award Assn. Women Surgeons, 1991. Mem. AMA (coun. sci. affairs), ACS (com. on cancer grad. med. edn. com., 2nd v.p. 1999, 2d v.p. 1999-2000), Am. Bd. Surgeons (bd. dirs. 1994—, chair 2001), Am. Assn. Endocrine Surgeons (v.p. 1992), Assn. for Surg. Edn. (pres. 1985), Corinthian Club. Office: SUNY Health Sci Ctr 750 E Adams St Syracuse NY 13210-1834 Office Phone: 315-464-6365. Business E-Mail: numannp@upstate.edu.

**NUNAMAKER, SUSAN SUN,** mathematics professor; d. Chin-tse and Jean Hwei-Lan Sun; m. Michael Edward Nunamaker; 1 child, Marina. BS in Math., U. Ill., Urbana-Champaign, 1982, BS in Civil Engring., 1982, MS in Applied Math., 1984. Rsch. asst. Ill. State Water Survey, 1979—81; tchg. and rsch. asst. U. Ill., 1982—86; math. prof. DeVry U., Addison, Ill., 1997—2006; math instr. Triton Coll., River Grove, Ill., 1997, Waubonsee CC, Sugar Grove, Ill., 2005—, Coll. DuPage, Glen Ellyn, Ill., 2006—; owner Sunflower Bear R & D, Urbana-Champaign, 1993—96, cons., 2006—. Computing analyst Minnow Bear Computers, Urbana-Champaign, 1984—93; engring. technician US Corps Engring. Rsch. Lab, Urbana-Champaign, 1979—80; instr. Waubimsee CC, Sugar Grove, Ill., 2006—. Recipient Book award, Harvard U., 1976, Lazarus Human Rels. award, Am. Jewish Cmty., 1977; Engring. scholarships, U. Ill., 1977, Math scholarships, 1978. Mem.: Ill. Math. Assn. CC, Math. Assn. Am., Am. Math. Soc. (assoc.). Home: 5 South 370 Vest Naperville IL 60563 Office: Coll DuPage 425 Fawell Blvd Glen Ellyn IL 60137 also: Waubonsee CC Route 47 at Waubonsee Dr Sugar Grove IL 60554 Office Phone: 630-942-2800 ext. 51498, 630-466-7900 ext. 3587, 312-671-9340. Personal E-mail: susan@nunamaker.com. Business E-Mail: nunama@cdnet.cod.edu.

**NUNES, DEVIN,** congressman; b. Tulare, Calif., Oct. 1, 1973; m. Elizabeth Tamariz. BS in Agrl. Bus., Calif. Poly. State U., 1995, MS in Agrl., 1996; BS, Coll. Sequoias. Calif. state dir. USDA; mem. U.S. Congress from 21st Calif. dist., 2003—; mem. Ways and Means com. Mem. Coll. Sequoias Bd. Trustees, 1996—2002; grad. Calif. Agr. Leadership Fellowship Program, 2000. Republican. Roman Catholic. Office: US Ho Reps 1013 Longworth Ho Office Bldg Washington DC 20515-0521

**NUNES, WINIFRED O.,** minister, educator; d. Jacob Albert Oliver and Katherine Collis Champion; children: Katharine Taylor, Julius Harper. A. U. Hartford, 1978. Ordained to ministry Pentecostal Assemblies of World, 1977. Paraprofl. Sch. Readiness, Hartford, Conn., 1966—67, tchr. presch., 1967—80; assoc. pastor Zion Apostolic Ch., Hartford, 1970—75; pastor New Testament Tabernacle, Bloomfield, 1988—. Author: Born & Bred in the Apostolic Way, 2004; contbr. articles to profl. jours. Mem.: Internat. Missionary & Christian Women's Aux. (pres. 1998—2004). Avocations: reading, travel, writing. Personal E-mail: pwnunes@aol.com.

**NUNEZ-LAWTON, MIGUEL G.,** financial analyst; b. Havana, Cuba, Feb. 8, 1949; came to US, 1964; s. Miguel Nunez-Cancio and Silvia Lawton-Alfonso. BSBA, Georgetown U., 1971, postgrad. in Econs., 1973. Asst. treas. Deltec Securities Corp., N.Y.C., 1971; debt specialist internat. econs. dept. World Bank, Washington, 1973-95; internat. cons. Miami, Fla., 1996—; World Bank del. Paris Club Debt Renegotiation for Senegal, 1982. UN Conf. in Trade and Devel. cons. Nat. Bank Angola, Luanda, 2000; chief tech.

adviser UN Conf. Trade and Devel. Bur. Treasury, Manila, 1989—90. Bd. dirs., treas. Friends of Art Mus. of the Americas, OAS, Washington, 1988-90; bd. dirs. Friends of Peru, 1991-1996, Friends of the Cuban Heritage Collection, U. Miami, 2003—; panel mem. The Lawrenceville Sch., 1992; mem. Presdl. Inaugural Com., Washington, 1997. Roman Catholic. Avocations: art collecting, genealogy. Home: 8860 SW 123rd Ct Apt K106 Miami FL 33186-4152 Office Phone: 305-606-0983. Personal E-mail: mnlawton@hotmail.com.

**NUNEZ OJEDA, ELPIDIO,** food distribution executive; b. Cuba; m. Olga M. Nunez; 1 child, Elpidio Nunez Jr. Founder, CEO Northwestern Meat, Inc., Miami, 1961—; founder Northwestern Selecta, PR, 1980—. Dir. Cuban Liberty Coun.; adv. bd. mem. First Union Nat. Bank. Mem.: Latin C. of C., Internat. Assn. Hispanic Businessmen. Office: Northwestern Meat Inc 2100 NW 23rd St Miami FL 33142 Office Phone: 305-633-8112. Office Fax: 305-633-6907.*

**NUNEZ-PORTUONDO, RICARDO,** investment company executive; b. N.Y.C., June 9, 1933; s. Emilio and Maria (Garcia) N-P.; m. Dolores Maldonado, Sept. 7, 1963; children — Ricardo Jose, Emilio Manuel, Eduardo Javier. LL.D., U. Havana, Cuba; postdoctoral in law, U. Fla., 1975. Bar: Cuba, Fla. Editor Latin Am. div. USIA, Miami, Fla., 1961-71, editor Washington, 1961-71; nat. dir. Cuban Refugee Program, Washington, 1975-77; pres. Cultural Pub., Inc., Miami, 1994—, Central Investment Trust, Coral Gables, Fla., 1977—; chmn. bd. Interstate Bank of Commerce, Miami, 1986-88; v.p. Century 21, Coral Gables, 1989—; adv. Miami-Dade County Commr. Jimmy L Morales, 1996—; litigation cons. Cohen & Kandell, P.A. Attorneys at Law, 1998—. Author: A Critique on the Linowitz Report, 1975, Cuba: La Otra Imagen, 1994, Un Procer Cubano, 1994, Cuban Refugee Program, The Early Years, 1995. Dir. Nat. Hispanic Scholarship Fund, San Francisco, 1978—; dir. COSSMHO, Washington, 1980—; trustee emeritus Fla. Internat. U., 1984—; pres. Mercy Hosp. Found., Miami, 1985—; bd. dirs. ARC, Greater Miami. Recipient numerous awards for civic contbns. including day named in honor Ricardo Nunez Day, Miami, 1975. Mem. Cuban Lawyers Assn., Cuban Acad. History, Metro. Club, Lyford Cay Club, Ocean Reef Club, Key Biscayne Yacht Club, Big Five Club, 200 Club. Republican. Roman Catholic. Office: PO Box 141720 Coral Gables FL 33114-1720*

**NUNN, ANDRE' RONALD,** surgeon, health facility administrator; s. Billy Ray and Mildred Morgan. MD, U. of Ala., Birmingham, 1990. Lic. Am. Bd. Surgery, Pa. Staff gen. surgeon Detroit Med. Ctr., 1995—; pres., CEO Detroit Surg. Specialists, P.C., 2001—. Clin. asst. prof. of surgery Wayne State U., Detroit, 2001—. Named one of Top Drs. in Detroit, Hour Mag., 2003; recipient Theodore McGraw Clin. Faculty Tchg. award, Wayne State U., 2001. Fellow: ACS (life); mem.: Soc. of Am. Gastrointestinal Endoscopic Surgeons (assoc.), Soc. of Laparoendoscopic Surgeons (assoc.), Am. Soc. for Bariatric Surgeons (assoc.; cert.), Mich. State Med. Soc. (assoc.), Detroit Med. Soc. (assoc.), Nat. Med. Soc. (assoc.). Office: Detroit Surg Specialists PC Ste 805 4160 John Rd Detroit MI 48201 Office Phone: 313-745-7454. Office Fax: 313-993-8625. Business E-Mail: arnunn@detroitsurgical.com.

**NUNN, CHARLES BURGESS,** retired religious organization administrator; b. Richmond, Va., May 1, 1931; s. Charles Burgess Sr. and Virginia Atkinson (Goode) N.; m. Helen Agnes Parker, Sept. 1, 1957; children: Patsy Virginia, Catherine Louise, Stephen Charles, Stewart Gavin. BA in Econs., Randolph Macon Coll., 1953; BD, Southwestern Bapt. Theol. Sem., 1959, MDiv, 1969; DMin, Pitts. Theol. Sem., 1979. Ordained to Gospel ministry, 1954. Pastor Warwick Rd. Bapt. Chapel, Richmond, Va., 1952-53, Garrett's Bluff Bapt. Ch., Arthur City, Tex., 1954-56, Plymouth Parish Bapt. Ch., Alexandria, Va., 1959-68, First Bapt. Ch., Bluefield, W.Va., 1968-77; exec. dir. missions Richmond (Va.) Bapt. Assn., 1977-97; adminstr., treas. So. Bapt. Conf./Assoc. Dirs. Missions, 1997—2003, ret., 2003. Trustee Bluefield (Va.) Coll., 1972-82, U. Richmond, Va., 1989-93; first v.p. Va. Bapt. Gen. Bd., Richmond, 1974-75; dir. Home Mission Bd., So. Bapt. Conv., Atlanta, 1976-84. Author: (children's book) Following Jesus, 1968. Commr. Bluefield (W.Va.) Urban Renewal Authority, 1971-74; chmn. Bluefield (W.Va.) Beautification Commn., 1972-73; pres. North Chamberlayne Civic Assn., Richmond, 1989-91. Recipient Disting. Svc. award City of Bluefield, 1970, Disting. Alumnus award Alumni Soc. Randolph Macon, Ashland, Va., 1992, Vol. Missions award Richmond Regional Devel. Coun. of the Fgn. Mission Bd., So. Bapt. Conv., 1995. Mem. Richmond Rotary Club (bd. dirs. 1990-92), Sandston Rotary Club, Pawleys Island Rotary Club, Omicron Delta Kappa. Avocations: travel, fishing, photography, baseball. Personal E-mail: cbnunnjr@aol.com.

**NUNN, GRADY HARRISON,** retired political science professor; b. Arlington, Tex., Apr. 12, 1918; s. William Roy and Floy Brooke (Dugan) N.; m. Ann Torrey Welsh, June 15, 1951 (dec. 1980); 1 child, Therese von Hohoff.; m. Virginia Cotton Chivington, Dec. 18, 1982. BA, U. Okla., 1939, MA, 1941; PhD (Penfield fellow), N.Y.U., 1961. Instr. N.Y.U., 1946-49; from instr. to assoc. prof. U. Ala., Tuscaloosa, 1949-65, prof., chmn. dept. polit. sci. Birmingham, 1969-83, prof. emeritus, 1983—; vis. asst. prof. Ind. U., 1960-61; asst. prof., assoc. prof. U. Pitts. at Ahmadu Bello U., Nigeria, 1964-68; assoc. prof. U. Pitts., 1968, Auburn U., 1968-69. Bd. dirs. Unitarian Universalist Service Com., 1978-84, v.p., 1981-82 Assoc. editor: Background on World Politics, 1957-62; Contbr. to: Readings in Government in American Society, 1949, Federalism in the Commonwealth, 1963, The Politics and Administration of Nigerian Government, 1965; editorial bd.: Jour. of Politics, 1971-74. Mem. Birmingham Regional Planning Commn., 1995-2000. Capt. F.A., AUS, 1942-46. Ford Found. Fgn. Area fellow, 1956-57 Mem. Am. Polit. Sci. Assn., So. Polit. Sci. Assn. (exec. council 1974-77) Royal Africa Soc., AAUP (pres. Ala. conf.) Phi Beta Kappa, Pi Sigma Alpha, Phi Eta Sigma, Alpha Tau Omega, Omicron Delta Kappa. Unitarian Universalist. Home: 805 Rockhurst Ln Birmingham AL 35209 Personal E-mail: ghnunn@aol.com.

**NUNN, KEN,** lawyer; b. Louisville, Mar. 22, 1940; s. Richard and Grace (Lynch) N.; m. Leah K. Blades, Aug. 19, 1962; children: Vicky A., David L. BS in Bus., Ind. U., 1964, JD, 1967. Bar: Ind. 1967, U.S. Dist. Ct. (so. dist.) Ind. 1967, U.S. Ct. Appeals (7th cir.) 1974, U.S. Supreme Ct. 1974. Pvt. practice, Bloomington, Ind. Office: 104 S Franklin Rd Bloomington IN 47404-5295

**NUNN, PATARICA DIAN,** poet; b. Arkadelphia, Ark., Aug. 10, 1951; m. Freddie Lee Nunn, Mar. 16, 1979; children: Katarica Lakisha, Roshonda Lanae, Ophelia Lorraine, Opal Laverne. Student, Ouachita Bapt. U., 1971—72. Dir. assistance operator Southwestern Bell Tel. Co., Hot Springs, Ark., 1978—2003; ret., 2003. Songwriter My Moment of Miles, Time, 1998, Mellow Drifting, 2002, Sassy Sassy Lady, 2003; author: (poetry) Sacred Memories, 1996, A True Mother's Love, 1997, A True Father's Love, 1998, Out in Left Field, 1998, A Breathe of Fresh Air, 2002. Bd. dirs., mem. adv. com. Nat. Libr. Poetry. Named to Internat. Poetry Hall of Fame, 1997, Internat. Hall of Fames's Mus. Mem.: Poetry Guild, Nat. Author's Registry. Democrat. Home: 4 Stillman Dr Little Rock AR 72209

**NUNN, ROBERT WARNE,** lawyer; b. Salem, Oreg., Sept. 20, 1950; s. Warne Harry and Dolores Nunn; m. Kandis Brewer; 1 child, Hayley Elisabeth. Student, U. Vienna, Austria, 1971; BS, Willamette U., 1972; MS in Acctg., Northeastern U., Boston, 1973, MBA, 2000; JD, U. Oreg., 1976. Bar: Oreg 1976, U.S. Dist. Ct. Oreg. 1977, U.S. Ct. Appeals (9th cir.) 1977, U.S. Supreme Ct. 1982, Wash. 1988. Ptnr. Schwabe, Williamson & Wyatt, Portland, Oreg., 1976-92; ptnr., chmn. corp. dept. Preston, Gates & Ellis, Portland, 1992-96; founder, mng. ptnr. Nunn Motschenbacher & Blattner LLP, Portland, 1996—. Dir. Oreg. State Bar Profl. Liability Fund, 1996—2004; spl. counsel Sussman Shankman LLP, 2001—. Mem. exec. com. Am. Leadership Forum, 1988-94, sr. fellow, 1989—; bd. mgrs. Multnomah Metro Br. YMCA, Portland, 1983-86, chmn., 1984-85; pres. Oreg. divsn. Am. Cancer Soc., Portland, 1986-87, bd. dirs., 1982-88; trustee Marylhurst Coll., Oreg., 1985-91, Willamette U., 1991—; trustee World Affairs Coun. Oreg. 1991-97, pres., 1995-96; bd. dirs. United Way of

Columbia-Willamette, Portland, 1984-87. Named Order of Red Sword, Am. Cancer Soc., 1985; fellow Am. Leadership, 1987. Mem. ABA, Oreg. Bar Assn. (past chmn. CPA joint com., past chmn. legal assts. and legal investigators com., cert. subcom., fee arbitration panel), Univ. Club, Multnomah Athletic Club (cert.). Republican. Lutheran. Avocations: computers, skiing, sailing. Office: Sussman Shank LLP 1000 SW Broadway Ste 1400 Portland OR 97205 Office Phone: 503-227-1111.

**NUNN, SAM (SAMUEL AUGUSTUS NUNN),** former senator, lawyer; b. Perry, Ga., Sept. 8, 1938; s. Samuel Augustus and Elizabeth (Cannon) N.; m. Colleen O'Brien, Sept. 25, 1965; children: Michelle, Brian. Student, Ga. Inst. Tech., 1956-59; AB, LL.B., Emory U., 1962. Bar: Ga. 1962. Legal counsel armed services com. U.S. Ho. Reps., 1963; mem. firm Nunn, Geiger & Rampey, Perry, Ga., 1964-73; mem. Ga. Ho. Reps., 1968-72; U.S. senator from Ga., 1972-96; ranking Dem. mem., chmn. armed svcs. com.; mem. govtl. affairs com., intelligence com., small bus. com.; ptnr. King & Spalding, Atlanta, 1997—2003; disting. prof. Ga. Inst. Tech., 1997—; co-chmn. Nuc. Threat Initiative, Washington, 2003—. Former ranking Dem., former chmn. Permanent Subcom. on Investigations of Govt. Affairs; bd. dirs. Chevron Texaco Corp., Coca-Cola Co., Dell Computer Corp., GE, Internet Security Systems Inc., Scientific-Atlanta; disting. prof. Sam Nunn Sch. Internat Affairs Ga. Tech. Office: Nuc Threat Initiative 1747 Pennsulvania Ave NW Ste 700 Washington DC 20006

**NUNNALLY, ALLEN C.,** lawyer; BA, Amherst Coll., 1999; JD, Boston U., 2002. Bar: Mass. 2003, D.C. 2005, U.S. Dist. Ct. Mass. 2003. Mng. editor Boston U. Jour. Sci. and Tech. Law, 2001—02; litigation assoc. Wilmer Cutler Pickering Hale and Dorr LLP, Boston, 2002—. Contbr. chapters to books, articles to profl. jours. Vol. legal counsel Kerry-Edwards Campaign/Dem. Nat. Com., 2004; bd. dirs. Friends of the Children, Boston, 2006—. Edward F. Hennessey scholar, Boston U. Sch. Law, 2002. Mem.: ABA, Mass. Bar Assn., Boston Bar Assn. Avocations: politics, reading, personal fitness, Boston sports enthusiast. Office: Wilmer Cutler Pickering Hale and Dorr 60 State St Boston MA 02109 Office Phone: 617-526-6242.

**NUNNELEY, JANELLE ANNETTE,** education educator; b. Bentonville, Ark., Jan. 30, 1953; d. Helen Francis and William Dudley Walker; 1 child, Robert Dennis. BS in Edn., U. Ark., Fayetteville. Cert. Teacher U. Ark., 1983. Tchr. Rogers Pub. Schs., Ark., 1999—. Office: Elmwood Jr HS 1600 S 13th St Rogers AR Office Phone: 479-631-3600.

**NUNNELLY, MARK EDWARD,** investor; b. Covington, Ky., Nov. 30, 1958; s. Donald Alfred and Lillian Ethel (Black) N.; m. Denise Marcel Dupre, Nov. 18, 1989; 1 child, Cameron. BA in History and Govt., Ctr. Coll. Ky., 1980; MBA, Harvard U., 1984. Legis. asst. U.S. Ho. of Reps., Washington, 1980; mem. brand mgmt. Procter & Gamble, Cin., 1980-82; mgmt. cons. Bain & Co., Boston, 1983-89; equity investor, mng. dir. Bain Capital, Boston, 1989—. Bd. dirs. Environ. Data Resources, Southport, Conn., Strategic Mapping, San Jose, Calif., Corp. Software, Boston, Houghton-Mifflin Co., Warner Music and DoubleClick, Inc., Domino's Pizza, 1998-. Mem. fin. bd. City Year, Boston, 1987; mem. alumni bd. Centre Coll., Danville, Ky., 1989—. Mem. Harvard Club.*

**NUNNIKHOVEN, THOMAS SPENCE,** statistician, consultant; b. Burlington, Iowa, June 19, 1947; s. Antonie Aart and Margaret Lois (Spence) Nunnikhoven; m. Kathleen Mae Smalley, Dec. 28, 1974; children: Amy Kathleen, Ryan Thomas. BA in Math., U. Iowa, 1968, MS in Stats., 1971; MS in Ops. Rsch., Case Western Reserve U., 1973, PhD in Ops Rsch., 1975. Sr. ops. rsch. analyst Hammermill Paper co., Erie, Pa., 1975-81, supr. ops. rsch., 1981-89; asst. prof. math. Pa. State U., Erie, 1989-92; sr. info. systems specialist Internat. Paper, Memphis, 1992-95, info. sys. cons., 1995-98, sr. info. sys. cons., 1998—2002, supply chain fellow, 2002—. Contbr. articles to profl. jours. Treas. Autism Soc. Am., Memphis, 1994—96, pres., 2001—03. With U.S. Army, 1969—71. Mem.: Informs, Am. Statis. Assn., Phi Beta Kappa. Achievements include development of method of finding optimal allocation to a health care reimbursement account; solved birthday problem for non-uniform birth frequencies. Home: 39 Red Thorn Cove Cordova TN 38018-7244 Office Phone: 901-419-7564.

**NUOVO, BETTY A.,** state representative; b. Englewood, NJ, Dec. 10, 1931; m. Victor L. Nuovo, 1953; two children. BS, Bucknell U., 1953. State rep. Vt. Ho. of Reps., Middlebury, 1981-90, 96—; pvt. law practice Middlebury, 1974—94. Jud. com. Ho. of Reps., 1981-88. chmn. 1985-88, chmn. jud. rules com. 1985-86, adminstrv. rules com. 1985-88, vice-chmn. 1987-88, ways and means com. 1989-90, Middlebury natural resources and energy com., 1996-2000, jud. com., 2001-02, agr. com., 2003-04, ways and means com., 2004—. Chair Vt. State Dem. Platform Com., Middlebury Charter Comm., Vt., Addison County Dem. Com.; bd. dirs., exec. bd. Addison County Regional Planning Com.; bd. selectmen Middlebury; bd. dirs. V.t. YMCA; mem. Middlebury LWV. Office: PO Box 1113 Middlebury VT 05753-0347 E-mail: bnuovo@leg.state.vt.us.

**NURENBERG, DAVID,** retired oil company executive; b. N.Y.C., Mar. 25, 1939; s. Abraham S. and Katherine G.; m. Brenda D. Schwait, Sept. 1963; children— Jill Suzanne, Brian Michael. BS in Marine Engring, U.S. Mcht. Marine Acad., 1960; MS in Indsl. Mgmt, Columbia U., 1963, PhD in Mgmt. Sci, 1965. With Exxon Corp., 1963-67; employee relations mgr. Esso Pappas, Athens, Greece, 1968-72; labor relations and compensation mgr. Esso Europe, London, 1972-77; corp. sec. Esso Eastern Inc., Houston, 1977-82; mgr. exec. compensation Exxon Corp., N.Y.C., 1982-90, mgr. compensation and exec. programs Irving, Tex., 1990-98; ret. Past mem. coun. exec. compensation Conf. Bd., past chmn.; adj. prof. Union Inst. Past mem. exec. edn. adv. bd. Wharton Sch., U. Pa.; past mem. adv. bd. Ctr. for Effective Orgns., U. So. Calif. Mem. Am. Compensation Assn. (bd. dirs., chmn., exec. comp. coun., bd. steering com.), Am. Contract Bridge League (Silver life master).

**NURICK, CARL J.,** writer, consultant, poet; b. Harrisburg, Pa., Mar. 29, 1934; s. Gilbert and Sylvia Nurick; m. Elizabeth Parker Nurick; children: Kim, Scott, Todd, Craig. BA, Pa. State U., 1955; postgrad., Mich. State U., Columbia U. Area v.p. AT&T, Phila., 1982—86; internat. v.p. Internat. Alliance, 1987—93; exec. v.p. Transnet, Huntington Valley, Pa., 1993; v.p. OutSource Internat., 1995—96; pres. and COO Vircom, West Chester, Pa., 1996—97; freelance author Tafton, Pa., 1998—; cons. world religions and military. Mem. MBA adv. bd. Pa. State U. and Bloomsburg U., 1990—98; mktg. adv. bd. Drexel U., Phila., 1974—78. Author: The Truth About Islam, 2003, Living To Die, 2003, Green Street Boy, 2006, poetry. Bd. dirs. Suburban Gen. Hosp., Norristown, Pa., 1979—80. Lt. USN, 1955—57, surface warfare officer USN, 1958—70. Mem.: Fairview Lake Assn., U.S. Naval Inst. Avocations: reading, fitness, boating, music.

**NURKIN, SIDNEY J.,** lawyer; b. Durham, N.C., Nov. 12, 1941; BSEE, Duke U., 1963, LLB, 1966. Bar: Ga. 1967. Mem. Powell, Goldstein, Frazer & Murphy; now sr. ptnr., corp. group Alston & Bird LLP, Atlanta. Mem. ABA (mem. com. on corp. laws, 1987—), Atlanta Bar Assn., Omicron Delta Kappa, Tau Beta Pi, Eta Kappa Nu. Office: Alston & Bird LLP One Atlantic Ctr 1201 W Peachtree St NW Atlanta GA 30309-3424 Office Phone: 404-881-7260. Office Fax: 404-881-7777. Business E-Mail: snurkin@alston.com.

**NURNBERG, CHARLES GORDON,** publishing executive; b. Newark, Nov. 16, 1947; s. Max and Eleanor (Gordon) N.; m. Barbara Ann Goldstein, Dec. 20, 1970; children: Jeremy, Peter, David. BA, Syracuse U., 1969. Proofreader Frederick Fell Pub., Inc., N.Y.C., 1969, editor, 1970-72, sales, 1972-74, sales mgr. 1974-75, v.p. sales, 1975-77, exec. v.p., 1977-78, pub., 1978; pub. paperbacks Sterling Pub. Co., Inc., N.Y.C., 1978-80, v.p. dir. mktg., 1980-82, sr. v.p., 1982-89, exec. v.p., 1990—2003, pres., 2003—, CEO, 2003—, pub., 2003—. Mem. Book Industry Study Group com., 1992-95. Mem. Assn. Am. Pubs. (mem. mktg. com. 1970-73, chmn. pubs. forum com. 1973-79), Marlboro Soccer Assn. (bd. dirs., coach 1974, boys

travel team). Avocations: writing, travel, exercise. Home: 25 Whitman Rd Morganville NJ 07751-1442 Office: 387 Park Ave S New York NY 10016-8810 Office Phone: 212-532-7160. Business E-Mail: cnurnberg@sterlingpub.com.

**NURNBERG, ROGER C.,** county official; b. Creston, Iowa, Jan. 31, 1943; s. Mansel and Harriet J. Nurnberg; m. JoAnn I. Stringham, Aug. 5, 1962; children: Kathryn A., Leah T., Stephani J. Student, Creston C.C., 1961—63. Cert. fire instr. I and II Okla. U., 1982, EMT Iowa, arson investigator Iowa. With S&L Clothing and Farm and Home Supply, Creston, 1961—64; letter carrier USPS, Creston, 1965—66; firefighter Creston Fire Dept., 1966—77, fire lt., 1977—96, fire chief, 1996—2000; emergency coord. Union County Emergency Mgmt., Creston, 2000—, E911 coord., 2000—. Author (editor): How to Install Dry Fire Hydrants, 1991; originator FireHousesoftware.com, 1990. Pres. 10,000 Crestonians, 2003—. Mem.: Union County Geneol. Soc., Creston Pyrotechnic Assn. (safety officer), Iowa Pyrotechnic Assn., Iowa Fireman's Assn., Masons (3d degree, 32d degree). Presbyterian. Avocations: travel, winemaking, geocaching, genealogy. Office: Union County Emergency Management Agency 208 W Taylor St Creston IA 50801 E-mail: ucema@mchsi.com.

**NURNBERGER, JOHN I., JR.,** psychiatrist, educator; b. N.Y.C., July 18, 1946; married; 3 children. BS in Psychology magna cum laude, Fordham U., 1968; MD, Ind. U., 1975, PhD, 1983. Diplomate Am. Bd. Psychiatry and Neurology. Resident in psychiatry Columbia Presbyn. Med. Ctr., N.Y.C., 1975-78, med. officer sect. psychogenetics, 1977-78; sr. staff fellow, outpatient clinic adminstr. sect. psychogenetics NIH, Bethesda, Md., 1978-83, staff psychiatrist, chief NIMH Outpatients Clinic, 1983-86, acting chief sect. clin. genetics, 1986; prof. psychiatry, dir. Inst. Psychiatric Rsch., rsch. coord. dept. psychiatry Ind. U. Med. Ctr., Indpls., 1986—; prof. med. psychiatry, neurobiology and med. genetics Ind. U. Grad. Sch., Indpls., 1987—; Joyce and Iver Small prof. psychiatry, dir. Inst. Psychiat. Rsch., Ind U., Indpls. Clin. cons. Cold Spring VA Hosp., 1986—; cons., lectr. in field. Editor-in-chief: Psychiatric Genetics; field editor: Neuropsychiatric Genetics; contbr. articles to profl. jours. NSF fellow, 1968; recipient NAMI Exemplary Psychiatrist award Nat. Alliance Mentally Ill, 1992, 94. Fellow Am. Psychiatric Assn., Am. Psychpathological Assn.; mem. AAAS, Am. Soc. Human Genetics, Internat. Soc. Psychiatric Genetics (bd. dirs.), Am. Coll. Neuropsychopharmacology, Soc. Light Treatment and Biol. Rhythms, Soc. Neursci., Assn. Rsch. in Nervous and Mental Disease, Soc. Biol. Psychiatry, Sigma Xi. Office: Ind U Sch Medicine Psychiatric Rsch Inst 791 Union Dr Indianapolis IN 46202-2873

**NURSE, SIR PAUL M.,** academic administrator; m. Anne Nurse; children: Sarah, Emily. BSc, U. Birmingham, 1970; PhD, East Anglia, 1973. Dir. rsch. Imperial Cancer Rsch. Fund, 1993-96, dir. gen., 1996—2002; chief exec. Cancer Rsch. U.K., London, 2002—03; pres. Rockefeller U., NYC, 2003—; pres. lab. yeast genetics and cell biology, 2003—, prof., dept. molecular, cellular and develop. biology, 2003—; Chair microbiology U. Oxford, 1988—93. Recipient Gairdner Internat. award, Gairdner Found., 1992, Royal medal Royal Soc., 1995, H. P. Heineken prize for biochemistry and biophysics Royal Netherlands Acad. Arts and Scis., 1996, Dr. Josef Steiner prize, Cancer Found., Bern, Switzerland, 1996, Alfred P. Sloan Jr. prize and medal, GM Cancer Rsch. Found., 1997, Albert Lasker award, basic med. rsch., USA, 1998, Berkan Judd award, 1998, Nobel Prize in Physiology or Med., The Nobel Found., 2001. Fellow: Am. Acad. Arts & Sciences, Royal Soc. (Copley medal 2005); mem.: NAS (foreign assoc.). Avocations: hiking, flying. Office: Rockefeller U 1230 York Ave New York NY 10021-6399 Business E-Mail: nurse@rockefeller.edu.*

**NUSBACHER, GLORIA WEINBERG,** lawyer; b. NYC, July 22, 1951; d. Murray and Doris (Togman) Weinberg; m. Burton Nusbacher, Aug. 4, 1974; 1 child, Shoshana. BA magna cum laude, Barnard Coll., 1972; JD with hons., Columbia U., 1975. Bar: N.Y. 1976. Assoc. Hughes Hubbard & Reed LLP, NYC, 1975-83, counsel, 1983-91, ptnr., 1991—. Lectr. in field. Mem. Columbia Law Rev.; contbr. articles to profl. jours. Troop leader, leader trainer Girl Scouts USA, 1991-97. Mem. ABA (employee benefits and exec. compensation com. 1987—, fed. regulation securities com., employee benefits, exec. compensation and sect. 16, 1983—, task force Sect. 16, 1991-97, vice-chair com. employee benefits and exec. compensation 2001-03, chair subcom. fed. and state securities laws of com. employee benefits and exec. compensation 1994-2001, 03-, mem. task force exec. compensation 1992-94). Office: Hughes Hubbard & Reed LLP 1 Battery Park Plz New York NY 10004-1482 Office Phone: 212-837-6719. Business E-Mail: nusbache@hugheshubbard.com.

**NUSBAUM, BERYL,** lawyer; b. Rochester, N.Y., Sept. 11, 1933; s. Shepard I. and Fan (Landes) N.; m. Joan E. Rosenthal, Aug. 3, 1958; children: Harris R., Mitchell S., Dena R. BA, Columbia Coll., 1955; LLB, Yale U., 1958. Bar: N.Y. 1958, U.S. Dist. Ct. (we. dist.) N.Y. 1959, U.S. Dist. Ct. (no. dist.) N.Y. 1999, U.S. Ct. Appeals (2d cir.) 1981, Fla. 1988. Assoc. Woods Oviatt Gilman Sturman and Clarke, Rochester, N.Y., 1959-65; ptnr. Woods Oviatt Gilman LLP, Rochester, 1966—, mng. ptnr. 1986-96. V.p. Temple Beth El, Rochester, 1972-75, pres. 1975-78. Sgt. U.S. Army, 1958-64. Mem. N.Y. Bar Assn., Monroe County Bar Assn. (past mem. com. on jud., past chmn. ethics com.). Republican. Jewish. Avocations: tennis, wildlife conservation. Home: 210 Hibiscus Dr Rochester NY 14618-4440 Office Phone: 585-987-2817. E-mail: bjnusbaum@woodsouiatt.com.

**NUSBAUM, EDWARD E.,** accounting company executive; BS summa cum laude, Ohio State U.; MS, Purdue U. CPA. Mem. audit staff Grant Thornton LLP, Chgo., 1978—86, ptnr., 1986, nat. dir. assurance svcs., 1993—97, mng. ptnr., 1997—99, interim exec. ptnr., 2001; CEO Grant Thornton, 2003—. Spkr. in field. Recipient Elijah Watts Sells award. Office: Grant Thornton 175 W Jackson Blvd Chicago IL 60604 Office Phone: 312-856-0200. Office Fax: 312-602-8099.

**NUSBAUM, JACK HENRY,** lawyer; b. Casablanca, Morocco, July 22, 1940; came to U.S., 1941; s. Simon and Regine (Kleefeld) N.; m. Ronni Danciger, June 10, 1962 (div. 1983); children: Lisa B., Gary D.; m. Margie Goldsmith, Feb. 5, 1984 (div. 1997). BS, U. Pa., 1962; JD, Columbia U., 1965. Bar: N.Y. 1965. Assoc. Willkie, Farr & Gallagher LLP, NYC, 1965-70, ptnr., 1971—, co-chmn., 1979-95, chmn., 1995—, leader Corp. and Fin. Svcs. Dept. Bd. dirs. W.R. Berkley Corp., Greenwich, Conn., GEV Corp., Greenwich, Fine Host Corp., Greenwich, Hirschl & Adler Galleries, Inc., N.Y.C., The Topps Co., Inc., N.Y.C., Pioneer Cos. Inc., Greenwich, Prime Hospitality Corp., Fairfield, N.J. Active The Robert Steel Found., N.Y.C., Prep for Prep, N.Y.C., The Joseph Collins Found., N.Y.C., Strategic Distbn. Inc., Greenwich. Mem. ABA, N.Y. State Bar Assn., N.Y. County Lawyers Assn. Home: 250 E 54th St New York NY 10022-4810 Office: Willkie Farr & Gallagher LLP 787 7th Ave New York NY 10019-6018 E-mail: jnusbaum@willkie.com.

**NUSIM, STANLEY HERBERT,** chemical engineer, consultant; b. N.Y.C., Oct. 2, 1935; s. Seymour and Ranna T. (Weiner) Nusim; m. Marcia Anne Borsig, Feb. 21, 1960; children: David Mark, Jill Wendi. BChemE, CCNY, 1957; MChemE, N.Y. U., 1960, PhD, 1967. Rsch. engr. Battelle Meml. Inst., Columbus, Ohio, 1956; researcher, chem. engring. rsch. and devel. Merck Rsch. Labs. Div., Rahway, NJ, 1957-68, sect. mgr., 1968-70; tech. svcs. mgr. Merck Chem. Mfg. Div., Rahway, 1970-73, mfg. mgr., 1973-80; dir. subsidiary projects Merck Internat. Div., Rahway, 1981-82, exec. dir. Latin Am., Far East, Near East ops., 1982-88; exec. dir. licensee, Latin Am., Far East, Asia ops. Merck Pharm. Mfg. Div., Rahway, 1989-92; exec. dir. licensee ops. worldwide Merck Mfg. Divsn. Merck & Co. Inc., Whitehouse Station, NJ, 1992-94; v.p. mfg. and ops. Therics Inc., Princeton, NJ, 1994-97; pres. S.H. Nusim Assocs., Inc., Aventura, Fla., 1994—. Mem. adv. bd. CCNY Sch. Engring., 1982—2004; bd. dirs. AGI Dermatics Inc., Freeport, NY, 1998—. Author: Kinetic Studies on C4 Hydrocarbon Systems, 1967; editor: Active Pharmaceutical Ingredients: Development, Manufacturing and Regulation, 2005. V.p. men's club Temple Beth Shalom, Livingston, N.J., 1975-78; rep.

to bd. edn. Livingston Home and Sch. Assn., 1982-83; bd. govs. Turnberry Isle Yacht and Racquet Club, Aventura, Fla., 1992-94. Mem. Am. Inst. Chem. Engrs. (bd. dir. N. Jersey sect. 1968-71, scholarship award 1955), Am. Chem. Soc., Tau Beta Pi, Garden State Yacht Club (bd. govs. 1987-88), Otis Woodlands Club (bd. dirs. 2002-2004). Achievements include U.S. and foreign patents on the continuous manufacture of halogenated acetone, development of "clean room" concepts for API manufacturing, development of sophisticated training techniques for sterile pharmaceutical manufacturing. Office Phone: 305-935-7576. E-mail: shn@pipeline.com.

**NUSS, BARBARA GOUGH,** artist; b. Washington, Apr. 11, 1939; d. Gaines Homer Gough and Edwerta Barbara (Beyer) Barber; m. Frederick A. Johnson, Sept. 30, 1968 (div. 1975); 1 child, Mark Eugene; m. Fred Dean Nuss, Dec. 18, 1982. BFA, Syracuse U., 1960; postgrad., Schuler Sch. Fine Arts, Balt., 1986—87. Art dir. Chappell's Dept. Store, Syracuse, NY, 1960-62, 66; mgr., illustrator Holman Anderson & Moore, Washington, 1967-70; art dir., advt. mgr. Ad-Media & Howard Advt. Assocs., Columbia, Md., 1970-75; acct. exec. Graphic Arts Inc., Alexandria, Va., 1975-77; sales mgr. The Jour. Newspapers, Washington, 1977-82; tchr., adult edn. Montgomery Coll., Rockville, Md., 1984-85; pvt. tchr. fine arts, Woodbine, Md., 1982-96; instr. Plein air painting workshop, 1998—2005. Chmn. Montgomery County Juried Art Exhibit, Rockville, 1988, Mid-Atlantic Regional Watercolor Exhibit, 1998—99; pres. Nuss Fine Arts, Inc., 1992—; judge Am. Landscape Show Art League Torpedo Factory, Alexandria, Va., 2002; judge Mountain State Forest Festival Fine Art Exhibition, Elkins, W.Va., 2002, Potomac Valley Watercolorists Ann. Juried Show, 2004, Mont. County Art Assn. Ann. Show, 2001, 04, 05. One-woman shows include Pa. State U., 1986, NIH, Bethesda, Md., 1989—90, Md. Nat. Capital Pk. and Planning Commn., 1991, Art League Gallery, Alexandria, 1992, Bendann Art Galleries, Towson, Md., 1999—2000, Troika Gallery, Easton, Md., 2004, Strathmore Hall Art Ctr., Bethesda, Md., 2004, Washington County Arts Coun. Gallery, Hagerstown, Md., 2004, Grand Style Gallery, Balt., 2004, Andrei Kushnir / Michele Taylor Gallery, N.Y.C., 2005, exhibited in group shows at Art League at the Torpedo Factory, 1987—92, 2002, Mid-Atlantic Regional Watercolor Exhbn., 1989 (Holbein award, 2006), Heritage Gallery Classical Realism, 1989—90, Art Barn Gallery, Washington, 1990, Carmen's Gallery, 1991—2002, Art Showcase 100 Md. Artists. 1991—92, Assn. pour la Promotion du Patrimoine Artistique Francais, Galerie Jean Lammelin, Argenteuil, France, 1991, Salmagundi Club 14th Ann. Exhbn., 1991, 18th Annual Exhbn., 1995, Thumb Box Exhbn., 2005, Atrium Gallery Georgetown U., Washington, 1991, 18th Ann. Exhbn., 1995, State House, Annapolis, 1996, World Trade Ctr., Balt., 1996, Bendann's Art Gallery, Towson, 1997—2002, Principle Gallery, Alexandria, 1998—2005, Miniature Painters, Sculptors and Gravers Soc. Washington, 1999, Addison/Ripley Fine Art Gallery, Washington, 1999, Rock Creek Gallery, 1999, 2001, Main St. Gallery, Annapolis, 1999—2000, Miniature Art Soc. Fla., 2000, Oil Painters Am., 2000—01, Troika Gallery, Easton, 2001—04, Washington County Arts Coun. Gallery, Hagerstown, 2001—04, Brazier Fine Art, Richmond, Va., 2002, Grand Style Gallery, Balt., 2002—04, Black Rock Ctr. for the Arts, Germantown, Md., 2003—04, Andrei Kushnir / Michele Taylor Gallery, Ellicott City, Md., and N.Y.C., 2003, MD Hall, Annapolis, Md., 2004, 2005, 2006, Washington County Mus. Fine Arts, Hagerstown, Md., 2006—, Represented in permanent collections Am. Coun. Edn., NIH, Bell Atlantic, Kiplinger Washington Editors, Fairhaven Retirement Cmty., Md. State Treas.'s Office, NIH; work represented in: Art from the Parks, How Did You Paint That?, 2000; author: 14 Formulas for Painting Fabulous Landscapes, 2004. Finalist still life competition, Artist's mag., 1996, landscape competition, 2003; recipient 1st prize for watercolor, C&O Canal Show, 1987, 1st prize for oil painting, Rockville Art League, 1987, Montgomery County Art Assn., 1983, 1989, Gaithersburg Fine Arts Assn., 1983, 1989, grand champion award for oil painting, Howard County Fair, 1989, Top 100 award for oil painting, Nat. Arts for Parks, 1989, 1991, 1992, 2001, 2006, Top 200, 1990, 1993, 1996, 2006, award of excellence, Washington Soc. Landscape Painters, 1999, 2005, Best in Show award, Nat. League Am. Pen Women, Md. Biennial Conv., 1999, 2003, 1st Prize Watercolor, 1st Prize Oils award, MAPAPA Paint Annapolis, 2003, Award of Excellence, 2004. Mem. Nat. League Am. Pen Women (sec. Bethesda, Md. 1989, treas. 2000-06, state treas. 2006), Balt. Watercolor Soc. (bd. dirs. 1997-99), Washington Soc. Landscape Painters (sec. 1999, pres. 2000-03), Salmagundi Club (NYC), Oil Painters Am. (assoc.). Avocations: crossword puzzles, quilting. Home: 3132 Cabin Run Woodbine MD 21797-7933 E-mail: barbara@barbaranuss.com.

**NUSS, JOANNE RUTH,** artist; b. Gt. Bend, Kans., May 2, 1951; d. Melvin Oliver and Ruth Helen (Brauer) Nuss. Student, Valparaiso U., Ind., 1969—71, U. Kans., 1972—73, U. Copenhagen, 1974; BA, Ft. Hays State U., 1976; MFA, Santa Fe Inst. Fine Arts, 1991. Lectr. Noon Edition Sta. KCMO-TV, Kansas City, 1981, Menoriah Hosp., Brookridge Elem. Sch., Jill Shurin Show Telecable 10, Kansas City, 1982, Barton County CC, Gt. Bend, Nelson-Atkins Mus., Kansas City, Mo., 1984; artist-in-residence Helen Wurlitzer Found., Taos, N.Mex., 1984, Taos, 90. One-woman shows include Bette Moses Gallery, Great Bend, 1980, Art Expo Ctr., San Francisco, 1981, Univ. Gall., Ft. Hays State U., 1985, Am. Legation Mus., Tangiers, Morocco, 1986, Inma Gallery, Dhahran, Saudi Arabia, 1994, Bab Rouah Gallery, Rabat, Morocco, 1996, Agora Gallery, Soho, New York, 2001, Amsterdam Whitney Internat. Fine Art Gallery, N.Y.C., 2003, others, exhibited in group shows at Second Internat. Signature Fair, Boston, 1980, Joan Cooke Gallery, Kansas City, Mo., 1983, Batz Lawrence Gallery, Kansas City, 1984, Galerie de Rond Point des Champs Elyssees, Paris, 1989, Tetouan & La Kabila Gallery, Tetouan, Morocco, 1991, N.Mex. Sculptors Guild, Fuller Lodge Art Gallery, Los Alamos, 1992, Hermosas Fine Arts Gallery, Durango, Colo., 1995, Tanjah Flandria Art Gallery, Tangiers, 1997—99, Shidoni Gallery, Tesuque, N.Mex., 1999—2002, Birger Sandzen Gallery, Lindsborg, Kans., 2000, Nat. Assn. Women Artists, Sarasota Visual Arts Ctr., 2000, U. No. Iowa, Cedar Falls, 2001 (1st pl.), 2001, 1st Pl. award Period Gallery, Omaha, Nebr., 2002), Coplan Gallery, Boca Raton, Fla., 2002, Attleboro (Mass.) Mus., 2002, Jeanette Hare Art Gallery, West Palm Beach, Fla., 2002, Attleboro (Mass.) Mus., 2003, Nat. Assn. Women Artists Fifth Ave. Gallery, NYC, 2003, Baker Arts Ctr., 2004, McDowell Arts and Crafts Assn., Shelby Arts, 2004—05, exhibitions include Nat. Assn. Women Artists, 2003, Baker Arts Ctr., 2004, 2005, Nat. Assn. Women Artists Travelling the Carolinas, Ashe County Arts, 2004—05, Pen & Brush 59th Annual Sculpture exhbn., N.Y.C., The Lawrence-Arnott Art Gallery, Marrakech, Morocco, 2005, 2006, Upstream People Gallery, Omaha, 2006, prin. works include archtl. project, Tangiers, 1988—90; featured artist Artist Spectrum Mag. Named 1st female fgn. artist commd. for archtl. major project, Tangiers, 1988—90, Internat. Profl. of Yr., Internat. Biog. Ctr., Cambridge, Eng., 2005; recipient Best 3-D Works award, Wichita Art Assn., 1983, 1st Kans. Artist Purchase award, Ft. Hays State U., 1985, 1st Pl. award, Nat. Exhbn., U. No. Iowa, 2001, Women of Achievement award, Am. Biog. Inst., Inc., 2004—05, Award of Excellence, 7th Annual All Media Internat. Juried Online Exhbn., Lipstream People Gallery, Omaha, 2005, Spl. Recognition award, Upstream People Gallery, 2006. Mem.: Kans. Sculptors Assn., Internat. Sculpture Ctr., Nat. Sculpture Soc., Nat. Assn. Women Artists, Internat. Platform Assn., N.Mex Women in Arts, Nat. Mus. Women in Arts. Avocations: travel, working with other artists, developing private sculpture garden. Office Phone: 505-988-2758.

**NUSS, LAWTON R.,** state supreme court justice; b. Salina, Kans., Dec. 30, 1952; m. Barbara Nuss; 5 children. BA in English and History, U. Kans., 1975, JD, 1982. Atty. Clark Mize & Linville, 1982—2002; special prosecutor City of Salina, 1994—96; justice Kans. Supreme Ct., Topeka, 2002—. Former employee U.S. Dist. Ct., Kans. Combat enigma officer USMC. Mem.: Kans. Assn. Def. Counsel (pres.), Kans. Bar Assn. (chmn. bd. editors jour.). Office: Kans Jud Ctr 301 SW 10th Topeka KS 66612-1507*

**NUSSBAUM, BENNETT,** printing/copying company executive; BS in Econs., U. Pa., 1969; MBA, Columbia U., 1971. CFO Kinko's Inc., Ventura, Calif., Burger King Corp., also exec. vice-pres.; sr. vice-pres., CFO Winn-Dixie Stores. Office: Winn Dixie Stores Inc 5050 Edgewood Ct Jacksonville FL 32254 Office Phone: 904-370-6655. Business E-Mail: bennettnussbaum@winn-dixie.com.

**NUSSBAUM, BERNARD J.,** lawyer; b. Berlin, Mar. 11, 1931; came to U.S., 1936; s. William and Lotte (Frankfurther) N.; m. Jean Beverly Enzer, Sept. 4, 1956; children— Charles, Peter, Andrew AB, Knox Coll., 1948-52; JD, U. Chgo., 1955. Assoc. Proskauer Rose Goetz & Mendelsohn, N.Y.C., 1955-56, Sonnenschein Nath & Rosenthal LLP, Chgo., 1959-65; sr. ptnr. Sonnenschein Nath & Rosenthal, Chgo., 1965—. Master bencher Am. Inns of Ct., 1986—; appointed to com. on civility 7th cir. U.S. Ct. Appeals, 1989-92. Editor U. Chgo. Law Rev., 1954-55; mem. nat. adv. bd. BNA Civil Trial Man., 1985—; contbr. articles to profl. jours. Mem. vis. com. U. Chgo. Law Sch., 1977-83. Served to capt. U.S. Army, 1956-59 Fellow Am. Bar Found., Ill. Bar Found. (charter); mem. ABA, Chgo. Bar Assn. (chmn. com. on fed. civil procedure 1968-69, mem. com. on judiciary 1970-76), Ill. Bar Assn. (council Antitrust sect. 1971-73, assembly del. 1972-80), U. Chgo. Law Sch. Nat. Alumni Assn. (pres. 1981-83). Avocations: skiing, bicycling. Office: Sonnenschein Nath & Rosenthal LLP 8000 Sears Tower 233 S Wacker Dr Ste 8000 Chicago IL 60606-6491 Office Phone: 312-876-8039. Business E-mail: bnussbaum@sonnenschein.com.

**NUSSBAUM, BERNARD W.,** federal official, lawyer; b. NYC, Mar. 23, 1937; m. Toby Nussbaum; 3 children. BA, Columbia U., 1958; LLB, Harvard U., 1961; LLD (hon.), George Washington Univ., 1993. Bar: N.Y. 1962, U.S. Dist. Ct. So. N.Y. 1964, U.S. Dist. Ct. Ea. N.Y. 1973, U.S. Ct. Appeals 2d cir. 1964, U.S. Supreme Ct. 1973. Asst. U.S. dist. atty. U.S. Dist. Ct. (so. dist.), N.Y., 1962-66; atty., then sr. ptnr. Wachtell, Lipton, Rosen & Katz, N.Y.C., 1966—; sr. staff atty. Judiciary Com., U.S. Ho. Rep., Washington, 1974; counsel to Pres. Clinton White House, Washington, 1993—94. Lectr. Columbia Law Sch. Note editor Harvard Law Review. Trustee Mt. Sinai Hosp., N.Y.C., Jewish Mus., Jewish Theological Sem. Am., Boys Brotherhood Rep. Recipient Torch of Learning lawyer's divsn. Am. Friends Hebrew U. Jerusalem, 1985; Sheldon travelling fellow Harvard U., 1961; Gould Award, Office of Appellate Def. Fellow Am. Bar Found.; mem. Assn. Bar City N.Y. (exec. com., v.p.), Fed. Bar Coun. (pres. 1991-93) Phi Beta Kappa. Office: Wachtell Lipton Rosen & Katz 51 W 52nd St New York NY 10019 Office Phone: 212-403-1266. Office Fax: 212-403-2266. Business E-Mail: BWNussbaum@wlrk.com.

**NUSSBAUM, LEO LESTER,** retired college president, consultant; b. Berne, Ind., June 27, 1918; s. Samuel D. and Margaret (Mazelin) N.; m. Janet Nell Gladfelter, Nov. 25, 1942; children: Felicity Ann, Luther James, Margaret Sue. BS, Ball State U., 1942, MA, 1949; PhD, Northwestern U., 1952; postgrad., U. Mich., 1963. Tchr. Monmouth H.S., Decatur, Ind. 1946-48; dean men, asst. prof. bus. Huntington (Ind.) Coll., Ind., 1948-51; dean coll. liberal arts, assoc. prof. edn. and psychology U. Dubuque, Iowa, 1952-60; dean coll., prof. edn. and psychology Austin Coll., 1960-67; dean coll., prof. psychology Coe Coll., 1967-82, pres., 1970-82, pres. emeritus, 1982—; dir. Acad. Sr. Profls. Eckerd Coll., 1983-87; dir. PEL-ASPEC Project, 1988-95; coord. faculty ASPEC Colleagues, St. Petersburg, 1992-97. Cons. pvt. practice St. Petersburg, Fla., 1982—; Fulbright lectr. U. Mysore, India, 1958-59; cons., evaluator So. Assn. Colls. and Schs., Atlanta, 1963-67, North Cen. Assn. Colls. and Schs., 1959-60, 67-82, dir. I.E. Industries and Iowa Electric Light and Power Co., Cedar Rapids, 1982-91, dir. emeritus, 1991-92. Contbr. articles to profl. jours. Bd. dirs. Cedar Rapids Symphony, 1968-70; mem. cabinet Cedar Rapids United Way, 1980-82; elder Presbyn. Ch., moderator Presbytery of S.W. Fla., 1989. Sgt. U.S. Army, 1942-46. Recipient Disting. Alumnus award Ball State U., 1976, Alumni Merit award Northwestern U., 1977. Mem. Assn. Colls. Midwest (chmn. 1975-77), Iowa Assn. Ind. Colls. and Univs. (chmn. 1976-77), Danforth Assocs., Rotary (Cedar Rapids pres. 1975-76), Phi Delta Kappa, Blue Key, Pi Gamma Mu Home: 6909 MI King St S # 336 Saint Petersburg FL 33705-6207 E-mail: lnussbau@tampabay.rr.com.

**NUSSBAUM, MARTHA CRAVEN,** philosophy and classics educator; b. NYC, May 6, 1947; d. George and Betty (Warren) Craven; m. Alan Jeffrey Nussbaum, 1969 (div. 1987); 1 child, Rachel Emily. BA, NYU, 1969; MA, Harvard U., 1971, PhD, 1975; LHD (hon.), Kalamazoo Coll., 1988, Grinnell Coll., 1993. Asst. prof. philosophy and classics Harvard U., Cambridge, 1975-80, assoc. prof., 1980-83; vis. prof. philosophy, Greek and Latin Wellesley (Mass.) Coll., 1983-84; assoc. prof. philosophy and classics Brown U., Providence, R.I., 1984-85, prof. philosophy, classics and comparative lit., 1985-87, David Benedict prof. philosophy, classics and comparative lit., 1987-89, prof., 1989-95; prof. law and ethics U. Chgo., 1995-96, prof. philosophy dept., 1995—, prof. Divinity Sch., 1995—, Ernst Freund prof. law and ethics Law Sch./Divinity Sch., 1996-99, assoc. mem. classics dept., 1996—, Rsch. advisor World Inst. Devel. Econs. Rsch., Helsinki, Finland, 1986-93; vis. prof. law U. Chgo., 1994. Author: Aristotle's De Motu Animalium, 1978, The Fragility of Goodness, 1986, Love's Knowledge, 1990, The Therapy of Desire, 1994, Poetic Justice: The Literary Imagination and Public Life, 1996, For Love of Country, 1996; editor: Language and Logos, 1983; (with A. Rorty) Essays on Aristotle's De Anima, 1992, (with A. Sen) The Quality of Life, 1993, (with J. Brunschwig) Passions & Perceptions, 1993, (with J. Glover) Women, Culture and Development, 1995, Poetic Justice, 1996, Cultivating Humanity, 1997, Sex and Social Justice, 1998. Soc. Fellows Harvard U. jr. fellow, 1972-75, Humanities fellow Princeton U., 1977-78, Guggenheim Found. fellow, 1983, NIH fellow, vis. fellow All Souls Coll., Oxford, Eng., 1986-87; recipient Brandeis Creative Arts award, 1990, Spielvogel-Diamondstein award, 1991; Gifford lectr. U. Edinburgh, 1993. Fellow Am. Acad. Arts and Scis. (membership com. 1991-93, coun. 1992-96), Am. Philos. Soc.; mem. Am. Philos. Assn. (exec. com. Ea. divsn. 1985-87, chair com. internat. coop., ex-officio mem. nat. bd. 1989-92, chair com. on status of women 1994-97), Am. Philol. Assn., PEN. Office: U Chicago The Law Sch 1111 E 60th St Chicago IL 60637-2776

**NUSSBAUM, MARTIN,** prosecutor; b. New York, NY, July 23, 1947; s. Molly Nussbaum; m. Kathleen Brennan; children: Caroline Deblyn, David Watson. JD, Columbia Law Sch., NY, 1970. Ptnr. Dechert LLP, New York, NY, 1996—. Home: 17 Midwood Dr Greenwich CT 06831 Office: Dechert LLP 30 Rockefeller Plaza New York NY 10112 Office Phone: 212-698-3596. Home Fax: 203-622-7299. Office Fax: 212-698-3599. E-mail: martin.nussbaum@dechert.com.

**NUSSBAUM, MICHAEL SCOT,** physician, medical educator; b. Cleve., Nov. 4, 1956; s. Fritz S. and Elaine (Sukenik) N.; m. Sue Ellen Weinstein, Aug. 6, 1983; children: Jaclyn, Rachel. BA, Northwestern U., 1977; MD, U. Pa., 1981. Intern dept. surgery U. Cin., 1981-82, resident dept. surgery, 1982-86, chief resident dept. surgery, 1985-86; dir. surg. edn. Jewish Hosp., Cin., 1986-90; asst. prof. surgery U. Cin., 1986-96, assoc. prof. surgery, 1996—, asst. prof. molecular and cellular physiology, 1991—; attending physician dept. parenteral and enteral nutrition U. Cin. Hosp., 1989—, dir. surg. endoscopy and laparoscopy, 1993—2000, chief sect. gen. surgery, 1999—2003, chief of staff, 2000—, vice chmn. clin. affairs, 2003—, asst. dean for hosp. affairs, 2003—. Med. records com. Jewish Hosp. Cin., 1986-88, med. incident rev. com., 1986-92, intensive care com., 1986-2000, CPR com., 1986-92, course dir. ACLS, 1987-92, chmn. nutrition support com., 1988-2000; chmn. adverse drug reaction com. U. Cin. Hosp., 1988-92, edn. coordinating com., 1990-93, oper. rm. adv. com. 1992-2000, patient care rev. com., 1992-2000, chmn. pharmacy and therapeutics com., 1992-2000, med. co-dir. collaborative care unit, 1993—, clin., tech. and support design team, 1994—, others; ACLS subcom. Am. Heart Assn.-Southwestern Ohio Chpt., 1988-95; affiliate faculty ACLS, 1988-95; assoc. examiner The Am. Bd. Surgery, 1990, 94, 96; trauma adv. com. Ohio Emergency Med. Svcs. Bd., 1993-2000. Editor-in-chief: The Mont Reid Handbook, The University of Cincinnati Surgical Manual, 1987; editl. bd. mem. Current Summaries in the Jour. Parenteral and Enteral Nutrition, 1991-97; contbr. chpts. to books and articles to profl. jours. Bd. mem. Yavneh Day Sch., Cin., 1992-95. Fellow ACS (com. on trauma, instr. advanced trauma life support 1987—, Ohio chpt. chmn. resident essay contest 1994—, sec. Ohio chpt. 1997-2000, chair local arrangements 1996 annual meeting); mem. Am. Soc. for Parenteral and Enteral Nutrition (liaison com. 1993-95), Am. Trauma Soc., Assn. for Acad. Surgery (com. on edn. 1989-91, nominating com. 1992, com. on issues 1992-94, councilor 1994-96), Assn. for Surg. Edn., Ctrl. Surg. Assn. (sec.

2006-2009), Cin. Acad. Medicine, Cin. Surg. Soc. (treas. 1990-92), Collegium Interatn. Chirurgia Digestivae, Mont Reid Surg. Soc. U. Cin., Ohio Soc. for Parenteral and Enteral Nutrition (dir.-at-large 1990, pres.-elect 1991, pres. 1991-92), Ohio State Med. Assn., Pancreas Club, Inc., Soc. Am. Gastrointestinal Endoscopic Surgeons (resident edn. com. 1998—, rsch. com. 2001—, membership com. 2001—), Soc. Critical Care Medicine, Soc. for Parenteral Alimentation, Soc. for Surgery of the Alimentary Tract, Surg. Infection Soc., Soc. Univ. Surgeons (com. on surg. edn. 1998-2002, chair 1999-2002), Am. Surg. Assn., Halsted Soc., Alpha Omega Alpha. Office: Univ Cin Dept Surgery PO Box 670558 231 Albert Sabin Way Cincinnati OH 45267-0558 Office Phone: 513-558-4014. E-mail: nussbaums@ucmail.uc.edu.

**NUSSBAUM, MICHEL ERNEST,** physician; b. LA, Nov. 7, 1947; s. Schymen and Jeannette Eleanor (Pequignot) N.; m. Joyce Wendy Laudon, Nov. 1, 1981; children: Eleanor, Anna. BA, Cornell U., 1969; MD, Free U. Brussels, 1977. Intern internal medicine NY Hosp. Queens, Flushing, 1977-78, resident, 1978-80, fellow gastroenterology, 1980-82, attending physician, 1982—; physician pvt. practice, Flushing, NY, 1982—; attending physician Flushing Hosp. Med. Ctr., 1987—; clin. instr. medicine Weill Med. Coll. Cornell U., N.Y.C., 1994-98, clin. asst. prof. medicine, 1998—; med. dir. Franklin Ctr. for Nursing and Rehab., Flushing, 1995-99. Dir. endoscopic svcs. N.Y. Hosp. Queens, 1990—, asst. dir. gastroenterology, 1998-2004, assoc. dir. gastroenterology, 2004—, pres. med. staff soc., 1992-96, chmn. med. bd., 1997-2003, trustee, 1998-2003 Fellow: ACP, Am. Gastroent. Assn., Am. Coll. Gastroenterology. Office: 142-43 Booth Memorial Ave Flushing NY 11355-5343 Office Phone: 718-886-1919.

**NUSSBAUM, PAUL STOWELL,** retired urologist; b. St. Louis, Mo., Sept. 25, 1930; s. Paul Beckman and Claire Stevenson Nussbaum; m. Joyce Lee Linebarger, May 21, 1955; children: Paul Stevenson, John Michael, David Matthew, Barbara Lee. Academic diploma, Castle Heights Mil. Acad., Lebanon, Tenn., 1948; AB in Biol. Scis., S.E. Mo. State Coll., Cape Girardeau, 1952; MD, U. Tenn. Coll. Medicine, Memphis, 1955. Cert. Am. Bd. Urology. Chief urology U.S. Army Hosp., Ft. Leonard Wood, Mo., 1961—64; pvt. practice urology Cape Girardeau, Mo., 1965—67; program dir. urology Scott White Meml. Hosp., Temple, Tex., 1967—77; pvt. practice urology Santa Fe, 1977—87; ret. Cons. urology U.S. Vets. Adminstrn., Marion, Ill., 1965—69, Temple, Tex., 1969—77. Author: (med. jour.) Surgery, Gynecology and Obstetrics. Maj. U.S. Army, 1957—64. Fellow: ACS; mem.: Am. Urol. Assn. (sr.), Masonic, Scottish Rite, Order of Ea. Star (Santa Fe #19, Past Patron). Republican. Methodist. Avocations: flying, hunting, fishing, sailing, golf. Home: 102 Pinehurst Meadowlakes TX 78654-6416

**NUSSBAUM, SAMUEL,** healthcare insurance company executive, medical educator; MD, Mt. Sinai Sch. Medicine. CEO health plan, pres. med. grp. BJC Health Sys., exec. v.p. med. affairs and sys. integration; positions to exec. v.p., chief med. officer Anthem, Inc., 2001—04; exec. v.p., chief med. officer WellPoint, Inc. Chmn. Nat. Com. Quality Health Care; chair Chief Med. Officer Leadership Coun. Am.'s Health Ins. Plan, bd. mem.; chmn. health care data and quality subcommittee Inst. Commn. on Excellence in Health Care; prof. clin. medicine Washington U. Sch. Medicine; adj. prof. Washington U. Olin Sch. Bus. Recipient Physician Exec. Award of Excellence, Am. Coll. Physician Execs. and Modern Physician mag., 2004. Mem.: Disease Mgmt. Assn. Am. Office: WellPoint Inc 120 Monument Cir Indianapolis IN 46204*

**NUSSLE, JAMES ALLEN,** congressman; b. Des Moines, June 27, 1960; s. Mark S. and Lorna Kay (Fisher) N.; m. Leslie J. Harbison, Aug. 23, 1986 (div. 1996); children: Sarah, Mark; m. Karen Chiccehitto. BA, Luther Coll., Decorah, Iowa, 1983; JD, Drake U., 1985. Bar: Iowa 1985. Pvt. practice law, Manchester, Iowa, 1986; states atty. Delaware County Atty., Manchester, 1986-90; mem. US Congress from 2d Iowa dist., Washington, 1991—, mem. house ways and means com., chmn. house budget com. Republican. Lutheran. Avocation: guitar. Office: US Ho Reps 303 Cannon Ho Office Bldg Washington DC 20515-1501 Office Phone: 202-225-2911. Office Fax: 202-225-5051.*

**NÜSSLEIN-VOLHARD, CHRISTIANE,** medical researcher; b. Magdeburg, Germany, Oct. 20, 1942; d. Rolf Volhard and Brigitte (Haas) Volhard. Diploma in Biochemistry, U. Tübingen, 1968, PhD, 1973; ScD (hon.), Yale U. Rsch. assoc. lab. of Dr. Schaller Max-Planck Inst. for Devel. Biology, Tübingen, 1972-74; postdoctoral fellow lab. of Dr. W. Gehring, Biozentrum, Basel, Switzerland, 1975-76; postdoctoral fellow lab of Dr. K. Sander U. Freiburg, 1977; head rsch. group European Molecular Biology Lab., Heidelberg, 1978-80; rsch. group leader Friedrich-Miescher Lab. Max-Planck-Gesellschaft, Tübingen, 1981-85; sci. mem. Max-Planck Assn., dir. Max-Planck Inst. for Devel. Biology, Tübingen, 1985-90, dir. genetics dept., 1990—. Hon. prof. U. Tübingen. Contbr. numerous articles to profl. jours. Recipient Albert Lasker Basic Med. Rsch. award Albert and Mary Lasker Found., 1991, Louisa Gross Horowitz prize Columbia U., 1992, Forderpreis award Deutschen Forschungsgemeinschaft, 1986, Franz Vogt prize U. Giessen, 1986, Carus medal German Acad. Leopoldine, 1989, Schering prize, Berlin, 1993, Rosenstiel medal Brandeis U., Nobel prize in physiology or medicine, 1995, L'oréal-UNESCO Tribute award (for UNESCO's 60th anniversary), 2006. Mem. European Molecular Biology Orgn., Berlin Brandenburgische Acad., Am. Philosophical Soc. Achievements include rsch. in using embryos, created a series of genetic screens that led to the identification of most of the genes responsible for the organism's body segment development, establishing that genes encode signaling molecules that tell cells where they are in the organism's overall structure and what their function is to be. Office: Max-Planck-Institut fur Entwicklungsbiologie Abt III Genetik D-72076 Tübingen Germany*

**NUSUM, JOHN BARRY,** professional soccer player; b. Mineola, NY, Mar. 18, 1981; s. John (former pro. soccer player, MISL and NASL) and Ellvera (Robinson) N. Grad. in Health and Exercise sci., Furman U., Greenville, SC, 2002. Forward Men's Soccer Team, Furman U., 1998—2002, Bermuda Nat. Team, 1999—. Mem. Umbro Select All-Star Classic, Ft. Lauderdale, Fla., 2000—01. Named first team All-American, NSCAA, 1999, 2000, All-Southern Conf. Player of Yr., 2001; recipient first team All-American, NSCAA, 2001, Finalist, Hermann Trophy, MO Athletic Club, 2001, Finalist, Player of Yr. award, 2001. 22nd player in the NCAA history to earn 2 First-team All-American Citations; All-time leader in points (161), Men's Soccer, Furman U., 2001; All-time leader in goals (61), Men's Soccer, Furman U., 2001. Office: Major League Soccer 110 East 42nd St 10th Fl New York NY 10017

**NUTBEAN, LEE,** multimedia designer, educator; b. Plymouth, Devon, Eng., June 4, 1971; s. James Alfred Nutbean and Vanessa Hooper; m. Neda Marefat Nutbean. B in Engring., U. Plymouth, 1996, BSc in Media Lab Arts with honors, 2000. Multimedia lectr. Plymouth Coll. Art and Design, 2000—; digital installation artist Submerge, Bristol, England, 2000—. Exhibitions include Port Elliot Lit Festival, 2005. Mem.: Brit. Interactive Media Assn. Personal E-mail: datahedz@o2.co.uk.

**NUTI, WILLIAM R.,** computer services company executive; married; 1 child. BS in Fin. and Economics, Long Island U., 1986. Various sales positions to sr. sales staff mem. IBM, 1982—88; sales mgr. Network Equipment Technologies, 1988—90, Netrix Corp., 1990—92; with Cisco Systems, 1992—2002, v.p. then pres. Greater Asia Pacific region, sr. v.p. Europe, Middle East and Africa ops. London, 1999—2001, sr. v.p. worldwide service provider bus. and US theatre ops. 2001—02; pres., COO Symbol Tech., Holtsville, NY, 2002—03, pres., CEO, 2003—05; pres. & CEO NCR Corp., Dayton, Ohio, 2005—. Bd. dirs. Opus 360, 1999—. Bd. dir. Fair Media Council; trustee Long Island U. Office: NCR Corp 1700 S Patterson Blvd Dayton OH 45479*

**NUTT, AMY ELLIS,** journalist; BA in English and Philosophy, Smith Coll., Mass.; MS in Philosophy, MIT; MS in Journalism, Columbia U. Feature writer The Star-Ledger, 1997—. Recipient non-deadline writing award, Am. Soc. Newspaper Editors, 2003, Science Journalism award, AAAS, 2004; Nieman Fellow, Harvard U., 2005. Office: Star-Ledger 1 Star Ledger Plz Newark NJ 07102-1200 Office Phone: 973-392-1794. Business E-Mail: anutt@starledger.com.

**NUTT, ROBERT L.,** lawyer, educator; b. New Castle, Pa., Mar. 30, 1945; s. James Earl and Dorothy Nutt; children: David, Jonathan. BA, Grove City Coll., 1967; JD, U. Pa., 1970. Bar: N.Y., Mass. Law clerk U.S. Ct. Appeals (2d cir.), N.Y.C., 1970-71; assoc. Ropes & Gray, Boston, 1971-79, ptnr., 1979—. Lectr. in law Boston U., 1989-98. Contbr. articles to profl. jours. Trustee Shore County Day Sch., Beverly, Mass., 1986-2001; moderator First Ch. of Christ, Marblehead, Mass., 1993-2000; trustee Grove City Coll., 1998—. Mem. ABA (bus. law sect. sec. com. on corp. laws), Boston Bar Assn. (bus. law sect. chair 1990-93). Congregationalist. Avocations: skiing, golf, upland bird hunting. Office: Ropes & Gray LLP One International Pl Boston MA 02110-2624 Office Phone: 617-951-7384. Business E-Mail: rnutt@ropesgray.com.

**NUTT, SANDRA KAY,** elementary school educator; b. Ashland, Wis., Dec. 3, 1955; d. Arthur Arnold and Myra Marie Riemer; m. Rickard Lee Nutt, June 14, 1975; children: Bonnie Lee, Katy Lynn. BA, Northland Coll., 1976; MS in Tchg. Reading, U. Wis., Superior, 1981. Cert. K-8 tchr. Wis., reading tchr. Wis. Kindergarten tchr. Mellen (Wis.) Sch. Dist., 1980—82; tchr. Ashland (Wis.) Sch. Dist., 1977—79; tchr. grades 1-2 South Shore Sch. Dist., Herbster, Wis., 1979—80; tchr. grades kindergarten, 1 and 6 Ondossagon Pub. Schs., Ashland, 1982—90; 1st grade tchr. Washburn (Wis.) Pub. Schools, 1990—, Title 1 and sage tchr., 2003—05. Adj. faculty mem. Northland Coll., Ashland, 1982—83; home trainer United Cerebral Palsy, Superior, 1978—79. Leader Brunswillow Busy Beavers 4-H Club, Marengo, Wis., 1988—2006; communicator Thrivent Fin. for Lutherans, Ashland, 2000—06; pres. and ch. rep. Luth. Brotherhood, Ashland, 1984—2000; advisor to youth group Zion Luth. Ch., Ashland, 2002—06, sec. ch. coun., mem. evangeliam bd., Sunday sch. tchr.,vacation bible sch. tchr. Named Fraser Tchr. of Yr., Washburn Sch. Dist., 1993, Vol. of Yr., Ashland County 4-H Parent Leader Orgn., 2004—05, Thrivent Fin. Vol. Yr., Luths. Northwoods, Superior Shores Chpt., Wis., 2005; recipient Thrivent Fin. Vol. Yr. award, Luth. Northwoods, Wis., 2006. Mem.: Washburn Edn. Assn. (treas. 2002—04), Wis. State Reading Assn., Internat. Reading Assn. Lutheran. Avocations: travel, hosting exchange students. Office: Washburn Pub Schs 411 W 8th St Washburn WI 54891 Office Phone: 715-373-6199.

**NUTTALL, RICHARD NORRIS,** management consultant, physician; b. Hamilton, Ont., Can., Feb. 7, 1940; s. James William and Margaret Gay (Walsh) N.; m. Ethel Jane Pickering, July 9, 1977; children: Andrew Richard, John Patrick. BSA, U. Toronto, 1961; MPA, Harvard U., 1964; MB, BS, U. London, 1974; TM, MPH, James Cook U., 2003; MCs, U. Western Ont., 2005. Cert. mgmt. cons. Zone dir. Health and Welfare Can., Prince Rupert, B.C., 1977-79, regional dir. Edmonton, Alta., 1980-82; pres. Rutland Consulting Group, Ltd., Vancouver, B.C., Canada, 1982-87, Richmond Assocs. Internat., Vancouver, 1988-90; med. health officer Govt. N.W. Ters., Yellowknife, B.C., Inc., Victoria, Canada, 1997—. Staff physician Royal Jubilee Hosp., Victoria Gen. Hosp. Fellow Am. Coll. Preventive Medicine, Am. Coll. Healthcare Execs., Can. Coll. Health Svc. Execs., Coll. Family Physicians Can. Office: 1494 Fairfield Rd Victoria BC Canada V8S 1E8 Office Phone: 250-598-5158.

**NUTTER, CAROL ANGELL,** academic librarian; b. Hinton, W.Va., Aug. 13, 1948; d. Woodrow Wilson and Sadie Eileen (Yancey) Angell; m. David Henan Nutter, May 31, 1969; children: Jon David, Matthew Jay. MS in Libr. Sci., Univ. Ky., 1978; MA, Morehead State Univ., 1984. Interlibr. loan librarian Camden-Carroll Libr. Morehead State Univ., Morehead, Ky., 1976-78, coord. reg. libr. svcs., 1978-86, reference librarian, 1986-89, head, reference dept., 1989—, asst. dir. pub. svcs., 2001—05, asst. dean for pub. svcs., 2005—. Mem. Am. Libr. Assn., Ky. Libr. Assn. (pres. 2004), Ky. Libr. Assn. Acad. Libr. Sect. (chair 2000-01), Ky. Libr. Assn. Libr. Instruction Roundtable (chair 1991-92). Avocations: singing, song writer. Office: Camden Carroll Libr Morehead State Univ Morehead KY 40351 Office Phone: 606-783-5110. Business E-Mail: c.nutter@moreheadstate.edu.

**NUTTER, DAVID GEORGE,** city planner; b. Manchester, Conn., Nov. 25, 1939; s. George Huitt and Catherine Lavina (Casey) N.; m. Ellen Marie Manfredonia, Sept. 7, 1968; children: Susan Katherine Bailey, Anne Amelia. BA in English cum laude, Tufts U., 1961; MS in Urban Planning, Columbia U., 1967. City planner Balt. City Planning Commn., 1967-69; dir. planning Charles Ctr.- Inner Harbor Mgmt., Inc., 1969-72, v.p., 1972-76; pvt. cons., 1976-83; dir. downtown mall mgmt. dist. Denver Partnership, Inc., 1983-85; exec. dir. Rochester Downtown Devel. Corp., NY, 1985-87; prin. Nutter Assocs., 1987-2000; dir. Salisbury-Wicomico Planning and Zoning Commn., Md., 2000—02; prin. Nutter Assocs., 2002—. Author: Selecting a Developer, 1983, Vienna-on-the-Nanticoke: The 2003 Greater Vienna Comprehensive Plan, 2003, Laurel of Delaware: The 2004 Greater Laurel Comprehensive Plan, 2004, Ellendale of the Forest:The 2004 Greater Ellendale Comprehensive Plan, 2004. Bd. dirs. Soc. Preservation of Fed. Hill, Balt., 1969-73, Arts for Greater Rochester, 1990-96, Nabb Rsch. Ctr. Delmarva History and Culture, Salisbury (Md.) U., 1998-2003, Lower Eastern Shore Heritage Com., 2000-2002; chmn. Town of Brighton (NY) Conservation Bd., 1992-95. Sgt. U.S. Army, 513th Army Intelligence Corps, 1962-65, Germany William F. Kinne fellow for travel in Europe, Columbia U., 1967. Mem. Am. Inst. Cert. Planners, Am. Planning Assn., Urban Land Inst. (assoc.). Nat. Hist. Trust, Chesapeake Bay Found., Canal Soc. of N.Y. State. Avocations: historical map and atlas collecting, American English and World history, hiking, swimming, travel. Home: 507C South Blvd Salisbury MD 21801 Office Phone: 443-260-2760. Personal E-mail: dnutter@aol.com.

**NUTTER, SUSAN K.,** librarian, academic administrator; b. Boston, Aug. 9, 1944; m. Joe Hewitt, 1982; stepchildren: Kirsten Elizabeth Hewitt(dec.), Stephen A. Hewitt. BS, Colby Coll., 1966; MLIS, Simmons Coll., 1968. Libr. intern to libr. Project INTREX MIT, 1966—73, assoc. head engring. libraries, assoc. dir. libraries collection mgmt. and technol. services, 1980—87; Coun. on Libr. Resources Academic Libr. Mgmt. Intern U. NC, Chapel Hill, 1979—80; dir. libraries NC State U., Raleigh, 1987—, vice provost, 1995—. Mem. steering com. NC Libraries for Virtual Edn. (NC LIVE); mem. exec. com., governing bd. Triangle Rsch. Libraries Network. Named Libr. of Yr., Libr. Jour., 2005; recipient Alumni Achievement Award, Simmons Coll., 1995, Hugh C. Atkinson Meml. Medal, Assn. College & Rsch. Libraries, 1999. Mem.: Assn. Rsch. Libraries (pres. 1993-1999). Office: DH Hill Libr NC State U Campus Box 7111 Raleigh NC 27695-7111 Office Phone: 919-515-7188. Business E-Mail: susan_nutter@ncsu.edu.*

**NUTTER, ZOE DELL LANTIS,** retired public relations executive; b. Yamhill, Oreg., June 14, 1915; d. Arthur Lee Lantis and Olive Adelaide (Reed) Lantis-Hilton; m. Richard S. West, Apr. 30, 1941 (div. Nov. 1964); m. Ervin John Nutter, Dec. 30, 1965. Assoc. in Bus., Santa Ana Jr. Coll., 1944. Cert. spl. emergency secondary tchr., Calif.; FAA cert. lic. commercial, instrument, single/multi engine land airplanes pilot. Promoter World's Fair & Comml. Airlines Golden Gate Internat. Expn., San Francisco, 1937-39; pirate theme girl, official hostess Treasure Island's World Fair, San Francisco, 1939-40; prin. dancer San Francisco Ballet, 1937-41; artist, 1941-45; program dir. Glenn County H.S., Willows, Calif., 1952-58; pub. rels. Monarch Piper Aviation Co., Monterey, Calif., 1963-65; pilot, pub. rels. Elano Corp., Xenia, Ohio, 1968-85. Bd. dirs. Nat. Aviation Hall of Fame, Dayton, Ohio, pres., chmn., 1989-92, bd. trustees, 1976—, chmn. bd. nominations, 1992—; bd. trustees Ford's Theatre, Washington, Treasure Island Mus., San Francisco; charter mem. Friends of First Ladies, Smithsonian, Washington, 1990-93. Assoc. editor KYH mag. of Shikar Safari Internat., 1985-87; contbg. columnist Scripps Howard San Francisco News, 1938. Bd. dirs. Cin. May

Festival, 1976-80, San Francisco Aero. Soc., 1997-; cen. com. Glenn County Rep. Party, Willows, 1960-64; state cen. com. Rep. Party, 1962-64; adv. bd. Women's Air & Space Mus., Dayton, 1987-94. Warrant officer, Civil Air Patrol, 1967-69. Recipient Civic Contbn. Honor award Big Brothers/Big Sisters, 1991, John Collier Nat. award Camp Fire Girls & Boys, 1988, Tambourine award Salvation Army, 1982, State of Ohio Gov.'s award for Volunteerism, 1992, Spirit of Innovation award Wright State U., 2001, Amb. award Wright Bros. Heritage Benefit, 2001, East Ann. Zoe Dell Nutter Dayton Air Show award, 2003. In grateful appreciation of contbn. 1909 Wright Flyer Monument award Inventing Flight (orgn. charted by Congress), 2003, Deeds-Kettering award Outstanding Contbn., Engrs. CLub Dayton, 2004; named Most Photographed Girl in World, News Burs. & Clipping Svcs., 1938-39. Mem., founder Dancers Over 40, NYC; Fellow Pres.'s Club U. Ky., Ohio State U., Wright State U.; mem. 99's Internat. Women Pilots Orgn. (life, hospitality chmn. 1968), San Francisco Aeronaut. Soc. (bd. dirs. 1997—), Monterey Bay Chapter 99's (mem. chmn. 1964-65), Walnut Grove Country Club, Rotary (Paul Harris fellow 1987), Shikar Safari Internat. (host com. 1976), Country Club of the North. Achievements include established ann. Zoe Dell Nutter Dayton Air Show award, 2003. Avocations: aviation, flying, horseback riding, hunting, shooting, fashion. Home: 986 Trebein Rd Xenia OH 45385-9534

**NUTTING, MAUREEN MURPHY,** historian, educator; b. NYC; d. Patrick Joseph and Marie (Clarke) Murphy; m. Theodore Michael Nutting, May 3 1975; children: Teresa, Andrew, Stephen, Eileen. BA in History, Fordham U., 1968; MA in Am. Studies, U. Notre Dame, 1969, PhD in History, 1975. Asst. prof. history Humboldt State U., Arcata, Calif., 1972—75, Chaminade U., Honolulu, 1975—77; asst. dir. minorities & women's scholarly & profl. interests Am. Hist. Assn., Washington, 1979—81; asst. prof. history U. Miami, Coral Gables, Fla., 1987—90, Seattle U., 1990—91; instr. history Seattle Ctrl. C.C., 1992—96; prof. history, chair North Seattle C.C., 1996—. Vol. Seattle Pub. Sch. Dist., 1982—86, 1990—98; chair local draft bd. U.S. Selective Svc., Seattle, 1998—, local draft bd., 1992—; trustee Nat. History Ctr., 2004—; vol. homeless ministry St. James Cathedral, Seattle, 1994—; bd. dirs. HistoryLink.org, 2005—. Rsch. Travel grant Asian Studies Devel. Program, East-West Ctr., China, 1996, India, 1995, Summer Inst. grant NEH, Hawaii, 1994, Brazil, 1998, Guatemala, Honduras and Mex., 2002, Trustees' Lifetime Learning award Seattle C.C. Dist., 1999; selected rsch. seminar Libr. of Congress, Am. Hist. Assn., C.C. Humanities Assn., Washington, 1999. Mem.: Coordinating Coun. for Women's History, We. Assn. Women Historians, Immigration and Ethnic History Soc. (program com. 1999—2002), C.C. Humanities Assn. (chair nat. conf. program 2001, Disting. Humanities Educator award 2005), Orgn. Am. Historians (com. on cmty.colls. 2006—), Am. Hist. Assn. (mem. coun. 2001—04, task force on pub. history 2001—, nat. history ctr. bd. 2004—, chair ann. meeting local arrangements com. 2005). Roman Catholic. Office: North Seattle CC 9600 College Way N Seattle WA 98103-3514 Office Phone: 206-526-7010. Business E-Mail: mnutting@sccd.ctc.edu.

**NUTZLE, FUTZIE (BRUCE JOHN KLEINSMITH),** artist, writer, animator; b. Lakewood, Ohio, Feb. 21, 1942; s. Adrian Ralph and Naomi Irene (Rupert) Kleinsmith; children: Adrian David, Arielle Justine and Tess Alexandra (twins); m. Halina Renatta Kleinsmith. Author: Modern Loafer, Thames and Hudson, 1981, (autobiography) Futzie Nutzle, 1983, Earthquake, 1989, Run the World: 50 Cents Chronicle Books, 1991; illustrator: The Armies Encamped Beyond Unfinished Avenues (Morton Marcus), 1977, Box of Nothing, 1982, The Duke of Chemical Birds (Howard McCord), 1989, Book of Solutions, 1990, Fact and Friction, 1990, Managing for the 90s, 1992, Soundbites for Success, 1994; feature cartoonist Rolling Stone, N.Y.C., 1975-80, The Japan Times, Tokyo and L.A., 1986-98, The Prague Post, Czechoslovakia, 1991-92; contbr. exhbns. include Inaugural, 1966, Cupola, 1967, Rolling Renaissance, San Francisco, 1968, 100 Acres, O.K. Harris 1971, N.Y.C., San Francisco Mus. Art, 1972, Indpls. and Cin. Mus. Art, 1975, Leica, L.A., 1978, Santa Barbara Mus. Annex, Calif., 1978, Swope, Santa Monica, West Beach Cafe, Venice, Calif., 1985, Les Oranges, Santa Monica, Correspondence Sch., NY Correspondence Sch., 1968-75, 1st Ann. Art-A-Thon, N.Y.C., 1985, Am. Epiphany with Phillip Hefferton, 1986, Polit. Cartoon Show, Braunstein, San Francisco, Komsomolskaya Pravda, 1988, retrospective Eloise Packard Smith, 1990, exemplary contemporary, Cowell, U. Calif. Santa Cruz, 1991, Silicon Graphics Inc., Computer Graphics for NAB, Las Vegas, 1993, Prague Eco-Fair, 1991; represented in pvt. and pub. collections (complete archives) Spl. Collections, McHenry Libr., U. Calif., Santa Cruz, Mus. Modern Art, N.Y.C., San Francisco Mus. Modern Art, Oakland Mus., San Francisco Mus. Cartoon Art, Whitney Mus. Am. Art, N.Y.C., Aromas (Calif.) Libr., San Juan Batista Libr. Address: Fools Gold 34A Polk St San Juan Bautista CA 95045 Office Phone: 831-623-9275. Personal E-mail: fnutzle@aol.com.

**NUVEMAN, STACEY,** Olympic athlete; b. Apr. 26, 1978; BA in Sociology, UCLA. Commentator Women's Coll. World Series, ESPN, 2003; mem. U.S. Women's Softball Team, Sydney Olympic Games, 2000, U.S. Women's Softball Team, Athens Olympic Games, 2004. Named NFCA/ Diamond Sports Div. I Catcher of the Yr., 2001, USA Softball Collegiate Player of the Yr., 2002, USA Softball Player of the Yr., 2002, Pac-10 Newcomer of the Yr., 1997, NFCA First-team All Am., 1997, 1999, 2001, 2002; named to All WCWS Tournament Team, 1997, 2002. Achievements include mem. NCAA Champion UCLA Bruins, Women's Coll. World Series, 1999; NCAA all-time career leader in home runs (90) and slugging percentage (.945); mem. Gold medal U.S. Nat. Team, ISF World Championships, 2003; second player in history named Pac-10 player of the yr. three times; mem. Gold medal U.S. Nat. Team, U.S. Cup, 2002; mem. Gold medal U.S. Nat. Team, Pan Am. Games, 1999, 2003; mem. U.S. Women's Softball Gold medal Team, Sydney Olympics, 2000.

**NUWER, HENRY JOSEPH (HANK NUWER),** journalist, educator; b. Buffalo, Aug. 19, 1946; s. Henry Robert and Teresa (Lysiak) N.; m. Alice May (Cerniglia), Dec. 28, 1968 (div. Mar. 1980); 1 child, Henry Christian; m. Jenine (Howard), Apr. 9, 1982 (div. 2004); 1 child, Adam.:m. Lizabeth Klein, Aug. 9, 2005. BS in English, SUNY, Buffalo, 1968; MA in English, Highlands U., 1971; PhD Equivalency, Ball State U., 1988; DHL, State Univ. Coll. NY, Buffalo, 2006. H.S. tchr., NY, 1968—69, N.Mex., 1970—71; freelance author, journalist, 1969—; asst. prof. Clemson U., SC, 1982—83; assoc. prof. Ball State U., Muncie, Ind., 1985—89; sr. editor Rodale Press, Emmaus, Pa., 1990—91; editor in chief Arts Ind. Mag., Indpls., 1993—95; assoc. prof. journalism U. Richmond, Va., 1995—97. Expert lectr. hazing, 1990—; hazing cons. NBC Movie-of-the-Week, Moment of Truth: Broken Pledges, Indpls., 1994, U.S. Dept. Edn., 2002—; adj. prof. journalism Ind. U. Sch. Journalism, Indpls., 1995—; Anderson U., 1998-2002; asst. prof. journalism, Franklin (Ind.) Coll., 2002—; nat. advisor NCAA study and survey on hazing in coll. athletic groups Alfred U., 1999. *Known internationally for his writings on hazing as a social problem, Hank Nuwer has lectured on hazing at U.S. universities such as Cornell, Dartmouth, Illinois, and Dartmouth. Expelled from high school and unruly as a young adult, he turned his life around and became a serious freelance journalist, educator, and author. As an educator, he is devoted to fraternity reform, a free student press and to helping at-risk youths with writing talent. His TV appearances include CNN Headline News, NBC Nightly News and ABC 20/20. His work recently cited internationally on BBC and in Die Zeit, New York Times, Newsweek, Sports Illustrated and U.S. News and World Report.* Author: Steroids, 1990, Broken Pledges: The Deadly Rite of Hazing, 1990; How to Write Like an Expert, 1995; The Legend of Jesse Owens, 1998; Wrongs of Passage, 1999, rev. edit., 2002; High School Hazing, 2000, To the Young Writer, 2002, The Hazing Reader, 2003, At the Crest, 2004; mem. editl. staff Reporter Dispatch, 1969-70, Chic Mag., 1976-77; contbr. articles to profl. jour. Grantee: Nat. Endowment for the Arts, 1976; Idaho Humanities Coun., 1985; Gannett Found., 1988; named New Mag. Adviser of Yr., Coll. Media Advisers, 1988; Disting. Alumnus, Buffalo State Coll., 1999. Mem.: Investigative Reporters and Editors, Soc. Profl. Journalists (3d pl. Best Bus. Article Ind. competition 2002), Alpha Lambda

Delta, Phi Kappa Phi. Democrat. Roman Catholic. Office: Franklin Coll Journalism Dept 101Branigin Blvd Franklin IN 46131-2598 also: Ind Univ Sch Journalism 902 W New York St ES 4104 Indianapolis IN 46202 Business E-Mail: hnuwer@hanknuwer.com.

**NUZUM, ROBERT WESTON,** lawyer; b. Evanston, Ill., Dec. 11, 1952; s. John Weston and Janet Marie (Talbot) N.; m. Julia Ann Abadie, Sept. 16, 1983. BS in Fin., La. State U., 1974, JD, 1977; LLM in Taxation, N.Y.U., 1978. Bar: La. 1977, D.C. 1979. Assoc. Office Chief Counsel, Washington, 1978-81, Jones, Walker, Waechter, Poitevent, Carrere & Denegre, New Orleans, 1981-85; ptnr. Jones, Walker, Waechter, Potevent, Carrere & Denegre, New Orleans, 1985-88, Deutsch, Kerrigan & Stiles, New Orleans, 1988-89, Phelps Dunbar, L.L.P. and predecessor firm, New Orleans, 1989—2003, Baker, Donelson, Bearman, Caldwell and Berkowitz, 2003—. Prof. law, state and local taxation Tulane U. Sch. Law, New Orleans, 1998—. Editor La. Law Rev., 1977; contbr. articles to profl. jours. Wallace scholar N.Y.U., 1978. Mem.: Tulane Tax Inst. (planning com. 1993—, tax specialization adv. commn.), New Orleans Bar Assn. (chmn. tax sect. 2001—), La. Bar Assn. (program chmn. tax sect. 1992—93, sec.-treas. 1993—94, vice chmn. 1994—95, chmn. 1995—96), Order of Coif. Republican. Roman Catholic. Avocations: golf, reading, fishing. Office: Baker Donelson Ste 3600 201 St Charles Ave New Orleans LA 70170 Business E-Mail: law@robertnuzum.com. E-mail: nuzumr@bellsouth.net.

**NUZZO, ANTHONY GERALD,** bank executive; b. New Haven, Aug. 9, 1951; s. Michael Anthony and Theresa Mary (Aitro) N.; m. Julie Nuzzo, Mar. 22, 1975; children: Beth, Michael, Cortney. BA, Boston Coll., 1973; MBA, Columbia U., 1975. CLU, cert. in long-term care. Brand asst. Procter & Gamble, Cin., 1975-76, sales rep., 1976, asst. brand mgr., 1976-77; asst. product dir. Johnson & Johnson, New Brunswick, NJ, 1977-78, spl. project dir., 1978-79, product dir. Milltown, NJ, 1979-82, group product dir., 1982-84; v.p. Am. Express Travel Related Svcs., NYC, 1984-87; v.p., exec. com. Am. Express Can., Inc., Markham, Ont., 1987-88; v.p. internat. mktg. Am. Express, NY, 1988; v.p. Chem. Bank, NYC, 1988-90, sr. v.p., 1990-91; pres., CEO Chem. Bank Del., Wilmington, 1991-92; pres., founder Advanced Mktg. Assocs., Inc., East Brunswick, NJ, 1992-93; pres., CEO Fidelity Trust Co., Salt Lake City, 1993-98, chmn., 1998-99; pres., CEO Fidelity TempWorks/TempSource, Boston, 1998-99; chmn., pres., CEO @Bank, Framingham, Mass., 1999-2000; pres., CEO Engage, Andover, Mass., 2000—01; pres., CEO, founder The Nuzzo Group, Inc., Wellesley, Mass., 2001—05; fin. adviser The Commonwealth Fin. Group, Newton, Mass., 2002—05; pvt. investor, mem. bd. dirs. Citizens Bank, Norwood, Mass., 2005—. Mem. Visa Mktg. Advisors, 1989—92, 1993—98. Editor: Physiology, 1984. Dir., co-chair, co-founder Citizens Against UnSafe Environments, East Brunswick, 1981-93; bd. dirs. Utah Bd. Fin. Instns., 1995-98. Named to PS&D Merchandising Hall of Fame Procter & Gamble, Cin., 1977, named Scholar of the Coll., Boston Coll., 1973; recipient Bus. Sch. Svc. award Columbia U., 1975, Excellence award Package Designer Coun., NYC, 1980, Clio Creative Excellence award Clio Adv. Body, NYC, 1981, Effie award, NYC, 1989. Mem. Boston Coll. Alumni Assn., Columbia Bus. Sch. Alumni Assn. (dir. NY club 1975), Utah Bankers Assn. (bd. dirs. 1996-98), Utah Assn. Fin. Svcs. (bd. dirs. 1993-98, treas. 1995-96). Avocations: golf, skiing, reading. E-mail: agnuzzo@aol.com.

**NWACHUKU, LEVI AKALAZU,** social sciences and behavioral studies educator; b. Okpala, Nigeria, Aug. 23, 1940; came to U.S., 1963; s. Moses Akalazu and Evangeline (Enwere-Uzo) N.; m. Ugochi Justina Nwachuku, Dec. 19, 1981; children: Uchenna, Nneka, Chimereze, Chinomso, Enyinna. BA, Lincoln U., Pa., 1967; MA, Howard U., 1969; PhD, Mich. State U., 1973. V.p. acad. Shorter Coll., Little Rock, 1977; assoc. prof. U. Mich., Flint, 1977-81, dir. Black studies, 1973-81; reader history U. Maiduguri, Nigeria, 1981-88; coord. African Am. studies Lincoln U., 1989-94, chair dept. history, 1993—, dean faculty social scis., 1994-97. Co-author: Troubled Journey: Nigeria Since the Civil War, 1994, Exploring the African-American Experience, 1995. Named Outstanding Male Faculty Mem., NAACP, 1995. Mem. Phi Alpha Theta, Alpha Phi Alpha. Home: PO Box 153 Lincoln University PA 19352-0153 Office: Lincoln U Lincoln University PA 19352

**NWAGBARAOCHA, JOEL ONUKWUGHA,** academic administrator, educator; b. Victoria, Cameroons, Nov. 21, 1942; came to U.S., 1964; naturalized, 1974; s. John O. and Christiana (Ihejeihu) N.; m. Patsy Coleman, Aug. 27, 1977; children: Jason, Jonathan, John, Eric. BS in Math., Norfolk State U., 1969, cert. in physics, 1969; EdM, Harvard U., 1970, EdD (Univ. fellow), 1972. Tchr. math. and physics Emmanuel Coll., Owerri, Nigeria, 1960-64; asst. dir. Manpower Rsch. Inst./Norfolk (Va.) State U., 1969-70; rsch. assoc. Harvard U. Grad. Sch. Edn., 1969-72; assoc. dir. co-op acad. planning program Inst. for Svcs. to Edn., Washington, 1972-74; dir. instnl. planning and mgmt. program, 1974-76, dir. divsn. acad. planning and faculty devel., 1976-78; assoc. prof. edn., v.p. planning and ops. analysis Morgan State U., Balt., 1978-87; v.p. acad. affairs Voorhees Coll., Denmark, S.C., 1987-80; pres. Barber-Scotia Coll., Concord, N.C., 1990-94; profl. edn., bus. adminstrn. Strayer U., Washingtn, 1994—, dir. grad. studies, 2000—02, dean grad. sch. Washington, 2005—. Dean Tacoma Park Campus, Strayer Coll., Washington; interim pres., Strayer U., 2006-; cons. in higher edn. planning and evaluation system devel., 1972—. Co-author: Operational Manual for ollege Planning Development, 1977, Planning Management and Evaluation System, 1979; mem. editl. bd. Spartan Echo, 1967-69; contbr. articles to profl. jours. Mem. AAAS, Am. Coun. on Edn., Nat. Coun. on Social Studies, Am. Assn. for Higher Edn., Am. Humanist Assn., Soc. for Coll. and Univ. Planning, Am. Assn. Univ. Adminstrs., Am. Mgmt. Assn., Higher Edn. Group of Washington, Smithsonian Nat. Assoc., Alpha Kappa Mu, Phi Beta Sigma, Beta Kappa Chi, Phi Delta Kappa. Home: 10928 Battersea Ln Columbia MD 21044-2701 Office: Strayer Univ Washington DC Campus 1133 15th St NW Washington DC 20005-2601 Business E-Mail: jon@strayer.edu.

**NWANGBURUKA, OKECHUKWU NKEM,** psychiatrist; b. Aba, Nigeria, Mar. 9, 1965; arrived in US, 1994; s. Joseph and Festa Nwangburuka; m. Iheoma B. Nwangburuka. MD, U. Maiduguri, Nigeria, 1988. Resident physician MCP/Hahnemann U. Hosps., Phila., 1995—98; clin. instr. Ohio State U., Columbus, 1998—2000; sr. psychiatrist Shasta County Mental Health, Redding, Calif., 2000—. Named Physician of the Yr., NRCC, 2005. Mem.: Nigeria Nat. Assn. USA, Central Calif. Acad. Child and Adolescent Psychiatry, Central Calif. Psychiatry Soc., North Valley Med. Assoc., Nigerian Med. Assn., Shasta Psychiat. Soc., Am. Acad. Child and Adolescent Psychiatry, Am. Psychiat. Assn. Office: Shasta County Mental Health 2640 Breslauer Way Redding CA 96001 Mailing: PO Box 493579 Redding CA 96049 Office Phone: 530-225-5200. Business E-Mail: onwangburuka@co.shasta.ca.us.

**NWOKOYE, PATRICK IKECHUKWU,** priest, researcher; b. Amawbia, Nigeria, Mar. 25, 1970; arrived in U.S., 1997; s. Anizoba and Nwakaego Nwokoye. BA, Lateran U., Rome, 1992, MA in Philosophy, 1994, PhD, 1997; MA, MDiv, Kenrick Sem. Theology, 2002. Ordained 2002. Clergy Diocese of Springfield-Cape Girardeau, Mo., 1997—. Tchr. Notre Dame H.S., Mo. 1999—2000; co-host talk show Raidue, Rome, 1995—96; parochial vicar Cathedral of St. Mary; chap. Notre Dame H.S.; Diocesan chap. for scouting. Youth dir. St. Mary Cathedral, Cape Girardeau, Mo., 1999—2000. Mem.: Internat. Lateran Assn., World Phenomenology Inst., Fellowship of Cath. Scholars. Roman Catholic. Avocations: soccer, ping pong/table tennis, basketball, ballet, hockey. E-mail: caritas@showme.net.

**NYBERG, ANNE MARIE,** secondary school educator; b. Grand Forks, ND, Dec. 8, 1953; d. George Wilford Blake and Kathryn Louise Leidall; m. Rand Lee Nyberg, Nov. 25, 1983. BS in Secondary Edn., Valley City State U., 1975. Tchr. Robinson Pub. Sch., ND, 1975—78, Gackle Pub. Sch., ND, 1978—80, Dakota H.S., Arthur, ND, 1980—99, No. Cass Pub. Sch., Hunter, ND, 1999—. Recipient Cass County Farm Bur. Tchr. of Yr., Cass County of ND Farm Bur., 2002, ND Tchr. of Yr., 1997, Cass County of ND Speech and Theater Assn., 2004, Tchr. of Yr., Dakota Sch. Dist., 1990, ND Speech Coach of the Yr., ND H.S. Activities Assn., 2002, Speech Coach of Yr., Region II, 1990, 1992, 1994, 1995, 1996, Play Dir. of Yr., 1990, 1999. Mem.: NEA, ND Reading Coun.,

ND Edn. Assn., Nat. Coun. Teachers of English, ND Speech and Theater Assn. (life). Roman Catholic. Avocations: reading, travel. Office: Northern Cass Pub Sch 16021 18th St SE Hunter ND 58048 Office Phone: 1-701-874-2322. Office Fax: 1-701-874-2422. E-mail: anne.nyberg@sendit.nodak.edu.

**NYBERG, DONALD ARVID,** oil industry executive; b. Ridgewood, N.J., Aug. 23, 1951; s. Arvid H. and Rita T. (Tenwick) N.; m. Susan Radis, Feb. 16, 1985; children: Matthew D., Ryan T. BA, St. Lawrence U., 1973; MBA, Harvard U., 1975. Mgr. marine ops. Standard Oil, L.A., 1982-83, mgr. ops. planning Cleve., 1984-85, dir. strategic studies, 1986; divsn. mgr. Brit. Petroleum, Ltd., London, 1987-88; v.p., gen. mgr. U.S. gas bus. BP Exploration, Houston, 1989, v.p., gen. mgr. tech., 1990, v.p. comml., 1991-94; pres., CEO BP Pipelines, Anchorage, 1991-94; pres. Marya Resources, Houston, 1994—; v.p. MAPCO, Tulsa, 1996; pres. Tesoro Marine Svcs., Houston, 1996—2003; CEO McDonough Marine, 2004—, bd. dirs., 2004—; CEO Champion Elevators, 2005—, bd. dirs., 2004—. Bd. dirs., exec. com. Boys and Girls Country Houston. Mem. Forest Club, Bentwater Country Club. Avocations: running, weightlifting, reading. Office: McDonough Corp 17500 Market St Channelview TX 77530 Office Phone: 281-452-5887. E-mail: dnyberg@marmac.net.

**NYBERG, STANLEY ERIC,** research scientist; b. Boston, Jan. 30, 1948; s. Leroy Milton and Anna Maria (Olson) N. PhD, SUNY, Stony Brook, 1975; MBA, Yale U., 1984. Postdoctoral fellow U. Calif., Berkeley, 1975-76; asst. prof. North Park Coll., Chgo., 1976-79, Barnard Coll., Columbia U., N.Y.C., 1979-82; sys. mgmt. Interactive Data Corp., Lexington, Mass., 1984-88, Dept. of Revenue, Commonwealth of Mass., Boston, 1988-2000; with Dept. of Environ. Protection, Commonwealth of Mass., 2000—01; registrar vital records and stats. Commonwealth of Mass., 2001—. Co-author: Human Memory: An Introduction to Research and Theory, 1982. Bd. dir. Childrens Home Cromwell, Conn., 1988-94, Decade Fund, Yale U. Sch. Mgmt., 1984-1985; ch. coun. Luth. Ch. of Redeemer, Woburn, Mass., 1991-1997, West Roxbury Rugby Football Club, 1984-1987; v.p., sec. L Street Running Club, South Boston, 1987—; mem. divsn. ecumenism New Eng. Synod, Evang. Luth. Ch. in Am., 1997—2002; bd. dir. Scandinavian Charitable Soc. Greater Boston, 2000—, v.p. 2002-2004, pres., 2004-06. Fellow Assn. Psychol. Sci.; mem. APA, Soc. Applied Rsch. in Memory and Cognition, Ea. Psychol. Assn., Midwestern Psychol. Assn. Personal E-mail: snyberg@aol.com.

**NYBORG, KENNETH WAYNE,** retired social sciences educator, small business owner; b. Mountain Lake, Minn., May 27, 1939; s. Lester C. and Clara E. Nyborg; m. Carol E. Nyborg; children: Glen, David, Solveig Kruse. BA, St. Olaf Coll., 1961; MSEd, Winona State U., 1970. Cert. life gen. secondary tchr. Calif. Tchr. Barstow (Calif.) Unified Sch. Dist., 1964—2002; bus. co-owner Nyborg's Music, Barstow, 1979—91. Dist. tech. lead Barstow Unified Sch. Dist., 1992—96; tech. lead Barstow H.S. 1994—98, dept. chair social studies, 1997—2001, co-chair WASC accreditation com., 1999—2001. Mem. Barstow C. of C., 1979—91. Named Small Bus. of Yr., Barstow C. of C., 1988, Tchr. of Yr., Barstow H.S., 2001. Mem.: Calif. Ret. Tchrs. Assn. (newsletter co-editor 2001—02). Lutheran. Avocations: reading, travel, golf, church choir, computers. Home: PO Box 1268 Barstow CA 92312-1268 Personal E-mail: knyb@hotmail.com.

**NYBORG, WESLEY LEMARS,** physics professor; b. Ruthven, Iowa, May 15, 1917; s. Isaac and Leva (Larson) N.; m. Beth Woolsey, Sept. 8, 1945; 1 dau., Elsa Beth. BA, Luther Coll., 1941; MS, Pa. State U., 1944, PhD, 1947. Asst. prof. physics Pa. State U., University Park, 1948-50; asst. prof. Brown U., Providence, 1950-54, asso. prof., 1954-60; prof. U. Vt., Burlington, 1960-86, acting chmn. physics dept., 1978-79, prof. emeritus, 1986—. Vis. scientist Oxford (Eng.) U., 1960-61, Univ. Coll., Cardiff, Wales, 1969, U. of Rochester, 1987; Exec. council Am. Inst. Ultrasound in Medicine, 1972-74, 76-78, chmn. bioeffects com., 1976-78; adv. bd. Bur. Radiol. Health, 1972-75; cons. FDA, 1976—; chmn. sci. com. 66 Nat. Council Radiation Protection and Measurements, 1980—; mem. working group on biol. effects ultrasound, WHO, 1982, 85, 88; mem. study sect. diagnostic radiology NIH, 1982-85; adv. mem. Rochester Ctr. for Biomed. Ultrasound, 1986; Lauriston S. Taylor lectr. Nat. Coun. Radiation Protection and Measurements, Bethesda, Md., 2001. Author: Intermediate Biophysical Mechanics, 1975; co-editor: Biological Effects of Ultrasound, 1985; Editorial bd.: Ultrasound in Medicine and Biology, Jour. Ultrasound in Medicine; internat. adv. editor: Ultrasonics; co-editor Proc. Symposium on Safety and Standardization in Med. Ultrasound, 2d World Fedn. Ultrasound in Medicine and Biology, 1989; contbr. to profl. jours. Recipient Presdl. recognition award Am. Inst. Ultrasound in Medicine, 1977, Univ. scholar award in physics. sci. U. Vt., 1984, Disting. Svc. award Luther Coll., 1996, Vt. Acad. Sci. and Engring., 1997, Lauriston S. Taylor Lectr. award 2001, P.P. Lele award, 5th Internat. Symposium, 2005; USPHS fellow MIT, 1956-57; research grantee NIH, 1955—. Fellow AAAS, Acoustical Soc. Am. (exec. coun. 1965-68, Silver medal 1990), Am. Inst. Ultrasound in Medicine (Joseph H. Holmes award 1985, W.J. Fry Lecture award 1990), Ultrasonic Soc. India (hon.); mem. NAS, Nat. Acad. Engrs., Am. Phys. Soc., Biophys. Soc., Am. Assn. Physics Tchrs., Sigma Xi, Sigma Pi Sigma. Home: 2 Stirling Pl Burlington VT 05401-2634 Business E-Mail: wesley.nyborg@uvm.edu.

**NYCE, JOHN DANIEL,** lawyer; b. York, Pa., Sept. 7, 1947; s. Harry Lincoln and Dorothy (Wagner) Nyce; m. Deborah Dvorak; children: Joshua David, Laura Kimberly. BA, SUNY, Buffalo, 1970; JD, U. Miami, 1973. Bar: Fla. 1973, U.S. District Ct. (so. dist.) Fla. 1973, U.S. Dist. Ct. (middle dist.), Fla. 1973, U.S. Ct. Appeals (5th and 11th cirs.) 1986, U.S. Supreme Ct. 1984. Assoc. Ralph P. Douglas, Pompano Beach, Fla., 1974, Coleman, Leonard & Morrison, Ft. Lauderdale, Fla., 1975-78; ptnr. Nyce and Smith, Ft. Lauderdale, 1979; sole practice Ft. Lauderdale, 1980—. Adj. prof. bus. law, internat. bus. law Lynn U., Boca Raton, Fla., 2001—. Author: Proof of God's Existence in the Seven C's and Christian Number of Lists, 2003. Mem. Social Register Ft. Lauderdale; mem. Broward County Right to Life, Operation Rescue, South Fla., Beach Street Aid to the Homeless of Ft. Lauderdale, Legis. Adv. Coun. on Adoptions, Nat. Right to Life Com., Inc.; founder, past pres., bd. dirs. Broward County Christian Lawyers Assn.; mem. Christian Legal Soc.; mem. exec. com. Broward County Rep. Party; Broward Citizens bd. U. Miami; mem. Conservative Caucus of Broward County; bd. dirs. Shepherd Care Ministries, Inc.; co-founder Christian Adoption Svcs. of Shepherd Care Ministries, Inc.; cert. trainer Evangelism Explosion III Internat., Inc.; legal counsel and evangelism trainer Coral Ridge Presbyn. Ch., Christ the Rock Cmty. Ch., First Bapt. Ch., West Hollywood, Fla., Calvary Chapel of Ft. Lauderdale Ch.; bd. dirs. Alliance for Responsible Growth, Inc. Mem.: Nat. Acad. Elder Law Attys., Attys. Title Ins. Fund, S.D. Rifle and Hunting Assn., U. Miami Alumni Assn., SUNY Buffalo Alumni Assn., Holiday Park Tennis Ctr., U.S. Tennis Assn., U. Miami Hurricane Club, Sports Fitness Clin., Palm Aire Golf and Country Club. Republican. Presbyterian. Office: PO Box 11071 Fort Lauderdale FL 33339-1071 Office Phone: 954-567-3305. E-mail: miami73jd@cs.com.

**NYCUM, SUSAN HUBBELL,** lawyer; BA, Ohio Wesleyan U., 1956; JD, Duquesne U., 1960; designated. Stanford U., Calif. Bar: Pa2, Calif. 1964, U.S. Supreme Ct. 1967. Sole practice law, Pitts., 1962-65; designer, adminstr. legal rsch. sys. U. Pitts., Aspen Sys. Corp., Pitts., 1965-68; mgr. ops. Computer Ctr., Carnegie Mellon U., Pitts., 1968-69; dir. computer facility Computer Ctr. Stanford U., 1969-72, Stanford Law and Computer fellow, 1972-73; cons. in computers and law, 1973-74; sr. assoc. MacLeod, Fuller, Muir & Godwin, Los Altos, LA and London, 1974-75; ptnr. Chickering & Gregory, San Francisco, 1975-80; ptnr.-in-charge high tech. group Gaston Snow & Ely Bartlett, Boston, NYC, Phoenix, San Francisco, 1980-86; mng. ptnr. Paio Alto office Kadison, Pfaelzer, Woodard, Quinn & Rossi, LA, Washington, Newport Beach, Palo Alto, Calif., 1986-87; sr. ptnr., chmn. U.S. intellectual property/info. tech. practice group Baker & McKenzie, Palo Alto, 1987—2002, mem. U.S. leadership team, 1987-97, mem. Asia Pacific regional coun., 1995—2002. Founder Tech. Disputes Resolution Svcs., Inc., 2002—; trustee EDUCOM, 1978-81. Internat. adv. com. for high tech. Ariz. State U. Law Sch., Santa Clara U. Law Sch., Stanford Law Sch., U. So. Calif.

Law Ctr., Harvard U. Law Sch., U. Calif.; U.S. State Dept. del. OECD Conf. on Nat. Vulnerabilities, Spain, 1981; invited spkr. Telecom., Geneva, 1983; lectr. N.Y. Law Jour., 1975—, Law & Bus., 1975—; Practicing Law Inst., 1975—; chmn. Office of Tech. Assessment Task Force on Nat. Info. Sys., 1979-80. Author:(with Bigelow) Your Computer and the Law, 1975, (with Bosworth) Legal Protection for Software, 1985, (with Collins and Gilbert) Women Leading, 1987; contbr. monographs, articles to profl. pubs. Fellow Am. Bar Found.; mem. Town of Portola Valley Open Space Acquisition Com., Calif., 1977; mem. Jr. League of Palo Alto, chmn. evening div., 1975-76 NSF and Dept. Justice grantee for studies on computer abuse, 1972-. Fellow Am. Bar Found., Assn. Computer Machinery (mem. at large of coun. 1976-80, nat. lectr. 1977—, chmn. standing com. on legal issues 1975—; mem. blue ribbon com. on rationalization of internat. propr. rights protection on info. processing devel. in the '90s 1990—, Hall of Fame 2004), Coll. Law Practice Mgmt. (trustee 2002—), Coll. Comml. Arbitration; mem. ABA (chmn. sect. on sci. and tech. 1979-80), Computer Law Assn. (v.p. 1983-85, pres. 1986—, bd. dirs. 1975—), Calif. State Bar Assn. (founder first chmn. econs. of law sect., vice chmn. law and computers com.), Internat. Bar Assn. (U.S. mem. computer com. of corps. sect.), Nat. Conf. Lawyers and Scientists (rep. ABA), Strategic Forum on Intellectual Property Issues in Software of NAS, Internat. Coun. for Computer Comm. (gov. 1998). Office: 35 Granada Ct Portola Valley CA 94028-7736 Office Phone: 650-888-7786. Business E-Mail: susan@nycum.net.

**NYDEGGER, RICK D.,** lawyer; b. Salt Lake City, Utah, Apr. 24, 1949; s. A. Don and Jean Virginia (Hansen) N.; m. Denise Winegar, Oct. 22, 1970; children: Dan L., Chad E., Kurt D., Brittney, Trent R. BSEE cum laude, Brigham Young U., 1974, JD cum laude, 1977. Bar: Utah 1977, US Dist Ct. (ctrl. dist.) Utah 1977, US Patent Office 1977, US Ct. Appeals (5th and 10th cirs.) 1980, US Supreme Ct. 1990, US Ct. Appeals (fed. cir.) 1994. Assoc. Fox, Edwards, & Gardiner, 1977-81, shareholder, dir., 1981-84; founding shareholder, dir., officer Workman, Nydegger, Salt Lake City, 1984—. Adj. prof. S.J. Quinney Coll. Law, U. Utah, 1988-99, J. Reuben Clark Law Sch., Brigham Young U., 1998-2002. Contbr. articles to profl. jours. Pres. Nat. Inventors Hall of Fame, 2000-05; bd. dirs. NIHF Found., 1998—, pres.; trustee Am. Intellectual Property Law Edn. Found., 2001-03. Named Hon. Alumnus of Yr., U. Utah, 2004, Alumnus of Yr., Brigham Young U., 2005. Fellow Am. Intellectual Property Law Assn. (founding mem., chmn. electronic computer law com. 1990-93, bd. dirs. 1993-96, editl. bd. quar. jour., vice-chmn. ad hoc com. PCT practice, 1994-98, nominations com. 1997, chmn. mid-winter Inst. 2000 planning com., 2d v.p. 2000-01, 1st v.p. 2001-02, pres. 2003-04); mem. Utah State Bar (chmn. patent, trademark, copyright sect. 1985-87), Fed. Cir. Bar Assn., US Supreme Ct. Hist. Soc. (10th cir. rep. 1993-94, Utah rep. 1992-93, 2005, trustee 2005-), Nat. Coun. Intellectual Property Law Assn. (chmn. 2000-01), Order of Coif. Office: Workman Nydegger 60 E South Temple Ste 1000 Salt Lake City UT 84111-1011 Office Phone: 801-533-9800. Business E-Mail: rnydegger@wnlaw.com.

**NYE, BILL S.,** research scientist, engineer, comedian, writer, inventor; b. Washington, Nov. 27, 1955; m. Blair Tindall, Feb. 3, 2006. BS in Mech. Engring., Cornell U., 1977; PhD in Sci. (hon.), Rennselaer Polytechnic Inst., Rochester, NY; PhD (hon.), Goucher Coll., Baltimore, Md. With Boeing Corp., Seattle, 1977—80, Marco, Seattle, 1980—81, Sundstrand Data Control, Redmond, Wash., 1981—86; lic. mech. engr. State of Washington, 1983—; cons. engr. US Dept. Justice, 1987—, Micro Encoder, Inc., 1987—, Avtech, 1987—; Frank H.T. Rhodes Class of '56 Univ. Prof. Cornell U., 2001—04. Established, promoter EarthDial Project; bd. dir. Mars Athena Exploration Team, Cornell U., 1998—2011, Denver Mus. Nature and Sci., 2001—, New Horizons Mission to Pluto, John Hopkins U., 2001—14. Originated Bill Nye-The Science Guy, KJR Radio, Seattle, 1986—92, writer, talent (TV comedy) Almost Live, KING TV, 1986—92, host, writer (video) Fabulous Wetlands, Washington State Dept. Ecology, 1988, writer, prodr., talent Bill Nye-The Science Guy (pilot and subsequent series) (Emmy awards for Best Performer, Best Writing and Producing, and Best Show), spokesperson, cons., on-air host Noggin TV (MTV Networks), 1999—, host (TV series) The 100 Greatest Discoveries (Science Channel), The Eyes of Nye (PBS); co-author: (book) Big Blast of Science, 1993, Bill Nye the Science Guy's Great Big Dinosaur Dig, 2002, Bill Nye the Science Guy's Great Big Book of Tiny Germs, 2005, Bill Nye the Science Guy's Great Big Book of Science: Featuring Oceans and Dinosaurs, 2005; author: Bill Nye the Science Guy's Big Blue Ocean, 1999, Bill Nye's Consider the Following: A Way Cool Set of Science Questions, Answers, and Ideas to Ponder, Mozart in the Jungle. Recipient Best Children's Live Action Show, Environ. Media Assn., 1994, 1996, 1997, Carl Sagan Candle in the Dark award for the Develop. of Critical Thinking, 1997, Gold Camera award, Internat. Film and Video Festival, 1997, Best Children's Live Action Show, Environ. Media Assn., 1998, Coun. for Elementary Sci. Internat. Sci. Advocate award, 2000, US Forest Svc. Disting. award for conservation. Mem.: Planetary Soc. (bd. dir. 1998—). Achievements include at Boeing Corporation, designed a hydraulic pressure resonance suppressor that is still flying on Boeing 747's; at Marco, designed equipment for oil slick skimming at sea, and for separation of water produced with oil in oil fields; at Sundstrand Data Control, designed oil well logging instruments, and an inertial navigation system for business jets; two patents on educational products-a magnifier made of water and an abacus that does arithmetic like a computer; patent pending on a device to help people learn to throw a baseball better; Won 28 Emmy awards in five years for writing and performing; and other designs as consulting engineer. Avocations: bicycling, baseball, Frisbee, inventing, especially with bikes. Address: c/o William Morris Agy Attn: Betsy Berg 1325 Avenue of the Americas New York NY 10019*

**NYE, DOROTHY MAE,** freelance journalist, educator; d. Robert Nathan and Marinda Josephine Nye; m. Joseph Arlo Westby, Nov. 20, 1955 (div.); children: Timothy Scott Westby, Pamela Kay Westby, Lisa Maureen Westby-Peltier, Thomas David Westby, Theodore Edward Westby, Erik Charles Westby. BA, U. Denver, 1999—2001, Combined Licensure & Master's Program, 2002—03. Administrator's Credential Nat. Assn. Edn. of Young Children (NAEYC) & Red Cross, 1993, Montessori Certification Nat. Ctr. for Montessori Edn., 1992. Asst. to v.p. of sales Morton Buildings, Morton, Ill., 1971—83; assoc. dir. of admissions Parks Coll., Denver, 1984—86; dir. of admissions Denver Tech. Coll., 1986—90; primary tchr. Montessori Inst., Houston, 1991—93; sales team mgr. Time Warner, Denver, 1993—96; counselor Open Door, Valley City, ND, 1996—99; communicatons specialist Theodore Roosevelt Medora Found., Medora, ND, 1999—2000; ednl. specialist for elderly Life Care of Am., Aurora, Colo., 2001—04; h.s. english tchr. Life Skills Charter Sch. of Colo. Springs, Denver. Com. for internat. program U. of ND & Mexican Universities, Valley City, ND, 1997—99. Com. monitor Majority Caucus Colo. Ho. of Representatives, Denver, 1993—95. Mem.: Pi Lambda Phi, Sigma Tau Delta. Office Phone: 719-471-0684. Business E-Mail: dnye@mylsc.net, dorothy.nye@lifeskillscenters.com. E-mail: grand_ma10@msn.com.

**NYE, ERIC W.,** English language and literature educator; b. Omaha, July 31, 1952; s. William Frank and Mary Roberta (Lueder) N.; m. Carol Denison Frost, Dec. 21, 1980; children: Charles William, Ellen Mary. BA, St. Olaf Coll., 1974; MA, U. Chgo., 1976, PhD, 1983; postgrad., Queens' Coll., Cambridge, England, 1979-82. Tutor in coll. writing com. U. Chgo., 1976-79, tchg. intern, 1978; tutor Am. lit. Cambridge (Eng.) U., 1979-82; asst. prof. English and religious studies U. Wyo., Laramie, 1983-89, assoc. prof., 1989—, dir. English honors program, 1985—89, 1992—93, 2002—04. Pres., bd. dirs. Plainview Tel. Co., Nebr.; hon. vis. fellow U. Edinburgh (Scotland) Inst. for Advanced Studies in the Humanities, 1987; guest lectr. NEH summer Inst., Laramie, Wyo., 1985, Carlyle Soc. of Edinburgh, 1987, Wordsworth summer Conf., Grasmere, Eng., 1988, cons. NEH. Contbr. articles and reviews to profl. jours. Elected mem. Wyo. Coun. for Humanities, 1992—96, mem. exec. com., 1993—94; mem. adv. bd. Wyo. Ctr. for the Book, 1995—, chair, 2006—; mem. Peripatetics, 1989—; leader Boy Scouts Am. Nat. Merit scholar St. Olaf Coll., 1970-74; Amb. fellow Rotary Found., 1979-80; grantee Am. Coun. Learned Socs., 1988; recipient Disting. Alumnus award Lincoln

(Nebr.) East H.S., 1986. Mem.: MLA (del. assembly 1991—93), Guild Book Workers, Bibliog. Soc. London (hon. treas. for N.Am. 2002—), Soc. History of Authorship, Reading, and Pub., Assn. Lit. and Linguistic Computing, Am. Acad. Bookbinding, Assn. Literary Scholars and Critics (life), Am. Trust for the Brit. Libr., Friends of Cambridge U. Libr. (life), Coleridge Soc. (life), Friends of Dove Cottage (life), Jane Austen Soc. N.Am. (life), Carlyle Soc. (life), Wyo. State Hist. Soc. (life), Tennyson Soc. (life), Charles Lamb Soc., Am. Friends of Cambridge U., Penn Club (London), Royal Oak Found., The Victorian Inst., Queen's Coll. Club (Cambridge), Phi Beta Kappa (rep. Triennial Coun. 1988, pres., v.p., sec. Wyo. chpt. 1988—, rep. Triennial Coun. 1994, 2000, 2003, 2006, 1988, Dedicated Svc. award 1997, Slater Tchg. award 2000). Home: 1495 Apache Dr Laramie WY 82072-6966 Office: U Wyo Dept English 3353 1000 E U Ave Laramie WY 82071 Office Phone: 307-766-6452. Business E-Mail: nye@uwyo.edu.

**NYE, ERLE ALLEN,** electric power industry executive, lawyer; b. Ft. Worth, June 23, 1937; s. Ira Benjamen N.; m. Alice Ann Grove, June 5, 1959; children: Elizabeth Nye Janzen, Pamela Nye Schneider, Erle Allen Jr., Edward Kyle, Johnson Scott. BEE, Tex. A&M U., 1959; JD, So. Meth. U., 1965. With Dallas Power & Light Co., 1960-75, v.p., 1975-80, Tex. Utilities Co. (dba TXU Corp.), Dallas, 1980, exec. v.p., 1980-87, pres., 1987-95, pres., CEO, 1995-97, chmn., CEO, 1997—2004, chmn., 2004—. TU Svcs., 1982-97, chmn., CEO, 1997—; Tex. Utilities Properties Inc., 1994, Tex. Utilities Commn., Dallas, 1995-97, chmn., CEO, 1997—; Tex. Utilities Fuel Co., 1982-97, chmn., CEO, 1997—; chmn. Tex. Utilities Australia Pty., Ltd., 1996—, chmn. and CEO ENSERCH Corp., Enserch Devel. Corp., Dallas, 1997—; chmn. Enserch Energy Svcs. Inc., 1997—; dir. The Energy Group PLC, London, 1998—; chmn. and CEO Tex. Energy Industries Inc., Dallas, 1997—, Southwestern Electric Svc. Co., 1997—, chmn. Lufkin-Conroe Comm. Co., 1997—, chmn. bd., CEO Tex. Utilities Integrated Solutions Inc., 1997—. Bd. dirs. Dallas Bar Found., 1980-83, Dallas Cen. Bus. Plan Com., 1980-83, Inroads/Dallas-Ft. Worth Inc., 1984-88, trustee Baylor Dental Coll., Dallas, 1985-94; mem. Dallas Together Forum, 1989—, Dallas Com. Fgn. Rels., 1991—, Bd. of Boys & Girls Clubs of Am., 1991—; The Dallas Found., 1991—; The Science Pl., Dallas, 1995-99; The Salvation Army's Dallas County Adv. Bd., 1995-99. Mem. ABA, Dallas Bar Assn., Tex. State Bar Assn., Dallas C. of C. (bd. dirs. 1991-95, vice chmn. 1992-95). Clubs: Engineers (pres. 1982-83), Northwood (Dallas), Northwood (hon.). Home: 6924 Desco Dallas TX 75225 Office: TXU Corp 1601 Bryan St Fl 41 Dallas TX 75201-3411

**NYE, JOSEPH SAMUEL, JR.,** political science professor, former dean; b. South Orange, N.J., Jan. 19, 1937; s. Joseph S. and Else (Ashwell) N.; m. Molly Harding, June 10, 1961; children— John Bundy, Joseph Benjamin, Daniel Tupper AB in Pub. Affairs, Princeton U., 1958; BA in Philosophy, Politics and Econs., Oxford U., Eng., 1960; PhD in Polit. Sci., Harvard U., 1964. Prof., govt. Harvard U., Cambridge, Mass., 1964—95, dean Kennedy Sch. Govt., 1995—2004, Disting. Svc. prof., 2004—; dep. undersec. state, security assistance, science & tech. U.S. Dept. State, Washington, 1977-79, cons., 1979; asst. sec. def., internat. security affairs U.S. Dept. Def., Washington, 1994—95; dean Harvard U. JFK Sch. of Govt., 1995—2004, Sultan of Oman prof. internat. relations, 2005—. Cons. Dept. Energy, Washington, 1979; U.S. rep. UN Adv. Bd. on Disarmament; chmn. Nat. Intelligence Coun., 1993-94; vis. prof. Belliol Coll., Oxford, Eng., 2005. Author: Pan Africanism and East African Integration, 1965, Peace in Paris: Integration and Conflict in Regional Organization, 1971 (with Robert O. Keohane) Power and Interdependence: World Politics in Transition, 1977, The Making of America's Soviet Policy, 1984, (with Graham Allison and Albert Carnesale) Hawks, Doves and Owls: An Agenda for Avoiding Nuclear War, 1985, Nuclear Ethics, 1986, Bound to Lead: The Changing Nature of American Power, 1990, (with Kurt Biedenkopf and Motoo Shiina) Global Competition After the Cold War: A Reassessment of Trilateralism, 1991, Understanding International Conflicts: An Introduction to Theory and History, 1993, The Paradox of American Power: Why the World's Only Only Superpower Can't Go It Alone, 2002, Soft Power: The Means to Success in World Politics, 2004, The Power: A Washington Novel; 2004; (with Yukio Satoh and Paul Wikinson) Addressing the New International Terrorism: Prevention, Intervention, and Multilateral Cooperation, 2003; co-editor: Canada and the United States: Transnational and Transgovernmental Relations, 1974, Energy and Security, 1980, Global Dilemmas, 1985, Seeking Stability in Space: Anti-Satellite Weapons and the Evolving Space Regime, 1987, On The Defensive? The Future of SDI, 1988, Fateful Visions: avoiding Nuclear Catastrophe, 1988, democracy.com?: Governance in a Networked World, 1999, Governance in a Globalizing World, 2000, For the People: Can We Fix Public Service, 2003. Recipient: US Dept. State Disting. Honor award, 1979; Rhodes scholar Oxford U., 1958-60, Montague Burton Professorship, U. Edinburgh, 1990, Intelligence Cmty. Disting. Service medal, 1994, Dept. Def. Disting. Service medal with Oak Leaf Cluster, 1995, Charles E. Merriam award Am. polit. Sci. Assn., 2003, Woodrow Wilson award Princeton U., 2004; fellow, Woodrow Wilson Internat. Ctr., Smithsonian Inst., 1993, Hon. fellow, Exeter Coll, Oxford, 1996. Fellow Am. Acad. Arts and Scis., Aspen Inst. for Humanistic Study (sr. fellow, 1983-93); mem. Amer. Assoc. for the Advancement of Science: Com. on Science, Arms Control, and Nat. Security, 1984-90, bd. dirs., Amer. Council on Germany, 1985-93, bd. govs., Atlantic Inst. for Internat. Affairs, 1974-77, Internat. Inst. Strategic Studies (council), Coun. Fgn. Rels. (bd. dirs.), Trilateral Commn., Am. Acad. Diplomacy. Office: Harvard U JFK Sch Govt 79 John F Kennedy St Cambridge MA 02138-5801 E-mail: joseph_nye@harvard.edu.

**NYE, LINDA PURCELL,** secondary school educator; d. George T and Sara Jane Purcell; m. Stephen Christopher Nye, Aug. 5, 2001; children: Levi, Clifton. MusB in Edn., U. of Puget Sound, Tacoma, Wash., 1975; MEd in Counseling, U. of Puget Sound, 1986; Cert. of Vocal Mastery, Austro-Am. Inst. of Edn., Vienna, Austria, 1972—73. Choir/drama teacher White River H.S., Buckley, Wash.; choir/drama tchr. Clover Pk. Sch. Dist., Lakewood, Wash., 1986—96; choir/drama/English tchr. Evergreen Sch. Dist., Vancouver, Wash., 1996—. Dir.: Best in the Northwest Festival (Best Dir., 1992); (plays) Grease (Outstanding Theatre Prodn. in Pierce County, 1989); choreographer (plays) He's Risen! (Best Artistic Design, 1993). V.p. Adelphian Concert Choir, pres., 1974—75; treas. Puyallup Bus. and Profl. Women, Puyallup, Wash., 1977—78. Named Outstanding Woman in Pierce County, Bus. and Profl. Women, 1979; recipient Inspirational award, Adelphian Concert Choir/ U. of Puget Sound, 1974; scholar Four Yr. Vocal scholar, U. of Puget Sound Sch. of Music, 1971—75. Fellow: NEA (assoc.); mem.: Am. Choral Dirs. Assn. (organizing chmn. women's hon. choir N.W. divsn. 1988), EEA, Wash. Edn. Assn., Music Educator's Nat. Conf. (assoc.; dist. pres. 1979—83, v.p. 1979—83, organizing chmn. all-N.W. choir), Mortar Bd. (life), Sigma Alpha Iota Alumnae Assn. (assoc.; pres. 1974—84, v.p. 1974—84, treas. 1974—84, Ruby Sword of Honor/ Nu Province Leadership Award 1976). Liberal. Avocations: travel, singing. Office Phone: 360-604-3200 x7079. Personal E-mail: lnye525@comcast.net. Business E-Mail: lnye@egreen.wednet.edu.

**NYE, RANDALL WAYNE,** music educator; s. John Barlow and Kathryn Viola Nye; m. Donna Sheryl Fraser, Mar. 18, 1995; 1 child, Benjamin Christopher. MusB, So. Meth. U., 1977, MusM, 1980. Educator Eastfield Coll., Mesquite, Tex., 2004—. Editor: The Guitar Ensemble; A Collection. Music scholar, So. Meth. U., 1974—77. Mem.: Dallas Classic Guitar Soc. (adv. bd. 1990—2003), Phi Theta Kappa. Office: Eastfield Coll 3737 Motley Dr Mesquite TX 75150 Personal E-mail: rnye@cccd.edu. Business E-Mail: randy.nye@dcccd.edu.

**NYE, WILLIAM ROGER,** psychologist; b. Haverhill, Mass., Oct. 23, 1940; s. Kenneth Enoch and Virginia Pauline (Cook) N.; childrens: Michael Shepherd Abowitz Nye; 1 stepson, Christopher J. Wells. BA, Yale U., 1962; MDiv, Union Theol. Sem., N.Y.C., 1965; PhD, Adelphi U., Garden City, N.Y., 1981. Lic. psychologist, N.Y. Pastor Ch. of the Evangel, Bklyn., 1965-77; asst. minister Plymouth Ch. of the Pilgrims, Bklyn., 1977-82; pastor All Souls Bethlehem Ch., Bklyn., 1983—2003; exec. dir. Blanton-Peale Counseling Ctrs., 1983—. Past pres. Met. Assn. N.Y. Conf. United Ch. of Christ,

1969—73. Pres. Bklyn. Cmty. and Housing Svcs., 1983—87, Vinmont Found., N.Y.C., 1988—. Mem. Am. Psychol. Assn. Democrat. United Ch. of Christ. Home: 888 E 19th St Brooklyn NY 11230-3108 Office Phone: 718-253-9001. E-mail: realbilnye@aol.com.

**NYENHUIS, JACOB EUGENE,** academic administrator; b. Mille Lacs County, Minn., Mar. 25, 1935; s. Egbert Peter and Rosa (Walburg) N.; m. Leona Mae Van Duyn, June 6, 1956; children: Karen J. Louwsma, Kathy J. Kurtze, Lorna J. Cook, Sarah Van Duyn N. AB in Greek, Calvin Coll., 1956; AM in Classics, Stanford U., 1961, PhD in Classics, 1963; LittD (hon.), Hope Coll., 2001. Asst. in classical langs. Calvin Coll., Grand Rapids, Mich., 1957-59; acting instr. Stanford (Calif.) U., 1962; from asst. prof. to prof. Wayne State U., Detroit, 1962-75, dir. honors program, 1964-75, chmn. Greek and Latin dept., 1965-75; prof. classics, dean for humanities Hope Coll., Holland, Mich., 1975-78, dean for arts and humanities, 1978-84, provost, 1984—2001, prof. and provost emeritus, 2001—; sr. rsch. fellow A.C. Van Raalte Inst., 2001—02, dir., 2002—. Cons. Mich. Dept. Edn., Lansing, 1971-72, Gustavus Adolphus Coll., St. Peter, Minn., 1974, Northwestern Coll., Orange City, Iowa, 1983, Whitworth Coll., Spokane, Wash., 1987, The Daedalus Project, 1988, Albion Coll., 2002-03, Kalamazoo Coll., 2003—04; reviewer NEH, Washington, 1986-87, panelist, 1991; reviewer Lilly Endowment, Indpls., 1987-89, U.S. Dept. Edn., 1993, Mich. Humanities Coun., 1999-2001, 2006; vis. assoc. prof. U. Calif., Santa Barbara, 1967-68, Ohio State U., Columbus, 1972; vis. rsch. prof. Am. Sch. Classical Studies, Athens, Greece, 1973-74, mng. com.; vis. scholar Green Coll. Oxford U., 1989; mem. editl. adv. bd. Christianity and The Arts, 1998-2001, chmn., 1999-2001. Co-author: Latin Via Ovid, 1977, rev. edit., 1982; A Dream Fulfilled: The Van Raalte Sculpture in Centennial Park, 1997; editor: Petronius: Cena Trimalchionis, 1970, Plautus: Amphitruo, 1970; author: Centennial History of 14th Street Christian Reformed Church, Holland, Michigan, 2002, Myth and the Creative Process: Michael Ayrton and the Myth of Daedalus, the Maze Maker, 2003; contbr. articles to profl. jours. Elder Christian Ref. Ch., Palo Alto, Calif., 1960—62, elder, clk. Grosse Pointe, Mich., 1964—67, Holland, Mich., 1976—85, v.p., 1988—91, exec. com. 1994—95; trustee Calvin Theol. Sem., 2001—. mem. exec. com., 2002—, v.p., 2003—; chmn. human rels. coun. Open Housing Com., Grosse Pointe, 1971—73. Mem. Am. Philol. Assn., Danforth Assocs. (chmn. regional com. 1975-77), Mich. Classical Conf. (1st v.p. 1965-66, pres. 1966-67), Mich. Coun. for Humanities (bd. dirs., 1976-84, 88-92, 96-99, chmn. 1980-82, Disting. Svc. award 1984), Nat. Fedn. State Humanities Couns. (bd. dirs. 1979-84, pres. 1981-83), Gt. Lakes Colls. Assn. (bd. dirs. 1991-93), Coun. on Undergrad. Rsch. (councilor-at-large 1993-99), Green Coll. Soc., Mortar Board, Phi Beta Kappa, Eta Sigma Phi. Democrat. Avocations: photography, carpentry. Office: Hope Coll Van Raalte Inst PO Box 9000 Holland MI 49422-9000 Office Phone: 616-395-7171. Business E-Mail: nyenhuis@hope.edu.

**NYERGES, ALEXANDER LEE,** museum director; b. Rochester, N.Y., Feb. 27, 1957; s. Sandor Elek and Lena (Angeline) N.; m. Kathryn Gray; 1 child, Robert Angeline. BA, George Washington U., 1979, MA, 1981. Intern The Octagon, Washington, 1976-79; archeol. asst. Smithsonian Instn., Washington, 1977; curatorial intern Nat. Mus. Am. History, 1978-79; adminstrv. asst. George Washington U., Washington, 1979-81; exec. dir. DeLand Mus. Art, Fla., 1981-85, Miss. Mus. Art, Jackson, 1985-92; dir. Dayton Art Inst., 1992—2006, Mus. Fine Arts, Dayton, 2006—. Mem. grants panel Nat. Endowment for the Arts, 1988—; field surveyor Inst. Mus. Svcs., Washington, 1985-88, nat. review panel, 1990-92; treas., bd. dirs. Volusia County Arts Coun., Daytona Beach, Fla., 1983-85. Author: Selections from the Permanent Collection, 1999, In Praise of Nature: Israel Adams and Photographers of the American West, The Harold W Shaw Collection: Pre Columbian Treasures, 2003, Edward Weston: A Photographer's Love of Life, 2004; contbr. articles to profl. jours. Bd. dirs. West Volusia Hist. Soc., 1984-85; pres. Miss. Hist. Arts and Letters, 1987-88; trustee Cultural Arts Ctr., DeLand, 1984-85, Miami Valley Cultural Alliance, 1993-95, Intermus. Conservation Lab., 1993-99, Montgomery County Arts and Culture Dist., 1994-2001; trustee, chmn. Dayton-Montgomery County Conv. and Visitors Bur. U.S. Dept. Edn. scholar, 1973. Mem. DeLand Area C. of C. (bd. dirs., tourist adv. com. 1984-85), Assn. Art Mus. Dirs., Am. Assn. Mus. (S.E. regional rep. to non-print media com. 1983-85, nat. legis. com. 1986-93), Miss. Mus. Assn., Southeastern Mus. Conf. (bd. dirs. 1991-92), Fla. Mus. Assn., Fla. Art Mus. Dirs. Assn., Cultural Roundtable (pres. 1993-95), Ohio Mus. Assn. (trustee 1993-98), Phi Beta Kappa. Avocations: photography, music, writing, sports, scuba diving. Office: Virginia Mus Fine Arts 700 N Blvd Richmond VA 23220 Office Phone: 937-223-5277, 804-340-1504. E-mail: anyerges@aol.com.

**NYGAARD, RICHARD LOWELL,** federal judge; b. Thief River Falls, MN, 1940; BS cum laude, U. So. Calif., 1969; JD, U. Mich., 1971. Mem. Orton, Nygaard & Dunlevy, 1972—80; judge Ct. Common Pleas, 6th Dist. Pa., Erie, 1981—88, US Ct. Appeals (3d Cir.), Erie, Pa., 1988—2005, sr. judge, 2005—; sr. lecturer Penn State Univ., 1999—2003. Councilman Erie County, Pa., 1977—81. With USNR, 1958—64. Mem.: ABA, Erie County Bar Assn., Pa. Bar Assn. Office: James A Byrne Courthouse 601 Market St Rm 2100 Philadelphia PA 19106 also: 17 S Park Row Ste B-230 Erie PA 16501-1164*

**NYHAN, LAWRENCE J. (LARRY),** lawyer; b. Chgo., May 16, 1955; BA, U. Chgo., 1977; JD, Loyola U., Chgo., 1980. Bar: Ill. 1980. Extern to Hon. Robert Eisen US Bankruptcy Judge, no. dist. Ill., 1979—80; now ptnr. bankruptcy law Sidley Austin LLP, Chgo., chmn. nat. and internat. corp. reorgn. and bankruptcy group, mem. exec. com. Office: Sidley Austin LLP 1 S Dearborn St Chicago IL 60603 Office Phone: 312-853-7710. Office Fax: 312-853-7036. Business E-Mail: lnyhan@sidley.com.

**NYHAN, MARY E.,** literature and language educator; children: Graham, Griffin. BA, SUNY, 1989; MEd, Plymouth State U., 1992. Tchr. English Inter-Lakes H.S., Meredith, NH, 1992—; Laconia Acad., 1998—2000. Sec. Little League, Laconia, 2005. Mem.: Nat. Coun. Tchrs. of English, N.H. Coun. Tchrs. of English. Avocations: hiking, rafting, reading, gardening. Office: Inter-Lakes High Sch 1 Laker Ln Meredith NH 03253

**NYHAN, WILLIAM LEO,** pediatrician, educator; b. Boston, Mar. 13, 1926; s. W. Leo and Mary N.; m. Christine Murphy, Nov. 20, 1948; children: Christopher, Abigail. Student, Harvard U., 1943-45; MD, Columbia U., 1949; MS, U. Ill., 1956, PhD, 1958; doctorate (hon.), Tokushima U., Japan, 1981. Intern Yale U.-Grace-New Haven Hosp., 1949-50, resident, 1950-51, 53-55; asst. prof. pediatrics Johns Hopkins U., 1958-61, assoc. prof., 1961-63; prof. pediatrics, biochemistry U. Miami, 1963-69, chmn. dept. pediatrics, 1965-69; prof. U. Calif., San Diego, 1969—, chmn. dept. pediatrics, 1969-86. Mem. FDA adv. com. on Teratogenic Effects of Certain Drugs, 1964-70; mem. pediatric panel AMA Council on Drugs, 1964-70; mem. Nat. Adv. Child Health and Human Devel. Council, 1967-71; mem. research adv. com. Calif. Dept. Mental Hygiene, 1969-72; mem. med. and sci. adv. com. Leukemia Soc. Am., Inc., 1968-72; mem. basic adv. com. Nat. Found. March of Dimes, 1973-81; mem. Basil O'Connor Starter grants com., 1973-93; mem. clin. cancer program project rev. com. Nat. Cancer Inst., 1977-81; vis. prof. extraordinario U. del Salvador (Argentina), 1982. Author (with E. Edelson): The Heredity Factor, Genes, Chromosomes and You, 1976; author: Genetic & Malformation Syndromes in Clinical Medicine, 1976, Abnormalities in Amino Acid Metabolism in Clinical Medicine, 1984, Diagnostic Recognition of Genetic Diseases, 1987; author: (with P. Ozand) Atlas of Metabolic Diseases, 1998; author: (with B. Barshop and P. Ozand) 2d edit., 2005; author: (with G. Hoffmann, J. Zschocke, S.G. Kahler and E. Mayatepek) Inherited Metabolic Diseases, 2001; editor: Amino Acid Metabolism and Genetic Variation, 1967, Heritable Disorders of Amino Acid Metabolism, 1974; mem. editl. bd.: Jour. Pediat., 1964—78, Western Jour. Medicine, 1974—86, King Faisal Hosp. Med. Jour., 1981—85, Annals of Saudi Medicine, 1985—87, mem. editl. coms.: Ann. Rev. Nutrition, 1982—86, mem. editl. staff: Med. and Pediat. Oncology, 1975—83. Served with U.S. Navy, 1944-46; U.S. Army, 1951-53. Nat. Found. Infantile Paralysis fellow, 1955-58; recipient Commemorative medallion Columbia U. Coll. Physicians and Surgeons, 1967, Guthrie award Am. Assn. Mental Retardation, 1998, Pool of

Bethesda award Bethesda Luth. Homes and Svcs., 1999. Fellow: Am. Acad. Pediat. (Borden award 1980, Lifetime Achievement award 1999); mem.: AAAS, Inst. Medicine of Nat. Acad. Scis., Biochem. Soc., Am. Coll. Med. Genetics, Am. Assn. Clin. Chemists, Am. Soc. Human Genetics (dir. 1978—81), Am. Soc. Clin. Investigation, Soc. Exptl. Biology and Medicine, Am. Inst. Biol. Scis., Am. Pediatric Soc., South African Human Genetics (hon.), Inst. Investigaciones Citologicas (Spain) (corr.), Soc. Francaise de Pediatrie (corr.), N.Y. Acad. Sci., Western Soc. Pediatric Rsch. (pres. 1976—77), Am. Soc. Pharmacology and Exptl. Therapeutics, Am. Assn. Cancer Rsch., Soc. Pediatric Rsch. (pres. 1970—71), Am. Chem. Soc., Am. Fedn. Clin. Rsch., Alpha Omega Alpha, Sigma Xi. Office: U Calif San Diego Dept Pediatrics # 0830 9500 Gilman Dr La Jolla CA 92093-0830 Office Phone: 619-543-5237. Business E-Mail: wnyhan@ucsd.edu.

**NYHUS, LLOYD MILTON,** retired surgeon, retired educator; b. Mt. Vernon, Wash., June 24, 1923; s. Lewis Guttorm and Mary (Shervem) N.; m. Margaret Goldie Sheldon, Nov. 25, 1949; children: Sheila Margaret, Leif Torger. BS, Pacific Luth. Coll., 1945; MD, Med. Coll. Ala., 1947; Doctor honoris causa, Aristotelian U., Thessalonika, Greece, 1968, Uppsala U., Sweden, 1974, U. Chihuahua, Mex., 1975, Jagallonian U., Cracow, Poland, 1980, U. Gama Filho, Rio de Janeiro, 1983, U. Louis Pasteur, Strasbourg, France, 1984, U. Athens, 1989. Diplomate Am. Bd. Surgery (chmn. 1974-76). Intern King County Hosp., Seattle, 1947-48, resident in surgery, 1948-55; practice medicine specializing in surgery Seattle, 1956-67, Chgo., 1967—; instr. surgery U. Wash., Seattle, 1954-56, asst. prof., 1956-59, assoc. prof., 1959-64, prof., 1964-67; Warren H. Cole prof., head dept. surgery U. Ill. Coll. Medicine, 1967-89, emeritus head, 1989—, prof. emeritus, 1993, founder Chgo., 2005, chair. gen surgery, 2006—; ret., 1993. Emeritus surgeon-in-chief U. Ill. Hosp.; sr. cons. surgeon Cook County, West Side VA, Hines VA hosps., Ill.; cons. to Surgeon Gen. NIH, 1965-69. Author: Surgery of the Stomach and Duodenum, 1962, 4th edit., 1986, named changed to Surgery of the Esophagus, Stomach and Small Intestine, 5th edit., 1995, Hernia, 1964, (book name change) Nyhus and Condon's Hernia, 5th edit., 2002, Chinese (Mandarin) edit., 2004, Abdominal Pain: A Guide to Rapid Diagnosis, 1969, 95, Spanish edit., 1996, Russian edit., 2001, Manual of Surgical Therapeutics, 1969, latest rev. edit., 1996, Mastery of Surgery, 1984, 3d edit., 1997, Spanish edit., 1999, Surgery Ann., 1970-95, Treatment of Shock, 1970, 2d rev. edit., 1986, Surgery of the Small Intestine, 1987; editor-in-chief Rev. of Surgery, 1967-77, Current Surgery, 1978-90, emeritus editor, 1991—; assoc. editor Quar. Rev. Surgery, 1958-61; editl. bd. Am. Jour. Digestive Diseases, 1961-67, Scandinavian Jour. Gastroenterology, 1966-97, Am. Surgeon, 1967-89, Jour. Surg. Oncology, 1969-89, Archives of Surgery, 1977-86, World Jour. Surgery, 1977-95; contbr. articles to profl. jours. Served to lt. M.C. USNR, 1943-46, 50-52. Decorated Order of Merit (Poland); postdoctoral fellow USPHS, 1952-53; recipient M. Shipley award So. Surg. Assn., 1967, Rovsing medal Danish Surg. Soc., 1973; Disting. Faculty award U. Ill Coll. Medicine, 1983, Disting. Alumnus award Med. Coll. Ala., 1984, Disting. Alumnus award U. Wash., 1993, 99; Guggenheim fellow, 1955-56. Fellow ACS (1st v.p. 1987-88), Assn. Surgeons Gt. Brit. and Ireland (hon.), Royal Coll. Surgeons Eng. (hon.), Royal Coll. Surgeons Ireland (hon.), Royal Coll. Surgeons Edinburgh (hon.), Royal Coll. Physicians and Surgeons Glasgow (hon.), Internat. Soc. Surgery Found. (hon., sec.-treas. 1992-2001); mem. Am. Gastroent. Assn., Am. Physiol. Soc., Pacific Coast Surg. Assn., Am. Surg. Assn. (recorder 1976-81, 1st v.p. 1989-90), Western Surg. Assn., Ctrl. Soc. Clin. Rsch., Chgo. Surg. Soc. (pres. 1974), Ctrl. Surg. Assn. (pres. 1984), Seattle Surg. Soc., St. Paul Surg. Soc. (hon.), Kansas City Surg. Soc. (hon.), Inst. Medicine Chgo., Internat. Soc. Surgery (hon. fellow 2001, pres. U.S. sect. 1986-88, pres. 34th World Congress 1991, internat. pres. 1991-93), Internat. Soc. for Digestive Surgery (pres. III world congress Chgo. 1974, internat. pres. 1978-84), Soc. for Surgery Alimentary Tract (sec. 1969-73, pres. 1974), Soc. Clin. Surgery, Soc. Surg. Chmn., Soc. U. Surgeons (pres. 1967), Duetschen Gesellschaft für Chirurgie (hon.), Polish Assn. Surgeons (hon.), L'Academie de Chirurgie (France) (corr.), Nat. Acad. of Medicine (France, Argentina and Brazil, hon.), Swiss Surg. Soc. (hon.), Brazilian Coll. Surgeons (hon.), Surg. Biology Club, Warren H. Cole Soc. (pres. 1981), Japan Surg. Soc. (hon.), Assn. Gen. Surgeons of Mex. (hon.), Columbian Surg. Soc. (hon.), Costa Rican Coll. Medicine & Surgery (hon.), Assn. Surgeons Costa Rica (hon.), Internat. Fedn. Surg. Colls. (hon. treas. 1992-99), Sigma Xi, Alpha Omega Alpha, Phi Beta Pi. Home: 310 Maple Row Northfield IL 60093-1036 Office: U Ill Coll Medicine Dept Surgery MC 958 840 S Wood St Chicago IL 60612-7322 Personal E-mail: lmn_23@msn.com.

**NYIKOS, STACY ANN,** publishing executive; d. Michael J. and Martha Nyikos; m. Rainer Kohrs, Dec. 1, 1994; children: Alysia Bella Kohrs, Sophia Johanna Kohrs. BA, U. Notre Dame, 1990; MA, Christian Albrecht U., Germany, 1994; PhD, U. Va., 2000. Gen. mgr. Stonehorse Pub, Tulsa, Okla., 2004—; stats. lab coord. U. Okla., Tulsa, 2004—; rsch. assoc. U. Okla, Tulsa, 2004—. Author: (children's lit.) Squirt, 2005, Shelby, 2006. Grantee, Fulbright Com., 1998—99; Dissertation Improvement grantee, NSF, 1999—2001, President's fellow, U. Va., 1995—98, Dumas Malone Traveling fellow, 1998—99. Liberal. Roman Catholic. Avocations: running, travel. Office: Stonehorse Pub LLC 10632 S Meml Ave 245 Tulsa OK 74133 Office Phone:     888-867-1927.     Office     Fax:     918-298-8182.     E-mail: snyikos@stonehorsepublishing.com.

**NYIRJESY, ISTVAN,** obstetrician, gynecologist; b. Budapest, Hungary, Nov. 14, 1929; came to U.S., 1954, naturalized, 1960; s. Sandor D. and Margit (Bertalan) N.; m. Michelle Shoepp, June 16, 1956; children— Francis, Paul, Christine. MD, Catholic U. Louvain, Belgium, 1955. Diplomate: Am. Bd. Ob-Gyn. Intern Cath. U. Louvain and Little Co. Mary Hosp., Evergeen Park, Ill., 1954-55; resident in gynecology obstetrics, 1960-63; chief obstetrical research Nat. Naval Med. Center, Bethesda, Md., 1966-68; ret., 1968; practice medicine specializing in Ob-Gyn Bethesda, 1968—. Clin. prof. Ob-Gyn Georgetown U., 1968—; cons. NIH, 1974—, FDA, 1977-88. Lit. editor Breast Disease: contbr. articles to med. jours.; author: Prevention and Detection of Gynecologic and Breast Cancer, 1994. Pres., Internat. Found. for Gynecol. Cancer Detection and Prevention, 1993—. Officer M.C. USN, 1956-68; advanced through grades to comdr. Recipient Sword of Hope pin Am. Cancer Soc., 1973, Vicennial medal Georgetown U., 1988. Fellow ACOG (Host award 1964), Hungarian Gynecologic Soc. (hon.), Internat. Coll. Surgeons; mem. Montgomery County (Md.) Med. Soc. (chmn. profl. edn. com. 1971-72), Am. Soc. of Breast Disease (past pres.), Assn. Profs. Ob-Gyn., Am. Soc. Reproductive Medicine, Washington Gynecol. Soc. (v.p. 1993-94, 1st v.p. 1994-95, pres. 1996-97). Office: 5301 Westbard Cir Ste 5 Bethesda MD 20816-1429 Office Phone: 301-654-0445.

**NYKROG, PER,** French literature educator; b. Copenhagen, Nov. 1, 1925; came to U.S., 1979; s. Kai S. Nathanson and Karen E. (Olsen) Nykrog; m. Vibeke H. Rasmussen, 1951 (dec. 1977); children: Thomas, Jakob; m. Usha Saksena Nilsson, Jan. 2, 1981. Grad., U. Copenhagen, 1952; PhD, U. Aarhus, Denmark, 1957. Asst. prof. U. Aarhus, 1953-57, prof., 1957-79; prof. French lang. and lit. Harvard U., Cambridge, Mass., 1979-98. Author: Les Fabliaux, 1957, La Pensée de Balzac, 1965, L'Amour et la Rose, 1986, La Recherche du Don perdu, 1987, Chrétien de Troyes romancier discutable, 1995. Mem. Royal Soc. Sciences. Denmark. Home: 243 Concord Ave Cambridge MA 02138-1360 Office: Harvard U Dept Romance Langs Boylston Hall Cambridge MA 02138 Business E-Mail: nykrog@fas.harvard.edu.

**NYLAND, WILLIAM LEWIS,** retired military officer; b. Coronado, Calif., Oct. 2, 1946; m. Brenda Petty; 3 children. BS in Biology, U. N.Mex., 1968; MS in Sys. Mgmt. R & D, U. So. Calif., 1980; student, Amphibious Warfare Sch., 1975, Navy Fighter Weapons Sch. (TopGun), 1977, Naval War Coll., 1981, Air War Coll., 1988. Commd. 2nd lt. USMC, 1968, advanced through grades to gen., 2002; comdr. VMFA-232, 1985—87, Marine Aviation Training Support Group, Pensacola, Fla., 1990—92; chief of staff 2nd Marine Aircraft Wing, 1992—94, asst. wing comdr., 1992—94, 2nd Marine Aircraft Wing, 1994—95; dep. dir. force structure & resources USMC Joint Staff (J-8), Washington, 1995-97; dep. commandr. gen. II Marine Expeditionary Force, Camp Lejeune, NC, 1997—98; commdg. gen. 2d Marine Aircraft Wing, MCAS, Cherry Point, NC, 1998—2000; dep. comdt. programs & resources USMC, 2000—01, dep. comdt. aviation, 2001—02, asst. comdt. Washington, 2002—05. Decorated Def. Disting.Svc. medal, Legion of Merit, Def. Meritorious Svc. medal, Meritorious Svc. medal, Air medal with 8 Strike/Flight awards, Joint Svc. Commendation medal. Office Phone: 703-966-9750. E-mail: spidernyland@aol.com.

**NYLANDER, JANE LOUISE,** museum director, educator, writer; b. Cleve., Jan. 27, 1938; d. James Merritt and Jeannette Cayford; m. Daniel Harris Giffen, 1963 (div. 1970); children: Sarah Louise, Thomas Harris; m. Richard Conrad Nylander, 1972: 1 child, Timothy Frost. AB, Brown U., Providence, R.I., 1959; MA, U. Del., Newark, 1961; postgrad., Attingham Summer Sch., Eng., 1970; PhD (hon.), New Eng. Coll., Henniker, N.H., 1994. Curator Hist. Soc. York County, Pa., 1961-62, N.H. Hist. Soc., Concord, 1962-69; instr. New Eng. Coll., Henniker, NH, 1964-65, Monadnock C.C., Peterborough, NH, 1966-69; curator of textiles and ceramics Old Sturbridge Village, Mass., 1969-85; adj. assoc. prof. Boston U., 1978-85; sr. curator Old Sturbridge Village, 1985-86; dir. Strawbery Banke Mus., Portsmouth, NH, 1986-92, Soc. for Preservation of New Eng. Antiquities, Boston, 1992-93, pres., 1993—2002, pres. emerita, 2002—. Adj. prof. art history and Am. studies Boston U., 1993—96; mem. adv. bd. Concord (Mass.) Mus., 1986—94, Wentworth-Coolidge Commn., 1991—96; mem. adv. com., 1996—2004; mem. adv. bd. John Nicholas Brown Ctr. for Am. Studies, Providence, 1995—2003; mem. adv. bd. dept. Am. decorative arts Mus. Fine Arts, Boston, 1971—99, Art of the Ams., 1999—2000; mem. adv. com. Lakes Region Conservation Trust, 2002—04, Charles S. Parsons Fund, 2004—; advisor house com. Moffatt Ladd House, 1973—; mem. adv. bd. Strawbery Banke Mus., 2004—, mem. steering com. Ctr. for Study of Cmty., 2004—05; cons. in field. Author: Fabrics for Historic Buildings, 4th edit., 1990, Our Own Snug Fireside: Images of the New England Home 1760-1860, 1993, paperback edit., 1994, Windows on the Past, 2000, The Art of Family, 2002; author: (with Richard C. Nylander) Fabrics and Wallpaper for Historic Buildings, 2005; mem. editl. bd.: Hist. N.H., 1993—, The Dublin Seminar, 1984—; contbr. numerous articles to profl. jours. Trustee Worcester (Mass.) Hist. Mus., 1978—84, Hist. Deerfield (Mass.) Inc., 1981—94, 2003—, chair strategic planning com., 2003—, hon. trustee, 1994—2003, Hist. Mass., Inc., 1991—93, Decorative Arts Trust, 1991—, Portsmouth Athenaeum, 1988—90, Japan Soc. N.H., 1988—92, Fort Ticonderoga, 2000—02; mem. adv. bd. New Eng. Heritage Ctr., 1993—2002; active State Ho. Adv. Com., Boston, 1984—85, Gov.'s Coun. for Wentworth Coolidge Mansion, Concord, 1964—66; mem. Com. for Preservation of N.H. State Flags, 1989—92; mem. H.F. duPont award com. Winterthur Mus., 1993—, mem. Mt. Vernon adv. com. for 1999, 1996—99; designator The Henderson Found., 1992—2004. Recipient Charles F. Montgomery prize, Decorative Arts Soc., 1985, Disting. Sophomore Book prize, Boston U., 1993, (with Richard C. Nylander) The Anne and Roger Webb award, Historic Mass., Inc., 1996, John F. Ayer award, The Bay State League, 2002, Boston History award, Bostonian Soc., 2003, award for outstanding contbn. to decorative arts, Iris Found., 2005, Lifetime Achievement award (with Richard C. Nylander), Victorian Soc. Am., 2005, Roll of Honor, Nat. Trust. Soc. Colonial Dames of Am., N.H., 2006. Mem.: N.H. Hist. Soc. (interpretation com. 2003—05, mem. exbns. and pubs. com. 2005—), Costume Soc. Am. (bd. dirs. 1977—83), New Eng. Hist. Geneal. Soc., N.H. Humanities Coun., Soc. Preservation of N.H. Forests, Soc. Winterthur Fellows, Mass. Hist. Soc., Portsmouth Athenaeum, Royal Oak Assn., Nat. Trust for Hist. Preservation, Am. Assn. for State and Local History (Cert. of Commendation 2001), Am. Antiquarian Soc., Castle Preservation Soc. (bd. dirs. 2003—, v.p. 2004—), Colonial Soc. Mass., Nat. Soc. Colonial Dames in N.H. (bd. dirs. 1967—73, program chair 2002—, Roll of Honor 2006), Friends of Hist. Deerfield, Friends of the Moffatt Ladd House, Lakes Region Conservation Trust, Brown Club N.H. (trustee 1988—93). Episcopalian. Home: 17 Franklin St Portsmouth NH 03801-4501 Personal E-mail: jane.nylander@verizon.net.

**NYMAN, MICHAEL LAWRENCE,** composer; b. London, Eng., Mar. 23, 1944; s. Mark and Jeanette N.; m. Aet Toome, May 16, 1970; 2 children. Attended, King's Coll., London, 1964-67; B.Mus., Royal Acad. of Music, 1965; attended, Conservatoire and Folklore Inst., Bucharest, 1965-66. Founder, MN Records, 2005. Music dir., composer, performer: (film scores) 1-100, 1977, A Walk Through H, 1977, Tom Philips, 1977, Vertical Features Remake, 1978, The Falls, 1980, Brimstone and Treacle, 1982, Frozen Music, 1983, Nelly's Version, 1983, The Draughtsman's Contract, 1983, The Cold Room, 1984, L'ange frenetique, 1985, A Zed and Two Noughts, 1985, Ballet Mechanique, 1986, The Disputation, 1986, Photographic Exhibits, 1987, Drowning By Numbers, 1988, La Traversee de Paris, 1989, The Cook, the Thief, His Wife, Her Lover, 1989, Monsieur, 1989, Prospero's Books, 1991, Les enfants volants, 1991, Le Mari de la Coiffeuse, 1991, The Piano, 1993; musical performer, composer: (theatre) The Masterwork/Award-Winning Fishknife, 1979, (ballets) Portraits in Reflection, 1985, And Do They Do, 1986, (dance works) The Fall of Icarus, 1989, Garden Party, 1990; composer: (ballets) A Broken Set of Rules, 1984, Touch the Earth, 1987, (dance works) Miniatures, 1989, (operas) The Man Who Mistook His Wife for a Hat, 1986, La Princesse de Milan, 1991, Letters, Riddles and Writs, 1992, (TV spls.) Act of God, 1980, The Man Who Mistook His Wife for a Hat, 1987, Fairly Secret Army Series 2, 1987, Dancing in Numbers, 1988, Touch the Earth, 1988, Out of the Ruins, 1989, Death in the Seine, 1989, Men of Steel, 1990, Letters, Riddles and Writs, 1991, The Final Score, 1992, The Fall of Icarus, 1992; author: (music criticism) Experimental Music: Cage and Beyond, 1975; recs. include The Convertibility of Lute Strings, 1993, For John Cage, 1993, Goodbye Frankie, Goodbye Benny, 1993. Office: care Screen Composer of Am 2451 Nichols Canyon Rd Los Angeles CA 90046-1734

**NYOKKA, SUZETTE,** artist, natural health educator; b. Meadowbrook, Pa., June 10, 1961; d. Barbara Louise and adopted d. Walter H. Schmitz; children: Thomas Ziemba children: Gaelen Ishi Nyokka Morrell, Emily Luna Rose Nyokka Morrell. BA, Calif. Inst. Integral Studies, 2001. Advanced Massage Therapies, Natural Health Educator Inst. of Ednl. Therapy, Heartwood Inst., 1988, cert. in Jin Shin Jyutsu 2005. Founder Heartwood Garden, Garberville, Calif., 1984—89; creator/artist Island Mt. Basketry, Garberville, 1986—; massage therapist/ educator Advanced Massage Therapies, Woodside, Menlo Park, Calif., 1989—2005, massage therapist/educator Garberville/Novato, 2005—; ednl. activist So. Humboldt Cmty. Sch. Dist., Garberville, 1984—; dir. Skyfish Sch. Permaculture Program, Garberville, 1997—; artistic dir. Teen's Radio, Redway, Calif., 2005—; instr. permaculture design, adj. advisor Skyfish Sch., Briceland, 1997—2005. Prodr.: (storytelling festivals) Live Performances; co-creator (cd) All Spirits Sing (Best Native Am. Rec., 1998). Devel. coord. Arts and Ecology Ctr., Garberville, Calif., 2005—; developmennt coord. KMUD Teen's Cmty. Radio, Garberville, Calif., 2004—05; vp So. Humboldt Youth and Cmty. Ctr., Garberville, Calif.; pres. Trees Found., Garberville, Calif., 1996—98; participant in a cross cultural sharing Nat. Storytelling Assn., San Francisco, 2002—02. Grant, Music For Little People Found., 2002, Humboldt Area Found., 2004, Calif. Inst. of Integral Studies, 2000. Mem.: So. Humboldt Cmty. Parks and Garden Club (life). Democrat-Npl. Avocations: reading, photography, language, film, travel. Home: 352 Meadowview Rd Garberville CA 95542 Office Phone: 415-250-1733. E-mail: suzette@asis.com.

**NYQUIST, CORINNE ELAINE,** librarian; b. Minnesota Falls, Minn., Nov. 1, 1935; d. Clair Francis and Ebba Ingeborg Johnson; m. Thomas Eugene Nyquist, Dec. 22, 1956; children: Jonathan Eugene, Lynn Marie. BA (cum laude), Macalester Coll., 1956; MALS, U. Minn., 1971; PhD (hon.), U. Albany, 2004. Asst. librarian U. Minn., Mpls., 1959-60, Evanston (Ill.) Pub. Library, 1960-64, Skokie (Ill.) Pub. Library, 1965-66; asst. librarian, research asst. Rhodes U., Grahamstown, Republic of South Africa, 1967; asst. librarian to librarian SUNY, New Paltz, 1968—, ombudsman, 1983-85; co-project dir. human rights documentation project Ford Found., 1986-88; cons. N.Y. State Edn. Dept., Albany, 2000-02; chmn. internat. librs. com. SUNY, 1984-86. Contbr. articles to profl. jours. Chmn. Town Dem. Com., New Paltz, 1984-86; organized SUNY Research Found., 1975, 84-86, Ford Found., 1986. Mem. ALA (chmn. human rights task force 1989-91, exec. internat. rels. task force 1987-92, interlibr. loan code revision com. 2006—), African Studies Assn., NY African Studies Assn. (co-editor newsletter 1974-99, v.p. 1991-92, pres. 1992-93), Ulster County Librs. Assn. (exec. com. 1984-94), Sojourner Truth Inst. (bd. 1997-2001), SUNY Librs. Assn., Beta Phi Mu. Avocations: reading, hiking, cross country skiing, travel. Office: SUNY Sojourner Truth Libr New Paltz NY 12561-2493 Home: 140 Huguenot St New Paltz NY 12561-1018 Office Phone: 845-257-3681. E-mail: nyquistc@newpaltz.edu.

**NYQUIST, JOHN DAVIS,** retired radio manufacturing company executive; b. Peoria, Ill., May 28, 1918; s. Eliud and Linnea (Widen) N.; m. Alice Schmidt, June 5, 1942; 1 child, Sarah Lynn. BS in Mech. Engring, U. Ill., 1941. With Collins Radio Co., Cedar Rapids, Iowa, 1941—, v.p., gen. mgr. Iowa region, 1965-69, v.p. operations, 1969-70, v.p., 1970-73, also dir.; ret., 1973; cons. Rockwell-Collins. Dir. Norwest Bank Iowa N.A. (formerly Peoples Bank & Trust Co.), Cedar Rapids. Bd. dirs. Am. Cancer Soc., YMCA, St. Lukes Hosp. Recipient award for outstanding achievement Am. Inst. Indsl. Engrs., 1966, Indsl. Engring. award, 1969, Coll. Engring. Alumni Honor award, 1977; both U. Ill.). Mem. Iowa Mfrs. Assn., Am. Mgmt. Assn., Am. Inst. Indsl. Engrs., IEEE, Cedar Rapids C. of C. (dir.) Clubs: Cedar Rapids Country. Home: 2115 1st Ave SE Cedar Rapids IA 52402

**NYQUIST, MAURICE OTTO,** retired federal agency administrator, scientist; b. Fairmont, Minn., May 30, 1944; s. Carl Arther and Wilda Yvette (Freitag) N.; m. Mary Maud Magee, Aug. 8, 1977; children: Gretchen, Beth. BS in Biology, Hamline U., St. Paul, Minn., 1966; MA in Biology, Mankato State U., 1968; PhD in Zoology, Wash. State U., 1973. Asst. prof. zoology Wash. State U., Pullman, 1973-74; scientist Nat. Park Svc., Lakewood, Colo., 1974-76, mgr., 1979-93; mgr., scientist Nat. Biol. Svc., Denver, 1993-96, USGS, Denver, 1996—2004; coord. Aurora Partnership, 1999—2003. Affiliate faculty Sch. Natural Resources, Colo. State U., Ft. Collins; mem. peer rev. coms. for academia, govt. and pvt. industry; agy. rep. Fed. Geographic Data Com., chair biol. data working group, mem. standards working group and coordination group, vegetation subcom. Dir. prodn. interactive computer exhibit on remote sensing for Denver Mus. Nat. History; contbr. sci. articles to profl. jours. Bd. dirs. Nat. Park Service Equal Employment Opportunity Com., Denver, 1981, chmn., 1982. Recipient Mgrs. award Nat. Park Service, Lakewood, 1981, Performance Commendation award, 1988, Excellence of Svc. Team awrd U.S Dept. Interior, 1999; NRA rsch. grantee, 1972. Fellow Am. Soc. Potogrammetry and Remote Sensing (exec. com., bd. dirs. 1988-90, v.p. 1992, pres.-elect 1993, pres. 1994, dir. remote sensing applications divsn. 1987-89); mem. Am. Congress on Surveying and Mapping (joint satellite mapping and remote sensing com.), The Wildlife Soc., ELAS Users Group (co-chmn. 1985-86, chmn. 1986-87), Sigma Xi. *Personal philosophy: We need to view the land as a community to which we all belong, instead of a commodity for individual gain. (adopted from Aldo Leopold's A Sand County Almanac, 1949).*

**NYQUIST, PAUL ALAN,** neurologist, researcher; b. Mpls., June 23, 1963; s. Russel Stanford and Marjorie Louise (Petrich) Nyquist; m. Christine Marie Nyquist; children: Tessa, Lindsey. BS in Zoology and Anthropology with distinction and high honors, U. Mich., 1986; MD with distinction, George Washington U., 1992, MPH, 1992. Diplomate Nat. Bd. Med. Examiners, Am. Bd. Neurology. Intern Nat. Naval Med. Ctr., Bethesda, Md., 1992—93; undersea med. officer Navy Med. Rsch. Inst., Bethesda, 1993—96; resident in neurology Mayo Clinic, Rochester, Minn., 1996—99; clin. fellow NIH Nat. Inst. Neurol. Diseases, Bethesda, 1999—2001; clin. fellow in intensive care medicine NIH Magnuson Clin. Ctr., Bethesda, 2001—03; asst. prof. medicine Va. Commonwealth U.; dir. stroke program Inova Fairfax Hosp.; asst. prof. neurology, anesthetic critical care, erebrovascular divsn. Johns Hopkins U. Hosp., Johns Hopkins Med. Sch., Balt., 2004—. Spl. vol., critical care unit NIH. Contbr. articles to profl. jours. Recipient Navy Health Profl. Scholarship, Young Investigators award, Am. Epilepsy Soc., 1999, Travel Fellow award, Am. Neurol. Soc., 2001. Mem.: Phi Eta Sigma, Alpha Omega Alpha. Avocations: deep sea diving, running. Office: 600 N Wolf St Baltimore MD 20817 Office Phone: 410-955-2611. Business E-Mail: pnyquis1@jhmi.edu.

**NYREN, NEIL SEBASTIAN,** publishing executive, editor; b. Boston, June 13, 1948; s. Karl Edwin and Dorothy Elizabeth (Smith) N.; m. Lois Miriam Sharfman, Oct. 11, 1970; 1 child, Alexander BA, Brandeis U. V.p. G.P. Putnam's Sons Pub., N.Y.C., 1997—; editor Random House Pubs., N.Y.C., 1974-77, Arbor House Pubs., N.Y.C., 1977-78; exec. editor Atheneum Pubs., N.Y.C., 1978-84; sr. editor G.P. Putnam's Sons Pub., N.Y.C., 1984-86, editor-in-chief, 1986—, pub., 1989—, sr. v.p., 1997—. Democrat. Jewish. Office: GP Putnam's Sons 375 Hudson St New York NY 10014-3658 Business E-Mail: nnyren@penguinputnam.com.

**NYROP, DONALD WILLIAM,** air transportation executive; b. Elgin, Nebr., Apr. 1, 1912; s. William A. and Nellie (Wylie) N.; m. Grace Cary, Apr. 19, 1941; children: Nancy, William, Karen, Kathryn. AB, Doane Coll., 1934; LL.B., George Washington U., 1939. Bar: D.C. 1938. Atty. Gen. Counsel's Office, CAA, Washington, 1939-41; exec. officer to chmn. CAB, 1942, chmn., 1952; rep. U.S. airlines; mem. ofcl. U.S. delegations Internat. Civil Aviation Orgn. Assemblies, 1946, 47; dep. adminstr. for ops. CAA, 1948-50, adminstr., 1950-51; chmn. CAB, 1951-52; pres. Northwest Airlines, Inc., 1954-78. Served with Air Transport Command USAAF, 1942-46. Decorated Legion of Merit. Mem.: Mpls. Club. Home: 4505 Golf Ter Minneapolis MN 55424-1510

**O, CAO K.,** cultural organization administrator; b. Vietnam; arrived in US, 1975; BS in Sociology, Cornell U., 1980; MS, Hunter Coll. Sch. of Social Work; attended, Columbia U. Former social worker and case mgr. NYC Dept. for the Aging, Vietnamese Am. Cultural Org.; develop. dir. Hamilton-Madison House, 1983—86; program developer NY State Office of Mental Health, 1986—88; consultant United Way of NYC, 1988—90. Exec. dir. Asian Am. Federation of NY, 1991—; vice chair 9/11 United Services Group; bd. mem. Museum of Chinese in Am., Hamilton-Madison House, Nonprofit Coordinating Com. of NY, Human Svc. Council of NYC; chmn. Coalition for New Philanthropy in NY, 2003—. Office: Asian Am Federation of NY 120 Wall St New York NY 10005

**O, KENNETH KYONGYOP,** engineering educator; s. Sang-Chol and Yong-Ae O; m. Hyun-Joo Nam, Dec. 28, 1991; children: Stephen Tae-Jin, Daniel Tae-Su, Andrew Tae-Yoon. BS, MS, MIT, 1984, PhD, 1989. Sr. process engr. Analog Devices Inc, Wilmington, Mass., 1989—94; prof. U. Fla., Gainesville, Fla., 1994—, Rsch. Found. Prof., 2004—06. Chief tech. officer Global Communication Device, North Andover, Mass., 2002—03. Recipient Faculty Partnership award, IBM, 1995, 1997, 2000, Copper Design Challenge award, Semiconductor Rsch. Corp., 1999, Career Devel. award, NSF, 1996, Copper Design Challenge award, Semiconductor Rsch. Corp., 1999, Materials Processing Ctr. fellow, MIT, 1985. Mem.: IEEE, Sigma Xi. Achievements include development of RF silicon bipolar process technology; first to show CMOS technology can be used to produce RF integrated circuits for WLAN applications which are competitive to those fabricated using the SiGe technology; development of Aaproaches to improve on-chip inductors and varactors in silicon integrated circuits; first to show on-chip antennas can be used for communication within and between IC's; development of Schottky diodes with cut-off frequency greater than 1 THz in CMOS technology; research in 200-GHz CMOS oscillator. It holds the highest operating frequency silicon based circuits. Office: U Florida Dept ECE 539 New Engineering Building Gainesville FL 32611 Office Phone: 352-392-6618. Office Fax: 352-392-8381. Business E-Mail: kko@tec.ufl.edu.

**OAK, CLAIRE MORISSET,** artist, educator; b. St. Georges, Quebec, Can., May 31, 1921; came to U.S., 1945; d. Louis and Bernadette (Coulombe) Morisset; m. Alan Ben Oak, July 2, 1947. Student, Ecole des Beaux Arts, 1938—42, Parsons Sch. Design, NYC, 1945, Art Students League, 1945—46. Staff artist Henry Morgan & R. Simpson, Montreal, 1942-45; artist illustrator W.B. Golovin Advt. Agy., N.Y.C., 1947-49; freelance illustrator Arnold Constable & Advt. Agy., N.Y.C., 1948-50, Le Jardin des Modes, Paris, 1950-51, May & Co., L.A., 1956, Katten & Marengo Advt., Stockton, Calif.,

1962-84; pvt. practice illustrator, designer San Joaquin Valley, Calif., 1984-92; art instr. San Joaquin Delta Coll., Stockton, 1973—. Owner Fashion Illustrator's Workshop, N.Y.C., 1953-54; instr. Bauder Coll., Sacramento, 1975-76; painting workshop leader Lodi Art Ctr., 1991—; watercolor workshop leader D'Pharr Painting Adventures, Virginia City, Nev., 1992; watercolor workshop Galerie Iona, Stockton, Calif., 1993—. Named S.B. Anthony Woman of Achievement in the Arts, U. Pacific, 1982. Mem. Stockton Art League, Lodi Art Ctr., Ctrl. Calif. Art League, The League of Carmichael Artists, Delta Watercolor Soc. (bd. mem. 1988—). Avocations: painting, drawing. Home: 2140 Waudman Ave Stockton CA 95209-1755 *You are a success in the visual arts if you teach others how to see.*

**OAKAR, MARY ROSE,** congresswoman; b. Cleve., Mar. 5, 1940; d. Joseph M. and Margaret Mary (Ellison) O. BA in English, Speech and Drama, Ursuline Coll., Cleve., 1962, LHD (hon.); MA in Fine Arts, John Carroll U., Cleve., 1966; LLD (hon.), Ashland U., 1978, Ursuline Coll., 1984, St. Mary's Notre Dame, 1989, Baldwin Wallace Coll., 1988; LHD (hon.), Trinity Coll., 1987. Instr. English and drama Lourdes Acad., Cleve., 1963-70; asst. prof. English, speech and drama Cuyahoga Community Coll., Cleve., 1968-75; mem. Cleve. City Council from 8th Ward, 1973-76, 95th-102nd Congresses from 20th Dist. Ohio, 1977-92; mem. Pepper Commn. on Long Term Health Care, chair subcom. internat. devel., fin., trade and monetary policy; chair task force on social security, elderly, women; chair subcom. on personnel and police; mem. banking, fin. and urban affairs com., select com. on aging, post office and civil service com., com. on house adminstrn., also numerous subcoms.; ptnr. Mary Rose Oakar and Assocs. Apptd. to Sec. Conf. to Establish Nat. Action Plan on Breast Cancer, 1994, by Pres. Clinton to bd. dirs. Bldrs., For Peace, 1994, to policy to White House Com. on Aging. Founder, vol.-dir. Near West Side Civic Arts Center, Cleve., 1970; ward leader Cuyahoga County Democratic Party, 1972-76; mem. Ohio Dem. Central Com. from 20th Dist., 1974; trustee Fedn. Community Planning, Cleve., Health and Planning Commn. Cleve., Community Info. Service Cleve., Cleve. Soc. Crippled Children, Public Services Occupational Group Adv. Com., Cuyahoga Community Coll., Cleve. Ballet, Cleve. YWCA. Recipient Outstanding Service awards OEO, 1973-78, Community Service award Am. Indian Center, Cleve., 1973, Community Service award Nationalities Service Center, 1974, Community Service award Club San Lorenzo, Cleve., 1976, Cuyahoga County Dem. Woman of Yr., 1977, Ursuline Coll. Alumna of Yr. award, 1977, awards Irish Nat. Caucus, awards West Side Community Mental Health Center, awards Am. Lebanese League, awards Cleve. Fedn. Am.-Syrian Lebanese Clubs, Breast Cancer Awareness award Nat. Women's Health Resource Ctr., 1989, 1st lay recipient Barbara Bohen-Pfeiffer award Italian-Am. Found. Cancer Rsch., 1989, Disting. Svc. award Am. Cancer Soc., 1989, Myrl H. Shoemaker award Ohio Dem. Party, 1992, Philip Hart award Consumer Fedn. Am., 1987; cert. appreciation City of Cleve.; Woman of Yr. award Cuyahoga County Women's Polit. Caucus, 1983; decorated Knight of Order of St. Ladislaus of Hungary, Women in Aerospace Outstanding Ach. award, Black Focus Woman of the Decade award. Office: 1888 W 30th St Cleveland OH 44113-3447

**OAKES, DENNIS,** lawyer, insurance company executive; b. 1951; AB, Hamilton Coll., 1973; JD, Cath. U. of Am., 1977. With Wolf, Block Schorr and Solis-Cohen, 1977—80, 1984—87; chief of staff Mayor of Phila., 1980—84; adminstrv. asst. Phila. Congressman William J. Green, 1973—77; spl. counsel Ronald O. Perelman, 1988—93; exec. dir., Acad. Medicine and Managed Care Forum Aetna Inc., 1996—2001, chief investor rels. officer, 2001—03, v.p. pub. policy, 2003—. Office: Aetna Inc 151 Farmington Ave Hartford CT 06156

**OAKES, DUWAYNE EARL,** retired principal; b. Fillmore, ND, May 28, 1926; s. Ralph William Oakes and Ella Catherine (Anderson) Baril; m. Elva Jean Jacobsen, Nov. 6, 1948; children: Jon, Robert, Kathleen, Mary. BA in Edn., Pacific Luth. U., 1952, MA, 1972. Tchr. DuPont Ft. Lewis Sch. Dist., Wash., 1952-59, prin., 1959, Clover Pk. Sch. Dist., Lakewood, Wash. 1959-71; ret., 1971. Author: God's Call to Communion, 1982; contbr.: National Poetry Library Anthology, 1995-96, God's Plan, 1999; inventor fishing rod socket. Inductee Internat. Poetry Hall of Fame, 1996. Mem.: Eagles Club, AmVets, Norwegian Lodge. Christian Socialist. Lutheran. Avocations: singing in church choir, Normanna Chorus. Home: 8515 94th St SW Lakewood WA 98498-4527

**OAKES, JAMES L.,** federal judge; b. Springfield, Ill., Feb. 21, 1924; m. Evelena S. Kenworthy, Dec. 29, 1973 (dec. Oct. 1997); m. Mara A. Williams, Jan. 1, 1999; m. Rosalyn Landon, Oct. 2, 2003; children. AB, Harvard Coll., 1945; LLB, Harvard U. Law Sch., 1947; LLD, New Eng. Coll., 1976, Suffolk U., 1980, Vt. Law Sch., 1995. Bar: Calif. 1949, Vt. 1950. Pvt. practice, Brattleboro, Vt.; spl. counsel Vt. Pub. Svc. Commn., 1959—60; counsel Vt. Statutory Revision Commn., 1957—60; mem. Vt. Senate, 1961—65; atty. gen. Vt., 1967—69; U.S. dist. judge, 1970—71; judge U.S. Ct. Appeals 2d Cir., Brattleboro, 1971—, chief judge, 1989—92. Adj. faculty Duke U. Law Sch., 1985—96, Iowa U. Coll. Law, 1993—97. Office: US Ct Appeals 204 Main St Brattleboro VT 05301 Office Phone: 802-254-5000.*

**OAKES, JEANNINE,** education educator; BA, San Diego State U., 1964; MA, Calif. State U., 1969; PhD in Edn., UCLA, 1980. Presdl. prof. in ednl. equity UCLA, dir. Inst. for Democracy, Edn. & Access, dir. All Campus Consortium on Rsch. for Diversity. Contbr. articles to profl. jours.; author: Keeping track: How schools structure inequality, 1985; co-author: Teaching to Change the World, 1998, Becoming Good American Schools: The Struggle for Civic Virtue in Education Reform, 1999. Recipient Disting. Achievement Award, Ednl. Press Assn. of Am., Ralph David Abernathy Award for Pub. Svc., So. Christian Leadership Conf., Multicultural Rsch. Award, Nat. Assn. Multicultural Edn., Jose Vasconcelos World Award in Edn., World Cultural Coun., 2002. Office: UCLA Grad Sch Edn Info Studies 1033D Moore Hall Los Angeles CA 90095 Office Phone: 310-825-2494. E-mail: oakes@ucla.edu.*

**OAKES, JUDY DIANNE,** real estate broker; b. Charleston, W.Va., Aug. 14, 1930; d. William E. and Betty A. Hager; m. Gary H. Oakes, Dec. 21, 1968; children: Scott E., Christina D. McDaniel, Brian M. Real estate sales Bishop Realtors, Cleve., 1973-82, Armstrong Realty, Riverside, Calif., 1986-88; real estate broker Remax All Stars, Riverside, Calif., 1988-94, Realty Exec., Riverside, Calif., 1994—2001. Named #1 Agt. in Co., Real Estate Sales, 1994—2002. Mem. Cert. Residential Specialist, Magnolia Ave. Bapt. Ch., Inland Valley Assn. Realtors (bd. dirs. 1995). Avocations: reading, gardening. E-mail: judy@judyoakes.com.

**OAKES, LESTER CORNELIUS,** retired electrical engineer, consultant; b. Knoxville, Oct. 11, 1923; s. Charles Vaughn and Maude Cornelia (Harrison) O.; m. Kathleen Clark, Dec. 27, 1947; children: Michael, Richard, Cynthia, Melissa. BS in E.E., U. Tenn., 1949, MS, 1962. Registered profl. engr., Tenn. Engr. Fairchild Engring. and Aircraft, Oak Ridge, 1949-51; engr. I&C div. Oak Ridge Nat. Lab., 1951-68, dep. head I&C div., 1968—, asst. dir. I&C div., 1971-90; cons. Oak Ridge Nat. Lab., electric Power Rsch. Inst., Nuclear Regulatory Commn., 1990—. Contbr. articles to profl. jours.; patentee in field. Served with USAF, 1943-46. Martin Marietta Corp. fellow. Fellow IEEE Presbyterian. Home: 710 Pleasant Hill Rd Maryville TN 37803-7337 Personal E-mail: lesoakes@aol.com.

**OAKES, NANCY,** chef, restaurant owner; Student, San Francisco Art Inst. Formerly chef Alexis, San Francisco; formerly chef, co-owner Barnacle, San Francisco, L'Avenue, San Francisco; chef, co-owner Boulevard, San Francisco, 1993—. Named Best Chef in Calif., James Beard Found., 2001. Office: Boulevard 1 Mission St San Francisco CA 94105

**OAKES, PAMELA R.,** retired elementary school educator; d. Frederick O. and Virginia Hoover Abrams; m. F. Michael Oakes, Oct. 4, 1958; children: Michael, Lisa Poole, Gigi Kershner, Gina Korsi. AA, Jefferson C.C., Louisville, 1971; BS in Edn., U. Louisville, 1979, postgrad., 1979—80, U. St.

Thomas, Houston, 1992—94. Cert. ESL and gifted and talented tchr. Tchr. spl. edn. Jefferson County Sch. Dist., Louisville, 1979—80; tchr. 5th/6th grade St. Thomas Acad., West Hartford, Conn., 1980—82; tchr. 5th grade Our Lady of Victory, Victoria, Tex., 1982—84, St. Gregory the Great, San Antonio, 1984—85; tchr. 2d grade Houston Ind. Sch. Dist., 1985—89; tchr. 5th grade Cypress-Fairbanks Ind. Sch. Dist., Houston, 1989—2005, ret., 2005. Demonstration tchr. Houston Ind. Sch. Dist., 1988; coord. spelling bee Matzke Elem. Sch., 1995—2005. Mem.: Tex. Edn. Assn., Ky. Cols., Kappa Delta Pi. Roman Catholic. Avocations: sewing, interior decorating. Home: 15027 Rain Shadow Ct Houston TX 77070 Office: Cypress-Fairbanks ISD Matzke Elem 13102 Jones Rd Houston TX 77070 Personal E-mail: pamoakeshouston@aol.com

**OAKES, ROBERT JAMES,** physics professor; b. Mpls., Jan. 21, 1936; s. Sherman E. and Josephine J. (Olson) O.; children: Cindy L., Lisa A. BS, U. Minn., 1957, MS, 1959, PhD, 1962. NSF fellow Stanford U., 1962-64; asst. prof. physics, 1964-68; assoc. prof. physics Northwestern U., 1968-70, prof. physics, 1970-76, prof. physics and astronomy, 1976—. Vis. staff mem. Los Alamos Sci. Lab., 1971-92; vis. scientist Fermi Nat. Accelerator Lab., 1975—, CERN, 1966-67; mem. Inst. for Advanced Study, Princeton, 1967-68; vis. scientist DESY, 1971-72; faculty assoc. Argonne Nab. Lab., 1982—; U.S. scientist NSF-Yugoslav joint program, 1982-92; panelist Nat. Rsch. Coun., 1990-98. A.P. Sloan fellow 1965-68; Air Force Office Sci. Rsch. grantee, 1969-71, NSF grantee 1971-87, Dept. Energy grantee, 1987—; named Fulbright-Hays Disting. prof. U. Sarajevo, Yugoslavia, 1979-80; recipient Natural Sci. prize China, 1993. Fellow Am. Phys. Soc., AAAS; mem. N.Y. Acad. Sci., Ill. Acad. Sci., Physics Club (Chgo.), Sigma Xi, Tau Beta Pi. Clubs: Physics (Chgo.). Office: Northwestern U Dept Physics 2145 Sheridan Rd Evanston IL 60208-0834 Office Phone: 847-491-5458

**OAKES, TERRY LOUIS,** apparel executive; b. Denver, June 12, 1953; s. Robert Walter and Stella Marie (Ray) O.; m. Cynthia Alison Bailey, Jan. 10, 1981; children: Madeleine Bailey, Robert Alan. BBA, So. Meth. U., 1975. Dept. mgr. Woolf Bros., Dallas, 1975-76; buyer I.K.O. Dry Goods, Denver, 1976-79, gen. sales mgr., 1979-81, exec. v.p., mdse. mgr., 1981-86; nat. sales mgr. Fresh Squeeze div. Bayly Corp., Denver, 1986-88; owner, pres. Bolderdash, Denver, 1988—. Tchr., mem. adv. bd. fashion mdse. divsn. Colo. Inst. Art., Denver, 1991-98. Bd. dirs. Cherry Creek North Bus. Improvement Dist., Vail Racquet Club, Vail, Colo. Mem. Vail Racquet Club (bd. dirs.). Democrat. Presbyterian. Home: 5390 S Geneva St Englewood CO 80111-6205 Office: Bolderdash 2721 E 3d Ave Denver CO 80206-4919 Business E-Mail: bolderdash@earthlink.net.

**OAKES, WALTER JERRY,** pediatric neurosurgeon; b. De Soto, Mo., July 10, 1946; s. Marvin Melton and Mildred Florene (Link) O.; m. Linda Helen Maas (div. Jan. 1985); 1 child, Kathleen Suzanne; m. Jean Evans, Dec. 1988; children: Matthew Marvin, Peter Clifford. BA in Chemistry, U. Mo., 1968; MD, Duke U., 1972. Diplomate Am. Bd. Neurol. Surgeons. Neurosurgery resident Duke U., Durham, NC, 1972-78, asst. prof. neurosurgery, 1979-90, assoc. prof. neurosurgery, 1991—, asst. prof. pediatrics, 1981-92, assoc. prof. pediatrics, 1992; pediatric neurosurgery resident U. Toronto Hosp. for Sick Children, Ont., Canada, July-Dec., 1975; registrar pediatric neurosurgery U. London Hosp. for Sick Children, England, Sept., 1978-Feb., 1979; prof. neurosurgery and pediat. U. Ala., Birmingham, 1992—; Dan Hendley chair pediatric neurosurgery, 2002—. Fellow: ACS. Office: Children's Hosp Ala 1600 7th Ave S Ste 400 Birmingham AL 35233-1785 Office Phone: 205-879-7754. Business E-Mail: wjomd@uab.edu.

**OAKLAND, RON,** violinist; MusB, Hartt Coll. Music, 1969; MusM, Juilliard Sch., 1975. Tchr. Calif. U., Washington, 1971—72, U. Md., College Park, 1975—76, The Dalton Sch., 1976—77, Chamber Music Conf. of the East, 1975—86; mem. Manhattan String Quartet, White Oak Chamber Ensemble, Bargemusic, Univ. Md. String Quartet, Interaction Artists. Concertmaster Am. Ballet Theatre, N.Y.C., 1980—; music dir. White Oak Dance Project (Mikhail Baryshnikov's Co.), Bolshoi Ballet Summer U.S. tours. Musician: (violinist solo appearances) Am. Ballet Theatre, White Oak Dance Project, N.Y. Chamber Symphony, Bennington Chamber Music Conf., Am. Symphony Orch., Bolshoi Ballet, many orchs. in U.S., Europe, S.Am., (prin. 2d) Am. Symphony Orch., 1976—82, Bklyn. Philharmonic, 1977—88, (concertmaster) Am. Ballet Theatre, 1991—, numerous others, —, recording for labels including EMI, DGG, Tournabout, Nonesuch. With USAF, 1969—72. Home: 70 Kovar St Bogota NJ 07603

**OAKLAND, SUZANNE N.J. CHUN,** state legislator; d. Philip S. and Mei-Chin Chun; m. Michael Sands Chun Oakland, June 11, 1994; children: Mailene Nohea Pua, Michael Sing Kamakau, Lauren Suzanne LeRong. BA in Comm. and Psychology, U. Hawaii. Adminstrv. asst. Au's Plumbing and Metal Works, 1979—90; cmty. svcs. specialist Hawaii State Senate, 1984; adminstrv. asst. Smolenski & Woodell, Attys. at Law, 1984—86; rsch. asst., office mgr. City Coun. mem. Gary Gill, 1987—90; state rep. House Dist. 27, 1990—96; state senator Senate Dist. 13, 1996—. Vice chair com. on health State Senate, 2003—, chair com. on human svcs., 2003—, com. on edn. and mil. affairs, 2005—, com. on higher edn., 2005—. Mem. Hawaii State Youth Vol. Bd., 1978—; bd. dirs. Honolulu Neighborhood Housing Svcs., 1986—88, 1989—, McKinley H.S. Found. and McKinley Alumni Assn. 1989—; mem. adv. bd. Lanakila Milti-Purpose Sr. Ctr., 1991—; com. The CHOW Project, 1992—; mem. Chung Wah Chung Kung Hui, 1991—; adv. bd. Sex Abuse Treatment Ctr., 1993—; vol. Legal Svcs. Hawaii, 1994—; bd. dirs. Susannah Wesley Cmty. Ctr., 2001—, Hawaii Housing Devel. Corp., 1993—; mem. Children's Trust Fund Adv. Coun., 1993—; bd. dirs. Liliha-Palama Bus. Assn., 1994—; mem. Hawaii Kids Count Coun., 1994—. Recipient Friend of Family award, Hawaii Assn. for Marriage and Family Therapy, 1998, Legislator of Yr. award, Mental Health Assn., 1999, Outstanding Legislator award, Hawaii Med. Assn., 1999, Legislator of Yr. award, Aloha State Assn. of Deaf, 1999, Hawaii State Chiropractic Assn., 2000, numerous other awards. Mem.: Hawaii Chinese Civic Assn., Chinese C. of C.

**OAKLEY, ANDREW ARTHUR,** journalist, educator; b. Chgo., Oct. 22, 1958; s. Arthur George and Dolores Margarite (Hernandez) O.; m. Suzanna Pinter, Sept. 7, 1985; children: Glen Matthias, Ryan Arthur. BS in Journalism, Northwestern U., 1980, MS, 1981. Reporter Woodstock (Ill.) Daily Sentinel, 1980-81; police reporter Herald-Palladium, St. Joseph, Mich., 1981-82; city hall reporter Daily Herald, Arlington Heights, Ill., 1982-84; instr. journalism Oakton C.C., Des Plaines, Ill., 1984-85; features editor North Shore Mag. Winnetka, Ill., 1985-86; news editor City and State, Chgo., 1986-93; journalism editor P.O. Publ. Co., Port Murray, NJ, 1993-2000; newsletter editor All Aboard for Hackettstown, NJ, 1996-98. Lectr. Northwestern U., Evanston, Ill., 1990-96; columnist Daily Herald, Arlington Heights, Ill., 1995-96; copy editor Full Time Dads Mag., Clifton, N.J., 1997-2000; corr. Daily Herald, Arlington Heights, 1995—. Author: Eighty-Eight, 1988, Issues Confronting City and State Governments, 1992, Beginning Journalism Packet, 1991; cons. editor P.O. Pub. Co., Skokie, Ill., 1988-92. Lifetime mem. N Club, 1980—; commr. Skokie Human Rels. Commn., 1987-94; advisor Mcpl. Alliance Lit. Club, 1997-98; U.S. Soccer Fedn. coach, referee, 1999—; edn. chmn. Charleston (Ill.) Alliance Ch., 2000-04; v.p. Blairstown Little League, 2005—. Mem. Medill Alumni Assn., Evanston Running Club. E-mail: nwarrenunited@aol.com.

**OAKLEY, CAROLYN LE,** state legislator, city manager, director; b. Portland, Oreg., June 28, 1942; d. George Thomas and Ruth Alveta Victoria (Engberg) Penketh; children: Christine, Michelle. BS in Edn., Oreg. State U., 1965. Education County (Oreg.) Schs., 1965-76; owner Linn County Tractor, 1965-90; mem. Oreg. Legis. Assembly, Salem, 1989—, asst. majority leader, 1993—, majority whip, 1994; apptd. regional dir. region 10 Dept. Health and Human Svcs., Seattle, 2002—. Mem. exec. bd. Oreg. Retail Coun., 1987-90. Chmn. Linn County Rep. Ctrl. Com., 1982-84; chmn. bd. dirs. North Albany Svc. Dist., 1988-90; chair Salvation Army, Linn and Benton Counties, 1987—; vice chmn. bd. trustees Linn-Benton C.C. Found., 1987—; pres. Women for Agr., Linn and Benton Counties, 1984-86; mem. STRIDE Leadership Round Table, 1991—; state chair Am. Legis. Exch.

Coun., 1991-96; nat. bd. dirs., 199-99, exec. com., 1995, 1st vice chair, 1998; mem. Edn. Commn. of the States, 1991—, com. policies and priorities, 1993—, steering com., 1998—, exec. com., 1998; mem. Leadership Coun. on Higher Edn., 1995—; mem. nat. policy bd. Danforth Found., 1995—; state dir., Women in Govt., 1996—; state dir., Nat. Order Women Legislators, 1993—; hon. mem. Linn-Benton Compact Bd., 1993—; active Linn County Criminal Justice Coun., 1994—; vol. Good Samaritan Hosp. Found., State Land Trust for Affordable Housing, Majestic Theater. Named Woman of Yr. Albany chpt. Beta Sigma Phi, 1970. Mem. Nat Conf. State Legislators (chmn. edn. com. 1992—), Albany C. of C. (bd. dirs. 1986-93, 96—), Linn County Rep. Women (legis. chmn. 1982-91), Greater Corvallis Rotary Club (bd. dirs.). Republican. Methodist. Avocations: gardening, camping, volunteering. Home: 3197 NW Crest Loop Albany OR 97321-9627 Office Phone: 541-928-7745. Personal E-mail: cloakley@juno.com.

**OAKLEY, DEBORAH JANE,** public health service officer, nursing educator; b. Jan. 31, 1937; d. George F. and Kathryn (Willson) Hacker; m. Bruce Oakley, June 16, 1958; children: Ingrid Andrea, Brian Benjamin. BA, Swarthmore Coll., 1958; MA, Brown U., 1960; MPH, U. Mich., 1969, PhD, 1977. Dir. teenage and adult programs YWCA, Providence, 1959-63; editl. asst. Stockholm U., 1963-64; rsch. investigator, lectr. dept. population planning U. Mich., 1971-77, asst. prof. cmty. health programs Ann Arbor, 1977-79, asst. prof. nursing rsch., 1979-81, assoc. prof., 1981-89, prof., 1989—2002, interim dir. Ctr. Nursing Rsch., 1988-90, acting dir. Ctr. Nursing Rsch., 1998, prof. emeritus, 2002—, interim dir. Health Asian Am. program, 2005. Vis. prof. Beijing Med. U., 1996—; prin. investigator NIII, CDC and pvt. found. funded rsch. grants and contracts on family planning, women's health and health care in China, mem. nat. adv. com. nursing rsch., 1993-97; mem. adv. workshop on Nat. Survey on Family Growth, 1994-97; co-chair Mich. Initiative for Women's Health, 1993-95. Author: (with Leslie Corsa) Population Planning, 1979; contbr. articles to profl. jours. Bd. dirs. Planned Parenthood Fedn. Am., 1975-80. Recipient Margaret Sanger award Washtenaw County Planned Parenthood, 1975, Outstanding Young Woman of Ann Arbor award Jaycees, 1970, Dist. Faculty award Mich. Assn. Gov. Bds., 1992, Blue Cross Blue Shield Found. of Mich. award for Excellence in Health Policy, 1996. Mem. APHA (chmn. population sect. coun.), Internat. Union Sci. Study Population, Midwest Nursing Rsch. Soc., Population Assn. Am., Delta Omega, Sigma Theta Tau (hon.). Democrat. Home: 5200 S Lake Dr Chelsea MI 48118-9481 Office: U Mich Sch Nursing Ann Arbor MI 48109-0482 Office Phone: 743-763-6730. E-mail: doakley@umich.edu.

**OAKLEY, FRANCIS CHRISTOPHER,** historian, educator; b. Liverpool, Eng., Oct. 6, 1931; arrived in U.S., 1957, naturalized, 1968; s. Joseph Vincent and Siobean (NiCurean) O.; m. Claire-Ann Lamenzo, Aug. 9, 1958; children: Deirdre, Christopher, Timothy, Brian. BA, Corpus Christi Coll., Oxford U., 1953, MA, 1957; postgrad., Pontifical Inst. Medieval Studies, Toronto, 1953—55; MA, Yale U., 1958, PhD, 1960; LLD, Amherst Coll., 1986, Wesleyan U., 1989, U. Notre Dame, 2006; LHD, Northwestern U., 1990, North Adams State Coll., 1993, Bowdoin Coll., 1993; LittD, Williams Coll., 1994. Mem. faculty Yale U., 1959-61, Williams Coll., Williamstown, Mass., 1961—, prof. history, 1970—2002, dean faculty, 1977-84, Edward Dorr Griffin prof. history of ideas, 1984—85, pres., 1985-94, pres. emeritus, 1994—, Edward Dorr Griffin prof. history of ideas, 1994—2002, prof. emeritus, 2002—; interim pres. Am. Coun. Learned Socs., 2002—03, pres. emeritus, 2003—; hon. fellow Corpus Christi Coll., Oxford U., 1991—; sr. fellow Oakley Ctr. Humanities, Williams Coll., 2002—. Vis. lectr. Bennington (Vt.) Coll., 1967; Sir Isaiah Berlin vis. prof. Oxford U., 1999-2000; Merle Curti lectr. U. Wis., Madison, 2001; Étienne Gilson lectr. Pontifical Inst. Medieval Studies, Toronto, 2002; mem. Inst. Advanced Study Princeton, 1981-82; assoc. Nat. Humanities Ctr., 1991; guest scholar Woodrow Wilson Internat. Ctr. for Scholars, 1994; chair bd. dirs. Am. Coun. Learned Socs., 1993-97; trustee Sterling and Francine Clark Art Inst., 1985—, pres. bd. trustees, 1998-2005; trustee MassMoCA Found., 1995-2004, Williamstown Art Conservation Ctr., 1995-98, Williamstown Theatre Festival, 1985-93; trustee Nat. Humanities Ctr., 1996-02, 2003—, chmn. bd. trustees, 2004—, Lake Forest Coll., 1997-2001; trustee Inst. Advanced Cath. Studies, 1998-2005, vice chair, 2002-05; mem. MassMoCA Cultural Devel. Commn., 1988—; mem. adv. coun. Ctr. for Study of Religion, Princeton U., 1999—. Author: The Political Thought of Pierre d'Ailly: The Voluntarist Tradition, 1964, Kingship and the Gods: The Western Apostasy, 1968, Council over Pope?, Towards a Provisional Ecclesiology, 1969, Medieval Experience: Foundations of Western Cultural Singularity, 1974, rev. England edit., The Crucial Centuries, 1979, Spanish edit., 1980, 95, Medieval Acad. edit., 1988, 93, The Western Church in the Later Middle Ages, 1979, rev. edit., 1985, 88, 91, Natural Law, Conciliarism and Consent in the Late Middle Ages, 1984, Omnipotence, Covenant and Order: An Excursion in the History of Ideas, 1984, Community of Learning: The American College and the Liberal Arts Tradition, 1992, Scholarship and Teaching: A Matter of Mutual Support, 1996, Politics and Eternity: Studies in the History of Medieval and Early Modern Political Thoughts, 1999, The Leadership Challenges of a College Presidency, 2002, The Conciliarist Tradition, 2003 (Roland H. Bainton History prize, 2004), Natural Law, laws of Nature and Natural Rights, 2005, Kingship: The Politics of Enchantment, 2006; editor: (with Daniel O'Connor) Creation: The Impact of an Idea, 1969, (with Bruce Russett) Governance, Accountability and the Future of the Catholic Church, 2003; contbr. articles to profl. jours. Lt. Brit. Army, 1955-57. Goldsmith's Co. London fellow, 1953-55, Social Sci. Rsch. Coun. fellow, 1963, Am. Coun. Learned Socs. fellow, 1965, 69-70, Weil Inst. fellow, 1965, Folger Shakespeare Libr. fellow, 1974, NEH fellow, 1976, 81-82, Mellon emeritus rsch. fellow, 2005, Academic fellow, Carnegie Corp. NY, 2003-05; recipient Wilbur Lucius Cross medal Yale Grad. Sch., 1997. Fellow Medieval Acad. Am. (pres. fellows 1999-2002), Am. Acad. Arts and Scis.; mem. Am. Hist. Assn., Am. Cath. Hist. Assn., (N.Y. History Soc., New Eng. Medieval Conf. (pres. 1983-04), The Century Assn., Am. Cusanus Soc. (adv. bd. 1997—). Democrat. Roman Catholic. Office: Williams Coll Oakley Ctr Humanities & Soc Sci Williamstown MA 01267 Office Phone: 413-597-2149. Business E-Mail: foakley@williams.edu.

**OAKLEY, GODFREY PORTER, JR.,** medical educator; b. Greenville, NC, June 1, 1940; s. Godfrey Porter and Carrie O.; m. Mary Ann Bryant, Sept. 2, 1961; children: Martha Gray, Susan Herndon, Robert Bryant. Student, Duke U., 1958-61; MD, Bowman Gray Sch. of Medicine, 1965; MS in Preventive Medicine, U. Washington, 1972. Diplomate Am. Bd. Pediatrics, Nat. Bd. Med. Examiners, Am. Bd. Preventive Medicine, Am. Bd. Med. Genetics. Intern in straight pediatrics Cleve. Met. Gen. Hosp., 1965-66, resident in pediatrics, 1966-68; sr. fellow in teratology and human embryology U. Washington Sch. of Medicine, Seattle, 1970-72; sr. fellow U. Washington Sch. Pub. Health and Community Medicine, Seattle, 1971-72; EIS officer leukemia sect. Ctrs. Disease Control and Prevention (CDC), Atlanta, 1968-70, chief etiology studies sect., bur. epidemiology, cancer and birth defects, 1972-81; chief birth defects br., chronic diseases divsn. Nat. Ctr. Environ. Health, Ctrs. Disease Control and Prevention, Atlanta, 1981-85, dir. divsn. birth defects and devel. disabilities, 1985-94; clin. asst. prof. pediatrics divsn. med. genetics Emory U., Atlanta, 1968-70, 72-85, clin. assoc. prof. gynecology-obstetrics divsn. med. genetics, 1981-85; mem. visiting med. staff Grady Meml. Hosp., Atlanta, 1974-84; vis. prof. epedemiology Rollins Sch. Pub. Health, Emory Univ., 1998—. Med. adv. bd. Ctrs. Disease Control & Prevention (CDC); mem. task force on predictors of hereditary desease or congenital defects NIH Consensus Conf., 1979; mem. genetics coordinating com. NIH/CDC; mem. adv. com. biometric and epidemiological methodology FDA/CDC; cons. bur. med. svcs. FDA; mem. Chronic Diseases Surveillance Working Group; mem. patient registry com. Cystic Fibrosis Found., med. adv. coun., 1978—; mem. drug experience coordinating com. Dept. Health, Edn. and Welfare; mem. genetics com. Ga. Dept. Human Resources, 1980—; ex-officio mem. disease diseases rev. and adv. com. Health Svcs. Adminstrn., 1981; mem. master community health program, interdisciplinary faculty com., curriculum com. Emory U.; mem. working group on heart disease epidemiology Nat. Heart, Lung and Blood Insts., 1978; mem. ad hoc com. on Alpha-fetoprotein Pub. Health Svc.; mem. profl. adv. coun. Spina Bifida Assn. Am., 1981—; mem.

WHO EURO-China Consultation, Beijing, China, 1983; lectr. in field. Mem. editorial bd. Pediatric & Perinatal Epidemiology, 1987-89; contbr. articles to profl. jours., chpts. to books. Nancy Lybrook Lasater scholar 1961-67; recipient Physician's Recognition award AMA, 1973-76, Outstanding Svc. medal Pub. Health Svc., 1981, Meritorious Svc. award, 1988, Spl. Recognition award, 1993, President's Excellence award Spina Bifida Assn. Am., 1988-89, Disting. Alumnus award U. Washington Sch. Pub. Health, 1990, Hebert L. Needleman award Am. Pub. Health Assn., 1996; named Person of Week, World News Tonight, 1996. Mem. Am. Acad. Pediatrics (past com. drugs/CDC liaison, com. genetics 1990, exec. com. 1990—, CDC rep. Ga. chpt. 1993), Am. Soc. Human Genetics, Am. Coll. Epidemiology, Am. Coll. Med. Genetics, Atlanta Genetics Soc., Greater Atlanta Pediatric Soc., Atlanta Obstetrical and Gynecological Soc. (assoc.), Soc. Epidemiologic Rsch., Soc. Pediatric Rsch., Teratology Soc. (pres. elect 1983-84, pres. 1984-85, editorial bd. Teratology 1978-83, edn. com. 1988), Internat. Clearinghouse Birth Defects Monitoring Systems (chmn. 1981-82, vice chmn. 1982-83, chmn. 1983-84), Pub. Health Leadership Inst., Alpha Omega Alpha, Inst. Medicine. Office: Rollins Sch Pub Health Emory U Dept Epedemiology 1510 Clifton Rd NE Atlanta GA 30322-4218

**OAKLEY, MARY ANN BRYANT,** lawyer; b. Buckhannon, W.Va., June 22, 1940; d. Hubert Herndon and Mary F. (Deeds) Bryant; m. Godfrey P. Oakley, Jr., Sept. 2, 1961; children: Martha, Susan, Robert. AB, Duke U., 1962; MA, Emory U., 1970, JD, 1974. Tchr. Winston-Salem/Forsyth County Schs., NC, 1961-65; assoc. Margie Pitts Hames, Atlanta, 1974-80; ptnr. Stagg Hoy & Oakley, Atlanta, 1980-83, Oakley & Bonner, Atlanta, 1984-90; pvt. practice, 1990-96; ptnr. Holland & Knight LLP, Atlanta, 1996—. Adj. prof. trial practice Ga. State U., 1986-95; adj. prof. pretrial Emory U. Law Sch., 1991, 95; bd. dirs. Nat. Employment Lawyers Assn., 1989-94; founding coord. NELA, Ga.; mem. Ga. Supreme Ct. Commn. on Racial and Ethnic Bias, 1994-95; mem. Ga. Bd. Bar Examiners, 1990-94, chmn., 1994. Author: Elizabeth Cady Stanton, 1972; mem. editl. rev. bd.: The Ga. Labor Letter, 1997—2001, notes and comments editor: Emory Law Jour., 1973—74; contbr. articles to law jours. Bd. dirs. Holland & Knight Charitable Found. Bd., 2002—, Atlanta Met. YWCA, 1975—79, 1st v.p., 1978—79; mem. Leadership Atlanta, 1979; bd. dirs. Ga. chpt. ACLU, 1981—83; bd. dirs. Ga. Legal Svcs. Program, 1991—98, Planned Parenthood Ga., 2006—; trustee Unitarian Universalist Congregation Atlanta, 1977—80, pres., 1979—80; mem. Unitarian Universalist Commn. Appraisal, 1980—85; bd. dirs. Unitarian Universalist Svc. Com., 1984—90, v.p., 1986—88, pres., 1988—90. Recipient Lifetime Commitment to Pub. Svc. award, Emory U. Sch. Law, 2005, Shining Star award, Atlanta Women's Found., 2006, Randolph Thrower award, Emory U. Sch. Law, 2005; Nat. Merit scholar, 1958. Fellow: Ga. Bar Found., Am. Bar Found.; mem.: ABA, Atlantic Vol. Lawyers Found. (adv. bd. 2006—), Ga. State Bar Disciplinary Bd. (investigative panel 1985—88, chmn. 1987—88), Ga. Assn. Women Lawyers (Kathleen Kessler award 1998), Atlanta Bar Assn., State Bar Ga. (chmn. individual rights sect. 1979—81, H. Sol Clark Pro Bono award 1996, Disting. Svc. award 1998), Am. Judicature Soc., Order of Coif, Phi Beta Kappa, Bleckley Inn of Ct. (pres. 1996—99). Home: 2224 Kodiak Dr NE Atlanta GA 30345-4152 Office: 1201 W Peachtree St One Atlantic Ctr Ste 2000 Atlanta GA 30309-3400 Office Phone: 404-817-8507. Business E-Mail: maryann.oakley@hklaw.com.

**OAKLEY, RICHARD PUTNEY,** investment banker; b. White Plains, N.Y., Apr. 8, 1920; AB, NYU, 1941. Partner Lehman Bros., N.Y.C., 1958-65; v.p., dir. One William St. Fund, N.Y.C., 1962-65; mgr. investment acct. Goldman, Sachs, 1965-66, partner, 1967-72; chmn. bd. Siff, Oakley & Marks, N.Y.C., 1973-77. Trustee No. Westchester Hosp. Center, 1977-82; chmn. bd. Mt. Pleasant Indsl. Devel. Agy., 1980— Chmn. Mt. Pleasant Zoning Bd.; trustee Pleasantville, 1950-52. Fellow Fin. Analysts Fedn.; mem. Nat. Assn. Bus. Economists, N.Y. Soc. Security Analysts, Westchester Assn. Tax Receivers (founder); Lodges: Rotary Internat. Home: 116 Meadow Rd Briarcliff Manor NY 10510-1135 Personal E-mail: roakley@mymailstation.com.

**OAKLEY, ROBERT LOUIS,** law librarian, educator; b. NYC, Nov. 6, 1945; s. Bert Tuttle Oakley and Allese (Duffin) Vestigo; m. Madeleine Cohen, Aug. 13, 1971 (div. 2002); children: Esther Shulamit, Daniel Isaac-Meir; m. Barbara DesRosiers, May 1, 2005 BA, Cornell U., 1968; MLS, Syracuse U., 1972; JD, Cornell U., 1976. Bar: N.Y. 1977, U.S. Dist. Ct. (no. dist.) N.Y. 1977. Assoc. dir. law libr. Cornell U., Ithaca, NY, 1976-79; dir. law libr., assoc. prof. Boston U. Law, 1979-82, Georgetown U., Washington, 1982-87, dir. law libr., prof., 1987—. Contbr. articles to profl. jours. Mem. Libr. of Congress, Network Adv. Com., 1986-92, 1995-99, copyright office study group on sec. 108 of Copyright Act; adv. nat. commn. on Preservation and Access, 1988-94; bd. dirs. Montgomery County (Md.) Pub. Librs. 1988-92. Mem. ABA, ALA, Am. Assn. Law Librs. (Washington Affairs rep. 1989—, mem. exec. bd. 1991-94, v.p. 1999-2000, pres. 2000-01), Assn. Am. Law Schs. Avocations: photography, music, amateur radio. Office: Georgetown U Law Ctr 111 G St NW Washington DC 20001-1417

**OAKS, SUNNY,** child and family advocate, consultant, lyricist; b. Cardston, Alta., Can., Aug. 21, 1944; d. Willard Glen Hansen and Priscilla Pearl Hansen-Wallace; m. Guy Eugene Williams (dec.); children: Shelley, Jason; m. Michael Oaks, Jan. 28, 1984; children: Brian, Anna, Bethany, Christen. Grad high sch., Moses Lake, Wash. Bus. leader Shaklee Wholesale Distbn., 1972—92; founder, dir. Adults Supporting Kids, Wenatchee, Wash., 1995—96, CARE for Kids, 1997—99; founder, CEO, dir. trainer. grant writer HOME Connection, 1998—99; pvt. practice East Wenatochee, 1999—2006. Mem. adv. bd. Home Connection, Care for Kids, Adults Supporting Kids. Author: Secrets, 1992; singer, composer: albums Sunny's Song, 1987. Recipient High Volume award, Shaklee; grantee, Cmty. Found., 1997, Cmty. Network, 1997—98, Target Stores, 1997—98, Washington Assn. Prevention of Child Abuse and Neglect, 1998, Alcoa, 2000. Mem.: Shaklee Pres.' Club (Altus award). Avocations: writing, music, sewing, swimming. E-mail: healthyhorizons@verizon.net.

**OATES, JOHN ALEXANDER, III,** medical educator; b. Fayetteville, NC, Apr. 23, 1932; s. John Alexander and Isabelle (Crowder) O.; m. Meredith Stringfield, June 12, 1956; children: David Alexander, Christine Larkin, James Caldwell. BS magna cum laude, Wake Forest Coll., 1953; MD, Bowman Gray Sch. Medicine, 1956. Intern, asst. resident medicine N.Y. Hosp.-Cornell U. Med. Center, 1956-58, 61-62; from clin. assoc. to sr. investigator Nat. Heart Inst., 1958-63; faculty Vanderbilt U. Sch. Medicine, Nashville, 1963—, prof. medicine and pharmacology, 1969—, Werthan prof. investigative medicine, 1974-84, chmn. dept. medicine, 1983-97, Thomas F. Frist Sr. prof. medicine, 1984—. Drug rsch. bd. Nat. Acad. Scis.-NRC, 1967-71; chmn. pharmacology and toxicology tng. com. Nat. Inst. Gen. Med. Scis., 1969-70; adv. coun. Nat. Heart, Lung and Blood Inst., 1985-89. Master ACP; fellow Am. Acad. Arts and Scis., Am. Assn. Advancement Sci.; mem. Am. Fedn. Clin. Rsch. (pres. 1970-71), Am. Soc. Clin. Investigation (v.p. 1976-77), Assn. Am. Physicians (pres. 1981-82), Am. Soc. Pharmacology and Exptl. Therapeutics (chmn. exec. com. divsn. clin. pharmacology 1967-69), Inst. of Medicine. Achievements include co-discovery of antihypertensive effect of methyldopa, elucidation of a number of interactions between drugs in man; research in biochemistry and pathophysiology of eicosanoids. Home: 2032 Sunset Hills Terr Nashville TN 37215 Office: Vanderbilt Med Ctr 536 RRB Nashville TN 37232-6602 Office Phone: 615-343-4845. Business E-Mail: john.oates@vanderbilt.edu.

**OATES, JOYCE CAROL,** writer; b. Lockport, NY, June 16, 1938; d. Frederic James and Caroline (Bush) O.; m. Raymond Joseph Smith, Jan. 23, 1961. BA, Syracuse U., 1960; MA, U. Wis., 1961. Instr. English U. Detroit, 1961-65, asst. prof., 1965-67; prof. English U. Windsor, Ont., Canada, 1967-87; writer-in-residence Princeton (N.J.) U., 1978-81, prof., 1987—. Author: (short story collections) By the North Gate, 1963, Upon the Sweeping Flood, 1966, The Wheel of Love, 1970, Marriages and Infidelities, 1972, The Hungry Ghosts, 1974, The Goddess and Other Women, 1974, Where Are You Going, Where Have You Been?: Stories of Young America, 1974, The Poisoned Kiss and Other Stories From the Portuguese, 1975, The Seduction and Other Stories, 1975, Crossing the Border, 1976, Night-Side, 1977, All the

Good People I've Left Behind, 1978, The Lamb of Abyssalia, 1980, A Sentimental Education: Stories, 1981, Last Days: Stories, 1984, Wild Nights, 1985, Raven's Wing: Stories, 1986, The Assignation, 1988, Heat: And Other Stories, 1991, Where is Here?: Stories, 1992, Haunted: Tales of the Grotesque, 1994, Will You Always Love Me? and Other Stories, 1995, The Collector of Hearts: New Tales of the Grotesque, 1998, Faithless: Tales of Transgressions, 2001, Small Avalanches: And Other Stories, 2003, I Am No One You Know, 2004, High Lonesome: Stories 1966-2006, 2006; (novels) With Shuddering Fall, 1964, A Garden of Earthly Delights, 1967 (Nat. Book award nomination 1968), Expensive People, 1967 (Nat. Book award nomination 1969), them, 1969 (Nat. Book award for fiction 1970), Wonderland, 1971, Do With Me What You Will, 1973, The Assassins, 1975, Childwold, 1976, The Triumph of the Spider Monkey, 1976, Son of the Morning, 1978, Unholy Loves, 1979, Cybele, 1979, Bellefleur, 1980 (LA Times Book award nomination 1980), A Sentimental Education, 1981, Angel of Light, 1981, A Bloodsmoor Romance, 1982, Mysteries of Winterthorn, 1984, Solstice, 1985, Marya, 1986, You Must Remember This, 1987, (as Rosamond Smith) The Lives of the Twins, 1987, American Appetites, 1989, (as Rosamond Smith) Soul-Mate, 1989, Because It Is Bitter, and Because It Is My Heart, 1990, (as Rosamond Smith) Nemesis, 1990, I Lock My Door Upon Myself, 1990, The Rise of Life on Earth, 1991, Black Water, 1992, (as Rosamond Smith) Snake Eyes, 1992, Foxfire: Confessions of a Girl Gang, 1993, What I Lived For, 1994 (PEN/Faulkner award nomination 1995), Zombie, 1995, First Love, 1996, We Were the Mulvaneys, 1996, Man Crazy, 1997, Devil's Half Acre, 1997, Come Meet Muffin!, 1998, My Heart Laid Bare, 1998, Broke Heart Blues, 1999, Starr Bright Will Be With You Soon, 1999, Blonde, 2000, The Barrens, 2001, Faithless: Tails of Transgression, 2001, Middle Age: A Romance, 2001, Big Mouth and Ugly Girl, 2002, I'll Take You There, 2002, Freaky Green Eyes, 2003, Rape: A Love Story, 2003, Where Is Little Reynard, 2003, The Tattooed Girl, 2003, Sexy, 2005, Missing Mom, 2005, The Female of the Species, 2006, (as Lauren Kelly) The Stolen Heart, 2005, Blood Mask, 2006, Black Girl/White Girl, 2006; (non-fiction) The Faith of a Writer: Life, Craft, Art, 2003; (poetry collections) Women in Love, 1968, Expensive People, 1968, Anonymous Sins, 1969, Love and Its Derangements, 1970, Angel Fire, 1973, Dreaming America, 1973, The Fabulous Beasts, 1975, Season of Peril, 1977, Women Whose Lives are Food, Men Whose Lives are Money: Poems, 1978, The Stepfather, 1978, Celestial Timepiece, 1981, Invisible Women: New and Selected Poems, 1970-1972, 1982, Luxury of Sin, 1983, The Time Traveller, 1987; (plays) The Sweet Enemy, 1965, Sunday Dinner, 1970, Ontological Proof of My Existence, 1970, Miracle Play, 1974, Three Plays, 1980, Daisy, 1980, Presque Isle, 1984, Triumph of the Spider Monkey, 1985, In Darkest America, 1990, I Stand Before You Naked, 1990, The Perfectionist and Other Plays, 1995; (essays) The Edge of Impossibility, 1972, The Hostile Sun: The Poetry of D.H. Lawrence, 1973, New Heaven, New Earth, 1974, Contraries: Essays, 1981, The Profane Art, 1984, On Boxing, 1987, (Woman) Writer: Occasions and Opportunities, 1988; editor, compiler: Scenes from American Life: Contemporary Short Fiction, 1973, (with Shannon Ravenel) Best American Short Stories of 1979, 1979, Night Walks, 1982, First Person Singular: Writer's on Their Craft, 1983, (with Boyd Litzinger) Story: Fictions Past and Present, 1985, (with Daniel Halpern) Reading and Fights, 1988, The Oxford Book of American Short Stories, 1992, The Sophisticated Cat: An Anthology, 1992,(editor)The Best American Mystery Stories 2005; editor (with Raymond Smith) Ontario Rev.; contbr. to nat. mags. including NY Times Book Rev., Mich. Quarterly Rev., Mademoiselle, Vogue, North Am. Rev., Hudson Rev., Paris Rev., Grand Street, Atlantic, Poetry, Esquire. Recipient O. Henry award, 1967, 73, Rosenthal award Nat. Inst. Arts and Letters, 1968, O. Henry Spl. award continuing achievement, 1970, 86, Award of Merit Lotos Club, 1975, St. Louis Lit. award, 1988, Rea award for the Short Story, 1990, Alan Swallow award for fiction, 1990, Nobel Prize in Lit. nomination, 1993; Guggenheim fellow, 1967-68, Nat. Endowment for the Arts grantee, 1966, 68. Mem. Am. Acad. and Inst. Arts and Letters. Office: care John Hawkins Agy 71 W 23rd St Ste 1600 New York NY 10010-4102 also: Princeton U Dept Creative Writing 117 185 Nassau St Princeton NJ 08544-0001*

**OATES, MARY JOSEPHINE,** historian, educator; b. Boston, Apr. 18, 1935; d. Thomas Francis and Mary (Folan) Oates. BA summa cum laude, Cath. U. Am., DC, 1963; MA, Yale U., 1964, PhD, 1969. Mem. Congregation of the Sisters of St. Joseph of Boston, 1952—; asst. prof. econs. Regis Coll., Weston, Mass., 1970—74, assoc. prof. econs., 1974—80, prof. econs., 1980—2000, econ. prof. econs., 2000—. Chair com. on internat. fellowships and awards AAUW, Washington, 1978—80, chair com. on fellowships to Am. women, 1983—85; mem. nat. adv. bd. Project on Religion and Am. Culture, Ind. U., Purdue U., Indpls., 1988—90; mem. com. on rsch. Nat. Fedn. of Congregations of Sisters of St. Joseph, U.S. and Can., St. Louis, 1988—96; cons. religion divsn. program Lilly Endowment, Indpls., 1992; mem. curriculum devel. project Ctr. for the Study of Philanthropy, CUNY, N.Y.C., 1996—99; chair com. on Cath. women U. of Notre Dame - Lilly Endowment Rsch. Initiative in Twentieth Century Studies in Am. Catholicism, Notre Dame, Ind., 1997—2000. Author: The Role of the Cotton Textile Industry in the Economic Development of the American Southeast, 1900-1940, 1975; editor: Higher Education for Catholic Women: An Historical Anthology, 1987; author: The Catholic Philanthropic Tradition in America, 1995 (Hon. Mention, Staley-Robeson-Ryan-St. Lawrence prize, Nat. Soc. of Fund Raising Execs., 1996), Catholic Philanthropy in America, Curriculum Guide, 1999; contbr. chpts. to books and articles to profl. and scholarly jours. Mem. history adv. bd. Mus. of Women's History - The Leadership Ctr., N.Y.C., 2000—; cons. U.S. CSC - Boston Region, 1971; mem. women's strategy group Giving New Eng., Associated Grant Makers, Boston, 2001—03; mem. ad hoc com. on stewardship Nat. Conf. of Cath. Bishops, Washington, 1990; mem. investment com. Congregation of the Sisters of St. Joseph of Boston, 1977—; mem. bd. dirs. Takayasu's Arteritis Assn., Bedford, NH, 1998—2002. Recipient Disting. Historian award, Conf. on the History of Women Religious, 2001; fellow Charlotte Dickson Fisher Fellowship, AAUW, 1966—67, Fellowship in Academic Adminstrn., Am. Coun. on Edn., 1969—70, Faculty Fellowship in Sci., Harvard U., NSF, 1976—77, Rsch. Fellowship, Mary I. Bunting Inst., Radcliffe Coll., 1980—81; grantee Kress Grant, Baker Libr., Harvard U. Grad. Sch. of Bus. Adminstrn., 1972, Rsch. Grant, Am. Philos. Soc., 1976, Curriculum Devel. Grant, Shelby Cullom Davis Found., 1978, Course Devel. Grant, Assn. of Am. Colls., 1986—89, Rsch. Grant, 1988, Lilly Endowment, 1988, 1990—92, Louisville Inst., 1997, Spencer Found., 2002—03. Mem.: Mass. Hist. Soc., Am. Cath. Hist. Assn. (chair, book prize com. 1997—98, 2d v.p. 2005), Econ. History Assn. (program com. 1971—73), Social Sci. History Assn. (program com. 1982, chair, book prize com. 1990—91), Assn. for Rsch. on Nonprofit Orgns. and Voluntary Action (book prize com. 2001), Orgn. of Am. Historians, Am. Hist. Assn., Phi Beta Kappa. Roman Catholic. Office: Regis Coll 235 Wellesley St Weston MA 02493 Office Phone: 781-768-7420. Business E-Mail: mary.oates@regiscollege.edu.

**OATES, STEPHEN BAERY,** retired historian; b. Pampa, Tex., Jan. 5, 1936; s. Steve Theodore and Florence (Baer) O.; divorced; children: Gregory Allen, Stephanie. BA magna cum laude, U. Tex., 1958, MA, 1960, PhD, 1968; Litt.D. (hon.), Lincoln Coll., 1981. Prof. history U. Mass., Amherst, 1971—98, Paul Murray Kendall prof. biography, 1980—98, adj. prof. English, 1981—98. Author: Confederate Cavalry West of the River, 1961, Rip Ford's Texas, 1963, Republic of Texas, 1968, Visions of Glory, 1970, To Purge This Land With Blood: A Biography of John Brown, 1970, Portrait of America, 2 vols., 1973, rev. edits., 2005, The Fires of Jubilee: Nat Turner's Fierce Rebellion, 1975, With Malice Toward None: The Life of Abraham Lincoln (Christopher award for outstanding lit., Barondess/Lincoln award N.Y. Civil War Round Table 1977), Our Fiery Trial: Abraham Lincoln, John Brown, and the Civil War Era, 1979, Let the Trumpet Sound: The Life of Martin Luther King, Jr., 1982 (Christopher award, Robert F. Kennedy Meml. Book award), Abraham Lincoln, The Man Behind the Myths, 1984, Biography as High Adventure: Life Writers Speak on Their Art, 1986, William Faulkner: The Man and the Artist, 1987, A Woman of Valor: Clara Barton and the Civil War, 1994, The Approaching Fury: Voices of the Storm, 1820-1861, 1997, The Whirlwind of War: Voices of the Storm, 1861-1865, 1998; contbr. articles and essays to periodicals; lectr. Presdl. Writers award, 1985; Master Tchr. award U. Hartford, 1985; Silver Medal award Case Council for Advance

and Support of Edn., Prof. of Yr., 1986, 87, Kidger award New Eng. History Tchrs. Assn., Nevins-Freeman award Chgo. Civil War Round Table, 1993; Guggenheim fellow, 1972; sr. summer fellow NEH, 1978. Fellow Tex. State Hist. Assn.; mem. Tex. Inst. Letters, Soc. Am. Historians, Am. Antiquarian Soc., Phi Beta Kappa. Office: U Mass Dept History Amherst MA 01003

**OATES, THOMAS R.,** university executive; married; 4 children. BA in English and Philosophy, St. Louis U., 1964, MA in English, 1970; postgrad., Am. Film Inst. Ctr., Beverly Hills, Calif., 1971; PhD in Am. Lit., St. Louis U., 1979. Coord., dir. program assts. and counselors upward bound pgm. Webster Coll., 1970-71, dir. media/journalism degree program, 1974-81, coord. MA program in media comms., 1975-81; chair, assoc. prof. dept. journalism St. Michael's Coll., 1981-85; campus dean U. Wis. Ctr., Richland Center, 1985-89; dir. U.S. ops. and acad. programs Coop. Assn. of States for Scholarships, Georgetown U., Washington, 1989-94; pres. Spalding U., Louisville, 1994—2002, Rocky Mountain Coll., Billings, Mont., 2002—. Mem. media adv. com. Mo. State Coun. of Higher Edn., 1977-79; mem. planning commn. State Dept. of Higher Edn., Baton Rouge, 1979-80; mem., rep. Mo.'s ind. colls. and univs. Cen. Ednl. Network Mo., 1979-81; mem. adv. bd. Tri-State Bilingual Tng. Program, St. Michael's Coll., 1981-83; mem. Vt. Cath. Press Assn. Bd., 1985-85; mem., appointed chair Internat. Edn. Coun., U. Wis. Sys., 1987-88, designer, author Ctr. of Excellence project, 1988; mem. acad. staff adv. bd., U. Wis. Ctr. Sys., 1987-89, chair acad. staff grievance com., 1988; mem. 9-person state commn. to develop criteria for legal evaluations of devel. projects reviewed under Act 250 environ. law, Vt., 1984-85; presenter on internat. ednl. regional and nat. meetings of various orgns. Author, designer: (slide-tape program on history of early French and English explorers in mid-west) Old Land, New Land, 1983; author, designer: (book) Images, Values, and Development in Crittenden County, 1984; prodr.: (documentary photographic study on 5 rural Alaskan comtys.) Images of Continuity, Images of Change, 1977; prodr., dir.: (16mm documentary film) The Faces of British Honduras, 1974. Grantee Mo. Coun. on Arts, 1972, 76, NEH, 1975, U. Alaska, 1978, Mo. Coun. on Humanities, 1979, Vt. Coun. on Humanities, 1981, IBM, 1982, U. Wis. Ext., 1988, Wis. Coun. for Humanities, 1989, Orgn. for Petroleum Exporting Countries, 1992, C.C.'s for Internat. Devel., 1992. Office: Spalding U 851 S 4th St Office Pres Louisville KY 40203-2188

**OATES, WILLIAM ARMSTRONG, JR.,** investment company executive; b. Pitts., July 27, 1942; s. William Armstrong and Margaret (Nichols) O.; m. Elizabeth Dick Macy, Sept. 7, 1968; children: Elizabeth N., Katherine M., Emily E.A. BA, Colby Coll., 1965; MBA, Harvard U., 1972. Asst. treas. Morgan Guaranty Trust, NYC, 1966—2004; pres. N.E. Investors Growth Fund, Boston, 1980—; ptnr. N.E. Investment Mgmt. Inc., Boston, 1984—. Dir. Horn Corp., Ayer, Mass., Furman Lumber Co., Boston, Clifford Inc., Bethel, Vt. Pres. bd. trustees Groton (Mass.) Sch., 1979; trustee, treas. Roxbury Latin Sch., West Roxbury, Mass., 2005; trustee Colby Coll., Waterville, Maine, 2005. 2d lt. Army N.G., 1966-70. Mem.: Country Club, Somerset Club, Harvard Club. Republican. Episcopalian. Home: 201 Village Ave Dedham MA 02026-4230 Office: NE Investment Mgmt Inc 150 Federal St Ste 1000 Boston MA 02110-1745

**OATIS-BALLEW, ROBIN LILLIAN,** psychologist, educator; d. Robert Oatis and Gloria Hawkins-Oatis; m. Andre Ballew, Dec. 17, 2004. BA, Fisk U., 1991; MS, Howard U., PhD, 1995. Psychotherapist Mt. Sinai Hosp., Chgo., 2000—03; psychologist pvt. practice Chgo., 2001—; asst. prof. Chgo. Sch. Profl. Psychology, 2003—, assoc. dir. tng., 2003—05, dir. tng., 2005—. Tutor adult literacy Delta Sigma Theta Learning Ctr., Chgo., 2003—; presenter Naomi Cohen Conf., Evanston, Ill., 2005. Edward Hawthorne fellow, Howard U., 1995—98. Mem.: Ill. Psychol. Assn., APA, Phi Beta Kappa. Baha'I. Avocations: knitting, reading, attending dramatic performances.

**OATWAY, FRANCIS CARLYLE,** corporate executive; b. Bermuda, Nov. 29, 1936; s. Charles Y. and Josephine (McLellan) O.; m. Ann Thomason; children— Stephen F., Karen E., Andrew C., Christopher M. BSBA, Boston Coll., 1960. CPA, Mass., N.Y., others. With Deloitte Haskins & Sells, N.Y.C. 1960-80, ptnr., 1970-80; v.p. taxation Continental Group, Inc., Stamford, Conn., 1980-81, v.p. treasury and taxation, 1981-82, v.p. fin., 1982-83, v.p., chief fin. officer, 1983; exec. v.p., pres., dir. Continental Forest Industries, Inc., Stamford, Conn., 1984-85; pres. Hargro Assocs., S. Pomfret, Vt., 1985—; pres., CEO, dir. Hargro Enterprises, Inc., S. Pomfret, 1985—. Chmn., CEO, bd. dirs. NER Data Products, Glassboro, N.J., 1985—; pres., bd. dirs. Covent Ins. Co. Ltd., Hamilton, Bermuda, 1980-85; chmn. bd., mng. dir. CCC Finanz A.G., Zug, Switzerland, 1980-85; mng. dir. Continental Group Overseas Fin. N.V., Curacao, Netherlands Antilles, 1981-85; bd. dirs. Suecia Ins. Co. Am., Tarrytown, N.Y., chmn. bd. Apple Syndicate Corp., Westport, Conn., 1983-85. Contbg. editor: Federal Income Taxation of Banks and Financial Institutions, 1968, Professional Responsibility in Federal Tax Practice, 1970; contbr. articles to fin. jours. Trustee Convent of Sacred Heart, Greenwich, Conn., 1979-83; mem. acctg. adv. bd. Columbia U. Grad. Sch. Bus., N.Y.C., 1982-86; mem. exec. com. Boston Coll. Wall St. Coun., 1989-2002; trustee Conn. Pub. Expenditure Coun., Inc., Hartford, 1984-85; mem. pres.'s adv. bd. Weston Sch. Theology, Cambridge, 1993-99. Mem. Woodstock Country Club, Orchid Island Golf and Beach Club, Quail Valley Golf Club (Fla.) Roman Catholic.

**O'BAIRE-KARK, MARIKA,** nurse, educator, poet, writer; b. Manila, Oct. 3, 1947; d. Gerald John and Giovanna (BelForti) Barry; m. Pieter Kark, Oct. 3, 2004; children from previous marriage: Matthew O'Baire, Alexei O'Baire, Rita O'Baire, D. Patrick O'Baire. Student, U. Conn., 1964—65; diploma, Ellis Hosp. Sch. Nursing, 1977; BSN, Russell Sage Coll., 1980, postgrad., 1983, postgrad., 1994; grad. ontological design, Logonet Inc. ODC-J, 1993; postgrad. humanities, Calif. State U., Dominguez Hills, 1995; postgrad., U. Dundee, 2000; postgrad. in Disaster and Emergency Mgmt., Touro U., 2005—; postgrad. in Writing, Stanford U., 2006—. RN NY, Calif.; lic. avatar master/wizard Star's Edge Internat. Tchr. English Lang. Inst., Taipei, Taiwan, 1971—73; team leader, staff nurse acute psychiatry Samaritan Hosp., Troy, NY, 1978—80; staff nurse pediat. ICU Albany Med. Ctr., NY, 1980—84, 1997—; rsch. nurse Commn. on Quality Care for Mentally Disabled, Albany, 1984; staff nurse Columbia-Greene Med. Ctr., Catskill, NY, 1984—89; night charge nurse Conifer Park, Scotia, NY, 1991—92; nursing educator St. Clare's Hosp., Schenectady, NY, 1992—96; adj clin. educator Albany Med. Ctr. So. Vt. Coll., Bennington, 1997—2001; nurse, specialized surg. pre-ICU, Stanford U. Hosp., 2005—. On-call nurse Cmty. Hospice Saratoga, NY, 1998—2004; founder Future Design: Create What You Prefer, Avatar Tech. & Skills, 2000, Favorite Nurses, Colonie, NY, 2002—; cons. Author: (novels) Dragon, 2002, Future Joyous, 2002, (short stories) About Love, (screenplays) Syin; contbr. articles to Echo Mag. Past vol. curriculum designer gifted and talented programs; firefighter Cazenovia, NY. Mem.: Ontological Design Cmty., Upstate Ind. Filmakers/Screenwriters, Childreach Plan Internat., Toastmasters Internat. Personal E-mail: mobaire@yahoo.com.

**OBAMA, BARACK H.,** senator, former state legislator; b. Honolulu, Hawaii, Aug. 4, 1961; m. Michelle Obama; children: Malia Ann, Natasha. BA in Polit. Sci., Columbia U., 1983; JD magna cum laude, Harvard U., 1991. Editor-in-chief Harvard Law Review; exec. dir. PROJECT VOTE!, Ill., 1992; atty. Miner, Barnhill & Galland, P.C., 1993—2004; mem. Ill. Senate Dist. 13, Springfield, 1997—2005; mem. judiciary & local govt. com Ill. Senate, Springfield, chmn., pub. health & human svcs. com.; US Senator from Ill., 2005—. Sr. lecturer U. Chgo. Law Sch.; keynote speaker Dem. Nat. Convention, Boston, 2004; mem. com. environment and public works US Senate, com. fgn. relations, com. veterans affairs. Author: Dreams From My Father: A Story of Race and Inheritance, 1995 (Publishers Weekly paperback bestseller list, 2005, Best Spoken Word or Non-Musical Album The Recording Acad., 2006), Audacity of Hope: Thoughts on Reclaiming the American Dream, 2006. Bd. dirs. Chgo. Lawyers Com. for Civil Rights Under the Law and Pub. Allies, Joyce Found., 1994—; chmn. Chgo. Annenberg Challenge; bd. dirs. Woods Fund Chgo., Ctr. for Neighborhood Tech. Named one of most influential people, TIME mag., 2005; recipient 40

Under 40 award, Crains Chgo. Bus., 1993, Monarch award for Outstanding Public Service, 1994, "Legal Eagle" award, IVI-IPO, 1995, Most Influential Black Americans, Ebony mag., 2006. Mem.: Cook County Bar Assn. Democrat. Ch. Christ. Office: US Senate B40B Dirksen Senate Office Bldg Washington DC 20510 also: John C Kluczynski Fed Office Bldg Ste 3900 230 South Dearborn St Chicago IL 60604-1480 Office Phone: 202-224-2854, 312-886-3506. Office Fax: 202-228-4260, 312-886-3514.*

**OBAMOGIE, MERCY A.,** physician; b. Lagos, Nigeria, Jan. 18, 1954; d. Godwin I and Janet E. (Amiolemen) O.; m. Abiodun O. Odunmbaku, June 20, 1980 (div. 1995); children: Abisola, Adenike, Abiodun. BS, Columbia U., 1980; MD, U. Medicine and Dentistry N.J., Piscataway, 1984; MPH, Johns Hopkins U., 1987; MBA, U. Calif., Irvine, 2000. Diplomate Am. Bd. Family Practice, Nat. Bd. Med. Examiners. Intern in internal medicine Muhlenberg Hosp., Plainfield, NJ, 1984-85; resident in gen. preventive medicine Johns Hopkins U., Balt., 1985-86; resident in family practice Georgetown U./Providence Hosp., Washington, 1986-89; pvt. practice Washington, Greenbelt, Md., 1989—; med. dir. Doctors Slim and Fitness Ctr., Greenbelt, 1996-98. Med. adv. bd. Metra Health Ins. Co., 1992-94; utilization com. Aetna Ins. Co., 1993-95, credentialing com., 1996; med. adv. com. United HealthCare, 1997; mem. planning com. Providence Hosp., Washington, 1996-98; with Prince George's Hosp. Ctr., Cheverly, Md., Howard U. Hosp., Washington, Doctors Cmty. Hosp., Lanham, Md., Providence Hosp., Washington; pres., med. dir. Mercy Med. Ctr., Benin City, Nigeria, 1996—; pres., CEO ASAKI Corp., Greenbelt, Md., 2000—. Contbr. articles to profl. jours. Home: 25 Atwood Ct Silver Spring MD 20906-2089 Office: 7323 Hanover Pkwy Ste A Greenbelt MD 20770-3617 Office Phone: 301-345-5900. E-mail: aimmercy@aol.com.

**O'BANION, DEBORAH MICHELLE,** school psychologist; b. Syracuse, NY, Apr. 12, 1958; d Donald Leroy and Daphne Francetta; m. Timothy Wilson O'Banion, Jan. 24, 1976. BS in Psychology, Tex. A&M U., 1996, MS in Sch. Psychology, 2002. Lic. specialist sch. psychology Tex. State Bd. Exam Psychologists. Sch. psychologist Wills Point Sch. Dist., Tex., 2001—. Avocations: home remodeling, hiking. Personal E-mail: tobdob@sbcglobal.net.

**OBBIE, MARK JOSEPH,** communications educator; b. Rochester, N.Y., May 16, 1959; s. Joseph S. and Patricia R. (O'Brien) O.; m. Nancy E. Lane, Oct. 2, 1982; children: Raema C., Dale M. BA, St. John Fisher Coll., 1980; MA, U. Mo., 1981. Reporter Tribune Chronicle, Warren, Ohio, 1982-83, Houston Post, 1983-86, Tex. Lawyer, Houston, 1987, mng. editor Dallas, 1987-88, editor, 1988-89, former editor, pub., 1989—98; former exec. editor Am. Lawyer, NYC, 1998; assoc. prof., communications Syracuse Univ., NY. Mem. Freedom of Info. Found. Tex., Soc. Profl. Journalists, Investigative Reporters and Editors. Avocations: reading, camping. Office: Public Communications Syracuse University Syracuse NY 13244 Office Phone: 585-298-1470. Business E-Mail: mjobbie@syr.edu.

**OBEAR, FREDERICK WOODS,** academic administrator; b. Malden, Mass., June 9, 1935; s. William Fred and Dorothea Louise (Woods) O.; m. Patricia A. Draper, Aug. 30, 1959 (dec. Dec. 1993); children: Jeffrey Allan, Deborah Anne, James Frederick; m. Ruth Crowley Sundell, Feb. 21, 1998. BS with high honors, U. Mass., Lowell, 1956, LHD, 1985; PhD, U. N.H., 1961. Mem. faculty dept. chemistry Oakland U., Rochester, Mich., 1960-81, prof., 1979-81, v.p. for acad. affairs, provost, 1970-81; chancellor U. Tenn., Chattanooga, 1981-97, univ. prof., chancellor emeritus, 1997—. Mem. nat. adv. panel Nat. Commn. on Higher Edn. Issues, 1981; mem. pres. commn. NCAA, 1991-94. Trustee Marygrove Coll., 1973-79. Am. Council Edn. fellow, 1967-68 Mem. AAAS, Am. Assn. State Colls. and Univs. (bd. dirs. 1992-96, chair 1995), Am. Chem. Soc., Am. Assn. Higher Edn., Sigma Xi. Roman Catholic. Office: 417H Fletcher Hall 615 McCallie Ave Chattanooga TN 37403-2504 Office Phone: 423-425-5281. Business E-Mail: frederick-obear@utc.edu.

**OBED, LEONORA RITA VILLEGAS,** writer; b. Manila, Philippines, May 22, 1971; arrived in US, 1973; d. Reynaldo Nera and Josefina Kalaw (Villegas) Obed. BA, St. Joseph's U., 1993; MA, U. Toronto, 1994; postgrad. in English Lit., U. Edinburgh. Spkr. in field. Author: The Invention of Candles, 2001, I Won't Send Roses, 2001, (plays) Epitome, 2003; contbr. articles to profl. jours. Mem.: Hopkins Soc., Yeats Soc., Oscar Wilde Soc. Home: 10 Michelle Ct Trenton NJ 08628-2924 Office Phone: 609-575-4959. Personal E-Mail: leonora.obed@hotmail.com.

**OBENHAUS, STEVEN LEE,** secondary school educator; b. Dallas, Aug. 30, 1958; s. Robert Edward and Betty Lee Obenhaus; m. Cindy Long Browning, June 12, 1992; children: Benjamin Christopher Long, Ann Elizabeth Long, Andrew David Long. BA, Lubbock Christian U., 1980, U. Mo., Kansas City, 1988, MA, 1995. Cert. secondary edn. Kans. Tchr. Leavenworth (Kans.) Sch. Dist., 1988—94, Olathe (Kans.) Sch. Dist., 1994—. Contbr. articles to profl. jours. Mapping, testing, and statis. analyst Maison de Naissance, Larnage, Torbeck, Haiti, 2004—06. Mem.: Math Assn. Am. (assoc.). Democrat. Achievements include research in using GIS to site new well locations in Haiti. Avocations: marathon racing, cheese tasting, winter backpacking. Home: 6718 Granada Ln Prairie Village KS 66208 Office: Olathe North HS 600 East Prairie Olathe KS 66061 Office Phone: 913-780-7140. Personal E-Mail: scobenhaus@kc.rr.com. Business E-Mail: sobenhauson@olatheschools.com.

**OBER, JOSIAH,** history educator; b. Brunswick, Maine, Feb. 27, 1953; s. Nathanial and Patricia Wilder (Stride) Ober. BA. U. Minn., 1975. MA, 1977; PhD, U. Mich., 1980. Asst. prof. history Mont. State U., Bozeman, 1980—84, assoc. prof., 1984—88, prof., 1988—90; prof. classics Princeton (NJ) U., 1990—, chmn. dept. classics, 1994—2001; prof. polit. sci. Stanford U., Calif., 2006—. Vis. prof. U. Mich., Ann Arbor, 1986—87; sr rsch. assoc Am Sch. Classical Studies Athens, Greece, 1981, Athens, 85. Athens, 85. Athens, 88; vis. lectr. Archeol. Inst. Am., 1985—87; Martin Classical lectr. Oberlin Coll., 1994; Magie chair in classics, 1994—; bd. dirs. Princeton U. Press, 1995—2000. Author: Fortress Attica, 1985. Mass and Elite in Democratic Athens, 1989, The Athenian Revolution, 1996, Political Dissent in Democratic Athens, 1998, Athenian Legacies, 2005; contbr. articles to profl. jours. Grantee. Am. Coun. Learned Socs., 1981, 1989, NEH. 1981, 1989, 1996, Nat. Humanities Ctr. NC, 1983—84, Ctr. Hellenic Studies, 1989—90, Guggenheim Found., 1996. Mem.: Am. Sch. Classical Studies, Am. Philol. Assn. (bd. dirs.), Archaeol. Inst. Am. Home: 55 Aiken Ave Princeton NJ 08540-5257 Office: Stanford U Dept of Polit Scis Palo Alto CA 94306 E-mail: jober@princeton.edu.

**OBER, RICHARD FRANCIS, JR.,** lawyer, director, banker; b. Balt., Dec. 12, 1943; s. Richard Francis and Caroline Fisher Ober; m. Carol Laycock Munger, Aug. 25, 1973; children: Julia Keyser Allen, Margaret Delancey. AB cum laude, Princeton U., 1965; LLB, Yale U., 1968. Bar: Md. 1968, Pa. 1970, N.J. 1977. Law clk. to chief judge Md. Ct. Appeals, Annapolis, 1968; assoc. Ballard, Spahr, Andrews & Ingersoll, Phila., 1969-75; gen. counsel Summit Bancorp, Trenton, NJ, 1975—2001; v.p., gen. counsel TerraCycle, Inc, Trenton, NJ, 2004—. Sec. Summit Bancorp, Princeton, 1978-2001, sr. v.p., 1982-88, exec. v.p., 1988-2001; bd. dirs. sec. Summit Credit Life Ins. Co., Summit Credit Corp.; sec. Summit Bank, Summit Leasing Co., Summit Venture Capital, Inc. Fire commr. South Brunswick (N.J.) Fire Dist. 3, 1981-85; Republican county committeeman, 1975-2004; v.p. Republican Assn. Princeton, 1995-96; trustee Princeton Day Sch., 1988-92, treas., 1988-92, vice-chmn., 1990-92; trustee Yale Law Sch. Assn. N.J.; first vice-chmn., dir N.J. Spl. Olympics; co-facilitator Trinity Jobseekers, 2005—. Mem. ABA, Bank Corp. Counsel Com. (mem. 1979-80), N.J Bar Assn. (gen. coun. 1982-85, 93-94, exec. com. banking law sect. 1979-94, sec. sect. 1980-81, vice-chmn. 1981-82, chmn. 1984-85, exec. com. pro bono com. 1982-85, vice-chmn. 1990-91, N.J. Corp. Counsel Assn. (sec. 1980-91, 2d v.p. 1982-85, pres. 1985-86, chmn. banking and fin. instns. com. 1984-85), Am. Bankers Assn. (exec. com. bank counsel unit 1990-95,

vice-chmn. 1993-94, chmn. 1994-95), N.J. Bankers Assn. (chmn. bank lawyers coun. 1993-94, chmn. legal and tax com. 1994-95), N.J. Bus. and Industry Assn. (legis. affairs com.), Pa. Bankers Assn. (legal affairs com.), Assn. Corp. Counsel, Princeton Bar Assn., Fin. Svcs. Roundtable, Lawyers Coun., Bedens Brook Club (Princeton). Episcopalian. Office Phone: 609-393-4252.

**OBER, RUSSELL JOHN, JR.,** lawyer; b. Pitts. June 26, 1948; s. Russell J. and Marion C. (Hampson) O.; children: Lauren Elizabeth, Russell John III; m. Sandi J. Antill. BA, U. Pitts., 1970, JD, 1973. Bar: Pa. 1973, U.S. Dist. Ct. (we. dist.) Pa. 1973, U.S. Tax Ct. 1982. U.S. Ct. Appeals (4th cir.) 1976, U.S. Ct. Appeals (3d cir.) 1979, U.S. Ct. Appeals (D.C. cir.) 1985, U.S. Ct. Appeals (2d cir.), 1990, U.S. Ct. Appeals (7th cir.) 1993, U.S. Supreme Ct. 1976, U.S. Ct. Appeals (6th cir.) 2000. Asst. dist. atty. Allegheny County, Pitts., 1973-75; ptnr. Wallace Chapas & Ober, Pitts., 1975-80, Rose, Schmidt, Hasley & DiSalle, Pitts., 1980-92, Meyer, Unkovic & Scott, Pitts., 1992—. Bd. dirs. Parent and Child Guidance Ctr., Pitts., 1983-90, treas., 1985-86, pres., 1986-88; bd. mgmt. South Hills Area YMCA, 1989-91; mem. Mt. Lebanon Traffic Commn., 1976-81; bd. dirs. Whale's Tale Youth Family Counseling Ctr., 1990-95. Mem. ABA (discovery com. litigation sect. 1982-88, ho. of dels. young lawyers div. 1982-83), Pa. Bar Assn. (ho. of dels. 1983-2004), Allegheny County Bar Assn. (chmn. young lawyers sect. 1983, bd. govs 1984, fin. com. 1984-88, mem. coun. civil litigation sect. 1991-93, judiciary com. 2004—), Nat. Bd. Trial Advocacy (diplomate), Acad. Lawyers Allegheny County (fellow 1983—, bd. govs. 1988-90) U. Pitts. Law Alumni Assn. (bd. govs. 1984-89, v.p. 1985-87, pres. 1987-88), Rivers Club Office: Meyer Unkovic & Scott 1300 Oliver Bldg Pittsburgh PA 15222 E-mail: rjo@muslaw.com.

**OBER, STUART ALAN,** investment advisor, writer; b. NYC, Oct. 2, 1946; s. Paul and Gertrude E. (Stollerman) Ober; m. Allison Craig; children: Erik Kenneth, Alexander Gabriel. BA, Wesleyan U., Middletown, Conn., 1968; postgrad., U. Sorbonne, Paris, 1972, CUNY, 1976—77. Accredited investment fiduciary auditor, cert. fraud examiner. Specialist tax investment Fidelity Mutual Life, N.Y., 1972—73; sr. assoc. mktg. ENI Corp., 1973; with mktg. and analysis J.F. Crowley and Co., Inc., 1974; co-mgr. Tax Investment Dept. Moseley, Hallgarten & Estabrook, N.Y., 1974; co-dir. mktg. NFC Petroleum, N.Y., 1975; specialist tax investment Loeb, Rhoades & Co., N.Y., 1976—77; divisional dir. Dept. Tax Investment Josephthal & Co., Inc., N.Y., 1977—78; founder, mgr. Dept. Tax Investment Bruns, Nordeman, Rea & Co., N.Y., 1978—79; pvt. practice cons. N.Y., 1979—81; founder, pres. Securities Investigations, Inc., Woodstock, NY, 1981—. Arbitrator Nat. Futures Assn., 2003—. Am. Arbitration Assn.; chairperson NASD, NYSE; cons. in field; expert witness in field; lectr. in field; -. Author: Everybody's Guide to Tax Shelters; editor-in-chief: Ober Income Letter, 1983-88; pub.: Tax Shelter Blue Book, 1983—. Bd. dirs., v.p. Woodstock Playhouse Assn., 1985-87; trustee Maverick Concerts, 1986—; chmn. Woodstock Arts and Cultural Com., 1988. Mem.: Inst. Cert. Fin. Planners (fin. products stds. bd. 1986—90, treas. 1988—90). Office: PO Box 888 Woodstock NY 12498-0888

**OBERBILLIG, MOLLY CASTLEMAN,** utilities executive; b. Gibraltar, Feb. 11, 1934; arrived in U.S., 1935; d. William Ferguson and Mary Castleman (Davis) Cavenaugh; m. Gary Joel Oberbillig, Nov. 8, 1961; children: Andrew Ferguson, Julie Anne. Student, Reed Coll., Portland, Oreg., 1951—53, Antioch Coll., Yellow Springs, Ohio, 1953—54, U. Wash., Seattle, 1954—55, San Jose State Coll., 1963—64. Conservation mgr. Mason County Pub. Utility Dist., 1975—90. Founding trustee Anne Williston Scholarship, Seattle, 1988—; sec. Mason County Fire Dist., Lilliwaup, Wash., 1979—81; founder youth diversity award Thurston County Cultural Diversity and Human Rights, 1995; charter mem. Nat. Women's History Mus.; mem. leadership coun. So. Poverty Law Ctr., 1992—; mem. Nordiska Folkhögskola Exhibition Team; continuing trustee Anne Williston Scholarship; vice chmn. Dem. Ctrl. Com., Shelton, Wash., 1991—92. Mem.: Thurston Coun. Cultural Diversity and Human Rights. Avocations: gardening, ethical investing, environmental concerns. Home: 1907 Parkwood Dr SE Olympia WA 98501

**OBERDORFER, JOHN L.,** lawyer; b. Lewes, Del., Feb. 19, 1944; AB, Dartmouth Coll., 1966; LLB, Yale U., 1969. Bar: Ohio 1969, D.C. 1972, US Ct. Appeals (several dists.), US Supreme Ct. Atty. office gen. counsel U.S. Dept. Trans., 1971-74; ptnr., chmn. Litigation dept. Patton Boggs LLP, Washington. Bd. dirs. Washington Lawyers Com. for Civil Rights Under Law 1981-, Washington Airport Task Force 1988-; mem. Clinton-Gore Transition Team, 1992. Contbr. articles to profl. jours. Reginald Heber Smith Law fellow 1969-71. Mem. D.C. Bar, Ohio State Bar Assn. Office: Patton Boggs LLP 2550 M St NW Washington DC 20037-1301 Office Phone: 202-457-6424. Office Fax: 212-457-6315. Business E-Mail: joberdorfer@pattonboggs.com.

**OBERFIELD, RICHARD ALAN,** oncologist; b. N.Y.C., July 29, 1932; s. George B. and Frances Oberfield; m. Valerie I. Oberfield, Feb. 14, 1954 (dec. Jan. 1980); children: Elizabeth A., Alice A.; m. Keren G. Oberfield, July 28, 1988. BA cum laude, Alfred U., 1953; MD, NYU, 1957. Lic. physician, Mass., N.Y.; diplomate Am. Bd. Internal Medicine. Intern Greenwich (Conn.) Hosp., 1957-58; USPHS sr. asst. surgeon venereal disease br. Detroit Receiving Hosp., 1958-60; tng. fellow pathology NYU Med. Ctr., N.Y.C., 1960-61; resident in medicine Dartmouth Med. Ctr. Affiliated Hosps., 1963-65; staff physician sect. med. oncology dept. internal medicine Lahey Clinic Med. Ctr., Burlington, Mass., 1965—, head sect. med. oncology dept. internal medicine, 1969-85. Hosp. appts. include New Eng. Bapt. Hosp., Boston, 1965—80, New Eng. Deaconess Hosp., Boston, 1965—97, Mary and Arthur R. Clapham Hosp. Lahey Clinic Med. Ctr., Burlington, 1980—97; chmn. emeritus sect. med. oncology dept. internal medicine Lahey Clinic Med. Ctr., Burlington, 1997—; clin. rsch. cons. dept. rsch., 1997—; ciin. instr. medicine Harvard Med. Sch., Boston, 1972—; asst. prof. medicine Tufts U. Sch. Medicine 2000 ; Contbr. numerous articles to profl. publs. Fellow ACP (Meade Johnson postgrad. scholar 1962-63); mem. AMA (Cert. Merit 1966), Internat. Assn. for Study of Lung Cancer (founding mem.), Nat. Bd. Med. Examiners (diplomate), Am. Assn. for Cancer Rsch., Am. Soc. Clin. Oncology, Am. Assn. for Cancer Edn., Mass. Med. Soc., Mass. Soc. Internal Medicine, New Eng. Cancer Soc., Mass. Soc. Clin. Oncologists. Avocations: piano, writing, running, reading. Office: Lahey Clinic Med Ctr 41 Mall Rd Burlington MA 01805

**OBERFIELD, SHARON ELEFANT,** pediatric endocrinologist: b. NYC, Aug. 14, 1950; d. Nicholas and Anna (Weiss) Elefant; m. Richard A. Oberfield; 2 children. AB in Biology, Cornell U., 1970, MD, 1974. Diplomate in pediatrics and pediatric endocrinology Am. Bd. Pediatrics. Intern in pediatrics The N.Y. Hosp., 1974-75, resident in pediatrics, 1975-76, fellow in pediatric endocrinology, 1976-79, asst. attending pediatrician, 1979-84; asst. attending pediatric endocrinology Meml. Sloan Kettering Cancer Ctr., N.Y.C., 1986—2001. Provisional pediatrician to outpatient dept. N.Y. Hosp., 1976-79; assoc. attending pediatrician St. Luke's-Roosevelt Hosp. Ctr., N.Y.C., 1984-91, Presbyn. Hosp., N.Y.C., 1991, Tisch Hosp., Bellevue Hosp., N.Y.C., 1992—; attending pediatrician Children's Hosp. of N.Y.-Presbyn. Hosp., 1998—; asst. attending pediatrician Meml. Sloan Kettering Cancer Ctr., 1979-84; asst. prof. pediatrics Cornell U. Med. Coll., N.Y.C., 1979-84, Columbia U. Coll. Physicians & Surgeons, N.Y.C., 1984-91, assoc. prof. clin. pediatrics, 1991, prof., 1998—; dir. pediat. endocrinology, 2004—. Grantee NIH, 1978-84, 2005-, Hoffman-LaRoche, 1985-89, Eli Lilly, 1986-92. Children's Brain Tumor Found., 1995-98; recipient Mitchell Spivak Meml. prize in pediatrics, 1974. Mem. Am. Med. Women's Assn. (citation 1974), N.Y. Acad. Scis., N.Y. Pediatric Soc., Soc. Pediatric Rsch., Endocrine Soc., Lawson Wilkins Soc., Pediatric Endocrinology, Alpha Omega Alpha. Office: Divsn Pediat Endocrinology 630 W 168th St PH-5E-522 New York NY 10032 Office Phone: 212-305-6559. Business E-Mail: seo8@columbia.edu.

**OBERHAUS, GEOFFREY LUTHER,** lawyer; b. Bowling Green, Ohio, Dec. 15, 1969; s. Luther and Cindy Oberhaus. BChemE, U. Detroit, 1992; JD, Rutgers U., 1998. Bar: Ohio 1998. Environ. engr. Occidental Chem. Corp., Burlington, NJ, 1992—98; assoc. Dinsmore & Shohl LLP, Cin., 1998—

Exec. bd. govs. River Soc., Dayton, Ohio, 2006—. Mem.: Am. Intellectual Property Owners Assn., Am. Intellectual Property Lawyers Assn. Office: Dinsmore & Shohl LLP 255 East 5th St Cincinnati OH 45202 Office Phone: 513-977-8623. Office Fax: 513-977-8141. Business E-Mail: geof.oberhaus@dinslaw.com.

**OBERHELMAN, HARRY ALVIN, JR.,** surgeon, educator; b. Chgo., Nov. 15, 1923; s. Harry Alvin and Beatrice (Babel) O.; m. Betty Jane Porter, June 12, 1946; children: Harry Alvin III, James I., Robert P., Thomas L., Nancy L. Student, Yale U., 1942-43; BS, U. Chgo., 1946, MD, 1947. Diplomate: Am. Bd. Surgery. Intern U. Chgo. Clinics, 1947—48, resident surgery, 1948—51, 1952—57; asst. prof., assoc. prof. surgery U. Chgo. Sch. Medicine, 1957—60; mem. faculty Stanford Sch. Medicine, Calif., 1960—, prof. surgery, 1964—95, emeritus prof. surgery, 1995—; med. dir. Stanford Internat. Med. Svc., 2006—. Mem. div. licensing Calif. Bd. Med. Quality Assurance, 1970-82 Author papers in field. Served with USAF, 1951-53. Mem. AMA, Calif. Med. Assn., Soc. Univ. Surgeons, Am., Western, Pacific Coast surg. assns., Soc. Alimentary Tract, Halsted Soc., Fedn. State Med. Bds. U.S. (bd. dirs. 1979-82) Home: 668 Cabrillo St Stanford CA 94305-8404 Office Phone: 650-736-7964. Personal E-mail: hoberhelman@hotmail.com.

**OBERING, TREY (HENRY A. OBERING),** federal agency administrator, career military officer; BS cum laude, U. Notre Dame, 1973; disting. grad. Squadron Officer Sch., Maxwell Air Force Base, 1977; MS in astronautical engring., Stanford U., 1980; grad., Defense Systems Mgmt. Coll., 1984; disting. grad., Air Command and Staff Coll, 1988, Indsl. Coll. of Armed Forces, 1993. Advanced through the ranks to lt. gen. USAF, 2004; student, undergraduate pilot training Craig Air Force Base, Ala., 1973—75; student pilot, F-4E Replacement Training Unit MacDill Air Force Base, Fla., 1975—76; operational F-4E pilot, chief aircraft maintenance unit, base exec. officer Moody Air Force Base, Ga., 1976—79; design mgr., space shuttle ground support; chief, space shuttle vehicle integration Vandenberg Air Force Base, Calif., 1980—82; engr. NASA Orbiter Project Kennedy Space Ctr., Fla., 1982—84; space shuttle project engr.; dir. shuttle engring. Western Space and Missile Ctr., Vandenberg Air Force Base, 1984—87; chief, spl. projects inspections Norton Air Force Base, Calif., 1988—90; program element monitor, Air Force Medium Space Launch Vehicles Program; dep. chief, Space Systems Div. Office of Sec. of Air Force for Acquisition, Washington, 1990—91; exec. officer to asst. sec. Office of Sec. of Air Force for Acquisition, the Pentagon, 1991—92; mission area dir., information dominance Office of Sec. of Air Force for Acquisition, 1999—2001; dep. dir., Acquisition and Tech. Group Defense Mapping Agency, Washington, 1993—96; prog. dir., spl. projects, Electronic Systems Ctr., Air Force Materiel Command Hanscom Air Force Base, Mass., 1993—96, dir., Expeditionary Forces Experiment System Program Office, 1997—99; dep., Force Structure Integration and Deployment; prog. dir., Battle Mgmt. Command and Control Missile Defense Agency, Washington, 2001—03; dir. Joint Nat. Integration Ctr., 2003—04, Missile Defense Agency, 2004—. Top Gun, Air-to-Air F-4E Replacement Training Unit. 2nd. lt. USAF, 1973, 1st lt., 1975, captain, 1977, major, 1986, lt. col., 1989, col., 1994, brigadier gen., 2000, major gen., 2004. Decorated Defense Superior Service Medal, Legion of Merit with oak leaf cluster, Meritorious Service Medal with three oak leaf clusters, Air Force Commendation Medal, Air Force Achievement Medal. Mailing: Military Defense Agency 7100 Defense Pentagon Washington DC 20301-7100*

**OBERKFELL, KEITH,** lawyer; b. St. Louis, Mar. 19, 1968; BA with highest distinction, Univ. Va., 1990; JD cum laude, Harvard Law Sch., 1993. Bar: Ill. 1993, NC 2000. Atty. Chapman and Cutler, Chgo., 1993—94, Vedder Price Kaufman Kammholz, Chgo., 1994—96, Mayer Brown Rowe and Maw LLP, Charlotte, NC, 1999—, ptnr., 2002—. Office: Mayer Brown Rowe & Maw LLP Ste 3800 214 N Tryon St Charlotte NC 28202 Business E-Mail: koberkfell@mayerbrownrowe.com.

**OBERLIN, EARL CLIFFORD, III,** securities brokerage company executive; b. Bryan, Ohio, Dec. 10, 1956; s. Earl Clifford II and Pauline Lois (Weber) O. BS in Acctg. and Fin., Miami U., Oxford, Ohio, 1979; MS, Cin. Coll., 1980; grad., Harvard Bus. Sch. CFP; CPA, PFS, Ohio; gen. securities prin., mcpl. bond prin., registered options prin. V.p. MFI Investments Corp., Bryan, 1977—80, treas., 1980—84, pres., chief exec. officer, vice chmn. Toledo and Bryan, 1984—; v.p. Merit Co., Bryan, 1979—87, pres., chief exec. officer, 1988—95; v.p. Oberlin-Ford, Inc., Bryan, 1979—87; vice-chmn. Oberlin and Ford, Inc., Bryan, 1979—95, pres., CEO, 1988—95; chmn. Sky Investments Corp., 1996—2000; chmn. bd. R&O Memls., Inc., 2000—; CEO Oberlin Fin. Corp., 2000—, Oberlin Fin. Mortgage Group, LLC, 2000—. Author: Building a High End Financial Services Practice, 2004; bi-weekly columnist Personal Investing for Women, 1987. Bd. dirs. Jr. Achievement NW Ohio Inc., 1989—; pres., bd. dirs. Jr. Achievement, Bryan, 1989-91. Jr. Achievement NW Ohio scholar, 1975. Mem. AICPA, Inst. CFP, Internat. Assn. Fin. Planning (broker/dealer coun., chmn.-elect 1991, chmn. 1992), Young Pres.'s Orgn., Nat. Assn. Securities Dealers (dist. 8 bus. conduct com. 1994-96, chmn. dist. 8 nominating com. 1999), Securities Ind. Regulatory Coun. on Continuing Edn., Toledo Club, Rotary (Paul Harris fellow), Eagles, Moose. Republican. Methodist. Avocations: sailing, skiing. Home: 127 Country Club Rd Bryan OH 43506-9139 Office: Oberlin Financial Corp PO Box 998 Bryan OH 43506-0998

**OBERLY, KATHRYN ANNE,** lawyer, diversified financial services company executive; b. Chgo., May 22, 1950; d. James Richard and Lucille Mary (Kraus) Oberly; 1 child. Michael W. Goelzer; m. Haynes B. Johnson, June 29, 2002. Student, Vassar Coll., 1967—69; BA, U. Wis., 1971, JD, 1973. Bar: Wis. 1973, D.C. 1981, N.Y. 1995. Law clk. U.S. Ct. Appeals, Omaha, 1973-74; trial atty. U.S. Dept. Justice, Washington, 1974-77, spl. asst., 1977-81, spl. litig. counsel, 1981-82, asst. to Solicitor Gen., 1982-86; ptnr. Mayer, Brown & Platt, Washington, 1986-91; assoc. gen. counsel Ernst & Young LLP, Washington, 1991-94, vice-chair, gen. counsel N.Y.C., 1994—. Bd. dirs. Appleseed Found., 2003—04. Named one of 50 Most Influential Women Lawyers in Am., Nat. Law Jour, 1998. Mem. ABA, Am. Law Inst. (coun. mem.), Am. Acad. Appellate Lawyers, Wis. Bar Assn., D.C. Bar Assn., NY Bar Assn. Democrat. Office: Ernst & Young LLP 5 Times Sq New York NY 10036 Office Phone: 212-773-2500. Business E-Mail: kathryn.oberly@ey.com.

**OBERMAN, IDA,** research and evaluation director, consultant; b. Brummen, Holland, Nov. 22, 1957; arrived in US, 1976; d. Heiko and Gertruida (Reesink) Oberman; m. Lis Cox, Mar. 7, 1999. BA, Swarthmore Coll., 1980; MA, Stanford U., 1983, PhD, 1998. Tchr. H.S. Green Meadow Waldorf Sch., Spring Valley, NY, 1984—87, Trinity Sch., NYC, 1987—92; found. officer Hewlett Found., Menlo Park, Calif., 1998—2001; dir. rsch. and evaluation Springboard Schs., San Francisco, 2002—. Mem. adv. com. Calif. Dept. Edn., 1998—2000, Alameda Unified Sch. Dist., Calif., 2002; mem. adv. bd. Dept. Edn., Calif. Co-author: Teacher Learning, 1996; author: Fidelity & Flexibility, 1998. Co-founder Waldorf-in-the-Mainstream, NYC, 1990, West Side Cmty. Sch., Harlem, NY, 1992. Scheffel grant, Germany. Mem.: Am. Edn. Rsch. Assn. (chair edn. and philanthropy spl. interest group 2001—). Avocations: pottery, swimming. Home: 516 Taylor Ave Alameda CA 94501 Office: Springboard Schs 181 Fremont San Francisco CA 94105

**OBERMAN, MICHAEL STEWART,** lawyer; b. Bklyn., May 21, 1947; s. Hyman Martin and Gertrude O.; m. Sharon Land, Oct. 8, 1975; 1 child, Abigail Land. AB, Columbia U., 1969; JD, Harvard U., 1972. Bar: N.Y. 1973, U.S. Dist. Ct. (so. and ea. dists.) N.Y. 1973, U.S. Ct. Appeals (2d cir.) 1973, U.S. Supreme Ct. 1976, Calif. 1981, U.S. Dist. Ct. (no. dist.) Calif. 1981, U.S. Ct. Appeals (9th cir.) 1981, U.S. Dist. Ct. (so. and cen. dists.) Calif. 1982, U.S. Ct. Appeals (5th cir.) 1989, D.C. 1992, U.S. Ct. Appeals (7th cir.) 1993. Law clk. to Hon. Milton Pollack, U.S. Dist. Ct., N.Y., 1972-73; assoc. Kramer Levin Naftalis & Frankel LLP, N.Y.C., 1973-79, ptnr., 1980—. Contbr. articles to profl. jours Recipient Nathan Burkan prize ASCAP, 1973. Mem. N.Y. State Bar Assn. (mem. ho. of dels. 1989-91, exec. com. comml.

and fed. litigation sect.). Office: Kramer Levin Naftalis & Frankel LLP 1177 Avenue of the Americas New York NY 10036-1003 Office Phone: 212-715-9294. Business E-mail: moberman@kramerlevin.com.

**OBERMANN, RICHARD MICHAEL,** governmental technology and policy analyst; b. May 21, 1949; s. Baird J. and Phyllis L. (Weber) Obermann; m. Grace Karaffa; children: Pearl Louise, John Baird. BS of Engring. in Aerospace and Mech. Scis. cum laude, Princeton U., 1971, PhD in Engring., Aerospace and Mech. Scis., 1977; MS of Engring. in Astronautics and Aeros., Stanford U., 1972; postgrad., Va. Poly. Inst. and State U., Am. U. With MITRE Corp., McLean, Va., 1977-88, engr. transp. systems analysis, transp. energy analysis, telecommunications, project leader, mem. tech. staff in communications and system design; sr. staff officer aeros. and space engring. bd. NRC, Washington, 1988-90, study dir. and analyst technol. and policy issues; mem. profl. staff for space automation. US Ho. of Reps. Com. on Sci., Space and Tech., Washington, 1990-95; minority staff dir., space and aeronautics subcom. US House of Reps. Com. on Sci., Washington, 1995—. Lectr. in field; presenter in field. Contbr. articles to profl. jours. Fellow AIAA (internat. activities com., pub. policy com.), Brit. Interplanetary Soc., Am. Astronaut. Soc. (bd. dirs., exec. com., internat. policy com.); mem. IEEE, AAAS, NY Acad. Sci., Asia Soc., Nat. Space Club, Pacific Telecomms. Coun., Women in Aerospace (bd. dirs.), Internat. Acad. Astronautics, World Affairs Coun. Avocations: languages, sports, trumpet.

**OBERMAYER, HERMAN JOSEPH,** newspaper publisher; b. Phila., Sept. 19, 1924; s. Leon J. and Julia (Sinsheimer) O.; m. Betty Nan Levy, June 28, 1955; children: Helen O. Levy-Myers, Veronica O. Atnipp, Adele O. Malpass, Elizabeth O. Weintraub. Student, U. Geneva, Switzerland, 1946; AB cum laude, Dartmouth Coll., 1948. Reporter L.I. Daily Press, Jamaica, NY, 1950-53; classified advt. mgr. New Orleans Item, 1953-55; asst. to pub. Standard-Times, New Bedford, Mass., 1955-57; editor, pub. Long Branch (N.J.) Daily Record, 1957-71, No. Va. Sun, Arlington, 1963-89; adj. prof. journalism U. Md., 1989-93; vis. lectr. U. West Indies, Jamaica, 1994-95; publ. com. Commentary Mag., 1989—. Pulitzer Prize juror, 1983, 84; lectr. in field; publs. mgmt. Hungary, Poland, Lithuania, Latvia, Estonia, Ukraine, Moldova, Slovenia, Macedonia, Russia, Croatia, Serbia, 1990-2002, Internat. Ctr. Journalists, 1992-2002. Author: Jews in the News, 2001, Soldiering for Freedom: A GI's Account of World War II, 2005; contbr. articles to popular mags., local newspapers. Bd. dirs. Monmouth Med. Ctr., 1958-71; exec. coun. Monmouth Boy Scouts Am., 1958-71, exec. com. Nat. Capital coun., 1971-79, v.p., 1974-77; mem. Va. Legis. Alcohol Beverage Control Study Commn., 1972-74; trustee Arlington (Va.) Bicentennial Commn., Am. Jewish Com. Cmty. Svc. award, 1986, nat. bd. govs., 1989-96, nat. coun., 1996—; trustee Jewish Inst. for Nat. Security Affairs, 1996—. With AUS, 1943-46, ETO. Rhineland Campaign Star; Recipient Silver Beaver award Boy Scouts Am., 1977, Knight Internat. Press fellow, 1994-95. Mem. Am. Soc. Newspaper Editors, So. Newspaper Pubs. Assn. (dir. 1981-84), Mont. Pelerin Soc., Nat. Press Club (Washington), Cosmos Club (Washington), Washington Golf and Country Club (Arlington, Va.), Dartmouth Club (N.Y.C.), Sigma Chi. Jewish. Rotarian. Personal E-mail: obenews@aol.com.

**OBERMEIER, TOM,** architectural firm executive; m. Tina Poe. BArch, U. Colo., MArch in Urban Design. Lic. Colo., Calif., Oreg., Ariz., Wyo., Wash., Tex., N.Mex., Utah, Idaho, cert. Nat. Coun. Archtl. Registration Bds. Founding prin. OZ Arch., Denver. Mem.: AIA. Achievements include invention of Cygnus Curtain Wall System. Office: OZ Architecture Inc 3012 Huron St Ste 100 Denver CO 80202

**OBERMEYER, THERESA NANGLE,** sociology educator; b. St. Louis, July 25, 1945; d. James Francis and Harriet Clare (Shafer) Nangle; m. Thomas S. Obermeyer, Dec. 23, 1977; children: Thomas Jr., James, Margaret, Matthew. BA, Maryville St. Louis, 1967; MEd, St. Louis U., 1970, PhD, 1975. Lic. real estate broker Alaska, 1979, cert. Type A teacher Alaska, 1979. Dir. student activities Lindenwood U., St. Charles, Mo., 1969—70; asst. dean of students Loyola Coll., Balt., 1972—73; asst. dir. student activities St. Louis C.C., Florissant Valley, 1973—78; dir. student activities U. Alaska, Anchorage, 1978—79; instr. sociology Chapman U., Anchorage, 1981—93; tchr. secondary McLaughlin Youth Ctr. for Juvenile Delinquents, 1984—90. Mem Anchorage Munic Health Commn., 1980—81; elected alt. coun. urban bd edn. Nat Sch. Bds. Assn., 1994; maj. party nominee US Senate Gen. Election, 1996; founder, mem. Alaska Women's Polit. Caucus, 1979—; elected Anchorage Sch. Bd., 1990—94, press., 1993. Recipient Fed Women's Equity Act, US Dept Educ Univ Alaska, 1978—79; fellow Fulbright, Project India, 1974, Project Jordan, 1977; grantee Title I, Univ Md and Loyola Col, 1972—73; scholar NDEA, 1968—70. Mem.: AAUW (bd. dirs. Anchorage br. 1980—81), DAR (regent col. John Mitchell chpt. 1992—94), Am. Soc. Pub. Adminstrn. (pres., bd. dirs. south ctrl. chpt. 1981). Avocations: athletics, swimming, horseback riding, skiing, running. Home and Office: 3000 Dartmouth Dr Anchorage AK 99508-4413 Office Phone: 907-278-9455. E-mail: tobermeyer@gci.net.

**OBERNAUER, MARNE, JR.,** technology industry executive; b. Lakehurst, NJ, July 1, 1943; s. Marne and Joan Carolyn (Strassburger) O.; m. Marion Fleck Gislason, Aug. 22, 1976 (div. Jan. 1996); children: Matthew Gene, Michael Sidney. BA, Yale U., 1965; MBA, Harvard U., 1972. With First Nat. City Bank (Citibank, N.A.), NYC, 1965-70, Donaldson, Lufkin & Jenrette, NYC, 1972-74, Devon Group, Inc., NYC and Stamford, Conn., 1974-98, pres., 1978, CEO, 1980-98, chmn. bd., 1986-98; vice chmn. Applied Graphics Techs., Inc., 1998—2003, also bd. dirs. Chmn. bd. dirs. Beverage Distbrs. Co. Trustee The Trinity Sch., The Obernauer Found., Inc.; bd. dirs. Com. for Responsible Fed. Budget. Mem.: Am. Bus. Conf. Found. for Econ. Growth (chmn.), Am. Bus. Conf., Assn. Yale Alumni (bd. dirs. 1999—2003, treas. 2002—03), Maroon Creek Club (Aspen), Century Country Club, Yale Club NYC. Office: Ste 1912 60 E 42d St New York NY 10165

**OBERNDORF, MARK ROBERT,** artist; b. N.Y.C., Feb. 8, 1961; m. Donna Teri Sabino, June 26, 1993; children: Mark Shane Sabino, James Layne Sabino. BS, Rider Coll., 1983. Numerous exhbns. Art educator Child Care Learning Ctr. At Hackensack U. Med. Ctr., NJ, 1998—2005, Wyckoff Pub. Schs., NJ, 2003—06. Avocations: mountain bicycle riding, plein air painting. Home: 533 Franklin Ter Wyckoff NJ 07481 Office Phone: 201-694-1379. Personal E-mail: obern@optonline.net.

**OBERNDORF, MEYERA E.,** mayor; m. Roger L. Oberndorf; children: Marcie, Heide. BS in Elem. Edn., Old Dominion U., 1964. Broadcaster Sta. WNIS, Norfolk, Va.; chair Pub. Libr. bd., Va.; mem. city coun. City of Virginia Beach, Va., 1976—, vice-mayor Va., 1986—88, mayor Va., 1988—. Mem. exec. bd. Tidewater coun. Boys Scouts Am.; bd. dirs. Va.Beach Pub. Libr., 1966-76, chmn. bd., 1967-76; past pres. Va. Muncipal League; bd. dir. Hampton Roads Partnership; Econ. Develop. Alliance; adv. com. Va. Inst. of Gov. Named 25 Most Dynamic Mayors in the US, Newsweek. Mem. AAUW, U.S. Conf. Mayors (trustee), Va. Mcpl. League (exec. bd.), Nat. League Cities (vice-chmn., mem. adv. bd., chair Energy, Environ., and Natural Resources Steering Com.), Princess Anne Women's Club; chair Standing Com. on Internat. Affairs. Jewish. Home: 5404 Challedon Dr Virginia Beach VA 23462-4112 Office: 2401 Courthouse Drive City Hall Bldg 1 Municipal Ctr Virginia Beach VA 23456 Office Phone: 757-427-4581. Office Fax: 757-426-5669. E-mail: moberndo@VBgov.com.*

**O'BERRY, CARL GERALD,** former military officer, electrical engineer; b. Lansing, Mich., Apr. 11, 1936; s. Gerald Ray and Edith Lenore (Watson) O'B.; m. Charlene Marice Bussche, June 21, 1958; children: Brian, Eileen, Kevin, Bradley, Kathleen. BSEE, N.Mex. State U., 1972; MS in Systems Mgmt., Air Force Inst. Tech., 1977. Commd. 2d lt. USAF, 1961, advanced through grades to lt. gen., 1993; commd. 2019 Communications Squadron, Griffiss AFB, NY, 1974-76; project engr. Rome Air Devel. Ctr., Griffiss AFB, 1979-81; asst. dep. chief of staff requirements Air Force Systems Command, Andrews AFB, Md., 1982-84; comdr. Rome Air Devel. Ctr., Griffiss AFB, 1984-86; joint program mgr. WWMCCS info. system Hdqrs. USAF, Wash-

ington, 1986-88; dir. command, control and communications U.S. European Command, Stuttgart, Fed. Republic Germany, 1988-90; dir. command control systems and logistics U.S. Space Command, Peterson AFB, Colo., 1990-92; command control comm. and computers DCS, HQ USAF, Washington, 1992-95; v.p. dir. strategic planning Motorola Space and Sys. Tech. Group, Scottsdale, Ariz., 1995-98; tech. cons. Def. Sci. Bd., Washington, 1998—; v.p., gen. mgr. govt. info. and comms. sys., space group The Boeing Co., Anaheim, Calif., 2000—05; ret. Exec. chair Network Centric Ops. Industry Consortium, 2004—. Mem. Air Force Assn., Armed Forces Communications-Electronics Assn., Soc. Logistics Engrs. Roman Catholic.

**O'BERRY, PHILLIP AARON,** retired veterinarian; b. Tampa, Fla., Feb. 1, 1933; s. Luther Lee and Marjorie Mae (Mahlum) O'B.; m. Terri Martin, July 31, 1960; children: Kelly, Eric, Holly, Danny, Andy, Toby. BS in Agr., U. Fla., 1955; DVM, Auburn U., 1960; PhD, Iowa State U., 1967. With Agrl. Rsch. Svc. USDA, 1956—2003, asst. to dir. vet. scis. div. Beltsville, Md., 1967-72; asst. dir. Nat. Animal Disease Ctr., Ames, Iowa, 1972-73, div. 1973-88, tech. transfer coord., 1988—2003; prin. scientist Office Agr. Biotech., USDA, 1988-90; ret., 2003. Adj. prof. Coll. Vet. Medicine, Iowa State U., 1973—; mem. expert panel livestock infertility FAO; sci. adv. com. Pan Am. Zoonosis Ctr., Buenos Aires; mem. Fed. Coun. Sci. and Tech.; mem. com. animal health, world food and nutrition study NRC; cons. Govt. of Italy, Govt. of Mex., USDA, Govt. of Egypt; mem. nat needs grad. fellowship rev. panel USDA, 1989-91, cons. agr. biotech. rsch. adv. com.; mem. sci. adv. bd. Biotech. R&D Corp., 1992-2001, sci. review bd. Am. Jour. Vet. Rsch., 1990-92; mem. USDA Patent Review Com., 1988-2003. Author 27 rsch. publs.; mem. editl. adv. bd. Food Safety mag. Recipient Cert. of Merit, Agrl. Rsch. Svc., 1972, 84, 2005, Alumni Merit award Iowa State Club of Chgo., 1982, Cert. Appreciation, 1988, Tech. Transfer award 1989, USDA, Disting. Alumnus award Auburn U., 1991; named Hon. Diplomate Am. Coll. of Vet. Microbiologists, 1995, Ames Citizen of the Yr., 2000, Iowa Gov.'s Vol. award, 2001. Mem. APHA, AVMA, AAAS, Nat. Assn. Fed. Vets., Iowa Vet. Med. Assn., N.Y. Acad. Scis., Conf. Rsch. Workers Animal Diseases, Am. Soc. Microbiology, Am. Assn. Lab. Animal Sci., U.S. Animal Health Assn., Am. Assn. Bovine Practitioners, Livestock Cons. Inst., Sigma Xi, Phi Zeta, Phi Kappa Phi, Gamma Sigma Delta (Alumni award Merit 1976), Alpha Zeta, Spades, Blue Key. Democrat. Home: 1612 Woodhaven Cir Ames IA 50010-4130 Personal E-mail: terrioberry@aol.com.

**OBERST, RICHARD B.,** military officer, hospital administrator; b. Wyo. BS in Zoology and Physiology, U. Wyo., 1972; MS in Microbiology, U. Pitts., 1975; PhD in Parasitology and Lab. Practices, U. N.C., 1985. Commd USN, 1975, advanced through grades to capt.; rschr. Malaria br. CDC, Atlanta; head microbiology Naval Regional Med. Ctr., Portsmouth, Va., Oakland; dir. lab. svcs. Navy Environ. Unit 6, Okinawa, Japan, 1977—79; head parasitology Naval Med. Rsch. Unit 2, Manila, Philippines, 1985; naval med. rsch. dir. Naval Med. Rsch. Inst., officer in charge Peru, dep. dir. infectious disease dept., product mgr. pharm. systems divs. Ft. Detrick, Md.; commdg. officer Naval Med. Rsch. Ctr., Silver Spring, Md., 1998—. Decorated Meritorious Svc. medal (2), Navy Commendation medal, Navy Achievement medal.

**OBERST, ROBERT JOHN,** financial analyst; b. Hackensack, N.J., Aug. 20, 1929; s. Bernard and Elsie (Schneider) O.; m. Ingrid Heilbut, Oct. 6, 1956; children: Jeanne, Robert John, Carl Edward. PhD in Fin. Mgmt., Columbia Pacific U., 1984. Cert. fin. planner, registered health underwriter. Spl. agt., mgr. Prudential Ins. Co. Am., Asbury Park, NJ, 1958-68; pres. Robert J. Oberst, Sr. & Assocs., Red Bank, N.J., 1969-92, chmn. bd., 1993—. Newspaper columnist Fin. Planning, 1986-87; prodr., host TV show Fin. Planning Today, 1983-93; contbr. articles to profl. jours. Pres. Monmouth-Ocean Devel. Coun., Manasquan, N.J., 1981-83; bd. dirs. Monmouth County coun. Boy Scouts Am., 1986-93; trustee Brookdale Coll. Found., Middletown, N.J., 1986-92; founder Palmetto State Shooting Ctr. LLC, 2003; mng.ptnr. of Gun Sch., Range, and Gun Retail Ctr. With USN, 1946-50. Recipient Silver Gull Service award Monmouth/Ocean Devel. Council, 1984. Mem. Inst. Cert. Fin. Planners (Fin. Planner of Yr. award 1977), Internat. Assn. Fin. Planning (bd. dirs. 1986-93, chmn. bd. dirs. 1992-93), Estate Planning Coun. (pres. 1971-72), Million Dollar Round Table (life), Nat. Assn. Life Underwriters, Red Bank C. of C. (bd. dirs.), Registry Fin. Planning Practitioners (chmn. 1987-88), N.J. Assn. Life Underwriters (state pres. 1969-70). Republican. Avocations: civil war history, bicycling, gourmet dining, theater, reading. Home: 2 Cottingham Rd Bluffton SC 29910-4714 Office: Robert J Oberst Sr & Assocs 218 Broad St Red Bank NJ 07701-2002 E-mail: rjo33@aol.com.

**OBERST, SHARON STOKES,** dancer, educator, choreographer; d. James H. and Betty Davis Stokes; m. John E.D. Oberst, Aug. 27, 1988; children: Carla Elizabeth, Ian Stokes. BS in Dance, Lamar U., Beaumont, Tex., 1984; MS in Dance, U. Oreg., Eugene, Oreg., 1987. Prof. dance We. Oreg. U., Monmouth, Oreg., 1987—, dir., choreographer Dept. Dance, 1987—, dir., choreographer Dept. Theater, 1987—. Reviewer: Register-Guard Newspaper, 1999—2006. Vol. Monmouth Elem. Sch., 1999—2006. Recipient Pres.'s award, We. Oreg. U., 2000, Passage Excellence in Tchg. award, 2006; grantee, 1999—2006. Mem.: Nat. Dance Edn. Orgn., Pedagogal Studies in Ballet Internat. (treas. coun. organized rsch. 2004—06). Avocation: reading. Office: Western Oreg Univ 345 N Monmouth Ave Monmouth OR 97361

**OBERSTAR, JAMES L.,** congressman; b. Chisholm, Minn., Sept. 10, 1934; s. Louis and Mary (Grillo) O.; m. Jo Garlick, Oct. 12, 1963 (dec. July 1991); children: Thomas Edward, Katherine Noelle, Anne-Therese, Monica Rose; m. Jean Kurth, Nov. 1993; stepchildren: Corinne Quinlan Kurth, Charles Burke Kurth, Jr. BA summa cum laude, St. Thomas Coll., 1956; postgrad. in French, Laval U., Que., Can.; MS in Govt. (scholar), Coll. Europe, Bruges, Belgium, 1957; postgrad. in govt, Georgetown U. Adminstrv. asst. Congressman John A. Blatnik, 1963-74; adminstr. Pub. Works Com. US Ho. Reps., 1971-74; mem. US Congress from 8th Minn. Dist., 1975—, ranking minority mem. transp. and infrastructure com. Mem. Am. Polit. Sci. Assn. Democrat. Office: US Ho Reps 2365 Rayburn Ho Office Bldg Washington DC 20515-2308

**OBERT, PAUL RICHARD,** lawyer, manufacturing executive; b. Pitts. s. Edgar F. and Elizabeth T. Obert. BS, Georgetown U., 1950; JD, U. Pitts., 1953. Bar: Pa. 1954, D.C. 1956, Ohio 1972, Ill. 1974, U.S. Supreme Ct. 1970. Sole practice, Pitts., 1954-60; asst. counsel H.K. Porter Co., Inc., Pitts., 1960—62, sec., gen. counsel, 1962-71, Addressograph-Multigraph Corp., Cleve., 1972-74; v.p. law Marshall Field & Co., Chgo., 1974-82, sec., 1976-82; v.p., gen. counsel, sec. CF Industries, Inc., Long Grove, Ill., 1982—, also officer, dir. various subs. Served to lt. col. USAF. Mem. ABA (corp. gen. counsel com.), Pa. Bar Assn., Allegheny County Bar Assn., Ill. Bar Assn., Chgo. Bar Assn., Am. Soc. Corp. Secs., Am. Retail Fedn. (bd. dirs. 1977-80), Georgetown U. Alumni assn. Pitts. Athletic Assn., Univ. Club (Chgo.), Delta Theta Phi. Office: CF Industries Inc 1 Salem Lake Dr Long Grove IL 60047-8401 Mailing: 115 Haverford Circle Pittsburgh PA 15228-2381

**OBERTON, WILLARD D.,** industrial supply company executive; Grad., St. Cloud Tech. Coll. V.p., COO Fastenal Co., Winona, Minn., 1997—2002, bd. dir., 1999—, v.p. COO, 2000—01, pres., COO, 2001—02, pres., CEO, 2002—. Bd. dir. Wincraft Inc., Donaldson Co. Inc. Trustee Coll. St. Benedict. Office: Fastenal Co 2001 Theurer Blvd Winona MN 55987*

**OBERWETTER, JAMES C.,** ambassador; b. Cuero, Tex., Nov. 3, 1944; m. Anita Oberwetter; children: Ellen, Rea, Brooke. BA in Journalism, U. Tex., Austin. Press sec. Rep. George H.W. Bush, US Ho. Reps.; 1970—81 and pub. Commn. on Alcohol and Drug Abuse, 1996—2001; sr. v.p. govtl. and pub. affairs Hunt Consol., Inc., 1974—2003; US amb. to Saudi Arabia US Dept. State, Riyadh, 2004—. Mem. comm. com. Petroleum Inst., commerce com. Recipient Lifetime Achievement award, Tex. Parent-Teachers Assn. Office: DOS Amb 6300 Riyadh Pl Washington DC 20521-6300*

**OBEY, DAVID ROSS,** congressman; b. Okmulgee, Okla., Oct. 3, 1938; s. Orville John and Mary Jane (Chellis) Obey; m. Joan Therese Lepinski, June 9, 1962; children: Craig David, Douglas David. BS in Polit. Sci., U. Wis., Madison, 1960; MA in Soviet Politics, U. Wis., 1962. Mem. Wis. State Gen. Assembly, 1963-69, asst. minority leader, 1967-69; mem. US Congress from 7th Wis. dist., 1969—, ranking minority mem. appropriations com., ranking minority mem. labor, health and human svcs., edn. and related agencies subcommittee. Mem. adminstrv. com. Wis. Dem. Com., 1960-62 Named Edn. Legislator of Yr., Rural div. NEA, 1968; recipient Legis. Leadership award Eagelton Inst. Politics, 1964, award of merit Nat. Coun. Sr. Citizens, 1976, citation for legis. statesmanship Coun. Exceptional Children, 1976. Democrat. Office: US Ho Reps 2314 Rayburn Ho Office Bldg Washington DC 20515-4907 Office Phone: 202-225-3365.*

**OBIOZOR, GEORGE ACHULIKE,** ambassador; b. Nigeria, Aug. 15, 1942; married. BA.in Polit. sci. and History, U. Puget Sound, Tacoma, Wash.; M in Internat. Affairs, Columbia U., NYC, 1971, M of Philosophy in Internat. Affairs, 1974, PhD in Internat. Affairs, 1976. Lectr. Pratt Inst., NYC, 1971—75; asst. prof., Polit. Sci. Medgar Evers Coll., CUNY, 1975—79; Ralph Bunche Rsch. Fellow in UN Grad. Ctr, CUNY, 1977—78; spl. asst. Office of Polit. Adviser to Pres., Nigeria, 1980—83; sr. rsch. fellow Nigerian Inst. of Internat. Affairs, Lagos, Nigeria, 1984—87; spl. adviser to Min. of Fgn Affairs Nigeria, 1988—99; spl. asst. to pres. of Nigeria, 1990; dir. gen Nigerian Inst. of Internat. Affairs, 1991—99; Nigerian amb. to Israel and high commr. to Cyprus, 1999—2003; amb. to U.S. Washington, 2004—. Chmn. Commonwealth Tech. Meeting, Abuja, 1996; vis. prof., Internat. Affairs, African Inst., Russian Acad. of Sci., Moscow, 1998. Author and editor of numerous prfl. books. Recipient Ugwumba 1 of Orlu, 1991; grantee Albert Schweitzer Fellowship, 1969—71, Alice Stetten Fellowship, Columbia Univ., Sch. of Internat. Affairs, 1969—71. Office: Embassy of Nigeria 3519 International Ct NW Washington DC 20008

**OBLINGER, JAMES L.,** academic administrator; b. Ashland, Ohio, Nov. 3, 1945; s. Richard Bruce and Pauline (Frary) Oblinger; m. Diana G. Oblinger; 4 children. BA in Bacteriology, DePauw U., Greencastle, Ind., 1967; MS in Food Tech., Iowa State U., 1970, PhD in Food Tech., 1972. Asst. prof. to prof. food sci. and human nutrition U. Fla., Gainesville, 1972-84; assoc. dean, dir. resident instrn. Coll. Agr., U. Mo., Columbia, 1984-86; assoc. dean, dir. acad. affairs Coll. Agr. and Life Sci., N.C. State U., Raleigh, 1986—97; dean, exec. dir. for agrl. programs N.C. State U., Raleigh, 1997—2003, provost, exec. vice chancellor for acad. affairs, 2003—04, chancellor, 2005—. Contbr. articles to profl. jours., chpts. to books. Recipient Award of Merit, Inst. of Food and Agrl. Scis., 1981, William V. Cruess Nat. Award, 1983, Disting. Educator Award, Nat. Assn. Colls. and Tchrs. of Agriculture, 1994. Mem. Inst. Food Technologists (Wm. V. Cruess Nat. Award Excellence 1983), Coun. for Agrl. Sci. and Tech. (pres. 1990—), Am. Assn. Higher Edn., Sigma Xi, Phi Kappa Phi, Gamma Sigma Delta, Phi Tau Sigma, Phi Epsilon Phi, Phi Beta Kappa. Episcopalian. Office: NC State U A Holladay Hall Campus Box 7001 Raleigh NC 27695-7101 Office Phone: 919-515-2191. E-mail: chancellor@ncsu.edu.

**O'BLOCK, ROBERT,** association executive, publishing executive; BS in Sociology, Pittsburg (Kans.) State U., 1972, MS in Sociology, 1973, EdS, 2001; PhD, Kans. State U., 1976; MA in Psychology, Newport U., 1998, PsyD in Psychology, 2000; MDiv, Trinity Coll., 2001, DMin, 2003; STD (hon.), St. Elins Sch. Orthodox Theology, 2003. Ordained deacon So. Episcopal Ch., 1999; ordained priest So. Episcopal Ch., 2002. Patrolman Frontenac (Kans.) Police Dept., 1971-73; probation officer Crawford County Juvenile Ct., 1973-74; supr. Children's Ct., 1974; adminstrv. asst. to dean student affairs/cmty. svc. Labette Cmty. Jr. Coll., 1976; dir. night sch. Marymount Coll., 1976; asst. prof. dept. adminstrv. justice Wichita State U., 1977-79; assoc. prof. dept. criminal justice/polit. sci. Appalachian State U., Boone, NC, 1979-89; prof. and chair dept. adminstrn. justice Coll. Ozarks, Point Lookout, Mo., 1989—93; exec. dir. Am. Coll. Forensic Examiners, Springfield, Mo., 1994—. Founder Am. Bd. Forensic Medicine, Am. Bd. Forensic Examiners, Am. Bd. Forensic Psychol.; lectr., cons. in field. Author: Criminal Justice Research Sources, 1983, 4th edit., 1992, (with others) Security and Crime Prevention, 2d edit., 1990, The 7 Steps to the Cure of Souls, 2005; founder, pub. The Forensic Examiner, Annals of the Am. Psychotherapy Assn., contbr. articles to profl. jours., holder 25 U.S. fed. trademarks. Adv. bd. Larnard State Hosp. Named Knight Chevalier, Sovereign Military Order of Temple of Jerusalem, 2001; grantee, Gov.'s Commn. on Criminal Adminstrn., 1976—77. Mem.: Am. Assn. Integrative Medicine (co-founder, CEO), Am. Coll. Forensic Examiners (founder), Am. Psychotherapy Assn. (founder, chmn., CEO). Office: 2750 E Sunshine St Springfield MO 65804-2047 Home: 3686 E Kingswood Dr Springfield MO 65809-4635 Office Phone: 417-881-3818. Personal E-mail: rloblock@aol.com.

**O'BLOCK, ROBERT PAUL,** management consultant; b. Pitts., Mar. 9, 1943; s. Paul Joseph and Mary Elizabeth (Galicic) O'B.; m. Megan Marie. BSME, Purdue U., 1965; MBA, Harvard U., 1967. Rsch. and tchg. fellow in fin., econs. and urban mgmt. Harvard U., 1967-70; assoc. in real estate mgmt. and fin. McKinsey & Co., Inc., Boston, 1969-78; gen. and mng. ptnr. Freeport Ctr., Clearfield, Utah, 1971—; prin. McKinsey & Co., Inc., Boston, 1979-84, dir., 1984-98, McKinsey Adv. Coun., Boston, 1998—. Vis. lectr. urban econs. Yale Law Sch., Princeton U.; cons. Mass., N.J. housing fin. agys., Rockefeller Assn., HUD, 1968-76; chmn. mgmt. com. Snowbird Lodge (Utah), 1974-86. Contbr. articles to profl. jours. Mem. nat. adv. bd. Snowbird Arts Inst., 1977-83; mem. budget com. N.Y. Pub. Libr., 1977-79; mem. adv. bd. Internat. Tennis Hall of Fame, 1986-89, bd. dirs. 1989-95; mem. bd. overseers Boston Symphony Orch., 1988-2000, vice-chmn. bd. overseers, 1992-95, chmn., 1995-2000, trustee, 2000—, vice chmn. bd. trustees, 2002—; trustee U.S. Ski Ednl. Found., 1989-2001, Park Sch., 1997—2003; bd. dirs. Bankstate, Inc. Mem. Devon Yacht Club, Maidstone Club, Nat. Golf Links Am., The Country Club (Brookline). Office: 60 Cramond Rd Chestnut Hill MA 02467-2803

**OBLOY, LEONARD GERARD,** priest; b. Cleve., Sept. 1, 1951; s. Henry Joseph and Ruth Elsie (Walter) Obloy. AB, Borromeo Coll. of Ohio, 1973; MDiv, St. Mary's Sem., 1977; SSL, Pontifical Bibl. Inst., Rome, 1983, postgrad., 1984. Ordained priest Roman Cath. Ch., 1977. Assoc. pastor St. Helen Parish, Newbury, Ohio, 1977-80, St. Rose of Lima Parish, Cleve., 1984-88; vice-rector Mt. St. Mary's Sem., Emmitsburg, Md., 1988-97, asst. prof. sacred scripture and computer sci., 1988-99, dir. aux. svcs., 1997-99; assoc. pastor St. Francis of Assisi Parish, Gates Mills, Ohio, 1999—2002; pastor St. William Parish, Euclid, Ohio, 2002—. Adj. prof. St. Mary's Sem., Cleve., 1984—88, Cleve., 1999—; dean grad. divsn. Cath. Distance U., Hamilton, Va., 1995—2003, dean emeritus, 2003—; guest lectr. Our Lady of Holy Cross Coll., New Orleans, 1998—2003; lectr. in field. Author, narrator pub. TV series And God Said, Witness; author various pamphlets, audio cassettes for Cath. Distance U. Mem.: IEEE Computer Soc., Vatican Radio, Sacred Congregation for Doctrine of Faith, Nat. Cath. Edn. Assn., Corp. for Pub. Broadcasting, Cath. Bibl. Fedn., NY Acad. Scis., Assn. Computing Machinery, GTO Assn. Avocations: computers, audio engineering, audio recording, auto mechanics. Office: St William Parish 367 E 260th St Euclid OH 44132 Office Phone: 216-731-1515. Business E-mail: lgobloy@aol.com.

**OBNINSKY, VICTOR PETER,** lawyer; b. San Rafael, Calif., Oct. 12, 1944; s. Peter Victor and Anne Bartholdi (Donston) Obninsky; m. Clara Alice Bechtel, June 8, 1969 (div. Oct. 30, 2003). BA, Columbia U., 1966; JD, U. Calif., Hastings, 1969. Bar: Calif. 1970. Sole practice, Novato, Calif., 1970-2001, Tiburon, Calif., 2001—2002, Sonoma, Calif., 2003—. Arbitrator Marin County Superior Ct., San Rafael, 1979—; superior ct. judge pro tem, 1979—; lectr. real estate and partnership law. Author: The Russians in Early California, 1966. Bd. dir. Calif. Young Reps., 1968-69, Richardson Bay San. Dist., 1974-75, Marin County Legal Aid Soc., 1976-78; baseball coach Little League, Babe Ruth League, 1970-84; mem. nat. panel consumer arbitrators Better Bus. Bur., 1974-88; leader Boy Scouts Am., 1970-84; permanent sec. Phillips Acad. Class of 1962, 1987—; mem. Phillips Acad. Alumni Coun., 1991-95; bd. cmty. advisors Buck Ctr. Rsch. on Aging, 1990-2001. Recipient Diploma of Honor, City Mus. Obninsk, Russia, 2004. Mem.: ABA, State Bar

Calif., Marin County Bar Assn. (bd. dirs. 1985—91, treas. 1987—88, pres.-elect 1989, pres. 1990), Sonoma Bar Assn., Russian Nobility Assn. Am., Inc., Phi Gamma Delta, Phi Delta Phi. Republican. Russian Orthodox. Home and Office: 21453 Shainsky Sonoma CA 95476-8412 Office Phone: 707-935-7422. Personal E-mail: vpobninsky@comcast.net. *An all-out intellectual attempt to understand baseball thoroughly may give sufficient insight to understand oneself; the so-called "designated hitter" rule should be abolished immediately.*

**OBOGEANU, MADALINA MARIA,** reporter; arrived in U.S., 1997; d. Vasile and Calina Obogeanu. BA in polit. sci, German studies (spl. hons.), Hunter Coll., N.Y., 2004. Analyst UNICEF, UN, N.Y.C., 2000; rsch. asst. Dept. Econ. Affairs, UN, N.Y.C., 2001; asst. prodr. Clear Channel, N.Y.C., 2003; rsch. analyst Hunter Coll., N.Y.C., 2004; reporter Instl. Investor, N.Y.C., 2004—. Mem.: German Academic Exch. Svc. (Scholarship 2002), The Acad. Polit. Sci. Avocations: tennis, skiing, reading. Office: Instl Investor Inc 225 Park Ave S New York NY 10003

**OBOLENSKY, IVAN,** investment banker, foundation administrator, writer; b. London, May 15, 1925; s. Serge and Alice (Astor) O. (parents Am. citizens); m. Claire McGinnis, 1949 (div. 1956); children: Marina Ava, Ivan Serge, David; m. Mary Elizabeth Morris, 1959; 1 child, Serge. AB, Yale U., 1947. Pres. Hotel Investments, Inc., NYC, 1950-58; dir. Silver Bear Inc., Atla., 1947—69; v.p., treas. Serge Obolensky Assocs., 1952-75; pres. Ivan Obolensky Inc. and Astor Books, Ivan Obolensky Inc., pubs., 1956-65; ptnr. A.T. Brod & Co., investment bankers, 1960—65, Dominick & Dominick Inc., investment bankers, 1965-70, Middendorf Colgate, investment bankers, 1970-73; v.p. C.B. Richard, Ellis/Moseley Hallgarten, investment bankers, 1974-81, Sterling Grace & Co., investment bankers, NYC, 1982-87; sr. v.p. Jesup, Josephthal & Co., investment bankers, NYC, 1987-90; principal Astor Capital Mgmt. Assocs. LLC, 1990—; v.p Capital Bank Assocs., NYC, 1990—, Shiclds & Co., NYC, 1990—. Bd. dirs. Gold Canyon Resources, 1996—, HiEnergy Technologies, 2005-06; cons. and lectr. in field. Author: Rogues' March, 1956; contbr. to Nihon Keizai Shimbun, Tokyo, on precious metals, 1985—, program com. NY Soc. of Security Analysts for pub., aerospace, metals and mining, nuc. power, oil and gas; contbr. articles to profl. publs. Bd. dirs. Police Athletic League, NYC, 1975-85, exec. com., 1980-85, 96—, U.S.O., 1987—2004, Audubon Canyon Ranch, Calif., 1989—, Tolstoy Found., 1994-2000, Soldiers', Sailors', Marines' and Airmen's Club, 1976—, pres., 1987-2000, chmn., ceo, 2000—, Russian Nobility Assn. in Am., 1990—, treas., 1991—, v.p., 1995—, Musicians Emergency Fund, 1985-93, pres.1987-92, Children's Blood Found., NY Hosp., 1952—, pres., 1981-95, pres. emeritus, 1995—; pres., dir. Josephine Lawrence Hopkins Found., 1971-2000, chmn., 2000-; pres. Whitemarsh Found., 1980-90, Masonic Toys for Tots Fedn., 2003-; bd. dirs. Masonic Brotherhood Found., 1996—. Lt. (j.g.) USNR, 1943-45, ret., 1980. Published works by James Agee: A Death in the Family and Tad Mosel: All the Way Home, which received Pulitzer prizes, 2 Caldecott awards. Mem. Am. Legion, Mil. Order Loyal Legion US (sr. vice-comdr. 1955, comdr. 1967-70), St. Elmo Soc., Met. Mus. Art (life), Knickerbocker Club, NY Yacht Club, New Eng. Soc. NY, St. George's Soc. NY, The Navy League, The Naval Inst., The Naval Order, Army and Navy Club, Explorer's Club, Masons (Holland #8 master 1981, dist. dep. grand master 1st Manhattan 1983-84, grand mstr. 1994-96), DeMolay (hon. mem.). Masonic Brotherhood Found. (chmn. fin. oversight com. 1999-, chmn. com. endowments, 2004-). Grand Lodge State of NY. Office: Shields & Co 140 Broadway New York NY 10005-1101 Office Phone: 212-320-3000. Personal E-mail: iobolensky@aol.com. Business E-Mail: ivan.obolensky@shieldsandco.com

**OBOLENSKY, MARILYN WALL (MRS. SERGE OBOLENSKY),** metals company executive; b. Detroit, Aug. 13, 1929; d. Albert Fraser and Christine (Frischkorn) Wall; m. Serge Obolensky, June 3, 1971. Student, Duschesne Jr. Coll., 1947. Chmn. bd. Wall-Colmondy Corp., Detroit, 1959-61, exec. sec., 1961—. Chmn. bd. Wall-Gases Inc., Morrisville, Pa., 1959-61; pres. Serge Obolensky Assocs. Bd. dirs. Heart and Lung Assn. N.Y.C., 1963—. Mem.: Bathing Corp. (Southampton, N.Y.), Southampton. Republican. Roman Catholic. Address: 45 Preston Pl Grosse Pointe Farms MI 48236-3035

**O'BOYLE, MAUREEN,** television show host; News prodr., anchor Sta. KREM-TV, Spokane, Wash.; reporter, prodr., writer, co-anchor Sta. WMAZ-TV, Macon, Ga.; nightside reporter, anchor Sta. WECT-TV, Wilmington, N.C.; morning news anchor Sta. WITN-TV, Washington, N.C.; anchor A Current Affair; anchor, sr. corr. Extra, Glendale, Calif., 1995-96, co-host, 1997—; host In Person With Maureen O'Boyle, 1996-97.

**O'BOYLE, ROBERT JOHN,** art educator; s. Patrick E. and Ann Elizabeth O'Boyle; m. Carrie Owen O'Boyle. BFA summa cum laude, Phila. Coll. Art; MFA summa cum laude, Rutgers U.; PhD, Union Inst. and U., Cin. Nat. bd. cert. tchr., cert. art therapist, tchr. of art K-12 NJ. Art tchr. Diocese of Trenton, Hopewell Valley HS, Pennington, NJ. Represented in permanent collections Vatican Collectiono of Contemporary Religious Art, Phila. Mus. Art; author: (poetry book) Night Psalms, 1989 (Shopard award), A Literary and Visual Art Study of the Iconography of "The Litany of Loretto", 1985 (Dean's award). Named Outstanding Secondary Tchr. of Art, Phila. U., 2001; recipient Gov.'s award for tchng. excellence, Presdl. medal, RI Sch. Art; grantee, Nat. Endowment for the Arts. Office Phone: 609-737-1411 ext 3650. E-mail: roboyle@hvrsd.k12.nj.us.

**OBRAMS, GUNTA IRIS,** clinical research administrator; b. Düsseldorf, Germany, Sept. 2, 1953; came to U.S., 1961; d. Robert and Olga (Baltins) O.; m. Malcolm DeWitt Patterson, Dec. 22, 1975; 1 child, Andrew McDougal Patterson. BS in Biology cum laude, Rensselaer Poly. Inst., 1977; MD, Union U., Albany, N.Y., 1977; MPH, Johns Hopkins U., 1982, PhD, 1988. Resident in obstetrics and gynecology Ea. Va. Grad. Sch. Medicine, Norfolk, 1977-78; community physician Southampton Meml. Hosp., Franklin, Va., 1978-81; resident in gen. and preventive medicine sch. hygiene and pub. health Johns Hopkins U., Balt., 1981-84, project dir., 1983-85, med. dir., 1985-86; med. officer divsn. cancer etiology Nat. Cancer Inst., Bethesda, Md., 1986-89, dep. chief, 1989-90, chief, 1990-96, dir. extramural epidemiology & genetics program, 1996-2001; mgmt. US Coast Guard Health Svcs., 2001—05; med. officer divsn. clin. resources NIH, Bethesda, 2005—. Editor: (with M. Potter) The Epidemiology and Biology of Multiple Myeloma, 1991; contbr. articles to profl. jours. With USPHS, 1987—. Recipient Nat. Cancer Inst. Nat. Rsch. Svc. award, 1981, Rsch. Career award Nat. Inst. Occupational Safety & Health; scholar Am. Med. Women's Assn., 1977. Mem. Phi Beta Kappa, Delta Omega, Alpha Omega Alpha. Office: DCRR NCRR NIH 6701 Democracy Blvd MSC-4874 Bethesda MD 20892

**O'BRIEN, ADRIENNE GRATIA,** communications educator; b. NYC, Nov. 19, 1935; d. John Robert and Regina C. (Murphy) O'B.; m. David G. Salten, Dec. 21, 1987. AB, Hunter Coll., NYC; MA, MA, Villanova (Pa.) U.; PhD, Syracuse U. Faculty Cabrini Coll., Radnor, Pa., 1962-68, dir. R & D, 1971-72; prof., chair MA program NY Inst. Tech., Old Westbury, 1974-78, dean Sch. Media and Arts, 1979-91, prof. comm. arts, 1992—. Pres. AID Assocs., NYC, 1972-74, Creative Cons., Port Washington, NY, 1992—; reviewer Nat. Coun. Humanities, Washington, 1981; pres. Women in Instrnl. Tech., Washington, 1981. Editor: Computer Based Training Today, 1987; prodr., dir. (video) Then and Now, 1995 (Communicator award, 1996), Legacy of Mother Ursula, 1996 (Communicator award, 1997), Maritime Mus. of L.I., founder, exec. prodr. L.I. News tonight, 1984; reviewer: Jour. Staff Devel., 1990. Mem. project steering com. Where Are the Women?, 2002; bd. dirs. Girl Scouts of Nassau County, 2002—. Named one of 90 Women for 90 Yrs., Girl Scouts of Nassau County; recipient Instrnl. Nat. Leadership award, Assn. Ednl. Comm. and Tech., Washington, 1989, Comm. award, Maritime Mus. L.I., 2001, L.I. Top 50 Women award, L.I. Bus. News, 2002, Lifetime Achievement award, Pub. Rels. Profls. L.I., 2005, Cmty. Svc. award, Patron of the Arts, NY, 2005, Women on the Job Achievement in Edn. award, 2005. Mem.: Women on the Job (v.p. 1995—2004), Alpha Epsilon Rho (hon.). Avocation: tennis. Office: NY Inst Tech Old Westbury NY 11568 Business E-Mail: aobrien@nyit.edu.

**O'BRIEN, ANNMARIE,** education educator; b. N.Y.C., Nov. 10, 1949; d. Hugh and Margaret (Doherty) O'B.; m. William James McGinty, Dec. 30, 1976; children: Michael Hugh, Liam Patrick. BS in Elem. Edn., Boston U., 1971; MS in Early Childhood Edn., Queens Coll., 1976; EdD in Ednl. Leadership, Portland State U., 1994. Tchr. St. Gerard Majella Elem. Sch., Hollis, N.Y., 1972-76, Lower Kuskokwim Sch. Dist., Bethel, Alaska, 1977-85; child sexual abuse prevention coord. Resource Ctr. for Parents and Children, Fairbanks, Alaska, 1986; grad. asst., project evaluator Portland (Oreg.) State U., 1989-92, student tchr. supr., 1992; prof. edn., rsch. assoc. Inst. Social and Econ. Rsch. U. Alaska, Anchorage, 1993-96; prin. Old Harbor Sch., Kodiak Island Borough Sch. Dist., Kodiak, Alaska, 1996-99; dir. curriculium and instr. Northwest Arctic Borough, Kotzebue, Alaska, 1999—2003; asst. supr. NW Artic Borough Sch. Dist., Kotzebue, Alaska, 2006—. Author: A Child Abuse Prevention Training Manual for Educators, 1976; co-author: The Academy for Future Educators Guidebook, 1992. Recipient scholarship Portland State U., 1991. Mem. ASCD, Kappa Delta Pi. Office: NWA BSD PO Box 51 Kotzebue AK 99752-0051 Office Phone: 907-442-3472 ext. 235. E-mail: aobrien@nwarctic.org.

**O'BRIEN, BEA JAE,** artist; b. Oshkosh, Wis., Dec. 4, 1940; d. Harry A. and Mammie Anna (Smith) Mac Farlane; m. John Walsh O'Brien, July 27, 1965; 1 child, John Christian. BA, U. Wis. Profl. artist B.J.'s Fine Arts, Moraga, Calif. Art included in various art publs.; exhibitions include Dennos Mus., Calif. Art & Wine Festival, 2001, Internat. Art Show, 2001, Valley Art Gallery, Calif., 2001—03, Calif. Art (3 awards), Internat. Art Show, Chgo., First Cyberspace Art Exhibit, New Zealand, Internat. Collage Constrn. Mus., Mexico City, one-woman shows include, Moraga, Calif., 1996—2001. Vol. children's art publ. Moraga Sch. Sys.; vol. local sch. projects Calif. Open Art Exhbits, 2003; vol. organizer Cmty. Art Gallery, Moraga Gallery, 2000—01; donated, vol Outreach Art Funds and Scholarships, Calif. Recipient 1st pl. award, Calif. Art and Wine Festival, 1999, Bay Area Art Festival, 1999, 2000. Mem.: Digital Image Art Career, Intuitive Layering Art Group, Valley Arts Ctr., Collage Artists Am., Nat. Collage Soc. (award 1997—99, 2004, signature), Internat. Soc. Exptl. Artists (Nautilus award 2003, signature), Lamorinda Arts Alliance, Coll. Art Am., Women in Arts Mus. (honor roll). Avocations: reading, volunteering. Office: BJs Fine Arts 34 Sea Pines Moraga CA 94556-1029 Office Phone: 925-376-8018. Personal E-mail: dancincollag7@yahoo.com.

**O'BRIEN, CATHERINE LOUISE,** museum administrator; b. NYC, July 21, 1930; d. Edward Denmark and Cathrine Louise (Browne) O'B.; m. Philip R. James (div.); m. Sterling Noel (div). BA, Finch Coll., 1952; postgrad, Williams Coll., 1954, Marymount Coll., 1954. Reprodn. mgr. Met. Mus. Art, N.Y.C., 1975—; dir. sales Simon Pearce Gallery, N.Y.C. Exhibited in group shows at Parrish Art Mus., Southampton, NY, 1965-70. Met. Mus. Art, NYC, 1975-85, Guild Hall Exhibit, East Hampton, NY, 1965-85. Mem. aux. Southampton Hosp., 1970-85; founder East Hampton Horse Show, Ladies Village Improvement Soc., East Hampton, 1970—; fair coms. St. James Ch., NYC, St. Luke's Ch., East Hampton, 1970-85; alumnae adv. bd. Marymount Coll., NYC, 1984-86, chmn. alumnae event, 1994; active Women's Nat. Rep. Club, NYC, John Drew Theater Co., Guild Hall, 1956-59; chmn. Landmark and Tree Planting Com. for Madison Ave. Assn., NYC, 1994—; mem. founding com. Internat. Debutante Ball, Waldorf Astoria, NYC, 1955; founding mem. Williamstown (Mass.) Theater, 1955; founder Parrish Art Mus. Players, Southampton, NY, 1955. Mem. DAR (founding; vice regent East Hampton chpt. 1974-85), Colonial Dames Am. (archives com. 1980-85), Daus. Brit. Empire (historian 1978-85), United Daus. Confederacy (state historian 1970-85), Daus. Colonial Wars (corr. sec. 1983-85), Sons and Daus. of Pilgrims (corr. sec. 1983-85), Victorian Soc., Soc. Mayflower Descs. (life), English Speaking Union, New Eng. Soc. (mem. ball com. 1983-86), Daus. of Cin. (historian 1979-85), Squadron "A", Devon Yacht, Maidstone, Southampton Yacht, Metropolitan Club (women's com., chmn. debutante ball 1980-84), Reciprocal/India House, St. Anthony Union League. Republican. Episopalian. Avocations: show horses, dogs. Home: 605 Park Ave New York NY 10021-7016 also: Seacote PO Box 1488 East Hampton NY 11937-0711 Office: Met Mus of Art 5th Ave New York NY 10028 also: Simon Pierce Gallery 500 Park Ave New York NY 10022-1606

**O'BRIEN, CHARLES H.,** retired lawyer, retired judge; b. Orange, N.J., July 30, 1920; s. Herbert Rodgers and Agnes Sidman (Montanya) O'B.; m. Anna Belle Clement, Nov. 9, 1966; children: Merry Diane, Steven Shawn (dec.), Heather Lynn. LLB, Cumberland U., 1947. Rep. Tenn. Legislature, Memphis, 1963-65, senator, 1965-67; assoc. judge Tenn. Ct. Criminal Appeals, Crossville, 1970-87; assoc. justice Tenn. Supreme Ct., 1987-94, chief justice, 1994-95; ret., 1995; pvt. practice, Crossville, 1995—. Bd. dirs. Lake Tansi Village Property Owners Assn., 1984-89, chmn., 1989. With U.S. Army, 1938-45, ETO, 1950, UN Command, Tokyo. Decorated Bronze Star, Purple Heart with oak leaf cluster. Fellow Tenn. Bar Found.; mem. Tenn. Bar Assn., Cumberland County Bar Assn., Am. Legion, Lake Tansi Village Chowder and Marching Soc. (pres.). Democrat. Avocation: outdoor activities.

**O'BRIEN, CHARLES HAROLD,** writer, priest; s. Erwin Joseph and Margaret Alice O'Brien; m. Elvy Astrid Setterqvist, Dec. 21, 1964. BA, Notre Dame U., 1951, MA, 1952; PhD, Columbia U., 1967. Instr. Ohio State U., Columbus, 1964—65, Skidmore Coll., Saratoga Springs, NY, 1965—66; asst. prof. Wittenberg U., Springfield, Ohio, 1966—72; prof. Western Ill. U., Macomb, 1972—94; author Williamstown, Mass., 1994—. Author: Ideas of Religious Toleration at the Time of Joseph II, 1969, (novels) Mute Witness, 2001, Black Gold, 2002, Noble Blood, 2004, Lethal Beauty, 2005. Vicar St. Paul's Episcopal Ch., Warsaw, Ill., 1984—88. With U.S. Army, 1945—47, Korea. Mem.: Am. Hist. Assn. Avocation: reading. Personal E-mail: obrien@bcn.net.

**O'BRIEN, CHRISTOPHER D.,** medical researcher, educator; BA, U Pa., 1985, PhD, 2003; MD, U. Conn., 1991. Diplomate in internal medicine, critical care and pulmonary disease Am. Bd. Internal Medicine, Nat. Bd. Med. Examiners. Resident in medicine Hosp. U. Pa., Phila., 1991—94, fellow pulmonary and critical care, 1995—99; instr. medicine physician-scientist pulmonary, critical care divsn. U. Pa. Sch. Medicine, Phila., 1999—2002, adj. asst. prof. pulmonary divsn., 2002—; dir. clin. rsch. AstraZeneca, Wilmington, Del., 2002—. Contbr. articles to profl. jours. Pres. U. Conn. Med./Dental Student Govt., 1988—89. Recipient Henry Christian award, Am. Fedn. for Med. Rsch., 2002; grantee Young Investigator award, Am. Heart Assn., 2001—02, KO*/MCSDA, NIH, 2002—; William Dyson Rsch. fellow, U. Pa., 1997—98, Parents Assn. scholar, U. Conn., 1989, Clark Meml. Academic scholar, Waterbury Med. Assn., 1990. Fellow: Am. Coll. Chest Physicians; mem.: Drug Info. Soc., Am. Physiologic Soc., Am. Thoracic Soc., Laennec Soc. Avocations: sailing, bicycling, running. Office: AstraZeneca LP DCC2 E3 1800 Concord Pike Wilmington DE 19850

**O'BRIEN, CLARE,** lawyer; b. Ireland, 1961; children: Una, Lucy. BA summa cum laude, Trinity Coll., 1982. Bar: Ireland, NY 1986, U.S. Dist. Ct. NY (so. dist.) 1987. Atty. Eugene F. Collins & Son, Brady & Tarpey, 1987—88, Shearman & Sterling LLP, NYC, 1988—95, mem., mergers & acquisitions group, 1989—, ptnr., 1995—. Bd. dirs. Am. Assn. Internat. Commn. Jurists. Named Dealmaker of Yr., Am. Lawyer mag., 2006. Office: Shearman & Sterling LLP 599 Lexington Ave New York NY 10022-6069 Office Phone: 212-848-8966. Office Fax: 212-848-7179. E-mail: cobrien@shearman.com.*

**O'BRIEN, CONAN,** talk show host, writer, performer; b. Brookline, Mass., Apr. 18, 1963; m. Liza Powel, Jan. 2002; children: Neve, Beckett. BA Am. Hist., Lit., Harvard U., 1985. Staff mem. The Harvard Lampoon, 1981-85 (pres. 1983, 84); head Conaco. Stage appearances with: The Groundlings (L.A.) 1985-87; writer, performer The Happy Happy Good Show (L.A.), Chgo.) 1988; writer (TV) Not Necessarily the News (HBO) 1985-87. Saturday Night Live, 1988-91 (NBC, Emmy Outstanding Writing in Comedy series 1989), Lookwell (NBC) 1991; writer, prodr. The Simpsons (Fox) 1991-93, The Wilton North Report (syndicated) 1987, Late Night with Conan O'Brien (NBC) 1993— (Best Writing in Comedy/Variety Show Writer's

Guild award 1997, TV award Writers Guild Am. 2000), host, Emmy Awards 2002; film appearances include Tomorrow Night, 1998, Barenaked in America, 1999, Vanilla Sky, 2001, Bewitched, 2005; TV appearances include (voice) The Simpsons, 1994, The Single Guy, 1996, Arli$$, 1996, (voice) Dr. Katz, Professional Therapist, 1997, Veronica's Closet, 1998, Spin City, 1998, LateLine, 1999, Space Ghost Coast to Coast, 1999, (voice) Futurama, 1999, Tomorrow Night, 1998, (voice) Robot Chicken, 2005. Named one of 25 Most Intriguing People, People Mag., 50 Funniest People Alive, Entertainment Weekly. Office: Late Night with Conan O'Brien NBC 30 Rockefeller Plz New York NY 10112-0002*

**O'BRIEN, DANIEL J.,** lawyer; b. Los Alamos, N.Mex., Nov. 18, 1951; BS, U. N.Mex., 1975, MBA, 1980, JD, 1983. Bar: N.Mex. 1983, Tex. 1993, U.S. Dist. Ct. N.Mex. 1984, U.S. Ct. Appeals (10th cir.) 1987. Ptnr. O'Brien & Ulibari, P.C., Albuquerque. Mem.: ABA, Albuquerque Bar Assn., N.Mex. Trial Lawyers Assn., N.Mex. Def. Lawyers Assn. (pres. 1999—2000), State Bar N.Mex. (bd. commrs. 1999—2000, v.p. 2002, pres. 2004). Office: O'Brien & Ulibari PC 6000 Indian Sch NE Ste 200 Albuquerque NM 87110 Office Phone: 505-883-8181.

**O'BRIEN, DANIEL WILLIAM,** lawyer, lumber company executive; b. St. Paul, Jan. 6, 1926; s. Daniel W. and Kathryn (Zenk) O'B.; m. Sarah Ward Stoltze, June 20, 1952; children: Bridget Ann, Daniel William, Kevin Charles, Timothy John. Student, U. Dubuque, 1943, Ill. State U., 1944; BSL, U. Minn., 1948, JD, 1949. Bar: Minn. 1949. Practice in, St. Paul, 1950—; partner Randall, Smith & Blomquist, 1955-65; of counsel Doherty, Rumble & Butler, 1965-99; pres., chmn. bd. dirs. F.H. Stoltze Land & Lumber Co., 1964—; pres. Maple Island, Inc., 1968—. Served to ensign USNR, 1943-46. Mem. Minn., Ramsey County bar assns., World Pres's. Orgn., Chief Execs. Orgn. Office: 2497 7th Ave E Ste 105 North Saint Paul MN 55109-2902 Home (Winter): 3951 S Placita de la Moneda Green Valley AZ 85614-5063 Address: 4734 Bouleau Rd White Bear Lake MN 55110-3355 E-mail: dwobrien@maple-island.com.

**O'BRIEN, DAVID MICHAEL,** law educator; b. Rock Springs, Wyo., Aug. 30, 1951; s. Ralph Rockwell and Lucile O'Brien; m. Claudine M. Mendelovitz, Dec. 17, 1982; children: Benjamin, Sara, Talia. BA, U. Calif., Santa Barbara, 1973, MA, 1974, PhD, 1977. Fulbright lectr. Oxford (Eng.) U., 1987-88; lectr. U. Calif., Santa Barbara, 1976-77; asst. prof. U. Puget Sound, Tacoma, Wash., 1977-79; Spicer prof. U. Va., Charlottesville, 1979—. Fulbright rschr. Tokyo, Kyoto, Japan, 1993-94, Fulbright chair, Bologna, Italy, 1999; jud. fellow U.S. Supreme Ct., Washington, 1982-83; Fulbriht lectr., Oxford U., England, 1987-1988; vis. postdoctoral fellow Russell Sage Found., N.Y.C., 1981-82; lectr. USIA, Burma, Japan, France, 1994-95. Author: Supreme Court Watch, 1991—, Constitutional Law and Politics, 2 vols., 6th edit., 2005, Storm Center: The Supreme Court in American Politics, 7th edit., 2005, To Dream of Dreams: Constitutional Politics in Postwar Japan, 1996, To Dream of Dreams: Religious Freedom in Postwar Japan, 1996, Animal Sacrifice & Religious Freedom, 2004; editor: Views from the Bench, 1985, Judges on Judging, 1997, Government by the People, 21st edit., 2005. Rappatour, jud. selection 20th Century Fund Task Force, N.Y., 1986-87. Tom C. Clark Jud. Fellow, Jud. Fellows Commn., Washington, 1983. Mem. ABA (Silver Gavel award 1987), Am. Judicature Soc., Am. Polit. Sci. Assn., Supreme Ct. Hist. Soc. (editl. bd. 1982—), Internat. Polit. Sci. Assn. Democrat. Avocations: painting, travel. Home: 916 Tilman Rd Charlottesville VA 22901-6338 Office: U Va 232 Cabell Hall Charlottesville VA 22901 Office Phone: 434-994-3358.

**O'BRIEN, DAVID PETER,** corporate director; b. Montreal, Que., Can., Sept. 9, 1941; m. Gail Baxter Cornell, June 1, 1968; children: Tara, Matthew, Shaun. BA in Econs. with honors, Loyola Coll., Montreal, 1962; BCL, McGill U., Montreal, 1965. Assoc. and ptnr. Ogilvy, Renault, Montreal, 1967-77; v.p. gen. counsel Petro-Can., Calgary, Alta., 1977-81, sr. v.p., 1982-85, sr. v.p. fin. and planning, 1982-85, exec. v.p., 1985-89; pres., CEO Noverco Inc., Montreal, 1989; chmn. bd. dirs., CEO PanCan. Petroleum Ltd., Calgary, 1990—95; pres., COO Can. Pacific Ltd., Montreal, 1995—96, chmn., pres., CEO Calgary, 1996—2001; chmn., CEO PanCan. Energy Corp., 2001—02; chmn. EnCana Corp., 2002—. Bd. dirs. Inco Ltd.; TransCan. PipeLines Ltd., Molson Coors Brewing Co.; chmn. Royal Bank Can., 2004—. Mem.: Calgary Golf and Country Club, Calgary Petroleum Club, Glencoe Club.

**O'BRIEN, DERMOT J.,** human resources specialist; b. Dublin; B of Fin.; Pace U. With Morgan Stanley; various positions Merrill Lynch; exec. v.p. human resources TIAA-CREF, N.Y.C., 2003—. Office: TIAA-Cref 730 3d Ave New York NY 10017

**O'BRIEN, DONALD EUGENE,** federal judge; b. Marcus, Iowa, Sept. 30, 1923; s. Michael John and Myrtle A. (Toomey) O'B.; m. Ruth Mahon, Apr. 15, 1950; children: Teresa, Brien, John, Shuivaun. LL.B., Creighton U., 1948. Bar: Iowa bar 1948, U.S. Supreme Ct. bar 1963. Pvt. practice law, Sioux City, 1948—61; asst. city atty., 1949—54; county atty. Woodbury County, Iowa, 1955—59; mcpl. judge Sioux City, Iowa, 1959-60; U.S. atty. No. Iowa, 1961-67; U.S. Dist. judge Sioux City, 1978—; chief judge U.S Dist. Ct. (no. dist.) Iowa, Sioux City, 1985-92, sr. judge, 1992—; pvt. practice law Sioux City, 1967—78. Rep. 8th cir. dist. ct. judges to Jud. Conf. U.S., 1990-97. Served with USAAF, 1942-45. Decorated D.F.C., air medals. Mem. Woodbury County Bar Assn., Am. Judicature Soc. Roman Catholic. Office: US Dist Ct PO Box 267 Sioux City IA 51102 0267 Office Phone: 712-233-3916. E-mail: Don_OBrien@iand.uscourts.gov.

**O'BRIEN, EDWARD IGNATIUS,** corporate financial executive, director, investor, lawyer; b. NYC, Sept. 15, 1928; s. Edward I. and Marguerite (Malone) O'B.; m. Margaret M. Feeney, June 29, 1957; children: Edward Ignatius III, Margaret Mary, Thomas Gerard, John Joseph. AB, Fordham U., 1950; LLB, St. John's U., 1954; grad., Advanced Mgmt. Program, Cornell U., 1965. Bar: N.Y. 1954. With firm Hale, Kay & Brennan, N.Y.C., 1954-55; with Bache & Co., Inc., N.Y.C., 1955-74, gen. counsel, 1960, gen. ptnr., 1964, sec., 1968, v.p., 1965-68, sr. v.p., mem. exec. com., 1969, exec. v.p., 1969, chmn. exec. com., 1971-74; pres. Securities Industry Assn., 1974-93; retired, 1993. Bd. dirs. 8 corps.; lectr. Am. Law Inst., Practising Law Inst., Am. Mgmt. Assn.; exch. ofcl. Am. Stock Exch., 1972; mem. adv. bd., mem. exec. com. Securities Regulation Inst., U. Calif., 1975—. Mem. Cardinal's com. Laity Cath. Archdiocese N.Y., mem. Cardinal's com. for edn.; chmn. Fordham U. Coun., 1971-73; bd. dirs. 3 non-profit orgns.; chmn. corp. devel. com. Fordham U.; trustee, chmn. bd. trustees Fordham Prep. Sch., 1975-77, Capt. USAR. Mem. N.Y. State Bar Assn., Am. Arbitration Assn. Soc. Internat. Law, Guild Cath. Lawyers, Securites Industry Assn. (chmn. publicly owned firms com. 1972), Nat. Assn. Securities Dealers (dist. com. 1973-74), Shenorock Shore Club (Rye, N.Y.), Town Club (Scarsdale, N.Y.), Met. Club (Washington). Home and Office: 12 Woods Ln Scarsdale N.Y. 10583-6408

**O'BRIEN, EDWIN FREDERICK,** archbishop; b. Bronx, NY, Apr. 8, 1939; BA, St. Joseph's Sem., Yonkers, N.Y., 1961, MDiv, 1964, MA, 1965; STD, Algelicum U., Rome, 1976. Ordained priest Roman Cath. Ch., 1965. Parish priest, chaplain U.S. Mil. Acad., West Point, NY, 1965—70; commd. 2d lt. U.S. Army, 1970, advanced through grades to capt., 1973, chaplain, 1970—73, 82nd Airborne Divsn., Ft. Bragg, NC, 1970—71, 173rd Airborne Brigade, 1st Calalry Brigade, Vietnam, 1971—72; post chaplain Ft. Gordon, Ga., 1972—73; assoc. pastor St. Patrick's Cathedral, NYC, 1976—81; vice chancellor Archdiocese NY, 1976—81, dir. comm., 1981—83, sec. Cardinals Terence Cooke, John J O'Connor, 1983—85; rector St. Joseph's Sem., Dunwoodie, NY, 1985—89, 1994—97, Pontifical N. Am. Coll., Rome, 1990—94; titular bishop Diocese of Tizica, 1996—99; auxillary bishop Diocese of N.Y., 1996—97; archbishop Archdiocese of Mil. Svcs., Washington, 1997—. Bd. dirs. Nat. Conf. Cath. Bishops, Basilica Nat. Shrine Immaculate Conception;

Trustee St. Joseph's Sem., Pontifical Coll. Josephinum; chmn. bd, trustees Pontifical N. Am. Coll. Mem.: Fellowship Cath. Scholars. Roman Catholic. Office: Mil Archdiocese PO Box 4469 Washington DC 20017-0469 E-mail: archbishop@erols.com.

**O'BRIEN, ELMER JOHN,** librarian, educator; b. Kemmerer, Wyo., Apr. 8, 1932; s. Ernest and Emily Catherine (Reinhart) O'B.; m. Betty Alice Peterson, July 2, 1966. AB, Birmingham So. Coll., 1954; Th.M., Iliff Sch. Theology, 1957; MA, U. Denver, 1961. Ordained to ministry Methodist Ch., 1957; pastor Meth. Ch., Pagosa Springs, Colo., 1957—60; circulation-reference librarian Boston U. Sch. Theology, 1961—65; asst. librarian Garrett-Evang. Theol. Sem., Evanston, Ill., 1965—9; librarian, prof. United Theol. Sem., Dayton, Ohio, 1969—96, prof. emeritus, 1996—; abstractor Am. Bibliog. Center, 1969—73; dir. Ctr. for Evang. United Brethren Heritage, 1979—96; acting libr. Iliff Sch. Theology, 2000—01. Chmn. div. exec. com. Dayton-Miami Valley Libr. Consortium, 1983—87; rsch. assoc. Am. Antiquarian Soc. 1990. Author: Bibliography of Festschriften in Religion Published Since 1960, 1972, Religion Index Two: Festschriften, 1960-69; contbg. author: Communication and Change in American Religious History, 1993, Essays in Celebration of the First Fifty Years, 1996; pub. Meth. Revs. Index, 1818-1985, 1989-91; contbr. articles to profl. jours. Recipient theol. and scholarship award Assn. Theol. Schs. in U.S. and Can., 1990-91; Libr. Staff Devel. grant Assn. Theol. Schs. in U.S. and Can., 1976-77, Rsch. grant United Meth. Ch. Bd. Higher Edn. and Ministry, 1984-85 Mem. ALA, Acad. Libr. Assn. Ohio, Am. Theol. Libr. Assn. (head bur. personnel and placement 1969-73, dir. 1973-76, v.p. 1977-78, pres. 1978-79), Am. Antiquarian Soc. (rsch. assoc. 1990), Delta Sigma Phi, Omicron Delta Kappa, Eta Sigma Phi, Kappa Phi Kappa. Clubs: Torch Internat. (v.p. Dayton club 1981-82, pres. 1982-83). Home: 4840 Thunderbird Dr Apt 281 Boulder CO 80303-3829 Personal E-mail: ejobr@aol.com.

**O'BRIEN, EVA FROMM,** lawyer; b. Herne, Germany, May 6, 1956; came to U.S., 1959; d. Georg and Eva (Aust) F.; m. John J. O'Brien, Feb. 12, 2000. BS in Chem. Engring., Syracuse U., 1978; JD, U. Houston, 1985. Bar: Tex. 1985, U.S. Dist. Ct. (so. dist.) Tex. 1987, U.S. Ct. Appeals (5th cir.) 1997. Engr. Chrysler Corp., Deer Park, Mich., 1978-79; process engr. Mobay Chem. Co., Baytown, Tex., 1980, ETI Engrs. Inc., Houston, 1981-82; engr. Petromas Inc., Houston, 1982-83; sr. chem. engr. NUS Corp., Houston, 1983-84; briefing clk., assoc. Hill Parker Franklin Cardwell & Jones, Houston, 1985-86; assoc. Fulbright & Jaworski LLP, Houston, 1986-93, ptnr., 1994—, and head, environ. law dept. Author, editor: Texas Environmental Law Handbook, 1989, 5th edit., 2000, (book chpt.) Environmental Aspects of Real Estate Transactions, 2d edit., 1999. Mem. ABA (co-chair real estate and probate sect., underground storage tank and RCRA com. 1994-95), Houston Bar Assn. (co-chair legal line com. 1988-90; sec. environ. law sect. 1991, vice-chair 1992, chair 1993). Office: Fulbright & Jaworski LLP 1301 McKinney St Ste 5100 Houston TX 77010-3031 Office Phone: 713-651-5151. Office Fax: 713-651-5246. Business E-mail: eobrien@fulbright.com.

**O'BRIEN, GEOFFREY PAUL,** editor, writer; b. N.Y.C., May 4, 1948; s. Joseph Aloysius and Margaret Dorothy (Owens) O'B.; m. Carly Francis O'Brien, Mar. 18, 1977; 1 child, Heather Sudent, Yale U., 1966—67. SUNY, Stony Brook, 1968—70. Editor Reader's Catalog, N.Y.C., 1987-91; exec. editor Libr. of Am., N.Y.C., 1992-97, editor-in-chief, 1998—. Author: Hardboiled America, 1981, Dream Time, 1988, A Book of Maps, 1989, The Phantom Empire, 1993, The Hudson Mystery, 1994, Floating City: Selected Poems, 1978-1995, 1996, The Times Square Story, 1998, Bardic Deadlines: Reviewing Poetry 1984-95, 1998, The Browser's Ecstasy, 2000, Castaways of the Image Planet, 2002, Sonata for Jukebox, 2004, A View of Buildings and Water, 2002, Red Sky Café, 2005; contbr. poetry, essays and revs. to profl. jours.; contbg. writer The Village Voice, 1982—90; editor: Frogpond, 1980—81; co-editor: Montemora, 1974—76. Recipient Writing award Whiting Found., 1988; fellow N.Y. Inst. Humanities, 1998—, John Simon Guggenheim Meml. Found., 1999, Rockefeller Found., 2002. Office: Libr of Am 14 E 60th St New York NY 10022-1006 Office Phone: 212-308-3360. Personal E-mail: BardicG@aol.com.

**O'BRIEN, GEORGE ALOYSIUS, JR.,** paper company executive; b. Port Arthur, Tex., Dec. 13, 1948; s. George Aloysius and Avril Colleen (Adkins) O'B.; m. Cynthia Jean McCaa, Aug. 16, 1973; children: Erin Colleen, Meghan Anne, Caitlin Jean. BS in Petroleum Engring., U. Tex., 1971, MBA, 1975. Engr. Tesoro Petroleum Corp., San Antonio, 1972-73; exec. asst. Mesa Petroleum Co., Amarillo, Tex., 1975-79; v.p., treas. Transco Energy Co., Houston, 1979-82; sr. v.p., chief fin. officer Spectrum Energy Co., Houston, 1982-83; v.p. Smith Barney Harris Upham & Co., Houston, 1984-86; 1st v.p. E.F. Hutton & Co., N.Y.C., 1986-88; v.p., dir. corp. devel. Internat. Paper Co., Purchase, NY, 1988-91, v.p. land and timber, sr. v.p. forest resources Savannah, Ga., 1997—2001; CFO Carter Holt Harvey Pulp, Paper & Tissue, Auckland, New Zealand, 1991-94, CEO, 1995-97; sr. v.p. forest products Internat. Paper Co., 1997—. Dir. Nat. Tree Trust, Savannah C. of C., United Way of Savannah, Arbor Day Found. Mem.: Savannah Harbour Golf Club. Republican. Roman Catholic. Avocations: golf, tennis, sailing.

**O'BRIEN, GEORGE DENNIS,** retired academic administrator; b. Chgo., Feb. 21, 1931; s. George Francis and Helen (Fehlandt) O'B.; m. Judith Alyce Johnson, June 21, 1958; children: Elizabeth Belle, Juliana Helen, Victoria Alyce. AB in English, Yale, 1952; PhD in Philosophy, U. Chgo., 1961. Tchr. humanities, Carnegie rsch. fellow U. Chgo., 1956-57; from instr. to asst. prof., asst. dean Princeton (N.J.) U., 1958-65; on leave in Athens, Greece, 1963-64; spl. honors seminars LaSalle Coll., spring 1963, fall 1964, spring 1965; assoc. prof. philosophy Middlebury (Vt.) Coll., 1965-71, prof., 1971-76, dean of men 1965-67, dean of coll., 1975-76, pres. Bucknell U., 1976-84, U. Rochester, NY, 1984-94; ret., 1994. Dir. Salzburg Seminar in Am. Studies. Author: Hegel on Reason in History, 1975, God and the New Haven Railway, 1986, What to Expect from College, 1991, All the Essential Half-Truths about Higher Education, 1997, The Idea of a Catholic University, 2002; contbr. articles to profl. jours. Trustee LaSalle Coll., Phila., 1965—; bd. dirs. Union Theol. Sem., 1985-90, Rsch. Librs. Group, 1994-96; chair Commonweal Found., 2002—. Fellow Am. Coun. Learned Socs., London, 1971-72; Nat. Phi Beta Kappa, 1996-97, Mem. Am. Philos. Assn., Phi Beta Kappa. Home: 153 Wildflower Ln Middlebury VT 05753-9172 Office Phone: 802-388-1376. Business E-mail: gdob@middlebury.edu.

**O'BRIEN, GERALD JAMES,** utilities executive; b. St. Paul, May 1, 1923; s. Dewey Joseph and Henrietta Elizabeth O'B.; m. Patricia Margaret McCorison, Feb. 23, 1946; children: Kathleen, Thomas, John, Andrew. Student, St. Thomas Coll., 1940-41, 45-46; B.C.S., Drake U., 1948. Staff acct. Haskins & Sells, Mpls., 1948-50; with Donovan Cos., Inc., St. Paul, 1950-81, sec., asst. treas., 1977-81; utility rate cons., 1981-84. Dir. Alumbaugh Coal Co., Donovan Constrn. Co., So. Tier Gas Corp., Gas Distbrs. Info. Service. Served with U.S. Army, 1942-45. Decorated Purple Heart. Address: 11111 River Hills Dr Apt 234 Burnsville MN 55337

**O'BRIEN, GREGORY MICHAEL ST. LAWRENCE,** academic administrator; b. N.Y.C., Oct. 7, 1944; s. Henry Joseph and Mary Agnes (McGoldrick) O'B.; m. Mary K. McLaughlin, Dec. 28, 1968; children: Jennifer Jane, Meredith Kathleen. BA with honors, Lehigh U., 1966; MA, Boston U., 1968, PhD, 1969. Educator in psychology Lab. Community Psychology, Harvard Med. Sch., Boston; dir. Human Svcs. Design Lab., Sch. Applied Social Scis., Case Western Res. U., Cleve., 1970-74; dean, prof. Sch. Social Welfare, U. Wis., Milw., 1974-78; provost, prof. psychology U. Mich.-Flint, 1978-80; prof. social work and psychology, v.p. acad. affairs U. South Fla., Tampa, 1980-83, provost, 1983-87, prof. mgmt., 1986-87; chancellor U. New Orleans, 1987—2003; interim supr. New Orleans Parish Schs., 1999; chancellor Argosy U., Chicago, Ill., 2004—; DeBlois Endowed Chair in Private/Public Initiatives U. New Orleans, 2004—. Evaluation research cons. Cambridge Dept. Health and Hosps. and USPHS, 1968; bd. dirs. WLAE-TV (PBS), Bank One New Orleans Region, Entergy New Orleans, Nat. Coalition for Advanced Mfg., Nat. Assn. State Univs. and Land-Grant Colls. Contbr. chpts. to books, articles to profl. jours. State of La. Econ. Devel. Coun.,

1997—; vice chmn. State of La. Film and Video Commn., 1993-94, mem., 1993—; chmn. Metro. Coun. Govts. MetroVision, 1992—; adv. mem. Bus. Coun. New Orleans and the River Region; bd. dirs. The Chamber/New Orleans and the River Region, 1988—; mem. Kellogg Commn. on Future of Land Grant Colls. and State Univs., 1996—. NIMH fellow, 1968-69 Fellow Am. Coll. Mental Health Adminstrs. (founding fellow, pres. 1984-86); mem. NCAA (chair pres. commn. 1992-93), Nat. Assn. Social Workers, Nat. Conf. Social Welfare, Soc. Gen. Systems Research, Am. Psychol. Assn., Am. Public Health Assn., Metrovision Partnership Found. (1992-93), Council Social Work Edn. (presdl. task force on structure of assn.), Indsl. Relations Research Assn. Roman Catholic. Office: Argosy U 2 First National Plz 20 S Clark St 3d Fl Chicago IL 60603 Home: 512 N Mcclurg Ct Apt 5407 Chicago IL 60611-4185

**O'BRIEN, H. MICHAEL,** lawyer; b. Auburn, NY, Feb. 10, 1954; BA cum laude, SUNY, Oswego, 1976; JD, Pace U., 1979. Bar: NY 1980, US Dist. Ct. So., Ea. & No. Districts NY, US Dist. Ct. Dist. NJ, registered: Japanese Ministry of Justice, 1989-92 (fgn. law solicitor). Ptnr. Wilson, Elser, Moskowitz, Edelman & Dicker LLP, White Plains, NYC. Mem.: ABA (tort & ins. sect.), Internat. Assn. Arson Investigators, Nat. Fire Protection Assn., Consumer Electronics Manufacturers Assn. (mfr.'s rep. to R-1 safety com.), Assn. Home Appliance Manufacturers (mfr.'s rep. to product liability task force/govt. rels. com.), Def. Rsch. Inst., Assn. Trial Lawyers of Am., NY State Trial Lawyers Assn., NJ State Bar Assn. Office: Wilson Elser Moskowitz Edelman & Dicker LLP 3 Gannett Dr White Plains NY 10604 Office Phone: 212-490-3000 ext. 4234. Office Fax: 212-490-3038. Business E-mail: obrienm@wemed.com.

**O'BRIEN, J. WILLARD,** lawyer, educator; b. N.Y.C., Oct. 19, 1930; s. J. Willard and Anna C. (Carroll) O'B.; m. Peggy J. O'Brien. BS, Fordham U., 1952, JD, 1957. Bar: N.Y. 1957. Assoc. Cahill, Gordon, Reindel & Ohl, N.Y.C., 1957-62; asst. prof. law Syracuse U. Coll. Law, 1962-65; prof. law Villanova (Pa.) U. Sch. Law, 1965-98, dean, 1972-83, dir. Connelly Inst. Law and Morality, 1983-95, dean and prof. of law emeritus, 1998—. Mem. Pa. Fed. Jud. Nominating Commn., 1977-80, vice chmn., 1978-80; mem. Pa. Law and Justice Inst., 1972-73, chmn. exec. com., 1973-75, pres., 1975-77 Editor-in-chief Fordham Law Rev, 1956-57. Bd. dirs. Nat. Inst. on Holocaust, 1984-85; bd. dirs. Phila. Coordinating Council on the Holocaust, 1983—2003. Served with USAF, 1952-54; Served with N.Y. Air N.G., 1954-58. Mem.: ABA, Pa. Bar Assn. Roman Catholic.

**O'BRIEN, JACK GEORGE,** artistic director; b. Saginaw, Mich., June 18, 1939; s. J. George and Evelyn (MacArthur Martens) O'B. AB, U. Mich., 1961, MA, 1962. Asst. dir. APA Repertory Theatre, N.Y.C., 1963-67, asso. dir., 1967-69; worked with San Diego Nat. Shakespeare Festival, 1969-82, A.C.T., 1970-80, Loretto Hilton, 1975, Ahmanson, Los Angeles, 1978-80, San Francisco Opera, Houston Grand Opera, Washington Opera Soc.; artistic dir. N.Y.C. Opera, 1982, Old Globe Theatre, San Diego, 1981—. Dir: (Broadway plays) Cock-A-Doodle Dandy, 1969, The Time of Your Life, 1975, Porgy and Bess, 1976, 1983, The Most Happy Fella, 1979, Two Shakespearean Actors, 1992, Damn Yankees, 1994—95, Getting Away With Murder, 1996, The Little Foxes, 1997, More to Love, 1998, The Full Monty, 2000—02 (Tony nom. best dir. of a musical, 2001), Imaginary Friends, 2003, Hairspray, 2002 (Tony award best dir. of a musical, 2003), Henry IV, 2003—04 (Tony award best dir. of a play, 2004); art. dir. (Broadway plays) Into the Woods, 1987—89, Rumors, 1988—90, The Piano Lesson, 1990—91, Two Trains Running, 1992, Redwood Curtain, 1993, Play On!, 1997, Oldest Living Confederate Widow Tells All, 2003. Mem. Actors' Equity, Am. Soc. Composers and Performers, Soc. Stage Dirs. and Choreographers, Dirs. Guild Am. Office: Old Globe Theatre PO Box 122171 San Diego CA 92112-2171

**O'BRIEN, JAMES ALOYSIUS,** foreign language educator; b. Cin., Apr. 7, 1936; s. James Aloysius and Frieda (Schirmer) O'B.; m. Rumi Matsumoto, Aug. 26,1961. BA, St. Joseph's Coll., 1958; MA, U. Cin., 1960; PhD, Ind. U., 1969. Instr. English, St. Joseph's Coll., Rensselaer, Ind., 1960-62; asst. prof. Japanese, U. Wis., Madison, 1968-74, assoc. prof., 1974-81, prof., 1981—2003, prof. emeritus, 2003—, chmn. East Asian langs and lit., 1979-80, 82-85, 1996—2000. Author: Dazai Osamu, 1975, Akutagawa and Dazai: Instances of Literary Adaptation, 1988; translator: Selected Stories and Sketches (Dazai Osamu), 1983, Three Works (Muro Saisei), 1985, Crackling Mountain and Other Stories (Dazai Osamu), 1989. Mem. MIddleton City Common Coun., 1996-2004. Ford Found fellow, 1965-66; Fulbright-Hays and NDEA fellow, 1966-68; Social Sci. Research Council fellow, 1973-74; Japan Found. fellow, 1977-78 Mem. Assn. Asian Studies, Assn. Tchrs. of Japanese (exec. com. 1981-84, dir. devel. 1981-83, pres. 1984-90) Home: 2533 Branch St Middleton WI 53562-2812 Office Phone: 608-262-2291. Business E-mail: jaobrie1@wisc.edu.

**O'BRIEN, JAMES D.,** language educator, communications executive; s. Eldon Sanford O'Brien and Catherine O'Briend. BA in Polit. Sci., St. Mary's Coll., Moraga, Calif., 1973; MA in Bilingual Edn., LaVerne Coll., Calif., 1984. Chair fgn. lang. dept Damien HS, LaVerne, 1984—; pres. O'Brien's Comm., Lake Arrowhead, Calif., 1998—. Author: (books and tapes) Beginning and Intermediate Spanish, 1990, 1992. Vol. Peace Corps, Guatemala, 1973—75. Named to Damien HS Hall of Fame. Roman Catholic. Avocations: soccer, baseball, sailing. Home: 2280 Damien Ave La Verne CA 91750 Office: Damien HS 2280 Damien Ave La Verne CA 91750 Office Fax: 909-596-6112. E-mail: obrien@damien-hs.edu.

**O'BRIEN, JAMES F.,** lawyer; b. Bklyn., Nov. 27, 1960; BS, Manhattan Coll., 1985; JD, Pace U., 1990. Bar: NY 1990, Conn. 1990, US Dist. Ct. No., So., Ea. & We. Districts NY, US Dist. Ct. Dist. DC, US Ct. Appeals 2nd Cir., US Supreme Ct. Ptnr. Wilson, Elser, Moskowitz, Edelman & Dicker LLP, White Plains, NYC. Mem.: ABA, Assn. of the Bar of the City of NY, NY State Bar Assn. Office: Wilson Elser Moskowitz Edelman & Dicker LLP 3 Gannett Dr White Plains NY 10604 Office Phone: 914-323-7000 ext. 4233. Office Fax: 914-323-7001. Business E-mail: obrienj@wemed.com.

**O'BRIEN, JAMES J.,** manufacturing executive; b. Circleville, Ohio; Degree in Acctg., Fin., Ohio State U., MBA. Exec. asst. to chmn. Ashland Inc., 1992—94; v.p., gen. mgr. branded mktg. Ashland Petroleum Co., 1994; v.p. Ashland Inc.; pres. Valvoline, 1995—2001; with Ashland Inc., 1976—, sr. v.p., 1997, group oper. officer, pres., COO, 2002, chmn., CEO, 2002—. Bd. dir. Humana Inc., 2006—. Nat. bd. dirs. Big Bros. Big Sisters Am.; adv. bd. sch. bus. Ohio State U.; chmn. bd. trustees Midway Coll. Ky. Mem.: Am. Chemistry Coun., Assn. Governing Bds. Univ. Colls. Office: 50 E River Ctr Blvd Covington KY 41012-0391*

**O'BRIEN, JAMES JEROME,** construction management consultant; b. Phila., Oct. 20, 1929; s. Sylvester Jerome and Emma Belle Filer (Fulforth) O'B.; m. Carmen Hiester, June 10, 1952 (div. Aug. 1, 1984); children: Jessica Susan, Michael, David; m. Rita F. Gibson, Nov. 1, 1984 BCE, Cornell U., 1952; postgrad., U. Houston 1957-58. Registered profl. engr., N.Y., N.J., Pa., Ga., Conn., Maine. Project engr. Rohm & Haas, Phila. and Tex., 1955-59, RCA Corp., Moorestown, N.J., Greenland and Alaska, 1959-62; cons. Mauchly Assocs., Fort Washington, Pa., 1962-65; founding ptnr., exec. v.p. Meridian Engring. Co., Phila., 1965-68; pres. MDC Systems, Cherry Hill, 1968-72; ptnr. James J. O'Brien P.E., Cherry Hill, 1972-77; pres. O'Brien-Kreitzberg & Assocs., N.Y.C., Pennsauken, San Francisco, 1977-80, chief exec. officer, 1980-89, chmn. bd. dirs., 1989-93, vice chmn., 1993—2002; cons. in field, 2002; prin. James J. O'Brien P.E., 2003—. Author: CPM in Construction Management-Scheduling by the Critical Path Method, 1965; co-author: CPM in Construction Management-Project Management with CPM, 6th edit., 2005, Management Information Systems-Concepts, Techniques and Applications, 1970, Management with Computers, 1972, Construction Inspection Handbook, 1974, 4th edit., 1997, Value Analysis in Design and Construction, 1976, Construction Delay-Risks, Rsponsibilities and Litigation, 1976, Preconstruction Estimating: Budget to Bid, 1994, Construction Documentation, 3d edit., 1995; co-author: Construction Man-

agement: A Professional Approach, 1974; editor: Recollections (L.D. Miles), 1987; author, editor: Scheduling Handbook, 1969, Contractor's Management Handbook, 1971, 2d edit., 1990, Standard Handbook of Heavy Construction, 3d edit., 1996, Construction Change Orders, 1998; contbr. articles to profl. jours. Lt. USN, 1952—55. Recipient Profl. Mgr. award, N.Y. Chpt. Soc. Advancement Mgmt., 1969. Fellow: ASCE (v.p. 1985, pres. South Jersey br. 1985, pres. N.J. sect. 1987—89, com. on quality in civil engring. profession 1990—97, Constrn. Mgmt. award 1976, Disting. Engr. South Jersey br. 1986), Cornell Soc. Engrs. (dean's adv. com. sch. civil and environ. engring. 1986—87), Constrn. Mgmt. Assn. Am. (bd. dirs. 1990—92, Fellow award 1993, Constrn. Mgr. of Yr. award N.Y.-N.J. chpt. 1994), Project Mgmt. Inst. (sec. 1971, v.p. 1972, pres. 1973, chmn. bd. 1974—75, project mgmt. profl. 1984, v.p. edn. 2002—, editor Time Mgmt. chpt. 3d edit. 2004, charter mem. Coll. Scheduling, award for contbn. to project mgmt. 1983, Fellow award 1989, Coll. Scheduling 1st Jim O'Brien Achievement in Life award 2005); mem.: Regional Alliance Small Contractors (bd. dirs. 1989—95), Port Authority NY and NJ, Miles Value Found. (bd. dirs. 1987—90, trustee 1990—99, bd. dirs. 1999), Soc. Am. Value Engrs. (v.p. N.E. region 1986—87, cert. value specialist, Fallon Value-in-Life award 1993, fellow 2005), Chi Epsilon, Tau Beta Pi. Home and Office: 2 Linden Ave Riverton NJ 08077-1124 Office Phone: 856-829-9480. Personal E-mail: jimobriendd527@aol.com.

**O'BRIEN, JAMES PHILLIP,** lawyer; b. Monmouth, Ill., Jan. 6, 1949; s. John Matthew and Roberta Helen (Cavanaugh) O'B.; m. Laurene Reason, Aug. 30, 1969 (div. 1980); m. Lynn Florsheim, Sept. 5, 1987 (dec. May 2005). BA, Western Ill., 1971; JD, U. Ill. 1974. Bar: Ill. 1974. Asst. atty. gen. State Ill., Springfield, 1974-75; jud. clerk Ill. Appellate Ct., Springfield, 1975-76; assoc. Graham & Graham, Springfield, 1976-81; corp. counsel Am. Hosp. Assn., Chgo., 1981-84; ptnr., chmn. health care dept. Katten, Muchin Rosenman, Chgo., 1984—. Task force med. malpractice reform legislation Am. Hosp. Assn., 1983-84, tax adv. com., 1987-91, tax reporting and compliance com., 1990-91; spkr. in field. Contbr. numerous articles to profl. jours. Recipient cert. recognition Ill. Dept. Children and Family Svcs., 1981; Edward Arthur Mellinger Found. scholar, Western Ill. U. 1971. Mem.: Am. Arbitration Assn. (Task Force Health Care Dispute Resolution 1982—84), Am. Health Lawyers Assn. Office: Katten Muchin Rosenman 525 W Monroe St Ste 1900 Chicago IL 60661-3693 Business E-mail: phillip.obrien@kattenlaw.com.

**O'BRIEN, JANE MARGARET,** academic administrator; b. Washington, Nov. 17, 1953; d. Thomas and Edith (Pedersen) O'B.; m. James A. Grube, June 28, 1975; children: William Howard Grube-O'Brien, Harold Thomas Grube O'Brien. BS in Biochemistry, Vassar Coll., 1975; PhD in Chemistry, U. Del., 1981. Rsch. asst. U. Vt., Burlington, 1978-79; asst. prof. chemistry Middlebury (Vt.) Coll., 1980-88, assoc. provost, 1988-89, assoc. prof. chemistry, 1988-91, dean of faculty, 1989-91; pres. Hollins Coll., Roanoke, Va., 1991—96, St. Mary's Coll., Md., 1996—. Ednl. chem. biology task force New Eng. Consortium Undergraduate Sci., 1988-91; project mgr. H. Hughes Med. Inst. Instl. Awards, 1988-91; mem. steering com. Sloan New Liberal Arts Initiative, 1988-91; bd. dir. Norfolk Southern Corp., So. Md. Navy Alliance, Nat. Outdoor Leadership Sch.; mem. NCAA Div. III Pres. Council. Implementation com. Vermont EPSCoR, 1989-91; bd. dirs. Coun. Ind. Colls. in Va., 1991-96, Va. Found. for Ind. Colls., 1991-96; ednl. adv. com. Rainforest All, 1991—; bd. dir. Md. Citizens for the Arts Found., Univ. Mobility. Grad. fellow U. Del., 1975-76, Kellogg fellow W.K. Kellogg Found., 1989-92, Internat. fellow Assoc. Am. Colls., 1990-91, Regional fellow finalist White House Fellowship, 1991; Eisenhower Fellow, 1999. Mem.: Phi Beta Kappa, Sigma Xi. Office: St Mary's College Office of the President 18952 E Fisher Rd Saint Marys City MD 20686-3001

**O'BRIEN, JOHN,** professional soccer player; b. LA, Calif., Aug. 29, 1977; With youth system Ajax Amsterdam, Netherlands, 1996—98; midfielder FC Utrecht, Netherlands, 1998—99, Ajax Amsterdam, Netherlands, 1999—2005, ADO Den Haag, Netherlands, 2005—06, CD Chivas USA, LA, 2006—. 31 caps, 3 goals U.S. Nat. Soccer Team, 1998—; mem. U.S. World Cup Team, 2002, 06. Office: US Soccer Fedn 1801 S Prairie Ave Chicago IL 60616*

**O'BRIEN, JOHN FEIGHAN,** investment banker; b. Cleve., Aug. 8, 1936; s. Francis John and Ann (Feighan) O'B.; m. Regina Quaid Harahan, June 27, 1959 (div. 1976); children: Regina, Victoria, Julie, John Jr.; m. Marilyn E. Schreiner, 1977. BS, Georgetown U., 1958. Salesman Appliance Mart, Cleve., 1958-59, ptnr., 1960-66; investment broker McDonald & Co. Investments, Cleve., 1966-71, ptnr., 1971-83; exec. v.p., 1983-88, mng. dir., 1988-91, sr. mng dir., 1993—. Bd. dirs. Hitchcock House, Cleve., 1978-89, Recovery Resources; chmn. Alcoholism Svcs. of Cleve., 1989-92, Alcohol and Drug-Addiction Svcs. Bd. of Cuyahoga County, 1992-98; trustee St. Edward H.S., Lakewood, Ohio, Alumnus of Yr., 1997, chmn. capital campaign, 1993-95; grand jury foreman Cuyahoga County, 2000. Named Good Fellow of Yr., Irish Good Fellows Club Cleve., 1996, Benefactor of Yr., St. Edward HS, 2003. Mem. Leadership Cleve., Greater Cleve. Growth Assn., Georgetown U. Alumni Assn. (alumni bd. senator, John Carrol award 1999), Westwood Country Club, Cleve. Yacht Club, Catawba Island Club, Lago Mar Club. Home (Winter): 1800 S Ocean Dr Fort Lauderdale FL 33316-3704 Office: McDonald & Co Investments 18500 Lake Rd Ste 300 Rocky River OH 44116-1744 Personal E-mail: jfeighanob@aol.com.

**O'BRIEN, J(OHN) PATRICK,** psychiatrist, educator; b. Washington, Aug. 25, 1941; s. John Francis and Gertrude Estelle (Offutt) O'B. BA magna cum laude, Yale U., 1963; MD, Johns Hopkins U., 1968. Diplomate Am. Bd. Psychiatry and Neurology. Intern U. Pa.-Phila. Gen. Hosp., 1970-71; resident Mass. Gen. Hosp., Boston, 1971-74, asst. in psychiatry, 1974-83, asst. psychiatrist, 1983—; clin. fellow psychiatry Harvard U., Boston, 1971-74, clin. instr. psychiatry, 1974-79, asst. clin. prof. psychiatry, 1979—. Lectr. Harvard Ext. Schs., Boston, 1985-88. Author: The Disorganized Mind, 1978, poems; translator: (jour.) Formations, 1987. Fellow Royal Soc. Medicine; Am. Psychiat. Assn., NY Acad. Scis., Mass. Psychiat. Assn., Yale Club Mass. Phi Beta Kappa. Democrat. Office: Mass Gen Hosp ACC 806C 15 Parkman St Boston MA 02114-3117

**O'BRIEN, JOHN WILFRID,** economist, educator, retired university president; b. Toronto, Ont., Can., Aug. 4, 1931; s. Wilfred Edmond and Audrey (Swain) O'B.; m. Joyce Helen Bennett, Aug. 4, 1956; children: Margaret Anne, Catherine Audrey. BA, McGill U., 1953, MA, 1955, PhD, 1962, LLD, 1976; postgrad., Inst. Polit. Studies, Paris, 1954; DCL, Bishop's U., 1976; LLD, Concordia U., 2004. Lectr. econs. Sir George Williams U., Montreal, 1954-57, asst. prof., 1957-61, assoc. prof., 1961-63, asst. dean U., 1961-63, dean arts, 1963-68, vice-prin. acad., 1968-69, prof., 1965-96, prin., vice chancellor, pres., 1969-74; rector, vice chancellor, pres. Concordia U., Montreal, 1974-84, rector emeritus, 1984—. Provincial ednl. TV com. Dept. Edn. Que., 1963-66, dep. chmn., 1965-66, mem. tchr. tng. planning com., 1964-66; mem. Gauthier Ad Hoc Com., Univ. Operating Budgets, 1965-68, Council Univs., 1969-76; pres. Conf. Rectors and Prins. Que. Univs., 1974-77; mem. council Assn. Commonwealth Univs., 1975-78; bd. dirs. Assn. Univs. and Colls., Can., 1977-79; mem. Conseil Consultatif sur l'Immigration, Que. Gov., 1977-79, Corp. Higher Edn. Forum, 1983-84; bd. govs. YMCA, 1969-89, Vanier Coll., 1973-79, Fraser-Hickson Inst., 1975-00, pres. 1989-92, Que. div. Can. Mental Health Assn., 1977-79, Montreal World Film Festival, 1985-2004; sec., treas., Cinematheque Can., 1988-96, bd. dirs.; sec., treas. World Film Fest. Found., 1989-96; exec. mem. Alliance Que., 1989-96, chmn., 1990-96, bd. dirs.; hon. mem. Corp. Higher Edn. Forum, 1984-00; hon. v.p. Que. Provincial council Boy Scouts Can., 1974-90; hon. councillor Montreal Mus. Fine Arts, 1969-2003. Author: Canadian Money and Banking, 1964, (with G. Lerner) 2d edit., 1969.

**O'BRIEN, JOHN WILLIAM, JR.,** management consultant; b. Bronx, NY, Jan. 1, 1937; BS, MIT, 1958; MS, UCLA, 1964. Sr. assoc. Planning Rsch. Corp., LA, 1962—67; dir. fin. systems group Syngeretic Scis., Inc., Tarzana, Calif., 1967—70; dir. analytical svcs. divsn. James H. Oliphant & Co., LA, 1970—72; chmn. bd., CEO, pres. Wilshire Assocs. (formerly O'Brien Assocs.

Inc.), Santa Monica, Calif., 1972—75; v.p. A.G. Becker Inc., 1975—81; chmn., CEO Leland O'Brien Rubinstein Assocs., 1981—97; mng. dir. Credit Suisse Asset Mgmt., NYC, 1997—2000; adj. prof. instn. U. Calif. Berkeley Haas Sch. Bus., 2000—. Recipient Graham and Dodd award Fin. Analysts Fedn., 1970, Matthew McArthur award Investment Mgmt. Consultants Assn., 2004; named Businessman of Yr. Fortune Mag., 1987. Mem.: Delta Upsilon. Home: 119 Jasmine Creek Dr Corona Del Mar CA 92625-1418 Office Phone: 510-643-1396. Business E-Mail: obrien@haas.berkeley.edu. E-mail: obrien@gmail.com.

**O'BRIEN, KATHLEEN L.**, special education educator; b. Oneida, NY, Aug. 31, 1975; d. Neal Patrick and Teresa Joan O'Brien. BS in Psychology, LeMoyne Coll., Syracuse, NY, 1997; MA of Edn., Cambridge Coll., Mass., 2006. Behavior specialist May Ctr., May Inst., Chatham, NJ, 1997—98; spl. edn. tchr. Albien Pub. Schs., NY, 1999—2000, Barnstable Pub. Schs., Hyanis, Mass., 2000—. Mentor Health Adventures Cape Cod Hosp., Hyannis, 2003—04. Mem. Barnstable Rep. Com., Hyannis, 2001—02. Republican. Roman Catholic. Avocations: tennis, volleyball, softball, music, reading. Home: 415 Cedar St West Barnstable MA 02668 Office: Barnstable Mid Sch 895 Falmouth Rd Hyannis MA 02601

**O'BRIEN, KENDRA ALLEN**, psychologist, researcher; b. Tachikawa, Japan, July 25, 1959; (parents Am. citizens); d. Jerry Eugene and Beverly Ann Allen; m. Daniel Kehaulani O'Brien, Apr. 19, 2002; 1 child, Pierce Keahi Aualii. BA, Colo. U., 1982; MA, Calif. Sch. Profl. Psychology, 1990, PhD in Clin. Psychology, 1997. Adolescent unit coord. Castle Med. Ctr., Kailua, Hawaii, 1988—88; addiction recovery aftercare coord. Vista Hill Hosp., San Diego, 1991—94; clin. rsch. coord. Damluji Bari Clinic, 1993—95; VA program specialist Nat. Ctr. Post Traumatic Stress, Honolulu, 1997—98; individual, family therapist C.A.R.E. Hawaii Inc., 1998—. With athletics dept. drug edn. San Diego State U., 1993—96; drug edn. addiction coms. Atlantic Richfield Co. Olympic Tng. Ctr., Chula Vista, Calif., 1994; adj. faculty Nat. U. San Diego, 1994—96. Named Most Innovative Intern, Met. Correctional Ctr. Fed. Bur. Prisons, San Diego, 1992. Mem.: APA, Hawaii Psychol. Assn., Gen. Soc. Mayflower Descs. (sec. 2001—03). Democrat. Methodist. Achievements include development of a drug education and consulting program that was used as a national model for effective education and intervention at an athletics conference in 1995. Avocations: photography, reading, scuba diving, running. Home: 485 Wana'ao Rd Kailua HI 96734 Office: CARE Hawaii Inc Ste 1003 677 Ala Moana Blvd Honolulu HI 96813-5417

**O'BRIEN, KEVIN D.**, medical educator; BS summa cum laude, U. Idaho, 1980; MD honors, U. Wash., 1984. Diplomate Am. Bd. Internal Medicine, Cardiovascular Diseases Am. Bd. Internal Medicine. Intern, resident U. Wash., Seattle, 1984—87, chief med. resident, 1987—88, assoc. prof. medicine, 1988—. Med. student rsch. fellow Fred Hutchinson Cancer rsch. Ctr., Seattle, 1981; attending physician U. Wash. Med. Ctr., Seattle, 1988—. Contbr. articles to profl. jours. Mem.: Am. Fedn. Med. Rsch. (pres. 2002—03). Office: Univ Wash Med Ctr Campus Box 356422 1959 NE Pacific St Seattle WA 98195-6422 Office Phone: 206-685-3930. Business E-Mail: cardiac@u.washington.edu.

**O'BRIEN, KEVIN J.**, lawyer; b. NYC, Mar. 12, 1934; s. George and Kathleen (Fox) O'B.; m. Winifred Gallagher, Aug. 23, 1958; children: Karen A., Kevin J., Susan M. BS, Fordham U., 1959; LLB, Columbia U., 1962. Bar: N.Y. 1962, U.S. Ct. Appeals (2d cir.) 1971, U.S. Dist. Ct. (so. dist.) N.Y. 1972, U.S. Tax Ct. 1972. Law clk. to presiding justice U.S. Ct. Appeals (2d. cir.), N.Y.C., 1962-63; assoc. Paul, Weiss, Rifkind, Wharton & Garrison, N.Y.C., 1963-70, ptnr., 1970—. Contbr. articles to profl. jours. Served with USN, 1952-55. Mem. N.Y. State Bar Assn. (exec. com. tax sect. 1979-83), Assn. Bar City N.Y. Office: Paul Weiss Rifkind Wharton & Garrison 1285 Ave of the Americas New York NY 10019-6065

**O'BRIEN, MARK STEPHEN**, pediatric neurosurgeon; b. West New York, NJ, Jan. 2, 1933; s. Mark Peter and Hannah (Dempsey) O'B.; m. Mary Morris Johnson, June 3, 1961 (div.); children: David, Derek, Marcia; m. Karen-Marie Sampson, June 1, 1984; children: Blythe, Blake, Lauren-Blair, Connor. AB cum laude, Seton Hall U., 1955; MD, St. Louis U., 1959. Diplomate Am. Bd. Neurol. Surgery, Am. Bd. Pediat. Neurol. Surgery. Intern St. John's Hosp., St. Louis, 1959-60, resident in surgery, 1960; resident in neurology Charity Hosp., New Orleans, 1962-63; resident in neurosurgery St. Vincent's Hosp., N.Y.C., 1963-64, resident in surgery, 1965; sr. resident, chief resident Cin. Children's Hosp., U. Cin., 1965-68, research fellow in neurosurgery, 1966-67, 67-68; NIH spl. fellow in neuroradiology Albert Einstein Coll. Medicine, N.Y.C., 1968-69; mem. faculty dept. surgery Emory U. Sch. Medicine, Atlanta, 1969—2003, prof. neurosurgery, assoc. prof. pediatrics, 1979—2003; chief neurosurgery Henrietta Egleston Hosp. for Children, Atlanta, 1971—2003; prof. neurosurgery U. Ark. for Med. Scis., Little Rock, 2005—. Trustee Elaine Clark Center for Exceptional Children; mem. med. adv. bd. Nat. Found., March of Dimes; trustee Henrietta Egleston Hosp. for Children; mem. profl. adv. panel Spina Bifida Assn. Am. Editorial bd. Pediatric Neurosurgery; contbr. chpts. to books, articles to med. jours. Served with USNR, 1960-62. Mem. Am. Assn. Neurol. Surgeons, Soc. Neurol. Surgeons, Congress Neurol. Surgeons, Internat. Soc. Pediatric Neurosurgery, Greater Atlanta Pediatric Soc., Med. Soc. Atlanta, AMA, ACS, Ga. Neurosurg. Soc., Am. Acad. Pediatrics, Am. Soc. Pediatric Neurosurgery, Pediatric Oncology Group, Am. Bd. Pediatric Neurol. Surgery (sec.), Acad. Pediatric Neurosurgeons. Home: 5720 Hawthorne Rd Little Rock AR 72207 Office: Ark Childrens Hosp 800 Marshall St Slot 838 Little Rock AR 72202 Office Phone: 501-364-1448. Personal E-mail: mobrien33@aol.com. Business E-Mail: obrienmark@uams.edu.

**O'BRIEN, MARY DEVON**, communications executive, consultant; b. Buenos Aires, Feb. 13, 1944; came to U.S., 1949, naturalized, 1962; d. George Earle and Margaret Frances (Richards) Owen; m. Gordon Covert O'Brien, Feb. 16, 1962 (div. Aug. 1987); children. Christopher Covert, Devon Elizabeth; m. Christopher Gerard Smith, May 28, 1983 BA, Rutgers U., 1975, MBA, 1976. Project mgmt. cert., 1989. Contr. manpower Def. Comm. divsn. ITT, Nutley, NJ, 1977-80, adminstr. program, 1977-78, mgr. cost, schedule control, 1978-79, voice processing project, 1979-80; mgr. project Avionics divsn. ITT, Nutley, 1980-81, sr. mgr. projects, 1981-93, cons. strategic planning, 1983-95; pres. Anamex, Inc., 1995—. Bd. trustees South Mountain Counseling Ctr., 1987-98, chmn. bd. trustees, 1994—; bd. dir. N.J. Eye Inst.; session leader Internet Conf., Florence, Italy, 1992; session moderator, panel mem. MES Conf., Cairo, Egypt, 1993, spkr., session leader Vancouver, 1994, keynote spkr. New Zealand, 1995; lectr. in field Author: Pace: System Manual, 1979, Voices, 1982; contbr. articles to profl. jours. and Maplewood Community calendar. Chmn. Citizens Budget Adv. Com., Maplewood, N.J., 1984-87, chmn. recreation, life, pub. svcs. 1982-83, 94-96, chmn. pub. safety, emergency svcs., 1983-84, chmn. schs. and edn., 1984-85, chmn. gen. gov. and fin., 1998-2000; first v.p. Maplewood Civic Assn., 1987-89, pres., 1989-91, 2000—, sec. 1993-94, bd. dirs., officer, 1984—; chmn. Maple Leaf Svc. award Com., 1987-89, 94—, Community Svc. Coun. of Oranges and Maplewood Homelessness, Affordable Housing, Shelter Com., 1988—; chmn. speaker's bur. United Way, 1989-93; bd. trustees United Way Essex and West Hudson Cmty. Svc. Coun., 1988—; v.p. mktg. United Way Community Svc. Coun. of Oranges and Maplewood, 1990-93, v.p. 1994; mem. Maplewood Zoning Bd. of Adjustment, 1983-95; officer, mem. exec. bd. N.J. Project Mgmt. Inst., 1985—, pres., 1987-88, 95-2000, v.p. adminstrn., 1994-95; bd. dirs. Performance Mgmt. Assn.; chmn. Charter Com.; chmn. Internat. Project Mgmt. Inst. Jour. and Membership survey, 1986-87, mktg. com., 1986-89, long range planning and steering com., 1987—; bd. dir. vice chmn. Coun. Chpt. Pres. Interaction Com., 1986-90, chmn., 1991—, pres. Internat. Project Mgmt. Inst., 1991, chmn., 1992, v.p. Region II, 1989-90; adv. bd. Project Mgmt. Jour., 1987-90, N.J. PMI Edit., 1987—; liaison officer, PMI internat. liaison to Australian Inst. of Project Mgmt. and Western Australia Project Mgmt. Assn.; apptd. fellow Leadership N.J., 1993—, Internat. Project Mgmt. Inst. and Performance Mgmt. Assocs.; mem. MCA/N.J. Blood Bank Drive; chmn. Maplewood Community Calendar,

1990-98; trustee community svc. coun. and edn. program United Way Essex and West Hudson, 1988—, also, chmn. leadership div., chmn. speakers bur., 1991— and mem. communications com.; mem. bd. dirs. Governing Inst. N.J.; chmn. Maplewood Rep. County Com., 1996—; chair, sec. Essex County Rep. County Com. Recipient Spl. commendation for Cmty. Svc. Twp. Maplewood, 1987; First Place award Anti-Shoplifting Program for Distributive Edn. Club Am., 1981, N.J. Fedn. of Women's Clubs, 1981, 82, Retail Mchts. Assn., 1981, 82; Commendation and Merit awards Air Force Inst. Tech., 1981; Pres.'s Safety award ITT, 1983; State award 1st Pl. N.J. Fedn. of Women's Clubs Garden Show, 1982; Cert. Spl. Merit award N.J. Fedn. of Women's Clubs, 1982, Disting. Contbn. award United Way, 1990, Pursuit of Exellence Cost Savs. Achievement award ITT Avionics, 1990, Maple Leaf award outstanding cmty. svc., 1992, Phoebe and Benjamin Shackelford award United Way, 1992, U.S. Ho. Reps. citation, 1992, N.H. Gen. Assembly Senate resolution Cmty. Leadership and Svc., 1992, resolution of Appreciation Township of Maplewood, Maplewood C. of C. Disting. Svc. award, 2005; N.J. Leadership fellow, 1993, awarded fellow of Internat. Project Mgmt. Inst., 1995. Mem. NAFE, Internat. Platform Speakers Assn., Grand Jury Assn., Telecomms. Group and Aerospace Industries Assn., Women's Career Network Assn., Nat. Security Indsl. Assn., Assn. for Info. and Image Mgmt., Internat. Project Mgmt. Inst. (liaison officer pres. 1991—, Outstanding Svc. and Contbrn. award 1986-87, Outstanding Pres. award 1988, Meritorious Svc. Recognition award 1989-1990), Performance Mgmt. Assn, Indsl. Rels. Rsch. Assn., ITT Mgmt. Assn., Rutgers Grad. Sch. Bus. Mgmt. Alumni Assn., Maplewood LWV (chair women and family issues com., voter registration bd. dir.), Maplewood Women's Evening Membership Div. (pres. 1980-82), Lions (Maplewood div. 1992-95, program chmn. 1991-92, treas. 1994-95, N.J. dist. 16E zone gov., chmn. 1992-93, 95-96, cabinet sec. internat. dist., region chmn. 1993-94, 96-98, trustee Eye Bank N.J., internat. dist. 16-E cabinet sec. 1994-95, dist. 16-E chmn. peace poster contest 1995-99, pres. Newark 1995-97, sec. 1997—, N.J. State chmn. youth outreach and quest 1995-98, internat. dist. 16-E gov., 1999—, dist. MD16 treas., 1999—, youth oppportunities chmn. N.J dist. MD-16, coun. chmn. 2003-2004, state advisor 2004-, trustee Eye Bank of Delaware Valley, sec.-treas. 2003-05, 3d vice chmn. 2005-). Home: 594 Valley St Maplewood NJ 07040-2616 Office: 21 Madison Plz Ste 152 Madison NJ 07940-2354

**O'BRIEN, MARY ELLEN CHRISTINA**, artist, educator; b. Caribou, Maine, Nov. 15, 1928; d. Richard Stephen and Caroline Elizabeth (McGuire) Sullivan; m. John Michael O'Brien, May 15, 1965; children: Maureen-Caroline, Kathleen. Cert. in arts, Cambridge Sch. of Design; student, Crafts Students League, 1958, Paul Puzinas Art Studio, 1959, Penland Sch. of Crafts, 1994. Freelance designer MIT and Harvard U., Cambridge, Mass., 1954-55; arts and crafts dir. Cambridge coun. Girl Scouts U.S., 1955, Spl. Svcs., U.S. Army, Ft. Devens, Mass., 1956-57, Ft. Totten, N.Y., 1957-61, Europe, 1961-64; art tchr. Red Feather Agys., Boston, 1955-56; freelance comml. artist Jordon March, Boston, 1955-56; art tchr. Most Holy Redeemer Sch., Tampa, Fla., 1971-78, Acad. of Holy Names, Tampa, 1986-94; art specialist City of Tampa, 1979-81. Pvt. tchr., 1981-86; creative art dir. polit. campaign Dem. Party, Tampa. 1970's. Cover design artist The Patron Sts., 1959; one-woman shows include Methodist Adminstrn. Bldg., Realistic Artist Gallery, Fed. Bank Bldg.; exhibitions include Busch-Reisinger Mus., Cambridge, Mass., 1955, Portland Art Mus., Maine, Art League L.I. Gallery Puzinas Studio, Gt. Neck, N.Y., Living Design Studio, Manchester, N.H., N.Y. Pub. Libr. Sys. Bayside Br., L.I., The Studio Gallery, L.I., N.Y., First Presbyn. Ch. Temple Terrace, Stewart Art Show, Gasparilla Outdoor Art Show, Lowry Park Outdoor Art Show, Vets. Adminstrn. Hosp., Fla., St. Joseph's Art Gallery, Fla., 1978, Rental Gallery of Tampa Bay Art Ctr., Fla., 1973, Mus. of Art., Fla., Performing Art Ctr., Fla., Fla. Craftsmen Gallery, St. Petersburg, and numerous others. Mem. delegation to Japan to observe art in schs. People to People Delegation, 1995; docent Mus. Art, 1974-85, 94—; vol. Performing Arts Ctr. Mem. Nat. League Am. Pen Women (pres. 1984-85, chair nat. art competition), Alpha Delta Kappa. Roman Catholic. Avocations: sewing, reading. Home: 10801 N Edison Ave Tampa FL 33612-6501

**O'BRIEN, MICHAEL J.**, lawyer; Ptnr. O'Sullivan LLP, Goodwin Procter LLC, 2002—03; sr. v.p., gen. counsel, sec. Omnicom Group Inc., NYC, 2003—. Office: Omnicom Group Inc 437 Madison Ave New York NY 10022 Office Phone: 212-415-3640. Fax: 212-415-3530.

**O'BRIEN, MORGAN EDWARD**, communications executive, lawyer; b. Washington, Dec. 14, 1944; AB Classical with honors, Georgetown U., 1966; JD, Northwestern U., 1969. Bar: Ill. 1969, Washington 1971. Lawyer Mobile Svcs. divsn. Common Carrier Bur. FCC, Washington, 1970-72; asst. bur. chief Spectrum Mgmt. Pvt. Radio Bur. FCC, Washington, 1976-87; co-founder, chmn. bd. Nextel Comm., Inc., Reston, Va., 1987-96, vice chmn. 1996—2005; co-founder, chmn., CEO Cyren Call Comms., McLean, Va., 2006—. Ptnr. Jones, Day, Reavis & Pogue, Washington, 1986-90; pvt. practice, Washington, 1979-90. Office: Cyren Call Comm 7601 Lewinsville Rd Ste 201 Mc Lean VA 22102 Office Phone: 703-760-4830. Business E-Mail: mobrien@cyrencall.com.

**O'BRIEN, MURROUGH HALL**, lawyer; b. Portland, Maine, July 23, 1945; s. Francis Massey and Constanze Kathryn (McDonnell) O'B. m. Johannah M. Hart, June 11, 1968; children: John David, Ellen Hart AB magna cum laude, Harvard U., 1969; JD, U. Maine, 1975. Bar: Maine 1975. Reporter, asst. city editor Evening Express, Portland, Maine, 1970-71; ptnr. firm Dunlap, Wood & O'Brien, Portland, Maine, 1975-80, Dunlap & O'Brien, Portland, Maine, 1980-85, Murrough H. O'Brien, Esquire, Portland, Maine, 1985—; exec. sec. Maine Jud. Coun., Portland, Maine, 1981-97. Pres. Portland Book Co. Mem. Keep Maine Scenic Com., 1974-79, So. Coastal Family Planning, Inc., Portland, 1975-79; mem. steering com. Study of the Future of Maine Legal Profession, 1983-89; mem. steering com. Gov.'s Commn. on Land Use Violation, 1983-84; treas. Coalition for Cruise Missile Reteconvalent, 1989; trustee, v.p. Portland Ministry at Large, 1990-96, pres., 1996-99. Served with USNR, 1969-70. Mem. Cumberland County Bar Assn. Democrat. Office: 149 Concord St Portland ME 04103 Office Phone: 207-774-4130.

**O'BRIEN, NANCY PATRICIA**, librarian, educator; b. Galesburg, Ill. Mar. 17, 1955; d. Leo Frederick O'Brien and Yvonne Blanche (Uhlmann) O'Brien Tabb; 1 child, Nicole Pamela. AB in English, U. Ill., 1976, MS in LS, 1977. Vis. instr. U. Ill., Urbana, 1977-78, asst. prof. libr. adminstrn., 1978-84, assoc. prof., 1984-91, prof., 1991—, serials bibliographer, 1977-78, social sci. bibliographer collection devel. div., 1979-81, project dir. Title II-C grant, 1987-88, acting head. and info. sci. libr., 1989-90, head Edn. and Social Sci. Libr., 1994—, coord. social scis. divsn., 1996—2000, Disting. Edn. and Behavioral Scis. Libr. 1997), Libr. Adminstrn. and Mgmt. Assn. (edn. and tng. com. pub. rels. sect. 1990-95), Resources and Tech. Svcs. Divsn. (micropub. com. 1982-85, chmn. 1983-85, cons. 1985-87). Office: U Ill Edn & Social Sci Libr 100 Main Libr 1408 W Gregory Dr Urbana IL 61801-3607 Office Phone: 217-333-2408. Business E-Mail: npobrien@uiuc.edu.

**O'BRIEN, ODESSA LOUISE**, protective services official; m. John Daniels O'Brien, May 30, 1964; children: James John, Jeanne Jacqueline, Kevin Raymond. B.Elective Studies, St. Cloud State U., 1975. Lic. pilot. Stewardess Northwest Airlines, St. Paul; personnel officer Minn. Wing USAF, 2001—03. Area rep. Youth for Understanding, Brainerd, Minn., 1979—82; v.p. Christian Women's Club, Brainerd, 1976—80; chmn. St. Francis Ch. Women's Guild, Brainerd, Minn., 1978—79; chmn. bd. St. Francis Parochial Sch., Brainerd, Minn., 1979—80; mem. coun. St. Francis Ch., Brainerd, Minn., 1979—80; adv. bd. Pine County Vo-Tech Sch., Pine City, Minn., 1967—71. Lt. col. USAF. Recipient Outstanding Woman of Collier County, Am. Bus. Women's Assn., 1983—85, Comdrs. Commendation, Naples Sr. Squadron, Civil Air Patrol, 1983, Grover Loening award, Minn. Wing Civil Air Patrol, Air Force Aux., Paul E. Garber award, Civil Air Patrol, 2003, Gill Robb Wilson award, 2004. Mem.: AAUW (life; pres. Naples br. 1983—85), Collier Automotive Mus. (sec. of vol. docents), Naples Woman's Club (internat. chmn.), Phi Theta Kappa (life). Roman Catholic. Avocations: bridge (Bronze Life Master), flying, travel, tennis, reading.

**O'BRIEN, ORIN YNEZ**, musician, educator; b. Hollywood, Calif., June 7, 1935; d. George Joseph and Marguerite Graham (Churchill) O'Brien. Studied with Frederick Zimmermann, Milton Kestenbaum and Herman Reinshagen; diploma, The Juilliard Sch., 1957. Double bassist N.Y.C. Ballet Orch., 1956—66, Saidenberg Little Symphony, Music Aeterna, Am. Symphony (with Stokowski), N.Y. Philharm., N.Y.C., 1966—; faculty Manhattan Sch. Music, N.Y.C., 1969—, Mannes Coll. Music, N.Y.C., 1988—, The Juilliard Sch., N.Y.C., 1990—, co-chair double bass dept., 1992—2002. Participant numerous chamber music festivals, including Marlboro; featured in 1st performances of Gunther Schuller Quartet for 4 double basses; artist for GM, CBS and RCA Recording cos. Mem.: Internat. Soc. Bassists, Am. Fedn. Musicians, The Bohemians. Avocations: reading, writing, cooking.

**O'BRIEN, PAT**, television personality; b. Sioux Falls, S.D., Feb. 14, 1948; m. Linda O'Brien, 1973; 1 child, Sean. Grad., U. S.D., 1970; postgrad., Johns Hopkins U. Prodn. asst. The Huntley-Brinkley Report; reporter WMAQ-TV, Chgo., KNXT-TV (now KCBS-TV), L.A.; host The Krypton Factor, 1981; anchor CBS Sports, 1981—97; host Overtime...with Pat O'Brien, 1990, How'd They Do That?, 1993—94; host (TV spls.) The Road to Olympic Gold, 1996, 2000; host CNBC coverage of the Sydney Olympics, 2000; corr. NBC coverage of the Utah Olympics, 2002; co-anchor Access Hollywood, 1997—2004; host NBC coverage of the Athens Olympics, 2004, The Insider, 2004—. Author: Talkin' Sports: A B.S.-er's Guide, 1998; columnist: N.Y. Daily News, Inside Sports, Live!, TV Guide, Ego, Men's Health, gadget editor: Gear Mag. Recipient newswriting award, L.A. Press Club, 1987. Office: Paramount Studios 5555 Melrose Ave Los Angeles CA 90038

**O'BRIEN, PATRICK MICHAEL**, library administrator; b. Newport, R.I., Mar. 17, 1943; s. Joseph Xavier and Loretta (DeCotis) O'B.; m. Roberta Luther, Nov. 27, 1977; children— Megan MacRae, Brendan Watters. BA in Eng. Lit., Merrimack Coll., North Andover, Mass., 1966; M.L.S., U. R.I. Kingston, 1965; MBA, Case Western Res. U., Cleve., 1983. Reference libr. Newsweek mag. N.Y.C., 1965-72; asst. dir. rsch. FIND/SVP, N.Y.C., 1972-74; head cen. libr., cultural ctr. Chgo. Pub. Libr., 1974-79; dir. Cuyahoga County Pub. Libr., Cleve., 1979-84; dir. librs. Dallas Pub. Libr., 1984-92; dir. Alexandria (Va.) Libr., 1992—. Mem. editorial bd. Handel's Nat. Directory for Performing Arts; contbr. articles to profl. jours. Participant, alumnus Leadership Dallas Program, 1984-85, Leadership Cleve. Program, 1981; mem. nat. adv. con. to Libr. of Congress; mem. adv. coun. Tex. State Libr., 1984-87; mem. info. svcs.; mem. com. Goals for Dallas, 1985; mem. exec. bd. univ. librs. So. Meth. U., 1985-93; bd. dirs. Urban Community Sch., Cleve., 1982-84, Mus. African-Am. Life and Culture, 1985-86; mem. client data base com. Dallas Assn. Svcs. to Homeless, 1988-90; mem. Latchkey Children's Task Force, 1985-90. Recipient Servant as Leader award City of Dallas, 1989, Disting. Alumnus award U. R.I. Grad. Sch. Libr. and Info. Studies, 1990. Mem. ALA (coun. mem. 1987-93, Am. Libr. Trustee Assn. (bd. dirs.), Pub. Libr. Assn. (pres. 1985-86), Pub. Libr. Systems Sect (pres. 1983), Tex. Libr. Assn. (legis com. 1986-92), Tex. Women's Univ. Sch. Libr. and Info. Studies Vis. Com., Tex. Ctr. for Book Dallas Pub. Libr., Cleve. Area Met. Libr. Systems (pres. bd. 1980), Chgo. Libr. Club (pres. 1978), D.C. Libr. Assn., Va. Pub. Libr. Dirs. Assn. (bd. dirs. 1994-96), Va. Libr. Assn., Online Computer Libr. Ctr. (bd. trustees 1992-98), The White House Conf. on Librs. and Info. Svcs. (del. 1991), Pub. Lib. Adminstrs. N.Tex. (pres. 1990-91), Dallas 40; Rotary of Alexandria Inst., 1996-97, pres. 2002-03, Rotarian of Yr. 2001), Alexandria Commn. on Info. Tech., Beta Gamma Sigma. Office: Alexandria Libr 5005 Duke St Alexandria VA 22304-2903

**O'BRIEN, PATRICK MICHAEL**, federal agency administrator; BA, U. Notre Dame; JD, U. Minn. Prin. dep. asst. atty. gen. legis. affairs U.S. Dept. Justice, Washington, counsel to dir. FBI, sr. counsel office of dep. atty. gen.; asst. sec. terrorist financing U.S. Dept. Treasury, Washington, 2005—. Office: US Dept of Treasury 1500 Pennsylvania Ave NW Rm 2058 Washington DC 20220 Office Phone: 202-622-0470. Office Fax: 202-622-7154.*

**O'BRIEN, PATRICK T.**, lawyer; b. NYC, Nov. 14, 1942; BS, Wheeling Coll., 1964; MA in Criminal Justice, John Jay Coll., 1976; JD cum laude, Univ. Miami, 1990. Bar: Fla. 1990, US Ct. Internat. Trade 1996. Spl. agent US Customs Svc.; now shareholder, prin., media, telecom. Greenberg Traurig LLP, Ft. Lauderdale, Fla. Mem.: ABA (Fla. regional subcom. on white collar crime), Fla. Bar Assn., Assn. Cert. Anti-Money Laundering Specialists, Interactive Gaming Counsel. Office: Greenberg Traurig LLP Ste 2000 401 E Las Olas Blvd Fort Lauderdale FL 33301-2296 Office Phone: 954-768-8221. Office Fax: 954 765-1477. Business E-Mail: obrienp@gtlaw.com.

**O'BRIEN, RAYMOND FRANCIS**, transportation executive; b. Atchison, Kans., May 31, 1922; s. James C. and Anna M. (Wagner) O'B.; m. Mary Ann Baugher, Sept. 3, 1947; children: James B., William T., Kathleen A., Christopher R. BS in Bus. Adminstrn., U. Mo., 1948; grad., Advanced Mgmt. Program, Harvard, 1966. Accountant-auditor Peat, Marwick, Mitchell & Co., Kansas City, Mo., 1948-52; contr., treas. Riss & Co., Kansas City, Mo., 1952-58; regional contr. Consol. Freightways Corp. of Del., Indpls., also, Akron, Ohio, 1958-61; contr. Consol. Freightways, Inc., San Francisco 1961—, v.p., treas., 1962-63, bd. dirs., 1966, v.p. fin., 1967-69, exec. v.p., 1969-75, pres., 1975—, chief exec. officer, 1977-88, 90-91, chmn., 1988—; now chmn. emeritus CNF Transportation. Pres. CF Motor Freight subs. Consol. Freightways, Inc., 1973; dir. Transam. Corp., Watkins-Johnson, Inc.; past chmn. WesternHwy. Inst., Champion Road Machinery, Ltd. Former mem. bus. adv. bd. Northwestern U., U. Calif., Berkeley; bd. dirs., regent, former chmn. bd. trustees St. Mary's Coll.; bd. dirs., regent Charles Armstrong Sch., 1991—; mem. Pres.'s Adv. Herbert Hoover Boys and Girls Club; dir. Boy Scouts Am. Bay Area Coun. Served to 1st lt. USAAF, 1942-45. Recipient Disting. Svc. Citation Automotive Hall Fame, 1991; named Outstanding Chief Exec. five times Financial World Mag. Mem. Am. Trucking Assn. (bd. dirs. Found., exec. com.), Pacific Union Club, World Trade Club, Commonwealth Club (San Francisco), Menlo Country Club. Office: 3240 Hillview Ave Palo Alto CA 94304

**O'BRIEN, RAYMOND VINCENT, JR.**, banker; b. Bronx, N.Y., Sept. 23, 1927; s. Raymond Vincent and Blanche (Harper) O'B.; m. Theresa Sweeney, Mar. 29, 1952 (dec. June 1981); children: Susan, Raymond, Christopher, Sean, Carol, Nancy Meisenzahl; m. Ellen Boyle, July 24, 1982. BA, Fordham U., 1951, JD, 1958; postgrad., Harvard U. Advanced Mgmt. Program, 1969. With Chase Manhattan Bank, N.A., N.Y.C., 1953-74; chief exec. officer, chmn. bd. Emigrant Savs. Bank, N.Y.C., 1978—93, pres., 1974-77. Bd. dirs. Internat. Shipholding Corp. Trustee Fordham U., 1979-92; chmn. bd. trustees Regis H.S., 1988-92; past chmn. Cmty. Bankers Assn., N.Y., Nat. Assn. Cmty. Bankers. Served with AUS, 1946-47, 51-53. Mem. Guild Cath. Lawyers, Navesink Country Club (Middletown, N.J.), Plantation Country Club (Ponte Vedra, Fla.), K.M., Friendly Sons St. Patrick. Republican. Roman Catholic. Home: 102 Lands End Ponte Vedra Beach FL 32082-3906

**O'BRIEN, RICHARD L(EE),** physician, educator, academic administrator; b. Shenandoah, Iowa, Aug. 30, 1934; s. Thomas Lee O'B. and Grace Ellen (Sims) Parish; m. Joan Frances Gurney, June 29, 1957; children: Sheila Marie, Kathleen Therese, Michael James, Patrick Kevin. MS in Physiology, Creighton U., 1958, MD, 1960. Diplomate Nat. Bd. Med. Examiners. Intern and resident Columbia med. divsn. Bellevue Hosp., N.Y.C., 1960-62; postdoctoral fellow in biochemistry Inst. for Enzyme Rsch., U. Wis., 1962-64; asst. prof. to prof. pathology Sch. Medicine, U. So. Calif., L.A., 1966-82, dep. dir. Cancer Ctr., 1975-80, dir. rsch. and edn. Cancer Ctr., 1980-81, dir. Cancer Ctr., 1981-82; dean Sch. Medicine Creighton U., Omaha, 1982-92, acting v.p. health scis., 1984-85, v.p. health scis., 1985-99, prof. health policy and ethics, Univ. prof., 2000—, dir. office of interprofl. edn., 2002—05. Vis. prof. molecular biology U. Geneva, 1973-74; mem. cancer control rsch. grants rev. com. NIH, Nat. Cancer Inst.; mem. Cancer Ctr. Support grant rev. com. Nat. Cancer Inst., 1984-88, chmn. 1987-88; co-chmn. United Way/CHAD Pacesetter campaign, 1988, 94; bd. dirs. Health Future Found., 2003—; cons. in field. Contbr. articles to profl. jours.; editor various profl. jours. Bd. dirs. Opera Omaha, 1994-2001, 04—, pres. 1998-2000, Opera Omaha Found., 2000—06, chmn., 2004—06. Capt. U.S. Army, 1964-66. Spl. fellow Nat. Cancer Inst., 1967-69; Combined Health Agys. Drive-Health Citizen of Yr., 1986. Mem. ACP, Am. Assn. Pathologists, Am. Assn. Cancer Rsch., Am. Assn. Cancer Edn., AAAS, Am. Assn. Cancer Insts. (dir. 1982-83), Am. Med. Colls. (chmn. MCAT evaluation panel 1987-88, liaison com. on med. edn., 1988-93, co-chmn. 1989-93, adv. panel Strategic Planning Health Care Reform 1992-96), Assn. Acad. Health Ctrs. (long-range planning com. 1986, 2000, nominating com. 1987, 96, Task Force Health Care Delivery 1992, mem. task force on leadership and instl. values 1993-99, bd. 1998-99), Am. Cancer Soc. (adv. com. Inst. Rsch. Grants 1977-80, Outstanding Leadership award, dir. Calif. divsn. 1980-82, dir. Nebr. divsn. 1992-96), Am. Hosp. Assn. (com. on med. edn. 1986-89), Alpha Omega Alpha. Home: 9927 Essex Dr Omaha NE 68114-3873 Office: Creighton Univ California At 24th Omaha NE 68178-0001 Office Phone: 402-280-2017. Business E-Mail: rlo@creighton.edu.

**O'BRIEN, ROBERT BROWNELL, JR.,** banker, consultant, yacht broker, opera company executive; b. NYC, Sept. 6, 1934; s. Robert Brownell and Eloise (Boles) O'B.; m. Sarah Lager, Nov. 28, 1958; children: Robert Brownell III, William Stuart, Jennifer. BA, Lehigh U., 1957; postgrad., NYU, Am. Inst. Banking. Asst. treas., credit officer, br. locations officer Bankers Trust Co., N.Y.C., 1957-63; v.p., dir. bus. devel. George A. Murray Co., gen. contractors, N.Y.C., 1964; also v.p. Bowery Savs. Bank, 1964-69; dir., chief exec. officer Fed. Savs. & Loan Ins. Corp., Washington, 1969-71; chmn. exec. com. Fed. Home Loan Bank Bd., 1969-71; v.p. Bowery Savs. Bank, N.Y.C., 1972; exec. v.p. First Fed. Savs. & Loan Assn., N.Y.C., 1973-75; chmn., chief exec. officer Carteret Savs. Bank, Morristown, 1975-91; also bd. dirs.; mng. dir. Printon Kane Group Inc., Short Hills, NJ, 1991-94; dir., former chief exec. officer Govs. Bank Corp., West Palm Beach, 1992-94; pres., CEO Hubert Johnson Inc., 1998—. Bd. dirs. Fed. Home Loan Bank N.Y., Govs. Bank Corp., Ocean Med. Ctr. Found., Ocean County Atty. Ethics Com.; vice chmn. 1st Mortgage Capital Corp., Vero Beach, Fla.; chmn. Neighborhood Housing Svcs. Am., 1972-91; vice chmn., bd. dirs. U.S. League Savs. Instns., Washington, O'Brien Yacht Sales. Contbr. articles to trade mags. Trustee Trinity Pawling Sch., Palm Beach County Housing Partnership, Lehigh U., Ocean Med. Found., Tuckerton Seaport; devel. cons. Ocean County Coll., Toms River, N.J.; chmn. Housing Opportunities Found.; trustee, pres. Toms River Seaport Soc., N.J. Mus. Boating; trustee, past chmn. Cmty. Found. of N.J., 1987—; trustee, pres. Bay Head Hist. Soc.; vice chmn., bd. dirs. Dalt Found.; chmn. adv. bd. Palm Beach Maritime Mus., Peanut Island, Fla.; active Nat. Commn. on Neighborhoods, The Kemp Commn.; past chmn., exec. dir. N.J. State Opera. Mem. Nat. Coun. Savs. Instns. (past chmn.), N.J. Savs. League (past chmn.), Essex County Savs. and Loan League (past chmn.), N.J. Savs. League (past chmn.), N.J. Hist. Soc. (past chmn.), Greater Newark C. of C. (bd. dirs.), N.J. C. of C. (bd. dirs.), Union League Club, Delray Beach Yacht Club (past commodore), New York Yacht Club, Morris County Golf Club, Somerset Hills Golf Club, Palm Beach Yacht Club, Bay Head Yacht Club (past commodore). Republican. Episcopalian. Home: 500 Club Dr Bay Head NJ 08742-5016 E-mail: bob@woodenboatsnj.com.

**O'BRIEN, ROBERT EMMET,** insurance company executive; b. St. Louis, Sept. 13, 1923; s. Algernon Francis Adams and Adeline (von Weisert) O'B.; m. Mary Lou Gallagher, July 20, 1946 (div. 1978); children: Robert Jr., Gardnar, Scott, Derek, Mary Berkeley; m. Marian Strong Achilles, June 30, 1983. BBA, St. Louis U., 1946, MBA, 1947. Prin., ptnr. R. Newman & R. O'Brien, St. Louis, 1946-52; mem. Lloyd's of London, 1952—; dir. Hunter Engring. Co., St. Louis, 1946-72, Atlas Mfg. Co., St. Louis, 1965-80, Narraganssett Corp., St. Louis and Moberly, Mo., 1965-80, Mid-America Coffee Co., St. Louis, 1970-75, Golden-Dipt Corp. and DCA (N.Y.), N.Y.C., 1948-1970; cons. internat. ins. The Law Firm of Honorable Wilbur D. Mills and Herman E. Talmadge, Washington, London, 1976—. Pres. North Atlantic Assurance Co. Ltd., London, 1962-75; elected hon. dir. Atlantic Coun. of the U.S. Treas. St. Louis Trust Coun., 1949-65; apptd. to Bd. Life Govs. Royal Hosp. Putney, West Hill, London, 1969; councillor The Athletic Coun. of U.S., Atlantic Coun. of U.S., Carnegie Found.; mem. U.S. Olympics (Ice) Speed Skating Team, 1939; trustee Errol Flynn Estate, Jamaica and London, 1959-64; mem. Hiberian United Svcs. Club, Dublin, Ireland. With AC U.S. Army, 1942-45, ETO, NATOUSA. Decorated DFC (Eng.). Mem. DAV (life), Royal Air Force Soc., Zurich Internat. Insurers (apptd.), Life Underwriters, Million Dollar Round Table (life), Mid-Atlantic Club, Royal Yacht Club Hobart Tasmania, Royal Yacht Club Tasmania, Army and Navy Club Washington (hon.), Devonshire Club (London), Irish Nat. (London), Liberal Club (London), Royal Jamacia Yacht Club (life), Mo. Athletic Club, Royal Yacht of Fiji, Royal Scots Mil. Club (Edinburgh), U.S. SAMOA Soc. So. Pacific, Bridlespur Hunt and Polo Club, Flying Tigers Club (life, China and DC) Home: 117 Old Wharf Rd North Chatham MA 02650-1129

**O'BRIEN, ROBERT JOHN, JR.,** public relations executive, former government official, air force officer; b. Wheeling, W. Va., Apr. 16, 1935; s. Robert John and Martha Virginia (Hunter) O'B.; m. Margaret Eugenia Schultz BS in Journalism, Northwestern U., 1957; MA in Journalism, U. Wis., 1970; grad., Indsl. Coll. Armed Forces, 1977. Comnd. officer U.S. Air Force, 1957, advanced through grades to col.; dir. pub. affairs N. Am. Air Def. Command, Colorado Springs, Colo., 1977-80, Air Force Systems Command, Camp Springs, Md., 1980-82; dir. def. info. Office Sec. Def., Washington, 1982-83, dep. asst. sec. def., 1983-86; dir. pub. rels., Washington McDonnell Douglas Corp., Arlington, Va., 1986-97; v.p. pub. rels. The Boeing Co., Arlington, Va., 1997-99. Decorated D.S.M., Legion of Merit, Bronze Star, Air medal, Honor medal (Republic Vietnam) Mem. Air Force Assn., Pub. Rels. Soc. Am., Aviation/Space Writers Assn., U.S. Space Found., Ret. Officers Assn., Williamsburg Nat. Golf Club (Williamsburg, Va.), Nat. Press Club. Republican. Methodist. Avocations: golf, stamp collecting/philately, model railroading.

**O'BRIEN, SOLEDAD,** news anchor; m. Brad Raymond; children: Sofia, Cecilia, Charlie, Jackson. Student, Harvard U. Prodr. Second Opinion, reporter Health Week in Review Sta. KISS-FM, Boston; assoc. prodr., newswriter Sta. WBZ-TV, Boston; prodr. NBC News, 1991—93; co-host The Know Zone Discovery Channel; chief East Bay bur. Sta. KRON-TV, San Francisco, reporter, 1993—96; co-host The Site, Nightly News, Weekend Today MSNBC, 1996—99; anchor, Weekend Today NBC, 1999—2003; co-anchor, American Morning CNN, 2003—. Recipient Emmy. Office: CNN 820 1st St NE Washington DC 20002-4243

**O'BRIEN, STEPHEN JAMES,** geneticist; b. Rochester, NY, Sept. 30, 1944; s. Bernard Carroll and Kathryn Marie O'Brien; m. Diane Louise Rockhill, Nov. 28, 1968; children: Mary, Meghan. BS, St. Francis Coll, Loretto, Pa., 1966; PhD, Cornell U., 1971. Postdoctoral fellow genetics-biochemistry Gerontology Rsch. Ctr., Balt., 1971-72; NIH postdoctoral fellow Nat. Cancer Inst., NIH, Bethesda, Md., 1972-73; staff fellow Lab. Viral Carcinogenesis, Nat. Cancer Inst., NIH, Bethesda, 1973-78, rsch. geneticist Frederick, Md., 1978-80, chief sect. of genetics, 1980—, acting chief, 1983-85; chief Lab.

---

Genomic Diversity Nat. Cancer Inst., NIH, Frederick, 1986—. Zoology and botany tchg. asst. St. Francis Coll., 1965-66; gen. genetics lab. instr. and lectr. Cornell U., 1966-71, biology and soc. tchg. asst., 1969-71, human genetics discussion leader, 1970-71; adj. prof. genetics George Washington U., 1974—; adj. grad. advisor dept. biology Am. U., 1979—, Hood Coll., 1982—; adj. prof. dept. zoology U. Md., 1982—, dept. biology Johns Hopkins U., 1982—; faculty affiliate dept. pathology Colo. State U., 1994—; affiliate prof. dept. biology George Mason U., 1994—; apptd. rsch. fellow Smithsonian Instn., Washington, 1982—; bd. trustees Am. Type Culture Assn., Rockville, Md., 1983—; apptd. exec. bd. Am. Type Culture Collection, Rockville, 1984—, sec.-treas. bd. trustees, 1987—; founder, co-dir. New Opportunities in Animal Health Scis., Ctr. for Wildlife Scis., Smithsonian Instn., 1985—; mem. cat specialist group Internat. Union for Conservation of Nature, Geneva, 1985—, mem. captive breeding specialist group species survival commn., 1986—; lectr. in field. Editor Isozyme Bulletin, 1975-78, Genetic Maps, 1980—; exec. editor Jour. Heredity, Am. Genetics Assn., 1987—; assoc. editor Genomics, 1987-91, Mammalian Genome, 1990—, Molecular Phylogenetics and Evolution, 1990—; guest editor Current Biology, 1993; jour. adv. bd. Cosmos, 1994; contbr. numerous articles to profl. jours. Mem. AAAS, Genetics Soc. Am., Am. Soc. Naturalists, Tissue Culture Assn., Am. Genetics Assn. (bd. dirs. 1984—, chmn. long range planning com. 1985—), Am. Assn. Zool. Pks. and Aquariums (advisor spl. survival plan-cheetah 1986—), N.Y. Acad. Sci., Cosmos Club. Achievements include research in molecular genetics, developmental and cell biology, genetics of oncology, viral oncology, immunology and reproductive physiology, molecular evolution, paleontology, cytology, populations genetics. Office: Nat Cancer Inst Lab Genomic Diversity Bldg 560 Rm 21-105 PO Box B Frederick MD 21702-1201 Office Phone: 301-846-1296. Office Fax: 301-846-1686. E-mail: obrien@ncifcrf.gov.

**O'BRIEN, STEPHEN MAZYCK, III,** lawyer; b. Louisville, Jan. 24, 1947; s. Stephen Mazyck O'Brien Jr. and Jane Hartman OBrien; m. Michele Marie Legris, May 20, 1972 (div. May 1993); children: Anne Chambers, William Teige; m. Sarah Catherine Sturgill, Dec. 3, 1994; children: John Patrick Jennings, Conor Francis. BA, U. Va., 1969; JD, U.Va., 1974. Bar: Ky. 74, Fla. 76, U.S. Dist. Ct. (ea. and we. dists.) Ky., U.S. Ct. Appeals (6th cir.). Assoc. McDonald, Alford & Roszell, Lexington, Ky., 1974—76; ptnr. Landrum & Shouse, Lexington, 1976—93; pvt. practice Lexington, 1993—2000; ptnr. Savage, Garmer, Elliott & O'Brien PLLC, Lexington, 2000—03, Garmer & OBrien, LLP, 2004—. 1st lt. U.S. Army, 1969—71, Vietnam. Home: 226 Henry Clay Blvd Lexington KY 40502 Office: Garmer & O'Brien LLP 141 N Broadway Lexington KY 40507 Office Phone: 859-254-9352. E-mail: sobrien@garmerobrien.com.

**O'BRIEN, STEVEN D.,** lawyer; b. Grand Island, Nebr., 1958; m. Becky O'Brien; children: Nick, Alex. BA, U. Nebr., Lincoln 1980; JD, George Washington U. Law Ctr., 1983. Bar: Nebr. 1983. Atty. Knudsen, Berkheimer, Richardson & Endacott, Lincoln, Nebr.; gen. counsel The Gallup Org., corp. counsel. Avocation: golf. Office: Gallup Org 901 F St NW Washington DC 20004*

**O'BRIEN, TERRENCE LEO,** federal judge; b. Lincoln, Nebr., Aug. 8, 1943; s. Leo James and Luella Mildred (Benting) O'B.; m. Dorothy Marguerite Driskill, Mar. 30, 1966; children: Sean Brendan, Heather Kathleen. BS in Acctg., U. Wyo., 1965, JD with honors, 1972. Bar: Wyo. 1972, U.S. Dist. Ct. Wyo. 1972, U.S. Ct. Appeals (7th and 10th cirs.) 1972, U.S. Ct. Appeals (8th, 9th and D.C. cirs.) 1973, U.S. Ct. Appeals (2d and 4th cirs.) 1974, U.S. Supreme Ct. 1975. Staff atty. Land and Natural Resources-U.S. Dept. Justice, Washington, 1972-74; ptnr. Omohundro & O'Brien, Buffalo, Wyo., 1974-80; judge 6th Jud. Dist. Wyo., Gillette, 1980—2001; pres. Visionary Communications Inc. 2000—01; private practice Wyo., 2001—02; judge U.S. Ct. Appeals (10th Cir.), 2002—. Justice of Peace Johnson County, Buffalo, 1975-80. Mem. Wyo. Community Coll. Commn., 1978-80. Capt. U.S. Army, 1966-69. Mem.: Rotary. Republican. Office: US Courthouse 2102 Carvey Ave Rm 200 Cheyenne WY 82001*

**O'BRIEN, THOMAS GEORGE, III,** lawyer; b. N.Y.C., Aug. 26, 1942; s. Thomas George Jr. and Margaret Patricia (Arctander) O'B.; m. Alison Marie Rich, Aug. 26, 1967; children: Christian Arctander, Kylin Stafford. AB magna cum laude, U. Notre Dame, 1964; LLB, Yale U., 1967; MA in Theology summa cum laude, St. Vincent de Paul Regional Sem., 2003. Bar: N.Y. 1967, Fla. 1988. Assoc. Carter, Ledyard & Milburn, N.Y.C., 1971-78; assoc. gen. counsel Frank B. Hall & Co. Inc., Briarcliff Manor, NY, 1978-79, v.p., sec., gen. counsel, 1979-86; exec. v.p., sec., gen. counsel CenTrust Savs. Bank, Miami, 1986-87; of counsel Steel Hector & Davis, Miami, 1987-88, ptnr. West Palm Beach, Fla., 1988—2001. Author: Florida Law of Corporations and Business Organizations, 1990, 92-98. Trustee Bus. Vols. for Arts, Miami, 1986—88, Fla. Repertory Theatre, West Palm Beach, 1989—91, chmn. 1990—91; vestry mem. Episcopal Ch., Bethesda-by-the-Sea, 1991—94, sr. warden Bethesda-by-the-Sea, 1992—94; bd. dirs. Palm Beach Fellowship Christians and Jews, 1993—97, sec., 1996—97; chmn. Diocesan Sch. Christian Studies Bd., 2003—; lay dep. Episcopal Ch. Gen. Conv., 2004—, mem. program, budget and fin. com., 2005—; mem. exec. bd. Episcopal Diocese of S.E. Fla., 2001—04, 2005—; bd. dirs. Bus. Devel. Bd. Palm Beach County, 1991—98, sec., 1992—93, chmn., 1993—94; bd. dirs. Directions 21st Century, 1995—98, chmn., 1996—98; bd. dirs. Toward a More Perfect Union, 2000—, sec., 2000—01, chair, 2003—05, sec., 2005—. Mem.: ABA (com. on legal opinions 1992—2001, negotiated acquisitions com. 1998—2001), Am. Soc. Corp. Secs. (sec. N.Y. regional group 1984—86), Fla. Bar Assn. (chmn. com. on opinion stds. 1988—95, mem. corps./securities law com. 1988—2002, vice-chmn. 1989—90, exec. coun. bus. law sect. 1989—93, chmn. 1990—91), PGA Nat. Club. Home: 272 Eagleton Estates Blvd Palm Beach Gardens FL 33418-8423 E-mail: tgobrien@adelphia.net.

**O'BRIEN, THOMAS HENRY,** former bank holding company executive; b. Pitts., Jan. 16, 1937; s. J. Vick and Georgia (Bower) O'B.; m. Maureen Sheedy; children: Thomas Henry, Lauren C., Timothy B. BS in Commerce, U. Notre Dame, 1958; MBA, Harvard U., 1962. Joined Pitts. Nat. Bank, 1962, v.p., 1967-73, sr. v.p., 1973-80, exec. v.p., 1980-83, vice chmn., 1983-84; bd. dirs., CEO PNC Fin. Corp., 1985—2000, also chmn. Pitts., 1988—2001; chmn. PNC Bank Corp., Pitts., 1988—, CEO, 1988-2000, chmn., 1988—2001; ret. Bd. dirs. Hilb, Rogal & Hamilton Co., Bell Atlantic Corp., Internat. Monetary Conf., Black Rock, Inc., Verizon Comm. Bd. dirs. United Way Southwest Pa., Extra Mile Found., Carnegie Museums of Pitts., Pitts. Opera, Allegheny Conf. Cmty. Devel., U. Pitts., Res. City Bankers; mem. Bd. visitors U. Pitts. Grad. Sch. Bus. Named Industrialist of Yr. Soc. Indsl. and Office Realtors, 1996. Mem. Assn. Res. City Bankers, Pa. Bankers Assn., Fox Chapel Golf Club. Clubs: Duquesne, Allegheny (bd. dirs.), Pitts. Field, Rolling Rock, Laurel Valley Golf. Roman Catholic. Avocation: golf.

**O'BRIEN, TIMOTHY ANDREW,** journalist, writer, lawyer, educator; b. NYC, July 11, 1943; s. Timothy Andrew and Hildegarde J. (Schenkel) O'B.; m. Maria de Guadalupe Margarita Moreno, Jan. 15, 1971; children: Theresa Marie, Tim A. BA in Comm., Harvard U., 1967; MA in Polit. Sci., U. Md., 1972; postgrad., Tulane U., 1974-75; JD, Loyola U., New Orleans, 1976. Bar: La. 1976, D.C. 1977, U.S. Supreme Ct. 1981. News writer, reporter, anchor WKBD-TV, Detroit, 1968-69, WTOP-TV, Washington, 1969-72, WDSU-TV, New Orleans, 1972-74, WVUE-TV, New Orleans, 1974-77; law corr. ABC News, 1977-99; corr. Cable News Network (CNN), 2001—. Leo Goodwin Prof. Law Southeastern U., 1997; disting. prof. law Hofstra U., Nova Sch. Law, 2000, St. Thomas Sch. Law, Miami, 2001, Nova U., 2002; disting. vis. prof. law, Nova Southeastern U., 1999, 2001, Loyola Sch. of Law, 2003. Contbr. articles to profl. jours. Bd. govs. Woodward Acad., College Park, Ga.; bd. visitors Loyola U. Sch. Law, 1997—. Recipient AP award for outstanding reporting of extraordinary event, 1976, New Orleans Press Club award for non-spot news reporting, 1976, Emmy award for documentary on D.C., 1969, ABA awards of merit, 1979 (2), 80, 85, Gavel award for documentary, 1980,

---

Nat. award for human rights reporting Women in Comm., 1981, Disting. Alumnus award Mich. State U., 1996. Mem. Am. Law Inst., Radio-TV Corrs. Assn. Washington, Am. Judicature Soc. (bd. dirs. 1991-97). Office: CNN 820 First St NE Washington DC 20002

**O'BRIEN, TIMOTHY JAMES,** lawyer; b. Detroit, Nov. 4, 1945; m. Hyon Baek, Jan. 31, 1970; children: Jean, Jane. AB, Yale U., 1967; JD, Harvard U., 1976. Bar: N.Y. 1977, Hong Kong, 1999. Assoc. Cleary, Gottlieb, Steen & Hamilton, N.Y.C., 1976-80; ptnr. Coudert Bros., N.Y.C. and Hong Kong, 1980—2005, mng. ptnr. Hong Kong office, 2002—05; sr. fgn. legal counsel Shin & Kim, Seoul, Republic of Korea, 2005—. Lectr. symposium on internat. investment Southwestern Law Found., 1995; dir. MetLife Korea, Ltd. Co-author: Corporate Governance in Korea at the Millennium, 2002; mem.: Harvard Law Rev., 1975—76; contbr. articles to profl. jours. Assoc. dir., vol. Peace Corps, Republic of Korea, 1967-73. Mem. ABA (co-chmn. conf. on Korea-U.S. trade and investment 1990-92), Assn. of Bar City of N.Y. (internat. law com., Asian affairs com. 1988—94), Korea Soc. (N.Y., sec., bd. dir. 1996-99). Office: Shin & Kim Ace Tower 1-170 Soonhwadong Chung-gu Seoul Republic of Korea Office Phone: +82-2-316-4221. Office Fax: +82-2-756-6226. E-mail: tjobrien@shinkim.com.

**O'BRIEN, TOM,** college football coach; b. Cin., Oct. 5, 1948; Cadet, Navy, 1970. Guards and centers coach Univ. Va., 1982—90, offensive coord., 1991—95; head football coach Boston Coll., 1996—. Second lt. USMC, 1971, maj. USMC. Recipient John F. Kennedy Mem. Nat. award, St. Patrick's Com., Holyoke, 2005. Office: BC Athletic Assn Conte Forum 140 Commonwealth Ave Chestnut Hill MA 02467 Office Phone: 617-523-3010.*

**O'BRIEN, WILLIAM J., III,** lawyer; BS, Holy Cross Coll., 1965; LLB, Yale U., 1969. Bar: N.Y. 1970, Mich. 1985. With Hughes Hubbard and Reed, N.Y.C. and Paris, 1969-75; asst. gen. counsel Chrysler Corp., Highland Park, 1983, assoc. gen. counsel, 1984, dep. gen. counsel, 1986, v.p., gen. counsel, sec., 1987; sr. v.p., gen. counsel DaimlerChrysler AG, 1998—2002, exec. v.p., gen. counsel, 2002—. Office: DaimlerChrysler Corp CIMS 485-14-96 1000 Chrysler Dr Auburn Hills MI 48326-2766

**O'BRIEN-PALMER, MICHELLE ANN,** educational writer, consultant; b. Long Beach, Calif., Apr. 8, 1954; d. Michael William O'Brien and Joanna Jacobson; m. Louis Gideon Palmer, Mar. 22, 1980; 1 child, Nicholas Gideon Palmer. BA, U. of Wash., 1979, MS, 1980; EdD, Fielding Grad. Inst., Santa Barbara, Calif., 2003. Co-pres., cons. Action Consulting, Kirkland, Wash., 1984—93; pres., edn. writer MicNik Publs., Inc., Woodinville, Wash., 1988—2003. Educator Group Health Coop., Seattle, 1980—83; author-in-residence Lake Washington Sch. Dist., Redmond, 1991—2001. Author: (ednl.text) How the Earth Works, (children's poetry book) Through My Eyes, (ednl. text) Poetry Projects with Pizzazz, Watch Me Grow (Rated Outstanding by Parents' Coun., 2001), Healthy Me, Sense-Abilities (Childrens' Lit. Choice award, 1999); writer, graphic designer: ednl. series Let's Learn About Story Elements: Book 1-Character, Book 2-Setting, Book 3-Plot (Benjamin Franklin award finalist in Edn., 1996), ednl. text Great Graphic Organizers, Beyond Book Reports, composer, musician: ednl. rec. Book-Talk: Singable Songs for Lifelong Readers. Mem.: ASCD, Alumni Assn. U. of Wash., Am. Ednl. Rsch. Assn., Internat. Soc. for Tech. in Edn. Achievements include research in The Effect of Learning Web Site Design on Higher-Order Thinking Skill Development in Fourth Grade Students. Personal E-mail: micnik@aol.com. E-mail: micnik.com.

**OBRINGER, DAVID C.,** archivist, educator; b. Pitts., Mar. 28, 1954; s. William John and Ruth Ann Obringer; m. Janice Ann McCensky, Oct. 16, 1982; children: Sean, Michael. BA in History, U. Pitts., 1976, MLS, 1988; MA in History, St. Bonaventure U., N.Y., 1987. Cert. archivist Acad. Cert. Archivists. Residential program dir. Children's Home, Bradford, Pa., 1977—87; info. asst. Carnegie-Mellon U., Pitts., 1987—88; ref. libr. Ind. U. S.E., New Albany, 1988—90; archivist Edinboro U., Pa., 1991—. Adj. history faculty Pa. State U., Erie, 2001—; cons. project archivist Lorain County C.C., Elyria, Ohio, 2001. Contbr. articles to profl. jours. Archivist Edinboro Area Hist. Soc., 1997—. Recipient Cmty. Svc. award, Greater Edinboro Area Roundtable, 2002; grantee, Pa. Hist. and Mus. Commn., 2002, Edinboro U., 1995. Mem.: Pa. Libr. Assn., Pa. Libr. Assn. (chair N.W. chpt. 1996), Assn. Pa. Coll. and Univ. Faculty (pres. Edinboro chpt. 2005—). Avocations: sailing, running, camping. Office: Edinboro University Library 200 Tartan Rd Edinboro PA 16444

**O'BRYAN, C. JILL,** visual artist, writer; b. Chgo., June 13, 1956; d. Robert Louis and Connie Clair (Johnson) O'B. BA, Macalaster Coll., St. Paul, 1978; student, Marchutz Sch. Painting, Aix-en-Provence, France, 1976-77, 81-82; MFA, San Francisco Art Inst., 1990; PhD, NYU, 1993-00. Freelance theatre set and costume designer, Boston, San Francisco, Aix-en-Provence, 1980-87; art instr. painting and drawing Exploratorium, San Francisco, 1984-85, San Francisco Art Inst. Extension Sch., 1988-90; graphic artist Jamison, Cawdrey, Benjamin Advt., San Francisco, 1984-90. N.Y. Observer, N.Y.C., 1991-92; art dir. Terry Pimsleur & Co., San Francisco, 1992-93; tchg. asst. art history, painting and drawing NYU, N.Y.C., 1993-95; documentarian, achivist Star Axis, N.Y.C., 1995—; adj. prof. women's studies NJCU, 2001. Exhibited works in shows at Jan Holloway Gallery, San Francisco, 1989, 91, Gallerie Annick Ketelle, Antwerp, 1993, 450 Broadway Gallery, N.Y.C., 1995, ABC No Rio Gallery, N.Y.C., 1998, 2000, 02, 04, 06, Rosenberg Gallery, N.Y.C., 1999, Lyon Bienelle, 2000, Ace Gallery, N.Y.C., 2001, Sideshow Gallery, Bklyn., 2003, 04, Kramarsky Found., N.Y.C., 2005-06; author: Carnal Art: Orlan's Refacing, 2005; contbr. articles to profl. jours. including N. Paradoxa Art Jour., Women/Performance, 2000, 2002; drawings published in Jáime la Vic, Artists to Artist, ABC No Rio Catalogue, N. Paradoxa', Time Capsule: A Concise Ency. by Women Artists. Office: 383 W Broadway New York NY 10012-4377 Business E-Mail: cjobryan@hotmail.com

**O'BRYAN, JAMES A.,** communications specialist, political organization administrator; BS, Boston U., 1978. Sen. U.S. V.I., 1985-87; dir. youth prevention program Dept. Human Svcs., V.I., 1987-90; press sec. to gov. of V.I. Office of Gov., 1990-95, asst. to gov. pub. affairs, 1999—2003, dist. dir. comms. for congresswoman Christian Christensen, 1997; adminstr. St. Thomas/Water Island, 2003—. Chmn. Dem. State Party, 1998—. Mem. Assn. State Dem. Chairs. Office: PO Box 501 St Thomas VI 00804-0501

**O'BRYAN, MARGARET SUNDBERG,** music educator; b. Potsdam, NY, Dec. 18, 1957; d. Randell Llewellyn and Marion Hamlin Sundberg; m. Thomas Henry O'Bryan, Aug. 25, 1984. MusB, Crane Sch. of Music, Potsdam, 1980; MusM, Crane Sch. of Music, 1986. Cert. tchr. music K-12 NY. Tchr. vocal music Somersworth City Schs., Somersworth, NH, 1980—81, Central Square (NY) Ctrl. Sch., 1983—84, Harpursville (NY) Ctrl. Sch., 1984—2001, St. Regis Falls (NY) Ctrl. Sch., 2001—. Dist. rep. Broome County Music Educators Assn., Harpursville, 1986—2001, county music festival chair; Chenango County vocal adjudicator Assn. Chenango Area Music Tchrs., Harpursville, 1988—2000, county music festival chair; mem. policy bd. St. Regis Falls Ctrl. Sch. Mem. St. Regis Falls Sports Boosters, PTO, St. Regis Falls, 2002—05, Olympic Chorus, Lake Placid, NY, 1980; founder, instr. Harpursville Juggling Club, 1998—2001, St. Regis Falls Juggling Club, 2002—. Regents scholar, NY State, 1976—80. Mem.: Franklin County Music Educators Assn. (chair vocal music festival 2006—), NY State United Tchrs., St. Regis Falls United Tchrs. (co-organizer benefit auction 2004), NY State Sch. Music Assn., Music Educators Nat. Conf., Internat. Jugglers Assn. Mem. Lds Ch. Avocations: juggling, genealogy, landscape photography, travel. Home: PO Box 109 Port Kent Rd Nicholville NY 12965 Office: St Regis Falls Ctrl Sch 92 N Main St Saint Regis Falls NY 12980 Office Phone: 518-856-9421. E-mail: mobryan@mail.fehb.org.

**O'BRYANT, DANIEL R.,** manufacturing executive; BS in Mgmt. Sci., Calif. State Polytechnic U., Pomona, Calif.; MBA, U. So. Calif. From dir. cap. planning to sr. v.p. fin., CFO Avery Dennison, Pasadena, Calif., 1990—2001, sr. v.p. fin., 2001—, CFO, 2001—. Office: Avery Dennison Corp Ctr 150 North Orange Grove Blvd Pasadena CA 91103-3596

**O'BRYANT, JOHN FREDERICK,** librarian, educator; b. Memphis, Feb. 28, 1949; s. Levy Richard and Una O'Neil (Cottrell) O'B.; m. Margaret St. Clair Martin, Sept. 22, 1973. BA in English Lit., Southwestern at Memphis, 1971; MLS, U. N.C., 1972. Cert. libr. Med. Libr. Assn., State of Va. Reference and serials libr. Carl A. Rudisill Libr. Lenoir Rhyne Coll., Hickory, N.C., 1973-75; head of audiovisual ctr. Claude Moore Health Sci. Libr. U. Va., Charlottesville, 1975-82; sci. bibliographer Sci. & Engring. Libr. U. Va., Charlottesville, 1982-84, asst. dir., 1984-95, coord. for WWW and instrnl. svcs., 1995—2003, libr. Applied Sci., Math. and Stats., 2003—. Adj. faculty bus. divsn. Piedmont Va. C.C., Charlottesville, 1984-89. Editor: (book) Va. Union List of Serials; author, editor: Principles of Managing AV Materials and Equipment, 1979; reviewer Libr. Jour., 1977-80; contbr. poetry to various publs.; arranger music. Reader Recording for the Blind, Charlottesville, 1975-83; bd. dirs Charlottesville Mcpl. Bd., 1985-91, 97, 2003—; prin. clarinetist Charlottesville Mcpl. Band, 1975-79—. Mem. Am. Soc. for Engring. Edn. (editor membership dir. 1995-97), HTML Writers Guild. Methodist. Avocations: music, writing, science fiction, steam locomotives, gardening. Office: Univ Va Sci & Engring Libr Clark Hall Charlottesville VA 22904-4124

**O'BRYON, JAMES FREDRICK,** defense consultant; b. Schenectady, N.Y., Oct. 1, 1941; s. Frederick Stanley and Elizabeth Mary O'B.; m. Margaret Adina Bell, Oct 23, 1965; children: Daniel, Douglas, Cris, Kera. BS in Math., King's Coll., Briarcliff, N.Y., 1964; MSA in Ops. Rsch., George Washington U., 1973; SM in Elec. Engring., MIT, 1975. Mathematician Ballistics Rsch. Lab. Aberdeen (Md.) Proving Ground, 1966-74, asst. to dir. Ballistics Rsch. Lab., 1975-76, ops. rsch. analyst smart munitions group Ballistics Rsch. Lab., 1976-79, chmn. red-on-blue working group Joint Tech. Coord. Group, 1979-85, chief combat survivability and tech. U.S. Army Materiel Systems Analysis Activity, 1985-86; asst. dep. undersec. def. Office Sec. Def., Washington, 1986-88, dir. live-fire testing, 1988-95, dep. dir. operational test and evaluation, 1995—2001; chmn. The O'Bryon Group, 2001—, Cons. Svc. Engring. Co., 2002—; cons. Inst. Def. Analysis, 2005—. Dir. Live Fire Test Program, Washington, 1986-2001; mem. Conventional Sys. Com., Washington, 1987—; panel mem. NAS, 2000-05, chmn. com. 2005—; newscaster, radio personality WRBS-FM, Balt., 1965-80; chmn. Mobius Bus. Solutions, 2002-04; cons. in field. Singer (albums) Until Then, 1968, Portrait of a Man, 1972, My Favorite Song, 1977, Celebration of Praise, 1982; co-author: Red-on-Blue Weapons, Effects, 1983, Lessons Learned From Live Fire Testing, 2006; contbr. over 75 articles to profl. jours. Active edn. coun. MIT, Cambridge, 1980—; bd. dirs. Internat. Bible Soc. Found., Colo., Sch. Ministries, Inc., 2004—; mem. adv. bd. N.Y. Theol. Sem. With U.S. Army, 1964-66. Named Outstanding Young Man in Am., Jaycees, 1970, Disting. Lectr., Def. Aquisition U., 1988. Fellow Ctr. Advanced Engring. Study MIT; mem. AIAA, NAS/NRC (com. mem., chmn.), Nat. Def. Indsl. Assn. (chmn. Test and Evaluation divsn.), internat. Test and Evaluation Assn., Sigma Xi. Home: 1608 S Tollgate Rd Bel Air MD 21015-5825 Office Phone: 443-528-2711. Business E-Mail: jamesobryon@obryongroup.com.

**O'BRYON, LINDA ELIZABETH,** broadcast executive; b. Washington, Sept. 1, 1949; d. Walter Mason Ormes and Iva Genevieve (Batrus) Ranney; m. Dennis Michael O'Bryon, Sept. 8, 1973; 1 child, Jennifer Elizabeth BA in Journalism cum laude, U. Miami. News reporter Sta. KCPX (now KTVX), Salt Lake City, 1971-73; documentary and pub. affairs prodr. Sta. WPLG-TV, Miami, Fla., 1974-76; producer, reporter, anchor, news dir. then v.p. for news and pub. affairs, exec. editor, sr. v.p. Nightly Business Report Sta. WPBT (PBS), Miami, 1976—. Recipient award Fla. Bar, Tallahasse, 1977, 2 awards Ohio State U., 1976, 79, award Corp. for Pub. Broadcasting, 1978, Econ. Understanding award Dartmouth Coll., 1980, award Fla. Bar, 1981, 1st prize Nat. Assn. Realtors, 1986, Bus. News Luminary award TJFR, 1990, Am. Women in Radio and TV award, 1995, 98, Disting. Achievement award Soc. Am. Bus. Editors and Writers, 2004; named Most Influential Woman Bus. News Exec., TJFR, 2001. Mem. NATAS (past bd. dirs. So. Fla. chpt., regional Emmy award), Radio-TV News Dirs. Assn. (past trustee). Republican. Roman Catholic. Avocations: aerobics, tennis, golf. Office: Sta WPBT 14901 NE 20th Ave Miami FL 33181-1121 Office Phone: 305-424-4050.

**OBSTFELD, MAURICE,** economics professor, consultant; b. Mar. 19, 1952; s. George Eliakim and Selma Giselle O. BA, U. Pa., 1973; MA, Cambridge U., Eng., 1975; PhD, MIT, 1979. Asst. prof. Columbia U., N.Y.C., 1979-81, assoc. prof. dept. econs., 1981-85, prof., 1985-86, U. Calif., Berkeley, 1989—, Class of 1958 prof., 1995—. Vis. scholar Fed. Res., Washington, 1981, 94, MIT, Cambridge, 1982, Stockholm U., 1988, 93, IMF, 1989; vis. prof. Tel-Aviv U., Israel, 1984, Harvard U., 1989-90; mem. econs. adv. panel NSF, 1983-84; rsch. assoc. Nat. Bur. Econ. Rsch., Cambridge; rsch. fellow Ctr. Econ. Policy Rsch., London. Co-editor: Financial Policies and the World Capital Market, 1983; author: (with others) International Economics: Theory and Policy, 1987, 4th edit., 1997, Foundations of International Macroeconomics, 1996, Global Capital Markets, 2004; mem. editl. bd. Jour. Monetary Econs., 1983—, Jour. Internat. Econs., 1985—, Internat. Econ. Rev., 1986—, Rev. Internat. Econs., 1992—; contbr. articles to profl. jours. Grad. fellow Danforth Found., 1973, Rsch. fellow Alfred P. Sloan, 1984; Rsch. grantee NSF, 1981, 84, 86, 88, 91, 94. Fellow Econometric Soc., Am. Acad. Arts and Sci.; mem. Am. Econ. Assn. (mem. editl. bd. jours. 1987—, mem. exec. com. 2003—). Office: Univ Calif Dept Econs Berkeley CA 94720-0001

**OCAL, TARKAN,** computer engineer; b. Ankara, Turkey, Dec. 1955; Attended, U. So. Miss., U. Minn., MG in Mechanical Design Engring., Trinity Coll., London. Junior drafter HAKO Minutemen Corp., St. Paul; designer apprentice Sperry-Univac, Honeywell, Hutchinson Technologies; junior engr. 3M Corp.; sr. engr. Matra-Manurhin Corp., Ft. Lauderdale; project engr. Dept. of Defense, Washington; founder, v.p. G&T TECH, Inc.; contractor Broward County Commn. Info. Techn., Fla.; sys. network analyst Broward County Commn. Info. Tech.

**O'CALLAGHAN, JERRY ALEXANDER,** federal agency administrator; b. Klamath Falls, Oreg., Feb. 23, 1922; s. Jeremiah Patrick and Marie Jane (Alexander) O'C.; m. Florence Marie Sheehan, Aug. 6, 1949; children—Jane Mary, Susan Margaret. BS with honors, U. Oreg., 1943, MA with honors, 1947; PhD, Stanford, 1951. Acting instr. history Stanford, 1951-52, U. Wyo., 1952-53; oil editor Tribune-Herald, Casper, Wyo., 1953-55; acting asst. prof. U. Wyo., 1955-56; legis. asst. to Senator Joseph O'Mahoney (Wyo.), 1956-60; exec. asst. to Senator Joseph Hickey(Wyo.), 1961; asst. dir. lands and minerals mgmt. Bur. Land Mgmt., Dept. Interior, 1961-62, asst. dir. plans and legislation, 1962-64, chief legislation and coop. relations, 1964-69, chief div. coop. relations, 1969-80, chief hist. studies, 1980-82, historian emeritus, 1982—. Author: Disposition of the Public Domain in Oregon, 1960, America 200—The Legacy of Our Lands, 1976. Bd. govs. St. Columba's Episc. Nursery Sch., 1959-71; vestryman Episc. Ch., 1964-68, outreach leader, 1985-90; lay ministry St. Columba's, 1990-2004. With AUS, 1943-46. Mem. Soc. of Forest History, Fed. Profl. Assn. (pres. 1972), Fossils, Phi Kappa Psi. Home: 5607 Chesterbrook Rd Bethesda MD 20816-1301

**O'CALLAGHAN, R.J. PATRICK,** lawyer; b. Mpls., Aug. 8, 1924; s. Robert Desmond and Claire Marie (Moe) O'C.; married Albina Julie Segish, June 4, 1949; children: Michael, Edward, Catherine, Diana, Robert, Daniel. BA, Drake U., 1949; JD, U. Denver, 1951. Bar: Colo. 1951, U.S. Dist. Ct. Colo. 1956, U.S. Tax Ct. 1971, U.S. Ct. Appeals (10th cir.) 1978. Pvt. practice law, Denver, 1952-53, Rangely, Colo., 1953-63; real estate broker Grand Junction, Colo., 1963-65; ptnr. Bellinger, Faricy, Tursi & O'Callaghan, Pueblo, Colo., 1965-73; pvt. practice law Pueblo, 1973-76; ptnr. Lattimer, O'Callaghan & Ware P.C., Pueblo, 1978-81; of counsel Quiet & Dice, Denver, 1981-83; pvt. practice law Pueblo, 1983—. Atty. Town of Rangely,

1953-63; bd. atty. Pueblo Bd. Realtors, 1971-82; instr. real estate U. Colo., 1968-79; sr. cert. valuer Internat. Real Estate Inst. Pres. Homes for Sr. Citizens Inc., Pueblo, 1978-80; pres. Mt. Carmel Credit Union, 1972-74; adv. bd. dirs. Pueblo Salvation Army, 1987-91. With USNR, 1943-46. Mem. ABA, Colo. Bar Assn., Pueblo County Bar Assn., Nat. Network Estate Planning Attys., Elks (exalted ruler Rangley Lodge No. 1907). Republican. Roman Catholic. Avocation: photography. Address: 125 E 7th Ste 100 Pueblo CO 81003-3407 Office Phone: 719-543-8371. E-mail: patoc@qwest.net.

**O'CALLAGHAN, THOMAS ALOYSIUS,** artist, librarian; b. Orange, N.J., Feb. 1, 1952; s. Thomas Aloysius O'Callaghan and Helen Elizabeth Crowther. BFA in Painting, Corcoran Sch. of Art, Washington, D.C., 1975; MFA in Painting, Am. U., Washington, D.C., 1980. Cert. Slide Curators Basic Tng. Coll. of Fine Arts, U. Tex. at Austin, 1989. Sr. mus. asst. for edn. Phillips Collection, Washington, 1980—84; assoc. slide libr. Nat. Gallery of Art, Washington, 1988—. Bd. mem. Internat. Artists Support Group, Washington, 1998—2001. Exhibited in group shows at 19th Area Exhbn., Corcoran Gallery of Art, Three Internat. Artists, Beethoven Society, Washington, Two Washingtonians, Two Europeans, Alex Gallery, Washington, Capital to Capital, Bonn, Germany, Alex Gallery, Washington, one-man shows include Alex Gallery, Wash., Blue Palette Art Gallery. Recipient Spl. Svc. Award, Nat. Gallery of Art, 1997; Scholarship for Grad. Art Study, Nat. Soc. of Arts and Letters, Wash., DC, 1976, Landscape Painting Fellowship, Artists for Environment Found. at the Del. Watergap, 1975, Robert H. Smith Fellowship, Nat. Gallery of Art, 1991. Mem.: Phi Kappa Phi. Avocations: writing, travel. Office: Nat Gallery of Art 4th St and Constn Ave NW Washington DC 20565

**OCAMPO, MANUEL,** artist; b. Philippines; Exhibitions include Corcoran Biennial, 1995, Kwangju Biennial, 1997, Biennale d'art Contemporain de Lyon, 2000, Berlin Biennale, 2001, Venice Biennale, 2001, Seville Biennale, 2004, Casa Asia, Barcelona, 2005, Lieu d'Art Contemporain, Sigean, France, 2005, exhibited in group shows at Asia Society, NYC, 1994, Setagaya Art Mus., Tokyo, 1997, Aldrich Mus. Art, 1998, LA County Mus. Art, 2000. Recipient Rome Prize, Am. Acad., 1995, award, Nat. Endowment for the Arts, 1996, Pollock-Krasner Found., 1995. Office: c/o Gray Kapernekas Gallery 526 W 26 St Ste 814 New York NY 10001*

**OCASIO-MELENDEZ, MARCIAL ENRIQUE,** history professor; b. San Juan, P.R., Aug. 22, 1942; s. Manuel C. and Amparo (Melendez) Ocasio; m. Mimi Rivera, Apr. 15, 1973 (div. 1976). BA, U. P.R., 1964, MA, 1977; PhD, Mich. State U., 1988. Tchr. sci. P.R. Dept. Edn., San Juan, 1966-67; tchr. sci., history Nyack (N.Y.) Schs., 1967-71; tchr. sci. Robinson Prep. Sch., Condado, P.R., 1971-72; instr. P.R. Jr. Coll., Rio Piedras, 1972-80; teaching asst. Mich. State U., E. Lansing, 1979-83; instr. history Caribbean U., Bayamon, P.R., 1983-85; instr. Inter Am. U., Bayamon, 1985-87, U. P.R., Rio Piedras, 1983-87; vis. asst. prof. Mich. State U., E. Lansing, 1987-88; asst. prof. history U. Mich., Flint, 1988-91; prof. history U. P.R., Rio Piedras, 1991—, dir. grad. program history, 1991-93, assoc. dean acad. affairs Coll. Humanities, 1993-95, dir. internat. rels., 1995—2001, chair, dept. history, 2004—; prof. Ctr. Advanced Grad. Studies P.R. and The Caribbean. Vis. prof. U. Zaragoza, Spain, 2001; bd. dirs. Spanish Speaking Info. Ctr., Flint; lectr. Universidad del Valle, Cali, Universidad de Los Andes, Bogota, Universidad Pedagogica Nacional, Tunja, U. del Norte Barranquilla, Colombia, Nat. U. Nicaragua, 2005; dir. Rockefeller Found. Caribbean 2000 Project, U. P.R., 1994-95, Urban Preservation Project of Rio Piedras, P.R., 1994-95; pres. P.R.'s Ist Hist. Preservation, 1999—; mem. editl. bd. Caribbean Studies, 1994-99. Author: Rio Piedras Notas, 1985, Las Americas, Su Tierra, Su Gente, 1997, Capitalism and Development, Tampico 1876-1924, 1998. Mich. State U. scholar 1981, urban affairs grantee, 1982-83; Fulbright scholar (Colombia) 1989, 90, 2001-; Fulbright scholar specialist, 2002—; NEH fellow, 1973, 78-79, 91, 2002-. Mem. Social Sci. Studies Assn., Coun. L.Am. History, Am. Hist. Assn., L.Am. Studies Assn., Assn. P.R. Historians (pres. 1995-97), Joint Border Rsch. Inst., Assn. Caribean Historians, Caribbean Studies Assn., Hispanic Coun. on Internat. Rels., Phi Alpha Theta. Office: Univ PR History Dept PO Box 23350 San Juan PR 00931-3350 Office Phone: 787-764-0000 3777. Personal E-mail: kokoroko9@hotmail.com. E-mail: mocasio@uprp.edu.

**OCCHIATO, MICHAEL ANTHONY,** municipal official; b. Pueblo, Colo. s. Joseph Michael and Joan Occhiato; m. Peggy Ann Stefonowicz, June 27, 1964 (div. Sept. 1983); children: Michael, James, Jennifer. BBA, U. Denver, 1961; MBA, U. Colo., 1984; postgrad., U. So. Colo. Cert. residential specialist. Sales mgr. Tivoli Brewing co., Denver, 1965-67, acting brewmaster, prodn. control mgr., 1967-68, plant mgr., 1968-69; adminstrv. mgr. King Resources Co., Denver, 1969-70; ops. mgr. Canners Inc., Pepsi-Cola Bottling Co., Pueblo, 1970-76; pres. Pepsi-Cola Bottling Co., Pueblo, 1978-82; gen. mgr. Pepsi-Cola Bottling Group div. PepsiCo., Pueblo, 1982, area v.p., 1982-83; ind. cons. Pueblo, 1983—; broker assoc. Sound Venture Realty, Pueblo, 1998-99, Jones Healy Better Homes & Gardens, 1998—. V.p. Colo. Soft Drink Assn., 1978, pres., 1979; regional dir. Pepsi Cola Mgmt. Inst. divsn. Pepsi Co., 1979-82; pres. Ethnic Foods Internat. dba Taco Rancho, Pueblo, Exodus 20, 1996—; chmn. Weifang (China) Sister City Del., 1991—; bd. dirs. Pueblo Diversified Industries, Pueblo Crime Stoppers, Pueblo Regional Bldg; rancher, 1976—; land devel. real estate broker assoc., 1996—. Mem. Pueblo City Coun., 1978—93, 2001—, pres., 1986—87, 1991; mem. Pueblo Bd. Health, 1978—80, Pueblo Regional Planning Commn., 1980—81, Pueblo Action Inc., 1978—80, Pueblo Planning and Zoning Commn., 1985; chmn. Pueblo Area Coun. Govts., 1980—82; mem. Pueblo Econ. Devel. Corp., 1983—91; chmn. fundraising Pueblo chpt. Am. Heart Assn., 1983—; active Earth Wise Pueblo, 1991; pres. Pueblo City Coun., 2002; active Pueblo Regional Bldg. Bd., 2003—; rep. in signing Sister City Agreement with Bergamo, Italy City of Pueblo, 2004; pres. Pueblo City Coun., 2006—; bd. dirs. Pueblo Urban Renewal Authority, 1993—, Pueblo Crime Stoppers, 2001—, El Pueblo Boys Ranch, pres. Colo. Soft Drink Assn., 1979—80, pres., 1980—81; del. 1st World Conf. Local Elected Ofcls. to UN Internat. Coun. for Local Environ. Initiative. Lt. USN, 1961—65. Mem. Soc. Emergency Med. Technicians Assn. (pres. 1975), Am. Saler Assn., Am. Quarter Horse Assn., Colo. Cattle Assn., Pueblo C. of C., Rotary, Pi Kappa Alpha (v.p. 1960). Home and Office: 11 Harrogate Ter Pueblo CO 81001-1723

**OCELLO, CLAUDIA BARBARA,** museum program director; b. Passaic, NJ, July 15, 1966; d. Fortunato and Adriana Concetta (Dominianni) Ocello. BA in Classical and Near Ea. Archaeology, Bryn Mawr Coll., 1988; BS in Mus. Edn., Bank St. Coll. Edn., 1993. Intern J. Paul Getty Mus., Malibu, Calif., 1993—94; coord. edn. and vol. Barnum Mus., Bridgeport, Conn., 1994—96; curator edn. NJ Hist. Soc., Newark, 1996—2005, dir. programand exhbns., 2005—06; asst. dir. for edn. and pub. programs Save Ellis Island, Inc., 2006—. Adj. prof. Seton Hall U., South Orange, NJ, 1997—; mem. adv. bd. NJ History Day, 1997—2005. Author: First Steps: A Scrapbook & Guide for Young Parents, 2002. Vol. project mgr. Jersey Cares, 1998—2003. Named Outstanding Educator, NJ History Day, 2004. Mem.: Mid-Atlantic Assn. Mus. (program com. 2006), Am. Assn. Mus. (Edn. Com. Excellence in Programming award 2002). Avocations: cooking, reading, yoga. Office: PO Box 571 268 Main St Gladstone NJ 07934 Office Phone: 408-781-9900. E-mail: cocello@saveellisisland.org

**OCHEJ, HELEN WANDA,** biologist, researcher, information scientist; b. Treysa, Germany, Oct. 3, 1946; d. Frank Ochej and Luba Kopytko; m. David R. Sutkoff; 1 child, Anne Q. Sutkoff. BA, Lycoming Coll., Williamsport, PA, 1968. Rsch. asst. McNeil Labs, Fort Washington, Pa., 1968—72, Max Planck Inst. Brain Rsch., Koln, Merheim, Germany, 1972—74, U. Rochester Cancer Ctr., Rochester, NY, 1975—85, supr. facility, 1980—85; contract med. indexer Kessler, Herner, Caelum, Rockville, Md., 1986—95; tech. info. specialist Nat. Libr. Medicine, Bethesda, Md., 1995—. Pres. Grad. Women Sci., Rochester, NY, 1978—79; focus group NLM Exhibit, Md., 2001—05; treas. Am. Soc. Indexers, Md., 2002—; treas., docent, sec. NLM Diversity Coun., 2004—06. Contbr. articles to profl. jours. V.p. Neighborhood Assn., Rochester, NY, 1978—79; adv. bd. Gifted and Talented Edn., Montgomery County, Md., 1991—95; active Seneca Valley Pony Club, Md., 1996—98.

Grantee Rsch. Grant, Max Planck Inst., 1972-1974. Mem.: Am. Soc. Indexers, DC Med. Writers Assn. Avocations: gardening, yoga, travel, hiking. Office: National Library of Medicine 8600 Rockville Pike Bethesda MD 20894 Office Phone: 301-402-6180. E-mail: helen.ochej@nlm.nih.gov.

**OCHMANEK, DAVID ALAN,** defense analyst; b. Oak Park, Ill., Apr. 10, 1951; s. Edwin Joseph and Phyllis Jean (Straass) O.; m. Barbara Jane Larson, June 16, 1973; children: James Edwin, Anne Skaaden. BS in Internat. Affairs, Polit. Sci., USAF Acad., 1973; MPA in Pub. Affairs and Internat. Rels., Princeton U., 1980. Fgn. svc. officer U.S. Dept. State, 1980-85; profl. staff The Rand Corp., 1985-93, 95—; dep. asst. sec. def. for strategy Washington, 1993-95; sr. def. analyst The RAND Corp., Washington, 1995—. Author: Military Operations Against Terrorist Operations Abroad, 2003, NATO's Future: Implications for U.S. Military Capabilities and Force Posture, 2000; co-author: (with Edward L. Warner III) Next Moves: An Arms Control Agenda for the 1990's, 1989, (with Christopher Bowie et al) The New Calculus, 1993, (with Zalmay Khalilzad) Strategic Appraisal, 1997, (with Edward Harshberger el at) To Find and Not to Yield, 1998, (with Anthony Lake) The Real and the Ideal, 2001; contbr. articles to profl. jours., chpts. to books. Capt. USAF, 1973-78. Lutheran. Office: The RAND Corp 1200 S Hayes St Arlington VA 22202-5050 Office Phone: 703-413-1100.

**OCHOA, ARTHUR J.,** lawyer, hospital administrator; b. LA, Calif., Sept. 16, 1968; s. Arthur P. and Josephine E. Ochoa; m. Daniele J. Worth. Jan. 25, 1998; children: Madeleine Worth, Eloise Worth. BA, U. of So. California, 1986—90; JD, Yale Law Sch., 1992—95. Bar: State of Calif. 1995. Policy coord. Youth Svc. Am., Washington, 1990—92; assoc. O'Melveny & Myers LLP, LA, Calif., 1995—98; atty. Irell & Manella LLP, Century City, 1998—2001; dir. planned giving Cedars-Sinai Med. Ctr., LA, 2001—04, sr. v.p. cmty. rels., 2004—. Mem. and sec., bd. of directors Youth Svc. Am., Washington, 1997—98; adj. faculty mem., mba program U. of Judiasm, LA, 2001—; adv. bd. mem. Neopets Found., Glendale, 2001—. Chmn. tax exempt orgn. com. LA County Bar Assn., 2004; mem., bd. of trustees Mexican Am. Bar Found., LA, 2002; chair tax expert orgn. com. LA County Bar Assn., 2004—05; mem. bd. trustees Am. Bar Assn., 2002—. Mem.: Nat. Eagle Scout Assn., Jonathan Club (L.A.), Yale Club N.Y.C., Phi Beta Kappa. Office: Cedars-Sinai Med Ctr 8700 Beverly Blvd Ste 2416 Los Angeles CA 90048 E-mail: ochoaa@cshs.org.

**OCHOA, ELLEN,** astronaut; b. L.A., May 10, 1958; d. Roseanne Ochoa; m. Coe Fulmer Miles; one son. BS in Physics, San Diego State U., 1980; MSEE, Stanford U., 1981, PhD in EE, 1985. Rsch. engr. Sandia Nat. Labs., Livermore, Calif., 1985—88; chief intelligent systems tech. br. NASA/Ames Rsch. Ctr./Moffet Field Naval Air Sta., Mountain View, Calif.; Astronaut NASA, Houston, 1991—, dep. dir., flight crew ops. Recipient two Space Act Tech Brief Awards, 1992, Space Flight Medals 1993, 1994, 1999, 2002; Outstanding Leadership Medal, 1995, Exceptional Svc. Medal, 1997, Women in Aerospace Outstanding Achievement Award, the Hispanic Engr. Albert Baez Award for Outstanding Tech. Contribution to Humanity, the Hispanic Heritage Leadership Award, San Diego State U. Alumna of the Year. Mem. Optical Soc. Am., Am. Inst. Aeronautics and Astronautics, Phi Beta Kappa, Sigma Xi, Pres. Commn. on the Celebration of Women in Am. History. Achievements include being the first female Hispanic astronaut chosen for Space Shuttle program. Office: NASA Johnson Space Ctr Astronaut Office Houston TX 77058

**OCHOA, LORENA,** professional golfer; b. Guadalajara, Mex., Jan. 15, 1981; d. Javier and Marcela. Attened, U. Ariz., 2000—02. Winner Franklin Am. Mortgage Championship, 2004, Wachovia LPGA Classic, 2004. Five-time U.S. 8-12 Jr. World Championship winner; NCAA Player of Yr., 2001; NCAA Freshman of Yr., 01; finished second NCAA Championships, 2001; finished first place Futures Tour money list, 2002. Recipient Nancy Lopez Award for outstanding amateur accomplishments, 2002, Louise Suggs Rolex Rookie of Yr., 2003, Nat. Sports Award, Mex., 2001. Achievements include Topped $1 million in earnings in 2002 and 2005. Avocations: triathalons, marathons, mountain climbing, tennis, basketball, accordion. Office: c/o LPGA 100 International Golf Dr Daytona Beach FL 32124-1092

**OCHOA, MANUEL, JR.,** oncologist; b. NYC, Apr. 22, 1930; s. Manuel and Maria (Diaz) O.; m. Suzanne Ellen Recca, Sept. 1, 1956; children: Elizabeth, Suzanne Elise. AB, Columbia Coll., 1951; MD, Columbia U., 1955. Diplomate Am. Bd. Internal Medicine; lic. physician, NY, Mass. Asst. in medicine U. Rochester Med. Sch., NY, 1958-61; instr. medicine, assoc., asst. prof. Columbia U., NYC, 1964-68; attending physician Meml. Sloan-Kettering Cancer Ctr., NYC, 1973—. Investigator Marine Biol. Lab., Woods Hole, Mass., 1965; assoc. prof. clin. medicine Cornell U., NYC, 1982-96, prof., 1996—; cons. Harlem Hosp. Ctr., NYC, 1966-68, Kingston Hosp., NY, 1970-85; vis. prof. U. Hawaii, Honolulu, 1971, U. Mex., Mexico City, 1979. Contbr. articles to profl. jours. Capt. USAF, 1956-58, ETO. Fellow Lalor Found., 1965. Fellow ACP, ACS. Republican. Roman Catholic. Achievements include discovery of genetic code and protein synthesis in cancer cells, cancer chemotherapy. Home: 82 E Middle Patent Rd Bedford NY 10506-2106 Office: Meml Sloan-Kettering Cancer Ctr 1275 York Ave New York NY 10021-6007 Office Phone: 212-639-8245.

**OCHOA, VANESSA JEANETTE,** academic administrator; b. LA, Nov. 13, 1976; BA in Chicano Studies, U. Calif., Berkeley, 1999; MA in Policy Analysis and Evaluation, Stanford U., Calif., 2003; postgrad., UCLA, 2003—. Student affairs officer Scholarship Resource Ctr. UCLA, 2004—. Author: Counter Stories of Students of Color in 'Privileged' Academic Environments, 2004. Outreach vol. U. Calif. Berkeley Alumni Assn., 2002—; mentor UCLA ASUL Vol. Orgn., 2004—05, Hispanic Scholarship Fund, 2005—. Recipient Gold shield, UCLA Alumnae, 2004—05; grantee Salvadorian Am. Leadership and Edn. grantee, 2003; scholar, USA Funds Access Edn., 2004—05; Pub. Employees Roundtable Pub. Svc. scholar, 2002, Hispanic Scholarship Fund grantee, 2003, UCLA fellow, 2003. Progressive. Avocations: travel, reading. Personal E-mail: vanessita1976@yahoo.com.

**OCHOA-BRILLEMBOURG, HILDA MARGARITA,** investment banker; b. July 8, 1944; BS in Econs., U. Catolica Andres Bello, Caracas, Venezuela; MPA, Harvard U.; postgrad. in fin., Harvard Bus. Sch. Chief investment officer, pension investment div. World Bank, 1976—87; mng. dir. Emerging Markets Investment Corp.; founder, pres., CEO Strategic Investment Group, 1987—. Bd. dirs. Harvard Mgmt. Co., Bank Fund Staff Fed. Credit Union, Gen. Mills, Inc., McGraw-Hill Inc.; treas. C.A. Luz Electrica de Venezuela, Caracas, 1967—71; lectr. U. Catolica Andres Bello, 1970; ind. cons. in econs. and fin. Published articles in Fin. Analyst Jour. and Pensions & Investments. Bd. dirs. Nat. Symphony Orch., Washington Nat. Opera, Cath. Charities Found.; chmn. bd. dirs. Youth Orch. of the Americas; mem. investment com. Rockefeller Family Fund; vice chair, Group of 50 Carnegie Endowment for Internat. Peace; mem. adv. com. Rockefeller Ctr. for Latin Am. Studies, The Hauser Ctr. at Harvard U., Small Enterprise Asst. Funds. Fulbright-Hays fellow. Office: 1001 19th St N 16th Fl Arlington VA 22209-1722 Office Phone: 703-243-4433.

**OCHS, CAROL REBECCA,** theologian, writer, theology studies educator, philosopher; b. N.Y.C., May 7, 1939; d. Herman and Clara Florence (Michaels) Blumenthal; m. Michael Ochs, Sept. 27, 1959; children: Elisabeth Amy, Miriam Adina. BA, CUNY, 1960, MA, 1964; PhD, Brandeis U., 1968. Philosophy lectr. CUNY, 1964-65; from asst. prof. to prof. philosophy Simmons Coll., Boston, 1967-92, prof. emerita, 1992—. Adj. faculty Grad. Sch. Union Inst., Cin., 1992—97, Hebrew Union Coll.-Jewish Inst. Religion, N.Y.C., 1994—97, dir. grad. studies, vis. prof. philosophy, 1997—2001, dir. grad. studies, adj. prof. Jewish Religious Thought, 2001—; cons. Inst. for Svc. to Higher Edn., Chestnut Hill, Mass., 1972, St. Mary's Coll., South Bend, Ind., 1980; scholar-in-residence Hollins Coll., Roanoke, Va., 1987, numerous temples and synagogues; mem. selection com. Kent Postdoctoral Fellowships Bunting Inst., Radcliffe Coll.; lectr. in field. Author: Behind the Sex of God: Toward a New Consciousness Transcending Matriarchy and

Patriarchy, 1977, Women and Spirituality, 1983, 2d edit., 1997, An Ascent to Joy: Transforming Deadness of Spirit, 1989, The Noah Paradox: Time as Burden, Time as Blessing, 1991, Song of the Self: Biblical Spirituality and Human Holiness, 1994, Jewish Spiritual Guidance, 1997, Our Lives as Torah: Finding God in Our Own Stories, 2001, Reaching Godward: Voices from Jewish Spiritual Guidance, 2004; contbr. articles to profl. jours. Mem. Jewish-Cath. Dialogue, Boston, 1989-93; mem. Cath.-Jewish com. Archdiocese of Boston, 1989-93. Fellow NEH, 1976, 88, Nat. Humanities Inst., U. Chgo., 1978-79, Danforth Found., 1981-86, Coolidge Rsch., Colloquium, 1985, Resource Theologian, 1995-99. Fellow Soc. for Values in Higher Edn. (bd. dirs. 1982-88, chair ctrl. com. 1985-87, 2003—, v.p. 2004-), Assn. for Religion and Intellectual Life (mem. editl. bd. 1986—). Office: Hebrew Union Coll 1 W 4th St New York NY 10012 Office Phone: 212-824-2267. Personal E-mail: cochs@earthlink.net.

**OCHS, MICHAEL,** editor, librarian, music educator; b. Cologne, Germany, Feb. 1, 1937; came to U.S., 1939, naturalized, 1945; s. Isaac Julius and Claire (Baum) O.; m. Carol Rebecca Blumenthal, Sept. 27, 1959; children— Elisabeth Amy, Miriam Adina BA, CCNY, 1958; MS, Columbia U., 1963; A.M., NYU, 1964; D.A., Simmons Coll., 1975. Cataloguer CCNY, 1963-65, lectr. in music, 1964; music libr. Brandeis U., Waltham, Mass., 1965-68, creative arts libr., 1968-74; asst. prof. libr. sci. Simmons Coll., Boston, 1974-78; libr. Eda Kuhn Loeb Music Libr., Harvard U., Cambridge, Mass., 1978-88, Richard F. French libr., 1988-92; lectr. music Harvard U., Cambridge, Mass., 1978-81, sr. lectr. music, 1981-92, also libr. cons., 1977-78; music editor W. W. Norton and Co., N.Y.C., 1992-2001; pres. Ochs Editl., 2001—. Libr. cons. Biblioteca Berenson, Florence, Italy, 1983, Columbia U., 1987; project dir. U.S. Répertoire International des Sources Musicales Manuscript Inventory Ctr. at Harvard U., NEH, Cambridge, Mass., 1985-88. Editor Notes, Jour. Music Libr. Assn., 1987-92, Music Librarianship in America, 1991; contbr. articles to profl. jours., 1976—. Mem. Am. Musicol. Soc. (bd. dirs. 2000-02), Internat. Assn. Music Librs. (pres. rsch. librs. br. 1987-90), Music Libr. Assn. (chmn. New Eng. chpt. 1968-69, chmn. com. on bibliog. description 1971-73, chmn. music libr. adminstrn. com. 1975-76, chmn. fin. com. 1976-78, bd. dirs. 1976-78, chmn. publs. com. 1983-87, pres. 1993-95). Office Phone: 212-987-1089. E-mail: mochsed@earthlink.net.

**OCHS, SIDNEY,** neurophysiology researcher, editor, writer; b. Fall River, Mass., June 30, 1924; s. Nathan and Rose (Kniaz) O.; m. Bess Ratner; children: Rachel F., Raymond S. Susan B. PhD in Physiology, U. Chgo., 1952. Rsch. assoc. Ill. Neuropsychiat. Inst., Chgo., 1952-54; rsch. fellow Calif. Inst. Tech., Pasadena, 1954-56; asst. prof. dept. physiology U. Tex. Med. Br., Galveston, 1956-58; assoc. prof. dept. physiology Ind U., Indpls., 1958-61, prof., 1961-94, prof. emeritus, 1994—. Author: Elements of Neurophysiology, 1965, Axoplasmic Transport and Its Relation to Other Nerve Functions, 1982, A History of Nerve Functions: From Animal Spirits to Molecular Mechanisms, 2004; founding editor, editor-in-chief Jour. Neurobiology, 1969-76, assoc. editor, 1977-86. With U.S. Army, 1943—45. Mem. Internat. Brain Rsch. Orgn., Internat. Soc. Neurochemistry, Internat. Soc. Hist. Neurosciences, Am. Physiol. Soc., Soc. Neurosci., Am. Soc. Neurochemistry, Peripheral Nerve Soc., Hist. Sci. Soc. Democrat. Jewish. Avocation: amateur radio. Office: Ind U Med Ctr Dept Cellular & Integ Physiology 635 Barnhill Dr Indianapolis IN 46202-5126 Office Phone: 317-274-7940. Business E-Mail: sochs@iupui.edu.

**OCHS, WALTER J.,** civil engineer, consultant; b. Springfield, Minn., May 20, 1934; s. Walter Minrod and Cleo (Schultz) O.; m. Connie Mae Strate, Sept. 15, 1956; children: Julie, Brian. BS in Agrl. Engring., South Dakota U., 1957. Registered profl. civil engr., Mich. Engr. in training USDA, Soil Conservation Svc., Watertown, S.D., 1957-58, project engr. Britton, S.D., 1958-61, area engr. Sioux Falls, S.D., 1961-63, asst. state conservation engr. East Lansing, Mich., 1963-66, state conservation engr., 1966-69, asst. state conservationist Saint Paul, Minn., 1969-71, nat. drainage engr. Washington, 1971-86; drainage advisor World Bank, Washington, 1986-96; internat. ind. water mgmt. cons., 1996—. Bd. dirs. Internat. Inst. for Land Reclamation and Improvement Postgrad Land Drainage Course, The Netherlands, 1990-98; particpated in. project work over 30 countries; mem. Internat. Commn. Irrigation and Drainage. Contbr. to profl. jours. Named Fed. Engr. of Yr., NSPE, 1982; recipient Outstanding Alumnus award S.D. State U., 1977, Outstanding Contbn. award Corrugated Plastic Tubing Assn., 1981, Svc. to the Profession award U.S. Com. on Irrigation and Drainage, 2004; named to Internat. Drainage Hall of Fame, 1996. Fellow: Am. Soc. Agrl. Engrs.; mem.: ASCE (chmn. drainage com. 1975—76, Royce J. Tipton award 2001). Office: 6731 Fern Ln Annandale VA 22003-1903 E-mail: wochs@hotmail.com.

**OCHSNER, JOHN LOCKWOOD,** thoracic-cardiovascular surgeon; b. Madison, Wis., Feb. 10, 1927; s. Edward William Alton and Isabel (Lockwood) O.; m. Mary Lou Hannon, Mar. 20, 1954; children: John L., John Hannon, Katherine Lockwood, Frank Hannon. MD, Tulane U., 1952. Diplomate Am. Bd. Thoracic Surgery (chmn. 1993-95), Am. Bd. Surgery, Am. Bd. Vascular Surgery. Intern Univ. Mich. Hosp., Ann Arbor, 1952-53, resident, 1953-54, Baylor U. Affilliated Hosp., Houston, 1956-58, 1958-59; chief surg. resident Tex. Children's Hosp., 1959-60; instr. Baylor U., Houston, 1960-61; mem. staff Ochsner Clinic, New Orleans, 1961—, chmn. dept. surgery, 1966-87, chmn. emeritus dept surgery, 1987—; clin. asst. prof. Tulane U., New Orleans, 1961-65, clin. assoc. prof., 1965-70, clin. prof. surgery, 1970—. Author: (with others) Coronary Artery Surgery, 1978. Pres. Thoracic Surgery Assn. New Orleans, 1967; image amb. City of New Orleans, 1982; bd. dirs. Internat. Trade Mart, New Orleans, 1983. Capt. USAF, 1954-56. Recipient award Life Mag., 1961, Golden Plate Acad. Achievement award, 1962, medal of honor, Ecuador, 1981. Mem. Internat. Soc. Cardiovascular Surgery (pres. N.Am. chpt. 1983-84, internat. pres. 1989-91), Am. Assn. Thoracic Surgery (sec. 1979-83, pres. 1992-93), New Orleans Surg. Soc. (pres. 1977-78), So. Surg. Assn. (pres. 1991), So. Assn. for Vascular Surgery (pres. 1983), Boston Club, La. Club, New Orleans Country Club, City Club, Alpha Omega Alpha. Republican. Home: 88 Audubon Blvd New Orleans LA 70118-5540 Office: Ochsner Clinic Found 1514 Jefferson Hwy New Orleans LA 70121-2483

**OCHSNER, OTHON HENRY, II,** importer, restaurant critic; b. Chgo., May 19, 1934; s. Othon Henry and Louise Catherine (Schlichenmaier) O. Pub. rels. staff Walgreen Co., Chgo., 1961-65; sales mgr. Porsche Car Imports, Northbrook, Ill., 1966-67; nat. sales mgr. Pirelli Tire Corp., N.Y.C., 1968-73; pres., CEO Ochsner Internat., Chgo., 1974—; mng. dir. Oberhallu Warehousing, Lake Buff, Ill. Bd.dirs., pres. Swiss-U.S.A. Racing Team, Chgo., 1976—. Author: Ochsner Pocket Guide to the Finest Restaurants and Hotels in the World, 12th edit.; author Ochsner Restaurant Newsletters, 1986—. Pres., exec. dir. Louise Catherine Schlichenmaier and Othon Henry Ochsner I Charitable Family Found., 2000—; founder Ochsner Art, Automobile, and Bicycle Mus., Lake Buff. With U.S. Army, 1957-59. Mem. The Am. Inst. Wine and Food, Am.-Swiss C. of C., Swiss-Am. Hist. Soc., Swiss Gourmet Soc. (pres. U.S. chpt.), Swiss Travel Club, Swiss Club Chgo., The Bagatelle Club, Conf. de la Chaine des Rotisseurs, Ordre des Canariers. Baptist. Avocation: visiting and reviewing world class french and swiss restaurants worldwide. Home: 701 Bluff Rd Lake Bluff IL 60044-2116 Office: Oberhallu Warehousing 86 Albrect Dr Lake Bluff IL 60044 Office Phone: 847-465-8200.

**OCKERBLOOM, RICHARD C.,** newspaper executive; b. Medford, Mass., Dec. 19, 1929; s. Carl F. and Helen C. (Haraden) O.; m. Anne Joan Torpey, Sept. 17, 1955; children: Catherine, Carl (dec.), Gail, Mark, John, Peter. BSBA, Northeastern U., 1952; D Pub. Svc. (hon.), Westfield State Coll., 1989; LLD (hon.), Northeastern U., 1995. With Boston Globe, 1948—; salesman, 1955-63, asst. nat. advt. mgr., 1963-70, nat. advt. mgr., 1970-72, asst. advt. dir., 1972-73, advt. dir., 1973-77, v.p. mktg. and sales, 1977-81, exec. v.p., 1981—, gen. mgr., chief operating officer, 1984-86, pres., chief operating officer, 1986-93, vice chmn., 1993-94; ret.; retired; chmn. bd. Met. Sunday Newspapers. Bd. dirs. Greater Boston Conv. and Visitors Bur., Winchester Hosp., United Way Mass. Bay; vice chmn. U.S. Army, 1952-54. Mem. Algonquin Club (pres.), Winchester Country Club, Phi Kappa Phi. Nat. Honor Soc. Home: 80 Arlington St Winchester MA 01890-3735

---

**OCKERMAN, HERBERT W.,** agricultural studies educator; b. Chaplin, Ky., Jan. 16, 1932; m. Frances Ockerman (dec.). BS with Distinction, U. Ky., 1954, MS, 1958; PhD, N.C. State U., 1962; postgrad., Air U., 1964-70, Ohio State U., 1974, postgrad., 1983, postgrad., 1987, postgrad., 2001, postgrad., 2003—05; PhD (hon.), Wyzial U., Poland, 2004. Asst. prof. Ohio State U., Columbus, 1961-66, assoc. prof., 1966-71, prof., 1971—. Former mem. Inst. Nutrition and Food Tech.; judge regional and state h. sci. fairs, 1965—, Ham Contest, Ky. State Fair, Sausage and Ham Contest, Ohio Meat Processing Groups; cons. Am. Meat Inst., 1977-88, USDA, 1977-2003, CRC Press., Inc., 1988—; bd. examiners U. Calcutta, 1987-88; examiner U. Mysore, India, 1990-97, U. We. Sydney, Australia, 2005, U. Newcastle, Australia, 2005; expert witness, various firms, 1992—; UN expert 95; expert cons. com. FAO/WHO, 2003; hon. mem. vet. med. faculty Assiut U., Egypt; adv. bd. Bull. Vet. Inst. Poland, 2004—; presenter, cons. in field. Contbr. more than 210 articles to profl. jours., more than 110 chpts. to books. Comdr. pilot USAF, 1955-58. Fisher Packing scholar; named Highest Individual in Beef Grading, Kansas City Meat Judging Contest, 1952, Hall of Disting. Alumni, U. Ky., 1995; recipient Am. Soc. Animal Sci. Meat Rsch. award Lilly Rsch. Labs., 1987, Appreciation cert. Ohio Assn. Meat Processors, 1987-2005, Profl. Devel. award Cahill Faculty, commendation Ohio Ho. of Reps., Merit Svc. badge Polish Govt., plaque Argentina Nat. Meat Bd., Animal Sci. award Roussel UCALF, France, U. Assiut, Egypt, Silver Platter award Nat. Meat Bd., Sec. Agr., Livestock and Fishery, Argentina, Svc. award Coun. Grad. Students, Pomerance Tchg. award, Outstanding Alumni award U. Ky., Outstanding Ednl. Achievements award Argentine Soc. Agr., Coop. award Vet. Faculty. U. Cordoba, Svc. award Panoma Legis. Br., Brazil; Vet. Faculty award U. Cordoba, Spain, 1982, 94, award Nat. Chung-Hsing U., 1982, 95, You Are The Best award INTA Sci., 1997, award Vet. Mus. Ciechanowcu, Poland, Internat. award Assn. Nat. Tech. en Alimentos de Mexico, Can. Inedst. Food Sci. and Tech., 1998, Appreciation plaque Republic of Argentina, 1999, Candle Stick of Knowledge award Ludhiana U., Punjab, India, 1999, Internat. award Am. Meat Sci. Assn., 1999, 2000, Appreciation plaque Am. Coll. Commerce, Taiwan, 1999, plaque Selcuk U., Turkey, 1999, Folklore and Cultural memento Sudanese Socs., Sudan U., 1999, Homage and Acknowledgment award Argentine Sec. Agr., 2000, Internat. award Am. Most. Sci. Assn., 2000, Most Honored Guest award Weifang, China, 2001, World History award Jhadong U., China, 2001, plaque Congress of Ham, Cordoba, Spain, 2001, Michal Oczapowski award Polish Acad. Sci., 2002, Sausage Maker award Poland, 2001, Great Educator award China, 2001, Silver Medallion award INTA Argentina, 2001, Pub. award Taiwan, 2002, Animal Sci. plaque, China, 2002, Food award China, 2002, Publ. award Dayeh U., Taiwan, 2003, Coop. award Cath. U., Argentina, 2004, Lifetime Achievement award PAU India, 2005 numerous others. Mem. NAS, NCR, ASTM, Am. Meat Sci. Assn., Am. Soc. Animal Sci. (Rsch. award 1987), Reciprocal Meat Conf., European Meeting of Meat Rsch. Workers, Polish Vet. Soc. (hon.), Inst. Food Technologists (nat. and OVS chpts.), Inst. Food Tech. (Internat. award 1998, 2000), Can. Meat Sci. Assn., Internat. Congress Meat Sci. and Tech., Rsch. in Basic Sci., Phi Beta Delta (Insts. 1987, pres. 1991, Internat. scholar award 1991, Internat. Faculty award 1991, Presdl. medallion award), Gamma Sigma Delta (Rsch. award 1977, Internat. award of merit 1988), Sigma Xi (outstanding advisor in coll. award 1995), Phi Beta Kappa (Outstanding Tchg. award 1997, Extension Diversity award 1997, Pomerene Tchg. Enhancement award 1997, Outstanding Internat. Faculty award 1997), Internat. Gamma Sigma Delta (Disting. Achievement Nat. award 1998), Phi Kappa Phi. Office: Ohio State U Meat Lab Animal Sci 2029 Fyffe Rd Columbus OH 43210-1007 Office Phone: 614-292-2201. Business E-Mail: ockerman.2@osu.edu.

**OCKEY, RONALD J.,** lawyer; b. Green River, Wyo., June 12, 1934; s. Theron G. and Ruby O. (Sackett) O.; m. Arline M. Hawkins, Nov. 27, 1957; children: Carolyn S. Ockey Baggett, Deborah K. Ockey Christiansen, David, Kathleen M. Ockey Hellewell, Valerie Ockey Sachs, Robert. BA, U. Utah, 1959, postgrad., 1959-60; JD with honors, George Washington U., 1966. Bar: Colo. 1967, Utah 1968, U.S. Dist. Ct. Colo. 1967, U.S. Dist. Ct. Utah 1968, U.S. Ct. Appeals (10th cir.) 1969, U.S. Ct. Claims 1987. Missionary to France for Mormon Ch., 1954-57; law clk. to judge U.S. Dist. Ct. Colo., 1966-67; assoc. ptnr., shareholder, v.p., treas., dir. Jones, Waldo, Holbrook & McDonough, Salt Lake City, 1967-91; pres. IntelliTrans Internat. Corp., 1992-94; mem. Utah Ho. of Reps., 1988-90, Utah State Senate, 1991-94; of counsel Mackey Price & Williams, Salt Lake City, 1995-98; asst. atty. gen. Utah, 1998—. Trustee SmartUtah, Inc., 1995-2002; trustee Utah Tech. Fin. Corp., 1995-98; lectr. in securities, pub. fin. and bankruptcy law. Mem. editl. bd. Utah Bar Jour., 1973-75; mem. staff and bd. editors George Washington Law Rev., 1964-66; contbr. articles to profl. jours. State govtl. affairs chair Utah Jaycees, 1969; del. state Rep. Convs., 1972-74, 76-78, 80-82, 84-86, 94-96, del. Salt Lake County Rep. Conv., 1978-80, 88-92; sec. Wright for Gov. campaign, 1980; legis. dist. chmn. Utah Rep. Party, 1983-87; trustee Food for Poland, 1981-85, pres., trustee Unity to Assist Humanity Alliance, 1992-95; bd. dirs. Utah Opera Co., 1991-94; trustee Utah Info. Tech. Assn., 1991-2000. Lt. U.S. Army, 1960-66, to capt. JAG, USAR, 1966-81. Mem. ABA, Utah State Bar Assn. (various coms.), Nat. Assn. Bond Lawyers (chmn. com. on state legislation 1982-85), George Washington U. Law Alumni Assn. (bd. dirs. 1981-85), Order of Coif, Phi Delta Phi. Home: 4502 Crest Oak Cir Salt Lake City UT 84124-3825 Office Phone: 801-366-0359. Business E-Mail: rockey@utah.gov.

**O'CONNELL, BRIAN,** public health service officer, educator, writer; b. Worcester, Mass., Jan. 23, 1930; s. Thomas J. and Mary (Carroll) O.; m. Ann C. Brown, July 11, 1953; children: Todd, Tracey, Matthew. BA, Tufts Coll., 1953; postgrad., Maxwell Sch. Citizenship and Pub. Adminstrn., 1953-54; also numerous hon. degrees. Field rep. Am. Heart Assn., Pa., 1954-56, Md. exec. dir., 1956—61, Calif. exec. dir., 1961—66; exec. dir. Nat. Assn. Mental Health, 1966-78, dir. emeritus, 1978—; pres. Nat. Council on Philanthropy, 1978-80; exec. dir. Coalition of Nat. Vol. Orgns., 1978-80; pres. Ind. Sector, 1980-95, founding pres., pres. emeritus, 1995—; adj. prof. vis. Tufts U., Medford, Mass., 1995—2006. Mem. U.S. Pres.'s Com. Employment of Handicapped, 1966-68; chmn. Liaison Group Mental Health, 1969-72. Author: Effective Leadership in Voluntary Organizations, 1976, Finding Values That Work: The Search for Fulfillment, 1977, America's Voluntary Spirit, A Book of Readings, 1983, The Board Members Book, 1985, Philanthropy in Action, 1987, Our Organization, 1987, Volunteers in Action, 1989, People Power: Service Advocacy, Empowerment, 1994, Board Overboard, 1995, Powered By Coalition: The Story of Independent Sector, 1997, Voices from the Heart: In Celebration of America's Volunteers, 1999, Civil Society: The Underpinnings of American Democracy, 1999, Fifty Years in Public Causes: Stories From a Road Less Traveled, 2005. Mem. Alumni Coun. Tufts U., 1970-80, trustee, 1988-2000, trustee emeritus, 2000—, chmn. pres. search com., 1992; trustee Points of Light Found., 1989-95; bd. dirs. Hogg Found., 1990-95; chmn. organizing com., 1st chmn. Civicus: World Alliance for Citizen Participation, 1992-96; bd. dirs. E.M. Kaufman Found., 1994—2003, The BridgeSpan Group, 1999—, The Cape Cod Found., 2003—. Recipient outstanding agy. prof. award United Way Am., 1979, Lincoln Filene Citizenship award, 1985, John W. Gardner Leadership award, 1994, Gold Key award Am. Soc. Assn. Execs., 1994, Chmns. award, NSFRE, 1994, The Tiffany award, 1998. Fellow Am. Pub. Health Assn., Nat. Acad. Pub. Adminstrn. (trustee 1993-2000), Nat. Com. Patients' Rights (chmn. 1975-77). Home: 50 Chase St Chatham MA 02633-2404

**O'CONNELL, BRIAN MICHAEL,** computer scientist, educator; b. Hartford, Conn., Nov. 2, 1960; s. Robert F. and Elizabeth S. O'Connell; m. Sarah E. Cox, Oct. 31, 2000. BA, Trinity Coll., Hartford, 1983; JD, U. Conn., 1987. Bar: Conn. 1988, U.S. Supreme Ct. 1992. Assoc. prof. ethics law, computing Ctrl. Conn. State U., New Britain, 1997—. Recipient Franklyn S. Haiman, Nat. Commn. Assn., 1999. Mem.: IEEE (pres. social implications tech. 2003, 2005), IEEE Computer Soc. (bd. govs. 2000—). Office: Central Conn State Univ 1615 Stanley St New Britain CT 06050 Office Phone: 860-832-2718. E-mail: oconnellb@ccsu.edu.

---

**O'CONNELL, CARMELA DIGRISTINA,** appraisal executive, consultant; b. Johnstown, Pa., Nov. 8, 1925; d. Salvatore and Josephine (Riggio) Digristina; m. Maurice F. O'Connell, Sept. 21, 1974 (dec. Feb. 1984); children: Geraldine, John, Bernard. Diploma, Eastern Secretarial Sch., N.Y.C., Sch. Interior Design. From typist to sec.-treas. Philip P. Masterson Co., N.Y.C., 1942-72; exec. v.p., bd. dirs. Masterson & O'Connell Inc., N.Y.C., 1972-80, cons., 1981—; founder, pres. N.Y. Appraisal Corp., N.Y.C., 1971-80; co-founder, pres. Park Ave. Appraisal, N.Y.C., 1981—. Mem. N.Y. Rep. Com., 1974—, Met. Opera Guild, N.Y.C., 1986; chmn. Ch. of Our Saviour, N.Y.C., 1986; mem. Ladies of Charity, Cath. Charities Archdiocese of N.Y., 1990; bd. dirs. 80 Park Avenue Condominiums, 1997—. Recipient Amita award for Bus. Woman of Yr., 1977, Lena Madesin Phillips award N.Y. League/Fortune 500 Bus. and Profl. Women, 1989. Mem. Nat. Fedn. Bus. and Profl. Women's Clubs Inc. (2d v.p. 1964, 1st v.p. 1966). Roman Catholic. Home: 2421 Old Collier Rd Land O Lakes FL 34639 Office Phone: 813-948-8941.

**O'CONNELL, DANIEL CRAIG,** psychologist, educator; b. Sand Springs, Okla., May 20, 1928; s. John Albert and Katherine (McGinnis) O'C. BA, St. Louis U., 1951, Ph.L., 1952, MA, 1953, S.T.L., 1960; PhD, U. Ill., 1963. Joined Soc. of Jesus, 1945; asst. prof. psychology St. Louis U., 1964-66, assoc. prof., 1966-72, prof., 1972-80, trustee, 1973-78, pres., 1974-78; prof. psychology Loyola U., Chgo., 1980-89, Georgetown U., Washington, 1990-98, emeritus, 1998—, chmn., 1991-96. Vis. prof. U. Melbourne, Australia, 1972, U. Kans., 1978-79, Georgetown U., 1986, Loyola U., Chgo., 1998-2003; Humboldt fellow Psychol. Inst. Free U. Berlin, 1968; sr. Fulbright lectr. Kassel U., W. Ger., 1979-80. Author: Critical Essays on Language Use and Psychology, 1988; contbr. articles to profl. jours. Recipient Nancy McNeir Ring award for outstanding teaching St. Louis U., 1969; NSF fellow, 1961, 63, 65, 68; Humboldt Found. grantee, 1973; Humboldt fellow Tech. U. of Berlin, 1987. Fellow: APA, Mo. Psychol. Assn.; mem.: AAAS, AAUP, Mo. Acad. Sci., N.Y. Acad. Sci., Psychonomic Soc., Eastern Psychol. Assn., Southwestern Psychol. Assn., Midwestern Psychol. Assn., Soc. Scientific Study of Religion, Psychologists Interested in Religious Issues, Phi Beta Kappa. Home: 4517 W Pine Blvd Saint Louis MO 63108-2109 Office Phone: 314-758-7143. Business E-Mail: doconnell@jesuits-mis.org. *Were it over, it would have been more than my expected share already. The challenge of learning to serve others has moved it along at a quick pace, and I am grateful that I have always received more than I've been able to give in return—from the Lord and from many good people.*

**O'CONNELL, DANIEL FRANCIS,** lawyer; b. Orange, NJ, May 5, 1943; BS with honors, Villanova U., 1965; JD, Rutgers U., 1968. Bar: NJ 1968, NY 1980, US Supreme Ct. 1980. Ptnr. Lanigan & O'Connell PC, Basking Ridge, NJ, 1969—85; ptnr. mng. ptnr. Shanley & Fisher PC, Morristown, NJ, 1985—99; ptnr., bus. fin. dept., ptnr.-in-charge Drinker Biddle & Reath LLP, Florham Pk., NJ, 1999—, mng. ptnr., mem. mgmt. com., 1999—. Dist. VII ethics com. Supreme Ct. NJ, 1978-83, sec., 1980-83; chmn. NJ Commn. Legal and Ethical Problems in the Delivery of Health Care, 1986-90. Mem. ABA (labor and employment law sect., antitrust law sect., health law sect. 1977—), NJ State Bar Assn. (labor law sect., health and hosp. law sect.), Somerset County Bar Assn. (exec. com. 1977-81, pres. 1979), Am. Health Lawyers Assn., Am. Hosp. Assn. Office: Drinker Biddle & Reath LLP 500 Campus Dr Florham Park NJ 07932-1047 Office Phone: 973-549-7160. Office Fax: 973-360-9831. Business E-Mail: daniel.oconnell@dbr.com.

**O'CONNELL, DANIEL JAMES,** lawyer; b. Evergreen Park, Ill., Aug. 14, 1954; s. Edmund J. and Kathryn J. (Hanna) O'C.; m. Nancy L. Eichler, March 21, 1992; children: Kelly Jacklyn, Kirby Kathryn. BS, Millikin U., 1976; JD, IIT, 1980; postgrad., DePaul U., 1981, U. Mich., 1997—2001, U. Ill., 1999— Bar: Ill. 1980, U.S. Dist. Ct. (no. dist.) Ill. 1980, U.S. Dist. Ct. (ctrl. dist.) Ill. 2000, U.S. Dist. Ct. Ariz. 1989. Ins. regulatory counsel Kemper Group, Long Grove, Ill., 1980-81, environ. claims counsel, 1981-82; sr. home office claim counsel Zurich Ins. Cos., Schaumburg, Ill., 1982-83; assoc. Clausen, Miller, Gorman et al, Chgo., 1983-86; ptnr. environ. toxic tort litigation O'Connell & Moroney, P.C., Chgo., 1986-90; ptnr. toxic tort litigation Burditt, Bowles & Radzius, Chgo., 1990-91; ptnr. Daniel J. O'Connell & Assocs., P.C., Elgin, Ill., 1991—2002, O'Connell & O'Sullivan, P.C., Elgin, Ill., 2002—03, Daniel J. O'Connell & Assocs., P.C., Elgin, Ill., 2003—. James S. Kemper Found. scholar, 1972—76. Mem.: ABA, APHA, AAAS, Ill. Bar Assn., Kane County Bar Assn., Def. Rsch. Inst., N.Y. Acad. Scis. Home: 177 Macintosh Ct Glen Ellyn IL 60137-6478 E-mail: doconn3@uic.edu.

**O'CONNELL, DAVID M.,** academic administrator, priest; b. Phila., Apr. 21, 1955; BPh magna cum laude, Niagara U., 1978; ThM, Mary Immaculate Seminary, 1981, DivM, 1983; PhD in Canon Law, Cath. U., 1987; Licentiate in Canon Law, Cath. U. Am., 1990. Ordained Cath. priest 1982. Religion tchr., dir. student activities Archbishop Wood H.S. for Boys, Warminster, Pa.; registrar, asst. acad. dean, asst. prof. philosophy, homiletics and canon law Mary Immaculate Seminary, Northampton, Pa., 1987—90; prof. theology St. John's U., Jamaica, NY, 1990—98, acad. dean, dean faculty Coll. Liberal Arts and Scis., 1991—98, assoc. v.p., 1996—98; interim acad. v.p. Niagara U., 1994—95; pres. Cath. U. Am., Washington, 1998—. Canonical cons. and ecclesiastical judge on the tribunals Diocese of Harrisburg, Pa., Diocese of Birmingham, Ala., Diocese of Scranton, Pa.; co-host, commentator during papal visit to U.S. CBS-TV, 1995; trustee Consortium Univs. Washington Met. Area. Contbr. articles to profl. jours. Trustee Cath. U. Am., St. John's U., Archbishop John Carroll H.S., Washington, Basilica of the Nat. Shrine of the Immaculate Conception; active Greater Washington Bd. Trade; mem. adv. bd. U. St.Thomas, St. Paul. Mem.: Assn. Cath. Colls. and Univs., La. Regional Canon Lawyers Assn., Canon Law Soc. Am. Office: Office Pres Cath Univ Am Nugent Hall 620 Michigan Ave NE Washington DC 20064 Office Phone: 202-319-5100. E-mail: cua-president@cua.edu.*

**O'CONNELL, EDWARD JAMES, JR.,** psychologist, educator, systems administrator, consultant; b. Sterling, Ill., Aug. 15, 1932; s. Edward James and Elizabeth E. (Clapham) O.; m. Pamelia Canon Floyd, Aug. 21, 1959; children— Edward James III, John Matthew BS in Psychology, Ill. Inst. Tech., 1958; MA in Psychology, Northwestern U., 1961, PhD in Psychology, 1962. NSF postdoctoral fellow Carnegie Inst. Tech., Pitts., 1962-63, asst. prof. psychology, 1963-65; psychology faculty Syracuse (N.Y.) U., NY, 1965-93, prof., 1975-93, prof. emeritus, 1993—. Cons. Rand Corp., Santa Monica, Calif., 1962-64, Abt Assocs., Boston, 1970-73, Marcy Psychiat. Hosp., N.Y., 1979-82 Served to cpl. U.S. Army, 1952-54 NSF predoctoral fellow, 1959-62; NSF postdoctoral fellow, 1962-63; Northwestern U. predoctoral fellow, 1958-59 Mem. Sigma Xi. Democrat. Avocations: billiards, computer programming. Address: PO Box 570 Cashiers NC 28717-0570 E-mail: ejoconn@dnet.net.

**O'CONNELL, HUGH MELLEN, JR.,** retired architect; b. Oak Park, Ill., Nov. 29, 1929; s. Hugh M. and Helen Mae (Evans) O'C.; m. Frances Ann Small, Apr. 13, 1957; children: Patricia Lynn, Susan Marie, Jeanette Maureen. Student mech. engring., Purdue U., 1948-50; BS in Archtl. Engring, U. Ill. 1953. Registered architect, Ariz., Calif., La., Nev., Nat. Council Archtl. Registration Bds. Designer John Mackel; structural engr. Los Angeles, 1955-57; architect Harnish & Morgan & Causey, Ontario, Calif., 1957-63; pvt. practice Ventura, Calif., 1963—69; architect Andrews/O'Connell, Ventura, 1970-78; dir. engring. div. Naval Constrn. Bn. Center, Port Hueneme, Calif., 1978-91, supervisory architect, 1991-93; ret., 1993. Mem. tech. adv. com. Ventura Calif., 1965-78; sec. Oxnard Citizens' Adv. Com., 1969-79, v.p., 1970-72, pres.; chmn. Oxnard Beautification Com., 1969, 74, Oxnard Cmty. Block Grant adv. com., 1975-76; mem. Oxnard Planning Commn., 1976-86, vice chmn., 1978-79, chmn., 1980-81. Mem. Oxnard Art-in-Pub. Places Commn., 1988-93, 2003—. Served with AUS, 1953-55. Mem. AIA (emeritus, pres. Ventura chpt. 1973), Am. Concrete Inst., Soc. Am. Registered Architects (Design award, bldg. cat. dir. 1970), Am. Legion, Soc. for Preservation and Encouragement of Barbershop Quartet Singing in Am. (chpt. pres. 1979, chpt. sec. 1980-83), Acad. Model Aeros. (#9190 1948—), Channel Islands Condors Club (treas. 1986-99), Sports Flyers Assn., Alpha Rho Chi (Anthemios chpt.). Presbyterian (elder 1963, deacon 1967). Lodges: Kiwanis (pres. 1969, div. sec. 1974-75), Elks. Home and Office: 520 Ivywood Dr Oxnard CA 93030-3527 Personal E-mail: hughoarch@msn.com.

**O'CONNELL, JACK,** school system administrator; b. Glen Cove, N.Y., Oct. 8, 1951; m. Doree O'Connell; 1 child, Jennifer Lynn. Student, Ventura Coll.; BA, Calif. State U., Fullerton; cert. secondary tchr., Calif. State U., Long Beach, 1975. Tchr. various high schs.; mem. Calif. State Assembly, 1982—94, Calif. State Senate, 1994—2002; state supt. pub. instrn. State of Calif., 2002—. Mem. Santa Barbara County Sch. Bd. Democrat. Office: Calif Dept Edn Ste 5602 1430 N St Sacramento CA 95814 Office Phone: 916-319-0800.

**O'CONNELL, JAMES F.,** anthropologist, educator; PhD in Anthropology, U. Calif., Berkeley, 1971. Rsch. fellow prehistory Australian Nat. U., 1973—78; faculty to prof. dept. anthropology U. Utah, Salt Lake City, 1978—. Chair dept. anthropology U. Utah, dir. Archaeol. Ctr. Contbr. articles to profl. jours., chapters to books. Fellow: NAS. Office: Dept Anthropology U Utah 270 S 1400 East Salt Lake City UT 84112-0060 E-mail: james.oconnell@anthro.utah.edu.*

**O'CONNELL, JAMES SHERIDAN,** physicist, researcher; b. Chgo., Jan. 15, 1932; BS, Beloit (Wis.) Coll., 1953; MS, U. Ill., 1955, PhD, 1961. Rsch. physicist Nat. Bur. Stds., Gaithersburg, Md., 1963-89; cons. Booz, Allen & Hamilton, Crystal City, Va., 1989-94; adj. prof. Frederick (Md.) C.C., 1994—; editor Am. Inst. Rsch., Washington, 1995—. Recipient Bronze medal Nat. Bur. Stds., 1988. Fellow Am. Phys. Soc. Home: 10716 Seneca Spring Way Montgomery Village MD 20886-3927

**O'CONNELL, JEANNE,** financial planner, insurance broker; b. Stoneham, Mass., Dec. 9, 1951; d. Kenneth Edward and Frances Evelyn (Matulewicz) O'C; 1 child, Ryan Sulloway. Student, U. Oreg., 1971-72; BFA cum laude, U. Mass.-Amherst, 1974, U. Calif.-Sacramento, summer 1973; postgrad., Northeastern U., 1975; MBA, Suffolk U., 1984. CPCU, CLU; chartered fin. cons.; assoc. in underwriting; enrolled agt. designation. Ins. clk. S.B. Swaim & Co., Boston, 1969-72, Hollis Perrin & Co., Boston, 1972; underwriting asst. Pub. Svc. Mut. Ins. Co., Newton, Mass., 1974-77; personal lines analyst Comml. Union Ins. Co., Boston, 1977-80, sr. personal lines analyst, 1980-83, tech. specialist, 1983-88; pvt. practice fin. cons., brokerage Boston, 1988—. Instr. ins. and fin. planning Ins. Libr. Boston, 1988—; speaker in field; ind. tax preparer; pub. arbitrator NASD, BBB, AMEX; founder, dir. Red Dragon Arts Coop., Boston, 1983; potter, artist Radcliffe Pottery Studio, Boston, 1980-85. Mem. exec. student adv. bd. Suffolk U., 1982—83, student liaison mem. between Exec. MBA Program and regular MBA Program and dean's adv. bd., coord. Exec. MBA Program Policy Seminar Weekend, 1983; v.p., trustee Friends Waltham Pub. Libr., 1998, 1999, asst. treas., 2000, 2000—; Fellow Nat. Tax Practice Inst.; mem. Internat. Assn. Fin. Planners, Nat. Soc. Enrolled Agts., Nat. Soc. Accts., Nat. Assn. Tax Preparers, Waltham Garden Club (photographer 1997—), Delta Mu Delta. Avocations: reading books on tape, photography, rubber stamps, gardening. Studio: 229 School St Waltham MA 02451-4546 Office Phone: 781-891-1721. Personal E-mail: reddragonart@yahoo.com.

**O'CONNELL, JEFFREY,** law educator; b. Worcester, Mass., Sept. 28, 1928; s. Thomas Joseph and Mary (Carroll) O'C.; m. Virginia Kearns, Nov. 26, 1960 (dec. 1994); children: Mara, Devin. Grad. cum laude, Phillips Exeter Acad., 1947; AB cum laude, Dartmouth Coll., 1951; JD, Harvard U., 1954. Bar: Mass. 1954, Conn. 1954, Va. 1983, hon. admittance to Ark. and Minn. bar. Instr. speech Tufts U., 1953-54; assoc. Sherburne, Powers & Needham, 1954-57, Hale & Dorr, Boston, 1958-59; asst. prof., then assoc. prof. law U. Iowa Coll. Law, 1959-62; assoc. dir. automobile claims study Harvard Law Sch., 1963-64; assoc. prof. law U. Ill. Coll. Law., 1964-65, prof., 1965-79; prof. law U. Va. Law Sch., 1980-83, John Allan Love prof., 1983-90, Samuel H. McCoy II prof., 1990—, Class of 1948 rsch. prof., 1994-97. Summer vis. prof. Northwestern U., 1963, U. Mich., 1966, 75, So. Meth. U., 1972, U. Tex., 1977, U. Wash., 1979; John Marshall Harlan vis. prof. N.Y. Law Sch., 1991; vis. fellow Centre for Socio-Legal Studies, Wolfson Coll., Oxford (Eng.) U., 1973, 79; Thomas Jefferson vis. fellow Downing Coll. Cambridge U., Eng., 1989; mem. U. Va. Ctr. for Advanced Study, 1980-83. Author: (with R.E. Keeton) Basic Protection for the Traffic Victim, 1965, After Cars Crash: The Need for Legal and Insurance Reform, 1967, (with Arthur Myers) Safety Last: An Indictment of the Auto Industry, 1966, (with R.E. Keeton, John McCord) Crisis in Car Insurance, 1968, (with Wallace Wilson) Car Insurance and Consumer Desires, 1969, The Injury Industry, 1971, (with Rita James Simon) Payment for Pain and Suffering, 1972, Ending Insult to Injury: No-Fault Insurance for Products and Services, 1975, (with Roger Henderson) Tort Law, No-Fault and Beyond, 1975, The Lawsuit Lottery: Only the Lawyers Win, 1979, (with C. Brian Kelly) The Blame Game: Injuries, Insurance and Injustice, 1986, (with Lester Brickman and Michael Horowitz) Rethinking Contingency Fees: A Proposal to Align the Contingency Fee System with its Policy Roots and Ethical Mandates, 1994, (with Peter Bell) Accidental Justice: The Dilemmas of Tort Law, 1997 Mem. Nat. Hwy. Safety Adv. Com., 1967-70; ednl. adv. bd. John Simon Guggenheim Found., 1973-87; bd. dirs. Consumers Union, 1970-76; mem. com. on competitive safeguards and med. aspects of sports NCAA, 1985-87. Served as 1st lt. USAF, 1954-57. Recipient Robert B. McKay award for ins. scholarship Tort and Ins. Practice sect. ABA, 1992; Guggenheim fellow, 1972-73, 79-80. Mem. ABA, Va. Bar Assn., Casque and Gauntlet, Farmington Country Club, Phi Beta Kappa, Psi Upsilon. Democrat. Roman Catholic. Home: 505 Oak Cir Charlottesville VA 22901-3220 Office: U Va Sch Law 580 Massie Rd Charlottesville VA 22903-1738 Office Phone: 434-924-7809. Business E-Mail: jo@virginia.edu.

**O'CONNELL, JOHN BERNARD, JR.,** medical educator, department chairman; b. Chgo., July 27, 1949; s. John B. O'C; m. Mary Owens, Jan. 12, 1980; children: Jessica, Moira, Claire, Sheila, John. BS, U. Ill., Chgo., 1971; MD magna cum laude, Loyola U., Maywood, Ill., 1974 Diplomat Nat. Bd. Med. Examiners Am. Bd. Internal Medicine, Am. Bd. Cardiovascular Disease. Intern Loyola U. Med. Ctr., Maywood 1975-76, resident in internal medicine, 1976-78, chief resident in internal medicine, 1977-78, fellow in cardiology, 1978-80, staff physician emergency dept., 1979-81, attending cardiologist, 1980-86, med. dir. Cardiac Transplantation Program, 1984-86; clin. instr. in medicine Loyola U. Stritch Sch. Medicine, Maywood, 1977-80, asst. prof. medicine, 1980-85, assoc. prof. medicine, 1985-86; asst. chief med. svc. Hines VA Hosp., Maywood, 1981-83; attending cardiologist LDS Hosp., Salt Lake City, 1986-91, U. Utah Med. Ctr., Salt Lake City, 1986-91; assoc. prof. medicine Sch. Medicine, U. Utah, Salt Lake City, 1986-91, 1991; attending physician Univ. Hosp., U. Miss. Med. Ctr., Jackson, 1991—97; prof. medicine U. Miss. Med. Sch., Jackson, 1991—97, chmn. dept. medicine, 1991—97, prof., chair dept. internal medicine Wayne State U., Detroit, 1997—. Cons. Salt Lake VA Med. Ctr., Salt Lake City, 1988-91, Primary Children's Med. Ctr., Salt Lake City, 1988-91; med. dir., chmn. exec. com. UTAH Cardiac Transplant Program, Salt Lake City, 1988-91; chmn. adv. bd. Exptl. Organ Transplantation Procedures, apptd. by Gov. of Ill., 1985-86; mem. working group on myocarditis Nat. Heart, Lung and Blood Inst., 1985; com. mem. Internat. Symposium Inflammatory Heart Disease, Snowmass, Colo., July, 1988; mem. sci. coun. Internat. Soc. and Fedn. Cardiology, 1990—; mem. spl. study sect. NIH, 1990; mem. sci. bd. Internat. Congress of Cardiology on Cardiovascular Pharmacotherapy and Cardiomyopathies, Greece, 1990; mem. adv. com. Miss. Health Scis. Info. Network, 1992-94; med. dir. Miss. Organ Procurement Agy., 1994—; mem. sci. com. Internat. Workshop on the Cardiomyopathies, LaCoruna, Spain, 1993. Co-editor (monographs): Myocarditis: Precursor of Cardiomyopathy, 1983, Drug Therapy of Dilated Cardiomyopathy and Myocarditis, 1988, Intrathoracic Transplantation 2000, 1993; mem. editorial bd. Jour. Heart and Lung Transplantation, 1986—, Internat. Jour. Cardiology, 1992—, Transplantation, 1993—; manuscript cons. numerous publs.; contbr. articles to profl. jours. Recipient Norris L. Brookens Outstanding Resident award Ill. Soc. Internal Medicine, 1978, Robert Kark, M.D. Rsch. award Chgo. Soc. Internal Medicine, 1981, Outstanding Young Citizen award Chgo. Jr. Assocs. Commerce and Industry, 1985, Shinshu U. medal Matsumoto City, Nagano, Japan,

1992; grantee Earl M. Bane Charitable Trust, 1979-83, Fraternal Order Eagles, 1983-86, BRSG, 1983-84, NHLBI, 1986-91, Deseret Found., 1987-91, Bristol Myers Squibb, 1988-91, Burroughs Wellcome, 1992—, Otsuka Pharm., 1993—, Smith Kline Beecham Pharm., 1993—. Fellow ACP, Am. Coll. Chest Physicians, Am. Coll. Cardiology (cardiac transplantation com. 1991—, conf. steering com. 1991-92), Am. Coll. Angiology; mem. AMA, AAAS, Assn. of Profs. of Medicine (bd. dirs. 1997—, treas. 1998-2001, pres.-elect 2001-02, pres. 2002-03), Am. Soc. Transplant Physicians (mem. tng. and manpower com. 1990—, mem. pub. policy com. 1993—, numerous others), N.Y. Acad. Scis., Internat. Soc. Heart and Lung Transplant (mem. sci. program com. 1987, 89, 90, councilor 1989-91, pres.-elect 1991-92, pres. 1993-94, past pres. 1993-94, others), Transplantation Soc., Assn. Profs. Medicine, Rsch., Miss. (bd. dirs.), Jackson Acad. Medicine, So. Soc. Clin. Investigation, Am. Fedn. Clin. Rsch. (sen. midwest sect. 1983-86), So. Soc. Clin. Rsch., Ctrl. Soc. Clin. Rsch., Miss. State Med. Assn., Ctrl. Med. Soc., Am. Heart Assn. (bd. dirs. West Cook County 1982-86, v.p. 1985-86, chmn. 1990-92, numerous others), United Network for Organ Sharing (mem. coalition on organ doning 1991-92, mem. thoracic com. 1992—, mem. sci. adv. com. 1993—), Alpha Omega Alpha. Office: Wayne State Univ UHC-2E 4201 Saint Antoine Detroit MI 48201 Home: 6150 Franklin Rd Bloomfield MI 48301-1556 Office Phone: 313-745-8244. Business E-Mail: joconell@med.wayne.edu.

**O'CONNELL, KEVIN,** lawyer; b. Boston, Sept. 4, 1933; s. Michael Frederick and Kathryn Agnes (Kelley) O'Connell; m. Mary Adams, July 14, 1990; children: Tiffany W., Elizabeth H., Dana A., Lisel E. AB, Harvard, 1955, JD, 1960. Bar: Calif. 1961. Assoc. firm O'Melveny & Myers, LA, 1960-63; asst. U.S. atty. criminal div. Ctrl. Dist. Calif., LA, 1963-65; staff counsel Gov. Calif. Commn to Investigate Watts Riot, LA, 1965-66; ptnr. Tuttle & Taylor, LA, 1966-70, Coleman & O'Connell, LA, 1971-75; pvt. practice law LA, 1975-78; of counsel firm Simon & Sheridan, LA, 1978-89; ptnr. Manatt, Phelps & Phillips, LA, 1989—. Adj. prof. law U. So. Calif. Law Sch., 2002—. Bd. editors Harvard Law Rev., 1958—60. Bd. dirs. Calif. Supreme Ct. Hist. Soc.; mem. Los Angeles County Dem. Ctrl. Com., Calif., 1973—74. Lt. USMCR, 1955—57. Recipient Best Lawyers in Am. Mem.: Am. Law Inst. Home: 426 N Mccadden Pl Los Angeles CA 90004-1026 Office: Manatt Phelps & Phillips Trident Ctr E Tower 11355 W Olympic Blvd Los Angeles CA 90064-1614 Office Phone: 310-312-4222. Business E-Mail: koconell@manatt.com.

**O'CONNELL, MARY-KATHLEEN,** lawyer; BA cum laude, Yale Univ. 1977; JD, NYU, 1981. Bar: Mass. 1981. With Goodwin Procter LLP, Boston, 1981—, ptnr., chair, trusts & estate planning practice, mem., investment com. Staff NYU Law Rev. Mem.: ABA, Estate Planning Coun., Women's Bar Assn., Mass Bar Assn., Boston Bar Assn. Office: Goodwin Procter LLP Exchange Pl 53 State St Boston MA 02109 Office Phone: 617-570-1391. Office Fax: 617-523-1231. Business E-Mail: moconnell@goodwinprocter.com.

**O'CONNELL, MAUREEN C.,** county official, former state legislator; m. Donald O'Connell; 1 child, Donald. BS in Health Care Adminstrn., St. Josephs Coll.; JD, St. John's U.; RN, Flushing Hosp. Med. Ctr. Mem. NY State Assembly, Dist. 17, 1998—2006; clk. Nassau Co., NY, 2006—. Mem. adv. bd. Nassau Cmty. Coll., Molloy Coll. Sch. of Nuring. Recipient Am. Jurisprudence award. Mem.: Oncology Nursing Soc., Nassau Co. Bar Assn., Am. Cancer Soc. Republican. Office: Nassau County Clk 1 West St Mineola NY 11501*

**O'CONNELL, MAURICE DANIEL,** lawyer; b. Ticonderoga, N.Y., Nov. 9, 1929; s. Maurice Daniel and Leila (Geraghty) O'C.; m. Joan MacLure Landers, Aug. 2, 1952; children: Mark M., David L., Ann M., Leila K., Ellen A. Grad., Phillips Exeter Acad., 1946; AB, Williams Coll., 1950; LLB, Cornell U., 1956. Bar: Ohio 1956. Since practiced in, Toledo; assoc. Williams, Eversman & Black, 1956-60; ptnr. Robison, Curphey & O'Connell, 1961-95, of counsel, 1996—; spl. hearing officer in conscientious objector cases U.S. Dept. Justice, 1966-68. Mem. complaint rev. bd. Bd. Commrs. on Grievance and Discipline of Supreme Ct. Ohio, 1987. Mem. Ottawa Hills Bd. Edn., 1963-66, pres., 1967-69; former trustee Toledo Soc. for Handicapped; past trustee Woodlawn Cemetery; past trustee Toledo Hearing and Speech Center, Easter Seal Soc.; mem. alumni council Phillips Exeter Acad. Served to 1st lt. USMCR, 1950-53. Fellow Ohio State Bar Found.; mem. NW Ohio Alumni Assn. of Williams Coll. (past pres.), Ohio Bar Assn., Toledo Bar Assn. (chmn. grievance com. 1971-74), Kappa Alpha, Phi Delta Phi. Clubs: Toledo. Home: 3922 W Bancroft St Toledo OH 43606-2533 Office: 9th Flr Four SeaGate Toledo OH 43604

**O'CONNELL, MIKE,** former professional sports team executive; b. Chgo., Nov. 25, 1955; m. Rosemary O'Connell; children: Kristen, Matthew, Gregory. Hockey player Ontario Hockey League, Canada, Chgo. Blackhawks, 1975—80, Boston Bruins, 1980—86, Detroit Red Wings, 1986—90; head coach San Diego Gulls, 1990—91, Providence Bruins, 1992—94; asst. gen. mgr. Boston Bruins, 1994—2000, v.p., 1998—2006, gen. mgr., 2000—06. Named to All Star Game, 1984; recipient Seventh Player award, WSBK-TV, 1984.

**O'CONNELL, PHILIP RAYMOND,** retired lawyer, paper company executive; b. N.Y.C., June 2, 1928; s. Michael Joseph and Ann (Blaney) O'C.; m. Joyce McCabe, July 6, 1957; children: Michael, Kathleen, Jennifer, David. AB, Manhattan Coll., 1949; JD, Columbia U., 1956; grad., Advanced Mgmt. Program, Harvard U., 1967. Bar: N.Y. 1956, U.S. Supreme Ct. 1961, Conn. 1988. Assoc. Dewey, Ballantine, Bushby, Palmer & Wood, N.Y.C., 1956-61, 62-64; gen. counsel, sec. Laurentide Finance Corp., San Francisco, 1961-62; gen. counsel Wallace-Murray Corp., 1964-66, div. mgr., 1966-70; prgm. chief exec. officer, dir. Universal Paperetch Corp., Hatfield, Pa., 1970-71; sec. Champion Internat. Corp., Stamford, Conn., 1972-90, v.p., 1979-81, sr. v.p., 1981-90. Mem. legal adv. com. N.Y. Stock Exch., 1985-88, corp. governance subcom., legal adv. com., 1985-94; chmn. lawyers steering com. corp. governance task force The Bus. Roundtable, 1981-87, mem., 1981-94. Mem. Champion Internat. Found., 1979-90; mem. bd. visitors Fairfield Univ. Sch. Bus., 1981-93, chmn., 1983-93; bd. dirs. Kearney-Nat. Corp., 1975-78. With USNR, 1951-54. Mem. Am. Soc. Corp. Secs. (hon.), chmn. 1988-89).

**O'CONNELL, RALPH ANTHONY,** dean, psychiatrist, educator; b. N.Y.C., Jan. 26, 1938; s. Ralph E. and Agnes H. O'Connell) O'C.; m. Jane Burke, June 15, 1963; children: Ralph E. III, Ellen C., John B. AB cum laude, Coll. of Holy Cross, Worcester, Mass., 1959; MD, Cornell U., 1963. Diplomate Am. Bd. Psychiatry and Neurology. Intern St. Vincent's Hosp. and Med. Ctr. N.Y., N.Y.C., 1963-64; resident, 1964, 67-69; rsch. psychiatrist, 1969-71; chief inpatient dept. psychiatry, 1971-76, clin. dir. and vice chmn. psychiatry, 1974-95; prof. psychiatry N.Y. Med. Coll., Valhalla, 1984—, dean and provost, 1996—. Editor-in-chief Comprehensive Psychiatry, 1983-96. Served to capt. U.S. Army, 1965-66. Fellow Am. Psychiat. Assn., N.Y. Acad. Medicine (trustee 1989—). Clubs: Univ. (N.Y.C.) Roman Catholic. Office: NY Med Coll Valhalla NY 10595 Office Phone: 914-594-4900.

**O'CONNELL, RICHARD (JAMES),** English literature educator, poet; b. NYC, Oct. 25, 1928; s. Richard James and Mary Ellen (Fallon) O'C.; BS, Temple U., 1956; MA, Johns Hopkins, 1957. Instr. English Temple U., Phila., 1957-61, asst. prof., 1961-69, assoc. prof., 1969-86; sr. assoc. prof., 1986-93, assoc. prof. emeritus, 1993; guest lectr. poetry dept. writing seminars Johns Hopkins U., 1961-74; participant Poetry in Schs. Program, Pa. Council Arts, 1971-73; Fulbright lectr. Am. lit. U. Brazil, Rio de Janeiro, 1960, U. Navarre, Pamplona, Spain, 1962-63. Served with USN, 1948-52. Recipient prize Contemporary Poetry Press, 1972. Mem. PEN, MLA, Assoc. Writing Programs, Walt Whitman Poetry Center (dir. 1975-84), Lit. Fellowship Phila. Author: From an Interior Silence, 1961, Cries of Flesh and Stone, 1962, New Poems and Translations, 1963; Brazilian Happenings, 1966, Terrane, 1967, Thirty Epigrams, 1971, Irish Monastic Poems (transl.), 1975, The Word in Time (selected transl. of Antonio Machado), 1975, Sappho (selected transl.),

1975, Lorca (selected transl.), 1976, Middle English Poems (transl.), 1976, More Irish Poems (transl.), 1976, Epigrams from Martial (transl.), 1976, One Hundred Epigrams from the Greek Anthology (trans.), 1977, Hudson's Fourth Voyage, 1978, The Epigrams of Luxorius (transl.), 1984, Temple Poems, 1985, Hanging Tough, 1986, Battle Poems, 1987, Selected Epigrams, 1990, Lives of The Poets, 1990, New Epigrams From Martial (transl.), 1991, The Caliban Poems, 1992, RetroWorlds, 1993 (translation) Simulations, 1993, Voyages, 1995, The Bright Tower, 1997American Obits, 2001, Fractals, 2002, Dawn Crossing, 2003; editor: Apollo's Day, 17th Century Songs, 1969; Atlantis Edits., 1962—, Poetry Newsletter, 1971-86. Home: 1147 Hillsboro Mile Apt 510 Hillsboro Beach FL 33062-1720 E-mail: rdzon@comcast.net.

**O'CONNELL, ROBERT FRANCIS,** physics professor; b. Athlone, Ireland, Apr. 22, 1933; came to U.S., 1958; s. William and Catherine (O'Reilly) O'C.; m. Josephine Molly Buckley, Aug. 3, 1963; children: Adrienne Molly, Fiona Catherine, Eimear Kathleen. BSc, Nat. U. Ireland, Galway, 1953, DSc, 1975; PhD, U. Notre Dame, 1962. Telecommunications engr. Dept. Posts and Telegraphs, Dublin, Ireland, 1954-58; scholar Inst. Advanced Studies, Dublin, 1962-63; systems analyst IBM, Dublin, 1963-64; sr. rsch. assoc. Inst. Space Studies, N.Y.C., 1966-68; asst. prof. physics La. State U., Baton Rouge, 1964-66, assoc. prof., 1966-69, prof., 1969-86, Boyd prof., 1986—. Editor for theoretical physics Hadronic Jour.; former bd. mem. Phys. Rev. A; contbr. articles to profl. jours. Named Disting. Rsch. Master, La. State U., 1975; NAS-NRC fellow, 1966-68, Sci. Rsch. Coun. (Eng.) sr. vis. fellow, 1976. Fellow Am. Phys. Soc.; mem. Am. Astron. Soc., Internat. Astronomy Union, Internat. Soc. Gen. Relativity and Gravitation. Republican. Roman Catholic. Avocation: tennis. Home: 522 Bancroft Way Baton Rouge LA 70808-480/ Office: La State Univ Dept Physics And Astronomy Baton Rouge LA 70803-0001

**O'CONNELL, THERESA AURORA,** title company executive; d. Marie G. Aurora; m. Robert G. O'Connell, Sept. 5, 1982; children: Lillian H., Abigail A., James K. BA in Polit. Sci., Upsala Coll., East Orange, NJ, 1980; JD, Seton Hall U., Newark, NJ, 1983. Cert.: NJ (atty. at law) 1984. Practicing atty., Montclair, NJ, 1995—2002; mgr. Resort Title Agy., Inc., Bluegreen Corp., Boca Raton, Fla., 2004—. Councilor at large Twp. of Montclair, NJ, 2000—02. Vice chair Planning & Zoning Bd., Coral Springs, Fla., 2003; mem. Zoning Bd., Montclair, NJ, 1998—2002; chairperson, funding subcommmittee, early childhood coun. Appointee of Montclair Bd. of Edn., Montclair, NJ, 1993—94. Named one of Women You Should Know in 2001, YWCA of Montclair North Essex, 2001; recipient Outstanding Svc. award, Clin. Program, Seton Hall Sch. Law, 1983, Partners in Performance Achievement award, Bluegreen Leadership Inst., 2005, Legendary Leadership 2005: Discover Your Toolbox Cert. of Graduation, 2005, Situational Leadership II Achievement award, Ken Blanchard Companies, 2006. Mem.: NJ. Assn. Women Bus. Owners, Essex Chpt. (v.p. 1996—97, Teal Heart Svc. award 1997—98), NJ. Assn. Women Bus. Owners (nom. Bus. Women of Yr., Essex County Chpt. 1998), NJ. League Municipalities. Office: Resort Title Agency Inc 4950 Communication Ave Ste 900 Boca Raton FL 33431 Office Phone: 561-443-8504. Office Fax: 561-443-8727. Business E-Mail: theresa.o'connell@bluegreencorp.com.

**O'CONNELL, VIRGINIA ADAMS,** science educator; m. Stephen Austin O'Connell. PhD, U. Pa., Phila. Asst. prof. Swarthmore (Pa.) Coll., 2001—. Office: Swarthmore College 500 College Avenue Swarthmore PA 19081 Office Phone: 610-328-8109.

**O'CONNELL, SISTER VIRGINIA M.,** school librarian; b. Boston, Apr. 26, 1930; d. Joseph and Katherine Walsh O'Connell. AB, Boston Coll., 1962; postgrad., Framingham State U.Tchr., libr. Marian High Sch., Framingham, Mass., 1969—84; tchr., bus mgr. Newton Cath. High Sch., 1984—88; pastoral assoc. St. Rose Parish, Chelsea, 1988—92; libr. Matignon High Sch., Cambridge, 1993—. Mem. adv. bd. Boston Coll. Advancement Studies, Chestnut Hill, 1993—; mem. adv. group Marian High Sch., 1994—96. Named Woman of Excellence, Mt. St. Joseph Acad., 1999. Mem.: LWV, Sisters St. Joseph Chorus, Mt. St. Joseph Acad. Roman Catholic. Avocations: travel, walking, reading. Home: 106 Waban St Newton MA 02458 Personal E-mail: oconnell2001@hotmail.com.

**O'CONNELL, WILLIAM EDWARD, JR.,** retired finance educator; b. NYC, Sept. 16, 1937; s. William Edward and Helen Margaret (Brazel) O'Connell; m. Janet Elinor Shields, Aug. 15, 1965; children: William Edward III, Cathleen Anne. AB, Manhattan Coll., Riverdale, N.Y., 1959; MBA, Columbia U., N.Y.C., 1961; DBA with honors, Ind. U., Bloomington, 1967; JD, Coll. William and Mary, Williamsburg, Va., 1974. Fin. analyst Pfizer, Inc., N.Y.C., 1962-64; asst. prof. U. Conn., Storrs, 1967-69; Morris prof. banking U. Va., Charlottesville, 1988; Chessie prof. bus. Coll. William and Mary, Williamsburg, Va., 1969—2005. Mem. faculty Va. Bankers Sch., Charlottesville, 1975—99, Stonier Grad. Sch. Banking, Newark, 1977—91, Bank Adminstrn. Inst., Madison, Wis., 1978—97; bd. dirs. C. & F Fin. Corp., Citizens & Farmers Bank. Author: Asset & Liability Management, 1979, Advanced Financial Planning, 1984, Financial Planning for Credit Unions, 1989, Strategic Financial Managment for Commercial Banks, 1993. Mem.: Fin. Mgmt. Assn., Am. Fin. Assn., Fords Colony Country Club, Omicron Delta Epsilon, Beta Gamma Sigma. Roman Catholic. Home: 102 Overlook Dr Williamsburg VA 23185-4434 Office: Coll William & Mary Sch Bus Williamsburg VA 23187-8795 Office Phone: 757-221-2893. Business E-Mail: william.oconnell@mason.wm.edu.

**O'CONNELL, WILLIAM EGAN,** English professor; b. Englewood, NJ, Oct. 20, 1957; s. John James and Carmel O'Connell; m. Elizabeth Allen, Sept. 25, 1998; children: Erin Madeline Kramer. John James V MA in Liberal Studies Wesleyan U, Middletown, Conn., 1989. English tchr. Stamford Cath. HS, Conn., 1982—90; English prof. Norwalk CC, Conn., 1992—. English chair Norwalk CC, Conn., 1998—2004. Recipient Merit award, Norwalk CC, 1998, 2001, Ednl. Excellence and Disting. Svc. award, Bd. Trustees of Conn. Cmty./Tech. Colls., 2003, Tchng. Excellence award, Nat. Inst. Staff Orgnl. Develop., U. Tex. Austin, 2006; fellow, NEH, 1991, 1999. Mem.: Assn. Lit. Scholars and Critics. Democrat. Roman Catholic. Home: 17 Valley Field S Sandy Hook CT 06482 Office: Norwalk Cmty Coll 188 Richards Ave Norwalk CT 06584 Office Phone: 203-857-7368. Personal E-mail: jocfift@yahoo.com. Business E-Mail: woconnell@ncc.commnet.edu.

**O'CONNELL, WILLIAM RAYMOND, JR.,** educational consultant, retired academic administrator; b. Richmond, Va., Jan. 4, 1933; s. William Raymond and Mary Helen (Wenenger) O'C.; m. Peggy Annette Tucker, June 29, 1957; 1 child, William Raymond III. B of Music Edn., Richmond Profl. Inst., 1955; MA, Columbia U., 1962, EdD, 1969; HLD (hon.), New Eng. Coll., 1995. Asst. to provost Richmond Profl. Inst., Va., 1955-57, dean of men, 1957-59, dean of students, dean of men, 1959-61; asst. to provost, dir. student info. ctr. Tchrs. Coll. Columbia U., NYC, 1962-65, rsch. assoc. inst. of higher edn. Tchrs. Coll., 1965-66; rsch. assoc. So. Regional Edn. Bd., Atlanta, 1966-69, dir. spl. programs, 1969-73, project dir., undergrad. edn. reform, 1973-79; dir. curriculum and faculty devel. Assn. Am. Colls., Washington, 1979-80, v.p. for programs, 1980-82, v.p., 1982-85; pres. New Eng. Coll., Henniker, NH, 1985-95, pres. emeritus, 1995—; vis. sr. fellow Assn. Am. Colls. and Univs., 1995—97; dir. health edn. and leadership program Nat. Assn. Student Pers. Adminstrs., 1996—2002, 2003—05. Cons. Coun. for Advancement Small Colls., 1975; adv. com. project on instnl. renewal through improvement of tchg. Soc. for Values in Higher Edn., 1975-78; evaluator NH Postsecondary Edn. Commrs., 1973-95, vice chmn., 1990-92, chmn., 1992-94; evaluator Nat. Ctr. for Rsch. to Improve Postsecondary Tchg. and Learning, 1987-90, New Eng. Assn. Schs. and Colls., 1988, 91; higher edn. rev. panel awards for pioneering achievements in higher edn. Charles A. Dana Found., 1988, 89. Author, editor: articles to profl. publs. Pres. Richmond Cmty. Amb. Project, 1958-60, bd. dirs., 1960-61; bd. dirs. Alumni Assn. Acad. divsn. Va. Commonwealth U., 1970-73; chmn. fundraising com. Atlanta Boys Choir, Inc., 1976-77, trustee 1978-79; trustee Atlanta Coun. for Internat. Visitors, 1973-76, 78-79; pres. UN Assn., Atlanta, 1976-77; steering com. Nat. Coun. chpt., divsn. pres. UN Assn. US, 1977-79, nat. coun.,

1980-90; steering com. Leadership Concord, 1992-95, chmn., 1994-95. Named Cmty. Amb. to Sweden Cmty. Amb. Project of the Experiment in Internat. Living, 1956. Fellow Royal Soc. of the Arts U.K. (life); mem. N.H. Coun. on World Affairs (bd. dirs. 1993-95), Greater Concord C. of C. (bd. dirs. 1989-93), Coordinating Coun. for Internat. Univs. (bd. dirs. 2001—), Va. Commonwealth U. Alumni Assn. (bd. dirs. 2006—), Phi Delta Kappa. Methodist. Avocations: antiques, travel. E-mail: wroconn@cox.net.

**O'CONNER, LORETTA RAE,** lawyer; b. Denver, Dec. 23, 1958; d. Ronald Lee and Norma Jareene (Warner) Barkdoll; m. George Ellis Bentley, Dec. 31, 1976 (div. 1979); m. Donald Hugh O'Conner, Feb. 3, 1987; children: Justin Lee, Brandon Craig. AS, Denver Acad. Ct. Reporting, 1983; BA summa cum laude, Regis U., 1992; JD, U. Colo., 1996. Bar: Colo., 1996. Ct. reporter, Denver, 1983-87; dist. ct. reporter Jud. Dept., State of Colo., Pueblo, 1987-91; ct. reporter Pueblo, 1991-93; student atty. Pueblo County Legal Svcs.; pvt. practice Pueblo, 1997—. With Jud. Dept. State of Colo. Chief justice Student govt. Ct. U. So. Colo., Pueblo, 1992; trained facilitator Kettering Found., Pub. Policy Inst., Dayton, Ohio, 1992; sec. So. Colo. Registered Interpreters for the Deaf, Pueblo, 1991; bd. dirs. Concerned Parents of Pueblo, 1999—2002. President's scholar U. So. Colo., 1991-92, Alumni Assn. scholar, 1991-92; grantee Kettering Found., 1992; Colo. Legislature grantee and scholar Regis U., 1992; Colo. Legislature grantee U. Colo. Sch. Law, 1993-95, Dean's scholar, Dazzo Scholar, King scholar U. Colo. Sch. Law, 1993-96. Mem.: ATLA, Pueblo County Bar Assn., Colo. Womens Bar Assn., Colo. Bar Assn., Colo. Trial Lawyers Assn., Walking Stick Assn. (sec. 2000—), Phi Delta Phi (clk. 1994—95), Golden Key. Avocations: reading, writing, community board memberships. Office: 9071 E Mississippi Ave Apt 13E Denver CO 80247-2019 Home: 9071 E Mississippi Ave Apt 13e Denver CO 80247-2019 Fax: (719) 584-2233.

**O'CONNOR, ABIGAIL ELIZABETH,** mathematician, educator, science educator; b. New Brunswick, N.J., Feb. 18, 1978; d. Samuel Margulies and Jennifer Alman Michaels; m. George O'Connor, Aug. 18, 2002; 1 stepchild, Nathan Edward. BA in Math., Rutgers U., 1999; MS in Applied Math., Rensselaer Poly. Inst., 2002; postgrad., Albany Law Sch., 2005—. Adj. math. lectr. Rutgers U., New Brunswick, NJ, 1999—2000; comml. pilot, flight instr. O'Connor Aviation, Inc., Albany, NY, 2000—01; owner, flight instr. No. Flight Acad., Inc., Scotia, NY, 2002—; instr. math. and physics Schenectady (N.Y.) County CC, 2002—03; instr. math Albany Coll. Pharmacy, NY, 2003—05. Presenter in field. Fellow, Claire Booth Luce Found., 2001—02. Mem.: Aircraft Owner and Pilot Assn., Am. Math. Soc. Avocations: alpaca farming, geology, home improvement, aviation. Home: 219 Verbeck Ave Schaghticoke NY 12154 Personal E-mail: abby@oconnorfarm.com.

**O'CONNOR, ANAHAD S.,** journalist; b. NYC, 1982; B, Yale U., 2003. Intern NY Times, 1999, CAP Advisors, St. Vincent's Hosp., Dublin; staff reporter Yale Daily News; health & fitness columnist NY Times. Writer: published in NY Times, 1999—. Office: NY Times Science & Health Desk 229 W 43rd St New York NY 10036 Office Phone: 212-556-7141. Office Fax: 212-556-7306.*

**O'CONNOR, BETTY LOU,** retired hotel executive, food service executive; b. Phoenix, Oct. 29, 1927; d. Georg Eliot and Tillie Edith Miller; m. William Spoeri O'Connor, Oct. 10, 1948 (dec. Feb. 1994); children: Thomas W., William K. (dec.), Kelli Anne. Student, U. So. Calif., 1946-48, Calif. State U., Los Angeles, 1949-50. V.p. O'Connor Food Svcs., Inc., Jack in the Box Restaurants, Granada Hills, Calif., 1983-93; pres. O'Connor Food Svcs., Inc., Granada Hills, Calif., 1994—., C.E.O. Foods, Inc., Victorville, Calif. Recipient Frannie award Foodmaker, Inc., Northridge, Calif., 1984, First Rate award, 1992. Mem. Jack in the Box Franchisee Assn., Spurs Hon. (sec. U. So. Calif. 1947-48), Associated Women Students (sec. U. So. Calif. 1946-47), Gamma Alpha Chi (v.p. 1947-48), Chi Omega. Republican. Roman Catholic. Avocation: sewing. Personal E-mail: clmocon@aol.com.

**O'CONNOR, BRIAN D. A.,** music educator, French horn musician; b. Albuquerque, Dec. 6, 1951; s. Joseph Fredrick and Mary Adger (King) O'Connor; m. Coral Lynn Johnson, Sept. 21, 1972 (dec. July 1993); 1 child, Sean Adger; m. Wendy Anne Gunby, July 14, 1995; 1 stepchild, Nicola G. Perry. Student, New Eng. Conservatory of Music, Boston, 1970—72; BFA, Calif. Inst. of the Arts, Valencia, 1973. Recording musician French horn L.A. Recording Orch., 1974—; prof. horn UCLA, 1998—. Horn clinician Calif. State Music Edn., L.A., 2001—; French horn performer Pacific Serenades, L.A., 2000—. UCLA Faculty Chamber Group, Westwood, 2001—. Musician (horn, soloist): (more than 1,900 films, including) Flicka, The Notebook, The Rock, Crimson Tide, Contact, Backdraft, Star Trek-First Contact, others, (films) Cinderella Man, (TV series) Star Trek, others, The Pacifier, Star Trek: Enterprise. Mem.: Recording Musicians Assn. of L.A. (pres. 1999—2005). Avocations: soccer, running, flying, bicycling. Office: 20335 Ventura Blvd Ste 400 Woodland Hills CA 91364 Personal E-mail: horn51@aol.com.

**O'CONNOR, CHARLES EDWARD, JR.,** state government official, lawyer; b. Phila., Feb. 21, 1960; s. Charles Edward O'Connor, Ruth Pauline Cardamone-O'Connor; m. Lori Marie Ruszkiewicz; 1 child, Charles Henry. BA, LaSalle Coll., Phila., 1982; JD, Widener U., Wilmington, Delaware, 1988. Election clk. County Commrs. Office, Phila., 1978—81; parcel post machine clk. U.S. Postal Svc., Phila., 1982—83; letter carrier Abington, Pa., 1983—85; bail interview supr. Common Pleas Ct. Phila., 1985—89; law clk. to Hon. John TJ Kelly Jr. Superior Ct. Pa., Phila., 1989—92, chief law clk. to Hon. John TJ Kelly Jr., 1992—97, dep. prothonotary for ea. dist. Pa., 1997—2005; exec. dir. 2001 Legis. Reapportionment Commn., Harrisburg, Pa., 2001—02. Mem. 2d Dist. Police Adv. Coun., Phila., 1998—2004, 24th Dist. Police Adv. Coun., 1989—92; counsel Summerdale Boys Club, Phila., 1993—97. Mem. 53d Ward Rep. Exec. Com., Phila., 1978—82, 25th Ward Rep. Exec. Com., Philadelphia, 1988—89; pres. Friends of Summerdale Civic Assn., Phila., 1999—2004. Mem.: Nat. Assn. Appellate Ct. Cks., Brehon Law Soc., Order Sons of Italy in Am., Grand Army of The Republic Mus., Pa. Hist. Soc., Custodes Pacis Lodge, Ancient Order of Hibernians (First Degree 2000). Roman Catholic. Avocation: Pennsylvania History, Neighborhood Cleanup/Graffiti Removal, Old Car Repair and Restoration, Urban Affairs. Home: 9040 Wesleyan Rd Philadelphia PA 19136-1113 Office: Superior Ct Pa 530 Walnut St Ste 315 Philadelphia PA 19106 Office Phone: 215-560-5795. Personal E-mail: Charles.O'Connor@pacourts.us. Business E-mail: fsmdcivic@aol.com.

**O'CONNOR, CHARLES P.,** lawyer; b. Boston, Sept. 29, 1940; m. Mary Linda Hogan; children: Jennifer, Amy, Austin, Catherine. Bachelors degree, Holy Cross Coll., Worcester, Mass., 1963; LLB, Boston Coll., 1966. Bar: Mass. 1966, D.C. 1968, U.S. Supreme Ct. 1974. Atty., gen. counsel's office NLRB, Washington, 1966-67; assoc. Morgan, Lewis & Bockius, LLP, Washington, 1968-71; ptnr. Morgan, Lewis & Bockius, Washington, 1971—2003, common. labor and employment law sect., 1996-99, mng. ptnr. Washington office, 1995-97; v.p., gen. counsel Maersk, Inc., 2003—. Gen. counsel Major League Baseball Player Rels. Com., N.Y.C., 1989-94. Contbr. numerous articles on labor and employment law to law jours. Spl. counsel elections com. U.S. Ho. of Reps., Washington, 1968-69. Fellow Coll. Labor and Employment Lawyers; mem. ABA, D.C. Bar Assn., Met. Club Washington, Belle Haven Country Club, N.Y. Athletic Club, Cape Cod Nat. Golf Club. Office: Maersk Inc 2 Giralda Farms Madison Ave Madison NJ 07940-0880 Home: 6237 Radcliff Rd Alexandria VA 22307-1143 Office Phone: 973-514-5014. Office Fax: 973-514-5003. Business E-mail: namlawmng@maersk.com.

**O'CONNOR, CHUCK (CHARLES O'CONNOR),** painter; b. Buffalo, 1943; Student, Pratt Inst., Bklyn., 1961—64; NY Studio Sch., 1964—66. Exhibited in group shows at Celebration, Lohin Geduld Gallery, NYC, 2005, 181st Ann.: An Invitational Exhbn. Contemporary Art, Nat. Acad. Mus., NYC, 2006. Grantee Fulbright fellowship. Mailing: c/o Lohin Geduld Gallery 531 W 25th St New York NY 10001-5501*

**O'CONNOR, DORIS JULIA,** not-for-profit fundraiser, consultant; b. Apr. 30, 1930; 1 child: Kim C. BA cum laude in Econs., U. Houston, 1975. Adminstrv. asst. Shell Cos. Found. Inc., N.Y.C., 1966-71, asst. sec. Houston, 1971-73, sec., 1973-76, sr. v.p., dir., mem. exec. com., 1976-93; prin. Doris O'Connor & Co., 1993—. Corp. assoc. United Way of Am., Washington, 1976-93; corp. advisor Bus. Com. of Arts, N.Y.C., 1976-91, del., 1982-87; dir. Ind. Sector, Washington, 1981-89, vice-chmn., 1983-87; mem. contbns. coun. Conf. Bd., N.Y.C., 1976-93; advisor Coun. of Better Bus. Burs., Washington, 1975-94, vice chmn., 1983-87; commr. adv. commn. on work-based learning, Dept. Labor, 1991-93; mem. Houston/Harris County Arts Task Force, 1991-93, Houston Ind. Sch. Dist. Task Force, 1991-93; trustee Houston Grand Opera, 1993-99, Houston Symphony Soc., 1993-99, Soc. Performing Arts, 1993-99, Cultural Arts Coun., 1993-96, Greater Houston Coalition Edn. Excellence, 1993-96; mem. adv. bd. Houston Zool. Soc., 1993-99; mem. Mus. Fine Arts, Houston. Mem. Houston Com. Fgn. Rels., Houston World Affairs Coun., Houston Philos. Soc., Plaza Club (bd. givs. 1987-89), Omicron Delta Epsilon. Office Phone: 713-522-3278.

**O'CONNOR, EDWARD GEARING,** lawyer; b. Pitts., May 5, 1940; s. Timothy R. and Irene B. (Gearing) O'C.; m. Janet M. Showalter, June 17, 1972; children: Mark G., Susan M. BA, Duquesne U., 1962, JD, 1965. Bar: Pa. 1965, U.S. Dist. Ct. (we. dist.) Pa. 1965, U.S.C. Appeals (3d cir.) 1968, U.S. Supreme Ct. 1976. Assoc. Eckert, Seamans, Cherin & Mellott, Pitts., 1965-72, ptnr., 1973-99, sr. counsel, 2000—. Mem. adv. com. on appellate ct. rules Supreme Ct. Pa., 1986—92, mem. procedure rules com., 1998—2004; bd. dirs., mem. audit com., compliance com. Federated Investors, Inc. Editor Duquesne U. Law Rev., 1964-65. Chmn. Hampton (Pa.) Twp. Planning Commn., 1986-87; mem. Hampton (Pa.) Twp. Zoning Hearing Bd., 1997—; bd. dirs. Duquesne U. Recipient Disting. Alumni award Duquesne U. Law Rev., 1985, Disting. Law Alumni award Duquesne U. Sch. Law, 1991, Disting. Svc. award Hampton Twp., 1991, McAnurlty Svc. award Duquesne U., 1992; named Century Club Disting. Alumni, Duquesne U., 1985. Fellow: Pa. Bar Found., Am. Bar Found.; mem.: Ally City Bar Found. (chair fellows com. 2000—01), Acad. Trial Lawyers Allegheny County (bd. govs. 1986—89, 1998—), Pa. Bar Assn. (ho. of dels. 1985—90), Pitts. Athletic Assn., Duquesne U. Alumni Assn. (pres. 1980—82, 1988—90, bd. govs. 1982—90, bd. dirs. 1988—89), Duquesne Club. Republican. Roman Catholic. Home: 4288 Green Glade Ct Allison Park PA 15101-1202 Office: Eckert Seamans Cherin & Mellott 600 Grant St Ste 44th Pittsburgh PA 15219-2702 Office Phone: 412-566-6053. Business E-Mail: eoconnor@eckertseamans.com.

**O'CONNOR, EILEEN J.,** federal agency administrator; Grad., Columbus State U., Cath. U. Corp. tax law specialist IRS; ptnr. Office Fed. Tax Svcs. Grant Thornton, 1984—99; officer for tax svcs. Aronson, Fetridge and Weigle, 1999—2002; asst. atty. gen. tax divsn. U.S. Dept. Justice, Washington, 2002—. Disting. adj. prof. law George Mason U. Law Sch.; adj. prof. law Georgetown U. Law Sch.; former tax cons. various acctg. firms. Mem.: Am. Inst. Cert. Pub. Accountants (past mem. tax. exec. com.), Fed. Bar Assn., DC Bar Assn. Office: US Dept Justice Tax Divsn 950 Pennsylvania Ave NW Washington DC 20530-0001

**O'CONNOR, FRANCIS PATRICK,** former state supreme court justice; b. Boston, Dec. 12, 1927; s. Thomas Lane and Florence Mary (Hagerty) O'C.; m. Ann Elizabeth O'Brien; children: Kathleen, Francis P., Brien T., Maureen T., Ellen M., Ann E., Jane C., Joyce E., Thomas J., Matthew P. AB, Holy Cross Coll., 1950; LLB, Boston Coll., 1953; JD (hon.), Suffolk U., 1983, New Eng. Sch. Law, 1984. Bar: Mass. 1953. Assoc. Friedman, Atherton, Sisson & Kozol, Boston, 1954-57, Mason, Crotty, Dunn & O'Connor, Worcester, Mass., 1957-73, Wolfson, Moynihan, Dodson & O'Connor, Worcester, 1974-75; judge Mass. Superior Ct., 1976-81; assoc. judge Mass. Supreme Ct., 1981-97, ret., 1997. Office: Supreme Judicial Court 1 Pemeberton Sq Ste 2-500 Boston MA 02108-1717

**O'CONNOR, FRANCIS X.,** financial executive; b. Bklyn., May 7, 1929; s. Richard B. and Mary (McCafferty) O'C.; m. Leona A. Windorf, June 30, 1951; children: Francis X., Edward K., Brendan T., Richard B. III, A. Bruce, Marianne, Margaret, Leona. BS, St. Peter's Coll., 1951. CPA, N.Y., N.J. Audit mgr. Coopers & Lybrand, N.Y.C., 1951-65; controller Ward Foods, Inc., N.Y.C., 1965-66, v.p. fin., CFO, 1966-72, also bd. dirs., 1968-73; v.p. fin., CFO UMC Industries, Inc., N.Y.C., 1973-76; v.p. fin. and corp. devel., CFO SKF Industries, Inc., King of Prussia, Pa., 1976-87; v.p. corp. fin. Moore & Schley Securities Corp., Morristown, NJ, 1987-89; mng. dir. Sterling Manhattan Corp. Investment Bankers, N.Y.C., 1989-93. Adv. bd. Boyden Cons. Corp. Mem. AICPA, AIM, N.Y. State Soc. CPAs. Fin. Excs. Inst., Nat. Conf. on Power Transmission (trustee), Machinery and Allied Products Inst. Fin. Coun., St. Peter's Coll. Alumni Assn. (trustee, past pres. Monmouth chpt.), Navy League of U.S., Spring Lake Golf Club, (past pres., trustee), Seaview Country Club (N.J.), Green Gables Croquet Club (past pres.), Legacy Golf Club (Ft. Pierce, Fla.), Yacht and Country Club (Stuart, Fla.). Home: 2355 NE Ocean Blvd Stuart FL 34996-2945 Office: 16 St Clair Ave Spring Lake NJ 07762

**O'CONNOR, SISTER GEORGE AQUIN (MARGARET M. O'CONNOR),** academic administrator, educator; b. Astoria, N.Y., Mar. 5, 1921; d. George M. and Joana T. (Loughlin) O'C. BA, Hunter Coll., 1943; MA, Catholic U. Am., 1947; PhD (NIMH fellow), NYU, 1964; LL.D. Manhattan Coll., 1983; D of Pedagogy (hon.), Dowling Coll., 1997; DHL, St. Francis Coll., 1997, St. Joseph's Coll., 1997. Mem. faculty St. Joseph's Coll. Bklyn., 1946—, prof. sociology and anthropology, 1966—, chmn. social sci. dept., 1966-69, pres., 1969-97; pres. emeritus. Fellow African Studies Assn.; mem. Anthrop. Assn.; Bklyn. C. of C. (dir. 1973-97), Alpha Kappa Delta, Delta Epsilon Sigma. Author: The Status and Role of West African Women: A Study in Cultural Change, 1964. Named one of N.Y. State Senate's Women of Distinction. Office: Saint Joseph's Coll 245 Clinton Ave Brooklyn NY 11205-3602 Office Phone: 718-636-6800. Business E-Mail: goconnor@sjcny.edu.

**O'CONNOR, G(EORGE) RICHARD,** ophthalmologist; b. Cin., Oct. 8, 1928; s. George Leo and Sylvia Johanna (Voss) O'C. AB, Harvard U., 1950; MD, Columbia U., 1954. Resident in ophthalmology Columbia-Presbyn. Med. Center, N.Y.C., 1957-60; research fellow Inst. Biochemistry, U. Uppsala, Sweden, 1960-61, State Serum Inst., Copenhagen, 1961-62; asst. prof. ophthalmology U. Calif., San Francisco, 1962-68, prof., 1972-84; Francis I. Proctor Found. for Research in Ophthalmology, 1970-84. Nat. adv. eye coun. NIH, 1974—78. Author: (with G. Smolin) Ocular Immunology, 1981; asso. editor: Am. Jour. Ophthalmology, 1976-81. Served with USPHS, 1955-57. Recipient Janeway prize Coll. of Physicians and Surgeons, Columbia U., 1954; Doyne medal Oxford U., 1984; NIH grantee, 1962-84 Mem. Am. Bd. Ophthalmology (sr. examiner), Assn. for Rsch. in Vision and Ophthalmology (trustee 1979-83, pres. 1982-83, Weisenfeld award 1990), Am. Ophthal. Soc., Calif. Med. Assn., Frederic C. Cordes Eye Soc., Pan Am. Ophthal. Assn., Faculty Club. Republican. Presbyterian. Home: 22 Wray Ave Sausalito CA 94965-1831 Office: U Calif Med Ctr 310 S San Francisco CA 94143-0001 Business E-Mail: richard.oconnor@ucsf.edu.

**O'CONNOR, JAMES, JR. (JIM O'CONNOR),** telecommunications industry executive; b. 1967; m. Julie O'Connor; 2 children. BA, JD, Georgetown Univ.; MBA, Northwestern Univ. Kellogg Sch. Bar: Ill. Mgmt. consultant AT Kearney; fell. White House, 1998; founder Motorola Ventures, Chgo., 1999; v.p., tech. incubation, commercialization Motorola, Chgo., 1999—. Adv. bd. mem. J.L. Kellogg Sch. Mgmt.; co-chmn. Chicagoland Entrepreneurial Ctr.; bd. mem. Chicagoland Chamber Commerce; founder Kellogg Corps, Field Mus. Assoc., Lyric Opera Aux. Bd.; mem. bd. Children's Home & Aid Soc., Chgo. Cities in Schools, Big Shoulders Bd. Recipient East Coast Athletic Conf. All-Star, GTE Academic All-American, CEO Volunteer award, Motorola, 2002, CEO outstanding Achievement

award, 2004; grantee Leadership Greater Chgo., 2000, Japan Leadership, 2000, Henry Crown Leadership, Aspen Inst., 2004. Mem.: Econ. Club Chgo., ABA. Office: Motorola Inc 1303 E Algonquin Rd Schaumburg IL 60196 Office Fax: 847-576-5372.*

**O'CONNOR, JAMES E.,** waste management executive; b. May 14, 1949; m. Cathy O'Connor; children: Kerry O'Connor Stiles, James, Kevin. BS, DePaul Univ., 1972. Staff acct. Waste Mgmt., Oakbrook, Ill., 1972-78, with, 1982-87, v.p. southeastern region, 1987-91, sr. v.p. N.Am., 1991-92, area pres., 1992-98; CEO Republic Svcs., Inc., Ft. Lauderdale, Fla., 1998—, chmn., CEO, 2003—. Bd. dirs. Broward Workshop, Children's Cardiac Found.; mem. bd. advisors Broward Econ. Devel. Coun., Broward County Make-A-Wish Found.; trustee Fla. Tax Watch, Mus. Art, St. Thomas Aquinas H.S. Found. Recipient Tree of Life award Jewish Nat. Fund, 1995. Office: Republic Svcs Inc 110 SE 6th St 28th Fl Fort Lauderdale FL 33301*

**O'CONNOR, JAMES G.,** auto company executive; With Ford Motor Co., 1964—, gen. mgr., parts & svcs. div., 1989—90; pres., COO Ford Motor Co. of Can. Ltd., 1990—92, pres., CEO, 1992—94; exec. dir., N Amer. mktg. ops. & plans Ford Motor Co., 1994—96, pres., Lincoln Mercury div., 1996—99, pres., Ford div., 1999—2002, group v.p., N. Amer. mktg, sales, & svcs., 2002—.

**O'CONNOR, JAMES JOHN,** retired utility company executive; b. Chgo., Mar. 15, 1937; s. Fred James and Helen Elizabeth O'Connor; m. Ellen Louise Lawlor, Nov. 24, 1960; children: Fred, John (dec.), James, Helen Elizabeth. BS, Holy Cross Coll., 1958; MBA, Harvard U., 1960; JD, Georgetown U., 1963. Bar: Ill. 1963. With Commonwealth Edison Co., Chgo., 1963-98, asst. to chmn. exec. com., 1964-65, comml. mgr., 1966, asst. v.p., 1967-70, v.p., 1970-73, exec. v.p., 1973-77, pres., 1977-87, chmn., 1980-98, CEO, also bd. dirs., 1998; chmn., CEO Unicom Corp., Chgo., 1994-98, ret., 1998. Bd. dirs. Corning, Inc., Trizec Properties, Inc., United Air Lines, Smurfit-Stone Container Corp. Bd. dirs. Lyric Opera, Joffrey Ballet, Helen Brach Found.; bd. dirs., trustee Mus. Sci. and Industry, Chgo. Symphony; past chmn. Met. Savs. Bond Campaign; trustee Northwestern U.; bd. dirs., past chmn. Chgo. Urban League, Chicagoland C. of C.; past chmn. bd. trustees Field Mus. Natural History; life trustee Adler Planetarium, Mus. Sci. and Industry; mem. exec. bd. Chgo. Area coun. Boy Scouts Am.; chmn. Cardinal Bernardin's Big Shoulders Fund; exec. v.p. The Hundred Club Cook County; dir., past pres. Cath. Charities; past chmn., hon. dir. Am. Cancer Soc., Chgo. Conv. and Tourism Bur. With USAF, 1960-63.

**O'CONNOR, JIM,** television host; Actor: (films) Mystic Pizza, 1988, This Is the Sea, 1997, Killing Cinderella, 2000, Undercover Brother, 2002, Sweet Home Alabama, 2002, Confessions of a Dangerous Mime, 2004, It's About Time, 2005; (TV series) Law and Order: Special Victims Unit, 2001, Rescue Me, 2004; co-host (TV series) USA Live, 1995, host All-American Festivals, Food Network, 2004, The Secret Life Of..., 2005.*

**O'CONNOR, JOHN DENNIS,** biology professor; b. Chgo., Mar. 20, 1942; married, 1964; 3 children. BS, Loyola U., Chgo., 1963; MS, DePaul U., 1966; PhD, Northwestern U., 1968. NIH fellow Mich. State U., East Lansing, 1968-70; asst. prof. biology UCLA, 1969-74, assoc. prof., 1974-77, prof. biology, 1977-81, chmn. biology, 1979-81, dean, life scis., 1981-87; vice chancellor for research, dean of grad. sch., prof. biology U. N.C., prof. biology Chapel Hill, 1988-91; chancellor, prof. biology U. Pitts., 1991-95; provost Smithsonian Instn., Washington, 1996-99, under sec. for sci., 2000—02; v.p. rsch., dean grad. studies U. Md., College Park, 2002—04, prof. biology, 2004—. Vis. prof. U. Nijmegen, Netherlands, 1975-76, Monash U., 1977. Fellow AAAS; mem. Am. Soc. Zoology, Soc. Devel. Biology, Am. Soc. Molecular Biology and Biochemistry, Bus. Higher Edn. Forum (vice chair 1994-96, chair 1996-98), Assn. Univs. for Rsch. in Astronomy (bd. dirs.). Office: U Md 2133 Lee Bldg College Park MD 20742-5121

**O'CONNOR, JOHN JOSEPH,** information technology manager; b. Smyrna, Tenn., June 1, 1959; s. John O'Connor and Dolores Jane (Bell) Brem; m. Lea Ann Bradford, Sept. 6, 1986; 1 child, Colleen Michelle. BS, Tex. A&M U., 1981. Cert. marine engr. 3rd asst. engr. Marine Engrs. Beneficial Assn., Houston, 1981-84; asst. engr. Biehl Ship Mgmt., Houston, 1984; balance technician Hickham Industries, Inc., LaPorte, Tex., 1984-86, prodn. scheduler/Sulzer, 1986-87, project engr./Sulzer, 1987-88, engring. mgr./Sulzer, 1988-89, ops. mgr./Sulzer Huntington Beach, Calif., 1989-93, sr. engr., corp. mergers and acquisitions La Porte, Tex., 1993-94; tech. and field svc. mgr. Sulzer Turbosys. Internat., Houston, 1994-98; engring. projects mgr. Hickham Industries, Inc., LaPorte, Tex., 1998—. Guest speaker Tex. A&M U., Galveston, Tex., College Station, Tex., 1981-89, U. Houston, 1986-89; moderator Power Machinery and Compressor Conf., Houston, 1989. Prin. engr. inventions in field (Achievement awards 1989); author: Steam Turbine Overhaul and Repair Specifications, 1994. Bd. dirs. Cedar Lawn Assn., pres., 1998-2001; bd. dirs. East End Presch., pres., 1998-99; bd. dirs. (pres.) Galveston Alliance of Island Neighborhoods, 1998-2003; adv. bd. Galveston Hist. Found., 1999. Recipient Outstanding Records in Engring., Gulf Oil Corp., Galveston, 1981. Mem. ASME (guest speaker convs.), Pacific Energy Assn. (guest speaker convs. 1990-92), Assn. of Former Students/Tex. A&M. Avocations: hiking, camping, travel, automotive restoration, litigation. Business E-Mail: john.oconnor@sulzerhickham.com.

**O'CONNOR, JOHN MORRIS, III,** retired humanities educator; b. Evanston, Ill., Sept. 21, 1937; s. John Morris and Clare Evelyn (Merrick) O'Connor; m. Mary Bittner, Dec. 30, 1960 (div.); 1 child, Emily; m. Miranda E. P. Ind, Aug. 14, 1971 (div.); 1 child, Amanda; m. Beate A. Schiwek, July 3, 2006. Student, Georgetown U., 1955—56; BA, Cornell U., 1959; MA, Harvard U., 1962, PhD, 1965. Instr. Vassar Coll., 1964-66, asst. prof. philosophy, 1966-68; asst. prof. Case Western Res. U., Cleve., 1968-70, assoc. prof., 1970-77; exec. sec. Am. Philos. Assn. U. Del., Newark, 1977-84, assoc. prof., 1977-83; asst. dir. programs Nat. Humanities Ctr., Research Triangle Park, NC, 1983-87; dean Sch. Humanities William Paterson Univ., Wayne, NJ, 1987—91, dean Sch. Humanities, Mgmt. and Social Scis., 1991-92, coord. spl. projects Office of Provost, 1992-93, prof. philosophy, 1992-2001; ret., 2001. Editor (with others): Introductory Philosophy, 1967, Modern Materialism, 1969, Moral Problems in Medicine, 1976; contbr. articles to profl. jours. Woodrow Wilson Nat. fellow, 1959—60. Home: 523 Guilford Ave Chambersburg PA 17201

**O'CONNOR, JOHN THOMAS,** civil engineering educator; b. N.Y.C., Feb. 11, 1933; married, 1966; 2 children. BCE, Cooper Union, 1955; MSCE, N.J. Inst. Tech., 1958; EngD, Johns Hopkins U., 1961. Sanitary engr. Elson T. Killam Sanit & Hydraulic Consulting Engrs., 1955-56; civil engr. George A. Fuller Constrn. Co., N.Y., 1956-57; sanitary engr. Parsons, Brinckerhoff, Quade & Douglas, 1957; from asst. prof. to prof. civil engring. U. Ill., Urbana-Champaign, 1961-75; prof. civil engring. U. Mo., Columbia, 1975-92, chmn. dept., 1975-89; chief Ill. State Water Survey, 1992-95; pres. H2O'C Engring., LLC, 1995—. Mem. ASCE, Am. Chem. Soc., Am. Water Works Assn., Am. Soc. Limnology and Oceanography, Water Environment Fedn. Achievements include research on drinking water treatment processes; removal of arsenic, microorganisms, organic substances, iron and manganese, radionuclides; wastewater treatment and disinfection; solid and hazardous waste site remediation. E-mial: Address: 2401 Tahoe Ct Columbia MO 65203-1444 Office Phone: 573-446-5595. Business E-Mail: john@h2oc.com. info@h2oc.com.

**O'CONNOR, JOSEPH A., JR.,** lawyer; b. NYC, Aug. 12, 1937; s. Joseph A. and Louise G. (Lucht) O'C.; children: Joseph A. III, Edward W. BA, Yale U., 1959; LLB, Columbia U., 1962. Bar: N.Y. 1963, U.S. Supreme Ct. 1968, Pa. 1973, Fla. 1978. Assoc. Davis, Polk & Wardwell, N.Y.C., 1963-72; ptnr. Morgan, Lewis & Bockius, Phila., 1972—2002, spl. coun., 2002—; exec. dir. E. Rhodes & Leona B. Carpenter Fedn., 2002—. Mem. ABA, N.Y. State Bar

Assn., Pa. Bar Assn., Fla. Bar Assn., Phila. Bar Assn., Assn. of Bar of City of N.Y. Clubs: Racquet (Phila.). Roman Catholic. Office: Morgan Lewis & Bockius LLP 1701 Market St Philadelphia PA 19103-2903

**O'CONNOR, KAREN,** political science professor, researcher, writer; b. Buffalo, Feb. 15, 1952; d. Robert J. and Norma (Wilton) O'Connor; m. Allen McDonogh, June 7, 1974 (div. 1986); 1 child, Meghan; m. Richard Cupitt, July 31, 1992. BA, SUNY, Buffalo, 1973, JD, 1977, PhD, 1979. Bar: Ga. 1978. Instr. polit. sci. Emory U., Atlanta, 1977—78, asst. prof., 1978—83, assoc. prof., 1983—88, prof., 1988—95, Am. U., Washington, 1995—2006, Jonathan N. Halfat disting. prof., 2006—. Editor Women & Politics, 1999—2004, Law & Policy, 1982—2005, Jour. of Politics, 1984—87, Am. Politics Quar., 1987—90; founder and dir. Women& Politics Inst., 1999. Author: Women's Organization's Use of the Courts, 1980; author: (with N.E. McGlen) Women's Rights, 1983; editor: Women and Congress, 2002; co-author (with McGlem): Women, Politics and American Society, 2004; co-author: (with L. Sabato) American Government, 9th edit., 2005; co-editor (with S. Brewer and M. Fisher): Gendering Politics, 2005; mem. editl. bd. Women, Politics & Public Policy; contbr. articles to profl. jours. Mem.: Nat. Capitol Area Polit. Sci. Assn. (pres. 2002—01), So. Polit. Sci. Assn. (pres. 2000—01), Women and Politics (pres. elect organized sect. 2005—), Am. Polit. Sci. Assn. (exec. coun. 1985—87), Cosmos Club. Home: 4383 Westover Pl NW Washington DC 20016-5555 Office: Dept of Govt American Univ 4400 Massachusetts Ave NW Washington DC 20016 Office Phone: 202-885-6237. Business E-Mail: oconn@american.edu.

**O'CONNOR, KARL WILLIAM (GOODYEAR JOHNSON),** retired lawyer; b. Washington, Aug. 1, 1931; s. Hector and Lucile (Johnson) O'C.; m. Sylvia Gasbarri, Mar. 23, 1951 (dec.); m. Judith Ann Byers, July 22, 1972 (div. 1983); m. Eleanor Celler, Aug. 3, 1984 (div. 1986), m. Alma Hepner, Jan. 1, 1987 (div. 1996); children: Blair, Frances, Brian, Brendan; m. Allie O'Connor, Jul. 15, 2000. BA, U. Va., 1952, JD, 1958. Bar: Va. 1958, D.C. 1959, Am. Samoa 1976, Calif. 1977, Oreg. 1993. Law clk. U.S. Dist. Ct. Va., Abingdon, 1958-59; practice law Washington, 1959-61; trial atty. U.S. Dept. Justice, Washington, 1961-65; dep. dir. Men's Job Corps OEO, Washington, 1965-67; mem. civil rights div. Dept. of Justice, chief criminal sect., prin. dep. asst. atty. gen., 1967-75, spl. counsel for intelligence coordination, 1975; v.p.; counsel Assn. of Motion Picture and Television Producers, Hollywood, Calif., 1975-76; assoc. justice Am. Samoa, 1976; chief justice, 1977-78; sr. trial atty. GSA Task Force, Dept. Justice, 1978-81; insp. gen. CSA, 1981-82; spl. counsel Merit Systems Protection Bd., Washington, 1983-86; U.S. atty. for Guam and the No. Marianas, 1986-89; pvt. practice Medford, Oreg., 1989—; Am. counsel O'Reilly Vernier Ltd., Hong Kong, 1992-93; ptnr. O'Connor & Vernier, Medford, Oreg., 1993-94; emeritus, 1994. Served with USMC, 1952-55. Mem. Oreg. Bar Assn., D.C. Bar Assn., Va. Bar Assn., Calif. Bar Assn., Am. Samoa Bar Assn., Soc. Colonial Wars, Phi Alpha Delta, Sigma Nu. Home: Box 126 6743 Griffin Ln Jacksonville OR 97530

**O'CONNOR, KATHLEEN MARY,** lawyer; b. Camden, Jan. 14, 1949; d. John A. and Marie V. (Flynn) O'C. BA, U. Fla., 1971, JD, 1981. Bar: Fla. 1981, U.S. Ct. Appeals (11th cir.) 1982, U.S. Supreme Ct. 1987. Atty. Walton, Lantaff, Schroeder & Carson, Miami, Fla., 1981-84, Thornton, Davis & Murray PA, Miami, 1984-98, Thornton, Davis & Fein, P.A., Miami, 2002—. Exec. editor U. Fla. Law Rev., 1981; contbr. articles to profl. jours. Legal advocate Miami Project to Cure Paralysis, 1992-97. Mem. ABA, Dade County Bar Assn. (chmn. appellate ct. com. 2004—), Def. Rsch. Inst., Fla. Def. Lawyers Assn., Am. Assn. for Women Lawyers (bd. dirs. Miami-Dade County chpt. 2002—), Fla. Bar (mem. appellate rules com. 2002—, cert. 1995—). Office: Thornton Davis & Fein PA 80 SW 8th St Ste 2900 Miami FL 33130 Home: 7445 SW 147 St Coral Gables FL 33158 Office Phone: 305-446-2646. E-mail: oconnor@tdflaw.com.

**O'CONNOR, KEVIN,** computer programing executive; BSEE with honors, U. Mich. Co-founder ICC Software Co., Atlanta, 1983—91; chief tech. officer, v.p. rsch. DCA, Atlanta, 1992—95; funded and built ISS Group, Atlanta, 1995, chmn. bd. dirs., 1995—; co-founder, chief exec. officer Internet Advt. Network, 1995—; co-founder, pres., chief exec. officer DoubleClick, NY, 1996—. Office: DoubleClick 111 Eighth Ave 10th Fl New York NY 10011 Office Phone: 212-683-0001, 212-271-2542. Office Fax: 212-287-1203.

**O'CONNOR, KEVIN,** electronics executive; b. 1958; Degree in Mgmt. Ariz. State U. With Sperry Flight Sys.; with Frito-Lay PepsiCo; various positions Dell Computer; sr. v.p. global human resources Iomega Corp., Axcelis Technologies; exec. v.p. Worldwide Human Resources Solectron Corp., Milpitas, Calif., 2002—. Mem.: Am. Compensation Assn., Asian Human Resource Alliance, Soc. Human Resources Mgmt., Am Lung Assn., North Shore C. of C., Boys and Girls Clubs Weber County. Office: Solectron Corp 777 Gibraltar Dr Milpitas CA 95035

**O'CONNOR, KEVIN JAMES,** prosecutor, lawyer; b. Hartford, Conn., May 3, 1967; s. Dennis Edmund and Mary Theresa (Leahy) O'Connor. BA, U. Notre Dame, 1989; JD, U. Conn., 1992. Conn. 1992, N.Y. 1993, U.S. Dist. Ct. Conn. (so. and ea. dists.) N.Y. 1994, U.S. Ct. Appeals (2d cir.) 1994. Law clerk Hon. William H. Timbers, U.S. Ct. Appeals (2d cir.), N.Y.C., 1992-93; assoc. Cahill, Gordon & Reindel, N.Y.C., 1993-95; sr. counsel Divsn. Enforcement U.S. Securities & Exchg. Commn., Washington, 1995-97; ptnr. Day Berry & Howard, Hartford, 1999—2002; US atty. dist. Conn. US Dept. Justice, 2002—. Adj. prof. George Washington U. Law Sch., Washington, 1996-97, U. Conn. Law Sch., 1998—. Republican. Roman Catholic. Office: Conn Finl Ctr PO Box 1824 New Haven CT 06508 Office Phone: 203-821-3700.*

**O'CONNOR, KEVIN JOHN,** psychologist, educator; b. Jersey City, July 18, 1954; s. John Lanning and Marilyn (Reynold) O'C.; m. Ryan Michael, Matthew Benham. BA, U. Mich., 1975; PhD, U. Toledo, 1981. Clin. psychologist Blythedale Children's Hosp., Valhalla, NY, 1980-83; dir. psychol. svcs. Walworth Barbour Am. Internat. Sch., Kfar Shmaryahu, Israel, 1983-84; adj. faculty dept. psychology Iona Coll., New Rochelle, NY, 1984; clin. psychologist No. Westchester Guidance Clinic, Mt. Kisco, NY, 1985; exec. dir., newsletter editor Assn. for Play Therapy, Fresno, Calif., 1982-97; cons. psychologist Fresno (Calif.) Treatment Ctr., 1986-87, Diagnostic Sch. for Neurologically Handicapped Children, Fresno, Calif., 1986-90; adj. faculty Pacific Grad. Sch. of Psychology, Palo Alto, Calif., 1997—2001, Calif. Sch. Profl. Psychology, Berkeley, Calif., 1988-89; prof. Alliant Internat. U., Calif. Sch. Profl. Psychology, Fresno, 1985—, dir. clinical PsyD and PhD programs, 1985—. Contbr. numerous publications and presentations in field. Named Psychologist of Yr. San Joaquin Psychol. Assn., 1994. Fellow APA; mem. Assn. for Play Therapy (dir. emeritus). Democrat. Avocations: travel, art, ceramics. Office: Calif Sch Profl Psych Alliant Internat U 5130 E Clinton Way Fresno CA 93727-2014 Office Phone: 559-253-2273. Business E-Mail: koconnor@alliant.edu.

**O'CONNOR, KEVIN THOMAS,** religious organization administrator; b. Dubuque, Iowa, Dec. 9, 1950; s. Francis John and Marion Helen (Rhomberg) O'C.; m. Abbie J. O'Connor, July 17, 1993; 1 child, Sean Francis. BS, Regis Coll., Denver, 1973. Spl. agt. Northwestern Mut. Life, Denver, 1973-78; account exec. Blue Cross/Blue Shield of Colo., Denver, 1978-82; pres., owner O'Connor Ins. Cons., Denver, 1982-92; dir. devel. Archdiocese of Denver, 1992-95, mgr. Cath. appeal, 1995-96; dir. devel. Archdiocese of L.A., 1996—2006; exec. dir. devel. Archdiocese of Washington, 2006—. Chmn. Regis Coll. Telefund, Denver, 1987-88, 90-91; treas., 1st vice chmn. Serra Trust Fund for Vocations, 1988-93, chmn., 1993-96; mem. fin. coun. St. James Parish, 1988-95, chmn. autumn bazaar, 1985, 87, mem. choir, 1993-95; sec. Mother Teresa Com., 1989; mem. choir St. Bede The Venerable, La Canada, Calif., 2001-06. Recipient Shane Serra Comm. award Serra Internat., 1989, Spl. Project award Dist. 6, 1986, 88, Spl. Recognition award, 1989, Outstanding Serran award, 1995, Jan Berbers award, 1996, Alumni Svc. award Regis Coll., 1997, Disting. Alumnus award Wahlert H.S., 1994. Mem.

Serra Internat. (trustee 1997-2003, sec. bd. 1998-2001, chmn. internat. vocation com. 2000-01, v.p. 2001-03, co-founder Pueblo chpt., 1992, Colo. Springs chpt., 1995, Greeley chpt., 1996, pres. Denver chpt., 1991-92, dist. 6 gov., 1995-96). Roman Catholic. Avocations: golf, tennis, mountain climbing, handball, running. Home: 3510 Fallenleaf Pl Glendale CA 91206-4803 Office: Archdiocese 5001 Eastern Ave Hyattsville MD 20782-3447 Office Phone: 301-853-4574. Personal E-mail: kevinabbie@charter.net. Business E-Mail: koconnor@adw.org.

**O'CONNOR, M. CAROL,** private school educator; b. Allentown, Pa. d. William J. and Mary C. Kurnig; m. Lawrence O'Connor, Apr. 20, 1975; children: Sarah, Maureen, Daniel. BA, Gwynnedd-Mercy Coll., Gwynnedd Valley, Pa., 1967. Roman Catholic. Home: 1710 Elmhurst Dr Whitehall PA 18052 Office: St Elizabeth Parish 618 Fullerton Ave Whitehall PA 18052

**O'CONNOR, MAUREEN,** state supreme court justice; b. Washington, Aug. 7, 1951; d. Patrick and Mary E. O'Connor; children: Alex, Ed. BA, Seton Hill Coll., 1973; postgrad., SUNY, 1975-76; JD, Cleve. State U., 1980. Pvt. practice, 1981-85; magistrate Summit County Probate Ct., 1985-93; judge Summit County Ct. of Common Pleas, 1993-95; prosecuting atty. Summit County, 1995-99; lt. gov., dir. Dept. Pub. Safety State of Ohio, 1999—2003; justice Ohio Supreme Ct., Ohio, 2003—. Dir. Summit County Child Support Enforcement Agy.; former chair Ohio Security Task Force, Building Security Review Com.; spkr. in field. Parishioner St. Vincent's Ch.; vol. Comty. Drug Bd., Am. Cancer Soc., bd. dirs.; bd. dirs. Victim Assistance, St. Edward Home, Fairlawn, Furnace St. Mission. Recipient MADD Law Enforcement award, 1997, Cleve. State Disting. Alumnae award for Civic Achievement, 1997. Mem. MADD, Nat. Dist. Attys. Assn., Nat. Child Support Enforcement Assn., Nat. Coll. Dist. Attys. Assn., Ohio Prosecuting Attys. Assn. (exec. com.), Ohio Family Support Assn., Atty. Gen.'s Prosecutor Liaison Com., Summit County Police Chiefs Assn., Summit Forum, Summit County Child Mortality. Republican. Office: Ohio Supreme Ct 65 S Front St Columbus OH 43215*

**O'CONNOR, MICHAEL E.,** lawyer; b. Syracuse, NY, Sept. 15, 1948; s. Leo T. and Geraldine (Hager) O'Connor; m. Margaret A. Soplop, June 3, 1972. AA, Auburn CC, NY, 1968; BA, SUNY, Buffalo, 1970; JD, Syracuse U., 1974. Bar: N.Y. 1975, U.S. Supreme Ct. 1983. Assoc. Coulter, Fraser, Bolton, Bird & Ventre, Syracuse, 1975-80, ptnr., 1981-90, Hancock & Estabrook, 1990-94, DeLaney & O'Connor LLP, 1994—. Pres. Onondaga Title Assn., 1979, Ctrl. N.Y. Estate Planning Coun., 1981; adj. prof. law U. Syracuse; pres. Most Holy Rosary Home Sch. Assn., 1985—86, Aurora of CNY, Inc., 1988—90. Bd. dirs. Syracuse Symphony Orch.; chmn. bd. CNY Cmty. Found.; pres. Citizens Found., Inc., 1983—85. Fellow: Am. Coll. Trust and Estate Counsel (state chair 1997—2002); mem.: ABA, Onondaga County Bar Assn. (chmn. estate and surrogates ct. com. 1981—87, bd. dirs. 1984—86), N.Y. State Bar Assn. (ho. of dels. 1982—85, chair elder law sect. 1999—2000, chair trusts and estates sect. 2005), Century Club of Syracuse, Lions (pres. 1984—85). Republican. Roman Catholic. Home: 154 Robineau Rd Syracuse NY 13207-1644 Office: DeLaney & O'Connor LLP One Lincoln Ctr Syracuse NY 13202 Office Phone: 315-476-8450. Personal E-mail: meoconnor1@twcny.rr.com.     Business     E-Mail: oconnor@delaneyoconnor.com.

**O'CONNOR, PAUL DANIEL,** lawyer; b. Paterson, NJ, Nov. 24, 1936; s. Paul Daniel and Anne Marie Christopher O'C.; children: Steven Paul, Sheryl Lynn, Laura Ann. BS in Engring, U.S. Naval Acad., 1959; LLB, U. Va., 1965. Bar: N.Y. 1965, Calif. 1995. Assoc. firm Winthrop, Stimson, Putnam & Roberts, N.Y.C., 1965-72, partner, 1972-80; sr. v.p. gen. counsel Singer Co., Stamford, Conn., 1980-86; chief exec. officer Citation Builders, 1986-95; trustee Valley Trusts, Oakland, Calif., 1986—; of counsel Clement, Fitzpatrick & Kenworthy, 2003—. 1st lt. USAF, 1959-62. Mem.: Sonoma County Bar Assn., Bar Assn. San Francisco, Assn. Bar City NY, Fairfield County Hunt Club. Office: 3333 Mendocino Ave Ste 200 Santa Rosa CA 95403 also: Valley Trusts 1939 Harrison St Ste 555 Oakland CA 94612-3586 Home: 1998 Broadway No 905 San Francisco CA 94109 Business E-Mail: poconnor@cfk.com.

**O'CONNOR, R. D.,** retired health services administrator; BS in Psychology and Sociology, U. So. Miss., 1960, MS Adminstrv. Pers., 1961, PhD Mgmt. and Orgnl. Comm., 1983. Asst. dean student affairs Holmes Jr. Coll., Goodman, Miss., 1961-64, Dept. Edn., Jackson, Miss., 1964-65; asst. adminstr. Hinds Gen. Hosp., Jackson, Miss., 1965-68; adminstr. Rankin Gen. Hosp., Brandon, Miss., 1968-76; v.p. Human Resources/ Mktg. Delta Mgmt. Systems, Metairie, La., 1976-79; asst. to pres. Bapt. Med. Ctr., Jacksonville, Fla., 1979-82; pres. RiverGroup Riverside Hosp., Rivercorp Inc., Riverside Found., Jacksonville, Fla., 1982-87; owner O'Connor & Assocs., Jacksonville, Fla., 1987-91; pres. Fla. 1st: Managed Health Care, Winter Haven, Orlando & Tampa, Fla., 1991-94; dir. orgn. devel. Mid Florida Med. Svcs. Inc., Winter Haven, Fla., 1994-97. Instr. U. So. Miss., Hattiesburg, Ms.; tchr., lectr. various univs., C.C.s, military acads.; grad. faculty coord. Webster U.; online instr. for univs. Contbr. articles to profl. jours. and books. Commr. Cleary Heights Sewer Dist., 1978-79; pres'. selective task force Induction Procedures, 1969; chmn. personnel com. San Jose Baptist Ch., 1981-86, strategic planning com., 1986-87; gov's com. Statewide Planning Vocat. Rehab., 1968; bd. dirs. Rankin County C. of C., 1970-73, exec. com., chmn. health affairs com., 1970-72, chmn. highway com. 1970-74, fin. com. 1971-73), Family Blood Assurance Program, 1972-77, v.p. 1977, Vol. Action Coun., 1973-76, United Givers Fund, 1973-76. With Army Security Agy., Air Nat. Guard, Med. Svc. Corps., ret. Fellow Am. Coll. Healthcare Execs. (life); mem. Fla. Hosp. Assn. (com. chmn. 1984), Greater Jacksonville Area Hosp. Coun. (chmn. 1985), Jackson-Vicksburg Hosp. Coun. (chmn. 1974), Nat. Assn. Mental Health (bd. dirs. 1973-74), Miss. Assn. Mental Health (pres. 1972-74), Miss. Hosp. Assn. (bd. dirs. 1973-76 exec devel com. 1974-75, mgmt engring. adminstrv. bd. 1979, fin. com. 1972-74, chmn. nominating com. 1971, coord. divsn. devel. pract. activity 1970.) Home: 12837 Julington Forest Dr E Jacksonville FL 32258-2294

**O'CONNOR, RALPH STURGES,** investment company executive; b. Pasadena, Calif., Aug. 27, 1926; s. Thomas Ireland and Edith Masury (Sturges) O'Connor; m. Alice Maconda Brown, Apr. 28, 1950; children: George Rufus, Thomas Ireland III, Nancy Isabel, John Herman. BA, Johns Hopkins U., 1951; postgrad., Harvard U., 1967. With Highland Resources, Inc., Houston, 1951-87, exec. v.p., 1961-64, pres., 1964-87; pres., CEO Ralph S. O'Connor and Assocs., Houston, 1987—. Chmn. bd. dirs. Amaud's Restaurant, New Orleans. Pres. Marian and Speros Martel Found., Houston, 1983—2003; trustee emeritus Rice U., Johns Hopkins U., Oldfields Sch., Glencoe, Md. With USAAF, 1943—46. Mem.: NAS, Presdl. Counselors, Houston Landmen's Assn. (past pres.), All Am. Wildcatters, Am. Assn. Petroleum Landmen, Johns Hopkins Instns., Players Club, River Oaks Country Club, Bayou Club. Home: 5627 Indian Cir Houston TX 77056-1006 Office: Ralph S O'Connor & Assocs 10000 Memorial Dr Ste 510 Houston TX 77024-3422    Office    Phone:    713-682-3441.    Personal    E-mail: ralphsoconnor@yahoo.com.

**O'CONNOR, ROD,** chemist, consultant, inventor; b. Cape Girardeau, Mo., July 4, 1934; s. Jay H. and Flora (Winters) O'C.; m. Shirley Ann Sander, Aug. 7, 1955; children: Mark Alan (dec.), Kara Ann, Shanna Suzanne, Timothy Patrick. BS, S.E. Mo. State Coll., 1955; PhD, U. Calif., Berkeley, 1958. Asst. prof. chemistry U. Omaha, 1958-60, Mont. State Coll., 1960-63; assoc. prof. chemistry Mont. State U., Bozeman, 1963-66; assoc. prof., coordinator gen. chemistry Kent (Ohio) State U., 1966-67; prof., dir. 1st year chemistry U. Ariz., Tucson, 1968-72; staff assoc. Adv. Council on Coll. Chemistry Stanford (Calif.) U., 1967-68; vis. prof. Wash. State U., Pullman, 1972-73; prof. chemistry Tex. A&M, College Station, 1973-86; pres. Texas ROMEC Inc., College Station, 1983-98; prof. environ. studies Baylor U., Waco, Tex., 1996-99. Cons. insect venoms Hollister-Stier Labs., Spokane, Wash., 1963-67; lab. separates editor W.H. Freeman Co., 1968-78; cdnl. cons. TUCARA-4 Media Resources, Inc., 1971-74; mem. Coll. Chemistry Cons. Service; vis. scientist, tour lectr. Am. Chem. Soc., 1970-86. Author: (with T. Moeller) Ions

in Aqueous Systems, 1972, Fundamentals of Chemistry, 1981, (with C. Mickey and A. Hassell) Solving Problems in Chemistry, 1981, (with L. Peck and K. Irgolic) Fundamentals of Chemistry in The Laboratory, 1981, (with T.E. Taylor and P. Glenn) Toward Success in College, 1981, (with A. Hassell and C. Mickey) Advanced Problems in Applied Chemistry, 2000; films Laboratory Safety, 1971; Contbr. articles to profl. jours.; patentee in field Recipient nat. teaching award Mfg. Chemists Assn., 1978; 4 regional teaching awards. Fellow AAAS, Am. Inst. Chemists, Sigma Xi; mem. Internat. Soc. Toxinology, Am. Chem. Soc. Office: Chem Consulting Svcs 1300 Angelina Cir College Station TX 77840-4855 Office Phone: 979-693-5804. E-mail: docroc34@hotmail.com.

**O'CONNOR, SANDRA DAY,** retired United States Supreme Court Justice; b. El Paso, Tex., Mar. 26, 1930; d. Harry A. and Ada Mae (Wilkey) Day; m. John Jay O'Connor, III, 1952; children: Scott, Brian, Jay. BA with great distinction, Stanford, III., 1950, LLB, 1952. Bar: Calif., Ariz. Dep. county atty., San Mateo, Calif., 1952—53; civilian atty. Q.M. Market Ctr., Frankfurt am Main, Germany, 1954—57; pvt. law practice Maryvale, 1958—60; asst. atty. gen. State of Ariz., 1965—69, state senator, 1969—75; chmn. com. on state, county and mcpl. affairs, 1972—73; senate majority leader, 1972—75; judge Maricopa County Superior Ct., Phoenix, 1975—79, Ariz. Ct. Appeals, 1979—81; assoc. justice US Supreme Ct., Washington, 1981—2006. Mem. Maricopa County Bd. Adjustments and Appeals, 1963—64, Ariz. Criminal Code Commn., 1974—76, Nat. Defense Adv. Com. on Women in Svcs., 1974—76; chmn. vis. bd. Maricopa County Juvenile Detention Home, 1963—64; chmn. Ariz. Supreme Ct. Com. to Reorganize Lower Cts., 1974—75, Maricopa County Superior Ct Judges Tng. and Edn. Com., 1977—79; vice chmn. Ariz. Select Law Enforcement Review Commn., 1979—80; served on Legis. Coun., Probate Code Commn., Ariz. Adv. Coun. on Intergovernmental Relations. Mem. bd. editors: Stanford (Calif.) U. Law Rev.; co-author (with H. Alan Day): (memoir) Lazy B: Growing Up on a Cattle Ranch in the American Southwest, 2002; author (with Dan Andreasen, illustrator): (children's books) Chico: A True Story from the Childhood of the First Woman Supreme Court Justice, 2005. Mem. adv. bd. Smithsonian Nat. Mus. Natural History, 2004—; mem., selection com. Okla. City Nat. Meml. and Mus., 2005—; co-chair nat. adv. coun. Campaign for Civic Mission of Schs., 2005—; mem. Cathedral Chpt. Wash. Nat. Cathedral, 1991—99. Named Woman of Yr., Phoenix Advt. Club, 1972, National Women's Hall of Fame, 1995; named one of Most Powerful Women, Forbes mag., 2005; recipient Ann. award, NCCJ, 1975, Disting. Achievement award, Ariz. State U., 1980, Gimble Nat. award, Gimble Phila. awards Com., 1982, Elizabeth Blackwell award, Hobart & William Smith Coll., 1985, award of Merit, Stanford Law Sch., 1990, OH State Law award, OH State U., 1992, Fordham Stein prize, Fordham U., 1992, Sara Lee Frontrunner award, 1997, ABA medal, 1997, Thomas Jefferson award of Law, U. Va., 1987, William Green award for Profl. Excellence, U. Richmond, 1990. Mem.: Anglo-Am. Exchange, Ariz. State Personnel Commn., Stanford Ct. Ethics (adv. bd. 2005—), Am. Soc. Internat. Law (adv. com. 2001—), Ariz. Women Lawyer's Assn., Nat. Assn. Women Judges, Ariz. Judges' Assn., Calif. Bar Assn., Maricopa County Bar Assn. (chmn. Lawyer Referral Svc. 1960—62), Ariz. Bar Assn. (former mem. Com. Legal Aid, former mem. Com. Public Relations, former mem. Com. Lower Ct. Reorganization, former mem. Com. Continuing Legal Edn.), ABA (exec. bd. Ctrl. European and Eurasian Law Initiative 1990—, exec. com. Mus. Law 2000—, adv. commn. Standing Com. on Law Library of Congress 2002—, mem. Commn. on Civic Edn. and Seperation of Powers 2005—), Adv. Com. for Judiciary Leadership Devel. Coun. (hon.).

**O'CONNOR, SHANNON LEIGH,** psychologist; b. Kansas City, Mo., Sept. 11; d. Dale Eugene O'Connor and Ella Rebecca Benson, William Frank Benson (Stepfather); m. Roby Scott Christian, Apr. 6, 2000; children: Daniel Scott Benson Christian, Claire Cavanaugh Culpepper Christian, Reece William James Christian. BA, Trinity Coll., Hartford, Conn., 1988; MA, U. of Rochester, 1992, PhD, 1994. Lic. psychologist Colo., Mo., Kans., Wis. Intern U. of Rochester, Strong Meml. Hosp., NY; fellow dept. psychiatry U. of Wis., Madison, 1994—96; rsch. coord. Nat. Jewish Med. and Rsch. Ctr., Denver, 1996—99; project mgr. Sprint, U. of Excellence, Overland Park, Kans., 1999—2001. Recipient Andrew Goodman fellowship in medicine, Dept. of Medicine, Nat. Jewish Med. and Rsch. Ctr., 1998, Chairman's Quality award, Teamwork award, U. of Excellence, Sprint Corp., 2001. Mem.: APA (assoc.), Colo. Psychol. Assn. (assoc.), Soc. for Indsl. and Orgnl. Psychology (assoc.).

**O'CONNOR, SHEILA ANNE,** freelance writer; b. Paisley, Scotland, Jan. 20, 1960; came to the U.S., 1988; d. Brian Aubrey Witham and Margaret Kirk (Reid) Davies; m. Frank Donal O'Connor, Aug. 9, 1986; children: David Michael, Andrew James, Christine Charlotte. BA in French and German, Strathclyde U., 1980, postgrad. diploma in office studies, 1981, MBA, 1992. Office asst. BBC, London, 1982-83; asst. to mng. dir. Unimatic Engrs. Ltd., London, 1983-84; freelance word processing operator London, 1984-88; staff asst. Internat. Monetary Fund, Washington, 1988-94; prin. Internat. Media Assn., Washington, 1988—. Co-author: Chocolate for a Woman's Spirit, 1999; contbr. articles to profl. jours. Mem. Am. Mktg. Assn., Bay Area Travel Writers Assn., Calif. Writers Club. Avocations: animals, travel. Home and Office: 1974 46th Ave San Francisco CA 94116-1005 E-mail: sheila.oconnor@juno.com.

**O'CONNOR, THOMAS EDWARD,** petroleum geologist, management consultant; b. Boston, Dec. 16, 1936; s. John Stephen and Lucille (Arnold) O'C.; m. Jeannette Canuel, June 30, 1962 (dec. Mar. 1976); children: Kevin Patrick, David Andrew, Shelley Elizabeth; m. Moufida Banawi, Apr. 28, 1977 (dec. July 2006); children: Tammer Thomas, Amr Adel Hammouda. BSc, Stanford U., 1958; MSc., U. Colo., 1961. Geologist Amoco Prodn. Wett, Denver, 1963-67, Amoco Netherlands, Utrecht, 1968-69, Amoco Europe, London, 1969-74; chief geologist Gulf of Suez Petroleum Co., Cairo, 1974-79; geol. mgr. Amoco Africa, Mid East, Houston, 1979-80; v.p. Aminoil, Houston, 1980-84; prin. petroleum engr. The World Bank, Washington, 1985-98; internat. petroleum mgmt. cons., 1998—; chmn. bd. dirs. Benchmark Oil & Gas AB, Stockholm, 2003—. Adj. prof. George Washington U. Grad. Sch. Polit. Mgmt., 2003—; Royal Sch. Mines, Imperial Coll., London, 2004—; presenter in field. Lt. USNR, 1960—63. Mem. Am. Assn. Petroleum Geologists (cert.), Houston Geol. Soc. Moslem. Home and Office: 937 5th St Camano Island WA 98282 Office Phone: 202-210-1305. Personal E-mail: teoconnor@aol.com.

**O'CONNOR, WILLIAM MICHAEL,** search company executive; b. Chgo., Sept. 28, 1947; s. Maurice Francis and Margaret (Brand) O'C.; m. Karen Jean Gipson, Jan. 30, 1972; children: Sean, Mary, William, David. BA in History, Loyola U., Chgo., 1970. Interviewer Ill. State Employment Svc., Chgo., 1970-73; ins. agt. Equitable Life Assurance Soc., Chgo., 1973-76; recruiting officer U.S. Army, Chgo., 1977-78; profl. employment rep. GTE Network Systems, Northlake, Ill., 1978-81; employment mgr. Molex, Inc., Lisle, Ill., 1981-85, Rand McNally & Co., Skokie, Ill., 1986; v.p. Richards Cons., Chgo., 1987-88; v.p., ptnr. Chestnut Hill Ptnrs., Deerfield, Ill., 1988-95; v.p. Kennedy & Co., Chgo., 1995-2001; pres. Edgewood Internat., Woodridge, Ill., 2001—. Mem. Art Inst. Chgo., Smithsonian Inst., Field Mus. Natural History, Rep. Nat. Com. 1984—. Lt. col. USAR, 1971-99. Decorated Chevalier, Sovereign Mil. Order of Temple of Jerusalem, 1998—. Mem. Res. Officers Assn., U.S. Armor Assn. (Order of St. George), Mil. Police Assn., 337th Cavalry Regiment (Order of the Spur), Bus. Mobilized for Loyola U. Roman Catholic. Home: 3018 Edgewood Pky Woodridge IL 60517 Office: Edgewood Internat 3018 Edgewood Pkwy Woodridge IL 60517 Office Phone: 630-985-6067. E-mail: wocatedgewood@aol.com.

**OCVIRK, OTTO GEORGE,** artist; b. Detroit, Nov. 13, 1922; s. Joseph and Louise (Ekle) O.; m. Betty Josephine Leise, June 11, 1949; children: Robert Joseph, Thomas Frederick, Carol Louise. B.F.A., State U. Iowa, 1949, M.F.A., 1950. Advt. artist apprentice Basse-Luckoff Advt. Agy., Detroit, 1941; engring. draftsman Curtiss-Wright Aircraft Corp., Buffalo, 1942; faculty Bowling Green (Ohio) State U., 1950—, assoc. prof., 1960-65, prof. art, 1965-85, prof. emeritus, 1985—. Exhibited in group shows at, Denver Mus.

Art, 1949, 50, 53, Detroit Inst. Art, 71948, 49, 50, 53, 56, Dayton (Ohio) Art Inst., 1950, 51, 56, Ohio State U., 1953, Walker Art Center, Mpls., 1948, 49, Library of Congress, Washington, 1949, Bklyn. Mus., 1949, Joslyn Mus., Omaha, 1949, Colorado Springs Fine Arts Center, 1949; represented in permanent collections, Detroit Inst. Arts, Dayton Art Inst., Friends of Am. Art, Grand Rapids, Mich., State U. Iowa, Iowa City, Bowling Green State U.; (Recipient 24 nat., regional juried art exhbn. awards 1947-57, others.); Author: (with R. Stinson, P. Wigg, R. Bone and David Cayton) Art Fundamentals — Theory and Practice, 1960-97, 7th edit., 8th edit., 1977, 9th edit., 2001, 10th edit., 2005. Scoutmaster Toledo Area council Boy Scouts Am., 1960-63, asst. scoutmaster, 1963-74, dist. commr., 1978-80. Served with AUS, 1943-46. Recipient Silver Beaver award Boy Scouts Am., 1976, Magnifico award Medici Circle, Bowling Green State U., 1987. Mem. Delta Phi Delta (hon.) Methodist. Home and Office: 231 Haskins Rd Bowling Green OH 43402-2206 *"Freedom for expression" keys creative thought into a productive whole.*

**ODAR, FUAT,** retired nuclear engineer; b. Harbin, China, May 8, 1934; arrived in U.S., 1957; s. Ibrahim and Hatice Odar; m. Zehra Agi, Oct. 9, 1979; m. Penelope Marie Hays, Dec. 28, 1959 (div. May 30, 1978); children: Deniz Ardelle, Holly Rosemarie. Diploma in engring, Tech. U., Istanbul, Turkey, 1956; PhD, Northwestern U., 1962, MS, 1958. Rsch. phys. scientist U.S. Cold Regions Rsch. Lab, Hanover, NH, 1962—74; nuclear engr. Westinghouse Electric Corp, West Mifflin, Pa., 1967—74; sr. reactor engr. U.S. Nuc. Regulatory Commn., Rockville, Md., 1974—2003; ret., 2003. Contbr. articles to profl. jours. Mem.: Am. Nuc. Soc. Personal E-mail: frankodar@earthlink.net.

**O'DAY, ANITA BELLE COLTON,** entertainer, musician, vocalist; b. Chgo., Dec. 18, 1919; d. James and Gladys (Gill) C. Singer, entertainer various Chgo. music clubs, 1939—41; singer with Gene Krupa's Orch., 1941—45, with Stan Kenton Orch., 1944, with Woody Herman Orch., 1945, Benny Goodman Orch., 1959; singing tours in US and abroad, 1947—; rec. artist Polygram, Capitol, Emily Records, Verve, GNP Crescendo, Columbia, London, Signature, DRG, Pablo. Million-seller songs include Let Me Off Uptown, 1941, And Her Tears Flowed Like Wine, 1944, Boogie Blues, 1945; appeared in (films) Gene Krupa Story, 1959, Jazz on a Summer's Day, 1960, Zigzag, 1970, Outfit, 1974, (TV shows) 60 Minutes, 1980, Tonight Show, Dick Cavett Show, Today Show, Big Band Bash, CBS Sunday Morning, CNN Showbiz Today, (documentary) Indestructable, 2006; author: High Times, Hard Times, 1981, rev. edit., 1989; performer 50 yr. Anniversary Concert Carnegie Hall, 1985, Avery Fisher Hall, 1989, Tanglewood, 1990, JVC Festival Town Hall, 1993, Rainbow and Stars, 1995, JVC Festival Carnegie Hall, 1996, JVC Festival Avery Fisher Hall, 1999, Hollywood Palladium, 1999, Blue Note, NYC, 2000, Atlas Supper Club, LA, 2000, Fez, NYC, 2001, Plush Room, San Francisco, 2002, Iridium, NYC, 2003-05, Blue Note, NYC, Jazz Alley, Seattle, 2003, Pizza-in-the-Park, London, 2004, New Paltz State Coll, NY, 2005; albums include Drummer Man, Kenton Era, Anita, Anita Sings The Most, Pick Yourself Up, Lady is a Tramp, An Evening with Anita O'Day, At Mr. Kelly's, Swings Cole Porter, Travelin' Light, All the Sad Young Men, Waiter Make Mine Blues, With the Three Sounds, I Told Ya I Love Ya Now Get Out, Uptown, My Ship, Live in Tokyo, Anita Sings the Winners, Incomparable, Anita 1975, Live at Mingos, Anita O'Day/The Big Band Sessions, Swings Rodgers and Hart, Time for Two, Tea for Two, In a Mellowtone (Grammy nomination 1990), At Vine St. Live, Mello'Day, Live at the City, Angel Eyes, The Night Has a Thousand Eyes, The Rules of the Road, Jazz Masters, Skylark, Swingtime in Hawaii, SS 'Wonderful (Carnegie Hall), Jazz Past Midnight, Compact Jazz, Let Me Off Uptown, The Complete Verve/Cleff Sessions, Ultimate Anita O'Day, After Midnight, Hi-Ho Trailus Bootwhip, Legends of the Swing Era, The Legacy Lives On, Finest Hour, Complete Signature and London Recordings, The Young Anita, Still Swinging, Indestructible, Live at Basin St. West. Jazz Masters fellow Nat. Endowment for Arts, 1997, Nat. Endowment fellowship; inductee Jazz Hall of Fame, Tampa, 1997. Mem. AFTRA, BMI, Screen Actors Guild. Office: 1010 Hillcrest Rd Glendale CA 91207-1542 Office Phone: 818-507-8918. E-mail: aeichler@earthlink.net. *From the time I was twelve or thirteen, my life was music. I never thought about being on top. I only wanted to be a part of the scene.*

**O'DAY, PATRICK MICHAEL,** sociologist, educator, criminologist, researcher; b. Chgo., Sept. 13, 1938; s. Leonard Lawrence O'Day and Marie Elizabeth Turnquist; m. Olga Minerva Ruíz (div.); 1 child from previous marriage, Dale. BA, Pan Am. Coll., Tex., 1966; MA, U. N.Mex., 1992, PhD, 1995. Vis. prof. N.Mex. Highlands U., Las Vegas, 1995—96; asst. prof. U. Tex., Edinburg, 1997—2002; vis. prof. Tamaulipas State U., Tampico, Mexico, 2002; assoc. prof. Lee P. Brown Criminal Justice Inst., Wiley Coll., Marshall, Tex., 2004—. Dir. Inst. for Latin Am. Policy Analysis, Coll. of NJ, Ewing, 1999—2001; mem. adv. bd. Organized Crime Obs., Geneva, 2000—02. Contbr. articles to profl. jours. Organizer Teamster for a Dem. Union, San Francisco, 1971—76. Fulbright fellow, U. Dept. State, Mex., 2002—03. Mem.: We. Soc. Criminology, Am. Soc. Criminology. Avocation: travel. Office: Wiley Coll Pemberton 150 711 Wiley Ave Marshall TX 75670

**O'DAY, PAUL THOMAS,** trade association executive; b. May 2, 1935; s. James Thomas and Jeannette Irene (Deschenes) O'D.; m. Nancy Frances Eitler, June 16, 1962; children: Kathleen, Maureen, Michael, Ellen. BA, Am. Internat. Coll., Springfield, Mass., 1958; JD, Georgetown U., 1963; MPA, Am. U., 1967; D of Pub. Adminstrn. honoris causa, Am. Internat. Coll., 1997. Bar: D.C. 1964, U.S. Supreme Ct. 1974. Patent examiner US Patent Office, Washington, 1959-62; exec. sec. panel high-speed ground transp., auto. air poll. Dept. Commerce, Washington, 1965-66, staff asst. to sec., 1967-69, exec. asst. to sec., 1969-71, dep. dir. bur. domestic commerce, 1972-74; dep. dir. Nat. Bus. Coun. for Consumer Affairs, Washington, 1971-72; cons. to Gen. Counsel GE, Fairfield, Conn., 1974-75; asst. trade rep. Exec. Office of the Pres., Washington, 1975-77; dep. asst. sec. US Dept. Commerce, Washington, 1978-84; pres. Am. Fiber Mfrs. Assn., Washington, 1984—. Chmn. Fiber Econs. Bur., 1984—; pres. Eisenhower World Affairs Inst. 1993-99, exec. com., 2000—. Corporator Am. Internat. Coll., 1974—; mem. governing coun. Shakespeare Theater Guild, 1989-2001. Recipient Constl. Law award Georgetown U. Law Ctr., 1962; Alumni award Am. Internat. Coll., 1970; Pres.'s Meritorious Exec. award., 1984; Nat. Inst. Pub. Affairs fellow Princeton U., 1964 Mem.: AAAS, NAM Assns. Coun. (bd. dirs. 2006—), Am. Chem. Soc., World Econ. Forum, Israel Bjorling Soc. USA (charter), O'Dea Clan Assn. (Corofin, Ireland), Fed. City Club, Cosmos Club. Home: 8261 Private Ln Annandale VA 22003-4471 Office: Am Fiber Mfrs Assn 1530 Wilson Blvd Ste 690 Arlington VA 22209

**ODDEN, ALLAN ROBERT,** education educator; b. Duluth, Minn., Sept. 16, 1943; s. Robert Norman and Mabel Eleanor (Bjornnes) Odden; m. Eleanor Ann Rubottom, May 28, 1966; children: Sarina, Robert. BS, Brown U., 1965; MDiv, Union Theol. Sem., 1969; MA, Columbia U., 1971, PhD, 1975. Tchr. N.Y.C. Pub. Schs., 1967-72; rsch. assoc. Teachers' Coll. Columbia U., N.Y.C., 1972-75; dir. policy Edn. Commn. of the States, Denver, 1975-84; prof. U. So. Calif., L.A., 1984-93, U. Wis., Madison, 1993—. Rsch. dir. Sch. Fin. Commns., Conn., 1974—75, SD, 1975—76, Mo., 1975—76, Mo., 1993, Mo., 94, NY, 1978—81, NJ, 1991—92, Ark., 2003, Ark., 2005—06, Wyo., 2005, Wyo., 05, Wyo., 06, Wash., 2005—06; co-dir. Consortium Policy Rsch. Edn.; cons. Nat. Govs. Assn., Nat. Conf. State Legislatures, U.S. Sec. Edn., U.S. Senate, U.S. Dept. Edn., many state legislatures and govs.; mem. task force sch. fin. equity adequacy and productivity NRC, 1996—99; ct. master Superior Ct. N.J. in Abbott V. Burke Sch. Fin. Case, 1997—98. Author: (book) Education Leadership for America's Schools, 1995; co-author: Financing Schools for High Performance, 1998, Paying Teachers for What They Know and Do, 1997, Paying Teachers for What They Know and Do, 2d edit., 2002, School Finance: A Policy Perspective, 1992, School Finance: A Policy Perspective, 3d edit., 2004, Reallocating Resources: How to Boost Student Achievement Without Spending More, 2001; editor: Education Policy Implementation, 1991, Rethinking School Finance, 1992, School-Based Financing, 1999; contbr. articles to profl. jours., chapters to books. Mem. L.A. Chamber Edn. and Human Resources Commn., 1986, Gov.'s Sch. Fin. Commn., Calif.,

1987, Calif. Assessment Policy Com., Gov.'s Edn. Task Force, Wis., 1996, Carnegie Corp. Task Force Edn. in the Early Yrs., 1994—96; mem. nat. rsch. coun. com. sch. fin. equity, adequcy and productivity, 1996—99; mem. Gov.'s Blue Ribbon Commn. State and Local Partnerships 21st Century, Wis., 2000. Grantee, Dept. Edn., Carnegie Corp., Spencer Found., Ford Found., Atlantic Philanthropic Svcs., Mellon Found., Carnegie Corp., Pew Charitable Trusts, Rockefeller Found. Mem.: Nat. Soc. Study Edn., Politics Edn. Assn., Am. Ednl. Fin. Assn. (pres. 1979—80), Am. Ednl. Rsch. Assn. Avocations: Lionel training collecting, youth soccer, baseball coach. Office: U Wis Sch Edn Wis Ctr Edn Rsch 1025 W Johnson St # 653E Madison WI 53706-1706 Home: 360 W Washington Ave Unit 1002 Madison WI 53703-2766 Business E-Mail: arodden@wisc.edu.

**ODDIS, JOSEPH ANTHONY,** health associations executive; b. Greensburg, Pa., Nov. 5, 1928; s. Giacinto and Felicetta (D'Amico) O.; m. Jeanne Trevena, July 10, 1954; children— Joseph Michael, Marie Theresa/ BS, Duquesne U., 1950; DSc (hon.), Mass. Coll. Pharmacy, 1975, Phila. Coll. Pharmacy and Sci., 1975, Albany Coll. Pharmacy, Union U., 1976, Duquesne U., 1989, Mercer U., 1995; LHD (hon.), L.I. U., 1991. Staff pharmacist Mercy Hosp., Pitts., 1950-51, asst. chief pharmacist, 1953-54; chief pharmacist Western Pa. Hosp., Pitts., 1954-56; staff rep. hosp. pharmacy Am. Hosp. Assn., Chgo., 1956-60; dir. div. hosp. pharmacy Am. Pharm., Washington, 1960-62; exec. v.p. Am. Soc. Health-System Pharmacists, Washington, 1960-98. Pres. Am. Soc. Hosp. Pharmacists Research and Edn. Found., 1986-98. Active Boy Scouts Am., Camp Fire Girls; Sec. Am. Soc. Health-System Pharmacists Research and Edn. Found., 1970-86. Served with AUS, 1951-53. Recipient 1st cert. Honor award Duquesne U. Sch. Pharmacy, 1969, named Outstanding Alumnus, 1978; recipient Harvey A.K. Whitney award Am. Soc. Hosp. Pharmacists, 1970, Julius Sturmer Meml. Lecture award Rho Chi soc. Phila., 1971, Howard C. Newton Lecture award 1977, Samuel Melendy Lecture award, 1978, Hugo H. Schaefer award, 1983, Reed and Alice Henninger Lecture award, 1984, Donald E. Francke medal, 1986, Remington medal award, 1990. Fellow AAAS; mem. Am. Pharm. Assn., Am. Soc. Hosp. Pharmacists, Am. Inst. History Pharmacy, Internat. Pharm. Fedn. (pres. hosp. pharmacy sect. 1977-81, v.p. 1984-86, pres. 1986-90), Drug Info. Assn., Am. Soc. Assn. Execs., Can. Soc. Hosp. Pharmacists (hon.), Soc. Hosp. Pharmacists Australia (hon.), Pharm. Soc. Gt. Britain (hon.), Pharm. Soc. Nigeria (hon.), Nat. Coun. Patient Info. and Edn. (sec. 1982-85), Israel Pharm. Soc. (hon.), Rho Chi, Kappa Psi (hon.), Duquesne U. Century Club (charter). Home: 6509 Rockhurst Rd Bethesda MD 20817-1661 Office: Am Soc Health-System Pharmacists 7272 Wisconsin Ave Bethesda MD 20814-4836

**ODDONE, PIERMARIA JORGE,** experimental particle physicist; b. Arequipa, Peru, Mar. 26, 1944; came to U.S., 1961; s. Pietro Giovanni and Maria Vittoria (Jona) O.; m. Barbara S. Oddone, Aug. 27, 1965; children: Gian Michele, Alessandra. BS in Physics, MIT, 1965; PhD in Physics, Princeton U., 1970. Postdoctoral fellow Calif. Tech. Inst., Pasadena, 1970-72, Lawrence Berkeley Nat. Lab., Calif., 1972-76, staff scientist Calif. 1976-78, sr. staff scientist Calif. 1978-87, dir. physics div. Calif., 1987-91, lab. dep. dir. Calif., 1990—2005; dir. Fermi Nat. Accelerator Lab., Batavia, Ill., 2005—. Head of the expti. program of the initial Positron Electron Project (PEP) Accelerator at Stanford Linear Accelerator Ctr.(SLAC), 1976-82; mem. of team that developed the Time Projection Chamber (TPC); science coord. in the TPC collaboration at the (PEP) at (SLAC), 1984-87; mem. Stanford Linear Accelerator Ctr. Sci. Policy Com., Calif. 1989-, Santa Cruz (Calif.) Inst. Particle Physics Adv. Com., 1989-91, U.S./Japan Com. for Cooperation in High Energy Physics, U.S. Peoples Republic of China Joint Com. on High Energy Physics, High Energy Physics Adv. Panel (HEPAP), 1991-, KEK Lepton Collider Adv. Com. Fellow Am. Phys. Soc. Achievements include rsch. in high energy physics; devel. of time projection chamber and asymmetric B-factory (a particle collider). Office: Fermilab PO Box 500 Batavia IL 60510-0500 Office Phone: 630-840-3211. Business E-Mail: PLOddone@lbl.gov. E-mail: pjoddone@fnal.gov.*

**O'DEA, J. DAVID,** psychologist, educator; b. Ellsworth, Kans., Feb. 17, 1924; m. Teresa Eleanor Cordova, June 21, 1980. BS in Psychology, Emporia State U., 1948, MS in Psychology, 1949; PhD in Psychology, Oreg. State U., 1952. Lic. psychologist Fla. Assoc. prof. Fla. State U., Tallahassee, 1953—56; sr. staff assoc. IBM, Dunedin, Fla., 1956—82. Cons. psychologist, Dunedin, 1982—92; vis. prof. Notre Dame U., South Bend, Ind., 1953, U. Va., Charlottesville, 1956, Oreg. State U., Corvallis, 1964, U. Miami, 1969—70; chmn. bd. Caladesi Nat. Bank, Dunedin, 1967—72, Clearwater (Fla.) Oaks Bank, Clearwater, 1973—82. Contbr., author: book Counseling Selected Readings, 1962; contbr. articles to profl. jours. and mags. Mem. adv. counsel for pres. Berea (Ky.) Coll.; bd. dirs. Dunedin Pub. Libr., 1991—. With USN, 1942—45, WWII. Named Ky. col., Hon. Order of Ky. Cols., 1982. Mem.: VFW, APA (licentiate; Fla. state pres. 1969—70), Ye Mystic Krewe of Neptune (charter mem. Tampa Bay, dir. 1979—), KC (4th degree, Family of Month 1980), Elks (life). Roman Catholic. Avocations: travel, reading, civil volunteering, genealogy. Home: 509 Baywood Dr S Dunedin FL 34698

**O'DEA, WILLIAM PATRICK,** research and development company executive; b. Jersey City, Feb. 20, 1959; s. William Patrick O'Dea Sr. and Blanche (Zakrzewski) O'Dea. BS in polit. sci., St. John's U., 1981; BS in criminal justice, Seton Hall Law Sch., 1982. Project mgr. Elizabeth (NJ) Devel. Co., 1993—94, UEZ dir., 1994—95, deputy exec. dir., 1995—. City coun. mem. City of Jersey City, 1985—93; freeholder County of Hudson, Jersey City, 1997—; mem. Jersey City Planning Bd., 1985—; v. chmn. Jersey City Edn. Devel. Co., 1985—89, PR Org. for Econ. Edn. Devel., Elizabeth, 1996—. Co-author: (plays) The Pitts, 2003 (Producer award, 2003), (screenplays) A Clown in Babylon, 1994 (Producer award, 1996); author: (plays) Therapy, 1993 (Producer award, 1993). Bd. mem. Friends of the Loew's, Jersey City, 2003; elected mem. NJ Dem. Com., Trenton, 2000—; bd. mem. Big Brother/Big Sister, Hudson County, 1997—. Recipient Advocate for People award, Christopher Columbus Found., 2003, Govt. award, NJ Dept. Com. Affairs Efficiency, 2005, Finalist, US Dept. Commerce, Excellence in Econ. Develop., EDA. Mem.: Knights of Columbus 475, Moose Lodge 266, Nat. Honor Soc. Democrat. Catholic. Achievements include directed nation's #1 Enterprise Zone program as selected by the Nat. Assn. of State Devel. agencies, 1998. Avocations: chess, mentor, playwriter, script writer, catechism thr. Home: 143 Mallory Ave Jersey City NJ 07304

**O'DEAR, CRAIG STEVEN,** lawyer; b. Quincy, Ill., June 26, 1957; s. H.C. and Martha Lou (Holbert) O'D.; m. Stephanie Doolin Patterson, Feb. 11, 1995. BS in Engring. Mgmt., U. Mo., Rolla, 1979; JD, Vanderbilt U., 1982. Bar: Mo. 1982, U.S. Dist. Ct. (we. dist.) Mo. 1982, U.S. Ct. Appeals (8th cir.) 1984, U.S. Ct. Appeals (10th cir.) 1988, U.S. Ct. Appeals (11th cir.) 1994. Indsl. engr. IBM Corp., Endicott, N.Y., summer 1979; summer assoc. Bass, Berry & Sims, Nashville, 1980, Stinson, Mag & Fizzell, Kansas City, Mo., 1981, Kirkland & Ellis, Chgo., 1981; assoc. Stinson, Mag & Fizzell, Kansas City, 1982-88, Bryan Cave LLP, Kansas City, 1988-89; ptnr., 1990—; mem. exec. com. Chmn. recruiting com. Bryan Cave, Kansas City, 1988-92, coord. litigation dept., 1994—, group leader product liability client svc., 1996—. Chmn. United Way Pacesetter Camp, Kansas City, 1985; mem. leadership devel. program Kansas City Tomorrow, Kansas City, 1990. Patrick Wilson scholar Vanderbilt U., 1979-82. Mem. Kansas City Club. Republican. Presbyterian. Avocations: flying, golf, running, photography. Office: Bryan Cave LLP 3500 One Kansas City Pl 1200 Main St Kansas City MO 64105-2122 Office Phone: 816-374-3207. E-mail: csodear@bryancave.com.

**ODELEIN, LYLE,** professional hockey player; b. Saskatchewan, Can., July 21, 1968; Defense Montreal Canadiens, 1989—96, Devils, 1996-99, 1999—2000, Coyotes, 1999—2000, Blue Jackets, 2000—02, Chgo. Blackhawks, 2002—. Recipient Stanley Cup, Montreal Canadiens, 1993. Office: Florida Panthers Office Depot Center One Panther Parkway Sunrise FL 33323

**ODELL, HERBERT,** lawyer; b. Phila., Oct. 20, 1937; s. Samuel and Selma (Kramer) O.; m. Valerie Odell; children: Wesley, Jonathan, James, Sarah, Samuel. BS in Econs., U. Pa., 1959; LLB magna cum laude, U. Miami, 1962;

LLM, Harvard U., 1963. Bar: Fla. 1963, Pa. 1968, D.C. 2002. Trial atty. tax div. U.S. Dept. Justice, Washington, 1963-65; assoc. Walton, Lantaff, Schroeder, Carson & Wahl, Miami, Fla., 1965-67; from assoc. to ptnr. Morgan, Lewis & Bockius, Phila., 1967-89; ptnr. Zapruder & Odell, Phila., 1989-98, Odell & Ptnrs., Phila., 1998-99, Miller & Chevalier, Chartered, Phila., 2000—. Adj. prof. U. Miami, Villanova U.; lectr. various tax insts. Contbr. articles to profl. jours. Ford fellow, 1962-63. Mem.: ABA, D.C. Bar Assn., Phila. Bar Assn., Pa. Bar Assn., Fla. Bar Assn., Harvard Club, Beta Alpha Psi, Omicron Delta Kappa, Phi Kappa Phi. Avocations: sailing, running, tennis, scuba diving, fishing. Office: Miller & Chevalier Ste 570 300 Conshohocken State Rd West Conshohocken PA 19428 Office Phone: 610-729-7810. Business E-Mail: hodell@milchev.com.

**ODELL, JAMES CALVIN,** history professor, theology studies educator; b. Weed, Calif., Nov. 23, 1951; s. Calvin Harry and Bessie Pearl (Matthews) Odell; m. Nancy Louise Everest, June 28, 1975; children: Abigail B. Cook, Rebekah L. Brooking, Rachel L. BS in Sem. Studies, We. Bapt. Coll., Salem, Oreg.: 1974; ThM in Hist. Theology, Dallas Theol. Sem., Tex., 1978; PhD in Bibl. Studies, Pensacola Christian Coll., Fla., 2000. Pastor Lafayette Bapt. Ch., Oreg., 1979—81; missionary Bapt. Mid. Missions, Cleve., 1984—99; prof. Crossroads Bible Coll., Indpls., 1987—. Chaplain USAR, 1983—. Author: Odells Kinfolk and Aquantinos, 2003. Lt. col. USAR, 1983—, Desert Storm, Bosnia, Kuwait. Avocation: genealogy. Office: Crossroads Bible Coll 601 N Shortridge Rd Indianapolis IN 46219

**O'DELL, NANCY,** television personality; b. Myrtle Beach, SC; d. Leonard and Betty Humphries; m. Richard O'Dell (separated). Grad, Clemson U. Reporter, anchor WPDE-TV, Myrtle Beach, SC; morning news anchor, crime reporter WCBD-TV, Charleston; co-anchor, investigative reporter WTVJ-TV, Miami; entertainment reporter A Current Affair, 1995—96; weekend co-anchor, weekday corr. Access Hollywood, 1996—99, co-anchor, 1999—; host Nashville Star, USA Network, 2003—. Contbr. reports NBC News's The Today Show and Dateline; host Emmys Pre-Show, Fox, 1999, Emmys Pre-Show, ABC, 2000; co-host Emmys Post Show, NBC, 2002, Hollywood Christmas Parade, 1999, 2000, 02, Tournament of Roses Parade coverage, NBC, 2001, 02, 03, 04, Golden Globes Arrivals Show, NBC, 2002, 03, 04, Miss USA, 2004. Actress (films) Scream 2, 1997, The Adventures of Ragtime, 1998, The Bachelor, 1999, Scream 3, 2000, Outta Time, 2002, (TV series) General Hospital, 1998, Days of Our Lives, 2002—03. Mem. Nat. Celebrity Cabinet, Am. Red Cross, 2002—; internat. bd. mem Best Buddies; Celebrity Amb. Childhelp USA; spokesperson March of Dimes. Named State SC Hall of Fame, 1998; recipient 2 AP Awards, 2 Soc. Profl. Journalists Awards, Spirit of Leadership Award, Best Buddies, 2002. Office: Access Hollywood NBC Studios 3000 W Alameda Ave Burbank CA 91523

**ODELL, PATRICK WAYNE,** mathematics professor; b. Watonga, Okla., Nov. 29, 1930; s. Max Vernon and Pamela (Massey) Odell; m. Norma Lou Maddox, Aug. 16, 1958 (dec. May 1980); children: James M., David L., Michael R.L., Julie K., Patricia L., Deborah L.; m. Dovalee Dorsett, Aug. 3, 1985. BS, U. Tex., 1952; postgrad., UCLA, 1953-54; MS, Okla. State U., 1958, PhD, 1962. Mathematician White Sands (N.Mex.) Proving Grounds, 1952-53, Kaman Nuclear, Albuquerque, 1958-59, U.S. Naval Nuclear Ordnance Evaluation Unit, 1959-62, Ling-Temco Vought Aeros., 1962; asst. prof. math. U. Tex., Austin, 1962-66; prof., chmn. dept. math. Tex. Technol. U., Lubbock, 1966-71, coordinator insts., dir. rsch., Coll. Arts and Sci., 1971-72; prof math. scis. and environ. scis. U. Tex., Dallas, 1972-88, prof. emeritus, 1988—; prof. emeritus math. sci. Baylor U., Waco, Tex., 1988—2001; exec. dean grad. studies and rsch. U. Tex., Dallas, 1972-75. Assoc. dir. Tex. Ctr. for Rsch., Austin, 1964—66; rsch. scientist Def. Rsch. Lab., 1963—65; cons. math. statistician, 1962—. Capt. USAF, 1953-57. Fellow: Am. Statis. Assn., Tex. Acad. Sci. (Disting. Tex. Scientist award 1994). Home: 1117 Deer Run Rd Valley Mills TX 76689 E-mail: pat_odell@baylor.edu.

**O'DELL, WALDEN WESLEY,** manufacturing executive; b. St. Louis, July 19, 1945; s. Walden W. and Nettie Ann (Chaffin)O'D.; m. Patricia Marie Gormley, Aug. 19, 1967; children: Micahael Thomas, Jennifer Mary, Patrick Brian, Kathleen Elizabeth. BS, St. Louis U., 1967, MS, 1970; MBA, Stanford U., Calif., 1972. Engr. Emerson Electrics-E&S, St. Louis, 1966-70; asst. to v.p. engr. Boise Cascade, St. Louis, 1971; engr., asst. to v.p., int. mgr., int. adminstr. Emerson Electric - Corp. Int., St. Louis, 1970-75; v.p. intl. Emerson Electric - Alco Controls, St. Louis, Emerson Electric - USEM, Milford, Conn., 1979-81; pres. Emerson Electric - Louisville Ladder, 1981-85, Emerson Electric - Krautkramer Branson, Lewistown, Pa., 1985-87, Emerson Electric Co., Lewistown, 1987—99, Diebold, Inc., North Canton, Ohio, 1999—2004, CEO Canton, Ohio, 1999—2005, chmn., 2000—05. Mem. Cin. Council on World Affairs, 1987—. Mem. Valve Mfrs. Assn., Hyde Park Country Club.*

**ODEN, JEAN P(HIFER),** special education educator; b. Chgo., May 2, 1936; d. Dillard James and Lena (Conner) Phifer; m. James Edward Oden, Apr. 26, 1959; 1 child, Eric James. BE, Chgo. Tchrs. Coll., 1958; MEd in Learning Disabilities, Chgo. State U., 1973; postgrad., Nat. Coll. Edn., Evanston, Ill., 1986—, cert. advance studies, 1987; EdD, Nat.-Louis U., 1995. Tchr. elem. schs. Chgo., 1958-73, tchr. learning disabilities elem. schs., 1973-81, cons. spl. edn., ind. edn. program facilitator, 1981; learning disability specialist Phillips High Sch., Chgo., 1982-87, Englewood High Sch., Chgo., 1987-94, Harold Washington Elem. Sch., Chgo., 1994-98. Mem. Ill. Guidelines for Learning Disabilities Devel. Com., Springfield, Ill., 1981-82, Com. to Devel. State Test for Learning Disabilities Tchrs., Springfield, 1986—; speaker Who's Who Congress, Cambridge, Eng., 1992; mem. del. to Vietnam, 1993, China, 1994, Oxford U., 1997, South Africa, 2001; mem. African Affairs Adv. Coun. to Chgo. Human Rels. Commn., 1999-, People to People Internat. Worldwide Conf., 2002—; chair edn. com. Chgo. Southside Br. NAACP, 2000, sec. 2003. Sec. Nat. Urban League N.Y.C. conf., 1980-2005, Chgo. Southside br., 2003—; mem. Congl. Victory Fund, Chgo., 1985, SCLC Met. Chgo., 1979-81, Mayoral Summit Parent-Community Coun. on Ednl. Reform, 1987—, Chgo. Mayor's Edn. Summit on Sch. Reform, 1988; charter mem. Rep. Presdl. Adv. Task Force, 1989, Rep. Inner Circle, 1991, Ctr. for Study of the Presidency, 1998; mem. Coalition Black Trade Unionists, 1991—, cons. pool Nat. Juvenile Justice Resource Ctr., 1991—, NAACP; state chair African Am. Econ. Devel. Task Force, Ill. Legis. Black Caucus, 1992—; bd. dirs., African Scientific Rsch. Mus. Inst., 2003. U.S. Dept. Edn. grantee, 1986; recipient Citizenship award Chgo. mayor, 1984, Cert. merit NAACP South Side Br., 1978; named state advisor U.S. Congl. Adv. Bd., 1985; speaker edn. seminar 19th Congress on Arts and Communicatiion, Cambridge, Eng. Mem. ASCD, LWV, NAACP (chair edn. com. 2000, sec. Chgo. Southside br., 2003), Minority Mainstream, United Neighborhoods Intertwined for Total Equality (founder, exec. dir., rschr.), Assn. for Citizens with Learning Disabilities, Coun. for Exceptional Children (liaison to state bd. Ill. Divsn. for Citizens with Learning Disabilities 1980), Spl. Edn. Tchrs. Assn. (1st pres., founder), Black Parents United for Edn. and Related Svcs. (founder), Kappa Delta Pi, Lehigh (Fla.) Country Club, Thousand Trails Club (Ottawa, Ill.). Mem. Carter C.M.E. Ch. Avocations: hiking, racketball, travel, camping. Fax: 773 821-4456. Business E-Mail: jeanoden@sbcglobal.net. *Personal philosophy: Those of us in society who are fortunate to reach levels of influence should share skills and talents with the less fortunate. A society which maintain masses of people in an undeveloped state is doomed to class conflict and cultural extinction. Those who don't study history are bound to repeat it.*

**ODEN, JOHN TINSLEY,** engineering educator, mathematician, consultant; b. Alexandria, La., Dec. 25, 1936; s. John James and Sara Elizabeth (Lyles) O.; m. Barbara Clare Smith, Mar. 19, 1965; children: John Walker, Elizabeth Lee. BS, La. State U., 1959; MS, Okla. State U., 1960, PhD, 1962; DSc (hon.), Tech. U. Lisbon, Portugal, 1986; Doctorate (hon.), Polytechnique de Mons, Belgium, 2000, Tech. U. Krakow, Poland, 2001, Ecole Normale Superior Cochan, 2006. Registered profl. engr., Tex., La. Teaching asst. La. State U., Baton Rouge, 1959; asst. prof. Okla. State U., Stillwater, 1961-63; sr. structures engr. Gen. Dynamics, Fort Worth, 1963-64; prof., head dept. engring. mechanics U. Ala., Huntsville, 1964-73; prof. U. Tex., Austin,

1973—, Carol and Henry Groppe prof. engring., Ernest and Virginia Cockrell chair in engring. Austin, 1987-93, Cockrell Family Regents prof. engring. 2, 1993—, assoc. v.p. rsch., 2003—. Prof. Coope U. Fed., Brazil, 1974; dir. Inst. Computational Engring and Sci., 2003, assoc. v.p. for rsch., 2003—; mem. Sci. Rsch. Coun. vis. scholar Brunel U., Eng., 1981; com. on computational mechanics NRC; chmn. U. S. Nat. Com. on Theoretical and Applied Mechanics, 1992-94; founder, CEO computational Mechanics Co., Inc., 1982-96; Peter O'Donnell Jr. chair in computer sys., 2003. Author, editor 45 books; editor Jour. Computer Methods in Applied Mechanics and Engring., 1980—; contbr. over 500 articles to profl. jours. Decorated Chevalier Ordre des Palms Academique (France); recipient rsch. award Southeastern Conf. on Theoretical and Applied Mechanics, 1978, Lohmann medal Okla. State U., 1991, Computational Mechanics Medal Japan Soc. Mech. Engrs., 1993, Presdl. Citation, U. Tex. Austin, 2004 Fellow ASCE (life; Outstanding Svc. award 1968, Walter Huber rsch. award 1973, Theodore von Karman medal 1992, Joe J. King Prof. Engring. award 1994), ASME (hon. mem., Worcester Reed Warner medal 1993, Timoshenko medal 1996), NAE, Soc. Engring. Sci. (pres. 1978, Eringen medal 1991, Hocott Rsch. award, 1992), Am. Acad. Mechanics (pres. 1990-94, Disting. Svc. medal 1995), Internat. Assn. Computational Mechanics (pres. 1990-94, Congress-Gauss-Newton medal 1994); mem. Soc. Indsl. and Applied Math., U.S. Assn. Computational Mechanics (pres. 1990-92, John Von Neumann medal 1993), Soc. Natural Philosophy, Nat. Acad. Engring. Mex., Nat. Acad. Engring. Brazil, World Innovation Found. (hon. 2004). Home: 7403 W Rim Dr Austin TX 78731-2044 Office: Univ Tex Austin ICES Campus Code CO200 Austin TX 78712

**ODEN, ROBERT A., JR.,** academic administrator; m. Teresa Oden; children: Robert, Katherine. BA in History and Lit., Harvard Coll.; MA in Religious Studies/Oriental Langs., Cambridge U.; MA in Theology, Harvard Divinity, 1972; PhD in Near Eastern Langs. and Lit., Harvard U., 1975; MA (hon.), Dartmouth Coll., 1987. Faculty Dartmouth Coll., 1975—89, prof., 1985—89, chair dept. of religion, 1988—; dir. founder Dartmouth's Humanities Inst.; headmaster Hotchkiss Sch., Lakeville, Conn., 1989—95; pres. Kenyon Coll., Gambier, Ohio, 1995—2002, Carleton Coll., Northfield, Minn., 2002—. Chmn. com. on orgn. and policy Dartmouth Coll., com. on admissions and fin. aid; lectr. in field. Author: The Bible Without Theology, 1987. Mem.: Conn. Assn. Ind. Schs. (bd. dirs.). Avocations: fishing, running, religious studies, archaeology. Office: Carleton Coll 1 North College St Northfield MN 55057 Office Phone: 507-646-4305. E-mail: president@acs.carleton.edu.*

**ODEN, ROBERT RUDOLPH,** surgeon; b. Chgo., Dec. 2, 1922; s. Rudolph J. E. and Olga H. (Wahlquist) Oden; m. Nancy Clow; children: Louise, Boyd, Beach, Lisbeth. BS, U. Ill., 1943; MD, Northwestern U., 1947, MS in Anatomy, 1947. Intern Augustana Hosp., Chgo., 1947-48, resident in surgery, 1948-49; resident in orthopaedics Hines Vets. Hosp., Chgo., 1949-51; resident in children's orthopaedics Shriner's Hosp., 1953-54; pvt. practice Chgo., 1954-57, Aspen, Colo., 1957—. Clin. assoc. prof. orthopedics U. Colo.; orthop. surgeon U.S. Olympic team., 1960, 72, 76, 80; founder, trustee Pitkin County Bank, 1983—. Assoc. editor: Clin. Orthopedics and Related Rsch. Founder Aspen Inst. Theol. Futures, 1978, Gt. Tchrs. and Preachers Series Episc. Ch., 1989; trustee U.S. Ski Ednl. Found., 1967—82, Aspen Valley Hosp., 1978—86; founder Aspen Orthop. and Sports Medicine Pub. Found., 1985; mem. organizing com. Aspen World Cup, 1976—92; founder Aspen Pitken Employee Housing, 1975. Named to Colo. Ski Hall of Fame, 2002, U.S. Ski Hall of Fame, 2002; recipient Biegan award Most Outstanding Svc. to U.S. Skiing, 1985, Halsted award, U.S. Ski Assn., 1987. Mem.: SICOT, ACS, Internat. Knee Inst., Internat. Soc. Knee, ACL Study Group, Internat. Ski Safety Inst., Am. Orthop. Soc. Sports Medicine (Hall of Fame 2004), Can. Orthop. Assn., Rocky Mountain Traumatologic Soc., Am. Assn. Bone & Joint Surgeons, Western Orthop. Assn., Internat. Coll. Surgeons, Am. Acad. Orthop. Surgeons, Phi Beta Kappa. Home: PO Box 660 Aspen CO 81612-0660 also: PO Box 172 Captiva FL 33924-0172 Office: 100 E Main St Aspen CO 81611-1778 E-mail: capoden@earthlink.net.

**ODEN, WALDO TALMAGE, JR.,** lawyer; b. Altus, Okla., May 17, 1929; s. Waldo Talmage Sr. and Lily Juanita (Clark) O.; m. Rebecca Jane Hazlitt, Mar. 25, 1951; children: Waldo Talmage, Timothy Patrick, Amy Germaine Lindley, Jonathan Andrew. BA, U. Okla., 1950, LLB, 1952, JD, 1970. Bar: Okla. 1952, U.S. Supreme Ct. 1960. Sole practice, Altus, 1952—; mem. Robinson & Oden, 1952-53, Oden & Oden, 1954-67, 70-81; mng. ptnr. Oden Oden & Derryberry, 1967-70; asst. atty. Jackson County, 1953-54; dir. Farmers & Mchts. Bank; instr. bus. law Western Okla. State Coll. 1956-59; instr., faculty coord. for criminology Altus AFB, 1958; instr. masters degree program Webster Coll., Altus AFB, 1975—; mem. Okla. Jud. Nominating Commn., 1967-71; lectr. agrl. law. County dir. Jackson County CD, 1959-68; chmn. Kicking Bird dist. Boy Scouts Am., 1969-78; del. Meth. Jurisdictional Confs., Meth. Gen. Confs.; lay leader Clinton Dist. of Okla. Conf. of United Meth. Ch., 1982-88; bd. dir. Gen. Bd. of Global Ministries, United Meth. Ch., 1984—; sec. exec. com. Meth. Series of Protestant Hour, 1968-72; chmn. dept. communications and pub. rels. Okla. United Meth. Conf., 1976-84; mem. United Meth. Nat. Bd. Higher Edn. and Ministry, 1980-84; mem. exec. com. W.W. and Rosa Woodworth Estate; pres. U. Okla. Wesley Found., 1947, Okla. Meth. Student Movement, 1948; mem. Okla. Humanities Com., 1976-79; campaign chmn. Jackson County Dem. Com., 1954-60; trustee Altus Libr. Bd., 1965-72; chmn. Okla. Bar Assn. Task Force on Farm Crisis, 1985—. Mem. ABA (chmn. agrl. law com. gen. practice sect. 1976-84, sec. gen. practice coun. 1982-83), Okla. Bar Assn. (chmn. gen. practice sect.), Jackson County Bar Assn., Assn. Trial Lawyers Am., Okla. Trial Lawyers Assn., Phi Delta Phi, Masons, Rotary (pres. 1959-60). Mem. staff Okla. Law Rev., 1950-52. Home: 913 E Elm St Altus OK 73521-4025 Office: PO Box J Altus OK 73522-1130

**ODEN, WILLIAM BRYANT,** bishop, educator; b. McAllen, Tex., Aug. 3, 1935; s. Charles Alva and Evea (Bryant) O.; m. Marilyn Brown, July 12, 1957; children: Danna Lee Oden Bowen, William Dirk, Valerie Lyn, Charles Bryant. BA, Okla. State U., 1958; MDiv, Harvard U., 1961, postgrad., 1964; ThD, Boston U., 1964; DD (hon.), Oklahoma City U., 1980; LHD (hon.), Centenary Coll., 1990. Ordained to ministry Meth. Ch., 1961. Pastor Aldersgate United Meth. Ch., Oklahoma City, 1963-69, St. Stephen's United Meth. Ch., Norman, Okla., 1969-76, Crown Heights United Meth. Ch., Oklahoma City, 1976-83; prof. Phillips Grad. Sem., Enid, 1976-88; pastor 1st United Meth. Ch., Enid, 1983-88; bishop United Meth. Ch., La., 1988-96, Dallas area, 1996—2004, Ecumenical del. to Lambeth Conf., 1998. Pres., United Meth. Coun. Bishops, 2000-01; pres. SCJ Coll. of Bishops, 1989-90; del. Gen. Conf., 1976, 80, 84, 88; chmn. Okla. Del. to Gen. and Jurisdictional Confs., 1984, 88; Jackson lectr. Perkins Sch. Theology, So. Meth. U., 1975, Wilson lectr. SCJ Bishop's Week, 1989; co-chair World Meth.-Anglican Dialogue, 1991-95; bd. dirs. Wesley Works Project; pres. Gen. Bd. Higher Edn. & Ministry, 1996-01; pres. commn. United Meth. Ch., 2000-04; Ecumenical officer, head communion, 2004-. Author: Oklahoma Methodism in the Twentieth Century, 1968, Liturgy as Life Journey, 1976, Wordeed: Evangelism in Biblical and Wesleyan Perspective, 1978; contbr.: Send Me: The Iteneracy in Crisis, 1991, Vision and Supervision, 2003. Trustee Oklahoma City U., 1980-88, Southwestern U., Winfield, Kans., 1983-88, Centenary Coll., 1988-96, Dillard U., 1988-96, So. Meth. U., 1996—2004. Named to U. Hall of Fame, Okla. State, 2003; recipient Outstanding Alumni award, Harvard Divinity Sch., 2005; Charles E. Merrill fellow, Harvard U., 2003. Mem. Am. Acad. Homiletics. Methodist. Avocations: writing, reading biographies, mountain climbing, backpacking. Office Phone: 214-768-1200. Personal E-mail: wbo8@earthlink.net.

**ODENHEIMER, ROBERT W.,** health care services company executive; Positions with Boeing Computer Services, MCI, CACI Internat. Inc.; now sr. v.p. info. tech. ops. and telecommunications Magellan Health Services, Inc., Avon, Conn. Named one of Premier 100 IT Leaders, Computerworld, 2005. Office: Magellen Health Services Inc 55 Nod Rd Avon CT 06001*

**ODENIGBO, INNOCENT CHUKWUNWIKE,** linguist, writer, consultant; b. Nri, Anambra State, Nigeria, Sept. 28, 1941; arrived in U.S., 1998; s. Lazarus Okonkwo and Rosaline Ama Odenigbo; m. Monica Chinwe Akpu, Oct. 6, 1996; m. Felicia Umekwulu Egesi, Sept. 26, 1967 (div. Sept. 16, 1996); children: Uchenna Zephyrina, Ifeanyi Innocent, Chukwuemeka John-Mary, Uzoamaka Assumpta. BA in Languages, U. de Grenoble, 1968—71; postgrad., U. Besancon, 1974—75. CIRNEA, Paris, 1990—94; PhD in Languages, Am. West U., 1999—2002; MBA, Dowling Coll., 2000—02. Lang. prof. Inst. of Mgmt. and Tech., Enugu, Nigeria, 1971—73; rsch. officer Nigerian Nat. Supply Co., London, 1973—78; sr. news presenter Nigerian TV Authority, Enugu, Nigeria, 1979—81; chief editor, anchorman Anambra Broadcasting Svc., Awka, Nigeria, 1983—98; pres. IMC Info. Services, Newark, 2003—. Cons. IMC Info. Services, Newark, 2003—. Author: (poetry) Thank God for America. Recipient Best Broadcaster award, Nigeria Union Journalists, 1984. Mem.: Soc. of Profl. Journalists, Internat. Soc. of Poets (Disting. Mem. 2000, 2001). Office Phone: 973-677-2665. E-mail: odenigbo5@aol.com.

**ODENWELLER, ROBERT PAUL,** philatelist, trade association administrator, retired pilot; b. Sept. 19, 1938; s. Charles Joseph and Robina Katharine (Watson) O.; m. Jane Blackistone Rawlings, June 24, 1965; 1 stepchild, Joy McCorriston; child, Liesl Hasbrouck. BS, U.S. Air Force Acad., 1960. Commd. USAF, 1956, advanced through grades to capt., 1963, resigned, 1956-66. Mem. Collectors Club Inc., N.Y.C., 1964—, gov. 1969—, program chmn., 1970-80, 2004—, mem. editl. bd., 1975—, sec. 1979-82, v.p. 1983-86, pres. 1987-90, trustee, 1992-98; trustee, vice chmn. then chmn. expert com. Philatelic Found., N.Y.C., 1970—; editor The Collectors Club Philatelist, 2005-. Author: The FIP Guide to Exhibiting and Judging Traditional and Postal History Exhibits, 1993; author, editor: Philatelic Vocabulary in Five Languages, 1978 (Vermeil medal 1979); editor: Opinions VI, 1992 (Gold medal), The Stamps and Postal History of Nineteenth Century Samoa, 2004 (Gold medal, Nat. Grand award, Internat. Gold medal, 2005, Spl. prize, 2005, Best in Show, 2005); contbr. articles to profl. pubs Recipient Grand Prix d'Honneur, Zeapex Orgn., 1980; selected to sign Roll of Disting. Philatelists, Brit. Philatelic Fedn., 1991, Alfred Lichtenstein Meml. award Collectors Club, N.Y., 1993, TWA Flight Ops. Meritorious Achievement award 1995, award of Excellence, 1995, 2000. Fellow Royal Philatelic Soc. London (spl. rep. for U.S. 2003—, conduct com. 2004—, Crawford medal, 2005), Royal Philatelic Soc. N.Z. (Collins award 2005); mem. Fedn. Internat. de Philatelie (pres. commn. traditional philately 1978-96; Grand Prix d'Honneur 1980, Svc. medal 1996, Rsch. medal 2006), Am. Philatelic Soc. (bd. dirs. 1981-84, 89-90, named Champion of Champions 1973, Luff award 1996, chmn. 2003-), Assn. Internat. Des Experts Philateliques (expert 1980-, bd. dirs. 1987-), Fedn. New Zealand Philatelic Socs., Grand Prix Club Internat. (sec., treas. 1980-89, bd. dirs. 1989-92, 94-00, v.p. 1994-96, pres. 1996-2002), Soc. Australasian Specialists (pres. 1969-72), U.S. Chess Fedn., European Acad. Philately. Republican. Episcopalian. Avocations: stamp collecting/philately, photography, languages, chess, bridge. Home: Chalon Round Top Rd Bernardsville NJ 07924 Office: Collector's Club Inc 22 E 35th St New York NY 10016-3806 Office Phone: 908-766-5460. Business E-mail: ccpeditor@cs.com.

**ODER, FREDERIC CARL EMIL,** retired aerospace transportation executive; b. L.A., Oct. 23, 1919; s. Emil and Katherine Ellis (Pierce) O.; m. Dorothy Gene Brumfield, July 2, 1941 (dec. Jan. 2004); children: Frederic E., Barbara Oder Debes, Richard W.; m. Doris S. Parrish, Sept. 24, 2005. BS, Calif. Inst. Tech., 1940, MS, 1941; PhD, UCLA, 1952. Commd. 2d lt. U.S. Army Air Force, 1941; advanced through grades to col. U.S. Air Force, 1960; ret., 1960; asst. dir. and program mgr. for research and engring. Apparatus and Optical div. Eastman Kodak Co., Rochester, NY, 1960-66; with Lockheed Missiles & Space Co., Sunnyvale, Calif., 1966-91, v.p., asst. gen. mgr. div. space systems, 1972-73, v.p., gen. mgr. div. space systems, 1973-84, exec. v.p., 1984—; cons., 1985-91. Mem. Def. Intelligence Agy. Sci. Adv. Com., 1972-76, assoc. mem., 1976-78; mem. Air Force Studies Bd., Assembly Engring., NRC, 1975-79, Def. Sci. Bd. Summer Study, 1975, Rev. Panel, 1979, Space Applications Bd., 1985-88. Contbr. articles to profl. jours. Decorated Legion of Merit; recipient Nat. Reconnaissance Pioneer. Fellow AIAA; mem. NAE, Masons, Sigma Xi. Episcopalian. Home: 50 Lake Rd Gloucester MA 01930-3972 E-mail: fceoder@aol.com.

**ODERMATT, ROBERT ALLEN,** architect; b. Oakland, Calif., Jan. 3, 1938; s. Clifford Allen and Margaret Louise (Budge) O.; m. Diana Birtwistle, June 9, 1960; children: Kristin Ann, Kyle David. BArch, U. Calif., Berkeley, 1960. Registered architect, Calif., Oreg., Nev., Colo., Hawaii; cert. Nat. Coun. Archtl. Registration Bds. Draftsman Anderson Simonds Dusel Campini, Oakland, 1960-61; architect James R. Lucas, Orinda, Calif., 1961-62, ROMA Architects, San Francisco, 1962-76, architect, pres., 1976-84; prin. ROMA Design Group, San Francisco, 1962-92; pres. The Odermatt Group, Berkeley, Calif., 1992—. Prin. spkr. Internat. Conf. on Rebuilding Cities, Pitts., 1988; mem. U.S. Design in Am. Program, Sofia, Bulgaria, Armenian Disaster Assn. Team, 1989, NA Collateral Internship Mgmt. Com.; prin. State of Calif. Bay Arera Facilities Plan, 1992, Greece Resort Privatization Program, 1993. Prin. designer U.S. Embassy, Bahrain, Grand Canyon Nat. Park, 1977, Yosemite Nat. Park, 1987; prin. planner hotel complex Westin Hotel, Vail, Colo., 1982, Kaanapali Resort, 1987, Las Montanas Resort, San Diego; master plan U. Calif., Berkeley, 1988, Kohanaiki and Mauna Lani resorts, 1989, Calif. State Strategic Real Estate Plan, 1992, Greek Resort/Marina Privatization Program, 1993, Tektronix Strategic Plan, 1994, United Labs, Manila Master Plan, 1995, State of Calif. Real Estate Orgn. Plan, 1996, Ford Island Pearl Harbor Master Plan, 1996, Pearl Harbor Visitor Ctr. Plan, 1997, Albiano Resort Study, 1998; master plans include Trefethen Vineyards, Bell Garden, Napa Valley Expo. Bd. dirs. Nat. Archtl. Accrediting Bd., 2003—, pres., 2005; mem. Santa Cruz Downtown Assessment, Eisenhower E. Plan, Alexandria, Va., Upper Potomac W. Plan, Alexandria, King St. Revitalization Study, Alexandria, 2004, Oakland Mayor's Com. on High Density Housing, 1982, Oakland Gen. Plan Congress, 1994; mem. waterfront plan adv. com. City of Oakland, 1996, Westpark Town Ctr., 2003, Koa Ridge Cmty., Oahu, Hawaii, King St. Retail Plan, Alexandria; mem. adv. com. Queen Emma Founds. Lands of Waikiki Plan, 2004—05. Recipient Leslie M. Boney Spirit of Fellowship award. Fellow AIA (dir. East Bay chpt. 1969-71, pres. 1980-81, dir. Calif. coun. 1979-81, Disting. Svc. award Calif. chpt., 1991, nat. dir. 1983-86, nat. v.p. 1986-87, chair AIA internat. steering com. 1993-94, graphic stds. adv. com. 1991-92, U. Calif. archtl. review comm. 1992-96, exec. com. Coll. Fellows 1996-98, vice chancellor Coll. Fellows 1999, chancellor 2000, East Bay medal 1997, Edward C. Kemper medal for outstanding svc. 2004), Am. Archtl. Found. (regent, bd. dirs.), Nat. Archt. Accreditation Bd. (pres.). E-mail: raomatt@aol.com.

**ODESCALCHI, EDMOND PÉRY,** international financial consultant, author; b. Budapest, Hungary, Oct. 11, 1928; came to U.S., 1950; s. Prince Bela and Princess Charlotte (de Bay) O.; m. Esther de Kando, Sept. 30, 1961; children: Daniel, Dominic. Student, Cornell U., 1951, U. Pa., 1956-57; MS in Econs., St. Andrews U., Scotland, 1959. Adminstrv. asst. French Govt., Baden, Fed. Republic Germany, 1948-50; world trade specialist IBM Corp., Poughkeepsie, NY, 1952-60, project mgr., 1960-74, devel. mgr. East Fishkill, NY, 1974; pres. Global Tech., Inc., N.Y.C., 1975-91. Internat. fin. cons., 1975-93. Author: The Global Arena, 1973, Faces of Reality, 1975, The Third Crown, 1997, The Evolution of Behavior, 2002; contbr. articles to profl. jours. Mem. Rep. Nat. Com., 1984—. Mem. Bus. Cons. Assn., Am. Mus. Natural History (assoc.), Internat. Platform Assn. Home and Office: 1020 Freedom Rd Pleasant Valley NY 12569-7636

**ODGERS, RICHARD WILLIAM,** lawyer; b. Detroit, Dec. 31, 1936; s. Richard Stanley and Elsie Maude (Trevarthen) O.; m. Gail D. Cassett, Aug. 29, 1959; children: Thomas R., Andrew B. AB, U. Mich., 1959, JD, 1961. Bar: Calif. 1962. Assoc. Pillsbury, Madison & Sutro, San Francisco, 1961—69, ptnr., 1969—87, 1998—2000; exec. v.p., gen. counsel Pacific Telesis Group, 1987-98; ptnr. Pillsbury Winthrop Shaw Pittman, San Francisco, 2001—. Exec. vice chmn., bd. dirs. Legal Aid Soc. Employment Law Ctr.; dir. Legal Cmty. Against Violence; dir., sec.-treas. Van Loben Sels/RembeRock Charitable Found.; bd. dirs. Immigrant Legal Resource Ctr., Fed. Dist. Ct. Hist. Soc.; mem. Calif. Legal Svcs. Trust Fund Commn. With USNR. Fellow Am. Bar Found., Am. Judicature Soc., Am. Coll. Trial Lawyers; mem. ABA, Am. Law Inst., Am. Coll. Law Practice Mgmt., Bar Assn. San Francisco (past dir.). Office: Pillsbury Winthrop Shaw Pittman 50 Fremont St San Francisco CA 94105 Office Phone: 415-983-1202. Office Fax: 415-983-1200. Business E-mail: richard.odgers@pillsburylaw.com.

**ODHIAMBO, EUCABETH A.,** education educator; d. Shaphan R. and Elizabeth A. Dulo; m. Lameck Odeck, Apr. 9, 1989; children: Damaris A., Edward O. BA in Edn., U. Ea. Africa, Kenya, 1988; MEd, Tenn. State U., 1999, EdD, 2003. Cert. secondary edn. tchr. Tchrs. Svc. Commn., 1984. Tchr. Nyabola Girls H.S., Oyugis, South Nyanza, Kenya, 1988—88; elem. sch. tchr. Maxwell Adventist Prep. Sch., Nairobi, Central Province, Kenya, 1988—91; tchrs.' aide Asian Inst. of Tech. Child Ctr., Bangkok, 1992—92; program officer Natural Resource Program at Asian Inst. of Tech., Bangkok, 1992—94; adminstrv. and mgr. Outsource Data Systems, Nairobi, Kenya, 1994—96; adminstrv. asst. Adventist Media Ctr., Nairobi, Kenya, 1996—97; grad. and tchg. asst. dept. tchg. and learning Tenn. State U., Nashville, 1997—2003; asst. prof. dept. tchr. edn. Shippensburg U., Pa., 2003—. Mem.: ASCD, World Coun. for Curriculum and Instrn. (N.Am. chpt.), Nat. Assn. for Multicultural Edn. Achievements include research in HIV/AIDS Curriculum implementation in Kenya and the US; problems associated with curriculum implementation and comfort level of teaching teaching HIV/AIDS topics; The typologies of successful and unsuccessful students in academic subjects using the perspectives of student metacognitive awareness and actions in a high school environment in Tennessee; Successful and Unsuccessful Students in the Context of Gardner's Multiple Intelligence Theory; An Investigation of Gardner's Theory of Multiple Intelligence in a High School Environment in Tennessee; Pre-service Teachers' Critical Reflections of an Urban Field Experience. Avocations: singing, jogging, sight seeing. Office Phone: 717-477-1198.

**ODIERNO, RAYMOND J.,** career military officer; b. Rockway, N.J. s. Raymond J. and Helen Odierno; m. Linda Odierno; children: Anthony, Kathrin, Michael. BS, U.S. Mil. Acad., West Point, N.Y., 1976; MS in Nuc. Effects Engring., N.C. State U.; MA in Nat. Security and Strategy, U.S. Naval War Coll. Commd. lt. U.S. Army, advanced through grades to lt. gen., 2004, nuc. rsch. officer, chief acquisition support divsn. Def. Nuc. Agy., 1986—87, various positions, commdr. 2d bat., 1992—94, commdr. artillery divsn. Ft. Hood, Tex., 1995—97, dir. requirements and force mgmt. Office Dep. Chief Staff Ops. and Plans Washington, commdg. gen., 4th Infantry Divsn. (Mechanized) Ft. Hood, Tex., 2002—04; asst. to the Chmn. of the Joint Chiefs of Staff US Dept. Def., Washington, 2004—06; commdg. gen. III Corps. & Ft. Hood U.S. Army, Ft. Hood, Tex., 2006—. Decorated Army Disting. Svc. medal, Def. Superior Svc. medal, Legion of Merit with 5 oak leaf clusters, Meritorious Svc. medal with 3 oak leaf clusters, Def. Meritorious Svc. medal. Office: US Army III Corps Fort Hood TX 76544

**ODLAND, STEVE,** consumer products company executive; BBA, U. Notre Dame, 1980; M in Mgmt., Northwestern U., 1981. Sr. v.p., gen. mgr. snacks divsn. Sara Lee, 1996—98, pres. bakery foodservice. divsn., 1997—98; pres., CEO Tops Markets, Inc., 1998—2000; COO Ahold USA, Inc., 2000—01; chmn., pres., CEO AutoZone Inc., Memphis, 2001—05; chmn., CEO Office Depot, Inc., Delray Beach, Fla., 2005—. Office: Office Depot Inc 2200 Old Germantown Rd Delray Beach FL 33445*

**ODLE, ROBERT CHARLES, JR.,** lawyer; b. Port Huron, Mich., Feb. 15, 1944; s. Robert Charles and Elizabeth Dagmar (Lassen) O.; m. Lydia Ann Karpinol, Aug. 2, 1969. BA, Wayne State U., Detroit, 1966; JD, Detroit Coll. Law, 1969, LLD (hon.), 1992. Staff asst. to pres. of U.S., 1969-71; dir. adminstrn. Com. Re-election of President, 1971-73; dep. asst. sec. HUD, 1973-76; Washington corp. affairs rep. Internat. Paper Co., 1976-81; asst. sect. Dept. Energy, 1981-85; ptnr. Weil, Gotshal & Manges, 1985—. Mem. Mich. Bar Assn., DC Bar Assn., Delta Theta Phi. Clubs: University (Washington), Republican. Roman Catholic. Home: 476 S Union St Alexandria VA 22314-3826 Office: Weil Gotshal & Manges LLP Ste 900 1300 Eye St NW Washington DC 20005 Office Phone: 202-682-7180.

**O'DOHERTY, BRIAN,** writer; b. Ballaghadereen, Ireland; came to U.S., 1957; m. Barbara Novak, 1960. MB BCh, Univ. Coll. Dublin, Nat. U. Ireland, 1952, DPH with honors, 1955; MS in Hygiene, Harvard U., 1958. TV host Invitation to art, Mus. Fine Arts, Boston, 1958-61; art critic N.Y. Times, 1961-64; host Dialogue, WNBC, 1961-64; vis. prof. Berkeley U., 1967; dir. visual arts Nat. Endowment for Arts, 1969-76, dir. media arts, 1976-94; dir. Millennium Projects, 1994-96. Art and architecture critic Today Program, 1971-77; adj. prof. Barnard Coll., 1969-96; editor-in-chief Art in Am., 1971-74; Univ. prof. fine arts and media L.I. U.-Bklyn. Campus, 1997—. Author: (art book) Object and Idea: A New York Art Journal, 1961-67, 1967; editor: (museum study) Museums in Crisis, 1972, (Art Book) American Masters, The Voice and the Myth, 1973, 2d edit., 1995, Inside the White Cube, 1986, revised edit., 1999, (novels) The Strange Case of Mile P., 1992 (Saggitarius award, 1993), The Deposition of Father McGreevy, 1999 (Booker prize short list, 2000); dir.: (films) Hooper's Silence, 1981; contbr. articles to profl. jours. Recipient Mpls. Citizens award, 1961, Eire Soc. Gold medal for contbns. to culture, 1963, Grand Prix Montreal Internat. Festival of Arts Film award, 1982, Emmy nominations, Smithsonian fellow, Royal Coll. Physicians Ireland (hon.); mem. Am. Irish Hist. Soc. (bd. dirs.), Whitney Mus. Am. Art (bd. dirs. 1996-2000), Coll. Art Assn. (life; Mather award 1964). Office: 15 W 67th St New York NY 10023-6226

**O'DOHERTY, SUSAN ANN,** psychologist, writer; b. Flushing, N.Y., Mar. 22, 1952; d. Dorothy and Cahir O'Doherty; m. William Steven Donnenberg, Nov. 27, 1975; 1 child, Benjamin Donnenberg. PhD, Adelphi U., 1992. Lic. psychologist N.Y., 1999, cert. hypnotherapist Bklyn Inst. Psychotherapy and Psychoanalysis, 2000. Pvt. practice, Bklyn., 1999—. Vol. psychologist Doctors of the World, N.Y.C., 2001—. Author: (weekly advice column) The Doctor is In, (short stories) Special Needs, 2005, From the Diary of Ethel Muggs, 2005, At Fairlawn, 2005, Spring to Fall, 2005, Land of the Silver Birch, 2006, The Tower, The Velvet Underground, 2005. Clk., peace and social action com. Bklyn. Friends Meeting, 2002—04. Mem.: APA. Democrat-Npl. Avocations: family life, reading, swimming, baking, travel. Office: 120 Remsen St Ste 1A Brooklyn NY 11201 Business E-mail: dr.sue@mindspring.com.

**ODOM, FLOYD CLARK,** surgeon; b. Cisco, Tex., 1946; MD, U. Tex., San Antonio, 1972. Diplomate Am. Bd. Colon & Rectal Surgery, Am. Bd. Surgery. Intern Bexar County Hosp., San Antonio, 1972-73, resident in gen. surgery, 1973-77; fellow in colon & rectal surgery Baylor Med. Ctr., Dallas, 1977-78; colorectal surgeon Presbyn. Hosp., Dallas, 1997—. Fellow ACS, Am. Soc. Colon and Rectal Surgeons. Office: 8220 Walnut Hill Ln Dallas TX 75231-4406 Office Phone: 214-739-5758.

**ODOM, JEROME D.,** academic administrator; BS, U. N.C., 1964; PhD in Inorganic Chemistry, Ind. U., 1968. Postdoctoral fellow U. Bristol, England, 1968—69; asst. prof. U. S.C., Columbia, 1969—74, assoc. prof., 1974—77, prof., 1977—, chair dept. chemistry, 1985—91, interim project dir. S.C. Alliance for Minority Participation, 1993—94, dean Coll. Sci. and Math., 1994—97, provost, exec. v.p. for acad. affairs, 1997—2004, chair strategic directions and initiatives com., 2001—02. Author five general chemistry textbooks; contbr. articles to profl. jours. Achievements include patents in field. Office: Chemistry Dept 102 Osborne Adminstrn Bldg Univ SC Columbia SC 29208

**ODOM, JUDY,** software company executive; b. 1952; BBA in Acctg., Tex. Tech. U., 1974. CPA. With Coopers & Lybrand, Dallas, 1974-76, Grant Thornton, Dallas, 1976-85; co-founder, owner Software Spectrum, 1983—2002, CEO, 1988—2002. Bd. dirs. Storage Tek, Leggett & Platt Inc., Harte-Hanks Inc. Named to, Computer Reseller News Industry Hall of Fame, 2003.

**ODOM, LAMAR JOSEPH,** professional basketball player; b. Jamaica, NY, Nov. 6, 1979; Student, UNLV; grad., U. Rhode Island, 2001. Player LA Clippers, 1999—2003, Miami Heat, 2003—04, LA Lakers, 2004—. Mem. US Olympics Basketball Team, Athens, Greece, 2004. Named to All-Rookie First Team, 2000. Office: c/o LA Lakers 555 N Nash St El Segundo CA 90245*

**ODOM, MARJORIE MILDRED MORGAN,** retired librarian; b. Lavernia, Tex., July 22, 1924; d. Andrew Jackson and Estella Fledia (Phillips) Morgan; m. Steven Odom, Jr. (dec.). Cert. in cosmetology, C.J. Walker Beauty Coll., 1943; BA in Libr. Sci., Our Lady of Lake U., San Antonio, 1964, MA in Edn., 1979. Ordained deacon Bapt. Ch., 1985. Mgr. Mme. C.J. Walker Beauty Salon, San Antonio, 1944—52; propr. Ross Hotel Beauty Salon, San Antonio, 1952—63; asst. supr. children's dept. San Antonio Pub. Libr., 1964—65; secondary sch. libr. San Antonio Ind. Sch. Dist., 1965—90; ret., 1990. Past sponsor Libr. Reading Club, San Antonio; past mem. Tex. Senator's adv. coun. on legis. affairs; del. Bexar County Presdl. Senatorial Dist. conv., 1984, 1988; mem. Dist. 19 Tex. Dem. conv., Ft. Worth, 1990; del. Dem. State Conv., El Paso, 2002; elected Dem. Precinct chair, 2002; del. Tex. State Dem. Convention, 2004; chmn. evangelism com. Corinth Bapt. Ch., San Antonio, 1983—86, mem. evangelism and witnessing team, 1984—, Sunday sch. tchr., 1983—; trainer Evangelism Explosion, 1987—. Recipient outstanding award analysis and design award, Kappa Pi Sigma, 1978, appreciation plaque, PTA, 1981, cert., Internat. Ctr. Learning, 1982—83, Nat. Sunday Sch. and Bapt. Temperance Union Congress, 1967—70. Mem.: NEA (life), San Antonio Area Ret. Tchrs. Assn. (scholarship com. 2004—05, telephone com. 2003—05). Democrat. Home: PO Box 8374 San Antonio TX 78208-0374

**ODOM, ROD D., JR.,** telecommunications industry executive; b. Miami; Grad., U. Fla. Acct. exec. So. Bell, West Palm Beach, Fla., 1972—83; dir. new venture planning Bellsouth Corp., 1983—2000, exec. v.p. network ops., 2000—02; pres. network svcs. Bellsouth Corp, Atlanta, 2002—. Bd. dirs. Oglethorpe U., Shelttering Arms, Piedmont Hosp., Fla. Found.; mem. engring. adv. bd. U. Fla. Methodist.

**ODOM, SARAH BERNICE,** elementary school educator; b. Orange, Tex., Dec. 17, 1965; d. William Ogden and Thelma Louise (Ball) Gilpatrick; m. Armond G. Odom, Jr., Dec. 15, 1978 (div. Oct. 1999); children: Wesley, Clinton, Cody. AS, Panola Jr. Coll., Carthage, Tex., 1989; BS in Edn. cum laude, U. Tex., Tyler, 1990; MEd in Edn., Lamar U., 2001. Cert. life elem. self-contained grades 1-8 tchr., life elem. reaing tchr. grades 1-8, life generic spl. edn. tchr. grades PK-12. Tchr. Mauriceville (Tex.) Middle, 1991—95, Little Cypress Jr. High, Orange, Tex., 1995—99, Little Cypress Intermediate, Orange, Tex., 1999—2001, Little Cypress Jr. High, Orange, Tex., 2001—. Nominee Disney's Am. Tchr. award. Avocations: reading, painting, writing, outdoor activities. Home: 502 Camellia Orange TX 77630 Office: Little Cypress Jr High 6765 Fm Rd 1130 Orange TX 77632

**ODOM, TERI WANG,** chemist; BS in chemistry, Stanford U., 1996; AM in chemistry, Harvard U., 1999, PhD in chemical physics, 2001, postdoctoral rsch., 2001—02. Asst. prof. dept. chemistry Northwestern U. Contbr. articles in profl. jours. Named one of Top 100 Young Innovators, MIT Tech. Review, 2004; recipient Prize for Young Chemists, IUPAC, 2001, Top Prize, Australian Jour. Chemistry, 2001, Victor K. LaMer award, ACS, 2003, Career award, NSF, 2004, NUE award, 2004; fellow, David and Lucille Packard, 2003; postdoctoral fellowship, NIH NRSA, 2001, Searle fellow, 2003. Mem.: Phi Beta Kappa. Office: Northwestern U Dept Chemistry 2145 Sheridan Rd Evanston IL 60208 Business E-Mail: todom@northwestern.edu.

**ODOM, WILLIAM ELDRIDGE,** career military officer; b. Cookeville, Tenn., June 23, 1932; s. John Albert and Callie Frances (Everhart) O.; m. Anne Weld Curtis, June 9, 1962; 1 child, Mark Weld. BS, U.S. Mil. Acad., 1954; MA, Columbia U., 1962, PhD, 1970; DSc (hon.), Middlebury Coll., 1987. Commd. 2nd lt. U.S. Army, 1954, advanced through grades to lt. gen., 1984; mem. U.S. Mil. Liaison Mission to Soviet Forces, Germany, 1964-66; from asst. prof. to assoc. prof. govt. U.S. Mil. Acad., West Point, 1966-69, 74-76; asst. Army attache U.S. embassy, Moscow, 1972-74; nat. security staff mem. White House, 1977-81; asst. chief of staff for intelligence Dept. Army, Washington, 1981-85; dir. Nat. Security Agy., Fort Meade, Md., 1985-88; sr. fellow Hudson Inst., 1988—. Adj. prof. polit. sci. Yale U., 1989—; mem. bd. dirs. Am. Sci. and Engring. Author: The Soviet Volunteers, 1973, On Internal War, 1992, Trial After Triumph, 1992, America's Military Revolution, 1993, (with Robert Dujarric) Commonwealth or Empire? Russia, Central Asia and The Transcaucasus, 1995, The Collapse of the Soviet Military, 1998, Fixing Intelligence, 2003, (with Robert Dujarric) America's Inadvertent Empire, 2004; contbr. articles to profl. jours. Trustee Middlebury Coll., 1987-97. Decorated Def. D.S.M. with oak leaf cluster, D.S.M. with oak leaf cluster, Legion of Merit, Nat. Security medal, Nat. Intelligence D.S.M.; grand cross Order of Merit with Star (Fed. Republic Germany); Order Nat. Security Merit (Republic of Korea), officer Nat. Order of Merit (France). Mem. Coun. on Fgn. Rels., Am. Assn. for Advancement of Slavic Studies, Internat. Inst. for Strategic Studies, Am. Polit. Sci. Assn., Acad. Polit. Sci., Am. Legion. Office: Hudson Inst 1015 15th St NW Ste 600 Washington DC 20005

**ODOM, WILLIAM GREG,** secondary school educator, music educator; b. Shawnee, Kans., June 8, 1972; s. James Brian and Billye Lynn Odom. BS in History and Music, Kans. State U., Manhattan, Kans., 2002; student, Ea. N.Mex. U., Poriales, N.Mex., 2002—. Dir. band Sierra Mid. Sch., Roswell, N.Mex., 2002—04, Roswell H.S., 2004—. Pvt. practice tchr. trumpet, Roswell, 2002—. Musician: Roswell Symphony Orch., 2002—, Roswell Cmty. Band, 2002—. Mem. bell choir 1st United Meth. Ch., Roswell, 2005—. Mem.: NEA, Ea. N.Mex. Music Educators, N.Mex. Music Educator Assn. Republican. Avocations: jazz, environment, wildlife. Home: 1611 N Ohio Roswell NM 88201 Office: Roswell High School 500 W Hobbs Roswell NM 88203

**ODONER, ELLEN J.,** lawyer; b. N.Y.C., Jan. 23, 1952; BA magna cum laude, Yale U., 1973; JD, Harvard U., 1977. Bar: N.Y. 1978. Mem. Weil, Gotshal & Manges, N.Y.C. Mem.: Assn. Bar City NY. Office: Weil Gotshal & Manges LLP 767 Fifth Ave New York NY 10153-0119 Office Phone: 212-310-8438. E-mail: ellen.odoner@weil.com.

**O'DONNELL, CATHERINE ROSE,** lawyer; b. South Charleston, W.Va., Feb. 15, 1964; d. Philip John and Madeline Marie Ripepi; m. Neil Taney O'Donnell, May 6, 1989; children: Neil Philip, Renata Marie. BA in Bus. and Econs., U. Pitts., 1984, JD, MBA, U. Pitts., 1987. Bar: D.C. 1988, Pa. 1988, U.S. Dist. Ct. (ea. dist.) Pa. 1988, U.S. Dist. Ct. (ctrl. dist.) Pa. 1990. Assoc. Drinker Biddle & Reath, Phila., 1988—90; assoc. to shareholder Elliott Reihner Siedzikowski & Egan, Scranton, Pa., 1990—2000; dist. justice Wilkes-Barre, Pa., 2000—02; assoc. O'Donnell Law Offices, Wilkes-Barre, 2002—. Mem. parish coun. St. Therese Ch., Wilkes-Barre, 1990—93, mem. fin coun., 2000—, cantor 2001—; bd. dirs Wyoming Valley Montessori Sch., Kingston, Pa., 1997—2000; pres. Wyoming Valley Montessori Sch. PTA, Kingston, Pa.; bd. dirs Osterhout Libr., Wilkes-Barre, 1999—2000, Cath. Youth Ctr., Wilkes-Barre, 1996—99, Wyoming Valley Habitat for Humanity, Kingston, 1991—93, Luzerne County LWV, Kingston, 1999—2000, Wyo. Sem. Lower Sch. Parents Assn., 2003—. Mem.: ATLA (social security disability sect. 2004—, bd. dir.), bd. dir. Pa. chpt.), Nat. Orgn. of Social Security Rep., Soical Security Disability Section, Northeast Trial Lawyers Assn., Lackawanna County Bar Assn., Wilkes-Barre Law and Libr. Assn., Pa. Trial Lawyers Assn., Pa. Bar Assn. Office: O'Donnell Law Offices 22 E Union St Wilkes Barre PA 18701 Office Phone: 570-821-5717. Business E-Mail: cro@odonnell-law.com.

**O'DONNELL, CHRIS,** actor; b. Winnetka, Ill., June 26, 1970; m. Caroline Fentress, Apr. 19, 1997; children Lilly Ann, Christopher Jr., Charles. BA in Mktg., Boston Coll., 1995. Actor: (films) Men Don't Leave, 1990, Fried Green Tomatoes, 1991, Scent of a Woman, 1992 (Golden Globe award nomination best supporting actor 1992), School Ties, 1992, The Three Musketeers, 1993, Blue Sky, 1994, Circle of Friends, 1995, Mad Love, 1995, Batman Forever, 1995, In Love and War, 1996, The Chamber, 1996, Batman & Robin, 1997, Cookie's Fortune, 1999, Vertical Limit, 2000, 29 Palms, 2002, Kinsey, 2004, (TV series) Head Cases, 2005; actor, prodr. The Bachelor, 1999; prodr. (TV films) The Triangle, 2001, Miracle on the 17th Green, 1999. Office: Creative Artists Agy care Josh Lieberman 9830 Wilshire Blvd Beverly Hills CA 90212-1804

**O'DONNELL, DENISE ELLEN,** lawyer, former prosecutor; BS in Polit. Sci., Canisius Coll., 1968; MSW, SUNY, Buffalo, 1973, JD summa cum laude, 1982. Bar: NY 1983, U.S. Dist. Ct. (we., no., ea. and so. dists.) NY, U.S. Ct. Appeals (2d cir.), U.S. Supreme Ct. Law clk. to Hon. M. Dolores Denman NY Appellate Divsn. 4th Dept., Buffalo, 1982-85; asst. U.S. atty. (we. dist.) NY, US Dept Justice, Buffalo, 1985-90, appellate chief, 1990-93, 1st asst. U.S. atty., 1993—97, U.S. atty., 1997-2001; ptnr. Gen. Litigation Practice Group, Hodgson, Russ, LLP, Buffalo, 2001—. Part-time instr. trial technique program SUNY, 1990—2002; lectr. ethics, evidence and trial practice Office Legal Edn.U.S. Dept. Justice, 1988—2000; lectr. NITA seminar Western NY Trial Acad., 1994, 98; mem. Atty. Gen.'s Adv. Com., 1999—2001, vice-chair, 2000—01; trustee SUNY Buffalo Found. Mem. Vol. Lawyers Program, 1997—2001; bd. dirs. NCCJ, 2000—; trustee SUNY Buffalo Found., 2004—; sec. Nat. Women's Hall of Fame, 2001—04, bd. dirs., 2001—. Fellow: N.Y. State Bar Found.; mem.: ABA, Nat. Assn. Former U.S. Attys. (bd. dirs.), Western NY Trial Lawyers Assn., Women's Bar Assn. State NY (founding mem. Western NY chpt. 1985), Bar Assn. Erie County (dep. treas. 1992—93, treas. 1993—94), West Side Rowing Club. Office: Hodgson Russ LLP One M&T Plz Ste 2000 Buffalo NY 14203-2931 Office Phone: 716-848-1314. Business E-Mail: dodonnel@hodgsonruss.com

**O'DONNELL, EDWARD JOSEPH,** bishop, retired editor; b. St. Louis, July 4, 1931; s. Edward Joseph and Ruth Mary (Carr) O'Donnell. Student, Cardinal Glennon Coll., 1949-53; postgrad., Kenrick Sem., 1953-57. Ordained priest Roman Cath. Ch., 1957, consecrated bishop, 1984; assoc. pastor in 5 St. Louis parishes, 1957-77; pastor St. Peter's Ch., Kirkwood, Mo., 1977-81; assoc. dir. Archdiocesan Commn. on Human Rights, 1962-70; dir. Archdiocesan Radio-TV Office, 1966-68, Archdiocesan Vocation Council, 1965; editor St. Louis Rev., 1968-81; vicar-gen. Archdiocese of St. Louis, 1981-84, aux. bishop, 1984-94; bishop emeritus Diocese of Lafayette, Lafayette, La., 1994—. Bd dirs Nat Cath Conf Interracial Justice, 1980—85; chmn Interfaith Clergy Coun Greater St Louis, 1963—67; NAACP, 1964—66; bd dirs Urban League St Louis, 1962—68. Named to Golden Dozen, Int Soc Weekly Newspaper Eds, 1970, 1977. Mem.: Nat Asn TV Arts and Scis, Cath Press Asn. Roman Catholic. Home: 6825 Natural Bridge Rd Saint Louis MO 63121-5314

**O'DONNELL, JAMES FRANCIS,** retired health scientist administrator; b. Cleve., July 22, 1928; s. John Michael and Mary Louise (Hayes) O'D.; m. Winifred Locke, Sept. 10, 1955; children— Anne Catherine, Patrick John, Mary Elizabeth BS in Biology, St. Louis U., 1949; PhD in Biochemistry, U. Chgo., 1957. Asst., then assoc. prof. biol. chemistry and exptl. medicine Coll. Medicine, U. Cin., 1957—68; grants assoc., divsn. rsch. grants NIH, Bethesda, Md., 1968—69; program dir. population and reprodn. grants br. Ctr. for Population Research, Nat. Inst. Child Health and Human Devel., NIH, 1969—71; asst. dir. divsn. rsch. resources NIH, Bethesda, 1971—76, dep. dir. divsn. rsch. resources, 1976—90, acting dir. divsn. rsch. resources, 1981—82, dir. Office of Extramural Programs, Office of the Dir., 1990-99; ret., 1999. Sci. cons. Commonwealth Health Rsch. Bd., Richmond, Va., 1999—. Served with U.S. Army, 1950-52 Home: 11601 Bunnell Ct S Rockville MD 20854-3603 Personal E-mail: jfwlodonnell@erols.com

**O'DONNELL, JAMES V.,** apparel executive; Mgmt. positions The Gap Inc., 1980—87, exec. v.p., bd. dir., 1987—92, COO, 1989—92; CEO Computer Aided Systems Inc., 1992—97; project cons. C. Everett Koop Found., 1997—2000; dir. merchant banking Colmen Capital Adv. Inc., 1997—2002; pres., COO Lyte Inc., 1999—2000; COO Am. Eagle Outfitters, Warrendale, Pa., 2000—03, bd. dir., 2000—, co-CEO, 2003, CEO, 2003—. Mem. adv. bd. Coll. Commerce & Fin. Villanova Univ. Office: American Eagle Outfitters 150 Thorn Hill Dr Warrendale PA 15086*

**O'DONNELL, JOHN LOGAN,** retired lawyer; b. Chgo., Mar. 6, 1914; s. William Joseph and Elizabeth (McLogan) O'D.; m. Mary Ellen Sipe, Sept. 2, 1939 (dec. Dec. 29, 1979); 1 son, John Logan; m. Michele G. Fischer, May 9, 1981. BA, Williams Coll., 1934; JD, Northwestern U., 1937. Bar: Ill. 1937, N.Y. 1943, D.C. 1977. Asso. firm Defrees, Buckingham, Jones and Hoffman, Chgo., 1937-38; staff atty. Office Gen. Counsel, SEC, 1938-41; instr. Cath. U. Law Sch., 1938-41; assoc. Cravath, Swaine & Moore, N.Y.C., 1941-52; ptnr. Olwine, Connelly, Chase, O'Donnell & Weyher, N.Y.C., 1952-91, of counsel, 1991, Twomey, Hoppe & Gallanty, N.Y.C., 1991—2003; ret., 2003. Bd. dirs. Near East Found., 1968-84. Fellow Am. Coll. Trial Lawyers; mem. Assn. Bar City N.Y., Am., Fed., bar assns., Beta Theta Pi, Phi Delta Phi. Clubs: Union, Univ., Williams, (N.Y.). Roman Catholic. Avocations: piano, sports. Home: 181 E 73rd St New York NY 10021-3549

**O'DONNELL, JOHN MICHAEL,** lawyer; b. Washington, Aug. 27, 1958; s. John M. and Mildred B. O'Donnell; m. Bonnie Humphrey, June 30, 1984; childrean Jack and Kate (twins). BA, U. Chgo., 1980; JD, U. Pa., 1983. Bar: Ill. 1983. Ptnr. Sonnenschein Nath & Rosenthal, Chgo., 1984-95; assoc. gen. counsel The Interlake Corp., Lisle, Ill., 1995-98; v.p., secretary, and general counsel Interlake Material Handling, Inc., Lisle, Ill., 1998—2004; dep. gen. counsel GKN, 2005—.

**O'DONNELL, KATHLEEN C.,** artist; b. Clifton, N.J., Nov. 15, 1919; d. George Francis and Alvina Rose (Munzell) Denzel; m. John Joseph O'Donnell, Feb. 17, 1942; children: John Joseph, Sharon Rose. BA cum laude, Montclair (N.J.) State Coll. Designer Denzell Mfg. Co., Passaic, NJ, 1937—38, clk., 1939—41; sec. Marschalk Ins., Clifton, NJ, 1941—42; clk. The Fair, Passaic, 1968—69; designer Arise Ministry, Lakewood, NJ, 1983—91; assoc. N.J. Bell, Clifton & Totowa, NJ, 1969—85. One-woman shows include Dwight Eisenhower Libr., Totowa, 1982, No. Lights Art Gallery, Clifton, 1985, YWHA, 1988, Fine Arts Ctr., Passaic, 1988, Denville Libr., 2003, Roxbury Pub. Libr., 2005, exhibited in group shows at Fine Arts Ctr., Passaic, 1983, 1988, Willowbrook Mall, Wayne, N.J., 1984, YWHA, Clifton, 1985, Clifton Libr., 1988, The Nathan's Art Gallery, West Paterson, N.J., 1994, Montclair Country Club, 1994, Montclair State U., 1995, 1998, Westbeth Gallery, N.Y.C., 1996, Caldwell (N.J.) Women's Club, 1999, Botto House, Haledon, N.J., 1999, Clifton Arts Ctr., N.J., 2001, Hamilton House, Clifton, 2002, Clifton Arts Ctr., 2003, 2004, Pub. Libr. Twp. of Roxbury, 2005, Roxbury Township Pub. Libr., 2005, 2006, The Atrium Gallery, Morris County Adminstrn. and Records Bldg., 2006, represented in numerous pvt. collections. Mem.: Roxbury Assn. Art, Clifton Assn. Artists, Bell Atlantic Pioneers. Roman Catholic.

**O'DONNELL, KATHLEEN MARIE,** lawyer; b. Methuen, Mass., Dec. 16, 1955; d. John Joseph and Helen Miriam (McCormack) O'D. BA magna cum laude, Wheaton Coll., Norton, Mass., 1977, JD cum laude, Suffolk U., 1980. Bar: Mass. 1981, U.S. Dist. Ct. Mass. 1982, U.S. Ct. Appeals (1st cir.) 1982. Instr. Suffolk U., Boston, 1980-82; assoc. Law Office Albert J. Marcotte, Lowell, Mass., 1982—. Bd. dirs. Greater Lowell Pastoral Counseling Ctr., 1987—; Greater Lowell Rape Crisis Ctr., Sohier Park Com., York, Maine, 1989—, co-chair, 1991—; bd. govs. Mass. Acad. Trial Attys. Mem. ABA, Mass. Bar Assn. (v.p. 2001, treas. 2002, pres.-elect 2003, pres. 2004), Mass. Acad. Trial Attys.(treas. 1995, pres. 1996), Greater Lowell Bar Assn. (treas. 1987, sec. 1988, v.p. 1989, pres. 1990), Assn. of Trial Lawyers of Am., Am. Bd. Trial Advocates, Phi Delta Phi. Democrat. Roman Catholic. Office: Law Office Albert Marcotte 45 Merrimack St Lowell MA 01852-1729

**O'DONNELL, KATHLEEN MARY,** social services administrator; b. Bklyn., Dec. 29, 1965; d. Maureen Grace O'D. BA in Psychology, Tchr. of Handicapped, Kean Coll. N.J., 1990; MS in Psychiat. Rehab., U. Medicine and Dentistry N.J., Newark, 2000. Cert. social worker, psychosocial rehab. practitioner; psychiat. rehab. practitioner. Nursing asst. Carrier Found., Belle Mead, N.J., 1988; tutor Kean Coll. N.J., Union, 1989; case mgr. Project Live, Inc., Newark, N.J., 1990-92, U. Medicine & Dentistry N.J., New Brunswick, 1992-2000. Vol. Childrens Specialized Hosp., Mountainside, NJ, 2003—, Make-a-Wish Found., NJ, 2000—. Mem. Internat. Assn. Psychiat. Rehab. Practitioners. Avocations: bowling, dance, music, travel.

**O'DONNELL, KEVIN,** retired metal products executive; b. Cleve., June 9, 1925; s. Charles Richard and Ella (Kilbane) O'Donnell; m. Ellen Blydenburgh, Aug. 16, 1965; children: Kevin, Susan, Michael, John, Maura, Neil, Megan, Hugh. AB, Kenyon Coll., Gambier, Ohio, 1947, PhD (hon.) in Law, 1980; MBA, Harvard U., 1947; PhD (hon.), Pusan Nat. U., Korea, 1970; PhD in Humanities (hon.), Ohio Wesleyan U., 1972. Gen. sales mgr. Steel Improvement & Forge Co., Cleve., 1947-60; mgmt. cons. Booz, Allen and Hamilton, Cleve., 1960-62; gen. mgr., dir. Atlas Alloys-Rio Algom Corp., Cleve., 1963-66; dir. Peace Corps, Seoul, Republic of Korea, 1966-70; dir. adminstrn. and fin., then acting dep. dir., 1970-71; assoc. dir. internat. ops. ACTION, 1971-72; exec. v.p. SIFCO Industries, Inc., Cleve., 1972-75, pres., chief oper. officer, 1976-83, pres., chief exec. officer, 1983-89, chief exec. officer, 1989-90, chmn., exec. comm., 1990-94; ret., 1994. Bd. dirs. Ctrl. Pk. Media Corp., N.Y.C., Doyle Pacific Industries, Ltd., Hong Kong; adv. dir. Plz. Group, Houston, Capital Strategies, Inc., Cleve. Mem. Washington Inst. Fgn. Affairs, Cleve. Coun. Fgn. Rels., chmn., 1979—82, CCWA, 1982—89; pres. Guest Ho., Inc., 1990—92; trustee Alcohol Svcs., Cleve., 1993—, Cleve. Coun. World Affairs, Nat. Peace Corps. Assn. Decorated Order Civil Merit Republic of Korea. Mem.: Harvard Bus. Sch. Alumni Assn. (dir. Boston 1991—94), Army-Navy Club (Washington), Westwood Country Club, Union Club, 50 Club, First Friday Club, Harvard Bus. Sch. Club Cleve., Knights of Malta (master knight). Republican. Roman Catholic. Avocations: golf, reading. Office Phone: 216-226-3505. Personal E-mail: kevodoncle@aol.com.

**O'DONNELL, LAURENCE GERARD,** retired managing editor; b. Bklyn., June 30, 1935; s. Thomas Edward and Dorothy (Clark) O'D.; m. Joan M. Coniglio, Jan. 9, 1960; children: Christopher, Carolyn, Jeffrey, Anthony. AB, Holy Cross Coll., 1957. Reporter Wall Street Jour., N.Y.C., 1958-66, chief Detroit Bur., 1966-74, asst. mng. editor, N.Y.C., 1974-77, mng. editor, 1977-83; assoc. editor Dow Jones & Co., Inc., N.Y.C., 1983-90, cons., 1991-99. Pres. Dow Jones Newspaper Fund, 1988-93; bd. dirs. Dow Jones Newspaper Fund; vis. lectr. Queens Coll/CUNY, 1992-99. Trustee Holy Cross Coll., 1982-90; mem. journalism adv. bd. Queens Coll./CUNY, 1989-2003; juror Pulitzer Prize, 1982, 83; bd. dirs. Interam. Press Assn., 1986-2001. Mem. Am. Soc. Newspaper Editors. Mem. Natl. adv. com., Robert Wood Johnson Found., 2002-. Office: Dow Jones Newspaper Fund PO Box 300 Princeton NJ 08543-0300

**O'DONNELL, LAWRENCE, III,** waste management executive; b. Houston, Dec. 14, 1957; s. Lawrence Jr. and Annell O'D.; m. Dare Boswell, May 22, 1981; children: Linley, Lawrence IV. BS in Archtl. Engring., U. Tex., 1980; JD cum laude, U. Houston, 1983. Bar: Tex. 1983. Assoc. Wood, Campbell, Moody & Gibbs, Houston, 1983-84; ptnr. Campbell & Riggs, Houston, 1984-91; dep. gen. counsel Baker Hughes Inc., Houston, 1991-94; v.p., gen. counsel Baker Hughes Oilfield Ops., Houston, 1993-95; corp. sec. Baker Hughes Inc., Houston, 1991-96, v.p., gen. counsel, 1995-2000; sr. v.p., gen. counsel, sec. Waste Mgmt., Inc., Houston, 2000-01, exec. v.p., gen. counsel, corp. sec., 2001—, exec. v.p. western ops., 2001—03, exec. v.p. ops. support, CAO, 2003—04, pres., COO, 2004—. Bd. dirs., mem. exec. com. Spring Br. Edn. Found.; bd. dirs. Am. Arbitration Assn., U. Tex. Med. Br.; mem. energy planning coun. State of Tex., 2004. Trustee. Houston Police Activities League.; adv. bd. Brookwood. Mem.: ASCE, ABA, Houston Bar Assn., Tex. State Bar, Order of Barons, Phi Delta Phi. Avocations: golf, sailing, skiing. Office: Waste Mgmt Inc 1001 Fannin St Ste 4000 Houston TX 77002-6711*

**O'DONNELL, PATRICK EMMETT,** lawyer; b. NYC, Mar. 17, 1937; s. Emmett and Lorraine Antoinette (Muller) O'D.; m. Janet Eve Marthorshead, Sept. 21, 1968; children: Patrick Justin, Hollace Tobin, Darcy Tanner. Student, Georgetown U., 1955-58; LLB, Am. Univ., 1962. Bar: D.C. 1962. Asst. corp. counsel City of Washington, 1962-69; spl. asst. to the pres. The White House, Washington, 1971-76; legal counsel to chmn. FCC, Washington, 1969-71; Washington counsel Gen. Electric Co., Washington, 1976-78, J.C. Penney Co., Inc., Washington, 1978-80; regional polit. dir. Howard Baker for Pres., Washington, 1980; asst. dir. legis. affairs Ronald Reagan for Pres., Washington, 1980-81; ptnr. O'Connor & Hannan, Washington, 1981; ptnr., legislative, govtl. affairs Venable LLP, Washington, 2001—. Vice chmn. fin. George Bush Com., Washington, 1988; economic affairs counsel Rep. Nat. Com., Washington, 1976-80; bd. dirs. Radio Marti (Presdl. Commn.), Washington, 1981-84. Mem. USO (bd. dirs. 1978-91). Republican. Roman Catholic. Office: Venable LLP 575 Seventh St NW Washington DC 20004 Office Phone: 202-344-4702. Office Fax: 202-344-8300. Business E-Mail: peodonnell@venable.com.

**O'DONNELL, PIERCE HENRY,** lawyer; b. Troy, NY, Mar. 5, 1947; s. Harry J. and Mary (Kane) O'Donnell; m. Dawn Donley, Mar. 17, 1995; children: Meghan Maureen, Brendan Casey, Courtney Dawn, Pierce Dublin, Aidan Yeats. BA, Georgetown U., 1969, JD, 1972; LLM, Yale U., 1975. Bar: D.C. 1973, U.S. Supreme Ct. Calif. 1978. Law clk. to Justice Byron R. White U.S. Supreme Ct; law clk. to Judge Shirley M. Hutstedler U.S. Ct. Appeals (9th cir.); assoc. Williams & Connolly, Washington, 1975-78; ptnr. Beardsley, Hufstedler & Kemble, L.A., 1978-81, Hufstedler, Miller, Carlson & Beardsley, L.A., 1981-82, O'Donnell & Gordon, L.A., 1982-87, Kaye, Scholer, Fierman, Hays & Handler, L.A., 1988-95, O'Donnell Shaeffer & Mortimer, L.L.P., L.A., 1996—. Exec. asst. U.S. Sec. Edn., 1979; spl. counsel Commn. Jud. Performance, San Francisco, 1979; chmn. Nat. Media, Inc., 1984—92. Co-author: (book) Fatal Subtraction: The Inside Story of Buchwald v Paramount, 1992, Toward A Just and Effective Sentencing System: Agenda for Legislative Reform, 1976; author: Dawn's Early Light, 2001, Funny You Asked About That, 2005, In Time of War, 2005; contbr. articles to profl. jours. Chmn. Friends Cal Tech YMCA, 1983—84, Verdugo-San Rafael Urban Mountain Park Fund, 1980—84; bd. dirs. Foothill Family Svcs., 1979—85, chmn., 1984—85; bd. dirs. Interfaith Ctr. To Reverse Arms Race, 1984—90, pres., 1987—88; mem. Econ. Round Table of L.A., 1979—, pres., 2000—01; chmn. Calif. Coast Baseball Acad., 2001—; mem. Santa Barbara Sheriff's Coun., 2003—; bd. dirs. Friends of Altadena Libr., 1979—81, Pasadena-Foothill Urban League, E. Altadena Little League, 1993—97. Fellow: Internat. Acad. Trial Lawyers; mem.: NAACP, PEN, Am. Coll. Trial Lawyers, Cal Tech Assocs., Am. Law Inst., Am. Bd. Trial Advocates, Sierra Club, Calif. Club, Gridiron Club (Georgetown U.), Bel Air Country Club. Episc. O'Donnell & Shaeffer LLP 550 S Hope 20th fl Los Angeles CA 90071-2027 Home: 735 Picacho Ln Santa Barbara CA 93108-1226 Office Phone: 213-532-2000. Business E-Mail: pod@oslaw.com

**O'DONNELL, ROSIE,** television personality, actress, comedienne; b. Commack, NY, Mar. 21, 1962; m. Kelli Carpenter, Feb. 26, 2004; children: Parker Jaren, Chelsea Belle, Blake Christopher, Vivienne Rose. Attended, Dickinson Coll., Boston Univ. Appearances include (TV series) Gimme A Break, 1986-87, Stand By Your Man, 1992, Women Aloud, 1992, Stand-up Spotlight, VH-1 (American Comedy award nomination best female performer in a TV special 1994, Cable ACE award nomination best entertainment host 1994); (TV) host The Rosie O'Donnell Show, 1995-2002 (Daytime Emmy awards 1997, 98, 99, 2000, 2001); (TV) co-host The View, 2006-; (TV films) The

Twilight of the Golds, 1997; (films) A League of Their Own, 1992, Sleepless in Seattle, 1993 (American Comedy award nomination best supporting female in a motion picture 1994), Another Stakeout, 1993 (American Comedy award nomination best actress in a motion picture 1994), Car 54, Where Are You?, 1994, I'll Do Anything, 1994, The Flintstones, 1994, Exit to Eden, 1994, Now and Then, 1995, Beautiful Girls, 1996, Harriet the Spy, 1996, A Very Brady Sequel, 1996 (uncredited), Wide Awake, 1996, Get Bruce, 1999, Jackie's Back, 1999, Tarzan, 1999 (voice), Flintstones in Viva Rock Vegas, 2000; Broadway shows include Grease, 1994, Seussical the Musical, 2001, Fiddler on the Roof, 2005; author: Find Me, 2002; editor: Rosie mag., 2000-2002; prodr.: Taboo (Broadway) 2003-2004; exec. prodr. (TV films) Kids are Punny, 1998, (films) Mina & the Family Treasure, 2004; actor, exec. prodr. (TV films) Riding the Bus with My Sister, 2005; guest appearances Ally McBeal, 1999, Third Watch, 2000, The Practice, 2000, Will & Grace, 2002, Judging Amy, 2003, Queer as Folk, 2005.

**O'DONNELL, TERRENCE,** lawyer; b. NYC, Mar. 3, 1944; s. Emmett and Lorraine (Muller) O'Donnell; m. Margaret Lynne Kidder; children: Stephanie T., Erin K., Victoria L. BS, U.S. Air Force Acad., 1966; JD, Georgetown Law Sch., 1971. Bar: D.C. 1971, U.S. Ct. Appeals (D.C. cir.) 1978, U.S. Ct. Appeals (4th cir.) 1987, U.S. Dist. Ct. Md. 1986, U.S. Ct. Mil. Appeals 1990, U.S. Ct. Fed. Claims, U.S. Supreme Ct., others. Commd. 2d lt. USAF, 1966, advanced through grades to capt., various positions Washington and Republic of Vietnam, 1966-72, resigned, 1972; spl. asst. Pres. of U.S., The White House, Washington, 1972-77; appointments sec. Pres. Ford, Washington, 1974-77; assoc. Williams & Connolly, Washington, 1977-82, ptnr., 1982-89; gen. counsel Dept. Def., Washington, 1989-92; ptnr. Williams and Connolly, Washington, 1992—; exec. v.p., gen. counsel Textron Inc., 2000—. Presdl. appointee to bd. visitors U.S. Air Force Acad., Colorado Springs, 1982-87, chmn., 1985-86; U.S. corr and rep. UN Program to Prevent Crime, Washington and N.Y.C., 1977-81; bd. dirs. IGI Inc., MLC Holdings. Trustee Gerald R. Ford Found., Grand Rapids, Mich., 1987—; mem. Adminstrv. Conf. U.S., 1991-92; mem. adv. com. U.S. Ct. Fed. Claims; mem. code com. U.S. Ct. of Mil. Appeals for the Armed Forces, 1993-95; bd. dirs. Falcon Found., 1988—. Decorated Bronze star; recipient Disting. Pub. Svc. medal Dept. of Def., 1992, Disting. Svc. award U.S. Atty. Gen., 1992. Mem. ABA, D.C. Bar Assn., Bar of U.S. Supreme Ct., and others. Home: 5133 Yuma St NW Washington DC 20016-4336 Office: Williams and Connolly 725 12th St NW Washington DC 20005-5901 Office Phone: 202-434-5678. Personal E-mail: todonnell@wc.com. Business E-Mail: todonnell@textron.com.

**O'DONNELL, TERRENCE,** state supreme court justice; b. Cleve., Feb. 11, 1946; m. Mary Beth O'Donnell; children: Terrence, Michael, Colleen, Nora. BA in Polit. Sci., Kent State U., 1968; JD, Cleve. State U., 1971. Bar: Ohio 1971. Instr. speech and debate Cuyahoga Cmty. Coll., 1968—70; instr. grades 7 & 8 St. Brendan Sch., North Olmstead, 1970; law clerk to Judge Justice J.J.P. Corrigan Supreme Ct. Ohio, 1971—72; law clerk to Judge John M. Manos and Judge V. Corrigan 8th Dist. Ct. Appeals, 1972—74; dir. program paralegal edn. David M. Myers Coll., 1974—76; atty. Marshman, Snyder & Corrigan, 1976—80; judge Cuyahoga County Ct. Common Pleas, 1980—95, 8th Dist. Ct. Appeals, 1995—2003; justice Ohio Supreme Ct., 2003—. Vis. judge counties throughout Ohio, 2003—; chmn. Ohio Legal Rights Svc. Commn.; instr. CPA bus. law rev. Cleve. State U.; instr. several continuing legal edn. programs; mem. Ohio Supreme Ct. Commn. on Professionalism. Past pres. Legal Eagles; former mem. bd. trustees Magnificat HS, Rocky River, past pres. Father's Club; exec. dir. emeritus St. Patrick's Day Parade, Cleve.; coach Little League Baseball, Rocky River; instr. pub. sch. religion program St. Bernadette Ch., Westlake; mem. St. Bernadette Parish, Westlake, Ohio; mem. bd. dirs. Our Lady Wayside. Mem.: Ohio Supreme Ct., Ohio State Bar Assn. (mem. pub. understanding law sect.), Cleve. Bar Assn. (chmn. law related edn. com., Pres.'s award 1989—99), Cath. Lawyer's Guild Cleve. (officer). Office: Ohio Supreme Ct 65 S Front St Columbus OH 43215-3431

**O'DONNELL, THOMAS LAWRENCE PATRICK,** lawyer; b. Taunton, Mass., Aug. 12, 1926; s. Patrick Francis and Ellen Balfe (Brady) O'D.; m. Carol Hodgdon, Feb. 16, 1952; children— Ellen, Thomas, Janet Gael, Christopher Hodgdon AB magna cum laude, Harvard U., 1947, LL.B., 1949. Bar: Mass. 1950. Assoc. Ropes & Gray, Boston, 1949-52, 54-61, ptnr., 1962-97, chmn., 1984-90, of counsel, 1998—. Dir. Rath & Strong, Inc., 1985-96. Trustee, Trustees of Reservations, 1970—, chmn. bd., 1975-76; bd. dirs. Mass. Land Conservation Trust, 1975-2002, chmn. bd., 1986-2002; bd. dirs. Mass. Taxpayers Found., 1972—, chmn. bd., 1977-79, 93-95, mem. exec. com., 1976—; bd. dirs Boston Mcpl. Rsch. Bur., 1965—, chmn. bd., 1967-72; mem. pub. pension task force Mass. Bus. Roundtable, 1983-86; bd. dirs., sec. Jobs for Mass., Inc., 1981-83; moderator Town of Hingham, 1967—; del. Rep. Nat. Conv., 1972, all Rep. State convs., 1960-94; overseer Harvard U., 1986-92; bd. dirs. United Way Mass. Bay, 1987—, mem. exec. com. 1993—, chmn. bd. 1997-2000. Lt. USNR, 1944-45, 52-54. Recipient Cushing award Labor Guild of Archdiocese Boston, 1973, Humanitarian award The Nat. Conf. Greater Boston, 1997, The Harvard medal, 1997; mem. Knights of Malta, 1983— Fellow Am. Bar Found.; mem. ABA, Mass. Bar Assn., Boston Bar Assn., Am. Arbitration Assn., Indsl. Rels. Rsch. Assn. (pres. Boston chpt. 1980), Harvard Alumni Assn. (bd. dirs. 1978-81; 1st marshal class of 1947). Clubs: Harvard of Boston (bd. govs. 1985-91), Union of Boston; Hingham Yacht, Comml. Roman Catholic. Home: 7 South Ln Hingham MA 02043-2446 Office: Ropes & Gray LLP 1 International Pl Boston MA 02110-2624 Office Phone: 617-951-7455. Business E-Mail: todonnell@ropesgray.com.

**O'DONNELL, WILLIAM DAVID,** retired construction firm executive; b. Brockton, Mass., Aug. 21, 1926; s. John Frank and Agnes Teresa (Flanagan) O'D.; m. Dixie Lou Anderson, Jan. 31, 1951; children— Craig Patrick, Ginger Lynn BS, U. N.Mex., 1953. Registered profl. engr., Ill., 1958. Engr. State of Ill., 1953-59; with Gregory-Anderson Co., Rockford, Ill., 1959—, gen. mgr. 1960-61, sec., 1961-81, pres., 1981-81, ret. Bd. dirs. Growth Enterprise, Davis Meml. Park, BankOne, Rockford. Dir. St. Anthony Med. Ctr., Youth Svcs. Network, Cath. Conf. of Ill.; bd. dirs Rockford YMCA, pres., 1984. Served with USN, 1943-47 Recipient Friend of the Boy award Optimist Club, 1966, Excalibur award for cmty. svc. Rockford Register Star, 1971; named Titan of Yr., Boylan H.S., 1974, Papal Knight Order of St. Gregory the Great; fellow Wisdom Hall of Fame. Fellow: NSPE, ASCE, Soc. Am. Mil. Engrs.; mem.: VFW (life), No. Ill. Bldg. Contractors, Amateur Trapshooting Assn., World Future Soc., Aircraft Owners & Pilots Assn., Balloon Fedn. Am., Am. Radar Soc., Nat. Sporting Clays Assn., Old Antarctic Explorers Assn., Forest Hills Country (Rockford), Metropolitan Club (Chgo.), Adventurers (Chgo.), Adventurers Club, Metropolitan Club, Forest Hills Country Club, Rotary (Service Above Self award 1972; v.p. Rockford chpt. 1983, pres. 1984), Rotary (v.p. Rockford chpt. 1983, pres. 1984, Svc. Above Self award 1972), Am. Legion (life), Tau Beta Pi, Chi Epsilon, Sigma Tau. Home: 2004 Bradley Rd Rockford IL 61107-1258 Office: PO Box 900 Rockford IL 61105-0900 Personal E-mail: odonnellbill@hotmail.com.

**O'DONNELL, WILLIAM JAMES,** engineering executive; b. Pitts., June 19, 1935; s. William James and Elizabeth (Rau) O'D.; m. Joanne Mary Kusen, Jan. 31, 1959; children: Suzanne, Janice, William, Thomas, Kerry, Amy. BSME, Carnegie Inst. Tech., 1957; MSME, U. Pitts., 1959, PhD, 1962. Jr. engr. Westinghouse Research Lab., 1957-58, asso. engr., 1958; with Westinghouse Bettis Atomic Power Lab., West Mifflin, Pa., 1961-70, adv. engr., 1966-70; pres., chmn. bd. O'Donnell & Assocs., Inc., Pitts., 1970—. Contbr. numerous articles on engring. and mechanics to profl. jours.; holder patents on processes and devices. Served with C.E. AUS, 1963-64. Recipient Machinery's Achievement award as outstanding mech. designer, 1957, Pi Tau Sigma Gold medal for achievements in engring., 1967, Pressure Vessel and Piping award ASME, 1996, Disting. Alumni award U. Pitts. Sch. Mech. Engring., 1996. Fellow ASME (nat. award for outstanding contbn. to engring. profession 1973, internat. award for best publ. in pressure vessels and piping 1988, Engr. of Yr. award 1988, Pressure Vessel and Piping medal 1994); mem. NSPE, AAAS, ASTM, Soc. Exptl. Mechanics, Am. Nuclear Soc., Am. Soc. Metals Internat.; The Minerals, Metals and Materials Soc., Sigma Xi.

Home: 121 Sunrise Ln Venetia PA 15367 Office: O'Donnell Consulting Engrs 2940 S Park Rd Pittsburgh PA 15102 Office Phone: 412-835-5007. Business E-Mail: wjo@odonnellconsulting.com.

**O'DONNELL II, BRIAN A.,** social studies educator; b. Niagara Falls, N.Y. MS in Secondary Edn., Niagara U., Niagra U., N.Y. Cert. secondary edn. Social Studies N.Y., 2002. Global history tchr. Niagara Falls City Sch. Dist., NY, 2002—. Mem.: Ancient Order of Hibernians. Office Phone: 716-278-5800.

**O'DONOVAN, CORMAC A.,** neurologist, educator; children: Katherine, Maura. BS, U. Coll. Galway, Ireland, 1982, MD, 1985. Assoc. prof. neurology Wake Forest U. Sch. Medicine, Winston-Salem, NC, 1995—. Med. dir. meg lab., dir. eeg and evoked potential labs., assoc. prof. internal medicine-cardiology Wake Forest U. Sch. Medicine. Fellow: Am. Clin. Neurophysiology; mem.: AMA, Am. Acad. Sleep Medicine, Irish Neurol. Assn., So. Epilepsy and Ctrl. EEG Soc., Am. EEG Soc., Am. Epilepsy Soc., Am. Acad. Neurology. Office: Wake Forest Univ Sch of Medicine Medical Center Blvd Winston Salem NC 27157 Business E-Mail: odonovan@wfubmc.edu.

**O'DONOVAN, LEO JEREMIAH,** former academic administrator, priest, theologian; b. NYC, Apr. 24, 1934; s. Leo J. O'Donovan Jr. AB, Georgetown U., 1956; Licentiate in Philosophy, Fordham U., 1961; STB, Woodstock Coll., 1966, Licentiate in Sacred Theology, 1967; ThD, U. Münster, Fed. Republic Germany, 1971; LittD (hon.), Sogang U., Seoul, 1993; DHL, Loyola Coll., 1991, Coll. St. Rose, 2000; MD (hon.), Georgetown U., 2001. Ordained to ministry Cath. Ch., 1966. Instr. philosophy Loyola Coll., Balt., 1961—63; asst. prof. Woodstock Coll., Woodstock, 1971—74; assoc. prof. Weston Sch. Theology, Cambridge, Mass., 1974—81, prof., 1981—89; pres. Georgetown U., Washington, 1989—2001, prof., 2001—. Provincial asst. formation Md. Province S.J., Balt., 1985—88; mem. Nat. Conf. Cath. Bishops, Washington, 1986—89; bd. dirs. The Riggs Nat. Bank, Walt Disney Co., 2001—, MedStar Health, Inc. Bd. dirs. U. Detroit Mercy, 1986—95; mem. Consortium of Univs. Washington Met. Area, 1989—2001, chair, 1994—96; mem. Fed. Cuty Coun., 1993—2001, Bus.-Higher Edn. Forum, 1989—2001, Nat. Coun. Arts, 1994—98, Consortium Fin. Higher Edn., 1990—98, chmn., 1995—97; mem. Am. Reads Stery Com., 1997—. Recipient Knight Comdr.'s Crodd, Germany; fellow, Danforth Found., 1956—71, vis. fellow, Woodstock Theol. Ctr.; grantee teaching grantee, Assn. Theol. Schs., 1978—79; scholar, Fulbright Found., U. Lyon, France, 1956—57. Fellow: Soc. Values in Higher Edn. (bd. dirs 1989—); mem.: Boston Theol. Soc., Assn. Cath. Colls. and Univs. (bd. dirs 1994—2000), Assn. Jesuit Colls. and Univs., Univ. Club. Office: Georgetown U 37th and O St NW Washington DC 20057-1789*

**ODORIZZI, MICHELE L.,** lawyer; b. Chgo., July 12, 1952; BA, Northwestern U., 1973; JD cum laude, U. Chgo., 1976. Bar: Ill. 1976, U.S. Ct. Appeals (7th cir.) 1976, U.S. Dist. Ct. (no. dist.) Ill. 1977, U.S. Supreme Ct. 1980, U.S. Ct. Appeals (4th, 9th, 10th cirs.). Ptnr. Mayer, Brown & Platt, Chgo. Office: Mayer Brown & Platt 190 S La Salle St Ste 3100 Chicago IL 60603-3441

**O'DOWD, CHARLES EDWYN,** physician; b. Nyack, NY, Oct. 12, 1962; s. Michael William and Helene Marie (Albert) O'D.; m. Barbara Ann Finan, May 18, 1991; children: Matthew, Patrick, Maureen, Caitlin. BS in Biology, Fordham U., 1984; MD, N.Y. Med. Coll., 1988. Diplomate Am. Bd. Internal Medicine. Resident physician Westchester County Med. Ctr., Valhalla, N.Y., 1988-91; attending physician Clarkstown Med. Assocs., New City, N.Y., 1991—. Mem. ACP, AMA, Med. Soc. State N.Y. Roman Catholic. Office: Clarkstown Med Assocs 200 E Eckerson Rd New City NY 10956-7153

**O'DOWD, DONALD DAVY,** retired university president; b. Manchester, NH, Jan. 23, 1927; s. Hugh Davy and Laura (Morin) O'D.; m. Janet Louise Fithian, Aug. 23, 1953; children: Daniel D., Diane K., James E., John M. BA summa cum laude, Dartmouth Coll., 1951; postgrad. (Fulbright fellow), U. Edinburgh, Scotland, 1951-52; MA, Harvard U., 1955, PhD, 1957. Instr., asst. prof. psychology, dean freshmen Wesleyan U., Middletown, Conn., 1955-60; assoc. prof., prof. of psychology, dean Univ. Oakland Univ., Rochester, Mich. 1960-65, provost, 1965-70; pres. Oakland U., Rochester, Mich., 1970-80; exec. vice chancellor SUNY, Albany, 1980-84; pres. U. of Alaska Statewide System, 1984-90. Carnegie Corp. fellow, 1965—66. Mem. APA, AAAS, Phi Beta Kappa, Sigma Xi. Home and Office: 801 A Senda Verde Santa Barbara CA 93105

**O'DOWD, SARAH A.,** lawyer; b. Manchester, NH, Sept. 7, 1949; AB, Immaculata Coll., 1971; MA, Stanford U., 1973, JD, 1977 Bar: Calif. 1978. Atty. Heller, Ehrman, White & McAuliffe, Palo Alto, Calif., 1978—; managing shareholder, Silicon Valley Office, 1995—99, firmwide practice chair, mem. exec. comm., 1999—2002. Mem. ABA.

**O'DRISCOLL, MARGARET MILLAR (PEGGY O'DRISCOLL),** real estate broker; b. Hollywood, Calif., Aug. 2, 1925; d. Russell Hartney and Marion Scott (Macarthur) Millar; m. William Harrington Walker, Jan. 10, 1949 (dec. Dec. 22, 1968); children: William Russell Walker, Elizabeth Howland, Hiram Scott Walker; m. James O'Driscoll, Oct. 17, 1970. Student UCLA, 1942-44. Lic. ins. solicitor, real estate broker, Calif. Salesman, Carol Smart Real Estate, Del Mar, Calif., 1966-68, Bernard & Assocs., Solana Beach, Calif., 1968-70; owner Town and Country Real Estate, Rancho Santa Fe, Calif., 1970—; pres. Peggy O'Driscoll Enterprises, Inc. Mem. publicity com. Rancho Santa Fe Republican Women, 1950-58; mem. San Dieguito Citizens Planning Group, 1977-78; mem. vestry St. Peter's Episcopal Ch. Del Mar, 1976-78; bd. dirs. Rancho Santa Fe Cmty. Svcs. Dist., 1982-85, chmn. 1983, mem., 1986—. Mem. San Dieguito Bd Realtors (v.p. 1980-82, pres. 1983-84), Calif. Assn. Realtors (hon. life mem., bd. dirs. 1981-86, ins. trustee 1982-86, regional v.p. dist. 29 1986), Rancho Santa Fe Cmty. Ctr., Rancho Santa Fe Hist. Soc. (bd. dirs. 1985-86), San Diego County Coun. Real Estate Bds., Rancho Santa Fe Club, The Country Friends, The Gold Diggers (San Diego, Gifts of Loving Donors), Garden Club (publicity chmn. 1965-74), Rancho Santa Fe Women's Golf Club (founding mem.). Home: PO Box 457 Rancho Santa Fe CA 92067-0457 Office Phone: 858-756-1422.

**ODUM, JEFFERY NEAL,** mechanical engineer; b. Bristol, Tenn., Sept. 11, 1956; s. Herschel S. and Minnie Lee (Carrier) O.; m. Stacy Elaine Ferrell, mar. 18, 1989; 1 child, Charles Wesley Ferrell. BSME, Tenn. Technol. U., 1978; MS in Engring., U. Tenn., 1983. Sr. project engr. TVA, Knoxville, 1978-81; sr. constrn. engr. Stone & Webster Engring. Corp., Boston, 1981-84; div. engr. E.I. DuPont de Nemours & Co., Aiken, S.C., 1984-89; engring. mgr. Flour Daniel, Greenville, S.C., 1989-92; mgr. of projects, Pharmaceutical Bus. Group CRS Sirrine Engrs., Inc., Raleigh, N.C., 1992-93; sr. project mgr. Gilbane Bldg. Co., Raleigh, 1993-95; dir. engring. Gilbane Process Group, Vacaville, Calif., 1995-98; biopharm. office leader Clark, Richardson and Biskup, Cons. Engrs., Cary, NC, 1998—2005; prin. NC Biosource, 2005—; dir. validation acad. NC Cmty. Coll. Sys. Author: Sterile Product Facility Design and Project Management, 1996, 2d edit., 2004, Large Scale Biomanufacturing, 2004, Advances in Large Scale Biomanufacturing-Capital Projects, 2004, Advanced Technologies For Biopharmaceutical Processing, 2005; contbr. articles to profl. jours Vol. Spl. Olympics, Habitat for Humanity; mem. bd. govs. U. Tenn., 2002—03. Recipient DuPont Engring. Achievement award 1986, 88, 89, Nat. Svc. Alumni award Univ. Tenn. Mem. Parenteral Drug Assn., Internat. Soc. Pharm. Engrs. (bd. dirs., pres. Carolina chpt. 1996-97, chair N.Am. Chpt. Coun. 1998, chair publs. com. 2000-01, chair chpt. excellence 2000-01, chair tng. 2002, Svc. award 1999, 2001, 2003, 2005, chmn. N. Am. edn. 2004, Richard Purdy Outstanding Achievement award 2002, edn advisor N.Am.), ISPE Trng. Faculty, U. Tenn. Nat. Alumni Assn. (pres. Augusta chpt. 1987-89, bd. govs.), Order Engr., Kappa Sigma Republican. Presbyterian. Avocations: sports, biking, cooking, writing, skiing. Office: NCBiosource 1213 Enoerbury Dr Raleigh NC 27614 Office Phone: 919-852-5400. E-mail: jodum@ncbiosource.com.

**O'DWYER, MARY ANN,** automotive executive; BS, DePaul U.; MS, Benedictine U. CPA. With Ernst and Young, McDonald's Corp.; various positions CC Industries (a Henry Crown Co.); sr. v.p. fin. ops., CFO Wheels, 1991—; sr. v.p. fin & ops., CFO Frank Consol. Enterprises. Office: Frank Consol Enterprises 666 Garland Pl Des Plaines IL 60016

**ODYA, GREGORY MATTHEW,** music educator, musician; b. Bloomington, Ind., Apr. 22, 1980; s. Charles Ervin and Martha Fortenberry Odya; m. Erin Catherine Stapleton, June 23, 2001. Degree in instrumental music edn., Ind. U., 2004. Lic. tchr. Ind. Weekend coord.; program asst. Christole, Inc., Bloomington, Ind., 2000—02; asst. program coord. Edgewood H.S. Marching Band, Ellettsville, Ind., 2000—03; instr. Bloomington H.S. North Marching Band, 2002; instrumental music arranger, instr. and performer Edgewood H.S. Show Choirs, 2002—04; assoc. instr. The PA Inst., MSD Lawrence Twp., Indpls., 2004; assoc. dir. of bands Decatur Ctrl. H.S. MSD Decatur Twp., Indpls., 2004—. Adjudicator Edgewood H.S. Contest of Champions, 2004. Music performer St. John the Apostle Cath. Ch., Bloomington, 2003—04. Mem.: Ind. State Tchrs. Assn., Music Educators Nat. Conf., Phi Lambda Theta, Golden Key, Nat. Soc. Collegiate Scholars. Avocations: running, swimming, music composition, music performance. Office Phone: 317-856-5288. Personal E-mail: gmodya@gmail.com.

**ODZA, RANDALL M.,** lawyer; b. Schnectady, May 6, 1942; s. Mitchell and Grace (Mannes) O.; m. Rita Ginness, June 19, 1966; children: Kenneth, Keith. BS in Indsl. and Labor Rels., Cornell U., 1964, LLB, 1967. Bar: N.Y. 1967, U.S. Ct. Appeals (2d cir.) 1970, U.S. Dist. Ct. (so. and ea. dists.) N.Y. 1969, U.S. Dist. Ct. (we. dist.) N.Y 1970. Assoc. Proskauer, Rose, Goetz & Mandelsolin, N.Y.C., 1967-69, Jaeckle, Fleischmann & Mugel, Buffalo, 1969-72, ptnr., 1972—. Past trustee, legal counsel, treas. Temple Beth Am; bd. trustees Buffalo Philharm. Orch. Soc. Recipient Honow award Western N.Y. Retail Mchts. Assn., 1980. Fellow Coll. Labor and Employment Lawyers; mem. ABA, Indsl. Rels. Rsch. Assn. Western N.Y., Erie County Bar Assn., N.Y. State Bar Assn. Office: Jaeckle Fleischmann & Mugel 12 Fountain Plz Rm 700 Buffalo NY 14202-2292 Office Phone: 716-843-3877. Business E-Mail: rodza@jaeckle.com.

**ODZE, ROBERT D.,** pathologist; s. Walter Karl Odze and Helen Natasha Minkis. BSc, McGill U., Montreal, 1980, MDCM, 1984. Cert. anatomic pathology. Staff pathologist Mount Sinai Hosp., Toronto, Canada; instr. pathology U. Toronto Med. Sch., Canada, 1991—93; cons. GI pathology New Eng. Deaconess Med. Ctr., Boston, 1994—99, Beth Israel Deaconess Med. Ctr., Boston, 1996—99; dir. GI pathology svc. Brigham and Women's Hosp., Boston, 1997—; assoc. prof. psychology Harvard Med. Sch., Boston, 1999—; cons. pathologist Dana Farber Cancer Inst., Boston, 2004—. Author, editor: Surgical Pathology GI Tract, Liver, Bilary Tract and Pancreas, 2003, assoc. editor: Am. Jour. Gastroenterology, 2003—, mem. editl. bd.: Human Pathology, 2001—, Gastrointestinal Endoscopy, 2001. Recipient MRC award, McGill U. Dept. Sci., 1980, CIBA prize for anatomy, McGill U. Med. Sch., 1981, MRC award, 1981, Joseph Morley Drake prize for pathology, 1982, Outstanding Surgery Student award, ACP and McGill U. Med. Sch., 1983, Pathology Finlayson Rsch. award, McGill U., 1988; grantee, Am. Coll. Gastroenterology, 1994—95, 1998—99, Stanley Robbins Rsch. Award, 1996—97; Univ. scholar, McGill U. Dept. Sci., 1981, Faculty scholar, McGill U. Med. Sch., 1982. Mem.: Arthur Purdy Stout Soc. Surg. Pathologists, U.S. and Can. Acad. Pathology Gastrointestinal Pathology Soc., U.S. and Can. Acad. Pathology, Am. Gastroenterol. Assn., Am. Coll. Gastroenterology, Crohn's Colitis Found. Am. Home: 1175 Chestnut St Newton MA 02464 Office: Brigham & Womens Hosp 75 Francis St Boston MA 02115

**OECHLER, HENRY JOHN, JR.,** lawyer; b. Charlotte, N.C., Apr. 9, 1946; s. Henry J. and Convere Jones (McAden) O. AB, Princeton U., 1968; JD, Duke U., 1971. Bar: N.Y. 1972, U.S. Ct. Appeals (2d cir.) 1974, U.S. Ct. Appeals (D.C. cir.) 1975, U.S. Ct. Appeals (8th cir.) 1986, U.S. Ct. Appeals (9th cir.) 1995. Assoc. Chadbourne & Parke, N.Y.C., 1971-80, ptnr., 1980—. Avocation: studying airline schedules. Office: Chadbourne & Parke 30 Rockefeller Plz Fl 31 New York NY 10112-0129

**OEFFNER, BARBARA DUNNING,** writer, educator, scriptwriter; b. Southampton, N.Y., Aug. 25, 1944; d. Walter Arnold and Grace Dominy (Werner) Renkens; m. Michael Arthur Dunning, Oct. 1, 1966 (div. June 1984); children: Brendan, Ania, Amie, Heidi, Matt; m. F. Thomas Oeffner, Oct. 2, 1991. BS in Journalism, Northwestern U., 1966; MLS and Info. Studies, Fla. State U. Film copywriter Ency. Britannica, Chgo., 1966-69; pub. rels. dir. Eldred Auctions, East Dennis, Mass., 1982-85; editor Sandscript, Cummaquid, Mass., 1975-95; ins. agt. State Farm Ins., Delray Beach, Fla., 1992-95; biographer Cape Cod Writers, Inc., Cummaquid, 1995—. V.p. Caribbean Coatings Corp., Moore Haven, Fla., 1996—, Native Am. Prodns., Palm Beach, Fla., 1994—; lectr. Glades County Hist. Soc. Author: (screenplay) The Cuban Accident, 1996; co-author: (screenplay) Chief, 1994; author: (book) Chief: Champion of the Everglades, 1995. Tchr. Meth. Bible Sch., Moore Haven, 1997; activities dir. Campers Club Am., Moore Haven, 1996-97. Grantee Mary Roberts Rinehart Found., 1975, Commonwealth of Mass.-Dept. of Arts and Humanities, 1984, Coord. Coun. Lit. Mags., 1976. Mem. DAR. Democrat. Avocations: water aerobics, line dancing, hiking, travel, gardening. Home: Box 1236 306 Yacht Club Way Moore Haven FL 33471-2809 Office: Hendry County Libr Coop 120 W Osceola Ave Clewiston FL 33440 Office Phone: 561-996-3453, 561-996-2304, 863-983-1493. Office Fax: 863-983-9194. Business E-mail: oeffnerb@pbclibrary.org, barbara.oeffner@clewiston.fl.gov.

**OEHLER, RICHARD WILLIAM,** lawyer; b. NYC, Nov. 24, 1950; s. John Montgomery and Florence Mae (Jahn) O.; m. Linda Tyson. BA, Dartmouth Coll., 1972, ID, Harvard U., 1976. Bar: Calif. 1976, Wash. 1987, D.C. 1988, U.S. Dist. Ct. (no. dist.) Calif. 1976, U.S. Dist. Ct. Wash. 1987, U.S. Claims Ct. 1979, U.S. Ct. Appeals (fed. cir.) 1982. Assoc. Pillsbury, Madison & Sutro, San Francisco, 1976-78; trial atty. U.S. Dept. Justice, Washington, 1978-87; of counsel Perkins Coie, Seattle, 1987-90, ptnr., 1990—. Mem. ABA, Nat. Contract Mgmt. Assn. (Spl. Achievement award 1990-92), Wash. State Bar Assn. Office: Perkins Coie 1201 3rd Ave Fl 40 Seattle WA 98101-3029 Office Phone: 206-359-8419. Business E-Mail: roehler@perkinscoie.com.

**OEHME, FREDERICK WOLFGANG,** medical researcher, educator; b. Leipzig, Germany, Oct. 14, 1933; arrived in U.S., 1934; s. Friedrich Oswald and Frieda Betha (Wohlgamuth) Oehme; m. Nancy Beth McAdam, Aug. 6, 1960 (div. June 1981); children: Stephen Frederick, Susan Lynn, Deborah Ann, Heidi Beth; m. Pamela Sheryl Ford, Oct. 2, 1981; 1 child, April Virginia. BS in Biol. Sci., Cornell U., 1957, DVM, 1958; MS in Toxicology and Medicine, Kans. State U. 1962; DMV in Pathology, Justus Liebig U., Giessen, Germany, 1964; PhD in Toxicology, U. Mo., 1969. Diplomate Am. Bd. Toxicology, Am. Bd. Vet. Toxicology, Acad. Toxicol. Scis. Resident intern, Large Animal and Ambulatory Clinic Cornell U., 1957-58; gen. practice vet. medicine, 1958-59; from asst. to assoc. prof. medicine Coll. Vet. Medicine Kans. State U., 1959-66, 69-73, dir. comparative toxicology labs., 1969—, prof. toxicology, pathobiology, medicine and physiology, 1996—; postdoctoral research fellow in toxicology, NIH U. Mo. 1966-69. Cons. FDA, Washington, Ctr. for Vet. Medicine, Rockville, Md.; cons. animal care com. U. Kans., Lawrence, 1969—76, Syntex Corp., Palo Alto, Calif., 1976—77; mem. sci. adv. panel on PBB Gov.'s Office, State of Mich., 1976—77; mem. Coun. for Agrl. sci. and Tech. Task Force on Toxicity, Toxicology and Environ. Hazard, 1976—83; cons., mem. adv. group on pesticides EPA, Cin., 1977—; expert state and fed. witness; advisor WHO, Geneva; presenter numerous papers to profl. meetings. Reviewer: Toxicology and Applied Pharmacology, Spectroscopy, numerous others. Mem. adv. coun. Cub Scouts Am., Eagle Scouts; mgr., coach Little League Baseball; active PTA; mem. Manhattan Civic Theatre; trustee Manhattan Marlin Swim Team; dir. meet Little Apple Invitational Swim Meet, 1984; mem. coun. Luth. Ch. Am., mem. sr. choir, numerous coms. Recipient Disting. Grad. Faculty award, Kans. State U., 1977—79, Dir.'s Letter of Commendation, FDA, 1983,

Kenneth P. DuBois award, Midwest Soc. Toxicology, 1991, Kenneth F. Lampe award, Am. Acad. Toxicology, 1993, John Doull award, Ctrl. States Soc. Toxicology, 1994, medal, Azabu U., 1994, Silver award, Aristotelian U., 1995, others; fellow, Morris Animal Found., 1967—69. Fellow: Am. Acad. Vet. and Comparative Toxicology (past sec.-treas., numerous coms.); Am. Acad. Toxicology (past pres., numerous coms.); mem.: NRC (subcom. on organic contaminants in drinking water, safe drinking water com., adv. ctr. on toxicology assembly life scis. 1976—77, panel on toxicology marine bd., assembly of engring. 1976—79), AVMA (com. on environmentology 1971—73, adv. com. coun. on biol. and therapeutic agts. 1971—74, Samuel Shiedy award 1999), Nat. Ctr. Toxicol. Rsch. (vet. toxicology rep. sci. adv. bd., sci. adv. bd. 1974—77), N.Y. Acad. Scis., Soc. Toxicologic Pathologists, World Fedn. Clin. Toxicology Ctrs. and Poison Control Ctrs. (past pres.), Soc. Toxicology (past pres., numerous coms., Edn. award 2003), Cornell U. Athletic Assn., Manhattan Square Dance Club, Cornell U. Crew Club, Sigma Xi, Phi Zeta, Omega Tau Sigma. Republican. Avocations: reading, writing, walking, travel. Home: 148 S Dartmouth Dr Manhattan KS 66503-3079 Office: Kans State Univ Comparative Toxicology Labs 1800 Denison Ave Manhattan KS 66506-5660 Office Phone: 785-532-4334. E-mail: oehme@vet.ksu.edu.

**OEHME, REINHARD,** physicist, researcher; b. Wiesbaden, Germany, Jan. 26, 1928; arrived in U.S., 1956; s. Reinhold and Katharina (Kraus) O.; m. Mafalda Pisani, Nov. 5, 1952. Dr. rer. nat., U. Goettingen, Germany, 1951; Diplom Physiker, U. Frankfurt am Main, Germany, 1948. Asst. Max Planck Inst. Physics, Goettingen, 1949-53; research asso. Fermi Inst. Nuclear Studies, U. Chgo., 1954-56; mem. faculty dept. physics and Fermi Inst., 1958—, prof. physics, 1964—; mem. Inst. Advanced Studies, Princeton, 1956-58. Vis. prof. Inst. de Física Teórica, São Paulo, Brazil, 1952-53, U. Md., 1957, U. Vienna, Austria, 1961, Imperial Coll., London, Eng., 1963-64, U. Karlsruhe, Fed. Republic Germany, 1974, 75, 77, U. Tokyo, 1976, 88; vis. scientist Internat. Centre Theoretical Physics, Miramare-Trieste, Italy, Brookhaven Nat. Lab., Lawrence Radiation Lab., U. Calif., Berkeley, CERN, Geneva, Switzerland, Max Planck Inst., Munich, Fed. Republic Germany, Rsch. Inst. for Fundamental Physics, Kyoto (Japan) U. Author articles in field, chpts. in books. Guggenheim fellow, 1963-64; recipient Humboldt award, 1974, Japan Soc. for Promotion of Sci. Fellowship awards, 1976, 88. Fellow: Am. Phys. Soc. Achievements include discovery of chargeconjugation non-invariance; formulation and proof of Edge of the Wedge theorem. Office: U Chgo Enrico Fermi Inst 5640 S Ellis Ave Chicago IL 60637-1433 Office Phone: 773-702-7299. E-mail: oehme@theory.uchicago.edu.

**OEHME, WOLFGANG WALTER,** landscape architect; b. Chemnitz, Germany, May 18, 1930; came to the U.S., 1957; s. Walter Gustav and Elisabeth Elsa (Neumann) O.; 1 child, Roland. Degree in horticulture, Bitterfeld Trade Sch., 1950; degree in landscape architecture, U. Berlin, 1954. Exch. student Waterer & Sons Nurseries, Bagshot, United Kingdom, 1954-56; landscape architect Baltimore County Planning, Towson, Md., 1958-65, The Rouse Co., Columbia, Md., 1965-66; asst. prof. U. Pa., Phila., 1962-64, U. Ga., Athens, 1965; pvt. practice Balt., 1965-74; CEO Oehme, Van Sweden and Assocs., Inc., Washington, 1974—. Co-author: Bold Romantic Gardens, 1990, Gardening with Water, 1995, Process Architecture, 1996, Gardening with Nature, 1997. Recipient Spl. Resolution for Disting. and dedicated vol. svc. Baltimore County Coun., 2003; mamed to Hall of Fame, Towson Devel. Corp., 1995; named Man of Yr., German Soc. Md., 1996. Fellow Am. Soc. Landscape Architects; mem. Perennial Plant Assn. (Disting. Svc. 1988), Garden Writers Assn. (Quill and Trowel award 1991). Mass. Hort. Soc. (George Robert White medal of honor 2002). Home: 511A W Joppa Rd Baltimore MD 21204-3819 Office: 800 G St SE Washington DC 20003-2816 Office Phone: 202-546-7575. Business E-Mail: oehme@ovsla.com.

**OEHNINGER, SERGIO C.,** endocrinologist, obstetrician, gynecologist; b. Montevideo, Uruguay, Oct. 24, 1952; s. Carlos F. Oehninger and Elena Gatti; m. Maria L. Fornella, Jan. 16, 1951; children: Sergio F., Juan S., Natalia, Matthew T. MD, U. of the Republic, Montevideo, Uruguay, 1980; MS, Rutgers U., 1991; PhD, U. Stellenbosch, Capetown, South Africa, 2002. Diplomate Uruguay. Prof. dept. of ob-gyn Ea. Va. Med. Sch., Norfolk, Va., 1998—, dir. reproductive endocrinology, The Jones Inst Reproductive Medicine, 2000—. Vis. prof. U. Stellenbosch, Capetown, South Africa, 1999—2002. Mem. editl. bd. Biology of Reproduction, 2000—02, Reproduction, U.K., 2000—02, Andrologia, Germany, Revista Latinoameri- can de Fertilidad y Reproduccion Humana; contbr. articles to profl. jours. Fulbright scholar, Rutgers U., 1980—81. Fellow: Am. Gynecol. Obstet. Soc. (assoc.); mem.: European Soc. Human Reproduction and Embryology (assoc.), Soc. for the Study of Reproduction (assoc.), Soc. for Gynecol. Investigation (assoc.), Am. Soc. Andrology (assoc.), Am. Soc. for Reproductive Medicine (assoc.). Office: Eastern Virginia Med Sch 601 Colley Ave Norfolk VA 23507 E-mail: oehninsc@evms.edu.

**OEI, LOK S.,** digital communications systems and DSP engineer, researcher; BSEE, U. Mich., 1973, MA in Math., 1973; DSc, Washington U., 1977. Mem. tech. staff Mitre Corp., McLean, Va., 1977—81; staff engr. Hughes Aircraft Co., Fullerton, Calif., 1981—86; prin. sys. engr. Lockheed Martin, Sunnyvale, Calif., 1986—94; sr. prin. engr. Boeing/Raytheon/Hughes Electronics Sys., El Segundo, Calif., 1994—. Mem.: IEEE, AIAA, Sigma Xi, Phi Kappa Phi, Eta Kappa Nu, Tau Beta Pi. Home: PO Box 1425 El Segundo CA 90245 Office: 2200 E Imperial Hwy El Segundo CA 90245 Office Phone: 310-334-3876. Personal E-mail: lsoei@ieee.org.

**OELBAUM, HAROLD,** lawyer; b. Bklyn., Jan. 9, 1931; s. Max and Betty (Molomet) O.; m. Nancy Rothkopf, June 28, 1968; children— Louise, Andrew, Jennifer. AB, Franklin and Marshall Coll., 1952; JD, Harvard, 1955; LL.M., N.Y. U., 1959. Bar: N.Y. 1955, Mass. 1960. Atty. Hellerstein & Rosier, Esqs., N.Y.C., 1955-59; gen. atty. Raytheon Co., Lexington, Mass., 1959-68; sr. atty. Revlon Inc., N.Y.C., 1968-72; pres., dir., mem. exec. com. Kane-Miller Corp., Tarrytown, N.Y., 1972—. Office: Kane Miller Corp 1991 Main St Ste 260 Sarasota FL 34236-5942

**OELBERG, DAVID GEORGE,** neonatologist educator, researcher; b. Waukon, Iowa, May 26, 1952; s. George Robert and Elizabeth Abigail (Kepler) O.; m. Debra Penuel, Aug. 4, 1979; children: Anna Elizabeth, Benjamin George. BS with highest honors, Coll. William and Mary, 1974; MD, U. Md., 1978. Diplomate in pediat. and in neonatal-perinatal medicine Am. Bd. Pediat. Intern U. Tex. Med. Br., Galveston, 1978-79, resident 1979-81, house pediat. staff, 1978-81; postdoctoral fellow in neonatal medicine U. Tex. Med. Sch., Houston, 1981-84, asst. prof. dept. pediat., 1984-90, assoc. prof., 1990-93; assoc. prof. pediat., head perinatal rsch. Ctr. Pediat. Rsch. Ea. Va. Med. Sch., 1993-2001, prof., interim chmn. dept. pediat. Ctr. Pediat. Rsch., 2001—, dir. divsn. neonatal-perinatal medicine. Mem. hosp. staff Hermann Hosp., Houston, 1983-93; physician Crippled Children's Svcs. Program, Houston, 1985-93; mem. hosp. staff Lyndon B. Johnson County Hosp., 1990-93; vis. prof. Wyeth-Ayerst Labs., 1992; med. dir. Office Rsch., Children's Hosp. of King's Daus., 1993—, v.p. for acad. devel., 2001—; med. dirs. Office of Rsch., Sentara-Norfolk Gen. Hosp., 1993—, pres. med. staff. Mem. editl. adv. bd. jour. Neonatal Intensive Care; contbr. articles to profl. jours.; ad hoc reviewer profl. jours.; patentee in field. Physician cons. Parents of Victims of Sudden Infant Death Syndrome, Houston, 1984; chmn. Instl. Animal Care and Use Com. Recipient award in analytical chemistry Am. Chem. Soc., 1974, NIH Clin. Investigator award NHLBI, 1989-94; rsch. grantee Am. Lung Assn., 1989-90, NIH, 1989-94. Fellow Am. Acad. Pediat. NY Acad. Scis.; mem. AMA, NAS, Soc. Exptl. Biology and Medicine, So. Soc. Pediatric Rsch. (councilor, mem. sec.-treas.), Soc. Pediatric Rsch. Achievements include development of a method for optical measurement of bilirubin in tissue. Home: 1624 W Little Neck Rd Virginia Beach VA 23452-4720 Office: Ea Va Med Sch Ctr Pediatric Rsch 855 W Brambleton Ave Norfolk VA 23510-1005 Office Phone: 757-668-7456. Business E-Mail: doelberg@chkd.org.

**OELBERG, ROBERT NATHAN,** landscape architect; b. Washington, May 7, 1956; s. George Robert and Elizabeth Abigail (Kepler) Oelberg; m. Katherine Jane Shoffner, Nov. 9, 2002; stepchildren: Forrest Dungan, Katelyn Dungan. BA in Art magna cum laude, Maharishi Internat. U., Fairfield, Iowa, 1981; M.Landscape Arch., U. Va., Charlottesville, 1985. Registered landscape architect, N.C. Landscape architect, sr. project mgr. Land Design Inc., Alexandria, Va., 1985-93; owner Robert N. Oelberg ASLA PA, Boone, NC, 1994—97, 1999—2005; dir. HMR Land Planning and Landscape Arch., Boone, 1997-99, v.p. planning Ginn NC region, 2005—. Chmn. Boone Country Dancers. With USMC, 1974-76. DuPont fellow, 1984. Mem. Am. Soc. Landscape Architects. Democrat. Episcopalian. Mailing: 432 Fawn Dr Boone NC 28607 Office: 389 Little Laurel Rd Ext Boone NC 28607 Office Phone: 828-263-5904. E-mail: boelberg@ginncompany.com.

**OELSNER, RICHARD S.,** lawyer; b. NYC, Jan. 23, 1951; BA, NYU, 1973, MA, 1976; JD, Fordham U., 1980. Bar: NY 1981, US Dist. Ct. Ea. Dist. NY, US Dist. Ct. So. Dist. NY. Ptnr. Wilson, Elser, Moskowitz, Edelman & Dicker LLP. NYC. Mem.: NY State Bar Assn. Office: Wilson Elser Moskowitz Edelman & Dicker LLP 23rd Fl 150 E 42nd St New York NY 10017-5639 Office Phone: 212-490-3000 ext. 2483. Office Fax: 212-490-3038. Business E-Mail: oelsnerr@wemed.com.

**OEMLER, AUGUSTUS, JR.,** astronomer, educator; b. Savannah, Ga., Aug. 15, 1945; s. Augustus and Isabelle Redding (Clarke) O.; children: W. Clarke, Bryan S. AB, Princeton U., 1969; MS, Calif. Inst. Tech., 1970, PhD, 1974. Postdoctoral assoc. Kitt Peak Nat. Obs., Tucson, 1974-75; instr. astronomy Yale U., New Haven, 1975-77, asst. prof., 1977-79, assoc. prof., 1979-83, prof., 1983-96, chmn. dept., 1988-96; dir. Carnegie Obs., Pasadena, Calif., 1996—2003, staff astronomer, dir. emeritus, 2003—. Contbr. articles to profl. jours. Alfred P. Sloan fellow, 1978-80 Mem. Am. Astronom. Soc., Internat. Astronom. Union Republican. Roman Catholic. Office: Carnegie Obs 813 Santa Barbara St Pasadena CA 91101-1232

**OERTEL, GOETZ KUNO HEINRICH,** physicist, professional society administrator; b. Stuhm, Germany, Aug. 24, 1934; arrived in US, 1957; s. Egon F.K. and Margarete W. (Wittek) O.; m. Brigitte Beckmann, June 17, 1960; children: Ines M.H. Oertel Downing, Carsten K.R. Abitur, Robert Mayer, Heilbronn, Fed. Republic Germany, 1953; vordiplom, U. Kiel, Fed. Republic Germany, 1956; PhD, U. Md. 1963. Aerospace engr. Langley Ctr. NASA, Hampton, Va., 1963-68, chief solar physics Washington, 1968-75, policy analyst for sci. advisor to Pres. and Office Mgmt. and Budget, 1974-75; head astronomy divsn. NSF, Washington, 1975; dir. def. and civilian nuc. waste programs U.S. Dept. Energy, Washington, 1975-83; acting mgr. sav. river ops. office Aiken, SC, 1983-84; dep. mgr. ops. office Albuquerque, 1984-85; dep. asst. sec. of energy for EH, Washington, 1985-86; pres., CEO Assn. Univs. for Rsch. in Astronomy, Inc., Washington, 1986-99; also bd. dirs. Assn. Univs. for Rsch. in Astronomy, Inc. (AURA, Inc.), Washington, disting. advisor, 2000—. Cons. Los Alamos Lab., N.Mex., 1987-92, Westinghouse Electric, 1988-99, Lampadia Found., Fundacion Andes of Santiago de Chile, Vitae Found. Sao Paulo, Brazil; bd. dirs. Inst. for Sci. and Soc., Ellensburg, Wash., IUE Corp.; mem. bd. internat. sci. orgns. NAS, 2001-; bd. mem. Sch. of Computational Sci., George Mason U., 1995—, chair, 2002-03, bd. mem. Coll. Sci., SC, 2006—; mem. Sch. for CODATA, 1993-03, chmn. 1997-00; US nat. del. CODATA ICSU, 1999-03; mem. peer rev. com. ASME 1996—; cons. conicyt, Govt. of Chile, 2000-, VITAE Found., Brazil, 2001-, Fundacion Andes, Chile, 2000-; chmn., bd. dirs. Ctr. of Excellence for Hazardous Materials Mgmt., Carlsbad, N.Mex., 2003-04; lifetime nat. assoc. Nat. Acads. Washington, 2003—; co-trustee FLF Trust, 2006—. Contbr. articles to profl. jours. Fulbright grantee, 1957; Exceptional Svc. medal NASA, 1973, Bronze medal Dept. Energy, 1983, Silver medal, 1985, Disting. Svcs. award NSF, 1999 Fellow AAAS, ASME (Dixy Lee Ray prize 2005); mem. Am. Phys. Soc., Am. Astron. Soc., Internat. Astron. Union, N.Y. Acad. Scis., Internat. U. Exch., Inc. (bd. dirs.), Cosmos Club (admissions com. 2004—), Sigma Xi. Lutheran. Achievements include patents in field. Avocations: exercise, chess, computing, genealogy. Address: 8833 Watts Mine Terr Potomac MD 20854-5439 Office Phone: 301-365-1061. Business E-Mail: goetz@oertel.org.

**OERTEL, MICHAEL,** researcher, medical educator; b. Berlin, May 6, 1971; arrived in U.S., 2001; s. Dieter and Heiderose Oertel. Diploma in Biology, U. Leipzig, 1995, PhD, 2000. Postdoctoral fellow Inst. Clin. Immunology U. Leipzig, Germany, 2000—01; rsch. assoc. Albert Einstein Coll. Medicine Yeshiva U., Bronx, NY, 2001—03; instr. medicine Marion Bessin Liver Rsch. Ctr., 2004—. Contbr. articles to profl. jours. Mem.: Am. Assn. for Study of Liver Diseases, German Transplantation Soc. Avocations: reading, music, chess, horseback riding, travel. Office: Albert Einstein Coll Medicine Yeshiva U Marion Bessin Liver Rsch Ctr 1300 Morris Park Ave Ullm 605 Bronx NY 10461 Office Phone: 718-430-3310. Business E-Mail: moertel@aecom.yu.edu.

**OERTEL, YOLANDA CASTILLO,** pathologist, educator; b. Lima, Peru, Dec. 14, 1938; came to U.S., 1966; d. Leonardo A. and Dalila (Ramirez) C.; m. James E. Oertel. Sept. 24, 1969. MD, Cayetano Heredia, Lima, 1964; Dr. honoris causa, U. Peruana Cayetano Heredia, 1999. Diplomate Am. Bd. Pathology (mem. test com. for cytopathology 1988-94). Internat. postdoctoral fellowship NIH, Bethesda, Md., 1966-68; asst. prof. pathology Sch. Medicine George Washington U., Washington, 1975-78, assoc. prof., 1978-84, prof., 1984-98, prof. emerita, 1998—. Adj. prof. pathology and lab. medicine MCP Hahnemann U. Sch. Medicine; cons. Registry Cytology Armed Forces Inst. Pathology, Washington, 1981—. Author: Fine Needle Aspiration of the Breast, 1987; contbr. chpts. to books, articles to profl. jours. Decorated comendador de la Orden Cayetano Heredia, 1999; recipient Francisco A. Camino prize Peruvian Med. Assn., 1965, cert. Meritorious Svc. Armed Forces Inst. Pathology, 1974; named Disting. Alumna Cayetano Heredia Med. Sch., 1989. Mem. Assn. Mil. Surgeons (hon.), Colombian Soc. Pathology (hon.), Argentinian Soc. Pathology (hon.), Peruvian Soc. Pathologists (hon.), Argentinian Soc. Cytopathology, (hon.), Am. Soc. Cytopathology, Internat. Acad. Pathology, Soc. Latinoamericana Patologia, Am. Soc. Clin. Pathologists (coun. on cytopathology 1982-88), Coll. Am. Pathologists, Arthur Purdy Stout Soc. Surg. Pathologists, Am. Thyroid Assn., Am. Thyroid Soc. Avocations: reading, opera. Office: Washington Hosp Ctr Pathology Dept Washington Cancer Inst 110 Irving St NW Washington DC 20010-2975 Office Phone: 202-877-2740. Office Fax: 202-877-0197. Business E-Mail: Yolanda.C.Oertel@medstar.net.

**OERTER, CYNTHIA LYNN,** medical technologist; b. Waupaca, Wis., Mar. 8, 1948; d. Lavern Charles and Geraldine Mae (Huffcut) Trinrud; m. Gregory Van Oerter, June 8, 1968; children: Nathan, Justin. BS, U. Wis., Oshkosh, 1971; MS, Cardinal Stritch Coll., 1993. Cert. Am. Soc. Clin. Pathologists. Med. technologist Mercy Med. Ctr., Oshkosh, Wis., 1970-76, Iola (Wis.) Hosp., 1978-86, wellness cons., 1985-86, Riverside Med. Ctr., Waupaca, Wis., 1986—95, med. technologist, hematology supr., insvc. coord., cons., 1987-95; pres. Pro Health Consul, Inc., Waupaca, Wis., 1994—; bus. ptnr., adminstr. Garden Park House, 1994—2000, owner, adminstr., 2000—; owner Back Door Bakery, 2003—, Secret Garden Cafe, 2003—. Tchr. Fox Valley Coll., Appleton, Wis., 1986, 87; organizer Overeaters Anonymous, Iola, 1985-89; owner Green Fountain Inn, 1995—. Mem. parent's com. for gifted and talented Waupaca Sch. Sys., 1984, charter mem. employment coun., 1989-92, mem. adv. com. guidance program K-12, 1992; vol. Nat. Wellness Inst., 1986-97, Am. Lung Assn., 1986-87; tchr. smokeless program Am. Inst. Preventative Medicine, 1988-93; com. mem. Main St. Design, 1999-2001. Mem. NAFE, Nat. Platform Assn., Am. Sch. Health Assn. (com. mem.), Waupaca S. of C (mem. tourism com. 2002—), Rotary (sec. 1996-98, bd. dirs. 1995-2004, pres. elect 1999-2000, pres. 2000-2001). Republican. Lutheran. Avocations: gardening, gourmet cooking, sailing, bible study, hobby farm. Business E-Mail: greenfountain@gglbbs.com.

**OESTERLE, ERIC ADAM,** lawyer; b. Lafayette, Ind., Dec. 2, 1948; s. Eric Clark and Germaine Dora (Seelye) O.; m. Carolyn Anne Scherer, Sept. 16, 1973; children: Adam Clark, Allison Margaret. BS, U. Mich., 1970, JD, 1973.

Bar: Ill. 1973, U.S. Dist. Ct. (no. dist.) Ill. 1973, U.S. Ct. Appeals (7th cir.) 1987, U.S. Supreme Ct. 1986. Assoc. Sonnenschein, Carlin, Nath & Rosenthal, Chgo., 1973—80; ptnr. Sonnenschein Nath & Rosenthal, Chgo., 1980—. Major gifts com. U. Mich. Law Sch., 2002—. Fellow Am. Bar Found.; mem. ABA, Ill. Bar Assn., Chgo. Bar Assn Home: 645 Lake Rd Glen Ellyn IL 60137-4249 Office: Sonnenschein Nath & Rosenthal 7800 Sears Tower 233 S Wacker Dr Ste 8000 Chicago IL 60606-6491 Business E-Mail: eoesterle@sonnenschein.com.

**OESTERLE, STEPHEN N.,** medical products executive, cardiologist, medical educator; b. LaGrande, Oreg., Mar. 3, 1951; BA summa cum laude, Harvard Univ., 1973; MD, Yale Univ., 1977. Intern & resident Mass. Gen. Hosp., 1977—80; fellowship in cardiology Stanford Univ., 1981—83; cardiologist Good Samaritan Hosp., LA, 1986—91; cardiologist, med. educator Georgetown Univ., 1991—92; assoc. prof. med. & dir. cardiac catheterization & coronary intervention labs Stanford Univ. Med. Ctr., 1992—98; assoc. prof. med. Harvard Med. Sch., 1998—2002; dir. invasive cardiology svc. Mass. Gen. Hosp., 1998—2002; sr. v.p. medicine & tech. Medtronic Inc., Mpls., 2002—. Office: Medtronic Inc 710 Medtronic Pkwy Minneapolis MN 55432-5604*

**OESTING, DAVID W.,** lawyer; b. Chgo., Aug. 6, 1944; AB, Earlham Coll., 1967; JD, Wash. U., 1970. Bar: Wash. 1970, Alaska 1981. Ptnr. in charge of Anchorage Office Davis Wright Tremaine, Anchorage, 1980—. Editor-in-chief Wash. U. Law Quarterly, 1969-70. Mem. ABA, Am. Coll. Trial Lawyers, Wash. State Bar Assn., Alaska Bar Assn., Anchorage Bar Assn., Order of Coif. Office: Davis Wright Tremaine 701 W 8th Ave Ste 800 Anchorage AK 99501-3467 Office Phone: 907-257-5300. Business E-Mail: daveoesting@dwt.com.

**OESTMANN, MARY JANE,** retired health science association administrator; b. Chgo., May 22, 1924; d. Charles Edward and Harriet Evelyn (Stoltenberg) O. BA in Math, Chemistry with honors, Denison U., 1946; MS, U. Wis., 1948, PhD, 1950; DSc (hon.), Denison U., 1975. Research chemist Inst. for Atom Energy, Oslo, 1954—55; vis. scientist AB Atom Energy, Stockholm, 1955—56; vis. prof. chem. dept. U. Iowa, Iowa City, 1957; sr. scientist Battelle Meml. Inst., Columbus, Ohio, 1957—61; assoc. chemist Argonne Nat. Lab, Ill., 1961—71; environ. project mgr. U.S. AEC, Washington, 1971—75; sr. radiation specialist U.S. Nuclear Regulatory Commn., Glen Ellyn, Ill., 1975—87; ret. Bd. dirs. U. Wis.-Madison Alumni Assn. of the So. Lakes, 1992—. Contbr. articles to profl. jours. Planning and zoning commn. Town of Burlington, 1991-2004; bd. trustees Plymouth Congl. UCC Ch. Burlington, 1993-96; mem. Art Inst. Chgo. Recipient UN Internat. Women's Yr. award Nuclear Regulatory Comm., 1975, Dist. Alumni citation Denison U., 1971. Fellow Am. Inst. Chemists, Am. Nuclear Soc. (bd. dirs. 1983-86); mem. Am. Chem. Soc., Inst. Environ. Sci. and Tech. (sr. mem.), Health Physics Soc. (sec.-treas. Midwest chpt. 1978, exec. com. 1983-86), NY Acad. Scis., Wis. Acad. Scis., Arts and Letters, Wis. Fedn. Rep. Women (1st Congl. Dist. 1990-2004), Nat. Parks Conservation Assn., Nat. Conservancy, Nat. Arbor Day Found., Am. Scandinavian Found., Burlington Woman's Club (treas., chair scholarship com. 1993—), Browns Lake Yacht Club (Burlington), Rep. Women Racine County-West Club (v.p. 1992-93, pres. 1994-2005, Anita Hunt award, Bovay award), Sigma Xi, Phi Beta Kappa, Sigma Delta Epsilon, Iota Sigma Pi Home: 2520 Cedar Dr Burlington WI 53105-9174

**OESTREICH, CHARLES HENRY,** retired university president; b. Columbus, Ohio, June 8, 1932; s. Henry F. and Martha (Schwartz) O.; m. Rhoda J. Haseley, Aug. 26, 1957; children: Martha, Mary, David. BS, Capital U., 1954; MS, Ohio U., 1956. PhD, 1961; LLD, Capital U. 1986. Instr. chemistry Va. Mil. Inst., 1956-57, Capital U., Columbus, 1960-62, asst. prof., 1962-64, assoc. prof., 1965-69; acad. dean Tex. Luth. U., Seguin, 1969-76, interim pres., 1976-77, pres., 1977-94, pres. emeritus Seguin, 1995—. Postdoctoral rsch. fellow Vanderbilt U., 1965-66 Bd. dirs., past pres. Mid-Tex. Symphony; bd. dirs. St. Luke's Health Ministries, Eden Home, Inc. Mem. Rotary (past pres. Seguin). Home and Office: 2269 S Abbey Loop New Braunfels TX 78130-8965 E-mail: charleso@satk.pp.com.

**OESTREICH, JAMES R.,** editor; Founder Opus magazine; editor High Fidelity; classical music & dance editor, critic NY Times, 1989—. Office: NY Times 229 W 43rd St New York NY 10036 Office Phone: 212-556-5825.*

**OETJEN, DAVID L. (JON DAVID DOUGLAS),** writer, film producer; b. Washington, Iowa, May 23, 1938; s. Walter Theodor Oetjen and Alyce Marie Peterson. BA, U. of Iowa, 1960. Prodr. Home Shopping Network, Clearwater, Fla.; broadcast prodn. dir. Barlow/Johnson Advt., Syracuse, Albany, Buffalo, Springfield, N.Y. and Mass., 1969—73; dir. of promotion, advt. mgr. Sta. WTVH-TV, Meredith Corp., Syracuse, NY, 1977—91. Prodr.: (TV series, television) Dari-Lean "Magic", 1971 (Chgo. Film Festival, 1971); author: (novels) Cody, A Boy's Odyssey, 2002, Place Out of Time, 2003, The American Boy, 2005, Deadly High School, 2006. Citizen's adv. Bayfront Med. Ctr., St. Petersburg, 1997—99; advisor Office of the Mayor, Syracuse, 1988—91, Syracuse (N.Y.) Symphony, 1988—90; prodr. Bring Them Home Alive-Missing Childrens' Clearing House, Tampa Bay. Recipient Silver Shaker award for Winterfest, CNY-Pub. Rels. Soc. Am., 1989, 1st Pl. TV Promotion award for Gimmie Five!, Syracuse Advt. Club, 1988, 1st Pl. TV Promotion award for Tell 'Em, 1989, Media award, CNY Parks and Recreation Soc., 1985, Award of Appreciation for svc. as dir. of broadcast promotion and publicity, AAU/USA Jr. Olympics, 1987. Mem.: Fiction Writers Roundtable, Broadcast Promotion Assn., Village Writers' Group. Home: 1617 Duran Dr The Villages FL 32162 Personal E-mail: dleeo@earthlink.net.

**OETTER, DOUG R.,** geography professor; BA in Geography, U. Wash., Seattle, 1985; MA in Geography, U. Ga., Athens, 1990; PhD in Geography, Oreg. State U., Corvallis, 2002. Asst. prof. Ga. Coll. & State U., Milledgeville, 2002—. Office: Dept of History Geography and Philoso GC&SU Box 047 Milledgeville GA 31061 Office Phone: 478-445-7379. Business E-Mail: doug.oetter@gcsu.edu.

**OETTGEN, HERBERT FRIEDRICH,** physician; b. Cologne, Germany, Nov. 22, 1923; came to U.S., 1958; s. Peter and Minna (Kaul) O.; m. Trudi Hesberg, Feb. 16, 1957; children: Hans Christoph, Joerg Peter, Anne Barbara. MD, U. Cologne, 1951. Diplomate Bd. Internal Medicine, Fed. Republic of Germany. Resident in pathology City Hosp., Cologne, 1952-54, resident in medicine, 1955-58; fellow Meml. Sloan-Kettering Cancer Ctr., N.Y.C., 1958-62, assoc. to assoc. mem., 1963-69, mem., 1972—, attending physician, 1971—; prof. medicine Cornell U. Med. Coll., N.Y.C., 1972—. Assoc. dir. Cancer Rsch. Inst., N.Y.C., 1985—. Author over 350 publs. in hematology, cancer rsch., immunology and clin. oncology. Recipient award for cancer rsch. Wilhelm Warner Found., Hamburg, Fed. Republic Germany, 1970, Lisec-Artz award Friedrich Wilhelm U., Bonn, Fed. Republic of Germany, 1982. Presbyterian. Avocations: violin, woodworking. Home: 48 Overlook Dr New Canaan CT 06840-6825 Office: Meml Sloan-Kettering Cancer Ctr 1275 York Ave New York NY 10021-6094 Office Phone: 212-639-7505. Business E-Mail: oettgenh@mskcc.org, hoettgen@licr.org.

**OETTINGER, ANTHONY GERVIN,** mathematician, educator; b. Nuremberg, Germany, Mar. 29, 1929; came to U.S., 1941, naturalized, 1947; s. Albert and Marguerite (Bing) O.; m. Marilyn Tanner, June 20, 1954; children: Douglas, Marjorie. AB, Harvard U., 1951, PhD, 1954; Henry fellow, U. Cambridge, Eng.. 1951-52; Litt.D. (hon.), U. Pitts., 1984. Mem. faculty Harvard, 1955—, assoc. prof. applied math., 1960-63, prof. linguistics, 1963-75, Gordon McKay prof. applied math., 1963—, chmn. program on info. resources policy, 1972—, mem. faculty of govt., 1973—2004, prof. info. resources policy, 1975—. Mem. command control comm. and intelligence bd. Dept. Navy, 1978-86; mem. sci. adv. group Def. Comm. Agcy., 1979-90; chmn. bd. visitors Joint Mil. Intelligence Coll., 1986—; chmn., dir. Nat. Intelligence Sci. Adv. Bd., 1994—; cons. Arthur D. Little, Inc., 1956-80, Office Sci. and Tech., Exec. Office of Pres., 1960-73, Bellcomm, Inc.,

1963-68, Sys. Devel. Corp., 1965-68, Nat. Security Coun., Exec. Office of Pres., 1975-81, Pres.'s Fgn. Intelligence Adv. Bd., 1981-90; chmn. Computer Sci. and Engring. Bd., Nat. Acad. Scis., 1968-73; mem. Mass. Cmty. Antenna TV Commn., 1972-79, chmn., 1975-79; mem. rsch. adv. bd. Com. for Econ. Devel., 1975-79; trustee Babbage Inst., 1991—; panel mem. Naval Studies Bd. NAS/NRC, 1993-95; mem. banking and fin. team Pres.' Commn. on Critical Infrastructure Protection, 1998; mem. Def. Sci. Bd., 2003—. Author: A Study for the Design of an Automatic Dictionary, 1954, Automatic Language Translation: Lexical and Technical Aspects, 1960, Run Computer Run: The Mythology of Educational Innovation, 1969, High and Low Politics: Information Resources for the 80s, 1977, Behind the Telephone Debates, 1988, Mastering the Changing Information World, 1993; editor: Proc. of a Symposium on Digital Computers and Their Applications, 1962; contbr. chpts. to The Information Resources Policy Handbook: Research for the Information Age, 1998. Fellow Am. Acad. Arts and Scis., AAAS, IEEE, Assn. Computing Machinery (mem. coun. 1961-68, chmn. com. U.S. Govt. Rels. 1964-66, editor computational linguistics sect. Commn. 1964-66, pres. 1966-68); mem. Soc. Indsl. and Applied Math. (mem. coun. 1963-67), Coun. on Fgn. Rels., Phi Beta Kappa, Sigma Xi. Clubs: Cosmos (Washington); Harvard (N.Y.C.). Home: 65 Elizabeth Rd Belmont MA 02478-3819 Office: Harvard U Maxwell Dworkin 125 33 Oxford St Cambridge MA 02138-2901 E-mail: anthony@deas.harvard.edu.

**OETTINGER, JULIAN ALAN,** lawyer, pharmaceutical executive; BS, U. Ill., 1961; JD, Northwestern U., 1964. Bar: Ill. 1964. Atty. SEC, 1964-67, Walgreen Co., Deerfield, Ill., 1967-72, sr. atty., 1972-78, dir. law, 1978-89, v.p., gen. counsel, corp. sec., 1989-2000, sr. v.p., gen. counsel, corp. sec., 2000—05.

**O'FARRELL, MARK THEODORE,** religious organization administrator; b. Milw., Apr. 13, 1948; s. Theodore Wolfred and Ernestine (Shelhammer) O.; m. Phillis Gilley, Sept. 18, 1948; children: Gwen, Kevin. BA, Columbia Bible Coll., 1970; DD, Toccan Falls Coll., 1996. Asst. pastor 1st Alliance Ch., Macon, Ga., 1970-71, sr. pastor Port Charlotte, Fla., 1981-86, Belle Glade (Fla.) Alliance Ch., 1971-81; asst. to dist. supt., ext. dir. Southeastern Dist. of Christian and Missionary Alliance, Orlando, Fla., 1986-93, dist. supt., 1993—2005; pres. Trinity Coll. Fla., New Port Richey, 2005—. Recipient Spiritual Aims award Kiwanis. Office: Trinity Coll Fla 2430 Welbilt Blvd New Port Richey FL 34655 E-mail: sedistrict@cmalliance.org

**OFFEN, RONALD CHARLES,** retired school librarian; b. Chgo., Oct. 2, 1930; s. Charles Henry and Ellen (Shirreffs) O.; m. Sharon Rae Nealy, Mar. 17, 1951 (div.); children: Deirdre, Eric; m. Rosine J. Franke, Aug. 20, 1966 (dec. Apr. 21, 2000); children: Michele, Darren P.; m. Beverly Kahling Drick, April 27, 2003. AA, Wright Jr. Coll., Chgo., 1950; MA, U. Chgo., 1967. Ins. investigator various ins. cos., Chgo., 1952-68; mng. editor Chicagoland Mag., Chgo., 1968-70; editor Automotive Fleet, Glenview, Ill., 1970-71; freelance editor, writer, author Chgo., 1971-78; sch. libr. Capistrano Unified Sch. Dist., Laguna Niguel, Calif., 1983-98; ret., 1998. Adminstr. theater co. The Peripatetic Task Force, Chgo., 1975-78. Co-editor Odyssey: Explorations in Poetry, 1956-58; exec. editor Lit. Times, 1975-78; co-author: (non-fiction) Dillinger: Dead or Alive?, 1970; author: (biographies) Cagney, 1973, Brando, 1974; (poetry) Putto as Bad Guy, 1963, Instead of Gifts, 1995, Questions, Answers, 1996, God's Haircut (And Other Remembered Dreams), 1999, Off-Target, 2006; editor: The Starving Poet's Cookbook, 1994; editor Free Lunch, 1989—. Chair James T. Farrell Centenary Com. Mem. Acad. Am. Poets (1st prize 1958), Authors Guild. Personal E-mail: ronoffen@yahoo.com.

**OFFENBERGER, ALLAN ANTHONY,** electrical engineering educator; b. Wadena, Sask., Can., Aug. 11, 1938; s. Ivy Viola (Hagglund) O.; m. Margaret Elizabeth Patterson, Apr. 12, 1963; children: Brian, Gary. BS, U. B.C., 1962, MS, 1963; PhD, MIT, 1968. Asst. prof. U. Alta., Edmonton, Can., 1968-70, assoc. prof., 1970-75, prof., 1975-95, prof. emeritus, 1996—. Cons. Lawrence Livermore (Calif.) Nat. Lab., 1996-2006, numerous univs., govts. and industries; vis. prof. U.K. Atomic Energy Agy., Abingdon, Oxon, Eng., 1975-76; project dir. Laser Fusion Project, Edmonton, 1984-91; mem. strategic adv. com. Nat. Fusion Program, Atomic Energy of Can. Ltd., Chalk River, Ont., 1987-96; vis. prof. U. Oxford, U.K., 1992, U. Osaka, Japan, 2000; served on several execs., bds. and sci. adv. and rsch. grant committees; hosted internat. scholars; invited lectr. at more than 120 internat. insts. and confs. Mem. editorial bd. Laser and Particle Beams, 1987-2004; contbr. over 150 sci. articles on lasers and plasma physics Killam Rsch. fellow Can. Coun., 1980-82. SERC rsch. fellow, Eng., 1992. Mem. Can. Assn. Physicists (exec. officer, v.p. elect 1987-88, pres. 1989-90), Am. Phys. Soc., Sigma Xi. Achievements include establishing a major center for high power laser research and development (particularly krypton fluoride lasers) for fusion energy and other applications. Home: 412 Lessard Dr Edmonton AB Canada T6M 1A7 Office: U Alta Dept Elec Computer Engring Edmonton AB Canada T6G 2V4 Office Phone: 780-492-3939. Business E-Mail: aao@ece.ualberta.ca.

**OFFER, STUART JAY,** lawyer; b. Seattle, June 2, 1943; m. Judith Spitzer, Aug. 29, 1970; children: Rebecca, Kathryn. BA, U. Wash., 1964; LLB, Columbia U., 1967. Bar: D.C. 1968, U.S. Tax Ct. 1968, Calif. 1972. Atty., advisor U.S. Tax Ct. Washington, 1967-68; assoc. Morrison & Foerster, LLP, San Francisco, 1972-76. ptnr., 1976—. Trustee Am. Tax Policy Inst. Served as capt. U.S. Army, 1968-72. Mem. ABA (chmn. taxation sect., corp. tax com. 1991-92. coun. dir. 1995-98. vice chmn. adminstrn. 1998-2000), Internat. Fiscal Assn. (regent), Am. Coll. Tax Counsel. Office: Morrison & Foerster LLP 425 Market St San Francisco CA 94105-2482 Office Phone: 415-268-7052. Business E-Mail: soffer@mofo.com.

**OFFERDAHL, JOHN ARNOLD,** former professional football player, food service executive; b. Wisconsin Rapids, Wis., Aug. 17, 1964; s. Arnold and Irene Offerdahl. Student, Western Mich. U. With Miami Dolphins, 1986—95; owner Offerdahl's Bagel Gourmet, 1990—95, Offerdahl's Cafe Grill, 2000—. Player NFL Pro Bowl, 1987, 88. Named to Pro-Bowl team 1986-90. Sporting News All-Star team, 1990. Office: Offerdahls Eat Fresh Co 929 Shotgun Rd Sunrise FL 33326*

**OFFIT, MORRIS WOLF,** investment company executive; b. Balt., Jan. 22, 1937; s. Michael and Rhea (Wolf) O.; m. Nancy Silverman, Nov. 26, 1959; children: Ned S., Daniel W. BA in History, Johns Hopkins U., 1957, LHD (hon.), 1996; MBA in Fin., U. Pa., 1959. V.p. investment dept. Mercantile Safe Deposit and Trust, Balt., 1960—68; gen. ptnr. Salomon Bros. Inc., N.Y.C., 1968-80; pres. Julius Baer Securities, N.Y.C., 1980-82; now CEO Offit Hall Capital Mgmt. LLC, 2002—; CEO Offit Assoc. Inc., NYC, 1983—2001. Trustee, former chmn. bd. trustees Johns Hopkins U.; chmn. adv. coun. Nitze Sch. Advanced Internat. Studies; trustee Jewish Mus., former chmn.; trustee Jewish Theol. Sem., Thirteen-WNET, United Jewish Appeal Fedn. N.Y., Am. Jewish Com. Mem. Coun. on Fgn. Rels. Office: Offit Hall Capital Mgmt LLC 65 E 55th St New York NY 10022

**OFFIT, SIDNEY,** writer, educator; b. Balt., Oct. 13, 1928; s. Barney and Lillian (Cohen) O.; m. Avodah Crindell Komito, Aug. 8, 1952; children: Kenneth, Michael Robert. BA, Johns Hopkins U., 1950; DHL (hon.), L.I. U., 1999. Editorial staff Mercury Publs., N.Y.C., 1952-53, Macfadden Publs., N.Y.C., 1953-54; contbg. editor Baseball mag., Washington, 1955-58; faculty NYU, 1964—2002; assoc. editor Intellectual Digest, 1970-72, sr. editor 1972-74; adj. prof. creative writing NYU, 1977—2003. Lectr. creative writing New Sch. U., 1965—; curator George Polk Awards for Journalism, 1977—; commentator Channel 5 TV, NYC, 1975-85, Channel 11 TV, 1992. Author: He Had it Made, 1959, The Other Side of the Street, 1962, Soupbone, 1963, Topsy Turvey, 1965, The Adventure of Homer Fink, 1966, The Boy Who Made a Million, 1968; short stories Not All the Girls Have Million Dollar Smiles, 1971; Only a Girl Like You, 1972, What Kind of Guy Do You Think I Am?, 1977, Memoir of the Bookie's Son, 1995; book editor: Politics Today, 1978-80. Selection com. Dist. Sch. Bd., NYC, 1968; exec. bd.

Lexington Democratic Club, 1957-60, NY Dem. County Com., 1966-; chmn. 19th Precinct Cmty. Coun. NYC, 1964-80. Recipient Disting. Alumni award Valley Forge Mil. Acad., 1961, Otty Cmty. Svc. award, 1975, Tchg. Excellence award NYU, 1981, commendation for achievment as teacher, scholar, communicator NY State Legislature, 1983, proclamation for contbns. to city, NYC Coun., 1983, Police Athletic League citation for svc. to children of NYC, 1991, 96, 2002, 04, Honors Convocation award Marymount Manhattan Coll., 1994, Detlev W. Bronk award Johns Hopkins Alumni Assn., 1994, Disting. Univ. Tchg. award New Sch. U., 2000, Poets and Writers award Writers for Writers, 2005 Mem. Tudor and Stuart Club, Authors Guild Found. (pres. 1993—), Authors Guild (coun. 1970-77, 79—, v.p. 1993-95), Authors League (nat. coun. 1976), Authors League Fund (v.p. 1998—, acting pres. 2004-05), Am. Ctr. PEN (exec. com. 1969, 2003—, v.p. 1970-74, internat. del. 1971-72, 74), Century Assn. Club (NYC), Coffee House Club (NYC). Home: 23 E 69th St New York NY 10021-4919 *I have been guided by a strong devotion to my family and friends and moderate ambition. In both these priorities I have been influenced by my parents. With my writing I have tried to fulfill my own needs, and for the most I have been satisfied by the reception. I do not aspire to fame or great fortune, and this leaves me free to enjoy the sharing of experiences with my friends and family. I consider myself a lucky man and this keeps me grateful to whatever forces there are that contrive man's fortune.*

**OFFNER, ERIC DELMONTE,** lawyer; b. Vienna, June 23, 1928; came to U.S., 1941, naturalized, 1949; s. Sigmund J. and Kathe (Delmonte) O.; m. Julie Cousins, 1955 (dec. 1959); m. Barbara Ann Shotton, July 2, 1961; 1 son, Gary Douglas; m. Carol Sue Marcus, Jan. 12, 1980 (dec. 1983) BBA, CCNY, 1949; JD in Internat. Affairs, Cornell U., 1952. Bar: NY 1952. Assoc. Langner, Parry, Card & Langner, N.Y.C., 1952-57; ptnr. Haseltine, Lake, Waters & Offner, N.Y.C., 1957-77; sr. ptnr. Offner & Kuhn, 1978-83; pvt. practice N.Y.C., 1965—74. Instr. George Washington U. Law Sch., Cornell U. Law Sch.; spl. prof. law Hofstra Law Sch., 1974-92; jazz disc jockey ProgressiveRadioNetwork.org. Author: International Trademark Protection, 1964, Japanese edit., 1977, International Trademark Service, Vols. I-III 1970, Vol. IV, 1972, Vol. V., 1973, Vol. VI, 1976, Vol. VII, 1981, Vols. I-VII, 2d edit., 1981, Legal Training Course on Trademarks, 1982; editor in chief: Cornell Law Forum, 1950-51; mem. editorial bd.: Trademark Reporter, 1961-64, 69-72; book reviewer Jour. Humanism and Ethical Religion; contbr. articles to profl. jours.; prodr. jazz concerts N.Y.C., 1996—, jazz video and jazz CDs. V.p. Riverdale Mental Health Clinic, N.Y.C., 1966-67; pres. Riverdale Mental Health Assn., 1967-69, Ethical Culture Soc., Riverdale-Yonkers, 1964-67, Ethical Cultural Retirement Soc., 1975-94; trustee Am. Ethical Union, 1967-73, Internat. Alliance of Holistic Lawyers; bd. dirs. Fit Kids; pres. The Sidney Bechet Soc., 1998. Mem. N.Y. Patent Law Assn. (assoc. editor Bull. 1961-66, gov. 1973-76), ABA, City N.Y. Bar Assn. (sec. 1962-64), U.S. Trademark Assn., World Peace Through Law (charter), Trademark Soc. Washington (charter), Inst. Trade Mark Agts. (London), Sidney Bechet Soc. Ltd. (pres. 1997—), Australian Patent Inst., Internat. Assn. Protection Indsl. Property, Nat. Coun. Patent Law Assn., Internat. Patent, Trademark Assn., Phi Alpha Delta. Home: 20 Joy Dr New Hyde Park NY 11040-1109 Office Phone: 516-627-6334. E-mail: eoffner@optonline.net. *Do unto others so as to elicit the best in them and thereby the best in yourself.*

**O'FLYNN, THOMAS M.,** investment company executive; m. Cheryl O'Flynn; 1 child. BA in Econ., Northwestern U., 1982; MBA, U. Chgo., 1986. Mng. dir. global power and utility group, head N.Am. region Morgan Stanley, 1986—2000; exec. v.p., CFO Pub. Svc. Enterprise Group, Newark, 2001—. Office: Pub Svc Enterprise Group Inc 80 Park Plz Newark NJ 07101*

**OFRI, DANIELLE,** internist; b. N.Y.C., Aug. 22, 1965; d. Zacharia and Marcia Kashdan Ofri; m. Benjamin Akman, Nov. 7, 1999; children: Naava Ofri-Akman, Noah Ofri-Akman, Ariel Ofri-Akman. BSc, McGill U., Montreal, Que., Can., 1986; MS, NYU, 1990, PhD, 1992, MD, 1993. Lic. physician N.Y. State. Resident physician Bellevue Hosp., N.Y.C., 1993—96; attending physician Bellevue Hosp./NYU Sch. Medicine, N.Y.C., 1998—. Dir. Anticoagulation Clinic Bellevue Hosp., N.Y.C., 2002—. Editor-in-chief, co-founder: lit. mag. Bellevue Lit. Rev., 2000—; author: (memoir) Singular Intimacies, 2003, (songs) (non-fiction) Incidental Findings: Lessons from My Patients in the Art of Medicine, 2005; assoc. chief editor: med. textbook Bellevue Guide to Outpatient Medicine, 2001 (AMWA Best Med. Textbook, 2002). Recipient Editors Prize for nonfiction, Mo. Rev., 2001, award, Best Am. Essays, 2001, 2005, Pushcart Prize nomination, 2002, award, Best Am. Sci. Writing, 2003, McGovern award, Am. Med. Writers Assn., 2005. Jewish. Avocations: writing, music, piano, literature. Office: Bellevue Hosp Md Clinic 462 1st Ave New York NY 10016 E-mail: danielle.ofri@nyu.edu.

**OFSTAD, EVELYN LARSEN BOYL,** retired primary school educator, radio personality, film producer; b. Laurel, Oreg., Sept. 11, 1918; d. Walter Winfred and Nellie Lyle (Gellatly) Larsen; m. Robert Morris Boyl (dec.); children: Kathleen Roberta Boyl, Robert Morris Boyl Jr., Shannon Gae Boyl, Brian Larsen Boyl; m. Olaf Ofstad, Nov. 15, 1988. BS, Oreg. State U., 1940; MS in Tchg., Portland State U., 1968. Cert. learning specialist. Radio announcer Sta. KOAC, Corvallis, Oreg., 1939-40; announcer, script writer Sta. KWIL, Albany, Oreg., 1940-42, operator, announcer, 1941-42; sec. Higgins Ship Bldg., New Orleans, 1943-44; elem. tchr. Portland Pub. Schs., 1968-71; learning specialist North Clackamas Schs., Milw., Ore., 1972-85, home instr. Milwaukie, Oreg., 1985-86. Prodr., actor (video travelogues) Portland Cable Access, 1987—; actor: Oreg. Sr. Theater, 1987—95, Plz. Players, 1999—. Co-leader Girl Scouts Am., Oak Grove, Oreg., 1954—55, Webelos Boy Scouts Am., 1956—57, 1970—71; videographer Ptnrs. Ams. Oreg., Costa Rica, 1990—91; head video prodn. Channel 29 In-House TV Ret., 1999—2004; prodr. biweekly travel show, 1999—; mem. synchronized swim team Holladay Park Plz., 2003—04. Mem. AAUW (pres. Albany chpt.) Avocations: painting, video production, travel, narration, script writing.

**OFTE, DONALD,** nuclear energy industry executive, consultant; b. NYC, Aug. 23, 1929; s. Sverre and Ingeborg Ofte; m. Margaret Mae McHenney, July 23, 1955; children: Marc Christian. Nancy Carolyn Appleby, Kirk Donald Jr. BA in Chemistry, Dana Coll., 1952; postgrad. study metall. engring., Ohio State U., 1958-60. Jr. chemist Inst. Atomic Rsch., Ames, Iowa, 1952-53; sr. rsch. chemist Monsanto Rsch. Corp., Miamisburg, Ohio, 1958-66; ops. engr. AEC, Miamisburg, 1966-69. br. chief, div. dir. ops. office Albuquerque, 1969-73, mgr. Pinellas area office Largo, Fla., 1973-79; mgr. Rocky Flats area office Dept. Energy, Golden, Colo., 1979-82. asst. mgr. devel. and prodn. Albuquerque, 1982-83, dep. mgr. ops. office, 1983-84; prin. dep. asst. sec. Dept. Energy Defense Programs, Washington, 1984-87; mgr. ops. office Dept. Energy, Idaho Falls, Idaho, 1987-89; mgmt. cons. Idaho Falls, 1990—92; v.p. govt. ops. United Engrs. & Constructors (Raytheon Engrs. & Constrn.), Denver, 1992-93; v.p. Adv. Scis., Inc., Albuquerque, 1993-94; pres. FERMCO (also known as Fluor Daniel, Fernald), Cin., 1994-96; chmn., bd. mgrs. Washington Group BWXT Oper. Svcs., LLC, 2004—05; nuc. mgmt. cons., 2005—. V.p. Fluor-Daniel, Inc., 1994—96; affiliate prof. Idaho State U., 1990—92; bd. dirs. Denver Fed. Exec. Bd., 1979—82. Author: (with others) Plutonium 1960, 1965, Physicochemical Methods in Metals Research; contbr. articles to profl. jours. on metallurgy and ceramics. Campaign chmn. United Way Pinellas, St. Petersburg, Fla., 1978; bd. dirs. Bonneville County United Way, Idaho Rsch. Found.; mem. adv. bd. Teton Peaks Council Boy Scouts of Am., 1987-92, Eastern Idaho Tech. Coll.; chmn. Excellence in Edn. Fund Com., 1990-92; vice chmn., bd. dirs. Rio Grande Ch. ARC, Albuquerque, 1982-84; trustee, bd. dirs. Nat. Atomic Mus., 1999—2003. Revival of Spirit award U.S.N., 1953-57. Recipient citation AEC for Apollo 12 SNAP 27 Radioisotope Generator, 1969, High Quality Performance award AEC, 1968, Group Achievement award NASA, 1972; Meritorious Svc. award Dept. Energy, 1985, Disting. Career Svc. award, 1989. Mem. Am. Chem. Soc. (emeritus), Am. Nuclear Soc., Am. Soc. Metals, Nat. Contract Mgmt. Assn., Am. Soc. Pub. Adminstrs., Suncoast Archeol. Soc., Idaho Falls C. of C. (bd. dirs., cmty. svc. award 1990), Rotary Internat. (Paul Harris fellow). Avocations: reading, bridge, gardening, golf. Home: 1129 Salamanca St NW Albuquerque NM 87107-5643 E-mail: dofte@aol.com.

**OFTENESS, OVE (O.V. MICHAELSEN),** writer, musician; b. Bergen, Norway, Mar. 2, 1954; came to U.S., 1954; s. Michael and Betsy Lydia (Vik) O.; m. Lois Marin Fischer, July 11, 1989 (div. Jan., 2002) Pvt. practice, 1973—. Author: Words at Play: Quips, Quirks and Oddities, 1998, The Word Play Almanac, 2002, Never Odd or Even: Palindromes, Anagrams & Other Tricks Words Can Do, 2005; musician (albums) Suzy Fischer and the Dinosaurs, 2005. Democrat. Avocation: collecting and preserving rare folk and rock recordings. Home: 1300 Roosevelt Ave Apt 506 Richmond CA 94801-2708

**OGAN, RUSSELL GRIFFITH,** real estate broker; b. Reading, Pa., Nov. 20, 1923; s. Russell John and Edna Gwendlyn (Griffith) O.; m. Gloria Mae Withers, Oct. 30, 1943; children: Susan Ann (Mrs. Greg Gunn), Russell Lee. Student, Wyomissing Polytech. Inst., 1942, Air Command Staff Coll., 1948; grad., Nat. War Coll., 1963. Commd. officer U.S. Army, 1942; advanced through grades to brig. gen. USAF, 1970; fighter squadron comdr. Dover AFB, Del., 1951; dir. combat operations (11th Air Div.), Ladd AFB, Alaska, 1951-53; dir. (Combat Operations Center), Hamilton AFB, Calif., 1953-56; with (Hdqrs. Air Def. Command), Ent AFB, Colo., 1956-60; dir. (Aerospace Def. Systems Office, Air Force Ballistic Missile Div.), 1960-62; from dep. dir. plans to comdr. Sector Operation Ctr. NATO, Germany, 1963-66; dep. dir. personnel data and records (USAF Mil. Personnel Center), Randolph AFB, Tex., 1966-68; comdr. 71st Missile Warning Wing, then vice comdr. (14th Aerospace Force), Ent AFB, Colo., 1968-71; dep. dir. personnel programs Hdqrs. USAF, Washington, 1971-72; dir. Prisoner of War and Missing in Action Affairs, Office Sec. Def., Washington, 1972 74; former pres. Vacation Interval Mktg.; real estate broker Fishermen's Village, Punta Gorda, Fla. Decorated D.S.M., Legion of Merit with bronze oak leaf cluster, Air medal with 1 silver and 1 bronze oak leaf cluster. Mem. Daedalians, T.R.O.A., Kingsway Country Club. Flew 62 missions as fighter pilot over France and Germany, 1944-45. Home (Winter): 12413 SW Kingsway Cir Lake Suzy FL 34269 Personal E-mail: ogan43@aol.com.

**OGATA, KATSUHIKO,** engineering educator; b. Tokyo, Jan. 6, 1925; came to U.S., 1952; s. Fukuhei and Teruko (Yasaki) O.; m. Asako Nakamura, Sept. 6, 1961; 1 son, Takahiko. BS, U. Tokyo, 1947; MS, U. Ill., 1953; PhD, U. Calif., Berkeley, 1956. Research asst. Sci. Research Inst., Tokyo, 1948-51; fuel engr. Nippon Steel Tube Co., Tokyo, 1951-52; mem. faculty U. Minn., 1956—; prof. mech. engring., 1961—; prof. elec. engring. Yokohama Nat. U., 1960-61, 64-65, 68-69. Author: State Space Analysis of Control Systems, 1967, Modern Control Engineering, 1970, 2002, Dynamic Programming, 1973, Ingenieria de Control Moderna, 1974, 1998, Metody Przestrzeni Stanow w Teorii Sterowania, 1974, System Dynamics, 1978, 2003, Engenharia de Controle Moderno, 1982, 2003, Teknik Kontrol Automatik, 1985, Discrete-Time Control Systems, 1986, 1995, Gendai Seigyo Riron, 1986, Dinamica de Sistemas, 1987, Solving Control Engineering Problems with MATLAB, 1994, Gendai Seigyo Kogaku, 1994, Designing Linear Control Systems with MATLAB, 1994, Kejuruteraan Kawalan Moden, 1996, Sistemas de Control en Tiempo Discreto, 1996, Projeto de Sistemas Lineares de Controle com MATLAB, 1996, Solucao de Problemas de Engenharia de Controle com MATLAB, 1997. Recipient Outstanding Achv. award Inst. of Tech., U. Minn., 1981, John R. Ragazzini Edn. award Am. Automatic Control Coun., 1999. Fellow ASME; mem. Sigma Xi, Pi Tau Sigma. Personal E-mail: kogata02@aol.com.

**OGAWA, JOICHI RAPHAEL,** director, consultant; b. Tokyo, July 2, 1958; arrived in U.S., 2002; s. Isamu and Yoshiko Ogawa. BA in Econs., Keio U., Tokyo, 1982, BA in Psychology, 1986, MA in Sociology, 1989, PhD in Human Rels., 1993. Tchr. Jogakukau Girls' HS, Tokyo, 1988—90; rschr. Inst. Behavioral Sci. Uchido Yoko Co. Ltd., Tokyo, 1989—90; lectr. Fukuoka Prefecture U., Tagawa-shi, Japan, 1992—93; mgr. info. planning divsn. Nippon Kouatsu Electric Co. Ltd., Obu-shi, Japan, 1993—97; gen. mgr. cons. Shinjuku Gen. Acctg. Firm, Tokyo, 1997—98; liaison mgr. O'Hara Coll. Bus. San Jose (Calif.) State U., 1997—2002; program coord. Palo Alto (Calif.) Ctr. Devel. Studies, Inc., 2002—. Rschr. human sensory Ministry of Internat. Trade and Industry, Tokyo, 1990—92; cons. Long Term Credit Bank, Tokyo, 1991—93; family psychologist Nagoya (Japan) Nat. Hosp., 1991—92; clin. psychologist Azabu HS, Tokyo, 1997—2000. Mem.: APA, Acad. Mgmt. Internat. Soc. Psychodynamic Studies Orgn. Office: Bay Process Cons Ctr Inc 322 S Abel St Milpitas CA 95035 Office Phone: 408-262-0306. Office Fax: 408-205-7517. E-mail: info@bayprocessconsultingctr.com.

**OGBONNAYA, CHUKS ALFRED,** entomologist, agronomist, environmentalist; b. Akoli-Imenyi, Abia, Nigeria, June 30, 1953; came to U.S., 1975; s. Alfred Agbaeze and Christy (Agubuche) Ogbonnaya; m. Joyce Elizabeth Belgrave, Mar. 30, 1985; children: Latoya, Oluchi, Kelechi, Chioma. BS, U. Nebr., 1979, PhD, 1985; MS, N.W. Mo. State U., 1981. Cert. profl. crop scientist, profl. agronomist. Lab. asst. U. Nebr., Lincoln, 1976-78, rsch. asst., 1978-80, 82-85, postdoctoral fellow, 1985; asst. prof., fellow Mountain Empire Coll., Big Stone Gap, Va., 1985-90, prof., 1990—, coord., prof. environ. sci. dept., 1986—, asst. dean, 1996—99. Disting. scholar-in-residence Pa. State U., summer 1990, vis. prof., 1990. Soccer coach Parks and Recreation, Big Stone Gap, 1989; mem. Va. Water Resources Statewide Adv. Bd., govt.-mined land reclamation adv. bd. Recipient Times Teaching award, 1990, Chancellor's Profs. award Va., 1990; Fulbright sr. scholar, 1993-94. Mem. Am. Soc. Agronomy, Crop Sci. Soc. Am., Entomol. Soc. Am., Acad. Sci., Va. Mining Assn. (Outstanding Contbn. to Comty. award 1993), Internat. Platform Assn., Phi Beta Kappa. Methodist. Avocations: tennis, soccer. Home: 520 Bays View Rd Kingsport TN 37660-3202

**OGBURN, HUGH BELL,** chemical engineer, consultant; b. Lexington, Va., July 13, 1923; s. Sihon Cicero Jr. and Bettie Mae (Bell) O.; m. Anne Wotherspoon, Mar. 2, 1946 (div.); children: Margaret Mathews Berenson. Scott A.; m. Nancy Wrenn Petersen, Sept. 5, 1974. BS, Princeton U., 1944, MS. 1947, PhD, 1954. Sect. dir. R&D dept. Atlantic Refining Co., Phila., 1950—61; mgr. process engring. M.W. Kellogg Co., N.Y.C., London. 1961—67; dir. rsch. and engring. Union Carbide Corp., N.Y.C., 1967—69; dir. new bus. devel. Weyerhaeuser Co., Tacoma, 1969—72; pres. H.B. Ogburn Assoc., Greenwich, Conn. and Honolulu, 1971—; v.p., dir. Incontrade Inc., Stamford, Conn., 1973—78; v.p. Pacific Resources Inc., Honolulu, 1978—83; chmn. Pacific Oasis, L.A., 1983—85. Dir. Danmore Corp., Planning Research Corp.; cons. AEC; prof. chem. engring. Drexel U., Phila., 1951-61 Contbr. articles to profl. jours.; patentee in field. Pres. bd. trustees Woman's Hosp., Phila., 1954-62, Kapiolani Women's and Children's Med. Ctr., 1980-90; mem. adv. bd. Princeton U., 1960-70. Served to lt. j.g. USNR, 1942-46, PTO. Mem. AIChE, Am. Chem. Soc., Research Engrs. Soc. Pacific (Honolulu) Club, Greenwich Field (Conn.) Club, Princeton (N.Y.C.) Club, Phi Beta Kappa, Sigma Xi, Tau Beta Pi. Republican. Presbyterian. Home and Office: 4340 Pahoa Ave Apt 16 A Honolulu HI 96816-5032 Office Phone: 808-732-6503. Business E-Mail: hbogburn@hawaii.rr.com.

**OGBURN, JOYCE,** library director; Libr. Old Dominion U., Yale U., Pa. State U.; assoc. dir. resources and collection mgmt. svcs. U. Wash. Librs., 1999—2005; dir. J. Willard Marriott Library U. Utah, Salt Lake City, 2005—. Mem.: ALA. Office: J Willard Marriott Libr 295 S 1500 E Salt Lake City UT 84112-0860 Office Phone: 801-585-9521. E-mail: joyce.ogburn@utah.edu.*

**OGBURN, NANCY WRENN,** civic volunteer; b. Honolulu, Sept. 16, 1926; d. Heaton Luse and Carolene (Cooke) Wrenn; m. Hugh Gerhard Petersen Jr., July 1, 1948 (div. 1972); children: Hugh G. Petersen III, Suzanne Elise Petersen, Monte Cooke Petersen, Alexander Wrenn Petersen; m. Hugh Bell Ogburn, Sept. 5, 1974. BA, Wellesley Coll., 1948. With outside sales dept. Harris Trust, Greenwich, Conn., 1974-78. Guide Hawaiian Mission Children's Soc., Honolulu, 1978-81, Lyon Arboretum; treas. Rep. precinct, Honolulu, 1993. Recipient Carey E. Quinn award, Am. Daffodil Soc., 1964, Roberta C. Waltrous award, Medal of Merit, Garden Club Am., 1966, Corning medal, 1991, 2006. Fellow Honolulu Acad. Arts; mem. Greenwich Garden

Club (non-resident, Horticultural Com. award (2)), Garden Club Honolulu (chmn. various coms., Horticultural Com. award). Republican. Episcopalian. Avocations: bridge, travel, hiking. Home: 4340 Pahoa Ave Apt 16A Honolulu HI 96816-5032

**OGDEN, BENJAMIN,** language educator; b. Merced, Calif., Jan. 16, 1960; s. Dale and Joy Ogden. ABD, Vanderbilt U., 1988—92. Asst. prof. of spanish Truman State U., Kirksville, Mo., 1992—, coord. of computing support for l&l, 1993—. Computer programmer (software development for spanish, var. computer programs).

**OGDEN, DANIEL MILLER, JR.,** public official, educator; b. Clarksburg, W.Va., Apr. 28, 1922; s. Daniel Miller and Mary (Maphis) O.; m. Valeria Juan Munson, Dec. 28, 1946; children: Janeth Lee Martin, Patricia Jo Hunter, Daniel Munson. BA in Polit. Sci., Wash. State U., 1944; MA, U. Chgo., 1947, PhD, 1949. From instr. to assoc. prof. Wash. State U., Pullman, 1949-61; staff asst. resources program U.S. Dept. Interior, 1961-64; asst. dir. U.S. Bur. Outdoor Recreation, 1964-67; dir. budget U.S. Dept. Interior, Washington, 1967-68; dean Coll. Humanities and Social Scis. Colo. State U., Ft. Collins, 1968-76; disting. vis. prof. Lewis and Clark Coll. and Portland (Oreg.) State U., 1977-78; dir. Office of Power Mktg. Coordination U.S. Dept. Energy, 1978-84; mgr. Pub. Power Coun., Portland, Oreg., 1984-88, ret., 1988. Mem. profl. staff com. interstate and fgn. commerce U.S. Senate, 1956-57; spll. asst. to chmn. Dem. Nat. Com., 1960-61; lectr. Mgmt. Devel. Ctrs., U.S. Office Pers. Mgmt., 1966-2004. Co-author: Electing the President, rev. edit., 1968, American National Government, 7th edit., 1970, American State and Local Government, 5th edit., 1972, Washington Politics, 1960, How National Policy is Made, 5th edit., 2004. Committeeman Wash. Dem. Ctrl. Com., 1952-56; chmn. Whitman County Dem. Ctrl. Com., 1958-60; chmn. 49th Legis. Dist. Dem. Com., 1990-94; chmn. Clark County Dem. Ctrl. com., 1994-98, 1999-2000, vice chair, 1998-99. With inf. U.S. Army, 1943-46. Mem. Phi Beta Kappa, Phi Kappa Phi, Pi Sigma Alpha, Sigma Delta Chi 96662-7435. Unitarian Ch. Home: 3118 NE Royal Oak Dr Vancouver WA 98662-7435 Office Phone: 360-254-8886.

**OGDEN, JAMES RUSSELL,** marketing educator, consultant, lecturer, writer; b. Paris, Ill., Nov. 4, 1954; s. Russell Lee and Marianne (Johnson) O.; children: David James, Anne Marie, Kari Kristine; m. Denise T. Alarid, 1989. B of Bus. Edn., Ea. Mich. U., 1978; MS, Colo. State U., 1981; PhD, U. No. Colo., 1986. With acctg. and fin. dept. Hydra-Matic Divsn. GM Motors, 1978; dir. mktg. Mich. Tech. Inst., 1979; grad. fellow Colo. State U., Ft. Collins, 1979—81, asst. mgr. family housing, 1979—81; placement counselor U. No. Colo., Greeley, 1981—83, instr. mktg., 1982—83; CEO, prin. The Doctors Ogden Group, LLC, Allentown, Pa., 1982—; chair advt. and mktg. dept., assoc. prof. Adams State Coll., Alamosa, Colo., 1983—89; dept. chair, prof. mktg. Coll. Bus. Kutztown U., Pa., 1989—, bd. bus. advisors Students in Free Enterprise Coll. Bus., 1996—. Interim dir. Small Bus. Devel. Ctr., Adams State Coll., 1988-89; adj. prof. Ctrl. Mich. U., Mt. Pleasant, 1987—; Cedar Crest Coll., Allentown, 1989—; Pa. State U., 1994-95, Nova Southeastern U., doctoral com. chair, Ft. Lauderdale, Fla., 1995—; spkr. in field; mktg. and advt. cons.; corp. trainer; textbook reviewer, editl. cons. Merrill Pub. Co., Allyn & Bacon, Inc., Richard Irwin, Inc., Macmillan Pub., John Wiley & Sons, Inc., Prentice-Hall, Houghton & Mifflin Co., Austen Press, Simon & Schuster; textbook reviewer Fairchild Books and Visuals, Inc.; tech. editor Rsch. and Edn. Assn.; doctoral com. mem. Nova Southeastern U., Drexel U., Phila., Pace U., NYC, Temple U., Phila.; bd. dirs. Z-Coil, Inc., Albuquerque; chmn. bd. The Group 8 Think Tank for Bus. and Edn., 2006—. Author: Developing a Creative and Innovative Integrated Marketing Communication Plan, 1998, The Power of Point-of-Purchase Advertising: Marketing at Retail, 2004, Retailing: Integrated Retail Management, 2005; co-author: The Best Test Preparation for the CLEP College-Level Examination Program Principles of Marketing, 1996, Retailing: Integrated Retail Management, 2005; contbg. author, editor: Principles of Business, 1991, Essentials of Advertising, 1992, rev. edit., 1994, Marketing's Powerful Weapon: Point-of-Purchase Advertising, 2001; editor: Essentials of Marketing, 1994; contbr. over 40 articles to profl. jours Treas. Com. to Elect Jorge Amaya County Commr., Colo., 1985, Bob Pastore for Senate Com.; senator Assoc. Student and Faculty Senate, Adams State Coll., 1984-85; bd. dirs. Am. Advt. Fedn. Acad. Com., 1991-97, Alamosa Personnel Bd., 1986-88, Alamosa County Devel. Corp., 1987-89, Alamosa Tourism Com., 1988-89, trustee bd. dirs. Creede Repertory Theatre, 1987-89; expert witness in tourism and mktg. State of Colo.; advisor team entries into Nat. Student Advt. Competition, Coll. World Series of Advt., 1989-90, 93—; trustee Dr. R.L. Ogden Meml. Scholarship, Colo. State U. Found., 1992—; faculty advisor Students in Free Enterprise Nat. Competition, 1997—, faculty advisor bus. adv. bd. Kutztown U. chpt. Recipient award for Excellence in Econ. Edn., Freedoms Found. Valley Forge, 1986, Capital award for contbn. to edn., Nat. Leadership Coun., 1991-92; named Outstanding Educator of Sch. Bus., Adams State Coll., 1987-88; Sam Walton fellow Students in Free Enterprise, 1997, 98, Outstanding Educator award, 1998. Fellow Direct Mktg. Assn.; mem. Am. Advt. Fedn. (faculty advisor 1987—, bd. dirs. acad. com. 1991-97), Western Mktg. Educators Assn. (paper reviewer), Nat. Guild Hypnotists (cert.), Acad. Mktg. Sci., Advt. Club N.Y., Point of Purchase Advt. Inst., Am. Collegiate Retailing Assn., Assn. Nat. Advertisers, Nat. Assn. Hispanic Profs. of Bus. Adminstrn. and Econs., New Eng. Bus. Adminstrn. Assn., Ctrl. Pa. Advt. Club, Phi Kappa Phi, Alpha Sigma Alpha (fin. advisor 1992—), Alpha Kappa Psi (dist. dir.). Democrat. Avocations: scuba, music, travel. Office: Kutztown U Coll Bus Dept Mktg Kutztown PA 19530 Office Phone: 610-683-4596. Business E-Mail: ogden@kutztown.edu.

**OGDEN, JOHN CLIFTON, III,** environmental scientist, director; b. Nashville, Tenn., Nov. 18, 1938; s. John Clifton Ogden, Jr. and Mary Ruth McKay; m. Maryanne Biggar, Sept. 12, 1975; m. Mary Ann Hollingsworth (div.); children: Laura Ann, Nicholas Alan. BA, George Peabody Coll., Nashville, 1961. Rsch. biologist Nat. Pk. Svc., Homestead, Fla., 1965—74; chair ecology working team, Man & the Biosphere Everglades team, 1993—94; coord. Fish & Wildlife Svc. wood stork recovery group, 1988—90, sr. rsch. scientist, 1988—95; mem. Fish & Wildlife Svc. crocodile recovery team Nat. Audubon Soc., Tavernier, Fla., 1974—78, sr. rsch. biologist, 1974—88, pres., Colonial Waterbird Assn., 1976—79, co-dir. Calif. condor recovery program Ventura, 1980—85, mem. Fish & Wildlife Svc. condor recovery team, 1980—88, dir. ornithol. rsch. unit Tavernier, Fla., 1986—88; adj. prof. U. Miami, Rosensteil Sch. Marine & Atmospheric Sci., 1996—2001; lead environ. scientist South Fla. Water Mgmt. Dist., West Palm Beach, 1995—2003; co-chair sci. coordination team South Fla. Ecosystem Restoration Task Force, West Palm Beach, 2003—04; chief environ. scientist South Fla. Water Mgmt. Dist., West Palm Beach, 2003—. Co-editor: (Everglades sci. rev.) Everglades. The Ecosystem and its Restoration, 1994; author: (two book chapts.) Monitoring Systems: Interdisciplinary Approaches, 2003; author: (lead coord.) 13 papers in Wetlands Jour., 2005; author: (and co-editor) (conf. proceedings) Wading Birds, National Audubon Society Report 7, 1972; author: (and sr. editor) Transactions North American Osprey Conference, 1978; author: (and co-editor) White Stork. Status and Conservation, 1980. Mem. Fla. Ornithol. Soc., 1986—88. Recipient Ann. Conservationist of Yr., Everglades Coalition, 1994, Disting. Svc. award, Colonial Waterbird Soc., 1996, Palladium medal, Am. Assn. Civil Engrs. & Nat. Audubon Soc., 1999, Charles Brookfield award for Exceptional Contbn. to South Fla. Conservation, Tropical Audubon Soc., 2004; fellow, Fla. State U., 1962—64, Am. Ornithologists Union, 1992. Mem.: Waterbird Soc. (life; pres. 1976—79). Democrat. Avocations: canoeing, hiking, birdwatching, collecting Florida landscape art, collecting orchids & palms. Home: 17390 Avocado Dr Homestead FL 33030 Office: S Florida Water Mgmt Dist 3301 Gun Club Rd West Palm Beach FL 33406 Office Phone: 561-682-6173. Personal E-mail: palmlodge@aol.com. Business E-Mail: jogden@sfwmd.gov.

**OGDEN, JONATHAN,** professional football player; b. Washington, July 31, 1974; BA in History, UCLA, 1996. Tackle Balt. Ravens, 1996—. Founder Jonathan Ogden Found.; bd. trustee's Urban League. Named First Team All-American, 1995, NFL First Team All-Pro, 2000; named to NFL Pro-Bowl, 1997—2005. Achievements include being a member of Super Bowl XXV Champion Baltimore Ravens, 2001; having his jersey number retired by UCLA, 1997. Office: c/o Baltimore Ravens 1101 Russel St Baltimore MD 21230

**OGDEN, MAUREEN BLACK,** retired state legislator; b. Vancouver, B.C., Nov. 1, 1928; came to U.S., 1930; d. William Moore and Margaret Hunter (Leitch) Black; m. Robert Moore Ogden, June 23, 1956; children: Thomas, Henry, Peter. BA, Smith Coll., 1950; MA, Columbia U., 1963; M in City and Regional Planning, Rutgers U., 1977. Researcher, staff asst. Ford Found., N.Y.C., 1951-56; staff assoc. Fgn. Policy Assn., N.Y.C., 1956-58; mem. Millburn (N.J.) Twp. Com., 1976-81; mayor Twp. of Millburn, N.J., 1979-81; mem. N.J. Gen. Assembly, Trenton, 1982-96. Chmn. Assembly Environment Com., N.J. Gen. Assembly; chmn. Energy and Pub. Utilities Com., Coun. State Govts., 1991-92; mem. adv. bd. Sch. Policy and Planning, Rutgers Univ., New Brunswick, N.J., 1992-96, vice chair Nat. Affairs and Legis. Com. Energy Sources. Author: Natural Resources Inventory, Township of Millburn, 1974. Bd. govs. N.J. Hist. Soc., Newark, 1992-2000; trustee N.J. chpt. The Nature Conservancy, 1994-99; hon. trustee Paper Mill Playhouse, Millburn, 1990—; former trustee St. Barnabas Med. Ctr., Livingston, N.J.; former pres. N.J. Drug Abuse Adv. Coun.; chair Gov.'s Coun. on N.J. Outdoors, 1996-99; mem. Palisades Interstate Park Commn., 1996-99; chair Garden State Preservation Trust, 1999—; co-chair policy com. N.J. Conservation Found., 2000—; mem. steering com. Highlands Coalition of NJ-NY-Conn. Recipient citation Nat. Assn. State Outdoors Recreation Liaison Officers, 1987, cert. appreciation John F. Kennedy Ctr. for the Performing Arts, The Alliance for Art Edn., 1987, disting. svc. award Art Educators N.J., 1987, ann. environ. quality award EPA Region II, 1988, citation Humane Soc. U.S., 1989 award N.J. Hist. Sites Coun., 1989, N.J. Sch. Conservation, 1990, pres.'s award The Nature Conservancy, 1995, pub. policy award Nat. Trust for Hist. Preservation, 1995. Mem.: Garden Club Am. (vice chair). Republican. Episcopalian. Home: 59 Lakeview Ave Short Hills NJ 07078-2240 E-mail: mrogden@worldnet.att.net.

**OGDEN, MAURICE B.,** retired minister, writer; b. Whizbang, Okla., Sept. 25, 1923; s. Arthur Omer Ogden and Hazel Mae Hartman; m. Ruth Lair Arnold (div.); 1 child, Michael Arnold; m. Kathryn Louise Freeman, June 3, 1990. BA in Letters and English, U. Okla., 1949. Freelance writer/editor, Oklahoma City, 1945—; tech. writer Paul Omohundro Co., Paramount, Calif., 1955—60; min. Unitarian Ch. Orange County, Anaheim, Calif. Creative writing instr. Coastline C.C., Fountain Valley, Calif., 1983—98, critical thinking instr., 1983—98. Author: Hangman, poetry, fiction, drama, short stories. With USAAF, 1942—43. Recipient O'Henry award for short stories, 1940. Green Party. Unitarian. Avocations: reading, cryptograms, crossword puzzles, sailing.

**OGDEN, PEGGY A.,** retired personnel director; b. N.Y.C., Mar. 21, 1932; d. Stephen Arnold and Margaret (Stern) O. BA with honors, Brown U., 1953; MA, Trinity Coll., Hartford, Conn., 1955. Asst. dir. YMCA Counseling Svc., Hartford, 1953-55; employment interviewer R.H. Macy & Co., N.Y.C., 1955; asst. pers. dir. Inst. Internat. Edn., N.Y.C., 1956-59; pers. advisor Girl Scouts U.S.A., N.Y.C., 1959-61; store and pers. mgr. Ohrbachs, Inc., N.Y.C., 1961-74; dir. pers. N.Y.C. Coll. Tech., CUNY, Bkyn., 1974-2000, ret., 2000. Arbitrator, mediator Better Bus. Bur., N.Y.C., 1988—; cons. Girl Scout Coun. N.Y., N.Y.C., 1988-89. Advocate Am. Diabetes Assn., 1999-2003; bd. dir. Project Eye to Eye, 2006—. Mem APA, AAAS, Am. Assn. U. Adminstrs., Women in Human Resources, N.Y. Pers. Mgmt. Assn. Home: 1100 Park Ave New York NY 10128-1202

**OGDEN, VALERIA MUNSON,** management consultant, state representative; b. Okanogan, Wash., Feb. 11, 1924; d. Ivan Bodwell and Pearle (Wilson) Munson; m. Daniel Miller Ogden Jr., Dec. 28, 1946; children: Janeth Lee Ogden Martin, Patricia Jo Ogden Hunter, Daniel Munson Ogden. BA magna cum laude, Wash. State U., 1946. Exec. dir. Potomac Coun. Camp Fire, Washington, 1964-68, Ft. Collins (Colo.) United Way, 1969-73, Designing Tomorrow Today, Ft. Collins, 1973-74; Poudre Valley Community Edn. Assn., Ft. Collins, 1977-78; pres. Valeria M. Ogden, Inc., Kensington, Md., 1978-81; nat. field cons. Camp Fire, Inc., Kansas City, Mo., 1980-81; exec. dir. Nat. Capital Area YWCA, Washington, 1981-84, Clark County YWCA, Vancouver, Wash., 1985-89; pvt. practice mgmt. cons. Vancouver, 1989—; mem. Wash. Ho. of Reps., 1991—2002, spkr. pro tempore, 1999—2002. Mem. adj. faculty pub. adminstrn. program Lewis and Clark Coll., Portland (Oreg.) State U., 1979-94; mem. Pvt. Industry Coun., Vancouver, 1986-95; mem. regional Svcs. Network Bd. Mental Health, 1993-03. Author: Camp Fire Membership, 1980. Mem. Wash. State Coun. Vol. Action, Olympia, 1986—90; county vice-chair Larimer County Dems., Ft. Collins, 1974—75; spkr. pro tem Wash. Ho. of Reps., 1999—2002; rep. Gov. Chris Gregoire S.W. Wash., 2005; mem. precinct com. Clark County Dems., Vancouver, 1986—88; treas. Mortar Bd. Nat. Found., Vancouver, 1987—96; bd. dirs. Clark County Coun. for Homeless, Vancouver, 1989—2004, chmn., 1994; bd. dirs. Wash. Wild Life and Recreation Coalition, 1995—2002, Human Svcs. Coun., 1996—2002, State Legis. Leaders Found., 2001—02; mem. adv. bd. Wash. State U., Vancouver, 2002—; chair arts and tourism com. Nat. Conf. State Legis., 1996—97, mem. exec. com., 2000—02; bd. dirs. Wash. State Hist. Soc., 1996—2006, Affordable Cmty. Environments, 1998—, Columbia Springs Environ. Edn. Ctr. Found., 2003—; pres. Nat. Order of Women Legislators, 1999—2001; chair Wash. State Interagy. Com. for Outdoor Recreation, 2003—, Wash. State Historic Preservation Fund, 2003—06, S.W. Wash. Ctr. for the Arts, 2003—; bd. dirs. Clark County Skill Ctr. Found., 2003, S.W. Wash. Child Care Consortium, 2003—. Named Citizen of Yr. Ft. Collins Bd. of Realtors, 1975, State Legislator of Yr., Wash. State Labor Coun., 2000, Citizen of Yr., Vancouver, Wash., 2002, First Citizen, Clark County, 2006; recipient Gulick award Camp Fire Inc., 1956, Alumna Achievement award Wash. State U. Alumni Assn., 1988; named YWCA Woman of Achievement, 1991. Mem. AAUW, Internat. Assn. Vol. Adminstrs. (pres. Boulder 1989-90), Nat. Assn. YWCA Exec. Dirs. (nat. bd. nominating com. 1988-90), Sci. and Soc. Assn. (bd. dirs. 1993-97), Women in Action, Philanthropic and Ednl. Orgn., Soroptimists, Phi Beta Kappa. Democrat. Avocations: hiking, travel. Home and Office: 3118 NE Royal Oak Dr Vancouver WA 98662-7435 Office Phone: 360-254-8886. Personal E-mail: repval@comcast.net.

**OGDON, MICHAEL WILLIAM,** minister, music educator; b. Bellingham, Wash., Dec. 11, 1959; s. William Edward Ogdon and Lee (Paul) Marilyn; m. R. Kerilyn Rosenberger, Feb. 18, 1984; children: Kelsey Lynn, Katie McKensie. BA, Biola U., 1981; MA, San Jose State U., 1986. Pastor worship and celebration Ch. at Rocky Peak, Chatsworth, Calif., 1987—90; pastor worship and media Palomar Cmty. Ch., Vista, Calif., 1990—93; assoc. pastor music and worship Scottsdale (Ariz.) Bible Ch., 1993—96; hospice chaplain, pastoral care Hospice Family Care, Phoenix, 1996—97; chmn. music and fine arts Ariz. Bible Coll., Phoenix, 1997—98; pastor worship arts Campus Bapt. Ch., Fresno, 1998—; prof. men's and women's chorus Calif. State U., Fresno, 2003—. Coach girls soccer team. Named Tchr. of Yr., Ariz. Bible Student Body, 1998. Avocations: soccer, computers.

**O'GEARY, DENNIS TRAYLOR,** retired engineering company executive; b. Waverly, Va., Feb. 20, 1925; s. King William and Mary Virginia (Traylor) O'G.; m. Alice Stuart Baum, Aug. 3, 1947; children: Dennis Patrick, Mary Alice O'Geary Eisenbarth, Christina O'Geary Bernstof. Surveying degree, Tri-State U., 1943; BS in Civil Engring., Ill. Inst. Tech., 1947. Resident engring trainee Va. Hwy. Dept., Richmond, 1947-50; civil engring. supt. Wiley Jackson Co., Roanoke, Va., 1950-57; engr., asst. estimator, project mgr., v.p. and asst. to area mgr. S.J. Groves & Sons Co., Mpls. and Springfield, Ill., 1957-77, v.p., area mgr., 1978-82, v.p., asst. divsn. mgr., divsn. estimator Atlanta, 1982-84; pres. Peabody S.W., Inc., Houston, 1984-85; v.p. Houston ops. J.D. Abrams, Inc., Austin, Tex., 1985-99; ret., 1999. Cons. J.D. Abrams, Inc. With USNR, 1943—46. Mem. ASCE (life), Am. Concrete Inst. (50 yr. mem.), Soc. Am. Mil. Engrs. (50 yr. mem.), Nat. Maritime Hist. Soc. Christian (Disciples Of Christ). Home: 15402 Cresent Oaks Ct Houston TX 77068-2079 E-mail: dennisalice@sbcglobal.net.

**OGG, WILSON REID,** lawyer, retired judge, poet, publishing executive, educator; b. Alhambra, Calif., Feb. 26, 1928; s. James Brooks and Mary (Wilson) Ogg. Student, Pasadena Jr. Coll., 1946; AB, U. Calif., Berkeley, 1949; JD, U. Calif., 1952; Cultural D in Philosophy of Law, World U. Roundtable, 1983. Bar: Calif. 1955. Assoc. trust dept. Wells Fargo Bank, San Francisco, 1954-55; pvt. practice Berkeley, 1955—. Instr. Taegu English Lang. Inst., 1954, 25th Sta. Hosp., Taegu, Republic of Korea, 1954; rsch. atty., legal editor dept. of continuing edn. Bar U. Calif., 1958—63; curator-in-residence, Pinebrook, 1964—2003; adminstv. law judge, 1974—93; real estate broker, cons., 1974—; trustee World U., 1976—80; dir. admissions internat. Soc. Phil. Enquiry, 1981—84; dep. dir. gen. Internat. Biog. Ctr., England, 1986—; dep. gov. Am. Biog. Inst. Rsch. Assn., 1986—; owner Pinebrook Press, Berkeley, Calif., 1988—2004; sci. faculty Cambridge U., 2000—. Author: The Enfolding Universe, 1995, Constitutional Law. Constitutional Crisis Facing American Democracy, 2005, Collective Essays of Wilson Ogg, 2005, numerous poems; contbr. articles to profl. jours. With AUS, 1952—54. Named to Internat. Poetry Hall of Fame, Nat. Libr. Poetry, 1997; recipient Internat. Peace prize, Auth. of United Cultural Conv., U.S., 2002, Auth. of United Culture Conv., U.S., 2005, 50 Yr. Commemorative medal, Albert Schweitzer Assn., 2003, The World Freedom medal, Am. Biog. Inst., 2006. Mem.: ACLU, ASCAP, ABA, VFW, AAAS, London Diplomatic Acad., Inst. Noetic Scis., Intertel, Calif. Soc. Psychical Study (pres., chmn. bd. 1963—65), Am. Arbitration Assn. (nat. panel arbitrators), San Francisco Bar Assn., State Bar Calif., Internat. Soc. Individual Liberty, Internat. Platform Assn., Faculty Club of the U. Calif. at Berkeley (emeritus), Men's Inner Cir. Achievement, Amnesty Internat., Marines Meml. Club, Elks, Shriners, Masons, Am. Legion. Unitarian Universalist. Office Phone: 510-845-7155. Fax: 510-540-6052. Business E-Mail: wilsonogg@cal.berkeley.edu.

**OGIER, WALTER THOMAS,** retired physics educator; b. Pasadena, Calif., June 18, 1925; s. Walter Williams and Aileen Vera (Polhamus) O.; m. Mayrene Miriam Gorton, June 27, 1954; children: Walter Charles, Margaret Miriam, Thomas Earl, Kathryn Aileen. BS, Calif. Inst. Tech., 1947, PhD in Physics, 1953. Research fellow Calif. Inst. Tech., 1953; instr. U. Calif. at Riverside, 1954-55, asst. prof. physics, 1955-60, Pomona Coll., Claremont, Calif., 1960-62, assoc. prof., 1962-67, prof. physics, 1967-89, prof. emeritus, 1989—, chmn. dept., 1972-89. Contbr. articles on metals, liquid helium, X-rays and proton produced X-rays to profl. jours. Served with USNR, 1944-46. NSF Sci. Faculty fellow, 1966-67 Mem. Am. Phys. Soc., Am. Assn. Physics Tchrs. (pres. So. Calif. sect. 1967-69), Tau Beta Pi. Home: 8555 San Gabriel Rd Atascadero CA 93422-4928 Business E-Mail: wogier@pomona.edu. E-mail: ogierwt@charter.net.

**OGILVIE, KELVIN KENNETH,** academic administrator, chemist, educator; m. Emma Roleen; children: Kristine, Kevin. BS with honors, Acadia U., 1964, DSc (hon.), 1983; PhD, Northwestern U., 1968; DSc (hon.), U. N.B., Can., 1991, McGill U., 1998. Assoc. prof. U. Man., Winnipeg, 1968-74; prof. chemistry McGill U., Montreal, 1974-88, Can. Pacific prof. biotech., 1984-87; bd. dirs. Sci. Adv. Bd., Biologicals, Toronto, Ont., 1979-84; dir. Office of Biotech. McGill U., 1984-87; prof. chemistry Acadia U., Wolfville, N.S., 1987—, v.p. acad. affairs, 1987—93, pres., vice-chancellor, 1993—2003. Invited lectr. on biotech. Tianjin, People's Republic of China, 1985; Snider lectr. U. Toronto, 1991; Gwen Leslie Meml. lectr., 1991; Centennial Mossman lectr. McGill U., 1998; mem. Nat. Adv. Bd. Sci. and Tech., 1994-95; chair selection com. Indsl. Postgrad. Scholarship program NSERCC, 1994; mem. Coun. N.S. Univ. Pres. 1993-2003; mem. Coun. of Applied Sci. and Tech. for N.S., 1988-93; mem. Nat. Biotech. Adv. Com., 1988-99; mem. Fisher Biotech. Adv. Ctr., Can., 1989-92; mem. sci. adv. bd. Allelix Biopharms., 1991-93; developer bd. NRC Inst. for Marine Biosci., 1990-93; mem. steering com. on biotech. labor Can., 1990-92; mem. Atlantic regional com. Prime Min.'s Awards for Tchg. Excellence in Sci., Tech. and Math., 1993-2004; chair regional planning forum for a pharm. industry, Atlantic Can., 1993; mem. Atomic Energy Control Bd., Can., 1997-99; chair sci. adv. bd. Quanta Nova Can., 1998-2001; mem. Can. Electronic Bus. Roundtable, 1999-2002, Can. Global Bus. Dialogue on Electronic Commerce, 1999, Coun. of Ministers Com. on Online Learning, 2000-01; mem. IBM Global Edn. Policy Coun., 2000-03, The Can. e-Bus. Initiative, 2002-04; chair Premier's Coun. on Innovation, N.S., 2003-06, AIMS Sci. fellow on Postsecondary Edn., 2004-; mem. bd. Gerome Can., 2005-. Mem. editl. bd. Nucleosides and Nucleotides, 1981-92; contbr. over 150 articles to profl. jours.; holder 14 patents. Bd. dir. Plant Biotech. Inst., 1987-90. Decorated Knight of Malta, 1985, Order of Can., 1991; named Hon. Col. 14th Air Maintenance Squadron, RCAF, 1995-2000; recipient Commemorative medal for 125th Anniversary of Confedn. Can., 1992, Buck-Whitney medal, 1983, Manning Prin. award, 1992, Queen Elizabeth Golden Jubilee medal, 2002; named to McLean's Honor Roll of Canadians Who Made a Difference, 1988; E.W.R. Steacie Meml. fellow, 1982-84; inducted into Discovery Ctr. Sci. and Tech. Hall of Fame, 2002. Fellow Chem. Inst. Can.; mem. Am. Chem. Soc., Ordre des Chemists of Que., Assn. Univs. and Colls. Can. (standing com. on rsch. 1993-2000), Atlantic Univ. Athletic Assn. (pres. 1995-97). Achievements include inventing of BIOLF-62 (ganciclovir), antiviral drug used worldwide; developer general synthesis of RNA; developer original 'gene machine'; developer complete chemical synthesis of large RNA molecules; developer Acadia Advantage Program. Home: PO Box 307 Canning NS Canada B0P 1HO Office: Acadia U Dept Chemistry Wolfville NS Canada B4P 2R6 E-mail: kelvin.ogilvie@acadiau.ca.

**OGILVIE, LLOYD JOHN,** clergyman; b. Kenosha, Wis., Sept. 2, 1930; s. Vard Spencer and Katherine (Jacobson) O.; m. Mary Jane Jenkins, Mar. 25, 1951. BA, Lake Forest Coll., 1952, Garrett Theol. Sem., 1956; postgrad., New Coll., U. Edinburgh, Scotland, 1955-56; D.D., Whitworth Coll., 1973; L.H.D., U. Redlands, 1974; D.Humanities, Moravian Coll., 1975; LLD, Ea. U., 1988. Ordained to ministry Presbyn. Ch., 1956; student pastor Gurnee, Ill., 1952-56; first pastor Winnetka (Ill.) Presbyn. Ch., 1956-62; pastor 1st, Presbyn. Ch., Bethlehem, Pa., 1962-72, 1st Presbyn. Ch., Hollywood, Calif., 1972—95. Preacher Chgo. Sunday Evening Club, 1963—1989, also frequent radio and TV personality weekly syndicated TV program Let God Love You. Chaplain US Senate, 1995-2003, ret. 2003. Author: A Life Full of Surprises, 1969, Let God Love You, 1974, If I Should Wake Before I Die, 1973, Lord of the Ups and Downs, 1974, You've Got Charisma, 1975, Cup of Wonder, 1976, Life Without Limits, 1976, Drumbeat of Love, 1977, When God First Thought of You, 1978, The Autobiography of God, 1979, The Bush Is Still Burning, 1980, The Radiance of the Inner Splendor, 1980, Congratulations, God Believes in You, 1981, Life as it Was Meant to Be, 1981, The Beauty of Love, The Beauty of Friendship, 1981, The Beauty of Caring, The Beauty of Sharing, 1981, God's Best for My Life, 1981, God's Will in Your Life, 1982, Ask Him Anything, 1982, Commentary on Book of Acts, 1983, Praying with Power, 1983, Falling into Greatness, 1983, Freedom in the Spirit, 1984, Making Stress Work For You, 1984, The Lord of the Impossible, 1984, Why Not Accept Christ's Healing and Wholeness, 1984, If God Cares, Why Do I Still Have Problems?, 1985, Understanding the Hard Sayings of Jesus, 1986, 12 Steps to Living Without Fear, 1987, A Future and a Hope, 1988, Enjoying God, 1990, Silent Strength, 1990, The Lord of the Loose Ends, 1991; gen. editor: Communicator's Commentary of the Bible, 1982; host: (TV and radio program) Let God Love You. Office: 1760 N Gower St Los Angeles CA 90028-5422

**OGILVIE, RICHARD IAN,** clinical pharmacologist; b. Sudbury, Ont., Can., Oct. 9, 1936; s. Patrick Ian and Gena Hilda (Olson) O.; m. Ernestine Taedel, Oct. 9, 1965; children — Degen Elisabeth, Lars Ian. MD, U. Toronto, 1960. Intern Toronto (Ont.) Gen. Hosp., 1960-61; resident Montreal Gen. and Univ. Alta. hosps., 1962-66; fellow in clin. pharmacology McGill U., Montreal, 1966-68, asst. prof. medicine, pharmacology and therapeutics, 1968-73, assoc. prof., 1973-78, prof., 1978-83, chmn. dept. pharmacology and therapeutics, 1978-83. Prof. emeritus U. Toronto, 2002-, clin. pharmacologist Montreal Gen. Hosp., 1968-83, dir. div. clin. pharmacology, 1978-83; prof. medicine and pharmacology U. Toronto, 1983—2002; dir. div. cardiology Toronto Western Hosp., 1983-88, div. clin. pharmacology, 1983-91; mem. pharm. grants com. Med. Research Coun. Can., 1977-82, chmn. 1980-82;

mem. med. adv. com. Que. Heart Found., 1976-82, chmn. 1977-81. Editor Hypertension Canada, 1989—. Bd. dirs. PMAC Health Care Found., 1986-92; hon. sec.-treas. Banting Research Found., 1984-87, mem. grant rev. coun., 1985-86 Decorated knight comdr. Sovereign Mil. Order St. John of Jerusalem, Knights of Malta, 1987, nat. chmn., recipient prize in med. ethics, 1988-98, sci. advisor to the prior, 1987—, Knight Grand Cross, 1990; jury mem. Can. Prix Galien, 1994-99; grantee Can. Kidney Found., J.C. Edwards Found., Med. Rsch. Coun., Que. Heart Found., Can. Found. Advancement Therapeutics, Conseil de la recherche en sante du Que. Fellow ACP, Royal Coll. Physicians of Can.; mem. Can. Soc. Clin. Investigation (coun. 1977-80), Can. Hypertension Soc. (bd. dirs. 1979-81, 89-94, 96—, v.p. 1991-92, pres. 1992-93, Disting. Svc. award, 2002), Can. Found. Advancement Clin. Pharmacology (dir. 1978-86), Canadian Soc. for Clin. Pharmacology (pres. 1979-82, Sr. Investigator award 1993), Internat. Union Pharmacology (coun. mem. clin. pharmacology sect. 1981-84, chmn. 1984-87), Pharm. Soc. Can., Can. Cardiovascular Soc., Am. Soc. Pharmacology and Exptl. Therapeutics, Am. Soc. Clin. Pharm., Toronto Hypertension Soc. (pres. 1988-98). Home: 79 Collard Dr King City ON Canada L7B 1E4 Office: Toronto Western Hosp 399 Bathurst St Toronto ON Canada M5T 2S8 Office Phone: 416-603-5176. Business E-Mail: ri.ogilvie@utoronto.ca.

**OGILVIE, T(HOMAS) FRANCIS,** marine engineering educator; b. Atlantic City, Sept. 26, 1929; s. Thomas Fleisher and Frances Augusta (Wilson) O.; m. Joan Husselton, Sept. 11, 1950; children: Nancy Louise, Mary Beth, Kenneth Stuart. BA in Physics, Cornell U., 1950; M.Sc. in Aero. Engring., U. Md., 1957; PhD in Engring. Sci., U. Calif., Berkeley, 1960; D in Naval Arch./Marine Engring. (hon.), Nat. Tech. U. Athens, 1996. Physicist, David Taylor Model Basin, Dept. Navy, Bethesda, Md., 1951-62, 64-67; liaison scientist Office of Naval Research, London, 1962-63; assoc. prof. naval architecture and marine engring. U. Mich., Ann Arbor, 1967-70, prof. fluid mechanics, 1970-81, chmn. dept. naval architecture and marine engring., 1973-81; prof. ocean engring. MIT, Cambridge, 1982-96, prof. emeritus, 1996—, head dept., 1982-94. Vis. prof. naval architecture Osaka (Japan) U., 1976; vis. prof. math. U. Manchester, Eng., 1976; founding mem. Ariz. Sr. Acad., Tucson, 1997. Contbr. articles to profl. jours. Recipient Meritorious Pub. Svc. award U.S. Dept. of Transp., 1982. Fellow Soc. of Naval Architects and Marine Engrs. (coun. 1977-82, exec. com. 1978-80, 83-84, William H. Webb medal 1989); mem. Sigma Xi, Phi Beta Kappa. Home: 7559 S Eliot Ln Tucson AZ 85747-9627

**OGILVY, GEOFF,** professional golfer; b. Adelaide, Australia, June 11, 1977; m. Juli Ogilvy. Profl. golfer Profl. Golf Assn., 2001—. Achievements include winning Tasmanian Open, 1998; runner-up five PGA events, winner two PGA events including the US Open, Winged Foot, 2006; winning WGC Accenture Match Play Championship at La Costa, 2006. Office: Pro Sports Mgmt PO Box 21 Suite 1 Dendy Plaza 1st Floor 26-34 Church St Brighton Victoria 3186 Australia Office Fax: 61 3 9592 5633.*

**OGINZ, RICHARD J.,** artist, educator; b. Phila., Feb. 17, 1944; s. Monroe and Malvina Oginz; m. Lori Starr, Jan. 26, 1984; children: Ben, Max; children: Alexandra, Sascha. BFA, Tyler Coll. Art and Design, 1966; MFA, U. Wis., 1968. Gregory fellow, artist-in-residence U. Leeds, England, 1970—73; head of sculpture Hornsey Coll. Art, Middlesex U., London, 1973—76; faculty mem. fine arts dept. Otis Coll. Art and Design, 1978—95. Adj. lectr. Chelsea Coll. Art, 1973—76, Portsmouth Polytechnic, 1973—76, Wimbledon Coll. Art, 1973—76; bd. dirs. LA Contemporary Exhbns., 1983—87; vis. artist Crossroads Sch. Arts and Scis., 1995—96; adj. prof. visual and performing arts dept. Glendale CC, 2001; instr. visual art dept. Louisville HS, 2001; adj. prof. art dept. Pierce CC, 2001; vis. lectr. dept. world arts and culture UCLA, 2005—06. Contbr. articles to mags., local newspapers; one-man shows include Pk. Sq. Gallery, Leeds, 1970, Serpentine Gallery, London, 1971, Drexel U., Phila., 1973, Leeds City Art Gallery, 1973, Molly Barnes Gallery, LA, 1980, Arco Ctr. Visual Art, 1983, Art Space Gallery, 1984, Ruth Bachofner Gallery, Santa Monica, Calif., 1991, 1993, Glendale CC, Calif., 1992, Sam Francis Gallery, Crossroads Sch., Santa Monica, 1995, LA County Mus. Art, 1997, Gallery Functional Art, Santa Monica, 1999, 2005, Jan Baum Gallery, LA, 2001, exhibited in group shows at Barnsdall Pk. Mcpl. Art Gallery, 1978, Ellie Blankfort Gallery, 1978, Parsons Sch. Design, NYC, 1979, LA Contemporary Exhbns., 1979, Kirk de Gooyer Gallery, LA, 1980, Md. Inst. Art, Balt., 1980, Santa Barbara Mus. Art, 1980, Nickle Arts Mus., U. Calgary, 1981—83, Palm Springs Desert Mus., Calif., 1981—83, Norman MacKenzie Gallery, U. Regina, 1981—83, Addison Gallery, Phillips Acad., Andover, Mass., 1981—83, Ill. State U., Normal, 1981—83, Madison Art Ctr., Wis., 1981—83, Dowtown Gallery, LA, 1981, Internat. Sculpture Conf., San Francisco, 1982, Stella Polaris Gallery, LA, 1982, LA County Mus. Art, 1983, 1992, 1994, 1996, Edge Gallery, Fullerton, Calif., 1983, Palos Verdes Cmty. Arts Assn., 1984, Loyola Law Sch., LA, 1984, Security Pacific Nat. Bank, 1984, Jr. Arts Ctr., 1984, Paulo Salvador Gallery, NYC, 1985, U. Art Mus., Calif. State U., Santa Monica, 1985, Welton Becket Arch. and Engrs., 1985, Guggenheim Gallery, Chapman Coll., Orange, Calif., 1985, U. So. Calif. Sch. Architecture Gallery, LA, 1986, Security Pacific Bank Gallery, 1987, Gallery Functional Art, Santa Monica, 1988, 1990, Evanston Art Ctr., Ill., 1988, Mobilla Gallery, Cambridge, Mass., 1989—90, Muckenthaler Cultural Ctr., Fullerton, Calif., 1989, San Francisco Internat. Airort, 1989, Std. Brands Gallery, Newport Beach, Calif., 1990, Venice, Calif., 1990, Contemporary Artist Svcs., LA, 1990, City of LA Gallery, Woodland Hills, 1991, Ruth Bachofner Gallery, Santa Monica, 1992, LA Mcpl. Gallery, 1993, Santa Monica Mus. Art, 1995, Crossroads Sch., Santa Monica, 1995, Armory Ctr. Arts, 1996, Venice, Calif., 1997, Millard Sheets Gallery, Pomona, Calif., 1997, Del Mono Gallery, Brentwood, Calif., 2000, Craft and Folk Art Mus., LA, 2001, Glendale CC Art Gallery, Calif., 2001, Pasadena City Coll. Art Gallery, 2002, Fisher Art Gallery, U. So. Calif., 2005, LA Internat. Airport, 2005, pub. commn., Junipero Serra State Office Bldg. Lobby Elevator Doors, LA, 1998. pub. collections, Madison Mus. Art, Wis., Nestle Corp., LA, Security Pacific Bank, Mika Corp., Michelin Corp., Paris, Wells Fargo Bank, LA, LA County Mus. Art, London Borough Camden, Ferens Art Gallery, Kinston-upon-Hull, Eng., Yorkshire Arts Assn., Eng., Bradford Mus., Yorkshire, Arts Coun. Gt. Britain, London, Leeds City Art Gallery, Yorkshire, numerous pvt. collections. Recipient Young Talent award, LA County Mus. Art, 1979; Faculty Devel. grant, Ford Found., 1976, 1978, Arts Visual Artist's Forum grant, Nat. Endowment Arts, 1984.

**OGLE, D. CLARK,** textiles executive; b. 1947; Buyer and numerous positions Super Valu, Eden Prairie, Minn., 1968-74; pres. W.Va. div. Fox Grocery Co., 1974-78; pres., COO, bd. dirs. Scrivner, Inc., 1978-87; pres., CEO Affiliated Food Stores, Keller, Tex., 1987-90; industry cons. Hoover, Ala.; CEO Peter J. Schmitt; pres., CEO various pvt. cos., 1987-96; mng. dir. KPMG Peat Marwick, LLP; pres., CEO Johnston Industries, Inc., 1998—. Office: Johnston Textile Industries 3101 23rd Dr Valley AL 36854-3042 Fax: 706-641-3159.

**OGLE, EDWARD PROCTOR, JR.,** investment advisor; b. Inglewood, Calif., Dec. 20, 1935; s. Edward Proctor and Allene Emma (Blumenthal) O.; m. Elizabeth Lovejoy Myers, Mar. 28, 1958; children: Kathryn Ogle Nava, Terry Ogle Nelson, Wendy Ogle Reeves. BA, U. So. Calif., 1964; MA, Claremont Grad. Sch., 1980. Cert. fin. planning practitioner. Zone mgr. Investors Diversified Svcs., Pasadena, Calif., 1964-66; asst. mgr. Merrill Lynch Pierce Fenner Smith, Pasadena, 1966-72; mgr. Clark Dodge & Co-Capital Place Dept., L.A., 1972-74; sr. v.p. Security Pacific Bank - Pacific Century Group, L.A., 1974-86; sr. v.p., registered prin. Brown Bros. Harriman & Co., L.A., 1986—2003; prin., cert. sr. advisor Philip V. Swan Assocs., 2003—. Author: (booklet) Role of Bank Trust Department, 1981; editor (booklet) Parade Operations Manual, 1992, 93. Com. sec. Tournament of Roses Assn., Pasadena, 1976—; mem. Town Hall of Calif., L.A., 1977—, Orange County World Trade Assn.; mem. exec. com. U.So. Calif. Alumni Assn., 2003—; chmn. bd. councilors U. So. Calif., 1998—, bd. govs., 2003—; mem. Rep. Presdl. Task Force, Orange County, Calif., 1984—; elder Presbyn. Ch. Recipient Corp. Fund Raising Cert. United Way, L.A., 1978-80, Exec. Mgmt. Cert. Claremont Grad. Sch., 1979, Mgmt. and Exec. Cert. Security Pacific Bank, L.A., 1981. Mem. Fin. Planning Assn., Drucker Ctr. Mgmt. Assn.,

Claremont Grad. Sch. Alumni Assn. (pres. 1984-86), Pasadena Bond Club, Bond Club L.A., Jonathan Club, City Club. Republican. Avocations: photography, golf, basketball, music, travel. Office Phone: 626-793-0377. E-mail: eogle@philipswan.com.

**OGLE, JAMES DAVID (DAVID OGLE),** lawyer; b. Kirksville, Mo., Mar. 23, 1968; s. John Charles and Elizabeth Ann Ogle; m. Laura Kerr Ogle, Aug. 14, 1993; children: Taylor, Jackson. BSc Okla. State U., Stillwater; JD, Okla. City U., Okla. Bar: Okla. 1997, US Dist. Ct. (no. and we. dists.) 1997, US Ct. Appeals (10th cir.) 1998, US Supreme Ct. 2004. Various sales, mktg. positions G.D. Searle, Skokie, Ill., 1990—93, Carter Healthcare, Okla. City, 1993—95; atty. Martin Law Office, Okla. City, 1995—2003, Ogle & Welch, P.C., Okla. City, 2003—. Spkr. in field. Mem., assoc. Okla. City Art Mus., Okla., 1997—2002; trustee Okla. County Law Libr. Mem.: Okla. County Bar Assn. (pres.), Okla. Criminal Def. Assn., Nat. Assn. Criminal Def. Lawyers (life). Office: Ogle & Welch PC 117 Park Ave 3d Fl Oklahoma City OK 73102 Office Phone: 405-232-9800. Office Fax: 405-232-1608.

**OGLE, ROBBIN SUE,** criminal justice educator; b. North Kansas City, Mo., Aug. 28, 1960; d. Robert Lee and Carol Sue (Gray) O. BS, Ctrl. Mo. State U., 1982; MS, U. Mo., 1990; PhD, Pa. State U., 1995. State probation and parole officer Mo. Dept. Corrections, Kansas City, 1982-92; collector J.C. Penney Co., Mission, Kans., 1990-92; instr. U. Mo., Kansas City, 1990-92; grad. lectr. Pa. State U., University Park, 1992-95; prof. criminal justice dept. U. Nebr., Omaha, 1995—. Author: Battered Women Who Kill: A New Framework, 2002, The Wienie Dog Adventure Series: The Great Ham Heist, 2005; contbr. articles to profl. jours. Athletic scholar Ctrl. Mo. State U., Warrensburg, 1978-82. Mem. AAUW, ACLU, NOW, Am. Soc. Criminology, Acad. Criminal Justice Scis., Am. Correctional Assn., Phi Kappa Phi. Avocations: reading, watching basketball, walking dog. Office: U Nebr Dept Criminal Justice 1100 Neihardt Lincoln NE 68588-0630 Home: 2410 N 99th St Omaha NE 68134-5642 Office Phone: 402-472-3677. Personal E-mail: rsogle@cox.net. Business E-Mail: rogle@mail.unomaka.edu.

**OGLESBY, ELAINE SUE,** elementary school educator; b. Rensselaer, Ind., Dec. 11, 1958; d. Richard E. and Lois I. Oglesby. BS in Natural Resources and Environ. Sci., Purdue U., 1981; MEd, Ind. U., 1988, MLS, 2005. Tchr. Indpls. Pub. Schs., 1986—2004, digital coach, 2004—. Recipient Shining Star, Indpls. Pub. Schs., 1993—94, Spirit of Harshman, Harshman Mid. Sch., 1998, Tchr. of the Yr. award, 2003, Top Ten Tchr. award, Indpls. Pub. Schs., 2003; grantee, Eli Lily Found., 1993. Mem.: Ind. Mid. Level Educators (assoc.), Nat. Mid. Sch. Assn. (assoc.), Ind. Libr. Fedn. (assoc.), Assn. Curriculum and Devel. (assoc.). Office Phone: 317-226-4030.

**OGLESBY, JENNIFER MARIE,** clinical psychologist, neuropsychologist; b. Rochester, N.Y., Sept. 21, 1966; d. Ellis James and Carolyn Marie Oglesby; m. Gordon Scott Freckleton; 1 child, David. BA, Cornell U., Ithaca, N.Y., 1988; MS, U. Fla., Gainesville, 1992, PhD, 1994. Diplomate Am. Bd. Profl. Psychology, bd. cert. in clinical neuropsychology Am. Bd. Profl. Psychology. Intern Greater Hartford Psychology, Newington, Conn., 1993—94; resident/fellow in clin. psychology/neuropsychology Norwalk Hosp., Conn., 1994—96, clin. psychologist, neuropsychologist, 1996—99, Neurobehavioral Inst. N.J., Raritan, 1999—2001, St. Lawrence Rehab. Ctr., Lawrenceville, 2001—. Co-sec. Antheil Elem. PTO, Ewing, NJ, 2004—. Recipient scholarship, Cornell U. Coll. Arts and Scis., 1984—88; grantee, Divsn. Sponsored Rsch., U. Fla., 1990, 1992. Mem.: APA, Internat. Neuropsychol. Soc., Am. Acad. Clin. Neuropsychology. Avocations: reading, exercise, gardening, travel, movies. Office: St Lawrence Rehab Ctr 2381 Lawrenceville Rd Lawrenceville NJ 08648 Office Phone: 609-896-9500 ext. 2277, 609-896-2515. Office Fax: 609-896-0698. E-mail: JOglesby@slrc.org.

**OGLESBY, JOSEPH WOODSON (MIKE ENGLISH),** writer, publishing executive; b. Louisville, Aug. 14, 1931; s. Joseph Woodson Oglesby, Sr. and Mary Lee (Wigginton) Oglesby; m. Marianna Bachmann, Sept. 4, 1971; 1 child, Shane Woodson. BA, U. Louisville, 1953. Staff writer Louisville Times, 1954—56, asst. editor, 1954—56; city editor New Albany Tribune, Ind., 1956—59; editor Frankfort Crusader, Ky., 1960, pub., 1960; investigative reporter Tonawanda News, North Tonawanda, NY, 1961—63; exec. editor Voice Newspapers, Louisville, 1964—70; pub., CEO Lucky Publs., Louisville, 1988—2000; freelance writer, 1970—. Founding mem. Ky. Thoroughbred Media, Lexington, Ky., 1990; pub. rels. adv. Nat. Kitchen Cabinet Assn., Louisville, 1970—72, Contact Lens Soc. of Am., Louisville, 1972. Author: (novels) The Devil's Disciple, 1977, Ghost Riders of the Staked Plains, (play) The Dodge, 1998 (nominee Pulitzer prize, 1999), (memoir) Dinner with D.W. Griffith and Other Memories, 2005, (children's book) The Marvelous Kingdom of Wee, 1976, monographs on Ky. history; contbr. articles to newspapers and magazines. Vice chmn. bd. dir. YMCA, St. Matthews, Ky., 1970; mem. bd. dir. Talbot Ho., Louisville, 1962; pub. rels. adv. Recovery, Inc., Louisville, 1960—62. Nominee Eclipse award, 1998; recipient Best Feature award, Ky. Press Assn., 1967, Short Story award, Writer's Digest, 1982, 1985; grantee, P.E.N. Internat. Ctr., NYC, 1983. Mem.: Nat. Turf Writers Assn., Mystery Writers Am., Authors Guild, Authors Legacy Soc., Hon. Order Ky. Cols., Omicron Delta Kappa. Democrat. Avocations: travel, history, thoroughbred handicapping, coin collecting/numismatics. Home: No 5 2312 Alta Ave Louisville KY 40205 Personal E-mail: novelistjosephoglesby@msn.com.

**OGLETREE, CHARLES J., JR.,** law educator; b. Calif., Dec. 31, 1952; m. Pamela Barnes, 1975; children: Charles III, Rashida. BA in Polit. Sci. Stanford U., 1974 MA in Polit. Sci., 1975, JD, Harvard U., 1978; LLD (hon.), NC Ctrl. U., New Eng. Sch. Law, Tougaloo Coll., Amherst Coll., 2002, U. Miami Sch. Law, 2003, Wilberforce U., 2003. Bar: DC 1979, US Supreme Ct. 1983. Staff atty. DC Pub. Defender Svc., training dir., 1982—83, trial chief, 1983—84, dep. dir., 1984—85; joined Jessamy, Fort & Ogletree, 1985; of counsel Jordan, Keys & Jessamy, Washington; lectr. law Harvard Law Sch., Cambridge, Mass., 1984, vis. prof. law from practice, 1985—89, Edward R. Johnston Lectr. Law, 1989, asst. prof. law, 1989—93, dir. Criminal Justice Inst., 1990, prof. law., 1993—, faculty dir. clin. programs, 1996, Jesse Climenko Prof. Law, 1998—, assoc. dean clin. programs, 2002—03, vice dean clin. programs, 2003, dir. Charles Hamilton Houston Inst. for Race and Justice, 2004—. Adj. prof. Am. U., Washington, 1983—85; moderator various nationally televised forums; guest commentator various nat. and local TV and radio programs. Co-author: Beyond the Rodney King Story: An Investigation of Police Conduct in Minority Communities, author: All Deliberate Speed: Reflections on the First Half-Century of Brown v. Board of Education, 2004; co-editor: Brown at 50: The Unfinished Legacy, 2004; contbr. articles to profl. jours., chapters to books. Chmn. bd. trustees U. DC; chmn. bd. dirs. B.E.L.L. Found.; mem. bd. trustees Stanford U., chmn. Stanford Fund. Named one of 100 Most Influential Lawyers in Am., Nat. Law Jour., 2000, 100 Most Influential Blacks in Am., Black Enterprise mag., 2003, Savoy mag., 2003; recipient Charles Hamilton Houston Medallion of Merit, Washington Bar Assn., 2001, Equal Justice Award, Nat. Bar Assn., 2002, Tribune Soc. Justice Award, Courts of NY State, 2003, Universal Humanitarian Award, NAACP, 2003. Office: Harvard Law Sch 1563 Massachusetts Ave Cambridge MA 02138 Office Phone: 617-495-5097. Office Fax: 617-496-3936. Business E-Mail: ogletree@law.harvard.edu.*

**OGLIARUSO, MICHAEL ANTHONY,** retired chemist, educator, actor; b. Bklyn., Aug. 10, 1938; s. Andrea and Anna (Bianco) O.; m. Basila Gallo, Apr. 2, 1961; 1 child, Michael Dana. BS, Poly. Inst. Bklyn., N.Y., 1960, PhD, 1965. Postdoctoral rsch. assoc. UCLA, 1965-67; asst. prof. chemistry Va. Poly. Inst. and State U., Blacksburg, 1967-72, assoc. prof., 1972-78, prof., 1978-95, assoc. dean Coll. Arts and Scis., 1984-95; ret. Coll. Arts and Scis.; profl. actor. Contbr. articles to profl. jours. Served with C.E. U.S. Army, 1960-61. Mem. Am. Chem. Soc., Va. Acad. Sci., Sigma Xi, Phi Lambda Upsilon. *I have been fortunate to be associated with the most personally rewarding profession available today, the professional education of young*

*men and women. This career is best suited to persons who wish to remain young in spirit, since regardless of your age you are always surrounded with students who are between 18 and 22 years old. This is the best way I know to remain spiritually young.*

**OGNIBENE, ANDRE JOHN,** internist, educator, retired military officer; b. NYC, Nov. 18, 1931; s. Morris S. and Josephine C. (Macaluso) O.; m. Margaret A. Haug, Apr. 21, 1957; children: Judy, Andrea, Adrienne, Marc, Eric. BA cum laude, Columbia U., 1952; MD, NYU, 1956. Diplomate Am. Bd. Internal Medicine, Am. Bd. Geriatrics, Am. Bd. Med. Mgmt. Intern in medicine Bellevue Hosp., NYC, 1956-57, resident in medicine, 1957-59; commd. capt. US Army M.C., 1957, advanced through grades to brig. gen., 1978; resident in medicine Manhattan VA Hosp., NYC and chief resident in medicine, 1959-60; chief med. service US Army Hosp., Nurnburg, Germany, 1961-62, chief dept. medicine, 1962-64; fellow in cardiology Walter Reed Gen. Hosp., Washington, 1964-65, asst. in cardiology, 1965-66, asst. chief dept. medicine, 1969-72; chief dept. medicine, chief profl. services US Army Hosp., Ft. Meade, Md., 1966-68; cons. in medicine Hdqrs. US Army, Vietnam, 1969; asst. chief dept. medicine Walter Reed Army Med. Ctr., 1970-72; from chief dept. medicine to dir. med. edn. Brooke Army Med. Ctr., Ft. Sam Houston, Tex., 1972-78, dir. med. edn., 1976-78, dep. comdr. and chief profl. services, 1976-78, comdr., commanding gen., 1978-81; hosp. dir. San Antonio State Chest Hosp., 1981-85; program dir. internal medicine Canton, Ohio, 1985-95; prof. medicine NE Ohio U., Rootstown, 1985-98, prof. emeritus, 1998—, chmn. dept. medicine, 1989-98, assoc. dean for med. edn., 1989—98; med. dir. Mercy Med. Ctr., 1995—98; v.p., treas. Majomed Corp., San Antonio, 1999—. Instr. medicine NYU, 1960; assoc. clin. prof. Georgetown U., 1970-72; clin. prof. U. Tex. Health Sci. Ctr., San Antonio, 1973-85, mem. postgrad. adv. com., 1977-78; mem. Instl. Rev. Bd., 1981-85; pres. Bexar Met. unit Am. Cancer Soc., 1984; dir. Eisenhower Nat. Bank; bd. dirs. Cancer Therapy and Rsch. Ctr.; chmn. South Tex. Epilepsy Found., 1985. Contbr. articles to med. publs. and chpts. to books; editor, prin. author Internal Medicine in Vietnam, Vol. II, 1982; editor-in-chief: Internal Medicine in Vietnam, vol. I, 1977. Trustee Regina Health Ctr., 1992-97; mem. med. adv. bd. Access Health Inc., 1998-2000. Decorated DSM, Legion of Merit; named among Am. Top Physicians, Consumer Rsch. Coun., 2003-05. Master ACP (laureate, master tchr.); fellow Am. Coll. Physician Execs. (cert.), Am. Coll. Angiology; mem. NY Acad. Scis., Am. Fedn. Clin. Rsch., Bexar County Med. Soc., Stark County Med. Soc., Assn. Profs. Medicine, Tex. Med. Found., Alpha Omega Alpha. Home and Office: 27671 Ramblewood St San Antonio TX 78261-2013 Personal E-mail: aognibene@satx.rr.com. *Compassion must remain the universal prescription in medical practice. Technology can provide no solutions in the absence of humanity.*

**OGNIBENE, FREDERICK PETER,** internist; b. Jamestown, NY, Aug. 30, 1953; s. Vincent Larry and Alma Linda (Martinelli) O. BA, U. Rochester, 1975; MD, Cornell U., 1979. Diplomate Am. Bd. Internal Medicine, Am. Bd. Internal Medicine-Critical Care. From intern to resident N.Y. Hosp./Cornell Med. Ctr., 1979-82; from med. to sr. staff fellow Critical Care Medicine Dept. NIH, Bethesda, Md., 1982-87, sr. investigator, 1987—, fellowship dir., 1998—2003. Assoc. clin. prof. George Washington U., Washington, 1996—; adj. assoc. prof. U. Md., 2000—; dir. clin. rsch. tng. program NIH, 2000—, dir. office clin. rsch. tng. and med. edn., 2003—. Manuscript reviewer; contbr. articles to profl. jours., chpts. to books. Mem. adv. bd. Washington Project of the Arts/ Corcoran; bd. dirs. Cultural Devel. Corp. D.C., 2003—, Curator's Cir. Hirshhorn Mus. and Sculpture Garden, 2004-. Capt. USPHS, 1985—. Fellow ACP, Am. Coll. Critical Care Medicine (chair credentials com. 1992-94, bd. regents 1994-2000); mem. Cornell U. Med. Coll. Alumni Assn. (bd. dirs.), Am. Fedn. Clin. Rschs. (nat. coun. 1987-95, sec.-treas. ea. sect. 1987-91, chair-elect 1991-92, chair 1992-93), Am. Fedn. Clin. Rsch. Found. (trustee), Soc. Critical Care Medicine (co-chair symposium 1998, governing coun. 2000-04, sec. 2004-05, pres. elect, 2006), Alpha Omega Alpha. Democrat. Roman Catholic. Avocations: travel, studying Italian language, collecting contemporary american art. Home: 1661 Crescent Pl NW Apt 308 Washington DC 20009 Office: NIH Rm BIL401 9000 Rockville Pike Bldg 10 Bethesda MD 20892 Office Phone: 301-496-9425, 301-402-0563. Business E-Mail: fognibene@nih.gov.

**O'GORMAN, JAMES FRANCIS,** art educator, writer; b. St. Louis, Sept. 19, 1933; s. Paul Joseph and Dorothy Frances (Hogan) O'G.; m. Jean Baer, Feb. 9, 1957 (div. 1987); children: Christopher, Harold, Michael (dec.), Samuel; m. Susan Danly, Aug. 1, 1998. BArch, Washington U., St. Louis, 1956; MArch, U. Ill., 1961; PhD, Harvard U., 1966. Grace Slack McNeil prof. Am. art Wellesley Coll., Mass., 1975—2004, prof. emeritus, 2004—. Author: H.H. Richardson and His Office: Selected Drawings, 1973, This Other Gloucester, 1976, H.H. Richardson, Architectural Forms for an American Society, 1987; Three American Architects: Richardson, Sullivan and Wright, 1865-1915, 1991, Living Architecture: A Biography of H.H. Richardson, 1997, Accomplished in All Departments of Art: Hammatt Billings of Boston, 1818-1874, 1998, ABC of Architecture, 1998, Connecticut Valley Vernacular: The Vanishing Landscape and Architecture of the New England Tobacco Fields, 2002; co-author: Principles of Architectural History, 1968, The Architecture of Frank Furness, 1973, American Architects and Their Books to 1848, 2001, The Makers of Trinity Church in the City of Boston, 2004. Phila. Athenaeum fellow, 1985. Mem.: Am. Antiquarian Soc. Office Phone: 207-892-6273. Business E-Mail: jogorman@wellesley.edu.

**OGRA, PEARAY L.,** pediatrician, educator; b. Srinagar, Kashmir, India, Mar. 19, 1937; came to U.S., 1961, naturalized, 1969; s. Govinda Kaul and Gunvati (Daftari) O.; children: Sanjay, Monica. MB, Christian Med. Coll., Ludhiana, India, 1961: Intern Binghamton (N.Y.) Gen. Hosp., 1962-63; resident H Chgo, 1963 64 N Y U Bellevue Med Center, 1964-66, fellow in infectious diseases, 1966-68; asst. prof. pediatrics SUNY, Buffalo, 1968-71, assoc. prof. pediatrics and microbiology, 1972-74, prof., 1974-91; John Sealy disting. chair, prof. U. Tex. Med. Br., Galveston, 1991-2000, chmn. dept. pediatrics, 1991-99; prof. pediatrics Children's Hosp., Buffalo, 2000—. Dir. divsn. virology Children's Hosp. Buffalo, 1969-81, chief dept. infectious diseases, 1970-91; dir. Clin. Labs. Children's Hosp., 1985-90; mem. study sect. NIH, 1979-85, maternal child health com., 1987-91; mem. conslt. Bd. Internat. Pediat. Rsch. Found., Inc., 1984-89; mem. com. on vaccines for 21st century Inst. of Medicine NAS, 1997-2000, com. in infant formula, 2002; adv. bd. Internat. Vaccine Inst., Seoul, Rep. Korea, 2003—. Recipient E. Mead Johnson award for Pediatric Research Am. Acad. Pediatrics, 1978; Kalhana award Kashmir Sci. Culture and Soc., 1984; Stockton Kimball award SUNY, 1985; Buswell fellow, 1968-71. Fellow Royal Soc. Medicine, Assn. Am. Physicians, Am. Acad. Pediatrics, Am. Acad. Microbiology; mem. Am. Soc. Clin. Investigation, Soc. Pediatric Rsch., Infectious Disease Soc. Am., Soc. Exptl. Biology and Medicine, Am. Assn. Immunologists, Am. Soc. Microbiology, AAAS, Am. Fedn. Clin. Rsch., Am. Assn. Soc. Virology. Home: 163 Troy Del Way Williamsville NY 14221-4505 Office Phone: 716-878-7407. Business E-Mail: pogra@upa.chob.edu.

**O'GRADY, BEVERLY TROXLER,** investment executive, counselor; d. Robert Andrew and Beverly Beam (Barrier) Troxler; m. Robert Edward O'Grady, Aug. 6, 1966. BA, Saint Mary's Coll., 1963; MA, Columbia U., 1965. Exec. v.p. Wilkinson & Hottinger Inc., N.Y.C., 1973-94, Helvetia Capital Corp., N.Y.C., 1987-94; pres. Wilkinson O'Grady & Co., Inc., N.Y.C., 1994—. Mem. adv. bd. Charles Schwab Fin., San Francisco, 1991-93. Active Women's Nat. Rep. Club, N.Y.C., 1991-94; trustee Saint Mary's Coll., Notre Dame, Ind., 2002—, Cristo Key H.S., N.Y.C., 2004— Mem. Assn. Investment Mgrs., N.Y. Soc. Security Analysts, Women's Bond Club (pres. 1992-94), Univ. Club. Office: Wilkinson O'Grady & Co Inc 520 Madison Ave New York NY 10022-4213

**O'GRADY, DENNIS JOSEPH,** lawyer; b. Hoboken, N.J., Nov. 16, 1943; s. Joseph A. and Eileen O'Grady; m. Mary Anne Amoruso, Sept. 9, 1966 (div. Apr. 1984); 1 child, Kara Anne. AB, Seton Hall Coll., 1965; MA, U. So. Calif., 1969; JD, Rutgers U., 1973. Bar: N.J. 1973, U.S. Ct. Appeals (3d cir.) 1975, U.S. Dist. Ct. N.J., U.S. Supreme Ct. 2000. Ptnr. Riker, Danzig, Scherer, Hyland & Perretti, Newark, Trenton and Morristown, NJ, 1974—

Adj. asst. prof. of bus. law St. Peter's Coll., Jersey City, 1973—; adj. prof. law Rutgers U. Law Sch., 1997—. Fellow: Am. Coll. Bankruptcy Lawyers; mem.: ABA (bus./bankruptcy sect.), NJ Turnaround Assn. (bd. dirs.), Am. Bd. Cert. (faculty subcom.), Am. Bankruptcy Inst. (health career subcom., bd. profl. cert.), Fed. Bar Assn., N.J. State Bar Assn. (debtor/creditor sect.). Democrat. Roman Catholic. Office: Riker Danzig Scherer Hyland & Perretti 1 Speedwell Ave Morristown NJ 07960-6823 Office Phone: 973-538-0800. E-mail: dogrady@riker.com.

O'GRADY, JOHN JOSEPH, III, lawyer; b. N.Y.C., Mar. 21, 1933; s. John Joseph and Terese (O'Rourke) O'G.; m. Mary E. McHugh, June 28, 1958; children: Glennon, Ellen, Carol, Paul. AB, Holy Cross Coll., 1954; JD, Harvard U., 1957. Bar: N.Y. 1958. Assoc. Cadwalader, Wickersham & Taft, N.Y.C., 1958-66, ptnr., 1966-96, counsel, 1997—. Office: Cadwalader Wickersham & Taft One World Fin Ctr New York NY 10281 Office Phone: 212-504-6000.

O'GRADY, MICHAEL J., federal agency administrator; B, Alfred U.; D in Polit. Sci., U. Rochester. Sr. analyst Biopartisan Commn. on the Future of Medicare; health analyst Senate Fin. Com.; sr. rsch. dir. Project Hope's Ctr. for Health Affairs; sr. health economist Joint Econ. Com., US Congress; asst. sec. for planning and evaluation HHS, Washington, 2003.

OGREAN, DAVID WILLIAM, sports association executive; b. New Haven, Feb. 7, 1953; s. Richard Berton and Dorothy (Nystrom) O.; m. Maryellen Harvey, Aug. 10 1974; children: Matthew David, Tracy Erin, Dana Marie. BA in English cum laude, U Conn., 1974; MS in Film, Boston U., 1978. Asa S. Bushnell intern Ea. Coll. Athletic Conf., Centerville, Mass., 1977—78; dir. pub. rels. Amateur Hockey Assn. U.S., Colorado Springs, Colo., 1978—80; mng. editor Am. Hockey and Arena mag., 1979—80; comm. rep. ESPN, Inc., Bristol, Conn., 1980—83, program mgr., 1983—88; asst. exec. dir. for TV Coll. Football Assn., Boulder, Colo., 1988—90; dir. broadcasting U.S. Olympic Com., Colorado Springs, 1990—93; exec. dir. USA Hockey, Colorado Springs, 1993—99, 2005—; chmn. Colorado Springs Sports Corp., 1996—97; dep. exec. dir. mktg. U.S. Olympic Com., Colorado Springs, 1999—2000; pres. CEO Colorado Springs Sports Corp., 2000—02. Chmn. legis. com. U.S. Olympic Com., 1997-99, 00-04; exec. dir. USA Football, 2002-05. Home: 4110 San Felice Pointe Colorado Springs CO 80906 Office: USA Hockey 1775 Bob Johnson Dr Colorado Springs CO 80906 Business E-Mail: daveo@usahockey.org.

OGRETMEN, BESIM, science educator, molecular biologist, researcher; b. Ankara, Turkey, Jan. 5, 1966; s. Necati and Ayse Ogretmen; m. Sarita Ogretmen, Nov. 6, 1993; children: Ari Cem, Talia Bahar. PhD, Ill. Inst. of Tech., 1989—94. Post-doctoral fellow The U. of Chgo., 1994—96; rsch. assoc. Med. U. of SC., 1996—2000, asst. prof., 2000—. Contbr. articles to profl. jours. Rsch. grant, Nat. Cancer Inst., 2002. Mem.: Am. Soc. for Biochemistry and Molecular Biology, Am. Assn. for Cancer Rsch. Office: Med U of South Carolina 173 Ashley Ave Dept of Biochemistry Charleston SC 29425

OGSBURY, JAMES STANLEY, III, neurosurgeon, educator; s. James Stanley and Lucile (Becker) Ogsbury; m. Kathleen McBride Ogsbury. BS, Denison U., 1965; MD, Cornell U. Med. Coll., 1969. Diplomate Am. Bd. Neurosurgery. Intern, resident N.Y. Hosp., N.Y.C., 1969—71; resident U. Colo. Health Sci. Ctr., Denver, 1973—77, clin. asst. prof. neurosurgery, 1977—; clin. neurosurgeon Luth. Med. Ctr., Wheat Ridge, Colo., 1977—, St. Anthony's Hosp., Denver, 1977—. Co-med. dir. Colo. Preferred Physicians Orgn., Inc., Wheat Ridge, 2002—. Maj. USAF, 1971—73. Mem.: Colo. Neurosurg. Soc. Avocations: skiing, bicycling. Office: Rocky Mountain Neurosurgery 3550 Lutheran Pkwy W Wheat Ridge CO 80033 Office Phone: 303-431-6678.

OGUL, MORRIS SAMUEL, political science professor, consultant; b. Detroit, Apr. 15, 1931; s. Jack and Sarah (Zimmerman) O.; m. Eleanor Simon, Aug. 26, 1954. BA, Wayne State U., 1952; MA, U. Mich., 1953, PhD, 1958. Instr. polit. sci. U. Pitts., 1957-59, asst. prof., 1959-64, assoc. prof., 1964-67, prof., 1967-98, prof. emeritus, 1998—. Cons. U.S. Ho. of Reps., 1973, 83, U.S. Office Personnel Mgmt., Washington, 1975—, U.S. Senate, 1977 Author: (with William J. Keefe) American Legislative Process, 1964, 7th edit., 1989, 8th edit., 1993, 9th edit., 1997, 10th edit., 2001, Congress Oversees the Bureaucracy, 1976. Carnegie Corp. research grantee, 1965-68 Mem. Am. Polit. Sci. Assn., Midwest Polit. Sci. Assn. (council 1982-84), Pa. Polit. Sci. Assn. Democrat. Home: 1500 Cochran Rd Apt 814 Pittsburgh PA 15243-1068 Office: U Pitts Dept Polit Sci 4614 Posvar Hall Pittsburgh PA 15260-7454 E-mail: morrissogul@comcast.net.

OGUNLESI, ADEBAYO O., investment banker; b. Nigeria; m. Amelia Quist-Ogunlesi; children: Geoffrey, Carl. BA with honors, Oxford U.; MBA, Harvard U., 1978, JD magna cum laude, 1979. Law clerk Thurgood Marshall, Assoc. Justice, 1980—81; former atty., corp. practice group Cravath, Swaine & Moore, NY; joined as an assoc. First Boston Corp., 1983, named dir., 1989, mng. dir., head of project fin., 1993—97; mng. dir., head of project fin. and global energy Credit Suisse First Boston LLC (First Boston Corp. acquired by Credit Suisse in 1997, now Credit Suisse First Boston), 1999—2002; global head, investment banking Credit Suisse First Boston, NYC, 2002—, mem. oper. com., exec. bd. Lectr. Yale U. Scho. Orgn. and Mgmt. Trustee St. Bernard's Sch., NYC. Named one of the 50 Most Powerful Black Executives in Am., Fortune Mag., 2002; recipient Nigerian Lawyers Assn. Merit award, 2002. Mem.: D.C. Bar Assn. Office: Credit Suisse First Boston 11 Madison Ave New York NY 10010-3629

OGUNLEYE, TOLAGBE MONUOLA, publishing executive, educator, small business owner, editor; b. Bayshore, NY, Mar. 8, 1952; d. Fleming Harry and Flora Henrietta Wright; m. Israel Ojo Ogunleye, Jan. 12, 1984; children: Yetunde Monifa, Imhotep Olufemi, Adeola Bolade, Babatunde Akhenaten, Oduduwa Omoegbo. B, U. of Buffalo, 1972—74, M, 1974—78; D, Temple U., 1989—95. Tchr. NYC Bd. of Edn., 1983—90; asst. prof. U. of Ariz., 1995—99; owner/editor Cowrie Pub. Co., Abingdon, Pa., 1999—; tchr. Sch. Dist. of Phila., 2001—; adj. faculty Chestnut Hill Coll., Phila., 2005—. Dancer Olatunji African Dance Co., NYC, 1976—82. Author: (book) The African Roots of Jumping the Broom, African American Names and their Meanings; contbr. articles. Founder Coalition for Academic Excellence, Phila., 1992—95. Recipient Outstanding African Am. Woman, Alpha Phi Alpha, 1998. Mem.: Dyebanyani Initiated Women's Soc. (life). Avocations: ceramics, travel. Office: Phone: 267-496-3730. Personal E-mail: tolagbeogunleye52@hotmail.com. Business E-Mail: ogunleyet@chc.edu.

OGURCAK, JANICE L., museum director, educator; b. Hershey, Pa., Jan. 4, 1956; d. Christian S. and Lillian K. Seaman; m. Richard S. Ogurcak, Aug. 27, 1977; children: Christiann Ogurcak Bodwell, Jesse. BJ, Pa. State U., 1977. News reporter Sun-Gazette, Williamsport, Pa., 1977—91, lifestyle editor, 1991—2005; mus. dir. Peter J. McGovern Little League Mus., Williamsport, Pa., 2005—. Coll. newspaper advisor Lycourier of Lycoming Coll., Williamsport, Pa., 2000—; adj. coll. instr. Lycoming Coll., Williamsport, Pa., 2002—. V.p. Am. Bus. Women's Assn., Williamsport, Pa. Named Woman of the Yr., Am. Bus. Women's Assn., 1991; recipient Story of the Yr. award, Am. Cancer Soc., Pa., 1992. Mem.: Am. Assn. for State and Local History, Internat. Assn. of Sports Museums and Halls of Fame, Internat. Sports Heritage Assn., Small Museums Assn., Pa. Fedn. of Museums and Hist. Orgns., Am. Assn. of Museums. Office: Peter J McGovern Little League Mus PO Box 3485 525 Rte 15 Hwy South Williamsport PA 17701 Office Phone: 570-326-1921.

OH, ALICE, art educator; b. Seoul, Republic of Korea, Aug. 10, 1967; d. Seayoung Oh and Ockja Jang; m. Christifer F. Portner; 1 child, Isabel J. Portner. BFA, Temple U., 1991; MFA, Yale U., 1994. Assoc. prof. Moore Coll. Art &Design, Phila., 1997—. Fellow, Dew Found., Phila., 2000, Pa.

Coun. Arts, 2004; grantee, The Ludwig Found., Phila., 2000. Mem.: Phila. Inst. Contemporary Art, Coll. Art Assn. Office: Moore Coll Art & Design 20th and the Pky Philadelphia PA 19103 Office Phone: 215-568-4515 4096. Business E-Mail: aoh@moor.edu.

OH, ALLEN JAMES, lawyer; b. Warren, Mich., Feb. 5, 1973; s. Kong Ping and Soo Khuan Oh; m. Tiffany Ann Millay, June 16, 2001; children: Madison Rose Kathleen, Mikyla Renee. BS in Elec. Engring., U. Mich., 1993; JD, U. Pa., 1996. Bar: Minn. 1996, Mich. 1998, U.S. Patent and Trademark Office 1998. Patent atty. Moore, Hansen & Sumner, PLLP, Mpls., 2003—. Bd. dirs. EECS Alumni Soc. U. Mich., Ann Arbor, Mich.; presenter in field. Mem.: IEEE, Minn. State Bar Assn. (mem. assembly 2005—), Tau Beta Pi, Eta Kappa Nu (v.p. 1992—93). Libertarian. Episc. Office: Moore Hansen & Sumner PLLP 225 South Sixth Street Suite 4850 Minneapolis MN 55402 Office Phone: 612-332-8200. Business E-Mail: ajoh@mhsiplaw.com.

OH, ANGELA E., lawyer; b. LA, Sept. 8, 1955; BA, UCLA, 1977, MPH, 1981; JD, U. Calif., Davis, 1986. Bar: Calif. 1986. Lawyer, 1987—. Lawyer del. 9th Cir. Jud. Conf., 1995-96, lawyer rep.; mem. Senator Boxer's Jud. Noms. Com. for Ctrl. Dist. Calif., 1994-95; bd. dirs. Calif. Women's Law Ctr., Lawyers Mut. Ins. Co.; mem. cmty. adv. bd. First Interstate Bank Calif.; spkr. in field. Contbr. articles to profl. jours. and newspapers. Spl. counsel to the Assembly Spl. Com. on the L.A. Crisis. Mem. ABA, State Bar Calif., Korean-Am. Bar Assn. So. Calif. (pres.). L.A. County Bar Assn. Office: 8th Fl 601 W Fifth St Los Angeles CA 90071 Office Phone: 213-225-5825.

OH, HYUNGSEON, power systems researcher; b. Seoul, Dec. 25, 1968; arrived in U.S., 1997; s. Soonkeun and Youngsoon (Song) Oh; m. Youjin Wang, Mar. 29, 1997; 1 child, Sooyoun. BA, Yonsei U., 1992; PhD, Cornell U., Ithaca, NY, 2005. Rsch. and tchg. asst. Cornell U., Ithaca, 1999—2001, power sys. rschr., 2005—. Reviewer Hawaii Internat. Conf. Sys. Scis., Kauai, Hawaii, 2005. V.p. student assn. Yonsei Ceramic Engring., Seoul, 1990—91; mem. YMCA. Primary acct. munitions, squad leader, 1994—96, Hongchun, Korea. Recipient Spl. award, Yonsei U., 1988. Home: 1804 Hasbrouck Apts Ithaca NY 14850 Office: Cornell U 428 Phillips Hall Ithaca NY 14850 E-mail: hso1@cornell.edu.

OH, JOHN KIE-CHIANG, political science professor, academic administrator; b. Seoul, Korea, Nov. 1, 1930; came to U.S., 1954, naturalized, 1971; s. Sung-Jun and Duk-Cho (Kim) O.; m. Bonnie Cho, Sept. 5, 1959; children: Jane J., Marie J., James J. BS, Marquette U., 1957; postgrad., Columbia U., 1957-58; PhD, Georgetown U., 1962. Asst. prof. St. Thomas Coll., St. Paul, 1962-66; assoc. prof. polit. sci. Marquette U., Milw., 1967-71, prof., chmn., 1971-77, dean grad. sch., 1977-85; acad. v.p. Cath. U. Am., Washington, 1985-89, Banigan scholar, prof. dept. politics, 1990-2001, prof. emeritus, 2001—. Adviser Republic of Korea Embassy, 2001—03; nat. chmn. Asian Sect. Fulbright Hays Program. Author: Korea: Democracy on Trial, 1968, (with Peter Cheng et. al.) Emerging Roles of Asian Nations in the 1980's, 1979, Democratization and Economic Development in Korea, 1990, Korean Politics: The Quest for Democratization and Economic Development, 1999, The Korean Embassy in America, 2003; contbr. articles to profl. jours. Chmn. scholarship com. World Affairs Coun., 1976-78; mem. Wis. Gov.'s Commn. for UN, Madison, 1971-74; chmn. Korean Studies com., Assn. Asian Studies, 1975-76. Grantee Hill Found., 1963, Relm Found., 1968, Social Sci. Rsch Coun., 1973, Am. Coun. Learned Socs., 1973. Mem. Am. Polit. Sci. Assn., Assn. Asian Studies, Internat. Polit. Sci. Assn., Midwest Conf. Asian Affairs (pres. 1970-71), Assn. Cath. Colls. and Univs. (bd. dirs. 1983-87), Indian Spring Country Club (bd. govs. 2000). Roman Catholic. Home: 8807 Maxwell Dr Potomac MD 20854-3123 Personal E-mail: jnboh@aol.com.

OH, JOONG-HWAN, sociologist; b. Ku-Chang, Kyungnam Province, Republic of Korea, Aug. 15, 1963; s. Bong-Ok Oh and Jung-Hwa Kim; m. Kyung-Hwa Lee, June 23, 1992; children: Jenny, Janet, Justin. BA, Pusan Nat. U., 1986; PhD, U. S.C., Columbia, 1993—99. Asst. prof., sociology Hunter Coll., N.Y.C., 1999—2003, assoc. prof., sociology, 2004—. Dir., grad. social rsch. program & acting dir., asian am. studies program Hunter Coll., 2003—05. Contbr. papers to profl. jours. and pubs. Office: Sociology Dept Hunter Coll 695 Park Ave New York NY 10021 Office Phone: 212-772-5643. Business E-Mail: joonghwan.oh@hunter.cuny.edu.

OH, JUNG HUN, computer engineer; b. Jeonnam, Korea (South), Dec. 25, 1971; s. Seung Ok Oh and Dong Jin Choi; m. Young Bun Kim, Dec. 1, 1972; 1 child, Yu Na. BS, Soongsil U., 1995, MS, 1997; postgrad., U. Tex., Arlington, 2003—06. Sys. engr. Jinro Industries, Seoul, Republic of Korea, 1997—98; sr. software engr. Willtech, Seoul, 1997—2002, Sk C&C, Seoul, Republic of Korea, 2002—03; rsch. scholar U. Tex., Arlington, 2004—. Software engring. tng. Satyam, Hyderabad, India, 2003; product adn. Willtech, Seoul, Korea (South), 1998—2002. Contbr. articles to profl. jours. Fellow Hermann Hellmu, U. Tex. at Arlington, 2003; scholar Grad. Study Abroad scholar, Korea Sci. and Engring. Found., 2003. Mem.: IEEE (assoc.), Internat. Assn. Engring. (assoc.). Democrat-Npl. Christian. Avocations: travel, golf, basketball. Office Phone: 817-272-7526.

OH, MARK EDWARD, minister; s. Kap Soo and Boonhak Oh; m. Rosemary McGuire, Aug. 20, 1965; children: Christopher Douglas, Jonathan David. BA, Keimyung U., 1958; MA, San Francisco Theol. Sem., 1963; MRE, New Orleans Bapt. Theol. Sem., 1964; MDiv, We. Sem. Portland, 1968; PhD, Calif. Grad. Sch. Theology, 1971; D of Ministry, Fuller Theol. Sem., 1988. Ordination Crescent-Bay Bapt. Assn., CA, 1968. Pastor Internat. Bible Ch., L.A., 1972—. Pres. Christ Bible Coll., L.A., 2001—. Mem.: Am. Assn. Christian Counselors (charter). Office Phone: 213-382-7925.

OH, MYOUNGHO, computer scientist, educator; b. Pusan, South Korea, Dec. 11, 1960; s. Suntae Oh and Bokcheol Baek; m. Kyungyoon Shim, Aug. 27, 1989; children: Hyunju, Hyunwoo. BS, Korea Mil. Acad., Seoul, 1984; MS, Oreg. State U., Corvallis, 1988; PhD, KAIST, Taejon, 1996. Chmn. dept. comp sci Korea Mil. Acad., 2000—04, assoc. prof. computer sci., prof. info. sci. Asst. mgr. acad. bd. Korea Mil. Acad., Seoul, 1990—91, asst. dir. computer ctr., 1997—98, dir. edni. development, 2005—. Author: (books) Introduction to Computer Science, Improvement of Computer Efficiency, Differential Equation, Computer Network, C Language, Practical Use of Computers, Computer Science; contbr. articles to profl. jours. Lt. col. South Korea Mil. Decorated True Soldier of Yr. Korean Army; recipient Honor Prize, Prime Min. of Korea, 1984, Edn. award, Korea Mil. Acad., 2001, Best Achievement Prof. award, 2002, 2003. Mem.: Korea Info. Soc., Korea Inst. of Mil. Sci. and Tech., Korea Math. Soc. Buddhism. Avocations: running, swimming. Office: Korea Mil Acad Dept Electronics & Info Nowon Gu PO Box 77 Gongneung Dong Seoul 139-799 Republic of Korea Office Phone: 02 2197 2877. Business E-Mail: mhoh@kma.ac.kr.

OH, SANDRA, actress; b. Nepean, Ont., Can., July 20, 1971; m. Alexander Payne, Jan. 1, 2003. Actor: (films) Double Happiness, 1994, Bean, 1997, The Princess Diaries, 2001, Big Fat Liar, 2002, Full Frontal, 2002, Long Life, Happiness & Prosperity, 2002, Rick, 2003, Under the Tuscan Sun, 2003, Break a Leg, 2003, Wilby Wonderful, 2004, Sideways, 2004 (Screen Actors Guild Award, outstanding performance by cast in motion picture, 2005), 8 Minutes to Love, 2004, Hard Candy, 2005, Break a Leg, 2005, Cake, 2005, 3 Needles, 2005, Sorry, Haters, 2005, The Night Listener, 2006; (TV series) Arli$$, 1996—2002 (CableACE Award, 1997), Grey's Anatomy, 2005— (Best Performance by an Actress in a Supporting Role in a Series, Mini-Series or Motion Picture Made for TV, Hollywood Fgn. Press Assn. (Golden Globe), 2006, Outstanding Performance by a Female Actor in a Drama Series, Screen Actors Guild award, 2006); (TV miniseries) Further Tales of the City, 2001.*

OH, SANGYOON, research scientist; b. Seoul, Republic of Korea, July 7, 1971; s. Choonjae Oh and Sunmin Park. BS in Engring., Sungkyunkwan U., Seoul, 1994; MS, Syracuse U., NY, 1999; PhD, Ind. U., Bloomington, 2006. Project engr. Hansol Paper Co., Seoul, Democratic Peoples Republic of Korea, 1995—96; rsch. asst. NE Parallel Archs. Ctr. Syracuse U.,

1999—2000; rsch. asst. computational sci. and info. tech. Fla. State U., Tallahassee, 2000—01; rsch. asst. cmty. grids lab. Ind. U., Bloomington, 2001—06, vis. rschr cmty. grids lab, 2006—. Contbr. articles to profl. jours. V.p. young adult group Korean United Meth. Ch., Bloomington, 2003—04, youth min., 2005—06. Pvt., 1991, Republic of Korea Mil. Grad. Rsch. scholar, Syracuse U., 1999—2000, Fla. State U., 2000—01, Ind. U., 2001—06. Mem.: IEEE. Achievements include design of handheld flexible representation architecture for web service on mobile devices; development of handheld message service for light weight messaging on mobile devices; tango interactive collaboration system; research in collaboration framework for universal accessibility. Avocations: golf, tennis, history. Office: Community Grids Lab 501 N Morton St Bloomington IN 47401 Office Phone: 812-856-0751.

OH, SEONGSHIK, physicist, researcher; b. Republic of Korea, May 31, 1970; BS with honors, Seoul Nat. U., Korea, 1992, MS, 1994; PhD, U. Ill., Urbana, 2003. Rsch. assoc. NIST, Boulder, Colo., U. Ill., 2003—04. 1st Lt. Korean Air Force, 1994—97, Korea. Recipient Outstanding Poster Presentation award, Dept. of Commerce, 2006; Academic Excellence scholarship, Bosung-Oh Scholarship Found., 1988-1990, Seoul Nat. U., 1990-1992, Ambassadorial scholarship, Rotary Internat. Found., 1997-2000. Achievements include development of first epitaxial qubit with a single-crystal tunnel barrier; invention of first microfabricated doping control scheme for mixed-valent metal oxides; discovery of unconventional superconductor-insulator transition in cuprates. Office: NIST Quantum Devices Group 81703 325 Broadway Boulder CO 80305 Office Phone: 303-497-4655. Office Fax: 303-497-4311. Business E-Mail: seongshik@gmail.com.

OH, SOOJIN SUSAN, elementary school educator; b. Seoul, Republic of Korea, July 7, 1980; d. Hyun Kyung and Eunsim Oh. BA summa cum laude, U. Pa., 2003, MS in Edn., 2004. Cert. tchr. elem. edn. Pa. Info. tech. asst. mgr. Coll. Ho. Computing, U. Pa., Phila., 1999—2003; acad. and career advisor U. Pa., Phila., 2000—03; product mgmt. intern Chubb Group of Ins. Cos., Washington, 2001; pub. svc. intern Korean Am. Coalition, Washington, 2001; tchg. asst. Wharton Sch., U. Pa., Phila., 2002—03; strategic mktg. intern Toyota Motor Corp., Torrance, Calif., 2002; rsch. analyst U. Pa. Grad. Sch. Edn., Phila., 2004; head tchr. grade 1 Abington Friends Sch., Jenkintown, Pa., 2004—; ednl. cons. Laurus Enterprise, 2005. Mem. math curriculum planning and devel. com. Abington Friends Sch., Jenkintown, Pa., 2004—, mem. acad. planning com., 2004—; internat. intern liaison; ethnographer Hist. Soc. Pa., Phila., 2004; transl., interpreter interviews, press confs., articles; presenter in field. Editor rev. bd.: Urban Edn. Jour.; editl. bd. Dear Theopilus Newsletter; contbr. articles to profl. jours. Local area coord. Habitat for Humanity, Reseda, Calif., 1995—99; liaison Tree People, Beverly Hills, 1995—99; chpt. mem. UNICEF, Phila., 2003—; curriculum developer Quo Vadis West Philly Edn. Outreach Program, Phila., 2004—; vol. nursery, maternity, oncology, pediat., newborn ICU Valley Presbyn. Hosp., Van Nuys, Calif., 1993—99; liaison Salvation Army, Canoga Park, Calif., 1995—99; pub. svc. intern Korean Am. Coalition, Washington, 2001—05; women's ministry, small group ministry leader Emmanuel Ch. in Phila., 1999—; pianist, ministry dir., youth group pres. Calvary Presbyn. Ch., Granada Hills, Calif., 1992—99. Recipient rsch. grant, Samuel S. Fels Fund, 2004, Penn Alumni scholarship, U. Pa., 1999—2003, Korean Ambassadorial scholarship, Embassy of Republic of Korea, 2003, Nat. Merit Commended scholar, Edn. Testing Svcs., 1999, Nat. AP scholar, 1999, Nat. Leadership and Svc. award, USAA Ednl. Found., 1997, rsch. grant, U. Pa. Grad. Sch. of Edn., 2004, All Am. scholarship, USAA Ednl. Found., 1996, Nat. Math. award, U.S. Acade. Achievement, 1997, UCLA Chancellor's scholarship, 1999, UCLA Alumni Assn. scholarship, 1999, U. Calif. Berkeley Regent's scholarship, 1999, Trustees' Scholarship, Boston U., 1999, Nat. Prudential Leadership Award, Prudential Fin., 1998, Toyota Cmty. scholarship, Toyota Motor U.S.A., 1999—2003, Tylenol Cmty. scholarship, Johnson & Johnson, 1999, Korean Am. scholarship, Korean Am. Scholarship Found., 2000, 2001, 2002, 2003, 2004, Ca. Golden State Scholar, Central Daily News scholar, 2001, Scott Kyungmo Kim Scholarship, 2004; scholar Korean Am. Student Leader of the Yr. award, Korean Heritage Found. Leadership award, Korean Sr. Citizens Mut. Club, 2001;, Korea Times Scholarship, 2000, 2002, Klingenstein Summer Inst. fellow, Columbia U. Tchrs. Coll., 2000. Mem.: North Am. Reggio Emilia Alliance (assoc.), Nat. Assn. for Edn. of Young Children (assoc.), Key Club Internat. (life; pres., v.p., dist. rep. 1995—99, Kiwanis Internat. Cmty. Leadership award 1999, Disting. Leader of the Yr. award 1995), Kiwanis (pres. local chpt. Key Club 1995—99), Pi Gamma Mu (life), Ephebian Honor Soc. (life), Golden Key Internat. Honor Soc. (life; pres. 2002—03), Psi Chi (life; pres., v.p., fin. dir. 2000—03). Achievements include research in educational policy, research and practice across K-12 schools and higher education institutions in China; key factors that facilitate effortless recall, accuracy and memory retention for simple multiplication; historical, cultural, and sociopolitical forces that have shaped the West Philadelphia neighborhood; featured in various newspapers such as: LA Times, Korea Times, Dong-A Daily News, Central Daily News. Avocations: photography, travel, interior design, literature, classical concerts. Office: Abington Friends Sch 575 Washington Ln Jenkintown PA 19046 Office Phone: 215-886-4350.

OH, SO-RYEOK, research scientist; b. Pusan, Republic of Korea, Nov. 20, 1970; arrived in U.S., 2001; s. Kum-Soon Jeon; m. Hyun-Ju Kim, Jan. 9, 1999; children: Hyoung-In, Joseph Soo-in. BS, Pusan Nat. U., 1997, MS, 1999; PhD, U. of Del., Newark, 2006. Rsch. assoc. Samsung, Changwon, Republic of Korea, 2000—01; rsch. asst. U. Del., Newark, 2001—06; postdoctoral fellow U. Mich., Ann Arbor, 2006—. Vis. scholar Australian Def. Force Acad., Canberra, Australia, 2004. Contbr. articles to profl. jours. Univ. campus leadership The Navigators, Pusan, 1990—93. Recipient Competitive Grad. fellowship, U. of Del., 2004, Rsch. Assistantship, 2002—05, Tchg. Assistantship, 2001—02, NSF Travel Award for IEEE Internat. Conf. on Robotics and Automation, Barcelona, Spain, 2005; grantee NSF Exch. Rsch. Grant, U. of NSW, ADFA, Australia, 2004. Mem.: ASME (Student Travel award for Am. Control Conf. 2005, ASME-DSCD Student Travel grants for 2004 ASME Internat. Mech. Engring. Congress and R&D Expo 2004), IEEE. Achievements include design of in-house 6DOF Cable Suspended Robot; flapping wing flying robots; research in dynamic modeling and robust controller design of a two-stage parallel cable robot; cable suspended planar robots with redundant cables: controllers with positive tensions; dual stage planar cable robot; dynamic modeling and design of a robust Controller with positive inputs; Feasible Workspace of a Set Point Controller for a Cable Suspended Robot with Input Constraints and Disturbances; Computationally Efficient Feasible Set Points Generation and Control of a Cable Robot. Home: 93 Amstel Ave E15 Newark DE 19711 Office: U Mich Marine Sys Lab Ann Arbor MI 48109-2145 Office Phone: 302-831-6536, 302-384-3929. Office Fax: 302-831-3619. E-mail: soryeok@yahoo.com.

OH, TAI KEUN, business educator, consultant; b. Seoul, Korea; came to U.S., 1958, naturalized, 1969; BA, Seiju U., 1957; MA, No. Ill. U., 1961; MLS, U. Wis., 1965, PhD, 1970; m. Gretchen Brenneke, Dec. 26, 1964; children: Erica, Elizabeth, Emily. Asst. prof. mgmt. Roosevelt U., Chgo., 1969-73; assoc. prof. Calif. State U., Fullerton, 1973-76, prof. mgmt., 1976—2001; assoc. prof. mgmt. emeritus, 2001—; vis. prof. U. Hawaii, 1983-84, 86, U. Nuertingen, Germany, 1996-97, 99; advisor Pacific Asian Mgmt. Inst., U. Hawaii; internat. referee Asia-Pacific Jour. Mgmt., 1990—; cons. Calty Design Rsch., Inc. subs. Toyota Motor Corp.; guest lectr. Chiba U. Commerce, Japan; cons., spkr. in field. Named Outstanding Prof., Sch. Bus. Adminstrn. and Econs., Calif. State U., Fullerton, 1976, 78. Tai Keun Oh received early tenure and jump promotion to full professor in 1976 before completing the regular probationary period at California State University Fullerton, which is regarded as one of the more rapid promotions in the California State University system. He helped over 100 organizations solve complex human resource and management problems over the course of his career and has served as consultant to Calty Design Research, one of Toyota Motor Corporation's think tanks, for over 25 years. Grandfather, Cung Sun Oh, was the first Western trained medical doctor in Korea; he came to the United States in 1902 to begin his education at Center College of Kentucky and completed his medical training at the University of Louisville in 1909. In Korea, he founded a Presbyterian church and high school in Kunsan and then pioneered in the area of social services by establishing Kyungsan orphanage in 1919 and a home for the elderly. In Seoul, he became associated with Severance Hospital and Yonsei University Medical School and eventually became its Korean president. He died at 85 as one of the most respected men in Korea. NSF grantee; 1968-69, recipient Exceptional Merit Svc. award Calif. State U., 1984, Meritorious Performance and Profl. Promise award Calif. State U., 1987. Editl. bd. Acad. Mgmt. Rev. 1978-81; contbg. author: Ency. Profl. Mgmt., 1978, Handbook of Management 1985; contbr. articles to profl. jours.; Mem. Acad. Mgmt Home: 2044 E Eucalyptus Ln Brea CA 92821-5911 E-mail: toh@fullerton.edu.

**OH, WILLIAM,** physician; b. The Philippines, May 22, 1931; came to U.S., 1958, naturalized, 1970; s. Bun Kun and Chay Suat (Lim) Oh; m. Mary Oh, June 4, 1960; children: Kenneth Albert, Kerstin Amy. MD, U. Santo Tomas, Phillipines, 1958; MA (hon.), Brown U., 1974; DSc (hon.), R.I. Coll., 1985. Diplomate Am. Bd. Pediatrics, Am. Bd. Neonatal Perinatal Medicine. Intern Deaconess Hosp., Milw., 1958-59; resident in pediatrics Michael Reese Hosp., Chgo., 1959-63; fellow in neonatology Kavolinska Inst., Stockholm, 1963-65; dir. neonatology Michael Reese Hosp., Chgo., 1965-69; dir. neonatology, assoc. prof. pediatrics UCLA, 1969-73, prof., 1973-74; prof. pediatrics and obstetrics Brown U., Providence, 1974-88, Sylvia Kay Hassenfeld prof. pediatrics, chmn. dept., 1989—2003; pediatrician-in-chief Women and Infants Hosp. of R.I., Providence, 1974—89, R.I. Hosp.; prof., chmn. dept. pediatrics Brown U. 1989—2003; prof. pediat. Women and Infants' Hosp., Brown U., 2003—. Mem. NIH study sect. on human embryology and devel., chmn., 1985-93, mem. pediatric test com. Bd. Med. Exam., 1985-89; mem. sub-bd. of neonatal-perinatal medicine Am. Bd. Pediatrics, 1982-88; chair com. on Fetus and Newborn, Am. Acad. Pediatrics; mem. Nat. Adv. Coun. for Child Health, 1995-99. Author book in field; contbr. chpts. to books, numerous articles to profl. jours.; editor profl. jour. Adv. com. Nat. Found. of March of Dimes. NIH grantee. Mem. Am. Pediatric Soc., Am. Acad. Pediatrics (fetus and newborn com. 1986-90), Soc. Pediatric Research, Perinatal Research Soc. (pres. 1981), Am. Inst. Nutrition, Fedn. Am. Socs. Exptl. Biology. Roman Catholic. Home: 24 Robbins Dr Barrington RI 02806-2612 Office: Dudley Providence RI 02905-4923 Office Phone: 401-274-1100. Business E-mail: woh@wihri.org.

**OH, YONGSEOK,** physicist; b. Mokpo, Jeonnam, Republic of Korea, Apr. 2, 1965; arrived in US, 2004; s. Deokgyo Oh and Chisook Kim; m. Jisoon Noh; 1 child, Suhoon. BS, Seoul Nat. U., Republic of Korea, 1987, PhD, 1993. Postdoctoral rsch. assoc. Taiwan Nat. U., Taipei, 1993—95; Alexander von Humboldt fellow Tech. U. of Munich, Garching, Germany, 1995—97; postdoctoral rschr. Seoul Nat. U., 1997—2000; postdoctoral rsch. fellow Inst. of Physics, Academia Sinica, Nankang, Taiwan, 2000; rsch. asst. prof. Yonsei U., Seoul, 2000—04; postdoctoral rsch. assoc. U. of Ga., Athens, 2004—. Office: U Ga Dept Physics and Astronomy Athens GA 30602 Office Phone: 706-542-2849. Office Fax: 706-542-2492. E-mail: yoh@physast.uga.edu.

**OH, YUN,** oncologist; s. Jai Keun Oh and Chung Hi Kang; m. Judy Hye-Young Jo, Mar. 23, 1996; children: Christopher Sae Joon, Richard Sae Jung. BA, Yale U., New Haven, Conn., 1984; MD, Dartmouth-Brown U., Providence, RI, 1988—88. Diplomate Providence, RI, 1988. Transitional internship in oncology Roger Williams Med. Ctr., Providence, 1988—89; gen. surgery resident George Wash. U. Hosp., Washington, 1989—92; clin. assoc. fellow Surgery Br., Nat. Cancer Inst., Bethesda, Md., 1992—94; internal medicine resident U. of Tex. Health Sci. Ctr., Houston, 1994—97, 1994—96; med. oncology fellow M.D. Anderson Cancer Ctr., Houston, 1997—2000, 1996—2000, asst. prof., thoracic med. oncology, 2000—; asst. prof. M.D. Anderson Cancer Ctr., Thoracic Med. Oncology. Organizer, lung cancer brain metastasis working group M.D. Anderson Cancer Ctr., 2005—. Recipient Clifton D. Howe award for Clin. Excellence, U. of Tex. M. D. Anderson Cancer Ctr., 1999—2000, Physician Scientist Tract, M.D. Anderson Cancer Ctr., 2000—03; Bioimmunotherapy Fellowship Tng. grant, Nat. Cancer Inst., 1998—2000. Mem.: Am. Soc. of Clinical Oncology, Am. Assn. for Cancer Rsch. Achievements include research in medical therapies for lung cancer brain metastases; novel treatments for oligometastatic lung cancer; yogurt bacteria for oral protein delivery; patents for therapeutic random sequence DNA; therapeutic sheared random DNA; research in clinical development of novel anti-cancer drugs. Office: MD Anderson Cancer Ctr Unit 432 1515 Holcombe Blvd Houston TX 77030 Office Phone: 713-792-6363. E-mail: ywoh@mdanderson.org.

**O'HAGAN, DESMOND BRIAN,** artist; b. Wiesbaden, Germany, July 17, 1959; Student, U. N.Mex., 1977—79; AA, Colo. Inst. Art, 1982. Graphic designer Hesdorfer-Hesse, Denver, 1982—85; pvt. practice Denver, 1985—. Contbr. articles to profl. jours.; one-man shows include Desmond Ottagam Studio, Denver, Colo., 1997—2006, E.S. Lawrence Gallery, Aspen, Colo., 2005, exhibitions include Pastel Soc. Am., Nat. Arts Club, NYC, 1987, 1988, 1997—99, Salmagundi Club, 1996, Colo. Gov.'s Invitational Art Show, Lovelane Mus., 2002—06, Pastel Soc. Am., Xi'an, China, 1997, Colo. History Mus., 1996—97, Represented in permanent collections Denver Pub. Libr., exhibited in group shows at Galleria Prova, Tokyo, 1998, Artists of America, Denver Rotary Club Show, 1996, 1997, 1998. Workshop instr., show judge Southeastern Pastel Soc., Ga., 2000, Pastel Soc. N.Mex., 2001, Pastel Soc. S.W., Tex., 2003. Recipient George Innes Jr. Meml. award, Salmagundi Club, 1996, Mrs. Pearl Kalikow award, Pastel Soc. Am., 1998, Prix'd Pastel award, Internat. Assn. Pastel Soc., 1999. Mem.: Internat. Assn. Pastel Soc. (master cir.), Colo. Pastel Soc., Pastel Soc. Am. (master pastelist). Avocations: billiards, running. Office Phone: 303-691-3736. E-mail: desmondohaganfineart@earthlink.net.

**O'HAGAN, JAMES JOSEPH,** lawyer; b. Chgo., Dec. 29, 1936; s. Francis James and Florence Agnes (Dowgiela) O'H.; m. Suzanne Elizabeth Weigand, June 28, 1958; children: Timothy, Karen, Peggy, Kevin. B in Commerce, De Paul U., 1958, JD, 1962. Sr. ptnr. O'Hagan Spencer, Chgo., 2006—. Mem. Cook County Pres.'s Com. on the Cts. for the 21st Century, chmn. suburban subcom., 1998—2000; lawyer Chgo. Claim Mgrs. Assn., 1992—; chmn. USLaw Network, Inc., 2001—03, mem. exec. com., bd. dirs. Mem. ABA, Ill. Bar Assn. Chgo. Bar Assn., Am. Bd. Trial Advocates, Internat. Assn. Def. Coun., Def. Rsch. Inst., Profl. Liability Underwriters Soc. Roman Catholic. Avocations: golf, tennis, physical conditioning, painting, reading. Office: O'Hagan Spencer 55 W Wacker Dr Ste 1400 Chicago IL 60601 Office Phone: 312-422-6121. Business E-mail: johagan@ohaganspencer.net.

**O'HAGAN, WILLIAM D.,** metal products manufacturing executive; Grad., Rutgers U., Harvard U. V.p., gen. mgr. NIBCO Inc.; with Cambridge-Lee Industries, Phelps Dodge Copper Products Co.; pres. Mueller Industries, Wichita, Kans., 1992—. Office: Mueller Industries Inc 8285 Tournament Dr Ste 150 Memphis TN 38125*

**O'HALLORAN, THOMAS ALPHONSUS, JR.,** retired physicist, retired researcher; b. Bklyn., Apr. 13, 1931; s. Thomas Alphonsus Sr. and Nora (Sheehan) O'H.; m. Barbara Joyce Hug, June 4, 1954; children: Theresa Joyce, Maureen Ann, Kevin Thomas, Patrick Joseph. Student, San Jose State U., 1948-50; BS in Physics & Math., Creighton U., 1953, MS in Physics, 1954; PhD, U. Calif., Berkeley, 1963. Rsch. asst. Lawrence Berkeley Lab., U. Calif., 1963-64; rsch. fellow Harvard U., Cambridge, Mass., 1964-66; asst. prof. physics U. Ill., Urbana, 1966-68, assoc. prof., 1968-70, prof., 1970-93, prof. emeritus, 1993—; vis. scholar U. Utah, Salt Lake City, 1990-93, rsch. prof. physics, 1993-97; ret., 1997. Vis. scientist Lawrence Berkeley Lab., U. Calif., 1979-80. Contbr. numerous articles on elem. particle physics to profl. jours. Lt. USNR, 1954-58. Guggenheim fellow, 1979-80. Fellow Am. Phys. Soc. Home: 4614 Ledgemont Dr Holladay UT 84124-4735

**OHAMA, GARY LOUIS,** dental ceramist; b. Abington, Pa., Dec. 9, 1948; s. Benjamin Saburo and Kuniko Hirokawa Ohama; 1 child from previous marriage, Jennifer Suzanne. BS, Pa. State U., 1971. Owner, ceramist Ohama

Dental Studio, Inc., Abington, 1973—91; finisher Nakashima Woodworkers, New Hope, Pa., 2000—02; dental ceramist Ft. Washington (Pa.) Dental Lab. 2002—. Cons., lectr. on dental ceramics N.Y. Dental Lab. Congress, Dentsply, Internat., Ney Co., Sterngold, Colo., others. Aikido instr. Served with USAR, 1971—77. Recipient Outstanding Alumni award, Pa. State U., 1982. Methodist. Achievements include development of internal translucency and effects of refractive index in dental ceramics; of special oil, and oil/polyurethane wood finishing processes. Avocation: Aikido instructor. Home: 207 Quigley Ave Willow Grove PA 19090 Office Phone: 212-628-4944.

**OHANIAN, BERNARD JAY,** writer, editor; b. Tokyo, Apr. 22, 1956; came to U.S., 1956; s. Abraham Sam and Bernadine Jeanette (Preis) O.; m. Catharine Greta Vollmer, July 2, 1983 (div. 1990); m. Kathleen Karen Kelly, Aug. 14, 1994; children: Rafael Kelly, Sofia Kelly. Student, U. Degli Studi, Pisa, Italy, 1977-78; BA, U. Calif., Berkeley, 1980. Editor Newsfront Internat., Oakland, Calif., 1978-81; editor-in-chief Mediafile, San Francisco, 1981-83; corr. RKO Radio, Rome, 1983-84; English lang. editor Inter Press Svc., Rome, 1983-84; sr. editor Rip N Read News Svc., San Francisco, 1984-85, Mother Jones mag., San Francisco, 1985-88; sr. editor, features MacWeek mag., San Francisco, 1988-89; editl. dir. RX Media Publs., Sausalito, Calif., 1989-90; mem. editl. staff Nat. Geographic mag., Washington, 1992-95, editl. dir. internat. edits. to assoc. editor, 1995—2006; editl. dir. AARP Publications. Freelance editl. cons., 1990—; vis. faculty mem. Sch. of Journalism U. Calif., Berkeley, 1990. Author (books) Baseball in America, 1991, A Day in the Life of Italy, 1990; editor (books) The Power to Heal, 1990, A Day in the Life of Ireland, 1991; caption writer (book) In Pursuit of Ideas, 1992; editorial cons., caption writer: The Face of Mercy, 1993. Bd. dirs. Media Alliance, San Francisco, 1986-93, pres., 1988-92. Recipient Best Feature Article award Western Publs. Assn., 1990. Mem. Am. Soc. Mag. Editors, U. Calif. Berkeley Alumni Assn. (life). Avocations: travel, basketball, photography, current affairs, opera. Office: AARP Publications 601 E St NW Washington DC 20049 Office Phone: 202-434-6804. Personal E-mail: bernardohanian@aol.com.

**OHANIAN, MIHRAN JACOB,** nuclear engineer, educator, dean, researcher; b. Istanbul, Turkey, Aug. 7, 1933; came to U.S., 1954, naturalized, 1967; s. Mark and Mary Catherine (Sayabalian) O.; m. Sandra Jean Blair, Apr. 22, 1962; children: Heather Jean Allen, Holly Lynn Welty. BSE.E. with high honors, Robert Coll. Engring. Sch., Istanbul, 1956; M.E.E., Rensselaer Poly. Inst., 1960, PhD in Nuclear Engring. and Sci., 1963. Lectr. nuclear engring. Rensselaer Poly. Inst., 1963, instr., 1958-62; asst. prof. nuclear engring. U. Fla., Gainesville, 1964-67, assoc. prof., 1967-70, prof., 1970-2001, prof. emeritus, 2001—, chmn. dept., 1969-79, assoc. dir. Engring. and Indsl. Expt. Sta., 1977-99, assoc. dean for rsch., 1979-90, assoc. dean for adminstrn. and planning, 1990-91, assoc. dean for rsch. and adminstrn., 1991-98, interim v.p. rsch., dean of grad. sch., 1998-99, pres. Rsch. Found., 1998-99, interim dean Coll. of Engr., assoc. v.p. Engring. and Indsl. Experiment Station, 1999-2001; sabbatical leave Inst. Energy Analysis, Oak Ridge, 1976-77, on assignment, 1977-78. Cons. Fla. Power Corp., Batelle Meml. Inst., Fla. Nuc. Assocs., Oak Ridge Nat. Lab., Inst. Energy Analysis, Argonne Nat. Lab., Savannah River Lab., U. Va., Tex. Higher Edn. Bd., NSF; U. Fla. rep. U.S. Nuc. Energy Inst., 1972-2001, mem. adv. coun., 1972-80; U. Fla. rep. to Oak Ridge Assoc. Univs., 1972-76; mem. engring. accreditation commn. Accreditation Bd. Engring. and Tech., 1984-88; mem. rev. com. reactor analysis and safety divsn. Argonne Nat. Lab., 1982-88, chmn. 1986-87, mem. rev. com. reactor engring. divsn., 1992-2001; mem. adv. com. Consol. Fuel Reprocessing Program Oak Ridge Nat. Lab., 1982-88; mem. com. on univ. rsch. reactors Energy Engring. Bd., NRC, 1986-88; mem. U.S. Dept. Energy's Adv. Com. on Nuc. Facility Safety (ACNFS), 1988-90; bd. dirs., chmn. Fla. Inst. Phosphate Rsch., 1990-2001. Contbr. articles to profl. jours. Trustee Fla. Defenders of the Environment, 1969-71, treas., 1969-70, mem., 1969-80. Recipient valor medal Am. Legion, 1966, Disting. Faculty award Fla. Blue Key, 1984; Alumnus fellow Rensselaer Poly. Inst., 1994. Fellow AAAS, Am. Nuclear Soc. (v.p., pres.-elect 1989-90, pres. 1990-91, bd. dirs. 1974-77, 84-93, vice chmn., chmn. edn. divsn. 1975-76, exec. com. nuclear fuel cycle divsn. 1978-81, mem. profl. devel. and accreditation com., chmn. tech. program of internat. conf. Washington, 1980, mem. nominating com. 1980-81, 87-88, chmn., 1991-92, exec. com., 1986-92, honors and awards com. 1997—, chmn. 2004—, Exceptional Svc. award 1980, adv. editor Nuclear Sci. and Engring. Jour. 1989— hon. chmn. ann. conf. 1997, hon. chmn. 10th Internat. Conf. on Robotics, 2004), Engr. Coun. Profl. Devel. (dir. 1976-78), Am. Assn. Engring. Soc. (awards com. 1985-86, bd. dir. 1990-91, exec. com. 1990-95, sec.-treas., 1992, chair-elect 1993, chair 1994, chair nominating com. 1995, chair awards com. 1996), Am. Soc. Engring. Edn. (adv. com. Ford Found. Resident Fellow Program 1971-79, sec.-treas. nuc. engring. divsn. 1981-82, vice chmn. 1982-83, chmn. 1983-84, projects bd. 1981-87, chmn. awards com. 1985-87; mem. Nat. Audubon Soc. (pres. 1965-66), Ret. Faculty U. Fla. Inc. (pres. 2004—05), Rotary (Paul Harris fellow), Sigma Xi, Tau Beta Pi (eminent engr.), Alpha Nu Sigma (pres. 1981-83), Eta Kappa Nu, Phi Kappa Phi, Epsilon Lambda Chi. Presbyterian. Home: 6095 Twin Lakes Rd Keystone Heights FL 32656-9728 Business E-Mail: johanian@ufl.edu.

**OHANJANIAN, RUZANNA,** clinical psychologist; d. Vladimir and Nina Ohanjanian; 1 child, Irene Gyulnazarian. BA in Linguistics & Lit. with honors, Leninakan Ednl. Inst., 1977; MA in Psychology, Yerevan P. State U., 1981; PhD, Moscow Acad. Scis., 1985; postdoctoral, U. San Francisco Med. Ctr., 1996. Cert. trauma specialist, Traumatic Incident Reduction Calif., 1991, lic. clin. psychologist Bd. Psychology, Calif., 1999. Clin. psychologist Dept. Pub. Health, San Francisco, 1998—2002, Family Svcs., Palo Alto, Calif., 1998—2002, Multilingual Psychology Cons., Mountain View, Calif., 1996—98, UCSF Med. Ctr., Mt. Zion Hosp., San Francisco. Nat. disaster team mem, Min. Health, Armenia, 1989—91; assoc. prof. Yerevan State U., Armenia, 1990—92, vis. prof., 1992; presenter State of World Forum, San Francisco, 1997; crisis mgmt. team mem. Family Enterprise Internat. Behavioral Health, 1999—. Contbr. over 30 publs. and presentations in field. Chmn. Irene Gyulnazarian Ednl. Fund for Armenia, Los Gatos, Calif., 2003—. Named Hon. Dr., Yereway State U., 2005; recipient Appreciation award, FEI Behavioral Health, 2000, Alaska Airlines, 2000, Make a Difference award, Total Employee Assistance and Mgmt., 2002, Employee Assistance Program Appreciation award, Pacific Care Behavioral Health. Mem.: APA, Armenian Profl. Soc. Avocations: painting, piano. Office: Ohanjanian Ruzanna POBox 320652 Los Gatos CA 95032 Personal E-mail: irachka2@hotmail.com.

**O'HANLON, NANCYANNE,** school librarian, educator; b. Chgo., Apr. 8, 1947; d. Irvin Walter and Edith Mary Nielsen; m. Timothy Patrick O'Hanlon, Aug. 24, 1968; 1 child, Matthew Aron. BA, So. Meth. U., 1968; MS in Libr. and Info. Sci., U. of Ill., 1983. Reference libr. Ohio State U. Librs., Columbus, Ohio, 1983—92; assoc. dir. Eisenhower Nat. Clearinghouse for Math. and Sci. Edn., Columbus, 1992—97; prof. Ohio State U. Libr., 1996—, instrm. libr., 1996—. Owner FoolProof Solutions Digital Pub., Columbus, 1995—2005. Recipient Web Access award, Ohio State U. Partnership Grant, 2001. Mem.: ALA (ref. adult svcs. divsn. 1989—90). Achievements include development of net.TUTOR (Online Instructional Program). Office: Ohio State University Libraries 1858 Neil Avenue Mall Columbus OH 43210 Business E-Mail: ohanlon.1@osu.edu.

**OHANNESSIAN, HARRY HAROUTUNE,** travel agency executive; b. Jerusalem, Jan. 5, 1919; s. Ohannes and Heripsimeh (Soultanian) C.; m. Eva Hamparsoumian, July 7, 1946 (div. Mar. 1978); children: John, Robert; m. Beatriz Araujo, Dec. 19, 1984. Matriculation, Brit. Govt., 1938; grad., London Sch. of Maths., 1940, London Sch. of Econ. Scis., 1942. Pres. Cedars Travel, Inc., N.Y.C., 1963—; chmn. Wataniyah Corp., N.Y.C., 1973-88; U.S.-Arab C. of C., N.Y.C., 1973-88; internat. commerce and bus. cons. to the middle east Stony Brook, N.Y., 1989—. Cons. in field. Decorated Knight (Order of St. John). Mem. St. George's Golf and Country Club, Stony Brook Club. Republican. Mem. Christian Ch. Avocations: tennis, swimming, gardening, music. Home: 9 Hillside Rd Stony Brook NY 11790-1002 Office: PO Box 120 Stony Brook NY 11790-0120 Office Phone: 718-446-4152.

**O'HARA, CATHERINE,** actress, comedienne; b. Toronto, Mar. 4, 1954; m. Bo Welch, 1992; children: Dylan, Matthew. Actress: films include After Hours, 1985, Heartburn, 1986, Beetlejuice, 1988, Dick Tracy, 1990, Betsy's Wedding, 1990, Home Alone, 1990, Little Vegas, 1990, There Goes The Neighborhood, 1992, Home Alone II: Lost In New York, 1992, (voice) The Nightmare Before Christmas, 1993, The Paper, 1994, Wyatt Earp, 1994, A Simple Twist of Fate, 1994, Tall Tale, 1995, Waiting for Guffman, 1996, The Last of the high Kings, 1996, (voice) Pippi Longstocking, 1997, Home Fries, 1998, The Life Before This, 1999, Surviving Christmas, 2004, Lemony Snicket's A Series of Unfortunate Events, 2004, Game 6, 2005, (voice) Chicken Little, 2005, (voice) Over the Hedge, 2006, Monster House, 2006; (TV films) The Last Polka, 1985, Hope, 1997, Late Last Night, 1999, The Wool Cap, 2004, (TV series) SCTV, 1976-1979 (Emmy award), Coming Up Rosie, 1976-77, The Steve Allen Comedy Hour, 1980, SCTV Network 90, 1981-82, (voice) Committed, 2001; dir.: (TV series) Dream On, 1990-96; writer Really Weird Tales, 1987; TV guest appearances The Simpsons Show, The Larry Sanders Show, 1992, The Outer Limits, 1995.*

**O'HARA, CYNTHIA O'CONNOR,** writer, columnist; b. New Hartford, N.Y., Sept. 17, 1963; d. Miles Joseph and Janice Louise O'Connor; m. Michael Timothy O'Hara, June 17, 1989; children: Colleen Meghan, Kelly O'Connor. Grad. Utica Sch. Commerce, 1984. Culinary instr. Bd. of Coop. Ednl. Svcs., New Hartford, 1996—; newspaper columnist Observer-Dispatch (Gannett News Svc.), Utica, NY, 1997—; TV personality numerous TV stas., 1997—. Spkr. N.Y.C. pub. librs., orgns., bus.; food demonstrator various stores, N.Y.C. Author: The Harried Housewife's Cookbooks, 1997; contbr. articles to mags. Leader Girl Scouts Am., Utica, N.Y., 1996-97. Mem. Internat. Assn. Culinary Profls., Mohawk Valley Businesswomen's Network. Roman Catholic. Avocations: cooking, gardening, reading. Office: The Harried Housewife PO Box 16 Whitesboro NY 13492-0016 Fax: 315-768-2714. E-mail: harried@borg.com.

**O'HARA, JOHN PATRICK,** lawyer, consultant; b. NYC, Jan. 11, 1930; s. Thomas James and Anne (Henry) O'H.; m. Mary Ann Leavey, Oct. 15, 1955; children: Ann O'Hara Carroll, Kathleen O'Hara Geary, Maureen O'Hara-Padden. BA in Acctg., St. John's U., NYC, 1952; JD, U. Balt., 1960. Bar: Md. 1960. Acct. Am. Cyanamid Corp., 1954—55; spl. agt. FBI, 1955-62; chief counsel, staff dir. emeritus subcom. on investigations and oversight Com. on Pub. Works and Transp., Ho. of Reps., Washington, 1962-86; dir. corp. security Flying Tiger Ln., L.A., 1986-89; ptnr. Burgess & O'Hara, Upper Marlboro, Md., 1990-91; cons. Legal Svcs. Corp., Washington, 1990-91, pres., 1991-94; cons. 1994—. 1st lt. USMC, 1952-1960. Decorated Nat. Def. Svc. medal, UN medal, Korean Svc. medal. Mem. Md. Bar Assn., Bolling AFB Officers Club, Marines Meml. Assn., Am. Legion. Home: 5904 Mount Eagle Dr Apt 911 Alexandria VA 22303-2539 also: 4490 Vincitor St Las Vegas NV 89135 E-mail: johnpohara@aol.com.

**O'HARA, JOHN PAUL, III,** orthopedic surgeon; b. Detroit, June 10, 1946; m. Randy Baird, Mar. 11, 1987; children: Riley Anne, Nolan Baird, Evan John. BA, U. Mich., 1968, MD, 1972. Resident U. Va. Med. Ctr., Charlottesville, 1973-77; fellow Nuffield Orthopaedic Ctr., Oxford, Eng., 1977; practice medicine specializing in orthopaedic surgery Southfield, 1978—; staff Providence Hosp., Southfield, Mich., 1978—, pres. elect med. staff, 1990, pres. med. staff, 1991; sect. chief orthopedics; pres. Porretta Orthopedic Ctr., 1996—, med. dir., 2001—; pres. Providence Med. Group. Pres. Providence Hosp. Med. Staff Research Found., 1984-85, bd. dirs., 1982—; bd. dirs. Mich. Master Health Plan, Southfield, 1982. Contbr. articles to profl. jours. Pres. Birmingham (Mich.) Little League Baseball. Recipient Disting. Alumni award Brother Rice High Sch., 1986. Fellow Am. Acad. Orthopaedic Surgery, Mid Am. Orthopaedic Soc.; mem. Detroit Orthopaedic Soc., Mich. Orthopaedic Soc., Detroit Acad. Orthopaedic Surgeons (past pres.), Oakland Hills Country Club (Birmingham, Mich.), Beverly Hills (Mich.) Club. Avocations: earthwatch vol., travel, sports. Home: 627 Waddington St Bloomfield Hills MI 48301-2346 Office: Providence Med Group 72255 Greenfield Rd #246 Southfield MI 48075

**O'HARA, KAREN ANN,** mathematician, educator; b. Long Beach, Calif., Oct. 30, 1971; d. Robert John and Penny Ann Bradford; m. Marc Edward O'Hara, July 25, 1992; children: Peyton Bryana, Auston Galen, Quinton Mathieu. BS in Math., Calif. State U., Fullerton, 1994; MS in Math., Vanderbilt U., 1996, PhD in Math., 2002. Asst. prof. math. High Point U., High Point, NC, 1999—. Mem.: Am. Women in Math., Am. Math. Assn., Math. Assn. of Am. Avocations: hiking, reading. Home: 6028 Weant Rd Archdale NC 27263 Personal E-mail: kohara@math.highpoint.edu.

**O'HARA, KEVIN J.,** information technology executive; Grad., Drexel U., 1983. Mgmt. staff Peter Kiewit Sons', Inc.; area mgr. Kiewit Network Tech., Inc.; v.p. network svcs. MFS Telecom.; pres. MFS Devel.; pres., CEO MFS Global Network Svcs.; COO Level 3 Comm., Inc., Broomfield, Colo., 1998—, pres., 2000—. Recipient Alumni Achievement award, Drexel U. Coll. Engring., 2001. Office: Level 3 Comm 1025 Eldorado Blvd Broomfield CO 80021*

**OHARA, NORIAKI,** hydrologist; b. Kawasaki, Japan, Aug. 17, 1973; s. Hiroyasu Ohara and Yoshimi Tsujino. PhD, U. Calif., Davis, 2003. Asst. devel. engr. U. Calif., Davis, 2004—. Recipient Best Paper award, Jour. Hydrologic Engring., 2006. Office: U Calif Davis 1 Shields Ave Davis CA 95616 Office Phone: 530-757-2207.

**O'HARA, PATRICIA ANNE,** dean, law educator; BA summa cum laude, Santa Clara U. 1971; JD summa cum laude, Notre Dame, 1974. Bar: Calif. 1974. Assoc. Brobeck, Phleger & Harrison, 1974—79, 1980—81; assoc. prof. law Notre Dame Law Sch., 1981, prof., 1990, v.p. student affairs, 1990—99, Joseph A. Matson dean, law educator, 1999—. Contbr. chapters to books, articles to law jours. Office: U Notre Dame 203 Law Sch PO Box 780 Notre Dame IN 46556-0780 Office Phone: 574-631-6789. Office Fax: 574-631-8400. E-mail: Patricia.A.O'Hara.3@nd.edu.

**O'HARA, PAUL P.,** mathematics professor; b. Dublin, Apr. 15, 1953; s. Frank O'Hara and Maura Farrell. PhD, UCLA, Los Angeles, 1991. Math. prof. NEIU, Chgo., 1993—. Treas. Focolare Movement, Chgo., 1982—2006. Achievements include research in establihed a 1-1 correspondence between metrics of general relativity and quantum mechanics. Office: Northeastern Ill Univ 5500 N St Louis Ave Chicago IL 60625 Office Phone: 773-442-5783. Home Fax: 708-848-6950. Personal E-mail: pohara@neiu.edu.

**O'HARA, ROBERT SYDNEY, JR.,** lawyer; b. Englewood, N.J., Apr. 26, 1939; s. Robert Sydney and Katharine (Drayton) O'Hara; m. Elizabeth Crocker, June 17, 1961 (div.); children: Jennifer, Isabelle; m. Bonnie Durkin, July 19, 1975. AB, Princeton U., 1960; JD, U. Pa., 1963. Bar: N.Y. 1964. Ptnr. Milbank, Tweed, Hadley & McCloy, N.Y.C., 1963—. Served to capt. AUS, 1963—65. Office: Milbank Tweed Hadley & McCloy 1 Chase Manhattan Plz Fl 47 New York NY 10005-1413

**O'HARA, SABINE U.,** academic administrator, dean, economist, educator; b. Ludwigsburg, W. Germany, Oct. 29, 1955; d. Wolfgang E. and Margarete Maier; m. Philip O'Hara, Mar. 17, 1983; children: Daniel, David, Dennis. Doctorate, U. Gottingen, Germany, 1984. Dir. pub. policy N.Y. State Coun. Chs., Albany, 1990—93; asst. prof. econs. Rensselaer Poly. Inst., Troy, NY, 1994—99, dir. grad. studies in econs., 1996—99; provost and prof. econs. Green Mountain Coll., Poultney, Vt., 1999—2002; v.p. acad. affairs and dean Concordia Coll., Moorhead, Minn., 2002—04; pres. Roanoke Coll., Salem, Va., 2004—. Lectr. in field. Author: (books) Economic Theory for Environmentalists, 1996; contbr. articles to profl. jours. Steering com. Downtown Revitalization Initiative, Poultney, 2001—02; bd. dirs. Girls Inc. of the Greater Capital Dist., Albany, NY, 1998—2000, Employee Ownership Project, Albany, 1997—2000; vice chair Schenectady Econ. Devel. Initiative, NY, 1994—97. Recipient Outstanding Paper award for excellence, Internat. Jour. Social Econs., 1996, 2000, Outstanding Svc. award, N.Y. State Coun.

Chs., 1997; grantee Rsch. grantee, Hewlett Found., Froehlich Found., Sloan Found. Mem.: Am. Econ. Assn., Internat. Assn. Feminist Econs., Assn. Social Econs., Internat. Soc. Ecol. Econs. Business E-Mail: ohara@roanoke.edu.

**O'HARA, THOMAS J.,** priest, academic administrator, educator; b. Hazleton, Pa., Mar. 16, 1949; s. Thomas John and Bridget Helen O'Hara. BA, King's Coll., Wilkes-Barre, Pa., 1971; MTh, U. Notre Dame, Ind., 1977; PhD, Am. U., Washington, 1988. Relief work Missionary Sisters of Charity, Dacca, Bangladesh, 1975; prof. English Notre Dame Coll., Bangladesh, 1975; assoc. pastor Our Lady of Good Counsel, Bklyn., 1977—82; chaplain Holy Cross Hosp., Silver Springs, Md., 1982—84; adj. prof. Am. U., 1987; prof. polit. sci. Philosophical Ctr. Jinja, Uganda, 1994—96, King's Coll., 1998—, assoc. v.p. academic affairs, 1996—99, pres., 1999—. Bd. dirs. St. Mary's Day Care Ctr., Wilkes-Barre, 1999—, Pa. Campus Compact, 2001; bd. trustees Stonehill Coll., North Easton, Mass., 1998—; mem. Geisinger South Wilkes-Barre Adv. Coun., 2006—. Contbr. articles to profl. jour. Bd. dirs. Greater Wilkes-Barre Chamber of Bus. and Industry, 2001—; adv. coun. Jewish Family Svc., Wilkes-Barre, 2004; bd. dirs. Diamond City Partnership, 2002—, St. Vincent de Paul kitchen, 1999—, Health NEPA Initiative, Scranton, 2004. Recipient Northeast Pa. award, Ethics Inst., 2003, Ny State award, NY State Dept. Juvenile Affairs, 1982, Ezamper award, U. Notre Dame Alumni Assn., 1997. Mem.: Pa. Soc., Delta Epsilon Sigma. Roman Catholic. Office: King s Coll 133 N River St Wilkes Barre PA 18711

**O'HARA, THOMAS PATRICK,** managing editor; b. Phila., July 15, 1947; s. Hugh James and Agatha Mary (Gilroy) O'H.; m. Juliet Munro, 1970 (div. 1974); m. Pamela Smith, Oct. 8, 1977; children: Rachel Kathleen, Patrick Graham. BA in English, Rutgers U., 1971; MA in Communications, U. Fla., 1974. Sports reporter Gainesville SUN, 1972-74; reporter Orlando (Fla.) Sentinel, 1974-76, Daytona Beach (Fla.) News Jour., 1976-78; various editing and reporting positions Miami (Fla.) Herald, 1978-86, city editor Palm Beach ed., 1985-86; asst. met. editor Palm Beach Post, West Palm Beach, Fla., 1986-87, met. editor, 1987-88, asst. mng. editor, 1988-89, mng. editor, 1989—2000, The Plain Dealer, Cleve., 2000—. Sgt. USAF, 1969-71. Home: 8890 Spring Valley Dr Broadview Heights OH 44147-2573 Office: The Plain Dealer 1801 Superior Ave Cleveland OH 44114 E-mail: tohara@plaind.com.

**O'HARA, VIRGINIA ANNE,** curator; b. Topeka, Kans., Dec. 9, 1956; d. David Edward and Anne Seaton (Milliken) Herrick; m. Christopher Evan O'Hara, Sept. 19, 1987; children: Evan Thomas, Peter Antony. Student, Beaver Coll. (now Arcadia Coll.), 1975—77; BFA in Art History, U. Kans., 1979, MA in Art History, 1985. Asst. curator Brandywine River Mus., Chadds Ford, Pa., 1986—91, assoc. curator, 1991—. Co-author: Howard Pyle: The Artist and His Legacy, 1987; author: Alexander Charles Stuart: Ship Portraits and Marine Paintings, 1997, Posters in the Age of Elegance, 1999, Monsters, Mickey, and Mozart: The Art of Maurice Sendak, 2003, Paul Revere's Ride and Longfellow's Legend, 2004. Mem.: Chester County Art Assn. Avocations: painting, crafts, music. Office: Brandywine River Mus PO Box 141 Chadds Ford PA 19317 E-Mail: vohara@brandywine.org.

**O'HARE, DEAN RAYMOND,** retired insurance company executive, director; b. Jersey City, June 21, 1942; s. Francis and Ann O'H.; m. Kathleen T. Walliser, Dec. 2, 1967; 2 sons, Dean, Jason. BS in Fin. Mgmt., NYU, 1963; MBA, Pace U., 1968. Underwriter trainee Chubb Corp., NYC, 1963-64, tax advisor, 1964-67, asst. v.p., mgr. corp. fin. devel., 1968-72, sr. v.p., mgr. corp. fin. devel. dept., from 1979, CFO, 1979-94, pres., 1986-88, chmn., CEO, 1988—2002, ret. Warren, 2002. Dir., chmn., audit com. Fluor Corp.; chmn. US Coun. Internat. Bus.; chmn. bd. SeaPass Solutions, HJ Heinz Corp., DFA Capital Mgmt., Proudfoot Consulting. The NJ Partnership; co-chmn. Hosp. Spl. Surgery, NYC; chmn., trustee fin. com. St. Benedict's Prep. Sch., Newark; trustee U. Dublin, Ireland, Intrepid Mus., NYC. Mem. The Links Club (N.Y.C.). Office Phone: 908-903-3565. Business E-Mail: dohare@chubb.com.

**O'HARE, JAMES RAYMOND,** energy executive; b. Evergreen Park, Ill., July 20, 1938; s. Raymond Clarence and Helen (Nickel) O'H.; m. Nan Jane Raleigh, Sept. 18, 1965; children: Joan, Daniel, Colleen, Patrick. BS, Marquette U., 1960; MBA, U. Calif. at Los Angeles, 1961. C.P.A., Ind., Ill., Ky., Calif., Tex. Mgr. Peat, Marwick, Mitchell & Co., Chgo., 1961-68, South Bend, Ind., 1968-69; controller Essex Internat., Inc., Fort Wayne, Ind., 1969-76, Am. Air Filter Co., Inc., Louisville, 1976-80; fin. v.p. and treas. Petrolane Inc., Long Beach, Calif., 1980-85; treas. Tex. Eastern Corp., Houston, 1985-87, v.p., treas., 1987-88; sr. v.p. fin. and adminstrn. Tex. Ea. Gas Transmission Co., Houston, 1988—89; v.p., CFO Enclean Inc., Houston, 1991—93; fin. cons., 1993—97; v.p., CFO Ascendant Healthcare Group, Inc., Houston, 1997, John March Ptnrs., Inc., Houston, 1998—2004, Sensor Microsystems, Inc., San Antonio, 2004; gen. ptnr. Connemara Ventures, LLC, The Woodlands, 2004. Controller Afras USA, Inc., 2005. Served with USNR, 1962-68. Mem. Evans Scholars, Fin. Execs. Inst., The Woodlands Country Club, Beta Gamma Sigma. Personal E-mail: johare@swbell.net.

**O'HARE, JOSEPH ALOYSIUS,** priest, editor-in-chief, former academic administrator; b. NYC, Feb. 12, 1931; s. Joseph Aloysius and Marie Angela (Enright) O'H. AB, Berchmans Coll, Cebu City, Philippines, 1954, MA, 1955; STL, Woodstock Coll., Md., 1962; PhD, Fordham U., 1968; DHL (hon.), Fairfield U., 1980, Rockhurst Coll., Kansas City, Mo., 1984, Ateneo de Manila U., 1990, CUNY, 1991, Coll. of St. Rose, Albany, NY, 1995, St. Francis Coll., Bklyn., 1996, St. Peter's Coll., 1997, Albertus Magnus Coll., 2004; DLitt (hon.), Coll. New Rochelle, 1984; D.D. (hon.), Muhlenberg Coll., 1998; DLitt (hon.), Fordham U., 2003. Joined S.J. 1948, ordained priest Roman Cath. Ch., 1961. Instr. Ateneo de Manila U., 1955-58, prof. philosophy, 1968-72; assoc. editor Am. Mag., N.Y.C., 1972-75, 2003—, editor-in-chief, 1975-84; pres. Fordham U., Bronx, NY, 1984—2003, Regis HS, N.Y.C., 2004—05. Author weekly column Of Many Things (Best Original Column award Cath. Press Assn. 1976, 78, 81, 84) Office Phone: 212-581-4640. Business E-Mail: johare@fordham.edu.

**O'HARE, SANDRA FERNANDEZ,** education educator; b. N.Y.C., Mar. 19, 1941; d. Ricardo Enrique and Rosario de Los Angeles (Arenas) Fernandez; m. S. James O'Hare, Oct. 12, 1963; children: James, Richard, Michael, Christopher. BA, Marymount Coll., 1962; MA, U. San Francisco, 1980. Cert. elem. and coll. tchr.; bilingual and lang. devel. specialist. Instr. adult edn., Guam, 1964-66, Spanish Speaking Ctr., Harrisburg, Pa., 1977-79; tchr. Colegio Salesiano, Rota, Spain, 1973-74, 84, Alisal Sch. Dist., Salinas, Calif., 1979—81, Liberty Sch., Petaluma, Calif., 1981-85, Cinnabar Sch., Petaluma, 1985—; instr. Chapman U., 1994-98; also summer migrant edn. programs, 1990-91. Instr. Santa Rosa (Calif.) Jr. Coll., 1982-83; mem. math. curriculum com. Sonoma County Office Edn., Santa Rosa, 1988; mem. Summer Sci. Connections Inst., Sonoma State U., 1994, Redwood Empire Math. Acad., summer 1995; mem. Sonoma County Math Project, 1995-96; summer '96 NEH stipend to Harvard U. Translator: Isabel la Catolica, 1961. Mem. Asian relief com. ARC, Harrisburg, 1975, Boy Scouts Am., Petaluma, 1983, Mechanicsburg, Pa., 1974, Monterey, Calif., 1971, Sonoma County Adult Literacy League, 1996—. Sarah D. Barder fellow Johns Hopkins U., 1990. Mem. NEA, AAUW (chair elem. founds. com. 1985-86), Calif. Assn. Bilingual Educators, Club Hispano-Americano Petaluma (pres. 1987-89), M3 Investment Club. Roman Catholic. Avocation: travel. Home: 1289 Glenwood Dr Petaluma CA 94954-4326 E-mail: funsohare@yahoo.com.

**OHASHI, SHOICHI,** business administration educator; b. Seto, Aichi, Japan, Mar. 7, 1932; s. Mitsuo and Yoshie Ohashi; m. Kimiko Ohashi, Nov. 20, 1957; 1 child, Reisaku MBA, Kobe (Japan) U., 1957, DBA, 1967. Acad. asst. Kansai U., Suita, Japan, 1957-60, lectr., 1960-63, assoc. prof., 1963-70, prof. bus. adminstrn., 1970-2000, vice dean students div., 1972-74, vice dean faculty commerce, 1977-78, dean faculty commerce, 1979-82, dean vocat. div., 1982-86, acad. v.p. 1986-92, dean of entrance divsn., 1993-99; prof., dean faculty tourism, acad. v.p. Osaka Meijo U., Kumatori, Japan, 2000—. Lectr. Osaka U. Fgn. Studies, 1968-74, Kobe U., 1971, Ritsumeikan U., Kyoto, Japan, 1971-73, Kwanseigakuin U., Nishinomiya, Japan, 1979-80,

94-97. Author: Theories on Works Community, 1966, Theory of Business Administration, 1992; co-author: Workers' Participation, 1979; co-editor: Information Society Business, 1988, Business Administration, 1991, Lexicon of Business Administration, 1994, An Inquiry into the Japanese Management, 1996. Researcher com. Rsch. Fund Commin. Japan Ministry Edn., 1987-89. Mem. Japan Soc. Bus. Adminstrn. (internat. com. 1980-83, exec. com. 1983-89, 92-95, v.p. 1995-98), Assn. for Comparative Study of Mgmt. (exec.com. 1980-84, pres. 1994-96), Soc. for the History of Mgmt. Theories (exec. com. 1993-96, v.p. 1996-99). Home: 5-40-602 Mukogawacho Takarazuka Hyogo 665-0844 Japan Office: Osaka Meijo U 5-3-1 Okubo-Minami Kumatori Osaka Japan *Books published as author, editor or co-editor since a first book in 1966, a dissertation book, until 1998 are 25. Being engaged these days in research into Japanese management system sponsored by Japan Ministry of Education and Japan Society for the promotion of Science. Recent accomplishments as Dean of Entrance Division include a successful increase of about 10% in applicants for Kansai University in 1997 entrance examination amid overall decrease of the applicable in Japan.*

**O'HEARN, ROBERT RAYMOND,** stage designer; b. Elkhart, Ind., July 19, 1921; s. Robert Raymond, Sr. and Ella May (Stoldt) O'H. BA, Ind. U., 1939-43; student, Art Students League, 1943-45. Designer Brattle Theatre, Cambridge, Mass., 1948-52; prof. stage design, chmn. design dept. Sch. Music Ind. U., 1989—. Instr. Studio and Forum Scenic Design, 1968-88. Stage designer: Broadway shows The Relapse, 1950, Loves Labor's Lost, 1953, Othello, Festival, 1955, The Apple Cart, Child of Fortune, 1956; asst. designer: Broadway shows Kismet, 1953, Pajama Game, 1955, My Fair Lady, 1956, West Side Story, 1958; designer: for film A Clerical Error, 1955; designer prodns. Central City Opera House, 1959-63, Opera Soc. Washington, 1958-61, L'Elisir D'Amore at Met. Opera House, 1960, Die Meistersinger, 1962, Aida, 1963; stage designer: As You Like It, Stratford, Conn., 1961, Troilus and Cressida, Stratford, 1961, Kiss Me Kate, Los Angeles Civic Light Opera, 1964, N.Y.C. Center, 1965, Samson and Delila, Met. Opera, 1964, La Sylphide, Am. Ballet Theatre, 1964, Italian Symphony, 1971, Adam Cochrane, Broadway, 1964, Pique Dame, Met. Opera, 1965, La Ventana, 1966, Die Frau Ohne Schatten, 1966, Porgy and Bess, Vienna Volksoper, 1965, Bregenzer Festspiele, 1971, Otello, Boston Opera, also Hamburg State Opera, 1967, Hansel and Gretel, Met. Opera, 1967, Nutcracker Ballet, San Francisco Ballet, 1967, L.A. Ballet, 1979, La Traviata, Santa Fe Opera 1968, Rosalinda, L.A. Civic Light Opera, 1968, Der Rosenkavalier, Met. Opera, 1969, Tallis Fantasia, N.Y.C. Ballet, 1969, Boris Godunov (unproduced), Met. Opera, 1970, Parsifal, Met. Opera, 1970, Porgy and Bess, Bregenz Festspiel, Austria, 1971, Falstaff, Marriage of Figaro, Gianni Schicci, Central City Opera House, 1972, Barber of Seville, 1973, The Enchanted, Kennedy Center, 1973, The Mind with the Dirty Man, Los Angeles, 1973, Midsummer Night's Dream, Central City Opera, 1974, Coppelia, Ballet West, 1974, Carmen, Strasbourg, 1974, The Pearl Fishers, Miami Opera, 1974, N.Y.C. Opera, 1980, Don Pasquale, Miami Opera, 1976, Scipio Africanus, Central City Opera, 1975, Swan Lake, Strasbourg, 1975, Marriage of Figaro, Met. Opera, 1975, Die Meistersinger, Karlsruhe, Germany, 1975, Girl of the Golden West, Houston Opera, 1976, N.Y.C. Opera, 1977, Vienna Staatsoper, 1976, Boris Godunov, Strasbourg, 1976, Der Rosenkavalier, Karlsruhe, 1976, Don Quixote, Ballet West, 1977, Die Meistersinger, Chgo. Lyric Opera, 1977, Adriana Lecouvreur, Miami Opera, 1978, La Boheme, 1978, Coppelia, Pacific N.W. Dance, Seattle, 1978, Andrea Chenier, N.Y.C. Opera, 1978, Der Rosenkavalier, Can. Opera Co., Toronto, 1978, Taming of the Shrew, Pa. State U., 1980, Die Fledermaus, Miami Opera, 1980, Tosca, Miami Opera, 1981, West Side Story, Bregenz Festspiel, Austria, 1981, Mich. Opera Theatre, 1985; Pique Dame, San Francisco Opera, 1982, La Traviata, Miami Opera, 1982, Of Mice and Men, Miami Opera, 1982, Carousel, Annie Get Your Gun, Miami Opera, 1984, Lucia di Lammermoor, 1984, L'Italiana in Algeri, 1985, Porgy and Bess, Met. Opera, 1985, West Side Story, Mich. Opera Theatre, 1985, Aida, Don Giovanni, Opera Colo., 1986, My Fair Lady, Mich. Opera Theatre, 1986, Samson and Delilah, Manon Lescaut Opera Colo., 1987, Annie Get Your Gun, Paper Mill Playhouse, 1987, Peter Grimes, Ind. U., 1987, Madama Butterfly, N.J. State Opera, 1990. Mem. vis. com. Costume Inst., Met. Museum. Recipient Robert L. B. Tobin award for lifetime achievement in theatrical design, 2005. Mem. United Scenic Artists. Home: 2604 E 2nd St Bloomington IN 47401-5351

**O'HERN, JANE SUSAN,** psychologist, educator; b. Winthrop, Mass., Mar. 21, 1933; d. Joseph Francis and Mona (Garvey) O'H. BS, Boston U., 1954, EdD, 1962; MA, Mich. State U., 1956. Instr. Mercyhurst Coll., 1954-55, Hofstra Coll., 1956-57, State Coll., Salem and Boston, 1957-60; asst. prof. Boston U., 1962-67, assoc. prof., 1967-75, prof. edn. and psychiat. (psychology), 1975-95, prof. emeritus, 1995—, chmn. dept. counseling psychology, 1972-75, 88-89, dir. mental health edn. program, 1975-81, dir. internat. edn., 1978-81, asst. v.p. internat. edn., 1981; prof. emeritus mental health and behavioral medicine program Boston U. Sch. Medicine, 2001—. Pres. ASSIST Internat., Inc., 1989—98; adv. bd, Internat. Study Cons., 1994—98; founder BettyBoston LLC, 2002—. Contbr. articles to profl. jours. Trustee Boston Ctr. Modern Psychoanalytic Studies, 1980-92. Recipient grants U.S. Office Edn., NIMH, Dept. of Def. Mem. Assn. Counselor Edn. and Suprs., Am. Counseling Assn., North Atlantic Assn. Counselor Edn. and Supervision (past pres.), Mass. Psychol. Assn., Am. Psychol. Assn., Mortar Bd., Pi Lamda Theta, Sigma Kappa, Phi Delta Kappa, Phi Beta Delta. Home: 111 Perkins St Apt 287 Boston MA 02130-4324 Office Phone: 617-414-2325. Personal E-mail: assistint@aol.com. E-mail: johern@bu.edu.

**OHGA, NORIO,** retired electronics executive; b. Numazu, Shizuoka, Japan, Jan. 29, 1930; s. Shoichi Ohga and Toshi Mizuno; m. Midori Matsubara, 1957. Grad., Tokyo Nat. U. Fine Arts and Music, 1953, Kunst U., Berlin, 1957; Dr hc music (hon.), Rochester U., 1996, McGill U., 1999. Cons., advisor Tokyo Tsushin Kogyo (later Sony Corp.), 1953-59; gen. mgr. tape recorder divsn., product planning divsn., indsl. design divsn. Sony Corp., Tokyo, 1959; originally trained as an amateur singer; bd. dirs. Sony Corp., Tokyo, 1964-72, mng. dir., 1972-74, sr. mng. dir., 1974-76, dep. pres., 1976-82, pres., chief oper. officer, 1982-89, pres. and CEO, 1989-95, chmn. and CEO, 1995-99, chmn., rep. dir., 1999-2000, chmn. bd., 2000—03, hon. chmn., 2003—; CEO Nobuyuki Idei. Sr. mng. dir. CBS/Sony Group, Inc., 1968-70, pres., 1970-80, chmn., 1980-91; chmn. Sony Corp. Am., 1988-98; vice chmn. Keidanren, 1998. Decorated Cmdr. Cross First Class of the Order of Merit of the Rep. of Austria, 1987, Medal of Honor with Blue Ribbon by J.M. the Emperor of Japan, 1988, Comdr.'s Cross Order of Merit of Germany, 1994, Officier de l'Ordre Nat. de la Legion d'Honneur France, 1996, Grande Ufficiale dell'Ordine Al Merito della Repubblica Italiana award Pres. Italian Republic, 1998, Grand Decoration of Honour in Silver with Star of the Rep. of Austria, 1999, Order of Panglima Jasa Negara of Malaysia, 1999, Knight Comdr.'s Cross (Badge and Star, FRG, 2001, First Class Order of the Sacred Treasure of Japan, 2001. Mem. Japan Fedn. Econ. Orgn. (vice-chmn. 1998), Tokyo C. of C. and Industry (vice chmn.). Avocations: yachting, flying. Office: Sony Corp 6-7-35 Kitashinagawa 6-chome Shinagawa-ku Tokyo 141 Japan also: Sony Corp Am 550 Madison Ave New York NY 10022-3211

**OHIRA, KAZUTO,** theatre company executive, writer; b. Hiroshima, Japan, Jan. 5, 1933; s. Kitaro and Ryo (Sugimoto) O.; m. Evelyn Lanham, Sept. 3, 1964 (div. Sept. 2005) BA, Waseda U., 1956. Theatre mgr. Toho's La Brea Theatre, L.A., 1961—63; gen. mgr. Toho Cinema, N.Y.C., 1963—64; publicity mgr. Towa Co., Ltd., Tokyo, 1965—69; rep., dir., mgr. Toho Internat. Inc., N.Y.C., 1969, CEO, 1988—97; pres. Internat. Cultural Prodn. Inc., N.Y.C. Prodr. (dance performance and drama) Yasuko Nagamine's Musume Dojoji, 1982, Mandara, 1985, (drama) Yukio Ninagawa's Media, 1987, Takarazuka Show at Radio City Music Hall, NY, 1989, Kanashibets U: Furano Group at La Mama, Takarazuka Dance Concert at Joyce Theater, 1992, Sotoba Komachi, Yasuko Nagamine and Co., Beauty of Tokyo, Met. Tokyo, City Ctr., N.Y., 1993, Virtue Senpo Sugihara, Danny Kay Theater, N.Y.C., 1997, Gen: Hiroshima Atom Bomb's Kid, Danny Kay Theater, N.Y.C., 1998, The Winds of God, Am. Pl. Theater, N.Y.C., 1999, Rent, Japan, 2000, Boonah, Come Down, N.Y.C., 2000, Thank You, Broadway at Lincoln Center, Alice Tally Hall, 2002; author: Broadway parts I and II, 1982, 2d edit., 1987, Broadway, Broadway, 1987, Performing Arts of New York, 1989,

Haiku Collection: Though The Travel is Short, The Charms of Broadway, 1994, Broadway Criticism: Walk on Broadway, 1995, Japanese transl. of Show Business Is No Business by Al Hirshfeld, 1997, Haiku Collection: Flower Garden, 2002. Bd. dirs. Japan Musical Award Com. in U.S.; chair bd. dirs. Saeko Ichinohe Dance Co., 1993-2002. Recipient 2d Fumiko Yamaji Cultural award, 1985, 1st Cultural Bridge award, 1998, Fgn. Min. Commendation award Japan, 2004. Avocation: golf. Address: 1-4-14-401 Nihonbashi Hama Cho Tokyo 103-0007 Japan Personal E-mail: ohkaz67@hotmail.com.

**OHIWEREI, GODWIN OISEOZOJE,** sociologist, educator; b. Ibadan, Oyo, Nigeria, July 15, 1956; arrived in U.S., 1976; s. Joel Wellington and Lyne Ohiwerei; children: A.J., Oise. BA, Dillard U., 1980; MA, So. U., Baton Rouge, 1980; PhD, La. State U., 1998. Assoc. prof. N.J. City U., Jersey City, 1990—, chmn. dept. sociology, 1996—. Author: The Effect of International Trade on Economic Development in Nigeria, 1988; editor: Developing Strategies for Excellence, 1996. Fellow, Nat. Coun. Black Studies, 1989, NEH, 1990. Mem.: Nat. Assn. Multicultural Edn., Am. Sociol. Assn., Ora-Ekpea Assn., Eghosa Alumni Assn. Episcopalian. Avocations: travel, reading. Office: NJ City Univ 2039 Kennedy Blvd Jersey City NJ 07305

**OHL, JOAN ESCHENBACH,** federal agency administrator; b. Harrisburg, Pa. m. Ronald E. Ohl. Grad., U. Del., 1967; EdM, SUNY, Buffalo, 1969; post grad., Pa. State U. Dir. women's housing Colo. Coll., Colo. Springs, 1969; positions at U. Ark., Pa. State U.; asst. to v.p. Fairleigh Dickinson U., Rutherford, NJ, 1975—82; v.p. Independent Coll. Fund of NJ; cons. to C.E. "Jim" Compton of FIVE-J Energy Inc. & Grafton Coal Co., 1984—93; sec. Dept. Health and Human Resources, W.Va., 1997—2001; commr. Adminstrn. Children, Youth and Families Adminstrn. Children and Families, HHS, Washington, 2002—. Bd. mem. W.Va. Health Care Cost Rev. Authority, 1993—97. Recipient Disting. West Virginian award, 2000, Joan E. Ohl Rural Health Leadership award, W.Va. Rural Health Assn., 2000, Leadership Award, Multi-CAP, Inc., 2000, Bateman Award, W.Va. Hosp. Assoc., 2000, Leadership Award, W.Va. Pub. Health Assoc., 2000. Office: HHS Adminstrn Children and Families 370 L'Enfant Promenade SW Washington DC 20447*

**OHLE, DAVID H.,** military career officer; b. Youngstown, Ohio, Oct. 16, 1944; m. Susan Thomas; children: Amanda, Darren. BS, U. Mil. Acad., 1968; MA in Social Sci., Ohio State U. Commd. officer US Army, 1968, advanced through grades to lt. gen., comdr. Ranger Co. Vietnam, comdr. inf. bn. Ft. Campbell, Ky., comdr. infantry brigade Schofield Barracks, Hawaii, asst. divsn. comdr. 1st Inf. Divsn. Ft. Riley, Kans., chief of staff of the Army chairholder Nat. War Coll., chief exec. svcs. divsn. Office of the Chief of Staff, exec. officer to the dep. chief of staff for ops. and plans, exec. officer to chief of staff of the Army, dir. La. Maneuvers Task Force, dep. comdt. U.S. Army Command and Gen. Staff Coll. Ft. Leavenworth, Kans., dir. Officer Pers. Mgmt. Sys. XXI Task Force, asst. dep. chief of staff for personnel, office of dep. chief of staff for personal Washington, 1997—98, lt. gen., dep. chief of staff for personnel, 1998—. Decorated Silver Star, three Legions of Merit, three Bronze Stars one with V device for valor, Def. Meritorious Svc. medal, two Air medals one with V device for valor. Office: US Army 300 Army Pentagon Washington DC 20310-0300

**OHLGREN, JOEL R.,** lawyer; b. Mpls., July 21, 1942; BA, UCLA, 1965, JD, 1968. Bar: Calif. 1969. Ptnr. Sheppard, Mullin, Richter & Hampton LLP. Fellow: Am. Coll. Bankruptcy; mem.: ABA, Internat. Insolvency Inst., Turnaround Mgmt. Assn., Am. Bankruptcy Inst., Fin. Lawyers Conf., Los Angeles County Bar Assn. (past chmn. comml. law and bankruptcy sect.), State Bar Calif. Office: Sheppard Mullin Richter & Hampton LLP 333 S Hope St Fl 48 Los Angeles CA 90071-1406 Office Phone: 213-620-1780. Business E-Mail: johlgren@sheppardmullin.com.

**OHLKE, AMANDA ANNE,** museum administrator, educator; b. Bethesda, Md., Aug. 8, 1964; d. Clarence Carl and Frances Nicholson O.; m. Michael Joseph Kapsa, Mar. 10, 2001; 1 child, Jeremy Clarence. M of Arts and Tchg., George Wash. U., Washington, DC, 1991. Edn. outreach specialist Md. Hist. Soc., Balt., 1991—94; adult programs coord. Nat. Bldg. Mus., Washington, 1994—96; assn. mgr. Mus. Trustee Assn., Washington, 1996—2001, exec. dir., 2001—04; mgr. adult edn. Internat. Spy Mus., Washington, 2004—. Bd. dirs. Cleve. Pk. Hist. Soc., Washington, D.C. Preservation League. Washington. Editor: (newsletter) Network. Mem. D.C. Preservation League, 1997—2003. Home: 3706 Reno Rd NW Washington DC 20008 Office: Internat Spy Mus 800 F St NW Washington DC 20004 E-mail: aohlke@spymuseum.org.

**OHLMEYER, DONALD WINFRED, JR.,** film and television producer; b. New Orleans, Feb. 3, 1945; s. Donald W. and Eva Clare (Bivens) O.; m. Linda Jonsson, 2003; children by previous marriage: Justin Drew, Christopher Brett, Todd Bivens, Kemper Perry. BA in Comms., U. Notre Dame, 1967. Pres. Roadblock Prodns., 1977—; chmn. bd., CEO Ohlmeyer Comms., L.A., 1982—92; pres. NBC West Coast, Burbank, Calif., 1993—2000. Adj. prof. Pepperdine U., 2002—. Assoc. dir. ABC Sports, N.Y.C., 1967-70, dir., 1971-72, prodr., 1972-77; dir. Olympic Games, 1972; prodr., dir. Summer and Winter Olympics, 1976; prodr. ABC Monday Night Football, 1972-76; exec. prodr. NBC Sports, N.Y.C., 1977-82; exec. prodr.: 1980 Olympic Games, Crime of Innocence, 1985, Under Siege, Bluffing It, 1987, Right to Die, 1987, Special Bulletin, The Golden Moment: An Olympic Love Story (also writer) 1980, Crazy in Love, 1992, Cold Sassy Tree, The Heroes of Desert Storm (also dir.) 1991; prodr.: The Emmy Awards Show, Fast Copy, Crimes of the Century, Lifestories; creator, dir.: MTV Awards Show, 1983-86, The Skins Game. Recipient 15 Emmy awards 1975-99, Cine Golden Eagle award, 1979, Miami Film Festival award 1979, award Nat. Film Bd., 1980, award Glaad Media, 1991, Humanities prize, 1983, 96. Mem. Dirs. Guild Am., Writers Guild Am., Acad. TV Arts and Scis., Bel-Air Club (Calif.), The Reserve (Indian Wells). Office: DWOCO Inc 10880 Wilshire Blvd Ste 920 Los Angeles CA 90024-4101

**OHLSON, DOUGLAS DEAN,** artist, educator; b. Cherokee, Iowa, Nov. 18, 1936; s. Lloyd E. and Effie O. (Johnson) O. BA, U. Minn., 1961. Prof. art Hunter Coll., N.Y.C., 1964—2001; ret., 2001. One man shows include Fischbach Gallery, N.Y.C., 1964, 66-70, 72, Susan Caldwell Gallery, N.Y.C., 1974, 76, 77, 79, 81, 82, 83, Portland (Oreg.) Ctr. for Visual Arts, 1977, Ruth Siegel Gallery, N.Y.C., 1985, 87, Andre Zarre Gallery, N.Y.C., 1985, 90, 92, 93, 95, 2000, Andre Zarre Gallery, N.Y.C., 2004, Gallery 99, Elaine Baker Gallery, Boca Raton, Fla., 2003, Miami, Fla., 1986, Nina Freudenheim Gallery, Buffalo, 1986, Jaffe Gallery, Miami, 1989, Elaine Baker Gallery, Boca Raton, 2003, Doug Ohlson 20 Years of Painting: 1982-2002,; group shows include Mus. Modern Art, N.Y.C., 1968, Tate Gallery, London, 1969, Whitney Mus., N.Y.C., 1969, 71, Corcoran Gallery, Washington, 1972, 73, UCLA, 1975, Born in Iowa: The Homecoming, 1986-87, Hunter Coll./Times Sq. Gallery, N.Y.C.; invitational Am. Acad. Arts and Letters, 1992, 94, 97, 2002; represented in permanent collections Met. Mus. Art, N.Y.C., Nat. Gallery Art, Washington, Am. Fedn. Art, Mus. Modern Art, Frankfurt, Fed. Republic Germany, Lowe Art Mus., Miami, Fla., Karl Ernst Osthaus Mus., Hagen, Germany, Mus. Contemporary Art, Helsinki, Mpls. Inst. Art, Dallas Mus., Bklyn. Mus., Whitney Mus., N.Y.C., Harvard Art Mus., Cambridge, Mass. Served with USMC, 1955-58. Guggenheim fellow, 1968; Creative Artists Public Service grantee, 1974; Nat. Endowment for Arts grantee, 1976 Home: 35 Bond St New York NY 10012-2426

**OHLY, D. CHRISTOPHER,** lawyer; b. N.Y.C., Nov. 7, 1950; s. Bodo Charles and Ellen Charlotte (Nekolla) O.; m. Karen Vanacek; 1 child, Sara Rebecca. AB, Johns Hopkins U., 1972; JD, U. Va., 1975. Bar: Md. 1975, U.S. Dist. Ct. Md. 1975, U.S. Ct. Appeals (1st, 2d and 4th cirs.), U.S. Tax Ct., U.S. Supreme Ct. Asst. U.S. Atty. U.S. Atty.'s Office, Balt., 1978-81; ptnr. Blank Rome LLP, Washington, 1999—. Contbr. articles to profl. jours. Mem. ABA, Md. Bar Assn., Am. Soc. Internat. Law, Phi Beta Kappa, Omicron Delta Kappa, Pi Sigma Alpha. Avocations: skiing, computers, amateur radio. Home:

5714 Saint Albans Way Baltimore MD 21212-2454 also: Village Chalet 5 Middle Ridge Rd South Londonderry VT 05155-9747 Office Phone: 202-772-5828. E-mail: Ohly@BlankRome.com.

**OHM, HERBERT WILLIS,** agronomy educator, agriculturist; b. Albert Lea, Minn., Jan. 28, 1945; s. Wilhelm Carl and Lena Ann (Finkbeiner) O.; m. Judy Ann Chrisinger, Aug. 8, 1964; children: Cari Lynn, David William. BS in Agrl. Edn., U. Minn., St. Paul, 1967; MS in Plant Breeding, N.D. State U., 1969; PhD in Plant Genetics and Breeding, Purdue U., 1972. Cert. agronomist. Asst. prof. Purdue U., West Lafayette, Ind., 1972-77, assoc. prof. agronomy, 1977-83, prof., 1983—2004, disting. prof., 2004—. Team leader Interdisciplinary Wheat and Oat Genetics and Breeding Program, West Lafayette, 1980—, Interdisciplinary Purdue/AID Devel. Program, Burkina Faso, West Africa, 1983-85; mgr. hard red winter wheat rsch. Pioneer Hi-Bred Internat., Inc., Hutchinson, Kans., 1980. Contbr. book chpts. Recipient Soils and Crops Merit award Ind. Crop Improvement Assn., 1988, Merit award Orgn. of African Unity, 1989, Meritorious Svc. award Sci., Tech. and Rsch. Commn., 1989, Agronomic Achievement award American Soc. of Agronomy, 1994, Sch. of Agr. Team award, 2000, Distinction cert. Purdue Agr. Alumni Assn., 2005. Fellow: AAAS, Crop Sci. Soc. Am. (chmn. divsn. 1991), Am. Soc. Agronomy; mem.: Am. Registry Cert. Profls. in Agrl. Crops and Soils (cert.), Coun. Agrl. Sci. and Tech., Nat. Oat Improvement Coun. (chmn.), Am. Oat Workers Conf. (chmn.). Avocations: woodworking, music. Office: Purdue U Dept Agronomy Lilly Hall Life Scis West Lafayette IN 47907-1150 Office Phone: 765-494-8072. Business E-Mail: hohm@purdue.edu.

**OHMAN, DIANA J.,** government agency administrator, former state official; b. Sheridan, Wyo., Oct. 3, 1950; d. Arden and Doris Marie (Carstens) Mahin. AA, Casper Coll., 1970; BA, U. Wyo., 1972, MEd, 1977, postgrad., 1979—. Tchr. kindergarten Natrona County Sch. Dist., Casper, Wyo., 1971-72; tchr. rural sch. K-8 Campbell County Sch. Dist., Gillette, Wyo., 1972-80, rural prin. K-8, 1980-82, prin. K-6, 1982-84, assoc. dir. instrn., 1984-87; dir. K-12 Goshen County Migrant Program, Torrington, Wyo., 1989; prin. K-2 Goshen County Sch. Dist., Torrington, Wyo., 1987-90; state supt. pub. instrn. State of Wyo., Cheyenne, 1991-94, secretary of state, 1995-98; dir. Dept. Def. Dep. Schs., Europe, 2002—. Chmn. Campbell County Mental Health Task Force, 1986-87; mem. Legis. Task Force on Edn. of Handicapped 3-5 Yr. Olds, 1988-89. State Committeewoman Wyo. Rep. Party, 1985-88. Recipient Wyo. Elem. Prin. of Yr. award, 1990; named Campbell County Tchr. of Yr. 1980, Campbell County Profl. Bus. Woman of Yr. 1984, Outstanding Young Woman in Am., 1983. Mem. Coun. of Chief of State Sch. Officers (Washington chpt.), Internat. Reading Assn., Wyo. Assn. of Sch. Adminstrs., N.Am. Securities Adminstrs. Assn., Kappa Delta Pi, Phi Kappa Phi, Phi Delta Kappa. Republican. Lutheran. Office: CMR 443 Box 111 APO AE 09096-9111

**OHMAN, E. MAGNUS,** cardiologist, educator; s. Karl-Erik Ohman and Maj-Britt Borjeson; m. Elspeth O'Reilly-Hyland, June 12, 1987; children: Edward, Elsa-Maria, Henry, Henry Kenneth. MB, BCh, MD, Royal Coll. of Surgeons in Ireland, Dublin, 1981. Asst. prof. of medicine Duke U. Med. Ctr., Durham, NC, 1991—96, assoc. prof. of medicine, 1996—2001, prof. of medicine, 2005—, U. of NC, Chapel Hill, NC, 2001—05. Dir. Heart Ctr. U. of N.C., Chapel Hill, 2001—05. Recipient Edith Walsh award, Brit. Med. Assn., 1985. Fellow: Am. Coll. Cardiology, European Soc. Cardiology, Royal Coll. Physicians of Ireland, Soc. of Cardiac Aniography and Intervention. Achievements include Methods patent for assessing reperfusion in heart attacks. Office: Duke Univ Med Ctr DUMC 3126 Erwin Rd Durham NC 27710 Office Phone: 919-681-2069. Office Fax: 919-681-4454.

**OHMAN, FRANKLIN ERIC,** ballet educator, choreographer; b. L.A., Jan. 7, 1939; s. Eric Ohman and Irene Iris Harsen; m. Gloria Isaksen, June 24, 1978 (div. Aug. 1984); 1 child, Johan Eric. Grad. h.s., Ontario, Calif., 1957. Dancer San Francisco Ballet, 1959—62, N.Y.C. Ballet, 1962—84; dir. N.Y. Dance Theatre, 1974—. Artistic dir. N.Y. Dance Theatre, 1974—; choreographer, tchr. Ohman Sch. Ballet, L.I., NY, 1980—; choreographer Boston Ballet, Am. Movie Classics (divsn. Rainbow Cablevision), Broadhollow Players, L.I.; tchr., choreographer Long Lake Performing Arts Camp, NY; ballet master Ballet Philippines, Manila, 2004; lectr.-demonstrations covering life of George Balanchine at pub. librs. and museums throughout N.Y. and Conn. Century of Balanchine 1904-2004; ballet tchr. St. Louis Ballet, 2004—05; completed 24th season Nutcracker, Hofstra U. Pvt. U.S. Army, 1961—67. Grantee, NY State Coun. on Arts, Suffolk County Office of Cultural Affairs. Avocations: painting, choreography, writing. Office: Ohman Sch Ballet Calvert Ave Commack NY 11725 Office Phone: 631-462-6266. Fax: 631-462-6361. Personal E-mail: frankohman@yahoo.com.

**OHNO, APOLO ANTON,** Olympic athlete; b. Seattle, May 22, 1982; Mem. U.S. Elite Short Track Speedskating Team. Named U.S. Champion, 1997, World Jr. Short Track Champion, 1999, World Cup Overall Champion, 2001, 500 meter champion, 2001, 1000 meter champion, 2001, 1500 meter champion, 2001; recipient U.S. Champion, 1999, 2001, 2002, 1500 meter Gold medal, 2002 Olympic Games, 1000 meter Silver medal, 1000 meter Bronze Medal, 2006 Winter Olympic Games, Men's Short Track Relay Bronze Medal, Gold Medal 500 meter Speed Skating, 2006 Winter Olympics. Achievements include was a national champion and record holder in indoor inline skating, earned a state championship as a swimmer in the breaststroke. Avocations: music, badminton, basketball, break dancing, friends. Address: US Speedskating PO Box 450639 Westlake OH 44145*

**OHNSORG, BRIAN GREGORY,** music educator, singer; b. Chaska, Minn., Aug. 26, 1974; s. Gregory Allen Ohnsorg and Claudia Ann Vierling; m. Shelley Ann Kuehn, Dec. 19, 1998; 1 child, Emily. BA in Music Edn., Gustavus Adolphus Coll., 1997; MusM in Vocal Performance, U. Minn., 2003. Tchr. Rogers HS Cold Spring, Minn. 1998—2001; vocal music prof. Gustavus Adolphus Coll., St. Peter, Minn., 2002—05; tchr. Jordan (Minn.) HS, 2005—. Dir., soloist Mt. Olivet Luth. Ch., Mpls., 2001—; singer Vocal Essence Ensemble, Mpls., 2001—; freelance tenor soloist, 2001—. Avocations: fishing, skiing, racquetball, golf. Home: 3000 W 88th St Bloomington MN 55431

**OHRENSTEIN, ROMAN ABRAHAM,** economist, educator, rabbi; b. Slomniki, Poland, June 12, 1920; arrived in U.S., 1951, naturalized, 1957; s. Joseph Barukh and Gena (Fiefkopf) O.; m. Ruth Silberstein, Aug. 30, 1953; children: Gena Ann, Ilana Rose. MA in Econs., U. Munich, 1948, PhD in Econs. cum laude, 1949, postgrad. in medicine, 1949—51; MHL, Jewish Theol. Sem. Am., 1955; postgrad., Columbia U., 1963—64. Ordained rabbi, 1955. Rabbi, Auburn, NY, 1955—57, Pittsfield, Mass., 1957—60, Atlanta, 1960—62, NYC, 1962—66; prof. econs. Nassau Coll., SUNY, Garden City, 1964-99, chmn. econs. dept., 1976-78, 82-84, prof. emeritus, 1999—, campus chaplain, 1970—; chaplain Nassau County Civic Preparedness, NY, 1965—; mem. Coll. Coun. Am. Coll. Jerusalem, 1967-73, prof. econs., 1968-73. Vis. prof. U. Newcastle, Australia, 1985, vis. rsch. prof., 1989; past chaplain Kiwanis, Police Dept. Cayuga County, NY, 1955-57, Mt. Sinai Hosp., NYC, 1963-64; mem. Coun. of Orgns., U.S.A., 1978-85; mem. spl. com. on Jewish law Rabbinical Assembly, 1971; condr. seminars U. Queensland, Sydney U., Nat. U., Australia, 1989, Sorbonne, Paris, 1990; lectr. guest spkr. Jewish civic and profl. orgns. Author: (series) Economic Thought in Talmudic Literature, 1968, 70, 83, 86, 87, 89, 91-93, 96, 2003 (citation Am. Biog. Inst. 1985), Inventories During Business Fluctuations, 1973, Inventory Control as an Economic Shock Absorber, 1975, Economic Analysis in Talmudic Literature, 1992, ed edit., rev. and enlarged, 2003; contbr. chpt. to anthology: Ancient and Medieval Economic Ideas, 1998; mem. editl. adv. bd. Internat. Rev. Econs. and Ethics; columnist Algemeiner Jour., NYC; contbr. articles to profl. jours. Mem. nat. exec. comm. Am. Profs. for Peace in the Mid. East, 1971-73; mem. adv. bd. Am. Acad. Alliance for Israel, 1995—. Recipient 1st Faculty Disting. Achievement award Nassau Coll., SUNY, 1992, 95, Citation of Excellence, Anbar Electronic Intelligence, Eng., 1996, Poineering Rsch. in Talmudic Economics, 1968; SUNY fellow, 1968, 70. Mem. Nat. Assn. Jewish Chaplains, Rabbinical Assembly NY Bd. Rabbis, Am. Econ. Assn., History of Econs. Soc., Assn. Social Econs., Learned Soc., NY Acad. Scis., Internat. Soc. for Intercommunication New Ideas, Literati Club (Eng.). Home: 28-74 208th

St Bayside NY 11360-2421 Personal E-mail: ohrenste@aol.com. *I kept my faith in God coupled with loyalty to tradition, sharpened my mind while maintaining discipline of the heart; tenacity in the face of adversity, turning stumbling blocks into stepping stones while never losing sight of life's supreme purpose: to leave the world a little better than I found it.*

**OHRN, NILS YNGVE,** chemistry and physics educator; b. Avesta, Sweden, June 11, 1934; came to U.S., 1966; s. Nils E. and Gerda M. (Akerlund) O.; m. Ann M.M. Thorsell, Aug. 24, 1957; children: Elisabeth, Maria. MS, Uppsala U., 1958, PhD, 1963, F.D., 1966. Research assoc. Uppsala (Sweden) U., 1963-66; assoc. prof. U. Fla., Gainesville, 1966-70, prof. chemistry and physics, 1971—, assoc. dir. Quantum Theory Project, 1976-77, dir. Quantum Theory Project, 1983-98, chmn. dept. chemistry, 1977-83. Editor: Internat. Jour. Quantum Chemistry, 1970—. Fulbright grantee Com. for Internat. Exchange of Scholars, Washington, 1961-63; recipient Bicentennial Gold medal King of Sweden, 1980; Fla. Acad. Scis. medal, 1984; named Tchr./Scholar of Yr., U. Fla., 2003-04. Fellow Am. Phys. Soc., Chaire Francqui Interuniversitaires Belgium; mem. Am. Chem. Soc. (Fla. award 1997), Royal Acad. Scis. Uppsala Sweden (fgn.), Finnish Acad. Scis. (fgn.), Royal Danish Acad. Scis. (fgn.), Sigma Xi, Phi Beta Kappa. Home: 1823 NW 11th Rd Gainesville FL 32605-5323 Office: U Fla Quantum Theory Project 2301 NPB Bldg # 92 Gainesville FL 32611-8435 Business E-Mail: ohrn@qtp.ufl.edu.

**OHRT, WILLIAM F.,** manufacturing executive; B in Acctg., Wayne State U., 1975; MBA in Fin., U. Detroit, 1981. Joined AlliedSignal, Inc., 1979, v p fin. AlliedSignal Turbocharging Sys., 1995—97; v.p. fin. ITT Automotive Elec. Sys., 1997—98; v.p., CFO truck group Navistar Internat. Transp. Corp., 1998—99; v.p., CFO Dura Automotive Sys., Inc., 2000—01; exec. v.p., CFO Walter Industries, Inc., Tampa, Fla., 2001—. Office: Walter Industries Inc 4211 W Boy Scout Blvd Tampa FL 33607

**OHS, KARL,** former lieutenant governor; b. Havre, Mont., Nov. 18, 1946; m. Sherri Ohs; children: Brad, Eric, Brian, Elizabeth. Student in Agrl. Econ., Mont. State U. Founder Mont. Agrl. Producers, Inc., 1988—; prin. owner AAA Storage, Helena, 1996—; rep. Mont. Ho. Reps., 1995—2001, majority whip, 1997—2001; lt. gov. State of Mont., Helena, 2001—05. Prin. negotiator Freeman standoff FBI, Jordan, Mont., 1996. Bd. dir. Harrison Sch. Bd., Mont., 1974—83. Recipient Lou Peters award, FBI, 1998.*

**O'HURLEY, JOHN,** actor; b. Kittery, Maine, Oct. 9, 1956; m. Eva LaRue Callahan, 1992 (div. 1994); m. Lisa Mesloh, Aug. 14, 2004. BA, Providence Coll., 1976. Owner Era Aviation, Alaska; part owner J. Peterman Co., bd. dirs.; principal ptnr. Heritage Capitol Advisors, Atlanta, Round One Investments, Los Angeles; investor Piccadilly Restaurants. Actor: (TV series) The Edge of Night, 1983—84, Loving, 1984—86, As the World Turns, 1988, The Young & the Restless, 1989—91, Santa Barbara, 1990—91, Scorch, 1992, General Hospital, 1992, Valley of the Dolls, 1994, A Whole New Ballgame, 1995, Seinfeld, 1995—98, Lost on Earth, 1997, Over the Top, 1997, Cursed, 2000—01, The Mullets, 2003—04; (TV films) Something is Out There, 1988, Billy the Kid, 1989, White Hot: The Mysterious Murder of Thelma Todd, 1991, Seduction: 3 Tales from the "Inner Sanctum", 1992, My Son is Innocent, 1996, The Secret, 1997, Murder Live!, 1997, Blood on Her Hands, 1998, Tempting Fate, 1998, Life of the Party: The Pamela Harriman Story, 1998, Wild Grizzly, 1999, Three Secrets, 1999; (films) Night Eyes II, 1992, Mirror Images, 1992, The Power Within, 1995, Love Stinks, 1999, Slammed, 2001, Firetrap, 2001, Race to Space, 2001, Teddy Bears' Picnic, 2002, Buying the Cow, 2002, Knuckle Sandwich, 2004; voice actor: (TV series) Mickey Mouse Works, 1999—2000; Buzz Lightyear of Star Command, 2000; House of Mouse, 2001—02; Duck Dodgers, 2003—; Father of the Pride, 2004; (films) Tarzan & Jane, 2002; host: (TV series) Extraordinary World of Animals, 1999; Get Golf with the PGA Tour!, 2000; contestant Dancing with the Stars, 2005; composer: (albums) Peace of Our Minds, 2005. Named one of sexiest men alive, People mag., 2005. Avocations: golf, tennis, carpentry, interior design, wine collection. Office: The J Peterman Company 1001 Primrose Ct Lexington KY 40511*

**OJALVO, MORRIS,** civil engineer, educator; b. NYC, Mar. 4, 1924; s. Nissim and (Fanny) O.; m. Anita Bedein, Dec. 26, 1948; children— Lynne, Joseph, Howard, Isobel. B.C.E., Rensselaer Poly. Inst., Troy, N.Y., 1944, M.C.E., 1952; PhD, Lehigh U., Bethlehem, Pa., 1960; JD, Ohio State U., Columbus, 1978. Bar: Ohio bar 1979. Draftsman Am. Bridge Co., Elmira, N.Y., 1946-47; tutor civil engring. CCNY, 1947-49; instr. Rensselaer Poly. Inst., 1949-51; asst. prof. Princeton U., 1951-58; research instr. Lehigh U., 1958-60; mem. faculty Ohio State U., 1960—, prof. civil engring., 1964-82, prof. emeritus, 1982—; vis. prof. U. Tex.-Austin, 1982-83. Author: Thin-Walled Bars With Open Profiles, 1990; contbr. papers in field; patentee warp restraining device. With USN, 1943—46. Mem.: ASCE, Structural Stability Rsch. Coun. Home and Office: 1024 Fairway Ln Estes Park CO 80517-7156 Office Phone: 970-577-0237. E-mail: morris_ojalvo@yahoo.com.

**OJEDA, JOSEPH A.,** psychotherapist; b. NYC, Mar. 25, 1950; s. Benigno Ojeda and Maria Luisa Ayala; children: Kenneth, Lorraine. D of Naturopathy, Westbrook U., Weirton, W.Va., 2004; PhD in Hypnotherapy, LaSalle U., Mandeville, La., 2002; DD, U. of Universal Life, Modesto, Calif., 1975; M in Holistic Healing, Westbrook U., 1996. Diplomate Am. Coll. Forensic Examiners, 1997, Am. Psychotherapy Assn., 1998, bd. cert. Am. Acad. of Experts in Traumatic Stress. Psychotherapist/clergy Counseling Ch. of the Universal Living God, Jamaica, NY, 1972—97; psychotherapist Holistic Healing, Hypnotherapy & Psychotherapy Family, Middletown, 1998—. Marriage officiant Counseling Ch. of the Universal Living God, 1976— pastoral counseling, 1976—; free counseling walk-in clinic, Counseling Ch. of the Universal Living God, 1972—97. Author: (book) Re-education & Reprogramming with Hypnotherapy..., 2001, Integration of Behavioral & Relaxation Approaches..., 2002, Application of Self-Hypnosis Reprogramming Procedure..., 2002. Recipient award for poem Mysterious Woman, Nat. Libr. of Poetry, 1997, Medal of Merit for cmty. involvement, Pres. Ronald Reagan, 1986, award letter for emergency control ctr. assistance, Commr. Joseph V. Terrenzio, Dept. of Hosp. Bur., 1970. Fellow: Am. Acad. of Experts in Traumatic Stress. Home and Office: 27 Sproat Street Middletown NY 10940 Personal E-mail: hypnotex@juno.com.

**OJEDA, NELSON A., II,** musician; b. LA, May 27, 1972; s. Nelson A. Ojeda Sr. and Martha E. Ojeda. MusB, Calif. State U., Fullerton, 1997, MusM, 1999; Diploma profl. studies, Manhattan Sch. of Music, 2004. Collaborative pianist Calif. State U., Long Beach, 1998—2001; prof. piano Mt. San Antonio Coll., Walnut, Calif., 2002—03; choir accompanist Via Magna, Madrid, 2005—, Univ. Politecnica, Madrid, 2004—; concert artist Vivace Concert Agy., Madrid, 2005—. State adjudicator Music Tchrs. Assn. Calif., 1997; nat. adjudicator Am. Coll. Musicians, 1999—; pianist Madrid Chamber Music Internat., 2005—. Translator (piano method book) Alfred Basic Piano Course, 2004. Finalist Ft. Collins (Colo.) Concerto Competition, 1998; recipient Grand prize, Music Assocs. Competition, Orange County, Calif., 1997, Spl. Recognitoin, La Peña Cubana, L.A., 2005. Achievements include Guest artist at David Dubal's World of Piano, Juilliard Sch., Lincoln Ctr. N.Y.C; concert tours in Asia and Europe; soloist with Pacific Symphony Orch. and Southwest Symphony. Avocation: Spanish, Italian, French. Home: 32464 Bergamo Ct Temecula CA 92592 E-mail: pianonelson@yahoo.com.

**OJEDA EISELEY, JAIME DE,** former Spanish ambassador, educator; b. Aug. 5, 1933; BL maxima cum laude in Law, U. Madrid, Spain, 1957; grad., Internat. Acad. of The Hague, The Netherlands; student, Naval War Coll. and Sr. Ctr. for Nat. Def. Studies, Madrid, Spain. Prof. polit. law Complutense U. Madrid, Spain, 1958; joined diplomatic svcs., 1958; served Embassy of Spain, Washington, 1962—69; min. counselor Peking, China, 1973—76; consul-gen. of Spain Hong Kong and Macao, 1976-79; fellow Ctr. Internat. Rels., Harvard U., Cambridge, Mass., 1979-80; dep. permanent rep. NATO, 1982-83, permanent rep., 1983-90; amb. to U.S.A., Spanish Embassy, Washington, 1990-97; pres. high level coun. fgn. affairs Min. F.A. Madrid,

1997; amb.-in-residence Shenandoah U., Winchester, Va., 1997—. Vis. scholar Johns Hopkins U., Washington, 1997; disting. adj. fellow CSIS, Washington, 1997. Translator: Alice in Wonderland and Through the Looking Glass, by Lewis Carroll, 1971—74, Spain and America: The Past and Future, 1994, El 98 en el Congreso y en la Prensa de los Estados Unidos, 1999. Lt. Reserve Marine Corps. Spanish Navy, 1957. Decorated Great Cross Mil. Merit, Great Cross of Civil Merit, Order of Charles III. Home: PO Box 57 3770 Leeds Manor Rd Markham VA 22643-1817 Office: Shenandoah U 1460 University Dr Winchester VA 22601-5195

**OJI, PAULINE E.,** secondary school educator; b. Ozuitem, Nigeria; arrived in U.S., 1995; d. Shedrack N. and Mercy O. Udah; m. Madumere Oji, June 1, 1995; children: Mercy A., Victoria O. BS in Chemistry, Univ. Port Harcourt, 1987; Spl. Edn., Coppin State Coll., 1999. Cert. spl. educator. Sub. tchr. Balt. City Pub. Sch., Balt., 1997—99; math. tchr. Woodbourne Ctr. Inc., Balt., 1997; sci. tchr. Strawbridge Sch., Balt., 2001—04, Woodlawn H.S., Balt., 2004—. Dept. chair Strawbridge Sch., Balt., 2001—02; mem. adv. com. John Hopkins Univ., 2003—. Facilitator (presentation) Picoturbine Windmills, 2001. Vol. Girl Scouts of Am. Troop 1536, Balt., 2003—; presenter Md. Assn. of Non Pub. Spl. Edn. Facilities, 2002, Md. Assn. of Non Pub. Spl. Edn. Facilitier, 2003; supporter Spl. Olympics, 2000—. Nominee Educator of the Yr., Ten Conf., 2001; recipient Gov. Citation, Md. Gov., 2000. Mem.: NEA, ASCD, Nat. Sci. Tchrs. Assn., Internat. Reading Assn., Coun. Exceptional Children (vol.), Md. State Tchrs. Assn. (vol.), Nat. Coun. for Tchrs. of Math., Md. State Coun. for Tchrs. of Math. Achievements include participated in Md. Educators Summer Rsch. Program. Avocations: reading, travel, dance, basketball, tennis. Home: 12 Hickory Nut Ct Baltimore MD 21236 Office: Balt County Pub Sch Woodlawn H S 1801 Woodlawn Dr Baltimore MD 21207 Office Phone: 410-887-1310. Personal E-mail: mvpeo@juno.com

**OJIMA, IWAO,** chemistry professor; b. Yokohama, Japan, June 5, 1945; came to U.S., 1983; s. Masaharu and Sumiko (Takatsuki) O.; m. Yoko Ogino, Apr. 24, 1971. BS, U. Tokyo, 1968, MS, 1970, PhD in Organic Chemistry, 1973. Rsch. fellow Sagami Inst. for Chem. Rsch., Japan, 1970-76, sr. rsch. fellow, group leader, 1976-83; assoc. prof. chemistry SUNY, Stony Brook, 1983-84, prof., 1984-91, leading prof., 1991-95, disting. prof., 1995—, chmn., 1997—2003; dir. Inst. Chem. Biology and Drug Discovery, 2003—. Editor: Catalytic Asymmetric Synthesis, 1993, 2d edit., 2000, Taxane Anticancer Agents, 1994, Biomedical Frontiers of Fluorine Chemistry, 1996, Anticancer Agents-Frontiers in Cancer Chemotherapy, 2001; contbr. numerous articles to profl. jours.; numerous patents in field. Named fellow J.S. Guggenheim Meml. Found., 1995-97. Fellow AAAS, N.Y. Acad. Sci.; mem. Am. Chem. Soc. (editl. adv. bd. 1995-2000, exec. com. divsn. organic chemistry 1998-2000, A.C. Cope Scholar award 1994, E.B. Hershberg award 2001), Chem. Soc. Japan (Nat. Young Investigator award 1976, Disting. Achievement award 1999), N.Y. Acad. Scis., Sigma Xi. Achievements include research in homogenous catalysis of transition metal complexes; asymmetric synthesis; organic synthesis by means of organometallic reagents; peptides and peptide mimetics; beta-lactam chemistry; organoflourine chemistry, medicinal chemistry especially in regard to enzyme inhibitors and taxane anticancer agents. Home: 41 Roslyn Ct Port Jefferson NY 11777-1462 Office: State U New York Dept Chemistry Stony Brook NY 11794-3400 Office Phone: 631-632-7947. Business E-Mail: iojima@notes.cc.sunysb.edu.

**OKA, TAKASHI,** journalist, consultant, educator; b. Tokyo, Oct. 21, 1924; s. William Masakazu and Fumiko Mary Oka; m. Hiroko Imai, Sept. 8, 1956; children: Megumi, Sakuya. B in Econs., Rikkyo U., 1947; BA, Principa Coll., 1950; MA, Harvard U., 1954. Asst. to fgn. editor Christian Sci. Monitor, Boston, 1954-59, fgn. corr. Hong Kong, Saigon, Moscow, 1959-68, Paris, London, Beijing, Tokyo, 1971-92; bur. chief Tokyo office NY Times, 1968-71; staff dir. internat. dept. New Frontier Party, Tokyo, 1994-98; Washington rep. Liberal Party of Japan, 1999—2002; vis. scholar Sigur Ctr. George Washington U., Washington, 1998-99, 2003—04. Rsch. assoc. Internat. Inst. of Strategic Studies, London, 1976-78; rsch. fellow Carnegie Endowment for Internat. Peace, 1992-95. Author: Prying Open the Door: Foreign Workers in Japan, 1995. Avocation: tennis. Home and Office: 800 25th St NW Washington DC 20037-2207

**OKA, TAKESHI,** physicist, physical chemist, astronomer, educator; b. Tokyo, June 10, 1932; arrived in U.S., 1981, naturalized, 2004; s. Shumpei and Chiyoko O.; m. Keiko Nukui, Oct. 24, 1960; children: Ritsuko, Noriko, Kentaro, Yujiro. B.Sc., U. Tokyo, 1955, PhD, 1960; DSc (hon.), U. Waterloo, 2001, Univ. Coll., London, 2004. Rsch. assoc. U. Tokyo, 1960-63; fellow NRC Can., Ottawa, Ont., 1963-65, asst., 1965-68, assoc., 1968-71, sr. rsch. physicist, 1971-80; prof. U. Chgo., 1981—, Robert A. Millikan disting. prof., 1989—; prof. Enrico Fermi Inst., 1993—2004, emeritus, 2004—. Mem. editorial bd. Chem. Physics, 1972-92, Jour. Molecular Spectroscopy, 1973—, Jour. Chem. Physics, 1975-77. Recipient Steacie prize, 1972; Earle K. Plyler prize, 1982, Norman McLean award U. Chog., 2004. Fellow Royal Soc. Can., Royal Soc. London (Davy medal 2004), Am. Phys. Soc., Optical Soc. Am. (William F. Meggers award 1997, Ellis R. Lippincott award 1998), Am. Acad. Scis. and Arts; mem. Am. Astron. Soc; Am. Chem. Soc. (E. Bright Wilson award, 2002). Office Phone: 773-702-7070. Business E-Mail: t-oka@uchicago.edu.

**OKADA, ISAMU,** finance educator, researcher; b. Kawasaki, Kanagawa, Japan, Jan. 6, 1973; s. Yaeko Okada. MA in Engring., U. Electro-Comm., Tokyo, 1997; PhD, U. Electro-Comm., 2000. Rsch. assoc. U. Electro-Comm., Tokyo, 2000—01; asst. prof. Soka U., Tokyo, 2001—05. assoc. prof., 2005—. Office: Soka Univ 1-236 Taugi Hachioji 192-8577 Japan

**OKADA, KAZUNORI,** research scientist; s. Mitsuo and Michiyo Okada; m. Eve Luckring. B of Engring., Nagoya U., Japan, 1992, MPhil, 1994; MS, U. of So. Calif., 1996, PhD, 2001. Rsch. assoc. U. of So. Calif., L.A., 2001—03; rsch. scientist Siemens Corp. Rsch., Princeton, NJ, 2003—06. Mem.: IEEE (assoc.).

**OKADA, RYOZO,** medical educator, researcher; b. Kiryu, Japan, July 20, 1931; s. Kenji and Sachi (Ishihara) O.; m. Shigeko Shindo, May 25, 1958; children: Kyoko, Taro. MD, Tokyo U., 1956, PhD, 1961. Intern then resident; asst. Tokyo U. Sch. Medicine, 1962-63; rsch. fellow Hektoen Inst. Cook County Hosp., Chgo., 1963-66; attending physician Yoikuin Hosp., Tokyo, 1966-68; assoc. prof. Sch. Med. Juntendo U., Tokyo, 1968-83, prof., 1983—97, prof. emeritus, 1997—; rector Gumma Paz Coll., 1998—2005, emeritus prof., 2005—; dir. Gumma Paz Rsch. Inst., 2005—. Councilor Cardiovasc. Inst. Roppongi, Tokyo, 1990—; com. in field. Contbr. chapters to books, articles to profl. jours. Bd. dirs. Shirane Kaizen Sch. Fellow: Japanese Geriat. Soc., Japanese Angiology Soc., Japanese Circulation Soc., Coun. Prevention Heart Disease, Am. Heart Assn., Internat. Electrocardiology, Am. Geriat. Soc., Internat. Cardiovasc. Pathology, Am. Diabetes Assn., Internat. Union Angiology; mem.: Sports Medicine Occupl. Medicine, Japanese Soc. Medicine. Avocation: travel. Office: Gumma Paz Rsch Inst 5-4 Iwaoshicho Takasaki Gunma 370-0044 Japan Home: 25-9 Asahigaoka Kanagawaku Yokohama 221-0814 Japan Office Phone: 027-310-7766.

**OKADA, SHIGERU,** medical educator, researcher; b. Okayama, Japan, Feb. 15, 1940; s. Keizo and Moyoko (Nishigaki) O.; m. Naoko Kobashi, Nov. 7, 1965; children: Satoru, Rie, Mari. MD, Okayama U., Japan, 1964, PhD, 1969. Chief pathologist Kyoto (Japan) City Hosp., 1977-80; rsch. Sch. Medicine Kyoto U., 1980-90; asst. Med. Sch. Okayama U., 1969-71, lectr., 1971-77; prof. Okayama U. Med. Sch., Japan, 1990—2001; dir. Isotope Ctr. Okayama U., Japan, 1995—2001, advisor to the pres. 1999—2001, prof., dean Sch. of Medicine, 2003—05, prof. emeritus, 2005—; prin. Tamano Inst. Med. Tech. and Nursing, 2005—. Head radiation protection com. Okayama U., 1991-2001; trustee Kake Edn:l. Inst., 2005—; vis. prof. Okayama U., 2005—. Contbr. articles to profl. jours. Mem. Japan Pathol. Soc. Tokyo, Japan Haematological Soc. Kyoto, Internat. Soc. Hematology, Japanese Cancer Assn. Tokyo, N.Y.

Acad. Sci. Office: Okayama U Grad Sch Medicine and Dentistry 2-5-1 Shikata Okayama 700-8558 Japan Office Phone: 81-86-235-7491. Personal E-mail: dragon40@beach.ocn.ne.jp. Business E-Mail: okadas@cc.okayama-u.ac.jp.

**OKAFOR, EMEKA,** professional basketball player; b. Houston, Tex., Sept. 28, 1982; BA in Finance, U. Conn., 2004. Player Charlotte Bobcats, 2004—. Mem. US Olympics Basketball Team, Athens, Greece, 2004. Named Most Outstanding Player, NCAA Final Four, 2004, Co-Nat. Player of the year, NABC, 2004, Big East Player of the Year, 2004, Defensive Player of the Year, 2004, Academic All-American first team, 2003—04, NBA Rookie of the Yr., 2005; named to All-American First Team, AP, 2004. Achievements include Mem.of NCAA Nat.Championship Team U. Conn Huskies, 2004; First ever draft pick (second overall) of expansion Charlotte Bobcats, 2004. Office: c/o Charlotte Bobcats 129 W Trade St Ste 700 Charlotte NC 28202*

**OKAFOR, VICTOR O.,** journalist, educator; s. Christopher C. and Grace I. Okafor; m. Victoria N. Morah, Aug. 26, 2000; 1 child, Emeka C. BA in Journalism, Ind. U., 1986, M in Pub. Affairs, 1988; PhD in African Am. studies, Temple U., Phila., 1994. Cert. online course designer and instr. e-Coll., 2001. Asst. prof. N.C. State U., 1994—95; assoc. prof. Ea. Mich. U., Ypsilanti, Mich., 1995—2004, prof., 2004—. Grad. instr. Temple U. Phila, 1989—94. Author: (book) Towards An Understanding of Africology, 2002. V.p. Black Faculty & Staff Assn. of Ea. Mich. U., Ypsilanti, 2003. Mem.: So. Conf. on African Am. Studies, Phi Kappa Phi. Achievements include design of Online Univ. courses. Avocations: writing, reading, travel. Office: Ea Mich Univ 620 Pray Harrold Ypsilanti MI 48198 Office Phone: 734-487-3460. Office Fax: 734-487-6891. Personal E-mail: victor.okafor@emich.edu.

**OKAMOTO, JEFFREY AKIRA,** psychiatrist; b. Abington, Pa., July 18, 1954; s. Allen H. and Yone (Watanabe) O.; m. Christina Royer Neff, Aug. 11, 1985; 1 child, Stephen Andrew. BS/Biology with honors, Ursinus Coll., 1976; MD, Pa. State Coll. Medicine, 1980. Diplomate Am. Bd. Psychiatry and Neurology. Resident in psychiatry U. N.C., Chapel Hill, 1984; staff psychiatrist Philhaven Hosp., Mt. Gretna, Pa., 1986—; clin. asst. prof. dept. family and cmty. medicine Pa. State U., 1991-93. Cons. staff Good Samaritan Hosp., Lebanon, 1986—; clin. instr. dept. psychiatry U. N.C., Chapel Hill, 1985-87. Named Chpt. Scholar Ursinus Coll., Collegeville, Pa., 1976. Mem. Am. Psychiat. Assn., Pa. Psychiat. Assn., Christian Med. Soc. Republican. Mennonite. Avocations: home computers, fishing, tennis, raquetball, photography. Home: 551 Hemlock Ln Lebanon PA 17042-9017 Office: Philhaven Hosp 283 S Butler Rd Mount Gretna PA 17064

**OKAMOTO, MARK P.,** pharmacist, educator, dean; b. Nov. 28, 1961; s. Takashi and Hisaye Okamoto; m. Eileen Okamoto. BS in Biology, UCLA, 1984; PharmD, U. So. Calif., 1988. Registered pharmacist Calif. Postdoctoral fellow U. So. Calif., LA, 1989—92; clin. pharm. scientist Kaiser Permanente, Downey, Calif., 1993—98; corp. dir. clin. affairs PHI Healthcare, Irvine, Calif., 1999—2000; assoc. prof. Western U. Health Scis., Pomona, Calif., 2000—, chair social and adminstrv. scis., 2005—, assoc. dean, 2005—. Cons. Internat. Soc. Pharmacoeconomics, Washington, 1998; grant reviewer Hong Kong Nat. Govt., 2005—. Mem. editl. bd. Annals Pharmacotherapy, 2003—; contbr. chapters to books, articles to profl. jours. Recipient Faculty Svc. award, U. So. Calif.; grantee, Calif. Healthcare Found., 2002. Mem. Am. Coll. Clin. Pharmacy, Rho Chi. Office: Western U Health Scis 309 E Second St Coll Plz Pomona CA 91766 Office Phone: 909-469-5587. Office Fax: 909-469-5428. E-mail: mokamoto@westernu.edu.

**OKAMOTO, SEIZO,** transportation executive; b. Wakayama, Japan, 1942; m. Tomoko Okamoto; 2 children. Degree in Engring., Osaka U., 1965. From engr. to pres., CEO Toyota Motor Mfg., Ind., Inc., Princeton, Ind., 1965—96, pres., 1996—, CEO, 1996—. Office: Toyota Motor Manufacturing Indiana Inc 4000 Tulip Tree Dr Princeton IN 47670 Mailing: PO Box 4000 Princeton IN 47670-4000

**OKAMURA, ARTHUR SHINJI,** artist, educator; b. Long Beach, Calif., Feb. 24, 1932; s. Frank Akira and Yuki O.; m. Elizabeth Tuomi, Aug. 7, 1953 (div.); children: Beth, Jonathan, Jane, Ethan; m. Kitty Wong, 1991. Student, Art Inst. of Chgo., 1950-54, U. Chgo., 1951, 52, 57, art seminar Yale, 1954. Faculty Ctrl. YMCA Coll., Chgo., 1956, 57, Evanston (Ill.) Art Center, 1956-57, Art Inst. Chgo., North Shore Art League, Winnetka, Ill., Acad. Art, San Francisco, 1957, Calif. Sch. Fine Arts, Ox Bow Summer Art Sch., Saugatuck, Mich., 1963, Calif. Coll. Arts and Crafts, Oakland, 1958-59, prof. arts, 1966-97, prof. emeritus, 1997—. lectr. watercolor painting, 1987; dir. San Francisco Studio Art, 1958; tchr. watercolor workshops, Bali, Indonesia, 1989, 92; lectr. in field. Author (with Robert Creeley): 1, 2, 3, 4, 5, 6, 7, 8, 9, 0, 1971; author: (with Robert Bly) Basho, 1972, Ten Poems by Issa, 1992; author: (with Steve Kowit) Passionate Journey, 1984; author: (with David Rosen and Joel Weishaus) The Healing Spirit of Haiku; author: Magic Rabbit, 1995, The Paper Propeller, 2000; one-man shows include Charles Feingarten Galleries, Chgo., 1956, 1958, 1959, San Francisco, 1957, Santa Barbara Mus. Art, 1958, Oakland Mus. Art, 1959, Legion Honor, San Francisco, 1961, Dallas, 1962, La Jolla (Calif.) Mus., 1963, U. Utah, 1964, San Francisco Mus. Art, 1968, Hanssen Gallery, 1968, 1971, Ruth Braunstein, San Francisco, 1981, 1982, 1984, 1986—88, 1990, 1994, 1997, 2000, 2003, Commonweal Gallery, Bolinas, Calif., 2001, exhibited in group shows at Pa. Acad. Fine Art, U. Chgo., U. Wash., U. Ill., Art Inst. Chgo., L.A. County Mus., Am. Fedn. Art, Denver Mus., NAD, De Young Mus., San Francisco, Knoedler Gallery, N.Y.C., Feingarten Galleries, Whitney Mus. Art, others; retrospective at Bolinas Mus., 2002, Claudia Chapline Galleries, Stinson Beach, Calif., 1995; Represented in permanent collections Art Inst. Chgo., Borg-Warner Collections, Chgo., Whitney Mus. Art, Santa Barbara Mus. Art, San Francisco Mus. Art, Ill. State Normal, Corcoran Mus., Nat. Collection Fine Arts, Smithsonian Instn., many others. Served as pvt. AUS, 1955-56. Recipient 1st prize religious art U. Chgo., 1953; Ryerson travelling fellow, 1954; Martin Cahn award contemporary Am. paintings Art Inst. Chgo., 1957; purchase award U. Ill., 1959; purchase award Nat. Soc. Arts and Letters, N.Y.C., 1960; Neysa McMein purchase award Whitney Mus. Art, 1960; Schwabacher-Frey award 79th Ann. of San Francisco Mus. Art, 1960 Mem.: Commonweal (bd. dirs. 1993—2002). Home: 210 Kale Rd Bolinas CA 94924 E-mail: arthurokamura@earthlink.net.

**O'KANE, BARBARA LYNN,** research psychologist; b. Jersey City, Sept. 7, 1950; d. Herbert and Pearl Clair Sandick; m. David Dean O'Kane, June 25, 1988; 1 child, Nathan Sean. BS, Suffolk U., 1976; PhD, Brandeis U., 1982. Rsch. psychologist U.S. Army Natick R&D Ctr., Natick, Mass., 1979-85; R&D insp. U.S. Army Material Command, Alexandria, Va., 1985-89; engring. rsch. psychologist U.S. Army Night Vision and Electronic Sensors Directorate, Ft. Belvoir, Va., 1985—. Author: (chpt.) Vision Models for Target Detection and Recognition, 1995; contbr. articles to profl. jours. Avocations: music, public speaking, creation science, skiing. Home: 6117 Burnett St Alexandria VA 22310-2662 Office: US Army Night Vision Lab Burbeck Rd Fort Belvoir VA 22060 Business E-Mail: okane@nvl.army.mil.

**O'KANE, MARGARET E.,** non-profit organization executive; children: Katie, Beth. BA in French, Fordham U., 1969; MHS in Health Adminstrn. and Planning, Johns Hopkins U. Sch. Hygiene and Public Health. Second grade tchr. St. Ambrose Sch., Bklyn., 1970-72; neurology rsch. asst. Children's Hosp., Boston, 1972-73; respiratory therapist St. Elizabeth's Hosp., Boston, U. Va. Med. Ctr., Charlottesville, Va., Children's Hosp., Washington, DC, 1973-78; program analyst office of planning, evaluation, legislation health svcs. adminstrn. U.S. Dept. Health and Human Svcs., Washington, 1979-81; rsch. assoc. intergovernmental health policy project (IHPP) The George Washington U., Washington, 1981-83; public health svc. fellow U.S. Dept. Health and Human Svcs. Nat. Ctr. for Health Svcs. Rsch., Washington, 1983-84, special asst. to dir., 1985-86; dir. med. dirs. divsn. Am. Assn. Health Plans (formerly Group Health Assn. of Am., Inc.), Washington, 1986-89; dir. quality mgmt. Group Health Assn., Inc., Washington, 1989-90; pres. Nat.

Com. Quality Assurance, Washington, 1990—. Elected mem. Inst. of Medicine, 1999. Named Health Person of Yr. Medicine & Health Jour., 1996; recipient Founder's award Am. Coll. Med. Quality, 1997. Office: Nat Com for Quality Assurance 2000 L St NW Ste 500 Washington DC 20036-4918

**OKAY, JOHN LOUIS,** management consultant; b. Emmett, Mich., Mar. 27, 1942; s. Stanley John and Mildred Isabell (Little) O.; m. Judith Ann Gerlach, Aug. 22, 1964; children: Stephen, Christopher, Douglas. BS in Agr., Mich. State U., 1964, MS in Agrl. Econs., 1967, PhD in Resource Econs., 1974. Agrl. economist U.S. Soil Conservation Svc., East Lansing, Mich., 1967-73, program analyst Washington, Mich., 1974-83, dir. info. systems, 1983-85; assoc. dir. info. systems USDA, Washington, 1985-91, dir. info. systems, 1991-95; dep. commr. Fed. Technology Svc., GSA, Falls Church, Va., 1995-97; sr. v.p. Fed. Sources Inc., McLean, Va., 1997-99; pres. J.L. Okay Cons., Oak Hill, Va., 1999—2003; ptnr. Topside Cons. Group, 2003—. Recipient Meritorious Exec. award Pres. of U.S., 1989, 97, Fed. Computer Week's Fed. 100 award, 1992, 1994, 1997, 2004. Mem. Armed Forces Comm. and Electronics Assn. (bd. dirs. 1994-98), Sr. Execs. Assn. (bd. dirs. 1989-98). Office: 2857 Fox Mill Rd Oak Hill VA 20171-1829 Personal E-mail: john.okay@verizon.net.

**OKECH, BERNARD ACHERO,** parasitologist, entomologist; b. Kenya, May 27, 1972; s. Samson Gibbs and Joyce Elizabeth Okech; m. Eva Livere Chweya; children: Craig Malinke Achero, Neville Fabu Achero. BSc with honors, Jomo Kenyatta U., Nairobi, Kenya, 1990—95; MSc in Parasitology, U. Nairobi, 1995—98; PhD in Med. Entomology, Kenyatta U, Nairobi, 1999—2004. Sr. rsch. scientist Kenya Med. Rsch. Inst., Nairobi, 1998—99; lectr. Inst. Tropical Medicine & Infectious Diseases, Nairobi, 2003—04; postdoctoral rsch. scientist Jichi Med. Sch., Minamikawachi-ken, Tochigi, Japan, 2004—05; vis. scientist Whitney Lab. U. Fla., St. Augustine. Home: 9505 Ocean Shore Blvd Saint Augustine FL 32080 Office: Univ Fla 9505 Ocean Shore Blvd Saint Augustine FL 32080

**O'KEEFE, DENISE SUSAN,** biomedical researcher; b. Melbourne, Victoria, Australia, June 1969; arrived in US, 1996, permanent resident, 2005; d. Kevin Joseph and Susan Knyvett O'Keefe; m. Dean John Bacich, Oct. 13, 2000; 1 child, Jackson Dean Bacich. BS with honors, La Trobe U., Melbourne, Australia, 1990; PhD in Medicine, U. Adelaide, Australia, 1995. Postdoctoral scientist Columbia U., NYC, 1996—97, Meml. Sloan-Kettering Cancer Ctr., NYC, 1997—99; project scientist, rschr. Cleve. Clinic Found., 1999—2002; asst. prof. urology U. Pitts., 2003—. Cons. Constella Group, Washington, 2006. Contbr. chapters to books, articles to profl. jours. Edwin Beer fellow in urology, NY Acad. Medicine, 2004—06, Prostate Health Coun. scholar, Am. Urol. Assn., 1999—2001. Mem.: Am. Assn. for Cancer Rsch. Achievements include patents for DNA Encoding the Prostate-Specific Membrane Antigen-Like Gene and Uses Thereof. Office: Univ Pittsburgh 5200 Centre Ave Ste G34 Pittsburgh PA 15232 Office Phone: 412-623-3916.

**O'KEEFE, EDWARD FRANKLIN,** lawyer; b. SI, NY, June 9, 1937; s. Francis Franklin and Bertha (Hall) O'K.; m. Toni Lynne McGohan; children: Kira Kathleen, Douglas Franklin, Andrew Franklin, Alison Elizabeth, Theadore William, Nigel Francis. AB, U. N.C., 1959; JD, U. Denver, 1961. Bar: Colo. 1962, N.C. 2000. Law clk. Colo. Supreme Ct., Denver, 1962-63; assoc. gen. counsel Hamilton Mgmt. Corp., Denver, 1966-69, sec., 1968-76, v.p. legal, gen. counsel, 1969-76; ptnr. Moye White, Denver, 1976—2006. Assoc. gen. counsel, sec. ITT Variable Annuity Ins. Co., Denver, 1969, v.p. legal, gen. counsel, 1969-70; sec. Hamilton Funds Inc., Denver, 1968-76 With USNR, 1963—66. Mem. Nat. Assn. Security Dealers (dist. conduct com., chmn. 1976), Colo. Assn. Corporate Counsel (pres. 1974-75)

**O'KEEFE, FRANCIS RONALD,** lawyer; b. Oct. 7, 1950; AB, Georgetown U., 1972; JD, Cleve.-Marshall Coll., 1977. Bar: Ohio 1977, U.S. Dist. Ct. (no. dist.) Ohio 1978, U.S. Supreme Ct. 2002. Pvt. practice, 1977—86; sec. and gen. counsel Broadview Fin. Corp., 1986—89; ptnr. Hahn, Loeser & Parks LLP, 1989—. Named Ohio Super Lawyer, Cin. mag., 2004, 2005; named to Best Lawyers in Am. in corp. law, 2001—; recipient Sindell Tort Competition prize, Cleve.-Marshall Law Sch., 1977. Mem.: ABA, Soc. Corp. Secs. and Governance Profls., Greater Cleve. Bar Assn., Ohio State Bar Assn., Delta Theta Phi (Article Most Useful to Practicing Attys. award 1977). Office: Hahn Loeser & Parks LLP 3300 BP Tower Cleveland OH 44114-2301 Office Phone: 216-274-2396. E-mail: frokeefe@hahnlaw.com.

**O'KEEFE, JAMES WILLIAM, JR.,** investment manager and banker; b. Troy, N.Y., Oct. 23, 1948; s. James William and Antoinnette (Shannon) O'K.; m. Ann Palmer Ghiglione, June 4, 1977; 1 child, Courtney Anne. BA, Georgetown U., 1970; MBA, Harvard U., 1972. Mng. dir. Morgan Stanley & Co. Inc., N.Y.C., 1972-87, Kidder, Peabody & Co. Inc., N.Y.C., 1987-92; CEO Aetna Realty Investors, Inc., 1993—96; CEO, Allegis Realty Investors, Hartford, Conn., 1996—99; mng. dir., head of global real estate UBS Global Asset Mgmt., 1999—. Pres., bd. dirs. Nat. Coun. Real Estate Investment Fiducaries. Mem. Urban Land Inst., Nat. Assn. Real Estate Investment Trusts, Nat. Realty Com., Pension Real Estate Assn., Nat. Assn. Real Estate Investment Mgrs., N.Y. Athletic Club, Fishers Island Club, Knickerbocker Club. Avocation: golf. Office: UBS Realty Investors LLC 242 Trumbull St Hartford CT 06103-1213

**O'KEEFE, JOHN DAVID,** brokerage house executive; b. N.Y.C., Nov. 16, 1941; s. Timothy J. and Agnes V. (Timlin) O.; m. Stefanie Carreau Keegan, Jan. 28, 1978; children: Douglas G., Hillary C., John M., Meredith B. BBA, Iona Coll., 1963; MBA, L.I. U., 1968. Analyst L.I. Lighting Co., Mineola, NY, 1965-69, Pershing and Co., N.Y.C., 1969-72; mng. dir. Kidder, Peabody and Co., Inc., N.Y.C., 1972-89; v.p. Smith Barney, N.Y.C., 1989—. Bd. dirs. Heisman Found. Sgt. USMC, 1963-65. Mem.: Touchdown Club of Am., Inc. (bd. dirs. 2001—), Union Club (N.Y.C.), Downtown Athletic Club (gov. 1986, 1988, chmn. Heisman Trophy com. 1987—88). Republican. Home: 31 Linden Tree Rd Wilton CT 06897-1613 Office: Smith Barney 200 Nyala Farms Rd Westport CT 06880-6267 Office Phone: 203-221-6082. Business E-Mail: john.d.okeefe@smithbarney.com.

**O'KEEFE, MICHAEL,** academic administrator, physicist; b. Mc Cloud, Minn. BS in Physics, Mathematics & Philosophy, Marquette U.; MS in Nuclear Physics & Mathematics, U. Pitts.; LittD (hon.), Hamline U. Pres. Consortium for Advancement of Pvt. Higher Edn., Washington, 1983—89; exec. v.p. & CEO McKnight Found., Mpls.; asst. sec. Fed. Dept. Health, Edn. & Welfare; human svcs. commr. State of Minn., 1999—2002; pres. Mpls. Coll. Art & Design, 2002—. Co-chmn. edn. program Aspen Inst., 1987—; bd. regents U. Minn., 1996—2002; bd. dirs. Minn. Pub. Radio. Office: Office of Pres Minneapolis College Art & Design 2501 Stevens Ave South Minneapolis MN 55404 Office Phone: 612-874-3785.

**O'KEEFE, MICHAEL DANIEL,** lawyer; b. St. Louis, Jan. 3, 1938; s. Daniel Michael and Hanoria (Moriarty) O'K.; m. Bonnie Bowdern, July 11, 1964; children: Collen Coyne, Daniel Michael. AB, LLB, St. Louis U., 1961; postgrad.; George Washington U., 1963. Bar: Mo. 1961, U.S. Ct. Appeals (8th cir.) 1961, U.S. Dist. Ct. (ea. dist.) Mo. 1961, Ill. 1975, U.S. Dist. Ct. (so. dist.) Ill. 1975, U.S. Ct. Appeals (5th and 7th cirs.) 1983, (10th cir.) 1995. Asst. cir. atty., St. Louis, 1961—62, 1964—65; pvt. practice, 1964-67; ptnr. Lucas, Murphy & O'Keefe, St. Louis, 1967-74, Thompson & Mitchell, St. Louis, 1974-96. Adj. prof. trial practice Sch. of Law, St. Louis U., 1992—. Editor: American Maritime Cases, 1985—. Trustee St. Louis U. Capt. USAF, 1962-64. Fellow Am. Coll. Trial Lawyers; mem. Internat. Assn. Def. Counsel, Fedn. Ins. and Corp. Counsel, Maritime Law Assn., Nat. Assn. Railroad Trial Counsel, Am. Law Inst. Democrat. Roman Catholic. Avocations: reading, tennis, fencing, archaeology, microbiology. Home: 372 Walton Row East Louis MO 63108-1909 Office: Thompson Coburn One US Bank Plz Saint Louis MO 63101-1643 Office Phone: 314-552-6092. Business E-Mail: mokeefe@thompsoncoburn.com.

**O'KEEFE, SEAN CHARLES,** academic administrator, former federal agency administrator; b. Monterey, Calif., Jan. 27, 1956; s. Patrick Gordon and Patricia Carlin O'Keefe; m. Laura Jean McCarthy, Oct. 7, 1978; children: Lindsey, Jonathan, Kevin. BA, Loyola U., New Orleans, 1977; MPA, Syracuse U., 1978; doctorate (hon.). Budget analyst U.S. Dept. Def., Washington, comtr., CFO, 1989—92, apptd. sec. of the Navy, 1992; profl. staff U.S. Senate Appropriations Com., Washington; staff dir. U.S. Def. Appropriations Subcommittee, Washington; asst. to sr. v.p. for rsch., dean grad. sch. Pa. State U., prof., bus. adminstrn. University Park; Louis A. Bantle Prof., business and govt. policy Maxwell Sch. Citizenship and Pub. Affairs, Syracuse U., 1996, endowed chair, 1996; dir., Nat. Security Studies Partnership, Syracuse U. and John Hopkins U., 1996; dep. dir. Office of Mgmt. & Budget, Washington, 2000—01; adminstr. NASA, Washington, 2001—05; chancellor La. State U. and A&M Coll., Baton Rouge, 2005—. Bd. dirs. J. Ray McDermott, S.A., New Orleans; trustee CNA Corp., Alexandria, Va.; bd. advisor Pa. State Applied Rsch. Lab., University Park; mem. com. Climate Change Sci. and Tech.; vis. scholar Wolfson Coll. U. Cambridge. Co-author: The Defense Industry in Post Cold War Era: Corporate Strategies and Public Policy Perspectives, 1998; contrib author Keeping the Edge: Managing Defense for the Future, 2000; contbr. articles to profl. jours. Staff rep. platform com. Rep. Nat. Com., New Orleans, 1988, advisor, Washington, 1994-97, mem. bd. adv. Naval Postgraduate Sch. Named one of Top 100 Irish Americans, Irish Am. Mag., 2003—04; recipient Disting. Pub. Svc. award, 1993. Fellow Nat. Acad. Pub. Adminstrn., Internat. Acad. Astronautics; mem. Bohemian Club San Francisco, Cavalry Club. Republican. Roman Catholic. Avocations: golf, fishing. Office: La State U Chancellor's Office 156 Thomas Boyd Hall Baton Rouge LA 70803 Office Phone: 225-578-6977. Fax: 225-578-5982. Business E-Mail: chan@lsu.edu.

**O'KEEFE, THOMAS MICHAEL,** academic administrator; b. St. Cloud, Minn., Mar. 25, 1940; s. Thomas William and Genevieve B. (McCormick) O'K.; m. Kathleen Marie Gnifkowski, Aug. 20, 1966; children: Steven Michael, Ann Catherine. Student, Marquette U., 1961-65, BS, 1965; MS in Nuclear Physics, U. Pitts., 1968; DHL, Hamline U., 1989. Dir. edn. planning HEW, Washington, 1969-70, dep. asst. sec., 1977-80; v.p. Carnegie Found. for Advancement of Teaching, Washington, 1980-83; pres. Consortium for Advancement Pvt. Higher Edn., Washington, 1983-89; exec. v.p. McKnight Found., Mpls., 1989-99; commr. Dept. Human Svcs., State Minn., St. Paul, 1999—2002; pres. Mpls. Coll. Art and Design, 2002—. Dir. Washington internships in edn. George Washington U., 1970-73; dir. policy analysis and evaluation U. Ill., Chgo., 1973-74, assoc. v.p. acad. affairs, 1974-77; head U.S. del. to Orgn. Econ. Coop. and Devel., 1979, 80; mem. Carnegie Forum on Edn. and the Economy, 1985-88; mem. N.J. Commn. on Ind. Higher Edn., 1986-88; mem. task force on ind. higher edn. Edn. Commn. States, 1987-89; co-chair Edn. Program, The Aspen Inst., 1987—. Contbr. articles to profl. jours.; contbg. editor: Change mag., 1985—2001; bd. dirs.: Editl. Project in Edn., 1984—93. Bd. dirs. The Edn. Resources Inst., Boston, 1987-94, Minn. Coun. on Founds., 1994-99, Minn. Pub. Radio, 1999—, Alliance Excellent Edn., 2004—; trustee Buena Vista Coll., Storm Lake, Iowa, 1984-90; mem. Coun. on Fgn. Rels., 1995-99; bd. regents U. Minn., 1996-02. Mem.: Mpls. Club. Democrat. Office: Mpls Coll Art and Design 2501 Stevens Ave S Minneapolis MN 55404 Business E-Mail: michael_okeefe@mcad.edu.

**O'KEEFE, VINCENT THOMAS,** clergyman, educational association administrator; b. Jersey City, Jan. 10, 1920; s. James and Sarah (Allen) O'K. AB, Georgetown U., 1943; MA, Woodstock Coll., 1945, Ph.L., 1944; Th.L., St. Albert de Louvain, Belgium, 1951; student, Muenster U., Germany, 1951-52; S.T.D., Gregorian U., Rome, 1954. Ordained priest Roman Cath. Ch., 1950. Instr. Latin and math. Regis High Sch., N.Y.C., 1944-47; assoc. prof. fundamental theology Woodstock Coll., 1954-60; acad. v.p. Fordham U., Bronx, NY, 1960-62, exec. v.p., 1962-63, pres. 1963-65, rector Jesuit community, 1984-88; gen. asst. to superior gen. Soc. of Jesus, Rome, 1965-83, v.p. spl. projects Jesuit Conf., 1988-90, superior, writer provincial residence Bronx, 1990-94; superior Am. House, N.Y.C., 1994-2000. Mem. regents exams. and scholarship center N.Y. State Dept. Edn.; pres., dir. mem. exec. com. Council Higher Ednl. Instns. of N.Y.C. Author: The History and Meaning of Ex Attrito Fit Contritus, 1957; Contbr. articles to religious publs., also book reviews. Dir. N.Y. World's Fair, 1964-65; Corp. Bd. mgrs. New York Bot. Garden; dir., mem. bd. Center Intercultural Formation, Cuernavaca, Mexico; trustee Fordham U. Fellow Royal Soc. Encouragement Arts Mfrs. and Commerce (London); mem. Council Cath. City N.Y., Religion Council Cath. Secondary Schs. Archdiocese of N.Y., Cath. Bibl. Assn., Cath. Theol. Assn. Am., Religion Ednl. Assn., NEA, Jesuit Ednl. Assn., Nat. Cath. Edn. Assn., Internat. Assn. Univs., Soc. Cath. Coll. Tchrs. Sacred Doctrine, Phi Beta Kappa. Roman Catholic. Office: 106 W 56th St New York NY 10019-3803 Office Phone: 212-581-4640.

**OKEIL, AYMAN M.,** educator; PhD, NC State U., 1995. Asst. prof. La. State U., Baton Rouge, 2003—. Vis. asst. prof. U. Ctrl. Fla., Orlando, 1998—2003. Mem.: ASCE, Am. Concrete Inst. Office: La State U Dept Civil & Env Eng 3502 CEBA Baton Rouge LA 70803 Office Phone: 225-578-7048.

**OKEKE, CHRISTIAN NWACHUKWU,** law educator; b. Obinofia, Enugu, Nigeria, June 8, 1941; s. Stephen Agueze and Sussana Nwaduvu Okeke; m. Justina Nwanago Okeke. LLM Summa Cum Laude, Kiev State U., Ukraine, 1969; PhD, Free U., Holland, 1973. Lic. Nigerian Coun. Legal Edn. Sr. Lectr. U. Nigeria, Enugu, Nigeria, 1974—85; pioneer dean emeritus Nnamdi Azikiwe U., Awka, Nigeria, 1985—91; dep. vice chancellor, dean of law emeritus Enugu State U. of Sci. Tech., Enugu, Nigeria, 1991—95; fellow MaxPlanck Inst., Heidelberg, Germany, 1994—95; law prof. Golden Gate U. San Francisco, 1996—. Ptr. ILegbune, Okeke & Co., Enugu, Nigeria, 1980—94; cons. African Network for Prevention of Child Abuse and Neglect, Enugu, 1974—; trustee mem. Internat. First Aid Soc., Enugu, 1974—. Author: Expansion of New Subjects of International Law, 1973, Controversial Subject of Contemporary International Law, 1974, Theory & Practice of International Law in Nigeria, 1986. Exec. dir. Internat. First Aid Soc., Inc., Antioch, Calif., 1994—. Rsch. fellowship, Hague Acad. of Internat. Law, 1970, fellowship, Cambridge U., England, 1971. Mem.: Nigerian Bar Assn., Nigerian Soc. of Internat. Law. Home: 4320 Mink Ct Antioch CA 94531 Office: Golden Gate U Sch of Law 536 Mission St San Francisco CA 94105 Office Phone: 415-442-6695. Office Fax: 415-442-6756. E-mail: cokeke@ggu.edu.

**O'KELLEY, WILLIAM CLARK,** federal judge; b. Atlanta, Jan. 2, 1930; s. Ezra Clark and Theo (Johnson) O'K.; m. Ernestine Allen, Mar. 28, 1953; children: Virginia Leigh O'Kelley Wood, William Clark Jr. AB, Emory U., 1951, LLB, 1953. Bar: Ga. 1952. Pvt. practice, Atlanta, 1957-59; asst. U.S. atty. No. Dist. Ga., 1959-61; partner O'Kelley, Hopkins & Van Gerpen, Atlanta, 1961-70; U.S. dist. judge No. Dist. Ga., Atlanta, 1970—, chief judge, 1988-94. Mem. com. on adminstrn. of criminal law Jud. Conf. U.S., 1979-82, exec. com., 1983-84, subcom. on jury trials in complex criminal cases, 1981-82, dist. judge rep. 11th cir., 1981-84, mem. adv. com. of fed. rules of criminal procedure, 1984-87; bd. dirs. Fed. Jud. Ctr., 1987-91, adv. com. history program, 1991-97, com. on orientation of newly appointed dist. judges, 1985-94; mem. Jud. Resources, 1989-94; mem. Jud. Coun. 11th Cir., 1990-96, exec. com. 1990-96; mem. Fgn. Intelligence Surveillance Ct., 1980-87; mem. Alien Terrorist Removal Ct., 1996—; corp. sec., dir. Gwinnett Bank & Trust Co., Norcross, Ga., 1967-70. Mem. exec. com., gen. counsel Ga. Republican Com., 1968-70; mem. fin. com. Northwest Ga. Girl Scout Coun., 1958-70. Served as 1st lt. USAF, 1953-57; capt. USAFR. Mem. Fed. Bar Assn., Ga. State Bar, Atlanta Bar Assn., Dist. Judges Assn. 5th Cir. (sec.-treas. 1976-79, v.p. 1977-78, pres. 1978-80), Lawyers Club Atlanta, Kiwanis (past pres.), Atlanta Athletic Club, Sigma Chi (named Significant Sig 1983), Phi Delta Phi, Omicron Delta Kappa. Baptist. Home: 550 Ridgecrest Dr Norcross GA 30071-2158 Office: US Dist Ct 1942 US Courthouse 75 Spring St SW Atlanta GA 30303-3309 Office Phone: 404-215-1530.

**O'KELLEY, WINNIE,** editor; m. Patrick McGeehan; 2 children. Grad., Northwestern U., 1984. Asst. copy desk chief Adv. Age, 1985; with Am. Banker, 1988; mng. editor Banking Week; dep. bus. editor, enterprise editor NY Times, NYC, 1993—. Recipient Best in Bus. for Overall Excellence Cert. Merit, Am. Bus. Editors and Writers, 2003. Office: New York Times 229 W 43rd St New York NY 10036 Office Phone: 212-556-7356. Office Fax: 212-556-7614.*

**OKEN, MARC D.,** retired bank executive; m. Celene Oken; 5 children. BSBA, Loyola Coll., Balt., Md., 1968; MBA, U. of West Fla., 1973. With Price Waterhouse, 1974—81, 1983—89; fellow Securities and Exchange Commn., 1981—83; principal fin. exec. Bank Am. Corp., Charlotte, NC, 1989—98, CFO, 1998—2005. Bd. dirs. Sonoco Products Co., Star Scientific, Inc., 2005—, Marsh & McLennan Cos. Inc., 2006—. Aviator USN, 1968—73, Vietnam. Office: 100 N Tryon St Ste 5120 Charlotte NC 28202*

**OKEN, ROBERT,** retired neuroscientist, consultant; b. N.Y.C., Oct. 15, 1929; s. Milton and Etta (Weiner) Oken. BA, NYU, 1949, PhD, 1958. V.p., dir. Oken Fabrics Inc., N.Y.C., 1959-68, 71-73; rschr., cons. U.S. Army, USN, Washington, Frederick, Md., 1955-56, Teller Environ. Sys., N.Y.C., 1969-70; businessman R.A. Siegel Galleries, N.Y.C., 1978-87; cons. to dir. N.Y. State Inst. Basic Rsch., S.I., 1991-93; cons. Gerex Biotech. P.L. McGeer, Vancouver, BC, Canada, 1994—98; ret., 1998. Editl. advisor NIMH, 2001—, Neurosci. Rsch., 1998—. Contbr. articles to profl. jours. Sci. advisor Lifer Environ. Group, Roxbury, NJ, 1984—87; vol. Dover (N.J.) Gen. Hosp., 1989—90. With U.S. Army, 1955—56. Recipient medal of achievement, Dover Gen. Hosp., 1990. Mem.: AAAS, Internat. Assn. Improvement Mental Health (advisor 2006), N.Y. Neuropsychology Group, N.Y. Acad. Scis., Am. Chem. Soc., Intertel, Mensa Internat., Am. Philatelic Soc., Phi Beta Kappa. Home and Office: PO Box 412 Hopatcong NJ 07843-0412 Office Phone: 973-770-0006. Personal E-mail: robertoken@nac.net.

**OKERLUND, ARLENE NAYLOR,** academic administrator, writer; b. Emmitsburg, Md., Oct. 13, 1938; d. George Wilbur and Ruth Opal (Sensenbaugh) Naylor; m. Michael Dennis Okerlund, June 6, 1959 (div. Apr. 1983); 1 dau., Linda Susan. BA, U. Md., 1960; PhD, U. Calif.-San Diego, 1969. Instr. sci. Mercy Hosp. Nursing Sch., Balt., 1959-63; prof. English San Jose (Calif.) State U., 1969—2005, dean humanities and arts, 1980-86, acad. v.p., 1986-93. Cons. Ednl. Testing Svc., Berkeley, Calif., 1976—80. Author: Elizabeth Wydeville: The Slandered Queen, 2005; editor San Jose Studies, 1975—80; contbr. articles on the humanities to profl. jours. Bd. dirs. World Forum Silicon Valley, Peninsula Banjo Band. Grantee NEH, 1979; grantee San Jose State U., 1971-72. Mem.: MLA (del. to assembly, west coast rep. 1976—77), Am. Beethoven Soc. (v.p. bd. dirs.), Calif. Coun. Fine Arts Deans (pres. 1984—86), Internat. Coun. Fine Arts Deans, Philol. Assn. Pacific Coast (sec.-treas. 1975—78). Democrat. Office: San Jose State U Dept English Washington Sq San Jose CA 95192-0090 Office Phone: 408-924-4425. Business E-Mail: okerlund@email.sjsu.edu.

**OKESON, JEFFREY PAUL,** dental educator, director; b. Newton, N.J., June 27, 1947; s. George Paul and Lois Wiley Okeson; m. Barbara Boian, Nov. 21, 1970; children: Brian Paul, Steven Tyler. BS, Ea. Ky. U., Richmond, 1969; DMD, U. Ky., Lexington, 1972; PhD (hon.), Fed. U. Espirito Santo, Brazil, 2001. Bd. cert. Amercian Bd. Orofacial Pain, 1994. Prof. dentistry Coll. Dentistry U. Ky., Lexington, founder and dir. orofacial pain ctr, 1977—, Chmn. dept. oral health sci. Coll. Dentistry U. Ky., Lexington, 2003—; cons. VA Dentistry, 1991—, USN, Bethesda, Md., 1994—. Author: The Clinical Management of Temporomandibular Disorders, Bell's Orofacial Pains, Orofacial Pain: Guidelines for Assessment, Diagnosis and Management. Named Outstanding Alumni of Yr., Phi Delta Theta, Ea. Ky. U. chpt.), 1994; named to Hall Disting. Alumni, Ea. Ky. U., 1991; recipient Disting. Alumnus award, Coll. Dentistry U. Ky., 2004. Fellow: Am. Coll. Dentists (assoc.); mem.: Spanish Soc. Craniomandibular Disorders (hon.; life), Catalana Dental Soc. Spain (hon.), South African Soc. Orthodontists (hon.), Ky. Pain Soc. (assoc.; nominating chmn. 2004—), Internat. Soc. Study of Pain (assoc.), Am. Bd. Orofacial Pain (assoc.; pres. 2004—), Am. Acad. Orofacial Pain (assoc.; pres. 1999—2000). Achievements include development of MS degree program in orofacial pain. Office: U Ky Coll Dentistry 800 Rose St Lexington KY 40536-0297 Office Fax: 859-323-9136. Business E-Mail: okeson@uky.edu.

**OKHAMAFE, IMAFEDIA,** philosophy and English educator; b. Otuo, Nigeria; s. Obokhe and Olayemi Okhamafe. Double PhD, Purdue U., 1984. Prof. philosophy and English U. Nebr., Omaha, 1993—. Office: U Nebr Annex 26 Omaha NE 68182-0001 also: U Nebr Philosophy Dept Omaha NE 68182-0001 E-mail: imafedia@unomaha.edu.

**OKIGBO, FRANKLIN C.,** engineering company executive; b. Lagos, Nigeria, Jan. 30, 1961; arrived in US, 1985; s. Alexandria and Veronica Okigbo; married, Sept. 11, 1998; children: Adaora, Nwando, Chinelo. BS in finance, So. Ill. U., 1990; MBA, Southeastern U., 1995; PhD in info. sys., Walden U., 2003. Cert. Network Assoc. Computer Info. Sys. Co., network profl. Computer Info. Sys. Co.; Microsoft Sys. Engr. Network engr. Social Security Office, Balt., sr. network engr., FAA, Wash.; pres., ceo Worldtech Inc., Hyattsville, Md., 1998—. Named one of 50 influential minority in bus., MBPN, 2002; recipient Outstanding Support with Golftrac Program, US Army. Mem.: Porter Ednl. Svcs. Avocations: volleyball, basketball, golf, tennis. Home: 13003 Englishturn Dr Silver Spring MD 20904 E-mail: franklin@worldtechinc.com

**OKIISHI, THEODORE HISAO,** mechanical engineering educator; b. Honolulu Jan 15, 1939; s. Clifford Munen and Dorothy Asako (Tokushima) U.; m. Rae Wiemers, May 28, 1963; children: Christopher Lane, Ethan Clifford, Mark William, Kenneth Edward. Student, U. Hawaii, 1956-57; BS, Iowa State U., 1960, MS, 1963, PhD, 1965. Registered profl. engr., Iowa, Ohio. From asst. prof. to prof., assoc. dean coll. engring Iowa State U., Ames, 1967—. Cons. on fluid dynamics Contbr. articles to profl. jours. Served to capt. C.E., U.S. Army, 1965-67 Decorated Joint Services Commendation award; named Outstanding Prof., Iowa State U. student sect. ASME, 1983, Mech. Engring. Dept. Prof. of Yr., Iowa State U., 1977, 86, 90; recipient award for research NASA, 1975; Ralph R. Teetor award Soc. Automotive Engrs., 1976, Engring. Coll. Superior Teaching award Iowa State U., 1987, Cardinal Key Iowa State U., 1991. Fellow ASME (Melville medal 1989, 98); mem. AIAA, Sigma Xi. Republican. Mem. Ch. of Jesus Christ of Latter-day Saints. Club: Osborn Research Home: 2940 Monroe Dr Ames IA 50010-4362 Office: Iowa State U 104 Marston Hl Ames IA 50011-0001 Office Phone: 515-294-4395. Business E-Mail: tedo@iastate.edu.

**OKIMOTO, GLENN MICHIAKI,** state official; b. Honolulu, Mar. 12, 1953; s. Sueo and Matsue (Kojima) O.; m. Hope Kayoko Okabe, Aug. 29, 1981; 1 child, Lauren. BS, U. Hawaii, 1976, MS, 1978, PhD, 1981, Cert. in Pub. Adminstrn., 1983. Economist Dept. of Transp., State of Hawaii, Honolulu, 1981-89, program analysis mgr., 1989-94, dep. dir., 1994—. Rsch. asst. U. Hawaii, Honolulu, 1976-81, lectr., 1987—; mgr. family bus., U. Hawaii, 1986—. Del. Dem. Party of Hawaii, Honolulu, 1996; speech contest judge Am. Legion, Honolulu. Mem. Govt. Fin. Officers Assn., Gamma Sigma Delta. Avocations: family, golf, tennis. Home: 94-243 Pulelo Pl Waipahu HI 96797-5051 Office: State of Hawaii Dept of Transportation 869 Punchbowl St # 54 Honolulu HI 96813-5036

**OKINAGA, LAWRENCE SHOJI,** lawyer; m. Carolyn Hisako Uesugi, Nov. 26, 1966; children: Carrie, Caryn, Laurie. BA, U. Hawaii, 1963; JD, Georgetown U., 1972. Bar: Hawaii 1972, US Dist. Ct. Hawaii 1972, US Ct. Appeals (9th cir.) 1976. Adminstrv. asst. to Congressman Spark Matsunaga, Honolulu, 1964, 65-69; law clk. to chief judge U.S. Dist. Ct. Hawaii, Honolulu, 1972-73; assoc. Carlsmith Ball, Honolulu, 1973-76, ptnr., 1976—. Mem. Gov.'s Citizens Adv. Com. Coastal Zone Mgmt., 1974—79; sec. Hawaii Bicentennial Corp., 1975—77, vice chmn., 1983—85, chmn., 1985—87; mem. Jud. Selection Commn., State of Hawaii, 1979—87, vice

chmn., 1986; mem. consumer adv. coun. Fed. Res. Bd., 1984—86; chmn. Jud. Conduct Commn., State of Hawaii, 1991—94; apptd. mem. Fed. Savs. and Loan Adv. Coun., Washington, 1988—89; mem. nat. adv. coun. U.S. SBA, 1994—2000; mem. adv. coun. Fed. Res. Bank, San Francisco, 1995—2002. Pres., bd. dirs. Moiliili Cmty. Ctr., Honolulu, 1965—68, 1973—86, trustee, 1993—; bd. dirs. Pub. Sch. Hawaii Found., 2004—; bd. visitors Georgetown U. Law Ctr., 1993—; trustee Kuakini Med. Ctr., 1984—88, 1989—96. Capt. USAFR, 1964—72, capt. USAFR, 1974—76. Mem.: ABA (ho. of dels. 1991—94, mem. standing com. jud. selection tenure and compensation 1993—96, mem. standing com. jud. independence 1999—2002), Am. Judicature Soc. (bd. dirs. 1986, treas. 1995—97, pres. 1997—99), Hawaii Bar Assn. (sec., bd. dirs. 1981), Georgetown U. Law Alumni Assn. (bd. dirs. 1986—91), Omicron Delta Kappa. Office: Carlsmith Ball PO Box 656 Honolulu HI 96809-0656 E-mail: lso@carlsmith.com.

**OKITA, GEORGE TORAO,** retired pharmacologist; b. Seattle, Jan. 18, 1922; s. Kazuo and Fusao (Mugurama) O.; m. Fujiko Shimizu, Nov. 29, 1958; children: Ronald Hajime, Sharon Mariko, Glenn Torao. Student, U. Cin., 1943-44; BA, Ohio State U., 1948; PhD, U. Chgo., 1951. Rsch. asst., rsch. assoc., instr., then asst. prof. U. Chgo., 1949-63; assoc. prof. Northwestern U. Med. Sch., 1963-66, prof. pharmacology, 1966—90, acting chmn. pharmacology, 1968—70, 1976—77; prof. emeritus molecular pharmacology and biol. chemistry, 1990—. Contbr. articles to profl. jours.; Asst. editor: Jour. Pharmacology and Exptl. Therapeutics, 1965-68. Served with AUS, 1944-46. NIH Postdoctoral fellow, 1952 Mem. AAAS, AAUP, Am. Soc. Pharmacology and Exptl. Therapeutics, Internat. Soc. Biochem. Pharmacology, Am Heart Assn., Cardiac Muscle Soc., Sigma Xi. Achievements include research in med. field. Home: 95-1058 Kihene St Mililani HI 96789 Personal E-mail: gtoki@aol.com.

**OKLAK, DENNIS D.,** real estate company executive; BS in Acctg. magna cum laude, Ball State U., 1977. CPA. Tax mgr. Duke Realty Corp., Indpls., 1986, contr., v.p., treas., exec. v.p., chief adminstv. officer, 1997—2002, co-COO, 2002—03, pres., COO, 2003—. Mem.: AICPA, Ind. CPA Soc. Office: Duke Realty Corp Ste 100 600 E 96th St Indianapolis IN 46240

**O'KON, JAMES ALEXANDER,** engineering company executive; b. N.Y.C., Aug. 8, 1937; s. A.C. and Rita O'Kon; m. Carol Ann Smith, 1988; children: Sean Fitzgerald, Katherine Shannon. BCE, Ga. Inst. Tech., 1961; MCE, NYU, 1970. Registered profl. engr., Tenn., N.Y., Mo., Conn., Ill., Fla., Tex., Miss., Calif., Ga., Mass., La. N.J., S.C., Ala., Ky., Va., N.C., Kans., Colo., Mich., Wyo. Hwy. engr. Ga. Hwy. Dept., Atlanta, 1960-62; structural engr. Robert & Co., Atlanta, 1962-64; project coord. So. Design, Spartanburg, SC, 1964-67; project engr. Crawford-Russell, Stamford, Conn., 1967-68, Farkas Barron Ptnr., N.Y.C., 1968-69; v.p. Lev Zetlin Assocs., N.Y.C., Atlanta, 1969-77; pres. O'Kon and Co. (formerly Lev Zetlin Assocs.), Atlanta, 1977-2000; v.p O'Kon divsn. RBA Group, Atlanta, 2000—03; pres. O'Kon & Co., Atlanta, 2003—. Mem. Bd. Constrn. Rsch. Ga. Tech. Author: Guidelines for Failure Investigation, 1989, Methodology For The Life Prediction of Buildings, 1989, Floating Factory to Produce Precast Concrete Components, 1973, Methods to Reduce Errors Due to Dependency on Computers, 1994, Bridge From the Past, 1995, Maya Intersite Scabe System, 1997, Error Avoidance in Light Weight Space Frames, 1999, Computer Design of Space Frames, 2000, Seismic Analysis of Large Structures, 2001, Maya Suspension Bridge, Yaxchilan, 2003. Recipient Grand award Builder's Mag., 1983, Archtl. Excellence award Am. Inst. Steel Constructors, 1984, Engring. Excellence award Am. Consulting Engrs. Coun. Ga., 1983, 88, Grand Award for Engring. Excellence, 1988-89, 91-93, USAF Air Mobility award, 1997, Nat. Grand prize Steel Joist Inst., 1999, Grand Nat. Design award Am. Inst. of Steel Constrn., 2000, Grand award ACEC, 2001. Fellow Explorers Club (nat. fellow), ASCE (chmn. tech. com. forensic engring.); mem. Am. Inst. Archaeology, Ga. Tech. Bldg. Rsch. Ctr. (Ga. Tech. continuing edn. com.), Bldg. Futures Coun., Soc. Am. Mil. Engrs., Smithsonian Inst., Am. Arbitration Assn. (panel of arbitrators). Democrat. Roman Catholic. Office: O'Kon & Co Inc 26104 Plantation Dr Atlanta GA 30324 Office Phone: 404-237-3018. E-mail: jamesokon@okon.com.

**OKONEDO, SOPHIE,** actress; b. London, Jan. 1, 1969; 1 child, Aoife. Grad., Cambridge U. Actor: (films) Young Soul Rebels, 1991, Go Now, 1995, Ace Ventura: When Nature Calls, 1995, The Jackel, 1997, This Year's Love, 1999, Mad Cows, 1999, Peaches, 2000, Once Seen, 2001, Dirty Pretty Things, 2002, Cross My Heart, 2003, Hotel Rwanda, 2004 (Oscar Nominee for Best Performance by an Actress in a Supporting Role, 2005, Nominee Image award for Outstanding Supporting Actress in a Motion Picture, 2005), Aeon Flux, 2005; (TV films) Age of Treason, 1993, Deep Secrets, 1996, Never Never, 2000, Sweet Revenge, 2001, Dead Casual, 2002, The Inspector Lynley Mysteries: In the Presence of the Enemy, 2003, Alibi, 2003, Whose Baby?, 2004, Born with two Mothers, 2005; (TV miniseries) Doctor Who: Scream of the Shalka, 2003; (TV series) Staying Alive, 1996, The Governor, 1996, In Defiance, 2000, Clocking Off, 2000.*

**OKOSHI-MUKAI, SUMIYE,** artist; b. Seattle; One-woman shows include Gallery Internat., N.Y.C., 1970, Miami Mus. Modern Art, 1972, Galerie Saison, Tokyo, 1982, St. Peter's Ch., Living Room Gallery, N.Y.C., 1987, Viridian Gallery, 1987, 1992, 1996, 1999, Port Washington (N.Y.) Pub. Libr., 1985, NAS, Washington, 1991—92, exhibited in group shows at Bergen Mus. Art and Scis., 1983, Am. Acad. Arts and Scis., 1984, Port Washington Pub. Libr., 1985, Hudson River Mus., 1985, Sao Paulo and N.Y. Culture Exch., 1988, Hyundai Gallery, Pusan, Korea, 1988, Gary Snyder Fine Art, N.Y.C., 2002, Represented in permanent collections The Mitsui & Co., N.Y., Hotel Nikko, Atlanta, Bank of Nagoya, N.Y., Palace Hotel, Guam Island, Port Washington Pub. Libr., Lowe Gallery-U. Miami, Miami Mus. Modern Art, Nat. Women's Edn. Ctr., Saitama-ken, Japan, NAS, Hammond Mus., North Salem, N.Y., The Jane Voorhees Zimmerli Art Mus., N.J., Asian Traditions Modern Expressions; included in Collage-Techniques, 1994. Mem. Nat. Women Artists Assn. (Belle Cramer award Zluta and Joseph Fund award, Ralph Mayer Meml. award, Doris Kreindler Meml. award 2002), Nat. Mus. Women in the Arts (charter mem. 1994).

**OKOUCHI-GUY, ALICIA,** performing arts educator; d. Lexine Okouchi-Anderson; m. Don Guy, July 14, 2000. BA, Loyola Marymount U., LA, 1995; MFA, U. Calif., Irvine, 1998. Asst. prof. U. Mo., St. Louis, 2003—05, Fullerton Coll., Calif., 2005—. Dir., choreographer St. Louis Steamers, 2004—05; tchr. master class, choreographer USA Pro and United Spirit Assn., Anaheim, Calif., 1987—; profl. freelance choreographer TV, film and video, LAa, Calif., 1999—; faculty senator U. Mo., St. Louis, 2004—05, Fullerton Coll., Calif., 2006—; dancer, choreographer LA Clippers. Artistic director (dance concert) Faculty and Friends Dance Concert, Physical Graffitti, (musical theatre) Cabaret (Achievement in Choreography from the John F. Kennedy Ctr. for the Performing Arts, Am. Coll. Theatre Festival, 2004), Pippin; dir.(choreographer): (dance concert) Faculty Dance Concert; author: (pamphlet) How to get an agent. Named Dance Educator of Yr., SCOPE, 2006. Mem.: Am. Coll. Dance Festival Assn., Nat. Dance Educators Orgn. Achievements include development of entire dance degree and curriculum for the new dance program at the University of Missouri.

**OKOUNKOV, ANDREI,** mathematics professor; b. Moscow, 1969; 2 children. BA in Math., PhD in Math. Moscow State U. Rsch. fellow, Dobrushin Math. Lab. Inst. for Problems of Info. Transmission, Russian Acad. Sciences; instructor U. Chgo.; asst. prof. U. Calif., Berkeley; prof., math. dept. representation theory Princeton U., 2002—. Mem. Inst. for Advanced Study, Math. Sciences Rsch. Inst., Berkeley. Recipient Sloan Research Fellowship, 2000, Fields medal, Internat. Math. Union, 2006. Office: Princeton U Dept Math 701 Fine Hall Washington Rd Princeton NJ 08544-1000*

**OKOYE, CHRISTIAN EMEKA,** professional football player; b. Enugu, Nigeria, Aug. 16, 1961; came to U.S. in 1982. Degree in phys. edn., Azusa Pacific U., 1987. With Kansas City Chiefs, 1987—92. Founder Christian

Okoye Found. Led NFL in rushing, 1989-90 season; named AFC player of the yr., Touchdown Club, Washington, D.C., also NFL Players' Assn.; named to Pro Bowl team, 1989, 91. Office: Christian Okoye Found PO Box 1323 Rancho Cucamonga CA 91701

**OKRENT, DANIEL,** writer; b. Detroit, Apr. 2, 1948; s. Harry and Gizella (Adler) Okrent; m. Cynthia Jayne Boyer, June 23, 1969 (div. Aug. 1977); m. Rebecca Kathryn Lazear, Aug. 28, 1977. BA, U. Mich., 1969; DHL, Mass. Coll. Liberal Arts, 1988. Editor Alfred A. Knopf, Inc., N.Y.C., 1969—73; editorial dir. Grossman Pubs., Inc., N.Y.C., 1973—76; editor-in-chief Harcourt Brace Jovanovich, N.Y.C., 1976—77; pres. Hilltown Press, Inc., Worthington, Mass., 1978—91, Tex. Monthly Press, Inc., Austin, 1978—83; editor New Eng. Monthly, Northampton, Mass., 1984—89; asst. mng. editor Life mag., N.Y.C., 1991—92, mng. editor, 1992—96; editor new media Time Inc., N.Y.C., 1996—99, editor-at-large, 1999—2001; pub. editor NY Times, 2003—05; dir. TESSCO Techs., Inc., 2004—. Columnist Esquire mag., N.Y.C., 1985—89. Author: Nine Innings: The Anatomy of a Baseball Game, 1985, The Way We Were: New England Then and Now, 1989, Great Fortune: The Epic of Rockefeller Center, 2003, Public Editor #1, 2006; co-author: Baseball Anecdotes, 1989; co-editor: The Ultimate Baseball Book, 1979; appeared in (films) Sweet and Lowdown, 1999, Wordplay, 2006, The Hoax, 2006. Commr. Nat. Portrait Gallery, 2001—, chmn., 2003—. Grantee Joan Shorenstein Ctr. on Press, Politics Public Policy fellowship, Harvard Univ., 2006. Mem.: Century Assn. Jewish. Office: 645 West End Ave New York NY 10025 Personal E-mail: okrent@gmail.com.

**OKRENT, DAVID,** engineering educator; b. Passaic, NJ, Apr. 19, 1922; s. Abram and Gussie (Pearlman) O.; m. Rita Gilda Holtzman, Feb. 1, 1948 (dec. June 2005); children: Neil, Nina, Jocelyn. ME, Stevens Inst. Tech., 1943; MA, Harvard, 1948, PhD in Physics, 1951. Mech. engr. NACA, Cleve., 1943-46; sr. physicist Argonne (Ill.) Nat. Lab., 1951-71; regents lectr. UCLA, 1968, prof. engring., 1971-91, prof. emeritus, rsch. prof., 1991—. Vis. prof. U. Wash., Seattle, 1963, U. Ariz., Tucson, 1970-71; Isaac Taylor chair Technion, 1977-78 Author: Fast Reactor Cross Sections, 1960, Computing Methods in Reactor Physics, 1968, Reactivity Coefficients in Large Fast Power Reactors, 1970, Nuclear Reactor Safety, 1981; contbr. articles to profl. jours. Mem. adv. com. on reactor safeguards AEC, 1963-87, also chmn., 1966; sci. sec. to sec. gen. of Geneva Conf., 1958; mem. U.S. del. to all Geneva Atoms for Peace Confs. Guggenheim fellow, 1961-62, 77-78; recipient Disting. Appointment award Argonne Univs. Assn., 1970, Disting. Service award U.S. Nuclear Regulatory Commn., 1985. Fellow Soc. for Risk Analysis, Am. Phys. Soc., Am. Nuclear Soc. (Tommy Thompson award 1980, Glenn Seaborg medal 1987), Nat. Acad. Engring. Home: 439 Veteran Ave Los Angeles CA 90024-1956 Business E-Mail: okrent@ucla.edu.

**OKSILOFF, CHRISTA,** technologist, educator; b. Berlin, Dec. 6, 1926; arrived in U.S., 1947, naturalized, 1952; d. Gustav Otto Uecker and Elisabeth Schulzek; m. Assen Oksiloff, 1953; 1 child, Assenka. Degree for kindergarten tchr., State Kindergarten Seminar, Berlin; degree for med. technologist, Norwegian Drs. Home and Hosp., Bkly. Dental asst. pvt. office, Berlin; medical technologist Shoregate Shopping Ctr., pvt. office; med. asst. Assen Oksiloff, MD, Willoughby, Ohio. Author: Art and Writing Exhbn., Passing on "Senior Wisdom", Frau Holle, Berlin in Crisis, 1945, The Journey of the Wedding Cake, 1996, Morris the Cat, 1996, Stigma, 1996, Seniors Childhood Memories of Christmas in Berlin, 1996, The Birthday Cake Surprise, 1997, Mt. St. Michel, 1997, Parents' Anguish, 1997, Teenage Carefree Summer Days, 1997, The Emigrants, 1998, The Gift Dogs Are, and Bring, 1998, Dedicated Teachers, 1998, Understanding in More Depth, 1998, The Remote Risk of Gardening, 1998, Floppy the Therapist, 1999, A Just Person, 1999, Blunder, 1999, The Inheritance, 1999, Albania Kosovo, 1999, Bulgaria One of the Balkans, 1999, Light Healing, 1999, The Cleanup, 1999, Grandpa, 1999, A Late Response, 1999, Renewal and Restoration, 2000, The Lure and Healing of the Sea, 2000, Spook, 2000. Mem.: Cleve. Mus. Art., Epworth United Meth. Ch. Univ. Cir., Cleve. Coll. Club. Avocations: writing, classical music, opera, travel, theater. Office Phone: 440-942-4342.

**OKTAVEC, EILEEN M.,** anthropologist, artist; b. Apr. 9, 1942; d. Albert W. and Margaret (O'Reilley) O. Student, Cooper Union, N.Y.C., 1960-61; BA in Anthropology, SUNY, Stony Brook, 1973; MA in Anthropology, U. Ariz., 1975, Instr. anthropology White Pines Coll., Chester, NH, 1975-76; art dir. Great Walks, Inc., Goffstown, NH, 1989—. Author: Answered Prayers: Miracles and Milagros Along the Border, 1995; photographs in: Great Walks of Acadia National Park and Mount Desert, 1990, Great Walks of Southern Arizona, 1991, Great Walks of Big Bend National Park, 1991, Great Walks of the Great Smokies, 1992, Great Walks of Yosemite National Park, 1993, Great Walks of Sequoia and Kings Canyon National Parks, 1994, Great Walks of Acadia National Park and Mount Desert Island, 1994, Great Walks of the Olympic Peninsula, 1999, The Woodland Garden, 1996; exhibited in group shows at Rockport (Mass.) Art Festival, 1977, 78, Berkshire Art Assn., Pittsfield, Mass., 1979, The Ogunquit (Maine) Art Ctr., 1982, 83, N.H. Art Assn., Manchester, 1985, Concord (Mass.) Art Assn., 1988, 91, 92, 96-98, Sharon (N.H.) Art Ctr., 1998. Winner Southwest Book award for Answered Prayers, 1997. Mem. Concord Art Assn., Sharon Arts Ctr. Home: 3151 Hazens Notch Rd Montgomery Center VT 05471-4408 Office Phone: 603-497-8020.

**OKTEM, OZGUR,** medical researcher; b. Kars, Turkey, Aug. 1, 1971; s. Lutfi and Fatma Oktem. MD, Erciyes U. Sch. of Medicine, Turkey, 1996. Cert. obstetrics and gynecology Marmara U. Hosp., 2001. Resideny obstetrics and gynecology Marmara U. Hosp., Istanbul, Turkey, 1997—2001; rsch. fellow in reproductive medicine Ctr. For Reproductive Medicine and Infertility, Weill Med. Coll. of Cornell U., New York, NY. Dir., chief attending clinician of obgyn Pendik Sifa Hosp., Istanbul, Turkey, 2001—03. Achievements include research in invitro growth and maturation of ovarian follicles. Home: 336 E 83rd St New York NY 10028 Office: Weill Med Coll Cornell U 515 E 71st St S Bldg 406 New York NY 10021 Office Phone: 212-746-1086. Office Fax: 212-746-8848. Personal E-mail: ozo2001@med.cornell.edu.

**OKUHARA, TETSU,** artist, photographer; b. L.A., Mar. 3, 1940; Student, U. Chgo., 1958-61, The Cooper Union, 1970-71. Lectr., workshop leader Otis Coll., L.A., Hartwick Coll., Oneonta, N.Y., NYU, Rutgers U., New Brunswick, N.J., Sch. Visual Arts, N.Y.C., New Sch., N.Y.C., Wesleyan U., Middletown, Conn, Cornish Inst., Seattle. Exhibited in one person and group shows at L.A. County Mus., 2002, Small Works, NYU, 1999, Fotomassan, Goteborg, Sweden, Chgo. Cultural Ctr., 1997, Gotland Konst Mus., Sweden, 1995, San Francisco Camera Work, 1994, Art Inst. Boston, 1994, Artist Space, N.Y.C., 1992, Chgo. Art Inst., 1991-92, Art in General, N.Y.C., 1990, Cleve. Mus. Art, 1978, San Francisco Mus. Modern Art, 1979, 2003, Tokyo Met. Mus. Photography, 2005, numerous others; represented in permanent collections Mus. Modern Art, N.Y.C., Met. Mus. Art, N.Y.C., Hasselad Collection, Goteborg, Sweden, Tokyo Met. Mus. Photography, Art Inst., Chgo., San Francisco Mus. Modern Art, L.A. County Mus., numerous others. Grantee Creative Artist Pub. Svc., 1973-74, 75-76, N.Y. Found. for the Arts, 1988-89, Nat. Endowment for the Arts, 1988-89, La Napoule Found./Nat. Endowment for the Arts, France, 1989, Intercambio, San Juan, P.R., 1991, James P. Phelan Art Award, San Francisco, 1993-94; Guggenheim fellow, 1975-76, N.Y. Found. for Arts fellow, 2000. Home: 202 E 42nd St New York NY 10017-5808 Office Phone: 212-986-0356. Personal E-mail: tetsuokuhara@yahoo.com.

**OKUN, DANIEL ALEXANDER,** environmental engineering educator; b. NYC, June 19, 1917; s. William Howard and Leah (Seligman) O.; m. Elizabeth Griffin, Jan. 14, 1946; children: Michael Griffin, Tema Jon. BS, Cooper Union, 1937; MS, Calif. Inst. Tech., 1938; ScD, Harvard U., 1948; ScD (hon.), UNC, 2000. Registered profl. engr., NC, NY. With USPHS, 1940-42; tchg. fellow Harvard U., 1946-48; with Malcolm Pirnie, NYC, 1948-52; from assoc. prof. dept. environ. scis. and engring. to prof. U. NC, Chapel Hill, 1952-73, Kenan prof. 1973-82, Kenan prof. emeritus, 1982—; head dept. environ. scis. and engring., 1955-73. Vis. prof. Tech. U. Delft, 1960-61, U. Coll., London, 1966-67, 73-75, Tianjin U. 1981; editor environ scis. series Acad. Press, 1968-75; cons. to industry, cons. engrs., govtl. agys. World Bank, WHO, UNDP, with spl. svc. in Switzerland, Israel, Jordan, Peru, Egypt, Colombia, Brazil, Venezuela, Thailand, Indonesia, Kenya, Singapore, Lesotho, Zambia, Tunisia, Australia, Taiwan, Bangladesh, Argentina, Chile, New Zealand, Jamaica, Guatemala, Turkey, Finland, Eng., Morocco, China, The Philippines, India, Singapore, Israel, Lesotho; environ. coun. Rohm & Haas Co., Inc., 1985-92; chmn. expert panel on NYC water supply EPA, 1992-93. Author: (with Gordon M. Fair and John C. Geyer) Water and Wastewater Engineering, 2 vols., 1966-68, Elements of Water Supply and Wastewater Disposal, 1971; (with George Ponghis) Community Wastewater Collection and Disposal, 1975; Regionalization of Water Management—A Revolution in England and Wales, 1977; editor: (with M.B. Pescod) Water Supply and Wastewater Disposal in Developing Countries, 1971; (with C.R. Schulz) Surface Water Treatment for Communities in Developing Countries, 1984; contbr. articles to profl. jours. Chmn. Chapel Hill Fellowship for Sch. Integration, 1961-63; adv. bd. Ackland Meml. Art Mus., 1973-78; bd. dirs. Warren Regional Planning Corp., 1971-77, Inter-Faith Coun. Housing Corp., 1975-83, NC Water Quality Coun., 1975-77; mem. adv. com. for med. rsch. Pan Am. Health Orgn., 1976-79; chmn. Washington Met. Area Water Supply Study Com., 1976-80, NAS-NRC; bd. sci. and tech. for internat. devel. NRC, 1978-81, vice chmn. environ. studies bd., 1980-83, chmn. water sci. and tech. bd., 1991-94; com. on human rights NAS, 1988-94; pres. Chapel Hill chpt. NC Civil Liberties Union, 1991-93. Maj. AUS, 1942-46, PTO. Decorated Philippine Liberation medal; recipient Harrison Prescott Eddy medal for rsch. Water Pollution Control Fedn., 1950, Gordon Maskew Fair award Am. Acad. Environ. Engrs., 1973, Thomas Jefferson award U. NC at Chapel Hill, 1973, Gordon Y. Billard award NY Acad. Scis., 1975, 1st Thomas R. Camp Meml. lectr. Boston Soc. Environ. Engrs., Gordon Maskew Fair medal Water Pollution Control Fedn., 1978, First Allen Hazen lectr. New Eng. Water Works Assn., 1990, Donald R. Boyd award Assn. Met. Water Agys., 1993, Jones award Chapel Hill cbpt. ACLU NC, 1998, Gano Dunn award for profl. achievement in sci. and engring. The Cooper Union, 2002; Friendship medal Inst. Water Engrs. and Scientists (Gt. Britain), 1984, Grand award Internat. Water Assn., 2006; NSF fellow, 1960-61; Fed. Water Pollution Control Adminstrn. fellow, 1966-67; Fulbright-Hayes lectr., Eng., 1973-74; Daniel A. Okun Disting. Professorship in Environ. Engring. established by U. NC, 1999. Mem. NAE, AAUP (pres. U. NC chpt. 1963-64), ASCE (hon., chmn. environ. engring. divsn. 1967-68, 1st Simon W. Freese award 1977, Lifetime Achievement award Environ. and Water Resources Inst. 2006), Am. Water Works Assn. (hon., NC Fuller award 1983, Best Paper award ednl. divsn. 1985, Abel Wolman award of Excellence 1991, Best Paper Water Resources Divsn. 1999), Inst. Medicine, Water Environ. Fedn. (hon., chmn. rsch. com. 1961-63, dir.-at-large 1969-72), Am. Acad. Environ. Engring. (pres. 1969-70, hon. diplomate, Kappe lectr. 1995), Assn. Environ. Engring. Profs. (Founders' award 1994), NC Pub. Health Assn. (Jarrett award 1994), U. NC Order of Golden Fleece), Sigma Xi (pres. U. NC chpt. 1968-69). Home: 750 Weaver Dairy Rd Apt 204 Chapel Hill NC 27514-1466 Office: ESE U NC CB 7431 Chapel Hill NC 27599-7431 Office Phone: 919-918-3500. Business E-Mail: dokun@unc.edu.

**OKUN, DEANNA TANNER,** federal official; m. Bob Okun; children: Rachel, Kelsi. BA in Polit. Sci., Utah State U.; JD, Duke U. Sch. of Law. Research assoc. Competitive Enterprise Inst., Washington; assoc. attorney and mem. of transit. Trade Group Hogan & Hartson law firm, Washington; legis. asst. to Senator Frank Murkowski US Senate, counsel for internat. affairs to Sen. Frank Murkowski, 1993—99; commr. U.S. Internat. Trade Comm., 1999—, vice chmn., 2000—02, 2004—06, chmn, 2002—04. Office: US Internat Trade Commission 500 E Street SW Washington DC 20436

**OKUN, HERBERT STUART,** diplomat, educator; b. NYC, Nov. 27, 1930; s. Irving and Ida Muriel (Levine) O.; m. Lorraine Joan Price, Dec. 5, 1954 (div. 1985); children: Jennifer, Elizabeth, Alexandra; m. Enid Curtis Bok, Dec. 27, 1990. AB with grand distinction, Stanford U., 1951; postgrad., Syracuse U., 1951—52, Princeton U., 1952; Hochschule fuer Politische Wissenschaft, Munich, 1956—57; MPA, Harvard U., 1959; M Naval Warfare, Naval War Coll., 1969. Mem. US Fgn. Svc., 1955—91, Munich vice consul, 1955—57; with Bur. Intelligence and Rsch., Dept. State Office Soviet Union Affairs, Washington, 1959-61, alt. dir., 1971-73; 2d sec. Am. Embassy, Moscow, 1961-63; consul, prin. officer Am. Consulate, Belo Horizonte, Brazil, 1964-65; 1st sec., prin. officer Am. Embassy, Brasilia, Brazil, 1965-66, counsellor embassy, prin. officer, 1967-68; assigned to Naval War Coll., 1968-69; spl. asst. to sec. of state Dept. State, Washington, 1969-71, dep. chmn. U.S. Del., U.S.-USSR Talks on Prevention Incidents at Sea, 1971-72; polit. advisor and spl. asst. for internat. affairs to comdr.-in-chief NATO So. Command, Naples, Italy, 1973-74; min.-counsellor, dep. chief mission Am. Embassy, Lisbon, Portugal, 1975-78; dep. chmn. U.S. del. Strategic Arms Limitation Talks with Soviet Union, Geneva, 1978-79; vice chmn. U.S. del. to trilateral U.S.-U.K.-USSR Talks on comprehensive test ban treaty, Geneva, 1979-80; amb. to German Dem. Rep. Berlin, 1980—83; amb.-in-residence Aspen Inst., Washington, 1983-85; amb., dep. permanent rep. of U.S. to the UN N.Y.C., 1985-89. Rep. of US to Gen. Assembly UN, to UN Security Coun., 1985-89, to Com. on Peaceful Uses of Outer Space, 1986-87, to Disarmament Commn. UN, 1985-89, to Commn. Human Rights, 1985-89, to com. on program and coordination of Econ. and Social Coun., 1987, 89; amb. in residence Carnegie Corp. NY, 1989-90; US mem. UN Sec. Gen's. Expert Group on Enhancing UN Structure for Drug Abuse Control, 1990, UN Internat. Narcotics Control Bd., Vienna, Austria, 1992-2002; founding exec. dir. Fin. Svcs. Vol. Corps, NYC, 1990-97; vis. lectr. Yale Law Sch., New Haven, 1991-2002; professorial lectr. in internat. rels., internat. law and instns. Johns Hopkins. U. Sch. Advanced Internat. Studies, Washington, 2002—; spl. adviser, dep. personal envoy of the sec. gen. UN, Yugoslavia and Nagorno-Karabakh, 1991-92; spl. adv., dep. co-chmn. Internat. Conf. on former Yugoslavia, 1992-93; UN mediator Dispute between Greece and former Yugoslav Republic of Macedonia, 1993-97; bd. dirs. World Rehab. Fund; adv. bd. Minority Rights Group USA; spl. advisor Carnegie Commn. on Preventing Deadly Conflict. Commr. U.S.-Poland Action Commn; mem. Internat. Coun., Found. Inter-Ethnic Rels., The Hague, Netherlands, 1995—; mem. Adv. Com., Human Rights Watch, N.Y., 1995—; mem. group internat. advisors Internat. Com. Red Cross, Geneva, 1996-2000; bd. overseers Curtis Inst. Music, Phila.; adv. bd. internat. security studies Yale U., New Haven; mem. adv. bd. Portuguese-Am. Leadership Coun.; bd. dirs. Internat. Ctr. N.Y., 2004-. Served with AUS, 1952-54. Recipient Meritorious Honor award Dept. of State, 1972, Superior Honor award Dept. of State, 1980, Presdl. Meritorious Svc. award, 1983. Mem. Am. Fgn. Policy (nat. com.), Am. Acad. Diplomacy, Lawyers Alliance World Security (nat. bd. dirs.), Washington Inst. Fgn. Affairs, Phi Beta Kappa. Home: 970 Park Ave 6-N New York NY 10028-0324

**OKUN, NEIL JEFFREY,** vitreoretinal surgeon; b. St. Louis, Nov. 21, 1957; s. Edward and Barbara J. (Braham) O.; m. Joan A. Sosnoff, May 19, 1984; children: David E., Sarah E. AB, Dartmouth Coll., 1980; MD, Washington U., 1984. Diplomate Am. Bd. Ophthalmology. Intern internal medicine Jewish Hosp. at Washington U., 1984-85; resident ophthalmology Washington U. Med. Ctr., St. Louis, 1985-88; fellow vitreoretinal Retina Cons., Ltd., Washington U., St. Louis, 1988-89; vitreoretinal surgeon Fla. Retina Inst., Jacksonville, Fla., 1990-91, Retina Assocs. Ctrl. Fla., Orlando, 1991—2004, Ctrl. Fla. Retina, Orlando, 2004—. Instr. dept. ophthalmology Washington U. Sch. Medicine, St. Louis, 1988-89; clin. asst. prof. dept. ophthalmology U. South Fla., Tampa, 1992—; chmn. dept. ophthalmology Fla. Hosp. Orlando, 1996-97 Recipient Upjohn Achievement award for endocrinology and metabolism Washington U. Sch. Medicine, St. Louis, 1984. Fellow ACS, Am. Acad. Ophthalmology; mem. AMA (Physician's Recognition award for continuing med. edn. 1992—), Am. Soc. Retina Specialists, Assn. for Rsch. in Vision and Ophthalmology, Fla. Med. Assn., Fla. Soc. Ophthalmology, Ctrl. Fla. Soc. Ophthalmology, Orange County Med. Soc., Vitreous Soc., Paul Cibis Club. Avocations: music, art. Office: Ctrl Florida Retina 2501 N Orange Ave Ste 401 Orlando FL 32804-4644 Office Phone: 407-896-1224.

**OKURA-MARSZYCKI, MINDY EMI,** editor; b. Honolulu, July 15, 1976; d. Gary and Gail Okura; m. Brian Marszycki, Mar. 27, 2004. BA in English and Psychology, Boston Coll., Chestnut Hill, Mass., 1998; MA in Pub., NYU, NYC, 2003; attending, St. John's U., Queens, NY, 2005—. Web content editor/mktg. assoc. PhysicianEd, Boston, 1998—2001; lit. agt. asst. Liza Dawson & Assocs., NYC, 2002; editl. asst. Columbia U. Press, NYC, 2002, Taylor and Francis, NYC, 2002; book editor Other Press, NYC, 2003—. Grad. Student Dean's fellow, NYU, 2001. Mem.: Young to Pub. Group, NYU Pub. Alumni Steering Com. Office: Other Press 2 Park Ave New York NY 10016 Office Phone: 212-414-0054.

**OKUWA, MAKOTO,** chef; b. Japan; Chef Sushi Tarp, Washington; head sushi chef Morimoto, Phila., 2006, NYC, 2006—. Named one of NYC's Rising Stars, StarChefs.com, 2006. Office: Morimoto 88 10th Ave New York NY 10011 Office Phone: 888-354-8842.*

**OLAFSON, FREDERICK ARLAN,** philosophy educator; b. Winnipeg, Man., Can., Sept. 1, 1924; s. Kristinn K. and Fredericka (Björnson) O.; m. Allie Lewis, June 20, 1952 (dec.); children— Peter Niel, Christopher Arlan, Thomas Andrew. AB, Harvard U., 1947, MA, 1948, PhD, 1951. Instr. philosophy and gen. edn. Harvard U., 1952-54; asst. prof. philosophy, then assoc. prof. Vassar Coll., 1954-60; assoc. prof. Johns Hopkins U., 1960-64; prof. edn. and philosophy Harvard Grad. Sch. Edn., 1964-71; prof. philosophy U. Calif., San Diego, 1971-91, chmn. dept., 1973-76, assoc. dean grad. studies and research, 1980-85. Author: Principles and Persons, 1967, Ethics and Twentieth Century Thought, 1973, The Dialectic of Action, 1979, Heidegger and the Philosophy of the Mind, 1987, What Is A Human Being?, 1995, Heidegger and the Ground of Ethics, 1998, Naturalism and the Human Condition, 2001. Served to lt. (j.g.) USNR, 1943-46. Mem. Nat. Acad. Edn. Home: 6081 Avenida Chamnez La Jolla CA 92037-7404 Business E-Mail: folafson@ucsd.edu.

**OLAFSSON, OLAF,** communications executive; b. Reykjavik, Iceland, 1962; Grad. in Physics, Brandeis U. With Sony Corp., 1985—97, founder, pres., CEO Sony Interactive Entertainment, Inc., 1991; bd. dirs. Advanta Corp., 1997, pres., 1998; vice chmn. Time Warner Digital Media Time Warner Inc., exec. v.p. NYC. Author: Absolution, 1994, The Journey Home, 2000, Walking Into the Night, 2003. Office: Time Warner Inc 1 Time Warner Ctr New York NY 10019-8016*

**OLAFSSON, OLAFUR JOHANN,** writer, media company executive; b. Reykjavik, Iceland, Sept. 26, 1962; s. Olafur Sigurdsson; m. Anna Olafsson; children: Arni, Olaf. Degree in physics, Brandeis U. Joined Sony Corp., San Jose, Calif., 1984; v.p., spl. projects Sony USA, N.Y.C., 1989—91; founder, pres., CEO Sony Interactive Entertainment Inc. (formerly Sony Electronic Pub. Co.), N.Y.C., 1991—96; pres. Advanta Corp., 1998—99; vice chmn. Time Warner Digital Media, N.Y.C., 1999—2003; exec. v.p. Time Warner Inc., N.Y.C., 2003—. Author: (short stories) Nine Keys, 1986, (novels) Marketplace of the Gods, 1988, Absolution, 1994, The Journey Home, 2000, Walking Into the Night, 2003, (plays) The Feast of Snails, 2002. Office: Time Warner Inc 75 Rockefeller Plz New York NY 10019-6990

**OLAGUNJU, AMOS OMOTAYO,** computer science educator, consultant; b. Igosun, Kwara, Nigeria, Nov. 27, 1954; came to U.S., 1980; s. Solomon Atoyebi and Ruth Ebun (Adegoke) O.; m. Janet; 1 child, Amanda. EdD, U. N.C., Greensboro, 1987; PhD, Kensington U., 1990; cert. in cryptography and info. systems, MIT, 1996, cert. in design and analysis experiments, 1999, cert. in digital comm. networks, 1999, cert. in bioinformatic principles, 2001. Cert. bioinformatic prins. MIT, 2001. Dir. mgmt. info. sys. Barber-Scotia Coll., Concord, NC, 1981-82; lectr. NC A&T State U., Greensboro, NC, 1982-87, asst. prof., 1987-90; mem. tech. staff Bell Comm. Rsch., Piscataway, NJ, 1986-90; vis. prof. Mich. State U., East Lansing, Mich., 1990-91; coord. acad. computing, assoc. prof. Del. State U., 1991-92, prof., chair dept. math. and computer sci., 1992—2001; collegiate prof. UMUC-Asia, 2001—02; prof. computer networking and applications St. Cloud State U., Minn., 2002—. Cons. NSF, Washington, 1991-93, Edn. Testing Agy., Princeton, NJ, 1995—. Author: Lecture Notes Series in Language C, Systems Programming, Database Systems, Theoretical Aspects of Computing, File Structures, Introduction to Computer Science and Scientific and Engineering Applications of Fortran, 1991-96; mem. editl. bd. Sci. World Jour., 2003—; contbr. articles to Software Metrics, Automatic Indexing, Perfect Hashing, Number Theory, Efficient Statis. Algorithms, Del. State News. Pres. Ahmadu Bello Assn. Computer Univ. Students, Zaria, Nigeria, 1976, Orgn. United Africans, Concord, NC, 1982. Recipient Queen's Grad. award Queen's U., Kingston, Ont., 1979; Navy-Am. Soc. for Engring. Edn. fellow, 1997, sr. fellow 1998, 2000. Mem. Internat. Assn. Sci. Tech. Devel. (reviewer 2001—), Assn. for Modelling and Simulation in Enterprises (program chair 1989-90, editor), Assn. for Computing Machinery (reviewer), NC Acad. Sci. (program chair 1991—, mem. editl. bd. 1999—) NY Acad. Sci. Achievements include invention of the Bell Communication research software report, analysis measurement system and generic administrative quantitative decision support system. Home: 1617 Highland Trail Saint Cloud MN 56301 Office Phone: 320-308-5696. Personal E-Mail: blessamos@yahoo.com.

**OLAH, GEORGE ANDREW,** chemist, educator; b. Budapest, Hungary, May 22, 1927; arrived in U.S., 1964, naturalized, 1970; s. Julius and Magda (Krasznai) Olah; m. Judith Agnes Lengyel, July 9, 1949; children: George John, Ronald Peter. PhD, Tech. U. Budapest, 1949, D (hon.), 1989; DSc (hon.), U. Durham, 1988, U. Munich, 1990, U. Crete, Greece, 1994, U. Szeged, Hungary, 1995, U. Veszprem, 1995, Case Western Res. U., 1995, U. So. Calif., 1995, U. Montpellier, 1996, SUNY, 1998, U. Pecs, Hungary, 2001, U. Debrecen, 2003. Mem. faculty Tech. U. Budapest, 1949—54; assoc. dir. Ctrl. Chem. Rsch. Inst., Hungarian Acad. Scis., 1954—56; rsch. scientist Dow Chem. Can. Ltd., 1957—64, Dow Chem. Co., Framingham, Mass., 1964—65; prof. chemistry Case Western Res. U., Cleve., 1965—69, C.F. Mabery prof. rsch., 1969—77; Donald P. and Katherine B. Loker disting. prof. chemistry, dir. Hydrocarbon Rsch. Inst., U. So. Calif., LA, 1977—. Vis. prof. chemistry Ohio State U., 1963, U. Heidelberg, Germany, U. Colo., 1969, Swiss Fed. Inst. Tech., 1972, U. Munich, 1973, U. London, 1973—79, Louis Pasteur U., Strasbourg, France, 1974, U. Paris, 1981; hon. vis. lectr. U. London, 1981—95; cons. to industry. Author: Friedel-Crafts Reactions, Vols. I-IV, 1963—64; author: (with P. Schleyer) Carbonium Ions, Vols. I-V, 1969—76; author: Friedel-Crafts Chemistry, 1973, Carbocations and Electrophilic Reactions, 1973, Halonium Ions, 1975; author: (with Goeppertau Prakash and J. Somer) Superacids, 1984; author: (with G. Prakash, R.E. Williams, L.D. Field and K. Wade) Hypercarbon Chemistry, 1987; author: (with R. Malthotra and S.C. Narang) Nitration, 1989; author: Cage Hydrocarbons, 1990; author: (with Wade and Williams) Electron Deficient Boron and Carbon Clusters, 1991; author: (with Chambers and Prakash) Synthetic Fluorine Chemistry, 1992; author: (with Molnar) Hydrocarbon Chemistry, 1995; author: (with Laali, Wang, Prakash) Onium Ions, 1998; author: A Life of Magic Chemistry, 2001; author: (with Goeppertau Prakash) Across Conventional Lines, 2003, Beyond Oil and Gas: The Methanol Economy, 2006; contbr. chapters to books, articles to profl. jours.; patentee in field. Recipient Alexander von Humboldt Sr. U.S. Scientist award, 1979, Calif. Scientist of Yr. award, 1989, Pioneer of Chemistry award, Am. Inst. Chemists, 1993, Mendeleev medal, Russian Acad. Scis., 1992, Nobel prize in Chemistry, 1994, Kapitsa medal, Russian Acad. Natural Scis., 1995, Order of the Hungarian Corvin-Chain, 2001, Albert Einstein medal, Russian Acad. Natural Scis., 2002, Bolyai prize, Hungarian Acad. Sci., 2002, Order of Merit with Cross of Star, Republic of Hungary, 2006; Guggenheim fellow, 1972, 1988. Fellow: AAAS, Chem. Inst. Can., Brit. Chem. Soc. (hon., hon./centenary lectr. 1978, Centenary lectr. 1978); mem.: NAS, Indian Nat. Acad. Sci. (fgn.), Can. Royal Soc., Royal Soc. Sci. Arts Barcelona, Royal Acad. Sci. and Arts, Am. Acad. Arts and Sci., Chem. Soc. Japan (hon.), Italy Chem. Soc. (hon.), Royal Chem. Soc. (hon.), Hungarian Acad. Sci. (hon.), Phila. Soc., Am. Chem. Soc. (award petroleum chemistry 1964, Leo Hendrik Baekeland award N.J. sect. 1966, Morley medal Cleve. sect. 1970, award Synthetic Organic Chemistry 1979, Roger Adams award in organic chemistry 1989, Arthur C. Cope award 2001, Priestley medal 2005), European Acad. Arts, Sci. and

Humanities, Royal Soc. London (fgn. mem.), Italian Nat. Acad. Sci. Lincei, Grand Cordon of the Order of the Rising Sun (Japan). Office: U So Calif Loker Hydrocarbon Rsch Inst Los Angeles CA 90007 Office Phone: 213-740-5976. Business E-Mail: olah@usc.edu. *America still is offering a new home and nearly unlimited possibilities to the newcomer who is willing to work hard for it. It is also where the "main action" in science and technology remains.*

**OLANSKY, SIDNEY,** retired dermatologist; b. Boston, Jan. 11, 1914; s. Samuel and Anna Olansky; m. Marian Elizabeth Freehafer, June 30, 1945; children: Leann, Alan, David, Sidney. BS, NYU, 1934; MD, Glasgow (Scotland) U., 1940. Diplomate Am. Bd. Dermatology. Intern Met. Hosp., N.Y.C., 1940-42; commd. officer USPHS, 1942, advanced through grades to med. dir., 1950; med. officer in charge Rapid Treatment Ctr., Washington, 1943-46; resident dept. dermatology Duke U. Hosp., 1946-48; pvt. practice dermatology Washington, 1948-50; dir. V.D. Rsch. Lab., Chamblee, Ga., 1950-55; assoc. prof. dermatology Duke U. Med. Ctr., 1955-59; prof. medicine, chief divsn. dermatology Emory U. Sch. Medicine, Atlanta, 1959-81, emeritus prof., 1981—; ret., 2006. Rschr. USPHS, Gallinger Meml. Hosp., 1948-50; mem. nat. serology adv. com. to Surgeon Gen. of Pub. Health Svc.; cons. 3rd Army Hdqs.; mem. med. sci. com. Dermatology Found. Contbr. articles to profl. jours. Fellow ACP; mem. AMA, Am. Acad. Dermatology and Syphilology (bd. dirs.), Am. Dermatol. Assn., Am. Venereal Disease Assn. (pres. 1971-72), Am. Fedn. Clin. Rsch., Med. Assn. Ga., Med. Assn. Atlanta, Southeastern Dermatol. Assn. (sec., pres. 1971-73), Atlanta Dermatology Assn. (pres. 1971-72). Avocations: reading, sports. Office: Sidney Olansky Md 3379 Peachtree Rd NE Ste 500 Atlanta GA 30326-1418

**OLASKY, MARVIN,** journalist, educator, editor; b. Malden, Mass., June 12, 1950; s. Eli and Ida (Green) O.; m. Susan Northway, June 27, 1976; children: Pete, David, Daniel, Benjamin. AB, Yale U., 1971; MA, U. Mich., 1974, PhD, 1976. Reporter The Bull., Bend, Oreg., 1971-72, Boston Globe, 1972; speechwriter Du Pont Co., Wilmington, Del., 1978-83; prof. U. Tex., Austin, 1983—. Vis. prof. Princeton U., 2004—05. Author: Prodigal Press, 1988, Abortion Rites, 1992, The Tragedy of American Compassion, 1992, Fighting for Liberty and Virtue, 1995, The American Leadrship Tradition, 1998, Compassionate Conservatism, 2000, The Religions Next Door, 2004, Scimitar's Edge, 2006, The Politics of Disaster, 2006; editor Turning Point Christian Worldview, 1987-95, Philanthropy, Culture and Soc., 1991-94; editor-in-chief World Mag., 1994—; syndicated columnist. Sr. fellow Acton Inst. for Study of Religion and Liberty. Presbyterian. Home: 4106 Firstview Dr Austin TX 78731-3904 Office: U Tex Sch Journalism Austin TX 78712

**OLAYAN, LUBNA S.,** finance company executive; b. Saudi Arabia; d. Suliman S. Olayan. BS in Agr., Cornell Univ.; MBA, Ind. Univ. With Morgan Guaranty, NYC, 1979—81; joined Olayan Group, Riyadh, Saudi Arabia, 1983—; now CEO Olayan Fin. Co., Riyadh, Saudi Arabia. Bd. dir. Olayan Investments Co. Establishment, Egyptian Fin. Co. (capital Union, Dubai, United Arab Emirates; non-exec. dir. Chelsfield, UK, WPP, UK; bd. trustees Arab Thought Found.; pres. Suliman S. Olayan Found. Named one of 100 Most Influential People, Time Mag., 2005, 50 Most Powerful Women, Fortune Mag, 2005; recipient Achievement award, Arab Bankers Assn. of N. Am., 2004. Mem.: World Econ. Forum (Women Leadership Initiative, Arab Bus. Coun. Exec. Com.), World Bank (World Links Adv. Coun.), INSEAD Internat. Coun. Office: Olayan Financing Co PO Box 8772 Riyadh 11492 Saudi Arabia*

**OLBERMANN, KEITH,** news analyst, former sportscaster; b. NYC, Jan. 27, 1959; BS in Comm. Arts, Cornell U., 1979. Sports reporter UPI Radio, N.Y.C., 1979-80, RKO Radio, N.Y.C., 1980-82, WNEW-AM, N.Y.C., 1980-83; nat. sports reporter, anchor CNN, N.Y.C., 1981-84, WCVB-TV, Boston, 1984; weeknight sports anchor, reporter KTLA-TV, L.A., 1985-88; sports commentator KNX-AM, L.A., 1996-91; sports anchor, host The Keith Olbermann Show KCBS-TV, L.A., 1988-91; weekend co-host ESPN Sports Radio, 1992-93; co-anchor, co-host SportsCenter ESPN, Bristol, Conn., 1992-97; co-anchor SportsNight ESPN2, 1993-94; anchor, exec. prodr. Fox Sports Net, 1998—2001; columnist Salon.com, 2002—03; host, Countdown with Keith Olbermann MSNBC, 2003—; co-host ESPN Radio, 2005—. Co-author (with Dan Patrick): The Big Show: Inside ESPN's Sport Center, 1997; author: The Worst Person in the World: And 119 More Strong Contenders, 2006. Recipient 11 Golden Mike awards Best Sportscaster, 1985, 86, 87, 88, 89, 90, Best Sportscast Calif. Radio and TV News Assn., 1985-91, Cable Ace award Best Sportscaster Nat. Acad. Cable Programming, 1995, Edward R. Murrow award, 2002; voted Calif. A.P. Sportscaster of Yr., 1985, 87, 89. Office: MSNBC Cable LLC 1 MSNBC Plz Secaucus NJ 07094*

**OLBRICK, VALERIE LYN,** management consultant, information technologist; b. Pitts., Feb. 9, 1959; d. Kenneth Donald and LaVerne Estelle (Aiken) O. BS, Grove City Coll., 1981. Sr. telecomm. analyst Timken Co., Canton, Ohio, 1981-85; network planning mgr. Leaseway Transp. Inc., Cleve., 1985-87; group mgr. Network Strategies, Fairfax, Va., 1987—88; sr. mgr. Ernst & Young, L.A., 1988—95, prin. N.Y.C., 1995, dir. tech. planning and deployment Internat. divsn., 1995—; CEO, pres. info. tech. cons. Olbneck & Assoc., 2001—. Avocations: sailing, skiing, bicycling, gardening, reading. Address: 106 Crestwood Dr Safety Harbor FL 34695

**OLCER, NURI YELMAN,** engineering researcher, educator; b. Gaziantep, Turkey, July 22, 1932; arrived in U.S., 1958; s. Samet and Besire Olcer. MS, Tech. U. Istanbul, 1956; PhD, Northwestern U., 1964. Rsch. engr. Ordnance Engring. Assocs., Chgo., 1960—66; assoc. prof. Ill. Inst. Tech., Chgo., 1966—69; mgr. engring. mechanics OEA, Inc., Des Plaines, Ill., 1970—84, v.p. engring. mechanics, 1984—97; cons., 1998—. Resident rsch. fellow Argonne Nat. Lab., Ill., 1962—64. Author: Recoilless Rifle Weapon Systems, 1976; contbr. articles to profl. jours.; Fulbright Scholar, 1958—59, Walter F. Murphy Rsch. fellow, Northwestern U. Tech. Inst., 1960—62. Mem.: AIAA, ASME (Calvin Rice Meml. scholar 1959), Soc. Engring. Sci., Am. Soc. Engring. Edn., Can. Math. Soc., N.Y. Acad. Scis., Soc. Nat. Philosophy, Math. Assn. Am., Am. Math. Soc., Am. Acad. Mech., Sigma Xi, Pi Tau Sigma. Avocations: rare book collecting, stamp collecting/philately, hiking, travel. Home: 9576 East Maplewood Cir Englewood CO 80111 Office Phone: 303-773-3659.

**OLCHYK, SAMUEL,** lawyer; b. Havana, Cuba, Feb. 26, 1960; married; 2 children. BBA, Univ. Tex., 1982, JD, 1985; LLM in Taxation, NYI, 1987. CPA Tex., 1985; bar: Tex. 1985, DC 1989. Tax counsel US Congress Joint Com. on Taxation, 1995—2003; ptnr., taxation, bus. transactions Venable LLP, Washington, 2003—. Contbr. articles to profl journals. Mem.: DC Bar Assn., State Bar Tex. Office: Venable LLP 575 Seventh St NW Washington DC 20004 Office Phone: 202-344-4034. Office Fax: 202-344-8300. Business E-Mail: solchyk@venable.com.

**OLCOTT, CORNELIUS, IV,** surgeon; b. Harlingen, Tex., 1942; s. Cornelius III and Margaret Ella (Dole) O.; m. Phoebe Swan Allen, Aug. 1, 1964; children: Cornelius V, Jocelyn Harrison. AB magna cum laude, Princeton U., 1963; MD, Columbia P&S, 1967. Diplomate Am. Bd. Surgery. Intern U. Calif. San Francisco, 1967-68, resident in surgery, 1968-74, fellow in vascular surgery, 1974-75; surgeon Stanford U. Hosp., Palo Alto, Calif., 1977—; prof. surgery Stanford U., 1993—; attending surgeon Lucille Packard Children's Hosp., Palo Alto, Calif., 1991—. Numerous clin. and faculty appointments, including attending surgeon Palo Alto VA Hosp., 1978—, Washington Hosp., Fremont, Calif., 1980-90, others. Contbr. articles to profl. jours., chpts. to books; presenter in field. Mem. Am. Coll. Surgeons (pres. No. Calif. chpt. 1984-85), Am. Trauma Soc., Naffziger Surg. Soc., Am. Acad. Surgery, San Francisco and Calif. Med. Assn., Internat. Cardiovascular Soc., No. Calif. Vascular. Soc., San Francisco Surg. Soc., Santa Clara County Med. Soc., Pacific Coast Surg. Assn. (pres.-elect), Soc. for Vascular Surgery, Soc. Clin. Vascular Surgery, Western Vascular Soc. Avocations: sailing, bicycling. Office: Stanford U Med Ctr Divsn Vascular Surgery Ret 2 No H-3630 Stanford CA 94305 Office Phone: 650-725-5227. E-mail: olcott@stanford.edu.

**OLCOTT, JOHN WHITING,** air transportation executive; b. Orange, NJ, Oct. 20, 1936; s. Egbert Whiting and Marion Richmond (Braillard) O.; m. Hope Bennett Phillips, May 14, 1966 (div. Feb. 1987); children: David Whiting, Bradley Phillips, Carter Howell; m. Isobel Waxman Ritter, Nov. 25, 1989. BS in Aero. Engring., Princeton U., 1960, MS in Aero. Engring., 1964; MBA in Gen. Mgmt., Rutgers U., 1970. Cert. Internat. Std. Bus. Aircraft Ops. Auditor Accreditation 2003, 2005. V.p. Linden (N.J.) Flight Svc., 1960-66; flight rsch. specialist Princeton (N.J.) U., 1966-68; v.p. corp. devel., sr. cons. Aero. Rsch. Assocs. Princeton, Inc., 1968-74; v.p., group pub., editorial dir. McGraw-Hill Aviation Week Group, Rye Brook, NY, 1973-92; pres. Nat. Bus. Aviation Assn., Inc., 1992—2003, Gen. Aero Co., Inc., 2003—. Rsch. engring. and devel. adv. com. FAA, 1990-03; mem. bd. govs. Flight Safety Found., 1992-00; bd. dirs. ARINC, Inc., Annapolis, Md., 1997-03, NASA, Aerospace Tech. Adv. Com., 1998-03; co-chair FAA Safer Skies Program, 1999-03; chmn. Be A Pilot, 2003-05; mem. Small Aircraft Transp. Sys. Coun. NASA, 2002-06; bd. dirs. Nat. Coalition for Aviation Mobility, 2004-06; chmn. Airbus Bus. Aviation Adv. Bd., 2005—; auditor Internat. Std. Bus. Aircraft Ops., 2003—. Crew chief, mem. New Vernon (N.J.) Vol. First Aid Squad, 1974-92; bd. dirs. Aviation Rsch. and Edn. Found., Washington, 1988-92; mem. bd. visitors Aircraft Owner and Pilots Assn. Air Safety Found., Frederick, Md., 1988-93; trustee Embry-Riddle Aero. U., Daytona Beach, Fla., 1988-93, 95-97; chmn. panel on gen. aviation and commuter tech. NASA, Washington, 1974-86; chmn. panel gen. aviation safety FAA, Washington, 1983-88; mem. New Vernon Bd. Adjustment, 2003—, integrated devel. team Joint Program and Devel. Office, airports and integrated product team Agile ATC Sys., 2005—. Recipient Meritorious Svc. award Flight Safety Found., 1983, 2003, Dir.'s award FAA Ctrl. Region, 1984, Am. Spirit award Nat. Bus. Aviation Assn., 2003, Commendation cert. FAA, 1984, Gill Robb Wilson award Embry-Riddle Aero. U., 1986, Journalism award Helicopter Assn. Internat., 1990, William F. Shea award for Disting. Contrbn. to Aviation, 2004, Turning Goals Into Reality award NASA, 2005, Langley Rsch. Ctr. Ctr. Team award NASA, 2005; inducted N.J. Aviation Hall of Fame, 2001. Mem.: Nat. Air Transp. Assn., Aircraft Owners and Pilots Assn., Soc. Exptl. Test Pilots, Nat. Bus. Aviation Assn., NJ Aviation Assn. (pres. 2005—06). Republican. Presbyterian. Office: Gen Aero Co Hangar One 1 Airport Rd Morristown NJ 07960 Office Phone: 973-734-9994. Business E-Mail: jack@generalaerocompany.com.

**OLCYZK, ED,** professional athletics coach; Hockey player Chgo. (Ill.) Blackhawks, 1983—87, 1998—2000, Toronto (Can.) Maple Leafs, 1987—90, Winnipeg Jets, 1990—92, 1995—96, N.Y. Rangers, 1992—95, LA (Calif.) Kings, 1996—97, Pitts. (Pa.) Penguins, 1997—98, head coach, 2003—05. Mem. Team USA Olympic Hockey Team, 1984, World Championships Tournament, 1985—87, 1989, Can. Cup Tournament, 1987, 91.

**OLCZAK, PAUL VINCENT,** psychologist, educator; b. Buffalo, May 25, 1943; s. Vincent Henry and Helen (Babula) O.; m. Marie Rose Oliveri, Oct. 20, 1973; children: Paul V. II, Patrick J., Drew M. MA, No. Ill. U., 1969, PhD, 1972. Clin. psychologist Family Ct. Psychiat. Clinic, Buffalo, 1975-77, cons. supervisory psychologist, 1977—; supr. psychol. svcs. Hopevale, Inc., Hamburg, NY, 1977-89; clin. psychologist Amherst (N.Y.) Police Dept., 1989—; asst. prof. psychology SUNY, Geneseo, 1977-83, assoc. prof. psychology, 1983-90, prof. psychology, 1990—, chairperson, 1999—; clin. psychologist child and adolescent psychiatry Niagara Falls Meml. Hosp., 1996—, clin. psychologist bariatric medicine program, 2002—; cons. psychologist Batavia (N.Y.) Sch. Dist. Co-editor: Community Mediation, 1991; contbg. author: The POI in Clinical Situations: A Review, 1991, Self-actualization-Polemics Surrounding Its Use, 1991; contbr. articles to profl. jours./publs. Mem. APA, Ea. Psychol. Assn., Midwestern Psychol. Assn., Psychonomic Soc., Soc. Exptl. Social Psychology, Internat. Assn. for Conflict Mgmt., Psi Chi, Sigma Xi. Home: 278 Troy Del Way Buffalo NY 14221-3358 Office: SUNY Dept Psychology Geneseo NY 14454 E-mail: olczak@geneseo.edu.

**OLD, HUGHES OLIPHANT,** theologian, minister; b. Redondo Beach, Calif., Apr. 13, 1933; s. Shadburne Edward and Emma Coulter (Oliphant) O.; m. Mary Chase McCaw, June 12, 1982; children: Hannah Chase, Isaac Houghton Chambers. BA, Centre Coll., 1955; BD, Princeton Theol. Sem., 1958; postgrad., U. Tubingen, 1964-66; ThD, U. Neuchatel, 1971. Ordained to ministry Presbyn. Ch., 1959. Minister Presbyn. Ch., Atglen, Pa., 1959-64; Faith Presbyn. Ch., West Lafayette, Ind., 1972-85; mem. Ctr. for Theol. Inquiry, Princeton, NJ, 1985—; prof. Erskine Theol. Sem., 2004—; dean Inst. Reformed Worship, 2004—. Lectr. Princeton Theol. Sem., 1998-2004. Author: Patristic Roots of Reformed Worship, 1975, Worship, 1984, enlarged edit. 2002, Shaping of the Reformed Baptismal Rite, 1992, Leading in Prayer, 1995, Themes and Variations for A Christian Doxology, 1992, The Reading and Preaching of Scripture in the Worship of the Christian Church, Vols. I and II, 1998, Vol. III, 1999, vol. IV, 2002, vol. V, 2004; contbr. numerous articles to scholarly jours. Fellow N.Am. Acad. Liturgy; mem. Union League Phila. Republican. Avocations: painting, music. Home: 818 Lower Ferry Rd Trenton NJ 08628-3501

**OLDAKER, GUY BROOKLYN, III,** lawyer; b. Washington, Aug. 18, 1950; s. Guy B. and Elisabeth H. Oldaker; m. Cynthia L. Keiser, Aug. 3, 1980; children: Guy B. IV, Mary Elisabeth. BA in Chemistry, U. Va., 1972; PhD in Chemistry, Va. Polytech. Inst. & State U., 1978; JD, W.Va. U., 1995. Bar: N.C. 1996, U.S. Dist. Ct. (mid. dist.) N.C. 1996. Tchr. Albemarle H.S. Charlottesville, Va., 1972—75; instr. Va. Polytech. Inst. and State U., Blacksburg, Va., 1977—78; sr. project mgr. Environmentalists, Inc., Raleigh, NC, 1978—85; sr. staff R&D chemist R.J. Reynolds Tobacco Co., Winston-Salem, 1985—92, cons., 1992—95; exec. dir. Ctr. for Indoor Air Rsch., Winston-Salem, NC, 1987—88; assoc. Gordon & Nesbit, PLLC, 1996—97; prt. practice Winston-Salem, 1996—. Asst. coach cross country and track Albemarle H.S., Charlottesville, Va., 1972—75; sci. illustrator prt. practice, Blacksburg 1978; environ. cons. Morgantown, NC, 1993—93; vocalist Piedmont Opera Theater, Winston-Salem, 2001—; expert witness. Contbr. articles to profl. jours. Pres. Winston-Salem Youth Symphony, 1997—99. Mem.: Forsyth County Criminal Def. Trial Lawyers Assn. (v.p. 2005), N.C. Acad. Trial Lawyers, Winston-Salem Symphony Chorale (treas.), Alpha Chi Sigma. Republican. Episcopalian. Achievements include patents for device for sampling indoor air. Avocations: running, reading, music, calligraphy, pen and ink drawing. Office: Ste 115 3410 Healy Dr Winston Salem NC 27103 Office Phone: 336-725-2346. Personal E-mail: oldakerg@bellsouth.net.

**OLDEN, KEVIN WILLIAM,** medical researcher; b. N.Y.C., Aug. 18, 1948; s. William and Josephine Olden; m. Sylvia Suikam Hom, Apr. 23, 1983; 1 child, Kimberly Jane. AB, NYU, 1971; MD, SUNY Downstate Med. Sch., 1976. Diplomate Am. Bd. of Internal Medicine with subspecialties in gastroenterology and addiction medicine, Am. Bd. of Psychiatry and Neurology. Intern categorical medicine UCLA-San Fernando Valley Med. Program, Sepulveda, Calif., 1976—77, resident internal medicine, 1977—79; resident psychiatry Mass. Gen. Hosp., Boston, 1979—81; postdoctoral fellow substance abuse and gastroenterology DVA Med. Ctr., Palo Alto, Calif., 1981—83; dir. alcohol rehab. unit Calif. Pacific Med. Ctr., San Francisco, 1983—86; asst. prof. medicine and psychiatry U. Calif., Davis, 1986—91, assoc. prof. medicine and psychiatry San Francisco, 1991—98, Mayo Med. Sch., Scottsdale, Ariz., 1998—2005; Levy prof. medicine, chair divsn. gastroenterology U. Ark., Little Rock, 2006—. Cons. Rome Internat. Working Teams on Functional GI Disorders, Rome, 1994—; fellow gastroenterology DVA Med. Ctr., Martinez, Calif., 1988—89; assoc. prof. medicine and psychiatry U. South Ala. Sch. Medicine, Mobile, 2005—06. Editor: (book) Handbook of the Functional Gastrointestinal Disorders, Chronic Abdominal Pain: A Comprehensive Approach; guest editor (med. jour.) Psychiat. Annals, Seminars in Gastroenterology, Jour. Psychosomatic Rsch., editl. bd. Am. Jour. Drug and Alcohol Abuse, Medicine and Psychiatry, Am. Jour. Gastroenterology. Med. advisor Internat. Found. for Functional Gastrointestinal Disorders, Milw., 1997—2003, Cyclic Vomiting Assn., Scottsdale, Ariz., 1998—2003; med. cons. Med. Bd. of Calif., San Francisco, 1986—98; med. advisor Physician Diversion Program State of Calif., 1986—97. Capt. USNR, 1978—2003. Recipient Harvard Macy scholar in Med. Edn., Harvard Med.

Sch., 2000, Clin. Scholar award, Am. Coll. of Gastroenterology, 1999, Outstanding Physician Educator (Rsch.), Mayo Clinic Scottsdale, 2000, Outstanding Physician and Educator, St. Mary's Med. Ctr., 1992—93, Clinician Engaged in Edn., Mayo Clinic Scottsdale, 1999—2000. Fellow: Acad. of Psychosomatic Medicine, ACP, Am. Coll. of Gastroenterology, Am. Psychiat. Assn.; mem.: Calif. Soc. Addiction Medicine (pres. 1990—92), Calif. Med. Assn. (chair chem. dependency 1986—98), Am. Gastroent. Assn. (pres. functional brain-gut rsch. group 2001—03). Avocations: fishing, scuba diving. Office: Univ Ark Sch Medicine 4301 W Markham Little Rock AR 72205-7199 Business E-Mail: kwolden@uams.edu.

**OLDENBURG, CLAES THURE,** artist; b. Stockholm, Jan. 28, 1929; arrived in US, 1936, naturalized, 1953; s. Gosta and Sigrid (Lindforss) O.; m. Patricia Joan Muschinski, Apr. 13, 1960 (div. Apr. 1970); m. Coosje van Bruggen, July 22, 1977. BA, Yale, 1951; student, Art Inst., Chgo., 1953—54. One-man shows include Judson Gallery, NYC, 1959, Reuben Gallery, 1960, Green Gallery, 1962, Sidney Janis Gallery, 1964—70, Galerie Ileana Sonnabend, Paris, 1964, Robert Fraser Gallery, London, 1966, Moderna Museet, Stockholm, 1966, 1977, Mus. Contemporary Art, Chgo., 1966, 1977, Irving Blum Gallery, L.A., 1968, Mus. Modern Art, NYC, 1969, Stedelijk Mus., Amsterdam, 1970, 1977, Tate Gallery, London, 1970, Pasadena (Calif.) Art Mus., 1971, Nelson-Atkins Mus., Kansas City, Mo., 1972, Art Inst. Chgo., 1973, Leo Castelli Gallery, NYC, 1974, 1976, 1980, 1990, Margo Leavin Gallery, LA, 1975—76, 1978, 1988—89, Walker Art Ctr., Mpls., 1975, 1992, Art Gallery Ont., Toronto, 1976, Ctr. Georges Pompidou, Paris, 1977, Rijksmus. Kröller-Muller Otterlo, 1979, Mus. Ludwig, Cologne, 1979, Wave Hill, Bronx, N.Y., 1984, Solomon R. Guggenheim Mus., NYC, 1986, 1995, Mus. Haus Esters Krefeld, Germany, 1987, Kunstmus., Basel, 1992, Pace Gallery, 1992, 1994, Nat. Gallery Art, Washington, 1995, Mus. Contemporary Art, LA, 1995, Kunst und Ausstellungshalle der Bundesrepublik Deutschland, Bonn, 1996, Hayward Gallery, London, 1996, Whitney Mus. Am. Art, NYC, 2002, two person show with Coosje van Bruggen, No. Ctr. Contemporary Art, Sunderland, 1988, Leeds City Art Gallery, 1988, Palais des Beaux-Arts, Brussels, 1988, IVAM Ctr. Julio González, Valencia, 1988, Galleria Christian Stein, Milan, 1990, Leo Castelli Gallery, NYC, 1990, 1990, Pace Gallery, 1994, Mus. Correr, Venice, 1999, Mus. Serralves, Porto, Portugal, 2001, Met. Mus. Art, NYC, 2002, PaceWildenstein, 2002, 2005, Frederick Meijer Gardens and Scupture Park, Grand Rapids, Mich., 2002, exhibited in group shows at Martha Jackson Gallery, NYC, 1960—61, Dallas Mus. Contemporary Art, 1962, Sidney Janis Gallery, NYC, 1962, 1964, Inst. Contemporary Arts, Lndon, 1963, Art Inst. Chgo., 1962—63, Mus. Modern Art, NYC, 1963, 1988, 1990—91, Washington Gallery Modern Art, 1963, Am. Pavilion, Venice, 1964, 1968, Moderna Museet, Stockholm, 1964, Whitney Mus. Am. Art, N.Y.C., 1964—66, NYC, 1968, 1970, 1974, 1981, 1984, 1999, Solomon R. Guggenheim Mus., 1965, Inst. Contemporary Art, Boston, 1966, Mus. Fridericianum, Kassel, 1968, 1972, 1977, 1982, Richard Feigen Gallery, Chgo., 1968—69, Minami Gallery, Tokyo, 1975, Mus. Contemporary Art, Chgo., 1980, Westfalisches Landesmus. Kunst und Kulturegeschichte, Munster, 1987, 1997, Venice Biennale, 1997, Mus. Nat. Modern Art, Ctr. Georges Pompidou, 1989, La Grande Halle-La Villette, Paris, 1989, Royal Acad. Arts, London, 1991, Mus. Contemporary Art, L.A., 1992, exhibited in group shows, Guggenheim Mus., NYC, 1993, Nat. Gallery, London, 2000, exhibited in group shows at others, Represented in permanent collections Solomon R. Guggenheim Mus., NYC, Mus. Modern Art, Albright-Knox Art Gallery, Guffalo, Ctr. Georges Pompidou, Stedelijk Mus., Tate Gallery, Mus. Ludwig, Moderna Museet, Rose Art Mus. Brandeis. U., Waltham, Mass., Oberlin Coll., Nat. Gallery Art, Canberra, Art Gallery Ont., Art Inst. Chgo., Hirshorn Gallery and Sculpture Garden, Whitney Mus. Am. Art, Mus. Contemporary Art, LA, others, exhibitions include public exhibitions and sculptures with Coosje van Bruggen Rijksmus. Kröller-Muller, Otterlo, The Netherlands, 1979, Nollen Plz. Civic Ctr., Greater Des Moines, Iowa, 1984, Vitra Internat. AG, Weil am Rhein, 1988, Mpls. Sculpture Garden, Walker Art Ctr., Mpls., 1990, Parc de la Villette, Paris, 1993, Ctrl. Gardens, Middlesbrough, Eng., 1994, Nelson-Atkins Mus. Art, Kansas City, Mo., 1996, Tokyo Internat. Exhbn. Ctr., 1996, Guggenheim Found., 2000, Piazzale Cadorna, Milan, 2000, Eindhoven, The Netherlands, 2001, Neumarkt Galerie, Cologne, Germany, 2001, High Mus., Atlanta, 2005; author: Store Days, 1967, Notes in Hand, 1971, Raw Notes, 1973, Multiples in Retrospect, 1991; author: (with Coosje van Bruggen) Claes Oldenburg: Sketches and Blottings Toward the European Desktop; Large-Scale Project, 1994, Claes Oldenburg Coosje van Bruggen, 1999, Down Liquidambar Lane: Sculpture in the Park, 2001, Images á la Carte, 2004. Recipient Sculpture award, Brandeis U., 1971, Skowhegan Sculpture medal, 1972, Am. Ann., Chgo. Art Inst., 1976, medal, AIA, 1977, Wilhelm-Lehmbrock prize, Germany, 1981, Wolf prize in arts (sculpture), Wolf Found., Israel, 1989, Creative Arts award, Brandeis U., Jack l. and Lillian Poses medal, 1993, Lifetime Achievement award, Internat. Sculpture Ctr., 1994, award, Rolf Schock Found., Stockholm, 1995, Nathaniel S. Saltonstall award, ICA, Boston, 1996, Nat. Medal Arts, Washington, 2000. Mem.: Am. Acad. Arts and Scis., Am. Acad. Inst. Arts & Letters.

**OLDENBURG, RICHARD ERIK,** auction company executive; b. Stockholm, Sept. 21, 1933; came to U.S., 1936, naturalized, 1959; s. Gösta and Sigrid Elisabeth (Lindforss) O.; m. Harriet Lisa Turnure, Dec. 17, 1960 (dec. Apr. 1998); m. Mary Ellen Meehan, June 11, 2003. AB, Harvard U., 1954. Mgr. design dept. Doubleday & Co., Inc., N.Y.C., 1958-61; mng. editor trade div. Macmillan Co., Inc., N.Y.C., 1961-69; dir. publs. Mus. Modern Art, N.Y.C., 1969-72, dir., 1972-94, dir. emeritus, hon. trustee, 1995—; chmn. Sotheby's North and South America, N.Y.C., 1995-2000, hon. chmn., 2000—06, cons., 2006—. Served with AUS, 1956-58. Home: 447 E 57th St New York NY 10022-3064 Office Sotheby's Inc 1334 York Ave New York NY 10021-8500

**OLDER, JAY JUSTIN,** ophthalmic plastic surgeon; b. Jersey City, N.J., Feb. 7, 1940; m. Lois Rosner; children: Benjamin, Jessica. AB, Rutgers U., 1961; MD, Stanford U., 1966. Diplomate Am. Bd. Ophthalmology. Intern, resident in internal medicine Cornell U./Bellevue Hosp. Ctr., N.Y.C., 1968; resident in ophthalmology Stanford (Calif.) U., 1973; fellow in ophthalmic plastic and reconstructive surgery Stanford U., San Francisco, 1974; prt. practice Tampa, Fla., 1974—. Clin. prof. ophthalmology U. South Fla. Coll. Medicine, Tampa, 1975—, dir. oculoplastic svc., 1974—99. Author: Eyelid Tumors: Clinical Diagnosis and Surgical Treatment, 1987, 2d edit., 2003. Fellow Am. Acad. Ophthalmology (Sr. Honor award 1995), Am. Soc. Ophthalmic Plastic and Reconstructive Surgery (pres. 1987, sec. 1983-84), ACS; mem. Phi Beta Kappa (v.p. Greater Tampa Bay Assn. 1995-96). Office: Older & Slonim Eyelid Inst 4444 E Fletcher Ave Ste D Tampa FL 33613-4937

**OLDERMAN, GERALD,** retired medical device company executive; b. N.Y.C., July 16, 1933; s. Cass and Hilda (Klein) O.; m. Myrna Ruth Schwartz, Aug. 3, 1958; children: Sharon, Neil, Lisa. BS in Chemistry, Rensselaer Poly Inst., 1958; MS Phys. Chemistry, Seton Hall U., South Orange, N.J., 1971, PhD, 1972. Rsch. chemist Nat. Cash Register, Dayton, Ohio, 1958-61; tech. mgmt. positions Johnson & Johnson, New Brunswick, N.J., 1961-75, dir. R & D, dir. surg. products hosp. divsn., 1972-75, v.p. R & D, Surgikos divsn., 1975-78; v.p. R & D, bd. dirs. Am. Convertors divsn. Am. Hosp. Supply corp., Evanston, Ill., 1978-85; v.p. internat. R & D Pharmaseal divsn. Baxter Healthcare Corp., Valencia, Calif., 1985-91; v.p. R & D, bd. dirs. cardiopulmonary divsn. C.R. Bard, 1991-96; cons. R.F. Caffrey & Assoc., Inc., Brownsville, Vt., 1996—; exec. v.p. R&D tech. and commercialization, bd. dirs. Quick-Med Techs., Inc., Wilmington, Del., 1998—. With USMC, 1954-56. Recipient Robert Wood Johnson medal, Johnson & Johnson, 1969. Fellow Am. Inst. Chemists; mem. Assn. Advancement Med. Instrumentation, INDA, Assn. Nonwovens Industry (bd. dirs., corp. rep. 1986, 87), Nat. Fire Protection Assn. (industry rep.), Am. Soc. Artificial Internat. Organs. Home: 17 Pickman Dr Bedford MA 01730-1009 Office: RF Caffrey & Assoc Inc PO Box 319 Brownsville VT 05037-0319 also: Quick Med Techs Inc 401 NE 25th Terr Boca Raton FL 33431 Office Phone: 781-271-9893. Personal E-mail: jolderman@aol.com.

**OLDERSHAW, LOUIS FREDERICK,** retired lawyer; b. New Britain, Conn., Aug. 30, 1917; s. Louis A. and Annie Louise (Bold) O.; m. Virginia Wakelin, Nov. 30, 1940; children: Peter W., Robert L., David L. AB, Dartmouth Coll., 1939; LLB, Yale U., 1942. Bar: Mass. 1946, Fed. 1947. Mem. legal staff Army Ordnance Dist., Springfield, Mass., 1942-43; with firm Lyon, Green, Whitmore, Doran & Brooks, Holyoke, Mass., 1947-49; ptnr. firm Davenport, Millane & Oldershaw, Holyoke, 1949-64; treas. Nat. Blank Book Co., Inc., Holyoke, 1964-65, pres., 1965-78, chmn. bd., 1978-83; group v.p., dir. Dennison Mfg. Co., Framingham, Mass., 1967-82; counsel Bulkley, Richardson & Gelinas, Springfield, Mass., 1983—2002, ret., 2002. Mem. editl. bd.: Yale Law Jour., 1941-42. Trustee Mt. Holyoke Coll., 1966-76, Greater Holyoke YMCA; bd. dirs. emeritus Holyoke C.C. Found., Sta. WGBY-TV. Lt. USNR, 1943-47. Mem.: Abenakee Club, Orchards Golf Club, Rotary, Colony Club, Longmeadow (Mass.) Country Club. Republican. Mem. United Congl. Ch. Home: 30 Bayon Dr South Hadley MA 01075 Office: Baybank Tower 1500 Main St Ste 2700 Springfield MA 01115-0001 Personal E-mail: louolder@aol.com.

**OLDFATHER, CHAD MICHAEL,** law educator; s. Guy M. and Catherine R. Oldfather; m. Lea Ann DeVillers, Sept. 3, 1994; children: Ada, Audrey, Laura. AB, Harvard U., 1990; JD, U. Va., 1993. Bar: Minn. 1994. Law clk. to Hon. Jane Roth U.S. Ct. Appeals (3d cir.), Wilmington, Del.; atty. Faegre & Benson, Mpls., 1994—99, 2000—02; asst. state pub. defender Minn. State Pub. Defender, Mpls., 1999—2000; assoc. prof. Oklahoma City U. Sch. Law, 2002—05, Marquette U. Law Sch., Miw., 2005—. Reporter ABA Study Group Pre-Judicial Edn., Chgo., 2004—05, 2005 Nat. Conf. Appellate Justice, Washington, 2005. Contbr. articles to profl. jours. Recipient Howard B. Eisenberg prize, 2004. Office: Marquette U Law Sch 1103 W Wisconsin Ave Milwaukee WI 53201 Office Phone: 414-288-8031. Office Fax: 414-288-6975. Business E-Mail: chad.oldfather@marquette.edu.

**OLDFIELD, BARNEY,** entertainment executive; b. Boston, June 28, 1956; s. Wilbur Joseph and Thelma Florence (Coombs) O. AB, Harvard U., 1979, Cert. Advanced Studies, 1981; Cert. Bus. Entertainment, NYU, 1996. Editor Musicians, 1979-83; copy editor Social Register Assocs., N.Y.C., 1983-87; advt. dir. Local Listings, N.Y.C., 1987-89; mkt. rep. Societa Italiana Luxor Oro, N.Y.C., 1989-90; bus. mgr. Al-Bab Internat., N.Y.C., 1990-92, McKenzie Internat., N.Y.C., 1992-96; gen. mgr. Angelika Entertainment, N.Y.C., 1996—; CEO Angelika Releasing, 1999—, Angelika.Com, 1999—; pres. Angelika TV.com, 2000—. Bd. dirs. Anthology Film Archives, N.Y.C., 1995—, Havana Film Festival in N.Y., Howl Arts Festival, SX Mobile Media, 2005; chair bd., coord. Harvard Ind. Film Group; mem. adv. com. Internat. Film and TV Exch., exec. prodr. New Filmmakers Series; exec. prodr. Metro Angelika Film Festival. Prodr.: Too Much Sleep, Zero Day, Another Deep Breath, All Ivy, Maniac 2; columnist: So. Voice newspaper, 1976—79; editor: Harvard Today, 1997—; prodr.: Maniac 2. Mem. Soc. Calif. Pioneers, San Francisco, 1981—. Mem. Friars Club of Calif., Harvard Club of N.Y., Harvard Club of Boston, Harvard Club of So. Calif., Harvard Faculty Club, Union League Club N.Y. Republican. Anglican. Avocations: squash, tennis. Office: PO Box 4956 New York NY 10185-4956 Office Phone: 212-410-9404, 213-840-6224. Office Fax: 213-477-2004. Business E-Mail: barney@angelikafilm.com.

**OLDFIELD, EDWARD HUDSON,** neurosurgeon, researcher; b. Mount Sterling, Ky., Nov. 22, 1947; s. Ellis Hudson Oldfield and Amanda Caroline Miller; m. Susan Shawler Wachs Oldfield, June 8, 1974; 1 child, Caroline Talbott. BA in Physics, U. Ky., 1969, MD, 1973. Diplomate Am. Bd. Neurol. Surgery. Pvt. practice, Lexington, Ky., 1980—81; senior staff fellow NIH, Bethesda, Md., 1981—83, dep. chief clin. neurosurgery, 1983—84, chief neurosurgery, 1984—. Med. dir. VHL disease Family Alliance, 1993—; adv. bd. brain cancer McDonnell Found., 1997—2004. Mem. editl. bd. Jour. Neurosurgery, 1994—2002. Recipient The Grass Award, Soc. Neurol. Surg., 1995, Farber Award, Am. Assn. Neurol. Surg., 1999. Achievements include patents in field of convective-enhanced drug distribution to the Central Nervous System; advances in the understanding and treatment of brain tumors, pituitary tumors, syringomyelia, spinal arteriovenous malformations, and drug delivery to the brain and spinal cord. Home: PO Box 309 Philomont VA 20131 Office: Nat Inst Health NINDS/SNB 10 Center Dr Rm 5D37 Bethesda MD 20892 Office Phone: 301-496-5728. Business E-Mail: eo10d@nih.gov.

**OLDFIELD, JAMES EDMUND,** retired nutrition educator; b. Victoria, BC, Can., Aug. 30, 1921; came to U.S., 1949; s. Henry Clarence and Doris O. Oldfield; m. Mildred E. Atkinson, Sept. 4, 1942; children: Nancy E. Oldfield McLaren, Kathleen E. Oldfield Sansone, David J., Jane E. Oldfield, Richard A. BSA, U. B.C., 1941, MSA, 1949; PhD, Oreg. State U., 1951. Faculty Oreg. State U., Corvallis, 1951-90, head dept. animal sci., 1967-83, dir. Nutrition Rsch. Inst., 1986-90; ret. 1990. Mem. nat. tech. adv. com. on water supply U.S. Dept. Interior, Washington, 1967-68; bd. dirs. Coun. for Agrl. Sci. and Tech., Ames, Iowa, 1978-84; mem. nutrition study sect. NIH, Bethesda, Md., 1975-80, 85-87; cons. Selenium Tellurium Devel. Assn., Grimbergen, Belgium, 1990-2002. Editor: Selenium in Biomedicine, 1967, Sulphur in Nutrition, 1970, Selenium in Biology and Medicine, 1987; author: Selenium in Nutrition, 1971, Selenium World Atlas, 1999. Served to maj. Can. Army, 1942-46, ETO. Decorated Mil. Cross Can.; recipient Klaus Schwarz medal Internat. Assn. Bioinorganic Scientists, 1998; Fulbright rsch. scholar U.S. Dept. State, 1974, Massey U., New Zealand. Fellow Am. Soc. Animal Sci. (pres. 1966-67, Morrison award 1972), Am. Inst. Nutrition; mem. Am. Chem. Soc., Am. Registry Profl. Animal Scientists (pres. 1990, editor: Profl. Animal Scientist 1993-96), Fedn. Am. Socs. Exptl. Biol., Pacific Fisheries Technologists (pres. 1966), Kiwanis (pres. 1964, lt. gov. 1986). Republican. Episopalian. Home: 1323 NW 13th St Corvallis OR 97330-2604 Office: Oreg State Univ Dept Animal Sci Corvallis OR 97331 Office Phone: 541-737-1894. Office Fax: 541-737-4174. Business E-Mail: james.e.oldfield@oregonstate.edu.

**OLDHAM, DARIUS DUDLEY,** lawyer; b. Beaumont, Tex., July 6, 1941; s. Darius Saran and Mary Francis (Carraway) O.; m. Judy J. White, Jan. 23, 1965; children: Steven, Michael BA, U. Tex., Austin, 1964; JD, U. Tex., 1966. Bar: Tex. 1966, U.S. Dist. Ct. (so., no., ea. and we. dists.) Tex. 1966, U.S. Supreme Ct. 1974, U.S. Ct. Appeals (3rd, 5th and 11th cirs.) 1968; cert. arbitrator and mediator. Assoc. Fulbright & Jaworski, Houston, 1966—74, ptnr., 1974—, mem. policy com., 1980—97, 2001—04, mem. exec. com., 1997—2000, mem. litigation mgmt. com., 1998—2004, chair, 2001—02. Mem. faculty grad. litigation program U. Houston; adv. com. Nat. Ctr. State Cts.; mem. chancellors coun. exec. com. U. Tex.; lectr. in field. Former mem. bd. editors Aviation Litigation Reporter, Personal Injury Def. Reporter, Internat. Ins. Law Rev.; contbr. articles to profl. jours. Adv. coun. Nat. Jud. Coll.; past liberal arts adv. coun. U. Tex.; past bd. dirs. FDCC Found., Houston Pops Orch. Fellow Am. Coll. Trial Lawyers (chair complex litigation and jud. com.), Tex. Bar Found. (life), Am. Bar Found. (life), Houston Bar Found. (life), Am. Bd. Trial Advs. (pres. Houston chpt. 1999); mem. ABA (mem. ho. of dels. 1996-98, chair tort and ins. practice sect. 1994-95, mem. coun. tort and ins. practice sect. 1988-98, presdl. emissary 1993-95, chmn. Standing Com. on Independence of the Judiciary 2001-04, chmn. Select Commn. on Jud. Campaign Fin. 2000-01, standing com. fed. jud. improvements, chmn. John Marshall award selection com. 2004-05), U. Tex. Law Sch. Alumni Assn. Exec. Com., 2003—, Tex. Bar Assn. (chmn. liaison fed. jud. com. 1989-90, pattern jury charges Vol. IV com. 1988-92), Tex. Young Lawyers Assn. (bd. dirs., chmn.), Fed. Def. and Corp. Counsel (pres. 1989-90, chmn. bd. 1990-91, exec. com. 1988-91), Tex. Assn. Def. Counsel, Maritime Law Assn. U.S., Am. Counsel Assn. (bd. dirs. 1982-83, 89-94), Def. Rsch. Inst. (chmn. aerospace com. 1984-87, Presdl. Achievement award 1987, bd. dirs. 1989-92, exec. com. 1991-92), Lawyers for Civil Justice (bd. dirs. 1988-98, chmn. 1998, exec. com. 1990-98, pres. 1997), Nat. Ctr. for State Cts., Lawyers Commn., U. Tex. Chancellors Coun. Exec. Com., River Oaks Country Club, Houston Ctr. Club, Sigma Chi (Significant Sig), Phi Delta Phi. Office: Fulbright & Jaworski 1301 Mckinney St 51st Fl Houston TX 77010-3031 Office Phone: 713-651-5397. Personal E-Mail: doldham@fulbright.com.

**OLDHAM, GRANVILLE MURL, JR.,** conductor, educator; b. Dyersburg, Tenn., Apr. 22, 1961; s. Granville Murl Oldham, Sr. and Theresa Fuller; BA in Music Edn., U. Pacific Conservatory Music, 1986; MA in Choral Conducting, San Jose State U., 1994; postgrad., U. So. Calif. Thornton Sch. Music, 2000—04. Asst. prof. U. Ala. Sch. Music, Tuscaloosa, 1994—99; lectr., condr. choral dept. U. So. Calif., Thornton Sch. Music, L.A., 2000—04; cathedral choir dir. Second Bapt. Ch., 2003—; heavenbound choir dir. Hollywood Presbyn. Ch., Hollywood, 2003—04; choral coord.; condr. L.A.'s Best After Sch. Arts Program, Calif., 2003—. Scholar, U. Pacific Sch. Edn., 1985—86. Mem.: Am. Choral Dirs. Assn. (assoc.; women's chorus chair 1996—98), Pi Kappa Lambda. Home: 748 S Orange Grove Ave Los Angeles CA 90036 Office: USC Thornton School of Music 840 West 34th Street Los Angeles CA 90089-0851 Office Phone: 213-748-0318. Personal E-mail: gmoldham@aol.com.

**OLDHAM, J. THOMAS,** lawyer, educator; b. Cleve., Jan. 20, 1948; s. Vern Lawrence and Pauline Adams (Drake) O.; m. Chaille Linn Cooper, Feb. 4, 1995. BA, Denison U., 1970; JD, UCLA, 1974. Bar: Calif. 1974, D.C. 1977, Tex. 1983. Pvt. practice, Beverly Hills, Calif., 1974-81; prof. law U. Houston, Beverly Hills, 1981—. Vis. prof. law U. Colo., 1984, George Washington U., 1988-89, Cambridge (Eng.) U., 1992, U.of Copenhagen, 1999; past chair family and juvenile law sect. Am. Assn. Law Sch. Author: Divorce Separation and the Distribution of Property, 1987, Texas Homestead Law, 1991, Texas Marital Property Rights, 1996, Family Law Cases and Materials, 1998, Child Support: The Next Frontier, 2000; mem. bd. editors Family Law Quar., Family and Children's Law Abstracts. Pres. Mus. Area Mcpl. Assn., 1986-90; bd. dirs. Main St. Theater, Houston, 1991-97. Mem. Houston Bar Assn. Office: U Houston Law Sch 4800 Calhoun St Houston TX 77204-0001 Business E-Mail: toldham@central.uh.edu.

**OLDHAM, JOHN MICHAEL,** physician, psychiatrist, educator; b. Muskogee, Okla., Sept. 6, 1940; s. Henry Newland and Alice Gray (Ewton) O.; m. Karen Joan Pacella, Apr. 24, 1971; children: Madeleine Marie, Michael Clark. BS in Engring., Duke U., 1962; MS in Neuroendocrinology, Baylor U., 1966, MD, 1967. Licensed physician N.Y., N.J., S.C., Tex.; diplomate in psychiat. and forensic psychiatry Am. Bd. Psychiatry and Neurology. Intern pediatrics St. Luke's Hosp., N.Y.C., 1967-68; resident psychiat. Columbia U. Dept. Psychiat., N.Y.S. Psychiatric Inst., N.Y.C., 1968-70; chief resident in psychiatry Columbia U., N.Y. State Psychiat. Inst., N.Y.C., 1970-71; grad. Columbia Psychoanalytic Ctr., N.Y.C., 1977; dir. psychiatric emergency svcs. Roosevelt Hosp., N.Y.C., 1973-74, dir. residency tng. dept. psychiat., 1974-77; dir. short term diagnostic and treatment unit N.Y. Hosp. Westchester Divsn., White Plains, NY, 1977-80, dir. divsn. acute treatment svcs., 1980-84; deputy dir. N.Y. State Psychiatric Inst., N.Y.C., 1984-89, acting dir., 1989-90, dir., 1990—2002; assoc. chmn. dept. psychiatry Columbia U. Coll. Physicians & Surgeons, N.Y.C., 1986-96, vice chmn., 1996-2000, acting chmn., 2000—02; chief med. officer N.Y. State Office Mental Health, Albany, 1989—2002; chmn. dept. psychiatry and behavioral sci. Med. U. SC, 2002—, exec. dir. Inst. Psychiatry, 2002—. From instr. clin. psychiatry to prof. clin. psychiatry Columbia U. Coll. P&S, 1974-96, 1998-96, Elizabeth K. Dollard profl clin. psychiatry medicine and law, 1996-2002; prof. psychiatry Med. U. S.C., 2002—; asst. prof. psychiatry Cornell U. Med. Coll., N.Y.C., 1977-83, assoc. prof. clin. psychiatry, 1983-84; attending staff dept. psychiatry Roosevelt Hosp., N.Y.C., 1973-77; assoc. attending in psychiatry, N.Y. Hosp., 1977-84, Presbyn Hosp., N.Y.C., 1984-88, attending in psychiatry, 1988-2002; tng. and supervising psychoanalyst Columbia Psychoanalytic Ctr., N.Y.C., 1983-2002; coord. med. student edn., dept. psychiatry Cornell U. Med. Coll., Westchester Divsn., White Plains, N.Y., 1977-84; coord. clin. clerkships in psychiatry Roosevelt Hosp., Columbia U. Coll. P&S, N.Y.C., 1974-77; spl. adv. bd. Freedom From Fear, Inc.; examiner Am. Bd. Psychiatry and Neurology; chmn. acute divsn. rsch. group, Westchester Divsn., N.Y. Hosp., 1981-84, co-project dir. borderline rsch. group, 1982-84, co-prin. investigator familial transmission DSM III personality disorders, 1982-84; prin. investigator personality disorders in bulimia, N.Y.S. Psychiat. Inst., 1985-90, structured DSM III assessment psychoanalytic patients, Columbia Psychoanalytic Ctr., 1986-91; co-prin. investigator validity DSM III R personality disorders, N.Y. State Psychiat. Inst., 1987-94; co-investigator NIMH, 1996—. Author: (with L.B. Morris) The Personality Self-Portrait, 1990; editor Jour. Psychia. Practice; editor bd. Jour. Personality Disorders; dep. editor Am. Psychiat. Pub., Inc.; mem. exec. editl. bd. Psychiat. Quar.; reviewer Arch Gen. Psychiatry, Am. Jour. Psychiatry, Psychiat. Svcs., Jour. of Neuropsychiatry; contbr. numerous articles to profl. jours.; presentations in field. Major USAF, 1971—73. Recipient John J. Weber prize Excellence in Psychoanalytic Rsch. Columbia Psychoanalytic Ctr., 1990, Dorothea Dix Award Mental Illness Found., 1996, Spl. Comm.'s award NY State Office Mental Health, 1997, Spl. Presdl. commendation Am. Psychiat. Assn., 1999, 2005, Payne Whitney Clin. award for Extraordinary Pub. Svc., 2002; Spl. Citation conferred by Governor George E. Pataki, State of NY, 2002; Paul Hoch award for Disting. Leadership, NY State Office Mental Health, 2002. Fellow Am. Coll. Psychiatrists (treas. 2004—), Am. Psychiat. Assn. (pres. N.Y. County dist. br., 1989-90, com. rsch. psychiat. treatment 1987-93, coun. rsch., steering com. practice guidelines, chmn. sci. program com. 1992-95, chmn. com. quality indicators 1999-2003, chmn. coun. quality care 2003—06), Am. Psychopath. Assn., N.Y. Acad. Medicine; mem. Am. Psychoanalytic Assn. (cert.), Assn. Psychoanalytic Medicine (pres. 1989-91), Internat. Psychoanalytical Assn., N.Y. Acad. Sci., N.Y. State Med. Soc., Assn. Rsch. Personality Disorders (bd. dirs.), Internat. Soc. for Study of Personality Disorders (pres. 2000—03), S.C. Psychiat. Assn. (pres. 2006—). Office: Med Univ SC Dept Psychiatry and Behavioral Sci PO Box 250861 67 President St Charleston SC 29425 Business E-Mail: oldhamj@musc.edu.

**OLDHAM, KIMBERLY ELISE See ELISE, KIMBERLY**

**OLDHAM, MAXINE JERNIGAN,** real estate broker; b. Whittier, Calif., Oct. 13, 1923; d. John K. and Lela Hessie (Mears) Jernigan; m. Laurance Montgomery Oldham, Oct. 28, 1941; 1 child, John Laurence. AA, San Diego City Coll., 1973; student Western State U. Law, San Diego, 1976-77, LaSalle U., 1977-78; grad. Realtors Inst., Sacramento, 1978. Mgr. Edin Harig Realty, LaMesa, Calif., 1966-70; tchr. Bd. Edn., San Diego, 1959-66; mgr. Julia Cave Real Estate, San Diego, 1973-74; salesman Computer Realty, San Diego, 1973-74; owner Shelter Island Realty, San Diego, 1974—. Author: Jernigan History, 1982, Mears Geneology, 1985, Fustons of Colonial America, 1988, Sissoms. Mem. Civil Svc. Commn., San Diego, 1957-58. Recipient Outstanding Speaker award Dale Carnegie. Mem. Nat. Assn. Realtors, Calif. Assn. Realtors, San Diego Bd. Realtors, San Diego Apt. Assn., Internationale des Professions Immobilieres (internat. platform speaker), DAR (vice regent Linares chpt.), Colonial Dames 17th Century, Internat. Fedn. Univ. Women. Republican. Roman Catholic. Avocations: music, theater, painting, genealogy, continuing edn. Home: 3348 Lowell St San Diego CA 92106-1713 E-mail: lilyham@coxs.com.

**OLDHAM, ROGER JAY,** plastic surgeon; b. Kokomo, Ind., Mar. 4, 1944; s. G. Robert and Betty Jean Oldham; m. Susan Marie Sheehan, June 21, 1969; children: Kathleen Elizabeth Oldham Lucenius, Brian Patrick, Brendan Robert. BS, Ball State U., 1965; MD, U. Ind., 1969. Diplomate Am. Bd. Plastic Surgeons. Intern George Washington U. Hosp., Washington, 1969—70, resident in gen. surgery, 1970—71; resident in plastic surgery U. Ill. Med. Ctr., Chgo., 1975—77; pvt. practice Bethesda, Md., 1977—. Instr. surgery U. Ill., Chgo., 1977; asst. clin. prof. surgery divsn. plastic surgery Georgetown U., Washington, 1978—; lectr. surgery George Washington U., Washington, 1982—. Lt. comdr. USN, 1971—73, Vietnam. Mem.: ACS, AMA, Am. Soc. for Aesthetic Plastic Surgery, Am. Soc. for Reconstructive Microsurgery, Plastic Surgery Ednl. Found., Am. Soc. Plastic and Reconstructive Surgeons (govt. rels. com. 1987), Nat. Capital Soc. Plastic Surgeons (exec. com. 1982—89, sec.-treas. 1984—85, v.p. 1986, pres.-elect 1987, pres. 1988), Montgomery County Med. Soc. (conv. del. 1983—85, membership com. 1982—84, nomination com. 1982—83). Home: 10704 Balantre Ln Potomac MD 20854 Office: 10215 Fernwood Rd Ste 412 Bethesda MD 20817 Office Phone: 301-530-6100.

**OLDHAM, TODD,** fashion designer; b. Corpus Christi, Tex., 1960; s. Jack and Linda Oldham. Founder Times 7, Dallas; founder, designer Todd Oldham, N.Y.C., 1989; design dir. Escada, Munich, 1994; dorm room furniture designer Target Corp., 2001—03; furniture designer La-Z-Boy Inc., 2002—. Host, dir. Todd Time MTV House of Style, 1993-96; guest Tracy Takes On with Tracy Ullman, 1994, The Nanny, 1996, Roseanne, 1996; designer spl. collection for Batman Forever, 1995, MTV's Choose or Lose bus, 1996, GM Bravada to raise money for cancer rsch., 1997; music video co-dir. (with Hype Williams) Maxi Priest's That Kind of Girl, 1996; music video dir. Us3's Come on Everybody, 1997. Active Design Industries Found. for AIDS, People for the Ethical Treatment of Animals, POWARS, Pet Pals. Recipient Rising Star award Internat. Apparel Mart, Dallas, 1991, Fashion Execellence award Internat. Apparel Mart, Dallas, 1993; named Designer of Yr. Calif. Fashion Industry Friends of AIDS Project, 1996. Mem. Coun. Fashion Designers Am. (Perry Ellis award for new fashion talent 1991). Office: Todd Oldham Store NY 120 Wooster St Frnt 3 New York NY 10012-5200

**OLDHAM, ALFRED MAURICE,** accountant, management consultant; b. London, May 12, 1948; s. Joseph and Dorothy O.; m. Marilyn Spiro, Jan. 16, 1983. MSc in Mgmt. Studies, U. Bradford, Eng., 1972; DBA, Henley Mgmt. Coll., 1997. Chartered acct., England. Gen. mgr. Europe The Torrington Co., Paris, 1983-87; dir. AMO Cons., Bath, Eng., 1987—. European contr. Measurex Corp., Datchet, Eng., 1979-82; asst. contr. North Europe, Norton Co., Welwyn Garden City, Eng., 1977-79; sr. corp. auditor Am. Express Co., N.Y.C. Editor: Handbook of Cost Management, 1998; author: Cost Management and its Interplay with Business Strategy and Context, 1999. Fellow Inst. Chartered Accts. in Eng. and Wales. Jewish. Avocations: music, antiques, mountain climbing, jogging. Office Phone: 44 7778 450080. E-mail: dramoldman@aol.com.

**OLDMAN, GARY,** actor; b. London, Mar. 21, 1958; m. Lesley Manville (div.); 1 child, Alfie; m. Uma Thurman, 1990 (div. 1992); m. Donya Fiorentino, Feb. 16, 1997 (div. Apr. 13, 2001); children: Gulliver Flynn, Charlie John. BA, Rose Buford Coll. Speech and Drama, 1979. Appearances include (TV movies) Meantime, 1984, Honest, Decent and True, 1985, Fallen Angels: Dead End for Delia, 1993 (Cable Ace award, Actor in a Dramatic Series), The Firm, 1988, Heading Home, 1991, Jesus, 1999; (TV miniseries) Who Was Lee Harvey Oswald, 1992; (video) Since I Don't Have You by Guns n' Roses, 1994; (films) Remembrance, 1982, Sid and Nancy, 1986, Prick Up Your Ears, 1987 (Brit. Acad. Film and TV Arts nomination 1988), Track 29, 1988, We Think the World of You, 1988, Criminal Law, 1988, Paris by Night, 1989, Chattahoochee, 1989, Henry & June, 1990, State of Grace, 1990, Rosencrantz and Guildenstern Are Dead, 1990, JFK, 1991, Bram Stoker's Dracula, 1992, True Romance, 1993, Romeo is Bleeding, 1993, The Professional, 1994, Immortal Beloved, 1994, Murder in the First, 1995, The Scarlet Letter, 1995, Basquiat, 1996, The Fifth Element, 1997, Air Force One, 1997, Lost in Space, 1998, Quest for Camelot (aka Magic Sword), 1998, The Contender (also exec. prodr.), 2000, Nobody's Baby, 2001, Hannibal, 2001, Interstate 60, 2002, The Hire: Beat the Devil, 2002, Sin, 2003, Harry Potter and the Prisoner of Azkaban, 2004, Who's Kyle, 2004, Batman Begins, 2005, Harry Potter and the Goblet of Fire, 2005; dir., author, prodr. Nil By Mouth, 1998; (theatre) Massacre at Paris, 1980, Chinchilla, 1980, Desperado Corner, 1980, A Waste of Time, 1980, Summit Conference, 1982, Rat in the Skull, 1984, The Pope's Wedding, 1984 (Drama Mag. Best Actor award 1985, Fringe Best Newcomer award 1985-86), The War Plays, 1985, The Desert Air, 1985, Women Beware Women, 1986, Real Dreams, 1986, Serious Money, 1987. Recipient Outstanding Brit. Film award Brit. Acad., Best Screenplay award Brit. Acad., Dirs. prize Edinburgh Festival Channel Four, Best Dir. prize Cannes Film Festival, Best Actor and Best Newcomer, Brit. Ind. Film Awards Best Actors. Office: c/o Douglas J Urbanski Douglas Mgmt Inc 5o5 N Robertson Blvd Los Angeles CA 90048-1730

**OLDMAN, TERRY L.,** museum director; BS, U. Kans., MA in Art Mus. Edn.; MS in Bus. Adminstrn., U. Hawaii. Interim asst. dir. Spencer Mus., Lawrence, Kans.; dir./curator edn. Mus. Art, Tallahassee; dir. Albrecht-Kemper Mus. Art, Saint Joseph, Mo., 1999—. USAF. Decorated Disting. Flying Cross, Bronze Star, Aerial Achievement Medal. Office: Albrecht-Kemper Mus Art 2818 Frederick Ave Saint Joseph MO 64506 E-mail: toldham@albrecht-kemper.org.

**OLDS, DAVID ANDREW,** food scientist, educator; b. San Francisco, Nov. 20, 1967; s. John Ward Olds, M.D. and Rosemary Burns Olds, D.A. Culinary Arts Degree, Des Moines Area C.C., Ankeny, Iowa, 1993; BS in Hotel, Restaurant and Instn. Mgmt., Iowa State U., Ames, 2002; MS in Foodsvc. and Lodging Mgmt., Iowa State U., 2004; postgrad., Kans. State U., Manhattan, 2004—. Cert. Hazard Analysis and Critical Control Point Kans. State U., 2004, ServSafe® food protection mgr. Nat. Restaurant Assn. Edn. Found., 2002. Cook Sheffield's Restaurant, Des Moines, 1984—86, Des Moines Art Ctr. Restaurant, Des Moines, 1986—91; sauté cook Embassy Club, Des Moines, 1988—90, French Quarter Bar and Restaurant, Des Moines, 1990—92, Met. Club, Des Moines, 1992—93; gen. mgr. Sheffield's West, Clive, Iowa, 1994—96; catering asst. Mary Miller Catering, Des Moines, 1993—97; sales assoc. A-Okay Antiques, West Des Moines, Iowa, 1997—2000; smokehouse cook Hickory Pk. Restaurant Co., Ames, 1997—2000; tchg. asst. Iowa State U., Ames, 2001—04; instr. Kans. State U., Manhattan, 2004—. Pres. Grad. Student Coun. - Kans. State U., Manhattan, 2006—. Contbr. articles to profl. jours. Participant Men's Conf. To End Violence Against Women, Ames, 2000; cook - vol. Ames Homeless Shelter, 2000—03; contbr. - grant writer Beyond Welfare, Ames, 2001; com. mem. All-University Theme Com. Mem., "Challenging Students to Become Their Best, " Iowa State U., 2001—02. Recipient Outstanding Grad. Asst. award, Golden Key, 2006, Top 2% of Graduating Class, Iowa State U., 2002; scholar Timothy R. Donoghue Grad. scholar, Kans. State U., 2004—05, Dr. Carol Shanklin scholar, Kans. State U. - Coll. of Human Ecology, 2005, L.M. & C.H. Beasley scholar, 2004, McKinley scholar, Iowa State U., 2003—04, Alice M. Ford scholar, 2002, NRAEF Undergraduate scholar, Nat. Restaurant Assn. Ednl. Found., 2001, Adult Student scholar, Iowa State U., 2001, Matthew Spencer Meml. scholar, 2001, Edalene Stohr Brown Meml. scholar, 2001. Mem.: Hotel, Restaurant and Instn. Mgmt. Club (treas. 2000—02), Grad. Foodsvc. and Hospitality Mgmt. Orgn. (chpt. v.p. 2004—05), Nat. Restaurant Assn. (assoc.), Internat. Assn. for Food Protection (assoc.), Inst. of Food Technologists (assoc.), Food Systems Mgmt. Edn. Coun. (assoc.), Coun. on Hotel, Restaurant, and Instn. Edn. (assoc.), Club Mgrs. Assn. of Am. (assoc.; chpt. treas. 2002—03), Iowa State U. Alumni Assn. (life), Kappa Omicron Nu (assoc.), Golden Key (assoc.), Phi Theta Kappa (assoc.), Phi Kappa Phi (life). D-Conservative. Episcopalian. Home: 2050 Kerr Dr Apt #Q27 Manhattan KS 66502-2407 Office: Kansas State University 110 Justin Hall Manhattan KS 66502-2407 Office Phone: 785-532-5513. Personal E-mail: mrdavidolds@hotmail.com. E-mail: daveolds@ksu.edu.

**OLDS, JACQUELINE,** psychiatrist, educator; b. Springfield, Mass., Jan. 4, 1947; d. James and Marianne (Ejier) O.; m. Richard Stanton Schwartz, Aug. 26, 1978; children: Nathaniel Leland, Sarah Elizabeth. BA, Radcliffe Coll., 1967; MD, Tufts U., 1971. Diplomate Am. Bd. Psychiatry and Neurology. Resident in adult psychiatry Mass. Mental Health Ctr., Boston, 1974; resident in child psychiatry McLean Hosp., Belmont, Mass., 1976, assoc. attending child psychiatrist, 1979—; psychiatrist-in-charge inpatient unit McLean Hall-Mercer Children's Ctr., Belmont, 1976-79; assoc. child psychiatry Beth Israel Hosp., Boston, 1979—; cons. in child psychiatry Mass. Gen. Hosp., Boston, 1994—. Instr. psychiatry Harvard U. Med. Sch, Boston, 1976-86; asst. prof. clin. psychiatry, 1986-2000, assoc. clin. prof. psychiatry, 2000—; cons. North Shore Mental Health Ctr., Salem, 1981-82. Author: Overcoming Loneliness in Every Day Life, 1996, Marriage in Motion, 2000, editor Clin. Challenges column in Harvard Rev. of Psychiatry; contbr. articles to profl. jours.; author (translator into Spanish): Matrimonio in Movimiento. Recipient Mentoring award Mass. Gen. Hosp. Dept. Child Psychiatry, 1998. Disting. fellow, Am. Psychiat. Assn.; mem. Mass. Psychiat. Soc. (ethics com. 1988-93,

mem. pub. affairs com. 1992—), Am. Acad. Child Psychiatry, Am. Psychoanalytic Assn., New England Coun. Child and Adolescent Psychiatry (bd. dirs.). Democrat. Avocations: piano, writing, cooking, watercolors. Office Phone: 617-547-5920.

**OLDS, JOHN WARD,** internist; b. Apr. 25, 1935; s. Thayer Stevens and Dorris (La Venture) O.; m. Rosemary Burns, July 10, 1957; children: David, James, Miriam. BS, Iowa State U., 1956; MD, U. Tenn., 1967. Diplomate Am. Bd. Internal Medicine, Am. Bd. Infectious Diseases, cert. physician exec. Intern San Francisco Gen. Hosp., 1967—68; resident, fellow U. N.Mex., 1968—72; practice internal medicine Des Moines, 1972—2002; dir. continuing med. edn. Iowa Meth. Med. Ctr., 1983—93, cons. infectious diseases, 1972—2002, attending physician, 1972—2002; asst. clin. prof. U. Iowa, Iowa City, 1978—95; co-dir. infectious disease and epidemiology Iowa Meth. Med. Ctr., 1985—93, dir. med. affairs, 1989—93; Medicare med. dir. for Iowa, 1993—97; Part A Medicare med. dir. for Iowa and S.D., 1997—2004; med. dir. Medicare RHHI, 1997—. Mem. Iowa Bd. Med. Examiners, 1987—93, vice chmn., 1991—93, med. advisor, 2005—. Contbr. articles to med. jour. Lt. USNR, 1956—61. Recipient Roche award, U. Tenn., 1966. Fellow: ACP, Infectious Diseases Soc. Am., Am. Coll. Physician Execs.; mem.: AMA, Iowa Found. Med. Care (dist. chmn. 1981—83, bd. dirs. 1985—), Iowa Med. Soc. (councilor 1980—84), Med. Libr. Club (pres. 1985—86). Avocation: squash. Office: 400 E Court Ave Des Moines IA 50309 Business E-Mail: jolds@cahabagba.com

**OLDSHUE, JAMES Y.,** chemical engineering consultant; b. Chgo., Apr. 18, 1925; s. James and Louise (Young) O.; m. Betty Ann Wiersema, June 14, 1947; children: Paul, Richard, Robert. BS in Chem. Engring., Ill. Inst. Tech., 1947, MS, 1949, PhD in Chem. Engring., 1951. Registered engr., N.Y. Chem. engr. Manhattan Project, Los Alamos, N.Mex., 1945-46; With Mixing Equipment Co., Rochester, NY, 1950-92, dir. research, 1960-63, tech. dir., 1963-70, v.p. mixing tech., 1970-92; pres. Oldshue Techs. Internat., Rochester, NY, 1992—; tchr. Sarasota (Fla.) Sch. Dist., 1992—, OASIS, Rochester Sch. Dist., NY, 1992—; pres. Pool Tech., Inc., 1968—. Adj. prof. chem. engring. Beijing U. Chem. Tech., 1992—; pres. mfr. Pool Tech. Inc., Sarasota, Fla. Author: Fluid Mixing Technology, 1983; contbr. chpts. and articles to books and jours. Chmn. budget com. Internat. div. YMCA; bd. dirs. Rochester YMCA. Served with AUS, 1945-46. Recipient 1st Disting. Svc. award N.E. YMCA Internat. Com., 1979, J.E. Purkynse medal Czech Republic Acad. Sci.; named Rochester Engr. of Yr., 1980. Fellow AIChE (pres. 1979, treas. 1983-89, chmn. 75th anniversary com. 1983, chmn. internat. activities com. 1989-92, Founders award 1981, Eminent Chem. Engr. award 1983, Svc. to Soc. award 1989, F.J. and Dorothy van Antwerpen award for Svc. to the Inst. 1999, centennial com. 2001-); mem. NAE, Am. Assn. Engring. Socs. (chmn. 1985, K.A. Roe award 1987), Am. Chem. Soc., Czech Soc. Chem. Engring. (hon.), World Congress Chem. Engrs. (v.p. 1986, pres. 1992-96), N.Am. Mixing Forum (chmn. 1990-93, Mixing Achievement rsch. award 1992), Interam. Confedn. Chem. Engrs. (sec. gen. 1991-93, v.p. 1993-95, pres. 1995-96), Victor Marquez award 1983), Rochester Engring. Soc. (pres. 1992-93, Rochester Engr. of Yr. 1980), UN Assn. of Rochester (pres. 2001-2003). Mem. Reformed Ch. in Am. (gen. program coun.). Achievements include design and scale-up procedures in field of fluid mixing. Home: 6140 Midnight Pass Rd Apt 502 Sarasota FL 34242 Office: 2250 Gulf Gate Dr Ste A Sarasota FL 34231 Office Phone: 941-924-8874. E-mail: ninetofive@juno.com.

**OLEA, HECTOR,** curator; m. Mari Carmen Ramirez. Independent curator, writer, translator. Co-curator (with Mari Carmen Ramirez) (exhibitions) Inverted Utopias: Avant-Garde Arts in Latin America, 2004 (Award for Best Thematic Mus. Show Nationally, Internat. Assn. Art Critics/USA, 2005); co-author (with Mari Carmen Ramirez): (book) Inverted Utopias: Avant-Garde Arts in Latin America, 2004.

**OLEARCHYK, ANDREW,** cardiothoracic surgeon, educator; b. Peremyshl, Ukraine, Dec. 3, 1935; s. Symon and Anna (Kravéts) O.; m. Renata M. (Sharan), June 26, 1971; children: Christina N., Roman A., and Adrian S. Grad., Med. Acad., Warsaw, Poland, 1961, U. Pa., 1970. Diplomate Am. Bd. Surgery, Am. Bd. Thoracic Surgery. Chief divsn. anesthesiology, asst. dept. surgery Provincial Hosp., Kielce, Poland, 1963-66; resident in gen. surgery Geisinger Med. Ctr., Danville, Pa., 1968-73; resident in thoracic, cardiac and vascular surgery Allegheny Gen. Hosp., Pitts., 1980-82; pvt. practice medicine splty. in cardiac, thoracic and vascular surgery Phila. and Camden, NJ, 1982—. Author: A Surgeon's Universe, 2003, 2d edit., 2006; contbr. articles to profl. jours. Achievements include description of mimicking of the subclavian steal syndrome (2004); application of the ultrasonic Doppler flow detector to localize an intramyocardial coronary artery to perform coronary artery bypass surgery on a beating heart in the presence of neoplastic pericarditis aiming to preserve cellular immunity (2003); recognition of a triad of the severe atherosclerosis of the aortic valve, a low incidence of coronary artery disease and rheumatic fever in patients with a congenital bicuspid aortic valve (2002); modification of a vertical reduction aortoplasty by a distal external synthetic grafting for surgical treatment of aneurysms of the ascending aorta (2002); treatment of a bullous emphysema of the lung by a conservative resection of bullae and a local application of a biological glue (2001); noted association between congenital diaphragmatic defect with peritoneopericardial communication and congenital bicuspid aortic valve (2000); applied a staged treatment of the left subclavian steal syndrome and coronary artery disease by the left carotid-subclavian and coronary artery bypasses (1999); establishing that in patients with coronary artery disease, the causes of congestive heart failure in those with a mild to moderate reduction of the left ventricular ejection fraction were hypertension, myocardial infarction or ishemic insufficiency of the mitral valve, and in those with severe reduction of the left ventricular ejection fraction were left ventricular dysfunction alone, or in combination with ischemic mitral regurgitation (1999); repair of a pseudoaneurysm of the ascending aorta on a beating heart (1997); ligation of bilateral coronary-pulmonary artery fistulas on a beating heart (1996); internal repair of the coronary sinus (Valsalva) aneurysm (1996); grafting of the internal thoracic to coronary arteries without touching the atherosclerotic ascending aorta, on cardiopulmonary bypass with a beating, warm and vented heart and bradycardia induced by beta-blockers (1994); design of Olearchyk R Triple Ringed Cannula Spring Clip to secure vein grafts over blunted cannulas in coronary artery bypass surgery (1989); combined right femoral and iliac retroperitoneal surgical approach to remove retained intraaortic balloon device (1989); technique a side graft during replacement of the ascending aorta in proximal aortic dissection (1989); intro. of endarterectomy and external prosthetic grafting of ascending and transverse aorta under hypothermic circulatory arrest (1987); first to combine insertion of the inferior vena cava filter with a protected iliofemoral venous thrombectomy (Olearchyk's operation, 1986); pioneering promotion of grafting of diffusely diseased coronary arteries with the internal thoracic artery (1980-82) and of the left anterior descending coronary artery sys. during resection of cardiac aneurysms (1979-80); used an inflated Foley balloon catheter to control hemorrhage from cardiac wounds and to infuse fluids through it to replace blood loss before and during suture repair (1978); description of a combined treatment of advanced gastric carcinoma by resection and chemotherapy (1975); recognized that alcoholism and smoking were common habits of patients with stomach cancer (1975); demonstration of safety of simultaneous use of fluothane and curare as gen. anesthesia (1966); description of combined treatment of advanced testicular seminoma with chemotherapy, resection and radiotherapy (1961). Address: 129 Walt Whitman Blvd Cherry Hill NJ 08003-3746 Office Phone: 856-428-0505. Personal E-mail: asolearchyk@yahoo.com.

**O'LEARY, DAN,** museum director; m. Hilary Bassett. PhD in art hist., Princeton U.; MBA in mktg and mgmt., U. Mich. Dir. Minn. Inst. Arts, Portland Mus. Art, Maine, 1993—. Office: Portland Mus Art Seven Congress Sq Portland ME 04101

**O'LEARY, DANIEL VINCENT, JR.,** lawyer; b. Bklyn., May 26, 1942; s. Daniel Vincent and Mary (Maxwell) O'L.; m. Marilyn Irene Gavigan, June 1, 1968; children: Daniel, Katherine, Molly, James. AB cum laude, Georgetown U., 1963; LLB, Yale U., 1966. Bar: Ill. 1967. Assoc. Wilson & Mc Ilvaine, Chgo., 1967—75, ptnr., 1975—87, Peterson & Ross, Chgo., 1987—94, Schwartz & Freeman, Chgo., 1994—95; of counsel Mandell, Menkes & Surdyk, LLC, Chgo., 1995—. Pres., bd. dirs. Jim's Cayman Co., Ltd.; pres. TV and Radio Purchasing Group Inc.; asst. sec. L.M.C. Ins. Co. Bermuda, 1990—; pres. Wagering Ins. N.Am. Purchasing Group Inc., 1997—. Lt. comdr. USNR, ret. Roman Catholic. Avocations: fishing, scuba diving. Office: Mandel Menkes LLC Ste 300 333 W Wacker Dr Chicago IL 60606 Office Phone: 312-251-1000. E-mail: doleary@mandellmenkes.com.

**O'LEARY, DAVID,** priest, theologian, educator; b. Lynn, Mass., Mar. 11, 1958; BA, St. John's Sem., Boston, 1981, MDiv, 1985; MEd, Boston Coll. 1986; STL, Weston Jesuit Sch. Theology, 1990; DPhil, Oxford U., Eng., 1999; cert. in Alcohol counseling/substance Abuse, Boston Coll Sch. Social Work, 1982; cert. in Spiritual Direction, St. Mary's Sem. and U., Balt., 1995; cert. in Human Sexuality, Christian Inst. for Study of Human Sexuality, Bosotn, 1995. Ordained priest Boston Archdiocese, 1985. From spl. edn. tchr. to dir. spl. edn. program St. John's Sem., Boston, 1977—81; rschr., film editor, and writer Office Religious Edn. Arcdiocese Boston, 1981—82; co-leader group therapy, case worker Brigham & Women's Hosp., Kenmore Sq. De-Tox, Boston, 1982—83; substance abuse counselor St. John/St. Hugh, Roxbury, Mass., 1983—84; deacon intern Immaculate Conception Ch., Malden, Mass., 1984—85; parochial vicar Immaculate Conception Parish, Everett, Mass., 1986-91; parochial vicar, dir. religious edn. St. Augustine's Parish, South Boston, 1991-93, St. Theresa's Ch., North Reading, Mass., 1993-95; asst prof. moral theology, spirituality, sexual ethics St. Mary's Sem. and U., Balt., 1995—; assoc. U. chaplain, dir. Cath. Ctr. Tufts U., Medford, Mass., 1998—2002, U. chaplain, 2002—, 2nd prof. Adj. faculty lectr. in moral theology and social ethics St. John's Sem. Pastoral Inst., 1991; vis. lectr. in social ethics USAF Acad., Denver, 1992, USAF Chaplain Sch., Squadron Oficer Sch.,Air Command and Staff Coll., Air War Coll., Maxwell AFB, Ala., summer, 1992; adj. faculty Christian Inst. for Study of Human Sexuality and St. Luke's Inst., Silver Springs, Md., 1995—98; theol. cons. Md. Cath. Conf. of Bishops and St. Luke's Inst., Silver Springs, Md., 1995—98; mem. Human Investigation Rev. Com. New Eng. Med. Ctr. and Tufts U., 1998; chmn. instn. rev. bd. Tufts U., Medford, Mass., 2001; elected to bd. ministry Harvard U., Cambridge, Mass., 2002. Author: (Book) A Vision of Catechesis for Today and Pointers on Catechetical Instruction, 1996, Roman Catholic Beliefs and Prayers: A Handbook for Those on a Spiritual Journey, 1999, The Roman Catholic Perspective on the Morality of Withdrawing or Witholding Food and Fluid Administered Artificially to an Individual in the Persistent Vegitative State, 2001, Seeking the Path of God's Justice: an Analysis of the U.S. Bishop's Letter on Economic Justice, 2001; contbr. articles to profl. jours. Recipient Exceptional Citizens Week for disadvantaged, Gilmanton, N.H., 1990-94; bd. dirs. Camp Giving summer camp for physically and mentally challenged, 2001. Chaplain, major USAF, 1982—94. Mem.: Nat. Assn. of Coll. and Univ. Chaplains, Cath. Theol. Soc. Am., Am. Acad. Religion, USAF Assn., Soc. Biblical Lit. Republican. Avocation: long distance running. Office: Office of Univ Chaplain Tufts U Goddard Chapel 3 The Green Medford MA 02155 Office Phone: 617-627-3427.

**O'LEARY, DEANNA KAY,** benefits compensation analyst, consultant; b. Corcoran, Calif., Feb. 14, 1967; d. Harold Devoe and Glenda Lea Hoppert; m. Michael Patrick O'Leary, Nov. 16, 1996. BA, U. Fresno, 2000. Cert. six sigma green belt 2003. Benefit analyst CIGNA HealthCare, Visalia, Calif., 1991—96, project specialist, 1996—99, sr. claims examiner, 1999—2000, process and orgn. evaluation analyst, 2000—02, sr. process and orgn. evaluation analyst, 2002—04, resource planner, 2004—. Author: inspirational short book, poems (Featured in Sparrowgrass Poetry Forum, 1996, featured in Famous Poets Soc., 2004), Don't Miss It - Reflections on the Journey of Life, 2003, The Cadence Of My Soul, 2005; composer, musician, singer (inspirational music) Beyond the Clouds. Trainer of ergonomics and time/motion economy City of Visalia, Visalia, 2002—02; asst. to vols. Youth Vision, Visalia, Calif., 2002—03; v.p. Children's Mus. of the Sequoias, Visalia, 2002—02; music dir., min. Tulare (Calif.) Missionary Bapt. Ch., 1998—, ins. com., 2001—03; ladies choir dir. Visalia Missionary Bapt. Ch., 1993—96; bd. mem. Imagineli Children's Mus., 2005—; vol. Gift of Life Found., Visalia, 2002—03, v.p., 2003—05; promoter and vol. Calif. Transplant Donor Network, Central Valley, Calif., 1996—2001. Recipient U. Merit award, Fresno Pacific U., 1999. Republican. Baptist. Avocations: writing inspirational and motivational works, songwriting and performing, enrichment of others, volunteer work, motion and time study. Home: 2602 S Silvervale St Visalia CA 93277 Office: CIGNA HealthCare 5300 W Tulare Ave Visalia CA 93277 Office Phone: 559-738-2153. Business E-Mail: kismet01@sbcglobal.net.

**O'LEARY, DENNIS SOPHIAN,** accrediting body executive; b. Kansas City, Mo., Jan. 28, 1938; s. Theodore Morgan and Emily (Sophian) O'L.; m. Margaret Rose Wiedman, Mar. 29, 1980; children: Margaret Rose, Theodore Morgan. BA, Harvard U., 1960; MD, Cornell U., 1964. Diplomate Am. Bd. Internal Medicine, Am. Bd. Hematology. Intern U. Minn. Hosp., Mpls., 1964-65, resident, 1965-66, Strong Meml. Hosp., Rochester, NY, 1966—67, chief resident and hematology, 1967—68; asst. prof. medicine and pathology George Washington U. Med. Ctr., Washington, 1971-73, assoc. prof., 1973-80, prof. medicine, 1980-86, assoc. dean grad. med. edn., 1973-77, dean clin. affairs, 1977-86; pres. Joint Commn. on Accreditation Healthcare Orgns., Oakbrook Terrace, Ill., 1986—. Med. dir. George Washington U. Hosp., 1974-85, v.p Univ. Health Plan, 1977-85; pres. D.C. Med. Soc., 1983. Chmn. editl. bd. Med. Staff News, 1975-80; contbr. articles to profl. jours. Founding mem. Nat. Capital Area Health Care Coalition, Washington, 1982; trustee James S. Brady Found., Washington, 1982-87; bd. dirs. Nat. Quality Forum, 2001—; Nat. Adv. Coun. Agy. for Healthcare Rsch. and Quality, 2002-04. Maj. U.S. Army, 1968-71. Recipient Community Service award D.C. Med. Soc., 1981, Key to the City, Mayor of Kansas City, Mo., 1982. Master ACP; fellow Am. Coll. Physician Execs.; mem. AMA (Resolution commendation 1981, Disting. Svc. award 2005), Am. Hosp. Assn. (del. 1984-86, Resolution commendation 1981), Internat. Club (Chgo.). Avocation: tennis.

**O'LEARY, HAZEL R.,** academic administrator, retired federal official, lawyer; b. Newport News, Va., May 17, 1937; d. Russell E. and Hazel (Palleman) Reid; m. John F. O'Leary, Apr. 23, 1980 (dec.); 1 child, Carl G. Rollins. BA, Fisk U., Nashville, 1959; JD, Rutgers U., Newark, 1966. Bar: N.J. 1967, D.C. 1985; cert. fin. planner. V.p., gen. counsel O'Leary & Assocs., Inc., Washington, 1981-89; pres. O'Leary & Assocs., Chevy Chase, Md., 1997—; exec. v.p. corp. affairs No. States Power Co., Mpls., 1989-93; administr., dep. administr. econ. regulatory commn. U.S. Dept. Energy, Washington, 1977—81, sec., 1993-97; COO Blaylock & Ptnrs., N.Y.C., 1997—2002; dir. Scottish Re Group Ltd., 2001—; pres. Fisk U., 2004—. Trustee AES Copr., ICF Kaiser, Inc. Trustee Morehouse Coll., Africare, Ctr. Democracy, Keystone Ctr. Mem. Phi Beta Kappa. Office: Fisk Univ 1000 17th Ave N Nashville TN 37208-3051 also: Scottish Re Group Ltd Crown House 3d Fl 4 Par la Ville Rd Hamilton HM 12 Bermuda

**O'LEARY, JOSEPH EVANS,** lawyer; b. Newton, Mass., Sept. 17, 1945; s. Cornelius Joseph and Dorothy Mary (Evans) O'L.; m. Carolyn Brady, Aug. 16, 1969; children: Caryn, Kevin, David, Catherine. AB, Boston Coll., 1967, JD, 1970; LLM, Georgetown U., 1974. Bar: Mass. 1970, Ill. 1974, N.Y. 1979. Assoc. Seyfarth, Shaw, Fairweather & Geraldson, Chgo., 1974-78, ptnr. N.Y.C., 1978-82; of counsel Choate, Hall & Stewart, Boston, 1982-83, a ptnr., 1983-99; ptnr. McDermott, Will, Emery, Boston, 1999—. Lt. USN, 1971-74. Mem. ABA, Mass. Bar Assn., Boston Bar Assn. Home: 23 Freeman St Harwich Port MA 02646 Office: McDermott Will Emery 28 State St Boston MA 02109-1775 Office Phone: 617-535-4000. E-mail: joleary@mwe.com.

**O'LEARY, MARION HUGH,** retired dean, chemist; b. Quincy, Ill., Mar. 24, 1941; s. J. Gilbert and Ruth Elizabeth (Kerr) O'L.; m. Sandra E. Eisemann, Sept. 5, 1964 (div. 1979); children— Catherine, Randall, Jessica; m. Elizabeth M. Kean, Jan. 24, 1981. BS, U. Ill., 1963; PhD, MIT, 1966. Asst. prof. chemistry U. Wis., Madison, 1967-73, assoc. prof., 1973-78, prof. chemistry and biochemistry, 1978-89; prof. and head dept. biochemistry U. Nebr., Lincoln, 1989-96; dean Coll. Natural Scis. and Math., Calif. State U., Sacramento, 1996—2006. Cons. Institut Pertanian Bogor, Indonesia, 1983-84; vis. prof. Universitas Andalas, Padang, Indonesia, 1984-85, Australian Nat. U., 1982-83. Author: Contemporary Organic Chemistry, 1976. Editor: Isotope Effects on Enzyme-Catalyzed Reactions, 1977. Contbr. articles to sci. publs. Grantee, NSF, U.S. Dept. Agr., Dept. Energy, NIH; Guggenheim Found. fellow, 1982-83; Sloan Found. fellow, 1972-74. Fellow AAAS; mem. Am. Chem. Soc., Am. Soc. Biochemistry and Molecular Biology. Home: 6428 Orange Hill Ln Carmichael CA 95608-4580 E-mail: moleary@csus.edu.

**O'LEARY, PATRICK J.,** manufacturing executive; BS in Acctg. and Law, U. Southampton, England. From acct. to ptnr. Boston (Mass.) Office Deloitte & Touche, 1978—88, ptnr. Boston (Mass.) Office, 1988—94; CFO, dir. Carlisle Plastics, Inc., 1994—96; v.p. fin., treasurer, CFO SPX, Charlotte, NC, 1996—. Office: SPX 13515 Ballantyne Corporate Pl Charlotte NC 28277

**O'LEARY, PAUL GERARD,** retired insurance company executive; b. Boston, June 22, 1935; s. Gerard Paul and Marie Agnes (Hennessey) O'Leary; m. Elizabeth Jane Pollins, Oct. 14, 1961; children: Paul Hennessey, William Gerard, Mary Elizabeth Conroy, James Daniel. AB cum laude, Harvard U., 1956; MRA, U. Pa., 1958. Alumni dir. Wharton Grad. Sch., U. Pa., Phila., 1958-60; asst. sec. Empire Trust Co., N.Y.C., 1960-65; sr. investment analyst Blyth & Co., Inc., N.Y.C., 1965-70; v.p. William D. Witter, Inc., N.Y.C., 1970-76, also bd. dirs.; investment sr. v.p. Prudential Ins. Co. Am., Newark, 1977—2002. Instr fin Univ Pa, 1957—60. V.p. Prudential Found., Newark, 1986—96. Mem.: Ireland House NYU, NY Hist. Soc., Boston Latin Sch. Alumni Assn., NY Property Ins. Underwriting Assn. (mem. investment com. 1994—2002), Ins. Inst. Hwy. Safety (mem. investment com. 1983—2002), Assn. Ins. and Fin. Analysts (pres. 1973—74), Am. Nuc. Insurers (chmn. investment com. West Hartford, Conn. 1989—96), Inst. Chartered Fin. Analysts, Am. Irish Hist. Soc. (NYC), Hobbyists Unltd. (Ridgewood, NJ), Harvard Club (NYC), Upper Ridgewood Tennis Club, Harvard Club (NJ) (pres. 1983—84). Roman Catholic. Avocations: tennis, philately, cartography, history. Home: 719 Belmont Rd Ridgewood NJ 07450-1300 Personal E-mail: ploleary@yahoo.com.

**O'LEARY, PRENTICE LEE,** retired lawyer; b. LA, May 6, 1942; BA, UCLA, 1965, JD, 1968. Bar: Calif. 1969. Ptnr. Sheppard, Mullin, Richter & Hampton, L.A., 1974—. Bd. dirs. Legal Aid Found. L.A., 1987—93, 2000—. Mem. ABA (bus. bankruptcy com.), State Bar Calif., Los Angles County Bar Assn. (chmn. bankruptcy com., chmn. comml. law and bankrupt sect. 1985-86), Am. Coll. Bankruptcy Profls., Order of Coif. Office: Sheppard Mullin Richter & Hampton 333 S Hope St Fl 48 Los Angeles CA 90071-1406

**O'LEARY, ROBERT J.,** retail executive; b. Bellefonte, Pa. m. Linda O'Leary; 2 children. BA in advt., Pa. State U., 1971. With advt. and pub. rels. divsns. United Techs. Corp., Hartford, Conn., IBM; v.p. pub. rels. and advt. Unisys, Blue Bell, Pa., 1988—94; gen. mgr. global pub. affairs Mobil Oil Corp., Fairfax, Va., 1995—2000; v.p. pub. affairs and comm. Bacardi Ltd., 2000; sr. v.p. global comm. Goodyear Tire & Rubber Co., Akron, Ohio, 2002—03; sr. v.p. pub. rels., comm., and govt. Sears, Roebuck & Co., Hoffman Estates, Ill., 2003—. Bd. visitors Pa. State U. Coll. Comm.; bd. trustees Found. Am. Comm. Alumni Fellow, Pa. State U. Office: Sears Roebuck & Co 3333 Beverly Rd Hoffman Estates IL 60179

**O'LEARY, SHARON,** obstetrician, gynecologist, researcher; MD, Mich. State U., East Lansing, 1990. Diplomate Am. Bd. Ob-Gyn, 1994. Pvt. practice Integrated Health Assocs., Ann Arbor, Mich., 1994—; residency program dir. St. Joseph Mercy Hosp., Ann Arbor, 1997—2005, rsch. dir., 2005—. Office Phone: 734-434-6200.

**O'LEARY, THOMAS MICHAEL,** lawyer; b. NYC, Aug. 16, 1948; s. James and Julia Ann (Connolly) O'L.; m. Luise Ann Williams, Jan. 13, 1978; 1 child, Richard Meridith. BA, CUNY, 1974; JD, Seattle U., 1977. Bar: Wash. 1977, U.S. Ct. Mil. Appeals 1978, U.S. Ct. Appeals (9th cir.), U.S. Supreme Ct. 1983. Dep. pros. atty. Pierce County, Tacoma, 1978; commd. 1st lt. U.S. Army, 1978, advanced through grades to capt., 1978; chief trial counsel Office of Staff Judge Adv., Ft. Polk, La., 1978-79; trial def. counsel, trial def. svc., 1979-81; chief legal advisor Office Insp. Gen., Heidelberg, Fed. Republic of Germany, 1981-82; sr. def. counsel Trial Def. Svc., Giessen, Fed. Republic of Germany, 1982-84; asst. chief adminstrv. law U.S. Army Armor Ctr., Ft. Knox, Ky., 1984-85, chief adminstrv. law, 1985, chief legal asst., 1985-86; ret. U.S. Army, 1996; sr. trial atty. Immigration and naturalization Svc., Phoenix, 1987; sector counsel, spl. asst. U.S. atty., U.S. Border Patrol, Tucson, 1987-90; enforcement counsel U.S. Immigration and Naturalization Svc., Tucson, 1990-95, asst. dist. counsel Phoenix litigation, 1995-97. Apptd. U.S. Immigration Judge, U.S. Immigration Ct., Imperial, Calif., 1997-2000, apptd. sr. U.S. Immigration Judge, Tucson, 2000—; adj. prof. Embry-Riddle Aero. U., Tucson, 2002- Decorated Purple Heart, Cross of Gallantry (Vietnam). Mem. Judge Advs Assn., Wash. State Bar Assn., Order Ky. Cols. (commd. col. 1985). Home: 9080 E 25th St Tucson AZ 85710-8675 Office: US Immigration Ct 1705 E Hanna Rd Ste 366 Eloy AZ 85231-9612 Office Phone: 520-466-3671.

**OLEJNICZAK, RONALD M,** corporate financial executive; B in acctg., Canisius Coll. CPA. Sr. audit mgr. Price Waterhouse; v.p.,mgr. fin. reporting and acctg. policy Shawmut Nat. Corp., 1992—95; dir. of corp. acctg. policy Aetna Inc., 1995—97, v.p., fin. reporting analysis, 1997—2001, v.p., contr., 2001—. Mem.: NY State Soc. of Cert. Pub. Accountants, Am. Inst. Cert. Pub. Accountants. Office: Aetna Inc 151 Farmington Ave Hartford CT 06156

**OLEJNICZAK, BERNARD CHARLES,** education educator; b. Green Bay, Wis., Aug. 23, 1930; s. Bernard Clement and Helen Josephine (LeClair) Olejniczak; m. Mary Jean Barrett-Terry, Oct. 13, 1956 (div. Dec. 1979); children: Ann Marie, Mary Rose, Patrick James, Thomas Bernard; m. Margaret Jean Olson, Sept. 19, 1980. BA in Philosophy, St. Norbert Coll., 1953; MA in Counseling, U. Wis., 1966. Tchr. in Latin, French and journalism Pulaski H.S., Wis., 1957—71; administr. Pulaski Elem. Schs., 1971—92; ednl. cons., 1993—96; tech. lectr. U. Wis., Oshkosh, 1996—. Chmn. curriculum U. Wis. Learning in Retirement, 1997—, 2004—. Editor (newsletter): Polish Heritage, 1993—, Wisconsin Counselor, 1995—2005. Pres. Village Bd., Pulaski, 1965—70; v.p. Bd. Edn., Pulaski, 1992—96; sec. Pulaski C. of C., 1958—64; pres. Brown County Libr. Bd., Green Bay, Wis., 1985—96, Nicolet Fed. Libr., Green Bay, Wis., 1987—92. Named Trustee of Yr., Wis. Libr. Assn., 1997; recipient Profl. Writing award, Wis. Counselors Assn., 1999. Mem.: Lions Club (newsletter editor, sec. 1993—2004), Phi Delta Kappa. Democrat. Roman Catholic. Avocations: reading, computers. Home: 1625 Graber St Oshkosh WI 54901 Office: Univ Wis Coll Edn 800 Algoma Blvd Oshkosh WI 54901 Business E-Mail: olejnicz@uwosh.edu.

**OLEJNICZAK, EDWARD THADDEUS,** research chemist; b. Milw., Oct. 20, 1954; s. Thaddeus and Erica Olejniczak; m. Catherine Anne Olejniczak; children: Rebecca, Jason. PhD, Harvard U., Cambridge, Mass., 1982. Rsch. scientist Abbott Labs., North Chicago, Ill., 1984—, group leader rsch. nmr, 2000—. Vol. Habitat for Humanity, Waukegan, Ill., Lake County Forest Preserve, Libertyville, Ill., 2000—06. Postdoctoral Fellowship, NIH, 2002—04. Mem.: AAAS. Achievements include patents for Process for Fragment Based Drug Design; Method to Screen Using 1D NMR. Office: Abbott Labs Abbott Park North Chicago IL 60040 Office Phone: 847-937-0298. Personal E-mail: edward.olejniczak@abbott.com.

**OLEMAUN, TOMMY,** Native American tribal leader; Pres. Native Village of Barrow Inupiat Traditional Govt. Office: Native Village of Barrow Inupiat Traditional Govt PO Box 1130 6970 Almaogak St Barrow AK 99723 Office Phone: 907-852-4411. Office Fax: 907-852-8844.*

**OLENCHAK, FRANK RICHARD,** music educator, musician; b. Scranton, Pa., Aug. 5, 1928; s. Francis Richard and Helen Anita Olenchak; m. Patricia Maye Ingram, June 15, 1949; children: Francis Richard III, Rebecca Lynn, Jeffrey Stuart. MusB, James Madison U., 1950; MEd, Pa. State U., 1957; CASE, postgrad., Johns Hopkins U., 1965; PhD in Music: Music Edn., U. Mich., 1977. Cert. music tchr. Md., Va. Supr. of music, band dir. Galax Pub. Schs., Va., 1950—54; dir. h.s. band Harford County Schs., Bel Air, Md., 1954—58, Balt. City Schs., 1958—61; tchr. elem. instrumental music Balt. County Schs., Towson, Md., 1961—66; emeritus prof. edn. and profl. devel. We. Mich. U., Kalamazoo, 1966—84; adj. coord. student tchg. Ea. Mich. U., Ypsilanti, 1984—85; dir., CEO Music on the Move of Mich., Ann Arbor, 1985—87; chair dept. of music Allen U., Columbia, SC, 1989—; CEO, record prodr. Myrtle Records, Columbia, 1997—. Postdoctoral rschr. Columbia U., 1981; vis. scholar U. Mich., Ann Arbor, 1981—82. Author: Exploratory Music, (periodical) The Instructor, 1968; editor: (newsletter) Michigan Association of Teacher Educators, (books) SchoolMATES, 3 vols., 1981, 1982, The Instructor, 1968. Choir dir. Trinity Luth. Ch., Columbia, 1999—2002; dir. of music 3d Luth. Ch., Balt., 1960—62. Recipient doctoral tchg. fellowship, U. of Mich., 1969—70, acad. scholarship, Shenandoah Conservatory of Music, 1947. Mem.: Am. Fedn. Musicians, Assn. Tchr. Educators (pres., comm. chair 1978—83, Meritorious Svc. award 1980), Phi Delta Kappa (pres. 1978—87, 1991—94, Disting. Svc. Key 1985). Achievements include Creator of NUMCOMPO, a system for teaching musical notation to children with no prior knowledge of music. Avocations: sports, bridge, checkers, record collecting, travel. Office: Allen U 1530 Harden St Columbia SC 29204 E-mail: myrtrec@earthlink.net.

**OLENDER, JACK HARVEY,** lawyer; b. McKeesport, Pa., Sept. 8, 1935; m. Lovell Olender. BA summa cum laude, U. Pitts., 1957, JD, 1960; LLM, George Washington U., 1961. Bar: DC 1961, US Supreme Ct. 1965, Md. 1966, Pa. 1985; diplomate Am. Bd. Trial Advocates, Inner Cir. Advocates. Pvt. practice, Washington, 1961-79; prin. Jack H. Olender & Assocs., P.C., Washington, 1979—. Contbr. articles to profl. jours. Active World Peace through Law, Washington. Named to Hall of Fame Nat. Assn. Black Women Attys., 1987, DC Hall of Fame, 2000, Washington Bar Assn. Hall of Fame, 2000, Nat. Bar. Assn. Hall of Fame, 2005; recipient Presdl. award Nat. Bar Assn., 1996, 2000, 02, 04, Advocate for Justice award Nat. Bar Assn., 2000, Internat. B'nai B'rith Pursuit of Justice award, 2001, named one of 30 Best Lawyers in Washington, Washingtonian survey mag., 2005, Champion Justice award Trial Lawyers Assn., DC, 2004, Charles Hamilton Houston medallian award Washington Bar Assn., 2005. Fellow Am. Coll. Trial Lawyers, Internat. Acad. Trial Lawyers and Inner Cir. Advs.; mem. Trial Lawyers Assn. Met. Washington (pres. 1969-1970); Am. Coll. Legal Medicine; ATLA, Nat. Bar Assn. (adv. for justice 2000), Am. Bd. Profl. Liability Attys. (sec. 1989—), Trial Lawyers Pub. Justice (bd. dirs.), Internat. Assn. Jewish Lawyers and Jurists (bd. dirs.), Bar Assn. DC (pres. 1999-2000). Office: Jack H Olender & Assocs PC 888 17th St NW Fl 4 Washington DC 20006-3939 Office Phone: 202-879-7777. Business E-Mail: jhop.c@olender.com.

**OLENDORF, WILLIAM CARR, JR.,** small business owner; b. Albany, N.Y., Oct. 3, 1945; s. William Carr Sr. and Mary Zilpha (Gillies) O.; m. Barbara Kay Cowan, Aug. 14, 1966; children: Mark, Julie, Jennifer. Student, Columbia Coll., 1964—65, So. Ill. U., 1965—66. Prodn. asst. Sta. WTTW-TV, Chgo., 1962-64; radio announcer Sta. WERX, Wyoming, Mich., 1967-68; sales rep. Sta. WCFL, Chgo., 1968-70, Sta. WJJD-AM & FM, Chgo., 1970-72; v.p. Promotion Network, Chgo., 1972-74; account exec. AVCO-TV, Chgo., 1974-76, Peters, Griffin & Woodward, Chgo., 1976-82, Petry TV, Chgo., 1982-83; owner, pres. Point South KOA Resort, Yemassee, S.C., 1983—. Commr. Point South Pub. Svc. Dist., 1987-88, Lowcountry & Resort Island Tourism Commn., 1994—; mem. tourism tax adv. bd. Jasper County, S.C., 1985—; chmn. Jasper County Hist. Preservation Commn., S.C. 1994-99; trustee S.C. Battleground Preservation Trust, Inc., 1994-98, 2003-2004; mem. Low Country Revolutionary War Trail Commn. Recipient S.C. Honor award for Historic Preservation, Palmetto Trust for Historic Preservation, S.C. Dept. Archives and History, 1997. Mem. Nat. Campground Owners Assn. (campground nat. adv. bd. 1989-93, Take Pride in Am. award 1992), Kampground Owners Assn. (S.C. regiona pres. 1994-97, Award of Merit 1990), S.C. Campground Assn. (pres. 1987-88), Point South Mchts. Assn. (pres. 1990—), Jasper County Hist. Soc., Jasper County C. of C. (bd. dirs. 2001-2003), Beaufort Yacht and Sailing Club. Republican. Episcopalian. Avocations: amateur radio operator, sailing. Home and Office: 14 Campground Rd Yemassee SC 29945-1760

**OLENDSKI, OLEG,** physicist; b. Grodno, Belarus, Mar. 10, 1964; s. Zbigniew Olendski and Anna Olendska. PhD, Belarussian State U., Minsk, 1992. Rsch. scientist Atomic and Molecular Engring. Lab., Minsk, 1992—98; math. developer Waterloo Maple Inc., Waterloo, Ont., 1998—99; rsch. scientist No. Digital Inc., 1999—2000, JDS Uniphase, Ottawa, 2000—02, Jackson State U., Miss., 2003—. Contbr. articles to profl. jours. Fellow, Chonnam Nat. U., Kwangju, 1995—96. Mem.: Am. Phys. Soc. Office: Jackson State University 1400 Lynch St Jackson MS 39217 Office Phone: 601-979-1391. E-mail: oleg.olendski@jsums.edu.

**OLENICOFF, IGOR,** real estate company executive; b. Russia, 1942; married; children: Andrei(?), Natalia. U in Corp. Fin., U. So. Calif., MBA, M in Statistics and Quantitative Analysis. Cons., corp. exec.; founder, pres. Olen Properties Corp., Newport Beach, Calif., 1973—. Named one of Forbes' Richest Americans, 2006. Office: Olen Properties Corp 7 Corporate Plaza Dr Newport Beach CA 92660 Office Phone: 949-644-6536.*

**OLER, KIM,** voice educator; b. NYC, July 24, 1954; s. Clarke Kimberly and Wendy Salmond Oler; m. Cecelia Jane Critchley, July 28, 1984; children: Elizabeth Critchley, Clarke Kimberly Oler III. BA, Yale U., 1976. Childrens choir dir. St. Edward the Confessor, Syosset, NY; dir. mixed chorus St. John's U., Queens, NY, 2003—. Composer: (musical) Little Women (Richard Rodgers award, 1998), The Enchanted Cottage (Jerry Bock award, 2003), (musical scoring) All My Children (ABC) (Emmy award, 2003, 2005), (musicals) Secret Garden, Buddy's Tavern, others (BMI Harrington award for Sustained Creative Achieve., 2002); composer: (lyricist) (choral) Blue Green Hills of Earth from MISSA GAIA. Alumni schs. com. Yale U., New Haven, 1996. Grantee, Lila Acheson Wallace Readers Digest, 1991. Mem.: BMI Lehman Engel Composers and Lyricists Workshop (life Jerry Harrington award for Sustained Creative Achieve. 2002). Home and Office: Helium Music 12 Brighton Pl Huntington NY 11743 Office Phone: 631-742-3179. Personal E-mail: kimoler@gmail.com.

**OLER, WESLEY M., IV,** portfolio manager; b. Washington, Apr. 13, 1955; s. Wesley Marion III and Virginia (Craemer) O.; m. Debra Brown, Apr. 16, 1993; children: Wesley V, Phoebe. BA, Yale U., 1978. CFA. Deputy mgr. instl. sales Brown Bros. Harriman & Co., Zurich, 1982-88, mgr. internat. bankers N.Y.C., 1988-95, sr. mgr. equity trading, 1995-99; sr. portfolio mgr., pvt. client group, 1999—. Mem. ITS/CAES subcom. Nasdaq Stock Market, N.Y.C., 1996—; mem. N.Y. Stock Exch., N.Y.C., 1998. Mem. Endowment Commn. Christ Ch., Greenwich, Conn. Mem. SAR (treas. 1995-96), Soc. Colonial Wars (coun. mem. 1993-94), Soc. Mayflower Descs., Securities Industry Assn. (mem. instnl. brokerage com. 1997—), N.Y. Soc. Security Analysts (mem. High Net Worth Investors Com.). Office: Brown Bros Harriman & Co 140 Broadway 5th Fl New York NY 10005 E-mail: wesley.oler@bbh.com.

**OLERUD, JOHN GARRETT,** professional baseball player; b. Seattle, Aug. 5, 1968; s. John E. Olerud. Student, Washington State U. Player Toronto Blue Jays, 1989-96, NY Mets, 1997-99, Seattle Mariners, 2000—04, New York

Yankees, 2004—, Boston Red Sox. Named to Am. League All-Star Team, 1993, 2001; recipient Am. League Gold Glove Award, 2000, 2002, 2003. winner A.L batting title, 1993. Office: c/o NY Yankees E 161st St and River ave Bronx NY 10452

**OLES, PAUL STEVENSON (STEVE OLES),** architect, educator; b. San Antonio, Sept. 26, 1936; s. Paul Stevenson Sr. and Suda (Willis) O.; m. Carole Simmons, Oct. 11, 1963 (div. 1991); children: Brian Thomas, Julia Oles Carr; m. Susan Thompson, Sept. 26, 1992. BArch, Tex. Tech U., 1960; MArch, Yale U., 1963. Registered architect, Mass. Draftsman The Architects Collaborative, Cambridge, Mass., 1963-65; Cambridge Seven Assocs., Cambridge, 1965-67; architect MIT, Cambridge, 1968-70; prin. architect Interface Architects, Newton, Mass., 1971—. Vis. faculty RISD, Providence, 1974-79; lectr. architecture Harvard Grad. Sch. Design, Cambridge, 1984-88, vis. scholar, 1989-91. Author: Architectural Illustration, 1979, Drawing the Future, 1988. Mem. vestry Episcopalian Ch., 1995-98. Named Loeb fellow Harvard Grad. Sch. Design, 1982. Fellow AIA (inst. honor 1983, fellow 1989), Boston Soc. Architects, Am. Soc. Archtl. Perspectivists (founder, pres. 1986-90, bd. dirs 1993-97, Hugh Ferriss Meml. prize 1996). Democrat. Avocations: music, painting, photography. E-mail: steve@psoles.com.

**OLESEN, ROBERT LIND OLE,** electrical engineer; s. Henning Lind and Birte Olesen; m. Janet Marie Reilly, Nov. 5, 1994; children: Peter Abner, Hannah Marie. BSEE, U. Mass., Amherst, Mass., 1980; MSEE, Poly. U., Bklyn., 1988; MBA with honors, Hofstra U., Hempstead, N.Y., 2006. Lic. ham radio operator FCC, 2003. Engr. Charles Stark Draper Lab., Boston, 1980—82, TRW Corp., San Jose, Calif., 1982—84; project engr. Eaton AIL Corp., Commack, NY, 1984—88; prin. engr. Mission Scis., Commack, NY, 1988—90, APS Corp., Commack, NY, 1990—91; staff scientist Target Sys. Tech. Corp., Stony Brook, NY, 1991—99; sr. mgr. InterDigital Comm. Corp., King of Prussia, Pa., 1999—. Adj. prof. Suffolk C.C., Selden, NY, 1995—96. Contbr. articles to profl. jours. Recipient CTO Patent award, InterDigital Comm. Corp., 2005. Mem.: IEEE, Am. Soc. Engring. Mgmt., Internat. Soc. Photographers (award 2006). Achievements include patents for wireless communications support for development of training programs. Avocations: photography, sailing, web site development. Home: 3 Country Club Dr Huntington NY 11743 Office: InterDigital Communications Corporation 2 Huntington Quadrangle Melville NY 11747 Office Phone: 631-622-4344. Personal E-mail: rolesen@mac.com.

**OLGAARD, ANDERS,** economics educator; b. Aabenraa, Denmark, Sept. 5, 1926; s. Axel O. and Anna Lebeck; m. Alice Christiansen, 1951; three children. Dr. Polit., Univ. Copenhagen, 1966. Civil servant Econ. Sec., 1953-60; prof. econs., Univ. Copenhagen, 1962-96; adviser in Malaysia, Harvard U. Devel. Adv. Service, 1968-69; mem. Econ. Council, 1966-68, chmn., 1970-76. Author: Growth, Productivity and Relative Prices, 1966; The Danish Economy, EEC Economic and Financial Series, 1980. Mem. Danish Econ. Assn. (pres. 1983-88). Home: 12 Lerbaekvej DK-2830 Virum Denmark Office: U Copenhagen Inst Econs Studiestraede 6 DK-1455 Copenhagen Denmark

**OLIAN, JOANNE CONSTANCE,** curator, art historian; b. N.Y.C. d. Richard Edward and Dorothy (Singer) Wahrman; m. Howard Olian; children: Jane Wendy, Patricia Ann Student, Syracuse U.; BA, Hofstra U., 1969; MA, NYU Inst. Fine Arts, 1972. Grad. internship Met. Mus., N.Y.C., 1973; asst. curator Mus. City of N.Y., 1974, curator costume collection, 1975—91; cons. curator Costume Collection, 1992—95, curator emeritus, 1995—. Lectr. Parsons Sch. Design; vis. lectr. Musée des Arts Decoratifs, Paris, summers, 1983—85; co-curator Art and fashion Nassau County Mus. Art, 2006. Author: The House of Worth: The Gilded Age, 1860-1918, 1982; editor: Authentic French Fashions of the Twenties, 1990, Everyday Fashions of the Forties, 1992, Children's Fashions from Mode Illustrée 1860-1914, 1994, Wedding Fashions, 1862-1912, 1994, Everyday Fashions 1909-1920, 1995, La Mode Illustrée, 1997, Victorian and Edwardian Fashions, 1998, 80 Godey's Full-Color Fashions Plates, 1838-1880, 1998, Full-Color Victorian Fashion, 1870-1893, 1999, Everyday Fashions of the Sixties, 1999, Parisian Fashions of the Teens, 2002, Everyday Fashions of the Fifties, 2002, Children's Fashions, 1900-1950, 2003; contbr. articles to profl. jours., chpts. to books Mem. Internat. Coun. Mus. (costume com.), Costume Soc. Am. (dir. 1976-79, 83-86), Fashion Group (bd. dirs. 1985-86), Centre Internat. d'Etude des Textiles Anciens, Cosmopolitan Club N.Y.C Home and Office: 2 Shepherds Ln Sands Point NY 11050 Personal E-mail: joanneolian1@aol.com.

**OLIAN, JUDY D.,** dean; b. Australia; BS in psychology, Hebrew U., 1974; MS in indsl. rels., U. Wis., 1977, PhD in indsl. rels., 1980. Lectr. to full prof. mgmt. and orgn. Robert H. Smith Sch. Bus., U. Md., 1979—2000, sr. assoc. dean, 1999—2000; fellow Am. Coun. Edn. Fellow to pres. U. Md., 1990—91, special asst. to pres., 1991—92, founder, dir. IBM-TQ Project, 1991—92; dean, prof. mgmt. Smeal Coll. Bus., Pa. State U., 2000—; dean-elect UCLA Anderson Sch. Mgmt., 2005—. Exec. com. Personnel and Human Resources divsn. Acad. Mgmt., 1984—87, 1991—94; exec. com. bd. dirs. Assn. to Advance Collegiate Sch. Bus., 2000—01. Author: (syndicated weekly column) About Business; past mem. editl. bd.: Jour. Quality and Mgmt., Acad. Mgmt. Review. Bd. dirs. The Second Mile, Penn State Fund. Recipient award for curriculum innovation, Md. Assn. for Higher Edn., 1996. Office: Dean's Office Smeal Coll Bus Adminstrn Pa State Univ 801-H Bus Adminstrn Bldg University Park PA 16802 Office Phone: 814-863-0448. Office Fax: 814-865-7064. Business E-Mail: jdo10@psu.edu.*

**OLIAN, ROBERT MARTIN,** lawyer; b. Cleve., June 14, 1953; s. Robert Meade and Doris Isa (Hessing) Olian; m. Terri Ellen Ruther, Aug. 10, 1980; children: Andrew Zachary, Alix Michelle, Joshua Brett. AB, Harvard U., 1973, JD, 1977, M in Pub. Policy, 1977. Bar: Ill. 1977, U.S. Dist. Ct. (no. dist.) Ill., U.S. Ct. Appeals (7th cir.) 1983, U.S. Dist. Ct. (no. dist. trial bar) Ill. 1992, U.S. Dist. Ct. (we. dist.) Mich. 1994, U.S. Dist. Ct. (cen. dist.) Ill. 2004. Assoc. Sidley & Austin, Chgo., 1977-84; ptnr. Sidley Austin LLP, Chgo., 1985—. Editor: (book) Illinois Environmental Law Handbook, 1988, 1997. Panel atty. Chgo. Vol. Legal Svcs., 1983—; bd. dirs. Friends IDF, 2003—; trustee North Shore Congregation Israel, 1990—, sec., 1995—96, v.p., 1996—2003, first v.p., 2004—05, pres., 2005—; mem. regional strategic/mktg. com. Alexian Bros. Ill., Inc., Elk Grove, 1985—88; mem. dean's alumni leadership coun. JFK Sch. Govt. Harvard U., Univ. Club (N.Y.C.), Columbia Club. Home: 860 5th Ave # 19J New York NY 10021-5856 also: 4 Rosebud Ln East Quogue NY 11942-3627 Office: The Chrysler Bldg 405 Lexington Ave New York NY 10174-1299 Office Phone: 212-554-7891. E-mail: polick@mosessinger.com.

**OLICK, PHILIP STEWART,** lawyer; b. NYC, Oct. 2, 1936; s. Jack and Anita (Babsky) O.; m. Alice D. Chait, Mar. 25, 1961; children: Jonathan A., Jeffrey K., Diana M. BA, Columbia U., 1957; LLB, NYU, 1960. Bar: N.Y. 1961, Mo. 1966. Ptnr. Benjamin, Galton, Robbins & Fink, N.Y.C., 1961-65; gen. counsel, v.p., sec. Nat. Bellas Hess, Inc., Kansas City, Mo., 1965-69, dir., 1970-76; ptnr. Burke & Burke, N.Y.C., 1970-73, Townley & Updike, 1973-89, Moses & Singer, 1989—. Bd. arbitrators N.Y. Stock Exch. Bd. dirs. Univ. Glee Club NYC, pres.; bd. dirs. Young Peoples Chorus NYC. With AUS, 1960-61. Mem. Assn. of Bar of City of N.Y., Univ. Club (N.Y.C.), Columbia Club. Home: 860 5th Ave # 19J New York NY 10021-5856 also: 4 Rosebud Ln East Quogue NY 11942-3627 Office: The Chrysler Bldg 405 Lexington Ave New York NY 10174-1299 Office Phone: 212-554-7891. E-mail: polick@mosessinger.com.

**OLIET, SEYMOUR,** endodontics educator, dean, dentist; b. Perth Amboy, NJ, July 12, 1927; s. Asher Jacob and Sarah Oliet; m. Sherry Roseff, July 2, 1949; children: Eric Jay, Amy Ellen Oliet Heller. Student, Rutgers U., 1945-46, 47-49; DDS with distinction U. Pa., 1953. Diplomate Am. Bd. Endodontics. Instr. oral medicine U. Pa. Dental Medicine U. Pa., 1953-56, assoc. oral medicine, 1956-61, asst. prof. oral medicine, 1961-65, assoc. prof. oral medicine, 1965-71, prof. oral medicine, dir. undergrad. endodontics, 1971-72, founding chmn. dept. endodontics, 1972-80, prof. endodontics,

---

interim chmn. endodontics, 1990-91, prof. emeritus, 1994—; attending dentist Albert Einstein Med. Ctr., Phila., 1953-60, sr. attending, chmn. endodontics, 1960-84; prof. endodontics Coll. Dental Medicine Nova Southeastern U., Ft. Lauderdale, Fla., 1996—, chmn. task force to estab. Dental Sch., 1995-96, founding dean Coll. Dental Medicine, 1996—2001, dean emeritus, 2001—. Cons. endodontics U.S. Army, Ft. Dix, N.J., and Walter Reed Army Hosp., Washington, 1955-80, VA Hosp., Phila., 1965-80; chmn. internat. to estab. I.B. Bender Endowment Fund, Israeli Endodontic Soc., Hebrew U., 1990-91; reviewer Jour. Am. Dental Assn., 1970—. Author: (with others) Endodontics Practice, 11th edit., 1988, Diagnosis and Treatment of Endodontic Emergences, 1981, Current Therapy in Dentistry, 1977, Diagnosis and Treatment Planning in Management of Diseases of the Pulp, 1963, Programmed Text Endodontics; editor Alpha Omega, 1956, (newsletter) Am. Assn. Endodontics, 1966-69; contbr. articles to profl. jours. Named Hon. Citizen of New Orleans; named to, Perth Amboy H.S. Hall of Fame, 1998, Seymour Oliet DDS Libr., dedicated at Nova Southeastern U., 2002; recipient Mayor's Citation, Perth Amboy, 1998. Fellow AAAS, Royal Soc. Health (Brit.), Internat. Assn. Dental Rsch., Am. Assn. Endodontists, Am. Coll. Dentists (sec.-treas. Phila. chpt. 1965-76, pres.-elect 1976-77, pres. 1976-77), Internat. Coll. Dentists, Phila. Coll. Surgeons; mem. ADA (life), Pa. Acad. Endodontics (founder, pres. 1977-79, adv. to pres. 1979), Phila. County Dental Soc. (membership com. 1954, indsl. dentistry com. 1954, chmn. sci. program com. 1963, chmn. essay and clins. com. 1964-65, chmn. mediation com. 1965-66, bd. govs. 1985-87, chmn. ad hoc com. ins. 1985-96, com. peer rev. 1985-96, com. on continuing edn. 1989-96, dir. liberty dental com. 1987-91, gen. chmn. 1991-92, chmn. awards and banquets 1988-89, dir. sci. exhibits and programs 1989-90, del. Pa. Dental Assn. 1985-96, 2005-, long-range planning com. 1993-96, historian, bd. govs. 1994-96), Brazilian Dental Soc. (hon.), N.Y. Acad. Sci., Am. Assn. Endodontists (arrangements com. 1958-60, libr. com. 1960-61, membership com. 1961-67, publ. chmn., editor newsletter, sci. 1966-69, sci. prof. chmn. 1970-71, bd. govs., exec. com. 1972-74, awards and hons. com. 1992-95), Eastern Dental Soc. (chmn. membership 1956-57, program com. 1957-59, chmn. publicity, editor 1957-59, sec. 1960-62, bd. dirs. 1958X, pres.-elect chmn. bd. govs. 1968-69, pres. 1969-70), Acad. Stomatology, Am. Assn. Dental Editors, Alpha Omega (Phila. alumni chpt., editor 1956, treas. 1956-60, adv. to alumni chpt., regent 1960-61, pres.-elect 1961-63, pres. 1963-64, nat. dept. marshall 1961-62). Avocations: tennis, golf, horseback trail riding, fishing. Office: Nova Southeastern U Coll Dental Medicine 3200 S University Dr Fort Lauderdale FL 33328-2018 Office Phone: 954-262-7333. Personal E-mail: sholiet@aol.com. Business E-Mail: soliet@nova.edu.

**OLIKER, DAVID WILLIAM,** healthcare management administrator; b. Elkins, W.Va., Mar. 29, 1948; married; 3 children. BA in Sociology and Anthropology, East Carolina U., 1970; MA in Social Anthropology, Am. U., 1973; Cert. in Healthcare Adminstrn., George Washington U., 1977. Health svcs. specialist United Mine Workers Am. Health and Retirement Funds, 1976-78; health planner Health Sys. Agy. Western Md., Cumberland, 1978-79; ops. mgr. Md.-Individual Practice Assn., Inc., Rockville, 1979-81; project dir. N.Y. Health Maintenance Plan, Inc., N.Y.C., 1981-82; pres., CEO MVP Health Plan, Schenectady, NY, 1982—, Preferred Care (merger with MVP Health Plan), Rochester, NY, 2005—. Mem. bd. dir. Schenectady 2000, Albany Colonie Regional C. of C., Twin Rivers Boy Scout Coun. Mem. APHA, Am. Assn. Health Plans, N.Y. State HMO Conf. (bd. dirs.), Nat. Managed Care Inc. (chmn.). Office: MVP Health Plan PO Box 2207 Schenectady NY 12301-2207 also: Preferred Care 259 Monroe Ave Rochester NY 14607*

**OLIKER, VLADIMIR,** mathematician, educator; b. Ulianovsk, Russia, Oct. 7, 1945; came to U.S. 1975, naturalized 1980; s. Yosef and Sonia (Bakelman) Oliker; m. Elena Matis, Mar. 20, 1969; children: Olga, Aviva, Yosef Matis. MS, Leningrad U., Russia, 1967; PhD, Leningrad U., 1971. Sr. researcher Hydrometeorological Inst., Leningrad, Russia, 1970-72; group leader Dept. Transportation, 1972-74; vis. prof. Temple U., Phila., 1975-77; assoc. prof. to prof. U. Iowa, Iowa City, 1977-80, 80-84; prof. math. Emory U., Atlanta, 1984—. Vis. mem. Math Scis. Research Inst., Berkeley, Calif., 1983; vis. prof. U. Florence, Italy, 1983, Technische U., Berlin, 1982, U. Heidelberg, Fed. Republic Germany, 1981 Contbr. articles to profl. jours. Jewish. Home: 1565 Adelia Pl NE Atlanta GA 30329-3805 Office: Emory U Dept Math And Computer Sci Atlanta GA 30322-0001 Business E-Mail: oliker@mathcs.emory.edu.

**OLIM, AUGUST SOUZA,** counselor; b. Honolulu, Aug. 11, 1940; s. Frank Souza and Hilda Lucy (Leong) O; m. Sharon Jean Warren, Dec. 28, 1963; children: Warren Kalani Olim, Tamera Meilani Olim. BA, U. N. Colo., 1958-63; MS, Pepperdine U., 1973-75. Cert. Exceptional Children (Life), Educable Mentally Retarded Gen. Elem. (Life), Pupil Pers. Ryan Adminstrn. Clear, Learning Handicapped. Tchr. Educable Mentally Retarded Centennial Intermediate, Norwalk-LaMirada, Calif., 1963-65, Walton Intermediate, Garden Grove, Calif., 1965-67; tchr. Learning Handicapped Ralston Intermediate, Garden Grove, Calif., 1967-70; tchr. Learning Disability Group Chapman Jr. High Sch., Garden Grove, Calif., 1970-74, 9th grade English tchr., 1974-76, 7th, 8th, 9th grade counselor, 1976-81; project facilitator Clinton Elem. Sch., Garden Grove, Calif., 1981-84; counselor, co-adminstr. Lake Continuation High Sch., Garden Grove, Calif., 1984-95; prin. Cook Elem., Jordan Spl. Edn., Garden Grove, Calif., 1988, Lincoln Adult Edn. Ctr., Garden Grove, Calif., 1992, Chapman Adult Edn., 1995—2000. Pres. Coun. for Exceptional Children, Orange County, Calif., 1976-80; regional dir. Pacific Am. Concerns HEW, Wash., 1977-81; treas. Asian/Pac/Islander Nat. Edn. Assn., Wash., 1977-81; v.p. Very Spl. Arts, So. Calif., 1989-90. Dir. Jr. Miss Pageant Fountain Valley (Calif.) Jaycees, 1970—72; treas., v.p. Fountain Valley Jaycees, 1972—74; state dir. Calif. Jaycees, 1975; dir. Jr. Miss Inc. Dist. Eight Jaycees Orange County, Calif., 1976; sch. bd. Speech Lang. Ctr., Buena Park, 1994—99; bd. Crippled Children Soc. Orange County, 1995—; bd. dirs. Ainahau o Kaleponi Hawaiian Civic Club, 1997—; co-founder Asian Pacific Islander Cultural Heritage Coun., 1999—. Recipient Life Hon. PTA Lampson, Garden Grove, Calif., 1967, Spoke award Fountain Valley (Calif.) Jaycees, 1972; named Outstanding State Dir. Calif. Jaycees, 1976, Outstanding Bd. Mem. Asian Pacific Islander Tchrs., HI, 1979. Mem. Calif. State Fedn. Coun. for Exceptional Children (mem. ethnic and multicultural concerns com.), Garden Grove Pupil Pers. Assn., Very Spl. Arts Calif., Spl. Olympics Beauty Pageant, Minority Affairs Commn. Nat. Edn. Assn., Interagy. for Legis. of Spl. Edn., Phi Delta Kappa. Roman Catholic. Avocations: music, tennis, cooking, gardening. Home: 6609 Sun Ray Dr Denton TX 76208

**OLIN, DAVID LIND,** conservator; b. Washington, D.C., Sept. 12, 1964; s. Charles Hilden and Jacquline Smith Olin. BA in Art History, U. Md., College Park, 1987, MA in Art History, 1991. Assoc. conservator Olin Conservation, Inc., Great Falls, Va., 1983—93, chief conservator, 1993—2005. Dir. Washington Conservation Gild, Washington, 1993—95; cons. U.S. GSA, Washington, 1993—2006; chief mural conservator U.S. Dept. Interior, Penthouse Renovation Project, Washington, 1996—98; conservation assessment reviewer Nat. Heritage Preservation, 1999—; chief murals conservator U.S. Nat. Archives Renovation Project, 2000—03; conservator Gettysburg Cyclorama Conservation, 2003—. Pres. Great Falls Citizen's Assn., 1999—2006, Great Falls Heritage Inc., 1999—2006. Recipient Noland award for Excellence, Mural Conservation and Hist. Preservation, AIA, Va. Soc., 1992, award of Excellence for Exhibit Installation, U.S. Nat. Archives, 2003; grantee, Kress Found. Fellow: Am. Inst. for Conservation; mem.: Internat. Inst. for Conservation (assoc.).

**OLIN, LAURIE DEWAR,** landscape architect, educator; BArch U. Wash., 1961. Lectr. to practice prof. landscape arch., regional planning Univ. Pa., 1976—; chair, landscape arch. dept., grad. sch. design Harvard Univ., 1982—86; prin. Hanna/Olin Ltd. landscape architects, Phila., 1976—96, Olin Partnership, Phila., 1996—. Prin. works include ARCO Hdqs., Newtown Sq., Pa., 1976, Johnson & Johnson Hdqs., Denver, 1977, Canary Wharf, London, 1985, LA County Mus. Art, 1987, Vila Olimpica, Barcelona, Spain, 1991, Nat. Gallery Sculpture Garden, Washington, DC, 1993, Toledo Mus. Art,

---

1995, Independence Nat. Historic Park, Phila., 1997, site design, Washington Monument, 2002. Recipient Bradford Williams medal for writing on landscape architecture, 1991. Fellow: Am. Acad. Arts and Sciences, Am. Soc. Landscape Architects; mem.: AAAL, Am. Inst. Architects (hon. Design medal 2005). Office: Olin Partnership Public Ledger Bldg Ste 1123 150 S Independence Mall W Philadelphia PA 19106 Office Phone: 215-440-0030. Office Fax: 215-440-0041.

**OLIN, LENA MARIA JONNA,** actress; b. Stockholm, Mar. 22, 1956; d. Britta Alice Holmberg; m. Orjan Ramberg (div.), 1 child, August; m. Lasse Hallstrom, Mar. 18, 1994, 1 child, Tora. Actress Royal Dramatic Theatre, Stockholm, Bklyn. Acad. Music; performances include (theater) The Alchemist, Paradisbarnen, Juno and the Peacock, Gross and Klein, Servitore Di Due Padrone, Restoration, King Lear, Nattvarden, Summer, A Dream Play, The Master and Margerita, Miss Julie; (films) The Adventures of Picasso, 1978, Karleken, 1980, Fanny and Alexander, 1982, Grasanklingar, 1982, After the Rehersal, 1984, Friends, 1988, The Unbearable Lightness of Being, 1988, Enemies, A Love Story, 1989, Havana, 1990, Mr. Jones, 1993, Romeo is Bleeding, 1994, The Night and the Moment, 1994, Lumiere et Compagnie, 1995, The Golden Hour, 1996, Polish Wedding, 1997, Hamilton, 1997, Night Falls on Manhattan, 1997, Planet 16, 1998, The Ninth Gate, 1999, Mystery Men, 1999, The Ninth Gate, 2000, Chocolat, 2000, Ignition, 2001, Queen of the Damned, 2002, Darkness, 2002, The United States of Leland, 2003, Hollywood Homicide, 2003, Casanova, 2005, Bang Bang Orangutang, 2005; (TV films) Gypsy Woman, 1977, After the Rehearsal, 1984, Wallenberg: A Hero's Story, 1985, Lady with dog, 1986, Komedianter, 1987, Hebriana, 1990, Hamilton, 2001; (TV series) Alias, 2002-03.*

**OLIN, MARILYN,** secondary school educator; b. Rochester, N.Y. BA in English, Nazareth Coll. Rochester, 1965; MS in English Edn., SUNY, Brockport, 1971. Nat. bd. cert. tchr. 1999. Tchr. Rochester Diocese Cath. Schs., 1965—68, Rochester Pub. Schs., Duval County (Fla.) Pub. Schs., 1972—, Paxon Sch. for Advanced Studies, Jacksonville, Fla., 1996—. Mem.: Nat. Forensic League, Nat. Bd. for Profl. Tchg. Stds. Office: Paxon Sch for Advanced Studies 3239 Norman E Thagard Blvd Jacksonville FL 32254 Office Phone: 904-693-7583 ext 161.

**OLIN, PETER JOEL,** landscape architect, educator; b. Hartford, Conn., Apr. 16, 1938; s. Hilding W. and Ruth A. Olin; m. Bonita E. Olin, June 22, 1977; 1 child, Zubi. BS, Cornell U., 1961; MLA, U. Mass., 1971. Cert. landscape arch. Minn., 1977. Landscape arch., Conn., 1970—74, Mass., 1970—74, Vt., 1970—74; prof., dir. Minn. Landscape Arboretum U. Minn., St. Paul, 1974—. Nat. pres. Coun. Educators in Landscape Arch., 1980—81; pres. Minn. Chpt. Am. Soc. Landscape Archs., St. Paul, Mpls., 1986; cons. in field. Office: Univ Minn Landscape Arboretum 3675 Arboretum Dr Chaska MN 55318 Office Phone: 952-443-1412.

**OLIN, WILLIAM HAROLD,** orthodontist, educator; b. Menominee, Mich., Mar. 7, 1924; s. Harold H. and Lillian (Hallgren) Olin; m. Bertha Spitters, May 6, 1950; children: William Harold, Paul Scott, Jon Edward. DDS, Marquette U., 1947; MS, U. Iowa, 1948. Asst. prof. orthodontics Univ. Hosps., U. Iowa, Iowa City, 1948, assoc. prof., 1963-70, prof., 1970-93, prof. emeritus, 1995—. Chmn. bd. dirs. Hills Bank. Author: (book) Cleft Lip and Palate Rehabilitation, 1960; contbr. articles to profl. jours. Fund raiser, participant Ops. Smile. Served to capt. U.S. Army, 1952—54. Mem.: Am. Acad. Sports Dentistry (bd. dirs., sec./treas. 1989—95), Am. Cleft Palate Assn. (pres. 1970), Iowa Orthodontic Soc. (pres. 1959), Midwest Orthodontic Soc. (pres. 1968—69), Angle Orthodontic Soc. Midwest (pres. 1982), Univ. Athletic Club (bd. dirs.), Rotary (pres. Iowa City). Republican. Methodist. Avocations: collecting political memorabilia, music box collecting, sports, travel, politics, coin collecting/numismatics. Home: 426 Mahaska Dr Iowa City IA 52246-1610 Personal E-mail: w.olin@mchsi.com.

**OLINER, ARTHUR AARON,** physicist, researcher; b. Shanghai, Mar. 5, 1921; s. Saul and Sarah (Schulsohn) O.; m. Frieda Ginsberg, June 16, 1946; children: Marian A., Eric J. BA, Bklyn. Coll., 1941; PhD, Cornell U., 1945; D (hon.), U. Rome, 2003, Polytech. U., 2005. Research assoc. Microwave Research Inst., Polytech. U. (formerly Poly. Inst. Bklyn.), 1946-53, mem. faculty, 1953—, prof. electrophysics, 1957—, head dept., 1966-71; dir. Microwave Research Inst., 1967-82, head dept. elec. engring. and electrophysics, 1971-74. Walker-Ames vis. prof. U. Wash., summer 1964; vis. prof. Cath. U. Rio de Janeiro, Brazil, summer 1973; vis. research scholar Tokyo Inst. Tech., spring 1978; vis. prof. Central China U. Sci. and Tech., Wuhan, spring 1980; vis. prof. U. Rome, fall 1982; tech. cons. to industry; dir. Merrimac Industries, West Caldwell, N.J.; chmn. adv. panel Nat. Bur. Standards, 1960-64. Contbg. author: Microwave Scanning Antennas, 1966; contbr. numerous articles to profl. jours.; mem. editorial bd.: Advances in Microwaves, 1966-73, Electronics Letters, 1969-75; co-editor: Phased Array Antennas, 1972; editor, contbg. author: Acoustic Surface Waves, 1978; co-editor, contbg. author: History of Wireless, 2005. Guggenheim fellow Ecole Normale Superieure, Paris, 1965-66; recipient Instn. premiem Instn. Elec. Engrs., London, 1963; citation for disting. rsch. Sigma Xi, 1974; honoree Spl. Session at Internat. Microwave Symposium, 1988. Fellow IEEE (Microwave prize 1967, Microwave Career award 1982, Centennial medal 1984, Disting. Educator award 1993, Heinrich Hertz Gold medal 2000, Millennium medal 2000), AAAS, Brit. Instn. Elec. Engrs.; mem. NAE, IEEE Microwave Theory and Techniques Soc. (hon. life, pres. 1959-60, nat. lectr. 1967, mem. publs. bd. 1971-74), Internat. Union Radio Sci. (mem. commn. B 1955—, chmn. U.S. commn. A 1959-62, co-chmn. U.S. commn. D 1983-88, mem. U.S. nat. com. 1985—, Van der Pol Gold medal 1990), Am. Phys. Soc., Optical Soc. Am. Home and Office: 11 Dawes Rd Lexington MA 02421-5926 E-mail: aao@merrimacind.com.

**OLINGER, ANGELA MARIE,** adult education educator; b. Eugene, Oreg., Nov. 14, 1965; d. Theodore Michael Colombo and Jean Annette Eyman; m. Jon Dru Olinger, June 29, 2003; children: Benjamin Michael Goff, Nicholas Keith Goff, Emily Rebecca Goff. AA, Ohio State U., 1994. Chemical Operations Specialist US Army Chem. Sch., 1986, Light Fighter Rite of Passage US Army, 7th Inf. Divsn. (Light), 1987, Basic Military Fire Suppression Nat. Wildlife Coordinating Group, 1994, Primary Leadership Development US Army, Pacific, 1996. Chem. ops. specialist U.S. Army, Ft. Ord, Calif., 1986—88; nuc. biol. chem. specialist Ohio Army N.G., Columbus, 1988—94; decontamination/bn. ops. U.S. Army, Ft. Riley, Kans., 1994—96, nuc. biol. chem. specialist Schofield Barracks, Hawaii, 1996—99, Ft. Lewis, 1998—99; instr. Madison Adult Edn., Mansfield, Ohio, 2002—. Author: (instructors manual) Civilian Nuclear Biological Chemical Protection Against Weapons of Mass Destruction. Sec. Vet. Connection, Akron, Ohio, 2000—01; vice pres./founder Colombo & Assoc. Emergency Preparedness and Safety Tng., Ashland, Ohio, 2002—05. Sgt/e-5 US Army, 1986—99, United States. Decorated Army Achievement medal U.S. Army, Army Commendation medal Ohio Army N.G., Nat. Svc. Def. medal, Humanitarian Svc. medal U.S. Army Force Command Mem.: Chem. Corp Rgt. (life). Achievements include U.S. Army expert qualifications M16A2 rifle. Avocations: diamond grading, gardening, reading. Office: Madison Adult Education 600 Esley Lane Mansfield OH 44905 Home: 4363 S Smith River Rd Reedsport OR 97467 Office Phone: 541-271-0882. Personal E-mail: angieolinger4@aol.com.

**OLINGER, CARLA D(RAGAN),** medical advertising executive; b. Cin., Oct. 8, 1947; d. Carl Edward and Selene Ethel (Neal) Dragan; m. Chauncey Greene Olinger, Jr., May 30, 1981. BA, Douglass Coll., 1975. Mgr. info. retrieval services Frank J. Corbett, Inc., N.Y.C., 1976—77; editor, proofreader, prodn. asst. Rolf W. Rosenthal, Inc., N.Y.C., 1977—78, copywriter, 1978—80, copy supr., 1980—82, v.p. copy dept., 1982—83; v.p., group copy supr., adminstrv. copy supr. Rolf W. Rosenthal, Inc., divsn. Ogilvy & Mather, 1984—89; v.p., assoc. creative dir. RWR Advt., 1989—; copy supr. Barnum & Souza, N.Y.C., 1990—92, Botto, Roessner, Horne & Messinger, Ketchum Comm., N.Y.C., 1992—95, Lyons Lavey Nickel Swift, N.Y.C., 1995—

Editor: Antimicrobial Prescribing (Harold Neu), 1979. Mem.: Nat. Inst. Social Scis., St. George's Soc. N.Y., Church Club N.Y. Office: Lyons Lavey Nickel Swift 220 E 42nd St New York NY 10017-5806

**OLINGER, CHAUNCEY GREENE, JR.,** investment company executive, editorial consultant; b. Long Beach, Calif., Jan. 16, 1933; s. Chauncey Greene and Cora Blount (Urquhart) O.; m. Carla R. Dragan, May 30, 1981. BA in Philosophy with honors, U. Va., Charlottesville, 1955; MA, Columbia U., NY, 1971. Cert. fin. planner Cert. Fin. Planning Bd. Standards. Coadjutant in philosophy Rutgers U., New Brunswick, NJ, 1968—72; rep. NY World Federalists, USA, NYC, 1970; dir. subcom. U.S. sec. of state adv. com. Dept. of State, Washington, 1972; editl. cons. Columbia U., NYC, 1973—82; editor, pres. Met. Rsch. Co., NYC, 1982—91; investment exec. First Albany, NYC, 1991—92, Janney Montgomery Scott LLC, NYC, 1992—. Sec. univ. seminar Columbia U., NYC, 1968—72, mem. increase corp. philanthropic giving com., 1980—83, founder, co-chmn. u. seminar, 1998—2004, chmn. u. seminar, 2005—. Editor: World Enough (Margaret Mead and Ken Heyman), 1975, A Celebration of Thanksgiving For the Life of I. I. Rabi, 1991, Columbia and the City: The University's Commitment to New York City, 1993, Courtney C. Brown: In Memory, 1995; author: New York City: An Economic Resource Profile, 1989, The I.I. Rabi Memorial Room, 1996. Pres. Fellowship of Young Churchmen, Episcopal Diocese of So. Va., 1950-52; trustee Cathedral Ch. St. John the Divine, 1988; nat. chmn. Coalition to Stop SST Environmental Damage, NY, 1975-78; pub. mem. human rights in rsch. com. NY Hosp.-Cornell Med. Ctr., 1975-80; pres. grad. faculty alumni Columbia U., NY, 1977-81, pres. student coun.Columbia U., NY 1963-64; bd. dirs. Bar Harbor (Maine) Festival, 1969-74, Bloomingdale House of Music, NYC, 1976 81. Lt. (j.g.) USN, 1955—58. Recipient Conspicuous Alumni Svc. medal Columbia U., 1980, Svc., Loyalty and Dedication award Grad. Faculty Alumni of Columbia U., 1988. Mem. Am. Philos. Assn., Nat. Inst. Social Scis. (dir. 1988-92, 2005—, pres. 2006-), Fin. Planning Assn., Pilgrims of the US, Am. Soc. Most Venerable Order of Hosp. of St. John of Jerusalem, St. Andrew's Soc. of the State of NY (sec. 1991-95), St. George's Soc. NY, Century Assn., Emeritus Profs. in Columbia (assoc.), The Ch. Club of NY (v.p. 1985-86, 88-89, 96-97, pres. 1997-2000, trustee 1983-89, 93-2000, 2001-24), Laymen's Club of the Cathedral of St. John the Divine (pres. 1988, gov. 1982—, 1st v.p. 2004—06), Ft. Ticonderoga Assn. Episcopalian. Avocations: reading, writing, walking, theater, ballet, sculpture. Office: Janney Montgomery Scott LLC 575 Lexington Ave New York NY 10022-6102

**OLINS, ROBERT ABBOT,** communications research executive; b. Cambridge, Mass., Sept. 25, 1942; s. Harry and Janice Olins; m. Irma Westrich, June 16, 1967; 1 son, Matthew Abbot. Student, Hobart Coll., 1961-62, San Francisco Art Inst., 1962; BA, U. Mass., 1967; postgrad., U. Tampa, 1968; MA, U. Mo., 1969, PhD, 1972. With Marstellar, 1972, N.W. Ayer, 1972, Post, Keys & Gardner, Chgo., 1973, Young & Rubicam, Chgo., 1973-76, mng. dir. comm. rsch. divsn., 1976-77; pres., CEO subs. Comm. Rsch. Inc., Chgo., 1978—, owner, chmn., 1979—. Pres., CEO Insights, Chgo., 1976—; assoc. prof. Howard Univ., 2004— Contbr. articles to profl. jours. Recipient Chgo./4 award for creative excellence, 1974; winner Chgo. Mackinac race, 1981; Am. Assn. Advt. Agys. grantee, 1968-71 Mem.: Mid North Assn. (bd. dirs., chmn. planning), Am. Mktg. Assn., Chgo. Yacht Club, Lake Mich. Yachting Assn., U.S. Sailing Club, Skyline Club. Avocations: skiing, sailing, power boating. Office Phone: 202-806-5119. Business E-Mail: rolins@howard.edu.

**OLIPHANT, CHARLES ROMIG,** retired physician; b. Waukegan, Ill., Sept. 10, 1917; s. Charles L. and Mary (Goss) R.; m. Claire E. Canavan, Nov. 7, 1942; children: James R., Cathy Rose, Mary G., William D. Student, St. Louis U., 1936-40, MD, 1943; postgrad., Naval Med. Sch., 1946. Intern Nat. Naval Med. Ctr., Bethesda, Md., 1943; pvt. practice medicine and surgery San Diego, 1947-99; ret., 1999. Bd. dirs. Midway Med. Enterprises; former chief staff Balboa Hosp., Doctors Hosp., Cabrillo Med. Ctr.; chief staff emeritus Sharp Cabrillo Hosp.; mem. staff Mercy Hosp., Children's Hosp., Paradise Valley Hosp., Sharp Meml. Hosp.; sec. Sharp Sr. Health Care, S.D., 1985-98; mem. exec. bd., program chmn. San Diego Power Squadron, 1985-95; charter mem. Am. Bd. Family Practice. Served with M.C., USN, 1943-47. Recipient Golden Staff award Sharp Cabrillo Hosp. Med. Staff, 1990; inducted into Wisdom Hall of Fame, 2003. Fellow Am. Geriatric Soc. (emeritus), Am. Acad. Family Practice, Am. Assn. Abdominal Surgeons; mem. AMA, Calif. Med. Assn., Am. Acad. Family Physicians (past pres. San Diego chpt., del. Calif. chpt.), San Diego Med. Soc., Pub. Health League, Navy League, San Diego Power Squadron (past comdr.), SAR, San Diego Yacht Club, Douglas County Scottish Soc. Home: Riverview Terr Unit # 109 1970 W Harvard Ave Roseburg OR 97470-2746

**OLIPHANT, PATRICK,** cartoonist; b. Adelaide, Australia, July 24, 1935; came to U.S., 1964; children: Laura, Grant, Susan. L.H.D. (hon.), Dartmouth Coll., 1981. Copyboy, press artist Adelaide Advertiser, 1953-55, editorial cartoonist, 1955-64; world tour to study cartooning techniques, 1959; editorial cartoonist Denver Post, 1964-75, Washington Star, 1975-81, L.A. Times Syndicate, 1965-80, Universal Press Syndicate, 1980—; represented by Susan Conway Gallery, Washington. Author: The Oliphant Book, 1969, Four More Years, 1973, An Informal Gathering, 1978, Oliphant! A Cartoon Collection, 1980, The Jellybean Society, 1981, Ban this Book, 1982, But Seriously Folks, 1983, The Year of Living Perilously, 1984, Make My Day, 1985, Between a Rock and a Hard Place, 1986, Up to There in Alligators, 1987, Nothing Basically Wrong, 1988, What Those People Need Is a Puppy, 1989, Fashions for the New World Order, 1991, Just Say No, 1992, Why do I Feel Uneasy?, 1993, Waiting for the Other Shoe to Drop, 1994, Off to the Revolution, 1995, Maintain The Status Quo, 1996, So That Where They Come From, 1997, Oliphant's Anthem, 1998, Are We There Yet?, 1999 Now We'll Have to Spray for Politicians, 2000, When We Can't See the Forest for the Bushes, 2001. Recipient 2d Place award as funniest cartoonist Internat. Fedn. Free Journalists in Fleet St., London, 1958, Profl. Journalism award Sigma Delta Chi, 1966, Pulitzer prize for editl. cartooning, 1967, Cartoonist of Yr. award Nat. Cartoonist Soc., 1968, 72, Best in Bus. award Washington Journalism Rev., 1985, 87, Premio Satira Politica award Forte de Marmi, 1992, Thomas Nast award, 1992. Office: Universal Press Syndicate 4520 Main St Ste 700 Kansas City MO 64111-7701

**OLIPHANT, URETZ JOHN,** physician, surgeon; b. Chgo., May 9, 1953; s. John and Letha (Fryson) O.; m. Mercidita DeJesus, Jan. 11, 1985; children: Michael, Jonathan, Kathryn. AB, Boston U., 1976; MD, U. Minn., 1983. Diplomate Am. Bd. Surgery. Fellow in trauma/critical care Ill. Masonic Hosp./U. Ill., Chgo., 1991-92; attending surgeon Carle Found. Hosp., Urbana, Ill., 1992—, head divsn. trauma, 1995—; clin. assoc. prof. dept. surgery U. Ill. Coll. Medicine, Urbana, 1994—, head dept. surgery, 1996—. Chmn. bd. dirs. Frances Nelson Cmty. Health Ctr., urbana, 1994—; chmn. Region 6 Trauma Com., Urbana, 1995-97. Founding mem. Nat. Safe Kids, Champaign, Ill., 1995—. Recipient Golden Apple Tchg. award U. Ill. Coll. Medicine, 1994, 95, 97, 99. Fellow ACS, Internat. Coll. Surgeons. Avocations: chess, basketball. Office: Carle Found Hosp 602 W University Ave Urbana IL 61801-2530 Office Phone: 217-383-3204. Business E-Mail: uretz.oliphant@carle.com.

**OLISA, NZEDEGWU ROBERT, III,** information technology executive, manufacturing executive; b. Onitsha, Nigeria, Aug. 5, 1967; arrived in US, 1971; s. Emeka Geoffrey and Ifey Stella Olisa. BSc, U. Jos, Nigeria, 1990; MS, U. Tex., 1996, MPA, 2006. Bd. cert. Am. Soc. Clin. Pathologists, 1996, Am. Acad. Microbiologists, 1999. Founder, CEO Biol. Apts. Corp., El Paso, Tex., 1998—. Guest scholar U. Tuebingen, Germany, 2002—04. Lt. comdr. USN, 2005. NIH Minority Biomed. Rsch. scholar, Howard U., 1998—2002. Conservative. Roman Catholic. Achievements include copyrights from US library of congress for electronic mail evaluation system for infectious disease surveillance; patents pending for braunmycris (olsiferol), a broad spectrum antimicrobial vaccine. Avocations: software development, jogging, travel. Home: Pmb 507 West University Ave El Paso TX 79968 Office: 7362 RemconCir #36 El Paso TX 79912 Personal E-Mail: nrolisa@olisa.org.

**OLITSKI, JULES,** artist; b. Snovsk, USSR, Mar. 27, 1922; came to U.S., 1923, naturalized, 1943; s. Jevel and Anna (Zarnitsky) Demikovsky; m. Gladys Katz, 1944 (div. 1951); 1 dau., Eve; m. Andrea Hill Pearce, Jan. 21, 1956 (div. 1974); 1 dau., Lauren; m. Kristina Gorby, Feb. 29, 1980. Postgrad., Nat. Acad. Design, NYC, 1939-42, Beaux Arts Inst., 1940-42, Ednl. Alliance, N.Y.C., 1947; student, Academie de la Grande Chaumiere, Paris, 1949-50; postgrad., Ossip Zadkine Sch. Sculpture, Paris, 1949; BA, NYU, 1952, MA, 1954; ArtsD (hon.), U. Hartford, CT, 1997, U New Hampshire, NH, 1998. Assoc. prof. art SUNY, New Paltz, NY, 1954-55; curator Art Ede. Gallery, NYU, 1955-56; chmn. fine arts div. C.W. Post Coll. L.I.U., Greenvale, NY, 1956-63; tchr. Bennington Coll., 1963-67. Exhibited in many one-man shows including Galerie Huit, Paris, 1951, Iolas Gallery, N.Y.C., 1958, French & Co., N.Y.C., 1959-61, Poindexter Gallery, N.Y.C., 1961-68, Bennington (Vt.) Coll., 1962, Kasmin, Ltd., London, 1964-75, 89, Galerie Lawrence, Paris, 1964, David Mirvish Gallery, Toronto, Ont., Can., 1964-78, Nicholas Wilder, L.A., 1966, Corcoran Gallery, Washington, 1967, 74, Am. Pavillion, Venice Biennale Art Exhbn., 1966, 88, Andre Emmerich Gallery, N.Y.C., 1966-96, Zurich, Switzerland, 1973-78, Met. Mus. Art, N.Y.C., 1969, Inst. Contemporary Art, U. Pa., 1968, 86, Lawrence Rubin Gallery, N.Y.C., 1969, 71, 72, 73, Knoedler Contemporary Art, 1973-77, 79, 81, 83, 85, 87, Dart Gallery, Chgo., 1975, FIAL, Paris, 1976, Berlinische Galerie, 1977, Downstairs Gallery, Edmonton, Can., 1980, 82, Janus Gallery, L.A., 1981, Gallery One, Toronto, 1980-90, Yares Gallery, Scottsdale, Ariz., 1986-89, Galerie Wentzel, Hamburg and Cologne, Fed. Republic Germany, 1975, 77, 81, 89, Mus. Fine Arts, Boston, 1973, 77, Whitney Mus. Am. Art, 1973, Galleria Dell'Ariete, Italy, 1974, Corcoran Gallery Art, 1974-76, Waddington Gallery, London, 1975, Galerie Templon, Paris, 1984-85, Hirshhorn Mus., Washington, 1977, Edmonton (Alta., Can.) Art Gallery, 1979, Martha White Gallery, Louisville, 1982, Harcus/Krakow Gallery, Boston, 1978, 81, 82, Harcus Gallery, Boston, 1984, 86, Meredith Long, Houston, 1981, 82, 87, 90, (retrospective) Fondation du Chateau de Jau, Perpignon, France, 1984, La Musee de Valence, France, 1985, Hokin Gallery, Palm Beach, Fla., 1988, Associated Am. Artists, N.Y.C., 1989, (retrospective) Buschlen/Mowatt Gallery, Vancouver, B.C., Can., 1990, Salander-O'Reilly Galleries, N.Y.C., 1990, 92, 94, Gallery Camino Real, Boca Raton, Fla., 1987, 88, 90, 92, 94, 95, 96, 97, Thorne-Sagendorph Art Gallery, Keene, N.H., 1993, 96, 99, Long Fine Arts, N.Y.C., 1994, 95, 97, 98, 99, U. Miami, Coral Gables, Fla., 1994, C.S. Schulte Gallery, Milburn, N.J., 1995, 97, Drabinsky Friedland Gallery, Naples, Fla., and Toronto, 1996, 97, 99, Dorthy Blau Gallery, Bay Harbor Island, Fla., 1996, 97, 2001, Hodecker Gallery, Waterville Valley, NH, 1997, Belknap Mills, Laconia, NH, 1997, Butler Institute, Youngstown, OH, 1997, 2000, Portland Museum, ME, 1998, Grimaldis Gallery, Baltimore, MD, 1998, Virginia Lynch Gallery, Tiverton, RI, 1998, 99, 2000, 2001, Gould Academy, Bethel, ME, 1998, Bernard Jacobsen Gallery, London (Paintings 1965-75), 1999, Marianne Friedland Gallery, Naples, Fla., 1999, 2000, 02 Galeria Metta, Madrid, 1999, Mary McGowan Fine Art, Concord, NH, 1999, Philharmonic Center for the Arts, Naples, FL, 1999, Annandale Galleries, Sydney, Australia, 2000, 2002, Charles Nodrum Gallery, Melbourne, 2000, The Butler Institute of American Art, Youngstown, OH, 2000, Ameringer-Howard Gallery, N.Y.C., 2000, Bunnington Gallery Notthingham Trent U., UK, 2001, Ameringer-Howard Fine Art, Boca Raton, FL, 2001, The Seventies: Painting and Sculpture, Paul Kasmin Gallery, 2006; exhibited in many group shows including Carnegie Internat., Pitts., 1961, 1965, Washington Gallery Modern Art, 1963, Los Angeles County Mus., 1964, Fogg Art Mus. Harvard, 1965, Pasadena Art Mus., 1965, Mus. Basel, Switzerland, 1965, 74, Whitney Mus. Am. Art, 1972, 73, Musée d'Art Contemporain, Montreal, 1973, Hirshhorn Mus., 1974, Corcoran Gallery Art, 1975, Everson Mus. Art, Syracuse, N.Y., 1976, Bass Mus., Miami, Am. Embassy, Madrid, 1984, Ft. Worth Art Mus., Mus. Art, Ft. Lauderdale, 1986, Joseloff Gallery, Hartford, Conn., 1994, Galerie Piltzer, Paris, 1994, N.Y. Studio Sch., N.Y., 1996, Andre Emmerich Gallery, N.Y.C., 1997, 1998, Suzanne Lemberg Usdan Gallery, Bennington College, VT, 1998, Yares Gallery, Scottsdale, Ariz., 1998, Mus. Fine Arts, Boston, 2000, Portland Mus., Oreg., 2001; represented in permanent collections including Mus. Modern Art, N.Y.C., Art Inst. Chgo., Whitney Mus., Corcoran Art Gallery, Nat. Gallery Can., Met. Mus. Art, N.Y.C., Bklyn. Mus., Hirshhorn Mus., Washington, Everson Mus. Art, Syracuse, N.Y., Mus. Fine Arts, Boston, Norman MacKensie Art Gallery, Regina, Can., Portland Mus., Oreg.;also pvt. collections; subject book Jules Olitski by Kenworth Moffett, 1981, Nat. Acad. Design, N.Y., 1993, illustrator of limited edition book, Small Mountains (with W.D. Wetherell), 2000. Recipient 2d prize Carnegie Internat. 1961, 1st prize Corcoran Biennial, Washington, 1967, Award for Distinction in the Arts Univ Union, U. S.C., 1975, The Milton and Sally Avery Disting. Professorship, Bard Coll., 1987; named Assoc. Nat. Academician Nat. Acad. of Design, 1993, named Distinguished Artist, Arkansas Celebration of the Arts, Hot Springs, Arkansas, 1996. Fellow AAAS, Nat. Acad. Arts and Scis. E-mail: jolitski@sover.net.*

**OLIVA, LAWRENCE JAY,** retired academic administrator, history professor; b. Walden, N.Y., Sept. 23, 1933; s. Lawrence Joseph and Catherine (Mooney) Oliva; m. Mary Ellen Nolan, June 3, 1961; children: Lawrence Jay, Edward Nolan. BA, Manhattan Coll., 1955; MA, Syracuse U., 1957, PhD, 1960; postgrad., U. Paris, 1959; DHL (hon.), Manhattan Coll., 1987; LLD (hon.), St. Thomas Aquinas Coll., 1988; DHL (hon.), Hebrew Union Coll., 1992; DLitt, Univ. Coll., Dublin, 1993; PhD, Tel Aviv U., 1994. Prof. history NYU, 1991—, assoc. dean, 1969—70, vice dean, 1970—71, dean faculty, 1971—72, dep. vice chancellor, 1970—75, v.p. acad. planning and services, 1975—77, v.p. acad. affairs, 1977—80, provost, exec. v.p. acad. affairs, 1980—83, chancellor, exec. v.p., 1983—91, pres., 1991—2002, pres. emeritus, 2002—. Author: Misalliance: A Study of French Policy in Russia during the Seven Years' War, 1964, Russia in the Era of Peter the Great, 1969; editor: Russia and the West from Peter to Kruschev, 1965, Peter the Great, 1970, Catherine the Great, 1971; contbr. articles to profl. jours. Trustee Inst. Internat. Edn., active Outrach Found., UN Assn. of N.Y. Adv. Coun., N.Y.C. Partnership, Assn. for Better N.Y., Am. Mus. Immigration; adv. bd. U. Athletic Assn.; bd. dirs. Chatham House, Royal Inst. Internat. Affairs, Am. Bd. Dirs. Coun. for U.S. and Italy Nat. Collegiate Athletic Assn., Pres.'s Commn.; adv. bd. Pres.'s Coun.; bd. dirs. N.Y. State Commn. on Nat. and Cmty. Svc. Recipient Medal of Sorbonne, U. Paris, 1992, Man. in Edn. award, Italian Welfare League, medal of honor, Ellis Island; fellow Fribourg fellow, 1959. Mem.: Irish-Am. Cultural Inst., Assn. Colls. and Univs. of State of N.Y., Am. Coun. Edn., Soc. Fellows NYU, Phi Gamma Delta, Phi Beta Kappa. Home: 33 Washington Sq W New York NY 10011-9154 Office: 60 Wash Square S 503 New York NY 10012

**OLIVA, MARICELA,** education educator; b. Weslaco, Tex., May 17, 1957; d. Jose Espiridion and Constancia (Garcia) O. BA, Yale U., 1980; MA, U. Houston, 1987; PhD, 1997. Dept. administr. U. Houston, 1985-90; program dir., asst. to commr., gender equity liaison Tex. Higher Edn. Coord. Bd., Austin, 1990-96; Dorothy Danforth Compton fellow U. Tex., Austin, 1996-97, asst. prof. El Paso, 1997—. Adv. bd. WICHE U.S. Mex. Ednl. Interchange Project, Denver, 1993-95. Cert. mediator Travis County Dispute Resolution Ctr., Austin, 1992-93; citizen's adv. panelist Congl. Office Tex. Dist. 16, El Paso, 1998—; faculty ptnr. Riverside H.S., El Paso, 1998—. Grantee Inst. Ednl. Renewal, Seattle, 1998—. Mem. Am. Ednl. Rsch. Assn., Assn. Study Higher Edn., Tex. Assn. Chicanos in Higher Assn. (legis. chair, sec. bd. dirs. 1993-95), Higher Edn. Adminstrn. Student Assn. Democrat. Avocations: music, arts. Home: PO Box 1394 Donna TX 78537-1394 Office: U Tex El Paso Dept Ednl Leadership 501 Educ El Paso TX 79968-0001

**OLIVARES-CUHAT, GABRIELA ANTONIA,** literature and language professor; b. Santiago, Chile, Apr. 2, 1968; d. Manuel Antonio Olivares and Rosa Ester Menchaca; m. Daniel R. Cuhat, May 23, 1998; children: Antoine Cuhat, Pascal Cuhat. BA in English Secondary Edn., Cath. U., 1990; MA in Liberal Arts, Purdue U., 1994, PhD in Liberal Arts, 1998. Tchr. high sch. English Colegio del Sagrado Corazon, Santiago, Region Metropolitana, 1990—90; tchg. asst. Spanish Purdue U., West Lafayette, Ind., 1992—98; asst. prof. Spanish Aquinas Coll., Grand Rapids, Mich., 1998—99, Cleve. State U., 1999—2004; tchr. Spanish, adv. Maquoketa (Iowa) H.S., 2005—06. Co-chair elect presdl. com. on the role and status of women Cleve. State U., 2003—, summer resident dir. study abroad program, 2002—03; grad. faculty

rev. com., 2003—04, student life com. mem., 2002—03, undergraduate advisor for spanish, 2001—03; Spanish immersion specialist Our Lady Guadalupe, Dubuque, Iowa, 2003—04; Spanish instr. N.E. Iowa CC, 2006—. Contbr. articles to profl. jours. Organizer ann. hispanic cmty. forums Cleve. State U., 2001—03; prin. investigator Cleve. Mcpl. Sch. Dist. and Cleve. State U., 2001—03. Recipient Walter J. Johnson award, Purdue U., 1997; grantee, Ctr. Tchg. and Learning, Cleve. State U., 2000, Ctr. Urban Child and Sch. Collaboration and Martha Holden Jennings, 2002, Purdue Rsch. Found., 1996—98; scholar, Am. Assn. Teachers Spanish and Portuguese, 2002. Mem.: Am. Assn. Tchrs. Spanish and Portuguese, Phi Kappa Phi, Delta Sigma Pi. Home: 1308 Danish Dr Cedar Falls IA 50613 Personal E-mail: niccspan@yahoo.com. Business E-mail: olivareg@nicc.edu, gabriela.olivares@uni.edu.

**OLIVE, DAVID MICHAEL,** journalist, editor; b. Toronto, Ont., Can., Nov. 9, 1957; s. Harold Leslie and Alison Linton (Black) O.; m. Margaret Anne O'Reilly, Feb. 13, 1982 (div. June 1992). B of Applied Arts in Journalism, Ryerson Polytech. U., 1979. Copy editor Toronto Life Mag., 1979-81; assoc. editor Can. Bus. Mag., Toronto, 1981-84; sr. writer Report on Bus. Mag., Toronto, 1984-87, Toronto Life Mag., 1988-90; editorial writer The Globe and Mail, Toronto, 1990-91, current affairs columnist, 1991-92, bus. ethics columnist, 1996-98; editor Report on Bus. Mag., 1991-97, sr. writer, 1997-98, Fin. Post, 1998, Nat. Post, Toronto, 1998—2001; bus. columnist Toronto Star, 2001—. Dir. Can. Ctr. for Ethics and Corp. Policy, 1988-91, Jessie's Ctr. for Teenagers, 1994—; pres. Jessie's Ctr. Non-Profit Homes Corp., 1994—; pres. Nat. Mag. Awards Found., 1988-90. Author: Just Rewards: The Case for Ethical Reform in Business, 1987, White Knights and Poison Pills: A Cynic's Dictionary of Business Jargon, 1990, Political Babble: The 1,000 Dumbest Things Ever Said by Politicians, 1992, Gender Babble: The Dumbest Things Men Ever Said About Women, 1993, Canadian Political Babble: A Cynic's Dictionary of Political Jargon, 1993, More Political Babble: The Dumbest Things Ever Said by Politicians, 1996, Canada Inside Out: How We See Ourselves, How Others See Us, 1996, No Guts, No Glory: How Canada's Greatest CEOs Built Their Empires, 2000, A Devil's Dictionary of Business Jargon, 2001, The Quotable Tycoon: A Treasury of Business Quotations, 2002. Recipient Silver, Nat. Mag. awards, 1987, Gold, 1988, hon. mention, 1983, 1985, 1987, 1989, 1996, Nat. Bus. Book awards, 2001, Nat. Newspaper awards, 2005. Mem. Can. Soc. Mag. Editors, Ethics Practitioners Assn. Can.

**OLIVE, KARL WILLIAM,** elementary education educator, secondary educator; b. Colorado Springs, Colo., Feb. 18, 1969; s. Kermit Floyd and Betty Jean (Anderson) O. BA in Studio Art, Centre Coll., Danville, Ky., 1991; MA in Art Edn., Western K. U., 1993; MA in Ceramics, U. Louisville, 2001. Studio glassblowing asst to Stephen Powell Centre Coll., 1990-91; art tchr., track coach Ft. Knox (Ky.) Cmty. Schs., 1991—. Elem. art edn. instr. Western Ky. U., 1995-99. Recipient Class A Coach of the Yr. in Track and Field, 2003. Republican. Methodist. Avocations: sports, stock market, ceramics. Office: Fort Knox H S Bldg 7501 Fort Knox KY 40121

**OLIVEIRA, CARLOS,** engineering educator; b. Fortaleza, Ceara, Brazil, Nov. 22, 1975; s. Raimundo Erialdo Silva and Maria Oliveira; m. Juliana Oliveira. PhD, U. of Fla., Gainesville, 2004. Asst. prof. Okla. State U., Stillwater, 2004—. Contbr. articles to profl. jours. Mem.: INFORMS. Office: Oklahoma State University 322 Engineering N Stillwater OK 74078

**OLIVER, AMIE,** artist, educator; b. Vaiden, Miss., Mar. 14, 1960; d. William Randolph III and Mable Sue (Vowell) O.; m. Harry Kollatz, Jr., June 20, 1996. BA, Miss. State U., 1982; MFA, Bowling Green State U., 1984. Tchg. asst. Bowling Green (Ohio) State U., 1982-84; assoc. prof. art Longwood Coll., Farmville, Va., 1986-97, Miss. State U., 1997—98. Summer faculty Tyler Sch. Art, Temple U., Phila., 1990, 92, 2000; adj. prof. U. Commonwealth U., 2001—; faculty Studio Sch. of the Va. Mus. Fine Art, 1998—; juror Scholastic Art Awards, Richmond, Va., 1994—; bd. dirs. 1708 Gallery, Richmond; resident, exhibiting artist Cité des Arts Internationale, 1994, 2004, 2006, Va. Ctr. for Creative Arts, 2000, 04, Oberpfalzerkunsterhaus, Germany, 2001. Art dir. (catalogues) Making a Mark, 1995, Artists of the Cite Internationale Des Arts, 1996, Gala 96, 1996; one-woman shows include The Painting Ctr., 2005, 06contbg. artist Soho 20, N.Y.C., Contemporary Art Ctr. of Va., Longwood Ctr. for the Visual Arts, Artists for Life, Richmond, 1988, Heart of Virginia, Farmville, Va., 1986-90, Visual Arts Ctr., Portsmouth, Va.; represented in permanent collections Va. Ctr. for Creative Arts, Longwood U., Rose Bower Vineyards, Thelonious Monk Jazz Inst., Med. Coll. Va. Named One of 8 Rising Art Stars WRIC-TV, 1996. Avocations: swimming, hiking, travel, reading, bicycle touring. Office: Va Commonwealth U PO Box 943062 927 W Franklin St Richmond VA 23284

**OLIVER, ANN BREEDING,** secondary school educator, art dealer; b. Hollywood, Fla., Sept. 21, 1945; d. Harvey James and Ruth (Lige) Breeding; 1 child, Anna Liege; m. Ted J. Oliver, June 29, 1996. BA in Fgn. Lang., U. Ky., 1967; MA in History of Art, Ohio State U., 1971. Curatorial intern Lowe Art Mus., Coral Gables, Fla., 1972; adj. faculty Fla. Atlantic U., Boca Raton, Fla., 1972-73, 78; lectr. Miami (Fla.) Dade C.C., 1974, with art-music workshop, 1980-81, lectr.-cons., 1972—, adj. faculty music dept., 1991; curator of edn. Ctr. for the Fine Arts, Miami, 1987-92, High Mus. of Art, Atlanta, Ga., 1992-96; Spanish tchr. Sprayberry H.S., Cobb County Bd. Edn., Marietta, Ga., 1997—. Mem. Artists in Edn. Panel, Ga. Coun. for Arts, 1994; field reviewer Inst. Mus. Svcs., 1994; adj. faculty in art history Kennesaw State U., Marietta, Ga., 1996—; Spanish tchr. Cobb County Bd. Edn., Atlanta, Spray H.S., Marietta, Ga; collector, dealer, historial so. folk art & outsider culture. Contbg. editor African Art: An Essay for Teachers, 1993; project mgr. and contbg. author: Rings, Five Passions in World Art: Multicultural Curriculum Handbook, 1996. Mem. Cobb County Com. for Fgn. Lang. Curriculum Alignment. Recipient Nat. award for graphics Mead Paper Co., 1989, Gold Medal of Honor publication design S.E. Mus. Educators Publ. Design, 1994. Mem. Am. Assn. of Mus., Inst. Mus. Svcs., Nat. Art Edn. Assn., Am. Coun. Tchrs. Fgn. Langs., Fla. Art Edn. Assn. (dir. mus. divsn.), Ga. Art Edn. Assn. (dir. mus. divsn., Mus. Educator of Yr. 1993), Fgn. Lang. Assn. of Ga. Home: PO Box 1032 Flat Rock NC 28731 Personal E-mail: oliverta@bellsouth.net.

**OLIVER, BRUCE LAWRENCE,** retired information systems educator; b. Westfield, Mass., Nov. 20, 1951; s. Ernest Lawrence and Elizabeth (Welchek) O. AS, Greater Hartford C.C., 1972; BS, U. Mass., 1974; MBA, U. Hartford, 1989. Cert. tchr. sec. and vocat. edn., Mass., Conn.; cert. asset protection and fin. privacy cons. Commit. sales Gordon Realty, Enfield, Conn., 1972—75; forestry tech. rsch. Dept. Environ. Protection State of Conn., Hartford, 1973—74; res. sales Forsman Realty, Enfield, 1975—77; substitute secondary tchr. Enfield Sch. Sys., 1975—78; collections mgr. New Eng. Bank & Trust, Enfield, 1978—79; ops. CCEC/McCullahg Leasing, Inc., S. Windsor, Conn., 1979—81; pres. Ollie & Ike's, Inc., Enfield, 1985—86; MBA Adj. U. Hartford, West Hartford, Conn., 1988—89; workstation engr. Travelers, Hartford, 1982—89; ret., 1989. V.p. 1st Class Expert Sys., Inc., Wayland, Mass., 1989—90, Microsoft Corp., Boston, 1991—94; cons., pres. Profl. Office Solutions, Enfield, 1994—2004; pres. New Venture Inc, Enfield, 1994—2004; owner nvi:Ednl. Multimedia Group, nvi: Webmaster Internet Devel.; del. leader Comparative Studies Assn., Internat. Cultural Exch. with China, Washington; pub. spkr. Spkrs. Bur., U. Hartford; vis. mem. faculty mgmt. info. sci. U. Hartford, 1989—91; instr. Sentry Real Estate Svcs., Inc., Enfield, Conn., 2003—. Author: A Novice's Guide to Personal Computer Buying, New Ventures to Egypt, New Ventures to China, Faith, Hope and Love: Coping With Life and Death. Gubernatorial appointee Conn. bd. trustees Reg. C.C.s, 1985-89; vice chmn. Student Affairs and Acad. Policies Bd., Hartford, 1987; chmn. trustee Conn. Data Processing Curriculum Com., Hartford, 1989; elected com. mem. Enfield Dem. Com., 1975; chmn. regional adv. coun. Asnuntuck C.C.; notary Pub. Conn., 1972—; gubernatorial appointee Conn. bd. trustees Cmty. Tech. Colls., 1990-93. Recipient CTM degree Toastmaster Internat., Hartford, 1987, State Farmer degree Conn. Future Farmers Am., DeKalb Agrl. Accomplishment award, cert. of recognition Bicentennial (USA) Commn., Enfield, 1976, Vigil Hon. BSA Order of the

Arrow, Hartford, 1972, Merit award State of Conn. Cmty.-Tech. Colls. Bd. Trustees, 1994. Mem. World Affairs Coun. of Hartford, Computer Soc. of IEEE, Am. Assn. for Artificial Intelligence, Assn. C.C. Trustees, Am. Assn. Cmty. and Tech. Colls., Microsoft AlumNet Assn., Internat. Platform Assn., Oldefield Farms Homeowners' Assn. (residence com. sec. 1990-91), Hartford County Soil and Water Conservation Dist., Nat. Press Club Found., Robert Schueller's Eagles Club, Masons, Hartford Club. Republican. Roman Catholic. Avocations: travel, refinishing antiques, tennis, hiking, real estate investment, photography. Home: 102 N Maple # 8A Enfield CT 06082 Office Phone: 800-387-5581, 800-387-5581. E-mail: Bruce@BruceLOliver.com, bruce@bruceloliver.com.

**OLIVER, DALE HUGH,** lawyer; b. Lansing, Mich., June 26, 1947; s. Alvin Earl and Jean Elizabeth (Stanton) Oliver; m. Sarah Elyse Sanders, Mar. 18, 2001; children: Nathan Corey, John Franklin. BA, Mich. State U., 1969; JD cum laude, Harvard U., 1972. Bar: DC 1973, Calif. 1991, US Dist. Ct. (DC dist.) 1973, US Ct. Appeals (DC cir.) 1976, US Supreme Ct. 1980, US Ct. Appeals (fed. cir.) 1983, US Ct. Claims 1983. Assoc., ptnr. Jones, Day, Reavis & Pogue, Washington, 1975—79; ptnr. Crowell & Moring, Washington, 1979—84; Gibson, Dunn & Crutcher, Washington, 1984—87, Jones, Day, Reavis & Pogue, Washington, 1987—92, Quinn Emanuel Urquhart & Oliver, L.A., 1992—. Editor: (jour.) Pub. Contracts Law, 1980—86; contbr. articles to profl. jours. Spl. counsel 1980 Presdl. Inaugural Com., Washington, 1980; commr. Calif. Arts and Cultural Commn., 2006—; bd. dirs. L.A. coun. Boy Scouts Am., 1991—. Capt. USAF, 1973—75. Mem.: ABA (com. chmn. pub. contract sect. 1979—), Pasadena Arts and Cultural Commn. (commr. 2006—), Nat. Security Indsl. Assn., Nat. Contract Mgmt. Assn., Harvard Law Sch. Assn., Mich. State U. Alumni Club of Washington (pres., dir. 1984—88). Office: Quinn Emanuel Urquhart & Oliver & Hedges 865 S Figueroa St Fl 10 Los Angeles CA 90017-2543 Office Phone: 213-624-7707. E-mail: daleoliver@quinnemanuel.com.

**OLIVER, DIANE FRANCES,** publisher, writer; b. NYC, Feb. 7, 1935; m. Ben Martin Oliver, Sept. 3, 1960 (div. 1973). BA, Syracuse U., 1955. Reporter Millinery Rsch. mag., NYC, 1956-58; with NYC Bur., London Daily Mail and London Daily Sketch, 1964-69; editor The Celebrity Bull., Celebrity Svc. Inc., NYC, 1971-78; pub. The Celebrity Bull., Phoenix, 1978—, owner Celebrity Svc. Ltd., London, 1978—. Former publicist Lake Lucerne (NY) Playhouse, Bklyn. Acad. Music, Statler Hilton Hotel, NYC. Author: Older Woman/Younger Man, 1975; columnist Palm Beach Social Pictorial mag., 1981-85. Avocations: music, ballet, films, theater, travel. Home: 44 Lennox Gardens London SW1X 0DJ England Office: Celebrity Service Ltd 4th Fl Kingsland House 122 124 Regent St London England W1B 5SA Office Phone: (020) 7439-9840. E-mail: celebritylondon@aol.com.

**OLIVER, DOMINICK MICHAEL,** business educator; b. Niagara Falls, N.Y., Apr. 12, 1962; s. Dominick Jr. and Priscilla (Prenatt) O.; m. Vicki Anne Sellig, May 18, 1991. AAS, Niagara County C.C., Sanborn, N.Y., 1982; BS in Bus., Niagara U., N.Y., 1984, MS in Edn., 1986. Lic. tchr. bus. and distributive edn., N.Y.; bus. sch. lic. bus., mgmt., acctg., gen. academics, N.Y. Temporary instr. Niagara County C.C., Sanborn, 1986-87; tchr. on spl. assignment LaSalle Sr. H.S., Niagara Falls, NY, 1986-87; instr. St. Joseph Parochial Elem. Sch., Niagara Falls, 1987-88; instr., acad. dean Kelley Bus. Inst., Niagara Falls, 1988-91; instr. Cheryl Fell's Sch. Bus., Niagara Falls, 1991-92; instr., advisor Bryant and Stratton Bus. Inst., Buffalo, 1992—99, sr. mentor, portfolio textbook curriculum com., 1996—99; sr. instr., math coordinator The Huntington Learning Ctr., 1999—2000; adj. instr. comp. sci. SUNY Buffalo, 2000—, Niagara County Cmty. Coll., 2001—; asst. prof. office mgmt. and admin. Erie Cmty. Coll., 2002—; with adult cmty. edn. program Kenmore-Town Tonawanda Sch. Dist., 2005—. Bus. mgr. Dove Artworks, Buffalo, 1996—; instr. Adopt-A-H.S., Seneca Vocat. H.S., Kensington H.S., Lafayette H.S., Riverside H.S., Buffalo, 1996-1999; evaluator Empire State Coll., 2003—. Life mem. Buffalo and Erie County Naval and Servicemen's Park, Buffalo, 1991—. Republican. Roman Catholic. Avocations: baseball, football, hockey, political history of US, reading. Home: 119 Wendover Ave Buffalo NY 14223-2731

**OLIVER, DONNA H.,** academic administrator, secondary school educator; AB, Elon Coll.; MEd, U. NC, Greensboro; MS, NC Agrl. and Tech. State U.; PhD, U. NC. Tchr. biology Hugh M. Cummings High Sch., Burlington, NC; v.p. academic affairs Bennett Coll., Greensboro, NC, 1989—. Office: Bennett College 900 E Washington St Greensboro NC 27401

**OLIVER, EDWARD CARL,** retired state legislator, retired insurance company executive, small business owner; b. St. Paul, May 31, 1930; s. Charles Edmund and Esther Marie (Bjugstad) O.; m. Charlotte Severson, Sept. 15, 1956; children: Charles E., Andrew T., Peter A. BA, U. Minn., 1955. Sales rep. Armstrong Cork Co., N.Y.C., 1955; registered rep. Piper, Jaffray & Hopwood, Mpls., 1958; mgr. Mut. Funds Inc., subs. Dayton's, Mpls., 1964, NWNL Mgmt. Corp. subs. Northwestern Nat. Life Ins. Co., Mpls., 1968-72, v.p., 1972-81, pres., dir., 1981-90; mem. Minn. State Senate, 1992—2003, asst. minority leader, 1998—2003; owner Oliver Fin., 2003—; Arbitrator/mediator, Nat. Assn. Securities Dealers Dispute Resolution, Inc., 1988—; bd. dir. 1st Minn. Bank, N.A. Mem. Gt. Lakes Commn., 1993—; bd. dirs. Minn. State Bar & Tax, 2003—. Mem. Internat. Assn. Fin. Planners (past pres. Twin City chpt., nat. governing com.), Psi Upsilon, Mpls. Athletic Club. Home: 20230 Cottagewood Rd Excelsior MN 55331-9300 Office: 401 2d Ave S Ste 429 Minneapolis MN 55401-2349 Office Phone: 612-259-0107. E-mail: oliverfinancial@earthlink.net.

**OLIVER, ELIZABETH KIMBALL,** historian, writer; b. Saginaw, Mich., May 21, 1918; d. Chester Benjamin and Margaret Eva (Allison) Kimball; m. James Arthur Oliver, May 3, 1941 (div. July 1967); children: Patricia Allison (dec.), Dexter Kimball. BA, U. Mich., 1940. Tchr. Dexter (Mich.) High Sch., 1940-41; libr. Sherman (Conn.) Libr. Assn., 1966-75; pres. Sherman (Conn.) Libr. Assn., 1983-84; writer, historian, 1976—. Reporter Sherman Sentinel, 1965-70; editor newsletter Sherman Hist. Soc., 1977-78; columnist Citizen News, Fairfield County, Conn., 1981-83. Author: History of Staff Wives-AMNH, 1961, Background and History of the Palisades Nature Association, 1964, History and Architecture of Grace United Methodist Church, 1990, Legacy to St. Augustine, 1993, Franklin W. Smith and His Casa Monica Hotel, 2000, Viewpoint of a St. Augustine Columnist, 2004; guest columnist Mandarin News, 1995-97; columnist St. Augustine Record, 1998-2005, Viewpoint of St. Augustine, 2004, Florida Impact--8 Biographical Sketches, 2004. Vol. N.Y. Hist. Soc., N.Y.C., 1961-65; treas. Coburn Cemetery Assn., Sherman, 1976-82; historian Greenbrook-Palisades Nature Assn., Tenafly, N.J., 1962-64; mem. St. Augustine Hist. Soc., Naromi Land Trust (life), Cedar Key Hist. Soc.; adv. bd. IBC (Eng.). Mem. AAUW, Friends of Libr. (life), Inst. Am. Indian Studies, Marjorie Kinnan Rawlings Soc. (charter), St. Augustine Woman's Club (archivist, cert. of appreciation 1990), Sherman Hist. Soc., Mandarin Hist. Soc., Smithsonian Nat. Mus. of the Am. Indian (charter). Republican. Congregationalist. Avocations: reading, piano, botany, dulcimer playing. Home: 2292 Commodores Club Blvd Saint Augustine FL 32080-9161 *There are four words which I endeavor to live up to in my work, my personal contacts and every day life. They are the guideposts which I use in all I do: love, courage, integrity and steadfastness.*

**OLIVER, FLORENCE BEATRICE,** secondary school educator; b. Lester, W.Va., June 6, 1949; d. Edward Lewis and Robert Ann (Leisure) Carter; m. Claude James Oliver, May 25, 1991. BS, West Chester State Coll., 1971, MEd, 1973; postgrad., Temple U., 1982—. Cert. secondary prin., social studies supr., Pa. Tchr. Sch. Dist. Phila., 1972—. Recipient Excellence in Teaching award Nat. Coun. Negro Women, 1992. Mem. Black Women's Ednl. Alliance, Student Coun. Advisors (v.p. 1992), Delta Sigma Theta (officer 1989—). Democrat. Baptist. Home: 360 E Meehan Ave Philadelphia PA 19119-1934 Office: Robert E Lamberton 7501 Woodbine Ave Philadelphia PA 19151-2798 Office Phone: 215-581-5647. E-mail: delta.girl.fbo@erols.com.

**OLIVER, GUILLERMO,** hospital administrator, researcher; b. Montevideo, Uruguay, Nov. 11, 1955; s. Juan Carlos Oliver and Yureidini Eugenia; m. Beatriz Sosa, Aug. 16, 1985; children: Mariana, Andres, PhD, U. Uruguay, Montevideo, 1990—92. Sr. scientist Max Planck Inst., Goettingen, Germany, 1992—96; group leader St. Jude Children's Rsch. Hosp., Memphis, 1992—. Spkr. in field. Grantee RO1, NIH, 1997—2006. Achievements include research in lymphatic vasculature development. Office: St Jude Children's Rsch Hosp 332 N Lauderdale Memphis TN 38105

**OLIVER, HARRY MAYNARD, JR.,** retired brokerage house executive; b. Kansas City, Mo., Jan. 21, 1921; s. Harry Maynard and Marie (Curtin) O. BA, Williams Coll., 1943. Pres. M.A. Gesner & Co., Marsh & McLennan Co., Chgo., 1947-88. Chmn. Chgo. Commn. for Sr. Citizens, 1960-69; mem. Chgo. Bd. Edn., 1966-69; pres. Vol. Agys. Chgo., 1956-86; mem. vis. com. Sch. Edn. and div. of social scis., U. Chgo.; pres., bd. dirs. Benton House Settlement, 1953-58; bd. dirs. Adult Edn. Council Greater Chgo., Nat. Fedn. Settlements and Community Centers, 1961-67; trustee Old Peoples Home Chgo., Pub. Sch. Tchrs. Pension and Retirement Fund Chgo., 1966-69, George M. Pullman Ednl. Found., Field Mus. Natural History, 1971-75. Served to lt. (j.g.) USNR, World War II. Mem. Chgo. Club, Racquet Club, Commonwealth Club, Tavern Club, Onwentsia Club (Lake Forest, Ill.), Chi Psi. Home: 1948 N Lincoln Ave Chicago IL 60614-5476 also: PO Box 1319 Big Pine Key FL 33043 also: New Richmond PO Box 100 Fennville MI 49408-0100

**OLIVER, JACK ERTLE,** geophysicist, educator; b. Massillon, Ohio, Sept. 26, 1923; s. Chester L. and Marie (Ertle) O.; m. Gertrude van der Hoeven, Apr. 16, 1964; children: Cornelia Oliver, Amy Oliver. AB, Columbia U., 1947, MA, 1950, PhD, 1953; DSci (hon.), Hamilton Coll., 1988. Rsch. asst., then rsch. assoc. Columbia, 1947-55, mem. faculty, 1955-73, prof. geology, 1961-71, chmn. dept., 1969-71, adj. prof., 1971-73; Irving Porter Church prof. engring. dept. geol. scis. Cornell U., 1971-93, prof. emeritus, 1993—, chmn. dept., 1971-81; chmn. exec. com. COCORP. Terrestrial physicist USAF Cambridge (Mass.) Rsch. Labs., 1951; dir. Inst. for Study of the Continents, 1981-88; cons. AEC, 1969-72, ACDA, 1962-74, USAF Tech. Applications Ctr., 1959-65; mem. Polar Rsch. Com., 1959-71, also nat. commn. uppermantle program, 1963-71; mem. panel solid earth problems NAS, 1962; mem. adv. com. U.S. Coast and Geodetic Survey, 1962-66, on seismology, 1960-72, chmn., 1966-70; mem. Geophysics Rsch. Bd., 1969-70; U.S. coord. 2d U.S.-Japan Earthquake Prediction Conf., Palisades, 1966; earth sci. panel NSF, 1962-65; mem. USAF Sci. Adv. Bd., 1960-63, 64-69; mem. geophysics adv. panel Office Sci. Rsch., USAF, 1961-74, chmn., 1966-68; U.S. del. Test Ban Conf., Geneva, Switzerland, 1958-59; intergovtl. meeting seismology and earthquake engring., mem. exec. com. IASPEI, 1968-71; mem. governing com. Internat. Seismol. Summary Commn., 1963-67, 75-76; mem. exec. com. UNESCO, Paris, France, 1964, U.S.-Japan Earthquake Prediction Conf., Tokyo, 1964; mem. UNESCO Joint Com. on Seismology and Earthquake Engring., 1965-71; chmn. exec. com. Office Earth Scis., NRC, 1976-79, Internat. Seismol. Centre, 1976-78; mem. U.S. Geodynamics Com., 1979-87, chmn., 1984-87; mem. Geol. Scis. Bd., Assembly of Math. and Phys. Scis., NRC, 1981-84; Cabot Disting. vis. scholar U. Houston, 1985-86; commn. on phys. scis., math. and resources NRC, 1987-90, commn. on geoscis., environ. and resources, 1990—. Served with USNR, 1943-46. Recipient Hedberg award Inst. for Study of Earth and Man, So. Meth. U., 1990. Fellow Am. Geophys. Union (pres. seismology sect. 1964-68, Walter H. Bucher medal 1981), Geol. Soc. Am. (coun. 1970-73, v.p. 1986, pres. 1987, Woollard medal 1990, Penrose medal 1998), Geol. Soc. London (hon.); mem. AAAS (chmn. geol. geog. sect. 1993), NAS, Seismol. Soc. Am. (pres. 1964-65, bd. dirs. 1961-70, 72-76, Eighth medal 1984), Soc. Exploration Geophysicists (Virgil Kauffman Gold medal 1983), European Union Geoscis. (hon. fgn. fellow), Sigma Xi. Home: 340 Savage Farm Dr Ithaca NY 14850 Office Phone: 607-255-2377. Business E-Mail: oliver@geology.cornell.edu.

**OLIVER, JAMIE,** chef, television personality; b. Essex, England, May 1, 1975; s. Trevor and Sally Oliver; m. Juliette Norton; children: Poppy, Daisy. Grad., Westminster Catering Coll., London. Head pastry chef Neal Street Restaurant, London, 1991—97; chef River Cafe, London, 1997—99; consulting chef Monte's, London, 2000; founder, owner Fifteen Restaurant, London, 2002—. Former columnist GQ mag.; former feature writer The Times Mag., London; designer cookware & tableware line Royal Worcester. Host, chef (TV series) The Naked Chef, 1999-2001 (BAFTA award 2001), Jamie's Kitchen, 2002-04, Oliver's Twist, 2004-, Jamie's School Dinners, 2006- (Best Factual Series award, Outstanding Presenter award, BAFTA 2006); author (cookbooks) The Naked Chef, 1999, The Return of The Naked Chef, 2000, Happy Days with The Naked Chef, 2001, Jamie's Kitchen, 2003, Jamie's Dinners, 2004, Jamie's Italy, 2005. Founder Fifteen Found., 2002. Decorated MBE; named GQ Man of the Yr., 2000; recipient GQ Best Chef award, 2000, Tatler Best Restaurant award (for Fifteen Restaurant), 2003, Excellence award, Tio Pepe Carlton London Restaurant Awards, 2003, Time Out special award for outstanding achievement, 2003, Glenfiddich Food and Drink award, 2003. Office: Fifteen Restaurant & Fifteen Found Westland Place London N1 7LP England also: c/o Penguin Publicity 80 Strand WC2R 0RL London England*

**OLIVER, JERRY ALTON,** former police chief; 5 children. BS in Criminal Justice, Ariz. State U., MS in Pub. Adminstrn., 1988; postgrad., Police Exec. Rsch. Forum, Washington. From patrolman to supr. Phoenix Police Dept., from supr. to asst. chief of police, 1971-90; dir. drug policy Memphis Mayors Office; chief of police Pasadena (Calif.) Police Dept., 1991—94, Richmond (Va.) Police Dept., 1995—2002, Detroit, Mich., 2002—03; spl. policy advisor Ariz. Atty. Gen., 2004—05; dep. dir. Ariz. Dept. Admin., 2005—. Founder Spl. Friends Project, Richmond, 1988—. Inductee Ariz. State U. Coll. Pub. Programs Hall of Fame, 1989; recipient Phoenix chpt. Image award NAACP, 1990, People of Yr. award Law Enforcement News, 1999, Richmonder of Yr. award Richmond Style Mag., 1999, U.S. Atty. Gen.'s award for outstanding contbns. to cmty. partnership for pub. safety, 2000, othrs. Office Phone: 602-542-0878. E-mail: jaoxfive@hotmail.com.

**OLIVER, JOHN PRESTON,** chemistry professor; b. Klamath Falls, Oreg., Aug. 7, 1934; s. Robert Preston and Agnes May (McCornack) O.; m. Elizabeth Ann Shaw, Aug. 12, 1956; children: Karen Sue Oliver Vernon, Roy John, Gordon Preston. BA, U. Oreg., 1956; PhD, U. Wash., 1959. Asst. prof. chemistry Wayne State U., Detroit, 1959-64, assoc. prof., 1964-67, prof., 1967—, assoc. dean R&D, Coll. Liberal Arts, 1987-91, acting dean, 1991-92, interim dean Coll. Sci., 1992-93, dep. provost, 1996—2003, v.p. for rsch., 2003—. Chmn. organizing com. XIV Internat. Conf. on Organometallic Chemistry. Mem. Ferndale (Mich.) Bd. Edn., 1984-88. Mem. Am. Chem. Soc., Detroit sect. Am. Chem. Soc., Sigma Xi. Office: Wayne State Univ 5057 Woodard Rm 6409 Detroit MI 48202-3489 Office Phone: 313-577-5600. Business E-Mail: jpo@wayne.edu.

**OLIVER, JOHN WILLIAM POSEGATE,** minister; b. Vincennes, Ind., Apr. 9, 1935; s. Dwight L and Elizabeth (Posegate) Oliver; m. Cristina Shepard Hope, Oct. 19, 1968; children: John William Posegate Jr, Sloan Christian Shepard. BA, Wheaton Coll., 1956; BD, Fuller Theol. Sem., 1959; ThM, So. Bapt. Theol. Sem., 1963; DD, Western Conservative Bapt. Sem., 1996. Ordained to ministry Presby Ch, 1962. Asst. pastor Covenant Presbyn. Ch., Hammond, Ind., 1964-66, Trinity Presbyn. Ch., Montgomery, Ala., 1966-69; pastor 1st Presbyn. Ch., Augusta, Ga., 1969-97, Trinity Presbyn. Ch., Montgomery, Ala., 1997-99; prof. preaching and practical theology Reformed Theol. Sem., Charlotte, NC, 1999—. Bd dirs Equip, Inc; moderator Cent Ga Presby, Presby Ch Am, 1976. Founder, trustee Westminster Schs, Augusta, 1972—97; bd. commrs. Augusta Housing Authority, vice chmn., 1976—93; trustee, chmn. bd. Columbia Internat. U., 1978—; dir. Bailey Manor Retirement Ctr., Clinton, SC, 1992—97; chmn. clergy Augusta United Way Campaign, 1974; exec. bd. clergy staff Univ Hosp, Augusta, 1975—76; bd. dirs. Mission to the World, Presbyn. Ch. Am, 1984—89, bd dirs, 1992—96; ministerial adv. bd. Ref. Theol. Sem., Jackson, Miss., 1978—85,

1989—93, Charlotte, 1996—99. Mem.: Evang Theological Soc, Wynlakes Country Club, Nassau Club, Kappa Sigma. Office: 2101 Carmel Rd Charlotte NC 28226-6318 Home: 731 Stanhope Ln Matthews NC 28105

**OLIVER, KIMBERLY,** Teacher of the Year; b. Wilmington, Del. BA in English Arts, Hampton U.; MEd in elem. edn., Wilmington Coll. Cert. Nat. Bd. Profl. Teaching Standards, 2004. Kindergarten teacher Broad Acres Elem., Silver Spring, Md., 2000—. Named Md. Teacher of the Year, 2006, Teacher of the Year, Coun. Chief State Sch. Officers, 2006; recipient Greenblatt Excellence Teaching award, Greenblatt Edn. Fund. Office: Broad Acres Elem Sch 13313 Old Columbia Pike Silver Spring MD 20903*

**OLIVER, LEANN MICHELLE,** government official; b. Eureka, Calif., Nov. 15, 1955; d. George L. and Laura Maxine (Jennings) O. BS, Willamette U., 1977; MPA, SUNY, Albany, 1980; cert., Nat. Comml. Lending Sch. of Am. Bankers Assn., Norman, Okla., 1982. Mgmt. trainee U.S. GAO, Albany, 1979-80; presdl. mgmt. intern U.S. SBA, Washington, 1980-83, fin. analyst, policy program devel., 1983-89, acting dir. Office Rural Affairs Econ. Devel., 1995, dir. divsn. Program Devel., 1995-2000, dep. assoc. adminstr. fin. assistance, 2000—05; dep. dir. program devel. Office Econ. Devel., 1989-92; dep. dir. Office Rural Affairs Econ. Devel., 1992-94; acting dir. One Stop Office, Capital Shop Project, 1994; acting dep., assoc. dep. adminstr. Entrepreneurial Devel., 2006—. Bd. dirs. Lafayette Fed. Credit Union, Washington, 1986—, treas., 1997-2000, asst. treas., 2000-04, treas., 2004—. Mem. Internat. Platform Assn. Roman Catholic. Office: SBA 409 3rd St SW Ste 8300 Washington DC 20416 Business E-Mail: le.oliver@sba.gov.

**OLIVER, LOUISE V.,** ambassador; m. Daniel Oliver; 5 children. BA with distinction, Smith Coll. Apptd. commr. Nat. Commn. on Children, 1989; pres. Oliver Mgmt. Consultants; permanent US rep. UNESCO, Paris, 2004—. Chmn. Philanthropy Roundtable, Washington, Intercollegiate Studies Inst.; co-founder New Atlantic Initiative; bd. dirs. Independent Women's Forum. Office: UNESCO 7 Place de Fontenoy 75352 Paris France Office Phone: 33-1-4524-7416. E-mail: parisunesco@state.gov.

**OLIVER, MADISON E.,** retired engineering executive, mechanical engineer; b. Hermosa Beach, Calif., Apr. 14, 1925; s. Eldon Seymour and Gertrude Helen Oliver; m. Virginia E. Kellis. BS Applied Sci., Chico State U., 1951; BSME, Wash. State U., 1953. Registered profl. engr. N.Mex., 1956. Staff mem. Sandia Corp., Albuquerque, 1953—56, sect. supr. Livermore, Calif., 1957—60; design engr. Aerojet Gen. Corp., Sacramento, 1960—63; dep. dir. pub. works Govt. of Am. Samoa, Pago Pago, 1963—67, dir. pub. works, 1967—69; project mgr. Parsons Hawaii (unit of Ralph M. Parsons Co.), Honolulu, 1970—74, sr. project mgr., mng. engr., 1974—82, gen. mgr., 1982—91; v.p. Parsons Overseas Co., Hawaii, 1990—91. Territorial bldg. ofcl. Govt. of Am. Samoa, Pago Pago, U. S. Territory of American Samoa, 1967—69; sec. bd. of dirs. Marine Dry Dock, Pago Pago, 1968—69; project mgr. New Saipan Internat. Airport, 1970—76, Trust Ter. of the Pacific Islands Airport Sys. Plan, 1975—76, New Guam Internat. Air Terminal, 1976—82; program dir. TRUK Capital Improvements, 1975—77; prin. project mgr., engring. design and constrn. Palau Hosp., 1988—91; spkr. in field. Mem. Pacific & Asian Affairs Coun., Honolulu, 1982—90; mem., transp. com. Chamber of Commerce, Honolulu, 1982—90; bd. dirs. Marina Towers Condominium, Honolulu, 1980—83, pres. bd. dirs., 1983—86. Motor machinist's mate first class USN, 1943—46, PTO. Recipient Airport Beautification Award, Saipan Internat. Airport, FAA, Saipan, No. Mariana Islands, 1976. Mem.: Soc. Am. Mil. Engineers, ASME, Toastmasters Internat. (gov., area VI, dist. 39 1963—63), Toastmasters Internat., Raconteur Club, Folsom, Calif. (pres. 1962—63), Masonic Lodge (Golden Veterans Award 2000). Avocation: golf, writing, and fishing. Home: 1821 Jansen Way Woodburn OR 97071

**OLIVER, MARY,** poet; b. Maple Heights, Ohio, Sept. 10, 1935; d. Edward William and Helen Mary (Vlasak) O. Student, Ohio State U., 1955—56, Vassar Coll., 1956—57. Chmn. writing dept. Fine Arts Work Ctr., Provincetown, Mass., 1972-84. mem. writing com., 1984; Banister poet-in-residence Sweet Briar Coll., 1991-95. William Blackburn vis. prof. creative writing Duke U., 1995; Catharine Osgood Foster prof. Bennington Coll., 1996-2001. Author: No Voyage and Other Poems, 1963, enlarged edit., 1965, The River Styx, Ohio, 1972, The Night Traveler, 1978, Twelve Moons, 1979, American Primitive, 1983, Dream Work, 1986, House of Light, 1990, New and Selected Poems, 1992, Vol. 2, 2005, A Poetry Handbook, 1994, White Pine, 1994, Blue Pastures, 1995, West Wind, 1997, Rules for the Dance, 1998, Winter Hours, 1999, The Leaf and the Cloud, 2000, What Do We Know, 2002, Owls and Other Fantasies, 2003, Why I Wake Early, 2004, Long Life, 2004, Blue Iris, 2004, New and Selected Poems, Vol. 2, 2005; contbr. to Yale U. Rev., Kenyon Rev., Poetry, Atlantic, Harvard mag., others. Recipient Shelley Meml. award, 1970, Alice Fay di Castagnola award, 1973, Cleve. Arts prize for lits., 1979, Achievement award Am. Acad. and Inst. Arts and Letters, 1983, Pulitzer prize for poetry, 1984, Christopher award, 1991, L.L. Winship award, 1991, Nat. Book award, 1992, Lannan award, 1998; Nat. Endowment fellow, 1972-73; Guggenheim fellow, 1980-81. Mem. PEN. Home: PO Box 619 Provincetown MA 02657-0619

**OLIVER, MATT,** publishing executive; V.p. prodn. San Antonio Express-News, 1993—2003; dir. productivity mgmt. Hearst Corp., newspaper div., San Antonio, 2003—05; exec. v.p. & gen. mgr. Houston Chronicle, 2005—.*

**OLIVER, NANCY LEBKICHER,** artist, retired elementary school educator; b. Stockton, Calif., 1939; d. John B. and Marjorie Lebkicher; m. Douglas C. Oliver, 1960; children: Charles, Elaine. BA with honors, San Jose State U., 1961. Summer playground dir. Recreation Dept., Redwood City, Calif., 1956-61; 1st grade tchr. Redwood City (Calif.) Elem. Sch. Dist., 1961-63; kindergarten tchr. Ukiah (Calif.) Unified Sch. Dist., 1963-67; assoc. tchr. kindergarten San Carlos (Calif.) Elem. Sch. Dist., 1976-81. Dept. store shopper Macy's, San Francisco, 1975-82; asst. hist. rsch., 2000—. Active White Oaks PTA, San Carlos, 1973-81; newsletter editor, 1978-81; leader Girl Scouts U.S.A., San Carlos, 1978-81; bd. dirs. Sequoia H.S. Ednl. Found., co-chmn., 2002-05, sec., 2005-; bd. dirs San Mateo County Hist. Resources Adv. Bd., 2003-; Sunday sch. dir. St. Peter's Episcopal Ch., Redwood City, 1973-78; mem. San Mateo County Sesquicentennial Com., 2005-06. Mem.: AAUW (pres. Willits br. 1966—67, San Carlos br. newsletter editor 1972—74, chmn. historic preservation sect. 1979—, editor historic tour booklet 1981, editor historic resources booklet 1989, co-pres. San Carlos br. 2002—04, dir.-at-large 2004—06, parliamentarian 2004—), Gift honoree 1976), SeriPrinters (serigrapher 1986—), San Carlos Heritage Assn. (founder and dir. 1995—), Sequoia H.S. Alumni Assn. (founding sec. and membership chmn 1985—, centennial coord. 1992—95, pres. 1996—98, sec. 2002—, newsletter editor 2003—, Unsung Hero award 1998), Internat. Order Rainbow Girls (grand officer Calif. 1957—58, mother advisor Redwood City 1987—89, quilt com. 1989—). Democrat. Episcopalian. Avocations: needle-crafts, historic preservation activities, walking, calligraphy, classical music. Home: 147 Belvedere Ave San Carlos CA 94070-4818

**OLIVER, NURIA,** computer scientist; b. Spain; BS, Tech. U. Madrid, 1992, MS, 1994; PhD in Media Arts & Scis., MIT, 2000. Rsch. asst. engr. Siemens F&E, 1992—93; software engr. Telefonica R&D, Spain, 1994—95; rsch. asst. Media Lab, MIT, 1995—2000; rsch. adaptive systems & interaction group Microsoft Rsch., 2000—. Named one of 40 Most Promising Young Spanish Persons, El Pais, 1999, Top 100 Young Innovators, MIT Tech. Review, 2004; fellow, La Caixa Found., 1995; Motorola fellow, 1997. Avocation: ballet. Office: Microsoft Rsch One Microsoft Way Redmond WA 98052-6399

**OLIVER, PATRICIA,** lawyer; b. Erie; m. Jim Oliver. BA in Polit. sci., Allegheny Collge; JD, Case Western Reserve U. Sch. Law, Cleve. Atty. Squire, Sanders & Dempsey, Cleve.; gen. counsel BB&T Corp, Winston-Salem, NC, 2004—. Recipient Rainmaker (community svc.), No. Ohio Live

Magazine, 2003, Profl. Woman of Excellence, Cleve. YMCA. Achievements include founder of Cleve.'s "Women in Family Bus." seminar series; pres. Children's Aid Soc. Office: BB&T Corp 200 W 2nd St Winston Salem NC 27101

**OLIVER, RAYMOND A.,** lawyer; b. Paterson, N.J., Feb. 26, 1951; s. Nicholas Joseph and Mona (Fayad) O.; m. Katherine Osborne McCullough, Aug. 27, 1977; children— Kristine Bettcher, Bennet Raymond, Lauren Anita. Student Emporia Coll., 1969-71; A.B., Loyola U., Chgo., 1973; postgrad NYU, 1974; J.D., John Marshall Law Sch., 1979. Bar: N.J. 1979, U.S. Dist. Ct. N.J. 1979, D.C. 1980. Clinic atty. Ill. Office Atty. Gen., Chgo., 1978-79; chief investigative staff, asst. to dir. Somerset County Consumer Affairs Office, Somerville, N.J., 1979; sole practice, West Paterson, N.J., and Washington, 1979—; instr. Taylor Bus. Inst., Plainfield, N.J., 1981. Mem. N.J. Bar Assn. (bd. dirs. adminstrv. law sect. 1983—, sec. adminstrv. law sect. 1985—, chmn. 1989—, editor adminstrv. law newsletter 1979—), Passaic County Bar Assn. (chmn. govt. law sect. 1983—, chmn. scholarship fund 1984—, chmn. constitutional law and civil rights com., chmn. internat. law com.), U.N. Internat. Progress Orgn., D.C. Bar Assn., Assn. Trial Lawyers Am. Democrat. Roman Catholic. Home: 88 Rose Pl Little Falls NJ 07424-3030

**OLIVER, ROBERT BRUCE,** retired investment company executive; b. Brockton, Mass., Aug. 1, 1931; s. Stanley Thomas and Helen (Sabine) O.; m. Sylvia E. Bell, Feb. 17, 1954; children: Susan Pamela, Robert Bruce. AB, Harvard U., 1953; postgrad., Bus. Sch., 1971, Boston U. Law Sch., 1955-57; MA, Mich. State U., 1958. Ret. chmn., pres., chief exec. officer John Hancock Income Securities Trust, Boston, 1989. Ret. chmn., pres., chief exec. officer John Hancock Investors Trust, John Hancock Bond Trust, John Hancock Growth Trust, John Hancock Tax Exempt Cash Mgmt. Trust, John Hancock Govt. Securities Trust, John Hancock Tax Exempt Income Trust, John Hancock Cash Mgmt. Trust, John Hancock Spl. Equities Trust, John Hancock Global Trust, John Hancock World Trust, John Hancock High Income Trust, John Hancock Tax Exempt Series Trust; chmn., dir. John Hancock Distbrs.; vice chmn., chief exec. officer John Hancock Advisers, Inc.; chmn., mng. dir. John Hancock Advisers Internat. Ltd. 1st lt. USMCR, 1953-55. Mem. Marine Corps League. Home: 9271 SW 29th Ave Gainesville FL 32608 Personal E-mail: rboliver72@aol.com.

**OLIVER, RONALD,** retired medical technologist; b. New Orleans, July 16, 1949; s. Wilbert and Everlina (Theard) Oliver; children: Nannette Marie, Joseph Byron. Diploma in bus. adminstrn., Meadows-Draughon Coll., 1972; AS in Environ. Health Tech., Delgado C.C., New Orleans, 1976; BS in Biology Edn., So. U., 1980, BS in Chemistry Edn., 1983; MA in Hosp. Adminstrn., Southwest U., 1986, PhD in Hosp. Adminstrn., 1987; cert. Charity Hosp. Sch. Nuc. Medicine, 1986; PhD in Pub. Health, Columbia State U., 1992; PhD in Health Adminstrn., Kennedy-We. U., 1993; PhD in Environ. Engring., Kensington U., 1994; PhD in Electrophysiology, Summit U., 1995. Med. technologist, supr. med. technologists Charity Hosp., New Orleans, 1969—95, ret., 1995; mem. faculty Pacific We. U., 1993—; rsch. scientist La. State U. Med. Ctr., New Orleans, 1999. Mem. faculty Tulane U. Pub. Health and Tropical Med. Sch., 1975-81, Kensington U., Glendale, Calif., 1990-92; rsch. scientist Tech. La. State U. Med. Sch., New Oreleans; ex-faculty, staff mem. Delgado C.C. Author 7 books, including A Primer in Electrocardiography with Technical and Some Evaluative Values, 1991, 2d edit., 1995, Electrocardiography, Theories, Applications and Practice, 1997; also articles. V.p. Friends of Amistad Rsch., Tulane U.; mem. U.S. Trade Adv. Bd., 1996. Recipient Outstanding Svc. award Charity Hosp., 1972, acknowledgement letter Nobel Found., 1992, cert. of acknowledgement Am. Pathologists, 1981, Am. Ex-mem. Assn. Profl. Cons.; candidate Pulitzer Prize, 1995. Mem. Am. Med. Technologists, Am. Coll. Healthcare Execs. (cert. of acknowledgement), La. Environ. Health Assn. Methodist. Achievements include over 30 copyrights in the field of electrophysiology in Library of Congress; discovered the sigma wave in electracardiography, the electrical alternan theory, the intracerebral-intracranial theories; patentee in field, 1 registered U.S. Dept. Commerce.

**OLIVER, SAMUEL WILLIAM, JR.,** retired lawyer; b. Birmingham, Ala., Apr. 18, 1935; s. Samuel William and Sarah C. Oliver; m. Anne Holman Marshall, Aug. 26, 1961; children: Sarah Bradley Oliver Crow, Samuel William III, Margaret Nelson Oliver Little. BS, U. Ala., 1959, JD, 1962. Bar: Ala. 1962, U.S. Dist. Ct. (no. dist.) Ala. 1963. Law clk. Supreme Ct. Ala., Montgomery, 1962-63, U.S. Dist. Ct. (no. dist.) Ala., Birmingham, 1963; assoc. Burr & Forman LLP, Birmingham, 1964-65, ptnr., 1966—2005, ret. 2005. Dir. Metalplate Galvanizing Inc., Birmingham, 1975-2004; mem. panel arbitrators comm. Am. Arbitration Assn., Atlanta, 1981-99. Chmn. bd. govs. The Relay House, Birmingham, 1985-89; mem. Leadership Birmingham, 1990; bd. dirs. Jr. Achievement Greater Birmingham, Inc., 1975-2003; mem. diocese coun. Episcopal Diocese Ala., Birmingham, 1981-85; chmn. bd. trustees Highlands Day Sch. Found., Inc., Birmingham, 1980-81; bd. dirs. Ala. Kidney Found., Birmingham, 1990-94. With U.S. Army, 1956-58. Mem. ABA (bus. law sect. 1965—, negotiated acquisitions com. 1990-2005, task force on model stock purchase agreement 1990-95, model asset purchase agreement 1994-2001, model joint venture agreement 1994-2003, corp. counsel com.), Southeastern Corp. Law Inst. (planning com. 1996-2005), Birmingham Bar Assn., Ala. Bar Assn., Monday Morning Quarterback Club, Rotary Club, Venture Club, Newcomer Soc. U.S Episcopalian.

**OLIVER, SANDRA,** art dealer, painter; b. Bronxville, N.Y., Apr. 2, 1941; d. Clarence Charles and Mary Bell E. (McTeique) Simoni; m. Paul Alan Williams, May 2, 1982; children: John Mortimer Wilson, Melissa Anne Wilson, PHilip Keith Wilson. BA, BFA, Marymount Coll., Tarrytown, NY, 1963. Art and art history tchr. N.Y.C. Sch. System, 1963-65; art tchr. Diocese Cath. Sch., Westchester, N.Y., 1963-65; comml. artist rep. Weston Conn., 1979-84; pres Sandi Oliver Weston, 1984—. Author catalog: American Impressionist Paul Williams: His Garden and His Oil Paintings, 1994. Recipient 1st prize Christmas Show, Pelham (N.Y.) C. of C., 1960, Bravo award, Revlon Corp., 1980, 1st prize, Braswell Galleries, 1998, honors, Westport Art Show, 2001, award, The Westport Downtown Merchants Assn., 2002, auction record (paintings), 1988—2001. Mem. New Eng. Appraisers Assn., Allied Arts Am. Inc., Am. Fedn. Artists, Nat. Mus. Women in Arts (charter mem.). Avocations: painting, antiques, gardening, walking, dog breeding. Home: 11 Tubbs Spring Dr PO Box 1203 Weston CT 06883-0203 Office: Sandi Oliver PO Box 1203 Weston CT 06883-0203 Office Phone: 203-226-4469. Fax: 203-226-4469. E-mail: sandioliver@aol.com.

**OLIVER, SOLOMON, JR.,** judge; b. Bessemer, Ala., July 20, 1947; s. Solomon Sr. and Willie Lee (Davis) O.; married; 2 children. BA, Coll. of Wooster, 1969; JD, NYU, 1972; MA, Case Western Res. U., 1974. Bar: Ohio 1973, U.S. Dist. Ct. 1976, U.S. Ct. Appeals (6th cir.) 1977, U.S. Supreme Ct. 1980. Asst. prof. dept. polit. sci. Coll. of Wooster, Ohio, 1972-75; sr. law clk. to Hon. William H. Hastie U.S. Ct. Appeals (3d cir.), Phila., 1975-76; asst. U.S. atty. U.S. Atty.'s Office, Cleve., 1976-82, chief civil divsn., 1978-82; spl. asst. U.S. atty., chief appellate divsn. Dept. Justice, Cleve., 1982, spl. asst. U.S. atty., 1982-85; prof. law Cleve. State U., 1982-94, assoc. dean faculty and adminstrn., 1991-94. Lectr. in law, trial practice Case Western Res. U., Cleve., 1979-82; vis. scholar Stanford U. Coll. Law, 1987; vis. prof. Comenius U., Bratislava, Czechoslovakia, 1991, Charles U., Prague, Czechoslovakia, 1991. Chair O.K. Hoover Scholarship com. Bapt. Ch., 1987-89; trustee Coll. of Wooster, Ohio, 1991-97, 2000—. Mem. ABA, Nat. Bar Assn. Office: 801 W Superior Ave Cleveland OH 44113-1838

**OLIVER, TERRY JAMES,** electronics engineer, educator, communications engineer; b. Greensboro, N.C., Sept. 5, 1949; s. William Alfred and Elizabeth Ellen (Baker) O.; m. Janice Marie Jones, Mar. 16, 1974 (div. May 1989); 1 child, Shonn Aaron; m. Janice Marie Meris, Nov. 25, 1990; children Jennifer G. Meris, Kelly Cervero. MS, St. John's U., 1981; PhD, Pacific Western U., 1985; AA, Thomas A. Edison State Coll., 1986, AS, 1987; BS, Regents Coll. U. State of N.Y., Albany, 1988. Cert. tchr., N.C.; sr. electronics technician, sr. biomed. electronics technician, video photographer, open water diver; lic.

trainer NC Dept. Pub. Instrn. Pub. edn. officer Civil Affairs and Signal Corps USAR, Greensboro, NC, 1975—79; comms.-electronic technician U.S. Army, 1968-75; sound systems engr. Soundak Engineered Systems, Greensboro, 1975-76; electronics tchr. Guilford County Sch. System, Greensboro, 1976-79; comm. electronics engr. U.S. Army, Washington, 1979-86; dir. prof. photoelectronics Randolph C.C., Asheboro, NC, 1986—99; prof. electronics, computers and telecomms. ECPI Coll. Tech., Greensboro, NC, 1999—2004. Faculty rep. N.C. Assn. Educators, Guilford County, N.C., 1976-79; cons. Guilford Tech. CC New Industry Tng., Greensboro, 1988-90. Mem. Guilford County PACE, 1977-79; party nominee N.C. Ho. of Reps., 1992, N.C. State Senate, 1996; candidate Guilford County Bd. Edn., 1993, N.C. State Senate, 1994; appt. ad large mem. Guilford County Bd. Environ. Quality, 1999-2004. With USAR, 1975-79. Mem. Nat. Soc. Profl. Engrs., Internat. Soc. for Optical Engrs., Soc. Am. Mil. Engrs., Photo Mktg. Assn. Democrat. Moravian. Avocations: scuba diving, tennis, bicycling, walking. Home: 7310 Shellford St Greensboro NC 27406-9165 E-mail: t_oliver5@bellsouth.net.

**OLIVER, THORNAL GOODLOE,** retired health care executive; b. Memphis, Aug. 26, 1934; s. John Oliver and Evelyn Doris (Goodloe) Mitchell; m. Pauline Reid, Oct. 1, 1959. B.S., Tenn. State U., Nashville, 1956; M.H.A., Washington U., St. Louis, 1973. Cert. nursing home adminstr., No. Asst. dir., King Meml. Hosp., Kansas City, Mo., 1973-75; evening mgr. Truman Med. Ctr., Kansas City, Mo., 1975-77; asst. adminstr. Mid-Am. Radiation Ctr. U. Kans. Coll. Health Sci., Kansas City, Kans., 1977-81; dir. CHS, Inc., Leawood, Kans., 1981-82; adminstr. Poplar Bluff Hosp., Mo., 1982-83; adminstr. The Benjamin F Lee Health Ctr., Wilberforce, Ohio, 1983-86; asst. clin. prof. Dept. Community Medicine, Wright State U., Dayton, 1986-89; asst. patent adminstr. Munson Army Hosp., Ft. Leavenworth, Kans., 1987-2004, ret., 2004; cons. Urban Health Assocs., Nashville, 1986-87, others. Contbr. articles to profl. jours. Served with U.S. Army, 1957-59, USAR, 1959-63. Fellow Am. Coll. Hosp. Adminstrs.; mem. Am. Hosp. Assn., Nat. Assn. Health Services Execs., Am. Med. Record Assn., Mo. League of Nursing Home Adminstrs. Home: 10641 N Grand Ave Kansas City MO 64155-1655

**OLIVER, WALTER M.,** human resources specialist; b. Decatur, Ill. B in Psychology, Whitworth Coll.; M in Human Resources Mgmt., Gonzaga U. Corp. personnel mgr., personnel rels. superintendent, labor rels. rep. Kaiser Aluminum and Chem. Corp., 1973—80; v.p. human resources Hoover Universal, Inc., 1980—85; v.p. orgnl. devel. to v.p. adminstrn. Johnson Controls, Inc., 1985—89, corp. v.p. human resources, 1989—94; sr. v.p. human resources Ameritech, 1994—2001; v.p. human resources and adminstrn. General Dynamics Corp., Falls Church, Va., 2001—02, sr. v.p. human resources and adminstrn., 2002—. Dir. Am. Family Ins. Co., Telect, Inc. Bd. trustees Nat. Pension Fund; trustee Whitworth Coll. Office: General Dynamics Corp 2941 Fairview Park Dr Ste 100 Falls Church VA 22042-4513 Office Phone: 703-876-3000. Office Fax: 703-876-3125.

**OLIVER, WILLIAM DONALD,** orthodontist; b. Montreal, Dec. 14, 1946; s. Austen William and Margaret Kay (Donald) O. BS in Physics, Mt. Allison U., 1962; DDS, McGill U., 1968; MSD in Orthodontics, U. Pa., 1970. Pres. Orthodontic Enterprises Internat., Geneva, 1973—78; orthodontist Barrington, RI, 1979—94; pvt. practice Everett, Wash., 1993—. Instr. Frankfurt Carolinium, 1972-74; witness Senate Armed Svcs. Com., 1975. Inventor Piezo Electric Bone Healing; contbr. articles to profl. jours. Mem. Olympic Ski Team, Squaw Valley, 1960. Served with USAF, 1970-73. Recipient Carter Meml. award, 1964, M.T. Dohan prize, 1966. Mem. ADA, Can. Assn. Orthodontists, Am. Assn. Orthodontists, European Orthodontic Soc., Can. Dental Assn., Fedn. Internat. d'Automobile (qualified and registered), Wash. State Soc. Orthodontists, Royal Ocean Racing Club. Republican. Office: 10812 19th Ave SE Everett WA 98208-5153 Office Phone: 425-338-5414. Business E-Mail: braces@seanet.com.

**OLIVER, WILLIAM JOHN,** pediatrician, educator; b. Blackshear, Ga., Mar. 30, 1925; s. John Wesley and Katherine (Schalwig) O.; m. Marguerite Bertoni, May 28, 1949; children: Ralph Scott, Catherine, Susan. Student, Ga. Southwestern Coll., 1942-43, Mercer U., 1943-44; MD cum laude, U. Mich., 1948. Diplomate Am. Bd. Pediatrics (examiner), Subsplty. Bd. Pediatric Nephrology. Intern, resident U. Mich. Med. Center, 1948-53; dir. pediatric labs., 1959-67; pvt. practice medicine specializing in pediatrics Ann Arbor, Mich., 1953—; instr. dept. pediatrics U. Mich., 1953-56, asst. prof., 1956-61, assoc. prof., 1961-65, prof., 1965, chmn. dept. pediatrics, 1967-79; chief pediatric service Wayne County Hosp., 1958-61. Co-chmn. task force on recent advances of coordinating com. on continuing edn. and recertification Am. Bd. Pediats. and Am. Acad. Pediats., 1977-80; mem. task force for pediatric rev. edn. program, 1980-88; mem. com. program for renewal certification in pediat. Am. Bd. Pediat., 1989-91; mem. exam writing com. for cert. pediatric nephrology, 1989-93, PRCP pilot test com., 1993-96; mem. rev. and question writing com. for Pediat. in Rev. Am. Acad. Pediat., 1991-97; cons. U. Riyadh, Saudi Arabia, 1980, Rsch. Rev. Com. on Pediat., 1989; ednl. cons. dept. pediat. Stanford U. Hosps., 1991-98; mem. self-assessment program for Pediat. in Rev., 1990-98; investigator adaptation primitive So. Ams. Indians, 1976—; African Pygmies, 1987—, worldwide primitive socs., 1997. Author: Primitive Peoples Without Salt, 1998, Amerindian Children: Mortality Study--Human Behavior and Evolution Society, 2005, child abuse study, 2006; mem. editl. bd. IRCS Jour. Med. Sci., 1975-90. Pres. Mich. Kidney Disease Found., 1969, Washtenaw County br. Mich. Childrens Aid Soc., 1964; trustee Ann Arbor Hands-On Mus., 1983-88; pres. bd. trustees Perry Nursery Sch. Ann Arbor, 1989-90 With USPHR, 1950-52. Fellow Am. Acad. Pediatrics (chmn. com. med. edn. 1974-80, chmn. coun. on pediatric edn. 1975-80, chmn. task force oversight of pediatric rev. and edn. program 1984-88, Clifford G. Grulee award 1979); mem. Soc. Pediatric Rsch., Midwest Soc. Pediatric Rsch. (pres. 1968), Am. Soc. Nephrology, Assn. Med. Sch. Pediatric Dept. Chairmen (mem. coun. 1977-79), Soc. for Exptl. Biology and Medicine, Am. Pediatric Soc., Alpha Omega Alpha, Gamma Sigma Epsilon. Home: 2892 Bay Ridge Dr Ann Arbor MI 48103-1704 Personal E-mail: wjoandmbo@aol.com.

**OLIVERI, EUGENE ALFRED,** gastroenterologist; b. N.Y.C., Apr. 30, 1937; children: Gregory, Lisa, Michelle. Student, Bklyn. Coll., 1954-56, 58-60; DO summa cum laude, Kansas City Coll., 1964; LHD, U. Health Scis., 2000; MSc, Trinity So. U., 2003. Diplomate Am. Bd. Internal Medicine, Am. Bd. Gastroenterology. Intern Detroit Osteo. Hosp., 1964-65; resident in internal medicine Botsford/Ziegler Hosps., 1965-67; fellowship in gastroenterology VA Hosp., East Orange, NJ, 1967-68; asst. dean Coll. Osteo. Medicine Mich. State U. Prof. dept. internal medicine sect. of gastroenterology Botsford Gen. Hosp., assoc. program dir. gastroenterology residency emeritus; mem., courtesy staff emeritus dept. of internal medicine Huron Valley Hosp. Trustee Pikeville (Ky.) Coll., 1994—, U. New Eng., Biddeford, Maine, 2001—. With U.S. Army, 1956—58. Recipient Highest Acad. Achievement award Mead-Johnson, 1964, Outstanding Alumni Achievement award U. for Health Scis., Coll. Osteo. Medicine, 1991, Dr. J.O. Watson Disting. Lecr. Ohio Osteo. Assn., 1991, Walter Patenge medal for humanitarian svc. MSU, 1999, Phillips medal Pub Svc., Ohio U., 2002; named Physician of Yr. Mich. chpt. Ileitis and Colitis Found., 1985, Botsford Profl. Staff, 1994. Fellow Am. Coll. Osteo. Internists (pres. 1982-83, Disting. Svc. award 1982, Disting. Lectr. award 1983); fellow Am. Coll. Internists (master); mem. Am. Osteo. Assn. (pres. 1999-2000, trustee mem. bd., Disting. Svc. certificat 2005), Mich. Assn. Osteo. Physician and Surgeons (pres. 1991-92), Oakland County Osteo. Assn., Am. Coll. Gastroenterology, Am. Soc. Gastrointestinal Endoscopy, Am. Soc. Addiction Medicine, Am. Osteo. Found. (bd. dirs., pres. bd. dirs., chair com. on awards), Mich. Osteo. Coll. Found. (chair, trustee, bd. dirs.), Crohn's and Colitis Found. Am. (Physician of Yr. 1991), Psi Sigma Alpha, Sigma Sigma Phi. Avocation: cooking. Home: 844 Old Milford Farms Milford MI 48381-3363 Personal E-mail: docoli@aol.com.

**OLIVERIO, PONZIO,** protective services official, educator; b. San Diego, Calif., June 14, 1958; s. Ponzio and Harriet Jean Oliverio; m. Amy Amber Edsall, Nov. 19, 1983; children: Giulia Marie, Giana. BA in Humanities, Thomas Edison Coll., Trenton, N.J., 1992; JD, U. San Diego Sch. Law, 1996. Bar: Calif. 1997; cert. in hostage negotiations FBI, 2004. Dep. sheriff San Diego County Sheriff, 1985—; prof. Nat. U., San Diego, 1999—; adj. faculty San Diego Regional Police Acad., 2000—; prof. U. Phoenix, San Diego, 2003—, faculty advisor; guest lectr., criminal procedure U. San Diego Sch. Law; instr. USN, Master-at-Arms Sch., San Diego. Uniform com. mem. San Diego Sheriff, 1993—95, process improvement team mem., 2003—, tng. officer. Columnist The Silver Star Holding Court, San Diego County Herald Cuff Links; co-author: (training manual) Crime-Free Mobile Housing Man., (anthology publ. in True Blue) Jimmy, 2004. Moot ct. judge U. San Diego Sch. Law, 2002—04; com. mem. State Bar Domestic Violence Com., Santa Ana, Calif.; facilitator Domestic Violence Restraining Order Clinic, San Diego, 1995—96. Recipient Letter of Appreciation, Calif. Dept. Corrections, 2000, Chula Vista, Calif. Police Dept., 2000, U.S. Border Patrol, 2001, Award of Exemplary Performance, San Diego Sheriff, 2000, Medal of Valor, 2001. Mem.: Statewide Calif. Coalition for Battered Women (assoc.), Dep. Sheriff's Assn. (assoc.), Fraternal Order of Police (assoc.). Conservative. Avocations: hunting, fishing. Home: 2208 Boulders Ct Alpine CA 91901 Personal E-mail: ponzio2@cox.net.

**OLIVER LEAHY TINEN KAEHLER, JEANNETTE** See LEAHY, JEANNETTE

**OLIVER-WARREN, MARY ELIZABETH,** retired library science educator, library and information scientist; b. Hamlet, N.C., Feb. 23, 1924; d. Washington and Carolyn Belle (Middlebrooks) Terry; m. David Oliver, 1947 (div. Feb. 1995). BS, Bluefield State U., 1948; MS, South Conn. State U., 1958; student, U. Conn., 1977. Cert. tchr., adminstr. and supr., Conn.; cert. pub. sch. substitute tchr., K-12, N.J. Media specialist Hartford Pub. Schs., Conn., 1952–86; with So. Conn. State U., New Haven, 1972—, asst. prof. Sch. Libr. Sci. and Instructional Tech., 1987—95, ret., 1995; substitute tchr. K-12 Windsor, Conn., 1999—2004; Grady County Pub. Schs., Cairo, Ga., 2004—. Mem. dept. curriculum com. So. Conn. State U. 1987-95, adj. prof., 1995—; cert. substitute tchr. Somerset County Pub. Schs., 1997—; cert. substitute tchr. Windsor, Conn. Sch. Sys., 1999–. Author: My Golden Moments, 1988, The Elementary School Media Center, 1990, Text Book Elementary School Media Center, 1991, I Must Fight Alone, 1991, (textbook) I Must Fight Alone, 1994. Mem. ALA, Conn. Ednl. Media Assn., Black Librs. Network N.J. Inc., Assn. Ret. Tchrs. Conn., Black and Hispanic Consortium, So. Conn. State U. Women's Assn., Cicuso Club (v.p.), Friends Club (v.p.), Delta Kappa Gamma, Alpha Kappa Alpha. Avocations: reading, music, piano, walking. Home: 1710 S Broad St Apt 35 Cairo GA 39828-3574

**OLIVIER, KATHY RICKS,** college basketball coach; b. Placentia, Calif. 1 child, Alexis. Student, Calif. State U., Fullerton; grad., U. Nev., 1982. Various coaching positions U. Nev., U. Calif.-Irvine, U. So. Calif., 1981-86; asst. coach UCLA Bruins, 1986; reached NCAA Sweet 16, 1991-92; head coach UCLA Bruins, 1993—. Achievements include finished 2nd in conf. (sch. record), 1997-98. Office: c/o Athletic Dept UCLA Women's Basketball PO Box 951361 Los Angeles CA 90095-1361

**OLIVIER, MICHAEL,** physiologist, educator; b. Neuss, Northrhine Westphalia, Germany, Dec. 5, 1966; s. Manfred Paul and Leonore Antonie Olivier; m. Claudia Scheiner, June 18, 1993; children: Deborah Alison, Eliana Carmel, Neriah Sarana. PhD, Cornell U., Ithaca, 1998. Postdoctoral rschr. Cornell U. Coll. Vet. Medicine, Ithaca, NY, 1998; rsch. assoc. Stanford U. Sch. Medicine, Calif., 1998—2001; asst. prof. physiology Med. Coll. Wis., Milw., 2001—04, assoc. prof. physiology, 2004—). Adj. prof. U. Wis., Whitewater, Wis., 2003—. Recipient Charles Epstein Rsch. award, Nat. Down Syndrome Soc., 2005, 2006. Mem.: Am. Soc. for Mass Spectrometry, North Am. Assn. Study of Obesity, Am. Soc. for Human Genetics. Roman Cath. Office: Med Coll Wis 8701 Watertown Plank Rd Milwaukee WI 53226 Office Phone: 414-456-4968. Office Fax: 414-456-6516. Business E-Mail: molivier@mcw.edu.

**OLIVOS, CLAUDIA,** artist, educator; d. Luis Olivos Olivos and Ximena Quiroga; 1 child, Julian. BFA in Painting, George Mason U., 1991, BA in Psychology, 1991; MFA, VCu. Coll., 2001. Counselor to adolescents Rappahanock Cmty. Svcs., Fredericksburg, Va., 1989—91, mental health counselor, 1991—97; housing counselor No. Va. Family Svc., Arlington, 1998—2000; faculty The Art League Alexandria, 1998—; owner Olivos ARt Studio LLC. Co-owner, dir. Internat. Visions Gallery, Washington, 1997—99; artist in residence Rappahanock Falls Acad., Fredericksburg, 1997—98, Key Elem. Sch., Arlington, 1999—; faculty Art Inst. Washington, Arlington; bd. mem. Teatro de la Luna, Arlington; guest artist various schs., 2001—. Cover of book, Coming Home, 1998, painting on cover, Anthology of Latin American Poetry, 2006, CD cover, Silence Beyond Octaves, 2000, numerous exhbns. Cmty. artist Streets of Arlington, 2000—, Cultural Affairs Dept., Arlington, Va., 2000. Office Phone: 703-237-7562. Business E-Mail: claudia@claudiaolivos.com.

**OLK, FREDERICK JAMES,** county official, legal assistant; b. Clintonville, Wis., Apr. 30, 1952; s. James Howard and Bernice Helen (Durben) O. Student, Inst. Comp. Polit.& Econ. Sys., 1973; BS in Liberal Arts, U. Wis. River Falls, 1976; cert., Wis. Sch. Real Estate, 1980. Notary pub., Ill. Libr. asst. U. Wis., Stevens Point and Oshkosh 1977 80; graduate libr. U.S. Dept. Justice, Oxford, 1980, editl. libr. The Chgo. Cath. newspaper Archdiocese Chgo., 1980—89; tax. examiner Cook County, Chgo., 1990—. Congl. intern U.S. Ho. of Rep., Washington, 1973; sales rep. Waupaca (Wis.) Pub. Co., 1978-79; freelance paralegal, Chgo., 1988—; security guard, account mgr. Glenbrook Security Svcs., Wheeling, Ill., 1988—; asst. reference libr. Cicero (Ill.) Pub. Libr., 1989; genealogy rschr. Lineage Search Assocs., Mechanicsville, Va., 1980-99; v.p. New World Credit Union, Chgo., 1981-86 Columnist Looking back Chgo. Cath., 1985-89. Tutor Mercy Home for Boys, Chgo., 1987—88; coord. Friends of Vatican Libr., Chgo., 1995—; mem. exec. bd. customer adv. coun. U.S. Postal Svc., Cicero, 1997—; Cicero rep. for Ill. 43d dist. Anti-Crime Adv. Bd., 1999—2001; precinct capt. Wis. and Ill. Rep. coms., 1973—; Rep. judge of election Cook County, 1980—; mem. Rome tour St. John Cantius Parish Resurrection Choir, 2001, sang at St. Peter's Basilica, 2001. Named adm. Nebr. Navy, State of Nebr., 1982, col. State of Ala., 1988, Internat. Citizen of Yr., Hutt River Province, Australia, 1995; recipient Legion of Merit Rep. Nat. Com., 1997, Order of the Arrow, Boy Scouts Am., 1971. Mem. Am. Soc. Notaries (life, chmn. govt. rels. 1984-85), Nat. Assn. Investigative Specialists, Am. Legion (life), Amtrak Hist. Soc. (asst. archivist 1994—), Chgo. Geneal. Soc. (life, bd. dirs. 1988-90), 20th Century R.R. Club (sec. 1994-98, Century Club 1996, dir. 1998-2000), KC (del. archdiocesan pastoral coun. 1996—, grand knight cardinal coun. 2001-03) Avocations: rail travel, genealogy, reading, music, stamp collecting/philately. Office: Cook County Clk 118 N Clark St Ste 434 Chicago IL 60602-1382 Office Phone: 847-452-3595.

**OLKINETZKY, SAM,** artist, educator, retired museum director; b. N.Y.C., Nov. 22, 1919; s. Isidor and Jennie O.; m. Sammie Lee Sturdevant, Dec. 20, 1959; children: Jov Shan, Tova Shana. BA, Bklyn. Coll., 1942; postgrad. Inst. Fine Arts, N.Y. U., 1946-47. Assoc. prof. art and humanities Okla. A&M U., Stillwater, 1947-57; vis. asst. prof. art U. Okla., Norman, 1957-58; assoc. prof. art Mus. of Art, 1959—; dir. Mus. Art U. Okla., Norman, 1959-83. Vis. prof. art and humanities U. Ark., Fayetteville, 1962-63, 67-68, Langston (Okla.) U., 1969-70; art com. Norman-McGee Industries, Inc.; advisor State of Okla. Visual Arts; mem. State Art Collection Com.; Mem. Norman Arts and Humanities Council One-man exhbns. include Arts Place II, Okla. Art Ctr., Firehouse Art Ctr., Norman, 1989; other exhbns. include Mus. Non-Objective Art, N.Y.C., Mus. Modern Art, N.Y.C.; 50-yr. Retrospective Exhbn., 1942-92, Norick Art Ctr., Oklahoma City, 1992; represented in permanent collections Mus. Art U. Okla., Philbrook Art Mus., Tulsa, Oklahoma City Mus. of Art.

Served with USAAF, 1942-45. Recipient Gov.'s Art award, 1981. Mem. Okla. Museums Assn. (pres. 1978-79), Internat. Council Museums, Mountain-Plains Museums Assn., Am. Assn. Museums, Art Mus. Assn.

**OLLER, JOHN W., JR.,** educator, writer; b. Las Vegas, N.Mex., Oct. 22, 1943; s. John W. and Betty Rickard Oller; m. Mary Anne Chavez, Oct. 19, 1952; children: Mark Louis, Laura Lynn Oller Murdoch, Stephen David, Ruth Marie. Gen. Secondary Tchg. Credential, Fresno State U., Calif., 1966; MA, U. Rochester, NY, 1968, PhD, 1969. Asst. prof. UCLA, 1969—71, assoc. prof., 1971—72, U. N.Mex., Albuquerque, 1972—80, prof., 1980—97; head dept.,prof. U. La., Lafayette, 1997—2004, Hawthorne regents prof. IV, 2004—. Disting. vis. prof. So. Ill. U., Carbondale, 1976—77. Author, editor: Methods that Work: A Smorgasbord of Ideas for Language Teachers (Mildenberger medal, 1984); co-author: Images that Work: Creating Successful Messages in Marketing and High Stakes Communication, (book & dvd-roms) Milestones: Normal Speech and Language Across the Life Span. Sec. Sertoma, Lafayette, 1999—2006. Office: Univ Louisiana at Lafayette PO Box 43170 Lafayette LA 70504-3170 Office Phone: 337-962-4649. Office Fax: 337-482-6195. Personal E-mail: joller@louisiana.edu. Business E-Mail: joller@louisiana.edy.

**OLLER, WILLIAM MAXWELL,** retired energy executive, retired military officer; b. Lancaster, Pa., Apr. 7, 1924; s. John Secrist and Mabel Margaret (Coffman) O.; m. Doris Seitz Greenleaf, June 15, 1946; children: Arthur G., J. Richard. BS, U.S. Naval Acad., 1946; MBA, George Washington U., 1960. Commd. ensign USN, 1946, advanced through grades to rear adm., 1972; svc. in Samoa, Philippines and Italy; exec. officer Naval Supply Ctr., Newport, R.I., 1966-67, Ships Parts Control Ctr., Mechanicsberg, Pa., 1970-72; comdr. Def. Fuel Supply Ctr., Alexandria, Va., 1972-76; comdg. officer Naval Supply Ctr., Norfolk, Va., 1976-77; gen. mgr. corp. supply and distbn. Champlin Petroleum Co., Houston, 1977-79, Ft. Worth, 1979-81; sr. v.p. Petroleum Ops. and Support Svcs., Inc., New Orleans, 1981-82, pres., 1982-84; spl. asst. to pres., CEO Kaneb Svcs., Inc., Houston, 1984-85; exec. v.p. Tex. Ea. Products Pipeline Co., Houston, 1986-90. Pres. Am. Leadership Forum, Houston, 1986. Decorated Legion of Merit with gold star, Meritorious Svc. medal with gold star, Joint Svc. Commendation medal. Home: 20510 Falcons Landing Circle # 1205 Sterling VA 20165

**OLLEY, ROBERT EDWARD,** economist, educator; b. Vendun, Que., Can., Apr. 16, 1933; s. Edwin Henry and Elizabeth (Reed) O.; m. Shirley Ann Dahl, Jan. 19, 1957; children— Elizabeth Anne, George Steven, Susan Catherine, Maureen Carolyn BA, Carleton U. Can., 1960; MA, Queen's U., Can., 1961, PhD in Econs., 1969. Vis. asst. prof. Queen's U., Kingston, Canada, 1967-68; asst. prof. econs. U. Sask., Saskatoon, Canada, 1963-67, 68-69, assoc. prof., 1969-71, 73-75, prof., 1975-93, prof. emeritus, 1993—; pres. Gen. Econs. Ltd., 1993—. Dir. rsch. Royal Commn. on Consumer Problems and Inflation, 1967-68; econ. advisor Bell Can., Montreal, Que., 1971-73, 78-79, Can. Telecom. Carriers Assn., 1978-85, Sask. Power Corp., 1980-83; econ. advisor AT&T, 1980-90, Waste Mgmt., Inc., 1990-92, SaskTel, 1989-93; chmn. adv. com. on consumer stds. Stds. Coun. Can., 1992-93; Can. rep. to ISO/COPOLCO, Geneva, 1992-93. Author, editor: Consumer Product Testing, 1979; Consumer Product Testing II, 1981; Consumer Credit in Canada, 1966; Economics of the Public Firm: Regulation, Rates, Costs, Productivity Analysis, 1983, Total Factor Productivity of Canadian Telecommunications, 1984; Consumer Reps. Conf. Procs., 1st-4th, 1982-91. Can. Found. for Econ. Edn., 1974-82, Can. Gen. Stds. Bd., 1977-81; v.p. Niagara-on-the-Lake Hosp. Found., 2000-03, bd. dirs., 1998-; Recipient Silver Jubilee medal Her Majesty The Queen, 1977, Can.'s Jean P. Carriere Exptl. Contbr. Vol. Standardization award, 1995. Mem. Royal Econ. History Soc., Royal Econs. Assn., Econ. History Assn., Am. Econ. Assn., Can. Econ. Assn., Consumers Assn. Can. (v.p. 1967-75, pres. 1975-77), Can. Stds. Assn. (dir., exec. com. 1971-93, vice chmn. 1985-87, chmn. 1987-89, Award of Merit 1995), Consumer's Assn. Found. Can. (v.p. 1989-95), Can. Comm. Rsch. Ctr. (dir. 1992-97), Internat. Telecom. Soc. (bd. dirs. 1986-2004), Shaw Guild, Niagara Hist. Assn. (bd. dirs. 1997-99), Niagara-on-the-Lake Golf Club (bd. dirs. 2001-05, v.p. 2002-05) Home and Office: PO Box 1440 374 Queen St Niagara-on-the-Lake ON Canada L0S 1J0 Office Phone: 909-468-0530. Personal E-mail: olley@niagara.com.

**OLLIE, PEARL LYNN,** artist, singer, lyricist; b. Highland Park, Mich., Oct. 15, 1953; d. Sam and Estelle Theresa Ollie; m. Christopher John Keyes, Nov. 29, 1975 (div. Nov. 1978); 1 child, Shane Michael Fiondella. Student, Henry Ford C.C., Dearborn, Mich., 1988—89, Soc. Arts and Crafts Coll., 1971—74, Ctr. for Creative Study, 1980—81. Tchr. ceramics Detroit Head Start, Mt. Zion, Mich., 1973; logo designer, platemaker, printer and painter Island Art Ctr., St. Simons Island, Ga., 1976—79; sec., receptionist High Performance Tube Inc., St. Simons Island, 1976—79; personal legal sec. State Senator Bill Littlefield, St. Simons Island, 1979; art coord., booking agt. Club Savoy Tivoli, San Francisco, 1979; tchr. at Redmond Hall, Skamokawa, Wash, 1980; artist Hollywood Costumes, Dearborn, 1980—90; account mgr. ins. Dr. Sheryl A. Ollie, Lynn, Mass., 1990; tchr. art Art in Nahant, Mass., 1991—97; staff artist, acting, costumes Creative Currents, Ferndale, Mich., 1990—. Make-up artist Paramount Costumes (was Hollywood Costumes), Dearborn; tchr. art and music St. Lukes Montessori Sch., Detroit; artist Mich. Art and Design, Detroit, Dearborn Awnings, Lincoln Park, Mich.; instr. Aups, Provence, France, 1997 Make-up artist TV commls. and shows, movies, commd. portrait artist, illustrator, guest (TV program) All Star Kids. Co-pres. Nahant PTO, Johnson Sch., 1991-92; tchr. 8th grade religious edn., vocalist area ch. chorus, choir dir. St. Anselms; vocal instr. Axis Music Musicians Inst.; instr. art, music and drama Hope of Detroit Acad Roman Catholic. Avocations: paint, sculpting, singing, writing, piano. Home and Office: The Cultured Pearl 840 Brevard Ave Rockledge FL 32955 Office Phone: 321-536-3523. Personal E-mail: pearlollieartist@yahoo.com.

**OLLINGER, W. JAMES,** lawyer; b. Kittanning, Pa., Apr. 5, 1943; s. William James and Margaret Elizabeth (Reid) Ollinger; m. Susan Louise Gerspacher, Oct. 20, 1979; children: Mary Rebecca, David James. BA, Capital U., Columbus, Ohio, 1966; JD, Case Western Res. U., 1968. Bar: Ohio 1968, US Dist Ct (no dist) Ohio 1971. Ptnr. Baker & Hostetler, Cleve., 1968—. Mem. Bentleyville Village Coun., Ohio, 1990—93; mayor Bentleyville, 1997—99. Mem.: Order of Coif, Phi Delta Phi. Office: Baker & Hostetler 3200 Nat City Ctr 1900 E 9th St Ste 3200 Cleveland OH 44114-3475 Office Phone: 216-861-7473. E-mail: jollinger@bakerlaw.com.

**OLLMANN, BRAD ERIC,** music educator; b. Merrill, Wis., Oct. 15, 1974; s. Richard Lee and Elayne Jeanette Ollmann. MusB, U. Minn., 1999; MA in Music Edn., U. St. Thomas, 2006. Elem. music tchr. Pky. Elem. Sch., St. Paul, 1999—2004, Mus. Magnet Elem. Sch., St. Paul, 2004—. Recipient Newberry Creativity award, U. Wis., Marathon Ctr., 1995; grantee, ECOLAB, 2005; scholar, Merrill Area Pub. Sch. Tchr. Assn., 1993, St. Paul Ret. Tchrs., Inc., 2003; Jean Sinor scholar, Midwest Kodaly Music Tchr. Assn., 2003. Mem.: Music Educators Nat. Conf., Orgn. Am. Kodaly Tchrs. (sec. Minn. chpt. 2004—), St. Paul Fedn. Tchrs. (cert.). Dfl. Avocations: travel, sports, reading, gardening. Home: 2048 Pathways Dr Saint Paul MN 55119-4670 Office: Museum Magnet Elem Sch 560 Concordia Ave Saint Paul MN 55103 Office Phone: 651-325-2600. Business E-Mail: brad.ollmann@spps.org.

**OLMERT, EHUD,** Prime Minister of Israel; b. Binyamina, Israel, Sept. 30, 1945; m. Aliza Olmert; 4 children. BA, LLB, Hebrew U. Jerusalem. Mem. Knesset, 1973—98, 2003—; min. minorities Govt. of Israel, 1988—90, min. health, 1990—92, min. comm., 2003—04, vice prime min., min. industry, trade & labor, 2004—06, acting min. fin., 2005, acting prime min., 2006, prime min., 2006—; mayor City of Jerusalem, 1993—2003. Mem. Kadima Party, 2006—. Named one of 100 Most Influential People, Time Mag., 2006. Office: Kinyat Ben Gurion 3 Kaplan St 91919 Jerusalem Israel*

**OLMOS, EDWARD JAMES,** actor; b. L.A., Feb. 24, 1947; m. Kaija Keel, 1972 (div.); m. Lorraine Bracco, Jan. 28, 1994 (div.); 2 children. AA in Sociology, East Los Angeles City Coll.; postgrad., Calif. State U., L.A.;

degree (hon.), U. Colo., Whittier Coll., Calif. State U., Fresno, Occidental Coll., Film Inst. Hollywood, Calif. Exec. dir. Lives in Hazard Ednl. Project, nat. gang prevention program. Performed in exptl. theater, L.A.; actor (play) Zoot Suit (Tony nominee, Los Angeles Drama Critics Circle award, Theatre World award), Broadway and Los Angeles, 1982, Triumph of the Spirit, 1989; actor, co-producer film Stand and Deliver, 1988 (nominee best actor Acad. Awards 1988); actor films Wolfen, 1981, Zoot Suit, 1981, Blade Runner, 1982, (also assoc. prodr., composer, music adapter) The Ballad of Gregorio Cortez, 1983, Saving Grace, 1986 (also prodr.) Stand and Deliver, 1988, Triumph of the Spirit, 1989, Talent for the Game, 1991, (also dir., prodr.) American Me, 1992, A Million to Juan, 1994, My Family, 1995, Caught, 1996, Selena, 1997, Death in Granada, 1997, The Wonderful Ice Cream Suit, 1998, The Wall, 1998, Gossip, 1999, (voice) The Road to El Dorado, 2000, Gossip, 2000, Jack and Marilyn, 2002; (TV series) Miami Vice, 1984-89 (Emmy award for best supporting actor in drama series 1985, Golden Globe award 1986); Battlestar Galactica, 2004-; (TV miniseries) The Fortunate Pilgrim, 1988, Menendez: A Killing in Beverly Hills, 1994, The Burning Season, 1995 (Golden Globe award for Best Supporting Actor in a TV Movie, Miniseries or Series 1994), Mirage, 1995, Slave of Dreams, 1995, Roosters, 1995, American Family, 2002, Battlestar Galactica, 2003, The Batman, 2004; (TV movies) The Princess and the Barrio Boy, 2000, The Judge, 2001, In the Time of the Butterflies, 2001; star ABC miniseries Dead Man's Walk (prequel to Lonesome Dove) 1996; co-star TV movie 12 Angry Men, 1997; prodr., dir. (TV documentary) Lives in Hazard, 1994, The Limbic Region, 1995. U.S. goodwill amb. UNICEF; nat. spokesman for voter registration, Juvenile Diabetes Found.; AIDS Awareness Found.; bd. dirs. Heal L.A., Recruiting New Tchrs., 20th Century Fund, UCLA Sch. Film and Theater, Miami Children's Hosp., L.A. Children's Hosp., Nat. Coun. on Adoption, Children's Action Netowrk, Hollywood Supports, Nat. Hispanic U., Plaza del Raza, Whittier Coll.; spkr. at numerous chs., charities and juvenile instns. throughout U.S. Address: Olmos Productions 18034 Ventura Blvd Ste 288 Encino CA 91316-3516 Office: AA Creative Artists Agency 830 Wilshire Blvd Beverly Hills CA 90210

**OLMSTEAD, CECIL JAY,** lawyer; b. Jacksonville, Fla., Oct. 15, 1920; s. Cecil Jay Sr. and Bessie (Irby) O.; m. Frances Hughes (dec. 2006); children: Cecil Jay III, Frank Hughes, Jane Olmstead Murphy, Amy Olmstead Vanecek. BA, U. Ga., 1950, LLB, 1951; Sterling Grad. fellow, Yale Law Sch., 1951-52; LLD (hon.), U. Hull, Eng., 1978. Bar: Ga. 1950, U.S. Supreme Ct 1964, D.C. 1978. Asst. to legal adviser Dept. State, counsel Mut. Security Agy., counsel Hoover Commn. on Orgn. Exec. Br. of Govt., 1952-55; prof. N.Y. U. Sch. Law, 1953-61; dir. Inter-Am. law Inst., 1958-61, adj. prof. law, 1959-61; atty. Texaco, Inc., N.Y.C., 1961-62, asst. to chmn. bd., 1962-70, v.p., asst. to chmn. bd., 1970, v.p., asst. to pres., 1970-71, v.p., asst. to chief exec. officer, 1971-73, exec. dept., v.p., 1973-80; mem. firm Steptoe & Johnson, Washington, 1980—. Vis. prof. Columbia U. Sch. Law, 1959; Wang Disting. vis. prof. St. Johns U., 1987-90; mem. adv. panel on internat. law to sec. state; adv. com. law of sea State Dept.; also adv. com. transnat. enterprise; U.S. del. UN Com. on Law of Sea, 1972-73; U.S. del. UN Conf. on Law of Sea, 1974-76; Eisenhower lectr. Nat. War Coll., 1973; mem. U.S. del. UN Conf. on Code of Conduct for Transnat. Corps., ann. 1984-90; mem. World Bank's panel of conciliators of the Internat. Ctr. for Settlement of Investment Disputes, 1988-95; vis. fellow All Souls Coll., Oxford U., 1988; vis. scholar Yale Law Sch., 1990-91. With USAF, 1943-46, 8th and 20th Air Forces. ETO, PTO. Recipient Gold medal City of Brussels (Belgium, 1973, Gold medal City of Paris (France), 1984; named Commdr. Brit. Empire (hon.), 1990. Mem. Internat. Law Assn. (pres. Am. br. 1966-73, pres. 1972-75, vice chmn. exec. coun. 1975-86, chmn. exec. coun. 1986-88, 1st Disting. Svc. award 2004), Am. Law Inst. (assoc. reporter Restatement of the Fgn. Rels. Law of the U.S., 1st edit. 1964, advisor 3d edit.), Coun. on Fgn. Rels., Washington Inst. Fgn. Affairs, Nat. Fgn. Trade Coun. (dir. 2004), Am. Coun. on Germany (hon. dir.), Coun. on Ocean Law (dir.), Knickerbocker Club, Yale Club, Fairfield County Hunt Club (Westport), Cosmos Club (Washington), Order of Coif, Phi Beta Kappa. Home: 4 Sprucewood Ln Westport CT 06880-4021 Office: 1330 Connecticut Ave NW Washington DC 20036-1704 Office Phone: 202-429-6483.

**OLMSTEAD, CLARENCE WALTER, JR.,** lawyer; b. Alexandria, Va., Jan. 24, 1943; s. Clarence Walter and Rhea Nancy (Donnelly) O.; m. Kathleen Frances Heenan, Sept. 7, 1973; children: Nicholas Heenan, Jonathan Heenan, Caitlin Heenan. AB, Stanford U., 1965; LLB, Columbia U., 1968. Bar: N.Y. 1970, U.S. Dist. Ct. (so. and ea. dists.) N.Y. 1970, U.S. Ct. Appeals (2d cir.) 1970, U.S. Supreme Ct. 1986. Law clk. to presiding judge U.S. Dist. Ct. (we. dist.) Wis., 1968-69; assoc. Shearman & Sterling, NYC, 1969-76, ptnr., 1976, of counsel. Bd. dirs. West Side Montessori Sch., N.Y.C., 1983-89, pres., 1985-87; mem. sch. com. Cathedral Sch., N.Y.C., 1992-95; trustee North Country Sch. Camp Treetops, 1992-95. Mem. ABA, N.Y. State Bar Assn., Assn. Bar City of N.Y., Phi Beta Kappa. Office: 599 Lexington Ave New York NY 10022

**OLMSTEAD, MARJORIE ANN,** physics professor; b. Glen Ridge, NJ, Aug. 18, 1958; d. Blair E. and Elizabeth (Dempwolf) Olmstead. BA in Physics, Swarthmore Coll., 1979; MA in Physics, U. Calif., Berkeley, 1982, PhD, 1985. Rsch. staff Palo Alto (Calif.) Rsch. Ctr. Xerox Corp., 1985-86; asst. prof. physics U. Calif., Berkeley, 1986-90, U. Wash., Seattle, 1991-93, assoc. prof., 1993-97, prof., 1997—, dir. nanotech. PhD program, 2000—. Prin. investigator sci. materials divsn. Lawrence Berkeley Lab., 1988—93. Contbr. articles to profl. jours. Named Presdl. Young Investigator, NSF, 1987; recipient Devel. award, IBM, 1986, 1987, Rsch. award, A. von Humboldt Found., 2000. Fellow: Am. Phys. Soc. (chair com. on status of women in physics 1999, Maria Goeppart-Mayer award 1996), Am. Vacuum Soc. (Peter Mark Meml. award 1994). Office: U Washington Dept Physics PO Box 351560 Seattle WA 98195-1560 Office Phone: 206-685-3031. E-mail: olmstd@u.washington.edu.

**OLMSTEAD, WILLIAM EDWARD,** mathematics professor; b. San Antonio, June 2, 1936; s. William Harold and Gwendolyn (Littlefield) Olmstead; m. Adele Cross, Aug. 14, 1957 (div. 1967); children: William Harold, Randell Edward. BS, Rice U., 1959; MS, Northwestern U., 1962, PhD, 1963. Mem. rsch. staff S.W. Rsch. Inst., San Antonio, 1959—60; Sloan Found. postdoctoral fellow Johns Hopkins, 1963—64; prof. applied math. Northwestern U., Evanston, Ill., 1964—, chmn. dept. engring. scis. and applied math., 1991—93. Vis. mem. Courant Inst. Math. Scis. NYU, 1967—68; faculty visitor U. Coll. London, 1973, Calif. Inst. Tech., 1987, 90; editor Options Prof. Newsletter, Spear Capital Mgmt., 2003—. Contbr. articles to profl. jours. Named Technol. Inst. Tchr. of Yr., 1980, Charles Deering McCormick prof., 1994—97; recipient Award for Tchg. Excellence, Northwestern Alumni Assn., 1993. Mem.: Am. Contract Bridge League (silver life master), Soc. Indsl. and Applied Math. (editl. bd. jour. 1997—), Am. Phys. Soc., Am. Math. Soc., Am. Acad. Mechanics, Soc. Engring. Sci. (bd. dirs. 1998—2000), John Evans Club, Sigma Tau, Tau Beta Pi, Sigma Xi. Episcopalian. Home: 153 E Laurel Ave #203 Lake Forest IL 60045 Office: Northwestern U Dept Engring Scis And Applie Evanston IL 60208-0001

**OLMSTEAD, JERAULD LOCKWOOD,** telephone company executive; b. Des Moines, Aug. 26, 1938; s. George Hamden and Virginia (Camp) O.; m. Mary Karen Autenrieth, June 20, 1962 (div. Dec. 1986); children: Scott H., Victoria L., Jerauld; m. Gisele A. Child, June 17, 1988. BS, Iowa State U., 1961; MBA, George Washington U., 1979; Cert. mgmt. accountant. Vice-pres. First Nat. Bank of Washington, 1969; v.p., dir. Intermediate Credit Corp., 1969-73, Internat. Gen. Industries, Inc., 1974-79, pres., dir., 1980-82, IB Credit Corp., 1982-85, N.Am. Communications, Inc., Bethesda, Md., 1985—. Sr. v.p., dir. Internat. Bank, 1978-85. Bd. govs. Iowa State U. Found., 1980—; chmn. corporate adv. bd. div. arts and humanities U. Md., 1982—; sec-treas. George Olmsted Found., 1970—. Served with U.S. Army, 1961-63. Decorated Knight of Malta, Order of St. John Mem. Fin. Execs. Inst., Mensa, Soc. Cincinnati, Soc. Sojourner Club, Bethesda Country Club, Beta Alpha Psi, Beta Gamma Sigma. Republican. Episcopalian. Home and Office: 7735 Arrowood Ct Bethesda MD 20817-2821 Office Phone: 301-365-7225.

**OLMSTED, THOMAS JAMES,** archbishop; b. Oketo, Kans., Jan. 21, 1947; BS in Philosophy, St. Thomas Sem. Coll., 1969; MA in Theology, 1977, PhD in Canon Law, 1979. Ordained priest Roman Cath. Diocese, 1973, ordained bishop Roman Cath. Diocese, 1999. Diocese. assoc. pastor Cathedral of Risen Christ, Lincoln, Nebr., 1973—76; asst. Secretariat of State of Holy See Pontifical N.Am. Coll., Rome, 1979—88; pastor St. Vincent de Paul Parish, Seward, Nebr., 1989—93; dean personal formation Pontifical Coll. Josephinum, Columbus, Ohio, 1993—97, rector, 1997—99; coadjutor bishop Diocese of Wichita, Kans., 1999—2001, bishop, 2001—03, Diocese Phoenix, 2003—. Com. mem. U.S. Conf. Cath. Bishops, 1999—; mem. adminstrv. com. U.S. Bishops, mem. com. consecrated life; bd.dir. Cath. Legal Immigration Network. Office: Diocese of Phoenix 400 East Monroe St Phoenix AZ 85004-2336

**OLNESS, KAREN NORMA,** medical educator; b. Rushford, Minn., Aug. 28, 1936; d. Norman Theodore and Karen Agnes (Gunderson) O.; m. Hakon Daniel Torjesen, 1962. BA, U. Minn., 1958, BS, MD, 1961. Diplomate Am. Bd. Pediat., Am. Bd. Med. Hypnosis, Develop. & Behavioral Pediatrics. Intern Harbor Gen. Hosp., Torrance, Calif.; resident Nat. Children's Hosp. Med. Ctr., Washington; asst. prof. George Washington U., Washington, 1970-74; assoc. prof. U. Minn., Mpls., 1974-87; prof. pediat., family medicine and internat. health Case Western Res. U., Cleve., 1987—. Named Outstanding Woman Physician, Minn. Assn. Women Physicians, 1987; recipient Christopherson award Am. Acad. Pediat., 1998, Aldrich award, Am. Acad. Pediat., 1999, Ann. award Soc. Devel. and Behavioral Pediat., 2003; named to Cleve. Med. Hall of Fame, 2000. Fellow Am. Acad. Pediat. (chair internat. health sect. 2001), Am. Acad. Family Physicians, Am. Soc. Clin. Hypnosis (pres. 1984-86), Soc. Clin. and Exptl. Hypnosis (pres. 1991-93); mem. Soc. for Devel. and Behavioral Pediat. (pres. 1991-92), Northwestern Pediat. Soc. (pres. 1977), Internat. Hypnosis Soc. (pres. 2003—). Office: Case Western Res U 11100 Euclid Ave Cleveland OH 44106-6038 Office Phone: 216-368-4368. Business E-Mail: karen.olness@case.edu.

**OLNEY, JOHN WILLIAM,** psychiatry professor; b. Marathon, Iowa, Oct. 23, 1931; married, 1957; 3 children. BA, U. Iowa, 1957, MD, 1963. Diplomate Am. Bd. Psychiatry, Am. Bd. Neurology. Intern Kaiser Permanente Found., San Francisco, 1963-64; resident, 1964-68; from instr. to assoc. prof. psychiatry Washington U., St. Louis, 1968-77. prof. psychiatry and neuropathology Sch. Medicine, 1977—. NIMH biol. sci. trainee Washington U., 1966-68; asst. psychiatrist Barnes Hosp., 1968—; cons. psychiatrist Malcolm Bliss Mental Health Ctr., 1968—; elected to Inst. Medicine/NAS, 1996. Recipient Wakeman award Rsch. Neurosci., 1992; co-recipient Charles A. Dana award for Pioneering Achievements in Health, 1994. Mem. APA, Am. Assn Neuropathology, Soc. Neurosci. Assn. Rsch. Nervous & Mental Disorders, Psychiatric Rsch. Soc. Achievements include research in role of excitatory neurotoxins in disorders of the nervous system. Office: Washington U Dept Psychiatry Sch Med Saint Louis MO 63110

**OLNEY, ROBERT STANBURY, III,** sportswriter and baseball analyst; BA in Jour., Vanderbilt Univ. Former sports feature writer, lead sports editor NY Times, NYC, 1998—2003; columnist ESPN The Mag., 2003—, ESPN.com; baseball analyst ESPN's Baseball Tonight, 2003—. Author: (sports books) The Last Night of the Yankee Dynasty, 2004. Office: ESPN ESPN Plz 935 Middle St Bristol CT 06010*

**OLOFSON, TOM WILLIAM,** technology company executive; b. Oak Park, Ill., Oct. 10, 1941; s. Ragnar V. and Ingrid E. Olofson; m. Jeanne Hamilton, Aug. 20, 1960; children: Christopher, Scott. Various mgmt. positions Bell Telephone Co. of Pa., Pitts., 1963-67; sales mgr. Xerox Corp., Detroit, 1967-68, nat. account mgr. Rochester, NY, 1968, mgr. govt. planning, 1969, mgr. Kansas City (Mo.) br., 1969-74; corp. v.p. health products group Marion Labs., Inc., Kansas City, 1974-78, sr. v.p., pres. Office Pres., 1978-80; exec. v.p., dir. Electronic Realty Assocs., Inc., 1980-83; chmn. bd., CEO Emblem Graphic Sys., Inc., 1983-88, EPIQ Sys., Inc., 1988—. Dir. DemoGraFX, Elinco Internat., Access Industries, Inc., Saztec Internat., Capital Ptnrs. Bd. visitors U. Pitts., Joseph M. Katz Grad. Sch. Bus.; past trustee Barstow Sch.; past chmn. bd. trustees Village United Presbyn. Ch.; chmn. Tom. W. and Jeanne H. Olofson Found., 2001-. Mem. Carlton Club (Chgo.), Kansas City Club, Omicron Delta Kappa, Sigma Chi. Republican. Presbyterian. Office: EPIQ Sys Inc 501 Kansas Ave Kansas City KS 66105-1309

**OLONI, ANTHONY OLUSHEGUN,** medical association administrator, director; s. James Bolaji and Deborah Funmi Oloni. MBBS, U. Ilorin, Nigeria, 1987; grad. cert. in Pub. Health Informatics, U. Ill., 2006, MPH in Informatics, 2004. Med. intern Mil. Hosp., Yaba, Lagos, Nigeria, 1988—89; med. rsch. assoc. Coll. of Medicine, U. Lagos, 1989—90; med. dir. Mc'Lonie Indsl. Clin., Lagos, 1990—92; pub. health cons. Phila. Dept. Pub. Health, 1994—99; pres., CEO, med. dir. Pub. Health Informatics Cons., Atlanta, 2000—; med. dir. Preventive Medicine Assoc., Atlanta, 2000—03. Directorship Nat. Black Leadership Initiative on Cancer, Phila., 1997—99; chaiman Metro-Atlanta Coalition for Cancer Awareness, Atlanta, 2001—02; dir., health adminstr. Project Flow, Mayors Office Cmty. Svcs.; chief health coord. Your Health. Recipient Ujama award for Cmty. Economics. Mem.: Am. Med. Informatics Assn. (assoc.). Achievements include design of patient electronic health record sys. Home: 1862 Hickory Creek Ct Acworth GA 30102 Office: Public Health Informatics Cons PO Box 2822 Acworth GA 30102 Office Phone: 678-354-6144. Home Fax: 678-355-0462. Business E-Mail: anthony.oloni.md@phicon.org.

**OLOPADE, OLUFUNMILAYO FALUSI (FUNMI OLOPADE),** geneticist, educator, oncologist, hematologist; b. Nigeria, Apr. 29, 1957; m. Christopher Sola Olopade; 3 children. MD with distinction, U. Ibadan, Nigeria, 1980. Diplomate Am. Bd. Internal Medicine, Am. Bd. Med. Oncology, Am. Bd. Hematology; lic. MD Ill., Ind. Med. officer Nigerian Navy Hosp.; intern in medicine, surgery, pediatrics, ob-gyn. Univ. Coll. Hosp., Ibadan, 1980—81; intern in internal medicine Cook County Hosp., Chgo., 1983—84, resident in internal medicine, 1984—86, chief resident in medicine, 1986; clin. instr. U. Ill. Abraham Lincoln Sch. Medicine, Chgo., 1986—87; postdoctoral fellow jt. sect. hematology/oncology U. Chgo., 1987—91, asst. prof. hematology/oncology, Pritzker Sch. Medicine, 1991—2002, mem. Cancer Rsch. Ctr., 1991—, mem. Cancer Biology com., 1994—, mem. Genetics com., 1996—, assoc. prof. medicine, prof. medicine and human genetics Ill., 2002—, dir. Ctr. for Clinical Cancer Genetics, Cancer Risk Clinic Ill., 1992—, dir. Hematology/Oncology Fellowship Program Ill., 1998—. Attending physician Cook County Hosp., Chgo., 1987; mem. steering com., cooperative family registry for breast cancer studies, Nat. Cancer Inst., also mem. adv. com. Cancer Genetics Network and bd. counselors; mem. adv. bd. Cancerandcareers.org; lectr. in field. Ad hoc reviewer Jour. AMA, Genes, Chromosomes and Cancer, Genomics, Human Molecular Genetics, Cancer Rsch., Blood, Molecular Carcinogenesis, Jour. Clin. Oncology, New Eng. Jour. Medicine; contbr. articles to profl. jours.; contbr. to book chpts. and abstracts on topics including genetics of cancer. Mem. med. adv. bd. Young Survival Coalition. Named a Top Doctor, Chicago Mag., 1997; recipient Sir Samuel Manuwa Gold medal for Excellence in Clin. Sciences, 1980, Scholar award, James S. McDonnell Found., 1992, Doris Duke Disting. Clin. Scientist award, 2000, Phenomenal Women award, 2003, People Are Today's Heroes (PATH), Gov. Rod R. Blagojevich, presented by First Lady Patti Blagojevich, State Ill., 2005, Heroes In Healthcare award, Access Cmty. Network, 2005, Am. Assn. Cancer Rsch. (AACR)-Minorities in Cancer Rsch. Jane Cooke Wright Lectureship, 2006; Ellen Roth Lebow Fellowship, Am. Assn. for Brain Tumor Rsch., 1990, MacArthur "Genius Grant" Fellow, John D. and Catherine T. MacArthur Found., 2005. Mem. AAAS, Am. Assn. Cancer Rsch. (membership credentialing com. 1994-95, program com. carcinogenesis subcom. 1993), Am. Soc. Clin. Oncology (mem. program com. subcom. tumor biology and genetics 1997, Young Investigator award, 1991), Am. Assn. Preventive Oncology, Women in Cancer Rsch., Am. Soc. Hematology, Am. Coll. Physicians, Am. Soc. Breast Disease, Am. Soc. Hematology, Assn. Am. Professors, Nigerian Med. Assn., Am. Cancer Soc. (adv. com. cancer control investigations, epidemiology, diagnosis, therapy

1994-97). Office: U Chgo Med Ctr 5841 S Maryland Ave # MC2115 Chicago IL 60637-1463 Office Phone: 773-702-1632, 773-702-6149. Office Fax: 773-702-0963. Business E-Mail: folopade@medicine.bsd.uchicago.edu.*

**O'LOUGHLIN, SANDRA S.,** lawyer; b. Buffalo, Jan. 15, 1942; BA summa cum laude, Rosary Hill Coll., 1973; JD cum laude, U. Buffalo, 1978. Bar: N.Y. 1979. Atty. Hiscock & Barclay, LLP, Buffalo, 1978-79, ptnr., 1990—. Chmn. character and fitness com. appellate divsn. 4th dept. 8th jud. dist. N.Y. Supreme Ct., 1986—2006; adj. prof. SUNY Law Sch., Buffalo. Note editor Buffalo Law Rev., 1977-78. Mem. Erie County Legis. Task Force Mental Health, 1979-81; mem. adv. bd. Congregation of Sisters of St. Joseph, 1987—. Mem. ABA (bus. law com. on securities), Nat. Assn. Bond Lawyers, N.Y. State Bar Assn. (ethics com. 1984-94, 2000-03, vice chmn. 1987-92, unauthorized practice of law com. 1998-2002, mem. com. on securities regulation 1999—, com. standards atty. conduct 2004—), Erie County Bar Assn. (ethics com. 1984-87, chmn. 1987-89, corp. law com. 1984, grievance com. 1993—). Office: Hiscock & Barclay LLP 1100 M&T Ctr 3 Fountain Plaza Buffalo NY 14203-1414 Business E-Mail: soloughlin@hiscockbarclay.com.

**O'LOUGHLIN, VALERIE DEAN,** medical educator; m. Robert O'Loughlin; 1 child, Erin. BS, Coll. William & Mary, Williamsburg, Va., 1985—89; MA, Ind. U., Bloomington, 1992, PhD, 1989—95. Assoc. prof. anatomy Med. Scis., Ind. U., Bloomington, 1995—, dir. undergraduate human anatomy, 1998—. Author: (textbook) Human Anatomy. Office: Med Sci Ind Univ 1001 E 3rd St Bloomington IN 47405 Office Phone: 812-855-7723.

**OLOWOKANDI, MICHAEL,** professional basketball player; b. Apr. 3, 1975, Student, U. Pacific, 1998. Guard, center L.A. Clippers, 1998—2002; player Min. Timberwolves, 2003—. Named to Schick All-Rookie Second Team, 1998—99. Achievements include recording 16 points and game-highs of 17 rebounds and 3 steals against the Vancouver Grizzlies; scored in double figures in six consecutive games; logged two double-doubles. Office: Min Timberwolves 600 First Ave N Minneapolis MN 55403

**OLPADWALA, PORUS,** architecture educator, dean; Bachelor's, U. Calcutta, 1962; MBA, Cornell U., 1972, MRP, 1976, PhD, 1979. Prof. dept. city and regional planning Arch., Art and Planning Cornell U., 1982—, dir. program internat. studies in planning, 1982—91, dir. grad. studies dept. city and regional planning, 1990—92, chair dept. city and regional planning, 1994—98, chair A.D. White profs.-at-large program, interim dean Coll. Arch., Art and Planning, 1998—99, dean Coll. Arch., Art and Planning, 1999—. Contbr. articles to profl. jours. Home: 319 Winthrop Dr Ithaca NY 14850 Office: Dean's Office Coll Arch Art and Planning Cornell U 129 Sibley Dr Ithaca NY 14853

**OLSCHWANG, ALAN PAUL,** lawyer, crossword puzzle author; b. Chgo., Jan. 30, 1942; s. Morton James and Ida (Ginsberg) O.; m. Barbara Claire Miller, Aug. 22, 1965; children: Elliot, Deborah, Jeffrey. BS, U. Ill., 1963, JD, 1966. Bar: Ill. 1966, N.Y. 1984, Calif. 1992. Law clk. Ill. Supreme Ct., Bloomington, 1966-67; assoc. Sidley & Austin and predecessor firm, Chgo., 1967-73; with Montgomery Ward & Co. Inc., Chgo., 1973-81, assoc. gen. counsel, asst. sec., 1979-81; ptnr. Seki, Jarvis & Lynch, Chgo., 1981-84, dir., mem. exec. com.; dir. Mitsubishi Electric & Electronics USA, Inc. and predecessors, N.Y.C., 1983-91, Cypress, Calif., 1991—. Mem. ABA, Am. Corp. Counsel Assn., Calif. Bar Assn., Ill. Bar Assn., Chgo. Bar Assn., N.Y. State Bar Assn., Bar Assn. of City of N.Y., Am. Arbitration Assn. (panel arbitrators). Office: Mitsubishi Elec & Electronics USA Inc PO Box 6007 5665 Plaza Dr Cypress CA 90630-0007 Business E-Mail: alan.olschwang@meus.mea.com.

**OLSEN, ALFRED JON,** lawyer; b. Phoenix, Oct. 5, 1940; s. William Hans and Vera (Bearden) O.; m. Susan K. Smith, Apr. 15, 1979. BA in History, U. Ariz., 1962; MS in Acctg., Ariz. State U., 1964; JD, Northwestern U., 1966. Bar: Ariz. 1966, Ill. 1966, U.S. Tax Ct. 1970, U.S. Supreme Ct. 1970; C.P.A., Ariz., Ill. cert. tax specialist. Acct. Arthur Young & Co., C.P.A.s, Chgo., 1966-68; dir. firm Ehmann, Olsen & Lane (P.C.), Phoenix, 1969-76; dir. Streich, Lang, Weeks & Cardon (P.C.), Phoenix, 1977-78; mgr. Olsen-Smith, Ltd., Phoenix, 1978—. Chmn. tax adv. commn. Bd. Legal Specialization, 1990-92. Bd. editors: Jour. Agrl. Law and Taxation, 1978-82, Practical Real Estate Lawyer, 1983-95. Mem. Phoenix adv. bd. Salvation Army., 1973-81. Fellow: Am. Coll. Tax Counsel, Am. Coll. Trust and Estate Counsel (state chair 2002—03, regent 2005—); mem.: ABA (chmn. com. on agr., sect. taxation 1976—78, chmn. CLE com. sect. taxation 1982—84), AICPA, Internat. Acad. Estate and Trust Law (exec. coun. 1994—99), Nat. Cattlemen's Assn. (tax com. 1979—88), Am. Law Inst. (life; chmn. tax planning for agr. 1971—82), Ariz. Estate Planning Coun. (pres. 1972—73), State Bar Ariz., Ariz. Soc. CPAs, Phi Beta Kappa, Phi Kappa Phi, Beta Gamma Sigma, Sigma Nu Internat. (pres. 1986—88). Office: 3300 Virginia Fin Pla 301 E Virginia Ave Phoenix AZ 85004-1218

**OLSEN, ASHLEY FULLER,** actress; b. Sherman Oaks, Calif., June 13, 1986; d. David and Jarnette Olsen, Mackenzie Olsen (Stepmother). Student, NYU, 2004—. Co-founder, prin. Dualstar Entertainment, Calif., 1993; co-editor-in-chief Mary-Kate and Ashley Mag. Launched clothing line with sister Mary-Kate, 2002. Actor: (films) To Grandmother's House We Go, 1992, Double, Double, Toil and Trouble, 1993, The Little Rascals, 1994, How the West Was Fun, 1994, It Takes Two, 1995, The Challenge, 2003, Charlie's Angels: Full Throttle, 2003; (TV films) Billboard Dad, 1998; (TV series) Full House, 1987—95, Two of a Kind, 1998; actor, prodr.: So Little Time, 2001; Mary-Kate and Ashley in Action!, 2001; actor, prodr., prodr.: (films) Switching Goals, 1999; actor, prodr. Passport to Paris, 1999; Our Lips are Sealed, 2000; Winning London, 2001; Holiday in the Sun, 2001, Getting There, 2002, When In Rome, 2002, New York Minute, 2004; (video series) The Adventures of Mary-Kate and Ashley; You're Invited to Mary-Kate and Ashleys; prodr.: (TV series) Tough Cookie, 2002, Fashion Forward: Spring 2001, 2001. Named one of 100 Most Powerful Women in Hollywood, Hollywood (Calif.) Reporter, 2003. Office: Dualstar Entertainment Group 1801 Century Park East Los Angeles CA 90067*

**OLSEN, BEN,** professional soccer player; b. Harrisburg, Pa., May 3, 1977; Attended, Univ. Va. Midfielder DC United, 1998—. 34 caps, 6 goals U.S. Nat. Soccer Team, 1998—; mem. U.S. World Cup Team, 2006. Named Player of the Yr., Soccer Am. mag., 1997, Humanitarian of the Yr., U.S. Soccer Found., 2003. Mailing: US Soccer Fedn 1801 S Prairie Ave Chicago IL 60616*

**OLSEN, CHRISTOPHER JOHN,** education educator; b. Fargo, N.D., Mar. 19, 1966; s. Richard Donald and Verna Jean Catherine Olsen; m. Jennifer Ann Ross, Mar. 18, 1995; children: Emma Catherine, Charlotte Ann, Ross Christopher. BA, N.D. State U., Fargo, N.D., 1988; MA, Univ. Nebraska, Lincoln, 1990; PhD, Univ. Fla., Gainsville, Fla., 1996. Asst. prof. Va. Wesleyan Coll., Norfolk, Va., 1996—99, Indiana State Univ., Terre Haute, Ind., 1999—2002, assoc. prof., chmn. dept., 2003—. Faculty advisor Phi Alpha Theta, Terre Haute, Ind., 1999—2005; mem. adv. bd. advanced placement U.S. History, 2005—06. Author: Political Culture and Secession in Mississippi: Masculinity Honor, and the Antiparty Tradition, 1830-1860, 2000, 2d edit., 2005, The American Civil War: A Hands-on History, 2006; contbr. articles to profl. jour. Grantee, Ind. State Univ., 2001—05; Mednick Rsch. grantee, Va. Found. Ind. Coll., 1998. Mem.: Southern Hist. Soc., Phi Beta Kappa. Democrat. Avocation: golf. Office: Indiana State Univ Dept Hist Terre Haute IN 47809 Office Phone: 812-237-2710. E-mail: colsen@isugw.indstate.edu.

**OLSEN, DAVID ALEXANDER,** insurance executive; b. Bklyn., Nov. 29, 1937; s. Alexander and Meile (Anderson) O.; m. Roberta Ruth Garverick, May 11, 1963; children: Bradford, Amy. With marine dept. Gt. Am. Ins. Co., N.Y.C. and Chgo., 1959-62; acct. exec. Johnson & Higgins, San Francisco, 1966-71, v.p., mgr. marine dept. Chgo., 1971-78, exec. v.p. Ill. br., 1978-79,

br. mgr., exec. v.p. Houston, 1979-80, chmn., bd. dirs. Tex. br., 1980-85, exec. v.p. N.Y.C., 1985-87, pres., COO, 1987-93, CEO, 1990-97, chmn., 1991—97; dir. Marsh & McLennan, N.Y.C., 1997—. Bd. dirs. U.S. Trust Corp. Trustee Bowdoin Coll., South St. Seaport Mus., Salisbury (Conn.) Congl. Ch., Vis. Nurse Assn., Landmark Vols. 1st lt. U.S. Army, 1960-62. Mem. India House, Sharon Country Club, Psi Upsilon. Avocations: art, photography, antiques, scuba diving, tennis, skiing.

**OLSEN, EDGAR OLIVER,** economics professor; b. New Orleans, La., Mar. 13, 1942; s. Edgar Oliver and Georgie Walker (Thompson) Olsen; m. Barbara Elliott Beasley, June 4, 1966; children: Robert Buckner, Melanie Guerry. BA, Tulane U., 1963; PhD, Rice U., 1968. Postdoctoral fellow Ind. U.-Bloomington, 1967—68; from asst. prof. to prof. U. Va., Charlottesville, 1970—83, prof., 1983—, chmn. dept. econs., 1993—96. Vis. assoc. prof. econs. U. Wis., Madison, 1975—76, vis. prof., 1982—84; economist Rand Corp., Santa Monica, Calif., 1968—70; vis. scholar HUD, Washington, 1978—79, cons., 1973—2003; bd. editors Am. Econ. Rev., Princeton, N.J., 1985—91; cons. GAO, Washington, 1999—2001; v.p. So. Econ. Assn., 2003—05. Contbr. articles to profl. publs. Congl. Testimony, 2001, 2003. Recipient Cert. Spl. Achievement, HUD, 1979; NIH fellow, 1983. Mem.: Am. Real Estate and Urban Econ. Assn., Am. Econ. Assn., Assn. Pub. Policy Analysis and Mgmt., So. Econ. Assn. Home: PO Box 400182 1606 Jamestown Dr Charlottesville VA 22904-4182 Office: U Va Dept Econs PO Box 400182 Charlottesville VA 22904-4182 Office Phone: 434-924-3443. Business E-Mail: eoo@virginia.edu.

**OLSEN, EDWARD JOHN,** geologist, educator, curator; b. Chgo., Nov. 23, 1927; s. Edward John and Elizabeth (Bornemann) O.; children— Andrea, Ericka. AB, U. Chgo., 1951, MS, 1955, PhD, 1959. Geologist Geol. Survey Can., 1953; U.S. Geol. Survey, 1954—, Canadian Johns-Manville Co., Ltd., 1956, 57, 59; asst. prof. Case Inst. Tech., also Western Res. U., 1959-60; curator mineralogy Field Mus. Natural History, 1960-91, chmn. dept. geology, 1974-78; research assoc. prof. dept. geophys. scis. U. Chgo., 1977—. Adj. prof. U. Ill., Chgo. Circle, 1970-91. Assoc. editor Geochim. et Cosmochim. Acta., 1985-91. Fellow Mineral. Soc. Am.; mem. Mineral. Assn. Can., Geochem. Soc., Meteoritical Soc. Achievements include spl. research stability relations of minerals in earth's mantle and meteorites. Home: 437 Wild Indigo Ln Madison WI 53717-2148 Office: U Chgo Dept Geophys Sci Chicago IL 60637

**OLSEN, ELISE,** dermatologist, researcher; BA, U. Tex., 1974; MD, Baylor U., 1978. Diplomate Am. Bd. Dermatology, N.C. Med. Bd. Asst. prof. Duke U., Durham, NC, 1985—91, assoc. prof., 1991—99, prof., 1999—. Cons. in field; mem. sci. adv. bd. NAAF, Calif.; mem. com. misconduct rsch. Duke U., Durham. Editor: Hair Disorders: Diagnosis & Treatment, 1984, 2003; assoc. editor: Derm Therapy, 1995—, asst. editor: Jour. Am. Acad. Dermatology, 1998—. Mem.: So. Consortium Dermatology (chmn. steering com. 1991—, pres., past pres.), Internat. Soc. Cutaneous Lymphomas, N.Am. Hair Rsch. Soc., N.C. Dermatologic Assn., Am. Dermatologic Assn. Office: Duke U Med Ctr Box 3294 DUMC Durham NC 27710

**OLSEN, FRANCES ELISABETH,** law educator, theorist; b. Chgo., Feb. 4, 1945; d. Holger and Ruth Mathilda (Pfeifer) O.; m. Harold Irving Porter, June 8, 1984. Cert., Roskilde (Denmark) Højskole, 1967; BA, Goddard Coll., 1968; JD, U. Colo., 1971; SJD, Harvard U., 1984. Bar: Colo. 1972, U.S. Dist. Ct. Colo. 1972. Law clk. hon. Arraj U.S. Dist. Ct. Colo., Denver, 1972; lawyer Am. Indian Movement, Wounded Knee, S.D., 1973; pvt. practice Denver, 1973-74; law prof. U. Puget Sound, Tacoma, Wash., 1975-79, St. John's U. Jamaica, N.Y., 1982-83, UCLA, 1984—. Vis. fellow New Coll., Oxford (Eng.) U., 1987; vis. prof. U. Mich., Ann Arbor, 1988, Harvard U., Cambridge, Mass., 1990-91, U. Berlin, Germany, 1995, Ochanomizu U., Tokyo, 1997, U. Tokyo, 1997, Cornell U., 1997, French U. Reunion, 2000, Hebrew U. Jerusalem, 2001, Haifa U., 2001, Tel Aviv U., 2001, 2002, Addis Ababa U., 2002, Bar Ilan U., 2002, Alberto Hurtado U., Santiago, Chile, 2004; sr. Fulbright prof. U. Frankfurt, Germany, 1991-92; overseas fellow Churchill Coll., Cambridge, Eng., 1997-99; mem. faculty law Cambridge U., 1997-99; del. UN 4th World Conf. on Women, Beijing, China, 1995, NGO Forum, Huairou, China, 1995. Co-author: Cases and Materials on Family Law: Legal Concepts and Changing Human Relationships, 1994; editor: Feminist Legal Theory I: Foundations and Outlooks, 1995, Feminist Legal Theory II: Positioning Feminist Theory Within the Law, 1995; contbr. articles to law revs. Named Outstanding Alumnus U. Colo., 1989. Mem. Assn. Am. Law Schs. (chair jurisprudence sect. 1987-88, chair women in law tchg. sect. 1995-96), Conf. on Critical Legal Studies, European Conf. Critical Legal Studies, Internat. Bar Assn. Avocations: scuba diving, kayaking, hiking. Office: UCLA Sch Law 405 Hilgard Ave Los Angeles CA 90095-1476 Office Phone: 310-825-6083. E-mail: olsen@law.ucla.edu.

**OLSEN, GLEN A.,** church musician, educator; b. Orange, NJ, Jan. 7, 1965; s. Peter Albert and Joan C Olsen; m. Amy Hastings, Aug. 6, 1988; children: Kristen A, Timothy C, Melissa C. BA, Wheaton Coll., 1983—87; MusM, Rutgers U., 1987—89; LittD, Drew U., 1998—2001, MA, 2006. Organist/choir dir. Heritage Bapt. Ch., West Orange, NJ, 1981—83; youth and music dir. North Fork Bapt. Ch., Mattituck, NY, 1983; organist Wheaton Christian Ref. Ch., Ill., 1985—87; min. of music and worship Montvale Evang. Free Ch., NJ, 1987—88; min. of music Lafayette Federated Ch., NJ, 1988—93; min. of music and worship Calvary Evang. Free Ch., Trumbull, Conn., 1993—95; dir. of choral activities Hawthorne Christian Acad., NJ, 1995—2005; dir. of music and organist United Meth. Ch., Madison, NJ, 1995—2005; adj. asst. prof. Drew U., Madison, NJ, 2001—; dir. music Calvary Bapt. Ch., Manhattan, NY, 2005—. Vol. Calvary Evang. Free Ch., Essex Fells, NJ, 1980. Recipient Outstanding Young Men of Am., 1989; Bard Thompson scholarship, Drew U., 2003—. Mem. Music Educators Nat. Conf., Am. Guild of English Handbell Ringers, Am. Guild of Organists, Fellowship of United Methodists in Music and Worship Arts, Am. Choral Directors Assn. Evangelical Free Church. Avocations: travel, architecture. Office Phone: 212-975-0170. Personal E-mail: olsenglen@aol.com.

**OLSEN, GREGORY H.,** fiber optic manufacturing executive, researcher; b. Bklyn., 1945; 2 children. BS in physics; BSEE in physics, Fairleigh Dickinson U., MS in physics magna cum laude; PhD in materials sci., U. Va., 1971. Tech. staff RCA Lab. (now Sarnoff Corp.), Princeton, NJ, 1972—83; founder, pres., CEO EPITAXX Inc. (acquired by Nippon Sheet Glass, 1990 and by JDS Uniphase, 1999), 1984; co-founder Sensors Unlimited, Inc. (acquired by Finisar Corp., 2000, bought back 2002), Princeton, 1991; pres., CEO Sensors Unlimited, Inc., Princeton, 1991—2000, 2002—, pres., 2000—02; chmn. bd. dirs. Sensors Unlimited, Inc.; officer, dir. Finisar Corp., 2000—02. Vis. scientist physics dept. U. Port Elizabeth, South Africa; lectr. in field; bd. dir. Princeton Power Sys., Achieve 3000, Eye Response Tech. Author over 100 papers, co-author several books on crystal growth and semiconductor devices; contbr. articles for trade jour. Investor NJ Tech. Coun. Venture Fund; adv. com. Princeton U., U. So. Calif. Photonics Ctr., U. Fla. Microelectronics Ctr., U. Va., City Coll. NY. Named Inventor Yr., NJ Inst. Tech., NJ Small Bus. Person Yr., US Small Bus. Adminstrn., Entrepreneur Yr., Arthur Young/Inc. Mag.; recipient Young Authors award, Am. Assn. Crystal Growth. Mem.: NJ Crystal Growth Assn., IEEE Laser & Electro-Optics Soc. (LEOS) (bd. gov., Aron Kressel award, named disting. leader), IEEE (fellow, named disting. leader), IEEE Electro, Electrochemical Soc., Internat. Soc. Optical Engring. (SPIE). Achievements include 12 US patents; named next Pvt. Space Explorer in 2003. Third civilian in history to visit the International Space Station (Soyuz TMA-7 spacecraft, Baikonur Cosmodrome, Kazakhstan) in 2005. Office: Sensors Unlimited Inc 3490 Rt 1 Bldg 12 Princeton NJ 08540-5914 Office Phone: 609-520-0610. Office Fax: 609-520-1663. Business E-Mail: golsen@sensorinc.com.

**OLSEN, HANS H.,** semiconductor company executive; BSEE, Copenhagen Tech. U.; MSEE, U. Copenhagen. Engring. and mgmt. positions Christian Rovsing A/S, Copenhagen, 1973—82; co-founder, CEO Electronic Designs, Inc., 1982—83; founder, CEO IChips Corp. (acquired by Paradigm Tech., Inc.), 1993—96; v.p. mktg. Paradigm Tech., Inc., 1996—97; v.p. graphics

mktg., v.p. N.Am. sales Trident Microsystems, 1997—98; v.p. ops. Pixelworks, Inc., Tualatin, Oreg., 1998—2001, exec. v.p., COO, 2001—. Office: Pixelworks Inc Ste 300 8100 SW Nyberg Rd Tualatin OR 97062

**OLSEN, HANS PETER,** lawyer; b. Detroit, May 21, 1940; s. Hans Peter and Paula M. (Olsen) O.; m. Elizabeth Ann Gayton, Sept. 14, 1968; children: Hans Peter, Heidi Susanne, Stephanie Elizabeth BA, Mich. State U., 1961; JD, Georgetown U., 1965; LLM, NYU, 1966. Bar: Mich. 1967, Pa. 1969, R.I. 1974. Law clk. Monaghan, McCrone, Campbell & Crawmer, Detroit, 1964, U.S. Ct. of Claims, Fed. Appellate Ct., Washington, 1966—68; assoc. Pepper, Hamilton & Scheetz, Phila., 1968—72; ptnr. Hinckley, Allen, & Snyder, Providence, 1974—. Adv. planning com. U. R.I. Fed. Taxation Inst.; continuing legal edn. adv. bd., tax symposium adv. bd. Bryant Coll.; mem. Gov.'s State Task Force, R.I. Pub. Expenditure Coun.; cons. Bur. Nat. Affairs; liaison Bar Assn. and North Atlantic region IRS; tax adminstrs. adv. com. R.I.; lectr. tax insts. and other profl. groups N.Y., L.A., Phila., Boston, R.I.; advisor R.I. Econ. Policy com. Contbr. numerous articles on taxation to legal jours. Fellow Am. Bar Found.; mem. ABA (sect. taxation, exempt orgns. com., subcom. healthcare, corp.-shareholders rels. com., partnerships com.), R.I. Bar Assn. (sect. taxation, sec.-treas. 1977-80, liaison with CPAs, specialization com., mem. various coms.), Providence C. of C., R.I. C. of C. (chmn. com. on bus. taxes and public spending, mem., past chmn. legis. action council), Mich. State Bar, Pa. State Bar. Home: 274 Olney St Providence RI 02906-2305 Office: 28 State St Boston MA 02109-1775 also: 43 N Main St Concord NH 03301-4934 also: 50 Kennedy Plz Ste 1500 Providence RI 02903 Office Phone: 401-274-2000. Personal E-Mail: hpeterolsen@cox.net. Business E-Mail: holsen@haslaw.com.

**OLSEN, HAROLD FREMONT,** lawyer; b. Davenport, Wash., Oct. 17, 1920; s. Oscar E. and Dorothy (Sprowls) O.; m. Jeanne L. Rounds, Aug. 30, 1942; children: Eric O., Ronald R., Margaret Ruth. BA, Wash. State U., 1942; LLB, Harvard U., 1948. Bar: Wash. 1948, U.S. Ct. Claims 1970, U.S. Supreme Ct. 1982; CPA, Wash. Instr. Oxford Bus. Sch., Cambridge, Mass., 1946-47; examiner Wash. State Dept. Pub. Utilities, 1948; with firm Perkins Coie (and predecessors), Seattle, 1949—, ptnr., 1954-88, of counsel, 1989—. Trustee Exec. Svcs. Corp. Wash., 1990-96. Bd. dirs. Northwest Hosp. Found., Northwest Hosp., 1980-90; trustee Wash. State U. Found., chmn. 1986-88; mem. adv. coun. Wash. State U. Sch. Bus. and Econs., 1978-90; trustee, mem. exec. com., pres. Mus. of Flight, 1991-92, chmn., 1993; trustee Horizon House, 1994-97. Maj. USAAF, 1942-45, NATOUSA, Mid. East, ETO. Decorated Silver Star. Mem. ABA, Wash. Bar Assn., Seattle Bar Assn., Aircraft Industry Assn. (chmn. legal com. 1957), Phi Beta Kappa, Phi Kappa Phi, Tau Kappa Epsilon, Rainier Club, Queenstown (New Zealand) Golf Club, Seattle Golf Club (pres. 1986-87). Sr. N.W. Golf Assn. Congregationalist. Home: 8875 Overlake Dr W Medina WA 98039-5347 Office: 1201 3rd Ave Ste 4500 Seattle WA 98101-3029 Office Phone: 206-359-8503. Personal E-mail: holsen@seanet.com. Business E-Mail: holsen@perkinscoie.com.

**OLSEN, HARRIS LELAND,** diplomat, writer, real estate company executive, educator; b. Rochester, NH, Dec. 8, 1947; s. Harries Edwin and Eva Alma (Turmelle) O.; m. Mimi Kwi Sun Yi, Mar. 15, 1953; children: Garin Lee, Gavin Yi, Sook Ja. AS, SUNY, Albany, 1983, BS, 1988; MA in Polit. Sci., U. Hawaii, 1990; PhD in Internat. Bus. Adminstrn., Kennedy Western U., Idaho, 1993. Enlisted USN, 1967, advanced through grades to, served in various nuclear power capacities Conn., 1971-76, Hawaii, 1976-87, ret., 1987; v.p. Waiono Land Corp., Honolulu, 1981-92, 1991-93-95; v.p. Asian Pacific Electricity, Honolulu, 1988-89, Kapano Land Assocs., Honolulu, 1988-92, 94-95, MLY Networks, Inc., Honolulu, 1989-99, THO Consultants Corp., 1991—2002, Clarix Internat. Corp., 1994; consulate gen. Papua New Guinea, 1996—2002. Staff cons. Mariner-Icemakers, Honolulu, 1982-84, Transpacific Energy Corp., Honolulu, 1982-84; dir. Asian Pacific Devel. Bank, 1983; sr. cons. Western Rsch. Assocs., Honolulu, 1984-87, 94-95; quality assurance cons. Asian Pacific, Inc., Honolulu, 1987-88; instr., lectr. Asian history and culture U. Chaminade in Honolulu, 1991; nuclear reactor plant specialist Pearl Harbor Emergency Recall Team, 1991-95; instr. nuclear reactor theory Pearl Harbor, Hawaii, 1992-95; v.p. Schwartz, Inc., 1992-98, dir. Schwartz Jewelry Sch., 1996-98; cons. Waiono/Kapano Devel. Co., 1993; bd. dirs., sec. Pacific Internat. Engring. Corp., 1993-94-95; Keiretsu sec. Global Ocean Cons., Inc. and Assocs., 1994-95; joint venture Premier Fisheries Pty. Ltd., Papua New Guinea, 1995-98; cons. BFD Devel. Group, 1995-96; co-drafter Nat. Tuna Industry Devel. Plan for Papua New Guinea, 1995; quality analyst, Pearl Harbor, 1995; rep. for Min. for Fisheries, Papua New Guinea, Bi-lateral Fisheries Access Rights Japan and Papua New Guinea, 1996-97, drafter Bi-Lateral Fishing Treaty Japan and Papua New Guinea, 1996; U.S. del. to 4th World Tuna Conf., Manila, 1995; U.S. del. to 5th Aquatic Coninent Conf., Maui, Hawaii, 1995, 6th, 1996; apptd. rep. Abau Electorate, Papua New Guinea Timber Sales, 1995-98; apptd. hon. consul gen. and trade rep., dep. trade min. for Govt. of Papua New Guinea in Honolulu, 1996-2001; bd. dirs. Island Art; cons. Pew Global Devel. Corp., 1998-99, Niugini Enterprises LLC, 1999-2001, Niugini Millenium Co., Ltd., 1999-2001. Author: The Price for Gold, 2002, Candi, 2003, Sialon, 2003, Small Prices, 2004, Silent, 2004, Emergence, 2005, Dark Water August, 2005; co-host: Hyscience Blog, 2005—; contbr. articles to profl. jours. Head coach USN Men's Softball, Honolulu, 1978-79; pres. Pearl Harbor (Hawaii) Welfare and Recreation Com., 1983-84; mem. Rep. Senatorial Inner Cir.; commd. hon. consul gen. Ind. State Papua New Guinea, 1996; mem. Consular Corps of Hawaii, 1997-2001. Named Alumnus of Yr., Kennedy Western U., 1993; recipient Citation of Leadership, Nat. Rep. Com., 1996, Letter of Commendation for Svc. During Aitape Tidal Wave Disaster in Papua New Guinea, 1998; selected to represent Hawaii at Presdl. Inauguration, Rep. Leadership U.S. Senate, 2001. Mem.: Nat. Assn. Scholars, Navy League, Delta Epsilon Sigma, Republican, Roman Catholic and Buddhist. Achievements include invention of alternate power supply sys. Avocations: chess, philosophy, japanese haiku poetry, native american cultures. Home and Office: 94 1025 Anania Cir Apt 56 Mililani HI 96789-2045 Personal E-mail: HarryTho@aol.com.

**OLSEN, JODY (JOSEPHINE K. OLSEN),** federal agency administrator; B, U. Utah; MSW, PhD, U. Md. Vol. Peace Corps, Tunisia, 1966—68, various positions incuding chief of staff, regional dir. North Africa, Near East, Asia and the Pscific, country dir. Togo, 1979—84, 1989—92; exec. dirs. Coun. Internat. Exch. of Scholars, 1992—97; sr. v.p., dir. Peace Corps, Washington, 1997—2002, dep. dir., 2002—, acting dir., 2006—. Office: Peace Corps 1111 20th St NW Washington DC 20526-0001*

**OLSEN, KATHIE LYNN,** science foundation director; b. Portland, Oreg., Aug. 3, 1952; d. Roland Berg and Gladys Elizabeth (Eldreth) O. BS, Chatham Coll., 1974; PhD, U. Calif., Irvine, 1979. Postdoct. fellow Harvard Med. Sch., Boston, 1979-80; rsch. scientist Long Island Rsch. Inst., Stony Brook, N.Y., 1980-83; rsch. asst. prof. SUNY, Stony Brook, 1982-85, asst. prof., 1985-89; assoc. program dir. NSF, Washington, 1984-86, program dir., 1988, leader neurosci., 1991; legis. fellow Brookings Instn., Washington, 1996—97; chief scientist NASA, 1999—2002; acting assoc. director, tech. Off. Science & Tech. Policy, Washington, 2002—05; dep. dir. NSF, Washington, 2005—. Adj. assoc. prof. George Washington U., Washington, 1989—; cons. editor Hormones and Behavior, 1988—. Contbr. articles to profl. jours, chapters to books. Recipient Dir. Superior Accomplishmentaward, NSF, Barry M. Goldwater Educator award, Am. Inst. of Aeronautics & Astronautics -Nat. Capital Section, Outstanding Leadership medal, NASA, Internat. Behavioral Neuroscience Soc. award, Soc. for Behavioral Endocrinology award, Barnard medal of Distinction. Mem. Soc. Neurosci., Endocrine Soc., Women in Neurosci., Sod. Study of Reproduction, Internat. Acad. Sex Rsch. Office: NSF 4201 Wilson Blvd Arlington VA 22230

**OLSEN, KENNETH HAROLD,** geophysicist, astrophysicist, historian; b. Ogden, Utah, Feb. 20, 1930; s. Harold Reuben and Rose (Hill) O.; m. Barbara Ann Parson, June 15, 1955; children: Susan L., Steven K., Christopher P., Richard S. BS, Idaho State Coll., 1952; MS, Calif. Inst. Tech., 1954, PhD, 1957. Grad. rsch. asst. Calif. Inst. Tech., Mt. Wilson and Palomar Obs.,

Pasadena, 1952-57; staff mem., group leader Los Alamos (N.Mex.) Nat. Lab., 1957-89, lab. assoc., 1989-95; geophys. cons. Lynnwood, Wash., 1989—. Vis. rsch. fellow Applied Seismol. Group, Swedish Nat. Def. Inst., Stockholm, Sweden, 1983; sr. vis. scientist fellow Norwegian Seismic Array, Oslo, Norway, 1983; vis. scholar Geophysics Program, U. Wash., Seattle, 1989-91. Author, editor: Continental Rifts: Evolution, Structure, Tectonics, 1995; contbr. articles to profl. jours. Mem. Am. Geophys. Union, Geol. Soc. Am., Seismol. Soc. Am., Am. Astron. Soc., Royal Astron. Soc. Home: 1029 187th Pl SW Lynnwood WA 98036-4986 Personal E-mail: barbolsen@verizon.net.

**OLSEN, M. KENT,** lawyer, educator; b. Denver, Mar. 10, 1948; s. Marvin and F. Winona (Wilker) O.; m. Shauna L. Casement; children: Kristofor Anders, Alexander Lee, Nikolaus Alrik, Amanda Elizabeth. BS, Colo. State U., 1970; JD, U. Denver, 1975. Bar: Colo. 1982, U.S. Dist. Ct. Colo. 1982, U.S. Tax Ct. Law clk. Denver Probate Ct., 1973-75; assoc. ptnr. Johnson & McLachlan, Lamar, Colo., 1975-80; assoc. Buchanan, Thomas and Johnson, Lakewood, Colo., 1981-82; William E. Myrick, P.C., Denver, 1982-83; referee Denver Probate Ct., Denver, 1983-89; ptnr. Haines & Olsen, P.C., Denver, 1989-95; pvt. practice Denver, 1995—2001; ptnr. Olsen & Traeger, LLP, 2001—. Adv. bd. Denver Career Coll., 1993—2004, Elder Law Inst., 1994—. Active Gov.'s Commn. on Life and the Law, Denver, 1991-2000; bd. dirs. Adult Care Mgmt., Inc., Denver, 1985-95, Colo. Guardianship Alliance, Denver, 1990-91, Arc of Denver, Inc., 1990—, pres., 1995-97, 2004—; bd. dirs. Colo. Fund for People with Disabilities, 1994—, pres., 1994-2000. Recipient Outstanding Vol. Svc. award Adult Care Mgmt., 1990, Outstanding Svc. award The Arc of Denver, 1991, Vol. Svc. award Colo. Gerontol. Soc., 1997, Pres.'s award Arc of Denver, 1998, 2002; named one of Colo. Super Lawyers, Law and Politics, 2006. Mem. ABA, Colo. Bar Assn. (past chair probate sect.), First Jud. Dist. Bar Assn., Nat. Acad. Elder Law Attys., Colo. Assn. Homes and Svcs. to the Aging, Denver Bar Assn., Denver Estate Planning Coun., Denver C. of C. Avocations: running, skiing, racquetball, art, hiking. Home: 3030 S Roslyn St Denver CO 80231-4153 Office: 650 S Cherry St Ste 850 Denver CO 80246-1805 Office Phone: 303-329-4670. Business E-Mail: mkolsen@olsentraeger.com.

**OLSEN, MARTIN E.,** obstetrician, educator; b. Morgantown, W.Va., 1959; m. Natalie Ann Maschmann, June 25, 1985; 1 child, Karen Rebeca. MD, Med. Coll. Ohio, 1981. Diplomate Am. Bd. Ob-Gyn., Am. Bd. Family Practice. Resident in family practice Akron (Ohio) Gen. Med. Ctr., 1985-88; resident in ob-gyn. U. Tenn., Chattanooga, 1989-91; mem. faculty E. Tenn. State U., Johnson City, 1992—, chmn. dept. ob-byn., 1999—; dir. residency program Johnson City Med. Ctr., 1994—. Contbr. articles to profl. jours. Office: PO Box 70569 Johnson City TN 37614-1707 Office Phone: 423-439-8097. Business E-Mail: olsen@etsu.edu.

**OLSEN, MARY-KATE,** actress; b. Sherman Oaks, Calif., June 13, 1986; d. David and Jarnette Olsen, Mackenzie Olsen (Stepmother). Student, NYU, 2004—05. Co-founder, prin. Dualstar Entertainment, LA, 1993—; co-editor-in-chief Mary-Kate and Ashley Mag. Launched clothing line with sister Ashley, 2002. Actor: (films) To Grandmother's House We Go, 1992, Double, Double, Toil and Trouble, 1993, The Little Rascals, 1994, How the West Was Fun, 1994, It Takes Two, 1995, The Challenge, 2003, Charlie's Angels: Full Throttle, 2003; (TV films) Billboard Dad, 1998; (TV series) Full House, 1987—95, Two of a Kind, 1998; actor, prodr.: (films) Switching Goals, 1999; Passport to Paris, 1999; Our Lips are Sealed, 2000; Winning London, 2001; Holiday in the Sun, 2001; Getting There, 2002; When In Rome, 2002; New York Minute, 2004; (TV series) So Little Time, 2001; Mary-Kate and Ashley in Action!, 2001; (video series) The Adventures of Mary-Kate and Ashley; You're Invited to Mary-Kate and Ashley's; prodr.: (TV series) Tough Cookie, 2002, Fashion Forward: Spring 2001, 2001. Named one of 100 Most Powerful Women in Hollywood, Hollywood (Calif.) Reporter, 2003. Office: Dualstar Entertainment Group 1801 Century Park East Los Angeles CA 90007*

**OLSEN, PATRICE ELIZABETH,** history professor, photographer; d. Albert R. and Mary Elizabeth Olsen. MA, U. Ill., Urbana, 1980; MA, Pa. State U., Univ. Pk., 1991, PhD, 1998. Asst. prof. Stephen F. Austin U., Nagadoches, Tex., 1998—2000, Ill. State U., Normal, 2000—06, assoc. prof., 2006—. Dir. Cuban study tours Dept. History Ill. State U., Normal, 2002—, dir. grad. studies, 2004—. Author: Artifacts of Revolution, 2006 (Lewis Hanke prize, 1999, Meyer prize, 2003). Named Outstanding Coll. Tchr., Coll. Arts and Scis. Ill. State U., 2004—05; recipient Faculty Tchg. Initiative award, Ill. State U., 2002—03. Mem.: L.Am. Studies Assn., Conf. L.Am. History, Southwest Conf. L.Am. Studies. Office: Ill State U Dept History 301 Schroeder Hall Normal IL 61790

**OLSEN, R. NILLS,** dean, law educator; BA, U. Wis., 1969; JD, Columbia U. Sch. Law, 1974. Law clerk to Chief Justice Thomas E. Fairchild Seventh Cir. U.S. Ct. Appeals, Chgo.; law lectr. and clin. fellow U. Chgo. Sch. Law; assoc. prof. U. Buffalo Law Sch., SUNY, 1978, vice dean, 1994—98, dean, 1998—, dir. clin. edn. Mem. Lewiston-Porter sch. bd.; bd. dirs. N.Y. State Environmental Activists, Environment Reserve Free Libr., Great Lakes United. Office: U Buffalo Law Sch SUNY 319 O'Brian Hall, N Campus Buffalo NY 14260-1100 E-mail: nolsen@buffalo.edu.

**OLSEN, RANDY J.,** university librarian; BA, Utah State U.; MLS, Brigham Young U., 1973, MPA, 1981. Univ. libr. Brigham Young U., 2002—. Office: Brigham Young U Harold B Lee Libr PO Box 26800 Provo UT 84602-6800 Office Phone: 801-422-2905. E-mail: randy_olsen@byu.edu.*

**OLSEN, REX NORMAN,** trade association executive; b. Hazeltown, Idaho, Apr. 9, 1925; s. Adolph Lars and Pearl (Robbins) O. B.J., BA in English, U. Mo., 1950. Editor Clissold Pub. Co., Chgo., 1950-54; copy editor Am. Peoples Ency., Chgo., 1955; asst. editor Am. Hosp. Assn., Chgo., 1956-59, mng. editor, 1959-64, dir. jours. div., 1964-69, dir. publs. bur., 1969-75, exec. editor, assoc. pub., 1975-79; v.p., meas. Am. Hosp. Pub., Inc., 1980-85; pres. Words Ltd., 1985—. Dir. publs. ETNA Comms., Chgo., 1997—. Served with USNR, 1943-46. Mem. Soc. Nat. Assn. Pubs. (sec. 1975-76, 2d v.p. 1976-77, 1st v.p. 1977-78, pres. 1978-79), Chgo. Bus. Publs. Assn. (dir. 1974-78, 4th v.p. 1978-79), Sigma Delta Chi. Home and Office: 5510 N Sheridan Rd Unit 12-A Chicago IL 60640-1630 Personal E-mail: rexorudy@aol.com.

**OLSEN, RICHARD GALEN,** biomedical engineer, consultant; b. Colorado Springs, Colo., Aug. 10, 1945; s. Floyd Edwin and Ruth Elizabeth (Robinson) O.; m. Karen Fidler Brubaker, June 17, 1973 (dec.); children: Kathryn Elizabeth, Nickolas Robert. BSEE, U. Mo., Rolla, 1968; MS, U. Utah, 1970, PhD, 1975. Registered profl. engr., Fla. Edgr. Bendix Corp., Kansas City, Mo., 1968-69; elec. engr. Naval Aerospace Med. Rsch. Lab., Pensacola, Fla., 1975-79; chief engring. systems divsn., 1979-82, head bioengring. divsn., 1982-94; head bioengring. dept. Naval Health Rsch. Ctr. Detachment, Brooks AFB, Tex., 1994-2000; cons. in bioelectromagnetics Pensacola, 2001—. Tech. cons. Naval Sea Sys. Command, Arlington, Va., 1989—91, Naval Surface Warfare Ctr., Dahlgren, Va., 1989—95, Armstrong Lab. USAF, 1991—99, Naval Command, Control and Ocean Surveillance Command, San Diego, 1996—97, Selicor, Inc., 2001—. Contbr. articles to profl. jours. and books. With U.S. Army, 1970-72. Recipient Fred A. Hitchcock award Aerospace Physiologust Aerospace Med. Assn., 1987, Award for Excellence in Tech. Transfer, Fed. Lab. Consortium, 2004; named Engr. of the Yr., N.W. Fla. Engrs. Coun., 1991. Mem. IEEE (sr., chmn. Pensacola sect. 1982-83, SCC-28 and SCC-34 coms. 1982-2000, cert. of appreciation 1983), Bioelectromagnetics Soc. (charter, editl. bd. 1990-96), Sigma Xi, Eta Kappa Nu, Tau Beta Pi, Phi Kappa Phi. Achievements include conducting the first shipboard measurements of specific absorption rate (SAR) and of electromagnetic pulse (EMP) induced body current; patents in RF medical device to treat vascular insufficiency, elastic wire conductor, RF coil for hypothermia resuscitation, RF dosimetry system, personal microwave and RF detector, and RF warming of submerged extremities. Home and Office: 1503 N Baylen St Pensacola FL 32501-2101 Personal E-mail: olsen116@bellsouth.net. *Live an ordinary life except in attainment.*

**OLSEN, RICHARD JAMES,** artist, educator; b. Milw., Nov. 15, 1935; s. Edward Marinus and Ann Frances (Larsen) Olsen; m. Nina Marsh Civilette-Olsen, July 25, 1969; children: Dayna Kim, Dawn Beth(dec.), Josh Keymar. BS, U. Wis., 1958, MFA in Painting and Printmaking, 1966. Tchg. asst. U. Wis., 1965-66; art tchr. grade 8 Winnequah Grade Sch., Monona, Wis., 1966-67; instr. printmaking Oper. Area Arts, Green Bay, Wis., 1967-69; from instr. painting and drawing to prof. emeritus U. Ga., Athens, 1969—2000, Gen. Sandy Beaver tchg. prof., 1998—2000, emeritus prof., 2001—; represented by Berman Gallery, Atlanta, 1986-97, Novus Inc., Atlanta, 1990—, Maurine Littleton Gallery, Washington, 1990, Miriam Perlman Gallery, Chgo., 1991, EDL & Assocs., Atlanta, 1994, Elements of Art, Columbus, Ohio, 1995, Ellen Wallace-Paushter, Art Cons., Chgo., 1999, Mercury Art Works, Athens, Ga., 2001—. Wrestling coach Monona Grove (Wis.) H.S., 1966-67; panelist Steinham Arts Festival St. Lawrence U., N.Y., 1987, Crossroads in Cultural Studies, Tampere, Finland, 1996; head praparator Reflexes and Reflections Russell Rotunda Capitol Hill, Washington, 1983, Lincoln Ctr., N.Y.C., 1984. One-man shows include Claywork Gallery, Atlanta, 1986, H. Smith Gallery U. SC, Spartanburg, 1991, Nat. Vietnam Vets. Art Mus., Chgo., 1999, Mercury Art Works, Athens, Ga., 2003, Floataway Complex, Atlanta, 2005, numerous group shows including most recently, exhibited in group shows at Peace Mus., Chgo., 2002, Aurora (Ill.) Hist. Ctr., 2003, U. N.Mex., 2004, Children of War, Nat. Vietnam Vets. Art Mus., 2005, Wis. Vets. Mus., Madison, 2006, Represented in permanent collections Nat. Vietnam Vets. Art Mus., Chgo., Nat. Mus. Fine Art, Hanoi, Vietnam., Ga. Mus. of Art, Athens, Ga. Ga. World Congress Ctr., Atlanta, U. Ga. Complex Carbohydrate Rsch. Ctr., Bank South Ga., Tifton, Ga.; featured (in over 150 mags.). With U.S. Army, 1959-63, Vietnam. Decorated Purple heart, 1963; Visual Arts fellow So. Arts Fdn./NEA, 1988; Sr. Faculty grantee U. Ga. Rsch. Found., Inc., 1991-93, 96-98, Individual Artist grantee Ga. Coun. Arts, 1993-94; recipient Purchase award 8th Annual Maine/Maritime Internat. Flatworks Exhibn., 1990, Merit award Three Works 29th Juried Exbhn., Lyndon House Arts Center, Athens, Ga., 2004. Mem. VFW, Mil. Order of the Purple Heart (comdr. 1990-2000), Vietnam Helicopter Pilots Assn. Home: 165 Springdale St Athens GA 30605-1237 Office Phone: 706-540-2937. Personal E-mail: richard.j.olsen@att.net.

**OLSEN, ROBERT C., JR.,** academic administrator, military officer; b. Bklyn. m. Maureen Olsen; 2 children. BS, USCG Acad., 1969; MS in Adminstrn., U. Naval Postgrad. Sch., Monterey, Calif., 1979; MA in Nat. Security and Strategic Studies, Naval War Coll., 1990. Commd. USCG, advanced through grades to rear admiral; exec. officer USCGC Madrona; comdg. officer various cutters USCG; comdt. of cadets USCG Acad.; asst. supt., maritime law enforcement and intelligence br. chief for 3d Coast Guard Dist. NY; mgr. surface forces Coast Guard Atlantic Area; detailer for officer assignments USCG Hdqrs., mem. tng. and edn. staff, dir. pers. mgmt.; supt., pres. USCG Acad., New London, Conn., ret., 2005; pres. Webb Inst., Glen Cove, NY, 2005—. Decorated Legion of Merit (3), Meritorious Svc. medal, Coast Guard Commendation medal (4), Humanitarian Svc. medal (2). Office: Webb Inst 298 Crescent Beach Rd Glen Cove NY 11542-1398 Office Phone: 860-444-8285.

**OLSEN, STEVEN KENT,** dentist; b. Spanish Fork, Utah, Nov. 20, 1944; s. Earl Clarence and Adela (Faux) O.; children: Curt, Christopher, Sara Kate, Vanessa BS, Brigham Young U., 1969; DDS, U. Pacific, 1974. Ptrn. practice dentistry in surg. and endodontics Brooks & Olsen, Salt Lake City, 1974—; gen. practice dentistry Steven K. Olsen, D.D.S., San Francisco, 1974-75; pres. S.K. Olsen, P.C., San Francisco, 1975—; ptnr. Olsen, H. & P., San Francisco 1977-83; instr. U. Pacific, San Francisco, 1978—. Chmn. bd. Am. Dentists Ins. Corp., Grand Cayman, W.I., 1978-81; instr. Stanford (Calif.) Inst., Chabot Coll. Inst., 1979-82; med. staff Latter-day Saints Hosp.; cons. Calif. Inst., San Francisco, 1981—; ptnr. J.B. Devel. Co., Russell Harris Restorations, Ryan Bott Restorations, Jason Herget Restorations, D.W. Mmgt. Co., Bob Steck Mgmt. Co., Dave Olsen & Co.; chmn. bd., pres. R.O.R., 1977-80; bd. dirs. Wilks & Topper, Inc., San Francisco, Curt Facchino Ltd., Woodside. Author: Accolade, 1963, (play) Lancer Ballade, 1963, (acad. course) World Religions, 1979; editor corr. course Calif. Inst., 1981. Recipient Good Citizenship medal SAR, 1963, Golden State award, 1988, others. Mem. Assn. Coll. of Physicians and Surgeons, ADA, Calif. Dental Assn., Utah Dental Assn., Physicians and Surgeons Club (San Francisco), Alpha Epsilon Delta. Home: 385 Old La Honda Rd Woodside CA 94062-2617 Office: 2 Embarcadero Ctr Promenade San Francisco CA 94111

**OLSEN, THOMAS RICHARD, SR.,** air force officer; b. Houston, June 28, 1934; s. Oscar Leonard and Catherine (Byers) O.; children: Thomas Richard Jr., Lisa Kendrick Olsen Wesolick; m. Jacquelyn Beasley Keels, June 28, 1998. BSME, Tex. A&M U., 1956; MS in Internat. Affairs, George Washington U., 1968. Mech. engr. Tex. Gas Corp., Houston, 1956; commd. 2d lt. USAF, 1957, advanced through grades to maj. gen., 1986; pilot trainee Greenville AFB, Miss., 1957-58; fighter pilot 326 FIS/526 FIS, U.S. and Fed. Republic Germany, 1958-65, 614 TFS/615 TFS, England AFB, La., 615 TFS, Phan Rang AB, Vietnam, 1966-67; instr. U.S. Naval Amphibious Sch., Coronado, Calif., 1968-71; fighter pilot 391 TFS, Mt. Home AFB, Idaho, 1971-72, squadron ops. officer, squadron comdr., 1972-74; chief rated officer Mgmt. Hdqrs. AFMPC, Randolph AFB, Tex., 1975-78; chief of staff Hdqrs. 9th Air Force, Shaw AFB, SC, 1978-79; dep. comdr. Hdqrs. 314th Air Div., Seoul, Republic of Korea, 1979-81; dir. ops. Hdqrs. 5th Air Force, Yokota AFB, Japan, 1981-82; wing comdr. 51 TFW, Osan AB, Republic of Korea, 1982-83; dep. dir. ops. Hdqrs. Pacific Command, Camp Smith, Hawaii, 1983-85; asst. chief of staff ops. Hdqrs. AFCENT, NATO, Brunsuum, The Netherlands, 1985-87; dep. comdr., chief of staff Hdqrs. 4 ATAF, NATO, Heidelberg, Fed. Republic Germany, 1987-89; vice comdr. Hdqrs. 9th Air Force, Shaw AFB, SC, 1989-91; dep. comdr. U.S. Cen. Command Air Forces (Desert Shield/Desert Storm), Riyadh, Saudi Arabia, 1990-91; ret., 1991. Exec. dir. Sumter Base Defense Com., 1994—. Mem. Optimist Club, Coronado, 1969-71. Mem. Air Force Assn., Ret. Officers Assn., Daedalians, Kiwanis, Rotary. Baptist. Home: 3030 Lowfalls Ln Sumter SC 29150-2337 Office Phone: 803-436-2574. Business E-Mail: tolsen@ftc-i.net.

**OLSEN-DUNBAR, JESSICA IDA,** sign language educator; b. Waterloo, Iowa, Dec. 7, 1977; d. Loren David and Deborah Ann Olsen; m. Stephen Leo Dunbar, Sept. 30, 1965. BA, U. No. Iowa, 2000; Master's, McDaniel Coll., 2003. Am. sign lang. instr. U. No. Iowa, Cedar Falls, 2000—. Club advisor Am. Sign Lang. Club of U. No. Iowa, Cedar Falls, Iowa, 2002—. Treas. Miss Deaf Iowa Pageant Com., 1997. Named Miss Deaf Iowa, 1995—97. Mem.: Iowa Assn. Deaf (assoc.), Miss Deaf Iowa Pageant Com. (assoc.), Cedarloo Assn. Deaf (assoc.; v.p. 1999—2001, del. 1999—2001). Office: University of Northern Iowa 1222 West 27th Street Cedar Falls IA 50614-0001 Home: 2212 Erik Rd Cedar Falls IA 50613-7948 Personal E-mail: jessicaiolsen@mchsi.com. E-mail: jessica.olsen@uni.edu.

**OLSEN-ESTIE, JEANNE LINDELL,** golf course owner; b. Everett, Wash., July 17, 1946; d. Carmen David Lindell and Violet Louise (Harrison) Johnson; m. Wayne William Olsen, Dec. 22, 1984 (dec. Apr. 1993); children: Kenda, Justin; m. John Gary Estie, Nov. 5, 1994. Grad., Lee Sch. Cosmetology, 1966, Everett Beauty Sch., 1968, Everett Plz. Sch. Cosmetology, 1987. With Marysville Police Dept., Wash., 1967—72, Durham Transp., 1979—87; owner, mgr. Olsen's Riverside Golf Course and Olsen's Golf Equipment, 1979—. Author of poems. Active Maryfest, Marysville, 1976-78; bd. dirs. Snohomish County Camp Fire Boys and Girls. Recipient Editors Choice award for outstanding achievement in poetry, 1999. Mem. Nat. Granite Ware Collectors, Everett Antique Club, Hummel Club Collectors,Everett Elks (officer lodge #479, Exalted Ruler of Yr. 2004). Achievements include pubished in third book of poetry; second woman Exalted Ruler of Elks Lodge #479 since 1899; Perfect Attendance Award, Elks Lodge, 2004. Avocations: golf, collecting and restoring antiques, singing. Home and Office: PO Box 5609 Everett WA 98206-5609

**OLSHAKER, MARK BRUCE,** scriptwriter, filmmaker; b. Washington, Feb. 28, 1951; s. Bennett and Thelma A. (Abramson) O.; m. Carolyn M. Clemente, Aug. 28, 1977. BA, George Washington U., Washington, 1972. Spl. correspondent St. Louis Post Dispatch, Washington Bur., 1974-75; writer, author, film maker Washington Area, 1972—. V.p. Unicorn Projects, Inc., Washington, 1983—, Mindhunters. Inc. Vienna, Va., 1995—; bd. dirs. Shakespeare Guild, Washington. Author: (novels) Einstein's Brain, 1981, Unnatural Causes, 1986, Blood Race, 1989, The Edge, 1994, The Mindhunters: Broken Wings, 1999; (anthology) Unusual Suspects, 1996; (non-fiction) The Instant Image, 1978; co-author (with John Douglas), Mindhunter, 1995 (Anthony award nomination, Brit. Gold Dagger nomination, Edgar nomination, Mystery Writers of Am.). Unabomber: On the Trail of America's Most-Wanted Serial Killer, 1996, Journey into Darkness, 1997, Obsession, 1998, The Anatomy of Motive, 1999, The Cases That Haunt Us, 2000; (with C.J. Peters) Virus Hunter, 1997; contbr. (textbook) Forensic Emergency Medicine; (screen writing) Stormchasers, 1995, (CINE Golden Eagle), The Edge, 1996 (TV Writing and Prodn.) We All Came to America, 1974, A Moment in Time, 1975, Patent Pending, 1975 (silver medal Inst. Film & TV Festival N.Y.), Lewis Mumford: Toward Human Architecture, 1979, Castle, 1983 (Am. Film Festival Red Ribbon), Cathedral, 1985 (Am. Film Festival Blue Ribbon, Cine Golden Eagle) Pyramid, 1988 (CINE Golden Eagle, Nat. Ednl. Film and Video Festival Gold Apple), What's Killing the Children?, 1990, Discovering Hamlet, 1990 (Am. Film Festival Red Ribbon, Bronze medal Inst. Film & TV Festival N.Y.), Mind of a Serial Killer, 1992 (Emmy nomination news and documentary 1993), Roman City, 1994 (Emmy award), Bridge, 1998, Mill Times, 2001, Bioterror: Dealing with a New Reality, 2001, Avoiding Armageddon, 2003, Flashpoints USA: God and Country, 2004; contbr. articles to newspapers, mags., wrote exhibition films for Nat. Park Svc., and Nat. Bicentennial Grand Parade, 1976. Media advisor, NEH, Corp. Pub. Broadcasting, Washington, 1984, 89, 91, 98, D.C. Comm. Arts and Humanities; hearing com. D.C. Ct. of Appeal Bd. on Profl. Responsibility, 1988-91. Mem. Am. Coll. Forensic Examiners, Writers Guild of Am. East, The Authors Guild, The Cosmos Club, Cosmos Club Found. (chmn.), English-Speaking Union. Office: PO Box 1957 Vienna VA 22183-1957

**OLSHAN, BERNARD,** artist; b. NYC, Jan. 31, 1921; Student, Am. Artists Sch., NYC, 1937—40, Ozenfant Sch. Fine Arts, 1945—47, Academie de la Grand Chaumiere, Paris, 1948—51. Cultural arts dir. Mosholu Montefiore YMCA/YWCA, NY; instr. Crafts Students League, 1953, NYC CC, 1965—69; teacher, dir., cultural arts dept. Mosholu Montefiore Cmty. Ctr., NYC, 1966—79; chmn., visual arts com. Amalgamated Houses, NYC, 1980—; faculty Nat. Acad., NYC, 1998—. One-man shows include Ward Eggelston Galleries, 1952, 1954, 1958, Grace Coll. Gallery, NY CC, 1969, exhibitions include Pearl St. Gallery, 1965, Whitney Mus., Dallas Mus. of Art. Served in U.S. Army, 1941—45. Recipient Emily Lowe award, 1950, Ralph Mayer Meml. award, 1984, 1987, Andrew Carnegie award, Nat. Acad. Design, 1999. Mem.: Fedn. Modern Painters & Sculptors, Nat. Acad. of Design (Academician), Am. Soc. Contemporary Artists. Office: National Academy Sch 5 E 89th St New York NY 10128 Office Phone: 212-996-1908. Office Fax: 212-426-1711.

**OLSHAN, JUDD DAVID,** environmental scientist; s. Marc Allen and Toni Peckham Olshan; m. Hannah Joy Spencer, Sept. 14, 2002. BA in Human Ecology, Coll. of the Atlantic, Bar Harbor, Maine, 1992; MA in Resource Mgmt., Ctrl. Wash. U., 1997; BA in History, SUNY Cortland, 2005. Lic. real estate salesperson Mass., 2001. Tour leader Trek Am., Gardena, Calif., 1994—2000; tchr. Nature's Classroom, Charlton, Mass., 1993—2000; program dir. Regional Environ. Coun., Worcester, Mass., 2000—02; program mgr. Cornell Coop. Ext., Ithaca, NY, 2002—03. Ranger Greater Worcester Land Trust, Worcester, Mass., 2001—02; chair Youth Environ. Svc. Corps Adv. Bd., Worcester, Mass., 2001—02. Mem., vol. Greater Worcester Land Trust, 2001—06, Lime Hollow Nature Ctr., Cortland, NY, 2002—06. Recipient Alumni Acheivment awards, SUNY Cortland Alumni Assn., 2004—05, All Coll. Writing award, 2005; fellow Univ. fellow, Syracuse U., 2005—; scholar Adult Learner scholar, SUNY Cortland, 2004. Mem.: Am. Hist. Assn. (assoc.), Alpha Sigma Lambda, Tau Sigma, Phi Alpha Phi, Phi Kappa Phi. Green Party. Avocation: back country canoeing. Office Phone: 315-223-2210. E-mail: jolshan@syr.edu.

**OLSHAN, REGINA,** lawyer; b. Kiev, Ukraine, 1964; m. Yves Cantin; children: Maxime, Gabrielle. AB cum laude, Harvard U., 1985; cert. in European Studies, Coll. d'Europe, 1986; JD, Yale U., 1989. Bar: Conn. 1991, N.Y. 1994. Law clk. Hon. José Cabranes U.S. Dist. Ct. Conn., 1989—90; atty. Skadden, Arps, Slate, Meagher & Flom LLP, N.Y., 1990—98, ptnr., 1998—. Scholar, Fulbright Found. Office: Skadden Arps Slate Meagher & Flom LLP Four Times Square New York NY 10036

**OLSHANSKY, BRIAN,** internal medicine and cardiology educator, researcher, physician; b. N.Y.C., Dec. 25, 1952; s. Murray and Phyllis (Macklin) O.; m. Darlene Marie Postaccchini, Nov. 20, 1989. Student, Columbia U., 1973; AB, Carleton Coll., Northfield, Minn., 1974; MD, U. Ariz., 1978. Diplomate Am. Bd. Internal Medicine, Am. Bd. Cardiovascular Medicine and Electrophysiology, Am. Bd. Electrophysiology. Intern in internal medicine Bellevue and NYU Hosps., N.Y.C., 1978-79, resident, 1979-81; fellow in cardiology U. Iowa Hosps., Iowa City, 1981-84; assoc. in medicine, staff physician U. Ala. Hosps., Birmingham, 1984-85, asst. prof. medicine, staff physician, 1985-86; asst. prof. medicine Case Western Res. U., Cleve., 1986-88; asst. prof., staff physician Loyola U. Med. Ctr., Maywood, Ill., 1988-90, assoc. prof., dir. rsch., staff physician div. cardiology, 1990—96, prof. medicine, 1996—2000; prof. of medicine U. Iowa Coll. Medicine, 2000—; dir. cardiac electrophysiology lab. Loyola U. Med. Ctr., Maywood, 1994—2000, dir. fellows training program clin. crdiac electrophysiology, 1994—2000; dir. cardiac electrophysiology U. Iowa Coll. Medicine, 2000—; dir. fellow training program clin. cardiac eletrophysiology U. Iowa Coll. of Medicine, 2000—. Reviewer, spkr. in field. Contbr. articles, 170 abstracts, more than 175 papers to med. jours., 26 chpts. to books; reviewer to numerous jours. including Am. Jour. Medicine, Am. Jour. Med. Scis., others; co-editor 2 books in field; guest editor to various jours.; contbg. editor CARDIO Mag., 1994-1995; co-author NASPEXAM for assoc. profls; mng. editor Medicine.com, 2000—; section editor to various electronic registry; edtl. bd. mem. to numerous jours., digests and mags. Rsch. fellow NSF, 1970, Henry R. Viets rsch. fellow, 1977, Am. Soc. Anesthesiologists, 1977; grantee Loyola Cardiovascular Inst., 1990, Am. Heart Assn. Metro. Chgo., 1992; Best Drs. in Am., 1996-2005. Fellow ACP, Am. Coll. Cardiology, Laennec Soc. (assoss.), Heart Rhythm Soc.; mem. Am. Heart Assn. (fellow clin. cardiology coun., rsch. fellow 1982), Am. Fedn. Clin. Rsch., N.Am. Soc. Pacing and Electrophysiology (abstract reviewer 1989-93), N.Y. Acad. Scis., Laonnec Soc. Home: 4344 Maier Ave SW Iowa City IA 52240-8410 Office: U Iowa Hosps 4426A JCP 200 Hawkins Dr Iowa City IA 52242 Office Phone: 319-356-2344. E-mail: brian-olshansky@uiowa.edu.

**OLSHANSKY, STUART JAY,** science educator; b. Detroit, Mich., Feb. 22, 1954; s. Abe and Pearl Olshansky; m. Sara Jane Turkin, Sept. 3, 1978; children: Jessica Ann, Ricky. BS in Psychology, Mich. State U., 1975; MA, U. Chgo., 1982, PhD, 1984. Rsch. assoc. Ctr. on Aging, U. of Chgo., Chicago, Ill., 1990—2000, prof. Sch. of Pub. Health, Chicago, Ill., 2000—. Author: The Quest for Immortality. Recipient Spl. Emphasis Rsch. Career award Nat. Inst. on Aging, 1992-1997, Ind. Scientist award, 1998-2003, Sr. Fulbright award, Fulbright, 2003-2008. Mem.: Gerontol. Soc. of Am. (assoc.). Achievements include research in modern development of the field of biodemography. Home: 400 Springside Ln Buffalo Grove IL 60089-1653 Office: U Ill 1603 W Taylor Chicago IL 60612 Office Phone: 312-355-4668. Home Fax: 847-537-7188. Business E-Mail: sjayo@uic.edu.

**OLSHEVSKY, GEORGE,** editor; b. Karlsruhe, Germany, June 12, 1946; arrived in U.S., 1947; s. George Eugene and Catherine Sergeyevna Olshevsky; m. Andrea Marie Matyas, Aug. 25, 1982. BSc, MIT, Cambridge, Mass., 1967; MSc, U. Toronto, Ontario, Can., 1970. Computer programmer U. Toronto Computer Ctr., Canada, 1967—77; freelance writer, publisher Official Marvel Comics Index, Toronto, San Diego, Calif., 1976—84; freelance writer The Official Index to Marvel Comics, N.Y.C, 1984—88, Dino Frontline Mag., Tokyo, 1992—96, Dino Press Mag., Tokyo, 2000—02; indexer self employed, 1989—. Author: (book) Mesozoic Meanderings #3,

2000; co-author (cons. with Howard Zimmerman): (children's book) Dinosaurs! The Biggest, Baddest, Strangest, Fastest, 2000; author: Encyclopedia of Dinosaurs, 2001; co-author (cons.): (childrens books series) Discovering Dinosaurs, 2002; contbr. articles to books and mags. on dinosaurs. Office: Publs Requiring Rsch PO Box 161015 San Diego CA 92176-1015 E-mail: dinogeorge@aol.com.

**OLSON, ALLISON W.,** social studies educator; b. Provo, Utah, Mar. 4, 1965; d. Donald Jex and Kelly (Duke) Woolley; m. Steven W. Olson, Dec. 15, 1986; children: Christopher, Cameron, Rylee, Paige. BS Elem. Edn. and Spl. Edn., Brigham Young U., Provo, 1988; postgrad., U. Phoenix. Cert. Social Studies Endorsement Colo. Dept. Edn. Resource specialist Highlands Elem. Sch. Salt Lake City Sch. Dist., 1988—89; resource specialist, tchr. 4th grade Bancroft Elem. Sch. LaMesa/Spring Valley Sch. Dist., San Diego, 1991—94; tchr. 5th grade Stafford Elem. Sch. Stafford County Schs., Va., 2000—03; tchr. 6th grade Heritage Elem. Sch. Douglas County Sch. Dist., Highlands Ranch, Colo., 2003—04; tchr. 8th grade AP Social Studies Liberty Mid. Sch. Cherry Creek Sch. Dist., Aurora, Colo., 2004—. Pvt. tutor, Salt Lake City, 1989—90; tutor Sylvan Learning Ctr., Spring Valley, Calif., 1994—96; mem. Excellence in Equity com. Liberty Mid. Sch., Aurora, 2005—06, coord. Social Studies Dept., 2005—06. Mem.: ASCD, Nat. Coun. Social Studies. Republican. Mem. Lds Ch. Avocations: boating, gardening, volleyball, basketball. Office: Liberty Mid Sch 2500 Dry Creek Rd Aurora CO 80016

**OLSON, BARBARA FORD,** physician; b. Iowa City, June 15, 1935; d. Leonard A. and Anne (Swanson) Ford; m. Robert Eric Olson, 1959 (div. 1973); children: Katherine Gee, Eric Ford, Julie Marie. BA, Gustavus Adolphus Coll., 1956; MD, U. Minn., 1960. Diplomate Am. Bd. Family Practice, Am. Bd. Geriat. Medicine, added qualification geriat. medicine. Intern St. Paul-Ramsey Med. Ctr., 1960-61; resident in anesthesiology U. Hosp. Cleve., 1961-62, U. Minn. Hosp., Mpls., 1962-63; pvt. practice anesthesiology St. Johns Hosp. and Devine Redeemer Hosp., St. Paul, 1963-67, Mercy Hosp., Coon Rapids, Minn., 1967-74; staff physician Oak Terrace Nursing Home, Minnetonka, Minn., 1974-88; staff physician, med. dir. geriatric evaluation clinic VA Med. Ctr., St. Cloud, Minn., 1988—. Pres. Alpha Epsilon Iota Med. Found., Mpls., 1980—86, bd.dirs., 1980—86, 2003—. Mem. Minn. Med. Assn., Minn. Women Physicians (pres. 1981-82, bd. dirs. 2003—). Office: VA Med Ctr 4801 8th St N Saint Cloud MN 56303-2015 Home: P O Box 27187 Minneapolis MN 55427 Business E-Mail: Barbara.Olson@med.va.gov.

**OLSON, BRUCE VAN,** music educator; b. Mpls., Mar. 23, 1961; s. Carl V. and Sandra L. Olson; m. Elizabeth Louise Guidry, Oct. 20, 1989; children: Grant, Luke. MusB, Concordia Coll., Moorhead, Minn., 1983; MusM, Calif. State U., Northridge, 1988. Band dir. Dinnba (Calif.) Pub. Schs., 1983—86, Cutler-Orosi Unified Schs., Orosi, 1989—92, Burnsville (Minn.) H.S., 1994—96, Anoka H.S., 1996—2002, Blaine H.S., 2002—. Trumpet Disneyland, Anaheim, Calif., 1983, No. Symphony Orch., Anoka, Minn., 2002—; dir. Continent Singers and Orch., Ventura, Calif., 1986—91. Orch. dir. LaCrescenta (Calif.) Bapt. Ch., 1986—88, Reedley Mennonite Brotherhood, 1990—92, Meadow Creek Ch., Andover, Minn., 2002—. Recipient J. Robert Hanson Music award, Concordia Coll., 1983. Mem.: Minn. Band Dirs. Assn., Music Educators Nat. Conf., Minn. Music Educators Assn. Evangelical. Avocations: boating, camping, fishing, reading. Office: Blaine HS 12555 Univ Ave NE Blaine MN 55434 Office Phone: 763-506-6570.

**OLSON, BYRON LOUIS,** biochemist, educator; s. Louis Nels and Mary Virginia Olson; m. Patricia Ann Thomas, June 28, 1969; children: Ann Marie, Michael David. BS, U. of Akron, 1964; PhD, Case Western Res. U., Cleve., 1970. Asst. prof. of preventive dentistry and biochemistry Ind. U. Schools of Dentistry and Medicine, Indpls., 1972—79, assoc. prof. of preventive and cmty. dentistry and biochemistry and molecular biology, 1979—92, prof. of oral biology, biochemistry and molecular biology, 1992—. Pres. faculty coun. Ind. U. Sch. Dentistry, 2000—01; chair faculty coun. campus planning com. Ind. U.-Purdue U., Indpls., 1997—99. Contbr. articles to profl. jours. Mem. and bd. chair Ind. Fedn. of Communities for Drug-Free Youth, Inc., Zionsville, 1991—95. 1st lt. U.S. Army, 1964—66. Recipient Tchg. Excellence awards, Ind. U. Sch. of Dentistry, 1997—99; grantee numerous grants. Mem.: Am. Assn. for Dental Rsch. (assoc.; pres. Ind. sect. 1991—92), Internat. Assn. for Dental Rsch. (assoc.), Royal Soc. of Chemistry (assoc.), Am. Dental Edn. Assn. (assoc.; chair biochemistry and nutrition sect. 1992—93, chair, oral biology sect 1997—99), Am. Chem. Soc. (assoc.; chair, Ind. sect. 1996), Omicron Kappa Upsilon (hon.; chpt. pres. 1998). Roman Catholic. Avocations: swimming, travel, reading, music, fishing. Home: 4994 Tudor Pl Carmel IN 46033 Office: Indiana Unviersity School of Dentistry 1121 W Michigan St Indianapolis IN 46202 Office Phone: 317-274-5419. E-mail: bolson@iupui.edu.

**OLSON, CAROL ANN,** retired librarian; b. Chgo., Dec. 16, 1945; d. Kenneth Carlyle and Marion Heath (Barkway) Nygaard; m. Ray Alan Olson, June 15, 1974; children: Eric Robert, Peter Alan. BA in History, Jamestown (N.D.) Coll., 1968; MALS, U. Minn., 1970. Acquisitions libr. Luther Sem. Library, St. Paul, 1971-97; catalog libr. Hamma Libr., Trinity Luth. Sem., Columbus, Ohio, 1998—2006; ret., 2006. Editor: (with others) Landings Across the Ocean, 1997. Church libr. rsch. roundtable, life mem. Vesterheim Norwegian-Am. Mus., Decorah, Iowa, Vesterheim Geneal. Ctr., Madison, Wis. Mem. Am. Theol. Libr. Assn., Minn. Theol. Libr. Assn., Minn. Libr. Assn., Libr. Rsch. Roundtable Divsn. Minn. Libr. Assn., Ohio Theol. Libr. Assn., Scandinavian Club Columbus, Sons of Norway, Romerike Lag and Landings Lag (editor Landings Lag newsletter 1984-94, genealogist Landings Lag 1995—, Voss Lag 1995-98), Beta Phi Mu (life). Lutheran. Home: 475 Doverwood Dr Reynoldsburg OH 43068-1166 Office: Hamma Libr Trinity Luth Sem 2199 E Main St Columbus OH 43209-3913 E-mail: caolson@copper.net.

**OLSON, CHARLES ERIC,** economist; b. Wausau, Wis., June 2, 1942; s. Roland Anthony and Lois (Erickson) O.; m. Pamela Ann Templin, July 1, 1967 (div. Oct. 1973); children: Sonja Anne, Erika Christine; m. Carole Emily Collesian, Dec. 1, 1973 (div. Oct. 1990); children: Cora Elizabeth, Sarah Emily; m. Jeanne Esther Katz, Apr. 14, 1991. Student, U. Wis., Marathon County, 1960-62; BBA with honors, U. Wis., Madison, 1964; MS, U. Wis., 1966, PhD, 1968. MALS, U. Wis., Madison, 1966-68; asst. prof. U. Md., College Park, 1968-71, assoc. prof. bus., 1971-76; sr. economist H. Zinder & Assocs., Washington, 1976-77, v.p., 1977-79, sr. v.p., 1979—80, pres., 1986-2000, Olson & Co., Inc., 1980-86; Tyser tchg. fellow R.H. Smith Sch. Bus. U. Md., College Park, 2000—. Cons. Devel. Adv. Service, atty. gens. N.C., Minn., Ky., Mass., Va. U.S. Postal Rate Commn., Dept. Def., numerous electric and gas utlities in U.S. and Can. Testified numerous pub. utility rate cases, before Senate Subcom. on Inter-govtl. Relations; mem. advisory com. research and devel. and energy conservation Fed. Power Commn., 1973-74, vice chmn. rate design task force, 1976—. Author: Cost Considerations for Efficient Electricity Supply, 1970; contbr. chpts. to books, articles to profl. jours. Mem. Prince Georges County (Md.) Citizens Airpark Advisory Com., 1970-71. Grantee Inst. Pub. Utilities, 1967-68; U. Md. 1970, 76. Mem. Transp. and Pub. Utilities Group. Home: 10822 Alloway Dr Rockville MD 20854-1503 Office: RH Smith Sch Bus Univ Md College Park MD 20742 Business E-Mail: colson@rhsmith.umd.edu.

**OLSON, DALE C.,** public relations executive; b. Fargo, ND, Feb. 20, 1934; s. Arthur Edwin and Edith (Weight) Olson Neubauer. Sr. v.p., prin., pres. motion picture divsn. Rogers and Cowan, Inc., Beverly Hills, Calif., 1967-85; prin. Dale C. Olson & Assocs., Beverly Hills, 1985—; mktg. dir. Hollywood History Mus., 2003. Cons. Filmex, L.A., 1972-83; U.S. del. Manila Film Festival, 1982-83. Editor L.A. edit. Theatre ann. Best Plays, 1963-67. V.p. Diamond Cir. City of Hope, Duarte, Calif., 1980-83; mem. adv. bd. Calif. Mus. Sci. and Industry, L.A., 1975-81; mem. bd. govs. Film Industry Workshops, Inc., 1965-80; pres. Hollywood Press Club, 1963-66; assoc. Los Angeles County Art Mus., 1981-83; bd. trustees Hollywood Arts Coun.; chair 1999 jury USA Film Festival, Dallas; cons. L.A. 2000. Recipient Golden Key, Pub. Rels. News, 1982, Les Mason and pub. svc. awards Publicists Guild,

Golden Satellite award for lifetime achievement Internat. Press Acad., 1999, Prism award for pub. svc. Entertainment Industries Coun., 2000, Named in his honor, Dale Olson Lobby, Actors' Fund L.A. Office, 2005. Mem. NATAS, Acad. Motion Picture Arts and Scis. (chmn. pub. rels. coordinating com. 1982—), Actors Fund Am. (chmn. western coun. 1991, trustee 1992, exec. com. 1998), Hollywood Arts Coun. (bd. dirs.), Pres.'s Club, Thalians. Lutheran. Office Phone: 323-876-9331. Personal E-mail: dolson2000@earthlink.net.

**OLSON, DAVID CARL,** physician; b. Sparta, Wis., Jan. 22, 1950; s. Oral Clifton and Ramona LaBelle Olson; m. Barbara Anne Roeming (div.); children: Emily Sullivan, Paul, Alexander. BA, U. Wis., Madison, 1972; MD, Med. Coll. Wis., Milw., 1986. Cert. AAFP, 2001. Physician Family Health Plan, Elm Grove, Wis., 1989—2002, Pro-Health, Brookfield, Wis., 2002—. Assoc. clin. prof. family and cmty. medicine Med. Coll. Wis. Pres. Med. Soc. Milw. County, 2004, mem. bd., 2005. Named Wis. Family Physician of Yr., 1995; named one of Best Drs. in Am., 2002, 2006, Am. Top Family Doctors, 2004—05. Mem.: Wis. Acad. Family Physicians (alternate del., pres., Family Physician of Yr. 1995). Unitarian Universalist. Avocations: jogging, movies. Office: 2085 N Calhoun Rd Brookfield WI 53005 Business E-Mail: dcolson@phci.org.

**OLSON, DAVID JOHN,** political science professor; b. Brantford, ND, May 18, 1941; s. Lloyd and Alice Ingrid (Black) O.; m. Sandra Jean Crabb, June 11, 1966; 1 dau., Maia Kari. BA, Concordia Coll., Moorhead, Minn., 1963; Rockefeller fellow Union Theol. Sem, N.Y.C., 1963-64; MA (Brooklings Instn. predoctoral research fellow 1968-69), U. Wis., Madison, 1966, PhD (univ. fellow 1967), 1971. Community planner Madison Redvel. Authority, 1965-66; lectr. U. Wis., 1966-67; from lectr. to asso. prof. polit. sci. Ind. U., Bloomington, 1969-76; prof. polit. sci. U. Wash., Seattle, 1976—2005, chmn. dept., 1983-88, Harry Bridges endowed chairlabor studies, 1992-94; bd. dirs. Harry Bridges Inst.; dir. Ctr. Labor Studies U. Wash., 1992-94; Disting. lectr. in labor studies San Francisco State U., 1994; prof. emeritus polit. sci. U. Wash., Seattle, 2005—. Vis. prof. U. Bergen, 1987, Harvard U., 1988-89, U. Hawaii, 1989, U. Calif., Berkeley, 1996. Co-author: Governing the United States, 1978, Commission Politics, 1977, To Keep the Republic, 1975, Black Politics, 1971; co-editor: Theft of the City, 1974. Named faculty fellow, Ind. U., 1973; recipient Disting. Tchg. award, 1973, Alumni Achievement award, Concordia Coll., 1998, S. Sterling Munro Disting. Tchg. award, 2005, Disting. Tchg. award. U. Wash., 2005, knight, Harold V of Norway, 2006. Mem. Am. Polit. Sci. Assn., Western Polit. Sci. Assn. (v.p. 1984, pres. 1985), Midwest Polit. Sci. Assn., So. Polit. Sci. Assn. Democrat. Lutheran. Home: 6512 E Green Lake Way N Seattle WA 98103-5418 Office: U Wash Dept Polit Sci Seattle WA 98195-0001 Office Phone: 206-543-7948. Business E-Mail: davidols@u.washington.edu.

**OLSON, DENNIS OLIVER,** lawyer; b. Seminole, Tex., Oct. 19, 1947; s. Edwin and Beulah Matilda (Strang) O.; m. Leonee Lynn Claud, Jan. 30, 1971; children: James Edwin, Stacy Rae. BA in English, U. Tex., 1969; JD, Tex. Tech U., 1974. Bar: Tex. 1974, U.S. Ct. Mil. Appeals 1974, U.S. Dist. Ct. (no. dist.) Tex. 1978, U.S. Dist. Ct. (we. dist.) Tex. 1978, U.S. Ct. Appeals (5th cir.) 1984, U.S. Supreme Ct. 1985, U.S. Dist. Ct. (ea. dist.) Tex. 2002. Commd. USMC, 1969, advanced through grades to capt., 1973, infantry officer various locations including Vietnam, 1969—74, judge advocate various locations, 1974—78, resigned, 1978; assoc. Carr, Evans, Fouts & Hunt, and predecessor, Lubbock, Tex., 1978—81, ptnr., 1981—85; pvt. practice Dallas, 1985—88; shareholder, co-chmn. bankruptcy sect. Godwin & Carlton, P.C., Dallas, 1989—94; ptnr. Olson Nicoud & Gueck, LLP and predecessor, Dallas, 1994—. Bd. dirs. Presbyn. Ctr. Doctors Clinic, Lubbock, 1983-85, United Campus Ministry, Tex. Tech U., Lubbock, 1984-85, Discovery Sch.of Canyon Creek, Richardson, 1999-2002; elder Canyon Creek Presbyn. Ch., Richardson, Tex.; treas., bd. dirs. Lubbock chpt. ARC, 1981-83; vol. Lubbock United Way, 1978-80. Decorated Bronze Star; named Outstanding Young Man of Am., 1983. Fellow Tex. Bar Found. (sustaining life); Dallas Bar Assn., Lubbock County Bar Assn. (bd. dirs. 1983-85), Tex. Young Lawyers Assn. (bd. dirs. 1981-83), Judge Advocates Assn. (bd. dirs. 1976-78), Lubbock C. of C. (grad. Leadership Lubbock program 1981), U. Tex. NROTC Alumni Found., (bd. dirs. 2001-), Phi Delta Phi. Home: 313 Forest Grove Dr Richardson TX 75080-1937 Office Phone: 214-979-7302. Business E-Mail: denniso@dallas-law.com.

**OLSON, DONALD RICHARD,** mechanical engineering educator; b. Sargent, Nebr., Dec. 26, 1917; s. Harry T. and Gyneth E. (Wittemyer) O.; m. Nancy Walker Benton, June 17, 1944; children: Walter H., Sally, Timothy W. BS, Oreg. State U., 1942; M.Engring., Yale U., 1944, D.Engring., 1951. Profl. engr., Conn. Asst. prof., asso. prof. mech. engring. Yale U., New Haven, 1951-62; prof. mech. engring. Pa. State U., University Park, 1962-83, prof. emeritus, 1983—; head underwater power plants Applied Research Lab., 1962-72, head dept. mech. engring., 1972-83; mem. engring. accreditation commn., 1979-82. Contbr. tech. papers in field to publs. Mem. ASME, Soc. Automotive Engrs. (dir. 1968-71), Sigma Xi. Home: 1930 Cliffside Dr State College PA 16801 E-mail: dro@psu.edu.

**OLSON, FERRON ALLRED,** metallurgist, educator; b. Tooele, Utah, July 2, 1921; s. John Ernest and Harriet Cynthia (Allred) O.; m. Donna Lee Jefferies, Feb. 1, 1944; children: Kandace, Randall, Paul, Jeffery, Richard. BS, U. Utah, 1953, PhD, 1956. Ordained bishop LDS Ch., 1962. Research chemist Shell Devel. Co., Emeryville, Calif., 1956-61; assoc. research prof. U. Utah, Salt Lake City, 1961-63, assoc. prof., 1963-68, chmn. dept mining. metall. and fuels engring., 1966-74, prof. dept. metallurgy and metall. engring., 1968-96, prof. emeritus, 1996—. Cons. U.S. Bur. Mines, Salt Lake City, 1973-77, Ctr. for Investigation Mining and Metallurgy Santiago, Chile, 1978; dir, U. Utah Minerals Inst., 1990-91. Author: Collection of Short Stories, 1985, (hist. book) Seymour Brunson: Defender of the Faith, 1998, (novel) Harriet Cynthia Allred Olson, 1995; contbr. articles to profl. jours. Del. State Rep. Conv., Salt Lake City, 1964; bishop, 1962-68, 76-82, missionary, 1988. With U.S. Army, 1943-46, PTO. Named Fulbright-Hayes lectr., Yugoslavia, 1974-75, Disting. prof. Fulbright-Hayes, Yugoslavia, 1980, Outstanding Metallurgy Instr., U. Utah, 1979-80, 88-89, Disting. Speaker U. Belgrade-Bor, Yugoslavia, 1974. Mem. Am. Inst. Mining, Metall. and Petroleum Engrs. (chmn. Utah chpt. 1978-79), Am. Soc. Engring. Edn. (chmn. Minerals div. 1972-73), Fulbright Alumni Assn., Am. Bd. Engring. and Tech. (bd. dirs. 1975-82). Republican. Achievements include research on explosives ignition and decomposition; surface properties of thoria, silica gels, silicon monoxide in ultra high vacuum; kinetics of leaching of Chrysocolla, Malachite and Bornite; electrowinning of gold; nodulation of copper during electrodeposition. Home: 1862 Herbert Ave Salt Lake City UT 84108-1832 E-mail: donnaolson1@mailstation.com.

**OLSON, GARY ROBERT,** banker; b. Milw., May 9, 1946; s. Ward Louis and Mary Jane (Brown) O.; m. Mia Kristina Sohn, Feb. 26, 1972; children: Kristin Anne, Brian Ward. Student, Loyola U., Rome, 1966-67; AB, Marquette U., 1968; M Internat. Mgmt., Am. Grad. Sch. Internat. Mgmt., Glendale, Ariz., 1973. Instr. Sogang Jesuit U., Seoul, 1968-70, Hankuk U. Fgn. Studies, Seoul, 1971-72; grad. asst. Am. Grad. Sch. Internat. Mgmt., 1972; credit analyst Chase Manhattan Bank, N.A., N.Y.C. and Tokyo, 1973-75, asst. treas. N.Y.C., 1975-77, 2d v.p. Madrid, 1977, Paris, 1977-80, v.p., mgr. Regional Banking Office Chgo., 1980-83; v.p., regional mgr. Case Nat. Corp. Svcs., San Francisco, 1983-87; sr. v.p. Chase Bank Ariz., Phoenix, 1987-90; v.p. Bklyn. and S.I. commercial mgr. Chase Manhattan Bank, N.A., Bklyn., 1990-93, v.p., team leader Nassau mid. mkt. mgr. Melville, L.I., 1993-97; mgr. corp. banking L.I. Dime Savs. Bank, Huntington Station, NY, 1997-99; sr. v.p. comml. banking Dime Savings Bank, 2000—. Advisor English program USIS, Seoul, 1969; alumni domestic counselor Am. Grad. Sch. Internat. Mgmt., 1990—, Marquette U., 1990—; vol. Spl. Olympics, Phoenix, 1988-89; fund drive capt. Phoenix Econ. Growth Corp., 1988; trustee, bd. dirs. Variety Pre-schooler's workshop, 1994—; bd. dirs. L.I. chpt. Robert Morris Assocs., 1994—, chmln., 1995—; trustee, bd. dirs., mktg. com., chmn.'s coun. Hecksher Mus., Huntington, N.Y., 1995—. Mem. Robert Morris Assocs. (assoc.), Econ. Club Phoenix, World Trade Club. Republican. Roman

Catholic. Avocations: reading, skiing, swimming, golf. Office: Washington Mutual Commercial Banking 3929 W John Carpenter Fwy Irving TX 75063-2909 E-mail: garyolson281@hotmail.com.

**OLSON, HAROLD ROY,** computer company executive; b. Escanaba, Mich., Apr. 8, 1928; s. Roy A. and Sara Calla Margarita (Carlson) O.; m. Angela Davis Hennessy, Sept. 26, 1959. BA in Journalism and Advt., Mich. State U., 1950. Mail clk. McCann Erickson Co., N.Y.C., 1950, 52-53; book promotion specialist, mgr. mag. promotion McGraw-Hill, N.Y.C., 1953-56; mgr. mag. promotion Reinhold Pub. Co., N.Y.C., 1956-58; space salesman McCall Corp., N.Y.C., 1959-60; pres. Visual Identity, Inc., N.Y.C., 1960-68; mktg. rep. Honeywell Info. Sys., Inc., N.Y.C., 1969-86; pres. Hal Olson's EDGE-BUY Express, Inc., 1986—. With U.S. Army, 1950-52. Republican. Episcopalian. Avocation: sailing.

**OLSON, HERBERT THEODORE,** trade association executive; b. Bridgeport, Conn., Feb. 9, 1929; s. Herbert Theodore and Inez Evelyn (Lindahl) O.; children: Christina, Victoria; m. Kathleen A. Harrison, Dec. 27, 1988. Student, Heidelberg Coll., 1947-49; AB, Ohio U., 1951, postgrad., 1951-52. Asst. to dean of men Ohio U., Athens, 1951-52; with Union Carbide Corp., 1952-71, mgr. employee rels., coord. pub. affairs N.Y.C., 1969-71; exec. v.p. Am. Assn. for Aging, Washington, 1971-75; dir. spl. projects Am. Healthcare Assn., Washington, 1975-79; pres. Promotional Products Assn. Internat., Irving, Tex., 1979-96, pres. emeritus, 1996—. Event coord.-supplier Stars Showcase, 1998-2000; mem. adv. bd. Allied Bank. Mem nat. exploring com., vice chmn. nat. events com., ann. meetings com., mem.-at-large nat. coun. Boy Scouts Am., 1980—; treas. U.S. Found. for Internat. Scouting, 1988—99, chmn. audit com., 1984—87, mem. internat. com., 1988—2003, mem. direct svc. coun. bd., 1997—2002; mem. long-term care for elderly rsch. rev. and adv. com. Dept. Health, 1972—77; mem. Longterm Care grant rev. com. HEW, 1972—77; mem. planning commn. City of Torrance, Calif., 1962—64, city councilman, 1964—67; chmn. Gov.'s Operation Leegit; mem. adv. bd. Irving Hosp.; chmn. bd. dirs. Irving Cancer Soc., 1997—; exec. bd. cir. 10 coun. Boy Scouts Am., 1979—; bd. mem. Irving chpt. Salvation Army, 2005, adv. coun.; mem. exec. bd. Circle 10 Coun., 1979—; mem. Irving Vistors and Cmty Bur., 2004—05; bd. dirs. Irving Conv. and Visitors Bur., 2001—, chmn., 2004—; bd. dirs. DFW Humane Soc., 2001—. Lord Baden Powell fellow, 1986; recipient Disting. Eagle award Boy Scouts Am., 1974, Silver Beaver award, 1968, Silver Buffalo award, 1998; named person of Yr. in Promotional Products in Counselor Mag., 1995, Hall of Fame Promotional Products Assn. Internat., 1997, Hall of Fame Can. Promo Prod. Assn., 1996. Mem. Meeting Planners Internat. (charter), Am. Soc. Assn. Execs., U.S. C. of C., Washington Soc. Assn. Execs., Nat. Assn. Exhibit Mgrs., Small Bus. Legis. Coun. (chmn. bd. 1993-95), Dallas Ft. Worth Soc. Assn. Execs. (v.p. 1985-87), Irving C. of C. (bd. dirs. 1999-2004), Am. Advt. Fedn., Am. Cancer Soc. (Irving chpt.), Tex. Soc. Assn. Execs., Las Colinas Country Club, Rotary (bd. dirs. 2004—), Masons, Shriners, Kiwanis (lt. gov.), DFW Humane Soc. Irving (bd. dirs. 2004—). Baptist. Home: 2910 Pacific Ct Irving TX 75062-4624 Office: 807 W Pioneer Dr Irving TX 75061

**OLSON, JACK CONRAD, JR.,** geriatrician; b. Muskegon, Mich., 1955; BS in Chemistry, Mich. State U., 1977, BA in English, 1977; MD, U. Mich., 1984. Bd. cert. internal medicine, bd. cert. geriatric medicine. Intern U. Wis. Hosps. and Clinics, Madison, 1984—85, resident internal medicine, 1985—87, fellow geriatrics, 1987—89; assoc. med. dir. Mendota Mental Health, U. Wis., 1989—92; dir. Windermere Sr. Health Ctr., U. Chgo., 1992—99; asst. clin. prof., fellowship dir. Rush U. Med. Ctr., Chgo., 1999—. Office: 1725 W Harrison St Ste 955 Chicago IL 60612 Office Phone: 312-942-7030. Business E-Mail: jolson@rush.edu.

**OLSON, JAMES (JIM OLSON),** telecommunications industry executive; BS in Elec. Engring., Univ. Calif. Davis; MS in Elec. Engring. Santa Clara Univ., MBA. Sr. mgmt., engring. mfg., mktg. Hewlett-Packard Co.; gen. mgr., Stanford Park Divsn. Hewlett-Packard, 1992; sr. v.p., gen. mgr., Wide Area Network Ops. 3Com Corp.; pres., CEO SkyStream Networks, 1997—. Spkr. in field. Office: SkyStream Networks 455 DeGuigne Dr Sunnyvale CA 94085-3890 Office Fax: 408-616-3404.*

**OLSON, JAMES RICHARD,** retired transportation executive; b. Alexandria, Minn., Mar. 11, 1941; s. Orie D. and Theresa Marie (Erickson) O.; m. Ronna Lee, Feb. 1, 1969 (dec.); 1 child, Trevor James. BS, N.D. State U., 1963; LLD, U. Minn., 1966; MBA, Harvard U., 1968. Asst. to v.p. finance Cargill Inc., Mpls., 1968-69; with Graco Inc., Mpls., 1969-75, v.p. finance, 1972-75; exec. v.p. finance Ponderosa System, Inc., Dayton, Ohio, 1975-77; v.p. planning Pillsbury Co., Mpls., 1977-79, v.p. restaurant group, 1979-80; group v.p.-restaurants The Carlson Cos., Inc., Mpls., 1981-83; exec. v.p., chief fin. and adminstrv. officer Schneider Nat., Inc., 1983-87, pres. van group, 1987-92, pres. transp. sector, 1992-98. Mem. Harvard Bus. Sch. Club Minn. (past pres.) Lutheran. Home: Winslow House 1103-100 2d St SE Minneapolis MN 55414-2157 Office Phone: 612-617-8869. Personal E-mail: jrolson1@att.net.

**OLSON, JAMES WILLIAM PARK,** architect; b. St. Louis, Oct. 6, 1940; s. James William Park; s. Louis Garfield and Gladys Helen (Schuh) O.; m. Katherine Fovargue, June 11, 1971; children: Park, Reed. BArch, U. Wash., 1963. Registered architect, Wash., Oreg., Calif., Ill., Colo., Hawaii, Ga., Fla. Ptnr. Olson Sundberg Kundig Allen Architects, Seattle, 1985—. Assoc. architect New Seattle Art Mus., 1991. Prin. works include Pike and Virginia Bldg. (AIA Honor award 1980), Seattle's Best Coffee Retail Locations (AIA Honor award 1984), Hauberg Residence (AIA Honor award 1997), Migy Institute Iehanisa, Denver (AIA Honor award 1998, AIA N.W. and Pacific Regional Merit award 1999, AIA We. Internat. Design award 2000), St. Mark's Cathedral Renovation (AIA Commendation award), Seattle (IFFRA award 1998, AIA citation 1998, AIA and Pacific Regional Merit award 2000), numerous residences nationwide; (subject of monologue) Monacelli Press: Architecture, Art and Craft. Bd. dirs. Ctr. Contemporary Art, Seattle, 1982-86, Artist Trust, Seattle, 1986-90, U. Wash. Henry Art Gallery, Seattle, 1986-92, Seattle Art Mus., 1996—. Recipient Best Architect award Seattle Mag., 1985. Fellow AIA; mem. NEA (juror). Avocation: art. Office: Olson Sundberg Kundig Allen Architects 159 South Jackson St 6th Fl Seattle WA 98104-2557 Office Phone: 206-624-5670. Business E-Mail: jim@olsonsundberg.com

**OLSON, JON PHILIP,** music educator, director, voice educator, actor; b. Oklahoma City, Feb. 5, 1971; s. Leslie John and Melanie Jane Olson; m. Betty (Betsy) Ruth Woodhams, Jan. 7, 2000; children: Megan Elizabeth Woodhams, Jonathan David. MusB, Okla. City U., 1993, MusM in Musical Theater Performance, 1997. Freelance actor Granbury Opera Ho., Tex., 1993, Casa Manana Theatre, Ft. Worth, 1998; cake decorator Homeland Foods, Oklahoma City, 1994—99; dir. music Selctman United Meth. Ch., Oklahoma City, 1997—98, Linwood United Meth. Ch., Oklahoma City, 1998—99; dir. music ministries Faith United Meth. Ch., Tulsa, Okla., 1999—2000, Mustang United Meth. Ch., Okla., 2001—. Actor: (theatrical prodn.) Camelot, H.M.S. Pinafore, West Side Story, Closer than Ever, A Little Night Music, 1776, The Unsinkable Molly Brown, The Pajama Game, Once Upon a Mattress, A Funny Thing Happened on the Way to the Forum, The Fantasticks; magician: The Magic Show at Frontier City; makeup designer Nine; The Phantom of the Opera (Yetson/Kopit); dir.: You're a goodman Charlie Borwn (revised), Joseph and the Amazing Technicolor Dream Coat; music dir.: Godspell; actor: (Operas) La Bohem, Faust; dir.: (play) Dracula; musician: (choral concerts) Canterbury Choral Society. Theatrical dir. Messiah Luth. Ch., Oklahoma City, 2004—05; mem.-at-large Ctrl. Okla. Ringers and Dirs., Oklahoma City, 2001—, pres., 2003—04. Mangager A. Margaret E. Petree scholarship, Okla. City U., 1990-1993, Homer S. Anderson scholarship, 1991-1993. Mem.: Okla. Music Educators Assn., Okla. Choral Dirs. Assn., Chorister's Guild, Music Educators Nat. Com., Am. Guild English Handbell Ringers, Am. Choral Dirs. Assn., Canterbury Choral Soc. R-Conservative. Methodist. Avocations: cooking, baking, model building, art, music. Office: Mustang United Methodist Church 211 W State Hwy 152 Mustang OK 73064 Personal E-mail: jonphilipolson@cox.net, maestromumc@aol.com.

**OLSON, KARL,** lawyer; b. San Francisco, Nov. 6, 1952; s. Leon and Reeva (Pearlstein) O.; m. Caroline M. Grannan, July 1, 1979 (div. Dec. 1982); m. Carolyn Ann Johnston, Jan. 1, 1990; children: Mark Johnson Olson, Jack Johnston Olson. BA, Sonoma State U., Rohnert Park, Calif., 1975; JD magna cum laude, U. Calif., San Francisco, 1982. Bar: Calif. 1982, U.S. Dist. Ct. (no. dist.) Calif. 1982, U.S. Ct. Appeals (9th cir.) 1983, U.S. Supreme Ct. 1990. Rsch. atty. to Justice Joseph Grodin Calif. Supreme Ct., San Francisco, 1982-83; assoc. Morrison & Foerster, San Francisco, 1983-86, Cooper, White & Cooper, San Francisco, 1986-89, prin., 1990-97, Levy, Ram & Olson, San Francisco, 1997. Contbr. articles to profl. jours. Precinct leader Dem. Party, San Francisco, 1988, 92, 96, 2000. Recipient James Madison award outstanding legal counsel, No. Calif. Soc. Profl. Journalists, 2005. Mem. State Bar Calif., Bar Assn. San Francisco (co-chmn. bench bar-media com. 1990—), Order of Coif, Thurston Honor Soc. Avocations: politics, journalism, sports. Office: Levy Ram & Olson 639 Front St 4th fl San Francisco CA 94111 Office Phone: 415-433-4949. E-mail: KO@lrolaw.com.

**OLSON, KEITH WALDEMAR,** historian, educator; b. Poughkeepsie, NY, Aug. 4, 1931; s. Ernest Waldemar and Elin Ingeborg (Rehnstrom) O.; m. Marilyn Joyce Wittschen, Sept. 10, 1955; children: Paula, Judy. BA, SUNY, Albany, 1957, MA, 1959; PhD, U. Wis., 1964; PhD (hon.), U. Tampere, Finland, 2000. Mem. history faculty Syracuse U., NY, 1963-66; mem. history faculty U. Md., College Park, 1966—; prof. history. Fulbright prof. U. Tampere, 1986-87, 2004, U. Oulu, Finland, 1993, U. Jyväskylä, Finland, 1994. Author: The G.I. Bill, the Veterans and the Colleges, 1974; Biography of a Progressive: Franklin K. Lane, 1979, Watergate: The Presidential Scandal That Shook America, 2003. Pres. Am. Scandinavian Found., Washington, 1977-79. Served with U.S. Army, 1952-54. U.S. Office Edn. grantee, 1965-66; U. Md. grantee, 1971, 76, 78. Mem. Am. Hist. Assn., Orgn. Am. Historians, Wis. Hist. Soc., Swedish Am. Hist. Soc., Finnish Hist. Soc. (hon.), Soc. Historians of Am. Fgn. Rels., Cen. Study of Presidency, Am. Scandinavian Assn. (pres. 1998-99). Unitarian Universalist. Home: 10746 Kinloch Rd Silver Spring MD 20903-1226 Office: U Md Dept History College Park MD 20742-0001 Office Phone: 301-405-4286. Business E-Mail: kwolson@umd.edu.

**OLSON, LEROY CALVIN,** retired educational administration educator; b. Kane, Pa., Mar. 7, 1926; s. Vernon Reinhold and Gertrude Viola Olson; m. Miriam Marie Vogler, June 19, 1954; children— David Lee, Thomas Edward, Steven Andrew. BS, Clarion State Coll., 1949; M.Ed., Pa. State Coll., 1950; Ed.D., Pa. State U., 1962; postgrad., U. Del., 1964-65. Tchr.-counselor Boiling Springs (Pa.) High Sch., 1950-52, Gordon Jr. High Sch., Coatesville, Pa., 1952-54; guidance dir. Cen. Dauphin Sch. Dist., Harrisburg, Pa., 1954-57; coordinator pupil personnel services, asst. supt. for instrn. and personnel, acting supt. Alfred I. duPont Sch. Dist., Wilmington, Del., 1957-65; prof. ednl. adminstrn. Temple U., Phila., 1965-92, prof. emeritus, 1992—. Cons. to schs. bds. and dists., also Nat. Wis., Pa. schs. assns. Contbr. articles to profl. jours. Trustee Luth. Ch., 1963-66, chmn. bd., 1976-78, chmn. various coms., discussion groups. Served with USNR, 1944-46, PTO. Recipient Disting. Alumni award, Clarion State Coll., 1972. Mem. Am. Personnel and Guidance Assn., AAUP, Am. Assn. Sch. Personnel Adminstrs., Assn. Supervision and Curriculum Devel., Council Profs. Instrn. Supervision, Nat. Staff Devel. Council, Am. Legion, Phi Delta Kappa, Phi Kappa Phi. Republican. Home: 211 Azalea Lane West Grove PA 19390 *God's gift of life is a marvelous thing. My attempt to make the best use of that gift is to try to live an integrated and balanced life. This means that active attention must be paid to the physical, social, spiritual, psychological, mental, and recreational aspects as well as to the work or career dimension. It also means we must share that gift through loving and caring about others.*

**OLSON, LYNDON LOWELL, JR.,** ambassador; b. Waco, Tex., Mar. 7, 1947; s. Lyndon Lowell and Frances (McLaughlin) O.; m. Nancy Swenson, Mar. 6, 1970 (div. Dec. 1980); m. Kathleen Woodward, Nov. 22, 1982. BA in Polit. Sci. and Religion, Baylor U., 1969, postgrad. Mem. Tex. Legislature, 1973-78; apptd. chmn. Tex. State Bd. Ins., Austin, 1979-81, 83-87, apptd. mem., 1981-83; pres. and chief exec. officer Nat. Group Ins. Cos., Waco, Tex., 1987—; chmn., CEO Travelers Ins. Holdings, N.Y.C., 1990-98; amb. to Sweden Stockholm, 1997. Bd. dirs. Central Nat. Bank; lectr. UN Conf. on Trade and Devel., Phillipines, 1985; mem. Expert Com. on Reinsurance for UN, Geneva, 1986-87; negotiator U.S.-Israeli Free Trade Agreement, 1986-87. Leader trade delegation People to People for Russia and People's Republic of China, 1985; chmn., bd. dirs. Tex. Arts Alliance, Austin, 1984, chmn. and pres. Tex. Opera Theater, Houston, 1980-82; mem. exec. com. Houston Grand Opera, 1985—; pres. Tex. Lyceum, The Woodlands, 1987; chmn. Baylor U. Honors Council, 1969; bd. dirs. Paul Quinn Coll., 1987; bd. trustees Scottish Rite Hosp. for Children, Dallas. Recipient Disting. Alumni award Baylor U., 1985, 98, Distinguished Pub. Servant award Tex. Med. Assn., 1986, Gates of Jerusalem award State of Israel, 1986; named Outstanding Pub. Ofcl. Tex. Mcpl. League, 1986, Disting. Grad. Waco Pub. Schs., 1998. Mem. Nat. Assn. Ins. Commrs. (pres. 1983),Baylor Alumni Assn. (pres. 1996), Am. Hosp. Paul Hereford Assn., Scottish Rite, Masons. Lodges: Masons. Democrat. Presbyterian. Office: Am Embassy Stockholm Dept State Washington DC 20521-0001

**OLSON, LYNN,** sculptor, painter, writer; b. Chgo., Mar. 23, 1952; s. Ellen (Nelson) Olson. Instr. direct cement sculpture workshops Montoya Art Studios, West Palm Beach, Fla., 1988—89, Alta. Sculptors Assn., Edmonton, Canada, 1990, Mendocino Art Ctr., Calif., 1992—93, Sierra Nev. Coll. Lake Tahoe, Incline Village, 1993, Lighthouse Art Ctr., Crescent City, Calif., 1990—96, Elisabet Ney Sculpture Conservatory, Austin, 1995, Tarrant County Jr. Coll., Ft. Worth, 1995, Art Students League Denver, 2000, Indpls. Art Ctr., 2002. Artist-in-residence St. Joseph Coll., 2000. Prin. works include Good Shepherd, Chy. Good Shepherd, Albion, Ind., Kneeling Figure, Manta Ray. World Concrete, Addison, Ill., Rose, Carter Meml., Chesterton, Ind., Redwood Tree, Lighthouse Art Ctr., Crescent City, Calif., George Bartholomew Meml., Bellefontaine, Ohio, Color Concerto, Purdue U., Hammond, Ind., Continuity III, Tower East, Shaker Heights, Ohio, Aluma Beam, Aluma Corp., Toronto, Amobius, St. Joseph Coll., Rensselaer, Ind., Flying Fish, Lake Sara, Effingham, Ill., Kim (stone sculpture), Irene Newhard portrait sculpture (cement), one-man shows include U. Ill., Chgo., 2001, 2006, No. Ind. Arts Assn., 1999, Munster, CCT Gallery, Evanston Hall, Northwestern U. Settlement, Chgo., 2000—, 18 Artists Gallery, Chesterton, Ind., Block Fine Arts, Inc., New Buffalo, Mich., Marion Coll., Indpls., 2003, Ill. Ctrl. Coll., East Peoria, 2003, U. Ill., Chgo., 2006, 2006, exhibited in group shows at Danada Sculpture Show, Cantigny Park, Wheaton, Ill., 1999—2001, Prairie Arts Coun., Rensselaer, Ind., 2000, Ind. U. N.W., 2001, Effingham's 3d Ann. Sculpture on Ave. Exhbn., Ill., 2001, McHenry CC, Crystal Lake, Ill., 2002, 4th Ann. Sculpture on Aves. Exhibit, Effingham, 2002, 5th Ann., 2003, 6th Ann., 2004, 7th Ann., 2005, 8th Ann., 2006, 15th Ann. Outdoor Sculpture Exhibit, Lawrence, Kans., 2002, Art Pub. Places, Cedar Rapids, Iowa, 2002, 2003, 2004, Torso, Delta State U., Cleveland, Miss., 2002, 5th Ann. Sculpture in Pk., White River State Pk., Indpls., 2003, Barrington (Ill.) Area Libr. Sculpture Garden, 2003, Tall Grass Arts Assn., Park Forest, Ill., 2004, Davlan Park, Mass. Ave. Urban Art Gallery, Indpls., 2004, U. Ill., Indpls., 2005—06, exhibitions include Effingham Cmty Com. Arts, Ill., 2005—06; author, pub.: Sculpting with Cement, 1981—2004; contbr. articles to profl. jours. Mem.: Am. Concrete Inst. (mem. com. 124 concrete aesthetics). Home and Office: Steelstone 4607 Claussen Ln Valparaiso IN 46383-1526 Office Phone: 219-464-1792.

**OLSON, LYNN,** editor; m. Steve Olson; 2 children. Grad., Yale U. Sr. editor Edn. Week, 1990—. Author: The School to Work Revolution: How Employers and Educators Are Joining Forces to Prepare Tomorrow's Skilled Workforce, 1997. Recipient award, Edn. Writers Assn., Nat. Assn. Secondary Sch. Prins., Internat. Reading Assn.; grantee, Alfred P. Sloan Found., N.Y., 1995. Mem.: Carnegie Found. for Advancement Tchg. (bd. mem.). Office: Editl Projects in Edn Inc Ste 100 6935 Arlington Rd Bethesda MD 20814-5233*

**OLSON, MARGARET,** music educator; d. Michael Sanders and Marilyn Shull Olson. MusB, U. N.C., 1993; MusM, U. Md., 1996; DMA, U. Iowa, 2001. Cert. instr. Kindermusik, 2002. Instr. voice Iowa Weslyan Coll., Mt. Pleasant, Iowa, 1998—99; tchng. asst. U. Iowa, Iowa City, 1999—2001; asst. prof. voice U. Tenn., Martin, Tenn., 2001—04; instr. voice Georgetown U., Washington, 2004—. Instr. in field. Contbr. articles to profl. jours. Grantee, Tenn. Arts Commn., 2002, 2003. Mem.: Nat. Assn. Singing, Coll. Music Soc.

**OLSON, MARIAN KATHERINE,** management consultant; b. Tulsa, Okla., Oct. 15, 1933; d. Sherwood Joseph and Katherine M. (Miller) Lahman; m. Ronald Keith Olson, Oct. 27, 1956 (dec. May 1991). BA in Polit. Sci., U. Colo., 1954, MA in Elem. Edn., 1962; EdD in Ednl. Adminstrn., U. Tulsa, 1969. Tchr. pub. schs., Wyo., Colo., Mont., 1956-67; tchg. fellow, adj. instr. edn. U. Tulsa, 1968-69; asst. prof. edn. Eastern Mont. State Coll., 1970; program assoc. rsch. adminstrn. Mont. State U., 1970-75; on leave with Energy Policy Office of White House then with Fed. Energy Adminstrn., 1973-74; with Dept. Energy and predecessor, 1975—, program analyst, 1975-79, chief planning and environ. compliance br., 1979-83; regional dir. Region VIII Fed. Emergency Mgmt. Agy., 1987-93; exec. dir. Search and Rescue Dogs of the U.S., 1993—. Pres. Marian Olson Assocs., Bannack Pub. Co Contbr. articles in field. Bd. dirs. Disaster Preparedness and Emergency Response Assn. Internat.; incorporator Jeffco Citizens League. Grantee Okla. Consortium Higher Edn., 1969, NIMH, 1974. Mem. Internat. Assn. Emergency Mgrs., Am. Soc. for Info. Sci., Am. Assn. Budget and Program Analysis, Assn. of Contingency Planners, Nat. Inst. Urban Search and Rescue (bd. dirs.), Nat. Assn. for Search and Rescue, Colo. Search and Rescue, Search and Rescue Dogs of U.S., Colo. Emergency Mgmt. Assn., Front Range Rescue Dogs, Kappa Delta Pi, Phi Alpha Theta, Kappa Alpha Theta. Republican. Home: 203 Iowa Dr Golden CO 80403-1337 Office: Marian Olson Assocs 203 Iowa Dr Ste B Golden CO 80403-1337 Personal E-mail: mlolson@ix.netcom.com.

**OLSON, MARK WALTER,** not-for-profit organization administrator, former bank executive; b. Fergus Falls, Minn., Mar. 17, 1943; s. Walter Roland and Agnes Marie (Peterson) Olson; m. Renee Irene Korda, July 5, 1980; children: Benjamin, Stephanie. BA in economics, St. Olaf Coll., 1965. Joined First Bank Sys., St. Paul, 1966, named officer, 1969; legis. asst. banking issues Congressman Bill Frenzel, Washington, 1971—72, dir. Minn. dist. office, 1974—76; with Andrews Allen Co., St. Paul, 1972—74; pres., CEO Security State Bank, Fergus Falls, Minn., 1976—88; ptnr. Ernst & Young LLP (formerly Arthur Young & Co.), 1988—99, nat. dir. regulatory consulting practice; staff dir. Securities Subcom., Banking, Housing and Urban Affairs com. US Senate, 2000—01; mem. bd. govs. Fed. Res. Sys., 2001—06, adminstrv. gov., 2002—06; chmn. Pub. Co. Acctg. Oversight Bd., 2006—. Bd. dirs. Pioneer Home, Fergus Falls 1977—86, Lake Region Hosp., Fergus Falls, 1978—88, Fergus Falls Area YMCA, 1977—83. Named a Disting. Alumni, St. Olaf Coll., 2003. Mem.: Am. Bankers Assn. (chmn. govt. rels. coun., bd. dirs 1982—84, pres. 1986—87), C. of C. (bd. dirs. 1980—84). Republican. Office: Pub Co Acctg Oversight Bd 1666 K St NW Washington DC 20006 Office Phone: 202-207-9100.

**OLSON, MYRNA RAYE,** education educator; b. Lakota, N.D., Mar. 11, 1947; d. Merlin W. and Ruby A. (Tufte) Munson; children: Nathan, Austin. BS in edn., No. Mont. Coll., 1969; MEd, Mont. State U., 1971; EdD, U. N.D., 1975. Prof. of higher edn., dir. of teaching and learning doctoral program, U. N.D.; tchr. Mont. Sch. for the Deaf and Blind, Gt. Falls, Mont., N.D. Sch. for the Blind, Grand Forks, ND. Spkr. in field of higher edn. Author: Collaboration Handbook for Educators, 1995, Women's Journeys Through Crisis, 1988, others. Named Chester Fritz Disting. Prof., U. N.D., 2003; recipient Humanitarian award, N.D. Coun. for Exceptional Children, 1999. Home: 3602 Chestnut St Grand Forks ND 58201-7654 Business E-Mail: myrna_olson@und.nodak.edu.

**OLSON, NORMAN FREDRICK,** food science educator; b. Edmund, Wis., Feb. 8, 1931; s. Irving M. and Elva B. (Rhinerson) O.; m. Darlene Mary Thorson, Dec. 28, 1957; children: Kristin A., Eric R. BS, U. Wis., 1953, MS, 1957, PhD, 1959. Asst. prof. U. Wis.-Madison, 1959-63, assoc. prof., 1963-69, prof., 1969-93, dir. Walter V. Price Cheese Research Inst., 1976-93; dir. Ctr. Dairy Research, 1986-93; disting. prof. U. Wis.-Madison, 1993-97, prof. emeritus, 1997—. Cons. to cheese industry, 1997—. Author: Semi-soft Cheeses; inventor enzyme microencapsulation; sr. editor Jour. Dairy Sci., 1996-2000. Lt. U.S. Army, 1953-55. Recipient Laureate award Nat. Cheese Inst., 1998, Disting. Svc. award Coll. Agrl. Life. Sci., U. Wis., 2002; named Highly Cited Rschr. ISI, 2002. Fellow Inst. Food Technologists (Macy award 1986), Am. Dairy Sci. Assn. (v.p. 1984-85, pres. 1985-86, Pfizer award 1971, Dairy Rsch. Inc. award 1978, Borden Found. award 1988, Hon. award 1997); mem. Inst. Food Technologists. Democrat. Lutheran. Avocation: cross country skiing. Home: 114 Green Lake Pass Madison WI 53705-4755 Office: U Wis Dept Food Sci Babcock Hall Madison WI 53706 Business E-Mail: nfolson@wisc.edu.

**OLSON, PAMELA FAITH,** lawyer, former federal agency administrator; b. Fargo, ND, July 6, 1954; d. Norman Clifford and Inga (Larson) O.; m. Grant Douglas Aldonas, Apr. 12, 1980; children: Nicole Helen, Kirsten Inga, Noah Grant. BA magna cum laude, U. Minn., 1976, JD, 1980, MBA, 1984. Bar: DC 1981. Instr. U. Minn., Coll. Bus. Adminstrn., Mpls., 1979; atty., Office of Chief Counsel, IRS US Dept. Treasury, Washington, 1981—86; assoc. Skadden, Arps, Slate, Meagher & Flom, LLP, Washington, 1986-90, ptnr., 1990—2001, 2004—; dep. asst. sec. for tax policy US Dept. Treasury, Washington, 2001—02, asst. sec. for tax policy, 2002—04. Bd. dirs. Tax Analysts, 2004-, So. Fed. Tax Inst., 2005-. Coun. mem. Resurrection Luth. Ch., Va., 2002-05; trustee Millenium Inst., 1993-99. Fellow Am. Bar Found., Am. Coll. Tax Counsel; mem. ABA (vice chmn. employment taxes com. 1988-90, chair employment tax com. 1990-92, com. on govt. rels. 1992—, com. on coms. 1992—, com. on women and minorities 1993—, com. on membership and mktg. 1993—, coun. dir. sect. on taxation 1993-95, vice chair sect. taxation 1995-98, chair-elect sect. on taxation 1999-00, chair sect. on taxation 2000-01), bd. dirs. retirement funds 2004-), Equipment Leasing Assn., DC Bar Assn. (chmn. legis. and regulations com.), U. Minn. Law Sch. Alumi Assn. (bd. dirs. 1992-97), Phi Beta Kappa. Avocations: children, volunteering, cooking, softball, skiing. Office: Skadden Arps Slate Meagher & Flom LLP 1440 New York Ave NW Ste 600 Washington DC 20005-6000

**OLSON, PETER,** publishing executive; b. Chgo., May 1, 1950; m. Candice Carpenter, Sept. 8, 2001. AB in History magna cum laude (hon.), Harvard Coll., 1972; JD cum laude, Harvard Law Sch.; MBA, Harvard Bus. Sch. Assoc. Baker & Botts, Wash., DC, 1976—77, Hamada & Matsumoto, Tokyo, 1977—79; officer, internat. group Dresdner Bank, Frankfurt, 1979—81, deputy mgr., corp. bus. dept. Tokyo, 1981—84, mgr., credit dept., 1984—87, v.p. planning dept., treasury div. Frankfurt, Germany, 1987—88; mgr. Bertelsmann AG, 1988, sr. v.p., Doubleday Book and Music Clubs Garden City, NY, 1989—90, pres., Bertelsmann, Inc., 1990—92, exec. v.p., CFO, Bantam Doubleday Dell Pub. Group, 1992—94; exec. v.p., chief admin. officer, Bantam Doubleday Dell Pub. Group, 1990—94; chmn, CEO Bertelsmann book group N. Am. Bertelsmann AG, 1994—98, mem. exec. bd., Bertelsmann Book AG, 1994—98, chmn., CEO, Random House Inc. N.Y.C., 1998—, exec. bd. mem., trade book pub. worldwide, 2001—. Exec. com. The Quills. Mem.: Phi Beta Kappa. Office: Random House Inc 1540 Broadway New York NY 10036-4039

**OLSON, PHILLIP ROGER,** naval officer; b. Elmhurst, Ill., June 23, 1939; s. Willard Clarence and Carol (Schulz) O.; m. Marsha Andrea Lippert, July 10, 1966; children: Christine Carole, Phillip Roger Jr. B in Naval Sci., U.S. Naval Acad., 1962; M in Physics, Naval Postgrad. Sch., 1968. Commd. ens. USN, 1962, advanced through grades to rear adm., 1987, instr. ship material readiness group Idaho Falls, 1978-81, commdg. officer USS Pharris (FF 1094) Norfolk, Va., 1981-83, commdg. officer USS Mississippi (CGN 40), 1983-86, sr. instr. ship material readiness group Newport, R.I., 1986-87; dep. dir. ops. Joint Staff, Washington, 1987-88; dep. dir. strategy & policy Joint Staff USN, Washington, 1988-89, comdr. logistics group two Norfolk,

1989-90, comdr. cruiser-destroyer group one San Diego, 1990-92, pres. bd. inspection & survey Norfolk, 1992-96; retired, 1996. Cons. on navy logistics support and operational engring.; exec. v.p. The Sigmon Group. Decorated Disting. Svc. medal. Mem. Surface Navy Assn. Lutheran. Avocations: golf, tennis.

**OLSON, RAY ALAN,** librarian; b. Yankton, SD, Mar. 26, 1946; s. Oliver Bernard Olson and Mabel Highland; m. Carol Ann Nygaard; children: Eric Robert, Peter Alan. BA in History and Philosophy, Augustana Coll., 1968; MDiv, Luther Theol. Sem., St. Paul, 1972; MA in Libr. Sci., U. Minn., 1974; ThM, Luther Northwestern Sem., St. Paul, 1985. Reference and pub. svcs. supr. Luther Theol. Sem., St. Paul, 1972-74; reference libr. Luther Northwestern Sem., St. Paul, 1974-89; acting libr. Luther Sem., St. Paul, 1975-76, 81-82, 88-89, pub. svcs. libr., 1989-96, interim libr., 1996; dir. Hamma Libr. Trinity Luth. Sem., Columbus, Ohio, 1996—. Co-editor: (with others) Landings Across the Ocean, 1997. Publicity chair Luth. Brotherhood Br. Bd., St. Paul, 1994-96. Mem.: Totenlag, Valdres Samband, Landings Laget (editor newsletter 1984—94, chair publs. com. 1994—2001), Am. Theol. Libr. Assn., Vesterheim Norwegian Am. Mus. (life), Ohio Theol. Libr. Assn. (life; pres. 1999—2001), Scandinavian Club Columbus. Avocations: reading, walking, genealogy, local history. Office: Hamma Libr Trinity Luth Sem 2199 E Main St Columbus OH 43209-2334 Office Phone: 614-384-4640.

**OLSON, RICHARD DAVID,** psychology professor; b. Reading, Pa., Oct. 10, 1941; s. Milton Stuart and Sarah Ellen (Moyer) O.; m. M. Gayle Augustine, Aug. 26, 1967. BA, U. Redlands, 1966; MS, St. Louis U., 1968, PhD, 1970. Lic. psychologist, La. Asst. prof. psychology U. New Orleans, 1970-74, assoc. prof., chmn. dept. psychology, 1974-79, prof., chmn. dept., 1979-81, assoc. dean Grad. Sch., 1981-82, dean, 1982-88, vice chancellor, 1984-88, rsch. prof., 1988—2000, prof. emeritus, 2000—; chmn. dept. psychology, 1995—2000. Cons. psychologist, New Orleans, 1973—2002; pres. Statis. Cons. of New Orleans, 1977-82 Editor: Learning in the Classroom, 1971, The Comma After Love, The Selected Poems of Raeburn Miller, 1994, The Collected Poems of Raeburn Miller, 1997; contbr. articles to profl. jours. Grantee HEW, 1976-81 Fellow APA, Am. Psychol. Soc.; mem. Soc. for Neuroscis., Am. Statis. Assn. Home: 40 Infinity Dr Poplarville MS 39470 Office: U New Orleans Dept Psychology Lake Front New Orleans LA 70148 Office Phone: 601-795-4838. E-mail: rolsonredoak@bellsouth.net.

**OLSON, RICHARD EARL,** lawyer, state legislator; b. Elmhurst, Ill., Apr. 24, 1953; s. Earl Leroy and Helen Ellen (Wanamaker) O.; m. Patricia Michelle McKinney, May 16, 1976; children: Shelley, Rachel, Eric. BA, U. Miss., Oxford, 1975; JD, So. Meth. U., 1978. Bar: N.Mex. 1978. Ptnr. Hinkle, Shanor, Hensley & Martin, Roswell, N.Mex., 1978—; mem. N.Mex. Ho. of Reps., 1989-95, mem. various coms. Bd. trustees Eastern N.Mex. Med. Ctr., 1995-98. Mem. Roswell City Coun., 1986—88, chmn. streets and alleys com., mem. various other coms.; past chmn. pastor parish rels. com. 1st United Meth. Ch., Roswell; bd. dirs. Assurance Home, 1990—98; pres. Assurance Home Found., 2000—; former bd. dirs. N.Mex. 1st; bd. dirs. N.Mex. Conf. Meth. Found., 2001—. Mem.: Def. Rsch. Inst., Order of Coif, Phi Kappa Phi. Republican. Home: 5003 Thunderbird Ln Roswell NM 88203-9386 Office: Hinkle Cox Eaton Coffield & Hensley PO Box 10 Roswell NM 88202-0010 Office Phone: 505-622-6510. Business E-Mail: rolson@hinklelawfirm.com.

**OLSON, ROBERT EDWARD,** coal mining executive; b. Phila., Aug. 5, 1927; s. Oscar E. and Marie B. (Kilgallon) O.; m. Jean Emilie Wadsworth, Dec. 31, 1955 (dec. Aug. 1997); children: Grace Olson, Nancy Olson Ashcraft, Karen Olson Culbertson. Student, U. Richmond, 1945, Duke U., 1945-46, U. Pa., 1946; BS in Mining Engring., Pa. State U., 1952. Registered profl. engr., Pa., W.Va. Indsl. engr. Island Creek Coal Co., Holden, W.Va., 1952-55; dir., treas., sr. assoc. Coal Standards, Inc., mgmt. cons., Charleston, W.Va., 1955-61; v.p. adminstrn. Rochester & Pitts. Coal Co., Indiana, Pa., 1961-81; pres., COO Valley Camp Coal Co., Oil City, Pa., 1981-86, vice chmn., dir., mem. exec. com. 1986-88, ret., 1988. Past pres., chmn., dir. Kanawha and Hocking Coal & Coke Co., Kelley's Creek and Northwestern R.R. Co., Valley Camp Coal Sales Co.; pres., chief exec. officer Gt. Lakes Coal & Dock Co.; chmn., dir. Donaldson Mine Co., Elm Grove Coal Co., Shrewsbury Coal Co., Helen Mining Co., Valley Camp of Utah Inc.; chmn., CEO Pa. and W.Va. Supply Co. Bd. dirs. United Way of Venango County, 1983-88; pres. bd. trustees Venango County Cmty. Area Found., 1988-94, former dir.; mem. Ind. County C. of C., 1973-81, pres., 1976-77; mem. vestry Christ Episc. Ch., Oil City, 1989-92, 98; charter mem. Haverford (Pa.) State Hosp. Task Force, 1999-2002; mem. Haverford Twp. Environ. Adv. Com., 2002-05. With USN, 1945-47. Mem. Am. Ind. Rotary (club pres. 1979-80), Merion Cricket Club, Theta Delta Chi, Sigma Phi Sigma.

**OLSON, ROBERT EUGENE,** physician, biochemist, educator; b. Minn., Jan. 23, 1919; s. Ralph William and Minnie (Holtin) O.; m. Catherine Silvoso, Oct. 21, 1944; children: Barbara Lynn, Robert E., Mark Alan, Mary Ellen, Carol Louise. AB, Gustavus Adolphus Coll., 1938; PhD, St. Louis U., 1944; MD, Harvard, 1951; MD (hon.), Chiang Mai U., Thailand, 1983. Diplomate: Nat. Bd. Med. Examiners, Am. Bd. Nutrition (pres. 1962-63). Postgrad. research asst. biochemistry St. Louis U. Sch. Medicine, 1938-43, asst. biochemistry, 1943-44, Alice A. Doisy prof. biochemistry, chmn. dept. biochemistry, 1965-82, disting. prof. medicine, 1966-72, prof. medicine, 1972-82; vis. prof. (sabbatical) dept. biochemistry U. Freiburg, Breisgau, West Germany, 1970-71; also Hoffman-La Roche Co., Basel, Switzerland, 1970-71; instr. biochemistry and nutrition Harvard Sch. Pub. Health, 1946-47; research fellow Nutrition Found., 1947-49, Am. Heart Assn., 1949-51, established investigator, 1951-52; house officer Peter Bent Brigham Hosp., Boston, 1951-52; prof., head dept. biochemistry and nutrition Grad. Sch. Pub. Health U. Pitts.; lectr. medicine Sch. Medicine, 1952-65; mem. panel malnutrition Japan-U.S. Med. Scis. Program, 1965-69; dir. Nutrition Clinic, Falk Clinic, 1953-65; mem. sr. staff Presbyn. Hosp.; dir. metabolic unit, 1960-65; mem. staff St. Louis U. Hosp., 1965-81; prof. biochemistry, prof. medicine, assoc. dean acad. affairs U. Pitts. Sch. Medicine, 1982-84; prof. medicine, prof. pharm. scis. SUNY-Stony Brook, 1984-90, prof. emeritus, 1990—; prof. pediatrics U. South Fla., Tampa, 1994—. Cons. Mercy Hosp. U. Pitts. Med. Center; assoc. in medicine St. Margaret's Meml. Hosp., Pitts., dir. metabolic unit, 1954-60; cons. divsn. rsch. grants USPHS, 1954-69, 72-76; dir. Anemia and Malnutrition Center, Chiang Mai, Thailand, 1967-77; vis. scholar dept. biochemistry Oxford (Eng.) U., 1961-62; vis. prof. dept. biochemistry U. Freiburg, West Germany, 1970-71; food and nutrition bd. NRC, 1977-83; adv. council Nat. Inst. Arthritis, Diabetes, Digestive and Kidney Diseases, 1981-85; William A. Noyes lectr. U. Ill., Urbana, 1980. Author: Perspectives in Biological Chemistry, 1970, Methods in Medical Research, 1970, Protein-Calorie Malnutrition, 1975, Balanced Nutrition, 1989; assoc. editor Nutrition Revs., 1954-56, editor, 1978-88; assoc. editor Am. Jour. Medicine, 1956, Circulation Rsch. 1956-76, Am. Heart Jour., 1958-65, Am. Jour. Clin. Nutrition, 1960-66, Methods in Med. Rsch., 1963-70, Biochem. Medicine, 1967-90, Molecular and Cellular Cardiology, 1967-78, Ann. Rev. Nutrition, 1979-84, editor, 1984-94; co-editor: Vitamins and Hormones, 1975-81; author 236 original sci. papers in peer-reviewed jours.; contbr. 114 chpts. in books and major reviews to profl. jours. Bd. dirs. Nat. Nutrition Consortium, 1977-81, Am. Council on Sci. and Health, 1984-91. Lt. (j.g.) USNR, 1944-46. Recipient Fulbright award, 1961-62, Guggenheim Found. award, 1961-62, 70-71, McCollum award, 1965, Joseph Goldberger award, 1974; named Atwater Meml. lectr., 1978; Geiger Meml. lectr., 1979, William A. Noyes lectr. U. Ill., 1980, H. Brooks James lectr. N.C. State U., 1981, Virginia Beal lectr. U. Mass., 1990. Fellow ACP, Internat. Acad. Cardiovasc. Scis., Am. Pub. Health Assn. (chmn. food and nutrition sect. 1960-61), Am. Inst. Nutrition (pres. 1982, Conrad Elvehjem award 1983), Royal Soc. Health (London), N.Y. Acad. Scis., Am. Fedn. Clin. Research, Am. Soc. Clin. Investigation, Boyleston Med. Soc., Am. Chem. Soc. (pres. biochemistry group Pitts. sect. 1960-61), Am. Soc. Biol. Chemists, Soc. Exptl. Biology and Medicine, Am.

Soc. Clin. Nutrition (pres. 1961-62, McCollum award 1965, Herman award 2002), Assn. Med. Sch. Depts. Biochemistry (pres. 1979-80), Pa., St. Louis, Allegheny County med. socs., Am. Soc. Study Liver Diseases, Phi Beta Kappa, Sigma Xi, Phi Lambda Upsilon, Alpha Omega Alpha, Alpha Sigma Nu. Clubs: Cosmos (Washington), Countryside Country Club (Clearwater, Fla.). Home: 2673 Camille Dr Palm Harbor FL 34684-2217 Office: U South Fla Dept Pediatrics 17 Davis Blvd Ste 200 Tampa FL 33606-3438 Office Phone: 813-259-8700. Personal E-mail: roberteolsonr@cs.com. Business E-Mail: rolson@hsc.usf.edu.

**OLSON, ROBERT GRANT,** lawyer; b. Ft. Dodge, Iowa, Mar. 29, 1952; s. Grant L. and R. June (Pohlmann) Olson; m. Cynthia Lynn Murray, Sept. 7, 1978; children: Brendon, Elisabeth, Jeffrey, Daniel. BS, Iowa State U., 1973; JD, U. Iowa, 1976. Bar: Mo. 1976, Ill. 1977. Ptnr. Thompson & Mitchell, St. Louis, 1976-92, Riezman & Blitz, P.C., St. Louis, 1992-2000, Stone, Leyton & Gershman, P.C., St. Louis, 2000—. Editor: Jour. Corp. Law, 1975—76. Vol. Habitat for Humanity, Gephardt for Pres. Campaign, 1988, Carnahan for Lt. Gov. Campaign, 1988, Carnahan for Gov. Campaign, 1992; arbitrator Better Bus. Bur., Taxpayer Assistance Program. Mem.: ABA, Met. St. Louis Bar Assn., Ill. Bar Assn., Mo. Bar Assn., Downtown St. Louis Lions Club (pres. 1990—91). Home: 424 E Jackson Rd Saint Louis MO 63119-4128 Office: Stone Leyton & Gershman 7733 Forsyth Blvd Ste 500 Saint Louis MO 63105-1817 Office Phone: 314-721-7011.

**OLSON, ROBERT HOWARD,** lawyer; b. July 6, 1944; s. Robert Howard and Jacquiline (Wells) O.; m. Diane Carol Thorsen, Aug. 13, 1966; children: Jeffrey, Christopher. BA in Govt. summa cum laude, Ind. U., 1966; JD cum laude, Harvard U., 1969. Bar: Ohio 1969, Fla. 1980, Ariz. 1985, Calif. 2001, U.S. Supreme Ct. 1973. Assoc. Squire, Sanders & Dempsey, L.L.P., Cleve., 1969, 70-71, 76-81, ptnr., 1981—, Phoenix, 1985—2002, Squire, Sanders & Dempsey, San Francisco, 2002—; sr. law clk. U.S. Dist. Ct., No. Dist., Ind., 1969-70; chief civil rights divsn. Ohio Atty. Gen.'s Office, Columbus, 1971-73, chief consumer protection, 1973-75, chief counsel, 1975, 1st asst. (chief of staff), 1975-76. Instr. Ohio State U. Law Sch., Columbus, 1974; Cen. Phoenix com. to advise city council and mayor City of Phoenix, 1987—89; bd. dirs. Orpheum Theater Found., 1989—2002, sec., 1989—90, pres., 1990—97, exec. com., 1997—99, The Ariz. Ctr. for Law in the Pub. Interest, 1989—2001, treas., 1992—93, 1997—2001, v.p., 1993—94; mem. Ariz. Ctr. for Disability Law, 1994—96, treas., 1994—95; mem. Valley Leadership Class XIV; rsch. com. Ariz. Town Hall, 1998—2002; mem. fin. com. Pub. Advs., Inc.; co-chair Calif. Pub. Fin. Conf., 2006. Contbr. articles to proff. jours. Bd. dirs. 1st Unitarian Ch. Phoenix, 1987-89, 98-2001, v.p., 1987-89, 2000-2001, pres. 1998-99; bd. dirs. 1st Unitarian Ch. Found., 1987-93, pres., 1990-93; exec. com. San Francisco (Calif.) Heartwalk, Am. Heart Assn., 2005. Named Arts Advocate of Yr. Bus. Vols. Arts/Phoenix, 1997. Mem. Ariz. State Bar Assn., Calif. Bar Assn., Phi Beta Kappa. Office: Squire Sanders & Dempsey LLP One Maritime Plaza Suite 300 San Francisco CA 94111-3492

**OLSON, ROBERT MARTIN,** plastic surgeon; b. Abington, Pa., Dec. 15, 1949; s. Carl Martin Olson and Jacqueline Mary O'Neill; m. Megan Evans Thomas, Dec. 30, 1982; children: Robert, Gwyneth, Nevin, Sonja. MD, U. Pa., 1974; ThM, New Brunswick Theol. Sem., 2004. Plastic surgeon Plastic Surgery Arts, New Brunswick, NJ, 1983—; clin. assoc., prof. surgery Robert Wood Johnson, New Brunswick, 1983—. Lt. col. USAR, 1988—96. Recipient Humanitarian award, Friends Health Connection, 2002, Middlesex County Music Soc., 2003, Svc. award, USAR, 1991. Episc. Office: 78 Easton Ave New Brunswick NJ 08901 Office Phone: 732-418-0700. Business E-Mail: rolson@psanj.com.

**OLSON, ROBERT WILLIAM,** writer, retired counselor; b. Chgo., Feb. 5, 1930; s. Milton Olaf Olson and Leonore Stillman; m. Seiko Itoyama, Jan. 16, 1955. BA, George Williams Coll., 1952; MA, U. Chgo., 1959; 7th yr. cert. counselor-cons., Oreg. State U., 1967. Tchr. 6th grade Matteson Elem. Sch., Ill., 1956—59; cons., sch. counselor elem. schs., jr. and sr. h.s., various cities Ill., Wash., 1959—91; instr. counseling U. Wash., Seattle, 1979—81; family counselor Seattle, 1980—91. Behavioral rschr., U. Wash., 1979-81. Author: Memories with a Christmas Attitude, 1994, Rich Memories with a Christmas Spirit, 2005; editor FOKUS Newsletter, 1998—; contbr. numerous articles to proff. counseling jours. Vol. Love and Forgiveness Seminar, Monroe Penitentiary, 1996—; bd. mem. Children Around the World Resource Ctr.; pres., King County (Wash.) Guidance Assn., 1978-79. With U.S. Army, 1952-56, Korea. Mem. NEA (life), Wash. Edn. Assn., Internat. Assn. Near-Death Studies, Full Gospel Businessmen Internat. (vol. King County Jail 1998—), Eastside Writers Assn. (hospitality chmn. 1999—), Northwest Christian Writers Assn. Avocations: ceramics, storytelling, swimming. Home and Office: 252 168th Ave SE Bellevue WA 98008 Office Phone: 425-747-3879. E-mail: membob@aol.com.

**OLSON, ROBERT WYRICK,** lawyer; b. Madison, Wis., Dec. 19, 1945; s. John Arthur and Mary Katherine (Wyrick) O.; m. Carol Jean Duane, June 12, 1971; children: John Hagan, Mary Catherine Duane. BA, Williams Coll., 1967; JD, U. Va., 1970. Assoc. Cravath, Swaine & Moore, N.Y.C., 1970-79; asst. gen. counsel Penn Cen. Corp., Cin., 1979-80, assoc. gen. counsel, 1980-82, v.p., dep. gen. counsel, 1982-87; sr. v.p., gen. counsel, sec. Am. Premier Underwriters, Inc. (formerly Penn Cen. Corp.), Cin., 1987-95; sr. v.p., gen. counsel and sec. Chiquita Brands Internat., Inc., Cin., 1995—. Mem. ABA. Office: Chiquita Brands Internat 250 E 5th St Ste 29 Cincinnati OH 45202-4119 E-mail: bolson@chiquita.com.

**OLSON, RONALD LEROY,** lawyer; b. Carroll, Iowa, July 9, 1941; s. Clyde L. and Delpha C. (Boyens) Olson; m. Jane Tenhulzen, June 21, 1964; children: Kristin, Steven, Amy. BS, Drake U., 1963; JD, U. Mich., 1966; Diploma Law, Oxford U., Eng., 1967. Bar: Wis. 1966, Calif. 1969. US Dist. Ct. (cen. dist.)/Calif. 1969, US Dist. Ct. (so. dist.)/Calif. 1971, US Ct. Appeals (9th cir.) 1974, US Ct. Appeals (10th cir.) 1980, US Ct. Appeals (5th cir.) 1982, US Supreme Ct. 1976, US Dist. Ct./Alaska 1983. Atty. civil rights divsn. US Dept. Justice, 1967; law clk. to chief judge David L. Bazelon US Ct. Appeals (DC cir.), Washington, 1967—68; ptnr. Munger, Tolles & Olson LLP, Los Angeles, Calif., 1968—; lawyer del. Am. 9th Cir. Conf., 1984—89; lectr. in field; mem. editorial bd. Alternatives, 1983—. Mem. bd. dirs. The Wash. Post Co., 2003—. Contbr. articles legal jour. Recipient Burton scholar, U. Mich.; fellow Am. Coll Trial Lawyers. Mem.: 9th Cir. Jud. Conf. (exec. com. 1984—89), Chancery, LA County Barristers (pres. 1976), Assn. Bus. Trial Lawyers (mem. adv. com. trial ct. improvement fund for Calif. jud. coun. 1988—), State Bar Calif. (bd. dir. 1985, v.p. 1986—87), LA County Bar Assn., Am. Arbitration Assn. (bd. dir. 1983, commil. panel 1983), LA Bar Found. (bd. dir. 1977), Am. Judicature Soc., Human Rights (editorial bd., publ. sect. ind. rights and responsibilities 1986—), Soviet Exchange Program (litig. sect. com. 1983—), ABA (litig. sect. council 1976, chmn. sp. com. on dispute resolution 1976—86, chmn. litig. sect. 1981—82, chmn. standing com. on fed. judiciary 1991—92), Am. Bar Found., Skid Row Housing Trust of LA (mem. 1986—), U. Mich. Law Sch. (com. visitors 1986—), Salzburg Seminar (bd. dir.), Legal Aid Found. LA (bd. dir. 1975—86, pres. 1984—85), Claremont U. Ctr. and Grad. Sch. (chmn. bd. fellows 1984—94), Sequoia Nat. Pk. Natural History Assn., Drake U. (trustee 1977), Ford Found. Oxford U., Alternatives (mem. editorial bd. 1983—88), LA Arts Festival (sec. 1985), Lawyers Alliance for Nuclear Arms Control (adv. com. Los Angeles and Orange Counties chpt.), Frat. of Friends of Music Ctr. (bd. dir., pres. 1978). Democrat. Episc. Office: Munger Tolles & Olson 355 S Grand Ave Fl 35 Los Angeles CA 90071-1560 E-mail: olsonrl@mto.com.

**OLSON, ROY ARTHUR,** retired government official; b. Dec. 8, 1938; s. Elof Herman and Beatrice Lorraine (Dolezal) O.; m. Elisabeth Rigge Behrens, June 24, 1967; children: Heather Elisabeth, Peter Roy. BS, Northwestern U., 1960. Lic. real estate salesman, Ill. Writer, editor Chgo. Am., 1956-68; pres. Roy Olson Pub. Rels. Co., Oak Park, Ill., 1968-70; asst. regional adminstr. SBA, Chgo., 1970-95; Chgo. spokesman Ill. Dept. Transp., 1995—2003. Bd. dirs. Am. Food Industries, Chgo., Covenant Village Retirement Ctr., Northbrook, Ill., Brandel Care Ctr., Northbrook. Home. Northbrook Covenant Ch., 1980-81, 97-2000. Mem. Soc. Proffl. Journalists,

---

Art Inst. Chgo., City Club (media com.), Execs. Club, Chgo. Press Club, Chgo. Headline Club (past dir. 1964-66), Northwestern Club. Home: 2015 Prairie St Glenview IL 60025-2824 E-mail: olsons2015@yahoo.com.

**OLSON, RUE EILEEN,** retired librarian; b. Chgo., Nov. 1, 1928; d. Paul H. and Martha M. (Fick) Meyers; m. Richard L. Olson, July 18, 1964; children: Catherine, Karen. Student, Herzl Coll., 1946-48, Northwestern U., 1948-50, Ill. State U., 1960-64, Middle Mgmt. Inst. Spl. Librs. Assn., 1985-87. Acct. Ill. Farm Supply Co., Chgo., 1948-59; asst. libr. Ill. Agrl. Assn., Bloomington, 1960-66, libr., 1966-86, dir. libr. svcs., 1986-96, ret., 1996. Bd. dirs. Corn Belt Libr. Sys., 1989-94, sec., 1991-94; mem. area com. Nat. Libr. Week, 1971, area steering com., 1972; mem. steering com. Illinet/OCLC, 1985-87; mem. adv. coun. of librs. Grad. Sch. Libr. Sci. U., Ill., 1976-79; mem. Ill. State Libr. Adv. Com. for Interlibr. Cooperation, 1979-80; del. Ill. White Ho. Conf. on Libr. and Info. Svcs., 1978; coord. Vita Income Tax Assistance, Bloomington, Ill., 1986-89, 95-99, preparer, 1978—2002; sec. Hawthorn Village Homeowner's Assn., 1995-2002, v.p., 2002—04; congl. sec. Good Shepherd Luth. Ch., 1990-2001, newsletter editor, 1994-96. Mem. Am., Ill., Bloom Valley (pres. 1970-71), Libr. Assns., Spl. Librs. Assn. (pres. Ill. chpt. 1977-78, first to be named Disting. Mem. food, agr. and nutrition divsn. 1989), Ill. OCLC Users Group (treas. 1988-90, bd. dirs. 1991-92), Internat. Assn. Agrl. Librs. and Documentalists, Am. Soc. Info. Sci., Am. Mgmt. Assn., USIN, Mended Hearts, Inc. (sec. Ill. chpt. 250, 1994-95, v.p. 1995-96, pres. 1996-98), Zonta (pres. 1987-89), Bloomington Club, Am. Heart Assn. (McLean County divsn., midwest affiliate, sec. 1998-2000). Home: 8 Aspen Ct Bloomington IL 61704-2781

**OLSON, SHEILA J.,** elementary school educator; b. Prairie Farm, Wis., Sept. 11, 1949; d. R. Spitzer and Tronrud; m. Olson, Mar. 21, 1970; children: Erin Olsen, Krissa, Dustin. BS, U. Wis. River Falls, 1971, MEd in proffl. devel., 2004. Cert. tchr. K-8. Tchr. Colfax Pub. Schs., Wis., 1971—75, Prairie Farm Pub. Schs., Wis., 1975—. Elem. rep. Conf. on Wis. Stds., Menomorie, Wis., 1999; chair Gifted and Talented Curriculum Com., Prairie Farm, 1992—94; leader Restorative Justice, Prairie Farm, 2002. Pompon adv. Prairie Farm H.S., 1976—86, 1995—99; township treas. Town of Stanford, 1982—92; dir. cherub choir Luth. Ch., Prairie Farm, 1983—88; adv. H.S. group Youth In Christ, Prairie Farm, 1993—2002. Mem.: Praise Band Choir United Luth. Ch., Naomi Ch. Cir. (pres. 1996—2005). Lutheran. Avocations: reading, gardening, crafts, music. Home: N13027 County Rd Vv Wheeler WI 54772 Office Phone: 715-455-1615.

**OLSON, STEPHEN M(ICHAEL),** lawyer; b. Jamestown, NY, May 4, 1948; s. Charles R. and Marilyn (Dietzel) O.; m. Linda C. Hanson, Aug. 24, 1968; children: Kevin, Darren. AB cum laude, Princeton U., 1970; JD, U. Chgo., 1973. Bar: Pa. 1973, U.S. Dist. Ct. (we. dist.) Pa. 1973, U.S. Ct. Appeals (3d cir.) 1975, U.S. Ct. Appeals (1st and D.C. cirs.) 1986, U.S. Ct. Appeals (7th cir. and 8th cir. 1988), U.S. Supreme Ct. 1986. Assoc. Kirkpatrick & Lockhart, Pitts., 1973-81, ptnr., 1981—. Mem.: ABA (rlwy/airline labor law com.), Allegheny County Bar Assn., Pa. Bar Assn., Princeton Alumni Assn. West Pa., Duquesne Club. Avocations: photography, bicycling. Office: Kirkpatrick & Lockhart Nicholson Graham LLC Henry W Oliver Bldg 535 Smithfield St Pittsburgh PA 15222-2312 Office Phone: 412-355-6496. Business E-Mail: solson@klng.com.

**OLSON, STEVEN R.,** lawyer; b. Baraboo, Wis., July 10, 1955; BS, Andrews U., 1978; JD, John Marshall Law Sch., 1982. Bar: Ill. 1982. Ptnr., chmn. Health Care Practice, mem. exec. com. Katten Muchin Zavis Rosenman, Chgo. Mem.: Am. Health Lawyers Assn. Office: Katten Muchin Rosenman LLP 525 W Monroe St Chicago IL 60661 Office Phone: 312-902-5640. Office Fax: 312-577-8954. E-mail: steven.olson@kattenlaw.com.

**OLSON, THEODORE BEVRY,** lawyer, former federal agency administrator; b. Chgo., Sept. 11, 1940; m. Barbara Kay Bracher, May 1996 (dec. Sept. 11, 2001); 2 children. BA, U. Pacific, 1962; LL.B., U. Calif.-Berkeley, 1965. Bar: Calif. 1965, D.C. 1982. Assoc. Gibson, Dunn & Crutcher LLP, Los Angeles, 1965—71, ptnr., 1972—81, 1984—2001, 2004—, co-chair, appellate & constitutional law practice group, 2004—; asst. atty. gen. US Dept. Justice, Washington, 1981—84, solicitor gen., 2001—04. Mem. Calif. Commn. on Uniform State Laws, 1972-74; del. Republican Nat. Conv., 1976, 80. Fellow Am. Acad. of Appellate Lawyers, Am. Coll. Trial Lawyers; mem. ABA, L.A. County Bar Assn. Republican. Office: Gibson Dunn & Crutcher LLP 1050 Connecticut Ave NW Washington DC 20036 E-mail: tolson@gibsondunn.com.

**OLSON, TODD ROWLAND,** anatomist, medical educator, consultant; b. Long Beach, Calif., Sept. 22, 1946; s. Junis Anora Gjertson and Vernon Benjamin Olsom; m. Lynn Airey Kimberly Davis, Sept. 0, 1969 (div. Dec. 0, 1975); m. Sarah Dame Whitten, May 0, 1995 (div. Oct. 0, 2005). AA, Long Beach City Coll., Calif., 1967; BA, U. Calif., Berkeley, 1970, MA, 1974; PhD, U. London, Eng., 1979. Lectr. Calif. State U., Sacramento, 1970—72, U. Coll. London, 1974—79; asst. prof. CCNY, 1979—85, assoc. prof., 1986—89; asst. prof. grad. sch. CUNY, 1980—85, assoc. prof. grad. sch., 1986—89; assoc. prof. Albert Einstein Coll. of Medicine, Bronx, NY, 1989—96, prof., 1997—. Author: (textbook) A.D.A.M. Student Atlas of Anatomy; co-author: Essentials of Clinical Anatomy, (ednl. software) A.D.A.M. Practice Practical - Medical Student Edition (Codie Award, 1997), A.D.A.M. Practice Practical - Undergraduate Edition (Codie Award, 1999). Educator bd. mem. NY State Bd. of Chiropractic, NY, 2001—06; state primary elector Presdl. Candidate Senator Paul Simon, NY, 1988—88; dist. leader Dem. Party, Pelham, NY, 1981—2006, town chairperson, 1985—89. Recipient Outstanding Tchr. of Yr., CUNY Med. Sch., 1989, Outstanding Preclinical Tchr. of Yr., Albert Einstein Coll. of Medicine, 2000, Outstanding Basic Sci. Tchr. of Yr., 1999. Fellow: Zool. Soc. of London; mem.: Associated Med. Schs. of NY (chair of anat. com. 1994—2006), Internat. Assn. of Med. Sci. Educators (treas. 1998—2002), Am. Assn. of Clin. Anatomists (treas. 2003—06), Am. Assn. of Clin. Anatomists (councilor 1994—96), Am. Assn. of Anatomists, Am. Assn. of Phys. Anthropologists, Primate Soc. of Gt. Britain (exec. mem. 1975—78), Sigma Xi, Phi Beta Kappa, Phi Kappa Phi. Democrat. Buddhist. Avocations: golf, travel, Shakespeare. Office: Albert Einstein Coll of Medicine 1300 Morris Park Ave Bronx NY 10461 Office Phone: 718-430-2847. E-mail: olson@aecom.yu.edu.

**OLSON, WALTER GILBERT,** lawyer; b. Stanton, Nebr., Feb. 2, 1924; s. O.E. Olson and Mabel A. Asplin; m. Gloria Helen Bennett, June 26, 1949; children: Clifford Warner, Karen Rae Olson. BS, U. Calif., Berkeley, 1947, JD, 1949. Bar: Calif. 1950, U.S. Dist. Ct. (no. dist.) Calif. 1950, U.S. Tax Ct. 1950, U.S. Ct. Appeals (9th cir.) 1950. Assoc. Orrick, Herrington and Sutcliffe (formerly Orrick, Dahlquist, Herrington and Sutcliffe), San Francisco, 1949-54, ptnr., 1954-88. Bd. dirs. Alltel Corp., Little Rock, 1988-94; mem. Commn. to Revise Calif. Corp. Securities Law, 1967-69, Securities Regulatory Reform Panel, 1978-80; mem. corp. security adv. com. Calif. Commr. of Corps, 1975-88. Editor-in-chief Calif. Law Review, 1948-49. Bd. dirs. Internat. Ho., Berkeley, 1981-86. With U.S. Army, 1943-46, ETO. Fellow Am. Bar Found.; mem. ABA (trust divsn. nat. conf. of lawyers and reps. of Am. Bankers Assn.), Calif. Bar Assn. (chmn. corps com 1975-76, exec. com. bus. law sect. 1977-78), San Francisco Bar Assn., U. Calif. Alumni Assn., Boalt Hall Alumni Assn. (bd. dirs. 1982-90, sec. 1985, v.p. 1987, pres. 1988), Order of Coif, Menlo Country Club (Woodside, Calif.), Pacific-Union Club. Home: 501 Portola Rd #8162 Portola Valley CA 94028-8616

**OLSON, WALTER JUSTUS, JR.,** management consultant; b. Paterson, NJ, July 27, 1941; s. Walter Justus and Viola Patricia (Trautvetter) O. BS, Brown U., 1964; MBA, Columbia U., 1967. CPA Va. Design engr. Rockwell Internat., Inc., Downey, Calif., 1964-65; mgmt. officer CIA, Washington, 1969-73; sr. cons. Booz, Allen and Hamilton, Inc., Washington, 1973-78; corp. planning coordinator Washington Gas Light Co., Washington, 1978-82; prin. Walter J. Olson & Assoc., McLean, Va., 1982-83; dep. asst. sec. for export adminstrn. U.S. Dept. Commerce, Washington, 1983-86; prin. Walter J. Olson & Assoc., Washington, 1986—; sr. rsch. analyst U.S. House Select

---

Com. Technology Transfer to PRC, Washington, 1998-99. Vice-chmn. fin. com. Fairfax County (Va.) Reps., 1982-83. Served to 1st lt., USAF, 1967-69. Mem. AICPA, Greater Wash. Soc. CPAs, Strategic Leadership Forum (pres. Washington chpt. 1990-91). Republican. Episcopalian. Home: 7348 Dartford Dr Mc Lean VA 22102-7348 Office: 8180 Greensboro Dr Ste 1070 Mc Lean VA 22102-3860 Office Phone: 703-356-6919. Personal E-mail: walterolson@mindspring.com.

**OLSON-HELLERUD, LINDA KATHRYN,** elementary school educator; b. Wisconsin Rapids, Wis., Aug. 26, 1947; d. Samuel Ellsworth and Lillian (Dvorak) Olson; m. H. A. Hellerud, 1979; 1 child, Sarah Kathryn Hellerud. BS, U. Wis., Stevens Point, 1969, tchg. cert., 1970, MST, 1972; MS, U. Wis., Whitewater, 1975; EdS, U. Wis., Stout, 1978. Cert. K-12 reading tchr., K-12 reading specialist, tech.and computer tng. Clk. U. Counseling Ctr. U. Wis., Stevens Point, 1965—69; elem. sch. tchr. Wisconsin Rapids, 1970—76; sch. counselor, 1976—79; dist. dir. elem. guidance, 1979—82; tchr. elem. and reading, 1982—. Instr. Summer Remedial Reading Program; cons. in field. Advocate Lit. Mentoring Program; adv. Moravian Ch. Sunday Sch. Mem.: NEA, Ctrl. Wis. Reading Assn., Internat. Reading Assn., Wood County Lit. Coun. (cons.), Wis. Reading Assn. Avocations: literacy activities, piano, technology, aerobics. Home: 120 11th St N Wisconsin Rapids WI 54494-5371 Office: Howe Elem Sch Wisconsin Rapids WI 54494

**OLSSON, ANN-MARGRET See ANN-MARGRET**

**OLSSON, BJÖRN ESKIL,** railroad supply company executive; b. Kristianstad, Sweden, Oct. 7, 1945; came to U.S., 1990; m. Cecilia Lindblad, July 6, 1968; children: Fredrik, Karin, Eva. M. Bus. and Adminstrn., U. Lund, Sweden, 1968. Internal auditor Kockums Mek. Verkstad, Malmö, Sweden, 1969-71, mgr. acctg., 1971-74; v.p. fin. and adminstrn. Kockums Industri, Söderhamn, Sweden, 1974-76, Linden Alimak, Skellefteå, Sweden, 1976-81, Sonessons, Malmö, 1981-82; pres. Sab-Nife, Malmö, 1982-87; v.p. corp. devel. Investment AB Cardo, Malmö, 1987-90; pres., CEO Harmon Industries Inc., Blue Springs, Mo., 1990—. Bd. dirs. BJ Papperats, Malmo, Green & Co., Malmö; mem. adv. bd. Ctrl. Mo. State U. Bus. Sch., Warrensburg, 1991—. Staff sgt. Swedish Army, 1964-65. Avocations: golf, skiing. Office: Harmon Industries Inc PO Box 600 Grain Valley MO 64029-0600

**OLSSON, CARL ALFRED,** urologist, department chairman; b. Boston, Nov. 29, 1938; s. Charles Rudolph and Ruth Marion (Bostrom) O.; m. Mary DeVore, Nov. 4, 1962; children: Ingrid, Leif Eric. Grad., Bowdoin Coll., 1959; MD, Boston U., 1963. Diplomate Am. Bd. Urology (trustee 1988-94, pres. 1993-94). Asst. prof. urology Boston U. Sch. Medicine, 1971-72, assoc. prof., 1972-74, prof., chmn. dept., 1974-80; dir. urology dept. Boston City Hosp., 1974-77; chief urology dept. Boston VA Med. Ctr., 1971—75; urologist-in-chief Univ. Hosp., Boston, 1971-80; John K. Lattimer prof., chmn. dept. urology Coll. Phys. and Surgs., Columbia U., N.Y.C., 1980—2005, chmn. emeritus, 2005—. Dir. Squier Urol. Clinic, urology service Presbyn. Hosp., N.Y.C.; lectr. surgery Tufts U. Sch. Medicine. Boston Interhosp. Organ Bank, 1976-79; mem. working cadre Nat. Prostate Cancer Project, Nat. Cancer Inst., 1979-84; mem. adv. coun. Nat. Inst. Diabetes, Digestive Disease and Kidney; mem. integration panel for prostate cancer rsch. Dept. of Def., 1998-2002, chmn., 2000-01. Editl. bd. Jour. Prostate, World Jour. Urology, Jour. Urodynamics and Neurourology, Jour. Urology; asst. editor Jour. Urology, 1978-2004; contbr. chpts. to books, articles to med. jours. Recipient Disting. Alumnus award Boston U., 1985. Fellow ACS; mem. Am. Urol. Assn. (coord. continuing med. edn. New Eng. sect. 1977-80, del. rsch. com., bd. dirs. 2001-06, exec. com. 2002-06, sec. 2002—, found. operating bd., 2005-06, Gold Cystoscope award 1979, Grayson-Carroll award 1971, 73, Hugh Hampton Young award 2001), Boston Surg. Soc. (exec. com. 1976-80), Am. Assn. Clin. Urologists, Am. Surg. Assn., Am. Assn. Genitourinary Surgeons (pres. elect 2006), Clin. Soc. Genitourinary Surgeons, Transplantation Soc., Soc. Urologic Oncology (pres. 1993), Soc. Pelvic Surgeons, Soc. Univ. Urologists (pres. 1990), N.Y. Sect. Am. Urol. Assn. (pres. 2002), AMA, Assn. Acad. Surgery, Am. Soc. Artificial Internal Organs, Am. Soc. Transplant Surgeons, Assn. Med. Colls., Can. Urol. Assn., Societe Internationale d'Urologie, Internat. Urodynamics Soc., Mass. Med. Soc., Soc. Govt. Urologists, Australasian Urol. Soc. (hon.), New Eng. Handicapped Sportsmen's Assn. (exec. com. 1977-81), U.S. Yacht Racing Union, Yacht Racing Union L.I. Sound, N.Y. Yacht Club, Cottage Park Yacht Club, Larchmont Yacht Club, Storm Trysail Club, Alpha Omega Alpha, Am. Found. Urol. Diseases (bd. dirs. 2002—05, exec. coun. 2002—05), NY Acad. Scis. (Valentine award medal 2006). Episcopalian. Office: Columbia-Presbyn Hosp Irving Pavilion 161 Ft Washington Av New York NY 10032-3702 Office Phone: 212-305-0100. Office Fax: 212-305-0106. Business E-Mail: CAO2@columbia.edu.

**OLSSON, NILS WILLIAM,** former association executive; b. Seattle, June 11, 1909; s. Nils A. and Mathilda (Lejkell) O.; m. Dagmar T. Gavert, June 15, 1940; children: Karna B., Nils G. and Pehr C. (twins). Student, North Park Coll., Chgo., Northwestern U., U. Minn., 1929-34; A.M., U. Chgo., 1938, PhD, 1949, U. Uppsala, Sweden, 1968; LHD, North Park Coll., Chgo., 1990. Admissions counselor, instr. Swedish North Park Coll., 1937-39; asst. Scandinavian U. Chgo., 1939-42, instr., 1945-50, asst. prof., 1950; mem. U.S. diplomatic service, 1950-67; 2d sec., pub. affairs officer Am. legation, Reykjavik, Iceland, 1950-52; attache, pub. affairs officer Am. embassy, Stockholm, Sweden, 1952-55, 1st sec., consul, 1955-57; pub. affairs adviser Dept. State, 1957-59; chief Am. sponsored schs. abroad, 1959-62; 1st sec. Am. embassy, Oslo, Norway, 1962-64, counselor for polit. affairs, 1964-66; diplomat in residence Ind. U., 1966-67; dir. Am. Swedish Inst., Mpls., 1967-73; exec. dir. Swedish Council of Am., 1973-84. Author: Swedish Passenger Arrivals in New York, 1820-1850, 1967, Swedish Passenger Arrivals in U.S. Ports (except New York) 1820-1850, 1979, Tracing Your Swedish Ancestry, 1974, (with Erik Wiken) Swedish Passenger Arrivals in the U.S. 1820-1850, 1995; editor: A Pioneer in Northwest America, 1841-1858, vol. I, 1950, vol. II, 1959, Veckobladet, 1934-35; editor, pub.: Swedish American Genealogist 1981—; editor: A Swedish City Directory of Boston 1881, 1986; contbr. to hist. and ednl. jours. Mem. bd. Evang. Covenant Hist. Commn., Chgo., 1958; asst. naval attache Am. legation, Stockholm, 1943-45. Served from lt. (j.g.) to lt. comdr. USNR, 1942-45. Decorated knight Order Vasa 1st class, knight comdr. Order North Star, Sweden; recipient Swedish Pioneer Centennial medal, 1948; King Carl XVI Gustaf Bicentennial Gold medal, Carl Sandburg medal Swedish Pioneer Hist. Soc., 1982, Charlotta medal Emigrant Inst. Växjö, Sweden; named Swedish Am. of Yr. Stockholm, 1969; recipient Hans Mattsson Plaque, Önnestad, Sweden, 1992; Victor Örnberg prize, Sweden, 1994. Fellow Geneal. Soc. (Finland), Geneal. Soc. (Sweden), Am. Soc. Genealogists; mem. Wermländska Sällskapet Stockholm (hon.), Nat. Geneal Soc., Carl Johan Soc. Sweden, Swedish-Am. Hist. Soc. (exec. sec. 1949-50, 57-68, pres. 1986-88), Royal Acad. Belles Lettres, History and Antiquities (Sweden, fgn. corr.), Pro Fide et Christianismo (Sweden, hon.), Royal Soc. Pub. Manuscripts Dealing with Scandinavian History (Sweden, fgn.). Address: 1620 Mayflower Ct Winter Park FL 32792 E-mail: nwolsson@mpinet.net.

**OLSSON-HUME, IRENA,** music educator; arrived in U.S., 1994; d. Dragogub D. and Gordana Bukvić; m. Jeremy Dale Hume, Sept. 5, 1999. MusB in Piano Performance summa cum laude, Oklahoma City U., 1998, MusM in Piano Performance with highest honors, 2000. Accompanist Performance Acad. Oklahoma City U., 1998—2000, piano instr., 1998—2002; owner, operator pvt. piano studio Oklahoma City, 2002—. Mem.: Ctrl. Okla. Music Tchrs. Assn., Okla. Music Tchrs. Assn., Music Tchrs. Nat. Assn., Alpha Chi, Pi Kappa Lambda.

**OLSTAD, ROGER GALE,** science educator; b. Mpls., Jan. 16, 1934; s. Arnold William and Myra (Stroschein) O.; m. Constance Elizabeth Jackson, Aug. 20, 1955; children: Karen Louise, Kenneth Bradley. BS, U. Minn., 1955, MA, 1959, PhD, 1963. Instr. U. Minn., Mpls., 1956-63; asst. prof. U. Ill., Urbana, 1963-64; mem. faculty U. Wash., Seattle, 1964—, assoc. prof. sci. edn., 1967-71, prof., 1971-95, asso. dean grad. studies Coll. Edn., 1971-85; prof. emeritus, 1995—. Chair environ. quality commn. City of Lake Forest

Park, Wash., 1997-2000, city coun., 2000—. Fellow AAAS; mem. NSTA (bd. dirs.) Wash. Sci. Tchrs. Assn. (pres. 1973-74), Nat. Assn. Rsch. Sci. Teaching (pres. 1977-78, bd. dirs.), N.W. Sci. Assn. (chmn. 1966-68), Assn. Edn. Tchrs. in Sci. (regional pres. 1966-68, pres. 1991-92), Nat. Assn. Biology Tchrs., Biol. Scis. Curriculum Study (chmn., bd. dirs. 1989-94), U. Wash. Faculty Club, Phi Delta Kappa. Home: 20143 53rd Ave NE Seattle WA 98155-1801 Office: U Wash Coll Edn Seattle WA 98195-0001 Office Phone: 206-364-3598. Personal E-mail: rolstad@earthlink.net. Business E-Mail: rolstad@u.washington.edu.

OLSZEWSKI, MARK ERIC, biomedical engineer, researcher; s. John George and Patricia Ann Olszewski; m. Carol Ann Persing. BS in Engring., U. Iowa, 2000, MS, 2002, PhD in Biomed. Engring., 2005. Formerly rsch. asst. dept. elec. and computer engring. U. Iowa, Iowa City; rsch. scientist Philips Med. Sys., Cleve., 2006—. Mem.: IEEE, Soc. for Indsl. and Applied Math., Internat. Soc. for Optical Engring. Office Phone: 440-483-2264. Personal E-mail: mark.olszewski@philips.com.

OLSZEWSKI, WOJCIECH, economist, mathematician; m. Anna Krystyna Kucharska; children: Maciej Wojciech, Adam Ignacy. Doktor Matematyki, Uniwersytet Warszawski, Warsaw, Poland, 1992; PhD in Econs., Princeton (NJ) U., 2001. Asst. prof. Northwestern U., Evanston, Ill., 2001—. Contbr. articles to profl. jours. NSF grantee. Home: 2742 Garrison Ave Evanston IL 60201 Office: Northwestern U 2003 Sheridan Rd Evanston IL 60208 Office Phone: 847-491-8482. Office Fax: 847-491-7001. Business E-Mail: wo@northwestern.edu.

OLTMAN, JOHN HAROLD, patent lawyer; b. Nov. 18, 1929; s. Peter Harold and Hazel Evelyn (Kelly) O.; m. Lita Marilyn Hagen, Aug. 16, 1952; children: David K., Laura G., John K. BS in Chem. Engring., U. Mich., 1952, JD, 1957. Bar: Ill. 1957, Ariz. 1964, Mich. 1965, Fla. 1968. Mem. firms Mueller & Aichele (Attys.), Chgo. and Phoenix, 1957—64, Barnes, Kisselle, Rasich & Choate (Attys.), Detroit, 1964—65, Settle, Batchelder & Oltman (Attys.), Detroit, 1965—67, Settle & Oltman (Attys.), Detroit and Ft. Lauderdale, 1967—72, Oltman and Flynn (Attys.), Ft. Lauderdale, 1972—90, Oltman, Flynn & Kublev, Ft. Lauderdale, 1990—. With USMC Res., 1952—54. Mem.: IEEE, ABA, Fla. Engring. Soc., Intellectual Property Law Assn. So. Fla., Am. Intellectual Property, Broward County Bar Assn., Fla. Bar Assn., Kiwanian (dir. Ft. Lauderdale Club 1972—74, 1977—78, pres. 1983—, chmn. Key Club 1970—78), Tau Beta Pi, Phi Eta Sigma. Office: 915 Middle River Dr Ste 415 Fort Lauderdale FL 33304-3561 Home: 168 Marion Oaks Golf Way Ocala FL 34473 E-mail: oltman@bellsouth.net.

OLUFOLABI, ADEYEMI JOHN, anesthesiologist; b. Colchester, Essex, England, Apr. 5, 1962; s. Festus Olufemi and Elsie Olufunke Olufolabi; m. Omolola Adenike Rogers, Dec. 17, 1988; children: Oluwatobi Olayemi, Oluwatosin Adebisi, Ifeoluwatomiwa Femi. MBBS, U. Ibadan, Nigeria, 1986; diploma in child health, Royal Coll. Paediatrics, London, 1993. Ho. officer Lagos U. Tchg. Hosp., Nigeria, 1986—87; sr. ho. officer Blackpool Victoria Hosp., England, 1988—90; registrar West Dorset Hospitals, Weymouth, 1990—91; sr. ho. officer Southampton U. Trust Hosp., 1991—92, sr. ho. officer pediatric surgery and neonatology, 1992—93; registrar Portsmouth Hosp. and Southampton U. Trust Hosp., 1993—95; sr. registrar Southampton U. Trust Hosp., 1995—97, 1998—99; asst. prof. anesthesiology Duke U., Durham, NC, 1999—. Instr. ACLS, Durham, 2005—; faculty tutor The Airway Course, Lake Oswego, Oreg., 2005—; vis. assoc. dept. anesthesilogy Duke U., 1997—98, quality improvement coord. obstetric anesthesia, 1999—, instr. neonatal resuscitation, 2005—. Contbr. articles to profl. jours. Bd. mem. Kybele, Winston Salem, NC. Fellow, Duke U., 2001—. Achievements include research in relieving pain during labor. Office: Duke U Dept Anesthesiology Erwin Rd Durham NC 27710 Office Phone: 919-681-6535. Office Fax: 919-668-6265. Business E-Mail: olufo001@mc.duke.edu.

OLUSEYI, HAKEEM MUATA, astrophysicist, educator; b. New Orleans, Mar. 13, 1967; s. James Edward and Elaine J. Plummer. PhD, Stanford U., Palo Alto, Calif., 2000. Grad. rsch. and tchg. fellow Stanford U., Palo Alto, 1993—99; sr. process engr. Applied Materials, Inc., Sunnyvale, Calif., 1999—2001; Ernest O. Lawrence postdoctoral fellow Lawrence Berkeley (Calif.) Nat. Lab., 2001—04; astrophysics rsch. fellow Gordon and Betty Moore Found., San Francisco, 2003—04; asst. prof. U. Ala., Huntsville, 2004—. Educator, mentor Cosmos Edn., Stanford, 2002—06; cons. Gordon and Betty Moore Found., San Francisco, 2004—05; adj. prof. physics Ala. A&M U., Huntsville, 2004—. Actor: (voice acting) Beat Generation series; voice acting, VH1 Download Your Love Valentines; actor: (voice acting) MTV.com various works; contbr. video webcast. Mentor North Ala. Ctr. for Ednl. Excellence, Huntsville, 2004—06. With USN, 1984—86. Named Top Physics Student, Tougaloo Coll., 1991; grantee Astrophysics Rsch. grantee, NASA, 2006—; Teagle scholar, Tougaloo Coll., 1986—87, Grad. Supplemental fellow, Nat. Consortium for Ednl. Excellence, 1991—95, Grad. Physics fellow, Stanford U., 1991—92, Grad. Student Rschrs. fellow, NASA, 1993—97, New Investigator in Earth-Sun Sys. Sci. fellow, 2006—, Astrophysics Rsch. grantee, NSF, 2005—. Mem.: Am. Assn. Physics Tchrs., Nat. Soc. Black Physicists (editor in chief 2003—06, Nat. Disting. Dissertation award 2002), Am. Astron. Soc., Kappa Alpha Psi (chpt. polemarch 1990—91). Achievements include patents for System, Method and Medium for Modeling, Monitoring and/or Controlling Plasma Based Semiconductor Manufacturing Processes; Monitoring of Film Characteristics during Plasma-EnBased Semiconductor Processing Using Optical Emission Spectroscopy; Method and Apparatus Employing Optical Emission Spectroscopy to Detect a Fault in Process Conditions of a Semiconductor System; Method of Etching Tungsten or Tungsten Nitride in Semiconductor Structures; Method of Etching Tungsten or Tungsten Nitride Electrode Gates in Semiconductor Structures – CIP; Method of Etching Tungsten or Tungsten Nitride Electrode Gates in Semiconductor Structures; High Selectivity and Residue Free Process for Metal on Thin Dielectric Gate Etch Application; patents pending for Method of Increasing Selectivity to Mask When Etching Tungsten or Tungsten Nitride; discovery of structures responsible for the Sun's Upper Transition Region emission. Avocations: travel, basketball, weightlifting, vocal artistry. Office: Univ Alabama Huntsville John Wright Dr OB 201C Huntsville AL 35899 Office Phone: 256-824-2490. Office Fax: 256-824-6873. Business E-Mail: oluseyh@uah.edu.

OLVER, JOHN WALTER, congressman; b. Honesdale, Pa., Sept. 3, 1936; s. Helen Fulleborn Olver; m. Rose Alice Richardson, Sept. 12, 1959; 1 child, Martha. BS, Rensselaer Poly. Inst., 1955; MS, Tufts U., 1956; PhD, MIT, 1961. Asst. prof. chemistry U. Mass., Amherst, 1962-67; mem. Mass. Ho. of Reps., Boston, 1969-72, Mass. Senate, 1973-91, U.S. Congress from 1st Mass. dist., 1991—, mem. com. on appropriations; mem. subcoms. on transp. and mil. constrn., mil. appropriations; whip-at-large Dem. Caucus. Contbr. articles to profl. jours. Democrat. Avocations: hiking, gardening, tennis. Office: US Ho Reps 1111 Longworth Ho Office Bldg Washington DC 20515-2101 Office Phone: 202-225-5335. Office Fax: 202-226-1224.*

OLVEY, PAMELA HAGAN, elementary school educator; b. Statesboro, Ga., Feb. 15, 1969; d. Franklin Donald and Shelvie Jean (Allen) Hagan; m. Bradley Alan Olvey, Oct. 11, 1997. BS in Edn., Ga. So. U., 1991, MEd, 1994. Tchr. 2d grade Marlow Elem. Sch., Guyton, Ga., 1992—95, Sand Hill Elem. Sch., Guyton, 1995—2000; tchr. 2-3rd grade Mill. Creek Elem. Sch., Statesboro, Ga., 2000—. Lead tchr. Partnership for Reform in Sci. and Math., Statesboro, 2004—06. Named Tchr. of Yr., Mill Creek Elem. Sch., 2002—03. Mem.: ASCD, Profl. Assn. Ga. Educators. Avocations: gardening, movies, reading, sunflower collector. Home: 1821 Stuckey Rd Statesboro GA 30461 Office: Mill Creek Elem Sch 239 Beasley Rd Statesboro GA 30461 Office Phone: 912-764-5979.

O'LYNN, ROBERT G., II, minister; b. Huntington, West Va., Dec. 2, 1978; s. Robert Gene and Carolyn Sue O'Lynn; m. Rachael Celeste Parsons, Dec. 21, 2002; children: Caleb Robert, Kyla Celeste. BA in Bible and Religion, Harding U., 2001; MA in Theol. Studies, Austin Grad. Sch. Theology, 2004.

Youth min. Rome Ch. of Christ, Proctorville, Ohio, 1998; min. staff mem. Coll. Ch. of Christ, Searcy, Ark., 1999—2000; preaching min. Wheeling Ch. of Christ, Ark., 2001—02; family life min. Bertram Ch. of Christ, Tex., 2003—05, dir. Stephens Ctr. Ministry, 2005—. Tchg. asst. Harding U., Searcy, Ark., 2001; dir. and co-founder Fisher's Men Ministries, Searcy, 1997—2002. Christian life columnist The Bertram Telegram, 2003—. Mem.: Christian Edn. Assn. Republican. Ch. Of Christ. Avocations: reading, golf, baseball. Office: Bertram Ch of Christ 215 West North St Bertram TX 78605 Office Phone: 512-355-2322. Business E-Mail: bertramcofc-rob@pgrb.com.

OLYPHANT, TIMOTHY, actor; b. Honolulu, Hawaii, May 20, 1968; m. Alexis Knief; 3 children. Student, U. So. Calif. Actor: (films) The First Wives Club, 1996, A Life Less Ordinary, 1997, Scream 2, 1997, Nineteen Ninety-Nine, 1998, Go, 1999, No Vacancy, 1999, Advice From a Caterpillar, 1999, The Broken Hearts Club: A Romantic Comedy, 2000, Gone in Sixty Seconds, 2000, Auggie Rose, 2000, Head Over Heels, 2001, Doppelganger, 2001, The Safety of Objects, 2001, Rock Star, 2001, Coastlines, 2002, Dreamcatcher, 2003, A Man Apart, 2003, The Girl Next Door, 2004; (TV films) Ellen Foster, 1997, When Trumpets Fade, 1998, Shadow Realm, 2002; (TV series) Deadwood, 2004—, (TV appearances) Mr. & Mrs. Smith, 1996, High Incident, 1997, Sex in the City, 1998, Night Visions, 2002, My Name Is Earl, 2006. Office: Internat Creative Mgmt 8942 Wilshire Blvd Beverly Hills CA 90211

OMAGU, DONALD, history professor; b. Lagos, Nigeria, May 26, 1967; arrived in U.S., 2004; s. John Odey and Elizabeth Akpana Omagu; m. Christina Ogeyi Omagu. BA in History with honors, U. Calabar, Cross River State, Nigeria, 1991, MA in History, 1997, PhD in History, 2000. Lectr. dept. history and internat. studies Calabar U., Nigeria, 2004; adj. asst. prof. African history Coll. S.I., NY, 2005, substitute asst. prof. African history, 2005—. A History of the Bekwarra People of the Upper Cross River Region, 1997; author: Regional Peace and Security: A Historical Perspective of the Role of Ecowas in Liberia & Sierra, 2001. Personal asst. adminstrn. Dep. Gov. Cross River State, Calabar, Nigeria, 2003—04. Recipient award of Excellence, Grad. Students Assn. Calabar U., 1995, 1997, 1999, Meritorious Svc. award, Student Union Govt. Calabar U., 1991. Mem.: N.Y. Hist. Soc., African Studies Assn., Am. Hist. Soc. Avocations: reading, writing. Office: College Staten Island Dept History 2800 Victory Blvd Staten Island NY 10314 Home: Apt 3A 1302 Rosedale Ave Bronx NY 10472

O'MALIA, MARY FRANCES, special education educator; d. Horace Emmett Fansler and Frances Fansler Kittle, Robert Blair Kittle (Stepfather); m. William Biff O'Malia, Nov. 8, 1980; children: Nohealani Marie, Shanice Francine. BA, Dominican U. of Calif., San Rafael, 1977; postgrad., Dominican U., 1977—83; postgrad. in Sch. Counseling, U. Nev., 1998—. Lic. tchr. Nev., 1979, cert. alcohol and drug abuse counselor Nev., 1999. Tchg- prin. Mineral County Sch. Dist., Hawthorne, Nev., 1986—88; spl. edn. tchr. Hawaii State Dept. of Edn., Holualoa, 1989—91; HIV/AIDS instr/trainer ARC: Hawaii State Chpt., Honolulu, 1992—97; substance abuse counselor Ctr. Behavioral Health, Reno, 1999—99; grad. tchg. asst. U. Nev., Reno, 1999—2001; spl. edn. diagnostician Washoe County Sch. Dist., Reno, 2001—03; spl. edn. tchr. Silver Stage Mid. Sch., Silver Springs, Nev., 2003—. Contbr. articles to profl. jours. Recipient Vol. of the Quarter, ARC, 1995, Distinguished Svc. award, Mineral County Sch. Dist., 1988. Mem.: Coun. for Exceptional Children. Catholic. Avocations: scuba diving, travel, computers, reading. Office: Silver Spring Mid Sch Silver Springs NV Office Phone: 775-423-6322. Business E-Mail: momalia@lyon.k12.nv.us.

O'MALLEY, BERT WILLIAM, JR., head and neck surgeon, educator, researcher; b. Pitts., Sept. 7, 1962; s. Bert. W. and Sally A. (Johnson) O'M.; m. Cheryl Anne Moore, Jan. 17, 1987; children: Bartley, Annette, Michael. Student, U. Notre Dame, 1980-81; BA in Biochemistry, U. Tex., 1984; MD, U. Tex., Dallas, 1988. Gen. surgery resident U. Tex. Southwestern, Parkland Meml. Hosp., Dallas, 1984-88; otolaryngology and head and neck surgery resident Baylor Coll. Medicine, Houston, 1988-90, clin. instr. dept. otorhino-laryngology, 1993-94; head and neck oncology and cranial base surgery fellow U. Pitts., 1994-95, clin. instr. dept otolaryngology and head and neck surgery, 1994-95; asst. prof. dept. otolaryngology—head and neck surgery Johns Hopkins U. Sch. Medicine, Balt., 1995, dir. gene therapy divsn., dept. otolaryngology-HNS, 1995—99, asst. prof. dept. oncology, 1996; chief otolaryngology U. Maryland, 1999—2003; prof., chmn. Dept. Otorhinolaryngology Sch. Medicine U. Pa., 2003—. Cons. head and neck gene therapy project GeneMedicine, Inc. The Woodlands, Tex.; lectr. dept. otolaryngology—head and neck surgery Grand Rounds, Greater Balt. Med. Ctr., 1995, U. Pitts., 1995, Johns Hopkins U., Balt., 1996, others; presenter in field. Contbr. book chpts.: Fundamentals of Molecular Biology and Gene Therapy, 1997, Surgery of the Anterior and Middle Cranial Base, 1997; contbr. articles to Transplantation Procs., Archives of Otolaryngology—Head and Neck Surgery, Human Gene Therapy, Seminars in Surg. Oncology, Cancer Rsch., others; reviewer: Otolaryngology—Head and Neck Surgery, Head and Neck, Cancer Rsch., Archives of Otolaryngology—Head and Neck Surgery, Clin. Cancer Rsch. Mem. AAAS, Am. Assn. for Cancer Rsch., Am. Soc. Gravitational and Space Biology, Am. Acad. Otolaryngology Head and Neck Surgery, Cell Transplant Soc. (founding mem.), Md. Soc. Otolaryngology. Roman Catholic. Achievements include patents pending for gene therapy to thyroid, somatic gene therapy. Office: U Penn Sch Medicine Otorhinolaryngology Dept 3400 Spruce St 5 Ravdin Bldg Philadelphia PA 19104

O'MALLEY, CARLON MARTIN, judge; b. Phila., Sept. 7, 1929; s. Carlon Martin and Lucy (Bol) O'M.; m. Mary Catherine Lyons, Aug. 17, 1957; children: Carlon Martin III, Kathleen B. O'Malley Aikman, Harry Tighe, John Todd, Cara M. O'Malley Colombo. BA, Pa. State U., 1951; LLB, Temple U., 1954. Bar: Pa. 1955, Fla. 1955, U.S. Supreme Ct. 1973. Practiced law, 1957-61; asst. U.S. atty. for Middle Dist. Pa., Dept. Justice, 1961-69, U.S. atty., 1979-82; ptnr. O'Malley & Teets, 1970-72, O'Malley, Jordan & Mullaney (and predecessor firms), 1976-79; pvt. practice Pa. and Fla., 1972-79, 82-87; judge Ct. Common Pleas of Lackawanna County (45th Judicial Dist.), 1987-97, sr. judge, 1998—. Dir. pub. safety City of Scranton, 1983-86; lectr. Lackawanna Coll., 1982-86. Editorial bd.: Temple Law Rev, 1952-53. Pres. Lackawanna County (Pa.) unit Am. Cancer Soc., 1966-67; bd. dirs. Pa. Cancer Soc., 1967-68, Lackawanna county chpt. ARC, 1967-69; mem. solicitation team, govtl. divsn. Lackawanna United Fund, 1963-68; chmn. profl. divsn. Greater Scranton (Pa.) YMCA Membership Drives; trustee Everhart Mus., Scranton, 1987—. Pilot USAF, 1955-57, Pa. N.G., 1957-59. Mem. Am. Judges Assn., Nat. Assn. Former U.S. Attys., Pa. Bar Assn., Lackawanna County Bar Assn. (bd. dirs., fin. sec.), Fla. Bar Assn., Country Club of Scranton, Elks (pres. Pa. 1978-79, judiciary com. 1985-89, justice Grand Forum 1991, 1995-97, chief justice 1992-93, nat. pres. 1997-98), K.C., Phi Kappa (pres.), Delta Theta Phi. Democrat. Office: Judges Chambers Lackawanna County Courthouse Scranton PA 18503 Office Phone: 570-963-6882.

O'MALLEY, JAMES TERENCE (TERRY), lawyer; b. Omaha, Nov. 24, 1950; s. John Austin and Mayme Bernice (Zentner) O'M.; m. Colleen L. Kizer, May 22, 1972; children: Erin C., Michael B., Patrick J. BA magna cum laude, U. Notre Dame, 1972; JD, Stanford U., 1975. Bar: Calif. 1975, Tex. 1998. Ptnr. Gray, Cary, Ames & Frye, San Diego, 1975-87, of counsel, 1987-91, ptnr., 1991—94; vice chmn., exec. v.p. gen. counsel Noble Broadcast Group, Inc., San Diego, 1987-91; ptnr. Gray Cary Ware & Freidenrich LLP, San Diego, 1994—2004, ptnr., 2004, mng. ptnr. US DLA Piper Rudnick Gray Cary US LLP, San Diego, 2005—. Pres. San Diego Taxpayers Assn., 1986—87; co-chmn. Mayor's City of the Future Health Care Task Force, San Diego, 1994—95; mem. C. of C. CEO Roundtable, San Diego, 1997—2002; adv. bd. Hildebrandt Internat., Inc., 2001; bd. dirs. San Diego Regional Econ. Devel. Corp., 1997—2002. Mem. Order of Coif, Sorin Soc. Avocations: jogging, music. Office: DLA Piper Rudnick Gray Cary Ste 1100 4365 Executive Dr San Diego CA 92121 Office Fax: 858-677-1401. Business E-Mail: terry.omalley@dlapiper.com.

O'MALLEY, JOHN DANIEL, lawyer, educator, banker; b. Chgo., Dec. 18, 1926; s. William D. and Paula A. (Skaugh) O'M.; m. Caroline Tyler Taylor, July 12, 1958; children: John Daniel, Taylor John. Grad., St. Thomas Mil. Acad., 1945; BS, Loyola U., Chgo., 1950, MA, 1952, JD, 1953; grad., U.S. Army Intelligence Sch., 1962, Command & Gen. Staff Coll., 1965. Bar: Ill. 1953, Mich. 1954, U.S. Supreme Ct. 1962. Asst. prof. law Loyola U., 1953-59, asso. prof., 1959-65; formerly spl. counsel and bond claims mgr. Fed. Ins. Co.; prof. law Loyola U. Grad. Sch. Bus., 1965—, chmn. dept. law, 1968-86. Trust officer, v.p. First Nat. Bank Highland Park (Ill.), Marina City Bank, Chgo., Hyde Park Bank & Trust Co., 1970-75; exec. v.p. Harris Bank Winnetka, Ill., 1975-95. Author: Subrogation Against Banks on Forged Checks, 1967, Common Check Frauds and the Uniform Commercial Code, 1969; Contbr. articles to profl. jours. and law revs. Served to maj. AUS, 1945-47, 61-62. Decorated Knight Grand Cross Papal Order of Holy Sepulchre, Knight Commdr. with star Constantinian Order of St. George (Italy), Knight of Malta. Mem. ABA, Chgo., Ill., Mich. bar assns., Chgo. Crime Commn., French Nat. Hon. Soc., Am., Chgo., bus. law assns., Mil. Govt. Assn., Order of St. Maurice and St. Lazarus (Italy, officer). Home: 1630 Sheridan Rd 6-L Wilmette IL 60091-1830 Office: Loyola U Ste 530 820 N Michigan Ave Chicago IL 60611-2147

O'MALLEY, KATHLEEN M., federal judge; b. 1956; AB magna cum laude, Kenyon Coll., 1979; JD, Case Western Reserve, 1982. Law clk. to Hon. Nathaniel R. Jones U.S. Ct. of Appeals, 6th circuit, 1982-83; with Jones, Day, Reavis & Pogue, Cleve., 1983-84, Porter, Wright, Morris & Arthur, Cleve., 1985-91; chief counsel, first asst. atty. gen., chief of staff Office of Atty. Gen., Columbus, 1991-94; district judge U.S. Dist. Ct. (Ohio no. dist.), 6th circuit, Cleve., 1994—. Vis. prof. U.S. Law Case Western Res. U. Mem.: ABA, FBA, Fed. Cir. Bar Assn., Anthony J. Celebrezze Inn of Ct., Order of Coif, Phi Beta Kappa. Office: US District Ct 801 W Superior Ave Cleveland OH 44113-1840

O'MALLEY, KEVIN FRANCIS, lawyer, writer, educator; b. St. Louis, May 12, 1947; s. Peter Francis and Dorothy Margaret (Cradick) O'M.; m. Dena Hengen, Apr.2, 1971; children: Kevin Brendan, Ryan Michael. AB, St. Louis U., 1970, JD, 1973. Bar: Mo. 1973, U.S. Ct. Appeals D.C. 1974, U.S. Ct. Appeals (8th cir.) 1979, Ill. 1993. Trial lawyer U.S. Dept. Justice, Washington, 1973-74, Los Angeles, 1974-77, Phoenix, 1977-78, asst. U.S. atty. St. Louis, 1978-83. Adj. prof. law St. Louis U., 1979—85; lectr. Ctrl. and Ea. European Law Initiative, Russian Fedn., 1996, Poland, 99. Author: (with Devitt, Blackmar, O'Malley) Federal Jury Practice and Instruction, 1990, 92, (with O'Malley, Grenig & Lee), 1999, 2000, 01; contbr. articles to law books and jours. Community amb. Expt. in Internat. Living, Prague, Czechoslovakia, 1968; bd. dirs. St. Louis-Galway (Ireland) Sister Cities. Capt. U.S. Army, 1973. Named one of Best Lawyers in Am., 2005—; recipient Atty. Gen.'s Disting. Svc. award, US Dept. Justice, 1977, John J. Dwyer Meml. Scholarship award, 1967—70. Fellow Am. Coll. Trial Lawyers; mem. ABA (chmn. govt. litigation counsel com. 1982-86, chmn. jud. com. 1986-87, chmn. com. on ind. and small firms, chmn. trial practice com. 1991-94, health care litigation 1994-98, mem. task force on fed. practice 2005—), Am. Law Inst., Met. Bar Assn. St. Louis (chmn. criminal law sect.), Nat. Inst. Trial Advocacy, Mo. Athletic Club. Roman Catholic. Office: Greensfelder Hemker & Gale PC 10 S Broadway Ste 2000 Saint Louis MO 63102-1747 Office Phone: 314-345-4753. Business E-Mail: ko@greensfelder.com.

O'MALLEY, MARTIN JOSEPH, mayor, lawyer, retired councilman; b. Jan. 18, 1963; m. Katie Curran; children: Grace, Tara, William, Jack. BA, Cath. U., 1985; JD, U. Md. Sch of Law, 1988. Asst. state's atty., Balt., 1988-90; staff asst. U.S. Congress; city councilman Balt., 1991—99; mayor, 1999—; pvt. practice law. Co-chmn. task force on fed.-local law enforcement U.S. Conf. Mayors. Former state field dir. Senator Barbara Mikulski Senate Campaign; former state coord. Senator Bob Kerrey Dem. Primary. chmn. Com. of Taxation and Finance, chmn. of Legislative Investment. Recipient Svc. to Humanity award Md. Jaycees, 1994. Mem.: Md. Bar Assn., Friendly Sons St. Patricks. Democrat. Catholic. Office: City Hall Rm 250 100 N Holliday St Baltimore MD 21202-3417 E-mail: mayor@baltimorecity.gov.*

O'MALLEY, SEAN PATRICK CARDINAL, Archbishop of Boston, cardinal; b. Lakewood, Ohio, June 29, 1944; s. Theodore and Mary Louise O'Malley. Student, St. Fidelis Sem., Herman, Pa., Capuchin Coll., Washington; MA in Religious Edn., Catholic U., Ph.D in Spanish & Portuguese, 1978. Ordained priest Roman Cath. Ch., 1970. Prof. Catholic U., Washington, 1969—73; exec. dir., Centro Catolico Hispano Archdiocese of Washington DC, Washington, 1973—78, episcopal vicar of priests serving Portuguese, Haitian & Hispanic communities, 1978-84; coadjutor bishop Diocese of St. Thomas, VI, 1984—85, bishop VI, 1985—92, Diocese of Fall River, Mass., 1992—2002, Diocese of Palm Beach, Fla., 2002—03; archbishop Archdiocese of Boston, Brighton, 2003—; elevated to Cardinal by Pope Benedict XVI, 2006—. Mem.: US Catholic Conf. of Catholic Bishops (chmn., Com. on Consecrated Life). Office: Archbishop of Boston 2121 Commonwealth Ave Brighton MA 02135-3192*

O'MALLEY, SUSAN, professional basketball team executive; d. Peter and Jan O'Malley. BS in Bus. and Finance, Mt. St. Mary's Coll., 1983. With Earl Palmer Brown Advt., 1983—86; dir. advt. Washington Bullets, 1986-87, dir. mktg., 1987-88, exec. v.p., 1988-91, pres., 1991-96, Washington Wizards, 1996—, Washington Sports and Entertainment, 1996—. Recipient American-ism Award, Alexandria-Olympic Boys and Girls Club, 1997, Adj. Prof. of Yr. Award, Georgetown U., 2002. Achievements include becoming first female president of an NBA franchise. Avocations: tennis, vacations. Office: Washington Wizards 718 7th St NW Washington DC 20001-3716

O'MALLEY, THOMAS ANTHONY, gastroenterologist, internist; b. St. Helens, Lancashire, Eng., Jan. 21, 1932; s. Michael and Margaret (Melia) O'M.; m. Margaret Mary O'Kane, Apr. 7, 1958 (dec. Apr. 1985); m. Marianne Rapier, Jan. 23, 1988; children: Anne, Patricia, Katherine, Jane, Margaret. MBChB, U. Liverpool, Eng., 1956; Lic. Medicine, U. State N.Y., 1964. Diplomate Am. Bd. Internal Medicine, State Bd. Med. Examiners Fla. House physician Royal Infirmary, Liverpool, 1956-57; house surgeon Royal Liverpool Children's Hosp., 1957; resident in medicine C.S. Wilson Meml. Hosp., Johnson City, NY, 1957-58; fellow internal medicine Lahey Clinic, Boston, 1958-59; USPHS trainee in gastroenterology U. Rochester (N.Y.), Strong Meml. Hosp., 1959-60; chief resident medicine/Segal Watson fellow gastroenterology Genesee Hosp., Rochester, 1960-61; gastroenterologist Cancer Clinic, Regina, Sask., Canada, 1963; asst. dir. med. edn. Genesee Hosp., U. Rochester, 1964—66; pvt. practice Rochester, NY, 1967—72; clin. asst. prof. medicine U. Rochester, 1967—72; clin. assoc. prof. medicine U. South Fla., Tampa, 1972—. Chief medicine Sarasota (Fla.) Meml. Hosp., 1973, Doctors Hosp., Sarasota, 1985. With RAF, 1961-62. Recipient Physician of Yr. award Doctors Hosp. Sarasota, 1985; listed among Best Dr.'s of Am., 1998. Fellow: ACP, Am. Coll. Gastroenterology; mem.: Cavalieri del Vini Nobili (amb. 1989—, pres. 1997—), Chevalier du Tastevin (comdr. 1985—), officieur comdr. 2001—). Office: O'Malley & Hall MD PA 2650 Bahia Vista St Sarasota FL 34239-2635 Office Phone: 941-366-8960.

O'MALLEY, THOMAS D., petroleum industry executive; b. N.Y.C., 1941; Grad., Manhattan Coll., 1963. Vice chmn., dir. Salomon, Inc. (formerly Phibro-Salomon, Inc.), N.Y.C.; former chmn., CEO, dir. Phibro Energy, Inc., Greenwich, Conn.; chmn. Argus Investments (formerly Argus Resources), Stamford, Conn., 1987; chmn., CEO Tosco Corp., Conn., 1989—2001; vice chmn., dir. Phillips Petroleum, 2001; CEO, pres., chmn. Premcor Inc., St. Louis, 2002—. Bd. dirs. PETsMART, Inc., 2002.

OMALU, BENNET IFEAKANDU, physician, consultant; arrived in US, 1994, permanent resident, 2006; MD, Coll. Medicine, U. Nigeria, Enugu, 1990; MPH in Epidemiology, U. Pitts., 2004. Diplomate anatomic pathology Am. Bd. Pathology, 2002, clin. pathology Am. Bd. Pathology, 2003, forensic pathology Am. Bd. Pathology, 2004, neuropathology Am. Bd. Pathology, 2005. House physician dept. pediat. Enugu Gen. Hosp., Nigeria, 1990; intern, gen. family practice U. Nigeria Hosp., Enugu, 1991—92; emergency rm.

physician Jos U. Hosp., Jos, Nigeria, 1992—94; vis. rsch. scholar dept. epidemiology U. Wash., 1994—95; pathology resident Harlem Hosp. Ctr., NYC, 1995—99; fellowship in forensic pathology Allegheny County Coroner's Office, Pitts., 1999—2000, assoc. forensic pathologist, 2000—02, attending forensic pathologist, 2002—, attending forensic neuropathologist, 2002—; fellowship in neuropathology U. Pitts. Med. Ctr., 2000—02; cons. forensic pathologist Cyril H. Wecht and Pathology Assoc. Inc., 2000—05, cons. neuropathologist, 2000—05; clinical assoc. prof. pathology U. Pitts. 2003—; cons. neuropathologist Conemaugh Mem. Hosp., Johnstown, Pa., 2003—. Prin. forensic cons. Neo-Forenxis, LLC, Pitts.; prin. health care mgmt. cons. BOGE, LP, Pitts.; adj. asst. prof. epidemiology Grad. Sch. Pub. Health, U. Pitts., Pitts., 2004—. Contbr. articles to profl. jours. Active St. Benedict the Moor Parish, Pitts., 1999—2006. Fellow: Nigerian Med. Dental Coun., Am. Coll. Epidemiology, Coll. Am. Pathologist, Am. Soc. Clinical Pathologists, Am. Assn. Advancement Sci.; mem.: AMA, Am. Soc. Investigative Pathology, Pa. Assn. Pathologists, Pa. Med. Soc., Alleghany County Pathology Soc., Am. Pub. Health Assn., Am. Assn. Pub. Health Physicians, US and Can. Acad. Pathology, Am. Acad. Forensic Scis., Am. Assn. Med. Examiners, Am. Assn. Neuropathologists, Am. Assn. Physician Execs. Conservative. Roman Catholic. Achievements include copyright ownership forensic case study series. Office Phone: 412-759-3597. Business E-Mail: bennet.omalu@neoforenxis.com.

**OMAN, HENRY,** retired electrical engineer, engineering executive; b. Portland, Oreg., Aug. 29, 1918; s. Paul L. and Mary (Levonen) O.; m. Winifred Eleanor Potter, June 17, 1944 (dec. Nov. 1950); m. Earlene Mary Boot, Sept. 11, 1954; children: Mary Janet, Eleanor Eva, Eric Paul. BSEE, Oreg. State U., 1940, MSFE, 1951. Registered profl. engr., Wash. Application engr. Allis Chalmers Mfg. Co., Milw., 1940—48; rsch. engr. Boeing Co., Seattle, 1948—63, engring. mgr., 1963—91; ret., 1991. Author: Energy Systems Engineering Handbook, 1986; co-author: Electric Bicycles, a Guide to design and Use, 2005; contbr. numerous articles to profl. jours. Mem. team that restarted amateur radio communication to the outside world from the People's Republic of China, 1981. Recipient prize paper award Am. Inst. Elec. Engrs., 1964. Fellow IEEE (founder power electronics sys. confs., 1970—, v.p. Aerospace and Electronics Sys. Soc. 1984-88, Harry Mimno award 1989, Third Millenium medal 2000, editor-in-chief Aerospace and Electronic Sys. mag. 1995-99/rated in top two by Inst. for Sci. Info.), AIAA (assoc. fellow); mem. AAAS (bd. dir. Pacific divsn.). Republican. Methodist. Achievements include development of concepts for solar power satellite which generates power in geo-synchronous orbit 24 hours per day and beams it to the Earth surface with a microwave beam; research in simple battery-powered electric bicycles for low-cost, pollution-free transportation in developing nations. Home: 19221 Normandy Park Dr SW Seattle WA 98166-4129 Personal E-mail: h.oman@ieee.org.

**OMAN, MARK C.,** bank executive; b. Cedar Falls, Iowa; B. U. No. Iowa. CPA. With Delooitte, HAskins & Sells, Des Moines, Norwest Corp., 1979; CEO Wells Fargo Home Mortgage, Inc., 1989—97, chmn., 1997—; exec. v.p. mortgage svcs. Norwest, 1997—98; group exec. v.p. home and consumer fin. Wells Fargo & Co., 2002—. Office: Wells Fargo & Co 420 Montgomery St San Francisco CA 94163

**OMAN, RALPH,** lawyer; b. Huntington, NY, July 1, 1940; s. Henry Ferdinand and Annamarie (Retelsdorf) O.; m. Anne K. Henehan, Oct. 21, 1967; children: Tabitha Russell, Caroline Adams, Charlotte Ericsson. Diploma, Sorbonne U., Paris, 1961; BA, Hamilton Coll., 1962; LLD, Georgetown U., 1973. Bar: D.C. 1973, U.S. Dist. Ct. Md. 1973, U.S. Ct. Appeals (4th cir.) 1974, U.S. Supreme Ct. 1977. Law clk. to U.S. Dist. Ct. judge U.S. Dist. Ct. Md., Balt., 1973-74; trial atty U.S. Dept. Justice, Washington, 1974-75; chief minority counsel patents, trademarks and copyrights subcom. U.S. Senate, Washington, 1975-77; legis. dir. Senator Charles Mathias, Washington, 1977-78; minority counsel judiciary com. U.S. Senate, Washington, 1978-81, chief counsel, staff dir. criminal law subcom., 1981-82, chief counsel patents, copyrights and trademarks subcom., 1982-85; register of copyrights U.S. Copyright Office, Washington, 1985-94; counsel Dechert Price and Rhoads, Washington, 1996—. Adj. prof. copyright law George Washington U.; speaker in field. Contbr. numerous articles to profl. jours. Served to lt. USN, 1965-70, Vietnam. Mem. ABA (chair authors com.), Fed. Bar Assn. (past pres. Capitol Hill chpt.). Episcopalian. Home: 1110 E Capitol St NE Washington DC 20002-6225 Office: Dechert Price and Rhoads 1775 Eye St NW Ste 1100 Washington DC 20006-2424 E-mail: ralph.oman@dechert.com.

**OMAN, RICHARD HEER,** retired lawyer; b. Columbus, Ohio, Jan. 4, 1926; s. B. R. Oman and Marguerite H. (Oman) Andrews; m. Jane Ellen Wert, Oct. 5, 1963; children: Sarah M., David W. BA, Ohio State U., 1948, JD, 1951; D in Cmty. Leadership (hon.), Franklin U., 2005. Bar: Ohio 1951. Atty. Ohio Nat. Bank, Columbus, 1951-55; ptnr. Isaac, Postlewaite, O'Brien & Oman, Columbus, 1955-71; dir. Columbus Found., 1955-77, counsel, 1955—2005; ptnr. Porter, Wright, Morris and Arthur (and predecessor firm), Columbus, 1972-89; of counsel Vorys, Sater, Seymour and Pease, Columbus, 1990, ptnr., 1991-96, of counsel, 1997—2004, ret., 2005. Mem. Columbus Airport Commn., 1960-64; trustee Reinberger Found., Cleve., 1980—, Columbus Acad., 1981-87, Grant Hosp., 1978-86, Harding Hosp., 1978-86; sr. warden Trinity Episc. Ch., 1985-88; counsel Columbus Jewish Found., 1985-2005, Wexner Ctr. Found., 1990-2005, Found. Cath. Diocese, Columbus, 2000-2005. Fellow Ohio State Bar Found.; mem. ABA, Am. Coll. Trust and Estate Counsel, Ohio State Bar Assn. (past mem. bd. govs. probate and trust law sect.), Columbus Bar Assn., Columbus Club, Rocky Fork Hunt and Country Club, Nantucket (Mass.) Yacht Club, Kit Kat Club. Republican. Episcopalian. Office: Vorys Sater Seymour & Pease LLP PO Box 1008 52 E Gay St Columbus OH 43215-3161 Fax: 614-714-4731. Office Phone: 614-464-6453. Business E-Mail: rhoman@vssp.com.

**OMAR, MOHAMMED A.,** engineering educator, consultant; BS in Mech. Engring., U. Jordan 2001; PhD, U. of Ky., 2005. Contbr. articles to profl. publs. (TVA fellow, Man of Yr., Medal of Honor, 2006). Recipient UN scholarship, 1996. Mem.: SAE (assoc.), SME (assoc.), SPIE (assoc.), ASNT (assoc.), ASME (assoc.). Achievements include patents pending for Infrared automated inspection system. Office: U Ky 151 RGAN Bldg Lexington KY 40506 Office Phone: 859 257 6336 80693. Business E-Mail: maomar2@uky.edu.

**O'MARA, JAMES WRIGHT,** lawyer; b. McComb, Miss., Jan. 7, 1940; s. Junior and Mary Jane (Wright) O'M.; m. Jeanette Walter, June 28, 1963; children: James W. Jr., Angela J. BA, U. Miss., 1962, JD with distinction, 1967. Bar: Miss. 1967. Ptnr. Butler, Snow, O'Mara, Stevens & Cannada, Jackson, Miss., 1967-97, chmn., 1990-97; sr. ptnr. Phelps & Dunbar, Jackson, Miss., 1997—. Vis. prof. Jackson Sch. Law, 1970-72. Editor-in-chief Miss. Law Jour., 1966-67. Pres. Jackson Prep. Sch., 1984-85, Woodland Hills Bapt. Acad., Jackson, 1973-84. Capt. U.S. Army, 1962-64. Fellow Miss. Bar Assn.; mem. ABA, Miss. Bar Assn., Am. Bankruptcy Inst., Miss. Bankruptcy Conf. (pres. 1980-81). Baptist. Home: 42 Eastbrooke St # I Jackson MS 39216-4714 Office: Phelps & Dunbar PO Box 23066 Jackson MS 39225-3066 E-mail: omaraj@phelps.com.

**O'MARA, JOHN ALOYSIUS,** retired bishop; b. Buffalo, Nov. 17, 1924; arrived in Can., 1940; s. John Aloysius and Anna Theresa (Schenck) O'Mara. Student, St. Augustine's Sem., Toronto, Ont., Can., 1944-51; JCL, St. Thomas U., Rome, 1953. Ordained priest Roman Cath. Ch., 1951. Mem. chancery Archdiocese of Toronto, Canada, 1953-69; pres., rector St. Augustine's Sem., Toronto, 1969-75; pastor St. Lawrence Parish, Scarboro, Ont., Canada, 1975-76; bishop Diocese of Thunder Bay, Ont., 1976-94, Diocese of St. Catharines, Ont., 1994—2002; ret., 2002. Pres. Ont. Conf. Cath. Bishops, 1986—92. Mem. Ont. Hosp. Svcs. Commn., 1964—69; bd. dirs. Ont. Hosp. Assn., 1961—65. Named Hon. Prelate of Papal Household with title Monsignor, 1954; Hon. fellow, U. St. Michael's Coll., Toronto, 1997. Mem.:

Cath. Health Assn. Ont. (bd. dirs. 1982—86, 1988—92, 1996—), Caht. Ch. Ext. Soc. (bd. dirs. 1992—96). Home: Holy Rosary Rectory 21 Queen St S Thorold ON Canada L2V 3M7 E-mail: h-rosary@computan.on.ca.

**OMASS, GEORGE A.,** federal agency administrator; b. Biloxi, Miss. Grad., U. Miss. Exec. v.p. Nat. Apt. Assn.; dir. Action Agy. Speakers Bur.; mem. com. on Post Office and Civil Svc. U.S. Ho. of Reps.; postal rate commr. U.S. Postal Rate Commn., 1997—2006, vice chmn., 2000—2001, chmn., 2006—. Mem. bd. govs. Nat. Rep. Club Capitol Hill; chmn. pastoral coun. Ch. of the Annunciation. Office: US Postal Commn 901 New York Ave NW Ste 200 Washington DC 20268-0001*

**OMASTA, MATTHEW J.,** artist, educator; s. John and Karen Omasta. BA in Drama, Ithaca (N.Y.) Coll., 2001; MA in Theatre Edn., Emerson Coll., 2006; student in Theatre for Youth, Ariz. State U., 2006—. Adminstr. Fla. Studio Theatre, Sarasota, Fla., 2004; instr. Emerson Coll., Boston, 2004—. Coach playwriting, dir. The Tremont St. Project, Boston, 2004—06; performer, coord. guest talent Walt Disney Entertainment, Lake Buena Vista, Fla. Dir.: (plays) The Mind/Body Dialogues, Songs for a New World. Grantee, Emerson Coll., 2005. Mem.: Southeastern Theatre Conf., New Eng. Theatre Conf., Assn. Theatre in Higher Edn., Am. Alliance Theatre in Edn. Independent. Avocations: theater, watersports, travel, writing.

**OMATSU, GLENN,** Asian American studies professor; b. Cleve., 1947; Grad., East Los Angeles Coll., U. Calif., Santa Cruz. Assoc. editor Amerasia Jour., 1985—2002; editor CrossCurrents, 1985—2002; prof. Asian Am. studies UCLA, Calif. State U., Northridge, Pasadena City Coll. Co-editor: Asian Americans: The Movement and the Moment, 2001. Mem. New Otani Workers Support Com., Koreatown Restaurant Workers Support Com. Recipient Cmty. Svc. award, Japanese Am. Hist. Soc. of So. Calif., Cmty. Activism award, Korean Immigrant Workers Advocates of L.A. Office: CSUN EOP 18111 Nordhoff St Northridge CA 91330-8366 Business E-Mail: glenn.omatus@csun.edu.

**O'MEALLIE, KITTY,** artist; b. Bennettsville, S.C., Oct. 24, 1916; d. Earle and Rosa Estelle (Bethea) Chamness; m. John Ryan O'Meallie, June 27, 1939 (dec. Apr. 26, 1974); children: Sue Ryan, Kathryn Bethea; m. Lee Harnie Johnson, Aug. 21, 1976. BFA, Tulane U., New Orleans, 1937; postgrad., Tulane U., 1954—59. One-woman shows include Masur Mus., Monroe, La., 1979, Marlboro County Mus. of S.C., 1975, Meridian Mus. ARt, Miss., 1981, 85; exhibited in group shows at New Orleans Mus. Art, Contemporary Art Ctr., Meadows Mus. Cushing Gallery, SE Ctr. for Contemporary Art, Art 80, Art Expo West, Art Expo 81; represented in permanent collections New Orleans Mus. Art, Ogden Mus. So. Art, Tulane U. Pan-Am. Life Ctr., Masur Mus. Art, Meridian Mus. Art. Nat. officer Newcomb Coll. Alumnae Assn., 1964-66; lectr. exhibitor for many charitable orgns. Recipient award WYES-TV, 1979, Hon. Invitational New Orleans Women's Caucus, 1986; winner NC cover art contest Continuing Care Ref. Guide, 2003; numerous awards and prizes in competitive exhibitions; grantee St. Charles Ave. Presbyn. Ch., New Orleans, 1995-96. Mem. Arts Coun. New Orleans, Fine Arts League Cary, Chi Omega Alumnae Assn. (pres. mothers' club 1964). Avocations: bird-watching, bridge. Home and Office: 158 Wee Loch Drive Cary NC 27511-3885 Office Phone: 919-481-9904.

**O'MEARA, CHRISTOPHER M.,** investment company executive; BA business administration, Georgetown U. CPA. Finance div. Lehman Bros. Holdings, 1994—95, asst. controller, 1995—2001, v.p., 2001—, financial controller, 2001—02, global controller, 2002—, CFO, 2004—. Office: c/o Lehman Bros 745 Seventh Avenue New York NY 10019*

**O'MEARA, JOHN CORBETT,** federal judge; b. Hillsdale, Mich., Nov. 4, 1933; s. John Richard and Karolyn Louise (Corbett) O'M.; m. Penelope Reinigier Appel, June 9, 1962 (div. Feb. 1975); children: Meghan Appel, John Richard, Corbett Edge, Patrick Fitzpatrick, Tighe Roberts; m. Julia Donovan Darlow, Sept. 20, 1975; 1 child, Gillian Darlow. AB, U. Notre Dame, 1955; LLB, Harvard U., 1962. Bar: Mich. 1962. Assoc. Dickinson, Wright, Moon, Van Dusen & Freeman, Detroit, 1962-70; mem. faculty U. Detroit, 1965-70; ptnr. Dickinson, Wright, Moon, Van Dusen & Freeman, Detroit, 1970-94, head of labor group, 1985-94; judge U.S. Dist. Ct., Detroit, 1994—. Bd. dirs. Mich. Opera Theatre, Detroit. Contr. articles to profl. jours. Fin. chmn. Dem. Party Mich., 1968-70; chmn. U.S. Cts. Comm. State Bar Mich., 1984-94. Lt. USN, 1955-59. Fellow Am. Coll. Trial Lawyers, Am. Bar Found.; mem. ABA, U.S. Supreme Court Bar, Am. Judicature Soc., Mich. State Bar Assn., 6th Cir. Court Appeals Bar (life mem., 6th Cir. Jud. Conf. 1986). Office: US Dist Ct 200 E Liberty St Ann Arbor MI 48104 Office Phone: 734-741-2106. Personal E-mail: omearajomear@sbcglobal.net.

**O'MEARA, NOEL P.,** priest, religious organization administrator; b. Gort, Galway, Ireland, Dec. 22, 1937; arrived in U.S., 1983; s. Thomas Joseph O'Meara and Moyna Theresa Pathe. BA, Nat. U. Ireland, Dublin, 1960, Higher Diploma, 1966; MEd, Trinity Coll., Dublin, 1973; PhD, Fordham U., 1987. Sr. dean Templeogue H.S., Dublin, 1966—73; provincial adminstr. Irish Province, Holy Spirit Order, Dublin, 1973—77; missionary priest Congreção do Espirito Santo, São Paulo, Brazil, 1977—83; fund raiser Brazil missions Brazil Spiritan Missions, N.Y.C., 1983—88; dir. Mission Agy. Svcs., N.Y.C., 1985; coord. Belem sector Archdiocese São Paulo, 1988—90; gen. sec. Congregation of Holy Spirit, Rome, 1990—93, provincial bursar Irish Province, Holy Spirit Order, 1994—2000, gen. bursar-adjoint, 2001—. Contbr. articles to profl. jours. Parish priest Cath. Ch., São Paulo, 1978—90; pres. Spiritan Found., Washington, 2001—; gen. bursar adjoint Congregation of Holy Spirit, 2001—; bd. dirs. Des Places Ednl. Trust, Dublin, 1997—2000; chmn. bd. dirs. Aidlink Ngo Dublin, 1996—2000. Mem. Fraternity of Sant. Egidio. Roman Catholic. Avocations: music, travel to underdeveloped countries, golf. Office: Spiritan Found 11411 Amherst Ave Silver Spring MD 20902

**O'MEARA, ONORATO TIMOTHY,** academic administrator, mathematician; b. Cape Town, Republic of South Africa, Jan. 29, 1928; arrived in U.S., 1957; s. Daniel and Fiorina (Allorto) O'M.; m. Jean T. Fadden, Sept. 12, 1953; children: Maria, Timothy, Jean, Kathleen, Eileen. B.Sc., U. Cape Town, 1947, M.Sc., 1948; PhD, Princeton U., 1953; LLD (hon.), U. Notre Dame, 1987. Asst. lectr. U. Natal, Republic South Africa, 1949; lectr. U. Otago, New Zealand, 1954-56; mem. Inst. for Advanced Study, Princeton, NJ, 1957-58, 62; asst. prof. Princeton U., 1958-62; prof. math. U. Notre Dame, Ind., 1962-76, chmn. dept., 1965-66, 68-72, Kenna prof. math., 1976-98, provost, 1978-96, provost emeritus, 1996—, Kenna prof. emeritus, 1998—. Vis. prof. Calif. Inst. Tech., 1968; Gauss prof. Göttingen Acad. Sci., 1978; mem. adv. panel math. scis. NSF, 1974-77, cons., 1960—. Author: Introduction to Quadratic Forms, 1963, 71, 73, 2000, Lectures on Linear Groups, 1974, 2d edit., 1977, 3d edit., 1988, Russian translation, 1976, Symplectic Groups, 1978, 82, Russian translation, 1979, The Classical Groups and K-Theory (with A.J. Hahn), 1989; contbr. articles on arithmetic theory of quadratic forms and isomorphism theory of linear groups to Am. and European profl. jours. Mem. Com. Intellectual and Cultural Affairs, 1962—, Commn. on Cath. Scholarship, 1997-99; life trustee U. of Notre Dame, 1996—. Recipient Marianist award U. Dayton, 1988; Alfred P. Sloan fellow, 1960-63. Mem. Am. Math. Soc., Am. Acad. Arts and Sci., Collegium (bd. dirs. 1992-96). Roman Catholic. Home: 1227 E Irvington Ave South Bend IN 46614-1417 Office: U Notre Dame Office of Provost Emeritus 255B Hurkey Hall Notre Dame IN 46556 Personal E-mail: omeara1227@sbcglobal.net.

**O'MEARA, PATRICK O.,** political science professor; b. Cape Town, South Africa, Jan. 7, 1938; came to U.S., 1964. s. Daniel and Fiorina (Allorto) O'M. BA, U. Capetown, 1960; MA, Ind. U., 1966, PhD, 1970; D (hon.), Nat. Inst. Devel. adminstrn., Bangkok, 2005. Dep. dir. African studies program, asst. prof. polit. sci. Ind. U., Bloomington, 1970-72, dir. African studies program, 1972—, assoc. prof. polit. sci. and pub. and environ. affairs, 1972-81, prof. polit. sci. and pub. and environ. affairs, 1981—, dean office of internat. programs, 1993—. Mem. Ind. Gov.'s Asia Delegation, 2005; cons. in field.

Author: Rhodesia: Racial Conflict or Coexistence?, 1975; editor (with Gwendolen M. Carter): Southern Africa in Crisis, 1977; editor: African Independence: The First Twenty-Five Years, 1985, Southern Africa: The Continuing Crisis, 1979, International Politics in Southern Africa, 1982; editor: (with Phyllis M. Martin) Africa, 1977, 3d edit., 1995; editor: (with C.R. Halisi and Brian Winchester) Revolutions of the Late Twentieth Century, 1991; editor: (with Howard D. Mehlinger and Matthew Krain) Globalization and the Challenges of a New Century, 2000; editor: (with Howard D. Mehlinger and Roxanna Ma Newman) Changing Perspectives on International Education, 2001; contbr. articles to profl. jours., chapters to books. Decorated Cross of St. George (Catalonia, Spain); recipient Medal of Warsaw U., 2001, Amicus Poloniae, Embassy of Poland, 2003, Founders award Soc. Coll. and Univ. Planning, 2005. Mem. African Studies Assn., Pi Alpha Alpha. Roman Catholic. Office: Ind U Bryan Hall 205 Bloomington IN 47405

**O'MEARA, SARA,** non-profit organization executive; b. Knoxville, Tenn., Sept. 09; m. Robert O'Meara (dec.); children: John Hopkins, Charles Hopkins (dec.); m. Robert Sigholtz, Nov. 1986 (dec.); stepchildren: Taryn, Whitney. Attended, Briarcliff Jr. Coll.; BA, The Sorbonne, Paris; D (hon.), Endicott Coll. Co-founder, chmn. &c., CEO CHILDHELP USA (formerly Children's Village USA), Scottsdale, Ariz., 1960—. Bd. dirs. Nat. Soc. for Prevention of Child Abuse and Neglect of Gt. Britain, Children to Children, Inc.; hon. com. mem. The Dyslexia Found., Inc.; mem. Mayor's adv. bd., Defense for Children Internat., Nat. Soc. Prevention Cruelty to Children, World Affairs Coun., Ariz. Found. Women Charter 100; bd. dirs. Internat. Alliance on Child Abuse and Neglect; sustaining mem. Spastic Children's League, past pres.; mem., past recording sec. Assistance League So. Calif. Recipient Cross of Merit, Knightly Order of St. Brigitte, 1967, Victor M. Carter Diamond award Japan-Am. Soc., 1970, Dame Cross of Merit of Order of St. John of Denmark, 1980, Official Seal of 34th Gov. Calif., 1981, Woman of Achievement award Career Guild, 1982, Women Making History award Nat. Fedn. Bus. Profl. Women's Clubs, 1983, Disting. Am. award for svc., 1984, Humanitarian award Nat. Frat. Eagles, 1984, Nat. Recognition award outstanding leadership Am. Heritage Found., 1986, Notable Am. award svc. to Calif., 1986, Dove of Peace award Pacific Southwest and Ctrl. Pacific Regions B'nai B'rith, 1987, Paul Harris fellow award Rotary Found., 1989, Internat. Collaboration to Prevention Child Abuse award HRH Queen of Eng., 1989, Living Legacy award Women's Internat. Ctr., 1989, Love and Help the Children award, 1990, Presdl. award, 1990, Kiwanis World Svc. medal, 1991, Women Who Make a Difference award Family Circle Mag., 1992, Outstanding Woman from Tenn. award Nat. Mus. Women in Arts, 1993, Nat. Caring award Nat. Caring Inst., 1993, Hubert Humphrey award Touchdown Club Washington, 1993, Lifetime Achievement award Nat. Charity Awards Com., 2001, Champions of Children award Nat. Children's Alliance, Sandra Day O'Connor award Ariz. Found. Women, 2004, Nobel Peace Prize nominee, 2005, numerous others. Mem. SAG, AFTRA, Victory Awards (exec. com.), Am. Biographical Inst. (nat. bd. advisors), Alpha Delta Kappa (hon.). Office: Childhelp USA 15757 N 78th St Scottsdale AZ 85260-1629 Office Phone: 480-922-8212.

**O'MEARA, THOMAS FRANKLIN,** priest, educator; b. Des Moines, May 15, 1935; s. Joseph Matthew and Frances Claire (Rock) O'M. MA, Aquinas Inst, Dubuque, Iowa, 1963; PhD, U. Munich, Germany, 1967. Ordained priest Roman Cath. Ch., 1962. Assoc. prof. Aquinas Inst. of Theology, Dubuque, Iowa, 1967-79; prof. U. Notre Dame, South Bend, Ind., 1981-84, William K. Warren prof. of theology, 1985—. Author 14 books, including: Romantic Idealism and Roman Catholicism, 1983, Theology of Ministry, 1985, revised edit., 1999, Church and Culture, 1991, Thomas Aquinas: Theologian, 1997, Erich Przywara, S.J., His Theology and His World, 2002, A Theologian's Journey, 2002. Mem. Catholic Theol. Soc. Am. (pres. 1980). Roman Catholic. Office: St Thomas Aquinas Priory 7200 Division St River Forest IL 60305 E-mail: tomeara@nd.edu.

**O'MEARA, VICKI A.,** lawyer; b. Mpls., May 13, 1957; d. James Michael and Joan Kathleen (Shepers) O'M.; children: Joseph O'Meara Masterman, Nicolas James Reisinger O'Meara. BA in Polit. Sci. cum laude, Cornell U., 1979; JD, Northwestern U., Chgo., 1982; MA in Environment & Natural Resource, George Washington U., Washington, 1987. Bar: Minn. 1982, D.C. 1983, Ill. 1989. Asst. to Army gen. counsel U.S. Army-Pentagon, Washington, 1982-86; spl. asst. to White House Counsel The White House Fellows Program, Washington, 1986-87; dep. exec. sec., domestic policy counsel, cabinent affairs The White House, Washington, 1987; dep. gen. counsel litigation and regional ops. U.S. EPA, Washington, 1987; ptnr. Jones, Day, Reavis & Pogue, Chgo., 1988-92, 93—; asst. atty. gen. U.S. Dept. Justice, 1992; exec. vice-pres., chief corp. ops., gen. counsel Ryder Systems Inc., Miami, Fla., pres. US Supply Chain Sol. Faculty mem. Army Logistics Management Inst., Ft. Lee, Va., 1982—86; guest lectr. Nat. ALI ABA progs., 1984—97; adj. prof. Union Inst., Cin., 1994—95. Author rev. Nat. Wetlands Newsletter, 1990; contbr. articles to profl. jours. Bd. dirs. Northwestern U. Alumni Assn., Chgo., 1988-90, Laidla Inc., 2003-04, Health Management Assn.; dir. Defenders of Property Rights, Zoological Soc. S.Fla.; mem. com. Chgo. Coun. Fgn. Rels, Cornell Pres. Coun. Women, Fla. Coun. Econ. Edn. Mem. Chgo. Econ. Club Chgo. (com. fgn. affairs). Office: Ryder System Inc 11690 NW 105th St Medley FL 33178-1103

**O'MEILIA, DAVID E.,** prosecutor, lawyer; b. July 1951; Grad. Okla. State U.; grad. in Law, Tulsa Coll. Atty. Tulsa County Dist. Atty.'s Office, 1980—84; asst. US. atty. US Atty.'s Office, Tulsa, Okla., 1986—96; atty. Nichols, Wolfe, Stamper, Nally, Fallis & Robertson, 1996—99; ptnr. Lyons, Clark, Danielson & O'Meilia, Tulsa, Okla., 1999—2002; US atty. (no. dist.) Okla. US Dept. Justice, 2002—. Office: US Attys Office 110 W 7th St Ste 300 Tulsa OK 74119*

**OMENN, GILBERT STANLEY,** academic administrator, internist; b. Chester, Pa., Aug. 30, 1941; s. Leonard and Leah (Miller) O.; m. Martha Darling; children: Rachel Andrea, Jason Montgomery, David Matthew. AB, Princeton U., 1961; MD, Harvard U., 1965; PhD in Genetics, U. Wash., 1972. Lic. Mass., Washington, Bd. Internal Medicine Part 1(1970), Part 2, (1972), Specialty Bd. Med. Genetics-Clin. Genetics, 1982. Intern Mass. Gen. Hosp., Boston, 1965-66; tchg. fellow in medicine Harvard U., 1966-67; rsch. assoc., Nat. Inst. Arthritis and Metabol Diseases NIH, Bethesda, Md., 1967-69; fellow, divsn. med. genetics U. Wash., 1969-71, asst. prof. medicine Seattle, 1971—74, assoc. prof. medicine, 1974—79, dir., Robert Wood Johnson Clin. Scholars Program, 1975—77, investigator Howard Hughes Med. Inst., 1976-77, prof. medicine, 1979-97, prof. environ. health, 1981—, chmn. dept. environ. health, 1981-83; dean U. Wash. Sch. Pub. Health and Cmty. Medicine, 1982-97, dean emeritus, 1997—; CEO health sys. U. Mich. Health Sys., Ann Arbor, 1997—2002; exec. v.p. med. affairs U. Mich., 1997—2002, prof. internal medicine, human genetics and pub. health, 1997—. Bd. dirs. Amgen, Rohm & Haas Co., CNAC, Population Svcs. Internat.; sci. adv. bd. 3M, Motorola, Divergence, Pac N.W. Nat. Lab.; attending staff, U. Hosp., Harborview Med. Ctr., VA Hosp, Providence Hosp., cons. staff, Children's Hosp. and Med. Ctr., Seattle, 1971-97; White House fellow/spl. asst. to chmn. AEC, 1973-74; asst. dir., 1977-78, assoc. dir., for Human Resources and Social and Economic Svcs, Office Sci. and Tech. Policy, The White House, 1977-80; assoc. dir. human resources Office Mgmt. and Budget, 1980-81; vis. sr. fellow Woodrow Wilson Sch. Pub. and Internat. Affairs, Princeton U., 1981; sci. and pub. policy fellow Brookings Instn., Washington, 1981-82; joint mem. Fed Hutchinson Cancer Rsch. Ctr., Seattle, 1983-; cons. govt. agys., Lifetime Cable Network; mem. Nat. Commn. on the Environment, Rene Dubos Ctr. for Human Environments, AFL-CIO Workplace Health Fund., Electric Power Rsch. Inst., Carnegie Commn. Task Force on Sci. and Tech. in Jud. and Regulatory Decision Making, adv. com. to dir., Ctrs. Disease Control, 1992-95, adv. com. Critical Technologies Inst., RAND; mem. Pres.'s Coun. U. Calif., 1992-97; chair, Pres. Congrl. Commn. on Risk Assessment and Risk Mgmt.; mem. Nat. Enterprise for the Environment. Co-author: Clearing the Air, Reforming the Clean Air Act, 1981. Editor: (with others) Genetics, Environment and Behavior: Implications for Educational Policy, 1972; Genetic Control of Environmental Pollutants, 1984; Genetic Variability in Responses to Chemical Exposure, 1984, Environmental Biotechnology;

Reducing Risks from Environmental Chemicals through Biotechnology, 1988, Biotechnology in Biodegradation, 1990, Biotechnology and Human Genetic Predisposition to Disease, 1990, Annual Review of Public Health, 1991-97, Clinics in Geriatric Medicine, 1992; mem. editl. bd. Jour. Protesme Research, Environ. Health Perspective; contbr. articles on cancer prevention, human biochem. genetics, prenatal diagnosis of inherited disorders, susceptibility to environ. agts., clin. medicine and health policy to profl. publs. Mem. Pres.'s Coun. on Spinal Cord Injury; mem. Nat. Cancer Adv. Bd., Nat. Heart, Lung and Blood Adv. Coun., Wash. State Gov.'s Commn. on Social and Health Svcs., Ctr. for Excellence in Govt.; chmn. awards panel Gen. Motors Cancer Rsch. Found., 1985-86; contbr. bd. Environ. Studies and Toxicology, Nat. Rsch. Coun., 1988-91; mem. Bd. Health Promotion and Disease Prevention, Inst. Medicine; mem. adv. com. Woodrow Wilson Sch., Princeton U., 1978-84; trustee Pacific Sci. Ctr., Fred Hutchinson Cancer Rsch. Ctr., Seattle Symphony Orch., Seattle Youth Symphony Orch., Seattle Chamber Music Festival, Santa Fe Chamber Music Festival, Univ. Mus. Soc., Ann Arbor, United Way Washtenaw County, 1972. Served with USPHS, 1967-69. U.S. Pub. Health Svc. Spl. Fellow, 1969-71, Nat. Genetics Found. Fellow, 1971-72, White House fellow, 1973-74; recipient Research Career Devel. award USPHS, 1972-76. Fellow ACP, AAAS (pres.-elect, pres., chmn. bd. dirs. 2006-), Hastings Ctr. Inst. Soc., Ethics and Life Sciences, Collegium Ramazzini; mem. Nat. Acad. Social Ins., Western Assn. Physicians, Inst. Medicine of NAS, White House Fellows Assn., Am. Soc. Human Genetics, Western Soc. Clin. Rsch., Assn. Am. Physicians, Am. Acad. Arts and Scis., Am. Assn. for Advancement of Humanities, Am. Occupational Medicine Assn., Phi Beta Kappa, Sigma XiAlpha Omega Alpha. Jewish. Home: 3340 E Dobson Ann Arbor MI 48105-2583 Office: Univ Mich Med Sch A510 Med Sci Res Bldg 1 1150 W Medical Center Dr Ann Arbor MI 48109-0656 E-mail: gomenn@umich.edu.

**OMER, GEORGE ELBERT, JR.,** orthopaedic surgeon, educator; b. Kansas City, Kans., Dec. 23, 1922; s. George Elbert and Edith May (Hines) O.; m. Wendie Vilven, Nov. 6, 1949; children: George Eric, Michael Lee. BA, Ft. Hays Kans. State U., 1944; MD, Kans. U., 1950; MSc in Orthopaedic Surgery, Baylor U., 1955. Diplomate Am. Bd. Orthopaedic Surgery, 1959, (bd. dirs. 1983-92, pres. 1987-88), re-cert. orthopaedics and hand surgery, 1983, cert. surgery of the hand, 1989. 2nd lt. U.S. Army, 1945; advanced through grades to col., 1967; ret. U.S. Army, 1970; rotating intern Bethany Hosp., Kansas City, 1950-51; resident in orthopaedic surgery Brooke Gen. Hosp., San Antonio, 1952-55, William Beaumont Gen. Hosp., El Paso, Tex., 1955-56; chief surgery Irwin Army Hosp., Ft. Riley, Kans., 1957-59; cons. in orthopaedic surgery 8th Army, chief orthop. surgery 121st Evacuation Hosp. Republic of Korea, 1959-60; asst. chief orthopaedic surgery, chief hand surgeon Fitzsimons Army Med. Center, Denver, 1960-63; dir. orthopaedic residency tng. Armed Forces Inst. Pathology at Walter Reed Army Med. Ctr., Washington, 1963-65; chief orthopaedic surgery and chief Army Hand Surg. Center, Brooke Army Med. Center, 1965-70; cons. in orthopaedic and hand surgery Surgeon Gen. Army, 1967-70; prof. orthopaedics, surgery, and anatomy, chmn. dept orthopaedic surgery, chief div. hand surgery U. N.Mex., 1970-90, med. dir. phys. therapy, 1972-90, acting asst. dean grad. edn. Sch. Medicine, 1980-81. Mem. active staff U. N.Mex. Hosp., Albuquerque, 1970—2005, chief of med. staff, 1984-86; cons. staff other Albuquerque hosps.; cons. orthopedic surgery USPHS, 1965-85, U.S. Army, 1970-92, USAF, 1970-78, VA, 1970-2000; cons. Carrie Tingley Hosp. for Crippled Children, 1970-99, interim med. dir., 1970-72, 86-87, mem. bd. advisor 1972-76, chair, 1994-96. Mem. bd. editors Clin. Orthopaedics, 1973-90, Jour. AMA, 1973-74, Jour. Hand Surgery, 1976-81; trustee Jour. Bone and Joint Surgery, 1990-99, sec., 1993-96, chmn., 1997-99; contbr. more than 300 articles to profl. jours., numerous chpts. to books. Decorated Legion of Merit, Army Commendation medal with oak leaf cluster; recipient Alumni Achievement award Ft. Hays State U., 1973, Recognition plaque Am. Soc. Surgery Hand, 1989, Recognition plaque N.Mex. Orthopaedic Assn., 1991, Recognition award for hand surgery Am. Osteo. Acad. Orthopaedics, 1982, Pioneer award Internat. Socs. for Surgery Hand, 1995, Rodey award U. N.Mex. Alumni Assn., 1997, Cornerstone award U. N.Mex. Health Scis. Ctr., 1997; recognized with Endowed Professorship U. N.Mex. Sch. Medicine, 1995; recognized with named Annual Orthop. Seminar and Alumni Day Brooke Army Med. Ctr., 1999. Fellow ACS, Am. Orthopaedic Assn. (pres. 1988-89, exec. dir. 1989-93), Am. Acad. Orthopaedic Surgeons, Assn. Orthopaedic Chmn., N.Mex. Orthopaedic Assn. (pres. 1979-81, 1999-2000), La. Orthopaedic Assn. (hon.), Korean Orthopaedic Assn. (hon.), Peru Orthopaedic Soc. (hon.), Caribbean Hand Soc., Am. Soc. Surgery Hand (pres. 1978-79), Am. Assn. Surgery of Trauma, Assn. Bone and Joint Surgeons, Assn. Mil. Surgeons U.S., Riordan Hand Soc. (pres. 1967-68), Sunderland Soc. (pres. 1981-83), Soc. Mil. Orthopaedic Surgeons, Brazilian Hand Soc. (hon.), S.Am. Hand Soc. (hon.), Groupe D'Etude de la Main, Brit. Hand Soc. (hon.), Venezuela Hand Soc. (hon.), South African Hand Soc. (hon.), Western Orthopaedic Assn. (pres. 1981-82), AAAS, Russell A. Hibbs Soc. (pres. 1977-78), 38th Parallel Med. Soc. (Korea) (sec. 1959-60); mem. AMA, Phi Kappa Phi, Phi Sigma, Alpha Omega Alpha, Phi Beta Pi. Achievements include pioneer work in hand surgery. Home: 316 Big Horn Ridge Rd NE Sandia Heights Albuquerque NM 87122 Office: U N Mex HSC Dept Orthop and Rehab MSC 10-5600 Albuquerque NM 87131 Office Phone: 505-856-6717. Personal E-mail: geoomer@juno.com.

**OMER, MARGARET VAUGHAN (PEGGY OMER),** retired computer technician, artist; b. Buffalo, Mar. 16, 1947; d. William Coleman and Elinor Burnett Vaughan; m. Farouk Ahmed Omer, Mar. 1, 1969; children: Sharif F., Sara Omer Kiriakos. Student, Antioch Coll., 1966—67, New Sch. Art, Toronto, 1967—69; AA Computer Sci., Monterey Peninsula Coll., Calif., 1995. MCSE plus internet. Computer coder Def. Lang. Inst., U.S. Govt., Presidio of Monterey, 1982—83, adminstrv. asst., 1984—91, computer specialist, 1991—2002; int., 2002; watercolor artist, 1982—. One-woman shows include over 80 original watercolors, Newburyport, Mass., 2005. Recipient 10 Exceptional Performance awards as Computer Specialist, NAA, 2004—. Mem.: Northshore Art Assn., Newburyport Art Assn., Jujitsu Am. (black belt 1993). Avocations: music, reading, swimming, travel. Office Phone: 978-388-0491. E-mail: peggyomer@peggyomer.com.

**OMER, ROBERT WENDELL,** hospital administrator; b. Salt Lake City, Feb. 10, 1948; s. Wayne Albert and Melva Bernice (Thunell) O.; m. Deborah Jackson, May 4, 1972;children: Melinda, Carmen, Creighton, Preston, Allison. BS in Biology, U. Utah, 1972; MHA, Washington U., St. Louis, 1975. V.p. St. Luke's Hosp., Cedar Rapids, Iowa, 1974-80; asst. administr. Franciscan Med. Ctr., Rock Island, Ill., 1980-82, Latter Day Saints Hosp., Salt Lake City, 1982-85, Clarkson Hosp., Omaha, 1985-93, v.p., COO, 1993-97; CEO Creighton St. Joseph's Clinics, Omaha, 1998-99; pres., CEO MCH Health Sys., Blair, Nebr., 1999—2001; CEO Cooper County Hosp., Boonville, Mo., 2002—03; rural health advisor U. Mo. Health Care, 2003—; CEO Pioneers Hosp., Meeker, Colo., 2003—. Bd. dirs. ARC, Heartland chpt. Omaha; bd. dirs. Nebr. Scanning Svcs. Lt. col. USAR, 1972. Fellow Am. Coll. Healthcare Execs. (regent); mem. Nebr. Hosp. Assn., Omaha C. of C. (Leadership Omaha award 1978), Omaha Healthcare Execs. Group (pres. 1989-90), Rotary (bd. dirs. 1990). Republican. Mem. Lds Ch. Avocations: jogging, history, bicycling, backpacking, racquetball. Home: PO Box 333 Meeker CO 81641

**OMHOLT, BRUCE DONALD,** product designer, mechanical engineer, consultant; b. Salem, Oreg., Mar. 27, 1943; s. Donald Carl and Violet Mae (Buck) Omholt; m. Mavis Aronow, Aug. 18, 1963 (div. July 1972); children: Madison, Natalie; m. Darla Kay Faber, Oct. 27, 1972; 1 child, Cassidy. BSME, Heald Coll. Engring., San Francisco, 1964. Real estate salesman R. Lea Ward and Assocs., San Francisco, 1962—64; sales engr. Repco Engring., Montebello, Calif., 1964; various mfg., engring. and mgmt. positions Ford Motor Co., Rawsonville, Saline, Owosso, Ypsilanti, Mich., 1964—75; chief engr. E.F. Hauserman Co., Cleve., 1975—77; dir. design and engring. Am. Seating Co., Grand Rapids, Mich., 1977—80; pres. Trinity Engring., Grand Rapids, Mich., 1980—81, Rohnert Park, Calif., 1981—. Cons. in mfg., carrier

rack apparatus, motorcycle improvements. Achievements include patents for a vertical mitre machine; a merchandise display unit; underwater breathing apparatus. E-mail: omholt@pacbell.ne.

**OMIDYAR, PIERRE M.,** Internet company executive; b. Paris, June 21, 1967; arrived in U.S., 1973; m. Pam Kerr; 2 children. BS in Computer Sci., Tufts U., 1988. With developer rels. Gen. Magic, Inc.; software developer Claris (subsidiary of Apple Computer), 1988—91; co-founder Ink Devel. Corp., 1991; founder, chmn. eBay, 1995—. Trustee Tufts U., mem. adminstrn. and finance com., mem., com. on trusteeship; trustee Santa Fe Inst. Co-founder, chair bd. dirs. Omidyar Found., 1998—; co-founder, CEO Omidyar Network; bd. dir. Meetup.com. Named one of World's Richest People, Forbes, 1999—, 50 Most Generous Philanthropists, Fortune Mag., 2005, Forbes Richest Americans, 2006; recipient Light on the Hill award (with Pam Omidyar), Tufts U. Office: eBay Inc 2125 Hamilton Ave San Jose CA 95125-5905*

**OMINSKY, ALAN JAY,** lawyer, medical educator; b. Phila., Apr. 7, 1938; s. Benjamin B. and Ida S. (Snydman) O.; m. Marlene Lachman, Nov. 1, 1992; 1 child, Sara. BA, U. Pa., Phila., 1958, MD, 1962, JD, 1988. Bar: Pa. 1989, U.S. Supreme Ct. 1994; cert. Am. Bd. Anesthesiology, Am. Bd. Psychiatry. Assoc. prof. anesthesiology U. Pa., Phila., 1972-88, assoc. prof. psychiatry, 1975-88; assoc. Bernstein Silver & Agins, Phila., 1089-96. Mem. ABA, Pa. Bar Assn., Phila. Bar Assn. (chiar medicolegal com. 1993-95, mem. sr. lawyers, state civil, and computer users coms.), Assn. Trial Lawyers Am., Pa. Trial Lawyers Assn., Phil. Trial Lawyers Assn., Am. Soc. Anesthesiologists, Am. Psychiat. Soc., Lawyers Club Phila., Phi Beta Kappa. Home: 233 S 6th St Apt 701 Philadelphia PA 19106-3751

**OMINSKY, HARRIS,** lawyer; b. Phila., Sept. 14, 1932; s. Joseph and Lillian (Herman) O.; m. Rosalyn Rita Rutenberg; children— Michelle, David. BS in Econs., U. Pa., 1953, LLB cum laude, 1956. Bar: Pa. 1956. Ptnr. Ominsky & Ominsky, Phila., 1958-64; ptnr. Blank, Rome, Comisky & McCauley, Phila., 1964—2003, Blank Rome LLP, 1964—2003; co-chmn. real estate dept. Blank, Rome, Comisky & McCauley, Phila., 1988-93. Lectr. Law Sch., Temple U., Phila., 1969-71, lectr. Real Estate Inst., 1996—. Author: Real Estate Practice: New Perspectives, 1996, Real Estate Practice: Breaking New Ground, 2001, If I'm Still Around, I Can't Be Dead, 2002, Real Estate Lore, 2006; contbr. columns to newspapers and mags.; contbr. numerous articles to profl. jours. Pres. bd. Phila. Singing City Choir, 1984-88; chmn. zoning com. Merion Civic Assn., Pa., 1984-91. Fellow Am. Bar Found.; mem. ABA (Harrison Tweed Spl. Merit award 1988, named Real Estate Lore, 2006), Pa. Bar Assn. (ho. of dels. 1984—2004), Pa. Bar Inst. (bd. dirs. 1981—, exec. com. 1986-93, v.p. 1988-89, pres. 1989-90, lectr., planner 1969—), Phila. Bar Assn. (chmn. real estate taxes subcom. 1984-85, real property sect. 1991-92, Leon J. Obermayer Edn. award 1989, Good Deed award real property sect. 1999), Am. Coll. Real Estate Lawyers (bd. govs. 1993-95), Order of Coif. Home: 526 Baird Rd Merion Station PA 19066-1302 Office: Blank Rome LLP One Logan Sq Philadelphia PA 19103-6998 Office Phone: 215-569-5668. Business E-mail: ominsky@blankrome.com.

**OMLAND, KIM MARIE,** music educator, department chairman; b. Ft. Meide, Md., Oct. 20, 1955; d. Delbert D. and Fran A. Aldinger; m. Gary Harold Omland, June 11, 1977; children: Laurie E., Patricia M., Scott C. BS in Music Edn. K-12, No. State U., Aberdeen, SD, 1977. Music tchr. Grant-Deuel H.S., Revillo, SD, 1977—81; music tchr. 7-12 band, choir Lac qui Parle Valley H.S., Madison, Minn., 1983—. Choir dir. Faith Luth. Ch., Madison, Minn., 1974—, music dir., 1977—. Lutheran. Avocations: travel, reading, directing, choreography. Home: 123 11th Ave Madison MN 56256 Office: Lac qui Parle Valley HS 2860 291st Ave Madison MN 56256 Office Fax: 320-752-4401. E-mail: komland@lqpv.org.

**OMMAYA, AYUB KHAN,** neurosurgeon, educator; b. Pakistan, Apr. 14, 1930; came to US, 1961, naturalized, 1968; s. Sultan Nadir and Ida (Counil) Khan; m. Ghalazala Nangiana, 1984; children: David, Alexander, Shana, Aisha, Iman, Sinan. MD, U. Punjab, Pakistan, 1953; MA, Oxford U., Eng., 1956; DSc (hon.), Tulane U. Diplomate Am. Bd. Neurol. Surgery. Intern Mayo Hosp., Lahore, Pakistan, 1953-54; resident in neurosurgery Radcliffe Infirmary, Oxford, Eng., 1954-61; vis. scientist NIH, Bethesda, Md., 1961-63, assoc. neurosurgeon, 1963-68, head sect. applied rsch., 1968-74, chief neurosurgery, 1974-79; clin. prof. George Washington U. Med. Sch., 1970—. Cons. VA, Armed Forces Radiobiology Rsch. Inst.; chmn. Inter-Agy. Com. for Protection Human Rsch. Subjects of Fed. Coordinating Coun. for Sci., Engring. and Tech., NAS; chmn. biomechanics adv. com. com. Nat. Hwy. Traffic Safety Adminstrn.; mem. adv. com. Nat. Ctr. Injury Control & Prevention, Atlanta; inaugural Lewin Meml. lectr. U. Cambridge, Eng., 1983; mem. adv. coun. CDC; Snively lectr. Am. Assn. Auto. Medicine, 1988; Ibn-Sina lectr. Islamic Med. Assn. N.Am. Contbr. articles to profl. jours.; inventor, patentee spinal fluid flow driven artificial organs for diabetes and degenerative diseases of the nervous system. Pres. Ctr. Integrative Neuroscience, Bethesda; v.p., dir. rsch. Cyborgan, Inc., Bethesda. Recipient J.W. Kirkdaldy prize Oxford U., 1956, Lifetime Achievement award Internat. Coll. Surgeons, 1996; recipient Sitara-I-Imtiaz for Achievements in Neurosurgery Govt. Pakistan, 1981; Hunterian prof. Royal Coll. Surgeons, 1968; Rhodes scholar, 1954-60 Fellow ACS, Third World Acad. Scis. (assoc., med. scis. com.), Royal Coll. Surgeons Eng.; mem. ASME (exec. affiliate), Soc. for Neurosci., Am. Assn. Neurol. Surgeons, Rsch. Soc. Neurosurgeons, Brit. Soc. Neurol. Surgeons, Am. Assn. Pakistani Physicians (pres.), Internat. Brain Rsch. Orgn. (life), Pan-Am. Med. Assn. Home: 8901 Burning Tree Rd Bethesda MD 20817-3007

**OMOLE, DUNCAN WAMBOGO,** information scientist, corporate communications specialist; b. Nairobi, Kenya, Mar. 18, 1973; arrived in U.S., 2003; s. Henry Omole Omero and Rosemary Akello Omole; m. Edwina Adhiambo Wambogo, Apr. 3, 1999; children: Kimberly Nyagaya, Davin Wambogo. BEd in Arts with 1st class honors, Kenyatta U., Nairobi, 1997. Info. officer Inst. French Rsch. in Africa, Nairobi, 1999—2000; project mgr. African Coun. Comm. Edn., Nairobi, 2000—01; cons. UN High Commn. for Refugees, Nairobi, 2002; info. analyst World Bank Group, Washington, 2003—. Recipient Spot award, World Bank, 2003, 2004, Recognition Cert., 2005; Ibiscus fellow, Fgn. Ministry Govt. of France, Paris, 1999. Mem.: Am. Soc. Info. Sci. and Tech. (program. chmn. 2004—05, chmn. internat. paper contest 2005—, chmn.-elect internat. info. issues 2005—). Avocations: Scrabble, badminton. Office: World Bank Group 1818 H St NW Washington DC 20433

**OMOLEWU, GABRIEL ADEBAYO,** business educator, researcher; b. Okeho, Oyo, Nigeria, Aug. 15, 1937; s. Samuel Aiyedogbon and Sarah Funmike Omolewu; m. Elizabeth Adejumoke Omolewu, Dec. 15, 1972; children: Daniel, Margaret, Sarah, Rachel, Deborah, Jacob, Samuel. BS Acctg., Wilberforce U., Wilberforce, OH, 1977; MBA, Wright State U, Dayton, Ohio, 1980; MS, Wright State U, 1981; D of Bus. Adminstrn., Internatl. Grad. Sch. U., 1986; PhD, The U of Akron, 2000. Instr. Wilberforce (Ohio) U, Wilberforce, Ohio, 1980—85, asst. prof. mgt., 1985—89, assoc. prof. of mgmt., 1989—2000, chair bus. and econ., 2000—02, assoc. prof. of mgmt., 2002—. Author: State and Local Govt. Employment in Dayton SMSA., Study of Relationship Between Print Promotion and Hiring of Minorities in Public Service Organizations, Presidency of Bishop Stokes Wilberforce U. Recipient Recognition for Tchg. Bus. Ethics, Gov. of Ohio, 1986, Nissan Fellowship award, Nissan Motors, 1991. Bapt. Avocations: real estate, Sunday school teacher, choir member, church deacon, reading. Office: Wilberforce U Walker Ctr 223 1055 N Bickett Rd PO Box 1001 Wilberforce OH 45384-1001 Office Phone: 937-708-5670.

**O'MORCHOE, CHARLES CHRISTOPHER CREAGH,** anatomist, surgeon, educator; b. Quetta, India, May 7, 1931; came to U.S., 1968; s. Nial Francis C. and Jessie Elizabeth (Joly) O.; m. Patricia Jean Richardson, Sept. 15, 1955; children: Charles Eric Creagh, David James Creagh. BA, Trinity Coll., Dublin U., Ireland, 1953, MB, BCh, BAO, 1955, MA, 1959, MD, 1961, PhD, 1969, DSc, 1981. Resident Halifax Gen. Hosp., England,

1955-57; lectr. in anatomy Sch. Medicine Trinity Coll., Dublin (Ireland) U., 1957-61, 63-65, lectr. in physiology, 1966-67, assoc. prof. in physiology, 1967-68; instr. in anatomy Harvard Med. Sch., Boston, 1962-63; vis. prof. physiology U. Md. Sch. Medicine, Balt., 1961-62, assoc. prof. anatomy, 1968-71, prof. anatomy, 1971-74; chmn. anatomy bd. State of Md., 1971-73; prof., chmn. dept. anatomy Stritch Sch. Medicine Loyola U., Maywood, Ill., 1974-84; dean Coll. Medicine, U. Ill., Urbana-Champaign, 1984-98, prof. anat. scis. and surgery, 1984-98, emeritus dean and prof., 1998—. WHO cons., vis. prof. physiology Jaipur, India, 1967, S.M.S. Med. Coll., U. Rajasthan, vis. prof. anatomy, 1971; vis. scholar U. Wash. Sch. Medicine, 2003—. Assoc. editor: Anatomical Record, 1978-98, Am. Jour. Anatomy, 1987-91, Lymphology, 2004—; contbr. articles to profl. jours. Elected fellow Trinity Coll., Dublin U., 1966; named faculty mem. of yr. Loyola U., Chgo., 1982. Mem. N.Am. Soc. Lymphology (v.p. 1982-84, pres. 1984-86, sec. 1993-98, Cecil K. Drinker award 1992), Am. Assn. Anatomy Chairmen (emeritus), Am. Assn. Anatomists (dir. placement svc. 1981-91), Internat. Soc. Lymphology (exec. com. 1987-95, pres. 1993-95, Presdl. award 2001), Alpha Omega Alpha. Mem. Church of Ireland. Home: 5645 NE Lincoln Rd East Poulsbo WA 98370-7756 Office: U Ill Coll Medicine 190 Med Sci Bldg 506 S Mathews Ave Urbana IL 61801-3618 Business E-Mail: cccom@uiuc.edu.

**OMOSHEYIN, ROTIMI,** electronics engineer, real estate company executive; b. Yaba, Labos, Nov. 4, 1960; arrived in U.S., 1982; s. Matthew and Eunice Olamita Omusheyin; m. Rochelle Smith, Oct. 27, 1990; children: Demetris, Rotimi, Dionte. BSc, Aero Space Inst., 1985; advanced cert., Harry S. Truman Coll., 1988. Lic. ins. agt. Ill.; real estate agt. Ill. Fgn. exch. specialist 1st Bank of Nigeria, Marina Lagos, 1979—82; sales cons. Century 21 Home Finder, Chgo., 1985—87; regional mgr. Al Williams and Assocs., Chgo., 1988—92; electronics specialist Marshall Field and Co., Chgo., 1986—; pres., CEO Binom Mgmt., Chgo., 1995—. Author: Monster Zunga, 1997. Amb.-in-chief Royal Amb. Bapt. Conv., Lagos, 1978. Mem.: Binom Club (pres. 1996—2000). Methodist. Achievements include invention of toddler cycle. Avocations: fishing, music, soccer, reading, travel. Home: 1455 W 115th St Chicago IL 60643 E-mail: Timiomo@yahoo.com.

**OMURA, GEORGE ADOLF,** medical oncologist; b. NYC, Apr. 30, 1938; s. Bunji K. and Martha (Pilger) O.; m. Emily Fowler, Dec. 27, 1962; children: June Ellen, Susan, Ann, George Fowler. BA magna cum laude, Columbia U., 1958; MD, Cornell U., 1962. Intern Bellevue Hosp., N.Y.C., resident, 1965-67; fellow Meml. Sloan Kettering Cancer Ctr., N.Y.C., 1967-70; asst. prof. medicine U. Ala., Birmingham, 1970-73, assoc. prof. medicine, 1973-78, prof. medicine, 1978-95, prof. emeritus, medicine, 1995—, prof. ob-gyn., 1991-95; v.p. clin. devel. BioCryst Pharms., Inc., Birmingham, 1995-99, med. dir., 1996-99; prof. emeritus, ob-gyn U. Ala., Birmingham, 1996—. Cons. Nat. Cancer Inst., 1975-97; chmn. Southeastern Cancer Study Group, 1983-87; cons. to FDA, 1994-95; cons. to pharm. industry, 2000—; prin. investigator cancer and leukemia Group B for Ala., 1986-95. Contbr. articles to profl. jours. Served with USNR, 1963-65. Am. Cancer Soc. jr. faculty clin. fellow, 1971-74. Fellow: ACP; mem.: Am. Assn. Cancer Rsch., Am. Soc. Hematology, Am. Soc. Clin. Oncology, Gynecol. Oncology Group (co-prin. investigator Ala. 1988—2003, bd. dirs. 2003—), Soc. Gynecologic Oncologists (hon.), Alpha Omega Alpha, Phi Beta Kappa. Home: 3621 Crestside Rd Birmingham AL 35223-1514 Office: University Sta Birmingham AL 35294-0001 E-mail: geoaomura@aol.com.

**ONAH, EJEMBI JOHN,** chemist, researcher; b. Aobidah, Benue, Nigeria, Apr. 4, 1963; s. Onah Isaac Ogbeh and Onyelu Oyijewu; m. Onyemowo Joy Okoh, Dec. 10, 1993; children: Owoicho-Oche children: Ihotu, Ijeyiko-woicho, Ehikowoicho. BSc in Chemistry, U. Jos, Nigeria, 1985, MSc in Applied Organic Chemistry, 1992; PhD summa cum luade, U. Tech., Dresden, Germany, 2001. Asst. lectr. Benue State U., Makurdi, Nigeria, 1993—96; vis. scientist Max Planck Inst., Golm, Germany, 1996—97; scientist/ph.d. student Inst. Polymer Rsch., U. Tech., Dresden, 1998—2001; rsch. assoc., post-doc Va. Poly. Inst. and State U., Blacksburg, 2001—02; vis. scientist Cornell U., Ithaca, NY, 2002—05; rsch. tech. dir. N.Am. Nanonige Corp., 2005—; pres., CEO Focus Nanotechnology Africa, 2005—. Vis. scientist NSF, 2002. Author: Questions and Answers in Chemistry; contbr. articles to profl. publs. Recipient USA Presdl. recognition, White Ho., 2004; scholar, KAAD, 1996; postdoctral fellow, Va. Poly. Inst. and State U., 2001. Mem.: AAAS, Am. Chem. Soc. Achievements include first to fabrication of film with the lowest dielectric constant of 1.5. Personal E-mail: eo42@cornell.edu.

**O'NAN, STEWART SMITH,** writer; b. Pitts., Feb. 4, 1961; BS, Boston U., 1983; MFA, Cornell U., 1992. Author: Snow Angels, 1994, The Names of the Dead, 1996, The Speed Queen, 1997, A Prayer for the Dying, 1999, Wish You Were Here, 2002, The Night Country, 2003, The Good Wife, 2005, (with Stephen King) Faithful: Two Diehard Boston Red Sox Fans Chronicle the Historic 2004 Season, 2004; contbr. to popular publs. Mailing: c/o David Gernert Co 136 East 57th St New York NY 10022

**ONDRASIK, JOHN,** songwriter; b. L.A. m. Carla Ondrasik; 2 children. BA in Applied Math., UCLA. Singer, pianist, guitarist, prodr. Five for Fighting, 1997—; columnist, "Hockey Rocks" Inside Hockey, 2004—. Singer, musician (albums) Message for Albert, 1997, America Town, 2000, Battle for Everything, 2004; prodr.: (soundtrack) We Were Soldiers, 2002. Nominee for Favorite Adult Contemporary, Artist, 30th Am. Music Awards.

**O'NEAL, E. STANLEY (STANLEY O'NEAL),** diversified financial services company executive; b. Roanoke, Ala., Oct. 7, 1951; m. Nancy A. Garvey; 2 children. BS, Kettering U., 1974; MBA, Harvard U., 1978. Analyst GM Corp., 1978—80, dir., 1980—82, treas. Spanish divsn. Madrid, 1982—84, asst. treas., 1984—87; dir. investment banking Merrill Lynch, 1986, mng. dir. investment banking, head global capital mkts. group, 1997, exec. v.p., co-head corp. and instl. client group, 1998, exec. v.p., CFO, 1998—2000, pres. U.S. pvt. client group, 2000—01, COO NYC, 2001—02, pres., 2001—, CEO, 2002—, chmn., 2003—. Bd. dirs. Merrill Lynch, 2001—, GM Corp., 2001—06, Financial Svcs. Roundtable. Bd. dirs. Nat. Urban League, Catalyst; trustee Ctr. Strategic & Internat. Studies, Washington DC; bd. dirs. NYC Partnership, Lower Manhattan Devel. Corp., Ronald McDonald House, NY; mem., adv. bd. The Bronx Prep. Sch.; trustee Buckley Sch.; overseer Meml. Sloan-Kettering Cancer Ctr. Recipient Corp. Exec. of the Yr., Black Enterprise, 2000, Achievement award, Exec. Leadership Coun., 2000, Most Influential Black Americans, Ebony mag., 2006. Office: Merrill Lynch 4 World Financial Ctr 250 Vesey St New York NY 10080*

**O'NEAL, EDGAR CARL,** psychology professor; b. St. Louis, Apr. 30, 1939; s. Clarence Edgar O'Neal and Alyce (Mullins) Redwine; m. Ellen Rose Luther, Aug. 31, 1963; children: Colleen Ruth, Patrick Blaine BA, Duke U., 1961; M.Div., Drew U., 1964; MA, U. Mo., 1968, PhD, 1969. Ordained to ministry United Meth. Ch., 1964. Minister Community Meth. Ch., Cold Spring Harbor, NY, 1962-65; NIMH fellow U. Mo., Columbia, 1966-69; asst. prof., assoc. prof. psychology Tulane U., New Orleans, 1969-76, chmn. dept. psychology, 1978-84, prof. psychology, 1977—99, John Madison Fletcher prof. psychology, 1999—. Editor: Perspectives on Aggression, 1976; mem. editl. bd. Jour. Personality and Social Psychology, 1991-97, Jour. Non-verbal Behaviour, 1991-94, Aggressive Behavior, 1995-2004; contbr. articles to profl. jours. Fellow APA (coun. 1982-85); mem. Sigma Xi, Sigma Chi. Democrat. Methodist. Home: 7219 O'Neil Dr Harahan LA 70123-4844 E-mail: edgar.oneal@cox.net, edgar.oneal@tulane.edu.

**O'NEAL, HANK,** theater producer, small business owner; b. Kilgore, Tex., June 5, 1940; s. Harold Lee and Sarah (Christian) O'N.; m. Shelley M. Shier, May 14, 1985. BA, Syracuse U., 1962. With CIA, Washington and N.Y.C., 1963-76; exec. v.p. Hammond Music Enterprises, N.Y.C., 1980-83; pres. owner Chiaroscuro Records Co./Downtown Sound recording studio, N.Y.C., 1970-80, 85—; exec. v.p. HOSS, Inc., N.Y.C., 1983—, Broadway Bound, Inc., 1998—. Instr. dept. head New Sch. for Social Rsch., N.Y.C., 1970-92; bd. dirs. The Jazz Found. Am., N.Y.C., The Jazz Gallery, N.Y.C.; chair bd.

govs. Jazz and Contemporary Music, New Sch. U.; pres. SOS Prodns., Wilkes Barre, Pa., 1987—. Author: Eddie Condon Scrapbook of Jazz, 1973, A Vision Shared, 1976, Berenice Abbott-American Photographer, 1982, Djuna Barnes 1978-81, 1990, Charlie Parker/The Funky Blues Date, 1995; author/photographer: The Floating Jazz Festival, 1985, The Ghosts of Harlem, 1997, Hank O'Neal, 2000, Gay Day, 2006; photographer: (books) Allegra Kent's Water Beauty Book, 1976, All the King's Men, 1990; prodr., cover photographer/designer numerous record albums, 1967—. Capt. U.S. Army, 1963-67. Recipient various awards and prizes for books. Mem. Phi Gamma Delta. Home: Glenside PO Box 101 Thornhurst PA 18424-0101 Office: Chiaroscuro Records 830 Broadway New York NY 10003-4827 Office Phone: 212-674-0265. Personal E-mail: chiarohank@aol.com.

**O'NEAL, JERMAINE,** professional basketball player; b. Columbia, S.C., Oct. 13, 1978; s. Angela Ocean. Basketball player Portland Trail Blazers, 1997—2000; forward ctr. Ind. Pacers, 2000—. Named to All-NBA Second Team, 2002—04, NBA All-Star Team, 2002—04. Achievements include youngest person to play in a NBA game, 1996. Office: Ind Pacers 125 S Pennsylvania Ave Indianapolis IN 46204*

**O'NEAL, KATHLEEN LEN,** communications executive, writer, management speaker, financial consultant; b. Ft. Riley, Kans., May 24, 1953; d. Leonard Arthur and Mary (Modlin) O'Neal. BS with honors, U. Mo., 1975; MBA, Calif. Coast U., Santa Ana, 1991. Cert. secondary teacher. Tchr. math. Killian Sr. H.S., Miami, Fla., 1975-78; mfg. supr. Western Electric Co., Lee's Summit, Mo., 1978-79, prodn. control supr., 1979-81; dept. mgr. Lee Wards Co., Independence, Mo., 1981-83; materials mgmt. specialist Northrup-Wilcox Electric, Kansas City, Mo., 1983-84; bus. resource planning mgr. AT&T, Lee's Summit, 1984-85, product mgr. Berkeley Heights, N.J., 1985-87, fin. mgr. Bedminster, N.J., 1987-89, info. sys. devel. mgr. Piscataway, N.J., 1989-90, sr. fin. mgr. Jacksonville, Fla., 1990-91, asst. treas., 1992-95, sr. procurement mgr., 1995-96, procurement system design dist. mgr., 1997-98, payroll dist. mgr., 1998—2001; pres Kathy O'Neal Speaks, Inc, 2001—; bd. mem., CFO and treas. Genesis Orlando Inc., 2003—05; treas. Parson Pub. Inc., 2004—05; CFO Avancen, LLC, 2005—. Faculty advisor to chair dept. digital game design and devel. bachelor's degree program Internat. Acad. Design and Tech., 2005—. Recipient Spec Recognition Award, United Way, 1980. Mem.: NOW, Osceola County C. of C. Avocations: reading, antique button collecting. Office: 1900 S Harbor City Blvd Ste 328 Melbourne FL 32901 Office Phone: 321-939-0982. Personal E-mail: kathyoneal@comcast.net. E-mail: kathy@mycfoforsuccess.com.

**O'NEAL, LYMAN HENRY,** biology educator; b. Princeton, Ind., Jan. 18, 1942; s. Henry and Eleanor Anne (Reibold) O'N.; m. Cynthia Sue Woods, June 13, 1964; children: Michael Lyman, Cheri Sue. BA, Oakland City U., 1963; MS, U. Minn., 1970, PhD, 1973. Secondary sch. tchr. Francisco HS, Ind., 1963-66; prof. biology Oakland City U., 1973-89, Edison Coll., Punta Gorda, Fla., 1989—. Rsch. asst. U. Minn., St. Paul, 1967-73; adj. prof. Henderson CC, Ky. 1982, Fla. So. Coll., Port Charlotte, 1989, Fla. Gulf Coast U., 1998—; bd. dirs. Ecol. Consortium Mid Am. Hancock Biol. Sta. Murray State U., 1982-89; mem. validation study panel Ind. State Dept. Edn., 1986; mem. Mote Marine Lab. Charlotte Harbor Adv. Coun., 1994—; mem. curriculum task force Fla. Gulf Coast U., 1994—. Contbr. articles to profl. jours. Mem. cmty. adv. bd. Fawcett Meml. Hosp. Mem. Am. Inst. Biol. Sci., Fla. Acad. Scis., Nat. Sci. Tchrs. Assn., Nat. Assn. Biology Tchrs. Avocations: bass guitar, painting, multimedia, canvassing. Home: 23 Amazon Dr Punta Gorda FL 33983-5208 Office: Edison Coll 26300 Airport Rd Punta Gorda FL 33950 Office Phone: 941-637-5614. Business E-mail: loneal@edison.edu.

**O'NEAL, MICHAEL RALPH,** state legislator, lawyer; b. Kansas City, Mo., Jan. 16, 1951; s. Ralph D. and Margaret E. (McEuen) O'N.; children from a previous marriage: Haley Anne, Austin Michael; m. Cindy Wulfkuhle, Apr. 9, 1999. BA in English, U. Kans., 1973, JD, 1976. Bar: Kans. 1976, U.S. Dist. Ct. Kans. 1976, U.S. Ct. Appeals (10th cir.) 1979. Intern Legis. Counsel State of Kans., Topeka, 1975-76; assoc. Hodge, Reynolds, Smith, Peirce & Forker, Hutchinson, Kans., 1976-77; ptnr. Reynolds, Peirce, Forker, Suter, O'Neal & Myers, Hutchinson, 1980-88; shareholder Gilliland & Hayes, P.A., Hutchinson, 1988—, mng. ptnr., 1999—2000; mem. Kans. Ho. of Reps., 1984, minority whip, 1991-92, majority whip, 1995-96; pres. Gilliland & Hayes, P.C., 1999-2000. Instr. Hutchinson C.C., 1977-88; mem. numerous coms. including most recently chmn. jud. com. Kans. Ho. Reps., 1997—, mem. fiscal oversight com., 1997—, tax, commerce, transp. and jud. budget com., 2003—, jud. br. budget com., 2003—, vice-chmn. ho. select com. sch. fin., 2005—. Vice chmn. Rep. Ctrl. Com., Reno County, Kans., 1982-86; bd. dirs. Reno County Mental Health Assn., Hutchinson, 1984-89, YMCA, 1984-86, Crime Stoppers (ex-officio), Hutchinson; chmn. adv. bd. dirs. Wesley Towers Retirement Cmty., 1984-96; mem. Kans. Travel and Tourism Commn., 1990-94; mem. bd. govs. U. Kans. Law Sch., 1991-94; mem. Kans. Sentencing Commn., 1997-2000, Tax Transp. Jud. Budget subcom., 2003-, Kans. Jud. Evaluation Commn., 2006—. Recipient Leadership award Kans. C. of C. and Industry, 1985; named one of Outstanding Young Men Am., 1986. Mem. ABA, Nat. Conf. State Legislatures (criminal justice com.), Kans. Assn. Def. Counsel, Def. Rsch. Inst., Kans. Bar Assn. (prospective legis. com., Outstanding Svc. award), Hutchinson C. of C. (ex-officio bd. dirs., Leadership award 1984), Am. Coun. Young Polit. Leaders (del. to Atlantic conf. biennial assembly), Kans. Jud. Coun., Commn. on Uniform State Laws. Avocations: basketball, tennis, golf. Home: 8 Windemere Ct Hutchinson KS 67502-2020 Office: Gilliland & Hayes PA 2d Flr Box 2977 20 W 2nd Ave Hutchinson KS 67504-2977 Office Phone: 620-662-0537. Business E-mail: mike@gh-hutch.com.

**O'NEAL, MIKE,** secondary school educator, state representative; b. Independence, Mo., Jan. 18, 1949; s Carl L and Mildred M. (Orth) O'Neal, m. Junnie Hoad; children: Tricia, Dennis, Katie. BS, Ctrl. Mo. State U., 1975. Tchr. Enid, Okla. Schs.; rep. Ho. of Reps. State of Okla., 1995—99, 2001—. Mem. appropriations and budget (subcom. on gen. govt. and transp.), common edn., pub, safey and homeland security, wildlife coms. Ho. of Reps., Okla., 2001—. Mem.: Enid (Okla.) C. of C. Republican. Office: 2300 N Lincoln Blvd Rm 502 Oklahoma City OK 73105 Home and Office: 1306 W Maine Enid OK 73703*

**O'NEAL, REAGAN See RIGNEY, JAMES JR.**

**O'NEAL, RODNEY,** automotive company executive; b. Dayton, OH, Aug. 27, 1953; s. James H. and Ida B. O'Neal; m. Pamela Estell O'Neal, Aug. 20, 1983; children: Heather Marie, Damien Cain. B Indsl. Adminstrn., GM Inst., 1976; MBA (Sloan fellow), Stanford U., 1991. Various engring. and mfg. pos. GM Inland Divsn., Dayton, Portugal, and Can., 1976—91; dir. indsl. engring. Chevrolet-Pontiac-GM of Can. Group, 1991—92; dir. mfg. GM Automotive Components Group Worldwide, Troy, Mich., 1992—94; gen. dir. warehousing and distbn. GM Svc. Parts Ops., 1994—97; v.p. GM, 1997—98; pres. Delphi Interior Systems, Troy, Mich., 1998—2000, exec. v.p. Safety, Thermal and Elec. Arch. sector, 2000—03; pres. dynamics, propulsion and thermal Delphi Corp., Troy, Mich., 2003—05, pres., COO, 2005—. Bd. dirs. Goodyear Tire & Rubber Co., 2004—, Delphi Corp., 2005—; mem. Exec. Leadership Coun. Recipient Svc. to HOPE. Recipient Lifetime Achievement in Industry award, Nat. Soc. Black Engineers, 2002. Office: World Hdqrs Delphi Corp 5725 Delphi Dr Troy MI 48098-2815

**O'NEAL, SHAQUILLE RASHAUN,** professional basketball player; b. Newark, N.J., Mar. 6, 1972; s. Philip A. Harrison and Lucille O'Neal; m. Shaunie Nelson, Dec. 26, 2002; children: Shareef Rashaun, Amira Sanaa, Shaquir Rashuan, Me'arah Sanaa. BS, La. State U., 2000; MBA, U. Phoenix, 2005. Center Orlando Magic, Fla., 1992—96, L.A. Lakers, 1996—2004, Miami Heat, 2004—. Mem. Dream Team II, 1994; Owner (Clothing line and Record label) TWIsM. Actor: (films) Blue Chips, 1994, Kazaam, 1996, Steel, 1997, The Wash, 2001, After the Sunset, 2004, The Year of the Yao, 2004, Scary Movie 4, 2006; performer: (albums) Shaq Diesel, 1993, Shaq Fu: Da Return, 1994, You Can't Stop the Reign, 1995, The Best of Shaquille O'Neal, 1996, Shaquille O'Neal Presents his Superfriends, Vol. 1, 2002. Named Co-MVP of NBA All-Star game, 2000, MVP of NBA All-Star game, 2004, Regular Season MVP (by media), 2000, NBA Finals MVP, 2000—02; named one of 50 Greatest Players in NBA history, 1996; named to All-Am. 1st team, Sporting News, 1990—91, NBA All-Star team, 1993—98, 2000—02, 2004—05, All-NBA 1st team, 1998, 2000—02, 2006, All-NBA 2nd team, 1995, 1999; recipient Rookie of Yr. award, NBA, 1993, Gold Medal, U.S. Olympic Team (Atlanta), 1996. Achievements include being first pick overall in draft, 1992, mem. of 3 consecutive championship teams, 2000-2002, NBA Scoring Champion, 1995, 2000; signed a five-year contract which gives Li Ning the right to produce and market a "Li Ning Shaq" line of professional basketball shoes and apparel only in China, 2006. Office: c/o Miami Heat American Airlines Arena 601 Biscayne Blvd Miami FL 33132*

**O'NEAL, STEPHEN V.,** lawyer; b. Bloomington, Ill., Mar. 23, 1953; AB, UCLA, 1975; JD, U. Calif. Boalt Hall Sch. Law, 1980. Bar: Calif. 1980, US Dist. Ct. (No. Dist.) Calif., US Dist. Ct. (Ea. Dist.) Calif. Ptnr., Construction & Govt. Contracts Practice Group Thelen Reid & Priest LLP, San Francisco, chmn. of firm, mem. exec. com. & partnership coun.; mng. ptnr. Mason Thelen Reid LLP. Assoc. editor Calif. Law Rev., 1979—80. Mem.: Calif. Bar Assn. (Real Property Law Sect.), Am Arbitration Assn., Bar Assn. San Francisco, ABA (Litig. Sect., Construction Industry Forum Com.). Office: Thelen Reid & Priest LLP 101 Second St Ste 1800 San Francisco CA 94105-3601 Office Phone: 415-369-7222. Office Fax: 415-371-1211. Business E-Mail: svoneal@thelenreid.com.

**O'NEAL, TATUM,** actress; b. Nov. 5, 1963; d. Ryan and Joanna (Moore) O'N.; m. John McEnroe, Aug. 1, 1986 (div. 1994); 3 children: Kevin, Sean, Emily. Student, pvt. schs. and tutors. Appearances include (films) Paper Moon, 1973 (Acad. award for best supporting actress), The Bad News Bears, 1976, Nickelodeon, 1976, International Velvet, 1978, Little Darlings, 1979, Circle of Two, 1981, Certain Fury, 1985, Prisioners, 1981, Certain Fury, 1985, Little Noises, 1992, Basquiat, 1996, The Scoundrel's Wife, 2002, The Technical Writer, 2003; (TV movies) 15 and Getting Straight, 1989, Woman on the Run: The Lawrencia Bambenek Story, 1993 (documentary) Award Show Awards Show, 2003; TV guest appearances include: Sex and the City, 2003, Celebrities Uncensored, 2003, 8 Simple Rules...for Dating My Teenage Daughter, 2004, Law & Order Criminal Intent, 2004, Rescue Me 2006-; performer, Dancing with the Stars, 2006; author: (book) A Paper Life: My Story, 2004.*

**O'NEAL-SERALATHAN, CRESCENTIA,** advocate; d. Andrew and Mary Patricia O'Neal; m. Muthiah Seralathan, Aug. 18, 1984; children: Ashanthi Meena Seralathan, Chithra Andasi Seralathan. JD, CWRU, Cleve., 1983. Sr. rschr. Roosevelt Ctr. Am. Policy Studies, Ill. Sch. Reform Project, Chgo., 1984; allocations mgr. United Way of Buffalo and Erie County, 1985—86; we. regional dir. N.Y. Civil Liberties Union, Buffalo, 1986—90; internat. fundraising and program devel. cons. Meendasi, Potomac, Md., 1990—. Planning com. U.N. 1985 Internat. Youth Yr., Washington, 1981—85; mem. task force women's issues N.Y. State Assembly, Albany, 1984—91; adv. bd. Erie County Task Force on Women, Buffalo, 1986—91, N.Y. State Divsn. of Human Rights, Buffalo, 1987—90, Erie County Task Force on Homeless, Buffalo, 1987—91; founder, chmn. We. N.Y. Coalition Against the Death Penalty, Buffalo, 1989—91; del. UN Internat. Conf. on Population and Devel., Cairo, 1994; planning com. UN 4th Internat. Conf. on Women, N.Y.C., 1994—95; del. UN 4th Internat. Conf. On Women, Beijing, China, 1995; fed. grant reviewer LCG, Washington, 2002—; e-commerce exec. Distinctly Yours, Potomac, Md., 2005—. Bd. dirs. Nat. Student Christian Leadership Consultation, Atlanta, 1981—85. Recipient Vol. Clearinghouse Vol. Activist award, Govt. of D.C., 1983, Congl. Cert. of Appreciation, U.S. Congress, Ho. Spkr. Thomas P. O'Neal, 1981, Cmty. Leader award, SCLC, 1989; L.B.J. Internship fellow, Congressman Walter E. Fauntroy, 1980. Mem.: UN Assn. (bd. dirs., resource and devel. com. chair 1994—2001). Avocations: jazz, reading, politics, movies, travel.

**O'NEIL, CAROLYN,** cable network executive, cable television host; BS in Nutrition and Dietetics cum laude, Fla. State U., MS in Nutrition cum laude. Registered dietitian. Registered dietitian outpatient edn. Peter Bent Bringham Hosp., Boston; consumer reporter Warner Cable TV, Boston; consumer reporter, news anchor WTVX-TV (CBS), West Palm Beach, Fla.; host On The Menu program CNN, Atlanta, 1982—, exec. prodr., sr. corr. food & health unit, 1982—. Recipient Journalistic Excellence awards Am. Heart Assn., James Beard awards, 1995, Outstanding Achievement in Broadcast Journalism award Am. Women in Radio and TV. Mem. Am. Dietetic Assn.

**O'NEIL, HAROLD FRANCIS,** psychologist, educator; b. Columbia, SC, Jan. 26, 1943; s. Harold Francis Sr. and Margaret Mary (Ryan) O'Neil; m. Eva L. Baker, Sept. 15, 1984; children: Tristan, Christopher. PhD, Fla. State U., 1969; MS, Hollins Coll., 1970. Asst., assoc. prof. U. Tex., Austin, 1971-75; program mgr. Def. Advanced Rsch. Projects Agy., Arlington Va 1975-78; from team chief in dir. Tng. Rsch. Lab. Army Rsch. Inst., Alexandria, Va., 1978-85; prof. U. So. Calif., L.A., 1985—. Cons. Army Rsch., 1985—, Inst. Def. Analyses, Alexandria, 1985—, Amry Sci. Bd., Washington, 1994—2001, Def. Sci. Bd. Task Force on Tng., Washington, 1999—2002. Editor: (book) Academic Press Education and Technology Series, 1977—92; editl. adviser Lawrence Erlbaum Assocs., Inc., Pubs., 1992—; contbr. chapters to books, articles to profl. jours.; founding editor Japanese Jour. Edn. Fellow: APA, Am. Psychol. Soc. Achievements include research in role of cognition and affect in computer-based instruction, role of motivation in testing, cross-cultural rsch. in Japan on the role of test anxiety and performance; Taiwan and Korea on the role of self-regulation anc achievement, games for tng; development of measures for metacognition, effort, and anxiety. Office: Univ So Calif 600 Wph University Park Los Angeles CA 90089-0001 Business E-Mail: honeil@usc.edu.

**O'NEIL, J. PETER (JAMES PETER O'NEIL),** elementary school educator, computer scientist; b. Rockville Center, N.Y., Apr. 2, 1946; s. Clement Lee and Frances Rita (Theis) O'N.; m. Carol Ann Sypniewski, June 8, 1968; children: Kelly Ann, Thomas Joseph. BA in Psychology, Loyola U., Chgo., 1968; MA in Sci. Edn., Webster Coll., St. Louis, 1972. Cert. elem. tchr. K-8, Mo., elem. tchr. K-8, Wis., dir. instruction, Wis. Tchr., student tchr. Sacred Heart Sch., Florissant, Mo., 1968-73; tchr. sci. Waunakee (Wis.) Mid. Sch., 1973-96, elem. tchr. K-8 sci. dept., chmn. K-12 dept., 1984-92; learning coord. Deforest (Wis.) Area Sch. Dist., 1992—2000. Dir. Waunakee Summer Sci. Program, 1975-91; dir. instrn./tech. Brodhead Wis., 1996-99; designer sci. curriculum computer CD-ROM programs Sci. Curriculum Assistance Program and Elem. Sci. Curriculum Assistance Program, 1990—; dir. instrn. DeForest (Wis.) Area Sch. Dist., 2000—; adj. prof. Viterbo U., 2003—; rsch. cons. IDEAS Wis., 2002—. Feature editor: Science Scope, 1989-96; contbr. over 30 activities and articles to profl. jours. Group worker settlement houses Chgo., St. Louis; mem. Parish Coun.; dir. Waunakee Area Edn. Found. Named Master Tchr. NSF, Waunakee, 1986-96; recipient Tchr. of Yr. award Waunakee, 1984, 90, 92, Kohl Found. award, 1992, Mid. Sch. Tchr. of Yr. award Wis., 1992-93. Mem.: Wis. Soc. Curriculum Designers, Am. Soc. Curriculum Designers. Roman Catholic. Avocations: computers, sports, writing, jogging. Home: 119 Simon Crestway Waunakee WI 53597-1721 Office: Deforest Area Sch Dist 520 E Holum St De Forest WI 53532-1316 Office Phone: 608-842-6531. E-mail: jponeil@deforest.k12.wi.us.

**O'NEIL, JOHN JOSEPH,** lawyer; b. Detroit, July 20, 1943; s. John J. and Dora J. (Collins) O'N.; children: Meghan, Kathryn. BA, Trinity Coll., 1965; LLB, U. Va., 1968. Bar: N.Y. 1969, U.S. Ct. Appeals (2d cir.) 1969, Fla. 1979, D.C. 1982. Assoc. Jackson & Nash, N.Y.C., 1968-71, Paul, Weiss, Rifkind, Wharton & Garrison, N.Y.C., 1971-77, ptnr., 1977—. Fellow Am. Coll. Trusts and Estates Counsel; mem. ABA (com. on spl. problems of aged), N.Y. State Bar Assn. (com. on taxation, trusts and estates sect.), Assn. Bar City N.Y. (com. on trusts and estates), Pi Gamma Mu. Office: Paul Weiss Rifkind Wharton & Garrison Ste 3221 1285 Avenue Of The Americas Fl 21 New York NY 10019-6064 Fax: 212-373-3379. E-mail: joneil@paulweiss.com.

**O'NEIL, MAUREEN,** think-tank executive; BA in Sociology, Carleton U., LLD (hon.), Wilfrid Laurier U. Pres. Internat. Devel. Rsch. Ctr., Ottawa, Ont., Canada, 1997—; interim pres. Internat. Ctr. for Human Rights and Dem. Devel.; pres. North-South Inst.; dep. min. citizenship Govt. Ont. Fellow Sch. Policy Studies Queen's U.; mem. internat. bd. govs. Ctr. for Internat. Governance Innovation; bd. dirs. Internat. Inst. for Democracy and Electoral Assistance; mem. Markle Found. Global Digital Opportunity Initiative. Chair bd. govs. Carleton U.; co-chair digital divide supervisory com. World Econ. Forum; mem. adv. bd. Min. Fgn. Affairs; chair Internat. Ctr. for Human Rights and Dem. Devel., Can. Found. for the Ams.; bd. mem. Inst. for Women, Law and Devel. Office: Internat Devel Rsch Ctr 250 Albert St PO Box 8500 Ottawa ON Canada K1G 3H9

**O'NEIL, MICHAEL C.,** lawyer; b. Pitts., Pa., Nov. 21, 1961; BA with high honors, Bklyn. Coll., 1986, JD with honors, DePaul Univ., 1989. Bar: Ill. 1989. Ptnr., chmn. Privacy Litigation practice group DLA Piper Rudnick Gray Cary, Chgo. Editor (articles & notes): DePaul Law Rev., 1988—89. Office: DLA Piper Rudnick Gray Cary Suite 1900 203 N LaSalle St Chicago IL 60601-1293 Office Phone: 312-368-4098. Office Fax: 312-236-7516. Business E-Mail: michael.oneil@dlapiper.com.

**O'NEIL, ROBYN,** artist; b. Omaha, 1977; Attended, Kings Coll., London, 1997; BFA, Tex. A & M- Commerce, 2000; attended, U. Ill., 2000—01. One-woman shows include These Are Pictures of Boats & Dinosaurs, Angstrom Gallery, Dallas, 2002, Even If It Shall Break Them: Prelude to a Solid Hope for Something Better, Clementine Gallery, NY, 2003, New Works, ArtPace, San Antonio, 2003, Bodybuilder & Sportsman, Chgo., 2004, Clementine Gallery, NY, 2005, exhibited in group shows at Bad Touch, Ukranian Inst. Modern Art, Chgo., 2002, Drawn II, Barry Whistler Gallery, Dallas, 2002, Summer Drawings, Mixture Gallery, Dallas, 2002, Super Nature, Inman Gallery, Houston, 2002, The Co. We Keep, 2003, Come Forward, Dallas Mus. Art, 2003, Am. Dream, Ronald Feldman Fine Arts, NY, 2003, Whim?, Angstrom Gallery, Dallas, 2003, Young Americans, Galerie Hof & Huyser, Amsterdam, The Netherlands, 2004, The Drawn Page, Aldrich Mus. Contemporary Art, Ridgefield, Conn., 2004, It's a Wonderful Life: Psychodrama in Contemporary Painting, Spaces, Cleve., 2004, Whitney Biennial, Whitney Mus. Am. Art, 2004. Artadia Grant, Fund Art & Dialogue, NY, 2003, Tex. Internat. Artist in Residence, ArtPace Found Contemporary Art, San Antonio, 2003. Mailing: c/o Whitney Museum American Art 945 Madison Ave at 75th St New York NY 10021

**O'NEIL, THOMAS,** dentist; b. Queens, NY; m. Chris O'Neil; 2 children. DDS, Columbia U., 1972; grad., Las Vegas Inst. Advanced Dental Studies. Resident Peninsula Hosp., Far Rockaway, NY, 1972—73; cosmetic dentist Tamarac, Fla., 1988—. Mem.: Broward County Dental Assn., Fla. Dental Assn., Fla. Acad. Cosmetic Dentistry, Internat. Assn. Oral Medicine & Toxicology, Am. Dental Assn., Dental Orgn. for Conscious Sedation, Am. Acad. Cosmetic Dentistry. Avocation: boating. Office: Ste 201 7707 N University Dr Tamarac FL 33321 Office Phone: 954-720-9570.

**O'NEIL, THOMAS FRANCIS, III,** lawyer; b. Fairfield, Conn., Apr. 8, 1957; s. Thomas F. Jr. and Carmen A. (Therrien) O'N.; m. Nancy D., Aug. 14, 1982; children: Caley Elizabeth, Patrick McGee. AB magna cum laude, Dartmouth Coll., 1979-79; JD, Georgetown U., 1979-82. Bar: Md. 1982, U.S. Dist. Ct. Md. 1983, U.S. Ct. Appeals (4th cir.) 1983, D.C. 1992, NY. Legis. asst. Congressman Stewart B. McKinney, Washington, 1980-82; law clk. Hon. Alexander Harvey II U.S. Dist. Ct. Md.; assoc. Venable, Baetjer & Howard, Balt., 1984-86; asst. U.S. atty. U.S. Dept. Justice, Balt., 1986-89; assoc. Hogan & Hartson, Balt., 1990-91, ptnr., 1992-95; chief litig. counsel MCI Comms. Corp., Washington, 1995-98; sr. v.p., chief legal counsel MCI, 1999—2001; sr. v.p., gen. counsel MCI Group, 2001—02; sr. ptnr. Piper Rudnick LLP, 2002—04; joint global leader legis. and regulatory group, chmn. govt. affairs practice group, chmn. govt. controversies practice group DLA Piper, Washington, 2005—. Bd. regents mem. Georgetown Univ., 2005—; mem., bd. visitors Georgetown Univ. Law Ctr., 1999—; mem. adv. bd. Georgetown Corp. Counsel Inst.; bd. govs. Fed. Bar Assn., Balt., 1992; ex officio trustee Walters Art Mus., 1995—96, trustee, 1997—2002; mem. adv. bd. Marbury Inst., 2000—02; pres. bd. trustees The Contemporary Mus., Balt., 2005. Contbr. articles to profl. jours. Recipient Chief Postal Insps. Spl. award U.S. Postal Svc., Washington, 1988, Letter of Commendation award Bur. of Investigation, Washington, 1989, Spl. Achievement award U.S. Dept. Justice, 1989. Mem. Internat. Bar Assn., Serjeants Inn Law Club. Republican. Roman Catholic. Office: DLA Piper 1200 19th St NW Washington DC 20036-2412 Office Phone: 202-861-6685. Office Fax: 202-223-2085. Business E-Mail: thomas.oneil@dlapiper.com.

**O'NEIL, THOMAS MICHAEL,** physicist, researcher; b. Hibbing, Minn., Sept. 2, 1940; married; 1 child. BS, Calif. State U., Long Beach, 1962; MS, U. Calif., San Diego, 1964, PhD in Physics, 1965. Rsch. physicist Gen. Atomic, 1965-67; prof physicis U. Calif., San Diego, 1967—. Mem. adv. bd. Inst. Fusion Studies, 1980-83, Inst. Theoretical Physics, 1983-86; mem. plasma sci. com. NRC, 1998—, chmn., 2001—, mem. bd. on physics and astronomy, 2001—. Assoc. editor Physics Review Letters, 1979-83; correspondent Comments Plasma Physics & Controlled Fusion, 1980-84. Alfred P. Sloan fellow, 1971; recipient Disting. Alumnus award Sch. Natural Sci. CSULB, 1985, Alumni Disting. Tchg. award UCSD, 1996. Fellow Am. Phys. Soc. (award for excellence in plasma physics 1991, James Clerk Maxwell prize 1996). Achievements include research in theoretical plasma physics with emphasis on nonlinear effects in plasmas and on non-neutral plasmas. Office: Dept Physics 9500 Gilman Dr La Jolla CA 92093-5003 E-mail: toneil@ucsd.edu.

**O'NEIL, WAYNE,** linguist, educator; b. Kenosha, Wis., Dec. 22, 1931; s. L.J. and Kathryn (Obermeyer) O'N.; married; children: Scott Leslie, Patrick Sean, Elizabeth Erla. AB, U. Wis., 1955, AM, 1956, PhD, 1960; AM (hon.), Harvard U., 1965. Asst. prof. linguistics and lit. U. Oreg., 1961-65; prof. linguistics and edn. Harvard U., 1965-68, lectr. edn., 1968-72, vis. prof. edn., 1978-86; prof. linguistics MIT, 1968—, chmn. lit. faculty, 1969-75, chmn. linguistics program, 1986-97, head dept. linguistics and philosophy, 1989-97. Lectr. human devel. Wheelock Coll., Boston, 1991—; lectr. Beijing Normal U., 1980, Beijing and Shanghai Fgn. Lang. Insts., 1981; lectr. linguistics Shandong (China) U., 1982-83; prof., 1984—; prof. Summer Inst. on Lang. Change, NEH, 1978; vis. prof. Tsuda Coll., Tokyo, 1983, Kanda U. Internat. Studies, Makuhari, Japan, 1997, Am. Indian Lang. Devel. Inst., 2000—, Kanazawa Inst. of Tech., Japan, 2001—; co-dir. MIT-Japan Sci. and Tech. mind articulation project, 1996—. Author: (in Chinese) English Transformational Grammar, 1981, Linguistics and Applied Linguistics, 1983, (with S.J. Keyser) Rule Generalization and Optionality in Language Change, 1985, (with S. Flynn) Linguistic Theory in Second Language Acquisition, 1988, (with S. Flynn and G. Martohardjono) The Generative Study of Second Language Acquisition, 1998, (with A. Marantz and Y. Miyashita) Image, Language, Brain, 2000, (with M. Honda) Understanding First and Second Language Acquisition, 2004; mem. editl. group Radical Tchr., 1975—. Mem. steering com. Resist, 1967—, Peoples Coalition for Peace and Justice, 1970-72; co-founder, mem. Linguistics for Nicaragua, 1985—. With U.S. Army, 1952-54. Fulbright fellow in Iceland, 1961; Am. Council Learned Socs. study fellow M.I.T., 1964-65; George Watson fellow U. Queensland, Brisbane, Australia, 1998. Mem. AAAS, Linguistic Soc. Am., Nat. Coun.

Tchrs. English, Am. Assn. Applied Linguistics, Assembly for the Tchg. English Grammar. Office: MIT Dept Linguistics and Philosophy Cambridge MA 02139-4307 Business E-Mail: waoneil@mit.edu.

**O'NEIL, WILLIAM FRANCIS,** academic administrator; b. Worcester, Mass., Mar. 26, 1936; s. John J. and Mary A. (Trahant) O'N.; m. Mary Elizabeth Dillon, Aug. 22, 1959; children: Kathleen, Mary Elizabeth. BS, Boston U., 1960; MEd, Worcester State Coll., 1963; diploma, U. Conn., 1970; EdD, Wayne State U., 1972; PhD in Pub. Edn. (hon.), Bridgewater State Coll., 2002; BFA (hon.), Montserrat Coll. Art, 1994. Tchr. Worcester Pub. Schs., 1960—68, cmty. sch. dir., 1968—73; assoc. prof., dir. community edn. devel. ctr. Worcester State Coll., 1973-75, dir. community svc., 1975—77, dean grad. and continuing edn., 1977—83, exec. v.p., 1983—85, Mass. Coll. Art, Boston, 1985—86, acting pres., 1986—87, pres., 1987—96; exec. officer Mass. State Coll. Coun. Pres., 1996—2002. Contbr. articles to profl. jours. Mem. Worcester Dem. City Com., Ward I Dem. Com., 1980-2005; pres., trustee Worcester Pub. Libr., 1977-82; mem. Mass. Bd. Libr. Commrs., 1984-89; bd. dirs. Worcester State Coll. Found., 2001—. Recipient Outstanding Alumni award field of edn. Worcester State Coll., 1996, citation Mass. Ho. of Reps., 1977, key City of Worcester, 1982; Mott fellow Charles Stewart Mott Found., 1971; Godine Cmty. Svc. medal, Mass. Coll. Art, 2002. Mem. Mass. Pub. Colls. and Univs. Pres. and Chancellors Assn. (chair 1991-92), Assn. Ind. Colls. Art and Design (bd. dirs. 1988-96), Mass. Cmty. Edn. Assn. (life; bd. dirs. 1972-77), Mass. State Colls. Pres. Assn. (chair 1992-93), Profl. Arts Consortium (v.p. Boston 1986-96, pres. 1993-94). Roman Catholic. Home: 47 Harvest Cir Holden MA 01520-3401 Business E-Mail: woneil@worcester.edu.

**O'NEIL, WILLIAM SCOTT,** publishing executive; V.p., portfolio mgr. William O'Neil Inc., L.A., 1992—. Office: Investors Bus Daily 12655 Beatrice St Los Angeles CA 90066-7303

**O'NEILL, ALBERT CLARENCE, JR.,** lawyer; b. Gainesville, Fla., Nov. 25, 1939; s. Albert Clarence and Sue Virginia (Henry) O'N.; m. Vanda Marie Nigels, Apr. 26, 1969; 1 child, Heather Marie. BA with high honors, U. Fla., 1962; LL.B. magna cum laude, Harvard U., 1965. Bar: Fla. 1965. Law clk. to judge U.S. Dist. Ct. (mid. dist.) Fla., Jacksonville, 1965-66; assoc. Fowler, White, Collins, Gillen, Humkey & Trenam, Tampa, Fla., 1966-69; ptnr. Trenam, Simmons, Kemker, Scharf & Barkin, Tampa, 1970-77; mem. firm Trenam, Kemker, Scharf, Barkin, Frye, O'Neill & Mullis (P.A.), Tampa, 1977—, also bd. dirs. Vis. lectr. law Stetson Law Sch., 1970-73; mem. adv. coun. IRS, 2001-03. Exec. editor Harvard Law Rev., 1964-65; contbr. articles to profl. jours. Mem. Fla. Gulf Coast Symphony, Inc., 1975-86, U. Fla. Found., Inc., 1976-84, 97-2001, 03-, Fla. Found., 2002-2005, Gator Boosters, Inc., 2002—. Mem. ABA (chmn. tax sect. 1992-93), Am. Law Inst., Am. Coll. Tax Counsel, Fla. Bar (chmn. tax sect. 1975-76), Am. Bar Retirement Assn. (pres. 2000-01, bd. dirs. 1995-04), Phi Beta Kappa. Office: Trenam Kemker Scharf Barkin Frye O'Neill & Mullis 101 E Kennedy Blvd Ste 2700 Tampa FL 33602-5150 Office Phone: 813-227-7437. Business E-Mail: aconeill@trenam.com.

**O'NEILL, BEVERLY LEWIS,** mayor, former college president; b. Long Beach, Calif., Sept. 8, 1930; d. Clarence John and Flossie Rachel (Nicholson) Lewis; m. William F. O'Neill, Dec. 21, 1952 LA, Long Beach City Coll., 1950; BA, Calif. State U., Long Beach, 1952, MA, 1956; EdD, U. So. Calif., 1977. Elem. tchr. Long Beach Unified Sch. Dist., 1952-57; instr., counsellor Compton (Calif.) Coll., 1957-60; curriculum supr. Little Lake Sch. Dist., Santa Fe Springs, Calif., 1960-62; women's advisor, campus dean Long Beach City Coll., 1962-71, dir. Continuing Edn. Ctr. for Women, 1969-75, dean student affairs, 1971-77, v.p. student svcs., 1977-88, supt.-pres., 1988—93, exec. dir. LBCC, 1983—; mayor City of Long Beach, Calif., 1994—. Advisor Jr. League, Long Beach, 1976—, Nat. Coun. on Alcoholism, Long Beach, 1979—, Assistance League, Long Beach, 1982—; bd. dirs. NCCJ, Long Beach, 1976—, Meml. Hosp. Found., Long Beach, 1984-92, Met. YMCA, Long Beach, 1986-92, United Way, Long Beach, 1986-92. Named Woman of Yr., Long Beach Human Rels. Commn., 1976, to Hall of Fame, Long Beach City Coll., 1977, Disting. Alumni of Yr., Calif. State U., Long Beach, 1985, Long Beach Woman of Yr. Rick Rackers, 1987, Assistance League Aux., 1987, Woman of Yr., Calif. Legislature 54th Dist., 1995; recipient Hannah Solomon award Nat. Coun. Jewish Women, 1984, Outstanding Colleague award Long Beach City Coll., 1985, NCCJ Humanitarian award, 1991, Woman of Excellence award YWCA, 1990, Community Svc. award Community Svcs. Devel. Corp., 1991, Citizen of Yr. award Exch. Club, 1992, Pacific Regional CEO award Assn. Community Coll. Trustees, 1992, EDDY award, 1999, Long Beach Excellence in Leadership, 1999. Mem. Assn. Calif. Community Coll. Administrs. (pres. 1988-90, Harry Buttimer award 1991), Calif. Community Colls. Chief Exec. Officers Assn., Rotary, Soroptimists (Women Helping Women award 1981, Hall of Fame award 1984), U.S. Conf. Mayors (trustee, 2001-), League Calif. Cities (pres. 2002-). Democrat. Office: Mayor Civic Ctr Plz 333 W Ocean Blvd Fl 14 Long Beach CA 90802-4604*

**O'NEILL, BRIAN,** science administrator; b. Bristol, Eng., Sept. 20, 1940; s. Raymond and Phyllis Mary (Marshall) O'N.; m. Alayne O'Neill, Aug. 31, 1969 (div. Sept. 1987); children: Allison Sarah, Stuart Douglas, Lesley Alexandra; m. Karen O'Neill, Feb. 20, 1988. BSc in Math. and Stats., Bath. U. Tech., 1965. Asscs. in stats. and ops. research Unilever Ltd., London, 1965-66; research assoc. Tech. Ops. Inc., Ft. Belvoir, Va., 1966-67; mgr. applied math. dept. Wolf Research & Devel. Corp., Riverdale, Md., 1967-69; v.p., sr. v.p., exec. v.p. Ins. Inst. for Hwy. Safety, Washington, 1969-85, pres., 1985—; v.p., sr. v.p., exec. v.p. Hwy. Loss Data Inst., Washington, 1969-85, pres., 1985—. Witness at numerous fed. and state hearings on hwy. safety and transp. Contbr. numerous articles to profl. jours.; also presentations at profl. confs. Mem. Am. Pub. Health Internat. Com. on Alcohol Drugs and Traffic Safety, Royal Statis. Soc., Soc. Automotive Engrs. Office: Ins Inst for Hwy Safety 1005 N Glebe Rd Ste 800 Arlington VA 22201-5759 Office Phone: 703-247-1500. Business E-Mail: boneill@iihs.org.

**O'NEILL, BRIAN,** national recreation area administrator; b. Washington, 1942; s. John and Virginia O'Neill; m. Marti Hendricks; 2 children. Student, U. Md., 1964. Joined Bur. Outdoor Recreation, Dept. Interior, 1965, mgr. Heritage Conservation and Recreation Svc. Albuquerque, 1973—81, San Francisco, 1973—81; asst. supt. Golden Gate Nat. Recreation Area, San Francisco, 1981—86, supt., 1986—; acting assoc. dir. Nat. Pk. Svc. Bd. mem. San Francisco Planning and Urban Rsch. Assn.; instr. Dale Carnegie & Assocs., 1975—77. Recipient Exec. Leadership award, Dept. of the Interior, 2004. Avocations: gardening, glasswork, sailboarding, body surfing, hiking. Office: Golden Gate Nat Rec Area Fort Mason Bldg 201 San Francisco CA 94123

**O'NEILL, BRIAN BORU,** lawyer; b. Hancock, Mich., June 7, 1947; s. Brian Boru and Jean Anette (Rimpela) O'N.; m. Ruth Bohan, Sept. 18, 1991; children: Dru Groves, Brian Boru, Maggie Byrne, Phelan Boru, Ariel Margaret. BS, U.S. Mil. Acad., 1969; JD magna cum laude, U. Mich., 1974; D in Pub. Svc. (hon.), Northland Coll., 1999. Bar: Mich. 1974, U.S. Dist. Ct. Minn. 1977, U.S. Ct. Mil. Appeals 1975, U.S. Ct. Appeals (6th cir.) 1975, U.S. Ct. Appeals (8th cir.) 1977, U.S. Ct. Appeals (Fed. cir.) 1983, U.S. Ct. Appeals (7th cir.) 1985, U.S. Ct. Appeals (10th cir.) 1986, U.S. Ct. Appeals (9th cir.) 1990, U.S. Ct. Appeals (D.C. cir.) 2005, U.S. Ct. Claims 1981, U.S. Supreme Ct. 1981. Asst. to gen. counsel Dept. Army, Washington, 1974-77; assoc., ptnr. Faegre & Benson, Mpls., 1977—. Mem. com. vis. Mich. Law Sch., 1994—; counsel Defenders of Wildlife, Washington, 1977—, also bd. dirs; counsel Sierra Club, Audubon Soc. Mng. editor: Mich. Law Rev., 1973—74. Advocate Am. Bd. Trial Advocates, 2004—; Capt. U.S. Army, 1969—77. Decorated Meritorious Svc. medal; named Environmentalist of Yr. Sierra Club North Star, 1982, 96, 97, 98; recipient William Douglas award Sierra Club, 1985, Trial Lawyer of Yr. award Trial Lawyers for Pub. Justice, 1995. Fellow Am. Coll. Trial Lawyers (regent 2003—), Internat. Acad. Trial Lawyers, Order of the Coif; mem. Am. Bd. Trial Advs. (adv. 2005—), Mpls.

---

Golf Club, Mpls. Athletic Club (pres.) Office: Faegre & Benson 2200 Wells Fargo Tower 90 S 7th St Ste 2200 Minneapolis MN 55402-3901 Office Phone: 612-766-8318. E-mail: boneill@faegre.com.

**O'NEILL, BRIAN DENNIS,** lawyer; b. Phila., Feb. 21, 1946; s. Harry William and Margaret Elizabeth (Miller) O'N.; m. Bonnie Anne Ryan, Aug. 17, 1968; children: Aimee Kathleen Fulchino, Catherine Margaret O'Sullivan. BA, Fla. State U., 1968, JD, 1971. Bar: Fla. 1971, D.C. 1975, U.S. Ct. Appeals (D.C. cir.) 1978, U.S. Ct. Appeals (5th and 11th cirs.) 1981, U.S. Ct. Appeals (10th cir.) 1985, U.S. Supreme Ct. 2003. Trial atty. Fed. Power Commn., Washington, 1972-75; assoc. Farmer, Shibley, McGuinn & Flood, Washington, 1975-80; mng. ptnr. DC office LeBoeuf, Lamb, Greene & MacRae LLP, Washington, 1980—, chmn. energy/utilities dept., co-chmn. Natural Gas Practice Group. Lectr. in field. Editorial bd. Energy Law Jour., Washington, 1983-84; contbr. articles to profl. jours. Bd. dirs. Immaculata Coll., Rockville, Md., 1989-91; bd. trustees Acad. of Holy Cross, Kensington, Md., 1994—; bd. visitors Fla. State U. Coll. of Law, 1994—. 2d lt. USAF, 1971-72. Mem.: ABA (chmn. coun., pub. utilities, comm. and transp. law sect.), Energy Bar Assn. (chmn. coms. 1983—84), Fla. Bar, Congl. Country Club (Bethesda, Md. bd. govs. 2002—), Phi Alpha Delta. Democrat. Roman Catholic. Office: LeBoeuf Lamb Greene & MacRae LLP 1875 Connecticut Ave NW Washington DC 20009-5728 Office Phone: 202-986-8012. Office Fax: 202-986-8102. Business E-Mail: boneill@llgm.com.

**O'NEILL, BRIDGET R.,** lawyer; b. 1963; BSBA, Georgetown U., 1985; JD, U. Wis., 1988. Bar: Wis. 1988, Ill. 1988, N.Y. 1992. With Sidley Austin Brown & Wood, Chgo., ptnr., 1996—. Office: Sidley Austin Brown & Wood Bank One Plz 10 S Dearborn St Chicago IL 60603

**O'NEILL, CHARLES K.,** lawyer; b. Mineola, NY, June 12, 1947; BA, U. Pa., 1969; JD, Fordham U., 1972. Bar: NY 1973, US Dist. Ct. (So. Dist.) NY 1974, US Dist. Ct. (Ea. Dist.) NY 1974, US Ct. Appeals (2nd Cir.) 1977, US Supreme Ct. 1979, US Ct. Appeals (DC Cir.) 1979, US Ct. Appeals (9th Cir.) 1980. Ptnr. Chadbourne & Parke LLP, NYC, mng. ptnr., mgmt. com., 1998—. Dir. Chadbourne & Parke Found. Lectr. in field; editor: Fordham Law Rev. Bd. dirs. Church Ave. Mcht. Block Assn. Inc. Legal Svcs., N.Y.C.; trustee NY Meth. Hosp. Mem.: Assn. Bar City NY, Fed. Bar Coun., NY State Bar Assn., ABA. Office: Chadbourne & Parke LLP 30 Rockefeller Plz Fl 31 New York NY 10112-0129 Office Phone: 212-408-5365. Office Fax: 212-541-5369. Business E-Mail: co'neill@chadbourne.com.

**O'NEILL, CHARLES KELLY,** marketing professional, retired advertising executive; b. Springfield, Mo., Apr. 2, 1933; s. Charles Chester and Frances (Kelly) O'N.; m. Kyoko Hirano, June 2, 1981. B.J., U. Mo., 1955. With Galvin-Farris-Alvine, Kansas City, Mo., 1957-58, copy chief, 1958; with Potts-Woodbury, Inc., Kansas City, 1958-61, chief time buyer, 1960-61; with Gardner Advt. Co., St. Louis, 1962-88, assoc. media dir., 1964-65, media dir., 1965-69, v.p., Chmn., 1976-78, corp. media dir., dir. co., 1969-88, v.p., 1976-78, pres., 1978-88; gen. mgr. Advanswers div., 1971-72; pres. Advanswers Media/Programming, Inc., 1973-78, chmn., 1978-88; v.p. Wells, Rich, Greene, N.Y.C., 1974-88, exec. v.p., 1979-88, dir., 1978-88; vice chmn. WRG-USA, 1981-88; chmn. O'Neill Mktg., Honolulu, 1988—; exec. v.p. Kyoko O'Neill, Inc., 1993—; dir. Colony Surf Ltd., Honolulu, 1990-94, chmn., bd. dirs., 1994. Bd. dirs. Waialae Iki Ridge Cmty. Assn., Honolulu, 1991—, 1st v.p., 1993-94. Lt. (j.g.) USN, 1955-57. Mem. St. Louis Advt. Club (gov. 1981-83), Outrigger Canoe Club (Honolulu), N.Y. Athletic Club, St. Louis Club, St. Louis Racquet Club, The Bridge (Navy League of the U.S.-Honolulu), Labrador Retriever Club of Hawaii, Sigma Chi, Alpha Delta Sigma. Episcopalian. Home: 1594 Hoaaina St Honolulu HI 96821-1345

**O'NEILL, DANIEL J.,** brewery company executive; b. Canada; BA, Carleton U., 1974; MBA, Queens U., 1976. With Colgate Palmolive, Toronto, 1976—79; sr. products mgr. insect control S.C. Johnson Wax, Racine, Wis., 1981—82, category mgr. Brazil, 1982—84, mktg. mgr., 1984—86, pres., gen. mgr. Venezuela, 1986—90, v.p. US consumer products, 1990—92, v.p. group business mgr. N.Am., 1992—93, v.p., group mng. dir. Europe Paris, 1993—94; pres. Campbell Canada Campbell Soup Co. Ltd., Toronto, 1994—95; pres. Campbell Sales Co., Camden, NJ, 1995—97, Campbell US Soup Division, 1996—97; pres., CEO Star-Kist Foods, Inc., 1997—99; exec. v.p. N.Am. sales & pres. Heinz S.Am. H.J. Heinz Co., Pittsburgh, Pa., 1997—99; exec. v.p., COO N.Am. brewing Molson Inc., 1999—2000, pres., CEO, 2000—. Bd. dirs. H.J. Heinz Co., 1988—99, Campbell Soup Co., 1994—97, Molson Inc., 1999—. Office: Molson Inc 1555 Notre Dame St E Montreal PQ H2L 2R5 Canada

**O'NEILL, HARRIET,** state supreme court justice; married, 2 children. BA, Converse Coll.; studied, U. Coll., Oxford, England; JD, U. S.C., 1982; PhD (hon.), Converse Coll., 2001. Practice law Houston; atty. Porter & Clements, Morris & Campbell; pvt. practice, 1982-92; judge 152d Dist. Ct., Houston, 1992—95; justice 14th Ct. Appeals, Houston, 1995—98, Tex. Supreme Ct., Austin, 1998—. Lectr. continuing edn. courses; adv. bd. CLE Inst., 1996; panelist Tex. Ctr. Advanced Jud. Studies., Austin, 1993. Contbr. articles to profl. publs. Mem. U. S.C. academic honors soc.; founder Jud. Outreach for Literacy Training. Named Appellate Justice of Yr., Tex. Assn. of Civil Trial & Appellate Specialists, 2002, 2006. Mem.: Harris County Bar Assn., ABA. Office: Supreme Ct PO Box 12248 Austin TX 78711-2248*

**O'NEILL, HARRY WILLIAM,** retired research market and opinion company executive; b. Atlantic City, Jan. 30, 1929; s. Harry William and Marian Elizabeth (Kuhl) O'N.; m. Carmel Gullo, Sept. 21, 1952; children: Sharon Ruth, Randal Bruce. BA, Colgate U., 1950; MS, Pa. State U., 1951. Lic. practicing psychologist, N.J. Research analyst Prudential Ins. Co., Newark, 1957-62; with Opinion Research Corp., Princeton, NJ, 1962-87, sr. v.p., 1970-73, exec. v.p., 1973-80, pres., 1980-85, vice chmn., 1985-87, NOP World, Princeton, NJ, 1988—2005. Mem. co-adj. faculty Rutgers U., 1959-64; vis. lectr. Woodrow Wilson Sch., Princeton U., 1980-82; mem. part-time faculty Rutgers U., 1999—2005. Editor Marketing Research: A Magazine of Management & Applications, 1988-93. Pres. Nat. Coun. Pub. Polls, 1984-94, trustee, 1994—; bd. dirs. Roper Ctr. for Pub. Opinion Rsch., 1984—, chmn., 1994—2004; bd. dirs. Am. Assn. Survey Rsch. Orgns., 1981-83, chmn., 1982-83; vice chmn. Rsch. Industry Coalition, 1993-94, chmn., 1994-95; bd. dirs. Market Rsch. Inst. Internat., 1999—2005; mem. Highland Park (N.J.) Human Rights Commn., 1973-77; bd. dirs. Del-Raritan Lung Assn., 1974-88, v.p., 1977-82, chmn., 1982-84; fin. chmn. Highland Park Rep. Orgn., 1977-89. With USAF, 1951-54. Recipient Maroon citation, Colgate U., 1975, induction into Market Rsch. Coun. Hall of Fame, 1997, Lifetime Achievement award, Coun. Am. Survey Rsch. Orgns., 2001. Mem. Am. Psychol. Assn., Ea. Psychol. Assn., Am. Assn. Pub. Opinion Rsch. (Outstanding Achievement award N.Y. chpt. 1997), Assn. Consumer Rsch., Am. Mktg. Assn., Market Rsch. Coun., Highland Park Rep. Club, Masons, Elks. Presbyterian. Personal E-mail: honeill536@aol.com.

**O'NEILL, JAMES ANTHONY, JR.,** pediatric surgeon, educator; b. N.Y.C., Dec. 7, 1933; m. Susan Pokorny; childen: James Anthony III, Elizabeth, Kathryn S. BS, Georgetown U., 1955; MD, Yale U., 1959. Diplomate Am. Bd. Surgery (bd. dirs. 1981-87, sr. 1988—), Am. Bd. Thoracic Surgery; lic. surgeon, Ohio, La., Tenn., Pa.; cert. instr. advanced trauma life support. Intern Vanderbilt U. Hosp., 1959-60, asst. resident, 1960-64, resident, instr. surgery, 1964-65; chief burn study divsn. U.S.A Surgl Rsch. Unit Brooke Army Med. Ctr., 1965-67; resident, USPHS fellow in pediatric oncology Columbus Children's Hosp., 1967-69; instr. pediatric surgery Coll. Medicine Ohio State U., 1967-69; asst. prof. surgery and pediatrics, chief pediatric surg. svc. Sch. Medicine La. State U., 1969-70, assoc. prof. surgery, chief sect. pediatric surgery, 1970-71; prof. surgery, chmn. dept. pediatric surgery Sch. Medicine Vanderbilt U., 1971-81, chief med. staff Med. Ctr., 1976-77; prof. pediatric surgery Sch. Medicine U. Pa., Phila., 1981-95, C.E. Koop prof. pediatric surgery, 1988-95; surgeon-in-chief Children's Hosp. Phila., 1981-95; chmn. of surgery, J.C. Foshee Disting. prof. surgery Vanderbilt U. Med. Ctr., Nashville, 1995—. Site visitor residency rev. com. for surgery AMA; mem.

---

trauma care subcom. med. adv. com. Phila. Emergency Med. Svcs. Coun.; surg. cons. U.S. Army Inst. Surg. Rsch., Ft. Sam Houston, Tex. Mem. editorial bd. Jour. Burn Care and Rehab., Jour. Enteral and Parenteral Nutrition, Jour. Surg. Rsch., Pediatrics, 1984—, Pediatric Emergency Care, 1984—, Pediatric Surgery, Pediatric Surgery Internat., 1988; mem. assoc. editorial bd. Jour. Pediatric Surgery; sect. editor Jour. Trauma, 1983—, Jour Vascular Surgery, 1992; contbr. 350 articles to med. jours. Mem. med. adv. bd. Hope Found.; mem. adv. bd. James Whitcomb Riley Rsch. Found., 1986-89; mem. standards com. State Pa. Found. for Trauma Care. Fellow Am. Acad. Pediatrics (surg., pediatric trauma care coord. Pa. chpt., sect. on oncology-hematology chmn. surg. sect. program com. 1975-77, adv. com. postgrad. edn. 1979-81, exec. com. surg. sect. 1977-80, chmn. 1980-81); mem. ACS (founding, cancer liason physician, Met. Phila. chpt., exec. com. trauma com. 1975-77, adv. coun. pediatric surgery 1977-83, 86-88, 90—, postgrad. edn. com. 1979-82, continuing edn. com. 1981-88, nominating com. 1986, regental ad hoc com. on legis issues in trauma in emergency med. svcs. 1987—, bd. govs. 1990—, coun. to study fiscal affairs coll. 1992-93, subcom. on burns, spl. soc. gov. from. AM. Pediatric Surg. Assn. 1992—, coun. on acad. surgery 1993—), v.p. Phila chpt. 1993-94), Am. Assn. for Surgery Trauma, Am. Trauma Soc. (bd. dirs. 1974-78), Am. Burn Assn., Am. Pediatric Surg. Assn. (sec. 1976-79, chmn. edn. com. 1984-87, pres.-elect 1987-88, pres. 1988-89, manpower, trauma and issues and ethics coms.), Am. Surg. Assn. (1st v.p. 1997-98), Assn. for Acad. Surgery (membership com. 1973-74), Soc. for Surgery Alimentary Tract, Soc. Univ. Surgeons (edn. com. 1974-75), Assn. Program Dirs. in Surgery (steering com. 1990-94), Internat. Soc. for Burn Injuries, Internat. Soc. Parenatal Nutrition, Brit. Assn. Pediatric Surgeons, S.E. Surg. Congress (program com. 1979-82, 1st v.p. 1998-99, pres. 1999-2000), So. Gut Club, So. Soc. for Pediatric Rsch., So. Surg. Assn., Tenn. Med. Assn. (del. 1976, 77), Tenn. Pediatric Soc., New Orleans Surg. Soc., Phila. Acad. Surgery, Phila Pediatric Soc., Coll. Physicians Phila. (coun. 1988-91), Portland Surg. Soc. (hon.), Nashville Surg. Soc., Davidson County Med. Assn., James D. Rives Surg. Soc., Halsted Soc. (bd. govs. 1986-89), Alpha Omega Alpha. Office: Vanderbilt Univ Med Ctr Dept Surgery 1001 Oxford House Nashville TN 37232-0001 Office Phone: 615-936-1290. Business E-Mail: james.oneill@vanderbilt.edu.

**O'NEILL, JAMES MARTIN,** venture capitalist; b. N.Y.C., Sept. 29, 1962; s. James and Bernice N. (Grogan) O'N.; m. Kimberly A. Mika, Nov. 19, 1998; children: Matthew M., Michael C., Liam J. BA in Govt. and Econs., Dartmouth Coll., 1984; MBA, Harvard Bus. Sch., 1990. V.p. Nat. Westminster Bank USA, N.Y.C., 1984-88; assoc. corp. fin. Merrill Lynch Internat. Ltd., London, 1990-91; gen. mgr. The Coca-Cola Co., Coca-Cola Poland Ltd., Warsaw, 1991—94; mng. dir. Czech Am. Enterprise Fund, Washington, 1994-95; CEO, mng. dir. DBG Devel. Capital Ea. Europe Ltd., Jersey, Channel Islands, 1995—2002, also bd. dirs.; mng. dir. corp. devel Metavante Corp. (W.O.S. Marshall & Isley Corp.), 2000—. Bd. dirs. DBG Osteuropa-Holding GmbH, Frankfurt. Em. European Venture Capital Assn. Avocation: travel. Home: 253 Pebble Creek Dr Barrington IL 60010-1367 Office: Metavante Corporate Development 4900 W Brown Deer Rd PO Box 240077 Milwaukee WI 53224-9004

**O'NEILL, JAMES PAUL,** psychiatrist; b. Elizabeth, N.J., Sept. 3, 1958; s. Paul James and Dorothy (Semansky) O'Neill; m. Patricia Anne Scott, Aug. 1989. BS in Biology, Niagara U., 1980; MD, U. N.E., Mex., 1984, U. Medicine & Dentistry NJ, 1985. Diplomate Am. Bd. Psychiatry and Neurology (added qualifications in addiction). Intern Jersey Shore Med. Ctr., Neptune, NJ, 1985-86; resident in psychiatry U. Medicine & Dentistry, Robert Wood Johnson Med. Sch., Piscataway, NJ, 1986-89, chief resident in psychiatry, 1988-89; pvt. practice Avon By The Sea, NJ, 1989—2003, Wall, NJ, 2003—. Attending psychiatrist Monmouth Med. Ctr., Long Branch, NJ; clin. asst. prof. psychiatry U. Medicine & Dentistry N.J., Robert Wood Johnson Med. Sch., Med. Coll. Pa., Drexel U. Coll. Medicine; profl. supporter Nat. Assn. Mental Illness. Contbr. articles to profl. jours. Mem. com. Gov.'s coun. Addictions Managed Care Round Table, 1992—93; adv. bd. Cath. Charities, Monmouth County, NJ. Named one of Am. Top Psychiatrists, Consumers Rsch. Coun. Am., 2003; recipient, 2004?; NIMH fellow, 1988. Fellow: Am. Psychiatrist Assn. (disting. fellow); mem.: AMA (N.J. del. to resident physician sect. 1987—89, Physician Recognition award 1991, 1994, 1997, 2000, 2003, 2006), Am. Coll. Psychiatry, Med. Soc. N.J. (del. Monmouth County 1990—), U.S. Life Saving Assn., Am. Soc. Addiction Medicine (cert.), Am. Acad. Addiction Psychiatry (N.J. chmn.), Monmouth Ocean County Psychiat. Assn. (pres.-elect 1998—99, pres. 1999—2000), N.J. Psychiat. Assn. (founding pres. resident physician sect. 1987—88, treas. 2000—01, sr. v.p. 2001—02, pres.-elect 2002, pres. 2003—04, chmn. addictive disorders treatment com., counselor, officer governing coun., chmn. strategic orgnl. long term planning com.), Manasquan Golf Club. Republican. Avocations: sports, travel. Office: 1540 Rt 138 Suite 307 Wall NJ 07719 Office Phone: 732-280-7555.

**O'NEILL, JOAN,** editor; Internat. bus. editor New York Times. Office: New York Times 229 W 43d St New York NY 10036 Office Phone: 212-556-5994. Office Fax: 212-556-1448.*

**O'NEILL, JOHN H., JR.,** lawyer; b. Bainbridge, Md., Oct. 20, 1946; s. John Hardin and Lois May (Schnepfe) O'N.; m. Vivian Lidwina Gemelli, Nov. 29, 1969; children: Eric Michael, David Christopher, Sean Timothy, Daniel Ryan. BS with distinction in Naval Engring., U.S. Naval Acad., 1968, grad. in Nuclear Power, 1969; JD, Yale U., 1976. Bar: Md. 1976, D.C. 1977, U.S. Supreme Ct., U.S. Dist. Ct. D.C.; lic. to supervise operation, maintenance naval nuclear propulsion power plants AEC. Commd. ensign USN, 1968; advanced through grades to lt. comdr., 1975; officer on nuclear submarines USN, 1968-73; resigned, 1973; ptnr., chmn. nuclear energy practice group Shaw Pittman LLP, Washington, 1976—2005; ptnr., leader regulatory dept., mng. bd. Pillsbury Winthrop Shaw Pittman LLP, Washington, 2005—. Counsel various nuclear industry cos.; cons. in field to fgn. govts. Trustee U.S. Naval Academy Found. Mem. ABA, Internat. Bar Assn., Internat. Nuclear Law Assn. Republican. Roman Catholic. Avocations: squash, tennis, skiing. Office: Pillsbury Winthrop Shaw Pittman 2300 N St NW Washington DC 20037-1128 Office Phone: 202-663-8148. Office Fax: 202-663-8007. Business E-Mail: john.o'neill@pillsburylaw.com.

**O'NEILL, JOHN JOSEPH, JR.,** retired chemicals executive; b. N.Y.C., Sept. 13, 1919; s. John Joseph and Margaret (Patterson) O'N.; m. Irene Ray, Apr. 18, 1940; children— Anne, Mary (Mrs. George Schuler). BS in Chem. Engring, Mo. Sch. Mines, 1940, Chem. Engr., 1951. Research engr. Western Cartridge Co., 1940-49; with Olin Industries, Inc., 1949-60, dir. prodn. explosives operations, energy div., 1959-60; with Olin Matthieson Chem. Corp., 1960-71, asst. to pres., 1963-64, staff v.p. planning, 1964-65, v.p. comml. devel., chems. group, 1965-67, corporate v.p. plastics, 1967-70, corporate v.p. product diverification, 1970-71; cons., 1971-72; exec. v.p., chief operating officer Kleer-Vu Inc., N.Y.C., 1972-76; v.p. planning and devel. Vertac Consol., 1976-77; chief exec. officer Vertac, Inc., 1977-78, cons., 1979-80, vice chmn. bd., chief oper. officer, 1980-81; cons., 1981—; pres. Jonco, Inc., 1984-89. Mem. bd. advisors Am. Express Sr. Card, 2001-2003. Contbr. articles to profl. jours.; patentee explosives, chemicals, ordnance items. Emeritus trustee St. Mary-of-Woods Coll., Terre Haute, Ind. Fellow Am. Inst. Chemists; mem. Am. Inst. Chem. Engring., Chemists Club (N.Y.C.). Clubs: Chemists (N.Y.C.). Home and Office: 7 Castlewood Ln PO Box 429 Pinehurst NC 28370-0429 Office Phone: 910-295-5503.

**O'NEILL, JUDITH D.,** lawyer; b. NYC, Dec. 9, 1945; BA in Romance Lang., Am. Univ. and Univ. Madrid, 1966; MA magna cum laude, Am. Univ., 1972; JD summa cum laude, Univ. Balt., 1975. Bar: Md. 1975, DC 1979, NY 2001, US Supreme Ct. 1976. Shareholder tech. media, telecom. Greenberg Traurig LLP, NYC. Founder, dir. Pan Am. Tech. Policy Forum. Contbr. articles to profl. journals. Mem.: ABA, Fed. Comm. Bar Assn., InterAm. Bar Assn. Office: Greenberg Traurig LLP MetLife Bldg 200 Park Ave New York NY 10166-1400 Office Phone: 212-801-9387. Office Fax: 212-801-6400. Business E-Mail: oneillj@gtlaw.com.

**O'NEILL, JUNE ELLENOFF,** economist; b. NYC, June 14, 1934; d. Louis and Matilda (Liebstein) Ellenoff; m. Sam Cohn, 1955 (div. 1961); 1 child, Peter; m. David Michael O'Neill, Dec. 24, 1964; 1 child, Amy. BA, Sarah Lawrence Coll., Bronxville, N.Y., 1955; PhD, Columbia U., 1970. Econs. instr. Temple U., Phila., 1965-68; rsch. assoc. Brookings Instn., Washington, 1968-71; sr. economist Pres.'s Coun. Econ. Advisors, Washington, 1971-76; chief human resources budget Congl. Budget Office, Washington, 1976-79; dir. rsch. assoc. The Urban Instn., Washington, 1979-86; dir. Office Policy and Rsch. U.S. Commn. Civil Rights, Washington, 1986-87; prof. econs. and fin., dir. Ctr. for Study Bus. and Govt. Baruch Coll., CUNY, 1987—; Morton Wollman Prof. Econs. Zicklin Sch. Bus. Baruch Coll., 1999—; dir. Congl. Budget Office U.S. Congress, Washington, 1995-99. Adj. scholar Am. Enterprise Inst., 1994-95, 99—; mem. Nat. Adv. Com., The Poverty Inst., U. Wis., 1988-95; chair bd. sci. counselors Nat. Ctr. for Health Stats., 2003—; mem. Nat. Bur. Econ. Rsch., 2004—. Contbr. articles to profl. jours. Mem. Am. Econs. Assn. (v.p. 1998-99), Nat. Acad. Social Ins. Republican. Jewish. Home: 420 Riverside Dr New York NY 10025-7773 Office: CUNY Baruch Coll Ctr Study of Bus and Govt 17 Lexington Ave New York NY 10010-5518 Office Phone: 646-312-3540. E-mail: june_oneill@baruch.cuny.edu.

**O'NEILL, KEVIN,** professional athletics coach; b. Jan. 24, 1957; m. Chelsea Hoffman; 1 child. BA in Edn., McGill U., 1979; EdM, Marycrest Coll., 1983. Head coach North County C.C., Saranac, NY, 1980—82, Marycrest Coll., 1982; asst. coach U. Del., 1983—85, U. Tulsa, Okla., 1985, U. Ariz., 1986—89; head coach Marquette U., 1989—94, U. Tenn., 1994—97, Northwestern U., Ill., 1997—2000; asst. coach N.Y. Knicks, 2000—01, Detroit (Mich.) Pistons, 2001—03; head coach Toronto (Can.) Raptors, 2003—04.

**O'NEILL, MARY JANE,** not-for-profit administrator, consultant; b. Detroit, Feb. 24, 1923; d. Frank Roger and Kathryn (Rice) Kilcoyne; m. Michael James O'Neill, May 31, 1948; children: Michael, Maureen, Kevin, John(dec.), Kathryn. PhB summa cum laude, U. Detroit, 1944; postgrad., U. Wis., 1949—50. Editor East Side Shopper, Detroit, 1939—45; club editor Detroit Free Press, 1945—48; reporter UP, Milw. and Madison, 1949; dir. pub. rels. Fairfax-Falls Church Cmty. Chest, Va., 1955—60; copy editor Falls Church Sun-Echo, 1958—60; freelance writer Washington, 1960—63; assoc. editor Med. World News, Washington, 1963—66; dir. publ. rels. Westchester Lighthouse N.Y. Assn. for Blind, 1967—71; dir. pub. edn. The Lighthouse, N.Y.C., 1971—73; dir. pub. rels., 1973—80; exec. dir., CEO Eye-Bank for Sight Restoration, Inc., 1980—2000; ret., 2000. Mem. N.Y. State Transplant Coun., 1991—2002; mem. instl. rsch. rev. bd. Manhattan Eye, Ear and Throat Hosp., 1981—; bd. dirs. N.Y. Organ Donor Network, 1997—2003, Pro Mujer, 1997—2003, mem. adv. coun., 2004—. Named to Top 100 Irish Ams., Irish Am. Mag., 1999. Mem.: Pan Am. Eye Bank Assn. (bd. dirs.), Women Execs. in Pub. Rels. (dir. 1982—88, pres. 1986—87, found. bd. dirs. 2001—), Eye Bank Assn. Am. (lay adv. bd. 1981—83, dir. 1983—86, pres. N.E. Region 1993—96, exec. com. 1994—96, EBAA Heise award 1997), Women in Comm. (pres. N.Y. chpt. 1980—81, treas. 2004—), Cosmopolitan Club. E-mail: maryjaneoneill@aol.com.

**O'NEILL, MICHAEL EDMUND,** law educator; b. Baldwin, Wis., Mar. 5, 1962; s. John Patrick and Eva Joyce O'Neill; m. Margaret Reba Stevens, June 1, 1991. BA summa cum laude, Brigham Young U., Provo, Utah, 1987; JD, Yale U., 1990. Bar: D.C., 1991, Wis., 1991. Law clk. to Hon. David B. Sentelle U.S. Ct. Appeals (D.C. cir.), Washington, 1990—91; appellate litigator U.S. Dept. Justice, Washington, 1991-94; gen. counsel U.S. Senate Judiciary Com., Washington, 1994-96, 97-98; law clk. to Justice Clarence Thomas U.S. Supreme Ct., Washington, 1996-97; asst. prof. George Mason Law Sch., Arlington, Va., 1998—2002, assoc. prof., 2002—. Commr., U.S. Sentencing Commn., 1999-2005. Bishop Ch. of Jesus Christ of Latter Day Saints, Balt., 1993-94. Mem. ABA. Mormon. Office: George Mason University School of Law 3301 N Fairfax Dr Arlington VA 22201-4426 Business E-Mail: moneill3@gmu.edu.*

**O'NEILL, MICHAEL J., JR.,** lawyer, insurance company executive; b. 1949; AB, Dartmouth Coll.; JD, Univ. Va. Bar: Pa. 1975. Sr. v.p. & counsel Chubb Corp., Warren, NJ. Office: Chubb Corp 15 Mountain View Rd Warren NJ 07059

**O'NEILL, MICHAEL JAMES,** editor, author; b. Detroit, Nov. 19, 1922; s. Michael J. and Ellen Mary (Dacey) O'Neill; m. Mary Jane Kilcoyne, May 31, 1948; children: Michael, Maureen, Kevin, Kathryn. BA, U. Detroit, 1946, LHD (hon.), 1977; postgrad., Fordham U., 1946—47. Writer Standard News Assn., N.Y.C., 1946—47; with UPI, 1947—56; Washington corr. N.Y. Daily News, 1956—66, asst. mng. editor, 1966—68, mng. editor, 1968—74, v.p., 1971—79, exec. editor, 1974—75, editor, 1975—82, exec. v.p., 1979—82, dir. Freelance writer; lectr., 1983—. Author (with L. Tanzer): The Kennedy Circle, 1961; author: (with K.M. Cahill) Preventive Diplomacy, 1996; author: China Today, 1976, Terrorist Spectaculars: Should TV Coverage Be Curbed, 1986, The Roar of the Crowd, How TV and People Power are Changing the World, 1993. Mem. Nat. Adv. Coun. Health Professions Edn., 1967—71; chmn. Fund of City of N.Y., 2003—06. With U.S. Army, 1943—45, ETO. Decorated Bronze Star; recipient Nat. Affairs Reporting award, Nat. Head-liner's, 1956. Mem.: Coun. Fgn. Rels., Am. Soc. Newspaper Editors (pres. 1981—82), Overseas Writers (pres. 1965), Century Club (N.Y.C. chpt.). Address: 23 Cayuga Rd Scarsdale NY 10583-6941

**O'NEILL, PAUL HENRY,** former secretary of the treasury; b. St. Louis, Dec. 4, 1935; s. John Paul and Gaynald Elsie (Irvin) O'N.; m. Nancy Jo Wolfe, Sept. 4, 1955; children: Patricia, Margaret, Julie, Paul Henry. BA, Fresno State Coll., 1960; Haynes Found. fellow, Claremont Grad. Sch., 1960-61; postgrad., George Washington U., 1962-65; MPA, Ind. U., 1966; DSc (hon.), Clarkson U., 1993; Georgetown U., 2005; D Pub. Svc. (hon.), Villanova U., 1997, California U. Pa., 1998; SD Bus. Leadership (hon.), Duquesne U., 1999; LHD (hon.), Calif. State U., 1999; D Pub. Svc. (hon.), U. Pitts., 2003; D Pub. Policy (hon.), Carnegie-Mellon U., 2003; PhD in Pub. Policy (hon.), Pardee RAND, 2004. Site engr. Morrison-Knudsen, Inc., Anchorage, 1955-57; systems analyst VA, Washington, 1961-66; budget examiner Bur. of Budget, Washington, 1967-69; chief human resources program div. U.S. Govt. Office of Mgmt. and Budget, Washington, 1969-70, asst. dir., 1971-72, assoc. dir., 1973-74, dep. dir., 1974-77; v.p. Internat. Paper Co., N.Y.C., 1977-81, sr. v.p., 1981-85, pres., 1985-87; CEO Alcoa Inc., Pitts., 1987-99, chmn., 1987-2000; founding co-chair Pittsburgh Regional Healthcare Initiative, 1997—2005; sec. U.S. Dept. Treasury, Washington, 2001—02; sr. advisor The Blackstone Group, L.P., N.Y.C., 2003—. Chmn. Pres.'s Edn. Policy Adv. Com., 1989—92; dir. Eastman Kodak, 2003—; bd. dirs. Ctr. for Global Devel., 2004—, Celanese Corp., 2004—, Nalco Co., Qcept, TRW Automotive Holdings, RAND, 2003—, mem. bd. of health, 2003—, bd. advisors. promising practices network, 2003—, former chmn.; sr. advisor The Blackstone Group, 2003—; mem. nat. bd. visitors Calif. State U., Fresno; mem. Nat. Quality Forum, 2003—. Trustee Coun. for Excellence in Govt., 2003—; mem. bd. visitors Heinz Sch., 2004—; active Riverlife Task Force, Pitts., 2003—; bd. dirs. Gerald R. Ford Found., 1981—, mem. audit com. Recipient Nat. Inst. Pub. Affairs Career Edn. award, 1965, William A. Jump Meritorious award, 1971, Health Quality award, Nat. Com. Quality Assurance, 2003; Fellow Nat. Inst. Pub. Affairs. Fellow Nat. Acad. Pub. Adminstrn.; mem. Am. Acad. Arts and Sci., Nat. Acad. Social Ins. (founding mem., hon. advisor), Inst. Electronics. (dir. 2003—). Republican. Methodist. Office: Ste 100 One North Shore Ctr Pittsburgh PA 15212 Office Phone: 412-553-1238. Personal E-mail: lindamurraypa@aol.com.

**O'NEILL, PAUL JOHN,** retired psychology educator; b. Taunton, Mass., Apr. 12, 1936; s. Clarence Bernard and Edna Mary (Burke) O'N.; 1 child, Maureen Kelly O'Neill. BA, St. Bonaventure (N.Y.) U., 1960; MA, Boston U., 1961; EdD, U. Ga., 1973. Lic. psychologist. Prof. psychology Jackson (Miss.) State U., 1972-93, dir. critical thinking and outcome measures program, 1987-93. Contbr. articles to profl. jours. With U.S. Army, 1954-56, Austria, Germany. Home: 239 NW North Shore Dr Kansas City MO 64151-1457 E-mail: pj31957@yahoo.com.

**O'NEILL, PHILIP DANIEL, JR.,** lawyer, educator; b. Boston, Sept. 19, 1951; s. Philip Daniel Sr. and Alice Maureen (Driscoll) O'N.; m. Lisa G. Arrowood, June 25, 1983; children: Alexander Edwin, Sean Matthew, Madeleine Clarice. BA, Hamilton Coll., 1973; JD cum laude, Boston Coll., 1977. Bar: Mass. 1977, N.Y. 1985, R.I. 1988. Assoc. Hale and Dorr, Boston, 1977—83, ptnr., 1983—87, Edwards Angell Palmer & Dodge LLP, Boston, 1987—. Adj. rsch. fellow John F. Kennedy Sch. Govt., Ctr. for Sci. and Internat. Affairs Harvard U., 1983—86; adj. prof. law Boston U., 1992, 2001—, Boston Coll., 1988—; cons. Arms Control and Disarmament Agy. U.S. Dept. Def., 1983—84; panelist in internat. and domestic legal programs; arbitrator in field; lectr. in field; Nomura lectr. Harvard U. Law Sch., 2005. Contbr. articles to profl. jours., chapters to books. Fellow Chartered Inst. Arbitrators (Eng.), Am. Bar Found.; mem. ABA (vice-chmn. nat. security and arms control com. 2002-05), Internat. Law Assn. (chmn. Am. br. arbitration com. 1985-89, rep. internat. arbitration com. 1989—), Boston Bar Assn. (chmn. internat. law sect. 1994-96, past chmn. internat. litig. and arbitration com.), Am. Soc. Internat. Law, Nat. Security Network. Home: 11 Blackburnian Rd Lincoln MA 01773-4317 Office: Edwards Angell Palmer & Dodge LLP 111 Huntington Ave Boston MA 02199-7613

**O'NEILL, ROBERT CHARLES,** inventor, consultant; b. Buffalo, Dec. 3, 1923; s. Albert T. and Helen (Lynch) O'N.; m. Agnes Balischak; 1 dau., Eileen Anne. BS in Chemistry, Rensselaer Poly. Inst., 1945; PhD in Organic Chemistry, MIT, 1950. Sr. chemist Merck & Co., Inc., Rahway, NJ, 1950-56, marketing devel. specialist, 1956-58; v.p. Stauffer Pharms. div. Stauffer Chem. Co., N.Y.C., 1958-61; v.p., dir. R & D Cooper Labs., Inc., 1961-70, exec. v.p., 1970-76, gen. mgr., 1975-76, pres., 1976-77, also dir. Cons. in field. Contbr. articles to profl. jours. Served with USNR, 1943-46. Mem. Am. Chem. Soc., Chemists Club N.Y. Achievements include patents in field. Home: 10 Whitlaw Close Chappaqua NY 10514-1008

**O'NEILL, RUSSELL RICHARD,** engineering educator; b. Chgo., June 6, 1916; s. Dennis Alysious and Florence Agnes (Mathurin) O'N.; m. Margaret Bock, Dec. 15, 1939; children: Richard A., John R.; m. Sallie Boyd, June 30, 1967. BSME, U. Calif., Berkeley, MSME, 1940; PhD, UCLA, 1956. Registered profl. engr., Calif. Design engr. Dowell, Inc., Midland, Mich., 1940-41; design engr. Dow Chem. Co., Midland, 1941-44, Airesearch Mfg. Co., Los Angeles, 1944-46; lectr. engring. UCLA, 1946-56, prof. engring., 1956, asst. dean engring., 1956-61, assoc. dean, 1961-73, acting dean, 1965-66, dean, 1974-83, dean emeritus, 1983—; staff engr. NAS-NRC, 1954; dir. Data Design Labs., 1977-86, dir. emeritus, 1986—. Mem. engring. task force Space Era Edn. Study Fla. Bd. Control, 1963; mem. regional Export Expansion Coun. Dept. Commerce, 1960-66, Los Angeles Mayor's Space Adv. Com., 1964-69; mem. Maritime Transp. Rsch. Bd., 1974-81; bd. advisers Naval Postgrad. Sch., 1976-84; mem. Nat. Nuclear Accreditation Bd., 1983-88; mem. accrediting bd. Dept. Energy, 1992—. Trustee West Coast U., 1981-90; bd. dirs. Western region United Way, 1982-90. Mem. NAE, Am. Soc. Engring. Edn., Sigma Xi, Tau Beta Pi. Home: 15430 Longbow Dr Sherman Oaks CA 91403-4910 Office: UCLA HSSEAS Box 951600 Los Angeles CA 90095-1600 Business E-Mail: russ@ea.ucla.edu

**O'NEILL, SHEILA,** principal; Prin. Cor Jesu Acad., St. Louis. Recipient Blue Ribbon award U.S. Dept. Edn., 1990-91. Office: Cor Jesu Acad 10230 Gravois Rd Saint Louis MO 63123-4099

**O'NEILL, THOMAS J. (TOM O' NEILL),** engineering company executive; b. Buffalo, July 22, 1952; AB, Dartmouth Coll., 1973, BE, 1974. With Parsons Brinckerhoff/Tudor, Atlanta, 1974-77, Tudor Engring. Co., Atlanta, 1978-92; pres., COO, CEO Parsons, Brinckerhoff, Quade, NYC, 1992—. Mem. Chief Executive Group, L.P., Montvale, NJ. Office: Parsons Brinckerhoff 1 Penn Plz Fl 2 New York NY 10119-0021 Office Phone: 212-465-5000. Office Fax: 212-465-5096.

**O'NEILL, THOMAS NEWMAN, JR.,** federal judge; b. Hanover, Pa., July 6, 1928; s. Thomas Newman and Emma (Cornpropst) O'N.; m. Jeanne M. Corr., Feb. 4, 1961; children: Caroline Jeanne, Thomas Newman, III, Ellen Gitt. AB magna cum laude, Catholic U. Am., 1950; LL.B. magna cum laude, U. Pa., 1953; postgrad. (Fulbright grantee), London Sch. Econs., 1955-56. Bar: Pa. 1954, U.S. Supreme Ct. 1959. Law clk. to Judge Herbert F. Goodrich U.S. Ct. Appeals (3d cir.), 1953-54; law clk. to Justice Harold H. Burton U.S. Supreme Ct., 1954-55; assoc. Montgomery, McCracken, Walker & Rhoads, Phila., 1956-63, ptnr., 1963-83; judge U.S. Dist. Ct. (ea. dist.) Pa., 1983—; counsel 1st and 2d Pa. Legis. Reapportionment Commns., 1971, 81. Lectr. U. Pa. Law Sch., 1973 Articles editor: U. Pa. Law Rev, 1952-53. Former trustee Lawyers Com. for Civil Rights Under Law; former mem. Gov.'s Trial Ct. Nominating Commn. for Phila. County; former mem. bd. overseers U. Pa. Mus.; mem. adv. bd. Civil War and Underground R.R. Mus. Phila. Fellow Am. Coll. Trial Lawyers; mem. Am. Law Inst. (life), Phila. Bar Assn. (chancellor 1976), Pa. Bar Assn. (gov. 1978-81), U. Pa. Law Alumni Soc. (pres. 1976-77), Pa. Conf. County Bar Officers (pres. 1981-82), Pa. Soc. of SAR (mem. bd.), Am. Inn of Ct. (founding chmn. U. Pa.), Order of Coif (pres. U. Pa. chpt. 1971-73), Merion Cricket Club, Edgemere Club, Broadacres Trouting Assn., Phi Beta Kappa, Phi Eta Sigma. Office: US Dist Ct 4007 US Courthouse 601 Market St Philadelphia PA 19106-1713 Office Phone: 215-597-2750.

**O'NEILL, WILLIAM LAWRENCE,** retired history professor; b. Big Rapids, Mich., Apr. 18, 1935; s. John Patrick and Helen Elizabeth (Marsh) O'N.; m. Elizabeth Carol Knollmueller, Aug. 20, 1960; children: Cassandra Leigh, Catherine Lorraine. AB, U. Mich., 1957; MA, U. Calif., Berkeley, 1958, PhD, 1963. Assoc. prof. history U. Colo., 1964—66; asst. prof. U. Wis., 1966—69, assoc. prof., 1969—71; prof. Rutgers U., New Brunswick, NJ, 1971—2006, ret., 2006. Vis. asst. prof. U. Pitts., 1963-64; vis. assoc. prof. U. Pa., 1969-70 summer Procession Era, 1967, Everyone Was Brave: The Rise and Fall of Feminism in America, 1969, rev. and repub. as: Feminism in America: A History, 1989, Coming Apart: An Informal History of America in the 1960's, 1971, 2005, The Last Romantic: A Life of Max Eastman, 1978, 2d edit., 1991, A Better World: The Great Schism: Stalinism and the American Intellectuals, 1982, repub. as: A Better World: Stalinism and the American Intellectuals, 1989, American High: The Years of Confidence, 1945-60, 1986, A Democracy at War: America's Fight at Home and Abroad in World War II, 1993. Nat. Endowment Humanities fellow, 1979-80 Mem.: Hist. Soc. Office: Rutgers U Dept History New Brunswick NJ 08903 Personal E-mail: wlohp@aol.com.

**O'NEILL, WILLIAM PATRICK,** lawyer; b. Joplin, Mo., Sept. 14, 1951; s. Fred Charles and Dorothy Isabel (Snyder) O'N.; m. Mary Louise Richardson, June 17, 1989. BA, U. Kans., 1973; JD, U. Mich., 1976. Bar: Ill. 1976, U.S. Dist. Ct. (no. dist.) Ill. 1976, U.S. Dist. Ct. D.C. 1982. Assoc. Kirkland & Ellis, Chgo., 1976-81, Sidley & Austin, Chgo., 1982-85, Skadden, Arps, Slate, Meagher & Flom, N.Y.C., 1986-87, Crowell & Moring, Washington, 1987-88, ptnr., 1988-2000, Latham & Watkins, 2001—. Gen. counsel Ill. Common Cause, Chgo., 1979-81. Editor, author: (with others) Successfully Acquiring A U.S. Business, 1990; editorial chmn. Antitrust Law Jour., 1984-89. Mem. University Club of Chgo. Office: Latham & Watkins 555 11th St NW Washington DC 20004-2595 E-mail: williamoneill@lw.com.

**O'NEILL, WILLIAM WALTER,** physician, educator; b. Nov. 24, 1951; BS, U. Mich., 1972; MD, Wayne State U., 1977. Diplomate Am. Bd. Internal Medicine, Am. Bd. Cardiology. Intern in internal medicine U. Wis., Madison, 1977-78; resident in internal medicine Wayne State U., Detroit, 1978-80; fellow U. Mich., Ann Arbor, 1980-82, instr. internal medicine, 1982-83, asst. prof., 1983-86, assoc. prof., 1986-87; dir. cardiac catheterization lab. U. Mich. Hosp., Ann Arbor, 1984-87; corp. chief cardiology William Beaumont Hosp., Royal Oak, Troy, Mich., 1987—. Attending cardiologist VA Hosp., Ann Arbor, 1982-90; chmn. govt. rels. subcom. Nat. Cardiovasc. Network; rsch. peer rev. com. Am. Heart Assn. Mich., 1988-89; chmn. publs. com. Mansfield Scientific Balloon Valvuloplasty Registry; bd. govs. William Beaumont Hosp. Rsch. Inst.; presenter in field. Author: Myocardial Revascularization by Coronary Angioplasty or Bypass Surgery During MI in Acute Myocardial Infarction: New Approaches to Evaluation and Therapy, 1986, (chpt.) Acute Coronary Intervention, 1987, Current Perspective in Coronary Care, 1987, Interventional Cardiovascular Medicine, 1994, Acute Coronary Care, 2d edit., 1995; co-author: (chpts.) Cardiovascular Review, 6th edit., 1985, 8th edit., 1987, Tissue Plasminogen Activator in Thrombolytic Therapy, 1987, Techniques and Applications in Interventional Cardiology, 1991, Atherectomy, 1992, Emergency Medicine: A Comprehensive Study Guide, 3d edit., 1992, Adjunctive Therapy for Acute Myocardial Infarction, 1992, Manual of Interventional CArdiology, 1992, Cura Intensiva Cardiologica, Primary Coronary Angioplasty in Acute Myocardial Infarction; author. co-author: (chpt.) Interventional Cardiovascular Medicine, 1994; editl. cons. Jour. Intervention Cardiology; mem. editl. bd. Catheterization Cardiovasc. Diagnosis; contbr. over 400 articles to profl. publs. Grantee Smith/Kline Beecham, 1989-90, 90—, Advanced Cardiovasc. Sys., Inc., 1988-90, 90—, Midwest Heart Rsch. Found., Abbott Labs., 1990—, Duke U., 1990—, William Beaumont Hosp. Rsch. Inst., 1990—. Fellow Am. Coll. Cardiology (chpt. sec.-treas. 1993-94, reimbursement com.), Am. Coll. Chest Physicians, Coun. Clin. Cardiology; mem. AMA, ACP, Internat. Andreas Gruentzig Soc. Office: William Beaumont Hosp 3601 W 13 Mile Rd Royal Oak MI 48073-6712

**ONEL, SUZAN,** lawyer; b. NYC, Sept. 29, 1964; d. Joseph and Miriam (Spitzer) O.; m. Keith B. Bickel, Sept. 8, 1990. BA with hons., U. Pa., 1986; JD, U. Va., 1990. Bar: Pa. 1990, D.C. 1991. Assoc. Arent, Fox, Kintner, Plotkin & Kahn, Washington, 1990-92, Hyman, Phelps & McNamara, Washington, 1992-94, McKenna & Cuneo, Washington; ptnr. Kirkpatrick & Lockhart Nicholson Graham LLP, Washington. Mem. Food and Drug Law Inst. Notes editor Va. Environ. Law Jour.; contbr. articles to profl. jours. Mem. facilities com. Williamsburg Condominium, 1994—; legal clk./investigator D.C. Pub. Defenders Svcs./Mental Health Divsn., D.C., 1988. Mem. ABA (past co-chmn. tech. assessment com.), Regulatory Affairs Profl. Soc., D.C. Bar Assn. Avocations: travel, photography, aerobics, bicycling, reading. Office: Kirkpatrick & Lockhart Nicholson Graham LLP 2d Fl 1800 Massachusetts Ave Washington DC 20036-1221 Office Phone: 202-778-9134. Office Fax: 202-778-9100. Business E-Mail: sonel@klng.com.

**ONES, DENIZ S.,** psychologist, educator; b. Istanbul, Turkey, Aug. 12, 1965; d. Somer and Ulker (Saime) Ones; m. Ates Haner, July 5, 1993; 1 child, Daria M. Haner. BA, Augustana Coll., 1988; PhD, U. Iowa, 1993. Asst. prof. U. Houston, 1993—96; Hellervik Prof. indsl. psychology U. Minn., Mpls., 1996—; founder Thetametrics LLP, Maple Grove, Minn., 2004—. Author: Handbook of Industrial, Work and Organizational Psychology. Recipient Cattell Award for Outstanding Early Career Contbns., Soc. of Multivariate Exptl. Psychology, 2003, Ernest J. McCormick Award for Disting. Early Career Contbns., Soc. for Indsl. and Orgnl. Psychology, 1998; Fellow of Divsn. 14 (Indsl. and Orgnl. Psychology), APA, 1999, Fellow of Divsn. 5 (Measurement, Stats., and Evaluation), 1998. Achievements include research in meta-analyses of integrity tests, managerial selection, police selection, employment testing. Office: Thetametrics LLP 6427 Ranchview Ln N Maple Grove MN 55311 E-mail: ones@thetametrics.com.

**ONESTI, SILVIO JOSEPH,** psychiatrist; b. San Francisco, Jan. 3, 1926; s. Silvio Joseph and Johanna (Kristoffy) O.; m. Jean Thomas, May 12, 1956; children: Sally Joanna, Stephen Thomas. BS, Stanford U., 1947; MD, McGill U., 1951. Diplomate Am. Bd. Psychiatry and Neurology. Instr. pediatrics Yale Med. Sch., New Haven, 1956-58; career tchr. psychiatry NIMH, Harvard Med. Sch., Beth Israel Hosp., Boston, 1963-65; head child psychiatry unit Beth Israel Hosp., Boston, 1965-73; dir. child and adolescent psychiatry McLean Hosp., Belmont, Mass., 1973-91, dir. Hall-Mercer Ctr. for children and adolescents, 1973-91; dir. child and adolescent psychiat. tng., 1973-92; dir. clin. svcs. McLean Hosp., Belmont, 1981-83; asst. prof. psychiatry Harvard Med. Sch., Boston, 1969—. Faculty Boston Psychoanalytic Soc. and Inst. Inc., Boston, 1971-81. Contbr. articles to profl. jours. With USN, 1944-46. Fellow Am. Psychiat. Assn., Am. Acad. Child and Adolescent Psychiatry, Am. Coll. Psychiatrists; mem. Group for Advancement of Psychiatry (fellow 1959-61, bd. dirs. 1987-89), Boston Psychoanalytic Soc. and Inst. Inc., Mass. Med. Soc., Alpha Omega Alpha. Home: 4 Gray Gdns W Cambridge MA 02138-2312 Office: McLean Hosp 115 Mill St Belmont MA 02478-1048 Office Phone: 617-855-2801.

**ONG, CHEE-MUN,** engineering educator; b. Ipoh, Perak, Malaysia, Nov. 23, 1944; came to U.S., 1978; s. Chin-Kok Ong and Say-Choo Yeoh; m. Penelope Li-Lok, July 17, 1971; children: Yi-Ping, Yi-Ching, Chiew-Jen. BE with honors, U. Malaya, 1967; MS, Purdue U., 1968, PhD, 1974. Registered profl. engr. Ind., Eng. Plant engr. Guinness Brewery, Malaysia, 1967; asst. lectr. U. Malaysia, 1968-73, lectr., 1976-78; rsch. asst. Purdue U., West Lafayette, Ind., 1973-74, vis. assoc. prof., 1975-76, assoc. prof., 1978-81, assoc. prof., 1981-85, prof., 1985—. Cons. SIMTECH, West Lafayette, 1978-85, L.A. Water and Power Co., 1986-88, Caterpillar, 1993-94, Franklin Electric, 1997-98, P Plus Corp., 1999-, PPlus, 1999-, Unibus, 2002. Author: Dynamic Simulation of Electric Machinery, 1998; contbr. articles to profl. jours. Fulbright-Hayes scholar, 1967-68; UNESCO fellow, 1969-70. Fellow Inst. Elec. Engrs. (U.K.); mem. IEEE (sr.). Avocations: gardening, fishing, reading. Office: Purdue U Dept Elec/Computer Engring West Lafayette IN 47907-1285 Business E-Mail: ong@ecn.purdue.edu.

**ONG, JOHN DOYLE,** former ambassador, retired manufacturing executive; b. Uhrichsville, Ohio, Apr. 29, 1933; s. Louis Brosee and Mary Edith (Liggett) O.; m. Mary Lee Schupp, July 20, 1957; children: John Francis Harlan, Richard Penn Blackburn, Mary Katherine Caine. BA, MA, Ohio State U., 1954; LLB, Harvard, 1957; LHD, Kent State U., 1982; HHD (hon.), Ohio State U., 1996; LHD (hon.), U. Akron, 1996; D Pub. svc. (hon.), SD State U., 2002. Bar: Ohio 1958. Asst. counsel B.F. Goodrich Co., Akron, 1961-66, group v.p., 1972-73, exec. v.p., 1973-74, vice chmn., 1974-75, pres., dir., 1975-77, pres., COO, 1978-79, chmn. bd., pres., CEO, 1979-84, chmn. bd., CEO, 1984-96, chmn. bd., 1996-97, chmn. emeritus, 1997—; U.S. amb. to Norway US Dept. State, Helsinki, 2002—05. V.p. exploring Great Trail coun. Boy Scouts Am., 1974-77; bd. dirs. Nat. Alliance of Bus., 1981-84; trustee Mus. Arts Assn., Cleve., Bexley Hall Sem., 1974-81, Case Western Res. U., 1980-92, Ft. Ligonier Assn., 1997-, Kenyon Coll., 1985-93, Hudson (Ohio) Libr. and Hist. Soc., pres., 1972-74; Western Res. Acad., Hudson, 1975-95, pres. bd. trustees, 1977-95; nat. trustee Nat. Symphony Orch., 1975-83, John S. and James L. Knight Found., 1995-2002; mem. bus. adv. com. Transp. Ctr. Northwestern U., 1975-78, Carnegie-Mellon U. Grad. Sch. Indsl. Adminstrn., 1978-83; life trustee U. Chgo., 1991—; chmn. Ohio Bus. Roundtable, 1994-97; trustee Ohio Hist. Soc. 1998-2002; dir. New Amn. Schs., 1991, chmn., 1998-2002. Mem. Ohio Bar Assn. (bd. govs. corp. counsel sect. 1962-74, chmn. 1970), Rubber Mfrs. Assn. (bd. dirs. 1974-84), Chem. Mfrs. Assn. (bd. dirs. 1988-91, 94-97), Conf. Bd., Bus. Roundtable (chmn. 1992-94), Bus. Coun., Portage Country Club, Union Club, Links, Union League, Ottawa Shooting Club, Met. Club, Rolling Rock Club, Castalia Trout Club, Phi Beta Kappa, Phi Alpha Theta. Episcopalian.

**ONG, LANCE ORION,** writer; b. San Francisco, June 10, 1963; s. Woodrow W. Ong and Jade Snow Wong. AA with honors, City Coll. San Francisco, 1987; cert. in mandarin proficiency, Nat. U. Singapore, 1993; BA magna cum laude, San Francisco State U., 1999. Travel agt. Jade Snow Wong Travel Svc., San Francisco, 1989—99; purchasing supr. Palace Hotel, San Francisco, 2000; writer, pub. Chromisphere Press, San Francisco, 2001—. Tutor, mentor U. Calif., Berkeley, 2003—. Author: From F to Phi Beta Kappa, 2004. Disaster relief vol. San Francisco Fire Dept., 2000; mentor Chinese Hist. Soc., 2002. Recipient Book of Yr. Bronze award, ForeWord Mag., 2004, Bookbuilders West 35th Ann. Book Show award, 2006. Mem.: Phi Beta Kappa (audit com. No. Calif. chpt. 1999—2003, recording sec. No. Calif. chpt. 2000). Achievements include invention of bicycle double brake actuating levers and handlebar. Avocations: travel, dance, hiking. Office: Chromisphere Press PO Box 470743 San Francisco CA 94147

**ONG, LAUREEN E.,** broadcast executive; b. NYC, Sept. 24, 1952; d. Douglas and Marion (Chin) Ong; m. Richard Ong. BA in math. and speech theater arts, Montclair State Coll., N.J., 1974; MA in comm., Columbia U., N.Y.C., 1977. Mgr. sales MTM TV Distbn. Group; acct. exec. WPVI-TV, Phila.; sales mgr. KRON-TV, San Francisco; sr. exec. Rainbow Programming, 1994—96; v.p. and gen. mgr. KSAZ-TV, Phoenix, 1997—98, WTTG-TV, Washington, 1998—2000; pres. and CEO Nat. Geog. Channel, Washington, 2000—. Mem.: Cable TV Adminstrv. and Mktg. Execs., Women in Comm. Women in Cable, Nat. Cable TV Assn. Lutheran. Office: Nat Geog Channel 1145 17th St NW Washington DC 20036

**ONG, MICHAEL KING,** mathematician, educator, bank executive; b. Manila, Philippines, Dec. 16, 1955; s. Sanchez and Remedios (King) Ong. BS in Physics cum laude, U. Philippines, 1978; MA in Physics, SUNY Stony Brook, 1979, MS in Applied Math., 1981, PhD in Applied Math., 1984. Asst. prof. Bowdoin Coll., Brunswick, Maine, 1984—91; sr. mathematician, fin. analyst Chgo. Rsch. & Trading Group Ltd., 1990—92; v.p., sr. rsch. analyst First Chgo. NBD, 1993—94; head market risk analysis unit First Chgo. Corp., 1994—, 1st v.p., head corp. rsch. unit, 1996—97; sr. v.p., head treasury bus. rsch. ABN-AMRO Bank, Chgo., 1997—, head of enterprise risk mgmt., 1999—2000; exec. v.p., chief risk officer Credit Agricole Indosuez, 2000—03; prof. fin. Stuart Grad. Sch. Bus. Ill. Inst. Tech., 2003—, dir. fin. program, exec. dir. Ctr. for Fin. Markets, Stuart Grad. Sch. Bus., 2003—. Adj. prof. fin. markets and trading program Stuart Sch. Bus. Ill. Inst. Tech., 1990—, bd. dirs. Carr Global Advs., 2000—. Author: Internal Credit Risk Models-Performance Measurement and Capital Allocation, 1999, Credit Ratings-Methodologies, Rationale and Default Risk, 2002, The Basel Handbook-A Guide for Financial Practitioners, 2004, Risk Management-A Modern Perspective, 2006; editor-in-chief Jour. Credit Risk, assoc. editor The RMA Jour., mem. editl. bd. Jour. Fin. Regulation & Compliance, Jour. of RISK, editor Jour. of Global Fin. Markets; contbr. articles to profl. jours. Mem. Am. Fin. Assn., Am. Math. Soc., Math. Assn. Am., Soc. Indsl. and Applied Math., Consortium for Math. and Its Applications, Am. Phys. Soc., Phi Kappa Phi. Avocations: writing, singing, travel, painting. Home: 2650 N Lakeview Ave Apt 4106 Chicago IL 60614-1833 Office: Ill Inst Tech Stuart Grad Sch Bus 565 W Adams St Chicago IL 60661-3691 Office Phone: 312-906-6568. Personal E-mail: michaelong123@aol.com. Business E-Mail: ong@stuart.iit.edu.

**ONG, NAI-PHUAN,** physicist, researcher; b. Penang, Malaysia, Sept. 10, 1948; came to U.S., 1967; s. Chin-Seng and Hooi Kean (P'ng) O.; m. Delicia Lai, Aug. 1982 BA, Columbia Coll., 1971; PhD Physics, U. Calif., Berkeley, 1976. Asst. prof. U. So. Calif., L.A., 1976—82, assoc. prof., 1982—84; prof. Princeton U., NJ, 1985—2003, Eugene Higgins prof. physics, 2003—. Cons. David Sarnoff Labs., Princeton, 1987-89. Co-discoverer (with Pierre Monceau) of Charge-Density-Wave conduction in metals; patentee in superconductivity, 1991; contbr. numerous articles to profl. jours Alfred Sloan fellow Sloan Found., 1982-84; recipient Kamerlingh Onnes prize for superdonductivity experiments, 2006. Fellow Am. Phys. Soc., Am. Acad. Arts & Sciences; mem. AAAS Office: Princeton Univ Dept Physics PO Box 708 Princeton NJ 08544-0708 Business E-Mail: npo@princeton.edu.

**ONGAN, NILGÜN ERDAL,** interior designer, architect, artist; b. Istanbul, Turkey, July 5, 1935; d. Galip and Fatma Zehra (Aliye) Erdal; m. Onay Ongan, July 18, 1981. Degree in interior arch., Fine Arts Acad., Istanbul, Turkey, 1957; Master degree (hon.), Rome Fine Arts Acad., 1963. Decorator TRT Ankara, 1968-80; asst. dir. TRT Istanbul, 1980-92; head decor and fgn. svcs. Interstar, Istanbul, 1992-95; dir. Kanal D, Istanbul, 1995-96; lectr. faculty comm., radio and TV dept. Istanbul U.; dir. HBB TV, Istanbul, 1996. Dir. decor, graphics chief Istanbul Turkish Radio TV, 1974. Decorator for theatrical and operatic prodns., including Hamlet, Rome, 1963, Falstaff, Rome, 1963, Gehrden Castle, Dortmund, Germany, 1963, (film) Bible, Rome, 1966; one-woman shows at Ankara Am. Culture Ctr., 1974, Istanbul Marmara Etap Hotel, 1979, Istanbul Italian Culture Ctr., 1990, Mandir Della Pace Congress, Assisi, Italy, 2000; group exhbns. include Club Internat. de Feminin, Paris, Vichy, Frankfurt, 1966, anniversary Fine Arts Acad. Soc., 2002, Galery Temore, 2002, Internat. Film Festival Antalya, 2002; represented in permanent collections in N.Am., Peru, Italy, Switzerland; designer oldstyle Turkish coffeehouse. Recipient Hon. Plaquette of High Merit, Turkish Radio TV, 1986. Mem. Fine Arts Soc., Fine Arts Acad. (mem. grads. assembly), Interior Architects Soc. Avocations: ceramics, drawing and sketching, decorating. Home: Kucuk Bebek Cad Nurhan Apt No 51/7 Kucuk Bebek Istanbul 80810 Turkey

**ONGLEY, LAURI,** mathematics professor; d. Lawrence and Evelyn Wilson; m. Mark Lee Ongley, May 19, 1984; children: Sarah, Ruth. BA, Anderson U., 1978; MA, U. Ky., 1980. Instr. Asbury Coll., Wilmore, Ky., 1981—83; tchg. assoc. U. Ky., Lexington, 1983—84; asst. prof. Asbury Coll., Wilmore, Ky., 1984—86; instr. Ind. State U., Terre Haute, 1992—94, Penn State Behrend, Erie, Pa., 1998, Edinboro (Pa.) U., 1998, 1999, 2000—04; lectr. Gannon U., Erie, Pa., 2004—05; instr. Allegany Coll. Md., Somerset, Pa., 2005. Contbg. author: Geometry: Applying, Reasoning, Measuring: Worked-Out Solution Key. Audit com. mem. Centerville (Pa.) United Meth. Ch., 1998—2000, fin. treas., 2003—05.

**ONISHI, YASUO,** environmental researcher; b. Osaka, Japan, Jan. 25, 1943; came to U.S., 1969; s. Osamu and Tokiko (Domukai) O.; m. Esther Anna Stronczek, Jan 22, 1972; children: Anna Tokiko and Lisa Michiyo. BS, U. Osaka Prefecture, 1967, MS, 1969; PhD, U. Iowa, 1972. Rsch. engr. U. Iowa, Iowa City, 1972—74; sr. rsch. engr. Pacific NW Nat. Lab., Richland, Wash., 1974—77, staff engr., 1977—2001, mgr. rsch. program office, 1984—92, chief scientist, 2001—05; mem. Yasuo Onishi Cons., LLC, 2006—. Adj. grad. faculty Wash. State U., Tri-Cities, 1993-2004, prof. 2005—. Co-author: Principles of Health Risk Assessment, 1985, others; contbr. articles to profl. jours.; featured on TV program NOVA. Recipient Best Platform Presentation award ASTM, 1979. Mem.: IAEA (advisor on environ. issues), NAS (com. mem. "Understanding Oil Spill Dispersants: Efficacy and Effects" 2004—05), ASCE (chmn. task com. 1986—96), Nat. Coun. Radiation Protection and Measurements (adj. mem. 1983—), Sigma Xi. Lutheran. Achievements include rsch. in bilateral USA/former USSR joint soil and environmental assessment of Chernobyl accident. Home and Office: 144 Spengler St Richland WA 99354-1971 Office Phone: 509-375-0454. Personal E-mail: yasuo.onishi@yahoo.com.

**ONLEY, SISTER FRANCESCA,** academic administrator; Prin. Nazareth Acad. H.S.; asst. to pres. Holy Family U., Phila., 1980—81, pres., 1981—. Chair Internat. Assn. of U. Pres., UN Commn. on Disarmament Edn., Conflict Resolution and Peace. Office: Holy Family U Grant and Franklin Aves Philadelphia PA 19114

**ONO, EIICHI,** engineering educator, researcher; BS in Agriculture, Meiji U., Kanagawa, Japan, 1990; MS in Agriculture and Biosystems Engring., U. Ariz., 1997, PhD, 2001. Rsch. assoc. The U. of Ariz., Tucson, Ariz., 2002—. Mem.: ASAE.

**ONO, KENT ALAN,** communications educator; b. Casper, Wyo., 1964; BA in English, DePauw U., 1987; MA in Comm., Mass U., 1988; PhD in Rhetoric, U. Iowa, 1992. Founder, Asian Am. cultural politics rsch. cluster U. Calif.-Davis, 1997, interim dir. MURALS undergrad. rsch. program, 1999—2000, co-founder & dir. cultural studies grad. program, 1999—2002; dir. & prof. Asian Am. studies and prof. commn. U. Ill., Urbana-Champaign, 2003—. Founder Commn. and Critical/Cultural Studies Jour.; former chair, critical and cultural studies Div. NCA, chair, Asian Pacific Am. Caucus, 1996—97, co-founder, Asian Am. studies, latino studies, and gay and lesbian studies div.; chair Asian Pacific Am. Caucus of Soc. for Cinema Studies, 1999—2001. Co-author: Shifting Borders: Rhetoric, Immigration, and Cali-

fornia's Proposition 187, 2002; co-editor: Enterprise Zones: Critical Positions on Star Trek, 1996. Grantee Ford Found. Diversity of Edu. Grant, 1990—91. Office: U Ill Inst Comm Rsch 228 Gregory Hall 810 S Wright St Urbana IL 61801

**ONOCHIE, FLORENCE N.,** accountant; b. Lagos, Nigeria, Apr. 27, 1961; arrived in U.S., 1987; d. Francis Wilcock E. and Mary Nwamaka E. Okolo; m. Henry Chuks Onochie; children: Chuks, Chizo, Kosi, Ndo's, Kenn. Degree in Fin., U. Tech. Enugu, Nigeria, 1985; BS in Acctg., U. Indpls., 1991. Reconciler Peoples Bank and Trust Co., Indpls., 1988—92; field examiner Ind. State Bd. Accounts, Indpls., 1992—94; acct., pres. HCO, Inc., Indpls., 1992—2001; auditor RGIS, Indpls., 1993—94; reconciler Bank One, Indpls., 1994; acct., pres. FNO, Inc., Indpls., 2001—. Mem. Inst. Bus. Fin. and Estate Planning. Former v.p. Rotary Club Nigeria; bd. mem. Profl. Womens Adv. Bd., Indpls., 2000. Named Woman of Yr., 2000, 2004. Mem.: NAFE, Greater Indpls. C. of C., Ind. Assn. Black Accts., Nat. Assn. Black Accts. (v.p. 2005—), Ind. Soc. Pub. Accts., Nat. Assn. Pub. Accts. Home: 8836 Worthington Cir Indianapolis IN 46278 Office: FNO Profl Svcs Inc Ste 130 3921 N Meridian St Indianapolis IN 46278 Office Phone: 317-872-3437.

**ONOFRIO, ROBERTO,** physicist, researcher; b. Rome, Jan. 14, 1963; s. Aurelio and Pierina (Rinaldi) O. Laurea degree, U. Rome, 1986, PhD in Physics, 1991. Postdoctoral fellow Nat. Inst. Nuclear Physics (I.N.F.N.), Rome, 1991; mem. faculty U. Padua, 1991—. Is. researcher dept. elec. engring. U. Rochester, N.Y., 1990-92, vis. researche r applied physics Stanford (Calif.) U., 1990; vis. researcher Moscow State U., 1991; vis. researcher MIT, 1997-2000, Los Alamos (N.Mex.) Nat. Lab., 2001—. Contbr. articles to profl. jours. Mem. Am. Phys. Soc., Amnesty Internat., Sigma Xi (MIT chpt.). Avocations: history, music, travel. Office: U Padua Dept Physics via Marzolo 8 35131 Padua Italy E-mail: onofrio@pd.infn.it.

**ONORATO, NICHOLAS LOUIS,** retired program director, economist; b. South Barre, Mass., Feb. 24, 1925; s. Charles and Amalia (Tartaglia) O.; m. Elizabeth Louise Settergren, July 19, 1947; children: Gary, Deborah, Nicholas, Jeffrey, Glenn, Charles (dec.), Lisa. BS in Pub. Relations, Boston U., 1951; MA in Econs, Clark U., 1952, PhD, 1959. Mem. faculty Becker Jr. Coll., Worcester, Mass., 1952-54; prof. econs. Worcester Poly. Inst., 1955-68, chmn. dept. econs., govt., bus., 1968-74, dir. Sch. Indsl. Mgmt., 1972-99; prof. emeritus Worcester (Mass.) Poly Inst., 1994. Vis. prof. Clark U., Worcester, 1964-66; fin. cons. Coz Chem. Co., Northbridge, Mass., 1959-95. Contbr. to newspapers and mags. Trustee Bay State Savs. Bank, Worcester. Served with USNR, 1943-46. Mem. Torch Club (pres. Worcester 1967, 87, 95). Home: 39 Knollwood Dr Shrewsbury MA 01545-3329

**ONOVWEROSUOKE, FRED,** music educator, musicologist; s. Fredrick Oberuvwu Onovwerosuoke Okonedo and Agnes Orukpesheke Onovwerosuoke; m. Wendy Kristin Hymes, Feb. 24, 1994; 1 child, Omena Benjamin Oberuvwu. Diploma in music theory, Principia Coll., Ill., 1991; MBA, Lindenwood U., St. Charles, 1993; PhD in Ethnomusicology and non-profit mgmt., Union Inst. & Univ., Cin., 2002—05. Founder & artistic dir. St. Louis African Chorus, St. Louis, Mo., 1994—; dir. Internat. Consortium for the Music of Africa & its Diaspora, New Orleans, La., 1999—. Editor The Voice of African Music, St. Louis, 1993—; music dir. Christ the King Luth. Ch., Kenner, La., 2003—. Prodr.: (cd/album) Live! At the Sheldon, 1991, AENaO: The Sacred Music of Harcourt-Whyte, 2001; author: (choral jour.) ACDA Choral Jour., 2002 (Mo. Arts Award, 2001); prodr.: (cd/album) MATESO! by the Muungano National Choir of Kenya, 2002, UVUMBUZI by The Boys Choir of Kenya, 2005; dir.: (choral workshops/clinics) African Choral Music Workshops. Dir., trustee Internat. Consortium for the Music of Africa and Diaspora; mem. NY African Chorus, N.Y.C., 2002—03, St. Louis African Chorus, St. Louis, 1994—2003; bd. mem. Musical Arts Soc. of New Orleans, 2003; mem. African Chorus, Inc., New Orleans, 2003. Grantee Grant, Regional Arts Commn., 1996-2003, Mo. Arts Coun., 1996-2003, NEA, 1999-2003. Mem.: Internat. Consortium for Music of Africa & its Diaspora (dir. 1999—2003), Internat. Soc.African-to-Am. Music (UK), Am. Choral Dirs. Assn., Am. Guild of Organists (New Orleans chpt.), The Am. Musicological Soc. Universalist. Achievements include first to New mode of artistic expression through African choral music. Avocations: travel, tennis, world music enthusiast, multiculturalist. Office: St Louis African Chorus 634 N Grand Blvd Ste 1143 Saint Louis MO 63103 Office Phone: 314-652-6800. E-mail: fredo@africanchorus.org.

**ONSTEAD, R. RANDALL, JR.,** food executive; m. Pam Onstead; 2 children. BA in mktg., Tex. Tech. U., 1978; attended mgmt. devel. program, Harvard U., 1986. Mng. dir. Chapman Ptnrs., LLC; CEO Garden Ridge Co., 2002—03; pres., CEO Randall's Food Markets, Inc., Houston. Bd. mem. Metro YMCA, York Christian Coll., York, Nebr., Randall's Food Markets, Topco Assoc., Inc., Mem. Care Sys. Office: Dominicks Finer Foods Inc 711 Jorie Blvd Oak Brook IL 60523

**ONTON, ANN LOUISE REUTHER,** chemist; b. Bridgeport, Conn., Sept. 29, 1943; m. Aare Onton, 1965; children: Alan David, Daryl John, Julie Ann. BS in Chemistry, Purdue U., 1965. Lab. chemist Great Lakes Chem. Corp., 1965-67; rsch. asst. Geigy Chem. Corp., 1967-70; abstractor Chem. Abstracts Svc., 1970-72; rschr. Cancer Prevention II Study, 1980-90; chemist Prototek Enzyme Sys. Products, 1992-93; rsch. assoc. Applied Biotech Concepts, Inc., 1995-98, Genaissance Pharms., 1999-2000; mgr. rsch. devel. and prodn. AllExcel, Inc., 2000—03; lab. asst. U. San Diego, 2003—05; lab. mgr. TheraCour Pharma, Inc., 2003—05; sr. scientist NanoViricides Inc., 2006—. NIH grantee, 1996, 97. Mem. NAFE, AAUW, Am. Chem. Soc., Assn. for Women in Sci. Achievements include co-inventor on patent pending for solubilization and targeted delivery of drugs with amphilphilic polymers; first to isolate, sequence and clone A Nidulans ahr asparaginase gene; development of novel materials and methods for improved electrophoresis and DNA sequencing technologies, development of methodologies for purification and testing of enzymes, U.S.A. Nat. and world medalist in Masters and Senior Olympic Swimming. Office: NanoViricides Inc 135 Wood St Ste 205 West Haven CT 06516-3700 Office Phone: 203-937-6137. Business E-Mail: annonton@snet.net.

**ONUFRIEV, ALEXEY,** science educator; s. Vlad and Irina Onufriev. PhD, Brown U., Providence, R.I., 1997. Asst. prof. Va. Tech., Blacksburg, 2003—. E-mail: alexey@vt.edu.

**ONUFROCK, RICHARD SHADE,** retired pharmacist; b. Colorado Springs, Colo., July 5, 1934; s. Frank and Mildred Joy (Overstreet) O.; m. Karen Faye Larson, June 15, 1958 (div. 1980); children: Richard Alan (dec.), Amy Mildred. BS in Pharmacy, U. Colo., 1961; diploma, Famous Artists Schs., 1963. Registered pharmacist, Colo., Ariz., South Africa. Pharmacist Aley Drug Co., Colorado Springs, 1961-75, St. Joseph Hosp., Denver, 1976-77, Navajo Nation Health Found., Ganado, Ariz., 1977-81, Kearny (Ariz.) Kennecott-Samaritan Hosp., 1984-85, NIH, Warren G. Magnuson Clin. Ctr., Bethesda, Md., 0988—2003; dir. pharmacy, chief pharmacist Tintswalo Hosp., South Africa, 1981-84; pharmacist, chief pharmacist Miami (Ariz.)-Inspiration Hosp., 1985-88. Instr. Coll. of Ganado, 1979-80; asst. in textbook revision and illustration U. Colo., 1961; cons. Heritage Health Care Ctr., Globe, Ariz., 1988, Gerson Lehrman Groups Coun. of Healthcare Advisors, 2004—. Illustrator Pharmacy for Nurses, 1961, Colo. Jour. of Pharmacy, 1962-64; illustrations exhibited Colo. Springs Fine Art Ctr., 1964-66, Gilpin County Art Assn., Central City, Colo., 1968-74, 1st Nat. Space Art Show, Denver, 1969. Dem. precinct committeeman, 1974-76; den leader Boy Scouts Am., com. mem., 1975-76; fireman, lt. Ganado Vol. Fire Dept., 1977-81; compassionate med. missionary Nazarene Ch., Tintswalo Hosp. Gazankulu, South Africa, 1981-84; bd. dirs. Friends of Libr., Kearny, 1985-87; active Grace Episcopal Ch. Mem.: Pharm. Soc. of S. Africa, Washington Met. Soc. Hosp. Pharmacists, Am. Soc. Hosp. Sys. Pharmacists, Am. Pharm. Assn., Delta Sigma Phi, Phi Delta Chi. Avocations: travel, bicycling, hiking, skiing, computers. Personal E-mail: pasquache@aol.com.

**ONUIGBO, MACAULAY AMECHI,** nephrologist, internist; b. Enugu, Nigeria, Mar. 17, 1958; came to U.S., 1994; m. Nnonyelum Onuigbo, Sept. 3, 1988; children: Mark, Victor, Chimdi. MB BS, U. Nigeria, 1981, MSc, 1988. Diplomate Am. Bd. Internal Medicine, Internal Medicine and Nephrologist, cert. nephrologist and transplant physician Luther Midelfort Mayo Health Sys., Eau Claire, Wis. Renal registrar Queen Elizabeth Hosp., Birmingham, Eng., 1988; asst. prof. medicine/nephrology U. Nigeria, Enugu, 1990-94; ISN nephrology rsch. fellow U. Tex. Health Sci. Ctr., Houston, 1994-96; resident Greater Balt. Med. Ctr., 1997-99; fellow in nephrology U. Md., Balt., 2000—02; nephrologist and transplant physician Luther Midelfort Mayo Health System, Eau Claire, Wis., 2002—; asst. prof. nephrology Mayo Clinic, Coll. Medicine Med. Sch., Rochester, Minn., 2005—. Diplomate Am. Bd. of Internal Medicine, 2000. Co-author: Handbook of Physiology, 1999; contbr. over 50 articles to profl. publs. Co-founder Cream Circle League, Enugu, 1990. E-mail: onuigbo.macaulay@mayo.edu, monuigbo27@hotmail.com.

**ONUKWULI, FRANCIS OSITA,** computer scientist, secondary school educator, mathematician; b. Warri, Nigeria, Aug. 5, 1955; arrived in U.S., 1977; s. Chief Mathias Nwafor and Mercy (Okonkwo) O.; m. Sandra Anthonia Mgbemena, Oct. 12, 1986; children: Francis Osita, Victor Chinedu, Anthony Tochukwu, Precious Chinenye. BS in Math. and Physics, Philander Smith Coll., Little Rock, 1981; MS in Computer Sci., Atlanta U., 1983; EdD in Ednl. Leadership Higher Edn., Clark Atlanta U., 1990. Billing and credit supr. Standard Bank Nigeria Ltd., Benin, 1975-77; tutor, counselor Philander Smith Coll., 1978-81; math. rsch. asst. Atlanta U., 1982-83; instr. computer sci. Spelman Coll., Atlanta, 1983-86; asst. prof. computer sci., mgr. computer and info. sci. lab. Morris Brown Coll., Atlanta, 1986-96, assoc. prof, chmn. computer sci. dept., 1991-92; gifted math. tchr. Lovejoy (Ga.) H.S., 1998—. Cons. PBT Engring. Co., Atlanta, 1985-86; judge Ga. Sci. Fair, 1989, 90, 93, 94, 95, 99, 2001. Co-author: Computer Applications for the Twenty-First Century; author microcomputer materials for calculus students. Named Man of Yr., Atlanta Met. Coll., 2002, Prof. of Yr., 2002, Coca Cola Tchr. of Yr., 2004—05, Tchr. of Yr., Lovejoy H.S., 2004—05; recipient Tchr. of the Yr. award, Parent-Tchr.-Student Assn., 2005—06. Mem. NSF (co-chair proposal review panelist 1989-90), Math. Assn. Am., Assn. Computing Machinery, Am. Math. Soc., Internat. Devel. Edn. Coun. (sec. 1987), Igbo Union (pres. Atlanta chpt. 1986-91), Umuoji Improvement Union (nat. v.p. U.S. and Can. 2000—04, pres. Atlanta chpt.), Anambra State Assn. (nat. edn. com. chmn.), Knights of Columbus (adv. Jonesboro coun. 2005-). Democrat. Roman Catholic. Home: 7544 Sedona Dr Jonesboro GA 30236-2740 Office: Lovejoy HS 1587 McDonough Rd Lovejoy GA 30250 Office Phone: 770-473-2920. Personal E-mail: Dronukwuli@aol.com. E-mail: fonukwuli@clayton.k12.ga.us.

**ONUSTOCK, MICHAEL R.,** manufacturing executive; BA in Bus. Adminstrn., U. Wash.; grad. exec. mgmt. program, Stanford U., 1987. Formerly with Boise Cascade; sales mgr. Willamette Industries, 1973—75, gen. mgr. paper, 1975—78, gen. mgr. pulp, paper and bd., 1978—79, v.p. Paper Group, 1980—88, exec. v.p. pulp and fine paper mktg., 1989—2002; sr. v.p. pulp and white paper Weyerhaeuser Co., Federal Way, Wash., 2002—. Mem. industry sector adv. com. Dept. of Commerce; mem. exec. com. AF&PA Printing and Writing Paper Bd., AF&PA Pulp Prodrs. Bd.; mem. internat. trade subcom. AF&PA. Bd. dirs. Wash. Pulp & Paper Found. Office: Weyerhaeuser Co 33663 Weyerhaeuser Way S Federal Way WA 98063-9777

**ONWUCHEKWA, MICHAEL O.,** accountant, educator; b. Ahaba, Nigeria; s. Joseph Oji and Ego Onwuchekwa; m. Miriam C. Onwuchekwa; 1 child, Sarah C. MBA, U. Ctrl. Ark., 1990. Auditor Divsn. Taxation, Newark, 1997—2000; prof. acctg. Gibbs Coll., Montclair, NJ, 2001—. Mem.: Nat. Assn. Accts., AICPA. Democrat. Avocations: jazz, travel, jogging, reading, electronics. Mailing: PO Box 10266 New Brunswick NJ 08906-0266 E-mail: mchekwas@optonline.net.

**ONWUDIWE, EBERE,** humanities educator, writer; s. Onwudiwe Simon and Nwangbede Magdalene Achigaonye; children: Chinwe, MbaMemme Ohiaeri, Obiawo. MA in Internat. Rels., Fla. State U., Tallahassee, MS in Econs., PhD in Polit. Sci. Sr. fellow program on ethnic & fed. studies U. Ibadan, Nigeria; prof. behavioral scis. Ctrl. State U., Wilberforce, Ohio, 1986—; columnist Newswatch Mag., Lagos, Nigeria. Cons. in field. Editor: (jour.) International Journal of African Studies, (books) Nigerian Federalism in Crises, Nigeria's Struggle for Democracy and Good Governance, The Management of the National Question in Nigeria, Afro-optimism, 2003; contbr. articles to profl. jours. V.p. Nigerian Scholars for Dialogue, Buffalo. Recipient Officer of Order of Mono, Govt. of Rep. of Togo, 2002. Avocations: tennis, soccer, travel, swimming, movies. Office: Ctrl State Univ 1400 Brush Row Rd Wilberforce OH 45384 Home Fax: 937-376-6257. Personal E-mail: eonwudiwe@csu.ces.edu.

**ONYEUKU, ALFRED EME,** small business owner, consultant; b. Aba, Nigeria, Apr. 30, 1948; arrived in U.S.A., 1974; s. Jeremiah and Violet Onyeuku; m. Felicia Nkpola Onyeuku, Dec. 12, 1987; children: Nasarachi, Chisom, Ngwanna, Udobi. BS, BA, U. Nebr., 1976; MBA, Sam Houston State U., 1978. Mgr. finance U.S. West Comms., Denver, 1980—95; self employed Buffalo Grove, Ill., 1995—97; sr. cons. Internat. Profit Assoc., Chgo., 1997—98; acct. adv. Parks Coll. South, Aurora, Colo., 1998—; mng. ptnr. Interglobe Svcs. Internat., Denver, 2001—. Chmn. fin. com. 100 Black Men of Denver, Denver, 1996—97; chmn. fin. Headstart, Omaha, 1987—91. Mem.: Acad. Mgmt. Avocations: tennis, reading business journals, public speaking. Office: Parks College 14280 E Jewell Ave Aurora CO 80012 Home: 225 Woodbyne Dr Fayetteville GA 30214-1295 E-mail: onyeuku@aol.com.

**ONYEWU, OGUCHI,** professional soccer player; b. Washington, May 13, 1982; Attended, Clemson Univ. Defender FC Metz, France, 2002—03, La Louviere, Belgium, 2003, Standard de Liege, Belgium, 2004—. 14 caps, 1 goal U.S. Nat. Soccer team, 2004—; mem. U.S. World Cup team, 2006. Mailing: US Soccer Fedn 1801 S Prairie Ave Chicago IL 60616*

**ONYIDO, JOHN CHIKE,** lawyer; b. Ihiala, Anambra State, Nigeria, Feb. 14, 1969; s. John Paul and Clara Chibuogu Onyido; m. Bertha Fountain-Onyido. LLM, U. Lagos, 1984; LLB, U. Benin, Nigeria, 1989; BL, U. Lagos, Nigeria, 1990; MS in Internat. law, U. Lagos, 1998. Bar: Nigerian Supreme Ct. 1990, N.Y. 2005; cert. notary pub. Nassau County, 2005. Assoc. ptnr. Allan * Ogunkeye, 1992—99; sr. assoc. counsel The Law Union, 1999—2001, head Dept. Intellectual Property Law and Litig., 1999—2001; ptnr. R.U. Metu and Assocs., 2001—05, Jones, Lewis & Simpson Ptnrs., 2001—. Author: (poems) www.Poetry.com, Collection of Poems (Pub. Poet Editor's Choice, 2005); contbr. articles to profl. jours. Named Resource Person on Fgn. Investment and Nigerian Intellectual Property Laws, South Africa, 2000, Poet amb., Internat. Soc. Poets, 2006; recipient Editor's Choice Poetry award, 2003. Mem.: ABA, Nigerian Bar Assn., Internat. Bar Assn., Am. Soc. Internat. Law, N.Y. County Lawyers Assn., N.Y. State Bar Assn., Human Rights Inst. (mem. African forum). Office: Pvt Legal Practice 888 N William St Baldwin NY 11510 Office Phone: 516-223-3523. Business E-Mail: johnchike@msn.com.

**OOI, TENG KEONG,** aerospace engineer, mechanical engineer; b. Penang, Malaysia, June 6, 1958; s. Leong Kee Ooi and Siew Poh Tan; m. Vivian Kcont-Salirrosas, Aug. 1, 1997. BS in aero. engring., Queen Mary Coll., U. London, England, 1981; MS in mech. engring., Okla. State U., 1983; MS in aviation mgmt., Embry-Riddle Aero. U., Fla., 1989; MS in indsl. engring., U. Ark., 1997; PhD in mech. engring., U. Ala. in Huntsville, 2002. Instr. Credential, Calif. CC, 1986. Lead engr. U.S. Army, Huntsville, Ala., 1996—. Adj. asst. prof. U. Ala., Huntsville, 1996—; vis. scholar dept. mech. and aerospace and elec. engring. UCLA, 2005—; vis. asst. prof. dept. aeros. and astronautics Stanford U., Calif., 2005—; adj. prof. dept. materials sci. and engring. Va. Polytech. Inst. and State U., Blacksburg, 2005—. Contbr. articles various profl. jours. With USAF, 1986—90, with USAF, 1993—2005, ens. USNR, 2005—. Decorated Achievement medal for Civilian Svc. US Army, Outstanding Unit award with Valor USAF, Achievement medal, Commendation medal;

recipient Group Achievement awards, NASA, Def. Recognition cert., Under Sec. Def. Mem.: Structural Engring. Inst., ASCE, Soc. of Exptl. Mechanics, Am. Acad. of Mechanics, Order of the Engr., Phi Kappa Phi. Achievements include research in modal testing of a lightweight cementitious structure and structural health monitoring of composite structure, and nano-sensor technology. Home: 4416 Kiger St Huntsville AL 35805 Office: UAH Dept of MAE Huntsville AL 35899

**OOLIE, SAM,** manufacturing and investment company executive; b. NYC, Aug. 11, 1936; s. Bernadt S. and Rose (Moyel) O.; m. Marjorie R. Oolie, Dec. 3, 1961; children: Janis Feldman, Caroline Gross, Tara. BS in Metallurgy, MIT, 1958; MBA, Harvard U., 1961. Chmn. Food Concepts, Inc., Rutherford, NJ, 1962-85; pres. CFC Venture Capital Corp., Fairfield, NJ, 1984-90; chmn. Oolie Enterprises, Upper Saddle River, NJ, 1985—; vice chmn. Am. Mobile, Inc., Secaucus, NJ, 1986-89; chmn. The Nostalgia Network, N.Y.C., 1987-90, New Thermal Corp., Keasbey, NJ, 1991-95, NoFire Tech., Inc., Upper Saddle River, NJ, 1995—. Bd. dirs. Converse Tech., N.Y.C., NCT Group (formerly Noise Cancellation Tech.), Stamford, Conn. Mem. exec. com. State of N.J.-Israel Commn., 1989-93; commr. Essex County Improvement Authority, 1987-88; trustee Coun. Jewish Fedns., 1986—; bd. govs. Haifa U., 1986-90, 93-95; trustee Garden State Cancer Ctr., 1989-96, Beth Israel Med. Ctr., 1990-96, Assn. Reform Zionists Am., 1990-97, Am. Joint Distbn. Com., 1990-98; pres. United Jewish Fedn. Met. West N.J., 1988-90; vice chmn. United Jewish Appeal, 1986-96; chmn. Beth Israel Health Care Found., 1993-96. Recipient Gates of Jerusalem award Boys Town of Jerusalem, 1990, Israel 40th Ann. medal State of Israel Bonds, 1988. Mem. Harvard Club. Avocations: golf, coin collecting/numismatics. Office: 21 Industrial Ave Upper Saddle River NJ 07458 Office Phone: 201-818-1291. E-mail: samoolie@cs.com.

**OONK, MARIAN BERNICE,** elementary school educator; d. Mildred Oonk. BA in English, Rhodes Coll., Memphis, 1968; M in Elem. Edn., U. N.C., Chapel Hill, 1970; Grad. Credit over Masters, Univ. Va., Charlottesville, 1989, Old Dominion U., Norfolk, 1970, William & Mary, Williamsburg, Va., 1989; Grad. Course over Masters, U. Tenn., Knoxville, 1998. Cert. Tchr. Tenn., Va. Third grade tchr. Arrowhead Elem., Virginia Beach, Va., 1970—76, Hermitage Elem., Virginia Beach, Va., 1977—90. Contbr. Tenn. state social studies conv. Mem. Hillwood Presbyn. Ch., Nashville, Nebr., 1992—2006. Recipient Va. Beach Tchr. of Yr., Va. Beach Sch. Sys., 1982. Mem.: Delta Kappa Gamma Internat. Soc. (corr.; v.p., rec. sec. 1979—2006). Home: 741 Darden Pl Nashville TN 37205 Office: Grassland Elem 6803 Manley Ln Brentwood TN 37027 Office Phone: 615-472-4480.

**OORT, ABRAHAM HANS,** meteorologist, researcher, educator; b. Leiden, The Netherlands, Sept. 2, 1934; came to U.S., 1961; s. Jan Hendrik and Johanna Maria (Graadt Van Roggen) O.; m. Bineke Pel, May 20, 1961; children: Pieter Jan, Michiel, Sonya. MS, MIT, 1963; PhD in Meteorology, U. Utrecht, The Netherlands, 1964. Rsch. meteorologist Koninklyk Nederlands Meteorologisch Instituut, De Bilt, Netherlands, 1964-66, Geophys. Fluid Dynamics Lab/NOAA, Washington, 1966-68, Princeton, NJ, 1968-77, sr. rsch. meteorologist, 1977-96, ret., 1996. Prof. dept. geol. and geophys. scis. Princeton U., 1971-96; Shiatsu tchr. Kushi Inst. for Macrobiotic Studies, Becket, Mass., 1999—. Author: Physics of Climate, 1992; contbr. monographs in field. 2nd lt. Netherlands Air Force, 1959-61. NATO sci. fellow MIT, Cambridge, 1961-63; 10th Victor P. Starr Meml. lectr. MIT, 1989; recipient Gold medal U.S. Dept. Commerce, Washington, 1979. Fellow N.Y. Acad. Scis., Am. Meteorol. Soc. (Jule G. Charney award 1993), Royal Meteorol. Soc.; mem. Am. Geophys. Union. Democrat. Avocations: sculpture, shiatsu, meditation.

**OOSTERHUIS, PAUL WILLIAM,** lawyer; b. Webster, Iowa, Nov. 5, 1946; m. Bronson Clayton, Jan. 21, 1978; children: Elizabeth, Christopher. BA magna cum laude, Brown U., 1969; JD cum laude, Harvard U., 1973. Bar: D.C. 1973, U.S. Tax Ct. 1989. Legislation staff atty. joint com. on tax. U.S. Congress, Washington, 1973-76, legislation counsel, 1977—78; assoc. Hogan & Hartson, Washington, 1979-80, ptnr., 1981-88; ptnr., internat. and corp. tax law Skadden, Arps, Slate, Meagher & Flom, LLP, Washington, 1988—. Adj. prof. lae Georgetown U. Law Ctr., 1977—83. Contbr. articles to profl. publs.; author and co-author (books and articles). Office: Skadden Arps Slate Meagher & Flom LLP 1440 New York Ave NW Ste 600 Washington DC 20005 Office Phone: 202-371-7130. Office Fax: 202-661-8232. Business E-Mail: poosterh@skadden.com.

**OOSTWOUDER, PETER HENRY,** physician; b. Sioux City, Iowa, June 27, 1956; s. Cornelius and Alice Theresa (Roghair) O.; m. Joanna Ruth Field, June 7, 1997; children: Christina Elaine, Cornelius Wayne, Emily Theresa, Andrew Jacob. BA cum laude, Washington U., St. Louis, 1978; MD, St. Louis U., 1982. Diplomate in family practice and geriatrics Am. Bd. Family Practice. Resident in family practice United Hosp., Clarksburg, W.Va., 1982-85; family physician Jasper Med. Svcs., Heidelberg, Miss., 1985-88, Ormond Family Physicians, Ormond Beach, Fla., 1989, Ctrl. Fla. Cmty. Clinic, Sanford, Fla., 1990—. Clin. assoc. prof. Nova Southeastern Sch. Osteo. Medicine, Ft. Lauderdale, Fla., 1997—. Contbr. articles to profl. jours. Mem. Am. Acad. Family Physicians, Mensa, Sigma Xi. Republican. Mem. St. Andrews Chapel. Avocations: photography, travel, scuba diving, stamp collection. Home: 198 Poinciana Ln Enterprise FL 32738-9371 Office: Ctrl Fla Family Health Ctr 2400 State Rd 415 Sanford FL 32771-6012 Office Phone: 407-322-8645. E-mail: oostwouder@pol.net.

**OPACICH, MILAN,** protective services official, musician; b. Gary, Ind., Apr. 12, 1928; s. Mile and Roza (Perpic) O.; m. Rosalyn Helen Nicolich, Oct. 20, 1951; 1 child, Karin Joann. Grad. h.s., Gary, Ind. Tool and die maker Gary Screw and Bolt Co., 1947-58; It. Gary Fire Dept., 1958-78; instr. Purdue U., NW, Hammond, Ind., 1978-80; luthier Merrillville, Ind., 1950—. Rev. panelist Ind. Arts Commn. Music, 2003; co-founder, N.W. Ind. Youth Tamburitza Orch., 2004; lectr. in field; guest on numerous radio and TV shows; instr. guitar building, repair Joblink/Inland-ispat-Mittel, 2005—. Author Tamburitza America, 2005; writer Serb World, USA, 1984-; exhbns. include Mall, Washington, 1976, Remwick Gallery, Washington, 1978, 79-80, Smithsonian Inst., Washington, 1981, Bailey Ctr., 1982, Balzekas Lithuanian Culture Mus., Chgo., 1988, Arie Crown Theater, Chgo., 1990, Old Town Sch. Music, 1998; represented in permanent collection Roy Acuff Mus., Nashville; recordings include Bleda Djeva, Kreni Kreni, Jamin with Julius, Drina and Mel Dokich, Vintage 59 and Patriotic Songs of the Serbs; featured in books, magazines and newspaper articles. Founder, co-dir. Tamburitza Orch. St. Sava Orthodox Ch., 1964-70; founder First Tamburitza Extravaganza, 1971—. Recipient Pres.'s award for 50 yrs. of beautiful Tamburitza music, 1999, Am. Slavic Assn. honoree, 2000, Nat. Heritage Fellowship award, 2004; Ind. Arts Commn. grant, 2000, Master Artist grant Traditional Arts Ind., 2003, Northwest Ind. Lifetime Achievement award, 2005, Ivy Tech. Cmty. Linkage award, 2005; inductee Tamburitza Assn. Am. Hall of Fame. Mem.: Assn. Stringed Instrument Artisans, Ea. Orthodox. Avocations: collecting 78-rpm records, rare vintage instruments, documenting historical data, photographs, memorabilia tamburitza orchs. Home and Office: 2255 Robinhood Blvd Schererville IN 46375-1847 E-mail: m.opacich@worldnet.att.net.

**OPALA, MARIAN PETER,** state supreme court justice; b. Lódz, Poland, Jan. 20, 1921; JD, Oklahoma City U., 1953, BSB in Econs., 1957, LLD (hon.), 1981; LLM, NYU, 1968; HHD, Okla. Christian U. Sci. & Arts, 1981. Bar: Okla. 1953, U.S. Supreme Ct. 1970. Asst. county atty., Oklahoma County, 1953—56; practiced law Oklahoma City, 1956—60, 1965—67; referee Okla. Supreme Ct., Oklahoma City, 1960—65; prof. law Oklahoma City U. Sch. Law, 1965—69; asst. to presiding justice Supreme Ct. Okla., 1967—68; administrv. dir. Cts. Okla., 1968—77; presiding judge Okla. State Indsl. Ct., 1977—78; judge Workers Compensation Ct., 1978; justice Okla. Supreme Ct., 1978—, chief justice, 1991—92. Adj. prof. law Okla. City U., 1962—, U. Okla. Coll. Law, 1969—; prof. law U. Tulsa Law Sch., 1982—; mem. permanent faculty Am. Acad. Jud. Edn., 1970—; mem. NYU Inst. Jud. Adminstrn.; mem. faculty Nat. Jud. Coll., U. Nev., 1975—; chmn. Nat. Conf. State Ct. Adminstrs., 1976-77; mem. Nat. Conf. Commrs. on Uniform State

Laws, 1982—. Co-author: Oklahoma Court Rules for Perfecting a Civil Appeal, 1969 Mem. Adminstrn. Conf. U.S., 1993-95. Recipient Herbert Harley award Am. Judicature Soc., 1977, Disting. Alumni award Oklahoma City U., 1979, Americanism medal Nat. Soc. DAR, 1984, ABA/Am. Law Inst. Harrison Tweed Spl. Merit award, 1987, Humanitarian award NCCJ, 1991, Jour. Record award, 1995, Constn. award Rogers State U., 1996, Jud. Excellence award Okla. Bar Assn., 1997, Leo H. Whinery Disting. Svc. award, 1999, Lifetime Achievement award Oklahoma City Univ. Sch. Law, 2000, First Amendment award FOI Okla., Inc., 2002; inductee Okla. Hall of Fame, 2000. Mem. ABA (edn. com. appellate judges conf. 1984-93), Okla. Bar Assn. (Earl Sneed Continuing Legal Edn. award 1988, Jud. Excellence award 1997), Okla. County Bar Assn., Am. Soc. Legal History, Oklahoma City Title Lawyers Assn., Am. Judicature Soc. (bd. dirs. 1988-92), Am. Law Inst. (elected), Order of Coif, Phi Delta Phi (Oklahoma City Alumni award). Office: Okla Supreme Ct State Capitol Rm 238 Oklahoma City OK 73105 Office Phone: 405-521-3839.

**OPARIL, SUZANNE,** cardiologist, researcher, educator; b. Elmira, N.Y., Apr. 10, 1941; d. Stanley and Anna (Penkova) Oparil. AB, Cornell U., 1961; MD, Columbia U., 1965. Diplomate Am. Bd. Internal Medicine. Intern in medicine Presbyn. Hosp., N.Y.C., 1965—66; sr. asst. resident in medicine Mass. Gen. Hosp., Boston, 1967—68, clin. and rsch. fellow in medicine, cardiac unit, 1968—71; asst. prof. medicine Med. Sch., U. Chgo., 1971—75, assoc. prof., 1975—77; assoc. prof. dept. medicine U. Ala., Birmingham, 1977—81, asst. prof. physiology and biophysics, 1980—81, assoc. prof., 1981—, prof. medicine, 1981—, dir. vascular biology and hypertension program, 1985—, prof. med. physiology and biophysics, 1993—. Mem. vis. faculty Nat. High Blood Pressure Edn. Program, 1974—, Joint Nat. Com. on Detection, Evaluation and Treatment High Blood Pressure, 1991; mem. bd. sci. advisors Sterling Drug, Inc., 1988—91; lectr. in field; Selkurt lectr. Ind. U. Sch. Medicine, 1994; hon. prof. Peking Union Med. Coll., 1994; Louis Gross-Harold Segall lectr. Jewish Gen. Hosp., Montreal, Que., 1995; Joy Goodwin Disting. lectr. Auburn U., 1996; A Ross McIntyre award U. Nebr., 1996. Author books on hypertension; editor: Am. Jour. Med. Scis., 1984—94; assoc. editor: Hypertension, 1979—83, mem. editl. bd.; 1984—, assoc. editor: Am. Jour. Physiology-Renal, 1989—91, mem. editl. bd.: Jour. Hypertension, 1989—98; contbr. over 450 articles to profl. jours., chapters to books. Recipient Young Investigator award, Internat. Soc. Hypertension, 1979, ann. award, Med. Coll. Pa., 1984; fellow, Am. Coll. Cardiology, 1992. Fellow: Am. Coll. Cardiology; mem.: AAAS, Am. Fedn. for Clin. Rsch. (midwest councillor 1974—75, nat. councillor 1975—78, sec.-treas. 1978—80, pres. 1981—82), Am. Soc. Physicians, So. Soc. for Clin. Investigation (Founder's award 1995), Soc. Exptl. Biology and Medicine (councillor 1993—), Am. Soc. for Clin. Investigation (sec.-treas. 1983—86), Am. Physiol. Soc. (clin. physiology advd. com. 1992—, Carl Ludwig disting. lectr. 2002), Am. Heart Assn. (coun. for high blood pressure rsch. 1973—, coun. on basic scis. 1978—, mem.-at-large, exec. com. 1979—81, chmn. Louis B. Katz Prize com. 1984—86, exec. com. 1985—90, vice chmn. 1986, v.p. Ala. affiliate 1986—87, pres.-elect Ala. affiliate 1987—88, pres. Ala. affiliate 1988—89, chmn. 1988—90, chmn. budget com. 1990—91, mem.-at-large bd. dirs. 1992, Lewis K. Dahl Meml. lectr. 1993, pres.-elect Ala. affiliate 1993—94, nat. pres.-elect 1993—94, nat. pres. 1994—, Arthur C. Corcoran Meml. lectr. 1998, Irving Page-Alva Bradley Lifetime Achievement award 2002), Assn. for Women in Sci., Am. Soc. Hypertension (sci. program com. 1990—92, pub. policy com. 1990—), Inter-Am. Soc. Hypertension, Endocrine Soc., Inst. Medicine of NAS (corr. com. on human rights 1992, chmn. com. adviser Dept. Def. 1993 Breast Cancer Rsch. Program), Phi Kappa Phi, Alpha Omega Alpha (mem. nat. bd. dirs., dir.-at-large 1991, treas. 1993), Sigma Xi, Phi Beta Kappa. Avocations: horseback riding, tennis, hiking, travel. Office: U Ala 703 S 19th St ZRB 1034 Birmingham AL 35294-0007 E-mail: soparil@uab.edu.

**OPAT, MATTHEW JOHN,** lawyer; b. Riceville, Iowa, Nov. 5, 1952; s. Wesley John and Dolores Genevieve (Ludwig) O.; m. Therese Ann Dusheck, Aug. 13, 1977; children: Michael, Kristin, Steven. BA in History, U. Iowa, 1974; JD, Hamline U., 1977. Bar: Iowa 1977, Minn. 1977. Prin. Opat Law Office, Chatfield, Minn., 1977—. Atty. Fillmore County, 1997-2003. Mem. Fillmore County Bar Assn. (pres. 1984-85), Minn. State Bar Assn. (bd. dirs. 1985-87), Tenth Dist. Bar Assn. (chmn. ethics com. 1989-96, pres. 2001-2002, 2004-2005) Office: 22 2nd St SE Chatfield MN 55923-1203 Office Phone: 507-867-4080.

**OPDAHL, VIOLA ELIZABETH,** secondary school educator; b. Watervliet, NY, Jan. 6, 1925; d. Leslie Rouse and Violetta Frances (O'Bryon) Woodruff; m. Robert Clarence Opdahl, Aug. 4, 1956. BA, Skidmore Coll., 1945; MS in Edn., Cornell U., 1951; postgrad., SUNY, Albany, 1951-93. Cert. tchr. social studies, guidance. Tchr. social studies New Lebanon Ctrl. Sch., Lebanon Springs, NY, 1945-50, Patchogue HS, 1951-55, Selkirk (NY) Sch. Dist., 1955-56, Kingston (NY) City Schs., 1956-58, secondary guidance, 1958-62, tchr. social studies, 1962-86; ret., 1986; coll. student tech. supr. SUNY, New Paltz, 1989-94; ret., 1994. Ad hoc syllabi and testing coms. NY State Edn. Dept., Albany, 1967—82; adj. instr. psychology Marist Coll., 1977—86. Author (with Robert Opdahl): A Shaker Musical Legacy, 2004. Spl. activities organizer Town of Hurley Spl. Events Com., 1988—. Named Outstanding Social Studies Tchr., Mid Hudson Soc. State Coun. NY, 1986; recipient Pres. award, Marist Coll., 1986, Dean's award, SUNY, New Paltz, 1989. Mem.: LWV, AAUW, Hurley Heritage Soc., Friends of Senate House. Avocations: reading, writing. Home: PO Box 218 431 Wynkoop Rd Hurley NY 12443-5108 Personal E-mail: velizabeth@msn.com.

**OPDYCKE, LEONARD EMERSON,** retired elementary school educator, publishing executive, writer; b. Boston, May 22, 1929; s. Leonard and Frances (Prescott) O.; m. Susan Wolcott, 1951 (div.); children: Susan, Deborah, Margot; m. Jeanne Bernhard 1967 (div.); children: Sarah, Frances; m. Sandra S. Auchincloss, 1976. BA, Harvard U., 1951; MA, U. Rochester, 1965. Tchr. Southfield Sch., Shreveport, La., 1952-53, Dedham (Mass.) Country Day, Harley Sch., Rochester, NY, 1956-64; dir. Poughkeepsie (NY) Day Sch., 1965-72; chair English dept. Rhinebeck (NY) HS, 1974-77; adj. prof. Marist Coll., Poughkeepsie, 1977-84, 93-95. Co-chair citizen's adv. com. Poughkeepsie Sch. Dist., 1994—2002. Author: French Aeroplanes before the Great War, 1999; editor, pub. WWI Aero, 1961—; pub. Skyways, 1987—. Bd. dirs. Cmty. Family Devel. Day Care Ctr., 1984—, Hudson River Housing, 2003—05. Mem. Phi Beta Kappa. Avocations: aviation history, linguistics, education. Home and Office: 15 Crescent Rd Poughkeepsie NY 12601-4405 Office Phone: 845-473-3679.

**OPDYKE, NEIL DONALD,** geology educator; b. Frenchtown, N.J., Feb. 7, 1933; BA, Columbia U., 1955; PhD, Durham (Eng.) U., 1958; DSc, U. Newcastle-upon-Tyne, 1982. Postdoctoral fellow Rice U., Houston, 1958-59, Australian Nat. U., 1959-60, U. Coll. Rhodesia and Nyasaland, Salisbury, Southern Rhodesia, 1960-63; rsch. assoc. Lamont-Doherty Geol. Observatory, 1964-66, sr. rsch. assoc., 1966-81; geology lectr. Columbia U., N.Y.C., 1967-69, adj. prof. geology, 1974-81; prof., geology U. Fla., 1981-88, prof. geology, 1994—. Vis. prof. U. Paris, 1989. Mem. editl. bd. Quaternary Rsch., 1982. Fulbright grantee, 1959, 77-78, 89. Fellow AAAS, Am. Geophys. Union (John Adam Fleming medal 1989, com. on pub. affairs 1990-91, geomagnetism and paleomagnetism sect. 1984-86, pres.); mem. NAS (geodynamics com. 1984-86), Am. Acad. Arts. and Scis., Geol. Soc. Am. (George P. Woollard award 1987, assoc. editor bull. 1983, day medal com. 1982), Geol. Soc. Australia (Stillwell award 1982). Office: U Fla Dept Geology PO Box B137 1112 Turlington Hall Gainesville FL 32611-7340

**OPEL, PAMELA LYNN,** elementary school educator; d. Richard Gene and Virginia Beaty Opel; 1 child, Thomas Wendolin. BA, U. So. Miss., 1977, MEd, 1997. Cert. Nat. Bd. Profl. Tchg. Stds. Educator Biloxi (Miss.) Pub. Sch., 1986—87, Vernon Parish Sch., Ft. Polk, La., 1987—90; tech. editor XMCO, Sterling Heights, Mich., 1991—94; educator Gulfport (Miss.) Sch. Dist., 1994—. Substitute tchr. Northside Ind. Sch. Dist., San Antonio, 1994—95; adj. faculty U. So. Miss., Long Beach, 1997—2004; chair 504 com., 2005—06; assessor Nat. Bd. Profl. Tchg. Stds., San Antonio, 2004—, Mobile, Ala., 2004—; editor, manuscript evaluator Corwin Press, 2006.

Grantee, Miss. Dept. Edn., 2003. Mem.: Miss. Profl. Educators Assn., Assn. Edn. Therapists, Phi Kappa Phi, Pi Lamba Theta, Phi Delta Kappa. Avocations: reading, sketching, travel, spelunking. Office: Gulfport Sch Dist 37 Pass Rd Gulfport MS 39507 Business E-Mail: popel@gulfportk12.ms.us.

**OPEL, WILLIAM,** medical research administrator; BA, Pepperdine U., 1968; MBA, U. So. Calif., 1993; PhD, Claremont Grad. U., 1998. Mem. staff Pasadena (Calif.) Found. Med. Rsch., Pasadena, Calif., 1961-63, rsch. assoc., 1964-70, asst. to dir., 1970-72, adminstr., 1972-76, exec. dir., 1976-82; acting exec. dir. Huntington Inst. Applied Med. Rsch., 1978-82; exec. dir. Huntington Med. Rsch. Inst., Pasadena, Calif., 1982—. Lectr. in technology, mgmt., Pepperdine U.; adj. prof. tech. mgmt. Claremont Grad. U. Mem. Beta Gamma Sigma, Phi Kappa Phi. Office: Huntington Med Rsch Insts 734 Fairmount Ave Pasadena CA 91105-3104*

**OPENDAK, IRENE,** academic administrator; d. Leonid and Rimma Fert; m. Michael Opendak; children: Roman, Maya. MS in Engring., Kalinin Poly. Inst. Mgr. of the dept. of data processing Info. Computing Ctr., Regional Trade Ministry, Leningrad, Russia, 1976—85; dir., coll. ops. and bus. services Bryn Mawr Coll., Bryn Mawr, Pa., 1997—; info. systems mgr. U. of Pa., Phila., 1990—97. Recipient Hon. award, Am. Astron. Soc., 1991, Leadership Recognition, IBM Corp., 2001, Achievement Recognition, Bryn Mawr Coll., 2000, 2001, 2002. Mem.: Nat. Assn. of Coll. and U. Bus. Officers. D-Conservative. Achievements include lead college team in implementation of core administrative system within unprecedented 18 months accelerated schedule; first in the United States converted 20+ years of historical advancement data. Avocations: travel, skiing, interior design. Office: Bryn Mawr Coll 101 North Merion Ave Bryn Mawr PA 19010

**OPENSHAW, JENNIFER,** finance company executive; BA in comm. studies, MBA in comm. studies, UCLA. Press sec. Calif. State Treas.; dir. media rels. ICN Pharm., 1995; sr. v.p. Bank One; v.p. investment mgmt. svcs. group Bank Am.; dir. investment svcs. Wilshire Assoc., 1999; founder, chmn., CEO, pres. Women's Fin. Network, 1999—2000; vice chmn. Women's Fin. Network at Siebert, 2000—. Fin. commentator Wise Women, Lifetime TV; corr. Money Expert, CBS-TV, LA; columnist Women & Money, CBS MarketWatch; featured on CNBC; featured in Bus. Week publ., Wash. Times publ.; adv. bd. Wyndham Hotels, MuchoInfo. Author: What's Your Net Worth? Click Your Way to Wealth, 2001. Commr. Little Hoover Commn., Calif. Recipient Tribute to Women and Industry award, YWCA, 2001. Mem.: Young Entrepreneurs Orgn. Office: WFN at Seibert 885 Third Ave Ste 1720 New York NY 10022

**OPFER, GEORGE J.,** federal agency administrator; b. N.Y.C., May 12, 1947; m. Elizabeth Opfer; 3 children. BS in Mgmt., St. John's U., 1969. With U.S. Secret Svc., spl. agt., treasury agt., asst. dir. Office of Investigations Washington; inspector gen. FEMA, Washington, 1994—2005, US Dept. Vet. Affairs, Washington, Del., 2005—. Recipient Presdl. Rank of Meritorious Exec. award Sr. Exec. Svc., 1992. Office: US Dept Veterans Affairs 810 Vermont Ave NW Rm 1114 Washington DC 20420*

**OPIE, CATHERINE,** photographer; b. Sandusky, Ohio, 1961; BFA, San Francisco Art Inst., 1985; MFA, CalArts, Valencia, 1988. One-woman shows include Mills Coll., Oakland, Calif., 1989, 494 Gallery, N.Y.C., 1991, Kiki Gallery, San Francisco, 1994, Jack Hanley Gallery, San Francisco, 1994, Galeria Massimo de Carlo, Milan, 1995, Parco, Tokyo, 1995, Richard Fonke Galerie, Ghent, Belgium, 1995, Richard Feigen Gallery, Chgo., 1996, Ginza Art Space, Tokyo, 1997, Suzanne Hilberry Gallery, Birmingham, Mich., 1997, Mus. Contemporary Art, L.A., 1997, Jay Gorney Modern Art, N.Y.C., 1998, Wood St. Gallery, Pittsburgh, 1999, Thread Waxing Space, NY, 2000; exhibited in numerous group shows, 1985—, latest being Santa Monica (Calif.) Mus. Art, 1992, 94, 95, Inst. Contemporary Art, Boston, 1993, Long Beach (Calif.) Mus. Art, 1994, Mus. Modern Art at Heide, Melbourne, Australia, 1994, Nat. Mus. Modern Art, Paris, 1995, Los Angeles County Mus. Art, 1995, Whitney Mus. Am. Art, N.Y.C., 1995, UCLA Armand Hammer Mus. Art and Cultural Ctr., 1996, Mus. Contemporary Art, Miami, Fla., 1996, Gröninger Mus., Gröningen, The Netherlands, 1996, Galerie Rodolphe Janssen, Brussels, 1996, Nat. Gallery, Athens, 1996, Guggenheim Mus., N.Y.C., 1997, St. Louis Art Mus., 1997, Milw. Art Mus., 1997, Mus. Contemporary Art, L.A., 1998, Stedelijk Mus., Amsterdam, The Netherlands, 1998, Whitney Biennial, Whitney Mus. Am. Art, 2004; represented in permanent collections Whitney Mus. Am. Art, Mus. Modern Art, San Francisco, Mus. Fine Arts, Boston, Mus. Contemporary Art, L.A., Los Angeles County Mus. Art, Long Beach Mus. Art, Gröninger Mus., Centro Cultural Arte Contemporaneo, Mexico City, Ctr. for Creative Photography, U. Ariz., Tucson; work represented in numerous publs. Office: Gorney Bravin Lee 322 W 72nd St # 6b New York NY 10023-2676

**OPIE, JOHN D.,** retired electric power industry executive; BSMetE, Mic. Coll. Mining & Tech., 1961. With magnetic materials bus. GE, 1961-64, various carboloy sys., 1964-73, nat. sales mgr. carboloy sys., 1973-74, gen. mgr. mining bus., 1974-75, gen. mgr. battery bus., 1975-77; gen. mgr. Lexan products divsn. GE Plastics, 1977-80, v.p. Lexan products divsn., 1980-82, pres. specialty plastics divsn., 1982-83; v.p. distbn. equipment bus. GE, 1983-86, sr. v.p., 1986; pres., CEO GE Lighting, 1986-95; vice chmn., exec. officer GE, 1995—2000; interim non-exec. chmn. The Stanley Works, New Britain, Conn., 2004. Bd. dirs. Delphi Corp., 1999—, The Stanley Works, 2000, Wal-Mart Stores Inc., 2003—06. Life Trustee Mich. Tech. U. Office: Delphi Corp 5725 Delphi Drive Troy MI 48098-2815*

**OPITZ, DONALD L.,** science historian; b. Chgo., June 23, 1969; s. Donald U. Opitz and Angeline L. Rispoli, Antoinette I. Opitz (Stepmother); life ptnr. Gregg J. Albrecht. BS, DePaul U., 1991; MLin., 1998, PhD, 2004. Dir. Women's Ctr. U. Minn., Mpls., 2001—02; dir. Gen. Coll. Math. Ctr., 2002—; asst. prof. DePaul U., Sch. New Learning, 2006—. Advisor Reentry Students' Orgn. U. Minn., Mpls., 2000—. Author: (pamphlet) Three generations in the Life of the Minnesota Women's Center: A History, 1960-2000; contbr. biographical dictionaries American National Biography, 2000—; books. Mem. OutFront Minn., Mpls., 1994—; bd. dirs. Calhoun-Isles Cmty. Band, Mpls., 2002—. Recipient vis. studentship, U. Cambridge, 2001; fellow, U. of Minn., 1991—92; grantee, NSF, 2001; scholar, DePaul U., 1987—91. Mem.: Brit. Soc. for History of Sci., Am. Hist. Assn., History of Sci. Soc. Dfl. Roman Catholic. Avocations: bicycling, French horn performance. Home: 134 Clyde Ave Evanston IL 60202 Office: DePaul U 25 East Jackson Blvd Chicago IL 60604

**OPOLKA, JAYME LYN,** medical writer, researcher; b. Iron Mountain, Mich., Nov. 8, 1977; d. Frank David and Suzan Ann Opolka. BS in Biol. Scis. summa cum laude, Mich. Technol. U., 1999; MS in Pharmacy Adminstrn. summa cum laude, U. Tex., 2001. Cert. pharmacy technician. Global outcomes profl. intern Pharmacia Corp., Kalamazoo, 2001—02; health outcomes vis. scientist Eli Lilly and Co., Indpls., 2002—03; med. writer Takeda Pharms. N.Am., Lincolnshire, Ill., 2003—04; brand sci. copywriter Corbett Accel Healthcare Group, Chgo., 2004; freelance copywriter, med. writer, med. educator, 2005—. Health outcomes cons. Eli Lilly and Co., Indpls., 1999—2003; adj. faculty Butler U., Indpls., 2003; grad. rsch. asst., cons. Office Quality Assurance for Tex. Long-Term Care Facilities, Tex. Dept. Human Svcs., 2000—03; presenter in field. Contbr. articles to profl. jours. Recipient numerous scholarships. Mem.: Am. Coll. Clin. Pharmacy, Internat. Soc. Pharmacoecons. and Outcomes Rsch. Democrat. Roman Catholic. Achievements include research in neuroscience, diabetes, women's health, ophthalmology. Avocations: travel, outdoor activities, crafts, photography. Home: 4630 River St Quinnesec MI 49876 E-mail: jlopolka@yahoo.com.

**OPPEDAHL, JOHN FREDERICK,** newspaper publisher, publishing executive; b. Duluth, Minn., Nov. 9, 1944; s. Walter H. and Lucille (Hole) Oppedahl; m. Alison Owen, 1975 (div. 1983); m. Gillian Coyro, Feb. 14, 1987 (div. 2002); 1 child, Max. BA, U. Calif., Berkeley, 1967; MS, Columbia U., 1968. Reporter San Francisco Examiner, 1967; reporter, asst. city editor

Detroit Free Press, 1968-75, city editor, 1975-80, exec. city editor, 1981, exec. news editor, 1981-82, asst. mng. editor, 1983; nat. and fgn. editor Dallas Times Herald, 1983-85, asst. mng. editor, 1985-87; mng. editor/news L.A. Herald Examiner, 1987-89; mng. editor Ariz. Republic, Phoenix, 1989-93; exec. editor Phoenix Newspapers, Inc., 1993-95; pub., CEO The Republic, 1996—2000; chmn., pub., CEO San Francisco Chronicle, 2000—03. Chmn. bd. The Daily Californian. Mem.: Am. Soc. Newspaper Editors. Personal E-mail: joppedahl@yahoo.com.

**OPPEDAHL, PHILLIP EDWARD,** computer company executive; b. Renwick, Iowa, Sept. 17, 1935; s. Edward and Isadore Hannah (Gangstead) O.; m. Sharon Elaine Ree, Aug. 3, 1957 (dec. Aug. 1989), m. Karen Suzanne Ungar, July, 4, 2004; children: Gary Lynn, Tamra Sue, Sue Ann, Lisa Kay. BS in Naval Sci., Navy Postgrad. Sch., 1963, MS in Nuclear Physics, 1971; MS in Sys. Mgmt., U. S.C., 1978. Commd. ensign U.S. Navy, 1956, advanced through grades to capt., 1977; with Airborne Early Warning Squadron, 1957-59, Anti-Submarine Squadron, 1959-65; asst. navigator USS Coral Sea, 1965-67; basig jet flight instr., 1967-69; test group dir. Def. Nuclear Agy., 1972-74; weapons officer USS Oriskany, 1974-76; program mgt. for armament Naval Air Sys. Command, Washington, 1977-79; test dir. Def. Nuclear Agy., Kirtland AFB, N.Mex., 1979-82, dep. comdr. 1982-83; pres., CEO Am. Systems, Albuquerque, 1983—. Bd. dirs. BASIS Internat., 1991—; command pilot Angel Flight, N.Mex. Author: Energy Loss of High Energy Electrons in Beryllium, 1971, Understanding Contractor Motivation and Incentive Contracts. Decorated Def. Superior Svc. medal; recipient Alumni Disting. Svc. award Waldorg Coll., 2006. Mem. Naval Inst., Aircraft Owners and Pilots Assn., Assn. Naval Aviation, Navy League. Lutheran.

**OPPENHEIM, ANTONI KAZIMIERZ,** mechanical engineer; b. Warsaw, Aug. 11, 1915; came to U.S., 1948, naturalized, 1954; s. Tadeusz and Zuzanna (Zuckerwar) O.; m. Lavinia Stephens, July 18, 1945; 1 dau., Terry Ann. Diploma in Engring., Warsaw Inst. Tech., London, 1943; PhD in Engring., U. London, 1945; Diploma of Imperial Coll., 1945; DSc, U. London, 1976; Dr. Honoris Causa, U. Poitiers, France, 1981, Tech. U., Warsaw, 1989, Imperial Coll., 1995. Registered profl. engr., Calif. Research asst. City and Guilds Coll., 1942-48, lectr., 1946-48; asst. prof. mech. engring. Stanford U., 1948-50; faculty U. Calif. at Berkeley, 1950—, prof. mech. engring., 1958-86, Miller prof., 1961-62, prof. emeritus, 1986—. Prof. assoc. Sorbonne, Paris, 1960-61, U. Poitiers, France, 1973, 80; staff cons. Shell Devel. Co., 1952-60. Editor-in-chief: Acta Astronautica, 1974-79; contr. articles to profl. jours., also monographs. Chmn. Heat Transfer and Fluid Mechanics Inst., 1958; IAA Com. on Gasdynamics of Explosions, 1968—; organizer Internat. Colloquia on Gas Dynamics of Explosions and Reactive Systems, 1967, 69, 71, 73, 75, 77, 79, 81, 83; mem. NASA, adv. com. fluid mechanics, 1963-69. Recipient Water Arbitration prize Inst. Mech. Engrs., 1948, Numa Manson medal Inst. for Dynamics of Explosions and Reactive Sys., 1981, Dionizy Smolenski medal Polish Acad. Scis., 1987, Alfred C. Egerton medal The Combustion Inst., 1988, Berkeley citation U. Calif., Berkeley, 1988; fellow Imperial Coll. Fellow Imperial Coll.; mem. U.S. Nat. Acad. Engring. Polish Acad. Scis. Achievements include contributions to compressible fluid flow, gas turbines and internal combustion engines, heat transfer, combustion, detonation and blast waves. Home: 54 Norwood Ave Kensington CA 94707-1119 Office Phone: 510-642-0211. Business E-Mail: ako@me.berkeley.edu.

**OPPENHEIM, CHARLES B.,** lawyer; b. N.Y.C., Oct. 18, 1962; s. Barry J. and Jean Elizabeth (Reeve) O.; m. Lydia Vitlacil, July 25, 1992; children: Calvin, Dean. BA, Cornell U., 1984; JD, Fordham U., 1988. Bar: Calif. 1988. Assoc. Skadden Arps et al., San Francisco, 1988-90, McDermott & Trayner, Pasadena, Calif., 1991-93, Weissburg and Aronson, L.A., 1993-95; ptnr. Weissburg & Aronson, L.A., 1996, Foley, Lardner, Weissburg & Aronson, L.A., 1996, Foley & Lardner LLP, L.A., 1996—. Co-editor: Health Care Law Sourcebook, 1995-2000; contr. articles to profl. jours. Bd. trustees The Accelerated Sch., L.A., 2000—. Recipient Nat. Philanthropy Day medallion, L.A., 2001. Mem. Am. Health Lawyers Assn., Calif. Soc. Healthcare Attys. Office: Foley & Lardner LLP 2029 Century Park E Ste 3500 Los Angeles CA 90067-3021 Office Phone: 310-975-7790. Business E-Mail: coppenheim@foley.com.

**OPPENHEIM, IRWIN,** chemical physicist, educator; b. Boston, June 30, 1929; s. James L. and Rose (Rosenberg) O.; m. Bernice Buresh, May 18, 1974; 1 child, Joshua Buresh. AB summa cum laude, Harvard U., 1949; postgrad., Calif. Inst. Tech., 1949-50; PhD, Yale, 1956. Physicist Nat. Bur. Standards, Washington, 1953-60; chief theoretical physics Gen. Dynamics/Convair, San Diego, 1960-61; assoc. prof. chemistry MIT, Cambridge, 1961-65, prof., 1965—. Lectr. physics U. Md., 1953-60; vis. assoc. prof. physics U. Leiden, 1955-56, Lorentz prof., 1983; vis. prof. Weizmann Inst. Sci. 1958-59, U. Calif., San Diego, 1966-67; Van der Waals prof. U. Amsterdam, 1966-67. Author: (with J.G. Kirkwood) Chemical Thermodynamics, 1961; editor: Phys. Rev. E, 1992-2001. Recipient Hildebrand award, 1998. Fellow Am. Phys. Soc., Am. Acad. Arts and Scis., Washington Acad. Sci.; mem. Phi Beta Kappa, Sigma Xi. Achievements include research in quantum statis. mechanics, statis. mechanics of transport processes, thermodynamics. Home: 140 Upland Rd Cambridge MA 02140-3623 Office: MIT 77 Massachusetts Ave #6-223 Cambridge MA 02139-4307 Office Phone: 617-253-1478. Business E-Mail: irwin@mit.edu.

**OPPENHEIM, JOOST J.,** allergist, immunologist, researcher; b. Venlo, The Netherlands, Aug. 11, 1934; MD, Columbia U., 1960. Diplomate Am. Bd. Allergy & Immunology. Intern King County Hosp., Seattle, 1960-61; resident U. Wash. Hosp., Seattle, 1961-62; fellow in immunology U. Birmingham, England, 1965-66; sr. investigator Lab. Biochemistry Nat. Inst. Dental Rsch., NIH, 1966, chief Cellular Immunology Sect., 1970—83; chief Lab. Molecular Immunoregulation Ctr. Cancer Rsch., Nat. Cancer Inst., Frederick, Md., 1983—, also head Cellular Immunology Group. Mem. Am. Acad. Immunology, Assn. Am. Physicians, Am. Soc. Clin. Investigation, Rsch. Soc. Office: Ctr Cancer Rsch Lab Molecular Immunology PO Box B Bldg 560 Rm 21-89A Frederick MD 21702-1201 Office Phone: 301-846-1551. Office Fax: 301-846-7042. E-mail: oppenhei@ncifcrf.gov.*

**OPPENHEIM, MARTHA KUNKEL,** pianist, educator; b. Port Arthur, Tex., June 25, 1935; d. Samuel Adam and Grace (Moncure) Kunkel; m. Russell Edward Oppenheim, June 18, 1960; children: Lauren Susan, Kristin Lee Oppenheim Mortenson. MusB with honors, U. Tex., 1957, MusM, 1959; diploma in piano, Juilliard Sch. Music, 1960; student, Am. Conservatory, Fontainebleau, France, 1956, student, 1958. Soloist Amarillo (Tex.) Symphony, Austin (Tex.) Symphony, U. Tex. Orch., San Antonio Symphony, Dallas Symphony, Heilbronner Kammer Orch., Heilbron, Germany. Solo and chamber music recitals in Tex., N.Y., France; mem. Halcyon Trio, 1974—77; tchg. asst. U. Tex., 1957—59, 1968—69; pvt. piano tchr., San Antonio, 1962—; pianist in duo with cellist Dan Zollars, 1991—. Recipient 1st place award, Internat. Piano Rec. Festival, Nat. Guild Piano Tchrs., 1956, 1956, Tuesday Mus. Club Young Artist Competition, 1956, 1st place award Young Artist Competition, Amarillo Symphony, 1959, 1st place award G.B. Dealey competition, Dallas Symphony, Dallas Morning News, 1959; scholar, U. Tex., Juilliard Sch. Music. Mem.: San Antonio Music Tchrs. Assn., Tex. Music Tchrs. Assn., Music Tchrs. Nat. Assn., Tuesday Musical Club (San Antonio, bd. dirs.), Pi Kappa Lambda, Sigma Alpha Iota. Presbyterian. Home and Office: 9118 E Valley View Ln San Antonio TX 78217-5160 E-mail: moppenheim@satx.rr.com.

**OPPENHEIM, ROBERT,** beauty industry executive; b. NYC, May 21, 1925; s. Hyman and Hannah (Lieberman) O.; m. Ruth Wigler, Feb. 7, 1954; children: Nancy Ellen, David Paul, Howard P. BS cum laude, Syracuse U., 1950. Product sales specialist McKesson & Robbins, Yonkers, NY, 1950-55; asst. sales mgr. Clairol, Inc., 1955-65; process. Salon div., 1976-83, chmn. Profl. Products div., 1983-87; dir. mktg. Haircolor div. Revlon, Inc., N.Y.C., 1960-68, dir. mktg. sales salon div., 1968-70; exec. v.p. Milton R. Barrie Co., Inc., 1970-71; pres. Oppenheim Communications, N.Y.C., 1987—. Pub. Beauty Salon Newsletter, N.Y.C., 1971—83, Salon Update,

1988—95, The Oppenheim Letter, 1988—95; mgmt. cons., 1988—; contbg. commentator Beauty Store Bus., 1998—2004, Profl. Beauty Mfr., 1998—99; bd. dirs. Cosmetology Advancement Found., 1995—98, Internat. Haircolor Exch., 1995—96. Author: 101 Salon Promotions, 1999. With AUS, 1942-44, ETO. Decorated Purple Heart; recipient Spirit of Life award City of Hope, 1989, Showman Wall of Fame award Internat. Beauty Show, 1994; inducted into Nat. Cosmetology Assn. Hall of Fame, 1994, Barber & Beauty Supply Inst. Hall of Leaders, 1998. Mem. Nat. Beauty and Barber Mfrs. Assn. (pres. 1984-85), Am. Beauty Assn. (pres. 1985-86), Masons. Address: 1755 York Ave # 22C New York NY 10128-6871 Office Phone: 212-600-1324.

**OPPENHEIMER, BONNIE LOU,** mathematics professor; b. Canton, Ohio, Dec. 2, 1955; d. Robert Earl and Elsie Marie (Rock) Sprankle; m. Seth F. Oppenheimer, Jan. 3, 1983; children: Albert Clark, Kathryn Rose. MusB and BS, Baldwin-Wallace Coll., Berea, Ohio, 1978; MA in Teaching, U. Chgo., 1979; MA, Miss. State U., 1991; PhD, U. Tex., 1992. Dept. chmn., tchr. math. Zion Benton Twp. HS, Ill., 1979-81; computer operator Interiors by Bruce, Park Ridge, Ill., 1981-82; tchr. Round Rock Ind. Sch. Dist., Tex., 1982-88; part-time faculty Austin C. C., Tex., 1985-88; tchr. Starkville HS, Miss., 1988—89, 1994—98; part-time faculty E. Miss. C. C., Mayhew, 1989, 1995—98; instr. math. Miss. State U., 1991, grad. teaching asst. in math, 1990-91; asst. prof. Delta State U., Cleveland, Miss., 1992-94; cons. Miss. State U. Tchr. Networking and Design Ctr., 1995—96; asst. prof. Miss. U. Women, Columbus, 1998—2003, assoc. prof., 2003—06, prof., 2006—. Prin. oboist Starkville Symphony Orch. Mem. Nat. Coun. Tchrs. Math., Math. Assn. Am., Am. Assn. U. Women, Kappa Delta Pi, Pi Lambda Theta, Kappa Mu Epsilon. Democrat. Jewish. Avocations: science fiction, needlecrafts. Home: 214 Hiwassee Dr Starkville MS 39759-2118 Office Phone: 662-329-7239. Business E-Mail: boppen@muw.edu.

**OPPENHEIMER, DEANNA WATSON,** bank executive; Degree cum laude in Polit. Sci. and Urban Affairs, U. Puget Sound. Mktg. and govt. rels. officer Washington Mutual Inc., Seattle, 1985—89, mgr. corp. relations div., 1989—93, exec. v.p., 1993—95, exec. v.p. Consumer Banking and Corporate Relations, 1995—2000, pres. Banking and Fin. Svcs. Group, 2000—03, overseer corp. R&D & corp. rels., 1999—2005, pres., consumer group, 2003—05; COO UK Banking Barclays PLC, London, 2005—. Bd. dir. Catellus Devel. Corp., U. Puget Sound. Pres. Seattle Children's Theatre Bd.; bd. dir. Corp. Coun. Arts, Greater Seattle YMCA. Named Person of Yr. Media Inc.; recipient Double Halo award, Seattle (Wash.) Advt. Fedn. Mem. Mktg. Comm. Execs. Internat. (pres.) Office: Barclays PLC 1 Churchill Place London E14 5HP England

**OPPENHEIMER, FRANZ MARTIN,** lawyer; b. Mainz, Germany, Sept. 7, 1919; s. Arnold and Johanna (Mayer) O.; m. Margaret Spencer Foote, June 17, 1944; children: Martin Foote, Roxana Foote, Edward Arnold. BS, U. Chgo., 1942; student, U. Grenoble, France, 1938-39; LL.B. cum laude (note editor Law Jour. 1945), Yale U., 1945. Bar: N.Y. 1946, D.C. 1955. Rsch. asst. com. human devel. U. Chgo., 1942-43; law clk. to Judge Swan, U.S. Circuit Ct. of Appeals, NY, 1945-46; assoc. atty. Chadbourne, Wallace, Parke & Whiteside, N.Y.C., 1946-47; atty. IBRD, Washington, 1947-57; individual practice law, 1958-59; ptnr. firm Leva, Hawes, Symington, Martin & Oppenheimer, 1959-83; Fort & Schlefer, Washington, 1984-94; pvt. practice Washington, 1995—2001; sr. of counsel Swidler Berlin Shereff Friedman (formerly Swidler & Berlin), Washington, 1996—2001; individual consulting and law practice, 2001—; atty. Internat. legal Inst., 2004—. Contbr. articles to profl. and other jours, chpts. to books. Bd. dirs. Internat. Student House; founding mem. Company of Christian Jews. Decorated officer's cross Order of Merit (Fed. Republic Germany), chevalier Nat. Order of Merit (France). Mem. ABA, Am. Soc. Internat. Law (hon. v.p., treas. 1964-76), Coun. Fgn. Rels., Yale Club, Century Assn. (N.Y.), City Tavern, Met. Club (Washington). Anglican. Home: 3248 O St NW Washington DC 20007-2847 Office Phone: 202-338-0225. Personal E-mail: franzmfmo@aol.com.

**OPPENHEIMER, MARTIN J.,** lawyer; b. Apr. 11, 1933; s. Julius and Sylvia (Haas) O.; m. Suzanne Rosenhirsch, July 3, 1958; children: Marcy, Evan, Joshua, Alexandra. BS with honors, U. Pa., 1953; LLB, Yale U., 1956. Assoc. Hays, Sklar & Hertzberg, Mendes & Mount; ptnr. Proskauer Rose Goetz & Mendelsohn, N.Y.C., 1958—. Contbr. articles to profl. jours. Chmn. City Ctr. of Music and Drama, Lincoln Ctr., N.Y.; vice chmn. N.Y.C. Opera, 1985—; bd. dir. 92nd St. YWCA, N.Y., 1985—, Lincoln Ctr. for Performing Arts, 1987—; bd. advs. Mailman Sch. of Pub. Health, Columbia U., 1991; chmn. Lincoln Ctr. Constituent Devel. Corp., 2001-02. English Fulbright scholar Goethe U., Frankfurt, Fed. Republic Germany, 1956-57. Home: 400 Claflin Ave Mamaroneck NY 10543-3906 Office: Proskauer Rose et al 1585 Broadway Fl 21-76 New York NY 10036-8299

**OPPENHEIMER, MAX, JR.,** foreign language educator, consultant; b. N.Y.C., July 27, 1917; s. Max and Louise (Pourfuerst) O.; m. Christine Backus, Oct. 14, 1942; children: Edmund Max, Carolyn Christine Oppenheimer Burns. Bachelier ès Lettres, U. Paris, 1935; BA cum laude, NYU, 1941; MA, UCLA, 1942; PhD, U. So. Calif., 1947. Instr. fgn. langs. San Diego State Coll., 1947-49; asst. prof. Romance langs. Washington U., St. Louis, 1949-51; assoc. prof. modern langs. Fla. State U., Tallahassee, 1958-61; prof., chmn. dept. Russian U. Iowa, Iowa City, 1961-67; prof. SUNY, Fredonia, 1967-76, prof. emeritus, 1976—, chmn. dept. fgn. langs., 1967-74; prof. English Yunnan Normal U., Kunming, Peoples Republic of China, 1985-86. Intelligence officer CIA, 1956—58. Author: Outline of Russian Grammar, 1962; translator: Theory of Molecular Excitons (Davydov), 1962, Theory of Ship Waves and Wave Resistance (Kostyukov), 1968, The Fake Astrologer (Calderón de la Barca), 1976, 94, The Lady Simpleton (Lope de Vega), 1976, Don Juan (Tirso de Molina), 1976, Swim First and Last, 1981, An Innocent Yank at Home Abroad, 2000, Is That What It Means?, 2004; contbr. articles to scholarly and profl. jours. Active YMCA, 1936—. Served to lt. col. M.I., AUS, 1942-46, 51-56, lt. col. Res. ret. Decorated Bronze Star; Fla. State U. grantee, 1961, Office Naval Rsch. grantee, 1965, SUNY grantee, 1973. Mem.: MLA, Am. Soc. Geolinguistics (pres. 1975—76), Mil. Officers Assn. Am., Am. Soc. Dowsers, Dobro Slovo, Am. Mensa Ltd., Elks, Phi Beta Kappa, Alpha Mu Gamma, Pi Delta Phi, Lambda Delta Phi, Sigma Delta Pi. Avocation: swimming. Home: 10963 W Coggins Dr Sun City AZ 85351-3346 Personal E-mail: maxojr@earthlink.net. *When you speak, always say what you think, not what you think you should say for the sake of expediency. Steadfastly, stubbornly, cling to your ideals, principles and beliefs, but be flexible enough to change whenever changing them reflects wisdom, not weakness or compromise. Avoid ego trips or being awed by your own alleged accomplishments.*

**OPPENHEIMER, MICHAEL,** physicist; b. Bklyn., Feb. 28, 1946; s. Harry and Shirley Oppenheimer; m. Leonie Haimson, Dec. 31, 1986; children: Chloe, Nathaniel. S.B., MIT, 1966; PhD, U. Chgo., 1970. Research fellow Harvard Coll., 1971-73; lectr. astronomy Harvard U., 1973-81; physicist Harvard-Smithsonian Center for Astrophysics, Harvard U., 1973-81, Environ. Def., N.Y.C., 1981—2001, chief scientist, 1996-2001; Albert G. Milbank prof. geoscis. and internat. affairs Princeton U., 2002—; dir. program on sci. tech. and environ. Mem. panel on atmospheric effects of aviation NRC, 1995—99, mem. panel on climate variability and change, 2005—06; lead author Intergovernmental panel on climate change. Author: Dead Heat: The Race Against the Greenhouse Effect, 1990; contbr. articles to profl. jours. Fellow, Union Carbide, 1969—70, A.F. Morrison, 1979, Guggenheim, 1978—79; vis. scholar, Russell Sage Found., 2005—06. Mem.: AAAS, Internat. Glaciological Soc., Am. Meteorol. Soc., Am. Geophys. Union, Am. Phys. Soc. Office: Princeton U Robertson Hall 448 Princeton NJ 08544 Business E-Mail: michael@princeton.edu.

**OPPENHEIMER, PAUL,** literature educator, poet; b. N.Y.C., May 1, 1939; s. Fred R. Oppenheimer and Gertrude Samuels; children: Julie Sarah, Ben. BA, Princeton U., 1961; MA, Columbia U., 1963, PhD, 1970. Lectr. Hunter Coll. CUNY, N.Y.C., 1964-67, lectr. poet-in-residence City Coll., 1967-70, from asst. prof. to assoc. prof. City Coll., 1970-84, prof. City Coll., 1984—; prof. comparative lit. The Grad. Ctr./CUNY, 2001—. Exch. prof., dir. CUNY

student exch. program Sorbonne nouvelle, Paris, 1984-85; exch. prof. U. North London, Eng., 1989-90, Univ. Coll. London German Dept., 1993, 95, 97, 99; Fulbright prof. U. Osnabrück, Germany, 1993-94. Author: Before a Battle and Other Poems, 1967, Beyond the Furies, 1985, The Birth of the Modern Mind: Self, Consciousness, and the Invention of the Sonnet, 1989, Evil and the Demonic: A New Theory of Monstrous Behavior, 1996, An Intelligent Person's Guide to Modern Guilt, 1997, Rubens: A Portrait, 1999, 2002, Blood Memoir, or the First Three Days of Creation, 1999, Infinite Desire: A Guide to Modern Guilt, 2000, The Flame Charts, new poems, 2002; translator: Till Eulenspiegel: His Adventures, 1972, 4th edit., 2001. Woodrow Wilson fellow, 1961-62, Alfred Hodder fellow, 1969-70, Fulbright sr. fellow, Germany, 1993-94; recipient Eisner Scholars award Rifkind Ctr. for the Humanities, 1998. Mem. Dante Soc. Am. Home: 50 W 67th St New York NY 10023-6227 Office: CCNY Dept English and Comparative Lit NAC 138 St and Convent Ave New York NY 10031 Also: The Graduate Ctr CUNY Dept Comparative Lit 365 Fifth Ave New York NY 10016 Office Phone: 212-650-6322. Personal E-mail: pauloppenheimer@hotmail.com.

**OPPENHEIMER, PETER,** computer company executive; BA with honors, Calif. Polytechnic U.; MBA with honors, U. Santa Clara. Former mgr. info. tech. cons. practice Coopers and Lybrand; former CFO automatic data processing Apple Computer Inc., controller Americas, 1996—97, v.p. worldwide sales controller to corp. controller Cupertino, Calif., 1997—2004, sr. v.p. fin., CFO, 2004—. Office: Apple Computer Inc 1 Infinite Loop Cupertino CA 95014 Office Phone: 408-996-1010.

**OPPENHEIMER, RANDY (MARK RANDALL OPPENHEIMER),** lawyer; b. Balt., 1952; AB summa cum laude, Harvard U., 1974; JD, U. Chgo., 1977. Bar: Calif. 1977. Ptnr., co-chair Entertainment, Sports, and Media practice O'Melveny & Myers LLP, LA. Mem.: ABA. Office: O'Melveny & Myers LLP 1999 Ave of Stars, 7th Fl Los Angeles CA 90067-6035 Office Phone:    310-246-6722.    Office    Fax:    310-246-6779.    E-mail: roppenheimer@omm.com.*

**OPPENHEIMER, SUZI,** state legislator; b. NYC, Dec. 13, 1934; d. Alfred Elihu Rosenhirsch and Blanche (Schoen) O.; m. Martin J. Oppenheimer, July 3, 1960; children: Marcy, Evan, Josh, Alexandra. BA in Econs., Conn. Coll. for Women, 1956; MBA, Columbia U., 1958. Security analyst McDonnell & Co., N.Y.C., 1958-60, L.F. Rothschild Co., N.Y.C., 1960-63; mayor Village of Mamaroneck, NY, 1977-85; mem. N.Y. State Senate, Albany, 1985—. Ranking mem. edn., mem. fin., transp., water resources, health, ethics, environ. conservation and banking coms., chmn. N.Y. State Women Legislators' Lobby, chmn. Senate Dem. Task Force on Women's Issues, treas. Legis. Women's Caucus, pres. Senate Club. Former pres. Mamaroneck LWV, Westchester County Mcpl. Ofcls. Assn., Westchester Mcpl. Planning Fedn. Recipient Humanitarian Svc. award Am. Jewish Com., 1988, Legis. Leadership award Young Adult Inst., 1988, Legis. award Westchester Irish Com., 1988, Hon. Svc. award Vis. Nurses Svcs., 1989, Humanitarian Svc. award Project Family, 1990, Meritorious Svc. award N.Y. State Assn. Counties, 1990, Friend of Edn. award N.Y. State United Tchrs., 1991, Assn. Health Care Providers award, 1993, Govtl. award Cmty. Opportunity Program, 1994, Spl. Recognition award Open Door Family Med. Group, 1995, Appreciation award, Careers for People with Disabilities, 1996, Dominican Sisters Family Health Svcs., 1996, Vets. Svc. award JWV, 1997; honoree Windward Sch. Ann. Dinner, 1992, Leadership award Westchester Dem. Com., 2003, Citizen of Yr. award NASW, 2003, Legal Advocacy award PACE Women's Justice Ctr., 2004, Lifetime Achievement award, The Guidance Ctr., 2004, Amigo award Hispanic Resource Ctr., 2005, others; named Legislator of Yr., N.Y. State Women's Press Club, Woman of Yr., Westchester ORT, 1990, Woman of Yr., Woman of the Yr., Bus. and Profl. Women's Club, 2001, Pub. Svc. award cmty. housing, 2002; honoree Wash. Housing Alliance Dinner, 2002, Hope Cmty. Svcs. Club, 2002, Westchester Fedn. Women's Clubs, 2002, Hadassah Westchester Chpt., 2005 Democrat. Jewish. Office: 222 Grace Church St Port Chester NY 10573-5168 Office Phone: 914-934-5250. E-mail: oppenhei@senate.state.ny.us.

**OPPER, BARBARA NEGRI,** financial economist; b. Torrington, Conn., Sept. 8, 1939; d. Albert Frederick and Anna (LaRocco) Negri; m. Franz Frederick Opper, Dec. 2, 1967 (dec. Mar. 1991); children: Gretchen Elizabeth, Stephen Frederick. BA, Conn. Coll., 1961; MA in Econs., U. Mich., 1965. Analyst Conn. Gen. Ins., Hartford, 1961-63; econ. rsch. assoc. Life Ins. Assn. Am., N.Y.C., 1965-66; corp. sec., dir. Krambo Corp., N.Y.C., 1966-67; economist Fed. Res. Bd., Washington, 1967—72, 1976—83; fin. economist Travelers Ins. Cos., Hartford, 1972-76; lectr. Mt. Holyoke Coll., South Hadley, Mass., 1975-76; chief officer, sr. mgr., advisor The World Bank, Washington, 1983—98; pres. ConFirm, Chevy Chase, Md., 1998—. Sec. Bank Fund Staff Fed. Credit Union, Washington, 1997—; advisor sovereign debt mgmt. U.S. Treasury, Office of Tech. Assistance, Washington, 2000—. Contbr. articles to Fed. Res. Bull. Bd. dirs. Washington Bach Consort, 1998—2004, pres. 2002-2004. Mem.: Cosmos Club, Phi Beta Kappa. Home: 7004 Meadow Ln Chevy Chase MD 20815

**OPPERMAN, JOHN R.,** lawyer; b. Charles City, Iowa, May 31, 1953; s. H. Herschel and LaVora M. (Fick) O.; m. Julianne Elizabeth Radkowski, June 12, 1976; children: Paul D., Lucas J. BS in Govt., U. S.D., 1975; JD, Harvard U., 1978. Bar: Maine 1978, U.S. Dist. Ct. Maine 1978, U.S. Supreme Ct. 1981. Assoc. to ptnr. Perkins, Thompson, Hinckley & Keddy, Portland, 1978-83; sr. v.p. legal dept. mgr. Banknorth Group, Inc., Portland, Maine, 1998—2000, exec. v.p., dep. gen. counsel, legal dept. mgr., 2000—. Lectr., panelist legal and fin. seminars; instr. paralegal program U. So. Maine, Portland, 1986-87. Contbr. articles to profl. pubns. Mem. Organizational com. Parkside Neighborhood Assn., Portland, 1979; del. Maine State Rep. Conv., Bangor, 1980; mem. adv. bd. Maine Alliance Arts Edn., Augusta, 1980-81; mem. govt. rels. com. Greater Portland United Way, 1980-83; trustee Ram Island Dance Ctr., Portland, 1980-81; trustee, advisor Portland Stage Co., 1981-91; mem. coun. 1st Luth. Ch., Portland, 1980-81, 88, pres., 1989-90; mem. City Mgrs.' Policy Adv. Com., Portland, 1987-94; trustee Portland Pub. Libr., 1997—; bd. dirs. Downtown Portland Corp., 1991—. Mem. ABA, Nat. Assn. Coll. and Univ. Attys., Maine State Bar Assn. (chmn. comml. law sect. 1992—), Maine Assn. Community Banks, Cumberland Club. Home: 25 Woodmont St Portland ME 04102-2708 Office: Banknorth Group Inc PO Box 9540 Portland ME 04112-9540 Office Phone: 207-761-8500. E-mail: jopperman@banknorth.com.

**OPPERMAN, ROSANNA RESENDEZ,** vice principal; b. LA, Apr. 06; d. Victor Thomas and Dolores Resendez Mendez; m. Daniel Charles Opperman, Aug. 3, 1974; children: Joshua Mendez, Timothy Mendez, Laura Mendez. BA in Exptl. Psychology, U. Calif., Santa Barbara, Calif., 1976; degree in Multiple Subject Tchg., Azusa Pacific Coll., 1979; MA in Ednl. Leadership, Calif. State U., 2005. Admin. Svcs. Credential 2003. From instr. to coord. ABE Program Fremont Sch. for Adults, Sacramento, 1989—2002, coord. ESL Program, 2002—04, Wasc accreditation co-chair, 2002—03; from coord. to vice prin. Winterstein & Bella Vista Adult Ctrs., Sacramento, 2004—; chair Wasc, 2000. Awards chmn. no. sect. Calif. Coun. Adult Edn., Sacramento, 1997—99, pres. no. sect., 1999—2000, v.p. no. sect., 1999—2000. Cmty. adv. co-chair Fremont Sch. for Adults, Sacramento, 1999—2000; caravans dir. Nazarene Ch., Sacramento, 1988. Recipient Outstanding Leadership award, Calif. Coun. Adult Edn., 1997—2001, Excellence in Tchg. award, 1998. Mem.: Adult Basic Educators (assoc.), Calif. Assn. Tchrs. English to Spkrs. Other Langs. (assoc.). Office: Winterstein & Sunrise Tech Adult Ctrs 900 Morse Ave Sacramento CA 95864 Office Phone: 916-979-8521.

**OPPERWALL, STEPHEN GABRIEL,** lawyer; b. Racine, Wis., Aug. 14, 1953; s. Raymond and Helen Bertha Opperwall; m. Kathleen O'Neill, Oct. 27, 1990; children: Christopher Stephen, Scott O'Neill. BA, Calvin Coll., 1975; JD, U. Santa Clara, 1981. Bar: Calif. 1981, U.S. Dist. Ct. (no., cen., and so. dists.) Calif. 1981, U.S. Tax Ct. 1994, U.S. Ct. Appeals (9th cir.) 1984; cert. specialist in creditor's rights Tchg. asst. U. Santa Clara (Calif.) Sch. Law, 1979; judge's law clk. U.S. Ct. Appeals, 9th Cir., San Francisco, 1980; assoc. Pitto & Ubhaus, San Jose, Calif., 1980-82, Germino, Layne & Brodie,

Palo Alto, Calif., 1982-87, Tarkington, O'Connor & O'Neill, San Jose, 1988-90, Smith & Smith, San Jose, 1990-92; pvt. practice Law Offices of Stephen G. Opperwall, Pleasanton, Calif., 1992—. Judge pro tem Santa Clara County Cts., 1986—, Alameda County (Calif.) Cts., 1992—; mem. adv. bd. Fremont (Calif.) Bank, 1996. Editor Santa Clara Law Review, 1980. Mem. bd. dirs. Fremont Symphony, 1994. Mem. Coml. Law League Am., Pleasanton C. of C. Avocations: golf, tennis, computers. Office: 4900 Hopyard Rd Ste 100 Pleasanton CA 94588-3149 Office Phone: 925-417-0300. E-mail: lawofcsgo@aol.com.

**OPPEY, MARK OFUSY**, career officer; b. Accra, Ghana, May 27, 1965; s. James and Juliana (Ogyerewaa) O.; m. Barbara Asamoah, Mar. 12, 1992; 1 child, Dorcas Darkoah. Lines and exch. operator, radio operator 1st Signal Regiment Burma Camp, Accra, Ghana, 1989—. Presbyterian. Avocations: football, hockey, sports, films, international news. Office: 1st Signal Regiment Dual Lines Blk E Burma Camp Accra Ghana

**OPRE, THOMAS EDWARD**, retired editor, retired film company executive; b. Evansville, Ind., Nov. 6, 1943; s. William Jennings and Ruth (Strouss) O.; children: Thomas Andrew, William Hartley. AB in Journalism, Ind. U., 1965. Writer sports and outdoors Decatur (Ill.) Herald and Rev., 1965-66; outdoor editor Detroit Free Press, 1966—91; field editor Midwest div. Field and Stream mag., 1971-81; editorial dir. Gt. Lakes Sportsman mag., 1972-75; editor-at-large and sports vehicles editor Outdoor Life mag., 1981-93; pres. Tom Opre Prodns., 1967—2004. Pres. TOP Safaris, Inc., 1986—2004. Author numerous articles in outdoor and travel fields. Recipient James Henshall award Am. Fish Tackle Mfrs. Assn., 1969, Teddy award Internat. Outdoor Travel Film Festival, 1973, Environ. award EPA, 1977, Nat. Writer's award Safari Club Internat., 1977, Deep Woods Writing award OWAA, 1977, Conservation Service award Ducks Unltd., 1977; World Wildlife Found. award, 1981; named to Internat. Fishing Hall of Fame, 1968, Conservation Communicator of Yr., 1985. Mem. Outdoor Writers Assn. Am. (past dir., pres., v.p., chmn. bd.), Assn. Gt. Lakes Outdoor Writers (past dir., chmn. bd., pres., v.p.), Mich. Outdoor Writers Assn. (v.p., pres., chmn. bd. dirs.), Alpha Tau Omega. Home and Office: 255 Powers Cv NE Marietta GA 30067-1503 Personal E-mail: topsafaris@aol.com.

**O'QUINN, APRIL GALE**, obstetrician, gynecologist, educator; b. Columbia, Miss., Apr. 21, 1936; d. R.V. and Anna Pauline (Cook) O'Q. Diploma, Scott and White Sch. Nursing, 1965; AA, Temple Jr. Coll., 1965; BS with honors, Baylor U., 1968; MD, U. Tex. Med. Br., 1971. Diplomate Am. Bd. Ob-Gyn. Intern U. Tex. Med. Br., Galveston, 1971-72, resident ob-gyn., 1972-75; fellow in oncology M.D. Anderson Hosp., Houston, 1976-78; practice medicine specializing in ob-gyn. Galveston, 1978-81, New Orleans, 1981—. Asst. prof. dept. ob-gyn. U. Tex. Med. Br., Galveston, 1975—81; mem. staff John Sealy Hosp., St. Mary's Hosp., Galveston, Tulane Med. Ctr., New Orleans Charity Hosp., Touro Infirmary, New Orleans; assoc. prof., dir. div. gynecol. oncology dept. ob-gyn. Tulane U. Sch. Medicine, New Orleans, 1981—85, prof., 1985—89, prof., chair dept. ob-gyn., 1989—. Fellow: ACOG, Willard R. Cooke Obstet. and Gynecol. Soc.; mem.: AMA, La. Med. Assn., Assn. Profs. in Ob-Gyn., Coun. Univ. Chmn. in Ob-Gyn., Soc. Gynecologic Oncologists, Felix Rutledge Soc. Orleans Parish. Republican. Baptist. Office: Tulane U Sch Medicine Dept Ob Gyn New Orleans LA 70112 E-mail: aoquinn@tulane.edu.

**O'QUINN, JOHN M.**, lawyer; b. 1941; JD magna cum laude, U. Houston, 1967. Bar: Tex. 1967, U.S. Dist. Ct. (so. and ea. dists.) Tex., U.S. Ct. Appeals (5th cir.) 1971, U.S. Supreme Ct. 1972. Founding ptnr. O'Quinn, Kerensky, McAninch & Laminack, Houston, 1981—. Mem. adv. com. Tex. State Supreme Ct., 1984-94; trustee U. Houston Law Found., 1985—; adj prof. law, Univ. Houston, So. Tex. Coll. Law, Tex. Southern Coll. Law. Regent U. Houston, 1993-1999. Honored by Nat. Law Jour. as one of 100 Most Influential Lawyers in U.S., 1994; named as mem. to Inner Circle of Advocates; named as one of 100 Legal Legends of Texas, Tex. Lawyer, and one of 5 Best Texas Trial Lawyers of the Century, Houston Chronicle. Am. Trial Lawyers Assn., Tex. Trial Lawyers Assn. (dir.), Houston Trial Lawyers Assn. (dir.), State Bar Tex., U. Houston Law Alumni Assn. (pres. 1978). Office: O'Quinn Kerensky & Laminack PC 2300 Lyric Centre 440 Louisiana St Houston TX 77002-1639

**O'QUINN, TERRY (TERRANCE QUINN)**, actor; b. Newberry, Mich., July 15, 1952; m. Laurie O'Quinn; 2 children. Grad., Iowa Univ., Ctrl. Mich. Univ. Actor: (TV films) FDR: The Last Year, 1980, Right to Kill, 1985, An Early Frost, 1985, Women of Valor, 1986, Between Two Women, 1986, A Mother's Request, 1987, When the Time Comes, 1987, Stranger on My Land, 1988, Guts and Glory, 1989, Roe vs. Wade, 1989, Kaleidoscope, 1990, Perry Mason: The Case of the Desperate Deception, 1990, The Last to Go, 1991, Son of the Morning Star 1991, Shoot First, 1991, Deliver Them from Evil, 1992, Trial, 1992, Sexual Advances, 1992, Wild Car, 1992, The Good Fight, 1992, Born Too Soon, 1993, Visions of Murder, 1993, MacShayne: Winner Takes All, 1994, Heart of a Child, 1994, Don't Talk to Strangers, 1994, Justice in a Small Town, 1994, A Friend to Die For, 1994, Ray Alexander: A Menu for Murder, 1995, On the Edge of Innocence, 1997, My Stepson, My Lover, 1997, Murder in a Small Town, 1999, Harsh Realm, 1999, Semper Fi, 2001, WW3, 2001, Hometown Legend, 2002, The Locket, 2002, Phenomenon II, 2003; (films) Heaven's Gate, 1980, Without a Trace, 1983, All the Right Moves, 1983, Places in the Heart, 1984, Mrs. Soffel, 1984, Mischief, 1985, Silver Bullet, 1985, Space Camp, 1986, The Stepfather, 1987, Black Widow, 1987, Pin, 1988, Jogger, 1988, Young Guns, 1988, Blind Fury, 1989, Stepfather II, 1989, The Forgotten One, 1990, Prisoners of the Sun, 1990, The Rocketeer, 1991, Company Business, 1991, My Samurai, 1992, The Cutting Edge, 1992, Tombstone, 1993, Lipstick Camera, 1994, Shadow Warriors, 1996, Primal Fear, 1996, Ghosts of Mississippi, 1996, Shadow Conspiracy, 1997, Breast Men, 1997, Rated X, 2000; (TV series) The Doctors, 1981, The X Files, 1998, JAG, 2000-2002, Alias, 2003-2004, The West Wing, 2004, Lost, 2004- (Outstanding Performance by an Ensemble in a Drama Series, Screen Actors Guild award, 2006); numerous TV series guest appearances. Mailing: care Touchstone TV Prodn Bldg #343 500 S Buena Vista Burbank CA 91521*

**ORAL, ELIF ARIOGLU**, endocrinologist, researcher; b. Istanbul, Turkey, Sept. 29, 1968; arrived in U.S., 1993; d. Ersin and Ulku Arioglu; m. Hakan Oral, June 30, 2001; children: Mert Hakan children: Kaan Tugrul. MD, Istanbul U., 1992. Diplomate Am. Bd. Internal Medicine, Am. Bd. Endocrinology and Metabolism. Intern dept. medicine Sinai Hosp., Detroit, 1993—94, resident dept. medicine, 1994—96; clin. assoc. diabetes br. NIDDK, NIH, Bethesda, Md., 1996—99, sr. fellow diabetes br., 1999—2002; asst. prof. dept. internal medicine divsn. endocrinology U. Mich. Med. Sch., Ann Arbor, 2002—. Clin. investiagor med. rsch. Efficacy of Leptin Replacement in the Treatment of Lipodystrophy. Contbr. articles to profl. jours. Named one of Jaycees Outstanding Young Persons of Turkey, Jaycees of Turkey, 1992; recipient Pilot and Feasibility grant, Mich. Diabetes Rsch. and Tng. Ctr., 2002. Mem.: Am. Assn. Clin. Endocrinologists, European Assn. for Study of Diabetes, Endocrine Sociaty, Am. Diabetes Assn., AMA. Achievements include research in Treatment of lipodystrophy syndromes in humans. Avocations: jogging, reading, music. Office Phone: 734-615-7271. Business E-Mail: eliforal@umich.edu.

**ORAM, ROBERT W.**, library administrator; b. Warsaw, Ind., June 11, 1922; s. George Henry and Lottie Mae (Gresso) O.; m. Virginia White, June 16, 1949; 1 child, Richard W. BA, U. Toledo, 1949; MS in Library Adminstrn., U. Ill., 1950. Asst. to librarian U. Mo.-Columbia, 1950-56; circulation librarian U. Ill.-Urbana, 1956-67, dir. pub. service, 1973-77, assoc. univ. librarian, 1971-79, acting univ. librarian, 1975-76; dir. Central Univ. Libraries So. Meth. U., Dallas, 1979-89, dir. emeritus, 1989. Mem. adv. com. Ill. State Library, Springfield, 1975-79 Contbr. articles to profl. jours. Exec. sec. Friends of So. Meth. U. Librs., 1980-89; former mem. bd. dirs. Urbana Free Libr., Lincoln Trails Libr. Sys., Champaign, Ill.; trustee Friends Austin (Tex.) Pub. Libr. 1994-99. Mem. ALA (life, pub. com. 1975-79), Friends of

Libraries U.S.A. (exec. bd. 1980-86), Ill. Library Assn. (treas. 1972-73), Democrat. Avocations: reading, music. Home: The Heritage 4409 Gaines Ranch Loop # 252 Austin TX 78735 E-mail: Roam1@austin.rr.com.

**ORANGE, CAROLYN**, education professor; b. St. Louis, July 11, 1948; d. William, Sr. and Alma M.; m. John H. Orange, Nov. 22, 1970; children: Traci, Timothy, Tisha. BA, Harris-Stowe Coll., 1970; MS, Washington U., St. Louis, 1977, PhD, 1991. Cert. tchr., Mo. Tchr. St. Louis Pub. Schs., 1970-77; asst. staff mgr. Southwestern Bell, St. Louis, 1977-80; program dir. Maritz Motivation, St. Louis, 1983-85; instr. Maryville U., St. Louis, 1986-88; tchg. asst. Washington U., St. Louis, 1990, motivation cons., 1987-91; asst. prof. St. Louis U., 1991-93, U. Tex., San Antonio, 1993—98, assoc. prof., 1998—2004, prof., 2004—. Cons. St. Louis Pub. Schs., 1992, San Antonio Ind. Sch. Dist., Tex., 1995-97, Region 13, San Antonio, 1995, 97-98; book reviewer Merrill Edn. Prentice Hall, 1997; vis. scholar Ednl. Testing Svc., 2005; presenter in field Author: 25 Biggest Mistakes Teachers Make and How to Avoid Them, 2000, The Quick Reference Guide to Educational Innovations, 2002, 44 Smart Strategies For Avoiding Classroom Mistakes, 2004; author/prodr.: (video) Using Peer Models to Teach Self-Regulation, 1996; contbr. articles to profl. jours. Publicity chair Ebony Fashion Fair, Chgo., 1996, 97, 99; mem. human rels. com. City of University City, St. Louis, 1992; bd. dirs. Greater San Antonio coun. Girl Scout U.S., 2003. Recipient four-year scholarship Harris Stowe State, St. Louis Pub. Schs., 1966-70, univ. fellow Washington U., St. Louis, 1975-77, 88-89, Spencer fellowship Woodrow Wilson Found., Chgo., 1990-91; named to San Antonio Women's Hall of Fame, 2004, others; vis. scholar Ednl. Testing Svc.; grantee in field. Mem. Am. Ednl. Rsch. Assn., Am Psychol. Soc., Serious About Money Investment Club (pres. 1995--), Phi Theta Kappa. Avocations: collecting costume jewelry, writing, painting, mentoring. Office: Univ Tex 6900 N Loop 1604 W San Antonio TX 78249-1130 Office Phone: 210-458-5417. Personal E-mail: jhorange2@swbell.net. Business E-Mail: carolyn.orange@utsa.edu.

**ORANGE, JORDAN SCOTT**, immunologist, educator, researcher; b. N.Y.C., N.Y., Jan. 29, 1968; s. Allan Herbert and Amy Lynn Orange; m. Katherine Rose Phillips, June 23, 2001; children: Audrey Hart, Marlaina Alyn. AB, Brown U., 1990, PhD, 1996, MD, 1997. Diplomate Am. Bd. Pediats., Am. Bd. Immunology and Allergy. Instr. Harvard Med. Sch., Boston, 2003; attending physician Children's hosp., Boston, 2003, Children' Hosp., Phila., 2003—; asst. prof. U. Pa. Sch. Medicine, Phila., 2003—. Dir. Jeffrey Modell Diagnostic Ctr. for Primary Immunodeficiency, Phila., 2004—. Recipient Dobular prize for Immunology Rsch., 2001; Ethyl Brach Foederer Fund fellow, 2004, Glaxo Smith Kline Immunology fellow, 2001. Fellow: Am. Acad. Pediatrics; mem.: Am. Acad. Asthma, Allergy and Immunology, Am. Assn. Immunologists. Office: Children's Hosp Phila 3615 Civil Ctr Blvd ARC 1216F Philadelphia PA 19104 Office Phone: 215-590-2549.

**ORANSKY, IVAN**, writer, editor; b. Nyack, N.Y., Aug. 20, 1972; s. Stanley Howard and Lesley Marsha Oransky. BA, Harvard U., 1994; MD, NYU, 1998. Editor-in-chief Praxis Post, N.Y.C., 2000—02; web editl. dir. The Scientist, Phila., 2002—04, dep. editor, 2004—, Adj. prof. NYU, N.Y.C., 2002—. Author: Insider's Guide to Medical Schools, 1999, Appleton & Lange's Review of Psychiatry, 6th edit., 2001, 8th edit., 2005, Common Symptom Answer Guide, 2005; contbr. The Lancet. Mem.: Online News Assn., Assn. for Health Care Journalists (nat. bd. dirs. 2002—), Am. Soc. Bioethics and Humanities, Nat. Assn. Sci. Writers. Personal E-mail: ivan-oransky@erols.com.

**ORBACH, RAYMOND LEE**, federal agency administrator, physicist, researcher; b. LA, July 12, 1934; s. Morris Albert and Mary Ruth (Miller) O.; m. Eva Hannah Spiegler, Aug. 26, 1956; children: David Miller, Deborah Hedwig, Thomas Randolph. BS, Calif. Inst. Tech., 1956; PhD, U. Calif. Berkeley, 1960; PhD in Policy Analysis (hon.), The Rand Grad. Sch., Santa Monica, Calif., 2002. NSF postdoctoral fellow Oxford U., 1960-61; asst. prof. applied physics Harvard U., 1961-63; prof. physics UCLA, 1963-92, asst. vice chancellor acad. change and curriculum devel., 1970-72, chmn. acad. senate L.A. divsn., 1976-77, provost Coll. Letters and Sci., 1982-92; chancellor U. Calif., Riverside, 1992—2002, chancellor emeritus, Disting. prof. physics emeritus, 2002—; dir. Office Sci. US Dept. Energy, Washington, 2002—06, under sec. for sci., 2006—. Mem. physics adv. panel NSF, 1970-73; mem. vis. com. Brookhaven Nat. Lab., 1970-74; mem. materials rsch. lab. adv. panel NSF, 1974-77; mem. Nat. Commn. on Rsch., 1978-80; chmn. 16th Internat. Conf. on Low Temperature Physics, 1981; Joliot Curie prof. Ecole Superieure de la Physique et Chimie Industrielle de la Ville de Paris, 1982, chmn. Gordon Rsch. Conf. on Fractals, 1986; Lorentz prof. U. Leiden, Netherlands, 1987; Raymond and Beverly Sackler lectr. Tel Aviv U., 1989; faculty rsch. lectr. UCLA, 1990; Andrew Lawson lectr. U. Calif., Riverside, 1992; mem. external rev. com. Nat. High Magnetic Fields Lab., 1994-01. Author: (with A.A. Manenkov) SpinLattice Relaxation in Ionic Solids, 1966; divsn. assoc. editor Phys. Rev. Letters, 1980-83, Jour. Low Temperature Physics, 1980-90, Phys. Rev., 1983-87; contbr. articles to profl. jours. Recipient Whitney M. Young Humanitarian award Urban League of Riverside and San Bernardino, 1998, El Sol Azteca award La Prensa Hispana, 2000, Disting. Alumni award Calif. Inst. Tech., 2005; Alfred P. Sloan Found. fellow, 1963-67; NSF sr. postdoctoral fellow Imperial Coll., 1967-68; Guggenheim fellow Tel Aviv U., 1973-74. Fellow AAAS (chairperson steering group physics sect.), Am. Phys. Soc. (chmn. nominations com. 1981-82, counselor-at-large 1987-91, chmn. divsn. condensed matter 1990-91); mem. NSF (mem. rsch. adv. divsn. materials 1992-93), Phys. Soc. (London), Univ. Rsch. Assn. (chair coun. pres. 1993), Sigma Xi, Phi Beta Kappa, Tau Beta Pi. Office: US Dept Energy 1000 Independence Ave SW Washington DC 20585 Office Phone: 202-586-0505. Personal E-mail: rorbach@earthlink.net.

**ORBEN, JACK RICHARD**, investment company executive, director; b. Bklyn., June 16, 1938; s. Stanley Souza and Helena Emily (Hall) O.; m. Patricia Wells, Dec. 17, 1960; children: Stacey Souza, Stephanie Anne, Bradford Richard. AA, Valley Forge, Pa., 1956; BA, Tufts U., Medford, Mass., 1960. Sales mgr. nat. accts. NY Tel Co., 1960—66; founder, exec. v.p. Facts, Inc., 1966—69; chmn., CEO Fiduciary Alliance, Inc., NYC, 1970—; chmn. Oaktree Asset Mgmt., LLC, NYC, 2004—03. Chmn., CEO, pres. Fiduciary Counsel, Inc., 1979-04; chmn. White Plains Charter Revision Commn.; mem. Fin. Com. City of White Plains; past pres. White Plains Child Day Care Assn., Thomas Slater Ctr.; past chmn., bd. dirs. YMCA Ctrl. and No. Westchester Mem. indsl. devel. agy. Town of Riverhead, N.Y. With USNG, 1960-66. Mem. Investment Advisors Assn., Am. Inst. Econ. Rsch., Larchmont Yacht Club, NY Yacht Club, Union League Club, Windemere Island Club, Univ. Club, Down Town Assn., The Econ. Club of NY, Inst. for Pvt. Investors, Fgn. Policy Rsch. Inst., The Pilgrims. Home: 61 Harbor Rd Riverhead NY 11901 Office Phone: 631-722-5649. E-mail: jrorben@aol.com

**ORBEN, ROBERT**, scriptwriter, writer; b. NYC, Mar. 4, 1927; s. Walter August and Marie O.; m. Jean Louise Connelly, July 25, 1945. Humor and speech writer for entertainment personalities, bus. execs., politicians, 1946—; writer Jack Paar Show, N.Y.C., 1962-63, Red Skelton Hour, Hollywood, Calif., 1964-70; editor Orben's Current Comedy, Wilmington, Del., 1971-89; cons. to Vice Pres. Gerald R. Ford, Washington, 1974; speechwriter Pres. Gerald R. Ford, Washington, 1974-75; spl. asst. to pres., dir. White House speechwriting dept., Washington, 1976-77; speaker on uses of humor in communication, 1977—. Author: 2500 Jokes to Start 'Em Laughing, 1979, 2100 Laughs for All Occasions, 1983, 2400 Jokes to Brighten Your Speeches, 1984, 2000 Sure-Fire Jokes for Speakers, 1986, Speaker's Handbook of Humor, 2000, others. Recipient World Humor award Workshop Libr. on World Humor, 1992, Humor award Gliner Humor Ctr., U. Md., 2005; Literary fellow Acad. Magical Arts, 1996. Mem. Writers Guild Am. Clubs: Nat. Press (Washington). Unitarian Universalist. Avocations: travel, theater. Home: 3709 S George Mason Dr Apt 205E Falls Church VA 22041-3700 *I have spent most of my lifetime creating laughter and consider it a lifetime well spent. Laughter is one of the glories of the human experience. It warms, amuses, instructs, and opens emotional doors. For me, laughter has been a living and a loving as well.*

**ORBISON, JAMES ARCHER, JR.**, cardiologist, surgeon; b. Dryden, Mich., Aug. 22, 1914; s. James Archer Sr. and Florence (Chamberlain) m. Pil-Sook Lee Orbison, Nov. 7, 1988; m. Helen Alice Bentley (dec.); children: Carole Ann Seeley, James Archer Obison III. Student, U. Denver, 1933—34; BA, U. Mich., 1937, MD, 1940. Diplomate Am. Bd. Internal Medicine, Am. Bd. Cardiovascular Disease, lic. physician Hawaii, Mich. Intern Harper Hosp., 1940—41; commd. 2d lt. US Army, 1941, advanced through grades to col., 1968; resident in internal medicine Oliver Gen. Hosp., Augusta, Ga., 1947—49; asst. prof. clinical medicine Med. Coll. Ga., Augusta, 1949—50; fellow in cardiovascular disease Walter Reed Gen. Hosp., Washington, 1951—52; asst. clin. prof. medicine U. Colo. Sch. Medicine, Denver, 1960—64; cons. tchg. internal medicine Queen's Med. Ctr., Honolulu, 1964—67, attending staff, 1967—; assoc. clin. prof. medicine U. Hawaii Sch. Medicine, 1967—; assoc. clin. prof. John Burns Sch. Medicine, Honolulu, 1967—88. Presenter in field. Contbr. articles to profl. jours. Decorated Commendation medal US Army, Legion of Merit, Am. Def. medal; recipient Cardiology Laureate award, Hawaii Heart Assn., 1988; grantee, US Army R & D Command, 1959. Fellow: Am. Coll. Cardiology (program com. annual meeting 1962, Hawaii gov. 1971—74); mem.: ACP (life; program com. Colo. regional meeting 1960—64, program com. annual meeting 1963, program com. Hawaii regional meeting 1964), Hawaii Med. Soc. (med. edn. com. 1971—, chronic illness com. 1973—), Assn. for Hosp. Med. Edn., Am. Soc. Clinical Pharmacology and Therapeutics, Am. Fedn. Clin. Rsch. (sr.), Honolulu County Med. Soc. (postgrad. com. 1970—), Hawaii Heart Assn. (bd. dirs. 1964—, 2d v.p. 1972—73, exec. com. 1972—, pres.-elect 1973—). Republican. Presbyterian. Avocations: fishing, tennis, golf, photography, football. Home. 15 Crecienta Ln Sausalito CA 94965

**ORBIT, WILLIAM (WILLIAM WAINWRIGHT)**, record producer; b. Eng., 1959; Hit records include Torch Song Wish Thing, 1984, Ecstasy, 1985, Exhibit A, 1987, Toward the Unknown Region, 1995, William Orbit, Orbit, 1987, Strange Cargo, 1984-87, Strange Cargo 2, 1990, Strange Cargo 3, 1993, Strange Cargo Hinterland, 1995, William Orbit The Best of Strange Cargos, 1996, The Electric Chamber Places in a Modern Style, 1995, Beth Orton Superpinkymandy, 1993, Caroline Lavelle Spirit, 1995, Bassomatic Set the Controls for the Heart of the Bass, 1990, and Science and Melody, 1997, Belinda Carlisle Belinda, 1986, Madonna Ray of Light (album, 1999 Grammy winner for best prodn.), 1998, Wishbone Ash Nouveau Calls, 1998, various Guerrilla Grooves Volume 1, 1991. TV and movie appearances include Rebellious Jukebox, 1983-84, Bachelor Party, 1984, Youngblood, 1986, Texas Chainsaw Massacre 2, 1986, Hot Shot, 1987, Heat, 1996, and Harald, 1997, Pieces in a Modern Style, 2000.

**ORCE, KENNETH W.**, lawyer; b. Yonkers, NY, Apr. 3, 1943; s. Edmund John and Helen (Mulcahy) Orce; m. Helene Mary Sparti, Aug. 20, 1966; children: Kenneth W., Kimberley J., Brian C. BS with honors, Manhattan Coll., 1965; LLB cum laude, Harvard U., 1968. Bar: NY 1969. Assoc. Cahill Gordon & Reindel LLP, NYC, 1968—76, ptnr., 1976—91, mem. exec. com., 1991—. Editor: Harvard Law Rev., 1966—68. Mem.: Down Town Assn., Hudson Nat. Golf Club, Met. Opera Club, Scarsdale Golf Club. Office: Cahill Gordon & Reindel LLP 80 Pine St Fl 17 New York NY 10005-1702 Office Phone: 212-701-3215. Office Fax: 212-378-2324. Business E-Mail: korce@cahill.com.

**ORCHARD, ROBERT A.**, system science educator; b. N.Y.C., Nov. 29, 1938; s. Francis A. and Vestal (Fudge) O.; m. Anna Lauria; children: Judith, Frank, Jeniffer; m. Gudrun Jandt; children: Kjen, Anna. BS in Math., Fairleigh Dickinson U., 1964; MS in Math., Stevens Inst., 1967, PhD, 1978. Mem. tech. staff Bell Labs., Murray Hill, N.J., 1964-67, mgr. R&D, 1972-83; assoc. prof. Fairleigh Dickinson U., Teaneck, N.J., 1967-72; prof. system sci. SUNY, 1980—; prof. CUNY, 1983—. Cons. AT&T, Bellcore, Fortune 500, etc., 1975—; trainer Inst. Advanced Systems, N.J., Germany, 1978—; hypnotherapist various insts., 1978—; corp. entepreneur trainer DEC Knowledge Engring., 1991. Contbr. articles to profl. jours. Fellow Internat. Assn. Neuro-Linguistic Programming; mem. Internat. Soc. Communicative Psychoanalysis and Psychotherapy, Internat. Soc. Systems Sci., Math. Assn. Am. Home: Vegesacker Strasse 3 28 Bremen Germany Office: Inst Advanced Systems PO Box 109 Hasbrouck Heights NJ 07604-0109

**ORCHARD, ROBERT JOHN**, theater producer, educator; b. Maplewood, N.J., Dec. 3, 1946; s. Robert Orchard and Beatrice (Gould) Todd; m. Pamela Marcy Pritchard, Sept. 6, 1969; children: Christopher, Katherine. Student, The Lawrence Acad., 1965; BA, Middlebury Coll., 1969; MFA, Yale U., 1972. Gen. mgr. Peterborough (N.H.) Players, 1967-70; asst. mng. dir. Yale Repertory Theatre, 1971-73, artistic administr., 1972-73; instr. Yale Sch. Drama, 1972-73; mng. dir. Yale Repertory Theatre and Sch. Drama, 1973-79, Am. Repertory Theatre, Cambridge, Mass., 1979—2002, exec. dir., 2002—. Assoc. prof., co-chmn. theatre adminstrn. tng. program Yale Sch. Drama, 1975-79; mng. dir. Loeb Drama Ctr., Harvard U., 1979-2000, dir., 2000—, mng. dir. Inst. for Advanced Theatre Tng., 1979-2002, exec. dir., 2002—; orgn. ptnr. Inst. Arts and Civic Dialogue at Harvard U. Former mem. bd. dirs. Theatre Commc. Group; pres. bd. Mass. Cultural Edn. Collaborative, Am. Arts Alliance, Peterborough Players, Cambridge Multi-Cultural Arts Ctrs.; former exec. com. League of Residents Theatres; chmn. NEA, Profl. Theatre Cos., Opera/Mus. Theatre Panels. Office: Am Repertory Theatre 64 Brattle St Cambridge MA 02138-3443

**ORCINO, LEONARD ANTHONY**, composer, conductor; b. Clev., Sept. 30, 1945; s. Leo Orcino and Belle Orcino, (nee, Apolitto). BS, MA, Case Western Res. U., 1981. Music dept. chair, dir. bands Lake Cath. H.S., Mentor, Ohio, 1971—77, Chardon (Ohio) City Sch., 1981—2003; owner Little Bear Music, music dir. Lakeland Coll. Jazz Impact, Kirtland, Ohio, 1975—85, North Coast Jazz Orch., Clev., 1978—81. Grantee, Case Western Res. 1979—80. Mem.: Music Educators Nat. Conf. (assoc.), Internat. Assn. Jazz Educators (life). Home: 11750 Parkwood Dr Chardon OH 44024 Office: Little Bear Music 11750 Parkwood Dr Chardon OH 44024 Personal E-mail: lenorcino@aol.com.

**ORCUTT, BEN AVIS**, retired social work educator; b. Falco, Ala., Oct. 17, 1914; d. Benjamin A. and Emily Olive Adams; m. Harry P. Orcutt, 1946 (dec.). AB, U. Ala., 1936; MA, Tulane U., 1939, MSW, 1942; DSW, Columbia U., 1962. Social worker ARC, Lagarde Gen. Hosp., New Orleans; social worker, acting field dir. Fort Benning (Ga.) Regional Hosp., 1942-46; chief social work svc. VA Regional Office, Phoenix, 1946—51; chief social work svc. unit outpatient office VA, Birmingham, Ala., 1954-57, 58; rsch. asst. Rsch. Ctr. Sch. Social Work, Columbia U. N.Y.C., 1960-62; asst. prof. social work, 1962, assoc. prof. social work, 1965-76, La. State U., Baton Rouge, 1962-65; prof. social work, dir. doctoral program U Ala., University, 1976-84; ret. Rsch. cons. Tavistock Centre, London, 1972; cons. sch. social work U. Houston, 1990, Troy State System, 1992. Author: Science and Inquiry in Social Work Practice, 1990, (with Harry P. Orcutt) America's Riding Horses, 1958, (with Elizabeth R. Prichard, Jean Collard, Austin H. Kutscher, Irene Seeland, Nathan Lefkowitz) Social Work with the Dying Patient and the Family, 1977, (with others) Social Work and Thanatology, 1980; editor: Poverty and Social Casework Services, 1974; mem. editl. bd. Jour. Social Work, 1982-84; contbr. articles to profl. books and jours. Mem. alumni bd. Sch. Social Work Columbia U., 1985—88, 1991—94. Recipient Centennial award for edn. Columbia U. Sch. Social Work, 1998; named to Ala. Social Work Hall of Fame, 1999; NIMH Fellow, 1957-60; Ben Avis Adams Orcutt doctoral scholar in social work named in her honor, U. Ala. Mem. Group for Advancement Doctoral Edn. (steering com., editor newsletter 1980-83). Episcopalian. Office: PO Box 870314 Tuscaloosa AL 35487-0314 Home: 1199 Valley View Dr Andalusia AL 36424

**ORDAL, CASPAR REUBEN**, retired cosmetics executive; b. Martell, Wis., May 5, 1922; s. Zakarias John and Sina Carlovna (Wulfsberg) O.; m. Ann Elizabeth Brady, June 7, 1947; Christopher Rolf, Peter Stuart. BS, Harvard Coll., 1946; M.P.A., Harvard U., 1947. Supr. central indsl. relations staff Ford Motor Co., Dearborn, Mich., 1947-53; dir. orgn. planning and mgmt. devel. Colgate-Palmolive Co., N.Y.C., 1953-65; v.p., gen. mgr. New Holland div.

Sperry Rand Corp., (Pa.), 1965-76; corp. v.p. personnel Norton Simon Inc., N.Y.C., 1976-78; sr. v.p. adminstrn. Max Factor & Co., Hollywood, Calif., 1978-85. Served to 1st lt. USAAF, 1943-46. Mem. Personnel Round Table (chmn. 1983-84), Am. Mgmt. Assn. (adv. coun. 1977-82), Lancaster (Pa.) Country Club, Phi Beta Kappa. Lutheran.

**ORDIN, ANDREA SHERIDAN,** lawyer; m. Robert Ordin; 1 child, M. Victoria; stepchildren: Allison, Richard. AB, UCLA, 1962, LLB, 1965. Bar: Calif. 1966. Dep. atty. gen. Calif., 1965-72; So. Calif. legal counsel Fair Employment Practices Commn., 1972-73; asst. dist. atty. L.A. County, 1975-77; U.S. atty. Central Dist. Calif. L.A., 1977-81; adj. prof. UCLA Law Sch., 1982; chief asst. atty. gen. Calif. L.A., 1983-90; sr. counsel Morgan, Lewis & Bockius, LA, 1993—. Mem. L.A. County Bar Assn. (past pres., past exec. dir.) Office: Morgan Lewis & Bockius 300 S Grand Ave Ste 2200 Los Angeles CA 90071-3109 Office Phone: 213-612-1090. Business E-Mail: aordin@morganlewis.com.

**ORDOG, TAMAS,** research scientist, educator; b. Nagykanizsa, Hungary, Feb. 8, 1964; arrived in U.S., 1992; s. Ferenc Ordog and Julianna Domjan; m. Katalin Malek; 1 child, Norbert. MD, U. Pecs, Hungary, 1988. Rsch. fellow neurophysiology rsch. group Hungarian Acad. Scis., Pecs, 1989—92; rsch. fellow U. Tex.-Houston Health Sci. Ctr., 1992—95, sr. rsch. fellow, 1995—97; rsch. asst. prof. U. Nev., Reno Sch. Medicine, 1997—2003, asst. prof., 2003—06; sr. assoc. cons. Mayo Clinic, Rochester, Minn., 2006—. Contbr. articles to profl. jours. Recipient Young Investigator award, Am. Motility Soc., 2000, 2002, Alvarez award, Internat. Electrogastrography Soc., 2005; grantee, Am. Motility Soc. and Janssen Pharmaceutica, 2002—03, NIH, 2002—; scholar, Republic of Hungary, 1984—88; rsch. fellow, Hungarian Acad. Scis., 1989—91. Mem.: AAAS, Am. Gastroenterol. Assn., The Endocrine Soc. Achievements include research in neuroendocrine regulation of reproduction; gastrointestinal pacemaking: Diabetic gastroenteropathy. Office: Stabile 7 Mayo Clinic 200 1st St SW Rochester MN 55905 Business E-Mail: ordog.tamas@mayo.edu.

**ORDONEZ, CHRISTINA ELIZABETH,** secondary school educator; b. Arlington Heights, Ill., Dec. 24, 1979; d. Jeffrey Allan and Karen Marie Butzen; m. Mark Christopher Ordonez, July 17, 2004. Degree in english edn., Ill. State U., 2002; degree in curriculum and instrn., Olivet Nazarene U., 2005. Asst. to asst. editor Dalkey Archive Press, Bloomington, Ill., 1999—2002; English tchr. Hoffman Estates (Ill.) HS, 2002—. Mem.: NEA, Ill. Edn. Assn., Ill. Assn. Tchrs. English, Nat. Coun. Tchrs. English. Avocations: technology, reading, movies, cooking, theater. E-mail: christina_ordonez@d211.org.

**ORDONEZ, FERNANDO IVAN,** adult education educator; b. Santiago, Chile, Nov. 23, 1970; s. Fernando Arturo Ordonez and Maria Gabriela Pizarro; m. Andrea Strauss, June 28, 2002; children: Tatiana, Sebastian. BS, U. Chile, 1996; PhD, MIT, 2002. Asst. prof. U. So. Calif., Los Angeles, 2002—. Contbr. articles to profl. jours. Fellow, Zumberge Rsch. Fund, U. So. Calif., 2003—05, Annenberg Ctr. Commn., U. So. Calif., 2005—; grantee, U. So. Calif., Calif. State U., Long Beach, Metrans Rsch. Ctr., 2003—05, NSF, 2004—. Mem.: Inst. Indsl. Engrs., Math. Programming Soc., Soc. for Indsl. and Applied Math., Inst. for Ops. Rsch. and the Mgmt. Scis. Achievements include research in optimization theory, sensitivity to data perturbation, applications in networked systems, such as wireless sensor networks, coordination of autonomous agents teams, and transportation. Avocations: running, soccer. Office: U So Calif 3715 McClintock Ave GER-240 Los Angeles CA 90089 Office Phone: 213-821-2413.

**ORDONEZ, MAGGLIO,** professional baseball player; b. Caracas, Venezuela, Jan. 28, 1974; Baseball player Chgo. White Sox, 1997—2004, Detroit Tigers, 2005—. Named to Am. League All-Star team, 1999—2003. Mailing: Detroit Tigers Comerica Pk 2100 Woodward Ave Detroit MI 48201*

**ORDORICA, STEVEN ANTHONY,** obstetrician, gynecologist, educator; b. N.Y.C., Jan. 4, 1957; s. Vincent and Rose (Goiricelaya) O. BA magna cum laude, NYU, 1979; MD, Stony Brook U., 1983. Diplomate Am. Coll. Obstetrics and Gynecology, speciality cert. maternal-fetal medicine; lic. Nat. Bd. Med. Examiners. Resident obstetrics and gynecology NYU-Bellevue Hosp. Ctr., 1983-87, fellow maternal-fetal medicine, 1987-89, instr. obstetrics-gynecology, 1989-91; clin. instr. obstetrics-gynecology NYU, 1986-89, asst. prof. ob/gyn., 1989—2001, clin. assoc. prof. ob/gyn., 2001—; dir. perinatal clinics and prenatal diagnostic unit Gouverneur Hosp., N.Y.C., 1989-94. Perinatal cons. Bellevue Hosp. Ctr., N.Y.C., 1989—; faculty mem. perinatal div. NYU Med. Ctr., 1989—; presenter in field. Contbr. articles to Surgery, Am. Jour. Obstetrics and Gynecology, Am. Jour. Perinatal, Surgery, Obstetrics and Gynecology, Jour. Reproductive Medicine, Acta Geneticae Medicae et Gemellologiae, Jour. Rheumatology. Named NYU scholar; recipient Founder's Day award, NYU, Wash. Sq. Alumni award. Mem. Am. Coll. Obstetrics and Gynecology, Soc. Perinatal Obstetricians, N.Y. Acad. Scis., N.Y. State Perinatal Soc., AMA, Phi Beta Kappa, Beta Lambda Sigma. Achievements include research in investigating aspects of maternal-fetal physiology. Office: NYU Med Ctr 530 1st Ave Ste 10Q New York NY 10016-6402

**ORDWAY, ELLEN,** biologist, educator, entomologist, researcher; b. N.Y.C., Nov. 8, 1927; d. Samuel Hanson and Anna (Wheatland) Ordway. BA, Wheaton Coll., Mass., 1950; MS, Cornell U., 1955; PhD, U. Kans., 1965. Field asst. N.Y. Zool. Soc., N.Y.C., 1950-52; rsch. asst. Am. Mus. Natural History, N.Y.C. 1955-57; tchg. asst. U. Kans., Lawrence, 1957-61, rsch. asst., 1959-65; asst. prof. U. Minn., Morris, 1965-70, assoc. prof. biology, 1970-85, prof., 1986-97, prof. emeritus, 1997, acad. advisor, 1997—. Cooperator, cons. USDA Bee Rsch. Lab., Tucson, 1971, Tucson, 83. Contbr. articles to profl. jours. Lectr. Morris area svc. clubs, 1972—2004; mgr. preserves Nature Conservancy, Mpls., 1975—; bd. dirs. county chpt. ARC, 1998—2003; vol. Stevens County Hist. Mus., 2005—; bd. dirs. U. Minn. Morris Retirees Assn. 1997—2003, sec., treas., 1998—2003. Mem.: AAAS, Ecol. Soc. Am., Internat. Bee Rsch. Assn., Kans. Entomol. Soc., Sigma Xi. Episcopalian. Avocations: travel, photography. Office: U Minn Div Sci And Math Morris MN 56267

**ORDWAY, FREDERICK IRA, III,** science educator, consultant, researcher, writer; b. NYC, Apr. 4, 1927; s. Frederick Ira and Frances Antoinette (Wright) O.; m. Maria Victoria Arenas, Apr. 13, 1950; children: Frederick Ira IV, Albert James, Aliette Marisol. SB, Harvard, 1949; postgrad., U. Alger, 1950, U. Paris, France, 1950-51, 53-54, U. Barcelona, Spain, 1953, U. Innsbruck, Austria, 1954, Air U., 1952-63, Alexander Hamilton Bus. Inst., 1952-58, Indsl. Coll. Armed Forces, 1953, 63; DSc (hon.), U. Ala., 1992. Various geol. engring. positions Mene Grande Oil Co., San Tome, Venezuela, 1949-50, Orinoco Mining Co., Cerro Bolivar, Venezuela, 1950, Reaction Motors, Inc., Lake Denmark, NJ, 1951-53; with guided missiles divsn. Republic Aviation Corp., 1954-55; pres. Gen. Astronautics Rsch. Corp., Huntsville, Ala., 1955-59, 65-66; v.p. Nat. R & D Corp., Atlanta, 1957-59; asst. to dir. Saturn Systems Office, Army Ballistic Missile Agy., Huntsville, 1959-60; chief space info. systems br. George C. Marshall Space Flight Ctr. NASA, 1960-64; prof. sci. and tech. applications Sch. Grad. Studies and Rsch., U. Ala. Rsch. Inst., 1967-73; cons. Sci. and Tech. Policy Office, NSF, 1974-75; cons. ops. analysis divsn. Gen. Rsch. Corp., 1974-75; asst. to adminstr. ERDA, 1975-77, Dept. Energy, 1977-94, policy/internat. affairs dir. spl. projects office, cons., 1994—; also participant internat. energy devel. program Office of Asst. Sec. Internat. Affairs, Dept. Energy, 1978-79. Cons. to industry, Ency. Britannica, Am. Coll. Dictionary of English Lang., M.G.M. film 2001: A Space Odyssey, 1965-66, Paramount Picture Corp., The Adventurers, 1968-69; internat. lectr. space flight and energy programs. Author: (with C.C. Adams) Space Flight, 1958, (with Ronald C. Wakeford) International Missile and Spacecraft Guide, 1960, Annotated Bibliography of Space Science and Technology, 1962, (with J.P. Gardner, M.R. Sharpe, Jr.) Basic Astronautics: An Introduction to Space Science, Engineering and Medicine, 1962, (with Adams, Wernher von Braun) Careers in Astronautics and Rocketry, 1962, (with Gardner, Sharpe, R.C.

Wakeford) Applied Astronautics: An Introduction to Space Flight, 1963, (with Wakeford) Conquering the Sun's Empire, 1963, Life in Other Solar Systems, 1965, (with Roger A. MacGowan) Intelligence in the Universe, 1966, (with W. von Braun) History of Rocketry and Space Travel, 1966, 1969, 75, L'Histoire Mondiale de l'Astronautique, 1968, 70, (with W. von Braun) Rockets Red Glare, 1976, (with C.C. Adams, M.R. Sharpe) Dividends from Space, 1972, Pictorial Guide to Planet Earth, 1975, (with W. von Braun) New Worlds, 1979, (with M.R. Sharpe) The Rocket Team, 1979, 82, 2d edit., 2003, (with F.C. Durant and R.C. Seamans) Between Sputnik and the Shuttle, 1981, (with E.M. Emme) Science Fiction and Space Futures, 1982, (with von Braun, Dave Dooling) Space Travel: A History, 1985, (with Ernst Stuhlinger) Wernher von Braun: Aufbrach in den Weltraum, 1992, Wernher von Braun: Crusader for Space (2 vols.), 1994, revised 1996, also single vol. edition, 1996, (with Randy Liebermann) Blueprint for Space, 1992, Visions of Spaceflight, 2001; editor: Advances in Space Science and Technology, vols. I-XII, 2 supplements, 1959-72, (with R.M.L. Baker, N.W. Makemson) Introduction to Astrodynamics, 1960, (with others) From Peenemünde to Outer Space, 1962, Astronautical Engineering and Science, 1963; mem. editl. bd.: IX Internat. Astronautical Congress procs., 2 vols, 1959, Xth Congress procs., 2 vols, 1960; guest editor: Acta Astronautica, 1985, 94, History of Rocketry and Astronautics, Vol. IX, 1989, Digital book Mars: Target for Tomorrow Microsoft Network & Internet, 1996; Co-developer of biographical film " He Conquered Space", Discovery channel, 1996, History of Astronautics Video, 1996, inter-active CD Rom, 1997, revised, 2001, interactive CD ROM and video versions) Mars: Past, Present, Future, 1998; contbr. (with others) numerous articles to profl. jours., US and fgn. encys., chpts. to books, sects. to others; organizer Blueprint for Space exhbn., 1991-95, US Space and Rocket Ctr., IBM Gallery of Sci. and Art, NASA Vis. Ctr., Houston, Spaceport USA, Cape Canaveral, Fla., Nat. Air and Space Mus., Washington, Va. Air and Space Ctr., Hampton exhibit Shaping The Vision contbns. Art Inst. Chgo., 2001, Bruce Mus. Art and Scis., Greenwich, Conn., 2001, Mus. Flight, Seattle, 2002, numerous others. Served with USNR, 1945. Recipient (with W. von Braun) diplôme d'honneur French Commn. d'Histoire, Arts et Letters, Paris, 1969,citation Arthur C. Clarke Found., 2005; commended for contbns. to U.S. Space and Rocket Ctr., Ala. Space Sci. Exhibit, U.S. Space Walk of Fame Found. Fellow: AAAS, AIAA (assoc.; history com. 1975—, internat. activities com. 1980—89, sel. com. hons. and awards 1996—, 2003 Centennial of Flight Ctr. 1998, Hermann Oberth award 1977, K.E. Tsiolkowski award 1988), Brit. Interplanetary Soc. (guest editor Jour. Brit. Interplanetary Soc. 1992—96); mem.: US Space and Rocket Ctr. (mem. Saturn V rocket restoration com., mem. mus. com., mem. 2d sci. adv. coun.), Acta Astronautica (guest editor 1994, 1997), Eurasian Acad. Scis., Nat. Space Soc. (bd. dirs. 1986—95, mem. publs. com. 1987—88, nominating com. 1990—92, bd. govs. 1997—, Ctr. for Lunar Rsch. com. 1998—), Am. Astron. Soc. (Emme award 1994, Nat. Space Club award 1997), Internat. Acad. Astronautics (history of astronautics com. 1983—, space activities and soc. com. 1986—, peer rev. com. 1995—, Luigi Napolitano Lit. award 1992), Arthur C. Clarke Found. (bd. dirs. 2000—, commendation 2005), Washington Golf and Country Club, Harvard Club NY, Cosmos Club (bd. mgmt. 1986—91, v.p. 1988—90, award 2001). Home and Office: 2401 N Taylor St Arlington VA 22207-4021 also: 3423 Lookout Dr SE Huntsville AL 35801 Personal E-mail: ordmars@aol.com.

**ORDWAY, JOHN DANTON,** retired pension fund administrator, lawyer, accountant; b. Mpls., Mar. 19, 1928; s. John Dunreath Ordway and Inez Adelaide (Stahl) Larson; m. Mary E. Bateman, June 16, 1951 (div. 1978); 1 child, David; m. Patricia A. Nagle, Dec. 27, 1996. BBA, Am. U., 1963, JD, 1965. CPA Minn.; bar: US Dist. Ct. DC 1966. Dir. ins. Nat. Automobile Dealers Assn., Washington, 1957—69; v.p. Edward H. Friend and Co., Washington, 1969—74; exec. v.p., CEO pension bd. United Ch. of Christ, NYC, 1974—96; ret., 1996. Mem. Planning Bd., Stamford, Conn., 1982—86. With U.S. Army, 1946—47. Mem.: AICPA, Black Hall Club (Old Lyme, Conn.), Quail Run Golf Club (Naples, Fla.), Westwood Country Club (Vienna, Va.), Kena Temple. Republican. Mem. United Ch. Of Christ. Home: 7520 Citrus Hill Ln Naples FL 34109

**O'REILLY, SIR ANTHONY JOHN FRANCIS,** media company executive, former food company executive; b. Dublin, May 7, 1936; s. John Patrick and Aileen (O'Connor) O'Reilly; m. Susan Cameron, May 5, 1962 (div.); children: Susan Cameron, Justine, Gavin, Caroline, Tony; m. Chryss Goulandris, Sept. 14, 1991. Student, Belvedere Coll., Dublin, Univ. Coll., Dublin, Wharton Bus. Sch. Overseas, 1965; BCL DCL (hon.), Ind. State U.; PhD in Agrl. Mktg. U. Bradford, Eng.; LLD (hon.), Wheeling Coll., 1974, Trinity Coll., Dublin, 1978; LL.D. (hon.), Allegheny Coll., 1983, De Paul U., Chgo., 1988; D in Bus. Studies (hon.), Rollins Coll., 1978; DHC in Civil Law (hon.), Ind. State U., 1980; DBA (hon.), Boston Coll., 1985; D in Econ. Sci. (hon.), Nat. U. Ireland, 1989. Indsl. cons. Weston Evans, 1958—62; personal asst. to chmn. Suttons Ltd., Cork, Ireland, 1960—62; lectr. dept. applied psychology Univ. Coll., Cork, 1960—62; dir. Robert McCowen & Sons Ltd., Tralee, Ireland, 1961—62; mng. dir. An Bord Bainne/Irish Dairy Bd., 1962—66; dir. Agrl. Credit Corp. Ltd., 1965—66, Nitrigin Eireann Teoranta, 1965—66; mng. dir., CEO Comhlucht Siuicre Eireann Teo. (Irish Sugar Co.) and Erin Foods Ltd., Dublin, 1966—69; joint mng. dir. Heinz-Erin Ltd. 1967—70; mng. dir. H.J. Heinz Co. Ltd., England, 1969—72; sr. v.p. N.Am. and Pacific H.J. Heinz Co., 1971—72, exec. v.p., COO Pitts., 1972—73, pres., COO, 1973—79, pres., 1979—96, CEO, 1979—98, chmn., 1987—2000, Waterford Wedgwood plc, 1994—; exec. chmn. Independent News & Media PLC, 2000—04, chief exec., 2004—. Chmn. Fitzwilliam Securities Ltd., 1971—77, Ind. Newspapers Plc, Atlantic Resources, Dublin; bd. dirs. Bankers Trust N.Y. Corp., 1980—90, Washington Post Co., 1987—94, London Tablet Found., Inc.. Starkist Foods Inc., Ore-Ida Foods, Inc.; founder O'Reilly Found., 1998—. Author: Prospect, 1962, Developing Creative Management, 1970, The Conservative Consumer, 1971, Food for Thought, 1972. Mem. Nat. Com. Whitney Mus. Art; bd. govs. Hugh O'Brian Found., L.A.; mem. coun. Rockefeller U., N.Y.C.; trustee U. Pitts., Com. for Econ. Devel.; bd. dirs. Assocs. Grad. Sch. Bus. Adminstrn. of Harvard U., Cambridge, Mass.; sr. bd. dirs. The Conf. Bd. Named Hon. Officer, Order of Australia, 1988. Fellow: Royal Soc. Arts, Brit. Inst. Mgmt.; mem.: Marks Club London, Exec. Coun. Fgn. Diplomats (bd. dirs.), Irish Mgmt. Inst. (coun.), Internat. Life Scis. Inst. Nutrition Found. (chmn., CEO coun.), Am. Irish Found., Grocery Mfrs. Am. (sec., bd. dirs.), Law Soc. Ireland (treas.), Inst. Dirs., Inc., Lyford Cay Club (Bahamas), Rolling Rock Club (Ligonier), Pitts. Golf Club, Allegheny Club, Duquesne Club, The Bd. Rm. (N.Y.C.), The Links, Union League, Les Ambassadeurs, Annabels, Univ. Club Dublin, Kildare St. Club, St. Stephens Green Club. Office: Independent News & Media PLC Independent House 2023 Bianconi Ave Naas Rd Dublin 24 Ireland*

**O'REILLY, BILL (WILLIAM O'REILLY JR.),** commentator, writer; b. NYC, Sept. 10, 1949; s. William and Angela O'Reilly; m. Maureen McPhilmy; children: Madeline, Spencer. BA in History, Marist Coll., Poughkeepsie, N.Y., 1971; MA in Broadcast Journalism, Boston U., 1976; MA in Pub. Policy, Harvard U., 1996. Tchr. H.S., Miami, Fla.; reporter WNEP-TV, Scranton, Pa., WFAA-TV, Dallas, KMGH-TV, Denver, WFSB-TV, Hartford, WCBS-TV, N.Y.C., 1980; fgn. correspondent CBS News; anchor CBS, Boston, ABC, Boston, KATU-TV, Portland; correspondent, The World News Tonight ABC, 1986—88; sr. correspondent Inside Edition, 1988, anchor, 1989—95; host, exec. prodr. FOX News Channel The O'Reilly Factor, 1996—; host Radio Factor, 2002—. Author: Those Who Trespass: A Novel of Television and Murder, 1998, The O'Reilly Factor: The Good, the Bad and the Completely Ridiculous in American Life, 2000, The No Spin Zone: Confrontations with the Powerful and Famous in America, 2001, Who's Looking Out for You?, 2003, The O'Reilly Factor for Kids: A Survival Guide for America's Families, 2004, Culture Warrior, 2006. Recipient Disting. Alumni award, Boston U., 2001. Office: FOX News Channel 1211 Avenue of the Americas New York NY 10036*

**O'REILLY, CHARLES TERRANCE,** university dean; b. Chgo., May 30, 1921; s. William Patrick and Ann Elizabeth (Madden) O'R.; m. Rosella Catherine Neilland, June 4, 1955; children: Terrance, Gregory, Kevin, Joan Bridget, Kathleen Ann. BA, Loyola U., Chgo., 1942, MSW, 1948; postgrad., U. Cattolica, Milan, Italy, 1949-50; PhD, U. Notre Dame, 1954. Instr. DePaul U., Chgo., 1948-49; asst. in psychology U. Cattolica, 1949-50; caseworker Cath. Charities, N.Y.C., 1953-54; exec. dir. Family Service, Long Branch, N.J., 1954-55; asst. prof. Loyola U., 1955-59; vis. lectr. Ensiss Sch. Social Work, Milan, 1959-60; asso. prof. U. Wis.-Milw., 1961-64; prof., asso. dir. U. Wis. Sch. Social Work, Madison, 1965-68; dean social welfare, v.p. acad. affairs SUNY-Albany, 1969-76; dean social work Loyola U., Chgo., 1976-92, dean emeritus, sr. prof., 1994—; vis. prof. sch. social work SS Maria Asunta, Rome, 1992-93. Author: OAA Profile, 1961, People of Inner Core North, 1965, Men in Jail, 1968, Italian Social Work Education 1946-1997, 1998, Italy's War of Liberation, 1998, The Enola Gay Controversy and the Smithsonian, 2004; contbr. articles to profl. jours. Pres. Community Action Commn. Dane County, Wis., 1967-68; bd. dirs. Council Community Services, Albany, Family and Children's Service, Albany; mem. adv. bd. Safer Found.; vice chmn. Ill. Pub. Aid Citizens Council. Served with AUS, 1942-46, 51-52. Fulbright scholar, 1949-50; fellow, 1959-60 Mem. AAUP, Nat. Assn. Social Workers. Roman Catholic. Home: 4073 Bunker Ln Wilmette IL 60091-1001 Office: Sch Social Work Loyola Univ Chicago IL 60611 E-mail: coreill@luc.edu

**O'REILLY, DAVID E.,** auto parts company executive; s. Charles Chub O'Reilly; 3 children. Grad., Drury Coll., 1971. With Southwestern Bell; joined O'Reilly Automotive, Springfield, Mo., 1972—, now co-chmn., CEO. Bd. dir. O'Reilly Automotive, 1993—; past chair Auto Value Inc. Mem. Springfield Catholic Schs. Devel. bd.; past pres. Drury Univ. Alumni Assn. Springfield YMCA. Mem.: Automotive Warehouse Distributors Assn. (past chmn.). Office: O'Reilly Automotive 233 S Patterson Springfield MO 65802 Office Phone: 417-862-6708.

**O'REILLY, DAVID J.,** oil industry executive; b. Dublin, Jan. 1947; BS ChemE, University Coll., Dublin, 1968, D (hon.) of Sci., 2002. Process engineer Chevron Corp., 1968—71, process engineer, operating assist., 1971—75, adviser, foreign operations, 1976—78, planning mgr., chemical div., 1979, mgr. agricultural chem., 1980—82, mgr. Salt Lake Refinery, 1983—85; mgr. manufacturing Chevron Chemical Co., 1985; gen. mgr. El Segundo Refinery, 1986—88; sr. v.p. Chevron Chemical Corp., 1989—90; v.p. Chevron Corp., 1991—94; pres. Chevron Products Co., San Francisco, 1994—98; dir., vice-chmn. Chevron Corp., San Francisco, 1998—2000, chmn. bd. dirs., CEO, 2000—01; CEO, chmn. ChevronTexaco Corp. (now Chevron Corp.), San Francisco, 2001—. Bd. govs. San Francisco Symphony, Bay Area Coun. Mem.: Am. Soc. Corp. Execs., Bus. Coun., Nat. Petroleum Coun., Am. Petroleum Inst. (treas., bd. dirs.). Office: Chevron Corp 6001 Bollinger Canyon Rd San Ramon CA 94583-2324*

**O'REILLY, HEATHER ANN,** Olympic athlete; b. East Brunswick, NJ, Jan. 2, 1985; Student, U.N.C. Mem. U.S. Women's Nat. Soccer Team, 2002—, U.S. Women's Olympic Soccer Team, Athens, 2004. Named National High School Player of the Yr., 2002; named to NCAA All-Tournament Team, 2003. Achievements include being a member of NCAA Champion University of North Carolina Tar Heels Women's Soccer Team, 2003; being a member of gold medal US Women's Soccer Team, Athens Olympic Games, 2004. Office: c/o US Soccer Federation 1801 S Prairie Ave Chicago IL 60616

**O'REILLY, JACKSON See RIGNEY, JAMES JR.**

**O'REILLY, JAMES THOMAS,** lawyer, educator, writer; b. NYC, Nov. 15, 1947; s. Matthew Richard and Regina (Casey) O'R.; children: Jean, Ann. BA cum laude, Boston Coll., 1969; JD, U. Va., 1974. Bar: Va. 1974, Ohio 1974, U.S. Supreme Ct. 1979, U.S. Ct. Appeals (6th cir.) 1980. Atty. Procter & Gamble Co., Cin., 1974-76, counsel, 1976-79, sr. counsel for food, drug and product safety, 1979-85, corp. counsel, 1985-93, assoc. gen. counsel, 1993-98; adj. prof. in adminstrv. law U. Cin., 1980-97, vis. prof. law, 1998—. Cons. Adminstrv. Conf. U.S., 1981-82, 89-90, Congl. Office of Compliance, 1995-96; arbitrator State Employee Rels. Bd.; mem. Ohio Bishops Adv. Coun., Mayor's Infrastructure Commn., Cin. Environ. Adv. Coun.; city coun. Wyo., Ohio. Author: Federal Information Disclosure, 1977, Food and Drug Administration Regulatory Manual, 1979, Unions' Rights to Company Information, 1980, Federal Regulation of the Chemical Industry, 1980, Administrative Rulemaking, 1983, Ohio Public Employee Collective Bargaining, 1984, Protecting Workplace Secrets, 1985, Emergency Response to Chemical Accidents, 1986, Product Defects and Hazards, 1987, Protecting Trade Secrets Under SARA, 1988, Toxic Torts Strategy Deskbook, 1989, Complying With Canada's New Labeling Law, 1989, Solid Waste Management, 1991, Ohio Products Liability Handbook, 1991, Toxic Torts Guide, 1991, ABA Product Liability Resource Manual, 1993, RCRA and Superfund Practice Guide, 1993, Clean Air Permits Manual, 1994, United States Environmental Liabilities, 1994, Elder Safety, 1995, Environmental and Workplace Safety for University and Hospital Managers, 1996, Indoor Environmental Health, 1997, Product Warnings, Defects & Hazards, 1999, Accident Prevention Manual, 2000, Food Crisis Management Manual, 2002, Police Racial Profiling, 2002, Homeland Security Deskbook, 2004, Ohio Tort Reform, 2005; mem. editl. bd. Food and Drug Cosmetic Law Jour.; contbr. articles to profl. jours. Trustee Regional Coun. of Govts.; mem. Hamilton County Dem. Ctrl. Com. With U.S Army, 1970—72. Mem. ABA (chmn. AD law sect.), FBA, Food and Drug Law Inst. (chair program com.), Leadership Cin. Democrat. Roman Catholic. Office: 24 Jewett Dr Cincinnati OH 45215-2648 Office Phone: 513-556-0062. Personal E-mail: joreilly@fuse.net. Business E-Mail: james.oreilly@uc.edu.

**O'REILLY, LAWRENCE P.,** auto parts company executive; s. Charles Chub O'Reilly; m. Nancy O'Reilly; 3 children. Grad., Drury Coll., 1968. Co-chmn., COO O'Reilly Automotive, Springfield, Mo. Dir. O'Reilly Automotive, 1993—. Big Brothers/Big Sisters; YPO; bd. trustees St. John's Regional. Health Ctr., Cath. Sch. Devel. bd. Mem.: Nat. Car Care Coun., Automotive Warehouse Distributors Assn. Office: O'Reilly Automotive 233 S Patterson Springfield MO 65802 Office Phone: 417-862-6708.

**O'REILLY, MARY,** environmental scientist, educator; b. NYC, Aug. 3, 1948; d. Luke Edward and Regina (Mahoney) O'Reilly; m. Jonathan Haney; children: Robert Brophy, Sara Brophy, Lena Brophy. Student, Fordham U., 1966—68; BS, U. Mich., 1970, MS, 1972, PhD, 1979. Rsch. asst. prof. Health Sci. Ctr., Syracuse, NY, 1979-84; environ. toxicologist Syracuse Rsch. Corp., 1984-86; pres. ARLS Cons., Inc., Syracuse, 1993—; sr. indsl. hygienist N.Y. State Dept. Labor, Syracuse, 1987—2000; environ. specialist N.Y. State Dept. Transp., Binghamton, 2000—. Adj. assoc. prof. SUNY Sch. Pub. Health, Albany, 1990—; dir. Am. Bd. Indsl. Hygiene, Lansing, Mich., 1995—2001; adj. prof. chemistry LeMoyne Coll., 2000; mem. Z10 com. Am. Nat. Stds. Inst., 2001—05, mem. sub bd. N.Y. State Inst Health and Environment, 2001—; bd. dirs. Am. Conf. Govt. Indsl. Hygienists, 2006—. Author: An Ergonomics Guide to VDTs, 1994; author: (with others) Occupational Ergonomics, 1996; co-author: ILO's Encyclopedia of Occupational Health and Safety, 1998, Implications of Hormesis for Industrial Hygienists, 2003, Health Risk Assessment at Brownfield Redevelopment Sites, 2003, Groundwater Effects from Highway Tire Shreds, 2004, others; contbr. articles to profl. jours. Mem. Syracuse Peace Coun. Mem.: Hormesis Soc., N.Y. State Assn. Transp. Engrs., Human Factors and Ergonomics Soc., Am. Assn. Govtl. Indsl. Hygienists, Am. Indsl. Hygiene Assn. Avocations: Karate, fly fishing, dance, folk harp. Home: 7705 Farley Ln Manlius NY 13104-9571 Office Phone: 607-721-8138. Personal E-mail: Mary_Brophy@sln.suny.edu. Business E-Mail: mbrophy@dot.state.ny.us.

**O'REILLY, MARY CATHERINE,** elementary school educator; b. St. Louis, Nov. 11, 1949; d. James C. and Ada C. (Stevens) Duke; m. Robert J. O'Reilly (div. 1992); children: Jennifer M., Lori C. BS in Edn., Ctrl. Mo. State U., 1973; MA, Maryville U., 1990. Cert. tchr. K-8, Mo. Elem. sch.

educator Ritenour Schs., St. Louis, 1973-98, ret., 1998. Councilwoman Hazelwood, Mo., 1996-2005; homecoming coord./alumni, Delta Zeta, 1997; bd. dirs. Ctrl. Mo. State U. Alumni, 1999—2005. Mem. Delta Zeta Alumni Assn. Avocations: gourmet cooking, civic improvement. Home: 5272 Ville Rosa Ln Hazelwood MO 63042-1662

**O'REILLY, MICHAEL,** corporate financial executive; BS, NYU; MBA, Pace U. Securities analyst investment dept. The Chubb Corp., 1969, chief investment officer, 1986, interim CFO, 2002—03, vice chmn., 2002—03, vice chmn. and CFO, 2003—. With U.S. Army, 1966—67, capt. USAR, 1968—71. Office: The Chubb Corp 15 Mountain View Rd Warren NJ 07059 Office Phone: 908-903-3764. Business E-Mail: moreilly@chubb.com.*

**O'REILLY, RICHARD JOHN,** pediatrician; b. Bklyn., Apr. 29, 1943; s. John Russell and Margaret (Cronin) O'R.; m. E. Jean Capitano, Nov. 1984; children from previous marriage: John, Steven. BS, Coll. Holy Cross, 1964; MD, U. Rochester, 1968. Diplomate Am. Bd. Pediatrics. Intern U. Minn. Hosp., Mpls., 1968-69; resident in pediatrics Children's Hosp. Med. Ctr. and Beth Israel Hosp., Boston, 1971-72; with dept. pediatrics Meml. Sloan Kettering Cancer Ctr., N.Y.C., 1973—; attending pediatrician, chmn. dept. pediatrics Meml. Hosp., N.Y.C., 1986—; mem. dept. immunology Sloan-Kettering Inst. Cancer Research; prof. pediatrics Cornell U. Med. Coll., 1980, Lila Acheson Wallace prof. pediatric research, 1980, Claire L. Tow, chair in pediat. oncology rsch., 2004; chief marrow transplantation svc. Meml. Sloan-Kettering Cancer Ctr., 1981—. Pres. Damon Runyon-Walter Winchell Cancer Fund, 1991-96. Editor-in-chief BBMT, 1995-2001; assoc. editor Cancer Rsch., Clin. Cancer Rsch., 1994-2002. Served with USPHS, 1969-71. Recipient Louise and Allston Boyer-Young Investigator award for clin. research, 1980, Boarhaave medal Leiden U., Pediat. Oncology award ASCO, Lifetime Achievement award ASEMT. Mem. AAAS, Am. Pediatric Soc., Am. Assn. Immunologists, Am. Acad. Pediatrics, Am. Assn. Pathologists, Soc. Pediatric Rsch., N.Y. Transplantation Soc., N.Y. Acad. Scis., Am. Assn. Clin. Radiology, Am. Soc. Hematology, Am. Soc. Blood and Marrow Transplantation (sec. 1993-95, v.p.-elect 1999, pres. 2001). Democrat. Roman Catholic. Achievements include first successful application of marrow transplantation from unrelated donors and from genetically mismatched donors, 1973. Office: Meml Sloan-Kettering Cancer Ctr 1275 York Ave New York NY 10021-6094

**O'REILLY, TERENCE JOHN,** lawyer; b. Farnborough, Eng., Apr. 12, 1945; came to U.S., 1960, naturalized, 1965; s. Arthur Francis and Doris Eileen (Burden) O'R.; m. Katharine Van Dyke Wallace, Sept. 26, 1970; children: Tobin Cooper, Matthew Wallace. BA, Loyola U., 1966; JD, U. Calif., Berkeley, 1969. Bar: Calif. 1970. Assoc. Voegelin, Barton, L.A., 1969-70, Walkup, Downing & Sterns, San Francisco, 1970-75; mem. Walkup, Shelby, Bastian, Melodia, Kelly & O'Reilly, San Francisco, 1975-87; prin. O'Reilly, Danko & Yamane, San Mateo, Calif., 1987—. Lectr. Kennedy Law Sch., Moraga, Calif., 1975-76, Inner Cir. of Advocates, 1998—; bd. govs. Consumer Attys. of Calif., 1995— bd. govs., diplomate Am. Bd. Profl. Liability Lawyers, 1989—. V.p. No. Calif. Rugby Football, San Francisco, 1975-80, bd. dirs., 1975—; trustee U.S. Rugby Football Found., 1987—; trustee The Philip Brooks Sch., 1986-89, Coun. of Bancroft Libr., U. Calif.; bd. dirs. San Francisco Traditional Jazz Found., 2002— Mem. Boalt Hall Alumni (bd. dirs. 1982-85), Assn. San Francisco Trial Lawyers (bd. dirs. 1985—), Assn. San Mateo Trial Lawyers (dir. 1992—, pres. 2003), Bohemian Club, Burlingame Country Club, Menlo Circus Club, Pacific Union Club. Roman Catholic. Office: 1900 O'Farrell St Ste 360 San Mateo CA 94403 E-mail: toreilly@oreillylaw.com

**O'REILLY, TIM,** computer book publishing company executive, open sourcer advocate; BA in Classics (cum laude, Harvard Coll.), 1975. Founder, pres. O'Reilly & Associates (now called O'Reilly Media, Inc.), Sebastopol, Calif., 1978—. Former bd. dir. Macromedia; bd. dir. CollabNet; spkr. in field. Co-author UNIX Text Processing (with Dale Dougherty and Howard Sams), 1987, (with Grace Todino) Managing UUCP and USENET, (with Valerie Quercia) The X Window System Users' Guide, (with Adrian Nye) The X Toolkit Intrinsics Programming Manual, (with Jerry Peek and Mike Loukides) UNIX Power Tools, (with Troy Mott) Windows 98 in a Nutshell; editor, (with O'Reilly & Associates) major contrbn. in the development of many of other titles, including UNIX in a Nutshell, Programming Perl, Sendmail, Essential System Administration, and The Cathedral and the Bazaar; O'Reilly Media Inc. published The Whole Internet User's Guide & Catalog (First popular book about the internet, selected by NY Pub. Libr. as one of the most signicant books of the 20th Century), 1992; introduced Safari Books Online (first web-native svc. for online book content), 2000; writer (web blog) radar.oreilly.com Recipient Industry Achievement award for advocacy on behalf of the open source community, InfoWorld, 1998. Mem.: Electronic Frontier Found. (bd. trustee), Internet Soc. (bd. trustee). Achievements include O'Reilly's Global Network Navigator site (GNN, sold to American Online in 1995) was the first web portal and the first true commerical site on the World Wide Web in 1993. Office: O Reilly Media Inc 1005 Gravenstein Hwy N Sebastopol CA 95472-2811 Office Phone: 707-827-7000. Office Fax: 707-829-0104.*

**O'REILLY, TIMOTHY PATRICK,** lawyer; b. San Lorenzo, Calif., Sept. 12, 1945; s. Thomas Marvin and Florence Ann (Ohlman) O'R.; m. Susan Ann Marshall, July 18, 1969; children: T. Patrick Jr., Sean M., Colleen K. BS, Ohio State U., 1967; JD, NYU, 1971. Bar: Pa. 1971, U.S. Dist. Ct. (ea. dist.) Pa. 1971, U.S. Dist. Ct. (mid. dist.) Pa. 1972, U.S. Ct. Appeals (3d cir.) 1977, U.S. Supreme Ct. 1988. Ptnr. Morgan, Lewis & Bockius, Phila., 1978—. Editor: Developing Labor Law, 1989; contrbr. articles to profl. jours. Bd. dirs. Notre Dame Acad. and Devon Preparatory Sch.; bd. govs. Aronimink Golf Club, J. Wood Platt Caddie Scholarship Trust, Applebrook Golf Club. Elected to Coll. of Labor and Employment Lawyers. Mem. ABA (chmn com on devel. of the law under the Nat. Labor Rels. Act, editor-in-chief The Developing Labor Law jour., elected mem. coun. labor and employment sect.), Pa. Bar Assn., Phila. Bar Assn., Ohio State U. Alumni Assn., Aronimink Golf Club (bd. govs.). Avocation: golf. Home: 1127 Cymry Dr Berwyn PA 19312-2056 Office: Morgan Lewis & Bockius 1701 Market St Philadelphia PA 19103-2903 Office Phone: 215-963-5470. Business E-Mail: toreilly@morganlewis.com.

**O'REILLY, WILLIAM R., JR.,** lawyer; b. 1955; m. Elizabeth Ross; children: Alex, Sam. BA summa cum laude with opt. honors, Tufts U., 1977; JD magna cum laude, Georgetown U., 1980. Bar: Mass. 1980. Assoc. to ptnr. Hale & Dorr, Boston, 1980—2004; ptnr., vice chmn. Real Estate Dept. Wilmer Cutler Pickering Hale & Dorr, Boston, 2004—. Mem. editl. bd. Georgetown Law Jour.; contrbr. articles to profl. jours. Trustee Tufts Univ., 2004—. Named a Mass. Super Lawyer, Boston Mag., 2004. Mem.: ABA, Mass. Bar Assn., Boston Bar Assn., Am. Coll. Real Estate Lawyers, Pension Real Estate Assn., Urban Land Inst., Real Estate Fin. Assn., Tufts Alumni Assn. (pres. 2000—02, Disting. Svc. award 2004), Tufts Alumni Council. Office: Wilmer Cutler Pickering Hale & Dorr 60 State St Boston MA 02109-1816 Office Phone: 617-526-6210. Office Fax: 617-526-5000. Business E-Mail: william.o'reilly@wilmerhale.com.

**OREM, CASSANDRA ELIZABETH (SANDRA OREM),** small business owner, educator, holistic health consultant and practitioner; b. Balt., Sept. 26, 1940; d. Ira Julius and Mabel Ruth (Peeples) O. Diploma, Ch. Home and Hosp. Sch. Nursing, 1962; BSN with honors, Johns Hopkins U., 1968; MSN, U. Md., 1972; cert., Balt. Sch. Massage, 1988; MA in Applied Psychology, U. Santa Monica, 1991, cert. in advanced applied psychology, 1992; cert., Waitley Masters Coaching Prog., 1996; postgrad., U. of the South, 2000—04. Staff, charge nurse Ch. Home and Hosp., Balt., 1962—63; asst. instr. Ch. Home and Hosp. Sch. Nursing, Balt., 1963—64, instr., 1964—70; student rschr., clin.-primary investigator U. Md. Sch. Nursing, Balt., 1971—72; clin. nurse specialist Johns Hopkins Hosp., Balt., 1972—77, rschr., clin. co-investigator, 1975, asst. dir. nursing, 1977—79, asst. adminstr., DON, 1979—87; clin. assoc. faculty Johns Hopkins U. Sch. Nursing, 1984—87; program dir., instr. intermediate massage course Balt. Sch. Massage, 1988—98, instr. advanced massage course, 1991—98, program dir. adv.

massage course, 1995—98, coord. curriculum devel., 1996—98; ptnr., educator UBP Assocs., 1990—91; pvt. practice Balt., 1986—2005. Pres. Nursing Edn. and Cons. Svc., Inc., Balt., 1976-78, Oasis Health Systems, Inc., Balt., 1987—; spkr. workshop facilitator, cons. profl. topics, Health and Wellness, Personal Growth, Time Mgmt., 1973—; mem. adv. bd. Integrative Medicine Nursing Consult Integrative Medicine Comm., 1999-2000; clin. and edn. cons. hosp. based massage and yoga St. Joseph Med. Ctr., 2000—. Author: (profl. booklet, audio publs.) Patient Education Book and Related Materials, 1977, Time Management/Organizing Sys., 1995; contrbr. chpts. and articles to profl. jours. Vol. Office on Aging, Balt., 1982-83, Boy Scouts Am., Balt., 1984-85, Cathedral of the Incarnation, Children's Peace Ctr., Balt., 2000-2001, Help Increase the Peace Program for/with Children, 2000-2004; sr. warden, lay pastor, Sunday sch. coord. and tchr. Ch. of Guardian Angel, Balt., 2006. Mem.: Ch. Home and Hosp. Sch. Nursing Alumni Assn. (treas. 1970—72, pres.-elect 1975—76), U. Md. Alumnae Assn., Sigma Theta Tau (Pi chpt.). Democrat. Episcopalian. Avocations: camping, photography, birding, music.

**OREMUS, STEPHEN,** composer; Grad., Berklee Coll. Music. Music dir.: Andrew Lippa's The Wild Party, Rent, regionally Into the Woods (Ordway), Dorian (World Premiere, Goodspeed), A Little Night Music, Jesus Christ Superstar (with Billy Porter and Emily Skinner), Nite Club Confidential (with Barbara Eden), The Radio City Music Hall Christmas Spectacular, vocal arranger, music supr.: Signed, Sealed, Delivered - The Music of Stevie Wonder, music supr., vocal arranger, orchestrator: Broadway plays Avenue Q, 2003; music supr., vocal arranger, orchestrator (Broadway plays) All Shook Up; music supr. arranger, orchestrator: Broadway plays tick,tick.BOOM!, musical dir.: Broadway plays Wicked, 2003. Office: Gershwin Theatre 222 W 51st St New York NY 10019 E-mail: storemus@earthlink.net.

**OREN, BRUCE CLIFFORD,** editor, artist; b. Mineola, N.Y., Aug. 31, 1952; s. Ralph and Berdene (Lands) O.; 1 child, Adam Nathaniel; m. Angela Malone Williams, Mar. 4, 1990. Student, U. Md., College Park, 1970-74. Archtl. sculptor Universal Restoration Inc., Washington, 1974-76; tech. illustrator Tex. Instruments, Stafford, Tex., 1976-77; graphic artist Houston Chronicle, 1977-79, photo editor, 1979-86, artist, 1986—, L.A. Times Syndicate, 1987-91. Named Best Art/Graphic, Hearst Newspapers, 1998, 2000; recipient Bronze medal, Soc. Newspaper Design, 1992, 1st Pl. Graphics award, Tex. Associated Press Mng. Editors, 2002. Jewish. Office: 801 Texas Ave Houston TX 77002-2904 Business E-Mail: bruce.oren@chron.com.

**ORENDER, DONNA,** sports association executive; m. M.G. Orender; children: Jacob, Zachary stepchildren: Morgan, Colleen. Grad., Queens Coll. NY, 1978; postgrad., Adelphi U. With ABC Sports, SportsChannel, NBA Entertainment, PGA Tour, 1988—2001, sr, v.p. strategic devel., 2001—05; pres. WNBA, NYC, 2005—. Hon. pres. PGA Am. Prodr.: Inside the PGA Tour. Office: WNBA Olympic Tower 645 Fifth Ave New York NY 10022 Office Phone: 212-688-9622, 212-750-9622.

**ORENGO-NANIA, SILVIA,** ophthalmologist; b. Detroit, June 24, 1961; d. Antonio and Christina Orengo; m. Jay Nania, Aug. 8, 1992; children: Christina Nania, Jason Nania, Julia Nania. Med. degree, Baylor Coll. of Medicine, Houston, 1983. Exec. eye care line Michael E. DeBakey Vets. Affair Med. Ctr., Houston, 1998—2006; prof. Baylor Coll. of Medicine, Houston, 2006—. Achievements include research in Central Corneal Thickness and Intraocular Pressure. Office: Cullen Eye Inst 6565 Fannin NC205 Houston TX 77030 Office Phone: 713-798-6100.

**ORENSTEIN, FRAN M.,** small business owner, writer; b. Bklyn., N.Y., Oct. 31, 1939; s. Nathan Gitterman and Gertrude Celia Chall-Gitterman; m. Walter Orenstein, Dec. 21, 1958 (div. Jan. 1977); children: James, Susannah, Peter. BA, Bklyn. Coll., 1960; MEd, Coll. N.J., 1976; EdD, Nova Southeastern U., 1993. Lic. tchr. N.Y., N.J., guidance N.J., Calif., cert. pub. mgr. N.J. Tchr. Pub. Sch. 256-N.Y.C. Bd. Edn., Bklyn., 1960—63, Hilltop Acad., Morganville, NJ, 1973—74; editor, writer Univ. Comms., Rahway, NJ, 1975—79; tchr., content specialist East Windsor (N.J.) Regional Schs., 1979—80; sr. rehab. counselor N.J. Divsn. Vocat. Rehab., Trenton, NJ, 1980—88; disability officer Americorps N.J. Dept. Edn., Trenton, NJ, 1990—2002; program devel. specialist N.J. Dept. Cmty. Affairs, Trenton, NJ, 1988—98, 2002—; Reiki master, founder Over the Rainbow Healing Arts. Presenter local, nat., and internat. confs. on gender equity in schs., violence prevention in schs., sexual harassment in schs and the workplace, and; cons., presenter Ednl. Visions Group, East Windsor, NJ, 1990—98. Author: editor: Bus. World for Women / Men mag., 1975—78 (Navy citation, 1977), SACC Talk, 1991—92. Campaign worker N.J. Dem. Party, NJ, 1992; founding bd. dirs. Cen. N.J. Breast Cancer Coalition, 2000—02, Am. Cancer Soc. Chpt. N.J. Breast Cancer Coalition, Manalapan, 1973—77, Freehold, 2000—; bd. dirs., newsletter editor Women's Agenda/N.J. Law, NJ, 1993—96; vol. bd. dirs. Susan B. Komen Race for the Cure, Princeton, NJ, 1995—99. Mem.: Soc. Children's Book Writers and Illustrators, Mensa (Ariz. proctor coord., S.C./Ga. proctor), Phi Delta Kappa, Kappa Delta Pi. Avocations: reading, gardening, writing children's books. Home: 268 Landing Ln Bluffton SC 29909-6091 Personal E-mail: frano1@davtv.com.

**ORENSTEIN, JAMES,** federal judge; Grad., Harvard U.; JD, NYU Sch. Law. Law clerk US Circuit Judge James Hunter, III; private practice, 1988—90; asst. US atty. US Dist. Ct. (Eastern Dist. NY), 1990—2001, magistrate judge, 2004—; ptnr. Baker & Hostetler, LLP, 2001—04. Adj. prof. NYU Law Sch., Fordham Law Sch. Office: 225 Cadman Plaza East Brooklyn NY 11201

**ORENSTEIN, MICHAEL (IAN ORENSTEIN),** philatelic dealer, columnist; b. Bklyn., Jan. 6, 1939; s. Harry and Myra (Klein) Orenstein; m. Linda Turner, June 28, 1964; 1 child, Paul David. BS, Clemson U., 1960; postgrad., U. Calif., Berkeley, 1960-61. Career regional mgr. Minkus Stamp & Pub. Co., Calif., 1964-70; mgr. stamp div. Superior Stamp & Coin Co., Inc., Beverly Hills, Calif., 1970-90; dir. stamp divsn. Superior Galleries, Beverly Hills, Calif., 1991-94; dir. space memorabilia Superior Stamp and Coin. Co., Inc., Beverly Hills, Calif., 1992-94; dir. stamp and space divsn. Superior Stamp & Coin an A-Mark Co., Beverly Hills, Calif., 1994-97; sr. buyer, appraiser Superior Stamp & Coin, 2001; co-founder, ptnr., prin., pres. AuroraGalleries Internat., 2002—04; pres. The Right Stuff Inc., 2001—. Cons. Office Insp. Gen. NASA, Nassau County Dist. Atty., NY, Regency Superior Auction Co. Columnist: L.A. Times, 1965—93; philatelic advisor/creator The Video Guide to Stamp Collecting, 1988; author: Stamp Collecting is Fun, 1990; contrbr. articles to publs. With U.S. Army, 1962—64. Recipient medal of Yuri Gagarin, Fedn. Supporting Russian Cosmonauts, 2002. Mem.: AIAA, Internat. Soc. Appraisers: Stamps, Space Memorabilia, Internat. Fedn. Stamp Dealers, Am. Philatelic Soc. (writers unit 1975—80, 1989—93), Confederate Stamp Alliance, German Philatelic Soc., C. Z. Study Group, Am. Stamp Dealers Assn. Republican. Avocation: fishing. Address: 19546 Minnehaha Northridge CA 91326 Office Phone: 818-368-6888. Personal E-mail: rightstuf@verizon.net.

**ORENSTEIN, WALTER ALBERT,** director; b. N.Y.C., Mar. 5, 1948; m. Diane Rauzin; children: Eliza Tema, Evan William. BS, CCNY, 1968; MD, Albert Einstein Coll. Medicine, 1972. Intern U. Calif., San Francisco, 1972—73, resident in pediat., 1973—74; EIS officer divsn. immunization CDC, Atlanta, 1974—76; med. epidemiologist divsn. immunization Ctr. for Disease Control, Atlanta, 1976—77; resident pediat. Childrens Hosp. L.A., 1977—78; fellow infectious diseases U. So. Calif. Med. Sch., 1978—80; resident preventive medicine Ctrs. for Disease Control and Prevention, Atlanta, 1980—82, chief surveillance and investigations sect., 1982—88, dir. divsn. immunization, 1988—94; nat. immunization program, 1993—2000; Assoc. Dir. Emory Vaccine Ctr. Emory Univ., 2004—. Cons. smallpox eradication program WHO, Uttar Pradesh, India, 1974—75; med. adv. bd. CDC, Atlanta, 1981—84; nat. vaccine adv. com., 1988—; clin. assoc. prof. dept. cmty. health Emory U. Sch. Medicine, 1985; adj. prof. The Rollins Sch. Pub. Health, 1992—2002; cons. and presenter in field. Mem. editl. bd.

Pediat. Infectious Disease Jour., 1987—2000; co-editor: Vaccines, 1999; contrbr. articles to profl. jours. Asst. surgeon gen. USPHS, 1995. Fellow: Pediat. Infectious Diseases Soc. (past chmn. publs. com., past mem. coun.), Infectious Diseases Soc. Am., Am. Acad. Pediats. (com. on infectious diseases 1989—, liaison mem., nat. vaccine adv. com.); mem.: APHA, Soc. for Epidemiologic Rsch., Am. Epidemiol. Soc. Office: Emory Sch of Medicine 1440 Clifton Rd Atlanta GA 30322

**ORENTLICHER, JOHN,** video research educator, artist; b. Roanoke, Va., June 7, 1943; s. Herman and Jeanette (Levin) O. BA, Goddard Coll., 1968; MFA, Sch. Art Inst. Chgo., 1970. Asst. prof. Ea. Mich. U., Ypsilanti, 1970-76; assoc. prof. Syracuse U., NY, 1976—, chmn. exptl. studios, 1978-81, chmn., prof. art media studies Coll. of Visual and Performing Arts, 1981-85, 87-89, chair dept. transmedia, 2005—. U.S. curator, 1st Internat. Video Festival Invitational, 1986, 2nd Internat. Video Festival, Mus. de Arte Medellin, Colombia, 1988; Fulbright Hays sr. lectr., Colombia, 1985; exec. producer WHAT-TV, Syracuse, 1983; video artist. Vol. Peace Corps, Aisen Province, Chile, 1964-66; curator 2d bi-annn. Internat. Video Festival, Medellin, Colombia. N.Y. State Coun. grantee, 1984, grantee Rockefeller Found., Nat. Endowment Arts; recipient ACE award. Avocations: music, antique boats. Home: 6074 Sewickley Dr Jamesville NY 13078-9464 Office: Syracuse U Dept Transmedia 102 Sheffer Bldg Syracuse NY 13244 Office Phone: 315-443-1033. E-mail: jorentli@syr.edu.

**ORESKES, IRWIN,** biochemistry educator; b. Chgo., June 30, 1926; s. Herman and Clara (Rubenstein) O.; m. Susan E. Nagin, June 18, 1949; children: Michael, Daniel, Naomi, Rebecca. BS in Chemistry, CCNY, 1949; MA in Phys. Chemistry, Bklyn. Coll., 1956; PhD in Biochemistry, CUNY, 1969. Cert. clin. lab. dir. NYC, NY State. Chemist Tech. Tape Co., Bronx, NY, 1949; technician NYU Sch. Medicine, 1950-51; phys. chemist Kingsbrook Jewish Med. Ctr., 1951-56; rsch. fellow Poly. Inst., NY, 1957-58; rsch. assoc. Mt. Sinai Hosp., NYC, 1959-68, dir. arthritis lab., 1961-90; rsch. asst. prof. Mt. Sinai Sch. Medicine, NYC, 1969-74, rsch. assoc. prof., 1974-91; assoc. prof. Hunter Coll. Sch. Health Scis., CUNY, 1969—74, prof., 1974—2002, prof. emeritus, 2002—, dean, 1977-80; mem. doctoral faculty in biochemistry Grad. Ctr., CUNY, 1970—2002, emeritus, 2002—. Vis. prof. Johns Hopkins U. Sch. Health Svcs., 1976-77; cons. to diagnostic reagent and instrument mfrs., 1953-; mem. Internat. Sci. Coun., Albert Einstein Rsch. Inst., Buenos Aires, 1969-79; mem. bd. examiners for clin. labs. NYC Dept. Health, 1973-75; sr. cons. Biotech. Rev. Assocs., 1983-92. Co-editor: Rheumatology for the Health Care Professional, 1991; contrbr. numerous articles to profl. jours. Served with U.S. Army, 1944-46. Nat. Inst. Arthritis and Metabolic Diseases grantee, 1961-69; Arthritis Found. grantee, 1961-65, 69, 72; Lupus Found. grantee, 1975-76; CUNY Found. grantee, 1982-83. Mem. Am. Chem. Soc., Am. Coll. Rheumatology, AAAS, NY Acad. Scis., Am. Assn. Immunologists, Am. Assn. Clin. Chemistry, Harvey Soc., Nat. Acad. Clin. Biochemistry, Acad. Clin. Lab. Physicians and Scientists, Clin. Immunology Soc., Sigma Xi, Phi Lambda Upsilon. Home: 670 West End Ave New York NY 10025-7313 Office: Hunter Coll Sch Health Sci 425 E 25th St New York NY 10010-2547 Office Phone: 212-481-5115. *I have always tried to live and work by the idea that strength is not harshness, caring is not sentimentality, and honesty is not vulnerability.*

**ORESKES, NAOMI,** science historian; b. NYC, Nov. 25, 1958; d. Irwin Oreskes and Susan Eileen Nagin Oreskes; m. Kenneth Belitz, Sept. 28, 1986; children: Hannah Oreskes Belitz, Clara Oreskes Belitz. BSc with honors, Imperial Coll., London, 1981; PhD, Stanford U., 1990. Geologist We. Mining Corp., Adelaide, Australia, 1981—84; rsch. and tng. asst. Stanford U., Calif., 1984—89; vis. asst. prof. Dartmouth Coll., Hanover, NH, 1990—91, asst. prof., 1991—96; assoc. prof. Gallatin Sch. NYU, 1996—98, U. Calif., San Diego, 1998—2005, prof., 2005—. Consulting geologist Western Mining Corp., 1984-90; consulting historian Am. Inst. Physics, N.Y.C., 1990-96. Author: The Rejection of Continental Drift, 1999, Theory and Method in American Earth Science, 1999; editor: Plate Tectonics: An Insider's History of the Modern Theory of the Earth, 2001; contrbr. articles to profl. jours. Recipient Lindgren prize Soc. Econ. Geologists, 1993, Young Investigator award NSF, 1994-99, George Sarton Lectr. award AAAS, 2004; fellow NEH, 1993. Mem. Geol. Soc. Am., History Sci. Soc. Jewish. Home: 14174 Bahama Cv Del Mar CA 92014-2901 Office: U Calif San Diego 9500 Gilman Dr La Jolla CA 92093-0104 Office Phone: 858-534-4695. Business E-Mail: noreskes@ucsd.edu.

**ORFALEA, PAUL,** printing, copying company founder, investment company executive; BS, Univ. So. Calif.; LLD (hon.), Babson Coll., Mass., 2004. Founder, CEO, chmn. Kinko's, Santa Barbara, Calif., 1970—2000, chmn. emeritus, 2000—04; co-founder West Coast Asset Mgmt., Ventura, Calif., 2000—. Lectr. Univ. So. Calif., Univ. Calif., Davis, Santa Barbara; adv. bd. Stone Canyon Venture Ptnrs. LP; bd. dir. Espresso Royale, DataProse; pub. spkr. Author (with Ann Marsh): Copy This: Lessons from a Hyperactive Dyslexic Who Turned a Bright Idea into One of America's Best Companies, 2005. Bd. trustee Univ. Calif. Santa Barbara Found. Named to CEO Hall of Fame; recipient Entrepreneur of Yr. award, Univ. So. Calif. Marshall Sch. Bus., 1998, Philanthropist of Yr., 2000, Conrad Hilton Entrepreneur award, 2001, Friend of Calif. Cmty. Colleges, 2003, R.O.S.E. award, Univ. So. Calif., 2003, Beta Gamma Sigma Medallion for Entrepreneurship, Sally award, Salvation Army, Ellis Island Medal of Honor. Office: West Coast Asset Mgmt Ste 1000 2151 Alessandro Dr Ventura CA 93001 Office Phone: 805-653-5333. Office Fax: 805-648-6466.

**ORFE, N. MICHAEL,** secondary school educator; b. Riverside, NJ, May 11, 1946; s. Norman Leo Orfe and Geraldine Laura Rementer; m. Gay Ann Anderten, June 30, 1984; children: Michael Joseph, Taryn Leigh Allean, K. C. BA in English and History, Montclair State U., NJ, 1968; MA in Am. Studies, Seton Hall U., 1973. Cert. supr., prin. NJ. English tchr. Scotch Plains Fanwood H.S., NJ, 1968—74, Mendham H.S., NJ, 1974—2000; supr. English Voorhees H.S., Glen Gardner, NJ, 2000—. Acad. dir. Summer Inst. for Gifted, Parsippany, NJ, 1999—2003. Author poems and short stories. Grantee, NEH, 2003. Mem.: Nat. Coun. Tchrs. English. Avocations: golf, basketball, hiking. Home: 6 Heather Hill Port Murray NJ 07865 Office: Voorhees HS Rt 513 Glen Gardner NJ 08826

**ORFIELD, ANTONIA MARIE,** optometrist, researcher; d. Alfred Anthony and Eva Swenson Stoll; m. Gary Allan Orfield, May 24, 1963; children: Amy Elizabeth, Sonia Marie, Rosanna Antonia. BA in History, Smith Coll., 1963; MAT in History/Social Studies, U. Chgo., 1966; BS in Visual Sci., Ill. Coll. Optometry, 1987, OD, 1989. Lic. Mass. Bd. Optometry. Optometrist Michael Reese HMO, Chgo., 1989—91, Eye Exam 2000, Chgo., 1989—91; behavioral optometrist Harvard U. Health, Cambridge, Mass., 1991—. Asst. prof. New Eng. Coll. Optometry, Boston, 1991—2000, dir. chief investigator, clin. preceptor Mather Sch. Vision and Learning Rsch./Svc. Clinic, 1993—99; pvt. practice behavioral optometrist, Cambridge, 1996—; spkr. in field. Contrbr. articles to profl. jours. Parent rep. Kenwood Acad. Sch. Coun., Chgo., 1989—91. Grantee, State Street Bank, N.E. Congress Optometry, Mass. Soc. Optometrists, Am. Found. Vision Awareness, Friends of the Sensorily Deprived. Fellow: Coll. Optometrists in Vision Devel., Am. Acad. Optometry; mem.: Neurooptometric Rehab. Assn. (charter), Internat. Coll. Applied Kinesiology. Democrat. Achievements include research in children in poverty have a great number of vision problems that interefere with learning; near point glasses can raise test scores; tracking problems are correlated with reading failures; vision therapy is correlated with improvement in grades. Avocations: study of homeopathic medicine, sports vision training, study of educational kinesiology, study of nutrition and vision, swimming. Office: Harvard Univ Health Svc 75 Mt Auburn St Cambridge MA 02138 also: Ste 205 678 Massachusetts Ave Cambridge MA 02139 E-mail: antoniaorfield@yahoo.com.

**ORFORD, ROBERT RAYMOND,** physician, consultant; b. Winnipeg, Manitoba, Can., Apr. 18, 1948; came to U.S., 1988; s. Robert Raymond and Sarah Gloria L. (Gullden) O.; m. Dale Laura Stuart, June 2, 1972; children: Carolyn Tiffany, Andrew Craig, Loren Brent. BS, McGill U., 1969, MD,

1971; MS, U. Minn., 1975; MPH, U. Wash., 1976. Assoc. prof. cmty. medicine U. Alberta, Edmonton, Can., 1978-88; dir. med. svcs. Govt. of Alberta, Edmonton, Can., 1979-81, exec. dir. occupational health svcs., 1981-85, deputy min. cmty. occupational health, 1985-88; med. dir. employee health U. Alberta Hosp., Edmonton, Can., 1988; sr. assoc. cons. Mayo Clinic, Rochester, Minn., 1988-91, cons. preventive medicine, 1991-96, Scottsdale, Ariz., 1996—. Asst. prof. Mayo Med. Sch., Rochester, 1988—; mem. Alberta Energy Resource Conservation Bd., 1988-89; chmn. divsn. preventive and occupl. medicine, dir. exec. health program, Mayo Clinic, Scottsdale, 1999—. Contbr. articles to profl. jours. Mem. Olmsted County Environ. Commn., Rochester, 1991-96, chair, 1994. Govt. of Can. Nat. Health fellow, 1975-76. Fellow Royal Coll. Physicians and Surgeons Can., Am. Coll. Occupational and Environ. Medicine (v.p. 2006—), Am. Coll. Preventive Medicine, Aerospace Med. Assn.; mem. Internat. Commn. Occupational Health Medicine (nat. sec. 2001—). Presbyterian. Avocations: languages, fitness, travel. Home: 15516 E Acacia Way Fountain Hills AZ 85268-3158 Office: Mayo Clinic Scottsdale Divsn Preventive Medicine 13400 E Shea Blvd Scottsdale AZ 85259-5499 Office Phone: 480-301-7379. Business E-Mail: rorford@mayo.edu.

**ORGAN, RITA C.,** museum administrator, consultant; b. Omaha, Aug. 7, 1965; d. Claude Harold and Elizabeth Lucille Organ. BFA, Calif. Coll. Arts & Crafts, 1987; attended, Ind. U., 1987—90. Curator African-Am. materials The Children's Mus., Indpls., 1990—96; dir. exhibits & collections CHW Mus. African-Am. History, Detroit, 1996—2000, Nat. Underground Railroad Freedom Ctr., Cin., 2000—04; exec. dir. Ind. Mus. African-Am. History, Indpls., 2004—. Bd. pres. Assn. African-Am. Mus., Detroit, 1999—2002; bd. mem. Assn. Study of African Am. Life and History, Washington, 2000—02; mem. nat. adv. bd. The Freedom Ctr., Cin., 2005—. Author: (preface) Black History Resource Guide, 1998. Mem.: Nat. Coun. Negro Women, Assn. Midwest Mus., Assn. African Am. Mus. Avocations: hiking, bicycling, cooking. Office: Ind Mus African Am History 39 W Jackson Pl Ste 75 Indianapolis IN 46225 E-mail: ro_imaah@sbcglobal.net.

**ORGEBIN-CRIST, MARIE-CLAIRE,** retired biology professor, department chairman; b. Vannes, France, Mar. 20, 1936; License Natural Scis., License Biology, Sorbonne, U. Paris, 1957; D. Scis., Lyons U., France, 1961. Stagiaire dept. biochemistry faculty medicine, Paris, 1957—58; stagiaire Centre Nat. de la Recherche Scientifique, Paris, 1958—60, attachee de recherche, 1960—62; research assoc. Population Council (Med. Div.), N.Y.C., 1962—63; research assoc. dept. ob/gyn Vanderbilt Sch. Medicine, 1963—64, research instr., 1964—66, asst. prof., 1966—70, assoc. prof., 1970—73, Lucius E. Burch prof. reproductive biology, 1973—2005, prof. dept. anatomy, 1975—2005; dir. Vanderbilt Sch. Medicine (Center Reproductive Biology Research.), 1973—2005, prof. emeritus, 2005—. Editor-in-Chief Jour. Andrology, 1983-89 Recipient Career Devel. award NIH, 1968-73, NIH Merit award, 1986,; Fogarty Internat. sr. fellow, 1977; Disting. Scientist award Am. Soc. Reproductive Medicine, 1996. Mem. Am. Assn. Anatomists, Am. Soc. Cell Biology, Am. Soc. Andrology (v.p. 1994-95, pres. 1995-96, Disting. Svc. award 1997, Disting. Andrologist award 1990). Internat. Com. on Andrology, Endocrine Soc., Soc. for Study Fertility (Eng.), Soc. for Study Reprodn., N.Y. Acad. Scis. Office: Vanderbilt U Sch Med Ctr Reproductive Biology Rsch Rm C-3306 MCN Nashville TN 37232-0001 E-mail: m-c.orgebin-crist@vanderbilt.edu.

**ORIANI, RICHARD ANTHONY,** metallurgical engineer, educator; b. El Salvador, July 19, 1920; arrived in U.S., 1929, naturalized, 1943; s. Americo and Berta (Siguenza) Oriani; m. Constance Amelia Gordon, June 26, 1949; children: Margaret, Steven, Julia, Amelia. B in Chem. Engring, CCNY, 1943; MS, Stevens Inst. Tech., 1946; MA, Princeton U., 1948, PhD, 1949. Lab. asst. CCNY, 1943; chemist Bakelite Corp., Bloomfield, NJ, 1943-46; instr. physics Miss Fine's Finishing Sch., Princeton, NJ, 1946-47; rsch. assoc. GE Rsch. Lab., Schenectady, 1949-59; asst. dir. U.S. Steel Corp. Rsch. Lab., Monroeville, Pa., 1959-80; prof. U. Minn., Mpls., 1980-89, dir. Corrosion Rsch. Ctr., 1980-87, prof. emeritus, dir. emeritus, 1989—. Cons. in field. Contbr. articles to profl. jours., chapters to books. Founder, mem. Foxwood Civic Assn., Monroeville, 1959—80; founder, v.p. Monroeville Pub. Libr., 1960—80. Recipient Alexander von Humboldt Sr. Scientist award, 1984, W. R. Whitney award, 1987. Fellow: Electrochemical Soc., Nat. Assn. Corrosion Engrs., N.Y. Acad. Scis., Am. Inst. Chemists, Am. Soc. Metals; mem.: AAAS, Am. Inst. Metall. Engrs., Am. Phys. Soc. Republican. Home: 4623 Humboldt Ave S Minneapolis MN 55409-2264 Office: U Minn 112 Amundson Hall 421 Church St SE Minneapolis MN 55455-0113 Office Phone: 612-625-5862. E-mail: orian001@umn.edu.

**ORICCHIO, MICHAEL,** editor; m. Renee Oricchio. Writer Washington Post, 1984; staff writer, editor San Jose Mercury News, 1987—2002; mng. editor NY Times Syndication Sales Corp, 2002—. Office: NY Times Syndication Sales Corp 14th Fl 122 E 42nd St New York NY 10168 Office Phone: 212-499-3314. Office Fax: 212-499-3382. E-mail: oricchio@nytimes.com.*

**ORIJI, GIBSON K.,** medical educator, medical researcher; b. Port Harcourt, Rivers, Nigeria, Dec. 13, 1960; arrived in U.S., 1981; s. Frank M. and Cecilia N. Oriji; m. Mary A. Bates, May 13, 1985; children: Gordon, Guyton, Gilbert. BSce/trf in Med. Tech., Rivers State U. Sci. and Tech., Port Harcourt, Nigeria, 1980; BS in Biology, Tex. So. U., 1983; PhD in Physiology, Howard U., 1992. Med. tech. bd. cert. Instr. dept. biology Tex. So. U., Houston, 1983—85; instr., grad. tchg. asst. dept. physiology and biophysics Howard U. Coll. Medicine, Washington, 1987—92; postdoctoral fellow Health Sci. Ctr., Coll. Medicine U. Tenn., Memphis, 1992—94; intramural rsch. fellow NIH, Bethesda, Md., 1994—98; asst. prof. biology William Paterson U., Wayne, NJ, 1998—. Sci. dir. Pre-Colege Acad. Program, Wayne, 1998—; adj. prof. biology Prince George's CC, Largo, Md., 1997—98, Largo, 2002. Sci. rsch. faculty liaison Pathways to Acad. Success, Wayne, 1998—2002. Biochemist Army Med. Svc. Commn. Corps. Res., 1997—, Walter Reed Army Med. Ctr., Washington. Grantee Rsch., Ctr. Rsch., 2002. Mem.: Am. Physiol. Soc. (sci. rsch. faculty liaison 1998—2002, Undergraduate Summer Rsch. 2001-2002). Office: William Paterson U 300 Pompton Rd Wayne NJ 07470 Business E-Mail: Orijig@wpunj.edu.

**ORING, STUART AUGUST,** audio-visual specialist, writer, photographer, researcher; b. Bronx, N.Y., Aug. 28, 1932; s. Irving and Helen Flora (Greenhut) O.; m. Mary Carolyn Barth, Aug. 22, 1957; children: Carlene Marie Oring, Sheri Alyce Oring. AAS, Rochester Inst. Tech., 1957; BFA, R.I. Tech., 1959; MA, Am. U., 1970. Photo lab asst. Nat. Geographic, Washington, summer 1957; photography asst. IJBecker, Nepo-Nuss Advt Photo, Studio Assocs. & Art Green Inc., N.Y.C., 1959-61; freelance photographer pvt. practice, Washington, 1961; indsl. photographer Vitro Corp., Rockville, Md., 1962-64; health photographer nat. Ctr. Radiol. Health, Rockville, Md., 1964-67; visual info. specialist ARS Info. div. USDA, Washington, 1967-69; audio visual specialist AV Ctr., Washington, 1969-71; photojournalist Office of Econ. Opportunity, Washington, 1971-74; visual info. specialist ASCS, U.S. Dept. Agr., Washington, 1974-94; ret., 1994. Mgr., owner ISIS Visual Comms.; photography tchr. Prince George's C.C., Largo, Md., 1975-96; guest lectr. U. Md. Balt. County, Catonsville, Corcoran Gallery of Art, Washington; spkr. in field. Author, editor and pub.: (textbook/gallery text) Understanding Pictures-A Teacher's Planning Guide, 1994, Understanding Pictures-Theories, Exercises and Procedures, 1990, rev. 1992, rev. 1995, A Beginner's Guide to Looking at Pictures, 1997; contbr. numerous articles to profl. jours.; photos published in books, mags., brochures, pamphlets. Photographer with U.S. Army, 1952-55. Recipient Cert. Recognition award Eastman Kodak Co., 1973, Nat. Ctr. Radiol. Health, Rockville, Md., 1965. Mem.: APA (divsn. 10 psychology and the arts, program spkr. 105th annm. conf., 108th ann. conf.), Inst. for Psychol. Study of Arts (program spkr.), Am. Soc. Psychopathology of Expression (bd. dirs.). Achievements include research and development of new approaches for analyzing and interpreting art and photographs. Home and Office: 2570 Redbud Ln Owings MD 20736-4308 Office Phone: 410-257-5709. E-mail: stuartoring@comcast.net.

**ORKAND, DONALD SAUL,** management consultant; b. NYC, Mar. 2, 1936; s. Harold and Sylvia (Wagner) O.; children: Dara Sue, Katarina Day; m. Kim Lim Sang, July 22, 2001; 1 child, Aaron J. BS summa cum laude, NYU, 1956, MBA, 1957, PhD, 1963. Statistician Western Electric Co., N.Y.C., 1956-58; group v.p. Ops. Rsch., Inc., Silver Spring, Md., 1960-69; pres. Ops. Rsch. Industries, Ltd., Ottawa, Ont., Canada, 1968-69; CEO Orkand Corp., Tysons Corner, Va., 1970—2004; ptnr. DC Ventures and Assocs. LLC, Mc Lean, Va., 2004—. Bd. dirs. U. Md. Found., Inc., College Park, 1993-2002. Bd. vis. Univ. Coll., 2002—; trustee Suburban Hosp., 1994-2000. 1st Lt. Ordnance Corps, USAR, 1958-60. Mem. Am. Econs. Assn., Am. Statis. Assn. Republican. Jewish. Avocations: reading, theater, travel, exercise. Office: Dc Ventures Associates PO Box 10625 Mc Lean VA 22102-8625

**ORKIN, JENNA,** writer; b. New York, NY; d. Harvey Orkin; 1 child, One. BA, Hunter Coll., NY; JD, NY Law Sch., NY; BA/MA, Oxford U., England. Interviewer Exploring Post One, New York, NY, 1984—86; educator Juilliard, New York, NY, 1978—83; press chairperson 911 Environ. Action, N.Y.C., 2002—04; founder World Trade Ctr. Environ. Orgn., 2002—. Moderator 1st Peak Oil Conf., N.Y.C., 2005.

**ORKIN, LOUIS RICHARD,** physician, educator; b. N.Y.C., Dec. 23, 1915; s. Samuel David and Rebecca (Rish) O.; m. Florence Fine, Mar. 5, 1938; 1 dau., Rita. BA, U. Wis., 1937; MD, NYU, 1941; AAS in Marine Tech., Kingsborough Coll., 1992. Intern Bellevue Hosp., NYC, 1942, resident anesthesiology, 1946-48; practice medicine specializing in anesthesiology Bronx, NY, 1946—48; dir. anesthesiology Backus Hosp., Norwich, Conn., 1948-50; asst. prof. anesthesiology NYU Coll. Medicine, 1950-55; prof., chmn. dept. anesthesiology Albert Einstein Coll. Medicine, 1955-82, Disting. univ. prof., 1982-86, dist. univ. prof. emeritus, 1986—. Vis. prof. depts. bioengring., anesthesiology U. Calif., San Diego, 1971; Cons. VA, USPHS, USN; mem. com. anesthesiology Nat. Acad. Scis., 1964-69; mem. com. anesthetic drugs FDA, Dept. Health, Edn. and Welfare, 1970— Author: Patient in Shock, 1965, Physiology of Obstetrical Anesthesia, 1969; Contbr. articles to profl. jours. V.p. and trustee Wood Library Mus. Served to capt. M.C. AUS, 1942-45. Decorated Bronze Star; honoree Albert Einstein Coll. Medicine, 2005. Fellow Am. Coll. Chest Physicians, NY Acad. Sci., NY Acad. Medicine, Am. Coll. Anesthesiology (past chmn. bd. govs.); mem. NY State Soc. Anesthesiologists (past pres.; Disting. Svc. award 2000). Home: 11 Stuyvesant Oval Apt 11F New York NY 10009-2001 Office Phone: 212-473-0023. Personal E-mail: Louis_Orkin@hotmail.com.

**ORLANDO, JOHN D.,** elementary school educator; b. Reading, Pa., Dec. 22, 1956; s. Anthony S. and Kathrine R. Orlando; life ptnr. Joseph A. Abba, Feb. 14, 1966. BS in Elem. Edn., Kutztown State Coll., 1978; EdM in Reading Specialist, Kuztown U. Pa., 1984. Tchr. Thomas H. Ford Elem. Sch., Reading, Pa., 1978—88, So. Mid. Sch., Reading 1988—2000; reading specialist Indian River Sch. Dist., Selbyville, Del., 2001—04, Sussex Tech. Sch. Dist., Georgetown, Del., 2004—. Avocations: physical fitness, spiritual expansion, travel. Home: 9 Somerset Rd Rehoboth Beach DE 19971 Office: Sussex Technical School District 17099 County Seat Hwy Georgetown DE 19947 Office Phone: 302-856-0961. Personal E-mail: jdo13579@aol.com. Business E-Mail: jorlando@sussexvt.k12.de.us.

**ORLANDO, LORI ANN,** medical researcher; d. Geraldine Sainthill and Roy Charles Orlando; m. Bradley F. Mann, May 19, 1995. BS, U. N.C., 1990—2001; MD, Tulane Med. Ctr., 1998; M in health sci., Duke U. Med. Sch., 2004. Diplomate Am. Bd. Internal Medicine. Resident in internal medicine Tulane Med. Ctr., New Orleans, 1998—2001, chief resident in internal medicine, 2001—02; internal medicine fellow Duke U. Med. Ctr., Durham, NC, 2002—04; assoc. in medicine, 2004—; rsch. assoc. Durham VA Med. Ctr., NC, 2002—. Contbr. articles to profl. jours. Recipient Rsch. internship, Harvard U., Brigham and Women's Hosp., Dept. of Pathology, 1987, Med. Student Achievement award, Endocrine Soc., 1998, Owl Club award for Outstanding Med. Resident, 2000, 2001, Outstanding Trainee award, Am. Fedn. for Med. Rsch., So. Sect., 2002. Mem.: Soc. of Gen. Internal Medicine (assoc.; chair planning com.). Achievements include research in describing chronic kidney disease in Va and evalauting interface between generalist and specialist care. Office Phone: 919-286-3399.

**ORLANDO, MARIA,** behavioral scientist; b. Boston, Jan. 18, 1965; d. Joseph Alexander and Ailene Cecilia Orlando; m. Philip Dennis Edelen, July 29, 2000. PhD, U. N.C., Chapel Hill, 1997. Asst. prof. and assessment specialist James Madison U., Harrisonburg, Va., 1997—98; psychometrician and behavioral scientist RAND Corp., Santa Monica, Calif., 1998—. Assoc. jour. editor Psychol. Assessment, 2004—. Mem.: APA, Psychometric Soc. Office: RAND Corp 1776 Main St Santa Monica CA 90407-2138 Office Phone: 310-393-0411. Office Fax: 310-260-8150. E-mail: orlando@rand.org.

**ORLANSKY, JULIAN DAVID,** magistrate; b. Drew, Miss., Oct. 5, 1930; s. Abram Hyman and Dora (Sklar) O.; m. Shirley Ruth Ettinger, May 27, 1954; children— Steven Daniel, Charles Lawrence, Linda Rachel. B.S. in Commerce, La. State U., 1952; LL.B., U. Miss., 1954. Bar: Miss. 1954, U.S. Dist. Ct. (so. dist.) Miss. 1954, U.S. Dist. Ct. (no. dist.) Miss. 1968, U.S. Ct. Appeals (5th cir.) 1971. Assoc. Taylor & Townsend, Drew, Miss., 1954-55; sole practice, Greenville, Miss., 1957-60; ptnr. Orlansky, Miller & Dean, Greenville, 1960-75; U.S. magistrate judge No. Dist. Miss., part-time 1970-75, full-time, 1975—. Pres. Hebrew Union Congregation, Greenville, 1975, Greenville United Fund, 1963; chmn. Salvation Army adv. bd., 1969. Served with U.S. Army, 1955-56. Mem. Washington County Bar Assn. (pres. 1972), Miss. State Bar, ABA, Nat. Conf. Fed. Trial Judges, Fed. Magistrate Judges Assn. (cir. dir. 1989—), Am. Inn of Ct. III, Greenville Area C. of C. (pres. 1970). Club: Kiwanis (pres. 1969). Contbr. articles to legal jours. Address: 1789 Camellia Dr Greenville MS 38701

**ORLEBEKE, WILLIAM RONALD,** retired lawyer, writer; b. El Paso, Tex., Jan. 5, 1934; s. William Ronald and Frances Claire (Cook) O.; children: Michelle, Julene, Daniel; m. Susan K. Nash, 2000. BA, Willamette U., 1956; MA, Kans. U., 1957; JD, Willamette U., 1966. Bar: Calif. 1966, US Dist. Ct. (no. dist.) Calif. 1967, US Ct. Appeals (9th cir.) 1967, US Ct. Appeals (7th cir.) 1989, US Dist. Ct. (no. dist.) Ill. 1989, US Dist. Ct. (so. dist.) Calif. 1989. Mem. staff Travelers Ins. Co., Sacramento, 1957-61; br. claim mgr. NY Life Ins. Co., 1961-62; branch claim mgr. Transamerica Ins. Co., San Francisco, 1962-63; assoc. Eliassen & Postel, San Francisco, 1966-69; ptnr. Coll, Levy & Orlebeke, Concord, Calif., 1969-77, Orlebeke & Hutchings, Concord, Calif., 1977-89; prin. Law Offices William S. Ronald Orlebeke, 1989-98; hearing officer Contra Costa County, Calif., 1981-98; arbitrator Contra Costa County Superior Ct., 1977-98, US Dist. Ct. No. Calif., 1978-98, Mt. Diablo Mcpl. Ct., 1987-89; ret., 1998. Judge pro tem Mt. Diablo Mcpl. Ct., 1973-75; criminology prof. Pioneer-Pacific Coll., 2002-03. Author: Orlebeke Family in Europe and America, 1570-1990, 1988, Don't Tell Me I Can't, 2003, (novels) Code Jeremiah, 2004, Lightning, 2004. Alumni bd. dir. Willamette U., 1978-81, trustee, 1980-81 scholar chmn. Concord Elks, 1977-79; del. Joint US/China Internat. Trade Law Conf., Beijing, 1987. With USMCR, 1952-59. Sr. scholar Willamette U., 1955-56; Woodrow Wilson fellow Kans. U., 1956-57, US Bur. Nat. Affairs fellow, 1966, others. Mem. SAR, Sons of Confederate Vets. (Merit award 1989), Sons of Union Vets. Civil War, First Marine Divsn. Assn., Order Ea. Star (worthy patron 1980), Masons (sec. Capitol Masonic Ctr., 2001-04, corp. sec. Oreg. Masonic Low Twelve Club, Inc 2005—, spl. trustee Oreg. chpt. 2006), Elks, Rotary (charter pres. Clayton Valley/Concord Sunrise club 1987-88, chmn. dist. 5160 Calif. membership devel. 1989-90, dist. gov. liaison dist. 5160 1990-92, dist. Rotarian of Yr. 1989-90, Paul Harris fellow 1988, 1992 dist. conf. chmn. benefactor 1990, Merit award 1990), Shriners (v.p. Salem Shrine Club 2005—). Republican.

**ORLIK, CHRISTINA BEAR,** music educator; b. Detroit, Nov. 10, 1945; d. Robert William and Olive Marie (Evans) Bear; m. Peter Blythe Orlik, Aug. 18, 1967; children: Darcy Anne, Blaine Truen. BS in Edn., Wayne State U., 1967, MS in Edn., 1969. Tchr. clarinet pvt. practice, Detroit, 1961-69; elem. band dir. City Recreation Dept., Troy, Mich., 1964-67; dir. bands Crary Jr.

High Sch., Waterford, Mich., 1967-69; instr. woodwind pvt. practice, Mt. Pleasant, Mich, 1970-84; dir. bands Montabella Jr. High Sch., Blanchard, Mich, 1974-76; substitute tchr. Mt. Pleasant Schs., 1976-84, libr. media profl., 1984-85, tchr. gen. music, 1985—, orch. dir., 1987—. Part-time instr. Ctrl. Mich. U. Tchr. Edn., 1989—91; organizing mem., mgr. Ctrl. Mich. Cmty. Band, Mt. Pleasant, 1973—75; clarinetist, bassoonist Alma (Mich.) Symphony Orch., 1973—86, Eddy Concert Band, Saginaw, Mich., 1973—2000; founder, mgr. Stringtacular Festival, 1991—. Tchr. Sunday sch. St. Andrew's Episcopal Ch., Clawson, Mich., 1966-67; treas., mem. chair LWV, Mt. Pleasant, 1972-73; chair Child Care Adv. Com., Mt. Pleasant, 1973-74. Mem. Am. String Tchrs. Assn. (program review grantee 1990), Mich. Edn. Assn., Mich. Sch. Band and Orch. Assn. (Dist. 5 Orch. Tchr. of Yr. 2000), Music Educators Nat. Conf. Association. Avocation: dance. Home: 613 Kane St Mount Pleasant MI 48858-1949 Office: West Intermediate Sch 440 S Bradley St Mount Pleasant MI 48858-3052

**ORLOFF, BARBARA-LEE MARGUERITE HEWITT,** social worker; b. N.Y.C., Feb. 18, 1944; d. Richard Elliott Hewitt and Elise Harriet (Hofer) DeMeritt; m. Jonathan Harris Orloff, Apr. 22, 1967 (div. May 1985); children: Aleksandr Monford, Piotr Richard. BA, Chatham Coll., Pitts., 1966; postgrad., Portland State U., 1988—90. Info. and referral specialist Info. and Vol. Svcs., Pitts., 1967—70; vol. coord. Friends of Tryon Creek State Park, Portland, Oreg., 1975—81, Oreg. State Parks, Salem, 1978, Portland Dept. Parks and Recreation, 1979; exec. dir. Friend of Tryon Creek State Park, Portland, 1985—88; social svc. coord. Lake Oswego Adult Ctr., Oreg., 1985—90; program dir. N.W. Housing Alternatives, Milwaukie, Oreg., 1990—. Mem. transitional housing continum of care bd. Clackamas County Social Svc.s, Oreg. City, Oreg., 1992—; vol. coord. book Guide to Urban Wilderness, 1978. Watercolor artist, photographer Monday Studio. Docent Portland Art Mus., 1970—74; opera evening vol. host Lake Oswego Adult Ctr., 1985—2001. Named Merit Mother of Oreg., Am. Assn. Mothers, Portland, 1991. Democrat. Episcopalian. Avocations: sailing, hiking, needlepoint, opera, literature. Home: 1400 SE Lava Dr # 14 Milwaukie OR 97222 Office: Northwest Housing Alternatives 2316 SE Willard St Milwaukie OR 97222 Office Phone: 503-654-1007 103. Business E-Mail: orloff@nwhousing.org.

**ORLOFF, CHET,** historian; b. Bellingham, Wash., Feb. 22, 1949; s. Monford A. and Janice (Diamond) O.; m. Wendy Lynn Lee, Sept. 20, 1970; children: Callman Labe, Hannah Katya, Michele Alison. BS, Boston U., 1971; BA, U. Oreg., 1971; MA, Portland State U., 1978. Tchr. Peace Corps, Afghanistan, 1972-75; asst. dir. Oreg. Hist. Soc., Portland, 1975-86, exec. dir., 1991-2000, Ninth Cir. Hist. Soc., Pasadena, Calif., 1987-91. Adj. prof. Portland State U.; prin. Oreg. History Works. Editor: Western Legal History, 1987-91, Law for the Elephant, 1992; sr. editor: Oreg. Hist. Quar. Commr. Met. Arts Commn., Portland, 1981-84, Portland Planning Commn., 1989-92; pres. Nat. Lewis and Clark Bicentennial Coun., 1996—; v.p. Portland Parks Bd. Mem. Phi Alpha Theta. Avocations: reading, tennis. Office: Oreg Hist Works 3332 NW Savier St Portland OR 97210

**ORLOFF, JONATHAN HARRIS,** engineering educator; b. N.Y.C., Apr. 30, 1942; s. Monford Arthur and Janice Diamond Orloff; m. Jean Clarice Scholtz, Aug. 19, 1993; children: Aleksandr, Piotr. BS, MIT, 1964; PhD, Oreg. Grad. Ctr., 1976. V.p. Elektros, Inc., Tigard, Oreg., 1970—74; prof. elec. engring. Oreg. Grad. Ctr., Beaverton, 1977—93; prof. elec. and computer engring. U. Md., College Park, 1993—2006. Dir. FEI Corp., Hillsboro, Oreg., 1986—96. Author: High Resolution Focused Ion Beams, 2003; editor: Handbook of Charged Particle Optics, 1996; contbr. over 85 articles to profl. jours. Recipient Presdl. Young Investigator award, NSF, 1984. Fellow: AAAS, IEEE; mem.: Cosmos Club. Avocations: photography, astronomy, cooking. Office: Univ Md Dept ECE College Park MD 20742 Office Phone: 301-405-5022. Office Fax: 301-314-9437. E-mail: jono@ece.umd.edu.

**ORLOV, YURI F.,** nuclear physicist, human rights activist; b. Aug. 13, 1924; With Moscow Inst. Theoretical and Experimental Physics, 1945—56, Yervan Physics Inst., Armenia, 1972, Inst. Terrestrial Magnetism and Dissemination, 1973; co-founder Moscow Chpt. Amnesty Internat., 1973; freelance work and wrote scientific filmstrips, 1973—77; physics prof. Cornell U., Ithaca, NY, 1986—; sr. scientist, Newman Lab. Nuclear Studies, physics dept. Contbr. several rsch. papers and articles on humna rights; author: (autobiography) Dangerous Thoughts, 1991. Recipient Nicholson medal for Humanitarian Svc., Am. Phys. Soc., 1995, Andrei Sakharov prize, 2005. Mem.: Am. Acad. Arts and Sciences. Founded the Moscow Helsinki Watch Group in 1976 to monitor Soviet adherence to the 1975 Helsinki human rights accord. Arrested in 1977, was incarcerated in the Siberian Gulag for some 10 years. In 1983, a letter written by the Austrian Chancellor Bruno Kreisky to the Soviet Leader Yuri Andropov asked for the release to Austria, the request was ignored. Finally released in 1986, stripped of Soviet citizenship and deported to the US as part of exchange for release of a Soviet spy. Office: Cornell U 229 Newman Lab Ithaca NY 14853 Office Phone: 607-255-3502. Office Fax: 607-254-4552. Business E-Mail: Yuri.Orlov@cornell.edu.*

**ORLOVSKY, DONALD ALBERT,** lawyer; b. Essex County, N.J., 1951; AB, Cornell U., 1973; JD, Rutgers U., 1976. Bar: Fla. 1976, U.S. Ct. Appeals (5th cir.) 1976, U.S. Dist. Ct. N.J. 1977, U.S. Supreme Ct. 1980, U.S. Ct. Appeals (11th cir.) 1981, U.S. Ct. Appeals (8th cir.) 2003. Assoc. Smathers & Thompson, Miami, 1976—77; ptnr. McCune, Hiaasen, Crum, Ferris & Gardner, P.A., Ft. Lauderdale, Fla., 1978—86, Kamen & Orlovsky PA, West Palm Beach, 1988—. Pres. bd. dirs. Comprehensive Alcoholism Treatment Program, Inc.; sec., bd. dirs. Fla. Lawyers Assistance, Inc., supervising monitor and counselor, 1991—. Author: Nova U. Law Review, 1977, U. Miami Law Review, 1978. Recipient All-Am. recognition in springboard diving, 1966-69; inducted Hall of Fame Newark Acad., Livingston, N.J., 1997. Mem. ABA, ATLA, Fla. Bar (civil procedure rules com. 1981), Acad. Fla. Trial Lawyers Episcopalian. Office: 1601 Belvedere Rd Ste 402 West Palm Beach FL 33406-1541 Office Phone: 561-687-8500. Personal E-Mail: dao4law@aol.com

**ORLOWSKY, MARTIN L.,** executive manager; b. N.Y.C., Dec. 7, 1941; s. Solomon and Sylvia (Levine) O.; m. Carolyn Louise Brady, Mar. 25, 1973; children— Daniel, Keith, Matthew. BA, Long Island U., N.Y.C., 1963. Media planner Compton Advertising, N.Y.C., 1968-69; media planner Young & Rubicam Inc., N.Y.C., 1969-71; v.p. media Grey Advertising, N.Y.C., 1971-76; sr. v.p., media and mktg. services Needham, Harper & Steers, N.Y.C., 1976-77; media dir. R.J. Reynolds Tobacco Co., Winston-Salem, N.C., 1977-80, dir. mktg. services, 1980-82, v.p. brand mktg., 1982-84, sr. v.p. mktg., 1984-85, exec. v.p., 1986; pres. Grocery div. Nabisco Brands, U.S.A., Parsippany, N.J., 1986—, Planters and Life Savers div. Nabisco Brands, U.S.A., Parsippany, N.J., 1987—, DKM Holdings, 1988-90; sr. v.p. mktg. Lorillard Tobacco Co., N.Y.C., 1990-92, exec. v.p. mktg. and sales, 1992-95, pres., 1995—, pres., CEO, 1999—. Vol., Peace Corps, Bolivia, 1963-65. Served to sgt. U.S. Army. Avocations: fishing, tennis. Home: 21 Loch Ridge Dr Greensboro NC 27408-3869

**ORM, SALLY S.,** music educator, consultant; d. Harvey Jacob and Lucille Mae Seyler; children: Jennifer E., Andrea. Student, Eastman Sch. Music. With FBI, Washington, 1970—75; co-owner, ptnr. All Things Music, LLC. Founder keyboard donations Orm Music Studios, Neenah, Wis., 2001—. Treas. Regional Domestic Abuse, Oshkosh, Wis., 1984—86, pres., 1988—88; treas. Audubon Soc., Appleton, 1985—86; Gold award coord. Fox Valley Area Girl Scouts, Appleton, Wis., 1995—99. Named Mem. of the Yr. award, Fox Valley Area Girl Scouts, 1999. Mem.: Wis. Music Tchrs. Assn. (chmn. found. 2006—), Music Tchrs. Nat. Assn., Fox Valley Keyboard Tchrs. (v.p. program dir. 1999—2003, Mem. of the Yr. award 2002), World Piano Pedagogy Conf., Keyboard Music Educators Assn. (adjudicator keyboard competition 2002—). Presbyterian. Avocations: gardening, travel. Office: Orm Music Studios 749 S Commercial St Neenah WI 54956 E-mail: sormusic@aol.com.

**ORMAN, LEONARD ARNOLD,** lawyer; b. Balt., June 15, 1930; s. Samuel and Bertie (Adler) O.; m. Barbara Gold, June 9, 1978; children: Richard Harold, Robert Barton. AB summa cum laude, U. Md., 1952, JD, 1955. Bar: Md. 1955. U.S. Ct. Appeals (4th cir.) 1956, U.S. Dist. Ct. Md. 1955, Ct. Appeals Md. 1955, U.S. Supreme Ct. 1977, U.S. Ct. Claims 1990, D.C. Ct. Appeals 1987. Law clk. Hon. Frederick W. Brune, Chief Judge Md. Ct. of Appeals, 1955-56; mem. dept. legis. reference Md. Legislature, 1957-58; mem. Gov.'s Commn. to Revise Criminal Code, 1958-59; pvt. practice law Balt., 1956—. Lectr. in trial tactics Mem. editl. bd. Md. Law Rev., 1953-55; contbr. articles to profl. jours. Pres. Young Dems. 2d Dist., Balt., 1960-63. With AUS, 1948-49; lt. col. USAF Res. ret. Rosco Pound Inst. fellow, trustee. Mem. Nat. Bd. Trial Advocacy (cert. civil trial adv.); Am. Bd. Trial Advs., Md. State Bar Assn., Balt. City Bar Assn., Nat. Coll. Trial Advocacy (trustee), ATLA (nat. committeeman 1976-80, bd. govs. 1985—, exec. com. 1988-90, chmn. orgn. rev. com., home office and budget com., orgn. and home office com., election com., key man com., past steering com., past publ. com., past ednl. adv. group 1989-90, chmn. Stalwarts Hall of Fame com., past vice-chair ABA-ATLA liaison com., M Club, co-chair conv. site planning com., co-chair polit. insight com., long-range planning com., auth-hwy. adv. com., toy safety conf., med. malpractice adv. com., product liability adv. com., co-chair home office capital improvements adv. com., co-chmn. conv. planning com. Washington, Wiedmann/Wysocki award 1989-90, 1996, 2002), Acad. Catastrophic Injury Attys., Trial Lawyers for Pub. Justice, Md. Trial Lawyers Assn. (bd. govs., pres. 1984-85, Lifetime Achievement award 2002), Order of Coif, Masons. Home: 2 Celadon Rd Owings Mills MD 21117-3010 Office: 26 South St Baltimore MD 21202-3215 Office Phone: 410-962-0400. Business E-Mail: lorman@triallaw.com.

**ORMAN, NANETTE HECTOR,** psychiatrist; b. Highland Park, Ill., Feb. 1, 1943; d. William Joseph and Agnes (Daly) Hector; m. John Christopher Orman, July 2, 1964; children: Laurel Anne, Nathaniel William. BA in Journalism, U. Calif., Berkeley, 1964; postgrad., Stanford U., 1978-81; MPH in Epidemiology, U. Calif., Berkeley, 1984, MS in Health and Med. Scis., 1985; MD, U. Calif., San Francisco, 1987. Diplomate Am. Bd. Psychiatry and Neurology; lic. physician, Calif. Psychiatrist San Jose (Calif.) State U., 1989-93; pvt. practice Los Altos, Calif., 1991—; staff El Camino Hosp., 1991-94, assoc. staff, 1994—; staff Stanford (Calif.) U. Hosp. and Med. Ctr., 1998—. Asst. clin. prof. Stanford (Calif.) U. Sch. Medicine, 1995—; oral bd. examiner Am. Bd. Psychiatry & Neurology, Deerfield, Ill., 1995—; chief resident in psychiatry, 1991; spkr. and cons. in field. Editor San Mateo County Planned Parenthood Assn. Newsletter, 1968-69. Bd. dirs. Mid-Peninsula Task Force for Integrated Edn., 1972-82, Psychiat. Found. No. Calif., 2001—; consumer mem. San Mateo County Mental Health Adv. Bd., 1987. Fellow Am. Psychiat. Assn. (disting., 2004; pub. info. com. 1989—); mem. No. Calif. Psychiat. Soc. (chair membership com. 1996-2002, pub. info. com., media spokesperson, moderator ann. meetings 1993-94), Nat. Alliance for the Mentally Ill, San Francisco Depressive and Manic Depressive Assn. Office: 851 Fremont Ave Ste 98 Los Altos CA 94024-5602

**ORMAN, SUZE,** news correspondent, writer; Cert. fin. planner. Account exec. Merrill Lynch, 1980—83; v.p. investments Prudential Bache Securities, 1983—87; dir. Suze Orman Fin. Group, 1987—97. Former fin. contbr. NBC News' Today; host QVC Fin. Freedom hour. Contbr. to Self mag.; author: (PBS spl.) The Road to Wealth; co-profl.: (PBS spl.) The Road to Wealth; host (PBS spl.) The Road to Wealth; author: (PBS spl.) The Courage to Be Rich; co-profl.: (PBS spl.) The Courage to Be Rich; host (PBS spl.) The Courage to Be Rich; author: (PBS spl.) The 9 Steps to Financial Freedom; co-profl.: (PBS spl.) The 9 Steps to Financial Freedom; host (PBS spl.) The 9 Steps to Financial Freedom; contbg. editor: O: The Oprah Mag.; host (nat. syndicated radio talk show) The Suze Orman Show; author: You've Earned It, Don't Lose It, 1995, The 9 Steps to Financial Freedom, 1997 (NY Times bestsellers), The Courage to Be Rich, 1999 (NY Times bestsellers, Motivational book award Books for a Better Life, 1999), The Road to Wealth, 2001 (NY Times bestsellers), The Money Book for the Young, Fabulous & Broke, 2005 (Publishers Weekly Bestseller). Named Top 30 Power Brokers Who Most Influenced Mutual Fund Industry and Affected Money, Smart Money mag., 1999, Outstanding Svc. Host for Suze Orman: For the Young, Fabulous & Broke, Nat. Acad. TV Arts and Sciences, Daytime Emmy award, 2006; named to 100th issue as those "who have revolutionized the way Am. thinks about money", Worth mag., 2001. Office: CNBC 2200 Fletcher Ave Ste 5 Fort Lee NJ 07024 Mailing: c/o Amanda Urban ICM 40 W 57th St New York NY 10019 Office Phone: 201-585-2183.

**ORMASA, JOHN,** retired utilities executive; b. Richmond, Calif., May 30, 1925; s. Juan Hormaza and Maria Inocencia Olondo; m. Dorothy Helen Trmble, Feb. 17, 1952; children: Newton Lee, John Trumble, Nancy Jean Davies. BA, U. Calif. Berkeley, 1948; JD, Harvard U., 1951. Bar: Calif. 1952, U.S. Supreme Ct. 1959. Assoc. Clifford C. Anglim, 1951—52, Richmond, Carlson, Collins, Gordon & Bold, 1952—56, ptnr., 1956—59; v.p. sys. gen. counsel Pacific Lighting Svc. Co. L.A., 1966—72; gen. atty., v.p., gen. counsel So. Calif. Gas Co., L.A., 1959—66; v.p. gen. counsel Pacific Lighting Corp. L.A., 1973—75, v.p., sec., gen. counsel, 1975; ret., 1975. Acting city atty. El Cerrito, Calif., 1952. With USN, 1943—46. Mem.: ABA, Richmond Bar Assn. (pres. 1959), Calif. State Bar Assn., Kiwanis (v.p. 1959). Republican. Roman Catholic.

**ORME, ANTONY RONALD,** geography educator; b. Weston-Super-Mare, Somerset, Eng., May 28, 1936; came to U.S., 1968; s. Ronald Albert and Anne (Parry) O.; m. Amalie Jo Brown, Nov. 18, 1984; children: Mark Antony, Kevin Ronald, Devon Anne. BA with 1st class honors, U. Birmingham, 1957, PhD, 1961. Lectr. Univ. Coll., Dublin, Ireland, 1960-68; mem. faculty UCLA, 1968—, prof. geography, 1973—, dean social scis., 1977-83. Cons. geomorphology various orgns., throughout U.S., 1968— Editor-in-chief Phys. Geography, Recipient Award of Merit Am. Inst. Planners, 1973; recipient Outstanding Service award USAF, 1977-80, Founders' medal Brit. Geom. Rsch. Group. Mem. Geol. Soc. Am., Assn. Am. Geographers (Disting. Career award), Assn. Geography Tchrs. Ireland (pres. 1964-68), Inst. Brit. Geographers, Internat. Geog. Union. Home: 5128 Del Moreno Dr Woodland Hills CA 91364-2426 Office: UCLA Dept Geography Los Angeles CA 90095-1524 Business E-Mail: orme@geog.ucla.edu.

**ORME, MARIANNE LINETTE,** librarian; b. Dekalb, Ill., Mar. 10, 1970; d. Tracy Eugene and Margaret Alma (Hanson) Koop; m. David James Orme, Dec. 22, 1990; children: Daniel, Jonathan. BA, Taylor U., 1991; MA, Trinity Evang. Div. Sch., 1994; MS in L.S., Pratt Inst., 1999. Libr. NY Pub. Libr., N.Y.C., 1995—99; reference libr. Ind. U., Kokomo, 2001; adult svcs. libr. Des Plaines Pub. Libr., Ill., 2001—. Web site developer Purdue U., West Lafayette, Ind., 2000. Book reviewer: Libr. Jour., 2000—; co-editor: The Scribe, 1992—94. Recipient Dist. Achievement award, Pratt Inst., 1999; Annual Conf. Student grant, No. Am. Serials Interest Group, 1999. Mem.: Ill. Libr. Assn., Am. Soc. of Info. Sci. and Tech., No. Am. Serials Interest Group, Beta Phi Mu Libr. Sci. Home: 814 N Summit St Wheaton IL 60187 Office: Des Plaines Pub Libr 1501 Ellinwood St Des Plaines IL 60016 E-mail: ormemlk@yahoo.com.

**ORMES, JONATHAN FAIRFIELD,** astrophysicist, researcher, educator; b. Colorado Springs, Colo., July 18, 1939; s. Robert Manly and Suzanne (Viertel) O.; m. Karen Lee Minnick, Dec. 26, 1960 (div.); 1 child, Laurie Kylee; m. Janet Carolyn Dahl, Sept. 12, 1964; children: Marina, Nicholas. BS, Stanford U., 1961; PhD, U. Minn., 1967. NRC assoc. Goddard Space Flight Ctr., NASA, Greenbelt, Md., 1967-69, astrophysicist, 1969, head cosmic radiations br., 1981-82, head nuclear astrophysics br., 1983-87, assoc. chief lab. for high energy astrophysics, 1987-90, chief lab. for high energy astrophysics, 1990-2000, project sci. for gamma ray astronomy obs., 1998—2004, dir. space scis., Denver 2004, dir. Denver 2004—; dir. Denver Rsch. Inst., 2005—. Acting head high energy astrophysics NASA hdqrs., Washington, 1982-83, mem. high energy astrophysics mgmt. ops. working group, 1975-83, cosmic ray program working group, 1984-91; com. on space and solar physics, com. on cosmic ray physics Nat. Acad. Sci., Washington, 1991-94; adj. prof. U. Md. Balt., 2000-, U. Utah, 2001—. Editor:

Essays in Space Science, 1987; assoc. editor astrophysics Phys. Rev. Letters, 1991-93; contbr. astrophysics Jour., Phys. Rev. Letters, Astronomy and Astrophysics. Trustee Paint Br. Unitarian Universalist Ch., Adelphi, Md., 1987-88, chair bd. trustees, 1989, numerous positions, 1972—. Recipient Meritorious Exec. Award (presdl. rank), 2001. Fellow: Am. Phys. Soc. (various divsn. offices); mem.: Am. Geophys. Union, Am. Astron. Soc. (sec.-treas. High Energy Astrophysics divsn. 1985—87), Internat. Astron. Union. Achievements include discovery of unusual isotopic abundance of Ne in galactic cosmic rays; research on composition and energy spectra of cosmic rays, antiprotons and gamma rays from the Milky Way galaxy. Office: U Denver Dept Physics & Astronomy Denver CO 80208-0001 Office Phone: 303-871-3552. Business E-Mail: jormes@du.edu, jonathan.ormes@du.edu.

**ORMOND, JULIA,** actress; b. Surrey, Eng., 1965; m. Rory Edwards (div. 1993); m. Jon Rubin, 1999. Grad., Webber Douglas Acad. Drama Art, 1988. Appeared in films The Baby of Macon, 1992, Legends of the Fall, 1994, Nostradamus, 1994, Captives, 1994, First Knight, 1995, Sabrina, 1995, The Prime Gig, 2000, Resistance, 2003; TV appearances include Traffik, 1990, Young Catherine, 1991, Stalin, 1992, The 67th Annual Academy Awards, 1995, Smilla's Sense of Snow, 1997, Sibirsky Tsiryulnik, 1998, (voice) Animal Farm, 1999, Varian's War, 2001, Iron Jawed Angels, 2004; stage appearances include Faith, Hope and Charity, 1989 (London Critics best newcomer award); producer: Calling the Ghosts, 1996. Recipient Female Star of Tomorrow award Sho West Awards, 1995.

**ORMOND, PAUL A.,** healthcare company executive; b. Aurora, Ill. B in economics with honors, Stanford U., 1971, MBA, 1973. Mem. corp. staff, positions with glass container divsn. Owens-Ill., Inc., 1973-77, nat. mktg. mgr. soft drinks, glass container divsn., 1977-78; mgr. Atlanta sales dist., glass container divsn. Owens-Ill. Inc., 1978-80, asst. gen. mgr. Gerresheimer Glas (internat. affiliate Owens-Ill. Inc.) Germany, 1980-82, v.p. glass container group, 1982-84, v.p. packaging ops., dir. market strategy and devel., 1984-91, corp. v.p., 1986-91; pres., CEO Health Care and Retirement Corp. (HCR) (subs. Owens-Ill. Inc.), Toledo, 1986-91; chmn., pres., CEO Health Care and Retirement Corp. (HCR) (now ind. co.), Toledo, 1991—98; pres., CEO HCR Manor Care Inc., Toledo, 1998—99, Manor Care, Inc., Toledo, 1999—, chmn., 2001—. Office: Manor Care 333 N Summit St Toledo OH 43604-2617*

**ORMSBY, ERIC LINN,** writer, educator; b. Atlanta, Oct. 16, 1941; s. Robert and Virginia (Haire) O.; m. Dorothy Louise Hoffmann, July 22, 1967; children: Daniel Paul, Charles Martin. BA summa cum laude, U. Pa., 1971; MA, Princeton U., 1973, PhD, 1981; MLS, Rutgers U., 1978. Near East bibliographer libr. Princeton (NJ) U., 1975-77, Near East curator libr., 1977-83; libr. dir. Cath. U. Am., Washington, 1983-86, McGill U., Montreal, Canada, 1986-96, assoc. prof. Inst. Islamic Studies, 1986-96, prof., 1996—2005; prof., chief libr. Inst. Ismaili Studies, London, 2005—. Cons. NYU, 1981-82; mem. libr. com. Mid. East Inst., Washington, 1985-87, Al Akhawayn U., Morocco, 1994-95, Saudi Arabian Monetary Agy., Riyadh, 1995-96; chmn. continuing edn. com. Washington Consortium, 1983-86; mem. bd. Ctr. Rsch. Librs., 1989-95. Author: Theodicy in Islamic Thought, 1984 (Choice Mag. award 1984), Bavarian Shrine and Other Poems, 1990 (QSPELL award for poetry 1991), (poems) Coastlines, 1992, (with others) Handlist of Arabic Manuscripts, 1986, For a Modest God: New and Selected Poems, 1997, (poems) Araby, 2001, (poems) Daybreak at the Straits, 2004, (essays) Facsimiles of Time, 2001; editor: Moses Maimonides and His Time, 1989; contbr. articles and book revs. to profl. jours., poetry and essays to various mags., including New Republic, New Yorker, Grand St., Shenandoah, The New Criterion, The Yale Rev., The Times Lit. Supplement, So. Rev. and Chelsea; weekly columnist N.Y. Sun, 2004-. Instr. Princeton Adult Sch., 1978-80: DAAD fellow German Acad. Exch., 1973-74; recipient Ingram Merrill award, 1993. Mem. Mid. East Librs. Assn. (v.p. 1981-82, pres. 1982-83), Societe des Amis de Jean de la Fontaine, Can. Assn. Rsch. Librs. (v.p. 1988-89), Can. Libr. Assn., Assn. pour l'Avancement des Scis. et des Techniques de la Documentation, Conseil des recteurs et des principaux des univs. du Québec, Sous-Comité des Bibliotheques (pres. 1989-91). Roman Catholic. Address: 22 Belsize Park Gardens Flat 2 London NW3 4LH England Office: Libr Inst Ismaili Studies 42-44 Grosvenor Gardens London SW1W 0EB England Office Phone: 44207 881 6027. E-mail: eric.ormsby@btinternet.com.

**ORNE, EMILY CAROTA,** psychologist, researcher; b. Boston, Sept. 7, 1938; d. Emil and Ruth (Farrell) Carota; m. Martin T. Orne, Feb. 3, 1962; children: Franklin Theodore, Tracy Meredith. BA, Bennington Coll., 1959. Rsch. assoc. Mass. Mental Health Ctr., Boston, 1963-64; rsch. psychologist Unit for Exptl. Psychiatry, Phila., 1964-79, sr. rsch. psychologist, 1979-83, co-dir., 1982—; rsch. assoc. psychology U. Pa. Sch. Medicine, Phila., 1983—. Trustee Inst. Exptl. Psychiatry Rsch. Found., Mass., 1964—, assoc. co-dir., 1987-97, exec. dir., 1998—; bd. dirs. False Memory Syndrome Found., 1995- Contbr. articles to profl. jours.; assoc. editor Internat. Jour. Clin. and Exptl. Hypnosis, 1977- Recipient Benjamin Franklin Gold medal Internat. Soc. Hypnosis, 1982, Roy M. Dorcus award Soc. Clin. and Exptl. Hypnosis, 1985, Bernard B. Raginsky award, 1993, Morton Prince award Soc. Clin. and Exptl. Hypnosis and APA, 1994 Avocations: fishing, swimming, reading. Office: U Pa Sch Medicine 1013 Blockley Hall 423 Guardian Dr Philadelphia PA 19104-6021

**ORNISH, DEAN,** medical association administrator, medical educator; MD, Baylor Coll. Medicine. Resident in internal medicine Mass. Gen. Hosp., Boston, 1981-84; clin. fellow in medicine Harvard Med. Sch., 1981-84; clin. prof. medicine U. Calif. San Francisco, 1984 - founder, pres. Preventive Medicine Rsch. Inst., Sausalito, Calif., 1984—; also bd. dirs. Physician cons. to Pres. Bill Clinton, U.S. Congress, others; U.S. bd. dirs. UN High Commn. on Refugees. Author: 5 books including Dr. Dean Ornish's Program for Reversing Heart Disease, 1990, Eat More, Weigh Less, 1993, Love & Survival: The Scientific Basis for the Healing Power of Intimacy, 1998; contbr. numerous articles to profl. jours. Bd. dirs. Quincy Jones Listen Up Found. Recipient Outstanding Young Alumnus award U. Tex., 1994, U.S. Army Surgeon Gen. medal, Beckmann medal German Soc. Prevention and Rehab. Cardiovascular Diseases, 1996. Mem. Calif. Acad. Medicine. Office: Preventive Med Rsch Inst 900 Bridgeway Sausalito CA 94965-2100 Fax: 415-332-5730. Office Phone: 415-332-2525. Business E-Mail: info@pmri.org.

**ORNT, DANIEL B.,** physician; b. Jan. 21, 1951; m. Jeanine Arden-Ornt. BA, Colgate U., 1973; MD, U. Rochester, 1976. Diplomate in internal medicine and nephrology Am. Bd. Internal Medicine, lic. physician N.Y., Ohio. Intern then resident U. Va., 1976—79; fellow in nephrology U. Mich., 1979—81; from sr. instr. medicine to assoc. prof. U. Rochester (N.Y.) Sch. Medicine and Dentistry, 1981—97, prof. medicine and pediat., 1997—; assoc. dean for clin. affairs Sch. Medicine, Case Western Res. U., Cleve., 2003—. Assoc. chmn. clin. svcs. dept. medicine U. Rochester, 1998—2000, vice-chmn. dept. medicine, 2000—03, acting chief divsn. gastroenterology, 2000, assoc. program dir. clin. rsch., 2001—02—03. Contbr. articles to profl. jours. Recipient Disting. Svc. award, Nat. Kidney Found., Inc., 1998. Fellow: ACP; mem.: Soc. for Clin. Trials, Am. Physiol. Soc., Am. Soc. Nephrology. Office: Case Western Res U Sch Medicine BRB 110 10900 Euclid Ave Cleveland OH 44106-4993 E-mail: dbo@case.edu.

**ORONA, JOSEPH RYAN,** information technology executive; b. Albuquerque, N.Mex., Aug. 10, 1967; s. Jose Ramon Jorge Orona and Maria Melinda Sanchez. BS in Aero. Studies, Embry-Riddle Aero. U., 1989. Pres. Retis Techs., Inc., Albuquerque, 1993—. Presdl. scholar, U. N.Mex. 1985. Mem.: Aircraft Owners and Pilots Assn. (life). Independent. Roman Catholic. Achievements include design of Scientific collaborative networks and data visualization. Avocations: flight, global travel, mountain biking, wine making, photography. Office: Retis Techs Inc PO Box 40305 Albuquerque NM 87196 Office Phone: 505-247-8129 202. Office Fax: 505-247-2473.

**OROPEZA, JENNY,** state official; b. Long Beach, Calif., Sept. 27, 1957; m. Tom Mullins. Mem. Long Beach Unified Sch. Dist. Bd. Edn., 1988—94; coun. mem. Long Beach City Coun., 1994—2000; state assembly mem. Dist. 55 Calif. State Assembly, 2000—. Mem. Latino Caucus. Democrat. Mailing: PO Box 942849 Rm 2148 Sacramento CA 94249 Office: One Civic Plaza Dr Ste 460 Carson CA 90745 Office Phone: 916-319-2055. Business E-Mail: assemblymember.oropeza@assembly.ca.gov.

**OROPEZA, PETER P.,** psychologist, consultant; b. Jourdanton, Tex., Jan. 30, 1975; s. Pio and Leticia Oropeza. BS, Angelo State U., 1996; MA, PsyD, Forest Inst. Profl. Psychology, 2000. Intern Fla. State Hosp., Chattahoochee, 1999—2000; clinical psychologist competency unit No. Tex. State Hosp., Vernon, 2001—04; pvt. practice Ft. Worth, 2003—. Staff psychologist, Ft. Dix, NJ, 2000—01; regional mental health cons. Job Corps, Dallas, 2004—. Contbr. articles to profl. jours. Mem.: APA, Ft. Worth Area Psychol. Asn., Nat. Hispanic MBA Soc., Soc. Cons. Psychology. Avocations: reading, travel, running, bicycling, art. Office: 210 W 6th St Ste 305 Fort Worth TX 76102 Office Phone: 817-850-9911.

**O'RORKE, JAMES FRANCIS, JR.,** lawyer; b. NYC, Dec. 4, 1936; s. James Francis and Helen (Weber) O'R.; m. Carla Phelps, Aug. 6, 1964. AB, Princeton U., 1958; JD, Yale U., 1961. Bar: N.Y. 1962. Assoc. Davies, Hardy & Schenck, 1962-69; ptnr. Davies, Hardy, Ives & Lawther, 1969-72, Skadden, Arps, Slate, Meagher & Flom, N.Y.C., 1972—. Dir. Clinipad Corp.; mem. adv. bd. Chgo. Title Ins. Co. N.Y. Trustee Mus. Am. Indian-Heye Found., 1977-80; dir. James Lenox House Assn., Inc., 1998-02. Mem. ABA, N.Y. State Bar Assn., Assn. Bar City N.Y., Am. Coll. Real Estate Lawyers, Princeton Club N.Y.C. Office: Skadden Arps Slate Meagher & Flom 4 Times Sq Fl 24 New York NY 10036-6595 Address: C/O Skadden Arps 4 Times Sq Rm 44200 New York NY 10036-6522 Office Phone: 212-735-2620. E-mail: jororke@skadden.com.

**OROSZ, RICHARD THOMAS,** lawyer; b. Painesville, Ohio, Dec. 26, 1942; s. Gabriel John and Helen Anna (Black) O.; m. Elizabeth Ann Dempsey, June 28, 1969; children: Karen, Gregory, Megan. BS, Lake Erie Coll., 1967; JD, Cleve. State U., 1970. Bar: Ohio 1971, U.S. Dist. Ct. (no. dist.) Ohio 1976., U.S. Supreme Ct. 1977. Sole practice, Painesville, 1971—; former acting judge Painesville Mcpl. Ct.; foreman Lake County Grand Jury, 1979. Tchr. MBA program Lake Erie Coll.; lectr. in field. Former trustee Morley Lib. Assn.; former mem. nat. alumni bd. Lake Erie Coll. Mem. ABA (mem. probate sect.), Ohio State Bar Assn. (mem. estate planning, trusts and probate sect.), Lake County Bar Assn. (former trustee, mem. probate com.), Lake County Law Libr. Assn. (sec. 1973-87), Painesville Exch. Club (past pres.), Elks Roman Catholic. Avocation: golf. Home: 7740 Mountain Ash Dr Mentor OH 44060-7421 Office: 56 Liberty St Ste 207 Painesville OH 44077-3361 Office Phone: 440-352-3324.

**O'ROURKE, C. LARRY,** lawyer; b. Colusa, Calif., Dec. 10, 1937; s. James Harold and Elizabeth Janice (Jenkins) O'R.; m. Joy Marie Phillips, May 22, 1965; children: Ryan, Paula, Alina. BSEE, Stanford U., 1959, MBA, 1961; JD, George Washington U., 1972. Bar: Va. 1971, D.C. 1974, Calif. 2002, U.S. Ct. Appeals (fed. cir.) 1973, U.S. Patent and Trademark Office 1971, U.S. Supreme Ct. Patent atty. Westinghouse Elec., Washington, 1969-70, Pitts., 1970-73; assoc. Finnegan, Henderson, Farabow, Garrett & Dunner, Washington, 1974-79, ptnr., 1979—, mng. ptnr. Palo Alto, Calif. Dir. Zest Inc., Md., 1988, chmn. bd. dirs., 1990-95; mem. George Washington Law Sch. I.P. adv. coun., mem. bd. dirs. Stanford Bus. Sch. Alumni and mem. devel. coun. Stanford GSB. Mem. ABA, Am. Intellectual Property Law Assn., Inter-Pacific Bar Assn. Democrat. Presbyterian. Office: Finnegan Henderson Farabow Garrett & Dunner 700 Hansen Way Palo Alto CA 94304-1016 Office Phone: 650-849-6640.

**O'ROURKE, JAMES LOUIS,** lawyer; b. Bridgeport, Conn., July 5, 1958; s. James G. and Margaret Elizabeth (Fesco) O'Rourke; m. Margaret C. DiCicco, Sept. 18, 1994. BS, U. Bridgeport, 1984, JD, 1987. Bar: Conn. 1988, U.S. Dist. Ct. Conn. 1989, Mashantucket Pequot Tribal Bar 1995, U.S. Supreme Ct. 1998. Pvt. practice, Stratford, Conn., 1987—. With USN, 1976—79. Mem.: ATLA, ABA, Greater Bridgeport Bar Assn., Conn. Bar Assn., Conn. Trial Lawyers Assn. Roman Catholic. Avocations: boating, gardening, fishing, bicycling, swimming. Office: The Barnum Profl Bldg 1825 Barnum Ave Ste 201 Stratford CT 06614-5333 Office Phone: 203-381-9800. Personal E-mail: js.orourke@snet.net.

**O'ROURKE, KATHLEEN ANN,** education educator; b. Chgo., Ill., Aug. 1, 1972; BS, Ea. Ill. U., Charleston, 1994; MS, Ea. Ill. U., 1995; PhD, U. Tenn., 1999. Geriatric cons. St. Mary's Health Sys., Inc., Knoxville, Tenn., 1996—99; instr. Carson-Newman Coll., Jefferson City, Tenn., 1998—2001; asst. prof. U. Tenn., Knoxville, 1999—2001; assoc. prof. Ea. Ill. Univ. Sch. of Family and Consumer Sci., Charleston, 2001—. Vol. Am. Cancer Society-Relay for Life, Charleston, Ill., 2005—06. Mem.: Kappa Omicron Nu (advisor 2002—06). Office: Ea Ill Univ 600 Lincoln Ave Klehm Hall Charleston IL 61920 Office Phone: 217-581-6350. Office Fax: 217-581-6090. Business E-Mail: kaorourke@eiu.edu.

**O'ROURKE, MARYLYN KAY,** counseling administrator, consultant; b. Perry, Okla., Aug. 28, 1942; d. George Howard and Mary Ellen Bocox; m. Robert Lloyd O'Rourke, Dec. 5, 1983 (dec. Jan. 1994); children: Roger Paul Hula, Rachel Adrienne Tiggelouen. BA, Okla. State U., 1971, MS, 1974, PhD, 1986. Lic. specialist sch. psychology Tex. Tchr. jr. high sch. edn. Ponca City Ind. Sch. Dist., Okla., 1971—73; psychometrist Regional Edn. Svc. Ctr., Cushing, Okla., 1974—77; sch. psychologist Tulsa World Tech. Sch., 1977—86, mgmt. cons. Birkman Internat., Houston, 1986—90; coord. fed. grants Kans. State Dept. Spl. Edn., 1990—92; lic. specialist sch. psychology Katy Ind. Sch. Dist., Okla., 1993—. Cons. and reviewer Tex. State Bd. Examiners of Psychologists, Austin, Tex., 2003; mgmt. cons., Houston, 1990—. Mem. Mayor's Commn. on Concerns of the Disabled, Tulsa, 1984—86; mem. adminstrn. bd. First Meth. Ch., Houston, 2003. Mem.: Coun. Exceptional Children, Tex. Assn. Sch. Psychologists (charter mem., chmn. 1993). Democrat. Avocations: yoga, ballroom dancing. Home: 12926 Kingsbridge Ln Houston TX 77077

**O'ROURKE, MAUREEN A.,** dean, law educator; BS summa cum laude, Marist Coll.; JD, Yale Law Sch. With IBM; assoc. prof. Boston U. Sch. Law, 1993—98, prof., 1998—, assoc. dean adminstrn., assoc. dean academic affairs, 2003—04, interim dean, 2004—. Vis. prof. Columbia U. Sch. Law, La Trobe U., Australia, 2002, U. Victoria Law Sch., British Columbia, British Virgin Islands. Co-author: Copyright in a Global Economy; contbr. articles to law jours. Recipient Metcalf Award, 2002. Mailing: Boston U Sch Law 765 Commenwealth Ave Boston MA 02215

**O'ROURKE, ROBERT A.,** physician, educator; b. San Francisco, Calif., June 12, 1936; m. Suzann Reiter, June 8, 1963; children: Michael, Kevin, Sean, Kathleen, Ryan. Student, Santa Clara U., 1954-55; BS, Creighton U., 1957, MD, 1961. Diplomate Am. Bd. Internal Medicine, Am. Bd. Cardiology. Straight med. internship Georgetown U. Hosp., Washington, 1961-62, jr. asst. resident internal medicine, 1962-63, sr. asst. resident internal medicine, 1963-64, med. houseofficer internal medicine, 1961-65, fellow cardiology dept., 1964-65, instr. in medicine cardiology, 1968-69; fellow U. Calif. Cardiovasc. Rsch. Inst., Washington, 1965-66; staff cardiologist Madagan Army Hosp., Washington, 1966-68; asst. prof. medicine cardiology coll. medicine U. Ariz., Tucson, 1969-70; asst. prof. medicine cardiology dir. clin. cardiology section, dir. heart station U. Calif., San Diego, 1970-73, assoc. prof. medicine cardiology, dir. clin. cardiology section, dir. coronary care unit, assoc. dir. myocardial infarction rsch. unit, 1973-76; acting chief medicine Audie L. Murphy Vets. Adminstrn. Hosp., 1977-78; Charles Conrad Brown disting. prof. cardiovasc. disease, dir. cardiovasc. divsn. U. Tex. Health Sci. Ctr., San Antonio, 1976—. Cons. in field for various hosps.; vis. professorships to various med. ctrs./univs. Mem. editl. bd.: Jour. Am. Coll. Cardiology, 1983-87, Am. Jour. Cardiology, 1976-81, 83—, Am. Heart Jour., 1980—

Clin. Cardiology, 1985—, Jour. Intensive Care Medicine, 1985—, Internat. Jour. Cardiology, 1981—, Annals of Internal Medicine, 1979-82, Med. Month, 1983—, Weekly Update: Cardiology, 1978-80, Cardiovasc. Medicine, 1976-80, Cardiologic Consultation, 1980—, Cardiovasc. Drugs and Therapy, 1989-90, Coronary Artery Disease, 1990—, Cardiology, 1990—, Jour. Heart Valve Disease, 1992, Current Problems in Cardiology, 1975—, assoc. editor, 1980-83, editor-in-chief, 1984—, Circulation, 1977-80, 81-83, 83-86, 86—, consulting editor, 1993, Yr. Book Cardiology, 1986-92, assoc. editor, 1986-92; assoc. editor: Jour. Applied Cardiology, 1985-90, Am. Jour. Cardiovasc. Pathology, 1985—. Recipient Sinsheimer award for Cardiovasc. Rsch., 1969-70; grantee from various sponsors. Fellow Am. Coll. Physicians, Am. Coll. Cardiology; mem. Am. Soc. Clin. Investigation, Am. Fedn. Clin. Rsch., Am. Heart Assn., Am. Physiological Soc., Assn. Army Cardiologists, Southern Soc. Clin. Rsch., Am. Soc. Echocardiography, Assn. U. Cardiologists, Alpha Omega Alpha, others. Office: The Univ Tex Health Sci Ctr VAH Rm C644 7703 Floyd Curl Drive San Antonio TX 78229-3900

O'ROURKE, THOMAS DENIS, civil engineer, educator; b. Pitts., July 31, 1948; s. Lawrence Robert and Adele Mildred (Moloski) O'R.; m. Patricia Ann Lane, Aug. 12, 1978; 1 child, Adele Christina. BSCE, Cornell U., 1970; MSCE, U. Ill., 1973, PhD, 1975. Geotech. engr. Dames & Moore, N.Y.C. 1970; rsch. asst. U. Ill., Urbana, 1970-75, asst. prof., 1975-78, Cornell U., Ithaca, NY, 1978-80, assoc. prof., 1981-87, prof., 1987-98, Thomas R. Briggs prof. engring., 1999—. Recipient Trevithick prize, Brit. Instn. Civil Engrs., 2002, Outstanding Paper award, Japan Gas Assn., 2003, Engr. Dist. Svc. award, U. Ill., 2005. Fellow: AAAS; mem.: ASTM (C.A. Hogentogler award 1976), ASME, NAE, ASCE (pres. Ithaca sect. 1981—82, chair exec. com. tech. coun. lifeline earthquake engr. 1998—99, Collingwood prize 1983, Huber prize 1988, C. Martin Duke award 1999, Stephen D. Bechtel pipeline engring. award 1997, Ralph B. Peck award 2005), U.S. Com. on Tunnelling Tech. (chmn. 1987—88), Internat. Soc. Rock Mechanics, Internat. Soc. Engring. Geology, Earthquake Engring. Rsch. Inst. (bd. dirs. 1998—2000, v.p. 2000, pres. 2002—04, Outstanding Paper award 1996). Home: 10 Twin Glens Rd Ithaca NY 14850-1041 Office: Cornell U Sch Civil Environ Engring 273 Hollister Hall Ithaca NY 14853-3501 Office Phone: 607-255-6470. Business E-Mail: tdo1@cornell.edu.

O'ROURKE, WILLIAM ANDREW, literature and language professor, writer; b. Chgo., Dec. 4, 1945; s. William Andrew and Elizabeth (Kompare) O'R.; m. Marion Teresa Ghilarducci, July 9, 1986; 1 child, Joseph Ghilarducci. BA, U. Mo. at Kansas City, 1968; M.F.A., Columbia U., 1970. Instr. journalism Kean Coll., Union, NJ, 1973; asst. prof. English Rutgers U., 1975-78, Mount Holyoke Coll., 1978-81, U. Notre Dame, Ind., 1981-87, assoc. prof. Ind., 1987-94, prof. Ind., 1994—. Writer-in-residence Thurber House, Columbus, Ohio, fall 1984 Author: The Harrisburg 7 and the New Catholic Left, 1972, The Meekness of Isaac, 1974, Idle Hands, 1981, Criminal Tendencies, 1987, Signs of the Literary Times: Essays, Reviews, Profiles 1970-92, 1993, Notts, 1996,Campaign America '96: The View From the Couch, 1997, Campaign America 2000: The View From the Couch, 2001, On Having a Heart Attack: A Medical Memoir, 2006; editor: On the Job, 1977. Fine Arts Work Ctr. fellow, Provincetown, Mass., 1970-72; recipient Creative Artists Pub. Svc. award N.Y. State Coun. on Arts, 1975; Nat. Endowment for Arts creative writing fellow, 1981-82, 90-91. Mem. Authors Guild, PEN Am. Ctr., Nat. Book Critics Cir. Office: U Notre Dame Dept English 356 O'Shag Notre Dame IN 46556 Office Phone: 574-631-7377.

OROZCO, GABRIEL, artist; b. Jalapa, Veracruz, Mex., 1962; Student, Escuela Nat. Arte Plasticas, 1981—84, Circulo de Bellas Artes, Madrid, 1986—87. Artist-in-residence DAAD, 1995. One-woman shows include Kanaal Art Found., Kortrijk, 1993, Galerie Crousel Robelin BAMA, Paris, 1993, Mus. Modern Art, N.Y.C., 1993, Mus. Contemporary Art, Chgo., 1994, Marian Goodman Gallery, N.Y.C., 1994, 1996, 1998, Musée d'Art Moderne de la Ville de Paris, 1995, 1998, De Cardenas, Milan, 1995, Galerie Micheline Szwajcer, Antwerp, 1995, DAAD Gallery, Berlin, 1995, Art Gallery Ont., Toronto, 1996, Staalichen Mus. am Kulturforum, Berlin, 1997, Stedelijk Mus., Amsterdam, 1997, Anthony d'Offay Gallery, London, 1997, Centro Fotográfico Alvarez Bravo, Oaxaca, Mex., 1998, St. Louis Mus. Art, 1998, exhibited in group shows at Ill. Encuentro Nacional de Arte joven, Inst. Nacional de Bellas Artes, Aguascalientes, 1983 (hon. mention), Museo U. del Chopo, Mexico City, 1984, Museo Carrillo Gil, 1985, Museo de Art Moderno, 1987, Am. de Arte y Cultura, Brasilia, 1989, Bronx Mus. Art, 1990, Pasadena Art Ctr., 1991, New Mus. Contemporary Art, N.Y.C., 1993, Marian Goodman Gallery, 1993, 1994, 1998, 2000—03, 2005, Margo Leavin Gallery, L.A., 1994, Zacheta Nat. Gallery Contemporary Art, Warsaw, 1996, Whitney Biennial, N.Y., 1997, Berlin Biennial, 1998, Phila. Mus. Art, 1999, Yokohama Triennale, Tokyo, 2001, Moving Pictures, Guggenheim Mus., 2002, Venice Biennial, 2003, Taipei Biennial, 2004, Guangzhou Triennial, 2005, Speaking with Hands, Mus Folkwang Essen, 2006. Office: care Marian Goodman Gallery 24 W 57th St New York NY 10019-3918 Fax: 212-581-5187.*

ORPHANIDES, GUS GEORGE, licensing executive; b. NYC, Jan. 27, 1947; s. Gus G. and Savesta (Agapetus) O.; m. Jeanne Wood, Feb. 3, 1968; children: Alyson, Paul, Lindsay. BS with honors, Hobart Coll., 1967; PhD, Ohio State U., 1972. Chemist E.I. Du Pont de Nemours & Co., Wilmington, Del., 1974—79, Beaumont, Tex., 1979—81, Air Products, Allentown, Pa., 1981—84, applications mgr., 1984—85, comml. mgr., 1985—88, rsch. mgr., 1988—91, sr. comml. devel. mgr., 1991—94, comml. devel. mgr., 1995—96, mgr. R&D, 1996—98, mgr. global tech. svc., 1998—2000, dir. applications devel., tech. svc., chem. tech., 2000—02, dir. intellectual asset mgmt. and licensing, 2002—. Contbr. articles to profl. publs.; patentee in field; developed new polymers for adhesives, non-wovens, paper coatings, polyurethane elastomers, rubber cross-linking. Phys. rehab. hosp. vol. in occupl. therapy. 1st U. S. Army, 1972-74. Decorated Army Commendation medal; recipient Army Cert. of Achievment, Raker Meml. award Good Shepherd Hosp.; N.Y. State Regents scholar, 1963-67. Mem. Am. Chem. Soc., Licensing Exec. Soc. Roman Catholic. Achievements include development of novel emulsion polymers and polymer intermediates, international technology transfer, new business creation technology licensing, contract negotiation, work process devel. and instituionalism, R&D project management, acquisition due diligence, lab-to-plant technology transfer, plant start-up, new products commercialization, new bus. start-up, work process devel., deal closure, acquisitions/divestments. Home: 4046 Providence Ct Schnecksville PA 18078-3524 Office: Air Products 7201 Hamilton Blvd Allentown PA 18195-1526 Office Phone: 610-481-6142. E-mail: orphangg@airproducts.com.

ORPHANIDES, NORA CHARLOTTE, ballet educator; b. NYC, June 4, 1951; d. M.T. and Mary Elsie (Tilly) Feffer; m. James Mark Orphanides, July 1, 1972; children: Mark, Elaine Orphanides Mastrosimone, Jennine. BA, CUNY, 1973; student, Joffrey Ballet Sch., N.Y.C., 1970-75; postgrad., Princeton Ballet Sch., 1976-86. Cert. speech and hearing handicapped tchr. With membership dept. M.M.A., N.Y.C., 1987—2002; mem. faculty Princeton (N.J.) Ballet Sch., 1983—, trustee emeritus, 1992—. Master tchr. ballroom dance. Mem. cast Princeton Ballet ann. Nutcracker, 1985-90, now Am. Repertory Ballet Co., 1993—; appeared in Romeo & Juliet, 1995-96, 2000. Fundraising gala chmn. Princeton Ballet, 1985, 86, 91-92, chmn. spl. events, 1987—, trustee, 1986—, chmn. Nutcracker benefit, 1990—, Dracula benefit, 1991, honoree, 1999; dept. chmn. June Fete to benefit Princeton Hosp., 1988, 90-92, 96, 2000, trustee, 1995-99; vol. Nat. Hdqrs. Recording for the Blind, 1991-93; dinner chmn. Nassau Ch. Music Festival, 1992, Handel Festival, Nassau U., 1993, Princeton Chamber Symphony, 1993; hon. chmn. Princeton Ballet Gala, 1993, Art First to benefit U. Med. Ctr., 2006; chmn. Christmas Boutique, Princeton Med. Ctr., 1993; trustee, Princeton Med. Ctr. Aux. Bd., 1992-2002, trustee 1995—, pres., 1997-99, past pres., 2000-2002; found. bd. dirs. U. Med. Ctr. Princeton, 2004—; choreographer Stuart Country Day Sch., Princeton, 1996-99, 2001; chmn. benefit dinner Eden Inst., 2000. Named honoree Princeton Ballet, 1999, recipient Edward R. and Irene D. Farley Cmty. Stewardship award Eden Inst. Found., 2003. Democrat. Avocations: piano, skiiing, tennis. Office: 301 N Harrison St Princeton NJ 08540-3512

ORR, A. SUMMEY, III, lawyer; b. Monroe, NC, 1960; AB, U. NC, Chapel Hill, 1983, JD, 1986. Bar: Ga. 1986, Ga. Ct. Appeals 1987, Ga. Supreme Ct. 1987, US Dist. Ct. (No. Dist. Ga.). Ptnr. Holland & Knight LLP, Atlanta, mem. dir. com. Mem.: State Bar Ga. (mem. real estate sect.), ABA (mem. real property, probate and trust sect.), Atlanta Bar Assn. (mem. real estate sect.), Internat. Coun. Shopping Ctrs., Nat. Assn. of Indsl. and Office Parks, Phi Delta Phi (magister 1985—86). Office: Holland & Knight LLP 1 Atlantic Ctr Ste 2000 1201 W Peachtree St NE Atlanta GA 30309 Office Phone: 404-898-8102. Business E-Mail: summey.orr@hklaw.com.

ORR, BOBETTE KAY, diplomat; b. Oak Park, Ill., Oct. 28, 1941; d. Robert Jay and Neta (Hoobler) Pottle; m. William Rucker Orr, Oct. 11, 1974; step children: Bridgette, Brietta, Alyson, William Jr. BA in Econs., Conn. Coll. for Women, 1963; student auditor Internat. Econs., London Sch. of Econs., 1964; postgrad. studies in Internat. Econs., George Washington U., 1964-65. Rsch. asst. C. of C. USA, Washington, 1965—66; country desk officer for Scandanavia U.S. Dept. Commerce, Washington, 1966—69, country desk officer for France, 1970—72, 1979—81, country desk officer for Belgium, Netherlands, Luxembourg, 1974—77, country desk officer for Japan, 1981—82; mkt. rsch. officer United States Trade Ctr., Stockholm, 1973, trade promotion officer London, 1977—78; asst. comml. attache Am. Embassy, Paris, 1982—87; comml. attache Am. Consulate Gen., Auckland, New Zealand, 1988—92, consul gen. Edinburgh, Scotland, 1992—95; comml. counselor Am. Embassy, London, 1995—99, Cairo, 1999—2002; regional dir. Africa, Near East, South Asia U.S. Dept. Commerce, Washington, 2002—04, 2006, regional dir. for Europe, 2005, regional dir. for Africa, Near East, South Asia, 2006—. Mem. bd. dirs. U.S. Dept. Commerce Fed. Credit Union, Washington, D.C., 1972-77, pres., 1976-77, mem. supervisory com., 1979-81; equal employment opportunity counselor for Greater Washington Met. Area, 1972-75; mission dir. for USDOC's Concrete Constrn. Techniques Seminar Mission to Hong Kong, Singapore, Malaysia, 1980; detailed to Office of Dir. Fgn. Comml. Svc. as evaluator of candidates for Fgn. Comml. Svc., 1981. Author: (with others) 10 pamphlet series, on free enterprise, The Power of Choice, 1966; contbr. to Bus. Am., 1966-81, Overseas Bus. Reports 1966-76 (Dept. Commerce publs.). Mem. Am. Women's Club of Edinburgh, (hon. pres.), The English Speaking Union. Avocations: skiing, bicycle riding. Home: PO Box 63 Great Falls VA 22066-0063 Office: USFCS/ITA Dept Commerce 14th and Constitution Ave NW Rm 2013 Washington DC 20230 Office Phone: 202-482-0368.

ORR, CAROLE, artist; b. Alexandria, Ind., June 10, 1933; d. Carl Victor and Marian Martha (Long) Coonse; m. Larry D. Ribble (dec. July 1953); m. Thomas LeRoy Orr, Nov. 10, 1950 (div. Oct. 1979); children: Karen Sue, Terri Ribble, David Thomas; m. Lev C. Hamblet Jr., Feb. 5, 1982 (div. Oct. 1998); stepchildren: James, Jean, Laura, Anne. Cert., Famous Artist Sch., Westport, Conn., 1956, Art Instrn. Schs., Mpls., 1962. Asst. art dir. La Gallerie du Mall, Houston, 1975—78; freelance fine artist Lantern Ln. Gallery, Houston, 1968—81, asst. mgr., design cons., 1979—81; artist Artist Showroom, Houston, 1982—. Participating artist Assistance Guild, Houston, 1968, Beaux Arts, Houston, 1968-70, Houston Gamma Phi Gallery, 1971-72, Houston Delta Gamma Found., 1978-81, Glassell Sch. of Art Houston, 1983; art instr. children's art Houston Park and Recreational Programs, 1964-68. One-woman shows include Nobler Gallery, Houston, 1967, Art Gallery, Pasadena, Tex., 1968, Gallarie La Rue, Austin, Tex., 1971, Gallery 12, Houston, 1972, Main St., Houston, 1974, La Galerie de Mall, Houston, 1976-78, Triumvirate Gallery, Santa Fe, N.Mex., 1980, Houshang's Gallery, Dallas, 1980-82, Battle Horn Galleries Ltd., Santa Fe, 1984, New Trends Inc., Santa Fe, 1985-88, Horizons Galleries, Houston, 1990-93, Houston C.C., 1992, Heinen Theatre, 1992, Windsor Gallery, Ft. Lauderdale, Fla., 1994; exhibited in group shows at Motorola Invitational, Houston, 1964, Assistance Guild Houston, 1968, Am. Gen. Bldg., Houston, 1968, Beaux Arts, Houston, 1968-70, Gamma Phi Gallery, Houston, 1971-72, Lantern Ln. Gallery, Houston, 1971-72, Delta Gamma Found., Houston, 1978-81, Glassell Sch. Art, Houston, 1983, New Trends Gallery Inc., Santa Fe, 1985-88, Pasadena (Tex.) Art Invitational, 1988, Double Tree Hotel, Houston, 1990, Horizons Gallery, Houston, 1990-93, Windsors Gallery, Dania, Fla., 1993, 2003, Magnolias Art Gallery, Town and Country Ctr., Houston, 2003-06, Bakery of the Poets, 2005—; T. Symington & Co. Interiors, Brenham, Tex., 2006. Art instr. adults Ch. of the Advent, Houston, 1968-70; adult edn. instr. arts Ch. Sch. Conf., Dept. Christian Edn., Trinity Ch., Diocese of Tex., Houston, 1969. Recipient Profl. Best Ann. Competition Art Instrn. Schs., Mpls., 1965; named Best-Selling Artist of Yr., 2001, Paintings DIRECT, N.Y.C., 2001, 03, Art on 5th, Austin, 2005, Diamond Domani Galleria, Houston, 2005, T. Sumington & Co. Interiors, Tex., 2006. Avocations: self-study in psychology, music, dance. Home and Office: Artist Showroom DBA 880 Tully Rd Apt 29 Houston TX 77079-5418

ORR, DENNIS PATRICK, lawyer; b. NYC, Dec. 29, 1952; s. Gerard Samuel and Mary Ellen (Dowd) O.; m. Laurie Louise Lawless, Jan. 15, 1977; children: Kathryn, Kristen, Megan, Matthew. BA, Boston Coll., 1975; JD, St. John's U., 1978. Bar: N.Y. 1979, U.S. Dist. Ct. (so. and ea. dists.) N.Y. 1979, U.S. Ct. Appeals (2d cir.) 1986. Assoc. Shearman & Sterling, N.Y.C., 1978-86, ptnr., 1987-97, Mayer, Brown & Platt, N.Y.C., 1997—. St. Thomas More scholar St. John's Law Sch., Jamaica, N.Y., 1975. Mem. ABA, N.Y. State Bar Assn. Roman Catholic. Office: Mayer Brown Rowe & Maw 1675 Broadway Fl 19 New York NY 10019-5820 Office Phone: 212-506-2690. Business E-Mail: dorr@mayerbrownrowe.com.

ORR, FRANK HOWARD, III, architect; b. Jasper, Ala., Sept. 4, 1932; s. Frank Howard Jr. and Lola Ruth (Lynch) O.; m. Nancy Gayle Gentry, Apr. 13, 1957; children: Mark Daniel, Steven Gentry, Karen Diann, Amy Ruth. B in Applied Art, Auburn U., 1961. Registered Ala., Ga., Ky., N.C., Tenn., Va. Miss. Assoc. architect Edwin A. Keeble Assocs., Nashville, 1962-70, Bianculli & Tyler, Inc., Chattanooga, 1970; prin. Frank Orr Architects, Nashville, 1970-76; pres., prin. Orr/Houk & Assocs. Architects, Inc., Nashville, 1976-2001; v.p. Hart Freeland Roberts, Inc. (merged with Orr/Houk), Brentwood, Tenn., 2001—04; prin. Frank Orr, AIA, Cons. Arch., 2004—. V.p. Hart Freeland Roberts, Inc., Brentwood, Tenn.; adj. faculty O'More Sch. Design, Franklin, Tenn., 1972—77, Nashville State Tech. Inst., 1978—79; guest lectr. Sch. Arch., Victoria U., Wellington, New Zealand, 1987; exam grader Nat. Coun. Archtl. Registration Bds., Ft. Lauderdale, Fla., 1985; guest lectr. Coll. Arch., Auburn U., 2001. Author: Professional Practice in Architecture, 1982, Scale in Architecture, 1985, Alabama Boy, An Architect's Memoir, 2006; author (column) Urban Life, Nashville Bus. Jour., 1995; editor, co-author: Notable Nashville Architecture 1930-1980; contbr. articles to profl. jours.; prin. works include Woodmont Bapt. Ch. (design commendation 1979, Design award of Merit 1990), Appalachian Ctr. for Crafts, Two Rivers Bapt. Ch. (design commendation 1979), 1st Bapt. Ch., Hendersonville, Tenn. (design award of merit 1992), First Bapt. Ch., Athens, Ala., First Bapt. Ch., Pasadena, Tex., Tenn. Bapt. Conf. Ctrs., Carson and Linden, First Baptist Ch., Joelton, Tenn., Lake Providence Missionary Baptist Ch., Nashville. Active Citizens com. Met. Nashville Gen. Plan, 1994; mem. Plan of Nashville Project, 2002—03; co-team leader Project Plan of Nashville, Nashville Civic Design Ctr., 2004—05; missionary trips, Guatemala, 1977, 1982, Mexico, 1980, Sierra Leone, 1985, 88, Poland, 1998, Brazil, 2000, Portugal, 2004. Mem.: AIA (Nat. Mid. Tenn. chpt. 1971—78, chmn. Gulf States design awards com. 1985, com. environ. edn. 1972—76), Tenn. Soc. Architects (sec.-treas. 1977), Nashville C. of C. (regional transp. com. 1993—94), Scarab Archtl. Honor Soc., Auburn U. Baptist. Avocations: drawing, writing. Office Phone: 615-319-2128. Personal E-mail: forr1@comcast.net.

ORR, FRANKLIN MATTES, JR., petroleum engineering educator; b. Baytown, Tex., Dec. 27, 1946; s. Franklin Mattes and Selwyn Sage (Huddleston) O.; m. Susan Packard, Aug. 30, 1970; children: David, Katherine. BSChemE, Stanford U., Calif., 1969; PhD in Chem. Engring. U. Minn., 1976, DEng (hon.), Heriot-Watt U., Edinburgh, Scotland, 2005. Asst. to dir. Office Fed. Activities EPA, Washington, 1970-72; rsch. engr. Bellaire Rsch. Ctr. Shell Devel. Co., Houston, 1976—77; head miscible flooding and gas injection N.Mex Petroleum Recovery Rsch. Ctr. N.Mex Inst. Mining and Tech., Socorro, 1978-84; assoc. prof. petroleum engring. Stanford U., Calif.,

1985-87, prof., 1987—; prof. chem. engring., 1994—, Keleen and Carlton Beal prof. petroleum engring., 1994—; dir. Global Climate and Energy Project, 2002—. Bd. dirs. Monterey Bay Aquarium Rsch. Inst., 1987—, Am. Geol. Inst. Found., 1997—2002, David and Lucile Packard Found., 1999—; interim dean Stanford U. Sch. Earth Scis., 1994—95, dean, 1995—2002; mem. adv. bd. Princeton U. Carbon Mitigation Initiative, 2004—; sr. fellow Ctr. Environ. Sci. and Policy Stanford U. Inst. Internat. Studies, 2005—; mem. com. to visit Earth and planetary scis. Harvard U., 2006—. Contbr. articles to profl. jours. Bd. dirs. Wolf Trap Found. for Performing Arts, 1988-94 Recipient Robert Earll McConnell award, AIME, 2001. Mem.: Soc. Indsl. and Applied Math., Soc. Petroleum Engrs. (Disting. Lectr. award 1988—89, Disting. Achievement award, Petroleum Engring. Faculty 1993), AAAS, AIChE, NAE. Office: Stanford U Dept Petroleum Engring 074 Green Earth Scis Bldg 367 Panama Str Stanford CA 94305-2220 E-mail: fmorr@pangea.stanford.edu.*

ORR, JAMES F., III, foundation administrator; b. Mpls., 1943; BA, Villanova U., 1962; MA, Boston U., 1969. With New Eng. Mchts. Bank, Boston, 1965-67, Bache & Co., N.Y.C., 1967-69; ptnr. Cardinal Mgmt. Co., Boston, 1969-75; exec. v.p., treas. Conn. Bank and Trust Corp., 1975-86; with UNUM, 1986-98, COO, pres.; chmn. bd., CEO UNUM Corp., 1987—99; also pres., chmn., CEO UNUM Life Ins. Co. (subs.), to 1999; pres., CEO United Asset Mgmt. Corp., Boston, 2000—01; chmn. bd. trustees Rockefeller Found., NYC, 2000—. Bd. dir. Mellon Fin. Corp., 2003—. Bd. trustees Bates Coll., Villanova Univ.; bd. overseers Harvard Sch. Pub. Health. Office: Rockefeller Found 420 Fifth Ave New York NY 10018-2702*

ORR, JAMES FRANCIS, marketing executive, information technology executive; b. Phila., Oct. 10, 1945; s. James F. Jr. and Dorothy (Gallagher) O.; m. Catherine Marie Reinholt; children: Kristin Leah, Lauren Beth, James Desmond. Student, Pa. State U., 1963-64, Rutgers U., Camden and New Brunswick, N.J., 1964-67. Various sales mgmt. positions Procter & Gamble, 1967-73, dist. mgr. White Plains, N.Y., 1973-76, nat. accounts mgr. Cin., 1976-78, sales div. mgr., 1978-81, sales merchandising mgr., 1981-82; sales dir. Procter & Gamble Ltd., Newcastle upon Tyne, Eng., 1982-85; v.p. sales Crush Internat. Inc., Cin., 1985-88; v.p. market devel. Matrixx Mktg. Inc. subs. Cin. Bell Inc., Cin., 1989-92, pres. and CEO, 1993—; COO Cincinnati Bell Inc.; pres Convergys Corp., Cin., 2000—05, chmn., CEO, 2000—. Mem. parents adv. coun. Hamilton Coll., Clinton, N.Y., 1989-91, vice chmn. Parents Fund, 1989-90, chmn., 1990-91; active Grad. Leadership Cin., class XVI, 1992-93. Mem. Direct Mktg. Assn., Soc. Consumer Affairs Profls., Greater Cin. C. of C., Coldstream Country Club (trustee), Melrose Club (Daufuskie Island, S.C.). Avocations: golf, theater, antiques, travel. Office: Convergys Corp PO Box 1638 Cincinnati OH 45201-1638

ORR, JENNIE MARIE (JENNIE THOMAS), family physician; b. Sioux City, Iowa, Feb. 16, 1952; d. J. Allen and Ione B. (Gronlund) O.; m. Daniel Joel Thomas, Aug. 23, 1980; children: Lorraine Marie, Joel Allen. BS in Computer Sci., Miss. State U., 1973, MD, 1976. Diplomate Am. Bd. Family Practice. Sub-intern pediatrics Grad. Med. Edn., Inc., Lansing, Mich., 1977; intern, resident family practice Cedar Rapids (Iowa) Med. Edn. Program, 1977-80; staff Allina Med. Clinic, Hastings, Minn., 1980—, corp. sec., 1984—88. Chmn. dept. obstetrics Regina Meml. Hosp., Hastings, 1986-90. Fellow Am. Acad. Family Practice. Lutheran. Office: Allina Med Clinic 1210 1st St W Hastings MN 55033-1085

ORR, JIM (JAMES D. ORR), editor, writer, publishing executive; b. Buffalo, Feb. 7, 1960; s. David James and Doris Kathleen (Wolos) O.; m. JoEllen Black, June 4, 1994. B in Journalism, Ind. U. of Pa., 1982, M in Comm., 1987. Station mgr. Sta. WIUP-TV, Ind., Pa., 1983-84; sports writer, news writer Ind. (Pa.) Gazette, 1984-88; reporter Stuart (Fla.) News, 1988-89; staff writer, columnist Gannett Rochester (N.Y.) Newspapers, 1989-96; staff writer The Bus. Jour., Fresno, Calif., 1997; sr. writer The Fresno Bee, 1998-99; features, spl. projects and weekend editor, page designer The Westerly (R.I.) Sun, 2000—03; editor, pub. Heartland Pub. Newspapers, Halstead, Kans., 2004—. Columnist Orrdinary People, 1994-95; freelance writer, publicist, 1996—. Moderator polit. debate Edu-Cable Corp., Greece, N.Y., 1993; panelist conf. New England Soc. Newspaper Editors, 2002. Recipient Agrl. Writing 1st Place award Penn-Ag Industries, 1985, 2d Pl. Keystone State Press award Pa. Newspaper Pub. Assn., 1987, 2 Writing awards Scripps Howard, 1989, award Gannett Enterprise Project, 1994, Cmty. Svc. award N.Y. Newspaper Pubs. Assn., 1994-95, 4 awards R.I. Press Assn., 2000-03, Cmty. Svc. award Kans. Press Assn., 2004 Home: 1004 11th Terr Halstead KS 67056

ORR, JO MILLER, music educator, voice educator; b. Magee, Miss., Sept. 19, 1945; d. Marvin Kavanaugh and Kathleen Bynum Miller; m. Benjamin Joseph Orr, Oct. 11, 1969; children: Anna Cayson, Megan Ewing. AA in Music, Hinds Jr. Coll., 1967; BM in Vocal Performance, U. South Miss., 1967; MM in Vocal Performance, U. Miss., Miss., 1980. Dir. First Presbyn. Ch., Tupelo, Miss., 1970—85, St. Luke UMC, 1987—; chmn. music edn. Itawamba CC, Fulton, Miss., 1997—98; pvt. voice tchr. Tupelo, 1998—. Adj. faculty Miss. U. Women, 2006. Singer: various symphonies in Miss. Vol. Tupelo Symphony. Recipient Woman of Distinction, Tupelo Area Bus. and Profl. Women's Club, 1994; grantee, Miss. Arts Commn., Jackson, Miss., 2002—04. Mem.: Miss. Fedn. of Music Clubs (pres. 2005—), Nat. Assn. of Tchrs. of Singing (pres. 1995—97), Fellowship United Meths. Music and Worship Arts (pres. 1992—94). Methodist. Avocation: interior decorating. Office Phone: 662-255-1593. E-mail: benorr1310@comcast.net.

ORR, JOSEPH ALEXANDER, educational administrator; b. West Palm Beach, Fla., Nov. 20, 1929; s. Joseph Alexander and Laura (Terry) O.; m. Addis W. Orr (div.); children: Eric, Pamela, Tracey; m. Linda F. Orr. BS, Fla. A&M U., 1951; MS, Mich. State U., 1963, MEd, Fla. Atlantic U., 1965; PhD, Fla. State U., 1972. Sci. tchr. Roosevelt Sr. H.S., West Palm Beach, Fla., 1953-68; counselor, coord. Adult Edn. Dept. Sch. Sys., Palm Beach County, Fla., 1960-72; dean of students Palm Beach H.S., West Palm Beach, 1968-70; asst. dean Fla. A&M U., Tallahassee, 1970-72; adj. prof. Fla. U. Bloomington, 1972-73; prin. Ctrl. Sr. H.S., Louisville, 1972-74, Jupiter (Fla.) H.S., 1974-78; adj. prof. Fla. Atlantic U., Boca Raton, 1978—; asst. supt. Palm Beach County (Fla.) Sch. Bd., 1978-84, assoc. supt., 1984-92, dep. supt., chief acad. officer, 2001—; exec. dir. Palm Beach County Sch. Adminstrs. Assn., 1992-2001. Chair State Adv. Bd. for Severely Emotionally Disturbed. Contbr. articles to profl. jours. Bd. dirs. Children's Home Soc. Fla., Palm Beach County Coun. Arts; past chair Health and Human Svcs. Bd., Palm Beach County, Inst. New Dimensions, Palm Beach C.C. Assn. Retarded Citizens, Inc., West Palm Beach; past pres. Scholastic Achievement Found. Palm Beach County, Edn. Found. Palm Beach County. Recipient Disting. Svc. award NEA, Pioneer award for excellence in pub. svc. Nat. Forum of Pub. Adminstrn., Outstanding Achievement award Fla. Assn. Cmty. Educators, Four Seasons award Nat. Assn. for Year Round Edn. Mem. ASCD, Fla. Assn. Sch. Adminstrs., Am. Assn. Sch. Adminstrs., Nat. Assn. Secondary Sch. Prins., Nat. Cmty. Edn. Assn. (Sch. Leadership award), Kiwanis Internat. Democrat. Episcopalian. Avocation: boating. Office: Palm Beach County Sch Adminstrs Assn PO Box 31511 Palm Beach Gardens FL 33420 Office Phone: 561-625-6918. E-mail: joeorr@usa.net.

ORR, JOSEPH NEWTON, recreational guide, outdoor educator; b. San Francisco, Oct. 25, 1954; s. James Neewah and Verna Louise (Butler) O. BA in Spanish, Sul Ross State U., 1981. Cert. swiftwater rescue technician, wilderness first responder, open water scuba diver, Grand Canyon river guide, Tex. master naturalist. Instr. astronomy lab. Sul Ross State U., Alpine, Tex., 1972-75; svc. sta. attendent, river guide Nat. Park Concessions, Big Bend Nat. Park, 1975-78; surveyor's aide Gila Nat. Forest U.S. Dept. Agriculture, N. Mex., 1979; instr. ESL Centro Universitario de Idiomas, Mexico City, 1981; English and Spanish tutor Ctr. Student Devel. Sul Ross State U., 1980-83; instr. ESL, Intensive Summer Lang. Tng. Inst. Alpine, Tex., 1980-83; ednl. cons. Chihuahuan Desert Rsch. Inst., Alpine, Tex., 1983; editor The Skyline (student newspaper) Sul Ross State U., 1984; interpreter, translator, guide Dr. John M. Miller, Mexico, 1980-85; guide in U.S., Mex., Belize, Guatemala and

Honduras for Far Flung Adventures, Terlingua, Tex., 1986-94, Remarkable Journeys, Houston, 1994-98; with Ceiba Adventures, Flagstaff, 1998—, Mountain Travel Sobek, 2005—. Active Grand Canyon River Guides, Friends of McDonald Obs., Chihuahuan Desert Rsch. Inst., Friends of Big Bend Nat. Park, Ctr. Big Bend Studies, Big Bend Natural History Assn. Mem. Internat. Dark Sky Assn., Grand Canyon Assn., Planetary Soc., Nat. Parks Conservation Assn., Sierra Club, Tex. Ornithol. Soc., Nat. Assn. Interpreters, Native Plant Soc. Tex. Democrat. Avocations: astronomy, archaeology, birding, camping, hiking. Home and Office: PO Box 1881 Alpine TX 79831 Office Phone: 432-386-2251. E-mail: josephorr@aol.com.

**ORR, KENNETH BRADLEY,** academic administrator; b. Charlotte, N.C., Mar. 15, 1933; s. Frank Wylie and Kate Harriett O.; m. Ruth Douglas Currie; children: Kevin, Jeffrey, Jonathan. BA, Duke U., 1954; MDiv, Union Theol. Sem., 1960, ThM, 1961; PhD, U. Mich., 1978; LittD, Carroll Coll., 1990; DD, Presbyn. Coll., 1997. Ordained to ministry, Presbyn. Ch., 1961. Minister West End Presbyn. Ch., Roanoke, Va., 1961-64; asst. to pres. Union Theol. Sem., Richmond, Va., 1964-68, v.p., 1968-74; pres. Presbyn. Sch. Christian Edn., Richmond, 1974-79, Presbyn. Coll., Clinton, S.C., 1979-97, pres. emeritus, 1997—; sr. v.p. John McRae & Assocs., Atlanta, 1997—. Past mem. coun. presidents Nat. Assn. Intercollegiate Athletics, Kansas City, Mo., chmn. S. Atlantic Conf., 1989—91; mem. nat. adv. com. on instnl. quality and integrity U.S. Dept. Edn., 1995—2001. Contbr. to religious and ednl. publs. Mem. Assn. Presbyn. Colls. and Univs. (pres. 1994, exec. com.), Coun. Ind. Colls. (bd. dirs. 1993-96), Laurens County C. of C. (past pres.), Kiwanis. Democrat. Avocations: reading, travel, tennis, classical music.

**ORR, LARRY L.,** economist; b. Terraville, S.D., Feb. 9, 1942; s. Leo Russell and Margery L. Orr; m. Kathleen L. Flanagan; children: Marilee Kay, David Jason, Elizabeth Chunyi, Natalie Rose. PhD, MIT, 1967. Asst. prof. econs. U. Wis., Madison, 1967—69; staff economist OEO, Washington, 1969—73; dir. office of income security policy rsch. U.S. Dept. Labor, Edn., and Welfare, Washington, 1973—80; fed. exec. fellow The Brookings Instn., Washington, 1976—77; dir., office tech. analysis U.S. Dept. Labor, Washington, 1980—82; chief economist Abt Associates Inc., Bethesda, Md.; guest scholar The Brookings Instn., Washington, 1995—96. Author: (book) Income, Employment, and Urban Residential Location (Named one of Outstanding Books in Indsl. Rels. and Labor Econs., Princeton U. Indsl. Rels. Sect., 1975), Social Experiments: Evaluating Public Programs with Experimental Methods; co-author (book) Does Training for the Disadvantaged Work?, Program Applicants as a Comparison Group in Evaluating Training Programs, mem. editl. bd. Evaluation and Program Planning, 1996—. Recipient Fed. Exec. award for govt. ofcl. who has done the most to improve applied social rsch., Coun. Applied Social Rsch., 1977, Citation of Merit, Coll. Scis. and Humanities, Iowa State U., 1982. Mem.: NAS (mem. com. on postsecondary edn. and tng. 1991—93), Assn. Pub. Policy Analysis and Mgmt. (policy coun. 1988—92). Avocations: scuba diving, golf, reading. Office: Abt Associates Inc 4550 Montgomery Ln Ste 800 Bethesda MD 20814

**ORR, MARCIA,** pre-school administrator, consultant; b. Anamosa, Iowa, Mar. 2, 1949; d. Harold Edward Eiben and Clara Elizabeth (Hubbard) E.; m. Robert J. Orr, Sept. 6, 1969; 1 child, Jennifer. Student, U. Iowa, 1977; BS, St. Xavier U., Chgo., 1981; MEd in Early Childhood Leadership, Nat. Louis U., 1996. Bookkeeper Monticello State Bank, 1967-69; exec. sec. Davenport Bank and Trust, 1969-73; asst. educator Elisabeth Ludeman Devel. Ctr., Park Forest, Ill., 1979; tchr. Flossmoor Hills (Ill.) Elem. Sch., 1980-1984; exec. dir. Co-Care, Inc., Park Forest, 1984-89; child devel. rschr., Flossmoor, Ill., 1989—; tchr. Nazarene Nursery Sch. and Kindergarten, Chicago Heights, Ill., 1991; child care ctr. cons. Matteson Sch. Dist. 162, Park Forest, 1991—; founder, exec. dir. Before and After Sch. Enrichment, Park Forest, 1991—; adv. mem. project early start Matteson Sch. Dist. 162, Park Forest, 1991—; home-sch. coord., 1992—. Grant writer Matteson Sch. Dist. 162 and Before and After Sch. Enrichment, Inc.; officer Boleo Childcare Ctr., Iowa City, 1975-77; mentor to dirs. child care programs early childhood edn. dept. Nat.-Louis U., Ill, 1994—; co-founder Reaching New Horizons, Inc., 1996—. Contbr. articles pub. to profl. jour. Tchr. religion Infant Jesus of Prague Ch., Flossmoor, Ill., 1982—; mem. Flossmoor PTO, 1987-89; music chmn. Dist. 161 PTO, 1980-90; exec. dir. Before and After Sch. Enrichment, Inc.; parent resource coord. Matteson Sch. Dist. 162. McCormick fellow, 1995—; recipient Golden Achievement award Nat. Sch. Pub. Rels. Assn., 2001; named Best Practices and Rsch. honoree Louis U., Evanston, Ill., 2001. Mem. NAFE, Nat. Assn. for Edn. Young Children (validator), Women Employed Orgn., Internat. Platform Assn., Parent Inst., South Suburban Small Bus. Assn. (charter). Democrat. Roman Catholic. Avocations: piano, classical music, travel. Home: 9411 Fox Run Ct Frankfort IL 60423-1380 Office: Before and After Sch Enrichment 210 Illinois St Park Forest IL 60466-1100 Office Phone: 815-464-8690. Business E-Mail: base@base-inc.net.

**ORR, RICHARD CLAYTON,** mathematician, retired securities trader; b. Oakland, Calif., Mar. 28, 1941; s. James Clayton and Helen (Kittle) Orr; children: Robert Clayton, Debra Orr Kostoff. AB in Math., Humboldt State Coll., Arcata, Calif., 1964; MA in Math., Syracuse U., 1966, PhD in Math., 1969. From asst. prof. to assoc. prof. SUNY, Oswego, 1969—81, chmn. dept. math.; pres. Contratrend, Inc., Lexington, Mass., 1981—84; v.p. rsch. John Gutman Investments Corp., New Britain, Conn., 1984—90; pres. Chronos Corp., Lexington, Mass., 1990—95; gen. ptnr. ROME Ptnrs., Marblehead, Mass., 1995—2003; mng. dir. Calibar, LLC, Glastonbury, Conn., 2000—04. Referee Market Technicians Assn., N.Y.C., 1989—2002, assoc. editor, 1985—89. Contbr. articles to profl. jours. Avocations: meteorology, hiking, sailing. Personal E-Mail: rco.calibar@comcast.net.

**ORR, ROBERT F.,** not-for-profit administrator, retired state supreme court justice; b. Norfolk, Va., Oct. 11, 1946; married; 4 children. AB, U. N.C., 1971, JD, 1975. Bar: N.C. 1975. Pvt. practice, Asheville, NC, 1975—86; judge N.C. Ct. Appeals, 1986—94; assoc. justice N.C. Supreme Ct., Raleigh, 1994—2004; exec. dir., sr. counsel N.C. Inst. of Constitutional Law, 2004—. Mem. N.C. Alcoholic Beverage Control Commn., 1985—86; adj. prof. appellate advocacy N.C. Ctrl. U. Sch. Law, 1989—2003, adj. prof. N.C. State constl. law, 2004. Mem. Asheville-Revitalization Commn., 1977—81, Asheville-Buncombe Hist. Resources Commn., 1980—81; bd. trustees Hist. Preservation Found. NC, 1982—85; mem. Nat. Park Sys. Adv. Bd., 1990—95, chmn., 1992—93; bd. visitors U. NC-Chapel Hill, 1993—97; mem. NCBAs Adminstrn. Justice Commn., 2004—; Gov.'s Crime Commn. With U.S. Army, 1968—71. Mem.: N.C. Bar Assn., 28th Jud. Dist., N.C. State Bar. Republican. Office: 225 Hillsborough St Ste 280 Raleigh NC 27603 Office Phone: 919-838-5313. Business E-Mail: orr@ncicl.org.

**ORR, SAN WATTERSON, JR.,** lawyer; b. Madison, Wis., Sept. 22, 1941; s. San Watterson and Eleanor Augusta (Schalk) Orr; m. Joanne Marie Ruby, June 26, 1965; children: San Watterson III, Nancy Chapman. BBA, U. Wis., 1963, JD, 1966. CPA Wis.; bar: Wis. 1966. Sec., tres., bd. dirs. Yawkey Lumber Co., Wausau, Wis., 1971—; pres. Forewood, Inc., Wausau, 1979—; also bd. dirs.; dir. Marshall & Ilsley Bank, Wausau, 1988—, Marshall & Ilsley Corp., 1994—; chmn. bd. Wausau Paper Corp., 1997—. Editor: U. Wis. Law Rev., 1962—63. Bd. dirs. Aytchmonde Woodson Found., Inc., Wausau, 1966—, Leigh Yawkey Woodson Art Mus., Inc., Wausau, 1981—; pres. Wausau YMCA Found., 2002, Nancy Woodson Spire Found., Inc., 2002, Wausau Health Found., Inc., 1998—; chmn. U. Wis. Found., Madison, 2003—05, chmn. emeritus; bd. dirs. Wis. Taxpayers Alliance, Madison, 1983—2006, Wis. Mfrs. and Commerce, 2001—04, Wausau YMCA Found., 1979—, Nancy Woodson Spire Found., Inc., 1980—, Wausau Health Found., Inc., 1981—, U. Wis. Found., Madison, 1991—, Wis. Policy Rsch. Inst., Milw., 1995—2006; mem. bd. regents U. Wis. Sys., Madison, 1993—2000, pres., 1998—2000; bd. dirs. Lynde and Harry Bradley Found., 2006—. Mem.: Am. Law Inst., Wis. Bar Assn., Ocean Club Fla., Country Club Fla., Minocqua Country Club. Office: Yawkey Lumber Co 500 3rd St Ste 602 Wausau WI 54403-4857

**ORR, STEVEN R.,** health facility administrator; b. 1947; Undergrad. degree, Macalester Coll.; M in Hosp. Adminstrn., U. Minn., 1973. Tchr., coord. master's degree program in hosp. adminstrn. U. Minn., 1974-76; v.p. corp. planning, v.p. managed and affiliated hosp. divsn. Fairfield Community Hosps., Mpls., 1976-81; COO Mid-Atlantic Health Group, 1981-83, adminstr. Monmouth Med. Ctr. Long Branch, N.J., 1981-83; ptnr., cons. Peat, Marwick, Main & Co., Mpls., 1984-88; chmn., pres., CEO Lutheran Health Systems, Fargo, N.D., 1988—.

**ORR, SUSAN PACKARD,** small business owner, foundation administrator; BA in Econs., Stanford U., 1968, MBA, 1970; MS in Computer Sci., N.Mex. Inst. Mining and Tech., 1984. Chmn. David and Lucile Packard Found., Los Altos, Calif.; CEO Telosa Software (formerly Tech. Resource Assistance Ctr.), Palo Alto, Calif., 1986—. Trustee Stanford U., 1998—. Office: The Packard Found 300 2nd St Ste 200 Los Altos CA 94022-3643

**ORR, TERRENCE S.,** dancer, ballet master, artistic director; b. Berkeley, Calif., Mar. 12, 1943; m. Cynthia Gregory (div.); m. Marianna Tcherkassky. Student, San Francisco Ballet Sch. With San Francisco Ballet, 1959-65; with Am. Ballet Theatre, NYC, 1965-97, soloist, 1967-72, rehearsal asst., 1970-73, prin. dancer, 1972-78, assoc. ballet master, 1973-78, ballet master, 1978-97; artistic dir. Pitts. Ballet Theatre, 1997—. Prodr. Royal Winnipeg Ballet, Nat. Ballet of Mexico, Teatro alla Scala in Millan, Nat. Ballet de Nancy in France, Teatro Colon in Buenos Aires, Pitts. Ballet Theatre, Boston Ballet, Ballet West, Dance Theatre of Harlem, N.Y.C. Ballet, Cleve./San Jose Ballet, San Francisco Ballet, Ballet Ariz., Sadler's Wells Royal Ballet, Paris Opera Ballet, Australian Ballet. Dancer (ballets) The Nutcracker, San Francisco Ballet, Fantasma, Divertissement d'Auber, Jeu des Cartes, Con Amore, Billy the Kid, Am. Ballet Theatre, Coppelia, La Fille Mal Gardee, Petrouchka, The River, Rodeo, Don Quixote, At Midnight, Dark Elegies, Fancy Free, Graduation Ball, Harbinger, Variations for Four, Pulcinella Variations, Brahms Quintet, Schubertiade, Mendelssohn Symphony, Polyandrion, Giselle, Swan Lake, La Sylphide, Gartenfest, Ontogeny; prodr., dir. Gala Performance, 1984; prodr.: La Sylphide, Rodeo; performer: Fancy Free; prodr.: Graduation Ball, Etudes, Billy the Kid, Fall River Legend, Giselle, Coppelia, Don Quixote, Swan Lake. Office: Pitts Ballet Theatre 2900 Liberty Ave Pittsburgh PA 15201-1511*

**ORR, ZELLIE,** entrepreneur, educator, writer, researcher; b. Holly Ridge, Miss., May 12, 1951; d. Leonard and Lucille Rainey; m. Foster G. Orr Jr., Feb. 28, 1976 (div. July 14, 1998); children: Kai A., Nia Haley. Student, L.A. City Coll., 1970—71, U. Calif., Northridge, 1971—73; cert., Airline Schs. Pacific, 1974, CMLS Inst., 1979; MA in Human Letters, U. Metaphysics, 1983. Cert. real estate salesperson, Ga., 1979, pub. notary, Ga, 1985. Personal lines underwriter Kemper Ins. Co., L.A., 1976—78, Comml. Union Ins. Co., Atlanta, 1980—82, Moore Group Ins. Co., Atlanta, 1982—85; lic. real estate agent Wofford Realty, Riverdale, Ga., 1979—85; owner Traffic Jam Lounge and Restaurant, Sunflower, 1986—89; documentation specialist Windsor Group, Atlanta, 1989—2001, mem. billing and collection mgmt. sys., 1991; pres., founder Comm. Unltd., Austell, Ga., 1995—. Mem. rsch. bd. advisors Am. Biog. Inst., Raleigh, NC, 1992—93. Co-author: Treasured Poems of America, 1989 (Editor's Choice award, 1989), The Best Poems & Poets of the 20th Century, 2000 (Editor's Choice award, 2000), Theatre of The Mind, 2003; author: numerous poems. Co-organizer Sunflower County Civil Rights and Cmty. Reunion, Indianola, 1999; founder Charles E. Scattergood Meml. Found., Marietta, Ga., 2000; mem. So. Poverty Law Ctr., Habitat for Humanity, Feed the Children. Recipient Cert. Appreciation, Superior Ct., Calif., 1976, Cert. Recognition, CME Ch., Indianola, 1999, Disting. Svc. award, Nat. Mus. of Tuskegee Airmen, 2004, Disting. Svc. and Dedication award, Alva N. Temple chpt. Tuskegee Airmen Inc., 2005, Presdl. award, Tuskegee Airmen, Inc., 2006. Mem.: NAACP, NAFE, Am. Metaphys. Drs. Assn., Nat. Trust Hist. Preservation, Nat. Mus. Women in Arts, Internat. Soc. Poets, Nat. Black MBA Assn. Avocations: stamp collecting/philately, reading, coin collecting/numismatics, antiques, chess. Home: 3285 Doyle Ln Marietta GA 30060 Office: Comm Unltd 3999 Austell Rd Ste 303 #158 Austell GA 30106 Personal E-Mail: orrs@artsonwheels.com. E-Mail: orrz@bellsouth.net.

**ORR-CAHALL, ANONA CHRISTINA,** museum director, art historian; b. Wilkes-Barre, Pa., June 12, 1947; d. William R.A. and Anona (Snyder) Boben; m. Richard Cahall. BA magna cum laude, Mt. Holyoke Coll., 1969; MA, Yale U., 1974, MPhil, 1975, PhD, 1979. Curator of collections Norton Gallery Art, West Palm Beach, Fla., 1975-77; asst. prof. Calif. Poly. State U., San Luis Obispo, 1978-81, Disting. prof., 1981; dir. art div., chief curator Oakland (Calif.) Mus., 1981-88; chief exec. officer Corcoran Gallery Art, Washington, 1988-90; dir. Norton Mus. Art, West Palm Beach, 1990—. Author: Addison Mizner: Architect of Dreams and Realities, 1974, 2d printing, 1993, Gordon Cook, 1987, Claude Monet: Am Impression, 1993; editor: The Art of California, 1984, The American Collection at the Norton Museum of Art, 1995. Office: Norton Museum of Art 1451 S Olive Ave West Palm Beach FL 33401-7162 Fax: 561-832-6529.

**ORRINGER, JEFFREY S.,** dermatologist, educator; b. Balt., Dec. 7, 1967; s. Mark B. and Susan M. Orringer; m. Kelly A. Orringer, May 1, 1994; children: Matthew J., Kate A. BA with honors, Brown U., 1990; MD, Harvard Med. Sch., 1994. Diplomate Am. Bd. Dermatology. Asst. prof. dept. dermatology, dir. Cosmetic Dermatology and Laser Ctr. U. Mich., Ann Arbor, 2002—. Contbr. articles to profl. jours. Patient-Directed Investigation grantee, Dermatology Found., 2001—02, Clin. Career Devel. grantee, 2002—05. Fellow: Am. Acad. Dermatology, Am. Soc. Dermatologic Surgery, Am. Coll. Mohs Micrographic Surgery and Cutaneous Oncology, Am. Soc. Laser Medicine and Surgery; mem.: Assn. Acad. Dermatologic Surgeons. Achievements include research in laser therapy and cosmetic dermatology. Office: U Mich Dept Dermatology 1500 E Medical Center Dr Ann Arbor MI 48109 Office Phone: 734 936 4193.

**ORRIS, DONALD C.,** freight transporation executive; b. BA, BS, Denver Univ. With Denver & Rio Grande We. Railroad; exec. positions, including pres., stacktrain and intermodal mktg. bus. APL; pres., COO So. Pacific R.R. (merged with Union Pacific R.R.); now chmn., CEO Pacer Internat., Concord, Calif. Named an Intermodal Founding Father, Univ. Denver Intermodal Transp. Inst. Office: Pacer Internat 2300 Clayton Rd Concord CA 94520 Office Phone: 887-917-2237.*

**ORRMONT, ARTHUR,** writer, editor; b. Albany, N.Y., July 3, 1922; m. Lora Orenstein, Oct. 6, 1956 (div. 1965); m. Leonie Rosenstiel, Aug. 22, 1995. Student, U. Ala., 1941, U. Mich., 1942-45, Cornell U., 1945; BA, U. Mich., 1945. Editl. dept. head Farrar, Straus & Co., N.Y.C., 1945-51; sr. editor Popular Libr., N.Y.C., 1951-55; exec. editor Fawcett Books, N.Y.C., 1955-57; pres., editl. dir. Author Aid Assocs., N.Y.C., 1967-97; v.p. Rsch. Assocs. Internat., N.Y.C., 1980-97; pres. Literary Cons., Albuquerque, 1997—. Lectr. creative writing CCNY, 1966, Columbia U., 1967; judge Hopwood Awards, U. Mich., 1999. Author: Love Cults and Faith-Healers, 1961, (with Capt. Marion Aten RAF) Last Train Over Rostov Bridge, 1962, Brit. edit., 1962, Indestructible Commodore Matthew Perry, 1962, Japanese edit., 1963, Amazing Alexander Hamilton, 1964, Portuguese edit., 1965, Master Detective: Allan Pinkerton, 1965 (Jr. Literary Guild selection), Chinese Gordon: Hero of Khartoum, 1966, Fighter Against Slavery: Jehudi Ashmun, 1966, Mr. Lincoln's Master Spy: Lafayette Baker, 1966, Diplomat in Warpaint: Chief Alexander McGillivray of the Creeks, 1967, Richard Burton, 1969, Brit. edit., 1969, James Buchanan Eads: The Man Who Mastered the Mississippi, 1970, (with Fr. Joseph Lauro) Action Priest, 1970, French edit., 1970, Requiem for War: The Life of Wilfred Owen, 1972; editor: (with Leonie Rosenstiel) Literary Agents of North America, 1984, 5th edit., 1995; editor Nat. Hall of Fame Biography series, 1970-72. With U.S. Army, 1942. Recipient Avery Hopwood award for short story U. Mich., 1943, 44, 45. Mem. Assn. Lit. Critics Scholars. Personal E-Mail: aokeet@earthlink.net.

**ORROCK, NAN,** state legislator; children: Jesse, Daniel. BA, U. Va., 1965. Mem. Ga. State Ho. of Reps., Atlanta, 1986—. Mem. Econ. Devel. Com., Indsl. Rels. Com., Ways and Means Com.; pres. Women Legislators' Lobby of WAND; past exec. dir. Fund for So. Cmties; bd. chair Ctr. for Policy Alternatives Exec. dir. Fund for So. Cmties. Mem. Unitarian Ch. Unitarian Ch. Home: 1070 Delaware Ave SE Atlanta GA 30316-2470 Office: Capitol Sq 612 Legislative Office Bldg Atlanta GA 30334 Office Phone: 404-656-0325. Business E-Mail: norrock@legis.state.ga.us.

**ORROCK, ROBERT DICKSON,** agricultural educator, state legislator; b. Fredericksburg, Va., Nov. 13, 1955; s. Welford and Cornelia (Houck) O.; m. Betsy Malinda Massey, Mar. 18, 1978; children: Robby, Lila, Welford. Student, Va. Poly. Inst. & State U., 1974-75, BS in Agrl. Edn., 1978; MS in Agrl. Edn., Va. State U., 1984-87; student, Germanna C.C., Locust Grove, Va., 1975-76. Agrl. edn. instr. Hanover County, Va., 1978, 86-91; vocat. edn. instr. Spotsylvania County, Va., 1978-85, 91—; sales rep. New Holland, Gordonsville, Va., 1985-86; announcer WFLS-Radio, Fredericksburg, 1988—. Vol. instr. Va. Game Commn.; past adv. bd. Rappahannock Electric Coop.; bd. mem. Rappahannock Emergency Med. Svcs. Coun., 1986—; mem. Ladysmith Vol. Rescue Squad, 1973—; deacon Bethany Bapt. Ch., Spotsylvania; treas. Caroline County (Va.) Rep Com., 1987-89; del. Va. Ho. Dels., Richmond, 1990—; bd. mem. Rappahannock Area Assn. Retarded Citizens, 1991—. Named Outstanding Educator, Tri-County Soil and Water Conservation, 1980-83, Va. State Dairyman's Assn., 1983, Va. Farm and Home Electrification Coun., 1987, named Outstanding Young Virginian, Va. Jaycees, 1994, Legislator of Yr., Va. Vocat. Assn., 1992; recipient Community Svc. award Fredericksburg Area Builders Assn., 1994. Mem. Va. Vocat. Agrl. Tchrs. Assn. (state pres. 1991-92). Republican. Baptist. Avocations: gardening, hunting, woodworking. Home: 12387 Nancy Wrights Dr Woodford VA 22580-2307

**ORSATTI, ERNEST BENJAMIN,** lawyer; b. Pitts., Nov. 14, 1949; s. Ernest Ubaldo and Dorothy Minerva (Pfeiffer) O.; m. Ingrid Zalman, May 3, 1975; 1 child, Benjamin E. BA, Marquette U., 1971; JD, Duquesne U., 1974; postgrad., Army Command and Gen. Staff Coll., 1984. Bar: Pa. 1974, U.S. Dist. Ct. (we. dist.) Pa. 1974, U.S. Ct. Appeals (3d cir.) 1977, U.S. Ct. Appeals (6th cir.) 1992, U.S. Ct. Appeals (4th cir.) 2006, U.S. Supreme Ct. 1978. Assoc. Jubelirer, Pass & Intrieri, Pitts., 1974-81, ptnr., 1981—. Contbg. editor: The Developing Labor Law, 4th edit., 1992—2002; chpt. editor The Developing Labor Law, 4th edit., 2002—; contbg. editor: Elkouri and Elkouri, How Arbitration Works, BNA, 2001—. Bd. dirs. Am. Italian Cultural Inst., Pitts., 1999—2004. Served to capt. U.S. Army, 1975, lt. col. USAR, ret. Mem. ABA, ACLU (legal com. 1996-2005), Am. Arbitration Assn., Pa. Bar Assn., Allegheny County Bar Assn. (profl. ethics com. 2000—), Am. Legion. Democrat. Roman Catholic. Home: 9343 N Florence Rd Pittsburgh PA 15237-4815 Office: Jubelirer Pass & Intrieri 219 Fort Pitt Blvd Pittsburgh PA 15222-1576 Office Phone: 412-281-3850. Personal E-Mail: eborsatti@aol.com. Business E-Mail: ebo@jpilaw.com.

**ORSILLO, JAMES EDWARD,** computer engineer, information technology executive; b. Elmira, N.Y., Oct. 30, 1939; s. Giacomo and Irene (Heppy) O.; 1 child, June Lynne. BEE, RCA Insts., 1962; BS in Elec. Engring. and Math., Ind. Inst. Tech., 1964; MS, Rensselaer Poly., 1968; BS in Nuclear Engring., Capital Radio Electronic Inst., 1974. Communications engr. Bell Telephone Labs., Holmdel, N.J., 1962-63; video engr. Westinghouse, Elmira, N.Y., 1965-66; computer engr. GE, Pittsfield, Mass., 1966-67; systems specialist Control Data Corp., Mpls., 1968-70; software specialist Computer Sci. Corp., Morristown, N.Y., 1970-72; prin. cons. Computer Cons. Assocs., Elmira, 1972-78; CEO ORTHSTAR, Inc., Elmira, 1974—; acquired Hughes Tng., Inc. Rail Simulation Bus., 1996—. Owner, pres. Shadowstand Properties, Inc. (FKA O-K Properties), Elmira, 1984—, Thundering Hooves Stables, Elmira, 1985—. Author: Mindstorm, 2004. Mem. IEEE, Am. Nuclear Soc., Soc. Indsl. and Applied Math., Am. Helicopter Soc., Army Aviation Assn. Am., Internat. Flying Engrs., USAF Assn., U.S. Naval League, U.S. Polo Assn. Republican. Achievements include invention of Integrated Data Acquisition System (IDAS), of Thread Algebra used in simulation development, of Extended Sentient Non-linear Ensemble (ESNE). Office: ORTHSTAR Inc Airport Corp Park PO Box 459 Big Flats NY 14814-0459 Office Phone: 607-562-2100. Business E-Mail: orsillo@orthstar.com.

**ORSINI, ERIC ANDREW,** military officer; b. Lodi, N.J., Jan. 7, 1918; s. Serafino and Valentina Lena (Dinino) O.; m. Mildred Jean Andre, Feb. 8, 1947; children: Donna Jean, Debra Jane. BS, Gen Edn. Devel., Fort Knox, Ky., 1948; student, Def. Sys. Mgmt. Coll., Ft. Belvoir, Va., 1978, Harvard U., 1982, George Washington U., 1986. Registered mech. engr. Commd. capt. armor U.S. Army, 1943, advanced through grades to col., 1965, transfer to Ordinance Corps., 1958, ret., 1971, appt. dep. asst. sec. for logistics, 1975—. Developer policy guidance mil. identification symbology technologies LOG-MARS, 1982; policy developer mil. ordnance/maintenance policies and procedures. Decorated Purple Heart, Silver Star, Bronze Star, Legion of Merit; named to Ordnance Hall of Fame, 1991; recipient Presdl. Meritorious Exec. award, 1991, 94, Logistics Emeritus award Nat. Security Indsl. Assn., 1999. Avocations: golf, fishing.

**ORSINI, ROSEMARY,** lawyer; b. Lodi, N.J., Aug. 21, 1955; d. Camillo Michael Orsini and Mary Margaret (Edell) Orsini. BA, U. Colo., Boulder, 1976; JD, U. Denver, Colo., 1992. Bar: Colo. 1993, Nebr. 1994, U.S. Dist. Ct.: Colo. 1994, U.S. Ct of Appeals: 10th Circuit 1998. Law clk. for justice Nebr. Supreme Ct., Lincoln, Nebr., 1993—94; shareholder Burg Simpson Eldredge Hersh & Jardine, P.C., Englewood, Colo., 1994—. Editor: U. Denver Law Review; contbr. Recipient Order of St. Ives, U. Denver, Coll. Law, 1993, Am. Jurisprudence awards in Administrative Law, Criminal Procedure, and Trusts and Estates. Fellow: Inns of Ct.; mem.: Interscholastic Trial Team, Plaintiff Emplyment Lawyers Assn., EEOC Liaison Com., Colo. Bar Assn., Nat. Employee Lawyers Assn., Arapahoe Bar Assn., Denver Bar Assn., Alzheimer's Assn., Phi Alpha Delta. Avocations: triathalon, mountain biking. Office: Burg Simpson Eldredge Hersh & Jardine P 40 Inverness Dr E Englewood CO CO Office Phone: 303-792-5595. Business E-Mail: rorsini@burgsimpson.com.

**ORSINI, TOM,** retired telecommunications company executive; Exec. v.p. Alltel Corp., Little Rock; ret., 1999. Office: Alltel Corp One Allied Dr Little Rock AR 72202 Address: 10 Town Plz Durango CO 81301-5104

**ORMSOND, GARETH IAIN,** lawyer, musician; b. Johannesburg, June 27, 1970; arrived in US, 1973; s. Garth Stanley and Patricia Maria Orsmond; m. Charlotte Mary Orsmond, Oct. 2, 1999; 1 child, Peter Kiran. BA, Yale U., 1992; JD, Lewis and Clark Coll., 1994; MusM in Jazz Performance, New Eng. Conservatory of Music, 1997. Bar: Mass. 1997, U.S. Dist. Ct. Mass. 2000. Atty. Rackemann, Sawyer and Brewster, P.C., Boston, 1998—. Contbr. chpt. to legal reference manual, articles to publs. Dir., clk. Westwood (Mass.) Land Trust, 2003—. Pub. Interest Law fellow, Northwestern Sch. Law, Lewis and Clark Coll., 1992—94. Mem.: ABA (natural resources, energy and environ. law sect.), Mass. Bar Assn. (property sect.), Urban Land Inst., Boston Bar Assn. (environ. law sect.). Office: Rackemann Sawyer & Brewster PC One Financial Center Boston MA 02111 Office Phone: 617-951-1117. Office Fax: 617-542-7437. Business E-Mail: gorsmond@rackemann.com.

**ORSON, BARBARA TUSCHNER,** actress; b. N.Y.C., May 19, 1929; d. Jonah Tuschner and Rebecca Traceman; m. Jay M. Orson, June 24, 1956; children: Beth-Diane, Theodore. Student, Dramatic Workshop, N.Y.C., 1948-50. Leading soubrette Am. Savoyards, N.Y.C., 1950-51, 53-55; actress Trinity Repertory, Providence, 1964-2002. Founding mem. Trinity Sq. Repertory Co., Providence, 1964—2001. Actress Edinburgh Festival, Scotland, 1968, Am. Repertory Theatre, Cambridge, Mass., 1981-85, Williamstown (Mass.) Theatre, 1985-89, Dallas Theatre Ctr., 1985, Yale Repertory Co., New Haven, Conn., 1991; appeared in: (films) Mission Hill, Code of Ethics, My One and Only, Swimming Upstream, Mr. North, Strangers in Transit (TV) theatre in America, Feasting with Panthers, Life Among the Lowly, House of Mirth, Camera Three, RI Demon Murder, Miller's Court, Conflict of Interest (Am. premiere) The Suicide, 1980, (world premiere) Grown Ups, 1981, God's Heart, 1995; founding mem., appeared in over 100 prodns. Trinity Sq.

Repertory Co., Providence, 1964—; (radio) House of Mirth, Masterpiece Radio Theatre with Jane Alexander; guest artist (Lady Macbeth), Brown U. Recipient Adrian Hall award, Trinity Repertory Co., RI, 2002. Mem. Am. Fedn. Radio and TV Artists, Screen Actors Guild, Actor's Equity Assn., Trinity Rep. Co. (founder). Home: 281 Hillside Ave Pawtucket RI 02860-6119

**ORSZAG, JONATHAN MARC,** economist, consultant; b. Boston, Apr. 15, 1973; s. Steven Alan and Reba Karp O.; m. Rica Rodman, June 17, 2000. AB, Princeton U., 1995; MSc, Oxford (Eng.) U., 1997. Econ. policy advisor The White House Nat. Econ. Coun., Washington, 1996-99; dir. policy and strategic planning U.S. Dept. Commerce, Washington, 1999—2000; mng. dir. Sebago Associates, Washington, 2000—, Competition Policy Assocs., Inc., Washington, 2003—. Mem. Calif. Workforce Investment Bd., Sacramento, 2000-03; mem. Calif. Tech. Adv. Group, Sacramento, 2000-03; adj. lectr. U. So. Calif., 2002-03. Recipient Leadership award, Corp. Enterprise Devel., 1999:, Marshall scholar, 1996. Mem. Pacific Coun. on Internat. Policy, L.A. World Affairs Coun., Asia Soc., Am. Econ. Assn., Am. Polit. Sci. Assn. Avocation: golf. Home: 5028 Warren St NW Washington DC 20016 Office: 1919 Pennsylvania Ave NW Washington DC 20006 Office Phone: 202-263-1444. E-mail: jorszag@competitionpolicy.com.

**ORSZAG, PETER RICHARD,** economist; b. Boston, Dec. 16, 1968; s. Steven Alan and Reba (Karp) O.; children: Leila Madeleine, Joshua Nathaniel AB summa cum laude, Princeton U., 1991; MS, London Sch. Econs., 1992, PhD, 1997. Econ. advisor Ministry of Fin., Moscow, 1992-93; staff economist Coun. Econ. Advisers, Washington, 1993-94; prof. rsch. staff London Sch. Econs., 1994-95; sr. economist Coun. Econ. Advisers, Washington, 1995-96, sr. adviser, 1996; sr. econ. advisor Nat. Econ. Coun., 1997, spl. asst. to pres for econ. policy, 1998; pres. Sebago Assocs., 1998—. Lectr. in econs. U. Calif., Berkeley, 1999—2000; rsch. assoc. Ctr. Retirement Rsch., Boston Coll., 2000—; Joseph A. Pechman sr. fellow in tax and fiscal policy The Brookings Instn., 2001—; co-dir. Tax Policy Ctr., 2003—; dir. Retirement Security Project, 2004—; rsch. prof. Georgetown U., 2005—; dir. The Hamilton Project, 2006—. Marshall scholar, 1991-92. Mem. Nat. Acad. Social Ins., Phi Beta Kappa. Office: The Brookings Instn 1775 Massachusetts Ave NW Washington DC 20036-2188 Business E-Mail: porszag@brookings.edu.

**ORSZAG, STEVEN ALAN,** applied mathematician, educator; b. N.Y.C., Feb. 27, 1943; s. Joseph and Rose (Siegel) O.; m. Reba Karp, June 21, 1964; children— J. Michael, Peter Richard, Jonathan Marc. BS, M.I.T., 1962; postgrad. (Henry fellow), St. John's Coll., Cambridge U., Eng., 1962-63; PhD, Princeton U., 1966. Mem. Inst. Advanced Study, Princeton, NJ, 1966—67; prof. applied math. MIT, 1967—84; prof. applied and computational math. Princeton U., 1984—98, dir., 1990—92, Hamrick prof. engring., 1989—98; Smith prof. math. Yale U., New Haven, 1998—, chmn. applied math., 1999—2003. Founder Flow, CHI, Ibrix, Inc., Vectek, Inc.; cons. in field. Author: Studies in Applied Mathematics, 1976, Numerical Analysis of Spectral Methods, 1977, Advanced Mathematical Methods for Scientists and Engineers, 1978; contbr. numerous rsch. publs. in field. A.P. Sloan Found. fellow, 1970-74, Guggenheim fellow, 1989-90. Fellow Am. Inst. Physics (Otto Laporte award 1991), AIAA (Fluid and Plasmadynamics award, 1986), Soc. Indsl. and Applied Math., Soc. Engring. Sci. (G.I. Taylor medal, 1995). Business E-Mail: orszag@math.yale.edu.

**ORTALDO, JOHN R.,** immunologist, researcher; b. West Chester, Pa., Apr. 22, 1945; BS, St. Francis Coll., Loretto, Pa., 1967; MS in Microbiology, Villanova U., 1969; PhD in microbiology/immunology, George Washington U., 1979. Mil. svc. in immunohematology Walter Reed Army Inst., 1969—71; microbiologist Dept. Agriculture, Dover, Del.; rsch. biologist Cellular and Tumor Immunology Sect., Lab. Cell Biology Nat. Cancer Inst., 1971, post-doctoral training Lab. Immunodiagnosis, named sr. investigator Lab Immunodiagnosis, 1980, head Natural Immunity Sect., Biol. Therapeutics Br. Frederick, chief Lab. Exptl. Immunology, 1985—. Mem.: Soc. Natural Immunology, Soc. Biol. Therapy, Reticuloendothelial Soc., Am. Assn. Immunology, Am. Assn. Cancer Rsch. Office: Lab Exptl Immunology Nat Cancer Inst at Frederick PO Box B Bldg 560 Rm 31-93 Frederick MD 21702-1201 Office Phone: 301-846-1323. Office Fax: 301-846-1673. E-mail: ortaldo@ncifcrf.gov.

**ORTEGA, MARIA A.,** security firm executive, educator; b. N.Y.C., Apr. 28, 1967; d. Humberto and Delia Margarita Ortega. BS, U. Chgo., 1992. Cert. Homeland Sec. Am. Coll. Forensic Examiners, 2003. Police officer N.Y.C. Police Dept., 1985—88; human resources mgr. Burns Internat. Security, N.Y.C., 1988—93; human resources mgr., dir. tng. Initial Security, N.Y.C., 1994—96; dir. human resources and tng. Command Security Svcs., N.Y.C., 1996—98; sr. program mgr. Opportunity Am., N.Y.C., 1998; pres., CEO Security Works Inc., N.Y.C., 1999—. Bd. dirs. N.Y. State Divsn. Criminal Justice Svc.; chmn. N.Y. State Divsn. Labor Latino JSEC, N.Y.C., 2000—. Named to Winner Circle, Burns Internat., 1989; recipient Rising Star award, N.Y. State Dept. Labor, 2000. Mem.: Nat. Assn. Chiefs of Police, ASIS Internat., Bklyn. C. of C. Avocations: basketball, music, reading, cooking. Office: Security Works Inc 41 Belknap Ave Yonkers NY 10710-5403 Office Phone: 718-780-4496.

**ORTEGO, GILDA BAEZA,** library director, educator; b. El Paso, Tex., Mar. 29, 1952; d. Efren and Bertha (Singh) Baeza; m. Felipe de Ortego y Gasca, Dec. 21, 1986. BA, Tex. Woman's U., 1974, PhD, 2001; MLS, U. Tex., 1976, postgrad., 1990-93; cert., Hispanic Leadership Inst., 1988. Stack maintenance supr. El Paso Pub. Libr., 1974-75; pub. svcs. libr. El Paso Community Coll., 1976-77; ethnic studies libr. U. N.Mex., Albuquerque, 1977-81; br. head El Paso Pub. Libr., 1981-82; dep. head Mex.-Am. Svcs., El Paso Pub. Libr., 1982-84; libr. Mex.-Am. Studies U. Tex. Libr., Austin, 1984—86; libr. Phoenix Pub. Libr., 1987-89; assoc. libr., west campus Ariz. State U., Phoenix, 1989-90; Proyecto Leer libr. Tex. Woman's U., Denton, 1991-92; dean divsn. learning resources Sul Ross State U., Alpine, Tex., 1992—99; dir. univ. libr., Tex. A&M U., Kingsville, 1999—. Speaker and cons. in field. Founding editor jour. La Lista, 1983-84; founding indexer Chicano Periodical Index, 1981-86; reviewer jour. Voices of Youth Advocates, 1988-90; contbr. poetry and articles to books and jours. Recipient Silver award, Nat. Commn. Library and Info. Sci., 1996. Mem. ALA (com. on standing of women in profession, com. on profl. edn.), MLA, Assn. for Libr. and Info. Sci. Edn., Tex. Libr. Assn., Ariz. State Libr. Assn. (pres. svcs. Spanish speaking Roundtable 1988-90), Reforma (pres. El Paso chpt. 1983, pres. Ariz. chpt. 1989-90, nat. v.p. 1993-94, natpres. 1994-95), Unltd. Potential, Inc. (treas. 1988-89), Hispanic Leadership Inst. Alumni Assn.

**ORTENBERG, ELISABETH CLAIBORNE See CLAIBORNE, LIZ**

**ORTENZIO, ROBERT A.,** health and medical products executive; V.p. Rehab Hosp. Svcs. Corp.; sr. v.p. Continental Med. Systems, Inc., Mechanicsburg, Pa., 1986—88, COO, 1988—95, pres., 1995—96; exec. v.p., dir. Horizon/CMS Healthcare Corp.; co-founder, pres., COO Select Medical, Mechanicsburg, Pa., 1997—2001, pres., 2001—04, CEO, 2001—. Bd. dir. US Oncology, Inc. Office: Select Medical 4716 Old Gettysburg Rd Mechanicsburg PA 17055 Office Phone: 717-972-1100.*

**ORTENZIO, ROCCO ANTHONY,** health facility administrator; b. Steelton, Pa., Nov. 28, 1932; s. Rocco and Minnie Ortenzio; m. Nancy Miller, Jan. 29, 1955; children: John, Robert, Martin. BS, West Chester U., 1955; postgrad., U. Pa., 1955—56. Pvt. practice phys. therapy, Harrisburg, Pa., 1957—69; founder, pres., CEO Rehab. Corp., Harrisburg, 1969—77, Pa. Health Corp., Mechanicsburg, Pa., 1977—79, Rehab. Hosp. Svc. Corp., Mechanicsburg, 1979—85; co-founder, chmn, CEO Continental Med. Sys., Inc. (merged with Horizon Healthcare Corp.), Mechanicsburg 1986—95, Select Medical, Mechanicsburg, Pa., 1997—2001, exec. chmn., 2001—. Bd.

**ORTIZ, ANGEL VICENTE,** church administrator; b. LA, Nov. 9, 1956; s. Benjamin and Petra (Santiago) O.; m. Michele Annette Gaunt, May 5, 1979; children: Angela Nicole, Michael David. BS in Bibl. Studies, Ft. Wayne (Ind.)

dirs. Continental Med. Sys., Inc., PNC, N.A., AMSCO Internat., Quorum Health Group, Inc. Mem.: World Pres. Orgn. Republican. Roman Catholic. Office: Select Material 4716 Old Gettysburg Rd Mechanicsburg PA 17055 Office Phone: 717-972-1100.

**ORTH, DAVID NELSON,** endocrinologist, educator, sculptor, potter; b. East Orange, N.J., Mar. 5, 1933; s. John Joseph and Marjorie Adelaide (Wauters) O.; m. Linda Diana D'Errico, June 9, 1979; children by previous marriage: John Randall (dec.), Jennifer Stewart, Julie Thomas. ScB in Chemistry, Brown U., 1954; MD, Vanderbilt U., 1962. Intern, Osler med. service Johns Hopkins Hosp., Balt., 1962-63, fellow in medicine, 1962-65; asst. resident John Hopkins Hosp., Balt., 1963-65; mem. faculty dept. medicine Vanderbilt U. Sch. Medicine, Nashville, 1965—, prof., 1975-98, prof. emeritus, 1998—, joint dir. endocrinology div. dept. medicine, 1968-81, dir. cancer research and treatment ctr., 1972-77, dir. div. endocrinology, 1984-96; sculptor and potter, 1998—. Scholar-in-residence Rockefeller Found. Bellagio Study and Conf. Ctr., Italy, 1989; vis. scientist Vollum Inst. for Advanced Biomed. Rsch., Oreg. Health Scis. U., Portland, 1993-94. Contbr. numerous articles in field of endocrinology to med. jours. Served with U.S. Navy, 1954-57. John and Mary R. Markle scholar, 1968-73; Howard Hughes Med. Inst. investigator, 1969-75 Mem. AAUP, AAAS, ACP, Assn. Am. Physicians, Am. Soc. Clin. Investigation, Endocrine Soc. (sec.-treas. 1989-94, pres. 1997-98), N.Y. Acad. Scis., Am. Fedn. Clin. Rsch., So. Soc. Clin. Investigation. Personal E-mail: orth@comcast.net.

**ORTINAU, DAVID JOSEPH,** marketing specialist, educator; b. Harvey, Ill., Dec. 14, 1948; s. Harold Raymond and Lois Agnice (Reich) O.; m. Shirley Keating, Aug. 15, 1975 (div. Nov. 1979); m. Renee Susan Hess, Apr. 30, 1983 (div. Aug. 1993). BS in Mgmt., So. Ill. U., 1970; MS in Bus. Adminstrn., Ill. State U., 1971; PhD in Mktg., La. State U., 1979. Sr. rsch. analyst, dir. projects Rabin Rsch. Co., Chgo., 1971-73; adminstrv. asst., instr. mktg. Coll. Bus., Ill. State U., Normal, Ill., 1973-76; grad. teaching assoc., instr. mktg. Coll. Bus., La. State U., Baton Rouge, Fla., 1976-79; from asst. prof. mktg. to assoc. prof. Coll. Bus., U. South Fla., Tampa, Fla., 1979-84; dir. mktg. and rsch. Market Rsch. Group, Tampa, Fla., 1980-83; assoc. prof. U. South Fla., Tampa, Fla., 1984-95, coord. PhD program dept. mktg., 1989-91, prof., 1995—. V.p. mktg. Neaves, Neaves and Ortinau, Normal, 1974-77. Co-author: Marketing Research: A Practical Approach in the New Millennium, 2000, Marketing Research: Within a Changing Information Environment, 2003, 3d edit., 2005; mem. editl. rev. bd. Jour. Acad. Mktg. Sci., 1989— (Disting. Merit award for Outstanding Reviewer 1992-93, Outstanding JAMS Rev. 1997-2000), Jour. Bus. Rsch., 2000— (Outstanding Editl. Rev. 2002); contbr. articles to profl. jours., including Jour. Acad. Mktg. Sci., Jour. Retailing, Jour. Bus. Rsch., Jour. Healthcare Mktg., Jour. Mktg. Edn., others. Recipient Disting. Merit award Advt. Fedn. SW Fla., 1983, Coba Outstanding Rsch. award U. South Fla., 1987, Outstanding Tchg. award, 1980, 81, 82, 86, 90, 95, 2001. Fellow Soc. for Mktg. Advances, 2001, (bd. dirs. 1998—, co-chair doctoral consortium 1998-99); mem. Am. Mktg. Assn. (doctoral consortium fellow 1978, keynote 1982—), Assn. Consumer Rsch., So. Mktg. Assn. (reviewer 1975—, chmn. 1976—, sec. 1990-91, treas. 1992-95, pres. elect 1995-96, pres. 1996-97, chmn. Svcs. Mktg. Customer Satisfaction Track Program 1990-92, co-chair doctoral consortium 1998, 99, Outstanding Articles award 1981, 86, 87, 90, 92), Soc. for Mktg. Advances Found. (bd. dirs., co-founder 2002—, pres. 2003—)Acad. Mktg. Sci. (reviewer 1988—, chmn. 1989, 92, Reviewer of Yr. 1992, session chair new tech. and retail store images at 1999, 2003 confs.), retailing svcs. mktg. track program chair, 2003, AMS conf. program co-chair 2004), Acad. Bus. Adminstrn. (track program chmn. 1993), Beta Gamma Sigma (pres. Fla. chpt. 1990-91). Avocations: sports, reading, gardening, the arts. Home: 2305 Windsor Oaks Ave Lutz FL 33549-5880 Office: U South Fla Mktg Dept Tampa FL 33620 Office Phone: 813-974-6236. Business E-Mail: dortinau@coba.usf.edu.

**ORTIQUE, REVIUS OLIVER, JR.,** retired judge; b. New Orleans, June 14, 1924; s. Revius Oliver and Lillie Edith (Gray) O.; m. Miriam Marie Victorianne, Dec. 29, 1947; 1 child: Rhesa Marie (Mrs. Alden J. McDonald). AB, Dillard U., 1947; MA, Ind. U., 1949; JD, So. U., 1956; LLD (hon.), Campbell Coll., 1960; LHD (hon.), Ithaca Coll., 1971; LLD (hon.), Ind. U., 1983, Morris Brown Coll., 1992, Loyola U. South, 1993, Dillard U., 1996, So. U. Law Ctr., 2005. Bar: La. 1956, U.S. Dist. Ct 1956, Eastern Dist. La 1956, U.S. Fifth Circuit Ct. of Appeals 1956, U.S. Supreme Ct 1964. Practiced in, New Orleans, 1956-78; judge Civil Dist. Ct. for Orleans Parish, 1978-92; assoc. justice La. Supreme Ct., 1993—94, ret., 1994; chmn. New Orleans Aviation Bd., 1994—2002. Lectr. labor law Dillard U., 1950-52, U. West Indies, 1986; formerly assoc. gen. counsel Cmty. Improvement Agy.; former gen. counsel 8th Dist. A.M.E. Ch.; former mem. Fed. Hosp. Coun., 1966, Pres.'s Commn. on Campus Unrest, 1970, Bd. Legal Svcs. Corp., 1975-83; chief judge civil cts. Orleans Parish, 1986-87; spkr. in field; U.S. alt. rep. to 54th Gen. Assembly UN, 1999-2000. Contbr. articles to profl. jours. Former pres. Met. Area Com.; former mem. Bd. City Trusts, New Orleans, New Orleans Legal Assistance Corp. Bd., Ad Hoc Com. for Devel. of Ctrl. Bus. Dist. City of New Orleans; bd. dirs. Cmty. Rels. Coun., Am. Lung Assn.; trustee Antioch Coll. Law, New Orleans chpt. Operation PUSH, 1981-84; pres. Louis A. Martinet Soc., 1959; active World's Fair, New Orleans, 1984, Civil Rights Movement, 1960-79; bd. dirs., exec. com. Nat. Sr. Citizens Law Ctr., L.A., 1970-76, Criminal Justice Coordinating Coun., UN Assn. New Orleans, 1980—; former mem. exec. bd. Nat. Bar Found.; mem. exec. com. Econ. Devel. Coun. Greater New Orleans; past chmn. Health Edn. Authority of La.; trustee, exec. com. Dillard U., 1965—; former mem. bd. mgmt. Flint Goodridge Hosp.; former adv. bd. League Women Voters Greater New Orleans; former men's adv. bd. YWCA; trustee AME Ch., former connectional trustee; former chancellor New Orleans Fedn. Chs.; bd. trustees Crimestoppers of New Orleans; mem. Com. for a Better New Orleans; bd. dirs. Nat. Legal Aid and Defender Assn.; trustee Civil Justice Found. 1st lt. AUS, 1943-47, PTO. Recipient Arthur von Briesen medal Disting. Svcs. Disadvantaged Ams. NLADA, 1971, Weiss award NCCJ, 1975, Brotherhood award NCCJ, 1976, Nat. Black Achievement award, 1979, Poor People's Banner award, 1979, His Personal Flag presented by 6 nat. poor people's groups at Nat. Client's Coun. Ann. Conv., San Diego, 1979, William H. Hastie award, 1983, Outstanding Citizen award Kiwanis of Pontchartrain, 1986, Civil Justice award, 1989, Daniel E. Byrd award NAACP, 1991, A.P. Tureaud Meml. medal La. State NAACP, 1993; Revius O. Ortique Jr. Law Libr. named in his honor, Lafayette, La., 1988; named Outstanding Young Man Nat. Urban League, 1958, Outstanding Person in La. Inst. Human Understanding, 1976, Citizen of Yr. Shreveport, 1993; named one of 100 Internat. Leaders as World Opinion Maker The Imperial Govt. of Japan, 1995. Mem. ABA (del., Legal Svcs. program, Nat. adv. coun., 1964-71, jud. divsn., Thurgood Marshall award 2000), Nat. Bar Assn. (pres. 1965-66, exec. bd., Raymond Pace Alexander award, jud. coun. 1987, William Hastie award 1982, Gertrude E. Rush award 1991, Thurgood Marshall award 2000), La. State Bar Assn. (former mem. ho. of dels., Lifetime Achievement award 1986, WTC award for Exceptional Internat. Distinction, 2001), Nat. Legal Aid and Defender Assn. (past pres., mem. exec. bd.), La. District Judges Assn., Am. Judicature Soc. (bd. dirs. 1975-79), Civil Justice Found. (trustee 1989-93), Louis A. Martinet Legal Soc., World Peace Through Law (charter mem.), Blue Key Honor Soc., Phi Delta Kappa, Alpha Kappa Delta. Home: 10 Park Island Dr New Orleans LA 70122-1229 *In 1989 the National Black Law Journal in cooperation with the UCLA Law Center published: Struggle: A Power Reserved to the People, which was distributed nationwide in commemoration of Black History month, the State of Louisiana thru the office of the Secretary of State has installed a life size portrait of Justice Ortique in the gallery of the State Archives, 1986-1994, 99. Appointed U.S. Alternate Representative to the 54th General Assembly of the United Nations, 2000. Delivered U.S. position on Taliban and terrorism before General Assembly. "With little or no effort on our part, life unfolds with opportunities and rewards, except that we permit our frailties to enslave our ambitions. I am grateful that there are only horizons.".*

Bible Coll., 1982. Ordained to ministry Christian and Missionary Alliance, 1987. Pastor, ch. planter Christian and Missionary Alliance, Chula Vista, Calif., 1983-90, supt. Spanish western dist. Escondido, Calif., 1991-96, also nat. conf. spkr., evangelist; asst. to the pres. for program devel. Nyack (N.Y.) Coll., 1996-97, v.p. student devel., dean students, 1997—2002; sr. pastor First Ch. Christian and Missionary Alliance, N.Y.C., 2002—. Republican. Mem. Christian And Missionary Alliance Ch. Avocations: camping, woodworking, refinishing, travel, teaching. Office Phone: 212-604-0300. Business E-Mail: angelortiz@firstchurchnyc.org.

**ORTIZ, ANTHONY,** hotel executive; b. Bronx, Feb. 19, 1969; s. Tony Ortiz and Elizabeth Mercado; m. Iris Elizabeth Alvarado, July 24, 1994; children: Tristan, Tyler. Student, Rockland C.C., Camden County Coll. Mgr. ops. Park Ridge Marriott, NJ, 1994—96, Newport Marriott, RI, 1996—98; event mgr. Walt Disney World, Orlando, 1998—2000; mgr. ops. Marriott Hotels, Phila., 2000—01, Sodexho, Vourhees, NJ, 2001—; pres., founder Deep Blue Films, Blackwood, NJ, 2003—. Avocations: reading, writing, movies. Office: 524 Neptune Bay #5248 Saint Cloud FL 34769 Office Phone: 407-929-2164.

**ORTIZ, ANTONIO IGNACIO,** public relations executive; b. Mexico City, Feb. 22, 1961; came to U.S., 1988; s. Antonio and Sylvia (Vega) O.; m. Socorro Chinolla, June 12, 1982. B of Bus., Autonoma U. Baja Calif., Tijuana, 1984. With acctg. dept. Bank of Atlantic, Tijuana, 1979-83; mgr. Aldaco, Tijuana, 1983-84; dir. pub. rels. Oh! Laser Club, Tijuana, 1984-88, Iguanas, Tijuana, 1988-90, Euebe, S.A., Tijuana, 1990-2000, R. Noble Enterprises, La Jolla, Calif., AAP, Inc., Chula Vista, Calif., SPD Transport Inc., Chula Vista. Cons. R.P. Noble Enterprises, La Jolla, Ca.; dir. pub. rels. R. Noble Enterprises, La Jolla, Calif., Chula Vista, Calif., 2000-; gen. ptnr. SPD Transport, Inc., Chula Vista, Calif., 2001-. Avocation: swimming. Home: PO Box 431859 San Diego CA 92143-1859 Office: 482 W San Ysidro Blvd #642 San Ysidro CA 92173

**ORTIZ, DAVID (DAVID AMERICO ORTIZ ARIAS),** professional baseball player; b. Santo Domingo, Dominican Republic, Nov. 18, 1975; Player Minn. Twins, 1997—2002, Boston Red Sox, 2003—. Mem. Dominican Republic Team, World Baseball Classic, 2006. Named ALCS MVP, 2004; named to Am. League All-Star Team, 2004, 2005, 2006; recipient Silver Slugger award, MLB, 2005, Hank Aaron Award, 2005. Achievements include being a member of World Series Champion Boston Red Sox, 2004. Office: Boston Red Sox 4 Yawkey Way Boston MA 02215-3496*

**ORTIZ, FELIX W.,** state legislator; b. La Playa de Salinas, P.R. m. Elba Ortiz; children: Felix, Daniel, Alberto. Student, U. P.R.; BS in Bus. Adminstrn., Boricua Coll., 1983; M in Pub. Adminstrn., NYU, 1986. Sr. budget analyst Office of Mgmt. and Budget, Adminstrn. of Criminal Justice, N.Y.C., 1988-90; adminstrv. mgr. Office of Mgmt. and Budget, Office of Bronx Borough Pres., 1990-95; assemblyman dist. 51 N.Y. State Assembly, Albany, 1995—. Mem. Cmty. Bd. 7, Bklyn., chair pub. safety com.; pres. 33d St. Block Assn., Nat. Hispanic Caucus State Legis.; mem. 72d Precinct Cmty. Coun.; mem. parish coun. Our Lady of Perpetual Help; mem. parent edn. task force Diocese of Bklyn.; mem. Sunset Park Health coun. Luth. Med. Ctr; bd. mem. Nat. Assn. Latino Elected and Appointed Officials. Served with U.S. Army, 1986-88. Mem.: Nat. Conference of State Legis. (NCSL), Council State Gov. (CSG). Office Phone: 518-455-3821.

**ORTIZ, FERNANDO, JR.,** commissioner; b. Havana, Cuba, Dec. 2, 1951; came to the U.S., 1961; m. Frances K. Ortiz; children: William, Fernando III. Attended, Miami-Dade C.C., 1972—74, U. Miami, Coral Gables, Fla., 1974—75, Fla. Internat. U., Miami, 1975—76; MD, U. Centro Estudios Technicos, Santo Domingo, Dominican Republic, 1981; postgrad, Syracuse U., postgrad., 1998—. Mgr. Ortiz Transp., Miami, 1981-84; ptnr. Astram, Syracuse, NY, 1984-91; bus. developer Rebuild Syracuse, Inc., 1991-92; coord. Urban Bus. Opportunity Ctr. City of Syracuse, 1992-96, sr. econ. devel. officer, 1996-2000, budget dir., 2000-01, commr. cmty. devel., 2001—. Mem. adv. bd. Greater Syracuse Small Bus. Loan Program, 1993-99; bd. dirs. Consol. Industries, Inc., Child Care coun. of Onondagy County; mem. educare com. Success By Six, 2000. Sec. bd. dirs. Onondaga Spanish Action League, Syracuse, 1994-95, 2003, pres., 1996-2000; Cultural Resources Coun., 1997-2000; active Onondaga Citizens League, Syracuse, 1995; bd. dirs. Syracuse Neighborhood Housing Svcs., 1997-2000, Met. Water Bd., 1998—, Leadership Greater Syracuse, 2000—, Jubilee Homes, 2001—; corp. mem. United Way Ctrl. N.Y.; mem. bus. and industry adv. bd. Onondaga C.C.; mem. Leadership Greater Syracuse Class of '93, alumni bd. dirs., 4-H mentor, 2001—; active F.O.C.U.S. Greater Syracuse, 1997—; sec. Syracuse Urban Renewal Agy.; bd. dirs. Syracuse Econ. Devel. Corp. Named Min. Small Bus. Adv. of Yr., U.S. SBA, Syracuse, 1995. Mem. Thursday Morning Roundtable. Avocations: reading, gardening, music. Home: 1412 Lemoyne Ave Syracuse NY 13208-1339 Office: City of Syracuse Dept Cmty Devel 201 E Washington St Rm 612 Syracuse NY 13202 Office Phone: 315-448-8620. Personal E-mail: fortiz@twcny.rr.com. Business E-Mail: fortiz@ci.syracuse.ny.us.

**ORTIZ, GUILLERMO,** banker; BA, Universidad Nacional Autonoma de Mexico; PhD Economics, Stanford U. Economist Ministry of the Presidency of Mex., 1971—72; mgr. & deputy mgr. Econ. Rsch. Bureau of Bank of Mex., 1977—84; exec. dir. IMF, 1984—88; undersecretary of finance and public credit, 1988—94; sec. telecommunications and transportation Zedillo Adminstrn.; sec. finance and public credit Mexican Fed. Govt., 1994—97; gov. Bank of Mex., 1998—. Instr. Univ. in Mex. and U.S. Author: books and papers on econ. and finance in specialized jour. and mag. Mem.: G-30. Office: Governor Banco de Mexico Avda 5 de Mayo 2 Centro 06059 Mexico City Mexico Office Phone: 5-237-2030. E-mail: gortiz@banxico.org.mx.

**ORTIZ, JAIME,** business educator; b. Santiago, Chile, Jan. 20, 1958; s. Sergio Ortiz and Pilar Arizabalo; m. Pamela Caballero, June 20, 1987; children: Maria Pamela, Maria Alejandra. BSc, U. Chile, Santiago, 1980, Diploma, 1981; MA, Inst. Social Studies, The Hague, The Netherlands, 1988; PhD, Va. Poly. Inst. and State U., 1993. Freelance bus. and econ. cons., Santiago, 1980—82; econ. analyst Inter-Am. Inst. Cooperation on Agriculture, Ecuador, 1983—85; mgmt. advisor Ecumenical Ch. Loan Fund, Quito, 1985—87; rsch. asst. dept. applied econ. Va. Tech. U., 1989—93; team leader Euroconsult B.V., Quito, Ecuador, 1994—95; sr. advisor COASER, Quito, 1995—96; internat. coord. Pre-investment Orgn. OPALC, Quito, 1996—97; gen. coord. Intern Am. Devel. Bank, Quito, 1997; faculty, dir. internat. programs Fla. Atlantic U. Coll. Bus., Boca Raton, 1998—; prof., exec. dir. internat. edn. William Paterson U., 2004—; assoc. v.p. internat. programs, prof. Tex. A&M Internat. U. Sr. mgmt. cons. Abastefrut S.A., Santiago, 1994, World Bank, Quito, 1995, GTZ gmbH, Quito, 1995, Inter Am. Devel. Bank, Caracas, Venezuela, 1996 Author: Small-scale Agriculture: Its Evolution in Ecuador, 1988, Small and Medium Enterprises as an Alternative to Macroeconomic Adjustments, 1997; contbr. articles to profl. jours., including Jour. Internat. Devel., Econ. Devel., Microfin., Am. Acad. Bus., Food Policy. Roman Catholic. Office: Tex A&M 5201 University Blvd Laredo TX 78041 E-mail: jortiz@tnniu.edu.

**ORTIZ, JOHN MICHAEL,** provost; BS, U. N.Mex., 1970, MA, 1971; PhD, U. N.C., 1981. Spl. edn. tchr., Albuquerque, 1969-72; instr. Appalachian State U., Boone, N.C., 1972, asst. prof. dept. spl. edn., 1972-75, assoc. prof. grad. faculty dept. spl. edn., 1976-81, interim dept. chair, assoc. dean grad. faculty, 1982-83, dept. chair, prof. grad. faculty, 1983-85, dir. Office Extension Instrn., prof. lang., 1985-90; prof. spl. edn., dean continuing edn., dir. summer sch. U. Southern Colo., 1990-93, assoc. provost, prof. spl. edn., 1993-95, interim provost, prof. spl. edn., 1995-96; assoc. provost, prof. spl. edn. Calif. State U., Fresno, 1996-97, provost, v.p. acad. affairs ad interim, prof. spl. edn., 1997-99, provost, v.p. acad. affairs, 1999—2003; pres. Calif. State Poly. U., Pomona, 2003—. Cons., evaluator North Ctrl. Assn. of Colls. and Scis., 1995-97; pres. N.C. Fedn. of the Coun. for Exceptional Children, 1984-85, state advisor 1979-80; spl. advisor Pres. Com. on Mental Retardation; presenter in field. Contbr. articles to profl. publs. Recipient numerous grants. Mem. ASCD, Am. Assn. of Higher Edn., Nat. U. Continuing Edn. Assn., Am.

Assn. for Adult and Continuing Edn., Assn. of the Severely Handicapped, Coun. for Exceptional Children. Office: Calif State U 5241 N Maple Ave MSTA 54 Fresno CA 93740-0001 Fax: 559-278-7987.

**ORTIZ, JOSEPH VINCENT,** chemistry professor, department chairman; b. Bethpage, N.Y., Apr. 26, 1956; s. José Vicente and Mary Davies (Bryant) O.; m. Karen Fagin, Dec. 16, 1979. BS, U. Fla., 1976, PhD, 1981. Rsch. fellow Harvard U., Cambridge, Mass., 1981-82; postdoctoral fellow Cornell U., Ithaca, N.Y., 1982-83; asst. prof. U. N.Mex., Albuquerque, 1983-89, assoc. prof., 1989-94, prof., 1994-96, Kans. State U., Manhattan, 1996—2004, dist. prof., 2004—; Ruth W. Mowlette prof. and chmn. chemistry and biochemistry Auburn U., Ala., 2006—. Mem. editl. adv. bd. Internat. Jour. Quantum Chemistry, 1994—98, 2001—, Jour. Chem. Physics, 2006—. Contbr. articles to profl. jours. Am. Soc. Engring. Edn. sr. rsch. fellow, 1986, 87; Assoc. We. Univs. rsch. fellow, 1991. Mem. AAAS, AAUP, Am. Chem. Soc., Am. Phys. Soc., Internat. Soc. for Theoretical Chem. Physics, World Assn. Theoretically Oriented Chemists. Achievements include development and applications of propagator theory in quantum chemistry; elucidation of electronic structure of anions, biomolecules, polymers, organometallics and clusters. Office: Auburn U Dept Chemistry and Biochemistry 179 Chemistry Bldg Auburn University AL 36849-5312 Office Phone: 334-884-4043.

**ORTIZ, MAYRA ZOE,** psychologist; b. Rio Piedras, Puerto Rico, Feb. 2, 1962; d. Guillermo Ortiz and Mirriam Cruz. PsyD, Yeshiva U., 2002. Lic. Psychologist NY. Psychologist Lincoln Med. Ctr., NY, 2001—02; psychologist, pvt. practice Bronx Lebanon Hosp., NY, 2002—04, Indsl. Medicine Assocs., 2004—. Mem.: NY State APA, APA.

**ORTIZ, PATRICK T.,** lawyer; b. 1950; BA, Coll. Santa Fe; JD, Georgetown U. Bar: N.Mex. 1976. Dep. gen. counsel ins. dept. N.Mex. State Corp. Commn., gen. counsel; asst. atty. gen. energy and utilities sect. Atty. Gen.'s Office, N.Mex.; staff counsel N.Mex. Public Svc. Commn., chief commn. counsel, commr.; atty. Mountain States Telephone & Telegraph Co.; chief counsel U.S. West Comm.; sr. v.p., gen. counsel, sec. PNM Resources, Albuquerque, 1991—. Bd. dirs. N.Mex. Bar Bus. Law Sect.; corp. exec. bd. Gen. Counsel Roundtable. Bd. trustees PNM Found.; pro bono counsel Challenge N.Mex.; bd. dirs. Archdiocese Santa Fe Catholic Found., Nat. Hispanic Cultural Ctr. Found. Named one of Most Influential Hispanics, Hispanic Bus. Mag. Mem.: Oliver Seth Am. Inn of Ct. (master of bench), Edison Elec. Inst. (mem. legal com.), Am. Gas Assn. (mem. legal com.). Office: PNM Resources Inc Alvarado Sq MS2822 Albuquerque NM 87158-0001

**ORTIZ, SOLOMON PORFIRIO,** congressman; b. Robstown, Tex., June 3, 1938; children: Yvette, Solomon P. Cert., Inst. Applied Sci., Chgo., 1962; student, Del Mar Coll., Corpus Christi, Tex., 1965—67, Nat. Sheriff's Tng. Inst., LA, 1977. Constable Neuces County, Tex., 1965—68, commr. Tex., 1969-76, sheriff Tex., 1977—83; mem. US Congress from 27th Tex. dist., 1983—, mem. resources com., mem. armed svcs. com., ranking minority mem. readiness subcommittee, dean Congl. Hispanic Caucus. Served in 61st Mil. Police Co. U.S. Army, 1960—62. Named Man of Yr., Internat. Order Foresters, 1981, one of Hispanic Bus. 100 Most Influential Hispanics in US, Hispanic Bus. Mag., 1999. Mem. Nat. Sheriff's Assn., Sheriff's Assn. Tex. Democrat. Office: US Ho Reps 2470 Rayburn Ho Office Bldg Washington DC 20515-4327 Office Phone: 202-225-7742.*

**ORTIZ, WILLIAM,** composer, music educator; b. Salinas, P.R., Mar. 30, 1947; s. William and Guillermina (Alvarado) O.; m. Candida, Mar. 26, 1988; children: Aleyda Enid, Nicole Samara, Amaya E. MusB, P.R. Conservatory of Music, 1976; MA in Composition, SUNY, Stony Brook, 1978; PhD in Composition, SUNY, Buffalo, 1983. Cons./auditor N.Y. State Arts Coun., N.Y.C., 1976-86; asst. dir. Black Mountain Coll. II, Buffalo, 1982-86; music advisor P.R. Symphony Orch., San Juan, 1988-90; prof. music U. P.R., Bayamon, 1986—; dir. humanities dept. U. P.R., Bayamon, 1997—. Dir./conductor, U. P.R. Band, Bayamon, 1986—, Grammy award nomination, 2001; music critic San Juan Star, 1993-94; composer-in-residence for Music-in-Motion program Atlantic Ctr. for the arts, 1996-97; artist-in-residence René Marquez Mid. Sch., 1999-2000. Composer: 124 E. 107th St., 1979 (Felipe Gutierrez Internat. Composition prize 1980), Llego la Banda, 1984 (Composers Guild Internat. Composition prize 1981), Dos Gritos y una Cancion, 1986 (Composition award Ateneo Puertorriqueno 1989), Tropicalizacion, 1999 (Grammy nomination 2001), others. Assoc. mem. Hispanic Womens League, Buffalo, 1982-86. Recipient commns. P.R. Symphony, San Juan, 1990, Camerata Caribe, San Juan, 1990, grants Inst. of Puerto Rican Culture, San Juan, 1990, P.R. Community Found., San Juan, 1990; Casals Festival, 1995, Orquesta Baja California, Mex., 1999, 2001; guest composer Festival Musica Nova, Sao Paulo, Brazil, 1988, Festival Latinoamericano de Musica, Caracas, Venezuela, 1991, 92, 94, 98, Am. Composers Orch. "Sonidos de las Americas," 1997, VIII Tribuna Musical para América Latina, Mex., 1997, Festival Iberoamericano de las Artes, 2004, 06. Mem. Am. Composers Alliance, Am. Music Ctr., Coll. Music Soc., Composers Alliance of Buffalo (pres. 1984), Assn. de Compositores Puertorriquenos. Home: Plaza de La Fuente 1275 Calle España Toa Alta PR 00953 Office: U PR Bayamon Gardens Sta Bayamon PR 00959 Office Phone: 787-786-2885. Personal E-mail: williamortizupr@yahoo.com.

**ORTIZ-BUTTON, OLGA,** social worker; b. Chgo., July 12, 1953; d. Luis Antonio and Pura (Acevedo) Ortiz; m. Dennis Vesley, Aug. 11, 1973 (div. 1976); m. Randall Russell Button, Nov. 3, 1984 (div. Oct. 1993); children: Josh, Jordan, Eli. BA, U. Ill., 1975; MSW, Western Mich. U., 1981. Cert. social worker sch. social worker, lic. master social worker, bd. cert. diplomate Am. Bd. Clin. Social Workers, 2005, Am. Bd. Clin. Social Workers, 2006. Social svcs. dir. Champaign County Nursing Home, Urbana, Ill. 1976; social svcs. and activity dir. Lawton (Mich.) Nursing Home, 1977; job developer Southwestern Mich. Indian Ctr., Watervliet, 1977-78; staff asst. New Directions Alcohol Treatment Ctr., Kalamazoo, 1978; counselor, instr. Alcohol Hwy. Safety, Kalamazoo, 1978-79; clin. social worker Mecosta County Community Mental Health, Big Rapids, Mich., 1981-84; program dir. substance abuse Sr. Svcs., Inc., Kalamazoo, 1984-85; sch. social worker Martin (Mich.) Pub. Schs., 1985-96, J.C. Huizenga Charter Schs., Grand Rapids, Mich., 1996—; owner, therapist Plainwell (Mich.) Counseling Ctr., 1989-98; co-dir. Everlasting Covenant Ministry, Kalamazoo, 1997—2003; owner Christian Counseling Ctr. PLC, 2004—. S.W. cons. Med. Pers. Pool, 1993-94; founder, owner Christian Coun. Ctr., 2003—. Vol. social worker Hospice-Wings of Hope, Plainwell, 1984-85; mem. Hospice Quality Rev. Bd., 1993-96; supporter Students Against Aparteid South Africa, Kalamazoo, 1979-81; mem. World Vision and Countertop Ptnr., 1984-90; mem., vol. Christian Life Ctr., Kalamazoo, 1996; sponsor, vol. People for Ethical Treatment of Animals, 1986-91; vol. helper Sparkies for Awana Club Ch., 1989-95; consortium mem. Mich. Post Adoption Svc. System, 1994-97; co-founder Everlasting Covenant Ministry, Kalamazoo, 1997; sch. social worker Nat. Heritage Acads., 1997-2004; founder Christian Counseling Ctr., 2002. Rural Mental Health grantee, NIMH, 1979—81. Mem.: NASW, Nat. Assn. Christian Social Workers, Am. Assn. Christian Counselors, Mich. Assn. Sch. Social Workers. Avocations: walking, gardening, cross country skiing. Home: 1339 Cadet Ln Kalamazoo MI 49009-1838 Office Phone: 269-343-2117. Personal E-mail: obutton@ureach.com.

**ORTIZ-CRUZ, BETHZAIDA,** physician, educator; b. Ponce, PR, Aug. 31, 1974; d. Manuel Antonio Ortiz-Correa and Ramonita Cruz-Roche; m. Armando Rivera-Santiago, June 13, 1998; 1 child, Amanda Rivera-Ortiz. BS, U. PR, Cayey, 1996; MD, Ponce Sch. Medicine, 2000. Diplomate Am. Bd. Family Medicine, 2003. cert. added qualifications in geriatric medicine Am. Bd. Family Medicine, 2004. Family medicine resident U. PR, Trujillo Alto, 2000—03; geriatric medicine physician San Lorenzo Family Medicine Ctr., PR, 2002—04; asst. prof. Ponce Sch. Medicine, 2004—; geriatric medicine physician PR Veterans Home, Juana Diaz, 2004—. Med. Com. Interns and Residents, San Juan, 2000—01; cmty. medicine and geriatric divsn. coord. Ponce Sch. Medicine, 2004—, mem. curriculum com. for the second yr.; geriatric cons. Cooperativa de Seguros de Vida de PR, San Juan, 2005—; mem. admissions com. family practice residency U. PR, Trujillo Alto; presenter in field. Contbr. articles to newspapers. Recipient Family Medicine Dept. Recognition award, Ponce Sch. Medicine, 2000, Family Medicine Residency Hospitalist Recognition award, U. PR Family Practice Residency, 2003, First prize Clin. Sci. Category, 2005; scholar Exceptional Fin. Need for Students with Interest in Primary Care, US Dept. Edn., 1998—2000. Mem.: AMA (Physician Recognition award 2004), Soc. Tchrs. Family Medicine, Am. Geriatric Soc., Am. Acad. Family Physicians. Roman Catholic. Avocations: reading, cooking, travel. Office: Ponce School of Medicine PO Box 7004 Ponce PR 00732 Office Phone: 787-840-0052. Office Fax: 787-848-1306. Business E-Mail: bortiz@psm.edu.

**ORTIZ RUIZ, AIDA M.,** university administrator, educator; d. Higinio and Joaquina (Ortiz) O.; m. William Ruiz; 1 child, Philip. BA, U. P.R., 1971; MA, NYU, 1973; MEd, Columbia U., 1988. Tchr. N.Y.C. Bd. Edn., 1972-74; instr. English Queens Coll., N.Y.C., 1974-78; lectr. English Hostos Community Coll., Bronx, N.Y., 1978-83, asst. dean of faculty, 1984-86, assoc. dean of academic affairs, 1988-91; coord. freshman yr. programs CUNY, 1991-93, assoc. dean academic affairs, 1998—2000. Mem. test of std. written English com. Coll. Bd., 1985-90; reader SAT Composition, GMAT, TOEFL-Test of Written English, 1990—; mem. coun. internat. edn. CUNY, 1989—, United Way campaign fund drive, 1990-95, mem. chancellors task force on writing, 1984-88, chair CUNY task force on transfer and articulation; grants administr. Title III, Vocat. Edn. Act, Ford Univ. C.C. Transfer Opportunity Program, Diamond Found. grant Minority Project for Tchg. Professions, 1993-95, Gear Up/BEA steering com., 1999—; CUNY coord. univ. skills immersion program, 1991-93; coord. Hostos Coordinated Freshmen Yr. Program, 1996—2002; bd. dirs. China Exch. Program; mem. Writing Across the Curriculum com. CUNY; cert. reader CUNY ACT and CUNY Coll. proficiency exam, 2000-06. Contbr. articles to profl. jours. Mem. Inst. for P.R. Policy, N.Y.C., 1986—, CUNY Women's Coalition, 1984—. Fellow Ford Found., 1971-73. Fellow ASCD, Acad. Affairs Adminstrs., Coll. Compositions and Comm., TESOL, Assn. Tchrs. English, Acad. for Humanities and Scis. Avocations: multi-ethnic literature, new media tech., Latino/U.S. literature. Office: Hostos Community Coll 500 Grand Concourse Bronx NY 10451-5323 Office Phone: 718-518-6769. Personal E-mail: aida.ruiz@mail.com. Business E-Mail: aortizruiz@hostos.cuny.edu.

**ORTIZ-WALTERS, ROWENA,** management educator; d. Ortiz and Rivera; m. Carl Allan Walters, May 14, 1999; 1 child, Ethan Andrew Walters. BS Chemistry, U. Conn., 1996; MBA, U. New Haven, 1999; PhD Mgmt., U. Conn., 2005. Chemist Uniroyal Chem. Corp., Middlebury, Conn., 1996—99; instr. bus. mgmt. U. Conn., Storrs, 2000—; asst. prof. entrepreneurship Quinnipiac U., 2004—. Asst. dir. Wolff Family Program in Entrepreneurship, Storrs, 2000—; pres. Mgmt. Doctoral Student Assn., 2001—02; advisor Quinnipiac U. Entrepreneurial Success team; presenter in field. Contbr. articles to profl. jours. Named Best Teaching Asst. of Yr., U. Conn., 2002, Best Student Tchr. of Yr., 2003; Summer Rsch grant, Quinnipiac U., 2005. Mem.: Mgmt. Doctoral Student Assn., Ea. Acad. Mgmt., Acad. Mgmt. Assn. (chair mentoring com., Best Symposium award 2004). Avocations: hiking, snowshoeing, reading, travel. Personal E-mail: rowena.ortiz-walters@quinnipiac.edu.

**ORTLIP, PAUL DANIEL,** artist; b. Englewood, NJ, May 21, 1926; s. Henry Willard and Aimee (Eschner) O.; m. Mary Louise Krueger, June 1981 (dec. May 2001); children from previous marriage: Carol, Kathleen, Sharon (dec.), Danielle (dec.), Michele. Diploma, Houghton Acad., 1944; student, Art Students League, 1947—49; diploma, Acad. la Grande Chaumiere, Paris, 1950; DFA (hon.), Houghton Coll., 1988. Tchr. Fairleigh Dickinson U., Teaneck, NJ, 1956-68, artist in residence, curator Rutherford, NJ, 1968-72. Official USN artist on assignment, Cuban missile crisis, Fla., 1963, Gemini 5 Recovery, Atlantic Ocean, 1965, Vietnam, 1967, Apollo 12 recovery, Pacific Ocean, 1969, Apollo 17 recovery, Pacific Ocean, 1972, Internat. Naval Rev., NY harbor, 1976, USCG Sta., Key West, Fla., 1985; mem. USN Art Coop. and Liason Com. Exhbns. include Salonde L'Art Libre, Paris, 1950, Nat. Acad. Design, 1952, Allied Artists of Am., NYC, Acad. Sci., Rundell Gallery, Rochester, NY, Montclair Art Mus., Hist. Mus, Lima, Ohio, Butler Art Inst., Youngstown, Ohio, Fine Arts Gallery, San Diego, State Capitol Bldg., Sacramento, Capitol Mus., Olympia, Wash., Mus. Gt. Plains, Lawton, Okla., Witte Meml. Mus., San Antonio, Nimitz Meml. Mus., Fredericksburg, Tex., Pentagon Collection of Fine Arts, James Hunt Barker Galleries, Palm Beach, Fla., Nantucket, Mass., NYC, Smithsonian Inst., Gallerie Vollem Breuse, Biarritz, France, Galerie Mouffe, Paris, Guggenheim Gallery, London, Wickersham Gallery, NYC, Soc. Illustrators, NYC; retrospective exhbn. Bergen Cmty. Mus., Paramus, NJ 1970, The Curzon Gallery, 1987, 88, 89, 93, 2003, Ardennes et de l'Eifel, Charleville Mézières, France, June-Sept. 1990; represented permanent collections including Salmagundi Club NYC, Houghton Coll., NY, Portrait Meml. J.F. Kennedy Life-, Fairleigh-Dickinson U., Nat. Air and Space Mus., Smithsonian Inst., Intrepid Sea-Air Space Mus., NYC, Hist. Mural Visitors Ctr., Palisades Interstate Pk., Ft. Lee, NJ, Vets. Med. Ctr., East Orange, NJ, USN Exhbn. Ctr., Washington Navy Yard, Am. Coll. Clin. Pharmacology, NYC, NJ U. Dentistry & Medicine, Newark, Bergen County Ct. House, Hackensack, NJ, Dickinson Coll., Carlisle, Pa., George Washingtogn Meml. Pk., Paramus, Marietta Coll., Ohio, Mcpl. Bldg., Ft. Lee, Navy League US, Arlington, Va., Nat. Archives and Records Adminstrn., Washington, (mural) Pub. Libr., Fort Lee, Bush Presdl. Libr., College Station, Tex., Underwater Demolition Team Seal Mus., Fort Pierce, Fla., Lynn U., Boca Raton, Fla. Served to sgt. U.S. Army, 1944-47, ETO, PTO, 1946-47. Recipient 1st prize Am. Artists Profl. League State Exhibit NJ chpt., Paramus, 1960, 1st prize U.S. Armed Forces Exhibit Far East, Seoul, Korea, Tokyo, 1946, Franklin Williams award, Salmagundi Club, NY, 1967, Outstanding Achievement award for oil painting, UBN, 1968, Artist of Yr. award, Hudson Artists, Jersey City Mus., 1970, Statue of Victory World Culture prize, Academia Italia, Parma, 1982, Men of Achievement medal Cambridge, Eng., 1990, Connaissance de Notre Europe Gold medal Charleville-Mézières, France, 1990. Mem. Allied Artists Am. (art coop. and liaison com. with USN), Nat. Soc. Mural Painters, Nat. Soc. Arts and Letters, Bergen County Artists Guild (pres. 1960-62), Portrait Soc. Am., Inc., Artists Fellowship, Inc., USCG Art Program, Art Students League NY (life), Navy League U.S., VFW (life), Am. Legion, Salmagundi Club (NYC, art chmn. 1979-81), Gov.'s of the Palm Beaches Club (Fla.). Office: Four Generations Art Gallery Paul D Ortlip Studio PO Box 4150 Vineyard Haven MA 02568 Office Phone: 508-693-5501. Business E-Mail: paulortlip@fourgenerationsart.com.

**ORTLOFF, GEORGE CHRISTIAN, SR., (CHRIS ORTLOFF),** journalist, state legislator; b. Lake Placid, NY, Sept. 20, 1947; s. Carl Jacob and Lillian Grace (Travis) O.; m. Ruth Mary Hart, Jan. 28, 1978; children: George Christian Jr., Jonathan Hart. BS, Rensselaer Poly. Inst., 1969; MA, U. Mich., 1975. Reporter, producer Sta. WUOM-FM, Ann Arbor, Mich., 1973-75; reporter Nat. Pub. Radio, 1973-75, Adirondack Daily Enterprise, Saranac Lake, NY, 1976-77, Sta. WNBZ-Am, Saranac Lake, 1975-77; pub. rels. dir. Ctr. for Music, Drama and Art, Lake Placid, 1975-76; pres. Macromedia, Inc., Lake Placid, 1976-82; anchor, mng. editor Sta. WPTZ-TV, Plattsburgh, NY, 1981-85; mem. N.Y. State Assembly, Albany, 1985—, ranking minority mem. Legis. Commn. on Sci. and Tech., 1987—, chmn. Rep. program com., 1993-98, vice-chair Rep. conf., 1999—2002, ranking minority mem. legis. task force redistricting, 1998—, mem. higher edn. budget com., 1998—, dep. minority whip, 2002, asst. minority leader, 2002—. Mem. health and human svcs. task force Am. Legis. Exch. Coun., 1994-97; N.Y. state chmn., 1997. Author: Lake Placid, The Olympic Years: 1932-80, 1976, A Lady in the Lake, 1985; reporter, producer (TV news series) "Special Segment", 1981-85 (N.Y. State Broadcasters Best Series award 1982, 83, 84, 85), (TV documentary) "A Time to Choose", 1985 (N.Y. State Broadcasters Best award 1986). Chief ceremonies 1980 Olympic Winter Games, Lake Placid, 1978-80; field asst. to congressman David O'B. Martin, Plattsburgh, 1981; chmn. Clinton County Rep. Com., 1995-2002; committeeman Essex County Rep. Com., 1980-81, NY Rep. State Com., 2003-; district com. mem. Plattsburgh City Repub. Com., 2003-; trustee Lake Placid Village, 1977-81, Olympic & Winter Sports Mus., 1980-84, Battle of Plattsburgh Assn., 1998-2001, St. Lawrence

Aquarium and Ecol. Ctr., 1997-2001, Adirondack Mus., 2001—; lay reader Episcopal Ch., Lake Placid and Plattsburgh, 1976-92. Mem. VFW, AMVETS, Am. Legion, North Vietnam Vets. Assn., Elks, Kiwanis (pres. Lake Placid 1980-81). Avocations: skiing, piano, trumpet, painting, woodworking. Home: 23 Morrison Ave Plattsburgh NY 12901-1417 Office: NY State Assembly 448 Legislative Office Bldg Albany NY 12248-0001 Office Phone: 518-455-5943. Business E-Mail: ortlofc@assembly.state.ny.us.

**ORTLUND, ANNE (ELIZABETH ANNE ORTLUND),** writer, musician; b. Wichita, Kans., Dec. 3, 1923; d. Joseph Burton and Mary Elizabeth (Weible) Sweet; m. Raymond Carl Ortlund, Apr. 27, 1946; children: Sherrill Anne, Margot Jeanne, Raymond Carl, Nels Robert. Student, Am. U., 1941—43; AA, Am. Guild Organists, 1944; MusB, U. Redlands, Calif., 1945. Organist Old-Fashioned Revival Hour and Joyful Sound, Radio World-Wide, 1960—75; spkr. Orgn. Renewal Ministries, Newport Beach, Calif., 1980—; composer hymns, anthems N.Y.C., 1963—77. Composer: Macedonia, 1966. 250 hymns; author: Up with Worship, 1975, Disciplines of the Beautiful Woman, 1977, The Gentle Ways of the Beautiful Woman, 1998, How Great Our Joy, 2001, Up With Worship, rev. and updated, 2001, A Fresh Start for Your Friendships, 2001; author: (with Raymond Carl Ortlund) The Best Half of Life, 1976, Discipling One Another, 1979, Children Are Wet Cement, 1981 (Christie award Christian Booksellers Assn., 1982), Joanna: A Story of Renewal, 1982, Building a Great Marriage, 1984; author: (with Raymond C. Ortlund) Staying Power, 1986, Disciplines of the Heart, 1987, Renewal, 1989, Confident in Christ, Disciplines of the Home, 1990, Fix Your Eyes on Jesus, 1991, My Sacrifice His Fire, 1993, In His Presence, 1995, Lord, Make My Life a Miracle, rev. and updated, 2002. Named Profl. Woman of Yr., Pasadena Bus. and Profl. Women, 1975; recipient SESAC award, Gospel Musicians, 1978. Home: 601 Lido Park Dr Apt 6E Newport Beach CA 92663-4403 Office: Renewal Ministries 4500 Campus Dr Ste 662 Newport Beach CA 92660-8828 Office Phone: 949-756-1313. E-mail: anne@ortlund.org.

**ORTMAN, DON L.,** principal; b. Battle Creek, Iowa, June 12, 1968; s. Lee Ortman and Peggy Fick. BA, Buena Vista U., Storm Lake, Iowa, 1991; MEd, N.W. Mo. State U., 1995. Tchr. Griswold CSD, Iowa, 1991—97; prin. Rock Valley CSD, Iowa, 1997—. Choir dir. Pioneer Meth. Ch., Rock Valley, Iowa. Recipient Outstanding Tchr. award, Aksarben, 1995, Prin. of Yr., Iowa, 2003, Adminstr. of Yr., Iowa Character Counts, 2005. Mem.: Sch. Adminstrs. Iowa, Iowa Reading Assn. (pres.). Home: 1222 Tenth Ave Rock Valley IA 51247 E-mail: dortman@nsd.org.*

**ORTMAN, GEORGE EARL,** artist; b. Oakland, Calif., Oct. 17, 1926; s. William Thomas and Anna Katherine (Noll) O.; m. Conni Whidden, Aug. 5, 1960 (dec.); 1 stepson, Roger Graham Whidden. Student, Calif. Coll. Arts and Crafts, 1947-49, Atelier Stanley William Hayter, 1949, Acad. Andre L'Hote, Paris, 1949-50, Hans Hoffman Sch. Art, 1949-50. Co-founder Tempo Playhouse, NYC, 1954; Instr. painting and drawing NYU, 1962-65; co-chmn. fine arts Sch. Visual Arts N.Y.C., 1963-65; artist-in-residence Princeton U., 1966-69, Honolulu Acad. Art, 1969; head painting dept. Cranbrook Acad. Art, Bloomfield Hills, Mich., 1970-92. One-man exhbns. include Tanager Gallery, 1954, Wittenborn Gallery, 1955, Stable Gallery, 1957, 60, Howard Wise Gallery, 1962, 63, 64, 66, 69, Gimpel-Weitzenhoffer Gallery, 1972 (all N.Y.C.), Swetzoff Gallery, Boston, 1961-62, Fairleigh Dickinson U., 1962, Mirvish Gallery, Toronto, Can., 1964, Walker Art Center, Mpls., 1965, Milw. Art Center, 1966, Dallas Mus. Art, 1966, Portland Mus. Art, 1966, Akron Inst. Art, 1966, U. Chgo., 1967, Princeton U. Art Mus., 1967, Honolulu Acad. Art, 1969, Reed Coll., 1970, Cranbrook Acad. Art, 1970, 92, Indpls. Mus. Art, 1971, J.L. Hudson Gallery, Detroit, 1971, Gimpel-Weitzenhoffer, N.Y.C., 1972, 73, Gertrude Kasle Gallery, Detroit, 1976, Lee Hoffman Gallery, Detroit, 1977, Flint (Mich.) Mus. Art, 1977; other one-man exhbns. include Cranbrook Mus. Art, 1982; exhibited numerous group shows including Whitney Mus. Am. Art Annual, 1962, 63, 64, 65, 67, 73, Carnegie Internat., Pitts., 1964, 67, 70, Jewish Mus., N.Y.C., 1964, Corcoran Mus., Washington, 1964, others; represented permanent collections, Walker Art Center, Mpls., Mus. Modern Art, Whitney Mus. Am. Art, (both N.Y.C.), Guggenheim Mus., N.Y.C., Albright-Knox Mus., Buffalo, NYU, Christian Theol. Sem., Indpls. Mus. Art, Cleve. Mus. Art, Mus. Am. Art, Washington, Honolulu Acad. Art, Newark Mus. Art, Container Corp. Am., Chgo. Ind. U. Music Bldg., Wausau (Wis.) Hosp. Center, Unitarian Ch., Princeton, Mfr. Hanover Trust Bldg., Albert Kahn & Assocs., Detroit, Renaissance Center, Detroit, Mich. State Univ. Performing Arts Ctr., East Lansing, Detroit Inst. Arts. Guggenheim fellow, 1965-66; Ford Found. grantee, 1966, Lee Krasner Found. grantee; One of five Am. artists selected for 1965 Japanese Bi-ann.; recipient Gov. N.J's Purchase award 2d ann. exhbn. art, 1967, Krasner Found. award, 2003; Best of Show Religion in Art Exhbn., Birmingham, Ala. 1966. Mem. Nat. Acad. of Design. also: Tim Hill Gallery 1527E 72d St Apt 12H New York NY 10021 Office Phone: 212-794-6551.

**ORTMEYER, CARL EDWARD,** retired demographer; b. Charles City, Iowa, Mar. 12, 1915; s. Arthur Herman and Sarah Emilie (Stoeber) O.; m. Anne Babuska O'Brien, Aug. 3, 1947 (dec. Dec. 15, 1995); 1 child, Kerry Michael; m. Ruth Forberg, Oct. 5, 1996. BA, U. Iowa, 1939; MS, Iowa State U., 1948, PhD in Rural Sociology, Demography, 1954. Rsch. assoc. bur. pub. health econs. Sch. Pub. Health U. Mich., Ann Arbor, 1954—56; sociologist Legis. Reference Svc., Libr. Congress, Washington, 1956—57; rsch. assoc. Social Security Adminstrn. U.S. Dept. HEW, 1957—58; rsch. assoc. Sch. Medicine Howard U., 1958—59; demographer Nat. Ctr. Health Statistics Pub. Health Svc. U.S. Dept. HEW, 1959—68, demographer Nat. Inst. Occpl. Safety and Health CDC, 1968—80. Vol. caregiver Benedictine Nursing Ctr., Mt. Angel, Oreg., 1990-96, Wesley Homes Health Ctr., Des Moines, Wash., 1996—; mem. Wesley Found., Ams. for Democratic Action. Sgt. U.S. Army, 1941-45. Travel grantee London Sch. Econs. Rockefeller Found., 1969. Fellow APHA AAAS, mem. N.Y. Acad. Sci. Democrat. Mem. United Meth. Ch. Avocation: dance. Home: 4532 Intelco Loop SE Woodland Ret 336 Lacey WA 98503 Personal E-mail: rortmeyer@aol.com.

**ORTNER, DONALD J.,** biological anthropologist, educator; b. Stoneham, Mass., Aug. 23, 1938; s. A.W. and Marie B. (Schweizer) O.; m. Joyce E. Walker, Sept. 4, 1960; children: Donald J. Ortner Jr., Allison A. May, Karen L. Ortner. BA, Columbia Union Coll., 1960; MA, Syracuse U., 1967; PhD, U. Kans., 1970; DSc (hon.), U. Bradford, England, 1995. Asst. curator Smithsonian Instn., Washington, 1969-71, assoc. curator, 1971-76, curator, 1976—, chmn. anthropology, 1988-92; acting dir. Nat. Mus. Natural History, Washington, 1994-96. Vis. prof. U. Bradford, 1988—; pres. Paleopathology Assn., 1999—2001. Author: (book) Identification of Pathological Conditions in Human Skeletal Remains, 1981, 2d edit., 2003; editor: How Humans Adapt, 1983; co-editor: Human Paleopathology, 1991. Mem. Am. Assn. Phys. Anthropology (mem. exec. com. 1987-90), Internat. Skeletal Soc., Paleopathology Assn. Office: Smithsonian Inst Nat Mus Natural History 10th & Constitution Ave NW Washington DC 20560-0001 Business E-Mail: ortner@si.edu.

**ORTNER, EVERETT HOWARD,** magazine editor, writer; b. Lowell, Mass., Aug. 25, 1919; s. Herman and Anne (Ehrenhaus) O.; m. Evelyn Frances Gelbman, Jan. 1, 1953. BA, U. Ark., 1939. Editor Popular Publs., N.Y.C., 1945-52; assoc. editor Popular Sci., N.Y.C., 1953-56, copy chief, 1956-70, group editor, 1970-76, mng. editor, 1976-80, editor, 1980-85. Pres. Brownstone Revival Coalition N.Y., 1968-76, chmn., 1986-2002, chmn. emeritus, 2002; founder, pres. Back to the City, Inc., N.Y., 1974-83, chmn. bd., 1983—; v.p. L.I. Hist. Soc., Bklyn., 1979-83; chmn. bd Preservation Vols. Inc., 2000—. L. U.S. Army, 1942-46, ETO. Recipient Cinderella award Bklyn. Union Gas Co., 1978, Honor citation Borough Pres. Bklyn., 1983, Disting. Citizen award City Louisville, 1979, Quality of Life award Kings County Hosp. Ctr. Bklyn., 1976, Spirit of Life award N.Y. Congl. Home, 1994, Excellence in Hist. Preservation award Preservation League NY State, 2002, Grassroots Preservation award Hist. Dists. Coun., 2002, Lifetime Achievement award Victorian Soc. in Am., 2005, Disting. Alumni award U. Ark., 2006, Lucy G. Moses Preservation award N.Y. Landmarks Conservancy, 2006. Mem. Overseas Press Club, Montauk Club, Ft. Hamilton Officers Club. Home: 272 Berkeley Pl Brooklyn NY 11217-3904

**ORTOLANO, RALPH J.,** engineering consultant; b. Phila., Apr. 12, 1931; BS in Marine Engring., U.S. Mcht. Marine Acad., 1954; MBA, Santa Clara U., 1969. Registered profl. engr., Calif. Engring. watch officer USN, 1954-56; sr. design engr. marine divsn. Westinghouse, Lester, Pa., 1956-64, Sunnyvale, Calif., 1964-69; mgr. project engring. corp. cost recovery dept. Litton Ship Systems, Inc., L.A., 1969-72; consulting engr., scientist So. Calif. Edison Co., Rosemead, Calif., 1972-92, chief cons., 1993—. Formed Turbine RESCUE, 1984; cons. more than 100 power cos., numerous others, U.S. and abroad; presenter seminars in the field. Contbr. more than 100 articles to profl. jours.; holder 22 U.S. patents in field. Recipient William R. Gould award SCE, 1992, Meritorious Alumni Svc. award USMMAAA, 1989, Outstanding Profl. Achievement award USMMAAA, 1994; named to USMMA Athletic Hall of Fame, 1990; USMMA rifle range named Ortolano Rifle and Pistol Range in honor of being selected to 1952 and 1953 All-Am. Rifle Teams, and 1952-54 All-Am. Pistol Teams, 1999. Fellow ASME (life, past dir. ASME-SCAC power chpt., past chmn. steam turbine com., past chmn. power divsn., mem. exec. com., co-chmn. steam turbine course 1984-99, George Westinghouse Gold medal 1991, past chmn. EEI steam turbine crack prevention task force). E-mail: turbinerescue@msn.com.

**ORTON, COLIN GEORGE,** medical physicist; b. London, June 4, 1938; came to U.S., 1966; s. Frederick G. and Audrey V. (Sewell) O.; m. Barbara G. Scholes, July 25, 1964; children: Nigel, Susanne, Philip. BS in Physics with honors, Bristol U., 1959; MS in Radiation Physics, London U., 1961, PhD in Radiation Physics, 1965; MA (hon.), Brown U., 1976. Diplomate Am. Bd. Radiology, Am. Bd. Med. Physics. Instr. London U. St. Barts' Hosp., 1961-66; assoc. prof. NYU Med. Ctr., 1966-75, Brown U., RI, 1975-81; prof., chief physicist Wayne State U., Harper Hosp., Detroit, 1981—2003. Dir. grad. program Wayne State U., 1981-2003. Author: Radiation Physics Review Books I, 1971, II, 1978; editor: Electron Treatment Planning, 1978, Progress in Medical Physics I, 1982, II, 1985, Radiation Dosimetry, 1986; editor Medical Physics, 1997-2004. Recipient Marie Curie Gold medal Health Physics Soc., 1987. Fellow Am. Assn. Physicists in Am. (pres. 1981, William D. Coolidge award 1993), Am. Coll. Med. Physics (chmn. 1985, Marvin D. Williams award, 1997), Inst. Physics London, Am. Coll. Radiology; mem. Internat. Orgn. for Med. Physics (sec. gen. 1988-94, pres. 1997-2000), Am. Brachytherapy Soc. (pres. 2001-02), Internat. Union Physics and Engring. Sci. in Medicine (pres. 2003-06, Merit award 2003). Avocations: golf, badminton, tennis, running, squash. Home: 15810 Lakeview Ct Grosse Pointe Park MI 48230-1806 Office Phone: 313-823-8079. E-mail: ortonc@comcast.net.

**ORTON, GEORGE FREDERICK,** aerospace engineer; b. Flushing, NY, Aug. 8, 1941; s. Harry and Evelyn (Brostrom) O.; m. Susan K., Dec. 21, 1962; children: Karen, Kevin, Kristen. BS in Aero. Engring., U. Md., 1964; MS in Engring. Mechanics, St. Louis U., 1971. Engr. propulsion McDonnell Douglas Co. (now The Boeing Co.), St. Louis, 1964-73, sr. engr. propulsion, 1973-77, unit chief propulsion, 1977-81, sect. chief propulsion, 1981-86, br. chief nat. aerospace plane, 1986-90, staff dir. nat. aerospace plane, 1990-92, dir. space programs, 1992-93, program mgr. Hypersonics Ctr. Excellence, 1993—, mem. air force sci. adv. bd., 2000—02. Mem. adv. bd. Ga. Inst. Tech., 1998—; guest lectr. USAF Acad., 2000—. Contbr. articles to profl. jours. Advisor Explorer Post 9005, St. Louis, 1980-87; sci. advisor University City (Mo.) Schs. Named to Acad. Disting. Alumni, U. Md., 2003; recipient Silver award, Boeing, 2004, world speed record for X-43A. Fellow AIAA (assoc., mem. liquid propulsion tech. com. 1980-84, 91-96, mem. hypersonics program com. 1994—, Best Paper award 1986), St. Louis Head Injury Assn. Methodist. Achievements include patent for propellant acquisition device for zero-g engine starts, patent for propellant resupply system, NASA technology cash award for work on shuttle auxiliary propulsion. Office: The Boeing Co PO Box 516 Mailcode S 2454055 Saint Louis MO 63166-0516 Office Phone: 314-232-7548. E-mail: george.f.orton@boeing.com.

**ORTON, KYLE,** professional football player; b. Nov. 14, 1982; s. Byron. BA in History, Purdue Univ., 2005. Quarterback Chgo. Bears, 2005—. Recipient Big Ten Offensive Player Yr, Sporting News, 2004. Office: Chgo Bears 1000 Football Dr Lake Forest IL 60045 Office Fax: 847-295-6600.*

**ORTTUNG, WILLIAM HERBERT,** chemistry professor; b. Phila., June 16, 1934; s. Elmer Herbert and Rosalind Orttung; married; children: Robert W., Mark. H. SB, MIT, 1956; PhD, U. Calif., Berkeley, 1961. Asst. prof. chemistry Stanford (Calif.) U., 1960-63, U. Calif., Riverside, 1963-69, assoc. prof., 1969-79, prof., 1979-94; emeritus prof., 1994—. Mem. AAAS, Am. Chem. Soc., Am. Phys. Soc. E-mail: worttung@att.net.

**ORUGUNTA, RAVEENDRA BABU,** pediatrician; s. Penchalaiah and Kamakshmamma Orugunta; m. Ramadevi Nanga, Mar. 30, 1994; children: Pranay, Abhinay. MB, BS, Sri Venkateswara U., Tirupati, India, 1991; MD in Pediat., U. of Health Scis., Andhra Pradesh, India, 1995; MD, Bklyn. Hosp. Ctr., 2005. Sr. resident physician in neurology Sri Venkateswara Inst. of Med. Scis., Tirupati, Andhra Pradesh, India, 1995—96; locum intern med. officer in pediatric emergency rm. Bustamante Hosp. for Children, Kingston, Jamaica, 1996—96; sr. resident med. officer in pediat. Savanna-La-Mar Pub. Gen. Hosp., Westmoreland, Jamaica, 1996—2002; house staff in pediat. (resident) The Bklyn Hosp. Ctr., 2002—04, chief resident in pediat., 2004—05; staff physician in pediat. Wyckoff Heights Med. Ctr., Bklyn., 2005—, attending pediatrician in pediatric emergency rm., 2005—. Mem.: Am. Acad. of Pediat. (assoc.). Home: 190 72nd St Apt 182 Brooklyn NY 11209 Office: Wyckoff Heights Med Ctr 374 Stockholm St Brooklyn NY 11237 Office Phone: 718-963-7272. Personal E-mail: orugunta@yahoo.com.

**ORULLIAN, B. LARAE,** bank executive; b. Salt Lake City, May 15, 1933; d. Alma and Bessie (Bacon) O. Cert., Am. Inst. Banking, 1961, 63, 67; grad. Nat. Mortgage Sch., Ohio State U., 1969-71; DHL (hon.), Whittier Coll., 2004. With Tracy Collins Trust Co., Salt Lake City, 1951-54, Union Nat. Bank, Denver, 1954-57; exec. sec. Guaranty Bank, Denver, 1957-64, asst. cashier, 1964-67, asst. v.p., 1967-70, v.p., 1970-75, exec. v.p., 1975-77, also bd. dirs.; chair, CEO, pres. The Women's Bank N.A., Denver, 1977-97, Colo. Bus. Bankshares, Inc., 1980-97; vice chmn. Guaranty Bank and Trust Co., Denver, 1997—, pres., bd. dirs. Lange Golf Co., Holladay (Utah) Bank; vice-chmn. bd. dirs. Frontier Airlines; bd. dirs. KBDI Channel 12TV; trustee Delta Dental Colo., 2005—. Treas. Girl Scouts U.S.A., 1981-87, 1st nat. v.p., chair exec. com., 1987-90, nat. pres., 1990-96; 1st vice chair world bd. World Assn. Girl Guides Girl Scouts, London. Recipient Woman Who Made a Difference award Internat. Women's Forum, 1994, Ultimate Woman of Colo. award, 2005, Women Enterprise award U. Denver, 2005; named to Colo. Women Hall of Fame, 1988; named Colo. Entrepreneur of Yr., Inc. Mag. and Arthyr Young and Co., 1989, Woman of Yr., YWCA, 1989, Citizen of Yr., EMC Lions Club, 1995, laureate Colo. Bus. Hall of Fame, 1999. Mem. Bus. and Profl. Women Colo. (3d Century award 1977, Unique Woman of Colo. 2005, Colo. Woman of Enterprise 2005), Internat. Women's Forum, Com. of 200. Independent. Latin Ch. Home: 6650 W 10th Pl Denver CO 80214 Office Phone: 303-296-9600.

**ORVICK, GEORGE MYRON,** religious organization administrator, minister; b. Hanlontown, Iowa, Jan. 9, 1929; s. George and Mabel Olina (Mandsager) O.; m. Ruth Elaine Hoel, Aug. 25, 1951; children: Daniel, Emily, Mark, Kirsten. AA, Bethany Luth. Coll., Mankato, Minn., 1948, candidate of theology, 1953; BA, Northwestern Coll., Watertown, Wis., 1957; postgrad., U. Wis. Ordained to ministry Evang. Luth. Synod, 1953. Pastor Our Saviour Luth. Ch., Amherst Junction, Wis., 1953-54, Holy Cross Luth. Ch., Madison, Wis., 1954-69; cir. visitor Evang. Luth. Synod, Mankato, 1964-69, v.p., 1969—70, pres., 1970—76, 1980—2002, dir. dept. archives and history, 2002—; bd. regents Bethany Luth. Coll., 1957—69. Author: Our Great Heritage, 1966; columnist: The Luth. Sentinel, 1982-2002. Lutheran. Home: 224 Terrace Dr Mankato MN 56001-4728 Office: Evang Luth Synod 6 Browns St Mankato MN 56001-6121 Office Phone: 507-344-7308. Business E-Mail: gorvick@blc.edu.

**ORVIS, KATHRYN S.,** science educator; m. John Orvis. BS - Botany and Lyman Briggs, Mich. State U., 1995; MS Plant Breeding and Genetics, U. Wis., 1997, PhD of Plant Breeding and Genetics, 2000. Grad. rsch. asst. U. Wis., Madison, 1995—2000; asst. prof. Dept. Youth Devel. and Agr. Edn., Horticulture and Landscape Arch. Purdue U., West Lafayette, Ind., 2000—. State coord. Jr. Master Gardener(R) Program, 2001—; state ext. specialist for plant related programs Ind. 4H Youth, West Lafayette, 2000—. Advisor (peer-reviewed jour. article) Genomics Analogy Model for Educators:from jumping genes to alternative splicing, A teaching model for biotechnology and genomics education. Grantee Outreach for Apple Functional Genomics Project, NSF, 2003—05. Mem.: AAAS, Am. Horticulture Soc., Nat. Assn. Ext. 4H Agts., Am. Soc. Horticulture Sci. Office: Purdue University 615 W State St West Lafayette IN 47907-2053

**ORWIG, MATTHEW DANE,** prosecutor, lawyer; b. Ardmore, Okla., Jan. 2, 1959; s. Richard R. and Mary E. (Pyle) O.; m. Melissa L. Vaughan, July 11, 1981; children: Joshua Matthew, Rachel Elizabeth, Jacob Andrew. BS, Tex. Tech. U., 1981, JD, 1984. Bar: Tex. 1985, U.S. Dist. Ct. (no. dist.) Tex. 1985, U.S. Ct. Appeals (5th cir.) 1985. Legal intern for no. dist. Tex. US Dept. Justice, Dallas, 1983; briefing atty. for judge US Dist. Ct., Lubbock, Tex., 1984-86; ptnr. Jones, Flygare, Galey, Moody and Brown, Lubbock, 1986-89; asst. US atty. (ea. dist.) Tex. US Dept. Justice, Dallas, 1989—2001, US atty. (ea. dist.) Tex., 2001—. Adj. prof. So. Meth. U. Law Sch., 1990—, Tex. Wesleyan U. Sch. Law, 1990—; legal advisor Exec. Office of U.S. Atty., Office of Legal Counsel, 1997—. Mem. ABA, State Bar Tex., Lubbock County Bar Assn., Lubbock County Young Lawyers Assn. (bd. dirs. 1987-89), Tex. Trial Lawyers Assn. Methodist. Office: US Attys Office 350 Magnolia Ave Ste 150 Beaumont TX 77701-2237*

**ORY, CARON,** biomedical researcher; m. Laszlo Ory. MSN, U. Phoenix, 1996. RN Calif., 1993. Rschr. Prescription Solutions, Irvine, Calif., 1999—2006. Achievements include research in diabetes and cardiovascular medicine. Office: Prescription Solutions 2300 Main Street Mail Stop CS57-404 Irvine CA 92614 Office Phone: 949-252-4345.

**ORY, STEVEN JAY,** physician, educator; b. Houston, Aug. 4, 1950; s. Edwin Marvin and Norma Gertrude O.; m. Kathleen Higgins, Jan. 10, 1981; children: Eleanor Claire, Edward Michael. BA, Washington and Lee U., 1972; MD, Baylor Coll., 1976. Diplomate Am. Bd. Obstetrics and Gynecology, subsplty. cert. in Reproductive Endocrinolgy and Infertility. Asst. prof. Duke U., Durham, NC, 1981-82, Northwestern U., Chgo., 1982-85; assoc. prof., cons. Mayo Clinic, Rochester, Minn., 1985-95, chmn. sect. reproductive endocrinology and infertility, 1985-95; pvt. practice reproductive endocrinology and infertility; mem. ob-gyn. staff Internat. U., Margate, Fla., 1995—; assoc. clin. prof. obstets. and gyn. U. Miami, Fla., 1999—. Assoc. dir. Am. Fertility Soc., Birmingham, Ala., 1986-87; bd. trustees Northwest Med. Ctr., Margate, Fla., 2003—. Asst. editor Fertility and Sterility, 1985-96; contbr. articles to profl. jours. Mem. Soc. for Humanism in Medicine (bd. dirs. 1999-2002, v.p 2004—05, pres.-elect 2006—), Am. Soc. Reproductive Medicine (chmn. practice com. 1998-2000, bd. dirs. 1999-2002, v.p 2004-05, pres.-elect 2005-06, pres 2006—), Soc. Reproductive Endocrinologists (sec.-treas., pres. 2001-02), Ft. Lauderdale Ob-Gyn. Soc. (pres. 1998-2000). Office Phone: 954-247-6200.

**OSAKI, MARK STEPHEN,** foundation administrator, writer; b. Sacramento, Oct. 7, 1952; s. Tadashi Melvin and Haruye (Murata) O. BA, U. Calif., Berkeley, 1974; PhD, Georgetown U., 1984. Assoc. dir. RAND Corp., Santa Monica, Calif., 1992-97, cons., 1997-2001; dir. devel. Disabled Sports USA Far West, Citrus Heights, Calif., 2000—. Comm. dir. U. Calif., 1984-90; dir. devel. Coro Found., San Francisco, 1996-97, Second Harvest Food Bank, San Jose, Calif., 1997-2000, Toigo Found., Sacramento, 1997-98. Author: Poetry of the Vietnam War, 1989, Men of Our Time: An Anthology of Male Poetry in Contemporary America, 1992. Nat. Endowment for Arts fellow, 1981, Alumni Scholar, Univ. Calif. Home: 6615 Fordham Way Sacramento CA 95831 Office: c/o Disabled Sports USA Ste 2540 6060 Sunrise Vista Dr Citrus Heights CA 95610 Personal E-mail: osakimark@comcast.net. Business E-Mail: mark@dsusafw.org

**OSAKWE, CHRISTOPHER,** lawyer, educator; b. Lagos, Nigeria, May 8, 1942; arrived in U.S., 1970, naturalized, 1979; s. Simon and Hannah (Morgan) Osakwe; m. Maria Elena Amador, Aug. 19, 1982; 1 child, Rebecca E. LLB, Moscow State U., Lomonosov, 1967; PhD, Moscow State U., 1970; JSD, U. Ill., 1974. Bar: Moscow 1967, Kazakhstan 1974. Prof. sch. law Tulane U., New Orleans, 1972-81, 86-88; Eason-Weinmann prof. comparative law, dir. Tulane U., Eason-Weinmann Ctr. Comparative Law, New Orleans, 1981-86; ptnr. Riddle and Brown, New Orleans, 1989—. Vis. prof. U. Pa., 1978, U. Mich., 1981, Washington and Lee U., 1986; vis. fellow St. Anthony's Coll. Oxford (Eng.) U., 1980, vis. fellow Christ Ch. Coll., 1988—89; vis. prof. Lomonosov Moscow State U., 1999—2005; cons. U.S. Dept. Commerce, 1980—85. Author: The Participation of the Soviet Union in Universal International Organizations, 1972, The Foundations of Soviet Law, 1981, Joint Ventures with the Soviet Union: Law and Practice, 1990, Soviet Business Law, 2 vols., 1991, The Russian Civil Code Annotated: Translation and Commentary, 2000; author: (with others) Comparative Legal Traditions in a Nutshell, 1982, Comparative Legal Traditions - Text, Materials and Cases, 1985, 2d edit., 1994, Comparative Law in Diagrams: General and Special Parts, 2000, 2d edit., 2002; editor: Am. Jour. Comparative Law, 1978—85. Carnegie fellow, Hague Acad. Internat. Law, 1969, Russian Rsch. fellow, Harvard U., 1972, USSR Sr. Rsch. Exch. fellow, 1982, Rsch. fellow, Kennan Inst. Advanced Russian Studies, 1988. Mem.: ABA, Soc. de Legis. Comparée, Supreme Ct. Hist. Soc., Am. Soc. Internat. Law, Am. Law Inst., Order of Coif. Republican. Roman Catholic. Home: 339 Audubon Blvd New Orleans LA 70125-4124 Office: 201 S Charles Ave Ste 3100 New Orleans LA 70170 Office Phone: 504-861-1272. Personal E-mail: osakwec@aol.com.

**OSANDER, JOHN,** secondary school educator; AB in English cum laude, Princeton U.; postgrad., U. Minn., Rider U., St. Thomas U. Macalester Coll., Yale U.; MEd in English Tchg. and Adminstrn., Harvard U. Cert. secondary sch. English and social studies tchr., cert. elem. and preschl. tchr., prin. and sch. adminstr. Tchr. Blake Sch., Mpls., 1957—59, Lincoln-Sudbury Regional H.S., Mass., 1961—63; dir. admissions Princeton U., 1963—71; rschr. Esptl. Work on Writing with Children, NJ, 1972—77; sr. dep. to the pres. Carnegie Found., 1990—97; writing vol. Mpls. schs., 2000—. Cons. in field; founding dir. tchr. recruitment and placement office N.J. State Dept. Edn., 1980—88; grant writer, NY, 1975—78. Author: (novels) Country Matters, 2000, Call Me Kick, 2002; contbr. lyrics for 3 pub. and recorded musicals. Founder Cmty. Theater, Lincoln-Sudbury. Mem.: Loft Literary Ctr., Playwrights' Ctr., Authors League Am., Dramatists Guild. Home: 9300 Collegeview Rd Apt 126 Minneapolis MN 55437-2168 E-mail: os5555@aol.com.

**OSBALDESTON, GORDON FRANCIS,** finance educator, retired federal agency administrator; b. Hamilton, Ont., Can., Apr. 29, 1930; s. John Edward and Margaret (Hanley) O.; m. Geraldine Reid, Oct. 3, 1953; children: Stephen, David, Robert, Catherine B.Commerce, U. Toronto, Ont., Can., 1952; MBA, U. Western Ont., London, 1953, LL.D., 1984, York U., Toronto, 1984, Dalhousie U., Halifax, N.S., 1985, Carleton U., Ottawa, Can., 1987. Fgn. service officer Dept. Trade and Commerce, Ottawa, 1953-54, vice consul, asst. trade commr. Sao Paula, Brazil, 1954-57, Chgo., 1957-60, consul, trade commr. Los Angeles, 1960-64, asst. dir., personnel trade commr. service Ottawa, 1964-66, asst. dir. ops. trade commr. service, 1966-67, exec. dir. trade commr. service, 1967-68; asst. dep. minister Dept. Consumer and Corp. Affairs, Ottawa, 1968-70, dep. minister, 1972-73; dep. sec. Treasury Bd. Secretariat, Ottawa, 1970-72, sec., 1973-76; dep. minister Dept. Industry, Trade and Commerce, Ottawa, 1976-78; sec. Ministry of State for Econ. Devel., Ottawa, 1978-82; undersec. of state Dept. External Affairs, Ottawa, 1982; clk. privy council, sec. to cabinet Privy Council Office, Ottawa, 1982-86; mem. Queen's Privy Coun. for Can., 1986; prof. emeritus Western Bus. Sch. U. Western Ont., 1986—. Bd. dirs. Can. Life Assurance Co., Can. Life Fin. Co., Great West Lifeco Inc., Great West Life Assurance Co., London Group Ins. Inc., London Life Co.; mem. Robarts Rsch. Coun., 2004. Author:

Keeping Deputy Ministers Accountable, 1989, Organizing to Govern, 1990. Decorated officer Order of Can., companion, 1997; recipient Outstanding Achievment award Can. Govt., 1981, Vanier medal Inst. Pub. Adminstrn., 1990. Mem. London Hunt and Country Club, Psi Upsilon Roman Catholic. Avocations: stamp collecting/philately, golf. Home: 1353 Corley Dr N London ON Canada N6G 4L4 Personal E-mail: gordon5304@aol.com.

**OSBERG, GREGORY JOHN,** publishing company executive; b. Jamestown, N.Y., June 12, 1957; s. John Raymond and Nancy (Jones) O.; m. Linda Burton, Aug. 22, 1981; children: Eric Burton, Alexander Gregory. BS in Mktg., Colo. State U., 1979. Regional mgr. Chilton Pub., Radnor, Pa., 1979-81; account mgr. U.S. News & World Report, N.Y.C., 1981-84, Fortune, N.Y.C., 1984-85; v.p. advt. sales U.S. News & World Report, N.Y.C., 1985-90; from advt. sales dir. to v.p. Newsweek, 1992—94, v.p., 1994—97; pres. sales and mktg. CNET, Inc., 1997—99; pres. Brass Ring, Inc., 1999—2000; exec. v.p. Newsweek, 2000—, worldwide pub., 2000—. Chmn. Careers in Communications, Pitts., 1980-81. Mem. Advt. Club N.Y., Lincoln Ctr. Ctr. Circle (exec. com.), Bedens Brook Club. Avocations: golf, tennis, squash, jogging, skiing. Office Phone: 212-445-5979. Office Fax: 212-350-4987. Business E-Mail: greg.osberg@newsweek.com.*

**OSBERG, TIMOTHY MICHAEL,** psychologist, educator, researcher; b. Buffalo, Aug. 11, 1955; s. John Carlton and Adeline Rose (Weichsel) O.; m. Debra A. Morreale, July 14, 1990; children: John Peter, Erika Evelyn. BA, SUNY, Buffalo, 1977, MA, 1980, PhD, 1982. Lic. psychologist NY. Intern VA Med. Ctr., Buffalo, 1981-82; asst. prof. Niagara U., NY, 1982-86; assoc. prof., 1986-90; prof., 1990—; pvt. practice Niagara U., Niagara Falls, NY, 1985—. Psychologist Optifast Weight Loss Program, Niagara Falls, 1989-92; editorial bd. Jour. Personality and Social Psychology, 1988-92, Teaching of Psychology, 1991-99, Jour. Correctional Edn., 1993-97, Jour. Clin. Psychology, 1999-2001; instr. Attica Correctional Facility, 1980-93; presenter in field. Contbr. articles to profl. jours. Vol. group leader pre-release program Attica (N.Y.) Correctional Facility, 1984-90, exec. com. Psychol. Assn. Western N.Y., Buffalo, 1982-87. Recipient Feldman-Cohen Meml. award SUNY, Buffalo, 1977, Disting. Faculty award Consortium of Niagara Frontier, 1993, Cmty. Svc. award Niagara County Mental Health Assn., 2000, Professionalism in Mental Health award Niagara County Mental Health Assn., 2004. Fellow APA; mem. Am. Psychol. Soc., Eastern Psychol. Assn., Soc. for Personality Assessment, Phi Beta Kappa. Democrat. Roman Catholic. Avocations: spectator sports, running, golf, bicycling, hockey. Home: 109 Hidden Oaks Ct Grand Island NY 14072-2575 Office: Niagara U Dept Psychology Niagara University NY 14109 Office Phone: 716-286-8524. Business E-Mail: tosberg@niagara.edu.

**OSBORN, DEVERLE ROSS,** insurance company executive; b. Leesburg, Ind., Sept. 29, 1925; s. Leland John and Beth (Bunnell) O.; m. Edith Helaine Germann, June 27, 1948 (dec. Mar. 1990); children: Bradford, Pamela, Andrea, Randall; m. Lillian C. Fellwock, Aug. 1990. Student, U. Notre Dame, 1944; BS in Air Transp. Engring., Purdue U., 1947. Spl. agt. FBI, Louisville, 1948, N.Y.C., 1948—53; agt. life ins. Conn. Mut. Life, N.Y., 1953—56, life ins. exec. Hartford, 1956—65, Allentown, Pa., 1965—70, Aid Assn. Luths., Appleton, Wis., 1970—78, Evansville, Ind., 1978—91; ret., 1991. Liaison State Legislators Justice Fellowship, Washington, 1982-85, chmn., 1989-92; fin. dir. Prescott, Ariz. Spl. Olympics, 1996-98; bd. dirs. Atlantic dist. Luth. Ch.-Mo. Synod, 1961-65, Habitat for Humanity, Evansville, 1991-92, Meals on Wheels, Prescott, 1997-2000, Prayer Family Internat., 1999-2002. Naval Aviation cadet, 1943-45, lt. (j.g.) res., 1950-60. Named Nat. Vol. Yr. Justice Fellowship, 1989. Mem. Soc. CLU (v.p., pres. local chpts. 1968,70), Gen. Agt. Mgr. Assn. (treas., v.p., pres. local chpts. 1966-68), Nat. Assn. Life Underwriters. Republican. Lutheran. Avocation: flying. Home: 5223 East Harvard Ct Columbus IN 47203 Personal E-mail: nrobso@sbcglobal.net.

**OSBORN, DONALD ROBERT,** lawyer; b. NYC, Oct. 9, 1929; s. Robert W. and Ruth C. (Compton) O.; m. Marcia (Lontz), June 4, 1955; (div.) children: David, Judith, Robert; m. Marie A. (Johnson), Sept. 11, 1986. BA, Cornell U., 1951; LLB, Columbia U., 1957. Bar: N.Y. 1957, U.S. Tax Ct. 1958, U.S. Ct. Claims 1961, U.S. Ct. Appeals (2d cir.) 1974, U.S. Ct. Appeals (8th cir.) 1974, U.S. Dist. Ct. (so. and ea. dist.) N.Y. 1975, U.S. Supreme Ct. 1975. Assoc. Sullivan and Cromwell, N.Y.C., NY, 1957—64, ptnr., 1964—96, sr. counsel, 1997—. Trustee Hamilton Coll., 1978-88, Mus. of Broadcasting, 1975-80; trustee, treas. Kirkland Coll., 1969-78; mem. coun. White Burkett Miller Ctr. Pub. Affairs, 1976-82; bd. dirs. Stevens Kingsley Found., 1967-2005; sec., treas. Dunlevy Milbank Found., 1974—; bd. dir. Spanel Found., 1978-88, CBS, Inc., 1975-80. Served in USN, 1951-54. Mem.: ABA, N.Y. State Bar Assn., Assn. of Bar of City of N.Y., Am. Bar Found., Scarsdale Golf Club, India House, Regency Whist Club, Country Club of the Rockies. Presbyterian. Home: 1049 Park Ave New York NY 10028-1061 Office: Sullivan and Cromwell 125 Broad St Fl 32 New York NY 10004-2498 Office Phone: 212-558-3724. Personal E-mail: dromao@aol.com.

**OSBORN, DONNA MARIE,** secondary school educator, mathematician; b. Huntsville, Ala., Oct. 4, 1950; d. John and Elma Osborn; m. Mark Levinthal, June 9, 1990. BA, Anderson Coll., Ind., 1972; MA, Purdue U., 1977. Tchr. math. Lafayette (Ind.) Sch. Corp., 1972—. Tchr. math. Billericay (England) Comprehensive Sch., England, 1979—80, Internat. Sch. Paris, 1991—92. Bd. dirs. CASA for Kids, Lafayette, 2005—06. Recipient Christa McAuliffe award, U.S. Dept. Edn., 1988, Presdl. Excellence in Tchg. Sci. and Math. award, NSF, 1996; scholar, Tandy Corp., 1996; Einstein Disting. Educator fellowship, U.S. Dept. Energy, 1999—2000.

**OSBORN, FREDERICK HENRY, III,** foundation executive; b. Phila., Dec. 31, 1946; s. Frederick Henry Osborn Jr. and Anne de Witt (Pell) O.; m. Anne Hampton de Peyster Todd, July 10, 1971; children: Frederick Henry IV, Elisabeth Van Cortlandt, Graham Livingston. Student in Econs., Princeton U., 1964-66; BA in Bus. Adminstrn., Colby Coll., 1971; postgrad., Nat. Planned Giving Inst., 1987, Philanthropy Tax Inst., 1988. Registered investment advisor. Pres. Call-Us, Inc., Edgartown, Mass., 1969-72; exec. v.p. Hall Labs., Boston, 1972-74; fin. officer Episcopal Diocese Mass., Boston, 1972-76; diocesan adminstr. Episcopal Diocese Maine, Portland, 1976-80; dir. adminstrn. Episcopal Diocese Conn., Hartford, 1980-86; dir. of devel. and planned giving Nat. Episcopal Ch., N.Y.C., 1987-94; dir. of devel. programs Episcopal Ch. Found., N.Y.C., 1995-97; dir. devel. The Nature Conservancy of N.Y., N.Y.C., 1997-99; dir. philanthropic svcs. Episcopal Ch. Found., 1999—. Bd. dirs. Living Music, Inc., Ulysses Co., William O. Benson Co., FAN Trusts, Oslands, Inc., Boscobel Restoration, Inc., Garrison Sta. Plz., Inc., Garrison Landing Assn., Covenant Svcs., Inc.; prin. Cat Rock Counsel, Garrison, N.Y., 1990—. Co-author: Planned Giving for the Episcopal Parish, 1989, Funding Future Ministry, 2000. Bd. dirs. The Giraffe Project, chmn. 1989-93, Alice Desmond & Hamilton Fish Libr.; chmn. bd. dirs. Hudson Highlands Land Trust; v.-chair., bd. dirs. Scenic Hudson, Berkeley Divinity Sch. Yale U., Nature Conservancy (lower Hudson chpt. 1994-97); trustee Tabor Acad., 1993-99, Cathedral Ch. St. John the Divine, chair Hudson Highlands Music Festival, 1994-96, 99-2001, The Constn. Island Assn., Soc. for Increase of the Ministry; trustee St. Francis Found., chair, 1999-2000. With U.S. Army, 1966-68, Vietnam. Mem. Nat. Soc. Fund Raising Execs., Nat. Planned Giving Assn., Nat. Environ. Le adership Coun., Planned Giving Group Greater NY, Social Investment Forum, Coun. Econ. Priorities, Social Venture Network, Century Assn. Constitution Is. Assn., St. Andrews Soc. NY, Highlands Country Club, NY Yacht Club, Portland Yacht Club, Dauntless Club, Garrison Yacht Club, Princeton Club (NY), Internat. Platform Assn., Yale Club (NY). Avocations: sailing, music, photography. Home: PO Box 347 Garrison NY 10524-0347 Office: The Episcopal Ch Found 815 2nd Ave New York NY 10017-4563

**OSBORN, JOHN EDWARD,** lawyer, pharmaceutical industry executive, former government official; b. Davenport, Iowa, Sept. 4, 1957; s. Edward Richard and Patricia Anne (O'Donovan) O.; m. Deborah Lynn Powell, Aug. 11, 1984; children: Delaney Powell, Keeley Rush. Student, Coll. William and Mary, 1975—76; BA, U. Iowa, 1979; cert., Georgetown U., 1980; JD, U. Va. 1983; cert. Wadham Coll., Oxford U., 1987; M Internat. Pub. Policy, Johns

Hopkins U., 1992; cert. Wharton Sch., U. Pa., 1994—95; postgrad., Princeton U., 1997—99. Bar: Mass. 1985, U.S. Supreme Ct. 2001. Staff U.S. Rep. Jim Leach, 1978, Congl. Budget Office, 1979—80, U.S. Senator John Heinz, 1981; law clk. to Hon. Albert V. Bryan U.S. Ct. Appeals (4th cir.), Alexandria, Va., 1983-84; assoc. McDermott, Will & Emery, Wash. and Chgo., 1981, Sidley & Austin, Chgo., 1982, Hale and Dorr, Wash. and Boston, 1983—88, Dechert Price & Rhoads, Phila., 1988-89; spl. asst. to legal adviser U.S. Dept. State, Washington, 1989-92; sr. counsel DuPont Merck Pharm. Co., Wilmington, Del., 1992-94, assoc. gen. counsel, 1994-96, v.p., assoc. gen. counsel, asst. sec., 1996—97; v.p. legal affairs Cephalon, Inc., Frazer and West Chester, Pa., 1997—98, sr. v.p., 1998—2005, gen. counsel, 1998—, sec., 1998—, exec. v.p., 2006—. Vis. lectr., exec. in residence Ross Sch. Bus. U. Mich., 1997—; vis. scholar East European studies Woodrow Wilson Internat. Ctr. for Scholars, Washington, 1991; vis. fellow politics, rsch. collaborator Princeton U., 2002—; Wharton fellow U. Pa., 2004—. Contbr. articles to profl. jours. and newspapers including NY Times, Wall St. Jour., Am. Jour. Internat. Law, Christian Sci. Monitor; articles editor Va. Jour. Internat. Law, 1982—83. Bd. advisors U. Pa. Inst. Law and Econs., Phila., 1999—; trustee Siasconset Beach Preservation Fund, 2004—, Tower Hill Sch., Wilmington, Del., 1997—, Del. Art Mus., 1999—2006; corp. exec. bd. Phila. Mus. Art. 2003—; bd. govs. East-West Ctr., Honolulu, 2004—; bd. dirs. Incept BioSystems, Inc., Ann Arbor, Mich., 2005—; bd. advisors U. Mich. Life Scis. Inst., Ann Arbor, 2005—; mem. Del. steering com. Bush-Cheney, 2004, 2000; del. Rep. Nat. Conv., San Diego, 1996; rsch. aide, speechwriter George Bush for Pres. Com., 1979—80, 1988. Recipient study grant, Andrew W. Mellon Found., 1999; Eisenhower fellow, Ireland and No. Ireland, 1998. Mem. Am. Law Inst., Coun. Fgn. Rels., Mortar Board, Greenville Country Club, Fieldstone Golf Club, Princeton Club N Y, Congl. Country Club, Met. Club Washington, Capitol Hill Club, Sankaty Head Golf and Beach Club, Siasconset Casino Assn., Bidermann Golf Club, Vicmead Hunt Club, Cosmos Club, Phi Beta Kappa, Phi Delta Phi, Omicron Delta Kappa, Omicron Delta Epsilon. Republican. Roman Catholic. Home: 5 Doe's Lane Way Ridge Wilmington DE 19807-1548 also: 75 Baxter Rd Siasconset MA 02564 Office: 41 Moores Rd Frazer PA 19355 Office Phone: 610-738-6337. Personal E-mail: jeosborn@princeton.edu. Business E-mail: josborn@cephalon.com.

**OSBORN, JOHN ROBERT,** retired engineering educator; b. Kansas City, Mo., Aug. 11, 1924; married, 1945; 3 children. BS, Purdue U., 1950, MS, 1953, PhD in Mech. Engring., 1957. Jr. engr. Thiokol Chem. Corp., 1950-51; asst. Purdue U., West Lafayette, Ind., 1951-57, from asst. prof. to assoc. prof. mechanical engring., 1957-61, prof., 1961-70, 71-79, prof. aero. and astronautical engring., 1980-89, prof. emeritus aero. and astronautical engring., 1989—2006; br. chief Ballistics Rsch. Lab. Aberdeen Proving Ground, 1970-71. Mem.: AIAA (assoc. fellow, Wyld Propulsion award 1995), Soc. Automotive Engrs. Achievements include research in combustion instability in rockets; high frequency response instrumentation; combustion in solid rockets and interior ballistics. Home: 40 Stayman Ct Lafayette IN 47905-4446 Personal E-mail: josborn@purdue.edu.

**OSBORN, JOHN SIMCOE, JR.,** lawyer; b. Louisville, Jan. 14, 1926; s. John S. and Ruby (Pinnell) O.; m. Mary Jo Fishback, Sept. 6, 1947; children— Robert, John, Donna LLB, U. Louisville, 1949. Bar: Ky. 1949, U.S. Dist. Ut. (ea. and we. dists.) Ky. 1952. Exec. v.p., gen. counsel Louisville Title Ins. Co., 1954-72; ptnr. Tarrant Combs & Bul!itt (name changed to Wyatt Tarrant & Combs 1980), Louisville, 1972—. Chmn. bd. Beargrass Corp. Capt. JAGC, U.S. Army, 1952-54. Fellow Am. Bar Found.; mem. Ky. Bar Assn., Louisville Bar Assn., ABA, Am. Land Title Assn., Am. Coll. Real Estate Lawyers, Rotary. Democrat. Lutheran. Office: Wyatt Tarrant & Combs 2800 Citizens Plz Louisville KY 40202 Office Phone: 502-589-5235.

**OSBORN, JOHN W.,** lawyer; b. Prescott, Ariz., 1951; BA magna cum laude, Mich. State U., 1972, JD, U. Pa., 1975. Bar: Ariz. 1975, NY 1980. Staff atty. divsn. of market regulation SEC, Washington, 1975-78, br. chief divsn. of market regulation, 1978-79; ptnr., head derivatives fin. products Skadden, Arps, Slate, Meagher & Flom LLP, NYC. Chmn. and spkr. Practicing Law Inst.; spkr. in field; primary and documentation contact for Skadden, Arps, Slate, Meagher & Flom, LLP Internat. Swap and Derivatives Assn. Mem.: Bar Assn. City NY (former mem. securities regulation com.). Office: Skadden Arps Slate Meagher & Flom 4 Times Sq New York NY 10036 Office Phone: 212-735-3270. Office Fax: 917-777-3270. Business E-mail: josborn@skadden.com.

**OSBORN, JUNE ELAINE,** pediatrician, microbiologist, educator, foundation administrator; b. Endicott, NY, May 28, 1937; d. Leslie A. and Dora W. (Wright) Osborn; children: Philip I. Levy, Ellen D. Levy, Laura A. Jana. BA, Oberlin Coll., Ohio, 1957; MD, Western Res. U., 1961; DSc (hon.), U. Med. Dental Sch. N.J., 1990, Emory U., 1993, Oberlin Coll., 1993, Rutgers U., 1994, Case Western Res. U., 1997, SUNY, Stony Brook, 1999, U. Wis., 2004; DMS (hon.), Yale U., 1992; LHD (hon.), Med. Coll. Pa., 1994. Intern, resident in pediatrics Harvard U. Hosp., 1961—64; fellow Johns Hopkins, 1964—65, U. Pitts., 1965—66; prof. med. microbiology and pediat. U. Wis. Med. Sch., Madison, Wis., 1966—84, prof. pediat. and microbiology 1974—84, assoc. dean Grad. Sch., 1975—84; dean Sch. Pub. Health U. Mich. Sch. Pub. Health, 1984—93; prof. epidemiology, pediat. and communicable diseases U. Mich. Sch. Pub. Health and Med. Sch., 1984—96, prof. emeritus, 1997—. Pres. Josiah Macy, Jr. Found., 1997—; mem. rev. panel viral vaccine efficacy FDA, 1973—79, mem. vaccines and related biol. products adv. com., 1981—85; mem. exptl. virology study sect. Divsn. Rsch. Grants, NIH, 1975—79; mem. med. affairs com. Yale U. Coun., 1981—86; chmn. life scis. associateships rev. panel NRC, 1981—84; mem. U.S. Army Med. R&D Adv. Com., 1983—85; chmn. working group on AIDS and the Nation's Blood Supply NHLBI, 1984—89; chmn. WHO Planning Group on AIDS and the Internat. Blood Supply 1985—86. Contbr. articles to profl. jours.; mem. editl. bd.: Jour. AMA, 2002—. Active task force in AIDS, Inst. of Medicine, 1986; adv. com. Robert Wood Johnson Found. AIDS Health Svcs. Program, 1986—91; nat. adv. com. on health of pub. program Pew and Rockefeller Founds.; active Global Commn. on AIDS, WHO, 1988—92; chmn. Nat. Commn. on AIDS, 1989—93; trustee Kaiser Found., 1990—98, Case Western Reserve U., 1993—97; nat. vaccine adv. com. HHS, 1995—98; adv. coun. Nat. Inst. on Drug Abuse, 1995—98; internat. adv. bd. Nat. Acads., 2002—05; bd. dirs. Legal Action Ctr., 1994—2001, Ctr. for Health Care Strategies, 1998—2003, The Mind Inst., 2003—05, US Pharmacopeia Bd., 2005—. Recipient NIH Pub. Svc. award, 2000, Scientific Freedom and Responsibility award, AAAS, 1994; grantee NIH, 1969, 1972, 1974—75, Nat. Multiple Sclerosis Soc., 1971. Fellow: Infectious Diseases Soc. Am., Am. Acad. Microbiology, Am. Acad. Arts and Scis., Am. Acad. Pediat.; mem.: Inst. Medicine (health promotion and disease prevention bd. 1987—90, coun. mem. 1999—2002), Soc. Pediat. Rsch., Am. Soc. Microbiology, Am. Soc. Immunologists. Office: Josiah Macy Jr Found 44 E 64th St New York NY 10021-7306 Office Phone: 212-486-2424.

**OSBORN, KATHY,** lawyer; b. Indpls., Oct. 18, 1963; m. Steven Pockrass, Apr. 30, 2004. BS in Biology magna cum laude, Ind. U., 1987, BA in Religious Studies summa cum laude, 1987, JD magna cum laude, 1999. Project mgr. Ind. Inst. Disability and Cmty., U., Bloomington, 1989—2000; clk. to Justices Frank Sullivan, Jr. and Myra Selby Ind. Supreme Ct., Indpls., 1999—2000; assoc. Baker & Daniels LLP, Indpls., 2000—. Pres. Youth Job Preparedness Program, Indpls., 2000. Mem.: ABA, 7th Circuit Bar Assn., Indpls. Bar Assn., Ind. Bar Assn. Avocations: travel, painting. Office: Baker & Daniels LLP 300 N Meridian St Suite 2700 Indianapolis IN 46204 Office Phone: 317-237-8261. Office Fax: 317-237-1000. Business E-mail: kathy.osborn@bakerd.com.

**OSBORN, KENNETH LOUIS,** financial executive; b. Belleville, Ill., Jan. 9, 1946; s. William Arthur and Louise Mary (Brueggemann) Osborn; m. Roberta Marie Vodicka, Oct. 23, 1971; 1 child, David Anthony. BBA, U. N. Mex., 1968. Auditor Ernst & Ernst, Albuquerque, 1968; budget mgr. Rockwell Internat., Chgo, 1970—74; mgr. internat. acctg. Allied Van Lines, 1974—76; fin. mgr. Sealy, Ill., 1976—79; sr. fin. analyst Newark Electronics, 1979—80, internat. dir. credit, 1980—82; bus. mgr. Prime Computer, Ill., 1982—90;

acctg. mgr. and CFO Flexonics, Inc., 1990—96; contr. and CFO Jackson Industries, Ill., 1996—. Fin. cons. Am. European Express. Rep. Nat. Com.; presdl. task force. With U.S. Army, 1968—70. Decorated Air medal. Mem.: Inst. Mgmt. Accts., Soc. Am. Baseball Rsch., Mensa Soc.

**OSBORN, KENNETHE C.,** banker; b. Sedro-Woolley, Wash., June 27, 1978; d. Mark and Elena B. Harp; m. Jeff C. Osborn, Sept. 9, 2000. BA in Acctg., We. Wash. U., 2000; grad., We. Sch. Intermediate Banking, 2004. Loan officer Skagit State Bank, Burlington, Wash., 2000—02, v.p. compliance officer, 2002—. Mem.: Am. Bankers Assn. (grad. compliance sch. 2002, grad. sch. compliance mgmt. 2004). Avocation: softball. Home: 627 State St Sedro Woolley WA 98284 Office: Skagit State Bank 301 E Fairhaven Ave Burlington WA 98233

**OSBORN, LA DONNA CAROL,** clergywoman; b. Portland, Oreg., Mar. 13, 1947; d. T.L. and Daisy (Washburn) O.; m. Cory A. Nickerson, Dec. 11, 1981; children: Tommy O'Dell, LaVona Thomas, Daneesa Dolan, Donald O'Dell. Student, Assemblies of God Coll., 1963; BA, Okla. City U., 1994; DD, Bethel Coll., 1995; Doctor of Humane Letters (hon.), Wesley Synod, 1998; MA, Oral Roberts U., 2000; D in Ministry, Am. Christian Coll. and Sem., 2001; DD, Zoe Univ., 2001. Fgn. mission corr., purchaser, personnel agt. Osborn Found., Tulsa, 1969-75, exec. asst., 1975-76, internat. gen. mgr., 1976-81, internat. editor-in-chief, 1981-86, corp. pres., 1986-93; assoc. pastor Internat. Gospel Ctr., Tulsa, 1986-89, sr. pastor, 1989-94, sr. pastor, overseer, 1994-97; founder, presiding bishop Internat. Gospel Fellowship, Tulsa, Okla., 1997—2006; v.p., CEO OSFO Internat., 1998—. Internat. minister, religious tchr., and motivational spkr. Nigeria, Kenya, Uganda, Colombia, Papua New Guinea, France, Russia, Belarus, Kazakhstan, Kyrgyzstan, Ukraine, Russia, Sweden, Eng., Brazil, Holland, Can., India, Zambia, Guatemala, Ecuador, China, Brazil, Mizoram, Guatemala, Mexico, U.S.; internat. spiritual advisor Christian Women's Fellowship Internat. Nigeria; founder Believers' Network Internat., Women's Internat. Network. Author: Jesus & Women, 2000, God's Big Picture, 2001, New Miracle Life Now, 2004, Peace is a Lifestyle, 2005; author: (and editor) Bible tng. courses. Republican. Home: 3111 E 89th St Tulsa OK 74137-3362 Office Phone: 918-743-0872. Personal E-mail: revldo@aol.com.

**OSBORN, MALCOLM EVERETT,** lawyer; b. Bangor, Maine, Apr. 29, 1928; s. Lester Everett and Helen (Clark) O.; m. Claire Anne Franks, Aug. 30, 1953; children: Beverly, Lester, Malcolm, Ernest. BA, U. Maine, 1952; postgrad., Harvard U., 1952-54; JD, Boston U., 1956, LLM, 1961. Bar: Maine 1956, Mass. 1956, U.S. Dist. Ct. Mass. 1961, U.S. Tax Ct. 1961, U.S. Claims Ct. 1961, N.C. 1965, U.S. Supreme Ct. 1979, U.S. Ct. Appeals (4th cir.) 1980, Va. 1991. Tax counsel State Mut. Life Assurance Co., Worcester, Mass., 1956-64; v.p., gen. tax counsel Integon Corp. and other group cos., Winston-Salem, NC, 1964-81; ptnr. House, Blanco & Osborn, P.A., Winston-Salem, NC, 1981-88; v.p., gen. counsel, dir. Settlers Life Ins. Co., Bristol, Va., 1984-89; ptnr. Malcolm E. Osborn, P.A., Winston-Salem, 1988—. Lectr. The Booke Seminars, Life Ins. Co., 1985-87; adj. prof. Wake Forest U. Sch. Law, Winston-Salem, N.C., 1974-82; disting. guest lectr. Ga. State U., 1965; guest lectr. NYU Ann. Inst. Fed. Taxation, 1966, 68, 75, 80; gen. counsel Blue Ridge Mutual Assn., Inc., Galax, Va., 1989—; adj. instr. bus. law Forsyth Tech. C.C., Winston-Salem, N.C., 2004—. Com. editor The Tax Lawyer, ABA, 1974-76; author numerous articles in field. Trustee N.C. Coun. Econ. Edn., 1968-76; bd. dirs. Christian Fellowship Home, 1972-80; co-founder Bereaved Parents Group Winston-Salem, 1978—. Mem. ABA (chmn. com. ins. cos. of taxation sect. 1980-82, chmn. subcom. on continuing legal edn. and publs. 1982-88), Am. Bus. Law Assn. (mem. com. fed. taxation 1968—, chmn. 1972-75), Assn. Life Ins. Counsel (com. on co. tax, tax sect. 1965—), N.C. Bar Assn. (com. taxation 1973—), Fed. Bar Assn. (taxation com. 1973—), Maine State Bar Assn., Va. State Bar Assn., Internat. Bar Assn. (com. on taxes of bus. law sect. 1973—), AAUP, Southeastern Acad. Legal Studies in Bus., Masons (Lincoln, Maine). Office: PO Box 5192 Winston Salem NC 27113-5192 Office Phone: 336-659-0613.

**OSBORN, MARVIN GRIFFING, JR.,** educational consultant; b. Baton Rouge, Sept. 7, 1922; s. Marvin Griffing and Mamie (Hester) O.; m. Sarah Fleming, Aug. 3, 1945; children: Jane Fleming, Charles Porter. BA, La. State U., 1942, MA, 1946; LLD, St. Xavier U., 1971; DHum, Phillips U., 1977. Pub. relations counsel La. State U., 1945-47, acting dir. pub. relations, 1947; assoc. prof., chmn. dept. journalism and dir. pub. relations Howard Coll. (now Samford U.), 1947-49; dir. pub. relations, lectr. journalism Miss. State Coll. (now Miss. State U.), 1949-53; dir. information Washington U., 1953-58, pub. relations adviser, 1955-58, dir. Devel. Funds, 1958-61; cons. coll. and univ. adminstrn., 1961—, including Drake, Duke, Phillips, Tampa, Tex. Christian univs., Atlantic Christian Coll. (now Barton Coll.), Bethany (W.Va.), Eckerd, Loretto Heights, St. Xavier U., Tenn. Wesleyan, Webster U., Hendrix, Mercy (Detroit), Bethel (Tenn.), McMurry U., St. Scholastica, Coker Coll., Christian Ch. Found., Nat. Meth. Found. Christian Higher Edn., Lexington Theol. Sem., Memphis Theol. Sem., Nat. Benevolent Assn. Christian Ch., Sisters of Loretto; interim pres. St. Xavier Coll. (now St. Xavier U.), 1968—69; pres. Marvin Osborn, Inc., 1979—94. Mem. planning com. Conf. for Advancement Understanding and Support Higher Edn., White Sulphur Springs, W.Va., 1958; mem. exec. com. program and arrangements com. Gen. Assembly Christian Ch., 1977, 87-89. Bd. dir. St. Louis Heart Assn., 1969-75, Fla. Christian Ctr., 1986-88; trustee Nat. City Christian Ch. Corp., 1981-85; mem. Christian Ch., bd. dir., exec. com., sec. divsn. higher edn., 1973-77, mem. panel to study fin. procedures of Christian Ch. (Disciples of Christ), 1987-89, Cypress Village Devel. Coun., Jacksonville, Fla., 1992-98, co-chair, 1992-98; chair first trustee ballot com. Cypress Village Residents Coun., 2005; mem. nat. fundraising com. Disciples World, 2002-04; mem. Fiers-Brown Soc. of Christian Ch. Found., 2003—. Served from lt. to capt. 20th Inf. Divsn. AUS, 1942-43, ETO. Recipient Harry T. Ice Disting. Svc. award for Excellence in Philanthropy, Christian Ch. Found., 1991. Mem. Am. Coll. Pub. Rels. Assn. (v.p. dists. 1951-52, v.p. membership 1952-53, sec.-treas. 1953-55, pres. 1959-60), Nat. Benevolent Assn. (amb. 1992-98), Soc. Profl. Journalists, Omicron Delta Kappa, Sigma Chi. Home: 13655 Myrica Ct Jacksonville FL 32224-6626

**OSBORN, MARY JANE MERTEN,** biochemist, educator; b. Colorado Springs, Colo., Sept. 24, 1927; d. Arthur John and Vivien Naomi (Morgan) Merten; m. Ralph Kenneth Osborn, Oct. 26, 1950. BA, U. Calif., Berkeley, 1948; PhD, U. Wash., 1958. Postdoctoral fellow, dept. microbiology NYU Sch. Medicine, N.Y.C., 1959-61, instr., 1961-62, asst. prof., 1962-63; asst. prof. dept. molecular biology Albert Einstein Coll. Medicine, Bronx, NY, 1963-66, assoc. prof., 1966-68; prof. dept. microbiology U. Conn. Health Ctr., Farmington, 1968—, dept. head, 1980—2002, prof. dept. molecular, microbial and structural biology, 2003—. Mem. bd. sci. counselors Nat. Heart, Lung and Blood Inst., 1975-79; mem. Nat. Sci. Bd., 1980-86; adv. coun. Nat. Inst. Gen. Med. Sci., 1983-86, divsn. grants NIGH, 1989-94, chair, 1992-94; trustee Biosci. Info. Systems, 1986-91, chair, 1990-91; mem. German Am. Acad. Coun., 1994-97; mem. space scis. bd. NRC, 1994-2000, chair com. space biology and medicine, 1994-2000; cochair com. on indications for waterborne pathogens, 2002-03. Assoc. editor Jour. Biol. Chemistry, 1973-80; contbr. articles in field of biochemistry and molecular biology to profl. jours. Mem. rsch. com. Am. Heart Assn., 1972-77, chair, 1976-77. NIH fellow, 1959-61; NIH grantee, 1962-95; NSF grantee, 1965-68; Am. Heart Assn. grantee, 1968-71 Fellow Am. Acad. Arts and Scis. (coun. 1988-91), NAS (coun. 1990-93, com. sci. engring. and pub. policy 1993-96); mem. Am. Acad. Microbiology (bd. govs. 1994-2000), Am. Fedn. Soc. Exptl. Biology (pres. 1982-83), Am. Soc. Biol. Chemists (pres. 1981-82), Am. Soc. Microbiology. Democrat. Office: U Conn Health Ctr Dept Molec Micro and Struct Biology MC3205 Farmington CT 06030-0001 Office Phone: 860-679-4206.

**OSBORN, SUSAN CHANEY,** writer, educator; b. Ft. Campbell, Ky., Jan. 7, 1953; d. Lawrence Elvie and Wilma Barbara (Powell) Howard; m. Nicholas Lourick, Aug. 1, 1976 (div. 1981); m. Steve Osborn, Mar. 20, 1993; 1 child. BS, Ga. State U., 1989; MS, U. Colo., 1997. Lic. tchr., Colo, pvt. occupational tchr., Colo. Owner, photographer Creative Assistance, Atlanta,

1979-89; educator St. Mary's Acad., Cherry Hills Village, Colo., 1989-90, Denver Pub. Schs., 1990-92; internet resource coord. Nat. Renewable Energy Lab., Golden, Colo., 1993-95; writer Diners Club Internat., Englewood, Colo., 1995-96; owner, writer, coord. Publs. Resolution, Denver, 1996—. Website advisor Colo. Dept. Pub. Health and Environment, Denver, 1998-99; advisor Houghton-Mifflin Co., Boston, 1992; mem. math. text seclection com. Denver Pub. Schs., 1991; cons. Hauser Chem. Co., Boulder, Colo., 1994. Author: Public Service Company Classroom Connection, 1992, photography manual. Art/photography dir. Boy's Club, Marietta, GA, 1987; art show sect. organizer Girl's Club, Atlanta, 1988; implementor Bear Creek Blvd. Civic Assn. Lakewood, Colo., 1995; pub. rels. coord. Resolve Rocky Mountain Area, Denver, 1996. Fellow Colo. Writing Project; mem. NEA, Golden Key. Avocations: creative writing, creative photography, theater, hiking, mountain biking. Office: Publs Resolution PO Box 37263 Denver CO 80237

**OSBORN, WILLIAM A.,** investment company executive; b. Culver, Ind., Oct. 14, 1947; married; 2 children. BA, Northwestern U., 1969, MBA, 1973. Joined No. Trust Corp., 1970, sr. exec. v.p., commercial banking Chgo., COO, 1993—95, pres., 1993—, chmn., CEO, 1995—. Bd. dirs. Caterpillar Inc., 2000—, Nicor, Inc., Tribune Co., 2001—; Class A dir. Fed. Reserve Bank Chgo. Bd. trustees Mus. Sci. and Industry, Chgo., Northwestern U., Chgo.; bd. dirs. Chgo. Symphony Orch., Northwestern Meml. HealthCare, Chgo. Urban League, Chgo. Horticultural Society, Lyric Opera Chgo., United Way Metropolitan Chgo.; bd. mgrs. YMCA Metropolitan Chgo.; advisory bd. J.L. Kellogg Grad. Sch. Mgmt., Northwestern. Mem.: Commercial Club of Chgo. (chmn., vice chmn civic com.), Chgo. United (bd. dirs.), Chgo. Coun. Foreign Relations (bd. dirs.), Financial Services Roundtable, Chgo. Club, Executives' Club (bd. dirs.), Economic Club (bd. dirs.). Office: No Trust Co 50 S Lasalle St Chicago IL 60675-0001

**OSBORN, WILLIAM GEORGE,** savings and loan association executive; b. Alton, Ill., Dec. 9, 1925; s. Ralph A. and Pauline J. (Horn) O.; m. Hilda M. Alexander, Aug. 12, 1950 (dec.); children: Barbara K., David A., Robert W., James A. BS in Math., Shurtleff Coll., 1947; certificate, Grad. Sch. Savs. and Loan, Ind. U., 1946-48; A.M. in Econs., St. Louis U., 1952. With Germania Fed. Savs. and Loan Assn., Alton, 1946-90, exec. officer, 1955-86, pres., 1964-86, chmn., 1981-86, chmn. trust com., 1982-86; pres. Fin. Service Assocs., Ft. Lauderdale, Fla., 1986—. Pres. Germania Fin. Corp., 1970-86; owner Fin. Guidance, Alton, 1951—; mem. Opportunities Unltd., 1954-58; instr. Am. Savs. and Loan Inst.; bd. dirs. Nat. Coun. Savs. Instns., Washington, 1984-86. Author: Savings and Loan Operating Policies Manual, 1960, Economic Factors Influencing Savings and Loan Interest Rates, 1962. Pres. Alton Wood River Community Chest, 1959; bd. dirs. Piasa Bird coun. Boy Scouts Am., 1961-88, Mississippi Valley Jr. Achievement, Alton Area United Fund, 1961-63; founder, bd. dirs., treas. New Piasa Chautauqua Ch. Assembly, 1982-86; treas. Lewis and Clark Community Coll. Found., 1976-86; bd. dirs., sec. Riverbend Civic Progress, 1984-86; elder Presbyn. Ch. Served to lt. (j.g.) USNR, 1943-46, 50-52. Mem. Nat. Assn. Bus. Economists, Nat. Economists Club, St. Louis Economists Club, Am. Inst. Mgmt., Masons, Shriners, Chautauqua (Ill.) Yacht Club. E-mail: Olazydaze@aol.com.

**OSBORNE, BARRIE M.,** motion picture producer; b. N.Y.C., Feb. 7, 1944; s. William Osborne and Hertha Schwarz; m. Micha Yun, July 30, 1969; 1 child, Danielle Kim. BA, Carleton Coll., 1966. Prodn. exec. New Regency Films, 1980-82; v.p. motion picture, producer Walt Disney Pictures, Burbank, Calif., 1985-87; ind. producer Los Angeles, 1987—. Prodr.(assoc. prodr.): (films) Cutter's Way, 1981, The Big Chill, 1983, Fandango, 1985; exec. prodr.: Peggy Sue Got Married, 1986, Child's Play, 1988, Dick Tracy, 1990, Wilder Napalm, 1993, China Moon, 1994, Rapa Nui, 1994, The Fan, 1996, The Matrix, 1999; prodr.: Face/Off, 1997, The Lord of the Rings: The Fellowship of the Ring, 2001 (AFI Movie of the Year, 2002, BAFTA Award for best film, 2002), The Lord of the Rings: The Two Towers, 2002, The Last Place on Earth, 2002, The Lord of the Rings: The Return of the King, 2003 (Academy Award for Best Picture, 2004). Served to 1st lt. U.S. Army, 1966-69, Korea. Mem. Dirs. Guild Am. Avocation: sailing.

**OSBORNE, BARTLEY PORTER, JR.,** aeronautical engineer; b. Akron, Ohio, Sept. 1, 1934; s. Bartley P. and Cordelia Inez (Sims) O.; m. Carol Ann Eubanks, Jan. 15, 1966; children: Roxane Elizabeth, Ashley Hamilton. BSME, Carnegie Mellon U., Pitts., 1956; MS in Aerospace Engring., U. So. Calif., 1962. Sr. stress analyst N. Am. Aviation, Columbus, Ohio, 1956-66; sr. design engr. Lockheed Aircraft, Burbank, Calif., 1966-70, project engr., 1970-74; staff specialist aeronautics and ocean vehicles Office Sec. of Def., Washington, 1974-78; engring. prog. mgr. Lockheed Aircraft, 1978-82, chief adv. design engr., 1982-85, chief engr. YF-22, 1985-87, dep. chief adv. design engr., 1987-89; prog. mgr. Lockheed Aero. Sys. Co., Burbank, 1989-90; v.p., engr. Lockheed Aero. Systems Co., Marietta, Ga., 1990-96, v.p. advanced concepts, 1996-97; retired; cons. Aerotec Solutions, 1998—. Chmn. NASA Aeronautics Adv. Com., 1994-97; chmn. Aerospace Coun. SAE, 1997-2002; chmn. program planning com. Quiet Supersonic, 2001-02; bd. dirs. Aerofon Corp., San Diego; guest lectr. Carnegie Mellon U., 2001, Calif. Inst. Tech., 2003. Pres. Chesterfield Mews Homeowners Assn., Fairfax, Va., 1977-78. 1st lt. U.S. Army, 1956-58. Pa. State schol., 1952; recipient Disting. Pub. Svc. medal U.S. Govt., 1997. Fellow Royal Aero. Soc., AIAA (assoc.); mem. L.A. Violin Cello Soc. Democrat. Avocation: cellist. Home: 405 White Horse Tel Palm Desert CA 92211-8947 Fax: 760-772-6842. Office Phone: 760-772-0582. Personal E-mail: spdfrk@aol.com. Business E-mail: aero21st@aol.com.

**OSBORNE, BURL,** publishing executive, editor; b. Jenkins, Ky., June 25, 1937; s. Oliver and Juanita (Smallwood) O.; m. Betty S. Wilks, Feb. 14, 1974; 1 son, Burl Jonathan. Student, U. Ky., 1955-57; BA in Journalism, Marshall U., 1960; MBA, L.I. U. Sch. Bus., 1984; A.M.P., Harvard Bus. Sch., 1984. Reporter Ashland (Ky.) Daily Ind., 1957-58; reporter, editor Sta. WHTN-TV, Huntington, W.Va., 1958-60; corr. AP, Bluefield, W.Va., 1960-62, statehouse corr. Charleston, W.va., 1963-64, corr. Spokane, Wash., 1964-67, news editor Denver, 1967-70; chief of bur. AP, Ky., 1970-72, AP, Ohio, 1972-74; asst. chief of bur. AP, Washington, Washington, 1974-76; mng. editor world hdqs. AP, N.Y.C., 1977-80; exec. editor Dallas Morning News, 1980-83, v.p., 1981, sr. v.p., editor, 1983-84, pres., editor, 1985-90, pub., editor, 1991—2001, pub. emeritus, 2001—. Bd. dirs. AP, chmn., 2002—; bd. dirs. J.C. Penney Co.; pres. publ. divsn. Belo Corp., 1995—2002; mem. journalism adv. coun. Knight Found., 1991—97; bd. dirs. Nat. Kidney Found., S.W. Transplant Alliance, Freedom Comms., Inc. Bd. dirs. Pulitzer Prize, 1986—95, co-chmn. bd. dir., 1994—95. Named Newspaper Exec. of Yr. Nat. Press Found., 1992; inducted to Ky. Journalism Hall of Fame, 1994; recipient Disting. Alumnus award Marshall U., 1997, Freedoms Found. Next Millinium award, 1999. Mem.: Newspaper Assn. Am. (bd. dirs. 1996—2004), World Assn. Newspapers (mem. exec. com. 1998—2001, bd. dirs.), So. Newspaper Pub. Assn. (bd. dirs. 1995—2003, pres. 2000—01), Tex. Daily Newspaper Assn. (bd. dirs. 1982—92, pres. 1993), Am. Press Inst. (chmn. 1988—93), Am. Soc. Newspaper Editors (bd. dirs. 1982—91, pres. 1990—91), Org. Profl. Journalists. Home: 3901 Turtle Creek Blvd Dallas TX 75219 Office: Dallas Morning News PO Box 655237 Dallas TX 75265-5237 E-mail: bosborne@belo.com.

**OSBORNE, CHARLES DAVID,** singer, composer, conductor; b. Suffern, NY, Aug. 14, 1949; s. Harold Clinton and Rosa Maria (Morales) Osborne; m. Kathryn Arden Stokes, Sept. 11, 1971; 1 child, Paul David. Attended in Bach Music, Voice, Hartt Coll. of Music, 1972; post grad. studies in opera, Juilliard Sch., 1974; diploma of Hazzanut with honors in musical composition and conducting, Jewish Theol. Sem., 1987, grad. studies in Jewish lit., 1988. Undergrad. asst. Hartt Coll. of Music, U. Hartford, 1970—71; faculty Jewish Theological Seminary of Am., 1987—88; staff N Am. Jewish Choral Festival, 1990—, IMUN Program, United Synagogue of Conservative Judaism, 1991; faculty Northeastern U., 1991—94; staff, Hazamir Nat. Jewish HS Chorus, 1993—; faculty, Prozdor Hebrew Coll. of Boston, HS Divsn., 1994—; faculty, cantorial program Hebrew Coll. of Boston, 2003—; founder, dir. Kol Rinah - The Jewish HS Chorus of Greater Boston, 1994—. Singer:

(Operas) Avery Fisher Hall, Carnegie Hall, Alice Tully Hall, Merkin Hall, The Jerusalem Theater; singer: (solo) (concerts and recordings) Zamir Chorale of Boston, The Zamir Chorale of NY, Selah and Jubal's Lyre; singer: (recordings with the Western Wind Vocal Ensemble) Birthday of the World (Parts I and II), (recordings) To Heal The Earth, various television and radio appearances; contbr. articles various profl. jours. Mem. bd. dirs Mazon – The Jewish Response to Hunger, 1994—2002; chmn. storage planning and recruitment coms. Cantors Assembly, 1991—94, 1996—98; chmn. Boy Scouts of Am. Viking Dist., 1998—; chaplain Philmont Scout Ranch, Boy Scouts of Am., 1991—95, 1998—; bd. dirs. Zamir Chorale of Boston, 1988—, Zamir Chorale Found., 1994—. Recipient Off-Off Broadway Theater award. Mem.: ASCAP, Assn. for Jewish Studies, Am. Soc. of Jewish Music, New England Holocaust Meml. Assn. (adv. bd. 1998—), Jewish Min. Cantors Assn. of New England (pres. 1990—94), Cantors Inst. Alumni Assn. (sec. 1990—92, pres. 1992—94), Newton Clergy Assn. Republican. Jewish. Achievements include first student to conduct svcs. at the Nat. Con. of the Cantors Assembly; first student to conduct Selichot svcs. at Jewish Theological Seminary. Avocations: astronomy, civil war, fire engine buff. Office: Congregation Adath Shir Rinah 321 Walnut St Box 263 Newton MA 02460 Office Phone: 617-395-5809. Office Fax: 617-558-8150. E-mail: cosborne@templeemanuel.com.

**OSBORNE, CLAUDINA ROSETTA,** financial analyst; b. Montserrat, Mar. 19, 1965; d. Joseph William and Mary Edith Osborne; 1 child, Bryan A. M. BS in health svcs. adminstrn., Herbert H. Lehman Coll., 1994; M in Pub. Adminstrn. and Fin., L.I. U., 2000. Fin. analyst AIG, N.Y.C., 1998—2001; sr. fin. analyst Primerica Fin. Svcs., N.Y.C., 1999-2000; ops. analyst Morgan Stanley Dean Witter, 2002—. Mem. MPA task force L.I. U., 1998-2000. Mem. Caribbean Women Orgn., Bronx, 1995-97; leader Boy Scouts of Am. 1995-97. Recipient Hiroshima Japanese scholarhip award Herbert Lehman Coll., 1993. Mem. NAFE, Am. Soc. for Pub. Adminstrn., N.Y. Women Agenda, Sigma Beta Delta. Episcopalian. Avocations: travel, reading, meeting people, tennis. Home: 2435 Boston Rd Bronx NY 10467 E-mail: dinaosborne@aol.com.

**OSBORNE, DONALD EUGENE,** performing company executive; b. San Francisco, Feb. 28, 1950; s. Cletus Eugene and Anne Osborne. MusB, San Francisco State U., MA, 1972. V.p. Mariedi Anders Artists Mgmt., San Francisco, 1972—75; dir. Calif. Artists Mgmt., San Francisco, 1976—. Mem.: Nat. Assn. Performing Arts Mgrs. & Agents (pres. 1995—96). Democrat-Npl. Office: Calif Artists Mgmt 564 Market St Ste 420 San Francisco CA 94104-5412 Office Phone: 415-362-2787. Business E-Mail: don@calartists.com.

**OSBORNE, DUNCAN ELLIOTT,** lawyer; b. Orange, N.J., May 24, 1944; s. Walter Dodd Osborne and Anne (Boaz) Treanor; m. Elizabeth May Bachman, Dec. 29, 1965; children: Ellen Osborne Ray, Mark Elliott, Michael Cleveland. BA, Stanford U., 1966; M. U. Tex., 1968, JD with honors, 1971. Bar: Tex. (cert. estate planning and probate law) 1971, U.S. Supreme Ct. 1975, U.S. Tax Ct. 1975, U.S. Fed. Ct. Claims 1997. Atty. Graves Dougherty, Austin, Tex., 1971-93, Osborne, Lowe, Helman & Smith L.L.P., Austin, 1993-2000, Osborne & Helman L.L.P., Austin, 2001—. Bd. dirs. Boatmen's Nat. Bank Austin, 1995-97, Hill Country Bank, Austin, 1998. Co-author, co-editor: Asset Protection: Domestic and International Law and Tactics; contbr. articles to profl. jours. Trustee Susan Vaughan Found., Houston, Still Water Found., Austin, Crail Found., Austin; chair bd. trustees St. Stephens Episcopal Sch., Austin, 1985-91, St. Andrews Episcopal Sch., Austin, 1978; dir. Touchstones Discussion Project, Annapolis, Md.; mem. Tex. Law Rev. Fellow Am. Coll. Trust and Estate Counsel (chair internat. estate planning com.), Coll. of State Bar of Tex.; mem. ABA, Internat. Tax Planning Assn., Internat. Bar Assn., Offshore Inst., Internat. Acad. Estate and Trust Law (v.p., exec. com.), Soc. Trusts and Estates Practioners, Tex. Bar Found., Asset Protection Planning Comm. (chair 1996-98)), Order of Coif Avocation: scuba diving. Office: Osborne & Helman LLP 301 Congress Ave Ste 1910 Austin TX 78701-2959 Office Phone: 512-542-2010. Business E-Mail: deosborne@osbornehelman.com.

**OSBORNE, JAMES ALFRED,** religious organization administrator; b. Toledo, July 3, 1927; s. Alfred James and Gladys Irene (Gaugh) O.; m. Ruth Glenrose Campbell, Nov. 26, 1945; 1 child, Constance Jean (Mrs. Donald William Canning). Grad., Salvation Army Coll., 1947; student, U. Chattanooga, 1954-55; D of Pub. Svc. (hon.), Gordon Coll., 1991. Corps officer Salvation Army, Magness, Nashville, 1947, Southside, Memphis, 1948, Owensboro, Ky., 1949-54, comdg. officer Chattanooga, 1954-61, city comdr. Miami, Fla., 1961-65, divisional comdr. Ky.-Tenn. Div., 1965-68, gen. sec. N.C. and S.C. Div., 1968-70, pub. rels. sec. 15 so. states, D.C. and Mex., 1970-71, divisional comdr. Md. and No. W.Va. Div., 1971-73, divisional comdr. Nat. Capital and Virginias Div. Washington, 1973-78, divisional comdr. Fla. Div. 1978-80, chief sec. Western Ter., 1980-84, nat. chief sec. Verona, NJ, 1984-86, territorial comdr. so. states Atlanta, 1986-89; nat. comdr., Republic of Marshall Islands, Guam, P.R., Virgin Islands Salvation Army USA, 1989-93. Chmn. Salvation Army Nat. Planning and Devel. Commn., 1974-76, 84-86; exec. bd. Vision Interfaith Satellite Network, Nat. Assn. Evangelicals, Christian Children's Fund Inc.; chmn. bd. Christian Mgmt. Assn., 1993-94; exec. com. religious alliance Against Pornography; rep. Salvation Army to numerous orgns. Bd. dirs. Nat. Law Ctr. for Children and Families; sec. Tenn. Conf. on Social Welfare, 1959, v.p.; 1960; pres. Fla. Conf. on Social Welfare, 1965; pres. Ky. Welfare Assn., 1970. Mem. Chattanooga Pastors Assn. (pres. 1958), Va. and W. Va. Welfare Confs., Rotary. Personal E-mail: jim@jarudsborne.com.

**OSBORNE, JAMES B., SR.,** academic administrator; b. Martin, Ky., Dec. 28, 1942; s. Mildred Louise and Willie Baisden Osborne; m. Nancy Luntsford, Jan. 13, 1948; children: James Baisden Osborne, Jr., Barton Christopher, Brian Samuel. Baisden, Morehead State U., 1966, Masters, 1968; Doctorate, East Tenn. State U., 1978. Football player N.Y. Giants, N.Y.C., 1966; faculty, head football coach Lees-McRae Coll., Banner Elk, NC, 1968—70; faculty, asst. football coach East Tenn. State, Johnson City, 1970—73; dir. for placement East Tenn. State Univ., Johnson City, 1974—79; dir. for coop. edn. U. Ala., Tuscaloosa, 1979—81; dir. for corp. rels. Ga. Inst. of Tech., Atlanta, 1981—88; v.p. for devel. Haggai Inst. for Leadership, Atlanta, 1988—89; v.p. for univ. advancement Med. Coll. of Ga., Augusta, 1989—2000; pres., CEO. Med. Coll. of Ga. Found., Inc., Augusta, 2000—. Dir. Jr. Achievement, Johnson City, Tenn., 1970—79; cons. Dept. of Edn., Washington, 1979—85. Bd. dirs. Hindman Settlement Sch., Ky., 2006—. Named Young Man of Yr., Jaycees, 1974; recipient Citation, Jr. Achievement, 1978, award, Coun. for Advancement and Support of Edn., 1987, 2000; grantee, NSF, 1979, U.S. Dept. of Edn., 1980. Mem.: Kiwanis Internat., Rotary Internat. Avocations: snow skiing, jogging. Home: 752 Eagleton Dr Augusta GA 30907 Office: Med Coll Ga Found Inc Alumni Ctr F1-1033 919 15th St Augusta GA 30912 Office Fax: 706-721-9324. Business E-Mail: josborne@mcg.edu.

**OSBORNE, JOAN (ELIZABETH),** singer, songwriter; b. Anchorage, Ky., July 8, 1962; d. Jerry and Ruth (Yunker) O. Student, NYU. Singer various blues clubs, N.Y.C. Albums include Soul Show, 1991, Blue Million Miles, 1993, Relish (includes One of Us), 1995 (7 Grammy nominations 1996, named No. 1 album Entertainment Weekly). Early Recordings, 1996.

**OSBORNE, JOHN L.,** academic administrator, educator; b. St. Catherines, Ont., Can., Aug. 28, 1967; s. John Barclay and Sharon Christine Osborne; m. Kelly Ilene Brewster, Aug. 6, 1988; children: Samuel, Riley, Seth. AA & AS, York Coll., Nebr., 1988; BS, Okla. Christian U., 1991. Tchg. cons. Mito Bd. of Ed., Japan, 1991—93; assoc. dir. Let's Start Talking, Ft. Worth, 1994—2000; dir. internat. prog. Okla. Christian U., 2000—. Cons. Let's Start Talking, 2000—, Internat. Edn. Network, Worland, Wyo., 2000—. Contbg. editor: (book) Global Perspectives, 2001, Culture Contact, 2002. Mem.: NAFSA.

**OSBORNE, JOHN WALTER,** historian, educator, author; b. Bklyn., Aug. 19, 1927; s. Douglas Walter and Gertrude Ann (Purcell) O.; m. Frances Patricia Hannon, Aug. 2, 1958; 1 son, David. BA, Rutgers U., 1957, MA (Louis Bevier fellow), 1959, PhD, 1961. Asst. prof. history Kean Coll. of N.J., 1961-63, N.J. Inst. Tech., 1963-64; asst. prof. Rutgers U., New Brunswick, NJ, 1964-66, assoc. prof., Phila., 1966-69, prof., 1969-93, prof. emeritus, 1993—. Author: William Cobbett-His Thought and His Times, 1966, The Silent Revolution: The Industrial Revolution in England as a Source of Cultural Change, 1970, John Cartwright, 1972; co-author: Cobbett in His Times, 1990; editor: Jour. of Rutgers U. Libraries, 1975-80; co-editor: A Grammar of the English Language, 1983; contbr. articles to profl. jours. Recipient Henry Browne award for disting. teaching Rutgers U., 1988; Am. Philos. Soc. grantee, 1966, 75 Home: PO Box 426 Ivoryton CT 06442-0426

**OSBORNE, JUDITH BARBOUR,** artist; b. Winnipeg, Man., Can., Oct. 14, 1950; came to U.S., 1952; d. John Anderson and Laura May (Jones) Barbour; m. Frederick Spring Osborne Jr., Feb. 15, 1986; children: Sheila, Thomas, Sophia, Jessica. BFA, Univ. of Arts, Phila., 1974; student, Vt. Studio Ctr., 1984-89; MFA, Pa. Acad. Fine Arts, Phila., 1997. Prin. Barbour CalliGraphics, Phila., 1976—2002; dir. publs. and publicity Phila. Conf. on Calligraphic Arts, Phila., 1982; mem. faculty Phila. Coll. Art (now U. of Arts), 1982-85, 92, 00, Drexel U., Phila., 1991—2002; faculty Innovations Internat. Calligraphy Conf., N.Y., 1987; exhbns. coord. Calleidoscope Internat. Calligraphy Conf., Trenton, NJ, 1993; guest lectr., workshop instr. Nantucket Island Sch. of Design and Arts, 2004. Guest curator Kamin Gallery, U. Pa., Phila., 1993, 95; exhbn. juror Phila. Calligraphers' Soc., 1989, 91, 94-95, 98, Phila. Sketch Club, 2002; spkr. 19th Internat. Calligraphy Conf., Guilford, Conn., 1999; lectr. in field. One-woman shows include Rourke Art Gallery, Moorhead, Minn., 1999, Phila. Art Alliance, 1999, Artists' House, 1998, 2000, 2002, Living Arts, Tulsa, Okla., 2000, Shipley Sch., Bryn Mawr, Pa., 2000, Delaware Ctr. for Contemporary Arts, 2004, Gallery Siano, Phila., 2004, Alexey von Schlippe Gallery, U. Conn, Avery Point, 2005, DeLong Gallery, Toronto, Can., 2005, West Liberty State Coll., W.Va., 2006, So. Vt. Arts Ctr., Manchester, 2006, Chester Gallery, Conn., 2006; exhibited in group shows at Nat. Arts Club, NYC, 1990, Pa. State Mus., Harrisburg, 1994, 2000-01, Am. Coll., Bryn Mawr, Pa., 1996, Nexus Found. for Today's Art, Phila., 1997, Del. Ctr. for Contemporary Art, 2002, Parallels Gallery, Phila., 2002, Tenri Cultural Inst., NYC, 2002, Shaanxi Mus., Xian, China, 2003, Ice House Gallery, Berkeley Springs, W.Va., 2004, Berman Mus. Art, Collegeville, Pa., 2004, Mobile (Ala.) Mus. Art, 2004, Calligrammes Gallery, Ottawa, Can., 2004-06, NY Hall Sci., Queens, 2005, Gallery One, Old Saybrook, Conn., 2005, Calif. State Polytechnic U., Pomona, Calif., 2006; represented in permanent collections Scripps Coll., Claremont, Calif., Mobile Mus. Art, Ala., Fed. Res. Bank Phila., Blue Cross, Rourke Art Gallery Mus., Moorhead, Barbour/Ladouceur Archs., Mpls.; also pvt. collections; collaborator Sophia Osborne Dance Assocs., 1999-2001, poet Jena Osman, 2001-04; contbr. articles to mags. and newspapers including Art Matters, 1997-2001, Letter Arts Rev., 2003. Recipient Best of Show Abington (Pa.) Art Ctr., 1990; Pa. Acad. Fine Arts fellow, Phila., 1997, Independence Found. fellow, 2001. Mem. Coll. Art Assn., Phila. Calligraphers' Soc. (bd. mem., publs. editor 1980-85), Inst. Noetic Scis. Avocation: metaphysics. Address: PO Box 4023 Old Lyme CT 06371-4023

**OSBORNE, LARRY NORMAN,** dean, consultant; b. Dayton, Ohio, Nov. 8, 1945; s. Edmund Arno and Helen Virginia Osborne; m. Sandra Kay Baer, 1968; 1 child, Nathaniel Earl. BS, Juniata Coll., 1970; MLS, U. Pitts., 1971, PhD, 1983. Staff announcer WFAD, Middlebury, Vt., 1967—69; staff photographer Dardanell Publs., Monroeville, Pa., 1970—71; cataloging libr. Idaho State U., Pocatello, Idaho, 1971—74; libr. dir. Clearfield County Pub. Libr., Curwensville, Pa., 1974—80; automation dir. Carlow Coll., Pittsburgh, 1980—83; asst. prof. U. Hawaii, Honolulu, 1983—2000; dean info. svcs. Chaminade U., Honolulu, 2000—. Author: (reference book) Library and Information Science Thesaurus, 1990; author: (textbook) Systems Analysis for Librarians and Information Professionals, 2000. Sgt. Army Inf., 1963—66, Mannheim Germany. Decorated Army Commendation medal US Army. Episcopalian. Office: Chaminade U 3140 Waialae Ave Honolulu HI 96816 Business E-Mail: losborn2@chaminade.edu.

**OSBORNE, LOUISE,** publishing executive; Pres. Osborne/Jenks Prodns., Inc., Wethersfield, Conn., 1979—. Office: care Osborne/Jenks Prodns Inc 936 Silas Deane Hwy Wethersfield CT 06109-4273

**OSBORNE, MARY GAGLIARDI,** elementary school educator, director; b. N.Y.C., Apr. 24, 1953; d. Victor Joseph and Margaret Louise Gagliardi; m. Cecil Edward Osborne, Aug. 11, 1979; 1 child, Margaret Victoria. BS, Wheelock Coll., Boston, 1975; MEd, U. South Fla., St. Petersburg, 1995. Cert. profl. educator Dept. Edn. Fla., 1975. Elem. tchr. Pinellas County Schs., Clearwater, Fla., 1977—; coord. Pinellas writing project Largo, 1989—; Writers camp coord. Poynter Inst. Media Studies, St. Petersburg, Fla. 1987—; adv. com. mem. Tampa Bay Area Writing Project, 1998—2001. Contbr. articles to profl. jours. Mem.: Internat. Reading Assn., Nat. Coun. Tchrs. English. Home: PO Box 686 Ozona FL 34660 Office: Pinellas County Schs 301 4th St SW Largo FL 33770 Office Fax: 727-588-5177.

**OSBORNE, MARY POPE,** writer; b. Ft. Sill, Okla., May 20, 1949; d. William Perkins and Barnette (Dickens) Pope; m. William R. Osborne, May 16, 1976. BA in Religion, U. N.C., 1971. Author: Run, Run, As Fast As You Can, 1982, Love Always, Blue, 1983, Best Wishes, Joe Brady, 1984, Mo to the Ocean, 1985, Last One Home, 1986, Beauty and the Beast, 1987, Favorite Greek Myths, 1988, American Tall Tales, 1990, The Many Lives of Benjamin Franklin, 1990, Moon Horse, 1991, George Washington, Leader of a New Nation, 1991, Spider Kane Mystery Series, 1992, 1993, Magic Tree House Series, 1992—, Haunted Waters, 1994, Molly and the Prince, 1994, Favorite Norse Myths, 1996, One World, Many Religions, 1996, Rocking Horse Christmas, 1997, Favorite Medieval Tales, 1998, Standing in the Light, 1998, The Life of Jesus, 1998, Adaline Falling Star, 2000, My Brothers Keeper, 2000, My Secret War, 2000, Kate and the Beanstalk, 2000, The Brave Little Seamstress, 2002, After the Rain, 2002, The One-Eyed Giant, 2002, The Land of the Dead, 2002, New Year's Bravest, 2002, Tales from the Odyssey, 2002, Happy Birthday, America, 2003, Magic Tree House Research Guides, 2000—, Magic Tree House Merlin Missions, 2000—, Sleeping Bobby, 2005, Pompeii: Lost and Found, 2006; co-author (with William Osborne): A Time to Dance, 2003. Recipient Disting. Alumna award, U. N.C., Chapel Hill, 1994, Distinctive Contbn. to Arts award, N.Y. Catholic Public Library; PEN, Authors League Fund (bd. dirs.), Authors Guild (pres. 1993—97). Office: Brandt & Brandt Lit Agy 1501 Broadway Ste 2310 New York NY 10036-5689

**OSBORNE, RICHARD DE JONGH,** mining and metals company executive; b. Bronxville, NY, Mar. 19, 1934; s. Stanley de Jongh and M. Elizabeth (Ide) O.; m. Cheryl Anne Archibald, Dec. 14, 1957; children: Leslie Coleman, Lindsay Vogel, Nicholas de J., Stanley de J. AB in Econs., Princeton U., 1956. With Cuno Engring. Corp., Meriden, Conn., 1956-60; fin., planning and mktg. exec. IBM Corp., Armonk, NY, 1960-69; investment adviser Sherman M. Fairchild, N.Y.C., 1969-70; exec. v.p. fin. and bus. devel., dir. Fairchild Camera & Instrument Corp., Mountain View, Calif., 1970-74; v.p. fin. ASARCO Inc. (formerly Am. Smelting & Refining Co.), N.Y.C., 1975-77, exec. v.p. 1977-82, pres., 1982-85, chmn., pres., CEO, 1985-99. Bd. dirs NACCO Industries, Inc., Tinker Found.; bd. dirs non-exec. chmn., bd. dirs. Datawatch Corp.; treas. Ams. Soc.; non-exec. chmn. Schering-Plough Corp; dir., non-exec. chmn. Southern Copper Corp. Mem.: Nat. Mining Assn. (non-dir.) Coun. Fgn. Rels., Econs. Club NY, River Club, Brook Club, Sakonnet Golf Club, John's Island Club. Home and office: 40 E 94th St Apt 32B New York NY 10128-0759 Personal E-mail: rdejo@att.net.

**OSBORNE, ROBERT STEPHEN,** automotive executive, lawyer; b. Montreal, Que., Can., Oct. 21, 1954; m. Martha Osborne; children: Tom, Sarah. AB magna cum laude, Harvard U., 1976, JD magna cum laude, 1979. Bar: Ill., 1979. Assoc. Kirkland & Ellis LLP, Chgo., 1979-85, ptnr., 1985—2002, Jenner & Block LLP, Chgo., 2002—, chair corp. practice; group v.p., gen.

counsel Gen. Motors Corp., 2006—. Gen. counsel, Lands' End, Inc., Dodgeville, Wis., 1986-95, corp. sec., sgl. asst. to bd. dirs., 1995-2002; adj. prof., U. Chgo. Law Sch., 2002-. Bd. dirs. Chgo. Shakespeare Theater, The Nature Conservancy of Alaska. Mem. ABA, Am. Soc. Corp. Secs., Internat. Bar Assn. Avocations: fly fishing, hiking. Office: Jenner & Block LLP One IBM Plz Chicago IL 60611 E-mail: rosborne@jenner.com.*

**OSBORNE, SEWARD RUSSELL,** writer; b. Catskill, NY, June 28, 1946; s. Seward Russell and Doris Virginia (Tompkins) O.; m. Jean Marie Shaver, June 22, 1968; children: Dean, Sarah. Historic site technician Senate House State Historic Site, Kingston, N.Y., 1976-77; contbg. editor Mil. Images, 1980—; contbg. author Mil. Collector & Historian, 1984—; historian Ulster County Civil War Round Table, 1994—; photographic cons. Arts and Entertainment Network, 1996. Cons. in field. Author: Holding the Left, The 20th New York State Militia at Gettysburg, July 1, 1863, 1990, The Saga of the Mountain Legion (156th N.Y. Vols.) in the Civil War and the Modest Hero Who Saved Our Flag, 1994, The Ninety Days Service of the 20th New York State Militia, 1998; editor: The Civil War Diaries of Col. Theodore B. Gates, 20th New York State Militia, 1991; contbr. articles to North South Trader's Civil War, 1970s, 1980s, Ulster County Gazette, 1970s, 1980s; photographic cons. Legacy TV Prodn. Three Days at Gettysburg, 1994. Active Friends of the Ulysses S. Grant Cottage; founder, dir. 120th Monument Restoration Fund, 1996-97; charter mem. Nat. WWII Meml., 2002—. Cited for erection 20th NY State Militia monument on the Gettysburg Battlefield, 1981, on the Battlefield of 2d Bull Run, Manassas, 1986, Rondout, NY, 2003. Fellow The Co. of Mil. Historians; mem. DAV (life), NRA, Ulster County Com. to Save the Grant Cottage (founder, chmn. 1990), N.Y. State Mil. Heritage Inst., 1997, Ulster County Geneal. Soc. (Civil War history cons.), Zadock Pratt Mus (hon. life), Kingston Area Libr. (Civil War history cons.), Friends of Nat. Parks at Gettysburg, Inc., Surratt Soc. (life), Gettysburg Battlefield Preservation Assn., Lexington Hist. Soc. (hon. life), Friends of Albany Rural Cemetery, Am. Legion, Sons of Union Vets., MOLLUS (Ulster County Hist. Soc. (hon. life). Born Again Christian. Avocations: historical sites, collecting Civil War artifacts, writing Civil War history. Home: 1329 County Road 2 Oliveridge NY 12461-5417 E-mail: info@ulsterguard.us.

**OSBORNE, TOM (THOMAS WILLIAM OSBORNE),** congressman, former college football coach; b. Hastings, Nebr., Feb. 22, 1937; m. Nancy Tederman; children: Mike, Ann, Susie. BA in Hist., Hastings Coll., Nebr., 1959; MA in Ednl. Psych., U. Nebr., 1963, PhD in Ednl. Psych., 1965. Flanker NFL Washington Redskins, 1959-61, NFL San Francisco 49ers, 1961-62; asst. football coach U. Nebr. 1962—67, receivers coach, 1967—71, asst. head coach, 1972, head football coach, 1973-97, prof. emeritus, 1998-2000; mem. US Congress from 3rd Nebr. Dist., 2001—, mem. agr. com., mem. edn. and the workforce com., mem. transp. and infrastructure com. Co-founder Osborne Endowment for Youth. Sgt. in US Army Nat. Guard and USAR, 1960—66. Named Big Eight Coach of Yr., 1975, 1978, 1980, Bobby Dodds Nat. Coach of Yr., 1978; recipient Policy Maker of Yr., Assn. Career and Tech. Edn., 2005. Mem.: Fellowship Christian Athletes. Republican. Meth. Achievements include coaching the U. Nebr. football team in several bowl games including the Sugar Bowl, 1971, Cotton Bowl, 1974, Astro-Bluebonnet Bowl, 1976, Liberty Bowl, 1977, Orange Bowl, 1979, 83, 84,89, 92-95, Sun Bowl, 1980; coached team to NCAA Divsn. IA Nat. Championship, 1994, 1995, 1997. Office: US Ho Reps 507 Cannon Ho Office Bldg Washington DC 20515-2703 Office Phone: 202-225-6435.*

**OSBOURNE, OZZY (JOHN OSBOURNE),** vocalist; b. Birmingham, Eng., Dec. 3, 1948; m. Thelma Mayfair, 1971 (div. 1981); children: Jessica Starshine, Louis Jon; m. Sharon Arden, 1982; children: Aimee Rachel, Kelly, Jack. Vocalist Black Sabbath band, 1969—79, solo career, 1980—. Albums Blizzard of Ozz, 1980, Diary of a Madman, 1981, Speak of the Devil, 1982, Bark at the Moon, 1983, The Ultimate Sin, 1986, Tribute, 1987, No Rest for the Wicked, 1988, Just Say Ozzy, 1990, No More Tears, 1991, Live & Loud, 1993, Ozzmosis, 1995, Ozzman Cometh, 1997, Down to Earth, 2001, Live at Budokhan, 2002, Essential Ozzy Osbourne, 2003, Under Cover, 2005, Interview Disc 97.7 Htz-Fm, 1999, albums (with Black Sabbath) Black Sabbath, 1969, Paranoid, 1970, Master of Reality, 1971, Volume 4, 1972, Sabbath, Bloody Sabbath, 1975, Sabotage, 1975, Technical Ecstasy, 1976, We Sold Our Soul For Rock and Roll, 1976, Never Say Die, 1978, Reunion, 1998, Past Lives, 2002, singles So Tired, 1984, (with Black Sabbath) Paranoid, 1970, appeared (films) Black Sabbath: Live, 1978, The Ultimate Ozzy, 2002 Osbourne: Bark at the Moon, Trick or Treat, 1986, Decline of Western Civilization Part II: The Metal Years, 2002 Osbourne: The Wicked Videos, 1988, Ozzy Osbourne: Don't Blame Me, 1992, The History of Rock 'N' Roll, Vol. 8, The Jerky Boys, 1995, Private Parts, 1997, Little Nicky, 2000, (TV films) Billy's Shout, 1991, (TV series) The Frank Skinner Show, 1996, South Park, 1997, The Osbournes, 2002—, Battle for Ozzfest, 2004—, (video) Ozzy Osbourne: Live and Loud, 1993, Black Sabbath: The Last Supper, 1999. Named to Rock and Roll Hall of Fame, 2006; recipient Grammy award, Best Heavy Metal Performance for I Don't Want to Change the World, 1994.

**O'SCANNLAIN, DIARMUID FIONNTAIN,** federal judge; b. NYC, Mar. 28, 1937; s. Sean Leo and Moira (Hegarty); m. Maura Nolan, Sept. 7, 1963; children: Sean, Jane, Brendan, Kevin, Megan, Christopher, Anne, Kate. BA, St. John's U., 1957; JD, Harvard U., 1963; LLM, U. Va., 1992; LLD (hon.), U. Notre Dame, 2002. Bar: Oreg. 1965, N.Y. 1964. Tax atty. Standard Oil Co. (N.J.), N.Y.C., 1963—65; oassoc. Davies, Biggs, Strayer, Sotel & Boley, Portland, Oreg., 1965—69; dep. atty. gen. State of Oreg., 1969—71, pub. utility commr., 1971—73; dir. Oreg. Dept. Environ. Quality, 1973—74; sr. ptnr. Ragen, Roberts, O'Scannlain, Robertson & Neill, Portland, 1978—86; judge U.S. Ct. Appeals (9th cir.), San Francisco, 1986—, mem. exec. com., 1988—89, 1993—94; mem. Jud. Coun. 9th Cir., 1991—93. Mem. U.S. Jud. Conf. Com. on Automation and Tech., 1990—; cons. Office of Pres.-elect and mem. Dept. Energy Transition Team (Reagan Transition), Washington, 1980—81; chmn. com. adminstrv. law Oreg. State Bar, 1980—81. Mem. coun. of legal advisors Rep. Nat. Com. 1981—83, mem., 1983—86; chmn. Oreg. Rep. Party, 1983—86; del. Rep. Nat. Convs., 1976, 1980, chmn. Oreg. del., 1984; nominee U.S. Ho. of Reps., 1st Congl. Dist., 1974; team leader energy task force Pres.'s Pvt. Sector Survey on Cost Control, 1982—83; trustee Jesuit H.S.; bd. visitors U. Oreg. Law Sch, 1988—; mem. citizens adv. bd. Providence Hosp., 1986—92. Maj. USAR, 1955—78. Mem.: ABA (sec. Appellate Judges Conf. 1989—90, exec. com. 1990—, chmn. 1994—95, chmn. jud. divsn. 2001—02), Fed. Judges Assn., Fed. Bar Assn., Multnomah Club. Roman Catholic. Office: US Ct Appeals 313 Pioneer Courthouse 555 SW Yamhill St Portland OR 97204-1396 Home: 700 SW 6th Ave # 313 Portland OR 97204-1417 E-mail: JudgeO'Scannlain@ca9.uscourts.gov.*

**OSE, DOUGLAS,** former congressman; b. Sacramento, June 27, 1955; m. Lynnda Ose; children: Erika, Emily. BS, U. Calif., Berkeley, 1977. Project mgr. Ose Properties, Sacramento, 1977-85; owner real estate devel. and investment co. 1986—; mem. U.S. Congress from 3d Calif. dist., 1999—2005; mem. agr., fin. svcs., and govt. reform coms., joint com. on printing. Former bd. dirs. Citrus Heights Chamber of Commerce, Citrus Heights Housing and Redevel. Commn.; mem. Citrus Heights Incorporation Project. Republican.

**OSEGUERA, PALMA MARIE,** retired career officer; b. Kansas City, Mo., Dec. 29, 1946; d. Joseph Edmund and Palma Louise (Utke) O'Donnell; m. Alfonso Oseguera, Jan. 1, 1977; stepchildren: Kristie M. Daniels, Michelle L. Nielson, Lori A. Kelley. BA in Phys. Edn., Marycrest Coll., 1969. Commd. 2d lt. USMC, 1969, advanced through grades to col., 1991; asst. Marine Corps exch. officer Hdqs. and Hdqs. Squadron, Marine Corps Air Sta., Beaufort, S.C., 1969-71; classified material control officer Hdqs. and Svcs. Battalion, Camp S.D. Butler, Okinawa, 1971-73; adminstrv. officer, asst. Marine Corps exch. officer Marine Corps Air Sta., El Toro, Santa Ana, Calif., 1973-76, Marine Corps exch. officer Yuma, Ariz., 1976-77; asst. Marine Corps exch. officer Hdqrs. and Support Bn., Marine Corps Devel. and Edn. Command, Quantico, Va., 1977-79; Marine Corps exch. officer Hqrs. Marine Corps, Washington, 1979-80; adminstrv. officer Marine Corps Air Base Squadon 46, Marine Air Group 46, Marine Corps Air Sta., El Toro, Santa Ana, 1981-83, Hdqs. and Maintenance Squadron 46, Marine Air Group 46, Marine Corps Air

Sta., El Toro, Santa Ana, 1983-85, Mobilization Tng. Unit Calif. 53, Landing Force Tng. Command, Pacific, San Diego, 1985-89, 3d Civil Affairs Group, L.A., 1989; dep. asst. chief of staff G-1 I Marine Expeditionary Force, Individual Mobilization Augumentee Detachment, Camp Pendleton, Calif. 1990-91; assoc. mem. Mobilization Tng. Unit Del. 01, Del., 1992-94; adminstrn. officer Mobilization Tng. Unit, CA-53, EWTG Pac, NAB, Coronado, San Diego, 1994-96; exch. officer MWRSPT ACT IMA Det MCB, Camp Pendleton, Calif., 1996-99; ret. from 30 yrs. commissioned svc. USMCR, 1999, Choir St. Elizabeth Seaton, Woodbridge, Va., 1978-80, St. Patricks, Arroyo Grande, Calif., 1990-94; vol. Hospice, San Luis Obispo, 1995-2000; active Los Osos (Calif.) Veteran's Events Com., 1994-2000; lector, Eucharistic min., Martha Min. St. Patrick's Cath. Ch., Arroyo Grande, 2004—. Mem. AAUW (past libr.), Marine Corps Assn., Marine Corps Res. Officer Assn., Marine Corps Aviation Assn. (12 dist. dir. 1987), Women in Mil. Svc. for Am., Woman Marine Assn., Marine Corps League. Republican. Roman Catholic. Avocations: skiing, gardening, reading, horseback riding, genealogy. Home: 728 Scenic Cir Arroyo Grande CA 93420-1617

**OSEI, JOSEPH,** education educator, minister; b. Kokofu, Ghana, Dec. 10, 1951; s. Paul Kwame Osei-Assibey and Kate Afiriyie Mensah; m. Victoria Adutwumwah; children: Lucy Osei-Asare, Georgina, Sussana, Miriam Jo, Emmanuel. BA in Philosophy and Religion, U. Ghana, 1981; MA in Philosophy, Ohio U., 1985; PhD, Ohio State U., 1991. Cert. Theology Meth. Ch., Ghana, 1978. Vis. prof. philosophy U. of South Fla., Tampa, 2000—01, Auburn U., Ala., 2001—. Acting chair, philosophy dept. U. of Ghana, Accra, 1995—99. Sec. Ecumenical Assn. of Third World Theologians, Accra, Ghana, 1994—99. Recipient First prize In Theology, Trinity Theol. Sem., Ghana, 1978; grantee Rsch. Grant, Ohio State U., 1990; tchg. award, Young Scholar's Program, 1990. Mem.: Am. Philos. Assn. Methodist. Achievements include first to Founder, African Christian Ch., Columbus, Ohio. Avocations: soccer, volleyball. Office: Auburn U 6080 Haley Ctr Auburn AL 36830 Home: 6540 Brookstone Ln Apt 210 Fayetteville NC 28314-8054 Office Fax: 334-844-2196. Personal E-mail: josephoseij@aol.com. E-mail: oseijos@auburn.edu.

**OSEN, GREGORY ALAN,** water conditioning company executive; b. Beloit, Wis., Mar. 14, 1951; s. Vincent Darryl and Mavis Lucille (Lasher) O.; m. Deborah Ann Churchill Bladorn, Jan. 29, 1972 (div. Jan. 1987); m. Christine Adel Dauenbaugh Pullnam, Oct. 8, 1987; children: Leah Michelle, Felicia Ann. BA in Music Edn. with honors, Milton (Wis.) Coll., 1973; postgrad., Cardinal Stritch Coll., 1985. Machinist, assembler Nat. Detroit, Rockford, Ill., 1973-78; sales tech. Ill. Water Treatment, Rockford, 1978-79, sales engr., 1979-80, dist. sales engr., 1980-85; sales mgr. Glegg Water Technologies, Guelph, Ont., Can., 1985-2000; v.p. mktg. & sales Process Equipment Unltd., Londonderry, N.H., 2000—. Pres. Seekers, Strawbridge Meth. Ch., 1995-96, mem. adminstrv. bd., 1996, mem. choir, 1995-96; trumpeter Harris County Big Band, 1993-95. Mem. Am. Water Works Assn., AIChe Avocations: auto racing, sports cars. Office: Process Equipment Unltd 46 Nashua Rd Bldg B Ste 9A Londonderry NH 03053 also: Glegg Water Conditioning 29 Royal Rd Guelph ON Canada N1H 1G2 Home: 3824 Sandy Hollow Rd Rockford IL 61109-2552 E-mail: peunh@aol.com.

**OSGOOD, CHARLES,** news broadcaster, journalist; b. N.Y.C., Jan. 8, 1933; s. Charles Osgood and Mary F. (Wilson) Wood; m. Jean Crafton, Dec. 5, 1973; children: Kathleen, Winston, Anne Elizabeth, Emily Jean, James Edward. BS, Fordham U., 1954; L.H.D. (hon.), St. Bonaventure U., 1977; PhD (hon.), Fordham U.; LLD, St. John's U. Program dir. Sta. WGMS, Washington, 1955—63; gen. mgr. Sta. WHCT, Hartford, Conn., 1963—64; reporter ABC Radio News, 1964—67; anchorman Sta. WCBS, 1967—71; corr. television and radio CBS, N.Y.C., 1971—; anchor CBS News Sunday Morning, 1994—. Author: Nothing Could be Finer Than A Crisis That Is Minor in the Morning, 1979, There's Nothing That I Wouldn't Do If You Would Be My POSSLQ, 1981-82; clin. asst. prof. psychiatry, clin. instr. family practice 1991, See You on the Radio, 1999. Recipient Sol Taishoff award for broadcasting excellence, Nat. Press Found., 2005. Mem.: AFTRA. Office: CBS News 524 W 57th St New York NY 10019-2924

**OSGOOD, CHRIS,** professional hockey player; b. Peace River, Alta., Canada, Nov. 26, 1972; Goalie Detroit Red Wings, 1991—2001, N.Y. Islanders, 2001—05, Detroit Red Wings, 2005—. Player NHLI All-Star Game, 1996. Named to WHL East All-Star 2d Team, 1990—91, Sporting News All-Star Team, 1996; recipient Bill Jennings Trophy, NHL, 1996. Office: c/o Detroit Red Wings 600 Civic Center Dr Detroit MI 48226-4408

**OSGOOD, CHRISTOPHER MYKEL,** radio sales executive; b. Northampton, Mass., Nov. 8, 1963; s. Robert Mansfield and Susanne (Mykel) Osgood; m. Angela Baxter; 1 child, Robert Marley. BS, Cornell U., 1989. Media rsch. mktg. analyst Vitt Media Internat., N.Y.C., 1988-89; acct. exec. KAOI AM/FM Radio, Maui, Hawaii, 1989-91, KTXH-TV, Houston, 1991-92; dir. advt. Oilers News, Browns News Illustrated, 49ers Report, Cleve., 1992-93; acct. exec. KRBE-FM, Houston, 1993-96, KLOL-FM, Houston, 1996-99; local sales mgr. KUCD-FM, Honolulu, 1999-2001; gen. sales mgr. KLOL-FM, Houston, 2001—03; local sales mgr. WSB-AM, Atlanta, 2003—05, gen. sales mgr., 2005—. Mem. sales adv. com. Radio Advt. Bur.; advanced competitive tng. coord. Radio Divsn. Cox Enterprises. Coach Bear Creek Basketball League, Houston, 1993—94. Mem.: Cornell Alumni Assn. Atlanta, Cornell Soc. Hotelmen. Home: 3333 Sulky Cir Se Marietta GA 30067-5074 Office: Newstalk 750 WSB 1601 W Peachtree St NE Atlanta GA 30309 Office Phone: 404-897-7562.

**OSGOOD, NANCY JEAN,** medical educator, writer; b. July 6, 1951; d. Jack Kent and Lois Emma (Stober) Luttrell; m. Raymond Clifford Jordan, Jr., Oct. 13, 1984. BA in Sociology and Spanish, Yankton Coll., 1972; MA in Sociology, Drake U., 1974; cert. in gerontology, Syracuse U. 1979; PhD in Sociology, 1979, Rsch. assoc. Syracuse Rsch. Corp., NY, 1975—78; asst. prof. SUNY, Cortland, 1979—80, Med. Coll. Va., Richmond, 1980—92, prof., 1992—. Mem. Nat. Com. on Vital and Health Stats., Washington, 1982—84. Author: Senior Settlers: Social Integration in Retirement Communities, 1982, Suicide in the Elderly: A Practitioner's Guide to Diagnosis and Mental Health Intervention, 1985, Suicide Among the Elderly in Long-Term Care Facilities, 1991; editor: Life after Work: Retirement, Leisure, Recreation and the Elderly, 1982; co-author: Seniors on Stage: The Impact of Applied Theatre on the Elderly, 1985, Suicide and the Elderly: An Annotated Bibliography and Review, 1986; co-editor: Dynamic Leisure Programming With Older Adults, 1987, The Science and Practice of Gerontology: A Multi-disciplinary Guide, 1989, Alcoholism and Aging: An Annotated Bibliography and Review, 1995, Treating Alcohol and Drug Abuse in the Elderly, 2002. Mem. selection com. King William H.S., Va., 1985; active Va. State Rehab. Bd., Am. Cancer Soc. Recipient acad. scholarship, Yankton Coll., 1969—72, N.Y. State Dept. Mental Hygiene Rsch. fellowship, 1974—75, Nat. Inst. Edn. award, 1975—78, NIMH award, 1977—79, Presdl. Invitation to White House, 1984, 1991; grantee Va. Commonwealth U., 1981—82. Fellow: Gerontol. Soc. Am.; mem.: Internat. Platform Assn., So. Gerontol. Soc., Am. Sociol. Assn., Am. Assn. Suicidology. Avocations: playing piano and clarinet, gourmet cooking, parrots. Home: PO Box 245 Manquin VA 23106-0245 Office Phone: 804-828-6077. Personal E-mail: nosgood@vlu.edu. Business E-mail: nosgood@mail2.vcu.edu.

**OSGOOD, RICHARD MAGEE, JR.,** electrical engineering professor, researcher; b. Kansas City, Mo., Dec. 28, 1943; s. Richard Magee and Mary Neff (Russell) O.; m. Alice Rose Dyson, June 25, 1966; children— Richard Magee, III, Nathaniel David, Jennifer Anne BS in Engring., U.S. Mil. Acad., 1965; MS in Physics, Ohio State U., 1968; PhD, MIT, 1973. Rsch. assoc. dept. physics MIT, Cambridge, Mass., 1969-72, rsch. staff Lincoln Lab., 1973-80, project leader Lincoln Lab., 1980-81; assoc. prof. applied physics and elec.engring. Columbia U., NYC, 1981-82, prof., 1982-91, Higgins prof., 1989—. Assoc. dir. Brookhaven Nat. Lab., Upton, NY, 2000—03; dir. Microelectronics Sci. Labs., 1984—90; mem. Army Sci. and Tech. Basic Energy Scis. Adv. Com., Def. Scis-Advanced Rsch. Projects Agy.; mem. Los Alamos Nat. Lab.; mem. ad hoc com. Air Force Sci. Adv. Bd. Editor: Laser Diagnostics and Photochemical Processing of Semiconductor Devices, 1983;

---

contr. articles to profl. jours.; patentee in field Served to capt. USAF, 1965-69 Recipient Samuel Burka award USAF Avionics Lab., 1968, Leos Travelling Lectr. award, 1986-87, Disting. Travelling Lectr. APS, R.W. Wood Prize, 1991, Optical Soc. Am.; John Simon Guggenheim fellowship, 1989. Fellow IEEE, Am. Phys. Soc., Optical Soc. Am. (R.W. Wood award, 1991); mem. Am. Chem. Soc., Materials Rsch. Soc. (councillor 1983-86), Optical Device Assn. (Japanese hon. lectr. 1990), Am. Phys. Soc. (travelling lecture-ship 1992). Office: Columbia U Radiation Lab New York NY 10027

**OSGOOD, ROBERT MANSFIELD,** lawyer; b. Elmira, NY, Jan. 27, 1942; s. Roland Lorenzo and Isabelle (Mansfield) O.; m. Janice Deakin, 1992; children: Christopher, Elisabeth, Abigail, Antonia. BA, Syracuse U., 1963, JD, 1968; postgrad. diploma in EC law, Kings Coll., London, 1994. Bar: N.Y. 1968, U.S. Dist. Ct. (no. dist.) N.Y. 1969, U.S. Dist. Ct. (so. dist.) N.Y. 1970, U.S. Ct. Appeals (2d cir.) 1971, U.S. Dist. Ct. (ea. dist.) N.Y. 1974, U.S. Ct. Appeals (D.C. cir.) 1976, U.S. Supreme Ct. 1977. Ptnr. Sullivan & Cromwell, N.Y.C. and London, 1968—. Fellow Am. Coll. Trial Lawyers; mem. Am. Law Inst. Office: Sullivan & Cromwell LLP 125 Broad St Fl 28 New York NY 10004-2489 also: 1 New Fetter Ln London E4A 1AN England Office Phone: 212-558-3710. Business E-mail: osgoodr@sullcrom.com.

**OSGOOD, RUSSELL KING,** academic administrator; b. Fairborn, Ohio, Oct. 25, 1947; s. Richard M. and Mary Russell Osgood; m. Paula Haley, June 6, 1970; children: Mary, Josiah, Micah, Iain. BA, Yale U., 1969, JD, 1974. Bar: Mass. 1974, U.S. Dist. Ct. Mass. (admitted to) 1976. Assoc. Hill & Barlow, Boston, 1974—78; assoc. prof. Boston U., 1978—80; prof. Cornell U., Ithaca, NY, 1980—88, dean law sch., 1988—98; pres. Grinnell Coll., Iowa, 1998—. Lt. USNR, 1969—71. Mem.: Selden Soc., Stair Soc., Mass. Hist. Soc. Office: Grinnell Coll 1121 Park St Grinnell IA 50112-1640 Office Phone: 641-269-3000. E-mail: osgood@grinnell.edu.

**OSGUTHORPE, JOHN DAVID,** otolaryngologist, educator; b. Fairbanks, Alaska, 1948; MD, U. Utah, 1973; grad., Med. Ed. in Otolaryngology. Intern UCLA, 1973-74, resident surgery, 1974-75, resident otolaryngology, 1975-78; prof. Med. U. SC, Charleston, SC, 1979—, surg. dir.; otolaryngologist Med. U. Hosp., Charleston, SC. Accreditation coun. Skull Base fellowship U. Zurich. Mem.: HNS, AMA (del. 1998—), Residence Rev. Comm., Sinus Allergy Health Partnership (bd. dir. 1998—, pres. 2004), Am. Rhinologic Soc. (bd. dir. 1998—2001, editor 1998—2001), Am. Laryngological Assn., Am. Acad. Otolaryngolic Allergy (pres. 1995), Am. Acad. Otolaryngology, Head and Neck Surgery (bd. dirs. 1997—, coord. continuing edn. 2000—), Disting. Svc. award 1995, 2004, Pres. award 2004). Office: Med Univ SC Dept Otolaryngology 150 Ashley Ave Charleston SC 29401-5803 Office Phone: 843-792-3533. E-mail: osguthjd@comcast.net.

**O'SHANICK, GREGORY JOHN,** physician, medical association administrator; b. Akron, Ohio, Nov. 22, 1953; s. Peter and Mary (Popadics) O'S; m. Alison Moon, Oct. 8, 1991; children: Beth, Peter, Van, Alexis, Drew. Student, Ohio State U., 1971-73; MD, U. Tex., Galveston, 1977. Cert. Am. Soc. Neurorehabilitation, 1993, Am. Soc. Neurorehabilitation, 2003, in psychosomatic medicine Am. Bd. Psychiatry and Neurology, 2006, diplomate in gen. psychiatry Am. Bd. Psychiatry and Neurology, 1983, and sr. disability analyst Am. Bd. Disability Analysts, 1996, lic. Va. State Bd. Med. Examiners, Tex. State Bd. Med. Examiners. Intern, dept. psychiatry Duke U. Med. Ctr., Durham, NC, 1977—78, resident, dept. psychiatry, 1978—80, chief resident, dept. psychiatry, 1980—81, fellow in consultation, liaison psychiatry, divsn. psychosomatic medicine, dept. psychiatry, 1980—81; asst. staff psychiatrist Meml. S.W. Hosp., Houston, 1981-84; assoc. The Hauser Clinic and Assoc., P.A., Houston, 1981-82; clin. asst. prof. psychiatry, clin. instr. family practice U. Tex. Health Sci. Ctr., Houston, 1981-82, asst. prof. psychiatry, assoc. dir. cons.-liason svc., 1982-84; asst. prof. psychiatry, dir. med./psychiatry svc. Med. Coll. Va., Richmond, 1984-89, asst. prof. rehab. medicine, 1985-89, dir. inpatient psychiarty svcs., 1987-90, co-dir. rehab. rsch. and tng. ctr. in brain injury, 1989-90, chmn. divsn. inpatient psychiatry, 1989-90, assoc. prof. psychiatry and rehab. medicine, 1989-91; attending physician VA Med. Ctr., Richmond, 1987-91; dir. Ctr. Neuro Rehab. Svc., Richmond, 1991—; assoc. med. dir. neurorehab. program Health South Med. Ctr., Richmond, 1993-96. Cons. neuropsychiatric PATE Rehab. Endeavors, Inc., Dallas, 1990-91; assoc. prof. dept. neurological surgery U. Va., 1998, rsch. Va. Inst. Neurological Inst., 1998; attending neuropsychiatrist U. Va. Med. Ctr., 1990; spl. cons. traumatic brain injury initiative Nat. Inst. Handicapped Rsch., 1986-87; assoc. prof. neurosurgery U. Va. Health Sci. Ctr.; mem. neuromed. adv. bd. N.E. Ctr. for Spl. Care, 1998-2000; presenter in field. Author: (with others) MMPI 168 Codebook, 1984; editor: Psychiatric Aspects of Trauma, 1986, Head Trauma Psychiatric Medicine, 1989; contbg. author: (with others) Neuropsychological Treatment of Head Injury, 1989, Principles of Medical Psychiatry, 1987, Community Reentry for Person with Traumatic Brain Injury, 1989, Psychiatric Aspects of Traumatic Brain Injury, 1994; editl. bd. Neurorehabilitation: An Interdisciplinary Jour.; contbr. articles, papers, book chpts., letters and editls. to numerous profl. jours. Mgr., coach Huguenot Little League, Chesterfield, Va., 1991-98; mem. selection com. Keep our Streets Safe and Sober, 1996; bd. dirs. Nat. Head Injury Found., 1989, chair psychiatry adv. com., 1988-90, mem. legis. com. profl. divsn., 1986-87, com. revise DSM-IV listings TBI, 1985, spl. cons., 1984; mem. task force dually diagnosed Southern Regional Edn Bd., 1986; mem. Va. Brain Injury Coun., 1987-2000, vice-chair, 1997-2000, chair, 1998-99; mem. adv. bd. Va. Head Injury Found., Inc., 1988-91; mem. task force cognitive retraining Gen. Assembly Commonwealth Va., 1992; mem. task force evaluate and modify traumatic brain injury program Woodrow Wilson Rehab. Ctr., Va., 1993; bd. dirs. Transitional Learning Cmty., Galveston, Tex., 1983-85, adv. bd. 1985-91; mem. com. psychol. edn. Am. Diabetes Assn., Houston onpt. 1983-84, mem.expert working group mild traumatic brain surgery-CDC, 2001; chmn. Blue Ribbon Panel brain injury and amusement park rider, 2002-03; cons. dopamine agonist therapy low response children following acquired brain injury, 2002-04, impact littermate psychol. stress in rats, 2003-04. Recipient Hamilton Ford award for Excellence, 1977, Appreciation cert., Tex. Head Injury Found., 1985, Appreciation cert., US Dept. Edn., 1987, Bus. Assoc. of Yr. award Shockoe Valley chpt., Am. Bus. Women's Assn., 1989; grantee UTHSCH, 1983, Roering Pharm., 1983-85, Va. Commonwealth Univ. Grants-In-Aid Program, 1985-89, DMHMR, 1987-88, 1988-89, 1989-90, 1990-91, NIDRR, 1986-89, 1988-89, 1989-90, 1989-93, 1992-93, Dept. Edn., 1991-92, NY State Dept. Edn., 1993, US Dept. Edn. RSA, 1995-96, Commonwealth Neurotrauma Initiative Adv. Bd., Va. Dept. Rehab. Svcs., 2002-05, NIH, 2003-04. Fellow Am. Psychiat. Assn. (disting., com. mem. life, accident and health ins. 1981-89, subcom. ins. code system 1983-84, task force traumatic brain injury 1990, assoc. editor Brian Injury: Jour. Internat. Brain Injury Assn. 1985-91, disting.); mem. AMA, Am. Neuropsychiat. Assn., Am. Soc. Neurorehabilitation, Brain Injury Assn. (med. dir. 1996—, bd. dirs. Rubin Rsch. Fund 1997), Assn. Medicine and Psychiatry, Am. Acad. for Cert. of Brain Injury Specialists (bd. dirs.), Psychiat. Soc. Va., Am. Acad. Neurology, Med. Soc. Va., World Fedn. Neurorehabilitation, Brain Injury Assn. Am., Sigma Xi, Mu Delta. Republican. Avocations: golf, skiing, travel, reading, Arabian horses. Office: Ctr Neurorehab Svc 11315 Polo Pl Midlothian VA 23113-1434 Office Phone: 804-897-1688. E-mail: gjocns@aol.com.

**O'SHAUGHNESSY, CHRISTOPHER T.,** lawyer; b. Princeton, N.J., Jan. 19, 1971; s. Thomas G. and Geraldine M. O'Shaughnessy; m. Renée M. Pilliod, Aug. 13, 1994; children: Michael J., Katherine Grace. BA, Ohio State U., 1993; JD, Capital U., Columbus, Ohio, 1997. Bar: Ohio 1998, U.S. Dist. Ct. (no. and so. dists.) Ohio 1999. Law clk. State of Ohio's Atty. Gen., Columbus, 1995, Ray, Alton, Todaro and Kirstein, LPA, Columbus, 1995—97, Lane, Alton & Horst, LLC, Columbus, 1997—98, atty. at law, 1998—, mem. profl. recruiting com. Atty., cons. Action Children Counsel Franklin County, Columbus, 1999—. Co-editor: (book) The ePolicy Handbook, 2001. Vol. Rep. John Kasich's Re-election, Columbus, 1990, Sen. Michael Dewine's Campaign, Columbus, 1992. Named one of Top Lawyers in Ctrl. Ohion, Bus. First The Verdict, 2005, Rising Stars, Ohio Super Lawyers, 2005. Mem.: Franklin Am. Inn of Ct., Ohio Acad. of Trial Lawyers,

---

Def. Rsch. Inst. Republican. Roman Catholic. Avocations: basketball, golf, music. Office: Lane Alton and Horst LLC 175 S Third St Columbus OH 43215 Business E-Mail: cto@lah4law.com.

**O'SHAUGHNESSY, JAMES PATRICK,** lawyer, consultant; b. Rochester, N.Y., Mar. 3, 1947; s. John Andrew and Margaret May (Yaxley) O'S.; m. Terry Lee Wood. BS cum laude, Rensselaer Poly. Inst., 1972; JD, Georgetown U., 1977. Bar: Va. 1977, Ohio 1979, Wis. 1987. Assoc. Squire, Sanders & Dempsey, Cleve., 1978-81; ptnr. Hughes & Cassidy, Sumas, Wash., 1981-84; patent counsel Kimberly-Clark Corp., Neenah, Wis., 1984-85; ptnr. Foley & Lardner, Milw., 1986-96; v.p., chief intellectual property counsel Rockwell Automation, Inc., Milw., 1996—2004; ind. cons. Mequon, Wis., 2004—. Founder Innovatech Co., 1996-2000; mem. tech. adv. coun. Ideation Internat., Inc., 1999-2004; mem. adv. bd. Licensing Econs. Rev., Intellectual Property Bus. Internat., 2002-04; mem. bd. visitors Georgetown U. Sch. Nursing, 1996-2000; bd. dir. Gemstar TV Guide Internat. Inc., comp. com., 2004—; lectr. in field. Contbg. author: Technology Licensing: Corporate Strategies for Maximizing Value, 1996, Profiting From Intellectual Capital: Extracting Value From Innovation, 1998; contbr. articles to profl. jours. Bd. dirs. Skylight Opera Theatre, 1991-92, Milw. Florentine Opera Co., 1999—, pres., 2002. With USN, 1964-68. Mem. CPR Inst. for Dispute Resolution (mediation/arbitration panel), Lic. Execs. Soc., Am. Intellectual Property Law Assn., Assn. Chief Patent Coun.; Disabled Am. Vets., Tau Beta Pi, Alpha Sigma Mu. Home and Office: 3207 W Donges Bay Rd Mequon WI 53092-5119 Office Phone: 262-512-9883.

**O'SHEA, ANNA BELLE MARIE,** music educator, liturgy administrator; b. Evergreen Park, Ill., Apr. 9, 1956; d. Joseph Bernard and Anna Belle Marie O'Shea. MusB, De Paul U., 1978; diploma in Pastoral Liturgy, St. Joseph's Coll., 2003, MA in Ch. Music and Liturgy, 2004. Pvt. flut instr., Chgo., 1976—; prin. flutist N.W. Ind. Symphony, Munster, Ind., 1977—88; freelance flutist Chgo., 1978—; founder, pres, dir. music Flutes Unlimited, Chgo., 1997—; dir. liturgy Mother McAuley HS, Chgo., 2005—. Mem. music staff Archdiocese Chgo., 2000—. Co-author: The Liturgical Flutist: A Method Book and More, 2005. Mem.: Nat. Flute Assn. (performer), Nat. Assn. Pastoral Musicians (clinician, bd. dirs. ensemble sect. 1999—). Roman Catholic.

**O'SHEA, CATHERINE LARGE,** marketing and public relations consultant; b. Asheville, N.C., Feb. 27, 1944; d. Edwin Kirk Jr. and Mary Mitchell (Westall) Large; m. Roger Dean Lower, Dec. 19, 1970 (dec. Sept. 1977); children: Thaddeus Kirk Lower and David Alexander Lower (twins, dec.); m. Michael Joseph O'Shea, Dec. 29, 1980 (div. 2001). BA in History magna cum laude, Emory U., 1966. Mktg. staff mem. Time Inc., N.Y.C., 1966-69; mktg. adminstr. Collier-Macmillan Internat., N.Y.C., 1970-71; circulation mgr. Coll. Entrance Exam. Bd., N.Y.C., 1971-73; spl. asst. to pres. Wayne Dressel Assocs. Exec. Search, N.Y.C., 1973-75; freelance writer, editor, pub. rels. Princeton, N.J., 1975-78; dir. constituency rels. Emory U., Atlanta, 1978-80; devel. assoc. U. Del., Newark, 1981-83; asst. to pres. Elizabethtown (Pa.) Coll., 1983-85; assoc. v.p. Beaver Coll., Glenside, Pa., 1985; cons. mktg. and pub. rels. Phila., S.C., Ga., 1985—. Lectr. in field. Co-author: 50 Secrets of Highly Successful Cats, 1994 (trans. German edit. Schnurrende Tyrannen by Manfred Sommer, 1996); editor Elizabethtown mag., 1983-85; contbr. articles to nat. mags. and profl. jours. Founder Helping Hands Internat.; founding trustee Newberry Opera House Found.; mem. founding com. Rachel Long-street Found., Jessye Norman Sch. of Arts. Mem. Mortar Bd., Phi Beta Kappa, Phi Mu.

**O'SHEA, DONALD C.,** physicist, educator, optical engineer; b. Akron, Ohio, Nov. 14, 1938; s. Donald Joseph and Sarah O'S.; m. Helen Rose Spustek, Oct. 20, 1962; children: Sean Stanley, Kathleen Susan, Sheila Sarah, Patrick Donald. BS, U. Akron, 1960; MS, Ohio State U., 1963; PhD in Physics, Johns Hopkins U., 1968. Rsch. fellow McKay Lab., Harvard U., Cambridge, Mass., 1968-70; asst. prof. Ga. Inst. Tech., Atlanta, 1970-75, assoc. prof., 1975-87, prof. physics, 1987—2004, prof. emeritus, 2004—. Author: Elements of Modern Optical Design, 1978; co-author: Introduction to Lasers and Their Applications, 1978; editor Optical Engring., 1998-99, 2001—; co-author Diffractive Optics, 2004; contbr. some 40 articles to profl. jours. Fellow Internat. Soc. Optical Engring. (sec. 1997, v.p. 1999, pres. 2000), Optical Soc. Am. (Esther Hoffman Beller award 1996). Democrat. Roman Catholic. Achievements include creation of the optics discovery kit for children; 3 patents in optical design. E-mail: doshea@prism.gatech.edu.

**O'SHEA, ERIN K.,** biomedical researcher; m. Doug Jeffery O'Shea. AB in biochemistry, Smith Coll., 1988; PhD in chemistry, MIT, 1992. Asst. prof. biochemistry and biophysics U. Calif., San Francisco, 1993—97, assoc. prof. biochemistry and biophysics 1997—2001, prof., vice chair biochemistry and biophysics, 2001—; asst. investigator Howard Hughes Med. Inst., 2000—. Chair sci. adv. bd. Boston U. Sch. Medicine, Dept. Genetics and Genomics, 2002—; mem. sci. adv. com. Ellen Hay Whitney Found., 2002—; chair external review com. Bauer Ctr. Genomics Harvard U., 2004. Pub. Libr. Sci., 2003—. Recipient Promega Early Career Life Sci. award, Am. Soc. Cell Biology, 2000, Irving Sigal Young Investigator award, Protein Soc., 2004; fellow, David and Lucile Packard Found., 1994. Fellow: Am. Acad. Arts and Scis.; mem.: NAS (mem. NTC com. on standards and principles in biol. rsch. 2002—, award in molecular biology 2001). Office: Howard Hughes Med Inst Harvard U Dept Molecular & Cellular Biology Bauer 307 7 Divinity Ave Cambridge MA 02138 Office Phone: 617-495-4328. Office Fax: 617-496-5425. Business E-Mail: Erin_OShea@harvard.edu.*

**O'SHEA, JAMES,** managing editor; Reporter US Army; reporter, fin. editor Washington corr. The Des Moines Register; reporter The Chicago Tribune, 1979—90, assoc. mng. editor for foreign and nat. news, 1990—95, dep. mng. editor for news, 1995—2001, mng. editor, 2001—. Bd. gov. Oversea Press Club Am. Office: Chicago Tribune 435 N Michigan Ave Chicago IL 60611 Business E-mail: jo'shea@tribune.com.

**O'SHEA, LYNNE EDEEN,** management consultant, educator; b. Chgo., Oct. 18, 1950; d. Edward Fisk and Mildred (Lessner) O'S. BA, BJ in Polit. Sci. and Journalism, U. Mo., MA in Info. Theory, 1971; PhD in Consumer Cultures, Northwestern U., 1978; postgrad., Sch. Mgmt. and Strategic Studies, U. Calif., 1988. Congl. asst., Washington, 1968—70; brand mgr. Procter & Gamble Co., Cin., 1971-73; v.p. Foote, Cone & Belding, Inc., Chgo., 1973-79; v.p. corp. comms. Internat. Harvester Co., Chgo., 1979-82; dir. mktg. comms. Arthur Andersen & Co., Chgo., 1983-86; v.p. bus. devel. Gannett Co., Inc., Chgo., 1987-94; pres., chief oper. officer Shalit Place L.L.C., 1995—98; exec. v.p. Mus. Broadcast Comm., Chgo., 1996-97; dir. A.T. Kearney, Chgo., 1994—2005; pres. Ill. Women's Forum, 2005—. Prof. mktg. U. Chgo. Grad. Sch. Bus., 1989-90, Kellogg Grad. Sch. Mgmt., 1983—84, 1994—95; co-chair Fed. Glass Ceiling Commn., 1991—95; exec.-in-residence, prof. Kellstadt Grad. Sch. Bus., DePaul U., 2003—03; bd. dirs. AskRex.com, Clark/Bardes Inc., Motown Snacks, Robison Securities/Fleet Bank, Internat. Leadership Forum. Bd. dirs. Off-the-Street Club, Chgo., 1977-86; adv. bd. U. Ill. Coll. Commerce, 1980-2000, Chgo. Crime Commn., 1987-90, DePaul U., 1989-95, Roosevelt U., 1994-2000, St. Mary's U., 1995-98; co-chair Fed. Glass Ceiling Commn., 1991-95, com. 21st century, 1992—. Recipient numerous Eagle Fin. Advt. awards, Silver medalist Am. Advt. Fedn., 1989; named Advt. Woman of Yr. Chgo. Advt. Club, 1989, One of Top 100 in Tech., 2003; fellow Internat. Leadership Forum, 2005—. Mem. Internat. Women's Forum (v.p. devel., v.p. comms., exec. com., bd. dirs.), Chgo. Network, Women's Forum Chgo., Women's Forum Mich., Social Venture Network, Execs. Club Chgo., Media Club (bd. govs. 1990-92), Women's Athletic Club Chgo. Office: 1703 Shoreline Dr Saint Charles IL 60174-5562 Office Phone: 847-778-8411. Personal E-mail: lynneoshea@juno.com.

**O'SHEA, PATRICK ALAN,** elementary school educator; s. Timothy and Elizabeth O'Shea; m. Michelle Rayne Varner; children: Patrick, Keegan, Finnegan, Shealin, Delaney. BS, Clarion U., Pa., 1992. Tchr. Northgate Sch.

Dist., Pitts., 1992—93, Seneca Valley Sch. Dist., Harmony, Pa., 1993—. Coach varsity football Laurel Sch. Dist., Newcastle, Pa., 2003—. Office: Seneca Valley Sch Dist 122 Seneca School Rd Harmony PA 16037

**O'SHEA, WILLIAM (BILL) T.,** telecommunications industry executive; b. Peabody, Mass. BEE, Lowell Technol. Inst., 1969; MEE, Northeastern U., 1970; grad., MIT. Joined Bell Labs., 1972; exec. dir. Info. Tech. divsn. AT&T, 1985—88, v.p. sys. mktg. and devel. computer sys., 1988—91; sr. v.p. network products group AT&T Global Info. Solutions (formerly NCR), 1991—93, sr. v.p. worldwide mktg. for computer bus., 1993—95; v.p. worldwide mktg. AT&T Global Info. Solutions, 1993—95; acting CEO NCR Corp., 1993; joined Lucent Techs., 1995, pres. network sys. internat. regions and profl. svcs., 1995—97, pres. bus. comm. sys., 1997—99, pres. data networking sys. group, 1999—99, exec. v.p., CEO enterprise networks group, 1999—2000, exec. v.p. corp. strategy and bus. devel., 2000—, chief tech. officer, 2001—; pres. Bell Labs., Murray Hill, NJ, 2001—. Office: Bell Labs 600 Mountain Ave New Providence NJ 07974

**OSHEROFF, DOUGLAS DEAN,** physics professor, researcher; b. Aberdeen, Wash., Aug. 1, 1945; s. William and Bessie Anne (Ondov) Osheroff; m. Phyllis S.K. Liu, Aug. 14, 1970. BS in Physics, Calif. Inst. Tech., 1967; MS, Cornell U., 1969, PhD in Physics, 1973. Mem. tech. staff Bell Labs., Murray Hill, NJ, 1972—82, head solid state and low temperature physics research dept., 1982—87; prof. Stanford (Calif.) U., 1987—, J.G. Jackson and C.J. Wood prof. physics, 1992—, chair physics, 1993—96, 2001—. Mem. Columbia Accident Investigation Bd., 2003. Co-recipient Simon Meml. prize, Brit. Inst. Physics, 1976; recipient Oliver E. Buckley Solid State Physics prize, 1981, Walter J. Gores award, 1991, Nobel prize in Physics, 1996; fellow John D. and Catherine T. MacArthur prize, 1981. Fellow: Am. Acad. Arts and Scis., Am. Phys. Soc.; mem.: NAS. Achievements include research in properties of matter near absolute zero of temperature; co-discovery of nuclear antiferromagnetic resonance in solid 3He, superfluidity in helium-3. Office: Stanford U Rm 150 Varian Physics Bldg 382 Via Pueblo Mall Stanford CA 94305-4060 Fax: 650-725-6544. E-mail: osheroff@stanford.edu.*

**OSHEROW, JACQUELINE SUE,** poet, English language educator; b. Phila., Aug. 15, 1956; d. Aaron and Evelyn (Victor) Osherow; m. Saul Korewa, June 16, 1965 (div. 2003); children: Magda, Dora, Mollie. AB Magna cum laude, Radcliffe Coll., Harvard U., 1978; postgrad., Trinity Coll., Cambridge U., 1978-79; PhD in English and Am. Lit., Princeton U., 1990. Prof. English C. Utah, Salt Lake City, 1989—. Author: (poetry) Looking for Angels in New York, 1988, Conversations with Survivors, 1994, With a Moon in Transit, 1996, Dead Men's Praise, 1999. Recipient Witter Bynner prize Am. Acad. and Inst. Arts and Letters, 1990; Ingram Merrill Found. grantee, 1990; Guggenheim fellow, 1997-98, Nat. Endowment for the Arts fellow, 1999—. Mem. Poetry Soc. Am. (John Masefield Meml. award 1993, Lucille Medwick Meml. award 1995, Cecil Hemley Meml. award 1992). Jewish. Office: U Utah Dept English 255 S Central Campus Dr Rm 3500 Salt Lake City UT 84112-0494 Office Phone: 801-581-7947, 801-581-6168. Business E-Mail: j.osherow@english.utah.edu.

**O'SHIELDS, CHARLIE,** marketing professional; s. John and Marlene O'Shields. BA in Studio Art (hon.), U. Mo., Kansas City, 1993. Creative dir. Lookandfeel new media, Kansas City, Mo., 1999—. Author: (children's book) The Curious Case of Miser Snoot and the Bibliomaniacs. Mem.: Am. Advt. Fedn. E-mail: coshields@lookandfeel.com.

**OSHIMA, JUNKO,** science educator, researcher; Mem. faculty U. Wash., Seattle, 1996—.

**OSHIMA, MICHAEL W.,** lawyer; b. Big Rapids, Mich., Apr. 4, 1957; s. Walter W. and Mitsue Oshima; m. Chiaki Tanaka, July 19, 2003. AB magna cum laude, Brown U., 1979; MA, Harvard U., 1984; JD, NYU, 1987. Bar: NY 1988, DC 1989. Sr. rsch. asst. Harvard U. John F. Kennedy Sch. Govt., Cambridge, Mass., 1981-84; assoc. Davis Polk & Wardwell, NYC, 1987-90, Arnold & Porter LLP, NYC, 1990-96, ptnr., 1997—, adminstrv. ptnr. N.Y. office, 1999—2005. Contbr. articles, reports to profl. publs. Bd. govs. Japanese Am. Nat. Mus., 2005—; bd. dirs. Asian Am. Arts Alliance, Inc., 2005—. Mem. Am. Sociol. Assn., Law and Soc. Assn., NY State Bar Assn., NYC Bar Assn. Business E-Mail: michael_oshima@aporter.com.

**OSHINSKY, DAVID M,** history professor, writer; PhD, Brandeis Univ., 1971. Prof. polit., cultural history Rutgers Univ., NJ, 1971—2002; now George Littlefield Prof. Am. History Univ. Tex., Austin, 2002—. Co-editor The Oxford Companion to United States History; co-author: American Passages: A History of the United States; author: A Conspiracy So Immense: The World of Joe McCarthy, 1983 (Hardeman Prize as best book about US Congress, NY Times Notable Book), Worse Than Slavery: Parchman Farm and the Ordeal of Jim Crow Justice, 1996 (Robert Kennedy Prize for contbn. to human rights, NY Times Notable Book), Polio: An American Story, 2005 (Pulitzer Prize for history, 2006). Office: Univ Tex Austin David M Oshinsky--GAR 206 1 Univ Station Austin TX 78712 Office Phone: 512-475-7230. Business E-Mail: oshinsky@mail.utexas.edu.*

**OSHINSKY, JEROLD,** lawyer; b. Jersey City, July 12, 1942; BA cum laude, Bklyn. Coll., 1964; LLB cum laude (Stone scholar), Columbia U., 1967. Bar: NY 1968, US Dist. Ct. (ea. dist.) NY 1968, US Ct. Appeals (2nd cir.) 1968, US Dist. Ct. (so. dist.) NY 1968, US Supreme Ct. 1971, US Dist. Ct. DC 1980, US Ct. Appeals DC Cir. 1980, US Ct. Appeals (5th cir.) 1975, DC 1980. Assoc. Chadbourne, Parke, Whiteside & Wolff, NYC, 1962—72; ptnr. Anderson Kill Olick & Oshinsky, 1972—96, Dickstein Shapiro Morin & Oshinsky, Washington, 1996—, mem. exec. com. Lectr. in field. Co-author: Practitioner's Guide to Litigating Ins. Coverage Actions; contbr. articles to profl. jours. Mem.: DC Bar Assn., NYC Bar Assn. (sec. adminstrv. law com 1972—74, chmn. adminstrv. law com. 1975—77), NY State Bar Assn., ABA. Office: Dickstein Shapiro Morin & Oshinsky 2101 L St NW Washington DC 20037-1526 Office Phone: 202-828-2251. Office Fax: 202-887-0689. Business E-Mail: oshinskyj@dsmo.com.

**OSHITA, JOHN TAKAO,** musician; Diploma, Edsbergs Musikinst., Sollentuna, Sweden, 1990; BA, Yale U., 1995; MA, N.E.C., music, 2003. Studio tchr. Am. String Tchrs. and Suzuki Assn., 2003—; string faculty Inst. of Art Music and Sci., Bellflower, 2004—; relief cellist L.A. Philharmonic Assn., 2001—03. Adjudicator, regional evaluations Am. String Tchrs. Assn., 2003, Music Tchrs. Assn. Calif. West Valley, 2003—04. Musician (relief cellist): L.A. Philharm. European Tour; musician: (soloist) (solo debut & televised documentary) Young Soloists Concert with Helsinborg Symphony Orch., 1989; musician: 432d Young People's Concert of the N.Y. Philharm., 1984. Named Presdl. Scholar in the Arts, Nat. Found. for Advancement in the Arts / Sec. of Edn., 1987; recipient Excellence in Musical Performance award, Com. on Asian/Pacific Am. Heritage / Hon. Mayor Tom Bradley, L.A., 1983, Dr. Shinya award, Japanese-Am. Assn. of N.Y., Inc., 1991; Juliette Esselborn Geier Meml. fellow, Tanglewood Music Ctr. Fellowship Program, 1988. Mem.: L.A. Violoncello Soc., Inc. (bd. dirs. 2000—04, treas. 2001—04).

**O'SHUGHNESSY, EDWARD JOSEPH,** urologist, retired medical educator; b. Bklyn., Jan. 18, 1922; s. Edward Joseph O'Shaughnessy and Lillian Daus; m. Virginia Mary Koch; children: Edward, Margaret, Kathleen, Mary. BSc, Holy Cross Coll., Worchester, Mass.; MD, St. Louis U.; MSc in Urology, U. Minn., Mpls.; MSc in Internat. Affairs, George Washington U., Washington, D.C.; MSc (hon.), U. Wash., Seattle. Diplomate Am. Bd. Urology. Assoc. prof. U. Wash., Seattle. Ret. Co-author: Burn Management, 1981; translator: Treatments des las Quenaduro, 1983. Co-founder U.S. Armed Forces Blood Bank. Col. med. corps. U.S. Army, Vietnam. Roman Cath. Avocations: travel, swimming. Home: 1434 Punahou St 617 Honolulu HI 96822

**OSIAS, RICHARD ALLEN,** corporate financial executive; b. NYC, Nov. 13, 1941; s. Harry L. and Leah (Schank) O.; children: A. Kimberly, Alexandra Elizabeth. Student, Columbia U., 1963; PhD, David Lipscomb U., 1988. Owner Osias Enterprises, Inc., numerous locations, 1953—98. Mem. bus. cabinet David Lipscomb U.; bd. dirs. Am. 21. Prin. works include city devel., residential and apt. units, developer City of Deer Park, LI, NY, founder, developer City North Lauderdale, Fla., founder, developer City of Lauderhill, Fla., complete residential housing communities, shopping centers, country clubs, golf courses, hotel chains, comprehensive housing communities; contributed Greystone Raquet and Tennis Club to Nolensville, Tenn.; owner, operator Coolsprings Exec. Plz., landmark office bldg., Internat. Common Market Shopping Complex and other office bldgs., shopping ctrs. in mid-southern region; co-author: South Florida Uniform Building Code; author: Prenuptial Bliss, 2003; columist: New York Daily Mirror, 1960s, 74-83, New York Herald Tribune, 1974-84. Mem. North Lauderdale City Coun., 1967—; mayor, 1968, police and fire commr., 1967—; hon. police chief NYC, Ft. Lauderdale, and Nashville Met. Police, 1994—; mem. Gold Cir., Atlanta Ballet; benefactor Atlanta Symphony Soc.; founder Boys Clubs Broward County, Tower coun. Pine Crest Prep. Sch.; v.p., bd. dirs. LaCiel Park Tower Condominium Assn.; bd. dirs. Tenn. Children's Home, MADD, Tenn. chpt., Tenn. Children's Home, Agape Children's Care Ctr., Nashville, 1993—; founding bd. dirs. AGAPE, Broward County chpt. Boys Club Am.; advisor to bd. dirs. Aviculture Microbiology Found., Inc. Recipient Best Am. House award Am. Home mag., 1962, Westinghouse award, 1968, Cert. of Merit for outstanding achievement and contbn. to City of Atlanta by Mayor Andrew Young, 1982; named Builder of Yr., Sunshine State Info. Bur., Fla. and Sunshine State Sr. Citizen, Fla., 1967-73, Builder of Month, Builder/Arch. Mag., 1992, Hon. Police Chief, Nashville, Tenn., 1995, N.Y.C., 1980; profiles on nat. and internat. media, including Dateline/CBS TV, NBC TV, CBS TV and Fuji Network (Japan). Mem. Fla. Sheriff's Assn., Ft. Lauderdale BBB, N.Y. BBB, Nashville BBB, Offshore Power Boat Racing Assn., Fraternal Order Police Assn. (pres.), U.S. C. of C., Fla. C. of C., Margate C. of C., Ft. Lauderdale C. of C., Smithsonian Instn., Soc. Founders U. Miami, Tower Coun., Columns Soc., Pinecrest Prep. Sch. (founder), Nat. Assn. Home Builders, Bankers Club (Miami, Fla.), Bankers Top of First Club, Quarter Deck Club (Galveston, Tex.), Boca Raton (Fla.) Yacht and Country Club, Maunalua Bay Club (Honolulu), Tryall Golf and Country Club (Jamaica), Top of the Home Club, Svc. Plus Club (France), Ensworth Red Gables Soc., Hawaii Loa Ridge Assn., Cannes Island Yacht Club, Canary Islands Yacht Club, Collier's Reserve Country Club (Naples, Fla.), Grey Oaks Country Club (Naples), Le Ciel Club (Naples; v.p. bd. dirs.), Hawaii Loa Ridge Assn. Personal E-mail: osias1@aol.com.

**OSICKA, TERESA D.,** health economist, consultant; arrived in US, 1998; d. Antoni Osicki and Apolonia Osicka; m. Andrzej Delegacz, Aug. 17, 2003. MA in Econs., U. Warsaw, Warsaw, Poland, 1990, diploma in Health Econs., 1991, U. Tromso, Norway, 1993; MS in Computer Sci., The Cath. U. Am., Washington, D.C., 2002. Sr. specialist health care Nat. Ctr. Health Sys. Mgmt., Warsaw, 1990—94; coord. health reform project Ministry Health and Social Welfare, Warsaw, 1991—93; chief specialist health care fin. Ministry Fin., Warsaw, 1994—99; database mgr. The Georgetown U., Washington, 1999—, rsch. asst. Med. Ctr., 1999—. Cons. UNESCO, Paris, 2005—, The World Bank, Washington, 2002—; fellow George Wash. U., 1998, Johns Hopkins U., Balt., 1999; lectr. in field. Contbr. articles to profl. jours. Recipient Cum Laude Poster award, Internat. Soc. Optical Engring. Med. Imaging, 2002, Hon. Poster award, 2003. Mem.: Assn. Health Care Mgrs. (v.p. 1991—93). Achievements include research in discrete wavelets transform application to the pulmonary nodules characterization on computer tomography (CT) scans with regard to their ability to discriminate benign and malignant nodules signals. Office: Georgetown University Medical Center 2115 Wisconsin Ave NW Washington DC 20007 Office Phone: 202-687-1572. Office Fax: 202-784-3479. Business E-Mail: osicka@isis.imac.georgetown.edu.

**OSINSKI, BRENDA CAROL,** music educator; b. Jeannette, Pa., May 29, 1965; d. David Earl and Frances Carol Lauffer; m. Joseph Allen Osinski, June 27, 1992; children: Joseph, Anna. B of Music Edn., Seton Hall U., 1987. Music educator Diocese of Greensburg, Pa., 1987—; asst. dir. music Immaculate Conception, Irwin, Pa., 1990—. Mem.: Westmoreland County Music Educators Assn.

**OSINSKI, KAY,** nursing educator, medical/surgical nurse; d. Harold and Barbara Lobred; m. Daniel Osinski, June 11, 1988; children: Mike Davis, Kyle. MSN, No. Ill. U., DeKalb Ill., 1980. CMSRN, Acad. Med.-Surg. Nursing, 2005. Asst. dean Baker U. Sch. Nursing, Topeka, 1990—. Ind. legal nurse cons., 1997—. Mem.: Sigma Theta Tau (awards com. chair 1999—2000, Excellence in Writing award (Eta Kappa chpt.) 2003). Office: Baker Univ Sch Nursing 1500 SW 10th St Topeka KS 66604 Office Phone: 785-354-5867. Business E-Mail: kay.osinski@bakeru.edu.

**OSINSKI, MARTIN HENRY,** healthcare consultant; s. Stanley and Shirley (Bobick) Osinski; m. Margie Osinski; children: Ashley, Brett. BBA in Acctg., U. Miami, Coral Gables, Fla., 1975, MBA, 1977. Cert. Accredited Valuation Analyst Nat. Assn. Cert. Valuation Analysts. Grad. asst. U. Miami, Fla., 1975-77; staff acct. Ernst & Ernst, CPA, Miami, 1977-78; asst. buyer, dept. mgr. Burdines Dept. Stores, Miami, 1978-80; buyer menswear Jefferson Ward Dept. Stores, Miami, 1980-82, Richway Dept. Stores, Atlanta, 1982-84; pres. Nat. Health Search, Inc., Miami, 1984-95; chief oper. officer MD Resources, Inc., Miami, 1989-95; prin. Am. Med. Consultants, Inc., Miami, 1996—. Mem. editl. adv. bd. Nephrology News and Issues, 2004—. Bd. dirs. Congregation Bet Breira, Miami 1994-98, 2002-. Mem.: Am. Soc. Nephrology, Nat. Assn. Physician Recruiters (bd. dirs. 1989—96, v.p. 1990—91, pres. 1991—, ethics com. 2001—, bd. dirs. 2004—, v.p. 2006, Presdl. award 1991, 2006), Iron Arrow Soc. U. Miami, Mens Club (pres. 1992—94). Office: Am Med Consultants Inc 11625 SW 110th Rd Miami FL 33176-3152 Office Phone: 305-271-9225. Personal E-Mail: amcmo@bellsouth.net.

**OSIPOW, LLOYD I.,** chemist, consultant; b. N.Y.C., Feb. 23, 1919; s. Joseph Osipow and Dorothy Schlossberg; m. Loretta Diana Mernyk, Aug. 1, 1941. BS, Columbia U., 1939. Rsch. dir. Foster D. Snell Inc., N.Y.C., 1948—69; pres. Omar Rsch. Inc., N.Y.C., 1969—74, Costech Inc., N.Y.C., 1974—92, OMS Holdings LLC, Boynton Beach, Fla., 1999—. Author: Surface Chemistry, 1962; contbr. chapters to books Encyclopedia of Chemistry, 3d edit., 1973. Sgt. U.S. Army, 1944—46, Japan. Mem.: Am. Chem. Soc. (emeritus mem.). Achievements include 40 patents in field; invention of non stinging waterproof mascara; development of process for the removal of silt, colloidal clay, from oil derived from the Athabasca tar sands. Avocations: golf, opera, reading. Home: 9875 Harbour Lake Cir Boynton Beach FL 33437 Personal E-Mail: LOsipow@aol.com.

**OSKIN, JOELLEN ROSS,** special education educator, school librarian; b. McKeesport, Pa., Apr. 26, 1943; d. Clarence Melvin Ross and Ada Mae Oliver; m. David William Oskin, Sept. 5, 1964; children: David William, Steven Ross. BS in Spl. Edn. magna cum laude, 1980, MLS So. Conn. U., 1987. Spl. edn. tchr. Greenwich (Conn.) Bd. Edn., 1980-89, Darien (Conn.) Bd. Edn., 1989—91; libr. Automated Kings Coll. Libr., Kings Coll., Auckland, New Zealand, 1992—94. Bd. dirs. Vis. Nurse/VNC Network, Wilton, Conn.; mem. adv. bd. Kids In Crisis, Greenwich, 2001—02. Mem.: AAUW. Avocations: golf, reading, travel.

**OSLER, GORDON PETER,** retired utilities executive; b. Winnipeg, Man., Can., June 19, 1922; s. Hugh Farquarson and Kathleen (Harty) O.; m. Nancy A. Riley, Aug. 20, 1948; children: Sanford L., Susan Osler Matthews, Gillian Osler Fortier. Student, Queen's U., Kingston, Ont., Can., 1940-41. Pres. Osler, Hammond & Nanton Ltd., Winnipeg, 1952-64, UNAS Investments Ltd., Toronto, Ont., Canada, 1964-72; chmn. Slater Steel Industries, Hamilton, Ont., Canada, 1972-86, N.Am. Life Assurance Co., Toronto, 1986-95, TransCan. Pipelines, Toronto, 1983-89, ret., 1993. Lt. Can. Army, 1942-45, ETO. Mem. York Club (Toronto), Everglades Club (Palm Beach, Fla.),

Manitoba Club (hon. life), Bath and Tennis Club (Palm Beach), Toronto Golf Club. Avocation: golf. Home: 17 Lamport Ave Toronto ON Canada M4W 1S7 Personal E-mail: gosler8660@aol.com.

**OSMAN, EDITH GABRIELLA,** lawyer; b. NYC, Mar. 18, 1949; d. Arthur Abraham and Judith (Goldman) Udem; children: Jacqueline, Daniel. BA in Spanish, SUNY, Stony Brook, 1970; JD cum laude, U. Miami, 1983. Bar: Fla. 1983, U.S. Dist. Ct. (so. dist.) Fla. 1984, US Dist. Ct. (mid. dist.) Fla. 1988, US Ct. Appeals (11th cir.) 1985, Fla. Supreme Ct. 1987, US Ct. Mil. Appeals 1990; cert. family law mediator Fla. Supreme Ct., civil mediator, Fla. Assoc. Kimbrell & Hamann, PA, Miami, 1984-90, Dunn & Lodish, PA, Miami, 1990-93; pvt. practice Miami, 1993-98; shareholder Carlton Fields, Miami, 1998—, practice group leader, family law divsn. Bd. dirs. Miami City Club, Supreme Ct. Historic Soc., So. Legal Coun., Fla. Women of Achievement (bd. dirs. leading atty). Mem. adv. com. for Implementation of the Victor Posner Judgement to Aid the Homeless, 1986-89. Recipient Breaking the Glass Ceiling award Ziff Mus., 2000, In the Company of Women award Dade County, 2000, Judge Mattie Belle Davis award, 2000, FAWL's Rosemary Barkett Achievement award, 1997, Outstanding Past Vol. Bar Pres.'s award, 1996, Women's Park Founders and Wall of Honor award, 2001; selected for photographic exhibit Florida Women of Achievement, 2000, South Fla.'s Top 250 Lawyers South Fla. Legal Guide, 2001, 02, 03, 04, 05; named 100 Women to Watch MIA metro mag., Fla. Trend, 2000, Women's Park Hall of Fame, 2001. Fellow Am. Bar Found., Fla. Bar Found.; mem. ABA (family law, alternate dispute resolution, Ho. of Dels. 1998—, standing com. on independence of judiciary 2000-03, standing com. bar svs. 2003-, house select com., 2004-), The Fla. Bar (budget com. 1989-92, 97-98, voluntary bar liaison com. 1989-90, spl. com. on formation of All-Bar Conf. 1988-89, chair mid-yr. conv. 1989, long range planning com. 1988-90, bd. govs. 1991-98, spl. commn. on delivery of legal svcs. to the indigent 1992-92, bus. law cert. com. 1995-96, practice law mgmt. com. 1995-96, chair program evaluation com., 1993-94, exec. com. 1992-93, 96-2000, rules and bylaws com., 1993-94, vice-chair disciplinary rev. com. 1994-95, investment com. 1994-95, vice-chair rules com. 1994-95, All-Bar Conf. chair 1997, chair grievance mediation com. 1997-99, pres.-elect 1998-99, pres. 1999-2000, exec. coun. family law sect. 2001—, vice-chair legis. 2001-2002, co-chair alternative dispute resolution com. 2003—, chair commn. legal needs of children, 2003-04, spl. commn. on disciplinary rev., 2003—, family law rules procedure com. 2003—, spl. com. succession planning), Dade County Bar Assn. (bd. dirs., ct. rules com. 1985-86, chmn. program com. 1988-91, bd. dirs., 1988—, 96-97, exec. com. 1987-88), Fla. Assn. Women's Lawyers Assn. (Dade County chpt. bd. dirs. 1984-85, treas. 1985-86, v.p. 1986-87, pres. 1987-88), Fla. Assn. Women Lawyers (v.p. 1988-89, pres. 1989-90), Fla. Bar Found. (dir. 1998-2001), Nat. Conf. Women's Bar Assn. (dir. nat. conf. 1990-91), Cuban Am. Bar Assn., Fla. Acad. Trial Lawyers, Dade County Trial Lawyers Assn., Nat. Conf. Bar Pres., So. Conf. Bar Pres., Leading Attys. (bd. dirs. 2000—), Iron Arrow Honor Soc., First Family Inns of Ct. Office: Carlton Fields PA 100 SE 2nd St Ste 4000 Miami FL 33131-2148 Office Phone: 305-530-0050. E-mail: eosman@carltonfields.com.

**OSMAN, LEE R.,** lawyer; b. 1965; BS in Mech. Engring., Colo. State U., 1988; JD, U. Denver, 1993. Bar: Colo. 1993, registered: US Patent and Trademark Office. Engr. Honeywell, ATMEL Corp.; atty., intellectual property group Holland & Hart, Denver; ptnr. Dorsey & Whitney LLP, Denver, 2000—, and chair, worldwide patent group, 2003—, head, intellectual property group, 2004—. Named one of 40 Under 40, Denver Bus. Jour., 2004. Mem.: Pi Tau Sigma. Office: Dorsey & Whitney LLP Ste 4700 Republic Plz Bldg 370 Seventeenth St Denver CO 80202-5647 Office Phone: 303-629-3434. Office Fax: 303-629-3450. Business E-Mail: osman.lee@dorsey.com.

**OSMANSKI, ADAM E.,** social studies educator; b. Oak Lawn, Ill., Dec. 29, 1976; s. Eugene Anthony and Diane Marie Osmanski; m. Jamie M. Bordner, July 16, 2004. BA, St. Xavier U., Chgo., 2000; MA, Governors State U., University Park, Illinois, 2001—03. Social studies tchr., coach Carl Sandburg HS, Orland Park, Ill., 2000—. Boys volleyball coach Carl Sandburg HS, Orland Park, Ill., 2000—, model UN sponsor, 2005—. Boys basketball coach, 2000—04; jr. high youth group instr. Parkview Christian Ch., Orland Park, Ill., 2005—06. Mem.: Nat. Coun. for Social Studies. Conservative. Avocations: basketball, fishing, golf, travel, hiking. Office: Carl Sandburg HS 13300 S LaGrange Rd Orland Park IL 60462 Office Phone: 708-671-3554. Personal E-mail: aosmanski@d230.org.

**OSMER-MCQUADE, MARGARET,** broadcast executive, journalist; b. N.Y.C. d. Herbert Bernard and Margaret Normann (Brunjes) O.; m. Lawrence Carroll McQuade, Mar. 15, 1980; 1 son, Andrew. BA, Cornell U., 1960. Assoc. producer UN Bur., CBS News, N.Y.C., 1962-69; producer 60 Minutes, N.Y.C., 1969-72; reporter, producer Bill Moyer's Jour., Pub. Broadcasting Service, N.Y.C., 1972-73. Reasoner Report, ABC News, N.Y.C., 1973-75; corr., anchor person Good Morning Am., ABC Morning News, Washington, 1975-77; corr. ABC TV News, Washington, 1977-79; v.p., dir. programs Council on Fgn. Relations, 1979-93; pres., CEO Qualitas Internat., N.Y.C., 1994—. Dir. Dime Savs. Bank, 1980—; cons. pub. broadcasting; mem. program com. Ditchley Found. Producer, reporter: TV news shows Come Fly A Kite (Nat. Press Photographer's award 1974), Kissinger, 1970, No Tears for Rachel, 1972, Calder: Master of Mobiles, 1975; moderator, producer World in Focus, publ. TV series for Coun. Fgn. Relations/Sta. WNYC, PBS, Worldnet, 1988-93. Mem. U.S. delegation World Conf. on Cambodian Refugees, Geneva, 1980; mem. Def. Adv. Com. on Women in the Service, 1978-82; trustee Cornell U.; mem. bd. overseers Cornell U. Med. Coll., pres.'s coun. Cornell Women; mem. program com. The Ritchley Found., 1994—, task force N.Y. Sch. Vols., 1994—; vol. Nat. Svc. Learning, 1994—. Recipient Peabody award Staff of 60 Minutes, 1970 Mem. NATAS, Coun. Fgn. Relations, program comm. The Mitching Found., Task Force N.Y. Sch. Vol., program com. Nat. Svc. Learning, vol. Nat. Svc. Learning. Clubs: Cosmopolitan, Century.

**OSMOND, DENNIS GORDON,** anatomist, researcher, medical educator; b. NYC, Jan. 31, 1930; s. Ernest Gordon and Marjorie Bertha (Milton) O.; m. Anne Welsh, July 30, 1955; children: Roger Gordon, Martin Henry, David Richard. BSc with first class honors, U. Bristol, Eng., 1951, MB, ChB, 1954, DSc, 1975. House surgeon Royal Gwent Hosp., Newport, England, 1954-55; house physician Bristol Royal Infirmary, 1955; demonstrator, lectr. anatomy U. Bristol, 1957-60, 61-64; instr. anatomy U. Wash., Seattle, 1960-61; assoc. prof. anatomy McGill U., Montreal, Que., Canada, 1965-67, prof., 1967-74, Robert Reford prof. anatomy, 1974-00, chmn. dept. anatomy and cell biology, 1985-95, Robert Reford emeritus prof. anatomy, 2000—. Vis. scientist Walter and Eliza Hall Inst. Med. Research, Melbourne, Australia, 1972-73; hon. sr. research fellow U. Birmingham, Eng., 1979; vis. scientist Basel Inst. Immunology, Switzerland, 1980, 96; Gaylord scholar Okla. Med. Rsch. Found., 1995. Contbr. numerous articles to profl. jours. Served with Royal Army Med. Corps, 1955-57. Fellow Royal Soc. Can.; mem. Am. Assn. Anatomists, Can. Assn. Anatomists, Anat. Soc. Gt. Britain and Ireland, Am. Can. assns. for immunology, Am. Assn. Immunologists, Internat. Soc. for Exptl. Hematology, Order of Can. Home: 1380 Revell Dr Manotick ON Canada K4M 1K8 Personal E-mail: dennisosmond@rogers.com.

**OSMOND, DONALD CLARK (DONNY OSMOND),** singer; b. Ogden, Utah, Dec. 9, 1957; s. George and Olive Osmond; m. Debra Glenn, May 8, 1978; 1 child, Donald Clark. Student, Brigham Young U. Performer (with): The Osmonds family singing group from age 4; performer: solo act, 1971—; co-star (TV series) Donny & Marie, 1976—79, 1998—, numerous TV guest appearances, appeared in (films) Goin' Coconuts, 1978, rec. artist: (with Marie) (albums) including Songs from Their TV Show, Donny Osmond Album, To You With Love, Donny, Portrait of Donny, Too Young, Alone Together, Disco Train, Donald Clark Osmond, (with Marie) I'm Leaving It All Up to You, Make The World Go Away, solo recordings include Donald Osmond (Soldier of Love), 1988, Eyes Don't Lie, 1990, Christmas at Home, Four (EP), 1997; performer: (Broadway plays) Little Johnny Jones, Joseph and the Amazing Technicolor Dreamcoat, 1995—98, Beauty and the Beast,

2006. Recipient (with Marie Osmond) Georgie award for best vocal team, Am. Guild Variety Artists, 1978. Mem. Lds Ch. Office: care The Osmonds Network 15 S 180 W Lindon UT 84042-1942*

**OSMOND, MARIE,** singer; b. Ogden, Utah, Oct. 13, 1959; d. George and Olive O.; m. Stephen Craig, 1982 (div.) m. Brian Blosil, 1986; children: Stephen James, Jessica Marie, Rachel. Student pub. schs., pvt. tutors. Appeared with The Osmond family singing group from age 7, solo act, 1973—;(TV co-star): Donny & Marie TV show, 1976-79, Donny & Marie Christmas Spl, 1979, Osmond Family Show, 1979, Osmond Family Christmas Show, 1980, Donny & Marie, 1998; (star TV spl.) Marie, 1981; appeared in TV series Maybe This Time, 1995, video Buster & Chauncey's Silent Night, 1998; (record albums) include (with Donny Osmond): Make the World Go Away, I'm Leaving It All Up To You; songs from their TV Show Goin Coconuts; (solo albums) include: Paper Roses, In My Little Corner of the World, Who's Sorry Now?, This Is The Way That I Feel, There's No Stopping Your Heart, 1985, I Only Wanted You, 1987, All In Love, 1988, Steppin' Stone, 1989, Twenty Five Hits-Special Collection, 1995; (#1 singles) include Meet Me in Montana (Best Country Duo of Yr. award with Dan Seals), 1986, You're Still New to Me, 1986, There's No Stoppin' Your Heart, 1986, I Only Wanted You, 1987, The Best Of, 1990; toured with Bob Hope, Persian Gulf, 1991; (co-author): Fun, Fame, and Family, 1973; Marie Osmond's Guide to Beauty, Health, and Style, 1980. Recipient (with Donny Osmond) Georgie award for best vocal team Am. Guild Variety Artists, 1978. Mem. Lds Ch.

**OSNOS, DAVID MARVIN,** lawyer, director; b. Detroit, Jan. 10, 1932; s. Max and Florence (Pollock) O.; m. Glenna DeWitt, Aug. 10, 1956; children: Matthew, Alison AB summa cum laude, Harvard U., 1953, JD cum laude, 1956. Bar: D.C. 1956 Assoc. Arent, Fox, Kintner, Plotkin & Kahn, Washington, 1956-61, ptnr., 1962—2002, chmn. exec. com., 1978-97, of counsel, 2003—. Bd. dirs. EastGroup Properties, Jackson, Miss., VSE Corp., Alexandria, Va., Washington Real Estate Investment Trust, Rockville, Md., Washington Wizards Basketball Club, Washington. Trustee Mt. St. Mary's Coll., Emmitsburg, Md., 1981-90; bd. dirs. Greater Washington Jewish Cmty. Found., Rockville, Md., Jewish Cmty. Ctr. Greater Washington, 1964-75. Avocations: tennis, music, enology. Office: Arent Fox 1050 Connecticut Ave NW Ste 600 Washington DC 20036-5339 Business E-Mail: osnosd@arentfox.com.

**OSNOS, PETER LIONEL WINSTON,** publishing executive; b. Bombay, Oct. 13, 1943; s. Joseph Lionel and Marta (Bychowski) O.; m. Susan R. Sherer, Aug. 18, 1973; children: Katherine Mason, Evan L.R. BA, Brandeis U., Waltham, Mass., 1964; MS in Journalism with honors, Columbia U., 1965. Editorial asst. I.F. Stone's Weekly, Washington, 1964-65; corr., editor Washington Post, 1966-84; v.p. assoc. pub. Random House Trade Books and pub. Times Books, Random House, Inc., NYC, 1984-96; cons. 20th Century Fund, 1996-97; founder, pub., chief exec. Public Affairs, 1997—2005, editor-at-large, 2005—. Contbr. articles to profl. publs. Bd. dirs. Human Rights Watch, chmn. Europe and Ctrl. Asia divsns.; co-chair Inst. for War and Peace Reporting, bd. dirs. U. Mich. Fellowship Journalists, 2000. Fellow NEH, 1973-74. Mem. Assn. Am. Pubs. (vice chmn. gen. pub. divsn. 1993-96), Coun. on Fgn. Rels., Century Club. Office: Pub Affairs 250 W 57th St New York NY 10107 Office Phone: 212-397-6666. Business E-Mail: peter.osnos@perseusbooks.com.

**OSOFF, JEFFREY ARLIN,** media company executive; b. Everett, Mass., June 5, 1936; s. Meyer and Minerva (Cogan) O. (dec.); m. Arlene Shuman, Sept. 23, 1962 (div. Jan. 1988); children: Judith Robin (dec.), David Eric; m. Donna M. Peyre-Ferry, May 26, 1997. BA, Bowling Green State U., 1958; MS, Columbia U., 1959. Reporter Boston Post, 1954-55, Boston Globe, 1955-64, rewriteman, 1962-63, acting asst. city editor, 1963-64; dir. News Bur. Brandeis U., Waltham, Mass., 1964-67, asst. dir. pub. affairs, 1967-69, dir. pub. affairs, 1969-76; chmn. bd. Jansson, Inc., Waltham, 1976-87; pres., chief exec. officer JAO Enterprises, Ltd., Lexington, Mass., 1987—; chmn. Dorian Enterprises, Ltd., 1992—, D & J Enterprises, Ltd., Lexington, Mass., 1995—; chmn. bd. Concannon's Inc., Marlborough and Wellesley, Mass., 1990—98. Lectr. in journalism and pub. rels. cons. First v.p. Dysuatonomia Found., NY; artist dept. fine art gift. State U. at Monterey, 1996; vis. faculty R.I. Sch. Design, Providence, 1993, Cleve. Art Inst., 1993; mem. adv. bd. Performance Space 122, N.Y.C., 1989—93, The New Mus., N.Y.C., 1996—98, Centro de Estudios Puertoriqueños at Hunter Coll., N.Y.C. 1996—98; lectr. in field. One-man shows include Hostos Ctr. Arts and Culture, Hostos C.C., Bronx, 1985, CU Art Galleries, U. Colo., Boulder, 1991, El Museo del Barrio, N.Y.C., 1991, U. Arts, Samuel S. Fleisher Art Meml., Phila., 1992, Mus. Am. Art, Acad. Fine Arts, 1992, Cleve. Inst. Art, 1993, Real Art Ways, Hartford, 1994, Storefront, 33 Broadway, Newark, 1995, Museo de Pedro Albizu, Campos, Chgo., 1996, Galerie OZ, Paris, 1996, Ronald Feldman Fine Art, N.Y.C., 1996, Otis Gallery, Otis Coll. Art and Design, Westchester, Calif., 1997, Ctr. Arts at Yerba Buena Gardens, San Francisco, 1997, South Bronx and Manhattan, N.Y., 1997, Museo Nacional Centro de Arte Reina Sofia, Madrid, 1998, Museo Alejandro Otero, Caracas, Venezuela, 1998, Hostos Art Gallery, Bronx, 1998, exhibited in group shows at Mus. Am. Art, Smithsoniann Instn., Washington, 1996, Whitney Mus. Am. Art at Champion, Stamford, Conn., 1997, Setagaya Art Mus., Tokyo, 1997, Africus Inst. Contemporary Art, Johannesburg, South Africa, 1997, The Bertha and Karl Leubsdorf Art Gallery, Hunter Coll., N.Y.C., 1998, Internat. Ctr. Photography Midtown, 1999, Galerie Jean-Luc & Takako Richard, Paris, 2000, Oakland Mus of Calif., 2002, Inst. Contemporary Art, Phila., 2004, Miami Art Mus., 2005, performances include, No Regrets, 1989, Broken Hearts, 1991, Historias, 1992, Familias, 1995, others, commns. include, Cafe Am., N.Y.C., 1990, Bklyn. Acad. Music, 1991, Represented in permanent collections El Museo del Barrio, N.Y.C., Nat. Mus. Am. Art, Phila., Newark Mus., Walker Ctr. Arts, Mpls., Wadsworth Atheneum, Hartford, Whitney Mus. Am. Art, N.Y.C. Recipient N.Y. Dance and Performance award, 1985, Louis Tiffany Comfort award, 1993, Mid-Atlantic Arts Found. Residency award, The Fabric Workshop, 1996, Internat. Assn. of Art Critics award, 1996; fellow Sculpture fellow, Nat. Endowment Arts, 1988, Artist fellow in sculpture, N.Y. Found. Arts, 1988, 1995, Intercultural Film/Video fellow, Rockefeller Found., 1993, Artist's fellow, Joan Mitchell Found., 1996—97, MacArthur fellow, John D. and Catherine T. MacArthur Found., 1999; Krasner Pollack Found. fellow, Theater Comm. Group and Nat. Endowment Arts fellow, 1990. Office: care Ronald Feldman Fine Arts 31 Mercer St New York NY 10013-2541*

**OSORIO, CLAUDIO E.,** computer company executive; Chmn., pres., CEO CHS Electronics, Miami. Office: Price Waterhouse Coopers 10 10th St NE #1400 Atlanta GA 30309-3906

**OSORIO, PEPON,** artist; b. Santurce, Puerto Rico, 1955; Student, U. Inter-Am., Rio Piedras, Puerto Rico, 1974; BS, Herbert H. Lehman Coll., 1978; MA, Columbia U., 1985. Artist-in-residence El Museo del Barrio, N.Y.C., 1989—91, The Fabric Workshop and Mus., Phila., Park Ave. Shelter Homeless Women, Artist/Homless Shelter, N.Y.C., 1993, Mus. Contemporary Art, L.A., 1993, Walker Art Ctr., Mpls., 1994, Ctr. Arts at Yerba Buena Gardens, San Francisco, 1996, Manchester Craftsmen's Guild, Pitts.; artist in residence dept. visual arts Rutgers U., Ctr. Innovative Print and Paper, New Brunswick, NJ, 1998; vis. artist dept. visual arts Skidmore Coll., Saratoga Springs, NY, 1998, Temple U., Tyler Sch. Arts, Phila., 1996; vis. artist Skowhegan (Maine) Sch. Painting and Sculpture, 1998, U. Hawaii, Honolulu, 1998; vis. artist dept. fine and pub. art Calif. State U. at Monterey, 1996; vis. faculty R.I. Sch. Design, Providence, 1993, Cleve. Art Inst., 1993; mem. adv. bd. Performance Space 122, N.Y.C., 1989—93, The New Mus., N.Y.C. Inst 1/ Cause Way Berkeley CA 94720 Office Phone: 510-642-0143.

**OSOWIEC, DARLENE ANN,** clinical psychologist, educator, consultant; b. Chgo., Feb. 16, 1951; d. Stephen Raymond and Estelle Marie Osowiec; m. Barry A. Leska. BS, Loyola U., Chgo., 1973; MA with honors, Roosevelt U., 1980; postgrad. in psychology, Saybrook Inst., San Francisco, 1985—88; PhD in Clin. Psychology, Calif. Inst. Integral Studies, 1992. Lic. clin. psychologist, Mo., Ill., Calif. Mental health therapist Ridgeway Hosp., Chgo., 1978; mem. faculty psychology dept. Coll. Lake County, Grayslake, Ill., 1981; counselor, supr. MA-level interns, chmn. pub. rels. com. Integral Counseling Ctr., San Francisco, 1983—84; clin. psychology intern Chgo.-Read Mental Health Ctr. Ill. Dept. Mental Health, 1985—86; mem. faculty dept. psychology Moraine Valley C.C., Palos Hills, Ill., 1988—89; lectr. psychology Daley Coll., Chgo., 1988-90; cons. Gordon & Assocs., Oak Lawn, Ill., 1989; adolescent, child and family therapist Orland Twp. Youth Svcs., Orland Park, Ill., 1993; psychology fellow Sch. Medicine, St. Louis U., 1994-95; pvt. practice Chgo., Geneva and St. Charles, Ill., 1996—; founder Maximum Potential, Chgo., 1996—. Contbr., author: Transpersonal Hypnosis, 1999. Ill. State scholar, 1969-73; Calif. Inst. Integral Studies scholar, 1983. Mem. APA (chair edn. and tng. com. divsn. 30 1998-2000, chair mem. svcs. 2001-05), Am. Psychol. Soc., Am. Women in Psychology, Ill. Psychol. Assn., Calif. Psychol. Assn., Mo. Psychol. Assn., Fla. Psychol. Assn., Am. Soc. Clin. Hypnosis, Chgo. Soc. Clin. Hypnosis, NOW (chair legal adv. corps, Chgo. 1974-76), Lincoln Park Bus. Devel. Inst. (chair program com. 2003—). Avocations: playing piano, gardening, reading, backpacking, writing. Office Phone: 630-845-8740. Personal E-mail: dr.osowiec@comcast.net.

**OSSANA, DIANA LYNN,** author, screenwriter; b. St. Louis, Aug. 24, 1949; d. Livio Aldo and Marian Yvonne O.; 1 child, Jennie Saria Inc., Tucson, 1993—. Co-author: (novel) Pretty Boy Floyd, 1994, Zeke and Ned, 1996; writer, exec. prodr.: (TV miniseries) Streets of Laredo, 1995, Dead Man's Walk, 1996, Johnson County War, 2002; screenwriter, prodr.; (films) Brokeback Mountain, 2005 (with Larry McMurty, Best Screenplay, Hollywood Fgn. Press Assn. (Golden Globe award), 2006, Theatrical Motion Picture, Producers Guild Am., 2006, Outstanding Film and Adapted Screenplay, British Acad. Film and TV Arts, 2006, Best Feature, Spirit Independent award, 2006, Adapted Screenplay, Acad. Motion Pictures Arts & Sciences, 2006) Recipient Teleplay of Yr. award Cowboy Hall of Fame, 1996, Teleplay of Yr. award Dallas Film Critics Assn., 1996. Mem. Pen Am. West (Tex. affiliation), Am. Acad. Poets, Internat. Crime Writers Assn., Women in Film.

**OSSENBERG, HELLA SVETLANA,** psychoanalyst; b. June 10, 1930; came to U.S., 1957, naturalized, 1964; d. Anatole E. and Tatiana N. (Dombrovski) Donath; m. Carl H. Ossenberg, June 7, 1958. Diploma langs. and psychology, U. Heidelberg, Germany, 1953; MS, Columbia U., 1968. Cert. Nat. Psychol. Assn. Psychoanalysis, 1977, diplomate Am. Bd. Examiners, lic. psychoanalyst; LCSW. Sr. psychiat. social worker VA Mental Hygiene Clinic, NYC, 1975—88; pvt. practice NYC, 1977—. Mem. Theodor Reik Cons. Center 1978—; field instr. Columbia U., Fordham U. schs. social work. Mem. NASW, Nat. Psychol. Assn. Psychoanalysis, Nat. Assn. Advancement Psychoanalysis, Coun. Psychoanalytic Psychotherapists. Office: 345 W 58th St New York NY 10019 Office Phone: 212-582-1515. E-mail: carolana77@juno.com.

**OSSER, DAVID NEAL,** psychiatrist, educator; b. NYC, Aug. 30, 1946; s. Abe A. and Edna (Meisel) Osser; m. Stephanie D. Fleischer; children: Reselin Emily, Daniel Alexander. BA, Amherst Coll., 1968; MD, SUNY, Syracuse, 1972. Intern in psychiatry U. So. Calif., LA, 1972-73; resident in psychiatry Mass. Mental Health Ctr. Harvard U., Boston, 1973-76; pvt. practice Needham, Mass., 1976—; assoc. prof. psychiatry Harvard U. Med. Sch., Boston, 1999—. Lectr. Tufts U. Med. Sch., 1978—, Taunton State Hosp., 1976—, Faulkner Hosp., 1976—, Beth Israel Hosp., 1984—, Brockton VA Med. Ctr., 1995—. Author: internet decision support software for psychopharmacology (www.mhc.com/Algorithms) (Internat. Neurosci. Found. prize, 2004); editor: schizophrenia: www.cogentmedicine.com; contbr. to pharmacol. websites, internat. psychopharmacology algorhythm project www.ipa-p.org, articles to profl. jours.; co-author: drug interaction website www.genel-ex.com. Recipient Lundbeck Internat. Neuroscience Found. prize, 2004, Journalism award, Kantar Found., 2001, award of excellence in edn., Internat. Psychopharm. Algorithm Project, 2006. Fellow: Am. Psychiat. Assn.; mem. Internat. Coll. Neuro-psychopharmacologium, Mass. Psychiat. Soc. (pres. 2001—02), Am. Soc. Clin. Psychopharmacology. Democrat. Jewish. Avocations: classical music, opera, piano, canoeing, hiking. Office: 150 Winding River Rd Needham MA 02492-1025 Office Phone: 508-977-3389.

**OSSERMAN, ROBERT,** mathematician, educator, writer; b. NYC, Dec. 19, 1926; s. Herman Aaron and Charlotte (Adler) O.; m. Maria Anderson, June 15, 1952; 1 son, Paul; m. Janet Adelman, July 21, 1976; children— Brian, Stephen. BA, NYU, 1946; postgrad., U. Zurich, U. Paris; MA, Harvard U., 1948, PhD, 1955. Tchg. fellow Harvard U., 1949-52, vis. lectr., rsch. assoc., 1961-62; instr. U. Colo., 1952-53; mem. faculty Stanford U., 1955-94, prof. emeritus, 1994—, prof. math., 1966—, chmn. dept. math., 1973-79, Mellon Prof. Interdisciplinary Studies, 1987-90; dep. dir. Math. Scis. Rsch. Inst., Berkeley, Calif., 1990-95, dir. spl. projects, 1995—. Mem. NYU Inst. Math. Scis., 1957-58, Math. Scis. Rsch. Inst., Berkeley,, 1983-84, head math. br. Office Naval Rsch., 1960-61; researcher and author publs. on differential geometry, complex variables, differential equations, astronomy, cosmology, especially minimal surfaces, isoperimetric inequalities. Author: Two-Dimensional Calculus, 1968, A Survey of Minimal Surfaces, 1969, 1986, Poetry of the Universe, 1995; author: (videos) Fermat's Last Theorem, 1994, Mathematics in Arcadia, 1999, Galileo: A Dialog, 2000; co-author (with Steve Martin): Funny Numbers, 2003; co-author: (with Michael Foale) (DVD) The Right Spin, 2005. Fulbright lectr. U. Paris, 1965-66; Guggenheim fellow, 1976-77; vis. fellow U. Warwick, Imperial Coll., U. London; recipient Comms. award Joint Policy Bd. for Math., 2003, Support of Sci. award Coun. Sci. Soc. Presidents, 2004. Fellow AAAS; mem. Am. Math. Soc. (Comm. award, 2003), Math. Assn. Am., Astrom. Soc. Pacific. Office: Math Sci Rsch Inst 17 Cause Way Berkeley CA 94720 Office Phone: 510-642-0143.

**OSSEWAARDE, ANNE WINKLER,** real estate company executive; b. Dallas, June 2, 1957; d. Lowell Graves and Ruth Lenore (Lind) Winkler; m. Kirk L Ossewaarde, Apr. 27, 1991. BBA in Fin. with honors, Emory U., 1979; MBA in Acctg. and Fin. with honors, U. Tex., 1983; MS in Real Estate Devel., MIT, 1988. Cert. comml. investment mem., Comml. Investment Real Estate Inst. Mgmt. trainee Citizens & So. Nat. Bank, Atlanta, 1979-81; banking assoc. Continental Ill. Nat. Bank, Chgo. and Dallas, 1983-85; asst. v.p., devel. assoc. Trammell Crow Residential, Dallas, 1985-87, Seattle, 1988-91; devel. mgr. Blackhawk Port Blakeley Cmtys., Seattle, 1991-93; v.p., real estate portfolio mgr. Aegon USA Realty, Atlanta, 1994-98; dir. UBS Brinson Realty Investors (formerly Allegis Realty Investors), Dallas, 1998—2000; exec. dir. asset mgmt. Morgan Stanley (formerly Lend Lease Real Estate Investments, Inc.), Atlanta, 2000—. Charles Harritt Jr. Presdl. scholar U. Tex., 1982, Alexander Grant scholar, 1982. Mem. Comml. Real Estate Women, MIT Ctr. for Real Estate Alumni Assn., Alpha Epsilon Upsilon. Methodist. Avocations: singing, photography, bicycling, reading. Home: 3170 Windsor Lake Dr Atlanta GA 30319

**OSSI, JAMES MATTHEW,** artist; b. Wyckoff, N.J., Jan. 7, 1947; s. Peter and (Hildegarde) O.; m. Diana Louise Wege (divorced); children: Sara, Peter; m. Marie Decarie, Aug. 18, 1997. Grad. in Indsl. Rsch., Parsons Sch. of Design, 1970. Sculptures located in The Mus. of Modern Art, N.Y.C., 1969, MIT Mus. Cambridge, Mass., 1983, Saibu Gas Mus., Fukuoka, 1989, math. dept. Princeton U., 1998, physics lobby MIT, 2000. Recipient numerous screenwriting awards, 2002—03. Home: 21 Baywater Dr Darien CT 06820 E-mail: james.ossi@earthlink.net.

**OSSOFF, ROBERT HENRY,** otolaryngologist, surgeon; b. Beverly, Mass., Mar. 25, 1947; s. Michael Max and Eve Joan (Kladky) G.; m. Lynn Spilman, 1984; 2 children: Leslin, Jacob. BA, Bowdoin Coll., 1969; DMD, Tufts U., 1973, MD, 1975; MS in Otolaryngology, Northwestern U., 1981. Diplomate Am. Bd. Otolaryngology. Intern Northwestern Meml. Hosp., Chgo., 1975-76; resident in otolaryngology and and maxillofacial surgery Northwestern U. Med. Sch., Chgo., 1976-80, NIH rsch. fellow dept. otolaryngology and maxillofacial surgery, 1977-78, clin. fellow in head and neck surgery, 1980-81; jr. faculty clin. fellow Am. Cancer Soc. Northwestern Med. Sch., Chgo., 1981-84; faculty practice, otolaryngology, head and neck surgery, laryngology and care of profl. voice Northwestern Med. Sch., Chgo., 1981—86, Vanderbilt U. Med. Ctr., Nashville, 1986—, prof., chmn. dept. otolaryngology, 1986—; exec. med. dir. Vanderbilt Voice Ctr., 1991—. Attending physician Cook County Hosp., Chgo., 1981—83, cons. physician, 1983—86; attending physician Northwestern Meml. Hosp, Chgo., 1981—86, Children's Meml. Hosp., Chgo., 1981—86; attending physician, chief otolaryngology svc. VA Lakeside Hosp., Chgo., 1982—85; attending physician, head divsn. otolaryngology head and neck surgery Evanston Hosp., 1983—86, chief divsn. otolaryngology, 1983—86; asst. prof. Northwestern U. Dental Sch., Chgo., 1980—86, Northwestern U. Med. Sch., Chgo., 1981—85, assoc. prof., 1985—86; attending surgeon, otolaryngologist-in-chief Vanderbilt U. Hosp., Nashville, 1986—, chief staff, 1995—97; attending surgeon VA Hosp., Nashville, 1986—; Guy M. Manness prof., chmn. dept. otolaryngology Vanderbilt U. Med. Ctr., Nashville, 1986—, assoc. vice chancellor health affairs, 1995—2005; assoc. dir. Vanderbilt Free-Electron Laser Ctr. Med. and Materials Rsch., Nashville, 1992—95; dir. Vanderbilt Bill Wilkerson Ctr. Otolaryngology Communication Scis., Nashville, 1997—. Sr. editor Lasers in Surgery and Medicine, 1987—94, editor-in-chief, 1995—2005, laryngology sect. editor Otolaryngology-Head and Neck Surgery, 2005—, mem. editl. bd. Clin. Laser Monthly, 1984—, Jour. Voice, 1987—, The Laryngoscope, 1988—2003, Jour. of Laser Applications, 1988—2004, Otolaryngology-Head and Neck Surgery, 1988—, mem. editl. adv. bd. Gen. Surgery News, 1990—97, assoc. editor Diagnostic and Therapeutic Endoscopy, 1992—2000; co-editor: Complications in Head and Neck Surgery, W.B. Saunders Co., 1993, The Larynx, Lippincott Williams and Wilkins, 2002; contbr. over 160 articles to profl. jours., 60 chpts. in books; editor, co-editor (8 books in field). Bd. dirs. Laser Inst. Am., 1984—90; dir. Am. Bd. Otolaryngology, 1995—; trustee Midwest Biolaser Inst., Chgo., 1981—86, Leadership Nashville, 1988—89. Recipient Nat. Rsch. Svc. award, NIH, 1977-78; Francis L. Lederer-Norval H. Pierce award, Chgo. Laryngol. and Otol. Soc., 1978, Hon. mem., 1986; Guest of Honor, First European Carbon Dioxide Laser Surgery Coruse and Workshop in Otolaryngology Head and Neck Surgery, Roskilde, Denmark, 1984; named a Prin. Investigator, NIH, 1977-78; Am. Cancer Soc., Ill. Divsn., 1981-82; VA Merit Rev., 1884-85; Nat. Cancer Inst., 1985-88; Office Naval Rsch., 1987-90, 91-94; A. Ward Ford Found., 1989-90. Fellow: ACS (bd. govs. 1996—2002, adv. coun. Otorhinolaryngology 1996—2003), Am. Laryngol. Assn. (chmn. rsch. support task force 1994—96, coun. mem. 1996—98, sec. 1998—2003, Daniel C. Baker Jr. lectr. 2001, v.p., pres. elect 2003—04, pres. 2004—05, Baker lectr. 2001, Guest of Honor 2002, Presdl. citation 2003, DeRoaldes medal 2004), The Triological Soc. (nat. nominating com. 1993, coun. mem. 1996—99, thesis advis. com. 1998—99, v.p. so. sect. 2002—03, coun. mem. 2002—03, 2005—, dir., CME 2005—), Am. Soc. Head and Neck Surgery (coun. mem. 1991—94); mem.: AMA, Soc. Univ. Otolaryngologists Head and Neck Surgeons (coun. mem. 2002—05, pres.-elect 2004—05, pres. 2005—), Assn. Academic Depts. Otolaryngology Head Neck Surgery (sec.-treas. 1996—98, pres. elect 1998—2000, pres. 2000—02, coun. mem. 2002—04), Am. Laryngol. Voice Rsch. Edn. Found. (bd. dirs. 1996—, sec. 2003—2003), Am. Bd. Otolaryngology (task force for new materials mem. 1985—89, assoc. examiner 1994—97, dir. 1995—), Cartesian Soc., Am. Broncho-Esophagological Assn. (coun. mem. 1987—90, treas. 1990—94, pres.-elect 1994—95, pres. 1995—96, Chevalier Jackson award 1997, Guest of Honor 2000), Soc. Head and Neck Surgeons, Am. Soc. Laser Medicine and Surgery (bd. dirs. 1985—88, chmn. program com. 1986—87, pres.-elect 1988—89, pres. 1989—90, nominating com. 1990—91, William B. Mark award 1992, Presdl. citation 2003), Am. Acad. Otolaryngology-Head and Neck Surgery (chmn. laser surgery com. 1983—89, chmn. self instl. package com. 1990—96, bd. dirs. 1992—95, coord. for devel. 2001—, Cert. of Honor 1984, Disting. Svc. award 1995, Presdl. citation 1999, Disting. Svc. award 2004, Presdl. citation 2005), Am. Acad. Oral Pathology, Am. Acad. Oral Medicine, Sigma Xi, Omicron Kappa Upsilon. Achievements include reestablishment of department of otolaryngology at Vanderbilt University Medical Center in 1986; establishment of the Vanderbilt Voice Center in 1991; establishment of an advanced training otolaryngology fellowship program at Vanderbilt University Medical Center in 1992. Avocations: boating, skiing, fly fishing, golf, photography. Office: Vanderbilt U Med Ctr Dept Otolaryngology 7302 Med Ctr E Nashville TN 37232-8783 Office Phone: 615-322-6326. Business E-Mail: robert.ossoff@vanderbilt.edu.

**OSTAR, ALLAN WILLIAM,** educational consultant; b. East Orange, NJ, Sept. 4, 1924; s. William and Rose O.; m. Roberta Hutchison, Sept. 10, 1949; children. Cert. engring., U. Denver, 1943; BA, Pa. State U., 1948; postgrad., U. Wis., 1949-55; LL.D., U. No. Colo., 1968, Eastern Ky. U., 1972, Whittier Coll., 1973; L.H.D., U. Maine, 1975; D.Letters, Central Mich. U., 1975; D.P.S., Bowling Green State U., 1975, R.I. Coll., 1983; D.Higher Edn., Morehead State U., 1977; L.H.D., Appalachian State U., 1977, No. Mich. U., 1978, Dickinson State Coll., N.D., 1979, Towson State U., 1980, Salem State Coll., 1980, Mont. Coll. Mineral Sci. and Tech., 1983, Ball State U., 1984; LL.D., U. Alaska, 1978, Ill. State U., 1983, Western Mich. U., 1984; D. Polit. Sci., Kyung Hee U., Korea, 1984; L.H.D., Fitchburg State Coll., 1986, Bridgewater State Coll., 1988, No. State Coll., 1988, Harris-Stowe State Coll., 1986; LLD, Edinboro U. Pa., 1987, Loch Haven U., Pa., 1989; LHD, No. Ariz. U., 1990, Shepherd Coll., W.Va., 1992, SUNY, 1993, Lincoln U., Mo., 1995. Dir. nat. pub. relations U.S. Nat. Student Assn., Washington, 1948-49; exec. asst. Commonwealth Fund, N.Y.C., 1952-53; asst. to dean extension div. U. Wis., 1949-52, dir. office communications services, 1954-58; dir. Joint Office Instnl. Research, Nat. Assn. State Univs. and Land Grant Colls., Washington, 1958-65; pres. Am. Assn. State Colls. and Univs., Washington, 1965-91, pres. emeritus, 1991—; sr. adv. Acad. Search Consultation Svc., 1991—. Adj. prof. edn. Pa. State U., 1990—. Co-author: Colleges and Universities for Change, 1987; contbr. chpts. in books. Mem. 42d (Rainbow) div., U.S. Army, 1943-46, Decorated 2 Bronze Stars with V, Combat Infantryman's badge; recipient Centennial award U. Akron, 1970, Fogelsanger award Shippensburg (Pa.) State Coll., 1974, World Peace Through Edn. medal Internat. Assn. U. Pres., 1975, Disting. Achievement award, U. So. Colo., 1979, Chancellor's award U. Wis., 1985, Chancellor's medal CUNY, 1986, Disting. Alumnus award Pa. State U., 1989, svc. award Coun. on Internat. Ednl. Exch., 1990, Chancellor's medal Internat. Svc. U. Ark., Little Rock, 1990, Disting. Pub. Svc. medal Dept. of Def., 1991; Alumni fellow Pa. State U., 1975. Unitarian-Universalist. Home: 404 Sandy Cove Tinton Falls NJ 07753

**OSTASZEWSKI, ALYCE VITELLA,** religion educator; b. Chgo., Apr. 24, 1936; d. Peter Anthony and Cleta Earline (Chastain) Indelli; m. Gerald Earl Nelson (div. 1967); children: Peter J., Maryalice C., William P., Paula A.; m. Stanley Joseph Ostaszewski; children: Vinson Shaw, Stacean V. Grad. high sch. Immaculata, Chgo., 1954. Tchr. religious edn. St. John the Evangelist Ch., Streamwood, Ill., 1962-68; tchr. religious edn., facilitator Rite of Christian Initiation of Adults, St. Thomas More Ch., Elgin, Ill., 1980-86; tchr. religious edn., young adult min. St. Julie Billiart Ch., Newbury Park, Calif., 1987-89, confirmation coord., 1990-91; confirmation asst. coord. St. Paschal Baylon Ch., Thousand Oaks, Calif., 1991-92; master chatechist basic faith formation program L.A. Diocese, Santa Barbara Region, 1990-93. Coun. mem. Santa Barbara Regional Conf., 1988-93; workshop spkr. Santa Barbara Regional Conf., 1992; confirmation tchr. Holy Cross Parish, Batavia, Ill., 1993-94; 3rd grade religion edn. tchr., 1994-96, Saturday ch. staff asst. 1997—; U. Dayton catechist formation program, 1997-98, 99, 00. Sec. Village of Streamwood Homeowners Assn., 1957-58; bd. dirs. Oak Ridge Estates Homeowners Assn., Newbury Park, Calif., 1986-88; lifetime mem. Streamwood Hist. Soc., 1993—; woman's team 7 C.R.H.P. Witness'er, 1994; mem. choir St. Thomas More, St. Julie Billiart, Holy Cross; vol. religion person program for McWayne Sch., Batavia, Ill., 1998-99. Recipient Bishop O'Neill award, 1999.

**OSTBERG, HENRY DEAN,** marketing executive; b. Bocholt, Germany, July 21, 1928; came to U.S., 1939, naturalized, 1945. s. Fred and Lotte (Hertz) O.; m. Sydelle Burns, Dec. 13, 1987; 1 child, Neal; stepchildren:

Elysa Bari, Brent Adam, Ross Jay. LLB, N.Y. Law Sch., 1950; MBA, Ohio State U., 1953, PhD, 1957. Pres. H.D. Ostberg Assocs., N.Y.C., 1950—; assoc. prof. mktg. NYU, 1954—63. Chmn. bd. Admar Group,Inc., 1960; dir. Self-Instructional Devel. Corp., Amherst Group, Porter Industries, Inc.; pres. Eastman Enterprises, Inc. Contbr. articles to profl. jours. Trustee Ostberg Found.; chmn. Givat Haviva Edn. Found. Capt. USAF, 1950—53. Jewish. Personal E-mail: hdousa@earthlink.net.

**OSTBY, FREDERICK PAUL, JR.,** meteorologist, retired government official, science administrator; b. New Haven, Jan. 20, 1930; s. Frederick Paul and Edna Maria (Kruckenberg) O.; m. Joanne Bernice Sorvig, Jan. 1, 1955 (div. 1989); children: Paul, Neil, Karen, Lynn; m. Barbara Richards, Mar. 17, 1989. BS in Meteorology, NYU, 1951, MS in Meteorology, 1960. Cert. Consulting Meteorologist. Meteorologist TWA, N.Y.C., 1953-54, Kansas City, Mo., 1955-56, N.E. Weather Service, Lexington, Mass., 1955, Travelers Weather Service, Hartford, Conn., 1956-60; research scientist Travelers Research Center, Hartford, 1960-70; meteorologist Nat. Weather Service, Silver Spring, Md., 1970-72; dep. dir. Nat. Severe Storms Forecast Center, Dept. Commerce, Kansas City, Mo., 1972-80; dir. Nat. Severe Storms Forecast Center, 1980-96; assoc. Climatological Cons. Corp., 1997—. Severe weather cons. The Weather Channel, 1997—98. Contbr. papers to profl. lit. Air weather officer USAF, 1951—53. Fellow Am. Meteorol. Soc. (council 1977-80, 84-87). Republican. Methodist. Home: 12537 Broadmoor St Overland Park KS 66209-3234 Office phone: 913-338-4222. Personal E-mail: fostby@sbcglobal.net.

**OSTBYE, TRULS,** medical researcher, educator; b. Norway, Dec. 15, 1954; arrived in U.S., 1999; m. Hemali Kulatilaka, 1984; children: Trevor, Adrian. MD, U. Bergen, 1979; MPH, Harvard U., 1983; PhD, U. Bergen, 2000; MBA, Edinburgh Bus. Sch., 2000. Exec. officer Directorate of Orgn. and Mgmt., Norway, 1981—84; spl. med. officer Nat. Inst. Pub. Health, Norway, 1984—85; lectr. U. Otago, New Zealand, 1985—86; Lalia B. Chase rsch. fellow Dalhousie U., Halifax, N.S., Canada, 1986—88; asst. prof. to prof. U. We. Ont., London, Canada, 1988—99; prof., vice chair rsch. Dept. Cmty. and Family Medicine Duke U., Durham, NC, 2000—. Contbr. more than 185 articles to profl. jours. Office: Duke U Dept Cmty and Family Medicine DUMC 2914 Durham NC 27710 E-mail: truls.ostbye@duke.edu.

**OSTEEN, JOEL,** minister; b. Houston; s. John and Dodie Osteen; m. Victoria Iloff, 1987; children: Jonathan, Alexandria. Student, Oral Roberts U., 1981—82. Prodr., creator John Osteen Television program, 1982—99; ordained, 1992; pres. and co-owner KTBU Channel 55, Houston, 1998—; sr. pastor Lakewood Church, Houston, 1999—. Author: Your Best Life Now: 7 Steps to Living at Your Full Potential, 2004. Achievements include ministering to the one of the largest and most diverse congregations in America; weekly television program appears on six cable networks and internationally in over 100 nations; aquired lease for the Compaq Center in Houston to accommodate growing congregation. Office: Lakewood Church PO Box 23297 Houston TX 77228 Office Phone: 713-635-4154. Office Fax: 713-635-4753.

**OSTEEN, LOUIS,** chef; b. Anderson, S.C. m. Marlene Osteen. Chef, owner Pawleys Island Inn, SC, 1980; chef Charleston Grill 1989—. Former mem. food bd. New Eng. Culinary Inst. Appearances Gourmet, Bon Appetit, Southern Living, GQ, Esquire, Saveur, Food & Wine, Town & Country, Great Chefs of the South. Bd. dirs. DiRoNa; founding co-organizer Charleston's Share Our Strength State of the Nation event. Nominee James Beard Found., 1996; named to Fine Dining Hall of Fame, Nation's Restaurant News A, 1994; recipient Great Am. Express Chef S.E. award, Ivy award, Restaurants & Institutions mag., Golden Dish award, Alan Richman, GQ's Mag.'s food and wine writer, 1994. Office: Louis's Restaurant 1228 E Morehead St Ste 100 Charlotte NC 28204-2889

**O'STEEN, WENDALL KEITH,** anatomist, neurologist, educator; b. Meigs, Ga., July 3, 1928; s. Wellna Hubert and Lillian (Powell) O'S.; m. Sandra Lynn Kraeer, July 30, 1983; children: Lisa Diane, Kerry Keith, Buckley Powell. BA, Emory U., 1948, MS, 1950; PhD, Duke U., 1958. Asst. prof. Emory U. Jr. Coll., Valdosta, Ga., 1948-49; instr. Emory U., Atlanta, 1950-51; prof. Emory U. Sch. Medicine, Atlanta, 1968-77; from asst. prof. to prof. med. br. U. Tex., 1958-67; asst. prof. Wofford Coll., Spartanburg, SC, 1951-53; prof., chmn. dept. neurobiology and anatomy, Bowman Gray Sch. Med. Wake Forest U., Winston-Salem, NC, 1977-93, prof. emeritus, 1993—. Mem. anatomy com. Nat. Bd. Med. Examiners, Phila., 1982-87. Contbr. over 150 articles to books, nat. and internat. jours. Lt. col. USAR. Recipient Golden Apple teaching award Med. Br. U. Tex., Galveston, 1967, Outstanding Tchr. award Emory U., 1973, Williams Disting. Teaching award Emory U., 1974, award for teaching excellence Bowman Gray Sch. Medicine, Wake Forest U. Mem. Am. Assn. Anatomists (exec. com. 1980-84, v.p. 1990-92), Assn. Anatomy Chairmen (exec. com. 1982-84, pres. 1990-91), So. Soc. Anatomists (pres. 1975-76), Soc. for Neurosci., N.C. Soc. Neurosci. (pres. 1980-81), Western N.C. Soc. Neurosci. (pres. 1987-88), Assn. Rsch. in Vision and Ophthalmology, Alpha Omega Alpha. Republican. Methodist. Avocations: gardening, music. Office: Wake Forest U Bowman Gray Sch Medicine Dept Neurobiology and Anatomy Winston Salem NC 27157-0001

**OSTEEN, WILLIAM L.,** federal judge; b. 1930; BA, Guilford Coll., 1953; LLB, U. N.C., 1956. With Law Office of W.H. McElwee, Jr., North Wilkesboro, N.C., 1956-58; pvt. practice Greensboro, N.C., 1958-59; with Booth & Osteen, Greensboro, 1959-69; U.S. atty. N.C. Attys. Office, Greensboro, 1969-74; ptnr. Osteen, Adams & Osteen, Greensboro, 1974-91; fed. judge U.S. Dist. Ct. (mid. dist.) N.C., Greensboro, 1991—. With USAR, 1958-51. Fellow Am. Coll. Trial Lawyers; mem. ABA, N.C. State Bar, N.C. Bar Assn. (mem. and chair subcom. N.C. sentencing commn.), U. N.C. Law Alumni Assn. Office: US Dist Ct PO Box 3485 Greensboro NC 27402-3485

**OSTENDORF, JOAN DONAHUE,** fund raiser, volunteer; b. Boston, Dec. 9, 1933; d. John Stanley and Genevieve Catherine (Morrissey) Donahue; m. Edgar Louis Ostendorf, Feb. 10, 1962; 1 child, Mary Elizabeth. BA, Marymount Coll., Tarrytown, N.Y., 1956; postgrad., Boston U., 1956. Tchr. Boston pub. schs., 1956-57, Waltham (Mass.) pub. schs., 1957-62. Trustee Cleve. Inst. Music, 1984—, mem. trustees coordinating coun., 1989; mem. Jr. League Cleve., 1964, 1st v.p. 1972-73; founder adv. coun. pub. rels. com. Cleve. Orch., 1974, 1st v.p. 1975-76; mem. del. assembly United Way, 1977-87; chmn. benefits Vis. Nurse Assn., 1987-88, March Dimes, 1982; trustee women's com. U. Hosps. Case Western Res. U. Med. Sch., 1974—; mem. nominating com. Inst. Music, 1990-91; 2d v.p. Music and Drama Club, 1991-93 (pres. 2001-2003), corresponding sec., 1993-95; chair Lyric Opera, 1992, Platform Assn., 1992—; pres. bd. trustees Cleve. Inst. Music, 1980-82, mem. women's com. 1980-82; mem. adv. bd. Women's Community Found., 1991—; v.p. Cleve. Internat. Piano Competition, 1994—; women's coun. Cleve. Mus., 1996. Mem. Internat. Platform Assn., Longwood Cricket Club, Intown Club, Chagrin Valley Hunt Club. Republican. Roman Catholic. Address: 3425 Roundwood Rd Chagrin Falls OH 44022-6634

**OSTENDORF, LANCE STEPHEN,** lawyer, educator, financial consultant; b. New Orleans, Aug. 16, 1958; 1 child, Christine Marie Ostendorf. BBA in Acctg. and Fin., Loyola U., 1976, JD, 1980. Bar: La. 1980, U.S. Dist. Ct. (ea. dist.) La. 1981, U.S. Dist. Ct. La., U.S. Supreme Ct. 1980, U.S. Dist. Ct. (we. and mid. dists.) La. 1983. Founder GO Entertainment, Inc. L.A., New Orleans,Balt./Washington, L.A./Orange County, San Diego/Riverside, Ostendorf, Tate, Barnett & Wells, PLC, L.A./Orange County, San Diego/Riverside, Houston, Balt., New Orleans. Treas., CFO La. State U. Med. Ctr. Found., New Orleans, 1992—; lectr. Lorman Ednl. Seminars; bd. dirs. La. State U. Med. Ctr. Found., New Orleans, tech. transfer com.; speaker and instr. Lorman Ednl. Svcs., Inc. Author: Insurance Law; contbr. articles to profl. jours. Mem. ABA, Fed. Bar Assn., Internat. Bar Assn., La. Bar Assn., Metairie Bar Assn., Maritime Law Assn., Comite Maritime Internat., Assn. for Transp. Law, Trucking Industry Def. Assn., Logistics and Policy, Assn. Average Adjusters of U.S., Jefferson Bar Assn., New Orleans Bar Assn., La. Restaurant Assn.,

Am. Trial Lawyers Assn., La. Bar Assn., Jefferson Bar Assn., Fifth Cir. Bar Assn., Def. Rsch. Inst., La. Trial Lawyers Assn., Law Def. Lawyers Assn., Houston Mariners Club, Southeastern Adm. Law Inst., St. Thomas Moore Club, La. Notary Soc., New Orleans South African Connection, Blue Key Honor Soc. Office: 708 Main St Ste 200 Houston TX 77002 Personal E-mail: lanceostendorf@yahoo.com. Business E-mail: lance.ostendorf@otbn-law.com.

**OSTER, GEORGE F.,** molecular biologist, environmental scientist; BS, US Merchant Marine Acad., 1961; PhD, Columbia U., 1967. Asst. prof. dept. mech. engring. U. Calif., Berkeley, 1972—73, prof. cell & devel. biology, dept. molecular & cellular biology, 1973—, prof. environ. sci., policy & mgmt., coll. natural resources, 1973—; prof. Miller Found., 1983—84, 2003; Oppenheimer prof. Los Alamos Nat. Lab., 1985. Mem. sci. adv. bd. Santa Fe Inst. Recipient Levy medal, Franklin Inst., 1971, 1974, Weldon Meml. prize, Oxford U., 1992—94; Postdoctoral Fellow, NIH, 1967—70, U. Calif Berkeley & Weitzmann Inst. Sci., 1969—71, Guggenheim Fellow, 1975—76, MacArthur Found. Fellow, 1985—90. Fellow: Am. Acad. Arts & Sciences; mem.: NAS. Office: U Calif Berkeley Dept Molecular & Cellular Biology 201 Wellman Hall Berkeley CA 94720-3112 Office Phone: 510-642-5277. Office Fax: 510-642-7428. Business E-mail: goster@nature.berkeley.edu.*

**OSTER, LEWIS HENRY,** manufacturing executive, industrial engineer, consultant; b. Mitchell, SD, Jan. 18, 1923; s. Peter W. and Lucy (Goetsch) Oster; m. Mary Mills, Aug. 17, 1948; children: David, Lewis, Nancy, Susan. BS in Engring., Iowa State U., 1948; MBA, Syracuse U., 1968. Registered profl. engr., Iowa. Mgr. Maytag Co., Newton, Iowa, 1953—59; sr. staff engr., mgr. Philco-Ford Corp., Phila., 1959—62; mgr. mech. and indsl. engring. Carrier Corp., Syracuse, NY, 1962—75; v.p. Superior Industries Internat., Van Nuys, Calif., 1981—. V.p., gen. mgr. Superior/Ideal, Inc., Oskaloosa, Iowa, 1975—; cons. in field. Author: MTM Application Manual, 1957. Leader Boy Scouts Am., Syracuse, NY, 1965—73; fund chmn. United Fund, Syracuse, 1965—73. Lt. col. USAFR, ETO. Decorated Purple Heart, DFC, Air medal with four oak leaf clusters. Mem.: Am. Inst. Indsl. Engrs. (pres. 1951—53), Ret. Officers Assn., Oskaloosa Country Club, Am. Legion, Elks.

**OSTER, ROSE MARIE GUNHILD,** foreign language professional, educator; b. Stockholm, Feb. 26, 1934; came to US, 1958; d. Herbert Jonas and Emma Wilhelmina (Johnson) Hagetorn; m. Ludwig F. Oster, May 17, 1956; children: Ulrika, Mattias. Fil. mag., U. Stockholm, 1956; PhD, Kiel U., Germany, 1958. Postdoctoral rsch. fellow linguistics Yale U., 1958-60, rsch. fellow Germanic langs., 1960-64, lectr. Swedish, 1964-66; mem. faculty U. Colo., Boulder, 1966-80, assoc. prof. Germanic langs. and lits., 1970-77, prof., 1977-80, chmn. dept., 1972-75, assoc. dean Grad. Sch., 1975-79, assoc. vice chancellor for grad. affairs Grad. Sch., 1979-80; dean for grad. studies and rsch. U. Md., College Park, 1980-83, prof. Germanic langs. and lits., 1980—, acting chair dept., 1997—2001. Mem. Fulbright Nat. Screening Com., Scandinavia, 1973, 83-87, chair, 1986-87; mem. selection com. Scandinavia Internat. Exch. of Scholars, 1982-86; cons. panelist Nat. Endowment for Humanities, 1975—; mem. bd. cons., 1980—; state coord. Am. Coun. on Edn., Colo., 1978-80, Md., 1981-83, dir. dept. leadership program, 1986-91; mem. exec. com. Assn. Grad. Schs., 1980-83; mem. dean's exec. com. African-Am. Inst., 1981-85; interim dir. Washington Sch. Psychiatry, 1994-95; cons. in field. Contbr. articles and revs. to profl. publs. Bd. dirs. Washington Sch. Psychiatry, Am.-Swedish Hist. Mus., Phila., Open Theatre, Washington; mem. nat. fellowship com. Am.-Scandinavian Found., 1997—; bd. trustees, 2001—. Carnegie fellow, 1974; grantee Swedish Govt., 1977, Am. Scandinavian Found., 1997, German Acad. Exch. Svc., 1983; recipient Translation prize Am.-Scandinavian Found., 1997. Mem. NOW, MLA (mem. Del. assembly 1995—), AAUP, Soc. Advancement Scandinavian Studies (pres. 1979-80), Am. Scandinavian Assn. of Nat. Capital Area (pres. 1983-86, 96—), Am.-Scandinavian Found., Am. Assn. Higher Edn. Home: 4977 Battery Ln Bethesda MD 20814-4931 Office: U Md Dept Germanic Studies College Park MD 20742-0001 Office Phone: 301-405-4096. Business E-mail: rmoster@umd.edu.

**OSTERBERG, EDWARD CHARLES, JR.,** lawyer; b. Honolulu, Jan. 1, 1942; s. Edward Charles and Emily Julia (Preston) O.; m. Susan Rhea Snider, Aug. 26, 1967; 1 child, Edward Charles III. BA, Northwestern U., 1963, JD cum laude, 1966; LLM in Taxation, So. Meth. U., 1972. Bar: Tex. 1966, Ill. 1966. Assoc. Vinson & Elkins, Houston, 1967-73, ptnr., 1974—. Reporter Internat. Fiscal Assn., Sydney, Australia, 1978, Barcelona, Spain, 1991. Contbr. articles to profl. publs. Mem. ABA (chmn. taxation com.), Houston Bar Assn. (chmn. taxation sect. 1987), Petroleum Club, Metro. Racquet Club. Methodist. Home: 11222 Wilding Ln Houston TX 77024-5308 Office: Vinson & Elkins LLP 1001 Fannin St Ste 3300 Houston TX 77002-6760 Office Phone: 713-758-2192. Business E-Mail: eosterberg@velaw.com.

**OSTERBERG, JAMES NEWELL See POP, IGGY**

**OSTERBROCK, DONALD E(DWARD),** astronomy educator; s. William Carl and Elsie (Wettlin) O.; m. Irene L. Hansen, Sept. 19. 1952; children: Carol Ann, William Carl, Laura Jane. PhB, SB, U. Chgo., 1948, SM, 1949, PhD, 1952, DSc (hon.), 1992, Ohio State U., 1986, U. Wis., 1997, Ohio U., 2003, U. Cin., 2004. Postdoctoral fellow, mem. faculty Princeton, 1952-53; mem. faculty Calif. Inst. Tech., 1953-58; faculty U. Wis.-Madison, 1958-73, prof. astronomy, 1961-73, chmn. dept. astronomy, 1966-67, 69-72; prof. astronomy and astrophysics U. Calif., Santa Cruz, 1972-92, prof. emeritus, 1993—. Dir. Lick Obs., 1972-81; mem. staff Mt. Wilson Obs., Palomar Obs., 1953-58; vis. prof. U. Chgo., 1963-64, Ohio State U., 1980, 86; Hill Family vis. prof. U. Minn., 1977-78. Author: Astrophysics of Gaseous Nebulae, 1974, James E. Keeler, Pioneer American Astrophysicist and the Early Development of American Astrophysics, 1984, Astrophysics of Gaseous Nebulae and Active Galactic Nuclei, 1989, (with Gary J. Ferland) 2d edit., 2006, Pauper and Prince: Ritchey, Hale and Big American Telescopes, 1993, Yerkes Observatory, 1892-1950: The Birth, Near Death and Resurrection of a Scientific Research Institution, 1997, Walter Baade: A Life in Astrophysics, 2001; co-author: (with John R. Gustafson and W.J. Shiloh Unruh) Eye on the Sky: Lick Observatory's First Century, 1988; editor: (with C.R. O'Dell) Planetary Nebulae, 1968, (with Peter H. Raven) Origins and Extinctions, 1988, (with J.S. Miller) Active Galactic Nuclei, 1989; Stars and Galaxies: Citizens of the Universe, 1990; letters editor Astrophys. Jour., 1971-73. With USAAF, 1943-46. Recipient Profl. Achievement award U. Chgo. Alumni Assn., 1982, Antoinette de Vaucouleurs Meml. lecture and medal U. Tex., Austin, 1994, Hans Lippershey medal Antique Telescope Soc., 1999, Alumni medal U. Chgo. Alumni Assn., 2000; Guggenheim fellow Inst. Advanced Studies, Princeton, N.J., 1960-61, 82-83, Ambrose Monnell Found. fellow, 1989-90, NSF sr. postdoctoral rsch. fellow U. Coll., London, 1968-69. Mem. NAS (chmn. astronomy sect. 1971-74, sec. class math. and phys. sci. 1980-83, chmn. class math and phys. sci. 1983-85, councilor 1985-88), Am. Acad. Arts and Scis., Internat. Astron. Union (vice commn. 34 1967-70), Royal Astron. Soc. (assoc., Gold medal 1997), Am. Astron. Soc. (councilor 1970-73, v.p. 1975-77, pres. 1988-90, vice chmn. hist. astronomy divsn. 1985-87, chmn. 1987-89, Henry Norris Russell lectr. 1991, LeRoy Doggett prize 2002), Astron. Soc. Pacific (chmn. history com. 1982-86, Catherine Wolfe Bruce medal 1991, bd. dirs. 1992-95), Wis. Acad. Scis. Arts and Letters, Am. Philos. Soc., Nat. Acad. Scis., Am. Acad. Arts and Scis., Wis. Hist. Soc., Mexican Acad. Scis. (corr.). Congregationalist. Home: 120 Woodside Ave Santa Cruz CA 95060-3422 Office Phone: 831-459-2605. Business E-Mail: don@ucolick.org.

**OSTERGAARD, JONI HAMMERSLA,** lawyer; b. Seattle, May 26, 1950; d. William Dudley and Carol Mae (Gillett) Hammersla; m. Gregory Lance Ostergaard, May 22, 1976 (div. 1985); 1 child, Bennett Gillett; m. William Howard Patton, Jan. 1, 1988; 1 child, Morgan Hollis; stepchildren: Colin W., Benjamin C. BS, U. Wash., 1972; MS, Purdue U., 1974; JD, U. Wash., 1980. Bar: Wash. 1980, U.S. Dist. Ct. (we. dist.) Wash. 1980, U.S. Ct. Appeals (9th cir.) 1981, U. S. Ct. Claims 1983. Clin. psychol. intern Yale Med. Sch., 1976-77; law clk. U.S. Ct. Appeals (9th cir.), Seattle, 1980-81; assoc. Roberts & Shefelman, Seattle, 1982-86, ptnr., 1987, Foster Pepper & Shefelman,

Seattle, 1988-92; sole practitioner Seattle, 1996—2003; dep. pros. atty. Snohomish County Prosecuting Attys. Office Civil Divsn., Everett, Wash., 2004—. Contbr. articles to profl. jours.; notes and comments editor Wash. Law Rev., 1979-80. Recipient Sophia and Wilbur Albright scholarship U. Wash. Law Sch., 1979-80, law sch. alumni scholarship U. Wash. Law Sch., 1978-79; NIMH. Avocations: gardening, reading. Office: Snohomish County Prosecuting Attys Office Civil Divsn 3000 Rockefeller Ave M/S 504 Everett WA 98201-4046 Office Phone: 425-388-3733. Office Fax: 425-388-6333. Business E-mail: jostergaard@co.snohomish.wa.us.

**OSTERGARD, PAUL MICHAEL,** philanthropy consultant; b. Akron, Ohio, Apr. 1, 1939; s. Paul and Janette Beryl (Laube) O.; m. Elizabeth K. McCombs, Jan. 1965 (div. Nov. 1971). AB magna cum laude, Case-Western Res. U., 1961; JD, U. Mich., 1964; MPA, Harvard U., 1969; diploma in hispanic studies, U. Madrid, Spain, 1960. Bar: Ohio 1964. Atty. US Steel Corp., Pitts., 1967—69; gen. atty. TWA Inc., NYC, 1969—71; v.p. administrn., sec., counsel Pa. Co. (now Penn Ctrl. Corp.), 1971—74, and subs. Buckeye Pipe Line Co., NYC, 1972—74; pub. affairs exec. GE, Fairfield, Conn., 1974—84; pres. GE Found., Fairfield, 1984—90; chmn., CEO, bd. dirs. Citigroup Found., NYC, 1990—99; pres. Com. to Encourage Corp. Philanthropy, NYC, 1999—2001; pres., CEO Jr. Achievement Internat., 2001—04. Bd. dirs. Master Card Found., Bond Market Found., Scholarship Am. Decorated Bronze Star, Legion of Merit (Vietnam); Univ. scholar, 1957-61; Littauer fellow, 1968-69 mem. Harvard Club, Wexford Plantation Club, Phi Beta Kappa, Omicron Delta Kappa. Episcopalian. Home: 29 Oxford Dr Hilton Head Island SC 29928

**OSTERHOFF, JAMES MARVIN,** retired telecommunications company executive; b. Lafayette, Ind., May 18, 1936; s. Abel Lyman and Mildred Paulene (Post) O.; m. Marilyn Ann Morrison, Aug. 24, 1958; children: Anne Michelle Bitsie, Amy Louise Olmsted, Susan Marie BSME, Purdue U., 1958; MBA, Stanford U., 1963. Staff asst. FMC Corp., San Jose, Calif., 1963-64; with Ford Motor Co., Dearborn, Mich., 1964-84; v.p. fin., CFO Ford Motor Credit Co., Dearborn, 1973-75; controller car ops. N. Am. Automotive Ops., Ford Motor Co., Dearborn, 1975-76, asst. controller, 1976-79; controller tractor ops. Ford Motor Co., Troy, Mich., 1979-84; v.p. fin., CFO Digital Equipment Corp., Maynard, Mass., 1985-91; exec. v.p., CFO U.S.West Inc., Englewood, Colo., 1991-95. Bd. dirs. Arkwright Mutual Ins. Co., FSA Ltd., GenCorp, Inc., Pvt. Sector Coun., Colo. Neurol. Inst., Goodwill Industries of Denver. Served to lt. (j.g.) USN, 1958-61. Recipient Disting. Engring. Alumnus award Purdue U.; named Outstanding Mech. Engring. Alumnus, Purdue U.

**OSTERKAMP, DALENE MAY,** psychology educator, artist; b. Davenport, Iowa, Dec. 1, 1932; d. James Hiram and Bernice Grace Simmons; m. Donald Edwin Osterkamp, Feb. 11, 1951 (dec. Sept. 1951). BA, San Jose State U., 1959, MA, 1962; PhD, Saybrook Inst., 1989. Lectr. San Jose (Calif.) State U., 1960—65, U. Santa Barbara (Calif.) Ext., 1970-76; prof. Bakersfield (Calif.) Coll., 1961-87, prof. emerita, 1987—; adj. faculty, counselor Calif. State U., Bakersfield, 1990—95. Gallery dir. Bakersfield Coll., 1964-72. Juried group shows include Berkeley (Calif.) Art, Ctr., 1975, Libr. of Congress, 1961, Seattle Art Mus., 1962. Founder Kern Art Edn. Assn., Bakersfield, 1962, Bakersfield Printmakers, 1976. Staff sgt. USAF, 1952-55. Recipient 1st Ann. Svc. to Women award Am. Assn. Women in C.C., 1989. Mem. APA, Assn. for Women in Psychology, Assn. for Humanistic Psychology, Calif. Soc. Printmakers. Home: PO Box 387 Glennville CA 93226-0387 Office: Calif State Univ Stockdale Ave Bakersfield CA 93309

**OSTERMAN, CATHERINE,** Olympic athlete; b. Apr. 16, 1983; Student, U. Texas. Mem. U.S. Women's Softball Team, Athens Olympic Games, 2004. Named USA Softball Player of the Yr., 2003, Big 12 Pitcher of the Yr., 2003, ESPY award, Best Female Coll. Athlete, 2006; named to First Team NFCA All-Am., 2003, All WCWS World Series Team, 2003. Achievements include mem. U.S. Elite Nat. Team, 2002; mem. Gold medal U.S. Nat. Team, U.S Cup, 2001; mem. Gold medal U.S. Nat. Team, Pan Am. Games, 2003; led U. Texas to Women's Coll. World Series, 2003.

**OSTERMANN, CURT,** lighting designer, educator; b. Detroit, July 20, 1952; s. G. William and Barbara Ostermann; life ptnr. Ralph W. Hanes, Nov. 19, 1977. BA with honors, U. Mich., Ann Arbor, Mich., 1974; MFA, NYU, N.Y.C., 1977. Cert. lighting designer United Scenic Artists Am., NY, 1976. Freelance lighting designer, N.Y., 1977—; lighting dir. The Maury Povich Show, N.Y., 1995—. Adj. prof. Tisch Sch. Arts NYU, N.Y., 1984—. Lighting designer: (plays) A Streetcar Named Desire; (Operas) X-The Life and Times of Malcolm X; Where the Wild Things Are; From the House of the Dead; lighting designer, scenic designer: (ballets) The Planets. Nominee Emmy award, 1997, 1998. Mem.: United Scenic Artists Am. Democrat. Episc. Avocations: landscape design, gardening, computers. Office: Curt Ostermann Lighting Design 170 W 73rd St 7B New York NY 10023-3008 Office Phone: 212-362-3965. Business E-Mail: gco1@nyu.edu.

**OSTERMEYER, MARYANN,** secondary school educator, writer; b. Indpls., Dec. 9, 1950; d. Kenneth Dale and Mary Ida Ostermeyer. AB in English, San Diego State U., 1972, M of History, 1981. Cert. secondary tchg.credential/Clad credential. Tchr. Cajon Valley Union Sch. Dist., El Cajon, Calif., 1975—; freelance writer San Diego County Office of Edn., 1983; curriculum writer Heritage Pub. Co., El Cajon, 1985—86; writer I Love a Clean San Diego, 1995—96; tchr. refugee students/ESL Internat. Rescue Com., San Diego, 1996—. Bd. dirs. Friends of Classics, San Diego; AVID dist. coord. Cajon Valley Union Sch. Dist., El Cajon, 1997—98; developer of dist. AVID programs Hillsdale Mid. Sch. and Cajon Valley Mid. Sch.; adv. comm., collaborator with Survivors of Torture Internat. Cajon Valley Mid. Sch., San Diego 2001—02; project tchr. rep. AJA; tchr. rep., collaborator San Diego Mus. of Photographic Art; writer curriculum San Diego (Calif.) Immigration Mus., 2005. Author: El Cajon: A Pictorial History, 1986, In My Heart and On My Mind, 2003; contbr. Hope True Stories of Answered Prayers Red Rock Press, 2003, ednl. curriculum Eranos, 1983, curriculum text San Diego World in Harmony - An Environmental Awareness Curriculum for Grades 7-12, 1994. Mem. El Cajon Hist. Soc.; tchr. rep. Cmtys. Against Substance Abuse, El Cajon, 1990—92; active Mercy Outreach; Bd. dirs. City of El Cajon Fire Dept., 2003—; Community Panel Representative - Vision 2000 City of EL Cajon Mayor's Recommendation Committee, El Cajon, CA, 1990—92. Recipient World of Difference Inst. OutstandingTchr. Recognition award, Anti-Defamation League, 1998, NEH Tchr. Summer Inst. Program, 1993, Outstanding Tchr. Yr. Emerald Mid. Sch./Cajon Valley Mid. Sch., PTA, 1985, 1991, Outstanding Tchr., Friends of Classics, 2003, Essay award, San Diego (Calif.) Immigration Mus., 2005. Mem.: DAR, Cajon Valley Ednl. Assn. Avocations: gardening, needlepoint, writing, dog walking, community philanthropic services. Home: 1114 Evilo St El Cajon CA 92021 Office: Cajon Valley Union Sch Dist 189 Roanoke Rd El Cajon CA 92021 Office Phone: 619-588-3092. Personal E-mail: magistrao@aol.com.

**OSTERTAG, ROBERT LOUIS,** lawyer; b. NYC, June 21, 1931; s. Frederick C. and Lillian (Bishop) O.; children: Thomas J., Daniel V., Debra A. BA, Fordham U., 1953; LL.B., St. John's U., Bklyn., 1956; LL.M., Georgetown U., 1960. Bar: N.Y. 1957, U.S. Dist. Ct. (so. dist.) N.Y 1969, U.S. Tax Ct. 1965, U.S. Ct. Mil. Appeals 1959, U.S. Supreme Ct. 1960. Atty. office chief counsel IRS, Washington, 1958-60; ptnr. Guernsey, Butts & Walsh, Poughkeepsie, NY, 1963-90, Guernsey, Butts, Ostertag & O'Leary, Poughkeepsie, NY, 1991-95, Ostertag, O'Leary & Barrett, Poughkeepsie, 1995—; adj. prof. paralegal studies Marist Coll., Poughkeepsie, 1975-91; adj. prof. Fordham U. Sch. of Law, N.Y.C., 1993—. Counsel Agr. Com., N.Y. State Assembly, 1967-68; mem. Gov.'s Jud. Screening Com., 1987-93; counsel to cons. and draftsman of proposed county charters and adminstrv. codes for Dutchess, Sullivan, Fulton, Orange and Onondaga Counties, N.Y., City of Poughkeepsie, N.Y., City of Beacon, N.Y.; mem. 9th Jud. Dist. Grievance Com., 1975-79, 9th Jud. Dist. Med. Malpractice Panel, 1975-91, mem. 9th Jud. Dist. Arbitration Panel, 1980—; mem. Chief Judges Com. on Pro Bono Legal Svc., 1992-93. Trustee Joseph F. Barnard Meml. Law Libr., Poughkeepsie, 1979—; dir. Hudson Valley Philharm. Soc., 1973—76; v.p., dir. High Tor Opera Co., 1967—70; dir. United Fund of Dutchess County, 1973—78; dir. Dutchess County chpt. Am. Heart Assn., 1975—81, 1984—89; trustee Sports Mus. Dutchess County, 1989—93, chmn., 1989—90; dir. Hudson Valley Stadium Corp., 1995—, chair, 1998—; cons. Charter Revision Commn., Beacon, 2002—03, Poughkeepsie Charter Rev. Commn., 1994; mem. Dutchess County (N.Y.) Charter Commn., 1966—67, Dutchess County Bd. Health, 1964—70, pres., 1966—70; chmn. Dutchess County Charter Revision Task Force, 1979—48; dep. supr. Town of Poughkeepsie, 1976; bd. dirs. Com. for Human Cts., 1975—99; dir. Std. Gage Co., 1972—88; mem. adv. coun. Pace U. Sch. Law, 1975—84; paralegal adv. coun. Marist Coll., 1975—. Served to capt. JAGC USAF, 1956—58. Recipient Recognition award Cen. Poughkeepsie Exch. Club, 1967, Marist Coll. Pres.'s award, 1991. Mem.: ABA (chmn. conf. of state bar gen. practice leaders of gen. practice sect. 1980—87, mem. coun. 1982—86, ho. of dels. 1985—98, Gavel awards com. 1989—, standing com. on solo and small firm practitioners 1992—95, standing com. on profl. discipline 2002—, Lifetime Achievement award Gen. Practice sect. 2004), Dutchess County Bar Assn. (sec. 1969—79, pres. 1984—85), N.Y. State Bar Assn. (ho. of dels. 1973—79, chmn. unlawful practice of law com. 1977—81, chmn. sect. on gen. practice of law 1980—82, ho. of dels. 1980—, chmn. com. on law office econs. and mgmt. 1982, exec. com. 1983—85, com. profl. ethics 1986—90, exec. com. 1986—93, pres. 1991—92, com. profl. ethics 1996—99, chmn. comm. on future of profession 1998, spl. com. on law governing firm structure and operation 1999—, com. profl. ethics 2000—), N.Y. Bar Found., Am. Bar Found., Hudson Valley Estate Planning Coun. (pres. 1965—66, dir. 1969—74), Delta Theta Phi. Home: 8 High View Rd Poughkeepsie NY 12603 Office: 17 Collegeview Ave Poughkeepsie NY 12603-2406 Office Phone: 845-486-4300. Personal E-mail: r.ostertag@verizon.net.

**OSTERWEIL, ADAM MATTHEW,** elementary school educator, writer; b. Plainview, NY, Apr. 26, 1972; s. Rheba Gerber and Michael Osterweil. BA, Cornell U., 1990—94; MA in liberal studies, Stony Brook U., 1995—96. Cert. Eng. Tchr. Secondary NY, 1998. UNIX sys. adminstr. Info. Tech., 1991—94; mid. sch. English tchr. The Springs, N.Y., 1996—. Author: (children's novel) The Comic Book Kid: Spring, 2001 (Walt Disney Adventures Best Book of the Yr. (Adventure category), Bank St. Coll. Best Children's Book of the Yr. (humor category), 2002), The Amulet of Komondor: Fall, 2003, The Lost Treasure of Talus Scree, 2005, (screenplays) The Comic Book Kid (adapted from own novel) (Scriptapalooza nat. screenwriting competition semi-finalist, 2003). Tchr. contract action com. mem. New York State Union of Teachers, East Hampton, NY, 1997—98. Recipient Nominated for the Walt Disney best tchr. of the yr. award, Walt Disney, 2001—02. Master: Springs Sch. Drama Club (play dir. 1996—99), Springs Sch. Video Game Club (club founder 1996—2004). Democrat. Avocations: treasure hunting, video games, collecting comic books, biking, cartooning. Office: Springs School 48 School St East Hampton NY 11937 Personal E-mail: adamost@optonline.net.

**OSTERYOUNG, JANET GRETCHEN,** chemistry professor; b. Pitts., Mar. 1, 1939; d. Arthur Roberts and Elizabeth Jane (Peebles) Jones; m. Bruce Ulrich, Aug. 16, 1967 (div. 1968); m. Robert Allen Osteryoung, Aug. 17, 1969; children: Anne Elizabeth, Adam Armstrong. BA, Swarthmore Coll., 1961; PhD, Calif. Inst. Tech., 1967. Asst. prof. chemistry Mont. State U., Bozeman, 1967-68; fellow Colo. State U., Ft. Collins, 1968-73, asst. prof. civil engring., 1969-73, asst. civil engring., microbiology, 1972-73, assoc. prof., 1973-78, assoc. prof. civil engring., rsch. chemist, 1978-79; assoc. prof. chemistry SUNY, Buffalo, 1979-82, prof., 1982-92, faculty exch. scholar, 1987-92; head dept. chemistry N.C. State U., 1992-94; prof. NSF, 1992—, dir. chemistry divsn., 1994—. Vis. prof. Colo. Coll., 1972, Calif. Inst. Tech., 1985; Guggenheim fellow, vis. prof. U. Southampton (Eng.), 1985-86; cons. Colo. State U., Ft. Collins, 1970-72, EG&G Princeton (N.J.) Applied, 1983—; dir. program chem. analysis NSF, Washington, 1977-78, mem. ad hoc rev. panel 1988. Co-author: Models in Chemical Science, 1971; assoc. editor Electrochemica Acta, 1986—; contr. over 180 articles to profl. jours.; patentee controlled-growth mercury drop electrode. Hon. Fulbright fellow, 1986; recipient Anachem award Soc. Analytical Chemists of Detroit, 1990, Schoellkopf medalist WNY-Am. Chem. Soc., 1992, ACS award in Electrochemistry-Electrochem. Soc., 1996. Fellow AAAS; mem., Internat. Soc. Electrochemistry (mem. divsn. 3 1985-88), Soc. Electroanalytical Chemistry (founding mem., pres. 1986-87, chmn. 1987-88), Am. Chem. Soc. (Garvan medal 1987, western N.Y. chpt., chmn. exec. com. 1981-89, Disting. Svc. award 1988), Soc. Applied Spectroscopy (Disting. Svc. award Niagara Frontier chpt. 1988), N.Y. Acad. Scis., Electrochem. Soc. (pres. Rocky Mountain sect. 1976-77), Fedn. Am. Scientists, Phi Beta Kappa, Sigma Xi, Iota Sigma Pi (Triennial Hon. mem.). Democrat. Episcopalian. Home: 4201 Wilson Blvd Ste 110 Arlington VA 22203-1859 Office: NC State U Dept of Chemistry PO Box 8204 Raleigh NC 27695-0001

**OSTFELD, GREGORY EDWARD,** lawyer; b. Houston, Tex., July 5, 1973; s. David Martin and Deedee Kessler Ostfeld. BA, George Wash. U., Washington, D.C., 1991—95; JD, U. Chgo. Law Sch., Ill., 1995—98. Bar: Ill. 1998. Clk. Judge W. Eugene Davis, Lafayette, La., 1998—99; atty. Althimer & Gray, Chgo., 1999—2003, Perkins Coie LLP, Chgo., 2003—05, Greenberg Traurig, LLP, Chgo., 2005—. Pro bono counsel Lambda Legal Def. Fund, Chgo., 2000—06; trustee Congregation Kol Ami, Chgo., 2001—04, pres., 2004—06. Mem.: Chgo. Bar Assn., Lesbian and Gay Bar Assn. of Chgo. Independent. Jewish. Avocations: cooking, flag football. Home: 1201 W Adams St #612 Chicago IL 60607 Office: Greenberg Traurig LLP 77 W Wacker Dr Ste 3000 Chicago IL 60601 Office Phone: 312-456-8400. Business E-Mail: ostfeldg@gtlaw.com.

**OSTLER, CLYDE W.,** banker; b. 1947; BA, U. Calif. San Diego, 1968; MBA, U. Chgo., 1976. With Touche Ross & Co., San Diego, 1970-71; with Wells Fargo Bank NA, San Francisco, 1971, v.p., 1977-81, sr. v.p., 1981-83, gen. auditor, 1983-85, exec. v.p. 1985-86, CFO, from 1986; with Wells Fargo & Co., San Francisco, 1971—, exec. v.p., CFO, from 1986, vice chmn., now group exec. v.p. internet svcs. Office: Wells Fargo & Co 420 Montgomery St San Francisco CA 94104-1205

**OSTLIND, DAN A.,** retired parasitologist; b. McPherson, Kans., June 19, 1936; s. Harry Dewey and Laura (Bartles) O.; m. Eleanor Ruth Ahlstedt, Oct. 5, 1958; 1 child, Dyanne Dee. MS, Kans. State U., 1962, PhD, 1966. Parasitologist Moorman Mfg. Co., Quincy, Ill., 1966-67; sr. rsch. parasitologist Merck & Co., Rahway, NJ, 1967-69, rsch. fellow, 1969-77, sr. rsch. fellow, 1977-86, sr. investigator, 1986-96. Office Phone: 908-236-9238. E-mail: stanton94@earthlink.net.

**OSTLING, PAUL JAMES,** corporate financial executive; b. Jamaica, N.Y., Sept. 22, 1948; s. John Carl and Margaret Ruth (Reilly) O.; m. Jane B. Mahler, June 1, 1974 (div. 1980); m. Julie Eileen Boyum, Feb. 20, 1982 (div. 1988); m. Danita Kay Hoover, May 3, 1991. BS in Math. and Philosophy, Fordham U., 1969, JD, 1973. Bar: NY 1974, US Dist. Ct. (so. and ea. dist.) NY 1974, US Ct. Appeals (2d cir.) 1974, US Ct. Appeals (4th, 5th, 9th, 10th, 11th cirs.) 1978. Assoc. Chadbourne Parke, NYC, 1973-77; asst. gen. counsel Authur Young & Co., NYC, 1977-79, assoc. gen. counsel, 1979-82, ptnr., assoc. gen. counsel, 1982, nat. dir. human resources, 1985-90; vice chmn. human resources Ernst & Young, NYC, 1990-94, assoc. gen. counsel, 1994-95; exec. ptnr. Ernst & Young Internat., NYC, 1995—2003, global COO, 2003—. Office: Ernst & Young 5 Times Sq New York NY 10036

**OSTLING, RICHARD NEIL,** journalist; b. Endicott, NY, July 14, 1940; s. Acton Eric Sr. and Christine Cathryn (Cumins) O.; m. Joan Elaine Kerns, July 8, 1967; children: Margaret Anne, Elizabeth Anne. BA, U. Mich., 1962; MS in Journalism, Northwestern U., 1963; MA in Religion, George Washington U., 1970; LittD (hon.), Gordon Coll., Mass., 1989. Reporter, copyreader Morning News and Evening Jour., Wilmington, Del., 1963-64; asst. news editor Christianity Today mag., Washington, 1965-67; news editor, 1967-69; staff corr. Time mag., N.Y.C., 1969-74, religion writer, 1975-94, sr. corr., 1994-98; broadcaster Report on Religion, CBS Radio, 1979-98; religion corr. Newshour with Jim Lehrer formerly MacNeil/Lehrer Newshour, 1991-98;

religion writer AP, N.Y.C., 1998—2006, freelance Bible columnist, 2006—. Author: Secrecy in the Church, 1974; co-author: Aborting America, 1979, Mormon America, 1999. Served with USNG, 1964-70. McCormick Found. fellow, 1962-63; recipient Supple, Templeton, Am. Acad. Religion and Wilbur awards for religion writing. Mem. Religion Newswriters Assn. (pres. 1974-76), Northwestern U. Alumni Hall of Achievement (charter), Phi Beta Kappa. Mem. Christian Reformed Ch. Home: 280 Hillcrest Rd Ridgewood NJ 07450-2400

**OSTLUND, H. GOTE,** marine biologist, educator; b. Stockholm, June 26, 1923; came to U.S., 1963; s. Sven and Ruth (Lundin) O.; m. Doris Beck, Sept. 30, 1950; children: Stellan, Goran. Fil Kand., U. Stockholm, 1949, Fil Lic., 1958; doctorate (hon.), U. Gothenburg, 1984. Research asst. U. Stockholm, 1944-46; tchr. Technol. Night Coll., Stockholm, 1946-51; research asst. Royal Inst. Tech., Stockholm, 1947, asst. instr., 1948-52; head of lab. Swedish Nitrogen Fertilizer Works, Ltd., 1952-54, Radioactive Dating Lab., Stockholm, 1954-63; asst. instr. Royal Inst. Tech., Stockholm, 1956-57; vis. research asso. prof. Inst. Marine Scis., U. Miami (Fla.), 1960-61, asso. prof. geochemistry, 1963-67, prof. marine and atmospheric chemistry Rosenstiel Sch. Marine and Atmospheric Sci., 1967-97, chmn. div. chem. oceanography, 1970-72, coordinator Geochem. Oceans Sects., 1976-86, mem. exec. com. Geochem. Oceans Sects., 1973-86, coordinator Transient Tracers in Ocean, 1977-85, prof. emeritus, 1997—. Assoc. editor: Revs. of Geophysics and Space Physics, 1974-76; mem. editorial bd.: Marine Chemistry, 1974-93; mem. adv. bd.: Tellus B; contr. articles to profl. jours. Served in Royal Swedish Air Force, 1943-44, 46. Mem. Am. Geophys. Union, Am. Meteorol. Soc., AAAS, Swedish Chem. Soc., Swedish Geophys. Soc., Fla. Acad. Scis. Office. U Miami 4600 Rickenbacker Cswy Miami FL 33149-1031 E-mail: gostlund@rsmas.miami.edu.

**OSTOVIC, VLADO,** engineering educator, researcher; b. Osijek, Croatia, May 25, 1954; s. Peter and Slavna Ostovic; m. Theresia Heil-Ostovic, July 23, 1977; children: Marko, Thomas. BSEE, U. Zagreb, Croatia, 1976, MSEE, 1978, PhD, 1982. Electric machines designer R. Koncar, Zagreb, 1978—82; rsch. asst. U. Zagreb, 1976—82; prof. U. Osijek, Croatia, 1982—87, U. Akron, Ohio, 1987—89; machine designer SISME SpA, Olgiate Comaco, Italy, 1989—91; sr. designer ABB Kraftwerke AG, Mannheim, Germany, 1991—96; prof. U. Applied Scis., Saarbruecken, Germany, 1996—. Cons. AJB Rsch., Sweden, 1996—98, Ford Motor Co., Dearborn, Mich., 1998—2002, Siemens, Germany, 2002—04. Author: (book) Dynamics of Saturated d. Machines, 1989, Computer-Aided Analysis of d. Machines, 1994. Recipient J. Lodcar Silver medal, U. Zagreb, 1982, univ. rsch. grant, Ford Motor Co., 2001. Mem.: IEEE (sr.). Achievements include patents for memory motors. Home: Muckensturmerstr 25 Weinheim 69469 Germany

**OSTRAGER, BARRY ROBERT,** lawyer; b. NYC, July 14, 1947; m. Pamela Goodman, Apr. 8, 1972; children: Anne Elizabeth, Katie, Jane. BA, City Coll. of CUNY, 1968, MA, 1973; JD, NYU Sch. Law, 1972. Bar: NY 1973, Calif. 1996, US Dist. Ct. (ea. dist.) NY, 1973, US Dist. Ct. (so. dist.) NY, 1973, US Dist. Ct. Conn., 1978, US Dist. Tex. 1986, US Dist. Ct. (no. dist.) NY 1993, US Ct. Appeals (2nd cir.) 1974, US Ct. Appeals (7th cir.) 1977, US Dist. Ct. (no. dist.) Calif. 1983, US Ct. Appeals (3rd cir.) 1984, US Ct. Appeals (9th cir.) 1985, US Ct. Appeals (4th cir.) 1989, US Ct. Appeals (6th cir.) 1993, US Supreme Ct. 1982, US Dist. Ct. (so. dist.) Calif. 1997, U.S. Ct. Appeals (D.C. cir.) 1997. Judicial clk. to Hon. Arnold Bauman US Dist. Ct. (So. dist.) NY, 1972—73; sr. litig. ptnr., co-head, litig. dept., mem. exec. com. Simpson Thacher & Bartlett, NYC, 1980—. Lectr. on fed. securities and insurance law. Co-author: Modern Reinsurance Law and Practice, 2nd edit., 2000, Handbook on Insurance Coverage Disputes, 12th edit., 2004; contr. articles to profl. jours. Named one of Top 10 Litigators, Nat. Law Jour., 2003. Mem. Am. Law Inst., Assn. of Bar of City of NY, ABA. Office: Simpson Thacher & Bartlett 26th Fl 425 Lexington Ave New York NY 10017-3954 Address: Simpson Thacher & Bartlett LLP 1999 Avenue of the Stars 29th Fl Los Angeles CA 90067 Office Phone: 212-455-2655. Home Fax: 310-407-7502; Office Fax: 212-455-2502. Business E-Mail: bostrager@stblaw.com.

**OSTRANDER, ELAINE A.,** federal agency administrator, geneticist; b. Syracuse, NY; BS, U. Washington, 1981; PhD, Oregon Health Sciences U., 1987. With Lawrence Berkeley Nat. Lab., Berkeley, Calif., 1991—93, Fred Hutchinson Cancer Rsch. Ctr., Seattle, 1993—2004; sr. investigator, chief, cancer genetics branch Nat. Human Genome Rsch. Inst., NIH, Bethesda, Md., 2004—, head, comparative genetics sect., 2004—. Affiliate prof., dept. of genome sci., sch. medicine and dept. biology, coll. arts and scis. U. Wash., Seattle; spkr. in field. Co-author more than 100 peer-reviewed publs. Office: Nat Human Genome Rsch Inst NIH Bldg 50 Rm 5351 50 S Dr MSC 8000 Bethesda MD 20892-8000 Office Phone: 301-594-5284. Office Fax: 301-594-0023. E-mail: eostrand@mail.nih.gov.*

**OSTRANDER, ROBERT EDWIN,** retired United Nations interregional advisor, petroleum company executive; b. Pitts., June 30, 1931; s. Robert Jesse and Elizabeth Raymond (Comstock) O.; m. Margaret Valentina Servello, Dec. 21, 1958; children: Robert Glen, Roseanne. BA, Cornell U., 1953. Cert. petroleum geologist; registered geol. scientist. Area reservoir engr. Mene Grande Oil Co., San Tome, Venezuela, 1956-61; dist. engr. Oasis Oil Co. of Libya, Tripoli, 1962-67; reservoir/petroleum chief engr. Occidental Oil of Libya, Tripoli, 1967-71; divsn. head Iranian Oil Consortium, Ahwaz, Iran, 1972-75; mgr. ops. Ultramar Co. Ltd., Mt. Kisco, NY, 1975-81; v.p. engring. Weeks Petroleum Lltd., Westport, Conn., 1982-85; mng. dir. Reomag Inc., South Salem, NY, 1980—. Cons. World Bank, Washington, 1991—; cons. UN Secretariat, 1991; advisor to govts. of China, India, others in Asia, Africa, Middle East; guest lectr. Asian univs., internat. seminars. Contbr. articles to profl. jours. Sec. Rep. Com., Town of Lewisboro; chair conservation adv. coun. Town of Lewisboro; pres. Ostrander Family Assn.; mem. Rep. Com. Westchester County; past. bd. dirs. Oakridge Condominium Assn., Vista, NY; fellow Herbert F. Johnson Mus. Art, Cornell U., 1999—. Served to 1st lt. US Army, 1953-55. Mem. Am. Assn. Petroleum Geologists, Soc. Petroleum Engrs., Holland Soc. NY. Address: 5715 State Route 89 Romulus NY 14541-9546 Personal E-mail: reomag@rochester.rr.com.

**OSTRANDER, THOMAS WILLIAM,** investment banker; b. Detroit, July 20, 1950; s. Roland J. and Sybil (Swartout) O.; m. Kelli Turner, Aug. 28, 2004; children: John Charles, Elizabeth Ann, Brian Thomas. BA, U. Mich., 1972; MBA, Harvard Bus. Sch., 1976. CPA., Mich. Staff acct. Ernst & Whinney, Detroit, 1972-74; sr. acct. Ernst and Whinney, Detroit, 1974, Cleve., 1975; assoc. Kidder, Peabody and Co., N.Y.C., 1976-78, asst. v.p., 1978-80; v.p. Kidder, Peabody and Co., N.Y.C., 1980-86; mng. dir. Kidder, Peabody and Co., N.Y.C., 1986-89, Salomon Bros., Inc., N.Y.C., 1989-97, Salomon Smith Barney, N.Y.C., 1997—2003, Citigroup Global Markets, Inc., N.Y.C., 2003. Bd. dirs., Westmoreland Coal Co.; mem. adv. bd. Paton Sch. Accountancy U. Mich., 1984-87,; mem. vis. com. Lit., Sci., and Arts Sch., 1988-90, 95- Pres. Ballet Hispanico, 1996- Mem. AICPA, Met. Club, Harvard Club, Hasty Pudding Club, Bond Club, Beaver Dam Winter Sports Club, and Theta Delta Chi Home: 18 Pheasant Run Old Westbury NY 11568 Office: Citigrp Global Markets Inc 388 Greenwich St New York NY 10013-2339

**OSTRANDER, WILLIS FREDERICK,** retired real estate appraiser; b. Berkeley, Calif., Apr. 23, 1926; s. Willis Frederick and Grace Jackson Ostrander; m. Nancy Majors Ostrander, Jan. 2, 1950; children: Margaret Jaffee, Frederick Adam, Daphne Grace Miller, John Ellery. BA, U Calif., 1948. Cert. MAI, SRA Appraisal Inst., 1994, State Certification Real Estate Appraisal State of Calif., 1996. Sales rep. Signal Oil Co. (Chevron), Alemeda, Calif., 1951—62; exec. v.p. Twin Pines Fed., Berkeley, 1962—84; pres. W.F. Ostrander & Assoc., Inc., Berkeley, 1984—2006; ret., 2006. Dir. East Bay chpt. Soc. Real Estate Appraisers, Calif., 1975—76. Contbr. articles to poetry mag.; author: The Hunchback and the Swan, 1978; editor: Blue Unicorn Mag., 1990—. Sec. Fair Housing and Fair Employment, Berkeley, 1965—.

With US Merchant Marines, 1944—45. Mem.: Berkeley Breakfast Club, Appraisal Inst. Democrat. Roman Catholic. Home and Office: 2360 Indian Saklan Dr # 3 Walnut Creek CA 94595 Office Phone: 925-930-9524. Personal E-mail: ostrand7@pacbell.net.

**OSTREM, WALTER MARTIN,** librarian, educator, consultant; b. Mpls., May 27, 1930; s. Oscar Martin and Helen Therese (Marcio) O.; m. Gertrud Franciska Tunkel, Aug. 6, 1956; children: Thomas, Paul, Francine. BA, U. Minn., 1953, MA, 1958; BS, Mankato State U., 1962, MS, 1964; postgrad., U. Mich., U. Iowa. Serials libr. Agr. Libr. U. Minn., 1958-59; acquisitions libr. Mankato State U., Minn., 1959-66, Eastern Mich. U., 1966-67; dir. media Iowa City Sch., 1967-69; libr. John F. Kennedy Sch., Berlin, 1969-73; disting. profl. libr. St. Paul Schs., 1973-90; libr. Open Sch. St. Pauls Schs., 1990-93; cons. in field. Librarian, educator, consultant; b. Mpls., May 27, 1930; s. Oscar Martin and Helen Therese (Marcio) O.; m. Gertrud Franciska Tunkel, Aug. 6, 1956; children— Thomas, Paul, Francine. B.A., U. Minn., 1953, M.A., 1958; B.S., Mankato State U., 1962, M.S., 1964; postgrad. U. Mich., U. Iowa. Serials librarian Agr. Library U. Minn., 1958-59; acquisitions librarian Mankato State U., Minn., 1959-66, Eastern Mich. U., 1966-67; dir. media Iowa City Sch., 1967-69; librarian John F. Kennedy Sch., Berlin, W.Ger., 1969-73; dist. profl. librarian St. Paul Schs., 1973-90; librarian Open Sch. St. Pauls Schs., 1990-93; cons. in field. Served to 1st lt. U.S. Army, 1954-55. Recipient Ency. Brit. 1st place Sch. Library Media System award, 1969. Mem. Minn. Ednl. Media Orgn., Am. Fedn. Tchrs., M Club, Phi Delta Kappa. Contbr. articles in field. Contbr. articles to profl. jours. Served to 1st lt. U.S. Army, 1954-55. Recipient Ency. Brit. 1st place Sch. Libr. Media System award, 1969. Mem. Minn. Ednl. Media Orgn., Am. Fedn. Tchrs., M Club, Phi Delta Kappa. Home: 5536 Harriet Ave Minneapolis MN 55419-1830 *Personal philosophy: I believe school libraries and school librarians are essential for increasing children's understanding of themselves and their society.*

**OSTRIKER, ALICIA SUSKIN,** poet; b. NYC, Nov. 11, 1937; d. David and Beatrice (Linnick) Suskin; m. Jeremiah P. Ostriker, 1958; children: Rebecca, Eve, Gabriel. BA, Brandeis U., 1959; MA, U. Wis., 1961, PhD, 1964. Asst. prof. Rutgers U., New Brunswick, NJ, 1965—68, assoc. prof., 1968—72, prof. English, 1972—2004; mem. faculty MFA program New Eng. Coll. Poetry, Henniker, NH, 2004—. Author: Vision and Verse in William Blake, 1965, Songs, 1969, Once More Out of Darkness, and Other Poems, 1974, A Dream of Springtime, 1979, The Mother/Child Papers, 1980, A Woman Under the Surface: Poems and Prose Poems, 1982, Writing Like a Woman, 1983, The Imaginary Lover, 1986 (William Carlos Williams prize Poetry Soc. Am. 1986), Stealing the Language: The Emergence of Women's Poetry in America, 1986, Green Age, 1989, Feminist Revision and the Bible, 1993, The Nakedness of the Fathers: Biblical Vision and Revisions, 1994, The Crack in Everything, 1996 (Nat. Book award finalist 1996, Paterson Poetry prize 1996, San Francisco State Poetry Ctr. award 1997), The Little Space: Selected and New Poems, 1998 (Nat. Book award finalist 1998), Dancing at the Devil's Party: Essays on Poetry, Politics, and the Erotic, 2000, The Volcano Sequence, 2002, No Heaven, 2005; editor: William Blake: Complete Poems, 1977. Nat. Coun. on Humanities grantee, 1968; NEA fellow, 1976-77, N.J. Arts Coun. fellow, 1982, Guggenheim Found. fellow, 1984-85, faculty fellow Rutgers Ctr. for Hist. Analysis, 1995-96, Rockefeller Found. fellow, 1982; recipient Strousse Poetry prize Prairie Schooner, 1986, Edward Stanley award Prairie Schooner, 1994, Anna David Rosenberg Poetry award, 1994, Best American Poetry award, 1996, Paterson prize, 1997, San Francisco State Poetry Ctr. award, 1997, Pushcart prize, 1999, Larry Levis prize 2001. E-mail: ostriker@rci.rutgers.edu.

**OSTRIKER, JEREMIAH PAUL,** astrophysicist, educator; b. NYC, Apr. 13, 1937; s. Martin and Jeanne (Sumpf) Ostriker; m. Alicia Suskin, Dec. 1, 1958; children: Rebecca, Eve; 1 child, Gabriel. AB, Harvard U., 1959; PhD, U. Chgo., 1964, degree (hon.), 1992; postgrad., U. Cambridge, Eng., 1964—65. Rsch. assoc., lectr. astrophysics Princeton U., Princeton, 1965—66, asst. prof., 1966—68, assoc. prof., 1968—71, prof., 1971—, chmn. dept. astronomy, dir. obs., 1979—95, Charles A. Young prof. astronomy, 1982—2002, provost, 1995—2001; Plumian prof. astronomy and exptl. philosophy U. Cambridge, England, 2001—04; dir. Princeton Inst. Computational Sci. and Engring., 2005—. Author: Development of Large-Scale Structure in the Universe, 1991; editl. bd., trustee Princeton U. Press; contbr. articles to profl. jours. Recipient Vainu Bappu Meml. award, Indian Nat. Sci. Acad., 1993, Karl Schwarzschild medal, Astronomische Gesellschaft, 1999, U.S. Nat. medal of Sci., 2000; fellow Alfred P. Sloan, 1970—72; NSF fellow, U. Chgo., 1960—64. Fellow: AAAS; mem.: NAS (counselor 1992—95, bd. govs. 1993—95), Royal Netherlands Acad. Arts and Scis. (fgn.), Am. Acad. Arts and Scis., Am. Philos. Soc., Internat. Astron. Union, Am. Astron. Soc. (councilor 1978—80, Warner prize 1972, Russel prize 1980), Royal Astron. Soc. (assoc. Gold medal 2004), Am. Mus. Natural History (trustee 1997—). Home: 33 Philip Dr Princeton NJ 08540-5409 Office Phone: 609-258-4267. Business E-Mail: ostriker@princeton.edu.

**OSTROFF, DAWN T.,** broadcast executive; b. Miami, Mar. 31, 1960; married. Exec. Kushner Locke; asst. 20th Century Fox, pres. devel.; exec., head programming Lifetime; pres. entertainment UPN. Office: UPN 11800 Wilshire Blvd Los Angeles CA 90025 E-mail: Dawn_Ostroff@upn.com.*

**OSTROFF, PETER I.,** lawyer; b. Washington, Dec. 15, 1942; BA, Washington U., 1964; JD, U. Chgo., 1967. Bar: Ill. 1967, Calif. 1970. Teaching fellow in law Monash U., Melbourne, Australia, 1968—69; law clk. to Hon. Shirley M. Hufstedler US Ct. Appeals (9th cir.), 1969-70; ptnr. comml. trial and litig. practice Sidley Austin Brown & Wood LLP, LA. mem. exec. com. Named one of Best Lawyers in Am. for Bus. Lldg., supplement to Am. Lawyer mag., 2003, LA's pit bull lawyers, LA mag. Mem. ABA (dir. divsn. substantive law 1982-83, chmn. comml. transations litigation com. 1976-80, coun. mem. 1980-83, chmn. computer litigation com. 1985—, dir. programs divsn. 1990—), State Bar Calif. (mem. exec. com. intellectual property sect. 1988-89, litig. sect. 1990—), La County Bar Assn. (bd. trustees 1974-76, chair human rights sect. 1975-76, mem. ethics com. 1982-84), Assn. Bus. Trial Lawyers (pres. 1988-89, mem. exec. com. litig. sect. 1990—). Office: Sidley Austin Brown & Wood LLP Fl 40 555 W 5th St Los Angeles CA 90013-1010 Office Phone: 213-896-6612. Office Fax: 213-896-6600. Business E-Mail: postroff@sidley.com.

**OSTROM, DON,** political science professor; b. Chgo., Mar. 9, 1939; s. Irving and Margaret (Hedberg) O.; m. Florence Horan, Jan. 13, 1972; children: Erik, Rebecca, Katherine. BA, St. Olaf Coll., Northfield, Minn., 1960; MA, Washington U., 1970, PhD, 1972. Prof. polit. sci. Gustavus Adolphus Coll., St. Peter, Minn., 1972—2004; state rep. Minn. Ho. of Reps., St. Paul, 1988-96; vis. prof. polit. sci. St. Olaf Coll., Northfield, 2004—. Co-editor: Perspectives on Minnesota Government and Politics, 1998. Democrat. Home: 2737 Ewing Ave S Minneapolis MN 55416 E-mail: dostrom@gac.edu.

**OSTROM, ELINOR,** political science professor, researcher; b. L.A., Aug. 7, 1933; d. Adrian and Leah (Hopkins) Awan; m. Charles Scott, Aug. 8, 1954 (div. 1961); m. Vincent Ostrom, Nov. 23, 1963. AB with honors, UCLA, 1954, MA, 1962, PhD, 1965; D in Economics (hon.), U. Zurich, 1999; D (hon.), Inst. Social Studies, The Hague, 2002, Luleå U. Tech., Sweden, 2005; DHL (hon.), U. Mich., 2006. Vis. asst. prof. dept. gov. Ind. U., Bloomington, 1965-66, asst. prof., grad. advisor, dept. gov., 1966-69, assoc. prof. polit. sci., 1974-91, Arthur F. Bentley prof. polit. sci., 1991—, prof., chmn. dept. polit. sci., 1980—84, acting chair dept. polit. sci., 1980-90, co-dir. workshop in polit. theory and policy analysis, 1973—, co-dir. Ctr. Study Instns., Population and Environ. Change, 1996—2006, prof. part-time Sch. Pub. and Environ. Affairs. Employment interviewer, asst. employee relations mgr. Godfrey L. Cabot, Inc., Boston, 1955-57; personnel analyst III U. Calif., LA, 1957-61; cons., Internat. Assn. Chiefs Police: Police Discipline Project, 1974-75; adv. bd. Nat. Evaluation Program Law Enforcement Assistance (Adminstrn.), Washington, 1975-76; mem. Nat. Adv. Panel, Nat. Acad. Pub. Adminstrn.; Neighborhood-Oriented Metropolitan

Gov., 1975-76, task force on criminal justice rsch. and devel. Nat. Adv. Com. on Criminal Justice Standards and Goals, 1975-76, Nat. Sheriffs Assn.: Study of Contract Law Enforcement, 1975-76; adv. panel Div. Policy Rsch. and Analysis, NSF, Washington, 1977-78, panel on Instl. Develop., 1985; rev. panel Polit. Sci. div. NSF, 1983-84; Interuniversity Consortium for Polit. and Social Rsch. Coun., 1983-85; adv. com. nat. urban policy NAS/NRC, 1985-88, panel on Common Property Resources Mgmt., 1985-86, Scientific Com. on Problems of the Environ., 1995-98; rsch. adv. com. U.S. AID, 1989-91; local gov. rsch. adv. bd., US Adv. Commn. on Intergovernmental Rels., 1985-88; adv. bd., Inst. for Policy Reform, 1993-96; bd. dirs. Beijer Internat. Inst. Ecol. Econs., Royal Swedish Acad. Scis., 1997-; academic adv. bd., Max-Planck-Inst. für Gesellschaftsforschung, 2000-; cons. in field. Co-author: Policing Metropolitan America, 1978, Local Government in the United States, 1988, Institutional Incentives and Sustainable Development: Infrastructure Policies in Perspective, 1993, Rules, Games, and Common-Pool Resources, 1994, The Samaritan's Dilemma, 2005, Seeing the Forest and the Trees, 2005; author: Governing the Commons, 1990, Crafting Institutions for Self-Governing Irrigation Systems, 1992, Understanding Institutional Diversity, 2005; editor: Strategies of Political Inquiry, 1982; co-editor: The Commons in the New Millennium: Challenges and Adaptations, 2003, Trust and Reciprocity: Interdisciplinary Lessons from Experimental Research, 2003, Jour. Theoretical Politics, 1987-95, People and Forests: Communities, Institutions, and Governance, 2000, Protecting the Commons: A Framework for Resource Management in the Americas, 2001, Foundations of Social Capital, 2003; mem. editl. bd. Am. Jour. Polit. Sci., Am. Polit. Sci. Review, Criminal Justice Review, Pub. Productivity Review, Publius; Quarterly Jour. Adminstrn., Sage Urban Affairs Ann. Review, Social Sci. Quarterly, Urban Affairs Quarterly, Ecol. Economics; contbr. articles to profl. jours. Grantee NSF, 1974-85, 87—, NIMH, 1977-81, U.S. Dept. Justice, 1978-82, AID, 1984-94, U.S. Geol. Survey, 1987-89, Ford Found., 1991—, FAO, 1992—, MacArthur Found., 1996-; recipient Frank E. Seidman Disting. award in Polit. Economy, 1997, Johan Skytte prize in Polit. Sci., Upsala University, 1999, Aaron Wildavsky Enduring Contbn. award for Governing the Commons, APSA, Pub. Policy Sect., 2000, John J. Carty award for the Advancement Sci., NAS, 2004, Sustainability Sci. award Ecol. Soc. Am., 2005, James Madison award Am. Polit. Sci. Assn., 2005. Fellow Am. Acad. Arts and Scis. (lifetime achievement award Atlas Econ. Rsch. Found., 2003), AAAS; mem. Pub. Choice Soc. (pres. 1982-84, co-chair, Duncan Black award Com., 1986-87, chair, Duncan Black award Com., 1990, exec. coun., 1982-), Am. Polit. Sci. Assn. (v.p. 1975-76, pres.-elect 1995-96, pres. 1996-97, chmn., several coms., 1978-88, mem., several coms., 1970-2002), Midwest Polit. Sci. Assn. (pres. 1984-85), Internat. Polit. Sci. Assn., Am. Econ. Assn., Internat. Assn. for Study Common Property (pres. 1990-91, program co-chair, 2000), Policy Studies Orgn., (nominating com., 1986-87, Miriam Mills award, 1996, Thomas R. Dye Svc. award, 1997), Am. Philos. Soc., Assn. for Politics and the Life Scis., NAS. Democrat. Home: 5883 E Lampkins Ridge Rd Bloomington IN 47401-9726 Office: Ind Univ Workshop in Polit Theory & Policy Analys 513 N Park Ave Bloomington IN 47408-3895 Office Phone: 812-855-0441. Office Fax: 812-855-3150. Business E-Mail: ostrom@indiana.edu.

**OSTROM, VINCENT A(LFRED),** political science professor; b. Nooksack, Wash., Sept. 25, 1919; s. Alfred and Alma (Knudson) Ostrom; m. Isabell Bender, May 20, 1942 (div. 1963); m. Elinor Awan, Nov. 23, 1963. BA in Polit. Sci., UCLA, 1942, MA in Polit. Sci., 1945, PhD in Polit. Sci., 1950. Tchr. Chaffey Union H.S., Ontario, Calif., 1943-45; asst. prof. polit. sci. U. Wyo., Laramie, 1945-48, U. Oreg., Eugene, 1954, assoc. prof. polit. sci., 1954-58, UCLA, 1958-64; prof. polit. sci. Ind. U., Bloomington, 1964-90, Arthur F. Bentley prof emeritus polit. sci., 1990—. Hooker disting. vis. scholar McMaster U., 1984-85; rsch. assoc. Bur. Mcpl. Rsch., 1950, Resources for Future, Inc., 1962-64; assoc. dir. Pacific NW Coop. Program in Ednl. Adminstrn., 1951-58; founding dir. Workshop in Polit. Theory and Policy Analysis, Ind. U., Bloomington, 1973—; cons. and lectr. in field. Author: Water and Politics, 1953, The Political Theory of a Compound Republic, 1971, 2nd rev. edit., 1987, The Intellectual Crisis in American Public Administration, 1974, 2nd edit., 1989, The Meaning of American Federalism, 1991, The Meaning of Democracy and the Vulnerability of Democracies, 1997; co-author: Understanding Urban Government, 1973, Local Government in the United States, 1988; co-editor: Comparing Urban Service Delivery Systems, 1977, Guidance, Control and Evaluation in the Public Sector, 1986, Rethinking Institutional Analysis and Development, 1988, 2d. edit. 1993; mem. bd. editors Publius, 1972—; mem. editl. bd. Constnl. Polit. Economy, 1989—, Nigerian Jour. Fin. and Human Resources Mgmt., 1996—, Internat. Jour. Orgn. Theory and Behavior, 1997—; contbr. articles to profl. jours. Program coord. Wyo. Assessors' Sch., 1946-48, Budget Officer's Sch., 1947-48; exec. sec. Wyo. League of Municipalities, 1947-48; cons. Wyo. Legis. Interim Com., 1947-48, Nat. Resources, Alaska Constitutional Convention, 1955-56, Tenn. Water Policy Commn., 1956; mem. founding bd. Com. on Polit. Economy of the Good Soc., 1990—. Grantee and fellowships Social Sci. Rsch. Coun., 1954-55, Ctr. Advanced Study in Behavioral Scis., 1955-56, Ctr. Interdisciplinary Rsch., 1981-82; co-recipient (with Elinor Ostrom) Lifetime Achievement award Atlas Economic Rsch. Found. Fund, 2003, Robert O. Anderson Sustainable Arctic award Inst. of the North 2003. Mem. AAAS, Am. Polit. Sci. Assn. (Spl. Achievement award for Significant Contbns. to Study of Federalism, 1991, Best Book on Federalism and Intergovtl. Rels. award 1999, John Gaus Disting. lecturer award 2005), Am. Econ. Assn., Am. Soc. Pub. Adminstrn., Pub. Choice Soc., Internat. Polit. Sci. Assn. Home: 5883 E Lampkins Ridge Rd Bloomington IN 47401-9726 Office: Ind U Workshop in Polit Theory 513 N Park Ave Bloomington IN 47408-3895 Office Phone: 812-855-0441. Business E-Mail: ghiggins@indiana.edu, workshop@indiana.edu.

**OSTROMENCKI, NANCY LEE,** music educator; b. Chgo., May 2, 1954; d. George Edward and Jeanette Ann Ostromencki; m. Joshua R. Weiksheimer, Feb. 12, 1987 (div. Feb. 1989). MusB, DePaul U., 1977. Tchr., pianist North Park Coll., Chgo., 1975—88, pvt. instrn., 1975—88, Rio Rancho High Sch, N.Mex., 1989—2001, pvt. instrn., Tucson, 2001—. Co-founder The Piano Education Page. Mem.: West Mesa Music Tchrs. Assn., Music Tchrs. Nat. Assn. Home: 6760 N Calle Lomita Tucson AZ 85704

**OSTROSKY-ZEICHNER, LUIS,** epidemiologist, educator, physician; s. Jose Ostrosky and Isabel Zeichner; m. Stephanie Lerner, May 25, 2002. MD, UNAM, Mexico City, 1995. Resident internal medicine Inst. Nal. Nutricion Salvador Zubiran, Mexico City, Distrito Federal, 1995—99; fellow infectious diseases Univ. of Tex.- Houston Med. Sch., 1999—2002; instr. medicine, 2002—03, asst. prof. medicine, 2003—; med. dir. epidemiology Meml. Hermann Healthcare Sys., 2005—. Med. dir. epidemiology Meml. Hermann Hosp., Houston, 2002—. Recipient 2d Prize Rsch. Award, Glaxo-Wellcome Found., 1999. Fellow: ACP. Achievements include research in Diagnosis, prevention, and treatment of invasive fungal infections; Hospital epidemiology and infection control. Office: Univ Texas- Houston Med Sch 6431 Fannin MSB 2 112 Houston TX 77030 Personal E-mail: lostrosky@hotmail.com.

**OSTROVSKY, LAWRENCE ZELIG,** lawyer; b. Cleve., June 1, 1956; s. Peter and Yetta Ostrovsky. BA, St. John's Coll., Annapolis, Md., 1978; JD, Lewis and Clark Coll., 1982. Bar: Ohio 1982, Alaska 1983. Assoc. Berger & Kirschenbaum, Cleve., 1982, Birch, Horton, Bittner, Pestinger & Anderson, Anchorage, 1983—87; spl. asst. to the commr. of natural resources Alaska Dept. Natural Resources, Anchorage, 1987—91; assoc. dir. for energy and public lands Alaska Gov. Office, Washington, 1991—94; asst. atty. gen. oil, gas, and mining sect., Alaska Dept. Law, Anchorage, 1994—. Mem. Commonwealth North, Anchorage, 1986, Alaska Bar Assn.(bd. of governors, 1998—, pres. elect, 2003, pres. 2004). Office: Alaska Dept Law 1031 W 4th Ave Ste 200 Anchorage AK 99501-1994 Business E-Mail: larry_ostrovsky@law.state.ak.us.

**OSTROW, JOSEPH W.,** advertising executive; b. NYC, Feb. 22, 1933; s. Meyer H. and Helen (Small) O.; m. Francine Lee Goldberg, Sept. 4, 1955; children: Elizabeth Sara, Peter Mathew, William Nathan. BS in Mktg., NYU, 1955. Researcher W.R. Simmons, N.Y.C., 1954-55; with Young & Rubicam,

N.Y.C., 1955-87, sr. v.p., dir. communication planning, 1972-73, exec. v.p., dir., dir. communications services, 1973-87, mem. N.Y. exec. com., U.S.A. bd. dirs.; pres., chief operating officer worldwide Direct Mktg. Group of Cos., 1983-84; exec. v.p., dir. media worldwide Foote, Cone & Belding Co., N.Y.C., 1987-94; pres., CEO Cabletelevision Advt. Bur., N.Y.C., 1994—2003; pres. Ostrow Cons., N.Y.C., 2003. Multichannel Advt. Bur. Internat.; hon. chair bd. dir. Cable Positive; past chmn. Traffic Audit Bur.; dir. Audit Bur. Circulations; bd. dir., past mem. exec. com. Advt. Info. Svc., Advt. Rsch. Found.; lectr. in field. Mem. nat. coun. Boy Scouts Am. Mem. Media Dirs. Coun. (past pres.), Am. Assn. Advt. Agys. (past vice chmn. media policy com.), Internat. Radio and TV Found. (bd. dirs.), Advt. Coun. (bd. dirs.), John Reisenbach Found. (bd. dirs.). E-mail: joe.ostrowconsulting@yahoo.com. *It is important that one continue to set goals that seem unachievable and at the same time live by standards that remain consistently high. The maintenance of integrity and adherence to principles which support it, are especially critical when dealing with consumer commercial persuasion. Anything less would be detrimental to the proper pursuit of both personal and business achievements.*

**OSTROW, STUART,** theatrical producer, educator, author; b. NYC; m. Ann Elizabeth Gilbert; children: Julie Elizabeth, Katherine Ann, John Stuart. Disting. univ. prof. theater U. Houston. Pres. Stuart Ostrow Found., Inc., Mus. Theater Lab.; founding mem. opera-mus. theatre panel NEA; mem. bd. overseers com. to visit Loeb Drama Ctr. Harvard U. Prodr.: We Take the Town, 1961, The Apple Tree, 1966, 1776, 1969, Scratch, 1971, Pippin, 1972, The Moony Shapiro Songbook, 1981, American Passion, 1983, M. Butterfly, 1988, La Bête, 1991, Face Value, 1993; prodr., dir.: Here's Love, 1963, Swing, 1980; author, producer: Stages, 1978; assoc. dir.: Chicago, 1975; author: A Producer's Broadway Journey, 1999, Thank You Very Much, 2002, Present At the Creation, Leaping in the Dark and Going Against the Grain, 2005 Mem. Pulitzer Prize Drama Jury; chmn. bd. trustees Inst. for Advanced Study in Musical Theatre. With USAF, 1952—55.

**OSTRY, SYLVIA,** academic administrator, economist; b. Winnipeg, Man., Can. d. Morris J. and B. (Stoller) Knelman; m. Bernard Ostry; children: Adam, Jonathan. BA in Econs., McGill U., 1948, MA, 1950; PhD in Econs., Cambridge U. and McGill U., 1954; also 19 hon. degrees. Lectr., asst. prof. econs. McGill U.; rsch. officer Inst. Stats., U. Oxford, Eng.; assoc. prof. U. Montreal, Can.; with dept. stats. Econ. Coun. Can., Ottawa, 1964-72, chmn., 1978-79; chief statistician Stats. Can., Ottawa, 1972-75; dep. minister consumer and corp. affairs Govt. Can., Ottawa, 1975-78, dep. minister internat. trade, coordinator internat. econ. relations, 1984-85, ambassador for multilateral trade negotiations, personal rep. of Prime Minister for Econ. Summit, 1985-88; chancellor U. Waterloo, 1991-96; head dept. econs. and stats. OECD, Paris, 1979-83; chmn. Ctr. for Internat. Studies U. Toronto, Ont., Can., 1990-97, disting. rsch. fellow Munk Ctr. for Internat. Studies, 1997—. Lectr. Per Jacobssen Found., 1987; chmn. nat. coun. Can. Inst. Internat. Affairs, 1990-95; western co-chmn. Blue Ribbon Commn. for Hungary's Econ. Recovery, 1990-94; mem. adv. bd. Inst. Internat. Econs., Washington; founding mem. Pacific Coun. on Internat. Policy; Volvo Disting. vis. fellow Coun. on Fgn. Rels., N.Y.C., 1989. Author: Governments and Corporations in a Shrinking World: The Search for Stability, 1990, The Threat of Managed Trade to Transforming Economies, 1993; co-author: (with Richard Nelson) Technonationalism and Technoglobalism: Conflict and Cooperation, 1995; co-editor: (with Karen Knop, Richard Simeon, Katherine Swinton) Rethinking Federalism: Citizens, Markets and Governments in a Changing World, 1995; New Dimensions of Market Access, 1995, (with Gilbert R. Winham) The Halifax G-7 Summit: Issues on the Table, 1995, Who's on First: The Post-Cold War Trading System, 1997, APEC and Regime Creation in the Asia-Pacific: The OECD Model?, 1998, Technology, Productivity and Multinational Enterprise, 1998, Intellectual Property Protection in the World Trade Organization: Major Issues in the Millennium Round, 1999, Globalization Implications for Industrial Relations, 1999, The Future of the World Trading System, 1999, Convergence and Sovereignty: Policy Scope for Compromise?, 2000, Regional Versus Multilateral Trade Strategies, 2000, Making Sense of it All: A Post Mortem on the Meaning of Seattle, 2000; The Uruguay Round North-South Grand Bargain: Implications for Future Negotiations, 2000, Regional Dominos and the WTO: Building Blocks or Boomerang?, 2000, Business, Trade and the Environment, 2000, The Changing Scenario in International Governance, 2000, Looking Back to Look Forward: The Multilateral Trading System after 50 Years, 2000, The WTO: Post Seattle and Chinese Accession, 2001, The WTO and International Governance, 2001, Dominos and the WTO: Building Blocks or Boomerang?, 2000, Business, Trade and the Environment, 2000, The Changing Scenario in International Governance, 2000, Looking Back to Look Forward: The Multilateral Trading System after 50 Years, 2000, The WTO: Post Seattle and Chinese Accession, 2001, The WTO and International Governance, 2001, Global Integration: Currents and Counter Current, 2003, What are the Necessary Ingredients for the World Trading Order?, 2003, External Transparency in Trade Policy, 2004, The World Trading System: In the Fog of Uncertainty, 2004, Summitry and Trade: What Could Sea Island Do for Doha?, 2004, External Transparency: The Policy Process at the National Level of the Two-level game, 2004; contbg. author: China and the Long March to Global Trade, 2003, Between Feast and Famine: Fixing Global Trade, 2004, The Future of the World Trading System: Beyond Doha, 2004, Global Integration: Currents and Counter-Currents, 2005, A Global Perspective on the Multilateral Trading System, 2006, What Are the Necessary Ingredients for the World Trading Order?, 2006, others; contbr. articles on empirical and policy-analytic subjects to more than 90 profl. publs. Decorated companion Order of Can., 1990; recipient Outstanding Achievement award Govt. of Can., 1987, Hon. Assoc. award Conf. Bd. of Can., 1992; Disting. vis. fellow Volvo, 1989-90. Fellow Royal Soc. Can.; mem. Group of Thirty, Inst. for Internat. Econs. (adv. bd.). Avocations: films, theater, contemporary reading. Office: Munk Ctr Internat Studies U Toronto 1 Devonshire Pl Toronto ON Canada M5S 3K7 Office Phone: 416-946-8927. Business E-Mail: sylvia.ostry@utoronto.ca.

**OSTWALD, MARTIN,** retired classicist; b. Dortmund, Germany, Jan. 15, 1922; arrived in U.S., 1946, naturalized, 1956; s. Max and Hedwig (Strauss) Ostwald; m. Lore Ursula Weinberg, Dec. 27, 1948; children: Mark F., David H. BA, U. Toronto, 1946; AM, U. Chgo., 1948; PhD, Columbia U., 1952; D (hon.), Fribourg U., Switzerland, 1995, Dortmund U., Germany, 2001. Instr. classics and humanities Wesleyan U., Middletown, Conn., 1950-51; from lectr. to asst. prof. Greek and Latin Columbia U., 1951-58; mem. faculty Swarthmore Coll., 1958—, prof. classics, 1966-92, prof. emeritus, 1992—; prof. classical studies U. Pa., 1968-92, prof. emeritus, 1992—. Vis. assoc. prof. Princeton (N.J.) U., 1964, mem. Inst. Advanced Study, 1974—75, 1981—82, 1990—91; vis. prof. U. Calif., Berkeley, 1969, Tel-Aviv U., 1996—; vis. fellow Balliol Coll. Oxford (Eng.) U., 1970—71, vis. fellow Wolfson Coll., 1987, 91; dir. fellowships-in-residence classics NEH, 1976—77; dir. d'etudes EHESS, Paris, 1991; mem. Inst. Advanced Studies, Tel Aviv, 1994, 2003. Translator: Nicomachean Ethics (Aristotle), 1962; author: (book) Nomos and the Beginings of the Athenian Democracy, 1969, Autonomia, Its Genesis and Early History, 1982, From Popular Sovereignty to the Sovereignty of Law, 1987, Anake in Thucydides, 1988, Oligarchia, 2000; author: (with T. G. Rosenmeyer and J. W. Halporn) The Meters of Greek and Latin Poetry, 2d edit., 1980; mem. editl. bd. Cambridge Ancient History, 1976—94; contbr. articles to profl. jours. Fellow, Am. Coun. Learned Socs., 1965—66, NEH, 1970—71, 1990—91; Fulbright Rsch. fellow, Greece, 1961—62, Guggenheim fellow, 1977—78, Lang. fellow, Swarthmore Coll., 1986—87. Fellow: AAAS; mem.: Soc. Ancient Philosophy, Classical Assn. Atlantic States, Classical Assn. Can., Am. Philol. Assn. (pres. 1986—87), Am. Philos. Soc., Soc. Promotion Hellenic Studies (hon.). Home: 408 Walnut Ln Swarthmore PA 19081-1137 E-mail: mostwal1@swarthmore.edu.

**OSTWALD, VENICE ELOISE VARNER,** librarian, educator, minister, writer; b. Denver, July 19, 1928; d. Earl Robert and Madeline (Shoemaker) Varner; m. Leonard F. Ostwald (div.). BA, U. Colo.-Boulder, 1946; MS, U. So. Calif., 1954. Librarian, tchr. Long Beach Pub. Schs., Calif., 1954-61; asst. prof. U. Oreg., Eugene, 1961-63; dir. libr. and audio-visual Hillsborough Pub. Schs., Calif., 1963-65; adminstrv. asst. to libr. dir. San Jose State U., 1965-67;

instrn. specialist/librarian DeAnza Coll., Cupertino, Calif., 1967-87, emeritus, 1987—. Founder, bd. dirs. Singles in Service, Santa Clara, Calif., 1972; co-founder Casa Serena Hospice, San Jose, 1981; pres. Spiritual Edn. Endeavors Publ. Co., 1985-; chmn. bd. SHARE Found., 1985—. Co-author 9 books under pseudonym Virginia Essene; lyricist songs include Part of Me, Oasis, Peru, Caliente, Hyano Cucarumba, Esclava. Mem. Beta Phi Mu, Kappa Delta. Office: SHARE Found 1556 Halford Ave # 288 Santa Clara CA 95051-2661 Office Phone: 408-248-8244. Business E-Mail: lovecorps@sharefoundationnetwork.com.

**O'SULLIVAN, CINDY MARIE,** mathematics professor; b. Blue Island, Ill., Dec. 22, 1956; d. Donald Edward and Frances Gloria Crawford; children: Michael, Ryan, Shannon. BS, No. Ill. U., 1979; M in Math. Edn., Olgethorpe U., Ga., 2000; M in Leadership, Kennesaw U., Ga., 2004. Cert. gifted edn. High sch. math tchr. Bremen High Sch., Midlothian, Ill., 1979—80, Elida High Sch., Ohio, 1980—81; substitute tchr. Grandville Sch. Dist., Mich., 1981; math tutor Huntington Learning Ctr., Mpls., 1987—88; substitute tchr. South Forsyth High Sch., Cumming, Ga., 1995—96; math tchr. South Forsyth Mid. Sch., 1996—99, Vickery Creed Mid. Sch., 1999—. State trainer Ga. Dept. Edn., Atlanta, 2004—05; math dept. chair Vickery Creek Mid. Sch., Cumming, 2000—; math curriculum trainer Forsyth County Schs., 2000—; featured participant Statewide Ednl. Video by Ga. Dept. Edn., Nat. Video by Phil Schlechty Group. Participant, money raiser Relay for Life, Cumming, 2003—05. Recipient Disney Am. Tchr. award, 2001, Honor Tchr., Atlanta Jour. Constitution, 2002, Tchr. of Year, Forsyth County Middle Sch., 2003. Mem.: Ga. Assn. Ednl. Leaders, Assn. Supervision and Curriculum Devel., Nat. Coun. Tchrs. Math. Avocations: reading, travel, exercise, fundraising, embroidery. Home: 4819 S Victor Ave Tulsa OK 74105

**O'SULLIVAN, DANIEL E.,** language educator; b. Worcester, Mass., Dec. 26, 1970; s. Daniel E. and Carol A. O'Sullivan; m. Patricia Mary Lucey; children: Marion Lucey, Colm Daniel. AB in French, Coll. of the Holy Cross, Worcester, 1992; MA in French, U. NC, Chapel Hill, 1994; PhD in French, Boston Coll., Chestnut Hill, Mass., 2000. Anglo-Am. book rev. editor Textual Cultures, 2004—. Author: Marian Devotion in Thirteenth-Century French Lyric, The French Review, Speculum; contbr. articles to profl. jours. Mem. AMOS Network Layfayette County, Oxford, Miss., 2004—05; social concerns com. St. John's Cath. Ch., Oxford, 2003—05. Faculty Rsch. fellow, U. Miss., 2004, 2006. Mem.: MLA, Soc. for Textual Scholarship (exec. bd. 2004—), Miss. Fgn. Languages Assn., Am. Assn. Tchrs. French, Southeastern Medieval Assn., Medieval Acad. Am., Phi Beta Kappa, Alpha Sigma Nu, Pi Delta Phi. Avocations: martial arts, Karate, Judo. Office: Univ Miss Bondurant Hall C115 University MS 38677-1848 Office Phone: 662-915-6693. Office Fax: 662-915-1086. Business E-Mail: dosulliv@olemiss.edu.

**O'SULLIVAN, EUGENE HENRY,** retired advertising executive, management consultant; b. Plainfield, N.J., June 8, 1942; s. Patrick J. and Helen (Callahan) O'S.; m. Tracy O'Sullivan; children: Meredith Heather, Charlie Hiromichi. BBA, U. Notre Dame, 1964. Media buyer Foote Cone Belding, N.Y.C., 1967-68; account exec., mgmt. supr. Group Dtr, N.Y.C.; exec. v.p., dir. client svcs. Young & Rubicam, N.Y.C., 1968-84; sr. v.p., group dir. Ogilvy & Mather, N.Y.C., 1984-87; exec. v.p. Hill, Holliday, Boston, 1986-87; exec. v.p., gen. mgr. McCann Erickson, N.Y.C., 1988-90; ret., 1990. Served to lt. (j.g.) USN, 1964-66. Mem. Lotos Club. Democrat. Home: 21 E 10th St New York NY 10003-5923 Office Phone: 212-614-9570. E-mail: eugeneo@earthlink.net.

**O'SULLIVAN, FRANCES K.,** computer company executive; BS, Univ. Va., 1980. With IBM, 1981—2005, gen. mgr., PC div.; sr. v.p., COO product group Lenovo, Purchase, NY, 2005—. Mem. engring. industry adv. bd. Univ. Va. Office: Lenovo Group The Ctr at Purchase 1 Manhattanville Rd Purchase NY 10577*

**O'SULLIVAN, JUDITH ROBERTA,** lawyer, writer, artist; b. Pitts., Jan. 6, 1942; d. Robert Howard and Mary Olive (O'Donnell) Gallick; m. James Paul O'Sullivan, Feb. 1, 1964; children: Kathryn, James. BA, Carlow Coll., 1963; MA, U. Md., 1969, PhD, 1976; JD, Georgetown U., 1996. Editor Am. Film Inst., Washington, 1974—77; assoc. program coord. Smithsonian Resident Assocs., Washington 1977—78; dir. instl. devel. Nat. Archives, Washington, 1978—79; exec. dir. Md. State Humanities Coun., Balt., 1979—81, 1982—84, Ctr. for the Book, Libr. of Congress, Washington, 1981—82; dep. asst. dir. Nat. Mus. Am. Art, Washington, 1984—87, acting asst. dir., 1987—89; pres., CEO The Mus. at Stony Brook, NY, 1989—92; exec. dir. Nat. Assn. Women Judges, Washington, 1993; clk. Office Legal Adviser U.S. Dept. State, Washington, 1994—96; trial atty. Atty. Gen.'s honors program U.S. Dept. Justice, 1996—, sr. trial atty. Criminal divsn., Domestic Security sect., 2002—; spl. asst. U.S. atty. U.S. Dist. (ea. dist.) Va., 1998—2002; asst. U.S. atty. U.S. Dist. Ariz., Tucson, 1999—2000. Summer assoc. Piper & Marbury, Balt., 1995; chair Smithsonian Women's Coun., Washington, 1988-89. Author: The Art of the Comic Strip, 1971 (Gen. Excellence award Printing Industry Am.); Workers and Allies, 1975; (with Alan Fern) The Complete Prints of Leonard Baskin, 1984, The Great American Comic Strip, 1991; editor Am. Film Inst. Catalogue: Feature Films, 1961-70, 1974-77; mem. editl. bd. Am. Film Inst. Catalog, 1979-1990. Trustee Child Life Ctr., U. Md., College Pk., 1971-74; chair Smithsonian Women's Coun., 1988-89. Univ. fellow, U. Md., 1967—70, Mus. fellow, 1970—71, Smithsonian fellow, Nat. Collection Fine Arts, Washington, 1972—73. Mem.: Mystery Writers of Am. (exec. bd. Mid-Atlantic br. 2003—), D.C. Bar Assn., Md. Bar Assn. Avocations: landscape painting, mystery writing.

**O'SULLIVAN, LAWRENCE JOSEPH,** retired financial consultant; b. Curragh, Ireland, Jan. 12, 1924; s. Florence Elizabeth (Heffernan) O'S.; m. Grace Ewart Logan, Dec. 24, 1947; children: Sharon, Lawrence, Maureen, James. BBA, St. John's U., Bklyn., 1953; postgrad., Coll. St. Rose, Elmira U. Sr. investment analyst Lionel D. Edie, Inc., N.Y.C., 1953-57; asst. v.p., editor Forbes IAI, Inc., N.Y.C., 1957-62; asst. v.p., registered rep. N.Y. G.C. Haas, N.Y.C., 1962-63; rsch. dir. Fin. Investment Adv. Svc., N.Y.C., 1963—70; pres. Financialite Corp., N.Y.C., 1963-80; ret. Instr. world history N.Y. State Edn. Sys., Bethpage, Hernando County Schs., Fla.; founder Star Stat Pubs., 1969; fin. liaison dept. US Navy to Congress Naval Appropriations Com., Adak, Alaska. Author: G.E. Graham, U.S. First Black International Spy, 1969, W.S. Schley, Theodore Roosevelt's Rogue Admiral?, 1985, A Centennial Salute to Watervliet, NY, 1995. Econ. cons. Hernando County Health Authority, Fla., 1979-82, chmn., 1983-84; dir. Watervliet (N.Y.) Hist. Club, 1995—, exec. dir., 1995; prodr., dir. performer Stage West Theater Group, Spring Hill, Fla., 1997—; comm. chmn. Cub pack Boy Scouts Am., Bethpage, 1960. With USNR, 1942-46. Decorated Liberation medal Philippines. Fellow Am. Fedn. Fin. Analysts (ret.); mem. N.Y. Soc. Security Analysts, DAV (life), VFW Roman Catholic.

**O'SULLIVAN, LYNDA TROUTMAN,** lawyer; b. Oil City, Pa., Aug. 30, 1952; d. Perry John and Vivian Dorothy (Schreffler) Troutman; m. P. Kevin O'Sullivan, Dec. 15, 1979; children: John Perry, Michael Patrick. BA, Am. U., 1974; JD, Georgetown U., 1978, postgrad., 1982-83. Bar: D.C. 1978. Ptnr. Perkins Coie, Washington, 1985-92, Fried, Frank, Harris, Shriver & Jacobson, Washington, 1993-97, Miller & Chevalier, Washington, 1997—2004; asst. dep. gen. counsel dispute resolution USAF, 2004—. Mem. adv. bd. Fed. Contracts Report, 1991-97, Govt. Contract Costs, Pricing & Acctg. Report, 1997-99; mem. faculty govt. contracts program George Washington U., 1993-99; lectr. in field. Contbr. Cost Reimbursement Contracting, 3d edit., 2005. Fellow Am. Bar Found.; mem. ABA (chair truth in negotiations com. 1991-94, chair acctg., cost and pricing com. 1996-2000, coun. sect. pub. contract law 1993-95). Office: 1777 N Kent St Arlington VA 22209 Business E-Mail: lynda.osullivan@pentagon.af.mil.

**O'SULLIVAN, MICHAEL,** writer, art critic; Staff writer, critic Washington Post, Washington, former writer, "Arts Beat" column; writer, "On Exhibit" column Washington Post Weekend Mag., Washington. Office: Washington Post 1150 15th St NW Washington DC 20071

**O'SULLIVAN, MICHAEL DAVID,** foundation executive; b. Pitts., Dec. 20, 1953; s. James C. and Gladys Vera (Erler) O'S.; m. Kathy Louise Lewis, Aug. 10, 1975; children: Caitlin Alaine, Kevin Patrick. BA, Ind. U. of Pa., 1975; MSW, MA in Pub. Policy, Ohio State U., 1980. Sr. div. dir. United Way, Columbus, Ohio, 1980-88, v.p. San Diego, 1988; assoc. dir. Riverside Meth. Hosps. Found., Columbus, Ohio, 1989—90, dir. major gifts, 1991—92, dir. devel., 1993, v.p. and COO, 1994—97; sr. v.p. Children's Hosp., 1997—2006; co-founder and dir. The Odysseus Group, 2006—. Treas. Huckleberry House, Inc., Columbus, 1993-97. Mem. Assn. Fund Raising Profls. (pres. elect 1998, pres. 1999), Ctrl. Ohio Planned Giving Coun. (pres. 1996-97), Estate Planning Group II, Rotary, Athletic Club Columbus. E-mail: osullim@aol.com.

**O'SULLIVAN, PATRICIA ANN,** principal, writer; b. Boston, Apr. 8, 1952; d. Robert Charles and Irene Emily Ritchie; m. Paul Francis O'Sullivan, Jr., June 16, 1974; 1 child, Paul Francis O'Sullivan, III. AS in Early Childhood Edn., Lasell Coll., 1972; BS in Behavioral and Social Scis., U. Md., 1992; postgrad., Bridgewater State Coll., 1994—95; MEd, Framingham State U., 1997. Cert. profl. educator Fla. Dept. Edn., 2001, instr. Mass. Dept. Edn., 1995. Instrnl. asst. Hayfield Elem. Sch., Alexandria, Va., 1988—91; resource tchr. Am. Sch. Bolivia, La Paz, 1992—94; elem. tchr. Internat. Am. Sch. Guatemala, Guatemala City, 1995—99, Sculptor Charter Sch., Titusville, Fla., 1999—2002, asst. prin., 2002—06, prin., 2006—. Internat. Sch. Guatemala rep. Basic Sch., Harrisonburg, Va., 1997—99; mentor tchr. Brevard County Sch. Bd., Viera, Fla., 2000—; Sculptor Sch. rep. Core Knowledge Found., Charlottesville, Va., 2002—; elem. rep. to dirs. adv. coun. Internat. Am. Sch. Guatemala, Guatemala City. Advisor Sculptor Charter Sch. Student Coun. Titusville; adminstrv. team rep. and program director's designee Brevard Innovative Charter Sch. Titusville, 2002. Named 1chr. of Yr., Brevard Innovative Charter Sch. 2000. Mem.: ASCD, Fla. Consortium Charter Schs., Fla. Assn. Sch. Administrs., Nat. Assn. Elem. and Mid. Sch. Administrs., Kapp Delta Pi. Avocation: reading. Office: Sculptor Charter School 1301 Armstrong Dr Titusville FL 32780 Office Fax: 321-264-9995. Personal E-mail: posullivan1@cfl.rr.com. Business E-Mail: o'sullivanp@brevard.k12.fl.us.

**O'SULLIVAN, PAUL KEVIN,** business executive, management and instructional systems consultant; b. Syracuse, N.Y., May 10, 1938; s. John Hugh and Helen Troy (Smith) O'S.; m. Lynda Troutman; children: Mary Kathleen and Karin Jennifer (twins), John Perry, Michael Patrick. A.B., Dartmouth Coll., 1960. Communications specialist Gen. Electric Co., Schenectady, N.Y., 1963-66; nat. inst. dir. Gen. Learning Corp., Washington, 1966-67; sr. con. ednl. systems. Aries Corp., McLean, Va., 1967-69; dir. profl. devel. Nat. Audio-Visual Assn., Fairfax, Va., 1969-74; exec. dir. Am. Soc. Tng. and Devel., Madison, Wis., 1974-80; sr. v.p. Sterling Inst., Washington, 1980-87, nat. account mgr. Orgnl. Dynamics, Inc., 1987-94; account exec. Zenger Miller, 1995-96, pres. The O'Sullivan Group, Inc., 1996—; staff dir. Nat. Audio-Visual Inst. for Effective Communications Ind. U., 1969-74; chief adminstr. Internat. Fedn. Tng. and Devel. Orgns., 1974-80; dir. Internat. Symposia for Tng. Communications in Switzerland, Australia and Middle East. Producer and dir. films and multi-media presentations; author communications and tng. courses, textbooks; contbr. articles to profl. jours. Served to lt. (j.g.), USNR, 1956-63. Recipient Honor medal for Literature Freedoms Found., 1963; Writers Gold Cup award Gen. Electric, 1966; Resolution for Outstanding Achievement Nat. Audio-Visual Assn., 1974, Pres.'s award for bus. achievement, 1989, 90, 91, 92, 93. Mem. Nat. Soc. for Performance and Instrn. (Presdl. citation 1977), Am. Soc. Assn. Execs. (Grand award for mgmt. achievement 1978), Am. Soc. Tng. and Devel. (hon. life).

**O'SULLIVAN, STEPHANIE L.,** federal agency administrator; With Office of Naval Intelligence, CIA, 1995—, assoc. dep. dir. sci. & tech., 2003—05, dep. dir. sci. & tech., 2005—. Office: Directorate of Science & Technology CIA Office Dir of National Intelligence Washington DC 20505*

**O'SULLIVAN, TERENCE M.,** labor union administrator; b. San Francisco; HS tchr.; mem. local 1353 Laborers Internat. Union of No. Am., Charleston, W.Va., 1974—, adminstr. W.Va. Laborers' Tng. Ctr., asst. to gen. pres., mid-atlantic regional mgr., v.p., gen. pres., 2000—; chmn., CEO Union Labor Life Insurance Co., 2003—. V.p. exec. coun. AFL-CIO, v.p. metal trades dept., v.p. bldg. and constrn. trades; chair pension fund of ctrl. and eastern Can. Laborers Internat. Union of No. Am., chair nat. (indsl.) pension fund, chair local union-dist. coun. pension fund, chair staff pension fund, chair death benefit fund, chair polit. league. Office: The Laborers' Union 905 16th St NW Washington DC 20006 Office Phone: 202-737-8320.*

**O'SULLIVAN, THOMAS J.,** lawyer; b. New Haven, Apr. 7, 1940; s. Thomas J. and Marjorie (Hession) O'S.; m. Anita Brady, Aug. 10, 1968; children: Kathleen, Margaret, Mary Tess, Anne Elizabeth. BA in History, Yale U., 1961; LLB, Harvard U., 1966. Bar: Conn. 1966, U.S. Dist. Ct. Conn. 1967, N.Y. 1967, U.S. Dist. Ct. (so. and ea. dists.) N.Y. 1967, U.S. Ct. Appeals (2d cir.) 1971, U.S. Supreme Ct. 1971, U.S. Dist. Ct. (no. dist.) N.Y. 1976, U.S. Ct. Appeals (11th cir.). 2004. Assoc. White & Case, N.Y.C., 1966-74, ptnr., 1974—. 1st lt. U.S. Army, 1961-63. Mem. ABA, N.Y. State Bar Assn., Assn. of Bar of City of N.Y., Internat. Bar Assn. Clubs: Milbrook (Greenwich, Conn.); Yale (N.Y.C.). Home: 56 Hillside Rd Greenwich CT 06830-4835 Office: White & Case Bldg Ll 1155 Avenue of The Americas New York NY 10036-2787

**OSVATH, LUDOVIC LAJOS,** minister; b. Lupoaia, Romania, July 22, 1938; arrived in US, 1980; s. Lajos and Anna (Feher) O.; m. Jolan Pacso, May 4, 1963; 1 child, Judith. Grad., Inst. Tech., Romania, 1954, Inst. Bus., 1957, Ady Endre Coll., 1978; student, Heritage Bapt. Inst., Cleve., 1986. Ordained to ministry Bapt.Ch., 1955. Preacher Bapt. Ch., Romania, 1955—, mem. coms. Egrespatak, Romania, 1955-65, treas., mem. com. Zalau Romania, 1965-73; pres. Hungarian Missionary Soc. Inc., Cleve., 1989—. Del. Romanian Bapt. Congress, Bucharest, Romania, 1978; maintenance exec. Sponge, Inc., Cleve., 1985—. Underground rep. Amnesty Internat., Romania, 1977-80; founding mem. Defenders of Religious Freedom and Ideas, Romania, 1978, persecuted and excluded from the country; mem. Internat. Christian Solidarity, Zurich, Switzerland. Mem. Christian Mgmt. Assn., Bocskai Cultural Soc. (sec. 1988—). Office Phone: 440-234-4329.

**OSVER, ARTHUR,** artist; b. Chgo., July 26, 1912; s. Harry and Yetta (Woodrov) O.; m. Ernestine Betsberg, Aug. 12, 1940. Student, Northwestern U., 1930-31, Art Inst. Chgo., 1931-36, Dartmouth U., 1997. Instr. art Washington U., St. Louis, 1960-83. Works exhbtd., Art Inst. Chgo., Pa. Acad. Art, Carnegie Inst., Whitney Mus., St. Louis Art Mus., Nelson Gallery, Atkins Mus., Corcoran Art Gallery, U. Ill. Ann., Mus. Modern Art, Met. Mus., others, works in permanent collections, Whitney Mus., Toledo Mus., Isaac Delgado Mus., Peabody Mus., Rio de Janeiro Mus.; artist in residence, U. Fla., 1954-55; trustee emeritus Am. Acad Rome, 1993, artist in residence, 1957-58, one man shows, Wilson Gallery, Chgo., 1940, Grand Central Moderns, N.Y.C., 1947, 49, 51, 56, U. Tenn., 1948, Syracuse U., 1949, Hamline U., 1950, U. Fla., 1951, 55, Fairweather-Hardin Gallery, Chgo., 1953, 55, 69, Dartmouth U., Hanover, N.H., 1997, St. Louis Art Mus., 2000, others. Recipient John Barton Paine medal Va. Mus., 1944, purchase prize U. Ill., 1949, Temple gold medal and purchase prize Pa. Acad., Prix de Rome, 1952, 53, J. Henry Schiedt prize Pa. Acad. Fine Arts, award Am. Acad. and Inst. Arts and Letters, 1991, Arts & Edn. Excellence in Painting award, Arts and Edn. Coun. Greater St. Louis, 1994, Andrew Carnegie Painting award, Nat. Acad. Design, 2003; James Nelson Raymond traveling fellow, 1936-38; Guggenheim fellow, 1950-51; sabbatical leave grantee Nat. Endowment Arts. Mem. Audubon Artists, Artists Equity. Address: 465 Foote Ave Webster Groves MO 63119-1502

**OSWALD, JAMES MARLIN,** education educator, researcher; b. Plainview, Tex., Aug. 17, 1935; s. James Buchanan and Eula Bea (Marlin) O.; m. Dorothy Anne Veigel, Dec. 27, 1956; children: Richard, Ramona, Roberta. BS, West Tex. State Coll., 1957, MA, 1958; EdD, Stanford U., 1970. Tchr., supr. Salt Lake City Pub. Schs., 1958-66; curriculum specialist Am. Insts. Rsch., 1966-68; staff assoc. Nat. Coun. Social Studies, 1968-69; asst. prof. social studies and social sci. edn. Syracuse (N.Y.) U., 1969-72; rschr.-writer, dir. global cultural studies edn. projects Am. Univs. Field Staff, 1972-75; asst. supt. instrn. East Penn Sch. Dist., Emmaus, Pa., 1975-78; field coord. Pa., Del. and N.J. citizen edn. Rsch. for Better Schs., Phila., 1978-80; instrnl. devel. specialist C.C. Phila., 1980-96; energy conservation cons., 1959—; edn. cons., 1963—. Propr. Energy Cons. and Main Line Stoves, 1972—, Fin. and Retirement Planning, 1980—, Macro/Micro Agro, 1992—, DudeSpa, 2002—; pres. N.Y. State Coun. Social Studies, 1971-72; co-founder, pres. Inst. Plant Based Nutrition, 1996—; nutrition educator, 1997—; career mentor, life coach, 2002—; phys. fitness trainer, karate coach, and model, 2002—; cons. in field Author: The Monroe Doctrine: Does It Survive?, 1969; Research in Social Studies and Social Science Education, 1972; co-author: Earthship, 1974, Planet Earth, 1976, Our Home, the Earth, 1980, Marco Polo Vegan Cuisine, 1998, Christopher Columbus Vegan Cuisine, 1999, Criteria for Nutritional Guidelines for Century 21, 1999, Ferdinand Magellan Vegan Cuisine, 2000, Commemoration of Heroic Produce Grower Sacrifices, Death and Survival on September 11, 2001, 2001, Garden of Eden Vegan Cuisine, 2003, Astronaut Vegan Cuisine, 2003, New York City Vegan Cuisine, 2003, Philadelphia Vegan Cuisine, 2003; introduced concepts of the snaggle-toothed curriculum, 1968, global cultural studies, 1972, humanself, 1972, zero runoff landscaping, 1979, veganomics, 1998, veganoccracy, 1998, veganagro, 1998, microagro, 2003; editor quar. newsletter Plant Based Nutrition, 1997—; contbr. articles to profl. jours. With U.S. Army, 1957-58, USAR, 1958-68. Recipient Sertoma Svc. to Mankind award, Salt Lake City, 1966; grantee Stanford U., NSF, U.S. Office Edn., Inst. Internat. Studies; Henry Newell fellow Stanford U., 1966-68; Fulbright-Hays SEAsia U. Singapore Study Program fellow, 1967. Mem. Am Vegan Soc. (life), Internat. Oak Soc., Vegan Organic Network Horticulture-Agr. (U.K.), Hastings-Halliburton Vegetarian Assn. (Can.), Inst. Nutrition Edn. and Rsch. (bd. advisor), Inst. Plant Based Nutrition, N.Am. Vegetarian Soc. (life), Toronto Vegetarian Assn., Main Line Vegan Soc. (founding pres.), Ctr. for Cancer Edn., Hindu Temple Soc. Am., Internat. Soc. Kirsna Consciousness, Food for Life Internat., Social Sci. Edn. Consortium (emeritus), Tex. Panhandle-Plains Hist. Soc. (life), Utah Hist. Soc. (life), Desc. Founders of Ancient Windsor (life), Windsor Hist. Soc. (life), Pa. Forestry Assn., Pa. Vegetable Growers Assn., Pa. Nut Growers Assn., Pa. Assn. Sustainable Agr., Vegetable Growers Assn. N.J., Stanford Club Phila., Keystone Trails Assn., Phi Delta Kappa (emeritus). Avocation: gardening. Home and Office: 333 Bryn Mawr Ave Bala Cynwyd PA 19004-2606 Office Phone: 610-667-6876.

**OSWALD, RUDOLPH A.,** economist; b. Milw., Aug. 4, 1932; s. Carl J. and Anne O.; m. Mary Louise Hurney BA, Holy Cross Coll., 1954; postgrad. (Fulbright scholar), U. Munich, W. Ger., 1954-55; MS, U. Wis., Madison, 1958; PhD in Econs., Georgetown U., 1965. Research and edn. dir. Internat. Assn. Fire Fighters, Washington, 1959-63; economist research dept. AFL-CIO. Washington, 1963-72, asst. dir. edn. dept., 1975-76, dir. research dept., 1976-96, economist-in-residence George Meany Ctr for Labor Studies, 1996—. Vis. prof. Cornell U., 1997, 99, 2000; rsch. dir. Svc. Employees Internat. Union, Washington, 1972-75, instr. GM-UAW Paid Ednl. Leave program, 2001-02; adj. prof. econs. George Washington U., 1966-75; mem. Fed. Employees Pay Coun., 1977-72, Sec. Navy's Adv. Bd. Edn. and Tng., 1975-78, Nat. Commn. Employment and Unemployment Stats., Fgn. Investment Adv. Com.; mem. adv. coun. Indsl. Labor Rels. Sch., Cornell U., 1981-85, 95-99, Sch. Bus. U. S.C. 1992-98; mem. consumer adv. com. SEC, 1994-98mem. labor rsch. adv. coun. Bur. Labor Stats.; mem. Pres.'s Adv. Com. on Trade, 1994-98; mem. adv. com. Ex-Im Bank, 1989-92; cons. Alliance for Ret. Ams., 2004-05. Bd. dirs. Nat. Industries for the Blind, 1965-71. Served with U.S. Army, 1956-57. Mem. Indsl. Rels. Rsch. Assn. (past pres.), Nat. Bur. Econ. Rsch. (dir.), Nat. Policy Assn. (life 1988-2003), Nat. Coun. on Econ. Edn. (dir. 1976-96). Home: 11804 Devilwood Dr Rockville MD 20854-3407 Office: George Meany Labor Studies Ctr 10000 New Hampshire Ave Silver Spring MD 20903-1706 E-mail: rudyo6@aol.com.

**OSWALT, ROY E.,** professional baseball player; b. Kosciusko, Miss., Aug. 29, 1977; m. Nichol Oswalt. Baseball player Houston Astros, 2001—. Named Rookie of Yr., Baseball Writers Assn. Am. (BBWAA) Houston chpt., Nat. League Championship Series MVP, MLB, 2005; named to TOPPS All-Rookie team, Nat. League All-Star Team, MLB, 2005; recipient Sporting News NL Rookie Pitcher of Yr. honors. Achievements include led Nat. League in wins (20), 2004. Office: Houston Astros Po Box 288 Houston TX 77001-0288*

**OTAL, MONICA D.,** music educator; d. Frank N and Amapola Otal. MusB, Oberlin Coll. Conservatory of Music, 1975; MusM, Johns Hopkins U., 1977. Music faculty Duke Ellington Sch. of the Arts, Washington, 1977—93; dir. of music Glenmont United Meth. Ch., Silver Spring, Md., 1988—; lectr. in music Morgan State U., Balt., 1993—99; assoc. prof. of music C.C. of Balt. County, Balt., 1999—; artistic dir. Ctrl. Md. Chorale, Laurel, Md., 2001—. Singer washington opera chorus, baltimore opera chorus. Artistic dir. Ctrl. Md. Chorale, Laurel, Md., 2001. ECISL grantee, C.C. of Balt. County, 2001. Mem.: Coll. Music Soc. (campus rep. 2001), Nat. Assn. of Teachers of Singing, Am. Choral Directors Assn. (chairperson repertoire and stds. com. for 2-yr. colls. 2000). Office: C C Balt County 7201 Rossville Blvd Baltimore MD 21237 Office Phone: 410-780-6726. Personal E-mail: divacoach1@comcast.com. E-mail: motal@ccbcmd.edu.

**OTALLAH, JOHN AUGUST,** school psychologist; b. Detroit, Oct. 18, 1948; m. Donna Ireland Otallah, Nov. 1, 1975; children: Nicole, Scott, Ashley. BA, U. Mich., 1970, MA, 1974; EdS, U Mich., 1979. Lic. sch. psychologist Va.; tchr. Va. Sch. psychologist Piedmont Regional Program, Culpeper, Va., 1975—77, Orange County Pub. Schs. Va., 1977—2000, Fauquier County Pub. Schs., Warrenton, Va., 2005—. Pvt. practice, Culpeper, 1982—89; adj. clin. instr. Inst. Clin. Psychology, U. Va., Charlottesville, 1982—94. Chmn. mental health adv. bd. Family Guidance Svcs. of Orange, 1982—84. Recipient Disting. Practitioner award, Va. Assn. Sch. Psychologists, 1983, Love and Dedication to Children award, Orange County Pub. Schs., 2004. Mem.: Va. Psychol. Assn., Nat. Assn. Sch. Psychologists, Culpeper Recreation Club (sec., bd. dirs. 1997—2002). Methodist. Home: 17158 Lakemont Dr Culpeper VA 22701 Office: Fauquier Count Pub Schs 430 E Shirley Ave Ste B Warrenton VA 20186

**OTANI, YURIKO L. (CHARKO),** artist; b. Pasadena, Calif., Mar. 11, 1931; d. Giichi and Shiki Nakamura; m. Herbert Otani, Nov. 24, 1959 (dec.); children: Diana R. Fuhrmann, Laura M., Glen K., Julia M. Otani Caruso; David E., Robert K. BFA, The Cooper Union Advancement Sci. and Art, 1976. Cert. tchr. Ramapo Coll., N.J. Graphic artist JJ Michaels, Little Ferry, NJ, 1981; art tchr. No. Valley Old Tappan HS, NJ, 1988—93; with prodn. dept. Cmty. Life, Westwood, NJ, 1993—97; graphic artist The Town Jour., Allendale, NJ, 1998, Rockland County Times, NY, 1998—2005. Guest lectr. WWII Japanese-Am. internment at local elem. & HS. Contbr. articles to newspapers and profl. jour. WWII internee, Tulare, Calif., Gila, Ariz.; guest lectr. WWII Japanese-Am. internments; contr. essays to local newspapers. Recipient Recognition award, Bergen County, 1991, Point of Light award, Pres. George H.W. Bush, 1991, Low Fund prize, Cooper Union, 1976, Tchr. Recognition award, Gov. of NJ. Avocations: art, quilting, swimming.

**OTELLINI, PAUL S.,** electronics company executive; b. San Francisco, Oct. 12, 1950; s. David Otellini; m. Sandy Otellini; 2 children. BA in Econs., U. San Francisco, 1972; MBA, U. Calif., Berkeley, 1974. Joined Intel Corp., Santa Clara, Calif., 1974, managed Intel's bus. with IBM Corp., 1980—85, gen. mgr. peripheral components ops., 1985—87, gen. mgr. Folsom Microcomputer Divsn., 1987—89, v.p. operating group, 1988, asst. to pres. (Andrew S. Grove), 1989, gen. mgr., microprocessor products group, 1990, corp. officer, 1991, exec. v.p., sales and mktg., 1992—98, sr. v.p., 1993—96, exec. v.p., 1996—2002, exec. v.p., gen. mgr., architecture group, 1998—2002, pres., COO, 2002—05, pres., CEO, 2005—. Bd. dirs. Intel Corp., 2002—. Office: Intel Corp 2200 Mission College Blvd Santa Clara CA 95052-8119 Office Phone: 408-765-8080. Office Fax: 408-765-9904.*

**OTHERSEN, HENRY BIEMANN, JR.,** surgeon, physician, educator; b. Charleston, S.C., Aug. 26, 1930; s. Henry and Lydia Albertine (Smith) Othersen; m. Janelle Lester, Apr. 4, 1959; children: Megan, Mandy, Margaret, Henry Biemann III. BS, Coll. Charleston, 1950; MD, Med. Coll. S.C., 1953. Diplomate Am. Bd. Surgery, Am. Bd. Thoracic Surgery, Am. Bd. Pediatric Surgery. Intern Phila. Gen. Hosp., 1953-54; postgrad. U. Pa., 1956-57; resident in gen. surgery Med. Coll. S.C., Charleston, 1957-62; resident in pediatric surgery Ohio State U. and Columbus Children's Hosp., 1962-64; research fellow Harvard U., Mass. Gen. Hosp., Boston, 1964-65; from asst. prof. to assoc. prof. pediatric surgery Med. U. S.C., Charleston, 1962—72, prof., 1972—, chief pediatric surgery, 1972-98; med. dir. Med. U. S.C. Hosp., 1981-85, Children's Hosp., 1985—2001, med. dir. profl. staff, 1996—2001, physician liaison documentation, 2002—03; acting chief surgery VA Hosp., 2002—04. Editor: The Pediatric Airway; mem. editl. bd. Jour. Pediatric Surgery, Jour. Parenteral and Enteral Nutrition; contbr. articles to profl. jours. Bd. Children's Hosp. Found; bd. dirs., pres. S.C. divsn. Am. Cancer Soc., 1977—79; bd. dir. SC Safe Kids. With USN, 1954—56, Korea. Fellow: ACS, Am. Acad. Pediat. (chair); mem.: Charleston County Med. Soc. (pres. 1981—83), Am. Trauma Soc., S.C Surg. Assn. (pres. 1991—92), Am. Surg. Assn., Brit. Assn. Pediatric Surgeons (overseas coun. 1995—99), Am. Pediatric Surg. Assn. (pres. 1998—99), Alpha Omega Alpha (councilor 1978—93). Republican. Lutheran. Achievements include first academic pediat. surgeon in SC; first to Established divsn. pediat. surgery and children's hosp. Med. U. SC. Avocation: water sports. Office: Pediatric Surgery PO Box 250613 96 Jonathan Lucas St Ste 418 CSB Charleston SC 29425 Office Phone: 843-792-3853. Business E-Mail: othershh@musc.edu. *A man ought to do what he thinks is right.*

**OTHMAN, TALAT MOHAMAD,** financial consultant, investment banker; b. Betunia, Palestine, Apr. 27, 1936; arrived in U.S., 1947, naturalized, 1954; s. Mohamad Racheed and Damelize Ahmed Othman; m. Haleema Othman; children: Joseph, Suad, Jamil, Rashid. Student, Northwestern U. With Harris Bank, Chgo., 1956—78, v.p., div. head, 1974—78; gen. mgr., CEO Saudi Arab Fin. Corp., S.A., Paris, 1978—83; pres. Dearborn Fin., Inc., Arlington Hts., Ill., 1983—95; chmn. Grove Fin. Inc., 1995—. Mem. adv. bd. Ovation Pharm., Inc.; bd. dirs. Bank One Wis. Corp., Milw., Harken Oil and Gas Co., Dallas, Pathogenesis Corp., Seattle; chmn. Dansk Internat. Designs, Inc., Mt. Kisko, NY, 1985—91, Goodson Polymer, Inc., Troy, Ohio, 1987—88. Contbr. chpts. to, articles and booklets. Bd. dirs. Inst. World Affairs, Milw., 1986—89, Khail Gibran Meml. com., Washington, 1987—89; pres. Islamic Cultural Ctr.; mem. adv. bd. Kennedy Sch. Govt. Harvard U.; mem. hon. bd. Mid East Studies Ctr. U. Chgo.; bd. dirs. St. Jude Children's Rsch. Hosp., 1991—, Ch. Alsac-Am. Lebanese Syrian Associated Charities. Recipient Outstanding Pres. award proclaiming Talat M. Othman Day in Ill., Nov. 1, 1997. Mem.: Forex Assn. of N.Am. (chmn., founding pres. Chgo. chpt. 1976, recipient plaque of Appreciation), Arab Bankers Assn. (pres. 1985—87, bd. dirs. 1984—89, recipient plaque of Appreciation), Mid. Am. Arab C. of C. (bd. dirs. 1974—78, founding pres. 1977, bd. dirs. 1984—91, recipient plaque of Appreciation), Chgo. Club. Moslem. Avocations: tennis, racquetball, reading. E-mail: grovefinancial@worldnet.att.net.

**OTIS, CLARENCE, JR.,** restaurant executive; BA magna cum laude, Williams Coll., 1977; JD, Stanford Univ., 1980. Atty., NY; investment banker First Boston, Kidder Peabody; mng. dir., co-head Mcpl. Securities group Chem. Securities; v.p., treas. Darden Restaurants Inc., Orlando, Fla., 1995-97, sr. v.p. investor rels., treas., 1997-98, sr. v.p. fin., 1998-99, sr. v.p., CFO, 1999—2002, exec. v.p., CFO, 2002, exec. v.p., pres. Smokey Bones div., 2002—04, CEO, 2004—. Bd. dir. St. Paul Travelers Ins., VF Corp.; mem. Exec. Leadership Council. Trustee Williams Coll.; bd. mem. Enterprise Fla. Inc., Preserve Eatonville Inc. Mem.: Phi Beta Kappa. Office: Darden Restaurants Inc 5900 Lake Ellenor Dr Orlando FL 32809*

**OTIS, JACK,** social work educator; b. N.Y.C., Feb. 13, 1923; s. Abraham Osipowitz and Esther (Goldberg) O.; children: Elisabeth H., Erich R., Greta M., Marcus H., Alicia. AB, Bklyn. Coll., 1946; MS in Social Work, U. Ill., 1948, M.Ed., 1955, PhD, 1957. Social worker Jewish Social Svc. Bur. Dade County, 1948-49; Psychiat. social worker Free Synagogue Social Service, N.Y. U., 1949-50; asso. prof. U. Ill., 1950-61; dep. dir. Office Juvenile Delinquency and Youth Devel., Dept. Health, Edn. and Welfare, 1961-65; dean Grad. Sch. Social Work U. Tex., 1965-77, prof. emeritus, 1993—. Cons. to govt., 1961—; presenter Internat. Coun. on Social Welfare, Inter-Univ. Consortium for Internat. Social Devel., Internat. Assn. Schs. Social Work, 1994; dep. dir. Pres.'s Com. Juvenile Delinquency and Youth Crime, 1961-65; spl. cons. for Am. social work edn. and rsch. European Ctr. for Welfare Tng. and Rsch., Vienna, Austria, 1976—; Dean Dan Sanders Meml. lectr. U. Ill., 1999. Author: (with George Barnett) Corporate Society and Education, 1961; contbr. article on child labor to Ency. Social Work, 1995. Bd. overseers Ctr. for Study Violence, Brandeis U., 1966-70; commencement spkr. U. Tex. Sch. Social Work, 2001. With AUS, 1943-46, PTO. Fulbright-Hays rsch.fellow Australia, 1977-78; established Dean Jack Otis Ann. Social Policy awards U. Tex., 2002. Mem. AAUP, Coun. on Social Work Edn. (commn. on accreditation), Philosophy of Edn. Soc., Nat. Assn. Social Workers (chair Calif. Task Force on Child Labor 2001-03); Am. Acad. Polit. and Social Sci., N.Y. Acad. Sci., Johannesburg Child Welfare Soc. (rsch. cons. South Africa chpt. 1990-91), Phi Kappa Phi (pres.). Office Phone: 949-240-9490. *The meaning of my life is whether I have added to the meaning of another's.*

**OTIS, JAMES, JR.,** architect; b. Chgo., July 8, 1931; s. James and Edwina (Love) O.; m. Diane Cleveland, Apr. 9, 1955; children: James III, Julie C., David C. BArch cum laude, Princeton U., 1953; postgrad., U. Chgo., 1955-57. Registered architect, Ill., Ariz., Colo., Ind Iowa, Wis, N Mex, Mo. Designer Irvin A Blietz Co., Wilmette, Ill., 1955-57; pres. Homefinders Constrn. Corp., Wilmette, 1957-59, O & F Constrn. Co., Northbrook, Ill., 1959-61; chmn. bd., chief exec. officer Otis Assocs., Inc., Northbrook, Ill., 1960-89; chmn., CEO Otis Co., 1981—. Bd. dirs. Banco Popular, Chgo., Trout & Grouse, Inc., OCO, Inc., Ranch Ptnrs., LLC. Prin. works include GBC Corp. Hdqrs., Schaumburg, Ill., AON Ins. Co. Corp. Hdqrs., Performing Arts Ctr., Northbrook, Ill., All State Regional Hdqrs., Skokie, Ill., Zurich Nat. Hdqrs.-Zurich Towers Schaumburg. Trustee Evanston (Ill.) Hosp., 1971-93, Better Govt. Assn., Chgo., Graham Found., 1984-86, Ill. Nature Conservancy; chmn. bd. trustees North Suburban YMCA, Northbrook, 1990-97; governing mem. Shedd Aquarium; bd. govs. Chgo. Zool. Soc.; mem. adv. bd. Cook County Forest Preserve Dist.; mem. founder's coun. Field Mus., Chgo. Lt. USNR, 1953-55. Mem. AIA, Nat. Coun. Archtl. Registration Bds., Urban Land Inst., Northwestern U. Assocs., Princeton Club (pres. 1971-72), Econ. Club, Commonwealth Club, Chgo. Club, Comml. Club, Glen View Golf Club, Old Elm Club, Coleman Lake Club, Angler's Club. Republican. Episcopalian. Office: Otisco 1450 American Ln Ste 1750 Schaumburg IL 60173-6010 Office Phone: 847-969-9000. Business E-Mail: jotisjr@otiscompany.com.

**OTIS, JOHN JAMES,** civil engineer; b. Syracuse, NY, Aug. 5, 1922; s. John Joseph and Anna (Dey) O.; m. Dorothy Fuller Otis, June 21, 1958; children: Mary Eileen Dawn, John Leon. B in Chem. Engring., Syracuse U., 1943, MBA, 1950, postgrad., 1951—55. Registered profl. engr., Ala., Tex. Jr. process engr. GM, Syracuse, 1951-53; prodn. engr., 1954-58, process control engr., 1958-59, process engr., 1960-61; engr., writer GE, Syracuse, 1961-63, configuration control engr. Phila., 1969; assoc. rsch. engr. Boeing Co., Huntsville, Ala., 1963-65; assoc. Planning Rsch. Corp., Huntsville, 1965-67; prin. engr. Brown Engring. Co. subs. Teledyne Co., Huntsville, 1967-69; mech. designer Drever Co., Beth Ayres, Pa., 1970-71; civil engr. U.S. Army Corps Engrs., Mobile, Ala., 1971-74, Galveston, Tex., 1974—. Lector; lay minister Roman Cath. Ch. Served with USNR, 1944-50. Mem. Am. Inst. Indsl. Engrs. (past v.p. Syracuse and Huntsville chpts.), Soc. Profl. Engrs. (dir. Galveston County chpt. 1976-79, sec.-treas. 1979-80, v.p. 1980-81, pres. 1982-83), Am. Legion, Tau Beta Pi, Phi Kappa Tau, Alpha Chi Sigma, Chi Eta Sigma. Home: 2114 Yorktown Ct N League City TX 77573-5056 Office: US Army Corps Engrs Jadwin Bldg 2000 Fort Point Rd Galveston TX 77550-3038 Office Phone: 409-766-3157. Business E-Mail: john.j.otis@usace.army.mil.

**OTIS, LEE (SARAH) LIBERMAN,** lawyer, educator; b. N.Y.C., Aug. 19, 1956; d. James Benjamin and Deen (Freed) L.; m. William Graham Otis, Oct. 24, 1993. BA, Yale U., 1979; JD, U. Chgo., 1983. Bar: N.Y. 1985, D.C. 1994. Law clk. U.S. Ct. Appeals (D.C. cir.), Washington, 1983-84; spl. asst. to asst. atty. gen., civil div. U.S. Dept. Justice, Washington, 1984-86, dep. assoc. atty. gen., 1986, assoc. dep. atty. gen., 1986; law clk. to Justice Antonin Scalia U.S. Supreme Ct., Washington, 1986-87; asst. prof. law George Mason U., Arlington, Va., 1987-89; assoc. counsel to the Pres. Exec. Office of the Pres., Washington, 1989-92; assoc. Jones, Day, Reavis & Pogue, Washington, 1993-94; chief judiciary coun. U.S. Sen. Spence Abraham, 1995-96; chief counsel subcom. on immigration Com. on the Judiciary, U.S. Senate, 1997-2000; gen. counsel U.S. Dept. Energy, 2001—05. Adj. prof. law Georgetown Law Sch., 1995, 96. Mem. Federalist Soc. for Law and Pub. Policy (founder). Republican. Jewish. Avocations: sailing, computers.

**O'TOOLE, AUSTIN MARTIN,** lawyer; b. Balt., Sept. 29, 1944; d. John Brian, Jr. and Helen Veronica O'T.; m. Valerie Sherlock O'Toole; children: Erin Ann, Austin Martin Jr. BBA, Coll. Holy Cross, 1957; JD, Georgetown U., 1963. Bar: N.Y. 1965, D.C. 1963, Tex. 1975. Law clk. to judge U.S. Ct. Appeals, Washington, 1962-63; assoc. White & Case, N.Y.C., 1963-74; sr. v.p., sr. counsel, sec. Coastal Corp., Houston, 1974—2001. Bd. editors Georgetown Law Jour., 1962-63. Bd. dirs. Nat. Coun. on Alcoholism and Drug Dependency, Inc., 2001—; charter mem., certificated mediator Inst. for Responsible Dispute Resolution, Houston, 2000—; bd. dirs. Houston Marathon Com., 1973—2002. Officer USMC, 1957—60. Mem. ABA, Am. Soc. Corp. Secs. (bd. dirs. 1982-85), State Bar of Tex., Houston Bar Assn. (past chmn. corp. counsel sect. 1979-80, chair elect ADR sect. 2006), Assn. Atty.-Mediators, Tex. Assn. Mediators. Home: 2200 Willowick (10-H) Houston TX 77027 Office: 509 Nineteenth St Galveston TX 77550 Office Phone: 409-763-3130. Personal E-mail: austinotoole@aol.com

**O'TOOLE, DEBORAH ANN,** lawyer; b. Balt., Sept. 29, 1944; d. Hamilton and Dorothy Hill Shea; m. Dennis Martin O'Toole, Aug. 17, 1963; children: Timothy, Terrence, Patrick, Erin. Student, Coll. William & Mary, 1962-63; BS in Psychology, Va. Commonwealth U., 1973; JD, U. Richmond, 1976. Assoc. McDonald & Crump, Richmond, Va., 1976-77; ptnr. Cowan & Owen, Richmond, Va., 1978—. Dir. Rainbow Games, Inc., Richmond, Va., 1994—. Mem. Met. Richmond Womens Bar Assn. (exec. bd. 1996-99), Chesterfield County Bar Assn. (exec. com. 2000-06, pres. 2004-05) Office: Cowan & Owen PO Box 35655 1930 Huguenot Rd Richmond VA 23235-4304 E-mail: dotoole@cowanowen.com.

**O'TOOLE, FRANCIS J.,** lawyer; b. Dublin, Feb. 10, 1944; came to U.S.A., 1960; s. Francis Herbert and Josephine (McCarthy) O'T.; m. Carole Ann Leland, Apr. 11, 1977; children: Kathleen, Kirra. AB, Harvard U., 1967; JD, U. Maine, 1970. Bar: Maine 1970, U.S. Supreme Ct. 1977, U.S. Dist. Ct. D.C., U.S. Dist. Ct. (ea. dist.) Va., U.S. Ct. Appeals (1st, 2d, 4th, 5th, 7th, 8th, 9th and 10th cirs.). Assoc. Fried, Frank, Harris, Shriver & Jacobsen, Washington, 1971-78, ptnr., 1978-92; Sidley & Austin, Washington, 1992—. Editor-in-chief U. Maine Law Rev., 1969-70; contbr. articles to profl. jours. Reginald Heber Smith fellow Calif. Indian Legal Services, 1970-71. Mem. ABA. Avocation: horse breeding and racing. Home: 7700 Burford Dr Mc Lean VA 22102-2105 Office: Sidley Austin Brown & Wood 1501 K St NW #LL Washington DC 20005-1401

**O'TOOLE, JAMES JOSEPH,** business educator; b. San Francisco, Apr. 15, 1945; s. James Joseph and Irene (Nagy) O'T.; m. Marilyn Louise Burrill, June 17, 1967; children: Erin Kathleen, Kerry Louise. BA, U. So. Calif., L.A., 1966; DPhil, Oxford U., Eng., 1970. Corr. Time-Life News Service, L.A., 1967-68, Nairobi, Kenya, 1967-68; mgmt. cons. McKinsey & Co., San Francisco, 1969-70; coordinator field investigations Pres.'s Comm. on Campus Unrest, Washington, 1970; spl. asst. to sec. HEW, Washington, 1970-73; prof. mgmt. U. So. Calif., L.A., 1973-93, Univ. Assocs. Chair of Bus., 1982-93; v.p. Aspen Inst., 1994-97; mng. dir. Booz-Allen & Hamilton Leadership Ctr., San Francisco, 1997—; rsch. prof. Ctr. for Effective Orgn., U. So. Calif., 1999—. Cons. news's com. work in Am. HEW, Washington, 1971-72; exec. dir. The Leadership Inst., 1990-93; bd. dirs. Radica Games. Prin. author: Work in America, 1973, Energy and Social Change, 1976; author: Work, Learning and the American Future, 1977, Making America Work, 1982 (Phi Kappa Phi prize 1982), Vanguard Management, 1985, The Executive's Compass, 1993, Leading Change, 1995, Leadership A to Z, 1999, Creating the Good Life, 2005, The New American Workplace, 2006; bd. editors: Ency. Britannica, 1981-87; editor: New Management, 1983-89, The American Oxonian, 1996-98. Active Project Paideia, Chgo., 1981-83. Rhodes scholar, 1966; recipient Mitchell prize Woodlands Conf., 1979. Mem. Phi Beta Kappa. Home: 23852 Pacific Coast Hwy Ste 364 Malibu CA 90265-4879 Office: U So Calif Ctr Effective Orgns Los Angeles CA 90089-0806 Business E-Mail: jim@jamesotoole.com

**O'TOOLE, JAMES MICHAEL,** history educator; b. Worcester, Mass., Feb. 25, 1950; s. George Augustine and Mildred Bercher (O'Grady) O'Toole. AB, Boston Coll., 1972; MA, Coll. William and Mary, 1973; MS, Simmons Coll., Boston, 1975; PhD, Boston Coll., 1987. Dep. archivist Commonwealth of Mass., Boston, 1974—77; archivist Roman Cath. Archdiocese Boston, 1978—86; asst. prof. history U. Mass., Boston, 1986—98; prof. history Boston Coll., Chestnut Hill, Mass., 1998—. Author: Guide to Archives of the Archdiocese of Boston, 1982, Understanding Archives and Manuscripts, 1990, Passing for White, 2002, Habits of Devotion, 2004; author/editor: Catholic Boston, 1985. Fellow Mass. Hist. Soc.; mem. Soc. Am. Archivists (exec. council 1988—, Lane award 1986), Am. Cath. Hist. Assn., Am. Hist. Assn., Orgn. Am. Historians, New Eng. Archivists (pres. 1981-82), New Eng. Hist. Assn. (pres. 2002-03). Democrat. Roman Catholic. Office: Boston Coll History Dept 140 Commonwealth Ave Chestnut Hill MA 02467 Office Phone: 617-552-8456. Business E-Mail: james.otoole@bc.edu.

**O'TOOLE, MICHAEL ANTHONY,** academic administrator; b. Phila., Feb. 20, 1950; s. George O'Toole, Jr. and Louise Mary Kopka; m. Mary Louise Castaldi, Jan. 8, 1977; children: Lara Nicole Castaldi, Daniel Peter Castaldi, Colin Peter Castaldi(dec.). AB magna cum laude, U. of Pa., 1972, MA, 1978; EdM, Columbia U., 1997. Info. specialist U.S. FDA, Rockville, Md., 1974; lectr. Abington Coll., Pa. State U., 1987—; tchr. La Salle Coll. H.S., Wyndmoor, Pa., 1974—2000, chmn. Dept. English, 1974—2000, dir. curriculum and summer sessions, 1989—2000; prin. Holy Ghost Prep. Sch., Bensalem, Pa., 2005—. Svc. bd. mem. La Salle Coll. II.S., Wyndmoor, Pa., 2000—05, dir. curriculum and summer sessions, 1974—2000, v.p. 2000—05; team editor NAIS Leading Edge Award, 2005—; reader Ednl. Testing Svc., Princeton, NJ, 1987—94; founder N.W. Cmty. Scholars Program. Editor: (alumni jour.) Explorer Mag., (profl. newsletter) Klingenstein Newsletter. Lay min. music St. Vincent De Paul Ch., Germantown, Pa., 1995—2001; bd. dirs. Face to Face, Inc., Phila., 2003. Recipient President's medal, La Salle Coll. H.S., 2005, Klingenstein Ctr. fellowship, Tchrs. Coll., Columbia U., 1994—95, fellowship in Am. Civilization, U. of Pa., 1978—79, Ford Fund scholarship, Ford Motor Co. Fund, 1968—72. Mem. Nat. Coun. Tchrs. of English, Nat. Assn. of Secondary Sch. Prins., Nat. Cath. Edn. Assn., Am. Studies Assn., Penn Club of N.Y. Independent. Roman Catholic. Avocations: bicycling, piano, music appreciation, swimming. Home: 810 Elkins Ave Elkins Park PA 19027 Office: Holy Ghost Prep Sch 2429 Bristol Pike Bensalem PA 19020 Office Phone: 215-639-2102.

**O'TOOLE, PATRICIA ELLEN,** writer, educator; b. Alpena, Mich., Oct. 10, 1946; d. Gordon Roy and Gertrude (McKenna) O'T. BA, U. Mich., 1968. Adj. asst. prof. Columbia U. Sch. Arts, NYC, 1995—2002, lectr., 2002—03, asst. prof., 2004—05, assoc. prof., 2005—. Author: The Five of Hearts: An Intimate Portrait of Henry Adams and His Friends, 1880-1918, 1990 (finalist, Pulitzer Prize and Nat. Book Critics Circle award), Money & Morals in America, 1998, When Trumpets Call: Theodore Roosevelt After the White House, 2005. MacDowell Colony fellow, 1988. Mem. AAUP, PEN, Am. Hist. Assn., Orgn. Am. Historians. Democrat. Office: Dept Arts Columbia Univ 404 Dodge MC 1804 2960 Broadway New York NY 10027-6902

**O'TOOLE, ROBERT JOHN, II,** telemarketing consultant; b. Binghamton, N.Y., Mar. 24, 1951; s. Robert John and Joan Ceclia (Martin) O'T.; m. Donna Sue Stevenson, Jan. 28, 1978 (div. 1984); 1 child, Irene Grace; m. Karen Irene Cady, Dec. 21, 1994. Student, Corning (N.Y.) C.C., 1969-71, SUNY, Brockport, 1970-71; BA, Wake Forest U., 1973; MBA, Southwestern Coll., 1986. Asst. dir. devel. Duvall Home for Children, DeLand, Fla., 1978-81; gen. mgr. Royale Art Advt., Odessa, Tex., 1981-82; v.p. Barnes Assocs. Advt., Odessa, 1982-84; Tex. Assn. for Blind Athletes, Austin, 1985-86; sales mgr. Los Amables Pub., Albuquerque, 1987-88; dir. devel. Albuquerque (N.Mex.) Help for the Homeless, 1988-91; chmn., CEO Advantage Ventures, Inc. (formerly Advantage Mktg., Inc.), Albuquerque, 1991—; CEO LaCourt, Medina & Sterling, Albuquerque, 1993-96. Cons. Nat. Child Safety Coun., Austin, 1985, Assn. Profl. Fire Fighters, Austin, 1985, Reynolds Aluminum, Austin, 1986, N.Mex. State Legis., 1990, Children's Charity Fund, 1996, N.Am. Found. for AIDS Rsch., 1992-93, N.Am. Pediatric AIDS Found., 1995. Author: Telemarketing Tickets, 1988, Fishing Secrets of the Florida Poachers, 1993; founder, editor: (newspaper) Albuquerque Street News, 1990; publisher: (newspaper) The New Mexican, 1991; contbr. articles to jours. Founder Permian Basin Rehab. Ctr., Odessa, 1983, Albuquerque (N.Mex.) Help for the Homeless, Inc., 1988. Recipient Cert. of Merit, Small Bus. Adminstrn., Odessa, 1984. Mem. Direct Mktg. Assn., Amnesty Internat. Avocations: historic building restoration, archeo-geomantics, travel. Office: Advantage Ventures Inc 1019 2nd St SW # B Albuquerque NM 87102-4124

**O'TOOLE, ROBERT JOSEPH,** retired manufacturing executive; b. Chgo., Feb. 22, 1941; s. Francis John O'Toole; children: William, Patricia, Timothy, Kathleen, John. BS in Acctg., Loyola U., Chgo., 1961. Fin. analyst A.O. Smith Corp., Milw., 1963-66, mgr. corp. fin. analysis and planning, 1966-68, contr. electric motor div. Tipp City, Ohio, 1968-71; mgr. dir. Bull Motors, Ipswich, England, 1971-74; gen. plant mgr. electric motor div. A.O. Smith Corp., Tipp City, 1974-79, v.p., gen. mgr., 1979-83, sr. v.p. Milw., 1984-85, pres., chief oper. officer, 1986-89, pres., 1989—2004, CEO, 1989—2005, also bd. dirs. Milw., and chmn. bd. dirs., 1992—2005. Bd. dirs. Briggs & Stratton Corp., Factory Mutual Ins. Co., Marshall & Ilsley Corp., Manufacturers Alliance/MAPI Inc.; mem. exec. com. TEC XIV, Milw., Mfrs. Alliance for Productivity and Innovation, Bus. Roundtable, Greater Milw. Com., Competitive Wis., Inc. Mem. Wis. Mgrs. and Commerce Assn. (exec. com.). Met. Milw. Assn. Commerce (bd. dirs.), Milw. Country Club, Univ. Club. Office: A O Smith Corp Ste 1001 11270 W Park Pl Milwaukee WI 53224-3690*

**O'TOOLE, STEPHEN JOSEPH,** special education educator; b. Chgo., June 24, 1960; s. Richard S. O'Toole and Frances L. Romeo; m. Victoria Susan O'Toole, Sept. 21, 2002. BA in Comm. Arts, St. Norbert Coll., 1982; MFA in Acting, U. Minn., 1986, EdM in Spl. Edn., 2000. Salesman Dayton Musical Corp., Mpls., 1985—89; actor, co-writer, co-prodr. Recovery Prodns., Mpls., 1989—94; tchr. Mpls. Pub. Sch., 1996—2004, Osseo Sch., Brooklyn Park, Minn., 2004—. Dir. Bismarck State Coll., 1991; actor, writer, prodr. Process Theatre Co., Mpls., 1992—2000; adv. Dakorn Communities, Inc., Robbinsdale, Minn., 1995—2001; tchr., dir. Century Coll., White Bear Lakes, Minn., 2004—05. Vol. tutor Minn. Literacy Soc., Mpls., 1991—94, English Learning Ctr., Mpls., 1998—, St. Stephen's Ch., Mpls., 1990—2000. Roman Catholic. Home: 1607 44th Ave N Minneapolis MN 55412

**O'TOOLE, TARA JEANNE,** medical educator, former federal agency administrator; b. Newton, Mass., May 3, 1951; d. Harold J. and Jeanne (Whalen) O'T. BA, Vassar Coll., 1974; MD, George Washington U., 1981; MPH, Johns Hopkins U., 1988. Diplomate Am. Bd. Internal Medicine, Am. Bd. Preventive/Occupational Medicine. Rsch. asst. Sloan-Kettering Cancer Inst., N.Y.C., 1974-77; resident in internal medicine Yale New Haven (Conn.) Hosp., 1981-84; physician Balt. Cmty. Health Ctrs., 1984-87; fellow in occupational medicine Johns Hopkins U., Balt., 1987-89; sr. analyst Office Tech. Assessment, Washington, 1989-93; asst. sec. energy for environ., safety and health US Dept. Energy, Washington, 1993-97; dep. dir. Johns Hopkins U. Ctr. Civilian Biodefense Studies, 1998—2001; dir., 2001—03; prof. medicine U. Pitts., 2003—; CEO Ctr. for Bio Security, U. Pitts. Medical Ctr., 2003—. Chmn. Bd. Fedn. Am. Scientists, 2004—. Democrat. Office: Ctr for Biosecurity The Pier IV Bldg 621 E Pratt St Ste 210 Baltimore MD 21202 E-mail: Totoole@upmc-biosecurity.org.*

**O'TOOLE, WILLIAM EDWARD, 3RD,** mathematics professor, computer science professor; b. Waynesboro, Pa., May 27, 1942; s. William Edward Jr. and Dora Alberta O'Toole; m. Annette Marie Smith, June 25, 1966 (div. July 15, 1977); m. Catherine Claire Bodin, Dec. 16, 1989; 1 child, Wendy Elizabeth Garilli. BS in Math. Edn., Mt. St. Mary's Coll., 1966; MA in Math., U. Md., 1975. Prof. math. and computer sci. Mt. St. Mary's U., Emmitsburg, Md., 1966—; sci. editor and prognosticator Gruber Almanack Co., Hagerstown, Md., 1969—. Computer cons. Nat. Inst. Stds. and Tech., Gaithersburg, 1969—91. Author: (textbook and software) GRASP: A Generic, Realistic Assembler Simulation Program, 1991—. Mem. Balt. Symphony Orch., Frederick, 1990—90. King Ferdinand III Sci. scholar, Diocese of Harrisburg, Pa., 1960—62. Mem.: Math. Assn. Am. Democrat. Roman Catholic. Avocations: travel, classical music, photography, computers and electronics. Office: Mount Saint Mary's U 16300 Old Emmitsburg Road Emmitsburg MD 21727-7799 Home Fax: 301-447-7403. Business E-Mail: otoole@msmary.edu.

**OTREMBA, GERALDINE MARIE,** congressional and international relations executive; b. NYC, Apr. 13, 1946; d. Frank Stanley and Beatrice Gloria (O'Malley) O.; m. Stanley F. Turesky, Oct. 26, 1975; children: Sarah, Catherine. BA St. John's U., 1967; MA, U. N.C., 1969, PhD, 1979. Dep. dir. ops. John F. Kennedy Ctr. for the Performing Arts, Washington, 1984-87, dir. planning, 1987-90, dir. ops., 1990-91, dir. govt. liaison, 1991-92, assoc. mng. dir., 1991-94; dir. congrl. rels. Libr. Congress, Washington, 1994—; exec. dir. Open World Leadership Ctr., Washington, 1999—2002; CEO Ctr. Russian Leadership Devel. (former Russian Leadership Program), Libr. of Congress, Washington, 2002. Chmn. Nat. Conf. Performing Arts Ctrs., 1990-93. Roman Catholic. Office: Congl Rels Office Libr Congress James Madison Meml Bldg 101 Independence Ave SW Washington DC 20540-4000 Office Phone: 202-707-7720.

**OTT, ATTIAT FARAG,** economist, educator; b. Cairo, June 18, 1935; m. David J. Ott (dec.); 1 child, Dana. BA in Econ. with highest honors, Cairo U., 1956; PhD, U. Mich., Ann Arbor, 1962. Assoc. prof., econ. So. Meth. U., 1965—68; vis. assoc. prof. U. Md., College Park, 1968—69; fiscal economist, office tax analysis U.S. Dept. Treasury, 1969; assoc. prof., econ. Clark U., Worcester, Mass., 1969—71; prof., 1971—; dir. Inst. Econ. Studies, 1980—. Vis. scholar Hoover Instn., Stanford U., 1977—78; adj. scholar Am. Enterprise Inst.; prin. investigator Fund for Pub. Policy Rsch.; mem. nat. com. and tax policy bd. Taxation with Representation, Washington. Author: Macroeconomic Theory, 1975, Federal Budget Policy, 1977, The Public Sector in the Global Economy, 2003; co-author: The Massachusetts Health Plan, 1988, Privatization and Economic Effiency, 1991, Public Sector Budgets: A Competitive Study, 1993; guest columnist Worcester Telegram and Gazette, mem. editl. bd. Jour. Econ. Devel., mem. editl. bd., guest editor Atlantic Econ. Jour.; contbr. articles to numerous profl. jours. Fellow, Olin Found., 1980—92; grantee, Am. Found., 1969—72, Hoover Instn., 1977—79; H.B. Earhart fellow, 1982. Home: 262 Salisbury St Worcester MA 01609-1641 Office: Clark U Dept Econs Worcester MA 01610 Office Phone: 508-793-7447. Business E-Mail: aott@clarku.edu.

**OTT, C(LARENCE) H(ENRY),** ambassador, accounting professor; b. Richmond, Mich., Jan. 20, 1918; s. Ferdinand and Wilhelmina (Radkte) Ott; m. Helen Louise McKay, Oct. 29, 1942 (dec. Apr. 1994); children: James Richard, Dennis McKay, Richard Darrel, Delene Michelle. BA, Valparaiso U., 1940; MBA, Northwestern U., 1970; PhD, Southeastern U., 1980. CPA N.Y., cert. mgmt. acct., N.Y. Chief acct. G.E. X-Ray Corp., Chgo., 1940—41; pub. budget officer Arthur Andersen & Co., Chgo., 1941—43; renegotiator contracts U.S. Army Air Corps, Chgo., 1943—45; internal auditor David Bradley Mfg. (Sears), Bradley, Ill., 1945—48; contr., treas. Manco Mfg. Co., Bradley, 1948—59; owner, operator Yellow-Checker Cab Co., Kankakee, Ill.,

1959—70; chmn. acctg., prof. Rochester Inst. Tech., NY, 1970—73, Southwestern Mich. Coll., Dowagiac, 1973—; citizen ambr. People to People Internat., Kansas City, Mo., 1992—. Curriculum advisor Southwestern Mich. Coll., Dowagiac, 1992—. Citizen ambr. People to People Internat., Bora Bora, Que., Canada, Cuba, China, Egypt, England, France, Galapagos Island, Greece, Greenland, Iceland, India, Israel, Italy, Japan, Moorea, Morocco, Portugal, Singapore, Tahiti, Turkey, Russia, Spain, Ecuador, Greek Islands, Hong Kong; del. to Russia to facilitate their transition to Dem. form of govt.; del. leader Wharton Sch. Fin. U. Pa., Phila., 1992. Mem.: Planning Execs. Inst. (spkr., chmn.), Inst. Cert. Mgmt. Accts., Nat. Assn. Accts., Pi Gamma Mu, Pi Kappa Alpha, Alpha Kappa Psi. Republican. Avocations: travel, golf, bowling, reading, exercise. Home: 30992 Middle Crossing Rd Dowagiac MI 49047-9268

**OTT, DAVID MICHAEL,** engineering company executive; b. Glendale, Calif., Feb. 24, 1952; s. Frank Michael and Roberta (Michie) O.; m. Cynthia Dianne Bunce. BSEE, U. Calif., Berkeley, 1974. Electronic engr. Teknekron Inc., Berkeley, 1974-79; chief engr. TCI, Berkeley, 1979-83; div. mgr. Integrated Automation Inc., Alameda, Calif., 1983-87, Litton Indsl. Automation, Alameda, 1987-92; founder, chmn. Picture Elements Inc., Berkeley, 1992—. Inventor method for verifying denomination of currency, method for processing digited images, automatic document image revision. Mem. IEEE, AAAS, Assn. Computing Machinery, Union of Concerned Scientists. Office: Picture Elements Inc 777 Panoramic Way Berkeley CA 94704-2538

**OTT, DORIS ANN,** librarian; b. Elgin, ND, Sept. 24, 1942; d. Oscar Edward Hirning and Lorraine Wilhelmina Gruebele; m. Richard Donald Ott, Nov. 21, 1998; m. Bennett Gordon Reinke, Sept. 1961 (div.); 1 child, Scott Bennett Reinke; m. James Lee Daugherty, June 1974 (div.). BS, Dickinson State U., 1964; MLS, George Peabody Coll., 1965. Lic. Ind. life tchr. Elem. tchr. Mott Pub. Schs., ND, 1963-64; asst. prof. Dickinson State U., ND, 1965-73; media specialist Minot Pub. Schs., ND, 1973-74; head tech. svcs. Bartholomew County Libr., Columbus, Ind., 1974-75; media specialist Rushville Pub. Schs., Ind., 1975-86; head interlib. loan ND State Libr., Bismarck, 1986-87, asst. state libr., 1987—2001, state libr., 2001—. Image cons. Beauty For All Seasons, 1984—. Mem. Humane Soc. Mem. ALA, N.D. Libr. Assn., Mountain Plains Libr. Assn. Avocation: image consulting. Office: ND State Libr 604 E Boulevard Ave Dept 250 Bismarck ND 58505-0800 Office Phone: 701-328-2492. Business E-Mail: dott@nd.gov.

**OTT, GILBERT RUSSELL, JR.,** lawyer; b. Bklyn., Apr. 15, 1943; s. Gilbert Russell Sr. and Bettina Rose (Ferrel) O.; m. Lisa S. Weatherford, Apr. 12, 1986; children: Gilbert R. III, Laura Elisabeth. BA, Yale U., 1965; JD, MBA, Columbia U., 1969. Bar: N.Y. 1970. Assoc. Chadbourne, Parke, Whiteside & Wolff, N.Y.C., 1969-72; LeBoeuf, Lamb, Leiby & MacRae, N.Y.C., 1972-78; assoc. sec., 1978-91, asst. v.p., 1978-79, v.p., 1979-86, mng. dir., 1986-91, sr. v.p., sec., 1992-96; v.p. Kidder, Peabody Group Inc., N.Y.C., 1989-96, asst. sec., 1986-96; exec. v.p., gen. counsel, sec. Rodman & Renshaw Capital Group, Inc., Chgo. and N.Y.C., 1996-98; counsel Cadwalader, Wickersham & Taft, N.Y.C., 1998-99; dep. gen. counsel Datek Online Holdings Corp., Jersey City, 1999—2002; chief legal officer instl. divsn. Ameritrade Holding Corp., Jersey City, 2002—05; dep. gen. counsel TD Ameritrade Holding Corp., Jersey City, 2006—. Mem.: Assn. Bar City of N.Y., Univ. Club, Piping Rock Club. Home: 260 Highwood Cir Oyster Bay NY 11771-3205 Office: 2600 Plaza 5 Jersey City NJ 07311 Office Phone: 201-761-5673. Business E-Mail: gott@ameritrade.com.

**OTT, JOHN HARLOW,** museum administrator; b. Ottawa, Ont., Can., Jan. 29, 1944; s. Thomas Gordon and Lois Elizabeth (Wright) O.; m. Lili Reineck, May 20, 1972; children— Jennie Elizabeth, Michael James Hutchins BA, Eastern Bapt. Coll., St. David's, Pa., 1966; MA, SUNY-Oneonta, 1975; postgrad. Mus. Mgmt. Inst., U. Calif., Berkeley, 1987. Curator Hancock Shaker Village, Inc., Pittsfield, Mass., 1970-72, dir., 1972-83; exec. dir. Atlanta Hist. Soc., 1983-91, B&O R.R. Mus., Inc., Balt., 1991-99, The Nat. Heritage Mus., Lexington, Mass., 1999—. Curator Ga. Hist. Soc., Savannah, 1983-87; mem. adv. bd. Concord (Mass.) Mus. Author: Hancock Shaker Village, 1976 Mem. Lexington Tourism Com. 2002—; bd. dirs. Devens Hist. Mus., 2001—03, bd. govs., 2003—; bd. dirs. Merimack Valley Conv. and Visitors Bur., N.E. Document Conservation Ctr., 2005—; pres. Cooperstown Grad. Program Alumni Assn., 2005—. Decorated Bronze Star; named mus. profl. of yr. in Ga., 1991, profl. of yr. Acad. for Travel, Hospitality and Tourism, 1996. Mem. Am. Assn. Mus. (accrediting officer 1982—), Am. Assn. for State and Local History, Mid-Atlantic Mus. Assn., Ga. Soc. Assn. Execs., Nat. Hist. Communal Socs. Assn. (pres. 1983-84), Nat. Soc. Fund Raising Execs. (bd. dirs. Ga. chpt. 1985-91, bd. dirs. Md. chpt. 1993), Balt. City C. of C. (bd. dirs., past chmn.), Md. Assn. History Mus. (bd. dirs. 1996), Freedom's Way Heritage Assn. (bd. dirs. 2000—), Lexington C. of C. (chmn. 2002-2004). Republican. Episcopalian. Office: The Nat Heritage Mus 33 Marrett Rd Lexington MA 02421-5703 Office Phone: 781-457-4102. E-mail: jott@monh.org.

**OTT, KARL OTTO,** nuclear engineer, consultant; b. Hanau, Germany, Dec. 24, 1925; arrived in U.S., 1967, naturalized, 1987; s. Johann Josef and Eva (Bergmann) Ott; m. Gunhild G. Göring, Sept. 18, 1958 (div. 1986); children: Martina, Monika; m. Birgit Fehse, May 1, 1995. BS, J. W. von Goethe U., Frankfurt, Germany, 1948; MS, G. August U., Göttingen, Fed. Republic Germany, 1953, PhD, 1958. Physicist Nuc. Rsch. Ctr., Karlsruhe, Germany, 1958-67, sect. head, 1962-67; prof. Sch. Nuc. Engring. Purdue U., West Lafayette, Ind., 1967-2001, prof. emeritus, 2000—. Cons. Argonne Nat. Lab., 1967—2001. Author: (book) Nuclear Reactor Statics, 1983, 2d edit., 1989, Nuclear Reactor Dynamics, 1985, Chinese edit., 1991. Recipient Disting. Appointment award, Argonne Universities Assn., 1973. Fellow: Am. Nuc. Soc. (Arthur Holly Compton award 1993). Office Phone: 765-494-5739. E-mail: kobott@sbcglobal.net.

**OTT, SHARON,** artistic director; Theatre dir.: The Wash, Yankee Dawy You Die; artistic dir.:Berkeley Repertory Theatre; now artistic dir. Seattle Repertory Theatre. Former bd. dirs. Theatre Comms. Group, v.p. Recipient Obie award, numerous others awards.

**OTT, WALTER RICHARD,** information technology executive; b. Bklyn., Jan. 20, 1943; s. Harold Vincent and Mary Elizabeth (Butler) Ott; m. Carla M. Narrett, May 27, 2002; children: Regina Winter Burrell, Christina W. Chiappetta, Walter R. Jr. BS in Ceramic Engring., Va. Poly. Inst. and State U., 1965; MS in Ceramic Engring., U. Ill., 1967; PhD in Ceramic Engring., Rutgers U., 1969; DSc (hon.), Alfred U., 1994. Research profl. engr., Pa. Process engr. Corning Inc. Buckhannon, W.Va., 1965-66; staff rsch. engr. Champion Spark Plug Co., Detroit, 1969-70; prof. engring. Rutgers U., New Brunswick, NJ, 1970-88; dean, assoc. provost N.Y. State Coll. Ceramics, Alfred, 1980-88; provost, chief acad. officer Alfred U., Alfred, 1988-2000; pres. Predictive Edge, Inc., West Orange, NJ, 1999—; v.p enrollment mgmt. Caldwell (N.J.) Coll., 2002—04. Rsch. assoc. Atomic Energy Commn.-E.I. duPont de Nemours, Aiken, S.C., 1971; cons. Haight & Hofeldt Inc., Chgo., 1984-88, Pillsbury, Mpls., 1977-79, Ctr. for Profl. Advancement, New Brunswick, 1971-79, Hammond (Ind.) Lead Products, 1970-80; bd. dirs. Victor (N.Y.) Insulator Inc., UNIPEG, 1987-88; treas. Alfred Tech. Resources N.Y.; bd. dirs. Grads Found., N.Y.C. Contbr. articles to profl. jours.; patentee in field. Recipient Ralph Teetor award N.Y. Soc. Automotive Engrs., 1973, PACE award Nat. Inst. Ceramic Engrs., 1975, Ann. award Ceramic Assn. N.J., 1980; named to Greaves Walker Roll, Keramos, 1991. Fellow Am. Ceramic Soc. (trustee 1980-83, v.p. 1988-89); mem. Ceramic Ednl. Coun. (pres. 1976-77), Ceramic Assn. N.Y. (treas. 1980-88, bd. dirs.), Ceramic Assn. N.J. (bd. dirs. 1974-80), Keramos (pres. 1982-84, Greaves-Walker Roll of Honor 1991), Tau Beta Pi. Avocations: tennis, sailing, reading. Home: 26039 Seminole Lake Blvd Punta Gorda FL 33955 Business E-Mail: ott@predictiveedge.com.

**OTT, WAYNE ROBERT,** environmental engineer; b. San Mateo, Calif., Feb. 2, 1940; s. Florian Funstan and Evelyn Virginia (Smith) Ott; m. Patricia Faustina Bertuzzi, June 28, 1967 (div. 1983). BA in Econs., Claremont McKenna Coll., 1962; BSEE, Stanford U., 1963, MS in Engring., 1965, MA in Comm., 1966, PhD in Environ. Engring., 1971. Commd. lt. USPHS, 1966, advanced through grades to capt., 1986; chief lab. ops. br. U.S. EPA, Washington, 1971—73, sr. systems analyst, 1973—79, sr. rsch. engr., 1981—84, chief air toxics and radiation monitoring rsch. staff, 1984—90; vis. scientist dept. stats. Stanford U., 1979—81, 1990—. Vis. scholar Ctr. for Risk Analysis and dept. stats., civil engring., Stanford U., 1990—93; sr. environ. engr. EPA Atmospheric Rsch. and Exposure Assessment Lab., 1993—95; cons. prof. civil engring. Stanford U., 1995—; dir. field studies Calif. Environ. Tobacco Smoke Study, 1993—95. Author: Environmental Indices: Theory and Practice, 1976, Environmental Statistics and Data Analysis, 1995, Exposure Analysis, 2006; contbr. articles to profl. jours. Decorated Commendation medal USPHS; recipient Nat. Statistician award, EPA, 1995. Mem.: Internat. Soc. Indoor Air Quality and Climate, Air and Waste Mgmt. Assn., Am. Soc. for Quality Control, Am. Statis. Assn., Internat. Soc. Exposure Analysis (v.p. 1989—90, Jerome J. Weselowski Internat. award for career achievement in exposure assessment 1995), Sierra Club, Theater Club, Jazz Club, Kappa Mu Epsilon, Tau Beta Pi, Sigma Xi, Phi Beta Kappa. Democrat. Achievements include development of nationally uniform air pollution index, first total human exposure activity pattern models; research in indoor air pollution, total human exposure to chems., stochastic models of indoor exposure to chems., stochastic models of indoor exposure, motor vehicle exposures, pers monitoring instruments and environ tobacco smoke. Avocations: hiking, photography, model trains, jazz. Home: 1008 Cardiff Ln Redwood City CA 94061-3678 Office: Stanford U Dept Stats Sequoia Hall Stanford CA 94305 Office Phone: 650-906-8442 Business E Mail: wott1@stanford.edu.

**OTTAWAY, JAMES HALLER, JR.,** newspaper publisher; b. Binghamton, N.Y., Mar. 24, 1938; s. James Haller and Ruth Blackburne (Hart) O.; m. Mary Warren Hyde, June 16, 1959; children— Alexandra, Christopher, Jay. Grad., Phillips Exeter Acad., 1955; BA, Yale U., 1960; DJournalism (hon.), Suffolk U., Boston, 1970; DBA (hon.), Southeastern Mass. U., 1984. Reporter, mgmt. trainee New-Times, Danbury, Conn., 1960—62, Times Herald-Record, Middletown, N.Y, 1962—63; editor Pocono Record, Stroudsburg, Pa., 1963—65; publisher New Bedford (Mass.) Standard-Times, 1965—70; pres. Ottaway Newspapers, Inc., Campbell Hall, NY, 1970—85, CEO, 1976—88, chmn. bd., 1979—2003, CEO, 1998—2003; ret. V.p. Dow Jones & Co., 1980-86, sr. v.p., 1986-2003, also bd. dirs.; dir., vice-chmn. AP, 1982-91. Past v.p. bd. trustees Phillips Exeter Acad.; trustee Am. Sch. Classical Studies at Athens, chmn., 1996-99; trustee, vice-chmn. Storm King Art Ctr., Mountainville, N.Y., World Wildlife Fund USA, 1993-96; trustee Bard Coll., 1996—; chmn. World Press Freedom Com., 1996—; treas. Internat. Commn. Transitional Justice, 2002—; chmn. Words Without Borders, 2004-; past pres., bd. dirs. Arden Hill Hosp. Found., Goshen, NY. Mem. Am. Newspaper Pubs. Assn., Am. Soc. Newspaper Editors. Episcopalian. Office: PO Box 401 Campbell Hall NY 10916-0401 Office Phone: 845-294-4902. E-mail: jimottaway837@yahoo.com.

**OTTE, PAUL JOHN,** academic administrator, consultant; b. Detroit, July 10, 1943; s. Melvin John Otte and Anne Marie (Meyers) Hirsch; children: Deanna Kropf, John. BS, Wayne State U., 1968, MBA, 1969; EdD, Western Mich. U., 1983. With Detroit Bank and Trust Co., 1965-68; teaching fellow Wayne State U., Detroit, 1968-69; auditor, mgr. Arthur Young & Co., Detroit, 1969-75; contr., dir. Macomb Community Coll., Warren, Mich., 1975-79, v.p. bus., 1979-86; pres. Franklin U. Columbus, Ohio, 1986—; prof. undergrad. and grad. programs, 1986—. Author various tng. manuals, 1982. Cpl. USMC, 1961-65. Teaching fellow Wayne State U., 1968-69. Mem. AICPA, Mich. Assn. CPAs (chmn. continuing profl. edn. com. 1980-82, leadership com. 1981-83), Nat. Assn. Coll. and Univ. Bus. Officers (acctg. prins. com. 1986), Assn. Ind. Colls. and Univs. Ohio (bd. dirs.), Greater Detroit C. of C. (leadership award 1983), Columbus C. of C. (info. svc. com.). Roman Catholic. Avocation: travel. Office: Franklin U 201 S Grant Ave Columbus OH 43215-5399

**OTTER, CLEMENT LEROY (BUTCH OTTER),** congressman; b. Caldwell, Idaho, May 3, 1942; s. Joseph Bernard and Regina Mary (Buser) O.; children: John Simplot, Carolyn Lee, Kimberly Dawn, Corinne Marie. BA in Polit. Sci., Coll. Idaho, 1967; PhD (hon.), Mindanao State U., 1980. Mgr. J.R. Simplot Co., Caldwell, Idaho, 1971-76, asst. to v.p. adminstrn., 1976-78, v.p. adminstrn., 1978-82, internat. pres., 1982—93; mem. Idaho House of Reps., 1973—77; lt. gov. State of Idaho, Boise, 1987—2001; mem. U.S. Congress from 1st Idaho Dist., 2000—; mem. transp. and infrastructure, resources and govt. reform, energy and commerce coms. Mem. Presdl. Task Force-AID, Washington, 1982—84, U.S. C. of C., Washington, 1983—84; com. mem. invest tech. devel. State Adv. Council, Washington, 1983—84; mem. exec. council Bretton Woods Com., 1984—. With Nat. Guard, 1968—73. Mem. Young Pres.' Orgn., Sales and Mktg. Execs., Idaho Assn. Commerce and Industry, Idaho Agrl. Leadership Council, Idaho Ctr. for Arts, Idaho Internat. Trade Council, Pacific N.W. Waterways Assn., N.W. Food Producers, Ducks Unltd, Safari Club Internat. (life). Clubs: Arid, Hillcrest Country. Lodges: Moose, Elks. Republican. Roman Catholic. Avocations: target shooting, art collecting, horse training, fishing. Office: US Ho Reps 1711 Longworth Ho Office Bldg Washington DC 20515-1201

**OTTER, JOHN MARTIN, III,** retired television advertising consultant; b. Pottsville, Pa., Nov. 26, 1930; s. John Martin and Ruth A. (Knipe) O.; m. Susan Morgan Eaves, May 21, 1960; children— John Martin, IV, Robert Marshal. BA, Cornell U., 1953. Comml. producer Arlene Frances Home Show, 1953-55; producer Dave Garroway Today Show, 1956-59; dir. spl. programs sales NBC-TV, 1959-61, v.p. nat. sales 1962-64, v.p. charge sales 1965-73; conn. sta. WNLT-TV, Practising Law Inst., also Dragonwk Prodns., 1973-75; v.p., dir. network programming SSC&B Inc., 1975-78; sr. v.p., dir. network programming SSC&B Lintas Worldwide, N.Y., 1978-84; sr. v.p. dir. nat. broadcast McCann-Erickson U.S.A., N.Y.C., 1984-88; sr. v.p. spl. projects McCann-Erickson Worldwide, N.Y.C., 1988; pres. RETTO Internat. Inc., N.Y.C., 1989-94; retired, 1994. Mem.: The Chatham Club, The Landings Yacht Club, The Landings Club. Republican. Episcopalian. Home: Four Seafarer's Cir Savannah GA 31411

**OTTERBOURG, ROBERT KENNETH,** public relations consultant, writer; b. N.Y.C., Jan. 26, 1930; s. Albert Marcus and Frances (Roset) O.; m. Susan Delman, Apr. 14, 1957; children— Laura Ann, Kenneth Douglas. BA, Colgate U., 1951; MS, Columbia U., 1954. Reporter, editor Fairchild Publs., N.Y.C., 1953-57; editor McGraw-Hill Pub. Co., 1957-59; v.p. pub. rels. Charles Mathieu & Co., 1959-61; pres. pub. rels. Otterbourg & Co., N.Y.C., 1962-69, 71—. Sr. v.p. Daniel J. Edelman, 1970. Author: It's Never Too Late, 1993, Retire and Thrive, 1995, 3d edit., 2003, Switching Careers, 2001; contbr. articles to profl. and consumer jours. Legis. asst. N.Y. State Senate, 1962-64; mem. exec. com. Columbia U. Sch. Journalism, N.Y.C., 1980-93, pres. exec. com., 1985-87; trustee Flat Rock Nature Ctr., pres., 1991-92; trustee Planned Parenthood Bergen County, 1985-88, v.p., 1986-88; trustee Urban League for Bergen County, 1988-93; chmn. Durham County Libr., 1997-99, Exec. Svc. Corps of the Greater Triangle; bd. dirs. Colgate U. Alumni Corp., 1969-73; bd. dirs., pres. Threshold, 2003; pres. Triangle Radio Reading Svc., 2004. 1st lt. USAF, 1951-53. Mem. Columbia U. Grad. Sch. Journalism Alumni Assn. (pres. 1985-87). Democrat. Jewish. Home and Office: 68 Beverly Dr Durham NC 27707-2224 Personal E-mail: rkotter@aol.com.

**OTTERNESS, TOM,** artist; b. Wichita, Kans., June 21, 1952; s. Garnet Otterness; m. Coleen Fitzgibbon; 1 child, Kelly. Student, Art Students League, 1970, Whitney Mus of Am. Art, 1973. One-person shows include Berggruen Gallery, San Francisco, 2004, Marlborough GAllery, 2004, 05, Skoto Gallery, 2003, Marlborough Gallery, Chelsea, NY, 2002, James Corcoran Gallery, Santa Monica, Brooke Alexander, N.Y., 1990, IVAM Centre Julio Gonzalez, Valencia, Spain, Portikus/Senckenbergmuseum,

Frankfurt, Germany, Haags Gemeentemuseum, The Hague, The Netherlands, 1991, The Mus. Modern Art, 1987, Nancy Drysdale Gallery, Washington, 1991, Brooke Alexander, N.Y., 1992, Galerie Weber, Muenster, Westfalen, Germany, 1993, John Berggruen Gallery, San Francisco, 1993, 99, Carnegie Mus. Art, Pitts., 1993, Gallery Contemporary Art, Krannert Art Mus., Champaign, Ill., 1994, MetroTech Ctr., Bklyn., 1995, Wichita Art Mus., 1995, Doris Freedman Plaza, 1995, Marlborough Gallery, N.Y., 1997, 2002, Marlborough Gallery, Madrid, Spain, 1999; exhibited in group exhibitions including Whitney Mus. Am. Art, N.Y.C., 1985, Marlborough Gallery, N.Y., 1995-96, Ubu Gallery, N.Y., 1995-96, Mus. Modern Art, NY, 1996, The White House, Washington, 1996, Detroit Inst. Arts, Mus. Fine Arts, Boston, Mpls. Inst. Arts, San Diego Mus. Art, Ctr. for the Fine Arts, Miami, 1996-97, John Berggruen Gallery, 1997, San Jose Mus. Art, Calif., 1997-98; pub. commns. include Edward R. Roybal Fed. Bldg., LA, 1991, Gov. Nelson A. Rockefeller Park, N.Y.C., 1992, State Libr., Munster, Germany, 1993, Roosevelt Island, N.Y., 1996, Mark O. Hatfield U.S. Courthouse, Portland, 1997, Cleve. Pub. Libr., 1998, Fed. Courthouse, Sacramento, 1999, Western Wash. U., Bellingham, 1999, Fed. Courthouse, Mpls., 1999, Hilton Times Sq. N.Y.C., 2000, MTA Arts for Transit, N.Y.C., 2000, Carl Sagan Discovery Ctr. 2000, Children's Hosp. Montefiore Med. Ctr., Bronx, MTA Arts for Transit, N.Y.C. 2002, Return of Four-Leggeds, N.W. Mus. of Art, Spokane, Wash., 2003, Mus. Beelden aan Zee, Scheveningen, The Netherlands, 2004, N.Y. Bot. Garden, Bronx, 2005, others; represented in pvt. and permanent collections including Bklyn. Mus., Carnegie Mus. Art, Guggenheim Mus., N.Y.C., Israel Mus., Jerusalem, IVAM Ctr. Julio Gonzalez, Valencia, Spain, Mus. Modern Art, N.Y.C., Whitney Mus. Am. Art, Miyagi Mus. Art, Sendai, Japan, Mus. Tamayo, Mexico City. Active Collaborative Project, Inc., NY, 1977-82. Fellow Nat. Endowment for the Arts, 1994. Studio. 80 4th St Brooklyn NY 11231-4821 E-mail: studio@tomotterness.net.

**OTTINGER, RICHARD LAWRENCE,** dean emeritus; b. N.Y.C., Jan. 27, 1929; s. Lawrence and Louise (Lowenstein) O.; children from previous marriage: Ronald, Randall, Lawrence, Jenny Louise; m. June Godfrey. BA, Cornell U., 1950; LLB, Harvard U., 1953. Assoc. Cleary, Gottlieb, Friendly & Hamilton, N.Y.C., 1955-56; ptnr. William J. Kridel, Law Firm, N.Y.C., 1956-60; second staff mem., dir. programs Peace Corps, L.Am., 1961-64; mem. 89th-91st Congresses, 1965-71, 94th-98th Congresses, 1975-85; profl. Pace U. Sch. Law, White Plains, N.Y., 1985—, dean, 1994—99, dean emeritus, 1999—. Chmn. bd. dirs. Environ. and Energy Study Inst., Washington, Legal Environl. Assistance Found., Tallahasse, Fla. Author: Environmental Costs of Electricity, 1990; co-author: Energy Law and Sustainable Development, 2003; co-author and co-editor The Law of Energy for Sustainable Development, 2005; co-editor Compendium of Laws on Energy for Sustainable Development, 2005; contbr. articles to profl. jours. Contract mgr. Internat. Coop. Adminstrn., 1960-61; organizer Grassroots to Action, 1971-73. Office: Pace U Sch Law 78 N Broadway White Plains NY 10603-3710 Office Phone: 914-422-4121. Business E-Mail: rottinger@law.pace.edu.

**OTTINO, JULIO MARIO,** engineering educator; b. La Plata, Buenos Aires, Argentina, May 22, 1951; came to U.S., 1976; naturalized, 1990; s. Julio Francisco and Nydia Judit (Zufriategui) O.; m. Alicia L. Löffler, Aug. 20, 1976; children: Jules Alessandro, Bertrand Julien. Diploma in Chem. Engring., U. La Plata, 1974; PhD in Chem. Engring., U. Minn., 1979; exec. program Kellogg Sch. Mgmt., Northwestern U., 1995. Instr. in chem. engring. U. Minn., Mpls., 1978-79; asst. prof. U. Mass., Amherst, 1979-83, adj. prof. polymer sci., 1979-91, assoc. prof. chem. engring., 1983-86, prof., 1986-91; Chevron vis. prof. chem. engring. Calif. Inst. Tech., Pasadena, 1985-86; sr. rsch. fellow Ctr. for Turbulence Rsch. Stanford (Calif.) U., 1989-90; Walter P. Murphy prof. chem. engring. Northwestern U., Evanston, Ill., 1991-2000, chmn. dept. chem. engring., 1992-2000; McCormick Inst. prof., 2000—; George T. Piercy Disting. prof. U. Minn., 1998, adj. prof. mech. engring., 2001—; dir. Northwestern Inst. Complex Sys., 2004—, dean Sch. Engring. and Applied Sci. Cons. to U.S. and European corps.; mem. tech. adv. bd. Dow Chem.; mem. bd. dirs. Coun. Chem. Rsch.; U. Minn.; Reily lectr. Notre Dame U., 2006; lectr. in field. Author: The Kinematics of Mixing: Stretching, Chaos and Transport, 1989; contbr. articles to profl. jours.; assoc. editor Physics Fluids A, 1991—; mem. editl. bd. Internat. Jour. Bifurc. Chaos, 1991—; assoc. editor Am. Inst. Chem. Engring. Jour., 1991-95, assoc. editor., 1995—; one man art exhibit, La Plata, 1974. Recipient Presdl. Young Investigator award NSF, 1984, Alpha Chi Sigma award AIChE, 1994, W.H. Walker award AIChE, 2001, E.W. Thiele award AIChE, Chgo., 2002; Univ. fellow U. Mass., 1988, J.S. Guggenheim fellow, 2001; Lacey lectureship Calif. Inst. Tech., 1994, Danckwerts lectureship Royal Instn., 1999, Robb lectr. Pa. State U. Fellow Am. Phys. Soc.; mem. AAAS, NAE, Am. Acad. Arts and Scis., Am. Chem. Soc., Am. Phys. Soc., Am. Soc. Engring. Edn., Sigma Xi (disting. lectr. 1997-99), Coun. for Chem. Rsch.(gov. bd. coun. 1999-2001). Achievements include research in granular dynamics, chaos, complex systems and mixing. Avocations: visual arts, painting. Home: 1092 Crescent Ln Winnetka IL 60093-1501 Office: Northwestern U Dept Chem Engring 2145 Sheridan Rd Evanston IL 60208-0834 Office Phone: 847-491-5220. Business E-Mail: jm-ottino@northwestern.edu.

**OTTO, BYRON LEONARD,** lawyer, state agency administrator; b. Battle Creek, Mich., Oct. 4, 1940; s. Henry John and Mildred Alice (Wagner) O. BBA, St. Edward's U., 1964, MBA, 1970; JD, U. Tex., 1968. Bar: U.S. Dist. Ct. (we. dist.) 1976. Staff atty. State Welfare Dept., Austin, Tex., 1968-75; sole practice Austin, Tex., 1975-77; assoc. James R. Sloan, Austin, Tex., 1978-79; adminstr. State Comptroller, Austin, Tex., 1980—; ret., 2000. Author articles and monographs. St. Edward's U. scholar, Austin, 1978. Mem. ABA, Tex. Bar. Democrat. Roman Catholic. Home: 4604 S Lamar Blvd Apt C202 Austin TX 78745-1358 E-mail: byron@austin.rr.com.

**OTTO, FRED DOUGLAS,** chemical engineering professor; b. Hadley, Alta., Can., Jan. 12, 1935; BSc, U. Alta., 1957, MSc, 1959; PhD in Chem. Engring., U. Mich., Ann Arbor, 1963. From asst. prof. to assoc. prof. U. Alta., Edmonton, 1962-70, chmn., 1975-84, prof. chem. engring., 1970-96, dean engring., 1985-94, prof. emeritus, 1996—; pres., CEO DB Robinson & Assocs. Ltd., 1998—2002. Mem. governing coun. NRC, 1991-94. Recipient Donald L. Katz award, Gas Processors Assn., 1998. Fellow: Can. Acad. Engring.; mem.: AIChE, Can. Coun. Profl. Engrs. (bd. dirs. 1997—2003), Assn. Profl. Engrs., Geologists and Geophysicists of Alta. (1st v.p. 1995—96, pres. 1996—97, Centennial award 1993), Can. Soc. Chem. Engrs. (pres. 1986—87). Office: 12319 52d Ave Edmonton AB Canada T6H 0P5 E-mail: fotto@interbaun.com.

**OTTO, JEAN HAMMOND,** journalist; b. Kenosha, Wis., Aug. 27, 1925; d. Laurence Cyril and Beatrice Jane (Slater) Hammond; m. John A. Otto, Aug. 22, 1946; children: Jane L. Rahman, Mary Ellen Takashima, Peter J.; m. Lee W. Baker, Nov. 23, 1973. Student, Ripon Coll., 1944-46. Women's editor Appleton (Wis.) Post-Crescent, 1968-68; reporter Milw. Jour., 1968-72, editorial writer, 1972-77, editor Op Ed page, 1977-83; editorial page editor Rocky Mountain News, Denver, 1983-89, assoc. editor, 1989-92, reader rep., 1992-99; endowed chair U. Denver, 1992-97. Founder, chmn. bd. trustees First Amendment Congress, 1979-85, chmn. exec. com., 1985-88, 89-91, pres. 1991-96, mem. bd. trustees, 1979-96; founding mem. Wis. Freedom of Info. Council. Recipient Headliner award Wis. Women in Communications, 1974; Outstanding Woman in Journalism award YWCA, Milw., 1977; Knight of Golden Quill Milw. Press Club, 1979; spl. citation in Journalism Ball State U., 1980; James Madison award Nat. Broadcast Editorial Assn., 1981; spl. citation for contbn. to journalism Nat. Press Photographers Assn., 1981; Ralph D. Casey award U. Minn., 1984; U. Colo. Regents award, 1985; John Peter Zenger award U. Ariz., 1988; Paul Miller Medallion award Okla. State U., 1990; Colo. SPJ Lowell Thomas award, 1990, Disting. Alumna award Ripon Coll., 1992, Hugh M. Hefner First Amendment Lifetime Achievement award Playboy Found., 1994; named to Milw. Press Club Hall of Fame, 1993, Freedom of Info. Hall of Fame, 1996. Mem.: Soc. Profl. Journalists (nat. freedom of info. com. chmn. 1977, pres.-elect 1978, pres. 1979—80, pres. Sigma Delta Chi Found. 1989—92, chair Found. 1992—94, First Amendment award 1981, Wells Key 1984), Am. Soc. Newspaper Editors (bd. dirs. 1987—92), Colo. Press Assn. (chmn. freedom of info. com. 1983—89), Assn. Edn. in

Journalism and Mass Communications (Disting. Svc. award 1984). Milw. Press Club (Hall of Fame 1993). Home: 2462 N Prospect #311 Milwaukee WI 53211 Personal E-mail: jottofirst@aol.com.

**OTTO, MARIE (BERTHA OTTO),** educational administrator, educational consulting company executive; b. Houston, July 11, 1930; d. Robert Lillard and Bertha Irene (Allen) Davis; m. Robert Lee Jr., Jan. 7, 1950; children: Lois Ann Otto Buschmann, Barbara Jeane Otto Hunt, Robert Lee Jr. Student, Tex. Christian U., 1947-49, Hardin-Simmons U., summers 1947, 49, 54; BA in Speech, Drama and Edn., Sul-Ross State U., 1954; postgrad., U. Wyo., 1961, U. Calif., Santa Barbara, 1962, Calif. State U., Northridge, 1964; MA, Calif. State U., Long Beach, 1969, postgrad., 1980-82. Lic. tchr., Tex., secondary tchr., Wyo., Calif.; lic. psychologist; lic. marriage and family counselor. Tchr. high schs., Tex., Wyo. and Calif., 1956-64; tchr., counselor Excelsior High Sch., Norwalk, Calif., 1964-66; counselor Neff High Sch., La Mirada, Calif., 1966-69; psychologist Huntington Beach (Calif.) Union High Sch. Dist., 1969-74, project mgr., dir. pupil pers., 1974-80, asst. supt., 1980-84, supt., 1984-88, supt. emeritus, 1988—. V.p. Poole-Young-Koehler Assocs., Inc., Long Beach, 1974-79; pvt. practice marriage and family counselor, Fountain Valley, Calif., 1970—; pres. Marie Otto Assocs., Fountain Valley, 1979—; supr. student tchrs. Chapman Univ. Orange, Calif., 1988—; sec.-treas., Ctr. for Teaching Thinking, Huntington Beach, 1991—. Mem. Fountain Valley Human Svcs. Com., Huntington Beach Human Resources Commn., state planning com. Girl Scouts U.S.A., Worland, Wyo., 1959-61; pres. Spl. Edn. Local Plan Orgn., 1983-84; bd. dirs. Humana Hosp. Huntington Beach, Golden West Coll. Found., Huntington Beach, Huntington Beach Community Clinic, Orange County chpt. ARC, Santa Ana, Calif, No on Drugs, 1988—; sec., treas. Ctr. for Teaching of Thinking, Huntington Beach, 1992—. Recipient numerous plaques including Fountain Valley Human Svcs. Com., 1979, City of Fountain Valley, 1975, 79, 88, City of Huntington Beach, 1988, Fountain Valley C. of C., 1988, City of Westminster, 1988, Orange Coast Coll., 1988, Golden West Coll., 1988, Ocean View Sch. Dist., 1988, Spl. Edn. Local Plan Orgn., 1984; named Woman of Yr., Soroptimist Club, Westminster, 1984, Disting. Alumnus, Grad. Sch. Edn. Calif. State U., Long Beach, 1988. Home and Office: 16689 Mount Hoffman Cir Fountain Valley CA 92708-2435

**OTTO, PETER,** information scientist, educator; b. Zurich, Switzerland, Apr. 29, 1956; s. Ferdinand Otto and Nelly (Mueller) Otto-Mueller; m. Judith Weber. PhD, U. Albany, NY, 2002. Asst. prof. Dowling Coll., Oakdale, NY, 2002—06; vis. fellow Cornell U., Ithaca, NY, 2004—; mng. ptnr. IPG Inc., Schenectady, NY, 2001—. Mng. dir. Ogilvy & Mather Healthcare, Zurich, Switzerland, 1991—99. Recipient Best Reader award, GSBA Zurich, Springer Verlag, 2002. Fellow: Sys. Dynamics Profls. (corr.); mem.: Sys. Dynamics Soc. (assoc.). Home: 410 Terrace Rd Schenectady NY 12306 Office Phone: 631-244-3192. Personal E-mail: po36@cornell.edu.

**OTTO, ROBERT L.,** information technology executive; Joined US Postal Svc., Washington, 1980, v.p. fin., v.p. info. tech., chief info. officer, chief tech. officer, 2003—. Mailing: US Postal Service Rm 2017 475 L'Enfant Plaza SW Washington DC 20260-4100 Office Phone: 202-268-6900. E-mail: robert.l.otto@usps.gov.*

**OTUNNU, OLARA A.,** international organization official; b. Mucwini (Chua), Northern Uganda, Sept. 1950; Attended, Makerere U., Kampala; exch. student, Oxford U.; Fulbright Scholar, Harvard U. Assoc. atty. Chadbourne and Parke, NY; asst. prof. law Albany Law Sch.; mem. Uganda Nat. Consultative Coun., 1979—80; permanent rep. of Uganda UN, 1980—85; pres. Security Coun., 1981; chmn. African Group, 1981; vice pres. Gen. Assembly, 1982—83; chmn. Contact Group on Global Negotiations, 1982—93, Common. on Human Rights, 1983—84, Gen. Assembly Credentials Com., 1983—84, Drafting Com. of the Ministerial Mtg. of Non-Aligned Countries, 1983; min. Fgn. Affairs of Uganda, 1985—86; vis. fellow Inst. Francais des Relations Internat., 1987—89; vis. prof. Am. U., Paris, 1987—89; pres. Internat. Peace Acad., 1990—97; special rep., sec. gen. for Children and Armed Conflict United Nations, 1997—2006. Mem. Internat. Task Force on Security Coun. Peace Enforcement; pres. Internat. Peace Acad.; mem. UN Group of Experts on New Concepts of Internat. Security, 1984—85, Commonwealth Group of Experts Study Group on the Security of Small States, 1984—85, Internat. Panel on Mgmt. and Decision-Making in the UN, 1986—87, Group on Rethinking Internat. Governance, 1986—90, Commn. on Global Governance, 1992—95, Carnegie Commn. on Preventing Deadly Conflict, 1994—. Bd. mem. Aspen Inst., Internat. Selection Commn. of the Philadelphia Liberty Medal, Carnegie Endowment for Internat. Peace, Aspen France, Coun. of African Advisors to the World Bank, Internat. Patrons of the Refugee Studies Programme, Oxford U., Aspen Italia; advisory com. Stockholm Internat. Peace Rsch. Inst.; bd. mem. Carnegie Corp. of NY, Hampshire Coll. Recipient Sydney Peace Prize, 2005. Office: UN Headquarters Rm S 3161 First Ave at 46th St New York NY 10017*

**OTWELL, RALPH MAURICE,** retired newspaper editor; b. Hot Springs, Ark., June 17, 1926; s. Walter Clement and Pearl Oda (Tisdale) O.; m. Janet Barbara Smith, July 18, 1953; children— Brian Thornton, Douglas Keith, David Smith. Student, U. Ark., 1947-48; BS, Northwestern U., 1951; postgrad. (Nieman fellow), Harvard, 1959-60. Reporter, telegraph editor So. Newspapers, Inc., Hot Springs, 1943-44, 47; asst. city editor Chgo. Sun-Times, 1953-59, news editor, 1959-63, asst. mng. editor, 1963-65, asst. to editor, 1965-68, mng. editor, 1968-76, editor, 1976-80, exec. v.p., editor, 1980-84. Mgmt. bd. newspaper div. Field Enterprises, Inc., 1967-84; lectr. Medill Sch. Journalism, Northwestern U., 1955— charter mem. Nat. News Coun. II, 1973 80; coord. Northwestern Inst. Learning in Retirement, 1992—. Trustee Garrett-Evang. Theol. Sem., 1965-79; Mem. nat. bd. Christian Social Concerns, United Meth. Ch., 1968-72; mem. bd. Community Renewal Soc., 1987-90, Chgo. Reporter, 1987-90, student publs. Northwestern U., 1968-72. Served to 1st lt. AUS, 1944-47, 51-53. Recipient Page One award Chgo. Newspaper Guild, 1964; named Ill. Journalist of Year No. Ill. U., 1974 Mem. Am. Soc. Newspaper Editors (chmn. ethics com. 1976-77), AP Mng. Editors Assn., Soc. Profl. Journalists (dir. 1966-71, sec. 1971-72, v.p. 1972-73, pres. 1973-74), Northwestern U. Alumni Assn. (dir. 1966-68, 91-93, sec. 1993-94, Merit award 1969, Svc. award 1995, chair seminar day com. 2001-2002), Sigma Delta Chi (pres. 1987-89), Kappa Tau Alpha, Econ. Club, Headline Club (pres. Chgo. chpt. 1965-66), Harvard Club Chgo., Chgo. Press Club (dir. 1968-77), Northwestern Club. Home: 2750 Hurd Ave Evanston IL 60201-1268 Personal E-mail: ralph@otwell.com.

**OU, YEN-CHUAN,** urologist; b. Taichung, Taiwan, Jan. 31, 1961; s. Wen-Guey and Haw (Jeng) Ou; m. Hui-Min Chen, Nov. 23, 1987; children: Hsien-Kuei, Hsien-Che, Hsien-Chi. B. Nat. Def. Med. Coll., Taipei, Taiwan, 1986. Resident Taichung Vets. Gen. Hosp., 1986—90, chief resident, 1990—91, urology specialist, 1991-92, 94—; chief urology Puli Vets. Hosp., Nan-Tou, Taiwan, 1993-94; rsch. assoc. U. Va., 1997—99, Inst. Medicine, Chung Shan Med. U., 2001—. Contbr. articles to profl. jours. Capt. Chinese Air Force, 1992-93. Nat. Sci. Coun. grantee, 1992. Mem. Urol. Assn. China, Assn. Andrology China, Surg. Assn. China. Mem. Nationalist Party. Avocations: ping pong/table tennis, basketball, travel, mountain climbing, music. Office: Taichung Vets Gen Hosp 160 SEc 3 Taichung-Kong Rd Taichung 407 Taiwan

**OUALLINE, VIOLA JACKSON,** psychologist, consultant; b. Edna, Tex., Oct. 17, 1927; d. S.R. Jackson and Myrtle Mae Wood; m. Charles M. Oualline Jr., Sept. 3, 1949; children: Stephen, Susan, Shari. BS, U. Houston, 1949; MS, North Tex. State U., 1962, PhD, 1975. Phys. therapist Herman Hosp., Houston, 1948-49; pvt. practice Austin, Tex., 1949-54; Miller Orthopedic Clinic, Charlotte, N.C., 1956-57; psychologist Dallas Easter Seal Soc., 1963-81, dir. psychology dept., 1981-93; pvt. practice, 1993—. Psychol. cons. Mesquite Ind. Sch. Dist., Tex., 1974—, Duncanville Sch. Dist., Tex., 1974-76, Grand Prairie Ind. Sch. Dist., Tex., 1976-79. Mem. Am. Psychol. Assn., Tex. Psychol. Assn., Dallas Psychol. Assn., Am. Assn. Counseling Devel., Coun.

for Exceptional Children, Chi Omega Mother's Club. Baptist. Avocations: reading, bicycle riding. Office: Site 208 11311 N Central Expy Dallas TX 75243-6729 Office Phone: 214-696-1079.

**OUDERKIRK, ANDREW J.,** corporate scientist; BS, No. Ill. U., 1978; PhD in Physical Chemistry, Northwestern U., 1983. With Universal Oil Products, DuPont; joined 3M Film and Light Mgmt., St. Paul, 1985, 3M corp. scientist. Mem.: NAE, Am. Chem. Soc. (Creative Invention Award 2004, Industrial Innovation Award 2003). Achievements include invention of 3M Multilayer Optical Film (MOF) technology. Office: 3M Corp Hdqs 3M Ctr Saint Paul MN 55144-1000*

**OUDIZ, RONALD,** cardiologist; MD, U. So.Calif., L.A., 1987—89. Diplomate Calif., 1989. Attending cardiologist Harbor-U.C.L.A. Med. Ctr., Torrance, 1995–2006. Home: 1124 W Carson St Torrance CA 90502 Office: 21840 S Normandie Ave Torrance CA 90502

**OULIANOV, DMITRI A.,** laser engineer; s. Natalia I. Oulianova and Anatoli M. Smolovich; m. Inessa D. Kobozeva, Nov. 18, 1995; 1 child, Angelina D. Oulianova. BS in Physics, Moscow Inst. Physics and Tech., Russia, 1995, MS in Applied Physics, 1997; PhD in Chemistry, U. Calif., Irvine, 2002. Postdoctoral fellow Argonne (Ill.) Nat. Lab., 2002—06; sr. product devel. engr. Spectra-Physics a Divsn. of Newport Corp., Mountain View, Calif., 2006—. Contbr. articles to profl. jours. Office: Spectra-Physics a Divsn Newport Corp 1335 Terra Bella Ave Mountain View CA 94043 Office Phone: 650-966-5833.

**OULTON, DONALD PAUL,** lawyer; b. Kingston, N.Y., July 22, 1930; s. Francis Terrance and Anne Agnes (Carrol) O.; m. Carol Jane Burke; children— David P., Nancy, Sarah, Carol. A.A. in Edn., Boston U., 1955; B.S. in Bus. Adminstrn., Boston U., 1958; J.D., Suffolk U., 1969. Bar: Mass. 1970, U.S. Dist. Ct. Mass. 1973, U.S. Supreme Ct. 1978, U.S. Ct. Appeals (1st cir.) 1980, U.S. Ct. Claims 1980, U.S. Tax Ct. 1980, U.S. Ct. Mil. Appeals 1981, U.S. Ct. Internat. Trade 1984, U.S. Ct. Appeals (fed. cir.) 1984. Contract negotiator Raytheon Corp., Bedford, Mass., 1959-65; chief negotiator claims Quincy Shipbldg. Div., Mass., 1965-72; assoc. div. counsel Quincy Shipbldg. 1970-72; asst. dist. atty. Middlesex County, Cambridge, Mass., 1972-75; contract negotiator Electronic Systems div. Office of Staff Judge Adv., U.S. Air Force, Hanscom AFB, Mass., 1974-76, chief atty. fgn. mil. sales, 1976-87; chief Internat. Law Br., 1987—2003. trial counsel Natick, Mass., Part-time, 1970—; real estate broker Mass. Realtors Assn., Boston, 1972—; ret. Air Force, 2003. Author: Inquests, 1973, Technology Transfer, 1983, Air Force Trivia, 1985, A Review of Executive Agreements From The Standpoint of Current Case Law, 1999, (with others) In Remembrance of Korea, 1987. Hearing officer Zoning Bd. Appeals, Natick, 1976; lectr. Western New Eng. Coll. Tchr. 9th grade, CCD, St. James Ch., Wellesley, Mass., 1976-83; bd. dirs., co-founder Shamrock Soc., Natick, Mass., 1976—; bd. dirs., counsel Little League, Natick, 1972-75, Mass. Korean War Meml. Com., 1988— Served with inf. U.S. Army, 1951-53, Korea. Named Outstanding Civilian Atty. of Yr., U.S. Air Force Systems Command, 1980; Outstanding Civilian Atty. of Yr., U.S. Air Force, Pentagon, 1980, Outstanding Civilian, Air Force Electronic Systems Div., 1983, US Senate Mil. & Govt. Svc. Honor, 2003. Mem. Am. Soc. Internat. Law, Air Force Assn., Middlesex Bar Assn., Mass. Bar Assn., Fed. Bar Assn., Mass. Police Chiefs Assn. Democrat. Roman Catholic. Club: Officers. Home: 54 Macarthur Rd Natick MA 01760-2938

**OUNDJIAN, PETER,** conductor, music director; b. Toronto, Canada; m. Nadine Oundjian; children: Lara, Peter. Grad. Royal Coll. Music, London; studied violin, Julliard Sch., NYC. First violinist Tokyo String Quartet, 1981—95; music dir. Nieuw Sinfonietta Amsterdam, 1998—2003; artistic dir., prin. condr. Caramoor Internat. Music Festival, Katonah, NY, 1995—; music dir. Toronto Symphony, 2004—. Vis. prof. Yale Sch. of Music; prin. guest condr. Colo. Symphony, 2003—; guest condr. San Francisco Symphony, Pitts. Symphony, Detroit Symphony, Houston Symphony, St. Louis Symphony, Nat. Symphony Orch., Cin. Symphony Orch., Konzerthaus, Berlin, City of Birmingham Symphony, NDR Hanover Symphony, Saarbrucken Radio Symphony, Zurich Tonhalle, Chgo. Symphony, LA Philharm.; guest artistic dir., condr. Mozart Festival; guest condr. Grand Teton Festival, 2005, Aspen Festival, 2005, Tanglewood Festivals, 2005. Recipient Gold medal for Most Disting. Student, Royal Coll. of Music, London, Stoutzker prize, First prize, Internat. Violin Competition in Vina Del Mar, Chile, 1980. Office: Toronto Symphony Orch 212 King St W, Ste 550 Toronto ON Canada M5H 1K5*

**OURISMAN, MANDELL J.,** automotive executive; b. Nov. 10, 1926; Student, U.S. Naval Acad., 1944, Georgetown U., 1947. Chmn., CEO Ourisman Automotive Enterprises, Marlow Heights, Md. Office: Ourisman Automotive Enterprises 4400 Branch Ave Temple Hills MD 20748-1802 Office Phone: 301-423-4028. Personal E-mail: mjo@ourismanchevrolet.com.

**OUROUSSOFF, NICOLAI,** architecture critic; Architecture critic LA Times, Calif., 1996—2004, NY Times, 2004—. Finalist 45th Ann. S. Cali. Journalism awards, 2003, Pulitzer Prize, 2003, 2004; recipient 46th Ann. S. Cali. Journalism awards, 2004. Office: NY Times Culture Desk 229 W 43rd St New York NY 10036 Office Phone: 212-556-1702. Office Fax: 212-556-1516.*

**OURSLER, FULTON, JR.,** editor, writer; b. West Falmouth, Mass., June 27, 1932; s. Fulton and Grace (Perkins) O.; m. Anne Noel Nevill, Nov. 29, 1954; children: Theresa Noel, Fulton III, Mark Nevill, James Randall, Carroll Grace. BA, Georgetown U., 1954. With Reader's Digest, Pleasantville, NY, 1956-87, book editor, 1968-70, sr. staff editor, 1970-72, asst. mng. editor, 1973, mng. editor, 1974-82, exec. editor, 1982-85, dep. editor-in-chief, 1986-87; editor-in-chief Guideposts mag., 1992—99; editor-in-chief, founding editor Angels on Earth mag., 1995-98, editl. dir., 1998-99; roving editor Guideposts mag., 2001—. Established: Fulton Oursler Meml. Collection, Georgetown U. Library.; editor: (commentary) Behold This Dreamer, 1964. Bd. dirs. Georgetown U. Library Assocs. Mem.: Friends of the Nyacks, Univ. Club. Home: 2 Laveta Pl Nyack NY 10960-1604 E-mail: tedlit@optonline.net. *Man makes two journeys in life: one in matter, the other in spirit. The first journey is outward and manifest; it leads to family, society, and career. The second journey is inward and invisible; it leads to the kingdom of God. The first journey is limited by logic, flesh, and time. The second is infinite, and its pathway is paradox. Self-preservation is the strongest instinct on the first journey; freedom, maturity, self-knowledge, power, and abundance seem to be important goals. But on the second journey, one learns that to find our truest selves, we must lose the sense of self; that to grow we must become as a child; that freedom is won by surrender, that the one counts for more than the many, that the meek are powerful, and the poor are rich. On both journeys, to gain life one must lose it, and be reborn.*

**OUSSANI, JAMES JOHN,** manufacturing executive; b. Bklyn., Jan. 3, 1920; s. John Thomas and Clara (Tager) Oussani; m. Lorraine G. Tutundgy, Apr. 25, 1954; children: James J., Gregory P., Rita C. BMechE, Pratt Inst., N.Y.C., 1942; JD (hon.), Lynn U., Boca Raton. Dir. rsch., mfg. Supertronic Co., N.Y.C., 1943—46; sr. ptnr. Perl-Oussani Machine Mfg. Co., NYC, 1946—49; founder Staplex Co., Bklyn., 1949, pres., 1949—. Exec. dir. Lourdes Realty Corp.; bd. dirs. Junios Corp.; prodr. air sampling equipment for radioactive fallout AEC, 1951—. Active Bur. Rsch. Air Pollution Control, Pres.'s Coun. on Youth Opportunity, Cardinal's Com. for Edn., Lumen Christi Found.; founder, bd. dirs. Oussani Found.; founder James J. & Lorraine G. Oussani Scholarship Coll. Boca Raton, Boca Raton; bd. overseers Lynn U., Boca Raton; trustee Ch. of Virgin Mary; founding mem. Lumen Christi-Palm Beach Diocese; cardinal's com. of laity, bishop's com. of laity; bd. dirs. St. Joan Arc Found., Boca Raton, Fla. Decorated knight of Jerusalem; recipient Blue Ribbon Mining award, Sch. Mgmt. award, Aerospace Pride Achievement award. Mem.: Office Equipment Assn., Nat. Stationery and Office Equipment Assn., Office Adminstrn. Assn., Adminstrv. Mgmt. Soc., Nat. Office Products Assn., Nat. Office Machine Dealers Assn.,

Nat. Office Machine Mfg. Assn., Office Execs. Assn., Bus. Equipment Mfrs. Assn., Our Lady Perpetual Help Holy Name Soc., Salaam Club, Mahopac Golf Club (Lake Mahopac, NY), Boca Raton Hotel and Resort Club, Internat. Club of Boca Raton, Knights of Holy Sepulchre, Knights of St. Gregory, Rotary, Knights of Malta. Achievements include invention of automatic electric stapling machine; patents in field. Home: 875 E Camino Real Boca Raton FL 33432

**OUSTERHOUT, DOUGLAS KENNETH,** plastic surgeon; b. Bellaire, Mich., Aug. 30, 1935; s. Kenneth and Naomi Ousterhout; children from previous marriage: Donald, Susan, Oliver, Thomas. Student, U. Colo., 1953—55; DDS, U. Mich., 1961, MD, 1965. Resident gen. surgery U. Med.; resident in plastic surgery Stanford U., Palo Alto, Calif., 1969—72; craniofacial tng. Dr. Tessier, Paris, 1972—73; clin. instr. U. Calif., San Francisco, 1973—86, clin. prof., 1986—. Editor: Aesthetic Contouring of the Craniofacial Skeleton, 1991; author: Cocktails for Two (AKA: Death Gets a Facelift), 1993. Capt. U.S. Army, 1966—68. Mem.: French Soc. Maxillofacial Surgeons, French Soc. Plastic, Reconstructive and Aesthetic Surgeons, Pan Pacific Surg. Assn. (pres. 1998—2000), Am. Soc. Maxillofacial Surgeons (pres. 1994—95), Internat. Soc. Craniofacial Surgeons, Am. Assn. Plastic Surgeons, Am. Soc. Plastic Surgeons, Equadorian Soc. Craniofacial Surgery (hon.), Japan Soc. Craniofacial Surgery (hon.). Avocations: piano, sculpting, gardening, travel. Home: 2640 Steiner St San Francisco CA 94115 Office: Ste 150 45 Castro St San Francisco CA 94114 Office Phone: 415-626-2888. E-mail: ousterht@cris.com.

**OUTCALT, DAVID LEWIS,** academic administrator, mathematics professor, consultant, musician; b. LA, Jan. 30, 1935; s. Earl Kinyon and Alberta Estes (Ferguson) Outcalt; m. Marcia Lee Beach, July 1, 1956 (dec.); children: Jeffrey David, Kevin Douglas, Gregory Mark, Eric Matthew. BA in Math., Pomona Coll., 1956; MA in Math., Claremont Grad. Sch., 1958; PhD in Math., Ohio State U., 1963; DPub in Adminstrn. (hon.), Kyung Hee U., Korea, 1984. Asst. prof. math. Clarement McKenna Coll., 1962-64; from asst. prof. to prof. U. Calif., Santa Barbara, 1964-80, chmn. dept. math., 1969-72, dean instrnl. devel., 1977-80; vice chancellor acad. affairs U. Alaska, Anchorage, 1980-81, prof. math., 1980-86, chancellor, 1981-86; prof. natural and applied sci. U. Wis., Green Bay, 1986-93, Hendrickson prof. econ. devel., 1994-98, chancellor, 1986—93, chancellor emeritus, 1998—. Pres. Mid-Continent Athletic Conf., 1990—91. Author: math. textbooks; contbr. articles to profl. jours. Mem. exec. bd. western Alaska coun. Boy Scouts Am., 1982—86, mem. exec. bd. Bay-Lakes Coun., 1987—97, v.p. exploring, 1988—92, v.p. ops., 1992—93, pres., 1993—94; mem. Anchorage Symphony Bd., 1986, Green Bay Symphony Bd., 1988—97, Weidner Ctr. Presents Bd., 1994—98; peer reviewer NCAA, 1994—99; trustee, v.p., treas. Kauai Internat. Theatre, 1998—2000; trustee Kauai CC Fund, 2000—05, trustee emeritus, 2005—; moderator bd. trustees Humana Hosp., Anchorage, 1982—83. Grantee, USAF Office Sci. Rsch., 1964—71, U. Calif., 1975—78, NSF, 1976—79. Mem.: Brown County Indsl. Devel. (pres. bd. dirs. 1994—97), Internat. Assn. Univ. Pres.'s (mem. exec. com. 1988—96, mem. N.Am. coun. exec. com. 1988—2002, newsletter editor 1994—95, mem. internat. com. tech. higher edn. 1996—2002), Math. Assn. Am., Greater Green Bay C. of C. (advance bd. 1987—97, bd. dirs. 1991—94, 1995—97), Rotary (bd. dirs. Kapaa club 1999—2004, pres. 2002—03, chair 2003—05, bd. dirs. Kapaa Found. 2003—05), Sigma Xi. Presbyn. Home: 1606 Palisades Dr Pacific Palisades CA 90272 Personal E-mail: outcaltd@verizon.net.

**OUTIN, MARY LOUISE,** business, multi-cultural history and geneology educator; b. Peak, S.C., July 18, 1948; d. Ralph T. Williams and Mary Frances Wicker-Outin, Theopolis Outin (Stepfather). BA in Bus. Adminstrn., Columbia Coll., Columbia, South Carolina, 1987; MEd, Lesley U., 1999; grad., S.C. Sch. Real Estate, 1986. Owner MO Businesses, Inc., Columbia, 2000—. N/A. Mem.: S.C. Afro-Am. Hist. and Geneal. Soc., Inc. (co-pub. rels. dir. 1998—2000), Am. Legion Aux. (Unit 219 2000). Avocations: family history research, genealogy, cooking, reading. Office: MO Businesses Inc P O Box 3393 Columbia SC 29230

**OUTLAW, LANNY F.,** gas company executive; B in Engring., S.D. Sch. Mines and Tech. Various positions Shell Oil Co., 1958-87, Western Gas Resources, Inc., Denver, 1987-96, exec. v.p. ops., bus. devel. and engring., pres., COO, 1996-99, CEO, pres., 1999—.

**OUTLAW, WANDA CECELIA,** priest; b. Washington, Oct. 17, 1954; d. Augustus King and Mary Lena (Booze) Brown; 1 child, Stephen Thomas Jr. Ordained priest 2002. Tng. mgr. Bur. ATF, Washington, 1989—; leadership, women's retreat leader African-Am. Cath. Congregation, Washington, 1993—, priest, 2002—. Preacher Women Uplifting Women Ministries, Washington, 2003—; designer, trainer LJR Group, Inc., Dallas, 2005—. Author: Woven Baskets on the Baobab Tree, In The Fulfillment. Active socks and sandwiches for the homeless Dynamic Crossroads, Washington, 2005; motivational spkr. Execs. of FEW, Balt., 2003—04. Mem.: NAACP (assoc.), NAFE (assoc.). Office: Imani Temple on Capitol Hill 609-611 Maryland Ave NE Washington DC 20002 Office Phone: 202-388-8155, Personal E-mail: wanda.outlaw@atf.gov. Business E-mail: noni.crowmother@verizon.net.

**OUTOLA, IISA EMMA JANIKA,** research scientist; b. Tuusula, Finland, Feb. 21, 1974; d. Rauno and Sinikka Maria Riekkinen; m. Petri Olavi Outola; 1 child, Max Olavi. MSc, U. Helsinki, Finland, 1997, PhD, 2002. Rsch. asst. Finnish Inst. Marine Rsch., Helsinki, 1995—97; rsch. scientist U. Helsinki, 1997—2002, Nat. Inst. Stds. and Technologies/U. Md., Gaithersburg, 2002—. Recipient Outstanding Doctoral Thesis award, U. Helsinki, 2002. Office: NIST 100 Bureau Dr Gaithersburg MD 20899 Office Phone: 301-975-4979.

**OUTWATER, JOHN OGDEN,** mechanical engineering educator; b. London, Jan. 2, 1923; came to U.S., 1924; s. John Ogden and Nenny (Boe) O.; m. Alice Hooker Davidson, Dec. 13, 1952; children— Anne Hooker, Catherine Boe (Mrs. Carl B. Colby), Rachel Brookfield (Mrs. Robert B. Lang), John Ogden III. BA, Cambridge U., Eng., 1943, MA, 1948; ScD, MIT, 1950; PhD, Cambridge, Eng., 1976. Registered profl. engr. Research engr. DuPont Co., 1950-52; project engr. Universal Moulded Products, 1952-53; indsl. liaison officer Mass. Inst. Tech., 1954-55; prof. mech. engring. U. Vt., Burlington, 1955—71, chmn., 1955-93, prof. emeritus, 1993—. Leader archaeol. expdns. Wenner-Gren Found., Central Mexico, 1954, Yucatan, 1955, Peru-Bolivia, 1957, Haiti, 1959; cons. non-metallic materials Naval Ordnance Lab., Nat. Acad. Scis., Monsanto Rsch. Corp., Smithsonian Instn., pres., Vt. Inst. Co., Inc. Author: (with others) Engineering Materials, 1959, Esplendor del Mexico Antigua; papers on metal cutting, plastics, archaeology, bones, ski safety, botany. Chmn. Vt. Instrument Co., Inc.; Mem. Vt. Conf. Econ. Growth; vestryman St. Paul's Cathedral, Burlington. Served as officer Brit. Army, 1943-47. Named Vt. Engr. of Year, 1970; grantee USPHS; Timken fellow MIT, 1950 Fellow ASME; mem. ASTM, Holland Soc., Vt. Soc. Engrs., Delta Psi, Tau Beta Pi. Achievements include patents for ski boot tension. Home: 62 Overlake Park Burlington VT 05401-4012 Office: 321 S Union St Burlington VT 05401-4595 Personal E-mail: jooutwater@aol.com.

**OUYANG, ANLI,** research scientist; s. Ouyang. PhD, Ohio State U., 2006. Rsch. assoc. East China U. Sci. and Tech., Shanghai, 1999—2002, Ohio State U., Columbus, 2002—. Recipient Chem. Engring. Grad. Student award Outstanding Acad. Achievements, Ohio State U., 2005; Tchg. Assoc. Excellence award, 2005; fellow, 2002—03, 2005—06. Mem.: AICE (assoc.), Am. Chem. Soc. (assoc.). Achievements include invention of Mass production of embryonic stem cells in fibrous bed bioreactor. Office: Ohio State U 140 West 19th Ave Columbus OH 43210 Office Phone: 614-292-4514.

**OUYANG, JUN,** electrical engineer, researcher; s. Shi Ouyang and Jinbing Peng; m. Hong Cai, July 31, 2005. PhD, U. Md., College Park, 2000—05. Grad. tchg. asst. Stevens Inst. Tech., Hoboken, NJ, 1999—2000, U. Md., 2000—01, grad. rsch. asst., 2001—05; sr. elec. integration engr. Seagate Tech., Rec. Head Operation, Bloomington, Minn., 2005—. Product devel., quality control Seagate Tech., 2005—. Contbr. papers to profl. jours. and

pubs. V.p., coord. of entertainment activities Chinese Student and Scholar Assn., U. Md., 2002—03. Named Outstanding Grad. Student Employee of Yr., U. Md., 2005; recipient Chinese Govt. award outstanding rsch., 2005. Mem.: Minerals, Metals & Materials Soc., Am. Soc. Metals, Materials Rsch. Soc., Am. Ceramic Soc. (First and second prizes ceramographic competition 2005). Office: Seagate Tech 7801 Computer Ave S Mailstop: NRW112 Bloomington MN 55435 Office Phone: 952-402-7926. Office Fax: 952-402-7063. Personal E-mail: jouyang2002@yahoo.com. Business E-mail: jun.ouyang@seagate.com.

**OUYANG, NORMA M.,** psychologist; arrived in U.S., 1985; m. Steve C. Ouyang, Jan. 1, 1970; children: Francis, Luke. BA, Nat. Taiwan Normal U., 1970; MBA, Pacific State U., 1988; MA, Azusa Pacific U., 1998, D of Psychology, 2003. Clin. psychologist Calif. Bd. Psychology. Founder, cons. Family Enrichment, Irvine, Calif., 1988—; with Orange County Health Care Agy., Westminster, 1999; intern U. Calif., Riverside, 2002—03; clin. psychologist Calif. State U., Fullerton, 2004—. Sr. group coord. Orange County Chimes Cath. Assn., Anaheim, Calif., 1989—93; asst. gen. mgr. Valone Computer Co., Irvine, 1988—93. Fellow, Calif. State U., Fullerton, 2003—04. Mem.: APA, Asian Faculty/Staff Assn., Am. Coll. Personnel Assn. Democrat. Roman Catholic. Avocations: reading, music, writing, travel.

**OUZTS, DAVID PERRY,** church music director, organist; b. Greenville, S.C., Nov. 30, 1962; s. Perry Cooper and Sara Owens Ouzts; life ptnr. Joseph Lee Middleton, Oct. 8, 1995. MusB, Furman U., Greenville, S.C., 1985; MusM, diploma in Sacred Music, diploma in Anglican studies, Yale U., 1987. Organist, choirmaster Trinity Episcopal Ch., Huntington, W.Va., 1987—90; dir. of music Congregation B'nai Sholom, Huntington, W.Va., 1988—90; assoc. dir. of music and fine arts St. Luke's United Meth. Ch., Houston, 1990—96; canon musician, liturgist Grace Episcopal Cathedral, Topeka, 1996—2001; dir. of music Ch. of Holy Communion, Memphis, 2001—. Liturgy and music cons. Episcopal Diocese of W.Va., Charleston, 1988—90; commn. on liturgy and music Episcopal Diocese of Kans., Topeka, 1997—2001; music dir. Memphis Girls Choir, 2002—. Mem. Rotary Club, Huntington, W.Va., 1987—89. Named to Order of Ky. Colonels, Commonwealth of Ky., 1989; Homozel Mickel Daniel Music scholarship, Furman U., 1981-85, Grad. Assistantship in Sacred Music, Yale Inst. of Sacred Music, 1985-87, Grad. Assistantship in Organ, Ind. U., 1990. Mem.: Hymn Soc. in the US and Can., Choristers Guild, Assn. of Diocesan Liturgy and Music Commns., Am. Recorder Soc., Am. Guild of English Handbell Ringers, Am. Choral Dirs. Assn., Royal Sch. of Ch. Music, Assn. of Anglican Musicians, Organ Hist. Soc., Am. Guild of Organists (dean 1988—90). Episcopalian. Avocations: walking, history, computers. Office: Church of Holy Communion 4645 Walnut Grove Rd Memphis TN 38117-2597 Business E-mail: douzts@holycommunion.org.

**OUZTS, EUGENE THOMAS,** minister, secondary education educator; b. Thomasville, Ga., June 7, 1930; s. John Travis and Livie Mae (Strickland) O.; m. Mary Olive Vineyard, May 31, 1956. BA, Harding U., Searcy, AR, 1956, MA, 1957; postgrad., Murray State U., KY, U. Ark., U. Ariz., Ariz. State U., No. Ariz. U. Cert. secondary tchr., Ark., Mo., Ariz.; cert. c.c. tchr., Ariz.; ordained minister Church of Christ, 1956. Min. various chs., Ark., Tex., Mo., 1957—65; tchr. various pub. schs., 1959—92; min. Ch. of Christ, Ariz., 1965—; 1st lt. CAP/USAF, 1980, advanced through grades to lt. col., 1989, chaplain Ariz., 1982—; asst. wing chaplain, 1985—. Adviser student activities Clifton (Ariz.) Pub. Schs., 1965-92; bd. dirs. Ariz. Ch. of Christ Bible Camp, Tucson, 1966-2005. Mem. airport adv. bd. Greenlee County, Clifton, Ariz., 1992—. Recipient Meritorious Svc. award, 1994, Exceptional Svc. award, 1997, Civil Air Patrol; named Ariz. Wing Chaplain of Yr 1984, Thomas C. Casaday Unit Chaplain of Yr., 1985, Ariz. Wing Safety Officer of Yr., 1989, Ariz. Wing Sr. Mem. of Yr., 1994, Southwest Region Sr. Mem. of Yr., 1995, Civil Air Patrol. Mem. Mil. Chaplains Assn., Air Force Assn., Disabled Am. Vets., Am. Legion, Elks. Democrat. Avocations: flying, building and flying model aircraft, reading. Home and Office: 739 E Cottonwood Rd Duncan AZ 85534-8108

**OVADIAH, JANICE,** not-for-profit developer, cultural organization administrator; m. Isaac Ovadiah; children: Meir Benjamin, Simha Victoria Miriam. BA, Washington U., St. Louis, 1965; MA, Columbia U., 1967, PhD, 1978. Dir. profl. study tours Am. Odysseys, Inc., 1973-84; escort, interpreter in French U.S. Dept. State, 1978-84; asst. to exec. dir. Meml. Found. for Jewish Culture, 1984-87; exec. dir. Congregation Shearith Israel/The Spanish & Portuguese Syn., N.Y.C., 1987—; Sephardic House, N.Y.C., 1987—2003; freelance cons., 2003—. Instr. French Rutgers U., New Brunswick, N.J., 1978-79; asst. to dir. of The Maison Franclase, Columbia U., 1970-72; instr. French Columbia U., 1968-70; lectr. in field. Author: (books) Toward a Concept of Cinematic Literature: An Analysis of Hiroshima, Mon Amour, 1983, The Far Away Island of the Grey Lady, 1979, others; contbr. articles to profl. jours. E-mail: jovadiah@aol.com.

**OVAERT, TIMOTHY CHRISTOPHER,** mechanical engineering educator; b. Chgo., Apr. 30, 1959; s. Walter Allen and Joyce Ann (Collins) O.; m. Valerie Mora, July 16, 1988; children: Teresa Noel, Christina Lynn. BSME, U. Ill., 1981; MEM, Northwestern U., 1985, PhD, 1989. Plant engr. Wells Mfg. Co.-Dura Bar Div., Woodstock, Ill., 1981-85; mech. engr. Nat. Inst. of Standards and Tech., Gaithersburg, Md., 1986; asst. prof. Penn State U., 1989-95; assoc. prof. Pa. State U., 1995-2000, prof., 2000, U. Notre Dame, Ind., 2000—. Assoc. editor ASME Trans., Jour. Tribology, 1998—2003. Traffic safety com. Borough of State College, Pa., 1992. Named Nat. Young Investigator, NSF, 1992. Office: U Notre Dame 374 Fitzpatrick Hall Notre Dame IN 46556 Office Phone: 574-631-9371.

**OVECHKIN, ALEXANDER,** professional hockey player; b. Moscow, Sept. 17, 1985; s. Tatiana and Mikhail. Left wing Dynamo Moscow (Russian Super League), Moscow, 2001—05, Wash. Capitals, 2005—. Left wing Team Russia, World Junior Championships, 2003—05, Team Russia, World Championships, 2004, 05, Team Russia, World Cup of Hockey, 2004; mem. Team Russia, Olympic Games, Torino, Italy, 2006. Named to First All-Star Team, NHL, 2006; recipient Calder Meml. Trophy, 2006. Achievements include being a member of gold medal Team Russia, World Junior Championships, 2003; being the first overall draft pick in NHL entry draft, 2004. Office: c/o Washington Capitals MCI Center 601 F Street NW Washington DC 20004*

**OVERBEY, KELLIE LYN,** actress; b. Cin., Nov. 21, 1964; d. George Edward and Jacquelyn (Arvin) Overbey. BS in Speech, Northwestern U., Evanston, Ill., 1986. Actress (Broadway plays) Buried Child, 1996, Present Laughter, 1996, Judgment at Nuremberg, 2001, QED, 2001, Twentieth Century, 2004, The Music Teacher, 2006, (off-Broadway plays) The Debutante Ball, Betty's Summer Vacation, Comic Potential, Gone Home, Hamlet, (plays) Bargains, Speed-The-Plow, New York Theatre, Melville Boys, Face Divided, The Second Coming, Mud People, (films) Misplaced, 1989, Defenseless, 1991, Outbreak, 1995, 35 Miles from Normal, 1997, Sweet & Lowdown, 1999, Love Thy Neighbor, 2002, (TV films) Equal Justice, 1990, Wife, Mother, Murderer, 1991, The Hunt for the Unicorn Killer, 1999, (TV series) That's Life, 1998, The Guiding Light, 1999—2000, (TV miniseries) The Stand, 1994. Avocation: knitting designer.*

**OVERBY, OSMUND RUDOLF,** art historian, educator; b. Mpls., Nov. 8, 1931; s. Oscar Rudolph and Gertrude Christine (Boe) O.; m. Barbara Ruth Spande, Mar. 20, 1954; children: Paul, Katherine, Charlotte. BA, St. Olaf Coll., 1953; B.Arch., U. Wash., 1958; MA, Yale U., 1960, PhD, 1963. Asst. in instruction dept. of history of art Yale U., 1959—62; rsch. architect Hist. Am. Bldgs. Survey, U.S. Nat. Park Service, 1960-61, summers 1959, 62, 63, 65, 68, 69, 70, 73, 85; lectr. dept. fine arts U. Toronto, Ont., Canada, 1963-64; faculty dept. art history and archaeology U. Mo., Columbia, 1964—, dept. chmn., 1967-70, 75-77, prof. art history, 1979-98, prof. emeritus, 1998—, dir. Mus. of Art and Archaeology, 1977-83. Vis. prof. dept. architecture U. Calif., Berkeley, 1980; Morgan prof. U. Louisville, 1989; vis. prof. dept. art history and archaeology Washington U., St. Louis, 1996; bd. advisors Nat. Trust for

Hist. Preservation, 1974-83; cons., panelist Nat. Endowment for Humanities, 1974—; bd. Mo. Mansion Preservation Commn., 1974-87; advisor Heritage/St. Louis Survey, 1974-76; counsellor to St. Louis Landmarks Assn. 1977—; chmn. Task Force on Hist. Preservation City of Columbia, 1977-78; cons. on hist. preservation; active Mo. Adv. Council on Hist. Preservation, 1967-82; lectr., exhibitor profl. confs. in field Author: Historic American Buildings Survey, Rhode Island Catalog, 1972, William Adair Bernoudy, Architect, Bringing the Legacy of Frank Lloyd Wright to St. Louis, 1999; co-author: Laclede's Landing, a History and Architectural Guide, 1977, The Saint Louis Old Post Office, A History and Architectural Guide to the Building and Its Neighborhood, 1979; co-author, editor: Illustrated Museum Handbook, A Guide to the Collections in the Museum of Art and Archaeology, University of Missouri-Columbia, 1982; editor in chief Buildings of the United States series, 1990-96; contrb. sects. to books, articles to profl. publs. in field. Served with U.S. Army, 1953-55. Recipient various fellowships and grants in field. Mem. Soc. Archtl. Historians (bd. dirs. 1968-73, 78-81, Jour. editor 1968-73, dir. Mo. Valley chpt., session chmn. ann. meeting 1976, v.p. 1982-86, pres. 1986-88, chmn. coms.), Mid-Continent Am. Studies Assn. (editorial bd. American Studies 1965-70), Midwest Art History Soc. (bd. 1975-78, gen. chmn. annual meeting 1977), Mid-Am. Coll. Art Assn. (session chmn. annual meeting 1975), Mo. Heritage Trust (pres. 1976-79, 81-83, bd. dirs. 1979—), Coll. Art Assn., Landmarks Assn. St. Louis. Lutheran. Home: 1118 W Rollins Rd Columbia MO 65203-2221 Office: U Mo Dept Art History & Archaeolo Columbia MO 65211-0001 Office Phone: 573-442-7882. Business E-Mail: overbyo@missouri.edu.

**OVERBYE, DAVID LAWRENCE,** dean, researcher; s. Vern Donald and Dorothy Ann Overbye; m. Lori Ann Nelson, Jan. 10, 1981; 1 child, Diane Marie. BSEE, U. Wis.; MSEE, MBA, U. Wis., Milw.; PhD in Elec. Engring., U. Ill., Chgo. Registered prof. engr., State of Wis., 1981. Various engr. and mgmt. Electric Utility Industry, Wis., 1981—93; faculty Keller Grad. Sch. Mgmt., Milw., 1988, program dir., 1993—96, dir. curriculum Oakbrook Terrace, Ill., 1996—2000, dir. acad. affairs, 2000—02; dean curriculum DeVry U., 2002—. Contrb. articles to profl. jours. Mem.: IEEE, Project Mgmt. Inst. Lutheran. Office: DeVry U One Tower Ln Oakbrook Terrace IL 60181 Office Phone: 630-990-1893. Office Fax: 630-574-1969. E-mail: doverbye@devry.edu.

**OVERGAARD, CORDELL JERSILD,** lawyer, rancher, director; b. Chgo., June 1, 1934; s. Kristin and Rose Marie (Jersild) Overgaard; m. Gail A. Gill, Sept. 5, 1959; children: Diane, Karen, Susan. BS with honors, U. Ill., 1957; LLB magna cum laude, Harvard U., 1960. CPA Ill.; bar: Ill. 1960. Assoc. Hopkins & Sutter, Chgo., 1960—67, ptnr., 1967—96, chmn. bus. fin. sect.; chmn., CEO SNG Internet Innovations LLC, 2005—. Dir. mem. exec. com. UPI, Inc., 1982—83; pres. Cmty. Cablevision, Inc., 1980—86, Gore-Overgaard Broadcasting, Inc., 1986—; pres. bd. trustees NorthCare, 1979—81; sec. Family Weekly, Inc., 1976—80; dir. Prudential Health Care Plan, Inc., 1980—89, Cahners Pub. Co., 1970—74; dir. v.p. Small Newspaper Group, Inc., 1981—; prin. mem. Rancho Paso Grande LLC (Rancho-PasoGrande.com); exec. com. mem. Paso Fino Horse Assn., 2005—. Editor: Harvard Law Rev., 1960. Mem. Ill. Bd. Ethics, 1976, chmn., 1976—80. Mem.: Chgo. Bar Assn. (chmn. corp. law com. 1972—73), February Group, Alpha Delta Phi, Beta Alpha Psi, Beta Gamma Sigma. Home: 11310 E Arabian Park Dr Scottsdale AZ 85259-4913

**OVERGAARD, WILLARD MICHELE,** retired political scientist; b. Montpelier, Idaho, Oct. 16, 1925; s. Elias Nielsen and Myrtle LaVerne (Humphrey) O.; m. Lucia Clare Cochrane, June 14, 1946; children: Eric Willard, Mark Fredrik, Alisa Claire. BA, U. Oreg., 1949; MA, U. Wis., 1955; PhD in Polit. Sci., U. Minn., 1969. Instr., Soviet and internat. affairs Intelligence Sch., U.S. Army, Europe, 1956-62, dir. intelligence rsch. tng. program, 1958-61; asst. prof. internat. affairs George Washington U., 1964-67; sr. staff polit. scientist Ops. Rsch. Inst., U.S. Army Inst. Advanced Studies, Carlisle, Pa., 1967-70; assoc. prof. polit. sci., chmn. dept., dir. Internat. Studies Inst., Westminster Coll., New Wilmington, Pa., 1970-72; prof. polit. sci. and pub. law Boise (Idaho) State U., 1972-94, chmn. dept., 1972-87, acad. dir. M.P.A. degree program, pers. adminstr., mem. humanities coun. interdisciplinary studies in humanities, 1976-87, prof. of pub. law emeritus, 1994—, dir. Taft Inst. Seminars for Pub. Sch. Tchrs., 1985-87, coord. Legal Asst. Program, 1990-95. Mem. comml. panel Am. Arbitration Assn., 1974—; mem. Consortium for Idaho's Future, 1974-75; adv. com. Idaho Statewide Tng. Program Local Govt. Ofcls., 1974-78; adv. group Gov. Idaho Task Force Local Govt., 1977; co-dir. Idaho State Exec. Inst., Office of Gov., 1979-83; grievance hearing officer City of Boise, 1981-85; arbitrator U.S. Postal Svc., 1988-90; cons. in field. Author: The Schematic System of Soviet Totalitarianism, 3 vols, 1961, Legal Norms and Normative Bases for the Progressive Development of International Law as Defined in Soviet Treaty Relations, 1945-64, 1969; co-author: The Communist Bloc in Europe, 1959; editor: Continuity and Change in International Politics, 1972; chief editor: Idaho Jour. Politics, 1974-76. Served with USAAF, 1943-45; with AUS, 1951-54; ret. maj. USAR. Named Disting. Citizen of Idaho, Idaho Statesman, 1979; Fulbright scholar, U. Oslo, 1949—50, Non-resident scholar, U. Wis., 1954—55, Adminstrv. fellow, U. Minn., 1955—56, Rsch. fellow, 1962—64. Mem. ABA (assoc.), Res. Officers Assn. (life), Am. Legion. Home: 2023 S Five Mile Rd Boise ID 83709-2316 Personal E-mail: wgaard@velocitus.net.

**OVERHAUSER, ALBERT WARNER,** physicist; b. San Diego, Aug. 17, 1925; s. Clarence Albert and Gertrude Irene (Pehrson) Overhauser; m. Margaret Mary Casey, Aug. 25, 1951; children: Teresa, Catherine, Joan, Paul, John, David, Susan, Steven. AB, U. Calif., Berkeley, 1948, PhD, 1951; DSc (hon.), U. Chgo., 1979; LLD (hon.), Simon Fraser U., 1998; DSc (hon.), Purdue U., 2005. Rsch. assoc. U. Ill., 1951-53; asst. prof. physics Cornell U., 1953—56, assoc. prof. 1956—58; supr. solid state physics Ford Motor Co., Dearborn, Mich., 1958—62, mgr. theoret. scis., 1962—69, asst. dir. phys. scis., 1969—72, dir. physics sci., 1972—73; prof. physics Purdue U., West Lafayette, Ind., 1973—74, Stuart disting. prof. physics, 1974—2004, Stuart disting. prof. emeritus, 2004—. With USNR, 1944—46. Recipient Alexander von Humboldt sr. U.S. scientist award, 1979, Nat. medal of Sci., Pres. of U.S., 1994. Fellow: Am. Acad. Arts and Scis., Am. Phys. Soc. (Oliver E. Buckley Solid State Physics prize 1975); mem.: NAS. Home: 236 Pawnee Dr West Lafayette IN 47906-2115 Office: Purdue U Dept Of Physics West Lafayette IN 47907 Office Phone: 765-494-3037. Business E-Mail: awo@physics.purdue.edu.

**OVERHOLT, HUGH ROBERT,** lawyer, retired military officer; b. Beebe, Ark., Oct. 29, 1933; s. Harold R. and Cuma E. (Hall) O.; m. Laura Annell Arnold, May 5, 1961; children: Sharon, Scott. Student, Coll. of Ozarks, 1951-53; BA, U. Ark., 1955, LL.B., 1957. Bar: Ark. 1957. Commd. 1st lt. U.S. Army, 1957, advanced through grades to maj. gen., 1981; chief Criminal Law Div., JAG Sch., Charlottesville, Va., 1971-73; chief personnel, plans and tng. Office of JAG, U.S. Army, Washington, 1973-75; staff judge adv. XVIII Airborne Corps, Ft. Bragg, NC, 1976-78; spl. asst. for legal and selected policy matters Office of Dep. Asst., 1978-79; asst. judge adv. gen. for mil. law Office of JAG, Washington, 1979-81, asst. judge adv. gen., 1981-85, judge adv. gen., 1985-89; atty. Ward & Smith, New Bern, NC, 1989—. Notes and comment editor Ark. Law Rev, 1956-57. Decorated Army Meritorious Service medal with oak leaf cluster, Army Commendation medal with 2 oak leaf clusters, Legion of Merit, Def. Meritorious Service medal, D.S.M. Mem. ABA, N.C. Bar Assn., Ark. Bar Assn., Assn. U.S. Army, Delta Theta Phi, Omicron Delta Kappa, Sigma Pi. Presbyterian. Office: Ward and Smith 1001 College Ct New Bern NC 28562-4972 Office Phone: 252-672-5462. Business E-Mail: hro@wardandsmith.com.

**OVERMAN, DEAN LEE,** lawyer, investor, writer; b. Cook County, Ill., Oct. 9, 1943; s. Harold Levon and Violet Elsa (True) O.; m. Linda Jane Olsen, Sept. 6, 1969; children: Elisabeth True, Christiana Hart. BA, Hope Coll., 1965; student, Princeton Sem. and U., 1965-66; JD, U. Calif., Berkeley, 1969; postgrad. in econs., U. Chgo., 1974, U. Calif. Bar: Ill. 1969, D.C. 1977. Law clk. to ptnr. D'Ancona, Pflaum et al., Chgo., 1970-75; White House fellow, asst. to v.p. Nelson Rockefeller, Washington, 1975-76; assoc. dir. Domestic

Council The White House, Washington, 1976-77; sr. ptnr. Winston & Strawn, Washington, 1977—. Cons. White House; spl. counsel to Gov. James Thompson, Springfield, Ill.; adj. faculty in secured financing U. Va. Law Sch., Charlottesville; vice chmn. J.F. Forstmann Co.; chmn. Holland Investment Co.; adj. fellow Ctr. for Strategic and Internat. Studies, 1993-95; vis. scholar, officer Harvard U., 1994-95; Templeton scholar Oxford U., 1999—2005, chmn. adv. bd. First Trust Portfolios, LP Author: Toward a National Policy on State and Local Government Finance, 1976, Effective Writing Techniques, 1980, (with others) Financing Equipment, 1973, Sales and Financing Under the Revised UCC, 1975, A Case Against Accident and Self Organization, 1997; monthly newspaper column Chgo. Daily Law Bull.; contrb. articles to profl. jours. Commencement spkr. Hope Coll., Holland, Mich., 1978; bd. dirs. Internat. Bus. Inst., White House Fellows Assn., Cmtys. in Schs., Inc.; adv. bd. The Beacon Group; former bd. dirs. U.S. Decathlon Assn. Reginald Heber Smith fellow U. Pa., 1969-70. Mme. Mensa, Intertel, ABA, Ill. Bar Assn., D.C. Bar Assn., Chgo. Bar Assn., Met. Club (D.C.), Internat. Philos. Enquiry, Triple Nine Soc., Burning Tree Club (Bethesda, Md.), Congl. Country Club (Bethesda), Harvard Club of N.Y.C., Macatawa (Mich.) Bay Yacht Club. Office: Glen Brook 4900 GlenGrook Rd NW Washington DC 20016

**OVERMIER, J. BRUCE,** psychology professor; s. James J. Wheelwright and Emma Annette (Carlton) Jacobson; m. Judith Ann Smith, Aug. 19, 1962; 1 child, Larisa Nicole. BA, Kenyon Coll., 1960; MA, Bowling Green State U., 1962; PhD, U. Pa., 1965; DSc (hon.), Kenyon Coll., 1990. Prof. psychology U. Minn., Mpls., 1965—. Mem. adv. bd. NSF, Washington, 1976-79, 86, USPHS, Washington, 1988-92. Author: (with others) Animal Learning: Survey and Analysis, 1979; editor: Affect, Conditioning and Cognition, 1985; cons. editor Jour. Exptl. Psychology, 1971-74, 88-2004; editor: Animal Research and Human Health, 2001; editor Learning and Motivation, 1973-76; mem. editl. bd. Behavioral Brain Rsch., 1979-84, Am. Psychologist, 1994-2000, Internat. Jour. Psychology, 1993-97; contrb. chpts. to books and articles to mags Grantee NIMH/NICHD, 1966-2003, NSF, 1966-83, 87-93; Fulbright Hays scholar, 1980, Scholar of the Coll., U. Minn., 1989-92; Fogarty Ctr. USPHS fellow, 1984, James McKeen Cattell Found. fellow, 1985, Joseph P. Kennedy found. fellow, 1989; recipient W. Horsely Gantt medal Pavlovian Soc., 2003, Outstanding Contributions award Minn. Psychol. Assn., 2004 Fellow APA (council 1987-97, pres. divsn. comparative psychology 1991, pres. divsn. experimental psychology 1993, bd. dirs. 1999-2004 pres. divsn. gen. psychology 2003, Disting. Svc. award 2005); mem. AAUP (local pres. 1981), Midwestern Psychol. Assn. (council 1984-87, pres. 1987), Psychonomics Soc. (sec.-treas. 1981-83, bd. govs. 1983-88), Internat. Union Psychological Sc. (exec. 1993-2004, pres. 2004—), Delta Kappa Epsilon Avocation: skiing. Office: Psychology Dept Univ Minn 75 East River Terr Minneapolis MN 55455 Office Phone: 612-625-1835. Office Fax: 612-626-2079. E-mail: psyjbo@umn.edu.

**OVERMYER, DANIEL LEE,** humanities educator; b. Columbus, Ohio, Aug. 20, 1935; s. Elmer Earl and Bernice Alma (Hesselbart) O.; m. Estella Velazquez, June 19, 1965; children: Rebecca Lynn, Mark Edward. BA, Westmar Coll., LeMars, Iowa, 1957; BD, Evang. Theol. Sem., Naperville, Ill., 1960; MA, U. Chgo., 1966, PhD, 1971. Pastor Evangel. United Brethren Ch., Chgo., 1960-64; asst. prof. dept. religion Oberlin (Ohio) Coll., 1971-73; prof. Asian studies U. B.C., Vancouver, Canada, 1973—2000, acting head religious studies, 1984-85, head Asian studies, 1986-91, prof. emeritus, 2000—. Vis. prof. Princeton (N.J.) U., 1983, U. Heidelberg, Heidelberg, Germany, 1993, Nat. Chengchi U., Taiwan, 2002; prof. Chinese U., Hong Kong, 1996—98; hon. prof. Shanghai Normal U., China, 1997—. Author: Folk Buddhist Religion, 1976, 2005, Religions of China, 1986; author: (with David Jordan) The Flying Phoenix, 1986; author: Precious Volumes: An Introduction to Chinese Sectarian Scriptures From the Sixteenth and Seventeenth Centuries, 1999; editor: Ethnography in China Today: A Critical Assessment of Methods and Results, 2002, Religion in China Today, 2003; editor spl. issue: The China Quar.; contrb. articles to encys. and profl. jours. Chmn. Sch. Consultative Com., Vancouver, 1976-77; coord. Vancouver Boys Soccer League, 1979-81; adult edn. coord. United Ch. Can., Vancouver, 1981-84; co-chmn. Endowment Lands Regional Park Com., 1987-90; co-chair China and Inner Asia Coun., Assn. Asian Studies, 1992—. With USNR, 1953-61. Recipient Killam faculty rsch. prize U. B.C., 1986, Killiam faculty tchg. prize, 2000; named Alumnus of Yr., U. Chgo. Divinity Sch., 2001; NEH fellow, 1978, 79, China Rsch. fellow, 1981, sr. fellow coun. humanities Princeton U., 1983, Wang Inst. Grad. Studies fellow, 1985-86. Fellow Royal Soc. Can.; mem. Am. Soc. Study Religion, Soc. Study Chinese Religions (pres. 1985-88), Assn. Asian Studies. Democrat. Methodist. Avocations: photography, swimming, hiking, gardening, birdwatching. Home: 3393 W 26th Ave Vancouver BC Canada V6S 1N4 Office: UBC Ctr Chinese Rsch Vancouver BC Canada V6T 1Z2 E-mail: eodano@shaw.ca.

**OVERMYER-VELAZQUEZ, MARK,** history professor; b. Chgo., July 22, 1970; s. Daniel Lee and Estella (Velazquez) Overmyer; life ptnr. Jordanna Hertz, Aug. 23, 1998; children: Sarai Dov Hertz-Velazquez, Maceo Ilan Hertz-Velazquez. BA, U. B.C., 1993; MA, MPhil, PhD, Yale U., 2002. Asst. prof. history U. Conn., Storrs, 2004—. Contbr. monographs. Doctoral Fellow, Toni Roothbert Found., 1999, Social Scis. and Humanities Rsch. Coun. Can., 1999, Ford Found. fellow, NRC, 2001, Andrew W. Mellon Postdoctoral fellow, Ctr. Humanities, Wesleyan U., 2003—04, Internat. Migration Inst. fellow, Social Sci. Rsch. Coun., 2004. Office: U Conn Dept History 241 Glenbrook Rd Storrs Mansfield CT 06269-2103 Office Phone: 860-486-5571.

**OVERSTREET, KAREN A.,** federal bankruptcy judge; BA cum laude, Univ. of Wash., 1977; JD, Univ. of Oregon, 1982. Assoc. Duane, Morris & Heckscher, Phila., 1983-86; ptnr. Davis Wright Tremaine, Seattle, 1986-93; bankruptcy judge U.S. Bankruptcy Ct. (we. dist.) Wash., Seattle, 1994—. Assoc. editor Oregon Law Review; dir. People's Law Sch.; mem. advisory com. U.S. Bankruptcy Ct. (we. dist.) Wash. Mem. Nat. Conf. of Bankruptcy Judges, Wash. State Bar Assn. (creditor-debtor sec.), Seattle-King County Bar Assn. (bankruptcy sec.), Am. Bar Assn., Wash. Women Lawyers Assn. Office: US Bankruptcy Ct 700 Stewart St Rm 7216 Seattle WA 98101 Office Phone: 206-370-5330.

**OVERSTREET, MARYANN ELIZABETH,** literature and language professor; b. Wahiawa, Hawaii, May 23, 1962; d. Frederick Heiskell and Dorothy Jean Overstreet; m. George Yule, July 26, 1994. BA in European Langs. and Lit., U. Hawaii, Honolulu, 1985, MA in German, 1989, PhD in Linguistics, 1995. Asst. prof. German U. Hawaii, Honolulu, 1998—2005, assoc. prof., chair German, 2005—. Contrb. articles to profl. jours. Recipient Excellence Tchg. award, Coll. Langs. Linguistics and Lit., 2000, Frances Davis award Excellence Undergrad.Tchg., U. Hawaii, 2001. Mem.: Am. Assn. Tchrs. German (v.p. Hawaii chpt. 2001—06), Internat. Pragmatics Assn. Office: University of Hawaii at Manoa 1890 East West Road Moore 483 Honolulu HI 96822 Office Phone: 808-956-4172. Office Fax: 956-9536.

**OVERTON, EDWIN DEAN,** retired campus minister, educator; b. Dec. 2, 1939; s. William Edward and Georgia Beryl (Fronk) O. BTh, Midwest Christian Coll., 1963; MA in Religion, Ea. N.Mex. U., 1969, EdS, 1978; postgrad., Fuller Theol. Sem., 1980. Ordained to ministry Christian Ch., 1978. Min. Christian Ch., Englewood, Kans., 1962-63; youth min. 1st Christian Ch., Beaver, Okla., 1963-67; campus min. Cen. Christian Ch., Portales, N.Mex., 1967-68, Christian Campus House, Portales, 1968—2005; acting chmn. religion dept. Ea. N.Mex. U., Portales, 2000, tchr. religion, philosophy, counseling, 1970—2005; ret. Dir. Campus Christian House, 1980-2005; farm and ranch partner, Beaver, Okla., 1963—. State dir. Beaver Jr. C. of C., 1964-65; pres. Beaver H.S. Alumni Assn., 1964-65; elder Cen. Christian Ch., Portales, 1985-88, 90-93; chmn. Beaver County March of Dimes, 1966; neighborhood chmn. Portales March of Dimes, 1997; pres. Portales Tennis Assns., 1977-78. Mem. U.S. Tennis Assn., Am. Assn. Christian Counselors, Ea. N.Mex. U. Faith in Life Com., Lions Club. Republican. Home: 1129 Libra Dr Portales NM 88130-6123 E-mail: campusmin@juno.com.

**OVERTON, LARRY DEAN,** music educator, musician; b. Alliance, Nebr., Aug. 8, 1937; s. Clarence Lloyd and Dorothy Iola Overton; m. Geraldine Overton, Aug. 29, 1959 (dec.); children: Michael, Daniel, Alan. BA in Music Edn., Nebr. State Coll., 1960; MMus, U. Nebr., 1964. Cert. State Adjudicator of Music 2005. Asst. music dir. Chadron (Nebr.) H.S., 1959—60; dir. music Madison (Nebr.) H.S., 1960—64; dir. orchs. Ft. Morgan (Colo.) Pub. Schs., 1964—2000. Guest conductor Colo. All-State Orch., 2000. Named Oustanding Music Educator, Chadron State Coll., 1988; named to Hall of Fame, Colo. Music Educators Assn., 1999, Colo. H.S. Activities Assn., 2002; recipient 25-Yr. Svc. award, Colo. Music Educators Assn., 1984, award, John F. Kennedy Alliance for Arts Edn., 1989, 30-Yr. Svc. award, Colo. H.S. Activities Assn., 1997, Hall of Fame, Chadron State Coll., 2002. Mem.: NEA, Nat. Harp Assn., Am. String Tchrs. Assn. (Distinguished Svc. award 1985), Nat. Sch. Orch. Assn. (Distinguished Pres. award 2002, Lifetime Svc. award 2004), Colo. Music Suprs. Assn., Colo. Music Educators Assn., Music Educators Nat. Conf., Morgan Edn. Assn., Colo. Edn. Assn., Elks. Methodist. Home: 614 Park St Fort Morgan CO 80701-2826

**OVERTON, MARCUS LEE,** performing arts association administrator, actor, writer; b. Calhoun, Ga., Aug. 13, 1943; s. Marcus Burt, Jr. and Eva Mae (Greene) Overton. BS in Speech and Theatre, Northwestern U., 1965. Actor, tchr. Southeastern Shakespeare Festival, Atlanta, 1965; actor, co. mgr. Eagles Mere Assocs. Repertory Co., Chgo., 1966; prodn. stage mgr. Lyric Opera Chgo., 1966-72; mgr. Ravinia Festival, Highland Park, Ill., 1973-77; performing arts program mgr. Smithsonian Instn., Washington, 1983-92; exec. dir., prod. dir. Spoleto Festival U.S.A., Charleston, SC, 1992 94; program prodn., host Who Do You Know S.C. Pub. Radio, Charleston, 1994-97; instr. theatre and arts mgmt. Coll. Charleston, 1995-97. Adv. panelist Nat. Endowments Arts, 1977—79, DC Commn. Arts and Humanities, 1989, 90, 92; narrator talking books Libr. Congress, Washington, 1982—83; bd. dirs. Performing Arts Assistance Corp., 1992—97; con. in field. Prodr.: Falstaff (LA Philharm.), 1981—82; prodr., host Spoleto Today, S.C. Pub. Radio, 1996—, Supertitles, San Diego Opera, 1999—2003; prodr.: Inside Spoleto, 2001— (Emmy award, 1984). Scholar, Northwestern U., 1961—65. Mem.: La Jolla Music Soc. (artistic adminstr. 2006—), Actors Alliance San Diego (bd. pres. 2001—02, chmn. 2003—06, announcer, program host XLNC1-FM 2004—). Avocations: travel, prehistoric cave art, motorcycle touring, linguistics, French culture. Address: 5581-A Adobe Falls Rd San Diego CA 92120 Office Phone: 858-459-3724. Personal E-mail: moverton@ljms.com.

**OVERTON, ROSILYN GAY HOFFMAN,** finance company executive; b. Corsicana, Tex., July 10, 1942; d. Billy Clarence and Ima Elise (Gay) Hoffman; m. Aaron Lewis Overton Jr., July 2, 1960 (div. Mar. 1975); children: Aaron Lewis III, Adam Jerome; m. Mardiros Hatsakorzian, 1991. BS in Math., Wright State U., Dayton, Ohio, 1972, MS in Applied Econs., 1973; postgrad., NYU, 1974—76. CFP. Rsch. analyst dept. Nat. Security Agy., 1962—67; bus. reporter Dayton Jour.-Herald, 1973—74; economist First Nat. City Bank, NYC, 1974, AT&T Co., 1974—75; broker Merrill Lynch, NYC, 1975—80; asst. v.p. E.F. Hutton & co., NYC, 1980—84; v.p., nat. mktg. dir. investment products Manhattan Nat. Corp., 1984—86; pres. R.H. Overton Co., NYC, 1986—; ptnr. Brown & Overton Fin. Svcs., 1987—. Named Businesswoman of Yr., NYC, 1976; fellow, Wright State U. Mem.: Internat. Assn. Fin. Planning (pres. NY chpt.), Inst. Cert. Planners, Mensa, Wright State U. Alumni Assn., Gotham Bus. and Profl. Womens Club, Zonta, Rotary Internat. Methodist. Office: 25418 Northern Blvd Ste 5 Little Neck NY 11362-1451

**OVITSKY, STEVEN ALAN,** musician, symphony orchestra executive; b. Chgo., Oct. 12, 1947; s. Martin N. and Ruth (Katz) O.; m. Camille Levy; 1 child, David Isaac. MusB, U. Mich., 1968; MusM, No. Ill. U., 1975. Fine arts dir. Sta. WNIU-FM Pub. Radio, Dekalb, Ill., 1972-76; program mgr. Sta. WMHT-FM Pub. Radio, Schenectady, NY, 1976-79; gen. mgr., artistic dir. Grant Park Concerts, Chgo., 1979-90; v.p., gen. mgr. Minn. Orch., Mpls., 1990-95; v.p., exec. dir. Milw. Symphony Orch., 1995-99, pres., exec. dir., 1999—2003; exec. dir. Santa Fe Chamber Music Festival, 2004—; owner Sotone Hist. Recordings. Panelist Ill. Arts Coun., Chgo. Artists Abroad, Nat. Endowment for the Arts; bd. dirs. Ill. Arts Alliance, Chamber Music Chgo.; hon. dir. Chgo. Sinfonietta. With U.S. Army, 1968-71, Korea. Mem. NARAS, Am. Symphony Orch. League. Jewish. Avocations: audio, record collecting, softball. Office: Santa Fe Chamber Music Festival PO Box 2227 Santa Fe NM 87504-2227 Office Phone: 505-231-8212.

**OVITZ, MICHAEL S.,** communications executive; b. Dec. 14, 1946; m. Judy Reich, 1969; children Christopher, Kimberly, and Eric. Grad., UCLA, 1968. With William Morris Agy., 1969—75; pres., bd. dir. Walt Disney Co., Burbank, Calif., 1995-97; co-founder, chmn. Creative Artists Agy., L.A., 1975-95; principal Artists Mgmt. Group, 1998—2002; owner, principal CKE Assocs., Beverly Hills, Calif., 1998—. Chmn. exec. bd. dirs. UCLA Hosp. and Med. Ctr.; bd. advisors Sch. Theater, Film and TV UCLA; bd. dirs. Livent, Inc., Gulfstream Aero. Corp., J. Crew Group, Inc., Opsware, Inc., Yankee Candle Corp. Exec. prodr.: Gangs of NY, 2002; exec. prodr.: Timeline, 2003. Trustee Mus. Modern Art, N.Y.C.; bd. govs. Cedars-Sinai Hosp., L.A.; mem. exec. adv. bd. Pediatric AIDS Found.; bd. dir. D.A.R.E. America; nat. bd. advisors, Children's Scholarship Fund. Named one of Top 200 Collectors, ARTnews Mag., 2004. Mem. Coun. Fgn. Rels., Zeta Beta Tau. Avocation: art collector. Office: 2601 Colorado Ave Santa Monica CA 90404-3518

**OWADA, HISASHI,** judge; b. Niigata, Japan, Sept. 18, 1932; s. Takeo and Shizuka (Tamura) O.; m. Yumiko Egashira, Oct. 7, 1962; children: Masako, Reiko, Setsuko. BA, U. Tokyo 1955; LLB, Cambridge U. Eng, 1959. Pvt. treaties div., 1974-76; pvt. sec. to Prime Min. of Japan, Tokyo, 1976-78; min. Japanese Embassy, Washington, 1979-81, Moscow, 1981-84; dir.-gen. treaties bur. and for law of sea Ministry Fgn. Affairs, 1984-87, dep. vice minister, 1987-88; amb., permanent rep. of Japan to OECD, Paris, 1988-89; dep. min. Ministry Fgn. Affairs, Tokyo, 1989-91; vice min. Fgn. Affairs of Japan, Tokyo, 1991-93; advisor Ministry Fgn. Affairs Japan, Tokyo, 1993-94; amb., permanent rep. of Japan to UN, 1994-98; prof. Waseda U., 1999—2003; advisor to Ministry Fgn. Affairs, Tokyo, 1999—2003; pres. Japan Inst. of Internat. Affairs, 1999—2003; sr. advisor to pres. of World Bank, 1999—2003; judge Permanent Ct. Arbitration, 2001—, Internat. Court Justice, Hague, Netherlands, 2003—. Adj. prof. U. Tokyo, 1963-88; vis. prof. Harvard U., Cambridge, Mass., 1979-81, 87, 89, 99-02; adj. prof. internat. law Columbia U., 1994-1998; Inge Rennert disting. vis. prof. NYU Global Law Sch., 1994—; acad. prop. advisor Hiroshima U., 2002—; hon. prof. Leiden U., 2006—. Author: Japanese Practice in the Field of International Law, 1984, From Involvement to Engagement, 1994, Diplomacy, 1996, A Treatise on International Relations, 2002. Bd. hon. trust U.N. Found., Ditchley Found.; mem. Inst. de Droit Internat. Mem. Japanese Assn. Internat. Law (exec. coun.). Avocations: skiing, mountain walking, music. Office: Internat Court of Justice Peace Palace 2517 KJ The Hague Netherlands Fax: 31 70 302 2409. Office Phone: 31 70302 23 23. E-mail: h.owada@icj-cij.org.

**OWEN, AMY,** library director; b. Brigham City, Utah, June 26, 1944; d. John Wallace and Bertha (Jensen) Owen. BA, Brigham Young U., 1966, MLS, 1968. Sys. libr. Utah State Libr., Salt Lake City, 1968—72, dir. reference svcs., 1972—74, dir. tech. svcs., 1974—81, dep. dir. 1981—87, dir., 1987—2003. Serials com. chmn. Utah Coll. Libr. Coun., Salt Lake City, 1975—77, exec. sec., 1978—84, mem. coun., 1987—2003; mem. staff Gov.'s Utah Sys. Planning Task Force, Salt Lake City, 1982; staff liaison Utah Gov.'s Conf. on Libr. and Info. Svcs., 1977—79, chmn. exec. planning com., 1990—91; mem. pres.'s adv. panel Baker & Taylor Co., Somerville, NJ, 1977—78; panelist U.S. Dept. Edn., 1992; mem. rsch. project adv. com. U. Wis. Sch. Libr. and Info. Madison, 1992—94; mem. adv. panel Nat. Commn. Libr. and INfo. Svcs., 1985; Alumni Honor lectr. Coll. Humanities Brigham Young U., 1990; cons., trainer in field. Contbr. chpts. to books; contbg. author: various manuals. Presdl. appt. mem. Nat. Mus. and Libr. Svcs. Bd., 2004; mem. coun. Utah Endowment for Humanities, 1986—91, vice chmn., 1987—88, chmn., 1988—90; trustee Bibliographic Ctr. for Rsch.,

1987—2003, mem. pers. com., 1988—89, chmn. person com., 1989—90, mem. nominating com., 1984, v.p. bd. trustees, 1989—91, pres., 1991—93; active Chief Officers of State Libr. Agys., 1987—2003, mem. stats. com. 1988—93, mem. network com., 1993—97, mem. state info. policy workshop com., 1988, bd. dirs., 1992—96; mem. com. Fedn. of State Humanities Couns., 1988; mem. coop. pub. libr. data sys. task force Nat. Commn. on Libr. and Info. Svcs., 1988—90; grant rev. panelist NEH, 1988, 1992, panel mem. reading and discussion groups, 1988; regional project mgmt. bd. mem. Intermountain Cmty. Learning and Info. Ctr. Project, 1987—90; mem. midcontinental regional adv. com. Nat. Libr. Medicine, 1991—94; mem. adv. com. Brigham Young U. Sch. Libr. and Info. Svcs., 1989—92. Named Libr. of Yr., Libr. Jour., 1990. Mem.: ALA (planning, orgn. and bylaws com. 1981—85, LITA divsn. Satellite Conf. Task Force mem. 1982, bd. dirs. ASCLA divsn. 1984—86, clene roundtable mem. com. 1984—86, fin. com. 1984—86, SLAS program com. 1984—86, ALA Office for Rsch. coop. pub. libr. data sys. adv. com. 1985—89, pres. program com. 1986, nominations com. 1986—87, PLA divsn. editor column 1987—89, PLA divsn. goals, guidelines and stds. com. 1987—90, nat. adv. bd. office comms. svcs., voices and visions project 1988—89, exec. bd. mem. 1988—90, PLA pub. libr. data svc. adv. com. 1988—91, fin. com. 1989—92, chair 1990—91, PLA non MLS involvement com. 1990—91, PLA Kellogg Phase III EIC project adv. com. chmn. 1990—92, PLA strategic issues and directions com. 1991—92, exec. bd. mem. 1993—94, bd. dirs. ASCLA divsn. 1993—96, fin. com. 1993—96, pres. ASCLA divsn. 1994—95, ASCLA Divsn. Profl. Achievement award 2004), Utah Partnership Edn. and Econ. Devel. (rsch. com. 1995—95), Utah Edn. Network (steering com. 1996—2003), Dynix Snowbird Leadership Inst. (nat. adv. bd. 1990—2002), Mountain Plains Libr. Assn. (rec. sec 1979—80, fin. com. 1982—84, Disting. Svc. award 1989), Utah Libr. Assn. (exec. bd. 1976—80, pres. 1978—79, Disting. Svc. award 2003, Spl. Svc. award 1989), Alpha Lambda Alpha, Phi Kappa Phi. Home: 4786 Naniloa Dr Salt Lake City UT 84117-5547

**OWEN, BRADLEY SCOTT,** lieutenant governor; b. Tacoma, May 23, 1950; s. Laural Willis; m. Linda Knoll, Jan. 20, 1983; children: Shanie, Dana, Mark, Sherrie, Adam, Royce. Student pub. sch., Germany. Rep. Wash. Ho. Rep., Olympia, 1976-82; senator Wash. State Senate, Olympia, 1983-96; lt. gov. State of Wash., Olympia, 1997—. Chmn. Legis. Com. on Economic Devel.; founder, pres. Strategies for Youth. Mem. Wash. State substance abuse coun., 1997—. Mem. Elks. Democrat. Office: Office Lt Governor 220 Legislative Bldg PO Box 40400 Olympia WA 98504-0400 Office Fax: 360-786-7749. E-mail: ltgov@leg.wa.gov.*

**OWEN, CHARLES THEODORE,** journalist, publisher; b. Beech Grove, Ind., June 14, 1941; s. James Robert and Helen Maurine (Sayre) O.; m. Kathleen Rose Dellaria, Apr. 29, 1967. AS in Journalism, Vincennes U., 1972; BA in Social Sci., Chapman U., 1976; MBA, Nat. U. San Diego, 1984. Enlisted U.S. Marine Corps, 1959-72, commd. 2d lt., 1973, advanced through grades to capt., 1979; combat journalist, photographer, Vietnam, 1967-68; dep. dir. Joint Pub. Affairs Office, Camp Pendleton, 1976-79; dir. Pub. Affairs Office, Marine Corps Recruit Depot, San Diego, 1980-81; dir. comm. and mil. affairs divsn. Greater San Diego C. of C., 1981-82, v.p. 1987—, bd. dirs., 1982-87; pres., pub. San Diego Bus. Jour., 1987-2004, pres., CEO Carlsbad (Calif.) C. of C., 2004—; host TV program North County Bus. Unfocus. Bd. dirs. San Diego Conv. and Visitors Bur., San Diego Econ. Devel. Corp.; econ. devel. advisor to Mayor of San Diego; presenter in field. Decorated Cross of Gallantry, Joint Svc. Commendation medal with Combat V (3 awards), medal of Honor 2d class (Vietnam); recipient Thomas Jefferson award, 1981. Republican. Pub. Newswriting Program Instruction, 1972. Office: 5934 Priestly Dr Carlsbad CA 92008 Office Phone: 760-931-8400.

**OWEN, CLARENCE B.,** construction materials manufacturing executive; BS in mech. engrng., La. Tech. U., 1972. Joined US Gypsum Co., Chgo., 1972, plant mgr., dir. tech. svcs.; v.p. oper. US Gypsum Co. Interiors; v.p. tech. svcs US Gypsum Co.; pres. mng. dir. US Gypsum Co. Europe; sr. v.p. US Gypsum Internat.; v.p., internat. tech. US Gypsum Co., v.p., chief tech. officer Chgo., 2003—. Office: United States Gypsum Industrial Products PO Box 803871 Chicago IL 60680-3871

**OWEN, CLAUDIA J.,** academic administrator; Pres., administr. Master's Touch Acad. Music, Kissimmee, Fla., 1996—. Office Phone: 407-846-8442.

**OWEN, CLIVE,** actor; b. Keresley, Warwickshire, Eng., Oct. 3, 1964; m. Sarah-Jane Fenton, Mar. 6, 1995; children: Hannah, Eve. Various stage roles including: Design for the Living, The Day in the Death of Joe Egg; actor: (films) Vroom, 1988, Close My Eyes, 1991, Century, 1993, The Turnaround, 1994, The Rich Man's Wife, 1996, Bent, 1997, Croupier, 1998, Greenfingers, 2000, The Hire: Ambush, Chosen, The Follow, Star, Powder Keg, 2001, Godsford Park, 2001, The Bourne Identity, 2002, The Hire: Hostage, Beat the Devil, Ticker, 2002, I'll Sleep When I'm Dead, 2003, Beyond Borders, 2003, King Arthur, 2004, Closer, 2004 (Golden Globe award for best supporting actor, 2005), Sin City, 2005, Derailed, 2005, The Pink Panther, 2006, Inside Man, 2006; (TV films) Precious Bane, 1989, Lorna Doone, 1990, Class of '61, 1993, The Magician, 1993, An Evening with Gary Lineker, 1994, Nobody's Children, 1994, Doomsday Gun, 1994, The Echo, 1998, Second Sight, 1999, Second Sight: Parasomnia, 2000, Second Sight: Kingdom of the Blind, 2000, Second Sight: Hide and Seek, 2000; (TV series) Capital City, 1989—90, Chancer, 1990, Sharman, 1996. Office: Creative Artists Agency c/o Kevin Huvane 9830 Wilshire Blvd Beverly Hills CA 90212-1815*

**OWEN, CYNTHIA CAROL,** sales executive; b. Ft. Worth, Oct. 16, 1943; d. Charlie Bounds and Bertice Vera (Nunley) Rhoads; m. Franklin Earl Owen, Oct. 20, 1961 (div. Jan. 1987); children: Jeffrey Wayne, Valeria Ann, Carol Darlena, Pamela Kay; m. John Edward White, Jan. 1, 1988 (div. Sept. 1991). Cert. Keypuncher, Comml. Coll., 1963; student, Tarrant County Jr. Coll., 1974-77; BBA in Mgmt., U. Tex., Arlington, 1981. Keypunch operator Can-Tex. Industries, Mineral-Wells, 1966-67; sec. Electro-Midland Corp., Mineral-Wells, 1967-68; exec. sec. to v.p. sales Pangburn Co., Ft. Worth, 1972-78; bookkeeper, sec. CB Svcs., Ft. Worth, 1978-82; project mgr. Square D Co., Ft. Worth, 1982—. Mem.: NAFE, NOW, AAUW. Baptist. Avocations: miniature golf, volleyball. Home: 1221 Pine Ridge Rd Roanoke TX 76262 Office: Square D Co 204 Airline Dr Ste 300 Coppell TX 75019-4663 Business E-Mail: cindy.owen@us.schneider-electric.com.

**OWEN, DANIEL THOMAS,** entrepreneur, venture capitalist; b. Dec. 6, 1947; s. Jesse Taylor and Loretta (Kirchner) O.; m. Margaret Wynne Chilton, Jan. 12, 1980; stepchildren: Margaret Anne Worsham Oden, Joseph Irion Worsham II. BA, U. Dayton, 1969. Dir. fundraising KERA-TV, Dallas, 1972-75; v.p. mktg. and programming Spectradyne, Inc., Dallas, 1975-87, exec. v.p., COO, 1987-89, internat. pres., 1989-90; founder, chmn. Focus Networks, Dallas, 1991-95; co-found. and gen. ptnr. HO2 Ptnr., Dallas, 1997—. Bd. dirs. Ignite Technologies, Inc., 2001-. Bd. dirs. North Tex. Pub. Broadcasting, Inc., 1994—. Mem. World Pres.'s Orgn. Episcopalian. Home: 3925 Potomac Ave Dallas TX 75205-2116 Office: HO2 Ptnrs Galleria Tower Two 13455 Noel Rd Ste 1670 Dallas TX 75240 E-mail: dan@ho2.com.

**OWEN, DENNIS P.,** lawyer; b. 1949; BS in Personnel Mgmt., No. Ill. U., 1973; JD, Loyola U., 1975. Gen. counsel Brand Insulations, Inc., Chgo.; dir. risk mgmt. Ligon Nationwide, Inc., Madisonville, Ky.; v.p. risk mgmt. Landstar Sys., Inc., Madisonville, Ky., 1989—2001, v.p., gen. counsel, asst. sec., 2001—. Mem.: ABA, Risk & Ins. Mgmt. Soc. Office: Landstar Sys Int 13410 Sutton Park Dr S PO Box 19135 Jacksonville FL 32224 Office Phone: 904-306-1723. Office Fax: 904-306-2539. E-mail: dowen@landstar.com.

**OWEN, DUNCAN SHAW, JR.,** internist, retired educator; b. Fayetteville, NC, Oct. 24, 1935; s. Duncan S. and Mary Gwyn (Hickerson) O.; m. Irene Lacy Rose, Oct. 22, 1966; children: Duncan Shaw III, Robert Burwell, Frances Gwyn. BS in Medicine, U. N.C., 1957, MD, 1960. Diplomate Am. Bd. Internal Medicine (proctor 1977-97). Intern Med. Coll. Va., Richmond, 1960-61; jr. asst. resident in medicine N.C. Meml. Hosp., Chapel Hill,

---

1961-62; asst. resident in medicine Med. Coll. Va., Richmond, 1964-65, fellow in rheumatic diseases, 1965-66; internal medicine and rheumatology physician Richmond, Va., 1966—; from instr. in medicine to assoc. prof. Med. Coll. Va., Richmond, 1966-78, prof. dept. internal medicine, 1978—; Taliaferro/Scott Disting. prof. internal medicine Med. Coll. Va., Va. Commonwealth U., 1989-2000, emeritus prof., 2000—; dir. residency tng. Med. Coll. Va. Hosp.; dir. rheumatology clinics. Dir. clin. tng. divsn. rheumatology, allergy, immunology, 1975-98, chmn. clin. activities comm., dept. internal medicine, 1970-90; chmn. med. adv. com. Richmond br. Arthritis Found., 1966-75, nat. patient edn. com., 1979-80; med. advisor Social Security Adminstrn., HHS, 1967-2004; co-chmn. arthritis project Va. Regional Med. Program, 1975-76; prodr. Your Health TV series Va. Ednl. TV, 1978-79; prodr. Update in Medicine, Good Morning Virginia TV show, 1980; cons. McGuire V.A. Contbr. articles to profl. jours.; assoc. editor: Va. Med., 1978-98; editl. reviewer Jour. AMA, 1979—, Arthritis Rheumatism, 1981-2004, Jour. Rheumatology, 1984—. Mem. usher's guild First Presbyn. Ch., Richmond, Va., 1966-70, deacon, 1974-77, chmn. of diaconate, 1976-77, elder, 1978—, chmn. witness com., 1978-80; co-chmn. physicians statewide capital funds campaign Va. Commn. U., 1986-87; bd. dirs. Mooreland Farms Assn., 1971-73, 77-81, Va. chpt. Arthitis Found., 1970-85; mem. Va. Mus., Richmond Symphony; bd. dirs. Richmond Area Health Care Coalition, 1980-84. Med. officer U.S. Army, 1962—63, Womack Army Hosp., Fort Bragg, NC, post surgeon, asst. divsn. surgeon U.S. Army, 1963—64, Camp Kaiser, Korea. Decorated Army Commendation medal; recipient Gerard B. Lambert award, 1974-75, Disting. Svc. award Arthritis Found., 1971, U. N.C., Chapel Hill, 1999; Nat. Inst. Arthritis and Metabolic Diseases fellow, 1965-66 Fellow ACP (Laureate award 1997), Am. Coll. Rheumatology; mem. AMA (expert on diagnostic and therapeutic tech. assessment program 1990-99), Am. Rheumatism Assn. (exec. com. 1979-80), Richmond Acad. Medicine (pres. 1982, chmn. bd. 1983, parliamentarian 1988-99), Med. Soc. Va. (com. on aging 1980-89, v.p. 1973, 75, del. 1972-99, scholarship com. 1980-89), Richmond Soc. Internal Medicine (bd. dirs. 1971-73), Met. Richmond C. of C. (bd. dirs. 1981-84), Jr. Clin. Club (emeritus), Custis Hunting and Fishing Club, Alpha Omega Alpha Honor Med. Soc. Presbyn. Achievements include development of techniques for arthrocenteses; cellophane tape polarizing microscopic compensator for identifying crystals in joint fluid. Avocations: hunting, fishing, photography, amateur radio. Home: 8910 Brieryle Rd Richmond VA 23229-7704 Personal E-mail: dowen75089@aol.com.

**OWEN, EDWARD ROGER JOHN (E. ROGER OWEN),** Middle Eastern studies professor, writer; MA, Oxford U., Eng., DPhil, 1964. Dir. Mid. East Ctr. St. Antony's Coll., Oxford U., England, emeritus fellow; A.J. Meyer Prof. Mid. Ea. History Harvard U., Cambridge, Mass., 1993—, dir. Ctr. Mid. Ea. Studies, 1996—99; dir. Contemporary Arab Studies Program, 1995—. Co-author (with Sevket Pamuk): (books) A History of the Middle East Economics in the 20th Century, 1998; author: Cotton and the Egyptian Economy, 1820-1914: A Study in Trade and Development, 1969, The Middle East in the World Economy 1800-1914, 1981, State, Power and Politics in the Making of the Modern Middle East, 1992, 2000, 2004, Lord Cromer: Victorian Imperialist: Edwardian Proconsul, 2004. Office: Harvard U Ctr Mid Ea Studies 1430 Massachusetts Ave Cambridge MA 02138

**OWEN, H. MARTYN,** retired lawyer; b. Decatur, Ill., Oct. 23, 1929; s. Honore Martyn and Virginia (Hunt) O.; m. Candace Catlin Benjamin, June 21, 1952; children: Leslie W., Peter H., Douglas P. AB, Princeton U., NJ, 1951; LLB, Harvard U., 1954. Bar: Conn. 1954, U.S. Ct. Appeals (2d cir.) 1961, U.S. Dist. Ct. Conn. 1962, U.S. Supreme Ct. 1963, U.S. Dist. Ct. Vt. 1975. Assoc. Shipman & Goodwin, Hartford, Conn., 1958-61, ptnr., 1961-94, of counsel, 1995-96; ret. Mem. Simsbury (Conn.) Zoning Bd. Appeals, 1961-67, Simsbury Zoning Commn., 1967-79; sec. Capitol Region Planning Agy., 1965-66; bd. dirs. Symphony Soc. Greater Hartford, 1967-73; trustee Renbrook Sch., West Hartford, Conn., 1963-72, treas. 1964-68, pres., 1968-72, hon. life trustee, 1972—; trustee Simsbury Free Libr., 1970-84; pres. Hartford Grammar Sch., 1987-98, trustee; corporator Hartford Hosp., 1984-96; vestry St. Alban's Ch., Simsbury, 1988-94; warden, vestry St. Paul's Ch., Brunswick, Maine, 1999-2001. Lt. USNR, 1954-62. Mem. ABA, Conn. Bar Assn., Hartford County Bar Assn., Am. Law Inst., U.S.N.C.C.) Club, Ivy Club (Princeton, NJ). Democrat. Episcopalian. Home: 80 Matthew Dr Brunswick ME 04011-3275 Personal E-mail: hmowen@gwi.net.

**OWEN, HENRY,** former ambassador, consultant; b. NYC, Aug. 26, 1920; AB, Harvard U., 1941. Economist Dept. State, Washington, 1946-55, mem. policy planning staff, 1955-62, dep. counselor, vice chmn. policy planning coun., 1962-66, chmn. coun., 1966-69; dir. fgn. policy studies Brookings Instn., 1969-77; personal rep. of Pres. U.S. with rank of ambassador to participate in preparations for summit meetings, 1977-81; sr. adviser Salomon Bros., 1981—2002; co-chmn. Capitol Ptnrs. for Edn., Washington, 2002—. Spl. adv. Pan-European Oil Pipeline Romania-Serbian-Croatia-Slovenia-Italy. Editor: Next Phase of U.S. Foreign Policy, 1971, (with Charles Schultze) Setting National Priorities, 1976. Served to lt. USN, 1942-46. Office: 2946 University Ter NW Washington DC 20016 Office Phone: 202-363-8370. Office Fax: 202-363-3492.

**OWEN, JANE DALE,** non-profit organization executive; d. Kenneth Dale and Jane Blaffer Owen; m. Per Arneberg; children: Ingrid Arneberg, Erik Arneberg. Attended, Bennington Coll., Vt. Founder, pres. Citizens' League for Environ. Action Now (CLEAN), Houston, 2000—. Bd. dir. Fedn. Am. Scientists; dealt with govt. agencies EPA, Harris County Pollution Control, Sierra Club, Citizen Environ. Coalition. Former exec. com. mem. Blaffer Gallery, mem. adv. bd., U. Houston; former exec. com. mem. Moores Sch. of Music Soc., U. Houston; recommended and funded the popular children's film program called "Family Flicks" Mus. Fine Arts, Houston; served on Mus. Fine Arts Film Com., Houston; avid supporter Houston SPCA, Planned Parenthood, Houston. Office: CLEAN 5120 Woodway Dr Ste 9004 Houston TX 77056 Office Phone: 713-524-3000.

**OWEN, JOE SAM,** lawyer; b. Gulfport, Miss., Dec. 31, 1948; s. Tofie and Amelia (Numnum) O., Sr.; m. Sandra Donohue, July 26, 1969; children— Ashley, Sam; m. 2d, Sherry Lynn Welch, Jan. 31, 1982; 1 child, Mitch. BA in History, U. Miss., 1970, JD, 1972. Bar: Miss. 1972, U.S. Dist. Ct. (no. and so. dists.) Miss. 1972, U.S. Ct. Appeals (5th cir.) 1974, U.S. Ct. Claims 1978, U.S. Tax Ct. 1978, U.S. Supreme Ct. 1978. Pvt. practice, Gulfport, Miss., 1972-82; ptnr. Blackwell, Owen & Galloway, Gulfport, Miss., 1982-83, Owen, Galloway and Dickinson, Gulfport, 1983-84, Owen and Galloway, Gulfport, 1984—; asst. dist. atty. Harrison, Hancock and Stone Counties, Miss., 1974-77; referee Harrison County Family Ct., Miss., 1971—. Mem. ABA, Miss. Bar Assn., Harrison County Bar Assn., Assn. Trial Lawyers Am., Miss. Trial Lawyers Assn., Am. Judicature Soc., Comml. Law League Am., Southeastern Bankruptcy Law Inst. Office: Owen & Galloway 1414 25th Ave Gulfport MS 39501-0673 Office Phone: 228-868-2821. E-mail: jso@owen-galloway.com

**OWEN, JOHN,** retired newspaper editor; b. Helena, Mont., June 10, 1929; s. John Earl and Ella Jean (McMillian) O.; m. Alice Winnifred Kesler, June 9, 1951; children— David Scott, Kathy Lynn. BA in Journalism, U. Mont., 1951. Sports editor Bismarck (N.D.) Tribune, 1953-55; wire editor Yakima (Wash.) Herald, 1956; with Seattle Post-Intelligencer, 1956-94, sports editor, 1968-80, assoc. editor, 1980-94, columnist, 1968-94. Author: Intermediate Eater Cookbook, 1974, Gourmand Gutbusters Cookbook, 1980, Seattle Cookbook, 1983, Great Grub Hunt Cookbook, 1989, Press Pass, 1994, Gluttony Without Guilt, 1997, Seattle Walks, 2000; also short stories. Served with AUS, 1951-52. Named Top Sports Writer in Wash. Nat. Sportswriters Orgn., 1966, 68, 69, 71, 74, 85, 88. Home: 611 Bell St Apt 4 Edmonds WA 98020-3065 E-mail: ieater@verizon.net.

**OWEN, JOHN ATKINSON, JR.,** internist, educator; b. South Boston, Va., Sept. 24, 1924; s. John Atkinson and Mary Helen (Carrington) O.; m. Wanda Earle Reamy, Nov. 29, 1952; children— John Atkinson III, Ryland R. BS, Hampden-Sydney Coll., 1944; MD, U. Va., 1948. Intern Cin. Gen. Hosp., 1948-49; resident, fellow U. Va. Hosp., 1950-52; rsch. fellow Duke Med.

---

Center, 1954-56; asst. prof. medicine Med. Coll. Ga., 1956-58, George Washington U. Med. Sch., 1958-60; mem. faculty U. Va. Sch. Medicine, 1960-96, prof., 1970-96, vice chmn. dept. internal medicine, 1972-74, James M. Moss prof. diabetes, sr. assoc. dean, 1995-96, prof. emeritus, 1997—. Mem. Va. Vol. Formulary Bd.; mem. exec. com. U.S. Pharmacopeia, 1970-75, pres., 1975-80, trustee, 1975-85. Mem. editorial bd.: Jour. Clin. Pharmacology, 1971-84; editor-in-chief: Hosp. Formulary, 1974-83. Served with USNR, 1942-45, 48-50, 52-53; capt. M.C. Res. Recipient Raven award U. Va., 1948; co-recipient Horsley Research prize, 1962, Walter Reed Disting. Achievement award, 1998; laureate ACP, 1998. Mem. AMA, ACP, Am. Fedn. Clin. Rsch., So. Soc. Clin. Investigation, Med. Soc. Va. (pres. 1990-91), Am. Diabetes Assn., Endocrine Soc. Presbyterian. (elder 1965—). Home: 106 Tally Ho Dr Charlottesville VA 22901-2034

**OWEN, LINDSAY ALEXANDER,** music director; b. Montgomery, Ala., May 26, 1976; d. David Earl and Charla Davis Alexander; m. Allan Lee Owen III, Oct. 28, 2000; 1 child, Langley Davis. MusB, Vanderbilt U., 1997; MusM, Belmont U., 2000. Music, drama dir. Camp Robindel, Centre Harbor, NH, 1996—97; tchg. asst. Vanderbilt U., Nashville, 1997—99; choir dir. First Presbyn. Ch., Nashville, 1997—99; piano, voice instr. Melody Music Studios, Franklin, Tenn., 1999—2001; music asst. First Presbyn. Ch., 1999—2001, assoc. dir. music Greensboro NC, 2001—. Mezzo-soprano Vanderbilt Opera Theatre, Nashville, 1994—96, Vanderbilt Chamber Singers, 1996—97; pres. Vanderbilt U. Concert Choir, 1996—97; mezzo-soprano Bella Voci, Nashville, 1997—2001, Sanctuary Choir First Presbyn. Ch., Nashville, 1997—2001; actress High Point (NC) Cmty. Theatre, 2002—05; mezzo-soprano Chancel Choir First Presbyn. Ch., Nashville, 2004—06. Mem.: Presbyn. Assn. Musicians (assoc.), Choristers Guild (assoc.), Am. Choral Director's Assn. (assoc.), Pi Kappa Lambda (assoc.), Alpha Omicron Pi (assoc.). Independent. Avocation: musical theatre. Home: 5517 Westerborne Dr Greensboro NC 27407 Office Phone: 336-478-4713. Personal E-mail: vandygrad97@hotmail.com.

**OWEN, MARC,** health products executive; b. Wales; Grad., Oxford U.; MBA, Stanford U., Calif. Sr. ptnr. McKinsey and Co., 1988—2000; pres., CEO MindCrossing, 2000—01; sr. v.p. corp. strategy and bus. devel. McKesson Corpn., San Francisco, 2001, exec. v.p. corp. strategy and bus. devel. Office: McKesson Corpn One Post St San Francisco CA 94104

**OWEN, MARY ANNE,** nuclear scientist, educator; m. Glenn Owen, Feb. 10, 1996. MS in Health Edn., Med. Coll. Ga., 2000. Registered nuc. technologist ARRT, 1993. Asst. prof. nuc. Med. Coll. Ga., program dir. nuc. medicine tech. Nat. com. rep. SE Chpt., Soc. of Nuc. Medicine. Author: Medical Case Studies in Nuclear Imaging. Mem.: Soc. of Nuc. Medicine (nat. com. rep. S.E. chpt. 2003—05, nat. edn. rep. 2004—05), Alpha Eta. Achievements include first to distant and blended learning for allied health science education. Office: Medical College of Georgia Department of BRT AE-1003 Augusta GA 30912 Office Phone: 706-721-3691.

**OWEN, MICHAEL LEE,** lawyer; b. LA, Aug. 17, 1942; s. Richard M. Owen and Betty Hamilton; m. Espy Bolivar-Owen. AB in Econ. with distinction, Stanford U., 1964; LLB, Harvard U., 1967. Bar: Calif., 1968, N.Y. 1968. Assoc. Reid & Priest, N.Y., 1967—69; mem. legal dept. Bank of Am. NT&SA, San Francisco, 1969—81; corp. sec. BRE Properties, San Francisco, 1970—75; v.p., assoc. gen. counsel Bank of Am. NT&SA, L.A., 1979—81; ptnr. and co-chair L.Am. practice group Paul, Hastings, Janofsky & Walker, LLP, L.A., 1981—. Vice chmn. adv. bd. Inst. for Internat. and Comparative Law, Ctr. Am. and Internat. Law (formerly Southwestern Legal Found.). Contbr. articles to profl. jours. regarding legal issues affecting financing and investment in Latin Amer. Bd. dirs. Constnl. Rights Found. Mem. US-Mex. Law Inst. (mem. adv. bd.). Office: Paul Hastings Janofsky & Walker LLP 515 S Flower St 25th Fl Los Angeles CA 90071-2228 Office Phone: 213-683-6214. Office Fax: 213-627-0705. Business E-Mail: michaelowen@paulhastings.com.

**OWEN, PAUL,** religious studies educator; b. Pocatello, Idaho, Sept. 21, 1970; s. Leon and Leona Owen; m. Alice Macmillan, Oct. 16, 1999. PhD, U. Edinburgh, Scotland, 2000. Asst. prof. Bible and religion Montreat Coll., 2001—. Contbr. articles to profl. jours. Recipient Overseas Rsch. scholarship, Brit. Govt., 1998-2000. Mem.: Soc. Bibl. Lit.

**OWEN, PRISCILLA RICHMAN,** federal judge; former state supreme court justice; b. Palacios, Tex., Oct. 4, 1954; BA, Baylor U., 1975; JD, Baylor U. Sch. of Law, 1977. Bar: Tex. 1978, U.S. Ct. Appeals (4th, 5th, 8th and 11th cirs.). Law clerk Sheehy, Lovelace & Mayfield, 1976—77; assoc. Andrews, Kurth, Campbell & Jones, 1978—85, ptnr., 1985—94; justice Supreme Ct. Tex., Austin, 1995—2005; judge U.S. Ct. Appeals (5th cir.), New Orleans, 2005—. Liaison to Tex. Legal Svcs. for Poor Spl. Supreme Ct. Tex., Supreme Ct. Adv. Com. on Ct.-Annexed Mediations. Bd. mem. Tex. Hearing & Service Dogs, A.A. White Dispute Resolution Inst.; advisory bd. mem. Federalist Soc. (Houston & Austin Chapter). Named Young Lawyer of Yr., Baylor U., Outstanding Young Alumna. Mem.: ABA, Am. Judicature Soc., Am. Law Inst. Office: US Courthouse 903 San Jacinto Blvd Rm 310 Austin TX 78701-2450*

**OWEN, RANDY YEUELL,** country musician, cattle rancher; b. Ala., Dec. 13, 1949; married; 3 children. Vocalist, guitarist with group Alabama, 1973—, also songwriter; albums include My Home's in Alabama, 1980, Feels So Right, 1981, Mountain Music, 1982 (Grammy award), The Closer You Get, 1983 (Grammy award), Roll On, 1984, Forty Hour Week, 1985, The Touch, 1986, Just Us, 1987, Alabama "Live", 1988, American Pride, 1992, Cheap Seats, 1993, Country Side of Life, 1993, Gonna Have A Party...Live, 1993, Greatest Hits, Vol. II, 1994, In Pictures, 1995, Super Hits, 1996, Dancin' on the Boulevard, 1997, 20th Century, 1999, Alabama for the Record, 2000, When It All Goes South, 2001, The Farewell Tour (live), 2003, Lady Down on Love, 2005. Group awards include: Country Music Assn. Instrumental Group Yr., 1981, 1982, Vocal Group Yr., 1981-83, Entertainer Yr., 1982-84 Acad. Country Music Vocal Group Yr., 1981-86, Entertainer Yr., 1982-86, Artist of Decade, 1989, Pioneer Award 2003, Am. Music Awards for Country Group Yr. & Favorite Country Group 1983, 1985, 1986, 1988-99, 2003, Recording Industry Assn. Am. Country Group of the Century, 1999, Am. Music Merit award, Spirit of Alabama medal, Pentagon 9/11 Medallion, 2003, named to Country Music Assn. Hall of Fame, 2005. Office: care Morris and Assocs 818 19th Ave S Nashville TN 37203-3202*

**OWEN, RICHARD,** federal judge; b. NYC, Dec. 11, 1922; s. Carl Maynard and Shirley (Barnes) O.; m. Lynn Rasmussen, June 6, 1960; children: Carl R., David R., Richard. AB, Dartmouth Coll., 1947; LLB, Harvard U., 1950; MusD (hon.), Manhattan Sch. Music, 1989. Bar: N.Y. 1950. Practiced in N.Y.C., 1950-74; assoc. Willkie Owen Farr Gallagher & Walton, 1950-53, Willkie Farr Gallagher Walton & Fitzgibbon, 1958-60; prvt. practice, 1960-65; ptnr. Owen & Aarons, 1965-66, Owen & Turchin, 1966-74; asst. U.S. atty. So. Dist. N.Y., 1953-55; trial atty. antitrust divsn. U.S. Dept. Justice, 1955-58; judge U.S. Dist. Ct. (So. Dist.), 1974-89, sr. judge, 1989—. Asst. prof. N.Y. Law Sch., 1951-53; adj. prof. law Fordham U. Sch. Law, 1996—. Composer, librettist operas Dismissed with Prejudice, 1956, A Moment of War, 1958, A Fisherman Called Peter, 1965, Mary Dyer, 1976, The Death of the Virgin, 1980, Abigail Adams, 1987, Tom Sawyer, 1989, Rain, 1997. Trustee Manhattan Sch. Music, N.Y.C.; founder, bd. dirs. Maine Opera Assn., 1975-85; pres., bd. dirs. N.Y. Lyric Opera Co. 1st It. USAAC, 1942-45. Decorated D.F.C. with oak leaf cluster, Air medal with 3 oak leaf clusters. Mem. ASCAP, Century Assn., Chelsea Yacht Club. Republican. Mem. Soc. Of Friends. Office: US Dist Ct US Courthouse 40 Centre St Room 2903 New York NY 10007-1501 Office Phone: 212-805-6155. E-mail: operaowen@aol.com.

**OWEN, ROBERT H.,** electronics executive; B in bus. and info. mgmt., Loretto Hts. Coll., 1983, M in bus., 1988. Info. services mgmt. positions at Burr-Brown Corp., Analog Devices, Inc., Syntex Corp.; dir. info. services

Microchip Tech., Inc., Chandler, Ariz., v.p. info. services, 1999—. Named one of Premier 100 IT Leaders, Computerworld, 2005. Office: Microchip Tech Inc 2355 W Chandler Blvd Chandler AZ 85224-6199 Office Phone: 480-792-7200.*

**OWEN, ROBERT HUBERT,** lawyer, real estate broker; b. Birmingham, Ala., Aug. 3, 1928; s. Robert Clay and Mattie Lou (Hubert) O.; m. Mary Dane Hicks, Mar. 14, 1954; children: Mary Kathryn, Robert Hubert. BS, U. Ala., 1950; JD, Birmingham Sch. Law, 1956. Bar: Ala. 1957, Ga. 1965. Methods and procedures analyst, supr. Ala. Power Co., Birmingham, 1952-58; assoc. Martin, Vogtle, Balch & Bingham, Birmingham, 1958-63; asst. sec. So. Services, Atlanta, 1963-69; sec. Southern Co., Atlanta, 1969-71, asst. treas., 1971-77; exec. v.p., sec., gen. counsel, dir. Proverbs 31 Corp., Atlanta, 1978-81, 90-97; broker Bob Owen Realty, Atlanta, 1990-97; pvt. practice law Marietta, 1978-85; v.p., gen. counsel Hubert Properties, 1985-86. Atlanta area rep. Inst. Basic Life Principles, 1970-80; elder Calvary Bapt. Ch., 1997—. Served to maj. USAF, 1951-52, 61-62. Mem.: Meteoritical Soc., Jasons, Phi Eta Sigma, Beta Gamma Sigma, Omicron Delta Kappa, Delta Chi, Delta Sigma Pi. Home and Office: 6590 Bridgewood Valley Rd NW Sandy Springs GA 30328-2906 Personal E-mail: roberthowen@bellsouth.net.

**OWEN, ROBERTS BISHOP,** lawyer, arbitrator; b. Boston, Feb. 11, 1926; s. Roberts Bishop and Monica Benedict (Burrell) O.; m. Kathleen Comstock von Schrader, Aug. 27, 1966; children— David Roberts, Lucy Leffingwell, William Atreus. Student, Dartmouth Coll., 1943-44; AB cum laude, Harvard U., 1948, LL.B. cum laude, 1951; Dip.C.L.S., Cambridge U., Eng., 1952. Bar: D.C. 1952, U.S. Ct. Appeals (D.C. cir.) 1953, U.S. Supreme Ct. 1958. Assoc. Covington & Burling, Washington, 1952-60, ptnr., 1960-79, 81—; the legal advisor U.S. Dept. State, Washington, 1979-81. Sr. advisor Sec. of State former Yugoslavia, 1995, arbitrator Fedn. Bosnia and Herzegovina, 1996-98; mem. Permanent Ct. Arbitration, The Hague, The Netherlands, 1980—86, 1993—98; mem. arbitration panel Internat. Ctr. for Settlement of Investment Disputes, 1995—; chair bd. dirs. Internat. Human Rights Law Group, 1996—99; mem. Claims Resolution Tribunal for Dormant Accounts in Switzerland, 1998—2000; sr. U.S. negotiator U.S.-Can. Pacific Salmon Treaty dispute, 1998; vice chair, sr. claims judge Claims Resolution Tribunal, 2001—02. Served to ensign USN, 1943-46. Fulbright scholar, 1951-52; recipient Disting Honor award Dept. of State, 1981, Sec. of State Disting. Svc. award, 1996, Sec. of Defense's medal for outstanding pub. svc., 1996. Fellow Am. Coll. Trial Lawyers; mem. ABA, Council Fgn. Relations, Am. Soc. Internat. Law (exec. council 1981-85). Clubs: Royal Ocean Racing (London); Metropolitan (Washington). Office: Covington & Burling PO Box 7566 1201 Pennsylvania Ave NW Washington DC 20004 Office Phone: 202-662-5254. Business E-Mail: rowen@cov.com.

**OWEN, STEPHEN LEE,** lawyer; b. Danville, Va., Mar. 25, 1952; s. L. Davis and Ann (Brodie) O.; m. Catherine Bryan Mabry; children: Hillary Brodie, Stephen Grayson, Mary Bryan, Davis Hammond, Edward Bloxton. BA, Hampden-Sydney Coll., Va., 1974; JD, Coll. of William and Mary, Williamsburg, Va., 1977. Bar: Va. 1977, Md. 1977, U.S. Tax Ct. 1978, U.S. Dist. Ct. Md., D.C. 1990. Assoc. Venable, Baetjer & Howard, Balt., 1977-84, ptnr., 1985-93, Piper & Marbury Rudnick & Wolfe, LLP, Balt., 1993-99; ptnr., chmn. Tax practice group DLA Piper Rudnick Gray Cary, Washington. Co-author: Federal Taxation of Estates, Gifts & Trusts, 1988; co-author newsletter Real Estate Tax Ideas, 1985—2001; contbr. articles to profl. jours.; editorial bd. Jour. Partnership Taxation, 1984-99, The Practical Tax Lawyer, 1985—, The Jour. Pass Through Entities, 1998—, Jour. of Real Estate Taxation. Bd. dirs. Balt. City Found., 1979-89, Balt. Zoo. Fellow Am. Coll. Tax Coun.; mem. ABA (v. chair ptnrships. com. taxation sect.), Am. Law Inst., Md. Bar Assn. (chmn. sect. of taxation 1989-90), Va. State Bar Assn., DC Bar Assn., Bar Assn. Balt. City, Real Estate Roundtable, Nat. Assn. Real Estate Investment Trusts, Balt. Country Club, Caves Valley Golf Club (bd. mem., Caddie Scholarship Found. bd. mem.). Avocation: golf. Office: DLA Piper Rudnick Gray Cary 1200 19th St NW Washington DC 20036-2412 Office Phone: 410-580-4230, 202-861-6240. Office Fax: 202-223-2085. Business E-Mail: stephen.owen@dlapiper.com.

**OWEN, THOMAS BARRON,** aerospace transportation executive, retired military officer; b. Seattle, Mar. 19, 1920; s. Thomas Barron and Ruth (Deane) O.; m. Rosemary Stolz, Dec. 24, 1944; children— Catherine Adams, Thomas Barron, James Rowell, Nancy Deane. BS cum laude, U. Wash., 1940; postgrad., U.S. Naval Postgrad. Sch., 1946-47; PhD in Chemistry, Cornell U., 1950; postgrad., U. Amsterdam, 1950-51, Indsl. Coll. Armed Forces, 1961-62, Harvard Grad. Sch. Bus. Adminstrn., 1964. Commd. ensign U.S. Navy, 1940, advanced through grades to rear adm., 1967, combat duty with Pacific Fleet, 1940-45; officer distbn. div. Bur. Naval Personnel, 1945-46; war armaments br. and mil. operations br. Office Naval Research, 1951-53; asst. repair supt. (hull) and prodn. analysis supt. Long Beach (Calif.) Naval Shipyard, 1953-57; dir. applied scis. div., dir. research and devel. planning div. Navy Bur. Ships, 1957-61; mil. asst. to dep. def. research and engring. engring. and chemistry, 1962-63; assigned Office Asst. Sec. Navy Research and Devel., 1963; dir. support services Naval Research Lab., 1963-65, dir., 1965-67; chief naval research, 1967-70; ret., 1970; asst. dir. nat. and internat. programs NSF, 1970-74; assoc. dean grad. affairs and rsch. Am. U., Washington, 1974-76, asst. provost, 1976-79; asst. adminstr. NOAA, Dept. Commerce, Rockville, Md., 1979-81; mgr. program planning Fairchild Space & Electronics Co., Germantown, Md., 1981-83; sr. dir. systems effectiveness Fairchild Space Co., Germantown, 1983-84, v.p. procurement, 1984-86. Author profl. papers. Decorated D.S.M., Silver Star, Bronze Star. Fellow AAAS; mem. Am. Chem. Soc., U.S. Naval Inst., Philos. Soc. Washington, Sigma Xi, Phi Kappa Phi, Phi Lambda Upsilon, Tau Beta Pi, Chi Psi. Clubs: Cosmos (Washington). Home: 415 Russell Ave Apt 109 Gaithersburg MD 20877 E-mail: wonkpop@aol.com. *Demand high standards of excellence for self and others. Achieve respect of others through own performance. Be direct; avoid circumspection. Develop empathy; listen, consider feelings and rights of others. Maintain philosophy of "Onward and Upward!".*

**OWEN, THOMAS LLEWELLYN,** investment company executive; b. Patchogue, NY, June 24, 1928; s. Griffith Robert and Jeanette Roberts (Hatfield) O. AB in Econs., Coll. William and Mary, 1951; postgrad., Columbia U., 1952, N.Y. Inst. Fin., 1960—62; MBA, NYU, 1966. Exec. trainee Shell Oil Co., N.Y.C. and Indpls., 1951-59, supr., 1958-59; petroleum and chem. investment analyst Paine, Webber, Jackson & Curtis, N.Y.C., 1959-62; sr. oil investment analyst DuPont Investment Interests, Wilmington, Del., N.Y.C., 1962-66, dir. rsch., 1964-66; v.p., sr. investment officer, mem. policy, investment coms. Nat. Securities and Rsch. Corp., N.Y.C., 1966-75, mutual fund portfolio mgr., 1972—75; sr. investment exec., v.p., investment mgr. F. Eberstadt & Co. and Eberstadt Asset Mgmt., Inc., N.Y.C., 1975-85, mem. policy com., 1979-85, also dir. portfolio rev. com.; sr. investment exec., portfolio mgr. Brown Brothers Harriman, N.Y.C., 1985-89; ptnr., CEO Owen Capital Mgmt., N.Y.C., 1989—. Contbr. chpt. "Oil and Gas Industries" to Financial Analysts Handbook, 1975. Former chmn. bd. trustees Congl. Ch. Patchogue, N.Y. Mem.: Investment Assn. NY, Assn. Investment Mgmt. and Rsch., Internat. Assn. Energy Economists, Nat. Assn. Petroleum Investment Analysts, Am. Petroleum Inst., Am. Econ. Assn., Oil Analysts Group N.Y., N.Y. Soc. Security Analysts, Phi Kappa Tau. Home and Office: 109 Namkee Rd Blue Point NY 11715

**OWEN, THOMAS WALKER,** banker, portfolio manager; b. Everett, Wash., June 7, 1925; s. Thomas Walker and Frances (Yantis) O.; m. Barbara May Neils, Oct. 20, 1951; children: Thomas W., Gerhard, Caroline, Jeffrey; m. Ingrid Lundgren, June 7, 1975. BA, U. Wash., 1949, MA in Finance, 1953; postgrad., Pacific Coast Banking Sch., 1956. Adminstrv. trainee Seattle Trust & Savs. Bank, 1949-54, asst. br. mgr., 1954-56, trust investment officer, 1956-57, mgr. investment dept., chmn. investment com., 1957-59; v.p., mgr. investment dept. Nat. Bank Wash., Tacoma, 1959-66, vice chmn., 1967-71; exec. v.p. bank adminstrn. Pacific Nat. Bank Wash., 1971-73; v.p. Reeder, Owen & Co., Inc., 1975-92; pres., chmn. Owen, Reeder, Inc., Merrill Lynch, 1991-92; bd. dirs. West One Bank Wash., Tacoma, 1981-93. Served with

AUS, 1943-45. Decorated Bronze Star, Purple Heart. Mem. N.W. Forum, Tacoma Club (past pres.), Tacoma Country and Golf Club, Phi Gamma Delta. Home: 11204 Tower Rd SW Lakewood WA 98498 Office Fax: 253-588-7483.

**OWEN, TONY QUINN,** investment company executive, horse trainer; b. Oklahoma City, Mar. 19, 1974; s. John Blair Owen and Margaret Ruth Wolford; 1 child, Danielle Kaye. AA in Architecture & Bus. Mhmt., Harrisburg C.C.; BA in Bus. and Fin. Mgmt., Northwestern U.; BA in Bus. Law, Villanova U., 1995. Cert. horse trainer. Gen. ptnr. Real Estate Lease Cons., Harrisburg, Pa., 1991—2002; architect Stonewall Golf Links, Elverson, 1992—94; pres., CEO Aztec Security Group, Carlisle, 1998—, Mystical Hannah Studios, 2005—, Stone Mountain Concrete, 2004—. Fin. advisor Loda Investment Group, Harrisburg, 2000—; equine instr. One Trick Pony, New Cumberland, 2000—02. Author: 26 Week Equitation Classes, 2003, OCD-Pieces of String, 2005. Asst. master counselor/chevaliar Order of DeMolay, Carlisle, 1987—; sec.youth aide panel Office Dist. Atty., Cumberland, 2004. Fellow: Am. Gemological Soc.; mem.: Pa. Guild of Craftsmen, Golf Soc. U.S., PGA Tour Ptnrs. Club. Avocations: horse training, skiing, cliff diving, hot air ballooning, golf. Home: 33 Village Ct Mechanicsburg PA 17050 Office Phone: 717-557-1293. E-mail: mysticalhannastudios@wildfun.com.

**OWEN, WILLIAM FRANKLIN,** academic administrator, former research and development company executive; b. Memphis, Nov. 11, 1955; m. Alice Crosby Owen; children: Lauren Leslie, William Franklin. MD, Tufts U., 1980. Cert. nephrology Am. Bd. Internal Medicine, 1985, internal medicine Am. Bd. Internal Medicine, 1984. Dir. dialysis svcs. Brigham and Women's Hosp., Boston, 1996—99; dir. Duke Inst. Renal Outcomes Rsch. Duke U. Med. Ctr., Durham, NC, 1999—2001; tenured prof. medicine Duke U. Sch. Medicine, Durham, 2001—01, adj. prof. medicine, 2002—; chief scientist Baxter Healthcare Corp., Renal, Deerfield, Ill., 2002—05; chancellor U. Tenn. Health Sci. Ctr., Memphis, 2005—. Chmn. internat. med. adv. bd. Nat. Kidney Found. Singapore, 1998; bd. sci. counsilors NIH, Bethesda, Md., 1998—2001; sci. adv. bd. U.S. Renal Data Sys., Bethesda, 2000—01; pres. Renal Physicians Assn., Bethesda, 2001—03; mem. medicare coverage adv. com. Ctrs. for Medicare and Medicaid Svcs., Balt., 2003—. Contbr. articles to profl. jours. Mem. site based com. Hillandale Elem. Sch., Durham, 1999—2000. Fellow, Robert Wood Johnson Found., 1985—89; grantee, NIH, 1984—. Avocation: astronomy. Office: U Tenn Health Sci Ctr Ste 220 62 South Dunlap Memphis TN 38163 Office Phone: 901-448-4796.*

**OWENDOFF, STEPHEN PETER,** lawyer; b. Morristown, N.J., Aug. 1, 1943; m.; 4 children. Student, Bowdoin Coll., 1966; BA, Kent State U., 1966; JD, Georgetown U., 1969. Bar: Ohio 1969. Assoc. Hahn Loeser & Parks and predecessor firms, Cleve., 1969-77; ptnr. Hahn Loeser & Parks (formerly Hahn, Loeser, Freedheim, Dean and Wellman), 1977—; mgmt. com. Hahn Loeser & Parks (formerly Hahn, Loeser, Freedheim Dean). Lectr. in field. Active Gesu Ch., University Heights, Ohio; mem. adv. bd. Learning About Bus., Inc.; past pres. Parmadale (Ohio) Adv. Bd.; bd. trustees, cmty. svcs. panel Fedn. Cath. Cmty. Svcs.; rep. United Way Assembly, Parmadale; bd. trustees LeBlond Housing Corp., Health Hill Hosp. Mem. Nat. Assn. Bond Lawyers, Nat. Assn. Coll. and Univ. Attys., Shaker Heights (Ohio) Country Club. Office: 3300 Bp Tower 200 Public Sq Cleveland OH 44114-2316

**OWEN-LEINERT, SUSAN HUFF,** voice educator, vocalist; b. Salisbury, NC, Sept. 6, 1958; d. James Bobby Huff and Mildred Clark Huff Simerson; m. Michael Leinert, Mar. 19, 1999. MusB, E. Carolina U., 1980; MusM, U. Tex., 1983. Opera singer Freelance, N.Y.C., 1985—95, Staatstheater Kassel, Germany, 1995—99, Staatstheater Darmstadt, Germany, 2000—02, Freelance, Duesseldorf, Germany, 2003—05; asst. prof. voice U. Memphis, 2005—; classical singer opera and concert Memphis, 2005—. Dir. Carolina Opera & Song Acad., Salisbury, NC, 2005—, Met. Opera Nat. Coun. Auditions, Memphis, 2005—. Singer: Der Ring des Nibelungen, Elektra, Tristan und Isolde, Der Fliegende Hollaender. Recipient First Pl. award, Met. Opera Nat. Coun., 1990, Opera Am., 1991, Sullivan Grant award, 1991. Mem.: Nat. Assn. of Tchrs. Singing (life). Office: U Memphis Rudi E Scheidt Sch Music Memphis TN 38152 Home: PO Box 22098 Memphis TN 38122 Office Phone: 901-678-4082. Business E-Mail: susan.owen-leinert@memphis.edu.

**OWENS, B. MITCHELL,** lab administrator; With GTE Tech. Products Divsn., Kayser-Roth Corp.; from dir. opers. to gen. mgr. Medtox Scientific Inc., 1988—2000, v.p., COO, 2000—. Office: Medtox Scientific Inc 402 County Rd D Saint Paul MN 55112

**OWENS, BILL,** governor; b. Ft. Worth, Tex., Oct. 22, 1950; s. Arthur and June Owens; m. Frances Owens; children: Monica, Mark, Brett. BA, Stephen F. Austin State U., 1973; MPA, U. Tex., 1975. With Touche Ross & Co., Gates Corp.; mem. Colo. Ho. Reps., 1983-89, Colo. State Sen., 1989-94; treas. State of Colo., 1994-98, gov., 1999—. Guest host Mike Rosen, Ken Hamblin and Chuck Baker talk shows; lectr. Russia. Contbr. more than 50 articles to profl. jours. Named One of Country's Ten Up-and-Coming leaders Robert Novak. Republican. Catholic. Office: Office of Governor 200 East Colfax Rm 136 Denver CO 80203 Office Phone: 303-866-2471. Office Fax: 303-866-2003. E-mail: governorowens@state.co.us.*

**OWENS, BIRDIE MURPHY,** retired music educator; d. Jesse and Emily Murphy; m. Eddie Lee Owens, July 1, 1969; children: Birdette, Eddie Jr., Heather. BS in Choral Music, SC State Coll., 1968, BS in Instrumental Music, 1968; MusM, Winthrop U., 1975. Chorus tchr. Guinyard Butler HS, Barnwell, SC, 1969—70, Rock Hill Sch. Dist. #3, SC, 1977—2004; gen. music tchr. Southside Elem. Sch., Lancaster, SC, 1970—73; music edn. work study tchr. Winthrop U., Rock Hill, SC, 1974—75; piano, voice chorus tchr. OASIS Performing Arts Sch., Charlotte, NC, 2004—; ret., 2004. Vol. World Vision Activities, Food for the Hungry Activities, Worldwide Christian Ministries; min. music Silver Mt. Baptist Ch., Charlotte, 1970—; husband and wife founder Bone of My Bone Flesh of My Flesh Marriage Ministry, 2003—. Mem.: Music Edn. Nat. Conf., Delta Sigma Theta. Democrat. Baptist. Avocations: reading, walking, jogging, singing, piano.

**OWENS, CECELIE ANN,** elementary school educator; b. Buffalo, N.Y., Apr. 26, 1962; d. Willa Mae Caver; 1 child, Joshua C. BS in Edn., Buffalo State Coll., NY, 1985, MS in Edn., 1999, Canisius Coll., 2004, degree in Sch. Dist. Adminstrn., 2004. Tchr. Buffalo (N.Y.) Pub. Schs., 1996—. Dir. camp Girl Scouts, Buffalo, 1985—90; dir. activities Nat. Youth Sports Program, Buffalo, 1999—. Named to Athletic Hall Fame, Athletic Dept., Buffalo (N.Y.) State Coll., 1998. Mem.: ASCD, Phi Delta Kappa. Avocation: basketball. Office: Buffalo Pub Schs Build Academy 91 Buffalo NY 14204 also: Buffalo Pub Schs City Hall Rm 720 Buffalo NY 14202

**OWENS, CHARLES VINCENT, JR.,** pharmaceutical executive, consultant; b. Kansas City, Mo., May 15, 1927; s. Charles Vincent and Helen (Barrett) O.; m. Cheryl Kreighbaum, Feb. 13, 1977; children: Melody, Kevin, Michael, John, Barbara. BS, U. Notre Dame, 1948; MS (Univ. fellow), U. N.C., 1949. Public health educator Richmond County (N.C.) Health Dept., 1949-51; with Miles Labs., Inc., Elkhart, Ind., 1951-82, pres. Ames Co. div., 1967-71, group v.p. profl. products group, 1971-77, exec. v.p. internat. ops., 1977-82; chmn., CEO Kyoto Diagnostics, Inc., 1982—85. Bd. dirs. Chronimed Inc.; CEO Genesis Inc., 1989—91. Bd. dirs. Elkhart YWCA, 1972-76, St. Jude Med. Inc., 1982-94; vice-chmn. Elkhart County Bd. Health, 1973-77; chmn. Child Abuse Task Force, Elkhart County, Ind., 1977-78; pres. Blue Crab Key Condo Assn., 1995-99, dir., 2003-04. With M.C., USAAF, 1945-47. Mem. Am. Public Health Assn., Health Industry Mfg. Assn. (dir.), Pharm. Mfrs. Assn., Nat. Pharm. Council (pres. 1970-71, dir. 1965-73), Am. Mgmt. Assn., Am. Diabetes Assn., Am. Assn. Diabetes Educators, Internat. Diabetes Fedn., Am. Soc. Med. Tech., Elcona Country Club (bd. dirs.), Nat. Home Dame Monogram Club (bd. dirs.). Republican. Roman Catholic. Office Phone: 574-264-9720.

**OWENS, CHUCK,** secondary school educator, broadcast technician; s. Lois Owens; m. Carolyn Sue Quillen, Oct. 5, 1980. BS in Social Studies, Lincoln Meml. U., Harrogate, Tenn., 1991; MEd, Cumberland Coll. Williamsburg, Ky., 1992. Tchr. Barbourville City Sch., Barbourville, Ky., 1992—99; social studies tchr./dept. chairperson Middlesboro H.S., Ky., 1999—. Broadcast engr. Cumberland Gap Broadcasting, Middlesboro, Ky., 1972—2006. With Ky. N.G., 1989—90. Mem.: NEA. Home: PO Box 2189 Middlesboro KY 40965 Office: Middlesboro High School 4404 W Cumberland Ave Middlesboro KY 40965 Office Phone: 606-242-8820. Personal E-mail: ceowens3@earthlink.net.

**OWENS, DANA** See QUEEN LATIFAH

**OWENS, DOUGLAS K.,** physician, researcher; s. Richard C. and Dorothy D. Owens; m. Sara H. Cody. BS, Stanford U., Stanford, California, 1978; MS, Stanford U., Stanford, Calif., 1991; MD, U. Calif., San Francisco, 1982. Diplomate Am. Bd. of Internal Medicine, 1985. Prof. medicine Stanford U., 2006—, assoc. prof. medicine, 1997—2006, asst. prof. medicine, 1991—97. Trustee Soc. for Med. Decision Making, Phila., 1995—97, pres., 1998—99; chair, clin. efficacy assessment com. ACP, Phila., 2005—. Recipient Rsch. Assoc. Career Devel. Award, Dept. Vet. Affairs, 1992-1995, Sr. Rsch. Assoc. Career Devel. Award, 1995 to 1999; Fellowship Health Care Rsch. and Health Policy, Stanford U., 1998-1991. Mem.: Soc. for Med. Decision Making (pres. 1998—99, Lee Lusted Prize 1991), ACP (chair, clin. efficacy assessment com. 2005), Phi Beta Kappa. Office: Stanford U 117 Encina Commons Stanford CA 94305-6019 Office Phone: 650-723-0933.

**OWENS, FRANK JAMES,** physicist; b. Dublin; came to U.S., 1947; s. Arthur Henry and Kathleen Mary (McKormack) O.; m. Janice Elizabeth Rourk, Sept. 8, 1971; 1 child. Arthur. BS, Manhattan Coll., 1962; MS, U. Conn., 1964, PhD, 1968. Space scientist NASA, Greenbelt, Md., 1964, 65; rsch. asst. dept. physics U. Conn., Storrs, 1965-68; rsch. physicist Dept. Army, Feltman Rsch. Lab., Picatinny, N.J., 1970-79; asst. tech. dir. Armament Rsch. and Devel. Command, Dover, N.J., 1979-80; chief molecular properties sect. Energetic Materials Lab., Picatinny, 1980-84, chief physics br., 1985-89; prof. physics Hunter Coll., CUNY, N.Y.C., 1989-90; mem faculty Grad. Sch. of CUNY, 1990—; sr. rsch. physicist Armament R&D Ctr., Picatinny, 1990—. Author: The New Superconductors, 1996, Electromagnetic Absorption in Copper Oxide Superconductors, 1999, Introduction to Nanotechnology, 2003; editor: Magnetic Resonance of Phase Transitions, 1979, Vibrational Spectroscopy of Phase Transitions, 1984; contbr. articles to profl. jours. Recipient Army R&D award, 1984, 95, 98; Sec. of Army fellow Office of Sec. of Army, 1989. Fellow Am. Phys. Soc.; mem. Park Lakes Tennis Club (pres. 1995—, bd. dirs.), Sigma Xi, Sigma Pi Sigma. Avocations: tennis, sailing. Office: Armament Rsch and Devel Ctr Bldg 3022 Picatinny Arsenal NJ 07806 Business E-Mail: fowens@pica.army.mil.

**OWENS, GUY,** retired neurosurgeon; b. Amarillo, Tex., Jan. 25, 1926; s. Guy Fitzhugh Owens and Mary Helen Virgin; m. Lillian Janet Parkinson, June 20, 1949; children: Victoria Ann, Guy Parkinson. BS, Tufts U., 1946; MD, Harvard U., 1950. Diplomate Am. Bd. Neurol. Surgery. Intern Vanderbilt U. Hosp., Nashville, 1950—51, resident in gen. surgery, 1954—57; asst. prof. Vanderbilt U., Nashville, 1958—62; assoc. prof. SUNY, Buffalo, 1963—68; prof. surgery, head dept. U. Conn. Med. Sch., Farmington, Conn., 1968—75; pvt. practice New Britain, Conn., 1975—2003; ret., 2003. Author: Neurologic and Neurosurgical Nursing, 1975; contbr. over 130 articles to profl. jours. Home: 41 Main St Farmington CT 06032-2229

**OWENS, HAROLD B.,** former state agency consultant; b. Knapp, Wis., Oct. 1, 1926; s. John Donald and Mabel Evelyn (Dunn) O.; m. Hazel Marie Allison, Feb. 18, 1956; children: Robert Bruce, Patrick Brian (dec.), Michael Shawn. Student, U. Mont., 1944, Rollins Coll., 1961—62, U. Hawaii, 1964—65. Airline transport pilot rating, FAA. Field rep. Puget Sound Power & Light, Kirkland, Wash., 1946—48; machinist Boeing Co., Seattle, 1948; commd. officer and pilot USAF, 1949, advanced through grades to col., 1979, ret., 1979; exec. dir. Tex. Soc. Energy Auditors, College Station, 1979—80; v.p. ops. Entek Assocs., Inc., College Station, 1979—88; aviation cons. Tex. Aeronautics Commn., Austin, 1983—89; rsch. assoc. Ctr. for Strategic Tech. Tex. A&M U. Sys., College Station, 1979—82; ret., 1992. Aviation instr. Bryan, Tex., 1979—; indd. energy cons., 1988—. Contbr. articles to profl. jours. Commr. Bryan Hist. Landmark Commn., 1993-96; mem. SCV, 2000—. With U.S. Army, 1944-46, ETO, with USAF, 1947-79, Korea, S.E. Asia. Decorated Legion of Merit, Bronze Star, Air Medal (7). Mem. Nat. Soc. Historic Preservation, Tex. Hist. Found., Nat. R.R. Hist. Soc. (nat. dir. 1988—), Air Force Assn. (charter; chpt. pres. 1980-82, v.p. S.E. region Tex. chpt. 1998-2000), Nat. Assn. Flight Instrs., Order of Daedalians, Tex. A&M Assn. Former Students, Century Club, Faculty Club, Coll. Station Noon Lion's Club, The Ret. Officers Assn., Aircraft Owner's and Pilots Assn., Quiet Birdmen, Sons of Confederate Vets. Republican. Avocations: flying, music, sports, travel. Home: 3207 Wilderness Rd Bryan TX 77807-3222 Office Phone: 979-777-3740. E-mail: tex@txcyber.com.

**OWENS, JAMES W.,** manufacturing executive; b. Elizabeth City, NC; PhD in Econs., NC State U., 1973. Corp. economist Caterpillar Inc., Peoria, Ill., 1972—75; chief economist Caterpillar Overseas S.A., Geneva, 1975—80; mgmt. positions, Acctg., Product Source Planning Depts. Caterpillar Inc., Peoria, 1980—87, mng. dir., P.T. Natra Raya Indonesia, 1987—90, pres., Solar Turbines Inc., 1990—93, v.p. group vics. divsn. Peoria, Ill., 1993-94, group pres., 1995—2003, vice chmn., 2003—04, chmn., CEO, 2004—. Bd. dir. Inst. Internat. Econ., Washington, Alcoa Inc., IBM. Mem.: Mfg. Council, Council on Fgn. Reln. Office: Caterpillar Inc 100 NE Adams St Peoria IL 61629*

**OWENS, JANA JAE,** entertainer; b. Great Falls, Mont., Aug. 30, 1943; d. Jacob G. Meyer and Bette P. (Sprague) Hopper; m. Sidney Greif (div.); children: Matthew N., Sydni C.; m. Buck Owens. Student, Interlochen Music Camp, 1959, Internat. String Congress, 1960, Vienna Acad. Music, 1963—64; BA magna cum laude, MusB magna cum laude, Colo. Womens Coll., 1965. Tchr. music Ontario Pub. Schs., Oreg., 1965—67, Redding Pub. Schs., Calif., 1969—74; entertainer Buck Owens Enterprises, Bakersfield, Calif., 1974—78, Tulsa, 1979—. Concertmistress Boise Philharm., Idaho, 1965—67, Shasta Symphony, Redding, 1969—74; founder Grand Lake Festivals, Inc., Tulsa, 1996—. Rec. artist (violinist, vocalist) Lark Records, 1978—. Avocations: skiing, tennis, swimming. Office: Jana Jae Enterprises Lark Record Prodns Inc PO Box 35726 Tulsa OK 74153-0726 Business E-Mail: janajae@janajae.com.

**OWENS, KATHLEEN C.,** academic administrator; married; 2 children. BS in Biology, Loyola U., Chgo.; MS in Edn. Biol. Scis., DePaul U., Chgo.; EdD in Curriculum and Instr., Loyola U., Chgo. Dean Lewis U., Romeoville, Ill., 1986—92; v.p. academic affairs St. Francis U., Loretta, Pa., 1992—2002; pres. Gwynedd-Mercy Coll., Gwynedd Valley, Pa., 2002—. Office: Gwynedd-Mercy Coll PO Box 901 1325 Sumneytown Pike Gwynedd Valley PA 19437-0901

**OWENS, LAURA,** painter; b. Euclid, Ohio, 1970; BFA, RI Sch. Design, 1992; MFA, Calif. Inst. Arts, Valencia, Calif., 1994; attended, Sch. Painting & Sculpture, Skowhegan, Maine, 1994. Represented in permanent collections, Guggenheim, NY, Centre Georges Pompidou, Paris, exhibitions include, Rosamund Felsen, Santa Monica, Calif., 1995, Painting Show, Regen Projects, LA, 1995, Palace, Beret Internat. Gallery, Chgo., 1997, Sadie Cole's Headquarters, London, 1997, Young Americans II, Saatchi Collection London, 1998, Gavin Brown's Enterprise, NY, 1998, Galerie Gisela Capitain Köln, Germany, 1999, Examining Pictures, Whitechapel Art Gallery, London, 1999, Original Language, Mus. Contemporary Art, Chgo., 2001, New Work, Isabella Stewart Gardner Mus., Boston, 2001, Urgent Painting, Musée d'Art

Moderne de la Ville de Paris, 2002, Laura Owens, Milw. Art Mus., 2003, the undiscovered country, UCLA Hammer Museum, LA, 2004, Whitney Biennial, Whitney Mus. Am. Art, 2004. Mailing: c/o ACME 6150 Wilshire Blvd #1 Los Angeles CA 90048

**OWENS, LAURA LEWIS,** lawyer; b. Atlanta, Sept. 27, 1960; BA cum laude, Furman U., 1982; JD cum laude, U. Ga., 1985. Bar: Ga. 1985. Ptnr., leader, product liability group Alston & Bird L.L.P., Atlanta. Mem. editl. bd. Ga. Jour. Internat. and Comparative Law, 1983-85, editor-in-chief, 1984-85; author: Annual Survey of Developments in International Trade Law, 1983. Mem. Atlanta Bar Assn., State Bar of Ga. Office: Alston & Bird 1 Atlantic Ctr 1201 W Peachtree St NW Atlanta GA 30309-3424 Office Phone: 404-881-7363. Office Fax: 404-881-7777. Business E-Mail: lowens@alston.com.

**OWENS, MAJOR ROBERT ODELL,** congressman; b. Memphis, June 28, 1936; m. Marie Cuprill; children: Christopher, Geoffrey, Millard, Carlos, Cecilia. BA with high honors in Math., Morehouse Coll., Atlanta, 1956; MLS, Atlanta U., 1957; grad. student, Columbia U. V.p. Met. Coun. Housing, 1964; chair Bklyn. Congress Racial Equality, 1964—66; cmty. coord. Bklyn. Pub. Libr., 1964—66; exec. dir. Brownsville Cmty. Coun., 1966; commr. NYC Cmty. Devel. Agy., 1968—73; dir. cmty. media libr. prog. Columbia U., 1973—75; mem. NY State Senate, 1975—82, US Congress from 11th NY dist., 1983—, mem. edn. and the workforce com., mem. govt. reform com., ranking minority mem. workforce protections subcommittee, chmn. select edn. and civil rights subcommittee, mem. progressive caucus. Mem. Internat. Commn. on Ways of Implementing Social Policy to Ensure Maximum Pub. Participation and Social Justice for Minorities, The Hague, Netherlands, 1972; keynote speaker White House Conf. on Librs., 1979. Pub. author and lectr. on libr. sci. Chmn. Dem. Ops. Com. Major R. Owens Day named in his honor, City Bklyn., 1971; named one of Most Influential Black Americans, Ebony mag., 2006. Mem.: ALA, NAACP. Democrat. Baptist. Office: US Ho Reps 2309 Rayburn Ho Office Bldg Washington DC 20515 Office Phone: 202-225-6231.*

**OWENS, MARVIN FRANKLIN, JR.,** oil industry executive, director; b. Oklahoma City, Feb. 20, 1916; s. Marvin Franklin and Lewis (Coley) O.; m. Jessie Ruth Hay, June 15, 1941; children: Marvin Franklin III, William Earl, Jack Hay. BS, U. Okla., 1937; postgrad., Rutgers U., 1960-62. Petroleum engr. Brit. Am. Oil Producing Co., Oklahoma City, 1937-41; chief petroleum engr. Bay Petroleum Corp., Denver, 1941-54; sr. v.p. Cen. Bank of Denver, 1954-81. Elder Presbyn. Ch., Denver. With U.S. Army, 1941-46; col. Res. ret. Mem. Cherry Hills Country Club. Home: 6513 S Glencoe St Centennial CO 80121

**OWENS, MELVIN;** public safety administrator, minister; s. Mary Faye Owens-Lyerly; m. Deborah Lynne Bell, June 18, 1977; 1 child, Kelvin Brian. BS, Faulkner U., 1992; MS, U. Ala., Tuscaloosa, 1996. Detective Auburn U. Police, Ala., capt., aux. svcs., 1988—97; dep. dir. dept. pub. safety Auburn U., 1997—2004, pub. safety adminstr., 2004—. Pastor Mt. Zion Bapt. Ch., LaFayette, 1991—2005; 1st v.p. Ala. Bapt. NE Dist. State Conv., Gadsden, Ala., 1996—2005; pres. East Ala. Congress Christian Edn., LaFayette, 1988—2005. Named one of Outstanding Young Men of Am., 1975, 1991. Mem.: FBI Nat. Acad. Assocs. (assoc.; pres. Ala. chpt.). Missionary Baptist. Avocations: reading, tennis. Office: Auburn Univ 215 South Donahue Dr Auburn University AL 36849 Office Fax: 334-844-2253.

**OWENS, ROBERT W.,** gas industry executive; Bus. Degree, Calif. Poly. State U., 1976; MBA, Northwestern U. From mktg. trainee to dist. mgr. Mobil Oil Corp., 1976—88; corp. planner Amerada Hess, 1988—89, mgr. East Coast Branded mktg. ops., 1989—94; v.p. mktg. and svcs. Ultramar Diamond Shamrock, 1994—97; joined Sunoco, Inc., Phila., 1997, v.p. East Coast mktg., 1997—2000, sr. v.p. mktg., 2000—, v.p. Midwest mktg., 2001—. Office: Sunoco Inc Ten Penn Ctr 1801 Market St Philadelphia PA 19103-1699

**OWENS, ROCHELLE,** poet, playwright; b. Bklyn., Apr. 2, 1936; d. Max and Molly (Adler) Bass; m. George Economou, June 17, 1962. Writer-in-residence, Brown U., 1989; tchr. U. Calif. 1982, U. Okla., 1985, 87, 88, U. Southwestern La., 1998, Tex. A&M Univ. Author: (plays) The String Game, 1965, Istanboul, 1965 (Obie award 1966), Futz, 1967, Homo, 1966, Beclch, 1966, Futz and What Came After, 1968, He Wants Shih, 1969, Farmers Almanac, 1969, The Queen of Greece, 1969, Kontraption, 1970, The Karl Marx Play, 1971, O.K. Certaldo, 1975, Emma Instigated Me, 1976, The Widow and the Colonel, 1977, Mountain Rites, 1977, Who Do You Want, Peire Vidal, 1978, Chucky's Hunch, 1981 (Obie award 1982), Who Do You Want, Peire Vidal, 1982, Plays by Rochelle Owens, 2000, (poetry) Not be Essence That Cannot Be, 1961, Salt and Core, 1968, I am the Babe of Joseph Stalin's Daughter, Poems from Joe's Garage, The Joe 82 Creation Poems, The Karl Marx Play & Others, The Joe Chronicles, Part 2, Four Young Lady Poets, 1962, Shemuel, 1979, French Light, 1984, Constructs, 1985, Anthropologists at a Dinner Party, 1985, Who Do You Want Peire Vidal, 1986, W.C. Fields in French Light, 1986, How Much Paint Does the Painting Need, 1988, Black Chalk, 1995, New and Selected Poems: 1961-1996, Rubbed Stones: Poems from 1960-1992, 1994, The Passersby, 1993, Wild River, Poems, 1999, Luca: Discourse on Life and Death, 2001, (radio play) Sweet Potatoes, 1979 (Obie award 1982); (The Passerby by Liliane Atlan (translation); feature film) Futz, 1969 (Obie award); North American Women's Drama From Colonial Times to Present, 2004; editor: (plays) Spontaneous Combustion (Obie award 1967); recs. include: From a Shaman's Notebook, 1968, The Karl Marx Play, 1974, Totally Corrupt, 1976, Black Box 17, 1979, (play) Three Front, 1990, (radio play) Guerre a'Trois, 1991; reading performances at St. Mark's Poetry Project, Mus. Modern Art, Guggenheim, Whitney Mus., Oxford U., Am. Coll., Paris, Kelly Writer's House, Pa.; host of The Writer's Mind; prodr. radio show, U. Okla.; (video) Oklahoma Too, 1987, How Much Paint Does the Painting Need, Black Chalk, 1995; prodr.: (CD ROM) N.Am. Women's Drama, 2004; reading performance: Am. Coll. Athens, Greece. Founding mem. N.Y. Theatre Strategy, Women's Theatre Coun. Ford Found. grantee, 1965, Creative Arts Pub. Svc. grantee, 1973, Nat. Endowment for Arts grantee, 1974, Rockefeller Found. grantee, 1974; Yale Sch. Drama fellow, 1968, Guggenheim fellow, 1971; honors N.Y. Drama Critics Cir.; Rockefeller Found. Guggenheim Resident, 1993; recipient Nomination in poetry Okla. Ctr. for the Book, 1995. Mem. Dramatists Guild, ASCAP. Achievements include being in anthologies. *Creativity and idealism have enabled me to pursue the world of ideas, transforming itself always into art.*

**OWENS, RONALD STEPHEN (RONN OWENS),** radio talk show host; b. N.Y.C., Oct. 17, 1945; s. Stanley S. Lowenstein and Monica (Frank) Owens; m. Jan Black; children: Sarah, Laura. BA with honors, Temple U., 1967, MA, 1969. Talk show host Sta. WCAU, Phila., 1968-70; Sta. WKAT, Miami Beach, Fla., 1970-71, Sta. WERE, Cleve., 1971-74, Sta. WRNG, Atlanta, 1974-75, KGO/ABC, San Francisco, 1975—. Hosted live radio call-in from S. Africa, 1985; author: Voice of Reason: Why The Left & Right Are Wrong, 2004. Bd. dirs. Am. Lung Assn., San Francisco. Named Top Radio Personality in San Francisco Bay Area, Oakland Tribune, 1986, One of the Top Radio Talk Show Hosts in USA Radio and Records, 1985, one of Top 25 Greatest Radio Talk Show Hosts of All Time, Talkers Mag., 2002; recipient Marconi Radio award for Major Market Personality of Yr., Nat. Assn. Broadcasters, 2003. Mem.: Concordia-Argonaut (San Francisco). Avocation: thoroughbred racing. Office: KGO-AM 3rd Fl 900 Front St San Francisco CA 94111-1427*

**OWENS, SUE GASTON,** retired middle school educator; b. Charleston, S.C., Nov. 6, 1955; d. Dearman Samuel and Harriet (Gaston) O. BS, Winthrop U., 1976; MEd, Converse Coll., 1981. Tchr. Whitlock Jr. H.S., Spartanburg, SC, 1977—2006; ret., 2006. Bd. dirs. Bethlehem Cmty. Ctr., Spartanburg, 1991-96; dist. rep. Wallace (S.C.) Family Life Ctr., 1992-97; cert. lay spkr. S.C. conf. United Meth. Ch., 1991—; pres. Spartanburg dist. United Meth. Women, 1993-96, coord. membership, nurture and outreach of S.C. conf., 1996-2000; mem. South Atlantic Regional Sch. of Christian Mission Planning Team, 1997-2000; dir. women's divsn. Gen. Bd. of Global Ministries, United Meth. Ch., 2000—, dir. gen. bd. global ministry, 2004—, exec. bd. women's

divsn., chair mission schs. and studies, exec. com. mem. and orgn. devel. sect., mem. mission edn., nominations and bylaws com. Mem. AAHPERD, NEA, S.C. Alliance for Health, Phys. Edn., Recreation and Dance, S.C. Edn. Assn.

**OWENS, SUSAN,** state supreme court justice; b. Kinston, NC, Aug. 19, 1949; d. Frank and Hazel Owens; children: Sunny Roloff, Owen Golden. BA, Duke U., 1971; JD, U. N.C., Chapel Hill, 1975. Bar: Oreg. 1975, Wash. 1976. Judge Dist. Ct., Western Clallam County, 1981—2001; chief judge Quileute Tribe, Lower Elwha S'Klallam Tribe; justice Wash. Supreme Ct., 2001—. Co-founder, chair Rural Courts Com., 1990; lecturer Jud. Coll., Nat. Coll. of Prosecuting Attorneys' Domestic Violence Conference. Co-author: Northwest Tribal Judges Domestic Violence Manual. Mem.: Dist. and Mcpl. Ct. Judges' Assn. (bd. dirs., sec.-treas., v.p., pres.-elect). Avocation: baseball. Office: Wash Supreme Ct PO Box 40929 Olympia WA 98504-0929

**OWENS, TERRELL ELDORAD,** professional football player; b. Alexander City, Ala., Dec. 7, 1973; s. Marilyn Heard; 1 child, Terique. BA in Merchandising, U. Tenn. Chattanooga, 1996. Wide receiver San Francisco 49ers, 1996—2003, Phila. Eagles, 2004—06, Dallas Cowboys, 2006—. Co-author (with Steven Singular): Catch This: Going Deep With the NFL's Sharpest Weapon, 2004; co-author: (with Jason Rosenhaus) T.O., 2006. Named All-Pro, 2001—02, 2004; named to Pro-Bowl team, 2000—04. Achievements include set NFL record for most receptions in one game (20), 2000. Office: Dallas Cowboys One Cowboys Pkwy Irving TX 75063*

**OWENS, VICKI PALMER,** elementary school educator, academic coordinator; d. Peggy Harvey and Robert Lee Richmond (Stepfather), Curry MacDonald Palmer; m. Tony Allen Owens, July 9, 1983. BS, Miss. State U., 1981. Cert. master reading tchr. Tex. 1st grade tchr. Whittier Elem. Sch./Houston Ind. Sch. Dist., Jacinto City, Tex., 1981—83, William Brown Miller Elem. Sch./Dallas Ind. Sch. Dist., 1984; 1st and 3rd grade tchr. J.P. Starks Elem. Sch./Dallas Ind. Sch. Dist., Dallas, 1985—91; 4th grade tchr. Gill Elem. Sch./Dallas Ind. Sch. Dist., Dallas, 1991—2003; master reading tchr. Charles A. Gill Elem. Sch., Dallas, 2002—; academic coord., 2004—. Named Tchr. of Yr., Gill Elem. Sch., 1994, Disney's Tchr., 2000. Mem.: ASCD, Nat. Coun. Tchrs. English, Internat. Reading Assn., Delta Kappa Gamma (ceremonies co-chmn. 2002—06). Office Phone: 972-749-8400.

**OWENS, WILBUR DAWSON, JR.,** federal judge; b. Albany, Ga., Feb. 1, 1930; s. Wilbur Dawson and Estelle (McKenzie) O.; m. Mary Elizabeth Glenn, June 21, 1958; children: Lindsey, Wilbur Dawson III, Estelle, John. Student, Emory U., 1947-48; JD, U. Ga., 1952. Bar: Ga. 1952. Mem. firm Smith, Gardner & Owens, Albany, 1954-55; v.p., trust officer Bank of Albany, 1955-59; sec.-treas. Southeastern Mortgage Co., Albany, 1959-65; asst. U.S. atty. Middle Dist. Ga., Macon, 1962-65; assoc., then ptnr. Bloch, Hall, Hawkins & Owens, Macon, 1965-72; judge U.S. Dist. Ct. for Mid. Dist. Ga., Macon, 1972—, now sr. U.S. dist. judge. Served to 1st lt., JAG USAF, 1952-54. Mem. State Bar Ga., Macon Bar Assn., Am. Judicature Soc., Phi Delta Theta, Phi Delta Phi. Clubs: Rotarian, Idle Hour Golf and Country. Republican. Presbyterian. Office: US Dist Ct PO Box 65 Macon GA 31202-0065 Office Phone: 478-752-3491.

**OWENS, WILLIAM ARTHUR (BILL OWENS),** telecommunications industry executive, retired military officer; b. Bismarck, N.D., May 8, 1940; s. Earl and Ruth (Arthur) O.; m. Monika Bastian, Sept. 30, 1967; 1 child, Todd. BS in Math., US Naval Acad., 1962; BA, MA in Politics, Philosophy and Econ., U. Oxford, Eng., 1974; MBA, George Washington U., 1976. Registered profl. engr. Commd. ensign USN, 1962, advanced through ranks to admiral, 1994, multiple assignments in nuclear submarines, 1962-77; comdg. officer USS Sam Houston (SSBN609), Honolulu, 1977-80, USS Corpus Christi (SSN705), New London, Conn., 1980-81, Submarine Squadron 4, Charleston, SC, 1984-85, Submarine Group 6, Charleston, SC, 1987-88; dir. office of program appraisal for the Sect. of the Navy Washington, 1988; sr. mil. asst. to Sec. Def., 1988—91; comdr. US 6th Fleet, Gaeta, Italy, 1990—91; dep. chief naval ops. for resources, warfare requirements and assessments Resources, Warfare Requirements & Assessments, Washington, 1991—93; vice-chmn. Joint Chiefs of Staff The Pentagon, Washington, 1993—96; vice chmn., pres., COO Sci. Applications Internat. Corp., 1996-98; joined Teledesic LLC, 1998, vice-chmn., co-CEO, 1999—2003, chmn., CEO, 2003—04; CEO Nortel Networks Corp., Brampton, Ont., Canada, 2004—05, vice-chmn., 2005—. Founder Extend America; bd. dirs. Daimler Chrysler AG, Nortel Networks Corp., 2002—; sr. advisor AEA Investors LLC; bd. dirs. Polycom, Inc. Author: Future of the Maritime Strategy, 1988, High Seas, 1994, Lifting the Fog of War, 2000; contr. articles on national security. Trustee Carnegie Corp.; mem. Carnegie Found., Brookings Instn., Fred Hutchinson Cancer Rsch. Ctr., Can. Coun. Chief Executives. Named 50 Most Powerful People in Networking, Network World, 2004; recipient Intrepid Salute award, Intrepid Foundation, 2004. Mem. Submarine League, U.S. Naval Acad. Alumni Assn., Oxford Soc., Coun. Fgn. Rels. Episcopalian. Avocations: golf, tennis.*

**OWENS, WILLIAM DEAN,** lawyer; b. Topeka, Kans., July 3, 1931; s. Claude and Melvina Owens; m. Doris McConnell, June 10, 1953; children: Steven D., Susan Bloom, Sarah Steele. BS in Bus., U. Kans., Lawrence, 1953, JD, 1968. Bar: Kans. 1968. Mgr. McConnell Lumber Co., Lawrence, 1955-65; ptnr. Hampton & Royce, L.C., Salina, Kans., 1968—2004. Trustee, chmn. Kansas Wesleyan U., Salina, 1990-99, Salina Regional Health Found., 1986-2004; trustee Eisenhower Found., 1999—. Capt. USMC, 1953-55, Japan. Fellow Kans. Bar Found.; mem. ABA, Kans. Bar Assn. Republican. Congregational. Avocations: golf, travel, woodworking. Home: 1707 Prestwick Dr Lawrence KS 66047 Office: Hampton & Royce LC 119 W Iron Ave 9th Flr Salina KS 67402-1247 E-mail: ddowens@sunflower.com.

**OWENS, WILLIAM DON,** anesthesiology educator; b. St. Louis, Dec. 12, 1939; s. Don and Caroline Wilhemena (Raaf) Owens; m. Patricia Gail Brown, Dec. 12, 1964; children: Pamela, David, Susan. AB, Westminster Coll., 1961; MD, U. Mich., 1965. Diplomate Am. Bd. Anesthesiology. Resident and fellow Mass. Gen. Hosp. and Harvard Med. Sch., Boston, 1969—72; instr. Harvard Med. Sch., Boston, 1972—73; asst. prof. anesthesiology Washington U. Sch. Medicine, St. Louis, 1973—76, assoc. prof., 1976—82, prof., 1982—2004, prof. emeritus, 2004—, chmn. dept., 1982—92. Trustee Barnes Hosp., St. Louis, 1987—89; bd. dirs. Anesthesia Found., 1994—, pres., 1999—; sec.-treas. Am. Bd. Anesthesiology, 1991—94, pres., 1995—96, bd. dirs., 1984—96, Found. Anesthesia Edn. and Rsch., 1990—95, pres., 1994—95; mem. Mo. State Bd. Healing Arts, 2003—04. Assoc. editor Survey of Anesthesiology, 1977—92; contbr. numerous articles to profl. jours. and chpts. to books. Served to lt. comdr. USN, 1966—69. Fellow: Am. Coll. Anesthesiology; mem.: Assn. Univ. Anesthesiologists, Acad. Anesthesiology, Internat. Anesthesia Rsch. Soc., Am. Soc. Anesthesiologists (bd. dirs. 1989—99, 1st v.p. 1995—96, pres. 1997—98). Office: Washington U Sch Med Dept Anesthesiology 660 S Euclid Ave Saint Louis MO 63110-1010 Office Phone: 314-362-4439.

**OWINGS, DONALD HENRY,** psychologist, educator; b. Atlanta, Dec. 7, 1943; s. Markley James and Loyce Erin (White) O.; m. Sharon Elizabeth Calhoun, Jan. 29, 1966; children: Ragon Matthew, Anna Rebekah. BA in Psychology, U. Tex., 1965; PhD, U. Wash., 1972. Asst. prof. psychology U. Calif., Davis, 1971—78, assoc. prof., 1978—83, prof., 1983—, chair dept., 1989—93. Editor: (with M.D. Beecher & N.S. Thompson) Perspectives in Ethology, Vol. 12: Communication, 1997, (with R.G. Coss & K.R. Henry) Introduction to Psychobiol., 1998, 99 (2nd edit.), 2003 (3rd edit.), (with C.M. Greene, L.A. Hart and A.P. Klimley) Jour. Comparative Psychology, Special Issue: Revisiting the Unwelt: Environments of Animal Communication, 2002; author: (with E.P. Morton) Animal Vocal Communication: A New Approach, 1998; contbr. articles to profl. jours., book chpts. NSF rsch. grantee, 1978-80, 82-84. Fellow Animal Behavior Soc.; mem. Internat. Soc. for Comparative Psychology, Internat. Soc. for Behavioral Ecology. Democrat. Avocations:

hiking, wildlife, travel, reading. Home: 815 Oeste Dr Davis CA 95616-1856 Office: U Calif Dept Psychology 1 Shields Ave Davis CA 95616-8686 Office Phone: 530-752-1673. Business E-Mail: dhowings@ucdavis.edu.

**OWINGS, JOHN R,** corporate financial executive; b. Chgo., 1949; BSc in acctg., No. Ill. U., 1971, MBA in fin., 1976. Sr. v.p., dir. fin., global telecom solutions segment Motorola Inc., 1998—2000, sr. v.p. fin., personal commn. segment, 2000—02; v.p., CFO Air Products, 2002—. Mem. exec. adv. coun. Coll. of Bus. at No. Ill. U., mem. bd. of exec. adv.

**OWINGS, MALCOLM WILLIAM,** retired management consultant; b. Cin., Feb. 5, 1925; s. William Malcolm and Margaret (Benvie) O.; m. Margie M. Gehiker, Sept. 4, 1948 (dec. June 2000); children: Lynn A., Sandra S., Wendy K., Cheryl M; m. Doris Marie Gorman, Aug. 23, 2002. BS in Bus. Adminstrn., Miami U., Oxford, Ohio, 1950, LL.D., 1976; A.M.P., Harvard U., 1975. With Continental Can Co., 1950-83, corp. v.p., from 1971; v.p., gen. mgr. pub. affairs Continental Packaging Co (Continental Group, Inc.), 1982-83; owner, pres. Owings Assocs., Inc., Pinehurst, NC, 1983-92. Dir. First Bank, Pinehurst, N.C.; adviser to Am. del. Internat. Tin Coun., 1978-82 Columnist The Pilot, Southern Pines, N.C., 1997-2004. Dean's assoc. exec. in residence Sch. Bus., Miami U., 1973, mem. alumni coun., 1958-65, mem. pres.'s devel. coun., 1965-69, mem. resource devel. bd., 1982; trustee Village of Thiensville, Wis., 1956-59; mem. N.C. Clean, 1985-94, chmn., 1986-93; bd. dirs. Barrington Area Devel. Coun., 1974-79, Sales Mgmt. Execs. Grad. Sch., Am. Soc. Environment, 1976, Keep Am. Beautiful, 1980-81, also chmn., 1990; chmn. Keep N.C. Beautiful Coun., Raleigh, 1988-92, Moore Meml. Hosp. Found., Pinehurse, N.C., 1986-89; mem. Moore Regional Hosp. Scroll Soc., 1991-94, chmn., 1992-93; chmn. Moore County (N.C.) Rep. Party, 1986-88; co-founder Rep. Presdl. Task Force; mem. U.S. Senate Bus. Adv. Bd., 1981-91; commr. Moore County, 1988-96, Youth Svcs., 1993-95; apptd. to N.C. Watershed Protection Adv. Com. by N.C. Environ. Mgmt. Commn., 1990-92; bd. dirs. Pub. Edn. Found., 1994-99, Ptnrs. for Children and Family, 1994-97, Drug-Free Moore County Inc., 1995-98, Dispute Settlement Ctr. of Moore County, 1995-97, Keep Moore County Beautiful, 1997—; mem. Moore County Bd. of Health, 1994-97; pres. Belle Meade Residents Assn., 2000. Recipient Cert. of Meritorious Svc. Miami U., 1967, Meritorious Svc. award Keep Moore County Beautiful, Inc., 1993-94; named Alumnus of Yr. Miami U., 1970; 1st Am. recipient Order of Apteryx Earth Awareness Found., 1971, Order of Long Leaf Pine. Mem. Ill. C. of C. (bd. dirs. 1976-78), Miami U. Alumni Assn. (nat. pres. 1964-65), Omicron Delta Kappa, Sigma Chi, Delta Sigma Pi Clubs: Pinehurst Country, Country of N.C. (Pinehurst). Home and Office: Belle Mead Retirement Resort 107 Caritas Ct Southern Pines NC 28387-2242 Personal E-mail: mal_owings@earthlink.net. *The Golden Rule - "treating others as thyself" is not only a cornerstone for success, it is the foundation of personal happiness. However, it is well to remember that none of this is possible without political freedom and the contingent responsibilities that freedom requires.*

**OWINGS, THALIA KELLEY,** elementary school educator; b. Franklin, N.H., Apr. 11, 1948; d. James Warren and Elizabeth Louise (Chadwick) Kelley; m. Alan Morritt, June 25, 1966 (div. June 25, 1990); children: Manderlee, Tiffany, Brooke; m. Frederick Richard Owings, Dec. 31, 1994; children: Jennifer, Lisa. AA, Harvard U. Ext., 1982, BA, 1989; student, Calif. State U., San Bernardino, 1996—2000. Cert. tchr., Calif., emergency tchr. Instr. CEA Internat., Providence, 1971-77; adminstrv. asst. Gulf Oil/Cumberland Farms, Norwood, Mass., 1989-91, So. Calif. Edison Co., Rosemead, Calif., 1991-96; substitute tchr. Palm Springs (Calif.) Unified Sch. Dist., 1996—2000. Tutor Calif. for Literacy!, Pasadena, Chino, and Palm Springs, Calif., 1991-96; applicant interviewer Harvard U.; mem. edn. com. Shelter From the Storm, 2000-03, tutor com. chair, 2000-03, vol. coord., 2002-03; leader Girl Scout jr. troops, 2004—. Mem. So. Calif. Harvard/Radcliff Club, Toastmasters Internat. (v.p. pub. rels. 1995-96), Edison's Roundtable. Avocations: screenplay writing, photography, bicycling, golf. Home: 78075 Ravencrest Cir Palm Desert CA 92211

**OWNBEY, VANCE SCOTT,** corporate financial executive; m. Elizabeth Dillon, Dec. 21, 1991. AA, Antelope Valley C.C., Lancaster, 1989; BS in Econs., Calif. Poly. State U., 1991; MBA, U. Phoenix, 1999. Fin. statement supr. Enterprise Rent A Car, Salt Lake City, 1995—2001; CFO Knight Mgmt. Ins. Svcs. LLC, LA, 2001—. Cons. in field. Co-chmn. United Way, Salt Lake City, 1998—99. 1st lt. infantry USAR, 1991—99. Mem.: AICPA, Internat. Who's Who of Bus., Inst. Mgmt. Accts., Nat. Soc. Accts. Republican. Avocations: travel, reading, music. Office: Knight Management Insurance Services LLC 4751 Wilshire Blvd Suite 111 Los Angeles CA 90010 Office Phone: 323-692-8904. Personal E-mail: vanceo-91@alumni.calpoly.edu.

**OWNBY, DENNIS RANDALL,** pediatrician, educator, allergist, researcher; b. Athens, Ohio, July 14, 1948; s. Dillard Ralph and Miriam (Lee) Ownby; m. Helen Louise Engelbrecht, May 24, 1970; children: David Randall, Kathryn Louise. BS, Ohio U., 1969; MD, Med. Coll. Ohio, 1972. Diplomate Am. Bd. Allergy and Immunology (bd. dirs. 1993-98, chair 1998, residency rev. com. 1995-2000), Am. Bd. Pediat., Nat. Bd. Med. Examiners. Intern and resident Duke U. Sch. Medicine, Durham, NC, 1972—74, asst. prof., 1977—80; staff physician Henry Ford Hosp., Detroit, 1980—97, dir. Allergy Rsch. Lab., 1986—97; prof. pediat. Case Western Res. U., Cleve., 1997; prof. pediat. and medicine Med. Coll. Ga., Augusta, 1998—. Clin. assoc. prof. pediat. U. Mich., Ann Arbor, 1980—86, clin. assoc. prof. pediat., 1986—95. Contbr. articles to med. jours., chpts. to books. Fellow: Am. Acad. Allergy, Am. Acad. Pediat. Office: Med Coll of Georgia Sect Allergy & Immunology BG-1019 Augusta GA 30912-3790 Office Phone: 706-721-3531. Business E-Mail: downby@mcg.edu.

**OWNBY, JERRY STEVE,** landscape architect, educator; b. Shawnee, Okla., Jan. 25, 1939; s. Hugh H. and N. Lorraine (Hopkins) O.; children by previous marriage: Gregory Steve, Mitchell Hugh; m. Arnola Closon, Dec. 19, 1971; 1 child, Steven Cory BS, Okla. State U., 1961; MS in Landscape Architecture, Kans. State U., 1964, M in Landscape Architecture, 1970. Coun. Landscape Archtl. Registration Bds. cert. and registered landscape architect, Ariz., Kans., Okla., Mo., Tex. Extension landscape architect Kans. State U., Manhattan, 1963-64, instr., 1969-70; landscape architect Beardsley & Talley, Seattle, 1964-65; extension specialist Okla. State U., Stillwater, 1965-69, from asst. prof. to prof. landscape architecture and coordinator landscape architecture, 1970-85; pvt. practice, 1985—. Chmn. Okla. Landscape Architect Registration Bd., 1980-85; mem. 1985 Expert Panel for Uniform Nat. Exam., 1984-85; gov.'s appointee Mo. Coun. Landscape Architects, 1991-97 Designs include Las Laderas residence, 1978 (Merit award 1981), Student Union courtyard Okla. State U., 1981 (Honor award 1983). Chmn. Oklahomans for Landscape Architecture, 1979-80; chmn., vice chmn. Stillwater Park and Recreation Adv. Bd., Okla., 1971-79. Recipient Outstanding Prof. award Okla. State U. chpt. Alpha Zeta, 1975, svc. award Stillwater City Commn., 1980, design awards Springfield Planning and Zoning Commn., 1988, 89, 90, 99, design award Springfield Environ. Adv. Bd., 1990, Gov.'s landscape design award for Andy Williams' Moon River Theatre, Branson, Mo., 1992, for Charley Pride Theater, Branson, 1995, design award Watershed Com., 1993; alumni fellow Kans. State U., 1995. Fellow Am. Soc. Landscape Architects (v.p. 1983-85, Okla. chpt. Svc. award 1980); mem. Nat. Coun. State Garden Clubs (accredited instr. 1964—), Nat. Coun. of Educators in Landscape Architecture, Mo. Assn. of Landscape Architects, Coun. Landscape Archtl. Registration Bds. (cert.), Phi Kappa Phi, Sigma Lambda Alpha. Republican. Baptist. Avocations: travel, photography, fishing. Home: 234 Sunset Cove # 108 Branson MO 65616-3604 E-mail: jsownby@aol.com.

**OWSLEY, DOUGLAS W.,** forensic osteologist, researcher, anthropologist; BS in Zoology, U. Wyoming, 1973; MS, U. Tenn., PhD in Anthropology, 1978. Assistantship, dept. anthropology U. Tenn., faculty mem. anthropology; faculty mem., dept. geography and anthropology La. State U.; assoc. curator, dept. anthropology Nat. Mus. of Natural History, Smithsonian Institution, 1987, divsn. head, divsn. physical anthropology Washington, curator, N.Am.

forensics. Lectr. in field assists law enforcement agencies in identifying human remains and in establishing cause of death. Office: Nat Mus Natural History Smithsonian Institution 10th St and Constitution Ave NW Washington DC 20560*

**OWSLEY, THOMAS L.,** oil industry executive; b. L.A., Oct. 27, 1940; AB, Harvard U., 1962; JD, U. N.C., 1969. Bar: Conn. 1969, D.C. 1973, U.S. Supreme Ct. 1973, Md. 1983. Assoc. Davis, Cheney & Chipman, 1969—70; atty. SEC, 1970—72; legis. asst. U.S. Sen. Robert P. Griffin, 1972—73; assoc. Purcell & Nelson, 1973—75; sr. v.p., gen. counsel, corp. sec. Martin Marietta Corp., 1976—82; pres. Crown Ctrl. Petroleum, Balt., 2003—. Lt. USN, 1962—66. Mem.: ABA, Am. Corp. Counsel Assn., Am. Soc. Corp. Secs., Md. State Bar Assn. Office: Crown Central Petroleum PO Box 1168 Baltimore MD 21201

**OWYANG, CHUNG,** gastroenterologist, researcher; b. Chung King, China, Nov. 20, 1945; arrived in Can., 1965; s. Chi and Ching-Ying (Fung) O.; m. Jeannette Lim; children: Stephanie, Christopher. BS with honors, McGill U., Montreal, Can., 1968, MD, 1972. Diplomate Am. Bd. Internal Medicine, Gastroenterology; lic. Gen. Med. Coun., U.K., Que., Can., Min. Med. lic. Mich. med. lic. Intern in internal medicine Montreal Gen. Hosp./McGill U., 1972-73, resident in internal medicine, 1973-75; clin. teaching fellow in internal medicine McGill U., 1974-75; fellow in gastroenterology Mayo Clinic and Found., Rochester, Minn., 1975-78; instr. internal medicine Mayo Med. Sch., Rochester, 1977-78; asst. prof. U. Mich., 1978-84, assoc. prof., 1984-88, assoc. chief divsn. gastroenterology, 1984-90, prof., 1988—, chief divsn. gastroenterology, 1991—, dir. med. procedures unit, 1992—. Assoc. dir. Gastrointestinal Peptide Rsch. Ctr., U. Mich., 1984-95, dir. 1996—; cons. Rsch. Coun. Janssen Pharmaceutica Inc., 1985—, Ann Arbor VA Med. Ctr., 1978—, NIH, Bethesda, Md., 1989-94, FDA, Bethesda, 1995—; H. Marvin Pollard chair in gastroenterology, U. Mich., 1996—; speaker, presenter in field. Co-author: Textbook of Gastroenterology, 1991, 2d edit. 1995, Atlas of Gastroenterology, 1992; mem. edit. bd. Pancreas, 1986—, Am. Jour. Physiology, 1988—, Regulatory Peptide Letter, 1988—, Gastroenterology, 1990—, guest editor, 1991—, Digestive Diseases, 1993—; contbr. numerous chpts. to books, articles to profl. jours., jours. refereed. Grantee in field. Fellow ACP; mem. Am. Assn. Physicians, Am. Soc. Clin. Investigation, Am. Gastroenterological Assn., Am. Pancreatic Assn., Am. Diabetes Assn., Am. Fedn. Clin. Rsch., Am. Motility Soc., Ctrl. Soc. Clin. Rsch., Internat. Assn. Pancreatology, Midwest Gut Club. Office: U Mich Med Ctr Divsn Gastroenterology PO Box 362 Ann Arbor MI 48106-0362

**OXARART, FRANK,** broadcast executive; Gen. mgr. Sta. KCBS-AM, San Francisco, 1989—. Office: KCBS Radioi SF 865 Battery St San Francisco CA 94111-1503

**OXENHANDLER, NEAL,** literature educator, writer; b. St. Louis, Feb. 3, 1926; s. Joseph and Billie (Lutsky) O.; m. Jean Romano (div. May 1976); children: Noelle, Daniel, Alicia; m. Judith I. Josel, Dec. 12, 1979; stepchildren: Rebecca, Marjorie Menza. AB, U. Chgo., 1948; MA, Columbia U., 1951; PhD, Yale U., 1955; MA (hon.), Dartmouth Coll., 1973. Lectr. French St. Louis U., 1951-52; asst. instr. Yale U., New Haven, 1952-54, instr., 1954-57; asst. prof. UCLA, 1957-60, assoc. prof., 1960-65, U. Calif., Santa Cruz, 1965-66, prof., 1966-69, Dartmouth Coll., Hanover, NH, 1969—, Edward Tuck prof., 1987—, chmn. dept. comparative lit., 1980—85, chmn. dept. French and Italian, 1987-91. Dir. NEH Summer Seminar in Comparative Lit., 1981. Author: Scandal and Parade: Theater of Jean Cocteau, 1957, Aspects of French Literature, 1961, French Literary Criticism: The Basis of Judgment, 1966, Max Jacob and Les Feux de Paris, 1964, (novel) A Change of Gods, 1962, Looking for Heroes in Post-War France, 1996, adv. editor Film Quar., Berkeley, 1958-91; mem. editl. com. U. Calif. Press, Berkeley, 1966-69; asst. editor French Rev., 1969-73; contbr. articles, revs., poetry and translations to profl. jours. With U.S. Army, 1941-43, ETO, PTO. Decorated Combat Inf. badge; Fulbright scholar, Italy, 1953; Cross-Disciplinary fellow Soc. for Values in Higher Edn., France, 1966, Guggenheim fellow, France, 1962, Inst. for Shipboard Edn., 1995. Mem. MLA (adv. editor proc. 1977-80), Assn. Literary Scholars and Critics, Assn. Hebrew Caths. Democrat. Roman Catholic. Home: # 502 97 Sunset Dr Sarasota FL 34236 Office: Dartmouth Coll Dept French Hanover NH 03755 Office Phone: 941-330-2086. Personal E-mail: nealoxen@aol.com.

**OXFORD, PATRICK C.,** lawyer; b. Beaumont, Tex., Aug. 15, 1942; BBA, U. Tex., 1966, JD with honors, 1967. Bar: Tex. 1967. Mng. ptnr. Bracewell & Giuliani LLP (formerly Bracewell & Patterson LLP), Houston. Mem. bd. dirs. BioHouston, Inc., M.D. Anderson Services Corp., Tex. Med. Ctr. Mng. editor Tex. Law Rev., 1966-67. Mem. Am. Coll. Mortgage Attys., State Bar Tex. Office: Bracewell & Giuliani LLP S Tower Pennzoil Place 711 Louisiana St Ste 2300 Houston TX 77002-2781 E-mail: patrick.oxford@bracewellgiuliani.com.

**OXLEY, MICHAEL GARVER,** congressman; b. Findlay, Ohio, Feb. 11, 1944; s. George Garver and Marilyn Maxine (Wolfe) Oxley; m. Patricia Ann Pluguez, Nov. 27, 1971; 1 child, Michael Chadd. BA in Govt., Miami U., Oxford, Ohio, 1966; JD, Ohio State U. Coll. Law, 1969. Bar: Ohio 1969, US Supreme Ct. 1986. Agt. FBI, 1969—71; atty. Oxley, Mallone, Fitzgerald & Hollister, 1971—81; mem. Ohio State Ho. Reps., 1973-81, US Congress from 4th Ohio dist., 1981—, chmn. fin. svcs. com. Recipient Taxpayer's Friend award, Nat. Taxpayers Union, Guardian of Small Bus. award, Nat. Fedn. Ind. Bus., Spirit of Enterprise award, US C. of C., Award for Mfg. Legis. Excellence, Nat. Assn. Mfrs., Jefferson award, Citizens for Sound Economy, Friend of the Family award, Nat. Security award, Am. Security Coun. Mem. ABA, Ohio Bar Assn., Findlay Bar Assn., Soc. Former Spl. Agts. FBI, Ohio Farm Bur., Sigma Chi., Rotary, Elks. Republican. Lutheran. Office: US Ho Reps 2308 Rayburn Ho Office Bldg Washington DC 20515-3504 Office Phone: 202-225-2676.*

**OXMAN, THOMAS ELLIOT,** psychiatrist; b. Denver, May 15, 1949; s. Albert Charles and Leah (Hurwitz) O.; m. Judy Ann Heldman, May 27, 1971; children: Elliot Warren, Robert Charles, Annaleah H. AB in Philosophy, Dartmouth Coll., 1971; MD, U. Colo., 1975. Diplomate in psychiatry and geriatric psychiatry Am. Bd. Psychiatry and Neurology; mem. test com. 1987-95). Intern Mt. Zion Med. Ctr., San Francisco, 1976; resident in psychiatry Dartmouth Med. Sch., Hanover, N.H., 1979, fellow in consultation/liaison and cancer psychiatry, 1979-80; asst. prof. psychiatry and family medicine U. Cin. Med. Ctr., 1980-83; asst. prof. Dartmouth Med. Sch., Hanover, 1983-87, assoc. prof. psychiatry and family and cmty. medicine, attending, 1987-95, prof., 1995—. Assoc. dir. consultation liaison psychiatry svc. Dartmouth Hitchcock Med. Ctr., Hanover, 1983-90, dir. geriatric psychiatry, 1988—, mem. sci. rev. com. Hitchcock Found., 1988-95; mem. Mental Disorders of Aging rev. group NIMH, 1995-99; med. dir. glenclift Home for the Elderly, NH, 1996-; assoc. chair MacArthur Found. Initiative on Depression in Primary Care, 2000-2007; ptnr. 3CM, LLC, 2006—. Editor Internat. Jour. Psychiatry in Medicine, 1996-2000, Online Abstract Svc. Am. Assoc. Geriatric Psychiatry, 2005-; contbr. articles to profl. jours Recipient Merrell Resident Rsch. award Dartmouth Med. Sch., 1978; Rufus Choate scholar Dartmouth Coll., 1971; Mental Health Acad. awardee NIMH, 1987-90, Aging, Social Support and Phys. and Emotional Disability grantee, 1990-95; MacArthur Found. and Hartford Found. Depression in Primary Care grantee, 1995—. Dist. fellow Am. Psychiat. Assn. (liaison com. on consultation/liaison psychiatry 1982-88,)bd. dirs. Am. Assn. Geriatric Psychiatry, 2002-2006; mem. Phi Beta Kappa. Avocations: running, conservation. Office: Dartmouth Med Sch Dept Psychiatry Lebanon NH 03756 Office Phone: 603-653-3556.

**OXNAM, PHILIP LINTON,** small business owner; b. Pomona, Calif., Nov. 5, 1945; s. Robert Fisher Oxnam and Dalys Oxnam Jaecker; m. JoAnne Buck, Sept. 30, 1989. BA, Norwich U., 1967; grad. Am. Acad. Dramatic Arts, 1972; student various acting schs., N.Y., L.A., 1972—82; grad., NYU, 1979. Lic. theatre arts tchr. Vt. Actor various orgns., N.Y., L.A., 1972—86; ind. casting

dir. NY, 1985—88; owner Acting Lab., NY, 1987—89; tchr. theatre arts Lamoille Union HS, Morrisville, Vt., 1990—2000; co-owner TRIXonSTIX skis, Warren, Vt., 2002—03; owner On the Edge Skis, Monument, Colo., 2002—04. Author: novels, plays and screenplays, 1990—99; co-creator (ski sports) TRIXonSTIX, 2002, creator (snow skis, snowboards) On the Edge Skis, 2003; dir.: (TV commercials), 2006. Figure skating performance coach, 1998—2003. 1st. lt. U.S. Army, 1968—70, U.S., Thailand. Named Ath. Hall of Fame soccer and swimming, Norwich U., Northfield, Vt., 2002; named to All New Eng. Soccer Team, Vt. All State Swimming Team. Mem.: Norwich U. Ath. Assn., Nat. Rifle Assn., Norwich U. Golden Goal Club, Norwich U. Blue Line Club, Tucson Nat. Country Club. Avocations: skiing, golf, figure skating, tennis.

**OXNAM, ROBERT BROMLEY,** trust company advisor; b. LA, Dec. 14, 1942; s. Robert Fisher and Dalys Elita (Houts) O.; children: Geoffrey Fisher, Deborah Elizabeth. BA, Williams Coll., 1964; MA, Yale U., 1966, PhD, 1969; LLD (hon.), Trinity Coll., 1994. Asst. prof. Trinity Coll., Hartford, Conn., 1969-74, assoc. prof., 1974-75, spl. asst. to pres., 1971-73; dir. China Coun. The Asia Soc., Washington, 1975-81, dir. Washington Ctr., 1979-81, v.p. NYC, 1979-81, pres., 1981—92; spl. corr. MacNeil/Lehrer NewsHour; sr. adv. Bessemer Trust Co., 1992—. Host and moderator 30-part series Asia: Half the Human Race, Sta. WCBS-TV, summer, 1979; mem. U.S. Nat. Com. for Pacific Econ. Coop.; bd. dirs. Clemente Global Growth Fund, Inc., First Philippine Fund Inc.; trustee, Rockefeller Brothers Fund, Armand Erpf Fund; vis. prof., Beijing Univ., global scholar, Ga. State Univ., Atlanta; chmn., US Trust for Chinese Sci. and Civilization at Needham Rsch. Inst., Cambridge Univ. Author: History and Simulation: Ch'ing Game, 1972, Ruling from Horseback, 1975; co-editor: Dragon and Eagle: U.S.-China Relations, 1978, China Briefing, 1979-82, (novel) Cinnabar, 1990, A Fractured Mind: My Life with Multiple Personality Disorder, 2005. Bd. dirs. Inst. for Shipboard Edn., Semester at Sea, U. Pitts. NDEA fellow, 1964-69, Ford Found. fellow, 1980, Williams Coll. Bicentennial medal, 1993. Mem. Coun. Fgn. Rels., Am. Assembly, Century Assn., Cosmos Club (Washington), Assn. Asian Studies, Nat. Com. on US-China Rels. Office: Rockefeller Brothers Fund 437 Madison Ave New York NY 10022 also: Sr Advisor Bessemer Securities 630 Fifth Ave New York NY 10111

**OXNARD, CHARLES ERNEST,** anatomist, anthropologist, biologist, educator; b. Durham, Eng., Sept. 9, 1933; arrived in Australia, 1987; s. Charles and Frances Ann (Golightly) O.; m. Eleanor Mary Arthur, Feb. 2, 1959; children: Hugh, David. BSc with 1st class honors, U. Birmingham, Eng., 1955, MB, BChir in Medicine, 1958, PhD, 1962, DSc, 1975. Med. intern Queen Elizabeth Hosp., Birmingham, 1958-59; rsch. fellow U. Birmingham, 1959-62, lectr., 1962-65, sr. lectr., 1965-66, court govs., 1958-66; assoc. prof. anatomy, anthropology and evolutionary biology U. Chgo., 1966—78, prof., 1970-78, gov. biology collegiate div., 1970-78, dean coll., 1973-77; dean grad. sch. U. So. Calif., Los Angeles, 1978-83, univ. rsch. prof. biology and anatomy, 1978-83, univ. prof., prof. anatomy and cell biology, prof. biol. scis., 1983-87; prof. anatomy and human biology U. Western Australia, 1987-98, dir. ctr. for human biology, 1989-99, head div. agr. and sci., 1990-92, prof. emeritus, 1998—, sr. rsch. fellow, 1998—; Leverhulme prof. U. Liverpool (U.K.), Univ. Coll., London, 2000—03; hon. prof. U. Hull, England, 2004—, Hull York Med. Sch., 2004—. Rsch. assoc. Field Mus. Natural History, Chgo., 1967; overseas assoc. U. Birmingham, 1988—; Lo Yuk Tong lectr. U. Hong Kong, 1973, 94, 97, 2003, hon. prof., 1978, Chan Shu Tzu lectr., 80, vis. scholar, 95, 96; Octagon lectr. U. Western Australia, 1987; Latta lectr. U. Nebr., Omaha, 1987; Stanley Wilkinson orator, 91; rsch. assoc. L.A. County Natural History Mus., 1984—, George C. Page Mus., L.A., 1986; vis. scholar Shaw Coll. Chinese U. of Hong Kong, 1995; bd. dirs. U. Western Australia Press, 1993—95; advisor on human biology World Sci. Pub. Co., 1993—; vis. prof. Northwestern U., Xian, China, 1999, U. York, England, 2003, hon. prof., 2004—, Hull York Med. Sch., 2004—; hon. prof. bioengring. U. Hull, 2004—. Author: Form and Pattern in Human Evolution, 1973, Uniqueness and Diversity in Human Evolution, 1973, Human Fossils: The New Revolution, 1977, The Order of Man, 1983, Humans, Apes, and Chinese Fossils, 1985, Fossils, Teeth and Sex, 1987, Anatomies and Lifestyles, 1990; series editor Recent Advances in Human Biology Series World Sci. Pub., Vol. I, The Origin and Past of Modern Humans, 1995, Vol. 2, Bone Structure and Remodeling, 1995, Vol. 3 The Origins and Past of Modern Humans: Towards Reconciliation, 1998, Vol. 4 The Natural History of the Doucs and Snub-nosed Langurs, 1998, Vol. 7 Morphometrics for the Life Sciences, 2000, Perspectives in Human Biology, Vol. 1 Genes, Ethnicity and Aging, 1995, Vol. 2 Humans in the Australasian Region, 1996, Vol. 3 Human Adaptability: Future Trends and Lessons from Past, 1998, Vol. 4, Is Human Evolution a Closed Chaptr, 1999, Vol. 4, Child Growth, Secular Trends and Continuing Human Evolution, Vol. 4, Dento-Facial Variation in Perspective, 1999, Vol. 5 Towards Consilience, 2000, Dedicatee, Shaping Primate Evolution, 2004; mem. editl. bd. Annals of Human Biology; cons. editor: Am. Jour. Primatology, Jour. Human Biology, Jour. Human Evolution: Australia com. mem. Ency. Britannica, 1991-99; bibliographic referee Britannica On-Line, 1994-99; contbr articles to anat. and anthrop. jours. Mem. Pasteur Found., 1988; bd. dirs. West Australian Inst. for Child Health, 1991-98; mem. electoral bd. Freemantle Hosp., 1991-94. Recipient Book award, Hong Kong Coun., 1984, S.T. Chan Silver medal, U. Hong Kong, 1980, Charles Darwin Lifetime Achievement award, Am. Assn. Phys. Anthropology, 2001; grantee, USPHS, 1960—71, NIH, 1974—87, NSF, 1971—87, Raine Found., 1988—91, Viertel Found., 1993—94, Australian Acad. Sci., 1995, Leverhulme Trust, Eng., 2003—06; Marie Curie Evan Rsch. Tng. grantee, 2005—, Marie Curie Palaeo Rsch. Tng. grantee, 2005—. Fellow N.Y. Acad. Sci., AAAS, So. Calif. Acad. Sci. (bd. dirs. 1985); mem. Chgo. Acad. Soc. (hon. life), Australasian Soc. for Human Biology (pres. 1987-90), Australia and New Zealand Anat. Soc. (pres. 1989-90), Gt. Britain and Ireland (councillor 1992-94), Nat. Health and Med. Rsch. Coun. (grantee 1994-97), Australian Rsch. Coun. (grantee 1988—), Med. and Health Infrastructure Fund, Western Australia (grantee 2001-03), Leverhulme Trust Rsch. Grant, 2003-06, Marie Curie awards 2005-), Soc. Study Human Biology (treas. 1962-66), Sigma Xi (pres. nat. lectr. 1990), Phi Beta Kappa (pres. chpt.), Phi Kappa Phi (pres., Book award 1984). Office: U Western Australia Nedlands WA 6009 Australia Business E-Mail: coxnard@cyllene.uwa.edu.au.

**OXNER, CATHERINE CANTRELL,** school psychologist, educator; d. H. Furman and Myra Cannon Cantrell; m. John Wilson Oxner, Oct. 29, 2005. BS, Wofford Coll., 1993; MA, Western Carolina U., 1995; PhD, U. S.C., 1999. Lic. sch. psychologist S.C. State Bd. Examiners, 2001. Sch. psychologist Lexington (S.C.) Sch. Dist. One, 1999—. Adj. prof. U. S.C., Columbia, 2002—. Mem.: S.C. Assn. Sch. Psychologists (profl. devel./program chair 2004—06, pres. 2003—04, com. chair 2000—06), Nat. Assn. Sch. Psychologists. Office Phone: 803-951-8315.

**OXNER, GEORGE DEWEY, JR.,** lawyer; b. Greenville, S.C., Dec. 31, 1933; s. George Dewey and Frances (Ruckman) O.; m. Louise Earle, Sept. 16, 1960; children: Frances, Dewey, Earle. BA, Washington & Lee U., 1956; LLB, U. S.C., 1959. Bar: S.C. 1959, U.S. Dist. Ct. S.C. 1959, U.S. Ct. Appeals (4th cir.) 1959. From assoc. to mng. ptnr. Haynsworth, Marion, McKay & Guerard, Greenville, 1959-98, ptnr., 1998—. Cochair Chief Justice's Commn. on the Profession. Fellow Am. Coll. Trial Lawyers, S.C. Def. Trial Attys. Assn. (pres. 1976), S.C. Bar Assn. (sec. 1997-98, treas. 1998—), sec. 1997-98, treas. 1998-99, pres. elect, 1999-2000, pres. 2000-2001 Home: 10 Parkins Lake Rd Greenville SC 29607-3668 Office: Haynsworth Sinkler Boyd PA 75 Beattie Pl Greenville SC 29601-2130 Office Phone: 864-240-3208. E-mail: doxner@hsbcowfarm.com.

**OXNER, GLENN RUCKMAN,** financial executive; b. Greenville, S.C., July 10, 1938; s. G. Dewey and Frances O.; m. Kathleen Gallagher, 1992. Student, Duke U., 1956-57; BS, U.S.C., 1961. Trainee stock bd. broker Alester G. Furman Co., Greenville, S.C., 1961, v.p., 1964-67, exec. v.p., 1967-75; pres. S.C. Securities Co., 1975-77; sr. v.p. Interstate Securities, Charlotte, N.C., 1977-82, exec. v.p., 1982-85; chmn. First Tryon Securities, Charlotte, 1986-89; mng. dir. Nations Bank Investment Banking Co., Charlotte, 1989-92; chmn. Edgar M. Norris & Co., Charlotte, 1992-2001; exec.

v.p. Scott & Stringfellow, Greenville, SC, 2001—04; pres. Belmont Corp., Greenville, SC, 2005—. Served with U.S. Army, 1957. Mem. Nat. Assn. Security Dealers (com. chmn. dist. 7 1974, gov. 1981-84), Security Industry Assn. (gov. 1974), Security Dealers Carolinas (pres. 1977). Home: 18 Woodland Way Cir Greenville SC 29601-3824 Office: Belmont Corp PO Box 313 Greenville SC 29602

**OXTOBY, DAVID WILLIAM,** academic administrator, chemistry professor; b. Bryn Mawr, Pa., Oct. 17, 1951; s. John Corning and Jean (Shaffer) O.. m. Claire Bennett, Dec. 17, 1977; children: Mary-Christina, John, Laura. BA, Harvard, 1972; PhD, U. Calif., Berkeley, 1975; DHL (hon.), Occidental Coll., 2005. Asst. prof. U. Chgo., 1977-82, assoc. prof., 1982-86, prof., 1986—2003, Mellon prof., 1987-92, dir. James Franck Inst., 1992-95, dean phys. scis. divsn., 1995—2003, William Rainey Harper prof., 1996—2003; pres., prof. chemistry Pomona Coll., Claremont, Calif., 2003—. Co-author: Principles of Modern Chemistry, 1986, Chemistry: Science of Change, 1990. Trustee Bryn Mawr Coll., 1989—, Tchrs. Acad. Math. and Sci., 1999-03, Toyota Technol. Inst., Chgo., 2002—, The Webb Schs., 2005-; mem. bd. govs. Argonne Nat. Lab., 1996-02, Astrophys. Rsch. Consortium, 1998-03; mem. bd. overseers Claremont Univ. Consortium, 2003-. Recipient Quantrell award U. Chgo., 1986, Alumni award of merit William Penn Charter Sch., 2003; Alfred P. Sloan Found. fellow, 1979, John Simon Guggenheim Found. fellow, 1987; Camille and Henry Dreyfus Found. tchr.-scholar, 1980. Fellow Am. Phys. Soc.; mem. Am. Chem. Soc., Am. Assn. Colls. and Univs. (bd. dirs. 2006—), Royal Soc. Chemistry (Marlow medal 1983), Phi Beta Kappa. Office: Office of the Pres Pomona Coll 550 N College Ave Claremont CA 91711 Office Phone: 909-621-8131.

**OYANA, TONNY J.,** geoscientist, educator; b. Kampala, Uganda, Apr. 20, 1968; arrived in U.S., 2000; s. Jerry Oyana Odongo and Mary Phoebe Oyana; m. Damalie M. Oyana, Feb. 4, 1992; 1 child, Owen Kiredi-Jean. BS in Biology and Geography, U. Dar-Es-Salaam, Tanzania, 1993; MS in Geog. Info. Sys., Environ. Planning, Nat. U. Ireland, Cork, 1996; PhD in Geog. Info. Sys., Geog. Info. Sci., SUNY, Buffalo, 2003. Biology and geography tchr. Jangwani Secondary Sch., Dar-es-Salaam, 1990—91, Kisitu Girls' Sch., Dar-es-Salaam, 1992; tchr., cons. SNV Netherlands Devel. Orgn., Tanzania and Uganda, 1993—94; tchg. asst. dept. geography Makerere U., Kampala, Uganda, 1993—95, lectr. dept. geography, 1996—98; child advocacy officer Nat. Coun. Children, Redd Barna, Norway, 1994; grad. tutor dept. geography U. Coll. Cork, 1995—96; rsch. fellow, project cons. Internat. Ctr. Tropical Agr., Colombia, 1997—98; tchg. asst. dept. geography U. BC, Vancouver, Canada, 1998—99; rsch. asst. dept. geography SUNY, Buffalo, 2000—02, postdoctoral fellow Ctr. Asthma and Environ. Exposure, 2003; asst. prof. geography info. sys. So. Ill. U., Carbondale, 2003—. Rsch./grad. asst. Nat. Ctr. Geog. Info. and Analysis, Sch. Medicine and Biomed. Scis., Ctr. Asthma and Environ. Exposure, SUNY, 2000—02; cons. in field. Reviewer: various jours. in field; contbr. articles to profl. publs., chpts. to books. Recipient U. Nairobi Collaborative Rsch. award, Ctr. Devel. Rsch., Denmark, 1995—97, Cross-Border Activities Rsch. award, UN Ctr. Regional Devel., 1995; postgrad. fellow, Dept. Fgn. Affairs, Dublin, Ireland, 1995—96. Mem.: Am. Assn. Geographers, Am. Acad. Sleep Medicine. Office: So Ill U 1000 Farner Carbondale IL 62901

**OYER, PAUL,** economist; b. Newark, Aug. 10, 1963; s. Calvin E. and Alice Cinader Oyer; m. Amy Friedman, July 25, 1992; children: David Friedman, Lucienne Friedman. BA, Middlebury Coll., Vt., 1985; MBA, Yale U., New Haven, Conn., 1989; PhD, Princeton U., NJ, 1996. Asst. prof. mgmt. and strategy Northwestern U., Kellogg Sch. Mgmt., Evanston, Ill., 1996—2000; assoc. prof. econs. Stanford U., Grad. Sch. Bus., Calif., 2000. Office: Stanford University Grad School of Bus 518 Memorial Way Stanford CA 94305 Office Phone: 650-723-2300.

**OYESIKU, NELSON MOBOLANLE,** neurosurgeon, neuroscientist; arrived in US, 1982; s. Nelson M. and Margaret M. Oyesiku; m. Lola M. Afolabi, Nov. 20, 1982; children: Angela, Linda, Nelson III. MD, U. Ibadan, Nigeria, 1979; MSc, U. London, 1982; PhD, Emory U., 1996. Diplomate Am. Bd. Neruol. Surgery. Intern Gen. Hosp., Laos, 1980; fellow in neurosurgery Lankenau Hosp, 1984, Harford Hosp., U. Conn., 1985—86, resident in gen. surgery, 1986—87; resident in neurosurgery Emory U., Atlanta, 1987—93, asst. prof. neurol. surgery, 1993—2000, assoc. prof. neurol. surgery, 2000—. Author: (book) Patient Care in Neurosurgery, 1990; contbr. chapters to books, articles to profl. jours. Bd. dirs. Brain Injury Assn. Ga., Atlanta, 1997—99, Med. Assn. Atlanta, 1997; trustee Emory U. Alumni Exec. Bd., Atlanta, 1997—2000; bd. dirs. Druid Hills Civic Assn., Atlanta, 1994—96. Recipient Augustus McCravey award, So. Neurosurg. Soc., 1992, Young Investigator award, Brain Trauma Found./AANS/CNS, 1994, Minority Med. Faculty Devel. award, Robert Wood Johnson Found., 1994, Clinician Investigator Devel. award, NIH, 1994; fellow Young Investigator Travel fellow, Internat. Stroke Congress, 1989; scholar Commonwealth scholar, Brit. Govt., 1981. Fellow: ACS; mem.: AMA, Ga. State Med. Assn., Pituitary Soc., Nat. Med. Assn., So. Neurosurg. Soc., Med. Assn. Atlanta (bd. dirs. 1997), Ga. Neurosurg. Soc. (sec.-treas. 2001—), Am. Assn. Neurol. Surgeons, Congress Neurol. Surgeons (exec. com. 1998, v.p., pres.-elect), Atlanta Soc. Episcopalian. Avocation: golf. Home: 1917 Durand Mill Dr NE Atlanta GA 30307

**OYLER, GREGORY KENNETH,** lawyer; b. Moses Lake, Wash., Sept. 16, 1953; s. Eugene Milton and Annetta Diane (Williams) O.; m. Evelyn Hartwell Wright, Oct. 18, 1986; 1 child, Elizabeth Atwood. AB, Princeton U., 1975; JD, Georgetown U., 1978; LLM, NYU, 1981. Bar: Pa. 1978, U.S. Tax Ct. 1978, U.S. Ct. Appeals (D.C. cir.) 1979, D.C. 1981, U.S. Supreme Ct. 1982, US Ct Fed Claims 1993, U.S. Ct. Appeals (fed. cir.) 1987. Law clk. to judges U.S. Tax Ct., Washington, 1978-80; assoc. Hamel & Park, Washington, 1981-85; ptnr. Hopkins & Sutter, Washington, 1985-95, Scribner, Hall & Thompson LLP, Washington, 1995—. Mem. adv. com. IRS Info. Reporting Program, 1993—94. Mem. ABA (tax sect., ins. com.), D.C. Bar Assn. (tax sect.), Fed. Bar Assn., Soc. Preservation Md. Antiquities (bd. dirs. 1991-97), Clark-Winchcole Found. (trustee 1999—). Office: Scribner Hall & Thompson LLP 1875 Eye St NW Ste 1050 Washington DC 20006-5441

**OZ, FRANK (FRANK RICHARD OZNOWICZ),** entertainer, film director; b. Hereford, Eng., May 25, 1944; s. Isidore and Frances Oznowicz. m. Robin Garsen, 1979; 2 children. Student, Oakland City Coll., 1962. Puppeteer with the Muppets, N.Y.C., 1963—; characters performed include The Mighty Favag (Saturday Night Live 1975-76), Miss Piggy, Fozzie Bear, Animal, Sam the Eagle for TV series The Muppet Show, Muppets Tonight!, 1996, films Muppet Treasure Island, 1996, Muppets From Space, 1999; voice of Bert, Grover, Cookie Monster for TV series Sesame Street, video Elmo Saves Christmas, 1996, film Adventures of Elmo in Grouchland, 1999, TV film Cinderelmo, 1999, TV series Play with Me Sesame, 2002; voice for CDROM: The Muppets Inside, 1996; voice film Monsters, Inc., 2001; v.p. Jim Henson Prodns., N.Y.C.; creative cons. feature film The Great Muppet Caper; appeared in films The Blues Brothers, 1980, Trading Places, 1983, Labyrinth, 1986, Innocent Blood, 1992, Blues Brothers, 2000; voice of Yoda in films The Empire Strikes Back, 1980, Return of the Jedi, 1983, Star Wars: Episode I-The Phantom Menace, 1999, Star Wars: Episode II-Attack of the Clones, 2002, Star Wars III-Revenge of the Sith, 2005, Zathura, 2005; dir. films The Dark Crystal (with Jim Henson), 1982, The Muppets Take Manhattan, 1984, Little Shop of Horrors, 1986, Dirty Rotten Scoundrels, 1988, What About Bob?, 1991, Housesitter, 1992, The Indian in the Cupboard, 1995, In & Out, 1997, Bowfinger, 1999, The Score, 2001, The Stepford Wives, 2004. Co-recipient Emmy award for outstanding comedy-variety or music program for The Muppet Show, 1978. Mem. AFTRA, Dirs. Guild Am., Writers Guild Am., Screen Actors Guild, Acad. TV Arts and Scis. Office: The Jim Henson Company 627 Broadway Fl 9 New York NY 10012-2612*

**OZ, MEHMET CENGIZ,** cardiac surgeon, writer; b. Cleve., June 11, 1960; s. Mustafa and Suna (Atabay) Oz; m. Lisa Oz; children: Daphne, Arabella, Zoe, Oliver. BA magna cum laude, Harvard U., 1982; MD, U. Pa., 1986; MBA, Wharton Bus. Sch., Phila., 1986; doctorate (hon.), Istanbul U. Cert. Am. Bd. Surgery, 1992, Am. Bd. Thoracic Surgery, 1994. Attending surgeon

NY Presbyn., Columbia U., NYC; physician, prof., vice chmn. surgery Columbia-Presbyn. Med. Ctr., 1993—, dir. Cardiovasc. Inst. and Complementary Medicine Program. Bd. dirs. Siga Corp.; host Second Opinion Show on Discovery Channel; med. class chmn. U. Pa. Med. Sch., 1982—83, med. sch. pres., 1984—85. Author: Healing from the Heart, 1998 (Best Book award Books Better Am.), Minimally Invasive Surgery (Doody award, 2000), Cardiac Assist Devices; co-author: You, the Owner's Manual: An Insider's Guide to the Body That Will Make You Healthier and Younger, 2005 (Best Seller), You, the Smart Patient: An Insider's Handbook for Getting the Best Treatment, 2006; contbr. chapters to books, articles to Newsweek and Oprah Mag., to profl. jours.; numerous network news appearances, guest host The Charlie Rose Show, host Second Opinion with Dr. Oz, guest appearances Oprah Winfrey Show. Named The Best and Brightest, Esquire mag., Doctor of Yr., Hippocrates mag.; named one of The Healers of the Millenium, Healthy Living mag.; named to Global Leaders of Tomorrow, World Econ. Forum; recipient Blakemore Rsch. Prize, Columbia U. Coll. Physician and Surgeon, 1988, 1989, 1990, Blakemore Rsch. award, 1991, P & S Club Outstanding, House Officer award, 1991, Prize Essay Award, Soc. Clin. Vascular Surgery, 1989, Rsch. award, Am. Soc. Laser Medicine and Surgery, 1991, Turkish-Am. of Yr., Assembly Turkish-Am. Assns., 1995, 25th Anniversary Silver award, Bastyr U., 2004. Mem.: Found. Advancement of Cardiac Therapies (Am. Turkish Soc. (bd. dirs.), Global Leader Tomorrow, World Econ. Forums, Am. Soc. Artificial Internal Organs, Am. Coll. Cardiology, Am. Heart Assn., Turkish-Am. Physicians Assn., Assn. Acad. Surgery, Internat. Soc. for Heart and Lung Transplantation, Am. Bd. Surgery, Am. Bd. Thoracic Surgery, Am. Assn. Thoracic Surgeons. Office: NY Presbyterian Hosp Columbia Univ 177 Fort Washington Ave MHB 7 435 New York NY 10032-3713 Office Phone: 212-305-4434. E-mail: mco2@columbia.edu.

**OZAKI, NANCY JUNKO,** performance artist, performing arts educator; b. Denver, Feb. 14, 1951; d. Joe Motoichi and Tamiye (Saki) O.; m. Gary Steven Tsujimoto, Nov. 12, 1989. BS in Edn., U. Colo., 1973; postgrad., U. Colo., Denver, 1977, Metro State Coll., 1982, Red Rocks C.C., 1982-83, U. No. Colo., 1982, U. N.Mex., 1985, U. No. Colo., 1988. Elem. tchr. Bur. Indian Affairs, Bloomfield, N.Mex., 1973—75, Aurora Pub. Schs., Colo., 1977—83, Albuquerque Pub. Schs., 1983—84, Denver Pub. Schs., 1984—87, Oak Grove Sch. Dist., San Jose, Calif., 1988—89, San Mateo City Elem. Dist., Calif., 1990—92; performing artist Japanese drums Young Audiences, San Francisco, 1992—93, Denver, 1994—97; performing artist Japanese drums Epcot Ctr. Walt Disney World, Orlando, Fla., 1993—97; co-dir., mgr., performer One World Taiko Japanese Drum Troupe, Denver, 1997—2001, Seattle, 2001—; artist-in-residence Washington States Arts Commn., 2003—. Mem. Touring Arts Roster, King County. Vol. worker with young Navajo children; co-sponsor girl's sewing and camping groups. Mem. Kappa Delta Pi (Theta chpt.). Avocations: reading, sewing, skiing, hiking, snorkeling. Office: PO Box 80158 Seattle WA 98108 E-mail: oneworldtaiko@earthlink.net.

**ÖZALP, NESRIN,** mechanical engineer, research scientist; d. Mehmet Orhan and Aysel Özalp. MS, Ege U., Izmir, Turkey, 1998, Stanford U., San Francisco, 2002; PhD, U. of Wash., Seattle, 2005. Rsch. asst. Stanford U., Mech. Engring. Dept., San Francisco, U. Wash., Mech. Engring. Dept., Seattle. Bd. mem. pres. rsch. adv. bd. U. Wash., Seattle, 2004—05; bd. mem. a Wash. State EPA, 2004; com. mem. provost's fund for innovation and redesign U. Wash.; sen. mech. engring. dept. Grad. and Profl. Students Senate, 2003—05; rep. grad. student Stanford U., San Francisco, 2001—02. Contbr. articles to profl. jours. Fellow, Pacific NW Nat. Lab. Mem.: ASME. Office Phone: 90 (546) 439 8880. Office Fax: 90 (232) 388 8562. E-mail: nesrin.ozalp@ege.edu.tr.

**OZANICH, RUTH SHULTZ,** artist, poet, retired elementary school educator; b. Calif., Feb. 12, 1915; d. Charles Andrew Shultz and Martha Viola Boring; m. Anton M. Ozanich, Nov. 1931; children: Antom M., Saralen Elaine, Marc Charles Dee. BEd, Fresno (Calif.) State U., 1956. Life cert. tchr. credential, Calif. Tchr. Beardsley Elem. Sch., Oildale, Calif., 1954-65, Sierra Vista Elem. Sch., Arvin, Calif., 1965-70; ret., 1970. Exhibited in group shows Bakersfield Art Assn. Gallery, Cunningham Gallery, Bakersfield, Kern County Fair, Calif. (numerous blue ribbons); contbr. poetry to anthologies. Elder Paiute Coun., Lake Isabella Calif.; treas. Mexican Am. Srs. Mem. Internat. Poetry Hall of Fame (life), Calif. Tchrs. Assn., Kern River Valley Poets and Writers Club (founder, past pres.), Bakersfield Art Assn. (founder, past treas.), Ladies Moose. Avocations: arts and crafts, reading, poetry, writing. Home: 5631 Caranor Rd Kent OH 44240-4206

**OZAWA, MARTHA NAOKO,** social work educator; b. Ashikaga, Tochigi, Japan, Sept. 30, 1933; came to U.S., 1963; d. Tokuichi and Fumi (Kawashima) O.; m. May 1959 (div. May 1966). BA in Econs., Aoyama Gakuin U., 1956; MS in Social Work, U. Wis., 1966, PhD in Social Welfare, 1969. Asst. prof. social work Portland (Oreg.) State U., 1969-70, assoc. prof. social work, 1970-72; assoc. prof. social work NYU, 1972-75; assoc. prof. social work Portland State U., 1975-76; prof. social work Washington U., St. Louis, 1976-85, Bettie Bofinger Brown prof. social policy, 1985—2003, Bettie Bofinger Brown Disting. prof. social policy, 2003—; dir. Martin N. Ozawa Ctr. Social Policy Studies, 2005—. Author: Income Maintenance and Work Incentives, 1982; editor: Women's Life Cycle: Japan-U.S. Comparison in Income Maintenance, 1989, Women's Life Cycle and Economic Insecurity: Problems and Proposals, 1989; editl. bd. Social Work, Silver Spring, Md., 1972-75, 85-88, New Eng. Jour. Human Svcs., Boston, 1987-95, Jour. of Social Work, Silver Spring, 1974-77, 91-95, 99-2003, Jour. Social Svc. Rsch., 1977-97, Children and Youth Svcs. Rev., 1991—, Social Work Rsch., 1994-97, Jour. Poverty, 1997-2004; co-editor-in-chief Asian Social Work and Policy Rev., 2005—. Grantee Adminstrn. on Aging, Washington, 1979, 84, NIMH, 1990-93. Mem. Nat. Assn. Social Workers (presdl. award 1999), Nat. Acad. Social Ins., Nat. Conf. on Social Welfare (bd. dirs. 1981-87), The Gerontol. Soc. Am., Soc. for Social Work and Rsch., Washington U. Faculty Club (bd. dirs. 1986-91). Avocations: photography, tennis, swimming, gardening. Home: 13018 Tiger Lily Ct Saint Louis MO 63146-4339 Office: PO Box 1196 Saint Louis MO 63130-4899 Office Phone: 314-935-6615. Business E-Mail: ozawa@wustl.edu.

**OZAWA, SEIJI,** conductor, music director; b. Shenyang, China, Sept. 1, 1935; s. Kaisaku and Sakura Ozawa; m. Kyoko Edo; m. Vera Motoki-Ilyin Ozawa; children: Seira, Yukiyoshi. Student, Toho Sch. Music, Tokyo, Japan, 1953-59; studies with, Hideo Saito, Eugene Bigot, Herbert Von Karajan, Leonard Bernstein; student at the invitation of Charles Munch, Tanglewood, 1959; DMus (hon.), U. Mass., New England Conserv. Music, Wheaton Coll. Music dir. Boston Symphony Orch., 1973—2002, Vienna State Opera, 2002—. One of three asst. condrs. N.Y. Philharm., 1961—62; music dir., season Ravinia Festival, 1964—68; music dir. Toronto Symphony Orch., 1965—69, San Francisco Symphony Orch., 1970—76; apptd. artistic advisor Tanglewood Festival, 1970; condr. Evening at Symphony Boston Symphony Orch., music advisor, 1972-73, Vienna State Opera, 1988, Saito Kinen Festival, Matsumoto, Japan, 1992; mem. internat. tour Dvorak Gala, Prague, 1993, Vienna Philharm. Asia, 1993, 96, 2000, Vienna Philharm. Europe, 1997, 98, 2000; mem. concert tour Berlin Philharm. Salzburg Festival; co-founder, artistic dir. Tokyo Opera Nomori, 2005—; opened music acad., Geneva, 2005—. Named a Chevalier de la Legion d'Honneur, Pres. France Jacques Chirac; named Laureate, Found. du Japan, 1988, Seiji Ozawa Hall for him, Tanglewood Music Ctr., 1994, Music Dir. Laureate, Boston Symphony Orch., 2002, Musician of the Yr., Musical America; recipient 1st prize, Internat. Competition Orch. Condrs., 1959, Koussevitzky prize, Tanglewood Music Ctr., 1960, Inouye award for Lifetime Achievement, 1964; conducting fellow, Tanglewood Music Ctr., 1959. Avocations: golf, tennis, skiing. Office: Veroza Japan Co Ltd 2F 6-13-21 Seijo Setagaya-ku Tokyo 157-0066 Japan Office Phone: +81-(0)3-5490-6805. Office Fax: +81-(0)3-5490-6985.*

**OZDOGANLAR, BURAK,** mechanical engineer, educator; m. Neslihan Ozdoganlar. MS in Aerospace Engring., Ohio State U., Columbus, Ohio, 1993, MS in Mech. Engring., 1995; PhD in Mech. Engring., U. Mich., Ann Arbor, Mich., 1999. Postdoctoral rsch. assoc. U. Ill., Urbana, Ill.,

1999—2001; sr. mem. tech. staff Sandia Nat. Labs., Albuquerque, 2001—04; asst. prof. mech. engring. Carnegie Mellon U., Pitts., 2004—. Grantee, NSF, 2006. Mem.: ASME (assoc.), Soc. Mfg. Engrs., Phi Kappa Phi. Office: Carnegie Mellon University 303 Scaife Hall 5000 Forbes Ave Pittsburgh PA 15213 Office Phone: 412-268-9890. Business E-Mail: ozdoganlar@cmu.edu.

**OZELLI, TUNCH,** economics professor; b. Ankara, Turkey, May 18, 1938; came to U.S., 1962; s. Sufyan and Saziye (Ozmorali) O.; m. Lale A. Baymur, Dec. 30, 1960 (div. Mar. 1972); children: Selva, Kerem; m. Nancy Ann Goldschlager, Feb. 3, 1974 (div. Dec. 1984); m. Meral Ozdemir, May 9, 1992. MBA, Fla. State U., 1963; PhD, Columbia U., 1968. Rsch. fellow Harvard U., Cambridge, Mass., 1969-70; econ. advisor Office Prime Minister, Ankara, 1970-72; prof. mgmt. N.Y. Inst. Tech., N.Y.C., 1972—. Spl. advisor State Planning Orgn., Ankara, 1989-92. Contbr. articles to profl. jour. Ford Found. scholar, 1963-64, Found. for Econ. Edn. fellow, 1968. Mem. Am. Econ. Assn., Middle East Studies Assn., Turkish Mgmt. Assn., Delta Mu Delta. Avocation: equestrian activities. Office: Dept of Economics NY Inst Tech Old Westbury NY 11568

**OZERDEM, UGUR,** medical researcher, educator; s. Suleyman and Teman Ozerdem. MD, Hacettepe U., 1993. Resident ophthalmology Hacettepe U. Sch. Medicine, Ankara, Turkey, 1993—97; fellow vitreous-retina surgery U. Calif., San Diego, 1998—2000; rsch. asst. prof. Burnham Inst., San Diego, 2002—03; asst. prof. La Jolla Inst. For Molecular Medicine, San Diego, 2003—. Sci. referee Ophthalmology Jour., Balt., 1999—, Investigative Ophthalmology and Visual Sci. Jour., Rockville, Md., 2004—, Jour. Clin. Investigation, 2005—; study sect. mem. Neurofibromatosis; sci. referee Arteriosclerosis, Thrombosis, and Vascular Biology Jour., 2005—. Sci. referee: various profl. jours.; contbr. articles to sci. jours. Recipient award, Am. Heart Assn. (New Investigator award 2002); mem.: Fedn. Am. Socs. for Exptl. Biology, Assn. for Rsch. in Vision and Ophthalmology, Am. Soc. for Investigative Pathology (corr.), Am. Assn. Cancer Rsch. (corr.), N.Am. Vascular Biology Orgn. Achievements include research in MMP inhibitors in PVR, pericyte tubes, vascular corrosion casting in mouse embryo; development of NG2/pericyte targeting, a novel method to measure interstitial fluid pressure in cancer. Office: La Jolla Inst Molecular Medicine 4570 Executive Dr Suite 100 San Diego CA 92121

**OZICK, CYNTHIA,** writer; b. NYC, Apr. 17, 1928; d. William and Celia (Regelson) O.; m. Bernard Hallote, Sept. 7, 1952; 1 dau., Rachel Sarah. BA cum laude with honors in English, NYU, 1949; MA, Ohio State U., 1950; LHD (hon.), Yeshiva U., 1984, Hebrew Union Coll., 1984, Williams Coll., 1986, Hunter Coll., 1987, Jewish Theol. Sem. Am., 1988, Adelphi U., 1988, SUNY, 1989, Brandeis U., 1990, Bard Coll., 1991, Spertus Coll., 1991, Skidmore Coll., 1992, Seton Hall U., 1999, Rutgers U., 1999, U. N.C., Asheville, 2000, NYU, 2001, Bar-Ilan U., Israel, 2002, Balt Hebrew U., 2004. Author: Trust, 1966, reissued, 2004, The Pagan Rabbi and Other Stories, 1971, Bloodshed and Three Novellas, 1976, Levitation: Five Fictions, 1982, Art and Ardor: Essays, 1983, The Cannibal Galaxy, 1983, The Messiah of Stockholm, 1987, Metaphor & Memory: Essays, 1989, The Shawl, 1989, Epodes: First Poems, 1992, What Henry James Knew, and Other Essays on Writers, 1994, Portrait of the Artist as a Bad Character, 1996, The Cynthia Ozick Reader, 1996, Fame & Folly, 1996, The Puttermesser Papers, 1997, (novel) Heir to the Glimmering World, 2004, The Din the Head: Essays, 2006; (plays) Blue Light, 1994, The Shawl, 1996; guest editor Best Am. Essays, 1998, Quarrel & Quandary: Essays, 2000, The Din the Head, Essays, 2006, Collected Stories, 2006; also poetry, criticism, revs., translations, essays and fictions in numerous periodicals and anthologies. Phi Beta Kappa orator, Harvard U., 1985. Recipient Mildred and Harold Strauss Living award Am. Acad. Arts and Letters, 1983, Rea award for short story, 1986, PEN/Spiegel-Diamonstein award for the Art of the Essay, 1997, Harold Washington Literary award City of Chgo., 1997, John Cheever award, 1999, Lannan Found. award for fiction, 2000, Koret Found. award for lit. studies, 2001, Nat. Book Critics Circle award for nonfiction, 2001; Lucy Martin Donnelly fellow, Bryn Mawr Coll., 1992, Guggenheim fellow, 1982. Mem. PEN, Authors League, Am. Acad. of Arts and Scis., Am. Acad. of Arts and Letters, Dramatists Guild, Académie Universelle des Cultures (Paris), Phi Beta Kappa.

**OZKAN, BETUL C,** education educator; BA, Ankara U., 1993; MA, Hacettepe U., Ankara, 1997, PhD, 2001. Post doctoral rsch. assoc. Iowa State U., Ames, 2001—03; asst. prof. U. West Ga., Carrollton, 2003—. Vis. rsch. scholar, Iowa State U., 2000—01, Fulbright Internship grantee, U.S. Dept. of State, 2000—02.

**OZKAN, UMIT SIVRIOGLU,** chemical engineering professor; b. Manisa, Turkey, Apr. 11, 1954; came to U.S., 1980; d. Alim and Emine (Ilgaz) Sivrioglu; m. H. Erdal Ozkan, Aug. 13, 1983. BS, Mid. East Tech. U., Ankara, Turkey, 1978, MS, 1980; PhD, Iowa State U., 1984. Registered profl. engr., Ohio. Grad. rsch. assoc. Ames Lab. U.S. Dept. Energy, 1980-84; asst. prof. Ohio State U., Columbus, 1985-90, assoc. prof. chem. engring., 1990-94, prof., 1994—, assoc. dean for rsch. Coll. Engring., 2000—05. Contbr. articles to profl. jours. French Ctr. NAt. Rsch. Sci. fellow, 1994-95; recipient Women of Achievement award YWCA, Columbus, 1991, Outstanding Engring. Educator Ohio award Soc. Profl. Engrs., 1991, Union Carbide Innovation Recognition award, 1991-92, NSF Woman Faculty award in sci. and engring., 1991, Engring. Tchg. Excellence award Keck Found., 1994, Ctrl. Ohio Outstanding Woman in Sci. & Tech., 1996, Pitts.-Cleve. Catalysis Soc. Outstanding Rsch. award, 1998, Achievement award Cen. Women Engring., 2002, Columbus Outstanding Rsch. award ACS, 2002, Fellow Am. Inst. Chemists; mem. NSPE, N.Am. Catalysis Soc., Am. Inst. Chem. Engring., Am. Soc. Engring. Edn., Am. Chem. Soc., Combustion Inst., Sigma Xi. Achievements include research in selective oxidation; electrocatalysis; in-situ spectroscopy; fuel reformulation; hydrodenitrogenation; hydrodeoxygenation; hydrodesulfurization; NO reduction; hydrogenation. Office: Ohio State U Chem Engring 140 W 19th Ave Columbus OH 43210-1110 Office Phone: 614-292-6623. E-mail: ozkan.1@usa.edu.

**OZOLINSH, SANDIS,** professional hockey player; b. Riga, Latvia, Aug. 13, 1972; Player San Jose Sharks, 1992—96, Colo. Avalanche, 1995—2000, Carolina Hurricanes, 2000—01, Fla. Panthers, 2001—03, Anaheim Mighty Ducks, 2002—06, NY Rangers, 2006—. Player NHL All-Star Game, 1994, 1997—98, 2000—03. Achievements include mem. Stanley Cup Champion Colo. Avalanche, 1995. Office: c/o NY Rangers 2 Pennsylvania Plaza New York NY 10121*

**OZOLS, ROBERT F.,** oncologist; b. Riga, Latvia, July 26, 1944; arrived in U.S., 1950; s. Robert and Marina Ozols; m. Jeanne E. Ozols, Nov. 11; children: Kristina, Mark, Robert. BS, U. Rochester, 1966, PhD, 1971, MD, 1974. Lic. physician Va., Pa., diplomate Am. Bd. Internal Medicine with subspecialty in med. oncology. Clin. assoc. Nat. Cancer Inst., Bethesda, Md., 1976—79; sr. investigator, attending physician, 1978—88, head exptl. therapeutics sect., 1984—88; chmn. med. oncology Fox Chase Cancer Ctr., Phila., 1988—93, sr. v.p. med. sci., 1993—, med. dir., 1993—; dir. Fox Chase Cancer Ctr./Temple U. Cancer Program, Phila., 1999—2005. Prin. investigator Gynecologic Oncology Group, Phila., 1989—; cons. oncologic drug adv. com. FDA, 1994—95; mem. ovarian cancer guidelines panel Nat. Comprehensive Cancer Network, 1995—. Contbr. articles over 300 articles to profl. jours., chpts. to books; editor: Drug Resistance in Cancer Therapy, 1989, 1993, Gynecology in Current Opinion in Oncology, 1989—99, Molecular and Clinical Advances in Anti-Cancer Drug Resistance, 1991, Current Problems in Cancer, 1991—95, Gynecologic Oncology, 1998, Yearbook of Oncology, 1995—99; co-editor: Carboplatin, 1990; guest editor Ovarian Cancer jour., assoc. editor Yearbook of Oncology, 1991—95, Cancer Rsch., 1986—, Cancer Investigation, 1988—, Current Opinion in Oncology, 1991—95, Jour. Exptl. Therapeutics and Oncology, 1994—, editl. bd. Internat. Jour. Gynecologic Cancer, 1990, Cancer Rsch., Therapy and Control, 1993—, Anti-Cancer Drugs, 1991, Internat. Jour. Oncology, 1993—, Anticancer Rsch., 1993—, Clin. Cancer Rsch., 1994, Cancer Treatment and Rsch., 1994—. Bd. dirs. Commonwealth divsn. Am. Cancer Soc., 1996—99. Recipient 25th Ann.

Bristol-Myers Squibb award for Disting. Achievement, 2002, 9th Claude Jacquillat award for achievement in oncology, 2001, Milken Family Found. award, 1990; grantee Comprehensive Cancer Ctr. Program, NIH, 2000—05, Spore in Ovarian Cancer, 1999—2009, 1998—2000, Ovarian Cancer Prevention Program, U.S. Army, 1998—2002. Mem.: Soc. Gynecologic Oncologists, Am. Soc. Clin. Investigation, Internat. Gynecologic Cancer Soc. (governing coun. 1987—90, sci. program com. 1997, 1999, edn. com 1999—2000, sci. program com. 2001, 2002, v.p. 2003—), Commd. Officers Assn., Am. Assn. Cancer Rsch., Am. Soc. Clin. Oncology, Alpha Omega Alpha, Sigma Xi. Office: Fox Chase Cancer Ctr 333 Cottman Ave Philadelphia PA 19111 E-mail: robert.ozols@fccc.edu.

**OZTURK, MEHMET CEVDET,** engineering educator; b. Ankara, Turkey, June 12, 1957; s. Necati Tevfik Ozturk and Fikret Kircali; m. Hatice Orun, Apr. 11, 1960; 1 child, Berk Orun. PhD, N.C. State U., Raleigh, 1988. Physics instr. English HS, Istanbul, Turkey, 1980—81; tchg. asst. Mich. Technol. U., Houghton, 1981—83; tchg. & rsch. asst. N.C. State U., 1983—88, prof., 1988—. Contbr. papers to profl. jours. and pubs. Presdl. Faculty fellow, NSF, 1995—2000. Achievements include first to propose the use of SiGe alloys in source/drain regions of nanoscale metal oxide field effect transistors; propose the recessed and in-situ doped SiGe source/drain junction technology as a replacement for ion-implantation. Office: NC State Univ Elec & Computer Engring Dept Raleigh NC 27695 Office Phone: 919-515-5245. Business E-Mail: mco@ncsu.edu.

**OZTURK, OZCAN,** electrical engineer, researcher; PhD, Pa. State U., University Park, 2006. Tchg. asst. U. Fla., Gainesville, 2000—02; rschr. Pa. State U., University Park, 2002—. Recipient Best Paper award, 12th Internat. Conf. on Parallel and Distributed Systems, 2006. Mem.: IEEE (assoc.). Achievements include design of memory hierarchy optimizer.

**OZTURK, YUSUF,** computer engineer, educator; b. Erzurum, Turkey, Sept. 7, 1961; arrived in U.S., 1996; s. Recep and Vasfiye Ozturk; m. Seckin Cankiri Ozturk, Jan. 1, 1964; children: Meric, Emre, Gulce. BS, Mid. East Tech. U., 1985; MS, Ege U., 1987, PhD, 1991. Asst. prof. Ege U., Izmir, Turkey, 1990—92, assoc. prof., 1992—96, San Diego State U., 1996—. Grantee, NSF, 2000, Intel, 2001, Nokia, Inc., 2005. Mem.: IEEE. Achievements include patents for a method of bus confirmation; a broadband cable harp. Avocations: basketball, bicycling, reading, swimming, travel. Office: 5500 Campanile Dr San Diego CA 92182 Office Phone: 619-594-4550. Business E-Mail: yozturk@mail.sdsu.edu.

**OZUMBA, BENJAMIN CHUKWUMA,** obstetrician, gynecologist, educator; b. Onitsha, Anambra, Nigeria, Mar. 21, 1954; s. Arthur Nwabunwanne and Alice chiebonam (Igebuike) O.; m. Chinelo Obianuju Udokwu, Jan. 29, 1994; children: Benjamin Chukwumdindu, Sarah Onyinyechukwu, Elizabeth Chimfunnanya, Rachel Chidinma. MB, BChir, U. Lagos, Nigeria, 1979; FMCOG, Post Grad. Med. Coll., Nigeria, 1987; MRCOG, Royal Coll. Ob.-Gyn., London, 1993; FICS, Internat. Coll. Surgeons, U.S., 1991; FWACS, W. African Coll. Surgeons, Lagos, Nigeria, 1993. Intern Lagos U. Tchg. Hosp., 1979—80; med. officer Coll. of Edn., Minna, Nigeria, 1980—81; sr. house officer Univ. Nigeria Tchg. Hosp., Enusu, 1981—82, registrar, 1982—83, sr. registrar, 1983—88, sr. lectr./ cons., 1988—93; prof. ob./gyn. U. Nigeria, Nsukka, 1993—, dean faculty med. scis. and dentistry, 2002—04, provost Coll. Medicine, 2004. Chmn. Enugu Med. Soc., 1993-95; coord. Tutorial System Internat., Nigeria, 1993-95; dean medicine U. Nigeria. Editor: Tropical Pediatrics and Child Health, 1999; assoc. editor Orient Jour. Medicine, 1988—, Nigerian Jour. Surgical Scis., 1991—; contbr. articles to profl. jours. V.p. Enugu chpt. Full Gospel Businessmen's Fellowship Internat., 1994-95, chpt. pres., 1997—; chmn. Harvest and Love Feast Com., Chapel of Redemption, Enugu, Nigeria, 1994-95. Takemi fellow Internat. Health Harvard U., 1995-96. Fellow Internat. Coll. Surgeons, W. African Coll. of Surgeons, Nigerian Postgrad. Med. Coll.; mem. AAAS (internat. mem.), Royal Coll. Obstetricians and Gynecologists. Born Again Christian. Achievements include measuring: serum concentrations of alphafetoprotein in mormal pregnancy and in pregnancy induced hypertensions; ivermectin levels in human breast milk. Office: Univ Nigeria Teaching Hosp Dept Ob-gyn Enugu Anambra Nigeria Mailing: 45 Duffield Dr South Orange NJ 07079 Personal E-mail: BenOzumba@hotmail.com.

**OZZIE, RAY (RAYMOND E. OZZIE),** computer software company executive; b. Nov. 20, 1955; B in Computer Sci., U. Ill., Urbana-Champaign, 1979. Sys. programmer Protection Mut. Ins. Co., 1972—73; technician dept. nuc. engring. U. Ill., 1974, sys. programmer PLATO project, 1974—79; co-founder Urbana Software Enterprises, 1978—79; with Data Gen. Corp., 1979—81; co-founder Microcosm Corp., 1981; with Software Arts, 1981—82, Lotus Devel., 1983—84; founder, pres. Iris Assocs., 1984—97; founder, chmn., CEO Groove Networks, Inc. (acquired by Microsoft Corp.), Beverly, Mass., 1997—2005; chief tech. officer Microsoft Corp., Redmond, Wash., 2005—06, chief software architect, 2006—. Adv. bd. mem., Live Labs (rsch. partnership between MSN and Microsoft Rsch.) Microsoft Corp., 2006—. Named Person of Yr., PC Mag., 1995, Disting. Alumnus, U. Ill., Urbana-Champaign; named one of Seven "Windows Pioneers", Microsoft Corp., Top Five Operators of the Century, Computer Reseller News; named to Computer Mus. Industry Hall of Fame, InfoWorld Hall of Fame; recipient W. Wallace McDowell award, IEEE Computer Soc., 2000. Mem.: NRC (mem. computer sci. and telecom. bd.), World Econ. Forum (gov. IT and telecom., honored as technology pioneer 2001), NAE. Achievements include first to field of collaboration technology; creator, developer Lotus Notes, 1984; instrumental in development of Lotus Symphony, TK!Solver and VisiCalc. Office: Microsoft Corp 1 Microsoft Way Redmond WA 98052-6399*

**O'BRIEN-AMICO, LEAH,** Olympic athlete; b. Sept. 9, 1974; m. Tommy Amico; 1 child. Mem. U.S. Women's Nat. Team, 1996—, U.S. Women's Softball Team, Atlanta Olympic Games, 1996, U.S. Women's Softball Team, Sydney Olympic Games, 2000, U.S. Women's Softball Team, Athens Olympic Games, 2004. Named Arizona State Woman of the Yr., 1997; named to First Team All-Am., 1994, 1995, 1997, All-College World Series Team, 1994, 1995, 1997. Achievements include mem. U.S. Women's Softball Gold medal Team, Atlanta Olympics, 1996, Sydney Olympics, 2000; mem. NCAA Champion Arizona Wild Cats, Women's Coll. World series, 1993, 1994, 1997; mem. Gold medal U.S. Nat. Team, ISF World Championships, 1998, 2002; mem. Gold medal U.S. Nat. Team, Pan-American Games, 1999, 2003.

**PAANANEN, VICTOR NILES,** language educator; b. Ashtabula, Ohio, Jan. 31, 1938; s. Niles Henry and Anni Margaret (Iloranta) P.; m. Donna Mae Jones, Aug. 15, 1964; children: Karl, Neil. AB magna cum laude, Harvard U., 1960; MA, U. Wis., 1964, PhD, 1967. Instr. English Wofford Coll., Spartanburg, SC, 1962-63; asst. prof. Williams Coll., Williamstown, Mass., 1966-68, Mich. State U., East Lansing, 1968-73, assoc. prof., 1973—82, prof. 1982—2002, asst. dean Grad. Sch., 1977-82, chmn. dept. English, 1986-94, prof. emeritus, 2002—. Vis. prof. Roehampton U., London, 1982, 96, hon. fellow, 92; mem. Harvard Inst. Learning Ret., 2006. Author: William Blake, 1977, 2d edit., 1996, British Marxist Criticism, 2000; contbr. articles to profl. and scholarly jours. Univ. fellow U. Wis., 1962, 63-64, Roehampton Inst. hon. fellow, London, 1992—; Harvard Nat. scholar, 1956-60. Home: 350 Revere Beach Blvd 5-5W Revere MA 02151-4851 E-mail: paananen@msu.edu.

**PAARSCH, HARRY J.,** economist, educator; b. Ashcroft, BC, Can., Aug. 29, 1959; arrived in U.S., 1996; s. Harry Horst and Betty Johanna Paarsch. BA honours, Queens U., Kingston, Can., 1980; MS, Stanford U., Palo Alto, Calif., 1983; AM, Stanford U., 1984, PhD, 1987. Asst. prof. U. B.C., Vancouver, Canada, 1987—92, U. We. Ont., London, Canada, 1992—95, assoc. prof., 1995—96, U. Iowa, Iowa City, 1996—2001, prof., 2001—. Author: An Introduction to the Structural Econometrics of Auction Data, 2006.

**PAAS, JOHN ROGER,** language educator; b. Chgo., Mar. 14, 1945; s. Walter V. and Doris (Marinoff) P.; m. Martha Clem White, Aug. 24, 1968; children: Emily, Anne. BA summa cum laude, Hamilton Coll., Clinton, N.Y., 1967; PhD, Bryn Mawr Coll., 1973. Part-time asst. prof. Bryn Mawr (Pa.) Coll., 1973-74; prof. German Carleton Coll., Northfield, Minn., 1974—, dept chair, 1985-88. Author: The German Political Broadsheet 1600-1700, 8 vols., 1985—, Effigies et Poesis: An Illustrated Catalogue of Printed Portaits with Laudatory Verses by German Baroque Poets, 2 vols., 1988; editor: Unbekannte Gedichte und Lieder des Sigmund von Birken, 1990, Hollstein's German Engravings, Etchings and Woodcuts, 1400-1700, vols. 38-41, 1994-95, Der Franken Rom: Nürnburgs Blütezeit in der zweiten Hälfte des 17 Jhts., 1995, Augsburg, die Bilderfabrik Europas, 2001, (with Wolfgang Harms, Michael Schilling and Andreas Wang) Illustrierte Flugblätter des Barock: Eine Auswahl, 1983; contbr. articles to profl. jours. Sgt. U.S. Army, 1969—71. Summer grantee German Acad. Exch. Svc., 1975, 78, 83, Andrew W. Mellon Found., 1976, Faculty Devel. grantee Bush Found., 1978, Carleton Coll., 1985, NEH grantee, 1990, 92-93; vis. fellow Beinecke Libr., Yale U., 1991, IREX fellow, 1978, Fulbright sr. rsch. fellow, 1988-89, Humboldt Rsch. fellow, 2000-01. Mem. Gutenberg Soc., Soc. German Renaissance and Baroque Lit., Internationaler Arbeitskreis für Barockliteratur, Frühe Neuzeit Interdisziplinär. Home: 107 College St Northfield MN 55057-2222 Office: Carleton College 1 N College St Northfield MN 55057-4044

**PAASWELL, ROBERT EMIL,** civil engineer, educator; b. Red Wing, Minn., Jan. 15, 1937; s. George and Evelyn (Cohen) P.; m. Rosalind Snyder, May 31, 1958; children: Judith Marjorie, George Harold. BA (Ford Found. fellow), Columbia U., 1956, BS, 1957, MS, 1961; PhD, Rutgers U., 1965. Field engring. asst. Spencer White & Prentis, Washington, 1954-56, engr. N.Y.C., 1957-59; rsch. scientist Davidson Lab., NJ, 1964; rsch. fellow Greater London Council, 1971-72; rsch. and teaching asst. Columbia U., 1959-62; asst. prof. civil engring. SUNY, Buffalo, 1964-68; chmn. bd. govs. Urban Studies Coll., 1973-76, assoc. prof., 1968-76, prof. civil engring., 1976-82; dir. Center for Transp. Studies and Research, 1979-82, chmn. dept. environ. design and planning, 1980-82; prof. transp. engring. U. Ill., Chgo., 1982-86, 89-90, dir. Urban Transp. Ctr., 1982-86; exec. dir. Chgo. Transit Authority, 1986—89; dir. transp. rsch. consortium, prof. civil engring. CCNY, 1990—, disting. prof., 1991—; dir. CUNY Inst. Urban Systems, 2000—. Faculty-on-leave Dept. Transp., 1976-77, cons., 1981—; v.p. Faculty Tech. Cons., Inc., Midwest Sys. Scis., Inc., 1982-86; dir. Urban Mass Transp. Adminstrn. Summer Faculty Workshop, 1980, 81; cons. transp. planning, energy and soil mechanics; spl. cons. to Congressman T. Dulski, 1973; vis. expert lectr. Jilin U. Tech., Changchun, Peoples Republic of China, 1985, hon. prof. transp., 1986—; bd. dirs. E'Escuto Archs. and Engrs., Chig, Hickling Co., Ottawa, Can., Transic Devel. Corp.; chmn. transp. steering adv. bd. Office of Tech. Assessment for Infrastructure and the Urban Core Project, 1994—; faculty Lincoln Inst. of Land Policy, 1994-95; vis. scholar Tel Aviv U., Israel, 1995—; arbitrator in productivity Met. Transp. Authority, N.Y.C., 1996—; mem. exec. com. Coun. on Transp., 1996—, NSF Ctr. for Infrastructure Sys.; cons. Coun. of North East Govs., 1997—; faculty "Conflict Resolution," NYU, 1998—; mem. exec. com. Inst. for Civil Infrastructure Sys. (NSF), 1998—; chair panel new paradigms in transit Transp. Rsch. Bd.; bd. dirs. Transit Stds. Consortium, chmn., 2000—, CUNY Sch. Profl. Studies, 2005—. Author: Problems of the Carless, 1977; contbg. author: Transport and Urban Development, 1995, Panels for Transportation Planning, 1997, Studies in Israel Planning, 1996, Dynamic Networks and Spatial Change, 1999, After the World Trade Center, 2002; editor: Site Traffic Impact Assessment, 1992; contbg. author: Decisions for the Great Lakes, 1982, World Book Encyclopedia, 1992, 93, 94, Transport and Urban Development, 1995, Israel Planning Studies, 1996, 97, Panels for Transportation Planning, 1997, New Contributions to Transportation Analysis in Europe, 1999, Policy Analysis of Transport Networks, 2005; mem. bd. editors Jour. Environ. Systems, 1974—, Transp., 1978—, Jour. Urban Tech., 1992—; contbr. articles to profl. jours. Mem. Buffalo Environ. Mgmt. Commn., 1972-74; mem. Area Com. for Transit, Mayor's Energy Adv. Bd., 1974, Block Grant Rev. Com., City of Buffalo; chmn. com. on transp., mem. rev. adv. bd. Rsch. and Planning Coun. Western N.Y.; mem. transp. com. Chgo. 1992 Worlds Fair; mem. citizens' adv. bd. Chgo. Transit Authority, 1985—; mem. strategic planning com. Regional Transp. Authority, 1985; mem. steering com. Nat. Transit Coop. Rsch. Program, 1991—, Borough pres. (Manhattan) Trans. Adv. Bd., Bronx Ctr. Devel. Project; bd. dirs. Transit Devel. Corp., 1992—; exec. bd. Transp. Coun., 1996—; mem. exec. com. Colin Powell Ctr.; bd. dirs. York Aviation Inst., 2003—; chmn. adv. bd. Cmty. Transp. Devel. Ctr., 2003—. Recipient Dept. Transp. award, 1977, Outstanding Alumnus award, 2003; SUNY faculty fellow, 1965-66 Fellow ASCE (past pres. Buffalo sect., chmn. steering com. 1992 splty. conf. traffic impact analysis, chair com. on peer rev. of pub. agys.); mem. AAAS, Transp. Rsch. Bd. (chmn. com. on transp. disadvantaged, mem. exec. com., peer rev. com. nat. transp. ctrs. 1988—), Inst. Transp. Engrs. (transit coun., exec. com., chmn. legis. policy com., rsch. com. surface transp. policy project 1995—), Coun. on Transp. (bd. dirs. 1996—), N.Y. Acad. Scis., Sigma Xi. Office: CCNY Marshak 917 135th St and Convent Ave New York NY 10031 Business E-Mail: paaswell@utrc2.org.

**PAAVO, JARVI,** conductor; b. Tallinn, Estonia; Studied under Leonard Bernstein; student in percussion and conducting, Tallinn Sch. Music; student under Otto-Werner, Max Rudolf, Curtis Inst. Music; student under Leonard Bernstein, L.A. Philharmonic Inst. Music dir. Cin. Symphony Orch., 2001—. Prin. guest conductor Royal Stockholm Philharmonic, City of Birmingham (Eng.) Symphony Orch., guest conductor N.Y. Philharmonic, Berlin Philharmonic, Munich Philharmonic, London Philharmonic, San Francisco Symphony, Phila. Orch. (Carnegie Hall debut), NHK Symphony, Tokyo Symphony, Israel Philharmonic, St. Petersburg Philharmonic, Orch. Filarmonica della Scala, L.A. Philharmonic, Philharmonic orch. and many others, (works by Bernstein) City of Birmingham Symphony Orch. Royal Stockholm Philharmonic Orch.; (recordings) with Estonian composers Part, Tuur, and Tubin) Searching for Roots, Sibelius' Kullervo, Lemminkainen Suite, (concerts with cellist Turls Mork); condr.: recs. with Cin. Symphony Orch. Office: Cin Symphony Orch 1241 Elm St Cincinnati OH 45210

**PABISCH, PETER KARL,** director, literature educator, humanities educator; b. Vienna, Apr. 17, 1938; came to U.S., 1969; s. Ernst and Gertrude (Engel) P.; m. Patricia Ann Trench, Nov. 25, 1959; 1 child, Angela. MA, U. Ill., 1971, PhD, 1974. Tchr. pub. schs., Vienna, 1959-69; dir. summer children's homes Vienna Social Welfare Sys., Italy, 1964-69; co-dir. German summer sch. U. N.Mex., Albuquerque, 1976—2003, from asst. prof. to assoc. prof., 1972-84, prof. German and European studies, 1984—2004, prof. emeritus, 2004—. Author: Austrian Poet H. C. Artmann, 1978, Modern German Lyrics, 1992, Cultural Study on Vienna, 2006, also 6 poetry books; editor 11 books on German, Swiss, and Austrian studies and on 250 years of J.W. Goethe, 1982—. Pres. Atlantic Bridge on the Camino Real, Inc., 1997—, Austrian-Am. Coun. of N.Mex., Inc., 1999— Decorated Order of Merit 1st Class (Germany), Gt. Order of Merit (Austria); named Best German Tchr., Am. Assn. Tchrs. of German, 1982, Outstanding German Educator, 2005; recipient Recognition award Goethe-Inst. Munich, 1995, poetry award Poetry in the Arts Inc., 1991, arts award Poetry in the Arts Inc., 1993, Friedestrom prize Internat. Dialect Archives, 2000; Check Point Charlie Found. scholar, 2005. Democrat. Roman Catholic. Avocations: skiing, scuba diving, playing music, travel, sketching. Home: 417 Jefferson St NE Albuquerque NM 87108-1279 Office: U N Mex German Program Fgn Langs and Lits Albuquerque NM 87131-0001 Office Phone: 505-277-5335. Business E-Mail: pabisch@unm.edu.

**PACALA, LEON,** retired professional society administrator; b. Indpls., May 3, 1926; s. John and Anna (Ferician) P.; m. Janet Lefforge, Dec. 28, 1947 (dec. July 1987); children: Mark, Stephen, James; m. Virginia Strasenburgh, Mar. 10, 1990. AB, Franklin (Ind.) Coll., 1949; BD, Colgate Rochester Div. Sch., 1952; PhD, Yale U., 1960; LLD (hon.), Nazareth Coll., 1980; LHD (hon.), Franklin Coll., 1987. Ordained to ministry Baptist Ch., 1952. Asst. prof. philosophy and religion DePauw U., 1956-61; participant study religion undergrad. coll. Lilly Found., 1957-59; assoc. prof. religion Bucknell U., 1961-68, prof., 1968-73, chmn. dept., 1961-64, dean, 1962-73; pres. Colgate Rochester (N.Y.) Div. Sch., pres. emeritus, 1995—; also Bexley Hall, Crozer

Theol. Sem., 1973-80; exec. dir. Assn. Theol. Schs. in U.S. and Can., 1980-91. Chair, founding mem. World Coun. Theol. Instns., 1986-2002; cons. acad. adminstrn. Beirut Coll. Women, 1972. Author: The Role of ATS in Theological Education, 1980-90, 1998; contbr. articles to profl. jours. Exec. com. Christian Faith in Higher Edn. Projects, 1965-68; trustee Franklin Coll., 1967-73, 98-2002; bd. dirs. Rohesters Jobs, Inc., 1973-80, Union Theol. Sem., N.Y.C., 1999—; trustee Rochester Area Colls., 1973-80; dir. Nat. Housing Ministries, Am. Bapt. Chs., 1976-80; mem. adv. bd. Colgate Rochester Div. Sch., 1997—. With USAAF, 1944-45. Internat. Rotary scholar, Louvain U., Belgium, 1952-53. Mem. Am. Conf. Acad. Deans (exec. com., treas., chmn., presiding officer 1973-74), Am. Assn. Higher Edn., Assn. Am. Colls. (commn. religion higher edn.), Assn. Theol. Schs. (com. accreditation), World Conf. Assns. Theol. Instns. (v.p. 1988-93), Am. Bapt. Assn. Sem. Adminstrs. (chmn 1975-80). Home: 56 Woodbury Pl Rochester NY 14618

**PACE, ANTONIETTA,** chemistry professor; b. Bklyn., May 20, 1976; d. Antonio and Mary Pace. BS in Biochemistry, Hofstra U., N.Y., 1998; MA in sci. edn., Columbia U., N.Y.C., 2002. Advanced Cert. in Administrn. and Suprvn. Hunter Coll., 2005. Chemistry tchr. LaGuardia Arts, N.Y.C., 1999—. Liberal. Roman Catholic. Avocations: travel, languages, art. Office: La-Guardia Arts 100 Amsterdam Ave New York NY 10023 Office Phone: 212-496-0700. Personal E-mail: coolnycteacher@yahoo.com.

**PACE, CAROLINA JOLLIFF,** communications executive, investor; b. Dallas, Apr. 12, 1938; d. Lindsay Gafford and Carolina (Juden) Jolliff; m. John McIver Pace, Jr., Oct. 7, 1961. Student, Holton-Arms Jr. Coll., 1956—57; BA in Comparative Lit., So. Meth. U., 1960. Promotional advisor, dir. season ticket sales Dallas Theatre Ctr., 1960—61; exec. sec. Dallas Book and Author Luncheon, 1959—63; promotional and instl. cons. Henry Regnery-Reilly & Lee Pub. Co., Chgo., 1962—65; pub. trade rep. various cos.; instl. rep. Don R. Phillips Co., Southea. area, 1965—67; Southwestern rep. Ednl Reading Svc., Inc.-Troll Assocs., Mahwah, NJ, 1967—72; v.p. multimedia divsn. Melton Book Co., Dallas, 1972—79; v.p. mktg. Webster's Internat., Inc., Nashville, 1980—82; pres. Carolina Pace, Inc., 1982—. Mem. adv. bd. Nat. Info. Ctr. of Spl. Edn. Materials; mem. materials rev. panel Nat. Media Ctr. for Materials of Severely-Profoundly Handicapped, 1981; mem. mktg. product rev. bd. LINC Resources, 1982, 83, 84, mktg. task force, 83, adv. bd., 87; reviewer spl. edn. U.S. Dept. Edn., 1975—79, 1985; rev. cons. HHS, 1982, 83, 84, 86; product rev. task force CEC, 1984, 85, 86; cons. Ednl. Cable Consortium, Summit, NJ, 1982—87. Prodr. ednl. videos; contbr. articles to profl. jours. Mem. adv. coun. Grad. Sys. Sch. Libr. and Info. Sci. Found., U. Tex., 1987—; co-vice chair Friends Highland Park Libr., 1989; mem. focus group City Dallas Growth Policy Plan; mem. art and design com. Downtown Ctrs.; active Dallas City Wide Parking Task Force, Ctrl. Transp. Forum Ctrl. Bus. Dist., Union Sta. Art & Design Com., Downtown Transfer Ctrs., Art and Design Com., West End Task Force, Ctrl. Bus. Dist. Task Force, Tex. Parking Assn.; co-founder Operation TexRec, 1990—91; bd. dirs. Transp. Mgmt. Assn., 1992—; chair Vanpool Use Study, 1995; budget chmn. Dallas County Sesquicentennial com., 1996; mem. adv. bd. Friends of Old Red Courthouse, 1997—, Trinity River Econ. Devel. Bd., 1998—; active Downtown Dallas: Vision 2020, 2001—02; mem. com. Trinity Commons Found., 2002—; active Downtown Dallas Task Force, Ctrl. Bus. Dist., West End, Individual Site Task Force, Dallas. Mem.: DAR (Jane Douglas chpt.), Coun. Exceptional Children (conf. spkr. 1981, dir. exhibitors com., chmn. publ. com. 1979 conf.), Pub. Rels. Soc. Am., Women in Comm., Assn. Spl. Edn. Tech. (nat. dir., v.p. publicity 1980—82), Assn. Ednl. and Comm. Tech., Internat. Comm. Industries Assn., Nat. Audio Visual Assn. (conf. panelist 1979), Downtown Dallas, Ctrl. Dallas Assn. (transp. com. 1996—, planning and greenspace com. 1998—), Dallas Plan (focus com.), Women's Nat. Book Assn., Dallas Founders, Friends of the West End (pres. 1988—), West End Assn. Dallas (chmn. subcom. on traffic and parking 1986—87, com. demographic study 1987—88), Downtown Transp. Mgmt. Assn. (adv. bd., chmn. vanpools subcom. 1995—, econ. devel. com. Trinity project 2000—, citizens adv. com. 2003—), Kimball Art Mus., Dallas So. Meml., Dallas Mus. Art, Dallas Zool. Soc., Dallas West End Hist. Dist. Assn., Tex. Parking Assn., Alpha Delta Pi. Presbyterian. Home: 4524 Lorraine Ave Dallas TX 75205-3613

**PACE, CHARLES ROBERT,** psychologist, educator; b. St. Paul, Sept. 7, 1912; s. Charles N. and Lenore (Lee) P.; m. Rosella Gaarder, Dec. 18, 1937; children: Rosalind, Jenifer. BA, De Pauw U., 1933; MA, U. Minn., 1935, PhD, 1937. Instr. in gen. coll. U. Minn., 1937-40; research asso. Am. Council Edn., 1941-42; research psychologist Bur. Naval Personnel, Navy Dept., 1943-47; mem. faculty Syracuse U., 1947-61, asso. dir., then dir. evaluation service center, 1947-52, asst. to chancellor, 1948-52, prof. psychology, chmn. dept., dir. psychol. research center, 1952-61; prof. higher edn. UCLA, 1961-82, prof. emeritus, 1982—. Mem. adv. coms. Am. Council Edn., Coll. Entrance Exam. Bd., Social Sci. Research Council. Author: They Went to College, 1941, (with M. E. Troyer) Evaluation in Teacher Education, 1944, The Junior Year in France, 1959, (with F.H. Bowles and J.C. Stone) How to Get Into College, 1968, College and University Environment Scales, 2d edit, 1969, Education and Evangelism, 1972, The Demise of Diversity?, 1974, Measuring Outcomes of College, 1979, Measuring the Quality of College Student Experiences, 1984, CSEQ: Test Manual and Norms, 1987, The Undergraduates, 1990. Post-doctoral fellow Rockefeller Found., 1940-41; fellow Center Advanced Study Behavioral Scis., 1959-60; recipient citation for meritorious civilian service Navy Dept., 1946, E.F. Lindquist award Am. Ednl. Research Assn. and Am. Coll. Testing Program, 1984, Suslow award for outstanding svc. Assn. for Instl. Rsch., 1989. Mem. APA, Am. Ednl. Rsch. Assn (Disting Rsch. award div. in postsecondary edn. 1992), Assn. for Study Higher Edn. (Disting. Career award 1989), Am. Assn. Pub. Opinion Rsch. Office Phone: 707-822-1204. E-mail: crp7001@axe.humboldt.edu.

**PACE, DAVID,** journalist; b. West Columbia, SC, 1950; B. in engring., Duke U.; M. in journalism, U. NC Chapel Hill. Reporter local newspapers, Tenn., Jacksonville (Fla.) Jour., AP, Montgomery, Ala., 1978—84; regional corr. for the Southeast AP Washington bur., 1984—99, supr. election projections, 1999—2006, news editor, 2006—. Co-recipient Presdl. award, AP Mng. Editors, 2000; recipient Gramling award for Achievement, AP, 2003. Office: AP Washington Bur 6th Fl 2021 K St Washington DC 20006-1082*

**PACE, DAVID A.,** lawyer; b. June 25, 1960; m. Tracy Pace. BS, U. Pa.; JD, Suffolk U., Boston. Bar: Mass. 1985. Joined Reebok Internat. Ltd., Canton, Mass., 1995, asst. gen. counsel, 1998—99, v.p. global alliances and endorsements, 1999—2000, general counsel, 2000—, v.p., 2001—, clerk. Office: Reebok Internat Ltd 1895 JW Foster Blvd Canton MA 02021

**PACE, DAVID A.,** human resources specialist, retail executive; BS, Cornell U., 1981. Various positions PepsiCo, Inc. and Tricon Global, 1981—99; sr. v.p. HomeGrocer.com, Seattle; exec. v.p., chief people officer i2 Technologies, Dallas, 2000—02; exec. v.p. ptnr. resources Starbucks Corp., Seattle, 2002—. Office: Starbucks Corp 2401 Utah Ave S Seattle WA 98134 Office Phone: 206-447-1575. Office Fax: 206-447-0828.

**PACE, ERIC DWIGHT,** retired journalist; b. NYC, Oct. 13, 1936; s. Eric and Eleanor Robertson (Jones) Paepcke; m. Suzanne Monique Wiedel, June 12, 1976 (div. Jan. 1987); children: Christine, Lydia. Grad., Phillips Exeter Acad., 1953; student, U. Heidelberg, Germany, 1955-56; BA magna cum laude, Yale, 1957; MA, Johns Hopkins, 1959. Reporter San Angelo (Tex.) Standard Times and Evening Standard, 1957-58; mem. staff Life mag., N.Y.C., 1959-61, assigned to Bonn, 1961, Paris, 1961-62; corr. Time mag., Bonn., 1962-63; Hong Kong, 1963-65; mem. staff New York Times, N.Y.C., 1965-66, assigned to Saigon, 1966, Cairo, 1966-69, Paris, 1969-70, Beirut, 1970-71, N.Y.C., 1971-74, Teheran, 1974-77, N.Y.C., 1977—2004. Author: (novels) Saberlegs, 1970, Any War Will Do, 1973, Nightingale, 1979; contbr. articles to Fgn. Affairs, also others. Served with AUS, 1957. Recipient George Polk Meml. award Overseas Press Club, 1968, Page One award N.Y.C.

Newspaper Guild, 1968 Mem. Mystery Writers Am., Crime Writers Assn. (Gt. Britain), Am. P.E.N. Clubs: Century (N.Y.C.), Squadron A (N.Y.C.). Home: 697 West End Ave Apt 11 E New York NY 10025

**PACE, GEORGE W.,** food products company executive; BA, U. N.C., MBA magna cum laude. Various sr. level. fin., sales and mktg. positions RJR Nabisco, 1986-88; sr. v.p. mktg. Del Monte Foods, San Francisco; v.p. sales, mktg. and distbrn. Rocco Inc., Harrisonburg, Va., 1992-96, CEO, 1996—, also bd. dirs.

**PACE, JAMES T.,** Internet company executive; b. Bonners Ferry, Idaho, Jan. 16, 1957; s. Robert Maurice and Hazel Marie (Jacob) Pace; m. Pamela Helen Dix, Oct. 7, 1985; children: Nicholas, Carolyn. BS in Bus. Adminstrn., U. Idaho, 1980; Russian proficiency cert., Def. Lang. Inst., 1985; Secondary Edn. tchg. cert., Gonzaga U., 1989; MLS, U. Wash., 1992. Cert. profl. libr. Wash. Sgt. U.S. Army, 1984—88. Mem.: Rotary Internat. Avocations: mountain climbing, whitewater kayaking, skiing. Office: PO Box 1309 Mccall ID 83638

**PACE, LEONARD,** retired management consultant; b. Torrington, Conn., Oct. 24, 1924; s. Anthony and Maria G. P.; m. Maureen Therese Murphy, Sept. 15, 1956; children: Leonard Anthony, Susan Maria, Daniel Graham, Thomas William, Mary Macaire, Cathleen Anne. Student, Syracuse U., 1943; BSM.E., U. Conn., 1949; postgrad., N.Y. U., 1951-52, Wayne U., 1955. Cert. mgmt. cons. With GAF, 1949-57, asst. to div. controller, 1954-57; with Deloitte Haskins and Sells, N.Y.C., 1957—, head N.Y. mgmt. adv. services, 1965-67, head Eastern region, 1967-76, nat. dir. mgmt. adv. services, 1976-85, chmn. internat. mgmt. adv. svcs. com. Served as officer, pilot USAAF, 1943-45. Mem. Am. Mgmt. Assn., Inst. Mgmt. Cons. (dir., chmn. profl. standards com.) Clubs: Baltusrol Golf, Union League, Circumnavigators. Home: 35 Little Wolf Rd Summit NJ 07901-3112

**PACE, NORMAN R.,** science educator, microbiologist; b. Washington, Ind., Sept. 20, 1942; BA, Ind. U., 1964; PhD, U. Ill., 1967. From asst. prof. to prof. biophysics and genetics U. Colo. Med. Ctr., 1974-84; prof. biology, then disting. prof. biology and chemistry Ind. U., Bloomington, 1975-97; prof. plant and microbial biology UCLA, Berkeley, 1996—99; prof., dept. molecular, cellular and dev. biology U. Colorado, Boulder, Colo., 1999—. Fellow AAAS, Am. Acad. Arts & Scis., Nat. Speleol. Soc., Am. Acad. Microbiology (award 1996), Am. Acad. Microbiology; mem. Am. Soc. Biol. Chemists. Office: U Colorado Dept of Molecular, Cellular & Dev Bio Boulder CO 80309-0347

**PACE, OLE BLY, III,** lawyer; b. 1939; AB, Ill. Wesleyan Univ., 1963; JD, Univ. Ill. Coll. of Law, 1966. Bar: 1966, US Dist. Ct., No. and Ctrl. Dist. Ill. Law clerk Appellate Ct. Justice A. J. Scheineman; spl. asst. atty. gen., 1968—80; ptnr. Ward, Murray, Pace & Johnson. Bd. dir. Northwestern Steel & Wire Co., First Nat. Bank, Sterling-Rock Falls, Ill., Mercantile Bank, Sterling-Rock Falls, Ill. Past pres. Sterling C. of C., Sinnissippi Mental Health Ctr. U.S. Army, 1958—60. Named one of the Best Lawyers in Am., 2003—04. Fellow: Ill. Bar Found.; mem.: ABA, Ill. Cmty. Coll. Attorneys Assn. (bd. mem., vice chair), Ill. Acad. of Lawyers (bd. regents, chancellor), Nat. Assn. of Coll. and Univ. Attorneys, Ill. Trial Lawyers Assn., Whiteside County Bar Assn. (past pres.), Ill. State Bar Assn. (bd. gov. 1995—2001, third v.p. 2001, pres. 2004, Bd. of Gov. award 1989), Order of Coif, Phi Delta Phi. Office: Ward Murray Pace & Johnson PC 202 Fifth St Sterling IL 61081

**PACE, ORLANDO LAMAR,** professional football player; b. Sandusky, Ohio, Nov. 4, 1975; Attended, Ohio State Univ. Lineman St. Louis Rams, 1997—. Donater Disadvantaged Kids; participant Spearheads Annual Offensive Line Thanksgiving Project, Chesterfield, Mo. Named to NFL Pro-Bowl, 1999—2005. Achievements include first to being the first player in college history to win two consecutive Lombardi awards, 1995, 1996; being the overall first pick in NFL Draft, 1997; being a member of Super Bowl XXXIV Champion St. Louis Rams, 2000. Office: 1 Rams Way Saint Louis MO 63045*

**PACE, PETER,** Chairman of the Joint Chiefs of Staff; b. Bklyn., Nov. 5, 1945; m. Lynne Ann Holden; children: Peter Jr., Tiffany Marie. BS, U.S. Naval Acad., 1967; MBA, George Washington U., 1972; student, USMC Command and Staff Coll., 1979-80; grad., Nat. War Coll., 1986; postgrad. in Nat. and Internat. Security, Harvard U. Commd. It. USMC, 1967, advanced through grades to gen., 2000; served in 2d Bns., 5th Marines, 1st Marine Divsn., Vietnam, 1968-69; ops. officer, Security Element Marine Aircraft Group 15, 1st Marine Aircraft Wing, Nam Phong, Thailand, 1972, exec. officer, 1972; asst. majors' monitor Hdqs. Marine Corps, Washington, 1973-76; ops. officer, 2nd Bn., 5th Marines, exec. officer, 3rd Bn., & divsn. staff sec. 1st Marine Divsn., Camp Pendleton, Calif., 1976—79; commdg. officer Marine Corps Recruiting Sta., Buffalo, 1980-83, 2nd Bn, 1st Marine Divsn., Pendleton, Calif., 1983—85; chief, ground forces branch Combined/Joint Staff, Seoul, Republic of Korea, 1986-87, exec. officer to asst. chief of staff, 1987—88; commdg. officer Marine Barracks, Washington, 1988—91; chief of staff, 2nd Marine Divsn. USMC, Camp Lejeune, NC, 1991—92, pres. Marine Corps. U., commdg. gen. Marine Corps. Combat Devel. Command Quantico, Va., 1992—94, dep. comdr. Marine forces Somalia, 1992—93, dep. comdr. Joint Task Force, 1993—94; dep. comdr., chief of staff US Forces Japan, 1994—96; dir. ops. (J-3) Joint Staff, Washington, 1996—97; comdt. USMC, Washington, 1997—2000; comdr. US So. Command, Miami, 2000—01; vice chmn. Joint Chiefs of Staff, US Dept. Def., Washington, 2001—05, chmn. 2005 . Decorated D.f.f. D.f.M., Def. Legion of Merit, Bronze Star with Combat V., Def. Superior Service medal, Def. Meritorious Service medal, Navy Commendation medal, Navy Achievement medal, Combat Action medal Office: Chmn of Joint Chiefs US Dept Def Pentagon Rm 2E873 Washington DC 20318*

**PACE, STANLEY DAN,** lawyer; b. Dayton, Ohio, Dec. 10, 1947; s. Stanley Carter and Elaine (Cutchall) Pace; m. Judy Roehm, Sept. 8, 1973; children: Stanley Carter, Barbara Roehm. BA, Denison U., Granville, Ohio, 1970; JD, U. Toledo (Ohio), 1975. Bar: U.S. Dist. Ct. (so. dist.) Ohio 1975, U.S. Dist. Ct. (no. dist.) Ohio 1977, U.S. Ct. Appeals (6th cir.) 1975. Atty. ARMCO Steel Corp., Middletown, Ohio, 1975-77; assoc. Spieth, Bell, McCurdy & Newell, Cleve., 1977-82, dir., 1982—, co-mng. dir., 1987—2005. Bd. dirs. Indsl. Rels. Resh. Assn., Cleve., 1985. Bd. dirs. Judson Retirement Cmty., Cleve., 1985; bd. dirs. Arthritis Found. N.E. Ohio, Cleve., 1984, Western Res. Hist. Soc., 1998. Mem.: ABA, Greater Cleve. Bar Assn., Ohio Bar Assn., 50 Club, Laurel Valley Golf Club, Chagrin Valley Hunt Club, Rolling Rock Club, Tavern Club, Pepper Pike Club, The Country Club. Office: Spieth Bell McCurdy & Newell 2000 Huntington Bldg Cleveland OH 44115 Office Phone: 216-696-4700. Business E-Mail: dpace@spiethbell.com.

**PACE, STEPHEN SHELL,** artist, educator; b. Charleston, Mo., Dec. 12, 1918; s. John C. and Ora K. (Reeves) P.; m. Palmina Natalini, Feb. 26, 1949. Student, Inst. Fine Arts, San Miguel, 1945-46, Art Students League, NYC, 1948-49, Grande Chaumiere, Paris, 1950, Inst. D'Arte Statale, Florence, Italy, 1951, Hans Hofmann Sch., NYC, 1951-52; ArtsD (hon.), U. So. Ind., Evansville, 2002, Maine Coll. Art, Portland, 2003. Artist in residence Washington U., 1959; instr. painting Pratt Inst., N.Y.C., 1961-69; artist in residence Des Moines Art Ctr., 1970; vis. artist U. Calif., 1968; assoc. prof. Bard Coll., 1969-71, Am. U., 1975-83; artist in residence U. So. Ind., Evansville, 2005. Artist in residence U. So. Ind., Evansville, 2005. One-man shows include Hendler Gallery, 1953, Artists Gallery, 1954, Poindexter Gallery, 1956, 57, Washington U., St. Louis, 1959, Holland-Goldowsky Gallery, Chgo., 1960, Howard Wise Gallery, Cleve., 1960, N.Y., 1960, 61, 63, 64, Dilexi Gallery, San Francisco, 1960, HCE Gallery, 1956-59, 61-63, 66, Dwan Gallery, L.A., 1961, Hayden Gallery, Cambridge, Mass., 1961, Kraby Gallery, Evansville, Ind., 1966, U. Calif., Berkeley, 1968, Graham Gallery, N.Y.C., 1969, Des Moines Art Ctr., 1970, U. Tex., Austin, 1970, Kansas City Art Inst., 1973, A.M. Sachs Gallery, N.Y.C., 1974, 76, 77, 78, 79, 81, 83, 85, Drew U., 1975, Bard Coll., 1975, Am. U., 1976, Roberto Polo Gallery,

Washington, 1976, New Harmony (Ind.) Gallery, 1977, Farm Gallery, Far Hill, N.J., 1978, Barbara Fiedler Gallery, Washington, 1980, Chastenet Gallery, Washington, 1981, Katharina Rich Perlow Gallery, N.Y.C., 1987, 89, 91, 94, 97, 98, 00, 02, 04, 06, Vanderwoude-Tananbaum Gallery, N.Y.C., 1991, U. N.C., Greensboro, 1991, Evansville Mus., 1992, Maine Coast Artists, Rockport, 1994-2006, Bates Coll. Mus., Lewiston, Maine, 1994, Union Coll., Schenectady, NY, 1999, A.J. Buecke Gallery, Northeast Harbor, Maine, 2001, Portland (Maine) Mus. Art, 2004, Farnsworth Mus., 2004; exhibited in group shows in U.S., Europe, Japan, Mid. East, India, Burma, Australia, New Zealand, Hawaii, Ctrl. and S.Am.; represented in permanent collections, Whitney Mus., Chrysler Mus., Norfolk, Va., Provincetown (Mass.) Mus., Evansville Mus., U. So. Ill., Carbondale, Michener Found., Walker Art Ctr., U. Calif., CIBA-Geigy Collection, Hallmark Collection, Bundy Art Gallery, U. N.C., Greensboro, Chase Manhattan Bank, Munson-Williams-Procter Inst., Utica, N.Y., Des Moines Art Ctr., Boston Mus. Fine Arts, Met. Mus., N.Y.C., Phillips Collection, Washington, Am. U., Washington, Corcoran Gallery, Washington, Curie Inst., Paris, Hirshhorn Mus., Washington, Bristol Myers Collection, Indpls. Mus., Portland (Maine) Mus., Bowdoin Coll. Mus., Brown U., Providence, Oberlin (Ohio) Coll. Mus., Farnsworth Art Mus., Rockland, Maine, Bates Coll. Mus., Lewiston, Maine, Nat. Mus. Am. Art, Washington, Columbus Mus. Art, Yale U., New Haven, U. of S. Indiana, Evansville, Union Coll., Schenectady, Newark Art Mus., N.J., U. No. Iowa, Cedar Falls, Colby Coll. Mus., Waterville, Maine, Rutgers U. Mus., NB, NJ, New Orleans Mus. Art, NAD, Baruch Coll., N.Y., U. Maine, Orono, U. Denver, Ogunquit (Maine) Mus., Fryeburg (Maine) Acad., Sweet Briar (Va.) Mus., Yeshiva U., NYC Served with AUS, 1941-45, ETO. Recipient Dolian Lorian award for promising Am. painters, 1954, Hallmark award, 1961, Am. Acad. Arts and Letters prize, 2004; grantee Creative Artists Pub. Svc. Program, 1973; Guggenheim fellow, 1980. Mem.: NAD (Benjamin Altman prize 1993, Edwin Palmer Marine prize 2001, William A. Paton prize 2005). Address: 345 W 29th St New York NY 10001-4780 Office Phone: 212-563-0249.

**PACE, THOMAS M.,** lawyer; b. Mesa, Ariz., Feb. 5, 1952; s. Lemuel Max and Ann (Green) P.; m. Vi Garrett Pace, Jan. 24, 1981; children: Melanie, Brittany. BA, Stanford U., 1973; JD, U. Ariz., 1976. Bar: Ariz.; cert. real estate specialist. Assoc. Martin, Feldhacker & Freidl, Phoenix, 1976-77, Trew & Woodford, Phoenix, 1977-78; ptnr. Hecker, Phillips & Hooker, Tucson, 1978-88; sr. ptnr. O'Connor Cavanagh, Tucson, 1988-95; pvt. practice Law Office of Thomas M. Pace, Tucson, 1995—. Mem. Mayor's Housing Task Force, Tucson, 1993; bd. dirs. Tucson Urban League, 1986-96; chmn. So. Ariz. Homebuilders Polit. Action Com., 1995, 96. Mem. So. Ariz. Homebuilders (tech. com). Stanford Club So. Ariz. Democrat. Office: 1670 E River Rd Ste 124 Tucson AZ 85718-8900 Office Phone: 520-322-5511. Business E-Mail: tom@pacelawaz.com.

**PACE, WAYNE H.,** communications executive; B in Accounting and Econs., Austin Peay State U.; M in Acctg., U. Ga. J.M. Tull Sch. Accountancy. Joined Price Waterhouse, 1970; exec. v.p. fin., adminstrv. officer Turner Broadcasting Sys., Atlanta, 1993—2001; vice chmn., CFO Turner Broadcasting Sys. (now Time Warner), Atlanta, 2001; exec. v.p., CFO Time Warner Inc, NYC, 2001—. Bd. dirs. Spl. Olympics of Ga. Recipient Disting. Alumnus award, U. Ga., 1988. Office: Time Warner Inc 75 Rockefeller Plaza New York NY 10019*

**PACELLE, WAYNE,** animal rights organization administrator; m. Kirsten Rosenberg. BA in History and Environ. Studies, Yale U., 1987. With anti-hunting group Fund for Animals, 1988—94; with Human Soc. U.S., Washington, 1994—, sr. v.p. comm. and govt. affairs, pres., 2004—. Spkr. in field; bd. dirs. Humane USA. Contbr. articles to newspapers. Named one of America's most important animal rights activists, LA Times, 1997.

**PACH, PETER BARNARD,** columnist, editor; b. Bklyn., Aug. 3, 1951; s. Stewart Warner and Constance (Barnard) P.; m. Kathleen Ann Megan, Sept. 7, 1985; children: Nell, Samuel. BA in English, Union Coll., 1973. Reporter Record Jour., Meriden, Conn., 1974-78, Wallingford bur. chief, 1978-83; Middletown bur. chief Hartford Courant, Conn., 1983-84, columnist Conn., 1984-95; mem. editorial bd. Hartford (Conn.) Courant, 1992—, town editls. editor, 2001—06, assoc. editor, 2006—. Vis. instr. Wesleyan U., Middletown, Conn., 1985—2003. Recipient First Bus. and Econ. Reporting award New England Press Ass., 1977. Mem. Dedham County and Polo Club. Avocations: running, skiing, golf, squash, gardening. Home: PO Box 46 Middle Haddam CT 06456-0046 Office: Hartford Courant 285 Broad St Hartford CT 06115-2510

**PACHECO, MANUEL TRINIDAD,** retired academic administrator; b. Rocky Ford, Colo., May 30, 1941; s. Manuel J. and Elizabeth (Lopez) Pacheco; m. Karen M. King, Aug. 27, 1966; children: Daniel Mark, Andrew Charles, Sylvia Lois Elizabeth. BA, N.Mex. Highlands U., 1962; MA, Ohio State U., 1966, PhD, 1969. Mem. faculty Fla. State U., 1968—71, U. Colo., 1971; prof. edn., univ. dean Tex. A&I U., Laredo, 1972—77; prof. multicultural edn., chmn. dept. San Diego State U., 1977—78; prof. Spanish and edn. Laredo State U., 1978—80; exec. dir. Bilingual Edn. Ctr., Kingsville Tex. A&I U., 1980—82; assoc. dean Coll. Edn. U. Tex., El Paso 1982—86, exec. dir. for planning, 1984; pres. Laredo State U., 1984—88, U. Houston-Downtown, 1986—97, U. Ariz., Tucson, 1991—97, U. Mo. Sys., Columbia, 1997—2002; ret., 2002. Cons. lang. divsn. Ency. Britannica, 1965—72; bd. dirs. Valley Nat. Bank Corp., Nat. Security Edn. Program, ASARCO, PNM Resources, Inc.; mem. exec. com. Bus.-Higher Edn. Forum. Co-editor: Handbook for Planning and Managing Instruction in Basic Skills for Limited English Proficient Students, 1983; prodr.: (videotapes) Teacher Training, 1976. Named, Most Prominent Am.-Hispanics Hispanic Bus., 1984, one of 100 Outstanding Hispanics Hispanic Bus., 1988, Man of Yr., Hispanic Profl. Action Com., 1991; recipient Disting. Alumnus award, Ohio State U., Columbus, 1984, Disting. Leadership in Higher Edn. award, Sec. of Edn. Richard Riley, 1997; Fulbright fellow, U. de Montepellier, France, 1962. Mem.; Tex. Assn. Chicanos in Higher Edn., Hispanic Assn. Colls. and Univs., Nat. Acad. Pub. Adminstrn., Am. Assn. State Colls. and Univs., Rotary, Phi Delta Kappa.

**PACHECO, SUSAN,** automotive executive; d. Jorge Pacheco; married; children: Alex, Adam. MBA, U. Detroit, 1989. Ford grad. tng. program Ford Motor Co., 1984—86, product design engr., 1986—89, supr. steering column and shiftsystem design and devel., 1989—92, program mgr. Ford Explorer special studies, 1992, chief program engr., pres. Ford Unlimited, dir. Mercury programs. Named one of 50 Most Important Hispanics in Bus. and Tech., Hispanic Engr. & Info. Tech. mag., 2003.

**PACHECO-FOWLER, VICTOR,** medical educator; b. Caracas, D.F., Venezuela, Jan. 15, 1960; MD, U. Carabobo, Valencia, Venezuela, 1987. Asst. clin. prof. Columbia U. Coll. Physician, NYC, 1996—; attending physician Columbia U. Med. Ctr., 1998—. Office: Columbia University Medical Center 622W 168th Street PH-137 New York NY 10032 Office Phone: 212-305-2995. E-mail: vp75@columbia.edu.

**PACHECO-RANSANZ, ARSENIO,** language educator, historian, educator; b. Barcelona, Feb. 8, 1932; s. Arsenio Pacheco and Jacoba Ransanz-Alvarez; m. Mercedes Olivella-Sole, Sept. 1, 1956; children: Arsenio-Andrew, David-George. MA, U. Barcelona, 1954, PhD, 1958. Tutor Colegio Mayor Hispan-oamericano Fray Junipero Serra, Barcelona, 1954-56; lectr. Hochschüle für Wirtschaft und Sozialwissenschaften, Nurnberg, Germany, 1956; asst. lectr. U. Glasgow, Scotland, 1957-59; lectr. U. St. Andrews, Scotland, 1960-70; vis. prof. U. Pitts., 1966; prof. Hispanic and Italian studies U. B.C., Vancouver, Canada, 1970-97, prof. emeritus, 1997—. Editor: Historia de Xacob Xalabin, 1964, Testament de Bernat Serradell, 1971, Varia fortuna del soldado Pindaro, 1975, Obres de Francesc de la Via, 1997; contbr. articles to profl. jours. Bd. dirs. Can. Fedn. Humanities, 1981-84. Fellow Royal Soc. Can.; mem. Can. Assn. Hispanists (pres. 1978-81), Asociacion Internacional de Hispanists, MLA, Assn. Hispanists Gt. Britain and Ireland, N.Am. Catalan Soc. (v.p.

1984-87, pres. 1987-90), Anglo Catalan Soc., Associacio Internacional de Llengua i Literatura Catalana. Roman Catholic. Office: U BC Dept French Hispanic Ital Vancouver BC Canada V6T 1Z1 Business E-Mail: arp@interchange.ubc.ca.

**PACHER, NANCY A.,** real estate company executive; Grad. cum laude, Georgetown U.; JD, Northwestern U. Atty. Katten Muchin Rosenman LLP, Chgo., 1975; sr. v.p., prin. Howard Ecker & Co.; COO US Equities Realty, Chgo., 1993—. Commr. City of Chgo. Plan Commn. Mem. editl. adv. bd.: Ill. Real Estate Jour. Named Broker of the Yr., Chgo. Sun-Times, 1986, 2004; named one of 100 Most Influential Women in Chgo., Crain's Chgo. Bus., 1996; named to Who's Who in Chgo. Bus., 2002, 20th Ann. Hall of Fame, Today's Chgo. Women. Mem.: ABA, Comml. Real Estate Orgn., Comml. Real Estate Exec. Women, The Chgo. Network (bd. chair 2005—06), Chgo. Bar Assn., Econ. Club Chgo., Phi Beta Kappa. Office: US Equities Realty Ste 400 20 N Michigan Ave Chicago IL 60602

**PACHINO, BARTON P.,** lawyer; BA in Pol. Sci. magna cum laude, Duke U.; JD cum laude, Northwestern U. Law Sch. Assoc. corp. counsel KB Home, 1987-89, corp. counsel, 1989-91, v.p., 1991-93, sr. v.p., gen. counsel, 1993—. Bd. dirs. Bet Tzecek Legal Svcs., former chmn. corp. law dept. section Century City Bar Assn. Mem. Am. Bar Assoc., Ca. Bar Assoc., L.A. County Bar Assoc. Office: KB Home 10990 Wilshire Blvd Fl 7 Los Angeles CA 90024-3913 E-mail: bpachino@kbhome.com.

**PACHMAN, FREDERIC CHARLES,** library director; b. Paterson, N.J., Apr. 16, 1952; s. Morris J. and Barbara M. (Haagen) P.; m. Donna Kearns, May 2, 1982; children: Rick, Kristina. BA, Syracuse U., 1973; MLS, Columbia U., 1976; cert., Rutgers U., New Brunswick, N.J., 1996. Libr. dir. Hamilton Twp. (N.J.) Pub. Libr., 1981-83, Middletown Twp. (N.J.) Pub. Libr., 1983-85, Monmouth Med. Ctr., Long Branch, N.J., 1985—. Mem. exec. bd. Hist. Soc. Ocean Grove, N.J., 1985-2003, Interagy. Coun. on Info. Resources for Nursing, N.Y.C., 1985-2003; cons. Caucus Archival Program Evaluation Svc., N.J., 1990—; mem. adv. com. on preservation and access N.J. State Libr., 1992-95. Contbr. articles to profl. jours. Asst. scoutmaster troop 32 Boy Scouts Am., River Plaza, N.J., 1993—. Mem. ALA, N.J. Libr. Assn., Med. Libr. Assn., League Hist. Socs. N.J., Mid Atlantic Regional Archives Conf., Acad. Health Info. Profls. (disting.) Monmouth Librs. Assn. (pres. 1985-86, 1999-2000), Order of the Arrow (brotherhood mem.). Avocations: backpacking, reading, historic preservation, archives, kayaking. Office: Monmouth Med Ctr 300 2d Ave Long Branch NJ 07740-6300 Office Phone: 732-923-6645. E-mail: fpachman@sbhcs.com.

**PACHOLCZYK, ANDRZEJ GRZEGORZ,** astrophysicist; b. Warsaw, Sept. 23, 1935; arrived in USA, 1962; s. Tadeusz and Natalia (Ugniewska) Pacholczyk; m. Mary Jane Driggs, Apr. 27, 1963; children: Tadeusz J., Helen L. Arnold, Hanna G. Zoucha, Elena M. Orosco, Michelle A. Weldy. MS astronomy, Warsaw U. Warsaw, Poland, 1956, MS physics, 1957, PhD astrophysics, 1961. Rsch. fellow Polish Acad. Sci., Warsaw, 1958—62; lectr. U. Warsaw, 1958—62; Italian Fgn. ministry fellow U. Turin, Italy, 1959—60; rsch. fellow Harvard U., Cambridge, Mass., 1963—64; from asst. prof. to prof., astronomer U. Ariz., Tucson, 1965—2001, prof. emeritus, 2001—. Vis. fellow Joint Inst. Lab. Astrophysics, Boulder, Colo., 1964—65; dir. Pachart Pub. House, Tucson, 1970—; sr. vis. fellow U. Sussex, Falmer, England, 1973; CNR vis. fellow Inst. Radio Astronomy, Bologna, Italy, 1973; vis. scientist Smidt Inst. Earth Physics, Moscow, 1962, Arecibo Ionospheric Obs., Arecibo, PR, 1968, Nat. Radio Astronomy Obs., Charlottesville, Va., 1976, Vatican Obs., Castelgandolfo, 1982, 84, 86, 88, Huazhong Normal U, Wuhan, PR, China, 1992, Swedish Inst. Space Physics, Umea, Sweden, 1998; CEO Pachart Found., Tuscon, Ariz., 1982—; vis. prof. U. Florence, Florence, Italy, 1982—83; bd. mem. Vatican Obs. Found., Tucson, 1986—89. Author: Radio Astrophysics, 1970, Radio Galaxies, 1977, A Handbook of Radio Sources, 1978, The Catastrophic Universe, 1984; pub. (jour.) Phil. in Sci., 1983—2003; contbr. articles in prof. jour. Bd. dirs. Forum on Theology and Sci. Newman Ctr., Tucson, 1991—2003. Fellow: Royal Astron. Soc.; mem.: Polish Astron. Soc., Internat. Astron. Union, Am. Astron. Soc. Roman Catholic. Avocations: classical organ, piano, poetry. Home: 1130 San Lucas Cir PO box 35542 Tucson AZ 85740 Office: Steward Observatory Univ of AZ Tucson AZ 85721

**PACHOLSKI, RICHARD FRANCIS,** securities trader, consultant, financial consultant; b. Seattle, June 18, 1947; s. Theodore Francis and Nellie (Tarabochia) P.; m. Dorothy Irene Nelson, May 25, 1974; children: Nicolas, Tara. BA cum laude, U. Wash., 1969, MBA summa cum laude, 1970. CPA Wash. Mgr. Arthur Andersen & Co., Seattle, 1970-76; v.p., contr. SNW Enterprises, Seattle, 1976-82; sr. v.p., treas., sec., dir. Seattle N.W. Securities, 1982-93; cons. Carl & Co., Portland, Oreg., 1984-88, Ellis & Carl Inc., Portland, Oreg., 1979-83; pres. R. Pacholski, P.C., Redmond, Wash., 1979—. Adj. prof. U. Wash., Seattle, 1976-80. Mem. AICPA, Nat. Assn. Securities Dealers (past bd. dirs. local dist.), Wash. Athletic Club, PacWest Club (Redmond, Wash.). Roman Catholic. Personal E-mail: pacholski@prodigy.net.

**PACHTER, IRWIN JACOB,** pharmaceutical consultant; b. N.Y.C., July 15, 1925; s. Nathan and Ethel Lillian (Thomases) P.; m. Elaine Anna White, Aug. 23, 1953; children: Wendy, Jonathan. BS, UCLA, 1947; MS, U. N.Mex., 1949; PhD, U. So. Calif., 1951; postgrad., U. Ill., 1951-52, Harvard U., 1952-53. Research chemist Ethyl Corp., 1953-55; asso. research chemist Smith Kline & French, 1955-62, asst. sec. head, 1962; dir. medicinal chemistry Endo Labs., 1962-66; dir. research Endo div. du Pont Co., 1967-70; v.p. research and devel. Bristol Labs. div. Bristol-Myers Co., 1970-82; lectr. Adelphi U., 1963-69. Contbr. articles to profl. jours.; patentee in field Trustee Gordon Research Conf., 1972-75; chmn. medicinal chemistry study group Walter Reed Inst. Research, 1975-77. Served with USN, 1944-46. Mem. Am. Chem. Soc. (chmn. div. medicinal chemistry 1974-76), Pharm. Mfrs. Assn. (chmn. research and devel. sect. 1975-76) Home: 101 Woodberry Ln Fayetteville NY 13066-1745 Personal E-mail: ijpac@aol.com.

**PACHTER, LEE M.,** pediatrician; b. Bklyn., Mar. 12, 1957; s. Harvey Leonard and Rosalind Blau Pachter; married Diedre Reynolds-Pachter; 1 child, Lauren. BA, Franklin and Marshal Coll., 1979; DO, Phila. Coll. Osteo. Medicine, 1983. Diplomate Am. Bd. Osteo. Physicians. Intern Metro. Hosp., Springfield, Pa., 1983-84; resident in pediatrics St. Christopher's Hosp. Children, Phila., 1984-87; fellow in pediatrics Children's Hosp. Phila., 1987-89; from asst. prof. to prof. pediats. and anthropology U. Conn. Sch. Medicine, Farmington, 1989—, head divsn. gen. pediat., 1999—. Trustee The Artists Collective, Hartford, Conn., 1989—. Fellow Am. Acad. Pediatrics, Soc. Applied Anthropology; mem. Am. Anthropol. Assn., Ambulatory Pediat. Assn., Soc. Rsch. and Child Devel., Soc. Applied Anthropology, Soc. for Pediat. Rsch. Office: St Francis Hosp & Med Ctr 114 Woodland St Hartford CT 06105-1208 Personal E-mail: Lpachter@comcast.net.

**PACHTER, MARC,** museum director; B summa cum laude, Univ. Calif., Berkeley; postgrad. Harvard Univ. Faculty Harvard Univ.; chief historian Smithsonian's Nat. Portrait Gallery, 1974—90, asst. dir., 1974—90, dep. asst. sec., external affairs, 1990—94, NPG dir., 2000—; acting dir. Smithsonian's Nat. Mus. of Am. History, 2001—02; former counselor to sec. Smithsonian Instn., 1995—2000. Chair Smithsonian's 150th Anniversary; sr. cons. various history documentaries; cons. Internat. Broadcasting; commentator CBS, Voice of Am., C-SPAN. Author/editor (books) Abroad in America: Visitors to the New Nation, Champions of American Sport, Documentary History of the Supreme Court, Telling Lives: The Biographer's Art, A Gallery of Presidents. Fellow Woodrow Wilson, Harvard Univ., five-yr. prize. Office: Nat Portrait Gallery Victor Bldg-Ste 8300 MRC PO Box 37012 Washington DC 20013-7012 Office Phone: 202-275-1740. Office Fax: 202-275-1887. Business E-Mail: pachterm@si.edu.

**PACI, RUTH A.,** freelance/self-employed writer; b. West New York, N.J., Mar. 7, 1928; d. Joseph Frederick and Theresa Becker Paci. BA in History and Polit. Sci., Fordham U., 1984; MA in Journalism, NYU, 1987. Adminstrv. officer, press officer U.S. Info. Agy., Washington and N.Y.C., 1951—86, dep. dir. Fgn. Press Ctr. N.Y.C., 1985—86; ret., 1986; freelance writer. Author: Down By the River and Under the Cliff, 1994, Dearest Friends, 2004, short stories and essays. V.p., trustee Edgewater Pub. Libr., 1995—; mem., founder Cultural and Hist. Commn. Edgewater, 2000—; hist. preservation advisory bd. Bergen County, 2004. Recipient Cert. of Commendation, Bergen County Bd. Chosen Freeholders, 2003, Hist. Preservation resolution, NJ Gen. Assembly, 2003, Career Achievement award, US Info. Agy., 1986. Roman Catholic. Avocations: travel, gardening, reading. Home: 24 Valley Pl Edgewater NJ 07020

**PACIESAS, WILLIAM SIMON,** astrophysicist, educator; b. Pottsville, Pa., Aug. 27, 1947; s. Simon J. and Alice A. (Bellis) P.; m. Dianne Strange, Apr. 28, 1986; children: Jack D. Darby, Rebecca M. Darby, Sylvia R., Roxanne H. BS magna cum laude, Seton Hall U., 1969; MS, U. Calif., San Diego, 1971, C.Phil., 1976, PhD, 1978. NAS/NRC resident rsch. assoc. NASA Goddard Space Flight Ctr., Greenbelt, Md., 1978-80; rsch. assoc. U. Md., College Park, 1980-82; asst. rsch. prof. U. Ala., Huntsville, 1982-88, assoc. rsch. prof., 1988-94, rsch. prof. astrophysics, 1994—. Editor: Gamma Ray Bursts, 1992; contbr. articles to profl. jours. Mem. AAAS, Am. Astron. Soc., Am. Phys. Soc., Internat. Astron. Union. Home: 1207 Bob Wallace Ave Huntsville AL 35801 Office: U Ala Dept Physics Huntsville AL 35899-0001 E-mail: william.paciesas@msfc.nasa.gov.

**PACIFICO, ALBERT DOMINICK,** cardiovascular surgeon; b. Bklyn., Sept. 24, 1940; s. Dominick Vincent and Amelia Catherine (Jannelli) P.; m. Vicki Lynne Overton, May 16, 1980; children: Albert D., Nicole M., Paul V. BS, St. Johns U., 1960; MD, N.J. Coll. Medicine, 1964. Diplomate Am. Bd. Surgery, Am. Bd. Thoracic Surgery. Med. intern Jersey City Med. Ctr., Seton Gall Coll. Medicine, 1964-65; asst. resident in surgery Mayo Clinic, Rochester, Minn., 1965-67; research fellow in surgery U. Ala., Birmingham, 1967-69, sr. resident, then chief resident surgery, resident in thoracic and cardiovascular surgery, 1968-72, mem. faculty dept. surgery, 1970—2006, prof. surgery, 1978-83, John W. Kirklin prof. cardiovascular surgery, 1983—2006, vice chmn. dept. surgery, 1990, dir. divsn. cardiothoracic surgery, 1984—2006, dir. Congenital Heart Disease Diagnosis and Treatment Ctr., 1985—2006. Mem. staff gen., thoracic and cardiovascular surgery Univ. Hosp., Birmingham, 1972-2006, VA Hosp., Birmingham, 1972-2006; mem. staff Children's Hosp., Birmingham, 1971-2006, chief gen., thoracic and cardiovascular surgery, 1984-2006. Author: (with others) Pediatric Cardiac Surgery, 1985, Cardiology, 1985, Textbook of Surgery, 13th edit., 1986, The Treatment of Congenital Cardiac Anomalies, 1986, Perspectives in Pediatric Cardiology, 1988, Current Therapy in Cardiothoracic Surgery, 1989, Decision Making in Surgery of the Chest, 1989, Cardiac Surgery: Cyanotic Congenital Heart Disease, 1989, Reoperation in Cardiac Surgery, 1989, others; mem. editorial bd. Am. Jour. Cardiology, 1983-2006, Heart and Vessel, 1985-2006, Jour. Cardiac Surgery, 1985-2006; cons. editorial referee Ala. Jour. Med. Scis., 1974-75; contbr. articles to med. jours. Fellow ACS, Am. Coll. Cardiology, Am. Surg. Assn.; mem. AMA, Ala. State Med. Soc., Jefferson County Med. Soc., Am. Heart Assn. (Paul Dudley White Internat. Svc. Citation 1977), Am. Assn. Thoracic Surgery, Soc. Thoracic Surgeons, Am. Surg. Soc., Internat. Coll. Pediatrics, John Kirklin Soc., Congenital Heart Surgeons Soc., Assn. Acad. Surgery, Ala. chpt. Mayo Clinic Alumni Assn., Panamanian Soc. Cardiology (hon.), Peruvian Soc. Thoracic and Cardiovascular Surgery (hon.), Soc. Nat. Inst. Cardiology Mex. (hon.), Cardiac Soc. Australia and New Zealand (corr.), Peruvian Soc. Cardiology (corr.), Alpha Omega Alpha. Republican. Roman Catholic.

**PACIFICO, JOSEPH CARL,** counselor; b. Grosse Ile, Mich., June 10, 1950; s. Carl Richard Pacifico and Mary Milano Campbell; m. Claire Lee Schlauch, Aug. 12, 1972; children: Mark Joseph, David Joseph. BS in Psychology, U. Md., 1972, MBA in Mktg., 1975; MS in Counseling Psychology, Loyola Coll., Balt., 1998. Lic. clin. profl. counselor Md., 2002. Acct. rep. Wallace Computer Svcs., Inc., Rockville, Md., 1975—99; master's level therapist Family and Marriage Therapy Ctr., Burtonsville, Md., 1998—2002, Christian Counseling Assocs., Inc., Columbia, Md., 1999—2002, clin. profl. counselor, 2002—. Leader, anger mgmt. group Christian Counseling Assocs., Inc., 2001—. Worship asst. Our Shepherd Luth. Ch., Columbia, Md., 1998—. Mem.: Christian Assocs. for Psychol. Studies. Avocations: photography, racquetball, tennis, ping pong/table tennis. Office: Christian Counseling Assocs Inc 9650 Santiago Rd # 101 Columbia MD 21045

**PACINO, AL (ALFREDO JAMES PACINO),** actor, film director, film producer; b. NYC, Apr. 25, 1940; s. Salvatore and Rose Pacino; children: Julie Marie, Anton, Olivia. Student, High Sch. of Performing Arts, Actors Studio. Formerly mail deliverer editorial offices Commentary Mag.; formerly messenger, movie theatre usher, bldg. supt.; co-artistic dir. The Actors Studio, Inc., N.Y.C., 1982-84. Served apprenticeship as actor, dir. and comedy writer in Off-Off Broadway theatres, Elaine Stewart's Cafe La Mama, Julian Beck & Judith Malina's Living Theatre; appeared in New Theatre Workshop prodn. of The Peace Creeps, Dec., 1966; joined Charles Playhouse, Boston, fall, 1967, and performed in New Theatre Workshop prodn. of America Hurrah and Awake and Sing; appeared in a one-act play Off Broadway The Indian Wants the Bronx, opened Astor Pl. Theater on Jan. 17, 1968 (Obie as best actor in Off-Broadway prodn. 1967-68); made Broadway debut in Does A Tiger Wear A Necktie?, 1969 (Tony award as best dramatic actor in a supporting role, named best promising new Broadway actor in a Variety poll of metropolitan drama critics); appeared in The Local Stigmatic at Actors Playhouse, N.Y.C., opening 1969; joined Repertory Theater of Lincoln Center, N.Y.C.; other plays include The Basic Training of Pavlo Hummel, Boston Repertory Theater, 1972, Camino Real, Richard III, 1973, 79, Jungle of Cities, 1979, The Connection, Hello Out There, Tiger at the Gates, American Buffalo, Julius Caesar, 1988, Salome, Chinese Coffee (also dir.) 2000, Circle in the Square, 1992, Dir. and Performer, Hughie, 1996; (films) Me, Natalie, 1969, Panic in Needle Park, 1971, The Godfather, 1972 (Best Actor award Nat. Soc. Film Critics, Acad. award nominee), Scarecrow, 1973, Serpico, 1973 (Golden Globe for best actor, Acad. award nominee), The Godfather, Part II, 1974 (BAFTA award for best actor, Acad. award nominee), Dog Day Afternoon (BAFTA award for best actor, Acad. award nominee), 1975, Bobby Deerfield, 1977, And Justice for All, 1979 (Acad. Award nomination), Cruising, 1980, Author! Author!, 1982, Scarface, 1983, Revolution, 1985, Sea of Love, 1989, Dick Tracy, 1990 (American Comedy award, Acad. award nominee), The Godfather Part III, 1990, Frankie and Johnny, 1991, Glengarry Glen Ross, 1992 (Acad. award nominee), Scent of a Woman, 1992 (Acad. award for best actor, Golden Globe for best actor), Carlito's Way, 1993, Two Bits, 1995, Heat, 1995, City Hall, 1996, (also prodr., dir., writer) Looking for Richard, 1996 (Dir. Guild of Amer. award for best dir. documentary), Donnie Brasco, 1997, Devil's Advocate, 1997, Chinese Coffee, 1999, The Insider, 1999, Any Given Sunday, 1999, People I Know, 2002, Simone, 2002, Insomnia, 2002, The Recruit, 2003, Gigli, 2003, The Merchant of Venice, 2004, Two for the Money, 2005; (TV miniseries) Angels in America, 2003 (Golden Globe for best actor, Screen Actors Guild Award for best actor, 2004, Emmy award Outstanding Lead Actor in a Miniseries or a Movie, 2004). Recipient Cecil B. DeMille Award Hollywood Fgn. Press. Assn., 2001, Am. Cinematheque Lifetime Achievement award, 2006. Office: Creative Artists Agy care Rick Nicita 9830 Wilshire Blvd Beverly Hills CA 90212-1804

**PACINO, MARIA ANTONIETA,** education educator, department chairman; d. Antonio Augusto Osorio de Carvalho and Maria da Conceicao Ponte (de Carvalho); m. Joe Louis Pacino, Dec. 2, 1974; children: Monique Caroline Morelli, Vanessa Paula Morelli. BA, Ball State U., 1977, MLS, 1981, EdD, 1988. Tchg. credential Ind., 1977. Tchr., libr. Muncie Cmty. Schools, Ind., 1978—90; asst. prof. sec. edn. Ball State U., Muncie, 1990—93; assoc. prof. edn. Azusa Pacific U., Calif., 1993—97, prof., dept. chair, 1997—. Spkr. in field. Contbr. articles to profl. jours., chapters to books.

Mem. Human Rels. Commn., Azusa, 1999—2000, Pub. Libr. Commn., Azusa, 2000—03; chair U. Diversity Comp., Azusa, 2004—. Mem.: ASCD, Nat. Assn. Multicultural Edn., Am. Ednl. Rsch. Assn. Roman Catholic. Avocations: reading, opera, music, travel, theater. Office: Azusa Pacific U P O Box 7000 Azusa CA 91702 Office Phone: 626-815-5367. Office Fax: 626-815-5416. Business E-Mail: mpacino@apu.edu.

PACK, MICHAEL, television producer, writer, director; b. N.Y.C., May 16, 1954; s. Harvey and Joy P.; m. Gina Cappo, Sept. 20, 1986. Student, Yale U., 1972-74, U. Calif., Berkeley, 1974-75, NYU, 1976. Staff editor R.A.I. (Italian TV Network), N.Y.C., 1976, Pathe News, N.Y.C., 1977; pres. Manifold Prodns., N.Y.C. and L.A., 1977—2003; sr. v.p. Corp. Pub. Broadcasting, 2003—06, co-chair internat. TV coun., 2003; independent film prodr., 2006—. Dir. Worldnet U.S. Info. Agy., 1992—93; mem. Nat. Coun. on Humanities. Assoc. producer (feature film) Never Pick Up A Stranger, N.Y.C. 1977; dir., writer (short drama) Hard Bargain, 1979 (CINE Eagle award); exec. producer, dir., writer (TV spl.) Hollywood's Favorite Heavy, 1987 (CINE Gold Eagle award 1987, Bronze award Houston Internat. Film Festival 1988); exec. producer (documentary) American Political Parties: The Republicans (part 2), 1988 (CINE Gold Eagle award 1989); producer, dir., writer (documentary) America's Political Parties: The Democrats, 1988 (Silver award Houston Internat. Film Festival 1989, 90, CINE Gold Eagle award 1989); producer, dir., writer (documentary) Fire From The Sun: The Search for Fusion Energy, 1989 (CINE Gold Eagle award 1990, Bronze award Houston Internat. Film Festival 1990, Red Ribbon award Am. Film and Video Festival 1991). Mem. Internat. Feature Projects, Internat. Documentary Assn., Internat. TV Assn.*

PACK, RUSSELL T., theoretical chemist; b. Grace, Idaho, Nov. 20, 1937; s. John Terrell and Mardean (Izatt) P.; m. Marion Myrth Hassell, Aug. 21, 1962; children: John R., Nathan H., Allen H., Miriam, Elizabeth, Quinn R., Howard H. BS, Brigham Young U., 1962; PhD, U. Wis., 1967. Postdoctoral fellow U. Minn., Mpls., 1966-67; asst. prof. Brigham Young U., Provo, 1967-71, assoc. prof., 1971-75, adj. prof., 1975-88; staff scientist Los Alamos (N.Mex.) Nat. Lab., 1975-83, fellow, 1983—, assoc. grp. leader, 1979-81. Vis. prof. Max Planck Institut, Gottingen, 1981; chmn. Gordon Rsch. Conf., 1982; lectr. in field. Contbr. articles to profl. jours. Named Sr. U.S. Scientist, Alexander Vol Humboldt Found., 1981. Fellow Am. Phys. Soc. (sec.-treas. div. Chem. Physics 1990-93); mem. Am. Chem. Soc., Sigma Xi. Mem. Ch. of Jesus Christ of Latter Day Saints. Home: 240 Kimberly Ln Los Alamos NM 87544-3526 Office: Los Alamos Nat Lab T 12 Ms # B268 Los Alamos NM 87545-0001 Business E-Mail: rtpack@lanl.gov.

PACKARD, JOHN MALLORY, physician, researcher; b. Saranac Lake, N.Y., Sept. 25, 1920; s. Edward Newman and Mary Bissell (Betts) P.; m. Ann Maurine Schoonover, June 15, 1944; children: Michael David, John Mallory, Ann Maurine, Mary Betts, Charles Edward, Kris Asvananda, Frank Schoonover, Charlotte Mellen. BA, Yale U., 1942; MD, Harvard U., 1945. Diplomate Am. Bd. Internal Medicine. Intern Presbyn. Hosp., N.Y.C., 1945-46; resident in internal medicine Peter Bent Brigham Hosp., Boston, 1948-49; practice medicine specializing in internal medicine and cardiology Pensacola, Fla., 1954-68; prof. medicine, asso. dean Med. Sch. U. Ala., Birmingham, 1968-76; exec. dir. Ala. Regional Med. Program, Birmingham, 1968-73; corp. v.p. med. edn. Bapt. Med. Centers, Birmingham, 1976-92; ret., 1992. Contbr. articles to med. jours. Served with USN, 1946-54. Fellow ACP, Am. Coll. Cardiology, AHA; mem. Jefferson County Med. Soc., Med. Assn. Ala., AMA, Am. Soc. Internal Medicine, Ala. Soc. Internal Medicine (pres. 1981-82), Alpha Omega Alpha. Republican. Episcopalian. Personal E-mail: jmpackard@juno.com.

PACKARD, JULIE, aquarium administrator; b. Los Altos Hills; d. David and Lucile Packard. Co-founder & exec. dir. Monterey Bay Aquarium, Monterey, Calif., 1984—, vice chair, bd of trustees, 1984—. Mem. Pew Oceans Commn. Bd. dirs. David and Lucile Packard Found., Monterey Bay Aquarium Rsch. Inst., Calif. Nature Conservancy. Recipient Audubon Medal for Conservation, 1998, Ted Danson Ocean Hero award, 2004. Office: Monterey Bay Aquarium 886 Cannery Row Monterey CA 93940-1023

PACKARD, PETER, retired internal medical educator; b. Evanston, Ill., Mar. 14, 1927; s. George and Marianna (Dickinson) P.; m. Jenifer Carr, Aug. 28, 1951 (div. 1969); m. Mary Jane P., Nov. 8, 1969; children: Patricia Ann Langlais, Charles Barklay Langlais, Georgia Packard, Caroline L. Gregger, Louise Moskowitz-Packard, Victoria P. Aase, Adam L. Packard. BA, U. Calif., Berkeley, 1945; MD, U. Calif., San Francisco, 1948. Diplomate Am. Bd. Internal Medicine. Intern San Francisco Gen. Hosp., 1948-49; vol. arzt fellow infectious diseases Children's Hosp., Zurich, 1949-50; asst. res. in medicine Franklin Hosp., U. Calif., San Francisco, 1950-51; capt., med. corps USAF, Riverside, Calif., 1951-53; asst. res. medicine Ft. Miley VA Hosp., San Francisco, 1953-54, U. Calif. Hosp., San Francisco, 1954-55; pvt. practice Mills Hosp., Peninsula Med. Lab., San Mateo, Burlingame, Calif., 1955-91. Med. dir., vice chmn. bd. dirs., Peninsula Med. Lab., Menlo Park, Calif., 1980-94; chief of medicine, chief of staff Mills Hosp., San Mateo, 1967-74; assoc. clin. prof. medicine, U. Calif. San Francisco, 1955—. Founding trustee, v.p. Mills-Peninsula Found., 1974-90, trustee emeritus, 1990—; pres., mem. bd. San Mateo County Heart Assn., 1964-74. Capt. M.C., USAFR, 1951-53, Korea. Mem. AMA, Calif. Med. Assn., San Mateo County Med. Assn. (various coms., bd. dirs., 1959-91), Am. Soc. Internal Medicine, Calif. Soc. Internal Medicine (del. off and on 1960-93), Calif. Soc. Medicine, U. Calif. San Francisco Assn. Clin. Faculty Avocations: tennis, golf, traveling, history, politics. Home and Office: 720 Seabury Rd Hillsborough CA 94010-6532

PACKARD, ROBERT GOODALE, III, urban planner; b. Denver, Apr. 12, 1951; s. Robert and Mary Ann (Woodward) P.; m. Jane Ann Collins, Aug. 25, 1973; children: Jessica Nelson, Robert Gregg. BA, Willamette U., 1973; M in Urban and Regional Planning/Community Devel., U. Colo., 1976. Project mgr. Environ. Disciplines, Inc., Portland, Oreg., 1973-75; asst. dir. planning Portland Pub. Schs., 1976-78; dir. planning Bur. of Parks, Portland, 1978-79; dir. planning and urban design Zimmer Gunsul Frasca, Portland, 1979-81, dir. project devel., 1981-84, mng. ptnr., 1984—. Co-author: The Baker Neighborhood/Denver, 1976. Contbr. articles to profl. jours. Trustee Willamette U., 1994; mem. City of Portland Waterfront Commn., 1982-83; mem. Mayor's Task Force for Joint Use of Schs., Portland, 1979-80; mem. Washington Park Master Plan Steering com., Portland, 1980-81; bd. dirs. Washington Park Zoo, 1983-86, pres. Arts Celebration Inc./Artquake, 1986—, New Rose Theatre, 1981-83; dir., pres Grant Park Neighborhood Assn., Portland, 1981-83; pres. Pioneer Square Bd., 1997-98; bd. mem. Regional Arts and Cultural Coun.; mem. Archtl. Found. Oreg., 1992; mem. crafts bd. Oreg. Sch. Arts. Recipient Spl. Citation, Nat. Sch. Bds. Assn., 1978; Meritorious Planning Project award Am. Planning Assn., 1980, Nat. Am. Planning Assn., 1981; Meritorious Design award Am. Planning Assn.; Honor award Progressive Arch., 1983. Mem. AIA (Architecture Firm award 1991, assoc.), Am. Planning Assn., Young Pres. Assn., Racquet Club, Arlington Club, City Club, Racquet Club. Home: 3313 SW Fairmount Blvd Portland OR 97201-1478 Office: Zimmer Gunsul Frasca Partnership 320 SW Oak St Ste 500 Portland OR 97204-2737

PACKARD, ROCHELLE SYBIL, elementary school educator; b. June 25, 1951; d. Dave Wallace and Jeanette (Goddy) P. BA in Early Childhood Edn., Point Park Coll., 1973; MEd in Elem. Edn., U. Pitts., 1975. Instrnl. II permanent tchg. cert., Pa. Substitute tchr. Pitts. Pub. Bd. Edn., 1973-77, tchr. kindergarten, 1st grade, 2d grade, 1977—92, tchr. kindergarten, 1992—. Chair Israel Day Parade, Pitts., 1981; mem. Hadassah, Pitts., 1983—; Pioneer Women, Pitts., 1982—, ORT, Pitts., 1975—. Mem. Pitts. Fedn. Tchrs. State Edn. Agy. Democrat. Jewish. Home: 4100 Lydia St Pittsburgh PA 15207-1135 Business E-Mail: rpackard@pghboe.net.

PACKARD, SANDRA PODOLIN, education educator, consultant; b. Buffalo, Sept. 13, 1942; d. Mathew and Ethel (Zolte) P.; m. Martin Packard, Aug. 2, 1964; children: Dawn Esther, Shana Fanny BFA, Syracuse U., 1964; MSEd, Ind. U., 1966, EdD, 1973. Cert. tchr. art K-12, N.Y. Asst. prof. art SUNY-Buffalo, 1972-74; assoc. prof. art Miami U., Oxford, Ohio, 1974-81, spl. asst. to provost, 1979-80, assoc. provost, spl. programs, 1980-81; dean Coll. Edn. Bowling Green State U., Ohio, 1981-85; provost and vice chancellor for acad. affairs U. Tenn., Chattanooga, 1985-92; pres. Oakland U., Rochester, Mich., 1992-95, prof. edn., 1995—, dir. higher edn. doc. cognate; sr. fellow, dir. tech. in edn. Am. Assn. State Colls. and Univs., 1995; coord. Nat. Coun. for Accreditation of Tchr. Edn., Washington, 1995—2001; acting dir. PhD program in end. leadership Oakland U., 2003—04. Cons. Butler County Health Ctr., Hamilton, Ohio, 1976-78, Univ. of the North, South Africa Project of the Am. Coun. on Edn., 1995; vis. prof. art therapy Simmons Coll., 1979, Mary Mount Coll., Milw., 1981; corp. adv. com. Corp. Detroit Mag., 1994-95. Sr. editor Studies in Art Edn. jour., 1979-81; mem. editl. adv. bd. Jour. Aesthetic Edn., 1984-90; editor: The Leading Edge, 1986; contbr. articles to profl. jours., chpts. to conf. papers Chmn. com. Commn. on Edn. Excellence, Ohio, 1982-83, Tenn. State Peformance Funding Task Force, 1988, Tenn. State Task Force on Minority Tchrs., 1988; reviewer art curriculum NY Bd. Edn., 1985; supt. search com. Chattanooga Pub. Schs., 1987-88; mem. Chattanooga Met. Coun., 1987-88, Chattanooga Ballet Bd., 1986-88, Fund for Excellence in Pub. Edn., 1986-90, Tenn. Aquarium Bd. Advisors, 1989-92, Team Evaluation Ctr. Bd., 1988-90; strategic planning action team Chattanooga City Schs., 1987-88, Siskin Hosp. Bd., 1989-92, Blue Ribbon Task Force Pontiac 2010: A New Reality, City of Pontiac Planning Divsn., 1992; steering coun., cultural action bd. Chattanooga, planning com United Way, 1987; Jewish Fedn. Bd., 1986-91; mem. coun. for policy studies Art Edn. Adv. Bd., 1982-91; ex-officio mem. Meadow Brook Theatre Guild, 1992-95; bd. chair Meadow Brook Performing Arts Co., 1992-95; chair World Cup Soccer Edn. Com./Mich. Host Com. 1993-95; bd. dirs. Ptnrs. for Preferred Future, Rochester Cmty. Schs., 1992-95, Traffic Improvement Assn. Oakland County, 1992-95, Oakland County Bus. Roundtable, 1993-95; Rochester C. of C. host com. chair on edn. World Cup, 1992-95; fin. adv. com. Jewish Fedn. Detroit, 1995-97; bd. dirs. United Way Southeastern Mich., 1992-95; bd. dirs. United Way Oakland County, 1992-95, Pontiac 2010: A New Reality, mayor's transition team city/sch. rels. task force: team evaluation leader Dept. of State Am. U. Bulgaria, 1995; bd. trustees Cohn's & Colitis Found., 1996-97; trustee Nat. Art Edn. Found., 2004—, chair fin. com.; steering coun. Nat. Forum Access to Democracy Project, 2004. Am. Coun. on Edn. and Mellon fellow Miami U., 1978-79; recipient Cracking the Glass Ceiling award Pontiac Area Urban League, 1992. Fellow Nat. Art Edn. Assn. (disting.); mem. Nat. Coun. Profs. of Ednl. Adminstrn. (technology com., 2000-03), Am. Assn. Colls. for Tchr. Edn. (com. chair 1982-85), Am. Art Therapy Assn. (registered), Nat. Art Edn. Assn. Women's Caucus (founder, pres. 1976-78, McFee award 1986), Am. Assn. State Colls. and Univs. (com. profl. devel. 1993-95, state rep. 1994-95), Econ. Club Detroit (bd. dirs. 1992-95), Rotary Club, Great Lakes Yacht Club (social chmn. 1996-97, ground chmn., bd. dirs. 1997-98), Phi Delta Kappa (Leadership award 1985), Nat. Assn. Profs. of Edn. Adminstrn. (com. chair 1998-), Great Lakes Yacht Club, 1995 (bd. dir. 1996-1998). Avocation: sailing. Home: 10471 Scout Trail White Lake MI 48386 Office: Oakland U 475 Education Bldg Rochester MI 48309-4423 Business E-Mail: packard@oakland.edu.

PACKARD BURNETT, NANCY, biologist; d. David Packard; m. Robin Burnett. BS in Biology, Stanford U., 1965; MS, San Francisco State. Former marine biologist Hopkins Marine Station; founder, marine biologist Monterey Bay Aquarium. Exec. prodr.: (TV films) The Shape of Life, 2002. Bd. dirs. Monterey Bay Aquarium Rsch. Inst.; adv. Whatcom Community Found.; vice chmn. David and Lucile Packard Found.; chmn. Sea Studios Found. Office: Sea Studios Found 810 Cannery Row Monterey CA 93940*

PACKER, BILLY, sports announcer (broadcast); b. Wellsville, NY, Feb. 25, 1940; m. Barbara Packer; 3 children. Graduated, Wake Forest Univ., 1962. Asst. basketball coach Wake Forest Univ., 1965; basketball announcer, ACC conference games Jefferson Pilot Sports, 1972, NBC Sports, 1974—81; basketball announcer, final four announcer CBS Sports, 1981—. Co-founder Tour DuPont, Buckler Challenger. Author: (sports books) Hoops, College Basketball's 25 Greatest Teams, History of the Final Four, Why We Win. Named to NC Hall of Fame, Wake Forest Hall of Fame, Nat. Basketball Hall of Fame, Nat. Polish Hall of Fame; recipient NC Sportscaster Yr. award. Office: CBS Sports 2200 W Cypress Creek Fort Lauderdale FL 33309*

PACKER, GEORGE, writer; Grad., Yale U., 1982. Staff writer The New Yorker, 2003—. Tchr. Harvard U., Columbia U., Sarah Lawrence Coll. Author: The Village of Waiting, 1988, 2001, Blood of the Liberals, 2000 (Robert F. Kennedy Book Award, 2001), The Fight Is for Democracy: Winning the War of Ideas in America and the World, 2003, The Assassins' Gate: America in Iraq, 2005 (Cornelius Ryan award for best nonfiction book, Overseas Press Club, 2006), (novels) The Half Man, 1991, Central Square, 1998; contbr. NY Times Mag., Dissent, Mother Jones, Harper's. Mem. Peace Corps, Togo. Recipient Overseas Press Club awards, 2003; Guggenheim Fellow, 2001—02. Office: New Yorker 4 Times Sq New York NY 10036*

PACKER, JAMES GOODWIN, library director, writer; b. Gunnedah, NSW, Australia, Dec. 11, 1954; s. Goodwin Edward Charles and Esme Hannah Packer. BA with honors, Australian Nat. U., Canberra, ACT, 1977; PhD in Australian Lit., U. Western Sydney, NSW, 1999. Diploma libr. and info. sci. Libr. Australian Inst. Music, Sydney, 1993, TAFE, NSW, Sydney, 1998—99; libr. mgr. WEA Sydney, 1999—. Dir. Interdisciplinary Database of Ideas and Theory in the Humanities, Sydney, 1994—95; cons. D&I Networks, Sydney 1997 Editor: (jour.) Sigmund, 1979, author: (book) The Gatesworth Dictionary of Modern Thought, 1984, Gatesworth's Game, 1986; contbr. multi-volumed series Dictionary of Literary Biography (Australian Literature 1914-1950; 1950-1975), 2002. Mem.: Australian Libr. and Info. Assn. (assoc. ALIA Acquisitions Essay award 1992). Avocations: martial arts, bush walking. Home: Fields Rd Macquarie Fields Sydney NSW 2564 Australia Office: WEA Sydney 72 Bathurst St Sydney NSW 2000 Australia Office Phone: 02 9264 2781. Office Fax: 02 9267 6988. E-mail: jim.packer@weasydney.nsw.edu.au.

PACKER, LINDA S., psychotherapist; b. NYC, July 30, 1941; d. Joseph Wolf Stark and Jean Carson; children: William Joseph, Andrew Landes. BA in English and Psychology with honors, NYU, 1972; CSW, NYU Sch. Social Work, 1987. Diplomate Am. Psychotherapy Assn.; LCSW Nat. Assn. Social Workers and SUNY Edn. Dept.; cert. Nat. Acad. Cert. Care Mgrs. Rsch. asst. alcoholic rsch. unit Silver Hill Found., 1972—75; intern clin. social worker Program for Devel. Human Potential, Bishop Ford H.S., 1985—86; intern clin. social worker outpatient psychiat. clinic Met. Hosp., 1986—87; psych. social worker N.Y. Svc. Program for Older People, 1987—88; sr. cons. Helena Internat., Morristown, NJ, 1988—89; psychiat. social worker Geriatric Psychiat. Inpatient Unit, 1989—92; psychiat. social worker adult psychiat. inpatient unit Mt. Sinai Hosp., N.Y.C., 1992—95; sr. assoc. Fine & Newcombie Assocs., N.Y.C., 1995—99; founder, dir. Prime Life Network, N.Y.C., 2000—. Cons., founder Care Mgrs. Consortium, N.Y.C., 2000—; pvt. practice, 1997—. Author: (article) Diseases of Nervous System, Am. Jour. Geriatric Psychiatry. Mem.: N.Y. State Soc. Clin. Social Work Psychotherapists, Nat. Assn. Social Workers, Nat. Assn. Pvt. Geriatric Care Mgrs., East Side Coun. on Aging, Am. Soc. on Aging, Am. Psychotherapy Assn., Am. Geriatric Soc. Avocations: gardening, reading, interior decorating. Office: PrimeLife Network 200 E End Ave #10-I New York NY 10128 Business E-Mail: plncsw@att.net.

PACKER, MARK BARRY, lawyer, financial consultant, foundation official; b. Phila., Sept. 18, 1944; s. Samuel and Eve (Devine) P.; m. Donna Elizabeth Ferguson (div. 1994); children: Daniel Joshua, Benjamin Dov, David Johannes; m. Helen Margaret (Jones) Klinedinst, July, 1995. AB magna cum laude, Harvard U., 1965, LLB, 1968. Bar: Wash. 1969, Mass. 1971. Assoc. Ziontz, Pirtle & Fulle, Seattle, 1968-70; pvt. practice Bellingham, Wash., 1972—. Bd. dirs., corp. sec. BMJ Holdings (formerly No. Sales Co., Inc.),

1977—; trustee No. Sales Profit Sharing Plan, 1977—; bd. dirs. Whatcom State Bank, 1995-98. Mem. Bellingham Planning and Devel. Commn., 1975—84, chmn., 1977—81; mem. shoreline subcom., 1976—82, capital improvements adv. com., 1999—2001; mem. Bellingham Mcpl. Arts Commn., 1986—91, landmark rev. bd., 1987—91; chmn. Bellingham campaign United Jewish Appeal, 1979—90; trustee, chmn. program com. Bellingham Pub. Sch. Found., 1991—96, Heavy Culture classic lit. group, 1991—, Jewish studies group, 1993—; trustee Kenneth L. Kellar Found., 1995—; mng. trustee Bernard M. & Audrey Jaffe Found.; Torah reader, trustee Frederick S. & Emma Gartner Charitable Trust, 1996—; pres. Congregation Eytz Chaim, Bellingham, 1998—2000; bd. dirs. Whatcom Cmty. Coll. Found., 1989—92. Recipient Blood Donor award ARC, 1979, 8-Gallon Pin, 1988, Mayor's Arts award City of Bellingham, 1993. Mem. Wash. State Bar Assn. (sec. dispute resolution, real property, probate and trust, com. law examiners 1992-94). Office: PO Box 1151 Bellingham WA 98227-1151 Business E-Mail: Packer@nas.com.

PACKER, MATTHEW JAMES, musician; b. Ann Arbor, Mich., Sept. 24, 1965; s. James Dale and Mary Leila Packer; 1 child, Janelle Nichole. B of Music Edn., Ctrl. Mich. U., 1987, MusM, 1995; D of Worship Studies, Inst. Worship Studies, 2004. Tchr. elem. music Lake Ville Cmty. Schs., Otisville, Mich., 1988—89; dir. music & Christian edn. Clare United Meth. Ch., 1990—99; dir. worship and music Fenton United Meth. Ch., 1999—2005. Mem. worship planning team Detroit Ann. Conf., 2000—. Ch. coord. Forgotton Man Mins., Flint, Mich., 2003—. Mem.: Am. Choral Dirs. Assn. Avocations: music, bicycling, stained glass, reading, weightlifting. E-mail: mpack65@yahoo.com.

PACKER, ZZ (ZUWENA), writer, literature educator; b. Chgo., Jan. 12, 1973; d. Rose; m. Michael Boros, 2001. BA, Yale U., 1994; MA in Creative Writing, Johns Hopkins U., 1995; MFA, U. Iowa, 1999. Tchr. various pub. schs., Balt.; Jones lectr. Stanford U.; vis. asst. prof. Writers' Workshop U. Iowa, 2003—04. Author: (short stories) Drinking Coffee Elsewhere, 2003. Recipient Ms. Giles Whiting award, 1999, Bellingham Rev. award, 1999; grantee, Rona Jaffe Writers Found., 1997; Wallace Stegner and Truman Capote fellow, Stanford U. Office: Univ Iowa Writers Workshop 102 Dey House 507 N Clinton St Iowa City IA 52242-1000

PACKERT, G(AYLA) BETH, retired lawyer; b. Corpus Christi, Tex., Sept. 25, 1953; d. Gilbert Norris and Virginia Elizabeth (Pearce) P.; m. James Michael Hall, Jan. 1, 1974 (div. 1985); m. Richard Christopher Burke, July 18, 1987; children: Christopher Geoffrey Makepeace Burke Packert, Jeremy Eliot Marvell Packert Burke. BA, La. Tech. U., 1973; postgrad., U. Ill., 1975—81, JD, 1985; MA, U. Ark., 1976. Bar: Ill. 1985, U.S. Dist. Ct. (no. dist.) Ill. 1985, U.S. Ct. Appeals (7th cir.) 1987, Va. 1988, U.S. Dist. Ct. (we. dist.) Va. 1989. Assoc. Jenner & Block, Chgo., 1985—88; law clk. U.S. Dist. Ct. Va. (we. dist.), Danville, 1988—89; asst. commonwealth atty. Commonwealth of Va., Lynchburg, 1989—95; pvt. practice Lynchburg, 1995—2002; English tchr. Paul Laurence Dunbar Middle Sch. for Innovation, Lynchburg, 2004—06. Notes and comments editor U. Ill. Law Rev., 1984-85. Mem. Phi Beta Kappa. Home: 3900 Faculty Dr Lynchburg VA 24501-3110 Office Phone: 434-522-3740.

PACKHAM, MARIAN AITCHISON, biochemistry professor; b. Toronto, Ont., Can., Dec. 13, 1927; d. James and Clara Louise (Campbell) A.; m. James Lennox Packham, June 25, 1949; children: Neil Lennox, Janet Melissa. BA, U. Toronto, 1949, PhD, 1954; DSc honoris causa, Ryerson Poly. U., 1997. Sr. fellow dept. biochemistry U. Toronto, 1954-58, lectr. dept. biochemistry, 1958-63, 66-67; rsch. assoc. dept. physiol. scis. Ont. Vet. Coll., U. Guelph, 1963-65; rsch. assoc. blood and cardiovascular disease rsch. unit U. Toronto, 1965-66, asst. prof. dept. biochemistry, 1967-72, assoc. prof., 1972-75, prof., 1975—, acting chmn. dept. biochemistry, 1983. Contbr. articles to profl. jours. Royal Soc. Can. fellow, 1991; recipient Lt. Govs. Silver medal Victoria Coll., 1949; co-recipient J. Allyn Taylor Internat. prize in Medicine, 1988. Mem.: Can. Soc. Biochemistry and Molecular and Cellular Biology, Can. Atherosclerosis Soc., Internat. Soc. Thrombosis and Haemostasis, Can. Soc. Hematology, Am. Soc. Hematology. Office: U Toronto Dept Biochemistry Toronto ON Canada M5S 1A8

PACOR, VICTOR J., diversified financial services company executive; MBA, Cornell U. Sr. v.p. Audio Divsns. JVC Co. Am.; with Sony Electronics, 1994—2004; pres. D&M Holdings, Suffern, NY, 2004—, COO, 2004—.

PACTER, PAUL ALLAN, accounting standards researcher; b. N.Y.C., Jan. 26, 1943; s. Bernard David and Hilda Libby (Margoles) P. BS, Syracuse U., 1964; PhD, Mich. State U., 1967. C.P.A., N.Y. Asst. prof. N.Y.U., 1967-69; rsch. mgr. KPMG, N.Y.C., 1969-73; exec. dir. Fin. Acctg. Standards Bd., Stamford, Conn., 1973-84; commr. fin. City of Stamford, 1984-90; prof. acctg., MBA program U. Conn., Stamford, 1990-96, adj. prof., 1982-84. Adj. prof. NYU, 1982-84; project cons. Fin. Acctg. Standards Bd., 1990-96; fellow Internat. Acctg. Standards Com., London, 1993-2000, dir., 2003—; bd. dirs. Deloitte Touche Tohmatsu, Hong Kong, 2000—. Consulting editor The Jour. of Accountancy, 1968-73 Chmn. Stamford Commn. on Human Rights, 1977-84, Stamford Film Commn., 1984-90; mem. Charter Revision Commn., Stamford, 1979-80, Gov.'s Tourism Coun., Conn., 1984-90, acctg. adv. coun. U. Conn., 1984-90; pres. N Stamford Dem. Club, 1983-84, treas., 1987-95; dir. Stamford Coliseum Authority, 1984-90, chmn. fin. com., 1984-90; dir. adv. coun. 1984-91; vice chmn. China Beijing Ctr for Actn Pacific Fin. and Acctg. Rsch., 2000—; treas. Conn. Tourism Assn., 1987-90, North Stamford Assn., 1993-94; bd. dirs. Stamford Ctr. for the Arts, United Way Stamford, Stamford Theatre Works, Stamford Cmty. Fund, Housing Devel. Fund of Fairfield County. Earhart Found. fellow Mich. State U., 1966-67; U.S. Office of Edn. grantee, 1967 Mem. AICPA, Am. Acctg. Assn. (coun.), N.Y. State Soc. CPA's, Beta Gamma Sigma, Beta Alpha Psi. Jewish. Office: Deloitte Touche Tohmatsu 88 Queensway Hong Kong Hong Kong Business E-Mail: ppacter@iasb.org.

PACUSKA, ALISON BRANDI, paralegal; b. Falmouth, Mass., May 23, 1974; d. Stephen C. and Margaret Anne (Nightingale) P. BA Internat. Studies, Am. U., 1996; MA in Russian Studies, George Washington U., 1999. Relocation asst. United Jewish Appeal Found., White Flint, Md., 1993—94; journalist First of Sept., Moscow, 1994; translator faculty of journalism Moscow State U., 1994; rsch. asst. Kennan Inst. for Advanced Russian Studies, Washington, 1995—96; logistics specialist Metrica, Inc., Arlington, Va., 1997—2000; litigation paralegal Armstrong, Westerman & Hattori, LLP, Washington, 2000—. Presenter U. Va. Grad. Symposium in Russian Studies, 1999. Contbr. articles to newspapers. Vol. Dem. Nat. Conv., Washington, 1993-94; participant CAAPS Peace Studies Student Conf., 1996. Presdl. scholar Am. U., 1992-94. Mem. Acad. Polit. Sci. Avocations: martial arts, music, marathons. Home: Apt 202 14134 Castle Blvd Silver Spring MD 20904-4662

PADALKA, GENNADY IVANOVICH, cosmonaut; b. Krasnodar, Russia, July 21, 1958; s. Ivan Vasilievich and Valentina Mefoievna Padalka; m. Irina Anatiolievna Ponomareva; children: Yulia, Ekaterina, Sonya. Grad., Eisk Mil. Aviation Coll., 1979. Commd., pilot and sr. pilot Russian Air Force, 1979, advanced through grades to col.; cosmonaut candidate Y.A. Gagarin Cosmonaut Tng. Ctr., Russia, 1989-91, test cosmonaut, 1991—, tng. for comdr. back-up crew for Mir 24/NASA-5, Russian-Am. program of 24th primary expdn., Pegasus Russian-French program/Euro-Mir program, 1996—97, tng. for primary crew comdr. for the space flight aboard the Soyuz-TM/Mir orbital complex (Expedition 26 Program), 1997—98, crew comdr. Soyuz-TM-28/Mir orbital complex Expedition 26 Russia, 1998—99, tng. for space flight Soyuz-TM transport as ISS contingency crew comdr., 1999—2000, tng. for space flight as ISS-4 back-up crew comdr., 2000—01; station commdr. ISS Expedition-9 crew, 2002; living and working aboard the ISS, Expedition-9 crew aboard Soyuz TMA-4 Baikonur Cosmodrome, Kazakhstan, 2004—.

First class pilot; instr. of gen. parachute tng. Named title of Russian Fedn. Test-Cosmonaut; recipient Star of Russian Fedn. Hero. Avocations: theater, diving, parachute sport. Office: Russian Space Agency 42 Shchepkinst 129857 Moscow Russia

**PADBERG, HELEN SWAN,** violinist; b. Shawnee, Okla. d. Frank P. and Birdie B. (Rudell) Swan; m. Frank Padberg, Feb. 6, 1943; children: Frank, Kristen. AA, Stephens Coll., 1938; MusB, U. Okla., 1940; MusM, Northwestern U., 1941; student, Jacques Gordon. Solo performances and concerts, 1932—; mem. faculty string quartet and symphony soloist Stephens Coll., 1937-38; violinist Oklahoma City Symphony Summer Concerts, 1940; soloist Northwestern U. Symphony, 1941; violinist USO Tours World War II, 1941-43; mem. Nat. Orchestral Assn. and Am. Youth Orch., N.Y.C., 1944-46; asst. concertmaster West Suburban Symphony, Chgo., 1947-48; mem. Chgo. Women's Symphony, Chgo. Civic Orch. and chamber music groups, 1947-51; violinist Ark. Piano Trio, 1952-58; concertmaster Ark. Symphony and Little Rock Philharm., 1953-57, Marjorie Lawrence TV Series, 1953-54; pvt. tchr. violin Little Rock, 1953-66; accompanist and performer on piano, harp. Pres. Ark. Med. Soc. Alliance, 1962-63, historian, 1963-94. Co-founder Little Rock Chamber Music Soc., 1954; pres. bd. dirs. Vis. Nurse Assn. of Pulaski County, Ark., 1967-69; bd. dirs. Internat. Visitors Ctr., Chgo., 1988—, Stephens Coll. Alumna Assn. Bd.; elder, trustee Presbyn. Ch.; docent Newberry Libr., Chgo., 1998—. Mem.: Mu Phi Epsilon, Internat. Women Assocs. (pres. 1988—91), Am. Opera Soc. Chgo. (v.p. and program chmn. 1981—82, pres. 1984—87), Am. Opera Soc. (historian 1987—), Am. Fedn. Musicians, Chgo. Harp Soc. (sec. 1979—84), Am. Harp Soc., English Spkg. Union (Chgo. br., bd. govs. 1997—), Musicians' Club of Women (Chgo. bd. dirs.), Women's Athletic Club of Chgo., Aesthetic Club (pres. Little Rock), Pi Beta Phi (pres. Little Rock Alumnae Club), Pi Kappa Lambda. Home: 175 E Delaware Pl Chicago IL 60611-1756

**PADDEN, PRESTON,** broadcast executive; b. Washington, Nov. 26, 1948; m. Barbara Padden; 3 children. Grad., U. Md.; JD, George Washington U. Asst. gen. counsel Metromedia Inc.; pres. Assn. of Ind. TV Sta. Inc.; with News Corp.; chmn., CEO Am. Sky Broadcasting, 1996; pres. ABC TV Network, N.Y.C., 1997-98; exec. v.p. govt. rels. The Walt Disney Co., Washington, 1998—. Bd. dirs. The Advt. Coun., Inc. Mem. Fedr. Comm. Bar Assn., Internat. Radio TV Soc. (bd. dirs.). Office: The Walt Disney Co 1150 17th St NW Ste 400 Washington DC 20036-4622

**PADDOCK, ANTHONY CONAWAY,** financial consultant; b. Paris, July 9, 1935; came to U.S., 1940; s. H. Watson and Mildred V. (Decker) P.; m. Wendy E. Brewer, Apr. 24, 1971. AB, Harvard U., 1957, JD, 1960; MBA, Columbia U., 1961. Bar: N.Y. 1961. Assoc. investment bank Merrill Lynch & Co., N.Y.C., 1961-69; v.p. Chase Manhattan Bank, N.Y.C., 1970-78. Standard Rsch. Cons., N.Y.C., 1978-84; mng. dir. Benchmark Valuation Cons., N.Y.C., 1978-84; prin. KPMG Peat Marwick, N.Y.C., 1984-96; mng. dir. Empire Valuation Cons., N.Y.C., 1997—. Adj. prof. NYU, 1979-90. Trustee Sun Capital Advisors Trust, 1998—. Mem. Assoc. for Corp. Growth, Inst. Mgmt. Cons. (cert.). Episcopalian. Home: 14 N Chatsworth Ave Larchmont NY 10538-2142 Office: Empire Valuation Cons 350 5th Ave Ste 5513 New York NY 10118-5513 Office Phone: 212-714-0122. Business E-Mail: acpaddock@empireval.com.

**PADEGS, ANDRIS,** electrical engineer, engineering company executive; b. Riga, Latvia, Mar. 27, 1929; s. Arturs and Vera Padegs; m. Mara Berzins, Aug. 28, 1954; children: Anita Bataraga, Gints, Sandra Slokenbergs. BA magna cum laude, Dartmouth Coll., Hanover, N.H., 1953, MS with highest distinction, 1954; PhD in Elec. Engring., Carnegie Inst. Tech., Pitts., 1958. Engring. positions Internat. Bus. Machines, Poughkeepsie, NY, 1958—68, mgr. processor architecture, 1968—69, mgr., architecture design & control, 1969—71, program mgr., systems architecture, 1971—87, program mgr., enterprise systems ctrl. architecture, 1987—92; pres. Infologistik Inc., Poughkeepsie, NY, 1992—. Cons. Padegs Consulting, Poughkeepsie, NY, 1992—2002; vice chmn. SWH-Technology, Riga, Latvia, 1994—2000; adv. bd. on computers Republic of Latvia, Riga, Latvia, 1991—. Contbr. more than 25 articles to profl. jours.; author: four U.S. patents. Pres. Latvian Found., Inc., Kalamazoo, 1980—82, Mid-Hudson Latvian Assn., Poughkeepsie, NY, 1972—75; exec. vice chmn. Latvian Cultural Assn. TILTS, Poughkeepsie, NY, 1976—. Recipient Three Star Medal (highest civilian medal granted by Republic of Latvia), Republic of Latvia, 2001. Mem.: IEEE (life), Latvian Acad. Scis. (elected fgn. mem., Grand medal 2004), Assn. Latvian Engrs. (v.p. 1986—92), Sigma Xi. Achievements include one of two authors of original IBM systems principles of operation; patents in field. Avocations: photography, singing, history. Home: 2 Merry Hill Rd Poughkeepsie NY 12603-3214 Home Fax: 845-462-8751. E-mail: apadegs@optonline.net.

**PADEN, HARRY,** municipal official; children: Shahara, Angela. Student, Am. U., 1971-73, Essex County (N.J.) Coll., 1981-83. Dir. social svcs. Unity Freedom Bapt. Ch., Newark, 1989-92; aide to freeholder pres. Essex County, 1992-96; code enforcement officer Township of Irvington, N.J., 1992-94, chief field rep. Office Neighorhood Preservation, 1994-98. Host, prodr. (cable T.V. program) Parent to Parent; contbg. writer Jersey Girl mag.; columnist Irvington Herald. Chmn. Irvington juvenile conf. com. Superior Ct.; v.p., former pres. PTA Irvington H.S.; program coord. Neighborhood Preservation, 1998—; parent coord. Essex County PTA; ednl. liaison mayor of Irvington; aide Irvington West Ward Council; celebrity reader Essex and Hudson County chpts. United Way; deacon, adminstv. asst. to pastor Unity Freedom Bapt. Ch., Newark; former mem. Irvington Bd. Edn. Named Irvington African Am. Male of Yr., 1994, One of 100 Most Influential in State, City News, 1997; recipient Pinnacle award Being Single mag., 1995, Spl. Civil award Irvington C. of C. Home: 31 Civic Sq W Apt 14 Irvington NJ 07111-2425 Office Phone: 973-580-2496. Personal E-mail: harry_paden@hotmail.com.

**PADEREWSKI, SIR CLARENCE JOSEPH,** architect; b. Cleve., July 23, 1908; BArch, U. Calif., 1932. Chief draftsman Sam W. Hamill, 1939-44; with Heitschmidt-Matcham-Blanchard-Gill & Hamill, 1943; prin. C.J. Paderewski, 1944-48; pres. Paderewski, Mitchell, Dean & Assoc., Inc. (and predecessor) San Diego, 1948-78. Instr. adult edn. San Diego city schs., 1939-44, U. Calif. extension div., 1945, 56; lectr. in field. Prin. works include Charactron Labs, Gen. Dynamics Corp., Convair, S.D., 1954, South Bay Elem. Schs., S.D., 1948-74; additions to El Cortez Hotel; including first exterior passenger glass elevator in the world and New Travolator Motor Hotel, S.D., 1959, Palomar Coll., San Marcos, 1951-80, San Diego County U. Gen. Hosp., San Diego Internat. Airport Terminal Bldgs., Fallbrook Elem. Schs., 1948-74, Silver Strand Elem. Sch., Coronado, Tourmaline Terrace Apt. Bldg., San Diego Salvation Army Office Bldg. Mem. adv. bd. Bayside Social Service Center, 1953-75, San Diego Polonia Newspaper, 1994—; mem. San Diego Urban Design Com.; adv. bd. Camp Oliver, 1963—, pres., 1975-76; bd. dirs. San Diego Symphony Orch. Assn., 1952-64, San Diego chpt. ARC, 1971-74; bd. dirs., chmn. coms.; pres. San Diego Downtown Assn., 1963—; bd. dirs. Nat. Council Archtl. Registration Bds., 1958-66, bd. dirs. other offices, 1961-64, pres., 1965-66, chmn. internat. relations com., 1967-68, Salvation Army, vice-chmn., 1989, life mem. adv. bd., 1993—, Copernicus Found., 1994—; mem. Calif. Bd. Archtl. Examiners, 1949-61, past pres., commr., 1961—; mem. Nat. Panel Arbitrators, 1957—. Nat. Council on Schoolhouse Constrn.; hon. chmn. Ignacy Jan Paderewski Meml. Com., 1991; adv. bd. S.D. Balboa Park Cmty. Endowment Fund, 1995—. Decorated Knight Order Polonia Restituta, Polish govt. in exile, 1982, recipient Commodore cross, 2002; recipient Award of Merit for San Diego County Gen. Hosp., San Diego chpt., AIA, 1961, Honor award for San Diego Internat. Airport Terminal, Honor award Portland Cement Co., Golden Trowel award Plastering Inst., 1958-60, 4 awards Masonry Inst., 1961, award Prestressed Concrete Inst., 1976, Outstanding Community Leadership award San Diego Downtown Assn., 1963-65, 80, Polish Engring. award for outstanding arch. and achievement, 2000, Gold award Engring. Soc., 2000, Outstanding Individual Polish Am. award Polish Ctr. of L.A., 2001. Fellow AIA (pres. San Diego chpt. 1948, 49, bd. dirs. 1947-53, chmn. several coms., spl. award 1977, Calif. Coun. Spl. award 1979, Calif. Coun. Disting. Svc. award 1982, Lifetime Achievement award 2000); mem. San Diego C. of C. (bd. dirs. 1959-62, 64-67), Am.

Arbitration Assn. (San Diego adv. coun. 1969—), Sister City Soc. (bd. dirs.), Lions (past pres. Hillcrest Club, Lion of Yr. 1990, fellow internat. found. 1991), Father Serra Club (charter, past pres.), Outboard Boating Club San Diego, Chi Alpha Kappa, Delta Sigma Chi. Home: 2837 Kalmia Pl San Diego CA 92104-5418

**PADGET, BARBARA JOHNSON,** elementary school educator; b. Greenwood, SC, Nov. 14, 1954; d. Charles Rush and Mildred (Faulkner) Johnson; m. Richard Edward Padget, July 15, 1977; children: William Richard, Benjamin Rush, Susan Elizabeth. BA, Clemson U., SC, 1975. Cert. tchr. SC. Tchr. Emerald Jr. HS, Greenwood, SC, 1976—77, Ashwood-Ctrl. HS, Bishopville, SC, 1977—78, Lugoff-Elgin Mid. Sch., Lugoff, SC, 1978—80, Gilbert HS, SC, 1980—93, Gilbert Mid. Sch., 1993—. Co-author: Curriculum for Methods of Teaching Cosmetologists, 1999. Vol. Ho. of Reps. campaign, Lexington, SC, 1988. Named Tchr. of Yr., 1978, 1993; recipient Achievement award, Gilbert Town Coun., 2004. Mem.: Nat. Coun. Social Studies, SC Coun. Social Studies. Avocations: reading, gardening, travel. Home: 1347 Beechcreek Rd Lexington SC 29072 Office: Gilbert Mid Sch 120 RiKard Cir Gilbert SC 29054

**PADGETT, CHRISTINE ELIZABETH KING,** education educator; b. Birmingham, July 11, 1978; d. Kim William and Carol Susan (Snyder) King; m. Michael Brandon Padgett, May 14, 2005. BS in Elem. Edn., Auburn U., 1999, PhD in Ednl. Psychology, 2004; MEd in Elem. Edn., U. Montevallo, 2000. Cert. tchr. Ala., Ga. Presch. tchr. CASA Sch., Birmingham, 1999—2000; tchr. West Point (Ga.) Elem. Sch., 2001—02; instr. Auburn (Ala.) U., 2002—04, adj. prof., 2004; asst. prof. U. West Ala., Livingston, 2005—. Spkr. in field. Childcare assoc. Asbury Meth. Ch., Birmingham, 1999—. Mem.: AAUP, APS, NEA, AAUW, Nat. Coun. Tchrs. Math., Nat. Coun. Tchrs. English, Nat. Coun. Social Studies, Nat. Sci. Tchrs. Assn., Assn. Childhood Edn. Internat., Soc. Info. Tech. and Tchr. Edn., Internat. Soc. Tech. Edn., Ala. Edn. Assn., Soc. Tchg. Psychology, Assn. Tchr. Educators, Phi Delta Kappa, Kappa Delta Pi, Phi Kappa Phi, Alpha Theta Chi. Avocations: scrapbooks, reading, photography, hiking, walking, crafts. Office: Univ West Ala UWA Sta 34 Livingston AL 35470 Home: 880 Country Rd 195 Clanton AL 35046 Office Phone: 205-652-3753. Business E-Mail: dr.kiki@auburnalum.org.

**PADGETT, CYNTHIA S.,** artist; b. Kansas City, Mo., Mar. 4, 1948; m. Charles Allen Padgett, June 10, 1967; children: Claire Padgett-Doane, Charles Alexander. BA, Goucher Coll., 1972; MA in Liberal Arts, Johns Hopkins U., 1983. Cert. instrument pilot. Docent The Walters Art Gallery, Balt., 1986-89; alumni bd. mem. Goucher Coll., Balt., 1993-95. One-woman show: A. Jain Marunouchi Gallery, NY, 1998, 99, 2000, 01, 03, 04; works exhibited at A. Jain Marunouchi Gallery, NYC, 1993—, Artshowcase, Balt., 1993, Internat. Contemporary Art Festival (NICAF), Yokohama, Japan, 1995, Tokyo, 1997, LINEART, Gent, Belgium, 2000, 01, Europ'art, Geneva, 2001, Art Phil., 2003; slide registries: Maryland Art Place, Nat. Mus. of Women in the Arts. Bd. mem. LWV, St. Petersburg, Fla., 1980-81, Balt., 1981-83; guide Nat. Aquarium, Balt., 1995—; bd. mem., pres. women's com. Historic Hampton, Inc., Towson, Md., 1995-97; chmn. Dulaney Valley, Md. Ho. and Garden Pilgrimage, 1996, 99; Mission Ch., 1992-95. Mem. Johns Hopkins Club, Goucher Club, DAR, Hamilton St. Club. Republican. Episc. Avocations: sailing, travel.

**PADGETT, GAIL BLANCHARD,** lawyer; b. Douglasville, Ga., Aug. 20, 1949; d. William David and Dorothy Rose (Bennett) P. BA, Ga. State U., 1971, MEd, 1974; JD, Georgetown U., 1981. Bar: Va., Ga., D.C., U.S. Supreme Ct. Tchr. Clayton Co. Bd. Edn., Jonesboro, Ga., 1971-77; spl. asst. to dir. Community Rels Svc., Chevy Chase, Md., 1977-81; gen. counsel, 1981-89, assoc. dir., 1989-96; asst. chief immigration judge U.S. Dept. Justice, Falls Church, Va., 1996—2004, U.S. Immigration Ct., Bradenton, Fla., 2004—. Recipient Disting. Svc. award Atty. Gen. of the U.S., 1992. Home: 9448 Discovery Terrace 102 Bradenton FL 34212 Office: US Immigration Ct 515 11th St West Ste 300 Bradenton FL 34205

**PADGETT, GREGORY LEE,** lawyer; b. Greenfield, Ind., May 9, 1959; s. William Joseph and Anna Katharine (Hyre) Padgett; m. Ruth Anne Dosworth, June 5, 1982; children: Joshua David, William Joel, Emily Xiao Lei. BA summa cum laude, DePauw U., 1981; JD, Northwestern U., 1984. Bar: Ill., U.S. Dist. Ct. (no. dist.) Ill. 1984, U.S. Ct. Appeals (7th cir.) 1986, Ind. 1988, U.S. Dist. Ct. (no. & so. dists.) Ind. 1988. Assoc. Kirkland & Ellis, Chgo., 1984-88, Baker & Daniels, Indpls., 1988-92; prtnr. Johnson, Lawhead, Buth & Pope, P.C., Indpls., 1992-2000; of counsel Barnes & Thornburg, Indpls., 2000—04; prin. Padgett Law, Indpls., 2004—. Adj. prof. Butler U., 1989—90. Mem. Marion County Prosecutor's Rev. Task Force, Indpls., 1991; pres., bd. dirs. Theatre on the Square, Indpls., 1994-95; mem. coun. Hope Evang. Covenant Ch., 1992-96; bd. dirs. Meridian St. Found., 1994-96; bd. dirs. Ind. Arts Chorale, 2003-. Mem. Ind. State Bar Assn., Indpls. Bar Assn. (exec. com. alternative dispute resolution sect.), Christian Legal Soc., Phi Beta Kappa. Avocations: theatre arts, vocal music, hiking, writing. Office: Padgett Law Ste 230 9000 Keystone Crossing Indianapolis IN 46240 Office Phone: 317-218-0316. Business E-Mail: gp@indianastatelaw.com.

**PADGETT, JOHN DAVID,** lawyer; b. Norfolk, Va., July 8, 1958; s. Royal Clayton and Phyllis (Hunt) Padgett; m. Lee Ann Hagy. BA with distinction, U. Va., 1980; JD, Washington & Lee U., 1983. Bar: Va. 1983, US Bankruptcy Ct. Ea. Dist. 1983, US Dist. Ct. Ea. Dist. Va. 1983, US Ct. Appeals 4th Cir. 1983. Ptnr. Jett, Berkley, Furr & Padgett (merged with McGuireWoods LLP), Norfolk, Va., 1983—93, McGuireWoods LLP, Norfolk, Va., 1993—, mng. ptnr. Norfolk office. Escheator City of Norfolk, Va., 1994—2003; gen. counsel Rep. Party of Va. Chmn. State Coun. of Higher Edn., Va., 1998—2001. Mem. Maritime Law Assn., Southeastern Admiralty Law Inst., Hampton Roads C. of C., Phi Delta Phi., Hampton Roads Fgn. Commerce Club, Norfolk Rotary Club Presbyterian. Avocations: baseball, golf, squash, book collecting, politics. Office: McGuireWoods LLP World Trade Ctr Ste 9000 101 W Main St Norfolk VA 23510-1655 Office Phone: 757-640-3779. Office Fax: 757-640-3968. Business E-Mail: jpadgett@mcguirewoods.com.

**PADGETT, NANCY WEEKS,** law librarian, consultant, lawyer; b. Newberry, S.C., June 3, 1932; d. Price John and Caroline (Weeks) P.; m. David Lazar, Aug. 6, 1953 (dec. May 19, 2002). BS, Northwestern U., 1953; MLS, U. Md., 1972; JD, Georgetown U., 1977. Bar: D.C. 1977. Asst. law libr. U.S. Ct. Appeals for D.C., Washington, 1972—74, supervisory law libr., 1974—84, circuit libr., 1984—. Mem. ALA, D.C. Bar Assn., Am. Assn. Law Librs. Home: 5301 Duvall Dr Bethesda MD 20816-1873 Office: US Ct Appeals for DC Cir Judges' Libr 5518 US Court House Washington DC 20001-5618 Office Phone: 202-216-7400.

**PADHI, RADHAKANT,** engineer; b. Berhampur, India, June 29, 1972; s. Niranjan and Santimala Padhi; m. Aseema Padhi, May 11, 2001. B in Engring., U. Coll. Engring., 1994; M in Engring., Indian Inst. of Sci., 1996; PhD, U. Mo., Rolla, 2001. Scientist DRDO-India, Hyderabad, 1996—97; lectr. U of Mo., Rolla, Mo., 2001—02, post doctoral fellow, 2001—. Contbr. articles to profl. jours. Mem.: SSI, ACSI, IEEE, AIAA. Avocations: movies, music. Office: Dept Aerospace Engring Indian Inst Sci Bangalore 560012 India Home: Vijnanapura Campus New Bel Rd Bangalore 560094 India Office Phone: +91-80-2293-2756. Personal E-mail: r_padhi@rediffmail.com.

**PADIAN, NANCY,** medical educator, epidemiologist; BA cum laude, Colgate U., 1974; MS in Reading Edn., Syracuse U., 1974; MPH, U. Calif. Berkeley, 1983, PhD in Epidemiology, 1987. Co-founder UZ-U. Calif. San Francisco Collaborative Rsch. Programme Women's Health, Zimbabwe, 1994; founder Women's Global Health Imperative, 2001; assoc. dir. rsch. U. Calif. San Francisco Global Health Scis., 2004; dir. AIDS Rsch. Inst. U. Calif. San Francisco; with Ob.-gyn. dept. U. Calif. San Francisco, co-dir. Ctr. Reproductive Health Rsch. and Policy, internat. expert heterosexual transmission HIV and other sexually transmitted infections, prof. dept. Ob.gyn. and reproductive scis., 2005—; with epidemiology dept. U. Calif. Berkeley.

Mem.: Inst. Medicine. Achievements include research in developing and evaluating female-controlled methods for disease prevention, such as the diaphram and microbicides, along with alternative strategies for fostering young women's economic independence; thus reducing their susceptibility to HIV, STIs, and unwanted pregnancies.

**PADILLA, JAMES JEROME (JIM PADILLA),** retired automotive executive; b. Detroit, June 13, 1946; s. David J. and Irene C. (Clos) P.; m. Alice M., Dec. 27, 1968; children: James Jr., Kathryn, Daniel. BSChemE, MS in Engring., U. Detroit, 1969, MA in Econ., 1970. Fuel econ. planning mgr. Ford Motor Co., Dearborn, Mich., 1977-78, engine planning engring. mgr. Detroit, 1979-80, engine controls dept. mgr., 1980-83, exec. engr., powertrain-electronics, 1983-85, chief engr., trim-chassis-elect-emissions, 1985, programs operations mgr., 1990, dir., small cars unit, 1991, exec. dir., engine and mfg., Jaguar Cars, Ltd., 1992—94, dir., performance luxury vehicle lines, 1994—96, pres., Argentina and Brazil operations, 1996—98, pres. S. Am. operations, group v.p., mfg. and quality, 1999—2001, group v.p., N. Am., 2001—02, exec. v.p. Detroit, 2002, pres. Americas, 2002—04, pres., COO, 2004—06, chmn. worldwide automotive operations, 2004—06. Spl. asst to sec., US Dept. Commerce, 1978-79; bd. dirs. Am. Supplier Inst., Dearborn. Pres. Civic Assn., Canton, Mich., 1972-74, Plymouth (Mich.) Sch. Bd., 1981-84; mem. Plymouth Parish Council, 1980-84, Plymouth Edn. Commn., 1980-85. Served to 2d Lt. USNG, 1970-76. White House fellow U.S. Govt., Washington, 1978-79, fellow, Nat. Acad. Engring., 2001-; rsch. grantee Dow Chem. Co., Detroit, 1968-69; recipient Engr. of the Year, Engineer Nat. Achievement Awards Conf., 2000, Ohtli medal from Mexican President Vincente Fox, 2004; named one of 50 Most Important Hispanics in Tech. & Bus., Hispanic Engr. & Info. Tech. mag., 2005. Mem. Soc. Automotive Engrs., Engring. Soc. Detroit. (selection com. U.S. Senate fellows 1982-84, named Outstanding Young Engr. 1980). Roman Catholic.*

**PADILLA, MARIO RENÉ,** literature educator, writer; b. Detroit, Oct. 4, 1949; s. Marcelino Ramos and Nina Consolata (Macioce) P.; children: Francesca, Miguel, Marcello, Gabriella; m. Christine Jasiorkowski; stepchildren: Trevor, Laura. BS, Ohio State U., 1971; MA, Loyola Marymount U., 1987; PhD, U. So. Calif., 1993. Prodn. supr. CBS TV, L.A., 1972-78; actor L.A., 1980—; prof. English lit. and creative writing, Latin Am. lit. Santa Monica (Calif.) Coll., 1994—. Author: Reaching Back for the Neverendings, 1993, Borges, Faulkner, Hemingway: Young Poets of Prose, 1993 (Fulbright award 1993); composer (ballet) The Harbinger of Evolution, 1980 (ASCAP award 1981), (song) I Found Love, (musical) Hercules on Normandie, 2006, and numerous other songs and ballets; actor including Mario on Falcon Crest, 1981-83, Jimmy Rivera on Hunter, 1991-92, officer Lopez in General Hosp., 2000, Dragnet, 2003 (films) Losin' It, 1983, Star Trek III, 1984. Capt. U.S. Army, 1971-72. Mem. ASCAP, MLA, Screen Actors Guild, Am. Fedn. TV Radio Artists, Actor's Equity. Avocations: Karate, soccer, basketball, coaching children's sports, reading. Home: 1211 Vienna Way Venice CA 90291-4026 Office Phone: 310-434-4064. Personal E-mail: Padilla_mario@smc.edu.

**PADILLA, SUE ANN,** librarian; b. Horton, Kans., Dec. 11, 1950; d. Moulder and Elva Mae (Grimes) Oaks; m. John H. Padilla (div.); children: Elizabeth, Matthew. BS in Edn., Kans. State Tchrs. Coll., 1972; MLS, Emporia State U., 1988. Tchr. Our Lady of Guadalupe Sch., Topeka, 1973-75, Topeka Pub. Schs., 1975-88; libr. Ida Long Goodman Meml. Libr., St. John, Kans., 1988—2001, Newton Pub. Libr., Newton, Iowa, 2001—. Contbg. author: Booktalk!3, Booktalk!4, Booktalk!5, The Booktalkers' Companion, Vol. 1, Booktalking the Award Winners, 1993-94, Booktalking the Award Winners: Young Adult Retrospective Volume, Booktalking the Award Winners 3. Bd. dirs. St. John Planning Commn., 1997-2001, St. John Hosp. Dist., 1991-92, St. John Sci. Mus., 1997-2001; chair Cmty. Arts Series, St. John, 1990—. Mem. ALA, Iowa Libr. Assn., Libr. Adminstrn. and Mgmt. Assn. (pres. 2005), Emporia State U. Alumni Assn. (bd. dirs. 1991-94), Lions Club (com. chair St. John's club 1990-2001), Kans. Ctr. for the Book (bd. dirs. 1999-2001), Arts Connection (bd. dir. 2001-), Jasper County Concert Assn. (bd. dirs. 2003-) Avocations: travel, antiques, cooking, gardening, reading. Home: 108 E 28th St S Newton IA 50208-2710 Office: Newton Pub Libr 100 N 3rd Ave W Newton IA 50208-0796

**PADMANABHAN, ANAND,** information technology executive; BS in Engring., Madras (India) U., 1989; MS, La. State U., 2002. Ednl. technologist, programmer Ctr. Ednl. Techs. NASA, Wheeling, W.Va., 1992—96; exec. dir. info. techs. Seton Hill U., Greensburg, 1996—98; chief info. officer, dir. Tenn. State U., Nashville, 1998—2000; chief info. officer Hunter Coll. CUNY, N.Y., 2000—, v.p. Hunter Coll., 2000—06; chief info. officer NYU Stern Sch. Bus., N.Y.C., 2006—. Contbr. articles to profl. jours. Mem.: IEEE, Soc. for Info. Mgmt., Assn. for Computing Machinery. Avocations: tennis, photography. Office: City Univ of New York - Hunter College 695 Park Ave New York NY 10021 Office Fax: 212-650-3399. Business E-Mail: anad@stern.nyu.edu.

**PADOS, DIMITRIS A.,** electrical engineer, educator; b. Athens, Greece, Oct. 22, 1966; arrived in U.S., 1990; s. Alexandros D. Pados and Anna E. Androvitsanea; m. Stella N. Batalama, Dec. 28, 1994; 1 child, Artemis Anna. BSc in Computer Sci. and Engring., U. Patras, Greece, 1989; PhD in Elec. Engring., U. Va., 1994. Asst. prof. U. La., Laffayette, 1994—97; assoc. prof. SUNY, Buffalo, 1997—. Rschr. Rsch. Found. SUNY, Buffalo. Contbr. articles to profl. jours. Recipient Internat. Conf. Telecom. Best Paper award, IEEE, 2001, Transactions Neural Networks Outstanding Paper award, 2003. Achievements include patents for circuitry and method for demodulating code division multiple access (CDMA) signals. Office: SUNY Dept Elec Engring 332 Bonner Hall Buffalo NY 14260 Office Phone: 716-645-3115 ext. 2134. Office Fax: 716-645-3656. Personal E-mail: dimitrisapados@aol.com. Business E-Mail: pados@eng.buffalo.edu.

**PADOS, FRANK JOHN, JR.,** investment company executive; b. Easton, Pa., Feb. 9, 1944; s. Frank John and Mary Helen (Pokrifscak) P.; m. Barbara Janselwitz, July 6, 1968; children— Frank John (dec.), Kelly Ann, Kristin, Matthew John, Kaitlyn. BA cum laude in Econs, Boston Coll., 1966; MBA, U. Pa., 1968. Securities analyst Tchrs. Ins. and Annuity Assn., N.Y.C., 1971-74, investment officer, 1975-77, v.p., 1977-78, sr. v.p., mgr. securities div., 1978-83; mng. dir. Trust Co. of the West, 1983-95; exec. v.p. Desai Capital Mgmt., N.Y.C., 1995—2003; mng. ptnr. Dublin Clark and Co., Greenwich, Conn., 2003—. Bd. dirs. Airoom, Inc. Served with U.S. Army, 1969-70. Decorated Bronze Star. Mem. Park Ave. Club. Roman Catholic. Home: 57 Thornley Dr Chatham NJ 07928-1360 Office: 485 W Putnam Ave Greenwich CT 06830 Office Phone: 203-629-2030. Business E-Mail: pados@dublinclark.com

**PADOVANI, ROBERTO,** communications executive; Degree, U. Padova, Italy; MS in Elec. and Computer Engring., PhD in Elec. and Computer Engring., U. Mass. With M/A-COM Linkabit, 1984—86; from mem. staff to exec. v.p., chief tech. officer QUALCOMM Inc., San Diego, 1986—2002, exec. v.p., 2002—, chief tech. officer, 2002—. Contbr. articles to profl. jours. Mem.: NAE, IEEE (Best Paper award 1991). Achievements include holds over 50 patents on wireless CDMA systems. Office: QUALCOMM Inc 5775 Morehouse Dr San Diego CA 92121*

**PADOVANO, ANTHONY JOHN,** fine arts educator, artist; b. Bklyn., July 19, 1933; s. Pasquale Anthony and Teresa (Pignataro) P.; m. Margaret Padovano, June 6, 1973 (div. 1981); children: Lea, Nicole, Roberto; m. Gerarda Santina Declement, Sept. 15, 1986; children: Francesca, Gina. BFA, Columbia U., 1957; MA, CUNY, 1960. Instr. U. Conn., Storrs, 1962-64; asst. prof. Columbia U., N.Y.C., 1964-71, Sarah Lawrence Coll., Bronxville, 1972-79; assoc. prof. Kingsborough Community Coll., Bklyn., 1983—. Tchr. U. Conn., Storrs, 1962-64, Columbia U., N.Y.C., 1964-70, Queens Coll., N.Y., 1971-73, Sarah Lawrence Coll., 1974-78, Lacoste, France, summers 1976-78, Kingsborough Coll., 1978-, Parsons Sch. Design, 1978-82, Art Students League, summers 1983, 84; Fulbright fellowship judge UN, N.Y.C., 2001, 02, 03. One-man shows include Lincoln Meml. Gallery, 1954,

Columbia U., 1957, Sculptors Studio, 1958, George Lester Gallery, 1962, Ruth White Gallery, 1962, Richard Feigen Gallery, 1964, U. Conn., 1964, Columbia U., 1965, Bertha Schaefer Gallery, 1968, Galerie Simmons Stern, 1968, Graham Gallery, 1972, 75, 79, 81, 82, I.F.A. Gallery, 1976, Alwin Gallery, 1978, Vorpal Gallery, 1986, 88, 90; exhbns. in group shows at Herron Mus. of Art, 1966, Newark Mus., 1969, Inst. Arts and Letters, 1976, Bard Coll., 1979; permanent collections, Newark Mus., Herron Gallery (Ind.), Storm King Art Ctr., Whitney Mus. Am. Art; author: The Process of Sculpture, 1981. Mem.: Audubon Artists (pres. 2002—). Office: Kingsborough CC 2001 Oriental Blvd Brooklyn NY 11235-2333

**PADOVANO, ANTHONY THOMAS,** theologian, educator, literature educator; b. Harrison, NJ, Sept. 18, 1934; s. Thomas Henry and Mary Rose (Cierzo) P.; m. Theresa Lackamp, 1974; children— Mark, Andrew, Paul, Rosemarie BA magna cum laude, Seton Hall U., 1956; S.T.B. magna cum laude, Pontifical Gregorian U., Rome, Italy, 1958, S.T.L. magna cum laude, 1960, S.T.D. magna cum laude, 1962; Ph.L. magna cum laude, St. Thomas Pontifical Internat. U., Rome, 1962; MA, NYU, 1971; PhD, Fordham U., 1980. Ordained priest Roman Cath. Ch., 1959. Asst. chaplain Med. Center, Jersey City, 1960; asst. St. Paul of the Cross Ch., Jersey City, 1962, St. Catharine Ch., Glen Rock, NJ, 1963; prof. systematic theology Darlington Sem., Mahwah, NJ, 1962-74; founding faculty mem., prof. lit. and philosophy Ramapo Coll., NJ, 1971—; prof. theology, religious studies Fordham U., 1973-93. Mem. Archdiocesan Commn. Ecumenical and Interreligious Affairs, 1965, Commn. Instrn. Clergy in Documents Vatican II, 1966; del. dialogue group Luth.-Roman Cath. Theol. Conversations, 1969; del.-at-large senate of priests Archdiocese of Newark; Danforth assoc., 1975—; Cath. pastor Inclusive Cmty. World Coun. Chs., 1986—; lectr. in field, also appearances on radio and TV; parish min. St. Margaret of Scotland, Morristown, NJ. Author: The Cross of Christ, the Measure of the World, 1962, The Estranged God, 1966, Who is Christ, 1967, Belief in Human Life, 1969, American Culture and the Quest for Christ, 1970, Dawn Without Darkness, 1971, Free to be Faithful, 1972, Eden and Easter, 1974, A Case for Worship, 1975, America: Its People, Its Promise, 1975, Presence and Structure, 1975, The Human Journey, 1982, Trilogy, 1982, Contemplation and Compassion, 1984, Winter Rain: A Play, 1985, His Name is John: A Play, 1986, Christmas to Calvary, 1987, Love and Destiny, 1987, Summer Lightening: A Play, 1988, Conscience and Conflict, 1989, Reform and Renewal, 1990, A Celebration of Life, 1990, The Church Today: Belonging and Believing, 1990, Scripture in the Streets, 1992, A Retreat with Thomas Merton, 1996, Hope is a Dialogue, 1998, Resistance and Renewal, 2002, Life Choices, 2004; editor: Centenary Issue Roman Echoes, 1959; editl. bd. The Advocate, 1966-73; contrbr. articles to mags., Padovano Papers, personal and profl. papers, Archives, U. Notre Dame. With Diocese Paterson Ecumenical Commn.; founding pres. Justice and Peace Commn., Diocese of Paterson, active Resigned Priests Com. Mem. Cath. Theol. Soc. Am., Mariological Soc. Am., Nat. Fedn. Priests Couns. (ofcl. rep. to Constl. Conv., Chgo. 1968), Corpus (pres.), Fedn. Christian Ministries, Internat. Fedn. of Married Cath. Priests (v.p. for N.Am.), North Atlantic Fedn. for Renewal Cath. Priesthood (bd. dirs.). Home: 9 Millstone Dr Morris Plains NJ 07950-1536 Office: Sch of Am Internat Studies Ramapo Coll NJ Mahwah NJ 07430 Personal E-mail: tpadovan@optonline.net. *People rather than ideas have been most formative in my life. More accurately, people, as they embodied certain ideas have proved most decisive. There is nothing more persuasive than an idea which becomes so vital that it transforms the person who proclaims it.*

**PADRNOS, DIANE E.,** language arts educator; b. Britton, S.D., July 9, 1942; d. Harry L. and Helen J. Nelson; m. Dennis R. Padrnos, Sept. 2, 1967; children: Michael, Beth, Lara. BS in Edn., No. State U., Aberdeen, S.D., 1964. Cert. S.D. Dept. Edn. Instr. bus./drama Sisseton (S.D.) Sch. Dist., 1964—65; press aide Sen. George McGovern, Washington, 1965—67, field rep. Mitchell, SD, 1967—69; counselor adult edn. Dakota Wesleyan U., Mitchell, 1977—80, dir. career planning/placement, 1980—88; real estate salesperson Century 21, Mitchell, 1988—95; instr. lang. arts Mitchell Sr. H.S., 1993—. Comty. vol. Mitchell C. of C.; active Heart Dr., MD Dr., Cancer Dr.; chair bd. dirs. Enchanted World Doll Mus., Mitchell; chair Corn Palace Devel. Com., Mitchell; mem. steering com. Mitchell Area Comty. Theatre; chairperson Oscar Howe Adv. Bd., Mitchell. Recipient S.D. Jr. C. of C. Person of Yr. award, 1973, Person of Yr. award, Beta Sigma Phi, 1973. Republican. Roman Catholic. Avocations: reading, travel. Home: 340 W McCabe Mitchell SD 57301

**PADULA, FRED DAVID,** filmmaker; b. Santa Barbara, Calif., Oct. 25, 1937; s. Fred and Mary (Adams) P.; married; 1 child. BA in Music, San Francisco State U., MA in Art, 1965. Adj. faculty U. Calif., San Francisco Art Inst., San Francisco State U.; artist-in-residence U. Minn., Mpls. Filmmaker: Ephesus, 1965 (1st pl. award San Francisco Internat. Film Festival, awards N.Y. Film Festival, Chgo. Internat. Film Festival, others), The Artist Speaks, Two Photographers: Wynn Bullock and Imogen Cunningham, Little Jews (Hippy Hill), Anthology of Boats, David and My Porch, Salmon River Run, El Capitan (awards: Grand Prize Festival Internat. de Film D'Aventure Uecue, La Plagne, France, Grand Prize Film Festival Internat. Montagna Esplorazione, Trento, Italy, Grand Prize Banff Festival of Mountain Films, Can., Grand Prize Mountain Film, Telluride, Colo., Gold medal Festival Internat. du Film Alpine, Les Diablerets, Switzerland; electronic music compositions include: Barking Dogs, Charnel Loops, others; one-man shows (photography) include San Francisco Internat. Airport, San Francisco Mus. Modern Art, Kalamazoo Inst. Arts, DeYoung Mus., San Francisco, San Fernando Valley State Coll., Bakersfield Coll., Wash. State U., West Chester Coll., Valhalla,N.Y., George Eastman House; represented in permanent collections Kalamazoo Inst. Arts, State of Calif., George Eastman House, San Francisco Internat. Airport, Crocker Art Mus., Oakland Mus. Art, 1004 Gallery, Port Towsend, Wash., New Horizons Nat. Bank Hdqs., San Rafael, Calif., SUNY/Westchester C.C., Valhalla, N.Y., Grace Mus., Abilene, Tex. Address: PO Box 254 Mill Valley CA 94941-1551

**PADULO, LOUIS,** university administrator; b. Athens, Ala., Dec. 14, 1936; s. Louis and Helen (Yarbrough) P.; m. Katharine Seamans, Jan. 28, 1963; children: Robert, Joseph. BSEE, Fairleigh Dickinson U., 1959; MSEE, Stanford U., 1962; PhD, Ga. Inst. Tech., 1966. Engr. design and devel. Radio Corp. Am., 1959-60; asst. prof. elec. engring. San Jose State Coll., 1962-63; asst. prof. math. Ga. State U., 1966-67; assoc. prof. Columbia U., summer 1969, Harvard U., summer 1970; asst. prof. Morehouse Coll., 1967-68, assoc. prof., chmn. dept. math., 1968-71; dir. exchange student program Stanford U., 1969-71, assoc. prof. elec. engring., 1971-75, assoc. prof. math., summers 1971-75, dir. MITE program, 1975; prof. elec. engring. and math., dean Coll. Engring. Boston U., 1975-88, assoc. v.p., 1986-87; pres. U. Ala., Huntsville, 1988-90; pres., chief exec. officer Univ. City Sci. Ctr., Phila., 1991-96, pres. emeritus, 1997—; chmn. Invictus, Phila., 1997—. Vis. assoc. prof. Stanford U., 1969-71; vis. prof. U. Tokyo, 1986-88, MIT, 1987-88, 90-91; vis. prof. mgmt. ENPC, France, 2002-; Reims Mgmt. Sch., 2001-; Fairleigh Dickinson U., 2002—, U. Pa., 2004-, Drexel U., 2005-; program dir. Inst. on Computers, Logic and Automata Theory, NSF, 1969; founder, dir. dual degree program Atlanta U. Ctr. and Ga. Inst. Tech., 1968-70; numerical analyst Airesearch Corp., L.A., 1969; vis. scientist MIT, 1990-91; bd. dirs. Nemawashi, Inc., Carver Fund, Tapelicator, Inc., Ovation Products, Inc., Knite, Inc., Atlantis Components, Inc., Light Media, Inc., Nucycle, Inc., Genpathways, Inc., Workwell, Inc. Author: System Theory, 1973, Minorities in Engineering, 1974; mem. editl. adv. bd. the Scientist, DiSyCom-Digital Sys. and Comm.; contbr. chpts. to books. Pres. Valley Found., Huntsville, Ala., 1988-89, Ala. Engring. Found., Huntsville, 1989, Consortium Advancement Affordable Distance Edn., 1997—; mem. task force Vision 2000, Huntsville, 1989; bd. dirs. North Ala. Intenat. Trade Assn., 1989, Ala. Supercomputer Network, 1989, Vision 2000, Am. Poetry ctr., 1992, Benjamin Franklin Tech. Ctr., 1991-97; pres. Higher Edn. Congress, 1992-2000; bd. dirs. U.S. Japan Soc., 1990—; adv. coun. United Negro Coll. Fund; trustee Fairleigh Dickinson U., 1989—, Presbyn. Found. Phila., 1993-2002, Phila. Fund for Edn., 1995-2001, Internat. House; vis. com. scis. engring. Tuskegee U., Coll. Engring. Drexel U., 1993-2004; mem. Huntsville Army Cmty. Rels. Coms.; bd. vis. schs. bus. Temple U., 1993-. Recipient Excellence in Sci. and Engring. Edn. award Nat.

Consortium for Black Profl. Devel., 1977, Reginald H. Jones Disting. Svc. award GE Found. and Nat. Action Coun. Minorities in Engring., 1983. Fellow IEEE, Am. Soc. Engring. Edn. (Western Electric Fund Excellence in Tchg. award 1973, Vincent Bendix award 1984, U.S. Interactive fellow 1997); mem. AAAS, ACM, Mass. Engrs. Coun., Math. Assn. Am., Union League of Phila. (life), NAACP (life), Penn Club (life). Office: Invictus 2020 Walnut St Apt 32A Philadelphia PA 19103-5645 Fax: 215-564-3988. E-mail: padulo@verizon.net.

**PAEZ, RICHARD A.,** federal judge; b. 1947; BA, Brigham Young U., 1969; JD, U. Calif., Berkeley, 1972. Staff atty. Calif. Rural Legal Assistance, Delano, Calif., 1972—74, Western Ctr. on Law and Poverty, 1974—76; sr. counsel Legal Aid Found. of LA, 1976—78, dir. litigation, 1978—79, act. exec. dir., 1980—81; judge LA Mcpl. Ct., 1981—94, superior ct, Los Angeles, 1993—94, U.S. Dist. Ct. (ctrl. dist.) Calif., LA, 1994—2000, U.S. Dist. Ct. (9th cir.), Pasadena, Calif., 2000—. Active Hollywood-Los Feliz Jewish Cmty. Ctr. Mem.: Calif. Jud. Coun., Mex.-Am. Bar Assn. LA County, LA County Bar Assn., Calif. State Bar Assn. Office: US Ct Appeals Richard H. Chambers US Courthouse 125 S Grand AveRm 204 Pasadena CA 91105-1652*

**PAGÁN, GILBERTO, JR.,** psychologist; b. San Juan, P.R., Dec. 30, 1950; s. Gilberto Sr. and Juanita (Quiñones) P.; m. Grissele Camacho, Aug. 6, 1972; children: Mariel, Loren. Exch. student, SUNY, Albany, 1969-70; BA in Psychology magna cum laude, U. P.R., 1972; MS in Devel. Psychology, Rutgers U., 1974, PhD in Clin. Psychology, 1984. Lic. psychologist, N.J.; cert. sch. psychology. Psychometrician Well Baby Clinic of New Brunswick, N.J., 1972-73; staff psychologist Community Orgn. for Mental Health and Retardation, Inc., Phila., 1976-77; intern in clin. psychology Multimodal Therapy Inst., Kingston, NJ, 1979-80; sch. psychologist New Brunswick Pub. Sch. System, 1980-83; mental health clinician Community Mental Health Ctr. U. Medicine and Dentistry N.J., Piscataway, 1983-93; sch. psychologist Perth Amboy Pub. Sch. Sys., 1993-95; pvt. practice clin. psychology Newark, 1988—; sch. psychologist Jersey City Pub. Sch. Sys., 1995-98, Elizabeth (N.J.) Pub. Sch. Sys., 1998—. Assoc. in psychiatry Univ. of Medicine and Dentistry of N.J., Piscataway, 1988-98; field supr. Rutgers U., New Brunswick, N.J., 1988—; cons. in field to clients including Bloomfield Pub. Sch. System, Div. of Youth and Family Svcs. of State of N.J., Project Head Start, Plainfield, N.J. Columnist San Juan Star, 1990-93, 97-98, El Hispano, Phila., 1977-78; contbr. profl. publs.; presenter in field. Pres. N.J. chpt. Nat. Com. for Puerto Rican Statehood, 1990-95; mem. U.S. Coun. for Puerto Rico Statehood, 2004-. NIMH fellow, 1978-79; predoctoral rsch. fellow Inst. for Rsch. in Human Devel., Divsn. Psychol. Studies of Ednl. Testing Svc., Princeton, N.J., 1974-75; recipient P.R. Psychol. Assn. award, 1972, Puerto Rican Action Bds. Parents Assn. award 1985; inducted into Nat. Honor Soc. in Psychology, 1973. Mem. APA, NEA, N.J. Edn. Assn., N.J. Psychol. Assn., Elizabeth Edn. Assn. Democrat. Roman Catholic. Office: 467 Mount Prospect Ave Newark NJ 07104-2907 Office Phone: 973-483-0448. E-mail: gpaganjr@comcast.net.

**PAGAN, KEITH AREATUS,** music educator, academic administrator; b. Beggs, Okla., June 7, 1931; s. Areatus and Opal Gail (Facker) P.; m. Betty Lois Wallace; children: Melva Joy, Lisa Lynne, Beryl Kay. B in Music Edn., Bethany Nazarene Coll., 1952; M in Music Edn., Okla. U., 1953; D in Music Edn. with honors, Ind. U., 1970. Asst. prof. music Bethany (Okla.) Nazarene Coll., 1952-53, 55-58; prof. music Pasadena (Calif.) Coll., 1961-76; acad. dean, v.p. acad. affairs Point Loma Nazarene Coll., San Diego, 1976-88, prof. music, chair dept. music., 1989—88. Dir. S.W. Music Symposium, San Diego, 1991—; cons. Sch. for Creative and Performing Arts, San Diego, 1990—, Chula Vista, Calif., 1992—; mem. vis. team Western Coll. Assn., Calif., 1977-82. Arranger (choral) To God be the Glory, (brass) Keith A. Pagan Brass Quintet Series, The King Shall Come; mem. editorial bd. Christian Scholars Rev., 1986—, EverGreen Morning Music Press. Trustee Christian Scholars Rev., 1994—; dir. music Village Ch., Rancho Santa Fe, Calif. With U.S. Army, 1953-55; v.p. Calif. Higher Edn. Assn., 1970-71. Recipient WHO award Calif. Higher Edn. Assn., 1971, Lawrence Vredevoe Disting. Leadership award 1986, Spl. Svc. to Music award Calif. Music Educators Assn., 1991; winner 4th ann. anthem contest Choral Condrs. Guild; grantee Danforth Found., 1960. Mem. Calif. Coll. and Univ. Faculty Assn. (state pres. 1969-70), Music Tchrs. Assn. Calif. (parliamentarian 1971-73), Western Assn. Schs. and Coll. (accreditation liaison 1976-88). Avocations: travel, photography. Home: 5875 Friars Rd #4316 San Diego CA 92110 Personal E-mail: keithpagan@earthlink.net.

**PAGAN, VICKI,** biology educator; b. Nashville, Tenn., Apr. 20, 1968; d. Wanda and Charles Waterston; m. Giuliano Pagan, July 13, 2005; BS, Tenn. Tech. U., 1990. Lic. Teacher Tenn. State Bd. of Edn., 1990. Sci. tchr. Sta. Camp H.S., Gallatin, Tenn., 2003—04, Macon County H.S., Lafayette, Tenn., 2004—. Mem. Tenn. Tax Revolt, Nashville, 1999—2002. Mem.: Delta Kappa Gamma. R-Consevative. Avocation: travel. Home: 3632 Oakdale Rd Westmoreland TN 37186 Office: Macon County High Sch 2550 Days Rd Lafayette TN 37083 Personal E-mail: vpagan@nctcwb.com.

**PAGANELLI, CHARLES VICTOR,** physiologist, educator; b. NYC, Feb. 13, 1929; s. Charles Victor and Mary Paganelli; m. Barbara Harriet Slauson, Sept. 18, 1954; children: William, Kathryn, Peter, Robert, John. AB, Hamilton Coll., Clinton, N.Y., 1950; MA, Harvard U., 1952, PhD, 1957. Instr. physiology U. Buffalo, 1958-60, asst. prof., 1960-63; assoc. prof. SUNY, Buffalo, 1963-71, prof. physiology, 1971-97, disting. svc. prof., 1997—. Interim chair SUNY, Buffalo, 1991-98, emeritus, 1998. Editor: Physiological Function in Special Environments, 1990; contbr. articles to profl. jours. Recipient Elliott Coues award Am. Ornithologists Union, 1981, Newman award 1998. Mem.: Am. Physiol. Soc., Gold Humanism Honor Soc., Phi Beta Kappa, Sigma Xi, Alpha Omega Alpha. Office Phone: 716-829-2918. Business E-Mail: cvp@buffalo.edu.

**PAGANI, ALBERT LOUIS,** aerospace system engineer; b. Jersey City, Feb. 19, 1936; s. Alexander C. and Anne (Salvati) P.; m. Beverly Cameron, Feb. 23, 1971; children: Penelope, Deborah, Michael. BSEE, U.S. Naval Acad., 1957; MBA, So. Ill. U., 1971. Commd. 2d lt. USAF, 1957, advanced through grades to col., 1978, navigator Lake Charles, La., 1957-63, pilot McGuire AFB, NJ, 1963-65, command pilot Anchorage, 1965-68, mgr. airlift Saigon, Vietnam, 1968-69, chief spl. missions Scott AFB, Ill., 1969-74; commd. tactical airlift group USAF Europe, Mildenhall, England, 1974-76, dep. comdr. Rhein Main Air Base Frankfurt, Germany, 1976-78; chief airlift mgmt. USAF Mil. Airlift Command, Scott AFB, Ill., 1978-81; dir. tech. plans and concepts, 1981, dir. command and control, 1982-85; ret., 1985; program mgr. Lockheed Missile and Space Co., Sunnyvale, Calif., 1985-94; dir. data applications, dir. adv. programs PAR Govt. Sys. Corp., New Hartford, NY, 1994-97; pres. Computer Solutions Group, NY, 1997—; prin. Beval Assocs., Inc., 1997—; CEO CSG, Canada, 1999—; dir. B-Net, NY, 1999—; prin., dir. Asset Trax, Inc., 2000—. V.p. Cath. Ch. Coun., Mildenhall, 1974, pres., 1975. Decorated Legion of Merit, Bronze Star, Air medal, Vietnam Cross of Gallantry. Mem. Nat. Def. Transp. Assn. (sr.), Soc. Logistics Engrs., Air Force Assn., Armed Forces Comm. and Electronics Assn., Air Lift Assn., Inst. Noetic Scis., Daedalions, Mensa. Avocations: woodworking, neurolinguistics, volunteer senior executive consulting. Home: 8592 Red Hill Rd Clinton NY 13323-4210 Personal E-mail: alpagani@bevalinc.com.

**PAGANI, MARK,** education educator, researcher; b. New York, NY, Mar. 29, 1960; s. Waldo and Bernice Pagani; life ptnr. Teresa Fields; children: Kyla Maria, Ruben Abraham. PhD, Pa. State U., 1998. Assoc. prof. Yale U., New Haven, Conn., 2002—. Achievements include research in paleoclimate. Office: Yale U 210 Whitney Ave New Haven CT 06520 Office Phone: 203-432-6275. E-mail: mark.pagani@yale.edu.

**PAGANO, CELESTE ANN,** social services coordinator; b. Bridgeport, Conn., Apr. 12, 1950; d. Peter Angelo and Carmella Marie (Carrafiello) P. AAS in Broadcast Journalism, Grahm Jr. Coll., Boston, 1970; BA magna cum laude, Fairfield U., Conn., 1997; MPA, NYU, 2000. Self employed real estate

investor, property mgr. Pagano-Albert, 1981—97; coord. cmty. rels., vol., bd. mem. Vol. Ctr. Greater Bridgeport, 1997—99; coord. program and vol. Interfaith Vol. Caregivers, 1999—2000; coord. program Bridgeport Supportive Housing Program, 2000—02; coord. domestic violence Ctr. for Women and Families, 2002—. Guest spkr. on discrimination Conn. Realtors Conv., Hartford, 1987. Mem. adv. bd. Coordinated Assessment and Referral for the Elderly Program, Bridgeport Hosp., 1999; steering com. mem. Caring Connections Program, Cath. Family Svcs., 2000-04. Recipient Outstanding Fair Housing Action award Bridgeport Fair Housing, 1986. Democrat. Avocations: writing, music, kayaking, cross country skiing. Home and Office: 56 Livingston St Bridgeport CT 06605-3303

**PAGANO, JO ANNE,** education educator; b. Rochester, N.Y., Dec. 30, 1946; d. John Richard and Marlyn Margaret (Mull) P.; m. William Arnold Gietz, Sept. 30, 1977 (div. May 1983); m. Bruce Peter Berlind, Jan. 17, 1985. BA, U. Rochester, 1973, MS, 1980, PhD, 1982. Assoc. prof. edn. Colgate U., Hamilton, N.Y., 1981—. Co-author: Preparing Teachers as Professionals, 1989; author: Exiles and Communities, 1990; mem. editl. rev. bd. Ednl. Theory, 1988-93; editor-in-chief JCT: Interdisciplinary Jour. Curriculum Studies, 1990—; contbr. articles to ednl. jours., chpts. to books. Grantee Ford Found., 1986. Mem. Am. Ednl. Rsch. Assn., Philosophy of edn. Soc., Am. Ednl. Studies Assn. (exec. bd. dirs. 1994, exec. coun. 1993—), Profs. of Curriculum, Nat. Women's Studies Assn. Home: PO Box 237 Hamilton NY 13346-0237 Office: Colgate U Edn Dept 13 Oak Dr Hamilton NY 13346-1383 Office Phone: 315-824-7253. E-mail: jpagano@mail.colgate.edu

**PAGANO, JOSEPH STEPHEN,** internist, researcher, educator; b. Rochester, N.Y., Dec. 29, 1931; s. Angelo Pagano and Marian (Vinci) Signorino; children: Stephen Reynolds, Christopher Joseph. AB with honors, U. Rochester, 1953; MD, Yale U., 1957. Resident Peter Bent Brigham Hosp. Harvard U., Boston, 1960-61; fellow Karolinska Inst., Stockholm, 1961-62; mem. Wistar Inst., Phila., 1962-65; from asst. to assoc. prof. medicine & microbiology U. N.C., Chapel Hill, 1965-73, prof., 1974—, dir. divsn. infectious diseases, 1972-75; founder, dir. U., N.C. Lineberger Comprehensive Cancer Ctr., Chapel Hill, 1974-97, dir. emeritus, 1997—. Attending physician U. Hosps., Chapel Hill; vis. prof. Swiss Inst. Cancer Rsch., Lausanne, 1970-71, Lineberger prof. cancer rsch., 1986—; mem. virology study sect. NIH, Bethesda, Md., 1973-79; recombinant DNA adv. com. USPHS, 1986-90; bd. dirs. Burroughs Wellcome Fund, 1993-2001, Wachovia Bank, Chapel Hill/Durham/Cary; chmn., adv. com. N.C. Cancer Coord. and Control, 1993—2004; Mclaughlin vis. prof. U. Tex. Med. Br., 1996; Norma Berryhill Disting. lectr. U. N.C., 1997; Harry Eagle lectr. Albert Einstein Coll. Medicine, 1997; Harry F. Dowling lectr. U. Ill. Sch. Med., 1991; Gertrude & Werner Henle lectr. in viral oncology, 1990, Joseph and Ruth McCartney Hauck lectr. Mayo Clinic, 2002; Japan Soc. for Head and Neck Cancer lectr. Kanazawa U., 2003; cons. Franklin St. Ptnrs., Chapel Hill, 1998. Mem. editorial bd. Jour. Virology, Jour. Immunology, Cancer Rsch., Jour. Gen. Virology, Antimicrobial Agts. and Chemotherapy, 1974-93; contbr. articles to profl. jours., chpts. to books. Mem. awards assembly GM Cancer Rsch. Found., 1997-2001. Recipient USPHS Rsch. Career award NIH, 1968-73, N.C. award in sci., 1996. Mem. Inst. of Medicine, Am. Assn. Cancer Rsch., Am. Assn. Cancer Insts. (bd. dirs. 1992-99, pres., chmn.), Internat. Assn. for Rsch. in Epstein-Barr Virus (pres. 1990-94), Chapel Hill Tennis Club (pres. 1980-82), Carolina Club (bd. dirs. 2002—), Baldhead Island and Shoals Club. Episcopalian. Avocations: tennis, squash. Home: 114 Laurel Hill Rd Chapel Hill NC 27514-4323 Office: U NC CB7295 Lineberger Comp Cancer Ctr Chapel Hill NC 27599-0001

**PAGANO, MICHELINA OLIMPIA,** art director, consultant, writer, script-writer; d. Domenico and Mary Pagano; m. Anthony Jude Parente. Grad. h.s., Floral Pk., N.Y. Dir. art Lintas Worldwide Advt., N.Y.C., 1986—88; dir. sr. art Wells, Rich, Greene, N.Y.C., 1988—93, N.W. Ayer & Ptnrs. Advt., N.Y.C., 1993—95; sr. v.p., group creative dir. D'Arcy Worldwide Advt., N.Y.C., 1996—2000; freelance creative dir., cons., 2000—. Instr. advt. Sch. Visual Arts, N.Y.C., 1989—90. Author: (novel) The Road To Jude, 2004, Grace of the Clouds, 2002, (children's book) The Magic Paint Box, 1990; co-author: (screenplay) The Blood Orange, 2006; writer and co-prodr. (short film) Two Shoes, dir., co-writer and co-prodr. Wishful Thinking, co-creator, dir., writer and co-prodr. Return of the Masterminds, dir., co-prodr. Mini Happy Returns, co-dir., co-writer, co-prodr. (music video) Suit for Jesus. Recipient Cannes Bronze Lion, Cannes Internat. Festival, 1988, Bronze medal, N.Y. Festivals Internat., 1991, Bronze Effie, Effie Awards, 1994, Golden Trailer award, 1999, Internat. Advt. award, London, 1991, award, Hollywood Spiritual Film and Book Festival, 2005. Mem.: Ind. Film Project (assoc.). E-mail: mickipagano@yahoo.com.

**PAGANO, RICHARD DONALD,** physical education educator, researcher; b. Phila., Jan. 17, 1951; s. Joe Thomas and Mary Irene Pagano; m. Anna Theresa Pagano, June 17, 1977; children: Lauren Ann, Ryan Richard. BS, East Stroudsburg U., 1973; MEd, West Chester U., 1981. Cert. tchr., Pa. Health and phys. edn. tchr. Upper Darby (Pa.) Sch. Dist., 1974—. Columnist Town Talk Newspaper, 1987—(Sportsman of Yr. 1999); author: Life of Fred Luehring, 1981, History of Delco Hall of Fame, 1988. Trustee Stuzebecker Found., 1998—; bd. dirs. Crozer-Keystone Healthplex Sports Mus., 1998—, Pa. Sports Hall of Fame, 1995—, Delaware County Athletes Hall of Fame Com., 1988—, sport historian, 1988—. Named to Delaware County Athletes Hall of Fame, 1991, Pa. Sports Hall of Fame, 1997, Ridley Twp. Old Timers Hall of Fame, 1991. Mem. Internat. Soc. Olympic Historians, AAPHERD. Avocations: sports research, writing, collecting sports books. Home: 1311 Donna Ave Woodlyn PA 19094-1126 Office: Westbrook Park Sch Westbrook Dr Clifton Heights PA 19018

**PAGAN ORTIZ, ALEX OMAR,** computer systems analyst, educator; b. Ponce, P.R., Dec. 8, 1967; s. Javier E. Pagan and Brunilda Ortiz Collazo. BS in Computer Sci., Sacred Heart U., 1993; MS in Computer Sci., Temple U., 1997. Computer scientist U.S. Dept. Def., Fort Meade, Md., 1998-99; sr. cons. Oracle Corp., Columbia, Md., 1999-2000; internal sys. engr. Digital Courier Techs., Clearwater, Fla., 2000-2001; data analyst Eli Lilly Export S.A., Hato Rey, PR, 2001—02; asst. prof. Daytona Beach C.C., 2002—. Faculty assoc. Johns Hopkins U., Washington, 1998-2000. Avocations: tennis, swimming. Office: Daytona Beach CC 1200 International Speedway Daytona Beach FL 32114 E-mail: aopagan@yahoo.com.

**PAGE, ALAN C.,** state supreme court justice; b. Canton, Ohio, Aug. 7, 1945; s. Howard F. and Georgianna (Umbles) P.; m. Diane Sims, June 5, 1973; children: Nina, Georgina, Justin, Khamsin. BA, U. Notre Dame, 1967; JD, U. Minn., 1978; LLD (hon), U. Notre Dame, 1993, St. John's U., 1994, Westfield State Coll., 1994, Luther Coll., 1995, U. New Haven, 1999; LHD (hon), Winston-Salem State U., 2000, Gustavus Adolphus Coll., 2003, U. Notre Dame, 2004. Bar: Minn. 1979, U.S. Dist. Ct. Minn. 1979, U.S. Supreme Ct. 1988. Profl. football player Minn. Vikings, Mpls., 1967-78, Chgo. Bears, 1978-81; assoc. Lindquist & Vennum, Mpls., 1979-85; special asst. atty. gen. employment law Minn. Atty. Gen.'s Office, St. Paul, 1985—87, asst. atty. gen., 1987—93; assoc. justice Minn. Supreme Ct., St. Paul, 1993—. Cons. NFL Players Assn., Washington, 1979-84. Commentator Nat. Pub. Radio, 1982-83. Founder Page Edn. Found., 1988. Named NFL's Most Valuable Player, 1971, one of 10 Outstanding Young Men Am., U.S. Jaycees, 1981; named to NFL Hall of Fame, 1988, Coll. Football Hall of Fame, 1993, Internat. Scholar-Athlete Hall of Fame, 2002; named one of 50 Greatest Sports Figures from Ohio Sports Illustrated, 1999; recipient NCAA Theodore Roosevelt award, 2004, Disting. Am. award Nat. Football Found. and Coll. Hall Fame, 2005. Mem. ABA, Minn. Bar Assn., Nat. Bar Assn., Hennepin County Bar Assn., Minn. Assn. Black Lawyers, Am. Law Inst. Avocations: running, biking. Office: 423 Minnesota Judicial Ctr 25 Rev Dr Martin Luther King Jr Blvd Saint Paul MN 55155-1500

**PAGE, ALBERT LEE,** soil science educator, researcher; b. New Lenox, Ill., Mar. 19, 1927; m. Shirley L. Jessmore, Sept. 14, 1952; children: Nancy, Thomas. BA in Chemistry, U. Calif.-Riverside, 1956; PhD in Soil Sci., U. Calif.-Davis, 1960. Prof. soil sci. U. Calif.-Riverside, 1960—. Dir. Kearney

Found., Univ. Calif.-Riverside, program of excellence in energy research Editor: Methods of Soil Analysis, 1983, Utilization of Municipal Wastewater and Sludge on Land, 1983, Heavy Metals in the Environment, 1977 With USN, 1944—52. Recipient Environ. Quality Research award Am. Soc. Agronomy, 1984, Disting. Teaching award U. Calif., Riverside, 1976, Disting. Svc. award USDA, 1991; Fullbright scholar, 1966-67; Guggenheim Meml. Found. fellow, 1966-67 Fellow AAAS, Am. Soc. Agronomy, Soil Sci. Soc. Am.; mem. Internat. Soil Sci. Soc., Western Soil Sci. Soc., Soc. Environ. Geochemistry and Health, Sigma Xi. Home: 5555 Canyon Crest Dr Apt 1F Riverside CA 92507-6443 Office: U Calif Dept Soil & Environ Sci Riverside CA 92521-0001 Office Phone: 951-827-3433. Business E-Mail: albert.page@ucr.edu.

**PAGE, BARBARA ROSE,** primary school educator; b. Piney River, Va., Sept. 21, 1940; d. Samuel C. and Tessie Morse Rose; m. Joseph Roland Sr. Page, Dec. 28, 1957 (dec.); children: Joseph Jr., Donna Gail, Janet Lee, Peyton Arthur, Jonathan Ralph. BA, Sweet Briar Coll., 1983. Cert. elem. tchr. Va. Sunday sch. tchr. St. James Bapt. Ch., Roseland, Va., 1958—95; tchr. Bethune Nursery Sch., Lynchburg, Va., 1983—84, Nelson County Pub. Schs., Lovingston, 1984—2000, tutor, 2000—. Vol. PTA, Nelson County, 1966—2000; musician Oak-Hill Bapt. Ch., Massie Mill, Va., 1958—72, Mt. Pleasant Sunday Sch. Conv., 1966—80, Mt. Olive Bapt. Ch., Amherst, Va., 1969—83; tchr. Sunday sch. and vacation Bible sch. Recipient Tchr. award, Monticello Area Cmty. Action Agy., 1989, Svc. award, Mahogany, Inc., 1990, St. James Bapt. Ch., 1998. Mem.: NAACP, Nelson County Hist. Soc., Habitat (bd. dir. 2003—05). Baptist. Avocations: piano, reading, writing, gardening.

**PAGE, CHERYL MILLER,** elementary school educator; BS in Social Sciences, Calif. Polytechnic State Univ., San Luis Obispo, Calif., 1975. Cert. health edn. specialist Nat. Commn. for Health Edn. Credentialing, 1993, Edn. Certification Program Calif. Polytechnic State Univ., San Luis Obispo, Calif., 1976. Elem. educator The Dalles Pub. Schs., The Dalles, Oreg., 1980—86, Salem-Keizer Pub. Schs., Salem, Oreg., 1986—95, middle sch. health educator, 1995—2002, health educator; prevention curriculum resource specialist Salem-Keizer Pub. Schs. Mid Valley Partnership. Named Oreg. Outstanding Elementary Health Educator, 1991, Oreg. Outstanding Secondary Health Educator of Yr., 1996, Vol. of Yr., Am. Cancer Soc., 1996; recipient Tambrands award, Am. Assn. Health Edn., 1996, Health and Safety Educator of Year, NW Divsn. AAHPERD, 1996. Mem.: Oreg. Alliance Health, Phys. Edn., Recreation and Dance (treas. 1992—96, pres. 2001—02), Oreg. Assn. for the Advancement of Health Edn. (sec./treas. 1990—92), Nat. Bd. for Profl. Tchg. Stds. (bd. mem.). Avocations: running, reading. Office: Salem-Keizer Sch Dist PO Box 12024 Salem OR 97309 Office Phone: 503-399-3101. E-mail: page_cheryl@salkerz.k12.or.us.

**PAGE, CLARENCE E.,** columnist; b. Dayton, Ohio, June 2, 1947; m. Lisa Johnson Cole, May 3, 1987; 1 child, Grady Jonathan. BS in Journalism, Ohio U., 1969. Reporter, asst. city editor Chgo. Tribune, 1969—80; dir. cmty. affairs dept. Sta. WBBM-TV, 1980—82, reporter, planning editor, 1982—84; columnist, mem. editl. bd. Chgo. Tribune, 1984—, Tribune Media Svcs., Washington, 1987—; essayist & frequent panelist NewsHour with Jim Lehrer, PBS; occasional panelist McLaughlin Group. Frequent guest Sta. WTTW-TV, Chgo. Tonight, Chgo. in Rev. Contbr. articles to profl. jours.; author: Showing My Color: Impolite Essays on Race & Identity, 1996; co-author (with Lenita McClain): A Foot in Each World: Essays & Articles, 1986, What Killed Lenita McClain? Essays on Living in Both Black & White Worlds, 1999. Participant 1972 Chgo. Tribune Task Force Series on Vote Fraud. Named to Chgo. Journalism Hall of Fame, 1992; recipient Pulitzer Prize for Chgo. Tribune Task Force on Voter Fraud, 1972, Edward Scott Beck award for overseas reporting, 1976, Cmty. Svc. award, Ill. UPI, 1980, James P. McGuire award, ACLU, 1987, Pulitzer Prize for commentary, 1989. Office: Tribune Media Svcs 1325 G St NW Washington DC 20005-3104

**PAGE, CURTIS MATTHEWSON,** minister; b. Columbus, Ohio, Oct. 24, 1946; s. Charles N. and Alice Matthewson P.; m. Martha Poitevin, Feb. 12, 1977; children: Allison, Charles, Abigail. BS, Ariz. State U., 1968; MDiv, San Francisco Theol. Sem., 1971, D Ministry, 1985. Ordained Presbyn. Ch., 1971. Pastor Ketchum (Idaho) Presbyn. Ch., 1972-80, Kirk O'The Valley Presbyn. Ch., Reseda, Calif., 1980-90; campaign dir. Kids 1st Edn. Reform Partnership, L.A., 1990-91; sr. pastor Orangewood Presbyn. Ch., Phoenix, 1991-93, First Meridian Heights Presbyn. Ch., Indpls., 1993—. Mem. com. Ch. Devel., Ind., 1995—; bd. dirs. Express Pub., Ketchum. Chmn. com. on preparation for the ministry, San Fernando, Calif., 1988-90; chmn. Ketchum City Zoning Commn., 1979-80; L.A. Mayor's Citizen's Adv. Task Force on Ethics, 1990; co-chmn. Voice Cmty. Orgn. L.A., 1988-90; chair Family CARES, Indpls., 1995—; founding pastor AliveTime, 1995; leading innovator in mainline Protestant worship and urban ministry. Avocations: tennis, skiing, coaching softball. Office: First Meridian Heights Pres 4701 Central Ave Indianapolis IN 46205-1828 E-mail: FMHPC@aol.com.

**PAGE, DANIEL BENNETT,** dean, musician; b. Jacksonville, Fla., Oct. 18, 1962; s. Jack and Tinka P. BA, Bates Coll., 1986; MFA, Brandeis U., 1995, PhD, 1996. Asst. dir. Cathedral Square Performing Arts Ctr., Jacksonville, 1979—83; staff assoc. Nat. Coalition Advs. Students, Boston, 1987—89; organist, choirmaster St. John's Ch., Winthrop, Mass., 1987—92, Parish of Good Shepherd, Newton, Mass., 1992—; acad. dean Longy Sch. Music, Cambridge, Mass., 1996—. Reviewer in field. Rev. panel Mass. Cultural Coun., Boston, 1998. Mellon Grad. fellow, 1989-94, Fulbright fellow Fulbright Commn., 1992-93, Brandeis U. fellow, 1994-95. Mem. Am. Guild Organists (sec. Boston chpt. 1997-98), Am. Musicological Soc., Renaissance Soc. Am., Royal Musical Assn., Assn. Anglican Musicians, Cambridge Soc. Early Music (bd. dirs. 1997—), Phi Beta Kappa. Democrat. Episcopalian. Office: 67 East St Pittsfield MA 01201-5313

**PAGE, DAVID SANBORN,** biochemist, educator, environmental scientist, consultant; b. Suffern, N.Y., June 1, 1943; s. William Kingman and Alice Malmgreen Page; m. Barbara Taylor, July 30, 1950; children: Matthew Taylor, Diana Taylor; 1 child, David Collingwood. BS, Brown U., 1965; DSc, Purdue U., 1970. Asst. prof. chemistry Bates Coll., Lewiston, Maine, 1971—74; prof. chemistry and biochemistry Bowdoin Coll., Brunswick, Maine, 1974—. Vis. scientist Skidaway Inst. Oceanography, Savannah, Ga., 1981, 2002, Plymouth (Eng.) Marine Lab., 1987—88, 1994—95; cons. in field; expert witness in field. Author: 2 Books; contbr. over 120 articles to profl. jours. Named to Charles Weston Pickard Chair Chemistry and Biochemistry, Bowdoin Coll., 1998; grantee, Various State, Fed. and pvt. sources, 1971—2005. Mem.: Hormesis Soc., Am. Chem. Soc., Soc. Environ. Toxicologists and Chemists, Am. Philatelic Soc. Office: Bowdoin College Chemistry Department 6600 College Station Brunswick ME 04011-8466 Office Phone: 207-725-3602. Personal E-mail: dpage@bowdoin.edu.

**PAGE, ERNEST,** retired medical educator; b. Cologne, Germany, May 30, 1927; came to U.S., 1936, naturalized, 1945; s. Max Ernest and Eleanor (Kohn) P.; m. Eva Veronica Gross, June 5, 1967; 1 son, Thomas J. AB, Calif., Berkeley, 1949; MD, Calif., San Francisco, 1952. Intern Peter Bent Brigham Hosp., Boston, 1952-53, resident, 1953-54, 57-58; research assoc. Harvard Med. Sch., 1957-65; assoc. prof. medicine and physiology U. Chgo. Med. Sch., 1965-69, prof. physiology, 1969-98, prof. emeritus, 1998—. Editor: (jour.) Am. Jour. Physiology: Heart and Circulatory Physiology, 1981—86; editor: (sects.) Handbook of Physiology Vol. I The Heart, 2002. Served with AUS, 1945-46. Established investigator Am. Heart Assn., 1959-65 Mem. Am. Physiol. Soc., Biophys. Soc., Am. Soc. Cell Biology, Soc. Gen. Physiologists, Assn. Am. Physicians. Home: 5606 S Harper Ave Chicago IL 60637-1832

**PAGE, FRANK S.,** head of religious order; b. Greensboro, NC; m. Dayle Page; children: Melissa, Lauren, Allison. BS in Psychology, Gardner Webb Univ.; MDiv, PhD, Southwestern Baptist Theological Seminary. Former pastor Southern Baptist Convention Church (SBC Church) Tex., SBC Church

No. Carolina, Warren Baptist SBC Church Ga., Taylor's First SBC Church So. Carolina; pres. So. Baptist Church, 2006—. Office: Southern Baptist Convention 1 Lifeway Plz MSN 146 Nashville TN 37234-1001*

**PAGE, FREDERICK WEST,** business consultant; b. East Orange, N.J., Oct. 19, 1932; s. Frederick West and Dorothy (Donham) P.; m. Miriam Lowell Jones, Feb. 14, 1959; children: William, Janet, Thomas, James. AB, Dartmouth Coll., 1954; postgrad., Wharton Grad. Sch. Bus., U. Pa., 1956-57; MBA, NYU, 1960. With Schering Corp. (now Schering-Plough), 1957-91, various mktg. positions, 1957-73, gen. mgr. animal health products, 1973-80, pres. U.S. Animal Health Products Div., 1980-83, v.p. pharm. ops., 1983-91; pres. Bus. Cons. Svcs., 1991—; dir. Immune Tech. Inc., 1996-98. Served with U.S. Army, 1954-56. Mem. Animal Health Inst. (exec. com. 1978-81, chmn. 1979-80) Clubs: Phi Kappa Psi. Republican. Home and Office: 22 Martin Rd West Caldwell NJ 07006-7419

**PAGE, GEORGE ALFRED, JR.,** lawyer; b. Evanston, Ill., June 30, 1932; AB, Princeton U., 1954; JD, Harvard U., 1959; LLM in Taxation, Boston U., 1964. Bar: Mass 1959. From assoc. to ptnr. Peabody & Arnold, Boston, 1959—79; sr. ptnr. Csaplar & Bok, Boston, 1979—90; pvt. practice Boston, 1990—. Lectr grad tax program Boston Univ Sch Law, 1974—77; gen counsel to bd dirs and sr mgmt Woodside Mgmt Sys Inc, Boston, 1978—87. 1st lt USAR, 1954—56. Mem.: ABA (mem. real property, probate and trust law sect.), Boston Bar Assn. (chmn. state tax com 1971—74, sect. taxation 1974—75, fed. tax com. 1980—82, sr. sect. 1994—96, mem. trusts and estates law sect., mem. estate planning com.). Home and Office: 1 Risley Rd Marblehead MA 01945-3720 Office Phone: 781-631-7243.

**PAGE, HARRY ROBERT,** business administration educator; b. Milw., Mar. 22, 1915; s. Harry Allen and Lydia (Rosendahl) P.; m. Jeanne Tompkins, Apr. 1, 1945; children: Patricia Jeanne, Margaret Berenice. AB, Mich. State U. 1941; postgrad., U.S. Army Command and Staff Coll., 1945-46, Indsl. Coll. Armed Forces, 1958-59; MBA, Harvard, 1952; PhD, Am. U., 1966. Served from 2d lt. to lt. col. U.S. Army, 1941-46; from lt. col. to col. USAF, 1947-61; exec. officer logistics directorate U.S. Joint Chiefs of Staff, Washington, 1959-61; asst. prof. bus. adminstrn. George Washington U., Washington, 1961-65, assoc. prof., chmn. dept., 1965-69, prof., chmn. dept. bus. adminstrn., 1970-74, assoc. dean, 1975-80, prof. emeritus, 1981—. Cons. Advanced Study program Brookings Instn., Washington, 1966-70, Ednl. Svcs. Inst., U.S. Postal Svc., 1985-92. Author: Church Budget Development, 1964, An Analysis of the Defense Procurement Program Decision-Making Process, 1966, Public Purchasing and Materials Management, 1980, rev. edit., 1989; co-author: Federal Contributions to Management, 1972. Chmn. task force edn. and tng. Commn. Govt. Procurement, 1972-73; bd. dirs., treas. Coun. Chs., Greater Washington, 1963-68; bd. dirs. Hunter Assocs. Lab., Inc.; deacon Rock Spring Congregational Ch., 1994-97. Decorated Air medal USAF, Purple Heart, Legion of Merit, Commendation medal USAF, U.S. Army. Fellow Nat. Contract Mgmt. Assn.; mem. Acad. Mgmt., Nat. Assn. Purchasing Mgmt., Internat. Fedn. Purchasing and Materials Mgmt., Harvard Bus. Sch. Assn., Air Force Assn., Nat. Parks and Conservation Assn. (trustee), Air Force Sgts. Assn. (trustee, chmn. scholarship bd. 1971—), Harvard Bus. Club, Sch. of Wash. Club (dir., pres. 1980-81), Alpha Phi Omega, Lambda Chi Alpha Alpha Mocha (pres.), Pi Sigma Alpha, Beta Gamma Sigma. Home: 3612 N Glebe Rd Arlington VA 22207-4317

**PAGE, JONATHAN ROY,** portfolio manager; b. Harrisburg, Pa., Sept. 10, 1946; s. John and Ellen (Smith) P.; m. Patrice Marie Margerm, May 17, 1975; children: Elizabeth, Gregory, Richard, Brian. BA, Dartmouth Coll., 1968; MBA, Tuck Sch. Dartmouth, 1969. Chartered fin. analyst. Investment officer Irving Trust Co., N.Y.C., 1970-75; portfolio mgr. to mng. dir., sr. portfolio mgr. Morgan Stanley Investment Mgmt., N.Y.C., 1975—. Mem. N.Y. Soc. Security Analysts, Fin. Analysts Fedn. Republican. Episcopalian. Avocations: tennis, golf, skiing, landscaping. E-mail: jonathan.page@morganstanley.com.

**PAGE, KENNETH R.,** lawyer; b. Rockville Centre, N.Y., May 20, 1946; s. Charles Herbert and Dorothy Emma (Koster) P.; m. Nancy McNeer Cummings, Oct. 27, 1973; children: Katherine Spessard Page, Taylor Benton Page; m. Deborah Ann Donovan, Feb. 14, 1998 AB cum laude, with distinction in Govt., Dartmouth Coll., 1968; JD, Cornell U., 1971. Bar: N.Y. 1972, U.S. Dist. Ct. (so. dist.) N.Y., U.S. Ct. Appeals (2d cir.) 1975, U.S. Tax Ct. 2000. Assoc. Cadwalader, Wickersham & Taft, N.Y.C., 1971-80; ptnr. Cole & Deitz, N.Y.C., 1980-83, Coudert Bros., N.Y.C., 1983—2005, head Trusts & Estates practice; ptnr. Baker & McKenzie, N.Y.C., 2005—. Trustee Family Dymanics, N.Y.C., 1976-86, Mus. Am. Folk Art, N.Y.C., 1976-86, Isaac H. Tuttle Fund., N.Y.C., 1980—; mem. Trustees of the Estate and Property of Diocesan Conv., N.Y.C., 1987-93, 94-2000, 01—. Mem. ABA, N.Y. State Bar. Assn., Union Club. Avocations: skiing, tennis, fishing, art. Office: Baker & McKenzie 1114 Ave of the Americas New York NY 10036-7710 Office Phone: 212-626-4806. Office Fax: 212-626-4120. Business E-Mail: kenneth.r.page@bakernet.com.

**PAGE, LARRY (LAWRENCE E. PAGE),** information technology executive; b. Ann Arbor, Mich., Mar. 26, 1973; s. Carl Victor and Gloria Page. BS in Computer Engring., U. Mich., 1995; postgrad., Stanford U. Co-founder Google, Inc., Mountain View, Calif., 1998, CEO, 1998—2001, pres. products, 2001—. Spkr. in field; spkr. World Econ. Forum; bd. dirs. Google, Inc. 1998—. Mem. nat. adv. com. U. Mich. Coll. Engring., Ann Arbor, Mich.; bd. trustee X Prize, 2005—. Co-recipient (with Sergey Brin) Marconi prize, 2004; named Global Leader for Tomorrow, World Econ. Forum, 2002, "Young Innovator Who Will Create the Future", MIT Tech. Review Mag., Innovator of Yr., R&D Mag., 2002, Persons of Week (with Sergey Brin) ABC World News Tonight, 2004; named one of World's 100 Most Influential People, Time Mag., 2005, Forbes Richest Americans, 2006; recipient Engring. Graduate award, U. Mich. Alumni Soc., Business Leader of Yr. for Google, Inc., Scientific American 50, 2005. Mem.: NAE, Eta Kappa Nu. Office: 1600 Amphitheatre PKWY #41 Mountain View CA 94043-1351 Office Phone: 650-623-4000. Office Fax: 650-618-1499.*

**PAGE, LARRY KEITH,** neurosurgeon, educator; b. Rayville, La., July 7, 1933; s. Ardie Lee and Edris Estelle (Chaney) P.; m. Joan Marie Doherty, Aug. 27, 1960; children: Matthew, Elizabeth, Jennifer. BS, La. State U., 1955, MD, 1958. Diplomate: Am. Bd. Neurol. Surgery. Intern Grad. Hosp., U. Pa., Phila., 1958-59; resident Children's Hosp. and Peter Bent Brigham Hosp., Boston, 1962-66; assoc. neurosurgeon Children's Hosp., assoc. surgeon Peter Bent Brigham Hosp., 1966-71; cons. Beverly Hosp., Mass., Robert Breck Brigham Hosp., Boston, Pondville Hosp., Boston, West Roxbury VA Hosp., Boston VA Hosp.; clin. instr. neurosurgery Harvard U., Boston, 1971-75; prof., vice chmn. dept. neurosurgery U. Miami, Fla., 1971-95, prof. emeritus Fla., 1995—, chief div. pediatric neurosurgery Fla., 1971-95; neurosurgeon VA Hosp., Miami, 1971-88, Jackson Meml. Hosp., Miami, 1971-95, dir. neurosurgery, 1994-95; chief neurosurgery Mt. Sinai Hosp., Miami, 1990-94. Cons. neurosurg. FDA, 1976-79, NASA, 1979-80 Mem. editorial bds., contbr. articles to profl. jours. Served to lt. USN, 1959-62. Mem. ACS, Am. Acad. Pediatrics, Am. Assn. Neurol. Surgeons, Internat. Soc. Pediatric Neurosurgery, Am. Soc. Pediatric Neurosurgery, Congress Neurol. Surgeons, Fellowship of Acad. Neurosurgeons, Internat. Neurosurg. Forum, Royal Soc. Medicine, Soc. for Rsch. in Hydrocephalus and Spina Bifida, New Eng. Neurosurg. Soc., Fla. Neurosurg. Soc. (pres. 1989-90), Mass. Med. Soc., Dade County Med. Assn., Internat. Palm Soc., Alpha Omega Alpha. Roman Catholic. Home and Office: 13845 SW 73rd Ct Miami FL 33158-1213

**PAGE, LESLIE ANDREW,** retired consumer products company executive; b. Mpls., June 5, 1924; s. Henry R. and Amelia Kathryn (Steinmetz) Page; m. DeEtte Abernathy Griswold, July 6, 1952 (div. Sept. 1975); children: Randolph, Michael, Kathryn, Caroline; m. Mary Ellen Decker, Nov. 26, 1976. BA, U. Minn., 1949; MA, U. Calif., Berkeley, 1953, PhD, 1956. Asst. microbiologist, lectr. U. Calif., Davis, 1956-61; cons. San Diego Zoological Soc. Zoo Hosp., 1957-60; microbiologist, research leader Nat. Animal Disease Ctr., USDA, Ames, Iowa, 1961-79; specialist in Chlamydial nomen-

clature and disease; med. text cons. Bay St. Louis, Miss., 1979-85; founder, pres., chmn. bd. Steri-Derm Corp., San Marcos, Calif., 1987—2005. Cons. McCormick Distilling Co., Weston, Mo., 1994—95. Editor: Jour. Wildlife Diseases, 1965—68, Wildlife Diseases, 1976; contbr. chpts. to textbooks, articles to profl. jours. Pres. Garden Island Cmty. Assn., Bay St. Louis, Miss., 1980—81; chief commr. East Hancock Fire Protection Dist., Bay St. Louis, 1982—83; treas. Woodridge Escondido Property Owners Assn., 1986—88; pres. Westminster Men's Group, Westminster Presbyn. Ch., Escondido, Calif., 2002. Fellow: Am. Acad. Microbiology; mem.: Am. Soc. Microbiology, Wildlife Disease Assn. (pres. 1972—73, Disting. Svc. award 1980, Emeritus award 1984), Les Families Pagé d'Amérique, Phi Zeta (hon.). Achievements include patent for Liquid Antiseptic Composition. Home: 2209 SE Pine Gate Cir Blue Springs MO 64014 Personal E-mail: lapage1234@hotmail.com.

**PAGE, LINDA KAY,** bank executive; b. Wadsworth, Ohio, Oct. 4, 1943; d. Frederick Meredith and Martha Irene (Vance) P. Student, Ohio U., 1976-77; grad. banking program, U. Wis., 1982-84; BA, Capital U. Asst. v.p., gen. mgr. Bancohio Corp., Columbus, 1975-78, v.p., dist. mgr., 1979-80, v.p., mgr. employee rels., 1980-81, v.p., divsn. mgr., 1982-83; commr. of banks State of Ohio, Columbus, 1983-87, dir. Dept. Commerce, 1988-90; pres., CEO Star Bank Ctrl. Ohio, Columbus, 1990—92; state dir. Rural Devel/USDA, 1993-2000; pub. svc. dir. City of Columbus, 2000—04; mgr. Nationwide Fed. Credit Union, 2004—. Bd. dirs. Clark County Mental Health Bd., Springfield, Ohio, 1982-83, Springfield Met. Housing, 1982-83, Pvt. Industry Coun. Franklin County, 1990-2000—, Ohio Higher Edn. Facilities Commn., 1990-93, Ohio Devel. Corp., 1995—; bd. advisers Orgn. Indsl. Standards, Springfield, 1982-83; trustee League Against Child Abuse, 1986-90; treas. Ohio Housing Fin. Agy., 1980-90; vice chair Fed. Res. Bd. Consumer Adv. Coun., 1989-91; trustee, treas. Columbus State C.C. Found., 1990-00, pres., 1997-99; bd. dirs. Columbus Urban League, 1992-98; mem. CompDrug Bd., 1998-00; mem. Mid Ohio Regional Planning Commn., 2000-04; devel. chair Ohio Coun. Econ. Edn., 2003-. Recipient Leadership Columbus award Sta. WTVN and Columbus Leadership Program, 1975, 82, Outstanding Svc. award Clark County Mental Health Bd., 1983, Giles Mitchell Housing award, 1996. Mem.: LWV (treas. edn. fund 1992—2000), Ohio Coun. Econ. Edn. (devel. chair 2004—), Womens Fund Ctrl. Ohio (grant reader 2003—05), Risk Mgmt. Assn., Women in Transp. (bd. trustees Ohio chpt. 2000, bd. dirs. 2002), Internat. Womens Forum, Am. Pub. Works Assn. (treas. Ohio chpt. 2000—04, govt. affairs com. 2002—03, treas. 2002—04), Ohio Mortgage Bankers Assn. (legis. commn. 1998), Ohio Devel. Assn., Ohio Bankers Assn. (bd. dirs. 1982—83, 1991—92), Conf. State Bank Suprs. (dist. chmn. 1984—85, sec.-treas. 1985—90, bd. dirs.), Women Execs. in State Govt., Am. Bankers Assn. (govt. rels. coun. 1990—92, cert.), Nat. Assn. Bank Women (pres. 1980—81), Rotary. Democrat. Avocations: reading, cultural arts, travel. Home: 1477 Sedgefield Dr New Albany OH 43054-9431 Personal E-mail: lpage@insight.rr.com.

**PAGE, LYMAN ALEXANDER, JR.,** physicist; b. San Francisco, Sept. 24, 1957; s. Lyman Alexander and Gillet (Thomas) P.; m. Elizabeth Olson, Feb. 12, 1990; children: William, James, Brent. BA with high honors in Physics, Bowdoin Coll., 1978; PhD in Physics, MIT, 1989. Rsch. technician Bartol Rsch. Found., Newark, Del., 1978-80; postdoctoral rsch. fellow MIT, 1989-90; instr. physics Princeton U., NJ, 1990-91, asst. prof. NJ, 1991-95, assoc. prof. NJ, 1995-98, prof. NJ, 1998—2005, Henry DeWolf Smyth prof., 2005—. Contbr. articles to sci. jours. Surdna fellow Bowdoin Coll., 1978, NASA grad. student rschrs. prog. fellow MIT, 1987-89, David and Lucile Packard fellow Princeton U., 1994; Rsch. Corp. Cottrell scholar Princeton U., 1994. Fellow: Am. Acad. Arts & Sci. Mem. Am. Phys. Soc., Am. Astron. Soc., NAS. Achievements include measurement of tiny spatial variations in the temperature of the radiation thought to be the afterglow of the big-bang. Office: Princeton U Dept Physics Jadwin Hall PO Box 708 Princeton NJ 08544-0708*

**PAGE, OSCAR C.,** academic administrator; b. Bowling Green, Ky., Dec. 22, 1939; s. Elizabeth Page; m. Anna Laura Hood, June 12, 1965; children: Kristen, Matt. BA in Social Sci., Western Ky. U., 1962; MA in History, U. Ky., 1963, PhD in Early Modern European History, 1967. Instr. history Western Ky. U., Bowling Green, 1964; asst. prof., asst. chair history dept. U. Ga., Athens, 1967-71; dean Wesleyan Coll., Macon, Ga., 1971-78; v.p. acad. affairs Lander Coll., Greenwood, S.C., 1978-86, acting pres., 1985, provost, v.p. acad. affairs, 1986-88; pres. Austin Peay State U., Clarksville, Tenn., 1988-94, Austin Coll., Sherman, Tex., 1994—. Bd. dirs.Clarksville Nations Bank. Bd. dirs. United Way, Sherman, 1994—98; mem. pres.'s commn. NCAA, 1990—94, mem. mgmt. coun., 1998—2002; bd. dirs. Meml. Hosp., Clarksville; pres. Assn. Tex. Colls. and Univs., 1998—99. Mem.: Sherman C. of C., Rotary Club. Office: Austin Coll 900 N Grand Ave Sherman TX 75090-4440

**PAGE, PATRICIA (PATTY) NEWTON,** real estate broker, real estate company executive; b. Nashville, Tenn., May 16, 1963; d. James Kelton and Alice (Clement) Cuff. Grad., Realtor Inst., 1999. Cert. affiliate broker North Ctrl. Inst., 1993, accredited credit buyer rep. Nat. Assn. Realtors, 2001, lic. real estate broker, cert. residential specialist. Sr. customer svc. rep. Comdata Corp., Brentwood, Tenn., 1981—92; realtor Century 21 ABC, Clarksville, Tenn., 1993—94, Lakeland Properties, Dover, Tenn., 1994—96; designated realtor Cherry Properties, Dover, Tenn., 1996—2003; owner, broker Patty Page Properties, LLC, 2004—. Mem.: Nat. Assn. Realtors (coun. residential specialist 2002). Methodist. Avocations: Continued Education, travel. Office Phone: 931-232-5082. Personal E-mail: PattyPage2000@aol.com.

**PAGE, PATRICK JOSEPH,** art educator; b. Highland Park, Ill., Sept. 6, 1975; s. Dennis and Carolyn Page. BS in History and Art Edn., Ball State U., Muncie, Ind., 1998, MA in Studio Art, 1999; post grad. in Modern Art History, Theory, and Criticism, Sch. Art Inst. Chgo., 2004—. Tchg. intern dept. history Ball State U., Muncie, Ind., 1996—97, grad. asst. mus. art, 1998—99; fine arts tchr. Lyons Twp. H.S., La Grange, Ill., 2004—. Curator New York and Paris: Generations in the Capitals of Modern Art Ball State U. Mus. Art, Muncie, Ind., 1999; juror 30th Ann. Hinsdale (Ill.) Fine Arts Festival, 2003. Grantee Undergraduate Creative Arts, Ball State U., 1998, Grad. Creative Arts, 1999; Presidental scholar, 1993—97, Alice Nichols Art Edn. scholar, 1997.

**PAGE, RANDALL,** state official; b. Mt. Vernon, Ohio, Feb. 18, 1967; s. James and Nancy Page; m. Melissa Rohrman, Feb. 16, 1991; children: Julie Anne, Jason Ryan. BS, Bob Jones U., Greenville, 1990. Dir. of pub. events Office of the Gov., Columbia, SC, 1995—99; exec. v.p. Jordan and McCallum Co., Greenville, SC, 1999—2001; legislative affairs dir. Office of the Lt. Gov., Columbia, SC, 2001—03, chief of staff, 2003—04; campaign mgr. Beasley for Senate, Columbia, SC, 2004; pres. South Carolinians for Responsible Govt., Columbia, SC, 2005—; sr. assoc. Richard Quinn & Assocs., Columbia, SC, 2004—05. Bd. dirs. Insights, Greenville, SC, 1994—2001; adv. bd. LifeEd, Greenville, SC, 2000—, Eagle Mil. Acad., Summerville, SC, 2006—; exec. bd. SC Citizens for Life, Columbia, 2001—. Cons. George W. Bush for Pres., Columbia, SC, 2000; fourth dist. chmn. SC Rep. Party, Columbia, 2001—03; bd. dirs. Kennerly Rd. Bapt. Ch., Irmo, SC, 2003—06, chmn. 2004—06; mem. exec. bd. Greenville County Libr. Sys., SC, 1999—2001; bd. dirs. Palmetto Family Coun., 2006—. Recipient Order of the Palmetto, Gov. David M. Beasley, SC., 1998, Hon. Order of Ky. Colonels, Gov. Paul Patton, Ky., 2003, Disting. Svc. award, Bob Jones U. Alumni Assn., 2006. Republican. Baptist. Avocation: swimming. Office: South Carolinians for Responsible Govt 1620 Gervais St Ste B Columbia SC 29201 Office Phone: 803-212-1051. Office Fax: 803-212-1052. Personal E-mail: govpage@sc.rr.com. Business E-Mail: randy@scrgov.org.

**PAGE, RAYMOND,** research and development company executive; b. Morgantown, W.Va., Nov. 12, 1965; s. Steven Lynn and Elene Page; life ptnr. Tanja Dominko. BS in Chem. Engring., W.Va. U., Morgantown, 1983—87, MS in Chem. Engring., 1987—89; PhD in Chem. Engring., Va. Poly. Inst. & State U., Blacksburg, 1989—92. Scientist & project mgr. PPL Therapeutics,

Inc., Blacksburg, Va., 1992—2000; sr. scientist Advanced Cell Tech., Worcester, Mass., 2000—01; chief sci. officer Cyagra, Inc., North Grafton, Mass., 2001—. Mem. Lions Internat., Southbridge, Mass., 2002—04. Mem.: Internat. Embryo Transfer Soc. (assoc.). Independent. Achievements include patents for Genetic Transformation of Animals; patents pending for Trans-differentiation of somatic cells; De-differentiation of Somatic Cells. Avocations: fly fishing, canoeing, camping. Office Phone: 508-765-0276. Personal E-mail: ray.page@verizon.net.

**PAGE, ROBERT EUGENE, JR.,** biology professor; PhD in Entomology, U. Calif., Davis, 1980. Mem. faculty dept. entomology Ohio State U., 1986—89, U. Calif., Davis, 1989—91, prof., 1991—2004, prof. emeritus, 2004; found. prof., founding dir. Ariz. State U. Life Scis., 2004—. Chair dept. entomology U. Calif., Davis, 1999—2004. Contbr. articles to profl. jours., chapters to books; co-editor: Genetics of Social Evolution, 1988; co-author: Queen Rearing and Bee Breeding, 1998. Recipient Alexander von Humboldt Sr. Scientist award, German Govt. Fellow: AAAS, Am. Acad. Arts & Scis.; mem.: Brazilian Acad. Sci. (fgn. mem.). Office: Sch Life Scis Life Scis E-Wing 427 E Tyler Mall Tempe AZ 85281 E-mail: Robert.Page@asu.edu.*

**PAGE, ROBERT HENRY,** retired engineering educator, researcher; b. Phila., Nov. 5, 1927; s. Ernest Fraser and Marguerite (MacFarl) P.; m. Lola Marie Griffin, Nov. 12, 1948; children: Lola Linda, Patricia Jean, William Ernest, Nancy Lee, Martin Fraser. BS in Mech. Engring. Ohio U., 1949; MS, U. Ill., 1951, PhD, 1955. Instr., research assoc. U. Ill., 1949-55; research engr. fluid dynamics Esso Research & Engring. Co., 1955-57; vis. lectr. Stevens Inst. Tech., 1956-57; dir. fluid dynamics lab., prof. mech. engring., 1957-61; prof. mech. engring., chmn. dept. mech., indsl. and aerospace engring. Rutgers-The State U., 1961-76, prof., research cons., 1976-79; dean engring. Tex.- A&M U., 1979-83, Forsyth prof., 1983-93, prof. emeritus mech. engring., 1994—; ret. 1994. Spl. research base pressure and heat transfer, wake flow and flow separation. Contbr. over 250 articles to profl. publs.; inventor impingement nozzles. Served with AUS, 1945-47, Pacific Theatre of Operations. Recipient Western Electric Found award Am. Soc. Engring Edn., 1968, Lindback Found. award, 1969, Disting. Alumnus award U. Ill., 1971, Disting. Svc. award, 1973, Life Quality Engring. award, 1974, James Harry Potter Gold medal, 1983, Ohio U. medal, 1983; named hon. prof. Ruhr U., Buchum, Fed. Republic Germany, 1984; named to Acad. Disting. Grads. Ohio U., 2001, Hall of Fame, Ctrl. H.S., Phila., 2002. Fellow AAAS, AIAA, ABET, Am. Astron. Soc. (chmn. nat. space engring. com. 1969-70, 72-76), Am. Soc. Engring. Edn. (Centennial medal 1993); mem. ASME (hon. mem. award 1988), Am. Phys. Soc., Pan Am. Acad. Engring. (charter). Home: 1905 Comal Cir College Station TX 77840-4818

**PAGE, RODNEY FRED,** lawyer; b. Pueblo, Colo., Oct. 27, 1946; s. Franklin H. and Ruth M. (Fetters) P.; m. Deborah Wolfe, Sept. 27, 1986; children: Allison, Tyler, Erin. BA, U. Ky., 1968; JD, Harvard Coll., 1971. Bar: D.C. 1971, Va. 1972. Assoc. Arent Fox Kintner Plotkin & Kahn, Washington, DC, 1971-79, ptnr., 1979-89, mng. ptnr., 1989-93; ptnr., mem. oper. group Bryan Cave LLP, Washington, DC. Corp. sec. Fairfax (Va.) Corp., 1988-92. Chmn. Fairfax County Sch. Bd., Fairfax, 1976-80; bd. dirs. Fairfax Dem. Bus. Adv. Com., 1987-90; trustee Greater Washington Bd. Trade VA-PAC, 1988—. Mem. ABA, D.C. Bar ASsn., Va. State Bar Assn., Tower Club (mem. bd. govs. 1989-90). Episcopalian. Office: Bryan Cave LLP 700 Thirteenth Street NW Washington DC 20005 Office Phone: 202-508-6002. E-mail: wfbavinger@bryancave.com.

**PAGE, RUFFNER,** bank executive; married; 3 children. BA in Philosophy and Psychology, Vanderbilt U., 1981; MBA, U. Va., 1986. With Remington Fund, 1986—89, Nat. Bank Commerce, 1989—93; from mem. staff to pres. McWane, Birmingham, Ala., 1993—. Bd. dir. Nat. Bank Commerce, Ala. Nat. Bancorporation, Protective Investment Co., O'Neal Steel, Inc. McWane Internat. Inc. Bd. dir. Ala. Symphony, Birmingham (Ala.) Mus. Art, Emmet O'Neil Lib. Found., Vulcan Pk. Found., Altamont Sch. Mem.: Rotary. Office: McWane 2900 Highway 280 Ste 300 Birmingham AL 35223

**PAGE, SALLY JACQUELYN,** university official, management educator; b. Saginaw, Mich., 1943; d. William Henry and Doris Effie (Knippel) P. BA, U. Iowa, 1965; MBA, So. Ill. U., 1973. Copy editor C.V. Mosby Co., St. Louis, 1965-69; editl. cons. Editl. Assocs., Edwardsville, Ill., 1969-70; rsch. adminstr. So. Ill. U., 1970-74, asst. to pres., affirmative action officer, 1974-77; officer of instn. U. N.D. Grand Forks, 1977—, lectr. mgmt., 1978—. Polit. comentator Sta. KFJM, Nat. Public Radio affiliate, 1981-90; mem. mayor's com. Employment of People With Disabilities, 1980-97. Contbr. articles to profl. jours. Chmn. N.D. Equal Opportunity Affirmative Action Officers, 1987-2003; chmn. NDUS Diversity Coun.; pres. Pine to Prairie coun. Girl Scouts U.S., 1980-85; mem. employment com. Ill. Commn. on Status of Women, 1976-77; mem. Bicentennial Com., Edwardsville, 1976, Bikeway Task Force, Edwardsville, 1975-77, Greater Grand Forks (N.D.) Bus. Leadership Network; bd. dirs. Grand Forks Homes, 1985—2003, pres., 1996-2001; mem. Civil Svc. Rev. Task Force, Grand Forks, 1982, civil svc. commr., 1983-98, chmn., 1984, 86, 88, 92, 96; ruling elder 1st Presbyn.; mem. Grand Forks Mayor's Adv. Cabinet, 1998-2000. Mem. AAUW (dir. Ill. 1975-77), PEO, Coll. and Univ. Pers. Assn. (rsch. and publs. bd. 1982-84), Soc. Human Resource Mgmt., Am. Assn. Affirmative Action, ADA Coords. Democrat. Presbyterian. Home: 3121 Cherry St Grand Forks ND 58201-7461 Office: U ND Grand Forks ND 58202 Business E-Mail: Sally-Page@mail.und.nodak.edu.

**PAGE, STEPHEN FRANKLIN,** aerospace transportation executive; b. LA, Jan. 21, 1940; s. Steve and Milla Theresa (Raditich) Page; m. Judith Kellyn children. Stephen D., Mark C., Kathryn K. BBA, Loyola U., L.A., 1962, JD, 1968. Bar: Calif. 1969; CPA, Calif. Prin. Deloitte, Haskins & Sells, L.A., 1962-72; v.p. sec., gen. counsel McCulloch Corp., L.A., 1972-76; pres. McCulloch Mite-E-Lite, L.A., 1976-79; v.p., controller, treas. Pacific Internat. Group (div. Black & Decker), L.A., 1979-81; v.p., treas. Ams. Internat. Group (div. Black & Decker), L.A., 1981-82, Black & Decker Mfg. Co., Towson, Md., 1982-85; v.p. fin., treas. Black & Decker Corp., Towson, 1985-90, exec. v.p., CFO, 1990-92; exec. v.p. United Techs. Corp., Hartford, Conn., 1993—97, CFO, 1993—97, 2002—, dir., vice chmn., 2002—; pres., CEO Otis Elevator Co., Farmington, Conn., 1997—2002. Bd. dirs. Augat, Inc., Mansfield, Mass, Lowe's Corp.; trustee, Loyola Marymount U. Pres. Associated Cath. Charities, Balt., 1987—, The Kennedy Inst., Balt., 1988—, chmn., INROADS for Greater Hartford and Springfield Inc. Mem. ABA, AICPA, Fin. Execs. Inst. (chmn. com. on internat. bus. 1987-89, vice chair 1990). Office: United Techs Corp United Techs Bldg Hartford CT 06101

**PAGE, TIM,** music critic, writer, producer; b. San Diego, Oct. 11, 1954; s. Ellis Batten and Elizabeth Latimer (Thaxton) Page; m. Vanessa Weeks, Mar. 3, 1984 (div.); children: William Dean, Robert Leonard, John Sherman; m. Julieta Stack, Oct. 12, 2002. Student, Tanglewood Music Ctr., 1970, 74, 75, Mannes Coll. Music, 1975-77; BA, Columbia U., 1979. Music critic Soho News, NYC, 1979-82; music writer N.Y. Times, NYC, 1982-87; music critic Newsday, NYC, 1987-95; writer, music critic Washington Post, 1995—. Artistic advisor St. Louis Symphony, 1999—2000; lectr. in field. Author: Music From the Road, 1992, William Kapell, 1992, Dawn Powell: A Biography, 1998, Tim Page on Music, 2001; editor: The Glenn Gould Reader, 1984; editor: (with Vanessa Weeks Page) Selected Letters of Virgil Thomson, 1988; editor: Dawn Powell at Her Best, 1994, The Diaries of Dawn Powell, 1995, Selected Letters of Dawn Powell, 1999, The Unknown Sigrid Undset, 2001; radio host WNYC-FM, 1981—92. Recipient Pulitzer prize for ciriticism, N.Y. Times, 1997. Mem.: The Century Assn. Office: Washington Post 1150 15th St NW Washington DC 20071-0002

**PAGE, WILLIAM MARION,** lawyer; b. Columbus, Ga., July 31, 1917; s. Roger McKeene and Louise Olivia (Seals) P.; m. Lucy Quillian Page, Feb. 8, 1941 (dec. 1982); children: John Roger, Jane Quillian Page McCamy, William Franklin (dec.); m. Barbara Brown Waddell, May 10, 1985 LLB, U. Ga., Athens, 1939, JD. Bar: Ga. 1938, U.S. Supreme Ct. 1955. Ptnr. Page

Scrantom Sprouse Tucker & Ford P.C., Columbus, Ga., 1939—. Bd. visitors U. Ga. Law Sch., 1969-74. With U.S. Army, 1941-46 Fellow: Lawyers Found. Ga., Am. Coll. Trial Lawyers; mem.: ABA, Columbus Bar Assn. (pres. 1946—47), Chattahoochee Circuit Bar Assn. (pres. 1948—49), State Bar Ga. (bd. govs. 1964—71), Chattahoochee River Club, Kiwanis. Home: 916 Overlook Dr Columbus GA 31906-3029 Office: PO Box 1199 Columbus GA 31902-1199 Business E-Mail: wmp@psstf.com.

**PAGE, WILLIS,** conductor; b. Rochester, NY, Sept. 18, 1918; Grad. with distinction, Eastman Sch. Music, Rochester., 1939. Mem. Rochester Philharm., 1937-40, Rochester Civic, 1939-40; prof. conducting Eastman Sch. Music, 1969-71. Guest condr. Sony concerts, Chiba, Japan, 1992. Mem. Boston Symphony Orch., 1940-55; prin. bass Boston Pops, 1947-55; condr. Cecilia Soc. Boston, 1952-54, New Orchestral Soc. Boston; assoc. condr. Buffalo Philharm., 1955-59; music dir./condr. Nashville Symphony Orch., 1959-67; music dir. Linwood Music Sch., 1955-59; 1st condr. Yomiuri Nippon Symphony, Tokyo, 1962-63; condr. Des Moines Symphony, 1969-71, Jacksonville (Fla.) Symphony Orch., 1971-83; founder, condr. St. John's River City Band, 1985-86; guest condr. Boston Pops, Toronto, Rochester Civic, Eastman-Rochester, Denver, Muncie, Jerusalem, St. Louis, Colorado Springs, Memphis, Hartford orchs., Yomiuri Nippon Symphony, 1988, 92; founding condr., exec. dir. First Coast Pops Orch., 1989; condr. all-state orchs. of N.Y., Iowa, Ky., Tenn., Fla., also national festivals; condr. 13 L.P. recordings including Symphony of the Air (Roger Williams soloist), Boston Festival Orch., Cook Labs., Nashville Symphony. Sgt. 95th inf. divsn. U.S. Army, 1943-45. Decorated Bronze Star; recipient Ford Found. European travel award, 1967. Address: 1567 Flanders Rd 302 Jacksonville FL 32207 Personal E-Mail: wpage11@comcast.net.

**PAGEL, ANDREW W.,** history educator; b. San Benito, Tex., June 17, 1972; s. Dennis W. Billings and Sue P. Pagel; m. Jill E. Eubank, June 1, 1996; children: Hadley D., Janie K. BA in History, Ky. Wesleyan Coll., Owensboro, 1994; MA in History, Murray State U., Ky., 2002. Nat. bd. tchr. cert. AYA SS/H Nat. Bd. for Profl. Tchg. Stds., 2005, cert. advanced placement U.S. history tchr. Coll. Bd., 2000, lic. nat. C coaching US Soccer Fedn., 1997. Us history tchr. Marshall County H.S., Benton, Ky., 1998—; social studies tchr. Calloway County H.S., Murray, Ky., 1997—98; social studies/sci. tchr. North Marshall Mid. Sch., Calvert City, Ky., 1995—97. Coaching adv. com. mem. Marshall County Soccer Assn., Calvert City, Ky., 2005—. Parks bd. mem. City of Calvert City, 2005—06. Writing fellow, Purchase Area Writers Project, 1998—. Republican. Baptist. Avocations: soccer, music, computer, travel. Home: 81 Woodfield Ln Calvert City KY 42029 Office: Marshall County High School 416 High School Rd Benton KY 42025 Office Phone: 270-527-1453. Business E-Mail: andrew.pagel@marshall.kyschools.us.

**PAGEL, PAUL STANLEY,** anesthesiologist; b. Madison, Wis., Dec. 6, 1957; s. Gerald Gordon and Mary Ellen (Young) P.; m. Judith A. May, Sept. 13, 1996. BS, Carroll Coll., 1979; MD, Med. Coll. Wis., 1986, MS, 1991, PhD, 1994. Intern St. Josephs Hosp., Milw., 1986-87; resident Med. Coll. Wis., Milw., 1987-90, instr. cardiac anesthesiology 1990—93, asst. prof., 1994—96, assoc. prof., 1996—99, prof. and dir. cardiac anesthesia, 1999—. Assoc. examiner Am. Bd. Anesthesiology. Contbr. articles to profl. jours.; editl. bd. Anesthesiology, Jour. of Cardiothoracic and Vascular Anesthesia. Rsch. Anesthesiology fellow Med. Coll. Wis., 1992-93, Rsch. fellow NIH, 1990-92. Office: Medical College Wisconsin MEB-M4280 8701 Watertown Plank Rd Milwaukee WI 53226 Business E-Mail: pspagel@mcw.edu.

**PAGET, JOEL HATHAWAY,** lawyer; b. Seattle, Mar. 21, 1945; s. John Bucher and Ruth (Hathaway) P.; m. Lorilee K. Nyholm, Aug. 13, 1966; children: Dene' Marie, Jeremy Hathaway. BA, Seattle Pacific U., 1967; JD, U. Wash., 1970. Bar: Wash. 1970, U.S. Dist. Ct. (we. dist.) Wash. 1971, U.S. Ct. Appeals (9th cir.) 1971, U.S. Supreme Ct. 1973, U.S. Tax Ct. 1972. Law clk. Wash. Ct. Appeals, Seattle, 1970-71; ptnr. Ryan, Swanson & Cleveland PLLC, Seattle, 1971—. Lectr. bus. law Seattle Pacific U., 1972-81. Contbr. articles to profl. jours. Bd. trustees Seattle Pacific U., 1972-2005, mem. alumni exec. bd., 1969—; sec.-treas. Christian Legal Soc. Puget Sound, Seattle, 1969-90; chmn. Seattle-King County Drug Commn., 1972-78; dir. Seattle Pacific Found., 1979—; bd. dirs. Seattle Pacific Credit Union, 1975-79; mem. Adv. Com. for Drug Abuse, Seattle, 1976-79; bd. dirs. Sammamish Bible Camp Assn., Seattle, 1974-77. Mem. Wash. State Bar Assn. (chmn. sect. taxation 1986-87, mem. bd. bar examienrs 1982-84), Am. Immigration Lawyers Assn. (chmn. Wash. chpt. 1984-85, mem. bd. govs. 1984-85), Harbor Club. Republican. Avocations: golf, swimming. Home: 16008 SE 24th St Bellevue WA 98008-5406 Office: Ryan Swanson & Cleveland PLLC 1201 3rd Ave Ste 3400 Seattle WA 98101-3034 Office Phone: 206-464-4224. Business E-Mail: paget@ryanlaw.com.

**PAGET, RUTH PENNINGTON,** academic administrator, educator; writer; b. Detroit, Dec. 12, 1963; d. Clarence and Beatrice May Pennington; m. Laurent Albert Paget, July 16, 1988; 1 child, Florence Isabelle Winifred. BA in East Asian Studies, U. Chgo., 1986. Mktg. mgr. T.L.I. Internat., Chgo., 1985—87; Japanese svcs. sec. Ernst & Young, Chgo., 1987—88; Japanese svc. coord. Deloitte & Touche, Paris, 1989—91; bilingual mkt. rschr. Chamberlain Rsch., Madison, Wis., 1996—97; focus group recruiter Martin Focus Groups, Va. Beach, Va., 1997—99; freelance reviewer Calif., 2000—; adminstrv. asst. Calif. State U., Monterey, Calif., 2002—. Author: The Edible Tao: Munching My Way Toward Enlightenment, 2003, Eating Soup with Chopsticks: Sweet Sixteen in Japan, 2003, Edible Alchemy: Making Life Magic, 2004, More Leisure than Money: Tales of a Military Wife in Virginia, 2005, China Hand: From the Great Wall to Olive Bull and Beyond, 2005; contbr. articles to publs.; to local newspapers; author: (global libr. column) Spl. Librs. Assn. San Francisco Bay Region. V.p. young execs. Am. C. of C., Paris, 1989—91; family group sec. USS Austin USN, Norfolk, Va., 1997—99; cross-cultural trainer Youth For Understanding, Paris, 1986—94, Chgo., 1986—94; v.p. Friends of Seaside Pub. Libr., 2004—05. Grantee, U.S.-China Peoples' Friendship Assn., 1979; Chrysler scholar, Youth for Understanding, 1980, U. Chgo. scholar, 1982—86. Mem.: Monterey Mus. Art, Oriental Art Soc., Alliance Francaise (bd. dirs., scholarship com.). Avocations: math, foreign languages, comparative religion, cooking, technology. Office: Calif State Univ Monterey 100 Campus Cr 82D Seaside CA 93955 Personal E-mail: rpenningtonpaget@aol.com, ruthmcfarland@aol.com. Business E-Mail: ruth_paget@csumb.edu.

**PAGHDIWALA, ABID F,** dentist; m. Seema Paghdiwala; 3 children. Grad., NJ Dental Sch., 1979. Pvt. practice dentist, 1979—. Mem.: Acad. Gen. Dentistry, Phila. County Dental Soc., Pa. Dental Assn., ADA. Office: Newtown Family Dentistry Tudor Sq 660 Newtown-Yardley Rd Newtown PA 18940 Office Phone: 215-504-4070. Office Fax: 215-504-4220. Business E-Mail: drafp@newtownfamilydentistry.com

**PAGLIA, CAMILLE,** writer, humanities educator; b. Endicott, N.Y., 1947; d. Pasquale John and Lydia (Colapietro) P. BA in English summa cum laude with highest honors, SUNY, Binghamton, 1968; MPhil, Yale U., 1971, PhD in English, 1974. Mem. faculty Bennington (Vt.) Coll., 1972-80; vis. lectr. Wesleyan U., 1980, Yale U., New Haven, 1980-84; asst. prof. humanities Phila. Coll. Performing Arts U. Arts, 1984—86, assoc. prof. humanities, 1987—91, prof. humanities, 1991—2000; Univ. prof. humanities and media studies U. Arts, Phila., 2000—. Spkr. in field. Author: Sexual Personae: Art and Decadence from Nefertiti to Emily Dickinson, 1990, Sex, Art, and American Culture, 1992, Vamps and Tramps: New Essays, 1994, Alfred Hitchcock's "The Birds", 1998, Break, Blow, Burn: Camille Paglia Reads Forty-Three of the World's Best Poems, 2005; columnist: Salon.com, 1995—2001; contbg. editor: Interview Magazine, 2001—. Mailing: Univ of the Arts 320 S Broad St Philadelphia PA 19102-4994 Office Phone: 215-717-6265.

**PAGLIARO, JAMES DOMENIC,** lawyer; b. Phila., Aug. 18, 1951; s. Domenic A. and Nancy I. (D'Amore) P.; m. Susan B. Boag, Aug. 25, 1973; children: Jamie C., Justin A. BA cum laude, LaSalle U., 1973; JD, Dickinson Law Sch., 1976. Bar: Pa. 1976, U.S. Dist. Ct. (ea. dist.) Pa. 1977, U.S. Ct. Appeals (3d, 4th, 8th, 9th and 10th cirs.) 1989, U.S. Supreme Ct. 1989. Regional atty. Gov. of Pa., Phila., 1976-79; sr. trial atty. office regional solicitor U.S. Dept. Labor, Phila., 1979-85; assoc. Morgan, Lewis & Bockius, LLP, Phila., 1985-88, ptnr. litigation, 1988—, mng. ptnr. litigation sect., 1999—. Chmn. Home & Sch. Bd. Norwood Acad., Chestnut Hill, Pa., 1983-87; vestry Hist. St. Paul's Ch., Elkins Park, Pa., 1993-94. Fellow Am. Coll. Trial Lawyers; mem. ABA, Pa. Bar Assn. (speaker continuing legal edn. 1987—), Phila. Bar Assn., Woolsach Honors Soc. Office: Morgan Lewis & Bockius LLP 1701 Market St Philadelphia PA 19103-2903 Office Phone: 215-963-5668. Business E-Mail: jpagliaro@morganlewis.com.

**PAGNANI, KEITH A.,** lawyer; b. NYC, 1964; BA, Dickinson Coll., 1986; JD, Cath. Univ. Law Sch., 1989. Bar: NY 1990, Conn. 1990. Joined Sullivan & Cromwell, NYC, 1989—, now ptnr., mergers & acquisitions and hiring ptnr. Office: Sullivan & Cromwell LLP 125 Broad St New York NY 10004-2498 Office Phone: 212-558-4000. Office Fax: 212-558-3588. Business E-Mail: pagnanik@sullcrom.com.

**PAGNI, ALBERT FRANK,** lawyer; b. Reno, Jan. 28, 1935; s. Bruno and Daisy Rose (Recami) Pagni; m. Nancy Lynne Thomas, Aug 12, 1961; children: Elisa, Michelle, Melissa, Michael. AB, U. Nev., 1961; JD, U. Calif., 1964. Bar: Nev. 1964. Assoc. Vargas, Dillon, Bartlett & Dixon, Reno, 1965—70; ptnr. Vargas & Bartlett and Jones Vargas, Reno, 1970—. Adv. bd. 9th Cir. Ct., chmn. adv. bd., 2006—; ct.-apptd. arbitrator; dist. ct. judge pro tem. Mem. Nev. Dist. Appeal Bd.; mem. hospice coun. St. Mary's Hosp.; mem. adminstrv. coun. U. Nev., 1974—81; treas. U. Nev. Legis. Commn., 1973—74, pres., 1975; bd. dirs. Better Bus. Bur. With U.S. Army, 1955—57. Recipient Outstanding Alumni award U. Nev., 1978. Master: Am. Inns Ct.; fellow: Am. Bd. Trial Advocates (nat. bd.), Nev. Law Found. (trustee, vice chair), Am. Coll. Barristers, Am. Coll. Trial Lawyers (state chair); mem.: ATLA, ABA, State Bar Nev. (bd. govs. 1976—87, v. chair 1984—85, pres.-elect 1985—86, pres. 1986—87), Am. Judicature Assn. (mediator, arbitrator 1990), Assn. Def. Counsel Calif. and Nev. (state chmn. 1983—85), Def. Rsch. Inst., Nev. Trial Lawyers Assn., Washoe County Bar Assn., Am. Softball Found. (bd. dirs.), Wolf Club, Order of the Coif. Office: 12th Fl 100 W Liberty St Fl 12 Reno NV 89501-1962 Office Phone: 775-786-5000.

**PAGNI, PATRICK JOHN,** mechanical engineering science educator, safety engineer; researcher; b. Chgo., Nov. 28, 1942; s. Frank and Helen P.; m. Carol DeSantis, Dec. 26, 1970 (div. Jan. 2000); children: Christina Marie, Catherine Ann, Patrick John Jr; m. Feriel Palmer, Mar. 21, 2003. B in Aeronautical Engring. magna cum laude, U. Detroit, 1965; SM, MIT, 1967, ME, 1969, PhD, 1970. Registered profl. mechanical engr., Calif., fire protection engr., Calif. Rsch. asst. MIT, Cambridge, 1965-70; asst. prof. dept. mech. engring. U. Calif., Berkeley, 1970-76, assoc. prof., 1976-81, prof., 1981—2003, prof. emeritus, 2003—, vice chmn. grad. study, 1986-89; acting assoc. dean Coll. Engring. U. Calif., 1990; assoc. faculty scientist Lawrence Berkeley Lab., 1976—. Vis. scientist Factory Mut. Research Corp., Norwood, Mass., 1980; cons. on fire safety sci. various orgns., 1972—; affiliate prof. fire protection engring. dept. Worcester Poly. Inst., 2000-03; vis. rsch. scholar U. Ulster, No. Ireland, 2000-03. Editor: Fire Science for Fire Safety, 1984, Fire Safety Science--Procs. of the First Internat. Symposium, 1986, Procs. of the Second Internat. Symposium, 1989; contbr. articles to profl. jours. Grantee NSF, NASA, Nat. Bur. Standards, Nat. Inst. Standards and Tech., U.S. Forest Svc., 1971—; Applied Mechanics fellow Harvard U., 1974, 77; Pullman Found. scholar, 1960. Mem. ASME, Am. Phys. Soc. (life), Combustion Inst., Soc. Fire Protection Engrs. (hon., Bono award for best paper 1999), Internat. Assn. Fire Safety Sci. (life mem., exec. com.), Tau Beta Pi, Pi Tau Sigma, Alpha Sigma Nu Democrat. Roman Catholic. Home: 1901 Ascot Dr Moraga CA 94556-1412 Office: U Calif Coll Engring Mech Engring Dept Berkeley CA 94720-1740 Office Phone: 925-376-4288. Business E-Mail: pjpagni@me.berkeley.edu.

**PAGON, ROBERTA ANDERSON,** pediatrician, educator; b. Boston, Oct. 4, 1945; d. Donald Grigg and Erna Louise (Goettsch) Anderson; m. Garrett Dunn Pagon Jr., July 1, 1967; children: Katharine Blye, Garrett Dunn III, Alyssa Grigg, Alexander Goettsch. BA, Stanford U., 1967; MD, Harvard U., 1972. Diplomate Am. Bd. Pediat., Am. Bd. Med. Genetics. Pediatric intern U. Wash. Affiliated Hosp., Seattle, 1972-73, resident in pediat., 1973-75; fellow in med. genetics U. Wash. Sch. Medicine, Seattle, 1976-79, asst. prof. pediat., 1979-84, assoc. prof., 1984-92, prof., 1992—. Prin. investigator, editor in chief GeneTests (www.genetests.org), Seattle, 1992—; mem. Am. Bd. Med. Genetics, 2002, 03; bd. sci. counselors Nat. Human Genome Rsch. Inst., NIH, 2000—04. Sponsor N.W. region U.S. Pony Club, 1985-94. Mem. Am. Soc. Human Genetics (bd. dirs. 2005—), Am. Coll. Med. Genetics, Western Soc. Pediat. Rsch., Phi Beta Kappa. Avocations: hiking, backpacking, horseback riding. Office: Gene Tests 9725 Third Ave NE Ste 602 Seattle WA 98115 Office Phone: 206-221-4674.

**PAGONIS, WILLIAM GUS,** retired army general; b. Charleroi, Pa., Apr. 30, 1941; s. Constantinos V. and Jennie (Kontos) P.; m. Cheryl Elaine Miller, June 14, 1964; children: Gust, Robert. BS, Pa. State U., 1964, MBA in Bus. Logistics, 1970. D in Pub. Svc. (hon.), Washington Jefferson Coll., 1997. Commd. 2d lt. U.S. Army, 1964, advanced through grades to lt. gen., 1991; comdr. 1097th Transp. Co. Vietnam 1968: div. transp. officer then corr officer 2d bn. 501st inf., 101st Airborne Div., Vietnam, 1970-71; pers. staff officer U.S. Army Mil. Pers. Ctr., Alexandria, Va., 1973-75; staff officer Office Chief of Legis. Liaison, Washington, 1975-76; comdr. 10th transp. bn. 7th Transp. Group, Ft. Eustis, Va., 1977-78; chief of staff 193d Inf. Brigade, Panama, 1980-81, comdr. Logistics Support Command, 1981-82; comdr. Div. Support Command, 4th Inf. Div., Ft. Carson, Colo., 1982-85; dir. transp., energy and troop support Office Dep. Chief of Staff for Logistics, Washington, 1989-90; comdg. gen. 22d Support Command, Dhahran, Saudi Arabia, 1990-91, 1990-92, 21st Support Command Europe, Germany, 1992-93; lt. gen., ret. U.S. Army, 1993; exec. v.p. logistics Sears & Roebuck Co., Hoffman Estates, Ill., 1993—. Author: Moving Mountains (Logistics Leadership and Management of the Gulf War), (one of top 30 best bus. books of 1992, top leadership book 1992 Soundview Exec. Book Summaries, 1992), 1992. Decorated D.S.M., Silver Star, Legion of Merit with oak leaf cluster, Bronze Star with 3 oak leaf clusters, Air medal with 2 oak leaf clusters, Meritorious Svc. medal with 4 oak leaf clusters, King Abdul Aziz 2d Class award Chief of Staff, Saudi Arabian Army, 1991, Kuwait Liberation medal Chief of Staff, Kuwait Army, 1992; recipient Merit and Honor award Govt. of Greece, 1991, Joseph C. Scheleen award Am. Soc. Transp. and Logistics, 1991, Man of Yr. award Modern Materials Handling, 1991, Grad. Man of Yr. award Alpha Chi Rho, 1991, AHEPA Man of Yr., 1992, Disting. Alumni award Pa. State U., 1994; named Hellenic Man of Yr., 1992; Pa. State U. fellow, 1992. Home: 202 Smalstig Rd Evans City PA 16033 Office: C&G Ranch LLC 202 Smalstig Rd Evans City PA 16033 Office Phone: 724-789-7680. Business E-Mail: pagonisg@genco.com.

**PAGTER, CARL RICHARD,** lawyer; b. Balt., Feb. 13, 1934; s. Charles Ralph and Mina (Amelung) P.; m. Judith Elaine Cox, May 6, 1978; 1 child by previous marriage: Corbin Christopher. AA, Diablo Valley Coll., 1953; BA, San Jose State U., 1955; LLB, U. Calif., Berkeley, 1964. Bar: Calif. 1965, D.C. 1977, U.S. Supreme Ct. 1976. Law clk. Kaiser Industries Corp., Oakland, Calif., 1963-64, counsel, 1964-70, assoc. counsel Washington, 1970-73, counsel Oakland, Calif., 1973-75, dir. govt. affairs Washington, 1975-76; v.p. sec., gen. counsel Kaiser Cement Corp., Oakland, Calif. 1976-88, cons., gen. counsel San Ramon, 1988-98, cons., 1998—. Author: (with A. Dundes) Urban Folklore from the Paperwork Empire, 1975, More Urban Folklore from the Paperwork Empire, 1987, Never Try to Teach a Pig to Sing, 1991, Sometimes the Dragon Wins, 1996, Why Don't Sheep Shrink When It Rains, 2000, A Sampling of Sacrelicious Folk Humor, 2005. Trustee Internat. Bluegrass Music Mus., Owensboro, Ky. With USNR, 1957—61, to comdr. USNR, 1978. Mem. Calif. Bar, Am. Folklore Soc., Calif. Folklore Soc., Calif. Bluegrass Assn. (founder, emer. bd. emeritus), Mariners Square Athletic Club. Republican. Home and Office: 17 Julianne Ct Walnut Creek CA 94595-2610

**PAI, SATISH UPENDRA,** publishing executive; b. Udupi, Karnataka, India, Nov. 26, 1941; s. Upendra Anantha and Parvathi Pai; m. Sandhya Satish, July 19, 1970; children: Nandana, Gautham. Dir. Manipal Press Ltd., 1960—; mng. dir. Manipal Media Network Ltd., 1989—. Editor Udayavani Daily, 1970, Tushara Mo., 1973, Roopathra Mo., 1976. Mem. Graphic Arts Tech. Found., IFRA, Fellow Inst. Printing. Avocations: stamp collecting/philately, photography, travel. Home: 38 Anant Nagar Manipal 576104 India Office: Manipal Media Network Ltd Udayavani Bld, Press Corner Manipal 576104 India Office Phone: 91-0820-2571151. Business E-Mail: satishpai@manipalmedia.com.

**PAIDOUSSIS, MICHAEL PANDELI,** mechanical engineering educator; b. Nicosia, Cyprus, Aug. 20, 1935; emigrated to Can., 1953, naturalized, 1976; s. Pandelis Aristeidis and Parthenope (Leptou) P. B in Engring., McGill U., 1958; PhD in Engring., U. Cambridge, 1963. Overseas fellow Gen. Electric Co., Erith, Kent, England, 1958-60; rsch. officer Atomic Energy of Can., Chalk River, Ont., 1963-67; with McGill U., Montreal, 1967—, prof., dept. mech. engring., 1976—, chmn., 1977-86, Thomas Workman prof., 1986—2000, Thomas Workman emeritus prof., 2000—. Cons. and rschr. in field. Author: 2 books; editor: Jour. Fluids and Structures; contbr. articles and books in field. Pres. Hellenic-Can. Solidarity Com. for Cyprus, 1974-80, Com. Pan-Can. de Solidarite pour Chypre, 1978-83; hon. consul gen. Republic of Cyprus, Montreal, 1983—. Recipient Brit. Assn. medal for high distinction in mech. engring., 1958, George Stephenson prize Inst. Mech. Engrs., 1976, commemorative medal for 125th ann. of Confederation of Can., 1993, medal Can. Congress Applied Mechs., 1995. Fellow Instn. of Mech. Engrs., ASME (Fluids Engring. award 1999), Can. Soc. Mech. Engring., Royal Soc. Can., Am. Acad. Mechanics, Can. Acad. Engring.; mem. Internat. Assn. Hydraulic Rsch., Internat. Assn. Structural Mechanics in Reactor Tech., Am. Acad. Mechanics (pres. 2005), Order Engrs. Que. Home: 2930 Edouard Montpetit #PH2 Montreal PQ Canada H3T 1J7 Office: 817 Ouest Rue Sherbrooke Montreal PQ Canada H3A 2K6 Office Phone: 514-398-6294. Business E-Mail: mary.fiorilli@mcgill.ca.

**PAIER, ADOLF ARTHUR,** computer company executive. director; b. Branford, Conn., Oct. 27, 1938; s. Adolf Arthur and Margaret Mary (Almond) P.; m. Geraldine Shnakis, Sept. 17, 1966; children: Nathaniel Jason, Andrew Joseph, Alena Catherine. AA. Quinnipiac Coll., 1958; BS in Econs., U. Pa., 1960. Audit mgr. Touche Ross & Co., Phila., 1960-67; pres., dir. Safeguard Scientifics, Inc., Wayne, Pa., 1967-92; chmn., CEO Healthworks Alliance, Inc., King of Prussia, Pa., 1992—2005; pres., CEO Novus Corp., Radnor, Pa., 1992—. Bd. dirs. Deltapaper, Levittown, Pa., Analytical Graphics, Malvern, Pa., Probaris Techs., Inc., Phila. Bd. dirs., treas. Univ. of Arts, Phila. bd. dirs. Lincoln Ctr. Family and Youth, Bridgeport, Pa.; bd. overseers U. Pa. Mus. Archaeology and Anthropology. Mem. Chief Execs. Orgn., Phila. Pres. Orgn., Phila. Country Club (bd. govs., treas.). Office: Novus Corp 5 Radnor Corp Ctr 100 Matsonford Rd Ste 520 Radnor PA 19087-4526 Office Phone: 610-964-9821.

**PAIGE, GLENN DURLAND,** political scientist, educator; b. Brockton, Mass., June 28, 1929; s. Lester Norman and Rita Irene (Marshall) P.; m. Betty Gail Grenier, Jan. 2, 1949 (div.); children: Gail, Jan, Donn, Sean, Sharon, Van; m. Glenda Hatsuko Naito, Sept. 1, 1973. Grad., Phillips Exeter Acad., 1947; AB, Princeton U., 1955; MA, Harvard U., 1957; PhD, Northwestern U., 1959; PhD (hon.), Soka U. 1992. Asst. prof. pub. administrn. Seoul Nat. U. 1959-61; asst. to assoc. prof. politics Princeton U., 1961-67; prof. polit. sci. U. Hawaii, Honolulu, 1967-92, prof. emeritus, 1992—. Author: The Korean Decision, 1968, The Scientific Study of Political Leadership, 1977, To Nonviolent Political Science, 1993, Nonkilling Global Political Science, 2002. Program chmn. Hawaii Gov.'s Conf. on Yr. 2000, 1970; faculty UN Univ. Internat. Leadership Acad., 1997; pres. Non-profit Ctr. for Global Nonviolence, 1994—. With U.S. Army, 1948-52. Decorated Commendation medal; recipient Seikyo Culture prize, 1982, Dr. G. Ramachandran award for internat. understanding, 1986, Anuvrat award for internat. peace, 1987, Jai Tulsi Anuvrat award, 1995; named Woodrow Wilson nat. fellow, 1955-56, Princeton U. Class of 1955 award, 1987, 3rd Gandhi Meml. lectr., New Delhi, 1990. Mem. Internat. Polit. Sci. Assn., Am. Polit. Sci. Assn. (Distng. Career award 200r, Hawaii Lifetime Peacemaker award 2005), Phi Beta Kappa. Home: 3653 Tantalus Dr Honolulu HI 96822-5033 Office Phone: 808-536-7442. E-mail: cgnv@hawaii.rr.com.

**PAIGE, HILLIARD WEGNER,** corporate financial executive, consultant; b. Hartford, Conn., Oct. 2, 1919; s. Joseph Wegner and Ruth (Hill) P.; m. Dorothea Magner, Dec. 8, 1945; children: Elizabeth, Deborah, Hilliard, Jr. BSME, Worcester Poly. Inst., 1941, D (hon.) of Engring., 1971. Sr. v.p. for aerospace and computer ops. GE, N.Y.C., 1941—71; pres. Gen. Dynamics, St. Louis, 1971—73; chmn., CEO Satellite Bus. Sys., Inc., Washington, 1973—76; vice-chmn. bd. Internat. Energy Assocs., Ltd., Washington, 1976—85; chmn. bd. H.A. Knott, Ltd., Silver Spring, Md., 1984—89. Vice-chmn. The Atlantic Coun. of U.S., 1987—, Gallager Marine Systems, Inc., 1993—. Patentee in field; contbr. articles to profl. jours. Mem. Def. Sci. Bd. U.S. Dept. Def., Washington, 1973-78; trustee Worcester Poly. Inst., Mass., 1974—. Recipient Pub. Service award NASA, 1969, Order of Merit Italy, 1970, Engr. of Year award Greater Phila. Engring Council, 1960 Fellow AIAA (founding dir.), Explorers Club (nat.); mem. NAE. Clubs: Metropolitan, Chevy Chase (Washington); Conquistadores del Cielo. Republican. Congregationalist. Avocations: skiing, tennis, scuba diving, golf. Home and Office: 5834 Williamsburg Landing Dr Williamsburg VA 23185 Office Phone: 757-220-2797. Office Fax: 757-220-2149.

**PAIGE, JEFFERY MAYLAND,** sociologist, educator; b. Providence, June 15, 1942; s. Charles Warren and Dorothy Frances (Rice) P.; m. Karen Ericksen, Apr. 30, 1966 (div. 1980). AB summa cum laude, Harvard U., 1964; PhD, U. Mich., 1968. Asst. prof. U. Calif., Berkeley, 1968-76; assoc. prof. U. Mich., Ann Arbor, 1976-82, prof., 1982—, dir. ctr for rsch. on social orgn., 1992-97; vis. scholar MIT, Cambridge, Mass., 1998. Vis. lectr. U. Ctrl. Am., San Salvador, El Salvador, 1990, Fla. Internat. U., Miami, 1992; internat. observer Nicaraguan Nat. Adv. Comm. on Atlantic Coast, Managua, 1986. Author: Agrarian Revolution, 1975 (Sorokin award 1976), Coffee and Power, 1997; co-author: The Politics of Reproductive Ritual, 1981. Fulbright fellow, 1990, Kellog fellow, 1991; rsch. grantee NSF, 1990-92. Mem. Am. Sociol. Assn. (coun. chair polit. econ. of world sys. sect. 1987-89), Latin Am. Studies Assn., Sociol. Rsch. Assn. Democrat. Avocations: hiking, skiing, sailing. Office: U Mich Dept Sociology Ann Arbor MI 48109

**PAIGE, KATHLEEN K.,** naval officer; b. Schenectady, N.Y., Aug. 31, 1948; m. David Tuma. BS, U. Mich., N.Y., 1970; MS. Naval Postgrad. Sch., 1976; grad., Def. Sys. Mgmt. Coll.; grad. program for execs., Cornell U. Commd. USN, advanced through grades to rear admiral; acquisition mgr. Navy's Std. Embedded Computer Resource Office; AEGIS C3 warfare officer USN; baseline mgr. combat sys. divsn. AEGIS Shipbuilding Program; chief engr. Naval Surface Warfare Ctr., Port Hueneme; tech. dir. AEGIS Program Office; comdr. Naval Surface Warefare Ctr., Arlington, Va., 1996-98, admiral, 1998—. Decorated Legion of Merit. Office: Naval Sea Systems Command SE#1100 1333 Isaac Hull Ave Washington DC 20376-1100

**PAIGE, RODERICK RAYNOR,** educational consultant, former secretary of education; b. Monticello, Miss., June 17, 1933; div., one child. BS, Jackson State U., 1955; MS, Ind. U., 1964, PhD, 1969. Head football coach Utica Jr. Coll., 1957—67, Jackson St. U., 1962—69; dean Coll. Edn. Tex. So. U., 1984—94, developer Ctr. Excellence in Urban Edn.; supt. Houston Ind. Sch. Dist., 1994—2000; sec. U.S. Dept. Edn., Washington, 2001—05; co-founder, chmn. Chartwell Edn. Group LLC, NYC, 2005—. Est. Ctr. for Excellence in Urban Edn., Tex. Southern U.; created Peer Exam., Evaluation, Redesign

(PEER) program. Co-author: A Declaration of Beliefs and Visions. Mem. NAACP; mem. adv. bd. Tex. Commerce Bank, Am. Leadership Forum. Recipient Harold W. McGraw, Jr. Prize in Edn., 2000; named Supt. of the Yr., Nat. Assn. Black Sch. Educators, 2000, Nat. Supt. Yr., Am. Assn. Sch. Administr. 2001. Mem. review coms. Tex. Edn. Agy., State Bd. Edn. Task Force H.S. Edn.; chair, Youth Employment Issues Nat. Com. Employment Policy U.S. Dept. Labor subcom.; mem. Nat. Assn. Advancement Colored People, Edn. Com. States, Coun. Great City Schs.(recipient Richard R. Green award for Outstanding Urban Educator, 1996). Office: Chartwell Education Group LLC Empre State Bldg Ste 7506 New York NY 10118 E-mail: paige@chartwelleducation.com.*

**PAIGE, VIVIAN JO-ANN,** accountant; b. Memphis, May 7, 1960; d. Charles Thomas and Mary Elizabeth (Manning) P. BS, Old Dominion U., 1981, MBA, 1994. CPA, Va. With IRS, Norfolk, Va., 1980-85; pres. Individual Returns Svcs. Inc., Norfolk, 1991-95; prin. Vivian J. Paige, CPA, P.C., 1986—; adj. instr. acctg. Old Dominion U., 2000—. Mem. acctg. dept. coun. Old Dominion U., 2000—. Bd. dirs. St. Columba Ecumenical Ministries, Inc., 1989-93, v.p. bd. dirs., 1990-91, pres. bd. dirs., 1992-93, Neighborhood Network steering com., 1996-2000, sec. Real Estate Bd. of Equalization, 1999-2001, bd. dirs. 2001-04, pres., 2002-05; co-founder Norfolk United Facing Race, 2001. With USAR, 1979-81. Mem. AICPA, NAFE, AAUW, NAACP, Urban Leauge, Va. Soc. CPAs. Avocations: music, singing, computers. Business E-Mail: vivian@vjpcpa.com.

**PAIK, HO JUNG,** physics professor; b. Seoul, Republic of Korea, Mar. 25, 1944; s. In Kee Paik and Young Pal Choi; m. Minja Koh Paik; children: Ellen Trina Jeong, Terri Wren. PhD, Stanford U., Calif., 1968—74. Rsch. assoc. Stanford U., 1974—78; asst. prof. physics U. Md., College Park, 1978—83, assoc. prof. physics, 1983—89, prof., 1989—. Disting. vis. scientist Jet Propulsion Lab., Pasadena, Calif., 2004—. Grantee Sloan fellowship, Sloan Found., 1981—83. Fellow: Am. Phys. Soc.; mem.: Assn. Korean Physicists Am. (pres. 2005—). Achievements include development of superconducting gravity gradiometer; research in precision tests of the laws of gravity. Office: Univ Md Dept Physics College Park MD 20742 Office Fax: 301-405-6087. Business E-Mail: hpaik@umd.edu.

**PAIK, JOHN KEE,** structural engineer; b. Seoul; came to U.S., 1955; s. Nam Suk and Kyong Ock (Yun) P.; m. Aine Fenoula Ievers, Feb. 20, 1970; 1 child, Brian Ievers Paik. BSCE. So. Meth. U., 1961; PhD, NYU, 1975. Lic. profl. engr. N.Y., N.J., Conn., Pa., Md., Mass., Vt., Ga., Fla., N.C. Chief engr. T.Y. Lin and Assocs., N.Y.C., 1960-67; chief structural engr. Soros Assocs., N.Y.C., 1967-68; sr. project engr. Stauffer Chem. Co., Dobbs Ferry, N.Y., 1975-77; prin. founder Paik and Assocs., Westchester County, N.Y., 1977—; chmn., founder The Future Home Tech. Inc., Port Jervis, N.Y., 1986—; chmn., pres. J.K.P. Constrn. Co. Inc., Mohegan Lake, N.Y., 1989—. Adj. assoc. prof. Grad. Sch. Engring. Manhattan Coll., Bronx, 1985; lectr. Grad. Sch. Engring. Polytech. U., Bklyn., 1973-85, Cooper Union, N.Y.C., 1972. Mem. ASCE, NSPE, Am. Inst. Steel Constrn., Prestressed Concrete Inst., N.Y Acad. Scis., Am. Concrete Inst., Post Tensioning Inst., Constrn. Specifications Inst., Am. Arbitration Assn. (dispute arbitrator, constrn.), So. Meth. U. Alumni Club (pres. 1964), Chi Epsilon. Republican. Methodist. Achievements include the design of over 200 million sq. feet of comml., residential, instl. structures including several highrise bldgs. over 40 stories in N.Y.C. and White Plains, N.Y. Home: Dyckman Dr Mohegan Lake NY 10547 Office: 16 Dyckman Dr Mohegan Lake NY 10547 Office Phone: 914-526-6500. Personal E-mail: jkpaik@optonline.net.

**PAIK, MYUNGHEE CHO,** statistician, educator; b. Seoul, Republic of Korea, Nov. 2, 1958; d. Seong-Yun Cho and Yong-Hee You; m. Yi Hyon Paik, Dec. 12, 1981; 1 child, Jane. PhD, U. Pitts., 1987. Prof. Columbia U., N.Y.C., 1988—. Author: (textbook) Statistical Methods for Rates and Proportions (Calderone Prize, 1989). Grantee, NIH. Mem.: Am. Statis. Assn. (regional adv. com. mem.). Home: 6 Farmington Ct Princeton Junction NJ 08550 Office: Columbia U 600 W 168th St New York NY 10032

**PAIK, YOUNHEE,** artist; b. Korea; BFA, Seoul Nat. U.; MFA, San Francisco Art Inst. Exhibitions include Gallery Hyundai, Seoul, Saint Peter's Church, NYC, Brenda Taylor Gallery, TOTAL Mus., Seoul, Kennedy Arts Ctr., Oakland, Calif., Nat. Mus. Contemporary Art, Seoul, San Jose Mus. of Art, San Jose. Calif., Eloise Pickard Smith Gallery, Santa Cruz, Calif., Art Mus. of South Tex., Venice Biennale, Nat. Mus. Modern Art, Mex., Triton Mus., Santa Clara, Calif., Represented in permanent collections Ho Am Art Mus., Byuck San Corp., Triton Mus., San Jose Mus., Korean Cultural Service Nat. Mus. Contemporary Art, Pacific Bell. Home: 448 W 37 St New York NY 10018*

**PAIKEDAY, THOMAS M.,** lexicographer, linguistic consultant; arrived in U.S., 1962, arrived in Can., 1964; m. Mary Kurien Kizhakethottam, Jan. 4, 1967; children: Anthony, Anne-Marie. LPH, Coll. of Jesuits, 1955; BA with 1st class honors, Madras Christian Coll., 1958; MA, U. Madras, 1960; postgrad, Boston Coll., 1962—63, U. Mich., 1963—64. Lectr. English St. Joseph's Coll., Tiruchy, Madras, India, 1958—59, Ramjas Coll. Delhi, India, 1960—61; copy editor Statesman, New Delhi, 1961—62; asst. lexicographer W.J. Gage Ltd.: Toronto, Ont., Canada, 1964—66; editor Ont. Min. Edn., Toronto, 1967—73; chief lexicographer Lexicography, Inc., Brampton, Ont., Canada. 1973—. Cons. Collier-Macmillan Can., Toronto, 1980-81, Can. advisor Collins Publs., Glasgow, Scotland, 1981-82. Chief editor Winston Interm. Dictionary, 1969, Compact Dictionary of Canadian English, 1970. Winston Canadian Dictionary, eiem. edit., 1975, New York Times Everyday Dictionary, 1982, The Penguin Canadian Dictionary, 1990, The User's Webster, 2000; author: The Native Speaker is Dead!, 1985; contbr. articles to profl. jours. Mem. Dictionary Soc. N.Am., MLA. Am. Dialect Soc., Am. Name Soc. Roman Catholic. Avocations: computer applications in lexicography, tennis, swimming. Office: Lexicography Inc 83 Sunny Meadow Blvd Brampton ON Canada L6R 1Z3 Office Phone: 905-790-7076. E-mail: thomaspaikeday@yahoo.ca.

**PAIN, BETSY M.,** lawyer; b. Albertville. Ala., Aug. 29, 1950; d. Charles Riley and Jean Faye (Rains) Stone; m. William F. Pain, Nov. 18, 1977 (div. July 30, 2003); children: Taylor Holland, Emily Anne Pain. AA, Northeastern Okla. A&M, Miami, 1970; BA, U. Okla., 1974, JD, 1976. Bar: Okla. 1977; U.S. Dist. Ct. (we. dist.) 1979. Staff atty. Okla. Dept. Corrections, Oklahoma City, 1978-79; gen. counsel Okla. Pardon and Parole Bd., Oklahoma City, 1979-84, exec. dir. 1983—88; corp. counsel Roberts, Schornick & Assocs., Inc., Norman, Okla., 1990-2000, Atkins Benham, Inc., 2002; chief legal officer The Benham Cos., LLC, Oklahoma City, 2002—. Editor: (newsletter) RSA Environ. Report, 1991—. With extended family program Juvenile Svcs., Inc. Cleveland County, Okla., 1983-91. Mem. NAFE, Okla. Bar Assn., Assn. Corp. Counsel, Phi Alpha Delta. Democrat. Methodist. Avocations: reading, needlecrafts, church activities. Office: The Benham Cos LLC 9400 N Broadway Oklahoma City OK 73114 Office Phone: 405-478-5353. E-mail: betsy.pain@benham.com.

**PAIN, GEORGE H.,** lawyer; b. Corry, Pa., Nov. 18, 1950; BA, BS cum laude, Bucknell U., 1973; JD cum laude, U. Conn., 1977; LLM, NYU, 1988. Bar: Conn. 1977, U.S. Dist. Ct. Conn. 1981, NY 1986, U.S. Dist. Ct. NY (We dist.) 1986, Ill. 1988. Assoc. Holland & Twachtman, Glastonbury, Conn., 1977—78; sr. counsel Environ. Law Inst., Washington, 1978—80; assoc. counsel Olin Chem. Group, Stamford, Conn., 1980—85; with Jaeckle, Fleischmann & Mugel, 1985—86; of counsel Olin Corp., East Alton, Ill., 1986—88, sr. counsel, 1988—91, chief counsel 1991—94, dep. gen. counsel, 1995—96; v.p., gen. counsel, sec. Primex Technologies Inc., St. Petersburg, Fla., 1997—2000; v.p., gen. counsel, asst. sec. Gen. Dynamics Ordinance and Tactical Systems Inc., St. Petersburg, Fla., 2001—02; v.p., gen. counsel, sec. Olin Corp., Norwalk, Conn., 2002—. Adj. prof. law Stetson U., 2001—02.

Mem. editl. adv. bd.: Environmental Law Reporter, 1982—91. Mem.: ABA, Am. Corp. Counsel Assn., Ill. State Bar Assn. Office: Olin Corp Legal Dept 190 Carondelet Plz Ste 1530 Clayton MO 63105 E-mail: ghpain@olin.com.

**PAINCHAUD, PHILLIP ANDRE,** metrologist; b. Somerville, Mass., Apr. 24, 1919; s. Phillip Andre Painchaud and Gertrude Marie Shanley; m. Josephine Daisy Wandschneider, Dec. 18, 1943 (dec. Feb. 1988); children: Phillip A. III, Denise Michele, Valerie Yvonne; m. Arlene Roberts Painchaud, July 12, 1992 (dec. Dec. 1999). Student, MIT and U. Ill., 1943, R.I. State Coll., 1938-41; BS in Engring., Pacific States U., 1947. Lic. profl. engr., Calif. Gen. supr. metrology Northrop Corp., Anaheim, Calif., 1948-65; dir. corp. stds. E-H Rsch. Labs., Oakland, Calif., 1965-70; sr. scientist Alcon Labs., Ft. Worth, 1970-71; dir. mktg. Metron Corp., Upland, Calif., 1971-72, 78-79; cons. Painchaud Cons., Brea, Calif., 1970—. Vice-chair Calif. Profl. Metrology Com., Sacramento, 1965—74; chair Gov.'s Commn. Metrology, Sacramento, 1967—68; mem. metrology adv. bd. Calif. State Poly. U., San Luis Obispo, 1970—76. Columnist The Std., 1993—. Mem. curriculum bd. Calif. State U.-Dominguez Hills, Carson, 1998—. With U.S. Signal Corps, 1942-45. Laureate Woodington award Meas. Sci. Conf. Inc., 1996; disting. vis. scholar Butler County C.C., 1996. Fellow Precision Measurements Assn. (co-founder 1958, exec. dir. 1980-89, life, pres. 1963-64), IEEE (life, sr. mem.); mem. Internat. Soc. Weighing and Measurements (life, sr. mem., gov. precision measurement divsn. 1997-99), Instrument Soc. Am. (life, sr. mem., dir. met. divsn. 1966-70), Am. Soc. for Quality (sr. mem.), ENG Club San Francisco. Avocations: computer operations, photography. Home and Office: 1110 W Dorothy Dr Brea CA 92821-2017 Office Phone: 714-529-6604. Office Fax: 714-529-1109. E-mail: painchaud4@cs.com.

**PAINE, ALAN,** poet; b. Panama City, Fla., Nov. 30, 1956; s. Charles Russell and Edna Pearl (Pierce) Williams. Student, Las Vegas, 1978—80, Taft Coll., 1975—77. Adj. prof. S. Nev. CC, Las Vegas, 1996—99; pres. Diogenes Prodns., Las Vegas, 2000—. Prodr., dir.; actor: (plays) What Happens to a Dream Deferred; author: (screenplays) Clear Skies on Tuesday, Shadow Chasers, The Love Child, What Kind of Fool, Ode to Madonna and Other Poems, 1991, numerous poems; actor: (plays) Raisin in the Sun, Don't Bother Me, I can't Cope, No Place to be Somebody; (films) No Not One. Counselor S. Nev. Suicide Prevention Ctr., Las Vegas, 1992. Recipient Golden Poet award, World Poetry, Inc., 1991, 1992, cert. of spl. recognition, Watermark Press, award of merit, Verses, cert. of honor, Hidden Springs Rev., Critics Choice award, Nat. Libr. Poetry, 1996, Editors Choice award, Poetry.com, 2006.

**PAINE, JAMES CARRIGER,** federal judge; b. Valdosta, Ga., May 20, 1924; s. Leon Alexander and Josie Carriger (Jones) P.; m. Ruth Ellen Bailey, Sept. 8, 1950; children: James Carriger, Jonathan Jones, JoEllen. BS, Columbia U., 1947; LL.B., U. Va., 1950, JD, 1970. Bar: Fla. 1950. Mem. firm Earnest, Lewis, Smith & Jones, West Palm Beach, Fla., 1950-54, Jones Adams Paine & Foster, 1954-60, Jones Paine & Foster, 1960-79; judge U.S. Dist. Ct. (so. dist.) Fla., West Palm Beach. 1979-92, sr. judge, 1992—. Bd. dirs., pres. Children's Home Soc. Fla., 1978-80; mem. bd. Episcopal Diocese S.E. Fla. Served to lt. USNR, 1943-47. Mem. Greater West Palm Beach C. of C. (pres. 1973-74), Palm Beach County Bar Assn. Democrat. Office: US Dist Ct 701 Clematis St West Palm Beach FL 33401-5101

**PAINE, MARLIN CRAIG,** band director; b. Allentown, Pa., Apr. 15, 1954; s. Jay Donald and Nancy Ann Paine; m. Mary Margaret Pfeiffer, June 14, 1975. BS, Hartwick Coll., 1976; MusM, U. Miami, Coral Gables, Fla., 1980: Band dir. Deposit (N.Y.) Cen. Schs., 1976—79, Parkland H.S., Orefield, Pa., 1980—82; dir. of bands Bangor (Pa.) H.S., 1982—. Mem. Allentown (Pa.) Band, 1982—; guest condr. band festivals, N.Y. and Pa. Mem.: Nat. Band Assn., Pa. Music Educators Assn. (mem. exec. bd. 1985—91, Citation of Excellence 1998). Office: Bangor H S 187 Five Points Richmond Rd Bangor PA 18013

**PAINE, ROBERT J.,** environmental scientist, consultant; s. Norman Emory and Jane T. Paine; m. Beth Stephanie Fuller, Aug. 4, 1979; children: Natalie, Nathan, Emory. BS in Atmospheric Sci., SUNY, Albany, 1973; MS in Meteorology, MIT, Cambridge, Mass., 1975. Cert. qualified environ. profl. Inst. Profls. Environ. Practice. Air quality scientist ENSR Corp., Westford, Mass., 1975—2004, tech. dir., 2004—. Com. mem. Medford Clean Energy Com., 2003—. Mem.: Air and Waste Mgmt. Assn. (chair meteorology com. 2000—03), Am. Meteorol. Soc. (chair com. on meteorol. aspects air pollution 1996—98, cert. consulting meteorologist 1983). Avocations: music, photography, gardening. Office: ENSR Corp 2 Technology Park Dr Westford MA 01886

**PAINE, ROBERT TREAT,** chemistry educator; b. Colorado Springs, Colo., Dec. 15, 1944; Robert T. and Marietta H. Paine; m. Bonnie Pauly Paine, Aug. 20, 1967; children: Andrew S., Matthew H., Joanna M. BS, U. Calif., Berkeley, 1966; PhD, U. Mich., 1970. Postdoctoral work Northwestern U., Evanston, Ill., 1970-72, Los Alamos (N.Mex.) Nat. Lab., 1972-74, cons., 1974—; asst. prof. U. N.Mex., Albuquerque, 1974-78, assoc. prof., 1978-82, prof., 1982—. Disting. prof., 2005—. Contbr. articles to profl. jours. Trainee NASA, 1966-69. Fellow AAAS; mem. Am. Chem. Soc. Office: U NMex Dept Chemistry Albuquerque NM 87131-0001 Office Phone: 505-277-1661. E-mail: rtpaine@unm.edu.

**PAINE, STEVEN L.,** school system administrator; m. Jackie Paine; 4 children. Grad., Fairmont State Coll.; MS in Ednl. Adminstrn., W.Va. U., PhD in Ednl. Leadership. Tchr. Harrison, Upshur and Morgan Counties, W.Va.; curriculum dir.; asst. prin.; prin.; county supt. Morgan County; dep. state supt. schs. W.Va. Dept. Edn., 2003—05, state supt. schs., 2005—. Recipient Milken Family Found. Nat. Educator Award. Office: W Va Dept Edn 1900 Kanawha Blvd E Charleston WV 25305 E-mail: dvermill@access.k12.wv.us.

**PAINE, WALTER CABOT,** journalist, consultant; b. Brookline, Mass., May 9, 1923; s. Richard Cushing and Ellen Eliot Paine; m. Ethel Landon Penzel, Dec. 1948 (div. Aug. 14, 1958); children: Michael, Christopher, Piera; m. Eleanor Cole Meyer, Aug. 27, 1959 (div. June 16, 1970); children: Alita. Benjamin; m. Barbara Ann Moyer, June 10, 1995. Student, St. John's Coll., Annapolis, Md., 1942—43; AB cum laude, Harvard U., 1949; postgrad., Columbia U., 1951. Cert. scuba diver, lic. capt. USCG, 1985. Assoc. editor Balt. Sunpapers, 1951—53; editor-in-chief, pubr. Valley News, West Lebanon, NH. 1956—80. Pres. Keene (N.H.) Pub. Co., 1955—80; dir. Chelsea Green Pub., White River Junction, Vt., 1995—; cons. Montshire Mus. Sci., Norwich, Vt., 1990—, founder, chmn., 1974—90. Trustee U Vt., Burlington, 1963—71. Sgt. USAF, 1943—46. Recipient Granite State award for outstanding pub. svc., N.H. State Univ. Sys., 1991. Avocations: ocean racing, marine research, music, poetry. Home: 213 Palmer Rd Enfield Center NH 03749 Office: Montshire Mus Sci 1 Montshire Rd Norwich VT 05055 Personal E-mail: verve@valley.net.

**PAINE, WILLIAM H.,** lawyer; b. 1961; BA cum laude, Amherst Coll. 1983; JD cum laude, Boston Univ., 1987. Bar: Mass. 1987. Ptnr., co-chmn. Securities Enforcement Litigation group Wilmer Cutler Pickering Hale & Dorr, Boston. Named a Mass. Super Lawyer, Boston Mag., 2004. Office: Wilmer Cutler Pickering Hale & Dorr 60 State St Boston MA 02109 Office Phone: 617-526-6134. Office Fax: 617-526-5000. Business E-Mail: william.paine@wilmerhale.com.

**PAINO, JAVIER E.,** physician; b. Lima, Peru, Mar. 5, 1965; arrived in U.S., 1989; s. Aldo L. Paino and Maria M. Scarpati. MD, Fed. Parana U., Brazil, 1990; PhD, George Washington U., 1996; postgrad., U. Miami, 1990—92; MSSM in /Neurosurgery, NYU, 1996—. Cert. Peruvian Coll. Physicians and Surgeons. Rescue diver Marine Corps, Lima, Peru, 1982—83; asst. prof. Stanley Kaplan, Washington 1992—96, Balt., 1992—96. Cons. new product devel. Peikard Labs., Lima, PR, Peru, 1989—95. Recipient Physician of Yr. award, Mt. Sinai Sch. Medicine,NYU, 2001; scholar, Brazilian Govt., 1983—89. Mem.: N.Y. Acad. Sci., Soc. for Neurosci., Am. Assn. Neurol. Surgery, N.Am. Skull Base Soc.

**PAINTER, BORDEN W.,** former academic administrator; BA in History, Trinity Coll., MA in History, 1959; PhD in History, Yale U., 1965; MDiv cum laude, Gen. Theol. Sem. Ordained Episc. priest. Asst. prof. history to prof. history Trinity Coll., Hartford, Conn., 1964—2004, chmn. history dept., 1974—79, 1989—93; sec. faculty, 1984—87, dean faculty, 1984—87, acting pres., 1994—95, 2003—04, pres. emeritus, 2004—. Chmn. bd. trustees, Cesari Barbieri Endowment for Italian Studies Trinity Coll., dir. Italian Programs, including Rome program and Elderhostel in Italy. Author: numerous publs. and papers. Recipient Mead History prize, 1955.

**PAINTER, JACK TIMBERLAKE,** civil engineer; b. Kincaid, W.Va., July 23, 1930; s. Troy Earl and Nannie Bell (Proffit) P. BSCE, W.Va. U., 1950, MSCE, 1955. Instr. civil engring. W.Va. U., 1950-51, 53-55; mem. faculty La. Tech U., Ruston, 1955—; prof. civil engring. La. Tech U., 1962-92; Alumni Found. prof. La. Tech U., 1977-78; prof. emeritus La. Tech U., 1992—. Vis. lectr. Manhattan Coll., Coll. Forestry, SUNY, Syracuse, Cornell U., U. Wis., summers 1954-60 Nat. pres. Circus Fans Assn. Am., 1967; lic. layreader Episcopal Ch. Served with USNR, 1951-52, comdr. res., 1966-90. Named Man of Year Omicron Delta Kappa, 1972, The Jack T. Painter Professorship in Engring. in his honor, 2003; Faculty fellow NSF, 1958—59. Fellow ASCE (life, 11 Outstanding Prof. award 1969-90); mem. Am. Congress Surveying and Mapping, La. Engring. Soc. (Charles M. Kerr Pub. Rels. award 1990), Am. Soc. Engring. Edn., Tau Beta Pi (Outstanding Prof. award 1963, 68, 74, 78), Chi Epsilon (Nat. Excellent Tchg. award 1985). Address: 101 Biel Lane New Bern NC 28562

**PAINTER, JOHN HOYT,** engineer; b. Winfield, Kans., Mar. 27, 1934; s. John Paul and Marjorie Marietta (Slack) P.; m. Joy Lou Vaughan, June 7, 1955; children: John Mark, Paul Burton, William Vaughan, Joy Lynn. BS, U. Ill., 1961, MS, 1962; postgrad., Coll. William and Mary, 1967—69; PhD, So. Meth. U., 1972. Apollo comm. engr.; tchr. astronauts Manned Spacecraft Ctr. NASA, Houston, 1962—65; sr. engr. Motorola Govt. Electronics divsn., Scottsdale, Ariz., 1965—67; rsch. engr. NASA Langley Rsch. Ctr., Hampton, Va., 1967—74; assoc. prof. elec. engring. Tex. A&M U., College Station, 1974—79, prof. elec. engring., 1979—, prof. computer sci., 1989—, prof. aerospace engring., 1999—. Pres. ALTAIR Corp. cons., College Station, 1980—; tchr. Christian eschatology seminars; adj. instr. Nat. Emergency Response and Rescue Training Ctr., 2003-. Author: The Church Visited, 2002; patentee digital signal processing and fuzzy logic. With USAF, 1953—58. Recipient Recognition cert. NASA, 1975; GE Found. fellow, 1962. Mem.: AIAA, IEEE (life). Avocation: radio operating. Office: Tex A&M U Dept Aero Engring College Station TX 77843-3141 Office Phone: 979-696-0429. Business E-Mail: painter@tamu.edu.

**PAINTER, MARK PHILIP,** judge; b. Cin., Apr. 6, 1947; s. John Philip and Marjorie (West) P.; m. Sue Ann Painter. BA, U. Cin., 1970, JD, 1973. Bar: Ohio 1973, U.S. Dist. Ct. (so. dist.) Ohio 1973, U.S. Supreme Ct. 1980. Assoc. Smith & Schnacke (now part of Thompson Hine), 1973-78; pvt. practice Cin., 1978-82; judge Hamilton County Mcpl. Ct., Cin., 1982-95, Ohio 1st Dist. Ct. Appeals, Cin., 1995—. Adj. prof. law U. Cin., 1990—; lectr. in field. Author: The Legal Writer: 40 Rules for the Art of Legal Writing, 2002, 3d edit., 2005; co-author: Ohio DUI Law, 1988, 15th edit., 2006, Ohio Appellate Practice, 2003, 3rd edit., 2005, William Howard Taft, 2004; mem. editl. bd.: Criminal Law Jour. Ohio, 1989—92; contbr. articles to profl. jours. Mem. bd. commrs. on grievances and discipline Ohio Supreme Ct., 1993—95; mem. Rep. Ctrl. Com., Cin., 1972—82; bd. dirs. Citizens Sch. Com., Cin., 1974—76; trustee Freestore Foodbank, Cin., 1984—90, Friends of William Howard Taft Birthplace, 2002—, Mary Jo Brueggeman Meml. Found., Cin., 1981—92. Recipient Superior Jud. Svc. award Ohio Supreme Ct., 1982, 84, 85, award for Superior Writing, Green Bag legal jour., 2005. Mem. ABA, Ohio State Bar Assn., Cin. Bar Assn. (trustee 1988-90), Am. Judges Assn., Am. Judicature Soc., Am. Soc. Writers on Legal Subjects, Potter Stewart Inn of Ct. (master of bench emeritus), Bankers Club. Home: 2449 Fairview Ave Cincinnati OH 45219-1170 Office: Ct of Appeals William Howard Taft Law Ctr 230 E 9th St Cincinnati OH 45202-2174 Office Phone: 513-946-3444. E-mail: JuqPainter@aol.com.

**PAINTER, NELL IRVIN,** historian, educator, writer; b. Houston, Aug. 2, 1942; BA, U. Calif., Berkeley, 1964; student, U. Bordeaux, France, 1962-63, U. Ghana, 1965-66; MA, UCLA, 1967; PhD, Harvard U., 1974. Teaching fellow Harvard U., Cambridge, Mass., 1969-70, 72-74; asst. prof. history U. Pa., Phila., 1974-77, assoc. prof., 1977-80; prof. history U.N.C., Chapel Hill, 1980-88, Princeton (N.J.) U., 1988-91, acting dir. Afro-Am. Studies Program, 1990-91, Edwards Prof. Am. History, 1991—. Russell Sage vis. prof. history Hunter Coll., CUNY, N.Y.C., 1985-86. Author: Exodusters: Black Migration to Kansas After Reconstruction, 1976, The Narrative of Hosea Hudson: His Life as a Negro Communist in the South, 1979, Standing at Armageddon: The United States 1877-1919, 1987, Sojourner Truth: A Life, A Symbol, 1996, Southern History Across the Color Line, 2002, Creating Black Americans, 2005; editor: Gender and Am. Culture Series; mem. editl. bd. Jour. Women's History, Ency. Americana; contbr. articles to profl. jours. Ford Found. fellow, 1971-72, Am. Coun. Learned Soc. fellow, 1976-77, Charles Warren Ctr. Studies in Am. History fellow, 1976-77, Radcliffe/Bunting Inst. fellow, 1976-77, Nat. Humanities Ctr. fellow, 1977-78, Guggenheim fellow, 1982-83, Ctr. Advanced Study in Behavioral Scis. fellow, 1988-89, Kate B. and Hall J. Peterson fellow Am. Antiquarian Soc., 1991, NEH fellow, 1992-93; recipient Ccoretta Scott King award AAUW, 1969-70, Grad. Soc. medal Radcliffe Coll. Alumnae, 1984 Candace award Nat. Coalition Unc Hundred Black Women, 1980, named U. Calif. at Berkeley Alumnae of Yr., 1989. Mem. Am. Coun. Learned Soc., Am. Antiquarian Soc., Am. Hist. Assn. (mem. program com. 1976-78, J. Franklin Jameson fellowship com. 1978-79, Beveridge and Dunning prizes com. 1985-87, mem. coun. 1991-93, Roelker Mentorship award 2001), Am. Studies Assn. (mem. internat. com. 1983-88, mem. nat. coun. 1989-92, mem. adv. coun. 1991-92), Assn. Study Afro-Am. Life and History (mem. program com. 1976, Carter G. Woodson award 2004), Assn. Black Women Historians (mem. rsch. com. 1980—, nat. dir. 1982-84, chair Brown pub. prize com. 1983-86, 88-91), Berkshire Conf. Women Historians (mem. program com. 1976), Inst. So. Studies (mem. exec. com. 1987-88), Orgn. Am. Historians (mem. com. status women 1975-77, mem. program com. 1977-79, 83-85, Frederick Jackson Turner award com. 1983, mem. exec. bd. 1984-87, chair ad hoc com. on minority historians 1985-87, chair Avery O. Craven award 1994-95), Nat. Book Found. (chair non-fiction jury, Nat. Book awards 1994), Social Sci. Rsch. Coun. (mem. com. social sci. pers. 1977-78), So. Hist. Assn. (chair Syndor prize com. 1991-92), So. Regional Coun. (mem. Lillian Smith Book prize com. 1986, mem. exec. com. 1987), Soc. Am. Historians (chair Parkman prize com. 1993—). Office: Princeton U History Dept Princeton NJ 08544-0001*

**PAINTER, RICHARD WILLIAM,** lawyer, educator; b. Phila., Oct. 3, 1961; s. William Hall and Marion (Homer) Painter; m. Karen Lindsley; children: Elizabeth Homer, William Hall II. BA, Harvard Coll., 1984; JD, Yale U., 1987. Bar: N.Y. 1989, U.S. Dist. Ct. (so. dist.) N.Y., Conn. 1990, U.S. Dist. Ct. Conn., U.S. Supreme Ct. Clk. Judge John T. Noonan, Jr. U.S. Ct. Appeals, San Francisco, 1987-88; assoc. Sullivan & Cromwell, N.Y.C., 1988-91, Finn Dixon & Herling, Stamford, Conn., 1991-93; assoc. prof. law Oreg. Sch Law, Eugene, 1993-97, dir. law and enterpreneurship ctr., 1994-97; prof. law U. Ill., Champaign, 1998—2005, Guy Raymond and Mildred Van Voorhis Jones prof., 2003—05; prof. law U. Minn., Mpls., 2005—; assoc. council to pres. (ethics) The White House, 2005—. Vis. prof. law Boston U., 1997, Cornell U. Ithaca, NY, 1997—98, Warren Knowles) vis. internat. govt. ethics U. Wis, 2001; vis. prof. U. Bielefeld, Germany, 1999, 2000, 01; vis. prof. law U. Mich., Ann Arbor, 2002; vis. scholar Humboldt U., Berlin, 2000, Harvard U. Ctr. European Studies, 2003—04. Co-author: Professional and Personal Responsibilities of the Lawyer, 1997, 2nd edit, 2001, Securities

Litigation and Enforcement, 2003; contbr. articles to profl. jours. Mem.: ABA, Am. Law Inst., Cosmos Club (Washington). Republican. Episcopalian. Avocation: classical music. Office Phone: 202-456-2608.

**PAINTER, ROBERT LOWELL,** surgeon, educator; b. Winchester, Ind., Jan. 13, 1934; s. Lowell Walter and Lillian Genevieve (Pierson) P.; m. Esther Lillian Reece, Sept. 21, 1957 (div. Sept. 1977); children: Elizabeth Haines, Bradley, Robert R., Andrew, Jane Macy-Painter; m. Nancy Sue Macy, Feb. 10, 1980. BA, Earham Coll., Richmond, Ind., 1955; MD, Ind. U., 1959. Intern and resident Hartford (Conn.) Hosp., 1959-65; resident Baylor U. Sch. Medicine, Houston, 1967-68; attending surgeon Day Kimball Hosp., Putnam, Conn., 1962-91; chmn. dir. surgery St. Francis Hosp., Hartford, 1991-98; med. practice, cons., 1999—2001. Cons. Hartford Hosp., 1969-99; assoc. prof. surgery U. Conn., 1991-99, anatomy instr., 2000—. Councilman Ct. Common Coun., Hartford, Conn., 2001—. Capt. USAF, 1965—67. Fellow ACS, Am. Coll. Physician Execs.; mem. New Eng. Surg. Soc., New Eng. Vasc. Soc., Soc. Thoracic Surgery. Republican. Avocations: hiking, gardening, bicycling, birdwatching.

**PAINTER, THEOPHILUS SHICKEL, JR.,** internist, allergist; b. Austin, Tex., Apr. 29, 1924; s. Theophilus Shickel and Anna Mary (Thomas) P.; m. Dorothy Bulkley, July 11, 1957; children: Dana Parkey, Amy Hur, Theophilus III. BA, U. Tex., 1944, MD, 1947. Diplomate Am. Bd. Internal Medicine, Am. Bd. Allergy and Immunology. Rotating intern Univ. Hosp., U. Mich., Ann Arbor, 1947-48, resident in internal medicine, 1948-51, fellow, jr. clin. instr., 1956-58; pvt. practice, Austin, Tex., 1958— Capt. USAF, 1951-53. Fellow ACP, Am. Coll. Allergy and Immunology, Am. Acad. Allergy and Immunology. Avocations: fishing, carving, hunting, painting. Home: 3222 Tarryhollow Dr Austin TX 78703-1639 Office: 800 W 34th St Ste 201 Austin TX 78705-1146 Office Phone: 512-454-5821. Personal E-mail: tspainterjr@cs.com.

**PAINTER, WILLIAM HALL,** law educator; b. Pitts., May 2, 1927; s. John Littleton Dawson and Eleanor Cramer (Hall); m. Marion Symmes Homer, July 9, 1955; children: Richard William, Edward Homer. AB, Princeton U., 1950; JD, Harvard U., 1954. Bar: N.Y. 1955. Assoc. Debevoise, Plimpton & McLean, 1954-58; teaching fellow Harvard U.Law Sch., Cambridge, Mass., 1958-59; prof. Villanova U. Law Sch., Phila., 1959-65; vis. prof. U. Mich. Law Sch., Ann Arbor, 1965; prof. U. Mo., Kansas City, 1965-71; spl. counsel, dir. study securities industry U.S. Ho. Reps., Washington, 1971-72; prof. U. Ill. Coll. Law, Champaign, 1972-81. Albert E. Jenner Jr. prof., 1981-87; Theodore Rinehart prof. emeritus of law George Washington U., Washington, 1987—. Author: Federal Regulation of Insider Trading, 1968, Corporate and Tax Aspects of Closely Held Corporations. 1971, 2d edit., 1981, Problems and Materials in Business Planning, 1975, 3d edit., 1994, The Federal Securities Code and Corporate Disclosure, 1979. Painter on Close Corporations, 1991; contbr. articles to legal publs. Mem. Ill. Bus. Corp. Act Revision Com., 1981-83. Mem. ABA (fed. securities commn. sect. corp., banking and bus. law, chmn. subcom. on legis. 1974-81), Assn. Am. Law Schs. (chmn. sect. bus. assn. 1976), Am. Law Inst., Phi Beta Kappa. Home: 6652 32d St NW Washington DC 20015 Office: George Washington U Nat Law Ctr 720 20th St NW Washington DC 20006-4306 E-mail: wpainter@main.nlc.gwu.edu.*

**PAINTON, RUSSELL ELLIOTT,** retired lawyer, retired mechanical engineer; b. Port Arthur, Tex., Dec. 5, 1940; s. Clifford Elliott and Edith Virginia (McCutcheon) P.; m. Elizabeth Ann Mullins, July 2, 1965 (div. Dec. 1977); 1 child, Todd Elliott; m. Mary Lynn Weber, May 9, 1981. BS in Mech. Engring., U. Tex.-Austin, 1963, JD, 1972. Registered profl. engr., Tex., 1972. Engr. Gulf States Utilities, Beaumont, Tex., 1963-66, Tracor, Inc., Austin, Tex., 1966-70, corp. counsel, 1973-83, v.p., gen. counsel, 1983-98, v.p., gen. counsel, corp. sec., 1991-98; atty. Brown, Maroney, Rose, Baker & Barber, Austin, 1972-73, Childs, Fortenbach, Beck & Guyton, Houston, 1973; corp. sec. Westmark Systems, Inc., Austin, 1990-91; sole practitioner, 1998—2005; ret., 2006. Gen. counsel Paramount Theatre for Performing Arts, 1977-83, 2d vice chmn., 1978-80, 1st vice chmn., 1980-82, chmn. bd., 1982-84, retiring chmn., 1984-85; mem. Centex chpt. ARC; mem. adv. bd. Austin Sci. Acad., 1985-88, 93-95; mem. adv. coun. Austin Transp., 1985-88; bd. dirs. Tex. Industries for the Blind and Handicapped, 1988-95, vice chmn., 1990-91; bd. dirs. Aransas County Ind. Sch. Dist. Found., 2002—, Key Allegro Homeowners Assn., 2002—, pres. 2004-06. Named Boss of Yr., Austin Legal Secs. Assn., 1981. Mem.: Rockport Yacht Club (rear commodore 2002, vice commodore 2003), Am. Electronics Assn. (chmn. Austin coun. 1985—86), Better Bus. Bur. (arbitrator 1983—), Nat. Chamber Litigation Ctr., Tex. Bar Assn. (treas. corp. counsel sect. 1982—83), ABA, Houston Yacht Club (order Blue Gavel, Austin Yacht Club (race comdr. 1968—69, treas. 1970—71, sec. 1972, 1975, vice commodore 1980, commodore 1981, fleet comdr. 1986), Delta Theta Phi. Republican. Episcopalian. Personal E-mail: sailor44@swbell.net.

**PAIR, JACKSON JARRELL,** computer scientist, media consultant; b. Augusta, Ga., Apr. 12, 1973; s. Charles Raymond and Kay Jarrell Pair. B of Computer Engring., Ga. Inst. Tech., Atlanta, BS in Internat. Affairs, MS in Human Computer Interaction, 1999. Dir. advanced projects Charmed Tech., Beverly Hills, Calif., 1999—2001; computer scientist Inst. Creative Techs., U. So. Calif., LA, 2001—. Mem.: IEEE, Assn. Computing Machinery. Personal E-mail: jarrell@acm.org.

**PAIROLERO, PETER CHARLES,** surgeon, educator; b. Bessemer, Mich., 1938; MD, U. Mich., 1963. Diplomate Am. Bd. Surgeons, Am. Bd. Thoracic Surgeons, Am. Bd. Gen. Vascular Surgeons. Intern St. Mary's Hosp., Duluth, Minn., 1963-64; resident gen. surgery Mayo Grad. Sch. Medicine, Rochester, Minn., 1966-71, fellow cerebral vascular rsch., 1968-69, resident thoraciccardio surgery, 1971-73; fellow cerebral vascular surgery Baylor U., Houston, 1973; chmn. American Board of Thorasic Surgery, 2001—; staff surgeon Mayo Clinic, Rochester, Minn., 1974—, chair vascular surgery, 1987—90, chair gen. thoracic surgery, 1989—93, chair cardiothoracic surgery, 1992—93, chair dept. of surgery, 1993—. Served in U.S. Army, 1964—66. Mem. AAAS, Am. Bd. Thorasic Surgery (chmn., 2001-). Office: 200 1st St SW Rochester MN 55905-0001

**PAISANO, STUWART,** Native American tribal leader; m. Catherine Paisano. Student, U. N.Mex.; grad. law enforcement acad. With Bernalillo County Sheriff's Dept.; gov. Pueblo of Sandia, 2000—. Office: Pueblo of Sandia 481 Sandia Loop Bernalillo NM 87004 Office Phone: 505-867-3317. Office Fax: 505-867-9235.*

**PAISLEY, BRAD,** musician; b. Glen Dale, West Virigina, Oct. 28, 1972; married. Grad., Belmont U., 1995. Musician: (albums) Who Needs Pictures, 1999, Part II, 2001, Mud On The Tires, 2003, Time Well Wasted, 2005 (Album of Yr., Acad. Country Music award, 2006). Founder The Brad Paisley Foundation, 2001—. Co-recipient with Chely Wright, Vocal Event of the Year, "Hard To Be A Husband, Hard To Be A Wife", Country Music Assoc. Award, 2001, with Alison Krauss, Music Video of Yr., Musical Event of Yr. "Whiskey Lullaby", 2004, with Alison Krauss, Video of Yr., Vocal Event of Yr., "Whiskey Lullaby", Acad. Country Music, 2005, with Dolly Parton, Most Inspiring Video of Yr. for When I Get Where I'm Going, CMT awards (Country Music TV), 2006, with Dolly Parton, Video of Yr. and Vocal Event of Yr. for When I Get Where I'm Going, Acad. Country Music award, 2006; recipient Video of the Yr., Song of the Yr., Single of the Yr., "He Didn't Have To Be", Country Music Assoc. Award, 2000, Male Vocalist of the Yr., 2000, 2001, Grammy Award for Best New Artist, 2001, Male Vocalist of the Year, Country Music Assoc. Award, 2002, Song of the Yr., Single of the Yr., Music Video of the Yr., "I'm Gonna Miss Her", 2002, Male Vocalist of the Yr., 2003, Grammy Award for Best Male Country Vocal Performance, "I'm Gonna Miss Her", 2003, Single of the Yr., Song of the Yr., Music Video of the Yr.,

"Celebrity", Country Music Assoc. Award, 2003, Collaborative Video of Yr. for the song Whiskey Lullaby, CMT Awards (Country Music TV), 2005. Office: William Morris Agency 1600 Division St Ste 300 Nashville TN 37203-2755*

**PAIVA, CLIFFORD ANTHONY,** physicist, consultant; b. Honolulu, Jan. 9, 1947; s. John Albert and Dorothy (Martin) P.; m. Jerrine Dunn, Oct. 15, 1972; children: Antonette, Alexander, Allison. Martin. BS in Geophysics, Christian Heritage Coll., El Cajon, Calif., 1978; MS in Astrogeophysics, Inst. Creation Rsch., El Cajon, Calif., 1988. Physicist Naval Warfare Assessment Ctr. Naval Weapons Sys., Seal Beach, Corona, Calif., 1979-83; physicist USAF Rsch. Lab. Rocket Propulsion Directorate Edwards AFB, Calif., 1986-91; physicist Naval Surface Warfare Ctr. Dahlgren (Va.) Divsn., 1991-2000; founder, pres. Battle Sci. Mgmt., California City, 2001—; engring. physicist, sr. infrared scientist SPIRAL Techs., Inc. Lancaster, Calif., 2002—. Mem. East Asia Working Group. Ctr. for Strategic and Internat. Studies, Washington, automatic target recognition working group Def. Advanced Rsch. Agy., Theater Missile Def. Asia Pacific sector, Washington; sr. councilor Atlantic Coun. U.S., Washington, mem. physicist for Global Underwater Search Team, Global Ridge, 2000. Contbr. articles to profl. jours. Tenor Masterworks Chorus, King George, Va., 1996-98, Fredericksburg (Va.) Master Chorale, 1996-98, Antelope Valley Master Chorale, 2000—. With USAF, 1965-69. Mem.: AIAA, Internat. Soc. Optical Engring./Penetrating Radiation Working Group, BSM Assn. (pres., founder), Am. Optical Soc., U.S. Naval Inst. Engrs., Creation Rsch. Soc., Optical Soc. Am., Internat. Soc. Optical Engrs. Am. Geophys Union, APS, U.S. Naval Intelligence Profl. (life). Republican. Assemblies Of God Ch. Achievements include development of advanced morphological target segmentation and extraction techniques, leading to accurate predictive computer simulations of threat target sets for ballistic missile defense; research in high energy lasers. Avocations: piano, guitar. Home and Office: Edwards AFB 159 Camp Fire Dr California City CA 93505 Office Phone: 760-373-1518. Personal E-mail: aanthony@as.net.

**PAJAK, DAVID JOSEPH,** lawyer, consultant; b. Buffalo, June 19, 1956; s. William H. and Theresa A. (Granato) P.; m. Peggy J. Fisher, Aug. 1, 1981; children: Andrew J., Karl W. BA, State Coll. Buffalo, 1978; JD, U. Buffalo, 1982. Bar: N.Y. 1983, U.S. Dist. Ct. (we. dist.) N.Y., 1991. Social svcs. counsel Genesee County Dept. Social Svcs., Batavia, N.Y., 1984-93; pvt. practice Corfu, NY, 1983—. Amherst, 1993—; town justice Town of Pembroke, NY, 1994—2005; with Genesee County Attys. Office, 2001—. Mem. legis. com. N.Y. Fed. on Child Abuse and Neglect, Albany, 1986—99, bd. dirs., 1987—89; cons. N.Y. Pub. Welfare Assn., Inc., Albany, 1987—92; pres. Social Svcs. Attys. Assn. N.Y. State, 1990—91; instr. Bill Adam's Martial Arts & Fitness Ctr., Buffalo, 1999—2002, Klassic Karate Studios, 1990—98, Filipino Karate Acad., 1989—90. Contbr. articles to profl. jours. Mem.: Genesee County Bar Assn., Erie County Bar Assn., N.Y. State Bar Assn. (chair com. on lawyer referral svcs. 2004—). Republican. Avocations: Karate, martial arts. Home: 17 E Main St Corfu NY 14036-9665 Office: 7170 Transit Rd Amherst NY 14221 Office Phone: 716-630-0400. E-mail: dave@davepajak.com.

**PAK, HYUNG WOONG,** community advocate; b. Ham-Hoong, Korea, Nov. 6, 1932; came to U.S., 1955, naturalized, 1968; s. Kyung-Koo and Myung-Sook (Lee) P.; m. Diana Lee Stenen Woodruff, 1975; children: Jonathan Tong-Hee, Michelle Hyun-Mi Lee. AB, U. Chgo., 1958. Editor and publisher Chgo. Rev., 1958-63, cons., 1963-65; assoc. editor Ency. Britannica Press, Chgo., 1963-64, sr. editor social scis. and humanities, 1964-66; ednl. dir. Bantam Books, Inc., N.Y.C., 1966-69; gen. mgr. sci. dept. Appleton-Century-Crofts/New Century, N.Y.C., 1970-72; v.p., editorial dir. D. Van Nostrand Co., N.Y.C., 1972-74, pres., 1974-76, Chatham Sq. Press, N.Y.C., 1976-83; pub. Urizen Books, Inc., N.Y.C., 1978-81; exec. v.p. Bus. Software Mag., Palo Alto, Calif., 1983-84; pub., editor Asian High-Tech. Report, 1984-90; exec. dir. The Philip Jaisohn Meml. Found., Inc., Phila., 1990-99; pres. Asian Cmty. Devel. Corp., 2000—. Fellow Hoover Instn., Stanford, Calif., 1984-85. Author: The Pacific Rim, 1990; columnist The Phila. Bus. Rev., 1993-99. Mem. Bd. Sch. Dist. Cheltenham Twp., Pa., 1987-94; mem. Asian task force Phila. Sch. Dist., 1988-95; co-chmn. bus. adv. com. Montgomery County, Pa., 1991-93; del. Citizens' Assembly for a Greater Phila., 1991-95; chmn. Pan Asian Assn. Greater Phila., 1992-96, mem. bd. fellowship commn., 1992-95; bd. dirs. Brandywine Art Ctr., 1995-99, vice chair, 1998-99; Pa. del. The White Ho. Conf. on Aging, 1995; trustee Abington Meml. Hosp. Found., 1995-2000; mem. cmty. adv. com. Keystone Mercy Health Plan, 1998-2002; bd. dirs. Nat. Conf. Cmty. and Justice, 2000-02. Mem. ACLU (life), AHA (mem. comms. com. 1998-2000, mem. Phila. All-Am. city host com. 1998-99), Phila. Mus. Art. Home: 1015 Sharpless Rd Elkins Park PA 19027-3040 Office: PO Box 7167 Elkins Park PA 19027-0167 Office Phone: 267-254-4234. Personal E-mail: hwpak1@gmail.com.

**PAK, SE RI,** professional golfer; b. Daejeon, Korea, Sept. 28, 1977; Professional golfer LPGA Tour, 1997—. Mem. KLPGA, 1996, 97. Recipient Rolex Rookie of Yr. award, South Korea Order of Merit 1998, Golf Writers Assn. of America Player of the Year, 1998, Vare Trophy 2003. Winner of 23 LPGA events including four Grand Slam titles. Won the LPGA championship 1998, 2002, 2006; won the U.S. Open 1998; won the du Maurier Classic 2001; first woman in 58 years to make cut in men's golf tournament, SBS Super Tournament on Korean tour (finished 10th overall); qualified for LPGA Hall of Fame, 2004. Address: LPGA 100 International Golf Dr Daytona Beach FL 32124-1082 Office Phone: 386-274-6200. Office Fax: 386-274-1099.

**PAKALA, JAMES COTTON,** library director, minister; b. Pitts., Mar. 6, 1944; s. William Elmer and Edythe Leona (Cotton) Pakala; m. Marie Denise Marchand, June 13, 1975; 1 child. Kent Marchand. BA, Shelton Coll., 1966; MDiv, Faith Theol. Sem., 1970; degree, Bibl. Theol. Sem., 1977; MS, Drexel U., 1979. Ordained minister Presbyn. Ch. Am., 1975. Dir. libr. Bibl. Theol. Sem., Hatfield, Pa., 1971—97, Covenant Theol. Sem., St. Louis, 1991—. Chaplain Pa. Army N.G., Phila., 1975—97. Lt. col. chaplain U.S. Army, 1975—97. Decorated Meritorius Svc. medal U.S. Army, Commendation medal, Meritorius Svc. medal; recipient President's award, Shelton Coll., 1966, William Allen Chamberlin award, Faith Theol. Sem., 1968. Mem.: ATLA, Am. Theol. Libr. Assn. (bd. dirs. 2004—), Mo. Libr. Assn. (bd. dirs. 1996—98), St. Louis (Mo.) Regional Libr. Network (mem. coun. 2000—03), SEPTLA (pres. 1985—87), MOBIUS (exec. com. 2001—05), Beta Phi Mu. Presbyn. Avocations: railroad buff, environmentalism. Office Phone: 314-434-4044.

**PAKENHAM, ROSALIE MULLER WRIGHT,** magazine and newspaper editor; b. Newark, June 20, 1942; d. Charles and Angela (Fortunata) Muller; m. Lynn Wright, Jan. 13, 1962; children: James Anthony Meador, Geoffrey Shepard; m. E. Michael Pakenham, Sept. 29, 2001. BA in English, Temple U., 1965. Mng. editor Suburban Life mag., Orange, NJ, 1960-62; assoc. editor Phila. mag., 1962-64, mng. editor, 1969-73; founding editor Womensports mag., San Mateo, Calif., 1973-75; editor scene sect. San Francisco Examiner, 1975-77; exec. editor New West mag., San Francisco and Beverly Hills, Calif., 1977-81; features and Sunday editor San Francisco Chronicle, 1981-87, asst. mng. editor features, 1987-96; v.p. and editor-in-chief Sunset Mag., Menlo Park, Calif., 1996—2001. Editl. cons., 2002—; tchr. mag. writing U. Calif., Berkeley, 1975—76; participant pubs. process course Stanford U., 1977—79; chmn. mag. judges at conf. Coun. Advancement and Support of Edn., 1980, judge, 84, Nat. Mag. Awards, 1998, 99, 2005. Contbr. numerous mag. articles, critiques, revs., Compton's Ency. Mem.: Internat. Assn. Culinary Profls., Am. Soc. Mag. Editors (nat. mag. awards judge, 1998, 99, 2005), Am. Newspaper Pubs. Assn. (Chronicle minority recruiter 1987—94, pub. task force for minorities in newspaper bus. 1988—89), Am. Assn. Sunday and Feature Editors (treas. 1984, sec. 1985, 1st v.p. 1986, pres. 1987, Hall of Fame 1999), Washington D.C. Women's Forum, Women's Forum West (bd. dirs. 1993—, sec. 1994), Internat. Women's Forum. Office Phone: 717-292-6969. Personal E-mail: RosalieMPakenham@aol.com. *Keep a sharp eye out for talent, recognize it and reward it, and everyone profits.*

**PAKTER, JEAN,** maternal and child health consultant; b. N.Y.C., Jan. 1, 1911; d. David and Lillian (Kunitz) P.; m. Arnold L. Bachman, Sept. 17, 1939 (dec. Dec. 1992); children: Ellen Bachman Mendelson, Donald M. Bachman. BS, NYU, 1931, MD, 1934; MPH, Columbia U., 1955. Diplomate Am. Bd. Pediat. Intern Mt. Sinai Hosp., N.Y.C., 1934-36, resident in pediat., 1937-39; pvt. practice, N.Y.C., 1939-43; dir. Bur. Dept. Health, Maternity, Newborn and Family Planning, N.Y.C., 1950-82; cons., lectr. maternity, child health Columbia U. Sch. Pub. Health, N.Y.C., 1984—, dep. dir. maternal and child health program, 1984-94, lectr. maternity, child health, 1970—. Contbr. numerous articles to profl. med. jours. Advisor March of Dimes, N.Y.C., 1975—. Recipient Fund for City of N.Y. Pub. Svc. award, 1974, Jacobi medal Mt. Sinai Hosp., 1975, N.Y. State Med. Soc. award, 2006. Fellow APHA (Martha May Eliot award 1990), Am. Acad. Pediatrics, N.Y. Acad. Medicine (trustee 1979-83), N.Y. Obstet. Soc. (assoc.); mem. Pub. Health Assn. N.Y.C. (bd. dirs. 1992-96, The Haven Emerson award 2006), Women's City Club, Alpha Omega Alpha. Avocations: concerts, opera, theater, reading. Home: 1175 Park Ave New York NY 10128-1211

**PAKULA, ANITA SUSAN,** dermatologist; b. LA, Nov. 20, 1961; BA, Pomona Coll., 1983; BS, Calif. Luth. Coll., 1985; MD, U. Calif., Irvine, 1988. Diplomat Am. Bd. Dermatology, NAt. Bd. Med. Examiners. Intern Evanston (Ill.) Hosp., 1988-89; resident Northwestern U. Med. Sch., Chgo., 1989-92; asst. clin. prof. dermatology UCLA MEd. Ctr., 1993—. Presenter in field. Contbr. articles to profl. jours. Fellow Am. Acad. Dermatology; mem. Soc. Pediatric Dermatology. Office: 267 W Hillcrest Dr Thousand Oaks CA 91360-4923

**PAKVASA, SANDIP,** physicist; b. Bombay, Dec. 24, 1935; came to U.S. 1961; s. Sirish V. and Sumitra (Surti) P.; m. Heide Miller, Nov. 19, 1978. BSc, M.S. U. Baroda, India, 1954; MSc, M.S. U. Baroda, 1957; PhD, Purdue U., 1966. Rsch. assoc. Syracuse (N.Y.) U., 1965-67; asst. prof. U. Hawaii, Honolulu, 1968-70, assoc. prof., 1970-73, prof. physics, 1974—. Vis. prof. U. Wis., Madison, 1978, 81, Nat. High Energy Physics Lab., Japan, 1983, 89, 2002, U. Melbourne, Australia, 1986, Tata Inst. Fund. Rsch., Bombay, 1983, 88; vis. assoc. CERN, Geneva, 1982; McMinn lectr. Vanderbilt U., 1996. Contbr. articles to profl. jours., chpts. to books. Japan Soc. for Promotion of Sci. fellow, 1981, 85. Fellow Am. Phys. Soc. Avocations: music, mysteries. Office: Univ Hawaii 2505 Correa Rd Honolulu HI 96822-2219 Office Phone: 808-956-2970. E-mail: pakvasa@phys.hawaii.edu.

**PAL, PRABIR KUMAR (SUNNY PAL),** lawyer; b. Chittagong, Bengal, India, Feb. 17, 1936; arrived in Can., 1969; s. Niranjan and Renuka (Mitter) P.; m. Nandinee Majumdar, Dec. 13, 1960; 1 child, Nobina Pal Robinson. BA in Law with honors, Cambridge U., 1958, MA, 1972; diploma in Indsl. Mgmt., Geneva U., 1964. Legal and fin. mgmt. positions Alcan Inc., in Can., Europe and Asia, 1959-99; v.p. chief legal officer, corp. sec., 1988-99; governance counsellor Flavell Kubrick LLP, lawyers, Ottawa, Canada, 1999-2005, Lang Michener LLP, Ottawa, 2005—. Bd. dir. Transparency Internat. Can. Inc., 1998-2004, Opera Lyra, Ottawa, 2000-05. Fellow Inst. Chartered Secs. and Adminstrs.; mem. Internat. Bar Assn., Rideau Club Ottawa. Avocations: photography, rowing. Office Phone: 613-232-7171. Business E-Mail: pkpal@langmichener.ca.

**PAL, PRATAPADITYA,** curator; b. Bangladesh, Sept. 1, 1935; came to U.S., 1967; s. Gopesh Chandra and Bidyut Kana (Dam) P.; m. Chitralekha Bose, Apr. 20, 1968; children: Shalmali, Lopamudra. MA, U. Calcutta, 1958, DPhil, 1962; PhD (UK Commonwealth Scholar), U. Cambridge, 1965. Rsch. assoc. Am. Acad. Benares, India, 1966-67; keeper Indian collections Mus. Fine Arts, Boston, 1967-69; sr. curator Indian and Southeast Asian art Los Angeles County Mus. Art, 1970-95, acting dir., 1979; vis. curator Indian and S.E. Asian art Art Inst. Chgo., 1995-2003; rsch. fellow Norton Simon Mus., Pasadena, Calif., 1995-2005. Gen. editor Marg Publs., Mumbai, 1993-; adj. prof. fine arts U. So. Calif., 1971-89; vis. prof. U. Calif., Santa Barbara, 1988, Irvine, 1994-95; William Cohn lectr. Oxford U., 1983; Catherine Mead meml. lectr. Pierpont Morgan Libr., N.Y.C., 1986; Ananda K. Coomaraswamy meml. lectr. Prince of Wales Mus., Bombay, 1987; D.J. Sibley prehistoric art lectr. U. Tex., Austin, 1989; Anthony Gardner meml. lectr. Victoria and Albert Mus., London, 1993, keynote spkr. 1st Internat. Conf. on Tibetan Art, 1994; mem. commr.'s art adv. panel IRS, Washington, 1986-96. Author: Vaisnava Iconology in Nepal, 1970, The Arts of Nepal, vol. 1, 1974, vol. 2, 1979, The Sensuous Immortals, 1977, The Ideal Image: Gupta Sculptures and its Influence, 1978, The Classical Tradition in Rajput Painting, 1978, Elephants and Ivories, 1981, A Buddhist Paradise: Murals of Alchi, 1982, Art of Tibet, 1983, Tibetan Painting, 1984, Art of Nepal, 1985, From Merchants to Emperors, 1986, Indian Sculpture, vol. 1, 1986, Icons of Piety, Images of Whimsey, 1987, Indian Sculpture, vol. 2, 1988, Buddhist Book Illuminations, 1988, Romance of the Taj Mahal, 1989, Art of the Himalayas, 1991, Pleasure Gardens of the Mind, 1993; Indian Painting, vol. 1, 1993, The Peaceful Liberators: Jain Art from India, 1994, A Collecting Odyssey, 1997, Divine Images, Human Visions, 1997, Tibet Change and Tradition, 1997, Desire and Devotion, 2001, Himalayas: An Aesthetic Adventure, 2003, Asian Art in the Norton Simon Museum, vols. 1 and 2, 2003, vol. 3, 2004; Painted Poems, 2004, Durga: Avenging Goddess Nurturing Mother, 2005. John D. Rockefeller III Fund fellow, 1964, 69, fellow NEA, 1974; Getty scholar, 1995-96. Fellow Asia Soc. (Bombay, hon.); mem. Asiatic Soc. (Calcutta, B.C. Law gold medal 1993, R.P. Chanda Centenary medal, 2003) Office Phone: 310-839-8547.

**PAL, RANADIP,** researcher; s. Dhirendra Chandra and Sabita Pal. B of Tech., Indian Inst. of Tech., Kharagpur, India, 2002; MS, Tex. A&M U., 2004. Rschr. Tex. A&M U., College Station, Tex., 2002—, phd student, 2004—. Recipient Nat. Math. Olympiad award, NBHM, India, 0997; Summer fellowship, Nat. Instruments, 1. Achievements include research in genetic network design. Office: Texas A&M Univ Zachry 09 College Station TX 77843 Office Phone: 979-862-8896. E-mail: ranadip@ece.tamu.edu.

**PAL, SUKUMAR,** immunologist, researcher; arrived in U.S., 1988; s. Kalipada and Parbati Pal; m. Sima Chaki, June 16, 1987; 1 child, Srijita Chaki. Degree, U. Calcutta, 1979, PhD, 1988. Postdoctoral fellow Johns Hopkins U., Balt., 1988-90; post grad. rschr. U. Calif., Irvine, 1990-91, jr. specialist, 1991-94, asst. specialist, 1994-2000, assoc. specialist, 2000—. Rschr. U. Calif., Irvine, 1990; parent site coun. Turtle Rock Elem. Sch., Irvine, 2002-04. Editor: Kheya Mag., Bengali Assn. So. Calif., 1995—; contbr. articles to profl. jours. Fight for Sight Rsch. fellow, Fight for Sight Inc, 1988-89, Equal Opportunity fellow, U. Calif., Irvine, 2001. Mem.: Am. Soc. for Microbiology (reviewer 2003—, Vector Labs. Young Investigator award 1995). Achievements include research in Engaged in chalmydial research for last 16 years, developed various animal models to study chlamydial infections in various hosts, developing vaccine to prevent from infection. Office: Univ Calif Irvine Dept Pathology Irvine CA 92697-4800 Office Phone: 949-824-7450.

**PALACIOS, ANTONIO,** mathematics professor; PhD, Ariz. State U., Tempe, 1987-95. Postdoctoral fellow U. Houston, Tex., 1996-99; rsch. scientist Hewlett Packard, Co., Fort Collins, Colo., 1995-96; assoc. prof., dept. math. San Diego State U., Calif., 1999—. Grantee, Dept. of Energy, 2000-03, Dept. Def., Space and Naval Warfare Ctr., 2005-06, NSF, 2005—. Achievements include patents pending for advanced dynamic magnetic sensors; multi-frequency oscillations for antennas and radar systems. Office: San Diego State Univ 5500 Campanile Dr San Diego CA 92128-7720 Office Phone: 619-594-6808. Office Fax: 619-594-6746.

**PALACIOS, LISA MAY,** academic administrator; b. Rochester, N.Y. d. Richard Alan and Nancy Mae Norton; m. Marcus Blake Palacios, Mar. 9, 2002. BA in Psychology, U. North Tex., 1995; MA in Psychology, San Francisco State U., 2004. Counselor Promise House, Dallas, 1992-95; residential counselor Nelson Ctr., Denton, Tex., 1995-96; rsch. asst. Pub. Rsch. Inst., San Francisco, 1997-98; sales rep., list broker Rsch. Mag., San Francisco, 1996-99; tchr. kindergarten Children's Courtyard, Plover Mound,

Tex., 2000-05; dir. recruitment and retention U. Tex., San Antonio, 2005—. Vol. Denton Humane Soc., 2004-05, Coppell (Tex.) Humane Soc., 2001-05, Soc. for Prevention of Cruelty of Animals, Dallas, 2003-06. Recipient TRIO Cert. Appreciation, 2005. Mem.: Nat. Assn. Grad. Admissions Profls. (presenter 2005-06), Tex. Assn. Grad. Admissions Profls. (com. mem. 2005-06), Am. Mktg. Assn. Avocations: music, dance, reading, hiking, camping. Home: 10410 Steuben Dr San Antonio TX 78249-600 Office: U Tex 6900 N Loop 1604 W San Antonio TX 78249-600

**PALACIOS, OLGA,** director; b. Bogotá, Colombia, July 6, 1964; d. Alvaro H. and Blanca L. (Gomez) Palacios; m. Heriberto Molinares, Feb. 2, 1985; children: Daniel, Francisco. BS in Ednl. Adminstrn., Fla. Nat. Coll., 1993. Asst. mgr. Comercial de Oriente, 1982-95; WIA project dir. Fla. Nat. Coll., 1997-2003, clin. rotation mgr., 1997-2003. Home: 6081 W 24th Ave #110 Hialeah FL 33016 Office: Fla Nat Coll 4425 W 20th Ave Hialeah FL 33012

**PALADE, GEORGE EMIL,** research scientist, educator; b. Jassy, Romania, Nov. 19, 1912; arrived in U.S., 1946, naturalized, 1952; s. Emil and Constanta Cantemir Palade; m. Irina Malaxa, June 12, 1941 (dec. 1969); children: Georgia Teodora, Philip Theodor; m. Marilyn G. Farquhar, 1970. Bachelor, Hasdeu Lyceum, Buzau, Romania; MD, U. Bucharest, Romania. Instr., asst. prof., then assoc. prof. anatomy Sch. Medicine, U. Bucharest, 1935-45; vis. investigator, asst. assoc., prof. cell biology Rockefeller U., 1946-73; prof. cell biology Yale U., New Haven, 1973-83, sr. research scientist, 1983-89; prof.-in-residence Med. Sch., U. Calif., San Diego, 1990-2001, dean sci. affairs, 1990-2001, prof. emeritus cellular and molecular med., 2001—. Contbr. articles to sci. jours. Recipient Albert Lasker Basic Rsch. award, 1966, Gairdner Spl. award, 1967, Horwitz prize, 1970, Nobel prize in physiology or medicine, 1974, Nat. Medal Sci., 1986. Fellow: Am. Acad. Arts Scis.; mem.: NAS, Royal Belgian Acad. Medicine, Romanian Acad., Leopoldina Acad. (Halle), Royal Soc. (London), Pontifical Acad. Sci. Achievements include correlated morphological and biochemical studies by electronmicroscopy and cell fractionation of subcellular components; discovery of ribosomes; discovery and elucidation of the secretory, exocytic pathway and studies on membrane biogenesis; discovery of and regulation of proteins and membrane traffic in animal eukaryotic cells.

**PALADINO, ALBERT EDWARD,** venture capitalist; b. N.Y.C., Aug. 4, 1932; s. Albert E. and Jennie (Fiato) Paladino; m. Dorothy M. Hayes (div. June 1979); children: Thomas A., Robert E., Catherine J., Paul F.; m. Susan Flynn, June 11, 1983. BS in Ceramic Engring., Alfred U., 1954, MS in Ceramic Engring., 1956; ScD in Materials Sci., MIT, 1962. Registered profl. engr., Mass. Staff mem. rsch. divsn. Raytheon Co., Waltham, Mass., 1955-59, mgr. materials and crystal growth lab., 1962-69, mgr. materials and techniques group microwave & power tube divsn., 1969-72, mgr. electronics materials group, 1972-75; program mgr. materials Office of Tech. Assessment U.S. Congress, Washington, 1975-78; asst. dir. tel. ops. tech. ctr. GTE Labs., Waltham, 1978-79; dep. dir. Office Energy Programs U.S. Dept. Commerce, Washington, 1979-81; mng. ptnr. Advanced Tech. Ventures, Boston, 1981-98. Bd. dir. TranSwitch Corp., Telaxis Comm. Corp., South Deerfield, Mass., 1988-2003, Electro-Scan Corp., Billerica, Mass., 1990-95, Onex Comm. Corp., 1999-2001, RF Micro Devices, Greensboro, NC, 1992—; telecom. bd. advisors Prism Ventures, 1997-2006, Early Stage Enterprises, 1997—; bd. advisers Battelle Ventures, 2004—; bd. dirs. Paladino & Co. Contbr. articles to profl. jours. Pres. West Needham (Mass.) Civic Assn., 1967-69; mem. Needham Town Meeting, 1973-74; trustee Alfred U., 1991—. Fellow: Am. Ceramic Soc. (chmn. basic sci. divsn. 1968-69, chmn. New Eng. sect. 1969-70, Disting. New Eng. Ceramic award) Achievements include patents in field. Avocations: painting, music, physical fitness, hiking, reading.

**PALANS, LLOYD ALEX,** lawyer; b. St. Louis, Aug. 6, 1946; s. Hyman Robert and Mae (Sherman) P.; m. Deborah Regn, Aug. 5, 1972; children: Emily Rebecca, Samantha Jane. BS, Tulane U., 1968; JD, U. Mo., 1972. Bar: Mo. 1972, US Dist. Ct. (ea. and we. dists.) Mo. 1972, US Ct. Appeals (8th cir.) 1972, US Ct. Appeals (5th cir.) 1974, US Supreme Ct. 1975, US Ct. Appeals (9th cir.) 1992. Ptnr. Kramer, Chused, Kramer, Shostak & Kohn, St. Louis, 1972-77, Blumenfeld, Marx & Tureen, P.C., St. Louis, 1978-81, Gallop, Johnson & Neuman, St. Louis, 1981-90, Bryan Cave, LLP, St. Louis, 1990—. Adj. prof. Washington U. Sch. Law, St. Louis, 1989—. Bd. dirs. St. Louis Chpt. ARC, 1987—, St. Louis Chpt. Leukemia Soc., 1988—, Combined Health Appeal Greater St. Louis, 1988—, Combined Health Appeal of Am., 1990. Fellow Am. Coll. Bankruptcy; mem. ABA, Mo. Bar, St. Louis Met. Bar Assn. Office: Bryan Cave LLP 1 Metro Sq 211 N Broadway Saint Louis MO 63102-2733 Office Phone: 314-259-2301.

**PALATNICK, FRANK SIDNEY,** educational consultant; b. Bklyn., Oct. 13, 1951; s. Abraham and Miriam Palatnick; m. Klara Alexandra Gliem, June 13, 1998 (div. June 2005). Assoc. Paralegal Sci., Ashworth Coll., 2003; postgrad., So. Calif. U. Profl. Studies, 2004—; cert., Nassau Acad. Law, 2003; cert. in spl. edn. law, Nat. Bus. Inst., 2004. Cert. real estate sales agt. NY, sch. bd. specialist N.Y. State Sch. Bd. Assn., 2005, ednl. testing svc. facilitator Nat. Sch. Leadership Stds., 2006. Paralegal Albert Grant Esq., Woodbridge, NJ, 1994-96; chief paralegal Oyster Bay Paralegal Assocs., Muttontown, NY, 1996-99; sr. assoc. Foresight Inst., Palo Alto, Calif., 2000-01; chief paralegal Glen Cove (NY) Paralegal Svcs., 2001-02; accreditation examiner Distance Edn. and Tng. Coun., Washington, 2002—. Mem. Presdl. Adv. Com. on Fed. Pay, Washington, 1981-82; Nassau County task force Office Mgmt. and Budget, Mineola, NY, 2002; substitute attendance tchr. Wyandanch Sch. Dist., L.I., 1997; substitute tchr. BOCES Nassau City, Greenlawn and Plainview, NY, 2000; chief cons. L.I. Degree Consulting Svc., Uniondale, NY, 2005; spkr., presenter in field. *Mr. Palatnick traveled to Beijing, China where he gave a lecture, which was filmed by the TV station of No. 8 Middle School, one of Beijing's best schools. A group of high school students along with one student from No. 8 Middle School collaborated on establishing a school devoted to the administrative concepts and practices discussed in Mr. Palatnick's lecture. While in Beijing, Mr. Palatnick also attended an invite-only wine reception and dinner in the Great Hall of the People, climbed the Great Wall, visited the Forbidden City, and stood in Tiananmen Square.* Assoc. editor: Nassau Lawyer, 2001—, asst. editor: The Flying Lady, 2000-02, contbg. editor: jour. Cardinal Points, 2000-02. Mem. U.S. Power Squadron, USCG Aux.; active People to People Amb. Program; poll taker Nassau County Dem. Com., Mineola, 2000. Nominee NYC Liberty Medal for Lifetime Achievement, 2005; named to Wall of Tolerance, Civil Rights Meml. Ctr., Ala., 2005; recipient Letter of Appreciation, Mayor of Glen Cove, 2001, Letter of Accomplishment, Supt. of Schs., Mineola, 2003, Letter of Acknowledgement of expertise in career devel., Cornell U., 2005. Mem.: ASCD (cert. assessment ednl. adminsrn.), ABA (individual rights and responsibilities com.), Am. Assn. for Adult and Continuing Edn., Assn. for Continuing Higher Edn., Edn. Writers Assn., Am. Coun. on Edn. (alumnus course evaluator tng.), N.Y. State Bar Assn., Nat. Career Devel. Assn. (alumnus career devel. facilitator tng.), Nat. Assn. Secondary Sch. Prins., Nat. Assn. for the Edn. Young Children, Coun. Adult & Experiential Learning (alumnus), Nat. Inst. Assessment Experiential Learning (alumnus), Am. Soc. Notaries, L.I. Paralegal Assn., Am. Mgmt. Assn., Suffolk County Bar Assn. (edn. law com., family law com., real estate com.), Nassau County Bar Assn. (publs. com., edn. law com., com. on coms., civil rights law com., med. legal com., cmty. and pub. rels. com., county clks. office), Foresight Inst. (sr.), Mensa, Amnesty Internat. Avocations: stamp collecting/philately, coin collecting/numismatics. Home: 233-38- 38 Dr Douglaston NY 11363 Personal E-mail: fpalatnick@msn.com.

**PALAZOTTO, ANTHONY N.,** aerospace engineering educator; b. Bklyn., Dec. 15, 1943; s. Andrew Anthony and Marie Palazotto; m. Helen Potosnak, June 11, 1960; children: Gary, Jane, Daniel, Terri, Christine, Loren, Sandra, Tracy. BCE, NYU, 1955, PhD in Engring., 1968; MCE, Bklyn. Poly. U., 1961. Registered profl. engr., Ohio. Cons. engr., 1955-68; prof. mech. engring. U. Bridgeport, Conn., 1968-75; prof. aerospace engring. Air Force Inst. Tech., Wright-Patterson AFB, Ohio, 1975—. Author: Nonlinear Shell

Analysis, 1992. Recipient Best Paper award, Aerospace Jour., 2004. Fellow: ASCE, Am. Acad. Mechanics (Best Paper award 1986), AIAA. Office: Air Force Inst Technology Dept of Aerospace Engineering Wright Patterson Afb OH 45433

**PALAZZI, JOSEPH LAZARRO,** manufacturing executive; b. New Haven, July 5, 1947; s. Joseph Anthony and Helen (Volosovich) P.; m. Lorna May Mickiewicz, May 27, 1978. BS in Acctg., Quinnipiac Coll., 1969; MBA, U. New Haven, 1973. CPA Conn.; cert. Turnaround Profl., 2005. Auditor Miter Carlson & Co.; mgr. budgets The Stanley Works, New Britian, Conn., 1972-76; mgr. planning Bangor Punta Corp., Greenwich, Conn., 1976-79; asst. corp. controller Pepperidge Farm, Norwalk, Conn., 1979-81, div. fin. services, 1981-82, group controller, 1982-83; corp. controller Plessey, Inc., White Plains, NY, 1983-84, v.p. finance, 1984-86, CFO, 1986-89; v.p. fin., CFO BTR Inc., Stanford, Ct., 1990-92; pres. Fasco Industries Inc., Chesterfield, Mo., 1992-98; CEO Fasco Motors Group, Chesterfield, Mo., 1998; mng. dir. Corp. Renewal Services, Inc. Mem. Rep. Town Com., Newtown, Conn., 1981; bd. dirs. Danbury Hosp., 1987-92. Served with U.S. Army, 1969—76. Mem. AICPA, Nat. Assn. Accts., Sigma Six Flying Club. Episcopalian. Avocations: sailing, tennis, golf, flying. Home: Corp Renewal Services Inc Ste 204 W 185 Plains Rd Milford CT 06460 Office Phone: 203-301-9901.*

**PALAZZO, ROBERT PAUL,** lawyer, accountant; b. LA, Apr. 14, 1952; s. Joseph Francis and Mickey Palazzo; m. Vivianne Palazzo. BA in Econs., UCLA, 1973; MBA, JD, U. So. Calif., 1976; postgrad., U. Oxford, Eng., 1979. CPA Calif., Colo.; bar: Calif. 1976, U.S. Dist. Ct. (so. dist.) Calif. 1977, U.S. Tax Ct. 1977, U.S. Ct. Appeals (9th cir.) 1978, U.S. Supreme Ct. 1980. Assoc. Graham & James, L.A., 1976-78; ptnr. Rader, Cornwall, Kessler & Palazzo CPAs, L.A., 1978-81, Palazzo & Kessler, L.A., 1978-81; pvt. practice L.A., Darwin, Calif., 1981—. Judge pro tem LA Mcpl. Ct., 1982—2000, L.A. Superior Ct., 2001—; alumni advisor UCLA, 1977—81, adv. and scholarship com., 1978—81; lectr. U. Oxford, 1979, U. So. Calif., L.A., 1986, Calif. Poly. Inst., Pomona, 1997; profl. adv. com. West L.A. Coll., 1993—96; session chair Medieval and Renaissance Conf. Ariz. State U., 2000—01, 2003; bd. dirs. Cons. Am. Oil. Co., Fin. Sys. Internat. Inc.; part-time faculty Moorpark Coll., Calif., 2004—; spkr. in field. Hist. cons. A&E Civil War Jour., (films) Death Valley Memories, hist. and archival cons. Echoes Through Death Valley, Chasing the Rainbow, hist. cons. (TV series) A&E Biography, Guns of Infamy, archival cons., hist. cons., prodr. Haunted History, Echoes Through Time Death Valley; editor: Gun Report; prodr.: (films) L.A. Bounty, the 20 Mule Team of Death Valley; (TV series) Magnificent Failures, 20th Century Infamous Guns; featured (TV series) Tales of the Gun, 1998—2000; contbr. articles to profl. jours. Treas. Italian Am. Civic Coalition; chmn. dist. bd. dirs. Darwin Cmty. Svcs., 1990—92; mem. ethics bd. Universal Autograph Collectors Club; founder Ohio History Flight Mus.; bd. dirs. Calif. Cancer Found., L.A., 1978—85, pres., 1979—80; bd. dirs. Friends William S. Hart Pk. and Mus., 1990—93, v.p. mus. rels. Mem.: NARAS, Ariz. Ctr. Medieval Renaissance Studies Conf. (chair 2000—01, 2003), So. Calif. Autograph Soc. (v.p.), S.E. Ohio Oil and Gas Assn., Medieval Acad. Am. (conf. session chair 2001—02), Am. Numismatic Assn. (dist. rep. Carson City 1981—82, L.A. 1982—83), Nat. Italian Am. Bar Assn., English Westerners Soc., Century City Bar Assn. (vice-chmn. estate planning, trust and probate com. 1979—80), Western Writers Assn., Italian Am. Lawyers Assn. (bd. govs. 1980—, 1st v.p 1984—88), L.A. County Bar Assn. (arbitration com., fee dispute resolution program), Death Valley History Assn. (life), Universal Autograph Collectors Club (mem. ethics bd., registered dealer review bd.), Mensa, Wig and Pen Club (London), Zeta Phi Eta, Phi Alpha Delta, Pi Gamma Mu, Beta Alpha Psi (pres. 1972), Omicron Delta Epsilon. also: 230 S Main St Darwin CA 93522 Office Phone: 805-777-7223.

**PALCHICK, BERNARD S.,** academic administrator, art educator; m. Lisa Palchick; children: Linnea, Benjamin. BA in Painting, Purdue U., 1967; MFA in Sculpture, RISD, 1971. Instr. art Kalamazoo Coll., 1972—74, asst. prof. art, 1974—79, assoc. prof. art, 1979—87, prof. art, 1987—, chair art dept., 1977—85, chair divsn. fine arts, 1982—95, dir. endowed artist-in-residence program, 1984—, assoc. provost, 1987—89, spl. asst. to pres. for comm., 1990, acting chair theatre dept., 1994—95, acting provost, 1996—97, v.p. for coll. advancement, 1997—, interim pres., 2004—. Mem. exhbns. selection com. Kalamazoo Inst. of the Arts, 1987—99, bd. mem., 1994—99, Plaza Arts Cir., Western Mich. U., 1999—. Mem.: Mich. Watercolor Soc., Watercolor USA Honor Soc., Coun. for Advancement and Support of Edn. Office: Kalamazoo Coll 1200 Academy St Kalamazoo MI 49006 E-mail: palchick@kzoo.edu.

**PALDUS, JOSEF,** mathematics professor; b. Bzi, Czech Republic, Nov. 25, 1935; arrived in Can., 1968; s. Josef and Ludmila (Danicek) P.; m. Eva Zdena Bajer, Jan. 26, 1961; 1 dau., Barbara Alice. MSc, Charles U., Prague, 1958, DrSc, 1995; PhD, Czechoslovak Acad. Sci., Prague, 1961; Drhc, Comenius U., Bratsilava, Slovakia. Research scientist Czechoslovak Acad. Scis., Prague, 1961-62, 64-68; postdoctoral fellow NRC, Ottawa, Canada, 1962-64; assoc. prof. applied math. U. Waterloo, Ont., Canada, 1968-75; prof. Ont., 1975-2001, disting. prof. emeritus Ont., 2001—; assoc. dir. Fields Inst., 1992-95. Vis. U. Rheims, 1973, U. Louis Pasteur, Strasbourg, France, 1975-76, 82-83, Cath. U., Nijmegen, Holland, 1981, Technion, Haifa, Israel, 1983, Max Planck Inst. for Astrophysics, Munich, Germany, 1997, 98, 99, 2005; vis. scientist NRC, Ottawa, 1966-68, Free U. Berlin, 1981; adj. prof. chemistry U. Fla., Gainesville, 1984—; fellow Inst. for Advanced Study, Berlin, 1986-87. Mem. editl. bd. Comtex Sci., 1981-83, Advances in Quantum Chemistry, 1986, Jour. Chem. Physics, 1987-89, Can. Jour. Chemistry, 1994-96, Internat. Jour. Quantum Chemistry, 1996; mem. adv. editl. bd. Internat. Jour. Quantum Chemistry, 1977-88, Theoretica Chimica Acta, 1988-94, Jour. Math. Chemistry, 1989; contbr. numerous articles to profl. jours., chpts. to books. Recipient prize Chemistry divsn., Czechoslovak Acad. Scis., 1962, 1967, J. Heyrovsky Gold medal, Czechoslovak Acad. Sci., 1992, Gold medal Faculty of Math and Physics, Comenius U., Slovakia, 1994, Alexander von Humboldt Sr. Scientist award, 1996, Charles U. Gold medal, Prague, Czech Republic, 2005; Killam Rsch. fellow, 1987—89, Fields Inst. for Rsch. in Math. Scis. fellow, 2002. Fellow Royal Soc. Can.; mem. Internat. Acad. Quantum Molecular Sci., Internat. Soc. Theoretical Chem. Physics (bd. dirs.), European Acad. Scis., Arts and Letters (corr.), Czech Learned Soc. (hon.), Am. Inst. Physics, NY Acad. Scis., Applied Math. Soc. Can. Roman Catholic. Office: U Waterloo Dept Applied Math University Ave Waterloo ON Canada N2L 3G1 Office Phone: 519-888-4567 ext. 6267. Business E-Mail: paldus@scienide.uwaterloo.ca.

**PALEN, J(OSEPH) JOHN,** social sciences educator; b. Dubuque, Iowa, Feb. 24, 1939; s. Joseph John Palen and Mary (Rowan) Toner; m. Karen Ann Doody, June 9, 1962; children: Joseph John, Elizabeth Ann, Ellen Marye. BA, U. Notre Dame, 1961; MS, U. Wis., Madison, 1963, PhD, 1967. Demographer UN, Addis Ababa, Ethiopia, 1971—72; assoc. prof. U. Wis., Milw., 1972—77, prof., 1977—80; vis. prof. Nat. U. Singapore, 1983—84; prof. sociology, chmn. dept. Va. Commonwealth U., Richmond, 1980—. Author: Gentrification, Displacement and Revitalization, 1984, Urban World, 7th edit., 2005, City Scenes, 2d edit., 1981, The Suburbs, 1995, Social Problems for the Twenty-First Century, 2001. Leader Boy Scouts Am., Wis., 1973-80; pres. Torch Club, 2006. Grantee, Rockefeller Found., 1985, NIH, 1980—82, Ford Found., 1979, NIMH, 1976, NSF, 1985; Sr. Fulbright scholar, Taiwan, 1992, Fulbright Disting. Lectr. and Chair in N.Am. Studies, U. Calgary, 1997, Fulbright scholar, Germany, 2002, Disting. scholar, Va. Commonwealth U., 1995. Mem. Fellow Am. Sociol. Assn., So. Sociol. Soc.; mem. Urban Affairs Assn. Avocations: hiking, canoeing, history. Home: 500 Gardiner Rd Richmond VA 23229-6919 Office: Va Commonwealth U Dept Sociology Richmond VA 23284 Office Phone: 804-828-2413. Business E-Mail: jjpalen@vcu.edu.

**PALEN, JOSEPH WILLIAM,** chemical process research company executive; b. Springfield, Mo., June 4, 1935; s. John Carlyle and Jean Allen (Gravely) P.; m. Louise Kibler, Sept. 13, 1956 (div. 1977); children: Patti, Joni, James; m. Kasdina Kasdan, June 4, 1977; children: Indradini, Indrasto, Indrastati. BS in Chem. Engring., U. Mo., 1957; MS in Chem. Engring., U.

Ill., 1965; PhD in Chem. Engrng., Lehigh U., 1988. Process design engr. Phillips Petroleum Co., Bartlesville, Okla., 1957-63; rsch. engr. Heat Transfer Rsch., Inc., Alhambra, Calif., 1965-68, asst., then assoc. tech. dir., 1968-86, prin. staff cons., 1988-90; prin. rsch. engr. Heat Transfer Rsch. Inc., College Station, Tex., 1992–2000, dir. rsch., 2000—; adj. prof. Bandung Inst. Tech., Indonesia, 1990-92. Patentee in field; editor: Heat Exchanger Sourcebook, 1986; contbr. to tech. publs. Lectr., UNESCO, Yugoslavia, 1981. Fellow AIChE (lectr. internat. heat transfer conf. 1986, D.Q. Kern award 1995); mem. Tau Beta Pi. Democrat. Baptist. Avocations: reading, exercise, music, personal computers. Office: Heat Transfer Rsch Inc 150 Venture Dr College Station TX 77845 Home: 5243 Olympic Cir Eugene OR 97402-6484

**PALERMO, ANTHONY ROBERT,** lawyer; s. Anthony C. and Mary (Palvino) P.; m. Mary Ann Coyne, Jan. 2, 1960; children: Mark Henry, Christopher Coyne, Peter Stuart, Elisabeth Megan McCarthy, Julie Coyne Lawther, Gregg Anthony. BA, U. Mich., 1951; JD, Georgetown U., 1956. Bar: DC 1956, NY 1957, U.S. Supreme Ct. 1961. Trial atty. U.S. Dept. Justice, Washington, 1956-58, asst. U.S. atty. N.Y.C., 1958-60, asst. U.S. atty. in charge Rochester, NY, 1960-61; ptnr. Brennan, Centner, Palermo & Blauvelt, Rochester, 1962-81, Harter, Secrest & Emery, Rochester, 1981-94, Hodgson, Russ, Andrews, Woods & Goodyear, LLP, Rochester, 1994-97, of counsel, 1998, Woods Oviatt Gilman LLP, Rochester, 1999—. Note editor Georgetown Law Jour., 1956. Bd. dirs. McQuaid Jesuit H.S., Rochester, 1978-84, St. Ann's Home, Rochester, 1974-2001; bd. dirs., sec. St. Ann's Found., Rochester, 1989-2001; trustee, charter chmn. Clients' Security Fund N.Y. (now Lawyer's Fund for Client Protection), 1981-90; chmn. Govs Jud. Screening Com. 4th Jud. Dept., mem. statewide com., 1987-89; chair magistrate selection com. U.S. Dist. Ct. (we. dist.) N.Y., 1995, 98; mem. N.Y. Chief Judge's Commn. on Jud. Salaries, 1997-2000; mem. N.Y. Office Ct. Adminstrn. Commn. on Fiduciary Appointments, 2004—. Fellow Am. Bar Assn., 1951—54. Fellow Am. Bar Found., N.Y. State Bar Found. (bd. dirs. 1978-91), Am. Coll. Trial Lawyers; mem. ABA (ho. dels. 1980-98, 2004—, state del. 1982-85, bd. govs. 1985-88, 1989-93, sec. 1990-93), N.Y. State Bar Assn. (pres. 1979-80, ho. dels. 1973-75, 77—), Monroe County Bar Assn. (pres. 1973, Rodenbeck award, 1998), Oak Hill Country Club. Roman Catholic. Avocations: golf, travel. Home: 38 Huntington Meadow Rochester NY 14625-1813 Office Phone: 585-987-2882. Business E-Mail: apalermo@woodsoviatt.com.

**PALERMO, GREGORY SEBASTIAN,** architect; b. Westfield, N.Y., Oct. 28, 1946; s. Sebastian and Frances Joan (Ciminella) P.;m. Olivia Madison; children: Mark Sebastian, Christopher Anthony. BArch, Carnegie Mellon U., 1969; MArch in Urban Design, Wash. U., 1976. Registered architect, Mo., Calif., N.Y., Iowa. Architect PGAV Inc., St. Louis, 1976-79; sr. v.p. HOK, Inc., St. Louis, 1980-87; sr. assoc. Mackey Assocs., St. Louis, 1987-89; v.p., prin. Stone Marraccini Patterson, St. Louis, 1989-91. Affiliate asst. prof. Washington U. Sch. Arch., 1984-90; vis. assoc. prof. Iowa State U. Dept. Arch., 1992-95, assoc. prof., 1995-2001, prof., 2001—, undergrad. program coord., 1996-98, assoc. chair undergrad. program, 1999—; chair Des Moines Archtl. Adv. Com., 1996-97; mem. Des Moines Gateway Planning Com., 1996. Editorial bd. Iowa Architect mag., 1992—, assoc. ed., 1995—. Mem. Light Rail Transit Rev. Com., 1985, St. Louis Mayoral Task Force, 1986; exec/coun. Arts in Transit Com., St. Louis, 1987—; chmn. design rev. com.,St. Louis Metrolink Transit System, 1989-91; chair Nat. AIA Edn. Task Force, 1990; mem. Leadership St. Louis, 1990-91, Archtl. Adv. Commn. city of Des Moines, 1992-2000. Fellow AIA (bd. dirs., nat. v.p., pres. Iowa chpt. 2004); mem. Nat. Archtl. Accreditation Bd (pres. 1993-94). Home: 2048 Pinehurst Dr Ames IA 50010-4561

**PALESKY, CAROL EAST,** tax accountant; b. Orange, N.J., May 13, 1940; d. Neil Norell and Marie R. Reiss; m. Jacob Palesky; children: Donna, Lewis. AB, Am. Inst., Pleasantville, N.J., 1973; postgrad., Am. Inst., Portland, Maine, 1980; student, Atlantic C.C., Mays Landing, N.J., 1971-73. With mgmt. First Nat. Bank of South Jersey (now First Fidelity), Pleasantville, NJ, 1967-74; loan officer Maine Savs. Bank, Portland, 1980-81; acct., owner East Acctg. Assocs., Topsham, Maine, 1985—. Pres. Sensible Tax Limits Coalition, 1995—. Treas., bd. dirs. Congl. Term Limits Coalition, Topsham, 1993—; bd. dirs. Maine Citizens Rev. Bd., Portland, 1992-94. Scholar Nat. Taxpayer Union, 1992, 94; recipient United to Serve Am. award, 1992. Mem. Nat. Assn. Small Business Owners, Maine Taxpayers Action Network (pres. 1990—), Topsham Taxpayer Assn. (pres. 1991—). Roman Catholic. Home and Office: 24 Sokokis Cir Topsham ME 04086-1615 Office Phone: 207-725-4539. E-mail: carol@clinic.net.

**PALESTRO, CHRISTOPHER J.,** physician; m. Lynnette V. Stevens, May 24, 1985; children: Christopher J., Sarah Alice, Alexander Steven, Lissette Halle, Vincent Giancarlo. MD, Universidad Autonoma de Guadalajara, Mex., 1975. Diplomate Am. Bd. Nuc. Medicine, 1982. Chief nuc. medicine Norwalk (Conn.) Hosp., 1982—85; nuc. medicine physician Mt. Sinai Med. Ctr., NYC, 1985—92; chief nuc. medicine L.I. Jewish Med. Ctr., New Hyde Park, NY, 1992—. Prof. nuc. medicine and radiology Albert Einstein Coll. Medicine, Bronx, NY, 1996—; past chmn. Am. Bd. Nuc. Medicine, 2006; mem. editl. bd. Quar. Jour. Nuc. Medicine and Molecular Imaging. Assoc. editor: Radiology, mem. editl. bd.: Quarterly Jour. Nuc. Medicine and Molecular Imaging, 2005; contbr. articles to profl. jours. including Jour. Nuc. Medicine, Radiology, RadioGraphics. Fellow: Am. Coll. Nuc. Physicians; mem.: Internat. Skeletal Soc., Radiol. Soc. N.Am., Soc. Nuc. Medicine. Office: Long Island Jewish Med Ctr 270-05 76th Ave New Hyde Park NY 11040 E-mail: palestro@lij.edu.

**PALEVSKY, MAX,** industrialist, director; b. Chgo., July 24, 1924; s. Isadore and Sarah (Greenblatt) P.; children: Nicholas, Madeleine, Alexander, Jonathan, Matthew. Ph.B., BS, U. Chgo., 1948; postgrad., U. Calif.-Berkeley, U. Chgo., UCLA, 1951-52. Mathematician Computer div. Bendix Corp., Los Angeles, 1952-56; v.p., gen. mgr. div. Packard Bell Electronics, Los Angeles, 1957-61; pres., chmn. bd. Sci. Data Systems; chmn. bd. Xerox Data Systems, Inc., El Segundo, Calif., 1961-72; dir. Xerox Corp., 1969-72, chmn. exec. com. of bd., 1969-72. Bd. dirs. Intel Corp., Santa Clara, Calif., Komag, Inc., Milpitas, Calif. Organized George McGovern's campaign for Pres. of U.S., 1972; organized and ran Tom Bradley's campaign for Mayor of L.A., 1973; mem. Folger com. Folger Shakespeare Libr., Washington, 1977—; mem. Dem. Adv. Com., 1968—; bd. dirs. ACLU, Constl. Rights Found.; trustee The Inst. for Advanced Study, Princeton U., 1980—. With USAAF, 1943-46. Office: 924 Westwood Blvd Ste 700 Los Angeles CA 90024-2928

**PALEVSKY, PAUL MARC,** nephrologist, educator; b. N.Y.C., Dec. 29, 1957; s. Gerald and Estelle (Moore) P.; m. Sharon Renee Roseman, Sept. 4, 1983; children: Hilary Ilana, Jason Michael. BS, Northestern U., 1979, MD, 1981. Diplomate Am. Bd. Internal Medicine, Am. Bd. Internal Medicine (Nephrology). Intern, resident Internal Medicine Hosp., U. Pa., Phila. 1981-84; fellow nephrology U. Pa., Phila., 1984-88, rsch. assoc., 1988-89; asst. prof. U. Pitts. Med. Sch., 1989-95, assoc. prof., 1995–2001, prof., 2001—. Chief Hemodialysis unit VA Pitts. Health Care Sys., 1989—, chief renal sect., 1993—; med. rev. ESRD Network 4, Pitts., 1989—. Contbr. articles to profl. jours. Fellow ACP, ACCP, Am. Soc. Nephrology; mem. Internat. Soc. Nephrology, Am. Soc. Nephrology, Am. Heart Assn. (Coun. on Kidney in Cardiovasc. Disease), Nat. Kidney Found., Alpha Omega Alpha. Home: 109 Bell Farm Ests Sewickley PA 15143-8367 Office: VA Pitts Health Care Sys University Dr Divsn Pittsburgh PA 15240 Office Phone: 412-688-6474. E-mail: palevsky@pitt.edu.

**PALEY, ALAN H.,** lawyer; b. Apr. 28, 1950; BA, Case Western Res. U., 1972; JD, NYU, 1975, LLM, 1976. Bar: NY 1976. Fellow securities inst. sch. law NYU, 1975-76; assoc. Debevoise & Plimpton, NYC, 1976—84, ptnr., 1984—, co-chair Securities Practice Group. Mem. Phi Beta Kappa. Office: Debevoise & Plimpton LLP 919 Third Ave New York NY 10022 Office Phone: 212-909-6694. Home Fax: 212-909-6386. E-mail: ahpaley@debevoise.com.

**PALEY, GERALD LARRY,** lawyer; b. Albany, N.Y., Sept. 11, 1939; s. Arthur and Mary (Peckner) P.; m. Joyce R., June 25, 1961 (div. June 1985); children: Jonathan, Eric, Suzanne; m. Sheryl Gae, Aug. 14, 1985. BA, Union Coll., 1961; JD with distinction, Cornell U., 1964. Bar: N.Y. 1964. Assoc. Nixon, Hargrave, Devans & Doyle, Rochester, NY, 1964-69; assoc. solicitor Dept. Labor, Washington, 1969-71; ptnr. Nixon, Hargrave, Devans & Doyle, Rochester, 1971-87, Phillips, Lytle, Hitchcock, Blaine & Huber, Rochester, 1987—. Author: Handbook of Federal Labor Relations Laws, 1981, Understand Employee Regulations, 1984. Mem. ABA. Republican. Jewish. Office: Phillips Lytle Hitchcock et al 1400 First Federal Plz Rochester NY 14614-1981 Office Phone: 585-238-2008.

**PALEY, GRACE,** author, educator; b. NYC, Dec. 11, 1922; d. Isaac and Mary (Ridnyik) Goodside; m. Jess Paley, June 20, 1942 (div. 1971); children: Nora, Dan.; m. Robert Nichols, 1972. Student, Hunter Coll., NYU. Formerly tchr. Columbia, Syracuse U.; ret. mem. lit. faculty Sarah Lawrence Coll., Stanford, Johns Hopkins, Dartmouth, CUNY. Author: The Little Disturbances of Man, 1959, Enormous Changes at the Last Minute, 1974, Leaning Forward, 1985, Later the Same Day, 1985, Long Walks and Intimate Talks, 1991, New and Collected Poems, 1992, The Collected Stories, 1994 (Nat. Book award nomination, 1994), Just As I Thought, 1998, Begin Again Collected Poems, 2000; contbr. stories to Atlantic, New Yorker, Ikon, Genesis West, others. Soc. N.Y. Greenwich Village Peace Center. Recipient Literary award for short story writing Nat. Inst. Arts and Letters, 1970, Edith Wharton award N.Y. State, 1988, 89, Rea award for short story, 1993, Vt. Gov.'s award for Excellence in the Arts, 1993, award for contbn. to Jewish culture Nat. Found. Jewish Culture; Guggenheim fellow; apptd. Vt. Poet Laureate, 2003—. Mem. Am. Acad. and Inst. Arts and Letters, Am. Acad. Arts and Scis. Office: PO Box 620 Thetford VT 05074-0620

**PALEY, RUSSELL ELIOT,** writer, small business owner; b. Annapolis, Md., May 23, 1969; s. Louis R and Rae Paley; m. Ronni L Krasin, July 3, 2001; 1 child, Max Andrew. BA with hons., Bryant Coll., Smithfield, R.I., 1991. Pres. Wealth Bldg. Publs., Woodbury, NY, 1995—, Wealth and Health Internat., Fla., 1991—. Author: (Book) Network Your Way to Millions, 1998. Personal E-mail: russnrole@aol.com.

**PALEY, VITALY,** chef, food service executive; Studied piano, The Juliard Sch.; grand diploma, French Culinary Inst. NY. Chef Union Sq Cafe, Remi, Chanterelle, Moulin de la Gorce. Recipient Best Chef: Northwest/Hawaii, The James Beard Found., 2005. Office: Paley's Place Bistro & Bar 1204 NW 21st Ave Portland OR 97209\*

**PALIA, ASPY PHIROZE,** marketing educator, researcher, consultant; b. Bombay, Nov. 27, 1944; arrived in US, 1973; s. Phiroze E. and Homai P. (Irani) P. BSME, U. Bangalore, 1966; MBA, U. Hawaii at Manoa, 1976; DBA, Kent State U., 1985. Sales engr. Larsen & Toubro Ltd., 1966—72, export sales engr., 1972—73; tchg. fellow Coll. Bus. Adminstrn. Kent State U., 1977—80, instr. Coll. Bus. Adminstrn., 1982—84; asst. prof. Coll. Bus. Adminstrn. U. Hawaii, Manoa, 1984—89, assoc. prof., 1990—95, prof., 1996—, pres. faculty coun., 1995—96; senator U. Hawaii Manoa Faculty Congress, 1996—98; sr. fellow dept. mktg. Nat. U. Singapore, 1998—99, vis. sr. fellow dept. mktg., 2000—02. Vis. prof. Coll. Mgmt. Nat. Sun Yat-sen U., Kaohsiung, Taiwan, 1992, Chulalongkorn U., Bangkok, 1992—93, 1997, 2003, 2005—06, U. Otago, New Zealand, 1995, Adminstrv. Staff Coll. India, Hyderabad, 1992, Indian Inst. Mgmt., Ahmedabad, 2000, Asian Inst. Tech., Bangkok, 2001; mem. U. Hawaii Manoa Ctr. for Teaching Excellence Faculty Adv. Group, 1991; mem. mktg. plan adv. com. U. Hawaii, Manoa, 1994, mem. honors and awards com., 1990—91, pres. faculty coun., 1995—96, mem. faculty adv. com. on acad. freedom, 1997; vis. scholar faculty bus. adminstrn. Nat. U. Singapore, 1991, Mktg. Inst. Singapore Exec. Devel. Seminars, 1991, 1994—95, 1997, Hong Kong Inst. Mktg. Exec. Devel. Seminar, 1996, Kathmandu Coll. Mgmt. Exec. Devel. Workshop, 2000; sr. fellow dept. mktg. faculty of bus. adminstrn. Nat. U. Singapore, 1998—99, vis. prof., 2000—02; affiliate faculty Japan Am. Inst. Mgmt. Sci., Honolulu, 1989—; vis. prof. Grad. Sch. Internat. Mgmt., Internat. U. Japan, Uhrasa, Yamato-machi, 1991, U. Internat. Bus. and Econs., Beijing, 1991, U. Kebangsaan Malaysia, Bangi-Selangor, Kuala Lumpur, Malaysia, 1991—92, Mt. Carmel Inst. Mgmt., Bangalore, India, 1997, Vietnam Nat. U., Hanoi Sch Bus., 2002, Singapore Mgmt. U., 2003—04; vis. scholar faculty bus. adminstrn. Boston Network Exec. Develop. Workshop, Bangkok, 2003; lectr., cons., presenter in field. Editor: (with Dennis A. Rondinelli) Project Planning and Implementation in Developing Countries, 1976; assoc. editor e-Services Quar., 1999—; contbr. articles to profl. jours. including Indsl. Mktg. Mgmt., Internat. Bus. Jour., Asia-Pacific Jour. Mgmt., Internat. Mktg. Rev., European Jour. Mktg., Fgn. Trade Rev., Internat. Rev. Econs. & Bus., others; chpts. to books; developer various mktg. decision support systems and decision-making tools for use in strategic market planning and in marketing simulations. Program rev. com. Pacific and Asian Mgmt. Inst., Acad. Internat. Bus., Assn. Bus. Simulation and Exptl. Learning, others; bd. examiners Nat. U. Singapore Sch. Postgrad. Mgmt. Studies, 1991; external examiner Bd. Grad. Studies, Nat. U. Singapore, 2001-2002; adv. bd. Soc. Coll. of Bus. Adminstrn. Alumni and Friends Exec. Com., 1991-93, Salvation Army Residential Treatment Facilities for Children and Youth Adv. Coun., 1989-96, vice chair, 1987-89; chair Salvation Army Family Treatment Svcs. Adv. Coun., 1997-98; mem. Salvation Army Honolulu Adv. Bd., 1997-98; treas., bd. dirs. Kings Gate Homeowners Assn., 1994-96; bd. advisors Ctr. for Nat. Competitiveness Inst. Indsl. Policy Studies, Korea, 1998—. Univ. fellow Kent State U., 1983; East-West Ctr. scholar East-West Ctr., 1973-75; Ednl. Improvement Fund grantee, 1989, Instrl. Travel and Devel. Fund grantee Office Faculty Devel. and Acad. Support, 1991, 95, joint rsch. grants U. Kebangsaan Malaysia Nat. U. Queensland, Australia, U. Otago, New Zealand, Lingnan Coll., Hong Kong; recipient Internat. Agreements Fund award Office Internat. Programs and Svcs., 1990-92, ORA travel award U. Rsch. Coun., 1986, 88-89, 91-92, 94-98. Mem. Am. Mktg. Assn. (academia editor Honolulu chpt. 1986-87), Acad. Internat. Bus. (chair Pacific Basin Region 1995, chair Pacific Basin chpt. 1996-2002, co-chair Asia Pacific Conf. 1997), Pacific Asian Consortium for Internat. Bus. Edn. and Rsch., Assn. for Bus. Simulation and Exptl. Learning, Pan-Pacific Bus. Assn. (charter), Mortar Bd. (Outstanding Educator award 1993, Mentor award 1995), East-West Ctr. Alumni Assn. U.S. (v.p. Hawaii chpt. 1987-89, ad campaign com. 1987-88), Beta Gamma Sigma (faculty assoc. sec.-treas. Alpha of Hawaii chpt. 1990—, Outstanding Svc. award 1992-93, Bd. Govs. Commitment to Excellence award 1997, Prof. of Yr. award 2003), Mu Kappa Tau, Pi Sigma Epsilon. Avocations: music, photography, swimming, reading, hiking. Home: 2724 Kahoaloha Ln # 1605 Honolulu HI 96826-3337 Office: U Hawaii Dept Mktg 2404 Malie Way Honolulu HI 96822-2223 Office Phone: 808-956-8642. Business E-Mail: aspy@hawaii.edu.

**PALILEO, HAZEL VALENCIA,** videographer; b. Pila, Laguna, Philippines, May 22, 1951; came to U.S., 1971, naturalized citizen, 1979; d. Lauro Gomez and Edna (Valencia) P. BFA in Photography and Media, Wright State U., 1976; student, DeVry Inst. Tech., 1995-97; diploma, Applied Multimedia Tng. Ctrs., 1998; cert. web designer, U. Calgary, 2002. Lab. tech. Valdhere Films, Inc., Dayton, Ohio, 1973-76; news photographer Sta. WDTN-TV, Dayton, 1977-79; videographer Sta. WKEF-TV News, Dayton, 1979-86, chief videographer, 1983-86; videographer, still photographer Wycliffe Bible Translators, Calgary, Alta., Can., 1986-92, co-mgr. media prodns. dept., 1990-92; video mgr., media coord. Cornerstone Comms., Calgary, 1992-94; photographer, videographer and multi media specialist freelance, Calgary, 1994—; media technician U. Calgary, 1998—. Videographer (TV news) Haviland Ave. Fire, 1984 (Emmy 1984). Recipient Best Video award Nat. Cath. Stewardship Conf., 1993. Mem. Aud. Bus. of Canada. Avocations: reading, photography, travel, walking. Business E-Mail: palileo@ucalgary.ca.

**PALIN, MICHAEL EDWARD,** actor, scriptwriter, writer; b. May 5, 1943; s. Edward and Mary P.; m. Helen M. Gibbins, 1966; 3 children. BA, U. Oxford, Eng., 1965. Writer, performer BBC Corp., 1965-69. Presenter in field. Actor, writer: (TV shows) Monty Python's Flying Circus, 1969-74, Ripping Yarns, 1976-80; (films) And Now for Something Completely Different, 1970, Monty Python and the Holy Grail, 1974, Monty Python's Life of Brian, 1978, Time Bandits, 1980, Monty Python's The Meaning of Life, 1982, American Friends, 1991; TV presenter, writer Great Railway Journeys of the World, 1980, Around the World in 80 Days, 1989, Pole to Pole, 1993, Palin's Column, 1994, Great Railway Journeys of the World, 1994, Full Circle, 1997, Michael Palin's Hemingway Adventure, 1999, Sahara with Michael Palin, 2002, Himalaya with Michael Palin, 2004; television presenter: Palin on Redpath, 1997, The Bright Side of Life, 2000, The Ladies Who Loved Matisse, 2003, Michael Palin & The Mystery of Hammershoi, 2005; actor: (TV shows) Three Men in a Boat, 1975, GBH, 1991; (films) Jabberwocky, 1976, A Private Function, 1984, Brazil, 1985, A Fish Called Wanda (Best Supporting Actor Brit. Acad. Film and TV Arts, 1989), Fierce Creatures, 1998; actor, writer and co-prodr.: The Missionary, 1982; writer (stage play) The Weekend, 1994; author: Monty Python's Big Red Book, 1970, Monty Python's Brand New Book, 1973, Dr. Fegg's Encyclopeadia of All World Knowledge, 1984, Limericks, 1985, Around the World in 80 Days, 1989, Pole to Pole, 1993, Pole to Pole: The Photographs, 1994, Hemingway's Chair 1995, Full Circle, 1997, Full Circle: The Photographs, 1997, Hemingway Adventure, 1999, Sahara, 2002, Himalaya, 2004; (children's books) Small Harry and the Toothache Pills, 1981, The Mirrorstone, 1986, The Cyril Stories, 1986. Co-recipient (with Monty Python) Michael Balcon award for outstanding contbn. to cinema, Brit. Acad. Film and TV Arts, 1987; named Book of Yr., Brit. Books awards, 2005; named to CBE New Yr.'s Honours List for Svc. to TV, Drama & Travel, 2000; recipient Lifetime Achievement award, Brit. Comedy Awards, 2002, Spl. award, BAFTA, 2005. Avocations: reading, running, railways. Office: 34 Tavistock St London WC2E 7PB England E-mail: paulbird@prominent-tv.co.uk.

**PALION, PETER THADDEUS,** financial planner; b. Warsaw, Jan. 14, 1966; came to U.S., 1982; s. Karol and Zofia (Biernacka) P.; m. Monica Witak, Jan. 18, 1992. Student, CUNY, 1984-85; CFP. Coll. Fin. Planning, Denver, 1993. Fin. cons. Shearson Lehman Bros., N.Y.C., 1987-88; fin. planner IDS Fin. Svcs., Inc., N.Y.C., 1988-94; pres., chmn. bd. dirs. Master Plan Advisory, Inc., N.Y.C., 1994—; registered rep., prin. various ind. broker dealers; registered prin. Comprehensive Asset Mgmt. and Servicing. Mem. NASD/SIPC, 2003—. Stock market cons. Polish Govt., Warsaw, 1990; guest spkr. on East European markets Voice of Am., Washington, 1990-93, on investments N.Y.C. Channel 31 Polish TV, 1991, CNNfn, 1997, 98, Neighborhood News 13; featured spkr. Times/Ledger Newspapers-IAFP Person Finance Day, 1998, 99, 2000; tchr. investment planning courses Hofstra U., 1999-2000. Author article series Kariera, 1990. Avocations: tennis, skiing, reading, motorsports. Office: Master Plan Advisory Inc 60 E 42nd St Fl 46 New York NY 10165-4699

**PALISI, ANTHONY THOMAS,** psychologist, educator; b. Rahway, NJ, Mar. 8, 1930; s. Anthony Francis and Marianne Catherine (Picone) P.; m. Dyane Cassidy, Apr. 19, 1954; children: Jane, Anthony Francis II, Phyllis, Damian-Marie. BS, Seton Hall U., 1951, MA, 1958; EdD, Temple U., 1973. Cert. secondary tchr., elem. prin., psychologist, rehab. counselor, N.J.; mem. Nat. Register Health Care Profls. in Psychology. Tchr., coach pub. schs., Rahway, 1953-60; sports editor Rahway News-Record, 1950-60; prin. elem. pub. sch. Franklin Twp., NJ, 1960-65; asst. prof. edn. Seton Hall U., 1965-73, assoc. prof., 1974-77, prof., 1977-82, acting grad. dean, 1976-77, dir., 1969-80, indsl. cons. group dynamics, 1967-97; pvt. practice psychology, 1977; dir. edn. divsn. FormTech Graphics, Inc., 1997—. Adj. faculty Brookdale C.C., 2005—, Prevention, Inc. Contbr. articles and short stories to profl. jours. and popular periodicals. Mem. Rahway Bd. Edn. 1961-62; trustee Rahway Libr., 1961-68, pres. 1967-68. Recipient award N.J. Sportswriters' Assn., 1953. Mem. APA, ACA, Am. Mgmt. Assn. (co-author video tng. program), N.J. Psychol. Assn., Assn. for Specialists in Group Work (mem. rsch. com. 1980-82), N.Y. Acad. Scis., Nat. Acad. Counselors and Family Therapists (chmn., exec. dir. 1988-93, co-editor Family Letter 1985-93), Nat. Register of Health Svc. Providers in Psychology, Am. Coll. Counselors., Clin. Hypnosis Soc. NJ. Roman Catholic. Office Phone: 732-223-5379. E-mail: atu74palisi@verizon.net.

**PALKOVIC, FRANCIS THEODORE,** artist, educator; b. Schenectady, N.Y., Dec. 25, 1957; s. Joseph Anthony and Loni Frieda Palkovic; m. Rie Shepherd, Apr. 8, 1994; children: Nathan Gene Whittington, Leah Hiromi Whittington, Elizabeth Whittington. MFA, N.Mex. State U., Las Cruces, 1993. Ceramics instr. Big Bend C.C., Moses Lake, Wash., 1998—, three dimensional design instr., 1999—, art appreciation instr., 1999—; lead instr. intro. to art Wash. On Line, Spokane, Wash., 2000—. Chair amateur exhbns. com. Moses Lake Mus. and Arts Ctr., Moses Lake, Wash., 2003—. One-man shows include Archetypal Angels ceramic sculpture, drawings, collages, Moses Lake Mus. and Arts Ctr., 2006, prin. works include Ink and Clay 30 Kellogg Gallery Pomona California (Limbo), Americas 2000 Minot North Dakota (Flybot 2), ceramic sculpture/ digital prints, Featured Artist at Seven Muses Gallery Tacoma, WA, ceramic sculptural installation, Alchemical Individuation, ceramic sculptures, The Just for Fun Exhibition Chase Gallery, Spokane, WA, exhibitions include Metempsychosis, Columbia Basin, 2004, 2005, 2006, traveling internat. mus. exhbn., Wenatchee Valley Mus., 2006. Performing artist Grant County Dem. Hdqs., Moses Lake, Wash., 2004. With USAF, 1976—82. Mem.: Coll. Art Assn. Green Party. Avocations: musical compositon, musical performing, writing, gardening, reading. Home: 2107 West Peninsula Dr Moses Lake WA 98837 Office: Big Bend Community College 7662 Chanute St Moses Lake WA 98837 Office Phone: 509-793-2275. Personal E-mail: ftpalkovic@excite.com. E-mail: franp@bigbend.edu.

**PALKOVIC, MICHAEL W.,** broadcast executive; With Times Mirror Cable Television, DirecTV Inc., El Segundo, Calif., 1990—, sr. v.p., CFO, 2001—04, exec., v.p., CFO, 2004—, DirecTV Group Inc., 2005—. Office: DirecTV Group 2250 E Imperial Way El Segundo CA 90245-0956\*

**PALL, ELLEN JANE,** writer; b. NYC, Mar. 28, 1952; d. David B. and Josephine H. (Blatt) P.; m. Richard Holmes Dicker, July 12, 1986; 1 child, Benjamin. BA, U. Calif., Santa Barbara, 1973. Freelance writer for several jours., 1987—. Staff assoc. Bread Loaf Writers Conf., Middlebury, Vt., 1986; instr. UCLA-Ext., 1980-83; adj. asst. prof. Fordham U./Coll. at Lincoln Ctr., N.Y.C., 1990-93. Author (under pen name Fiona Hill): The Trellised Lane, The Wedding Portrait, The Practical Heart, Love in a Major Key, Sweet's Folly, The Autumn Rose, The Love Child, The Stanbroke Girls, 1981, The Country Gentleman, 1987; author: (as Ellen Pall) Back East, 1983, Among the Ginzburgs, 1996, Corpse de Ballet, 2001, Slightly Abridged, 2003; contbr. articles to N.Y.Times Mag., N.Y. Times Arts & Leisure, New Yorker mag., Chgo. Tribune, Washington Post; book reviewer. Shane Stevens fellow, Bread Loaf Writer's Conf., Vt., 1983. Mem. Am. PEN (freedom to write com.). Office: care Mary Evans Inc 242 E 5th St New York NY 10003-8501 Business E-Mail: ellen@ellenpall.com.

**PALLADINO-CRAIG, ALLYS,** museum director, educator; b. Pontiac, Mich., Mar. 23, 1947; d. Stephan Vincent and Mary (Anderson) Palladino; m. Malcolm Arnold Craig, Aug. 20, 1967; children: Ansel, Reed, Nicholas. BA in English, Fla. State U., 1969; M.Z., 1967; grad., U. Toronto, Ont., Can., 1969; MFA, Fla. State U., 1978, PhD in Humanities, 1996. Editorial asst. project U. Va. Press, Charlottesville, 1970-76; instr. English Inst. Franco Americain, Rennes, France, 1974; adj. instr. Fla. State U., Tallahassee, 1978-82, dir. Four Arts Ctr., 1979-82, dir. U. Mus. of Fine Arts, 1982—, prof. mus. studies. Mem. grad faculty Mus. Studies Cert. Program Fla. State U. Curator, contbg. editor: Nocturnes and Nightmares, Monochrome/Polychrome, Chroma, High Roads & Low Roads-Anthems, Dirges, Myths; contbg. editor: Body Language; guest curator, author: Mark Messersmith: New Mythologies; curator, editor Albert Paley--Sculpture, Drawings, Graphics and Decorative Arts, Trevor Bell: A British Painter in America, and Trial by Fire: Contemporary Glass; curator, author: The Abridged Walmsley--Selections from the Career of William Aubrey Walmsley, co-curator, contbg. author: Terrestrial Forces; author: Jack Nichelson: Micro-Theatres, Alexa Kleinbard: Talking Leaves, Jake Fernandez--Ethereal Journeyman, Jim Roche-Sense of Place; curator: Athanor I-XXV, 1980—; Represented in permanent collections Fla. Ho. of Reps., Barnett Bank, IBM. Individual artist fellow Fla. Arts Coun., 1979

Mem. Am. Assn. Mus., Fla. Art Mus. Dirs. Assn. (sec. 1989-91), Phi Beta Kappa. Democrat. Avocation: antiques. Home: 1410 Grape St Tallahassee FL 32303-5636 Office: Fla State U Mus of Fine Arts 250 Fine Arts Bldg Tallahassee FL 32306-1140 Business E-Mail: apcraig@fsu.edu.

**PALLAI, DAVID FRANCIS,** publishing executive; b. NYC, Nov. 7, 1950; s. Alfiero and Clara Aurora (Dignani) P.; m. Jean Therese Leary, June 25, 1977; children: Matthew Gian, Jeremy Michael. BA, Boston Coll., 1972, MA, 1974, Yale U. 1981. Sales rep. Prentice Hall, Inc., Englewood Cliffs, NJ, 1976-77, field editor, 1977-78; acquisitions editor Allyn & Bacon, Inc. Boston, 1978-80; sr. editor PWS Pubs., Boston, 1980-87, Addison-Wesley Pub. Co., Reading, Mass., 1987-88, exec. editor, 1988-90; v.p., pub. Acad. Press, Cambridge, Mass., 1990-94; pres., founder Charles River Media, Inc., Rockland, Mass., 1994—2005; pres. Charles River Media (an imprint of Thomson Delmar Learning), Rockland, Mass., 2005—. Com. mem. Duxbury (Mass.) Hist. Commn., 1984-87. With USNG, 1972-78. Mem. Math. Assn. Am., Mensa, KC, Harvard Club, Yale Club of Boston. Republican. Roman Catholic. Avocations: softball, model shipbldg. Home: 10 Downer Ave Hingham MA 02043-1132

**PALLAM, JOHN JAMES,** lawyer; b. Cleve., May 19, 1940; s. James John and Coralia (Gatsos) P.; m. Evanthia Venizelos, Nov. 29, 1969; 1 child, Alethea. BA, Case Western Res. U., 1962; JD, Ohio State U., 1965. Bar: Ohio 1965, U.S. Ct. Claims 1969, U.S. Ct. Mil. Appeals 1969, U.S. Supreme Ct. 1970. Law clk. to presiding justice Cuyahoga County Ct., Cleve., 1965-66; assoc. Burke, Haber & Berick, Cleve., 1970-73; corp. atty. Midland Ross Corp., Cleve., 1973-80, corp. counsel, 1980-87; v.p., gen. counsel Brush Engineered Materials Inc., Cleve., 1987—. Guest lectr. Nat. Foundry Assn., Chgo., 1986—. Contbr. articles on labor and environ. matters to jours. Legal advisor Am. Hellenic and Prog. Assn., Cleve., 1966—. Served to capt. JAGC U.S. Army, 1966-70, Vietnam. Decorated Bronze Star with oak leaf cluster. Mem. Ohio Bar Assn. (committeeman 1984—), Cleve. Bar Assn. (merit svc. award 1972), Hellenic Bar Assn., Hellenic Univ. Club, Rowfant. Greek Orthodox. Avocations: history, antiques, golf, rare books, railroading. Office: 17876 Saint Clair Ave Cleveland OH 44110-2602

**PALLASCH, B. MICHAEL,** lawyer, director; b. Chgo., Mar. 30, 1933; s. Bernhard Michael and Magdalena Helena (Fixari) P.; m. Josephine Catherine O'Leary, Aug. 15, 1981; children: Bernhard Michael III and Madeleine Josephine (twins). BS, Georgetown U., 1954; JD, Harvard U., 1957; postgrad., John Marshall Law Sch., 1974. Bar: Ill. 1957, U.S. Dist. Ct. (no. dist.) Ill. 1958, U.S. Tax Ct. 1961, U.S. Ct. Claims 1961, U.S. Ct. Appeals (7th cir.) 1962. Assoc. Winston & Strawn, Chgo., 1958-66, resident mgr. br. office Paris, 1963-65, ptnr. Chgo., 1966-70, sr. capital ptnr., 1971-91; sr. ptnr. B. Michael Pallasch & Assocs., 1991—. Corp. sec. Tanis, Inc., Calumet, Mich., 1972-2000, Greenbank Engring. Corp., Dover, Del., 1976-91, C.B.P. Engring. Corp., Chgo., 1976-91, Arthur Andersen Assocs., Inc., Chgo., 1976-98, Chgo. Cutting Svcs. Corp., 1977-88, L'hotel de France of Ill., Inc., Chgo., 1980-85, Water & Effluent Screening Co., Chgo., 1988-91. Bd. dirs. Martin D'Arcy Mus. Medieval and Renaissance Art, Chgo., 1975—; bd. dirs. Katherine M. Bosch Found., 1978—; asst. sec. Hundred Club of Cook County, Chgo., 1966-73, bd. dirs., sec., 1974—. Served with USAFR, 1957-63. Decorated Knight of Merit with silver star Sacred Mil. Constantinian Order of St. George of Royal House of Bourbon of Two Sicilies, Grand Officer with gold and silver stars Sovereign Mil. Order of Temple of Jerusalem; named Youth Mayor, City of Chgo., 1950; recipient Outstanding Woodland Mgmt. Forestry award, Monroe County (Wis.) Soil and Water Conservation Dist., 1975. Mem. Ill. Bar Assn. (tax lectr. 1961), Advs. Soc., Field Mus. Natural History (life), Max McGraw Wildlife Found., English Speaking Union. Clubs: Travellers (Paris); Saddle and Cycle (Chgo.). Roman Catholic. Home: 737 W Hutchinson St Chicago IL 60613-1519 Office: 35 W Wacker Dr Ste 4700 Chicago IL 60601-1614 *Personal philosophy: We define and measure success in various ways: achievement, position, wealth: and attribute it to the application of various attributes but is there any degree of success that we can achieve that is worthier than the knowledge that we have faithfully served those who depend upon and trust in us?.*

**PALLIN, SAMUEL LEAR,** ophthalmologist, educator, medical director; b. NYC, May 8, 1941; s. Irving and Gertrude (Lear) P.; children: Daniel Jay, Marla Jean, Laura Jane; m. Karen K. King, 2004. BA, Hofstra U., 1963; MD, SUNY, Bklyn., 1968. Diplomate Nat. Bd. Med. Examiners, Am. Bd. Ophthalmology. Intern L.I. Jewish Med. Ctr., 1968-69; resident Bklyn. Eye and Ear Hosp., 1972-75; prin. The Lear Eye Clinic, Ltd., Sun City, Ariz., 1975—, Phoenix, 1998—; asst. prof. dept. ophthalmology Sch. Medicine Midwestern U., 1997—; with White Dog Ranch, LLC, Tonopah, Ariz., 2005—; physician supr., med. dir. Arizona State Prison Complex, Perryville, 2005—. Mem. staff Walter O. Boswell Meml. Hosp., Del E. Webb Meml. Hosp., St. Luke's Med. Ctr., Thunderbird Samaritan Hosp.; presenter in field. Patentee in method of making self-sealing episcleral incision. Trustee Congr. Beth El Endowment Fund, 1987; mem. exec. bd. Ariz. chpt. Israel Bonds, 1988; lt. mounted unit cmty. svcs. posse Maricopa County Sheriff's Office, 1996—. With USAF, 1969-71. Mem. AMA, ACS, Am. Cataract and Refractive Surgery, Am. Acad. Ophthalmology, Ariz. Med. Assn., Ariz. Easter Seal Soc. (bd. dirs. 1989, life dir.), Maricopa County Med. Assn., Lions, hon. mem. Mex. Ophthalmology Soc. N.E., Mex. Intraocular Implant Soc., Ctrl. Mex. Ophthalmol. Soc. Office: 33537 N Highland Ave Tonopah AZ 85354 Office Phone: 602-957-6799. Business E-Mail: whitedogranch2@earthlink.net.

**PALLMEYER, REBECCA RUTH,** judge; b. Tokyo, Sept. 13, 1954; arrived in U.S., 1957; d. Paul Henry and Ruth (Schreiber) Pallmeyer; m. Dan P. McAdams, Aug. 20, 1977; 2 children. BA, Valparaiso U., Ind., 1976; JD, U. Ill., Chgo., 1979. Bar: Ill. 1980, U.S. Ct. Appeals (7th cir.) 1980, U.S. Ct. Appeals (11th and 5th cir.) 1982. Judge clk. Minn. Supreme Ct., St. Paul, 1979-80; assoc. Hopkins and Sutter, Chgo., 1980-85; judge, administrv. law Ill. Human Rights Commn., Chgo., 1985-91; magistrate judge U.S. Dist. Ct. (No. Dist.), Chgo., 1991-98, dist. judge, 1998—. Mem. jud. resources com. Jud. Conf. U.S., 1994—2000. Nat. adv. com. Christ Coll., Valparaiso U., 2001—; bd. dirs. Augustana Ctr., 1990—91. Recipient Profl. Achievement award, Chgo.-Kent Coll. of Law, 2002, Alumni Achievement award, Valparaiso U., 2002, President's Award for Disting. Svc., N.W. Suburban Bar Assn., 2003. Mem.: FBA (bd. mgrs. Chgo. chpt. 1995—2004), Chgo. Bar Assn. (chair devel. law com. 1992—93, bd. mgrs. 2004—06, David C. Hilliard award 1990—91), Fed. Magistrate Judges Assn. (bd. dirs. 1994—97), Womens Bar Assn. Ill. (bd. mgrs. 1995—98), Valparaiso U. Alumni Assn. (bd. dirs. 1992—94). Lutheran. Avocations: choral music, sewing, running. Office: US Dist Ct 219 S Dearborn St Ste 2178 Chicago IL 60604-1877 Office Phone: 312-435-5636.

**PALLONE, FRANK, JR.,** congressman, lawyer; b. Long Branch, NJ, Oct. 30, 1951; m. Sarah Hospodor; 3 children. BA cum laude in Hist. and French, Middlebury Coll., Vt., 1973; MA in Internat. Rels., Tufts U. Sch. Law and Diplomacy, Mass., 1974; JD, Rutgers U. Sch. Law, NJ, 1978. Bar: Fla., NJ, NY, Pa. Coastal law specialist NJ Marine Adv. Svc., 1980—81; asst. prof. sea grant ext. prog. Cook Coll.-Rutgers U., NJ, 1980—81; counsel Monmouth County Protective Svcs. for the Elderly, NJ; instr. Monmouth County Cmty. Coll.; maritime atty. NYC, 1982—84; mem. City Council, Long Branch, NJ, 1982-88, NJ Senate, 1984-88, US Congress from 6th NJ dist., 1988—, mem. energy and commerce com., resources com., ranking minority mem. fisheries, conservation, wildlife and oceans subcommittee. Co-chair Congl. caucus on Armenian issues US Congress, founder Congl. caucus on India and Indian Am.; chair Dem. caucus task force on health and medicare. Named Consumer Hero, Consumer Fedn. Am., 1997, Legislator of Yr., NJ Acad. Ophthalmology, 1998, Outstanding Legislator of Yr., VFW, 1999; recipient Cancer Advocacy award, Cancer Inst. NJ, 1998, Internat. Yr. of Ocean award, Clean Ocean Action, 1998. Democrat. Roman Catholic. Office: US Ho Reps 420 Cannon Ho Office Bldg Washington DC 20515-3006 Office Phone: 202-225-4671.*

**PALLOTTA, JOHANNA ANTONIA (JOHANNA STEPHEN),** endocrinologist, educator; b. Boston, May 7, 1937; d. John and Antonia (Lanni) P.; m. Michael John Stephen, Aug. 13, 1966; children: Jacqueline, Antonia, Michael, Andrew. BS in Chemistry magna cum laude, Boston Coll., 1958; MD, N.Y. Med. Coll., 1962. Diplomate Am. Bds. Internal Medicine, Endocrinology and Metabolism; lic. N.Y., Mass., Calif. Intern St. Elizabeth's Hosp., Boston, 1962-63; resident in medicine N.Y. Med. Coll. Metro. Hosp., N.Y.C., 1963-64; resident in medicine, fellow radioisotope svc. VA Hosp., Bronx, 1964—66; fellow metabolism and endocrinology Yale U. Sch. Medicine, New Haven, 1966-67; instr. medicine Harvard Med. Sch., Boston, 1967-69, Beth Israel Deaconess Hosp. Harvard Med. Sch., 1969-70; asst. prof. medicine Harvard Med. Sch., 1970—2003, assoc. prof. medicine, 2004—. Tutor med. scis. Harvard Med. Sch., 1972-73; dir. endocrinology clinic Beth Israel Deaconess Hosp., Boston, 1967—, dir. radioimmunoassay lab., 1972-83, clin. cons., 1984—, asst. in medicine, 1967-69, assoc. in medicine, 1969-70, asst. physician, 1970-79, assoc. physician, 1979-87, sr. physician, 1987—, dir. clin. rsch. ctr. core radioimmunoassay lab., 1984-93; cons. staff Mount Auburn Hosp., Cambridge, 1974-90; mem. numerous other coms., 1969—. Rschr. in field; contbr. articles to profl. jours. Named Carl Shapiro scholar, BIDMC-Harvard Med. Sch., 2000—; recipient S. Robert Stone Harvard Med. Sch.-BIDMC tchg. award, 1998. Fellow: ACP, Am. Assn. Clin. Endocrinologists; mem.: Am. Fedn. Clin. Rsch., Am. Thyroid Assn., Endocrine Soc., Harvard Aesculapian Club, Alpha Omega Alpha. Roman Catholic. Home: 16 Fresh Pond Ln Cambridge MA 02138-4616 Office: Beth Israel Hosp Harvard Med Sch 330 Brookline Ave Boston MA 02215-5491 Office Phone: 617-667-4016. Business E-Mail: jpallott@bidmc.harvard.edu.

**PALLOTTI, MARIANNE MARGUERITE,** foundation administrator; b. Hartford, Conn., Apr. 23, 1937; d. Rocco D. and Marguerite (Long) P. BA, NYU, 1968, MA, 1972. Asst. to pres. Wilson, Haight & Welch, Hartford, 1964-65; exec. asst. Ford Found., N.Y.C., 1965-77; corp. sec. Hewlett Found., Menlo Park, Calif., 1977-84, v.p., 1985—. Bd. dirs. N.Y. Theatre Ballet, N.Y.C., 1986-98, Austin Montessori Sch., 1993, Djerassi Resident Artists Program, 1998—, Mexican Mus., 1999—; mem. women's adv. com., nat. coun.World Wildlife Fund, 1997—; mem. program com. Ind. Sector, Washington, 1998—. Mem. Women in Founds., No. Calif. Grantmakers. Office: William and Flora Hewlett Foundation 2121 Sand Hill Rd Menlo Park CA 94025-6903

**PALLOZOLA, CHRISTINE,** not-for-profit executive; b. St. Louis, Mar. 28, 1952; BS, U. Mo., 1974. Purchasing and sales mgmt. computer industry, Mo., 1984-92; exec. dir. Cahokia Mounds Mus. Soc., Collinsville, Ill., 1993—2001, dir. spl. events, mktg. Arts and Edn. Coun., 2001—04; exec. dir. Am. Acad. Physician and Patient, St. Louis, 2004—. Sec. Businesspersons Between Jobs, St. Louis, 1998—2004. Mem.: Assn. Fundraising Profls. Home: 150 Burtonwood Ballwin MO 63011

**PALM, CHARLES GILMAN,** academic administrator; b. Havre, Mont., Apr. 25, 1944; s. Victor F. and Laura (McKinnie) P.; m. Miriam Willits, Sept. 15, 1968. AB, Stanford U., 1966; MA, U. Wyo., 1967; MLS, U. Oreg., 1970. From asst. archivist to dep. dir. Hoover Instn. Stanford (Calif.) U., Palo Alto, Calif., 1971—90; dep. dir. Hoover Instn. Stanford U., 1990—2001, dep. dir. emeritus, 2002—. Adv. bd. Calif. Hist. Records, 2006—. Co-author: Guide to Hoover Institution Archives, 1980, Herbert Hoover, Register of His Papers in the Hoover Institution Archives, 1983. Mem. Calif. Heritage Preservation Commn., Sacramento, 1988-2005, vice chmn., 1993-97, chmn., 1997-2004; mem. Nat. Hist. Records and Publs. Commn., Washington, 1990-96; mem. history and edn. ctr. adv. bd. ARC, 1994-2005; trustee Golden State Mus. Corp., 1997-2004. Fellow: Soc. Am. Archivists; mem.: Soc. Calif. Archivists (pres. 1983—84), Bohemian Club. Republican. Office: Hoover Instn Stanford CA 94305

**PALM, GREGORY K.,** lawyer, investment company executive; b. Binghamton, N.Y., Sept. 25, 1948; m. Susan Palm; children: Jennifer, Katherine, Eleanor, James. SB, MIT, 1970; MBA, JD, Harvard U., 1974. Bar: N.Y. 1977, DC 1978. Law clk. to Hon. Henry J. Friendly US Ct. Appeals (2nd cir.); law clk. to Justice Lewis F. Powell US Supreme Ct.; assoc. Sullivan & Cromwell, 1976—82, ptnr., 1982—92; gen. counsel, co-head, legal dept. Goldman Sachs LP, NYC, 1992—99; exec. v.p., gen. counsel, co-head of legal dept. Goldman, Sachs & Co., NYC, 1992—. Mem. Harvard Law Rev. Mem.: Am. Law Inst., DC Bar. Office: Goldman Sachs and Co Legal Dept 37th Fl 1 New York Plz New York NY 10004

**PALM, MARY EGDAHL,** mycologist; b. Mpls., Jan. 27, 1954; d. Lauren and Mary E.; children: Natalie Elizabeth, Christopher Steven. BA in Biology, St. Olaf Coll., 1976; MSc in Plant Pathology (mycology), U. Minn., 1979, PhD in Plant Pathology (mycology), 1983. Lab. asst. St. Olaf Coll. Biology Dept., Northfield, Minn., 1974, tchg. asst., 1975-76; rsch. asst. U. Minn. plant pathology dept., Mpls., 1976-83; post doctoral rsch. assoc., 1983-84; mycologist (botanist GS12) USDA/APHIS biol. assessment and support staff, Beltsville, Md., 1984-91; mycologist scientific svcs. USDA/Animal and Plant Health Inspection Svc., Beltsville, 1991—, mycologist, dir. morphology, molecular and biochem. diagnostics lab., 2006—. Instr., coord. seminars and tng. sessions for USDA and ednl. sci. group, 1982—; adj. assoc. prof. plant pathology Pa. State U., State College, 1995. Co-author: Deuteromycetes and Selected Ascomycetes That Occur On or In Wood: An Indexed Bibliography, 1979, An Indexed Bibliography and Guide to Taxonomic Literature, 1988, A Literature Guide for the Identification of Plant Pathogenic Fungi, 1987, Fungi on Rhododendron: A World Reference, 1996, Mycology in Sustainable Development: Expanding concepts, Vanishing Borders, 1997, Cultivation and Diseases of Proteaceae: Leucodendron Leucospermum, and Protea, 2004; contbr. articles to profl. jours. Recipient St. Olaf Coll. Hon. Biology scholarship, 1976, Disting. Alumnus Dept. Plant Pathology U. Minn., 1999; grantee U. Minn. Computer Ctr. 1979, 80, 81, 82, V.P Gores Hammer award, 1998. Fellow Mycological Soc. Am.(sec. 1991-94, Am. Inst. Biol. Scis. rep. 1994—, v.p. 1995-96, pres.-elect 1996-97, pres. 1997-98, other coms.); mem. Am. Phytopathol. Soc. (chairperson mycology com. 1988, 89, vice chairperson 1987, mem. 1985, 86, regulatory plant pathology com. 1993—, organizer, moderator colloquium on systematics of plant pathogenic fungi 1987), L.Am. Mycol. Assn. (U.S. liaison), Internat. Assn. Plant Taxonomy (co-chair of com. on fungi and lichens 1986, 87, 88). Office: USDA Rm 329 B-011A 10300 Baltimore Ave Beltsville MD 20705-2350 Office Phone: 301-504-5327. Business E-Mail: mary.palm@aphis.usda.gov.

**PALMA, JACK D.,** lawyer; b. NYC, Sept. 15, 1946; BA, Allegheny Coll., 1968; JD with honors, U. Denver, 1974. Bar: Colo. 1975, Wyo. 1976. Ptnr. Holland & Hart, Cheyenne, Wyo., 1984—. Mem. ABA, Colo. Bar Assn., Wyo. State Bar, Order St. Ives. Office: Holland & Hart PO Box 1347 Cheyenne WY 82003-1347 Office Phone: 307-778-4200. E-mail: jpalma@hollandhart.com.

**PALMAZ, JULIO C.,** radiologist; b. Argentina; m. Amalia Palmaz. MD, Nat. Univ. La Plata, Argentina, 1971. Vascular radiologist, chief of angiography San Martin U. Hosp., La Plata, Argentina, 1974—83; chief of angiography & spl. procedures U. Tex. Health & Sci. Ctr., San Antonio, 1983, Stewart R. Reuter disting. prof., chief cardiovascular & interventional radiology, Ashbel Smith prof., 2006—. Co-owner Palmaz Vineyards, Napa, Calif., 1997—. Mem. editorial bd. Circulation. Named to Nat. Inventors Hall of Fame, 2006; recipient Honor award for Excellence in Endovascular Innovation, Internat. Soc. Endovascular Surgery, 2002, Presdl. Disting. Scholar award, U. Tex. San Antonio, 2003. Achievements include invention of intravascular stent, 1988. Office: U Tex Health Ctr at San Antonio Dept Radiology 7703 Floyd Curl Dr MS 7800 San Antonio TX 78229 also: Palmaz Vineyard 4029 Hagen Rd Moraga CA 94556 Office Phone: 210-567-5564. Office Fax: 210-567-5541. E-mail: palmaz@uthscsa.edu.*

**PALMEIRO, RAFAEL CORRALES,** professional baseball player; b. Havana, Cuba, Sept. 24, 1964; Degree in Comml. Art, Miss. State U. Baseball player Chgo. Cubs, 1986-88, Tex. Rangers, 1988—93, 1999—2003, Balt. Orioles, 1994-98, 2004—. Named Nat. League All-Star Team, 1988, Am. League All-Star Team, 1991, 1998, 1999; recipient Gold Glove award, 1997-1999; led Am. League in runs (124), 1993; hit 500th career home run, May 10, 2003; had his 3,000th career hit, July 15, 2005 Office: c/o Baltimore Orioles Camden Yards 333 W Camden St Baltimore MD 21201

**PALMER, ADAM P.,** lawyer; b. 1975; BA, Valparaiso U., 1997; JD, Duquesne U., 2000; MA, U. Hawaii, 2003. Bar: 2000. Assoc. U.S. Navy Judge Advocate Gen. Corps, 2000—03, Collins & Lay LLP, Columbia, SC, 2003—05; staff atty. Nat. Ctr. for Missing & Exploited Children, 2005, sr. atty., dir. office legal counsel, 2005—. Office: Nat Ctr for Missing and Exploited Children 699 Prince St Alexandria VA 22314-3117*

**PALMER, ANN THERESE DARIN,** lawyer; b. Detroit, Apr. 25, 1951; d. Americo and Theresa (Del Favero) Darin; m. Robert Towne Palmer, Nov. 9, 1974; children: Justin Darin, Christian Darin. BA, U. Notre Dame, 1973, MBA, 1975; JD, Loyola U., Chgo., 1978. Bar: Ill. 1978, U.S. Supreme Ct. 1981. Intern Wall Street Jour., Detroit, 1974; freelancer Time Inc. Fin. Pubs., Chgo., 1975—77; extern, Midwest regional solicitor U.S. Dept. Labor, 1976—78; tax atty. Esmark Inc., 1978; counsel Chgo. United, 1978—81; ind. contractor Legal Tax Rsch., 1981—89; fin. and legal news contbr. Chgo. Tribune, 1991—, Bus. Week, 1991—, Automotive News, 1993—97, Crain's Chgo. Bus., 1994—2000; contbg. editor Registered Rep, 2002—. Mem.: Chgo. Club. Home: 1570 Christina Ln Lake Forest IL 60045

**PALMER, ARNOLD DANIEL,** professional golfer; b. Youngstown, Pa., Sept. 10, 1929; s. Milfred Jerome and Doris M. Palmer; m. Winnie Walzer, Dec. 20, 1954 (dec. Nov. 1999); children: Peggy Palmer Wears, Amy Palmer Saunders; m. Kathleen Gawthrop, Jan. 26, 2005. Student, Wake Forest Coll., LLD, 1970. Profl. golfer, 1954—; businessman, entrepreneur, 1960—. Nat. spokesman Sears Can., Rolex, Golf mag., Lexington Furniture, Callaway Golf, Capital Mercury, Encore Bank, Invacare, Timing Inc., Cessna, Ketel One, Administaff, Spectrum Brands, Ez-Go; nat. spokesman, spectrum bd. Jacobsen, Pennington Seed, Electronic Arts, Luna Vineyards, Golf Channel. Author: Arnold Palmer's Golf Book, 1961, Portrait of a Professional Golfer, 1964, My Game and Yours, 1965, rev. edit., 1983, Situation Golf, 1970, Go for Broke, 1973, Arnold Palmer's Best 54 Holes of Golf, 1977, Arnold Palmer's Complete Book of Putting, 1986, Play Great Golf, 1987, (with Thomas Hauser) A Personal Journey, 1994, (with James Dodson) Arnold Palmer, A Golfer's Life, 1999, Playing by the Rules, 2002, Arnold Palmer, Memories, Stories, and Memorabilia, 2004. Served USCG, 1951—54. Recipient numerous golf awards including Bob Jones award U.S. Golf Assn., William D. Richardson award Golf Writers Assn. Am., Herb Graffis award Nat. Golf Found.; Presdl. medal of Freedom, 2004; named Sportsman of Yr. Sports Illustrated mag., 1960, Player of Yr. Profl. Golfers assn., 1960, 62, AP Athlete of Decade, 1969; Profl. Golfers Assn. Tour Money Leader, 1958, 60, 62, 63; elected to World Golf Hall of Fame, Profl. Golfers Assn. Hall of Fame. Mem. Latrobe (Pa.) Country Club, Laurel Valley Golf Club, Rolling Rock Club (Ligonier, Pa.), Bay Hill Club, Duquesne Club (Pitts.). Winner of over 90 major golf tournaments since 1955, including Masters Championship, 1958, 60, 62, 64, U.S. Open, 1960, U.S. Amateur, 1954, Brit. Open, 1961, 62. Home and office: PO Box 52 Youngstown PA 15696-0052 Office Phone: 724-537-7751.

**PALMER, BEN M.,** gas industry executive; With Arthur Andersen, Atlanta; sr. v.p., CFO, treas. EQ Svcs. Inc., Atlanta; CFO RPC Inc., Atlanta, 1996—. Office: RPC Inc 2170 Piedmont Rd NE Atlanta GA 30324-4135

**PALMER, BEVERLY BLAZEY,** psychologist, educator; b. Cleve., Nov. 22, 1945; d. Lawrence E. and Mildred M. Blazey; m. Richard C. Palmer, June 24, 1967; 1 child, Ryan Richard. PhD in Counseling Psychology, Ohio State U., 1972. Lic. clin. psychologist, Calif. Adminstrv. assoc. Ohio State U., Columbus, 1969—70; rsch. psychologist Health Svcs. Rsch. Ctr. UCLA, 1971—77; commr. pub. health L.A. County, 1978—81; pvt. practice clin. psychology Torrance, Calif., 1985—; prof. psychology Calif. State U., Dominguez Hills, 1973—. Author: Interpersonal Skills for Helping Professionals Online Course, 2001, 04, reviewer manuscripts for numerous textbook pubs; contbr. numerous articles to profl. jours. Recipient Proclamation, County of L.A., 1972, 1981, Outstanding Prof. award, Calif. State U., 1995; Fulbright Sr. scholar, Malaysia, 2001, Fulbright scholar, Borneo, 2001, Fulbright Sr. scholar, Malaysia, 2004—05, Fulbright scholar, Barbados, 2005. Mem. APA. Office: Calif State U Dominguez Hills Dept Psychology Carson CA 90747-0001 Office Phone: 310-373-6691. Business E-Mail: bpalmer@csudh.edu.

**PALMER, BRIAN EUGENE,** lawyer; b. Mpls., May 16, 1948; s. Eugene Philip and Virginia Breeze (Rolfshus) P.; m. Julia Washburn Morrison, Dec. 29, 1972; 1 child, Julia Hunter. AB, Brown U., 1970; JD, William Mitchell Coll. of Law, 1974. Bar: Minn. 1974, U.S. Dist. Ct. Minn. 1975, U.S. Dist. Ct. (ea. dist.) Wis. 2001, U.S. Ct. Appeals (8th cir.) 1980, U.S. Ct. Fed. Claims 1984, U.S. Supreme Ct. 1980. Asst. pub. defender Hennepin County Pub. Defender, Mpls., 1974-78; assoc. Dorsey & Whitney LLP, Mpls., 1978-82, ptnr., 1983—2004, of counsel, 2005—. Home: 1190 Lyman Ave Wayzata MN 55391-9671 Office: Dorsey & Whitney LLP 50 South Sixth St Ste 1500 Minneapolis MN 55402-1498 Office Phone: 612-340-2797. E-mail: palmer.brian@dorsey.com.

**PALMER, CARSON,** professional football player; b. Fresno, Calif., Dec. 27, 1979; BA in Pub. Policy, U. So. Calif., 2002. Quarterback Cin. Bengals, 2003—. Founder Carson Palmer Foundation. Named to AFC Pro Bowl Team, 2005; recipient Heisman Meml. Trophy, Heisman Trophy Trust, 2002. Office: c/o Cincinnati Bengals 1 Paul Brown Stadium Dr Cincinnati OH 45202*

**PALMER, CATHERINE E.,** lawyer; BA, Boston Coll., 1977; JD, Catholic Univ., 1980. Bar: NY 1981. Asst. US atty., chief of criminal divsn. US Attorney's Office, Ea. Dist. NY, 1985—94, spl. assignment asst. US atty., 1996—98; ptnr. Latham & Watkins, NYC, 1994—96, 1998—, and chair, white collar practice and ptnr. chair, global litig. dept. Office: Latham & Watkins Ste 1000 885 Third Ave New York NY 10022-4834 Business E-Mail: catherine.palmer@lw.com.

**PALMER, CHARLES F.,** lawyer; b. Rome, Ga., 1957; BS cum laude, Univ. Ga., 1979; JD, Emory Univ., 1986. Bar: Ga. 1986. Assoc. Troutman Sanders LLP, Atlanta, 1986—94, ptnr., telecom. tech., govtl. law, transp., 1995, and practice group leader, govtl. law. Editl. bd. Emory Law Jour., 1985—86. Mem.: State Bar Ga. (chmn., Young Lawyers Sect., legislative affairs com. 1992—93, adv. com. on legislative activity 1992—93), Gamma Sigma Delta, Phi Kappa Phi. Office: Troutman Sanders LLP Bank of America Plz Ste 5200 600 Peachtree St NE Atlanta GA 30308-2216 Office Phone: 404-885-3402. Office Fax: 404-962-6647. Business E-Mail: charles.palmer@troutmansanders.com.

**PALMER, CHARLIE,** chef, restaurant manager; b. N.Y. married; 4 children. Student, Culinary Inst. Am. Former exec. chef The River Café, NYC; chef, owner Aureole, NYC, 1986—; owner numerous other restaurants including Aureole at Mandalay Bay Resort and Casino, Las Vegas, Nev., Charlie Palmer Steak, Las Vegas, Astra, NYC, Métrazur, NYC, Kitchen 22, NYC, Charlie Palmer Steak, Washington, Dry Creek Kitchen, Sonoma, Hotel Healdsburg, Sonoma. Author: (books) Great American Food, 1996, Charlie Palmer's Casual Cooking, 2001, Art of Aureole, 2003. Recipient Restaurant & Institutions IVY award, 1997, James Beard award for best chef in NY, 1997, James Beard award for Who's Who of Food & Beverage in Am., 1998, Food Arts Silver Spoon award for outstanding service, 2003. Office: Charlie Palmer Group 34 E 61st St Ste 2A New York NY 10021

**PALMER, CHARLOTTE MARIE,** writer; d. Floyd Bell Morgan and Louise Lillian May; m. George Saxon Palmer, Feb. 26, 1988; m. Robert Jon Probst, Nov. 25, 1978 (dec. Mar. 24, 1987); children: Rose Michele Watson, Tina Louise Witt, Frederick Ray Berretta Jr. Cert., Chgo. Nat. Assn. Dance Masters, 1955, Dance Masters Am., Miami, Fla., 1963, So. Dance Masters Assn., Memphis, 1961. Dir., choreographer Charlotte Morgan Sch. Dance, Memphis, 1954—67; writer, corr. Memphis Press Scimitar, Greenville, Miss., 1967—69; v.p. Probst Media Comm., Jupiter, Fla., 1981—88; freelance writer Tallahassee, 1987—. Chmn., founder Dance Promotions, Memphis, 1962—67; mktg. v.p. Fla. TV PBS Network, Jupiter, 1981—82. Prodr.: (films) The Apprentice. Docent Fla. Governor's Mansion, Tallahassee, 1995—2003; sec. Myers Pk. Neighborhood Assn., Tallahassee, 1988—2002; regent, vice regent DAR, Ft. San Luis, Tallahassee, 1987—2002. Recipient Curtains Up award, Ft. Lauderdale Civic Ballet, 1974, Disting. award, Dollars Against Diabetes, Blueprint for Cure, 1987, President's award, Fla. Heritage Found., 1991, 1992. Mem.: Capital Med. Alliance, St. Mary's Cir., St. John's Episcopal Ch., Fla. State Sch. Theater (patrons bd. mem. 1995—2003). Republican. Episcopalian. Avocations: gardening, directing productions, stage, film, and dance, poetry.

**PALMER, CHRISTINE (CLELIA ROSE VENDITTI),** vocalist, educator, musician; b. Hartford, Conn., Apr. 2, 1919; d. John Marion and Immacolata (Morcaldo) Venditti; m. Raymond Smith. Oct. 5, 1949 (div. June 1950); m. Arthur James Whitlock, Feb. 25, 1953. Student, Mt. Holyoke Coll., 1937-38, New Eng. Conservatory of Music, 1941-42; pvt. studies, Boston, Hartford, N.Y.C., Florence and Naples, Italy; RN with honors, Hartford Hosp. Sch. Nursing, 1941. Artist-in-residence El Centro Coll., Dallas, 1966-71. Pvt. vocal instr.-coach, specializing in vocal technique for opera, mus. comedy, supper club acts, auditions, Dallas, 1962-94; voice adjudicator San Francisco Opera Co., 1969-72, Tex. Music Tchrs. Assn., 1964-75, others; lectr. in field; appearances with S.M. Chartocks' Gilbert and Sullivan Co. Leading operatic soprano N.Y.C. Opera, Chgo., San Francisco, San Carlo, other cities, 1944-62, N.Y. Town Hall Concert, 1951; soloist with symphony orchs. maj. U.S. Cities, 1948-62; soloist Marble Collegiate Ch., Holy Trinity Ch.; coast-to-coast concert tour, 1948; numerous appearances including St. Louis MUNY Opera, Indpls. Starlight Theatre, Lambertville Music Circus; soloist Holiday on Ice, 1949-50; TV performer, including Home Show on NBC, Telephone Hour on NBC, Holiday Hotel; performer various supper clubs, N.Y.C., Atlanta, Bermuda, Catskills, others, including Number One Fifth Avenue, The Embers, The Carriage Club, Viennese Lantern. Hon. mem. women's bd. Dallas Opera Assn.; mem. adv. bd. Tex. Opera News; mem. Tex. Music Tchrs. Cert. Bd., Collegiate Chorale, Don Craig Singers, The Vikings; mem. women's bd.; Dallas Bapt. Univ. Oliver Ditson scholar, 1942; recipient Phi Xi Delta prize in Italian, 1937; named Victor Herbert Girl, ASCAP; Spl. Recognition Gold book of Dallas Soc. Mem. Nat. Assn. Tchrs. of Singing (pres. Dallas chpt. 1972-74), Nat. Fedn. Music Clubs, Tex. Fedn. Music Clubs, Dallas Fedn. Music Clubs (pres. 1972-74), Dallas Symphony League, Dallas Music Tchrs. Assn. (pres. 1971-72, Tchr. of Yr. 1974), Thesaurus Book Club (pres. 1990-91, 97-98), Friday Forum (Dallas, bd. dirs.), Dallas Women's of C., Eagle Forum, Pub. Affairs Luncheon Club, Dallas Fedn. Music Club, Pro Am., Wednesday Morning Choral Club, Dallas Knife and Fork Club, Prestoncrest Rep. Club. Presbyterian. Home: 6232 Pemberton Dr Dallas TX 75230-4036

**PALMER, CHRISTOPHER E.,** lawyer; BA cum laude, St. John's Univ., Minn., 1982; JD magna cum laude, Georgetown Univ., 1986. Bar: Minn. 1986, DC 1988. Ct. law clerk US Dist. Ct., DC; ptnr. Shea & Gardner (merged with Goodwin Procter LLP); ptnr.,chair, bus. law dept. Goodwin Procter LLP, Washington, 2004—. Articles editor Georgetown Law Jour. Office: Goodwin Procter LLP 901 New York Ave NW Washington DC 20001 Office Phone: 202-346-4253. Office Fax: 202-346-4444. Business E-Mail: cpalmer@goodwinprocter.com.

**PALMER, CRAIG,** digital music and media company executive; BSEE, U. Wis. Mktg. positions with Hewlett-Packard, 1982—89; several sr. mktg. positions Cadence Design Systems, 1989—94; several v.p. positions Aspect Development (acquired by i2), 1994—2000; chmn., pres., CEO eWanted; pres., CEO Gracenote, Emeryville, Calif., 2003—. Spkr. in the field; spkr. Global Wireless Forum, Jupiter Plug-In. Office: Gracenote Hdqs 2000 Powell St Ste 1380 Emeryville CA 94608 Office Phone: 510-547-9680. Office Fax: 510-547-9681.

**PALMER, CRUISE,** newspaper editor; b. Kansas City, Kans., Apr. 9, 1917; s. Thomas Potter and Margaret Scroggs (McFadden) P.; m. Dorraine Humphreys, Sept. 7, 1946; children: Thomas Crise, Martha D. Sprague. BS in Journalism, Kans. State U., 1938. With Kansas City (Mo.) Star, 1938—, news editor, 1963-64, mng. editor, 1965-66; exec. editor, bd. dirs. Star and Times, 1967—78, cons., 1978—. Bd. dirs. Purtec Systems, Inc. Author: Bosses of the News Room, 1927-2006, 2003. Mem. bd. govs. Am. Royal Live Stock and Horse Show Assn., 1967-91; bd. dirs. ARC, 1978-91, Kansas City Mayor's Corps Progress, 1978-91; found. trustee Kans. State U.; trustee Kansas City Sister Cities Commn., 1978-91. Served to lt. (j.g.) USNR, 1943-46. Recipient Distinguished Service award Kans. State U., 1967; First Place award Pro-Am. Southgate Open Golf Tournament, 1973; Second Place award Pro-Am. Hawaiian Open, 1973, 85; Third Place, 1981; First Place award Jim Colbert Celebrity Tournament, 1981, First Place Team award Kansas City area Am. Cancer Soc. Golf Tournament, 1986. Mem. Am. Soc. Newspaper Editors, Soc. Profl. Journalists, Kansas City Sr. Golf Assn., Kansas City Press Club (pres. 1953-54, 64-65, permanent trustee, pres. scholarship found. 1989), Kansas City Club, Chiefs Red Coat Club, Milburn Golf and Country Club, Beta Theta Pi (Greater Kansas City Beta of Yr. 1980). Episcopalian (former vestryman and lay reader). Home: Lakeview Retirement Village 14100 W 90th Ter Apt 504 Lenexa KS 66215-5430 Office: 1729 Grand Ave Kansas City MO 64108-1413

**PALMER, DAN M.,** finance company executive; b. Memphis, 1943; BBA, U. Memphis, 1966; cert. in Exec. Program, Dartmouth U., 1979. Founder Electronic Fleet Sys., 1982—90; CEO Concord Computing Corp. (formerly Electronic Fleet Sys.), 1990—2003; co-CEO Concord EFS, Inc. (formerly Concord Computing Corp.), Memphis, 2003—, bd. dirs. Named Debit Exec. of Yr., Credit Card Mgmt. Mag., 2000; named one of Top 10 Leaders & success CEOs, Investors Bus. Daily, 2001. Mem.: Memphis Soc. Entrepreneurs. Office: Concord 7000 Goodlett Farms Pkwy Ste 200 Cordova TN 38016-4917

**PALMER, DAVE RICHARD,** retired military officer, academic administrator; b. Ada, Okla., May 31, 1934; s. David Furman and Lorena Marie (Clardy) P.; m. LuDelia Clemmer, Apr. 13, 1957; children: Allison J., Kersten. BS, U.S. Military Acad., 1956; MA in History, Duke U., 1966; postgrad., Army War Coll., 1972-73; PhD (hon.), Duke U., 1990. Commd. U.S. Army, 1956, advanced through grades to lt. gen.; mem. faculty dept. history U.S. Mil. Acad., 1966-69; mem. staff (Pentagon), 1973-76, Joint Chiefs of Staff, 1979-81; comdr. Baumholder Mil. Community, W. Ger., 1981-83; dep. comdt. Command and Gen. Staff Coll., Ft. Leavenworth, Kans., 1983-85; comdg. gen. 1st Armored Div., W.Ger., 1985-86; supt. U.S. Mil. Acad., 1986-91, ret., 1991; pres. Walden U., 1995-99; CEO Walden Corp., 1999-2000. Author: The River and the Rock, 1969, The Way of the Fox, 1975, Summons of the Trumpet, 1978, 1794-America, Its Army, and The Birth of the Nation, 1994, First in War, 2000, Provide for the Common Defense, 2001, Washington and Arnold, 2006. Bd. dirs. Walden U., 1992-2001. Decorated Legion of Merit (3); Bronze Star (2), D.S.M.(2); named Disting. Grad., U.S. Mil. Acad., 2005. Mem. Assn. U.S. Army, Armor Assn., Mil. History, Soc. Cin. Personal E-mail: lucpalmer4@cs.com.

**PALMER, DAVID GILBERT,** lawyer; b. Lakewood, NJ, Jan. 10, 1945; s. Robert Dayton and Lois (Gilbert) P.; m. Susan Edmundson Walsh, Aug. 17, 1968; children: Jonathan, Megan. AB, Johns Hopkins U., 1967; JD, U. Colo., 1970. Bar: Colo. 1970, U.S. Dist. Ct. Colo. 1970, U.S. Ct. Appeals (9th and 10th cirs.) 1970, U.S. Supreme Ct. 1970. Ptnr., mng. ptnr., chmn. litig. dept. Holland & Hart, Denver, 1970-87; ptnr., mng. ptnr. Gibson, Dunn & Crutcher,

Denver, 1987-97; mng. ptnr. Zevnik, Horton, Palmer, Denver, 1997-2001; mng. shareholder Greenberg Traurig LLP, Denver, 2001—. Chmn. N.W. region Am. Heart Assn., Dallas, 1986—, bd. dirs., 1986—, sec., 1990—, nat. chmn., 1992-93; pres., bd. dirs. Colo. Heart Assn., Denver, 1974; bd. dirs. C.H. Kempe Nat. Ctr. for Prevention of Child Abuse, Denver, 1984-90, pres., 1989-90; bd. dirs. Goodwill Industries, Denver, 1981-84, Metro Denver Econ. Devel. Corp., 2004—; mem. coun. of advisors U. Colo. Med. Sch., 2004—. Mem. ABA, Colo. Bar Assn., Denver Law Club, Univ. Club of Denver (pres. 2004-05), Mile High Club. Office: Greenberg Traurig Tabor Ctr 1200 17th St Ste 2400 Denver CO 80202 Office Phone: 303-572-6539. Office Fax: 303-572-6540. Business E-Mail: palmerdg@gtlaw.com.

**PALMER, DAVID SCOTT,** political scientist, educator; b. Boston, July 16, 1937; s. Walter S. and Jean (Stuart) P.; m. Sarah Crawford, 1966 (dec. Nov. 1985); children: Walter Scott, Henry Crawford, Asa MacAdam; m. Diane Nagel, 1998. BA in Internat. Studies cum laude, Dartmouth Coll., 1959; MA in Hispanic Am. Studies, Stanford U., 1962; PhD in Comparative Govt., Cornell U., 1973. Vol. leader Peace Corps, Peru, 1962-64; asst. dean freshmen, asst. to dir. admissions Dartmouth Coll., Hanover, NH, 1964-68; from instr. to asst. prof. dept. govt. Bowdoin Coll., 1972-76; professorial lectr. Sch. Advanced Internat. Studies Johns Hopkins U., Washington, 1977-88; assoc. dean for programs Fgn. Svc. Inst., Dept. State, 1984-88, chair Latin Am. and Caribbean studies, 1976-88; prof. polit. sci. Boston U., 1988—, prof. internat. rels., 1990—, assoc. chair undergrad. studies internat. rels. dept., 1997-99, chair dept. polit. sci., 1998-2001, dir. Latin Am. studies program, 1991-94, 2004—05. Vis. lectr. Princeton U., 1978—79, Georgetown U., 1985; vis. scholar Inter-Am. Dialogue, 2001—02. Author: Peru: The Authoritarian Tradition, 1980, (with Kevin Middlebrook) Military Government and Political Development: Lessons from Peru, 1975 (with Robert Wesson and others) The Latin American Military Institution, 1985; editor, contbr.: Shining Path of Peru, 1992, 2d edit., 1994, U.S. Relations with Latin America during the Clinton Years, 2006; contbr. chpts. to books, articles and revs. to profl. jours. Bd. visitors Tucker Found., Dartmouth Coll., 2005—; mem. Fulbright nat. screening com., 2005—. Recipient Meritorious Honor award U.S. Dept. of State, 1981; Daniel Webster nat. scholar, 1955-59; Edward John Noble Found. leadership grantee 1959-62; Fulbright fellow, 1998. Mem. Latin Am. Studies Assn. (exec. coun. 1983-86), New Eng. Coun. Latin Am. Studies (exec. com. 1989-98, 2000—, pres. 1993-94), Phi Beta Delta, Phi Kappa Phi, Sigma Delta Pi. Home: 69 Waverley St Belmont MA 02478-1958 Office: Boston U 152 Bay State Rd Boston MA 02215-1501 Office Phone: 617-353-9388. Business E-Mail: dspalmer@bu.edu.

**PALMER, DENISE E.,** publishing executive; b. Seymour, Ind., Feb. 12, 1957; m. Gregory G. Palmer. BA, U. Dayton, 1977; MS in Mgmt., Northwestern U., 1984. Sr. auditor Coopers & Lybrand, Dayton, Ohio, 1977—80; corp. auditor Tribune, 1980—86, planning analyst. 1983—86, mgr. planning, 1986—88; dir. fin. WGW Radio, Chgo., 1988—93, sta. mgr., 1993; dir. fin. Chgo. Tribune, Chgo., 1994—95, v.p. fin. & adminstrn., 1996—97, v.p. fin. strategy & fin., 1996—97, v.p. devel., strategy, fin., 1998—2000; pres., CEO CLTV, Oakbrook, Ill., 2000—02; pres., pub., CEO Balt. Sun, 2002—06; pres., pub. Tampa Tribune, 2006—. Bd. mem. Greater Baltimore Com., 2003—, Econ. Alliance of Greater Baltimore, 2003—, Md. Bus. Roundtable for Edn., 2003—; bd. visitors U. Md. Baltimore County, 2003—; mem. adv. bd. U. Dayton; mem. Fedn. Women's Assn., Coun. of 100 Women. Office: Tampa Tribune 202 Parker St Tampa FL 33606*

**PALMER, DENNIS DALE,** lawyer; b. Alliance, Nebr., Apr. 30, 1945; s. Vernon D. Palmer and Marie E. (Nelson) Fellers; m. Rebecca Ann Turner, Mar. 23, 1979; children: Lisa Marie, Jonathan Paul. BA, U. Mo., 1967, JD, 1970. Bar: Mo. 1970, U.S. Dist. Ct. (we. dist.) Mo. 1970, U.S. Ct. Appeals (8th and 10th cirs.) 1973, U.S. Supreme Ct. 1980. Staff atty. Legal Aid Soc. Western Mo., Kansas City, 1970-73; assoc. Shughart, Thomson & Kilroy, P.C., Kansas City, 1973-76, ptnr., bd. dirs., 1976—. Contbr. articles on franchise and employment law to legal jours. Bd. dirs., chmn. legal assts. adv. bd. Avila Coll., Kansas City, 1984-87. 2d lt. U.S. Army, 1970. Mem. ABA (litigation com. 1980, forum com. on franchising 1987), Mo. Bar Assn. (antitrust com. 1975—, civil practice com. 1975—), Kansas City Bar Assn. (chmn. franchise law com. 1987—), Univ. Club. Avocations: jogging, golf, tennis, outdoor activities, reading. Home: 13100 Canterbury Rd Leawood KS 66209-1700 Office: Shughart Thomson & Kilroy 12 Wyandotte Plz 120 W 12th St Fl 17 Kansas City MO 64105-1902

**PALMER, DERYCK A.,** lawyer; b. NYC, Nov. 21, 1956; BA, Syracuse U., 1978; JD, U. Mich., 1982. Bar: NY 1984. Ptnr., bus. fin. restructuring dept. Weil, Gotshal & Manges LLP, NYC. Adj. prof. law NY Law Sch.; mem. Bureau Nat. Affairs Adv. Bd., Bankruptcy Law Reporter. Co-author: Restructuring: The Search for Value in a Troubled Enterprise, 1993, History of Bankruptcy Law in the Second Circuit, 1995. Bd. dirs. Boys & Girls Harbor, Inc., Insol Internat., Greater NY Couns. Boy Scouts Am., UJA-The Ednl. Alliance, Maplewood Village Alliance, Syracuse U., Cleveland Clinic Found., Coalition Consumer Bankruptcy Debtor Edn. Named one of Am. Top Black Attys., Black Enterprise, 2003. Fellow: Am. Coll. Bankruptcy; mem.: ABA, NY State Bar Assn. Office: Weil Gotshal & Manges LLP 767 Fifth Ave New York NY 10153 Office Phone: 212-310-8721. Office Fax: 212-310-8007. Business E-Mail: deryck.palmer@weil.com.

**PALMER, DOUGLAS HAROLD,** mayor; b. Trenton, N.J., Oct. 19, 1951; s. George H. and Dorothy (Vaughn) P. BS in Bus. Mgmt., Hampton U., 1973. With C.V. Hill Co., Trenton; civil svc. worker N.J. Dept. Motor Vehicles, Trenton; dir. Community Schs. Trenton; asst. dir. Trenton Bd. Edn., dir. purchasing; small bus. owner Trenton; mayor City of Trenton, 1990—, bd. dirs. ARC, Urban League Met. Trenton, Forum Project, Rider Coll. Ednl. Opportunity Fund Program, We, Inc., Cancer Inst. N.J., NAACP, treas.; freeholder Dem. Party Mercer County, 1981-91; mgr. West End Little League, Trenton, 1965-75, treas., 1975—. Named Outstanding Young Man Am., Del. Valley United Way Bd.; recipient Fai Ho Cha award Omega Psi Phi; recipient City Livability award, US Conf. of Mayors, Twenty Year Alumnus award, Hampton U., Spirit of St. Francis award, St. Francis Hosp., Equal Justice medal, Legal Svcs. NJ, State of Israel Peace medal award, 1993, Tending the Garden State, Cmty. Develop. Leadership award, Worldworks Found. NJ, 1993. Baptist. Office: 319 E State St Trenton NJ 08608-1809*

**PALMER, DOUGLAS S., JR.,** lawyer; b. Peoria, Ill., Mar. 15, 1945; AB cum laude, Yale U., 1966; JD cum laude, Harvard U., 1969. Bar: Wash. 1969. Mem. Foster Pepper & Shefelman PLLC, Seattle, 1975—2002, Hillis Clark Martin & Peterson, P.S., Seattle, 2002—. Office: Hillis Clark Martin & Peterson PS 500 Galland Bldg 1221 Second Ave Seattle WA 98101-2925 Office Phone: 206-623-1745.

**PALMER, EARL FRANK,** minister; b. McCloud, Calif., Nov. 26, 1931; s. Lewis Ward and Myrtle Horey Palmer; m. Shirley Elizabeth Green, June 14, 1958; children: Anne, Jonathan, Elizabeth. BA, U. Calif., 1953; BDiv, Princeton Theological Seminary, 1956; DDiv (hon.), Whitworth Coll., 1987. Min. of students U. Presbyn. Ch., Seattle, 1956—64; head min. Union Ch. of Manila, Malati, Philippines, 1964—70, First Presbyn. Ch., Berkely, Calif., 1970—91, U. Presbyn. Ch., Seattle, 1991—. Mem., bd. trustees Princeton Theological Seminary, Princeton, NJ, New Coll., Berkeley, Calif.; mem., bd. gov. Regent Coll., Vancouver, Canada. Author: The Preacher's Commentary, 1982, Old Law - New Life, 1984, 1 & 2 Thesalonians, Good News Commentary, 1983, Alive From The Center, Commentary on 1&2 Corinthians, The Preacher's Commentary on 1,2,3, John, Revelation, The Enormous Exception, Commentary on the Sermon on the Mount, A Faith That Works, The Book That John Wrote, Commentary on the Gospel of John, Laughter in Heaven, The Parables of Jesus, Love Has Its Resons, Salvation by Surprise, Commentary on the Book of Romans, Sign Posts, The Search for Values, Prayer, Between Friends, Integrity, Commentary on the Book of Philippians, The Book That James Wrote, 24 Hour Christian, The Humor of

Jesus. Recipient Dist. Alumnus award, Princeton Theological Seminary, 1999. Presbyn. Avocations: hiking, reading, mountain climbing. Home: 4416 50th Ave NE Seattle WA 98105 Office: U Presbyn Ch 4540 15th Ave NE Seattle WA 98105 E-mail: earl@upc.org.

**PALMER, EDWARD KENT,** charitable organization executive; b. Jacksonville, Ill., Aug. 10, 1960; s. Richard Edward and Bette Louise (Wheaton) P. B cum laude, U. Wis., Green Bay, 1982; M cum laude, Sangamon State U., 1987. Rsch. participant Argonne (Ill.) Nat. Lab., 1982; rsch. asst. Clemson (S.C.) U., 1982-83; constrn. worker Brethren Vol. Svc., Oklahoma City, 1984-85; radio chemist Ill. Dept. Nuclear Safety, Springfield, 1985-87; microcomputer specialist Koinonia Ptnrs., Americus, Ga., 1987-89; tech. support specialist Habitat for Humanity, Americus, 1989—. Singer Ga. Southwestern Civic Chorus, Americus, 1990; dir. N.E. Wis. Food Coop., Green Bay, Wis., 1980, Soc. for Environ. and Ednl. Devel., Jacksonville, Ill., 1977. Mem. Sumter Squares. Democrat. Mem. Ch. of the Brethren. Avocations: preaching, teaching sunday school, reading. Home: 130 S Dudley St Americus GA 31709-3445

**PALMER, EDWARD L.,** psychologist, educator, writer; b. Hagerstown, Md., Aug. 11, 1938; s. Ralph Leon and Eva Irene (Brandenburg) P.; children: Edward Lee, Jennifer Lynn. BA, Gettysburg Coll., 1960; BD, Luth. Theol. Sem., Gettysburg, 1964; MS, Ohio U., 1967, PhD, 1970. Asst. prof. Western Md. Coll., Westminster, 1968-70, Davidson Coll., NC, 1970-77, assoc. prof. NC, 1977-86, chair, 1985—99, prof. NC, 1986—. Watson prof. NC, 1991—. Guest rschr. Harvard U., Cambridge, Mass., 1977; vis. scholar UCLA, 1984, UNC Chapel Hill, 1991, U. Exeter, 2000, U. Ala., 2005; cons. Council on Children, Media, Merchandising, 1978-79, 1st Union Bank Corp., Charlotte, N.C., 1975-79; NSF proposal reviewer, 1978—. Editl. reviewer Jour. Broadcasting and Electronic Media, 1978—, editl. bd. Media Psychology; editor: Children and the Faces of TV, 1980, Faces of Televisual Media, 2003; author: Children in the Cradle of TV, 1987; contbr. to Wiley Ency. of Psychology, 1984, 2002, Lawrence Erlbaum Assocs., 1991, Sage Pub., 1993-96; author jour. articles and book chpts. Sec. Mecklenburg Child Devel. Assn., Davidson and Cornelius, N.C., 1974-78; bd. mem. pub. radio Sta. WDAV, 1970-90, Telecomms. task force Rutgers U., 1981. Recipient Thomas Jefferson Tchg. award Robert Earl McConnell Found., 1993. Mem. APA, Am. Psychol. Soc., Assn. Heads Depts. Psychology (chair 1994-96), Am. Psychol. Assn. (task force on advt. and children 2001-03), Southeastern Psychol. Assn., Southeastern Soc. Social Psychologists, Phi Beta Kappa (pres. Davidson chpt. 1985-86). Avocations: sunrise and sunset walks, poetry, bird watching, music composition and performance. Office: Davidson Coll PO Box 7007 Davidson NC 28035-7007 Office Phone: 704-894-2882. E-mail: edpalmer@davidson.edu.

**PALMER, FRANCIS ROGER, III,** plastic surgeon; Grad. (hon.), San Diego State U.; MD, U. Calif. Irvine Sch. Medicine. Cert. Am. Bd. Facial Plastic and Reconstructive Surgery, bd. eligible Am. Bd. Cosmetic Surgery. Resident, head and neck surgery U. So. Calif.-LA County Med. Ctr.; fellow Am. Acad. of Facial Plastic and Reconstructive Surgery, Am. Acad. Cosmetic Surgery; dir. facial plastic surgery, head and neck surgery dept. U. So. Calif. Sch. Medicine, 1991—; dir. Beverly Hills Internat. Ctr. for Aesthetic Surgery. Spkr. in field. Guest appearances CNN, ABC, CBS, NBC, FOC, KTLA News, Gabrielle, Hard Copy, GMTV, and Good Day Britain, featured in Cosmopolitan, LA Times, NY Times, Liz Smith's Column and several others. Named one of The World's Best Aesthetic Plastic Surgeons, Tatler Mag. Office: Beverly Hills Internat Ctr for Aesthetic Surgery 8500 Wilshire Blvd Ste 900 Beverly Hills CA 90211 Office Phone: 310-652-9583. Office Fax: 310-652-0009. E-mail: drpalmer11@aol.com.*

**PALMER, GARY JAMES,** public policy research and education executive; b. Haleyville, Ala., May 14, 1954; s. J.C. and Mae (Lacy) P.; m. Marjorie Ann Cushing, Nov. 19, 1983; children: Claire Elaine, Kathleen Corrie, Robert William. BS in Ops. Mgmt./Mgmt. Sci., U. Ala., 1977. Gen. mgr. Palmer Truss Co., Hodges, Ala., 1977-78; bus. mgr. Bradford and Co., Birmingham, Ala., 1979-80; cost engr. Combustion Engring., Birmingham, Ala., 1980-81; cost engr., project control engr. Rust Internat., Birmingham, Ala., 1981-89; co-founder, state coord. Ala. Policy Inst., Birmingham, 1989-90, exec. dir., 1990-93, pres., 1993—. Speaker and writer in field. Contbr. articles to profl. jours. Bd. dirs. State Policy Network, 1992-98, pres., 1996-98. Named to Outstanding Young Men of Am.; 1989; recipient Roe award, 2002, State Policy Network. Mem.: Rotary. Presbyn. Avocations: hunting, fishing, golf, history, skiing. Office: Ala Policy Inst 402 Office Park Dr Ste 300 Birmingham AL 35223-2434

**PALMER, IRENE SABELBERG,** retired dean, retired nursing educator, genealogist; b. Franklin, N.J., May 28, 1923; d. John Joseph and May (Heiser) Sabelberg. BS, N.J. State Tchrs. Coll., 1945; diploma, Jersey City Med. Center Sch. Nursing, 1945; MA, NYU, 1951, PhD, 1963. Edn. dir. Diploma Schs. Nursing N.J. and Mass, 1948—52; ednl. dir. Glenn Dale (Md.) Hosp. and D.C. Dept. Pub. Health, 1956, dir. nursing svc. and edn., 1956—61; assoc. clin. prof. nursing Georgetown U., Washington, 1960—61; USPHS trainee, 1961—62; assoc. chief nursing svc. for rsch. VA Hosp., San Francisco, 1963—64; rsch. nurse cons. divsn. nursing HEW and USPHS Nursing Rsch. Field Ctr., San Francisco, 1964—66; asst. dean and assoc. prof. nursing U. Colo. Sch. Nursing, Denver, 1966—68; dean and prof. nursing Boston U. Sch. Nursing, 1968—74; prof. Hahn Sch. Nursing U. San Diego, 1974—91, prof. emeritus, 1991—; founding dean Hahn Sch. Nursing, U. San Diego, 1974-87, dean emeritus, 1988—. Lectr. Classical Alliance of the Western States, Uskudar, Turkey, 1994, Italy, 1995. Editor: Nursing Clinics of North America, 1970, Contbr. articles to profl. jours. Served to capt. Nurse Corps U.S. Army, 1953-56. Internat. Nightingale scholar; Nat. Health Svc. fellow; recipient Excellence in Nursing Scholarship award Orgn. Nurse Execs., 1993. Fellow Nat. League Nursing (bd. visitors 1977-87), Am Acad. Nursing; mem. ANA, Am. Assn. History Nursing, Am. Colls. Nursing (hon.), Boston U. Nursing Archives, German Rsch. Assn. (pres. 1995), Sigma Theta Tau (Leadership award Zeta Mu chpt. 1986, Excellence in Nursing award 1991).

**PALMER, JAMES DANIEL,** information technology educator; b. Washington, Mar. 8, 1930; s. Martin Lyle and Sarah Elizabeth (Hall) P.; m. Margret Kupka, June 21, 1952; children: Stephen Robert, Daniel Lee, John Keith. AA, Fullerton Jr. Coll., 1953; BS (Alumni scholar), U. Calif., Berkeley, 1955. MS, 1957; PhD, U. Okla., 1963; DPS (hon.), Regis Coll., Denver, 1977. Chief engr. Motor vehicle and Illumination Lab. U. Calif., Berkeley, 1955-57; assoc. rsch. engr. U. Okla., Norman, 1957-63, prof., 1963-66, asst. to dir. Rsch. Inst., 1960-63, cons. Rsch. Inst., 1966-69, dir. Sch. Elec. Engring., 1963-66, dir. Systems Rsch. Center, 1964-66; dean sci. and engring., prof. elec. engring. Union Coll., Schenectady, 1966-71; pres. Met. State Coll., Denver, 1971-78; rsch. and spl. programs adminstr. Dept. Transp., Washington, 1978-79; v.p., gen. mgr. rsch. and devel. div. Mech. Tech., Inc., Latham, NY, 1979-82; exec. v.p. J.J. Henry Co., Inc., Moorestown, NJ, 1982-85; BDM internat. prof. info. tech. George Mason U., Fairfax, Va., 1985-95, prof. emeritus, 1995—; software cons., 1995—. Bd. dirs. J.J. Henry Co., Inc., cons. Sym Mgmt. Co., Boston, Higher Edn. Exec. Assocs., Denver, PERI, Princeton; adj. prof. U. Colo. Co-author: (with A.P. Sage) Software Systems Engineering, (with Aseltine, Beam and Sage) Introduction to Computer Systems, Analysis, Design and Application. Bd. dirs., exec. v.p. adv. com. U.S.A. Vols. for Internat. Tech. Assistance, 1967-83, exec. v.p., 1970-71, chmn. exec. com.; trustee, vice chmn. Nat. Commn. on Coop. Edn.; mem. exec. policy bd. Alaska Natural Gas Pipeline, 1978-79; trustee Auraria Higher Edn. Program, Denver; mem. Fulbright fellow Selection Com., Colo.; bd. mgrs., mem. exec. com. Hudson-Mohawk Assn. Colls. and Univs., trustee, chmn. bd., 1970-71; adv. com. USCG Acad., 1972-82, chmn. adv. com., 1979-82; mem. Colo. Gov.'s Sci. and Tech. Adv. Coun.; pres. Denver Cath. dirs. U. Okla. Rsch. Inst.; chair bd. dirs. Tri-City Vols. Inc., 2004—; mem. adv. com. Mile-Hi Red Cross. With USMC, 1950-51. Named James D. Palmer scholarship in his honor, George Mason U., 2002; recipient U.S. Coast Guard medal, 1983; Centennial scholar, Case-Western Res., 1981. Fellow

IEEE (exec. and adminstrv. coms., v.p. long-range planning and finance, chmn. com. on large scale systems, Joseph E. Wahl Outstanding Career Achievement award 1993, Millennium medal 2000); mem. Systems, Man and Cybernetics Soc. (pres., Outstanding Contbns. award 1981), alumni assns. U. Calif. and U. Okla., Inst. Internat. Edn. (bd. dir. Rocky Mt. sect.), Soc. Naval Architects and Marine Engrs., Am. Soc. Engring. Edn., Am. Mil. Engrs., N.Y. Acad. Sci., Navy League, Sigma Xi, Eta Kappa Nu, Pi Mu Epsilon, Alpha Gamma Sigma. Home: 860 Cashew Way Fremont CA 94536-2646 Office: George Mason U Sch of Info Tech & Engring Fairfax VA 22030 E-mail: jdpalmer@ix.netcom.com.

**PALMER, JAMES F.,** corporate financial executive; BS, Southeast Mo. State, 1971. Sr. v.p., CFO McDonnell Douglas Corp., 1995—97; pres. Boeing Shared Services Group The Boeing Co., 1997—2000, sr. v.p.; pres. Boeing Capital Corp., 2000—03; exec. v.p., CFO Visteon Corp. Office: Visteon Corp One Village Ctr Dr Belleville MI 48111-5711 Office Phone: 734-710-2020.*

**PALMER, JANE G.,** music educator; d. William Edgar and Mildred Irene (Anthony) Galbraith; m. Merrill Jay Palmer, Dec. 26, 1972; 1 child, Brittany Leigh. BA in Edn., U. North Fla., 1977, MA in Edn., 1981. Music resource tchr. Duval County Pub. Schs., Jacksonville, Fla., 1997—99; choral dir. Fletcher Sr. HS, Neptune Beach, Fla., 1999—. Chmn. performing arts dept. Fletcher HS, 2002—. Choir mem., soloist Palms Presbyn. Ch., Jacksonville, 1976—, mem. pastoral nominating com., 2005—06. Named Tchr. of Yr., San Pablo Elem. Sch., Jacksonville, 1993, Fletcher H.S., 2003; recipient Tchr.'s Choice award, Pine Forest Elem., Jacksonville, 1991. Mem.: Am. Choral Dirs. Assn., Fla. Vocal Assn. (dist. chmn., adjudicator), Music Educators Nat. Conf. Avocations: travel, reading. Office: Fletcher HS 700 Seagate Ave Neptune Beach FL 32266 Office Phone: 904-247-5905 ext 152. Office Fax: 904-247-5920. E-mail: palmerj3@educationcentral.org.

**PALMER, JASON MICHAEL,** research and development company executive; b. Aberdeen, Md., Dec. 1, 1971; s. Lonnie Eugene and Diane Marie (Whalen) Palmer. Degree, U. Va., 1993, Harvard Business Sch., 1999. Pres. Corner Meal Plan, Inc., Charlotesville, Va., 1993—96; dir., founder Bridgepath, Inc., Berkeley, Calif., 1997—98; CEO Maxpost Network, Inc., Cambridge, Mass., 1998—2001; product mgmt. Microsoft, Inc., Redmond, Wash., 2002—04; v.p. bus. devel. Schoonet, Inc., N.Y.C., NY, 2004—. Dir. Citizenjoe.org, N.Y.C., NY, 2003—. U. Va., Currey Grad Sch. of Edn., Charlotesville, Va., 2005—. Home: 1 Sheridan Sq 3F New York NY 10014 E-mail: jpalmer@mba1999.hw.edu.

**PALMER, JEFFERY DEAN,** systems engineering manager, consultant; b. Monroe, La., Apr. 11, 1960; s. Kenneth Dean and Martha Jean Palmer; m. Sharman Ann Taylor. BSEE, La. State U., Baton Rouge, 1983. EIT La., 1983, cert. reliability engr., Am. Soc. for Quality, 1998. Engr. General Dynamics, Fort Worth, Tex., 1983—90, Nagoya, Japan, 1991—92; sys. engr. mgr. Lockheed Martin, Fort Worth, 1993—. Mem.: Am. Soc. for Quality. Avocation: guitar playing. Home: 228 Valley Ranch Rd Weatherford TX 76087 Office: Lockheed Martin 1000 Lockheed Blvd Fort Worth TX 76108 Personal E-mail: plmrjd@aol.com. Business E-Mail: jeff.d.palmer@lmco.com.

**PALMER, JEFFRESS GARY,** hematologist, educator; b. Bklyn., Oct. 7, 1921; s. William Ware and Margaret Lee (Boswell) P.; m. Jane Ann Cartwright, Feb. 2, 1951; children: Kristin Cartwright, Julie Mitchell. BS, Emory U., 1942, MD, 1944. Intern N.C. Bapt. Hosp., 1944-45; resident in medicine Emory U., Atlanta, 1947-49; fellow hematology U. Utah, Salt Lake City, 1949-52; from asst. prof. to prof. medicine U. N.C., Chapel Hill, 1952—, ret., 1985. Capt. M.C. AUS, 1945-47. Mem. AAAS, AAUP, AMA, Am. Fedn. for Clin. Rsch., So. Soc. for Clin. Investigation, N.Y. Acad. Scis., Am. Soc. Hematology. Home: Morgan Creek Rd Chapel Hill NC 27517 Personal E-mail: jgpal@med.unc.edu.

**PALMER, JESSICA,** diversified financial services company executive; Head of risk mgmt. for corp. and investment banking group Citigroup, NYC, 2003—. Named one of 25 Women to Watch, US Banker mag., 2005. Office: Citigroup 767 5th Ave New York NY 10153*

**PALMER, JOCELYN BETH,** volunteer; b. Salina, Kans., Dec. 19, 1927; d. Paul Franklin and Josie Murtle (Schultz) Swartz; m. Gerald Keith Palmer, Dec. 28, 1952; children: David, Paula, Brian, April. AA, Christian Coll., Columbia, Mo., 1947; BS with honors, Kans. State U., 1949; MA, U. Iowa, 1951. Grad. asst. presch. U. Iowa, Iowa City, 1949-51; instr. U. Ill., Urbana, 1951-52; co-dir. child devel. ctr. Long Beach (Calif.) City Coll., 1954-56. Mem. task force Early Childhood Edu., 2000-01. Tchr. trainer, presch. tchr., cons., chmn. nursery com., elder, deacon Presbyn. Ch.; mem. Com. to Develop Stds. for Presch. Handicapped, Salina, 1981-83; pres., bd. dirs. # 305 Salina Sch. Dist., 1975-87; com. chair, bd. dirs. St. Francis Boyd Home, Salina, Ellsworth, 1984-87; bd. dirs. YWCA, 1993-97; bd. dirs. Asburg Hosp. Aux., 1993-96, sec. 1994-96; mem. com. planning early childhood edn. USD 305. Mem. Clippership Mariners (chaplain 1991-93, logkeeper 1994-95, 2000-01, skipper 1997, chaplain, 2002-03), Saline County Med. Alliance (bd. dirs. 1992-96, 98-2000), Twentieth Century Forum (courtesy chmn. 1989-93, 2000—), PEO (pres. 1989-91, 94-95, treas. 1993-95), Salina Downtown Lioness (bd. dirs. 1988-89, 91-93, program chair 1997, pres. 2000-03), Phi Kappa Phi, Omicron Nu. Republican. Avocations: sewing, reading, music, swimming.

**PALMER, JOHN ANTHONY, III,** secondary school educator, music educator, language educator; b. Worcester, Mass., May 18, 1955; s. John Jr. and Barbara (Dufresne) P. BA in Spanish, Worcester State Coll., 1977, MEd in Ednl. Adminstrn., 1988. Cert. Spanish, French, German and music tchr., Mass. Tchr., head dept. fgn. langs. Mahar Regional Sch., Orange, Mass., 1979-88; tchr. French, Spanish and German, Doherty Meml. H.S., Worcester, 1993-99, Burncoat Sr. High, 1999—. Adj. prof. Spanish, Worcester State Coll., 1988-90, Fla. Atlantic U., 1991-93, Quinsigamond Cmty. Coll., 1997—; instr. voice Worcester Poly. Inst., 1979-81; cantor Ch. of St. Peter, 1977-81, Worcester Eglise Notre Dame des Canadiens, Worcester, 1981-83; adjudicator vocal auditions All-State Music Educators Conf., 1988. Tenor soloist Regis Coll., Boston, Worcester Poly. Inst., 1988, Worcester Chorus, Salisbury Singers, Simmons Coll., Boston, Ft. Lauderdale Opera Co., Opera Worcester, Smith Coll., North Hampton, Wells Coll., Aurore, N.Y. Mem. ASCD, Am. Coun. Tchrs. Fgn. Langs., Nat. Assn. Secondary Sch. Prins., Mass. Assn. Sch. Supts., Mass. Fgn. Lang. Assn., Sigma Delta Pi. Democrat. Roman Catholic. Home: 14 Waterford Dr Botany Bay Worcester MA 01602 E-mail: jpalmerIII@aol.com.

**PALMER, JOHN BERNARD, III,** lawyer; b. Ft. Wayne, Ind., May 18, 1952; s. John Bernard and Dorothy Alma (Lauer) P. BA, Mich. State U., 1974; JD, U. Mich., 1977. Bar: Ill. 1977, US Dist. Ct. (no. dist.) Ill. 1977, US Ct. Appeals 2002, US Tax Ct. 1979, US Ct. Claims 2001. Assoc. Mayer Brown & Platt, Chgo., 1977-80, Hopkins & Sutter, Chgo., 1980-83, ptnr., 1983-2001, Foley & Lardner LLP, Chgo., 2001—, chmn. taxation practice group. Adj. prof. Ill. Inst. Tech.- Kent Coll. of Law, Chgo., 1984—. Mem. ABA (tax sect.). Office: Foley & Lardner LLP 321 N Clark St Chicago IL 60610 Office Phone: 312-832-4575. Business E-Mail: jpalmer@foley.com.

**PALMER, JOHN DERRY,** physiology educator; b. Chgo., May 26, 1932; s. John and Florence (Eley) P.; m. Carla Bianchi, Sept. 15, 1960; 1 child, John Charles. BA, Lake Forest Coll., 1957; MS, Northwestern U., 1959, PhD, 1962. Asst. prof. U. Ill., Chgo., 1961-63; fellow NSF, U. Bristol, Eng., 1963-64; prof., dept. chmn. NYU, 1964-74; prof. U. Mass., Amherst, 1974—, dept. chmn., 1974-80. Edit. bd. Marine Behavior and Physiology, 1988—, Chronobiology Internat., 1986—; author: Textbook of Modern Biology, 1968, The Biological Clock: Two Views, 1970, Biological Clocks in Marine Animals: The Control of Physiological and Behavioral Tidal Rhythms, 1974, An Introduction to Biological Rhythms, 1976, (with others) Biological Rhythms and Living Clocks, 1977, Human Biological Rhythms, 1983, The

Biological Rhythms and Clocks of Intertidal Animals, 1995, The Living Clock, 2000, The Biological Clock, 2003; contbr. articles to profl. jours. With U.S. Army, 1953-55. Fellow AAAS, Explorers Club; mem. Internat. Soc. of Chronobiology, Nat. Assn. of Scholars, Marine Biol. Lab., Phi Beta Kappa, Sigma Xi (pres., v.p., treas. N.Y. chpt., Disting. Rschr. award 1968). Avocation: trout and saltwater fishing. Office: U Mass Dept Biology 611 North Pleasant St Amherst MA 01003 Office Phone: 413-545-4400. Business E-Mail: ftodd@bio.umass.edu.

**PALMER, KIMBERLY ANNE,** director; b. Lansing, Mich., June 5, 1959; d. Stan A Clapp and Ann Jedrzejek; m. Neil Raymond Palmer, June 26, 1982; children: Amanda, Ethan, Sean. BS, Mich. State U., 1982. Cert. tchr. State Dept. Of Edn., 1982. Corp. and institutional trust officer Manufactures Bank Of Detroit, 1986—90; secondary sci. tchr. Lansing Pub. Schs., Mich., 1994—2000; Curriculum, Instrn., and Assessment Coord. K-12 Math and Sci. South Lyon Cmty. Schs., South Lyon, Mich., 2000—. Cons. State Of Mich. MEAP Office - Sci. Content Adv. Com., Lansing, Mich., 1999—; contbg author - MICLiMB State Of Mich. Dept. Of Educaiton, Lansing, 2000—01. Mem. Howell Band Boosters, Mich., 2003—04. Recipient NEWMAST, NASA, 1998. Mem.: ASD, Mich. Sci. Tchrs. Assn., Oakland Rsch., Evaluation, And Assessment Com., Nat. Coun. For Tchrs. Of Math., NSTA. Office: South Lyon Community Schools 345 S Warren St South Lyon MI 48178 Office Phone: 248-573-8114. E-mail: palmerk@slcs.us.

**PALMER, LARRY GARLAND,** music educator, writer, musician; b. Warren, Ohio, Nov. 13, 1938; s. Gerald Leroy and Esther Garland Palmer. MusB, Oberlin Coll., Ohio, 1960; MusM, Eastman Sch. Music, 1961, MusD, 1963. Head Dept. Fine Arts St. Paul's Coll., Lawrenceville, Va., 1963—65; prof. music Norfolk (Va.) State U., 1965—70; prof. harpsichord and organ So. Meth. U., Dallas, 1970—. Author: Hugo Distler and his Church Music, 1967, Harpsichord in America: A 20th-Century Revival, 1989, paperback edit., 1993; musician: The Harpsichord Now and Then, 1975, Organ Works of Hugo Distler, 1978, Dedication Recital, Fisk Organ opus 101, 1993, Larry Palmer /Harpsichord/ Bach, 1994, Harpsichord Recital, 1997, Music of Rudy Davenport, 1999, Dos Prados: Larry Palmer Plays the 1762 Oldovini Organ in the Meadows Museum, SMU, 2001; harpsichord editor: The Diapason, 1969—, contbg. author: The New Grove Dictionary of Music, The Grove Dictionary of Opera. Mem.: Am. Guild Organists (dean Norfolk chpt. 1968—70, dean Dallas chpt. 1977—79), Southeastern Hist. Keyboard Soc. (pres. 2004—). Avocations: reading, cooking. Office: Southern Methodist University Meadows School of the Arts Dallas TX 75275 Office Phone: 214-768-3273. E-mail: lpalmer@smu.edu.

**PALMER, LARRY ISAAC,** lawyer, educator; b. 1944; AB, Harvard U., 1966; LLB, Yale U., 1969. Bar: Calif. 1970. Asst. prof. Rutgers U., Camden, N.J., 1970-73, assoc. prof., 1973-75, Cornell U., Ithaca, N.Y., 1975-79, prof. law, 1979—2002, vice provost, 1979-84, v.p. acad. programs, 1987-91, v.p. acad. program and campus affairs, 1991-94; endowed chair Dept. Urban Health Policy U. Louisville, 2003—. Vis. fellow Cambridge U., 1984-85. Author: Law, Medicine, and Social Justice, 1989, Endings and Beginnings: Law, Medicine and Society in Assisted Life and Death, 2000. Mem. Am. Law Inst. Office: Inst Bioethics Health Law and Policy Sch Medicine 501 E Broadway Ste 310 Univ Louisville Louisville KY 40292 E-mail: lip1@cornell.edu.

**PALMER, LARRY LEON,** foundation administrator, former ambassador; b. Augusta, Ga. BA, Emory U., 1970; MEd in African History, Tex. So. U., 1973; EdD in Higher Edn., Ind. U., Bloomington, 1978. Vol. Peace Corps., Liberua, West Africa, 1971—73; joined Foreign Svc., 1982; vice consul Dominican Republic, 1982—84; personnel officer Montevideo, Uruguay and Asuncion, Paraguay, 1984—86; staff asst. to asst. sec. African Affairs US Dept. State, 1986—87, counselor for adminstrn. Freetown, Sierra Leone, 1987—89, personnel officer Seoul, Republic of Korea, 1991—94, counselor for adminstrn. Dominican Republic, 1994—98, dep. chief of mission to chargé d'affaires Quito, Ecuador, 1999—2002, US amb. to Honduras Tegucigalpa, 2002—05; pres. Inter-Am. Found., Arlington, Va., 2005—. Asst. dir. fin. aid U. Va., Charlottesville, 1973—74; prof. hist. Cuttington Coll., Suakoko, Liberia, 1974—76, Wake Forest U., Winston Salem, NC, 1978—81; Pearson fellow, asst. to pres. U. Tex., El Paso, 1989—91. Office: Inter-Am Found 901 N Stuart St, 10 Fl Arlington VA 22203 Office Phone: 703-306-4301.*

**PALMER, LOUIS THOMAS,** pathologist; b. Omaha, Dec. 12, 1937; s. Harry Calvin and Helen Irene (Hansen) P.; m. Rosario Garcia, Dec. 28, 1977; children: Ria Charrise, Ryan Christopher. BS, Wash. State U., 1960; MS, Kans. State U., 1965; PhD, U. Minn., 1968. Cert. plant pathologist; cert. pest control operator, Fla. Plant pathologist Rockefeller Found., Mex. and India, 1968-71; extension plant pathologist U. Nebr., Lincoln, 1971-75; plant pathologist Internat. Rice Rsch. Inst., Sukamandi, Indonesia, 1975-79; dir. United Fruit Co., La Lima, Honduras, 1979-81; field devel. biologist E.I. duPont de Nemours, Campinas, Brazil, 1982-85; mgr. Madera, Calif., 1985-88; cons. Checchi & Co., Dhaka, Bangladesh, 1988-91; field rsch. mgr. Calif. Agriculture Rsch., Kerman, Calif., 1992; plant pathologist Harris Moran Seed Co., Ruskin, Fla., 1992—94, Pioneer Vegetable Genetics, Ruskin, Fla., 1995—96; pres., owner Tropical Foliage Inc., Wimauma, Fla., 1997—. Part-time faculty U. Fla., Plant City, 2003—; adj. prof. Fla. So. Coll., Lakeland, 2004—; part-time pest control operator Ct. Fla. Landscaping Co., Tampa, 2004—05. Contbr. articles to profl. jours. Advisor Boy Scouts Am., Campinas, 1983-85, councilor, Madera, 1985-88, leader Tiger Club, Dhaka, 1988-90, cubmaster, 1990-91, den. leader, Madera, 1991-92, asst. den leader Brandon, 1993, asst. scoutmaster Brandon, Fla., 1994—. Carl Raymond Grey scholar Union Pacific R.R., 1955, Carl J. Erickson scholar Benton County, Washington, 1956. Mem.: Am. Legion (1st vice comdr. Brandon post 2002—). Roman Catholic. Avocations: photography, swimming. Home: 1343 Monte Lake Dr Valrico FL 33594-8109 Office: Tropical Foliage Inc 5202 Bonita Dr Wimauma FL 33598 E-mail: cremlap@gmail.com.

**PALMER, LYNNE,** writer, astrologer; b. El Centro, Calif., Dec. 14, 1932; d. Clarence Lee and Paquita Mae (Hartley) Hafer; m. Bruno Cazzaniga, Mar. 13, 1964 (div. 1965); m. Sidney Latter, Nov. 29, 1997 (dec. Oct. 2004). Student, Ch. of Light, 1957-62, Calif. Sch. Escrows, L.A., 1960; theatre mgmt. degree, Mus. Arenas Theatres Assn., N.Y.C., 1963. Asst. teller Western Mortgage, L.A., 1957-58; head teller Sutro Mortgage Svc., L.A., 1958-61; freelance astrologer N.Y.C., 1961-92, Las Vegas, Nev., 1962—; owner, operator, tchr. astrology sch. N.Y.C., 1970-72; owner Star Bright Pubs., Las Vegas, 1996—. Spkr. in field; interviewed in N.Y. Post and other major newspapers and mags. including Life and Oggi (Italy), Veja (Brazil), Wall St. Jour., People Mag., Globe, Die Welt am Sonntag (West Germany), New Woman Mag., Forbes. Author: Prosperity, Nixon's Horoscope, Astrological Almanac, Astrological Compatibility (Profl. Astrologers award 1976), Horoscope of Billy Rose, ABC Basic Chart Reading, ABC Major Progressions, ABC Chart Erection, Pluto Ephemeris (1900-2000), Daily Positions, Is Your Name Lucky For You?, Do-It-Yourself Publicity Directory, Your Lucky Days and Numbers, Money Magic, Astro-Guide to Nutrition and Vitamins, Gambling to Win, The Astrological Treasure Map, Dear Sun Signs, Are You Compatible With Your Boss, Partner, Coworkers, Employee, Client?, Bet to Win, Special Report: USA Under Attack, Lucky Days and Winning Numbers; columnist: Self, House Beautiful, Gold; record album: Cast and Read Your Horoscope; TV appearances include The Johnny Carson Tonight Show, What's My Line, 60 Minutes, CBS News Night Watch, Cosmos (BBC), Sci. Series (Italian TV), Fantastico (Brazilian TV), Japan TV, News (Nippon), Do We Really Need It? (ASAHI), The World is Calling (Uranai); contbr. articles to mags. and newspapers. Mem. AFTRA, Am. Fedn. Astrologers (cert.). Avocation: travel. Home: 850 E Desert Inn Rd Apt 912 Las Vegas NV 89169 Office: Lynne Palmer 1155 E Twain Ave Ste 108-248 Las Vegas NV 89169 Office Phone: 800-615-3352. Business E-Mail: lynnepalmer@lynnepalmer.com.

**PALMER, MARILYN JOAN,** English composition educator; b. Mahoning County, Ohio, Mar. 3, 1933; d. Rudolph George and Marian Eleanor Wynn; m. Richard Palmer, Nov. 10, 1956 (dec. 1987); children: Ricky, Larry, Kevin.

Phys. therapy cert., UCLA, 1954, BS, 1955; MA in Philosophy, Ohio State U., 1969; PhD, U. Okla., 1996. Phys. therapist Neil Ave. Sch. for Handicapped, Columbus, Ohio, 1968-69; instr. philosophy Ohio State U., Columbus, 1969; instr. English Youngstown (Ohio) State U., 1970-71; writer, editor The Economy Co., ednl. publs., Oklahoma City, 1977-81; grad. asst. in English U. Okla., Norman, 1981-87, lectr. in English, 1988-90, tech. writing instr. ind. studies, 1988-97. Free-lance editing and cons.; cons. for on-line CD-ROM to accompany a textbook, 2002. Author: Technical Writing for Science, Business and Industry, 1988, An Enthymeme as a Platform for Understanding Audience Values, 1997; editor: Kindergarten Keys Teacher's Guidebook, 1982, author parochial supplement, 1982. Fund-raiser Easter Seal Soc., 1965-68; den mother coord. Boy Scouts Am., 1966, 67. Dept. Energy grantee, 1976. Mem. AAUP, Am. Phys. Therapy Assn., Soc. for Women in Philosophy, Alpha Xi Delta (nat. editor Quill 1984-86). Office Phone: 405-447-6495. Personal E-mail: doclynn@cox.net.

**PALMER, MICHAEL,** poet; b. NYC, 1943; Author: (books of poetry) Blake's Newton, 1972, The Circular Gates, 1974, Without Music, 1977, Notes For Echo Lakes, 1981, First Figure, 1984, Sun, 1988, At Passages, 1996, The Lion Bridge: Selected Poems 1972-1995, 1998, The Promises of Glass, 2000, Codes Appearing: Poems 1979-1988, 2001, Company of Moths, 2005, Recipient Wallace Stevens award, Acad. Am. Poets, 2006. Office: c/o Acad Am Poets Ste 604 584 Broadway New York NY 10012-5243*

**PALMER, PAMELA S.,** lawyer; BA, U. Calif., Irvine, 1978; JD, U. So. Calif., 1982. Bar: Calif. 1982. Jud. clk. to Hon. Walter Ely, U.S. Ct. Appeals (9th cir.); with Heller, Ehrman, White & McAuliffe, L.A., ptnr., 1992—96, Latham & Watkins, L.A., 1996—. Office: Latham and Watkins LLP 633 W Fifth St Ste 4000 Los Angeles CA 90071

**PALMER, PATRICK ASA,** retired bank executive, finance educator; b. Amherst, N.S., Can., Mar. 29, 1943; s. James Asa and Evelyn Elizabeth (Hatt) P.; m. Margaret Ann Teixeira, Feb. 8, 1964; children: Mark, Ingrid, Petrina, Kara-Lynn. B in Commerce with honors, U. Windsor, Ont., Can., 1970; FICB, U. Toronto, 1972. Mgr. mktg. program Royal Bank of Can., Toronto, Ont., 1976-78, mgr. nat. bus. met., 1978-79, mgr. comml. markets, 1979-81, v.p. comml. mktg. and svcs. Ont., 1981-82, v.p. comml. mktg. Can., 1982-83, v.p. planning, comml. banking and nat. accounts, 1983-86, v.p. sales and svcs. Can., 1986-88, v.p. corp. mktg. and sales, 1988-89, v.p. retail banking, 1989-94; sr. v.p. channel mgmt. RBFG, 1994-97; pres. Where Eagles Soar, Inc., 1997—. Lectr. Sheridan Coll., Oakville, Ont., 1979-81, George Brown Coll., Toronto, 1979; bd. dirs. Janes Family Foods Ltd., Kinfolk Mgmt. Inc., Penetangore Ridge, Inc; mem. adv. bd. Mphasis. founder Cappy Ride, Motorcycle Charity Ride; past bd. dirs. Ont. Export, Inc., C. of C., Ont., C. of C., CDN C. of C., Gov. Gen.'s Can. study conf., U. Windsor, CDN Tourism Assn. Econ. Devel. Assn. Can., CDN Tourism Mgmt. Ctr., other non-profit orgns.; mem. devel. bd. Windsor/Essex Hosp. Found. Contbr. articles to profl. jours. Recipient Can. 125 medal, U. Windsor Clark award, Alumni award Merit, Double Gold medalist, U. Windsor, 1970. Mem. Alliance for Ont. Univs. (hon.). Home: 8078 8th Line RR # 4 Kenilworth ON Canada NOG 2E0 Office: Where Eagles Soar Inc 5720 Timberlea Blvd Ste 201 Mississauga ON Canada L4W 4W2 E-mail: pat@whereeaglessoar.com.

**PALMER, PATRICK EDWARD,** radio astronomer, educator; b. St. Johns, Mich., Dec. 6, 1940; s. Don Edward and Nina Louise (Kyes) P.; m. Joan Claire Merlin, June 9, 1963; children: Laura Katherine, Aidan Edward, David Elijah. SB, U. Chgo., 1963; MA, Harvard U., 1965, PhD, 1968. Radio astronomer Harvard U., Cambridge, Mass., 1968; asst. prof. astronomy and astrophysics U. Chgo., 1968-70, assoc. prof., 1970-75, prof., 1975—. Vis. assoc. prof. astronomy Calif. Inst. Tech., Pasadena, 1972; vis. radio astronomer Cambridge (Eng.) U., 1973; vis. rsch. astronomer U. Calif., Berkeley, 1977, 86; vis. scientist Nat. Radio Astronomer Obs., 1980-2005. Contbr. articles on radio astron. investigations of comets and interstellar medium to tech. jours. Recipient Bart J. Bok prize for contbns. to galactic astronomy, 1969, Alfred P. Sloan Found. fellow, 1970-72, Helen B. Warner prize, 1975. Fellow AAAS (chmn. sect. D astronomy 1984); mem. AAUP, Am. Astron. Soc. (chmn. nominating com. 1981, mem. publs. bd. 1985-86, mem. Warner Prize selection com. 1977-78), Royal Astron. Soc., Internat. Astron. Union, U. Chgo. Track Club. Home: 5549 S Dorchester Ave Chicago IL 60637-1720 Office: Univ Chgo Astronomy & Astrophysics Ctr 5640 S Ellis Ave Chicago IL 60637-1433 Office Phone: 773-702-7972. E-mail: ppalmer@oskar.uchicago.edu.

**PALMER, PAUL RICHARD,** school librarian, archivist, curator; b. Cin., Jan. 21, 1917; s. Gardiner O. and Sarah Ellen (Christy) Palmer. BA, U. Cin., 1949; MS, Columbia U., 1950, MA, 1955. Asst. br. libr. Bklyn. Pub. Libr., 1950-51; libr. Columbia U., N.Y.C., 1951-67, libr. sch. libr. svc., 1968, libr., curator Brander Matthews Dramatic Mus., 1969-73, bibliographer Avery Archtl. Libr., 1974, curator Columbiana Collection, 1974—. Cons. Am. Libr. Assn., Chgo., N.Y.C., 1954—59. Contbr. articles to profl. jours. Founder fund for collection and preservation of filsm stills and formats Mus. Modern Art. Fellow: Pierpont Morgan Libr.; mem.: VFW, Manuscript Soc., Licoln Ctr. Film Soc., Soc. Hist. Preservation, French Inst., Am. Film Inst., Theatre Libr. Assn. (exec. coun. 1970—74), St. George Soc. N.Y., Mus. Modern Art, Am. Mus. Britain, Met. Mus. Art, Ch. Club N.Y., Grolier Club, Order St. John of Jerusalem, Phi Beta Kappa. Episcopalian.

**PALMER, PHILIP EDWARD STEPHEN,** radiologist; b. London, Apr. 26, 1921; MBBS, U. London, 1944, DMR, 1946, DMRT, 1947; MD (hon.), U. Tirgu Mures, Romania, 2004. Intern, then resident Westminster Hosp.; cons. radiologist West Cornwall (Eng.) Hosp. Group, 1947-54; sr. govt. radiologist Matabeleland, Rhodesia-Zimbabwe, 1954-64; prof. radiology U. Cape Town, South Africa, 1964-68; prof. U. Pa., 1968-70; prof. diagnostic radiology and vet. radiology U. Calif., Davis, 1970—. WHO cons. in field. Author: The Imaging of Tropical Diseases, 1980 and 2nd edit.; contbr. 200plus articles to profl. publs. Recipient German Röentgen award, 1993, 1st Béclère medal Internat. Soc. Radiology, 1996, 1st Antoine Béclère lectr. Internat. Soc. Radiology, 1996, Presdl. award Radiol. Soc. N.Am., 2000. Fellow Calif. Radiol. Assn., Royal Coll. Physicians (Edinburgh), Royal Coll. Radiologists (Eng.), Romanian Soc. Radiol. and Nuclear Med.; mem. Brit. Inst. Radiology, Brit. Med. Assn., Calif. Med. Assn., Internat. Skeletal Soc., Assn. Univ. Radiologists, Radiol. Soc. N.Am. (Spl. Pres.'s award 2000), Kenya Radiol. Soc., South African Coll. Medicine, Egyptian Soc. Radiology and Nuclear Medicine, Yugoslav Assn. for Ultrasound, West African Assn. Radiologists. Address: 821 Miller Dr Davis CA 95616-3622

**PALMER, R. SCOTT,** lawyer; b. Albany, N.Y., Nov. 8, 1944; s. Roger Alan and Alma Jane (Farley) P.; m. Linda Lee Westphal, Sept. 8, 1968 (Dec 1980); children— Mahri Westphal, David Scott, Roger Alan; m. Jane Amerena, Mar. 9, 1981; 1 son, John Robert Winfield. B.A., U. Mich., 1966; J.D. cum laude, U. Miami, 1976. Bar: Fla. 1976, U.S. Dist. Ct. (mid. dist.) Fla. 1977, U.S. Dist. Ct. (no. dist.) Fla. 1981. Asst. state atty. 9th Jud. Circuit, Orlando, Fla., 1976-79; chief field counsel Fla. Dept. Law Enforcement, Tallahassee, 1980-81, chief exec. investigations, 1981-82; chief prosecutor Statewide Grand Jury of Fla., Exec. Office of Gov., Tallahassee, 1982-86; assoc. Rumberger, Kirk, Caldwell, Cabiness & Burke, Orlando, 1986—; adj. prof. criminal justice Valencia Coll., Orlando, 1977-80; instr. Organized Crime Inst., Orlando, 1980-86, Fla. State U., 1986. Contbr. articles to legal jours. U. Miami Sch. Law Scholar, 1973-76. Mem. ABA. Democrat. Roman Catholic. Home: 301 Timbercove Cir Longwood FL 32779-2559

**PALMER, RICHARD N.,** state supreme court justice; b. Hartford, Conn., May 27, 1950; BA, Trinity Coll., 1972; JD with high honors, U. Conn., 1977. Bar: Conn. 1977, U.S. Dist. Ct. Conn. 1978, D.C. 1980, U.S. Ct. Appeals (2d cir.) 1981. Law clk. to Hon. Jon O. Newman U.S. Ct. Appeals (2d cir.), 1977—78; assoc. Shipman & Goodwin, 1978—80; asst. U.S. atty. Office U.S. Atty. Conn., 1980—83, 1987—90, U.S. atty., 1991, chief state's atty.,

1991—93; ptnr. Chatigny and Palmer, 1984—86; assoc. justice Conn. Supreme Ct., Hartford, 1993—. Mem. Phi Beta Kappa. Office: Connecticut Supreme Ct 231 Capitol Ave Hartford CT 06106-1548 Office Phone: 860-757-2115.

**PALMER, RICHARD WARE,** retired lawyer; b. Boston, Oct. 20, 1919; s. George Ware and Ruth French (Judkins) P.; m. Nancy Fernald Shaw, July 8, 1950; children: Richard Ware Jr., John Wentworth, Anne Fernald. AB, Harvard U., 1942, JD, 1948. Bar: N.Y. 1950, Pa. 1959. Sec., dir. N.Am. Mfg. Co., Natick, Mass., 1946-48; assoc. Burlingham, Veeder, Clark & Hupper, Burlingham, Hupper & Kennedy, N.Y.C., 1949-57; ptnr. Rawle & Henderson, Phila., 1958-79; co-founder, ptnr. Palmer, Biezup & Henderson, Phila., 1979—97, of counsel, 1998—2004; ret., 2004. Sec. Underwater Technics, Inc., Camden, NJ, 1967-85; adv. on admiralty law to U.S. del. Inter-Govtl. Maritime Consultative Orgn., London, 1967, U.S. del. 30th-34th internat. confs.; mem. U.S. Shipping Coord. Com., Washington legal sub com., 1967—; titular mem. Comité Maritime Internat.; v.p., sec., bd. dirs. Phila. Belt Line R.R., Mather (Bermuda) Ltd. Editor: Maritime Law Reporter. Mem., permanent adv. bd. Tulane Admiralty Law Inst., Tulane U. Law Sch., New Orleans, 1975—; trustee Seamen's Ch. Inst., Phila., 1967—2001, pres., 1972—84; mem. exec. com. Harvard Law Sch. Assn., Phila., 1986—2005; bd. dirs. Havrford (Pa.) Civic Assn., 1972—85, pres., 1976—79; consul for Denmark State of Pa., 1980—91, consul emeritus, 1992—. Lt. comdr. USNR, 1942—46. Fellow World Acad. Art and Sci. (treas. 1988-2002); mem. ABA (former chmn. stdg. com. on admiralty and maritime law 1978-79), N.Y.C. Bar Assn., Phila. Bar Assn., Maritime Law Assn. U.S.(chmn. limitation liability com. 1977-83, 2d v.p. 1984-86, 1st v.p. 1986-88, pres. 1988-90, immediate past pres. 1990-92), Assn. Average Adjusters USA and Gt. Britain, Port of Phila. Maritime Soc., Consul Assn. Phila., Colonial Soc. Pa. (treas. 2003-05, bd. govs. 2005—), Danish Order of Dannebrog, Merion Cricket Club, Phila. Club, Rittenhouse Club, Geneal. Soc. Pa. (bd. dirs. 1997-2002, v.p. 2003-04, bd. dirs. 2005—), Harvard Club NYC and Phila. (exec. com. 1983-86, 94-97). Republican. Episcopalian. Home: 432 Montgomery Ave Haverford PA 19041-1527 Home Fax: 610-649-7824.

**PALMER, ROBERT BAYLIS,** librarian; b. Rockville Centre, NY, Apr. 5, 1938; s. John Frederick and Marion (Baylis) P.; divorced; 1 child, Michele Palmer Fracasso. AB, Kenyon Coll., Gambier, Ohio, 1960; MS in L.S, Simmons Coll., Boston, 1965; MA in English, Middlebury Coll., Vt., 1965. Tchr. Brooks Sch., North Andover, Mass., 1960-65, libr., 1961-65; acting libr. Columbia Coll., 1965-66; asst. to dir. libraries Columbia U., 1965-67; dir. Barnard Coll. Libr., 1967-81. Fulbright lectr. Tribhuvan U. Library, Kathmandu, Nepal, 1972-73, Kathmandu, 1980; vol. lectr. USIS, library cons., Asia, 1976; Fulbright lectr. Wuhan, Peoples Republic China, 1984-85; library cons., advisor, Peoples Republic China, 1986-87, Zanzibar, Tanzania, 1988; lectr., cons. Kenya, Ethiopia, Zimbabwe, 1988; English lang. escort officer US Dept. State, 1989—. Mem. ALA. Address: 190 Riverside Dr New York NY 10024-1008 *Life rocks by developing an informed skepticism towards life in general and politics in particular, by thanking your teachers before it is too late, and by always having a plan B.*

**PALMER, ROBERT J.,** corporate financial executive; m. Trish Palmer; 2 children. BS in computer info. sys., Tulane U. Assoc. dir., student sys. Tulane U., New Orleans; sr. cons. Lawyers Title Ins. Corp., a LandAmerica subsidiary, 1990—93, v.p., dir. sys. devel. support, 1993—94, sr. v.p., 1994—2000; pres. Elliptus Tech., Inc., 2000; Exec. v.p., chief info. officer LandAmerica Fin. Group, Inc., 2002—. Avocations: boating, golf, fishing. Office: LandAmerica Fin Group Inc 101 Gateway Ctr Pkwy Richmond VA 23235-5153

**PALMER, ROBERT LESLIE,** lawyer; b. Porterville, Calif., Apr. 10, 1957; s. Harrison Rowe and Margaret Elizabeth (Witty) P.; m. Huisuk Kim, Feb. 1, 1986; 1 child, Aaron Rowe. BA, Tulane U., 1979; JD, Georgetown U., 1982. Bar: D.C. 1982, U.S. Ct. Mil. Appeals 1985, Tex. 1987, Ala. 1987, U.S. Dist. Ct. (no. dist.) Ala. 1987, U.S. Ct. Appeals (11th cir.) 1987, U.S. Supreme Ct. 2005, U.S. Dist. Ct. (mid. dist.) Ala. 2006; registered lobbyist, Ala. Assoc. Lewis Martin Burnett & Dunkle, P.C., Birmingham, Ala., 1987-89, Lewis and Martin, Birmingham, Ala., 1989-90, Martin, Drummond and Woosley, Birmingham, 1990-91, bd. dirs., 1991-92, Martin, Drummond, Woosley and Palmer, Birmingham, 1992-95; atty. Environ. Litig. Group, P.C., Birmingham, Ala., 1995—. Ala. del. 6th Joint Conf. between Korea and S.E. U.S., Kyongju, Republic of Korea, 1991, 7th Joint Conf., Atlanta, 1992; founder, dir. pres. Ala. Legal Reform Found.; asst. scoutmaster Boy Scouts Am., 2003—; bd. dirs. Jimmie Hale Mission, 2005—. Capt. JAGC, U.S. Army, 1983-87, USAR, 1987-91. Recipient commendation Republic of Korea Ministry of Justice, 1984. Mem. ATLA, Ala. Trial Lawyers Assn. (exec.com.), Tex. Trial Lawyers Assn., Christian Legal Soc., Phi Beta Kappa, Omicron Delta Kappa. Independent. Baptist. Home: 1408 E Whirlaway Helena AL 35080-4102 Office: Environ Litig Group PC 3529 7th Ave S Birmingham AL 35222-3210 Office Phone: 205-328-9200. Business E-Mail: bob@elglaw.com.

**PALMER, ROBERT TOWNE,** lawyer, bank executive; b. Chgo., May 25, 1947; s. Adrian Bernhardt and Gladys (Towne) P.; m. Ann Therese Darin, Nov. 9, 1974; children: Justin Darin, Christian Darin. BA, Colgate U., 1969; JD, U. Notre Dame, 1974. Bar: Ill. 1974, D.C. 1978, U.S. Supreme Ct. 1978. Law clk. to Hon. Walter V. Schaefer Ill. Supreme Ct., 1974-75; assoc. McDermott, Will & Emery, Chgo., 1975-81, ptnr., 1982-86, Chadwell & Kayser, Ltd., Chgo., 1987-88, Connelly, Mustes, Palmer & Schroeder, Chgo., 1988-89; of counsel Garfield & Merel Ltd., Chgo., 1990-2000. Adj. faculty Chgo. Kent Law Sch., 1975—77, Loyola U., 1976—78; adv. com. Fed. Home Loan Mortgage Corp., 1988—89; bd. dirs. Ctrl. Fed. Savs. & Loan Assn. of Chgo., chmn., COO, 2000—; dir. Chgo. Assn. Fin. Insts., 2001—03, sec., 2002—03; mem. Chgo. Crime Commn. 2001, dir. 2002. Contbr. articles to legal jours. and textbooks. Mem. ABA, Ill. State Bar Assn. (Lincoln award 1983), Chgo. Bar Assn., Chgo. Club, Dairymen's Country Club, Lambda Alpha. Office: Central Fed Savs 1601 W Belmont Ave Chicago IL 60657-3044

**PALMER, ROGER FARLEY,** pharmacology educator; b. Albany, N.Y., Sept. 23, 1931; m. Nelida Santiago, Apr. 1994. BS in Chemistry, St. Louis U., 1953; postgrad., Tulane U., 1955-56, Woods Hole Marine Biology Lab., 1956; MD, U. Fla., 1960. Intern Johns Hopkins Hosp., 1960-61, resident in medicine, 1961-62; asst. dept. biochemistry U. Fla., Gainesville, 1957; asst. medicine Osler Med. Service, 1960-62; instr. pharmacology and therapeutics U. Fla., 1962, asst. prof. pharmacology and medicine, 1964-67, assoc. prof. pharmacology and medicine, 1967-69, prof. medicine, chief div. clin. pharmacology, 1969-70, 71-82; prof., chmn. dept. pharmacology, prof. medicine U. Miami, Fla., 1970-81, clin. prof. medicine, 1982. Chmn. pharmacology sect. Nat. Bd. Med. Examiners, 1977—81; cons. Nat. Acad. Scis. Editorial bd. Pharmacol. Revs.; assoc. editor Advances in Molecular Pharmacology; ad hoc editor Am. Heart Jour.; editor Horizons in Clinical Pharmacology, 1976; author abstracts; contbr. over 100 articles to profl. jours. Served with USAR. Mosby scholar, 1957-60; Markle scholar in acad. medicine, 1965-70; recipient Basic Sci. Teaching award U. Miami, 1975-76; Meritorious Service medal Am. Heart Assn., 1972; citation for meritorious Service So. Region Am. Heart Assn., 1979; Visitante Distinguido award, Costa Rica, 1979; Outstanding Tchr. award U. Miami, 1982. Mem. Am. Coll. Clin. Pharmacology, Am. Fedn. Clin. Rsch., Am. Therapeutic Soc. (prize essay award 1970), Am. Soc. Pharmacology and Exptl. Therapeutics (emeritus), N.Y. Acad. Scis., So. Soc. Clin. Investigation, U.S. Pharmacopeia Revision Com., Internat. Study Group Rsch. Cardiac Metabolism, Am. Soc. Internal Medicine, Royal Soc. Health, Key Biscayne Yacht Club (bd. govs. 1994-97, fleet surgeon 1999-2000), Sigma Xi. Office: 240 Crandon Blvd Ste 215 Key Biscayne FL 33149-2009 Office Phone: 305-361-8655. Personal E-mail: palmerpebbles@aol.com.

**PALMER, ROGER RAYMOND,** finance educator; b. N.Y.C., Dec. 31, 1926; s. Archibald and Sophie (Jarnow) P.; m. Martha West Hopkins, June 7, 1986; children by previous marriage: Kathryn Sue, Daniel Stephen, Susan Jo.

BS, U. Wis., 1949; MBA, Cornell U., 1951; postgrad., NYU, 1951-54. Auditor, Ernst and Ernst, CPA's, N.Y.C., 1953-54; auditor Gen. Dynamics Corp., 1956-60; mgr. corp. audits Tex. Instruments, 1960-64; auditor 1st Nat. Bank, St. Paul, 1964-68, v.p. planning, 1968-69, v.p., comptr., 1969-75, sr. v.p., contr., 1975-82; chmn. dept. fin. Coll. of St. Thomas (now U. St. Thomas), St. Paul, 1996—; prof. emeritus U. St. Thomas, 2005—. Dir. First Met. Travel, Inc.; guest lectr. U. Minn., 1966; conf. leader, speaker, 1996— Contbr. articles to publs. Bd. dir. Waterford (Conn.) Civic Assn., 1959-60, Friends of St. Paul Pub. Library, 1967, Mpls. Citizens League; chmn. bd. dirs. Film in the Cities, 1983-85; mem. acctg. adv. council U. Minn.; trustee, chmn. fin. com. Hazelton Found. With U.S. Maritime Svc., 1945-47; with U.S. Army, 1954-56. Mem. Inst. Internal Auditors (pres. So. New Eng chpt. 1957-60, edn. chmn. Dallas 1961, Twin City chpt. 1965-66), Nat. Assn. Accts. (dir. Norwich, Conn. chpt. 1958-60), Nat. Assn. Accountants (St. Paul chpt. 1967), Assn. Bank Audit, Control and Operation, Am. Inst. Banking, Fin. Execs. Inst., Planning Forum (pres. Twin Cities chpt. 1984-85), Univ. Club (St. Paul). Clubs: St. Paul Athletic. Home: 415 Oak Ridge Dr San Marcos TX 78666 Business E-Mail: rrpalmer@stthomas.edu.

**PALMER, RUSSELL EUGENE,** investment company executive, retired dean; b. Jackson, Mich., Aug. 13, 1934; s. Russell E. and Margarite M. (Briles) P.; children: Bradley Carl, Stephen Russell, Russell Eugene, III, Karen Jean. BA with honors, Mich. State U., 1956; D in Comml. Sci. (hon.), Drexel U., 1980; MA (hon.), U. Pa., 1984; PhD (hon.), Chulalongkorn U., 1988, Free U. Brussels, 1989, York Coll., 1989. With Touche Ross & Co., N.Y.C., 1956-83, mng. ptnr., CEO, 1972-82, also bd. dirs., exec. coms.; mng. dir., CEO Touche Ross Internat., 1974-83; dean, Reliance prof. mgmt. and pvt. enterprise Wharton Sch. U. Pa., 1983-90, CEO. Bd. dirs. Honeywell Internat., Inc. Mem. Pres.'s Mgmt. Improvement Coun., 1979—80; mem. adv. bd. Salvation Army, past mem. nat. adv. bd.; former mem. adv. coun. Women's Way; bd. dirs. UN Assn. U.S.A.; former mem. adv. panel Comptr. Gen. U.S.; former chmn. bd trustees U. Pa. Health Care Sys.; trustee Acctg. Hall of Fame U. Pa.; bd. dirs. Joint Coun. Econ. Edn., 1978—83, United Fund Greater N.Y., 1980—83; mem. Bus.Com. Arts, 1977—83; bd. dirs. SEI Ctr. for Advanced Studies in Mgmt.; former mem. adv. coun. Sch. Internat. and Pub. Affairs Columbia U., Grad. Sch. Bus. Stanford U.; mem. assocs. coun. Bus. Sch. Oxford U.; mem. U.S. Sec. Labor's Commn. on Workforce Quality and Labor Market Efficiency; pres. Fin. Acctg. Found., 1972-82; pub. mem. Hudson Inst. Recipient Gavin Meml. award Beta Theta Pi, 1956, Disting. Community Svc. award Brandeis U., 1974, Outstanding Alumnus award Mich. State U., 1978, Humanitarian award Fedn. Jewish Philanthropies, 1979, Disting. Aux. Svc. award Salvation Army, 1979, LEAD Bus. award, 1984, Good Scout award Phila. coun. Boy Scouts Am., 1987. Mem. Merion Cricket Club, Conf. Bd. (bd. dirs.), Beta Gamma Sigma (mem. bd. govs.), Presbyterian. Office: The Palmer Group 3600 Market St Ste 530 Philadelphia PA 19104-2649 Office Phone: 215-243-2590. Business E-Mail: rpalmer@palmer-group.com.

**PALMER, SAMUEL COPELAND, III,** lawyer; b. Phila., June 9, 1934; s. Samuel Copeland Jr. and Vivian Gertrude (Plumb) P.; divorced; children: Samuel C. IV, Sarah Anne, Bryan Douglas. Grad., Harvard Sch., Los Angeles, 1952; student, Yale U., 1953; AB, Stanford U., 1955; JD, Loyola-Marymount U., Marymount, 1958. Bar: Calif. 1959, U.S. Dist. Ct. (cen., ea. and so. dists. Calif.) 1959, U.S. Ct. Appeals (9th cir.) 1970, U.S. Supreme Ct. 1971. Dep. city atty., Los Angeles, 1959-60; assoc. firm Pollock & Deutz, Los Angeles, 1960-63; ptnr. firm Pollock & Palmer, Los Angeles, 1963-70, Palmer & Bartenetti, Los Angeles, 1970-81, Samuel C. Palmer III, P.C., 1981-85; ptnr. Thomas, & Snell, 1985—. Adj. prof. Calif. State U., Fresno, 1993. Trustee Western Ctr. Law and Poverty; bd. dirs. Big Bros./Big Sisters, Fresno, Arte Ams., Lively Arts Found., Nat. Sleep Found., Vols. in Parole; pres., bd. dirs. Poverello House; founder, pres. Fresno Crime Stoppers. Mem. ABA, State Bar Calif. (disciplinary subcom., bar examiners subcom.), Fresno County Bar Assn. (pres., bd. dirs. 1988-93), Pickwick Soc., Am. Bd. Trial Advocates, Chancery Club, Downtown Club, Calif. Club, Fig Garden Tennis Club, Rotary, Delta Upsilon, Phi Delta Phi. Office: Gilmore Wood Vinnard 7108 N Fresno St Ste 410 Fresno CA 93720-2953 Home: 9323 N Saybrook Dr Apt 117 Fresno CA 93720-0830 E-mail: spalmer@thomasnell.com.

**PALMER, STACY ELLA,** periodical editor; b. Middletown, Conn., Oct. 25, 1960; d. Marvin Jerome Palmer and Eileen Sondra (Cohen) Palmer Burke. B in Liberal Arts and Internat. Rels., Brown U., 1982. Asst. editor Chronicle of Higher Edn., Washington, 1982-86, sr. editor, 1986-88; news editor Chronicle of Philanthropy, Washington, 1988-93, mng. editor, 1993-98, editor, 1998—. Bd. dirs. Brown Alumni Monthly, Providence, 1988-91, vice chmn., 1991-93, mem. 1996—, chmn., 2003. Mem.: Brown U. Alumni Assn. (bd. govs. 1997—2001), Brown Club Washington (bd. dirs. 1993—99, pres. 1994—99). Avocations: swimming, bicycling, travel. Home: 3513 30th St Washington DC 20008 Office: Chronicle of Philanthropy 1255 23rd St NW Washington DC 20037-1125

**PALMER, STUART HUNTER,** sociology educator; b. NYC, Apr. 29, 1924; s. Herman G. and Beatrice (Hunter) P.; m. Anne Barbara Scarborough, June 22, 1946; 1 dau., Catherine. BA, Yale U., 1949, MA, 1951, PhD, 1955; LHD (hon.), Daniel Webster Coll., 1997. Asst. to dean Yale Coll., New Haven, 1949-51; instr. sociology New Haven Coll., 1949-51, 53-55; faculty U. NH, Durham, 1955—, prof., 1964—, chmn. dept. sociology and anthropology, 1964-69, 79-82, dean Coll. Liberal Arts, 1982-95, dir. London program, 1995-96. Disting. vis. prof. SUNY, Albany, 1970-71; vis. behavioral scientist NH Divsn. Mental Health; vis. prof. U. Sussex, Eng., 1976, U. Ga., 1977; cons. U.S. Office Edn., USPHS, U.S. Office Delinquency and Youth Devel., Dept. Justice, mem. adv. com. for sociology Com. on Internat. Exch. of Persons; mem. exec. com. NH Gov.'s Commn. on Crime and Delinquency; co-chmn. Internat. Symposium on Univs. in Twenty-First Century; co-chmn. Internat. Confs. on Stress Rsch., Nat. Commn. Arts and Scis. Author: Understanding Other People, 1955, A Study of Murder, 1960, (with Brian R. Kay) The Challenge of Supervision, 1961, Deviance and Conformity, 1970, (with Arnold S. Linsky) Rebellion and Retreat, 1972, The Violent Society, 1972, The Prevention of Crime, 1973, (with John A. Humphrey) Deviant Behavior, 1980, Role Stress, 1981, Deviant Behavior: Patterns, Sources, and Controls, 1990, The Universities Today, 1998; contbr. articles to profl. jours. Chmn. bd. trustees Daniel Webster Coll., New Eng. Aero. Inst. Served to lt. AC AUS, 1942-45; Served to lt. AC USAF, 1951-53. Decorated Air medal with 3 oak leaf clusters; fellow Henry Page. Mem. Am. Sociol. Assn., Ea. Sociol. Soc., Internat. Sociol. Soc., Internat. Soc. Criminology, Internat. Soc. Forecasters, Am. Assn. Colls., Coun. for Liberal Learning, Am. Assn. Higher Edn., Coun. Colls. Arts and Scis., Nat. Assn. State Univs. and Land-Grant Colls., AAAS, Am. Acad. Polit. and Social Scis., NY Acad. Scis., Am. Assn. Suicidology, Soc. Cross-Cultural Rsch., Am. Soc. Criminology, Assn. Gov. Bds. Univs. and Colls., Phi Beta Kappa (hon.), Sigma Xi, Alpha Kappa Delta. Home: 38A Emerson Rd Durham NH 03824-2110 *Be honest with yourself.*

**PALMER, THOMAS HOWARD, JR.,** retired surgeon; b. Cambridge, Mass., Apr. 19, 1924; s. Thomas Howard and Elizabeth Agnes (Higgins) P.; m. Mary Ellen Herlihy, Feb. 20, 1954; children: Thomas H. III, Edward H., Anne M., David A., James L. Student, Harvard U., 1942-44; MD cum laude, Tufts U., 1948. Diplomate Am. Bd. Surgery. Intern City Hosp., Boston, 1948-49; resident surgery New Eng. Med. Ctr., Boston, 1949-50, 52-55; staff surgeon Ea. Maine Med. Ctr., Bangor, 1955-89, chief of surgery, 1967-74, 80-85; med. staff pres. Ea. Maine Med. Ctr., Bangor, 1973-75. Dir. Ea. Maine Healthcare, Bangor, 1982—2003; bd. dirs. Maine Peer Rev. Bd. (Med.) Bangor, 1988-89. Contbr. articles to med. jours. Trustee Ea. Maine Med. Ctr., Bangor, 1955-89; bd. dirs. Eastern Maine Charities, 1995—2003. Lt. USN, 1943-45, 50-52, Korea. Henry B. Humphrey scholar Harvard U., 1942; Charlton Rsch. fellow Tufts U. Med. Sch., 1950; recipient Disting. Svc. award Ea. Maine Healthcare, 1987. Fellow ACS (pres. Maine chpt. 1969-70); mem. New Eng. Surg. Soc., Maine Med. Assn., Penobscot Med. Soc., Alpha Omega Alpha. Roman Catholic. Avocations: writing, gardening. Home: 332 Garland St Bangor ME 04401-5543

**PALMER, TODD MICHAEL,** ecologist, educator; b. Berkeley, Calif., Aug. 30, 1967; s. Parker J. and Sarah Ann Palmer; m. Rayne Kristine Hurzeler, Sept. 10, 2005. PhD, U. Calif., Davis, 2001. Postdoctoral assoc. Ctr. fPopulation Biology, Davis, Calif., 2001—05; mem. faculty zoology U. Fla., Gainesville, 2006—. Dir. Kenya Wildlands Program, Nanyuki, Laikipia District, 2001—06. Contbr. articles to profl. jours.; rschr.; featured on Discovery Channel, ScienceNews, Natural History Magazine, and Conservation in Practice and in textbook Ecology. Grantee, NSF, US Fish and Wildlife Svc. Mem.: Sigma Xi. Republican. Office: U Florida 223 Bartram Hall Box 118525 Gainesville FL 32611 Personal E-mail: tmpalmer@ucdavis.edu. Business E-Mail: tmpalmer@zoo.ufl.edu.

**PALMER, TONY,** marketing executive; BS, Monash U., 1986; MBA, Internat. Mgmt. Inst., 1989. Bus. devel. mgr. PA Cons. Group, 1986—91; sr. cons. LEK Partnership, 1991—92; joined Mars Confectionery, Australia, 1992—95; mktg. mgr. CSR Refined Sugars, Australia, 1995—96; regional dir., mktg. and mgmt. Minute Maid div. Coca-Cola Co., Australia, 1996—2000; pres. natural, frozen and warehouse-club bus. Kellogg Co., mng. dir. England; chief mktg. officer Kimberly-Clark Corp., Dallas, 2006—. Office: Kimberly-Clark Corp 8611 Lemmon Ave Dallas TX 75209*

**PALMER, VENRICE ROMITO,** lawyer, educator; b. Springfield, Mass., Jan. 11, 1952; s. Venrice Wellesley and Mildred Adlay (Foster) P. Higher diploma, U. Besançon, France, 1973; AB maxima cum laude, King's Coll., Wilkes-Barre Pa., 1971; JD, Harvard U., 1977. Bar: N.Y. 1978, U.S. Dist. Ct. (so. and ea. dists.) N.Y. 1979, Ill. 1986, Calif. 1997. Spl. asst. atty. gen. Office N.Y. Atty. Gen., N.Y.C., 1977-79; staff atty. SEC, N.Y.C., 1979-82, br. chief, 1982-83, spl. trial counsel, 1983-85, acting asst. regional adminstr., 1984-85; sr. counsel Sears, Roebuck and Co., Hoffman Estates, Ill., 1985-97, Bank of Am., San Francisco, 1997-99; counsel McCutchen, Doyle, Brown & Enersen, LLP, San Francisco, 1999—2002, Bingham McCutchen LLP, San Francisco, 2002—. Guest lectr. St. John's U. Bus. Sch., N.Y.C., 1984; lectr. Practicing Law Inst., N.Y.C., 1995—, Glasser LegalWorks, Little Falls, N.J., 1997—, Am. Soc. Corp. Secs., 1997-99, Nat. Bus. Inst., Eau Claire, Wis., 2000—. Contbr. articles to various law publs. Recipient cert. of appreciation N.Y. State Bar Assn., 1978, Benaglia award King's Coll., 1974. Mem.: ABA, Calif. State Bar Assn. (mem. fin. instns. com. 2000—03), Alpha Mu Gamma, Delta Epsilon Sigma. Avocations: opera, ballet, reading. Home: 1200 Gough St Apt 7A San Francisco CA 94109-6616 Office: Bingham McCutchen LLP Three Embarcadero Ctr San Francisco CA 94111 E-mail: venricepalmer@bingham.com.

**PALMER, VICKI R.,** food products executive; b. Memphis; m. John E. Palmer; 1 child, Alexandria. B in Econs. and Bus. Adminstrn., Rhodes Coll., 1975; MBA in Fin., U. Memphis, 1980. Corp. loan officer First Tenn. Bank.; head pension investment FedEx, mgr. corp. fin.; mgr. pension investments Coca-Cola Co., 1983—86; asst. treas. Coca-Cola Enterprises Inc., 1986—93, v.p., 1993—99, treas., 1993—, sr. v.p., spl. asst. to CEO, 1999—, bd. dirs., 2001—. Bd. dirs. Spelman Coll., Rhodes Coll., Woodward Acad., First Tenn. Nat. Corp. Named one of 20 Women of Power and Influence in Corp. Am., Black Enterprise Mag., 100 Black Women of Influence, Atlanta Bus. League, 1998; recipient Disting. Alumni award, U. Memphis Alumni Assn. Office: Coca-Cola Enterprises 2500 Windy Ridge Pkwy Atlanta GA 30339

**PALMER, WENDY,** professional basketball player; b. Aug. 12, 1974; BA in History, U. Va., 1996. Forward Oviedo, Spain, 1996—97, WMBA - Utah Starzz, Salt Lake City, 1997—99, Detroit Shock, 1999—. Named to, All-Am., 1995, 1996. Avocations: horseback riding, music. Office: 2 Championship Auburn Hills MI 48326

**PALMER, WILLIAM JOSEPH,** accountant; b. Lansing, Mich., Sept. 3, 1934; s. Joseph Flammin Lacchia and Henrietta (Yagerman) P.; m. Judith Pollock, Aug. 20, 1960 (div. Nov. 1980); children: William W., Kathryn E., Leslie A., Emily J.; m. Kathleen Francis Booth, June 30, 1990; stepchildren: Blair T. Manwell, Lindsay H. Manwell. BS, U. Calif., Berkeley, 1963. CPA. With Coopers & Lybrand, 1963—80, mng. ptnr. Sacramento, 1976—80; ptnr. Arthur Young & Co., San Francisco, 1980—89, Ernst & Young, San Francisco, 1989—94; prof. U. Calif., Berkeley, 1994—. Bd. dirs. Dutra Group; chair constrn. industry group Coopers & Lybrand, 1973-80, Arthur Young, 1980-89, Ernst & Young, 1989-94; guest lectr. Engring. Sch. Stanford U., 1976; lectr. Golden Gate Coll., 1975. Author: Businessman's Guide to Construction, 1981, Construction Management Book, 1984, Construction Accounting and Financial Management, 5th edit., 1994, Construction Litigation-Representing The Contractor, 1992, Construction Insurance, Bonding and Risk Management, 1996. Bd. dirs. Sacramento Met. YMCA, 1976-82, KXPR, Sacramento 1976-85, V.p., 1979-82; bd. dirs. Sacramento Symphony Found., 1977-80; asst. state fin. chmn. Calif. Reagan for Pres., 1980. Lt. USN, 1953-59. Mem. AICPA (vice chmn. com. constrn. industry 1975-81), Nat. Assn. Accts. (pres. Oakland/East Bay chpt. 1972, Man of Yr. 1968), Calif. Soc. CPAs, Assn. Gen. Contractors Calif. (bd. dirs. 1971-74), World Trade Club, Del Paso Country Club, Sutter Club, Lambda Chi Alpha. Roman Catholic. Avocations: antique boats, golf, book collecting, pipe collecting. Home: PO Box 60405 Sacramento CA 95860-0405 Office: Ernst & Young 560 Mission St San Francisco CA 94105-2907 Office Phone: 415-894-8500. Personal E-mail: kathypalm@hotmail.com.

**PALMERLEE, APRIL WAHLESTEDT,** management consultant; b. Cheverly, Md., Apr. 9, 1968; d. James Anthony Pazienza and Beth Lewisa Catherwood; m. Claes R. Wahlestedt, June 15, 1991 (div. July 1996); m. David Luke Palmerlee, May 28, 2000. BS in Fgn. Svc., Georgetown U., 1989; M Internat. Affairs, Columbia U., 1999. Program asst. Spanish Inst., N.Y.C., 1990-92; spl. asst. Oscar de la Renta, Ltd., N.Y.C., 1992-94, 95-96; rschr. Bank Credit Analyst, Montreal, Que., Can., 1994-95; dir. comms. Coun. on Fgn. Rels., N.Y.C., 1996—2002; sr. coord. internat. women's issues U.S. Dept. State, Washington, 2002—03; dir. Potomac Ptnrs. Party, Ltd., Woolahra, Australia, 2004—; vis. fellow Ctr. for Ind. Studies. Republican. Episcopalian. Business E-Mail: apalmerlee@yahoo.com.

**PALMIERI, DORA ANN,** retired language educator; b. Monmouth, Ill., Dec. 31, 1943; d. Gust John and Ruth Ida Douffas; m. Ronald Ernest Naedele, Feb. 3, 1966 (dec. Sept. 30, 1966); 1 child, Ronnann Naedele-Risha; m. Frank William Palmieri, Jan. 2004. BA in English, Milligan Coll., 1966; MA in English, E. Tenn. State U., 1974. Cert. tchr. Miss., Tenn., N.C., Md., Fla. Editor/asst. editor Courier And Gateway Newspapers, Suitland, Md., 1966—69; English tchr. Long Beach (Miss.) HS, 1969—74, Garinger HS Night Program, Charlotte, NC, 1974—76; curriculum specialist, English instr. Ctrl. Piedmont CC, Charlotte, 1976—81; mgr. tng. and devel. Control Data Corp. and Comml. Credit Corp., Charlotte, Balt., 1980—87; program designer, rschr. Rutledge Coll. Sys., Charlotte, 1987—88; assoc. prof. Daytona Beach (Fla.) CC, 1990—. Lead tchr. adult HS English Daytona Beach CC, 1998—. Co-author: Ecology: The Living World, 1996; author: English All Around Us, vols. 1-4, 1999—2003, Vols. 2, 3, 4. Singles' lay min. South Daytona Christian Ch., 1990—2001. Named Lay Person Of The Yr., Kiwanis Port Orange And South Daytona, 1996. Mem.: Fla. Assn. CCs, Nat. Coun. Tchrs. English. Avocations: photography, theater, writing, crafts, movies. Personal E-mail: hollyhilla@hotmail.com.

**PALMIERI, VICTOR HENRY,** lawyer, director, investment advisor; b. Chgo., Feb. 16, 1930; s. Mario and Maria (Losacco) P.; children: Matthew B., John W.; m. Cathryn Connors, July 6, 1990. AB in History, Stanford U., 1951, JD, 1954. Bar: Calif. 1954. Assoc. O'Melveny & Myers, L.A., 1955-59; exec. v.p. Janss Investment Corp., L.A., 1959-63, pres., 1963-68; chmn. Pa. Co. and its subs. Great S.W. Corp., 1969-77; chmn. bd. Palmieri Co., N.Y.C., 1969—. Chmn. PHL Corp., Inc. (formerly Baldwin-Unitaed Inc.), Phila., 1983—87; trustee, CEO Colo. Ute Electric Assn., Inc., 1990—92; spl. dep. rehabilitator Confedn. Life Ins. Co., 1994—98; dep. rehabilitator, CEO Mut. Benefit Life Ins. Co., 1991—94; pres., CEO MBL Life Assurance Corp., 1994—95; chmn. AlixPalmieri Assocs., 1997—99; bd. dirs. Mullin Cons., Inc., vice chmn., 2002—; bd. dirs. M Fin. Holdings Inc., M Benefit Solutions, M Fin.

Investment Advisors, Trenwick Am. LLC, LA Universal Pre-Sch. Ambassador-at-large, U.S. coord. refugee affairs Dept. State, 1979—81; chmn. Am. Learning Corp., 1970—85; dep. exec. dir. Nat. Adv. Commn. on Civil Disorders, 1967—68; mem. Coun. on Fgn. Rels.; trustee Rockefeller Found., 1979—89; pres., bd. dirs. Lincoln Ctr. Theater, 1985—89; chmn. Overseas Devel. Coun., 1985—91; bd. trustees The Police Found., 1996—2002. Office: Mullin Cons Inc 644 S Figueroa St Los Angeles CA 90017 Business E-Mail: victor.palmieri@mullinconsulting.com

**PALMINTERI, CHAZZ,** actor; b. Bronx, NY, May 15, 1952; m. Gianna Ranaudo, June 6, 1992; children: Gabriella Rose, Dante Lorenzo. Actor: (theatre) The Guy in the Truck, 1982, Broadway, 1983, The King's Men, 22 Years, The Flatbush Faithful, 1985; actor, author: (TV films) Peter Gunn, 1990, Boss of Bosses, 2001; (TV series) Kojak, 2005—; (films) Oscar, 1991, Bullets Over Broadway, 1994 (Academy award nomination best supporting actor, 1994), The Perez Family, 1994, The Usual Suspects, 1995, Jade, 1995, Faithful, 1996, Diabolique, 1996, Mulholland Falls, 1996, Scar City, 1998, Hurly Burly, 1998, Cadaveri eccellenti, 1998, Company Man, 1999, Analyze This, 1999, Poolhall Junkies, 2002, Just Like Mona, 2003, One Last Ride, 2003, Noel, 2004, In the Mix, 2005. A Guide to Recognizing Your Saints, 2006, Running Scared, 2006, Push, 2006, Little Man, 2006, (voice) Stuart Little, 1999, Hoodwinked, 2005; playwright, actor (theatre) A Bronx Tale, 1989, screenwriter, actor (films), 1993; actor, prodr.: (films) Dante and the Debutante, 1996. Office: care Hilda Queally William Morris Agy 151 El Camino Dr Beverly Hills CA 90212

**PALMISANO, SAMUEL J.,** information technology executive; b. Baltimore, July 29, 1951; m. Gaier Notman; 4 children. BA in History, Johns Hopkins U., 1973. Joined IBM, Balt., 1973, various sales, mktg. and prod. devel. positions, 1973—89, exec. asst. to IBM CEO John F. Akers, 1989; sr. mng. dir. ops. IBM Japan, 1991; pres., CEO Integrated Systems Solutions Corp., IBM subs., 1993—96; sr. v.p., group exec. IBM Personal Systems Group, 1997, IBM Global Svcs., 1998, IBM Enterprise Systems Group, 1999; pres., COO IBM, White Plains, NY, 2000—02, pres., CEO, 2002—, chmn., 2003—. Bd. dirs. IBM, 2000—, ExxonMobil Corp., 2006—. Trustee Johns Hopkins U. Recipient Disting. Alumni award, Johns Hopkins U., 2003. Avocations: golf, history, jogging, skiing. Office: IBM 1133 Westchester Ave White Plains NY 10604*

**PALMORE, JOHN STANLEY, JR.,** retired lawyer; b. Ancon, C.Z., Aug. 6, 1917; s. John Stanley and Antoinette Louise (Gonzalez) P.; m. Eleanor Anderson, July 31, 1938 (dec. 1980); 1 child, John Worsham (dec.); m. Carol Pate, Jan. 1, 1982. Student, Western Ky. State Coll., 1934-36; LL.B. cum laude, U. Louisville, 1939. Bar: Ky. 1938. Practice law, Henderson, 1939-42, 47-59; judge Ct. Appeals Ky. (name changed to Supreme Ct. Ky. 1975), 1959-82, chief justice, 1966, 73, 77-82; practice law Frankfort, Ky., 1983-84; ptnr. Palmore & Sheffer, Henderson, 1984-86; sr. counsel Jackson & Kelly, Lexington, Ky., 1986-92; ret., 1992. City pros. atty., Henderson, 1949-53, city atty., 1953-55; commonwealth's atty. 5th Circuit Dist. Ky., 1955-59 Served to lt. USNR, 1942-46, 51-52. Mem. VFW, Ky. Bar Assn., Am. Legion, Ky. Hist. Soc., Frankfort Country Club, Lexington Club, Frankfort Rotary Club (pres. 1993-94), Masons, Shriners, Elks, Phi Alpha Delta. Episcopalian (past vestryman, sr. warden). Home: 2310 Peaks Mill Rd Frankfort KY 40601-9437

**PALMORE, RICK (RODERICK A. PALMORE),** lawyer; b. Pitts., Feb. 14, 1952; s. Jefferson and Sophie (Spencer) Palmore; m. Lynne Avril Janifer, June 3, 1978; children: Jordan, Adam. BA, Yale U., 1974; JD, U. Chgo., 1977. Bar: Pa. 1977, Ill. 1982. Assoc. atty. Berkman Ruslander Pohl Lieber & Engel, Pitts., 1977-79; asst. U.S. atty. U.S. Atty's Office, Chgo., 1979-82; assoc. atty. Wildman Harrold Allen & Dixon, Chgo., 1982-86, ptnr., 1986-93, Sonnenschein Nath & Rosenthal, Chgo., 1993-96; v.p., dep. gen. counsel Sara Lee Corp., Chgo., 1996-99; sr. v.p., gen. counsel, sec., 1999—2004, exec. v.p., gen. counsel, sec., 2004—. Commr. Oak Park Plan Commn., 1988—, chair, 1994—; lectr. Youth Motivation Program Chgo. Coun. Commerce & Industry 1989—; chair Oak Park Pub. Art Adv. Com., 2002—; bd. dirs. Pub. Interest Law Initiative, Legal Assistance Found. Chgo., Chgo. Bd. Options Exch., 2002—, Noreen Investments, 2003—, United Way Met. Chgo., 2003—. Named one of Outstanding African-Am. Businessmen, Dollars & Sense mag., 1991. Mem. ABA (monirity ptnrs. conf. 1991—), Nat. Bar Assn., Cook County Bar Assn., Chgo. Bar Assn. (bd. dirs. 1992-94, co-chmn. minority clerkshop program 1991-92), Chgo. Com. on Minorities in Law Firms (bd. dirs. 1990-92), Chgo. Bar Found. (bd. dirs. 1993-94). Mem. Trinity United Ch. Of Christ. Avocations: running, biking, tennis, reading. Home: 507 N Euclid Ave Oak Park IL 60302-1617 Office: Sara Lee Corp Three First National Plaza Chicago IL 60602 Office Phone: 312-726-2600.

**PALMS, JOHN MICHAEL,** academic administrator, physicist; b. Rijswijk, The Netherlands, June 6, 1935; naturalized, 1956; s. Peter Joannes and Mimi Adele (DeYong) P.; m. Norma Lee Cannon, June 2, 1958; children: John Michael, Danielle Maria, Lee Cannon. BS in Physics, The Citadel, 1958, DSc (hon.), 1980; MS in Physics, Emory U., 1959; PhD, U. N.Mex., 1966. Commd. 2d lt. USAF, 1958, retired capt. Res., 1970; lectr. physics dept. U. N.Mex., 1959-60; instr. physics dept. USAF Acad., 1961-62; staff mem. Western Electric Sandia Lab., 1961-62, U. Calif. Los Alamos Sci. Lab., 1962-66, Oak Ridge Nat. Lab., 1966; asst. prof. Emory U., Atlanta, 1966-69, assoc. prof., 1969-73, chmn., assoc. prof. dept. physics, asso. prof radiology dept. Med. Sch., 1973-74, prof., chmn. dept. physics, 1969-74, dean Coll. Arts. and Scis., 1974-80, acting chmn. dept. math. and computer sci., 1976-77, v.p. arts and scis., acting chmn. dept. anthropology, 1979-80, acting dean Emory U. Computing Ctr., 1979-80, acting dir. Emory U. Computing Ctr., 1980-82, v.p. acad. affairs, 1982-88, interim dean Grad. Sch., 1985-86, Charles Howard Candler prof. nuclear, radiation and environ. physics, 1988-90; pres., prof. physics Ga. State U., Atlanta, 1989-91, U. S.C., Columbia, 1991—92. Chmn. bd. Assurant Inc., 2003-, Inst. for Def. Analyses; bd. dirs. Fortis, Inc., N.Y.C., Exelon Corp., Chgo., NCAA, Simcom Internat. Holdings, Inc., Atlanta, Computer Task Group, Assurant, 1990-; adv. com. Oak Ridge Nat. Lab. 1985-89; mem. nat. nuclear accredititng bd. Inst. Nuclear Power Ops., 1985-91, mem. nat. adv. coun., 1997-2001; mem. panel for semicondt. detectors NAS/NRC, 1963-74; cons. Acad. Natural Scis., Phila., Hughes, Inc., Santa Barbara, Calif., Tennelec, Inc., Three Mile Island Environ. Study, TRW Space Sys. Divsn., L.A., Ga. Dept. Human Resources, Nat. Cancer Inst.; mem. high tech. task force Atlanta C, of C. Contbr. articles on nuclear, atomic, med. and environ. physics to profl. jours. Mem. adv. bd. The Citadel, Oak Ridge Nat. Lab.; mem. exec. bd. Atlanta Area Coun. Boy Scouts of Am., 1989-90; mem. cmty. rels. bd. U.S. Penitentiary, Atlanta, 1989-90; mem. Internat. Def. Analyses, Wesleyan Coll., 1984-89, Pace Acad., 1984-89, St. Joseph's Hosp., Atlanta, 1987-89. Ga. Rsch. Alliance, 1989-89; mem. S.C. Univs. Edn. Found., Devel. Found. and Rsch. Found., S.C. Rsch. Inst. Bds.; bd. dirs. Civic-Atlanta Partnership Bus. and Edn., Inc., 1988-90, United Way; chair Rhodes scholar selection com., 1987, S.C., 1995-99; bd. dirs. Nat. Merit Scholarship Corp. Mem. AAAS, Am. Phys. Soc., Am. Assn. Physics Tchrs., IEEE (Nuclear Sci. Group), Am. Nuclear Soc., Am. Coun. Edn., Coun. Provosts and Acad. V.P.s, Am. Conf. Acad. Deans, Soc. Nuclear Medicine, Health Physics Soc., Greater Columbia C. of C. (bd. dirs.), Rotary, Columbia C. of C., Phi Beta Kappa, Sigma Xi, Phi Kappa Phi, Omicron Delta Kappa, Sigma Pi Sigma. Home and Office: Pres U SCO Osborne Bldg Columbia SC 29208-0001*

**PALMS, ROGER CURTIS,** writer, educator, minister; b. Detroit, Sept. 13, 1936; s. Nelson Curtis and Winifred Jessie (Bennett) P.; m. Andrea Sisson, Aug. 22, 1959; children— Grant Curtis, Andrea Jane BA, Wayne State U., 1958; B.D., Eastern Baptist Sem., Phila, 1961, M.Div., 1971, D.D., 1977; MA, Mich. State U., 1971. Ordained to ministry Am. Bapt. Chs., 1961. Pastor Ronceverte Bapt. Ch., W.Va., 1961-64; pastor 1st Bapt. Ch., Highland Park, NJ, 1964-67; chaplain Am. Bapt. Student Found., Mich. State U., East Lansing, 1967-73; assoc. editor Decision mag. Billy Graham Evang. Assn., Mpls., 1973-76, editor, 1976-98. Lectr. in field. Author: Enjoying the Closeness of God, 1989, Let God Help You Choose, 1989, An Unexpected Hope, 1998, Effective Magazine Writing, 2000, Your Best Years, 2003,

others; newspaper columnist Trustee No. Bapt. Theol. Sem., 1973— Mem. Evang. Press Assn. (pres. 1991-93). Baptist. Personal E-mail: rcpalms@aol.com. *Investing in people's spiritual lives, giving time and counsel, will bring multiplied results for generations. It is one of the most far-reaching ways I can put faith to work.*

**PALOMAR, DANIEL PEREZ,** electrical engineer; b. Barcelona, Apr. 28, 1975; arrived in U.S., 2004; s. Domingo Perez Casals and Mercedes Palomar Perez. PhD in Elec. Engring., Tech. U. Catalonia, Barcelona, 2003. Rsch. asst. Tech. U. Catalonia, 1999—2003; Fulbright rsch. fellow Princeton (NJ) U., 2004—. Vis. rschr. Tellecomms. Tech. Ctr. Catalonia, Barcelona, 2000, Stanford (Calif.) U., 2001—02, U. Rome-La Sapienza, 2003—04; guest rschr. Royal Inst. Tech., Stockholm, 2003. Grantee, Catalan Govt., 1999—2002, Fulbright Commn., 2004—; travel grantee, Catalan Govt., 2001, Socrates-Erasmus scholar, European Union, 1998. Office: Princeton U B-311 Engring Quadrangle Princeton NJ 08544 Home: 40 Princeton Ave Princeton NJ 08540 Business E-Mail: danielp@princeton.edu.

**PALOMARES, RONALD S.,** psychologist; PhD, Tex. A&M U., College Station. Cert. psychologist Tex. State Bd. Exam. Psychologists. Asst. prof. Tex. Woman's U., Denton, 1995—2000; asst. exec. dir. APA, Washington, 2000—. Capt. USAF, 1984—88, F.E. Warren AFB. Office: APA 750 1st St NE Washington DC 20002-4242

**PALOMBELLA, ANTHONY LEWIS,** biology professor; b. San Francisco, Aug. 1, 1961; s. Michele Vincent and Mary Elisabeth Palombella; m. Monica Severin, Aug. 6, 1988; children: Laura Jane, Mark William. BA in Genetics, U. Calif., Berkeley, 1983; MA in Cell and Molecular Biology, San Francisco State U., 1989; PhD in Molecular, Cellular and Devel. Biology, U. Colo., Boulder, 1997. Instr. biology Monmouth U., West Long Branch, NJ, 1997—98, vis. asst. prof. biology, 1998—99; asst. prof. biology Longwood U., Farmville, Va., 1999—. Office: Longwood Univ 201 High St Farmville VA 23909 Office Phone: 434-395-2646. Personal E-mail: palombella@earthlink.net. Business E-Mail: palombellaal@longwood.edu.

**PALOMBO, LISA,** artist; b. Providence, Mar. 1, 1965; d. Joseph Christopher Palombo and Catherine Ann Walsh. BFA, R.I. Sch. Design, 1987. Featured artist: (books) The Best of Oil Painting, 1996, Exploring Color, 1998. Recipient honors recognition Artist's Mag., 2003, 2004. Mem.: Oil Painters of Am., N.J. Am. Artists Profl. League. Studio: Lisa Palombo Studios 55 Mountain Ave Caldwell NJ 07006 Office Phone: 973-364-0280. E-mail: art@lisapalombo.com.

**PALSER, BARBARA F.,** retired botanist; b. Worcester, Mass., June 2, 1916; d. G. Norman and Cora A. (Munson) P. AB, Mt. Holyoke Coll., 1938, A.M., 1940, D.Sc. (hon.), 1978; PhD, U. Chgo., 1942. From instr. to prof. botany U. Chgo., 1942-65; from assoc. prof. to prof. botany Rutgers U., New Brunswick, NJ, 1965-83, dir. grad. program in botany, 1973-80; adj. prof. botany U. Mass., Amherst, 1991—. Erskine fellow U. Canterbury, Christchurch, N.Z. 1969; vis. prof. Duke U., Durham, N.C., fall 1962; vis. research fellow U. Melbourne, Parkville, Victoria, Australia, fall 1984-85 Author lab. manual Principles of Botany, 1973, also numerous research papers in bot. jours.; bot. adviser Ency. Brit., Chgo., 1958-59; editor Bot. Gazette, Chgo., 1960-65 Named Outstanding Tchr., Rutgers Coll., 1977 Mem. Bot. Soc. Am. (sec. 1970-74, v.p. 1975, pres. 1976, Merit award 1985), Torrey Bot. Club (pres. 1968), Internat. Soc. Plant Morphologists, N.J. Acad. Scis. (pres. elect 1987-88, pres. 1988-89, Outstanding Svc. award 1985, 90). Avocations: hiking, stamp collecting/philately, photography. Home: Rockridge Retirement Cmty 37 Coles Meadow Rd #303 Northampton MA 01060

**PALSHO, DOROTHEA COCCIOLI,** information services executive; b. Phila., Pa., June 9, 1947; d. John Charles and Dorothy Lucille (Decker) Coccioli; m. Edward Robert Palsho; children: Christopher, Ryan and Erica (stepchild). BS, Villanova Univ., 1976; MBA, Temple Univ., 1977. V.p. info. svc. Dow Jones and Co., Princeton, NJ, 1977-97, pres. bus. info. svc., 1995-97, v.p. interactive pub. N.Y.C., 1997—2002, v.p. electronic pub, 2000—02, v.p. stragetic mktg., 2002—. Named to Class of Women Achievers, YWCA Acad. of Women Achievers, 1985. Avocation: sports. Office: Dow Jones and Co Inc 200 Liberty St New York NY 10281

**PALTER, ROBERT MONROE,** humanities educator; b. N.Y.C., June 19, 1924; s. Meyer and Mildred (Gilder) Palter; m. Ruth Rappeport, July 15, 1945 (div. 1953); 1 child, Alixe Daphne Cielo; m. Toni Ann Inman, Apr. 5, 1955 (div. 1977); children: Geoffrey Meyer, Jennifer Thorn Allan, Nicholas Trask, Adam Finch; m. Annette B. Weiner, May 21, 1979 (div. 1982). AB, Columbia U., 1943; PhD, U. Chgo., 1952. From instr. to assoc. prof. phys. scis. and philosophy U. Chgo., 1949-64; prof. philosophy and history U. Tex., Austin, 1964-82; Dana prof. history of sci. Trinity Coll., Hartford, Conn., 1983-91, prof. emeritus, 1991—. Author: (book) Whitehead's Philosophy of Science, 1960, The Duchess of Malfi's Apricots and Other Literary Fruits, 2002; editor: Toward Modern Science, 1961, The Annus Mirabilis of Sir Isaac Newton, 1971. With U.S. Army, 1944—46. Mem.: Phi Beta Kappa.

**PALTROW, GWYNETH,** actress; b. L.A., Sept. 28, 1972; d. Bruce Paltrow and Blythe Danner; m. Chris Martin, Dec. 5, 2003; children: Apple Blythe Alison Martin, Moses Martin. Student, U. Calif. Santa Barbara. Grad. Spence Sch., N.Y.C., 1990. Spokesmodel Estee Lauder. Appeared in films: Shout, 1991, Hook, 1991, Malice, 1993, Flesh and Bone, 1993, Mrs. Parker and the Vicious Circle, 1994, Jefferson in Paris, 1995, Moonlight and Valentino, 1995, Seven, 1995, The Pallbearer, 1996, Emma, 1996, Hard Eight, 1996, Sliding Doors, 1998, Out of the Past, 1998 (voice), Great Expectations, 1998, Hush, 1998, A Perfect Murder, 1998, Shakespeare in Love, 1998 (Academy Award for Best Actress, Golden Globe for Best Actress), The Talented Mr. Ripley, 1999, Duets, 1999, The Intern, 2000, Bounce, 2000, The Anniversary Party, 2001, The Royal Tenenbaums, 2001, Shallow Hal, 2001, Possession, 2002, View From the Top, 2003, Sylvia, 2003, Sky Captain and the World of Tomorrow, 2004, Proof, 2005; TV films: Cruel Doubt, 1992, Deadly Relations, 1993; Theatre: Picnic, The Adventures of Huck Finn, Sweet Bye and Bye, The Seagull, Proof. Mem. Screen Actors Guild (Outstanding Performance with others). Office: Creative Artists Agy c/o Rick Kurtzman 9830 Wilshire Blvd Beverly Hills CA 90212-1804 also: Screen Actors Guild 5757 Wilshire Blvd Los Angeles CA 90036-3635

**PALUMBO, ANTHONY,** education educator; b. N.Y.C., Dec. 4, 1938; s. John and Lucy Palumbo; m. Ellen Eskridge Palumbo, Aug. 27, 1960; children: Anna Baltrusaitis, Frank, Gordon. BA, St. John's U., 1960, MS, 1963; PD, Hofstra U., 1976, EdD, 1980. Tchr. reading, English Plainedge Pub. Schs., Massapequa, NY, 1960—98. Adj. prof. edn. St. Francis, Bklyn., 1990—92, N.Y. Inst. Tech., Greensoe, 1996—99, CW Post, Brentwood, 2001—; cons. in field. Author novels, short stories; contbr. articles to profl. jours. Mem.: Internat. Reading Assn., Mystery Writers Am. Achievements include patents for an underwater cutting rod. Home: 95 Le Baum Ave Amityville NY 11701

**PALUMBO, ANTHONY JOHN,** lawyer; AB, Cornell U., Ithaca, NY, 1996—2000; JD, Benjamin N. Cardozo Sch. Law, NYC, 2000—03. Bar: NJ 2003, NY 2004. Assoc. Hartman & Craven LLP, NYC, 2004—. Contbr. articles to profl. jours. Mem.: ABA, NY State Bar Assn., Internat. Trademark Assn. Office: Hartman & Craven LLP 488 Madison Ave New York NY 10022 Office Fax: 212-688-2870. Business E-Mail: apalumbo@hartmancraven.com.

**PALUMBO, BENJAMIN LEWIS,** public relations executive, consultant; b. Boston, Mar. 4, 1937; s. Guido Americo and Stella Marie (Lombardo) P.; m. Magdalene Julia Palinczar, Nov. 18, 1961; children: Matthew, Jason, Guy. BA, Rutgers U., 1959, MA, 1961. Adminstrv. asst. to Gov. Richard J. Hughes, NJ, 1963-65; dir. rsch. N.J. Dem. Com., Trenton, 1965-66; asst. to commr. N.J. Dept. Transp., Trenton, 1966-70; asst. dean Woodrow Wilson Sch. Princeton (N.J.) U., 1970—71; adminstrv. asst. to Senator Harrison Williams, U.S. Senate, Washington, 1971-73, staff dir. U.S. Ho. Dem. caucus, 1975-77, Ho.

subcom. on govt. activities and transp., 1977-78; nat. campaign dir. Bentsen for Pres., Washington, 1973-75; dir. fed. govt. rels. Phillip Morris, Inc., Washington, 1978-83; chmn., CEO Palumbo & Cerrell, Inc., Washington, 1983—, pres., bd. dirs., 2005—. Pres. Nyumbani Child of God Hospice and Orphanage, bd. dirs., John Mott Found. Mem.: N.J. State Soc., Am. League Lobbyists, Nat. Dem. Club, Rutgers Club Washington, Nat. Press Club. Democrat. Roman Catholic. Office: 1717 K St NW Ste 1050 Washington DC 20036-5346 Office Fax: 202-466-9009. Business E-Mail: bpalumbo@covad.net.

**PALUMBO, JAMES FREDRICK,** finance company executive; b. Everett, Mass., Nov. 30, 1950; s. Bruno James and Lillian Elizabeth (Picardi) P.; m. Nancy Laurie Richards, July 24, 1976; children: Elizabeth Richards, Andrew Reid, Alexander Thomas. BA, Lake Forest Coll., 1973; MBA, Washington U., 1975. Market surveillance analyst Nat. Assn. of Securities Dealers, Washington, 1975-76, asst. treas., 1976-78; regional rep. Student Loan Mktg. Assn., Washington, 1978-79, mgr., 1979-81, dir., 1981-82, asst. v.p., 1982-83, v.p., 1983-87; sr. v.p. Connie Lee Mgmt. Svcs. Corp., Coll. Constrn. Loan Ins. Assn., Washington, 1987-95; with N.Y. Life Ins. Co., N.Y.C., 1995-2001, N.Y. Life Securities Inc., N.Y.C., 1995-2001; prin. Treasury Investment Svcs., Reston, Va., 1999—2003; mng. dir. TransCapital Group, Reston, 1999—2003, sr. mng. dir., 2003—04; v.p. RyanLabs Fund Mgmt. LLC, 2003—; registered broker Bedminster Fin. Group, 2003—06; prin. Dynamic Capital Ptnrs. LLC, 2006—. Participant Govt.-Univ.-Industry Rsch. Roundtable, Washington, 1986; chmn. Palumbo Properties L.L.C.; chmn. Capital Holdings Ltd., Great Falls, Va. Actor popular and children's theater, 1973-76. Chmn. sports announcers com. D.C. Spl. Olympics, Washington, 1986, 87, D.C. Regional Counsel, Lake Forest Coll., Washington, 1976-80; mem. Elliott Soc. membership com. Washington U., 1986—, Great Falls (Va.) Hist. Soc., Great Falls Citizens Assn., 1996—; bd. govs. Lake Forest Coll., 1978-82, trustee, 1992-99; trustee Abruzzo and Molise Heritage Soc., 2002-03. Mem.: Washington Soc. Investment Analysts, Nat. Assn. Ins. and Fin. Advisors, Assn. for Investment Mgmt. and Rsch., Great Falls Swim and Tennis Club (bd. dirs. 1988—91), Alpha Psi Omega. Avocations: polo, horseback riding, painting. Office: Dynamic Capital Ptnrs 8120 Woodmont Ave Ste 960 Bethesda MD 20814 Office Phone: 301-229-8400. Business E-Mail: jpalumbo@dyncap.com.

**PALUMBO, MATTHEW ALOYSIUS,** marketing executive; b. Queens, NY, Sept. 17, 1961; s. John Christopher and Seiko (Murakami) P. BS, Cornell U., 1986; MBA in Mktg. Mgmt., St. John's U., 1990. Mortgage clk. Salomon Bros., Inc., N.Y.C., 1986; mut. fund adminstr. Bank of N.Y. Co. Inc., N.Y.C., 1986-88; copywriter Pierce Assocs., N.Y.C., 1988-90; dir. mktg. cons. Palumbo Assocs., S.I., 1989-90; adj. prof. St. John's U., S.I. 1990; mktg. dir., copy dir. Flaghouse Inc., Mt. Vernon, NY, 1990-93; spl. projects mgr., group product mgr. Global Computer Supplies, Port Washington, NY, 1993-97; dir. product mktg. Cyberian Outpost, Kent, Conn., 1997—2000; pres. Palumbo Consultants, Kent, 2000—. Guest lectr. Am. direct mktg. techniques Sheffield Halleron U. (Eng.), 1993; guest lectr. designed and acquired funding Cornell U., Ithaca, 1992—. NY State Regents scholar, 1979, Annette Brodsky scholar, 1988. Mem. Am. Assn. MBA Execs., Cornell Asian Alumni Assn. (v.p. alumni affairs 1993-95), Cornell ILR Alumni, Direct Mktg. Club N.Y., Cornell Club N.Y., Cornell Club Fairfield County, Cornell U. Quadrangle Club, Beta Gamma Sigma. Avocations: reading, sports, music.

**PALUMBO, MICHAEL,** investment company executive; b. 1966; Ptnr. Third Millenium Investment Firm, Chgo., 1996—. Named one of Top 100 Fin. Traders in the World, Trader Monthly, 2004, 40 Under Forty, Crain's Bus. Chgo., 2005. Office: Third Millenium Trading LLC 100 S Wacker Dr Chicago IL 60606*

**PALUMBO, MICHAEL J.,** air transportation executive; b. N.Y.C. BA in history, Marquette U., 1968; MBA, Fairleigh Dickinson U., 1977. Dir., banking & fin. analysis Pan Amer. World Airways, 1977—80, dir., corp. fin., 1980—81, asst. treas., 1981—83; v.p., treas. Western Airlines, 1983—84, sr. v.p., fin. & treas., 1984; v.p., treas. TransWorld Airlines, Inc., St. Louis, 1994—96, sr. v.p., CFO, 1996—99, exec. v.p., CFO, 1999—2001, Delta Air Lines, Inc., Atlanta, 2004—05.

**PALUMBO, ROBERT CRAIG,** sports medicine physician, director, not-for-profit developer; BA, Cornell U., Ithaca, N.Y., 1982; MD, Rutgers U., Piscataway, New Brunswick, N.J., 1986. Lic. physician Nat. Bd. of Med. Examiners, Pa., 1996, diplomate Am. Bd. Orthop. Surgery, 1996. Resident gen. surgery Robert Wood Johnson Med. Sch. (formerly Rutgers Med. Sch.), New Brunswick, NJ, 1988—92, resident orthop. surgery 1992—93; fellow sports medicine Union Meml. Hosp., Balt., 1993—94; attending physician Orlando Orthopaedic Ctr. Lucerne Med. Plz., Orlando, Fla., 1994—98, Celebration Orthopaedic & Sports Medicine Inst., Fla., 1998—2002; dir. Orthop. Specialists Sports Medicine Inst. Found. Orthop. Assoc. Allentown, Pa., 2002—. Team physician Browns Gym Metro Gymnastics Jr. Olympic Tng. Ctr., Orlando, 1994—2002, Orlando Ballet (formerly the So. Ballet Theater), Orlando, 1996—2002, LGE Sports Medicine Inst., Orlando, 1996—2002, Orlando Columbia Sundogs Soccer Team, Fla., 1997; orthopaedic team leader Walt Disney World Marathon Med. Tent, Orlando, 1997—2002; team physician Orlando Rays Baseball Team (Seattle Mariners & Tampa Bay Devil Rays) AA Farm Club, Orlando, 1997—98, Walt Disney World Wide World of Sports, Orlando, 1997—2002, U.S. Nat. Women's Soccer Team, 1997—, Orlando Nighthawks Soccer Club, Fla., 1998, World Telehealth InPlay Sports Health Mgmt., NFL Players Assn., 1998—; Cirque De Soleil La Nouba, Orlando, 1998—2002, Parkettes Nat. Tng. Ctr., Allentown, 2002—, Muhlenberg Coll. Athletics, Allentown, 2003—; reviewer The Am. Jour. of Sports Medicine, 2002—; med. dir. Orlando Regional Health Sys. Ctr. Performing Arts, Orlando, 1996—2002; cons. in field. Scholar, Cornell U., 1978—82. Mem.: AMA, Fla. Med. Assn., Internat. Assn. Dance Medicine and Sci., Am. Orthop. Foot and Ankle Soc. (mem. endoscopy and arthroplasty com.), Arthroscopy Assn. N.Am., Am. Coll. Sports Medicine, Am. Orthop. Soc. Sports Medicine, Am. Acad. Orthop. Surgeons (mem. sports medicine com., mem. sports medicine evaluation com.). Orange County Med. Soc. Avocations: fishing, exercise, photography. Office: OAA Orthopaedic Specialists 250 Cetronia Road Allentown PA 18104 Office Phone: 610-973-6200.

**PALUMBO, RUTH ANN,** state legislator; b. Lexington, Ky., July 7, 1949; d. James Keith and Dorothy Calvin (Carrier) Baker; m. John Anthony Palumbo II, June 29, 1974; children: John A. III (dec.), Joseph Edward, James Thomas, Stephen Baker. BA in Secondary Edn., U. Ky., 1972. Sales Chez Lissette Boutique, Leysin, Switzerland, 1966; sales, shoes Purcell's Dept. Store, Lexington, Ky., 1966-70; organist Ctrl. Bapt. Ch., Lexington, Ky., 1968; clk. Good Samaritan Hosp., Lexington, Ky., 1968-73; sec. Dr. Joseph Keith, Lexington, Ky., 1971-73; senate clk. aide Ky. Gen. Assembly, Frankfort, Ky., 1974; pub. rels. Palumbo Properties, Lexington, 1974-92; state rep. Ky. Gen. Assembly, 1991—. Mem. LWV, Lexington, 1990-92, Ky. Women's Polit. Caucus, Louisville, 1991-92, NAt. Order Women Legislators, Washington, 1992; sec. Ctrl. Ky. Caucus, Lexington, 1991-92. Mem. Greater Lexington Dem. Women, fin. v.p., 1982; mem. Nat. Order of Women Legislators, Washington, 1992; legis.liaison ACS Breast Cancer Detection Task Force, Ky., 1992; adv. coun. Bryan Sta. Youth Svcs. Ctr., Lexington, 1992; ballt chmn. Lexington Philharmonic Women's Guild, 1990; govt. affairs Am. Symphony Orch. League Vol. Coun., Washington, 1992; bd. dirs. Philharmonic Women's Guild, pres., 1988-89; bd. dirs. Lexington Philharmonic Soc. Recipient Dorothy Moomaw Miles Svc. award Sayre Sch., 1986, Govs. Vol. Activist award Gov. Wallace G. Wilkinson, 1989, named Lexington's Outstanding Young Woman Bluegrass Jr. Woman's Club, 1982, Leadership Lexington C. of C., 1988, Leadership Am. Found. for Women's Resources, Washington, 1989. Fellow U. Ky. Devel. Coun.; mem. Jr. League LExington (sec. 1989-90), Prof. Women's Forum, Gamma Phi Veta (pres. 1980-82). Baptist. Avocations: playing piano, singing, collecting stamps, music boxes, family. Home: 10 Deepwood Dr Lexington KY 40505-2106 Office: House of Reps State Capitol Annex Rm 370B Frankfort KY 40601*

**PAMIES, RUBENS JOHN,** dean; s. George and Lillian Pamies. MD, SUNY at Buffalo, Sch. of Medicine, 1982—86. AAMC Health Services Researach Institute ACP, 2004, diplomate Nat. Bd. Examiners, Am. Bd. Internal Medicine. Dir. and founder of minority affairs U. of South Fla. Coll. of Medicine, 1994; vice chancellor for academic affairs U. of Nebr. Med. Ctr., 2004—; program dir. Mt. Sinai Med. Ctr., Cleve., 1994—94; assoc. dean for academic programs and student affairs Case Western Res. U. Sch. of Medicine, Cleve., 1994—2000; chmn. and prof. Meharry Med. Coll., Nashville, 2000—03; prof. of medicine Vanderbilt U. Sch. of Medicine, Nashville, 2001—03; chief of svc. Met. Nashville Gen. Hosp., 2000—03; prof. of internal medicine U. of Nebr. Med. Ctr., 2004—, dean of grad. studies, 2004—. Author: (text book) Multicultural Medicine And Health Disparities. Mem. Va.-Nebr. Alliance, Richmond, Va., 2004, Joslyn Art Mus., Omaha, 2004. Grant, Nat. Heart, Lung, & Blood Inst., 2002, scholarship, Case Western Res. U. SOM, 2000—. Mem.: ACP, AMA, Assn. of Am. Med. Colleges, Internat. Soc. of Hypertension in Blacks, Assn. of Academic Minority Physicians. Achievements include research in early clinical exposure and its effect on performance in the third year clearkship. Office: Univ of Nebr Med Ctr 987810 Nebraska Med Ctr Omaha NE 68198-7810 Office Phone: 402-559-5130. Office Fax: 402-559-7845. Personal E-mail: rpamies@unmc.edu.

**PAMPLIN, ROBERT BOISSEAU, SR.,** retired textile manufacturing executive; b. Sutherland, Va., Nov. 25, 1911; s. John R. and Pauline P. (Beville); m. Mary K. Reese, June 15, 1940; 1 child, Robert Boisseau Jr. BBA, Va. Poly. Inst. & State U., 1933; postgrad., Northwestern U., 1933-34; LLD (hon.), U. Portland, Oreg., 1972; LHD (hon.), Warner Pacific Coll., 1976. With Ga.-Pacific Corp., Portland, 1934-76, sec., from 1936, adminstrv. v.p., 1952-55, exec. v.p., 1955-57, pres., 1957-67, chmn. bd., chief exec. officer, from 1967; ret., 1976; with R.B. Pamplin Corp., 1957—, chmn. bd., CEO, to 1996, Mt. Vernon Mills Inc. (subs. R.B. Pamplin Corp.), Greenville, S.C., retired, 1996. Office: R B Pamplin Corp Ste 2400 805 SW Broadway Portland OR 97205-3341

**PAMPLIN, ROBERT BOISSEAU, JR.,** manufacturing company executive, minister, writer; b. Augusta, Ga., Aug. 3, 1941; s. Robert Boisseau and Mary Katherine (Reese) P.; m. Marilyn Joan Hooper; children: Amy Louise, Anne Boisseau. Student, Va. Poly. Inst., 1960-62, BSBA, 1964, BS in Acctg., 1965, BS in Econs., 1966; BS (hon.), Va. Tech., 2001; LHD (hon.), Va. Poly. Inst., 1995, Pacific U., 2001; DHL (hon.), Va. Poly. Inst., 1995; MBA, U. Portland, 1968, LLD (hon.), 1972, MEd, 1975; MA, Western Conservative Bapt. Sem. (name now Western Sem.), 1978, DMin, 1982, D (hon.) of Sacred Letter, 1991, MA, 2000; PhD, Calif. Coast U.; DHL (hon.), Warner Pacific Coll. 1988; LLD (hon.), Western Baptist Coll., 1989, George Fox U., 2005; cert. in wholesale mgmt., Ohio State U., 1970; cert. labor mgmt., U. Portland, 1982; cert. in advanced mgmt., U. Hawaii, 1975; DD (hon.), Judson Baptist Coll., 1984; DBA (hon.), Marquis Giuseppe Scicluna Internat. U. Found., 1986; LittD (hon.), Va. Tech. Inst. and State U., 1987, LHD (hon.), Western Seminary, 1991; DD, Western Evang. Sem., 1994; DBA (hon.), U. S.C., 1996; D Pub. Svc., DHL (hon.), U. Puget Sound, Pacific U., 1999, 2001; BS in Bus. Adminstrn. (hon.), Va. Inst. Tech., 2001. Pres., CEO R.B. pamplin Corp., Portland, Oreg., 1964—. Chmn. bd., CEO Columbia Empire Farms Inc., Lake Oswego, Oreg., 1976—, Pamplin Comms.; chmn. bd., CEO Mt. Vernon Mills Inc.; pres., CEO Ross Island Sand & Gravel; lectr. bus. adminstrn. Lewis and Clark Coll., 1968-69; adj. asst. prof. bus. adminstrn., U. Portland, 1973-76; pastor Christ Cmty. Ch., Lake Oswego; lectr. in bus. adminstrn. and econs. U. Costa Rica, 1986, Va. Tech. Found., 1986; chmn. bd. dirs. Christian Supply Ctrs. Inc.; prof. with tenure U. Portland, 1999. Author: Everything is Just great, 1985, The Gift, 1986, Another Virginian: A Study of the Life and Beliefs of Robert Boisseau Pamplin, 1986; author: (with others) A Portrait of Colorado, 1976, Three in One, 1974, The Storybook Primer on Managing, 1974, One Who Believed, Vol. I, 1988, vol. II, 1991, Climbing the Centuries, 1993, Heritage the Making of an American Family, 1994, American Heroes, 1995, Prelude to Surrender, 1995, Alaska Gold, 1998, Robert Reese, 1998; editor: Oreg. Mus. Sci. and Industry Press, 1973; trustee Oreg. Mus. Sci. and Industry Press, 1971, 1974—; editor: Portrait of Oregon, 1973; editor: (with others) Oregon Underfoot, 1975. Trustee Lewis and Clark Coll., 1989—, chmn. bd. trustees, 1988-96; life trustee 1996-; hon. life pres. Western Conservative Bapt. Sem.; chmn. regents Western Sem., 1994; mem. nat. adv. coun. on vocat. Edn., 1975—; mem. Western Interstate Com. on Higher Edn., 1981-84; co-chmn. Va. Tech. $50 Million Campaign for Excellence, 1984-87, Va. Tech. Found., 1986—, Va.-Oregg. State Scholarship Commn., 1974—, chmn. 1976-78; mem. Portland dist. adv. coun. SBA, 1973-77; mem. rewards rev. com., City of Portland, 1973-78, chmn., 1973-78; bd. regents U. Portland, 1971-79, chmn. bd., 1975-79, regent emeritus, 1979—; trustee Oreg. Episc. Schs., 1979, Linfield Coll., U. Puget Sound, 1989—; dr. pub. svc., U. Puget Sound, 1999; chmn. bd. trustees Portland Art Mus., 2003-05. Named Outstanding Philanthropist of Yr. award, Nat. Soc. Fund Raising Execs., 1997, Western Conservative Bapt. Sem. Lay Inst. for Leadership, Edn. Devel. and Rsch. named for R.B. Pamplin Jr., 1988, Textile World's Top 10, 1999, Portland First Citizen, Portland Met. Assn. Realtors, 1999, Parents of Yr., Juvenile Diabetes Found., 2001, Entrepreneur of Yr., Oreg. Entrepreneur Forum, 2001, Va. Tech. Coll. Bus. Adminstrn. renamed R.B. Pamplin Coll. Bus. Adminstrn. in his honor, U. Portland Sch. Bus. renamed Dr. Robert B. Pamplin, Jr. in his honor, Civil War Preservationist of Yr., Civil War Preservation Trust, 2003, Vol. of Yr., Vols. of Am., 2006; named one of 20 Most Influential Execs. Past 20 Yrs., Bus. Jour.; recipient Disting. Alumnus award, Lewis and Clark Coll., 1974, ROTC Disting. Svc. award, USAF, 1974, bronze medal, Albert Einstein acad., 1986, Disting. Leadership medal, Freedoms Found., Disting. Bus. Alumnus award, U. Portland, 1990, Nat. Caring award, Caring Inst., 1991, Pride of Portland award, Portland Lions Club, Hero Athlete award, 1994, Herman Lay Entrepreneurship award, 1995, Thomas Jefferson award, Oreg. Hist. Soc., 1998, Aubrey R. Watzek award, Lewis and Clark Coll., 1998, Leadership award, Portland Living Man, 1998, Unique Contbns, to Comme. award, Portland Advt. Fedn., 2001, Oliver Wendell Holmes, Jr. award for Civil War Preservationist of Yr., 2001, Govs. Arts award, 2001, Legacy award, Civil War Preservation Trust, 2003, Gov.'s Gold award as Oregonian of Achievement, 2003, Corp. Citizenship award, Woodrow Wilson Internat. Ctr. for Scholars, 2005. Mem. Acad. Mgmt., Delta Epsilon Sigma, Beta Gamma Sigma, Sigma Phi Epsilon, Waverley Country Club (pres. 2003-04), Arlington, Multnomah Athletic Clubb, Capitol Hill Club, Greenville Country Club, Poinsett Club, Eldorado Country Club, Thunderbird Country Club, Rotary. Republican. Episcopalian. Office: RB Pamplin Corp Inc Ste 2400 805 SW Broadway Portland OR 97205-3341

**PAMPUSCH, ANITA MARIE,** foundation administrator; b. St. Paul, Aug. 28, 1938; d. Robert William and Lucille Elizabeth (Whaley) P. BA, Coll. of St. Catherine, St. Paul, 1962; MA, U. Notre Dame, 1970, PhD, 1972. Tchr. St. Joseph's Acad., St. Paul, 1962-66; instr. philosophy Coll. of St. Catherine, St. Paul, 1970-76, assoc. acad. dean, 1979, acad. dean, 1979-84, pres., 1984-97; Am. Council Edn. fellow Goucher Coll., Balt., 1976-77; pres. Bush Found., St. Paul, 1997—. Bd. dirs. St. Paul Cos.; head Women's Coll. Coalition, 1988-91. Author: (book rev.) Philological Quarterly, 1976; contbr. articles to profl. jours. Mem. adv. com. Instl. Leadership project, Columbia U., 1986—; dist. chmn. Rhodes Scholarship Selection com., No., Neb., Minn., Kans., N.D., S.D.; 1987—; exec. com. Women's Coll. Coalition, Washington, 1985—. Mem. Coun. for Ind. Colls. (bd. dirs. 1987—, chair 1991—), Am. Philos. Assn., St. Paul C. of C. (bd. dirs. 1986—), St. Paul's Athletic Club, Mpls. Club, Phi Beta Kappa. Roman Catholic. Avocations: swimming, camping, reading, music. Home: 161 Stonebridge Rd Saint Paul MN 55118

**PAN, CHAI-FU,** engineering educator; b. Loshon, Szechwan, China, Sept. 8, 1936; arrived in U.S., 1960; s. I-Chen Pan, Shih-Liang Shih; m. Maria Chia-Yao Shih, Aug. 18, 1962; children: Lawrence, Mariette. BS in Chem. Engring., Nat. Taiwan U., 1956; PhD in Phys. Chemistry, U. Kans., 1966. Assoc. prof. Ala. State U., Montgomery, 1966—71, prof., 1971—91, prof. emeritus, 1991—. Contbr. numerous articles to profl. jours. Recipient Rsch. award, Ala. State U., 1985; grantee MISIP grantee, NSF, 1985. Fellow: Am. Inst. Chemists; mem.: Am. Chem. Soc. (referee), Phi Lambda Upsilon. Achievements include development of Pan equations; research in methods to

study hydrophilic and hydrophobic phenomena in electrolyte solutions. Avocations: reading, writing, gardening, photography. Home: 2420 Wentworth Dr Montgomery AL 36106 Personal E-mail: ppan@charter.net.

**PAN, DEMING,** chemistry professor; b. Shanghai, May 9, 1944; arrived in U.S., 1988; d. Han Qing Pan and Jiang Zou; 1 child, Xiaosheng Huang. BSChemE, Tian Jing U., China, 1966; MSChemE, Chem. Engring. Inst. East China, 1983; MS in Inorganic Chemistry, Kent State U., Ohio, 1993, PhD in Phys. Chemistry, 1995. Chem. engr. Shanghai Rsch. Inst. Materials, 1983—88; tchg. asst. chemistry Kent State U., 1988—93, vis. asst. prof., 1996—98; prof. chemistry Mid-Plains CC, North Platte, Nebr., 1998—. Contbr. articles to profl. publs. Mem.: Am. Chem. Soc. Office Phone: 308-535-3743. E-mail: dpan@mpcc.edu.

**PAN, GUOQUAN VICTOR,** mathematics professor, computer science educator; b. Guangzhou, China, Feb. 26, 1962; arrived in U.S., 1986; s. Yi Hong Pan and Mei Liang; children: Elizabeth, Phillip. BS, Guangzhou U., 1980; MA, Jinan U., Guangzhou, 1986; PhD, U. South Fla., Tampa, 1990. Vis. prof. U. Calif., Riverside, 1990—92, La State U., Shreveport, 1992—93; prof. dept. math. and computer sci. Barry U., Miami Shores, Fla., 1993—. Office: Barry University Dept Math and Computer Sci 11300 NE 2d Ave Miami FL 33161-6628

**PAN, HENRY YUE-MING,** clinical pharmacologist, cardiologist; b. Shanghai, Dec. 27, 1946; came to U.S. 1969; s. Chia-Liu and Siu-Ging (Sung) P.; m. Mary Agnes Tse; children: Lincoln Jonathan, Gregory Kingsley. BSc, McGill U., 1969; MS in Toxicology, U. Hawaii, 1973, PhD in Pharmacology, 1974; MD, U. Hong Kong, 1979. Rsch. asst. U. Hawaii, Honolulu, 1969—74, tchg. asst., 1970—74; med. officer Queen Mary Hosp., Hong Kong, 1979—81; asst. prof. medicine U. Hong Kong, 1981—85; vis. asst. prof. Stanford U., Calif., 1983—85; from asst. clin. pharmacology dir. to exec. dir. clin. rsch. Squibb Inst. Med. Rsch., Princeton, NJ, 1985—91; v.p. clin. rsch. Bristol-Myers Squibb Pharm. Rsch. Inst., Princeton, 1991—92; v.p. clin. R & D DuPont Merck Pharm. Co., Wilmington, Del., 1992—93; sr. v.p. drug devel., 1993—96, exec. v.p. R & D, 1996—97; pres. MDS Pharm. Svcs., 1997—99; pres., CEO, mng. ptnr. Integrated Drug Devel. Svcs. and Pharmacologics, LLC, Morristown, NJ, 1998—2000; mng. dir. VennWorks LLC, N.Y.C., 2000—01; CEO VennWorks, Research Triangle Park, NC, 2000—01; exec. v.p., chief med. officer Neurocrine Bioscis., Inc., San Diego, 2001—06; chief scientific officer Prometheus Therapeutics and Diagnostics, 2006—. Bd. dir. Predict, Inc., Proband, Inc.; chmn. EastWest Pharm. Internat. LLC. Contbr. articles to profl. jours. Stanford Asian Med. Fund grant, 1983-85. Fellow: Am. Soc. Angiology, Inst. Biol. and Clin. Investigation, Acad. Medicine N.J., Am. Coll. Cardiology, Am. Coll. Clin. Pharmacology, Am. Heart Assn. Coun.; mem.: AMA, AAAS, Soc. Chinese Biologists in Am. (chmn. biopharm. divsn.), Royal Coll. Physicians (faculty pharm. medicine), Assisted Profl. Sleep Soc., Am. Acad. Pharm. Physicians, Am. Fedn. Med. Rsch., Am. Soc. Pharmacology and Exptl. Therapeutics, Am. Soc. Clin. Pharmacology and Therapeutics, Am. Assn. Pharm. Scientists. Roman Catholic. Avocations: tennis, golf, bicycling, music, reading. Home: PO Box 675552 Rancho Santa Fe CA 92067 Office: Prometheus Therapeutics and Diagnostics 9410 Carroll Pk Dr San Diego CA 92121 Office Phone: 858-617-7683. Personal E-mail: henrypan@att.net. Business E-Mail: hpan@neurocrine.com.

**PAN, LIANG RU,** physicist, researcher; b. Szechuan, China, Apr. 24, 1917; arrived in U.S., 1947; s. Min Gau Pan and Yun Dou Chong; m. Zhong De Ding, Apr. 7, 1960; children: Luanne, Feng. BS, Nat. Southwest U., China, 1943; MS, Va. Polytech. Inst., 1950; PhD, Cornell U., 1956. Assoc. prof. Chinese Acad. Sci., Beijing, 1956—78; assoc. editor The Chinese Jour. Mechanics, Beijing, 1957—60; prof. Chinese Acad. Sci., Beijing, 1978—. Vis. sr. scientist Blockett Lab. Imperial Coll., London, 1986; vis. sr. scientist Lab. Plasma Studies Cornell U., Ithaca, NY, 1987. Contbr. articles to profl. jours. Recipient award, Beijing (China) Soc. and Tech. Assn., 1986, State Dept., China, 1993. Mem.: N.Y. Acad. Scis., Beijing (China) Soc. Plasma Sci. and Tech. (founder 1978—, vice chmn. 1978—). Avocations: exercise, bridge, travel, television.

**PAN, NING,** engineering educator; s. Bao Pan and Xiangyu Wu; m. Hualin Huang, July 13, 1983; 1 child, Kathleen Lin. PhD, Donghua U., 1982—85. Fellowship, Textile Inst., 1994. Mem.: The Fiber Soc. (licentiate; pres. 2001—02, Disting. Lectr. 1998). Achievements include pioneer work in several areas of fibrous materials science. Office: U of Calif at Davis One Shields Ave Davis CA 95616 E-mail: npan@ucdavis.edu.

**PAN, RONG,** engineering educator; b. Kaifeng, China, Dec. 22, 1973; US, 1997; s. Yinqi Pan and Tongli Li; m. Ying Hua Chen. BS in Materials Sci., Shanghai Jian Tong U., 1995; MS, Fla. A&M U., 1999; PhD in Indsl. Engring., Pa. State U., 2002. Asst. prof. U. of Tex. at El Paso 2002—; rsch. asst. Pa. State U., 1999—2002; engr. Newcom Co., State Coll., 2000; quality cons. Gen. Nutrition Products, Greensville, SC, 1999; rsch. asst. Fla. A&M U., 1997—98; quality tech. GE, Nausha, China, 1995—97. Mem.: Inst. for Ops. Rsch and Mgmt, Inst. of Indsl. Engring., Am. Soc. Quality. Office: U Tex at El Paso Dept Indsl Engring 500 W University Ave El Paso TX 79968 Office Phone: 915-767-5780. Business E-Mail: rpan@utep.edu.

**PAN, VIVIEN L.,** obstetrician, gynecologist; parents Han S. and Jane S. Pan. BS, U. Calif., Berkeley, 1992; MD, Chgo. Med. Sch., 1996. Diplomate Am. Bd. Ob-Gyn., Am. Bd. Obstetrics and Gynecology. Resident, obstetrics and gynecology U. Pitts. 1996—2000; fellowship, maternal-fetal medicine U. So. Calif., Los Angeles, 2000—03, asst. prof., 2003—04; pvt. practice maternal fetal medicine Mission Viejo, Calif., 2004—. Contbr. articles various profl. jours. Mem.: Soc. Maternal Fetal Medicine, Am. Coll. Obstetrics and Gynecology, Alpha Omega Alpha.

**PAN, WILLIAM KUANG-YAO,** research scientist; s. Peter Naw-Yank and Carolyn Louise Pan; m. Sophia Theadora Papadeas, Aug. 20, 2005; 1 child, Zoe. BA, Boston Coll., 1994; MPH, Emory U., 1997; MS, U. of NC, Chapel Hill, 1999, DpH, 2003. Coord. - cardiomyopathy and transplant dept. Brigham and Women's Hosp., Boston, 1994; intern - epidemiology program office Ctr. for Disease Control and Prevention, Atlanta, 1995—96, intern - dept. of unintentional injury prevention, 1997—97; environ. scientist EPA, Human Studies Divsn., Chapel Hill, 1998—98; post-doctoral rsch. fellow Carolina Population Ctr., 2003—04, Johns Hopkins U., Dept. of Internat. Health, Balt., 2004—05; asst. scientist Johns Hopkins U. Bloomberg Sch. of Pub. Health, 2005—. Cons. UNICEF, Beijing, 1996, Program Against Micronutrient Malnutrition, Atlanta, 1995—96. Contbr. chapters to books, articles to profl. jours. Recipient Travel award, Mellon Found., 2001, Tinker Pre-Dissertation Travel award, Inst. for Latin Am. Studies, 2000; grantee Travel award, UNC Dept. of Biostatistics, 1999—2002, US Population Projections using European Indicators of Population Growth, Zero Population Growth, 1997—98; Mindel C Sheps fellow in Math. Demography, U. of NC at Chapel Hill, 2003, GIS & Population Sci. Tng. Program Travel grant, U. of Calif. at Santa Barbara & NIH, 2005. Mem.: APHA (sec. elect of the stats. sect. 2005—), Internat. Union for the Sci. Study of Population, Am. Statis. Assn., Population Assn. of Am. Avocations: soccer, camping, travel, fishing. Office: Johns Hopkins U 615 N Wolfe St Rm W5508 Baltimore MD 21205 Office Phone: 410-502-2141. Home Fax: 410-502-6733; Office Fax: 410-502-6733. Business E-Mail: wpan@jhsph.edu.

**PAN, YI,** computer science educator; b. Wujiang, Jiangsu, China, May 12, 1960; came to U.S., 1987; s. Jun and Xiuzhen (Fei) P.; m. Hong Miao, Aug. 4, 1986; children: Marissa, Anna. BEng, Tsinghua U., Beijing, 1982, MEng, 1984; MSc, U. Pitts., 1988, PhD in Computer Sci., 1991. Rsch. asst. Tsinghua U., 1982-86; tchg. asst. U. Pitts., 1987-89, tchg. fellow, 1989—91; asst. prof. computer sci. U. Dayton, Ohio, 1991-96, assoc. prof. Ohio, 1996-2000; assoc. prof. computer sci. Ga. State U., Atlanta, 2000—, now chair computer sci. Director of Graduate Studies in Computer Science University of Dayton, Dayton, 1998—2000. Contbr. articles to profl. jours. Recipient Rsch. Oppor-

tunity award NSF, 1995, Investment Competition Fund award Ohio Bd. Regents, 1996, World Acad. Scis. Achievement award, 2002; Mellon Found. fellow 1990, Summer Rsch. fellow U. Dayton Rsch. Coun., 2000, Air Force Office for Sci. Rsch., JSPS fellow, 1998. Mem.: IEEE (sr.; Secretary of the IEEE Computer Society Dayton Chapter 1996—97, IEEE Computer Society Distinguished Visitor Program Speaker 2000). Home: 615 Summer Breeze Ter Alpharetta GA 30005-6431 Office: Ga State U Computer Sci Dept 34 Peachtree St Ste 1450 Atlanta GA 30303 E-mail: pan@cs.gsu.edu.

**PANAGIDES, JOHN,** pharmacologist; b. NYC, Aug. 15, 1944; s. Chris and Sophie (Marmar) P.; m. Kathleen Ann Heimann, July 9, 1967; children: Christopher, Melissa, Adrienne. BS, CCNY, 1966; MS, U. N.C., 1968; PhD, SUNY, Buffalo, 1972. Rsch. assoc. Rockefeller U., N.Y.C., 1972-73; sr. scientist Lederle Labs., Pearl River, NY, 1973-83; sr. clin. monitor Ayerst Labs., N.Y.C., 1983-87; dir. clin. projects, CNS Organon Pharms. USA Inc., 1987-99, sr. dir. clin. projects, CNS, 1999—. Contbr. articles to profl. jours. NDEA Title IV fellow, Chapel Hill, 1966-68. Mem. AAAS, Am. Soc. Pharmacology and Exptl. Therapeutics, Am. Coll. Neuropsychopharmacology, N.Y. Acad. Scis. Achievements include development of haemophilus influenza vaccine, 23-valent pneumococcal vaccine, fenbufen, Iodine, cotazym, cotazym-S, zymase, remeron. Home: 7 Catawba Dr West Nyack NY 10994-2304 Office: Organon Pharms USA Inc 56 Livingston Ave Roseland NJ 07068 E-mail: j.panagides@organonusa.com.

**PANAGIS, PETE,** writer; b. N.Y.C., Aug. 23, 1952; s. Lycourgos and Elizabeth Panagis; m. Evanthia Mentonis, Sept. 2, 1973; children: Penelope, Lee. BA, Bklyn. Coll., 1974; postgrad., Bklyn Coll., N.Y.C. 1974. Lic. rea estate broker Poh's Inst., 1974. Tchr. Soterios Ellenas Parochial Sch., Bklyn., 1973—75; real estate broker Ionian Realty, Bklyn., 1975—83; gen. ptnr. Sheridan Sq. Restaurant, N.Y.C., 1983—89; gen. mgr. Del's Inc., Old Bridge, NJ, 1989—91, Charlie Brown's Steak House, Mountain Side, NJ, 1991—97; writer Freelance, South Amboy, NJ, 2001—. Contbr. articles to profl. jours. Basketball coach Old Bridge Basketball, Old Bridge, NJ, 1995—96; baseball coach Cheesequake Baseball, Old Bridge, NJ, 1988—95; basketball coach Soterios Ellenas Parochial Sch., Bklyn., 1973—75. Mem.: Ahepa (assoc.). R-Liberal. Greek Orthodox. Avocations: swimming, travel, reading, excercise. Personal E-mail: ntana@aol.com.

**PANAGOPOULOS, PANAGIOTIS NIKOS,** physicist, researcher; b. Athens, June 6, 1958; s. Nikos and Maria Panagopoulos; m. Anastasia Moustakali, Jan. 5, 1965; children: Maria-Magdalini, Nick. BSc in Physics, U. of Ioannina, Greece, 1982; PhD (hon.), Nat. Tech. U. Athens, 1987. Cert. in digital tech. Elkepa, Greece, 1990. Faculty Ednl. Lab. Phys. Sci. Ministry of Edn., Mandra, Greece, 2000—06; physics tutor Hellenic Open U., Patra, Greece, 2005—. Rschr. Nat. Tech. U. of Athens, 1999—. Sgt. arty., 1987—88, Greece. Scholar Rsch: scholar, Greek Govt., 1982—86, 2003—06. Mem.: EEF. Achievements include research in passive sinks of vibrational energy. Office: Educational laboratory of Phys Sciences Omirou & Diomidous Attici Mandra 19600 Greece Office Phone: 2105001920. Personal E-mail: panago58@otenet.gr. E-mail: mail@ekfe-dytik.att.sch.gr.

**PANAGOS, STEVEN GREGORY,** food products executive; b. Royal Oak, Mich., Nov. 18, 1961; s. George William and Anna (Pappas) P.; m. Joan Kwiatkoski. BS in Acctg., U. Mich., 1983. CPA; cert. insolvency reorganization acct. Sr. acct. KMG Main Hurdman, Stamford, Conn., 1984-86; corp. contr. Van Wagner Comms., Inc., N.Y.C., 1986-88; prin. Zolfo Cooper, LLC, N.Y.C., 1988—; pres., COO Krispy Kreme Doughnuts Inc., 2005—. Mem. adv. bd. CDC Techs., Inc., Newtown, Conn., 1990—, Contract Rec. Co., N.Y.C., 1996—, Eaton Life Ins. Co., N.Y.C., 1995-96. Mem. Patterson Club. Greek Orthodox. Avocations: golf, tennis. Home: 73 Sasco Hill Rd Fairfield CT 06430-6346 Office: Zolfo Cooper LLC 7th Fl 292 Madison Ave Fl 7 New York NY 10017-6307 also: Krispy Kreme Doughnut Corp PO Box 83 Winston Salem NC 27102

**PANAGOTIS, DAVID TIMOTHY,** editor; b. Wash., Pa., Aug. 11, 1951; s. Timothy George Panagotis and Betty Louise King-Panagotis; m. Marie Nancy Granato (dec.). BA, Marist Coll., 1991. Ct. aide NY State Supreme Ct., Queens, NY, 1982—84; data mgmt. specialist Hill & Knowlton Inc., N.Y.C., 1986—87; asst. keyboard specialist Hudson River State Hosp., Hudson River Regional Office, Poughkeepsie, NY, 1988—89; libr. Marist Coll. Lib., Poughkeepsie, 1989—91; sr. editor Awakening, Newsletter, Poughkeepsie, 1995—. Author various poet verse titles; songs: Vol. No. Dutchess Hosp., Rhinebeck, NY, 1992—94; pres. Distributive Edn. Clubs of Am., Ocala, Fla., 1968. Mem.: Acad. Am. Poets, Am. Fedn. State, County and Mcpl. Employees, Nat. Geog. Soc., Am. MENSA Ltd., Alpha Sigma Lambda. Democrat. Avocations: music appreciation, theology, philosophy, poetry.

**PANARESE, WILLIAM C.,** civil engineer; b. Framingham, Mass., Mar. 6, 1929; s. Angelo and Stephanie (Di Profio) P. BSCE, Purdue U., 1952. Structural research engr. Assn. Am. Railroads, Chgo., 1952-55; with Portland Cement Assn., Chgo. and Skokie, Ill., 1957-76, 80-94, mgr. concrete tech. sect., 1973-76, assoc. mgr. bldg. constrn. sect., 1980-83, mgr. bldg. tech. dept., 1983-86, mgr. constrn. info. services dept., 1987-94. Author, editor: Concrete Floors on Ground, 1983, Transporting and Handling Concrete, 1987, The Homeowner's Guide to Building with Concrete, Brick and Stone, 1988, Cement Mason's Guide, 1990, Concrete Masonry Handbook for Architects, Engineers, Builders, 1991, Fiber Reinforced Concrete, 1991, High Strength Concrete, 1994, Design and Control of Concrete Mixtures, 2002, Performance of Architectural Concrete Panels in the PCA Outdoor Display, 2004, Environmental Performance of Concrete, 2005, Concrete Floors and Mixtures, 2005, Specifier's Guide to Durable Concrete, 2005; author, editor Concrete Finisher's Guide, 2006; author, editor: other bldg. guides and handbooks; editor: Concrete Constrn. mag., 1976—80, Concrete Tech. Today newsletter, 1980—94. Served with C.E. U.S. Army, 1955-57. Fellow Am. Concrete Inst. (coms. 302 on constrn. of concrete floors and slabs, 332 on residential concrete work, chmn. 332 1984-88), Chi Epsilon. Roman Catholic. Avocations: music, walking, tennis, skiing, writing. Home and Office: 1625 Glenview Rd Unit 304 Glenview IL 60025-2973 Office Phone: 847-729-5885. Personal E-mail: wmpanarese@aol.com.

**PANASYUK, GEORGE YURYEVICH,** physicist, researcher; b. Leningrad, Russia, Apr. 20, 1955; s. Yuriy Pavlovich and Galina Ivanovna Panasyuk. MS, Leningrad State U., 1979, candidate of Scis. (Soviet PhD) in Plasma Physics, 1984; PhD in Condensed Matter Physics, Kent State U., 2003. Rschr. St. Petersburg State U., Russia, 1979—97; rsch. asst. dept. physics Kent State U., Ohio, 1997—2003; rsch. assoc. Liquid Crystal Inst., Kent State U., 2003; postdoctoratal rschr. dept. bioengring. U. Pa., Phila., 2004, rsch. assoc. dept. bioengring. 2005—. Tchr. atomic physics Leningrad State U., 1981—83; tchr. math. Leningrad Trade and Commerce Inst., 1987—90; referee for sci. jours. Physical Rev. Letters, Applied Optics, Jour. Quantitative Spectroscopy and Radiative Transfer, Physics Essays, U.S. and Can., 2002—; referee for fund Internat. Assn. European Cmty., European Union's Mem. States, 2003—. Author: (articles) Physical Rev. E, Applied Physics, Physics Letters A, Jour. Physics D, other jours. (rsch. award, Kent State U., 2002, Internat. Sci. Found. award, 1993), (invention) Two Coordinate Angular Position Sensor (patent, 1990). Grantee advanced liquid crystalline optical material grant, NSF, 1998—2001, liquid crystal based beam steering device and optical telescopes grant, NASA, 2003, modeling and improvement for pi-cell type devices for active matrix liquid crystal display applications grant, Samsung Elect., So. Korea, 2003. Mem.: Am. Phys. Soc. (pres. 1999—), Soc. Info. Display (pres. 2001—), Internat. Liquid Crystal Soc. (pres. 1999—). Office: Univ Pa Dept Bioengring 3320 Smith Walk Philadelphia PA 19104 Office Phone: 215-746-3018. Office Fax: 215-573-2071. Business E-Mail: georgey@seas.upenn.edu.

**PANAYOTOV, CHRISTO ANGELOV,** research scientist, consultant; arrived in U.S., 1990; s. Angel Panayotov Angelov and Elena Christova Panayotova; m. Iliana Nicolova Gospodinova-Panayotova, Sept. 6, 1988. Degree in Chem. Engring., Tech. U., Sofia, Bulgaria, 1953; PhD (hon.), Tech.

U., Budapest, Hungary, 1959; DSc (hon.), Humboldt U., Berlin, 1972. Prodn. mgr. Pharmachim, Sofia, 1953—67; dep. trade commr. Bulgarian Trade Commn., N.Y.C., 1967—70; chmn. Biotech. Com. Bulgarian Govt., Sofia, 1970—75; dept. chair, full prof. Nat. U., Sofia, 1975—89; chief trade officer Bulgarian Trade Commn., Toronto, Canada, 1989—92; engring. cons. R&D Bioindustries, Leveling and Engring. Svcs., LLC, Toronto, 1992—96; dir. R&D Bausch & Stroebel Machine Co., Clinton, Conn., 1996—2004. Rep. of Bulgaria European Union Biotechnology, Frankfurt, Germany, 1980—85; chmn. sci. Policy Com. World Union Scientists, Paris, 1980—85; sr. adviser World Food Program-Internat. Inst. for Applied Sys. Analysis, Vienna, 1982—84; mem. adv. bd. Nobel Prize Com. on Chemistry, Stockholm, 1982—85; mem. Biotech. Com. State of Conn., United States, 1998—; cons. pharm. industry, 2004—. Editor: Acta Biotechnologica, 1982—86; author: Enzyme Production and Their Practical Application, 1969, Biotech Industry and Science, 1972, Technology of the Antibiotic Industry, 1975, Technology and Utilization of Food Supplements, 1976, Praxis of Pharmaceutical Synthesis, 1982, Protein Biosynthesis, 1986, 12 sci. books in bio-organic chemistry; contbr. articles to profl. sci. jours. Mem.: AIChE, AAAS (cert. of recognition 2001). Achievements include patents in field. Avocations: ecology, reading, sports. Home: 106 Cow Hill Rd Clinton CT 06413 Personal E-mail: c_angelov@yahoo.com.

**PANCHALAVARAPU, POORNACHANDRA RAO,** industrial engineer, consultant; s. Purushotham and AdiLakshmi Panchalavarapu; m. SriPadmaja S Ogirala; children: Manoj, Niraj. PhD, Case Western Res. U., 2000. Logistics engr. Schneider Logistics Inc., Green Bay, Wis., 1998—2001, lead logistics engr., 2001—03, sr. logistics engr., 2003—. Contbr. articles to profl. jours.; mem. editl. bd.: Internat. Jour. Indsl. Engring., 2000—03. Mem.: Inst. Ops. Rsch. and Mgmt. Sci. Hindu. Avocation: travel. Home: 2980 Conesta Dr Green Bay WI 54311 Office: Schneider Logistics Inc 3101 South Packerland Drive Green Bay WI 54313 Personal E-mail: ppc_rao@yahoo.com. E-mail: panchalavarapur@schneider.com.

**PANDE, ANURAG,** researcher; s. Mahesh Chandra and Bhawna Pande. B in Tech., Indian Inst. Tech., Mumbai, 2002; MS, U. Ctrl. Fla., Orlando, 2003; PhD, U. Ctrl. Fla., 2005. Grad. rsch. asst. U. Ctrl. Fla.-CATSS, 2002—05, adj. faculty, rsch. assoc., 2005—. Gen. sec. hall of residence Hostel 7 Indian Inst. Tech. Bombay, 2001—02. Provost's fellow, U. Ctrl. Fla., 2002—03, Presdl. Doctoral fellow, 2003—05, CATSS fellow, 2004. Hindu. Achievements include development of real-time crash 'prediction' system for freeways based on data from Interstate 4 in Orlando. Avocations: politics, music, sports. Office: U Ctrl Fla-CATSS Engring II 4000 Central Florida Blvd Orlando FL 32816 Office Phone: 407-823-4902. E-mail: anurag@mail.ucf.edu.

**PANDEL, ROBIN MCEWAN,** elementary school educator; d. Joseph Charles and Ruth Mae McEwan; m. Praxiteles Ted Pandel, Oct. 16, 1980; children: Praxiteles Jr., Katherine. BS in Music Edn., SUNY, Potsdam, 1978; MusM, West Chester U., Pa., 1980. Cert. tchr. Pa. Piano instr. Neumann Coll., Aston, Pa., 1985—89; vocal music tchr grades 1-5 West Chester Area Sch. Dist., Pa., 1990—. Organist St. Luke's Greek Orthodox Ch., Broomall, Pa., 1987—97, choir dir., 1997—2005; organist Clergy Liaty Greek Orthodox Ch., Phila., 2000. Mem.: Pa. Music Edn. Assn., Music Educators Nat. Conf., Daus. of Penelope. Greek Orthodox. Avocation: reading.

**PANDEY, JANARDAN P.,** agronomist, educator; BSc with honors in Biology, G.V. Pant U. of Agr. and Tech., India, 1967; MS in Agronomy, U. Wis., 1970, PhD in Genetics and Plant Breeding, 1972. Postdoctoral fellow U. Wis., Madison, 1972—73, U. Conn., Storrs, 1973—74; vis. scientist Case Western Res. U., Cleve., 1975; postdoctoral fellow Med. U., 1975—76, instr. dept. microbiology and immunology, 1976—78, asst. prof., 1978—83, assoc. prof., 1983—88, prof., 1988—. Mem. editl. bd. Disease Markers, 1983—2001; co-editor: Experimental and Clinical Immunogenetics, 1984—2002; contbr. over 169 articles to profl. jours. Grantee, Dept. of Energy, 2004—, U. Nebr., 2005—, NIH/NIDA, 2003—05. Office: Medical Univ of South Carolina Dept Microbiology/Immunology Charleston SC 29401

**PANDEY, RAMESH CHANDRA,** chemist, chemicals executive; b. Naugaon, Uttranchal, India, Nov. 5, 1938; arrived in US, 1967; s. Gauri Dutt and Jivanti Pandey. BSc, U. Allahabad, India, 1958; MSc, U. Gorakhpur, India, 1960; PhD, U. Poona, India, 1965. Jr. rsch. fellow CSIR Nat. Chem. Lab., Poona, 1960-64, rsch. officer, 1965-67; scientist organic divsn., 1970-72; rsch. assoc. dept. chemistry U. Ill., Urbana, 1967-70, vis. scientist, 1972-77; sr. scientist fermentation program Nat. Cancer Inst. Frederick (Md.) Cancer Rsch. Facility, 1977-82, head chem. sect., 1982-83; sr. scientist Abbott Labs., North Chicago, Ill., 1983-84; pres. Xechem, Inc., Melrose Pk., Ill., 1984-90, pres., CEO, dir. tech. devel. New Brunswick, NJ, 1990—2003; chmn., CEO, pres. Xechem Internat. Inc., 1994—2004, chmn., CEO, 2004—; chmn., CEO, pres. Xetapharm Inc., 1996—. Cons. Washington U. Sch. Medicine, St. Louis, 1976-85, LyphoMed, Inc., Melrose Park, 1984-85; vis. prof. Waksman Inst. Rutgers U., Piscataway, NJ, 1984-86; mem. life sci. adv. bd. NJTC, 1999—; mem. statewide adv. com. bd. mgrs. NJ Agri. Exptl. Sta., Rutgers State U. NJ in Biotechnology, 2002—; founder G.D. Padney Ayurved U., New Brunswick, NJ. Mem. editl. bd. Internat. Jour. Antibiotics, 1986—; patentee graft thin layer chromatography; several US and internat. patents for the isolation and purification of antiobiotics and anticancer agents. Mem. Middlesex County (NJ) Work Force Investment Bd., 1999—; mem. adv. com. for sci. transfer and sci. tech. program Middlesex County Coll., Edison, NJ, 1999-2001. Fellow Am. Inst. Chemists; mem. Am. Chem. Soc., Am. Soc. Microbiology, Am. Soc. Mass Spectrometry, Am. Assn. Cancer Rsch., Am. Soc. Hosp. Pharmacists, Am. Soc. Pharmacognosy, Am. Indsl. Microbiology, NY Acad. Scis., Indian Sci. Congress Assn., Am. Acad. Ayurvedic Medicine (founder, exec. trustee), Rotary Club (Paul Harris fellow 1996—, pres. New Brunswick club 1999-2000). Office: Xechem Internat Inc New Brunswick Tech Ctr 100 Jersey Ave Ste B-310 New Brunswick NJ 08901-3200 Office Phone: 732-247-3300. Business E-Mail: ramesh@xechem.com.

**PANDIT, VIKRAM S.,** investment banker; b. Bombay, 1957; married; 2 children. BS, Columbia U., 1976, MBA, 1980, PhD, 1986. Fin. prof. Columbia U.; mng. dir. Morgan Stanley & Co., 1990—94; head of equity derivatives Morgan Stanley Group Inc., 1994—96; head of instl. equity divsn. Morgan Stanley, 1997—2000, co. pres., COO instl. securities divsn., 2000—03, pres. COO, instl. securities divsn., 2003—05; founding ptnr. Old Lane Capital Mgmt. LLC, 2005—. Bd. dirs. NASDAQ, 2000—03, NYC Investment Fund.*

**PANDO, JESUS,** education educator; b. El Paso, Jan. 26, 1956; s. Antonio and Gloria Pando; children: Jacquelyn Claire Keeper, Daniel Eric. PhD, U. Ariz., 1997. Asst. prof. Chgo. State U., Chgo., 2000—02; assoc. prof. DePaul U., Chgo., 2002—. Author several articles in scientific jours. Chateaubriand Post-Doctoral Fellowship, Edn. Office of Embassy of France, 1997, Post-Doctoral Fellowship, NSF, 1998. Mem.: Soc. for Advancement of Chicanos and Native Americans in Sci. (program com. 2005—06), Nat. Soc. of Hispanic Physicists (treas. 2004—06). Office: DePaul Univ 2219 N Kenmore Chicago IL 60614 Office Phone: 773 325 4942. Office Fax: 773 325 7334. Business E-Mail: jpando@depaul.edu.

**PANDOLFI, FRANCES,** health facility administrator; b. NYC, Sept. 7, 1944; d. Frank Pandolfi and Rose McGinn; m. Edmund Lewiska Menelik Bobbitt, May 19, 1973. BA, Vassar Coll., 1965; MPA, NYU, 1990. Health planner N.Y.C. Dept. City Planning, 1965-74; planner West Midlands County Coun., Birmingham, Eng., 1974-81, dir. recreation and tourism planning, 1981-85, dir. strategic planning, 1985-86; dep. dir. housing coord. N.Y.C. Mayor's Office, 1987-89; dir. nurses housing N.Y.C. Health & Hosps. Corp., 1989-92, exec. asst. to v.p., 1992-94, asst. 1994-97; chief of staff N.Y.C. Health and Hosps. Corp., 1998-2001, chief info. officer, 2001—. Dir. Women in Housing and Fin., N.Y.C., 1990-96. Mem.: Am. Soc. Pub. Adminstrn. Office: NYC Health & Hosps Corp 125 Worth St New York NY 10013-4006 Office Phone: 212-788-3437. Business E-Mail: pandolff@nychhc.org.

**PANE, NATALIA,** policy and research analyst, strategic planner; b. Princeton, NJ, Apr. 21, 1970; d. Michael Anthony and Frances H. Pane; m. Douglas Tyrka, May 30, 2005. BA, Miami U., Oxford, Ohio, 1992; MA, U. Del., 1997; MBA, U. Md., 2004. Prin. rsch. analyst Am. Insts. Rsch., Washington, 1997—. Office: Am Insts Rsch 1000 Thomas Jefferson St Washington DC 20007 Office Phone: 202-403-5335. E-mail: npane@air.org.

**PANEK, WILLIAM DOMINICK,** systems engineer executive; b. Pert Amboy, NJ, Jan. 14, 1970; s. Richard William Panek and Marjaree Marie Mayne; m. Crystal Marie Pellerin, Feb. 11, 1995; children: Paige children: Alexandria. Assoc. degree, Computer Learning Ctr., 1994. MCSE Microsoft, 1997, Microsoft, 2001, cert. trainer Microsoft, 1997, database adminstr. Microsoft, 2000, network assoc. Cisco Corp., 2000. Microsoft cert. instr. The Associates, Shrewsbury, Mass., 1997—98; pres. Stellacon Corp, Farmington, NH, 1998—. Cons. MicroScript, Danvers, Mass., 1994—2000. Firefighter/EMT; spl. advisor to the chmn. Bus. Adv. Coun., Washington, 2002—03. E4 USAF, 1988—92, Spain. Recipient NH Businessman Yr., Bus. Adv. Coun., 2003. Mem.: AOPA (corr.), NRA (assoc.). R-Consevative. Roman Catholic. Avocations: pilot, hunter, scuba. Home and Office: Stellacon Corp 18 Polliwog Ln Farmington NH 03835

**PANERIO, ROBERT MAJOR, SR.,** music educator, composer; b. Roslyn, Wash., June 28, 1929; s. Major Annible and Margaret Beatrice (Hunter) Panerio; m. Charlotte Ruth Klein, June 10, 1950; children: Deborah Jo, Robert Major Jr. BA in Edn., Ctrl. Wash. U., 1953, BA, 1953, MusM in Edn., 1958; postgrad., Eastman Sch. Music, 1963. Supr. instrumental music Moses Lake (Wash.) Pub. Sch., 1953—62; head arts and humanities Big Bend Coll., Moses Lake, 1962—63; prof. music Ctrl. Wash. U., Ellensburg, 1963—91. Composer: Marauders, Nocturne, Ensenada, Concert March, Passacaglia, Pastorale, Two Contemporary Songs for Children, The Beepers' March, Theme for Band, Concert Suite for Bank, Brassology, Quartal Quartet, Dark Blue, Beguine for Orchestra, Softly. Named Disting. Univ. Prof., Ctrl. Wash. U., 1982; named to Wash. Music Educators Hall of Fame, 1998; recipient Am. Bandmasters Composition award, 1975. Mem.: Am. Soc. Composers, Authors and Publishers, Music Educators Nat. Conf. (adj. clinician). Home: 1309 Radio Rd Ellensburg WA 98926

**PANERO, HUGH EDWARD,** broadcast executive; b. NYC, Feb. 26, 1956; s. Julius and Renee (Rubin) P.; m. Mary Beth Durkin, June 21, 1987; 1 child, Sofia. BA in Govt. & Sociology, Clark U., Worcester, Mass., 1978; MBA, Baruch Coll., N.Y.C., 1989. Dep. bur. chief CableVision Mag., N.Y.C. 1980-82; v.p. mktg. Time Warner Cable of N.Y.C., 1982-93; pres., CEO Request Television, Denver, 1993—98; pres., CEO, dir. XM Satellite Radio Holdings Inc., 1998—. Mem.: Cable Television Adminstrv. and Mktg. Soc. Office: XM Satellite Radio Holdings Inc 1500 Eckington Pl NE Washington DC 20002-2194 Office Phone: 202-380-4000. Office Fax: 202-380-4500.*

**PANES, JACK SAMUEL,** publishing executive; b. N.Y.C., Apr. 6, 1925; s. Max S. and Sophie (Levine) P.; m. Pearl Shaine, Dec. 25, 1949; children— Stephanie Jill, Michael Jonathan. BA, Bklyn. Coll., 1947; MS in Journalism, Northwestern U., 1949. Editor, pub. The Howe Service, Inc., N.Y.C., 1949-54; founder, pub. Publs. for Industry, N.Y.C., 1955—, Panes Publs., Inc., N.Y.C., 1959—; owner Drug Products Display Service Advt. Co., N.Y.C., 1955—, Supplies for Industry Co., N.Y.C., 1956—; pres. Senap Devel. Corp., Great Neck, N.Y., 1972—. Pres. Russell Woods Civic Assn., Great Neck. Served with inf. AUS, 1942-45, ETO. Decorated Silver Star medal, Bronze Star medal. Mem. 94th Infantry Divsn. Assn. (pres.), Deadline Club, Sigma Delta Chi. Home: 21 Russell Woods Rd Great Neck NY 11021-4644 Office: Panes Publications Inc Great Neck NY 11021 Office Phone: 516-487-0990.

**PANETH, DONALD JOSEPH,** editor, writer; b. NYC, Feb. 28, 1927; s. Irving and Maud (Kramer) P.; m. Elma Olans, Apr. 10, 1949 (dec. 1987); children: Thea, Ira. BBA, CCNY, 1948; postgrad., Columbia U., N.Y.C., 1949-50. Reporter NY Times, 1947-49; freelance journalist NYC, 1950-56, 73-75, 77-83, 94—; rewriteman Daily Mirror, NYC, 1956-63; copy editor Morning Telegraph, NYC, 1964-65, L.I. Press, Queens, NY, 1975-77; staff writer Med. Tribune, NYC, 1966-72; editor-in-chief News Dictionary: People, Places, Events, 1977-80; editor, writer Yearbook UN, NYC, 1986-93; documents editor UN Office Conf. Svcs., NYC, 1993-94; recruiting asst., crew leader US Bur. Census, 2000; UN corr. N.Y. Indypendent, 2002—. Adj. lectr. English York Coll., CUNY, 1983-86; cons. study lit. far right extremist groups US, Anti-Defamation League, NY, 1995-96. Author: William Bazi-otes: A Lit. Portrait, 1961, Current Affairs Atlas, 1979, The Ency. of Am. Journalism, 1983; contbr. articles to Commentary mag., The Nation, Village Voice, Current Biography, Peacework, WorldPaper, others; work included anthologies Commentary on the American Scene, 1953, New York City Folklore, 1956. Mem. Am.-Scandinavian Found., NY Soc. Libr. Avocation: reading. Home and Office: 240 Cabrini Blvd Apt 1E New York NY 10033-1113

**PANETTA, JOSEPH DANIEL,** biotechnologist, director; b. Syracuse, N.Y., Mar. 1, 1954; s. Salvatore and Josephine Mary (Sbardella) P.; m. Karin Ann Hoffman, Oct. 21, 1978; children: Lauren Marie, Christopher Daniel. BS, LeMoyne Coll., 1976; MPH, U. Pitts., 1979. Environ. protection specialist EPA, Washington, 1979-82, sr. policy analyst, 1982-84; project leader Schering Corp./NorAm Chem Co., Wilmington, Del., 1984-85; mgr. regulatory affairs agrchems. divsn. Pennwalt Corp., Phila., 1985-88; mgr. corp. regulatory affairs Mycogen Corp., San Diego, 1988-90, dir. corp. regulatory affairs and quality assurance, 1990-92, dir. corp. regulatory, environ. affairs San Diego, 1992-97, v.p. govt. and pub. affair, 1998-99; pres., CEO BIOCOM, San Diego, 1999—. Bd. dirs. Gene Therapy Sys., San Diego (Calif.) Econ. Devel. Corp.; chmn. agr. and environment subcom. Internat. Bioindustry Forum; guest lectr. biotech. U. Calif., San Diego, and Calif. Western Law Sch.; advisor bd. on agr. NAS; mem. San Diego Pub. Utilities Adv. Commn., 2002—; adv. Com. Calif. Food Biotech., 2002-2004, U. Calif. Sch. Pharm. Sci., San Diego, Calif., 2003—; mem. adv. coun. Keck Grad. Inst., 2003—; vice chmn. Coun. State Biotech Assocs., 2002—, chmn. Coun. State Biotechnology Assn., 2004-. Columnist San Diego Daily Transcript, 1999—; contbr. articles to profl. jours. Mem. Rep. State Com. Del., 1987; bd. dirs. San Diego Work Force Partnership; mem. exec. com. Calif. Cmty. Colls. Econ. Devel. Network; mem. adv. bd. UCSD-Connect; bd. dirs. San Diego C. of C.; commissioner San Diego City Pub. Utilities commn., 2002—. Mem. Am. Crop Protection Assn. (chmn. com. biotech.), Nat. Agrl. Chems. Assn. (mem. registrations com. 1986-89), Biotech. Industy Orgn. (mem. food and agr. steering com., chmn. bipesticides com., internat. affairs com.), Calif. Indsl. Biotech. Assn. (mem. agrl. affairs com.), Am. Chem. Soc. (mem. agrl. div.), Am. Seed Trade Assn. (chmn. steering com. biotech.), Gov.'s Biotech. Coun. (Calif.), San Diego C. of C. (mem. pub. policy com.), San Diego Workforce Partnership (mem. youth coun.). Roman Catholic. Avocations: yachting, skiing, classical piano. Home: 5459 Shannon Ridge Ln San Diego CA 92130-4808 Office: BIOCOM San Diego 4501 Executive Dr San Diego CA 92121-3025 Office Phone: 858-455-0300. E-mail: jpanetta@biocom.org.

**PANETTA, LEON EDWARD,** former White House chief of staff, former congressman; b. Monterey, Calif., June 28, 1938; s. Carmelo and Carmelina Panetta; m. Sylvia Marie Varni, July 14, 1962; children: Christopher, Carmelo, James. BA magna cum laude, U. Santa Clara, Calif., 1960, LL.B., JD, 1963. Bar: Calif. bar 1965, U.S. Supreme Ct. 1965, U.S. Dist. Ct. (no. dist.) Calif. 1965, U.S. Ct. Appeals 1965. Legis. asst. to US Sen. Thomas Kuchel, Washington, 1966-69; dir. US Office Civil Rights, HEW, Washington, 1969-70; exec. asst. to mayor NYC, 1970-71; ptnr. Panetta, Thompson & Panetta, Monterey, 1971-76; mem. agr. com. 95th-103d Congresses from 17th Calif. dist., 1976—84, adminstrn. com., 1976—84, com. dep. majority whip budget issues, mem., 1977-93, chmn. budget com., 1989—92, also com. dep. majority whip for budget issues, chmn. select com. hunger, chmn. 95th Congress New Mems. Caucus, vice chmn. Caucus Vietnam Era Vets. in Congress, mem. Pres.'s Com. Fgn. Lang. and Internat. Studies; dir. Office Mgmt. & Budget Exec. Office of the Pres., Washington, 1993-94; chief of staff to Pres. The White House, Washington, 1994-97; founder Panetta Inst.,

Calif. State U., Monterey bay, Seaside, Calif., 1998—. Co-author: Bring Us Together, 1971. Counsel Monterey Regional Park Dists.; counsel NAACP, 1971-76; bd. trustees U. Santa Clara Law Sch.; founder Monterey Coll. Law; mem. Monterey County Dem. Cen. Com., 1972-74; v.p. Carmel Valley Little League, 1974-75; spl. advisor chancellor Calif. State U.; presdl. prof. pub. policy Santa Clara U.; former mem. bd. dirs. NY Stock Exch., chmn. com. rev. bd. dirs., co-chair corp. governance and listing stds. com. bd. dirs.; mem. nat. rev. bd. US Conf. Cath. Bishops; former trustee Nat. Steinback Ctr., Nat. Marine Sanctuary Found., 2005-; former mem. U. Calif. Santa Cruz Found., 2005-; nat. bd. advisors Ctr. Nat. Policy, 2005-; former chmn. Oceans Commn., 2005-; DCO-chair Joint Ocean Commn. Initiative; mem. Iraq Study Group, 2006-; mem. Task Force on Immigration and Am.'s Future, 2005-; bd. dirs. Blue Shield Calif., 2005-, IDT, 2005-, Zenith, 2005-, Connetics, 2005-, Bread for the World, 2005, Close Up, 2005-. Served with AUS, 1964-66. Recipient Army Commendation medal, 1966, Lincoln award NEA, 1970, A. Philip Randolph award, 1971, Disting. Svc. award NAACP, 1972, Bread for World award, 1978, 80, 82, 91, Nat. Hospice Orgn. award, 1984, Golden Plow award Am. Farm Bur. Fedn., 1988, 91, Pres.'s award Am. Coun. on Tchr. of Fgn. Langs., 1991, Coastal and Ocean Mgmt. award Coastal Zone Found., 1991, Food Rsch. and Action Ctr. award, 1991, Disting. Pub. Svc. medal Ctr. Study Presidency, 1995, Peter Burnett award disting pub. svc., 1993, Spl. Achievement award Nat. Italian Am. Found., 1997, John H. Chafer Coastal Stewardship award, 2001, Spl. Achievement award Santa Clara U. Sch. Law, 2002, Julius A. Stratton award coastal leadership, 2003, Coastal Stewardship award Aquarium of the Pacific, 2006, Lifetime Achievement award Nat. Marine Sanctuary Found., 2006, Paul Peck Presdl. award Smithsonian Instn. Nat. Portrait Gallery, 2006; named Lawyer of Yr., Law Sch. U. Santa Clara, 1970. Mem.: Calif. Bar Assn. Roman Catholic. Office: The Panetta Inst Calif State U Monterey Bay 100 Campus Ctr Bldg 86E Seaside CA 93955-8000 Office Phone: 831-582-4200. Business E-Mail: info@panettainstitute.org.

**PANETTA, MICHAEL JON,** retired state agency administrator, writer; b. Lansing, Mich., Sept. 9, 1949; s. Frank Anthony P. and Elizabeth Virginia Rocchetti; m. Susan Marie Cottrill, May 1, 1971; children: Mary Elizabeth Panetta-Lowe, Michelina Anne Panetta-Cantu, Joseph Andrew. AA, Lansing (Mich.) C.C., 1970; BA, Mich. State U., East Lansing, 1971, MS, 1972, MA equivalency, 1988, DPhil, 2000. Cert. paramedic Mich., lic. emergency med. technician Mich.; pvt. detective Mich. Fed. Manpower administr. Manpower Area Planning Coun., Lansing, Mich., 1970—73; spl. agent med. fraud auditor State of Mich., Lansing, 1973—78, supr. fed. food stamp program, 1977—78, emergency med. svcs. program specialist, 1978—89, program specialist Gov.'s Coun. Environ. Quality, 1989—90, departmental policy and procedure specialist, 1990—91, fin. specialist, contract administr. child and family health programs, 1991—2002; prof. Spring Arbor U., Lansing, 2001—02; pvt. practice, cons., 2003—. Dir. youth and vet. program Nat. Alliance of Businessmen, Lansing, 1970—73; suggestion award program administr. Mich. Dept. Pub. Health, Lansing, 1990—91. Author: Leader Behavior & Member Response in an Institutional Setting, 1972, Citizens Perceptions of Police & Community Policing, 2000, pamphlets, booklets, guides. Co-founder, pres., v.p. Citizen's to Save Lansing Mich., Lansing, 1992—99; founder Citizens to Save Vets. Civic Ctr., Lansing, 1992—99; co-founder, v.p. Citizens Against the Rain Tax of Lansing, Lansing, 1994—2000. Recipient award, Soc. Study Social Problems Columbia U., 1986; scholar grad. rsch. scholarship, Mich. State U. Bd. Trustees, 1971. Fellow: Am. Lit. Assn.; mem.: Nat. Assn. Welfare Adminstrs., NRA, Mich. State U. Alumni Assn. (life), KC (assoc.; grand knight Richard coun. 1988—90, assoc. mem. Msgr. John A. Gabriels coun., charter grand knight Msgr. John A. Gabriels coun. 1993—95, Knight of Yr. Richard Coun. 1989, Top Proposer of Yr. Richard Coun. 1990, Knight of Yr. Msgr. John A. Gabriels Coun. 1993—95, Papal medallion 1992, Star Coun. award, Columbian award, Founders award 1993—95), Alpha Kappa Delta (life). Republican. Roman Catholic. Avocations: teaching, writing, travel, bicycling, camping.

**PANG, DARREN,** hockey analyst, retired professional hockey player; b. Ottawa, Ont., Can., Feb. 17, 1964; m. Lynn Pang; children: Tyler, Samantha. Goaltender Chgo. Blackhawks, 1984—89, ret., 1990, post game show host, 1990—92, pre game show host, 1992—97; guest analyst Norris Divsn. playoffs ESPN, 1988; color analyst, studio analyst, reporter Ctrl. Collegiate Hockey Assn. (CCHA) SportsChannel, Chgo., 1989-94; analyst Internat. Hockey League games Prime Network, 1989-93; NHL game analyst ESPN2, 1993—2005, analyst NHL 2Night; ice level reporter Nagano Olympic Games, CBS, 1998, Salt Lake City Olympic Games, NBC, 2002; color commentator Phoenix Coyotes, 2005—; part-time playoff analyst TSN. Goalie coach Notre Dame U., 1996—99, U. Ill.-Chgo. Flames, Ctrl. Collegiate Hockey Assn., 2002—04. Named to NHL All-Rookie team, 1988. Office: c/o Phoenix Coyotes Hockey Club 5800 W Glenn Dr, Ste 350 Glendale AZ 85301*

**PANICEK, DAVID,** radiologist; b. Johnson City, NY, Oct. 7, 1954; MD, Cornell U., 1980. Cert. diagnostic radiology 1984. Intern Lenox Hill Hosp., N.Y.C., 1980—81; resident NY Hosp. Cornell Med. Ctr., N.Y.C., 1981—84; radiologist U. Hosp., Syracuse, NY, 1984—88; asst. prof. radiology SUNY Health Sci. Ctr., Syracuse, 1984—88, Cornell U. Med. Coll., 1988—93; radiologist Meml. Sloan-Kettering, N.Y.C., 1988—; assoc. prof. radiology Cornell U. Med. Coll., 1993—98, prof. radiology, 1999—. Fellow: Am. Coll. Radiology; mem.: Am. Roentgen Ray Soc., Radiological Soc. N.Am., Internat. Skeletal Soc. Office: Meml Sloan-Kettering Cancer Ctr 1275 York Ave New York NY 10021-6007

**PANICH, DANUTA BEMBENISTA,** lawyer; b. East Chicago, Ind., Apr. 9, 1954; d. Fred and Ann Stephanie (Grabowski) B.; m. Nikola Panich, July 30, 1977; children: Jennifer Anne, Michael Alexei. AB, Ind. U., 1975, JD, 1978. Bar: Ill. 1978, U.S. Dist. Ct. (no. dist.) Ill. 1978, U.S. Dist. Ct. (ctrl. dist.) Ill. 1987, U.S. Ct. Appeals (7th cir.) 1987, U.S. Dist. Ct. (no. dist.) Ind. 2001, U.S. Dist. Ct. (ea. dist.) Mich. 2003, U.S. Ct. Appeals (6th cir.) 2003, U.S. Dist. Ct. (so. dist.) Ill., 2004. Assoc. Mayer Brown & Platt, Chgo., 1978-86, ptnr., 1986—2001, Mayer Brown Rowe & Maw, LLP, Chgo., 2002—. Bd. dirs. Munster (Ind.) Med. Rsch. Found., 1990—, Pub. Interest Law Initiative, 2003—. Mem. ABA, Fed. Bar Assn., Ill. Bar Assn. Republican. Roman Catholic. Office: Mayer Brown Rowe & Maw LLP 71 S Wacker Dr Chicago IL 60606 Office Phone: 312-701-7198. Business E-Mail: dpanich@mayerbrownrowe.com.

**PANICHAS, GEORGE ANDREW,** language educator, critic, editor; b. Springfield, Mass., May 21, 1930; s. Andrew and Fotini (Dracouli) P. BA, Am. Internat. Coll., Springfield, Mass., 1951, LittD (hon.) 1984; AM, Trinity Coll., Conn., 1952; PhD, Nottingham U., Eng., 1962. Instr., English and comparative lit. U. Md., College Park, 1962-63, asst. prof., 1963-66, assoc. prof., 1966-68, prof., 1968-92. Mem. Richard M. Weaver fellowship awards com., 1984-88, Ingersoll Prizes Jury Panel, 1986; vis. prof. conf. on Irving Babbitt: Fifty Years Later, 1983. Author: Adventure in Consciousness: The Meaning of D.H. Lawrence's Religious Quest, 1964, Epicurus, 1967, The Reverent Discipline: Essays in Literary Criticism and Culture, 1974, The Burden of Vision: Dostoevsky's Spiritual Art, 1977, The Courage of Judgment: Essays in Criticism, Culture and Society, 1982, The Critic as Conservator: Essays in Literature, Society, and Culture, 1992, The Critical Legacy of Irving Babbitt: An Appreciation, 1999, Growing Wings to Overcome Gravity: Criticism as the Pursuit of Virtue, 1999, Joseph Conrad: His Moral Vision, 2005; editor: (with G.R. Hibbard and A. Rodway) Renaissance and Modern Essays: Presented to Vivian de Sola Pinto in Celebration of His Seventieth Birthday, 1966, Mansions of the Spirit: Essays in Literature and Religion, 1967, Promise of Greatness: The War of 1914-1918, 1968, The Politics of Twentieth-Century Novelists, 1971, The Simone Weil Reader, 1977, Irving Babbitt: Representative Writings, 1981, (with C. G. Ryn) Irving Babbitt in our Time, 1986; Modern Age: The First Twenty-Five Years. A Selection, 1988, In Continuity: The Last Essays of Austin Warren, 1996, The Essential Russell Kirk. Selected Essays, 2006; editl. advisor Modern Age: A Quar. Rev., 1971-77; assoc. editor, 1978-83, editor, 1984—; adv. bd. Continuity: A Jour. of History, 1984-88, Humanitas,

1993—; contbr. articles and revs. to profl. jours. Mem. Acad. Bd. Nat. Humanities Inst., 1985—; trustee Found. for Faith in Search of Understanding, 1987. Grantee Earhart Found., 1982, Henry Regnery award, 2003. Fellow Royal Soc. Arts (U.K.). Eastern Orthodox. Home and Office: PO Box Ab College Park MD 20741-3025 Office Phone: 301-779-6894. *In a profane age of unrest and breakdown, it is not enough for the critic to be purely and simply critical. He must work to conserve what is timeless, time-tested, time-honored. He must fight for causes he believes in, even if they appear to be lost causes. The critic's burden of responsibilty is also his vision of order.*

**PANISH, MORTON B.,** retired physical chemist; b. N.Y.C., Apr. 8, 1929; s. Isidore and Fanny (Glasser) P.; m. Evelyn Wally Chaim, Aug. 20, 1951; children: Steven, Paul, Deborah. Student, Bklyn. Coll., 1946-48; BS in Chemistry, Denver U., 1950; MS in Chemistry, Mich. State U., 1951, PhD in Phys. Chemistry, 1954. Chemist Oak Ridge (Tenn.) Nat. Lab., 1954-57; mem. tech. staff RAD div. AVCO Corp., Wilmington, Mass., 1957-61, sect. chief, 1961-64; mem. tech. staff Bell Telephone Labs. (now Bell Labs.), Murray Hill, NJ, 1964-69, dept. head, 1969-86, disting. mem. tech. staff, 1986-92; cons., 1992—2003. Mem. com. on microgravity rsch. NRC, 1991-96, mem. com. on future of space sci. rsch. priorities, 1994-95, space studies bd., 1996-98; mem. com. on human rights NAS, 1996-02. Co-author: Heterostructure Lasers, 1978, Gas Source Molecular Beam Epitaxy, 1993; contbr. numerous articles to profl. jours.; patentee in field. Mem. dean's adv. bd. Coll. Natural Sci., Mich. State U., 1990-95. Recipient Electrochem Soc. Electronics Divsn. award, 1972, Solid state medal, 1979, C&C Found. prize, Japan, 1986, Internat. Crystal Growth award Am. Assn. Crystal Growth, 1990, John Bardeen award The Minerals, Metals and Materials Soc., 1994, The Kyoto prize, 2001. Fellow IEEE (Morris N. Liebmann Meml. award 1991), Am. Phys. Soc.; mem. Nat. Acad. Engring., Nat. Acad. Scis. Avocation: photography. Home and Office: 52 Baldwin Rd Freeport ME 04032 Personal E-mail: mort@att.net.

**PANITCH, RONALD LOUIS,** lawyer; b. Newark, Feb. 10, 1941; BSME, NJ Inst. Tech., 1962; JD, Georgetown U., 1965. Patent examiner US Patent and Trademark Off., 1962; mng. ptnr. Panitch, Schwarze, Jacobs & Nadel, P.C., Phila., 1983; now ptnr.-in-charge Phila. Akin Gump Strauss Hauer & Feld LLP. Course chmn. ABA Am. Law Inst., Phila., 1990—. Assoc. editor Georgetown Law Jour. Named one of Best Lawyers in Phila., Phila. Mag., 1994, 1999; recipient Alumni Achievement Honor Roll medal, NJ Inst. of Tech., 2001. Mem. Phila. Bar Assn., Pa. Bar Assn., Phila. Patent Law Assn., Am. Intellectual Property Assn., Am. Law Inst. Office: Akin Gump Strauss Hauer & Feld LLP One Commerce Sq Ste 2200 2005 Market St Philadelphia PA 19103-7013 Office Phone: 215-965-1300. Office Fax: 215-965-1210. Business E-Mail: rpanitch@akigump.com.

**PANITZ, DANIEL R.,** psychologist, consultant; b. Bklyn., Aug. 1, 1945; s. Daniel Panitz and Lilian Victor. BA in Psychology, Rutgers U., 1963; MA in Psychology, New Sch., 1967; PhD candidate, NYU, 1972. Chief psychologist N.Y. State Narcotic Addiction Control, 1970—79; psychologist N.Y. State Alcoholism divsn., 1980—89; dir. Human Svcs., 1990—2004; project dir. Hope Internat. Ministeries, 2004—05; dir. Eagle Ministeries, 2005. Mem. editl. bd.: Am. Jour. Family Therapy, 1990—; composer (album): Songs Carried on Angel's Wings, 2001, In God We Trust, 2002; author: Poem, 2001. Named Humanitarian of the Yr., U.S. Congress, 2002, NY Gov. Mem.: Internat. Soc. Arts Acad. Scis. Achievements include coord. rescue efforts 9/11; participated rescue efforts Hurricanes Katrina and Rita; coord. rescue efforts Pakistan volcano. Avocation: writing. Office: 3840 Hillsboro Blvd Deerfield Beach FL 33442

**PANITZ, LAWRENCE,** physician; b. Apr. 30, 1928; s. Max and Gussie (Gorenstein) Panitz; m. Adrienne Ruth Luke, June 20, 1965; children: Jennifer, Michael. BA, NYU, 1962; MD, Upstate Med. U., Syracuse, 1966. Diplomate Am. Bd. Family Practice. Intern St. Joseph's Hosp., Syracuse, NY, 1966—67; pvt. practice gen. medicine Elmsford, NY, 1967—90, Hawthorne, NY, 1968—. Affiliated with Docs Physicians Beth Israel Med. Ctr., N.Y.C., Shrub Oak, NY, Hartsdale, NY, Larchmont, NY, Yonkers, NY, Thornwood, NY, Crestwood, NY, New City, West Haverstraw, NY; mem. staff New Rochelle Hosp., NY, St. Agnes Hosp., White Plains, NY, Westchester County Med. Ctr., Valhalla, NY, N.Y. Dobbs Ferry Hosp., Beth Israel Hosp. Med. Ctr., N.Y.C., Sound Shore Med. Ctr., Phelps Meml. Hosp., North Tarrytown, NY, dep. dir. dept. family practice; dir. Elmsford Med. Ctr.; police surgeon, Tarrytown, North Tarrytown, Sleepy Hollow, Elmsford, Town of Greenburgh; med. dir. Margaret Chapman Sch. Exceptional Child, Hawthorne; med. dir. prin. rschr. Clin. Tech. Assoc., Elmsford, CNS Bioservices, Pleasantville, NY; physician Westchester County Correctional Health Dept., Valhalla; sch. physician, Elmsford; cons., expert witness Vogel & Rosenberg, N.Y.C., Britcher, Leone & Roth, LLC, Glen Rock, NJ; cons. on malpractice litig. for law firms. With U.S. Army, 1946—48, with U.S. Army, 1982—88, lt. col. Med. Corps USAR. Fellow: AMA, Am. Acad. Family Physicians; mem.: Westchester Acad. Medicine, Westchester County Med. Soc., Med. Soc. State of N.Y., Masons, Shriners. Jewish. Home and Office: Riveredge 3 David Ln Yonkers NY 10701-1122 Office: 132 S Central Ave Elmsford NY 10523 Office Phone: 914-968-6135. E-mail: lp711md@aol.com.

**PANKAU, CAROLE,** state senator; b. Aug. 13, 1947; m. Anthony John Pankau Jr.; 4 children. BS, U. Ill., 1981. Mem. Ill. House of Rep., 1993—2004, Ill. Senate from 23th dist., 2004—. Mem. DuPage County (Ill.) Bd., 1984-92; committeeman Bloomingdale Twp. Rep. Precinct 70; mem. Keeneyville (Ill.) Sch. Dist. 20; vice chair Bloomingdale Twp. Rep. Orgn. also: One Tiffany Pointe Bloomingdale IL 60108 Office: 105-K State House Springfield IL 62706 E-mail: carole@pankau.org.

**PANKEN, PETER MICHAEL,** lawyer; b. N.Y.C., Dec. 30, 1936; s. Harold Ira and Sylvia Rita (Haimes) P.; m. Beverly Muriel Giubbini, June 19, 1960; children: Naomi, Molinda. BA cum laude, Haverford Coll., 1957; LLB magna cum laude, Harvard U., 1962. Bar: N.Y. 1962, U.S. Dist. Ct. N.Y. 1962, U.S. Ct. Appeals (2d cir.) 1969, (3d cir.) 1988, (10th cir.) 1989, (7th cir.) 2003, U.S. Supreme Ct. 1989. Assoc. Paul Weiss Rifkind Wharton Garrison, N.Y.C., 1962-66, Poletti Freiden Prashker Feldman & Gartner, N.Y.C., 1966-67, Parker Chapin Flattau & Klimpl, N.Y.C., 1967-72, ptnr., 1973-99, chair employment and labor law dept., 1986-99; mem. Epstein Becker & Green PC, N.Y.C., 1999—. Editor: Harvard Law Rev., 1961-62; author: A State-by-State Survey of the Law of Religion in the Workplace, 2001; contbg.: Employment Law Desk Book for Human Resources Professionals; editor-in-chief ALIABA Resource Materials: Employment and Labor Law; mem. bd. editors The Practical Litigator; contbr. articles to profl. jours. Pres., bd. dirs. Fedn. of Handicapped, N.Y.C., 1984-92; bd. dirs. Fedcap Rehab. Svcs., 1993—; pres. metro N.Y. chpt. Soc. for Human Resource Mgmt., 1990-92, gen. counsel, 1993-2003. Mem. ABA (labor and employment sect., com. on NLRB law, contbg. editor The Developing Labor Law), NY State Bar Assn. (labor and employment law sect., continuing legal edn. com.), Am. Law Inst.-ABA (chmn. employment and labor law programs), Am. Law Inst. (com. on restatement of agy. and restatement of employment law), Soc. for Human Resource Mgmt. (com. on employment practices 1990-99). Office: Epstein Becker & Green PC 250 Park Ave Ste 1200 New York NY 10177-1211 Office Phone: 212-351-4840. Business E-Mail: ppanken@ebglaw.com.

**PANKEY, GEORGE ATKINSON,** internist, educator, researcher; b. Shreveport, La., Aug. 11, 1933; s. George Edward and Annabel (Atkinson) P.; m. Patricia Ann Carreras, Sept. 22, 1972; children: Susan Margaret, Stephen Charles, Laura Atkinson, Edward Atkinson. Student, La. Poly. Inst., 1950-51; BS, Tulane U., 1954, MD, 1957; MS, U. Minn., 1961. Diplomate Am. Bd. Internal Medicine, Am. Bd. Infectious Disease. Intern U. Minn. Hosps., 1957-58, resident in internal medicine, 1958-60, Mpls. VA Hosp., Mpls. Gen. Hosp., 1960-61; practice medicine New Orleans, 1961—; ptnr. Ochsner Clinic, New Orleans, 1968-99; asst. vis. physician Charity Hosp. La., New Orleans, 1961-63, vis. physician, 1962-75, sr. vis. physician, 1975-95; cons. infectious diseases Ochsner Clinic Found., 1963—, head sect. infectious diseases, 1972-94, dir. infectious disease training program, 1972—94, dir. infectious disease rsch., 1999—; instr. dept. medicine, div. infectious diseases

Tulane U. Sch. Medicine, New Orleans, 1961-63, clin. instr., 1963-65, clin. asst. prof. medicine, 1965-68, clin. assoc. prof., 1968-73, clin. prof., 1973—; clin. prof. dept. medicine La. State U. Sch. Medicine, 1979—; clin. prof. oral diagnosis, medicine and radiology La. State U. Sch. Dentistry, 1983—; dir. Nat. Found. for Infectious Diseases, 2004—. Cons. World Health Info. Services Inc., 1974, Federal Air Surgeon, 1997—; dir, founder Century Nat. Bank, New Orleans; mem. medicine test com. Nat. Bd. Med. Examiners, 1979-83; mem. infectious diseases adv. bd. Hoffman-LaRoche, 1982—; dir. Nat. Found. Infectious Diseases, 2004—. Author: A Manual of Antimicrobial Therapy, 1969; co-author: (with Charles W. Gross and Michael G. Mendelsohn) Contemporary Diagnosis and Management of Sinusitis, 1997, 4th edit., 2004, (with Julia Garcia-Diaz and Layne O. Gentry) Contemporary Diagnosis and Management of Diabetic Foot Infections, 2006; editor: Infectious Diseases Digest, 1983-95, So. Med. Assn. Program for Infectious Diseases Dial-Access, 1983-92, Ochsner Clinic Reports on Serious Hosp. Infections, 1985—, Ochsner Clinic Reports on Geriatric Infectious Diseases, 1990-93, Ochsner Clinic Reports on the Mgmt. of Sepsis, 1991-93, Infectious Disease Clinics of N.Am., 1994, co-editor: (with Geoffrey A. Kalish) Outpatient Antimicrobial Therapy - Recent Advances, 1989; contbg. editor: Antimicrobial Therapy Guide, 17th edit., 2005; mem. editl. bd. Nat. Infectious Disease Info. Network, 1983; mem. editl. adv. bd. Compendium Continuing Edn. in Dentistry, 1984—, Quinolones Bull., 1985-93, Ochsner Jour., 1999—, Infectious Disease News, 2001—; contbr. numerous articles to profl. jours. Dir. Camp Fire Inc.; Pres. New Orleans Young Republican Club, 1969-71; adv. bd. Angie Nall Sch. Hosp., Beaumont, Tex.; trustee Nall Found. for Children, Beaumont. Recipient cert. merit Am. Acad. Gen. Practice, 1969, 70 Master ACP-ASIM (laureate award La. chpt. 1997); fellow Am. Coll. Preventive Medicine, Infectious Disease Soc. Am. (Clinician award 1996), Am. Coll. Chest Physicians, Royal Soc. Medicine; mem. Am. Soc. of Transplantation, Assn. Contamination Control (chpt. pres. 1968-70), Am. Fedn. Med. Rsch., So. Med. Assn. (certificate of award 1970), Am. Soc. Internal Medicine (del. ann. meeting 1971-72), Am. Soc. Microbiology, Am. Thoracic Soc., New Orleans Acad. Internal Medicine (pres. 1977-78, 96-97), AMA, Aerospace Med. Assn., Am. Soc. Tropical Medicine and Hygiene, Am. Venereal Disease Assn., Am. Soc. Parasitologists, Internat. Travel Medicine Soc., La. Soc. Internal Medicine (pres. 1972-73), La. Med. Soc., La. Thoracic Soc. (chmn. program com. 1968, governing council 1976-80), Surg. Infection Soc., Immunocompromised Host Soc., Musser Burch Soc., Orleans Parish Med. Soc., N.Y. Acad. Scis., Pan Am. Med. Assn. (diplomate mem. sect. internal medicine 1971, sect. pres. infectious diseases and virology 1978-85), SAR, Huguenot Soc. Founders Manakin in Colony of Va., Aviation Med. Examiner, Masons (32 deg), Shriners. Home: 5910 Prytania St New Orleans LA 70115-4348 Office: Ochsner Clinic Found 1514 Jefferson Hwy New Orleans LA 70121-2483 Office Phone: 504-842-4006. Personal E-mail: gpankey@ochsner.org.

**PANKO, JESSIE SYMINGTON,** education educator; b. Jan. 19, 1935; Student, Hunter Coll., N.Y., 1959-62; BA, MS, SUNY, 1969; PhD, Syracuse U., 1974. Tchr. Anderson Elem. Sch., Mariana Islands, Guam, 1964-65; tchr. Herman Ave. Elem. Sch., Auburn, NY, 1969-71; asst. prof. edn. dept. SUNY, Cortland, NY, 1971-76, Utica, Rome, NY, 1974-76; asst. prof. applied scis. dept. Loop Coll., Chgo., 1976-77; assoc. prof. social scis. dept. Truman Coll., Chgo., 1977-81; dir. student teaching St. Xavier Coll., Chgo., 1976—94, dir. undergrad. edn., 1977-79, dir. grad. edn., 1979-81, prof. edn. ctr., 1981-83, dir. grad. prog. in edn., 1983-86, dir. edn. ctr., 1986-89, dean sch. edn., 1989-92. Bd. dirs. Queen of Peace, Acad. of Our Lady; mem. com. grad. programs St. Xavier Coll., 1986-89, title com. coun., 1976-94, early childhood adv. bd., 1976-92. Moffett SUNY scholar, 1969. Mem. AAUP, ASCD, Am. Assn. Colls. of Tchr. Edn. (instnl. rep. 1987-92), Assn. Ind. Liberal Arts Colls. of Tchr. Edn. (instl. rep. 1986-92), Ill. Assn. of Tchr. Edn. in Pvt. Colls. (instnl. rep. 1985-98), Ill. Assn. Colls. Tchr. Edn. (coll. rep. 1981-98, sec. 1990-92), Assn. Tchr. Educators, Nat. Assn. Educatos Young Children, Ill. Dirs. Student Tchg., Chgo. Consortium Dirs. Student Tchg. (chairperson 1976-79), Ill. Assn. Tchr. Educators, Chgo. Area Dir. Student Tchg. (chmn. 2002-04), Pi Lambda Theta, Kappa Delta Pi. Office: St Xavier U 3700 W 103rd St Chicago IL 60655-3105 Office Phone: 773-298-3215. Business E-Mail: panko@sxu.edu.

**PANKOV, GRADIMIR KRUNISLAV,** ballet artistic director; b. Skopje, Macedonia, Yugoslavia, Oct. 25, 1938; s. Krunislav Ivan Pankov and Dragica Isak (Mihajlovska); m. Margret Maria Kaufmann, Dec. 30, 1980. Baccalaureat, Josip Broz Tito Gymnasium, Skopje, 1956; diploma, State Conservatory of Dance & Music, Skopje, 1957. Dancer Nat. Theatre Macedonia, Skopje, 1956-63; guest artist Nat. Theatres, Belgrade, Zagreb, Sarajevo, 1963-67; soloist City Theatres, Nuremberg, Karlsruhe, Wuppertal, Fed. Republic Germany, Theater Am Gärtnerplatz, Munich, 1967-74, Nat. Theatre, Mannheim, Fed. Republic Germany, 1974-76; ballet master City Theatre, Dortmund, 1976-80; artistic dir., tchr. Netherlands Dance Theatre Jr. Co., The Hague, 1980-81; artistic dir. Nat. Ballet of Finland, Helsinki, 1981-84; artistic dir., tchr. Cullberg Ballet, Stockholm, 1984-88; artistic dir. Ballet du Grand Theatre, Geneva, 1988-96, Les Grands Ballets Canadiens de Montreal, 2000—. Dancer (ballets) Mercutio in Romeo and Juliet, 1963, title role in Petrushka, 1965, title role in Pulcinella, 1971, The Faun in Afternoon of a Faun, 1975, choreographer (Operas) Eugene Onegin, 1977, Carmen, 1978, Don Giovanni, 1978. Office: Les Grands Ballets Canadiens de Montreal 4816, rue Rivard Montreal PQ H2J 2N6 Canada

**PANKOVE, JACQUES ISAAC,** retired physicist, researcher; b. Chernigov, Russia, Nov. 23, 1922; came to U.S., 1942, naturalized, 1944; s. Evsey Leib and Miriam (Simkine) Pantchechnikoff; m. Ethel Wasserman, Nov. 24, 1950; children: Martin, Simon. BSEE, U. Calif., Berkeley, 1944, MGEE, 1948; PhD in Physics, U. Paris, 1960. DSc (hon.), Nat. Poly. Inst., Grenoble, France, 2000. Mem. tech. staff RCA Labs., Princeton, NJ, 1948-70, physicist, fellow, 1970-85; prof. U. Colo., Boulder, 1985-93, prof. emeritus, 1993—, Hudson Moore Jr. Univ. prof., 1989-93, program mgr. materials and devices Ctr. for Optoelectronic Computing Systems, 1986-89; Disting. Rsch. fellow Nat. Renewal Energy Lab. (formerly Solar Energy Rsch. Inst.), 1985-93; v.p. for rsch. and tech. Astralux, Inc., 1992—2004; ret. Vis. McKay lectr. U. Calif., Berkeley, 1968-69; vis. prof. U. Campinas, Brazil, 1975; Disting. vis. prof. U. Mo., Rolla, 1984; participant NAS sci. exch. program with Romania, 1970, Hungary, 1972, Yugoslavia, 1976. Mem. hon. editl. bd. Solid State Electronics, 1970-94, Solar Energy Materials, 1984—, Optoelectronics, 1986-95; regional editor Crystal Lattice Defects and Amorphous Materials, 1984-90; author: Optical Processes in Semiconductors, 1971, 75, (ednl. film) Energy Gap and Recombination Radiation, 1962; editor: Electroluminescence, 1977, Display Devices, 1980, Hydrogenated Amorphous Silicon, 1984; co-editor: Hydrogen in Semiconductors, 1991, Wide Bandgap Semiconductors, 1992, III-Nitrides, 1997, Gallium Nitride Vol. I, 1998, Vol. II, 1999; designer: laser sculpture, Bklyn. Mus., 1968; contbr. articles to profl. jours.; patentee in field. Trustee Princeton Art Assn., 1970-82; mem. Experiment-in-Arts-and-Tech., Berkeley, 1968-69. Served with U.S. Army, 1944-46. Recipient RCA achievement awards, 1952, 53, 63, Faculty Rsch. award U. Colo. Coll. Engring. and Applied Sci., 1997, Rank Prize award Optoelectronics, 1998; David Sarnoff scholar, 1956, Disting. Alumnus award U. Calif., Berkeley, 2000. Fellow IEEE (J. J. Ebers award 1975, assoc. editor Jour. Quantum Electronics 1968-77, mem-at-large IEEE awards bd. 1992-95), Am. Phys. Soc.; mem. AAAS, Nat. Acad. Engring. (hon.), Materials Rsch. Soc., Sigma Xi. Home: 809 10th St Boulder CO 80302-7551

**PANNALA, SREEKANTH,** aerospace engineer; m. Venkat Narayan and Chandrakala Pannala; m. Maria Laura Cavallero, Aug. 29, 2005. B in Aerospace Engring., Indian Inst. Tech., Kharagpur, 1993; MS in Aerospace Engring., Ga. Tech, Atlanta, 1994; PhD in Aerospace Engring., Ga. Inst. Tech., Atlanta, 2000. Summer internship Aero. Devel. Establishment, Bangalore, Karnataka, India, 1991; grad. student asst. Ga. Tech, Atlanta, 1993—99; post-doctoral rsch. fellow Oak Ridge Inst. Sci. and Edn./Oak Ridge Nat. Lab., Tenn., 1999—2001; summer intern Defence R & D Lab., Hyderabad, Andhra Pradesh, India, 1992; rsch. staff mem. Oak Ridge Nat. Lab., Tenn., 2001—. Contbr. articles to profl. jours., chapters to books. Grad.

student sen. Ga. Tech, Atlanta, 1995—96; vol. Centennial Olympics, 1996, Paralympics, 1996; founder ASHA and Child Relief and You chpts. Ga. Tech, 1996—96; walk coord. Vibha, Sunnyvale, Calif., 1998—98, project monitoring coord., 2004—, nat. walk advisor, cons., 1999—; philanthrophy chair India Club Ga. Tech, 1997—98. Recipient Person Yr., India Club Ga. Tech, 1998; fellow, ORISE, 1999—2000, 2000—01. Mem.: AIChE, Siam Sac. Achievements include research in open source multiphase flow software; development of realistic simulation models for reacting two-phase flows in order to achieve more efficient and controllable spray combustion; reduced order model for bubbling fluidized beds; a detailed simulation model for simulating spouted bed coaters for nuclear fuel particles. Office: Oak Ridge Nat Lab Bldg 6012 MS-6367 RM-101 Oak Ridge TN 37831 Office Phone: 865-574-3129. Office Fax: 865-574-0680. E-mail: pannalas@ornl.gov.

**PANNELL, THIERRY EDGARD,** engineer, information technology manager; s. Frank James Pannell and Emiliene Eugenie Omont. AAS, Brookdale C.C., 1989; BS, So. Ill. U., 1991; MS, Regis U., 2003. Lic. gen. radio operators radar endorsement, FCC, 1991, cert. broadcast engr., Soc. of Broadcast Engrs., 1991, sr. electronics technician, ETA/Iowa State U., 1990, cert. electronics technician, ISCET, 1991. Electronics mechanic U.S. Navy, Colts Neck, NJ, 1983—88; electronics technician U.S. Marine Corps, Cherry Point, NC, 1988—90, U.S. Army Yuma Proving Ground, Yuma, Ariz., 1990—93; grad. tchg., rsch. asst. Ill. State U., Normal, Ill., 1993—94; electromagnetic test technician Delco Electronics, Kokomo, Ind., 1995; electromagnetic interference, electromagnetic compatability technician Ford Motor Co., Dearborn, Mich., 1996—98; sr. electro-mechnical technician Barry Controls, Brighton, Mass., 1998; assoc. electro-magnetic interference compatibility engr. Sundstrand Aerospace, Rockford, Ill., 1998—2000; hardware engr. Rockwell Automation, Mayfield Heights, Ohio, 2000; info. tech. analyst Caterpillar, Inc., Lafayette, Ind., 2004; train controls sys. engr. GE Rail, Erie, Pa., 2004—06. Cons. 24 Hour Club, Kokomo, Ind., 1999—2003, ClearView Windows, Hastings, Nebr., 2004. With U.S. Army, 1974—78. Mem.: Internat. Soc. Profl. Electronics Technicians (assoc.). Achievements include development of computer applications. Home: 1701 E Empire St Ste 360 #140 Bloomington IL 61704 Office Phone: 765-437-2588.

**PANNER, OWEN M.,** federal judge; b. 1924; Student, U. Okla., 1941-43, LL.B., 1949. Atty. Panner, Johnson, Marceau, Karnopp, Kennedy & Nash, 1950-80; judge, now sr. judge U.S. Dist. Ct. Oreg., Portland, 1980—, sr. judge, 1992—. Recipient Am. Bd. Trial Advocates Trial Lawyer of Yr., 1973. Mem. Am. Coll. Trial Lawyers, Am. Bd. Trial Advs., Order of Coif. Office: US Dist Ct 1000 SW 3rd Ave Ste 1207 Portland OR 97204-2942

**PANNETON, JEAN M.,** vascular surgeon; MD, U. of Montreal, Can., 1987. Lic. surgery Am. Bd. of Surgery, gen. surgery Royal Coll. of Physicians and Surgeons of Can., spl. competence in Vascular Surgery Royal Coll. of Physicians and Surgeons of Can., lic. vascular surgery Am. Bd. of Surgery. Clin. lectr. U. of Glasgow, Scotland, 1994—95; asst. prof. of surgery U. of Man., Winnipeg, Canada, 1995—97, Mayo Clinic Coll. of Medicine, Rochester, Minn., 1997—2002, assoc. prof. of surgery, 2002—04; assoc. prof. of clin. surgery Ea. Va. Med. Sch., Norfolk, Va., 2004—. Dir. of clin. rsch. in vascular surgery Mayo Clinic, Rochester, 2002—04. Contbr. articles to profl. jours., chpts. to books. Named Surg. Subspecialty Tchr. of the Yr., Mayo Clinic Grad. Sch. of Medicine, 2000; recipient Prix B.G. Bourgeois Award for Excellence in Surgery, U. of Montreal, 1987, Ctr. Hospitalier de la Baie des Chaleurs Found. scholarship, 1984, Prix Pierre Masson, U. of Montreal, 1983, Excellence in Tchg. Recognition award, Mayo Clinic Coll. of Medicine, 1999—2000, Walter C. MacKenzie, Johnson & Johnson / Ethicon award, Royal Coll. of Physicians and Surgeons of Can., 1994, R.S. McLaughlin Found. fellowship, McLaughlin Found. and U. of Montreal, 1994, Lange Med. Publ. award, U. of Montreal, 1987, Mosby Award for Scholastic Excellence, 1987, Prix E.P. Lachapelle for Scholastic Excellence, 1987, Merck Sharp and Dohme Award for Scholastic Excellence, 1987, Prix T. Parizeau for Excellence in Surgery, 1987. Fellow: ACS, Royal Coll. Surgeons of Can.; mem.: Internat. Soc. for Cardiovasc. Surgery, Internat. Soc. for Endovascular Specialists, Can. Assn. of U. Surgeons, Soc. for Clin. Vascular Surgery, Priestley Soc., Peripheral Vascular Surgery Soc. (intern. program com. 2002—02), Mayo Alumni Assn., Med. Soc. of Va., Chesapeake Med. Soc., Societe Francaise d'Angiologie (cons. of internat. com. 2003—06), Soc. for Vascular Surgery, Christian Med. and Dental Assn., Internat. Union of Angiology (sec. N.Am. chpt. 2002—06), Midwestern Vascular Surg. Soc., Societe de Chirurgie Vasculaire de Langue Francaise, Am. Assn. for Vascular Surgery, Can. Soc. for Vascular Surgery, European Soc. for Vascular Surgery (corr.). Achievements include research in Endovascular repair of aortic aneurysms. Office: Vascular and Transplant Specialists Ste 8620 600 Gresham Dr Norfolk VA 23507 Office Phone: 757-622-2649. Office Fax: 757-961-4992. Business E-Mail: jpanneton@vascularandtransplant.com.

**PANNKE-SMITH, PEGGY,** insurance company executive; b. Chgo., Oct. 26; d. Victor E. and Leona (O'Leary) Stich; m. Craig D. Smith, July 18, 1998; children from previous marriage: Thomas Scott, David Savonne, Heidi Mireille, Peter. V.p. long term care ins. Sales & Seminars, Des Plaines, 1986-90; pres., founder Nat. Consumer Oriented Agy., Des Plaines, 1990—. Cons. on long-term care ins. The Travelers, Tchrs. Inc. & Annuity Assocs., others; spkr. Exec. Enterprises, NYC, 1988—93. Columnist Sr. News, Vital Times, Daily Herald, Sr. Connection, Sr. Marketplace News, Prime Time for Seniors, Pioneer Press, Boulder Daily Camera, Longmont Times-Call, Aurora Sun, Mature Times Lifestyles, 50 Plus Marketplace. Sponsor Ill. Alliance for Aging, Chgo., 1990—, Ill. Assn. Homes for Aging, 1990-91; bd. govs. St. Matthew Luth. Home, Park Ridge, Ill., 1993-95. Recipient Spkrs. awards Health Ins. Assn. Am., Washington, 1990, Ret. Officers Assn., Glenview, Ill., 1991, 93, Nat. Assn. Sr. Living Industries, Denver, 1992, Exec. Enterprises, NYC, 1993, Gov.'s Conf. on Aging, Chgo., 1996, Golden Harvest Long Term Care award Ret. Officers Assn., 2001, Nat. awards UNUM, 2001, AIG 2002, Conseco, 2000, Allianz, 2002, Mut. of Omaha, 2003, Presidents Club, Lincoln Benefit. Mem.: Internat. Soc. for Retirement Planning, Am. Soc. on Aging, Mature Am., Nat. Coun. on Aging (ad hoc com.), Ctr. for Applied Gerontology, Nat. Assn. Long Term Care Profl., Nat. Assn. Sr. Living Industries, Friends of the Colo. Trail, Colo. Mountain Club, Boulder C. of C., Park Ridge C. of C., Kiwanis (bd. dir. Park Ridge 1992—98, pres. 1996—97, Boulder pres. 2006—), Am. Mensa (program dir. in Ill. 1983—85, Colo. chpt. 1999—, pres. Boulder chpt. 2003—). Avocations: showshoeing, travel, sketching wildflowers, hiking, trekking the Colorado Trail. Office: Nat Consumer Oriented Agy 2200 E Devon Ave Ste 303 Des Plaines IL 60018-4505 also: Cherry Creek 300 S Jackson St Denver CO 80209-3176 also: 4450 Arapahoe Ave Boulder CO 80303-9123 also: 250 Parkway Dr 150 Lincolnshire IL 60069 also: 1900 E Golf Rd 950 Schaumburg IL 60173 Office Phone: 800-554-1996. Business E-Mail: NCOAmmp@sbcglobal.net. E-mail: MyBestLTC@sbcglobal.net.

**PANOFF, STEPHEN EDWARD,** music educator; b. Washington, May 24, 1961; s. Robert and Kathleen Dorothy Panoff. BS in Math. and Music, Coll. of William and Mary, Williamsburg, Virginia, 1984; MusM Edn., Shenandoah U., Winchester, Va., 1997. Cert. postgrad. profl. tchr. Va., 2001. Asst. dir. of bands Tabb (Va.) H.S., 1984—96; dir. of bands Tallwood H.S., Virginia Beach, 1996—. Adjudicator Fiesta-Val Music Festivals, Richmond, Va., 1985—86; dir. Brass Menagerie, Tabb, Va., 1990—96; asst. dir. Shenandoah U. Fine Arts Camp, Winchester, Va., 1997—2001. Contbr. world premiere musical composition Ascensions, 1992; dir.(conductor): (musical performance) Heroes, Lost and Fallen, 2000, To Those Who Serve, 2001, (music performance to honor 9/11 victims) Band-aide, 2001, (conductor) (musical performance) Danzas Brillantes, 2002. Basketball rules interpreter Peninsula Bd. #125, Newport News, Va., 2000—02, basketball ofcl., 1985—2002. Nominee for Disney Am. Tchg. Award, 1999—2002. Mem.: Internat. Jazz Educators Assn., Va. Band and Orch. Dirs' Assn., Va. Music Educator Assn. Roman Catholic. Avocation: golf. Office: Tallwood HS 1668 Kempsville Rd Virginia Beach VA 23464 Personal E-mail: spanoff@cox.net. E-mail: sepanoff@vbcps.k12.va.us.

**PANOFSKY, WOLFGANG KURT HERMANN,** physicist, researcher; b. Berlin, Apr. 24, 1919; arrived in U.S., 1934, naturalized, 1942; s. Erwin and Dorothea (Mosse) Panofsky; m. Adele DuMond, July 21, 1942; children: Richard, Margaret, Edward, Carol, Steven. AB, Princeton U., 1938; PhD, Calif. Inst. Tech., 1942; DSc (hon.), Case Inst. Tech., 1963, U. Sask., 1964, Columbia U., 1977, U. Hamburg, Germany, 1984, Princeton U., 1983, Yale U., 1985, U. Beijing, 1987, U. Rome, 1988; degree (hon.), Uppsala U., Sweden, 1991. Mem. staff mem. radiation lab. U. Calif., 1945-51, asst. prof., 1946-48, assoc. prof., 1948-51; prof. physics Stanford U., 1951-62, prof. Stanford Linear Accelerator Ctr., 1962-89, prof. emeritus, 1989—; dir. Stanford (High Energy Physics Lab., Stanford Linear Accelerator Center), 1962-84, dir. emeritus, 1984—. Am. del. Conf. Cessation Nuclear Tests, Geneva, 1959; mem. Pres.'s Sci. Adv. Com., 1960—64; cons. Office Sci. and Tech., Exec. Office Pres., 1965—73, U.S. ACDA, 1968—81; mem. gen. adv. com. to White House, 1977—81; mem. panel Office Sci. and Techl. Policy, 1977; with nat. defense rsch. Calif. Inst. Tech. and Los Alamos, 1942—45; mem. JASON, 1965—; chmn. bd. overseers Superconducting Supercollider Univs. Rsch. Assn., 1984—93; mem. com. to provide interim oversight Dept. Energy nuclear weapons complex NAS, 1988—89; mem. panel on nuclear warhead dismantlement and special materials control Dept. Energy, 1991—92; mem. Commn. on Particles and Fields Internat. Union Pure and Applied Physics, 1985—93. Decorated officier Legion of Honor; named Calif. Scientist of Yr. 1966; recipient Lawrence prize, AEC, 1961, Nat. med. of Sci., 1969, Franklin medal, 1970, Ann. Pub. Svc. award, Fedn. Am. Scientists, 1973, Enrico Fermi award, U.S. Dept. Energy, 1979, Shoong Found. award for sci., 1983, Hilliard Roderick prize Sci., AAAS, 1991, Matteucei medal, 1997. Fellow: Am. Phys. Soc. (pres. 1974); mem.: AAAS, NAS (mem. com. on internat. security and arms control 1985—, chmn. com. 1985—93, mem. scis. com. on scholarly comm. with China 1987—92), Chinese Acad. Scis. (fgn.), Nat. Acad. Lincei (Italy), Russian Acad. Scis., French Acad. Scis. (fgn.), Am. Philos. Soc. (pres. 1974—75), Sigma Xi, Phi Beta Kappa.

**PANSINI, MICHAEL SAMUEL,** financial analyst, tax specialist; b. Molfetta, Italy, July 12, 1928; arrived in U.S., 1935; s. Ralph and Isabel (Cirilli) P.; m. Anna D'Angelo, June 5, 1949 (div. 1970); children: Elizabeth, Valerie, Michael; m. Elizabeth Bischoff, Oct. 3, 1970 (div. Feb. 1992); 1 child, Elissa Michelle. BS, NYU, 1950, MBA, 1952, LL.M., 1960; LL.D., Fordham U., 1956. Bar: N.Y. 1956, U.S. Tax Ct. Tax mgr. Pfizer Corp., N.Y.C., 1951-64; asst. treas. Hooker Chem. Corp., N.Y.C., 1964-69; treas., dir. United Indsl. Corp., N.Y.C., 1969-72; sr. v.p., gen. counsel Beker Industries Corp., Greenwich, Conn., 1972-87; pres., dir. Panmer, Inc., 1987—; tax, fin. cons., 1987—; v.p. corp. counsel Champion Energy Corp. and affiliates, 1991-93, Champion Holdings Co. and affiliates, 1993-96. V.p., chmn. various coms. Tax Exec. Inst., N.Y.C., 1963-72; pres., dir. Fed. Tax Forum, Inc., N.Y.C., 1961-72; dir. Intelligent Bus. Communications Corp. Mem. Rep. Town Com. 19th Dist., Stamford, Conn., 1993—; commr., vice chmn. Econ. Devel. Commn., Stamford, 1994—; bd. dirs. Stamford Sr. Ctr., 2000—; bd. dir., treas. Women's Bus. Devel. Ctr., Inc., 2003—, Food Bank of Lower Fairfield County, 2004—. Mem. North Stamford Assn. (bd. dirs. 1999—2005, v.p. 2000, pres. 2001), Sr. Men's Assn. Stamford (dir., 2d v.p.). Republican. Home and Office: 76 Lawrence Hill Rd Stamford CT 06903-2120

**PANTALEO, PETER S.,** lawyer; BA, Univ. Wis., 1971; JD with honors, Univ. ND, 1976. Bar: Pa. 1976, ND 1977, DC 1989. Atty. Verner Liipfert Bernhard McPherson and Hand; ptnr. Piper Rudnick, Washington, 2002—04; ptnr., chair labor and employment law practice group DLA Piper Rudnick Gray Cary LLP, Washington, 2005—. Editor-in-chief ND Law Rev.; lectr.; contbr. articles to profl. jours. Mem.: ABA, Inst. of Directors, London. Office: DLA Piper Rudnick Gray Cary LLP 1200 Nineteenth St NW Washington DC 20036-2412 Office Phone: 202-861-3956. Office Fax: 202-223-2085. Business E-Mail: peter.pantaleo@dlapiper.com.

**PANTANO, DANIELE,** poet, educator; b. Langenthal, Bern, Switzerland, Feb. 10, 1976; U.S. s. Giuseppe Pantano and Katharina Wiest; m. Nicole Renée Boyer, June 23, 1997; children: Fiona, Giacomo. BA in Philosophy, U. South Fla., 2003, MA in Creative Writing, 2005. Instr. U. South Fla., Brandon, 2003—, Writing Ctr. coord., 2005—. Adj. prof. Fla. So. Coll., 2006—. Office: U South Fla 527 Emberwood Dr Brandon FL 33511

**PANTEL, GLENN STEVEN,** lawyer; b. Plainfield, N.J., Sept. 25, 1953; s. Donald and Sarah Libby (Pearlman) P.; m. Lisa Pamela Krop, June 28, 1981; 1 child, Adam Scott. AB, Johns Hopkins U., 1975; JD, U. Pa., 1978. Bar: N.J. 1978, U.S. Dist. Ct. N.J. 1978, Pa. 1978, Fla. 1980, U.S. Ct. Appeals (3d cir.) 1982. Law clk. to presiding judge U.S. Dist. Ct. (so. dist.), Miami, Fla., 1978-79; from assoc. to ptnr. Shanley & Fisher P.C., Morristown, NJ, 1979-99, also bd. dirs.; ptnr. Drinker Biddle and Reath LLP, Florham Park, NJ, 1999—. Trustee, mem. scholarship com. 200 Club of Somerset County. Mem. ABA, Fla. Bar Assn., N.J. Bar Assn., Morris County Bar Assn., Phi Beta Kappa. Avocations: skiing, sailing. Home: 3 Cross Way Mendham NJ 07945-3120 Office: Drinker Biddle & Reath LLP 500 Campus Dr Florham Park NJ 07932-1047

**PANTHAKI, ZUBIN JAL,** medical educator, plastic surgeon; b. Bombay, Feb. 26, 1968; arrived in U.S., 2000; s. Jal Minocher Panthaki and Nergish Nanabhoy Sethna. B in Engring., McGill U., 1991, MD, 1995. Diplomate Am. Bd. Plastic Surgeons, cert. for hand surgery Am. Bd. Plastic Surgeons, lic. N.H., Calif., Fla. Surgery resident McGill U., Montreal, 1995—2000; microsurgery and hand surgery fellow Buncke Clinic, San Francisco, 2000—01; asst. prof. plastic surgeon U. Miami, Fla., 2001—05; assoc. program dir. plastic surgery residency Univ. Miami. Cons. Miami Children's Hosp., 2001—05, Cedar's Hosp., Miami, 2001—05, Jackson Meml. Hosp., Miami, 2001—05; assoc. program dir. plastic surgery U. Miami, 2005—. Book editor: Jour. Craniofacial Surgery, 2004—05. Vol. Interplast, 2003—. Capt. med. engrs., 1987—2000, Can. Fellow: Royal Coll. Surgeons; mem.: Miami Soc. Plastic Surgeons (v.p. 2006—), Fellow Am. Coll. Surgeons, Fla. Soc. Plastic Surgeons, Nat. Bd. Med. Examiners, Am. Soc. Plastic Surgeons. Avocation: computers. Home: 1800 Sunset Harbour Dr Apt 2215 Miami Beach FL 33139 Office: Univ Miami Jackson Meml 1611 NW 12th Ave ET-3019 Miami FL 33136 Office Phone: 305-585-5285. Office Fax: 305-324-7384. Business E-Mail: zpanthaki@med.miami.edu.

**PANTOJA, JUAN LUIS,** hospital administrator, educator; b. Caracas, Venezuela, July 12, 1963; s. Luis Ramon Pantoja and Luisa Ramona Rodriguez; m. Marianella Seijas, Dec. 29, 2001; children: Luis Alejandro, Alexandra. MD, U. Autonoma Guadalajara, Jalisco, Mex., 1989; MS in Health Svcs. Adminstrn., Nova Southeastern U., Davie, Fla., 1991. Utilization rev. McKesson Health Solutions, Fla., utilization mgmt. McKesson Health Solutions, Fla., healthcare risk mgmt. Fla. Risk Mgmt. Inst. Med. dir. Fed. Assist, Miami, 2001—05; coord. clin. admissions Kindred Hosp., Ft. Lauderdale, Fla., 2005—. Cons. medical billing V&L Med. Billing, Miami, 2000—02; adj. faculty Broward C.C., Coconut Creek, Fla., 2003—. Contbg. author: Manual de Emergencias Medicas, 1990. Contbr. Emmaus Group, Miami, 1999. Recipient Outstanding Acad. Achievements award, Miami Dade C.C., 1980—82. Mem.: South Fla. Healthcare Exec. Forum, Am. Coll. of Healthcare Execs. Avocations: history, travel, cooking. Office Phone: 954-356-5136.

**PANTOLIANO, JOE,** actor; b. Hoboken, NJ, Sept. 12, 1951; s. Dominic and Mary Pantoliano; m. Morga Kester, 1979 (div. 1985); 3 children; m. Nancy Sheppard, Feb. 18, 1994; 1 child. Actor: (stage prodns.) Brothers, 1982, Orphans, 1983, One Flew Over the Cuckoo's Nest, Italian American Reconciliation, The Death Star, Visions of Kerouac, (feature films) The Godfather Part II, 1974, The Idol Maker, 1980, Monsignor, 1982, Risky Business, 1983, Eddie and the Cruisers, 1983, The Mean Season, 1985, Goonies, 1985, Running Scared, 1986, The In Crowd, 1987, The Squeeze, 1987, Scenes from the Goldmine, 1987, Amazon Women on the Moon, 1987, La Bamba, 1987, Empire of the Sun, 1987, Midnight Run, 1988, Downtown, 1990, The Last of the Finest, 1990, Short Time, 1990, Zandalee, 1991, Used People, 1992, Three of Hearts, 1993, The Fugitive, 1993, Baby's Day Out,

1994, Calendar Girl, 1994, Steal Big, Steal Little, 1995, Bad Boys, 1995, Bound, 1996, Top of the World, 1997, Self Storage, 1997, Tinseltown, 1997 (also assoc. prodr.), The Tax Man, 1998, U.S. Marshals, 1998, The Life Before This, 1999, Black and White, 1999, Tinseltown, 1999, The Matrix, 1999, Ready to Rumble, 2000, Memento, 2000, Silver Man, 2000, (voice) Cats & Dogs, 2001, The Adventures of Pluto Nash, 2002, A Piece of My Heart, 2002, Daredevil, 2003, Bad Boys II, 2003, 5-25-77, 2003, Second Best, 2004 (also prodr.), A Piece of My Heart, 2004, (voice) Racing Stripes, 2005, The Check Up, 2005, The Moguls, 2005, (voice) The Easter Egg Adventure, 2005, Larry the Cable Guy: Health Inspector, 2006; (TV movies) More Than Friends, 1978, Alcatraz: The Whole Shocking Story, 1980, Destination: America, 1987, El Diablo, 1990, One Special Victory, 1991, Through the Eyes of a Killer, 1992, (voice) Olive, the Other Reindeer, 1999, (TV mini-series) From Here to Eternity, 1979, Robert Kennedy and His Times, 1985, (TV spl.) Mr. Roberts, 1984 (TV Series) Free Country, 1978, The Fanelli Boys, 1990-91, Sugar Hill, 1999, The Sopranos, 2001-02 (Emmy award best sup. actor drama, 2003), Dr. Vegas, 2004-05; writer, dir. (films) Just Like Mona, 2003; TV appearances include Tales From the Crypt, Amazing Stories, L.A. Law, The Hitchhiker, NYPD Blue, Arliss$, Hill Street Blues, The Hitchhiker, Highlander, The Marshal. Avocations: skiing, jogging, shopping. Office: UTA care Lisa Hellerman 9560 Wilshire Blvd Fl 5 Beverly Hills CA 90212-2401*

**PANTUSO, VINCENT JOSEPH,** food service consultant; b. Charleston, W.Va., Aug. 13, 1940; s. Fortunato F. Pantuso and Josephine Malcom (Ginestra) Pantuso Messer; m. Carol Barber, Dec. 10, 1964 (div. 1976); children: Lisa, Barbara, Tina; m. Nancy Josephine Chellman, Sept. 30, 1978 (div. 1995). Student, Drexel U.; BSBA, St. Joseph's U., 1968; postgrad., Rollins Coll., 1984-85. Asst. mgr. Marriott Hotels, Inc., Bethesda, Md., 1962-64; v.p. sales mktg. ARA Services, Inc., Phila., 1964-72; sr. v.p. Interstate United Corp., Chgo., 1972-84; pres. V.J. Pantuso Services, Inc., Orlando, Fla., 1984—, New Vista Services, Inc., 1988-97. Mem. Nat. Assn. Concessionaires (bd. dirs. 1982—, pres. 1989-91, chmn. 1991-94, Master Concessionaire, Chgo. 1985), Nat. Assn. Food Equipment Mfrs. (doctorate 1989). Republican. Episcopalian. Avocation: fishing. Home: Apt 5 120 Monarch Cir Casselberry FL 32730-2718 Office Phone: 407-539-0000.

**PANUSKA, CAROLYN MARIE,** science educator; b. Balt., Aug. 13, 1947; d. Howard Charles and Niala Marie Overman; children: Elizabeth Shrader, Jonathan, Mark. BA in Chemistry, Mt. St. Agnes Coll./Loyola, Balt., 1969; MSc in Chemistry, Morgana State U., Balt., 1981. Adminstrv. I cert. Towson U., Balt., 2001. Lab. technician Md. State Dept. Health, Balt., 1969, Bexar County Health Dept., San Antonio, 1970; tchr. West Jr. H.S., Blytheville, Ark., 1970, Immaculate Concept Sch., Blytheville, 1971, The Catholic H.S., Balt., 1979—85; tchr., dept. chair Loyola Blakefield, Balt., 1985—95, Balt. County Pub. Sch., 1995—. Instr./subject area coord. Johns Hopkins Ctr. for Talented Youth, Balt., 2000—05. Co-author: (book) Chemistry in the Environment, 1989; curriculum writer: Balt. Pub. Schs. Ecology of Md. and Chesapeake Bay. Mem. Chesapeake Bay Found., Annapolis, Md., 1979—. Named Woodrow Wilson Master Tchr., Camille & Henry Dayfur Found., Princeton, N.J., 1989; recipient scholarship, Nat. Audubon Soc., 1996. Mem.: NSTA, Nat. Audubon Assn. Roman Catholic. Avocations: camping, canoeing, skiing, bicycling. Office: Balt County Pub Schs 5401 Kenwood Ave Lutherville MD 21093 Business E-Mail: cpanuska@bcps.org.

**PANUSKA, JOSEPH ALLAN,** retired academic administrator; b. Balt., July 3, 1927; s. Joseph William and Barbara Agnes (Preller) P. BS, Loyola Coll., Balt., 1948; PhD, St. Louis U., 1958; STL, Woodstock Coll., 1961; LLD (hon.), U. Scranton, 1974; LHD (hon.), Marywood Coll., 1992; D of Health (hon.), Trnava U., Slovakia, 1997. Joined S.J., 1948; ordained priest Roman Cath. Ch., 1960. Instr. dept. physiology Emory U. Sch. Medicine, 1962-63; asst. prof. biology Georgetown U., 1963-66, assoc. prof., 1966-72, prof., 1973; provincial, bd. dirs. Jesuit Conf. Md. Province (S.J.), 1973-79; acad. v.p., dean faculties, prof. biology Boston Coll., 1979-82; pres. U. Scranton, Pa., 1982-98, pres. emeritus, 1998—2004; rector Jesuit Ctr. 1988—2003; pres. emeritus, 2004—. Mem. Pa. Commn. Ind. Colls. and Univs., 1982-98 mem. exec. com., treas., 1987-91, vice chmn., 1988-89, chmn., 1990-91; mem. Pres.'s Commn., NCAA, 1989-90; spiritual dir. Scranton Ctrl. City Ministerian, bd. dirs., 2003—. Mem. editl. bd. Crybiology, 1968-88, editor-in-chief, 1971-74; contbr. chpts. to books, articles to sci. rsch. jours. Mem. corp. Am. Found. Biol. Rsch., 1967-85, pres. bd. dirs., 1974-79, v.p., 1979-83; trustee Loyola Coll., 1979-85, St. Joseph's U., 1979-84, U. Scranton, 1970-73, 1982-98, St. Peter's Coll., 1971-72, Woodstock Coll., 1973-76, Fordham U., 1982-88, Cambridge Ctr. for Social Studies, 1973-79 (pres. 1973-79), Corp. Roman Cath. Clergymen, 1973-79 (pres. 1973-79); rector Jésuit Cmty. at Georgetown U., 1970-73; bd. dirs. United Way Pa., 1985-87, Scranton Prep. Sch., 1984-90, Scranton Area Found., 1997-98, John Carroll U., 1992-98, Nat. Inst. Environ. Renewal, 1992-98, Woodstock Theol. Ctr., Washington, 1998-2001, St. Joseph's Prep. Sch., Phila., 1998-2001, Alvernia Coll., 2001—, Ctrl. Scranton (Pa.) Ministerium, 2004—; chmn. Pa. Commn. for Ind. Colls. and Univs., 1990-91; bd. visitors Panuska Coll. Profl. Studies, U. Scranton, 1998-; pres. emeritus, spiritual dir. and advancement Campus Ministry. NIH postdoctoral fellow, 1962-63; recipient Danforth Found. Harbison prize for disting. tchg., 1969, B'nai B'rith Americanism award, 1997, recipient from 2001, Michelini award Outstanding Svc. to Higher Edn. AICUP (Assoc. Ind. Coll. and U. Pa.), 2001; vis. fellow St. Edmunds Coll., Cambridge U., 1969; college named J.A. Panuska Coll. of Profl. Studies, Univ. at Scranton, Interfaith Person of Yr. Scranton Ctrl. City Ministerium, 2004. Mem. Assn. Jesuit Colls. and Univs. (bd. dirs. 1982-98, treas. 1993-96), Pa. Assn. Colls. and Univs. (exec. com., adv. com. to State Bd. Edn. 1990-91). Home and Office: Jesuit Cmty U Scranton Scranton PA 18510-4623 Office Phone: 570-941-6594. Business E-Mail: panuskaj1@scranton.edu. *In order to be happy in a leadership role and to succeed in it, I have to possess a sense of coherence with my life values. I also need to recognize that my own activity makes a real difference in the empowerment of others so that there is a multiplier effect which extends me beyond my own person and activity.*

**PANUTHOS, PETER J.,** federal judge; b. NY, 1943; BS, Bernard Baruch Sch. Bus., CUNY; diploma, Bryant Coll., Providence, RI, 1966; JD, Suffolk U. Law Sch., Boston, 1969; LLM in Taxation, Boston U. Sch. Law, 1972. Bar: DC, admitted to: Supreme Jud. Ct., Mass., US Supreme Ct. Trial atty., asst. dist. counsel Boston Office of Chief Counsel, IRS, 1970—83; spl. trial judge US Tax Ct., 1983—92, chief spl. trial judge, 1992—. Adj. prof. Bentley Coll., Boston, Catholic U. of Am., Columbus Sch. Law, David A. Clarke Sch. Law, U. of DC; mem. law rev. Suffolk U. Law Sch. Mem.: ABA, Inns of Ct., Fed. Bar Assn. Office: US Tax Ct 400 Second St NW Washington DC 20217

**PANWAR, SHIVENDRA SINGH,** education educator, researcher; b. Delhi, India, Dec. 15, 1959; came to U.S., 1981; s. Surendra Singh and Lakshmi (Singh) P.; m. Shruti Kumari, Apr. 8, 1988. B Tech., Indian Inst. Tech., Kanpur, India, 1981; MS, U. Mass., Amherst, 1983, PhD, 1986. Tchr., rsch. asst. U. Mass., Amherst, 1981-85; asst. prof. Poly. U., Bklyn., 1985-90; assoc. prof. Poly U., Bklyn., 1990—2003, prof., 2003—. Vis. scientist IBM Rsch., Yorktown Heights, N.Y., 1987; spl. cons. AT&T Bell Labs., Holmdel, N.J., 1988; dir. N.Y. State Ctr for Adv. Tech. in Telecom., 1996—. Co-author TCP/IP Essentials: A Lab Based Approach, 1994; contbr. articles to profl. jours. Recipient Rsch. Initiation award NSF, Washington, 1989 Mem. IEEE (sr., tech. com. computer comms., Leonard G. Abraham prize 2004), Sigma Xi, Tau Beta Pi. Hindu. Office: Polytechnic Univ Six Metrotech Ctr Brooklyn NY 11201-2907

**PANY, KURT JOSEPH,** finance educator, consultant; b. St. Louis, Mar. 31, 1946; s. Joseph Francis and Ruth Elizabeth (Westerman) P.; m. Darlene Dee Zabish, June 3, 1971; children: Jeffrey, Michael. BSBA, U. Ariz., 1968; MBA in Mgmt., U. Minn., 1971; PhD in Accountancy, U. Ill., 1977. CPA, Ariz., cert. fraud examiner. Staff auditor Arthur Andersen & Co., Mpls., 1968-69; Touche Ross & Co., Phoenix, 1971-73; teaching asst. U. Minn., Mpls., 1969-71; teaching asst. U. Ill., Urbana, 1972-76; asst. prof. acctg. Ariz. State U., Tempe, 1977-81, assoc. prof., 1981-85, Arthur

Andersen/Don Dupont prof. acctg., 1985-91. Mem. acctg. and auditing standards com. State of Ariz., Phoenix, 1989—; reviewer Jour. Acctg. and Pub. Policy, 1983—. Contbg. author: CPA Exam. Rev., 1983—; co-author: Principles of Auditing, 1988—, Auditing, 1993—; co-editor Auditing: A Jour. Practice and Theory, 1984-88; mem. editl. bd. Advances in Acctg., 1982—, Jour. Acctg. Edn., 1983—; reviewer Acctg. Rev., 1984—, ad hoc editor, 1989—; contbr. numerous articles to profl. jours. Active various child-related orgns. Peat, Marwick, Mitchell & Co. Found. grantee, 1985. Fellow AICPA (auditing stds. divsn. 1989-90, acctg. lit. selection com. 1989-90, acctg. lit. awards com. 1979-83, mem. auditing stds. bd. 1995—); mem. Am. Acctg. Assn. (tech. program com. 1980-81, chairperson Western region auditing sect. 1981-83, acctg. lit. nominating com. 1982-84, 88-89, acctg. lit. selection com. 1989-90, dir. auditing stds., chmn. auditing stds. com. 1990-93), Ariz. Soc. CPA's (auditing stds. com. 1978-81, ethics com. 1981-84). Avocation: baseball. Address: 7445 S Rita Ln Tempe AZ 85283-4792 Office: Ariz State U Sch Accountancy Tempe AZ 85287 Business E-Mail: kpany@cox.net, kurt.pany@asu.edu.

**PANZARINO, SAVERIO JOSEPH,** physician; b. East Orange, N.J., Nov. 29, 1930; s. Joseph Saverio and Pasqua (Binetti) P.; m. Suzanne Laico, Apr. 24, 1934; children: Laura, Kathleen. BA, Columbia Coll., 1952; MD, U. Rome, 1957. Diplomate Am. Bd. Pediat. Surgery. Intern St. Vincent's Hosp., N.Y.C., 1957-58; resident in gen. surgery Manhattan VA Hosp., N.Y.C., 1958-62; fellow in pediat. surgery Hosp. for Sick Children, London, 1962-63; pvt. practice, 1963-90; ret.; clin. assoc. surgery Columbia Coll. Physicians and Surgeons, N.Y.C., 1980-90. Part-time med. legal cons., 1990—. Recipient Bowen Brooks scholarship N.Y. Acad. Medicine, 1962. Fellow ACS; mem. AMA, Am. Acad. Pediats. Home and Office: 53 Sentinel Dr Basking Ridge NJ 07920-4231

**PANZER, MARY CAROLINE,** historian, museum curator; b. Flint, Mich., May 29, 1955; d. Milton and Caroline Alice (Weis) P. BA, Yale U.; MA, Columbia U., 1980; PhD, Boston U., 1990. Asst. prof. U. Kans., Lawrence, 1989-91; curator photographs Spencer Mus. Art, Lawrence, 1989-91; asst. dir. SMART Mus. Art U. Chgo., 1991; curator photographs Nat. Portrait Gallery Smithsonian Instn., Washington, 1992-2000; ind. historian N.Y.C., 2000—; adj. faculty NYU, 2002—, Hunter Coll., CUNY, 2003. Author: Philadelphia Naturalistic Photography, 1982, Rudolf Eickemeyer, Jr. and the Art of the Camera, 1986, Mathew Brady and the Image of History, 1997, Halsman: A Retrospective, 1998, Brady 55, 2001, Hine 55, 2002 Separate, But Equal, 2002, Nickolas Muray and Miguel Corarrubias, 2004, Things as They Are: Photojournalism in Context Since 1955, 2005 (winner Infinity award, 2006); contbg. editor Am. Photo, 2002. Mem. Am. Studies Assn., Coll. Art Assn., Oracle, Mid-Atlantic Radical Historians Orgn., Orgn. Am. Historians.

**PANZERA, ANTHONY,** artist; BS, SUNY, New Paltz; MFA, So. Ill. Univ., Carbondale. Teacher, fine arts, Hunter Coll., CUNY, 1968—, Bklyn. Coll., NY Acad. of Art; co-dir. Art in Florence/Rome Summer program; fresco instr. RI Sch. of Design; now faculty Nat. Acad., NYC. Mem. Abbey Mural Com. Nat. Acad. One-man shows include Bates Coll., Lewiston, Maine, Marsh Art Gallery, Richmond, Va., Colgate Univ. Art Gallery, Hamilton, NY, Ariz. State Univ. Mart Mus., Tempe, exhibited in group shows at Nat. Acad. Annuals, Century Assn., Leubsdorf Gallery, Laurel Tracy Gallery, Red Bank, NJ, NJ State Mus., Trenton, Robert Wilson Gallery, Nantucket, Represented in permanent collections Bristol-Myers Squibb Collection, Princeton, Jane Voorhees Zimmerly Art Mus., New Brunswick, NJ, others; contbr. articles on art history to Art World Mag. Office: National Acad Faculty 5 E 89th St New York NY 10128 Office Phone: 212-996-1908. Office Fax: 212-426-1711.

**PAO, CHIA-VEN,** mathematics professor; b. Ho-hsien, China, Aug. 10, 1933; s. Chuan-S. and Shyu-Xi Pao; m. Mei-Shan K. Pao; children: Gene S., Bing S., Phillip S. BS, Nat. Taiwan U., 1959; M, Kans. State U., 1962; PhD, U. Pitts., 1968. Engr. Westinghouse Elec. Co., Pitts., 1962—67; tchg. asst. U. Pitts., 1967—68, rsch. assoc., 1968—69, asst. prof., assoc. prof., 1969—79; prof. N.C. State U., Raleigh, 1979—2002, prof. emeritus, 2002—. Pres. Cen-Condo Corp., Raleigh, 1984—89; chmn. Cen Karlay Ptnrship., Raleigh, 1986—93. Contbr. over 150 articles to profl. jours. Mem.: Fedn. Nonlinear Analysis. Avocations: music, ballroom dancing, travel, reading. Office: NC State U Dept Math Box 8205 Raleigh NC 27695 Business E-Mail: cvpao@math.ncsu.edu.

**PAOLANTONIO, SAL,** sports correspondent; b. Queens, N.Y. BA in History, SUNY, Oneonta, 1977; M in Journalism, NYU, 1978. Reporter Albany Times Union; host Sat. Morning Sports Page Sta. WIP-AM, Phila., 1993-95; reporter Inquirer News Tonight Sta. WPHL-TV, Phila., 1994-95; polit. reporter Phila. Eagles Phila. Inquirer, 1985-93, beat reporter Phila. Eagles, 1993-95; NFL SportsCenter corr. ESPN, 1995—; NFL Columnist ESPN.com, 2003—. Author: The Last Big Man in Big City America, 1993. With USN, 1979-83. Recipient Mng. Editor's award for enterprise reporting AP, 1985, Sports Editor award for Reporting, 1994. Office: care ESPN ESPN Plz 935 Middle St Bristol CT 06010*

**PAOLINI, CLAIRE JACQUELINE,** dean, educator; b. Newton, Mass., May 19, 1934; d. Frank and Angelina Landro; m. Gilberto Paolini, June 18, 1960; children: Angela J., John F. BA, Boston U., 1956; MA, Middlebury (Vt.) Coll., 1958; PhD, Tulane U., 1982. Instr. Spanish U. Mass., Amherst, 1956-60, U. New Orleans, 1970-75; from dir. internat. student affairs to assoc. dean Loyola U., New Orleans, 1975-83, assoc. dean arts and scis., 1983-97; dean coll. arts and scis., prof. spanish Sacred Heart U., Fairfield, Conn., 1997—. Author: The Narrative Art of Domingos Monteiro, 1979, Valle-Inclán's Modernism: Use and Abuse of Religious and Mystical Symbolism, 1986; editor: LA CHISPA '95: Selected Proceedings, 1995, LA CHISPA '97: Selected Proceedings, 1997; co-editor: La CHISPA '99: Selected Proceedings, 1999; assoc. editor: LA CHISPA '93: Selected Proceedings, 1993; mem. editl. bd. LA CHISPA, 1983, 85, 87, 89, NACADA Jour., 1995-97. V.p. Soc. Espanola, New Orleans, 1977-81, bd. mem. 1976-97. Nat. Assn. Academic Affairs Administrators (Administrator of Yr. award 1996-97), Modern Lang. Assn., Council Colls. Arts Scis., Am. Assn. Tchrs. Spanish and Portuguese, Coll. Consortium Internat. Studies (bd. mem. 1997—), Am. Assn. Higher Edn. Home: 3 Gregory Farm Rd Easton CT 06612-2049 Office: Sacred Heart Univ 5151 Park Ave Fairfield CT 06825-1000 Office Phone: 203-396-8020. Business E-Mail: paolinic@sacredheart.edu.

**PAOLINI, GILBERTO,** literature educator; b. L'Aquila, Italy; naturalized citizen, 1954; s. John and Assunta Angela P.; m. Claire Jacqueline Landro; children: Angela Janet, John Frank. BA, Buffalo, 1957, MA, 1959; postgrad., Middlebury Coll., summer 1960, 61; PhD, Minn., 1965. Lectr. Spanish Rosary Hill Coll., Buffalo, 1957-58; instr. Italian and Latin lit. U. Mass., Amherst, 1958-60; instr. Spanish and Italian Syracuse U., 1962-65, asst. prof., 1965-67; assoc. prof. Spanish lit. Tulane U., New Orleans, 1967-76, prof. comparative lit., 1976—; dir. Tulane scholars and honors program, 1981-83, chmn. colloquia dept., 1981-83. Originator Spanish Culture Week, New Orleans, 1977, 79; chmn. adv. com. Jambalaya program Nat. Endowment Humanities, New Orleans, 1975-80; Spanish essay reader Ednl. Testing Svc., Princeton, 1979-85; founder, gen. Chmn. La. Conf. on Hispanic Langs. and Lits., 1981, 83, 85, 87, 89, 93, 95, 97, 99. Author: Bartolome Soler: novelista: Procedimientos estilísticos, 1963; An Aspect of Spiritualistic Naturalism in the Novel of B.P. Galdos: Charity, 1969, La Vita Transeciare nel Contado Aquilano, 2003; mem. editl. bd.: Forum Italicum, 1967-71, Critica Hispanica, 1979—, Discurso Literario, 1985—, Letras Peninsulares, 1987—, Ojáncano, 1994—; assoc. editor South Central MLA Bull, 1978-80; editor: La Chispa: Selected Procs., 1981-99, Papers on Romance Literary Relations, 1983; cons. editor South Central Rec., 1988-99; contbr. articles to profl. jours. With AUS, 1952-54, USAF, 1954-57. Recipient Disting. Service award Sociedad Espanola, 1979, Knight Cross of Order of Isabel the Catholic, 1984; subject of Festscrift Studies, Honor of Gilberto Paolini, 1996. Mem. MLA, AAUP, Am. Assn. Tchrs. Spanish and Portuguese (chmn. pub. rels. com. 1981-86, pres. La. chpt. 1979-81, 88-89), Am. Assn. Tchrs. Italian, Am. Assn. Advancement Humanities, Soc. for Lit. and Sci., Asociacion Internacional de Hispanistas, Southeastern Am. Soc. 18th Century

Studies (exec. v.p.), Assn. Internat. Galdosistas, Soc. Literatura Española del Siglo XIX, Phi Sigma Iota, Sigma Delta Pi (v.p. for S.W. 1989-92). Office: Tulane Univ 304 Newcomb Hall New Orleans LA 70118 Business E-Mail: gpaolini@tulane.edu.

**PAOLINO, RONALD MARIO,** clinical psychologist, consultant, psychopharmacologist, pharmacist; b. Providence, Mar. 15, 1938; s. Lawrence and Mary Corinne (Guglielmi) P.; m. Eileen Frances Quimby, June 18, 1960; children: Lisa Katherine, David Lawrence. Student, Providence Coll. 1955—56; BS in Pharmacy, U. R.I., 1959, MS, 1961; PhD in Pharmacology/Toxicology, Purdue U., 1963; postdoctoral studies Exptl. Psychology, Yale U., 1963—65; doctoral studies in clin. psychology, Purdue U., 1972—74; postdoctoral studies in existential analytic psychotherapy, Okla. Inst. Existential Analysis and Psychotherapy, 1974—75; Hostage Negotiation, FBI, 1991, Advanced Hostage Negotiation, 1995; Crisis Negotaition, FBI Acad., 1994; MA (hon.), Brown U., 1977. Lic. psychologist, R.I., pharmacist R.I.; nat. registered health svc. provider in psychology; cert. arbitrator; cert. nat. registered group psycho-therapists; cert. edn. provider N.Y.; diplomate Am. Bd. Forensic Examiners, Am. Bd. Forensic Medicine. Intern dept. psychiatry and behavioral scis. U. Okla. Health Scis. Ctr., 1974—75, NIMH fellow in clin. psychology, 1974-75; David Ross predoctoral fellow dept. pharmacology/toxicology Purdue U., West Lafayette, Ind., 1961—63, assoc. prof. psychopharmacology, 1967—74; NIMH postdoctoral fellow in psychology dept. psychology Yale U., 1963—65; asst. prof. pharmacology U. Conn. Sch. Pharmacy, 1965—67; coord. group psychotherapy tng. program Brown U. Program in Medicine, 1983—85, assoc. prof. psychiatry and human behavior, 1976—90; pvt. practice; chief drug dependency treatment program VA Med. Ctr., Providence, 1975—87, dir. biofeedback clinic, 1977—87, primary hostage negotiator, 1991—. Psychiatric cons. VA Police, alternative Dispute Resolution Mediator, New Eng. Veterans Integrated Svc. Network, 1996—, pain mgmt. bd., 1999—; mem. Pharmacology and Therapeutic Agts. Com., 1979-87, VA Med. Ctr., coord. VA Contracted Half-Way Project for Substance Dependent Vets., 1981-85, chmn. Pain Mgmt. Task Force, 1984-85, mem. Supervisory Level Pharmacy Profl. Standards Bd., 1990—, mem. Mgmt. Suicidal and Violent Patient Task Force, 1990-91, chmn. Com. Prevention & Mgmt. of Disturbed Behaviors, 1991—, chief crisis mgmt. program, 1993-96, advisor FBI Hostage Negotiations, 1991—, instr. R.I. State Police Acad., 1994, Instr., Drug Recognition Experts Recert PRGM, R.I. Dept Health, 1995, Faculty, Law Enforcement Mgmt. Command Sch. U.R.I. 1991—, Va. Nat. Law Enforcement Tng. Ctr., 1997; chmn. Outpatient Psychiatry Svcs. Reorganization Task Force, 1991, mem. VA DOD Desert Storm Emergency Plan Com., 1991; advisor OSHA Dept. Labor for Violence in the Work Place, 1994-95; mem. E. Prov. Clergy & Mental Health Providers Alliance, 1995—; mem. substance abuse and prevention grant application rev. com. R.I. Adv. Coun. on Substance Abuse, 1982-92, prevention, edn. and tng. com. on substance abuse, 1981—, chmn. 1981-82; adj. assoc. prof. psychology, U. R.I., 1982—, clin. assoc. prof. pharmacy U. R.I., 1998—; mem. planning com. State Conf. on Substance Abuse in the Hispanic Community, 1986; mem. alcohol awareness commn. Episc. Diocese of R.I., 1983-85; gubernatorial appointee Gov.'s Permanent Coun. on Drug Abuse Control, 1978-82; mem. rev. com. for funding of state drug abuse programs R.I. Single State Agy. on Drug Abuse, R.I. Dept. Mental Health Retardation and Hosps., 1978-82; cons. Nurses Renewal Com., 1980-81, substance abuse prevention edn. for elem. sch. children R.I. chpt. ARC, 1977, mem. suicide prevention steering com., 1977; mem.Interagy. Drug Abuse Steering Com., Lafayette, Ind. 1969-72; bd. dirs. Providence VA Med. Ctr. Credit Union; mem. bd. cert. for alcoholism counselors R.I. Assn. Alcohol Counselors, 1979-81; mem. Gov.'s Task Force on Substance Abuse at Adult Correctional Instn., 1977-78, Gov.'s Task Force on Mental Health Svcs. at Adult Correctional Instn., 1977-78, chmn. reclassification of inmates com., 1977-78; chmn. com. on edn. and cert. biofeedback practioners Conn. Biofeedback Soc., 1977-78; summer faculty fellow U. Conn., 1967; vis. scientist lectr. Assn. Am. Colls. Pharmacy, 1972-73; cons. to bus., unions, law enforcement. Author: (2 chpts.) Drug Testing: Issues and Options, 1991; contbr. 37 articles to profl. jours. Bd. dirs. R.I. chpt. Samaritans Internat. Suicide Prevention Orgn., 1978-84; v.p. Experience Jesus Inc.; mem. com. adv. bd. Cpina Bifida Assn. R.I., 1980-83; mem. R.I. East Bay Interfaith Mental Health Alliance; congressman appointee (Patrick J. Kennedy); mem. veterans adv. commn., 1995—. Recipient Citation award for svc. and contbns. to formulation of state policy for treatment and prevention of drug abuse Gov. R.I., 1983, Letter of Commendation, Gov.'s R.I. Adv. Coun. on Substance Abuse, 1986, vc. Recognition award DAV, 1990, Spl. Contbn. award Providence VA Med Ctr., 1990, 98, 99, 2000, Outstanding Performance award, 1991, 92, 93, 94, 97, cert. appreciation for continued excellence in patient care, 1999; named to Cranston Hall of Fame, 2001. Fellow Am. Coll. Forensic Examiners; mem. AMA, Am. Psychotherapy Assn., Am. Soc. Pharmacology Exptl. Therapeutics, Internat. Brain Rsch. Orgn., Internat. Narcotic Enforcement Officers Assn., R.I. Group Psychotherapy Soc. (pres. 1991-93, continuing edn. dir. psychologists 1990-95, exec. bd. 1986—, tng. faculty 1985—, co-dir. tng. 1986-87, tng. adv. bd. 1985-86), R.I. Psychol. Assn. (chmn. substance abuse ins. subcom. 1986-87, rep. Gov.'s Coun. on Mental Health State Plan Com. 1982-84), Hostage Negotiators Am. Office: Mental Health and Behavioral Scis Svc VA Med Ctr Providence RI Mail: ronald.paolinophd@med.va.gov.

**PAOLOZZI, JENNIFER,** elementary school educator; b. Providence, Nov. 10, 1982; d. Walter Benjamin and Laure Jean Paolozzi. BS, Salve Regina U., 2004. Cert. ESL. After sch./night program asst. Sullivan Sch., Newport, RI, 2002—05; circulation asst. Salve Regina U., Newport, 2003—04; tchr. 1st and 2d grade Newport Pub. Schs., 2004; tchr. 2d grade Cranston (RI) Pub. Schs., 2004—05; tchr. 1st grade New Haven (Conn.) Pub. Schs., 2005—. Mem.: Internat. Reading Assn. Avocations: softball, swimming, reading. E-mail: paolozzj@yahoo.com.

**PAOLUCCI, ANNE ATTURA,** playwright, poet, literature educator, educational consultant; b. Rome; d. Joseph and Lucy (Guidoni) Attura; m. Henry Paolucci(dec.). BA, Barnard Coll.; MA, Columbia U., PhD, 1963; D (hon.), Lehman Coll., CUNY, 1995. Mem. faculty English dept. Brearley Sch., N.Y.C., 1957—59; asst. prof. English and comparative lit. CCNY, 1959—69; rsch. prof. St. John's U., Jamaica, NY, 1969—75, prof. English, 1975—77, acting head dept. English, 1973—74, chmn. dept. English, 1982—91, dir. doctor of arts degree program in English, 1982—97; ednl. cons.; editl. cons. Bagehot Coun. Fulbright lectr. in Am. drama U. Naples, Italy, 1965-67; spl. lectr. U. Urbino, summers 1966-67, U. Bari, 1967, univs. Bologna, Catania, Messina, Palermo, Milan, Pisa, 1965-67; disting. adj. vis. prof. Queens Coll., CUNY; bd. dirs. World Centre for Shakespeare Studies; spl. guest Yugoslavia Ministry of Culture, 1972; rep. U.S. at Internat. Poetry Festival, Yugoslavia, 1981; founder, exec. dir. Coun. on Nat. Lits., 1974—; mem. exec. com. Conf. Editors Learned Jour.-MLA, 1975—85; del. to Fgn. Lang. Jours., 1977—85; mem. adv. bd. Commn. on Tech. and Cultural Transformation, UNESCO, 1978—80; vis. fellow Humanities Rsch. Centre, Australian Nat. U., 1979; rep. U.S. woman playwright Inter-Am. Women Writers Congress, Ottawa, Ont., Can., 1978; organizer, chmn. profl. symposia, meetings; TV appearances; hostess Mag. in Focus, Channel 31, N.Y.C., 1971-72; mem. N.Am. Adv. Coun. Shakespeare Globe Theatre Ctr., 1981—; mem. Nat. Social Fellows Program Fellowship Bd., 1985—87; mem. Nat. Garibaldi Centennial Com., 1981; trustee Edn. Scholarship, Grants Com. of NIAF, 1990-94; guest spkr. with E. Albee Ohio No. State U., 1990; Apptd. by Pres. Reagan to Nat. Coun. on Humanities, 1986-1993; One of the 10 top Women in Bus. in Queens, 2003. Author (with H. Paolucci) books, including: Hegel On Tragedy, 1962, new edition, 2001, From Tension to Tonic: The Plays of Edward Albee, 1972, new edit., 2000, Pirandello's Theater: The Recovery of the Modern Stage for Dramatic Art, 1974, 2d edit. 2002, Henry Paolucci: Selected Writings on Literature and the Arts; Sci. and Astronomy; Law, Govt., and Pol. Sci., 1999, Dante's Gallery of Rogues, 2001, Do Me a Favor (and other short stories), 2001 (nominated for the Pulitzer Prize), Poems Written for Sbek's Mummies, Marie Menken, and Other Important Persons, Places, and Things, 1977, Eight Short Stories, 1977, Sepia Tones, 1985, 2nd edit. 1986, In Wolf's Clothing, 2004; plays include: Minions of the Race (Medieval and Renaissance Conf. of Western Mich. U. Drama award 1972), video

version, 2002, Cipango!, 1985, pub. as book, 1985, 86, videotape excerpts, 1986, revision, 1990; performed NYC and Washington, 1987-88, Winterthur Mus., U. Del., 1990; The Actor in Search of His Mask, 1987, Italian translation and prodn., Genoa, 1987, The Short Season, Naples, 1967, Cubiculo, NY, 1973, German translation, Vienna, 1996, mini-prodn. of Minions of the Race, The Players, 1999, video prodn. 2002, In the Green Room (play), 1999, Three Short Plays, 1995, Slow Dance to Samara,; editor with introduction: Readings in the Divine Comedy, 2006; poems Riding the Mast Where It Swings, 1980, In the Green Room (orig. play), 1999; Gorbachev in Concert, 1991, Queensboro Bridge (and other Poems), 1995 (Pulitzer prize nominee 1995-96), Terminal Degrees, 1997; contbr. numerous articles, rev. to profl. jour.; editor, author intro. to: Dante's Influence on Am. Writers, 1977; gen. editor tape-cassette series China, 1977, 78; founder Coun. on Nat. Lit.; gen. editor series Rev. Nat. Lit., 1970-2000, CNL/Quar. World Report, 1974-76, semi-ann., 1977-84, ann., 1985-2000; full-length TV tape of play Cipango! and ednl. TV with original music by Henry Paolucci, 1990, grant Queens Pub. TV for 48 Min Videotape of award-winning play, Minions of the Race, 2003, About Thomas More, Thomas Cromwell, and Cardinal Thomas Wolsey, 2003-04; featured in PBS psl. Italian-Americans II: A Beautiful Song, 1998; translations of Selected Poems by Giacomo Leopardi (with Thomas Bergin), 2004 (Italian Ministry Fgn. Affairs prize 2005), The Woman in Dante's "Divine Comedy" and Spenser's "Faerie Quene", 2005; editor: Background of the "Divine Comedy", 2006. Pres. Reagan appointee Nat. Grad. Fellows Program Fellowship Bd., 1985—86, Nat. Coun. Humanities, 1986—. Ann. award FIERI, 1990; bd. dirs. Am. Soc. Italian Legions of Merit, chmn. cultural com., 1990—; bd. dirs. Italian Heritage and Culture City-wide com., Feb.—; mem. Columbus. Countdown 1992 Fedn.; mem. Gov. Cuomo's Heritage Legacy Project for Schs., 1989—; trustee CUNY, 1996—, chairwoman bd. trustees, 1997—99; mem. adv. com. on edn. N.Y. State Senate, 1996—. Decorated cavaliere Italian Republic, commendatore Order of Merit (Italy); named one of 10 Outstanding Italian Ams. in Washington, awarded medal by Amb. Rinaldo Petrignani, 1986; recipient Notable Rating for Mags. in Focus series N.Y. Times, 1972, Woman of Yr. award Dr. Herman Henry Scholarship Found., 1973, Amita award, 1970, award Women's Press Club N.Y., 1974, Gold medal for Quincentenary Can. trustee NIAF, 1990, ann. awards Consortium of Italian-Am. Assns., 1991, Am.-Italian Hist. Assn., 1991, 1st Columbus award Cath. Charities, 1991, Leone di San Marco award Italian Heritage Coun. of Bronx and Westchester Counties, 1992, Children of Columbus award Order of Sons of Italy in Am., 1993, 1st Nat. Elena Cornaro award Order of Sons of Italy, 1993, Golden Lion award, 1997, Can.'s Gold medal Christopher Columbus Can. Commn., 1992, Ann. award Am. Italian Cultural Roundtable, 1997, Am. Italian Tchrs. Lifetime Achievement award, 1997, Italian-Am. Legislator's award, Albany, 1997, N.Y. State Italian-Am. Legis. Lifetime Achievement award, 1997, Columbus Citizens Fedn. Ann. award, 1997, Italian Welfare League award, 1998, Queens Coun. on Arts award, 1998, N.Y. State Conservative Party Bronx com. award, 1998, Woman of Distinction award Kingsborough C.C./CUNY, 1999, Woman of Distinction award N.Y. State Senate, 2000, prize Italian Ministry Fgn. Affairs, 2005; named one of "Ten Top Queens Women in Bus.", 2003; Columbia U. Woodbridge hon. fellow, 1961-62; Am. Coun. Learned Socs. grantee Internat. Pirandello Congress, Agrigento, Italy, 1978; Women of the First Woodbridge fellow Dept. English and Comparitive Literature, Columbia U., 2005. Mem. Internat. Shakespeare Assn., Shakespeare Assn. Am., Renaissance Soc. Am., Internat. Comparative Lit. Assn., Am. Comparative Lit. Assn., MLA, Am. PEN, Hegel Soc. Am., Dante Soc. Am. (v.p. 1976-77), Am. Found. Italian Arts and Letters (founder, pres.), Pirandello Soc. (pres. 1978-85), Am. Soc. Italian Legions of Merit (bd. dir. 1990-93). Achievements include pioneering work in multi-comparative literary studies. *My own first practical premise has been to organize every task (even routine chores) so that there is always time and energy for whatever important projects come up. There is enough room in the day for doing a number of things—and for creating "space" every so often to do one's own special work (writing fiction or poetry or plays, in my case). Organization is all-important; but perhaps the basic premise in intellectual things is organic growth, letting "in" those things that are meaningful because they already suggest an intrinsic pattern. In my case, I discovered long after the projects had been themselves had taken shape and had been published, that I had been tending for a number of years more and more exclusively toward drama and dramatic criticism and theory. Well, that, obviously, was my own potential "law" organizing from within my various interests. One must continue to allow for new interests to revitalize those already familiar.*

**PAONE, PETER,** artist; b. Phila., Oct. 2, 1936; s. George and Angelina (Vitrella) P.; m. Alma Alabilikian, 1976. BA, Phila. Mus. Coll. Art, 1958. Head graphics dept. Fleisher Art Meml., 1959—62; instr. Phila. Mus. Coll. Art, 1959—66, Positano Art Sch., Italy, 1961—64, Pa. Acad. Fine Arts, 1978—, chmn. graphics dept., 1978; instr. Pratt Inst. One-man shows include Grippi Gallery, 1959—61, Phila. Print Club, 1961—64, Ft. Worth Mus., 1963, Clydie Jessop Gallery, London, 1968, David Gallery, Houston, 1970—72, Kennedy Gallery, NYC, 1970—72, Robinson Gallery, Houston, 1978—79, Hooks Epstein Gallery, 1978, 1980—83, Pa. Acad. Fine Arts, 1983, Phila. Print Club, 1983, Hooks Epstein Gallery, 1985, 1987—88, 1990, Rider Coll., NJ, 1991, Ryder Coll., Pa., 1991, Merlin Verlag, Hamburg, Germany, 1996, Dresden, Germany, 1996, Pascal Robinson Gallery, Houston, 2000, exhibited in group shows at Poets, Phila. Mus. Art, 1960—61, Contemporary Am., 1961, Lehigh U., Pa., 1962, Bklyn. Mus., 1962, Poets, Phila. Mus. Art, 1963, Paris Biennial, 1963, Dallas Mus., 1964, Otis Art Inst., LA, 1964, Syracuse U., NY, 1964, La Escuela Nacional, Mexico City, 1967, Vanderbilt U., 1967, NY World's Fair Exhbn., Pakistan, 1967, 176 Anniv. Nat. Acad. Design, NYC, 2001, Poets, Nat. Acad. of Design Mus., 2003, Jersey City Mus., 2004, James A. Michener Mus., Doylestown, Pa., 2004, Lancaster Mus., 2006. Represented in permanent collections Libr. Congress, Washington, DC, Phila. Mus., Art, NY Mus, Modern Art, Princeton Univ., Phila. Libr., Gen. Mills, Phila. Print Club, Rosenwald Collection, Carl Sandburg Meml. Libr., Syracuse U., Ft. Worth Mus., Victoria and Albert Mus., Brit. Mus., Art Inst. Chgo., Yale U. Recipient award of merit Phila. Print Club, 1983, Painting prize Nat. Acad., 1997; Tiffany Found. grantee, 1962, 64; John Simon Guggenheim fellow, 1965-66; grantee Penn Council for the Arts, 1985, Nat. Portrait Gallery, Washington. Mem. NAD. Home: 1027 W Westview St Philadelphia PA 19119-3718 Personal E-mail: ppaone@aol.com. *Somewhere between the world of realism and surrealism, there is a world that deals with the reality of relationships, favoring the substance of the imagination rather than the substance of everyday vision. Objects that seemingly have no real relationship to each other in their existence are juxtaposed in the life of the artist. They have touched each other and have become part of the vision, and in turn have become his iconography. There is no urgency in this vision. The private reality has always been there and always will be. The viewer is allowed to question his knowledge of it, and in doing so, he often is uneasy and bewildered before the assemblage. This, at first, implies fantasy; this is not true. Instead, this is a reconstruction of reality, not an escape from it.*

**PAPA, JOSEPH C.,** pharmaceutical executive; BS in Pharmacy, U. Conn.; MBA in Mktg. and Fin., Northwestern U. Kellogg Grad. Sch. Mgmt. Pharmacist; with Geneva Pharms., Ciba Geigy Pharms., Novartis Pharms. Corpn.; pres. US ops. Searle Pharms.; pres. global country ops. N.Am. Pharmacia Corpn.; pres., COO DuPont Pharms., Watson Pharms. Inc., 2001—04; grp. pres. Pharm. Technologies and Svcs. Cardinal Health, 2004—. Office: Cardinal Health 7000 Cardinal Pl Dublin OH 43017*

**PAPA, MARK GARY,** oil and gas industry executive; b. Monroeville, Pa., Sept. 16, 1946; s. Mark W. Papa and Jean Feiler; m. Susan Berryman, Dec. 21, 1970; 1 child, Christine. BS in Petroleum Engring., U. Pitts., 1968; MBA in Econs./Fin., U. Houston, 1980. Registered profl. engr., Tex. Various petroleum engring. supervisory & engring. positions Conoco, Inc., various locations, 1968-81; divsn. prodn. coord. Belco Petroleum, Houston, 1981-82, mgr. ops., 1982-83; v.p. drilling and prodn. Belnorth, Houston, 1983-84, sr. v.p. drilling and prodn., 1984-85; sr. v.p. ops. Enron Oil & Gas, Houston 1986—94, pres. N.Am. ops., 1994—98, pres., 1996—99, COO, 1997—98, CEO, 1998—99; chmn., CEO EOG Resources, 1999—. Bd. dir. Oil States Internat., Magellan Midstream Partners; chmn. U.S. Oil & Gas Assn. Mem.

Soc. Petroleum Engrs., Am. Assn. Petroleum Geologists, Natural Gas Supply Assn., Tex. Ind. Prodrs. Royalty Orgn. Avocation: tennis. Office: EOG Resources 333 Clay St PO Box 4362 Houston TX 77002

**PAPA, VINCENT T.,** insurance company executive; b. N.Y.C., Dec. 11, 1946; s. Frank R. and Carmela (Farruggia) P.; m. Karen Ann Conroy, July 4, 1969; children: Kimberly, Jennifer, Kristen. AA, Nassau C.C., 1967; BBA, Hofstra U., 1969. CPA, N.Y. Staff acct. Arthur Andersen & Co., N.Y.C., 1969-72; comptr. Finserv Corp., N.Y.C., 1972-80; sr. v.p. Orion Capital Corp., N.Y.C., 1980-99; chmn. bd. dirs. Wm. H. McGee & Co. Inc., N.Y.C., 1995-99; CEO NYMAGIC Inc., 1999. Mem. AICPAs, Am. Mgmt. Assn. (mem. ins. and risk mgmt. coun.), N.Y. State Soc. CPAs.

**PAPACHRISTOU, COSTAS JOHN,** physicist, researcher; b. Athens, July 16, 1957; s. John C. and Katherine (Luckmas) Papachristou. BS in Physics, U. Athens, 1981; PhD, Brigham Young U., 1987. Postdoctoral assoc. Brigham Young U., Provo, Utah, 1987—88; faculty Ctr. Naval Edn. for Petty Officers, Athens, 1988—89; faculty dept. physics Naval Acad. Greece, Piraeus, 1989—. Course dir. Athens Inst. Tech., 1989-93, 96—. Contbr. articles to profl. jours. John E. Anderson scholar Brigham Young U., 1981-87. Mem. N.Y. Acad. Scis., Sigma Xi, Phi Kappa Phi. Avocations: music, poetry. Office: Naval Acad Greece Dept Physics 18539 Piraeus Greece Office Phone: 30-210-4581616. Business E-Mail: papachristou@snd.edu.gr.

**PAPADAKIS, CONSTANTINE N.,** academic administrator, civil engineer, educator; b. Athens, Greece, Feb. 2, 1946; came to U.S., 1969; s. Nicholas and Rita (Masciotti) P.; m. Eliana Apostolides, Aug. 28, 1971; 1 child, Maria. Diploma in Civil Engring., Nat. Tech. U. Athens, 1969; MS in Civil Engring., U. Cin., 1970; PhD in Civil Engring., U. Mich., 1973. Registered profl. engr., Ohio, Greece. Engring. specialist, geotechnical group Bechtel, Inc., Gaithersburg, Md., 1974-76, supr. and asst. chief engr. geotechnical group Ann Arbor, Mich., 1976-81; v.p., bd. dirs. water resources div. STS Cons. Ltd., Ann Arbor, 1981-84; v.p. water and environ. resources dept. Tetra Tech-Honeywell, Pasadena, Calif., 1984; head dept. civil engring. Colo. State U., Ft. Collins, 1984-86; dean Coll. Engring. U. Cin., 1986-95, dir. Groundwater Rsch. Ctr., 1986-95; dir. Ctr. Hill Solid and Hazardous Waste Rsch. Ctr. EPA, Cin., 1986-93; pres. Drexel U., Phila., 1995—. Adj. prof. civil engring. U. Mich., 1976-83; cons. Gaines & Stern Co., Cleve., 1983-84, Honeywell Europe, Maintal, Fed. Republic of Germany, 1984-85, Arthur D. Little, Boston, 1984-85, Camargo Assocs., Ltd., Cin., 1986, King Fahd U. Rsch. Inst., Dhahran, Saudi Arabia, 1987, King Abdulaziz City for Sci. and Tech., Riyadh, Saudi Arabia, 1991, Henderson & Bodwell Cons. Engrs. Inc., 1991, Cin. Met. Sewer Dist., 1992, Ohio River Valley Water Sanitation Commn., 1994; acting pres. Ohio Aerospace Inst., 1988-90; interim pres. Inst. Advanced Mfg. Scis. Ohio Edison Tech. Ctr., 1989-90; bd. govs. Edison Materials Tech. Ctr., 1988-95; adv. bd., founding mem. Hamilton County Bus. Incubator, 1988-95; bd. dirs. Nat. Commn. for Coop. Edn., U. City Sci. Ctr., Ben Franklin Tech. Ctr., WHYY Inc., Fidelity Fed. Bank, Opera Co. of Phila., Corcell, Inc., Greater Phila. First, Hellenic Coll./Holy Cross Acad. Author: Problems on Strength of Materials, 1968, Sewer Systems Design, 1969; editor: Fluid Transients and Acoustics, 1978, Pump-Turbine Schemes, 1979, Small Hydro Power Fluid Machinery, 1982; Megatrends in Hydraulics, 1987; contbr. more than 65 articles to profl. jours. Mem. Greater Cin. C. of C. Blue Chip Campaign for Econ. Devel. Task Force, 1988-93, bd. dirs. Bus. Assistance Ctr., 1989-95; mem. Ohio Coun. on Rsch. and Econ. Devel., 1988, Ohio Sci. and Tech. Commn. Adv. Group, 1989-90, 92-95; coun. mem. St. Nicholas Ch. Parish, Ann Arbor, 1981-84; mem. City of Ft. Collins Drainage Bd., 1984-86; bd. dirs. Dan Beard coun. Boy Scouts Am., 1995, Intelligent Vehicle Hwy. Soc. Ohio, 1994-95; bd. dirs. Liberty Bell Coun. of the Boy Scouts of Am., 1994; Recipient Horace W. King scholarship civil engring. dept. U. Mich., 1971-73, 6 Bechtel Merit awards, 1974-79, Young Engr. of Yr. award Mich. Soc. Profl. Engrs., Ann Arbor, Mich., 1982, Disting. Engr. award Engrs. and Scientists Cin. Tech. Soc. Coun., 1989, Acad. of Achievement in Edn. award Am. Hellenic Ednl. Progressive Assn., 1995, Hellenic Univ. Club of Phila. Achievement award, 1996, Krikos Disting. Hellene Leader award, 1996. Fellow ASCE (pres. Ann Arbor br. 1980-81, pres.-elect Mich. sect. 1983-84, hydraulics divsn. publ. com. 1980-83), ASME (chmn. fluid transients com. 1978-80, mem. fluids engring. divsn. awards com. 1981-84), Am. Soc. Engring. Edn.; mem. NSPE (legis. and govt. affairs com. 1994-95, chair profl. engrs. in edn. divsn. 1995), Order of the Engr., Internat. Assn. for Hydraulic Rsch., Ohio Engring. Tech. Coun. (chmn.-elect 1989-91), Rotary, Sigma Xi, Chi Epsilon, Tau Beta Pi. Greek Orthodox. Avocations: photography, classical music, travel, swimming, racquetball. Home: 75 Crestline Rd Wayne PA 19087-2611 Office: Drexel Univ Main Building 310 3141 Chestnut St Philadelphia PA 19104-2875 Office Phone: 215-895-2100. E-mail: papadakis@drexel.edu.*

**PAPADAKIS, EMMANUEL PHILIPPOS,** physicist, consultant; b. NYC, Dec. 25, 1934; s. Philippos E. and Helen (Eastman) P.; m. Stella Christopher, Sept. 4, 1960; children: Susan H., Philip E., Christopher E., Nicholas E. BS in Physics, MIT, 1956, PhD in Physics, 1962; M.M. in Mgmt., U. Mich., 1979. Mem. tech. staff Bell Telephone Labs., Allentown, Pa., 1962-69; dept. head Panametrics, Inc., Waltham, Mass., 1969-73; prin. staff engr. Ford Motor Co., Detroit, 1973-75, supr., 1975-87; ptnr. E&S Antiques, 1978—; pres. Quality Sys. Concepts Inc., 1991—; assoc. dir. Ctr. for Nondestructive Evaluation, Iowa State U., Ames, 1988-95. Adj. prof. Northeastern U. ext., Waltham, 1970-73, elec. engring. and computer engring. Iowa State U., 1988-95; cons. quality, NDT, TQM, ISO-9000, acoustics and ultrasonic testing evm., 1969-73, 88—. Contbr. numerous articles on electronics, ultrasonics, acoustics, nondestructive testing and quality to profl. jours.; tech. editor Materials Evaluation, 1988—; reviewer various jours. in physics, testing materials and sci. instrumentation; guest editor for Academic Press, 1995-2000; reviewer proposals to various govtl. agencies; patentee in field. Fellow: IEEE, Am. Soc. for Nondestructive Testing (Mehl honor lect. 1979, tutorial award 1993), Acoustical Soc. Am. (Biennial award 1968); mem.: ASTM, Am. Soc. Quality, Am. Phys. Soc., Sigma Xi. Achievements include developing method and instrument for measuring ultrasonic velocity, method for bonding thin slabs to substrates, instrument for sheet metal texture determination, method using DSSS in ultrasonic flaw detection, method to calculate effect of quality on profitability quantitatively, new economic field of nanoeconomics. Office: QSC Inc 379 Diem Woods Dr New Holland PA 17557-8800 Office Phone: 717-355-2142. Personal E-mail: epp34@comcast.net.

**PAPADAKIS, PANAGIOTIS AGAMEMNON,** corporate financial executive; b. Athens, Greece, Mar. 29, 1935; s. Agamemnon Ioannou and Anna Karyatis (Kyriakopoulou) P.; m. Alexandra Argyropoulou, July 12, 1959. Student, U. Athens, 1953-57. Registered rep., Del., Athens, Greece, Zurich, Switzerland, Chgo., NY, DC, 50 other countries. Pub., owner newspaper Peristeri, Athens, 1953-64; owner, gen. dir. printing house, advt. office, ins. agy., Athens, 1953-64; leader Nat. Radical Party Youth, Athens, 1958-59; founder, gen. dir. Servis Advt., Athens, 1963-78, Book-Servis, Athens, 1974-78; pres. Investments Promotions and Assocs. of Chgo., Athens, 1979-85; chmn. Internat. Investments World Co. Inc., Athens and Zurich, 1985—, Internat. Bus. Co. Inc., Internat. Comml. Co. Inc., Athens and Zurich, 1985—, Papadakis Internat. Fin. Co. Inc., Guarantor Co. Inc., Athens and Zurich, 1992—, Internat. Banker Fin. Co. Inc., Athens and Zurich, 1992—. Chmn. Internat. Pap Financing and Investment Group, Vaduz Liechtenstein and US, Konekt Financing Investment Group AG; chmn., pres. 30 companies in several countries. Author, editor: Historical Biography of President Karamanlis, 1974-77; author: Why the Revolution of 21 April 1967 Happened, 1968; author numerous articles in Recently Humanity '93, Human Rights. Mem. Democracy Party, Christian Orthodox Ch. Mem. Internat. C. of C., Assn. Bus. Leaders Inc., London Diplomatic Acad., Comml. and Indsl. Chamber Athens, Greece. Mem. New Democracy Party. Christian Orthodox. Office: Internat Invest World Co Inc PO Box 140 88 115 10 Athens Greece also: Bahnhofstrasse 52 8001 Zurich Switzerland also: 24 Pontou St Ilisia 115 28 Athens Greece Office Phone: 0030-210-7795444. Business E-Mail: papgroup@otenet.gr.

**PAPADAKOS, NICHOLAS PETER,** retired state supreme court justice; b. Hoboken, NJ, Jan. 24, 1925; s. Petros and Olga (Christopoulou) P.; m. Roula Sakellariou, 1950; children: Peter, James, Thomas BA, Dickinson Coll., 1949; LLB, Columbus Law Sch., Washington, 1952. Bar: DC 1952, Pa. 1957, US Supreme Ct. 1975. Atty. Dept. Labor, Washington, 1950-55; office mgr. Pa. Dept. Labor, McKeesport, 1955-57; pvt. practice McKeesport, Pa., 1957-75; judge Ct. of Common Pleas, Pitts., 1976-84; justice Pa. Supreme Ct., 1984-95. Solicitor Versailles Sch. Dist., McKeesport, Pa., 1964-65, Port Vue Borough, Pa., 1969-75; City of McKeesport, 1974-75; instr. in bus. law Pa. State U.-McKeesport, 1960-75; mem. nat. panel arbitrators Am. Arbitration Assn., 1986. Trustee Hellenic Coll./Holy Cross Greek Orthodox Sch. of Theology; mem. charter rev. com. Greek Orthodox Archdiocese Am.; del. World Coun. Hellenes Abroad; Laic chmn. Greek Orthodox Diocese of Pitts.; past mem., past chmn. U.S. Selective Service Bd., McKeesport, Pa., early 1970s; bd. dirs. Mendelssohn Choir, Pitts. Sgt. A.C., U.S. Army, 1943-46; PTO Recipient Ellis Island Medal of Honor, Gold medallion Chapel Four Chaplains Dept. Pa. Mil. Order Purple Heart, 2003. Mem. Pa. State Trial Judges Conf., Greek-Am. Progressive Assn., Am. Hellenic Ednl. Progressive Assn., Tall Cedars Club, Optimists Club, Lions, Elks, Masons. Democrat.

**PAPADEMOS, LUCAS,** bank executive; Gov. Bank of Greece, Athens, 1994—2002; v.p. European Ctrl. Bank, Frankfurt, Germany, 2002—. Mailing: European Central Bank Postfach 16 03 19 D-60066 Frankfurt Germany

**PAPADIAS, CONSTANTINOS BASIL,** electrical engineer; b. Athens, Jan. 16, 1969; s. Basil C. and Vassiliki B. Papadias. Diploma of elec. engring., Nat. Tech. U. Athens, 1991; PhD with highest honors, Ecole Nat. Supérieure des Télécomms., Paris, 1995. Cert. engr., Tech. Chamber of Greece. Mem. tech. staff Bell Labs. Wireless Rsch. Lab., Holmdel, NJ, 1997—2002, tech. mgr., 2002—. Mem. steering bd. Wireless World Rsch. Forum. Author: (book chpt.) Multiple Antenna Transceivers for Wireless Communications, 2002, (stds. contbns.) Downlink improvement through Space-Time Spreading, 1999 (Inclusion in cdma-2000 std. for 3G wireless comms., 1999); contbr. articles to profl. jours. Mem. Hellenic Assn. at Stanford (HELL.A.S), Stanford, 1995—97. Recipient FITNESS project on smart antennas rsch., European Commn., 2001—03, award for grad. studies abroad, Eugenides Found., Greece, 1991, award for top class undergrad. records, Nat. Bursaries Found. Greece, 1990, Bell Labs. Pres.'s Gold award, 2003, Young Author Best Paper award, IEEE Signal Processing Soc., 2003. Mem.: IEEE (sr.), Tech. Chamber of Greece. Achievements include patents for detectors for CDMA systems. Avocations: guitar, swimming, tennis, reading. Office: Bell Labs Lucent Techs Rm R-202B 791 Holmdel-Keyport Rd Holmdel NJ 07733-0400 Business E-Mail: papadias@lucent.com.

**PAPADIMITRIOU, DIMITRI BASIL,** economist, educator, academic administrator; b. Thessaloniki, Greece, June 9, 1946; came to U.S., 1965, naturalized, 1974; s. Basil John and Ellen (Takas) P.; m. Rania Antonopoulos. BA, Columbia U., 1970; PhD, New Sch. U., 1986. V.p., asst. sec. ITT Life Ins. Co. N.Y., N.Y.C., 1970-73; exec. v.p., sec., treas. William Penn Life Ins. Co. N.Y., N.Y.C., 1973-78, also dir.; exec. v.p., provost Bard Coll., 1978—; Jerome Levy prof. econs., 1978—; exec. dir. Bard Ctr., 1980—; pres. Levy Econs. Inst., 1988—; disting. scholar Shanghai Acad. Social Scis., 2002. Adj. lectr. econs. New Sch. U., 1975-76; fellow Ctr. for Advanced Econ. Studies, 1983; Wye fellow Aspen Inst.; bd. dirs. William Penn Life Ins. Co. N.Y.; bd. govs. Levy Econs. Inst., 1986—; mem. subcoun. capital allocation Competitiveness Policy Coun., 1998-2000; mem., vice-chmn. Congrl. Commn. to Rev. the Trade Deficit, 2000-02; mem. adv. com. Women's World Banking; radio econs. commentator Sta. WAMC, NPR, PRI, Money Radio, Marketplace. Author: Employment Policy Community Development and the Underclass, 1997, Employment Policy: Theory and Practice, 1998; co-author: Community Development Banking, 1993, A Path to Community Development, 1993, An Alternative in Small Business Finance, 1994, Monetary Policy Uncovered: The Federal Reserve's Experiment with Unobservables, 1994, Targeting Inflation: The Effects of Monetary Policy on the CPI and Its Housing Component, 1996, The Fed Should Lower Interest Rates More, 1998, What to Do With the Surplus, 1998, How Can We Provide for the Baby Boomers in their Old Age?, 1999, Can Social Security Be Saved, 1999, Fiscal Policy for the Coming Recession, 2001, Is Personal Debt Sustainable?, 2002, Understanding Deflation: Treating the Disease not the Symptom, 2003, Is Deficit-Financed Growth Limited? Policies and Prospects in An Election Year, 2004, How Fragile is the US Economy?, 2005, The United States and Her Creditors: Can the Symbiosis Last?, 2005, Are Housing Prices Household Debt and Growth Sustainable?, 2006, Can the Growth in the US Current Account Deficit be Sustained?, 2006; editor, contbr. Profits, Deficits and Instability, 1992, Aspects of Distribution of Wealth and Income, 1994, Stability in the Financial System, 1996, Modernizing Financial Systems, 2000, Employment Policies: Theories and Evidence, 2001, Induced Investment and Business Cycles, 2004, The Distributional Effects of Government Spending and Taxation, 2006; co-editor, contbr.: Poverty and Prosperity in the USA in the Late Twentieth Century, 1993, Financial Conditions and Macroeconomic Performance, 1992; bd. editors Challenge, Rev. of Income and Wealth; book reviewer Econ. Jour., Ea. Econ. Jour. Trustee, treas. Am. Symphony Orch. Mem. Am. Econ. Assn., Royal Econ. Soc., Am. Fin. Assn., Econ. Club N.Y., The Bretton Woods Com., European Econ. Assn., Eastern Econ. Assn., Econ. Sci. Chamber of Greece, Assn. for Evolutionary Econs. Home and Office: Bard Coll Annandale On Hudson NY 12504 Office Phone: 845-758-7426.

**PAPADONIKOLAKIS, ANASTASIOS,** orthopedist, surgeon; s. Ioanna Pentarakis and Petros Rouggeri (Stepfather). MD, Ioannina, Greece, 1999, PhD, 2003. Diplomate NC, 2005. Resident Wake Forest Med. Ctr., Dept Orthopaedic Surgery, Winston Salem, NC, 2005—. With Greek Mil., 2003—04. Recipient Gold award, Wake Forest U., Dept. Surg. Sci., 2004; fellow, Wake Forest Med. Ctr., Dept Orthopaedic Surgery, 2004—05. Mem.: NC Med. Bd. (licentiate). Achievements include research in distal radius fractures, 3D joint kinematics (first study to prove rotational instability of the knee during walking after anterior cruciate ligament disruption-American Journal of Sports Medicine). Personal E-mail: papadonik@hotmail.com.

**PAPADOPOULOS, GREGORY MICHAEL,** computer scientist, educator; b. Oakland, Calif., Apr. 30, 1958; s. Michael Nicholas and Imogen (Sherman) P.; m. Elizabeth Ann Woellner, Nov. 26, 1982; children: Michael Gregory, Kathryn Elizabeth. BA in Systems Sci., U. Calif.-San Diego, 1979; MS in Elec. Engring. and Computer Sci., MIT, 1983, PhD in elec. engring., 1988. Programmer Scripps Inst. Oceanography, La Jolla, Calif., 1977-79; devel. engr. Hewlett-Packard, Inc., San Diego, 1979-81; sr. research scientist Honeywell, Inc., Mpls., 1981-84; co-founder, chief syss. architect PictureTel Corp., Danvers, Mass., 1984-86; co-founder, chief tech. officer A.I. Architects, Inc., Cambridge, 1985-88; project mgr. MIT lab. for computer sci., 1988-90, asst. prof. elect. engring. and computer sci., 1990-93, assoc. prof., 1993-95; sr. architect Thinking Machines Corp., Cambridge, 1993-94; chief scientist server sys. engring. Sun Microsystems Computer Co., Santa Clara, Calif., 1994-95, chief tech. officer, enterprise servers and storage group, 1995-96, v.p., tech. and advanced develop., chief tech. officer, 1996-98, v.p., chief tech. officer, Sun Microsystems Inc., Santa Clara, Calif., 1998-2000, sr. v.p., chief tech. officer, 2000-02, exec. v.p R&D, chief tech. officer, 2002-; also bd. dir., 2002-. Dir. Ergo, Inc., 1989-90 (also co-founder); co-founder Exa Corp.; rsch. fellow Charles Stark Draper Labs., Cambridge, 1981-83; vis. prof. elec. engring. and computer sci., MIT, 2002-03; mem. President's bd. on Sci. and Innovation, U. Calif.; tech. advisor BP, Alien Technologies. Contbr. articles to profl. jours. Pres. Meml. chpt. Am. Field Service, Houston, 1975-76; bd. trustee Anita Borg Inst. for Women and Tech. Recipient Spl. distinction award Nat. Forensic League, 1976, Presdl. Young Investigators award, Nat. Sci. Found., U. Calif. Regents scholar, 1978. Mem. AAAS, Search for Extrterrestrial Intelligence (chmn. bd.), Phi Beta Kappa, Sigma Xi. Avocations: bicycle touring; soccer, diving. Office: Sun Microsystems 4150 Network Cir Santa Clara CA 95054 Office Phone: 650-960-1300. Office Fax: 408-276-3804.*

**PAPAEFTHYMIOU, GEORGIA C.,** physicist, educator; b. Athens, Greece, Sept. 24, 1946; arrived in US, 1964; d. Christos and Chrysoula Papaefthyiou; children: Hrysoula Davis, Stephanie Davis. BA in Physics, Barnard Coll., NYC, 1968; MA in Physics, Columbia U., NYC, 1974, PhD in Physics, 1976. Physicist F. Bitter Magnet Lab., MIT, Cambridge, Mass., 1976—99; prof. physics Villanova (Pa.) U., 1999—. Peer reviewer, panel reviewer NSF, Washington. Contbr. articles to profl. jours. Grantee, Office Naval Rsch., 1996, NSF, 2000—. Mem.: Materials Rsch. Soc., Am. Phys. Soc. Office: Villanova U Dept Physics 800 E Lancaster Ave Villanova PA 19085 Office Phone: 610-519-4883.

**PAPAGEORGIS, JACK,** small business owner; b. Gaitani, Zakynthos, Greece, Feb. 19, 1933; came to U.S., 1951; s. Anastasios and Eftihia P.; m. Maria Papageorgis, Oct. 1, 1959 (div. Sept. 1993); 1 child, Marie D. BS, Seton Hall U., 1974, Cert. in Internat. Bus.; 1983; MBA, Fairleigh Dickinson U., 1978, Seton Hall U., 1987. Gen. helper Libby's Lunch, Paterson, NJ, 1951-54, cook, 1954-56, counterman, 1956-58, mgr., 1958-63; co-owner, sec., treas. Libby's A Corp., Paterson, NJ, 1963-83, co-owner, pres., 1983-85; officer Passaic County Sheriff's Dept., Paterson, NJ, 1985-88; family svc. specialist III Divsn. Youth Family Svc., Newton-Pompton Lakes, NJ, 1990-92; food svc. assoc. Sodexho-Marriott William Paterson U., 1993—. Active St. Nicholas Greek Orthodox Ch., 1970—. Mem. Am Hellenic Progressive Assn. (25th anniversary award 1992), Panzakynthian Brotherhood (sec., v.p.). Home: 441 Preakness Ave Paterson NJ 07502-1100

**PAPAI, BEVERLY DAFFERN,** retired library director; b. Amarillo, Tex., Aug. 31, 1949; d. Clarence Wilbur and Dora Mae (Henderson) Daffern; m. Joseph Andrew Papai, Apr. 3, 1976. BS in Polit. Sci., West Tex. State U., Canyon, 1972; MSLS, Wayne State U., 1973. Head extension dept. and Oakland County Subregional Libr. The Farmington Cmty. Libr., Farmington Hills, Mich., 1973-79, coord. adult svcs., br. head, 1980-83, asst. dir., 1983-85, dir., 1985—2005; ret., 2005. Cons. U.S. Office of Edn., 1978, Battelle Meml. Inst., Columbis, Ohio, 1980; presenter in field; libr. cons. 2005-. Contbr. articles to profl. jours. Bd. dirs. Mich. Consortium, 1987-91; bd. dirs. Oakland Literacy Coun., 1998—, vice chair, 2000-01, chair, 2001—; trustee Libr. of Mich., 1989-92, vice chair, 1991, 97-98, chair, 1992; del. White House Conf. on Librs. and Info. Svcs., 1991; founder, treas., fiscal agt. METRO NET Libr. Consortium, 1993—; mem. edn. com. Child Abuse and Neglect Coun. of Oakland County, 1998-2000; mem. Commn. on Children, Youth and Families, 1996—, Multiracial Cmty. Coun., 1995—; chair Edn. and Tng. Com., 2000—04. Recipient Athena award Farmington/Farmington Hills C. of C. and Gen. Motors, 1994, Chairperson's Rainbow award, 2001, Spl. Recognition award Oakland County, 2004; Amarillo Pub. Libr. Friends Group fellow, 1972, Wayne State U. Inst. Gerontology fellow, 1972. Mem. ALA (officer), Mich. Libr. Assn. (chair specialized libr. svcs. roundtable 1975, chair conf. program 1982, chair pub. policy com. 1988-89, chair devel. com. 1994-95, chair ann. conf. and program coms. 1995-96, pres. 1996-97, Loleta D. Fyan award 1975, Libr. of Yr. award 2004), LWV of Mich., Farmington Exch. Club, Coun. on Resource Devel. Democrat. Roman Catholic. Home: 6805 Wing Lake Rd Bloomfield Hills MI 48301-2959 Personal E-mail: papaibev@farmlib.org.

**PAPAKOSTAS, ACHILLEAS,** telecommunications engineer, researcher; b. Larissa, Greece, Sept. 23, 1967; came to U.S., 1990; s. Ioannis and Dimitra Papakostas; m. Sheila Ann Papakostas, Apr. 27, 1996; children: Maria Margarita, Demitra Eleni, Erini Gianna. MS, U. Mass., 1993; PhD, U. Tex., Dallas, 1996. Cert. engr., Greece. Telecom. engr. NEC Am., Irving, Tex., 1996—2005; wireless engr. Telephia, Inc., Richardson, Tex., 2005—. Contbr. articles to profl. jours. Tchr. Greek Orthodox Ch., Dallas, 1994-97; pres. Hellenic Cultural Soc. Dalls, 1996-97. Mem. IEEE, Greek Tech. Chamber, Soc. Indsl. and Applied Math. Avocations: reading, teaching greek, bicycling. Business E-Mail: apapakostas@telephia.com.

**PAPALAS, MARY MARGARET,** school psychologist; b. Warren, Ohio, Jan. 12, 1954; d. Joseph John and Elizabeth Jane Dziak; m. Michael Andrew Ognibene, Apr. 15, 2006; 1 child, Ben Adam. AA in Gen. Studies, Kent State U., 1992, BA, 1996, MA, 1998, Ednl. Specialist, 2000. Lic. School Psychologist Ohio, 2001. Sch. psychologist Ashtabula Ednl. Svc. Ctr., Ohio, 2001—, Niles City Schools, Ohio, 2001—. Mem.: Cleve. Assn. of Sch. Psychologists (assoc.), Ohio Assn. of Sch. Psychologists (assoc.), Nat. Assn. Sch. Psychologists (assoc.), AAUW (assoc.). Office Phone: 330-652-4929.

**PAPALIA, DIANE ELLEN,** humanities educator; b. Englewood, NJ, Apr. 26, 1947; d. Edward Peter and Madeline (Borrin) P.; 1 child, Anna Victoria Finlay. AB, Vassar Coll., 1968; MS, W.Va. U., 1970, PhD, 1971. Asst. prof. child and family studies U. Wis., Madison, 1971-75, assoc. prof., 1975-78, prof., 1978-87, coord. child and family studies, 1977-79. Adj. prof. psychology in pediatrics U. Pa. Sch. Medicine, 1987-89. Author (with Sally W. Olds and Ruth D. Feldman): A Child's World: Infancy Through Adolescence, 1975, Human Development, 1978, with Sally W. Olds and Ruth D. Feldman: 10th edit., 2006;; author: (with Harvey Sterns, Cameron J. Camp & Ruth D. Feldman) Adult Development and Aging, 1996, 3rd edit., 2006; author: (with Dana Gross and Ruth D. Feldman) Child Development: A Topical Approach, 2003; co-author: Psychology, 1985, 2d edit., 1988; contbr. articles to profl. jours. NSF fellow, 1971, Am. Coun. on Edn. fellow, 1979-80; U. Wis. grantee. Fellow: Gerontol. Soc.; mem.: APA, Nat. Coun. Family Rels., Soc. Rsch. in Child Devel., Am. Psychol. Soc., Author's Guild, Psi Chi. Home: Apt 6D 253 W 73d St New York NY 10023 Office Phone: 212-724-4244. Personal E-mail: depapalia@aol.com.

**PAPALIA, ROCCO DOMINIC,** food products executive; b. Walnut Creek, Calif., Sept. 19, 1960; s. Rocco and Carolyn Therese (Corker) P.; children: Dominique Therese, Rocco Anthony. BSChemE, Princeton U., 1982. Engr. Procter & Gamble, Cin., 1982-83, group leader, 1983-87, sect. head, 1987-89; group mgr. Frito-Lay Tech., Dallas, 1989-93; dir. tech. Frito-Lay, Dallas, 1993; head rsch. and devel. tech. PepsiCo, Inc. Indsl. adv. bd. Tex. A&M U. chem. engring. dept., 1992—. Inventor shampoo dispenser. Recipient Textile Vets. Assn. award, 1982. Office: Frito Lay 7701 Legacy Dr Plano TX 75024-4099*

**PAPANEK, GUSTAV FRITZ,** economist, educator; b. Vienna, July 12, 1926; s. Ernst and Helen Papanek; m. Hanna Kaiser, June 13, 1947; children: Thomas H., Joanne R. Papanek Orlando. BA in Agrl. Econs., Cornell U., 1947; MA in Econs. Harvard U., 1949, PhD, 1951. Economist, dep. dir. program planning for Asia, tech. coop. adminstrn. Dept. State, 1951-53; from econ. adv. to dir. adv. group to planning commn. Harvard U., Pakistan, 1954-58, from dep. dir. to dir. devel. adv. svc. Cambridge, Mass., 1958—70, dir. adv. group to planning commn. Indonesia, 1971—73; prof. econs. Boston U., 1974-92, prof. emeritus, 1992—, chmn. dept., 1974-83, interim dir., 1977-80, dir. Ctr. Asian Devel. Studies, 1983-90, dir. Asian program, 1991-92; pres. Boston Inst. Developing Econs., Ltd. (BIDE), 1987—; dir., cons. team devel. studies to planning commn. Govt. of Indonesia, 1987—89; dir. policy adv. team to Federated States of Micronesia, 1995—2002. Cons. econ crisis Govt. of Indonesia, 1998—2002; co-dir. pro-poor growth study U.S. AID, 2002—03; cons. in field. Author: (book) Pakistan's Development: Social Goals and Private Incentives, 1967, The Indonesian Economy, 1980, Development Strategy, Growth Equity and the Political Process in Southern Asia, 1986; co-author: Decision Making for Economic Development, 1971, The Indian Economy, 1988, others; contbr. articles to profl. jours. With U.S. Army, 1944—46. Grantee, Ford Found., AID, World Bank, UN Devel. Program, UN Univ., HEW, Asian Devel. Bank. Mem.: Pakistan Econ. Assn., Asian Studies (pres. New Eng. conf. 1975—77), Assn. Comparative Econ. Studies (pres. 1982), Soc. Internat. Devel. (past mem. exec. com.), Am. Agrl. Econs. Assn., Am. Econs. Assn. Home and Office: 2 Mason St Lexington MA 02421-6315 Office Phone: 781-862-7776. E-mail: papanek@bide.com.

**PAPAPOLYMEROU, JOHN,** engineering educator; b. Athens, Greece; married. PhD, U. Mich., 1999. Assoc. prof., dept. elect., comm. engr. U. Ariz., Tucson, 1999—2001; asst. prof. Ga. Tech., Sch. of Elect. Comm. Engring.,

Atlanta, 2001—. Recipient Best Paper award, 3rd Internat. Conf. Microwave Millimeter-Wave Tech., 2002, Career award, NSF, 2002. Mem.: IEEE, Am. Soc. Engring. Edn. Office: Ga Tech Sch Elect Comm Engring 777 Atlantic Dr Atlanta GA 30332-0250 E-mail: papapol@ece.gatech.edu.

**PAPARELLA, LEON RALPH,** psychotherapist, consultant; b. Providence, Dec. 31, 1944; s. Ralph A. and Eleanor Paparella; m. Jacqueline Z. Anderson, Sept. 19, 1987 (div. Aug. 5, 1993). BA, RI Coll., Providence, 1967; MSW, Howard U., Washington, 1969; cert. in group psychotherapy, Washington Sch. Psychiatry, 1972. Lic. psychotherapist Md., Washington, Va. Social worker Cmty. Mental Health Ctr., Washington, 1969—72; psychotherapist Inst. Marriage and Family Rels., Annandale, 1972—74, Va. Cmty. Mental Health Ctr., Fairfax, 1974—78, Treatment Ctr. Washington Sch. Psychiatry, 1977—90; pvt. practice Washington, 1973—. Mem. faculty Washington Sch. Psychiatry, 1974—; cons. Walter Reed Army Hosp., 1984—; support group specialist Parkinson Found. Nat. Capital Area, Washington, 1999—; dean Nat. Group Psychotherapy Inst., 2004—; presenter in field. Named Social Work Mentor of the Yr., Walter Reed Army Hosp., 2002; recipient appreciation, Washingotn Sch. Psychiatry, 1994, Social Work commendation, Walter Reed Army Hosp., 1997. Mem.: NASW, Mid-Atlantic Group Psychotherapy Assn., Nat. Registry Certified Group Psychotherapists, Am. Group Psychotherapy Assn. Avocations: singing, sports.

**PAPAS, IRENE KALANDROS,** English language educator, poet, writer; AA with highest honors, Balt. C.C.; BA magna cum laude, Goucher Coll., 1968; MA in English Lang. and Lit., U. Md., 1974, postgrad., 1980—. Lic. theology profl. Tchr./tutor various schs., Balt., 1965—; tchr. theology U. Md. Free Univ., College Park, 1979—; author/pub. Ledger Publs., Silver Spring, Md., 1982—; TV producer Arts and Humanities Prodns., Silver Spring, 1991—. Lectr. in English, philosophy, Montgomery Coll., Goucher Coll.; instr. English Composition, World Literature, U. Md., College Park, 1968—; adj. faculty various colls.; White House duty, 1997—. Author: Irene's Ledger Songs of Deliverance, 1982, Irene's Ledger Song at Sabbatyon, 1986, Small Meditations, Leaves for Healing, 1996; prodr./dir. tv. progs. Election judge, Montgomery County (Md.) Suprs. Bd. of Elections, 90's; tutor in literacy, 1989, 90. Recipient First Prize Arts and Culture Category Smithsonian Inst., 1991; honored 6th Annual Awards Ceremony Montgomery Community, 1991. Mem. AAUP, Internat. Platform Assn., Nat. Poetry Assn., Phi Beta Kappa. Democrat. Greek Orthodox. Avocations: art/iconography, calligraphy, music, needlepoint. Office: PO Box 10303 Silver Spring MD 20914-0303

**PAPATHOMAS, GEORGIA NIKOLAKOPOULOU,** technology executive; b. Kato Achaia, Greece, Sept. 11, 1950; d. Andreas and Corina (Fotopoulou) Nikolakopoulos; m. Thomas Vergil Papathomas, Aug. 15, 1976; children: Lia Natassa, Alexander Vergil. BS in Engring. Sci., Columbia U., 1973, MS in Engring. Sci., 1974, PhD in Engring. Sci., 1978; cert. in bus. devel., U. Pa., 1994; cert. in strategic mktg., Harvard U., 1995. Mem. tech. staff Bell Labs., Murray Hill, NJ, 1978-84, supr. Whippany, NJ, 1984-90, program mgr., 1990-93; dir. strategy AT&T, Morristown, NJ, 1993-96, dir. ops. Bedminster, NJ, 1996—2002; v.p. network solutions Lucent Tech., 1998—2002; v.p. info. tech. Pfizer, 2003—. Sloan Found. rsch. fellow, N.Y.C., 1974. Mem. ASCE, Soc. Women Engrs., Sigma Xi. Business E-Mail: georgia.papathomas@pfizer.com.

**PAPAYANNOPOULOU, THALIA,** hematologist, oncologist, educator; arrived in US, 1964; MD, U. Athens Sch. Medicine, Greece, 1961, DSci, 1965. Resident medicine, dept. clinical therapeutics & Hematology U. Athens, Athens, Greece, 1962—64; postdoctoral trainee cell biology & tissue culture, pathology dept. U. Wash., Seattle, 1965—67, NIH fellow, sr. fellow hematology div., 1968—73, asst. prof. medicine & hematology, 1974—78, assoc. prof. medicine & hematology, 1979—84, full prof. medicine & hematology, 1984—. Mem. Seattle Cancer Care Alliance. Recipient G. J. Stewart award honoring women in Biomedical Sciences, Temple U. Sch. Medicine, 2001. Fellow: Am. Acad. Arts & Sciences; mem.: Am. Soc. Heamatology (W. Dameshek prize 1990). Achievements include research in regulation of hemoglobin production, development of hematopoietic stem cells, and mechanisms of stem cell trafficking. Office: U Wash Hematology Div Box 357710 1959 NE Pacific St HSB K-136 Seattle WA 98195-7710

**PAPAZIAN, DENNIS RICHARD,** historian, educator, commentator; b. Augusta, Ga., Dec. 15, 1931; s. Nahabed Charles and Armanouhe Marie (Pehlevanian) P.; m. Mary Arshagouni. BA, Wayne State U., 1954; MA, U. Mich., 1958; NDG, Moscow State U., 1962; PhD, U. Mich., 1966. Head dept. social and behavioral scis. U. Mich., Dearborn, 1966-69, head div. lit., sci. and the arts, 1969-73, assoc. dean acad. affairs, 1973-74; dir. Armenian Assembly Am., Washington, 1975-79; dir. grad. studies U. Mich., Dearborn, 1979-85, prof. history, dir. Armenian Rsch. Ctr., 1985—. Fellow Ctr. for Russian and East-European Studies, U. Mich., Ann Arbor, 1982-92; chmn. bd. dirs. Mich. Ethnic Heritage Studies Ctr., U. Mich., 1987-92. Author: St. John's Armenian Church, 1974; editor: The Armenian Church, 1983, Out of Turkey, 1994; editor Jour. of Soc. Armenian Studies, 1994—. Bd. dirs. Armenian Apostolic Soc., Southfield, Mich., 1968-78; chmn. bd. dirs. Alex Manoogian Found., Taylor, Mich., 1969-77; mem. evaluation team Ind. Schs. Assn. Ctrl. States, Chgo., 1985; polit. commentator WXYZ-TV, ABC, Detroit, Southfield, 1984—, WWJ-Radio, Detroit, 1984—; bd. dirs. Southeastern Mich. chpt. ARC, 1988-98, chmn. internat. svcs. com., 1988-98, disaster and mil. family svcs. com., 1988-98; mem. NJ Commn. on Holocaust Edn. Scholar/diplomat U.S. Dept. State, Washington, 1976; grantee NEH, Washington, 1977, AID, Washington, 1978. Mem. AAUP (chpt. pres. 1962-65), Nat. Assn. Armenian Studies and Rsch. (bd. dirs. 1961-91), Nat. Ethnic Studies Assn. (bd. dirs. 1976-85), Am. Hist. Assn., Soc. Armenian Studies (pres. exec. com. 1988-91, 97—, sec./treas. exec. com. 1991-97), Am. Assn. Advancement of Slavic Studies, Am. Acad. Polit. Sci., Armenian Students Assn. (Arthur S. Dadian Armenian Heritage award 1993), Knights of Vartan. Armenian Orthodox. Avocations: reading, travel. Home: 9 Blueberry Dr Woodcliff Lake NJ 07677 Office: U Mich 4901 Evergreen Rd Dearborn MI 48128-1491 Office Phone: 313-593-5181. Business E-Mail: papazian@umich.edu.

**PAPE, GLENN MICHAEL,** lawyer, financial planner; b. Aug. 20, 1954; s. Gilbert Thomas and Janine Elizabeth (Beheyt) P.; m. Nancy Ann Vaske, Apr. 7, 1979 (div. 2006); children: Katherine Jo, Courtney Johanna. BA in Classics, U. Chgo., 1978, MBA, 1981; JD, DePaul U., 1979. Bar: Ill. 1979; CPA, Ill. 1979, Calif. 1979, CLU, Ill. 1979, cert. fin. planner Ill., 1979; cert. investment mgmt. analyst, 1998. Cons. tax divsn. No. Trust Co., Chgo., 1980-81, fin. planner, 1981-82; fin. counselor Continental Ill. Nat. Bank, Chgo., 1982—84; tax mgr. Arthur Andersen & Co., Chgo., 1984-88; v.p., ptnr. Fin. Related Svcs., Ayco Co., L.P., Albany, N.Y., 1988-96; ptnr., nat. svc. leader broad market fin. planning svcs. Ernst & Young, Chgo., 1996—2005, area mkt. leader, 2003—05. Developer Money in Motion Fin. Edn. System; mem. bd. govs. Cert. Fin. Planning Standards, 2000-2005; chair bd. of stds. Cert. Fin. Planning, 2005 Active Five Hosp. Homebound Elderly Program, Chgo., 1981; treas. Chamber Music Coun., Chgo., 1982. Mem. AICPA (accredited pers. fin. specialist), Nat. Spkrs. Assn. (cert. spkg. profl.). Office: Ernst & Young 560 Mission St San Francisco CA 94105 Home: 211 Monte Diablo Ave San Mateo CA 94401 Office Phone: 408-390-6814. Personal E-mail: glenn_pape@hotmail.com.

**PAPE, PATRICIA ANN,** social worker, consultant; b. Aurora, Ill., Aug. 2, 1940; d. Robert Frank and Helen Louise (Hanks) Grover; children: Scott Allen, Debra Lynn. BA in Sociology, Northwestern U., 1962; MSW, George Williams Coll., 1979. Cert. addictions counselor, Ill.; lic. clin. social worker, sch. social worker, Ill. Pvt. practice family counseling, 1979—; coord. community resources DuPage Probation Dept., Wheaton, Ill., 1977-80; dir. The Abbey Alcoholism Treatment Ctr., Winfield, Ill., 1980-81; prin. Pape & Assocs., Wheaton, 1982—; dir. alcoholism counselor trng. program Coll. of DuPage, Glen Ellyn, Ill., 1982-87. Chgo. affiliate Employee Assistance Program, 1982—; cons. Luth. Soc. Services Ill., 1979-80. Contbr. articles to profl. jours. Mem. alcohol drug task force Ill. Synod Luth. Ch. Am., Chgo., 1985—. Named Woman of Yr., Entrepreneur Women in Mgmt., Oak Brook,

Ill, 1986, Social Worker of Yr. Fox Valley Dist., 1998. Mem. Assn. Labor-Mgmt. Adminstrs. Cons. Alcoholism (women's issues com. 1984—), Acad. Cert. Social Workers, Am. Assn. Marriage Family Therapists, Nat. Assn. Soc. Workers, Women in Mgmt. Home: 1330 Shagbark Ln Wheaton IL 60187 Office: Pape & Assocs 618 S West St Wheaton IL 60187-5038

**PAPE, STUART M.,** lawyer; b. Paterson, NJ, Dec. 24, 1948; BA, U. Va., 1970, JD, 1973. Bar: Va. 1973, DC 1980, US Ct. Appeals (6th cir.) 1975, US Supreme Ct. 1976. Law clk. to Hon. Leonard Braman Superior Ct. DC, 1973-74; exec. asst. to commr. FDA, 1979; mng. ptnr., Food & Drug Law, Legis. Affairs practices, mem. exec. com. & mgmt. com. Patton Boggs LLP, Washington. Contbr. articles to profl. jours. Mem. ABA (com. food and drug law, sect. adminstrv. law 1973-2002), Va. State Bar, DC Bar. Office: Patton Boggs LLP 2550 M St NW Washington DC 20037-1350 Office Phone: 202-457-5240. Office Fax: 202-457-6315. Business E-Mail: spape@pattonboggs.com.

**PAPE, WILLIAM JAMES, II,** newspaper publisher; b. Waterbury, Conn., Aug. 14, 1931; s. William B. and Helen (Cronan) P.; m. Patricia Moran, Oct. 15, 1959; children: William B. II, Andrew J. BS, U.S. Naval Acad., 1953; MBA, Harvard U., 1959; LHD (hon.), Teikyo Post U., 1991. Commd. ensign USN, 1953, advanced through grades to lt., 1955, resigned, 1957; asst. treas. Ea. Color Printing Co., Waterbury, 1959-63, pres., treas. Avon, Conn., 1977-87; v.p., asst. treas. Am.-Republican Inc., Waterbury, 1963-64, asst. publisher, comptroller, v.p., treas., 1964-72, pres., 1972—, pres., 1972-98; pub. Republican-Am., 1972—, editor 1988—; also bd. dirs.; v.p., asst. treas. & dir. Paper Delivery, Inc., 1972—. Bd. dirs. Platt Bros., Waterbury, Bd. dirs. Conn. Coun. Freedom of Info., 1968-88, Conn. Bus. and Industry Assn., 1980-83, Naugatuck Valley Devel. Corp., Regional Action Coun., Waterbury, 1991; bd. dirs. Conn. Citizens for Ind. Modernization, pres., 1973-75; bd. dirs. Waterbury YMCA, 1970-78, trustee, 1972-2001, chmn. trustees, 1976-85; trustee Northeast Utilities, 1974-2001, Greater Waterbury Health Network Inc., 1993-95; mem. Conn. Pub. Expenditure Coun. Inc., 1974-77, dir. Conn. policy and econ. coun., 1994-2000; trustee Teikyo Post U., 1976-96; grants com. Waterbury Found., 1980-87; pub. affairs com. Waterbury Hosp., 1984-90, past trustee; incorporator Conn. Found. for Open Govt. Inc.; active Conn. Legislature Commn. to Study Modernization and Unification of Cts., 1973-75, Citizens for Better Govt. Through Reorganization, 1977. Mem. Am. Judicature Soc. (assoc. dir. 1975-76), New England Newspaper Assn. (Conn. bd. govs. 1983-87), Conn. Bar Assn. (task force conflict of interest 1979), Conn. Daily Newspaper Assn. (pres. 1970, exec. com. 1971-91), Waterbury C. of C. (exec. com., v.p. 1975, chmn. 1977-79, dir. 1964-2001, vice-chmn. transp. 1981-2001), Navy League U.S. (comms. bd. 1982), Waterbury Club, Madison Beach Club, Highfield, Liverpool Nautical Rsch. Soc., Am. Legion, Vet. Foreign Wars. Republican. Roman Catholic. Avocations: sailing, firearms, walking, carpentry. Home: Old Sherman Hill Rd Woodbury CT 06798 Office: Waterbury Republic Amer PO Box 2090 389 Meadow St Waterbury CT 06722-2090 E-mail: wjpape@rep-am.com.

**PAPELBON, JON,** professional baseball player; b. Baton Rouge, La., Nov. 23, 1980; Pitcher Red Sox minor league sys., 2003—05, Boston Red Sox, 2005—. Recipient Sarasota Red Sox Pitcher Yr., 2004. Achievements include two-time minor league All-Star, 2004-2005; holds record for fewest bases thrown by a rookie pitcher in first month, 2006. Office: Boston Red Sox 4 Yawkey Way Boston MA 02215-3496*

**PAPELL, HELEN GERTRUDE,** poet, retired librarian; b. N.Y.C., Apr. 8, 1924; d. Henry and Anna (Gimpel) Sobel; m. Robert Papell, June 1, 1949; 1 child, David H. BA, U. Mo., 1949; MLS, Pratt Inst., 1969; cert. profl. pub. libr., SUNY, 1973. Libr. trainee Bklyn. Pub. Libr., 1967-69, libr., storyteller, puppeteer, sr. libr., supervising libr., 1969-84; libr., cataloger Jewish Women's Resource Ctr. Nat. Coun. Jewish Women, N.Y.C., 1984-98; ret., 1998. Puppeteer in librs., schls., chs., st. fairs, N.Y.C., Bklyn., 1969-84. Author: (poems) Talking with Eve, Leah, Hagar, Miriam, 1996, Caretaker's Mask, 2003; contbg. editor Jewish Women's Lit. Ann. Grantee Poets and Writers, 1991, 93. Mem. Nat. Coun. Jewish Women, Phi Beta Kappa. Avocations: reading judaica, folklore and mysteries, visiting museums, attending plays. Home: 720 W End Ave New York NY 10025-6299 E-mail: helenpapell@aol.com.

**PAPENFUSE, EDWARD CARL, JR.,** archivist, state official; b. Toledo, Oct. 15, 1943; m. Sallie Fisher; children: Eric, David. BA in Polit. Sci., Am. U., 1965; MA in History, U. Colo., 1967; PhD, Johns Hopkins U., 1973. Assoc. editor Am. Hist. Rev., Washington, 1970-73; asst. archivist Md. Hall of Records, Annapolis, 1973-75, archivist, 1975—, commr. land patents, 1975—. Author: In Pursuit of Profit: The Annapolis Merchants in the Era of the American Revolution, 1975, (with others) Biographical Dictionary of Maryland Legislators, 1635-1789, 1974, (with others) Maryland: A New Guide to the Old Line State, 3d edit., 1999, Doing Good to Posterity, 1995, Maryland State Archives Atlas of Historical Maps of Maryland, 1608-1908, 2003; contbr. articles and revs. to profl. jours. Mem. Johns Hopkins U. Med. Archives. NEH grantee; recipient Disting. Svc. award to State Govt. Nat. Gov.'s Assn., 1985, Marylander of Yr. award Md. Colonial Soc., 1985. Fellow Soc. Am. Archivist, Md. Hist. Soc., Am. Antiquarian Soc. Home: 206 Oakdale Rd Baltimore MD 21210-2520 Office: Md State Archives 350 Rowe Blvd Annapolis MD 21401-1686 Office Phone: 410-260-6401. E-mail: edp@mdsa.net.

**PAPER, LEWIS J.,** lawyer, educator; b. Newark, Oct. 13, 1946; s. Sidney and Dorothy (Nieman) P.; m. Jan Clachko, Sept. 4, 1972; children: Lindsay, Brett. BA, U. Mich., 1968; LLM, Harvard U., 1971; JD, Georgetown U., 1972. Bar: D.C. 1971, N.J. 1975, Md. 1984. Fellow Inst. Pub. Interest Representation Georgetown U. Law Sch. Washington, 1971-72; staff atty. Citizens Commn. Ctr., Washington, 1972-73; legis. counsel to Sen. Gaylord Nelson U.S. Senate, 1973-75; assoc. atty. Lowenstein, Sandler, Brochin, Kohl & Fisher, Newark, 1975-78; asst. gen. counsel FCC, Washington, 1978-79, assoc. gen. counsel, 1979-81; ptnr. Grove Engelberg & Gross, Washington, 1981-86, Keck, Mahin & Cate, 1986-95, Dickstein, Shapiro, Morin & Oshinsky LLP, Washington, 1995—. Adj. prof. law Georgetown U. Law Sch., Washington, 1983-86. Author: John F. Kennedy: The Promise and the Performance, 1975, 79, Brandeis: An Intimate Biography, 1983, Empire: William S. Paley and the Making of CBS, 1987, Deadly Risks, 2006; contbr. articles to newspapers, mags., and profl. jours. Office: Dickstein Shapiro Morin & Oshinsky LLP 2101 L St NW Washington DC 20037-1526 Office Phone: 202-828-2265. Business E-Mail: lpaper@dsmo.com.

**PAPERNIK, JOEL IRA,** lawyer; b. NYC, May 4, 1944; s. Herman and Ida (Titefsky) Papernik; m. Barbara Ann Barker, July 28, 1972; children: Deborah, Ilana. BA, Yale U., 1965; JD cum laude, Columbia U., 1968. Bar: NY 1969. Assoc Shea & Gould, N.Y.C., 1968—76, ptnr, 1976—91; ptnr., chmn. corp. and securities dept., mem. mgmt. com. Squadron, Ellenoff, Plesent & Sheinfeld, N.Y.C., 1991—2000; ptnr., mem. opinion com. Mintz, Levin, Cohn, Ferris, Glovsky and Popeo PC, N.Y.C., 2000—05. Lectr. various panels. With 11th Spl. Forces USAR, 1967-73. Mem.: ABA (sect. corp. law), Negotiated Acquisitions Com., Tri-Bar Opinion Com., Assn. Bar City N.Y. (securities regulation com. 1992—95, chmn., lectr., corp. law com.), N.Y. State Bar Assn. (lectr. various panels, securities law com.), N.Y. Biotech. Assn. (bd. dirs. 2005—), Yale Club. Office: Mintz Levin Cohn Ferris Glovsky and Popeo PC 666 3rd Ave New York NY 10017-4011 Office Phone: 212-692-6774. Business E-Mail: jpapernik@mintz.com.

**PAPISOV, MIKHAIL I.,** chemist; b. Moscow, USSR, June 11, 1955; came to U.S., 1991; s. Ivan M. Papisov and Valeria I. Naidich; m. Elena A. Tokareva, Aug. 23, 1986; children: Vera M., Eugenia M. MS in Chemistry, Moscow State U., 1982; PhD in Biochemistry and Biology, Inst. Exptl. Cardiology, Moscow, 1988. Rsch. scientist Nat. Cardiology Rsch. Ctr., Moscow, 1988—91; assoc. chemist Mass. Gen. Hosp., Boston. Sci. founder, cons. Mersana Therapeutics, Cambridge, Mass., 2002—. Recipient Outstanding Pharm. Paper, Controlled Release Soc., 1995; grantee Several Rsch. grants, U.S. Govt., The Whitaker Found., Pharm. Industry, 1996—2006.

Mem.: Controlled Release Soc., Am. Chem. Soc. Achievements include U.S. and foreign patents in the areas of pharmacology and biomaterials. Home: PO Box 441 Winchester MA 01890 Office: Mass General Hosp 55 Fruit St Boston MA 02114-2696 Office Phone: 617-724-9655.

**PAPITTO, RALPH RAYMOND,** manufacturing executive; b. Providence, Nov. 1, 1926; s. John and David (David) P.; m. Norma J. Ewart, June 10, 1943 (div.); children: Andrea (Mrs. Harry Crump), Aurelia (Mrs. William Young), David John; m. Barbara Auger, Apr. 1982. BS in Finance, Bryant Coll., Providence, 1947, DSc Bus. Adminstrn. (hon.), 1987; student, Boston U. Law Sch., 1948-49; DSc Bus. Adminstrn. (hon.), Roger Williams Coll., 1985; LLD (hon.), New Eng. Inst. Tech., 1985, Suffolk U., 1986, New England Inst. Tech. With Arthur Andersen & Co. and Ernst & Ernst, Providence, 1948-51; exec. v.p. fin. Ritz Products, Inc., Providence, 1951-55; founder, pres., chmn., dir. Glass-Tite Industries, Inc., Providence, 1956-63, chmn. bd., 1963—, also bd. dirs.; founder, chief exec. officer, pres., chmn. Nortek Inc., Providence, 1967-90, bd. dirs.; Chair and CEO AFC Cable Systems, Inc., Providence, 1993—. Bd. dirs. Hi-G, Inc. Fin. dir. Town of Johnston, R.I., 1955-59; trustee Roger Williams U., Bristol, R.I., chmn. bd. trustees, 1972—; bd. dirs. Meeting St. Sch. Retarded; mem. Gov.'s Blue Ribbon Commn., Roger Williams Hosp.; mem. Aurora Civic Assn. Named Man Yr. in R.I., R.I. C. of C., 1961. Mem. Alpine Country Club (pres. 1966-68, 92—), Jockey Club, Surf Club, LaGorce Country Club (Fla.). Office: AFC Cable Systems Inc 50 Kennedy Plz Providence RI 02903-2393 Office Phone: 401-453-2000. Fax: 401-453-2009.

**PAPP, HARRY,** science association administrator; Pres. Ariz. Zool. Soc., The Phoenix Zoo, from 1995, now former pres. also: Phoenix Zoo 455 N Galvin Pkwy Phoenix AZ 85008-3431 Office: L Roy Papp and Assoc LLP 2201 E Camelback Rd 227B Phoenix AZ 85016-9028

**PAPP, LASZLO GEORGE,** retired architect; b. Debrecen, Hungary, Apr. 28, 1929; came to U.S., 1956; m. Judith Liptak, Apr. 12, 1952; children: Andrea, Laszlo-Mark (dec. 1978). Archtl. Engr., Poly. U. Budapest, 1955; MArch, Pratt Inst., 1960; D of Liberal Arts, Tech. U. Budapest, 1998. Designer Harrison & Abramovitz, Architects, N.Y.C., 1958—63; ptnr. Whiteside & Papp, Architects, White Plains, NY, 1963—67; pres. Papp Architects, P.C., White Plains, 1967—96, chmn., 1996—2005; exec. dir. Urban Redevel. Commn., Stamford, Conn., 2001—05. Adj. prof. U. Debrecen, Hungary, 1999—; chmn. Planning and Zoning Commn., New Canaan, Conn., 2004—. Mem. Pres.'s Adv. Com. on Pvt. Sector Initiatives, 1980-85; mem. adv. com. Westchester C.C., 1971-75, Iona Coll., New Rochelle, N.Y., 1982-87, Norwalk State Tech. Coll., 1983-95; v.p. Clearview Sch., 1985-89, pres., 1990-91; mem. Town Coun. New Canaan, Conn., 1993-99; chmn. Planning and Zoning Commn., New Canaan, 2004—. Fellow AIA (reg. dir. 1983-85); mem. Internat. Union Architects (rep. habitat com. 1986-90), N.Y. State Assn. Architects (v.p. 1977-80, pres. 1981), Am.-Hungarian Engrs. Assn. (bd. dirs. 1978-90), Am. Coun. World Fedn. Hungarians (pres. 1993-97, regional pres. 1996-2000), Hungarian Assn. (vice pres. 1958-60), Westchester County C. of C. (bd. dirs. 1968-71, vice chmn. bd. for area devel. 1983-89, chmn. bd. dirs. 1989-90), Am.-Hungarian C. of C. (charter 1989—). Home: 1197 Valley Rd New Canaan CT 06840-2428 Personal E-mail: papparch@aol.com.

**PAPPAGALLO, MARCO,** neurologist, pain medicine specialist; b. Senigallia, Italy, Sept. 30, 1957; arrived in U.S., 1986; s. Sergio Pappagallo and Fiorella Capomagi. MD, U. Rome, 1982. Diplomate in neuology Am. Bd. Psychiatry and Neurology, in pain mgmt. Am. Bd. Med. Specialties. Clin. instr. Johns Hopkins Hosp., Balt., 1993—95; asst. prof. dept. neurology and neurosurgery Johns Hopkins Sch. Medicine, Balt., 1995; assoc. prof. dept. neurology NYU Sch. Medicine, N.Y.C., 1999—; dir. Pain Treatment Ctr. Hosp. for Joint Diseases, Mt. Sinai-NYU Health, N.Y.C., 1999—; dir. NYU Pain Treatment Ctrs., Hosp. for Joint Diseases, NYC, 1999—2003; dir. divsn. chronic pain Beth Israel Med. Ctr., 2003—. Assoc. prof. neurology and anesthesiology Albert Einstein Coll. Medicine, Bronx, NY. Achievements include invention of therapeutic method with capsaicin; therapeutic method with capsaicin and capsaicin analogues. Office: Beth Israel Med Ctr 10 Union Sqare East Ste 5L New York NY 10003

**PAPPAGALLO, MICHAEL V.,** realty company executive; b. 1958; Grad. summa cum laude, Iona Coll., New Rochelle, N.Y. Sr. mgr. audit group KPMG Peat Marwick; with GE Capital, mgr. fin. bus. devel. team Vendor Fin. Svcs. unit, mgr. fin. reporting and practices, CFO comml. real estate fin. and svcs.; CFO Kimco Realty Corp., New Hyde Park, N.Y., 1997—. Office: Kimco Realty Corp PO Box 5020 3333 New Hyde Park Rd #100 New Hyde Park NY 11042-0020 Fax: (516) 869-9001.

**PAPPAJOHN, JOHN G.,** venture capitalist; b. St. Luke's, Greece, July 31, 1928; s. George and Maria (Zanios) P.; m. Mary; children Ann Vassiliou. BSc, U. Iowa, 1952. Owner Pappajohn Ins. Agy., Mason City, Iowa, 1953-59; pres., founder Guardsman Life Investors, Inc., Des Moines, 1962-69; cofounder, v.p. Guardsman Life Ins. Co., West Des Moines, Iowa, 1962-69; pres. Equity Dynamics Inc., Des Moines, 1969—, Pappajohn Capital Resources, Inc., Des Moines, 1969—. Bd. dirs. United Systems Tech., Dallas, Optimumcare Corp., La Jolla, Calif., Galagen, Inc., BioCyst, Inc., Neose Pharms., Drug Screening Systems. Horatio Alger Assn., Leadership 100. Trustee Anatolia Coll., Thessalonia, Greece, 1988, Pine Manor Coll., Boston, 1990, U. Iowa Found., Iowa City, 1990; mem. adv. bd. Kennedy Ctr. for Performing Arts, Washington, 1986, 90; philanthropic causes with wife: John Pappajohn Bus. Bldg., Univ. Iowa Sch., Pappajohn Pavilion, Univ. Iowa Hosp. and Clinics, John and Mary Pappajohn Clin. Cancer Ctr., founder, John and Mary Pappajohn Scholarship Fund, 1997; organizer, financer Univ. Iowa Pappajohn Entrepreneurial Ctrs. at five different univs. and colls. in the state of Iowa; funder, NIACC Pappajohn Bus. Bldg., Mason City, Iowa, 2001; active mem. Nat. Com. of the Performing Arts; mem. trustee coun., collectors com., Nat. Gallery Art, Washington, DC.; dir. Hirshhorn Mus., Washington, DC; mem. nat. com., Whitney Mus., NYC; hon. trustee, Des Moines Art Ctr., Iowa; bd. visitors Univ. Iowa; mem. Greek Orthodox Archdiocese Exec. Com., 2001-04; coun. mem. Greek Orthodox Archdiocese of Am.; associated with JF Kennedy Ctr. for Performing Arts, Washington, D.C., former mem. advisory bd. Recipient Spl. Achievement award Big Bros., 1972, Big Bro. of Yr. award, 1974, Oscar D. Schmidt Iowa Bus. Leadership award, U. Iowa Coll. Bus., 1993, Horatio Alger award, Horatio Alger Assn., 1995, Brotherhood award, Iowa Region Nat. Conf. of Christian and Jews, 1997, Beta Gamma Sigma Medallion for Entrepreneur of Yr., 1997, Hellenic Hertiage Achievement award, 1997, Meredith Willson Heritage award, 1998, Ellis Island Medal of Honor, 2000, Greek Orthodox Archon award, 2000, Univ. Iowa Homecoming Honored Guest, 2002; Finkbine award, U. Iowa Bus. Sch., 2004; named Iowa Bus. Leader of Yr., 1993; named to Iowa Hall of Fame, 1996, Central Iowa Bus. Hall of Achievement, 1999; named one of Top 200 Collectors, ARTnews Mag., 2004, 2006. Mem. U. Iowa Alumni Assn. (pres.' club), Des Moines Club, Embassy Club, Univ. Club, Order AHEPA, Masons, Shriners, Phi Gamma Delta. Republican. Greek Orthodox. Avocations: Collector of Modern and Contemporary Art, wines, philanthropy. Office: Pappajohn Capital Resources 2116 Financial Ctr Des Moines IA 50309-3908 Address: John Pappajohn Entrepreneurial Ctr Curris Bus Bldg Stes 5 & 264 U Northern Iowa Cedar Falls IA 50614-0130*

**PAPPALARDO, A. JOHN,** former prosecutor, lawyer; BA in Govt., Bowdoin Coll., 1971; JD, Suffolk Univ., 1974. Asst. dist. atty. Off. of Dist. Atty., Norfolk County, 1975—78; Chief, Public Integrity Unit Off. of Atty. Gen., Commonwealth of Mass., 1981, spl. investigator,spl. commn., 1978—81; asst. US atty. Dept. Justice, 1981—86, Chief, Public Corruption Unit, US Attys. Off., 1986—87; dep. atty. gen., chief criminal bur. Off. Atty. Gen., Commonwealth of Mass., Boston, 1987—89; 1st asst. US atty, Dist. of Mass. Dept. Justice, 1989—92, US atty, Boston, 1992—; now co-mng. shareholder Greenberg Traurig LLP, Boston. Office: Greenberg Traurig LLP Third Fl One International Place Boston MA 02110 Office Phone: 617-310-6000. Office Fax: 617-310-6001. Business E-Mail: pappalardoj@gtlaw.com.

**PAPPALARDO, ROSA GLORIA,** secondary school educator; b. Bklyn., Mar. 10, 1932; d. Angelo Charles and Rose (Paternostro) Borgia; m. Leonard Thomas Pappalardo, Apr. 16, 1955; children: Marianne, Leonard, Charles, Roseanne. BS, NYU, 1952, MA, 1953; postgrad., Seton Hall U., 1980-81, Rutgers U., 1984. Cert. supr. of art K-12, N.J., N.Y. Art edn. tchr. Islip (N.J.) Bd. Edn., 1953—54; Herricks (N.Y.) Bd. Edn., 1954-57, 61-62; tchr. spl. edn. Passaic Assn. for Mentally Retarded, Passaic, NJ, 1958—60; supr. art/home edn. Randolph (N.J.) Twp. Schs., 1962—95; adj. prof. Jersey City State Coll., 1971—98, N.J. State U., Trenton, 2002—03; prof. Jersey City State U., 2002—. Art cons.; developer Leadership Curriculum, Jersey City U.; presenter in field. Co-author art and math. curricula for Randolph Twp. Schs. K-12; contbr. chpt. to books Recipient numerous svc. awards, recognition awards, awards for art edn. and art adminstrn. Fellow: Art Educators N.J. (Disting., pres.); mem.: NABA (pres.), Art Adminstrs. N.J. (pres.), N.J. Art Educators, Arts Coun. of Morris Area (planning com. 2002, Chinese, U.S. and Croatia exhibits), Kiwanis, Delta Zeta (pres.), Phi Delta Kappa. Republican. Roman Catholic. Avocations: swimming, visual arts. Home: 312 Mountain Way Morris Plains NJ 07950-1910 Office: 73 Evans Ln Lake Placid NY 12946-1605

**PAPPAS, ALCESTE THETIS,** consulting company executive, educator; b. Dix Hills, N.Y., May 5, 1945; d. Costas Ernest and Thetis (Hero) P.; m. Sylvan V. Endich, Sept. 13, 1987. AB, U. Calif.-Berkeley, 1967, PhD, 1978; EdM, Harvard U., 1969. Cert. guidance counselor, Mass., secondary sch. tchr., Mass. Dir. student-young alumni affairs Calif. Alumni Assn., Berkeley, 1969-71; dir. residential programs U. Calif., Berkeley, 1971-73, dir. housing and childcare, 1973-79; sr. cons., mgr. Peat, Marwick, Mitchell & Co., N.Y.C., 1979-80, 80-82, sr. mgr., 1982-84; ptnr. in charge edn., other instns. Peat, Marwick, Main & Co., N.Y.C., 1984-93; pres., CEO Pappas Cons. Group, Inc., Greenwich, Conn., 1993—. Spkr. in field. Author: Reengineering Your Non-Profit Organization: A Guide to Strategic Transformation, 1996; contbr. articles to profl. jours., author monographs. Mem. Merola Opera Bd., San Francisco, 1978-80, Calif. Alumni Council, 1976-79; bd. overseers Regents Coll., 1988-89; bd. dirs., mem. fin. com. Hellenic Coll. and Holy Cross Sch. Theology, Brookline, Mass., 1983-87, Seabury Western Theol. Sem., Evanston, Ill., 1983-89; bd. dirs. N.Y. Chiropractic Coll., 1986-88, Com. on Econ. Devel., 1986-88, Greek Orthodox Archdiocese Council, N.Y.C., 1985-89; bd. dirs., vice chmn. St. Basil Acad., 1983-87; bd. dirs., mem. exec. com. YWCA, N.Y.C., 1985-90, Catalyst, 1988-90; chairperson capital campaign com. U. Calif., Berkeley, exec. v.p. exec. coun. Coll. Letters and Sci.; trustee Clark U., 1993-95, U. Calif. Found., 1993-99; bd. dirs. Nat. Coun. for Rsch. on Women, 1996-98; mem. adv. bd. Grad. Sch. Edn. U. Calif., Berkeley, 2005—. Named mem. Acad. Women Achievers, YWCA, N.Y.C., 1984; recipient award Nat. Mgmt. Assn., 1997. Mem. Mid. States Assn. Schs. and Colls. (bd. dirs., fin. com. 1984-89, planning com. 1988-89), Order of the Ky. Colonels, Mortar Bd., Pi Lambda Theta, Prytanean. Avocations: opera, gourmet cooking, travel, photography. Office: 68 Southfield Ave Stamford CT 06902-7237 Office Phone: 203-357-7058.

**PAPPAS, BARBARA ESTELLE,** biblical studies educator, author; b. Chgo., July 26, 1941; m. George G. Pappas, Sept. 20, 1964; children: Dheanna Pappas Fikaris, Michele Pappas Glavanovits, Laina Pappas Krabbe. BA in Early Ch. Fathers, DePaul U., Chgo., 2004. Lay asst. Holy Apostles Ch., Westchester, Ill., 1976—. Sec., lectr. Diocese of Chgo. Religious Edn. Commn., 1982—; founder, dir. Holy Apostles Resource Ctr., Westchester, 1984—. Author: Are You Saved?, The Orthodox Christian Process of Salvation, 4th edit., 1997, The Christian Life in the Early Church and Today, Commentaries on Paul's Epistles to the Corinthians, Vol. I, 2d edit., 2004, Vol. II, 1998, God's Bubbly, Gurgly, Overwhelming, Overflowing Love, 2000, First and Second Corinthians: A Study of Paul's Letters, 2005. Mem. teenage curriculum com. Greek Orthodox Archdiocese. Mem.: ASCD. Greek Orthodox. Home: 379 Arboretum Cir Wheaton IL 60187 E-mail: ayspappas@comcast.net.

**PAPPAS, CHARLES NICHOLAS, III,** dentist, educator; b. Phila., Jan. 14, 1936; s. Charles Nicholas, Jr. and Marie (Pero) Pappas; m. Edith Basedow, Aug. 24, 1974. Student, U. Colo., 1953—55; DDS, Northwestern U., 1959. Assoc. practice dentistry, South Weymouth, Mass., 1962; pvt. practice dentistry Weymouth Heights, Mass., 1962—65; public health dentist Dept. Health and Hosps., Boston, 1965—70; assoc. practice Weymouth, 1965—68, Brookline, Mass., 1969; practicing clin. dentist Harvard U., 1970—71, clin. instr. operative dentistry 1967—71; clin. rsch. asst. Forsyth Dental Ctr., 1972; asst. prof. restorative dentistry U. Pa., 1972—83; dentist Dept. Pub. Health, City of Phila., 1984—. Clin. instr. Tufts U., 1965. Author: The Life and Times of G.V. Black, 1983, (pamphlet) Self-Control of Tooth Decay, 1967; contbr. articles to profl. publs. Program, fund-raising chmn. Phillips Brooks Club Boston Trinity Ch., 1965—66. Capt. AUS, 1960—62. Recipient Earle Banks Hoyt award for excellence in tchg., 1980. Mem.: AAAS, ADA, Christian Dental Soc., NY Acad. Scis., Pa. Assn. Dental Surgeons, Mass. Dental Soc., Philadelphia County Dental Soc., Harvard Odontological Soc., Yale Libr. Assocs., U.S. Submarine Vets WWII (assoc. Cert. of Appreciation 1982), Goethe Soc. New Eng., English-Speaking Union, 4001 Lit. Union (founder, faculty advisor), New Haven Colony Hist. Soc., Hist. Soc. Pa., Ill. State Hist. Soc., G.V. Black Soc., Northwestern U. of Delaware Valley Club (pres. 1978), Xi Psi Phi, Lambda Chi Alpha. Home: 5723 Charles St Philadelphia PA 19135-3806 Office: City of Phila Dist Health Ctr # 10 Dental Clinic 2230 Cottman Ave Philadelphia PA 19149

**PAPPAS, DAVID CHRISTOPHER,** lawyer; b. Kenosha, Wis., Mar. 18, 1936; s. theros and Marion Lucille (Piperas) P.; m. Laurie Jean LeCauffrey, Nov. 26, 1966 (div.), 1969; children: Christopher David, Andrea Lynn; m. Nancy Marie Pratt, June 11, 1983 (div. 1998). BS, U. Wis., 1959, JD, 1961. Bar: Wis. 1961, U.S. Dist. Ct. (ea. and we. dists.) Wis., 1965, U.S. Supreme Ct. 1971; lic. master mariner. Asst. corp. counsel Racine County (Wis.), 1961; atty., advisor U.S. Dept. Labor, Washington, 1961-62; staff atty. U.S. Commn. Civil rights, Washington, 1962-63; asst. city atty. City of Madison (Wis.), 1963-65; atty. pvt. practice, Madison, 1965—. Chmn. Madison Mayor's Citizen Adv. Com., 1964-65; pres. Wis. Cup Assn., Madison, 1965; c0-chmn. 2d Congl. Dist. Humphrey for Pres., Madison, 1972. Recipient commendation for Supreme Ct. work Madison County Coun., 1965, commendation resolution City of Madison, 1965. Mem. Wis. Bar Assn., Dane County Bar Assn., Wis. Acad. Trial Lawyers, Am. Assn. Trial Lawyers, Lawyer-Pilot Bar Assn. (master mariner), Gt. Lakes Hist. Soc., Madison Club, South Shore Yacht Club (Milw.). Home and Office: 1787 Strawberry Rd Deerfield WI 53531-9779 Office Phone: 608-256-7900. E-mail: mooney@midplains.net.

**PAPPAS, EDWARD HARVEY,** lawyer; b. Midland, Mich., Nov. 24, 1947; s. Charles and Sydell (Sheinberg) P.; m. Laurie Weston, Aug. 6, 1972; children: Gregory Alan, Steven Michael. BBA, U. Mich., 1969, JD, 1973. Bar: Mich. 1973, U.S. Dist. Ct. (ea. dist.) Mich. 1973, U.S. Dist. Ct. (we. dist.) Mich. 1980, U.S. Ct. Appeals (6th cir.) 1983, U.S. Supreme Ct. 1983, U.S. Ct. Appeals (3d cir.) 1994, U.S. Ct. Appeals (1st cir.) 2002. Ptnr. firm Dickinson & Wright, P.L.L.C., Detroit and Bloomfield Hi, Mich., 1973—. Mediator Oakland County Cir. Ct., Pontiac, Mich., 1983—; hearing panelist Mich. Atty. Discipline Bd., Detroit, 1983—, mem. bus. tort subcom. Mich. Supreme Ct. Com. Std. Jury Instrns., 1992-94; bd. commrs. State Bar Mich., 1999-, v.p., 2006-. Trustee Oakland Community Coll., Mich., 1982-90, Oakland-Livingston Legal Aid, 1982-90, v.p., 1982-85, pres., 1985-87; trustee, adv. bd. Mich. Regional Anti-Defamation League of B'nai B'rith, Detroit, 1983-90; planning commr. Village of Franklin, Mich., 1987-91, chmn. 1989-91, councilman 1991-92, chmn. charter com., 1993-94; chmn. State Bar Mich. Long Range Planning com.; pres.-elect Oakland County Bar Assn., 1996-97, pres., 1997-98, chmn. Jud. Selection Task Force, 1997; bd. dirs. Franklin Found., 1989-92; trustee The Oakland Medication Ctr., 1992-96; treas. State Bar of Mich., 2004-05. Master Oakland County Bar Assn. Inn of Ct.; fellow Mich. State Bar Found., Oakland Bar-Adams Pratt Found., ABA Found., Am. Coll. Civil Trial Mediators; mem. ABA, Fed. Bar Assn., State Bar Mich. (co-chmn. nat. moot ct. competition com. 1974, 76, com. on legal aid, chmn. standing com. on atty. grievances 1989-92, comml. litig. com., civil procedure com. 1992-94, bd. commrs. 1999—, treas.

2004-05, sec. 2005-06, v.p. 2006—), Oakland County Bar Assn. (vice-chmn. CLE com., chmn. CLE com. 1985-86, mediation com. 1989-90, chmn. mediation com. 1990-91, bd. dirs. 1990-98, chmn. select com. Oakland County cir. ct. settlement week 1991, chmn. strategic planning com. 1992-93, editor Laches monthly mag. 1986-88, co-chair task force to improve justice systems in Oakland County 1993—, pres.-elect, bd. dirs. 1996-97, pres. 1997-98), Am. Judicature Soc., Mich. Def. Trial Lawyers, Def. Rsch. and Trial Lawyers Assn. (com. practice and procedure), B'nai B'rith Barristers. Home: 32223 Scenic Ln Franklin MI 48025-1702 Office Phone: 248-433-7228. Business E-Mail: epappas@dickinsonwright.com.

**PAPPAS, EFFIE VAMIS,** language educator, finance educator, writer, poet, artist; b. Cleve., Dec. 26, 1924; d. James Jacob and Helen Joy (Nicholson) Vamis; m. Leonard G. Pappas, Nov. 3, 1945; children: Karen Pappas Morabito, Leonard J., Ellen Pappas Daniels, David James. BBA, Western Res. U., 1948; MA in Edn., Case Western Res. U., 1964; postgrad., 1964—68; MA in English Lit., Cleve. State U., 1986; postgrad., Ind. U. Pa., 1979—86. Cert. elem. and secondary tchr. Ohio. Tchr. elem. schs., Ohio, 1963-70; office mgr. Cleve. State U., 1970-72, adminstr. pub. rels., 1972-73; med. adminstr. Brecksville (Ohio) VA Hosp., 1974-78; lectr. English, econs./bus. mgmt., math., comm., composition Cuyahoga CC, Cleve., 1978-92. Tchg. asst. Case Western Res. U., 1979—80; lectr. bus. comm. Cleve. State U., 1980; participant in sci. and cultural exch. dels. Am. Inst. Chemists, China, 1984, Russia, 89. Feature writer: The Voice, 1970—78, editor, writer: Cleve. State U. newsletter and mag., 1970—73. Cub scout leader Boy Scouts Am., Brecksville, 1960; mem. local coun. PTA, 1965—70; sec. St. Paul's Coun., 1990—91; mem. membership com. St. Paul Ladies Philoptohos, 1990—; active Women's Equity Action League, 1995—2003; mem. Greater Cleve. Learning Project; Sunday sch. tchr., mem. choir Brecksville United Ch. of Christ, 1975—76, mem. bd. missions, 1966—67, mem. membership com., 1993; mem. planning com. edn. Case Western Res. U.; mem. 75th Anniversary steering com. Cleve. Coll. Recipient Editor's Choice award for outstanding achievement in poetry, Nat. Libr. Poetry, 1995, 2000; grantee, Cuyahoga CC, 1982. Mem.: AARP, AAUW (del. meetings, regis. chair 1993—94, co-chair Cleve. br. 1994, 1996—97, legis. chair 1997—98), NAFE, NAE (life named to Nat. Women's Hall Fame), Ohio Edn. Assn. (rep. assembly Columbus 1994, 1999—2001, 2002—03), N.E. Ohio Edn. Assn. (licentiate), Nat. Mus. Women in Arts (hon. roll. mem.). Avocations: travel, art, legal studies, theater, correspondence with national and international friends. Home: 8681 Brecksville Rd Brecksville OH 44141-1912

**PAPPAS, ERIC CHARLES,** director; b. NYC, Mar. 10, 1950; s. Robert Lester and Betty Pappas; children: Jesse, Angelea. BS in Econ. Theory, Wagner Coll., NYC, 1972; MA in English, Va. Tech., 1987, EdD in English Edn., 1990. Furniture designer, furniture maker, Ithaca, NY, 1973—81; composer, singer Blacksburg, Va., 1979—85; dir., founder Va. Dept. Corrections Sch., Floyd, 1980—82; lit. instr. Va. Tech., Blacksburg, 1985—93; founder, dir. Va. Tech. Engring. Ctr., Blacksburg, 1993—2003; founder, dir. Inst. Higher Order Thinking James Madison U., Harrisonburg, Va., 2003—. Cons., spkr. in field. Songwriter, singer (record album) All Your Heart, 1983, founder (academic jour.) Cutting Ed, 2001—; contbr. articles to engring. jours.; editor: Managing Quality and Productivity, 1988; author: A Rural Community Organizer's Manual, 1988. Founding organizer Ithaca (NY) Farmer's Market, 1973—78; cmty. organizer Coalition of Am. Electric Consumers, Va., 1980—82; chair Va. Tech. Commn. on Outreach, Blacksburg, 2001—03. Named Artist of Mo., Swamp Records, 2003; grantee, Honeywell Internat., 1994—2002, State Coun. of Higher Edn., Richmond, Va., 1997. Mem.: AAUP, Am. Soc. Engring. Edn., Phi Kappa Phi (pres. Va. Tech. chpt. 1990—92). Office: James Madison U ISAT 117 MSC 4102 Harrisonburg VA 22807 Office Phone: 540-568-1694. Office Fax: 540-568-2761. E-mail: pappasec@jmu.edu, epappas@cisat.jmu.edu.

**PAPPAS, G. CHRIS,** electronics engineer; b. Galveston, Tex., Sept. 3, 1956; s. Patrick Henry and Maragret Jean Pappas. BSEE, U. Tex., 1984; MSEE, Tex. Tech U., 1987. Mem. tech. staff Hughes Aircraft Co. Electron Dynamics Divsn., Torrance, Calif., 1987—90; elec. engr. Superconducting Super Collider Lab., Dallas, 1990—94; group leader Brookhaven Nat. Lab., Upton, ND, 1994—96; electronics engr. Stanford Linear Acclerator Ctr., Menlo Park, Calif., 1996—. Contbr. articles to profl. jours. Democrat. Achievements include development of solid state modulators for accelerator radio frequency applications; solid state modulators for beam injection and extraction; design of fast pulsed magnets for beam injection and extraction; invention of a taped wound pulse forming network. Avocations: skiing, sailing, mountain climbing, rock climbing. Office: Stanford Linear Accelerator Center 2575 Sanhill Rd Menlo Park CA 94025 Office Phone: 650-926-3813. Personal E-mail: chrispappas@netscape.net. Business E-Mail: pappas@slac.stanford.edu.

**PAPPAS, GEORGE DEMETRIOS,** anatomist, cell biologist, educator; b. Portland, Maine, Nov. 26, 1926; s. James and Anna (Dracopoulos) Pappatheodoros; m. Bernice Levine, Jan. 14, 1952; children: Zoe Alexandra, Clio Nicollette. BA, Bowdoin Coll., 1947; MS, Ohio State U., 1948, PhD, 1952; DSc (hon.), U. Athens, Greece, 1988. Vis. investigator Rockefeller Inst., N.Y.C., 1952-54; assoc. in anatomy Coll. Physicians and Surgeons, Columbia U., N.Y.C., 1956-57, asst. prof. anatomy, 1957-63, assoc. prof., 1963-66; prof. anatomy Albert Einstein Coll. Medicine, Yeshiva U., N.Y.C., 1967-77, prof. neurosci., 1974-77, vis. prof. neurosci., 1977-97; prof., head dept. anatomy and cell biology U. Ill. Coll. Medicine, Chgo., 1977-96, prof. cell biology and psychiatry, 1996—. Trustee Marine Biol. Lab., Woods Hole, Mass., 1975-81. Author: (with others) The Structure of the Eye, 1961, Growth and Maturation of the Brain, vol. IV, 1964, Nerve as a Tissue, 1966, The Thalmus, 1966, Pathology of the Nervous System, vol. 1, 1968, Structure and Function of Synapses, 1972, Methodological Approaches to the Study of Brain Maturation and Its Abnormalities, 1974, Advances in Neurology, vol.12, 1975, The Nervous System, vol. 1 The Basic Neurosciences, 1975, Cellular and Molecular Basis of Synaptic Transmission, 1988; contbr. over 250 articles to profl. jours.; former mem. editl. bd. Anatomical Record, Biol. Bull., Brain Rsch., Jour. Neurocytology, Microvasculature, Neurol. Rsch. Arthritis and Rheumatism Found. fellow, 1954-56; recipient Career Devel. award Columbia U., 1964-66; Rsch. grant NIH. Fellow AAAS, N.Y. Acad. Scis., Inst. Medicine Chgo.; mem. Am. Soc. Cell Biology (pres. 1974-75), Am. Assn. Anatomists (chmn. pub. policy com. 1981-82, Henry Gray award 2003), Assn. Anatomy Chmn. (exec. com. 1978-80, pres. 1981-82), Electron Microscopy Soc. Am. (program chmn. 1984-85), N.Y. Soc. Electron Microscopy (mem. 1967-68), Soc. for Neurosci. (pres. Chgo. chpt. 1985-86), Harvey Soc., Internat. Brain Rsch. Orgn., Cajal Club, Sigma Xi. Achievements include patents for method inducing analgesia by implantation of cells releasing neuroactive substances. Home: Apt 512 S 680 N Lake Shore Dr Chicago IL 60611 Office: U Ill Psychiat Inst MC 912 1601 W Taylor St Chicago IL 60612-4310 Office Phone: 312-413-4562. Business E-Mail: gdpappas@uic.edu.

**PAPPAS, JAMES PETE,** university administrator; b. Price, Utah, June 30, 1939; s. Pete S. and Dia P. (Metrakis) P.; m. Peggy Ann Kunz, Aug. 30, 1964; children: C. Jennifer, Peter T. AS in Psychology, Coll. Eastern Utah, 1959; BA in Psychology, U. Utah, 1961; MS in Counseling Psychology, Ohio U., 1964; PhD in Clin. Psychology, Purdue U., 1968; cert. in Mgmt., Stanford U., 1979; cert. in adminstrn., Harvard U., 1985. Asst. dir. counseling ctr. U. Utah, Salt Lake City, 1969-72, dir. ctr. for acad. advising, assoc. dean liberal edn., 1975-78, assoc. dean divsn. of continuing edn., 1978-87; prof. ednl. psychology and liberal studies U. Okla., Norman, 1987—, v.p. for univ. outreach; dean Coll. of Continuing Edn., 1994-00, Coll. of Liberal Studies, 2000—. Author: (book) Windows of Opportunity: Preparing University Based Residential Continuing Education for the Twenty-First Century, 1992, The University's Role in Economic Development: From Research to Outreach, 1997; co-author: (workbook) Promotional Techniques, 1987. Mem. Norman Econ. Devel. Coalition, 1996—; state chmn. Utah Endowment for Humanities, 1985-88; pres. Norman Arts and Humanities Coun., 1994-95. Recipient St. Paul award Greek Orthodox Ch. of N. Am., Denver, 1990, Christopher Outstanding Leadership and Bittner Svc. awards U. Continuing Edn. Assn.; inductee Internat. Adult and Continuing Edn. Hall of Fame, 1997. Mem. Am.

Assn. Counseling and Devel. (nat. senator 1975-77), Assn. Acad. Affairs Adminstr. (bd. dirs. 1977-78), Adult Edn. Assn. (bd. dirs. 1979-82), Univ. Continuing Edn. Assn. (pres. 1996-97, Julius M. Nolte award 2006), Nat. Assn. State Univs. and Land Grant Colls. (bd. dirs. 1994-97), Assn. Grad. Liberal Studies Programs (bd. dirs. 2002—). Avocations: reading, community service, writing, sports, travel. Office: Coll Continuing Edn 1700 Asp Ave Rm 111 Norman OK 73072-6407

**PAPPAS, MARGENE,** retired music educator; d. Eugene Wallace and Marietta Joan Kirkwood; m. Peter Michael Pappas, Dec. 30, 1973. BS, U. Ill., Champaign-Urbana, 1969, MS, 1973. Tchr. Oswego Dist. 308, Ill., 1969—2006; band dir. Oswego Cmty. Band, 1994—2006; ret., 2006. Guest conductor Ill. All-State Band, 2001. Contbr. articles to NBA Jour. Named to Hall of Fame, Phi Beta Mu, Ill. Chpt., 2003; recipient Studs Terkel Humanitarian award, Village of Oswego, 2002, Sudler Legion of Honor, John Philip Sousa Found., 2003, John P. Paynter Lifetime Achievement award, Quinlan and Fabish Music Co., 2006. Mem.: Bands of Am. (adv. bd. 2001—), Ill. Music Edn. Assn., Am. Sch. Band Dirs. Assn., Nat. Band Assn. (bd. dirs. 2000—06). Achievements include directing the HS Wind Symphony performance at 2004 IMEA All-State; directing Oswego HS Marching Band in the 2005 Tournament of Roses; Margene Pappas Day named in her honor Village of Oswego, May 28, 2006. Avocations: travel, reading, music, hiking, cross stitch. Home: 2469 Lakeside Dr Aurora IL 60504 Office Phone: 630-636-2050. E-mail: tntohsband@aol.com.

**PAPPAS, MARJORIE L.,** library studies educator; b. Adrian, Mich., Oct. 4, 1938; d. Raymond C. Spielman and Adalene E. Dickey, Alfred Dickey (Stepfather); children: David J, Mark J. BS, U. Toledo, 1961; MEd, Miami U., Oxford, Ohio, 1977, PhD, 1987. Sch. libr. Watts Mid. Sch., Centerville, Ohio, 1970—78; dir. tech. and librs. Troy (Ohio) City Schs., 1978—85; asst. prof. Wright State U., Dayton, Ohio, 1986—95; assoc. prof. U. No. Iowa, Cedar Falls, 1995—98, vis. prof. online, 1998—2001; assoc. prof. Ea. Ky. U., Richmond, 2001—04; adj. prof. Mansfield U., Mansfield, Pa., 2004—05; assoc. prof. sch. libr. and Dept. Info. Tech. Mansfield (Pa.) U., 2005—, chmn. sch. libr. and Dept. Info. Tech., 2005; freelance writer, cons. Danville, Ky., 2005—. Pres., cons. C L Assocs., Inc., Danville, Ky., 1999—2000. Author: (information process model) Pathways to Knowledge, 1997, Searching Electronic Resources, 1998, Pathways to Knowledge and Inquiry Learning, 1998; contbr. articles to profl. jours. Recipient Edgar Dale award, Assn. Ednl. Comm. and Tech., 1995. Mem.: ALA, Ky. Sch. Media Assn., Am. Assn. Sch. Librs. (regional dir. 1993—96), Ohio Ednl. Libr. Media Assn. (life award of merit 2001), Delta Kappa Gamma. Home: 426 Cloverdale Dr Danville KY 40422 Business E-Mail: mlpappas@adelphia.net.

**PAPPAS, MICHAEL,** former congressman; b. New Brunswick, N.J., Dec. 29, 1960; Mem. U.S. House of Reps., Washington, 1996-98. Mem. Nat Security com., Small Bus. com., Govt. Reform and Oversight Com.; vice chmn. Civil Svc. subcom. Govt. Reform and Oversight com.; mem. Caucus on Hellenic Issues; freeholder Somerset County, dep. dir. 1986, 87, 92, 96, freeholder dir., 1998, 93; chmn. Somerset County Bd. Social Svcs., 1986-96; past liaison Somerset County Agriculture Devel. Bd.; mem. Franklin Township Coun., 1982-87, mayor, 1983-84. Trustee Somerset Med. Ctr.; Rep. candidate for Congress in N.J., 1999—. Recipient Disting. Svc. award Somerville Area Jaycees, 1992; named Outstanding Young Citizen, N.J. Jr. C. of C., 1993. Mem. Somerset County 4-H Assn. (Outstanding Svc. award 1994), Franklin Township Lions Club (Citizen of Yr. 1988), Ctrl. Jersey Club of the Deaf, Inc., Order AHEPA.

**PAPPAS, MILTON J.,** venture capitalist; b. Cleve., Nov. 13, 1928; s. John Milton and Helen Stajos Pappas; m. Christine Kanillos, Nov. 7, 1953; children: Jeannine, William. BBA, Case Western Res. U., 1950; LLB, Cleveland Marshall Law Sch., 1956. Bar: Ohio 1956; cert. Inst. Chartered Analysts. Trust investment officer Cleve. Trust Co., 1954-60; fin. analyst Merrill Turben & Co., Cleve., 1960-62; sr. v.p. First of Mich., Detroit, 1962-66; v.p. Drexel, Harrman Ripley, N.Y.C., 1966-70, Euclid Ptnrs., N.Y.C., 1970—. Bd. dirs. IntraLinks, Inc., N.Y.C., Cubic Wafer, Inc., Austin, Tex. Lt. (j.g.) USCG, 1952-54. Mem. N.Y. Venture Capital Forum. Greek Orthodox. Avocations: opera, ballet, theater, travel, jogging. Office: Euclid Ptnrs Corp 45 Rockefeller Plz Ste 3240 New York New York 10111-0999 Business E-Mail: milton@euclidsr.com.

**PAPPAS, PHILIP JAMES,** real estate company executive; b. Chgo., Sept. 29, 1954; s. Nicholas James and Ann (Nicholson) P.; m. Ana Lucia Sant'Anna; children: Tiago, Marcelo, Amanda. BA, Shimer Coll., 1975. Mgr. Cook County Hosp., Chgo., 1975-77, purchasing agt., 1977-81; pres. L.G. Properties, Chgo., 1980—, Tiamar Real Estate, 1990—. Docent Chgo. Architecture Found., 1976-78. Pres. Lincoln Park Builders Assn., 1997-99, Lake View Developers, 1988-89; trustee Shimer Coll., 1997-2003. Recipient 1st pl. award for best interior restoration Nat. Trust for Hist. Preservation, 1991. Mem. Nat. Assn. Realtors, Oxford Union Soc. (life), Chgo. Assn. Realtors (Good Neighbor award 1992, 96, 99-2004), Owassippe Staff Assn. Boy Scouts Am. (life). Greek Orthodox. Office: LG Properties 3654 N Lincoln Ave Chicago IL 60613-3536

**PAPPAS, SANDRA LEE,** state senator; b. Hibbing, Minn., June 15, 1949; m. Neal Gosman, 1976; 3 children. BA, Met. State U., 1986; MPA, Harvard U., 1994. Mem. Minn. Ho. of Reps., St. Paul, 1984-90, Minn. Senate, St. Paul, 1990—. Part-time coll. instr. Mem. Dem. Farmer Labor Party. Home: 182 Prospect Blvd Saint Paul MN 55107-2136 Office: Minn State Senate 120 State Capitol 75 Martin Luther King Jr Blvd Saint Paul MN 55155-1601 Office Phone: 651-296-1802.

**PAPPAS, TOM,** Olympic track and field athlete; b. Sept. 6, 1976; Attended, Lane Community Coll., Oregon, 1995—97; BA in Recreation & Leisure studies, U. Tenn., 1997—99. Decathlete Team USA, Sydney Olympic Games, 2000, Team USA, Athens Olympic Games, 2004. Named SEC Outdoor Track Athlete of the Yr., 1999. Achievements include U.S. Outdoor National decathlon champion, 2003; Set new single meet record with 8,784 points. Office: c/o USOC One Olympic Plz Colorado Springs CO 80909

**PAPPAS-SPEAIRS, NINA,** financial planner, educator; d. Steve E. and Martha (Hicks) Kalfas; m. Harry J. Pappas, 1951 (div.); children: John J., Nicholas S., Vivian E. Pappas Unger, Mark A., Carol A. Pappas Siegel; m. Mitchell F. Speairs, 1992 (dec. 2001). BS, U. Cin., 1950; MA, Northwestern U., 1957; PhD, U. Ill., 1960. Faculty St. Mary's H.S., Chgo., Sch. Dist. 102, LaGrange, Ill., U. Ill., Chgo., 1969-79, U. Tex., Arlington, 1979-82, Tex. Wesleyan Coll., Ft. Worth, 1982-83; realtor Merrill Lynch Realty, Ft. Worth, 1983-84; fin. planner Cigna Corp., Irving, Tex., 1984-90; pvt. practice fin. planning and investments, Ft. Worth, 1990—. Organizer, condr. 1st U.S. Olympic Acad., Chgo., 1977; collaborator Internat. Olympic Acad., Olympia, Greece, 1977, guest lectr., 77, 78; chief of mission to Greece U.S. Olympic Com., 1977; guest lectr. Nat. Olympic Acad. Republic of China, 1982. Author: History and Development of the International Olympic Academy: 1927-1977, 1978; editor: Perspectives of the Olympic Games, 1979; also articles. Vice chair edn. coun. U.S. Olympic Com., 1977—85; sch. bd. Dist. 107, LaGrange, Ill., 1971—74. Recipient Silver Medal Internat. Olympic Acad., Olympia, Greece, 1981. Mem. Lecture Found., Symphony League, Opera Guild (pres. 1982-83), Round Table, Ft. Worth Woman's Club, Women's Wednesday Club (pres. 2003-04), River Crest Country Club, Ft. Worth Boat Club, Ridglea Rejebian Club, Carousel Club. Republican. Greek Orthodox. Avocations: golf, reading, sailing, dance. Home: 7705 Lake Highlands Dr Fort Worth TX 76179-2809

**PAPPERT, JERRY (GERALD J. PAPPERT),** lawyer, former state attorney general; m. Ellen Pappert; 2 children. Grad. with honors, Villanova U., 1985; JD, Notre Dame U., 1988. Atty. Duane, Morris and Hecksher, Phila., 1988—96; first deputy atty. gen. State of Pa., Harrisburg, Pa., 1996—2003,

acting atty. gen., 2003—04, atty. gen., 2004—05; ptnr. Ballard, Spahr, Andrews & Ingersoll LLP, Phila., 2005—. Office: Ballard Spahr Andrews & Ingersoll LLP 51st Fl 1735 Market St Philadelphia PA 19103

**PAPPS, BRUCE WILLIAM,** financial analyst, investment company executive; b. Mt. Kisco, N.Y., Jan. 19, 1962; s. Ernest W. and Annette (Lazration) P. BS in Econs., U. Pa., 1985. CFA Designation, 2000. Pres., CEO Papps Capital Group, Inc., N.Y.C., 1996—. Adj. prof. SUNY, Valhalla, 1996—98. Mentor P.R.I.D.E., Harlem, N.Y., 1996-98. Mem. N.Y. Soc. Securities Analysts (mem. com.), Merrill Lynch Pres.'s Club, Wharton Club. Avocations: sky diving, scuba diving, boating, skiing. Office: Papps Capital Group Inc 67 Wall St Ste 2211 New York NY 10005-3101 Office Phone: 888-727-7769. E-mail: CEO@papps.com.

**PAPROCKI, THOMAS JOHN,** lawyer, priest; b. Chgo., Aug. 5, 1952; s. John Henry and Veronica Mary (Bonat) P. BA, Loyola U., Chgo., 1974; student Spanish lang. study, Middlebury Coll., 1976, student Italian lang. study, 1987; MDiv, St. Mary of the Lake Sem., 1978; student Spanish lang. study, Instituto Cuannahuac, 1978; Licentiate in Sacred Theology, St. Mary of the Lake Sem., 1979; JD, DePaul U., 1981; JCD, Gregorian U., Rome, 1991; student Polish lang. study, Cath. U. Lublin, Poland, 1989, Jagiellonian U., Cracow, Poland, 2000. Bar: Ill. 1981, U.S. Dist. Ct. (no. dist.) Ill. 1981, U.S. Supreme Ct. 1994. Assoc. pastor St. Michael Ch., Chgo., 1978-83; pres. Chgo. Legal Clinic, 1981-87, 91—; exec. dir. South Chgo. Legal Clinic, 1981-85, bd. dirs., 1987—; adminstr. St. Joseph Ch., Chgo., 1983-86; vice-chancellor Archdiocese of Chgo., 1985-92, chancellor, 1992-2000; adj. faculty Loyola U. of Law, 1999—; pastor St. Constance Parish, 2001—03; Titular Bishop of Vulturara, Aux. Bishop of Chgo., Episc. Vicar, Vicariate IV Archdiocese of Chgo., 2003—; Archbishop's liaison for health and hosp. affaris, 2003—; v.p. Ill. Health Care Assn., 2005—. Senator Presbyteral senate Archdiocese of Chgo., 1985-87, mem. Presbyteral coun., 1992-2000, mem. Cardinal's cabinet, 1992-2000, sec. coll. consultors, 1992-2000, chmn. incardination com., 1991-2000, chmn. policy devel. com., 1998-2000, chmn. Fgn. Priests Initiative, 1998-2000; asst. to the Gen. Sec., Vatican Synod of Bishops, Spl. Assembly for Am., Rome, 1997, cardinal's del. to profl. rev. bd., 1991-2003, chmn. profl. conduct adminstrv. com., 1991-2002; bd. dirs. Cath. Conf. Ill., 1985-87. Mem. editl. adv. bd. Chgo. Cath. Newspaper, 1984-85; contbr. articles to profl. jours. Bd. dirs. United Neighborhood Orgn., Chgo., 1982-85, S.E. Community Youth Svc. Bd., Chgo., 1985, Ctr. for Neighborhood Tech., Chgo., 1986-87, Chgo. Area Found. for Legal Svcs., 1994-2002; active Chgo. Cmty. Trust Com. on Children, Youth and Families, 1991-2002, Ill. Family Violence Coordinating Coun., 1994—. Recipient Humanitarian award Polish Am. Congress, 1997, Alumni award for Outstanding Pub. Svc., DePaul Coll. of Law, 2001; named Man of Yr., Nat. Advs., 1999. Fellow Leadership Greater Chgo.; mem. ABA Assn., Chgo. Bar Assn. (bd. mgrs. 1999-2001, Maurice Weigle award 1985), Advs. Soc. (award of merit 1996), Cath. Lawyers Guild, Canon Law Soc. Am., Polish Am. Leadership Initiative (bd. dirs. 2001—), Polish Am. Assn. (bd. dirs. 1998—), The Chgo. Jr. Assn. Commerce and Industry (Ten Outstanding Young Citizens award 1986), Union League Club of Chgo., Pi Sigma Alpha, DePaul U. Alumni Assn. Avocations: hockey, running, reading. Office: Aux Bishop of Chgo 1400 S Austin Blvd Cicero IL 60804 Office Phone: 708-329-4040. Business E-Mail: tpaprocki@archchicago.org.

**PAPS, BETTY LOU,** nursing educator; b. Chrisman, Ill., Nov. 17, 1937; d. Robert Bertram Bonwell and Katherine Carol (Hess) Buchanan; m. Peter George Paps, Apr. 22, 1989 (dec.); children: Jill Stuebe Thompson, Nena Carol Mihailovic. RN, Lakeview Hosp. Sch. Nursing, 1958; BSN, U. Ill., Chgo., 1965; MSN, DePaul U., 1970; PhD, LaSalle U., 1998. Nurse educator Danville Jr. Coll., Ill., 1963-65, Chgo. Pub. Schs., 1966-68, Mt. Sinai Hosp. Sch. Nursing, Chgo., 1970; prof. nursing Kennedy King Coll., Chgo., 1970—96; chief nurse Aeromedical Evacuation Squadron, 1980—92, troop comdr. Persian Gulf War, 1991; evaluator Nat. League Nursing, 1994—98. Col. USAFR, 1974—95. Decorated Commendation award, Air medal, Meritorious Svc. award, Southeast Asia award, Kuwait Liberation medal, Chief Nurse's badge, Chief Flight Nurse award, Nat. Def. medal. Mem.: Air Force Assn., Res. Officers Assn., Aerospace Med. Assn., Am. Legion, VFW. Personal E-mail: bpaps@aol.com.

**PAPY, CHARLES C., III,** lawyer; b. Miami, Fla., Feb. 16, 1952; s. Charles C. and June (Marlow) Papy; m. Anne Lang, Aug. 6, 1977; children: Jennifer, Ryan, Alyson, Douglas. BBA, U. Miami, 1974, JD, 1977. Bar: Fla., U.S. Dist. Ct. So. Dist. Fla. Atty. Papy Poole & Weissenborn, Miami, 1977-83; ptnr. Papy Weissenborn & Papy, Miami, 1983-92, Eckert, Seamans, Cherin & Mellott, Miami, 1992—98, Duane Morris LLP, Miami, 1998—, mng. ptnr. Miami office. Appointee Jud. Nominating com., Miami, 1986-90, Health Fin. com. Dade County, Miami. Presbyterian. Avocations: fishing, hunting, sports. Office: Duane Morris LLP 200 S Biscayne Blvd Miami FL 33131-2397 Office Phone: 305-960-2222. Office Fax: 305-960-2201. Business E-Mail: ccpapy@duanemorris.com.

**PAPYRIN, ANATOLII NIKIFOROVICH,** physicist, researcher; b. Novosibirsk, Russia, Apr. 2, 1942; s. Nikifor Vasilievich Papyrin and Kaleria Sergeevna Chirkovskaya; children: Margarita Anatolievna Vartanyan, Veronica Anatolievna Pavrina. PhD, State U., Tomsk, Russia, 1971; MS, State Tech. U., Novosibirsk, Russia, 1965. Sr. rschr. K Tech. Corp., Albuquerque, 2000—; sr. rschr. assoc. Penn State U. State Coll., Pa., 1997—2000; visiting prof. McGill U., Montreal, Canada, 1990—91; assoc. prof. State U., Novosibirsk, Russia, 1972—85, prof., 1985—90; sr. scientist, head of lab. ITAM of RAS, Novosibirsk, Russia, 1971—97; research asst. Nuclear Physics, Novosibirsk, Russia, 1965—71. Coord. Metallurgical Plant, Novosibirsk, Russia, 1986—89; cons. ASB Ind. Inc., Barberton, Ohio, 1996—97, Round Table Group, Inc., Wash., DC, 2001—; mem. Cold Spray Consortium. Author: (book) Supersonic Two-Phase Flows, 1980 (SB of RAS award). Methods of Experimental Physics, 1981; contbr. articles to jour. Mem. Social Coun. Edn., Novosibirsk, Russia, 1981—86. Mem.: ASM Internat. Achievements include invention of gas dynamic spraying method. Avocations: basketball, tennis, music. Office: K Tech Corp 1300 Eubank Blvd SE Albuquerque NM 87123-3336

**PAQUE, RONALD EDWARD,** molecular immunologist; b. Green Bay, Wis., Apr. 29, 1948; s. Edward Alphonse and Lucille Rose (Aerts) P. BS, Wis. State Coll., 1960; MS, U. Wis., 1963; PhD, U. Ariz., 1966. Project asst. U. Wis., Madison, 1961-62, rsch. asst., 1962-63; trainee fellow U. Ariz., Tucson, 1963-66; assoc. dir. Cancer Chemotherapy Dept., Microbiol. Assocs., Bethesda, Md., 1966-68; USPHS postdoctoral fellow U. Ill., Chgo., 1968-70; asst. prof. U. Ill. Med. Sch., Chgo., 1970-74; assoc. prof. molecular immunology U. Tex. Health Sci. Ctr., San Antonio, 1974-86, prof., 1987—. Exec. dir. Nat. Coalition to End Peer Rev., 1986-90; mem. NIH Clin. Study Sect., Washington, 1979-82, Pres.'s Panel on Biomed. Rsch., 1975-76; cons. NIAID Rsch. Trends in Mycology, Washington, 1977-80; newsletter editor Singles Profl. Network, 1988-90. Dir. Community Outreach, San Antonio, 1988. With USMCR, 1956-62. U. Ariz. scholar, 1966; NIH Recognition awardee, 1983. Mem. AAAS, Am. Soc. Microbiology, Am. Assn. Cancer Rsch., Am. Assn. Immunologists, Fedn. of Am. Socs. for Exptl. Biology, Mensa, Sigma Xi, Beta Beta Beta. Republican. Avocations: skiing, shooting, hunting, fishing, writing. Home: 5700 N Knoll San Antonio TX 78240-2252 Office: Univ of Tex Health Sci Ctr 7703 Floyd Curl Dr San Antonio TX 78284-6200

**PAQUET, GARY LEE,** elementary school educator; b. Marquette, Mich., Feb. 28, 1963; s. Herbert Russell and Rena Ann McEachern. MusB, No. Mich. U., 1985; MA in Child Devel., Mich. State U., 1995. Music tchr. grades K-5 Algonac (Mich.) Cmty. Schs., 1985—93, tchr. 3d grade, 1993—. Prin. Pte. Tremble Elem. Sch., 2004—. Conductor Rainbow Singers Cmty. Honor Choir, Port Huron, Mich., 1998—99; soloist Schubert Male Chorus, Port Huron, Mich., 1998—2001. Mem.: Algonac Edn. Assn. (bldg. reps. 1996—99, exec. bd. 1998—99, pres. 2003—). Avocation: art. Home: 362 4th St Marysville MI 48040 Office: Algonac Cmty Schs 9541 Phelps Rd Algonac MI 48001 Office Phone: 810-794-3022 1602.

**PAQUETTE, JACK KENNETH,** management consultant, writer, historian; b. Toledo, Ohio, Aug. 14, 1925; s. Hector J. and Nellie (McCormick) P.; m. Jane Russell, Sept. 13, 1947; children: Jan Eriksen, Mark Russell, Mary Beth, John Eric. Student, Baldwin-Wallace Coll., 1943-44, Marquette U., 1944; BA, Ohio State U., 1949, MA, 1951; postgrad., Wayne State U., 1966. Editor monthly pub. Bur. Motor Vehicles, Ohio, 1947-49; asst. city editor, copy editor Ohio State Jour., 1949-51; copywriter Owens-Ill., Inc., Toledo, 1951-53, copy chief mktg. dept., 1953-55, asst. advt. mgr. mktg. dept., 1955-59; advt. mgr. Owens-Ill., Inc. (Libbey div.), 1959-61; mgr. advt. and sales promotion Owens-Ill., Inc. (Libbey products), 1961-64, mgr. customer mktg. services glass container div., 1964-67, dir. corporate orgn. planning, 1967-69, v.p. adminstrv. div., dir. corp. relations, 1969-70, corporate v.p., dir. corp. relations, 1970-80, corp. v.p., asst. to chmn. bd., 1980-84, cons., 1984-86; pres. Paquette Enterprises, 1984—; owner The Trumpeting Angel, antiques, 1985—. Mem. advt. bd. Cresset Chem. Co., 1987—. Author: A History of Owens-Illinois Inc., (1818-1984), 1985, The Glassmakers, 1994, Blowpipes, 2002, A Boy's Journey Through the Great Depression, 2005. Bd. dirs. Toledo YMCA, 1970-74, Vis. Nurse Svc., 1970-73, Children's Svcs., Lucas County, 1973-80, Toledo coun. Boy Scouts Am., trustee, v.p. fin., 1978-84; trustee Owens Tech. Coll. Found, 1978-81; mem. Advt. Club Toledo, 1951-75, trustee, 1960-62; hon. bd. dirs. Greater Toledo area chpt. ARC, 1970—; mem. advt. bd. Mercy Hosp., Toledo, 1981-84, Mary's Adult Day Care Ctr., 1989-93, St. Anthony's Children's Ctr., 1993, Mid-Coast Hosp., Brunswick, Maine, 1998—; mem. pub. rels. com. Cath. U. Am., 1979-82; chmn. U.S. Savs. Bonds, Lucas County, 1977-79; trustee Bowling Green State U. Found., 1976-83, pres., 1980-82; mem. Nat. Commn. on a Free and Responsible Press, 1980-83; v.p. trustee, Toledo Repertoire Theatre, 1984-88; trustee Crosby Gardens, 1983-89, chmn. 1987 88; trustee Toledo Bot. Gardens, 1989-90, chmn. emeritus and hon. lifetime trustee, 1990—; mem. pres.'s coun. Toledo Mus. Art, Bowling Green State U.; trustee Riverside Hosp. Found., 1984-94, chmn. 1986-89; mem. Juvenile Justice Adv. Bd., 1986-87; advisor R.B. Hayes Presdl. Ctr., 1990-92. With USNR, 1943-46, PTO. Recipient Gold Key award Pub. Rel. News, 1970, Silver Anvil award Pub. Rel. Soc., 1971, 72; named to Toledo Clean Hall of Fame, 1983. Mem. Soc. Profl. Journalists (co-founder Columbus and Toledo chpts.), Ohio Mfrs. Assn. (v.p., trustee 1969-84), Keep Am. Beautiful, Inc. (nat. chmn., exec. com., 1978-84, chmn. emeritus, mem. nat. adv. coun. 1984—), Bus. Com. for the Arts (corp. liaison 1980-84), U.S. C. of C. (cons. affairs com. 1980-84), Western Lake Erie Hist. Soc. (life, trustee 1998-2003), USN Armed Guard Assn., Sampson WWII Navy Vets. Assn., OSU Alumni Assn. (life), Maine Maritime Mus., Toy Soldier Collectors of Am. Soc., Toledo Glass Club, Fostoria Glass Club, Toledo Press Club (founding trustee), Toledo Club, Torch Club (trustee), Rotary (Paul Harris fellow), U.S. Navy League, Am. Legion (Toledo post), Pi Sigma Alpha. Home and Office: 2355 Parliament Sq Toledo OH 43617-1256

**PAQUETTE, WILLIAM ARTHUR,** historian, educator; b. Lawrence, Mass., Aug. 6, 1947; s. Arthur Conrad Paquette and Dorothy Lucille Root; m. Sylvia Lois Kreps, June 14, 1969 (div. 1987). BA, Grove City Coll., Pa., 1969; MA, Duquesne U., Pitts., 1971; PhD, Emory U., Atlanta, 1994. Tchr. Acad. Holy Cross, Kensington, Md., 1972—75, chmn. dept. social sci. 1973—75; from adj. prof. to prof. history Tidewater C.C., Portsmouth, Va., 1975—94, prof., 1994—. Grad. tchng. asst. Duquesne U., Pitts., 1969—71; adj. prof. history Old Dominion U., Norfolk, Va., 1975—78, Spelman Coll. Atlanta, 1983—84, adj. prof., 1989—90; adj. prof. history Ga. Perimeter, Atlanta, 1983—84; adj. prof. edn. Emory U., Atlanta, 1989—90; project historian NEH, 1979—82, 1995—96, 2000—02; reviewer ETS, 1995—2002; chmn. chancellor's prefix review com. Va. CC. Sys., Richmond, 1998—2000; nat. co-editor history Merlot Project, 2000—; mem. adv. bd. history digital project Nat. Humanities Alliance, 2000—, Gale Group Pubs., 2003—; ProQuest Pubs., 2004—, Prentice-Hall, 2004—, Houghton Mifflin, 2005—; cons. in field; grants reviewer Dept. Edn., 2004—; edn. reviewer Nat. Gallery of Art, 2004—; mem. adv. bd. H-NET. Author: U.S. Colored Troops from Lower Tidewater in the Civil War, 1992, Encyclopedia of African-American Civil Rights, 1992, Ready Reference: Censorship, 1997, Great Events from History, North America Series, 1997, The War of 1812: An Encyclopedia, 1998, Dictionary of World Biography: 20th Century, 1999, Biographical Encyclopedia of Twentieth Century World Leaders, 1999, Encyclopedia of the U.S. Supreme Court, 2000, Encyclopedia of America's Historic Sites, 2000, Putting the World into World History textbooks, Teaching History, 2001, Great Events: 1900-2001, 2002, World Education Encyclopedia, 2002, World Press Encyclopedia, 2003, A Taste of Merlot: The Multimedia Resources for Historians and Others, Perspectives, 2003; co-author: Instructor's Guide to the Teaching of American History, 1979, Readings in Black and White, 1982, Suffolk: A Pictorial History, 1987, Dictionary of World Biography: Renaissance, 1998, Encyclopedia of North America, 1998, Teaching History, A Journal of Methods, 2001; photographer Fashion Doll Wardrobe, 2002; contbr. articles to profl. jours. Mem. adv. bd. US Com. World Food Day, 1999—; commr. Mus. Fine Arts, Portsmouth, Va., 1997—2002; mem. adv. bd. Fest. of the Book, 1998—2004; adv. bd. H-NET, 2005—. Fellow Summer fellow, NEH, 1985; grantee Study grant, Tidewater C.C., 1992—93; summer grant Am. Cities and Pub. Spaces, NEH, 2005—06, Gilder-Lehrman fellow, U. Va., 2005. Mem.; Va. Political Scientists, History of Edn. Soc., Comparative and Internat. Edn. Soc., US Capitol Hist. Soc., Internat. Standing Conf. History Edn., Am. Ednl. Rsch. Assn., Am. Coun. Quebec Studies, Cmty. Coll. Humanities Assn. (v.p. 1991—93, bd. dirs. 1993—97, Disting. Svc. award 1997), Orgn. Am. Historians (com. cmty. coll. 2002—, chmn. 2004—05), Am. Hist. Assn. (Nancy Roelker Mentorship com. 1997—2000, chmn. 1999—2000, joint com. adj. 2000—04), Mayflower Soc. Va. (asst. historian 1992—93, historian 1993—98, dep. gov. gen. 2004—). Avocations: stamp collecting/philately, photography, travel, genealogy. Office: Tidewater CC 7000 Coll Dr Portsmouth VA 23703 Home: 13565 Filly Ct Gainesville VA 20155 Office Phone: 757-822-2386. Business E-Mail: wpaquette@tcc.edu

**PAQUIN, ANNA,** actress; b. Winnipeg, MB Canada, July 24, 1982; d. Brian and Mary Paquin. Actor: (films) The Piano, 1993 (Academy Award best supporting actress, 1993, Golden Globe nomination best supporting actress, 1993), Jane Eyre, 1995, Fly Away Home, 1996, Amistad, 1997, A Walk on the Moon, 1988, Hurly-burly, 1998, Begin the Beguine, 1998, Sleepless Beauty, 1998, A Walk on the Moon, 1999, She's All That, 1999, X-Men, 2000, Almost Famous, 2000, Finding Forrester, 2000, Buffalo Soldiers, 2001, Darkness, 2002, 25th Hour, 2002, X2: X-Men United, 2003, Steamboy, 2004, The Squid and the Whale, 2005, X-Men: The Last Stand, 2006; (TV films) Member of the Wedding, 1997, Hercules (voice only), 1988, All the Rage, 1999, (voice) Joan of Arc, 2005,: (plays) After Ashley, 2005. Office: Double Happy Talent c/o Gail Cowan PO Box 9585 Wellington New Zealand also: William Morris Agy One William Morris Pl Beverly Hills CA 90212*

**PAQUIN, EDWARD H., JR.,** retired state legislator, not-for-profit developer; b. Bennington, Vt., Feb. 12, 1953; s. Edward H. Sr. and Alice Marie P.; m. Patricia LaRose, July 4, 1981 (div. Dec. 2005); 1 child, Katherine Marie BA, U. Vt., 1975. Various positions including silversmith and factory worker; builder; rep. Vt. Gen. Assembly, Montpelier, 1991—2002; exec. dir. Vt. Protection and Advocacy, Inc., Montpelier, 2002—. Dir. summer camp for low-income rural children CAMP!; bd. dirs. Vt. Ctr. Ind. Living. Recipient Victory award Nat. Rehab. Hosp., 1991. Democrat. Baptist. Home: PO Box 219 Fairfax VT 05454-0219 Office: Vt Protection and Advocacy Inc 141 Main St Ste 7 Montpelier VT 05602

**PAQUIN, THOMAS CHRISTOPHER,** lawyer; b. Quincy, Mass., Feb. 12, 1947; s. Henry Frederick and Rita Marie (St. Louis) P.; m. Jean Jacqueline O'Neill, Aug. 5, 1972; children: Martha, Edward. BS in Acctg., Bentley Coll., 1969; JD, U. Notre Dame, 1974. Bar: Mass. 1974, U.S. Dist. Ct. Mass. 1976. Tax atty. Coopers and Lybrand, Boston, 1974-76; assoc. Cargill, Masterman & Cahill, 1976, Wilson, Curran & Malkasian, Wellesley, 1976-77; ptnr. Bianchi and Paquin, Hyannis, 1977-98; shareholder, dir. Quirk and Chamberlain, P.C., Yarmouthport, 1998—2001; of counsel Quirk, Chamberlain & Marsh, P.C., 2002—04; pvt. practice Barnstable, Mass., 2004—; pub. adminstr. Barnstable County, 2006—. Bd. dirs., chmn. nominating com. Elder

Svcs. Cape Cod and Islands, Inc., Dennis, Mass., 1986-91; bd. dirs., corporator Vis. Nurse Assn. Cape Cod Found., Inc., Dennis, 1988-97; pres. Life Svcs. Inc., 1991-95; bd. dirs. Woodside Cemetery Corp., 1998—, pres., 1999—. Mem. Bass River Golf Commn., Yarmouth, Mass., 1980-83, chmn., 1982-83; chmn. Yarmouth Golf Course Bldg. Com., 1985-89; mem. hearing com. bd. Bar Overseers of the Supreme Jud. Ct., 1989-95; bd. dirs. Project Coach, Inc., 1990-97; conciliator Barnstable Superior Ct., 1992—, Barstable Dist. Ct., 2000—; trustee, asst. treas. Cape Symphony Orch., 1999-2004, chmn. fin. com., 2003-04. Fellow Mass. Bar Found.; mem. ABA, Mass. Bar Assn. (del. 1986-87, mem. com. on bicentennial U.S. Constn. 1986-88, fee arbitration bd. 1985-86, chmn. spkrs. and writers subcom. 1986-88), Barnstable County Bar Assn. (chmn. seminar com. 1979-83, mem. exec. com. 1981-84, v.p. 1984-86, pres. 1986-87), Estate Planning Coun. Cape Cod (exec. com. 1985-98, sec. 1991-93, pres.-elect 1993-95, pres. 1995-97), Mass. Conveyancers Assn., Mid-Cape Men's Club (v.p. 1992, pres. 1993), Cummaquid Golf Club (dir. 2003-). Office: PO Box 1145 3010 Main St Barnstable MA 02630-1145 Personal E-mail: thomaspaquin@verizon.net.

**PARA, GERARD ALBERT,** lawyer, real estate broker, consultant; b. Oak Park, Ill., June 27, 1953; s. Bruno Joseph and Bernice Agnes Para; m. Gayle Louise Keegan, Sept. 15, 1979; children; Eric, Teresa. BA with honor, De Paul U., 1973, JD, 1976. Bar: Ill. 1977, U.S. Dist. Ct. (no. dist.) Ill. 1977, U.S. Ct. Appeals (7th cir.) 1977, Fed. Trial Bar. 1984; lic. real estate broker, Ill., 1981. Jud. law clk. Ill Appellate Ct. (1st dist.), Chgo., 1977-78; divsnl. counsel Household Internat. Franchisor Divsns., Prospect Heights, Ill., 1978-85; v.p Bannockburn (Ill.) Pk. Concepts, Inc., 1986-93; dir. real estate ops., asst. gen. counsel Ben Franklin Stores, Carol Stream, Ill., 1994-96; v.p., gen. counsel DiMucci Devel. Corp., Palatine, Ill., 1996-97; gen. counsel Urban Investment Trust Inc., Chgo., 1998-99; prin. Franchise ESQ.sm, Lincolnshire, Ill., 1999—; arbitrator 19th Jud. Cir., Lake County, Ill., 1999—, 18th Jud. Cir., DuPage County, Ill., 2000—, Cir. Ct. of Cook County, Ill., 2000—; candidate 19th Jud. Cir. Judge, Dem. Party, Lake and McHenry Counties, Ill., 2002. Real estate broker, Long Grove, Ill., 1987—; franchise cons. Elliotts' Off Broadway Deli, Oak Brook, Ill., 1993—; interim exec. dir. YWCA of Rockford, Ill., 2006—. Editor: Medical Malpractice, 1975, Trial Technique, 1975. Asst. coach Little League Buffalo Grove Recreation Assn., Ill., 1988—2000; asst. scoutmaster Boy Scouts Am., Long Grove, 1995—; interim exec. dir. YWCA Rockford, Ill., 2006—. Mem. ABA, Internat. Coun. Shopping Ctrs., Internat. Corp. Real Estate Execs. (bd. dirs. Chgo. chpt. 1999-2002), Chgo. Bar Assn., Internat. Franchise Assn., Coun. Franchise Suppliers. Roman Catholic. Avocations: lap swimming, boating, scuba diving, weightlifting. Office: Franchise ESQ sm 125 Shelter Rd #450 Lincolnshire IL 60069 Office Phone: 847-634-2175. Personal E-mail: franchiseesq@aol.com.

**PARAD, RICHARD BARRY,** pediatrician, researcher; b. Boston, Sept. 29, 1955; s. Sidney and Edna Parad; m. Judy Ann Estroff, Nov. 16, 1951; children: Rebecca Estroff, Matthew Alexander Estroff. BA, Wesleyan U., Middletown, Conn., 1977; MD, U. Calif., La Jolla, 1981; MPH, Harvard U., Boston, Mass., 1997. Diplomate Am. Bd. of Pediat., 1986. Neonatologist Harvard Newborn Medicine, Brigham and Women's Hosp., Boston, 1987—2006; assoc. prof. pediat. Harvard Med. Sch., Boston, 2006. Co-dir. Mass. Cystic Fibrosis Newborn Screening Program, Boston, 1999—; dir. clin. rsch. dept. newborn medicine Brigham and Women's Hosp., Boston, 2006. Fellow: Am. Acad. of Pediat.; mem.: Soc. for Pediatric Rsch. Achievements include research in Newborn Respiratory Disorders, Cystic Fibrosis, C1 Inhibitor defects and Cystic Fibrosis Newborn Screening. Office: Brigham and Women's Hosp 75 Francis St Boston MA 02115 Office Phone: 617-732-8405.

**PARADA, LUIS FERNANDO,** science educator; b. Santa Fe de Bogota, Colombia, July 18, 1954; came to the U.S., 1993; s. Alfonso and Clara Parada. BS, U. Wis., 1979; PhD, MIT, 1985. Postdoctoral fellow Pasteur Inst., Paris, 1985-87; group leader Nat. Cancer Inst., Frederick, Md., 1988-91, sect. chief ABL, 1991-94; prof., dir. Ctr. Devel. Biology U. Tex. Southwestern Med. Ctr., Dallas, 1994—, Dana and Richard C. Strauss disting. chmn. in devel. biology, 1994—; dir. Kent Waldrep Ctr. for Basic Rsch. on Nerve Growth, 1997—, Southwestern Bell disting. chair in basic neurosci. rsch., 1998—; prof. Amer. Cancer Soc., 2003. Mem. sci. adv. bd. Rett Syndrome Found., N.Y., 1999—, Christopher Reeve paralysis Found., N.Y.C., 1996—; mem. sci. adv. coun. Damon Runyan-Walter Winchell Cancer Fund., N.Y.C., 1998—, Nat. Neurofibromatosis Found., N.Y.C., 1997—; chmn. bd. sci. counselors Nat. Inst. Neurol. Disorders and Stroke, Bethesda, Md., 1999—; mem. bd. sci. counselors Nat. Cancer Inst., Bethesda, 1995-99; rschr. in field. Patentee in field. Peter A. Steck Memorial ward, Soc. for Neuro-Oncology, 2000 Mem. Amer. Assn. for the Advancement of Science, Soc. for Neuroscience, Amer. Assn. for Cancer Rsch, Soc. for Develp. Biology. Office: U Tex Southwestern Med Ctr 5323 Harry Hines Blvd Dallas TX 75390-9133

**PARADISE, LOUIS VINCENT,** education educator, dean; b. Scranton, Pa., Apr. 19, 1946; s. Louis Benjamin and Lucille P.; children: Christopher, Gabrielle,Victoria. BS, Pa. State U., 1968; MS, Bucknell U., 1974; PhD, U. Va., 1976. Lic. psychologist, profl. counselor; cert. sch. psychologist. Assoc. prof. Cath. U. Am., Washington, 1976-83; prof. edn., chmn. edn. leadership U. New Orleans, 1983-90, dean Coll. Edn., 1990-92, univ. vice chancellor, provost, 1992-94, exec. vice chancellor, provost, 1994—2003, prof. Dept. Ednl. Leadership, Counseling, and Found., 2003—. Author: Ethics in Counseling and Psychotherapy, 1979, Questioning: Skills for the Helping Process, 1979, Counseling in Community College, 1982. 1st lt. U.S. Army, 1968-72. DuPont scholar U. Va., 1974. Mem. APA, ACA (ethics com. 1986-89), Am. Edn. Rsch. Assn., So. Assn. Counselor Edn. Chmn. ethics com. 1988-89), Acad. Counseling Psychology, Chi Sigma Iota (founding chpt. pres. 1985 07) Roman Catholic. Avocations: running, bicycling, music. Office: U New Orleans Dept Ednl Leadership Counseling & Found New Orleans LA 70148-0001 Business E-Mail: louis.paradise@uno.edu.

**PARAMESWARAN, RAJU,** accountant; b. Aymanam, India, Oct. 5, 1955; s. Raghunatha Iyer and Rajalakshmi Raghunathan; m. Ramaa Ramharith, June 3, 1981; 1 child, Arun. BSc, U. Kerala, India, 1972—75. Chartered acct., Inst. Chartered Accts. India, 1979, CPA Botswana Inst. Accts., 1990. Chmn. Moores Rowland, Gaborone, Botswana, 1981—; dir. Drawtech Pty, Ltd., Lobatse, Botswana, 1995—2005; founder, dir. Flotek, Lobatse, 1999—; Budgetax, Ft. Myers, Fla., 2003—; Capri-Budgetax, Chennai, India, 2003—. Contbr. articles to profl. jours. Chmn. BOCCIM-Lobatse Bus. Coun., Lobatse, 2004—05. Mem.: Rotary Club Lobatse (pres. 1993—94, Paul Harris Fellow 2004).

**PARAN, MARK LLOYD,** retired lawyer; b. Cleve., Feb. 1, 1953; s. Edward Walter and Margaret Gertrude (Ebert) P. AB in Sociology cum laude, Harvard U., 1977, JD, 1980. Bar: Ill. 1980, Mass. 1986, Tex. 1993. Assoc. Wilson & McIlvaine, Chgo., 1980-83, Lurie Sklar & Simon, Ltd., Chgo., 1983-85, Sullivan & Worcester, Boston, 1985-92; pvt. practice Boston, 1992, Euless, Tex., 1992—2002. Mem. ABA, State Bar Tex. Avocations: tornado hunting, severe thunderstorms, photography. Home and Office: 1050 W Ash Ln Apt 1015 Euless TX 76039-2171 Office Phone: 817-684-0725. Personal E-Mail: f6tornado@comcast.net.

**PARAZYNSKI, SCOTT E.,** astronaut; b. Little Rock, Ark., July 28, 1961; m. Gail Marie Vozzella; 2 children. BS in Biology, Stanford U., 1983, MD with honors, 1989. Intern Brigham and Women's Hosp., 1990; resident in emergency medicine Denver; astronaut NASA, Houston, 1992—; crew rep. for extravehicular activity, Astronaut Office Mission Devel. Br., crew rep. for space shuttle, space station, dep. Astronaut Office ISS Br. Author numerous publs. in the field of space physiology. Team coach for the Philippines Olympic Winter Games, Calgary, Canada, 1988. Recipient Predoctoral Tng. award in cancer biology, NIH, 1983, NASA-Ames Cert. of Recognition, 1990, Space Station Team Excellence award, 1996, NASA Exceptional Svc. medal, 1998, 1999, NASA Space Flight medal, 1994, 1997, 1998, 2001, NASA Disting. Svc. medal, 2002, Ellis Island Family Heritage award in Technology, Statue of Liberty-Ellis Island Found., Inc., 2005. Mem.: Aircraft

Owners and Pilots Assn., Exptl. Aircraft Assn., Assn. Space Explorers, Wilderness Med. Soc. (Rsch. award 1991), Am. Soc. Gravitational and Space Biology, Aerospace Med. Assn., Am. Alpine Club. Achievements include logged over 2,000 flight hours in a variety of aircraft; logged over 1,019 hours in space; 20 hours EVA; crew STS-66 (1994), STS-86 Atlantis (1997), STS-95 Discovery (1998) and STS-100 Endeavour (2001); mission specialist reassigned from mission STS-118 to STS-121 to Internat. Space Station, 2006; competed on the US Development Luge Team and was ranked among the top 10 competitors in the nation during the 1988 Olympic Trials; served as an Olympic Team Coach for the Phillippines during the 1988 Olympic Winter Games in Calgary, Canada. Avocations: mountain climbing, rock climbing, flying, scuba diving, skiing, woodworking, nature photography. Office: Astronaut Office/CB NASA Johnson Space Ctr Houston TX 77058*

**CUMMARD, JOHN CLEO,** music educator; b. Oskaloosa, Iowa, July 17, 1945; s. John Melvin and Verda Louella May Parcell; m. Cathy Kay Hardy, Sept. 30, 1990;; children: Kent Bradley, Khristina Lynn. BS, NE Mo. St U., Kirksville, MO, 1967; MA, Truman St U., Kirksville, MO, 1968; MS, Ctrl. Mo. St U., Warrensburg, MO, 2000; DMA, U. Mo., Kansas City, MO, 1990. DESE-Life Certification Mo., Orff Schulework Level J Mo., Elementary Administration-DESE Mo. Band dir. Rich Ctrl. H.S., Olympia Field, Ill., 1967—69, Tipton Cmty. Sch., Tipton, Iowa, 1969—72, Maynard (West Ctrl.), Maynard, Iowa, 1972—73, Carl Junction R-I Schools, Carl Junction, Mo., 1973—73; choir dir. Meml. H.S., Joplin, Mo., 1980—82; music and instrumental music tchr. Joplin R-8, Joplin, Mo., 1982—88; elem. music tchr. Kans. City Sch. Dist., Kansas City, Mo., 1990—; adj. prof. Longview CC, Lee's Summit, Mo., 1992—. Music critic Pk. Forest Star, Park Forest, Ill., 1967—69; trumpet player Chgo. Hgts Symphony, Chicago Heights, Ill., 1967—69; member-european tour Mid Am. Jazz & Concert Band-Coe Coll., Cedar Rapids, Iowa, 1972; member-mexican tour Kans. City Symphony Chorus, Kansas City, Mo., 1988; mem. Mid. Sch. Music Curriculum Committe, Joplin, Mo., 1984, Profl. Devel. Com., Kansas City, Mo., 1990—2000, Kans. City Sch. Dist. Core Curriculum and Textbook Com., Kansas City, Mo., 1999—2000. Camelot cast mem. Joplin Little Theater, Joplin, Mo., 1983—83; asst. condr. Carthage Cmty. Band, Carthage, Mo., 1985—87; mem. Blue Springs Summer Musical Orch., Blue Springs, Mo., 1990—95. Recipient Cowlgill & Blair Incentive Award, SW Mo. Teachers Assoc, 1986, Phi Kappa Phi, Ctrl. Mo. St U., 2000. Mem.: Mo. Music Educators Assn., Music Educators Nat. Conf. Southern Baptist. Avocations: music listening, music listening, landscaping, instrument and vocal music performance. Home: 5433 Appleton Ave Raytown MO 64133 Office: Kansas City School District 12th & McGee Kansas City MO 64109 Personal E-mail: john_parcell2003@yahoo.com

**PARCELLS, BILL (DUANE CHARLES PARCELLS),** professional football coach; b. Englewood, N.J., Aug. 22, 1941; m. Judith Parcells; children: Suzy, Jill, Dallas. BA, Wichita State U., 1964. Asst. coach Hastings Coll. (Nebr.), 1964, Wichita State U. (Kans.), 1969, U.S. Mil. Acad., 1966—69, Fla. State U., Tallahassee, 1970—72, Vanderbilt U., Nashville, 1973—74, Tex. Tech U., Lubbock, 1975—77; head coach U.S. Air Force Acad., Colorado Springs, Colo., 1978; asst. coach New Eng. Patriots, NFL, 1980, N.Y. Giants, NFL, 1981—82, head coach, 1983—91; NFL studio analyst NBC Sports, 1991—92; head coach New England Patriots, NFL, 1993—97, NY Jets, 1997—2000, chief football ops., 2000—01; head coach Dallas Cowboys, 2003—. Achievements include head coach, Super Bowl Champion New York Giants, 1986, 1990. Office: Dallas Cowboys One Cowboys Pkwy Irving TX 75063*

**PARCELLS, FREDERICK R.,** underwriter; b. Chgo., May 14, 1957; s. Charles Hubbard and Winifred Elaine (Summer) P. AA, Barton County C.C., Great Bend, Kans., 1977; BA in Fin., U. Ill., 1980; MBA, Ind. U., 1985. CFP, CPCU; assoc. in risk mgmt., assoc. in reinsurance/Ins. Inst. Am. Actuarial trainee CNA Ins., Chgo., 1980-81; actuarial technician Sentry Ins., Stevens Point, Wis., 1982-83; scouting intern The Buffalo Bills, Orchard Park, Fredonia, N.Y., 1984; underwriting trainee Kemper Group, Chgo., 1986-87, casualty underwriter Chgo. and St. Louis, 1987-88; acct. underwriter Northbrook P&C Ins. (subs. Allstate), Chgo., 1988-91; sr. account underwriter Northbrook Property and Casualty Ins., Chgo./Rolling Meadows, 1991; sr. underwriter Allstate Ins., South Barrington, Ill., 1991-95; product analyst CNA Ins. Cos., Chgo., 1995-97; sr. splty. exec. underwriter Interstate Ins. Group, Chgo., 1997-2000; sr. underwriter Apex Ins. Mgrs., 2001—. Asst. chmn. civic affairs com., Cambridge Forest Assn., Lincolnshire, Ill., 1980-81; treas. Santa Claus Anonymous, Chgo., 1990-91, 91-92, pres., 1992-93; vol. duplex constrn. Habitat for Humanity, Chgo., 1988, 89. Mem. CPCU Soc. (sec. Chgo. chpt. 1994-95, bd. dirs./pub. rels. chmn. 1993-94, mem. nat. underwriting sect. com. 1994-2003, com. chair, 2001-03, treas. Chgo. chpt. 1995-96, v.p. Chgo. chpt. 1996-97, pres. Chgo. chpt. 1997-98, pres. 1998-2000). Presbyterian. Home: 1957 Barnhill Dr Mundelein IL 60060 Office: Apex Ins Mgrs LLC 500 W Madison St Ste 450 Chicago IL 60661 E-mail: fparcells@apexamerican.com

**PARCHOMOVSKY, GIDEON,** law educator; LLB, Hebrew U. Jerusalem, 1993; LLM, U. Calif., Berkeley, 1995; JSD, Yale U., 1998. Law clk. to Hon. Eliahu Mazza Supreme Ct. of Israel, 1993—94; asst. prof. law U. Pa. Law Sch., Phila., 2002—04, prof. law, 2004—. Vis. prof. Fordham Law Sch., 1998—2002, Yale Law Sch., 2000, 02. Contbr. articles to law jours. Office: U Pa Law Sch 3400 Chestnut St Philadelphia PA 19104 Office Phone: 215-898-1603. E-mail: gparchom@law.upenn.edu.

**PARDE, DUANE ARTHUR,** association executive; BA in Polit. Sci History, U. Kans Legis rsch. assn. mgmt. Am. Legis. Legis., Topeka, 1986-87; dir. state legis. rsch. Am. Legis. Exchange Coun., Washington, 1989-92; dir. state affairs Coun. Affordable Health Ins., Alexandria, Va., 1992-95; chief of staff Am. Legis. Exchange Coun., Alexandria, 1995-96, exec. dir., 1996—. Bd. adv. Kans. Pub. Policy Inst. Mem. Am. Soc. Assn. Exec. Office: Am Legis Exchange Coun 1129 20th St NW #500 Washington DC 20036-3479

**PARDEE, ARTHUR BECK,** biochemist, educator; b. Chgo., July 13, 1921; s. Charles A. and Elizabeth B. (Beck) Pardee; m. Ruth Sager (dec.); m. Ann Goodman; children: Michael, Richard, Thomas. BS, U. Calif., Berkeley, 1942; MS, Calif. Inst. Tech., 1943, PhD, 1947; D (hon.), U. Paris, 1993. Merck postdoctoral fellow U. Wis., 1947—49; mem. faculty U. Calif., Berkeley, 1949—61, assoc. prof., 1957—61; NSF fellow Pasteur Inst., 1957—58; prof. biology, chmn. dept. biochem. scis. Princeton (NJ) U., 1961—67, prof. biochemistry, 1961—75, Donner prof. sci., 1966; prof. Dana Farber Cancer Inst. and biochem. pharmacology dept. Harvard Med. Sch., Boston, 1975—. Co-author: Experiments in Biochemical Research Techniques, 1957; editor: Biochemica et Biophysica Acta, 1962—68; contbr. over 500 articles to publs. Mem. nat. adv. coun. Am. Cancer Soc., 1967—71; trustee Cold Spring Harbor Lab. Quantitative Biology, 1963—69. Named Princess Takamatu lectr., 1990, hon. faculty mem., Nanjing U., 1999; recipient Young Biochemists travel award, NSF, 1952, Krebs medal, Fedn. European Biochem. Socs., 1973, Rosenstiel award, Brandeis U., 1975, 3M award, Fedn. Am. Socs., Exptl. Biology, 1980, CIIT prize, 1993, Disting. Alumnus award, Calif. Inst. Tech., 1999; fellow, Internat. Inst. for Advanced Studies, 1999. Fellow: AAAS; mem.: NAS (editl. bd. proc. 1971—73, com. on scis. and pub. policy 1973—76), Chem. Industry Inst. Toxicology (Founders award, Boehringer-Mannheim award 1998), Ludwig Inst. Cancer Rsch. (sci. com. 1984—), Japanese Biochem. Soc., Am. Philos. Soc., Am. Soc. Microbiologists, Am. Assn. Cancer Rsch. (pres. 1985—86), Am. Soc. Biol. Chemists (treas. 1964—70, pres. 1980—81), Am. Chem. Soc. (Paul Lewis award 1960). Office: 44 Binney St Boston MA 02115-6013 Office Phone: 617-632-3372. Business E-Mail: arthur_pardee@dfci.harvard.edu.

**PARDEE, OTWAY O'MEARA,** computer scientist, educator; b. Seattle, June 26, 1920; s. Otway and Mary Gertrude (O'Meara) Pardee; m. Marilynn Lowrie, Aug. 9, 1946; children: Irene, Loraine, Suzanne. BS in Elec. Engring., U. Wash., 1941; PhD in Elec. Engring., Stanford U., 1948. Instr. math. Syracuse U., NY, 1948-52, asst. to assoc. prof. NY, 1952-69, dir. Computing Ctr. NY, 1962-69, prof. computer sci. NY, 1969-86, prof.

emeritus, 1986—. With USNR, 1944–46. Mem.: IEEE, AAUP (pres. Syracuse U. chpt. 1960), Am. Phys. Soc., Math. Assn. Am., Am. Math. Soc., Assn. Computing Machinery (chmn. Syracuse chpt. 1963), Tau Beta Pi, Sigma Xi. Avocations: camping, photography. Home: 843 Maryland Ave Syracuse NY 13210-2502 Office: Syracuse U Ctr for Sci and Tech Ste 2-175 Syracuse NY 13244-0001 Business E-Mail: oopardee@syr.edu.

**PARDEE, SCOTT EDWARD,** securities dealer; b. New Haven, Oct. 11, 1936; s. William Durley and Catherine (Eames) P.; m. Aida Milagros Fuentes Tavarez, Jan. 29, 1966; 1 child, Alan Alexander. BA, Dartmouth Coll., 1958; PhD, MIT, 1962. Research asst. Fed. Res. Bank, Boston, 1959-62; teaching asst. in econs. MIT, Cambridge, Mass., 1961-62; research economist Fed. Res. Bank N.Y., N.Y.C., 1962-66, mgr. rsch. dept., 1967-70, asst. v.p. fgn. dept., 1970-74, v.p. fgn. dept., 1974-79; tchr. banking and fin. NYU, 1965-67, Am. Inst. Banking, 1969-72; adj. prof. Grad. Sch. Bus. Columbia U., N.Y.C., 1972-75; dep. mgr. fgn. ops. Fed. Res. System Open Market Account, 1975-79, mgr. fgn. ops., 1979-81; exec. v.p., dir. Discount Corp. N.Y., N.Y.C., 1981-86; dir. Am. Internat. Group, 1982-86; vice chmn. Yamaichi Internat. Am. Inc., N.Y.C., 1986-88, chmn., 1988-95, sr. advisor, 1995-97; sr. lect., exec. dir. Fin. Rsch. Ctr., MIT Sloan Scool of Mgmt., 1997-99; adj. prof. Grad. Sch. of Business, U. Chicago, Chicago, Ill., 1997-98; Alan R. Holmes prof. of monetary econs. Middlebury Coll., Vt., 2000—. Bd. dirs. Renaissance Holdings, Ltd. Author: A Study of Inter-City Wage Differentials, 1962. Trustee Woodrow Wilson Fellowship Found., 1994—; mem. Coun. on Fgn. Rels., 1995—. Woodrow Wilson fellow MIT, 1958-59; recipient Dr. Louis M. Spadaro award Fordham U., 1980 Mem. Phi Beta Kappa. Home: 250 South End Ave New York NY 10280-1074 Office: Middlebury Coll Econs Dept Middlebury VT 05753

**PARDEN, CINDY MARIA,** elementary school educator; b. Pensacola, Fla., Aug. 6, 1957; d. Leroy and Helen Lorene (Earnest) Rigby; m. Stephen Anthony Parden, July 11, 1998. AA, Pensacola Jr. Coll., 1977; BS, U. West Fla., 1979; MEd, U. South Ala., 1987. Cert. elem. tchr., Ala. Tchr. 4th-5th grades Escambia City Sch. Bd., Pensacola, Mobile (Ala.) City Schs., tchr. 4th grade, tchr. 1st grade and basic skills. Named one of 2,000 Notable Am. Women, 1994, 1996, 2000, 2002, 2,000 Outstanding People of 20th Century, 1995, 1996; named to Dictionary of Internat. Biography, 1994, 1995, 1996, 1998, Internat. Directory of Disting. Leadership, 1994, 1996, 2001, 2002. Mem. NEA (del. 1992-95), Assn. Classroom Tchrs., Ala. Edn. Assn. (state del. 1988-95), Mobile Edn. Assn. Home: 250 Border Dr E Mobile AL 36608-2752

**PARDEN, ROBERT JAMES,** engineering educator, management consultant; b. Mason City, Iowa, Apr. 17, 1922; s. James Ambrose and Mary Ellen (Fahey) P.; m. Elizabeth Jane Taylor, June 15, 1955; children—Patricia Gale, James A., John R., Nancy Ann. BS in Mech. Engring, State U. Iowa, 1947, MS, 1951, PhD, 1953. Reg. profl. engr. Iowa, Calif.; lic. gen. contractor Calif. Indsl. engr. LaCrosse Rubber Mills, 1947-50; assoc. dir. Iowa Mgmt. Course, 1951-53; assoc. prof. indsl. engring. Ill. Inst. Tech., 1953-54; prof. engring. mgmt. Santa Clara U., 1955—, dean Sch. Engring., 1955-82; prin. Saratoga Cons. Group (Calif.), 1982—. Mem. Sec. Navy's Survey Bd. Grad. Edn., 1964 Mem. Saratoga Planning Commn., 1959-61. Served to 1st lt., Q.M.C. AUS, 1943-46. Named to Silicon Valley Engring. Hall of Fame Silicon Valley Engring. Coun., 1993. Mem. ASME (chmn. Santa Clara Valley sect. 1958), Am. Soc. Engring. Edn. (chmn. Pacific N.W. sect. 1960), Am. Inst. Indsl. Engrs. (edn. chmn. 1958-63, dir. ASEE-ECPD affairs 1963-68), Nat. Soc. Profl. Engrs., Engrs. Council Profl. Devel. (dir. 1964-65, 66-69), Soc. Advancement Mgmt., ASEM, Sigma Xi, Tau Beta Pi. Roman Catholic. Home: 19832 Bonnie Ridge Way Saratoga CA 95070-5010 Office: Santa Clara U Sch Engring Santa Clara CA 95053-0001 Office Phone: 408-554-4984. Personal E-mail: bobparden@comcast.net. Business E-Mail: rparden@scu.edu.

**PARDES, HERBERT,** health facility executive, psychiatrist, educator; b. Bronx, N.Y., July 7, 1934; s. Louis and Frances (Bergman) P.; m. Juidith Ellen Silber, June 9, 1957; children: Stephen, Lawrence, James. BS, Rutgers U., 1956; MD, SUNY-Downstate Med. Center, Bklyn., 1960; DSc (hon.), SUNY, 1990. Straight med. intern Kings County Hosp., 1960-61, intern & resident in psychiatry Bklyn., 1961-62, 64-66; asst. prof. psychiatry Downstate Med. Ctr., Bklyn., 1968-72, prof., chmn. dept., 1972-75; dir. psychiat. svcs. Kings County Hosp., Bklyn., 1972-75; prof., chmn. dept. psychiatry U. Colo. Med. Sch., 1975-78; dir. psychiat. svcs. Colo. Psychiat. Hosp., Denver, 1975-78; dir. NIMH, Rockville, Md., 1978-84; asst. surgeon gen. USPHS, 1978-84; prof. psychiatry Columbia U., N.Y.C, 1984—, chmn. dept., 1984; dir. Psychiat. Svc. Presbyn. Hosp. (now Columbia Presbyn. Center of NY Presbyn. Hosp.), NYC, 1984-89; dir. NY State Psychiatric Inst., 1984—89; v.p. for health scis., dean faculty medicine Columbia U., NYC, 1989—99; pres., CEO NY-Presbyn. Hosp. and Healthcare Systems, NYC, 2000—. Bd. trustees Healthcare Leadership Coun. Contbr. articles to med. jours. Pres. sci. bd. Alliance for Rsch. on Schizophrenia and Depression. Capt. M.C., AUS, 1972-74. Named Ann. Hon. Lectr. Downstate Med. Ctr. Alumni Assn., 1972; recipient Alumni Achievement medal, 1980, William Menniner award ACP, 1992, Dorothy Dix award Mental Illness Fedn., 1992, Vester Mark award, 1994, Salmon award, 1996. Mem. Assn. Am. Med. Colls. (chair 1995-96), Am. Psychiat. Assn. (v.p. 1986-88, pres. 1989-90, Disting. Svc. award 1993), Inst. Medicine, Am. Psychoanalytic Assn., Coun. of Deans (adminstrv. bd., chair-elect 1993-94, chair 1994-95), Assoc. Med. Schs. NY (pres. 1995-2000), Phi Beta Kappa, Alpha Omega Alpha. Office: NY Presbyn Hosp Pres and CEOs Office 161 Ft Washington Ave New York NY 10032 also: NY Presbyn Hosp 525 E 68th St New York NY 10021 Office Phone: 212-305-8000. Business E-Mail: pardesh@nyp.org.*

**PARDO, JANETTE M.,** archivist, librarian; b. Passaic, NJ, May 22, 1970; d. Jesus and Gladys Pardo. BA, Rutgers U., Newark, 1992, MLS, 2001. Libr. Wayne Pub. Libr., NJ, 1995—. Archival cons. Caucus Archival Projects Evaluation Svc., Trenton, NJ, 2001—. Mem.: ALA, Romance Writers Am., Soc. Am. Archivists, Mid-Atlantic Regional Archival Conf. Democrat. Roman Catholic. Avocation: writing. Office: Wayne Pub Libr 461 Valley Rd Wayne NJ 07470 Personal E-mail: jpardo22@yahoo.com.

**PARDO, ROBERT,** game designer, video game software company executive; V.p. game design Blizzard Entertainment, Irvine, Calif. Accredited to the following games Everquest, Voyage, 1994, Cyberia, 1994, Whiplash, 1995, Descent, 1995, Tempest X3, 1996, Mortal Kombat Trilogy, StarCraft: Brood War, 1998, StarCraft, 1998, Warcraft II: Battle.net Edition, 1999, StarCraft 64, 2000, Diablo II, 2000, Diablo II (Collector's Edition), 2000, Kingdom Under Fire, 2001, Warcraft III: Reign of Chaos, 2002, Warcraft III: The Frozen Throne, 2003, lead designer World of Watercraft, 2004 (WIRED Rave award-Games, 2006). Named one of 100 Most Influential People, Time Mag., 2006. Office: Blizzard Entertainment PO Box 18979 Irvine CA 92623*

**PARDUE, A. MICHAEL,** retired plastic and reconstructive surgeon; b. Nashville, June 23, 1931; s. Andrew Peyton and Ruby (Fly) P. BS, Sewanee U. of the South, 1953; MD, U. Tenn., 1957. Resident in gen. surgery Pittsfield (Mass.) Affiliated Hosps., 1966; resident in plastic surgery N.Y. Hosp./Cornell Med. Ctr., 1968; plastic surgeon A. Michael Pardue, M.D., Thousand Oaks, Calif., 1968-98; ret., 1995. Lt. comdr. USN, 1956-62. Fellow ACS; mem. Am. Soc. Plastic Surgeons, Am. Soc. Aesthetic Plastic Surgery, Calif. Soc. Plastic Surgeons. Episcopalian. Avocations: fly fishing, skiing, golf, horses, African safaris. Home: PO Box 4677 Tubac AZ 85646-4677 Also: 3217 Augusta Dr Bozeman MT 59715-8792

**PARDUE, BILL,** publishing executive; Grad., Harvard Law Sch. Atty. Wiley, Rein and Fielding, Washington; business exec. Baltimore Sun; journalist, exec. Assoc. Press; editor Denver Post; mktg. dir. The Washington Post; CEO U.S. Corp. and Fed. Markets divsn. Lexis-Nexis, Miamisburg, Ohio, 2000—; pres., Intelligence Unit Gartner, Inc., Stamford, Conn., 2004—. Office: Gartner Inc 56 Top Gallant Rd Stamford CT 06904

**PARDUE, DWIGHT EDWARD,** venture capitalist; b. North Wilkesboro, N.C., Aug. 3, 1928; s. Gilbert F. and Nina (Glass) P.; m. Annie Eller, Mar. 24, 1951; children: Richard S., Dwight E. Cert., Clevenger Bus. Coll., 1956. Dir. warehousing Lowe's Co., Inc., North Wilkesboro, 1956-57, store mgr. Sparta, NC, 1957-59, Richmond, Va., 1959-70, regional v.p. North Wilkesboro, 1970-75, sr. v.p. store ops., 1975-78, exec. v.p. sales and store ops., 1978-86, sr. exec. v.p., 1986-90; pres., investor D. Pardue & Assocs., Wilkesboro, NC, 1990—. Mem. steering com. Home Ctr. Leadership Coun., Nat. Home Ctr. Home Improvement Congress and Exposition, 1983—86; bd. dirs. Northwestern Nat. Bank, Inc., Wilkesboro, NC, Integrity Fin. Corp., Hickory, NC; chmn. bd. Cmty. Bancshares, Inc., Wilkesboro, 1992—2002. Served with U.S. Army, 1950-52. Mem. Jefferson Landing Golf Club, Masons. Office Phone: 336-667-9411. E-mail: dep0013@aol.com.

**PARDUE, MARY-LOU,** biology professor; b. Lexington, Ky., Sept. 15, 1933; d. Louis Arthur and Mary Allie (Marshall) P. BS, William and Mary Coll., 1955; MS, U. Tenn., 1959; PhD, Yale U., 1970; D.Sc. (hon.), Bard Coll., 1985. Postdoctoral fellow Inst. Animal Genetics, Edinburgh, Scotland, 1970—72; assoc. prof. biology MIT, Cambridge, 1972—80, prof., 1980—, Boris Magasanik prof. biology, 1995—. Summer course organizer Cold Spring Harbor Lab., NY, 1971—80; mem. rev. com. NIH, 1974—78, 1980—84, nat. adv. gen. med. scis. coun., 1984—86; sci. adv. com. Wistar Inst., Phila., 1976—2004; mem. health and environ. rsch. adv. com. U.S. Dept. Energy, 1987—94; bd. trustees Associated Univs., Inc., 1995—97; mem. Burroughs Wellcome Adv. Com. on Career Awards in Biomed. Scis. 1996—2000, now bd. dirs.; chair Inst. of Medicine Com. on Biol. Basis of Sex and Gender Differences, 1999—2001. Mem. editl. bd.: profl. jours.; contbr. articles to profl. jours. Mem. rev. com. Am. Cancer Soc., 1990-93, Howard Hughes Med. Inst. Adv. Bd., 1993-2000. Recipient Esther Langer award Langer Cancer Rsch. Found., 1977, Lucius Wilbur Cross medal Yale Grad. Sch., 1989; grantee NIH, NSF, Am. Cancer Soc. Fellow AAAS, NAS (chmn. genetics sect. 1991-94, coun. 1995-98), Am. Acad. Arts and Sci. (coun. mem. 1992-96); mem. NRC (bd. on biology 1989-95), Genetics Soc. Am. (pres. 1982-83), Am. Soc. Cell Biology (coun. 1977-80, pres. 1985-86), Phi Beta Kappa, Phi Kappa Phi, Sigma Xi. Office: MIT Dept Biology 68-670 77 Massachusetts Ave Dept 68-670 Cambridge MA 02139-4307 Office Phone: 617-253-6741. E-mail: mlpardue@mit.edu.

**PARÉ, JOCELYN MARIE,** elementary school educator, consultant; b. New Bedford, Mass., Aug. 15, 1948; d. Armand Bernard and Helene Yvonne Paré. AA, Coll. Alameda, Calif., 1973; BA in Phys. Ed. and Kinesiology, U. Calif., Berkeley, 1976; MEd in Phys. Edn., St. Mary's Coll., Moraga, Calif., 1981; APE Credential, Calif. State U., Hayward, 1981. Nursery sch. tchr. Rochester Clothes Factory, New Bedford, Mass., 1967—68; nurse in charge Bristol Nursing Home, New Bedford, 1969—72; undercover security Naval Air Sta., Alameda, Calif., 1972; nurse Oakland Nursing Registry, Calif., 1973; social dir. asst. S. Shore Beach Tennis Club, Alameda, 1973—85; recreation instr. Alameda Adult Sch., 1974—76; remedial phys. edn. tchr. Mt. Diablo Unified Sch. Dist., 1973—78; adapted phys. edn. tchr., specialist W. Contra Costa Unified Sch. Dist., Richmond, 1978—. Pvt. practice health practitioner Source of Wholeness, Alameda, 1998—. Contbr. articles to profl. pubs. Tchr. leader People to People, 1996—; mem. ministries St. Joseph Basilica, Alameda, 1972—. Recipient You Make a Difference award, Parents of Students With Disabilities, Cerritos, Calif., 1998, Tchr. Excellence award, W. Contra Costa Unified Sch. Dist., 2000. Mem.: Touch For Health Internat., Brain Gym Internat., Alpha Delta Kappa (v.p. 2004—06), Alpha Phi. Roman Catholic. Avocations: crew, marathon running, travel, crafts, photography. Home: 1710 Chapin St Alameda CA 94501 Office: W Contra Costa Unified Sch Dist 1108 Bissett Ave Richmond CA 94805

**PARE, JOHN Z.,** lawyer; b. Chgo., Oct. 1968; m. Pamela Pare. BA, U. Fla., 1991; JD, George Washington U., 1995. Bar: Fla. 1995, US Dist. Ct. Mid. Dist. Fla. 1998, US Dist. Ct. So. Dist. Fla. 1999. Asst. state atty., Fla., 1995—98; atty. pvt. practice, 1998—2000; assoc. gen. counsel Hughes Supply Inc., Orlando, Fla., 2000—03, sr. v.p., gen. counsel, 2003—. Adj. prof. Ctrl. Fla. Criminal Justice Inst., 1998. Bd. dirs. Big Brothers Big Sisters of Ctrl. Fla. Mem.: Assn. of Corp. Counsel, The Fla. Bar, Orange County Bar Assn. Office: Hughes Supply Corp Office 1 Hughes Way #100 Orlando FL 32805-2232

**PARE, MICHAEL,** actor, singer; b. Bklyn., Oct. 9, 1958; m. Lisa Katselas, 1980 (div. 1988); m. Marisa Roebuck, 1986 (div. 1988); m. Marjolein Pare, 1992; 1 child. Actor: (films) Eddie and the Cruisers, 1983, The Philadelphia Experiment, 1984, Streets of Fire, 1984, Instant Justice, 1986, The Women's Club, 1987, World Gone Wild, 1988, Eddie and the Cruisers II: Eddie Lives!, 1989, Dragonfight, 1990, Moon 44, 1990, The Dark Sun, 1990, The Closer, 1990, Sunset Heat, 1991, The Last Hour, 1991, Killing Streets, 1991, Blink of an Eye, 1992, Into the Sun, 1992, Point of Impact, 1993, Warriors, 1994, Lunacrop, 1994, The Dangerous, 1994, Deadly Heroes, 1994, Village of the Damned, 1995, Raging Angels, 1995, Coyote Run, 1996, Bad Moon, 1996, Merchant of Death, 1997, 2103: The Deadly Wake, 1997, Strip Search, 1997, Hope Floats, 1998, Back to Even, 1998, October 22, 1998, The Virgin Suicides, 1999, Men of Means, 1999, Peril, 2000, Space Fury, 2000, A Month of Sundays, 2001, Red Serpent, 2002, Blackwoods, 2002, Heart of America, 2003, Fate, 2003, Two Faced, 2005, Crash Landing, 2005, BloodRayne, 2005, (TV series) The Greatest American Hero, 1981-83, Houston Knights, 1987, Starhunter, 2001, (TV movie) Houston Knights, 1987, Empire City, 1991, Triplecross, 1995, Carver's Gate, 1995, The Malibu Branch, 1996, The Colony, 1996, Falling Fire, 1998, Sanctimony, 2000. Office: Slade Grant Hartman Hartman 9019 Dorrington Ave Los Angeles CA 90048-1712 also: GVA Talent Agency Inc 9229 Sunset Blvd Ste 320 West Hollywood CA 90069*

**PAREDES, JAMES ANTHONY,** anthropologist, educator; b. NYC, Sept. 29, 1939; s. Antonio Paredes Piñeiro and Mildred Olene (Brown) P.; m. Anna Hamilton, Nov. 25, 1959 (div. 1984); children: J. Anthony Jr., Anna Teresa P. Lesinski, Sara Caroline P. Campbell; m. Elizabeth Dixon Purdum, Aug. 10, 1985 (div. 1994): 1 stepchild, David Joseph Plante; m. Aileen Dimitroff Deutsch, July 24, 2003. BA, Oglethorpe U., 1961; MA, U. N.Mex., 1964, PhD, 1969. Rsch. coord. Upper Miss. Mental Health Ctr., Bemidji, Minn., 1964-67; asst. prof., acting dir. Am. Ind. Studies Bemidji State Coll., 1967-68; community devel. specialist U. Minn. Agrl. Extension Svc., Bemidji, 1967-68; asst. prof. dept. anthropology Fla. State U., Tallahassee, 1969-74, assoc. prof., 1974-78, prof., 1979-99, emeritus prof., 1999—, chmn. dept., 1974-77, 84-90; chief ethnography and Indian affairs S.E. regional office Nat. Park Service, Atlanta, 1999—2006. Adj. prof. dept. anthropology U. Fla., Gainesville, 1979—; cons. Nat. Marine Fisheries Svc., Galveston, Tex., 1987-88, Bur. Indian Affairs, Washington, 1985, 92, Fed. Recognition Panel, Assn. on Am. Indian Affairs, N.Y.C, 1987-88. Author: Indios de los Estados Unidos Anglosajones, 1992; editor: Anishinabe: Six Studies of Modern Chippewa, 1980, Indians of the Southeastern United States in the Late 20th Century, 1992; co-editor: Classics of Practicing Anthropology: 1978-1998, 2000; co-editor: Anthropologists and Indians in the New South, 2001; series editor: Contemporary American Indian Studies; author or co-author numerous articles, chpts. in books, revs. Mem. Sci. and Statis. Com., Gulf of Mex. Fishery Mgmt. Coun., Tampa, Fla., 1978-88. Recipient svc. award Poarch Creek Indians, 1990, Woodrow Wilson Found. fellow U. N.Mex., 1961-62; Nat. Inst. Mental Health predoctoral fellow U. N.Mex., 1968-69; Rockefeller Ctr. for Study of So. Culture and Religion fellow, Fla. State U., 1978. Fellow Am. Anthrop. Assn. (exec. bd. 2004—), Soc. for Applied Anthropology (assoc. editor 1983-88, pres. 1993-95); mem. So. Anthrop. Soc. (pres. 1988-89), Fla. Acad. Scis. (sect. chair 1984-85), Sigma Xi (Fla. State U. chpt. pres. 1977-78). Democrat. Avocation: walking. Personal E-mail: janthonyparedes@bellsouth.net.

**PAREENE, ALEX E.,** political blog editor; b. July 23, 1985; Attended, NYU. Guest editor Gawker Media, 2004—06; co-editor Wonkette.com, 2006, editor, 2006—. E-mail: tips@wonkette.com.*

**PAREKH, DHIRAJLAL GOKALDAS,** electrical engineer; b. Mumbai, Maharasthra, India, May 20, 1945; s. Gokaldas Bhagwandas and Lilavatiben Gokaldas Parekh; m. Nirulata Dhirajlal Parekh, July 6, 1973; children: Parag Dhirajlal, Monica Dhirajlal. MSEE, Ga. Inst. Tech., 1970; MBA, Fla. Inst. Tech., 1986. Profl. engr., Ga., 1974. Supervisory mech. engr. Edgewood (Md.) Chem. Biol. Ctr., Edgewood, 1982—. Bd. dirs. Cinemaya Media, N.Y.C., 1999—. Am. Desi Mag., Cockeysville, Md.; founder, chmn. Indian Sch. Performing Arts, Lutherville, Md., 2002—; founder Internat. Sch. Performing Arts, Balt., 2002—; founder, ptnr. A.C. Birox. Internat. Prodr.: (film) Wings Of Hope (Cineview Internat. Film Festival, 2000), Bawandar (San Jose Internat. Film Festival, 2001); author: (book) Reality Check Happiness And Success; exec. prodr.: (tv serial) Dollar Bahu. Author acad. excellence Gujarati Samaj, Balt., 1994—97; founder Internat. Sch. Performing Arts; founding mem. Greater Balt. Temple, Balt., 1989—98; mem. World Gujarati Conf., College Park, Md., 1994, founder, convenor, 2006, convenor Edison, NJ, 2006; founder Olympics Performing Arts For World Peace. Named Internat. Poet, 1995; recipient Civilian Svc. award, Soldier Chem., Biol. Command, 1993, Army Materieal Command, 1995, Pravasi Excellence award, Ind. Orgn., Delhi, 2004, Prodr. award, TV Asia, 2005. Achievements include patents for biological classifier system; office organizer; electro-magnetizing of polymers for decontamination. Home: 9 Westspring Way Lutherville MD 21093 Personal E-mail: dparekh001@yahoo.com.

**PARELES, JON,** music critic; Copy editor Crawdaddy!, NYC, 1977, music editor; asst. music editor Rolling Stone; music writer Village Voice; freelancer NY Times, 1982, chief popular music critic. Author: The Rolling Stone Encyclopedia of Rock and Roll, 1983. Office: NY Times Culture Desk 229 W 43rd St New York NY 10036 Office Phone: 212-556-7304. Office Fax: 212-556-1516.*

**PARENT, MARY,** film company executive; Past agt. trainee ICM; dir. develop. to v.p. prodn. New Line Cinema, 1994—97; sr. v.p. prodn. Universal Pictures, Universal City, Calif., 1997—2000, exec. v.p. prodn., 2000—01, co-pres. prodn., 2001—03, vice chmn., worldwide prodn., 2003—05, prodr., 2006—. Exec. prodr.: (films) Set It Off, 1996, Trial and Error, 1997, Pleasantville, 1998; prodr.: You, Me and Dupree, 2006; prodn. mgr.: Dangerous Ground, 1997. Named one of 100 Most Powerful Women in Entertainment, Hollywood Reporter, 2004. Office: 100 Universal City Plaza Universal City CA 91608*

**PARENT, RICHARD EARL,** education educator, consultant; b. Dayton, Ohio, Mar. 4, 1950; s. Winton Adrian and Edith Elizabeth Parent; m. Arlene Eck, July 1, 1989; children: Kimberly Rose, John Winton. BS, U. Dayton, Ohio, 1972; MS, PhD, Ohio State U., Columbus, 1977. Pres. The Computer Animation Co., Columbus, 1980—85; assoc. prof. Ohio State U., Columbus, 1985—. Achievements include development of modeling of human figure including early model of human musculature and lip sync animation. Office: Ohio State Univ 2015 Neal Ave Columbus OH 43210 Office Phone: 614-292-0055. Office Fax: 614-292-2911. Business E-Mail: parent@cse.ohio-state.edu.

**PARENT, RODOLPHE JEAN,** retired Canadian air force officer, pilot; b. Thurso, Que., Can., June 16, 1937; s. Eugène Jean and Eliane Marie (Raby) P.; m. Michelle Marie Masse, Aug. 10, 1963; children— Stéphane, Nathalie, Cynthia Student, Coll. Militaire Royal de St-Jean, 1958-61; B.Sc., Royal Mil. Coll. Can., Kingston, Ont., 1963. Commd. Royal Can. Air Force, 1958; advanced through grades to brig.-gen., 1984; joined 425 Squadron for ops. on CF-101 aircraft Bagotville, Que., 1966-69; worked for Directorate of Recruiting and Selection at Nat. Def. Hdqrs., Ottawa, Ont., Canada, 1969-71; chief of ops. 433 Tactical Fighter Squadron, Bagotville, 1972-75, Can. Forces Base Bagotville, 1975-76; comdg. officer 433 Tactical Fighter Squadron, 1976-80; asst. dir. personnel careers Nat. Def. Hdqrs., Ottawa, 1980-81; base comdr. Can. Forces Base Lahr, Federal Republic Germany, 1981-83; commandant Coll. Militaire Royal de Saint-Jean, Que., 1983-86; dir. gen. personnel careers other ranks Nat. Def. Hdqrs., Ottawa, 1986-89; def. attaché Paris, 1989-92; ret., 1992. Decorated Order of Mil. Merit, Order of St. John of Jerusalem Roman Catholic. Avocations: hockey, tennis, windsurfing. E-mail: rudy.michelle@sympatico.ca.

**PARENTE, ROBERT BRUCE,** electrical engineer, consultant; b. Sept. 10, 1936; s. Almerico Elmer and Royda (Boyd) P.; m. Rozalinda Thelma Saturnio, May 28, 1977; children: Jennifer Dee, Jessica Dale, Jacquelyn Dawn. BSEE, MIT, 1959, MS in Engring., 1959, EE, 1961, PhD, 1966. Registered profl. engr., Calif. Instr. elec. engring. MIT, Cambridge, 1959-65; asst. prof. engring. UCLA, 1965-70; mgr. electric power sys. Sys. Devel. Corp., Santa Monica, Calif., 1970-72, dir. planning, 1973-75, dep. dir. energy devel., 1975-76; sr. cons. Theodore Barry & Assocs., L.A., 1976-78; propr. Parente & Assocs., mgmt. cons., L.A., 1978—. Expert witness before utility commns.; cons. to U.S. and fgn. electric power cos. Author: Electric Power Pools, 1983; contbr. articles to profl. jours.; patentee in field. Res. lt. sheriff L.A. County Sheriff's Dept., 1976—. Mem. IEEE, Inst. Mgmt. Scis., Ops. Rsch. Soc. Am., Sigma Xi, Tau Beta Pi, Eta Kappa Nu, Hex-Alpha, Theta Chi. Office: 2715 Angelo Dr Los Angeles CA 90077-2142 Office Phone: 310-271-4248.

**PARENTE, WILLIAM JOSEPH,** political science professor; b. Chgo., July 7, 1937; s. Salvatore S. and Genevieve (Rooney) P.; m. Diane Alpern, Nov. 30, 1963; children: Elizabeth, Margaret, William Joseph, Caroline, Rebecca, Catherine, Abigail, Christopher, Natalya. AB cum laude, Xavier U., Ohio, 1961; PhD (Woodrow Wilson fellow, Woodrow Wilson dissertation fellow), Georgetown U., 1970. Woodrow Wilson intern Wilberforce (Ohio) U., 1965-66; asst. prof., chmn. polit. sci. dept. Antioch Coll., 1966-69, assoc. dean faculty, 1969-70; dean Coll. Arts and Scis., U. Scranton, Pa., 1970-85, assoc. prof. polit. sci., 1970-73, prof., 1973—; Fulbright scholar Chulalongkorn U., Bangkok, Thailand, 1985-86, Inst. for Policy Studies, Washington, 1986-87. Mem. nat. Fulbright screening com. for East Asia, Southeast Asia; mem. adv. com. Inst. Internat. Edn.; cons. on world affairs to Peace Corps. Author articles in field. Fellow Inst. Acad. Deans, 1971, Inst. Ednl. Mgmt., Harvard Bus. Sch., 1972, Fulbright fellow, Korea, 1974, Indonesia, 1978, Germany, 1980, Thailand, 1985-86, fellow NEH Seminar, U. Va., 1976, Harvard U., 1985, Columbia U., 1988, George Mason U., Va., 1990, UCLA, 1991, U. Mich., 1992, William and Mary, 1993, U. Iowa, 1994, U. Accra, Ghana, 1996; scholar-diplomat program State Dept., 1970, 73; vis. scholar in humanities NYU, 1989; named Tchr. of Yr. Chulalongkorn U., 2006. Fellow Union Experimenting Colls. and Univs., Inst. for Policy Studies, Soc. for Religion in Higher Edn.; mem. Am. Polit. Sci. Assn., Assn. Jesuit Colls. and Univs. (chmn. conf. on internat. edn. 1981-85), Alpha Sigma Nu (nat. sec.-treas. 1979-82, nat. pres. 1983-85), Pi Sigma Alpha, Eta Sigma Phi, Alpha Sigma Lambda, Tau Kappa Alpha, Phi Alpha Theta. Roman Catholic. Home: 1608 Summit Pointe Scranton PA 18508-1034 Office: U Scranton Coll Arts & Sciences Scranton PA 18510 Office Phone: 570-941-7644. Business E-Mail: parentew1@scranton.edu.

**PARET, PETER,** historian; b. Berlin, Apr. 13, 1924; s. Hans and Suzanne Aimée (Cassirer) P.; m. Isabel Harris, Sept. 23, 1961; children: Suzanne Aimée, Paul Louis Michel. BA, U. Calif., Berkeley, 1949; PhD, U. London, 1960, DLitt, 1992; LittD, U. S.C., 1995; HHD, Coll. of Wooster, 1996. Resident tutor, delegacy of extramural studies Oxford U., 1959-60; research assoc. Center of Internat. Studies, Princeton U., 1960-62, 63; vis. assoc. prof. U. Calif., Davis, 1962-63, assoc. prof., 1963-66, prof., 1966-69; prof. history Stanford U., 1969-79, Raymond A. Spruance prof. internat. history, 1977-86; Andrew W. Mellon Prof. in humanities Inst. Advanced Study, Princeton, N.J., 1986-97, Andrew W. Mellon Prof. in humanities emeritus, 1997—. Mem. Inst. for Advanced Study, Princeton, 1966-67; fellow Ctr. for Advanced Study in Behavioral Scis., Stanford, Calif., 1968-69; vis. fellow London Sch. Econs., 1972-73; NEH fellow, 1979-80; sr. fellow Hoover Instn., Stanford U., 1988-93. Author: (with John Shy) Guerrillas in the 1960's, 1962, French Revolutionary Warfare from Indochina to Algeria, 1964, Yorck and the Era of Prussian Reform, 1966, Clausewitz and the State, 1976, rev. edit., 2006; The Berlin Secession, 1980, Art as History, 1988, (with Beth Irwin Lewis and Paul

Paret) Persuasive Images, 1992, Understanding War, 1992, Imagined Battles, 1997, German Encounters with Modernism, 1840-1945, 2000, An Artist against the Third Reich: Ernst Barlach, 1933-1938, 2003; editor, translator: (with Michael Howard) On War (C. v. Clausewitz), 1976, (with Daniel Moran) Historical and Political Writings (C. v. Clausewitz), 1992; editor: Frederick the Great, 1968, Frederick the Great: A Historical Profile, 1972, Sisyphus or the Limits of Education, 1973, The Age of German Liberation, 1977, Berliner Secession, 1981, Makers of Modern Strategy, 1986, (with Ekkehard Mai) Sammler, Stifter & Museen, 1993. Served with inf. U.S. Army, 1943-46. Decorated Officer's Cross, Order of Merit, Germany. Fellow AAAS, Royal Hist. Soc., Leo Baeck Inst., London Sch. Econs. (hon.); mem. Am. Philos. Soc. (Jefferson medal), Hist. Kom zu Berlin, Soc. for Mil. History (Samuel Eliot Morison and Moncado prizes), Clausewitz Gesellschaft (hon.). Office: Sch Hist Studies Inst Advanced Study Princeton NJ 08540 Office Phone: 609-734-8344. Business E-mail: paret@ias.edu.

**PARETS, PAUL L.**, music educator; b. Bangor, Maine, Apr. 29, 1942; s. J. P. and Berneta L. Parets; children: Timothy E. VanderGraaff, Meredith Anne. B of Music Edn., Cen. Mich. U., 1965; postgrad., U. Mich., 1980—83, U. Md., 1980—83. Cert. tchr. Del. Band dir. Sacred Heart H.S., Mt. Pleasant, Mich., 1965—66, Croswell (Mich.)-Lexington H.S., 1966—76; band dir., politics/govt. educator Alexis I. duPont H.S., Greenville, Del., 1976—. Mem. city coun. City of Delaware City, 1998—2006; assoc. mem. Rep. Nat. Com. Named Del. Tchr. of Yr., State of Del., 1987; named to 50 Who Make a Difference, SBO Mag., 2003, 2004; recipient Order of the 1st State, Gov. Michael Castle, 1987. Mem.: Music Educators Nat. Conf. (state pres. 1984—86, Disting. Music Educator award 1988). Anglican. Avocations: astronomy, travel. Home: PO Box 711 Delaware City DE 19706 Office: Alexis I duPont H S 50 Hillside Rd Greenville DE 19807

**PARETSKY, SARA N.**, writer; b. Ames, Iowa, June 8, 1947; d. David Paretsky and Mary E. Edwards; m. S. Courtenay Wright, June 19, 1976; children: Kimball Courtenay, Timothy Charles, Philip William. BA, U. Kans., 1967; MBA, PhD, U. Chgo., 1977. Mgr. Urban Resch Ctr., Chgo., 1971-74, CNA Ins. Co., Chgo., 1977-85; writer, 1985—. Author: (novels) Indemnity Only, 1982, Deadlock, 1984 (Friends of Am. Writers award 1985), Killing Orders, 1985, Bitter Medicine, 1987, Blood Shot, 1988 (Silver Dagger award Crime Writers Assn., 1988), Burn Marks, 1990, Guardian Angel, 1992, Tunnel Vision, 1994, Ghost Country, 1998, Hard Time: A V.I. Warshawski Novel, 1999, Total Recall, 2001, Blacklist, 2003 (Gold Dagger, Brit. Crime Writers Assn.), Fire Sale, 2005 (Publishers Weekly Bestseller hardcover fiction list, 2005), also numerous articles and short stories. Pres. Sisters in Crime, Chgo., 1986-88; dir. Nat. Abortion Rights Action League Ill., 1987—; mentor Chgo. inner-city schs. Named Woman of Yr. Ms mag., NYC, 1987; recipient Mark Twain award for disting. contbns. to Midwestern lit., 1996, Lifetime Achievement award, Private Eye Writers Am., 2005, Cartier Diamond Dagger for Lifetime Achievement, Brit. Crime Writers Assn., 2005. Mem. Crime Writers Assn. (Silver Dagger award 1988), Mystery Writers Am. (v.p. 1989), Authors Guild, Chgo. Network Achievements include being the founder of two scholarships at U. Kans. Office: c/o Dominick Abel Lit Agy #1B 146 West 82nd St New York NY 10024 Business E-mail: viwarshawski@mindspring.com.*

**PARHAM, ELLEN SPEIDEN**, nutrition educator; b. Mitchells, Va., July 15, 1938; d. Marion Coote and Rebecca Virginia (McNiel) Speiden; m. Arthur Robert Parham, Jr., Dec. 16, 1961; children: Katharine Alma, Cordelia Alyx. BS in Nutrition, Va. Poly. Inst., 1960; PhD in Nutrition, U. Tenn., 1967; MSEd in Counseling, No. Ill. U., 1994. Registered dietitian. ic. clin. profl. counselor. Asst. prof. to prof. nutrition No. Ill. U., DeKalb, Ill., 1966—2003, coord. programs in dietetics, 1981—86, 1990—2003, coord. grad. faculty sch. family, consumer, nutrition scis., 1985-87, interim chair Sch. Applied Health Professions, 2005—. Cons. on nutrition various hosps., clins. and bus., Ill., 1980-88; founder, dir. Horizons Weight Control Program, DeKalb, 1983-91; founder, leader "Escaping the Tyranny of the Scale" Group, 1994—; co-chair Nutrition Coalition for Ill., 1989-90; instr., mgr. Blue Chicory Arts, 1986—; adj. counselor Ctr. for Counsel, Family Svc. Agy. of DeKalb County. Bd. editors Jour. Nutrition Edn., 1986-90, 97—2005, Jour. Am. Dietetic Assn., 1991-97; contbr. articles to profl. jours. Recipient Fisher award, No. Ill. U. Coll. Health and Human Svcs., 2001, Sullivan award, 2002. Mem. Am. Inst. Nutrition, Soc. Nutrition Edn., Am. Dietetic Assn. (named Ill. Outstanding Dietetics Educator 2001, Excellence in Dietetics Edn. award 2001), Soc. Nutrition Edn. (treas. 1991-94, chair divsn. nutrition and weight realities 1995-96, chair jour. com. 2002—05, Weight Realities Cert. of Achievement 1999), N.Am. Assn. Study Obesity. Avocations: painting in watercolor, gardening, reading. Business E-mail: eparham@niu.edu.

**PARHAM, THOMAS DAVID**, education educator; b. Chgo., Sept. 6, 1963; s. Thomas David and Marion Cordice Parham. BS, U.S. Naval Acad., Annapolis, 1985; MA, Regent U., Va. Beach, 1992, PhD, 1995. Cert. Surface Warfare Officer U.S. Navy, 1988. Commd. officer U.S. Navy, Washington, 1985—92; writers' prodn. asst. Family Prodns., Inc., Va. Beach, 1993—94; supr. pub. Viacom Consumer Products, Hollywood, 1995—96; writers' asst. CBS Prodns., Salt Lake City, 1996—97, Paramount Pictures, Hollywood, 1997—99; asst. prof. Biola U., La Mirada, Calif., 1999—2002; assoc. prof. Azusa (Calif.) U., 2002—. Tech. cons. Paramount Pictures, Hollywood, 1999—2002; adv. bd. Act One, Inc., Hollywood, 2000—. Author: (play) Inside Out, Steeple Chasers; dir.: (play) The Skin of Our Teeth, Dinner with Friends; contbr. book; author: (TV episode) Big Brother Jake, 1994, JAG, 1998; exec. prodr.: (student film) Giver Her Away. Planning com. Reel Spirituality, Pasadena, Calif., 2002; writer-in-residence Lake Ave. Ch., Pasadena, Calif., 1996—2005. Lt. USN, 1985—92. Mem.: Popular Culture Assn., Nat. Comm. Assn., Comic-Con Internat Writers Guild of Am, Independent, Southern Baptist. Avocations: comic books, singing, swimming, travel, weightlifting. Office: Azusa Pacific Univ/Theater-Film-TV 901 E Alosta Ave Azusa CA 91702 Office Phone: 626-815-6000 5219. Office Fax: 626-815-2045. Business E-mail: tparham@apu.edu.

**PARHAM, VALERIE DEFOREST BYRON**, artist; b. Cambridge, Mass., Jan. 25, 1953; d. Donald Cameron and Mary deForest Pierce Byron; m. Anthony Bruce Parham, Oct. 30, 1990; children: Victoria deForest, Corrina Bess. Grad., Buckingham Sch., Cambridge, 1968; pvt. classes in painting, 1968—74. Lay missionary Holy Spirit Assn. for Unity of World Christianity, N.Y.C. and Washington, 1974—95; Am. for peace-Ghana Family Fedn. for World Peace and Unification, N.Y.C., 1974—2000. Vol. Rep. presdl. campaigns. Republican. Mailing: 236 Princeton St Jefferson MA 01522 Office Phone: 508-829-2809. E-mail: deforestbyron@hotmail.com.

**PARHAM-HOPSON, DEBORAH**, health programs administrator; BSN, U. Cin., 1977; MS in Pub. Health, U. NC, 1979, PhD in Pub. Health, 1990. Rear adm. USPHS Commd. Corps.; dep. assoc. adminstr. Health Resources and Svcs. Adminstrn., HIV/AIDS Bur., HHS, 2000—02, acting assoc. adminstr., 2002, assoc. adminstr., 2002—. Office: US Dept Health and Human Svcs Health Resources Svcs Adminstrn 5600 Fishers Ln Rm 7-05 Rockville MD 20857 Office Phone: 301-443-1993. Business E-mail: dparham@hrsa.gov.

**PARHI, KESHAB KUMAR**, electrical and computer engineering educator; b. Balasore, Orissa, India, June 15, 1959; came to U.S., 1983; s. Budhiram and Kamalini Parhi; m. Jagruti Mahapatra, Dec. 11, 1988; children: Megha, Rahul B Tech., Indian Inst. Tech., Kharagpur, 1982; MSEE, U. Pa., 1984; PhD, U. Calif., Berkeley, 1988. Tchg. and rsch. asst. U. Pa., Phila., 1983—84; postgrad. rschr. U. Calif., Berkeley, 1984—88; mem. tech. staff T.J. Watson Rsch. Ctrs. IBM, Yorktown Heights, NY, 1986. AT&T Bell Labs., Holmdel, NJ, 1987; asst. prof. U. Minn., Mpls., 1988—92, assoc. prof., 1992—95, prof., 1995—, Edgar F. Johnson prof., 1997—, Disting. McKnight U. prof., 2000—. Tech. dir. DSP Sys., Broadcom Corp., Irvine, Calif., 2000-02; vis. rschr. NEC Computer Comm. Lab., Kawasaki, Japan, 1992, 96-97; cons. AT&T Bell Labs., 1987, U.S. West Sci. and Techs., Boulder, Colo., 1989 Editor Jour. VLSI Signal Processing, 1993—; contbr. articles to profl. jours Recipient NSF Young Investigator award, 1992, Eliahu Jury award U. Calif., Berkeley, 1987, Demetri Angelakos award U. Calif., Berkeley, 1987, Fred-

erick Emmons Terman award Am. Soc. Engring. Edn., 2004; IBM grad. fellow, 1987-88. Regents fellow U. Calif., 1986-87 Fellow IEEE (assoc. editor trans. on cirs. and sys. 1990-91, editor-in-chief 2004-05, assoc. editor trans. on signal processing 1993-95, assoc. editor trans. on cirs. and sys. part II 1995-97, 2002-03, trans. on VLSI syss. 1997-98, signal processing letters 1997-99, signal processing mag. 2003-2004, signal processing soc. paper award 1991, Browder J. Thompson Meml. Prize Paper award 1991, W.R.G. Baker prize 2001, Kiyo Tomiyasu Tech. Field award 2003), Cirs. and Sys. Soc. (bd. govs. 2005—, Guillemin-Cauer award 1993, Darlington award 1994, Golden Jubilee medal 1999, Disting. lectr. 1994-99, Design Automation Conf. Best Paper award 1996) Avocations: swimming, gardening, hiking, travel. Office: U Minn Dept Elec/Computer Engring 200 Union St SE Minneapolis MN 55455-0154 Office Phone: 612-624-4116. E-mail: parhi@uma.edu.

**PARIENTE, BARBARA J**, state supreme court justice; b. N.Y.C., Dec. 24, 1948; m. Frederick A. Hazouri; 3 children. Grad. with high honors, Boston U., 1970; JD with highest honors, George Washington U., 1973. Bar: Fla. 1973; cert. civil trial lawyer Fla. Bar; cert. Nat. Bd. Trial Advocacy. Law clk. to hon. Norman C. Roettger, Jr. U.S. Dist. Ct. (so. dist.) Fla., 1973-75; assoc. Cone Wagner Nugent, 1975—77, ptnr., 1977—83, Pariente & Silber, P.A., 1983; pvt. practice, 1983—2001; judge U.S. Ct. of Appeals (4th dist.), 1993-97; justice Fla. Supreme Ct., Tallahassee, 1997—, chief justice, 2004—06. Participant Twenty-First Century Justice Conf.; mem. Jud. Ctr. Grievance Com., 1989-92, chair, 1990-92; mem. nominating com. State Ct. (15th cir.), 1980-84. Bd. dirs. Fla. Bar Found.; mentor Take Stock in Children, 1992-2003; mem. Cities in Schs. mentoring program, 1993, Palm Beach County Commn. on Status of Women; vol. judge Palm Beach County Youth Ct. Program; past chair Supreme Ct. Steering Com. on Families and Children in the Courts Fla. Supreme Ct.; liaison Supreme Ct. Task Force on Treatment-Based Drug Cts., 1999-2004; mem. nat. judges adv. com. Balanced and Restorative Justice Project Dept. Justice. Recipient award for disting. svc. to the arts Palm Beach County Bar Assn., 1987, Civil Litigation Pro Bono award Legal Aid Soc., 1993, Lifetime Achievement award Palm Beach County Jewish Feds., 1998, Disting. Jud. Svc. award Fla. Coun. on Crime and Delinquency, 2000, Breaking the Glass Ceiling award Jewish Mus. Fla., 2002, Fla. Bar Assn. Family Law Sect. Chair Family Law Visionary award, 2004, William M. Hoevelor Jud. award, 2004, Good Govt. award Palm Beach County LWV, 2005. Mem. ABA (mem. Coalition for Justice 2000-03, Law Day Speech award 1998), Nat. Assn. Women Judges, Am. Inns. of Ct. (founding mem. Palm Beach County chpt.), Acad. Fla. Trial Lawyers (bd. dirs., chair Spkr.'s Bur. program 1984-87, outreach com. 1991-92, co-chair Workhorse Seminar 1991-92), Assn. Trial Lawyers Am. (vice chair profl. rsch. and devel. dept. 1980-82, chair comml. litig. sect. 1984-85, women's trial lawyer caucus 1986-87; mem. ethics com. 1989-90, conv. planning com. 1992-93), Fla. Assn. Women Lawyers (Lifelong Dedication award 2000), Order of Coif. Office: State Supreme Ct of Florida 500 S Duval St Tallahassee FL 32399-1925 Business E-mail: supremecourt@flcourts.org.*

**PARIHAR, PRADEEP SINGH**, sports medicine physician; s. Shildhwaj Singh Parihar and Basanti Singh; m. Sunita Singh, June 3, 1996; children: Siddharth Singh, Parth Singh. MD, SS Med. Coll., India, 1989. Diplomate Am. Bd. Of Sports Medicine, 2006. Assoc. orthop. surgeon Gandhi Meml. Hosp. and SS Med. Coll., Rewa, Mp, India, 1995—2000; assoc. rsch. asst. Southwestern U., Dallas, 2002—05; resident in family medicine East Tenn. State U., Johnson City, 2002—05; fellow in sports medicine St. Vincent Health Ctr., Erie, Pa., 2005—. Sec. Orthop. Assn. Dist. Chpt., Rewa, Mp, India, 1996—98. Mem. St. Vincent Charity Union, Erie, Pa. Recipient Best Comedian award, SS Med. Coll. and APS U. India, 1985. Mem.: Am. Coll. Of Sports Medicine, Am. Med. Soc. Of Sports Medicine, Am. Acad. Of Family Physicians. Achievements include patents pending for crutches. Avocations: running, field hockey, soccer. Home: 5420 Cider Mill Rd Erie PA 16509 Office: St Vincent Health Ctr 2314 Sassafras St Erie PA 16509 Office Phone: 814-452-5092. Home Fax: 814-217-0416; Office Fax: 814-866-0697. Personal E-mail: parihar2@hotmail.com. E-mail: pparihar@svhs.org.

**PARIKH, JAY R.**, radiologist; s. Rajendra Somalal and Minaxi Rajendra Parikh; m. Niyati Jay Patel, July 5, 1992; children: Viraj, Parikh Rajan, Miti. MD, U. Ottawa, Ontario, Can., 1990. Cert. physician exec. Am. Coll. of Physician Execs., 2005. Med. dir. Women's Diagnostic Imaging Ctr., Seattle, 2001—. Pres. Nat. Consortium of Breast Ctrs., Warsaw, 2005—; cons., sci. adv. panel Hologic, Bedford, Mass.; med. advisor Confirma, Kirkland, Wash., 2005—. Contbr. articles to profl. jours. Asst. troop leader, pack 624 Boy Scouts Am., Seattle, 2005—06. Named Honorary Texan, Gov. Tex., 2006; Leadership Conf. scholar, WSMA, 2004. Fellow: Soc. of Breast Imaging, Royal Coll. of Physicians and Surgeons of Can. (licentiate); mem.: Alaska State Soc. Radiol. Technologists, Wash. State Med. Assn. (bd. trustee 2004—), Pacific NW Radiol. Soc. (1st. v.p. 2003—), Wash. State Radiol. Soc. (pres. 2004—), Hawaii Breast Soc. (hon.; life), Hawaii Radiol. Soc. (hon.), Am. Assn. of Radiologists of Indian Origin (life), Ariz. State Soc. Radiol. Technologists (life), Western Wash. Mammography Soc. (hon.), Radiol. Soc. of N.Am., Am. Roentgen Ray Soc., King County Med. Soc., Am. Coll. of Physician Executives, Am. Coll. of Radiology (clin. image rev., nat. mammography accreditation program 2005—, clin. image rev. nat. breast ultrasound accreditation program 2006—). Office: Women's Diagnostic Imaging Center 1221 Madison St Seattle WA 98104 Office Phone: 206-215-3939. Office Fax: 206-215-3909. E-mail: jay.parikh@swedish.org.

**PARIKH, JEANNINE LUBOLD**, physician; b Pittsfield, Mass, Aug 2, 1970; d. Charles Frank Lubold, Jr and Sandra Pemble Lubold; m. Manish Parikh, Oct. 13, 1996; children: Zachary Manish, Cameron Nayan. BS, Stonehill Coll., North Easton, Mass., 1992; MS, St. George's U., Grenada, W.I., 1997. Diplomate Am. Bd. of Family Practice, 2003. Family practice resident St. Joseph Med. Ctr., Yonkers, NY, 1998—2001; family practitioner Brewster Family Medicine, Brewster, NY, 2003—05, King's Dau. Med. Ctr., South Point, Ohio, 2005—. Mem.: Am. Acad. Family Practice (assoc.). Democrat-Npl. Roman Catholic. Avocations: photography, running, decorating. Office: King's Daughter Medical Center 384 County Rd 120 S South Point OH 45680 Office Phone: 740-894-2080.

**PARIKH, MIHIR**, consumer products company executive; PhD, U. Calif., Berkeley. Various mgmt. positions IBM, N.Y.C., San Jose, Calif., Hewlett-Packard Labs., Palo Alto, Calif.; pres., CEO ASYST technologies, Inc., Fremont, Calif., 1984—, chmn., 1992—. Contbr. articles to profl. jours. Office: ASYST Technologies Inc 48761 Kato Rd Fremont CA 94538-7313

**PARIKH, NEEL**, library director; b. Pitts., Apr. 20, 1948; d. John White and Virginia Kellogg Kingston; m. Mihir Parikh, Dec. 28, 1968 (div. July 1975). BA in Polit. Sci., U. Calif., Berkeley, 1970, MLS, 1971. Branch mgr. Alameda County Libr., various, Calif., 1977-84; coord. children's svcs. San Francisco Pub. Libr., 1984-90, chief branch librs., 1990-94; dir. Pierce County Libr. Sys., Tacoma, Wash., 1994—. Chair adv. bd. Libr. Coun. Wash., Olympia, 1996—2002, chair Mayor's Adv. Coun. on Child Care, San Francisco, 1985-90; mem. steering com. Calif. Libr. Networking Task Force, San Francisco, 1992-93; instr. U. Calif., Berkeley, 1990; pres. Pierce County AIDS Found., Tacoma, Wash., 1995-2002; bd. dirs. Commns. on Children, Youth and Their Families, Tacoma, 1993-96. Contbr. articles to profl. jours. Mem. Am. Leadership Forum, Tacoma, 1998—; Lakewood's Promise exec. bd., Tacoma, 1997-2001, 2005—; pres., bd. dirs YWCA, Pierce County, 2003-2005, Fund for Women and Girls Adv. Com., 2001-06. Recipient Merit award Calif. Assn. Tchrs. Eng., San Francisco, 1989, Golden Rule award J.C. Penney, San Francisco, 1989. Mem. ALA (John Cotton Dana award 1988, councillor 1999—), Calif. Libr. Assn. (pres. 1992), Washington Libr. Assn. (exec. bd. 1995-97), Women Libr. Workers (nat. pres. 1978-79), Urban Librs. Coun., City Club Tacoma, Tacoma Rotary. Avocations: reading, rafting, gardening. Office: Pierce County Library System 3005 112th St E Tacoma WA 98446-2200 Office Phone: 253-536-6500 ext. 114. Business E-mail: neelp@pcl.lib.wa.us

**PARINS, ROBERT JAMES**, professional football team executive, judge; b. Green Bay, Wis., Aug. 23, 1918; s. Frank and Nettie (Denissen) P.; m. Elizabeth L. Carroll, Feb. 8, 1941; children: Claire, Andrée, Richard, Teresa, Lu Ann. BA, U. Wis., 1940, LL.B., 1942. Bar: Wis. Supreme Ct. 1942. Pvt. practice, Green Bay, Wis., 1942-68; dist. atty. Brown County, Wis., 1949-50, cir. judge Wis., 1968-82, res. judge Wis., 1982—; pres. Green Bay Packers, Inc., 1982-90, chmn. bd., 1990-92; hon. chmn. bd., 1992-94. Mem.: Wis. State Bar Assn. Roman Catholic.

**PARIS, DAVID ANDREW**, dentist; b. Milw., Jan. 16, 1962; s. John Baptistia and Geraldine Louella (Grosso) P. BA, UCLA, 1985, DDS, 1989. Oral surgery extern VA, Phoenix, 1989; primary practitioner Alexis Project L.A. Dental Clinic, 1990-94; assoc. M. Marchese D.D.S., Sun Valley, Calif., 1990-92, D. Pickrell DMD, West Hollywood, Calif., 1992-94, Dental Arts Assocs., Milw., 1994-95, Family Dental Ctr., Milw., 1994-96; pvt. practice Elm Grove, Wis., 1996—. Mem. ADA, Wis. Dental Assn., Calif. Dental Assn., Acad. Gen. Dentistry, Delta Sigma Delta. Avocations: cello, Italian language. Office Phone: 262-784-7770.

**PARIS, DAVID C.**, academic administrator, political scientist, educator; b. Rochester, N.Y. married; 3 children. Grad., Hamilton Coll., 1971; PhD, Syracuse U. Mem. faculty Hamilton Coll., Clinton, NY, 1979—; James S. Sherman prof., assoc. dean faculty, acting dean faculty, 2000—01, v.p. acad. affairs, dean faculty, 2001—. Author: Ideology and Education Reform: Themes and Theories in Public Education, 1995. Office: Hamilton College 198 College Hill Rd Clinton NY 13323

**PARIS, DEIDRE EILEEN**, artificial intelligence researcher, educator; b. Hammond, Ind., Oct. 7, 1968; d. Elizabeth Paris and Dillard Paris Jr. BSEE, So. U., Baton Rouge, 1992; Masters of Sci., Pub. Policy, Ga. Inst. Tech., 1996; MS in Elec. Engring., Ga. Inst. of Tech., 1994; PhD in Civil & Environ. Engring., Ga. Inst. Tech., 2002. Rschr. Constrn. Rsch. Ctr., Ga. Inst. of Tech., Atlanta; fellow GE Med. Sys., Milw., 1991—93, Army Environ. Policy Inst., Atlanta, 1995—97; rschr. Lawrence Livermore Nat. Lab., Livermore, Calif., 1997; asst. prof. Clark Atlanta U., Atlanta, 2002—04; faculty rschr. Oak Ridge Nat. Lab., Tenn., 2003; rsch. participant (NRC) Nuc. Regulatory Commn., Washington, 2004—05; adminstr. fellow NASA Marshall, Ala., 2004—; prof. coll. engring., architectgure & phys. sci. Tuskagee U. Adminstr. fellow Nasa Marshall Space Flight Ctr., Huntsville, Ala., 2002—04; presenter in field. Author; (exbhn.) 17th Internal Symposium on Polymer Analysis and Characterization; contbr. chapters to books. Resident adv. Atlanta Mut. Housing Assn., Atlanta, 2000—03; grad. senator for civil engring. Ga. Inst. Tech. Student Govt. Assn., 1997—99; coord. ReJOYce In Jesus Ministries, LA, 1995—2001; contractor selection com. mem. Hist. Dist. Devel. Corp., 2003—04. Fellow, NASA, ASEE, 2004, GEM, 2003-2006; scholar Ga. Tech Bd. of Regents, Ga. Bd. of Regents, 1999—2001, GM, 1988—91, Motorola Corp., 1992; Adminstv. fellow, NASA, 2004—06, Presdl. Fellow, Ga. Inst. Tech., 1996—2000. Mem.: ASCE (assoc.), Am. Soc. of Civil Engring. (assoc.). Independent. Avocations: dance, reading, exercise. Home: 3672 Hawthorn Ct Auburn AL 36830 Office: Tuskegee U Coll Engring Architecture & Phys Sci 305 Luther Foster Hall Tuskegee Institute AL 36088 Office Phone: 404-429-9469. Home Fax: 256-544-8280; Office Fax: 256-544-8480. Personal E-mail: deidreparis@yahoo.com. E-mail: deidre.e.paris@msfc.nasa.gov.

**PARIS, GORDON A.**, publishing executive; b. 1953; Head of investment banking TD Securities Inc.; sr. v.p. Toronto-Dominion Bank, 2000—02; pres. & CEO Hollinger Internat. Inc. (name changed to Sun-Times Media Group, 2006), NYC, 2003—06, chmn., 2004—. Mng. dir. TD Securities Inc., 1996—2002; dir. Warrantech Corp., 1998—; mng. dir. Berenson & Co., 2002—06, adv. dir., 2006—. Office: Sun-Times Media Group 350 North Orleans St Chicago IL 60654 also: Berenson LLP 135 W 50th St New York NY 10020 Office Phone: 212-586-5666.*

**PARIS, KATHLEEN**, secondary school educator; Biology tchr. Bethel High Sch., Spanaway, Wash. Named Wash. State Biology Tchr. of Yr., 1993; recipient Presdl. award in secondary sci., 1997. Office: Bethel High Sch 22215 38th Ave E Spanaway WA 98387-6824

**PARIS, NORMA JEAN**, psychologist, educator; b. Muskogee, Okla., Jan. 15, 1937; d. Howard Charles and Eleanor Ruth Lewis; m. Barney McKinley Paris, Jr., Feb. 17, 1957; children: Donna Katherine Paris Willis, Cynthia Elizabeth Paris Bickham, Barney McKinley Paris III(dec.). BA summa cum laude, La. State U., 1975, specialist, 1985, MEd, 1977, PhD, 1997; Edn. Specialist in Counseling, La. Tech. U., 1980. Tchr. Bossier Parish Sch. Bd., Bossier City, La., 1975—84, sch. psychologist, 1984—87, Caddo Parish Sch. Bd., Shreveport, 1987—2001; spl. lectr. Centenary Coll. La., Shreveport, 2001—. Psychol. advisor Compassionate Friends, Shreveport, 1981—92; cons. Children's Advocacy Ctr. Task Force, Shreveport, 1996—98; presenter in field. Bd. mem. Juvenile Justice Bd. Dirs., Shreveport, 1996—2000; exec. bd. mem. Caddo-Bossier Mental Health Assn. Bd. Dirs., Shreveport, 1996—2000. Mem.: La. Sch. Psychologists Assn. (exec. bd. mem. 2001—, La. Sch. Psychologist of Yr. 2001), Assn. Tchr. Educators, Internat. Reading Assn., Mensa. Republican. Baptist. Avocations: bridge, puzzles, water aerobics, travel. Home: 4406 Curtis Loop Bossier City LA 71112

**PARIS, STEVEN MARK**, application developer; b. Boston, May 26, 1956; s. Julius Louis and Frances (Keleishik) Paris. BS, Rensselaer Poly. Inst., 1978; MS, Boston U., 1980. postgrad., 1980-84. Sr. software engr. Prime Computer Inc. Framingham, Mass., 1978-82, sr. analyst Computervision Corp., Bedford, Mass., 1982-84; prin. engr. Lotus Devel., Inc., Cambridge, Mass., 1984-88; pres. Tri-Millennium Corp., 1988-91; sr. rschr. Tech. Edn. Rsch. Ctr., Cambridge, 1990-93; prin. engr. Beyond, Inc., Burlington, Mass., 1993, Bus. Matters Inc., Waltham, Mass., 1994—96; v.p. engr. Ambit, Inc., Brighton, Mass., 1996—2002; v.p. product implementation Health Allianze, Inc., Andover, Mass., 2003—. Civil def. capt. City of Somerville, Mass., 1984—. Recipient 1st prize, Boston Sci. Fair, 1973, 1974, 3d prize, State of Mass. Sci. Fair, 1973, 2d prize, 1974. Mem.: IEEE, Boston Computer Soc., Assn. Computing Machinery, Planetary Soc. Jewish.

**PARISH, J. MICHAEL**, lawyer, mutual fund executive, writer; b. Decatur, Ill., Nov. 9, 1943; s. John Mitchell and Gladys Margaret (Daulton) P.; m. Susan Lee Sgarlat, July 24, 1976 (div.); m. Ellen R. Harnett, Dec. 3, 1991; children: Margaret Ruth, William Walter. AB cum laude, Princeton U., 1965; LLB, Yale U., 1968. Assoc. LeBoeuf Lamb et al, N.Y.C., 1968-73; ptnr., 1974-89, Winthrop Stimson Putnam & Roberts, N.Y.C., 1989-95, Thelen, Reid & Priest, N.Y.C., 1995—2002, Wolf, Block, Schorr & Solis-Cohen, N.Y.C., 2002—03. Chmn. bd. dirs. Forum Funds, Portland, Maine, Core Trust. Contbr. stories and poetry to mags. Dir. PBS Am. Poetry Project, 1985-90; coord. Yale Law Sch. Clinton Election com.; class sec. Princeton Class of 1965. Univ. scholar Princeton U., 1965, Nat. scholar Yale U., 1968. Avocation: creative writing. Home: 443 1st St Oradell NJ 07649-1705 Office Phone: 201-634-0812. E-mail: mparish@alumni.princeton.edu.

**PARISH, JAMES MICHAEL**, medical educator; MD, U. Ill., Chgo., 1978. Diplomate Am. Bd. Internal Medicine, 2nd Bd. Pulmonary Medicine. Pulmonary and critical care specialist Sharp Rees-Stealy Med. Group, San Diego, 1984—87; cons. pulmonary med. Mayo Clinic, Scottsdale, Ariz., 1987—. Fellow: ACP, Am. Acad. Sleep Medicine, Am. Coll. Chest Physicians; mem.: AMA, Am. Thoracic Soc. Achievements include research in sleep disorders. Office: Mayo Clinic 13400 Shea Blvd Scottsdale AZ 85259 Office Phone: 480-301-8000.

**PARISH, JAMES ROBERT**, writer, cinema historian; b. Cambridge, Mass., Apr. 21, 1944; s. Fred Arthur and Ann Lois (Magilevy) P. BA, U. Pa., 1964, LLB, 1967. Pres. Entertainment Copyright Rsch.Co. Inc., N.Y.C., 1967-68; film reporter, reviewer, interviewer Variety, Motion Picture Daily, 1968-69; entertainment publicist Harold Rand & Co., 1969-70; free-lance writer, publicist, film book cons., film reviewer, novelist, 1970—; acquisition editor

Renaissance Books, 1996-99. Author: (with P. Michael) The Emmy Awards: A Pictorial History, 1970, The Fox Girls, 1971, The Great Movie Series, 1971 (with A.H. Marill) The Cinema of Edward G. Robinson, 1972, The Slapstick Queens, 1972, The Paramount Pretties, 1972, (with R. Bowers) The MGM Stock Company, 1973, Actors TV Credits, 1950-72, 73, Good Dames, 1973, (with M.R. Pitts) The Great Spy Pictures, 1973, The RKO Gals, 1973, (with S. Whitney), The George Raft File, 1973, (with M.R. Pitts) Film Directors: A Guide to Their American Pictures, 1974, Hollywood's Great Love Teams, 1974, (with S. Whitney) Vincent Price Unmasked, 1974, The Great Movie Heroes, 1975, (with D. Stanke), The Glamour Girls, 1975, The Debonairs, 1975, (with L. DeCarl) Hollywood Players: The Forties, 1975, (with J. Ano) Liza! (The Liza Minnelli Story), 1975, (with M.R. Pitts) The Great Gangster Pictures, 1975, The Elvis Presley Scrapbook, 1975, (with W. Leonard) Hollywood Players: The Thirties, 1976, (with D. Stanke) The All Americans, 1976, Film Directors: A Guide for Western Europe, 1976, Great Child Stars, 1976, The Jeanette MacDonald Story, 1976, (with D. Stanke) The Leading Ladies, 1977, (with M.R. Pitts) The Great Science Fiction Pictures, 1977, Film Actors Guide: Western Europe, 1977, The Elvis Presley Scrapbook (update), 1977, (with M. Trost) Actors TV Credits: Supplement One, 1977, (with M.R. Pitts) Hollywood on Hollywood, 1978, (with R. Braff et al.) Hollywood Character Actors, 1978, (with G. Mank and D. Stanke) The Hollywood Beauties, 1978, (with W. Leonard) The Funsters, 1979, (with D. Stanke) The Forties Gals, 1980, (with G. Mank) The Hollywood Reliables, 1980, The Great American Movies Book, 1980, (with G. Mank) The Best of MGM, 1981, (with M.R. Pitts) The Great Spy Pictures II, 1986, (with M.R. Pitts) The Great Gangster Pictures II, 1987, (with M.R. Pitts) The Great Western Pictures II, 1988, Black Action Pictures from Hollywood, 1989, (with M.R. Pitts) The Great Science Fiction Pictures II, 1990, (with V. Terrace) Complete Actors TV Credits, 1990, (with M.R. Pitts) Hollywood Songsters, 1990, updated edit., 2002, The Great Cop Pictures, 1990, Prison Pictures from Hollywood, 1991, (with M.R. Pitts) Hollywood's Great Musicals, 1992, (with D. Stanke) Hollywood Baby Boomers, 1992, Prostitution in Hollywood Film, 1992, The Hollywood Death Book, 1992; Let's Talk: America's Favorite Talk Show Hosts, 1993, Gays and Lesbians in Mainstream Cinema, 1993, Hollywood's Celebrity Death Book, updated and expanded, 1994, Ghosts and Angels on the Hollywood Screen, 1995, Today's Black Hollywood, 1995, Pirates and Seafaring Swashbucklers, 1995, The Great Child Stars, 1996, The Unofficial "Murder She Wrote" Casebook, 1997, Rosie: Rosie O'Donnell's Biography, 1997, updated edit., 1998, Whoopi Goldberg: From Poverty to Mega Stardom, 1997, updated edit., 1999, Jason Biggs, 2000, The Hollywood Book of Death, 2001, Gus Van Sant, 2001, Hollywood Bad Boys, 2002, Jet Li, 2002, The Encyclopeida of Ethnic Groups in Hollywood, 2002, Hollywood Divas, 2002, The Hollywood Book of Love, 2003, Whitney Houston, 2003, Steven Spielberg, 2004, The Hollywood Book of Scandals, 2004, Tom Hanks, 2004, Stephen King, 2004, Halle Berry, 2004, Twyla Tharp, 2005, Denzel Washington, 2005, Stan Lee, 2005, Katie Couric, 2005, Katharine Hepburn: The Untold Story, 2005, Jim Henson, 2006, Gloria Estefan, 2006, Fiasco: A History of Hollywood's Iconic Flops, 2006, The Hollywood Book of Breakups, 2006, (with Allan Taylor) Career Opportunities in Writing, 2006, (with Allan Taylor) Career Opportunities in Television and Cable, 2006; assoc. editor: The American Movies Reference Book, 1969, TV Movies, 1969, The Great American Movie Book, 1980. Mem. Phi Beta Kappa. Avocations: docent, reading, writing. Address: 4338 Gentry Ave Unit 1 Studio City CA 91604-1764 E-mail: jrparish@sbcglobal.net. *To succeed in one's ambitions requires an unyielding avoidance of other people's skepticisms.*

**PARISH, MICHAEL J.,** controller; b. Augusta, Ga., Dec. 28, 1973; s. John G and Barbara Q Parish; m. Sandy Kay Marshall, July 19, 1997; children: Lily Ann children: Sydney Katherine. BBA in Acctg. Augusta State U., Ga., 1997. Cert. profl. mgr., Inst. of Profl. Mgrs./James Madison U., 2004, state fin. mgr., U. of Ga./ Carl Vinson, 1998. Acct. Hawk Firm, Augusta, Ga., 1994—97; dir. of fin. Augusta Tech. Inst.-JTPA, Augusta, 1997—98, Augusta Reg. Airport, Augusta, 1998—2001; contr./dir. of human resources Progress Rail Augusta Divsn., Augusta, 2001—02; contr. Xytex Corp., Augusta, 2002—. Fin. cons. Progress Rail Svc.-Augusta Divsn., 2002—03. Mem. Com. to Elect County Sheriff, Evans, Ga., 1996—97. Mem.: Inst. of Mgmt. Accts., Inst. of Cert. Profl. Mgrs. Office: Xytex Corporation 1100 Emmett St Augusta GA 30904 Office Phone: 706-733-0130. Business E-Mail: mparish@xytex.com.

**PARISH, NORMAN,** artist, art gallery director; b. New Orleans, Aug. 26, 1937; B in Painting, Sch. of Art Inst. of Chgo., 1960. Draftsman to asst. project leader, to project leader to supr. of computer-aided drafting; founder, dir. Parish Gallery, Washington, 1991—. Contbr. to Wall of Respect, Chgo., 1967. Office: Parish Gallery 1054 31st St Washington DC 20007 Office Phone: 202-944-2310. Business E-Mail: parishgallery@bigplanet.com.

**PARISH, RICHARD LEE,** engineer, consultant; b. Kansas City, Mo., May 31, 1945; s. Charles Lee and Ruth (Duncan) P.; m. Patricia Ann Erickson, June 2, 1968; children: Christie Lynn White, Kerry Anne Parish-Philp. BS in Agrl. Engring., U. Mo., 1967, MS in Agrl. Engring., 1968, PhD, 1970. Registered profl. engr., Ohio. Asst., then assoc. prof. engring. Univ. Ark., Fayetteville, 1969-74; mgr. mech. research and devel. O.M. Scott & Sons Co., Marysville, Ohio, 1974-83; assoc. prof., then prof. La. State U., Baton Rouge, 1983-97; prof. Hammond Rsch. Sta., 1995—. Cons. in equipment patents, equipment safety, product liability, personal injury, design and evaluation; expert witness testimony in agrl. and hort. equipment, patents, 1984—. Contbr. over 100 articles to profl. jours.; patentee in field. Bd. dirs. Agrl. Devel. Found. Recipient Quality award, ITT, 1979, Doyle Chambers award for excellence in rsch., La. State U. Agrl. Ctr., 2001; NSF fellow, 1967—69. Mem. Am. Soc. Agrl. Engrs. (chmn. agrl. chem. application com. 1982-83, chmn. power and machinery divsn. program com. 1986-87, chmn. cultural practices equipment com. 1994-95, chmn. fruit and vegetable prodn. engring. com. 1999-2001), La. Vegetable Growers Assn., Am. Soc. Hort. Sci. Republican. Baptist. Avocations: old tractors, gardening, woodwork, bicycling. Home: 21135 Highway 16 Amite LA 70422-4733 Office: Hammond Rsch Sta 21549 Old Covington Hwy Hammond LA 70403-0533 Office Phone: 985-543-4125. Business E-Mail: dparish@agcenter.lsu.edu.

**PARISH, SHARON DENISE,** music educator, director; b. Pasadena, Tex., Nov. 4, 1952; d. Verble William and Gladys Francille Parish; m. Scott Robert Hagy (div.); 1 child, Robert Michael; 1 child, Joshua Nathaniel Bowlin. AA, San Jacinto Coll., 2000; MusB magna cum laude, Houston Bapt. U., 2004. Legal sec., rsch. asst. various law firms, Houston, 1971—96; pvt. practice tchr. piano Houston, 1996—; music tchr. Pasadena Ind. Sch. Dist., Houston, 2005—; asst. choral dir. Thompson Intermediate Sch. Author: Clef Notes - the Pilgrims Gift to the New World, 2002, Clef Notes- Nicolai Paganini Il Virtuoso Italiano piu Grande, 2003. Mem.: Tex. Music Educators Assn., Alpha Chi (life). Avocations: sailing, animals, theater, travel. Home: 14719 Sun Harbor Dr Houston TX 77062 Office: 12900 Almeda Genoa Rd Houston TX 77034 Office Phone: 713-948-4230. Business E-Mail: sparish@pasadenaisd.org.

**PARISH, WILLIAM HENRY,** lawyer; b. Oakland, Calif. July 28, 1954; s. Harry and Elaine Katherine (Triplett) P.; m. Kathryn Annette, Aug. 14, 1976; children: Michael Erik, Jennifer Christine, Melissa Ann. AA, Hartnell Coll., 1974; BA, Calif. State U., 1977; JD, U. Pacific, 1980. Bar: Calif. 1980, U.S. Dist. Ct. (ea. dist.) Calif. 1980, U.S. Ct. Appeals (9th cir.) 1980, U.S. Supreme Ct. 1990. Assoc. Cavalero, Bray, Geiger & Rudquist, Stockton, Calif. 1980-82, ptnr., 1982-87; Bray, Geiger, Rudquist, Nuss & Parish, Stockton, Calif., 1987; prin. Law Offices of William H. Parish, Stockton, Calif., 1987—96, Parish & Nelson, A Profl. Corp., Stockton, Calif., 1997—2002, Parish & Small, A Profl. Corp., Stockton, Calif., 2003—. Mem. ABA (litigation sect. 1980—), Order of Coif, Am. Heart Assn., San Joaquin County, mem. bd. dirs. (2001-), pres. (2002-). Office: Parish & Small Profl Corp 1919 Grand Canal Blvd Ste A-5 Stockton CA 95207

**PARISI, CHERYL LYNN,** art educator; b. Hackensack, N.J., Aug. 26, 1955; d. Elza A. and Constance Leah (Sculley) Sockey; m. Albert J. Parisi, Apr. 18, 1981; 1 child, Christopher Thomas. BA, Fairleigh Dickinson U., 1977; MA in Art Edn., Columbia U., N.Y.C., 2005. Cert. tchr., N.J. Piano instr., Bergen County, N.J., 1972-79; art tchr. Meml. Sch., South Hackensack, N.J., 1979-80, Hackensack Mid. Sch., 1980-84, Nellie K. Parker Sch., Hackensack, 1984—. Exhibited in group shows at The Jacob Javits Conv. Ctr., N.Y.C., 1990, The Designer Craftsmen's Gallery, New Brunswick, N.J., 1993, Gloucester County Coll., Sewell, N.J., 1993, Johnson and Johnson Corp., Titusville, N.J., 1993, Arts Coun. Princeton, N.J., 1993, Montclair State U., Upper Montclair, N.J., 1992, 94, Old Cultural Ctr. juried Small Works Show, Demarest, N.J. 2004, Macy Gallery. T.C., Columbia U., 2004, James Howe Gallery, Union, N.J., 2005, Art Ctr. No. NJ, 2006, James Howe Gallery, Kean U., Union, N.J., 2006; mem. panel for selection of educators for the NEH seminar Am. and Brit. Children's Lit., Princeton, 1999; author, co-dir. children's musical Claude Monet: A Bridge to the Past, 1999. Recipient Art Educator Achievement award Fantasy Fund Inc. at the Cathedral of St. John the Divine, N.Y.C., 1992; grantee Hackensack Edn. Found., 1991; grantee Hackensack Small Grants Program, 2003, Hackensack Rotary Club, Art Educators of N.J., 2004, Target Corp., 2004; NEH fellow Princeton U., 1991. Mem. Art Educators N.J. (chairperson 1993 Yr. of the Am. Craft 1991-93, publicity 50th anniversary conf. 1990; pres. Bergen County chpt. 1984-86, Achievement award 1989), Nat. Art Edn. Assn. Avocation: reading. Home: 167 Godwin Ave Wyckoff NJ 07481-2004 Office: Nellie K Parker Elem Sch 261 Maple Hill Dr Hackensack NJ 07601-1497

**PARISI, LEAH EVANS,** dean, nursing educator, lawyer; d. Leslie Malcom and Elizabeth Stoughton Evans; m. Alfonso Parisi, Oct. 6, 1990; stepchildren: Anne Marie, Joseph, Nancy, Paula; m. Ronald Katz (div.). BSN, Ohio State U., Columbus, 1962; MA in Healthcare Adminstrn., Lindenwood Coll., L.A., 1975; EdD in Instl. Mgmt., Pepperdine U., L.A., 1982; JD, Loyola Law Sch., L.A., 1985. Bar: Calif. 1985; RN Ohio, 1962, N.Y., 1967, Tex., Ontario, Can., 1989, S.C., 1999, Calif., 1989, CRNA, Am. Assn. Nurse Anesthetists, 1965. Nurse anesthetist cardiac surgery Cleve. Clinic, Cleve., 1960—67, Baylor Coll. Medicine, Houston, 1967—73; dir. nurse anesthesia program Martin Luther King Gen. Hosp., L.A., Calif., 1973—74, UCLA Sch. Medicine, 1973—85; attorney med. malpractice and staff privileges law Rushfeld Shelley & Drake, 1985—88; prof. sch. nursing Faculty Health Scis. McMaster U., Hamilton, Ontario, Canada, 1989—99; instr. legal asst. and paralegal program Tech. Coll. Lowcountry, Beaufort, SC, 2000—, dean bus. tech., 2000—. Adj. assoc. prof. dept. anesthesiology UCLA Sch. Medicine, 1974—85; ednl. cons. and sr. on- site visitor Am. Assn. Nurse Anesthetists, Chgo., 1975—85; prof. sch. nursing Faculty Health Scis. McMaster U., Hamilton, Ontario, 1989—99; invited vis. faculty U. Nebr., Lincoln, Henry Ford Hosp. U. Detroit, U. So. Calif., L.A.; invited participant McMaster U. Faculty Health Scis. Program Academic Leaders, Hamilton, Ontario; dir. Hummingbird Enterprises, Hilton Head, SC. Contbr. to conf. proceedings, chapters to books, scientific papers, articles to profl. jours. Bd. mem. St. Josephs Villa, Hamilton, Ontario, 1992—99. Recipient Helen Lamb award Educator of Yr., Am. Assn. Nurse Anesthetists, 1984, Alumni Assn. Ann. award, Ohio State U., Nurse Anesthesia Program, 1985, Faculty Tchg. Excellence award, McMaster U. students, 1999, hon. mention Ann. Grad. Student Supr. award, McMaster U. Mem.: ABA. Achievements include established first graduate nurse anesthesia program in nurse anesthesia U.S. Office: Tech Coll Lowcountry 921 Ribaut Rd Beaufort SC 29910 Office Phone: 843-525-8278. E-mail: lparisi@tcl.edu.

**PARISI, VALERIE MARIE,** dean, medical educator; b. Bklyn. m. Gary Strong. BS in Biology, Brown U., 1972, MD, 1975; MPH, U. Calif. Sch. Pub. Health, 1980; MBA, U. NC, 2004. Lic. Calif., 1979, Tex., 1984, NY, 1994, NC, 1998, diplomate Nat. Bd. Med. Examiners, 1976, Am. Bd. Ob-gyn., 1981, Am. Bd. Ob-gyn. Divsn. Maternal-Fetal Medicine, 1987. NIH rsch. fellow, Dept. Chemistry and Physics Brown U., Providence, 1970, Noyes Found. rsch. fellow, Dept. Sociology & Divsn. Reproductive Biology and Medicine, 1971; Noyes Found. rsch. fellow, Dept. Ob-gyn. Women and Infants Hosp. RI, Providence, 1972; intern in categorical gen. surgery Brown U. Affiliated Hospitals, RI Hosp., Providence, 1975—76; resident in ob-gyn. Women and Infants Hosp. of RI, Providence, 1976—79; fellow divsn. maternal-fetal medicine, Dept. Ob-gyn. U. Colo. Health Sci. Ctr., Denver, 1982—83, U. Wis. Ctr. for Health Sciences, Madison, 1983—84; instr. Dept. Human Growth and Reproduction Brown U., 1976—79; lectr., divsn. maternal child health U. Calif. Sch. Pub. Health, Berkeley, 1980—81; clin. instr. Dept. Ob-gyn. and Reproductive Sciences, U. Calif., San Francisco, 1980—81, clin. asst. prof., 1981—82; asst. prof. Dept. Ob-gyn. U. Colo. Health Sci. Ctr., Denver, 1982—83, U. Wis. Health Sci. Ctr., Madison, 1983—84; asst. prof. Dept. Ob-gyn. and Reproductive Sciences U. Texas Med. Sch., Houston, 1984—89, assoc. prof. Dept. Ob-gyn. and Reproductive Sciences, 1989—94, dir. divsn. maternal-fetal medicine, 1984—94, asst. prof. Dept. Pediatrics, 1987—89, assoc. prof. Dept. Pediatrics, 1989—94, co-dir. maternal-fetal medicine fellowship program, 1987—94; vis. prof. Dept. neonatology Dept. Pediatrics U. Cin. Med. Ctr., 1991—92; prof. & chair Dept. Ob-gyn. and Reproductive Medicine U. Med. Ctr. at Stony Brook, NY, 1994—97; Robert A. Ross prof. & chair Dept Ob-gyn. U. NC, Chapel Hill, 1997—2004, residency program dir. Dept. Ob-gyn., 1999—2004, rsch. fellow Cecil G. Sheps Ctr. for Health Sciences Rsch., 2003—; dean medicine U. Tex. Med. Branch, Galveston, 2004—; chief acad. officer, v.p. acad. program adminstrn. and services, 2004—06, advisor, Health personnel Providence Neighborhood Health Centers, RI, 1977—79; dir. Ob-gyn. Services Bristol County Cmty. Med. Ctr., RI, 1977—79; dir. gynecological services Brown U. Student Health Services, 1978—79; consulting staff Letterman Army Med. Ctr., Presidio of San Francisco, 1979—82; attending staff Kaiser Found. Hosp., Oakland, Calif., 1980, San Francisco, 1980—82; clin. staff Moffitt Hosp. U. Calif. San Francisco Med. Ctr., 1980—82; med. dir. Ambulatory Care Ctr. Dept. Ob-gyn. U. Colo. Health Sci. Ctr., Denver, 1982—83; attending staff Madison Gen. Hosp., Wis., 1983—84, U. Wis. Clin. Sciences Ctr., Madison, 1983—84; consulting staff St. Mary's Med. Ctr., Madison, Wis., 1983—84; attending staff Hermann Hosp., Houston, 1984—94, dir. Maternal-Fetal Spl. Care Unit, 1985—92, obstetrical dir. labor and delivery, 1987—88, Houston, 1992—94, med. dir. Family Ctr., 1992—94; consulting staff St. Joseph's Hosp., Houston, 1987—94, Meml. Southwest Hosp., Houston, 1990—94; active staff Lyndon Baines Johnson Hosp., Houston, 1990—94; ob-gyn. chief U. Hosp., Stony Brook, NY, 1994—97; consulting staff Southampton Hosp., NY, 1995—97, St. Charles Hosp., Port Jefferson, NY, 1996—97; obstetrician-gynecologist-in-chief NC Women's Hosp., Chapel Hill, 1997—2004; attending staff Dept. Ob-gyn REX Hosp., 2002—04. Bd. dirs. Am. Bd. Family Practice, 1999—2004; fin. and investment com., nominating com. Am. Bd. Med. Specialties, 2004; basic examiner Am. Bd. Obstetrics and Gynecology, 1990—, maternal and fetal medicine examiner, 1992—, divsn. maternal and fetal medicine, 1996—2002, bd. dirs. and divsn. chief maternal and fetal medicine, 1998—2002, exec. com., 1999—2002, fin. com., 2004—; mem. Coun. on Residency Edn. in Ob-gyn., 1995—2000; bd. dirs. Planned Parenthood of Suffolk County, 1994—97; exec. bd. Western Perinatal Collaborative Group, 1986—92, chair membership com., 1986—88, vice pres. & pres.-elect, 1988—90, pres., 1990—92. Fellow: Am. Gynecologic and Obstetrical Soc. (nominating com. 1992, fellowship com. 1992—95), Am. Assn. Advancement Sci.; mem.: Tex. Perinatal Assn., Tex. Med. Found., Tex. Med. Assn., Tex. Assn. Obstetricians and Gynecologists, Soc. for Study of Reproduction, Soc. Obstetric Anesthesia and Perinatology (bd. dirs. 1995—99), Soc. for Maternal Fetal Medicine (bd. dirs. 1989—92, scientific program chair 1993, pres.-elect 1993—94, pres. 1994—95), Soc. Gynecological Investigation, Perinatal Rsch. Soc. (exec. coun. 1993—95), NY Obstetrical Soc., Internat. Soc. for Study of Hypertension in Pregnancy, Nat'l Foundation for Gynecological and Obstetrical Soc., Harris County Med. Soc., Assn. Reproductive Health Professionals, Assn. Professors of Gynecology and Obstetrics, Am. Med. Women's Assn., AMA, Am. Coll. Obstetricians and Gynecologists (patient edn. com. 1989—91, scientific program com. 1993, edn. commnn. 1995—97), Sigma Xi. Office: Office of Dean Univ Tex Med Branch Galveston 301 University Blvd Galveston TX 77555-0133

**PARISOTTO, GLORIA,** publishing executive, poet, writer; b. São Paulo, Brazil, July 4, 1938; came to U.S., 1980; d. Luiz and Antonia (Guimarães) P.; m. Onofre Pereira Mendonca, Dec. 13, 1954 (div. 1980); children: Marco Antonio, Marco Tulio, Maria Emilia. Degree in tchg., Inst. Fernando Costa, Prudente, 1954; student, Brazilian Acad. Fine Arts, Rio de Janeiro, 1985. Cert. tchr., Brazil. Tchr. Sch.-Pres. Bernardes, São Paulo, Brazil, 1954-56, Maristas H.S., Parana, P.R., 1954-66; hosp. supr. Sanatory Maringa Ltd., Parana, P.R., 1955-90; pres. Sunrising Publ. Co., N.Y.C., 1991—. Author: Learning Portuguese without a Teacher, 1991, The Extraterrestrial and the Blue Planet, 1992, My Poems (3 langs.), 1992; (poems) The Flower (Poet of Merit award Am. Poetry Assn. 1990), Mother (Poet of Merit award Internat. Poetry soc. 1991); contbr. poetry to numerous anthologies; one-woman art show at Cricket Club, Nfianii, U.S., 1981; exhibited art in group shows at Assn. de Criticos y Comentaristas de Arte, Miami, Fla., 1981, Hispanic Heritage Festival, Miami, 1981, Internat. Festival, Nhan-@, 1982, Nouvelle Gailerie, Geneva, Switzerland, 1983, UNESCO, Paris, 1984, Brazilian Artists Show, Rio de Janeiro, 1985, Internat. Expo, N.Y.C., 1986, Internat. Art Expo, Montreal, Que., Can., 1986, Pub. Libr., Gt. Neck, N.Y., 1987 (Excellence medal), Am. Embassy, Brasilia, Brazil, 1987, House of Spain, Rio de Janeiro, 1987, Lever House, N.Y.C., 1987, Mcpl. Gallery, São Paulo, 1989, Lincoln Ctr. Cork Gallery, N.Y.C., 1989, Icaro Gallery, N.Y.C., 1990, Epiphany Gallery, N.Y.C., 1990, Vanderbilt Mus., L.I., N.Y., 1992, Rio Design Ctr. Gallery, 1993 (hon. mention), Portal Gallery, São Paulo, 1993, Who's Who Artists, Edinburgh, Scotland, 1994, IPS's Conv. Art Show, Washington, 1995, Art Show, Capetown, South Africa, 1995, Am. & Internat. Bio Ctr., San Francisco, 1996, Oxford (Eng.) Gallery, 1997. Rep. abroad Brazilian Ecology Assn., Rio de Janeiro, 1988, Pan Am. Writers Assn., Brazilian Acad. Fine Arts, Rio de Janeiro, 1988. Recipient Bronze medal L'Amounier Gallery, Rio de Janeiro, 1981, Hebrew Cmty., Rio de Janeiro, 1981, Silver medal Brazilian Assn. Drawing and Visual Arts, Rio de Janeiro, 1982, Mil. Assn. Art Show, Rio de Janeiro, 1982, Gold medal Internat. Blenal, Rio de Janeiro, 1983, Ho. of Reps., Rio de Janeiro, 1983, Planetarium Gallery, Rio de Janeiro, 1984, Nat. Acad. Fine Arts, Rio de Janeiro, 1985, Palace "Espelho D'Agua", Belem, Portugal, 1986, Civil Police Acad., Rio de Janeiro, 1986, Gold Palette award Exhbn. Brazilian Artists, Salvador, Bahia, Brazil, 1987, Editor's award Nat. Libr. of Poetry, Washington, 1993, 94, Excellentia Order of Merit award, 1995, 1st prize award Famous Poetry Soc., Calif., 1996; semi-finalist nat. contest Internat. Poetry Soc.; named Poet of Merit, Internat. Poetry Assn., Washington, 1990, 91, 92. Mem. Nat. League Am. Pen Women, Inc., Internat. Platform Assn., Writers and Poets Soc., Acad. Am. Poets, Française-Italian Cultural Inst. Avocations: tennis, gym, travel, reading, music. Home and Office: 150 W 56th St Apt 3407 New York NY 10019-3843

**PARIZEK, ELDON JOSEPH,** geologist, educator; dean; b. Iowa City, Apr. 30, 1920; s. William Joseph and Libbie S. P.; m. Mildred Marie Burger, Aug. 9, 1944; children— Richard, Marianne, Elizabeth, Amy. BS, U. Iowa, 1942, MS, 1946, PhD, 1949. Instr. U. Iowa, 1947-49; asst. prof. geology U. Ga., 1949-54, asso. prof., 1954-56, U. Kansas City, 1956-63; prof. U. Mo., Kansas City, 1963—, chmn. dept. geoscis., 1968-78; dean U. Mo. (Coll. Arts and Scis.), 1979-86. Served with USN, 1942-45. Fellow Geol. Soc. Am.; mem. AAUP, Assn. Mo. Geologists, AAAS, Sigma Xi. Roman Catholic. Achievements include research, numerous publs. on mass wasting, slope failure, underground space, geology of West Mo. Home: 6913 W 100th Shawnee Mission KS 66212 Office: 5100 Rockhill Rd Kansas City MO 64110-2481

**PARK, ALICE MARY CRANDALL,** author, genealogist; b. Loda, Ill., Oct. 4, 1901; d. Frederick Adam and Sarah Elizabeth (Clemens) Crandall; m. Lee I. Park, Aug. 29, 1925 (dec. Aug. 24, 1978); children: Lee Crandall, Nancy Park Kern. BS, U. Chgo., 1924. Tchr. U. Chgo. Lab. Sch., 1924-25; genealogy rschr. Washington, 1925—2006. Author: Park/e/s and Bunch on the Trail West, 1974, rev. edit., 1982, Schenck and Related Families in New Netherland, 1992, One Crandall Family 1651-1996, 1996, supplement, 1999, Our Immigrant Ancestors from Scotland: George Smith and His Wife, Mary Baird and Their Descendants, 2002. Pres. Falls Church (Va.) PTA, 1941-42, LWV, Fairfax County, Va., 1947-48. Mem. DAR, Nat. Soc. Colonial Dames Am., Nat. Soc. Sons and Daughters of Pilgrims, Nat. Soc. Daughters Am. Colonists, Friends Holland Soc., Nat. Huguenot Soc., Nat. Soc. U.S. Daughters 1812, Soc. Daughters Holland Dames: Descs. Ancient and Hon. Families of New Netherland, Chevy Chase Club, Met. Club, Farmington Country Club. Avocations: gardening, travel, cooking, music. Home: Washington, DC. Died May 21, 2006.

**PARK, BARBARA,** writer; b. Mt. Holly, NJ, Apr. 27, 1947; m. Richard A. Park, 1969; 2 children. Attended, Rider Coll., 1965—67; BS, U. Alabama, 1969. Author: (children's books) Don't Make Me Smile, 1981, Operation: Dump the Chump, 1982 (Tennessee Children's Choice Book award, 1986), Skinnybones, 1982, Beanpole, 1983, Buddies, 1985 (Parents' Choice award, 1985), Kid in the Red Jacket, 1987 (Library of Congress Book of the Yr., 1987), Almost Starring Skinnybones, 1988, Mother Got Married: and Other Disasters, 1989, Rosie Swanson, 1991, Junie B. Jones and the Stupid Smelly Bus, 1992, Junie B. Jones and Her Big Fat Mouth, 1993, Junie B. Jones and a Little Monkey Business, 1993, Junie B. Jones and Some Sneaky Peeky Spying, 1994, Mick Harte Was Here, 1995, Junie B. Jones and the Yucky Blucky Fruitcake, 1995, B. Jones Loves Handsome Warren, 1996, Junie B. Jones and that Meanie Jim's Birthday, 1996, Junie B. Jones Loves Handsome Warren, 1996, Junie B. Jones has a Monster Under Her Bed, 1997, Junie B. Jones is Not a Crook, 1997, Junie B. Jones is a Party Animal, 1997, Junie B. Jones Smells Something Fishy, 1998, Junie B. Jones is a Beauty Shop Guy, 1998, Psst! It's Me...the Bogeyman, 1998, Junie B. Jones is Almost a Flower Girl, 1999, Junie B. Jones and the Mushy Gushy Valentine, 1999, Junie B. Jones has a Peep in her Pocket, 2000, Junie B. Jones is Captain Field Day, 2001, Junie B. Jones is a Graduation Girl, 2001, Junie B. Jones: First Grader, 2001, Junie B. First Grader: Boss of Lunch, 2002, Junie B. First Grader: Toothless Wonder, 2002, Top Secret, Personal Beeswax: A Journal by Junie B., 2003, Junie B. First Grader: Cheater Pants, 2003, Junie B. First Grader: One-Man Band, 2003. Recipient Young Hoosier award, 1985, Milner award, 1986. Office: c/o Random House 1745 Broadway New York NY 10019

**PARK, CHAN HO,** professional baseball player; b. Kongju, South Korea, June 30, 1973; Grad., Hanyang U., South Korea. Player LA Dodgers, 1994—2001, Tex. Rangers, 2002—05, San Diego Padres, 2005—. Player Korean Nat. Team, World Baseball Classic, 2006. Named a mem. of the All-Tourney Team (pitcher), World Baseball Classic, 2006. Achievements include becoming the first South Korean to ever reach 100 Career Wins in the majors; 3 saves (1st in tournament) in the World Baseball Classic 2006, 3 games finished (3rd in tournament, 0.00 (10.0 innings) earned run average (2nd in tournament). Office: San Diego Padres PO Box 122000 San Diego CA 92112-2000 Office Phone: (619) 795-5000.*

**PARK, CHAN HYUNG,** cell biologist, physician; b. Seoul, Korea, Aug. 16, 1936; s. Chung Suh and Yoon Sook Yuh; m. Mary Hyungrok Kim, Apr. 16, 1966; 1 child, Christopher Myungwoo. MD, Seoul Nat. U., 1962, MS, 1964; PhD, U. Toronto, 1972. Diplomate in internal medicine and med. oncology Am. Bd. Internal Medicine. Asst. prof. U. Kans. Med. Ctr., 1974—80, assoc. prof., 1980—86, prof., 1986—; chief divsn. oncology/hematology, dept. internal med. Tex. Tech U. Health Scis. Ctr., 1989—94; dir. Cancer Ctr. Samsung Med. Ctr., Seoul, 1994—2001, head divsn. hematology/oncology dept. medicine, 1994—99; sr. rsch. scientist Ctr. for Improvement of Human Functioning Internat., Inc., Wichita, Kans., 2001—. Transl. novel from German to Korean; mem. editl. bd. Jour. Nutrition, Growth and Cancer, 1986-87; mem. editl. bd. Internat. Jour. Hematology, 1999—; contbr. articles to biomed and sci. jours. Recipient Rsch. Career Devel. award USPHS, NIH, 1979-84. Fellow: ACP; mem.: Am. Soc. Hematology, Internat. Soc. Exptl. Hematology, Am. Soc. Clin. Oncology, Am. Assn. Cancer Rsch. Home: 611 S 291 ST Federal Way WA 98003 Office: The Ctr for the Improvement Human Functioning Internat Inc 3100 N Hillside Wichita KS 67219 Personal E-mail: chanhpark@hotmail.com, park.chanh@gmail.com. Business E-Mail: cbpark@brightspot.org.

**PARK, CHANDO,** materials scientist, researcher; b. Seoul, South Korea, Oct. 15, 1971; s. Keunsuh Park and Kyungja Bae; m. Jeongwoo Ko, Mar. 11, 1971; 1 child, Joonho. BS, Korea U., Seoul, 1996; MS, KAIST, Daejeon, 1999, Carnegie Mellon U., Pitts., 2001, PhD, 2004. Cert. material sci. engr., Pa., 2004. Asst. rschr. LG Philips LCD Rsch. Ctr., Anyang, Kyoungkido, Republic of Korea, 1999—2000; rschr. Carnegie Mellon U., Pitts., 2004—. Contbr. articles to profl. jours. Sgt. 1st Signal brigade, 1991—94, Korea. Recipient Suklim scholar, KAIST, 1999, Yongpung award, Yongpung Moongo, 1990. Achievements include research in Fe3O4 based magnetic tunnel junction; MgO based magnetic tunnel junction; crystallization of hydrogenated amorphous/microcrystalline bilyers; metal induced lateral crystallization; metal induced crystallization. Office: Carnegie Mellon University 5000 Forbes Ave Pittsburgh PA 15213 Office Phone: 412-268-5430.

**PARK, CHONG S.,** computer company executive; BA in Mgmt., Yonsei U.; MA in Mgmt., Seoul Nat. U.; MBA, U. Minn.; PhD in Mgmt., Nova Southeastern U. Chmn., pres., CEO Axil Computer, Inc., 1993—95; pres., CEO Hynix Semiconductor Am., Inc., 1996—2000, chmn., 1996—2002; pres., CEO, chmn. Hynix Semiconductor, Inc., 2000—02; pres., CEO Maxtor Corp., Milipitas, Calif., 1995—96, chmn., 1996, CEO, 2004—06. Chmn. MMC Tech. (Maxtor subs.), 1996—2000; bd. dir. Dot Hill Sys. Corp., ChipPAC, Seagate Tech., 2006—. Mailing: Seagate Technology Bd Directors 920 Disc Dr Scotts Valley CA 95066-4544*

**PARK, CHUNG IL,** retired librarian; b. Chang-won, Korea, Aug. 25, 1938; s. Zung S. and Bong-y (Choo) P.; m. Jung Yoo, Aug. 30, 1969; children: Charlotte, June. Andrew. BA, Yonsei U., 1961; MLS, U. So. Calif., L.A., 1971; postgrad., U. Ill., 1975. Librr. mem. faculty Malcolm X Coll., Chgo., 1972—2002; ret., 2002. Compiler, editor: (books) Best Sellers and Best Choices 1980-83, Best Books by Consensus 1984-88, Advertisement Digest: Library and Information Services, 1979; editor COINT, 1980-88; contbr. articles to profl. jours. Mem. ALA, Am. Fedn. Tchrs. Avocation: automobile travel. Home: 4384 N Indianhead R Hernando FL 34442 E-mail: ci_park@yahoo.com.

**PARK, CYNTHIA,** sociology educator, consultant; b. Schenectady, N.Y., Feb. 7, 1925; d. Robert Hiram and Miriam Elizabeth Park; m. Robert Wentworth Christy (div.). BA, New Sch. Social Rsch., 1959; MS in Secondary Social Studies, Yeshiva U., 1961; MA in Sociology, Hunter Coll., CUNY, 1969; postgrad., New Sch. U., 1970—75. Permanent lic. secondary social studies N.Y.C. and N.Y. State. Tchr. h.s. sci. and social studies N.Y. Bd. Edn., N.Y.C., 1961, tchr. h.s. social studies Brandeis H.S., 1962—66; tchr. Nassau C.C., L.I., NY, 1970; instr. sociology Bloomfield (N.J.) Coll., 1967—70, Quinnipiac Coll., New Haven, 1971—73, U. New Haven, West Haven, Conn., 1973—75; ind. cons. N.Y.C., 1975—77. Cons. Paulo Mesdag Gruppe Rec. Yale U. Archives; owner 98 1/2 McDougal St., N.Y.C., 1951; dir. Coop Gallery, N.Y.C., 1960—65, Westerly Gallery, N.Y.C. Prodr.: (mus. recs.) Music of Finland. Local campaign worker Lexington Dem. Club, N.Y.C., 1963—67. Recipient Fulbright grant to Finland, 1959—60, grants in field. Mem.: Soc. Ethnomusicology, Ind. U., Am. Sociol. Assn., Violoncello Soc., Am. Fedn. Musicians. Democrat. Episcopalian. Avocations: art, violincello, singing. Home: 965 Lexington Ave New York NY 10021

**PARK, DAVID ALLEN,** physicist, researcher; b. NYC, Oct. 13, 1919; s. Edwin Avery and Frances (Paine) P.; m. Clara Justine Claiborne, Aug. 18, 1945; children: Katharine, Rachel, Paul, Jessica. AB, Harvard, 1941; PhD, U. Mich., 1950. Instr. Williams Coll., 1941-44; ops. research on radar countermeasures Harvard U. and Eng., 1944-45; instr. U. Mich., 1950; mem. Inst. Advanced Study, Princeton, 1950-51; mem. faculty Williams Coll., 1952-88, prof. physics, 1960-88, emeritus, 1988—; sr. vis. Cambridge (Eng.) U., 1962-63; vis. lectr. U. Ceylon, 1955-56, 72, Mass. Inst. Tech., 1966; vis. prof. U. N.C., 1964. Author: Quantum Theory, 1964, 3d edit., 1991, Contemporary Physics, 1964, Strong Interactions, 1966, Classical Dynamics and Its Quantum Analogues, 1979, 2d edit., 1990, The Image of Eternity, 1980, (with P.J. Davis) No Way, 1987, The How and the Why, 1988, The Fire Within the Eye, 1997, The Grand Contraption, 2005. Fellow Am. Phys. Soc.; mem. Internat. Soc. for Study Time (pres. 1973-76). Office: Williams Coll Dept Physics Williamstown MA 01267 Business E-Mail: dpark@williams.edu.

**PARK, DAVID WILLIAM,** humanities educator; b. Geneva, Ill., Oct. 4, 1971; s. William Oliver and Lois Ann Park; m. Sarah Ann Conner, May 23, 1998. BS, Northwestern U., Evanston, Ill., 1989—93; PhD, U. Pa., Phila., 1994—2001. Adj. prof. U. Ill., Chgo., 2001—03; asst. prof. Lake Forest Coll., Ill., 2003—. Editor: (book) Media Research and Its Histories; contbr. articles to profl. jours. Mem.: Assn. Internet Rschrs., Nat. Comm. Assn. (chmn. Franklyn S. Haiman award com. 2005—), Internat. Comm. Assn. Office: Lake Forest Coll 555 N Sheridan Rd Lake Forest IL 60045-2399 Office Fax: 847-735-6193. Business E-Mail: park@lakeforest.edu.

**PARK, EDWARD CAHILL, JR.,** retired physicist; b. Wollaston, Mass., Nov. 26, 1923; s. Edward Cahill and Fentress (Kerlin) P.; m. Helen Therese O'Boyle, July 28, 1951. AB, Harvard U., 1947; postgrad., Amherst Coll., 1947-49; PhD, U. Birmingham, Eng., 1956. Instr. Amherst (Mass.) Coll., 1954-55; mem. staff Lincoln Lab., Lexington, Mass., 1955-57, Arthur D. Little, Inc., Cambridge, Mass., 1957-60, group leader electronic systems Santa Monica, Calif., 1960-64; sr. staff engr., head laser system sect. Hughes Aircraft Co., Culver City, Calif., 1964-68, sr. scientist El Segundo, Calif., 1986-88; mgr. electro optical systems sect. Litton Guidance and Control Systems, Woodland Hills, Calif., 1968-70; sr. phys. scientist The Rand Corp., Santa Monica, 1970-72; sr. scientist R&D Assocs., Marina Del Rey, Calif., 1972-1986, cons., 1986-89; sr. tech. specialist Rockwell Internat. Anaheim, Calif., 1989-94. Contbr. articles to profl. jours.; patentee in field. Served to 1st lt. USAAF, 1943-46. Grantee Dept. Indsl. and Sci. Research, 1953. Fellow Explorers Club (sec. So. Calif. chpt. 1978-79); mem. IEEE, Soc. Archtl. Historians, Acad. Am. Poets, Sigma Xi. Clubs: 20-Ghost (Eng.), BMW Car Club Am., Mercedes Benz Club Am. Democrat. Avocations: music, art, architecture, gardening, classic cars. Home: 932 Ocean Frnt Santa Monica CA 90403-2410

**PARK, ELIZABETH HASKELL,** librarian, educator; d. Henry Cummings and Lois Ogren Haskell; m. Melburn Robert Park, June 11, 1966; children: Geoffrey Haskell, Carolyne Elizabeth. BA, Stanford U., 1966; MLS, SUNY, Buffalo, 1972; MS, Memphis State U., 1989. Librr. Gardenville Elem. Sch., West Seneca, NY, 1972—73; reference librr. Lansing (Mich.) C.C., 1980—82; asst. bus. librr. Mich. State U., Lansing, 1982—83; reference librr. U. Memphis, 1983—95, head reference dept., 1995—. Co-author: Charging and Collecting Fees and Fines: A Handbook for Libraries, 1998; contbr. articles to profl. jours., chpt. to book. Mem.: ALA, Mich. Librr. Assn., Tenn. Librr. Assn., Assn. Coll. and Rsch. Librrs., Kappa Delta Phi, Beta Phi Mu. Office: U Memphis 126 Ned R McWherter Library Memphis TN 38152 Office Phone: 901-678-8214. Business E-Mail: ehpark@memphis.edu.

**PARK, GRACE,** professional golfer; b. Seoul, South Korea, Mar. 6, 1979; Attended, Ewha Women's U., 2003, Ariz. State U. Winner Kathy Ireland greens.com Championship, 2000, Home Depot Championship, 2001, Cisco Ladies World Matchplay Championship, 2002, Michelob Light Championships, 2003, Kraft Nabisco Championship, 2004. Non-voting mem. LPGA Exec. Com., 2004. Recipient Am. Jr. Golf Assn (AJGA) Player of Yr., 1994, 1996, Rookie of the Yr., LPGA, 2000. Avocation: shopping. Office: c/o LPGA 100 International Golf Dr Daytona Beach FL 32124-1092*

**PARK, HEE-JUNG (HEE JONG PARK),** professional golfer; b. Seoul, Korea, Feb. 27, 1980; Profl. golfer Korean LPGA, 1998—2000, LPGA Tour, 2000—. Winner Australian Jr. Championship, 1996, 97, 98. Achievements include winning several Korean LPGA events including Sports Seoul Ladies Open, 1998, Indonesian Ladies Open, 1999; winner LPGA events including Williams Championship, 2001, Sybase Big Apple Classic, 2002. Avocations: movies, music, video games. Office: LPGA 1000 International Golf Dr Daytona Beach FL 32124-1092*

**PARK, HYOSANG,** music educator; b. Seoul, Republic of Korea, Nov. 8, 1972; arrived in US, 1996; d. Sukkil Park and Minja Lee. BA, Sungkyul U., Republic of Korea, 1995; MusM, Westminster Choir Coll., Princeton, N.J., 2001. Adminstr. Sungkyul U., Kuynggy, Republic of Korea, 1996; accompanist Monmouth Square U. Med. Ctr., Eatontown, NJ, 1997—2000; music dir. Emburg Meth. Ch., Little Silver, NJ, 2000—02; accompanist Arbertor Choir, Trenton, NJ, 2000; music dir. First Presbyn. Ch., Freehold, NJ, 2002—; music tchr. St. Jerome Cath. Sch., W. Long Branch, NJ, 2001—05. Bell ringer Reverberation, Plumsteadville, Pa., 2003. Musician: (CD) Christmas at Westminster, 1999, Christ Church I, 2001, Christ Church II, 2002. Mem.: Am. Choral Dirs. Assn., Am. Guild of Organists, Am. Guild of English Handbell Ringers, Am. Dirs. of Assn. Home: 6 Dickinson Ln East Windsor NJ 08520 Personal E-mail: pianistpark@aol.com. E-mail: sangpark118@yahoo.com.

**PARK, JAE HYUN,** mechanical engineer, researcher; b. Daegu, Republic of Korea, Dec. 2, 1973; arrived in U.S., 2002; s. Ki Dong Park and Yun Sun Sohn; m. Eun Ha Cho, Sept. 4, 2004. BS, Korea Advanced Inst. Sci. and Tech., Daejeon, 1996, MS, 1998, PhD, 2002. Vis. scholar Japan Aerospace Exploration Agy. (formerly Nat. Aerospace Lab. Japan), Chofu, Tokyo, 2000; post doctoral rsch. assoc. Tex. A&M U., College Station, 2002—03; post doctoral rsch. assoc., Beckman Inst. for Advanced Sci. and Tech., U. Ill., Urbana, 2003—. Reviewer AIAA Jour., Reston, Va., 2003—, Infrared Sci. and Tech., N.Y.C., 2003—, ASME Jour. Fluids Engring., NYC, 2004—. Contbr. articles to profl. jours., chapters to books. Recipient Silver Prize award, Samsung Electronics, 1996; fellow, Japan Internat. Sci. and Tech. Exch. Ctr., 2000, Korea Sci. and Engring. Found., 2002. Mem.: APS, ASME, AIAA. Achievements include research in nanofluidics, microfluidics, space propulsion; rarfied gas dynamics; acoustics and micro/nano-scale heat transfer. Home: #7-104 401 W Curtis Rd Urbana IL 61801 Office: U Ill Beckman Inst 405 N Mathews Ave Urbana IL 61801 Office Phone: 217-244-4353. Office Fax: 217-244-4333. E-mail: jaepark@uiuc.edu, ccami1202@gmail.com.

**PARK, JEFFREY BRYAN,** controller; b. Tampa, Fla., Nov. 20, 1951; s. William H. Jr. and Mary W. (Pounds) P.; m. Kathaleen Barbara Mace, Feb. 4, 1973; children: Shawn M., Amber M. BS in Acctg., Calif. State U., Sacramento, 1973. Cost analyst Antioch (Calif.) Mill-Crown Zellerbach, 1973-76; planning analyst Crown Zellerbach Corp., San Francisco, 1976-77, fin. analyst, 1977-78; controller Crown Zellerbach Multiwall Bag Div., Antioch, 1978-79, Crown Zellerbach Bogalusa (La.) Mill, 1979-84; group controller Crown Zellerbach Gaylord Container Group, San Francisco, 1985-86; v.p., corp. controller Gaylord Container Corp., Deerfield, Ill., 1986—. Mem. Fin. Exec. Inst. Avocation: golf. Home: 701 Paddock Ln Libertyville IL 60048-3734 Office: Gaylord Container Corp 500 Lake Cook Rd Deerfield IL 60015-5609

**PARK, JIN-SUK,** lawyer; s. Dou-Sik and In-Sun Park; m. Audre L. Hodge; 1 child, Jaeya. B of Art, Biology, Johns Hopkins U., 1996; JD, MBA, Boston U., 2001. Bar: NY 2002, DC 2005, US Patent and Trademark Office 2002. Assoc. Clifford Chánce US LLP, NYC, 2002—04, Akin Gump Strauss Hauer & Feld LLP, Washington, 2004—. Office: Akin Gump Strauss Hauer & Feld LLP 1333 New Hampshire Ave NW Washington DC 20036 Office Phone: 202-887-4465. Business E-Mail: jspark@akingump.com.

**PARK, JOHN,** financial consultant; b. Seoul, Korea, Nov. 29, 1925; came to U.S., 1949; s. Young-Kee and In-Oak P.; m. Nancy A. King, Dec. 21, 1961 (div. Nov. 1969); children: John K., Ben C.; m. Kwi Yong Lee, Aug. 14, 1990; 1 child, Angela L. AB, Coll. St. Thomas, 1953; MA, U. Nebr., 1955, PhD, 1959. Chmn., dept. econs., bus. Tarkio (Mo.) Coll., 1957-62; sr. prof. econs., bus. Clarkson Coll., Potsdam, N.Y., 1962-65, Northeast Mo. State U., 1965-67; prof. bus. econs. Southwest Mo. State U., 1967-70; chmn., dept. econ., bus. adminstrn. Frostburg (Md.) State U., 1970—93, prof., econs., bus. adminstrn., 1970—78. Investment advisor, Met. Securities Corp., St. Louis, 1966-70. Mem. Am. Econs. Assn., Am. Fin. Assn., Nat. Assn. Securities Dealers, Am. Assn. Polit. Social Scis., Eastern Fin. Assn., Fin. Mgmt. Assn., Alpha Kappa Delta, Pi Gamma Mu. Republican. Methodist. Avocation: classical music. Home and Office: PO Box 3436 451 Beacon Knoll Ln Fort Mill SC 29708-3436

**PARK, JOHN THORNTON,** retired academic administrator; b. Phillipsburg, N.J., Jan. 3, 1935; s. Dawson J. and Margaret M. (Thornton) P.; m. Dorcas M Marshall; June 1, 1956; children: Janet Ernst, Karen Daily. BA in Physics with distinction, Nebr. Wesleyan U., 1956; PhD, U. Nebr., 1963. NSF postdoctoral fellow Univ. Coll., London, 1963-64; asst. prof. physics U. Mo., Rolla, 1964-68, assoc. prof. physics, 1968-71, prof., 1971-2000, prof. emeritus, 2000—, chmn. dept. physics, 1977-83, vice chancellor acad. affairs, 1983-85, 86-91, interim chancellor, 1985-86, 91-92, chancellor, 1992-2000, chancellor emeritus, 2000—; ret., 2000. Vis. assoc. prof. NYU, 1970-71; pres. Talema Electronics, Inc., St. James, Mo., 1983-99, Tortran Corp., 1990—; prin. investigator NSF Rsch. Grants, 1966-92; bd. dirs. Mo. Tech. Corp., Jefferson City, Mo., 1994—, Mo. Enterprise, 1990—, Phelps County Bank, 1997—. Contbr. articles to profl. jours. Recipient Most Disting. Scientist award Mo. Acad. Sci., 1994. Fellow Am. Phys. Soc. (mem. divsn. elec. and atomic physics); mem. Am. Assn. Physics Tchrs., Rotary. Methodist.

**PARK, JOON BU,** biomedical engineer, researcher, educator; b. Pusan, Republic of Korea, June 20, 1944; arrived in U.S., 1964; s. Sung Sub and Jung Ju (Kim) P.; m. Hyonsook Yoo, Apr. 15, 2000; children: Misun, Yoon Ho, Yoon Il, Lajong. Student, Seoul Nat. U., 1962—64; BS, Boston U., 1967; MS, MIT, 1969; PhD, U. Utah, 1972. NIH postdoctoral fellow U. Wash., Seattle, 1972—73; vis. asst. prof. U. Ill., Urbana, 1973—76; asst. prof. assoc. prof. Clemson U., SC, 1976—81; prof. Tulane U., New Orleans, 1981—83; prof. biomed. engring. U. Iowa, Iowa City, 1983—. Advisor, cons. FDA, Rockville, Md., 1980—. Author: Biomaterials: An Introduction, 1979, 2d edit., 1992, Biomaterials Science and Engineering, 1984, Biomaterials: Principles and Applications, 2002; contbr. over 120 articles to profl. jours. Fellow Am. Inst. Med. and Biol. Engring.; mem. Soc. for Biomaterials (founding mem.), Biomed. Engring. Soc., Orthop. Rsch. Soc., NY Acad. Scis. Achievements include patents in field. Home: 1810 Country Club Dr Coralville IA 52241-1183 Office: Univ Iowa Dept Biomed Engring Iowa City IA 52242 Office Phone: 319-335-5636. Business E-Mail: joon-park@uiowa.edu.

**PARK, JU-HYEONG,** environmental scientist, public health service officer; b. Seoul, Republic of Korea, Feb. 21, 1964; s. Bong-Wan Park and Seung-Rae Jeong; m. Yeonmi Kim; children: Elliot Sang-Hyun, Reena Joon-Hee. BS in Agr. Chemistry, Seoul Nat. U., Suwon, Republic of Korea, 1986; MPH, Seoul Nat. U., Republic of Korea, 1988; MS in Pub. Health, Harvard U., Boston, 1995, DSc in Pub. Health, 1999. Cert. Am. Bd. Indsl. Hygiene, 2002. Rsch. assoc. Sch. Pub. Health Harvard U., 1999—2000; sr. svc. fellow Nat. Inst. Occupl. Safety and Health, Morgantown, W.Va., 2000—. Adj. prof. W.Va. U., Morgantown, W.Va., 2006—. Contbr. articles to profl. jours. Third pvt. Dae-Duk Bn. Korean Army, 1988—90. Recipient Best Paper award; scholar, Indoor Air Jour.; scholarship, Taejeon HS Alumni Assn., 1981, Korea Occupl. Safety and Health Agy., 1996—98. Mem.: Am. Indsl. Hygiene Assn. (assoc.). Home: 106 Meadow Ridge Morgantown WV 26505 Office: Ctr Disease Control Niosh 1095 Willowdale Road Morgantown WV 26505 Office Phone: 304-285-5967. Office Fax: 304-285-5820. Personal E-mail: ymi52@msn.com. Business E-Mail: gzp8@cdc.gov.

**PARK, LEE CRANDALL,** psychiatrist; b. Washington, July 15, 1926; s. Lee I. and Alice (Crandall) P.; m. Barbara Ann Merrick, July 1, 1953; children: Thomas Joseph, Jeffrey Rawson; m. Mary Woodfill Banerjee, Apr. 27, 1985; stepchildren: Stephen K., Scott K. Grad., Putney Prep. Sch., Vt.; BS in Zoology, Yale U., 1948; MD, Johns Hopkins U., 1952. Diplomate Nat. Bd. Med. Examiners, Am. Bd. Psychiatry and Neurology. Intern medicine Johns Hopkins Hosp., Osler Clinic, Balt., 1952-53; resident psychiatry USN Hosp., Oakland, Calif., 1953-54, Henry Phipps Psychiat. Clinic, Johns Hopkins Hosp., Balt., 1955-59, asst. psychiatrist, 1955-59, staff psychiatrist, 1959—, staff dept. medicine, 1970—, hon. staff dept. medicine, 1991—, dir. psychiat. outpatient svcs. and community psychiatry program, 1972-74, asst. dir. clin. svcs. dept. psychiatry, 1973-74, mem. departmental coun., 1974-76. Fellow psychiatry Johns Hopkins U., 1955-59, faculty in psychiatry, 1959—, assoc. prof., 1971—, physician charge psychiat. svcs. student health svc., 1961-73; vis. psychiatrist Balt. City Hosp., 1960-61; co-prin., prin. investigator NIMH Psychopharmacology Rsch. Br. Outpatient Study of Drug-Set Interaction, 1960-68, co-dir. (with Eugene Meyer) Time-Limited Psychotherapy Rsch. Grant, 1969-73; pvt. practice psychiatry, 1964—; cons. Met. Balt. Assn. Mental Health, 1961-63, Bur. Disability Ins., Social Security Adminstrn., 1964-81; attending staff Seton Psychiat. Inst., 1966-73, exec. bd., 1970-73; staff Sheppard and Enoch Pratt Hosp., 1974—. Co-author: A Primer on Mental Disorders: A Guide for Educators, Families and Students, 2001; contbr. articles and chpts. to profl. jours. and books. Served to lt. M.C., USNR, 1953-55, div. psychiatrist 1st Marine Div., Korea, staff psychiatrist USN Hosp., Camp Pendleton, Calif., 1954-55; mem. Md. Interdisciplinary Coun. for Children and Adolescents, 1978-98, treas., 1980-87. Fellow: AAAS, Am. Psychiat. Assn. (mem. assembly 1983—93, Psychiat. Rsch. Network 1994—2002, Disting. life fellow); mem.: AAUP, AMA, Johns Hopkins Med. and Surg. Assn., Balt. County Med. Assn., Balt. City Med. Soc., Med. and Chirurg. Faculty Md., Group Therapy Network, N.Y. Acad. Scis., Soc. Psychotherapy Rsch., Md. Psychiat. Soc. (pres. 1978—79), Md. Assn. Pvt. Practicing Psychiatrists, Am. Assn. Pvt. Practicing Psychiatrists, Am. Coll. Neuropsychopharmacology, Am. Soc. Adolescent Psychiatry, Internat. Soc. Study Personality Disorders, Am. Psychosomatic Soc., Md. Found. Psychiatry (bd. dirs. 1995—2003, pres. 2000—03), Nat. Assn. Scholars, St. George's Soc., Avery Assn., Denison Soc., Crandall Assn., Van Kouwenhoven-Conover Assn., Van Voorhees Assn., Parke Soc., Nat. Soc. Sons and Daus. of Pilgrims (gov. State of Md. 2006—), Gen. Soc. War 1812 (pres. State of Md. 2004—06, v.p. gen. 2006—). Nat. Huguenot Soc. (surgeon gen. 2005—), Descendants Mexican War Vets, Sons Union Vets. Civil War, SAR (surgeon State of Md. 2006—), Gen. Soc. Colonial Wars. S.R. (bd. mgrs. State of Md. 2006—), Yale Club NYC, Farmington Country Club, Met. Club (Washington), Johns Hopkins Club, Chevy Chase (Md.) Country Club, Phi Beta Pi. Republican. Episcopalian. Achievements include research in borderline and narcissistic conditions, long-term effects of childhood emotional abuse and neglect, psychotherapy; interrelationships of psychotherapy and pharmacotherapy; genesis and nature of social and personal and emotional intelligence. Home: 308 Tunbridge Rd Baltimore MD 21212-3803 Office: 1205 York Rd Ste 35 Lutherville Timonium MD 21093-6268 Office Phone: 410-321-1276. E-mail: lpark3@jhmi.edu.

**PARK, LELAND MADISON,** librarian; b. Alexandria, La., Oct. 21, 1941; s. Arthur Harris and Jane Rebecca (Leland) P. Student, McCallie Sch., 1957—59; AB, Davidson Coll., 1963; MLS, Emory U., 1964; postgrad., Simmons Coll., 1968; AdvM in Libr. Sci., Fla. State U., 1973, PhD, 1974. Reference librr. Pub. Librr. of Charlotte and Mecklenburg County, NC, 1964-65; head reference and student pers. Davidson (N.C.) Coll. Librr., 1967-70, asst. dir., 1970-75, dir., 1975—2006. Cons. coll. service network So. Assn. Colls and Schs.; vis. lectr. Emory U., summer 1972; temporary instr. Fla. State U., 1973; librr. cons.; conf. spkr.; chmn. state adv. com. Librr. Svcs. and Constrn. Act, 1975-79. Mem. N.C. State Librr. Commn., 1983-85, 87-92, chmn., 1989-92; mem. Davidson (N.C.) Town Appearance Commn., 1986-93, 98—, Hist. Preservation Commn., 1994-96; mem. editl. bd. CHOICE, 2003-06. Editor Southeastern Librarian, 1976-78; acad. sect. editor N.C. Libraries, 1972-77; contbr. articles to profl. jours. Mem. Wake County Citizens for Better Librrs., N.C., 1965-67; sec. com. libr. affairs Piedmont U. Ctr., 1969-70, chmn., 1970-72; mem. nat. bd. coms. NEH, 1976-2006; clk. mission com. St. Alban's Episcopal Mission, Davidson, N.C., 1969-72, layreader, 1970-75, treas., 1975-86; bd. dirs. statewide computer libr. resource network NC-LIVE, 1997—2006. Recipient H.W. Wilson Librr. periodical award, 1979, Alumni Achievement award The McCallie Sch., 1989, Order of Long Leaf Pine presented by N.C. Gov. James G. Martin, 1993. Mem. ALA, Southeastern Librr. Assn. (chmn. coll. and univ. sect. 1976-78, exec. bd. 1976-78), N.C. Librr. Assn. (2d v.p. 1975-77, 1st v.p. 1981-83, pres. 1983-85), Metrolina Librr. Assn. (pres. 1969-71), Mecklenburg County Librr. Assn. (treas. 1969-70), Soc. of Cin. (2d v.p. Ga. Soc. 1982-83), SAR, Mil. Order World Wars, Raleigh Jaycees (chmn. civic com. 1965-67), Res. Officers Assn., SCV, Soc. Colonial Wars, S.C. Huguenot Soc., Rotary, Beta Phi Mu, Sigma Nu, Omicron Delta Kappa. Home: PO Box 777 235 Ney Circle Davidson NC 28036-0777 Office Phone: 704-894-2155. E-mail: lepark@aol.com.

**PARK, MARINA H.,** lawyer; b. Pasadena, Calif., Nov. 6, 1956; BA with honors, Univ. Calif., Berkeley, 1978; JD, Univ. Mich., 1982. Bar: Calif. 1983. Mng. ptnr. Pillsbury Winthrop LLP, Palo Alto, Calif., 1999—2005; ptnr., Emerging Growth & Tech. practice & mng. ptnr. Pillsbury Winthrop Shaw Pittman, Palo Alto, Calif., 2005—. Office: Pillsbury Winthrop Shaw Pittman 2475 Hanover St Palo Alto CA 94304-1114 Office Phone: 650-233-4770. Office Fax: 650-233-4545. Business E-Mail: marina.park@pillsburylaw.com.

**PARK, MARY WOODFILL,** information consultant, librarian, writer; b. Nevada, Mo., Nov. 20, 1944; d. John Prossor and Elizabeth (Devine) Woodfill; m. Salil Kumar Banerjee, Dec. 29, 1967 (div. 1983); children: Stephen Kumar, Scott Kumar; m. Lee Crandall Park, Apr. 27, 1985; stepchildren: Thomas Joseph, Jeffrey Rawson. BA, Marywood Coll., 1966; postgrad., Johns Hopkins U., 1983, Goucher Coll., 1986. Asst. to dir. U. Pa. Librrs., Phila., 1968-69; investment librr. Del. Funds, Phila., 1969-71; investment officer Investment Counselors Md., Balt., 1980-84, 1st Nat. Bank Md., Balt., 1984-85; founder Info. Consultancy, Balt., 1985—. Lectr Loyola Coll., Balt., 1991-92, Cath. U., 1993. Author: InfoThink—Practical Strategies for Using Information in Business, 1998; editor, contbr. to profl. pubis. Vol. Internat. Visitors' Ctr., Balt., 1979-80, 91; del. White House Conf. on Librrs.; v.p. bd. dirs. Friends of Goucher Libr., 1988-90; mem. industry applications com. Info. Tech. Bd., State of Md., 1993-96; mem. info. tech. com. of the Tech. Coun., Greater Balt. Com., 1993-98. Named One of Md.'s Top 100 Women, Warfield's Bus. Publn., 1996. Mem.: DAR, MD Women's Health Initiative, Huguenot Soc. Md. (1st v.p. 2003—05), Nat. Huguenot Soc., Md. Found. for Psychiatry (bd. dirs. 1998—), Assn. Ind. Info. Profls., Info. Futures Inst., Spl. Librrs. Assn. (pres. Md. chpt. 1991—92, v.p. network coord. coun. Sailor project 1993—95, govt. rels. chair 1998—2003, publ. rels. chair 2003—), Daus. of Colonial Wars, Nat. Soc. Daus. Am. Colonists (Md. state 1st vice regent 2003—05, regent Joppa Trail chpt. 2003—05), Nat. Soc. Colonial Dames XVII Century (state rec. sec. 2003—05, 2d v.p. 2005—), Nat. Soc. of the Sons and Daus. of the Pilgrims, Nat. Soc. of U.S. Daus. of 1812 (Md. state rec. sec. 2003—05), Nat. Soc. Dames Ct. Honor, Colonial Dames Am., Nat. Instal. Geneal. Rsch. Alumnae Assn., Soc. of Daughters of Holland Dames, Descendants of Ancient and Honorable Families of New Netherland (coores. sec. 2003—), Friends of New Netherlands, Three Arts Club Homeland, Hamilton St. Club (bd. dirs. 1989—92). Episcopalian. Office: The Information Consultancy 308 Tunbridge Rd Baltimore MD 21212-3803 Business E-Mail: mwpark@informationconsultancy.com.

**PARK, MYUNG KUN,** medical educator; b. Suhung, Hwanghae, Republic of Korea, Sept. 30, 1934; arrived in U.S., 1962; s. Jung-Jin and Sonnyu (Lee) Park; m. Issun Kim, Jan. 21, 1967; children: Douglas Yongwoon, Christopher Yongchul, Warren Yongsun. Diploma, Seoul Nat. U., Republic of Korea, 1956, MD, 1960. Intern Vassar Brothers Hosp., Poughkeepsie, NY, 1962—63; pediat. resident Georgetown U., Washington, 1963—64; chief resident Univ. Hosp., Morgantown, W.Va., 1964—65; pediat. cardiology fellow U. Wash., ington, Seattle, 1965—68; asst. prof. U. Kans. Coll. Medicine, Kansas City, 1973-76; assoc. prof. U. Tex. Med. Sch., San Antonio, 1976-83, prof., 1983—2003, prof. emeritus, 2003—; prof., chmn. pediat. Arabian Gulf U. Med. Coll., Bahrain, 1995-98. Author: (book) How to Read Pediatric ECG, 1982, 3d rev. edit., 1992, Pediatric Cardiology for Practitioners, 1984, 4th rev. edit., 2002, The Pediatric Cardiology Handbook, 1991, 3d rev. edit., 2002; contbr. articles to profl. jours. Postdoctoral fellow, NIH, 1965—68, Rsch. fellow, 1971—73, Rsch. grantee, Maternal and Child Health Bur., 1991—95. Fellow: Am. Acad. Pediat., Am. Coll. Cardiology; mem.: Soc. Pediatric Rsch., Sigma Xi. Personal E-Mail: drmpark@satx.rr.com.

**PARK, MYUNGKARK,** publishing company owner; b. Kangwon Do, Republic of Korea, July 24, 1950; came to U.S., 1977; m. Hyunmi Suh, July 17, 1977; 1 child, Brian. BS, Seoul Nat. U., Repubic of Korea, 1972; MS, Wayne State U., 1979; postgrad. Wash. State U., 1979—83, Kent State U., 1983—85, U. Cin., 1985—87. Teaching asst. Seoul Nat. U., 1974-76; tchr. physics Jeonnong Girl's Mid. Sch., 1976-77; teaching and rsch. asst. Wayne State U., Detroit, 1977-79; tchg. and rsch. asst. Wash. State U., Pullman, 1979-83, Kent (Ohio) State U., 1983-85, U. Cin., 1985-87, Southern Ohio Coll., 1987—88; pres., owner Prompter Publs., Cin., 1988-90, 1990—. Author and editor several books and jours.; contbr. over 750 articles to profl. jours. and rsch. notebooks. 1st lt. Republic of Korea Army, 1972-74. Nat. scholar, 1962-68, 70-72, Hamchoon scholar, 1968-70, tchg./rsch. asst. scholar, 1977-87, Am. Vacuum Soc. scholar, 1989, The Knoller Physics-Chemistry scholar 1977-78; faculty fellow Wayne State U., 1977-79. Mem. AAAS, Am. Phys. Soc., Am. Math. Soc., Korean Phys. Soc., Phi Theta Kappa, Pi Sigma Alpha. Home: PO Box 167 Chongnyangni Tongdaemoon-gu Seoul 130-650 Republic of Korea

**PARK, NO-HEE,** dean, academic administrator; b. Jan. 30, 1944; m. Yu Bai Yuly, 1969; 1 child, Jennifer. DDS, Seoul Nat. U., 1968, MSD, 1970; PhD, Med. Coll. Ga., 1978; DMD, Harvard U., 1982. Postdoctoral fellow in oral biology and pharmacology Med. Coll. Ga., 1975—78; rsch. assoc., Eye Rsch. Inst. Harvard Med. Sch., Boston, 1978—80, instr., dept. ophthalmology, 1978—82, asst. scientist, Eye Rsch. Inst., 1980—82, assoc. scientist, Eye Rsch. Inst., 1982—83; asst. prof., oral biology and pathophysiology Harvard U. Sch. Dental Medicine, Boston, 1982—83; assoc. prof., oral biology UCLA Sch. Dentistry, L.A., 1984—85, prof., 1985—, assoc. dean rsch., 1997—98, dean, 1998—; assoc. dir. UCLA Dental Rsch. Inst., L.A., 1986—90, dir., 1995—, UCLA Wound Healing Rsch. Ctr., L.A., 1997—. Contbr. articles to profl. jours.; ad-hoc reviewer for various publs., 1990—, editl. bd. Internat. Jour. Oncology, 1996—, Electronic Jour. Biotechnology, 1997—, editor-in-chief Internat. Jour. Oral Biology, assoc. editor Odontology, 2000—. Mem.: Internat. Assoc. for Dental Rsch. (Selection Com. for Distinguished Scientist in Oral Medicine 2001—), Friends of NIDCR (Exec. Com. 2001—), Am. Assn. for Dental Schools Coun. of Deans Exec. Com., Am. Dental Assn., Calif. Dental Assn., Tissue Culture Assn., Am. Assn. for Cancer Rsch., Am. Dental Edn. Assn., Am. Assn. for Dental Schools, Am. Soc. for Microbiology, Am. Assn. for the Advancement of Sci., Internat. Assn. for Dental Rsch., Internat. Coll. Dentistry, Omicron Kappa Upsilon Dental Soc. Achievements include research in the role of telomerase in oral carcinogenesis, gene therapy for oral cancer, molecular mechanism of replicative senescence in normal human oral keratinocytes and viral and chemical oncogenesis; cellular proto-oncogenes and tumor suppressor genes, cell cycle and DNA repair, and antiviral chemotherapy. Office: UCLA 10833 Leconte Ave Rm 53-038 Los Angeles CA 90095*

**PARK, PENNY SHERAN,** retired elementary school educator; b. Tulare, Calif., July 13, 1948; d. Sheridan Lee Roy Harris and Jeanne Avril Lightbody. AA, Coll. of the Sequoias, Visalia, CA, 1968; B in Music Edn., U. of Pacific, 1971; M in Music Edn., U. Calif., Fresno, 1980. Registered music therapist Nat. Assn. Music Therapy, 1971. Music therapist mental health wing Emmanual Hosp., Turlock, Calif., 1971; music therapist Brandel Manor Nursing Home, Turlock, 1971, Kings County Mental Health Day Treatment Ctr., Hanford, Calif., 1971—77; self-employed Hanford, 1977—85; music therapist Lee Richmond Sch. -Spl. Edn., Hanford, 1979—84; resource tchr.-music The Learning Ctr., Hanford, 1984—85; tchr. Hanford Elem. Sch. Dist., 1985—2006; ret. 2006; pvt. music studio cafe.com, Anmona, Calif., 2006—. Consulting music therapist, music educator various, Hanford, 1977—79; program developer Kings County Supt. Schs.-Spl. Edn., 1979—84; chorale instr. Hanford Elem. Sch. Dist., 1985—90; trainer The Activities In Math & Sci. Found.- Fresno (Calif.) Pacific Coll., 1987—92. Author: Five Merry Santas, 1992; editor: Community Treasures, 2000. Mem.: Hanford Elem. Tchrs. Assn., Calif. Tchrs. Assn., Ea. Star (25 year pin 1997). Avocations: writing, reading, music, scrapbooks, computer games.

**PARK, ROGER COOK,** law educator; b. Atlanta, Jan. 4, 1942; s. Hugh and Alice (Cook) Park; m. Rosemarie J. Lilliker, June 14, 1967 (div. 1979); 1 child, Matthew; m. Suzanne Nicole Howard, Feb. 18, 1984; stepchildren: Sophie Currier, Nicolas Currier. BA cum laude, Harvard U., 1964, JD magna cum laude, 1969. Bar: Mass. 1969, Minn. 1973. Law clk. to Hon. Bailey Aldrich U.S. Ct. Appeals (1st cir.), Boston, 1969-70; with Zalkind & Silverglate, Boston, 1970-73; prof. Law Sch. U. Minn., Mpls., 1973-95, Fredrikson and Byron prof. law, 1990-95; Disting. James Edgar Hervey prof. law Hastings Coll. Law U. Calif., San Francisco, 1995—. Vis. prof. Law Sch. Stanford U., Palo Alto, Calif., 1977, Sch. Law Boston U., 1981—82, Law Sch. U. Mich., Ann Arbor, 1984; bd. dirs. Ctr. Computer-Aided Legal Instrn., 1982—96; reporter adv. group Civil Justice Reform Act, Dist. Minn.; mem. evidence adv. com. Minn. Supreme Ct., 1988—95. Author: Computer Aided Exercises in Civil Procedure, 1979, 2d edit., 1995, Waltz and Park Casebook on Evidence, 8th edit., 1994; author: (with Leonard and Goldberg) 10th edit., 2005; author: Evidence Law, 1998, 2d edit., 2004; author: (with McFarland) Trial Objections Handbook, 1991, 2d edit., 2001; contbr. articles to profl. jours. 1st Lt. U.S. Army, 1964—66, Vietnam. Mem.: ABA (mem. rules criminal procedure and evidence com. criminal justice sect. 1988—, mem. subcom. fed. rules evidence), Am. Assn. Law Schs. (chairperson evidence sect. 1994), Am. Law Inst. Office: Hastings Coll Law 200 Mcallister St San Francisco CA 94102-4707

**PARK, ROY HAMPTON, JR.,** advertising executive; b. NC, 1938; s. Roy Hampton and Dorothy Goodwin (Dent) P.; m. Elizabeth Tetlow Parham; children: Elizabeth P. Fowler, Roy H. III. BA in Journalism, U. N.C., 1961; MBA, Cornell U., 1963. Sr. acct. exec., rsch. bd. exec., advt. planning dir., J Walter Thompson Co., N.Y.C. and Miami, 1963-70; v.p. mktg. and account mgmt. Kincaid Advt. Agency divsn. First Union Nat. Bank Corp., Charlotte, NC, 1970-71; v.p. Park Outdoor Advt., Ithaca, NY, 1971-75; v.p. advt. and promotion Park Broadcasting Inc., Ithaca, 1975-81, 1993-95; mng. editor Park Comm. Newsletter, Ithaca, 1976-81; mng. dir. Agrl. Rsch. Advt. Agy., Ithaca, 1976-81; v.p., gen. mgr. Park Outdoor Adv., 1981-84; pres., CEO, dir. Park Outdoor Advt. of N.Y. Inc., 1984—; pres. Outdoor Advt. Coun. N.Y. Inc., 1986-91, chmn., dir., 1992-95; dir., sr. v.p. RHP Inc., 1994-96, RHP Properties Inc., 1994-96. Mem. region I planning bd. Inst. Outdoor Advt., 1984—86. Dir. Boyce Thompson Inst. for Plant Rsch. Inc., 1995-2001, dir., vice chmn. 2002—; trustee, v.p. Park Found. Inc., 1995-2002; pres., chmn. Triad Found., Inc., 2003—; trustee Cornell U., 1991—; mem. adv. coun. Johnson Grad. Sch. Mgmt., 1996—, named to Johnson Hall Hon., 1999—; bd. vis. U. N.C. Sch. Journalism and Mass Comm., 1994—; chmn. Ithaca Assembly Cotillion, 1979-81; dir. pub. rels. Tompkins County Conf. and Tourist Coun., 1976; exec. com. Tompkins County Rep. Fin. Com., 1983-84; chmn. fin. com. MacNeil for Assembly, 1984-86, co-chmn. 1978-82; bd. dir. Tompkins County Coun. Arts, 1976; chmn. pub. rels. com. United Way Tompkins County, 1973-74, loaned publicity exec., 1972; bd. dir., chmn. publicity dr. Jr. Olympics, 1973-74; dir. pub. rels. United Fund Raleigh, N.C., 1971; fin. com. Spl. Children's Ctr., 1979; founding mem. alumni exec. com. Cornell U., 1984-88. Recipient Disting. Alumnus award, U. N.C., 2005. Mem. Tompkins County C. of C. (chmn. legis. action com. 1976, acting chmn. nominating com. 1976, chmn. sign ordinance com., 1975-76, pub. rels. coun. 1976, Project of Yr. award 1974, Recognition award 1975), Charlotte C. of C. (pub. rels. com. 1970-71), Boque Banks Beach Preservation Assn., Ithaca Yacht Club, Ithaca Country Club, Boca Bay Pass Club, Gasparilla Inn Beach and Tennis Club. Office: Park Outdoor Advt PO Box 4680 Ithaca NY 14852-4680 Office Phone: 607-257-1477. Business E-Mail: roy.park@parkoutdoor.com.

**PARK, SAM-KOO,** transportation executive; BA in Econs., Yonsei U. 1967. Exec. dir. internat. trading Samyang Tire Indsl. Co., 1967-68; mng. dir. Korea Synthetic Rubber Indusl. Co., 1968-73, Kumho & Co., 1973-74, pres. L.A. br., 1974-79, v.p. 1979-80, pres., 1980—; pres., CEO Asiana Airlines, Inc., 1991—. Office: Asiana Airlines Inc 3530 Wilshire Blvd Ste 1450 Los Angeles CA 90010-2328 also: Kang Seo Ku Osai Dong 47 157 600 Asaiana Town Seoul Republic of Korea

**PARK, SEOK-KYUN,** civil engineer, educator; b. Seoul, Oct. 10, 1961; s. Keum-Churl and Chae-Bong (Kim) P.; m. Hyun-Joo Na, May 10, 1985; 1 child, Jeong-Min. BE, U. Hanyang, Seoul, Korea, 1984, M in Engring., 1986; PhD, U. Tokyo, 1996. Asst., tchr. U. Hanyang, Seoul, 1984-86; rschr. Ssangyong Rsch. Ctr., Daejeon, 1986-94, sr. rschr., project mgr., 1995-96; postdoctoral fellow U. Tokyo, 1996-97; lectr. Korea Infrastructure Safety and Tech. Corp., Goyang, 1998—; asst. prof. U. Daejeon, 1998—. Vis. prof. Ssangyong Rsch. Ctr., Daejeon, 1998—; expert advisor Korea Inst. of Contrn. Tech., Seoul, 1998—; cons. prof. Korea Infrastructure Safety and Tech. Corp., Goyang, 1999—; design cons. Adv. Com. of Cheonju City Hall, 1999-2001; mem. internat. exchange com., U. Daejeon, 1999—; hon. supr. Subway Constrn. Hdqs. Daejeon City, 2000-2005; mem. Asian Model Code Com.; exec. sec. study com. smart concrete structures, study com. repair and reinforcement of concrete structures, tech. com. concrete structure instrumentation com. Korea Concrete Inst., 2001-04; mem. tech. coun. of Chungmam provincial govt., 2001-03. Author: Evaluation and Repair of Concrete Structures, 1998, Design and Maintenance of Civil Structures, 2000, Concrete Engring., 1989; postdoctoral rsch. assoc. tchr. U. Hanyang, 1989, grand prize, Ssangyong Cement Ind. Co. Ltd., 1993. Mem. Japan Soc. Civil Engrs. (Best Presentation award 1995, 96), Japan Concrete Inst., Korea Concrete Inst., Korean Soc. Civil Engrs., Korea Inst. for Structural Maintenance Inspection, Taeduk Sci. Forum. Achievements include patent for ultrasonic measurement system for concrete setting time; radar image processing system for non-destructive evaluation of concrete; composite material of high tenacity and non-retraction grouting material which includes powder of wasted tire and powder of plastic. Home: 115-1401 Nurie APT Wolpyung-dong Seo-gu Taejon 302-280 Republic of Korea Office: U Daejeon Dept Civil Engring 96-3 Yongwoon-dong dong-gu Daejeon 300-716 Republic of Korea E-mail: skpark@dju.ac.kr.

**PARK, THOMAS JOSEPH,** biology researcher, educator; b. Balt., June 8, 1958; s. Lee Crandall and Barbara Ann (Merrick) P.; m. Stephanie Suzanne Reynolds, June 22, 1985; 1 child, Nicholas Timothy. BA in Psychology, Johns Hopkins U., 1982; MSc in Exptl. Psychology, U. Md., 1984, PhD in Exptl. Psychology, 1988. Postdoctoral fellow Inst. Cellular and Molecular Embryology, Paris, 1989; postdoctoral rsch. assoc. dept. zoology U. Tex., 1989—94; asst. prof. dept. biol. scis. U. Ill., Chgo., 1994—2000, assoc. prof. dept. biol. scis., 2000—. Contbr. articles and chpts. to profl. jours. and books. Grantee NIMH, 1986-88, Nat. Ctr. Sci. Rsch., Paris, 1989, NIH, 1989-90, 1997-2003, Nat. Orgn. Hearing Rsch., 1996-97; Alexander von Humboldt Rsch. fellowship, Zool. Inst., U. Munich, 1993-94, Max Planck Inst. Neurobiology, Munich, 2001-02. Mem. AAAS, Soc. Neurosci., Assn. Rsch. in Otolaryngology. Achievements include research in neurobiology of sensory information processing and sensorimotor integration. Office: Univ Ill Chgo Dept Biol Sci Neurobiology Group 840 W Taylor St Chicago IL 60607

**PARK, WILLIAM ANTHONY (TONY PARK),** lawyer; b. Blackfoot, Idaho, June 4, 1934; s. William Clair and Thelma Edelweiss (Shear) P.; m. Elizabeth Taylor, Aug. 26, 1961 (div.); children: Susan E., W. Adam, Patricia A.; m. Gail Chaloupka, Aug. 6, 1983. AA, Boise Jr. Coll., 1954; BA, U. Idaho, 1958; JD, U. Idaho, 1963. Bar: Idaho 1963. Sole practice, Boise, Idaho, 1963-70, 82-83; atty. gen. State of Idaho, 1971-75; ptnr. Park & Meuleman, Boise, 1975-81, Park & Burkett, Boise, 1983-84, Martin, Chapman, Park & Burkett, Boise, 1984-90, Park, Costello & Burkett, Boise, 1990-93, Park, Redford, Thomas & Burkett, Boise, 1994-97, Park, Thomas, Burkett & Williams, Boise, 1997-99; of counsel Huntley Park (formerly Huntley, Park, Thomas, Burkett, Olsen & Williams), Boise, 1999—. Chmn. Idaho Bicentennial Commn., 1971—77; bd. dirs. ACLU, Idaho, 1996—2000, pres. Idaho, 1997—99; chmn. Idaho State Dem. Party, 1998—99; bd. dirs. Radio Free Europe/Radio Liberty, Inc., 1977—82, Am. Lung Assn., 1978—90, Am. Lung Assn. Washington/Idaho, 1976—96, pres., 1991—95, 2002—04, bd. dirs., 1999—. With U.S. Army, 1956—58. Recipient Disting. Svc. award. Home: 706 Warm Springs Ave Boise ID 83712-6420 Office: PO Box 2188 Boise ID 83701-2188 Office Phone: 208-345-7800. Personal E-mail: gchaloupka@msn.com. Business E-Mail: wap@huntleypark.com.

**PARK, WILLIAM H(ERRON),** finance company executive; b. Mononga-hela, Pa., Sept. 19, 1947; s. William M. and Marjorie (Herron) P.; m. Mary Cornell, June 25, 1977; children: William H., Douglas C. BS in Indsl. Engring. with distinction, Cornell U., 1969, MBA, 1970. Engr. True Temper Corp., Geneva, Ohio, 1970-72; with Price Waterhouse & Co., Boston, 1972-82; exec. v.p., CFO United Asset Mgmt. Corp., Boston, 1982—2001; v.p. The UAM Funds, 1982—2001; pres., CEO Prizm Capital Mgmt., 2001—05; CEO Structured Capital Ptnrs., 2005; vice chmn. Comml. Indsl. Fin. Corp., 2006—. Bd. dirs. No. Light Asset Mgmt.; bd. trustees Eaton Vance Group of Mut. Funds, 2003—. Treas., trustee Tower Sch. in Marblehead, 1982—92; trustee Proctor Acad., 1998—2006; bd. dirs. Nat. Com. to Preserve Social Security and Medicare, 1997—2005, chmn., 2000—03; bd. dirs. The Chautauqua Found., Inc., 1992—2005, dir., 1996—2005. Home: 3 Fort Sewall Ter Marblehead MA 01945-3505 Office: Structured Capital Ptnrs Inc 150 Federal St Boston MA 02110 Personal E-mail: parkwilliam@comcast.net.

**PARK, WILLIAM LAIRD,** agricultural studies educator, dean; b. Mar. 29, 1931; s. William D. and Ardella (Laird) Park; m. Ann Payne, Aug. 7, 1953; children: Leslie, David W., Wayne I., Andrea, John L. BS, Utah State U., 1957, MS, 1958; PhD, Cornell U., 1963. Dep. chief coop. tech. NY/NJ Milk Mktg. Adminstrn., N.Y.C., 1958—65; assoc. prof. agrl. econs. Rutgers U., New Brunswick, NJ, 1965—68, chmn. dept. agrl. econs. and mktg., 1970—75; sr. agrl. economist Devel. and Resources Corp., Sacramento, 1969—70; chmn. dept. agrl. econs. Brigham Young U., Provo, Utah, 1977—83, prof., 1983—, assoc. dean agr., 1988—98, dir. Agrl. Sta., 1995—98, ret., 1998. Pres. Ag-Econ Rsch. Assocs., Orem, Utah, 1978—; bd. dirs. N.E. Agrl. Econs. Coun., 1972—77; cons. agr., agribus. Author: Estimating Demand and Price Structures by Residual Analysis, 1970; author: numerous bulls., reports on dairy econs., feasibility analysis, internat. econ. devel.; contbr. articles to profl. jours. Cpl. U.S. Army, 1953-55. Mem.: Am. Agrl. Econs. Assn., Western Agrl. Econs. Assn., Phi Kappa Phi, Sigma Xi. Republican. Mem. Lds Ch. Home: 7807 White Pine Way Sandy UT 84094-0256

**PARK, WILLIAM WYNNEWOOD,** law educator; b. Phila., July 2, 1947; s. Oliver William and Christine (Lindes) Park. BA, Yale U., 1969; JD, Columbia U., 1972; MA, Cambridge U., 1975. Bar: Mass. 1972, DC 1980. Law practice, Paris, 1972-79; prof. law Boston U., 1979—, dir. Ctr. Banking Law Studies, 1990—93. V.p. London Ct. Internat. Arbitration; vis. prof. U. Dijon, France, 1983—84, Inst. U. Hautes Etudes Internat., Geneva, 1983, U. Hong Kong, 1990; arbitrator Claims Resolution Tribunal Dormant Accts., Switzerland, 1998—2002, Internat. Commn. Holocaust Era Ins. Claims, London. Author: International Chamber of Commerce Arbitration, 3d edit., 2000, International Forum Selection, 1995, International Commercial Arbitration, 1997, Arbitration in Banking and Finance, 1998, Income Tax Treaty Arbitration, 2004, Arbitration of International Business Disputes, 2006; gen. editor: Arbitration Internat.; contbr. articles to profl. jours. Trustee Mass. Bible Soc.; sr. warden King's Chapel, Boston. Fellow, Selwyn Coll., Cambridge, Eng., 1975—77. Fellow: Coll. Comml. Arbitrators, Chartered Inst. Arbitrators (U.K.); mem.: ABA (chmn. internat. dispute resolution com.). Home: 36 King St Cohasset MA 02025-1304 Office: Boston Univ Law Sch 765 Commonwealth Ave Boston MA 02215-1401 Office Phone: 617-353-3149.

**PARK, WON KUK,** foundation administrator; b. Bukchang Dong, Chung-Ku, Korea, Mar. 24, 1929; s. Jun Seop and Kum Sun (Song) P. BA in Economics, Sungkyunkwan U., Seoul, Korea, 1957; MA in Economics, Am.

U., 1960; PhD in Economics, Kyunghee U., Seoul, Korea, 1975; PhD (hon.), Caldwell Coll., 1997. Asst. prof. Duksung Women's U., Seoul, Republic of Korea, 1961-63, assoc. prof. 1965-67, v.p., 1965-70, prof., 1967-77, pres., 1970-77, chmn. bd. trustees Duksung Sch. Found., 1979—2001; asst. prof. Kyunghee U., Seoul, Republic of Korea, 1963-65; v.p. Korean Pvt. Ednl. Found., Seoul, Republic of Korea, 1987-90, Korean Assn. for Univ. Found., Seoul, Republic of Korea, 1987-92. Dir. Korean Pvt. Ednl. Found., Seoul, 1978—, Korean Assn. for Univ. Found., 1987—. Chmn. bd. trustees Jungam Found. of Culture in Korea, 2002—. Recipient Choon Kang award, Republic of Korea, 1995. Mem. Korean Sect. World Edn. Fellowship (v.p. 1987—), The Seoul Ctrl. Club of Good Will.

**PARK, YONG JIN,** lawyer; b. Daejeon, Korea, Oct. 13, 1953; BA Coll. Bus. & Economics, Yonsei U., Korea, 1976; MBA, NYU, 1982; JD, Pa. State U. 1988. Bar: NY 1989, US Dist. Ct. Ea. Dist. NY, US Dist. Ct. No. Dist. NY. Ptnr. Wilson, Elser, Moskowitz, Edelman & Dicker LLP, NYC. Mem.: ABA. Office: Wilson Elser Moskowitz Edelman & Dicker LLP 23rd Fl 150 E 42nd St New York NY 10017-5639 Office Phone: 212-490-3000 ext. 2864. Office Fax: 212-490-3038. Business E-Mail: parky@wemed.com.

**PARK, YONIL,** mathematician; b. Yosu, Korea (South), Oct. 10, 1971; m. Sang Kim, Feb. 24, 2001; children: Jeanne Kim, Jireh Kim. PhD in Indsl. Engring., Korea Advanced Inst. Sci. and Tech., 2000. Staff scientist NIH, Bethesda, Md., 2000—. Office: NIH 8600 Rockville Pike Bethesda MD 20894 Office Phone: 301-402-1438.

**PARK, YOUNG H.,** dean; b. Kyung-Buk, Korea, Aug. 5, 1937; s. Won K. Park and Tae S. Lee; m. Jong-Hwa Park, Oct. 20, 1967; children: Grace, David. BD, Presbyn. Gen. Assembly Theol. Seminary, 1961; BA in English Lit., Kyung Hee U., Seoul, 1963; BD, Covenant Theol. Sem., St. Louis, 1967, M in Theology, 1968; MA in Bibl. Lit., St. Louis U., 1973; PhD in Theology, Calif. Grad. Sch. Theol., 1978. Lic. Midwestern Presbytery, 1970. Minister First Presbyn. Ch., St. Louis, 1970—83; prof. New Testament Chongshin U., Seoul, 1983—86, pres., 1986—92; dean grad. sch. Midwest Theol. U., St. Louis, 1992—93, acad. dean, 2002—; pres. Taeshin Christian U., Taegu, Republic of Korea, 1994—2002. Author: Exegetical Principles of N.T., 1988, A Study of Christological Titles, 1990. Avocations: classical music, reading, walking, travel. Home: 1322 Creve Coeur Mill Saint Louis MO 63146 Office: Midwest Univ 851 Parr Rd Wentzville MO 63385 Personal E-mail: younghpark@sbcglobal.net.

**PARKE, DAVID ALAN,** lawyer; b. Marlboro, Mass., May 23, 1953; s. Richard Alan Parke and Barbara Ann Morse; m. Patrice Ann Meacham, Aug. 5, 1955; 1 child, Geoffrey David. BA, U. Pa., Phila., 1975; JD, Georgetown U., Washington, 1979. Bar: Mass. 1980. Ptnr. Bulkley, Richardson and Gelinas LLP, Springfield, Mass., 1980—. Bd. dirs. Safety Coun. Western New England, Inc., Springfield, 2004—. Author: Forming a Massachusetts Corporation Under Chapter 156D, 2005. Mem. fin. com. Town of Wilbraham, Mass., 2005—. Mem.: Mass. Bar Assn. (mem. bus. law sect. coun. 2004—). Office: Bulkley Richardson and Gelinas LLP 1500 Main St Springfield MA 01115 Office Phone: 413-272-6257.

**PARKE, DAVID WILKIN, II,** ophthalmologist, educator, health facility administrator; b. Columbus, Ohio, May 19, 1951; s. David William Parke and Eunice Joyce Erikson; m. Julie Diane Thorne, Sept. 15, 1975; children: David W. III, Laura Thorne, Lindsey Diane. AB, Stanford U., 1973; MD, Baylor Coll. Medicine, 1977. Diplomate Am. Bd. Ophthalmology. Resident in internal medicine Baylor Coll. Medicine, Houston, 1977-78; resident in ophthalmology, 1978-81, fellow in med. retina, 1981-82, asst. prof., 1983-90, assoc. prof., 1990-92; fellow diseases and surgery of the retina and vitreous Med. Coll. of Wis., 1982-83; prof., chair dept. ophthalmology U. Okla., Oklahoma City, 1992—; pres., CEO McGee Eye Inst., Oklahoma City, 1992—. Chmn., bd. dirs. Medem, Inc., 2004—; vice chair Ophthalmic Mut. Ins. Co., 2005—. Active Okla. Econ. Devel. Found., 1992, Okla. Health Ctr. Found., 1992—; trustee Presbyn. Health Found., 1995-2006, Casady Sch., 1997-2004, vice chair, 1999-2004; mng. dir. Stephenson Laser Ctr., 1996—; bd. mgrs. Okla. Health Alliance, 1995-97; dir. Oklahoma City C. of C. Fellow: Am. Acad. Ophthalmology (assoc. sec. 1983—92, trustee 2000—, sr. sec. for ophthalmic practice 2002—; Honor award 1980, Sr. Honor award 1998); mem.: Am. Soc. Ret. Specialists, Retina Soc., Assn. Univ. Profs. Ophthalmology (trustee 2003, pres. 2001—02), Greater Oklahoma City C. of C. (bd. dirs. 1998—99, 2004—), Alpha Omega Alpha. Office: Dean A McGee Eye Institute 608 Stanton L Young Blvd Oklahoma City OK 73104-5065 E-mail: david-parke@ouhsc.edu.

**PARKE, M. LESLIE,** artist; b. White Plains, N.Y., July 2, 1952; d. William More and Mildred Louise P. BA, Bennington Coll., 1974, MA, 1976. Lila Wallace-Reader's Digest Artist-in-Residence, Giverny, France, 1994. Exhibited in group shows at Centro Cultural Recoleta, Buenos Aires, Argentina, Galerie Etienne Causans, Paris, A.I.R. Gallery, N.Y.C., Schick Art Gallery, Skidmore Coll., Saratoga Springs, N.Y., St. Lawrence U., Canton, N.Y., 1994, U. West Fla., Pensacola, 1994, Arnot Art Mus., Elmira, N.Y., 1994, Austin (Tex.) Mus. Art at Laguna Gloria, 1994, others; solo exhbns. include Mus. of the Southwest, Midland, Tex., San Diego Sports Mus., Gremillion Fine Arts, Houston, Gibsone Jessop Gallery, Toronto, Can., others. Recipient Honor award Visual Arts award Interfaith Forum Art & Archtl., Washington, 1992, Itzhak Sankowsky award Main Line Art Ctr., Haverford, Pa., 1994; grantee George Sugarman Found., 2005.

**PARKE, M(ARGARET) JEAN,** retired business owner, editor; b. Akron, Ohio, Aug. 23, 1920; d. Lawrence William and Rosella (Washburn) Beat; m. Harry Morris Parke, July 25, 1942; children: Richard Blake, Catherine Jean. BA magna cum laude, U. Toledo, 1942, MA, 1959. Adminstrv. asst. Dist. Office Price Adminstrn., Toledo, 1943-45; editing cons. Century Press, Toledo, 1955-72; cons. women's progs. U. Toledo, 1973-75; reports editor Price-Waterhouse & Co., Cleve., 1976-78; fin. officer, ptnr. Parke Supply Co., Avon Lake, Ohio, 1980-86, co-owner, sec. Woodlark Farms, Inc., George-town, Ky., 1978-94. Bd. trustees, past pres. Avon Lake Pub. Libr., 1981-90, Friends of the U. Toledo Libr., past pres. 1971-74; founding trustee Friends of Toledo-Lucas county Pub. Libr., 1970-73; trustee Avon Lake Pub. Libr. Found., Inc., 1991-97; organizer, past pres. Parkview Hosp. Evening Guild, Toledo, 1953; incorporator, sec. Ch. Women United of Toledo area, 1963-66; bd. dirs. LWV, Sylvania, Ohio, Avon Lake; mem. Friends of Avon Lak Libr. Jean Parke Conf. Rm. named in her honor Avon Lake Pub. Libr., 1981. Mem. AAUW (past pres., bd. dirs. Toledo br. 1981-90, Ednl. Found. Prog. honoree 1981), Avon on the Lake Garden Club, U. Toledo Alumni Assn. (trustee, officer Blue T award 1981), Chi Omega Alumnae Toledo (officer), Chi Omega Alumnae Ohio (state bd. dirs. 1983-85, Outstanding Ohio Chi Omega Alumna 1982). Republican. Episcopalian. Avocations: travel, great books, theater, college football, needlecrafts. Home: 32821 Tanglewood Ct Avon Lake OH 44012-1540

**PARKE, ROBERT LEON,** retired communications executive; b. Jersey City, Aug. 28, 1940; s. Edwin Gager and Alice Elizabeth (Servis) P.; m. Geraldine R. Pavlick, Sept. 2, 1967; children: Cheryl Lynn, Tracy Ann, David Scott. Grad. high sch. Jersey City. Asst. bookkeeper Snow-Kist Frozen Foods, Jersey City, 1964-67; contr. Imperial Cartage Co., Inc., Jersey City, 1969-79; mgr. logistic svcs. Vista United Telecommunications, Lake Buena Vista, Fla., 1980-2000; ret. 2000. Corp. sec. Imperial Warehouse Co., Inc., Jersey City, 1968—79, Arbe Transfer Co. Inc., 1968—79; v.p. Cole Foods, Inc., Jersey City, 1968—79. Spl. min. of the eucharist Diocese Orlando, Fla., 1992; vol. Give Kids The World, Kissimmee, Fla., 1992-98; mem. Pemberton Twp. Zoning Bd., Browns Mills, N.J., 1977-79; trustee, bd. dirs. Browns Mills Improvement Assn., 1974-79; life trustee Rebecca Worf Meml. Fund Browns Mills, N.J., Parke Soc., S.E. Milw.; hon. trustee Am. Indian Relief Coun.; founding mem. Nat. Law Enforcement Officers Mus., 2002. Recipient Cert. Appreciation Am. Indian Relief Coun., 1996, 97, 98, 99, 2000, hon. trustee, 1999, 2000; recipient spl. recognition award masters degree program in Nat. Security Studies, Grad. Sch. of Georgetown U., 1996; Bob Parke day proclaimed by Twp. of Pemberton, 1979, Customer Appreciation Award GN Netcom/Unex, 1997, Partners in Excellence Award Walt Disney Co., 1997. Mem.: Nat. Assn. Purchasing Mgmt. (scholarship for continued edn., Ctrl. Fla. Most Supportive Mem. 1994, accrediated purchasing practitioner cert. 1998), Nat. Assn. Purchasing Mgmt. Ctrl. Fla. (named scholar), Am. Soc. Notaries, Fla. Notary Assn. (hon.), Nat. Notary Assn., Fla. Sheriffs Assn. (life), Winthrop Soc., Nat. Soc. Sons and Daus. of Pilgrims, Soc. Sons and Daus. Am.'s First Families (life), Soc. Descs. of the Colonial Clergy (life), KC (mem. coun.). Personal E-mail: rlparke828@aol.com. *Everyone can have a dream, but only those that care and show perseverance will achieve success.*

**PARKE, TERRY RICHARD,** state legislator; b. Pittsfield, Ill., Feb. 21, 1944; m. Joanne Toombs; 2 children. BS, 1970. Mem. Ill. Ho. of Reps. from 44th dist., 1985—. Rep. spokesman ins. com., mem. telcom. com.; mem. labor com.; mem. consumer protection, mem. environment and energy com., mem. environ. health com.; co-chmn. Ill. Commn. on Govt. Forecasting and Accountability; mem. Employee Suggestion Award Bd.; past pres. Elgin Area Life Underwriters. Exec. comm. Bus. and Labor Am. Legis. Exch. Coun. Past Pres. and Nat. Coun. of Ins. Legis.; past pres. N.W. Schaumburg Assn. Commerce and Industry; bd. dirs. Boy Scouts Northwest Suburban Coun.; past mem. Girl Scouts Crossroads Coun. Mem. Rotary (past pres. Schaumburg club). Republican. Office: 220 State House Springfield IL 62706-0001 also: 837 W Higgins Rd Schaumburg IL 60195 Home: 6098 Delaney Dr Hoffman Estates IL 60192-4811 Office Phone: 847-882-0270. Personal E-mail: cityparkxx@yahoo.com.

**PARKEL, JAMES G.,** former health association administrator; BS in elec. engring., U. Denver; LLD (hon.), Am. Grad. Sch. Internat. Mgmt. Exec. mgmt. IBM Internat. Found., 1961—93; pres.-elect AARP, 2000—02, pres., 2002—04. Chair AARP Andrus Found.; mem. bd. councilors Andrus Gerontology Ctr., U. So. Calif. Mem. Madison Coun. Libr. of Congress; former pres. and CEO Junior Achievement Internat.; former chair Junior Achievement Westchester; former nat. bd. mem. Junior Achievement; bd. dirs. Danbury Hosp., New Fairfield Cmty. Trust, Am. Grad. Sch. Internat. Mgmt. Mem.: Soc. Human Resource Mgmt. (past nat. chair).

**PARKER, ALAN (WILLIAM) (SIR ALAN PARKER),** film director, writer; b. London, Feb. 14, 1944; s. William Leslie and Elsie Ellen Parker; m. Annie Inglis, July 30, 1966 (div. 1992); children: Lucy Kate, Alexander James, Jake William, Nathan Charles; m. Lisa Moran, Dec. 16, 2001. Student Brit. schs. Advt. copywriter, 1965—67; dir. TV commls., 1968—78. Author: (screenplay) Melody, 1968; (novels) Bugsy Malone, 1975, Puddles in the Lane, 1977, The Sucker's Kiss, 2003; author, dir.: No Hard Feelings, 1972, Our Cissy, 1973, Footsteps, 1973, Bugsy Malone, 1975 (5 Brit. Acad. awards), Come See the Paradise, 1990; dir.: The Evacuees (Brit. Acad. award, Internat. Emmy award, Press Guild U.K. award), Midnight Express (6 Golden Globe awards, 3 Brit. Acad. awards, 2 Oscar awards), Fame, 1980 (Brit. Acad. award, Golden Globe award, 2 Oscar awards), Shoot the Moon, 1982, Pink Floyd-The Wall, 1982, Birdy, 1984 (Grand Prix Spl. du Jury, Cannes Film Festival), A Turnip Head's Guide to the British Cinema, 1986 (British Press Guild award), Angel Heart, 1987, Mississippi Burning, 1988 (Oscar award), The Commitments, 1991 (4 BAFTA awards), The Road to Wellville, 1994, Evita, 1996 (3 Golden Globe awards), Angela's Ashes, 1999, The Life of David Gale, 2003. Recipient 4 Brit. Acad. awards. Mem.: Acad. Motion Picture Arts and Scis., Dirs. Guild Gt. Britain, Writers Guild Am., Writers Guild Gt. Britain, Dirs. Guild Am., Brit. Film Inst. (chmn. 1997—99, chmn. UK Film Coun. 1999—2004), Brit. Acad. Film and TV Arts. Office: care Michael Wimer Creative Artists Agy 9830 Wilshire Blvd Beverly Hills CA 90212-1804

**PARKER, ALAN JOHN,** veterinary neurologist, educator, researcher; b. Portsmouth, Eng., Oct. 28, 1944; arrived in U.S., 1969, naturalized, 2002; s. William Barton and Emily (Begley) P.; m. Heather Margaret Nicholson, Oct. 30, 1971; children: Alyxander John, Robert William. BSc with honors, Bristol U., 1966, BVSc with honors, 1968; MS, U. Ill., 1973, PhD, 1976. Diplomate Am. Coll. Vet. Internal Medicine-Neurology, European Coll. Vet. Neurology. Intern Vet. Coll., U. Calif.-Davis, 1969—70; instr. vet. clin. medicine U. Ill. Urbana, 1970—71, 1972—76, asst. prof., 1976—77, assoc. prof., 1977—82, prof., 1982—2000, prof. emeritus, 2001—. Cons. pharm. cos., seminar presenter; cons. in neurology Berwyn Vet. Hosp., Chgo., 1973—, Lake Shore Animal Hosp., Chgo., 1998-2003. Contbr. numerous articles to sci. jours., chpts. to books. Active Boy Scouts Am., Champaign, Ill., 1982—; active Presbyn. Ch., Monticello, Ill., 1979—. Recipient Vigil Honor and Founder's award Order of the Arrow, Silver Beaver award Boy Scouts Am.; sci. grantee various orgns., 1972-2003. Mem. AVMA, Am. Animal Hosp. Assn., Ill. Vet. Assn., Ill. State Vet. Assn. Republican. Office: 2845 S Harlem Ave Berwyn IL 60402

**PARKER, ALICE,** composer; b. Boston, Dec. 16, 1925; d. Gordon and Mary (Stuart) P.; widowed; children: David, Timothy, Katharine, Mary, Elizabeth. BA, Smith Coll., Northampton, Mass., 1947; MS, Juilliard Sch., N.Y.C., 1949; MusD (hon.), Hamilton U., 1979, Macalester Coll., St. Paul, 1989, Bluffton Coll., Ohio, 1991, Westminster Choir Coll., Princeton, N.J., 1996. Arranger Robert Shaw Chorale, N.Y.C., 1948-66; artistic dir. Melodious Accord, N.Y.C., 1985—. Tchr., workshop leader Westminster Choir Coll., Princeton, N.J., summers, 1972-98; McDonald chair Emory U., 2003. Composer 4 operas, 41 cantatas, 8 song cycles and numerous anthems and suites. Recipient composer's award ASCAP, 1968—, AGO Disting. Composer of the Yr., 2000, Barlow Endowment, 1992, spl. award Nat. Endowment Arts, 1976, Gottschalk award Pioneer Valley Symphony, 2003, Lifetime Achievement award Choral Arts New Eng., 2004. Fellow Hymn Soc., Hymn Soc. Am. (conf. composer in res., 2006); mem. Am. Choral Dirs. Assn. (ea. divsn. conf. dedicated in her honor 2006), Am. Condrs. Guild, Chorus Am. (Founders award 1994), Am. Music Ctr., Sigma Alpha Iota. Office: Melodious Accord Inc Park West Sta PO Box 20801 New York NY 10025-1523

**PARKER, ALICE JEANNE,** music educator; b. Janesville, Wis., Jan. 13, 1950; d. Edward Judson and Doris Leone Rood; m. R. Michael Parker, June 13, 1971; children: Rachel Marie Mackintosh, Anna Elizabeth Mackintosh, Brandon Robert. MusB in En., Colo. State U., Fort Collins. Cert. music tchr. Colo. Elem. music tchr. Scotch Plains (NJ) / Fanwood Sch. Dist., 1974—76, Riverdale Elem. Sch., Thornton, Colo. Camp dir. Denver Seventh Day Bapt. Ch., Lakewood, Colo., 2004—. Edn. grantee, Adams 12 Five Star Sch. Dist., 1988—91. Republican. Baptist. Avocations: reading, travel. Home: 1091 Russell Blvd Thornton CO 80229 Office: Riverdale Elem Sch 10724 Elm Dr Thornton CO 80233 Office Phone: 720-972-3581.

**PARKER, BARBARA ANNE,** education educator, social studies educator; b. Mount Vernon, Ohio, Oct. 16, 1956; d. Ervin Eugene and Sylvia Anne McCoy; m. Thomas Sutton Parker, Oct. 24, 1981; children: Sarah Kristine, Angela Nicole. BSN, Bowling Green State U., Ohio, 1979; MA in Edn., Ohio State U., Columbus, 1989—92. RN Ohio, 1979; cert. tchr. Ohio, 1998. Office nurse Am. Health Network, Fredericktown, 1985—88; tchr. Fredericktown Local Schs., 1992—. Social studies chairperson Fredericktown Intermediate Sch., 2003—. Contbr. articles to profl. jours. Deaconess First Bapt. Ch., Fredericktown, 2006—; adult Sunday sch. tchr. Avocation: scrapbooks. Office Phone: 740-694-2966.

**PARKER, BARRINGTON D., JR.,** federal judge, lawyer; b. Washington, Aug. 21, 1944; BA, Yale U., 1965, JD, 1969. Bar: N.Y. 1971. Law clk. to Hon. Aubrey E. Robinson, U.S. Dist. Ct. for D.C., Washington, 1969-70; assoc. Sullivan & Cromwell, N.Y.C., 1970-77; ptnr. Parker Auspitz Neesemann & Delehanty, P.C., N.Y.C., 1977-87, Morrison & Foerster, N.Y.C., 1987-94; judge U.S. Dist. Ct. for so. dist. N.Y., White Plains, 1994—2001, U.S. Ct. Appeals (2nd Cir.), N.Y. 2001—. Bd. dirs., v.p. NAACP Legal Def. and Educational Fund, Inc., 1980—; com. on grievances, com. on civil discovery U.S. Dist. Ct. (so. dist.) N.Y., 1983—; com. on pre-trial phase civil cases U.S. Ct. Appeals (2nd cir.) 1983—. Trustee Governance Inst., Green-

wich Acad., South Africa Legal Svcs. and Legal Edn. Project, Inc.; successor trustte an mem. Yale Corp. Mem. ABA, Fed. Bar Coun., Assn. Bar City N.Y. (com. on the judiciary 1978-82, exec. com. 1982-86, nominating com. 1987), Coun. on Fgn. Rels. Office: US Courthouse 300 Quarropas St Rm 633 White Plains NY 10601-4150 also: Thurogood Marshall US Courthouse 40 Foley Square New York NY 10007 also: US Courthouse Two Stamford Plz 281 Tresser Blvd Stamford CT 06901*

**PARKER, BRENT MERSHON,** retired medical educator, internist, cardiologist; b. St. Louis, July 3, 1927; s. William Bahlmann and Florence (Mershon) P.; m. Martha Shelton, Aug. 1, 1953; children: Martha Parker Burgess, Elizabeth, Margaret. MD cum laude, Wash. U., St. Louis, 1952. Diplomate Am. Bd. Internal Medicine. Intern and asst. resident N.Y. Hosp.-Cornell, N.Y.C., 1952-54; asst. resident, fellow Barnes Hosp., Wash. U., St. Louis, 1954-57; cardiology sect. chief VA Hosp., U. Oreg., Portland, 1957-59; asst. prof. to assoc. prof., co-dir. cardiovascular div., chief adult cardiac catherization Wash. U. Sch. Medicine, St. Louis, 1959-73; prof. medicine U. Mo., Columbia, 1973-89, prof. emeritus, 1989-94, chief of staff, assoc. dean, 1976-82, chief of cardiology, 1983-89. Mem. colloquium faculty Merck, Sharp and Dohme, West Point, Pa., 1980-86. Author or co-author 58 papers in referred jours., 6 book chpts., teaching papers. others. Bd. dirs. St. Louis Heart Assn., 1962-73, v.p. 1972-73; bd. dirs. Mo. Heart Assn., 1965-75, pres. 1970-71. Served with USN, 1945-46. Recipient Arthur Strauss award St. Louis Heart Assn., 1973, 3 teaching awards U. Mo. Sch. Medicine, 1974, 75, 86, Preventive Cardiology Acad. award, Nat. Heart Lung and Blood Inst., 1982 87, Alumni Achievement award Washington Univ. Sch. Medicine, 1992; Brent Mershon Parker professorship estab. in honor U. Mo., 1989. Fellow ACP, Am. Coll. Cardiology (Mo., Kans. council rep. 1973-77), Clin. Cardiology Soc. Am. Heart Assn.; mem. Am. Fedn. Clin. Research, Cen. Soc. for Clin. Research, Alpha Omega Alpha, Sigma Xi. Episcopalian. Avocations: choral singing, jogging, camping, back packing.

**PARKER, C. ALLEN,** lawyer; b. Jacksonville, Fla., Feb. 17, 1955; BA magna cum laude, Duke Univ., 1977; MA, Univ. Chgo., 1980; JD magna cum laude, Columbia Univ., 1983. Bar: NY 1985. Law clk., Hon. Amalya L. Kearse US Ct. of Appeals, 2nd Cir.; assoc. Cravath Swaine & Moore LLP, NYC, 1984—90, ptnr., corp., 1990—. Mem: NY State Bar Assn. Office: Cravath Swaine & Moore LLP Worldwide Plz 825 Eighth Ave New York NY 10019-7475 Office Phone: 212-474-1765. Office Fax: 212-474-3700. Business E-Mail: aparker@cravath.com.

**PARKER, CATHERINE L.,** theater educator; b. Warren, Mich., Dec. 12, 1973; d. Carl and Elinor Russo; m. Nathan T. Parker; 1 child, Owen Travis. MA, Ea. Mich. U., Ypsilanti, 1996—99; asst. prof. theatre Rochester Coll., Rochester Hills, Mich., 1997—. Worship team leader Heritage Ch. Christ, Clawson, Mich., 2005—06. Office: Rochester Coll 800 W Avon Rd Rochester Hills MI 48307 Business E-Mail: cparker@rc.edu.

**PARKER, CLEA EDWARD,** retired university president; b. Talisheek, La., Apr. 2, 1927; s. William A. and Lutritia (Davis) P.; m. Peggy Ann Faciane, June 21, 1953; children: Brian, Stephen, Karen, Robin. BA, Southeastern La. U., 1948; M.Ed., La. State U., 1952, Ed.D., 1965. Coach, tchr. Rugby Acad., New Orleans, 1948-50; tchr., prin., supr. instr., dir. curriculum and instrn. St. Tammany Parish Sch. Bd., 1950-67; prof. edn., head dept. student teaching Nicholls State Coll., Thibodaux, La., 1967-68; acting pres. Southeastern La. U., Hammond, 1968, pres., 1968-80, pres. emeritus, 1980—86. Liaison La. State Dept. Edn., Higher Edn. and Bds. for Edn. in La., 1986; vis. lectr. La. State U. at NC, 1965-69; past pres. St. Tammany Parish Tchrs. Assn., La. Assn. Supervision and Curriculum Devel.; past pres. elementary dept. La. Tchrs Assn.; chmn. Pres.'s Coun. La. Bd. Edn., 1972-73; v.p. Conf. La. Colls. and Univs., 1973-74, pres., 1974-75; pres. elect Gulf South Conf., 1974-75, pres., 1975-76; mem. Steering Com. on Curriculum Devel. and Revision for Career Edn. for State La., 1973; mem. adv. council for State Plan for Career Edn.; 1973 Mem. planning com. Gov.'s Conf. on Aging, 1976; v.p. chpt. 15 La. Good Samaritans, 1987-88; bd. dirs. Assn. for Retarded Citizens, pres.-elect, 1981; mem. Zemurray Park Recreation Commn., Hammond, 1992-95; chmn. bd. dirs. Lallie Kemp Meml. Hosp., 1993-94; bd. dirs. Lallie Kemp Med. Ctr., 1994—, chmn., 1994-95. With USCGR, 1945, 93-94. Named Hon. State Farmer La., 1970, Disting. Alumnus of Yr., Southeastern La. U. Alumni Assn., 1977, 91, 92; inductee La. Spl. Olympics Hall of Fame, 1998. Mem. Am. Assn. State Colls. and Univs. (com. on nat. svc. 1972-73, task force on aging 1975-76, 78-79, nominating com. 1977—, state Rep. for La. 1979—, com. agr. renewable resources and rural devel. 1979-80, Svc. to Edn. award 1980), Hammond C. of C., La. Assn. for Sch. Execs., Ozone Ramblers Camping Club (pres. 1988), KC (lectr. 1982, 85, 90-91, chancellor 1983-84, 87—, dep. grand knight 1995-96), Rotary (bd. dirs. Hammond, internat. svc. dir. 1972), Phi Delta Kappa, Kappa Delta Pi. Home: 10 Golden Dr Hammond LA 70401-1010 Personal E-mail: ceparker10@bellsouth.net.

**PARKER, DAVID G.,** music educator, music publisher; s. Herbert G. and Carol M. Parker; m. Linda O. Owens, June 3, 1978; children: Rebeccah Anne Downs, Sarah Elizabeth. BS in Edn., Bob Jones U., 1978; MA in Voice Performance, Bob Jones U., Greenville, SC, 1980; doctoral degree of Musical Arts in Voice Performance, U. Mich., Ann Arbor, 1985. Cert. McClosky vocal technician McClosky Inst. Voice, 2006. Prof. voice and music tech. Bob Jones U., Greenville, 1985—; baritone soloist Bob Jones U. Orchestra, 2002, 2004, bass soloist, 2005; pres., CEO C & L Enterprises, Inc., Greenville, 1986—; CoilTech, Pickens, SC, 1995—, SacredSheetMusic.com, Pickens, 2006—. Vocal pedagogy Wilds Music Conf., Brevard, NC, 1999—2006; bass soloist Greenville Symphony Orch., 2004, baritone soloist, 05; bass soloist Clemson U. Orch., SC, 2005. Composer: (choral octavo) Silent Night, I Will Love the Lord, Softly and Tenderly, Be Thou My Vision, (vocal solo) Only Fear the Lord, Trust and Obey, New Life, Worthy is the Lamb. V.p. New Town Mountain Sch. Homeowner's Assn., Pickens, 1999—2001, pres., 2001—03; asst. music dir. Hampton Pk. Baptist Ch., Greenville, 1996—2006; music dir. Westgate Baptist Ch., Spartanburg, SC, 2006—. Mem.: Nat. Assn. Tchrs. of Singing. R-Consevative. Avocations: writing and arranging music, golf, hiking, woodworking. Home: 308 Wandering Way Pickens SC 29671 Office: Bob Jones Univ 1700 Wade Hampton Blvd Greenville SC 29614 Office Phone: 864-242-5100. Business E-Mail: daparker@bju.edu. E-mail: david@sacredsheetmusic.com.

**PARKER, DAWN CASSANDRA,** social sciences educator; PhD, U. Calif.-Davis, 2000. Asst. prof. George Mason U., Fairfax, Va., 2003—. Grantee, NSF, 2004—. Office Phone: 703-993-4640.

**PARKER, DEAN E.,** lawyer; s. Samuel and Mother Parker; m. Bonnie R. Parker; children: Samuel (20), John (17). Degree in Bus. Adminstrn., U. Wis., Madison, Wis., 1976, JD, 1979. Bar: Ill., Wis., Minn. Assoc. Hinshaw & Culbertson LLP, Chgo., 1979—84, ptnr., 1984—, regional dir., 1995—. Fellow: Phi Kappa Phi, Beta Gamma Sigma; mem.: ABA. Home: 588 Cherokee Lake Forest IL 60045 Office Phone: 312-704-3117.

**PARKER, DENNIS GENE,** former sheriff, martial arts instructor; b. Kansas City, Kans., Jan. 5, 1956; s. Billy Gene and Lola Ruth (Martens) Parker; m. Brenda Jean Hamre, June 30, 1972 (div. 1989); children: Heatheryn Ruth, Jessica Elise. Student, U. Kans., 1984. Nat. accredited police firearms instr. and expert., police side handle baton instr. Martial arts instr. Northland Tai-Ryuku, Kansas City, Mo., 1974-84; anti-terrorist/hostage rescue specialist ITC CITRO, 1977—80; anti-terrorist team mem. USNSAD, Mid. East, 1980—81; police cpl. Atchison (Kans.) Dept. Police, 1984-90; estate investigator Am. Rsch. Bur., L.A., 1990; sheriff Atchison County, Kans., 1990-94; instr. martial arts, including Shito-Ryu Okinawa-TE, Tang Soo Do Mu Duk Kwon, Chinese Wu-Shu Chin Na. Bd. dirs. Atchison County Community Corrections; team mem. Atchison County Multidisciplinary Child Protection Team, 1992—; bd. dirs. N.E. Kans. Drug Task Force, Oskaloosa, 1990-91. Author: Surviving the Badge, 2005. Bd. dirs. N.E. Kans. Community Action Program, Atchison, 1991—, Atchison Area Drug Task Force, 1993—. Recipient Silver Star for Bravery Am. Police Hall of Fame, 1992, Honor

award, 1992, John Edgar Hoover Meml. award Nat. Assn. Chiefs of Police and Police Hall of Fame, 1993, State of Kans. medals of valor, 1992, 93, Pres.'s Nat. medal of patriotism, 1993, APD Life Saving award and commendation, 1987, knight chevalier medal Am. Police Hall of Fame, 1992, Medal of Valor Atchison County, 1992, U.S. Cold War Recognition award, 2000. Mem. World Black Belt Bur., Sandan-3d Level Black Shito-Ryu Okinawa Te. Baptist. Home and Office: 5125 NW Parkdale Rd Kansas City MO 64151-3205 Office Phone: 816-505-0949. Personal E-mail: dparker20@kc.rr.com.

**PARKER, DENNIS REY,** finance educator; b. Toledo, Ohio, Oct. 18, 1944; s. Jess Revere and Elizabeth Elaine Parker; m. Cheryl Lynn Yerxa (div.); children: Lane Stephen, Paige Reylynn, Amber Elaine. BA in Spanish, Calif. State U., Fullerton, 1967, MA in Linguistics, 1973; postgrad., U. San Francisco, 1988. Cert. secondary and bilingual crosscultural tchr. Tchr. Corona Sr. H.S., Calif., 1967—75; resource tchr. Corona-Norco Unified Sch. Dist., 1975—77, bilingual program dir., 1977—80; cons. Calif. Dept. Edn., Sacramento, 1980—86, adminstr., 1986—2000; faculty sch. mgmt. program UCLA, 2000—. Developer REACH statewide reading network, Calif.; developer strategic schooling model of edn. reform. Mem.: ASCD, Calif. Assn. Bilingual Edn., Internat. Reading Assn. Democrat. Avocations: guitar, singing, motorcycling, horse training and riding. Home: 11656 County Rd 92B Zamora CA 95698 Office: 924 33d St Sacramento CA 95816-4411

**PARKER, DEREK,** architectural firm executive; Chmn., sr. prin. Anshen & Allen Archs. Inc., San Francisco, 1993—; chmn. Anshen Dyer, London. Mem. design rev. com. U. Calif., Berkeley; practicum faculty doctoral program U. Hawaii; adv. faculty for doctoral program Coll. Arch., Ga. Tech.; bd. mem. Ctr. for Health Design; mem. bd. on infrastructure and constructive environment NRC, 2003—. Fellow: AIA, Am. Coll. Healthcare Archs.; mem.: Royal Inst. Brit. Archs. Office: Anshen & Allen Archs Inc 901 Market St San Francisco CA 94103

**PARKER, DIANA LYNNE,** restaurant manager, special events director; b. Eureka, Calif., June 21, 1957; d. Carol Dean and Lynne Diane (Havemann) P. BA in English, Humboldt U., Arcata, Calif., 1981, postgrad., 1982—84. Lic. real estate agent, Calif. Retail clk. Safeway, Inc., Eureka, 1977-84; caterer, owner TD Catering, Eureka, 1982-84; asst. buyer Macy's Calif., San Francisco, 1984-85; realtor Mason-McDuffie, Alameda, Calif., 1985-87; host, Rotunda Restaurant Neiman Marcus, San Francisco, 1987-89, asst. mgr. Rotunda Restaurant, 1989—96, dir. spl. events, 1989—96, mgr. dining room Rotunda Restaurant, 1996—. Mem.: Nat. Assn. Catering Execs., San Francisco Visitor and Conv. Bur., Women Chefs and Restauranteurs, Mus. Modern Art, Commonwealth Club Calif. Republican. Avocations: gourmet cooking, art, antiques. Office: Rotunda at Neiman Marcus 150 Stockton St San Francisco CA 94108-5807 Office Phone: 415-362-4777.

**PARKER, DONNA TULLY,** elementary school educator, department chairman; b. Oak Hill, W.Va., Nov. 30, 1960; d. Donald Cameron and Elizabeth Ann Tully; 1 child, Megan Elizabeth. B in Elem. Edn., Marshall U., Huntington, W.Va., 1983; MEd, Lesley U., Cambridge, Mass., 2006. Cert. mid. sch. studies S.C., gifted and talented cert. S.C. Elem. tchr. Winyah Acad., Georgetown, SC, 1984—86, Coastal Acad., Myrtle Beach, SC, 1986—87; mid. sch. tchr. Horry County Sch. Dist., Conway, SC, 1989—; social studies dept. chairperson St. James Mid. Sch., Myrtle Beach, 2004—. Recipient S.C. VFW History Tchr. of the Yr. award, VFW Post Murrells Inlet, 2001. Mem.: PTSO (corr.), S.C. Mid. Sch. Assn. (life Mid. Sch. Magic award 1991). Democrat. Baptist. Avocations: travel, swimming, water-skiing, skiing. Home: 122 Ashton Cir Myrtle Beach SC 29588 Office: Saint James Mid Sch 9775 Saint James Rd Myrtle Beach SC 29588 Office Phone: 843-650-5543.

**PARKER, DOUG See PARKER, W.**

**PARKER, DOUGLAS MARTIN,** retired lawyer, writer; b. Chgo., Mar. 6, 1935; s. Lewis Wallace and Elaine (Schulz) P.; m. Angela Macintosh, June 5, 1965; children: Heather Louise, Melissa Meredith. AB, Cornell U., 1956, LL.B., 1958. Bar: N.Y. 1959, U.S. Supreme Ct. 1966, D.C. 1969. Assoc. Mudge Rose Guthrie Alexander & Ferdon, N.Y.C., 1958-59, 62-69, ptnr., 1977-94, of counsel, 1995; ptnr, Lankler & Parker, Washington, 1969-73; with Office of Counsel to Pres., 1973; dep. gen. counsel HUD, 1974-77. Author: Ogden Nash: The Life and Work of America's Laureate of Light Verse, 2005. Served to capt. U.S. Army, 1959-62. Republican. Congregationalist. E-mail: dmparker@capecod.net.

**PARKER, EDWIN BURKE,** communications executive; b. Berwyn, Alta., Can., Jan. 19, 1932; m. Frances G. Spigai, 1976; children: David Kendall, Karen Liane. BA, U. B.C., Can., 1954; MA, Stanford U., 1958, PhD in Mass Comms., 1960. Staff reporter Vancouver (Can.) Sun., 1954-55; info. officer U. B.C., Vancouver, 1955-57; rsch. asst. Inst. Comms. Rsch. Stanford U., 1957-60, asst. prof., 1962-63, assoc. prof., 1963-71, prof., 1971-79; vp. Equatorial Comms. Co., 1979-85, chmn. bd. dirs., 1986-87; pres. data networks divsn. CONTEL, 1987-88; pres. Parker Telecomm., Gleneden Beach, Oreg., 1989—. Asst. prof. Communications U. Ill., Urbana, 1960-62. Ctr. fro Advanced Studies in Behavioral Sci. fellow, 1969-70. Office: Parker Telecommunications PO Box 402 Gleneden Beach OR 97388-0402 Office Phone: 541-764-3058. E-mail: edparker@teleport.com.

**PARKER, ELIZABETH RINDSKOPF,** dean, law educator; b. Detroit, Dec. 2, 1943; d. Arthur C. and Kathryn G. (Rodgers) Roediger; m. Peter E. Rindskopf, May 25, 1968; 1 child, m. Robert Parker. BA in Philosophy cum laude, U. Mich., 1964, JD, 1968. Bar: Ga. 1968, U.S. Dist. Ct. (no. dist.) Ga. 1969, U.S. Ct. Appeals (5th cir.) 1969, U.S. Supreme Ct. 1971, U.S. Ct. Appeals (6th cir.) 1972, U.S. Ct. Appeals (3rd cir.) 1974, U.S. Ct. Appeals (4th cir.) 1977, U.S. Ct. Appeals (9th cir.) 1978, D.C. 1979. Reginald Heber Smith fellow, mng. atty. Emory Legal Svcs., Atlanta, 1968-71; ptnr. Moore, Alexander & Rindskopf, Atlanta, 1971-74; dir. New Haven Legal Assistance Assn., Inc., 1974-76; dep. dir. Lawyers Com. Civil Rights Under Law, Washington, 1978-78; ptnr. Cohen, Vitt & Annand, Alexandria, Va., 1978-79; acting asst. dir. mergers and joint ventures, dep. asst. dir. health care Bur. of Competition, Fed. Trade Commn., 1979-81; of counsel Surrey & Morse, Washington, 1981-84; gen. counsel Nat. Security Agy., Washington, 1984-89; prin. dep. office of the legal adviser US Dept. State, Washington, 1989-90; gen. counsel CIA, Washington, 1990-95; of counsel Bryan Cave, LLP, 1995—99; gen. counsel U. Wis. Sys., 1999—2002; dean, prof. law U. Pacific Sch. Law, Sacramento, 2003—. Co-operating atty. NAACP Legal Def. and Edn. Fund, Inc., 1971-74; trustee Monterey Inst. Internat. Studies. Contbr. articles to profl. jours. Bd. dirs. Austen Riggs Psychiat. Hosp. Mem. ABA (standing com. law and nat. security, counsel sect. internat. law and politics, adv. bd. Ctr. and Eastern European Law Initiative), Coun. Fgn. Rels, NAS (com. mem. Roundtable on Sci. Comm. and Nat. Security & Commn. on Sci. Comm. and Nat. Security. Office: U of Pacific McGeorge Sch Law 3200 Fifth Ave Sacramento CA 95817 Office Phone: 916-739-7151. E-mail: elizabeth@pacific.edu.

**PARKER, ELLIS D.,** retired military officer; b. Adams, Tenn, Nov. 1, 1932; s. Ellis A. and Lorene (Qualls) P.; m. Judy C. Matthews, Dec. 24, 1952; children: Donald S., Phillip R., David B. BS in Psychology, U. Nebr., 1972; MPA, Shippensburg U., 1979; LLD (hon.), Miles U., 1989. Rated aviator FAA. Commd. 2d lt. U.S. Army, Republic of Korea, 1957, advanced through ranks to lt. gen., 1992, aviation officer, comdr. 17th aviation brigade Republic of Korea, 1978-80; dir. requirements army staff Pentagon, Washington, 1980-83; asst. divsn. comdr. 101st airborne divsn. U.S. Army, Ft. Campbell, Ky., 1983-84; commdg. gen. Army Aviation Ctr. Sch. Ft. Rucker, Ala., 1984-89; dir. army staff Pentagon, Washington, 1989-92; bd. dirs. Can. Aviation Electronics, 1993—; chmn. & CEO Can. 1993. Bd. dirs. Mesa Airlines, Doss Aviation, Colorado Springs; chmn., bd. dirs. Hammer Constrn. Co., Sanson, Ala.; bd. dirs. Aereus Internat., Enterprise, Ala. Contbr. articles to profl. jour. Chmn. Fort Rucker Mus. Found., 1995—; adv. bd. Troy U., Dotham, 1992—; chair retiree coun. for chief of staff U.S. Army, 1993-99;

co-chair Dept. of Def. Retiree Coun., 1994-99. Decorated D.S.M. with oak leaf cluster, D.F.C., Legion of Merit, Bronze Star with two oak leaf clusters, Meritorious Svc. medals, 23 Air medals; named to Hall of Honor Bd. by Gov. Ala., 1993—, chmn. Bd. of dirs., Enterprise Cals. C of C. Mem.: Army Assn. Am., Enterprise C. of C. (chmn bd. 1995—), Assn. U.S. Army (mem. exec. com. Ft. Rucker chpt. 1994, named to Army Aviation Hall of Fame 1994), Ret. Officers Assn. (1st vice-chmn.), Army Aviation Assn. Am. (pres.., Order of St. Michel, Gold 1992), Enterprise Rotary Club (Paul Harris fellow). Republican. Avocations: flying, hunting, fishing, volunteering in community. Home and Office: 128 Deer Run Strut Enterprise AL 36330-7812

**PARKER, ELLIS JACKSON, III,** lawyer, broadcaster; b. Haleyville, Ala., Oct. 2, 1931; s. Ellis J. and Elizabeth (Funderburg) P.; m. Nancy Elizabeth Bealer; children: Francis Hill, Ellis Stuart Student, U.S. Mil. Acad., West Point, N.Y., 1953—57; AB, U. Ala., 1958, LLB, 1960, JD, 1961; diploma, Droit Compare, Luxembourg, 1959; cert., Acad. Internat. Law, Hague, Netherlands, 1960. Bar: Ala. 1960, U.S. Tax Ct. 1960, U.S. Supreme Ct. 1966, U.S. Ct. Appeals D.C. 1972, Md. Ct. Appeals 1973, U.S. Ct. Claims 1977. Legis. atty. IRS, Washington, 1961—62; chief of staff to U.S. Congressman Grant Ala., 1963—64; pvt. practice Birmingham, Ala., 1964—84; spl. advisor to Pres. Richard Nixon White House, Washington, 1968—69; v.p., counsel Birmingham Broadcasting Co., 1964—83; ptnr. Taylor, Smith & Parker Law Office, Upper Marlboro, Md., 1970—86; prin., owner Ellis J. Parker, Law Office, Washington, 1986—. V.p., sec. Constrn. Components Corp., Upper Marlboro, Md., 1968-72; pres. Washington-Ala. News Reports, Washington, 1980-01, Parker Real Estate, Birmingham, Bealer-Parker, LLC, Washington; chmn. bd. Blackbelt Broadcasting Co., Selma, Ala., 1986-2000; founding mem. Women's Nat. Bank, Washington; CEO Birmingham Broadcasting Co.; ptnr. Linden Radio Joint Venture, Faunsdale, Ala., 1969-89; pres., bd. dirs. 17th St LLC, N.B. Devel. Co. LLC, Washington, 2006, Hartford E. Bealer Devel. Corp. LLC, Washington Mem. Presdl. Inaugural Com., inaugural protocol officer V.p. Agnew, 1968; mem. steering com. Rep. Party, Balt., 1972; chmn. bd. trustees Prince George's Hist. and Cultural Trust, Upper Marlboro, 1974; chmn. bd. advisors Prince George's Equestrian Ctr., Upper Marlboro, 1980; founder, pres. bd. dirs. Hospice of Prince George's County, Upper Marlboro, 1982; mem. Upper Marlboro Devel. Com. Mem. IEEE, ABA, FCC Bar Assn., Fed. Bar Assn., Inter-Am. Bar Assn., Ala. Bar Assn., Md. Bar Assn., D.C. Bar Assn., Nat. Assn. Broadcasters, Ala. Broadcasters Assn., Balt. Coun. Fgn. Affairs. Assn. Grads. U.S. Mil. Acad., Chevy Chase Club, Md. Club, St. Andrews Soc., Met. Club, Ala. Alumni Assn., Scabbard and Blade (chmn. nat. alumni coun. 1986-2006), Pi Kappa Alpha, Sigma Delta Kappa. E-mail: Home: Chateau Rambouillet 2165 Ibis Island Palm Beach FL 33480 E-mail: eparker124@aol.com.

**PARKER, EUGENE NEWMAN,** retired physicist, retired educator; b. Houghton, Mich., June 10, 1927; s. Glenn H. and Helen (MacNair) Parker; m. Niesje Meuter, 1954; children: Joyce, Eric. BS, Mich. State U., 1948, DSc (hon.), 1975; PhD, Calif. Inst. Tech., 1951; DHC in Physics and Math. (hon.), U. Utrecht, The Netherlands, 1986; DHC in Theoretical Physics (hon.), U. Oslo, 1991. Instr. math. and astronomy U. Utah, 1951—53, asst. prof. physics, 1953—55; mem. faculty physics U. Chgo., 1955—95, prof. dept. physics, 1962—95, prof. dept. astronomy and astrophysics, 1967—95, prof. emeritus, 1995—. Author: Interplanetary Dynamical Processes, 1963, Cosmical Magnetic Fields, 1979, Spontaneous Current Sheets in Magnetic Fields, 1994, Conversations on Electric and Magnetic Fields in the Cosmos, 2006. Recipient Space Sci. award, AIAA, 1964, Chapman medal, Royal Astron. Soc., 1979, Gold medal, 1992, Disting. Alumni award, Calif. Inst. Tech. 1980, Karl Schwarzschild award, Astronomische Gesselschaft, 1990, Bruce medal, Astron. Soc. Pacific, 1997, medal, Assn. Internat. Devel. Nice (France) Obs., 1997, Kyoto prize, Inamori Found., 2003, Maxwell prize, plasma physics divsn., Am. Phys. Soc., 2003. Mem.: NAS (H. K. Arctowski award 1969, U.S. Nat. medal of Sci. 1989), Norwegian Acad. Sci. and Letters, Am. Geophys. Union (John Adam Fleming award 1968, William Bowie medal 1990), Am. Astron. Soc. (Henry Norris Russell lectr. 1969, George Ellery Hale award 1978). Achievements include development of theory of the origin of the dipole magnetic field of Earth; prediction and theory of the solar wind and heliosphere; theoretical basis for the X-ray emission from the Sun and stars. Home: 1323 Evergreen Rd Homewood IL 60430-3410 E-mail: parker@odysseus.uchicago.edu.

**PARKER, EVA ANNETTE,** librarian; b. North Island, Calif., Nov. 27, 1950; d. R.L. and Eva Mae (Helm) Peters; m. Darrell Dwight Parker, Nov. 9, 1970; children: Geoff, Jenny. BS, Okla. Christian Coll., 1974; MEd, Southwestern Okla. State U., 1984. Cert. libr. media specialist. Tchr. Summer Safari program Oklahoma City Zoo, 1973; libr., tchr. Leedey (Okla.) Pub. Sch., 1983-87; prof. Draughon Tng. Inst., Wichita Falls, Tex., 1988-89; tchr. Region IX Edn. Svc. Ctr., Wichita Falls, 1990; libr. media specialist Vernon (Tex.) Mid. Sch., 1990—2003; libr. Burgess Elem. Sch., Wichita Falls, Tex., 2004—; tchr. art and sci. Vernon Kids Kollege, 1999—. Tutor Vernon Intermediate Sch., 1993—; del. alt. to NEA, Leedey, 1987; storm spotter for City of Grandfield, Okla. Contbg. author: What America's Teachers Wish Parents Knew, 1993; contbr. article to profl. jour. Tchr. Bible sch. Ch. of Christ, Iowa Park, Tex., 1987-93, Grandfield, Okla., 1994—; vol. ARC, Wichita Falls, 1987-93; coach bowling Spl. Olympics, 1992-93; coach track and field Spl. Olympics, Vernon, 1993—; bd. mem. Harvest Playhouse; spl. olympics coach. Libr. improvement grantee Okla. State Dept. Edn., Leedey, 1984, Sch.-to-Work grantee, 1996-2001. Mem. Tex. Libr. Assn., Assn. Tex. Profl. Educators, P.E.O. (pres. Okla. orgn.). Avocations: rock collecting, painting, calligraphy, reading, music. Home: 1303 W 1st St Grandfield OK 73546 Office: Kate Burgess Elem Lang and Prep Acad 3106 Maurine St Wichita Falls TX 76306 Office Phone: 940-716-2850. Personal E-mail: annettep_1@yahoo.com.

**PARKER, EVERETT CARLTON,** clergyman; b. Chgo., Jan. 17, 1913; s. Harry Everett and Lillian (Stern) P.; m. Geneva M. Jones, May 5, 1939; children: Ruth A. (Mrs. Peter Weiss), Eunice L. (Mrs. George Kolczun, Jr.), Truman E. AB, U. Chgo., 1935; BD magna cum laude, Chgo. Theol. Sem., 1943, Blatchford fellow, 1944-45, DD, 1964, Catawba Coll., Salisbury, N.C., 1958; L.H.D., Fordham U., 1978, Tougaloo Coll., 1987; LLD, Coll. St. Elizabeth, 2000. Pastor Waveland Ave. Congl. Christian Ch., 1943; asst. pub. service and war program mgr. NBC, 1943-45; founder-dir. Protestant Radio Commn., 1945-50; lectr. communication Yale Div. Sch., 1946-58, dir. communications research project, 1950-54; dir. Office Communication United Ch. Christ, 1954-83; sr. research assoc., adj. prof. Fordham U., 1983—; founder citizen movement to protect minority rights in media, 1963—. Chmn. broadcasting and film commn. Nat. Coun. Chs., 1969-72, gen. bd., 1966-72; chmn. Study Commn. on Theology, Edn. and Electronic Media, 1985-87; founder Found. for Minority Interests in Media, 1985—, treas., 1985—; Hispanic Telecommunications Network, 1986-2004; adv. com. on advanced TV svcs., Consumer Adv. Group FCC, 1988-92 Producer-dir.: nat. TV programs including series Off to Adventure, 1956, Tangled World, 1965; originator: series Six American Families, PBS-TV, 1977; Author: Religious Radio, 1948, Film Use in the Church, 1953, The Television-Radio Audience and Religion, 1955, Religious Television, 1961, (with others) Television, Radio, Film for Churchmen, 1969, Fiber Optics to the Home: The Changing Future of Cable, TV and The Telephone, 1989, Social Responsibility of Television in the United States, 1994. Recipient Human Relations award Am. Jewish Com., 1966, Faith and Freedom award Religious Heritage Found., 1966, 77, Alfred I. DuPont-Columbia U. award pub. service in broadcasting, 1969; Roman Cath. Broadcasters Gabriel award pub. service, 1970; Lincoln U. award significant contbn. human relations, 1971; Racial Justice award Com. for Racial Justice, United Ch. Christ, 1973; Leadership award Coun. for Christian Social Action, 1973; Public Svc. award Black Citizens for a Fair Media, 1979, Pioneer award World Assn. for Christian Commn., 1988, award for Ecumenical Leadership Nat. Coun. Chs., 2000, Ellul award Media Ecology Assn., 2004 Mem.: Yale (N.Y.C.). Home: 11 Midland Ave White Plains NY 10606-2828 Office: Fordham University Dept Communications Bronx NY 10458 Office Phone: 914-393-4854. E-mail: ecparker92@msn.com.

**PARKER, GARY DEAN,** manufacturing executive; b. Omaha, Mar. 27, 1945; s. Norman and Dolores (Pierce) P.; m. Joanne Baker, Aug. 27, 1966; children: Jason E., Rodney R. BS in BA, Nebr. Wesleyan U., BS in Econs. Dir. sales Lindsay Mfg. Co., Nebr., 1971-73, v.p. sales-mktg. Nebr., 1973-76, sr. v.p. Nebr., 1976-78, exec. v.p. Nebr., 1978-83, pres., 1983—, dir., 1977—. Pres. Irrigation Assocs., Silver Springs, Md., 1981-82, dir., 1978-83; dir. Irrigation Found. & Research, Silver Springs, 1978— Mem. Nebr. Mfg. Assn. (pres. 1982-83), Delta Omicron Epsilon Lodges: Elks. Office: Lindsay Mfg Co PO Box 156 Lindsay NE 68644-0156

**PARKER, GEORGE ERNEST,** mathematics educator; b. Willimantic, Conn., Nov. 4, 1940; s. J. Ernest and Alice C. (Costello) P.; m. Cynthia Ann Nucci Parker, Oct. 16, 1965; children: Kimberly, Geoffrey, Christopher. BS, Ea. Conn. State U., 1964; MA, Wesleyan U., 1971, student, 1973, 81, 84, 85, 86, U. Conn., 1982, 83, 89. Cert. secondary sch. tchr. math, sci., Conn. Math. tchr. Valley Regional H.S., Deep River, Conn., 1964-65, Sweeney Sch., Willimantic, Conn. 1965-66, Coventry (Conn.) H.S., 1966-76; math dept. head Edwin O. Smith Sch., Storrs, Conn., 1976—2002. Lectr. secondary math. edn. U. Conn., Storrs, 1976—87, supr. student tchrs.; adj. prof. Ea. Conn. State U., Willimantic, 1982—90, 2002—; cons. curriculum Project to Increase Mastery Math. & Sci., Middletown, Conn., 1984—; pres. Foxbrush Consultants; del. US-China Jt. Edn. Conf., Beijing, 2005. Author: (with others) Computer Integrated Lessons for the Math Classroom, 1989, Math Connections Book III, 1995. V.p. Conn. Jr. Soccer Assn., 1970-75; pres. Mansfield (Conn.) PTA, 1984-86. G.E. Vanguard Fellow, 1984; recipient Outstanding Tchr. award MIT, 1992, Presidential award Nat. Found. Sci., 1994. Mem.: Nat. Coun. Tchrs. Math. (state rep. 1968—), Assn. Tchrs. Math. in Conn., Assn. Tchrs. Math. in New Eng., Conn. Coun. Suprs. Math. (pres. 1995—2001, exec. bd. 1990—), Math. Assn. Am., Conn. Soccer Coaches Assn. (pres., founder 1973—77). Roman Catholic. Avocations: running, reading, hiking, boating, soccer referee.

**PARKER, GERALD M.,** osteopath, researcher; b. Olean, N.Y., Nov. 20, 1943; s. Richard and Kathleen (Manwaring) P.; m. Linda Kay Stuart, Dec. 28, 1968; children: Kimberly, Gerald, Cassandra, Kevin. BA, Western Wash. U., 1965; DO, Kirksville Coll. Osteopathy & Surgery, 1969. Intern Art Centre Hosp., Detroit, 1969-70; ptnr. Doctor's Clinic, Amarillo, Tex., 1970. Dir. S.W. Inst. Preventive Medicine, Amarillo, 1978—, Hyperbaric Oxygen Ctr., Amarillo, 1979—; appeared on That's Incredible TV show, 1982. Contbr. articles to profl. jours. Pres. S.W. Amarillo Little Dribblers Assn., 1979—; coach Girls Nat. Champion Basketball Teams, 1981, 83-87, 89. Named Physician of Yr., Nat. Rep. Com. Physician Adv. Bd., 2003. Fellow Am. Acad. Med. Preventics; mem. S.W. Acad. Preventive Medicine (pres. 1980—), Am. Osteo. Assn. Methodist. Avocation: athletics. Office: Doctors Clinic 4714 S Western St Amarillo TX 79109-5950 Office Phone: 806-355-8263.

**PARKER, GERALD WILLIAM,** internist, health facility administrator, retired military officer; b. Susquehanna, Pa., Oct. 22, 1929; m. Susan Emerson, May 4, 1985. BS, Union Coll., Schenectady, 1951; MD, N.Y. Med. Coll., 1955. Diplomate Nat. Bd. Med. Examiners, Am. Bd. Internal Medicine; lic. physician, N.Y., Tex., D.C. Intern Ellis Hosp., Schenectady, 1955-56; resident internal medicine Wilford Hall, USAF Med. Ctr., San Antonio 1958-61; resident in gastroenterology Water Reed Army Med. Ctr., Washington, 1965-66; commd. capt. U.S. Air Force, 1956, advanced through grades to brig. gen., 1980, retired, 1986; chair dept. medicine USAF Hosp., Clark AFB, Philippines, 1967-69; chief internal medicine Malcolm Grow USAF Med. Ctr., Andrews AFB, Wash., 1969-70, chair dept. medicine, 1970-72, Wilford Hall USAF Med. Ctr., Lackland AFB, Tex., 1972-75, dir. hosp. services, 1975-77; comdr USAF Hosp., Torrejon Air Base, Spain, 1977-78; dep. dir. med. plans and resources Office of Surgeon Gen. USAF, Washington, 1978-80, dir. med. plans and resources, 1980-81; dir. med. inspection AF Inspection and Safety Ctr., Norton AFB, Calif., 1981-83; dep. surgeon gen. for ops. AF Med. Service Ctr., Brooks AFB, Tex., 1983-85; dir. prof. affairs and quality assurance Office of Surg. Gen., USAF, Washington, 1985-86; dep. dir., chief profl. services King Health Ctr., U.S. Soldiers and Airmens Home, Washington, 1986-97, ret., 1997. Clin. prof. medicine U. Tex. Health Scis. Ctr., San Antonio, 1972-77; adj. prof. Health Care Scis., George Washington Univ., 1987-97; clinical prof. medicine Uniformed Svcs. Univ. of Health Scis., 1988-97. Trustee, Hampshire Country Sch., 2000—; mem. Rindge (N.H.) Planning Bd., 2000—, Rindge Conservation Commn., 2000—04, Rindge Hist. Soc., 2000—; Rindge health officer, 2001—. Decorated Air Force D.S.M. with oak leaf cluster, Legion of Merit with oak leaf cluster, Bronze Star, Air Medal with oak leaf cluster, ACP Laureate award, 1996, Air Force Civilian Outstanding Svc. medal. Fellow ACP; mem. Soc. AF Physicians, Alpha Omega Alpha. Personal E-mail: gengwparker@aol.com.

**PARKER, GORDON ARTHUR,** chemistry professor; b. Monroe, Mich., July 6, 1936; s. David W. and Ruth A. (Schweizer) P.; m. Judy K. Elkins, Feb. 25, 2006. BS, U. Mich., Ann Arbor, 1958; MS, Wayne State U., Detroit, 1962, PhD, 1966. Tchr. sci. Milam (Mich.) Area Schs., 1958-61, Robichand High Sch., Woodhaven, Mich., 1962-63; asst. prof. U. Toledo, 1965-72, assoc. prof., 1972-82, prof. chemistry, 1982-86, prof. chemistry and pharmacy practice, 1986-92; lectr. U. Mich., Dearborn, 1992—. Sci. advisor local sch. dists. N.W. Ohio, 1985-92. Contbr. articles to profl. jours., chpts. to books. Mem. Am. Chem. Soc., Sigma Xi Office: U Mich-Dearborn Dept Natural Scis 4901 Evergreen Rd Dearborn MI 48128-2406 Home: 908 Wright Ln Milan MI 48160-1466 Office Phone: 313-593-5488. Business E-mail: gparker@umich.edu.

**PARKER, H. LAWRENCE,** investor, retired rancher, retired investment banker; b. Portchester, N.Y., June 16, 1926; s. Raeburn H. and Alice (Lawrence) P.; m. Eleanor Sage, Mar. 3, 1951 (div. 1967); children: Katherine, Richard, Michael, Douglas (dec.); m. Regine Hawes, Nov. 15, 1994. BA, Yale U., 1949. With Morgan Stanley & Co., N.Y.C., 1950—, prin. 1959-75, mng. dir., 1975-83, adv. dir., 1984—; pres. Morgan Stanley Can. Ltd., 1976-79, chmn., 1979-84, ret. Mem. adv. bd. on edn. and tng. Sec. Navy, 1985-87; dir. Jupiter (Fla.) Med. Ctr. Found., vice chmn., 2002—. Trustee Green Mountain Valley Sch., Waitsfield, Vt., 1981-91. Served with USMC, 1944-46. Mem. Investment Bankers Assn. Am. (bd. govs. 1966-70, pres. 1969), Nat. Assn. Securities Dealers (gov. 1981-84), Sublette County Hist. Soc. (trustee 1987-91), Blind Brook Club, Augusta (Ga.) Nat. Golf Club, Jupiter (Fla.) Island Club, Seminole Golf Club, Ekwanok Country Club. Home: One Angas Trail Hobe Sound FL 33455 Office Phone: 212-762-8865. E-mail: thepard@aol.com.

**PARKER, HARRY LEE,** retired army officer, academic administrator; b. Birmingham, Ala., Feb. 20, 1944; s. Guy Milburn and Grace (Lee) P.; m. Sheri Lynn Pogue (div. Oct. 1973); children: John Lee, Suzanne Grace, Stephen Scott; m. Melanie Louise Cox, Apr. 20, 1979; 1 child, Christopher Robert. BA, Miss. State U., 1966; MS, Johns Hopkins U., 1980; postgrad., U.S. Army Command & Staff Coll., 1982. Commd. 2d lt. U.S. Army, 1966, advanced through grades to lt. col., 1967; maintenance officer 85th Maintenance Bn., Hanau, Germany, 1967—69; commanding officer 143d Engr. Co. and A Co. 34th Engr. Bn., Long Binh, Vietnam, 1969-70; chief plans and ops. divsn. Dir. Logistics, Ft. Rucker, Ala., 1971—73; supply and maintenance officer 97th Signal Bn. NATO, Mannehim, Germany, 1973—76; asst. materiel officer 8th Maintenance Bn., Grossaheim, Germany, 1977; tng. evaluator HQ 1st US Army, Ft. Meade, Md., 1978—81; logistics coord. Cuban Task Force, Ft. Indiantown Gap, Pa., 1980; project officer Dept. Def., Project Office Mobile Electric Power, Washington, 1982—85; exec. officer 193d Support Bn., Ft. Clayton, Panama, 1986—87; chief divsn. maintenance U.S. Army South, Ft. Corozol, Panama, 1987—88; prof. mil. Sci. Army ROTC Miss. State U., Starkville, 1988—90; ops. officer 101st area support group, Guardian City, Saudia Arabia, logistics officer, 1st Corps Support Command, XVIII Airborne Corps., Damman, Saudi Arabia, 1990—91; career/coop. edn. counselor Ctrl. Fla. C.C., Ocala, 1992—95; educator Seminole County Pub. Sch. Sys., Fla., 2000—02; asst. registrar, 2004—. Elder Presbyn. Ch. Decorated Bronze Star with oak leaf cluster, Meritorious Svc. medal with two oak leaf clusters, Army Commendation medal with four oak leaf clusters.

Mem. Mil. Officers Assn. Am. (life), Am. Legion, Sigma Chi (life). Presbyterian. Avocations: woodworking, flying, scuba diving, boating, computers. Home: 895 Palmetto St Oviedo FL 32765 Office Phone: 407-823-2392. E-mail: hleepark@bellsouth.net.

**PARKER, HENRY GRIFFITH, III,** insurance executive; b. Plainfield, N.J., Oct. 27, 1926; s. Henry Griffith and Ruth Martin (Van Auken) P.; m. Audrey Lansing Turner, May 11, 1957; children: Henry Griffith, IV, Elizabeth Wright. AB, Princeton U., 1948; postgrad., U. Pa. Sch. Law. With Chubb & Son, Inc., 1949-97, v.p., 1968-70, sr. v.p., dir., 1971-92, mng. dir. 1986-92; cons. to chmn., 1992-97; v.p. Fed. Ins. Co., 1968-73, sr. v.p., 1973-91; v.p. Vigilant Ins. Co., 1966-91, mgr. internat. div., 1967-84; chmn. Parker Assocs., Madison, NJ, 1997—. Adv. bd. Firemark Global Ins. Fund II, L.P., 1997—; bd. dirs. Alliance Assurance Co. Am. NYC, Sun Ins. Office Am. Inc., NYC; mem. industry sector adv. com. on svcs. US Dept. Commerce, Washington; bd. dirs. Nat. Fgn. Trade Coun., chmn. declarations com., 1974-81, chmn. ins. com., 1976-81; chmn. internat. policy com. US C. of C., 1970-73; chmn. US del. XII-XIII-XX-XXII Hemispheric Ins. Conf., Chile, 1969, Paraguay, 1987, Panama, 1985, Buenos Aires, 1989; chmn. Internat. Ins. Adv. Coun., Washington, 1970-73, 85-90, chmn. Internat. Com. Am. Ins. Assn., 1991-93; mem. NJ Commn. on Internat. Trade, 1986—; chmn. bus. adv. com. bus. coun. UN, 1988—; mem. adv. bd. Liaison Office Peoples Ins. Co. China, 1986-94. Appeared on numerous TV and radio programs; contbr. articles to profl. jours. Chmn. bd. Overlook Hosp., Summit, NJ, 1973-80; trustee Drew U., Madison, 1974—. Lt. (j.g.) USNR, 1944-46. Recipient Internat. Ins. award US C. of C., 1981, Disting. Service award Internat. Ins. Council, 1988. Mem. Nat. Assn. Ins. Commrs. (chmn. internat. adv. com.), Am. Ins. Assn. (chmn. internat. com.), Downtown Assn. Club (NYC), Princeton Club (NYC), River Club (NYC), Devon Yacht Club, Morris County (NJ) Golf Club, Hillsboro Club (Fla.), Psi Upsilon. Republican. Episcopalian. Office: Parker Assocs 38 East Ln Madison NJ 07940-2652

**PARKER, JAMES AUBREY,** federal judge; b. Houston, Jan. 8, 1937; s. Lewis Almeron and Emily Helen (Stuessy) P.; m. Florence Fisher, Aug. 26, 1960; children: Roger Alan, Pamela Elizabeth. BA, Rice U., 1959; LLB, U. Tex., 1962. Bar: Tex. 1962, N.Mex. 1963. With Modrall, Sperling, Roehl, Harris & Sisk, Albuquerque, 1962-87; judge U.S. Dist. Ct. N.Mex., Albuquerque, 1987—2000, chief judge, 2000—03. Mem. Standing Commn. on Rules of Practice and Procedures of U.S. Cts., 1993-99, N.Mex. Commn. on Professionalism, 1986-2004; bd. vis. U. N.Mex. Law Sch., 1996-2000; bd. dirs. Fed. Jud. Ctr. Articles editor Tex. Law Rev., 1961-62. Mem. Fed. Judges Assn., Am. Judicature Soc., Am. Bd. Trial Advocates, N.Mex. Bar Assn. (Outstanding Judge award 1994), Albuquerque Bar Assn. (Outstanding Judge award 1993, 00, 500 Leading Judges in Am.), Order of Coif, Chancellors, Phi Delta Phi. Avocations: ranching, fly fishing, running, skiing. Office: US Dist Ct 421 Gold S W 6th Fl Albuquerque NM 87102-2277 Mailing: PO Box 669 Albuquerque NM 87103 Office Phone: 505-348-2220. Office Fax: 505-348-2225. Business E-mail: jparker@nmcourt.fed.us.

**PARKER, JAMES FRANCIS,** former air transportation executive, lawyer; b. San Antonio, Jan. 1, 1947; s. Raymond Francis and Libbie Olivia (Dusek) P.; m. Patricia Elaine Lorang, May 15, 1971; children: James, Jennifer. BA with hons., U. Tex., 1969, JD with hons., 1971. Bar: Tex., U.S. Dist. Ct. (ea., we., so. no. dists.) Tex., U.S. Ct. Appeals (5th and 11th cirs.), U.S. Supreme Ct. Law clk. to presiding judge U.S. Dist. Ct., Austin, Tex., 1972-76; asst. atty. gen. State of Tex., Austin, 1976-79; atty. Oppenheimer, Rosenberg, Kelleher & Wheatley, San Antonio, 1979-86; v.p., gen. counsel SW Airlines Co., Dallas, 1986—2001, vice chmn., CEO, 2001—04. Mem. ABA, Tex. Bar Assn. Democrat. Lutheran.

**PARKER, JAMES JOHN,** engineer, marketing professional; s. John J. and Marjorie (Grohmann) P.; m. Mary P. Nash, Oct. 21, 1972; children: Elizabeth Ann Parker Fahey, John James, Patricia Mary. BSEE, Marquette U., 1971; BSBA, Elmhurst Coll., 1982; MBA, U. Chgo., 1987. Student engr. Motorola Consumer Products, Franklin Park, Ill., 1968—70, engring. assoc., 1972—74; co-op engr. Warwick Electronics, Niles, 1971—72; sr. engr. R&D Quasar Electronics, Inc., Franklin Park, 1974—76; sr. project engr. Motorola Data Products, Carol Stream, 1978—79, Zenith Electronics Co., Glenview, 1979—82, mgr. market rsch., 1982—85, mgr. sect., 1985—86, mgr. program, 1988—95; mgr. displays Zenith Data Sys./Groupe Bull, Buffalo Grove, 1995—96; v.p. mktg. AVC Tech, Niles, 1996—97; mgr. product planning Telular, Inc., Vernon Hills, 1997—98; mgr. product mktg. Motorola BCS/SBNS, Schiller Park, 1998—2001; sr. cons. Pro-Team Cons., Palatine, 2001—03; dir. engring. Graphic Solutions Internat., Burr Ridge, Ill., 2003—. Faculty Wright Jr. Coll., Chgo., 1975-80. Mem. editl. bd. Electronic Products Mag., 1976-77; contbr. to conf. and forums. Adviser Jr. Achievement, Chgo., 1972-78; treas. Immaculate Conception Parish Christian Svc. Commn., 1988-91; vol. Pub. Action to Deliver Shelter, 1987-2000; alderman 5th ward Elmhurst, 1993-2005; vice-chmn. fin. com. City of Elmhurst, 1995-2003, chmn. pub. works and bldg. com. 2003-05, vice-chmn. telecom. and tech. adv. group, 1997. Mem. IEEE Midcon. (vice-chmn. pub. rels. 1979, chmn. spl. exhibits 1981, vice-chmn. spl. exhibits 1983), Hon. Order Ky. Cols., Internat. Microelectronics and Packaging Soc., Tech. Assn. Graphic Arts, Delta Mu Delta (hon.) Roman Catholic. Avocations: ham radio, flying. Home: 421 Berkley Ave Elmhurst IL 60126-3706 Office: Graphic Solutions Internat 311 Shore Dr Burr Ridge IL 60527 Business E-mail: jimparker@ameritech.net.

**PARKER, JAMES WESLEY,** former naval officer, investment company executive; b. Portsmouth, Va., July 31, 1917; s. Charles Wesley Parker and Dempsey Elizabeth Darden; m. Mary Elizabeth Mara, Oct. 12, 1946; children: Diane Marie Wright, Susan Gertrude Kennelly. BA, Elon U., 1939; MBA, Stanford U., 1951. Registered securities broker, life ins. agent, Calif.; real estate agt., Calif.; registered fin. cons.; accredited estate planner. Commd. ensign USN, 1940, advanced through grades to capt., 1959; ret., 1962; v.p., gen. mgr. so. divsn. Montgomery Bros., Inc., L.A., 1962—66; dir. comm. Master Charge, Western States Bancard Assn., 1967—70; ops. mgr. Nat. BankAmericard, 1971—73; v.p. Bank of Am., 1974—87, Bank of Calif., 1987—92, Pacific Trust Co., 1992—94, Comerica Bank, 1994—95, Kelmoore Investment Co., Palo Alto, Calif., 1996, exec. v.p., 1997—2002, cons., 2002—03. Bd. dirs. Diablo Valley Estate Planning Coun., Walnut Creek, Calif., 1986-95, Planned Giving Coun. Santa Cruz County, Calif., 1993-94, Tri-Valley Estate Planning Coun., 1989-2002, pres. 1996; mem. Santa Clara County Estate Planning Coun., 1988-2002, Estate Planning Coun. So. Alameda County, 1988-92, Santa Cruz County Estate Planning Coun., 1989-2002, San Mateo County Estate Planning Roundtable, 1989-98, Silicon Valley Planned Giving Coun., 1992-, No. Calif. Planned Giving Coun. 1997-2002, Fin. Planning Forum, 1988-, Peninsula Estate Planning Coun., San Mateo, Calif., 1980-, pres. 1996-98, Tri-Valley Estate Planning Coun. 1996; active East Bay Estate Planning Coun., Oakland, Calif., 1991-, pres. 1997-98; bass Calvarymen Gospel Quartet; big band saxaphonist, clarinetist Elon Coll and USS Kasaan Bay; violinist Norfolk Symphony Orch., 1934-35, Bethel Ch. Orch., San Jose, Calif. Mem. Fin. Planning Assn. (bd. dirs. Silicon Valley chpt. 1997-99), Nat. Assn. Estate Planners Couns., Inst. Cert. Investment Mgmt. Cons., Alameda County Bar Assn. (estate planning probate sect. 1988-93), San Mateo County Bar Assn. (estate planning probate sect. 1983-95), Santa Clara County Bar Assn. (estate planning probate sect. 1988-2002), Pi Gamma Mu, Alpha Pi Delta. Avocations: golf, photography, music. Home: 20278 Kilbride Dr Saratoga CA 95070 Office: Kelmoore Investment Co 2471 E Bayshore Rd # 501 Palo Alto CA 94303

**PARKER, JEFFREY SCOTT,** law educator; b. Alexandria, Va., Sept. 6, 1952; s. Clarence Franklin and Mary Florence (Partlow) P. B in Indsl. Engring., Ga. Inst. Tech., 1975; JD, U. Va., 1978. Bar: N.Y. 1979, U.S. Dist. Ct. (ea. and so. dists.) N.Y. 1979, U.S. Ct. Appeals (3d cir.) 1981, U.S. Ct. Appeals (2d cir.) 1984, U.S. Supreme Ct. 1984, U.S. Ct. Appeals (fed. cir.) 1985, U.S. Ct. Appeals (4th cir.) 1992, U.S. Ct. Appeals (D.C. cir.) 1997. Assoc. Sullivan & Cromwell, N.Y.C., 1978-86, Sacks Montgomery, N.Y.C. 1986-87; dep. chief counsel U.S. Sentencing Commn., Washington, 1987-88; of counsel Sacks Montgomery, N.Y.C., 1988-90; assoc. prof. law George

Mason U Sch. Law, Arlington, Va., 1990-94; prof. George Mason U. Sch. Law, Arlington, Va., 1994—; assoc. dean acad. affairs, 1994-96. Cons. counsel U.S. Sentencing Commn., Washington, 1988-89. Contbr. articles to law revs.; mem. editorial bd. Va. Law Rev., 1976-78. Mem. ABA, Assn. of Bar of City of N.Y., N.Y. State Bar Assn., Am. Law and Econs. Assn., Am. Econs. Assn., Am. Judicature Soc. Office: George Mason U Sch of Law 3401 Fairfax Dr Arlington VA 22201-4411 E-mail: jparke3@gmu.edu.

**PARKER, JENNIFER MERRI,** writer, editor, educator; b. Ft. Riley, Kans., Jan. 6, 1967; BA, Harvard U., 1989. Lic. educator Miss. Assoc. editor Urban Family Mag., Jackson, Miss., 1993—95; sr. editor Urban Family/Reconcilers Mag., Jackson, 1995—98; news editor Christian Ref. Ch. Pub., Grand Rapids, Mich., 2000—02; assoc. editor AgapePress, Tupelo, Miss., 2003—. Instr. Miss. Gov.'s Sch., Columbus, 1993, Columbus, 2005, Sylvan Learning Ctr., Tupelo, 2005—; bd. dirs. Arts pub., Chgo. Mem. staff Am. Family Assn., Tupelo, 2005—; arts pub. A Small Garlic Press, Chgo., 1995—2005. Recipient Disting. Alumnus award, West Point Sch. Dist., 1997, David McCord Book prize, Harvard U., 1992, Higher Goals in Christian Journalism award, Evang. Press Assn., 2003. Mem.: Associated Ch. Press (assoc.), Harvard Club of Miss., Mensa. Avocations: writing, teaching, photojournalism, reporting. Office: AgapePress 107 Parkgate Dr Tupelo MS 38803 Office Phone: 662-844-5036 319. E-mail: jparker@agapepress.org.

**PARKER, JOEL LOUISE,** nursing administrator; d. Hattie Louise and Joe Nmn Williams. BS in nursing, Tex. Christian U., 1975—77; MS in human resources, Golden Gate U., 1988—90; MS in nursing informatics, U. Md., 1997—99, postgrad., 1997—99. CPA; cert. nursing informatic ANCC, 2001. Dept. head, oper. rm. Naval Hosp., Jacksonville, Fla., 1999—2003; dir. ctrl. credentials quality assurance sys. Resources II Program Office, Falls Church, Va., 2003—. Clin. coord., oper. rm. Nat. Naval Med. Ctr., Bethesda, 1994—97; charge nurse pacu/gen. surgery Naval Hosp., Okinawa, Japan, 1991—94; charge nurse ent Naval Hosp. Camp Lejeune, 1988—91; relief charge nurse sicu Veterans Adminstrn. Hosp., Dallas, 1983—87; oper. rm. staff nurse St. Joseph's Hosp., Fort Worth, 1987—88. Pres. ushers bd. First Bapt. Ch. Of Mandarin, Jacksonville, 2000—02. Comdr. USN, 2003—05. Decorated Navy/Marine Corps Achievement medal, Naval Officers Disting. Svc. award, Navy and Marine Corps Overseas Svc. ribbon, Global War on Terrorism Expeditionary medal, Navy Fleet Marine Force ribbon, Joint Meritorious Unit award, Navy Unit Commendation, Meritorious Unit Commendation, Nat. Def. Svc. medal. Mem.: Nat. Naval Officers Assn. (life; pres. 1995—97, Disting. Svc. award 1996), Sigma Theta Tau. Democrat. Bapt. Personal E-mail: texjop@yahoo.com.

**PARKER, JOHN FRANCIS,** retired lawyer; b. L.A., Aug. 17, 1928; s. Ignatius Francis and Helen Mary P.; m. Mary Ann Kirkpatrick, Dec. 26, 1950; children: Kathleen Ann, John Patrick. BA cum laude, Loyola U., L.A., 1950; JD, UCLA, 1953; LLD, Southwestern U., 1975. Bar: Calif. 1953, U.S. Dist. Ct. (so. dist.) Calif. 1953, U.S. Ct. Mil. Appeals 1954, U.S. Supreme Ct. 1965, U.S. Ct. Appeals (9th cir.) 1982. Atty. Title Ins. & Trust Co., L.A., 1956-57, State Compensation Ins. Fund, L.A., 1957-58; assoc. Herlihy & Herlihy, L.A., San Bernardino, 1958-63; pvt. practice San Bernardino, Pomona, Calif., 1962-63; ptnr. Parker & Dally, San Bernardino, Pomona, Calif., 1964-77; pres. Parker & Dally PC, San Bernardino, Pomona, Calif., 1977-94; ret., 1994. Adj. prof. law Southwestern U., L.A., 1956-64, pres., chmn. bd. trustees, 1969-75, trustee, exec. com., 1956-97, trustee emeritus, 1997—; workers compensation judge, San Bernardino, 1994-97. 1st lt. JAG, U.S. Army, 1953-56. Mem. ABA, Calif. Bar Assn. Republican. Roman Catholic.

**PARKER, JOHN VICTOR,** judge; b. Baton Rouge, Oct. 14, 1928; m. Mary Elizabeth Fridge, Sept. 3, 1949; children: John Michael, Robert Fridge, Linda Anne. BA, La. State U., 1949, JD, 1952. Bar: La. 1952. Atty. Parker & Parker, Baton Rouge, 1954-66; asst. parish atty. City of Baton Rouge, Parish of East Baton Rouge, 1956-66; atty. Sanders, Downing, Kean & Cazedessus, Baton Rouge, 1966-79; chief judge U.S. Dist. Ct. Middle Dist. La., Baton Rouge, 1979—. Vis. lectr. law La. State U. Law Sch. With JAG U.S. Army, 1952—54. Mem.: ABA, Baton Rouge Bar Assn. (past pres.), La. State Bar Assn. (past mem. bd. govs.), Am. Arbitration Assn., Am. Judicature Soc., Baton Rouge Country Club, Kiwanis (past pres.), Masons (32 degree), Order of Coif, Phi Delta Phi. Democrat. Office: Russell B Long Fed Bldg and Courthouse 777 Florida St Ste 355 Baton Rouge LA 70801-1717

**PARKER, JOSEPH CORBIN, JR.,** pathologist, educator, department chairman; b. Richmond, Va., Aug. 1, 1937; s. Joseph Corbin and Alice Cabell (Horsley) P.; m. Patricia Hugh Singleton, June 24, 1961; children: John Randolph, Nancy Jordan. BA, Va. Mil. Inst., 1958; MD, Med. Coll. Va., 1962; MS in Pathology, U. Minn., 1968. Fellow in pathology Mayo Clinic, Rochester, Minn., 1963-68; fellow in neuropathology Duke U., Durham, NC, 1968—69, asst. prof., 1969-70, Harvard U., Boston, 1970-71; assoc. prof. U. Ky., Lexington, 1971-75; prof. U. Miami, Fla., 1975-81; dir. neuroscience lab. U. Tenn., Knoxville, 1981—86, assoc. dean, prof., 1981—83, prof. pathology and med. biology; prof., chmn. dept. pathology U. Mo., Kansas City, 1986—92, U. Louisville Sch. Medicine, 1992—2002, chair, prof., 2002—. Bd. dirs. Truman Med. Ctr., Kansas City, Mo., Hosp. Hill Health Svc., Kansas City; cons. Ky. Stroke Assn., Stroke Coun. Author 4 chpts. in books; contbr. more than 170 articles to profl. jours. Bd. dirs. Multiple Sclerosis Soc., Knoxville, Tenn., 1985, Alzheimers Assn., Kansas City, 1988-91. With Med. Corp, USAR, 1958-67. Recipient 1st Jackson -Hope medal Va. Mil. Inst., 1958; Caldwell award Alzheimers Assn., 1986. Fellow Am. Assns. Neuropathology, Am. Soc. Clin. Pathology, Coll. Am. Pathology, Assn. Clin. Scientists (pres. 2000); mem. So. Med. Assn., Am. Acad. Neurology, Am. Assn. Neurol. Surgeons, Univ. Pathologists (pres. 1993-01). Republican. Unitarian Universalist. Achievements include discovery of autosomal recessive neonatal adrenal leuko-distrophy, and types of cerebral mycoses at autopsy. Home: 4606 Wolf Creek Pky Louisville KY 40241 5500 Office: U Louisville Sch Medicine Dept Pathology Louisville KY 40292-0001 Office Phone: 502-852-6515. Business E-mail: jcpark01@gwise.louisville.edu.

**PARKER, JOSEPH MAYON,** retired publishing executive; b. Washington, NC, Oct. 11, 1931; s. James Mayon and Mildred (Poe) Parker; m. Lauretta Owen Dyer, Mar. 23, 1957; children: Katherine Suzanne, Joseph Wilbur. Student, Davidson Coll., 1949-51; BA, U. N.C., 1953, MPA, 1992; postgrad., Carnegie Inst. Tech., 1955-56. From mgr. print divsn. to pres. Parker Bros., Inc., Ahoskie, NC, 1956—77, pres., CEO, 1977—2001; ret., 2001. Editor, columnist: 5 cmty. newspapers; panelist (TV series) NC This Week, 1986—89. Treas. Chowan Graphic Arts Found., Murfreesboro, NC, 1971—90, pres., 1990—92; mem. Ind. Devel. Commn., 1974—86; dir. Gov.'s Hwy. Safety Program, 1993—2001; vice chmn. N.C. Goals and Policy Bd., Raleigh, 1977—84; pres. Com. of 100, Winton, NC, 1984—87; chmn. Northeastern N.C. Tomorrow, Elizabeth City, 1981—84, sec., 1984—90; del. Dem. Nat. Conv., N.Y.C., 1980, platform com., 1988; dist. chmn. N.C. Dem. Ctrl. Com., 1980—82, 2005—; bd. dirs. Wake Dem. Men, 2004—; exec. com. State Dem., 2005—; pres. NC Meth. Bd. Pub., 2004—06; trustee Pitt County Meml. Hosp., 1980—88. With U.S. Army, 1953—54, col. USAR, 1954—88. Mem.: Roanoke Island Hist. Assn. (vice-chmn. 1987—89), Nat. Newspaper Assn. (state chmn. 1976—83), NC Press Assn., East NC Press Assn. (past pres.), Soc. Profl. Journalists, Ea. NC C. of C. (past chmn.), NC Order of Long Leaf Pine, Rotary. Democrat. Methodist. Avocations: golf, reading. Home: 4500 Connell Dr Raleigh NC 27612-5600 E-mail: jpark4173@aol.com.

**PARKER, KEVIN JAMES,** electrical engineer, educator; BS in Engring. Sci. summa cum laude, SUNY, Buffalo, 1976; MSEE, MIT, 1978, PhD, 1981. Rsch. assoc. lab. for med. ultrasound MIT, Cambridge, 1977-81; asst. prof. dept. elec. engring. U. Rochester, NY, 1981-85, assoc. prof., 1985-91, assoc. prof. dept. radiology, 1989-91, prof., 1992—, chair, 1992-98, dean sch. engring. & applied scis., 1998—, William F. May Prof. Engring., 2005—. Com. mem. Internat. Symposium Ultrasound Imaging, 1989—; dir. Rochester Ctr. Biomedical Ultrasound, 1990—. Mem. editl. bd. Ultra. Med. Biology, 1989—; contbr. articles to profl. jours. Named IBM Supercomputing Contest finalist, 1989; recipient Ultrasound Medicine and Biology prize, World Fed.,

1991, Outstanding Innovation award, Eastman Kodak Co., 1991; fellow, NIH, 1979; Lilly Tchg. fellow, 1982. Fellow: IEEE, Am. Inst. Ultrasound Medicine (ethics com. 1987—90, stds. com. 1990—93, bd. govs. 1996—99, Joseph P. Holmes Pioneer award 1999); mem.: Acoustical Soc. Achievements include patents in field of 13 patents, liscened by several companies in field of engring. Office: Univ of Rochester Sch Engring & Applied Scis Lattimore Bldg Rm 309 Rochester NY 14627-0076

**PARKER, KEVIN T.,** computer software company executive; BS in Acctg., Clarkson U. With O'Neil Data Sys., Toshiba Am. Info. Sys., CalComp, Price Waterhouse; contr. sys. product divsn. Std. Microsystems; sr. v.p. fin. and adminstrn. Fujitsu Computer Products Am., 1996—99; sr. v.p., CFO Aspect Comm. Corp., 1999—2000, PeopleSoft, Inc., Pleasanton, Calif., 2000—02, exec. v.p. fin. & adminstrn., CFO, 2002—04, co-pres., 2004; CEO Deltek Systems Inc., Herndon, Va., 2005—. Office: Deltek Systems Inc 13880 Dulles Corner Ln Herndon VA 20171 Office Phone: 703-734-8606. Office Fax: 703-734-1146.

**PARKER, LETITIA,** secondary school educator; b. Waukegan, Ill., Jan. 12, 1947; d. Robert Edwin and Lettie M. Parker. AA, Gulf Park Coll., Long Beach, Miss., 1970; BS, Fla. State U., 1972, MS, 1975. Tchr. St. John Elem. Sch., Quincy, Fla., 1972—75, LaFayette Art Ctr., Tallahassee, 1975—76, Henry County Sch., Collinsville, Va., 1976—79, Milton (Wis.) HS, 1979—. Regional chair WAEA Visual Art Classic Competition U. Wis., Whitewater, Wis., 1992—2002. Bd. dirs. Hunziker Endowment Bd., 2000—04. Mem.: AAUW, Wis. Art Edn. Assn. (bd. dirs. 1979—2005, Pres. award for svc. 1990, 2002), Nat. Art Edn. Assn. Christian Scientist. Avocations: travel, theater. Office: Milton High Sch 114 W High St Milton WI 53563 E-mail: parkerl@mail.milton.k12.wi.us.

**PARKER, LYNDA CHRISTINE RYLANDER,** secondary school educator; b. Bremerton, Wash., Apr. 21, 1949; d. Richard Algot and Marian Ethelyn (Peterson) Rylander; m. Joseph Hiram Parker, Feb. 7, 1981; 1 child, Joseph Hiram IV. BA in English, Sociology, Pacific Luth. U., 1971, MA in Ednl. Administrn., 1981, prin.'s credential, 1982, postgrad. Tchr. lang. arts Cen. Kitsap Schs., Silverdale, Wash., 1971-74; tchr. English gifted Okanagan Schs., Kelowna, B.C., Can., 1974-78; tchr. lang. arts gifted Federal Way (Wash.) Schs., 1978-86; tchr. lang. arts, remedial reading, humanities gifted Bethel Sch. Dist., Spanaway, Wash., 1986—. Counselor Okanagan Sch. Dist., Kelowna, 1974-78; advisor Ski Club, Cheerleaders, Svc. Club, Pep Club, Kitsap Schs., Silverdale, 1971-74, Cheerleaders, Pep Club, Svc. Club, Ski Club, annual, newspaper, class advisor, Okanagan Sch. Dist., Kelowna, 1974-78, newspaper, Cheerleaders, Bethel Schs., Spanaway, 1986—; multimedia, at-risk program, gifted program, 1996; presenter of workshops for parents, tchrs., adminstrs., 1988—. Named Christa McAuliffe Outstanding Tchr. of Yr. State of Wash., 1988, Walmart Tchr. of Yr., 2004. Mem. NEA, ASCD, NAFE, Nat. Assn. Secondary Sch. Prins., Wash. Edn. Assn., Wash. Assn. Secondary Sch. Prins., Bethel Educators Assn. Republican. Lutheran. Avocations: piano, skiing, body building. Home: 1721 169th Street Ct S Spanaway WA 98387-9141 Personal E-mail: stefanlay@aol.com.

**PARKER, LYNDA MICHELE,** psychiatrist; b. Sept. 28, 1947; d. Albert Francis and Dorothy Thomasina (Herriott) P. BA, C. W. Post Coll., 1968; MA, NYU, 1970; MD, Cornell U., 1974; postgrad., N.Y. Psychoanalytic Inst., 1977-82. Diplomate Am. Coll. Forensic Examiners. Intern N.Y. Hosp., N.Y.C., 1975; resident in psychiatry Payne Whitney Clinic, N.Y.C., 1975-78; psychiatrist-in-charge day program Cabrini Med. Ctr., N.Y.C., 1979-96; from instr. psychiatry to asst. prof. Cornell U. Med. Coll., 1979-96; instr. psychiatry N.Y. Med. Coll., 1978-96; assoc. prof., regional chair dept. psychiatry Tex. Tech. U. Health Scis. Ctr., Amarillo, 1996-99, No. region dir. correctional mental health scis., 1999—2002, clin. dir. PAMIO, 1999—2002; pvt. practice, 2002—. Assoc. prof. pharmacy practice in psychiatry Tex. Tech U. Sch. Pharmacy, 1996-99; psychiat. cons. Bldg. Service 32BJ Health Fund, 1983-89, Inwood House, N.Y.C., 1983-86, Time-Life Inc., 1986-96, Ind. Med. Examiners, 1986-96, Epilepsy Inst., 1986-87, asst. med. dir., 1987-88, med. dir., 1988; int. med. examiner Rep. Health Care Rev. Sys. Mem. adv. bd. St. Bartholomew Community Presch., N.Y.C., 1990-96. Martin Luther King Jr. scholar, NYU, 1968—70. Mem.: AAUW, Tex. Med. Assn., Tex. Soc. for Psychiat. Physicians, Am. Womens Med. Assn., Am. Psychiat. Assn. Episcopalian. Office: 1616 S Kentucky Ste C-200 Amarillo TX 79102 Office Phone: 806-457-9200. Personal E-mail: LyParker@aol.com.

**PARKER, MARILLA J.,** school psychologist; b. Durant, Okla., Feb. 2, 1955; d. Charles B. Ladd and C. Joyce (Grimes) Ladd; m. Ricky E. Parker, July 28, 1979; children: Stuart E., Stephanie J. BA, in Edn., Southeastern Okla. State U., 1981, MEd in Counseling, 2000; Cert. in Sch. Psychol. Svcs., East Ctrl. U., Ada, OK, 2003. Lic. Psychologist Okla. State Bd. of Edn., 2003, School Counselor Okla. State Bd. of Edn., 2000, cert. tchr. music Okla. State Bd. of Edn., 1981. Vocal music dir. Atoka Pub. Schs., Atoka, Okla., 1981—84, Caddo Pub. Schs., Caddo, Okla., 1988—91, Rock Creek Pub. Schs., Bokchito, Okla., 1991—98; sch. counselor Caney Pub. Schs., Caney, Okla., 2000—. Co-chair SE All-District Honor Choir, Durant, Okla.; adv. coun. Kiamichi Tech. Ctr., Atoka, Okla., 2001—. Mem.: Okla. Music Educators Assn. (coord. region G 1997—98), Music Educators Nat. Conf., Okla. Sch. Psychologists Assn., Nat. Assn. Sch. Psychologists, Psi Chi. Office Phone: 580-889-6608.

**PARKER, MARION HAWKINS,** retired librarian; b. Lawrenceville, Va., June 6, 1912; d. John Lee and Alice Louise (Pearson) Hawkins; m. Ammie Parker, Jr., Dec. 6, 1959; children: Anthony, Johnnye, Kenneth. Student, Hampton Inst., 1958-59; AA cum laude, Orange County C.C., 1971; BS in Elem. Edn., SUNY, New Paltz, 1974; MLS, LI U., 1976. Cert. elem. tchr., pub. libr., sch. libr. media specialist NY. Clk., head children's dept. libr. Newburgh Free Libr., NY, 1964-86; libr. media specialist West Sr. Sch., Primary Sch., 1986-87, Vails Gate High Tech Magnet Sch., 1987—2000; ret., 2000. Lectr. Supreme Ct. Heroines Jericho. Author (with Stella Denton): 1776: A Bicentennial Bibliography, 1976. Bd. dirs. United Fund Meals on Wheels, fundraising chmn.; chmn. bd. dirs. Head Start East Orange County; past chmn. Bd. Christian Edn., Ebenezer Bapt. Ch. Mem.: NY Libr. Assn., Newburgh Area Zonta Club (past pres., Supreme Grand Ct. Heroines Jericho supreme lectr.), Rose Seven Seals (past state dep.), Royal and Exalted Order Amaranth (past supreme grand assoc. matron, past state dep.), Order Ea. Star (past grand matron, past 1st v.p. supreme coun. grand chpt., Star of Hope). Democrat. Home: 414 Bingham Rd Marlboro NY 12542-5921 E-mail: mott1@juno.com.

**PARKER, MARK G.,** retail executive; BS, Pa. State Univ., 1977. With Nike Inc., 1979—, designer, develop. mgr. Exeter, NH, 1979—80, mgr., advanced product design, 1980—81, dir. design concepts & engring. Beaverton, Oreg., 1981—82, dir. footwear design, 1982—83, mgr. footwear mktg., 1983—85, head, spl. design project teams, 1985—87, div. v.p. footwear rsch., design, develop., 1987—88, corp. v.p. rsch. design & develop., 1988—93, v.p. consumer prod. mktg., 1993—98, v.p., gen. mgr. global footwear, 1998—2001, pres. Nike Brand, 2001—06, pres., CEO, 2006—. Avocations: running, rock climbing, mountain biking, sailing, kayaking, drawing, painting, collecting art. Office: Nike Inc One Bowerman Dr Beaverton OR 97005-6453*

**PARKER, MARSHA MARIE,** dean, actress; b. St. Charles, Mo., Aug. 13, 1949; d. Anthony Gregory and Stella Julia Hollander; m. Ronald E. Parker, Oct. 20, 1979. BA, Lindenwood U., St. Charles, 1971; MFA, Lindenwood U., 1987. Dir. vol. svcs. St. Louis State Sch. and Hosp., 1971—73; dep. juvenile officer 11th Jud. Cir., St. Charles, 1973—76; dir. pers. St. Charles City-County Libr., 1976—87; dir. evening grad. admissions Lindenwood U., St. Charles, 1987—90, dir. alumni svcs., 1990—93, dean fine and performing arts, 1993—. Dir., prodr., actress various plays. Author: (plays) A Christmas

Carol - adaptation, 1993. Mem. Higher Edn. Coun.-Theatre, St. Louis, 2004—; adv. bd. The Foundry, St. Charles, 2004—05. Named Outstanding Tchr., Emerson Elec., St. Louis, 1996. Democrat. Roman Catholic. Office: Lindenwood University 209 S Kingshighway Saint Charles MO 63301

**PARKER, MARY LOU,** lawyer; b. Brockton, Mass., Nov. 16, 1945; BA, Immaculata Coll., Pa., 1967; JD cum laude, Seton Hall U. Sch. of Law, South Orange, N.J., 1975; LLM in Taxation, NYU, 1989. Bar: N.J. 1975, Fla. 1983. Law clk. to Hon. Worrall F. Mountain Supreme Ct. N.J., 1975-76; ptnr. Pitney Hardin LLP, Morristown, NJ, 1982—. Notes editor Seton Hall Law Review, 1974-75; author, Increased Cost of Dying in New Jersey, New Jersey Lawyer, 2002, Estate Administration Checklist, NJSBA Real Property, Probate and Trust Law Section Newsletter, 2003. Named NJ Super Lawyer for trusts and estates, 2005, Best Lawyer in Am. for 2006. Fellow Am. Coll. Trust and Estate Counsel, Am. Bar Found.; mem. ABA, N.J. State Bar Assn. (bd. consultors real property probate and trust law sect. 1986—, chmn., real property, probate and trust law section 1991-92), Fla. Bar Assn., N.J. State Bar Found. (trustee, 1993, sec., 1994, pres. 1995-96), Northwestern N.J. Estate Planning Coun. (pres. 1982-83), Morris County Bar Assn.(named Profl. Lawyer of Yr., 2005) Office: Pitney Hardin LLP PO Box 1945 Park Ave at Morris County Morristown NJ 07962-1945 Office Phone: 973-966-8061. Business E-mail: mparker@pitneyhardin.com.

**PARKER, MARY-LOUISE,** actress; b. Ft. Jackson, S.C., Aug. 2, 1964; 1 child, William Atticus. Attended, Bard Coll. Actress: (theatre) Hay Fever, 1987, The Misci., 1988, The Art of Success, 1989, The Importance of Being Earnest, 1989, Prelude to a Kiss, Broadway, 1990-91 (Theatre World award, Clarence Derwent Award, Tony nomination, 1990), Babylon Gardens, 1991, How I Learned to Drive, 1997 (Lucille Lortel Award for outstanding actress, OBIE Award, 1997), Proof, Broadway (Tony award for best actress in a play, 2001); (films) Signs of Life, 1989, Longtime Companion, 1990, Grand Canyon, 1991, Fried Green Tomatoes, 1991, Mr. Wonderful, 1993, Naked in New York, 1994, The Client, 1994, Bullets Over Broadway, 1994, Boys on the Side, 1995, A Portrait of a Lady, 1996, Reckless, 1995, Murder in Mind, 1997, The Maker, 1997, Let the Devil Wear Black, 1998, Goodbye, Lover, 1998, Five Senses, 1999, Pipe Dream, 2002, Red Dragon, 2002, The Best Thief in the World, 2004, Saved!, 2004, Romance & Cigarettes, 2005, others; (TV movies) Too Young the Hero, 1988, A Place for Annie, 1994, Sugartime, 1995, Legalese, 1998, Saint Maybe, 1998, The Simple Life of Noah Dearborn, 1999, Cupid & Cate, 2000, Master Spy: The Robert Hanssen Story, 2002, Miracle Run, 2004, Vinegar Hill, 2005; (TV miniseries) Angels in America, 2003 (Golden Globe for best supporting actress 2004, Emmy award, Outstanding Supporting Actress in a Miniseries or a Movie, 2004); (TV series) Ryan's Hope, 1975, West Wing, 2001-05,(Emmy nomination, 2002), Weeds, 2005- (Best Performance by an Actress in a TV Series-Musical or Comedy, Hollywood Fgn. Press Assn. (Golden Globe award), 2006. Office: William Morris Agy care Scott Henderson 151 S El Camino Dr Beverly Hills CA 90212-2775*

**PARKER, MEL,** editor; b. N.Y.C., Feb. 11, 1949; s. David Parker and Mollie (Kantorowicz) Lederman; m. Diane Nancy Goldberg, June 27, 1971; children: Emily, David. AB, Rutgers U., 1971; AM in English, NYU, 1973. Editl. rschr. Esquire Mag., N.Y.C., 1973; grad. asst. NYU Dept. English, 1974-77; adj. lectr. CUNY, 1977-78; editor Leisure Books, N.Y.C., 1978-81; sr. editor Playboy Paperbacks, N.Y.C., 1981-82, Berkley Pub. Group, N.Y.C., 1982-85, exec. editor, 1985-86, editor-in-chief, 1986-87; v.p. editor-in-chief Warner Paperbacks, 1987-90, pub., 1990-96; sr. v.p. Warner Books, N.Y.C., 1998-99, sr. v.p., editor-in-chief Book-of-the-Month Club, 1999-2000; sr. v.p., editl. dir. Bookspan, 2000—03; pres. Mel Parker Books, LLC, 2004—. Co-chair exec. pub. com. United Jewish Appeal Fedn.; mem. faculty Stanford Pub. Course, 1997-98. Mem. Jerusalem Book Fair Com., 1997-99. Mem. Assn. Am. Publs. (chmn. trade exec. com. 1997-99), Book Table, Pub. Lunch Club (sec.-treas. 2000-01, v.p. 2001-02, pres. 2002-03). Office Phone: 718-788-0080. Business E-Mail: mel@melparkerbooks.com.

**PARKER, MELISSA BERNICE,** advertising executive; d. Marzine Parker, Sr. and Moretha Parker. BS in Agrl. Econs., U. Calif., Davis, 1995; MBA, Calif. State U., Hayward, 2000. Cert. notary pub. Calif.; lic. Realtor Calif., property mgmt. Calif. Apt. Assn. Property mgr. M & M Parker & Assocs., Oakland, 1991—; banking officer Citibank F.S.B., San Francisco, 1995—96; sr. claims rep. Farmers Ins. Exch., Pleasanton, Calif., 1996—2000, Richmond, Calif., 1996—2000; applied materials Human Resources Exec. Program, Santa Clara, Calif., 2000; advt. exec. SBC Calif., Oakland, 2001—04, Valley Yellow Pages, Hayward, Calif., 2004—05, Hilltop Learning Corp., 2004—, Jack London Square Realty, Inc., 2005—. Photo journal dvd, Celebrations Article Oakland Tribune Marzine & Moretha Parker Sr. Co-chair Taylor Meml. United Meth. Ch. Ann. Woman's Day; with Marilyn Hickey Ministries; mem. U. Calif.-Davis. Mem.: NAFE, So. Poverty Law Ctr., Pres.'s Cir., Alfred Lepure Soc., Delta Sigma Theta (life). Democrat. United Methodist. Home: 2625 Alcatraz Ave Ste 350 Berkeley CA 94705 Office: 311 Oak St Ste 116 Oakland CA 94607 Office Phone: 510-459-9062. Personal E-mail: parkermel@aol.com. Business E-Mail: melissa.parker@jacklondonrealty.com.

**PARKER, MICHAEL D.,** chemicals executive; BSChemE, U. Manchester (Eng.); MBA, Manchester Bus. Sch. With organics R & D Dow Internat., Freeport, Tex., 1968, prodn. engr., field sales position Birmingham, Eng., 1972-75, dist. sales mgr., 1975-77; product mktg. mgr. Epoxy resins Dow Europe, 1977, dir. mktg. inorganic chems., dir. mktg. organic chems., comml. dir. functional products dept., 1983-84; gen. mgr. splty chems dept. Dow U.S.A., Midland, Mich., 1984-87, group v.p. chems. and hydrocarbons, 1993-95; comml. v.p. Dow Pacific, Hong Kong, 1987-88, pres., 1988-93; pres. bus. v.p. chems. Dow N.Am., Midland, 1995—96; exec. v.p. Dow Chem. Co., Midland, 1996—2000, pres., CEO, 2000—, also bd. dirs. Bd. dirs. Dow Corning Corp. Bd. dirs. Nat. Legal Ctr. Pub. Interest. Mem. Nat. Assn. Mfrs. (bd. dirs.), Am. Plastics Coun. (bd. dirs.), Am. Chemistry Coun.

**PARKER, NANCY KNOWLES (MRS. CORTLANDT PARKER),** publishing executive; b. Buffalo, Aug. 30, 1929; d. Ward Emerson and Barbara Louise (Bull) Knowles; m. Cortlandt Parker, Sept. 8, 1951; children: Elizabeth, Cortlandt, Stephen, Nancy Gray. Student, Chevy Chase Jr. Coll., 1949. Copy girl Washington Evening Star, 1947-49; reporter Newark Evening News, 1949-51; asst. pub. rels. dir. Newark Cmty. Chest, 1951-52; writer Suburban Life mag., Summit, NJ, 1952-55; co-founder, assoc. editor, then editor Observer Tribune, Mendham, NJ, 1955-59; cmty. living editor Recorder Pub. Co., Bernardsville, NJ, 1959-84, v.p., 1960—2002. pub. emeritus, 2002—; editor, pub. New Eng., Finger Lakes, L.I. and Va. Wine Gazettes, 1988—. Pres. Greenvale Vineyards, Portsmouth, R.I. Past trustee Somerset Hills Cmty. Chest, North Jersey Tng. Sch., Totowa, Morris-Somerset chpt. UN Assn., Bonnie Brae Ednl. Ctr., Millington, NJ. Vis. Homemaker Svc. Somerset County; trustee, bd. dirs. Camp Brett-Endeavor, Clinton, NJ, Morristown (NJ) Meml. Hosp.; mem. Glen Manor House Com., Portsmouth, RI; sec. New Eng. Wine Coun Mem. LWV (chair voters svc. Morris County chpt. 1954-55), Bus. and Profl. Women, Nat. Soc. Arts and Letters, Southeastern New Eng. Grape Growers Assn., Jr. League, Pen and Brush NYC, Friends of Whitehall, Colonial Dames in Am. (past bd. dirs. RI chpt.), Newport (RI) Garden Club (bd. dirs., past pres.), English Speaking Union (bd. dirs. Newport br. 1990-2000), NJ Hist. Soc. (adv. coun. Newark chpt.) Home: 582 Wapping Rd Portsmouth RI 02871-5306 Office: Greenvale Farm & Vineyard 582 Wapping Rd Portsmouth RI 02871-5306 also: 17 Morristown Rd Bernardsville NJ 07924-2312

**PARKER, OLIVIA,** photographer; b. Boston, June 10, 1941; d. Harvey Perley and Barbara Ellen (Churchill) Hood; m. John Otis Parker, Apr. 4, 1964; children: John Otis, Helen Elizabeth. BA, Wellesley Coll., 1963. Tchr. photog. workshops, 1975—. Photographer (monographs) Signs of Life, 1978, Under the Looking Glass, 1983, Weighing the Planets, 1987; portfolios of black and white photographs Ephemera, 1977, Lost Objects, 1980; one-woman shows include Vision Gallery, Boston, 1976, 1977, 1979, 1982, 1983, 1986, 1987, Friends of Photography, Carmel, Calif., 1979, 1981,

Marcuse Pfeifer, N.Y.C., 1980, 1983, George Eastman House, Rochester, N.Y., 1981, Art Inst. Chgo., 1982, Photo Gallery Internat. Tokyo, 1983, 1984, 1987, Fotografie Forum Gallery, Frankfurt, Germany, 1985, Lieberman and Saul, N.Y.C., 1988, Mus. Photgraphic Arts, San Diego, 1988, Photographers' Gallery, London, 1990, Brent Sikkema, N.Y.C., 1990, 1991, Parco, Tokyo, 1991, ICAC/Weston, 1992, Vision, San Francisco, 1993, Robert Klein, Boston, 1993, 1996, 1999, 2005, Wooster Gardens, N.Y.C., 1996, (with Jerry Uelsmann) Isabella Stewart Gardner Mus., Boston, 1997, Huntington (W.Va.) Mus. of Art, 2000, Lancaster (Pa.) Mus. of Art, 2000, Toledo (Ohio) Art Mus., 2002, Visual Arts Ctr. Coll. of Santa Fe, 2003, Edelman Gallery, Chgo., 2004, exhibited in group shows at Mus. Fine Arts, Boston, 1978, 1992, 1993, 1996, 1999, Chgo. Art Inst., 1978, Internat. Ctr. Photography, N.Y.C., 1985, 1987, Fogg Art Mus. Harvard U., 1989, Aldrich Mus. Contemporary Art, 2004, Represented in permanent collections Mus. Modern Art, N.Y.C., Art Inst. Chgo., Boston Mus. Fine Arts, Victoria and Albert Mus., London, TV documentary, Africans in America, 1998. Trustee Art Inst. Boston, 1992—; bd. dirs. MacDowell Colony, 1988—. Recipient Wellesley College Alumnae Achievement award, 1996; Artists Found. fellow, 1978. Mem.: Soc. for Photog. Edn., Chilton Club. Office: Robert Klein 4th Fl 38 Newbury St Fl 4 Boston MA 02116-3210 E-mail: glasslight@mac.com. *I am interested in the way people think about the unknown. New ideas form, the old are shattered, and sometimes old ideas pop up among the new like graffiti on a wall. All is uncertainty and change, but optimists and bingo players are on the look out for moments of perfect knowledge and perfect cards.*

**PARKER, PETER D.M.,** physicist, educator, researcher; b. N.Y.C., Dec. 14, 1936; s. Allan Ellwood and Alice Francis (Heywood) P.; m. Judith Maxfield Curren, Dec. 27, 1958; children: Stephanie, Gregory, Gretchen. BA, Amherst Coll., 1958; PhD, Calif. Tech., 1963. Physicist Brookhaven Nat. Labs., Upton, NY, 1963-66; prof. Yale U., New Haven, 1966—. Office: Yale U Physics Dept Wright Nuclear Structure 272 Whitney Ave New Haven CT 06520-8124 Office Phone: 203-432-3099. E-mail: peter.parker@yale.edu.

**PARKER, R. JOSEPH,** lawyer; b. St. Louis, June 29, 1944; s. George Joseph and Ann Rosalie Parker; m. Theresa Gaynor, Aug. 26, 1967; children: Christa Michele, Kevin Blake. AB, Georgetown U., 1966; JD, Boston Coll., 1969. Bar: Ohio 1969. Law clk. to judge U.S. Ct. Appeals (6th Cir.), Akron, Ohio, 1969-70; assoc. Taft, Stettinius & Hollister, Cin., 1970-78, ptnr. Arbitrator Am. Arbitration Assn., Cin., 1980—; faculty Nat. Inst. for Trial Advocacy, 1990—; faculty advanced trial advocacy program IRS, 1993. Editor Law Rev. Am. Survey Mass. Law, 1967-69; contbg. author: Fed. Civil Procedure Before Trial-6th Circuit. Bd. dirs. West End Health Ctr., Inc., Cin., 1972-76, Legal Aid Soc. Cin., 1982-85; chmn. bd. dirs. Vol. Lawyers for Poor Found., Cin., 1986-88; master Am. Inn of Court, 1984—. Fellow Am. Coll. Trial Lawyers; mem. Ohio State Bar Assn., Cin. Bar Assn., Cin. Country Club, Order of Coif. Democrat. Roman Catholic. Office: 425 Walnut St Ste 1800 Cincinnati OH 45202-3759 E-mail: parker18002000@yahoo.com.

**PARKER, RAYMON PHILIP,** dean; s. Harry Burnham Parker and Doris Mabel Alexander; children: Luke Harry, Jacob Randolph. BA, Plymouth State Coll., Plymouth, N.H., 1977; MA, U. of R.I., 1979. Asst. dir. for cmty. life Phillips U., Enid, Okla., 1979—83; dir. of student activities SUNY New Paltz, 1983—85; assoc. dean of the coll. Vassar Coll., Poughkeepsie, NY, 1985—. Cons. Anti-Defamation League, N.Y.C., NY, 1993—. Recipient Patsy Morley Outstanding Programmer award, Nat. Assn. for Campus Activities, 1995, Founders awards, 1996. Mem.: Nat. Assn. Campus Activities (chmn. bd. dirs. 1988—89, hon. trustee 1992—). Office: Vassar College 124 Raymond Ave Poughkeepsie NY 12604-0715 Office Phone: 845-437-5370. Office Fax: 845-437-7801. E-mail: raparker@vassar.edu.

**PARKER, RICH,** lawyer; b. St. Paul, 1948; AB summa cum laude, U. Calif. Davis, 1970; JD, U. Calif., Los Angeles, 1974. Bar: Calif. 1974, DC 1980. Clerkship with Hon. William Matthew Byrne, Jr. US Dist. Ct., Ctrl. Dist. Calif., 1974—75; former sr. dep. dir. FTC, 1998—99, former dir., Bur. Competition, 1999—2001; ptnr. O'Melveny & Myers LLP, Washington, 2001—, chair antitrust/competition. Comment editor U. Calif. Los Angeles Law Review, 1973—74; contbr. articles to profl. jours. Mem.: DC Bar, ABA (annual mtg. chair 1996—98, spring mtg. chair, antitrust sect. 2002), Phi Kappa Phi, Order of the Coif, Phi Beta Kappa. Office: O'Melveny & Myers LLP 1625 Eye St NW Washington DC 20006 Office Phone: 202-383-5380. Office Fax: 202-383-5414. Business E-Mail: rparker@omm.com.

**PARKER, RICHARD DAVIES,** law educator; b. Boston, Apr. 3, 1945. BA, Swarthmore Coll., 1967; JD, Harvard U., 1970. Bar: Mass. 1973. Law clk. to Judge J. Skelly Wright, US Ct. Appeals DC Cir., 1970-71; law clk. to Assoc. Justice Potter Stewart, US Supreme Ct., 1971-72; atty. Children's Def. Fund, Cambridge, Mass., 1973-74; asst. prof. law Harvard Law Sch., Cambridge, 1974-79, prof., 1979—98, Paul W. Williams prof. criminal justice, 1998—. Author: The People Rule: A Constitutional Populist Manifesto, 1994. Office: Harvard Law Sch 1563 Massachusetts Ave Cambridge MA 02138 Office Phone: 617-495-7925. Office Fax: 617-496-4913. Business E-Mail: parker@law.harvard.edu.

**PARKER, RICHARD WILSON,** lawyer, retired rail transportation executive; b. Cleve., June 14, 1943; s. Edgar Gael and Pauline (Wilson) P.; m. Helen Margaret Shober, Jan. 3, 1998; children from previous marriage: Brian Jeffrey, Lauren Michelle, Lisa Christine. BA in Econs. cum laude, U. Redlands, 1965; JD cum laude, Northwestern U., 1968. Bar: Ohio 1968, Va. 1974. Assoc. Arter & Hadden, Cleve., 1968—71; asst. gen. atty. Norfolk & Western Ry. Co., Cleve. and Roanoke, Va., 1971-74, asst. gen. solicitor Roanoke, 1974-78, gen. atty., 1978-84, Norfolk So. Corp., 1985-88, sr. gen. atty., 1988-93, asst. v.p. real estate, 1993-99, v.p. properties, 1999-2000, v.p. real estate, 2000—03. Mem. ABA, Va. State Bar, Norfolk-Portsmouth Bar Assn. Presbyterian. Office: 3 Commercial Pl Norfolk VA 23510-2108

**PARKER, ROBERT ALLAN RIDLEY,** federal agency administrator, astronaut; b. NYC, Dec. 14, 1936; s. Allan Elwood and Alice (Heywood) P.; m. Joan Audrey Capers, June 14, 1958 (div. 1980); children: Kimberly Ellen, Brian David Capers; m. Judith S. Woodruff, Apr. 2, 1981. AB, Amherst Coll., 1958; PhD, Calif. Inst. Tech., 1962. NSF postdoctoral fellow U. Wis., 1962-63, asst. prof., then assoc. prof. astronomy, 1963-74; astronaut NASA, Johnson Space Ctr., 1967-91; dir. policy plan Office Space Flight, NASA Hdqs., Washington, 1991, dir. space ops. utilization program, 1992-97; dir. NASA Mgmt. Office, JPL, Pasadena, Calif., 1997—. Mem. support crew Apollo XV and XVII, mission scientist Apollo XVII, program scientist Skylab program, mission specialist for Spacelab 1, 1983, ASTRO-1, 1990. Mem. Am. Astron. Soc., Phi Beta Kappa. Office: NMO 180 801 JPL 4800 Oak Grove Dr Pasadena CA 91109-8001 Business E-Mail: rparker@nmo.jpl.nasa.gov.

**PARKER, ROBERT ANDREW,** artist; b. Norfolk, Va., May 14, 1927; s. William Clay and Harriet (Cowdin) P.; m. Dorothy Lane Daniels, Nov. 20, 1948; children: Christopher, Anthony, Eric, Geoffrey, Nicholas. BAE., Sch. Art Inst. Chgo., 1952; student, Atelier 17, N.Y.C., 1952-53. Tchr. Parsons Sch. Design, N.Y.C., 1969. Lectr. Pa. State U., 1981, Bklyn. Mus., 1981, New Sch. for Social Rsch., 1982, Phila. Coll. Art, 1982, Am. U., 1984, R.I. Sch. Design, 1984, NAD, 1985, Sch. Visual Arts, 1985, Skowhegan Sch. Painting and Sculpture, 1965, Sch. of Visual Arts, 1960-70, Syracuse U., 1975, Parsons Sch. Design, N.Y.C., 1980-85, Pratt Inst. 1985. Illustrated: handcolored ltd. edits. Marianne Moore poems, 1962; one-man shows include, Roko Gallery, N.Y.C., 1954, 55, 56, 58, World House Gallery, N.Y.C., 1961, Terry Dintenfass Gallery, N.Y.C., annually 1965—, Kilkenny Arts Festival, Ireland, Bklyn. Mus., 1983, Jay Gallery, N.Y.C., Gallerit, Stockholm, 1984, Mattatuck Mus., Waterbury, Conn., 1985, Wash. U., St. Louis, 1985, Munson Gallery, Santa Fe, 1985; group exhbns. include Watercolors, Drawings and Prints, Met. Mus., 1952, Young Am. Print Makers, Mus. Modern Art, 1953, Young Am., Whitney Mus., 1957, Recent Acquisitions, Mus. Modern Art, 1957, Laon Mus., Aisne, France, 1956, New Sch. Social Research, 1965, 72, Gallery Modern Art, N.Y.C., 1965, Mus. Modern Art, 1966, Herron Mus. Art,

Indpls., 1967, Bklyn. Mus., 1968, 69, Kennedy Galleries, N.Y.C., 1974, Neuberger Mus., SUNY at Purchase, 1974, AAA Galleries, N.Y.C., 1976, 84, Inst. Contemporary Art, Boston, 1976, Ind. U. Mus., 1977, NAD, N.Y.C., 1977, 79, SUNY at Potsdam, 1977, Butler Inst. Am. Art, Ohio, 1987, Green Mountain Gallery, N.Y.C., 1979, Squibb Gallery, Princeton, 1979, Pratt Inst. Graphics Ctr., Bklyn., 1979, Ark. Fine Arts Ctr., 1982, 84, Redding (Calif.) Mus., 1984, Sylvan Cole Gallery, N.Y.C., 1985, Flinn Gallery, 2004; represented in permanent collections Mus. Modern Art, Whitney Mus., Met. Mus., Bklyn. Mus., Am. Acad. Arts and Letters, Morgan Library, Dublin Mus., Los Angeles County Mus.; included in pvt. collections Joseph Hirshhorn, Monroe Wheeler, William Lieberman, Roy Neuberger, Marianne Moore, Mrs. John D. Rockefeller III, Sir Basil Goulding, Bart., Winthrop Paul Rockefeller, King Gustaf XVI of Sweden, Queen Sylvia, Charles, Prince of Wales, Her Highness Elizabeth, the Queen Mother; artist in residence, Sch. Visual Arts, N.Y.C., 1968; drawings and paintings for film Lust for Life, 1955; illustrator, Action Jackson, 2002; illustrator for film The Days of Wilfred Owen, 1966; illustrator for poetry of Keith Douglas for film How to Kill, 1980; numerous sets, backdrops and costumes. Assoc. Nat. Acad. Served with USAAF, 1945-46. Recipient Richard and Hinda Rosenthal award Nat. Inst. Arts and Letters, 1962; grantee Tamarand Lithography Workshop, Los Angeles, 1967; John Simon Guggenheim Found. fellow, 1969-70.

**PARKER, ROBERT BROWN,** writer; b. Springfield, Mass., Sept. 17, 1932; s. Carroll Snow and Mary Pauline (Murphy) P.; m. Joan Hall, Aug. 26, 1956; children: David, Daniel. BA, Colby Coll., 1954; MA, Boston U., 1957, PhD, 1971; LittD (hon.), Northeastern U., 1987. Various bus. and advt. positions, N.Y.C. and Boston, 1956-62; lectr. Boston U., 1962-64; mem. faculty Lowell (Mass.) State Coll., 1964-66, Bridgewater State Coll., 1966-68; asst. prof. English Northeastern U., Boston, 1968-73, assoc. prof., 1973-76, prof., 1976-79. Lectr. Suffolk U., 1965-66; co-chmn. Parker-Farman Co., 1960-62. Author: (with others) The Personal Response to Literature, 1970, (with Peter L. Sandberg) Order and Diversity: The Craft of Prose, 1973, Godwulf Manuscript, 1974, God Save the Child, 1974, (with John R. Marsh) Sports Illustrated Weight Training, 1974, Mortal Stakes, 1975, Promised Land, 1976 (Edgar Allan Poe award for best novel Mystery Writers Am. 1976), The Judas Goat, 1978, (with Joan Parker) Three Weeks in Spring, 1978, Wilderness, 1979, Looking for Rachel Wallace, 1980, Early Autumn, 1981, A Savage Place, 1981, Surrogate: A Spenser Short Story, 1982, Ceremony, 1982, The Widening Gyre, 1983, Love and Glory, 1983, Valediction, 1984, The Private Eye in Hammett and Chandler, 1984, A Catskill Eagle, 1985, Parker on Writing, 1985, Taming a Seahorse, 1986, Pale Kings and Princes, 1987, Crimson Joy, 1988, Playmates, 1989, (with Raymond Chandler) Poodle Springs, 1989, Stardust, 1990, Perchance to Dream, 1990, A Year at the Races, 1990, Pastime, 1991, Double Deuce, 1992, Paper Doll, 1993, Walking Shadow, 1994, All Our Yesterdays, 1994, Spenser's Boston, 1994, Thin Air, 1995, Chance, 1996, Small Vices, 1997, Night Passage, 1997, Sudden Mischief, 1998, Trouble in Paradise, 1998, Family Honor, 1999, Hush Money, 1999, Hugger Mugger, 2000, Potshot, 2001, Gunman's Rhapsody, 2001, Widow's Walk, 2002, Shrink Rap, 2002, Melancholy Baby, 2004 (Publishers Weekly Bestseller list), Double Play, 2004, Bad Business, 2004, Stone Cold, 2004, Cold Service, 2005, Appaloosa, 2005, School Days, 2005; (novels/teleplays) Walking Shadow, 2001, Thin Air, 2000; screenwriter with Joan Parker: (TV movies) Blues for Buder, 1988, High Rise, 1988, Spenser: Ceremony, 1993, Spenser: Pale Kings and Princes, 1993, Spenser: Small vices, 1999, Poodle Springs, 1998; contbr. cons.: (TV series) Spenser: For Hire, 1985-88, A Man Called Hawk, 1989-90. Served with U.S. Army, 1954-56. Recipient Grand Master award, Edgar Mystery Writers Am., 2002. Mem. Writers Guild Am. Avocations: jogging, weightlifting. Office: care Putnam Publicity 375 Hudson St New York NY 10014

**PARKER, ROBERT CHAUNCEY HUMPHREY,** clergyman, publishing executive; b. NYC, Apr. 6, 1941; s. Robert Humphrey and Edith Louise (Corya) P. Student, U. Va., 1960—61, student, 1962—63; diploma, Inst. Psychorientology, Laredo, Tex., 1973. Ordained to ministry Ch. of Antioch-Malabar Rite, 1975. Law clk. Shearman & Sterling, NYC, 1961-62; owner Parker's Pronto-Pups Inc., NYC, 1962-64; asst. to pres. U.S. Packaging, NYC, 1964-66; asst. nat. sales mgr. Elliott Svc. Co. Inc., Mt. Vernon, NY, 1966-67; pres., cons. Lenfield Assocs. & Cons., NYC and Washington, 1967-71; founder, pres. Occult Comm. Corp., NYC, Washington, and Danbury, Conn., 1967-76; New Awareness Corp., London and Mpls., 1973-81; dir., resident min. The Healing Ctr. at St. Patricia's, Inver Grove Heights, Minn., 1975; lectr., min. Ch. of Antioch-Malabar Rite, 1975—; editor New Awareness News, 1975—2006; founder, pres. Parker/Tofte Comm., Robert Parker Assocs., Minnetonka, Minn., 1977—2005; pres., CEO Am. Energy & Alcohol Corp., Mpls., 1981-84. Cons. Boat Owners Assn. U.S., Washington, 1967-70, Durance Co., 1994-95; rschr., cons. Am. Marine Corp., Marblehead, Mass.; pres. Field Harmonics Rsch. Group Inc., 1993-97, New Awareness Spkrs. and Pub. Group, Inc., 1997-2005; cons., spkr. in field. Author: Watergate Flight 553, 1974, Reabsorption Energy, 1975, Finding Your Own Four-Leaf Clover, 1993; author Telsa Newsletter, 1979; editor New Awareness Mag., 1973-75, (newsletter) Sunbeams; editor, pub. New Awareness News and Book News, 1977—2006, New Awareness Computer News, 1995—2006, psychic/parapscychology internat. trade jours., 1971-75; designer, pub.: Henry's Hilarious One Liners, 1991, Henry's Just a Chuckle, 1992, Henry's Just a Laugh, 1992, Henry's Just a Witticism, 1992; contbr. articles to profl. jours.; featured on Dimension WCCO-TV, 1991, 93, Forbes Mag., 1996, Elizabeth Smart Recovery, Sta. WCCO-TV, 2003, Ruth Koscielak Show, Sta. KCCO-AM, 2003, Smart Predictions 100% Correct, 2003; host (cable) Astrology and Mind, Etc., 1994-96; syndicated columnist; ongoing guest WUO-AM, 2006. Bd. dirs. Toutorsky Entl. Found., Washington, 1988—91. Mem. Nat. Press Club (Washington), Internat. Telsa Soc. Inc., Knickerbocker Greys Vet. Corps (NYC), Browning Sch. Alumni Assn. (NYC), Lenox (Mass.) Sch. Alumni Assn. Avocations: reading, travel. Home and Office: Box 387 Excelsior MN 55331-0387 Office Phone: 952-936-9974. Personal E-mail: rchparker@aol.com.

**PARKER, ROBERT M., JR., (BOB PARKER),** wine critic, writer; b. Balt., July 23, 1947; m. Patricia Parker; 1 child, Maia. BA in History, U. Md., College Park; JD, U. Md., Balt., 1973. From sr. atty. to asst. gen. counsel Farm Credit Banks of Balt., 1973—84; founder, writer, pub. The Wine Advocate (formerly The Baltimore-Washington Wine Advocate), Parkton, Md., 1978—. Author Bordeaux, 1985 (Glenfiddich Award, 1986, Goldene Feder, 1993, Moët Hennessy Wine and Vine Comm. Award, 1993), 2d edit. 1991 (Internat. Assn. of Cooking Profls. Award, 1992), 3rd edit., 1998, 4th edit., 2003, Parker's Wine Buyer's Guide, 1987, 2nd edit., 1989, 3rd edit., 1993, 4th edit., 1995, 5th edit., 1999, 6th edit., 2002, The Wines of the Rhone Valley and Provence, 1987 (Tastemaker's Award, 1989, Wine Guild's Wine Book of Yr. Award, 1989), Burgundy, 1990 (Moët Hennessy Wine and Vine Comm. Award, 1993), The Wines of the Rhone Valley, 1997, The World's Greatest Wine Estates: A Modern Perspective, 2005, contbg. editor Food and Wine Mag., contbr. The Field, wine critic L'Express mag., columnist BusinessWeek, 2006—. Named Marylander of Yr., Loyola Coll., 1992, Chevalier, Ordre Nat. du Merite, 1993, Légion d'honneur, 1999, Officer, 2005, Hon. Citizen of Châteauneuf-du-Pape, 1995, Wine and Spirits Profl. of 1997, James Beard Found., 1998, Comdr., Italy's Nat. Order of Merit, 2002. Office: The Wine Advocate PO Box 311 Monkton MD 21111 Office Phone: 410-329-6477. Office Fax: 410-357-4504. E-mail: wineadvocate@erobertparker.com.*

**PARKER, SARA ANN,** librarian, consultant; b. Cassville, Mo., Feb. 19, 1939; d. Howard Franklin and Vera Irene (Thomas) P. BA, Okla. State U., 1961; M.L.S., Emporia State U., Kans., 1968. Adult svcs. librarian Springfield Pub. Libr., Mo., 1972-75, bookmobile dir. Mo., 1975-76; coord. S.W. Mo. Libr. Network, Springfield, 1976-78; libr. developer Colo. State Libr., Denver, 1978-82; state librarian Mont. State Libr., Helena, 1982-88, State Libr. Pa., Harrisburg, 1988-90; Pa. commr. librs., dep. sec. mktg. State Libr. Pa., Harrisburg, 1990-95; state libr. State of Mo., Jefferson City, 1995. Cons. and lectr. in field. Author, editor, compiler in field; contbr. articles to profl. jours. Svc., Western Coun. State Librs., Reno, 1984-88, mem. Mont. State Data Adv. Coun., 1983-88, Mont. Telecommunications Coun., 1985-88, WLN Network Coun.,

1984-87, Kellogg ICLIS Project Mgmt. Bd., 1986-88; mem. adv. com. Gates Libr. Initiative, 1998—2005; mem. OCLC Strategic Directions and Governance Study Adv. Coun., 2000-01, webjunction adv. coun., 2003—. Recipient Pres.'s award, Nature Conservancy, 1989, Friends award, Pa. Assn. Ednl. Comms. and Techs., 1989, Friend of Sch. Librs. award, Mo. Sch. Librs. Assn., 2000, Bohley Libr. Cooperation award, 2001; fellow Inst. Ednl. Leadership, 1982. Mem. ALA, Chief Officers State Libr. Agys. (pres. 1996-98), Mont. Libr. Assn. (bd. dirs. 1982-88), Mountain Plains Libr. Assn. (sec. chmn. 1980, pres. 1987-88, chair MOREnet adv. coun. 2004—). Home: PO Box 554 Jefferson City MO 65102-0554

**PARKER, SARAH ELIZABETH,** state supreme court chief justice; b. Charlotte, NC, Aug. 23, 1942; d. Augustus and Zola Elizabeth (Smith) P. AB, U. N.C., 1964, JD, 1969; LHD (hon.), Queens Coll., 1998. Bar: N.C. 1969, U.S. Dist. Ct. (mid., ea. and we. dists.) N.C. Vol. U.S. Peace Corps, Ankara, Turkey, 1964-66; pvt. practice Charlotte, 1969-84; judge N.C. Ct. Appeals, Raleigh, 1985—92; assoc. justice N.C. Supreme Ct., Raleigh, 1993—2005, chief justice, 2006—. Bd. visitors U. N.C., Chapel Hill, 1993—97; pres. Mecklenburg County Dem. Women, Charlotte, 1973; N.C. ct. commr., 1999—; bd. dirs. YWCA, Charlotte, 1982—85. Recipient Disting. Woman of N.C. award, 1997, Woman of Achievement award Nat. Fedn. Women's Clubs, 1997, Humanitarian award N.C. Assn. of Black County Officials, 2003; Named Judge of Yr., N.C. Women Attorneys Assn., 2002. Mem. ABA, Inst. Jud. Adminstrn., N.C. Bar Assn. (v.p. 1987-88), Mecklenburg County Bar (sec.-treas. 1982-84), Wake County Bar Assn., N.C. Internat. Women's Forum, Women Attys. Assn. (Gwyneth David Pub. Svc. award 1986). Episcopalian. Office: NC Supreme Ct PO Box 1841 Raleigh NC 27602-1841

**PARKER, SARAH JESSICA,** actress; b. Nelsonville, Ohio, Mar. 25, 1965; m. Matthew Broderick May, 1997; 1 child: James. Launched fragrance Lovely perfume, 2005. Actress: (theatre) The Innocents, 1976, The Sound of Music, 1977, Annie, 1978, The War Brides, 1981, The Death of a Miner, 1982, To Gillian on Her 37th Birthday, 1983, 84, Terry Neal's Future, 1986, The Heidi Chronicles, 1989, How to Succeed in Business Without Really Trying, 1996, Once Upon a Mattress, 1996; (films) Rich Kids, 1979, Somewhere Tomorrow, 1983, Firstborn, 1984, Footloose, 1984, Girls Just Want to Have Fun, 1985, Flight of the Navigator, 1986, L.A. Story, 1991, Honeymoon in Vegas, 1992, Hocus Pocus, 1993, Striking Distance, 1993, Ed Wood, 1994, Miami Rhapsody, 1995, If Lucy Fell, 1996, Mars Attacks!, 1996, The First Wives Club, 1996, Extreme Measures, 1996, 'Til There Was You, 1997, The Substance of Fire, 1996, (voice) A Life Apart: Hasidism in America, 1997, Isn't She Great, 1999, Dudley Do-Right, 1999, State and Main, 2000, Life Without Dick, 2001, Strangers with Candy, 2005, The Family Stone, 2005, Failure to Launch, 2006; (TV movies) My Body, My Child, 1982, Going for the Gold: The Bill Johnson Story, 1985, A Year in the Life, 1986, The Room Upstairs, 1987, Dadah Is Death, 1988, The Ryan White Story, 1989, Twist of Fate, 1989, In the Best Interest of the Children, 1992, The Sunshine Boys, 1995, Sex and the Matrix, 2000, (TV series) Square Pegs, 1982-83, A Year in the Life, 1987-88, Equal Justice, 1990-91, Sex and the City, 1998-2004 (Best Supporting Actress Golden Globe award 1999, 2000, 01, 02, 04, Emmy nominee for Outstanding Lead Actress 1999-2002, Outstanding Performance by Female Actor in Comedy Series award 2001, Emmy award Outstanding Lead Actress in a Comedy Series, 2004), (TV pilots) The Alan King Show, 1986; guest appearances The Ben Stiller Show, 1992, The Larry Sanders Show, 1992; co-exec. prodr. Sex and the City. Nat. amb. U.S. Fund for UNICEF. Office: Creative Artists Agy care Jane Berliner 9830 Wilshire Blvd Beverly Hills CA 90212-1804*

**PARKER, SASHA SMILKA,** medical educator, nurse, consultant; b. Neustadt, Holstein, Germany, Nov. 3, 1947; arrived in US, 1952; d. Blagoje Blazo and Sofia Soka Dragic; life ptnr. Richard A. Polemeni; 1 child, Peter Joseph. Student, Ind. U., 1978; AS in Nursing, Broward CC, 1982. Lic. massage therapist Fla., cert. electrologist Fla.; RN Fla.; cert. facial specialist Fla. Asst. surg. adminstr. Am. Med. Inst. Surgery, Ft. Lauderdale, Fla., 1988—89; surg. adminstr. Eye Care & Surgery Ctr., Ft. Lauderdale, 1989—91; clin. supr. Spl. Care Home Health, 1991—97; pres., CEO Gem Homecare Svcs., Inc., Ft. Lauderdale, 1997—2005, Eclectic Skin Inst., LLC, Ft. Lauderdale, 1998—2003; pres., CEO, CFO Esthetic Skin Inst., Inc., 2003—. Cons. Innovative Health Svcs., Inc., Ft. Lauderdale, 1997—; faculty spa mgmt. and hospitality program U. Calif., Irvine, Calif. Vol. Women in Distress, Ft. Lauderdale, Adult Congregate Living Assn., Ft. Lauderdale. Named Ultimate Nurse, Ultimate Nurses, Inc., 2004, Businesswoman of Yr., Nat. Rep. Congrl. Com., Inc., 2004, 2005; recipient Spotlight Entrepreneur award, Nursing Spectrum, 2004. Mem.: Am. Massage Therapy Assn., Nat. Bus. Adv. Coun., Fla. Electrology Assn., Fla. Nurses Assn., Assn. Med. Esthetic Nurses (pres., founder 2004). Avocations: dancing, travel, music, cooking. Office: Esthetic Skin Inst Inc 1120 S Fed Hwy Ste 4 Fort Lauderdale FL 33316 Office Fax: 954-463-4459. Personal E-mail: sashas@bellsouth.net.

**PARKER, SUSAN BROOKS,** health facility administrator; b. Newport, NH, Nov. 7, 1945; d. Ronald Elliott and Elizabeth Louise (Wiggins) P.; m. Allen D. Avery, 1967 (div. 1978); children: Jeffrey Roberts Avery, Mark Brooks Avery. BS in English and French, U. Vt., 1968; MSW/MSP, Boston Coll., 1978. EMT Vt., 1973-76. Resort hotel mgr., retail buyer Avery Vt. Inns, 1967-75; aftercare psychiat. social worker Orange County Mental Health, Bradford, Vt., 1974-76; exec. dir. Grafton County Planning Coun., Lebanon, NH, 1978-80, N.H. Developmental Disabilities Planning Coun., Concord, NH, 1980-87; commr. Dept. of Mental Health, Augusta, Maine, 1987-89; assoc. commr. U.S. Social Security Adminstrn., Balt., 1989-93; sec. gen. Rehab. Internat., NYC, 1993—98; sr. adv., interim dir. disability program Internat. Labor Office, Geneva, 1998—2002; dir. policy and rsch. Office Disability Employment Policy U.S. Dept. Labor, Washington, 2002—. Cons. Nat. Gov.'s Assn., Washington, 1985-86, Office of Health and Devel. Svcs., Washington, 1987; bd. dirs. Nat. Assn. Devel. Disabilities, Washington, 1983-87, Ctrl. NH Mental Health Ctr., Concord, 1985-87, World Com. Disability, Washington, 1997—, Roeher Inst., Toronto, 1997-2000, Orah.com, Geneva, 2002—, NH Devel. Disabilities Coun., 2002—05; hon. coun. Rehab. Internat., mem. World Assembly, NYC, 1998—. Author: (poetry) Scheme, 1965, Jamaican Collection, 1973; contbr. articles to newspapers and profl. jours. Pres. Parent Tchr. Orgn., Fairlee, Vt., 1972-73; founder and dir. Fairlee Ford Sayre Ski Program, Dartmouth Coll. Skiway, Fairlee, 1972-76, United Way, Concord, 1983-86; bd. dirs. PTO Rundlett Jr. H.S., Concord, 1982-85; pres. U.S. Coun. for Internat. Rehab., Washington, 1993. Recipient Assn. Retarded Citizens Children's Disability Pub. Policy award, 1992, Kathryn C. Arneson award from People to People, 1992, Commr.'s citation for outstanding efforts in developing policy U.S. Social Security Adminstrn., 1992, Commn.'s citation for outstanding exec. leadership, 1993, Secretary's Performance award U.S Dept. Labor, 2003-2005, Sec.'s Exemplary Achievement award, 2003, 2006; named Outstanding Alumnae Boston Coll., 1991. Avocations: skiing, gardening, canoeing, reading, film and performing arts.

**PARKER, TERRY S.,** telecommunications industry executive; Pres. GTE Mobil Comms., GTE Telecommunicatins, 1991—93; sr. v.p. GTE Corp., 1993—96; pres., COO CellStar Corp., Carrollton, Tex., 1995—96, dir., 1995—, CEO, 2001—; pres., CEO Teletnetics, 2000—01. Office: Cellstar Corp 1730 Briercroft Ct Carrollton TX 75006

**PARKER, THERESA ANN BOGGS,** special education educator, music educator; b. Spencer, W.Va., Jan. 16, 1947; d. Harry Clay and Betty Jean (Richards) Boggs; m. Larry Glen Parker, Apr. 29, 1967; children: Carey Ann, Jill Renee, Timothy Preston, Jeremy David, Leanna Michelle. AA in Secretarial Studies, Glenville State Coll., 1967, BA in Music Edn., 1970; MA in Spl. Edn., Coll. Grad. Studies, 1991; EdS in Ednl. Leadership, W.Va. Grad. Coll., 1996. Cert. tchr. Pvt. practice piano tchr., Spencer, 1967—; sub. tchr. Roane County Schs., Spencer, 1970—71, tchr. spl. edn., 1987—2001, tchr. music K-8, 2001—02, tchr. spl. edn., 2002—06, tchr. music K-8, 2006—, educator team mem.-parent/educator resource ctr., 1989—2002; sub. tchr. Marietta City Schs., Ohio, 1986; adminstr. Sand Hill Day Care Ctr., Reno, Ohio, 1986—87. Spl. edn. rep. W.Va. Dept. Edn., Charleston, 1995-98; dir.

Safetytown Roane County, Spencer, 1989-93. Author: (with others) Selected Teaching Models Integrated with West Virginia's Academic Model for Gifted Education, 1991; poet with works appearing in Echoes of Yesteryear, America at the Millennium, 2000, Enlightened Shadows, Miracles of Nature, Best Poems and Poets of 2001, The Road That Never Ends, Internat. Libr. Poetry. Chmn. Cub Scout Pack Boy Scouts Am., Reno, 1983-87, dist. trainer, Parkersburg, W.Va., 1986-87, chmn. Boy Scout Troop, Spencer, 1987-91; Roane County rep. to Clay Ctr. for Arts Charleston, 2005—; organizer First Bapt. Ch. Diabetes Sup. Group, 1995—. Safetytown grantee W.Va. Dept. Edn., Roane County, 1989, grantee W.Va. Edn. Fund, Roane County, 1992, W.Va. Edn. Fund, Clover Sch., 1992, Diabetes Support Group grantee Benedium Found., Roane and Calhoun/Jackson Counties, 1995, Youth and Edn. grantee Tri-County Partnership, Inc., 1998, W.Va. Humanities Coun., 2000-01, 05, The Edn. Alliance, 2004, 05, Exceptional Tchg. Techniques award RESA V, 2005; named Tchr. of Yr. Spencer Middle Sch., 1999-2000. Mem. MENC, ASCD, W.Va. Profl. Educators, Blue Grass Riding Club, Lions (program chmn., pres. 1997-98, dist. Leo chmn. 1998-00, chmn.). Flag Day/Peace Poster contest 2000-2001), Roane Arts and Humanities Coun. (charter, pres. 2000—), W.Va. Celtic Soc., Cultural Diversity Soc. Democrat. Baptist. Avocations: reading, sewing, playing piano. Home: 5754 Charleston Rd Walton WV 25286 Office: Roane County Schs 102 Chapman Ave Spencer WV 25276 Office Phone: 304-927-6415. Personal E-mail: partheresa6410@aol.com.

**PARKER, TOM,** state supreme court justice, lawyer; b. Montgomery, Ala., Aug. 19, 1951; s. Tom Parker and Gloria Parker Pennington; m. Dottie James. BA, Dartmouth Coll., 1973; JD, Vanderbilt U., 1978; attended, U. Sao Paulo Sch. of Law, Brazil. Prtnr. Parker & Kotouc; asst. atty. gen. State of Ala.; legal adviser, to Chief Justice Ala. Supreme Ct.; dep. administrative dir., gen. counsel Ala. Ct. System, 2001—03; assoc. justice Ala. Supreme Ct., 2004—. Former special projects mgr. Found. for Moral Law. Founding exec. dir. Ala. Family Alliance (now Alabama Policy Institute), Ala. Family Advocates. Grantee Rotary Internat. Fellowship, U. São Paulo Sch of Law, Brazil. Office: Ala Supreme Ct 300 Dexter Ave Montgomery AL 36104-3741*

**PARKER, TONY,** professional basketball player; b. May 17, 1982; Guard San Antonio Spurs, Tex., 2001—. Basketball player Team France, European Championships, 2001, 03. Named Champion of French Champions, L'Equipe, 2003. Achievements include member, NBA Championship Team, 2005; has appeared in more playoff games before 24th birthday than any player in NBA history. Office: San Antonio Spurs One SBC Ctr San Antonio TX 78219*

**PARKER, TOWANA D.,** entrepreneur, director; d. John Richard Martin and Bernice Eason; m. Towana D. Parker, Sept. 25, 1976; children: Tanaya S., Yoshaundala S., Edmond II M., Gabriel T. Child Evangelism Metro Child Evangelism, 1985. Entrpreneur Special-T Uniform & Embroidery, Detroit, 1995—; pres. Ladies of Destiny and Purpose Internat., 1997—; exec. dir. Destiny and Purpose Cmty. Outreach, 1999—. Host (television interviewing) Public Report Host, mentor-role model (mentoring (young women 13-18 at risk) Role Model - Mentor (Several from Mayor, State Rep, Youth home & Gov. of State, 2004); contbg. writer. Master puppeteer Kings Kids Puppet Ministry, Detroit, 1986—2004; mem. Detroit Exch. Club, 2004—. Grantee, Detroit Empowerment Zone Devel. Corp., 2002-2004, City of Detroit Neighborhood Opportunity Fund, 2004-2005. Office Phone: 313-533-1931. Home Fax: 313-535-8810; Office Fax: 313-533-1932. Personal E-mail: ladyteedp@aol.com. E-mail: dapco7outreach@aol.com.

**PARKER, TREY,** animator; b. Conifer, Colo., Oct. 19, 1969; s. Randy and Sharon Parker. Attended, Colo. Univ. Dir., writer: (films) American History, 1992; prodr., dir., writer, voice of various characters The Spirit of Christmas (also titled Jesus vs. Frosty), 1992; The Spirit of Christmas (also titled Jesus vs. Santa), 1995 (Los Angeles Film Critics Assn. award for Best Animation, 1997); dir., writer, actor Your Studio and You, 1995; prodr., dir., writer, composer, actor Alfred Packer: The Musical (also titled Cannibal! The Musical), 1996; dir.: For Goodness Sake II, 1996; creator, exec. prodr., dir., writer, composer (TV series) South Park, 1997—, voice of Mr. Mackey, Satan, Randy Marsh, Ned Gerbalnski, Mr. Hankey, Officer Barbrady, and others (CableACE award for Animated Programming Special or Series, 1997); prodr., dir., composer, actor: (films) Orgazmo, 1997; composer, actor BASEketball, 1998; prodr., dir., writer, composer (films) South Park: Bigger Longer & Uncut, 1999 (Los Angeles Film Critics Assoc. award for Best Music, 1999, New York Film Critics Circle award for Best Animated Film, 1999, MTV Movie award Best Musical Performance, 1999); exec. prodr.: (films) How's Your News?, 1999; exec. prodr., writer, creator, composer (TV series) That's My Bush, 2001; prodr., dir., writer, composer: (films) Team America: World Police, 2004; exec. prodr., singer: albums Chef Aid: The South Park Album, South Park: Bigger, Longer and Uncut, Mr. Hankey's Christmas Classics, Timmy and the Lords of the Underworld. Office: c/o Comedy Central 1775 Broadway 10th Fl New York NY 10019

**PARKER, VIRGINIA MARIE,** language educator; b. Boston, Aug. 31, 1950; d. Thomas Gurney Sr. and Marguerite Mary (O'Sullivan) P. BA, Emmanuel Coll., 1972; postgrad. studies in English, Lincoln Coll. U. Oxford, (Eng.) Bread Loaf Sessions, summers 1987-89; MA, Middlebury Coll., 1989. Cert. secondary English tchr., Mass. Vol. Jesuit Vol. Corps N.W., Seattle, 1972-73; tchr. English Blue Hills Regional Tech. Sch., Canton, Mass., 1973—, sch. newspaper advisor, 1973—75. Editl. cons. competency-based vocat. ednl. curriculum Dept. Edn./Occupl. Divsn., Commonwealth of Mass., 1984-88; nat. honor soc. advisor, screening com. mem. William A. Dwyer Chpt., Blue Hills, Canton, 1986-88, 1994-97; mediation trainee, advisor Sch. Mediation Assocs., 1993, 2000-03 Ch. lector, religious educator, youth retreat facilitator various parishes, 1970—; grad. master tchr. program Office of Religious Edn., Archdiocese of Boston, 1977. Mem. NEA, Nat. Coun. Tchrs. English, Mass. Vocat. Assn., Mass. Tchrs. Assn., Blue Hills Ednl. Assn. (sec. 1977-78), Mass. Audubon Soc., Alden Kindred Am., Irish Culture Ctr. Democrat. Roman Catholic. Avocations: travel, theater, beach walking, genealogy, cemetary haunting. Home: 80 Parks St Duxbury MA 02332-4831 Office: Blue Hills Regional Tech Sch 800 Randolph St Canton MA 02021-1358 E-mail: vparker@bluehills.org.

**PARKER, W. DOUGLAS (DOUG PARKER),** air transportation executive; m. Gwen Parker; 3 children. BA in Econ., Albion Coll., 1984; MBA, Vanderbilt U., 1986. Various fin. mgmt. positions Am. Airlines, 1986—91; v.p., fin. planning and analysis, v.p., asst. treas. Northwest Airlines; sr. v.p., CFO Am. West Holdings, 1995—99, exec. v.p., corp. group, 1999—2000, pres., COO, 2000—01, chmn., pres., CEO, 2001—05, US Airways Group Inc., Tempe, Ariz., 2005—. Recipient Disting. Alumnus award, Vanderbilt U. Owen Grad. Sch. Mgmt., 2004. Methodist. Office: US Airways 111 W Rio Salado Pkwy Tempe AZ 85281*

**PARKER, WALTER BRUCE,** arctic research specialist, consultant; b. Spokane, Wash., Aug. 11, 1926; s. Bruce Velorus and Lucille Kathryn (Chessman) P.; m. Patricia Isabelle Ertman, Jan. 28, 1946; children: Sandra Wassilie, Patrick B., Jeffrey K., Douglas S., Lisa M. BA in History, U. Alaska, Fairbanks, 1964; DSc, U. Alaska, Anchorage, 1998. Air traffic controller FAA, 1946-64, evaluation officer Anchorage, 1964-66, analyst Washington, 1966-68, planner Anchorage, 1968-70; sr. planner Fed. Field Com. for Alaska, Anchorage, 1970-71; rsch. assoc. U. Alaska, Anchorage, 1971-74; commr. Alaska Dept. Hwys., Juneau, 1974-76; chmn. Alaska Fed./State Land Use Planning Commn., 1976-79; disting. practitioner in residence U. Alaska, Anchorage, 1979-80; chmn. Alaska Oil Spill Commn., 1989-90; pres., cons. transp. and telecom. sys. Parker Assocs., Inc., Anchorage, 1971—; commr. U.S. Arctic Rsch. Commn., Anchorage, 1995—2001. Sr. fellow Inst. of the North, 2000—; mem. marine bd., com. on advances in pilotage and navigation NRC, 1991-94, North Pacific rsch. bd., 2000-04, Oil Spill Recovery Inst. bd., 1999-; chmn. Alaska Hazardous Substance Spill Coun., 1991-95; chmn. Arctic Coun. Circumpolar Infrastructure Task Force, 2000—. Author: Alaska and The Law of the Sea, 1974, Alaska People's and Alaska Lands, 1977; contbr. reports to profl. publs. Chmn. Alaska Conserva-

tion Soc., Anchorage, 1969-71; Alaska Humanities Forum, Anchorage, 1987-93, Anchorage Parks and Recreation Coun., 1971-74; active Alaska Bd. Fish and Game, Juneau, 1971-74; chmn. Prince William Sound Sci. Ctr., 1996-2004, chmn.; assemblyman Anchorage Borough, 1971-74. With USN, 1944-46. Mem. Am. Soc. Pub. Administrn. (chmn. Alaska chpt. 1971-73). Democrat. Avocations: skiing, dog mushing and breeding, gardening. Home: 3724 Campbell Airstrip Rd Anchorage AK 99504-4422 Office Phone: 907-343-2444. E-mail: wbparker@gci.net.

**PARKER, WILLIAM,** education educator; b. Savannah, Ga., May 23, 1965; s. William Robert and Carolyn Parker; m. Maria Susanne Meza-Keuthen, Aug. 4, 1989. PhD, U. Nebr., 1992. Asst. prof. Duke U. Med. Ctr., Durham, NC, 1993—. Co-author: more than 80 sci. articles. Mem. local and state leadership Royal Rangers, Durham, 1981—2006. Grantee, NIH. Mem.: Fedn. Am. Socs. for Exptl. Biology, Protein Soc., Sigma Xi Sci. Rsch. Soc., AAAS, Am. Soc. Transplant Surgeons, Am. Chem. Soc. Achievements include discovery of new model for host-bacterial interactions in the gut; new model for evaluation of the hygiene hypothesis; evidence for universal protein folding mechanism proposed by Valerie Lim; new member of the family of antibodies that includes isohemagglutinins. Home: 1023 Wells St Durham NC 27707 Office: Duke Univ Med Ctr DUMC Box 2605 Durham NC 27710 Office Phone: 919-681-3886. Business E-Mail: bparker@duke.edu.

**PARKES, WALTER F.,** film company executive; b. Bakersfield, Calif. m. Laurie MacDonald; 2 children. AB in Anthropology, Yale U.; student, Grad. Sch. Comm., Stanford U. Pres. Amblin Entertainment, 1994; co-head, dir. motion pictures Dreamworks Pictures, 1995—. Prodr., dir.: (films) The California Reich, 1975 (nominated Acad. Award, spl. citation Cannes Film Festival); prodr.: Volunteers, 1985, True Believer, 1987, Awakenings, 1990 (nominated best picture, 1990), Men in Black, 1997, The Peace Maker, 1997, Gladiator, 2000, Artificial Intelligence, 2001; prodr.: (films) The Time Machine, 2002; prodr.: (films) Minority Report, 2002, Men in Black II, 2002, Road to Perdition, 2002, The Tuxedo, 2002, The Ring, 2002, Catch Me If You Can, 2002, The Terminal, 2004, Lemony Snicket's A Series of Unfortunate Events, 2004, The Ring Two, 2005, The Island, 2005, Just Like Heaven, 2005; exec. prodr.: (TV series) Birdland, 1994, Men in Black: The Series, 1997; (films) Littler Giants, 1994, Twister, 1996, The Trigger Effect, 1996, Amistad, 1997, Deep Impact, 1998, Small Soldiers, 1998, Mask of Zorro, 1998; writer: WarGames, 1983 (nominated best original screenplay, 1983); prodr., writer: (films) Sneakers, 1992 (nominated Acad. Award, spl. citation Cannes Film Festival). Named one of 50 Most Powerful People in Hollywood, Premiere mag., 2004—05. Office: DreamWorks SKG 1000 Flower St Glendale CA 91201 Office Phone: 818-733-7000. Office Fax: 818-695-7574.

**PARKHURST, BEVERLY SUSLER,** lawyer, administrative law judge; b. Decatur, Ill. d. Sewell and Marion Susler; m. Todd S. Parkhurst, Aug. 15, 1976. BA with honors, U. Ill., 1966, JD. Private. Bar: Ill. 1969, U.S. Dist. Ct. (no. dist.) Ill. 1969, U.S. Ct. Appeals (7th cir.) 1975, U.S. Supreme Ct. 1980. Asst. U.S. atty. U.S. Atty.'s Office U.S. Dist. Ct. (no. dist.) Ill., Chgo., 1974-78, exec. asst. U.S. atty., 1978-81; pvt. practice law Offices of Beverly Susler Parkhurst, Chgo., 1982-86; trial judge Cir. Ct. Cook County, 1996-98; of counsel Witwer, Poltrock & Giampietro, Chgo., 1997—2003, Hedlund & Hanley LLC, 2003—04; appt. fed. administr. law judge, 2004—. Faculty Nat. Inst. of Trial Advocacy; bd. dirs. Internat. Forum Travel and Tourism Advs., vice chmn. 2d Internat. Conf., Jerusalem, 1986, regional chmn. 3d Internat. Conf., San Francisco, 1987; chmn. inquiry bd. Ill. Atty. Registration and Disciplinary Commn., 1985-87; guest lectr. legal ethics Washington U., St. Louis, 1986; lectr. on travel law, fed. civic procedures and med. malpractice; adj. prof. John Marshall Law Sch., 1999—; recipient Jud. Disput Resolution. Contbr. articles to profl. jours.; spkr. in field. Mem. Ill. Toll Hwy. Adv. Com., 1985-90; bd. dirs. Ill. Soc. for Prevention of Blindness, Cook County Ct. Watchers, Chgo. State U. Found., 1997—2003. James scholar U. Ill., 1962-66; recipient Spl. Achievement award U.S. Dept. Justice, 1978, Dir.'s award, 1981, Cert. of Profl. Achievement in Mediation, DePaul U. Dispute Resolution Ctr.; U.S. Utility Patent grantee 1984. Mem. ABA (chmn. subcom. alternatives to discovery litigation sect. 1985-87), Ill. Bar Assn. (com. profl. responsibility), Women's Bar Assn., Fed. Bar Assn., Chgo. Bar Assn. (chmn. judiciary commn. 1988-90, bench bar symposium 1988-91, exec. com. Alliance for Women), Nat. Inst. Trial Advocacy (faculty N.E. region), Lincoln Inn of Ct. (v.p.), Legal Club of Chgo. Avocations: scuba diving, swimming, cooking. Office: Fed Administr Law Judge Chicago IL 60603

**PARKHURST, CAROLYN,** writer; b. 1971; BA, Wesleyan U.; MFA in creative writing. m. U. Author: The Dogs of Babel, 2003 (Best Fiction Book Fort Worth Star-Telegram, 2003, Notable Book New York Times, 2003), (short stories) (included in) North Am. Review, Minn. Review, Hawaii Review, Crescent Review. Office: c/o Douglas Stewart Curtis Brown Ltd 10 Astor Pl New York NY 10003

**PARKHURST, CHARLES LLOYD,** electronics executive; b. Nashville, Aug. 13, 1943; s. Charles Albert Parkhurst and Dorothy Elizabeth (Ballou) Parkhurst Crutchfield; m. Dolores Ann Oakley, June 6, 1970; children: Charles Thomas, Deborah Lynn, Jere Loy. Student, Hume-Fogg Tech. Coll., 1959—61; AA, Mesa Community Coll., 1973; student, Ariz. State U., 1973—76. Mem. design staff Tex. Instruments, Dallas, 1967; mgr. design Motorola, Inc., Phoenix, 1968—76; pres. LSI Cons., Inc., Tempe, Ariz., 1976—85, LSI Photomasks, Inc., Tempe, 1985—94, Charles Parkhurst Books, Inc., Prescott, Ariz., 1994—; founder IC Photomask, LLC, Chandler, Ariz., 2002—. Founder IC Photomask. Designer 1st digital watch chip, 1973. Mem. Rep. Congl. Leadership Coun., Washington, 1988; life mem. Rep. Presdl. Task Force, 1990. Served as cpl. USMC, 1961-64. Mem. Ariz. State U. Alumni Assn. (life), Antiquarian Booksellers Assn. Am. Digital Achievements include th sign of the world's first digital watch chip. Office: Charles Parkhurst Books Inc PO Box 10850 Prescott AZ 86304-0850

**PARKHURST, TED A.,** publishing executive; b. Cadillac, Mich., Dec. 27, 1947; s. Ted Archie and Rose Mary (Flemming) P.; m. Elizabeth Smith, June 27, 1981; 1 child, Lucy Rose. Student, Harding U., 1966-69; BA in History, U. Ark., Little Rock, 1970. Pers. mgr. C. Finkbeiner, Inc., Little Rock, 1970-77; writer Little Rock, 1977-79; cons. writer Little Rock Sch. Dist., 1979-80; pres., founder August House, Inc., Little Rock, 1979—. Author: What Giants Eat, 1979, The Get-Even Fairy, 1981; editor: A Fruitbowl of Rhinos, 1979. Resource person, vol. Vols. in Pub. Schs, Little Rock 1982—; chair coun. on ministries 1st United Meth. Ch., Little Rock, 1988-89, chair bd. stewards, 1989-90; v.p. Univ. History Inst., Little Rock, 1991-92, pres. 1992-96, bd. dirs., 1988-96. Recipient Disting. Svc. award Coll. Arts and Humanities and Social Scis., U. Ark. at Little Rock, 1994. Mem. Pubs. Assn. of the South (bd. dirs. 1985-86, v.p. 1986-87, 96-97, pres. 1987-88, 97—), S.E. Booksellers Assn. (bd. dirs. 1988-90), South Ctrl. Booksellers Assn. (bd. dirs. 1990—, v.p. 1991-93). Avocations: reading, movies, watercolor. Office: August House Inc 201 E Markham St Little Rock AR 72201-1627

**PARKHURST, TODD SHELDON,** lawyer; b. Evanston, Ill., Mar. 8, 1941; s. Don A. and Ruth Ellen (Sheldon) P.; m. Karen Judy Huckleberry, Sept. 2, 1968 (dec. Sept. 1969); m. Beverly Ann Susler, Aug. 15, 1976. BS in Gen. Engring., U. Ill., 1963; JD, U. Pa., 1966. Bar: Ill. 1968, U.S. Dist. Ct. (no. dist.) Ill. 1968, U.S. Dist. Ct. (ea. dist.) Wis. 1989, U.S. Ct. Appeals (7th cir.) 1977, U.S. Ct. Appeals Fed. Cir. 1978, U.S. Ct. Mil. Appeals, 1968, U.S. Patent and Trademark Office, 1968. U.S. Supreme Ct. 1973. Assoc. Wolfe, Hubbard, Voit & Osann, 1968-72; assoc. and ptnr. Trexler, Wolters, Bushnell & Fosse, Chgo., 1972-84; ptnr. Jenner & Block, Chgo., 1984-87; ptnr., mgr. intellectual property practice Schiff Hardin & Waite, Chgo., 1987-96; ptnr. Gardner, Carton & Douglas, 1996-98, Hill & Simpson, Chgo., 1998-2000; ptnr., mgr. intellectual property practice Holland & Knight, Chgo., 2000—. Adj. prof. John Marshall Law Sch., Chgo., 1980-84, Ill. Inst. Tech.-Chgo. Kent Law Sch., 1989—. Contbr. articles to profl. jours. Mem. Lifeline Pilots, Inc., pres. 1994-96; hearing officer Ill. Pollution Control Bd., 1972-96. Capt. Corps of Engrs. U.S. Army, 1966—68. Mem. Am. Intellectual Property Law Assn., Licensing Execs. Soc., Chgo. Bar Assn., Patent Law Assn. Chgo., Chgo. Lit. Club (pres. 1989-90), Adventurers Club Chgo. (sec. 1988).

Methodist. Avocations: flying, scuba diving, photography, theatrical acting. Office: Holland & Knight 131 S Dearborn Ste 3000 Chicago IL 60603 Office Phone: 312-263-3600. E-mail: todd.parkhurst@hklaw.com.

**PARKHURST, VIOLET KINNEY,** artist; b. Derby Line, Vt., Apr. 26, 1926; d. Edson Frank and Rosa (Beauchiene) Kinney; student Sch. Practical Arts, Boston, 1941-42, Baylor U., Waco, Tex., 1943, Calif. State U., Los Angeles, 1950-51; m. Donald Winters Parkhurst, Apr. 10, 1948. Fgn. corr. 5 Brazilian mags., 1946-53; tech. illustrator, 1954-55; owner five galleries including Ports of Call, San Pedro, Calif.; artist, specializing in seascapes; work included in permanent collection of Stockholm Mus., many pvt. collections including Presidents Richard M. Nixon, Ford, Reagan, Bush, Gov. Wilson, Mayor of Kobe, Japan, Mayor Yorty of L.A., Rory Calhoun, Barbara Rush, Jim Arness, David Rose, President Hu of China, 2005; one-shows shows at prominent galleries; numerous paintings published. Winner 30 blue ribbons for art. Fellow Am. Inst. Fine Arts. Mem. Ch. of Religious Sci. Author: How to Paint Books, 1966; Parkhurst on Seascapes, 1972. Paintings reproduced on covers South West Art, Arizona Living, Hollywood Bowl Easter Sunrise Service program; ltd. edit. prints published, also ltd. edit. plates. The first artist in the world invited to present a painting to Pres. Jiang Zemin, Beisin, China, 2002; the first western artist to have a painting in China Nat. Mus. of Fine Arts and the Hall of the People. Office: Parkhurst Gallery Ports of Call Village San Pedro CA 90731 E-mail: violet@parkhurstartgalleries.com.

**PARKIN, FERN AGNES MARVEL,** medical/surgical nurse, nursing educator; b. Pocatello, Idaho, Nov. 22, 1931; d. Clarence J. and May Agnes Cuppett; m. Jesse James Marvel, Apr. 16, 1948 (div. Aug. 28, 1973); children: Alexa Ann Adams, Marco Lewis Marvel, Jill Lynn Osburn; m. William Heber Parkin, Jan. 4, 1991. AA, L.A. Harbor Coll., Wilmington, Calif., 1967; B in Vocat. Edn., Calif. State U., Long Beach, Calif., 1978. RN Calif., Idaho, Ariz., Wyoming, Wash., cert. adult cardiopulmonary resuscitation, Calif., coronary care. Staff nurse, clinic nurse Kaiser Found. Hosp., Harbor City, Calif., 1964—65, 1967—69; charge nurse Bishop Randal Hosp., Lander, Wyo., 1970, Needles Hosp., Calif., 1971, Icelandic Rest Home, Blaine, Wash., 1971—, Shuksans Nursing Home, Bellingham, Wash., 1971—72; nursing instr. LA Unified Sch. Dist., 1973—78; charge nurse Pacific Hosp., Long Beach, Calif., 1972—74; acting head nurse L.A. Harbor Gen. Hosp., Torrance, Calif., 1974—76; LVN nurse instr. YWCA Job Corp, LA, 1976—77; intensive care and coronary care nurse Profl. Nurses Bur., Long Beach, Calif., 1971—77; psychiatric facilitation instr. Atascadero State Hosp., Calif., 1979; dir. staff devel. Paso Robles Convalescent, Calif., 1987—88; welfare missionary Church of Jesus Christ of LDS, Ormoc, Cebu, Bohol, Philippines, 1988—90; charge nurse Twin Cities Convalescent Ctr., Templeton, Calif., 1990—92. Portraits, Pres. Aquina, Pres. Ronald Regan. Counselor relief soc. Ch. Jesus Christ LDS, Wilmington, 1973, mem. choir Pocatello, Idaho, 1969; pres. PTA, Nampa, Idaho, 1962—63. Mem.: Alpha Gamma Sigma. Democrat. Mem. Lds Ch. Avocations: painting, writing, reading. Home: 200 N PO Box 220667 Centerfield UT 84622

**PARKIN, GERARD FRANCIS RALPH,** chemistry educator, researcher; b. Middlesbrough, Cleveland, Eng., Feb. 15, 1959; s. Ralph and Clementine (Gill) P.; m. Rita K. Upmacis. BA with honors, Oxford (Eng.) U., 1981, MA, 1984, PhD, 1985. NATO/SERC (U.K.) postdoctoral rsch. fellow Calif. Inst. Tech., 1985-88; asst. prof. Columbia U., N.Y.C., 1988-91, assoc. prof., 1991-94; prof., chmn. chemistry dept., 1994—; chmn. dept. chemistry, 1999—2002. Contbr. numerous articles to profl. jours. Recipient Camille and Henry Dreyfus Tchr.-Scholar award, 1991, award in pure chemistry Am. Chem. Soc., 1994, Corday Morgan medal Royal Soc. Chemistry, 1995, Organometallic Chemistry award, 2004; A.P. Sloan rsch. fellow; NSF Presdl. faculty fellow, 1992—. Roman Catholic. Achievements include discovery that bond stretch isomerism in an artifact. Office: Columbia U 116th St And Broadway New York NY 10027

**PARKIN, JAMES LAMAR,** retired otolaryngologist, educator; b. Salt Lake City, June 2, 1939; s. Elmer Lamar and Mary Ilene (Soffe) Parkin; m. Bonnie Dansie, July 1, 1963; children: Jeffrey, Brett, Matthew, David. BS, U. Utah, 1963, MD, 1966; MS, U. Wash., 1970. Diplomate Am. Bd. Otolaryngology. Resident in otolaryngology U. Wash., Seattle, 1968—72; practice medicine specializing in otolaryngology Salt Lake City, 1972—; chmn. divsn. otolaryngology U. Utah Sch. Medicine, Salt Lake City, 1974—93, prof. surgery, 1981—, acting chmn. dept. surgery, 1984—84, 1993—94, chmn., 1994—96, prof. emeritus, 2004—. Pres. med. bd. Univ. Med. Ctr., Salt Lake City, 1983—85, chmn. exec. com. faculty practice orgn., 1994—96, assoc. v.p. health scis., 1996—97, v.p. sch. medicine alumni 2003—, v.p. med. alumni, 2003—, chmn. centennial com., 2005—; bd. govts. Utah Med. Ins. Assn., Salt Lake City, 1979—81. Guest editor Ear, Nose and Throat Jour., 1982, assoc. editor Archives of Otolaryngology. Leader Boy Scouts Am.; bishop Ch. of Jesus Christ of Latter-Day Saints, Salt Lake City, 1983—86, stake pres., 1986—96, pres. Eng. London South Mission, 1996—2000. Recipient Honor award, Am. Acad. Otolaryngology, 1980. Fellow: ACS, Am. Neurotology Soc., Am. Soc. Laser Medicine and Surgery, Am. Otol. Soc., Am. Plastic and Reconstructive Surgery, Am. Laryngol, Rhinol. and Otol. Soc.; mem.: Collegium Aesculapium (pres. 2005—), Soc. Otolaryngology-Maxillofacial Surgery (pres. Utah chpt. 1979), Am. Cancer Soc. (pres. Utah chpt. 1984—86), Soc. Univ. Otolaryngologists (pres. 1984—85), Assn. Acad. Depts. Otolaryngology (chmn. nat. faculty survey com. 1980—90, sec.-treas. 1982—84, pres. 1986—88). Home: 2390 Bernadine Dr Salt Lake City UT 84109-1206 Office: U Utah Health Scis Ctr 50 N Medical Dr Salt Lake City UT 84132-0001 Personal E-mail: parkin2slc@earthlink.net.

**PARKIN, STUART STEPHEN PAPWORTH,** materials scientist; IBM fellow IBM Almaden Rsch. Ctr., San Jose, Calif., 1983—. Recipient Internat. prize for new materials Am. Phys. Soc., 1994, C.V. Boys prize Inst. Physics, London, 1991, Inaugural Outstanding Young Investigator award Materials Rsch. Soc., 1991, Europhysics prize Hewlett-Packard, 1997, Instl. Applications of Physics prize Am. Inst. Physics, 1999-2000, Humboldt award, 2005; named Innovator of Yr., R&D Mag., 2001. Fellow AAAS, IEEE, Am. Phys. Soc., Royal Soc. London, Inst. Physics (London). Office: IBM Almaden Rsch Ctr 650 Harry Rd San Jose CA 95120-6099 E-mail: parkin@almaden.ibm.com.

**PARKINS, FREDERICK MILTON,** dental educator, dean; b. Princeton, N.J., Sept. 8, 1935; s. William Milton and Phyllis Virginia (Plyler) P.; m. Carolyn V. Rude; children: Bradford, Christopher, Eric. Student, Carleton Coll., 1953-56; D.D.S., U. Pa., 1960; MSD. in Pedodontics, U. N.C., Chapel Hill, 1965; PhD in Physiology, 1966. Fellow pedodontics U. N.C., 1965-67; asst. prof. pedodontics U. Pa., 1967-68, dir. Dental Aux. Utilization program, chmn. pedodontics, 1968-69; assoc. prof., head pedodontics U. Iowa, Iowa City, 1969-72, prof., head pedodontics, 1972-75; asst. dean acad. affairs U. Iowa (Coll. Dentistry), 1974-75, assoc. dean acad. affairs, 1975-79, dir. continuing edn., 1975-77; prof. pedodontics, dean Sch. Dentistry, U. Louisville, 1979-85, prof. pediatric dentistry 1985—2003, prof. pediatric dentistry emeritus, 2003—. Mem. Hillenbrand Fellowship advg. com. Am. Fund Dental Health, 1980-85; cons. Div. Dental Health USPHS, 1969-72; dental cons., med. staff Children's Hosp. Phila., 1968-71; med. staff Kosair Children's Hosp. Louisville, 1983—; cons., mem. pedodontic adv. com. Council Dental Edn., 1974-80, chmn. pedodontic adv. com., 1978-80, cons. council on legislation, 1978-79; dental cons. Aux. Utilization VA, 1968-69; cons. Bur. Health Resources Devel., 1974-76, Dept. Army, 1980-, numerous others Assoc. editor Jour. Preventive Dentistry, 1973-79, mem. editl. bd., 1980-83; editl. reviewer Jour. Pediatrics, 1969-, Jour. Dental Edn. 1978-, Jour. AMA, 1979-; assoc. editor Jour. Clin. Preventive Dentistry, 1979-84; mem. editl. bd. Jour. Clin. Laser Medicine and Surgery, 1999-; contbr. chpts. to textbooks, articles to profl. publs Bd. govs. Youth Performing Arts Coun., Louisville-Jefferson County Sch. Dist., 1980-89, pres., 1986-88; bd. govs. Regional Cancer Ctr., U. Louisville, 1979-84, Univ. Hosp., 1979-84; mem. human studies com. U. Louisville, 1988-90. Robert Wood Johnson Congl. fellow Inst. of Medicine, 1977-78; USPHS postdoctoral fellow, 1963-67; NIH grantee, 1971-75; Recipient Earle Banks Hoyt Teaching award, 1969 Fellow AAAS, Am. Acad. Pediat. Dentistry (chmn. rsch. com. 1972-73, Ann. Rsch.

award 1968, chmn. advanced edn. com. 1974-75, chmn. dental care programs com. 1978-80); mem. ADA, Am. Coll. Dentistry, Am. Soc. Dentistry for Children (exec. bd. Iowa unit 1969-75, award com. 1973-76, edn. com. 1974-77, chmn. rsch. adv. com. 1973-76), Biophys. Soc., Internat. Assn. Dental Rsch., N.Y. Acad. Dentistry, Ky. Dental Assn. (exec. bd. 1979-85, Am. Assn. Dental Schs. (coun. deans 1979-85, chmn. pedodontics sect. 1976, chmn. continuing edn. sect. 1979, legis. com. 1978-83), Louisville Dental Alumni Assn. (bd. govs. 1979-84), Am. Assn. Dental Rsch. nat. affairs com. 1978-85), Acad. Laser Dentistry (co-chmn. rsch. and edn. 1997, chair 1998-2003, bd. dirs. 1997-2003, cert. com.), T.H. Maiman award for excellence in dental laser rsch.), U.S. Power Squadron (bd. govs. 1987-93, sec. 1989, adminstrv. officer 1990, exec. officer 1991, comdr. 1992), Aircraft Owners and Pilots Assn., Omicron Kappa Upsilon (pres. Wa. chpt. 1991-92), Rotary. Unitarian Universalist. Home: 6424 Marina Dr Prospect KY 40059-8846 Office: U Louisville Sch Dentistry Dept Orth and Pediatric Dentistry Rm 240N Louisville KY 40292 Office Phone: 502-852-1334. Business E-Mail: fmpark01@louisville.edu.

**PARKINSON, BRADFORD WELLS,** astronautical engineer, educator; b. Madison, Wis., Feb. 16, 1935; s. Herbert and Metta Tisdale (Smith) P.; m. Virginia Pinkham Wier, Nov. 26, 1977; children: Leslie, Bradford II, Eric, Ian, Bruce, Jared Bradford. BS, U.S. Naval Acad., 1957; MS, MIT, 1961; PhD, Stanford U., 1966; grad. (disting.), USAF Command and Staff Coll., 1969, Naval War Coll., 1972. Commd. 2d lt. USAF, 1957, advanced through grades to col., 1972; divsn. chief AF Test Pilot Sch., 1966-68; chair dept. astronautics and computer sci. USAF Acad., 1969-71; dir. engring. ABRES, 1972; program mgr. NAVSTAR GPS, 1972-78; ret. USAF, 1978; prof. mech. engring. Colo. State U., Ft. Collins, 1978-79; v.p. advanced engring. Rockwell Internat., Downey, Calif., 1979-80; gen. mgr., v.p. Intermetrics, Inc., Cambridge, Mass., 1980-84; prof. emeritus, assoc. dir. gravity probe-B Stanford (Calif.) U., 1984—; CEO, pres. Trimble Navigation Ltd., 1998-99. Chair adv. coun. JPL NASA; dir. Trimble Navigation Ltd., Sunnyvale, Calif., NTV, Cambridge; past chair bd. dirs. Aerospace Corp., El Segundo, Calif. Decorated Def. Superior Svc. medal, AF Commendation medal with oak leaf cluster, Meritorius Svc. medal, Presdl. Unit citation, Bronze Star, Legion of Merit, Air medal with oak leaf cluster; recipient Pub. Svc. award, Disting. Pub. Svc. award, NASA, 1984, Thurlow award Inst. Navigation, 1986, Burka award, 1987, Kepler award, 1991, Aerospace Contbn. to Soc. award, 1991, Goddard medal, von Karman Lectureship AIAA, 1996, Magellan Premium, Am. Philos. Soc., 1997, Gold medal Space Tech. Hall of Fame of U.S. Space Found., 1998, Williams Space medal Soc. Logistics Engrs., 1996, ASME medal, 2004; named to National Inventors Hall of Fame, 2004. Fellow AIAA, Royal Inst. Navigation (Gold medal 1983), Inst. Navigation, IEEE (Kirchner award 1986, Pioneer award 1994, Sperry award 1999, Simon Remo medal); mem. AAS, NAE (Charles Stark Draper Prize, 2003), Internat. Acad. Astronautics, Sigma Xi, Tau Beta Pi. Avocations: hiking, skiing, sailing. Office: Stanford U 4085 Mail Code Stanford CA 94305 Home: 2360 Camino Edna San Luis Obispo CA 93401

**PARKINSON, DIAN,** actress; Student, Lee Strasberg Studio, LA. Talk show hostess The Women's Side; appeared on TV shows The Price is Right, The Tonight Show Starring Johnny Carson, Vegas, Bob Hope's Desert Classic, The Bob Hope Christmas Show (Emmy Award Citation); model on cover of Bert Stein, Master of Contemporary Photography, Cosmopolitan mag., commls., posters, billboards, other mags. Named Miss U.S.A.

**PARKINSON, JAMES THOMAS, III,** investment consultant; b. Richmond, Va., July 10, 1940; s. James Thomas and Elizabeth (Hopkins) P.; m. Molly O. Owens, June 16, 1962 (div. June 1998); children: James Thomas, Glenn Walser; m. Caroline Smith Pyle, Oct. 10, 1998. BA, U. Va., 1962; MBA, U. Pa., 1964. Trainee Chem. Bank, N.Y.C., 1964—66; assoc., corp. fin. dept. Blyth & Co., Inc., N.Y.C., 1966-69; v.p., corp. fin. dept. Clark Dodge & Co., Inc., N.Y.C., 1969—72; pvt. practice investment mgmt. N.Y.C., 1972—85, Va., 1987—; v.p. Pleasantville Industrial Advisors, Inc., N.Y.C., 1986—87. Instr. corp. fin. Ind. U., 1966-68; bd. dirs. Bowles Fluidics Corp. Sr. warden Ch. of Holy Trinity, N.Y.C., 1978-87; trustee Am. Bible Soc., 1980—, Funds, Episcopal Diocese of Va., 2000-06, Diocesan Missionary Soc., 2006—, Mus. Bibl. Art, N.Y.C., 2005—. With AUS, 1966-68. Mem. Univ. Club (N.Y.C.), Va. Country Club. Republican. Episcopalian. Home and Office: PO Box 2247 Middleburg VA 20118-2247

**PARKINSON, JOHN S.,** information technology executive; Degree in math., Exeter U., Eng., degree in info. sciences. Joined Ernst & Young LLP, England, 1985, moved to US, 1991, head global solutions team, chief technologist global ecommerce group, dir. innovation and strategy Americas region, sr. ptnr. strategy & corp. devel. group; now v.p., chief technologist Americas region Capgemini. Named one of Top 25 Most Influential Consultants, Consulting Mag., 2003, Premier 100 IT Leaders, Computerworld, 2005. Office: Capgemini US Ste 1800 750 7th Ave New York NY 10019*

**PARKINSON, ROBERT L., JR.,** medical products executive, health facility administrator; BBA, MBA, Loyola U., Chgo. With Abbott Labs., Abbott Park, Ill., 1976, v.p. European ops., 1990-93, sr. v.p. chem. and agrl. products, 1993-95, pres. internat. divsn., 1995-98, bd. dirs., 1998, pres., COO, 1999-2001; dean Loyola U. Chgo.'s Sch. of Bus. Adminstrn. and Grad. Sch. of Bus., 2002—04; chmn., CEO Baxter Internat., Inc., 2004—. Chmn. Geneva (Switzerland) Proteomics, 2001; bd. trustees Healthcare Leadership Coun. Bd. dirs. Northwestern Mem. Hosp., Northwestern Mem. Found. Office: Baxter Internat Inc One Baxter Pkwy Deerfield IL 60015 Office Phone: 847-948-2000.*

**PARKINSON, WILLIAM CHARLES,** physics professor, researcher; b. Jarvis, Ont., Can., Feb. 11, 1918; came to U.S., 1925, naturalized, 1941; s. Charles Franklin and Euphemia Alice (Johnston) P.; m. Martha Bennett Capron, Aug. 2, 1944; children: Martha Reed, William Reid. BSE, U. Mich., 1940, MS, 1941, PhD, 1948. Physicist Applied Physics Lab., Johns Hopkins U., 1942-46, OSRD, 1943-44; mem. faculty U. Mich., 1947-; prof. physics, 1958-88, prof. emeritus physics, 1988—, dir. cyclotron lab., 1962-77; mem. subcom. nuclear structure NRC, 1959-68; mem. nuclear physics sub panel mgmt. and costs nuclear program, 1969-70; adv. panel physics NSF, 1966-69. Cons. grad. sci. facilities, 1968, chmn. postdoctoral fellowship evaluation panel, 1969, cons. to govt. and industry, 1955—Quondam mem. Trinity Coll., Cambridge, Eng. Recipient Ordnance Devel. award Navy Dept., 1946; Fulbright research scholar Cavendish Lab., Cambridge U., 1952-53 Fellow Am. Phys. Soc.; mem. N.Y. Acad. Scis., Biophys. Soc., Grad. "M" Club (awarded hon. "M" 1991), Flounders Water Polo, Sigma Xi, Phi Kappa Phi, Kappa Kappa Psi. Achievements include invention of automatic judging and timing for swim meets, fast neutron spectroscopy using cyclotrons; development of high resolution nuclear spectroscopy with cyclotrons. Home: 1600 Sheridan Dr Ann Arbor MI 48104-4052 Office: Univ Mich Dept Physics Ann Arbor MI 48109 Office Phone: 734-764-3458. Business E-Mail: wcpark@umich.edu.

**PARKISON, AIMEE DAWN,** language educator, writer; d. Reid and Paula Parkison. BA in English, Okla. State U., 2000; MFA in English, Cornell U., 2002. Asst. prof. U. N.C., Charlotte, 2004—. Author: (short stories) The Upstairs Album, 2001 (Jack Dyer Fiction prize, 2001), Van Windows, 2003 (Writers at Work fellowship, 2003), Warnings, 2004 (Kurt Vonnegut Fiction prize, 2004), Woman with Dark Horses, 2004 (Starcherone Fiction prize, 2004). James C. McCormick fellow in fiction, Christopher Isherwood Found., 2005. Mem.: Associated Writers Program. Personal E-mail: aimeeparkison@hotmail.com.

**PARKS, ARVA MOORE,** historian; b. Miami, Fla., Jan. 19, 1939; d. Jack and Anne (Parker) Moore; m. Robert Lyle Parks, Aug. 19, 1959 (div. May 1986); children: Jacqueline Carey, Robert Downing, Gregory Moore; m. Robert Howard McCabe, June 20, 1992. Student, Fla. State U., 1956-58; BA, U. Fla., 1960; MA in History, U. Miami, Coral Gables, 1971; LLD (hon.), Barry U., 1996. Tchr. Rolling Crest Jr. H.S., West Hyattsville, Md., 1960-63;

Miami Edison Sr. H.S., Fla., 1963-64; grad. asst. U. Miami, Coral Gables, 1964-65; tchr. Everglades Sch. for Girls, Miami, 1965-66; cons., 1966-70; free-lance rsch. historian Miami, 1970-86; adj. prof. U. Miami, Coral Gables, 1986-87; pres. Arva Parks & Co., Miami, 1986—. Cons. thematic and interpretive rsch. and design Harry S. Truman Little White House, Key West, Fla., 1989-91; pres. Centennial Press, 1991—. Author: Miami the Magic City, 1981, rev. edit., 1991, The Forgotten Frontier, 1977 (rev. edit. 2004), Harry Truman and the Little White House in Key West, 1991, Miami: Then and Now, 1992, The Pathway to Greatness, 2001; co-author: (with Gregory M. Bush) Miami: The American Crossroad, 1996, (with Carolyn Klepser) Miami Then & Now, 2002, George Merrick's Coral Gables, 2006; editor Tequesta Jour. Hist. Soc. Fla., 1986-95; writer: (film) Our Miami: The Magic City, 1994. Bd. advs., Nat. Trust for Hist. Preservation, 1984-93, chmn. so. region, 1990-91, Fed. Adv. Coun. Hist. Preservation, 1995-2003; trustee Miami-Dade C.C., 1984-90, U. Miami, 1994—; bd. dirs. Louis Wolfson Media History Ctr., Miami, 1985-90, Orange Bowl Com., 1989—, Bapt. Health Systems of Miami, Inc., 1992—, Dade Found., 1997-2004, Drs. Hosp. Bd., 2004—; cmty. adv. Dade Heritage Trust, Miami, 1988-97, mem. Bi-Racial Tri-Ethnic Adv. Bd., Miami, 1984-99, New World Sch. Arts (exec. com.), Miami, 1986-90, Bok Sanctuary Bd., 2005—, City of Coral Gables Mus. Bd., 2005-; chmn. Vizcaya Trust, 1998-2004; pres. Fla. Forum, 2003-05; chair City of Miami Planning Adv. Bd., 2005—; bd. dirs. Internat. Women's Forum, 2005—. Recipient Historic Preservation award AIA, 1993, Outstanding Women of History award Cuban Am. Women's Club, 1992, Women Helping Women award Soroptimists, 1992, Am. History award DAR, 1987, Pathfinder's award Women's Com. 100, 1985, Outstanding Citizen award Coral Gables C. of C., 1983, Outstanding Preservationist award Dade Heritage Trust, 1983, Good Faith award Black Archives and Rsch. Found., 1981, Mus. of Sci. award, 1981, Cmty. Headliner award Women in Comm., 1980, Humanitarian award Urban League Guild, 1980, award City of Coral Gables Hist. Preservation Bd., 1978, Women of Impact award Cmty. Coalition for Women's History, 1996, Cmty. Star award Family Counseling Svcs. of Greater Miami, 1996, Edward T. Foote Alumnae of Distinction award U. Miami, 2002, Henriette Harris award Dade Heritage Trust, 2004; named to Alumni Hall of Fame Dade County Pub. Schs., 1985, Fla. Women's Hall of Fame, 1986, one of Women Who Made a Difference YWCA, 1988, City Miami Women's Hall Fame, 1996, Woman of Distinction award Soroptimist Internat. of Ams., Woman of Distinction award Girl Scouts Am., 1996, Alumni Women Distinction U. Fla., 1997, Tebeau prize Fla. Hist. Soc. for Am. Crossroad, 1997, Theodore Gibson Unity award, 1999, Vizcayans Cultural Millennium award, 1999, Miami Herald Spirit of Excellence award, 1999, Joseph R. Narot Cmty. Svc. award, 2003, Olympian award Olympia Theater at Gusman Ctr., 2006, Julia Tuttle award Commn. on the Status of Women, City of Miami, 2006. Mem. Internat. Women's Forum, Jr. League. Democrat. Methodist. Avocation: photography. Home and Office: 1601 S Miami Ave Miami FL 33129-1103 Office Phone: 305-854-8087. Personal E-mail: arvamiami@bellsouth.net.

**PARKS, DONALD LEE,** mechanical engineer, human factors engineer; b. Delphos, Kans., Feb. 23, 1931; s. George Delbert and Erma Josephine (Boucek) P.; m. Bessie Lou Schur, Dec. 24, 1952; children: Elizabeth Parks Anderson, Patricia Parks-Holbrook, Donna, Charles, Sandra Parks-Bennett. Student, Kans. Wesleyan U., 1948-50; BSME, BSBA, Kans. State U., 1957, MS in Psychology, 1959. Cert. profl. ergonomist. Elem. tchr., 1950-51; with Kans. State U. Placement Svc., 1959-57; human factors engr., sys. engr. Boeing Co., Seattle, 1959-90, sr. specialist engr., 1972-74, sr. engring. supr., 1974-90; pres. D-Square Assocs. Engring. Cons., 1990-95, Venture Worlds, 1995—. Adj. lectr. UCLA Engring. Extension, 1989—; cons., lectr. in field; participant workshops on guidelines in profl. areas, NATO, NSF, Nat. Acad. Sci., NRC, Contrb. over 80 articles to profl. publs., 8 book chpts. Mem. Derby (Kans.) Planning Commn., 1961-62, chmn., 1962; del. King County (Wash.) Rep. Conv., 1972. With AUS, 1952-54. Mem. ASME, APA, Human Factors Soc. (Puget Sound Pres.'s award 1969), Elks. Presbyterian. Home: 6232 127th Ave SE Bellevue WA 98006-3943

**PARKS, GARRY LEE,** military officer; b. Huntingdon, Pa., Mar. 9, 1947; m. Earlene Knight; children: Garry Lee Jr., Tamara Anne. BS, The Citadel, 1969; MA, Pepperdine U., 1973, Naval War Coll., 1987. Commd. 2d lt. USMC, 1969, advanced through grades to lt. gen., 2001; platoon comdr., co. exec. officer 1st Reconnaissance Bn. 1st Marine Divsn., Vietnam; co. comdr. 2nd Bn., 3rd Marines; aide-de-camp to comdg. gen. 1st Marine Brig., Kaneohe Bay, Hawaii; co. officer U.S. Naval Acad., 1979-81; comdg. officer recruiting sta. USMC, Raleigh, NC, 1982-85; joint program and budget coordination officer Requirements and Programs divsn. USMC Hdqrs.; exec. officer, then comdg. officer 2nd Bn. 5th Marines, 1st Marine divsn.; officer in charge spl. ops. tng. group USMC, Okinawa, Japan, 1990-91; comdg. officer, camp comdr. Camp Hansen, 1992; dir. presentation team USMC, 1993; chief of staff Marine Forces Pacific, Camp H.M. Smith, 1993-94; comdg. gen. USMC Recruit Depot, Western Recruiting Region, San Diego, 1995-97; dep. dir. politico-mil. affairs global, multi-lateral issues The Pentagon, Washington, 1997-98; comdg. gen. Marine Corps Recruiting Command, Quantico, Va., 1998-2001; dep. comdt. Manpower and Res. Affairs, 2001—/res./CEO SC Credit Union League, Irmo, SC, 2004—. Decorated Dist. Svc. medal, Legion of Merit, Bronze Star, Def. Superior Svc. medal. Office: SC Credit Union League 7440 Broad River Rd Irmo SC 29063 Business E-Mail: gparks@sccul.org.

**PARKS, HAROLD RAYMOND,** mathematician, educator; b. Wilmington, Del., May 22, 1949; s. Lytle Raymond Jr. and Marjorie Ruth (Chambers) P.; m. Paula Sue Beaulieu, Aug. 21 (div. 1984); children: Paul Raymond, David Austin; m. Susan Irene Taylor, June 6, 1985; 1 stepchild, Kathryn McLaughlin. AB, Dartmouth Coll., 1971; PhD, Princeton U., 1974. Tamarkin instr. Brown U., Providence, 1974-77; asst. prof. Oreg. State U., Corvallis, 1977-82, assoc. prof., 1982-89, prof. math., 1989—, chmn. dept. math., 2001—04. Vis. assoc. prof. Ind. U., Bloomington, 1982-83. Author: Explicit Determination of Area Minimizing Hypersurfaces, vol. II, 1986, (with Steven G. Krantz) A Primer of Real Analytic Functions, 1992, 2d edit., 2002, (with G. Musser, R. Burton, W. Siebler) Mathematics in Life, Society and the World, 1997, 2d edit., 2000, (with Steven G. Krantz) The Geometry of Domains in Space, 1999, (with Krantz) The Implicit Function Theorem: History, Theory, and Applications, 2002; contbr. articles to profl. publs. Cubmaster Oregon Trail Coun. Boy Scouts Am., 1990-92. NSF fellow, 1971-74. Mem. Am. Math. Soc., Math. Assn. Am., Soc. Indsl. and Applied Math., Phi Beta Kappa. Republican. Mem. Soc. Of Friends. Home: 33194 Dorset Ln Philomath OR 97370-9555 Office: Oreg State U Dept Math Corvallis OR 97331-4605 Office Phone: 541-737-5166. Business E-Mail: parks@math.orst.edu.

**PARKS, J. MICHAEL,** data processing executive; b. Independence, Mo., Dec. 29, 1950; s. Emory C. and Lorene (Belt) P.; m. Maureen C. Weston; children: Christopher Michael, Daniel John. BS in Edn., U. Kans., 1973. Sales rep. Ingersoll-Rand Corp., Kansas City, Mo., 1973-75; sales rep., then sr. v.p. First Data Resources/Am. Express Info. Svcs. Co., Omaha, San Francisco, Boston, Atlanta, 1976-88; chief exec. officer Call Interactive (joint venture of Am. Express Info. Svcs. Corp. and AT&T), Omaha, 1989—93; pres. First Data Resources, 1993—94; chmn., pres., CEO Alliance Data Systems, Dallas, 1997—. Bd. dirs. Commerce Bank Omaha, Data Transmission Network Inc., Am. Express Info. Svcs. Corp., WATS Mktg. of Am. Inc. Chief YMCA Indian Guide Program, Omaha, 1988-89; Cub Scouts den leader local chpt. Boy Scouts Am., Omaha, 1989—. Methodist. Avocations: golf, tennis, camping. Office: Alliance Data 17655 Waterview Pkwy Dallas TX 75252*

**PARKS, JAMES WILLIAM, II,** public facilities executive, lawyer; b. Wabash, Ind., July 30, 1956; s. James William and Joyce Arlene (Lillibridge) P.; m. Neil Ann Armstrong, Aug. 21, 1982; children: Elizabeth Joyce, Helen Frances, James William III. BS, Ball State U., 1978; JD, U. Miami, 1981. Bar: La. 1981, U.S. Dist. Ct. (ea. dist.) La. 1981, U.S. Ct. Appeals (5th and 11th cirs.) 1981. Fla. 1982, U.S. Dist. Ct. (mid. dist.) La. 1982. Atty. Jones, Walker, Waechter, Poitevent, Carrere et al., New Orleans, 1981-83, Foley & Judell, New Orleans, 1983-88, McCollister & McCleary, pc, Baton Rouge, 1988-95;

pres., CEO La. Pub. Facilities Authority, Baton Rouge, 1995—. Mem. AICPA, Nat. Assn. Bond Lawyers, La. State Bar Assn., Fla. Bar Assn., Assn. for Gifted and Talented Students, Baton Rouge (treas. 1994-96, pres.-elect 1996-97, pres. 1997-98), Soc. La. CPA (govt. acctg. and auditing com. 1994-95), Nat. Assn. Higher Edn. Facilities Authorities (bd. dirs. 1996-2001, v.p. 1997-99, pres. 1999-2001), Nat. Coun. Health Facilities Fin. Authorities (bd. dirs. 2004—, treas. 2004—), Coun. of Devel. Fin. Agys. (bd. dirs. 2002—), La. Assistive Tech. Access Network (bd. dirs. 2001—, chmn. 2004—), La. Pub. Health Inst. (bd. dirs. 2005—). Avocations: travel, computers. Home: 5966 Tennyson Dr Baton Rouge LA 70817-2933 Office: La Pub Facilities Authority 2237 S Acadian Thruway Ste 650 Baton Rouge LA 70808-2380 Office Phone: 225-923-0020. E-mail: jameswsparks2@hotmail.com, parks@lpfa.com.

**PARKS, JEAN ANNE,** retired acute care nurse; b. Grand Rapids, Mich., Aug. 3, 1940; d. Edwin Charles and Ruth Katherine (Skellenger) Paepke; m. Charles Wilbur Parks, Nov. 24, 1961; children: Charles Edwin, Catherine Ann, Michael Allan. Diploma in Nursing with highest honors, Blodgett Meml. Hosp., 1961; BS summa cum laude in Health Studies, Western Mich. U., 1987; MA magna cum laude in Health and Humanities, Mich. State U., 1994. RN. Staff nurse Blodgett Meml. Hosp., Grand Rapids, 1961—62; nurse Ctrl. Mich. Cmty. Hosp., Mt. Pleasant, 1962—64; med.-surg. staff Blodgett Meml. Hosp., 1964—70, part-time staff, 1979—2003; part-time Medicaid evaluator for Kent County, Mich. Dept. Pub. Health, Lansing, 1987—88. Mem. Grand Rapids Symphony Chorus, 1987—2003. Baptist. Avocations: travel, music (toured with chorus to several countries).

**PARKS, JOE BENJAMIN,** entrepreneur, retired state legislator; b. McAlester, Okla., Dec. 17, 1915; s. James Allen and Mary Florence (Youngblood) P.; m. Florence M. Evans, Oct. 25, 1941; children: Anne, Kathryn. BS in Pub. Adminstrn., Okla. State U., 1939. Divsn. dir. U.S. VA, Washington, 1946—56; spl. asst., cons. U.S. GSA, Washington, 1957—58; mgr. dist. EDP divsn. RCA Corp., Washington, 1959—65; mgr. Ea. region Dashew Bus. Machines, Arlington, Va., 1966—68; assoc. adminstr. social and rehab. svc. U.S. Dept. HEW, Washington, 1969—73; dir. mktg. govs. sys. divsn. Booz, Allen & Hamilton, Washington, 1974—75; ptnr. Forbes & Parks, Dover, NH, 1976—2002, PatPar, Inc., 1990—; mem. N.H. State Legislature, Concord, 1984—92, chmn. joint com. on elderly affairs, 1987—92, mem. com. on health, human svcs. and elderly, 1987—90; chmn. subcom. mileage and electronic roll call, 1989—90; vice chmn. legis. adminstrn. com., 1990—91; mem. appropriations com., 1991—92; propr. Portsmouth Athenaeum, Portsmouth, NH, 1992—. Corporator Wentworth Douglas Hosp., Dover, 1980-89; pres. Berr Par, Inc., 1994—. Columnist Nat. Antiques Rev., 1975-77, Boston Globe N.H. Weekly 1987-88, Foster's Daily Democrat (Dover, N.H.), 1988-90; freelance writer, 1990—. Vice-chmn. NH State Rep. Com., 1987-88; chmn. Strafford County, NH, Reps., 1988; Strafford County campaign mgr. George W. Bush for Pres., 1999-2000; bd. dirs. Coastal Maine Bot. Garden, 2001-05, Rockingham Bot. Garden, 2005—. Decorated Bronze Star; recipient Lawmakers award for disting. environ. svc. Sierra Club, 1990, NH State award New England Wildflower Soc., 1998; named Norris Cotton Rep. of Yr., 1993; Paul Harris fellow Rotary Internat. Found., 1998. Mem. Am. Rhododendron Soc. (pres. Mass. chpt. 1995-96, Bronze medal 1992, 2003, Silver medal, 2006). Congregationalist. Avocation: plant breeding. Home and Office: Parkwood Farm 195 Long Hill Rd Dover NH 03820-6108

**PARKS, KATIE MAE,** human services manager; b. Hubbard, Tex., Feb. 15, 1922; d. Sylvester and Janice Ruth Toliner; m. James Parks, Feb. 15, 1947 (dec.); children: Joe Keith, Sheryl Janice. Student, Tex. Tech. U. Unit mgr. Meth. Hosp., Lubbock, Tex., 1966—87; outreach specialist Tex. Tech. Wellness Ctr., Lubbock, Tex., 1994—. Bd. mem. Cmty. Health Clinic, Lubbock, Tex., Lubbock (Tex.) Art Commn. Author: (book) Why? - Poetry, 1971, History of African American In Lubbock, 2002. Adv. bd. mem. Martin Luther King, Lubbock, Tex., 1970—; bd. mem. Neighborhood Assn., Lubbock, Tex., 2001—03; pres. Usher Unit #2 Missionary Bapt. Ch., Sunday sch. tchr.; assists Missionary Soc. Nominee Tex. Women Hall of Fame, Gov. Ann Richards, Woman of Yr., Delta Sigma Theta, Clinton's Vol. award. Democrat. Baptist. Avocation: writing. Home: 2402 Cedar Ave Lubbock TX 79404

**PARKS, KIZZY MARIE,** psychology professor; b. Southfield, Mich., May 22, 1979; d. Arthur R. and Kathy J. Parks. BA in Psychology, Alfred U., 2001; MS in Psychology, Fla. Inst. Tech., 2003, postgrad. Adj. instr. Fla. Met. U., Melbourne, Fla., 2004—; adj. instr. online Brevard CC, Melbourne, 2003—. Mem.: APA (assoc.), Soc. for Occupl. Health Psychology (assoc.), Soc. for Indsl. and Orgnl. Psychology (assoc.), Assn. for Psychol. Sci (assoc.). Personal E-mail: kizwiz@hotmail.com.

**PARKS, LLOYD LEE,** oil industry executive; b. Kiefer, Okla., Dec. 9, 1929; s. Homer Harrison and Avis Pearl (Motes) P.; m. Mary Ellen Scott, Aug. 20, 1948; children: Connie Jo, Karyn Ann, Rebecca Lee. Student, Okla. State U., 1948-50, Tulsa U., 1950-51, Harvard U. Bus. Sch., 1965. Acct. Deep Rock Oil Corp., 1951-54; chief acct. Blackwell Oil & Gas Co., Tulsa, 1954-60, sec. treas., 1960-62; v.p., controller Amax Oil & Gas Inc., Houston, 1962-67, pres., CEO, 1968—92; v.p. Amax, Inc., 1975-92; pvt. practice oil and gas and real estate investment Salado, Tex., 1992—. Served with AUS, 1946-48, 50-51. Mem.: Ind. Petroleum Assn. Am. (dir.), Union Club, Wildflower Country Club (Temple, Tex.). Republican. Office: PO Box 1021 Salado TX 76571-1021 Personal E-mail: llparks9@aol.com. *Work hard, work smart and believe in yourself. You can and will be successful; if you want to be.*

**PARKS, MICHAEL CHRISTOPHER,** journalist, educator; b. Detroit, Nov. 17, 1943; s. Robert James and Rosalind (Smith) P.; m. Linda Katherine Durocher, Dec. 26, 1964; children: Danielle Anne, Christopher, Matthew. AB, U. Windsor, Ont., Can., 1965. Reporter Detroit News, 1962-65; corr. Time-Life News Service, N.Y.C., 1965-66; asst. city editor Suffolk Sun, Long Island, NY, 1966-68; polit. reporter, foreign corr. The Balt. Sun, Saigon, Singapore, Moscow, Cairo, Hong Kong, Peking, 1968-80; fgn. corr. L.A. Times, L.A., Peking, Johannesburg, Moscow, Jerusalem, 1980-95, dpty. fgn. editor, 1995-96, mng. editor, 1996-97, editor, 1997-2000, v.p., 1996-97, sr. v.p., 1997-98, exec. v.p., 1998-2000; v.p. Times Mirror Co., 1998-2000; prof. Annenberg Sch. Comm. U. So. Calif., L.A., 2000—02, dir. Annenberg Sch. Journalism, 2002—; prof. journalism, 2002—. Disting. fellow Pacific Coun. Internat. Policy, 2000-02, dir. 1998-; dir. L.A. Jewish Jour., 2004-. Recipient Pulitzer prize, 1987. Mem. Am. Soc. Newspaper Editors, AP Mng. Editors, Pacific Coun. Internat., Policy, Radio-TV News Dirs., Soc. Profl. Journalists, Athenaeum (Pasadena, Calif.), Coun. on Fgn. Rels., US Naval Inst., City Club (L.A.), Nat. Press Club. Office: Annenberg Sch U So Calif Los Angeles CA 90089-0281 Office Phone: 213-740-0638. E-mail: mparks@usc.edu.

**PARKS, MICHAEL JAMES,** editor; b. Spokane, Wash., June 3, 1944; s. Floyd Lewis and Marie (McHugh) Parks; m. Janet K. Holter, Aug. 12, 1967; children: Michael J., Gregory F. Sarah M. BA, Seattle U., 1966. Reporter The Seattle Times, 1966—74, fin. editor, 1974—77; pub., editor Marple's Pacific N.W. Letter, Seattle, 1977—. Bd. govs. Seattle U. Alumni Assn.; trustee Seattle Rotary Svc. Found. Fellow, Am. Press Inst., N.Y.C., 1973. Mem.: Rotary. Roman Catholic. Avocations: opera, reading, swimming, walking. Office: Marples NW Letter Ste 200 117 W Mercer St Seattle WA 98119-3960 Personal E-mail: michaeljparks@gmail.com. E-mail: info@marples.com.

**PARKS, PATRICIA JEAN,** lawyer; b. Portland, Oreg., Apr. 2, 1945; d. Robert and Marion (Crosby) Parks; m. David F. Jurca, Oct. 17, 1971 (div. 1976). BA in History, Stanford U., 1967; JD, U. Pa., Phila., 1970. Bar: N.Y. 1971, Wash. 1974. Assoc. Milbank, Tweed, Hadley & McCoy, N.Y.C., 1970-73; Shidler, McBroom, Gates & Lucas, Seattle, 1974-81, ptnr., 1981-90, Preston, Thorgrimson, Shidler, Gates & Ellis, Seattle, 1990-93; pvt. practice Seattle, 1993-99; spl. counsel Karr Tuttle Campbell, Seattle, 1999—. Active Vashon Allied Arts; former bd. dirs. Seattle chpt. Western Pension and Benefits Conf. Mem.: ABA, Pension Roundtable, Seattle-King County Bar Assn., Wash. Women Tax, Wash. State Bar Assn. (past chair gift and estate tax com.), Wash. Native Plant Soc., Wash. Athletic Club. Avocations: kayaking, hiking, contra dancing, birdwatching. Office: 1201 3rd Ave Ste 2900 Seattle WA 98101-3284 Office Phone: 206-224-8094. Business E-Mail: pparks@karrtuttle.com.

**PARKS, ROBERT HENRY,** consulting economist, educator; b. New Orleans, Sept. 20, 1924; s. Charles Samuel and Amelia (England) P.; m. Inta Kondrats, Sept. 20, 1958 (div.); children: Karen E., Robert R., Alison J.; m. Annette Fiechter, Dec. 10, 1982 (div.). AB in Econs., Swarthmore Coll., 1949; MA, PhD in Econs., U. Pa., 1958. Economist Econ. Forecasting div. Gen. Electric Co., 1958-61; dir. econ. research Life Ins. Assn. Am., 1961-68; chief economist Maj. Wall St. Investment Firms, 1968-80; pres. Robert H. Parks & Assocs., Inc., N.Y.C., 1980—; cons. to instnl. investment officers; prof. fin. Wharton Sch., U. Pa., 1957—58, Pace U., 1980—. Adj. prof. fin. Baruch Sch., CUNY, Lehigh U. Author: The Witch Doctor of Wall Street, 1996, Unlocking the Secrets of Wall Street, 1998, Prometheus; contbr. articles to profl. jours. Democrat. Home: Scarborough Manor 6M-2 PO Box 307 Scarborough NY 10510

**PARKS, ROBERT MYERS,** appliance manufacturing company executive; b. Nevada, Mo., July 18, 1927; s. Cecil R. and Marcella (Myers) P.; m. Audrey Lenora Jones, June 18, 1955; children— John Robert, Janet M. Parks Huston. BS, U. Mo., 1949; MBA, Harvard U., 1952. Asst. dept. mgr. Jewett & Sherman Co., Kansas City, Mo., 1949-50; staff cons. Harbridge House, Inc., Boston, 1952; v.p. Electronic Splty. Co., Inc., Los Angeles, 1952-57; founder, chmn. bd. Parks Products, Inc., Hollywood, Calif., 1957—; pres. Generalist Industries, Inc., Hollywood, 1960-73. Chmn. bd. Shaver Corp. Am., L.A., 1965—; lectr. mktg. UCLA Extension divsn., 1960-61. Contbr. articles to profl. jours.; patentee in field. Active YMCA; bd. dirs. Hollywood Presbyn. Med. Center Found., Presbyn. Homes Found.; mem. dean's adv. council U. Mo. Bus. Sch., mayor's task force on L.A. River Cahuenga Pass Coalition. With USNR, 1944-45. Named in his honor Grad. Bus. Sch., U. Mo. Mem. Sales and Marketing Execs. Assn., C. of C., Navy League, World Affairs Council, Calif. Caballeros, Rangers, Vaqueros del Desierto, Los Caballeros, Rancheros Visitadores, E Clampus Vitus, Delta Sigma Pi, Sigma Chi. Clubs: Mason (Shriner), L.A. Breakfast, Braemar Country, Saddle and Sirloin. Presbyterian. Home: 7421 Woodrow Wilson Dr Los Angeles CA 90046-1322 Office: 3611 Cahuenga Blvd Hollywood CA 90068-1205 Office Phone: 323-876-5454.

**PARKS, SUSAN JANE,** artist; b. Chattanooga, Tenn., Feb. 19, 1957; d. James Bennett and Clara Jane (deLoach) P. BFA, Middle Tenn. State U., 1979; postgrad. cert., Banff Ctr. Sch. Fine Arts, 1982-84; cert. apprenticeship, Appalachian Crafts Ctr., 1984-85. Studio mgr. The Banff Ctr., Alberta, Can., 1982-84, Appalachian Crafts, Smithville, Tenn., 1984-85; custom jewelry J.A. Designs and Crabtree Jewlers, Chattanooga, Tenn., 1985-90; art specialist Hunter Mus., City Parks Hamilton County Schs., 1990—; art coord. Creative Discovery Mus., Chattanooga, 1995-96; art tchr. Cleve. City Schs. 1996—. Designer, sculpture 212 Market St., Chattanooga, 1992—; designer edn. puppets and costumes Tenn. Aquarium, Chattanooga, 1992—; cons.; designer city decoration project World U., Edmonton, Alb., Can., 1983 Vol., bd. dirs. Hunter Mus., Chattanooga, 1992-93; art selection adv. com. Ross's Landing, Chattanooga, 1989-90. Recipient 3rd Pl. Second Nat. Fiber Arts Competition, 1989, 1st Pl. Color, The Spectrum of Expression, 1986; scholarship The Banff Ctr., 1982-84; named Best of Metals Artist-Craftsman Assn., 1977. Mem. Assn. for Visual Artists, Scenic City Kite Club. Avocations: kite-flying, swimming, learning about and trying new art forms, camping and gardening. Home: 611 Barton Ave Chattanooga TN 37405-4301

**PARKS, SUZAN LORI,** playwright; b. Fort Knox, KY, 1964; d. Donald and Francis Parks; m. Paul Oscher, 2001. BA, Mount Holyoke Coll., 1985. Guest lecturer Pratt Institute, N.Y.C., 1988, U. Mich., Ann Arbor, Mich., 1990, Yale U., New Haven, 1990—91, NYU, 1990—91; prof. of playwriting Eugene Lang Coll., N.Y.C., 1990; writer-in-residence New School for Social Research (now New School U.), N.Y.C., 1991—92; dir. Theater Projects Calif. Inst. Arts, Valencia, 2000—. Author: (plays) The Sinner's Place, 1985, Betting on the Dust Commander, 1988, Imperceptible Mutabilities in the Third Kingdom, 1990 (Obie award, 1990), Devotees in the Garden of Love, 1992, The Death of the Last Black Man in the Whole Entire World, 1992, The America Play, 1993, Venus, 1996 (Obie award, 1996), In the Blood, 1999, Topdog/Underdog, 2001 (Pulitzer Prize for drama, 2002), (screenplays) Anemone Me, 1990, Girl 6, 1996, (novels) Getting My Mother's Body, 2003. Recipient Rockefeller Foundation grant, 1990, N.Y. Found. for the Arts grant, 1990, Whiting Found. Writers award, 1992, Ford Found. grant, 1995, CalArts/Alpert award, 1996, PEN-Laura Pels award, 2000; fellow MacArthur Found., 2001, Guggenheim Found., 2000; grantee Mary E. Woolley fellowship, 1989, Naomi Kitay fellowship, 1989, Nat. Endowment for the Arts playwriting fellowship, 1990—91. Office: Calif Inst Arts 24700 McBean Pkwy Valencia CA 91355

**PARK SPENCER, KAREN LYNN,** architect, apparel designer; b. Brookville, Pa., Apr. 30, 1963; d. John Joseph Park, Roselyn Ann Park; m. Michael Vincent Spencer. A Specialized Tech., Triangle Tech. Coll., 1986. Cert. interior design 1995, lic. real estate Pa., 1993, cert. kitchen specialist 1988, quality control mfg. housing 1988. Space planner & cad drafter Pace Design, McLean, Va., 1986—86; cad drafter and quality control Strattan Homes, Strattanville, Pa., 1986—88; store planner Penn-Traffic Riverside Engring., DuBois, 1988—95; designer K.T.H. Architects, 1995—96; drafting coord. C-Cor Elecs., State College, 1996—97; mech. engr. D.L. Martin (for Schindler Elevator Corp.), Mercersburg, 1997—98; sr. project mgr. Noelker & Hull Architects, Chambersburg, 1998—2000. Cons. Park Places, Chambersburg, 1995—2002; drafting shadow Riverside Engring., DuBois, 1988—95; real estate Sarvey, Brookville, 1993—94; elec. tech. Strattan Homes, Strattanville, 1987—88. Author: (Poetry) Application of Pen and Thought, 1997 (Editors Choice Award, 1998), Perceptions in Harmony, 1998 (Editors Choice Award, 1999), Dawn of Silence, 1998 (Editors Choice Award, 1999), Last Good-byes, 1998 (Editors Choice Award, 1999), America at the millenium - The Best Poems and Poets of the 20th Century, 2000 (Editors Choice Award, 2001). Vol. Brookville Civic Club, Brookville, 1992—95, Vols. for Charity, DuBois, 1992—95; asst. Girl Scout of Am., Brookville, 1972—76; helper 4-H, Home & Dairy, Brookville, 1971—76; tchr. The Presbyn. Ch. Brookville, Brookville, Pa., 1991—95; facilitator Alpha program The Presby. Ch. Falling Spring, Chambersburg, Pa., 2001—02. Mem.: Order of Ea. Star. Presbyterian. Avocations: poetry, art, swimming, travel.

**PARKYN, JOHN WILLIAM,** editor, writer, columnist; b. London, Dec. 7, 1931; came to U.S., 1967; citizen, 1973; s. James R. and Eva M. (Dix) P.; m. Sybil (Judy) Hetherington; 1 child, Elaine. Student, Dulwich Coll., 1943-48. Staff writer Bus. Mag., London, 1954-56; writer-editor Amalgamated Press, London, 1956-58; features editor Woman's Illustrated mag., London, 1958-60; staff writer Internat. Pub. Corp., London, 1960-61; editor Westward mag. Daily News Ltd., London, 1961-64; assoc. editor Daily Telegraph mag., London, 1964-66; features editor King mag. Europress, Ltd., London, 1966-67; assoc. editor Tropic mag. Miami (Fla.) Herald, 1967-69; editor Tropic mag., 1969-77; editor Calif. Today mag. San Jose (Calif.) Mercury News, 1977-83; editor Sunshine: The Mag. of South Fla. Sun-Sentinel Co. (subs. Tribune Co.), Ft. Lauderdale, Fla., 1983-96; columnist S. Fla. Sun-Sentinel, 1997—2005; exec. editor, sr. writer Vero Beach (Fla.) Mag., 1998—; columnist, feature writer City & Shore mag., 2000—05; exec. editor Tropical Home mag., 2006—. Cons. Het Parool newspaper, Amsterdam, 1965. Contbr. numerous articles to Am. and European mags. Chmn. Sunday Mag. Editors Conf., Louisville, 1973. With RAF, 1950-52. Recipient Outstanding Use of Editl. Color award Editor & Pub. mag., 1974, 75, 77, Nat. Headliner award, 1976, 79; named Editor Best Weekly Mag. in State Fla. Press Club, 1985-93, 95. Office Phone: 772-231-8199. Personal E-Mail: johnparkyn@aol.com.

**PARLAMIS, MICHAEL FRANK,** civil engineer, construction executive; b. Bklyn., May 29, 1940; s. Frank Michael and Phyllis (Burnago) P.; m. Marguerite Koskinas, Aug. 21, 1966; children: Franklin, Christine, Alexander.

BSCE, MIT, 1962, BS in Indsl. Mgmt., 1962; MSCE, Stanford U., 1963. Registered profl. engr., N.Y. Engr. Port Authority of N.Y. and N.J., 1963-64; asst. to chief engr. George A. Fuller Co., N.Y.C., 1964-67; pres. Frank Parlamis Inc., Bklyn., 1968—, Parlamis Bros. Inc., Bklyn., 1968—, Hermes Constrn. Corp., Bklyn., 1968—; ptnr. City Path LLC, City Jam LLC, 128 MAC LLC, 128 MAPP LLC. Author: CPM/PERT As Basis for Management Information Systems in Building Construction, 1966, Regulation of Building Construction in the City of New York, 1967, Greece and the Panama Canal, 1988. Chmn. expansion program Greek Orthodox Cathedral St. John the Theologian, Tenafly, N.J., 1978—; mem. Leadership 100 of the Greek Orthodox Ch.; Archon of the Ecomenical Patriarcate, Greek Orthodox Ch.; mem. ednl. coun. MIT; trustee Frank Parlamis Sr. Citizens Ctr., Jamaica, NY, Space Camp Turkey, Izmir; founder St. John the Theologian Peace Meml. Gymnasium; exec. dir. St. John the Theologian World Peace Inst. Recipient Ellis Island medal of honor, 2002, Gold Key award for best engineered restaurant in USA, Internat. Hotel, Motel an Restaurant Show, 1992. Mem. Am. Hellenic Progressive Assn., Bklyn. Tech. Rsch. Found. (life), Tau Beta Pi, Chi Epsilon. Republican. Avocations: engineering and religious history, peace advocacy, ecumenical religious activities. Home: 128 Downey Dr Tenafly NJ 07670-3006 Office: 328 Atlantic Ave Brooklyn NY 11201-5804 Office Phone: 718-875-6744. Business E-Mail: parlamis@alum.mit.edu.

**PARLE, BERTHA IBARRA,** writer; b. El Paso, Tex., Nov. 14, 1947; d. Arnulfo and Bertha (Soto) Ibarra; m. Dennis Jerome Parle, Aug. 16, 1969; children: Joseph, Mónica, Angélica Attended, Loretto Acad., 1965; BA in French, Spanish, U. Tex., El Paso, 1968; MA in Spanish, U. Kans., Lawrence, 1970, H.S. tchg. cert., 1971; postgrad. courses in French, U. Houston, 1990—95. Bilingual tchr. Kans. Remedial Edn. Program, Sharon Springs, 1967, 71, 72; Spanish tchr. Ottawa (Kans.) H.S., 1971-74; ESL instr. North Harris Coll., Houston, 1977-83; modern lang. prof. N. Harris Montgomery C.C. Dist., Houston, 1983-97, head lang. inst., 1997—2002. Cultural cons.; sponsor Hispanic students North Harris Coll. and Montgomery Coll., 1983-97, organizer Hispanic cultural events, 1983—, sponsor Cath. Newman Club, 1985-95; lectr., slide show The Nahua Mexica Legacy, 1994-96; participant in field seminars; NEH and Fulbright Ecuador field experience. Author numerous poems; Spanish poetry publ. in Tejidos, Grito al Sol, 1972-94. Hispanic leader St. Leo's Cath. Ch., Houston, 1982-92; del. People to People Am. Program to S. Africa, 2000. Recipient Tchg. Excellence award North Harris Coll., 1997, Excellence award Nat. Inst. for Staff and Orgn. Devel., 1998; Am. Coun. Tchrs. Fgn. Langs. summer scholar U. Montreal, 1999. Mem. AAUW, Am. Coun. Tchrs. Fgn. Langs., Computer Assisted Lang. Instn. Consortium, Am. Assn. C.C. Women, Tex. Fgn. Lang. Assn., Inst. Hispanic Culture., North Harris United Faculty. Avocations: creative writing, study of indigenous language cultures, hispanic students and hispanic issues in the community. Office: North Harris Coll 2700 W Thorne Dr Houston TX 77073 Office Phone: 281-618-5546. Business E-Mail: bertha.parle@nhmccd.edu.

**PARLIER, GREG H.,** military officer, engineer, research scientist; b. San Luis Obispo, Calif., May 10, 1952; s. Merton B. and Kathleen F. Parlier; m. Judy D. Olson, Aug. 30, 1975; children: Jamie Lynn, Timothy Scott, Steven Hugh. BS, U.S. Mil. Acad., 1974; MS, Naval Postgrad. Sch., 1983; MA, Georgetown U., 1988; postgrad., USMC Command and Staff Coll., 1988—89, U. Va., 1992, U.S. Army War Coll., 1995—96; PhD, Wesleyan U. 2004. Registered profl. engr., Va.; master parachutist, army strategist, battle staff officer. Vulcan and redeye platoon leader 3-4 ADAR, 82d Airborne Divsn., Ft. Bragg, NC, 1975—76; exec. officer Battery C, 3-4 ADAR, 82d Airborne Divsn., 1976—77, Battery C, 2-71 ADA, 31st ADA Brigade, Republic of Korea, 1977; battery comdr. Battery C, 3-4 ADAR, 82d Airborne Divsn., 1979—81; asst. prof. dept. engring. U.S. Mil. Acad., West Point, NY, 1983—86; chief officer plans U.S. Army Mil. Pers. Ctr., Alexandria, Va., 1986—88, 3-4 ADAR ops. officer, 1989—90, exec. officer, 1990—91; G-3 air def. element XVIII Airborne Corps, Ft. Bragg, 1991—92; bn. comdr. 5-2 ADAR, 69th ADA Brigade, V Corps, Crailsheim and Bamberg, Germany, 1992—94; chief resource plans and analysis divsn. Office of the Chief of Staff U.S. Army, Washington, 1996—98; dir. program analysis and evaluation U.S. Army Recruiting Command, Ft. Knox, Ky., 1998—2002; dir. for transformation U.S. Army Aviation and Missile Command, Redstone Arsenal, Ala., 2002—03; sr. rsch. scientist U. Ala., Huntsville, 2003—05; def. analyst Inst. for Def. Analysis, 2004—; sr. sys. analyst Sci. Applications Internat. Corp., 2005—; v.p. strategic planning Rsch., Sys., and Analytical Engring., Inc., 2005—. Pres. ops. Rsch. Soc. Am., 2005. Sr. tactical comdr. McKee Barracks, Crailsheim, 1993; vice chmn. Bamberg (Germany) Scholarship Com., 1993—94; mentor Georgetown U. ROTC, Washington, 1996—98. Col. US Army, 1997. Decorated Bronze Star U.S. Army, Legion of Merit; named 8th FLAK, 1st German Mountain Divsn., 1994, Dept. of the Army Rsch. Analyst of the Yr., 1987; recipient German Efficiency Badge (Gold), Bundeswehr (German Army), 1999, 2001, plaque of appreciation, Korean Nat. Assembly, 1978, Can. Parachutist Badge, Can. Forces, 1977, USMC CSC Disting. Grad. and Gen. Clifton B. Cates award, 1989, Jim and Rafer Johnson Outstanding Athlete Award, Kingsburg H.S. Faculty and Coaches, 1970; Nat. Def. Fellow, MIT, 1994—95. Mem.: Mil. Ops. Rsch. Soc. (Grad. Rsch. award 1983), Inst. Ops. Rsch. and Mgmt. Scis., 82nd Airborne Divsn. Assn. (life), Sigma Xi. Avocations: reading, classical music, sports. Home: 255 Avian Ln Madison AL 35758-6863 Personal E-Mail: gparlier@knology.net. Business E-Mail: greg.h.parlier@saic.com.

**PARLOW, CYNTHIA MARIA,** professional soccer player; b. Memphis, May 8, 1978; BS in Nutrition, U. N.C., 1998. Profl. soccer player Atlanta Beat, 2001—03. Mem. U.S. Women's Nat. Soccer Team, 1996—, U.S. Under-20 Nat. Team, Nordic Cup championships, Denmark, 1997, U-16 Nat. Team pool. Named All-ACC and ACC Rookie of Yr., 1995, Soccer Am. Freshman of Yr., 1995, Most Valuable Player, 1995 Under 17 U.S. Nat. Soccer nat. tournami nt, World Cup Champion, 1999; recipient Gold medal, Centennial Olympic Games, 1996, Herman Trophy, Mo. Athletic Club Player of Yr. award, 1997, Silver medal, Sydney Olympic Games, 2000. Achievements include helped U. N.C. to NCAA Championship 1996, 97; 1st-Team All-ACC selection in 1997; named to 1997 NCAA All-Tournament Team. Office: US Soccer Fedn 1801-1811 S Prairie Ave Chicago IL 60616

**PARMA, EDWARD SCOTT,** engineer, surgeon; b. Montgomery, Ala., May 17, 1963; s. George Edward and Marie Little Parma; m. Victoria Mathison; children: Edward Scott, Catherine Mathison. BS in engring., Auburn U., 1981—86; MBA, U. of Ala. at Birmingham, 1987—93; MD, U. of Ala. Sch. of Medicine, 1994—98. Design engr. SCI Systems, Huntsville, Ala., 1986—90; project engr. So. Rsch. Technologies, Birmingham, Ala., 1990—92; systems engr. Rust Internat., Birmingham, 1992—94; internal medicine resident Bapt. Health Sys., Birmingham, 1998—99; ophthalmology resident Tulane Health Sciences Ctr., New Orleans, 1999—2002; vitreoretinal surgery fellow Retina Specialists of Ala., 2002—. Chief resident Tulane U. Dept. of Ophthalmology, New Orleans, 2001—02. Musician: Ala. All-State Band (First Chair Trumpet State of Ala., 1981); singer: Performed with DisneyWorld Voices of Liberty; contbr. articles to profl. jours. Humanitarian liaison Montgomery Coun. on Aging, Ala., 1981—85; staff mem. Frazer United Meth. Ch., Ala., 1981—85. Mem.: AMA, Jefferson County Med. Soc., La. Med. Soc., Ala. Med. Soc., Am. Acad. Of Ophthalmology, Beta Gamma Sigma, Upsilon Pi Epsilon, Tau Beta Pi, Sigma Pi Epsilon. Methodist. Achievements include design of space computer hardware currently in geosynchronous orbit supporting intercontinental ballistic missile tracking; design of in-flight missile computer to process real time tracking video; discovery of genetic mutation causing blindness in a large 3000 member pedigree dating to 1793. Avocations: weightlifting, tennis, music. Office: Retina Specialists Of Alabama 1201 11th St South Birmingham AL 35205

**PARMAL, PAMELA ANN,** curator; b. Milw., May 3, 1959; d. Edward Paul and Dolores Parmal; m. William Coyle Van Siclen, Nov. 23, 1954. MA in Mus. Studies, Fashion Inst. Tech., N.Y.C., 1985—87. Assoc. curator, costume and textiles Mus. Art, RISD, Providence, 1987—98; curator of textile and fashion arts Mus. Fine Arts, Boston, 1998—2004, David and Roberta Logie curator of textile & fashion arts, dept. head, 2005—. Author (contributing): (exhibition catalogue) From Paris to Providence; author: (curator) (exhibition

and book) Samplers from A to Z; author: (curator and author) (exhibition and catalogue) Geoffrey Beene; author: (contributing) Beene by Beene, (collections catalogue) MFA Highlights: Textile and Fashion Arts; author: (curator) (exhibition and book) Fashion Show. Grantee Exhbn. Planning grant, NEH, 1996—97, 1997—98. Mem.: Centre Internat. des Etudes des Textiles Anciens (directing coun. mem. 2005), Textile Soc. Am. (pres. 2004—06). Office: Museum Fine Arts 465 Huntington Ave Boston MA 02115 Home Fax: 617-262-6549; Office Fax: 617 369-3707. Business E-Mail: pparmal@mfa.org.

**PARMAN, STEPHEN WAYNE,** science educator; b. Texas City, June 1, 1972; BA, Harvard U., Cambridge, Mass., 1990—94; PhD, MIT, Cambridge, 1994—2001. Postdoctoral fellow Harvard U., 2003—05; lectr. Durham U., England, 2005—. Recipient MSA Disting. Lecture Series award, Mineral. Soc. Am., 2006—. Mem.: Am. Geophys. Union. Achievements include research in constraints on the thermal evolution of the Earth from ancient lavas; discovery of first measurement of helium partitioning in olivine. Home: 45 York Crescent Durham DH1 5PT England Personal E-Mail: stephen.parman@durham.ac.uk.

**PARMAN, SUSAN MORRISSETT,** anthropologist, writer; b. Middletown, Conn., Aug. 17, 1945; d. Lee Ferguson and Edith Rosalie (Morrissett) Parman; m. Jacob Pandian, May 11, 1972; 1 child, Georgina Morrissett Pandian. BA, Antioch Coll., 1967; PhD, Rice U., 1972. Asst. prof. anthropology Calif. State U., Hayward, 1972-76; lectr. anthropology various colls. and univs., Calif., 1976-88; prof. anthropology Calif. State U. Fullerton, 1988—, chair dept. anthropology, 1996—2006; v.p., chair bd. Human Rels. Area Files Yale U., New Haven, 2006—. Cons. Holt, Rinehart & Winston, 1985—, Harcourt, Brace Jovanovich Pubs., 1985—, Prentice Hall Publ., Wadsworth/Thompson, Berg Press, Pluto Press. Author: Scottish Crofters, 1990, 2d edit., 2005, Dream and Culture, 1991, Europe in the Anthropological Imagination, 1997; (with J. Pandian) The Making of Anthropology, 2004; contbr. articles to profl. jours NEH rsch. fellow, Scotland, 1983, 92; Calif. State U. Found. grantee, 1991-95, NSF grantee, 1995, 98 Fellow Soc. Antiquarians of Scotland; mem. Am. Anthrop. Assn., Soc. for the Anthropology of Europe (publs. chair 1992-96, pres. 2000-02) Democrat. Office: Calif State U Fullerton Dept Anthropology Fullerton CA 92834 Home: 5345 Avenida El Cid Yorba Linda CA 92887-3127 Office Phone: 714-278-2844. Business E-Mail: sparman@fullerton.edu.

**PARMAR, PARMINDER,** education educator; b. Mhow, Madhya Pradesh, India, Oct. 20, 1956; arrived in US, 1994, permanent resident, 2005; BSc, G.B. Pant U. of Agr. and Tech., Pantnagar, India, 1977; MSc, Punjab Agrl. U., Ludhiana, Punjab, India, 1980; PhD, U. Conn., Storrs, 2000. Part time tchr. (child devel.) Punjab Agrl. U., Ludhiana, Punjab, India, 1980—82, asst. prof. (child devel.), 1982—94; rsch. asst. Pa. State U., University Park, 1994—96, faculty; grad. rsch. asst. U. of Conn., Storrs, Conn., 1996—2000, rsch. assoc./adj. tchr., 2000—02. Sec. child devel. soc. Punjab Agrl. U., Ludhiana, Punjab, India, 1986—90. Researcher (research presentation) Stress among College Students (Profl. Devel. Award, 2003). Pres. Assn. for Rsch. on Asian Indian Communities, National, 2005—06; sec., treas. Internat. Soc. for Interpersonal Acceptance Rejection, 2006—; pres. Indian Assn. of Pa./Ny., Clarks Summit, Pa., 2005—06. Recipient David and Joyce Mark Tresseller Profl. Devel. award, 2003, Adv. Bd. Excellence in Tchg. award, 2005. Mem.: Internat. Soc. for the Study of Behavioral Devel. (corr.). Office: Pennsylvania State University 120 Ridgeview Dr Dunmore PA 18512 Office Phone: 570-963-2530.

**PARMELEE, ARTHUR HAWLEY, JR.,** pediatric medical educator; b. Chgo., Oct. 29, 1917; s. Arthur Hawley and Ruth Frances (Brown) P.; m. Jean Kern Rheinfrank, Nov. 11, 1939; children: Arthur Hawley III, Ann (Mrs. John C. Minahan Jr.), Timothy, Ruth Ellen. BS, U. Chgo., 1940, MD, 1943. Diplomate Am. Bd. Pediatrics (examiner 1966—). Intern U.S. Naval Hosp., Bethesda, Md., 1943-44; extern Yale Inst. Child Devel., 1947, New Haven Hosp., 1947-48, L.A. Children's Hosp., 1948-49; mem. faculty UCLA Med. Sch., 1951—; prof. pediat., 1967-88, prof. emeritus, 1988, dir. divsn. child devel., 1964-88; mem. Brain Rsch. Inst., 1966-88, Mental Retardation Rsch. Ctr., 1970-88. Rsch. prof. pediat. U. Göttingen, Germany, 1967-68; mem. com. child devel. rsch. and pub. policy NRC, 1977-81; cons. Nat. Inst. Child Health and Human Devel., 1963-70, Holy Family Adoption Svc., 1949-80. Author articles, chpts. in books. Trustee Los Angeles Children's Mus., 1979. Served with USN, 1943-47. Recipient C. Anderson Aldrich award in child devel., 1975; Commonwealth fellow Centre de Recherches Biologiques Neonatales, Clinique Obstetricale Baudelocque, Paris, 1959-60; fellow Ctr. Advanced Study in Behavioral Scis., Stanford U., 1984-85; hon. lectr. Soc. for Developmental and Behavioral Pediat., 1996. Mem. AMA, Am. Pediat. Soc., Soc. Pediat. Rsch., Western Soc. Pediat. Rsch., Am. Acad. Pediat. (chmn. com. sect. child devel. 1966), Assn. Ambulatory Pediat. (mem. coun. 1966-69), Soc. Rsch. in Child Devel. (pres. 1983-85, Disting. Sci. Contbns. to Child Devel. award 1993), Assn. Psychophysiol. Study of Sleep, Los Angeles County Med. Soc., Phi Beta Kappa. Home: 764 Iliff St Pacific Palisades CA 90272-3927 Office: Univ Calif Dept Pediatrics Los Angeles CA 90024

**PARMELEE, WILLIAM DOUGLAS,** financial executive, accountant; b. Providence, Aug. 16, 1957; s. Lyman Malcolm and Dorothy (Baird) P.; m. Luann Moody, Aug. 23, 1980. BSBA, U. N.C., 1979. CPA, N.C. Sr. mgr. Ernst & Young, Raleigh, NC, 1979—88; v.p., contr. Qualex, Inc., Durham, NC, 1988—2000; CFO Nat. Gypsum Co., Charlotte, NC, 2000—. Dir., treas. Carolina Excellence, Inc., Wake Forest, N.C., 1988—. Pres. Theatre in the Park, Raleigh, 1992-93; treas. N.C. Consumers Coun., Chapel Hill 1987 03; elder, treas. Hudson Meml. Prosbyn. Ch., Raleigh, 1986-89; elder Wake Forest Presbyn. Ch., 1991-92. Mem. AICPA, N.C. Assn. CPAs (health care com. 1985-88), Inst. Mgmt. Accts., Fin. Execs. Inst. Mem. AICPA, N.C. Assn. CPA's (health care com. 1985-88). Democrat. Avocations: team sports, gardening, theater, reading fiction, music. Office: Nat Gypsum 2000 Rexford Rd Charlotte NC 28211 E-mail: wdparmelee@nationalgypsum.com.

**PARMESE, GABRIEL J.,** corporate financial executive; s. James and Martha (Phillips) Parmese; m. Ann C. Mullen, Oct. 20, 2000; children: Norah, Jimmy. BSc in Commerce and Fin., Rider U.; MBA, N.H. Coll., 1987. V.p. fin., corp. contr. Art Tech., Cambridge, Mass., 2001—04; CFO SynQor Inc., Boxboro, Mass., 2004—. Corp. contr. Applix, Westbrough, Mass., 2000—01. Active homeless shelter activities and abuse programs, 1993—2005. Mem.: Fed. Executives Inst. (assoc.). Conservative. Achievements include public reporting, turn around and operational efficiency expert for US based companies. Office: SynQor Inc 155 Swanson Rd Boxboro MA 01719 Office Phone: 978-849-0600. Business E-Mail: gabrielparmese@synqor.com.

**PARMET, HARRIET ABBEY L.,** literature educator; b. Phila., July 22, 1928; d. Jacob and Belle Cecil (Popolow) Leibowitz; m. Sidney B. Parmet, June 7, 1950; children: Howard B., Jonathan L. AB, Temple U., 1950, MS, 1960; B in Hebrew Lit., Gratz Coll., 1979; PhD in English, Lehigh U. Cert. secondary edn. tchr., Pa. Tchr. Hebrew Temple U., Phila., 1946-50, Beth Israel, Phila., 1946-51; tchr. English and social studies Gillespie Jr. High Sch., Phila., 1950-55; tchr. Hebrew and Jewish history Temple Beth El, Allentown, Pa., 1964-77; tchr. Hebrew and Israeli lit. Lehigh U., Bethlehem, Pa., 1976—95; prof. emeritus, 1995. Hillel co-advisor, mem. exec. bd. Lehigh U., 1976—. Author: The Terror of Our Days: Four Am. Poets Respond to the Holocaust, 2001; contbr. articles to profl. jours. Vice pres. Temple Beth El Sisterhood, Allentown, 1973-75; mem. exec. bd. Jewish Family Svc., Allentown, 1988—; bd. dirs. Women's Proft. Jewish Fedn., Allentown, 1973-75. Coolidge Colloquim fellow, 1986, Givat Haviva Rsch. fellow, 1987; named Outstanding Alumna Gratz Coll. Cetenial Celebration. Mem. Women's Studies Consortium, Lehigh Valley Assn. Ind. Colls., Am. Jewish Congress (pres. Allentown chpt. 1970), Assn. Jewish Studies, Nat. Assn. Hebrew Profs., Temple U. Alumni Assn. (Disting. Alumni award 1995), Gratz Coll. Alumni Assn., Hadassah (life). Home: 1118 N 28th St Allentown PA 18104-2908 Office: Lehigh U Modern Lang Dept Maginnes Hall # 9 Bethlehem PA 18015-3206 Office Phone: 610-758-3090. Business E-Mail: hlpo@lehigh.edu.

**PARMET, HERBERT SAMUEL,** historian, writer; b. N.Y.C., Sept. 28, 1929; s. Isaac and Fanny (Scharf) P.; m. Joan Kronish, Sept. 12, 1948; 1 child, Wendy. BS, SUNY, Oswego, 1951; MA, Queens Coll., 1957; postgrad., Columbia U., 1958-62. Prof. history Grad. Sch. CUNY, 1968-95, disting. prof. history, 1983-95, prof. emeritus, 1995—. Cons. ABC-TV, N.Y.C., 1983, KERA-TV, Dallas, 1986-91, WGBH-TV, Boston, 1988-91. Author: Aaron Burr: Portrait of an Ambitious Man, 1967, Never Again: President Runs for a Third Term, 1968, Eisenhower and the American Crusades, 1972, The Democrats, 1976, Jack: The Struggles of John F. Kennedy, 1980, JFK: The Presidency of John F. Kennedy, 1983, Richard Nixon and His America, 1990, George Bush: The Life of a Lone Star Yankee, 1997, Presidential Power: From the New Deal to the New Right, 2001. Cpl. U.S. Army, 1952-54. Grantee, NEH, 1987. Fellow Soc. Am. Historians; mem. Am. Hist. Assn., Orgn. Am. Historians, Authors Guild. Avocation: photography. Home: 36 Marsten Ln Hillsdale NY 12529-5816 Personal E-mail: herbertparmet@yahoo.com. E-mail: hparmet@taconic.net.

**PARMET, ROBERT DAVID,** historian, educator; b. N.Y.C., Dec. 11, 1938; s. Isaac and Fanny (Scharf) Parmet; 1 child, Andrew Charles. BA, CCNY, 1960; MA, Columbia U., 1961, PhD, 1966. Fellow CCNY, 1960-62, lectr., 1962-65; asst. prof. Newark State Coll., Union, NJ, 1965-67, CUNY, Jamaica, NY, 1967-70, assoc. prof., 1971-77, chmn. dept. history, 1972-75, prof., 1978—. Author: Labor and Immigration in Industrial America, 1981, rev. edit., 1986, The Master of Seventh Avenue: David Dubinsky and the American Labor Movement, 2005; co-author: American Nativism 1830-1860, 1971, rev. edit., 1979; contbr. articles to encys., profl. jours. Fellow, Woodrow Wilson Nat. Found., 1960, CUNY, 1994. Mem.: Labor and Working Class History Assn., Immigration History Soc., Am. Jewish Hist. Assn., So. Hist. Assn., N.Y. Labor Hist. Assn. (mem. exec. bd. 1990), Conn. Hist. Soc., Acad. Polit. Sci., Orgn. Am. Historians, Am. Hist. Assn., Phi Alpha Theta. Democrat. Jewish. Avocations: photography, travel, musical theater, baseball. Home: 1 Highland Pl Great Neck NY 11020 Office: York Coll CUNY 94-20 Guy R Brewer Blvd Jamaica NY 11451 Office Phone: 718-262-2644. Business E-Mail: parmet@york.cuny.edu.

**PARMLEY, JAY,** political organization administrator; Assoc. in arts, Northeastern A&M Coll.; B in pub. adminstrn., U. Okla., MPA. Mem. DNC Exec. Com., Okla. Dem. Party Exec. Com.; nat. pres. Young Dems. of Am., 1999—2001; chmn. Okla. Dem. Party, 2001—. Asst to pres. U. Okla., 1993—95; chancellor's student rels. liaison Okla. State Regents for Higher Edn., 1995—97; dir. Oklahoma City Downtown Coll. Consortium, 1997—2001; mem. adv. bd. Okla. State U.-Oklahoma City Pub. Svc. Degree Program. Recipient Outstanding Alumnus award, Northeastern Okla. A&M Coll., 2001. Democrat. Office: 4100 N Lincoln Blvd Oklahoma City OK 73105 Office Phone: 405-427-3366. E-mail: chair@okdemocrats.org.

**PARMLEY, RICHARD TURNER,** pediatric hematologist, oncologist; b. Madison, Wis., Sept. 10, 1949; BA, U. Va., 1970; MD, Med. U. S.C., 1973. Diplomate in pediatrics and in pediatric hematology/oncology Am. Bd. Pediatrics; diplomate in hematopathology Am. Bd. Pathology. Intern Med. U. S.C., Charleston, S.C., 1973, resident in pediats., 1974-75; fellow in pediat. hematology-oncology St. Jude Children's Rsch. Hosp., Memphis, 1976-77, U. Ala., Birmingham, 1977; clin. fellow in med. oncology bone marrow transplant svc. Fred Hutchinson Cancer Rsch. Ctr., Seattle, 1986; dir. electron microscopy and histology unit inst. dental rsch. U. Ala., Birmingham, 1978-83, assoc. scientist Comprehensive Cancer Cancert Ctr., 1978-83, asst. prof. pediats. and pathology, 1978-82, assoc. prof. pediats., 1982-83; assoc. prof. pediats. and pathology U. Tex. Health Sci. Ctr., 1983-88, prof. pediats., 1988-94; dir. divsn. pediat. hematology/oncology Carolinas Med. Ctr., Charlotte, NC, 1994—2000; clin. prof. pediat. U. N.C., Chapel Hill, 1994—2000; mem. med. staff Spartanburg (S.C.) Reg. Med. Ctr., 2000—; clin. prof. pediat. Med. Univ. SC, Charleston, 2000—. Mem. Am. Soc. Pediatric Hematology/Oncology, Am. Acad. Pediat., Am. Pediatric Soc., Soc. Pediatric Rsch., Alpha Omega Alpha. Office: Spartanburg Regional Med Ctr Dept Med Edn 101 Eastwood St Spartanburg SC 29303 Office Phone: 864-560-6287. Personal E-mail: rparmley@srhs.com.

**PARNAFES, ITZIK,** Internet company executive; Co-founder, R&D mgr. Class Data Sys. (acquired by Cisco Networks, 1998); co-founder, v.p. products Kagoor Networks; sr. dir. product mgmt. Juniper Networks (formerly Kagoor Networks). Spkr. in field; consul. in field. Office: Juniper Networks 1194 No Mathilda Ave Sunnyvale CA 94089-1206 Office Fax: 408-745-2100.*

**PARNELL, CHARLES L.,** speechwriter; b. Myrtis, La., Feb. 13, 1938; s. Forrest L. and Dorothy D. (Jones) P. BA, Rice U., 1960; M Bus. and Pub. Adminstrn., Southeastern U., 1977. Commd. ens. USN, 1960, advanced through grades to comdr., 1975, ret., 1987; speechwriter Mead Data Cen., Dayton, Ohio, 1987-89, Nationwide Ins. Co.; Columbus, Ohio, 1989-90; exec. speechwriter Miller Brewing Co., Milw., 1990-96; speechwriter, Milw., 1996-98; exec. speechwriter, Dallas, 1998—. Contbr. articles to profl. jours.; frequently quoted in leading speech-related publs.; speeches used as models in 8 college level textbooks in U.S. and Can. Mem. U.S. Naval Inst., Mil. Officers Assn., World Future Soc. Avocations: reading, writing, travel. Home and Office: 1311 Brittany Ln Mansfield TX 76063-4013

**PARNELL, FRANCIS WILLIAM, JR.,** otolaryngologist; b. Woonsocket, RI, May 22, 1940; s. Francis W. and Dorothy V. (Lalor) P.; m. Diana DeAngelis, Feb. 27, 1965; children: Cheryl Lynn, John Francis, Kathleen Diana, Alison Anne, Thomas William. Student, Coll. Holy Cross, 1957-58; AB, Clark U., 1961; MD, Georgetown U., 1965. Diplomate: Nat. Bd. Med. Examiners, Am. Bd. Otolaryngology. Intern Univ. Hosps., Madison, Wis., 1965-66, resident in gen. surgery, 1966-67, otolaryngology, 1967-70; pvt. practice medicine specializing in otolaryngology San Rafael, Calif., 1972-75, Greenbrae, Calif., 1978—2000; chmn., pres., CEO Parnell Pharms., Larkspur, Calif., 1982—. Cons. corp. med. affairs 1978-82; corp. med. dir. Becton, Dickinson & Co., Rutherford, N.J., 1976-78; clin. instr. U. Calif. at San Francisco, 1972-75, asst. clin. prof., 1975-76; Alt. del., U.S. Del. 27th World Health Assembly WHO, Geneva, 1974. Contbr. articles to profl. jours. Candidate Calif. State Assembly, 1988; bd. dirs. Marin Coalition, 1990-96, 97-01, chmn., 1986-87; trustee Ross (Calif.) Sch. Dist., 1981-89; mem. governing bd. Marin Cmty. Coll. Dist., 1995-03, pres., 1999-00, 02-03; dir. Coll. Marin Found., 2004-, pres., 2006-. Maj. M.C. AUS, 1970-72, lt. col. M.C., USAR, 1985-93. Fellow ACS (gov. 1988-94), Am. Acad. Otolaryngology. Home: PO Box 998 Ross CA 94957-0998 Office: 1100 S Eliseo Dr Greenbrae CA 94904-2017 Office Phone: 415-256-1800.

**PARNELL, THOMAS ALFRED,** physicist; b. Lumberton, N.C., Nov. 24, 1931; s. Johnathan Alfred and Lula Beale (Lashley) P.; m. Elizabeth G. Brite, June 4, 1955; children: Marc Thomas, Gina Ann. BS in Physics, U. N.C., 1954, MS in Physics, 1962, PhD in Physics, 1965. Rsch. adj., dept. physics U. N.C., Chapel Hill, 1962-65; ops. analyst U.S. Air Force Europe, Wiesbaden, W. Ger., 1965-66; asst. prof. physics Marshall U., Huntington, W.Va., 1966-67; physicist NASA-Marshall Space Flight Center, Huntsville, Ala., 1968—99, chief astrophysics br., 1969-98; prin. rsch. scientist, dir. high energy photonics lab U. Ala., Huntsville, 1999—. Mem. editorial bd. Radiation Measurements; contbr. articles to profl. jours. Served to capt. USNR, 1954-91. Recipient Exceptional Sci. Achievement medal, Outstanding Leadership medal NASA, U.S. Antarctic Svc. medal. Mem. Am. Phys. Soc. Home: 907 Corinth Cir SE Huntsville AL 35801-2064 Office Phone: 256-961-7845. Business E-Mail: tom.parnell@msfc.nasa.gov.

**PARNELL-BOOTH, RUBY SHEREE,** science educator; b. Chgo., Dec. 24, 1964; d. Lillian Bernice Qualls; m. Andre Booth, Aug. 17, 1996; 1 child, Monet Sheree Booth. BS, Ala. State U., Montgomery, 1987; MEd, Loyola U., Chgo., 2000. Lic. secondary edn. State of Ill., ednl. adminstrn. and supervision State of Ill. Tchr. Chgo. Pub. Sch., 1990—. Mem. Am. Fedn. Tchrs., Nat. Coun. Tchrs. Math., NSTA. Office Phone: 773-534-6176. Personal E-mail: rsparnellbooth@hotmail.com. E-mail: rsparnell-booth@cps.k12.il.us.

**PARNES, ANDREW H.,** financial executive; V.p. fin., treas., CFO Standard Pacific Corp., Costa Mesa, Calif., 1996—. Office: Standard Pacific Corp 15326 Alton Pkwy Irvine CA 92618-2338

**PARO, JEFF,** publisher; b. 1959; married; 2 children. BA in Internat. Afairs and Econs., U. Colo. Various advtg. sales and mktg. positions Sports/Leisure mag. divsn., past nat. sales mgr. Tennis mag./The Tennis Co. NY Times, 1982-95; nat. sales mgr. Times Mirror Mags., Inc., NYC, 1995, pub. Field & Stream mag., Outdoor Life mag, Outdoor Explorer Mag.; group pub. AOL Time Warner's Time4Media; pres. Time's Outdoor Co., 2000—01; sr. v.p. and group pub. dir. PRIMEDIA Enthusiast Media, NY, 2002—. Bd. dir. Nat. Forest Found. Office: Primedia Enthusiast Media 260 Madison Ave New York NY 10016

**PAROBEK, DREW THOMAS,** lawyer; b. Lorain, Ohio, Oct. 22, 1957; s. James Stephan and Opal Ann (Kitchens) P.; m. Julie Gail King, Aug. 19, 1983; children: Emily Elizabeth, Andrew Thomas Jr., James Craig. BA summa cum laude, Vanderbilt U., 1980, JD, 1984. Bar: Ohio, U.S. Dist. Ct. (no. and so. dists.) Ohio. Ptnr. Vorys, Sater, Seymour & Pease, Columbus, 1984—; law clk. Ohio Supreme Ct., Columbus; 1985. Examiner State of Ohio Bd. Bar Examiners, Columbus, 1991-94. Contbr. articles to law rev. Trustee Worthington (Ohio) Pub. Libr., 1991-93, Cleve. chpt. Juvenile Diabetes Found.; active Columbus Area Leadership Program, 1991-92; mem. bd. trustees Clev. Bar Assn., Clev. Zoo. Soc. Bay Soccer Club, Contemporary Youth Orches. Mem. ABA, Ohio State Bar Assn., Clev. Bar Assn., Vanderbilt All Stars. Avocations: civil war history, country music, guitar, golf. Office: Vorys Sater Seymour & Pease 2100 One Cleveland Ctr 1375 E 9th St Cleveland OH 44114-1724 Office Phone: 216-479-6162. E-mail: dtparobek@vssp.com.

**PARODE, ANN,** lawyer; b. LA, Mar. 3, 1947; d. Lowell Carr and Sabine Parode. BA, Pomona Coll., 1968; JD, UCLA, 1971. Bar: Calif. 1972, U.S. Dist. Ct. (so. dist.) Calif. 1972, U.S. Ct. Appeals (9th cir.) 1975, U.S. Supreme Ct. 2000. Assoc. Luce, Forward et al, San Diego, 1971-75; gen. counsel, exec. v.p., sec. San Diego Trust & Savs., 1975-94; with First Interstate Bank, 1994—97; campus counsel U. Calif., San Diego, 1997—. Judge pro tem San Diego Mcpl. Ct., 1978—84; campus counsel U. Calif., San Diego, 1997—. Bd. dirs. San Diego Cmty. Found., 1989-97, chmn., 1994-96; bd. dirs. The Burnham Inst., 1995-2001, Girard Found., 1990-. Mem. Calif. Bar Assn. (corp. law com. 1980-83, client trust fund commn. 1986-90, chmn. 1989-90), San Diego County Bar Found. (comdr. bd. dirs. 1979-86, 98-2001, pres. 1980-83), San Diego Bar Assns. (bd. dirs. 1977-81, v.p. 1977-78, 80-81, treas. 1979-80), Law Libr. Justice Found. (pres. 1994). Office Phone: 858-822-1236. Business E-Mail: aparode@ucsd.edu.

**PARR, CAROLYN MILLER,** federal judge; b. Palatka, Fla., Apr. 17, 1937; d. Arthur Charles and Audrey Ellen (Dunklin) Miller; m. Jerry Studstill Parr, Oct. 12, 1959; children: Kimberly Parr Trapasso, Jennifer Parr Turek, Patricia Audrey Smith. BA, Stetson U., 1959; MA, Vanderbilt U., 1960; JD, Georgetown U., 1977; LLD (hon.), Stetson U., 1986. Bar: Md. 1977, U.S. Tax Ct. 1977, D.C. 1979, U.S. Supreme Ct. 1983. Gen. trial atty. IRS, Washington, 1977-81, sr. trial atty. office of chief counsel, 1982; spl. counsel to asst. atty. gen. tax divsn. U.S. Dept. Justice, Washington, 1982-85; judge U.S. Tax Ct., Washington, 1985-2000, sr. judge, 2000—. Nat. Def. fellow Vanderbilt U., 1959-60; fellow Georgetown U., 1975-76; recipient Spl. Achievement award U.S. Treasury, 1979. Mem. ABA, Md. Bar Assn., Nat. Assn. Women Judges, D.C. Bar Assn. Office: US Tax Ct 400 2nd St NW Washington DC 20217-0002

**PARR, GRANT VAN SICLEN,** surgeon; b. NYC, Dec. 30, 1942; s. Ferdinand Van Siclen and Helene H. P.; m. Helen Mushat Frye, July 1, 1967; children: Kathleen Gage, Helen Johnston. AB with honors, Wesleyan U., 1965; MD, Cornell U., 1969. Diplomate Am. Bd. Thoracic Surgery, Am. Bd. Surgery. Intern, resident U. Hosps. of Cleve., 1969-71; resident in surgery U. Ala. Hosps., Birmingham, 1971-74, chief resident in surgery, 1974-75, resident in cardiovascular and thoracic surgery, 1975-77; practice medicine specializing in thoracic surgery Hershey, Pa., 1978-82; mem. staff Presbyn.-U. Pa. Med. Ctr., Phila., 1982-88, chief div. Thoracic surgery, 1984-88, acting chmn. Dept. Surgery, 1988, chief cardiovascular surgery, 1984-88; asst. prof. cardiothoracic surgery M.S. Hershey Med. Center, Hershey, Pa., 1987-88; chief cardiovascular surgery Morristown (N.J.) Meml. Hosp., 1988-97, co-chmn. dept. cardiovasc. scis., 1997—2004, chmn. dept. cardiovasc. medicine, 2004—; med. dir. Cardiac Svc. Line, 2004—; asst. prof. Pa. State U., 1978-82; clin. assoc. prof. surgery Pa. U., 1982-89; assoc. prof. clin. surgery Columbia U., 1992—. Chief cardiovasc. surgery Overlook Hosp., 1988—, Morristown Meml. Hosp., 1988-98; chmn. cardiovasc. surgery Atlantic Health Sys., 1998—, trustee, 1998-2006, med. dir. cardiac svcs., 2004—. Contbr. articles to profl. jours. Fellow Am. Coll. Cardiology, ACS, Am. Coll. Chest Physicians, Phila. Coll. Physicians; mem. AMA, Internat. Cardiovascular Soc., Assn. of Acad. Surgeons, Am. Assn. Thoracic Surgery, Phila. County Med. Soc., Soc. Thoracic Surgeons, Soc. Critical Care Medicine Pa., Thoracic Surg. Soc., John W. Kirklin Soc., Pa. Med. Assn., N.J. Soc. Thoracic Surgery, N.Y. Soc. Thoracic Surgery, Morris County Golf Club, NYU Club, Beaverkill Trout Club. Office: 100 Madison Ave Morristown NJ 07960-6136 Office Phone: 973-971-5597. Business E-Mail: gparr@atlantichealth.org.

**PARR, JAMES ALLAN,** literature professor; b. Ritchie County, W.Va., Oct. 7, 1936; s. James William and Virginia Alice (Bragg) P.; m. Franciszka Duda, May 4, 1957 (div. 1967): 1 child, Jacqueline; m. Carmen Salazar, Aug. 19, 1968 (div. 1980); m. Patricia Catherine Brinck, June 28, 1985. BA, Ohio U., 1959, MA, 1961; PhD, U. Pitts., 1967. Prof., chmn. Murray (Ky.) State U., 1964-70; prof. U. So. Calif., Los Angeles, 1970-90, U. Calif., Riverside, 1990—. Dir. Nat. Def. Edn. Act Inst., summers, 1966, 67, 69. Author: Don Quixote: An Anatomy of Subversive Discourse, 1988, Confrontaciones calladas, 1990, After Its Kind: Approaches to the Comedia, 1991, Don Quixote, Don Juan and Related Subjects, 2004, Don Quixote: A Touchstone for Literary Criticism, 2005; editor: Critical Essays on Juan Ruiz de Alarcon, 1972, El Burlador de Sevilla, 1991, On Cervantes: Essays for L.A. Murillo, 1991, Don Quixote, 1998; editor jour. Bull. of the Comediantes, 1973-98 Recipient Phi Beta Kappa award, Ohio U., 1960, Mellon fellowships, U. Pitts., 1961-63, Del Amo fellowship, U. So. Calif., Los Angeles, 1977, 84, 89, Fulbright, 1991. Mem. MLA, Am. Assn. Tchrs. of Spanish and Portuguese, Internat. Assn. Hispanists, Cervantes Soc. Am. (pres.). Avocation: travel. Home: 421 Elmwood Dr Pasadena CA 91105-1358 E-mail: cervantista@aol.com.

**PARR, ROBERT GHORMLEY,** chemistry professor; b. Chgo., Sept. 22, 1921; s. Leland Wilbur and Grace (Ghormley) P.; m. Jane Bolstad, May 28, 1944; children: Steven Robert, Jeanne Karen, Carol Jane. AB magna cum laude with high honors in Chemistry, Brown U., 1942; PhD in Phys. Chemistry, U. Minn., 1947; D (hon.), U. Leuven, 1986, Jagiellonian U., 1996. Asst. prof. chemistry U. Minn., 1947-48; mem. faculty Carnegie Inst. Tech., 1948-62, prof. chemistry, 1957-62, Johns Hopkins U., 1962-74, chmn. dept., 1969-72; William R. Kenan, Jr. prof. theoretical chemistry U. N.C., Chapel Hill, 1974-90, Wassily Hoeffding prof. chem. physics, 1990—. Vis. prof. chemistry, mem. Ctr. Advanced Study, U. Ill., 1962; disting. vis. prof. SUNY, Buffalo, Pa. State U., 1967; vis. prof. Japan Soc. Promotion Sci., 1968, 79, U. Haifa, 1977, Free U., Berlin, 1977, Duke U., 1996-97; Firth prof. U. Sheffield, 1976; Coochbehar prof. Indian Assn. Cultivation of Sci., 1990; Sandoval Vallarta prof. UAM-Iztapalapa, 1992; chmn. com. postdoctoral fellowships in chemistry NAS-NRC, 1961-63; chmn. panel theoretical chemistry Westheimer com. survey chemistry NAS, 1964; mem. coun. Gordon Rsch. Conf., 1974-76; mem. Commn. on Human Resources, NRC, 1979-82; mem. coun. Inst. for Molecular Sci., Okazaki, Japan, 1986-88; bd. trustees Inst. for Fundamental Chemistry, Kyoto, Japan, 1986—. Author: Quantum Theory of Molecular Electronic Structure, 1963, Density-Functional Theory of Atoms and Molecules, 1989, also numerous articles.; Assoc. editor: Jour. Chem. Physics, 1956-58, Chem. Revs. 1961-63, Jour. Phys. Chemistry, 1963-67, 77-79, Am. Chem. Soc. Monographs, 1966-71, Theoretica Chimica Acta,
1966-69, 92-96; Chinese Chem. Letters, 1998—; bd. editors: Jour. Am. Chem. Soc, 1969-77; adv. editorial bd.: Internat. Jour. Quantum Chemistry, 1967—, Chem. Physics Letters, 1967-79. Recipient Outstanding Achievement award U. Minn., 1968, N.C. Disting. Chemist award, 1982; fellow U. Chgo., 1949; research assoc., 1957; Fulbright scholar U. Cambridge, Eng., 1953-54; Guggenheim fellow, 1953-54; NSF sr. postdoctoral fellow U. Oxford (Eng.) and Commonwealth Sci. and Indsl. Research Orgn., Melbourne, Australia, 1967-68; Sloan fellow, 1956-60, N.C. award in sci., 1999. Fellow AAAS, Am. Phys. Soc. (chmn. divsn. chem. physics 1963-64); mem. NAS (award in chem. scis., 2004), AAUP, Am. Chem. Soc. (chmn. divsn. phys. chemistry 1978, Irving Langmuir award in chem. physics 1994), Am. Acad. Arts and Sci., Indian Nat. Sci. Acad., Internat. Acad. Quantum Molecular Sci. (pres. 1991-97), Phi Beta Kappa, Sigma Xi, Phi Lambda Upsilon, Pi Mu Epsilon. Home: 701 Kenmore Rd Chapel Hill NC 27514-2019 Office: U NC Dept Chemistry Chapel Hill NC 27599-3290 Office Phone: 919-962-1577.

**PARR, ROYSE MILTON,** retired lawyer, writer; b. Elk City, Okla., Sept. 11, 1935; s. Clinton Riley and Caroline (Royse) Parr; m. Sheila Ann Harshaw, May 28, 1960; children: Clinton Howard, Reagan Royse. BS, Okla. State U., 1958; JD, U. Tulsa, 1964. Bar: Okla. 1964. Rsch. scout Jersey Prodn. Rsch. Co., Tulsa, 1960-64; atty. Sun Oil Co., 1964-70, White Shield Corp., 1970-71; sec., atty., asst. gen. counsel MAPCO, Inc., Tulsa, 1971-97; gen. counsel, dir. Seminole Pipeline Co., 1989-97. Lectr. in field. Co-author: Glory Days of Summer: The History of Baseball in Oklahoma, 1999, Allie Reynolds: Super Chief, 2002, Native Americans in Sports, 2004. Vice chmn. Tulsa County Election Bd., 1973—97; pres. Ret. Sr. Vol. Program, 1982—83. Served to 1st lt. U.S. Army, 1958—60, capt. USAR, 1960—63. Mem.: ASME, ABA, Soc. Am. Baseball Rsch., Am. Soc. Corp. Secs., Tulsa County Bar Assn., Okla. Bar Assn., Soc. Petroleum Engrs., Oaks Country Club, Phi Delta Phi. Republican. Methodist.

**PARR, VIRGINIA HELEN,** retired librarian; b. Mansfield, Ohio, May 23, 1937; d. Bernard Franklin and Frances Cole (Downes) P.; m. Marvin E. Lickey, June 14, 1959 (div. 1972); children: Sarah Elizabeth, David Andrew, Rachel Alison; m. Laurence E. Steadman, Nov. 27, 1993. AB, Oberlin Coll., 1959; AM, U. Mich., 1961; MLS, U. Oreg., 1973. English and social studies tchr. Whittier Jr. High Sch., Livonia, Mich., 1961-64; libr. U. Oreg. Libr., Eugene, 1973-79, head edn. and psychology, 1979-80, acting asst. univ. libr. for pub. svcs., 1980-82; head reference, rsch. and instrn. svcs. U. Cin., 1982-89, reference librr., bibliographer, 1989—2002, ret., 2002—. Chair, mem. budget com. Eugene Sch., 1976-79. Founding editor: Behavioral and Social Scis. Libr., 1978; contbr. articles to profl. jours. Bd. dirs. Eugene Jr. Symphony Assn., 1979-82; mem. adv. bd. various mental health groups, Eugene, 1971-79. Mem. Assn. Coll. and Rsch. Librs. of ALA (various offices edn. and behavioral sci. sect. 1977-86, numerous coms. reference and adult svcs. divsn. 1981-92), Beta Phi Mu, Pi Lambda Theta. Democrat. Episcopalian. Avocations: reading, classical music, travel. Home: 5532 S Shore Dr 12F Chicago IL 60637-1990 E-mail: v_parr@sbcglobal.net.

**PARRA, DEREK,** Olympic athlete; b. San Bernardino, Calif., Mar. 15, 1970; Mem. U.S. Elite Long Track Speedskating Team. Named U.S. Allround Overall Champion, 2000, Allround World Championships Men, 2003; recipient 5000-meter Silver medal, 2002 Olympic Games, 1500-meter Gold medal, ranked 10th in 5000m, World Single Distance Championships, 2003, ranked 5th in 1500m, 2003, ranked #16 in 10000m, 2003. Achievements include set world record for 1500m, Salt Lake City, 2002; first Mexican-American to compete in and medal in Winter Olympics. Address: US Speedskating PO Box 450639 Westlake OH 44145

**PARRA, RAUL O.,** urologist, educator; arrived in U.S., 1954; s. Raul F. and Olena Parra; married; 3 children. MD, U. Seville, Spain, 1980. Diplomate Bd. Urology. Chmn. urology St. Louis (Mo.) U., 1989—99, Mayo Clinic, Jacksonville, Fla., 1995—2002; dir. urologic cancer surgery Oreg. Health and Sci. U., Portland, 2002—04; chmn. urology Cooper Health Sys., Robert Wood Johnson Sch. Medicine, Camden, NJ, 2004—. Author med. papers, book chpts., and textbooks. Office: Cooper Urology 3 Cooper Plz Camden NJ 08103 Office Phone: 856-963-3577. Business E-Mail: parra-raul@cooperheadth.edu.

**PARRA, ROSENDO G.,** computer company executive; B in Mktg., Univ. Md. Various sales, mgmt. positions GRiD Sys. Corp.; joined Dell Corp., 1993, sr. v.p., US Pub. Sector, sr. v.p., worldwide home and small bus. group, now sr. v.p., Americas. Named one of Most Important Hispanics in Tech., Bus., Hispanic Engineer and Info. Tech. mag., 2005. Office: Dell Americas One Dell Way Round Rock TX 78682*

**PARRA-ARANGUREN, GONZALO,** judge; b. Caracas, Venezuela, Dec. 5, 1928; Degree juridical and political studies, Ctrl. U. Venezuela, 1950; degree, Inter-Am. Law Inst., NYU; LLD, Ludwig-Maximilians U., Munich. Prof. Ctrl. U. Venezuela, Caracas, 1956—96, Andrés Bello Cath. U., Caracas, 1957—96; judge 2d Ct. of 1st Instance Fed. Dist. and State of Miranda, Caracas, 1958-71; 1st assoc. judge Chamber of Cassation Supreme Ct. of Justice, Caracas, 1988-92, alt. judge, 1992—96; judge Internat. Ct. Justice, The Hague, Netherlands, 1996—. Mem. nat. group for Venezuela Permanent Ct. of Arbitration, The Hague, 1985—; arbitrator, Venezuela and abroad; mem. legal adv. com. Ministry of Fgn. Affairs, 1984-96, Nat. Congress, 1990-96; mem. Acad. Polit. and Social Scis. of Caracas, 1966—, pres., 1993-95; mem. Inst. of Internat. Law, 1979—; Venezuelan rep. several sessions of The Hague Conf. on Pvt. Internat. Law. Author: (books) Die Regel "Locus Regit Actum" und die Fromen der Testamente, 1955, La Nacionalidad Venezolana Originatia, vols. I and II, 1964, La Constitucion de 1830 y los Venzolanos por Naturalizacion, 1969, La Influencia del Matrimonio sobre la Nacionalidad de la Mujer en la Legislacion Venezolana, 1983, Ensayos de Derecho Procesal Civil Internacional, 1986, Estudios de Derecho Mercantil Internacional, 1998, others. Office: Internat Ct of Justice Peace Palace 2517 KJ The Hague Netherlands Business E-Mail: mail@icj-cij.org.

**PARRAGUIRRE, RONALD DAVID,** state supreme court justice; b. Reno, July 8, 1959; s. Paul Charles and Iris Mae (Bleick) P.; m. Leslie, 2 children. BBA, San Diego State U., 1982; JD, U. San Diego, 1985. Bar: Pa. 1986, Nev. 1986, D.C. 1987. Legis. assist. U.S. Senator Paul Laxalt, Washington, 1985-86; counsel subcom. on criminal law, judiciary com. U.S. Senate, Washington, 1986-87; lawyer Parraguirre & Parraguirre, Las Vegas, Nev., 1987-91; mcpl. ct. judge Dept. 6 City of Las Vegas, 1991-99; dist. ct. judge Eighth Jud. Dist. Ct., Clark County, Nev., 1999—2004; justice Nev. Supreme Ct., 2004—. Mem. Nev. State-Federal Jud. Council, Nev. Supreme Ct. State Ct. Funding Com.; former mem. Nev. Supreme Ct. Jud. Election Practices Com. Mem. ABA, ATLA, Am. Judges Assn., Nev. Judges Assn., Nev. State Bar Assn. (mem. multi-jurisdictional task force com.), Clark County Bar Assn. (former exec. bd. mem.) Republican. Lutheran. Avocations: skiing, racquetball, hunting, fishing. Office: Nev Supreme Court 201 S Carson St Carson City NV 89701-4702*

**PARRAMORE, BARBARA MITCHELL,** education educator; b. Guilford County, N.C., Aug. 29, 1932; d. Samuel Spencer and Nellie Gray (Glosson) Mitchell; m. Lyman Griffis Worthington, Dec. 23, 1956 (div. 1961); m. Thomas Custis Parramore, Jan. 22, 1966 (dec. Jan. 2004); children: Lisa Gray, Lynn Stuart. AB, U. N.C., Greensboro, 1954; MEd, N.C. State U., 1959; EdD, Duke U., 1968. Counselor, tchr. Raleigh City Schs., 1954-59, sch. prin., 1959-65; prof. dept. of curriculum and instrn. N.C. State U., 1970-96, prof. emeritus, 1996—. Acad. specialist Office Internat. Edn., U.S. Info. Svcs., sec. sch. initative program, The Philippines, 1987. Author: The People of North Carolina, 1972, 3rd edit. 1983. Japan Inst. Social and Econ. Affairs fellow, 1980; N.C. AAUW award for juvenile lit., 1973, Holladay medal for excellence N.C. State U., 1994. Mem. ASCD, N.C. ASCD (pres. 1994-96), N.C. Coun. for Social Studies (pres. 1985-87), Assn. Tchr. Educators, Delta Kappa Gamma, Kappa Delta Pi. Home: 5012 Tanglewood Dr Raleigh NC 27612-3135

**PARRAVANO, AMELIA ELIZABETH (AMY BETH PARRAVANO),** recording industry executive; b. Providence, Apr. 5, 1951; d. Olindo Luigi and Violet Carmella (Russo) Izzo; m. Grimaldo Antonio Parravano, July 4, 1979; children: Peter Paul, Paula Elizabeth. AA, Roger Williams Coll., 1972; student, RI Coll., 1972—73, Oral Roberts U., 1986. Owner, operator Aura Arts & Crafts, Cranston—RI, 1985-88; pres. Peridot Caprice Rec. Artist, Cranston, 1990—; president, owner Peridot Records; music pub.; host, prodr. cable TV show Amy Beth Presents!. Freelance artist Artist Letters League, Cranston, 1992—; singer (Amy Beth), songwriter, musician. Active PTA, Cranston, 1991-92; artist mem. RI State Coun. Arts, Providence, 1986-92; active Pawtucket (RI) Arts Coun., 1986-92. Named Ky. Col.; named to Rockabilly Hall Fame. Mem. Am. Soc. Composers, Authors Pubs., Songwriters Guild Am., Gospel Music Assn., County Music Assn., Country Music Showcase Internat., Broadcast Music Inc. (pub.), Retirement Entertainment Orgn., Internat. Fan Club Assn., Greater So. Country Music Assn. (state rep. RI). Avocations: golf, bicycling, entertaining at children's parties, painting, poetry. Home: 17 Woodbine St Cranston RI 02910-1916 Personal E-mail: amybeth_e@yahoo.com.

**PARRCOTT, DORIAN LEE, II,** music educator; b. Neptune, N.J., Nov. 23, 1965; s. Dorian Roderick and Yvonne Dorothy Parrcott; m. Carla Yvette Smith, July 9, 1999. BA Music Edn. and Performance, Trenton State Coll., Ewing, N.J., 1988. Cert. tchr. N.J. Dir. mid. sch. band Neptune Twp. Bd. Edn., NJ, 1988—98; dir. mid./h.s. band North Plainfield Bd. Edn., NJ, 1998—. Cons. in field; soloist Monmouth Symphony, 1989—99. Mem.: N.J. Educators Assn., N.J. Music Educators (clinician 1990), Musicians Local 802/873/399. Avocations: motorcycling, music, tennis. Home: 105 DeMott Ln Somerset NJ 08873 Office: North Plainfield Pub Schs 34 Wilson Ave North Plainfield NJ 07060

**PARRESOL, BERNARD ROSS,** research scientist, statistician; b. Washington, Sept. 15, 1953; s. Thomas and Rita Delores P.; m. Lisa Leigh Morton-Barbé, May 5, 1995; children: Sarah Marie Barbé, Christine Pamela Barbé. BS with honors, Mich. State U., 1977; M of Applied Stats., La. State U., 1983, PhD, 1998. Reg. forester, N.C. Br. mgr. James M. Vardaman & Co. Forestry Cons., Shreveport, La., 1977-80; rsch. assoc. dept. explt. stats. La. State U., Baton Rouge, 1983-86; math. statistician USDA Forest Svc., New Orleans, 1986-95, Asheville, NC, 1996—. Stats. cons. Internat. Inst. Tropical Forestry, Rio Piedras, P.R., 1987-2002; guest lectr. Nanjing (China) Forestry U., 1994, 97, U. de Tras-os-Montes e Alto Douro, Portugal, 1998, 2002, 2003, Universidad Autonoma de Nuevo Leon, Mex., 2001, Univeridad de Santiago de Compostela, Spain, 2002, Beijing Forestry U., 2003; adj. prof. U. Fla., 1999-2002, U. Tenn., 2005—. Guest assoc. editor Forest Sci., 1999-2000, assoc. editor Southern Jour. of Applied Forestry, 2002—; contbr. Encyclopedia of Envirometrics; contbr. articles to profl. jours. Officer La. Indian Heritage Assn., 1988-92; mem. organizing com. Nanjing Internat. Wetland Symposium, 2002. Recipient Dir.'s award for internat. programs USDA Forest Svc. So. Rsch. Sta., 2002, Chief's Global Stewardship award USDA Forest Svc., 2003; Rockefeller Found. scholar, 1990; grantee Smithsonian Tropical Rsch. Inst., Panama, 1992, U.S. Office Internat. Coop. and Devel., Chile, 1993; Humanities scholar La. Endowment for Humanities, 2000, 02. Mem. Am. Statistical Assn., Soc. Am. Foresters, Internat. Soc. Tropical Foresters. Avocation: American Indian culture. Office: USDA Forest Svc PO Box 2680 Asheville NC 28802-2680 Office Phone: 828-259-0500. Office Fax: 828-257-4840. Business E-Mail: bparresol@fs.fed.us.

**PARRETT, SHERMAN O.,** lawyer; b. Cin., Jan. 8, 1943; s. Earl and Ruby (Angel) P.; m. Rosalind K. Brooks, Sept. 21, 1985; children: Laura, Samantha. BSEE, U. Cin., 1965; JD with honors, George Washington U., 1969. Bar: Calif. 1970, D.C. 1975, Ariz. 1992. Assoc. Flehr, Hohbach et al., San Francisco, 1970-73; ptnr. Cushman, Darby & Cushman, Washington, 1973-86, Irell & Manella, L.A., 1986-91, Streich Lang, Phoenix, 1991-94, Snell & Wilmer, Phoenix, 1994-98. Address: 2818 SE 19th Ave Cape Coral FL 33904 E-mail: parretts@aol.com.

**PARRETT, WILLIAM G.,** accounting company executive; m. Diane Parrett; six children. BA, St. Francis Coll., NY, 1967. Joined predecessor firm Deloitte & Touche LLP, 1967, named ptnr., 1977, ptnr. Stamford, Conn., group mng. ptnr. NY, regional mng. ptnr. tri-state, mng. ptnr., now sr. mng. ptnr.; co-founding chmn. global fin. services industry practice Deloitte Touche Tohmatsu, regional mng. ptnr. Americas, now CEO, 2003—. Mem. bd. Japan Soc., US-Japan Bus. Coun. Bd. trustees Carnegie Hall, United Way of Am.; nat adv. bd. Nat. Underground R.R. Freedom Ctr.; trustee Cath. U. Am.; internat. councillor Ctr. Strategic and Internat. Studies. Mem. Econ. Club NY, Am. Inst. CPAs, Com. to Encourage Corp. Philanthropy, G100 CEO Forum, Transatlantic Bus. Dialogue, US Coun. Internat. Bus.(chmn. 2005-). Office: Deloitte Touche Tohmatsu 1633 Broadway New York NY 10019-6754*

**PARRICK, GERALD HATHAWAY,** communications and marketing executive; b. Cushing, Okla., Oct. 27, 1924; s. Gerald H. and Phyllis A. (Sheppard) B.; m. Gail V. Straney, Dec. 5, 1984; children: Gerald Hathaway III, Candace Anne. BJ, U. Mo., 1948. Creative account exec. George Knox & Assoc., Oklahoma City, 1948-51; account exec. Batten, Barton, Durstine & Osborn, San Francisco, 1952-60; account dir. McCann-Erickson, L.A., 1960-67, v.p. Portland, Oreg., 1967-72; dir. comm. Pacific Power Co., Portland, 1972-77, spl. asst. to chmn. bd., 1977-79; pres. Entreepublic Comm., West Linn, Oreg., 1979—; Bailey/Parrick, Inc., Portland, 1981-84, Parrick/Milpacher, Inc., Portland, 1984-85, The Layle Clinic Inc., Portland, 1984-90, K-KQR Inc., 1990-93 Author! A 20th Century Miracle, 1981, touched by a Miracle, 1997. Mem. Oreg. Advt. Rev. Bd., 1974-75. Capt. AUS, 1943-45, 51-52, ETO. Named Oreg. Advt. Man of Yr., Oreg. Advt. Club, 1971. Mem. Am. Advt. Fedn. (chmn. edn. western region 1973-74), Portland Advt. Fedn. (pres. 1974-75), Toastmasters (pres. 1966-67) (Encino, Calif.), Kappa Tau Alpha. Home: 17185 Carlson Ct Lake Oswego OR 97034-5802 Personal E-mail: jergail@aol.com.

**PARRILLO, JOSEPH EDISON, JR.,** allergist, immunologist, cardiologist; b. Paterson, N.J., Jan. 5, 1947; MD, Cornell U., 1972. Diplomate Am. Bd. Allergy and Immunology, Am. Bd. Internal Medicine, Am. Bd. Cardiology. From intern to resident in medicine Mass. Gen. Hosp., Boston, 1972-74, fellow in cardiology, 1978-80; resident in medicine N.Y. Hosp.-Cornell Med. Ctr., N.Y.C., 1977-78; resident in alleregy & immunology and infectious disease Clin. Ctr. Nat. Inst. Allergy and Immunology Disease, Bethesda, Md., 1974-77; med. staff Rush-Presbyn.-St. Lukes Med. Ctr., Chgo.; chief divsn. cardiology and critical care medicine Rush Heart Inst. Mem. Am. Coll. Cardiology, Am. Fedn. Clin. Rsch., Am. Heart Assn., Am. Soc. Clin. Immunology, Am. Coll. Critical Care Medicine, Am. Coll. Chest Physicians, Soc. Critical Care Medicine, Alpha Omega Alpha. Office: Cooper Univ Hosp Dorrance Bldg 3d Fl One Cooper Plaza Camden NJ 08103

**PARRINO, ROBERT,** finance educator; b. N.Y.C., Sept. 4, 1957; s. Dominick Paul Parrino and Gertrude (Rainer) Wieczorek; m. Emily Allen Parrino, July 12, 1980. BSChemE, Lehigh U., Bethlehem, Pa., 1979; MBA, Coll. William and Mary, 1980; MS, U. Rochester, 1991, PhD in Fin., 1992. CFA. Sr. analyst Marriott Corp., Bethesda, Md., 1984-85; pres Sprigg Lane Fin. Corp., Charlottesville, Va., 1985-88; faculty dept. fin. U. Tex., Austin, 1992-96, 97—; faculty U. Chgo., 1996-97. Founding mng. dir. Hicks, Muse, Tate & Furst Ctr. for Pvt. Equity Fin., Austin; mem. adv. bd. visitors Mary Baldwin Coll., Staunton, Va., 2002—. Contbr. articles to profl. jours. Capt. U.S. Army, 1981-84, lt. col. USAR. ret. Mem. CFA Inst. (cand. curriculum com. 1994-99), Am. Econ. Assn., Fin. Mgmt. Assn., Am. Soc. Appraisers 1988-96 (Richmond chpt. treas. 1987-88), Beta Gamma Sigma. Office: McCombs Sch Bus Dept Fin CBA 6 222 U Tex at Austin Austin TX 78712-1179 Office Phone: 512-471-5788. E-mail: parrino@mail.utexas.edu.

**PARRIS, MARK ROBERT,** former ambassador, policy advisor; b. Mpls. m. Joan Elizabeth Gardner; 2 children. BS magna cum laude, Georgetown U., 1974. With Fgn. Svc., 1972-77, polit. counselor Moscow, 1982-85, dir. Office Soviet Union Affairs, 1985-88; dep. chief mission U.S. Embassy, Tel Aviv, 1989-92; spl. asst. pres., sr. dir. Nat. Security Coun., Washington, 1995-97; amb. to Turkey Ankara, 1997—2000; sr. fgn. policy advisor Baker, Donelson, Bearman and Caldwell, Washington, 2000—. Counselor Turkish Rsch. Program The Washington Inst., 2002—; bd. chmn. Am. Friends of Turkey; bd. mem. Am. Turkish Coun. Mem. policy bd. Una Chapman Cox Found., U.S.-Israel Edn. Found. Phi Beta Kappa. Office: Baker Donelson Bearman and Caldwell 6th Fl 555 Eleventh St Washington DC 20004

**PARRIS, MARK S.,** lawyer, professional athletes consultant; b. Caldwell, Wash., Mar. 22, 1957; s. Wayne Wesley and Helen (Padgett) P. BA, Gonzaga U., 1980; JD, U. Wash., 1983. Bar: Wash. 1983, U.S. Dist. Ct. (we. dist.) Wash. 1983, (ea. dist.) Wash. 1989, U.S. Dist. Ct. (ea. dist.) Wash. 1989, U.S. Ct. Appeals (9th cir.) 1990. Assoc. Syrdal, Danelo, Seattle, 1983-88, Heller, Ehrman, White & McAuliffe, Seattle, 1988-90, ptnr., 1990—. Cons. Athlete Cons. Svcs., Seattle. Pres., Athletes That Care, Seattle; vol. Lake City Legal Clinic, Seattle, Children's Hosp., Seattle. Avocations: cricket, golf, squash, mountain climbing. Office: Heller Ehrman White & McAuliffe 721 5th Ave 6100 Columbia Ctr Seattle WA 98104-7043

**PARRIS, SALLY NYE,** real estate agent; b. Evanston, Ill., Apr. 5, 1946; d. Harry Gale Nye Jr. and Bettye (Herb) Sollitt; m. Thomas Baxter Parris, Mar. 25, 1988 (div. Sept. 1985); 1 child, Samantha Ross. AA, Bradford Jr. Coll., 1966; BS in Secondary Edn., Northwestern U., 1968; cert. real estate, Conn. Real Estate Inst., Norwalk, 1985. Lic. real estate agt., Conn. Dir. girls phys. edfn. Latin Sch. of Chgo., 1967-68; dir. Greenwich (Conn.) YWCA, 1972-79; English tchr. Inlingua Sch. Langs., Stamford, Conn., 1981-84; real estate agt. Curtis Assocs., Realtors, Greenwich, Conn., 1985—. Chair profl. divsn. United Way, Greenwich, 1995-98, chair real estate sect. profl. divsn., 1993-94, co-chair campaign kickoff Septemberfest, 1985-99, co-chair Greenwich Pro-Am. Lit. Vol. Benefit, 1995—; v.p., bd. dirs. YMCA, Greenwich, 1993—, chair spl. events com., 1994—, co-chair annual campaign, 1998; bd. dirs., benefit chair Cmty. Answers, Greenwich, 1994—; co-chair 350th Yr. parade Town of Greenwich, 1990; mem. benefits com. Literacy Vols., 1991-93. Recipient Vol. Recognition award Literacy Vols. Am., 1996, Town of Greenwich, 1991, United Way of Greenwich, 1985-97, Thomas Shepard award, 1995, 96. Mem. Conn. Assn. Profl. Women, Greenwich Bd. Realtors (advisor pub. rels. 1985-87, grievance com. 1999), Riverside Yacht Club (winter mem., social register 1960—), Greenwich Country Club (paddle tennis com. co-chmn. 1984-86, quar. editor 1982-86). Republican. Episcopalian. Avocations: swimming, racquet sports, golf, sporting clays, needlepoint. Office: Colwell Banker/Curtis Assocs 278 Sound Beach Ave Old Greenwich CT 06870-1626

**PARRISH, CARL E.,** artist, educator; b. Cuthbert, Ga., Jan. 21, 1945; s. Carl Edward and Frances Allen Parrish; m. Sarah Carter, Dec. 22, 1966 (div. Dec. 1976); 1 child, Rebecca Carter. AB cum laude, Harvard U., 1967; MA, Emory U., Atlanta, 1972. Head liberal arts dept. Atlanta Coll. of Art, 1997—. Rschr. Helike (Greece) Archeol. Project, 2004. Author: (plays) Jimmy!, 1993. Head protocol Alex. Coliseum, Internat. Olympic Com., Atlanta, 1996; vol. Caretta Rsch. Project for sea turtle preservation, 2003, 2005. Grantee Rsch. grantee, Atlanta Coll. Art, Sorbonne, 2002, Atlanta Coll. Art, Oxford U., Eng., 2001, Study grantee, Atlanta Coll. Art, Harvard U., 2000. Mem.: Archeol. Inst. Am., Nat. Assn. Schs. Art and Design, Caretta Rsch Project (vol. sea turtle preservation), Coll. Art Assn. (mem. nat. edn. com.), Harvard Club of Boston, Harvard Club of N.Y.C., Harvard Faculty Club, Harvard Club of Ga. (scholarship com. 1992—95, v.p. membership 1994—96). Avocation: bridge. Office: Atlanta College of Art 1280 Peachtree St NE Atlanta GA 30309

**PARRISH, CHARLES,** lawyer; BA in History with honors, U. Va.; JD, U. Houston Law Sch. State Bar Tex. V.p., gen. counsel, sec. Tesoro Corp., San Antonio, 1994—2005, 2005—. ABA Office: Tesoro Corp 300 Concord Plz Dr San Antonio TX 78216-6999

**PARRISH, EDWARD ALTON, JR.,** electrical and computer engineering educator, academic administrator; b. Newport News, Va., Jan. 7, 1937; s. Edward Alton and Molly Wren (Vaughn) Parrish; m. Shirley Maxine Johnson, Oct. 26, 1963; children: Troy Alton, Gregory Sinton. BEE, U. Va., 1964, MEE, 1966, DScEE, 1968. Registered Tenn., Va. Group leader Amerad Corp., Charlottesville, Va., 1961—64; asst. prof. elec. engring. U. Va., Charlottesville, 1968—71; assoc. prof. elec. engring., 1971—77, prof. elec. engring., 1977—86, chmn. dept. elec. engring., 1978—86; dean, centennial prof. electrical engring. Vanderbilt U., Nashville, 1987—95; pres., prof. elec. and computer engring. Worcester Poly. U., 1995—. Cons. U.S. Army, Charlottesville, Va., 1971—77, ORS, Inc., Princeton, NJ, 1973—74, Sperry Marine Systems, Charlottesville, 1975—76, Hajime Industries Ltd., Tokyo, 1978—84. Contbr. articles to profl. jours. With USAF, 1954—58. Grantee numerous rsch. grants. Fellow: IEEE (bd. dirs. 1990—91, v.p. ednl. activities 1992—93, engring. accreditation commn. 1989—96, exec. com. 1991—96, officer 1993—94, chmn. elect 1994—95, chmn. 1995—96, past chmn. 1996—97, editor-in-chief IEEE Computer 1995—98), ABET (bd. dirs. 2000—); mem.: IEEE Computer Soc. (sec. 1997, v.p. 1978—81, pres. 1988), Tau Beta Pi, Eta Kappa Nu, Sigma Xi. Baptist. Avocations: music, woodworking. Office: Office of Pres Worcester Polytechnic Institue 100 Institute Rd Worcester MA 01609-2247 E-mail: eap@wpi.edu.

**PARRISH, FRANK JENNINGS,** retired food products executive; b. Manassas, Va., Dec. 29, 1923; s. Edgar Goodloe and Alverda (Jennings) Parrish; m. Lorene Lomax, Feb. 11, 1944 (div. Apr. 1984); children: Edgar Lee, Julia Lorene; m. Mary Jane Biser, Aug. 25, 1984. Student, Va. Poly. Inst., 1942-43; grad., Indsl. Coll. Armed Forces, 1972. Pres. Manassas Frozen Foods, Inc., 1946—2001; pres., mgr. Cert. Food Buyers Svc., Inc., 1953—2001; pres. First Nat. Acceptance Co., 1966—2001; ret., 2001. V.p. Manassas Ice & Fuel Co. Chmn. bd. N. Va. coun. Am. Heart Assn., 1987—88, mem. inaugural com., 1961, vice-chmn. inaugural parade com.; chmn. bd. trustees Meth. Ch., 1958—66; mem. bus. adminstrn. com. No. Va. TC. Maj. USAF, 1943—46, CBI, comdr., dr. 909 TAC Airlift Group USAF, 1969—73, mobilization asst. DCS plans and opts. hdqrs. USAF, 1973—79, ret. brig. gen. USAF, 1983. Decorated Legion of Merit, Air medal. Mem.: Va. Assn. Meat Processors (pres. 1986—90), Hump Pilots Assn., Va. Frozen Foods Assn. (past pres., dir.), Nat. Inst. Locker and Freezer Provisioners Am. (past pres.), Kiwanis. Methodist. Home: 9107 Park Ave Manassas VA 20110-4350 *Do unto others as you would have them do unto you.*

**PARRISH, JILL NIEDERHAUSER,** state supreme court justice; BA, Weber State U., 1982; JD, Yale U., 1985. Bar: Utah 1985, 10th Cir. Ct. Appeals 1987, U.S. Supreme Ct. 2000. Clk. Hon. David K. Winder U.S. Dist. Ct., Utah, 1985; atty. Parr, Wadddoups, Brown, Gee & Loveless, Salt Lake City, 1986—90, shareholder, 1990—95; asst. U.S. atty. Civil Divsn. U.S. Dist. Ct., Utah, 1995—2003; justice Utah Supreme Ct., Salt Lake City, 2003—, mem. tech. com., judicial performance evaluation com., 2003—. Supr. Fin. Litigation Unit US Attys. Office. Mem.: Fed. Bar Assn. (pres.) Office: Utah Supreme Ct PO Box 140210 Salt Lake City UT 84114-0210*

**PARRISH, JOHN EDWARD,** state appellate judge; b. Lebanon, Mo., June 10, 1940; s. Folie and Thelma (Osborn) P.; m. Claudia Barbee, Sept. 1, 1962; 1 child, Mark Everett. BBA, U. Mo., 1962, JD, 1965. Acct. Arthur Andersen & Co., St. Louis, 1965-66; ptnr. Phillips & Parrish, Camdenton, Mo., 1968-73; prosecuting atty. Camden County, Camdenton, 1969-73; circuit judge State of Mo., Camdenton, 1973-1990, judge Mo. Ct. Appeals (southern dist.), 1990—; mem. State Adv. Group on Juvenile Justice, Jefferson City, Mo. 1981—; Bd. dirs. Lake Regional Health Sys., Osage Beach, Mo., 1977—, pres. 1983-85, 1991-93, 1999-2001. Capt. U.S. Army, 1966-68. Mem. Mo. Bar Assn., Mo. Coun. Juvenile Ct. Judges (pres. 1978-79), Mo. Jud. Conf.

(exec. coun. 1980-87, 92-94), Nat. Coun. Juvenile and Family Ct. Judges, Nat. Juvenile Ct. Found Inc. (trustee 1987-90). Mem. Methodist. Office: MO Ct Appeals 300 Hammons Pky Springfield MO 65806 Business E-Mail: john.e.parrish@courts.mo.gov.

**PARRISH, KARL JOSEPH,** judge, lawyer; b. Wilmington, Del., Oct. 5, 1927; s. Edwin T. Parrish and Mary C. Ivory; m. Marian E. Purdy, June 7, 1958; children: Matthew, Michael, Mark. BA, Miami U., 1951; MS, U. Pa., 1953; JD, Temple U., 1966. Dir. liquor commn., Del., 1965—67; atty. Wilmington, Del., 1967—78; judge Family Ct. of State, Del., 1978—91. Editor: Gallitzin, 1998. Bd. mgrs. Am. Cath. Historians, Phila., 1980—95; pres. Old Bohemia, Warwick, Md. With USMC, 1945—47. Democrat. Roman Catholic. Avocation: history. Home: 3211 Romilly Rd Wilmington DE 19810

**PARRISH, LORI NANCE,** property appraiser; b. Evansville, Ind., July 31, 1948; m. Geoffrey Brown; children: Gary Brown, Brandi Schmidt. Student, Fin. Inst. Sch., 1968, Fla. Atlantic U., 1969, Clemson U., 1982, Fla. Internat. U., 1988; LHD (hon.), Keiser Coll., 1996; postgrad., U. Ctrl. Fla., 1996—98. Cert. Retail Nurseryman Nova/Davie Cmty. Sch., Fla., 1975, in Credit and Collections Broward CC, Fla., 1980, in Quality Cir. Fla. Atlantic U., 1986, in Target Mgmt. Selection Fla. Internat. U., 1988, County Commrs. Cert. in Fin. Mgmt. Fla. Counties Found., Fla. Assn. Counties, 1997, County Commrs. Cert. in County Govt. Law Fla. Counties Found., Fla. Assn. Counties, 1998, County Commrs. Cert. in Ethics Fla. Counties Found., Fla. Assn. Counties, 1998. Toll operator So. Bell Telephone Co., 1966-68; adminstrv. asst. appraisal and constrn. Loan Dept. Hollywood Fed. Savings & Loan Assn., 1968—72; acct., qualifying agt. Victor Purdo Painting Co., 1972-81; fin. mgr. CRG, Inc., 1982-83; bookkeeper I county and vocat. Sch. Bd. Broward County, South Plantation HS, 1983-84; commr. dist. 5 Broward County, Fla., 1988—2004, vice-chair, 1989—90, 1996—97, chair, 1990—91, 1997—98, 2001—02, property appraiser, 2005—. Citizen's adv. bd. mem., City of Cooper, 1976-77, pers. rev. bd. mem., 1976-77; mem. Property Appraisal Adjustment Bd., 1984-90, 91-94, vice chair, 1987-88, chair 1989-90, 1993-94, 95-96; mem. South Fla. Coordinating Coun., 1985-, Criminal Justice Planning Coun., 1988-2004, Human Svcs. Com., 1988-2004, Broward Econ. Devel. Bd., 1988-89, chair 1991-92; mem. Courthouse Security Com., 1990-93, Pub. Health Trust Com., Environment, Energy Land Use Steering Com., 1991-2004, Health Steering Com. 1989-90, 94-95, Overall Econ. Devel. Planning Com., 1988-90, Met. Planning Orgn., 1988-90, 92-2004, HIV Health Planning Coun., 1992-93, Broward Edn. Planning Initiative Com., Legal, Legis. Subcommittee, 1993, Resource Recovery Bd. 1994-95, 2002-03, vice chair, 1992, chair, 1993, Tourist Devel. Coun. 1997, 2001; mem. select com. water policy, Fla. Assn. Counties', 1995-96, elderly task force mem., 1995; bd. govs. Fort Lauderdale C. of C., 1987-88, 90-91; adv. bd. mem. Water Supply, 1988-94, chair 1991-92; Brady Brigade recruiter, Nat. Orgn. Disability, 1991-93; chair NACO's Subcommittee on Aging, 1993; chair Cooper City Election Reform Com., 1993-94; bd. mem. Cmty. Health Purchasing Alliance, 1993-96; bd. dirs. Fla. Assn. Counties, 1988-2001, South Fla. Regional Transp. Authority, Tri-County Commuter Rail Authority, 1988-2004, vice chair, 1996-97, chair 1997-98; vice chair Broward County Planning Coun., 1991-92, mem. 2002-; spl. projects coord. Davie/Cooper City C. of C.; adminstrv. asst. to bldg. ofcl. City of Cooper City, 1972-81; landscape contractor, owner Earthy Interiors; v.p. Lake Shore Motel and Swap Shop, Inc., 1994-2003, 3290 Sunrise Investments, Inc., 1994-2003, 3291 Sunrise Investments, Inc. (dba Swap Shop), 1994-2003, Fla. Drive-In Theater Mgmt. Inc. 1994-2001, COO Millennium Hollywood's City Pl., 1994-2003; v.p., sec., treas. Swap Shop Mgmt. LLC, 2001-; founder Broward Workshop Criminal Justice Com. Regional Transp. Orgn. Bd. 1996-2003; served on other coms., bds, orgns. Adv. bd. Broward County Libr., 1979-85, Mommas and Poppas of Cooper City High, 1982-90, Broward C.C. Women's Programs Adv. Com., 1981-82; sec. Cooper City Elem. Sch. Adv. Com., 1979-80, chair 1980-82, South Ctrl. Area Adv. Com., 1982-83, sec., 1981-82; legis. chair Broward County Libr. Adv. Bd., 1982-84; active Broward County Sch. Bd., 1984-88, vice-chair, 1986-87, chair, 1987-88; bd. dirs. Pembroke Pines Human Resource Ctr. Adv. Com., 1984-88; hon. mem. Broward County Police Benevolent Assn., 1992-; served on other various civic bds. and coms. Recipient Lifetime Membership award Broward County Phys. Edn. Tchrs., 1988, VIP Female award West Broward Dem. Club, 1988, Lifetime Membership award Young Dems., 1988, Outstanding Svc. award Lauderhill Regular Dem. Club, 1988, Disting. Svc. award Plantation Dem. Club, 1988, Disting. and Dedicated Svc. award Broward County Deputies Assn., 1989, 92, Spl. Achievement award Jefferson-Jackson, 1990, Friend of ARC award Assn. Retarded Citizens of Broward, 1990, Tribute to Success award Pembroke Pines Dem. Club, 1991, Leadership and Dedication award Children's Svcs. Bd., 1991, Desert Storm Family Support award 1991, Disting. Svc. award Women in Distress, 1991, 92, Appreciation award Mus. Archaeology, 1992, Ann. Appreciation award N.W. Federated Woman's Club, 1992, Mother's Day award Rainbow Crusaders, 1992, Environ. Appreciation award Sunshine Ranches Homeowners Assn., 1992, Woman Leadership award Assn. Retarded Citizens, 1992, Coconut Creek Disting. Svc. award, 1994, Conservation Legislator of Yr. award Broward County Airboat, Halftrack, Conservation Club, 1994, Honoree Sunrise Regular Dem. Club, 1994, Legislator of Yr. award Broward County Fire Fighters and Paramedics, 1994, Woman of Yr. award Plantation Dem. Club, 1995, Humanitarian of Yr. award Soref Jewish Cmty. Ctr., 1995, Pres.'s award Broward County Fair, 1996, award Manatee Survival Found. 1996, Dream Maker award Jr. League Greater Fort Lauderdale, 1996, Junie Portis Helms award Dolphin Dem. Club, 1996, Par Excellence award Miramar High Cmty. Sch., 1997, Recognition award North Dade C. of C., 1997, Par Excellence award Miramar High Cmty. Sch., 1997, Criminal Justice Image award Cmty. Reconstruction Inst., 1998, Govtl. Dream Builder award Children's Harbor, 1999, Ray Lisanti Meml. award Gays United to Attack Repression and Discrimination, 1999, Gracias award Hispanic Unity, 1999, Polit. Leader of Yr. award The Vanguard Chronicle, 1999, Environ. Merit award EPA, 2000, Third Ann. Student Life Achievement Corp. Ptnr. of Yr. award Nova Southeastern U., 2002, 2002 Arts Collaboration award 13th Ann. ArtServe Encore awards, Karl Clark Cmty. Involvement award, 2002, Commr. Leadership award Fla. Local Environ. Resource Agencies, 2002, Spirit of Excellence award South Broward Chpt. Am. Bus. Women's Assn., 2002, Edee Greene Good Egg award, 2002, Humanitarian award LWV, 2002, Medallion award Unsung Heroine People with AIDS Coalition Broward County, 2002, Dem. Elected Women Honoree N.W. Dem. Club, 2002, Contbn. to Cmty. award, Pine Island Ridge Civic Orgn. award, 2003, Outstanding Svc. award Engring. Profession Broward Chpt. Fla. Engring. Soc., 2003, Women of Valor Broward County award David Posnack Jewish Cmty. Ctr., 2003, Outstanding Svc. award Washington Pk. Neighborhood Preservation and Enhancement Dist., 2003, South Fla. Commuter Svcs. Transp. Leadership award, 2004, David Posnack Hebrew Day Sch. Lifetime Achievement award, 2004, Outstanding Pub. Ofcl. award Fla. Assn. Mus., 2004, 05, Pub. Svc. award Davie Merchants and Indsl. Assn., 2005, Cert. Appreciation Coral Springs C. of C., 2005, Cert. Appreciation Poinsettia Heights Civic Assn., 2005; nominee Feminist of Yr. Fedn. Pub. Employees, 1987; finalist Woman of Yr. Govt., 1987; named Woman of Yr. City of Hope, 1989, Hon. Conch and Citizen of Fabulous Fla. Keys, 1991, Woman of Yr. Metro Broward Fire Fighters, 1992, Dem. of Yr. Jefferson-Jackson, 1992, Woman of Yr. Women in Distress, 1993, Environ. Legislator of Yr. Environ. Coalition of Broward County, 1993, Polit. Alliance of Yr. Dolphin Dem. Club, 1999, Humanitarian of Yr. E.A.S.E. Found., 2001, Woman of Yr. South Fla. Mus. Natural History and Pyramid Soc., 2002; named to Broward County Women's Club Hall of Fame, 1997; Paul Harris fellow Rotary Found. Rotary Internat. Davie Rotary Club, 1997. Mem. ALA, Southeastern Libr. Assn., Davie/Cooper City Friends of Libr. (founder), Ft. Lauderdale Friends of Libr., Broward County Friends of Libr., Amalgamated Transit Union (hon. life mem.), Naval Air Sta., Ft. Lauderdale Hist. Assn. Democrat. Office: Broward County Property Appraiser 115 S Andrews Ave Ste 111 Fort Lauderdale FL 33301-1801 Office Phone: 954-357-6830. Business E-Mail: lori@bcpa.net.

**PARRISH, MARK,** health products executive; B. U. Calif., Berkeley. Various gen. mgmt. and sales positions Foxmeyer Health Corpn., Gen. Med. Coun., Bergen Brunswig Corpn., Proctor & Gamble Co.; exec. v.p. sales and mktg. Cardinal Health, Inc., 1997—99, exec. v.p. retail sales and mktg., 1999—2001, pres. medicine shoppe internat., 2001—03, group pres. pharm. supply chain svcs., 2003—; exec. v.p., 2003—. Office: Cardinal Health Inc 7000 Cardinal Pl Dublin OH 43017

**PARRISH, MAURICE DRUE,** museum executive; b. Chgo., Mar. 5, 1950; s. Maurice and Ione Yvonne (Culmens) P.; m. Gail Marie Sims, Sept. 2, 1978; children: Theodore, Andrew, Brandon, Cara. BA in Arch., U. Pa., 1972; MArch, Yale U., 1975. City planner City of Chgo., 1975-81; architect John Hiltscher & Assocs., Chgo., 1981-83, Barnett, Jones & Smith, Chgo., 1983-84; zoning adminstr. City of Chgo., 1984-87, bldg. commr., 1987-89; dep. dir. Detroit Inst. of Arts, 1989-97, interim dir., 1997-99, exec. v.p., 1999—. Bd. dirs. Arts League of Mich., Detroit, 1994-97, Mosaic Youth Theatre Detroit, 2000—, chmn., 2002—; co-chmn. Mayor's Affordable Housing Task Force, Chgo., 1984-89; chmn. Chgo. Elec. Commn., 1988-89; mem. Chgo. Econ. devel. Commn., 1987-89; pres. St. Philip Neri Sch. Bd., Chgo., 1981-85, South Shore Commn., Chgo., 1982-84. King Chavez Parks fellow U. Mich., 1991, H.I. Feldman fellow Yale U., 1972; Franklin W. Gregory scholar Yale U., 1974, Nat. Achievement scholar U. Pa., 1968. Mem. Am. Assn. Mus., Am. Assn. Mus. Adminstrs., Constrn. Specifications Inst., Lambda Alpha. Avocations: sailing, chess, reading, astronomy. Office: Detroit Inst of Arts 5200 Woodward Ave Detroit MI 48202-4094 E-mail: mparrish@dia.org

**PARRISH, OVERTON BURGIN, JR.,** pharmaceutical corporation executive; b. Cin., May 26, 1933; s. Overton Burgin and Geneva Opal (Shinn) P. BS, Lawrence U., 1955; MBA, U. Chgo., 1959. With Pfizer Inc., 1959-74; salesman Pfizer Labs., Chgo., 1959-62, asst. mktg. product mgr. N.Y.C., 1962-63, product mgr., 1964-66, group product mgr., 1966-67, mktg. mgr., 1967-68, v.p. mktg., 1969-70, v.p., dir. ops., 1970-71; exec. v.p. domestic pharm. div. Pfizer Pharms., 1971-72; exec. v.p., dir. Pfizer Internat. Divsn., 1972-74; pres., chief operating officer G.D. Searle Internat., Skokie, Ill., 1974-75, pres., chief exec. officer, 1975-77; pres. Worldwide Pharm./Consumer Products Group, 1977-86; pres., chief exec. officer Phoenix Health Care, Chgo., 1987—; chmn., CEO, bd. dirs. Wis. Pharmiacal Co., Inc., 1990-96; co-chmn. Inhalon Pharms., 1991-95, also bd. dirs.; chmn. ViatiCare Fin. Svcs. LLC, 1993—, also bd. dirs.; chmn., CEO, bd. dirs. The Female Health Co., 1996—. Bd. dirs., chair Abiant Inc. Author: The Future Pharmaceutical Marketing; International Drug Pricing, 1971. Trustee Mktg. Sci. Inst.; trustee Food and Drug Law Inst., 1979-86, Lawrence U., 1983-87, 98—. Served to 1st lt. USAF, 1955-57. Mem. Beta Gamma Sigma, Phi Kappa Tau. Home: 505 N Lake Shore Dr Chicago IL 60611-3427 Office: Phoenix Health Care 515 N State St Chicago IL 60610- Office Phone: 312-595-9833. Personal E-mail: oparrish@aol.com.

**PARRISH, ROBERT ALTON,** retired pediatric surgeon, educator; b. Augusta, Ga., Sept. 10, 1930; s. Robert Alton and Thelma Elizabeth (Roney) P.; children: Joyce Ann, Cynthia Ann. AB, Mercer U., 1951; MS, U. Ga., 1953; MD, Med. Coll. Ga., 1956. Diplomate: Am. Bd. Surgery. Intern Bapt. Meml. Hosp., Memphis, 1956-57; resident in surgery U. Tenn., Memphis, 1957-62; gen. surgeon Med. Coll. Ga., Aususta, 1962-64, asst. prof. surgery Augusta, 1964-67, assoc. prof., 1967-70, prof. pediatric surgery, chief pediatric surgery 1970-93, prof. emeritus pediatric surgery, 1993—. Cons. to hosps. Named Outstanding Tchr. of Yr. Med. Found. Ga., Med. Coll. Ga., 1966 Fellow ACS; mem. Am Assn. Surgery of Trauma, So. Surg. Assn., Am. Acad. Pediatrics, Alpha Omega Alpha, Phi Sigma, Alpha Epsilon Delta Methodist. Home: 433 Scotts Way Augusta GA 30909-3134

**PARRISH, STEPHEN B.,** psychotherapist; b. Alexandria, Va., Dec. 13, 1948; s. Matthew Denwood and Virginia John Parrish; children: Virginia, Shawn, David, Daniel, Thomas. BA in German, Brigham Young U., 1973; EdM in Edn. Adminstrn., Mo. Sate U., 1977; PhD in Edn., Loyola U., 1990; PhD in Clin. Psychology, So. Calif. U., 1999. Dir. cons. med. edn. Hahnemann U. Med. Sch., Phila., 1990—91; dir. clin. svcs. Malcolm Eaton Enterprises, Freeport, Ill., 1991—92; dir. spl. svcs. Queens Coll., Flushing, NY, 1992—93; dir. clin. tng. Phoenix House, Hauppauge, NY, 1993—96; dir. vocat. svcs. Postgrad. Ctr. Mental Health, N.Y.C., 1996—98; dir. med. svcs. tng. Adminstrn. Children's Svcs., N.Y.C., 1998—2000; exec. dir. Bushwick Geographic Inc., Bklyn., 2000—. Pvt. practice, 1992—. Contbr. articles to profl. jours.; prodr.: Lt. USAF, 1973—77. Grantee, U.S. Dept. Edn., 1992. Mem.; APA, Internat. Soc. Social Svcs., Am. Soc. Group Psychotherapy and Psychodrama. Mem. Lds Ch. Avocation: mountain climbing. Office Phone: 718-574-5100. Personal E-mail: cephaloid@aol.com.

**PARRISH, STEVEN C.,** consumer products company executive; BA in Polit. Sci., U. Mo., 1972, JD, 1975. Joined Philip Morris Cos., 1990, sr. v.p. external affairs, gen. counsel, 1992—94, sr. v.p. worldwide regulatory affairs, 1994—95; sr. v.p. corp. affairs Altria Group, Inc., NYC, 1995—. Vice chmn. bd. dirs. Safe Horizon; bd. dirs. Stamford Symphony Orch. Office: Altria Group Inc 120 Park Ave New York NY 10017-5592

**PARRISH, THOMAS KIRKPATRICK, III,** marketing consultant; b. Richmond, Va., May 18, 1930; s. Thomas Kirkpatrick and Sally Cary (Friend) P.; divorced; children: Linn Cary, Wayne Elizabeth, Susan Scott, Thomas Kirkpatrick IV. AB, Princeton U., 1952. Product mgr. Vick Chem. Co., N.Y.C., 1955-58; v.p. Benton & Bowles Advt. Agy., N.Y.C., 1958-65; pres. Am. Chicle Co. div. Warner-Lambert Co., Morris Plains, NJ, 1965-70, Life Savers Inc. div. Squibb Corp., N.Y.C., 1970-73, Lanvin-Charles of Ritz Inc. subs. Squibb Corp., N.Y.C., 1974-76; dir. parent co. Squibb Corp., 1974-77; group dir. new bus. devel. Gillette Co., Boston, 1977-78; exec. v.p. SSC & B, Inc., N.Y.C., 1978-81; sr. assoc. Am. Cons. Corp., 1982-86; prin. The Parrish Co., N.Y.C., 1986—. Mem. N.Y. State Republican Com., 1962-63; bd. dirs. YMCA Ctr. for Internat. Mgmt. Studies, N.Y.C., 1970-85. Served to lt., jr grade USN, 1952-55. Home: 138 Fiddlers Green Waitsfield VT 05673 Office Phone: 802-496-6360.

**PARRISH, WILLIAM M.,** lawyer; b. Springfield, Mass., Feb. 8, 1953; BA with honors, U. Tex., Austin, 1975, JD, 1978. Bar: Tex. 1978, US Dist. Ct. No. & We. Districts Tex. 1978, US Ct. Appeals 5th & 11th Circuits 1978. Named ptnr. Jenkins & Gilchrist, P.C., 1983, now shareholder, litig. practice group Austin, Tex., firm v.p. bd. dirs. Mem. ABA, Tex. State Bar Assn., Dallas Bar Assn., Travis County Bar Assn., Phi Beta Kappa, Omicron Delta Kappa. Office: Jenkens & Gilchrist PC 401 Congress Ave Ste 2500 Austin TX 78701 Office Phone: 512-499-3893. Office Fax: 512-499-3810. Business E-Mail: bparrish@jenkens.com.

**PARRISH-ST. JOHN, FLORENCE TUCKER,** writer, retired federal agency administrator; b. Greenville, Miss., Nov. 12, 1925; d. Victor Amos and Martha Buchannan (Binkley) Denslow; m. Joseph Nathaniel Tucker Jr., Nov. 9, 1946 (dec. Dec. 1955); children: Joseph Nathaniel Tucker III, Frederick Steven Tucker, James Denslow Tucker; m. Noel Francis Parrish, June 25, 1983 (dec. Apr. 1987); m. Adrian St. John, Jan. 29, 1998. Diploma in piano, Ward-Belmont Coll., Nashville, 1945; studied piano with Michael Field, N.Y.C., 1945—46; B of Music Edn., Delta State U., 1960; MS in Counseling, U. So. Miss., 1971; EdD in Human Resources, George Washington U., 1983. Tchr. music Gulfport Pub. Schs., Miss., 1959—63; recreation therapist VA Hosp., Gulfport, 1964—70; edn. counselor USAF, Miss. and Japan, 1971—74, edn. svcs. officer Kunsan, Republic of Korea, 1974—75; asst. dir. sr. tng. CAP Nat. Hdqrs., 1975—77; EEO officer D.C. Dept. Labor, 1977—80; bur. chief complaints processing and adjudication, EEO U.S. Geol. Survey, Reston, Va., 1980—82; mgr. human resources Dept. Interior, 1982—84; internat. torum coord. Inspire 85 Pres.'s Com. on Employment of Handicapped, 1985; commr., chmn. edn. and cultural affairs com. Alexandria Commn. on Aging, Va., 1985—88, sec., 1987—88; lead scholar pilot project Nat. Coun. Aging. Mem. adv. bd. Inst. Conflict Analysis and resolution George Mason U., 1993—, vice chair adv. bd. Inst. Conflict Analysis and

resolution, 1995—97, chmn. adv. bd. Inst. Conflict Analysis and resolution, 1998—2000, adv. bd. mem. emeritus, 2003—. Feature writer on aging issues: Alexandria Gazette-Packet, 1986—92; feature writer Hurricane Katrina and White House Presdl. Families, 2006; contbr. articles to profl. jours. Pianist/organist Sr. Living Cmty., The Fairfax, Ft. Belvoir, Va., 2003—, The Fairfax. Mem.: Nat. Press Club (sr. rep. NPC trip to China and Hong Kong 1998, events com., chmn. oral history com., dir. videos and taped programs, presenter 13 panel programs, Vivian award 1998, 1999, 2000, 2002, 2003), Va. Assn. on Aging, World Affairs Coun., Women in Comm., Nat. Tuskegee Airmen Inc. Orgn., Smithsonian Assocs., Friends of Kennedy Ctr., Ret. Officers Assn., Miss. Soc. Washington, Am. Inst. Wine and Food, NATO Def. Coll. Ancients Assn., USAF Assn. (v.p. for cmty. programs Gen. Charles Gabriel chpt. 1991—98, Pres.'s award 1998, Woman of Distinction award Thomas Anthony chpt.), Washington Opera Guild. Home: 9110 Belvoir Woods Pky Apt 118 Fort Belvoir VA 22060-2717 Office Phone: 703-799-4355. Personal E-mail: fpstjohn@msn.com.

**PARR-JOHNSTON, ELIZABETH,** economist, consultant; b. NYC, Aug. 15, 1939; d. Ferdinand Van Siclen and Helene H. Parr; m. David E. Bond, Dec. 28, 1962 (div. July 1975); children: Peter V.S., Kristina Aline; m. Archibald F. Johnston, Mar. 6, 1982; children: James, Heather, Alexandra, Margaret. BA, Wellesley Coll., 1961; MA, Yale U., 1962, PhD, 1973; postgrad., Harvard U., 1986; DLitt, U. NB, 2004. Various positions Govt. of Can., Ottawa, Ont., Canada, 1973-76, INCO Ltd., Toronto, 1976-79; chief of staff, sr. policy advisor Ministry of Employment and Immigration, Govt. of Can., 1979-80; various positions Shell Can. Ltd., Calgary, Alta., Canada, 1980-90; pres. Parr-Johnston & Assocs., Calgary, 1990-91; pres., vice-chancellor Mt. St. Vincent U., Halifax, Nova Scotia, N.S., Canada, 1991-96, The U. New Brunswick, Fredericton, Canada, 1996—2002; pres. Parr Johnston Econ. and Policy Cons., Chester Basin, N.S., Canada, 2002—. Instr. U. We. Ont., London, 1964—67, U. B.C., Vancouver, 1967—71; vis. scholar Wesleyan U., Middletown, Conn., 1971—72; acad. rsch. assoc. Carleton U., Ottawa, 1972—73; bd. dirs. Nova Scotia Power, Emera Ltd., Bank of Nova Scotia, Social Rsch. and Demonstration Corp., Can. Found. Sustainable Devel. Tech., Can. Millennium Scholarships Found., Coun. Can. Acads.; spkr. and presenter in field; mem. Fed. Expert Adv. Panel on Equalization, 2005—06; bd. dirs. Coun. Can. Acads. Mem. editl. bd. Can. Econ. Jour., 1980—83; contbr. articles to profl. jours. Planning chmn. John Howard Soc., 1980—84; mem. policy adv. com. C.D. Howe, 1980—85; mem. Ont. Econ. Coun., 1981—84, Fed. Expert Adv. Panel on Equalization, 2005; bd. dirs. Dellcrest Home, 1980—84, Calgary S.W. Fed. Riding Assn., 1985—91, The Learning Ctr., Calgary, 1989—91, Halifax United Way, 1991—92, North/South Inst., 1992—96, Can. Unity Coun., 1993—2005, Vol. Planning N.S., 1992—93, Social Sci. Human Rsch. Coun., 1995—98, FPI Ltd., 1996—2001, Empire Co., 1994—2002, Symphony Nova Scotia, Nat. Theatre Sch. Recipient Canada 125 medal, Queen's Jubilee medal; Hon. Woodrow Wilson fellow, 1962. Mem. Assn. Atlantic Univs. (chair 1994-96), Assn. Univs. and Colls. in Can. (bd. dirs., mem. exec. com. 1994-96), Women in Acad. Adminstrn. (adv. bd. 1991-96), Calgary Coun. Advanced Tech. (exec. 1990-91), Can. Econs. Assn., Inst. Pub. Adminstrn. Can., Sr. Women Acad. Adminstrs. Can., Assn. Commonwealth Univs. (former mem. exec. com.), Phi Beta Kappa. Anglican. Avocations: golf, travel. Home: PO Box 219 Chester Basin NS Canada B0J 1K0 Office Phone: 902-275-3436. Personal E-mail: EPJ@chesterbasin.com

**PARROTT, DENNIS BEECHER,** retired insurance company executive; b. St. Louis, June 13, 1929; s. Maurice Ray and Mai Ledgerwood (Beecher) P.; m. Vivian Cleveland Miller, Mar. 24, 1952; children: Constance Beecher, Dennis Beecher, Anne Cleveland. BS in Econs., Fla. State U., Tallahassee, 1954; postgrad., Princeton U., 1964; MBA, Pepperdine U., 1982. With Prudential Ins. Co. Am., 1954-74, v.p. group mktg. L.A., 1971-74; sr. v.p. Frank B. Hall Cons. Co., L.A., 1974—83; v.p. Johnson & Higgins, L.A., 1983-95; exec. v.p. Arthur J. Gallagher & Co., L.A., 1995-98; ret., 1998. Spkr. in field. Chmn. Weekend with the Stars Telethon, 1976-80; chmn. bd. dirs. United Cerebral Palsy/Spastic Children's Found., L.A. County, 1979-82, chmn. bd. govs., 1982-83; bd. dirs. Nat. United Cerebral Palsy Assn., 1977-82, pres., 1977-79; bd. dirs. L.A. Emergency Task Force, 1992; mem. cmty. adv. coun. Birmingham High Sch., Van Nuys, Calif., 1982-85; sect. chmn. United Way, L.A., 1983-84; bd. dirs. The Betty Clooney Found. for Brain Injured, 1986-88; mem. com. to fund an endowed chair in cardiology at Cedars-Sinai Med. Ctr., 1986-88; adv. coun. Family Health Program, Inc., 1986-88; bd. deacons Bel Air Presbyn. Ch., 1990-92, chmn., 1991-92, elder, 1993-96; mem. adv. coun. Blue Cross Calif., 1996-98; chmn. Danny Arnold Meml. Golf Classic at Riviera Country Club benefitting John Wayne Cancer Inst., 1997. 1st lt. AUS, 1951-53. Named Tournament Champion, Sunkist Invitational Golf Tournament, 1995. Mem. Am. Soc. CLUs, Internat. Found. Employee Benefits, Mchts. and Mfrs. Assns. 44th Ann. Mgmt. Conf. (chmn. 1986), Employee Benefits Planning Assn. So. Calif., L.A. Club, Woodland Hills Country Club, Jonathan Club (L.A.). Republican. Presbyterian. Home: 17023 Encino Hills Dr Encino CA 91436-4009 Personal E-mail: CallParrott@aol.com.

**PARROTT, LINDA SUSAN,** chemistry educator; b. Birmingham, Ala., May 4, 1951; d. John D. Latham and Theresia Ann Hocutt; m. James Richard Parrott, June 12, 1971; children: Theresia Elisabeth De Iorio, Mary Ashley Young. BS, U. Memphis, Tenn., 1973; MEd, William Carey Coll., Gulfport, Miss., 2000. Tchr., asst. prin. Temple Christian Acad., Gulfport, Miss., 1987—98; tchr. Ocean Springs H.S., 2000—. Writing cons. Live Oak Writing Project, Long Beach, Miss., 2002. Author: (short stories) Hooked on Teaching. Tchr. Sunday sch. Robinson Rd. Bapt. Ch., Gulfport, 1995. Mem.: Miss. Sci. Tchrs. Assn. Liberal. Baptist. Avocations: reading, travel, swimming, needlecrafts. Home: 15317 Saint Charles St Gulfport MS 39503 Office: Ocean Springs High Sch PO Box 7002 Ocean Springs MS 39566-7002 Office Phone: 228-875-0333. Business E-Mail: lparrott@ossd.k12.ms.us.

**PARROTT, WANDA SUE,** writer, journalist; b. Kansas City, Mo., Feb. 12, 1935; d. William Raymond and Lois Marie (Cain) Childress; m. Edward Anthony Cyriacus Parrott, Dec. 16, 1962 (div. 1971); 1 child, Edward Anthony. AA, Citrus Coll., 1957; journalism cert., L.A. Evening Adult Coll., 1968; PhD in Comms., Colegium Orthogenesis, 1961; DD in Comparative Religion, Universal Life Ch., 1974. Tech. writer aerospace industry, So. Calif., 1965-67; journalist Hearst Corp./L.A. Herald-Examiner, 1967-74, Daily News subs. Chgo. Tribune, 1977-79, Assoc. Valley Publs., 1980-82, Sr. Living Newspapers, 1992-2000. Co-prodr. Golden Words, 1993-2006; co-author: How to Try Your Own Case in Court...And Win!, 1997, There's A Spirit in the Kitchen, 2001; author: Springing Soliloquy- The Trail of Tears-Missouri, 2004 Co-founder, prodr. nat. ann. Sr. Poet Laureate Poetry Competition; founder Springfield Writers' Workshop, 1992; founder Amy Kitchener's Angels Without Wings Found. Recipient Gold Kettle award, Salvation Army, 1994—2005. Fellow Ancient Mystical Order Rosae Crucis (master of lodge 1984-85), Springfield Writers' Guild (bd. dirs., past pres.), Mo. Writers' Guild (past sec.-treas.), Book Publicists of So. Calif., Mo. State Poetry Soc. (hon. life), Nat. Trail of Tears Assn Personal E-mail: amykitchenerfdn@hotmail.com

**PARRS, MARIANNE M.,** paper and lumber company executive; b. NYC, 1945; m. Walter Parrs; 3 children. Grad., Brown U. Joined Internat. Paper Co., 1974, sector controller, printing papers Purchase, NY, staff v.p., worldwide responsibility tax planning and compliance, CFO, sr. v.p., 1995—99, exec. v.p. adminstrn., info. tech. and human resources Stamford, Conn., 1999—, CFO, 2005. Bd. dir. Liaison Tech. (formerly Forest Express), CIT Group, 2003—. Bd. dir. Women's Forum. Office: Internat Paper Co 400 Atlantic St Stamford CT 06921 Fax: 914-397-1650. Office Phone: 203-541-8000.*

**PARRY, DALE D.,** newspaper editor; BS in Journalism cum laude, Ball State U., Muncie, Ind., 1981. Feature writer Richmond (Ind.) Palladium-Item, 1981-84, Cin. Enquirer, 1984-86; editor Today section The Dallas Morning News, 1987-90; assignment editor The Way We Live sect. Detroit Free Press,

1990-92, dep. features editor, 1992-94, features editor, 1993-96, asst. mng. editor, 1997-2000, dep. mng. editor, 2001—. Mem. Am. Assn. Sun. and Feature Editors. Office: Detroit Free Press 600 W Fort St Detroit MI 48226-2706

**PARRY, LANCE AARON,** publishing executive; b. Allentown, Pa., Sept. 4, 1947; s. Harwood Clayton Bachman and Iola Mary (Johnson) P.; m. Virginia Eleanor Ford, Apr. 24, 1971; children: Halloran Lee, Christine Ford. BS in English Edn., Kutztown U., 1969; MS in Journalism, W.Va. U., 2003. With Call-Chronicle Newspapers, Allentown, 1970-81, mng. editor, 1979-81; asst. news editor The Phila. Inquirer, 1981-82, systems editor, 1982-84, night news editor, 1984-86, news editor daily edit., 1986-87, news editor Sunday edit., 1987-89, sr. editor/systems and tech., 1989-93, page design dir., 1993-94, features news editor, 1994-96, news editor Sunday edit., 1996-98, features news editor, 1998—2004, news editor, 2005, sr. news editor, 2005—. Recipient 1st Place award for front page design Pa. Newspaper Pubs. Assn./Pa. Soc. Newspaper Editors, 1985, 87, 88, Disting. Alumnus award Kutztown U., 1992; Sigma Delta Chi scholar, 1969. Mem. Soc. Profl. Journalists, Pen and Pencil Club. Democrat. Presbyterian. Home: 16 Salisbury Ln Malvern PA 19355-2836 Office: The Phila Inquirer 400 N Broad St Philadelphia PA 19130-4099

**PARRY, ROBERT WALTER,** chemistry professor; b. Ogden, Utah, Oct. 1, 1917; s. Walter and Jeanette (Petterson) P.; m. Marjorie J. Nelson, July 6, 1945; children: Robert Bryce, Mark Nelson. BS, Utah State Agr. Coll., 1940; MS, Cornell U., 1942; PhD, U. Ill., 1946; DSc (hon.), Utah State U., 1985, U. Utah, 1997. Rsch. asst. NDRC Munitions Devel. Lab. U. Ill., Urbana, 1943-45, tchg. fellow, 1945-46; mem. faculty U. Mich., Ann Arbor, 1946-69, prof. chemistry, 1958-69; Disting. prof. chemistry U. Utah, Salt Lake City, 1969-97, prof. emeritus, 1997—. Chmn. bd. trustees Gordon Rsch. Conf., 1967-68; cons. in field. Founding editor Inorganic Chemistry, 1960-63. Recipient Mfg. Chemists award for coll. tchg., 1972, Sr. U.S. Scientist award Alexander Von Humboldt-Stiftung, West Germany, 1980, First Govs. medal of Sci., State Utah, 1987. Mem. AAAS (chmn. chemistry sect. 1983), Internat. Union Pure and Applied Chemistry (chmn. U.S. nat. com., chmn. com. tchg. chemistry 1968-74), Am. Chem. Soc. (bd. editors jour. 1969-80, dir. 1973-83, pres.-elect 1981, pres. 1982, Disting. Svc. to Inorganic Chemistry award 1965, Disting. Svc. to Chem. Edn. award 1977, Utah award Utah sect. 1978, Priestly medal 1993), Sigma Xi. Achievements include research in structural problems of inorganic chemistry and incorporation results into theoretical models, chemistry of phosphorus, boron and fluorine. Home: 5002 Fairbrook Ln Salt Lake City UT 84117-6205 Office: U Utah Dept Chemistry 315 South 1400 East Salt Lake City UT 84112-0850 Office Phone: 801-581-7022. Business E-Mail: parry@chem.utah.edu.

**PARRY, SCOTT BRINK,** psychologist; b. Reading, Pa., Sept. 4, 1932; s. George Raymond and Claire (Blackburne) Parry; m. Joan SantAntonio; 1 child, Christiana Claire. BA, Princeton U., 1954; MS, Boston U., 1960; PhD, NYU, 1969. Account exec. Hill & Knowlton Inc., N.Y.C., 1960-62; editor Harcourt, Brace, Jovanovich, N.Y.C., 1962-64; ptnr. Parry & Robinson, Inc., N.Y.C., 1964-66; mgr. N.Y.C. office Sterling Inst., 1966-71; v.p., pres., chmn. Tng. House, Inc., N.Y.C., Princeton, 1971—; prof. comms. Mercer County (N.J.) C.C., 2000—05. Educ. cons. UNESCO, Paris, Nigeria, 1963, Ghana, 64; mem. adv. bd. Training Mag. Lakewood Publs., 1988—92; adj. prof. NYU, 1968—74; spkr. convs. and meetings in 17 countries on 6 continents; cons. to more than 50 Fortune 500 cos. Author: (book) The Story of Handbells, 1957, A Handbell Handbill, 1963, From Managing to Empowering, 1993, The Managerial Mirror, 2 vols, 1997, Evaluating the Impact of Training, 1997, Training for Results, 2000, 46 training books; contbr. articles to profl jours and newspapers. Lt U.S. Army, 1957—59. Named Hon Chmn, 25th Anniversary Am Guild English Handbell Ringers, 1979; named to Human Resource Develop Hall of Fame, 1999; recipient Best Training Product Award, Human Resource Exec, 1990, 1994. Mem.: ASTD, Instructional Sys Asn, Int Soc Performance Improvement, Int Fedn Training and Develop Orgns. Republican. Presbyterian. Avocations: music (harpsichord, organ, carillon); collecting and restoring antiques, renovating buildings. Office: Training House 96 Bear Brook Rd Princeton NJ 08540-6246 E-mail: jsparry@erols.com

**PARRY, TIMOTHY R.,** lawyer; b. Syracuse, N.Y., July 28, 1954; s. Edward Lee and Ruth (Thomas) P.; m. Isabelle Eckmayer, Aug. 30, 1980; children: Ryan Edward, Ian Andrew. BS, Ariz. State U., 1976; JD, U. Cin., 1980. Bar: Ohio 1980, Fla. 1983, U.S. Dist. Ct. (so. dist.) Ohio 1981, U.S. Dist. Ct. (so. and mis. dists.) Fla. 1983, U.S. Ct. Appeals (11th cir.) 1984. Law clk. to judge John D. Holschuh U.S. Dist. Ct. (so. dist.) Ohio, Columbus, 1980-81; asst. atty. gen. Ohio Atty. Gen.'s Office, Columbus, 1981-83; assoc. Harter, Secrest & Emery, Naples, Fla., 1983-88, ptnr., 1989—96; dir. v.p., asst. gen. counsel Health Mgmt. Associates, Naples, Fla., 1996—97, sr. v.p., gen. counsel, sec., 1997—. Past pres., Cath. Social Svcs. Collier County, Naples, Fla. 1988—, adv. bd. Mem. Fla. Bar Assn. (20th jud. cir. bar grievance com. 1989—), Collier County Bar Assn. (bd. dirs. 1989—), Ohio Bar Assn. Office: Health Mgmt Associates 5811 Pelican Bay Blvd Naples FL 34108-2710

**PARRY, WILLIAM DEWITT,** lawyer; b. Hartford, Conn., June 4, 1941; s. William Brown and Mary Elizabeth (Caton) p.; m. Andrea Hannah Lewis, June 30, 1973; children: Sara, Jessica. BA, U. Mass., 1963; JD, U. Pa., 1966. Bar: N.J. 1987, Pa. 1967, U.S. Dist. Ct. (ea. dist.) Pa. 1974, U.S. Ct. Appeals (3d cir.) 1980, U.S. Ct. Appeals (9th cir.) 1998, U.S. Supreme Ct. 1980. Assoc. Shapiro, Cook & Bressler, Phila., 1966-67; asst. dir. ABA joint com on continuing legal edn. Am. Law Inst., Phila., 1967-73; assoc. Lowenschuss Assocs., Phila., 1973-85; of counsel Weiss, Golden & Pierson, Phila., 1985-88; pvt. practice Phila., 1988; ptnr. Rubin, Quinn, Moss & Patterson, Phila., 1989-93; pvt. practice Phila., 1993—. Lectr. in field. Author: Understanding and Controlling Stuttering: A Comprehensive New Approach Based on the Valsalva Hypothesis, 1994, 2000; editor U. Pa. Law Rev., 1964-66, The Practical Lawyer, 1967-73. Founder Phila. area chpt. Nat. Stuttering Project, 1985; bd. dirs. Nat. Stuttering Assn., 1996-2002; trustee Unitarian Soc. Germantown, Phila., 1983-86. Mem.: ATLA, ABA, Pa. Trial Lawyers Assn., Phila. Bar Assn., Pa. Bar Assn. Democrat. Avocations: acting, writing. Home: 520 Baird Rd Merion Station PA 19066-1302 Office: 1608 Walnut St Ste 900 Philadelphia PA 19103-5451 Office Phone: 215-735-3500. Personal E-mail: wdparry@aol.com.

**PARRY-JONES, RICHARD,** automotive executive; b. Wales, 1951; Mech. engring. (hon.), Univ. Salford, Manchester, 1973; D (hon.), Loughborough Univ., 1995. Apprentice Ford's European Product Group, 1969; leading role in devel. of the 1981 European Escort Ford Motor Co., 1981, apptd. mgr. small car programs, 1982, v.p. European vehicle ctr. Dearborn, Mich., 1994—98, group v.p. global product devel. and quality, 1998—2001, chief tech. officer, 2001—. Vis. prof. Dept. of Aero. and Automotive Engring. at England's Loughborough U., 2001. Named Exec. Engr.of Ford's Technol. Rsch. in Europe, 1985, Chief Engr. for Vehicle Rngring., 1991, Man of the Yr., Bit. publ. Autocar, 1994, U.S. mag. Automobile, 1997, sr. exec. for Mazda oversight on Nov. 15, 2001; recipient Golden Gear Award, Wash. Motor Press Assn., 2001, Mktg. Statesman of the Yr., Sales and Mktg. Executives of Detroit. Fellow: Inst. of Mech. Engineers, Royal Acad. Engineers. Office: Ford Motor Co One American Rd Dearborn MI 48126-1899

**PARSA, FEREYDOUN DON,** plastic surgeon; b. Tehran, Iran, May 20, 1942; came to U.S., 1970; s. Issa and Zahra (Bayat) P.; m. Touri Akhlaghi, June 17, 1972; children: Natalie, Alan, Sean. MD, Lausanne U., Switzerland, 1969. Diplomate Am. Bd. Plastic Surgery. Chief of plastic surgery, prof. surgery U. Hawaii, Honolulu, 1981—. Contbr. articles to profl. jours. Mem. AMA, Am. Soc. Plastic Surgeons, Hawaii Med. Assn. Avocation: painting. Office: U Hawaii 1329 Lusitana St Honolulu HI 96813-2429 also: U Hawaii Sch Med Surgery 1329 Lusitana St 807 Honolulu HI 96813-2421 Personal E-mail: hawaiiplasticsurgery@yahoo.com.

**PARSHALL, GEORGE WILLIAM,** chemist, researcher; b. Hackensack, Minn., Sept. 19, 1929; s. George Clarence and Frances (Virnig) Parshall; m. Naomi B. Simpson, Oct. 9, 1954; children: William, Jonathan, David. BS, U. Minn., 1951; PhD, U. Ill., 1954. Rsch. chemist E.I. duPont de Nemours & Co., Wilmington, Del., 1954—65, rsch. supr., 1965—79, dir. chem. sci., 1979—92, cons., 1992—2004, mem. com. on environ. mgmt. techs., 1994—97; mem. chem. stockpile disposal com. NRC, Washington, 1992—98, mem. non-stockpile com., 1998—99, 2001—06, mem. chem. weapons adv. com., 2004—. Bd. chem. sci. NRC, Washington, 1983—86; Reilly lectr. Notre Dame U., 1980; Ipatieff lectr. Northwestern U., 1994; mem. sci. adv. bd. Phoenix S&T, 2002—. Author: (book) Homogeneous Catalysis, 1980, Homogeneous Catalysis, 2d rev. edit., 1992; editor: Inorganic Syntheses, 1974, Jour. Molecular Catalysis, 1977—80. Recipient Ballar Inorganic Chemistry medal, U. Ill., 1976, Alumni Achievement award, 2005. Mem.: NAS, Am. Acad. Arts Scis., Am. Chem. Soc. (award in inorganic chemistry 1983, award leadership in chem. rsch. mgmt. 1989), Inst. Chemists (Chem. Pioneer award 1992, Gold medal award 1995), Guild Episcopal Scholars (treas. 1994—99). Episcopalian. Home: Apt 806 2401 Pennsylvania Ave Wilmington DE 19806 Personal E-mail: gparshall@aol.com.

**PARSHALL, GERALD,** journalist; b. St. Paul, Apr. 24, 1941; s. William Elmer and Evelyn (Steckling) P.; m. Sandra Grant, Dec. 20, 1970. BA, U. Minn., 1963; MA, U. Mich., 1964; grad. fellow, U. Chgo., 1966-67. Reporter York (Pa.) Gazette and Daily, 1968, Balt. Evening Sun, 1968-71; Capitol Hill staff U.S. News & World Report, Washington, 1971-77, sr. editor, 1977-79, asst. mng. editor, 1979-90, sr. writer, 1990-99, contbg. editor, 1999—2004. Mem. Exec. Com. of Periodical Corrs., U.S. Congress, 1974-80, chmn., 1979-80 Served to 1st lt. U.S. Army, 1964-66. Recipient Front Page award Washington-Balt. Newspaper Guild, 1971, Silver Gavel award ABA, 1983 Home: 1004 Congress Ln Mc Lean VA 22101-2116 Personal E-mail: gparshall@verizon.net.

**PARSHALL, KAREN VIRGINIA HUNGER,** mathematician; b. Virginia Beach, Va., July 7, 1955; d. Maurice Jacques and Jean Kay (Wroton) Hunger; m. Brian J. Parshall, Aug. 6, 1978. BA, U. Va., 1977, MS, 1978; PhD, U. Chgo., 1982. Asst. prof. math. Sweet Briar (Va.) Coll., 1982-87, U. Ill., Urbana, 1987-88; asst. prof. math. and history U. Va., Charlottesville, 1988-93, assoc. prof. math. and history, 1993—99, prof. math. and history, 1999—. Author: (with David Rowe) Emergence of American Mathematics Research Community, 1994; (with others) Experiencing Nature, 1997, James Joseph Sylvester: Life and Work in Letters, 1998, (with others) Mathematics Unbound: The Emergence of an International Mathematical Community, 1800-1945, 2002; Years Ago editor Mathematical Intelligencer, N.Y.C., 1990-93; book rev. editor Historia Mathematica, San Diego, 1990-93, mng. editor, 1994-95, editor, 1996-99; contbr. articles to Archive for History Exact Scis., History of Sci., Jour. of the History of Biology, Archives internationales d'histoire des sciences, Annals of Sci., Historia Mathematica, Notices of the Am. Math. Soc., Am. Math. Mo., Revue d'histoire des mathématiques. Scholars award NSF, 1986-87, 90-93, NSF VPW award, 1996-97; John Simon Guggenheim Found. fellow, 1996. Mem. Am. Math. Soc., History Sci. Soc., Math. Assn. Am., Académie Internationale d'histoire des sciences (corr.), Phi Beta Kappa. Office: U Va Depts Math and History Dept Mathematics P O Box 400137 Charlottesville VA 22904

**PARSKY, GERALD LAWRENCE,** lawyer; b. West Hartford, Conn., Oct. 18, 1942; s. Isadore and Nettie (Sanders) P.; m. Susan Haas, June 26, 1966; children: Laura, David; m. Robin Cleary, Jan. 27, 1980. AB, Princeton U., 1964; JD, U. Va., 1968. Bar: N.Y. 1969, D.C. 1974, Calif. 1983. Assoc. Mudge Rose Guthrie & Alexander, N.Y.C., 1968-71; spl. asst. to under sec. U.S. Treasury Dept., Washington, 1971-73, exec. asst. to dep. sec. Fed. Energy Office, 1973-74, asst. sec. internat. affairs, 1974-77; sr. ptnr. Gibson, Dunn & Crutcher, L.A., 1977-90; of counsel Gibson, Dunn & Cruther, 1990-92; chmn. Aurora Capital Ptnrs., 1990—. Bd. dirs. James A. Baker III Inst. Pub. Policy. Trustee George Bush Presdl. Libr. Found., 1993—, Ronald Reagan Presdl. Found., 1995—; bd. dirs. Music Ctr. Found., 1998—. Recipient Alexander Hamilton award U.S. Treasury, 1976, Woodrow Wilson award, 2000. Mem. ABA, Coun. Fgn. Rels., N.Y. Princeton Club, Calif. Club, Racquet Club N.Y., Rolling Rock Club, Rancho Santa Fe Golf Club. Office: Aurora Capital Group 10877 Wilshire Blvd Ste 2100 Los Angeles CA 90024-4376

**PARSLEY, HENRY NUTT, JR.,** bishop, academic administrator; b. Memphis, Tenn. m. Rebecca Knox Allison; 1 child, Henry Nutt III. B in English magna cum laude, U. of the South, 1970; MDiv, Gen. Theol. Sem., N.Y.C., 1973. Asst. rector Trinity Ch., Myrtle Beach, SC, St. Philip's Ch., Charleston, SC; rector St. Paul's Ch., Summerville, SC, Christ Ch., Charlotte, NC; bishop Episcopal Diocese Ala., 1999—; chancellor U. of the South, Sewanee, Tenn. 2003—. Avocations: reading, fishing. Office: Univ of the South 735 University Ave Sewanee TN 37383

**PARSLEY, STEVEN DWAYNE,** title company executive; b. Monrovia, Calif., Dec. 31, 1959; BBA magna cum laude, U. Albuquerque, 1985. Lic. agt. to issue title ins. N.Mex. Data processing asst. Orion Corp., Albuquerque, 1978-79; title searcher N.Mex. Title, Albuquerque, 1979; various positions Rio Grande Title Co., Albuquerque, 1979-84, v.p., mgr. title ops., 1984-91, sr. v.p., escrow officer, 1992-94, exec. v.p., 1994-99; pres. Dona Ana Title Co., Las Cruces, N.Mex., 1999—. Bd. dirs. N.Mex Land Title Trust Fund. Mem. state apptd. Title Ins. Task Force State of N.Mex.; mem. Affordable Housing Round Table. Presdl. scholar, U. N.Mex, 1978. Mem.: Las Cruces Homebuilders Assn., N.Mex Land Title Assn. (pres. 1997—98, past v.p.). Avocations: ragtime piano, running. Home: 746 Oro Viejo Las Cruces NM 88011-8071 Office: Dona Ana Title Co 425 S Telshor Blvd Ste B Las Cruces NM 88011-8237 Office Phone: 505-521-5800, Personal E mail ssppiano@msn.com. Business E-Mail: stparsley@donaanatitle.com.

**PARSON, EDWARD A.,** law educator; Grad. U. Toronto, U. BC; PhD in public policy, Harvard U. Prof. law U. Mich. Law Sch., Ann Arbor, 2003—. Mem. synthesis team US Nat. Assessment of Impacts of Climate Change; cons. Internat. Inst. for Applied Systems Analysis, UN Environment Prog., Office of Tech. Assessment of US Congress, Privy Coun. Office of Govt. Can., White House Office of Sci. and Tech. Policy; leader Environ. Treads Project Govt. Can. Author: Governing the Environment: Persistent Challenges, Uncertain Innovations, 2001, Protecting the Ozone Layer: Science and Strategy (Harold and Margaret Sprout Award, 2004); co-author: The Science and Politics of Global Climate Change; contbr. articles to law jours. Mem.: NAS (mem. Com. on Human Dimensions of Global Change). Office: U Mich Law Sch 432 Hutchins Hall 625 S State St Ann Arbor MI 48109-1215 Office Phone: 734-763-6133, 734-763-9375. E-mail: parson@umich.edu.

**PARSONS, ALEXANDRA CLARE,** literature and language educator; b. London, Sept. 3, 1975; arrived in U.S., 1976; d. Andrew and Carol Parsons. BA in English cum laude, Wellesley Coll., 1997; MA, Columbia U., Tchrs. Coll., 2001. Permanent tchg. cert. NY, 2001. TV rsch. analyst Katz Media, Seltel, Inc., NYC, 1997—98; broadcast assoc. CBS News Prodns., NYC, 1998—99; media rels. publicity coord. ABC News, NYC, 1999; asst. kindergarten tchr. Marymount Sch., NYC, 1999—2000; English tchr. The Nightingale-Bamford Sch., NYC, 2001—. Scholar, Japan Fulbright Meml. Fund, 2005. Mem.: Nat. Coun. Tchrs. English, Assn. Tchrs. Ind. Sch., Kappa Delta Pi.

**PARSONS, ANDREW JOHN,** management consultant; b. Kingston, Surrey, Eng., July 22, 1943; arrived in US, 1968; m. Carol Ann Iannucci; children: Alexandra, Katherine. BA, MA, Oxford U., 1965; MBA, Harvard U., 1970. Acct. exec. LPE/Leo Burnett, London, 1965—68; from strategic planning dir. to v.p. mktg. Prestige Group Ltd. div. Am. Home Products, N.Y.C. and London, 1970-76; v.p. mktg. Kurzweil Computer Products div. Xerox Corp., Cambridge, Mass., 1979-80; assoc. McKinsey & Co., Inc., N.Y.C., 1981—, prin., 1982-88, dir. consumer industries sector, mktg. ctr., sr. ptnr., 1988-2000, dir. emeritus, 2004—; chmn. Kantar Group of WPP, PLC, 2001-03.

Underwriting mem Lloyds of London, 1986—; chmn. Gulliver Growth Ptnrs. LLC, 2001—; with McKinsey Adv. Coun., 2001—04; adv. bd. aQuantive, Inc., 2002—05, Quaero, Inc.; pres. Smithfield Estates LLC, 2002—; bd. dirs. A.T. Cross Co., IXI Corp., ENR Svcs., Inc., UST Inc., BuySafe, Inc. Contbr. articles to profl jours. Mem. adv. bd. Salvation Army, Greater NY, 1983—, chmn. adv. bd., 1993—97; gov. United Way of Tri-State, 2003—; bd. dirs. United Way, N.Y.C., 1988—; trustee Sarah Lawrence Coll., Bronxville, NY, 1993—2001. Scholar Baker, Harvard Bus Sch, 1970. Mem.: Shelter Harbor Golf Club, Weekapaug Golf Club, Watch Hill Yacht Club, Siwanoy Country Club. Home: 56 Hereford Rd Bronxville NY 10708-5408 also: 2 Arraquat Rd Westerly RI 02891 E-mail: andrew_parsons@mckinsey.com.

**PARSONS, ANNE,** performing company executive; m. Donald Dietz; 1 child. BA, Smith Coll., 1980. Staff Nat. Symphony Orchestra, Wash., DC, 1981—83; orchestra mgr. Boston Symphony Orchestra, 1983—91; gen. mgr. Hollywood Bowl, LA, 1991—98, NY City Ballet, 1998—2004; exec. dir. Detroit Symphony Orchestra, 2004—. Fellow Am. Symphony Orchestra League, 1980—81. Office: Detroit Symphony Orchestra Max M Fisher Music Ctr 3711 Woodward Ave Detroit MI 48201

**PARSONS, DANIEL LANKESTER,** pharmaceutics educator; b. Biscoe, NC, Sept. 10, 1953; s. Solomon Lankester and Doris Eva (Bost) P. BS in Pharmacy, U. Ga., Athens, 1975, PhD, 1979. Asst. prof. pharmaceutics U. Ariz., Tucson, 1979-82; asst. prof. Auburn U., Ala., 1982-86, assoc. prof. Ala., 1986-91, chmn. divsn Ala., 1990—, prof. Ala., 1991—. Cons. Wyeth-Ayerst, Phila., 1989—93, Technomics, Ardsley, NY, 1990—93 Murty Pharm., Lexington, Ky, 1996—99; presenter in field. Author (with G.V. Betageri and S.A. Jenkins): Liposome Drug Delivery Systems, 1993. Named Disting. Alumni, Sandhills Coll., 1990, Tchr. of Yr., Pharmacy Student Coun., 1987, Grad. Faculty Mem. of Yr., Grad. Student Orgn., 1994, Prof. of Yr., Kappa Psi Fraternity, 2000. Mem. Am. Pharm. Assn., Am. Assn. Pharm. Scientists, Phi Kappa Phi, Kappa Psi (advisor 1990-95, nat. grad. devel. com. 1993-95, nat. scholarship com. 1995-99, nat. grand coun. dep. com. 1997—, Svc. award 1990, 95, Advisor award 1992). Achievements include research in plasma protein binding of drugs, effects of perfluorochemical blood substitutes on such binding, and development of orally disintegrating tablets. Office: Auburn U Sch Pharmacy Auburn AL 36849 Business E-Mail: parsodl@auburn.edu.

**PARSONS, DONALD FRANCIS,** judge; b. Phila., June 28, 1948; BSEE cum laude, Lehigh U., 1970, MA, 1972; JD, Georgetown U., 1977. Bar: Del. 1977. Law clk. to Hon. James L. Latchum U.S. Dist. Ct. Del., 1977-79; ptnr. Morris, Nichols, Arsht & Tunnell, Wilmington, Del., 1979—2003; vice chancellor Del. Ct. of Chancery, Wilmington, 2003—. Case and note editor Georgetown Law Jour., 1976-77. Mem. ABA, N.Y. Patent Law Assn., Phila. Patent Law Assn., Am. Intellectual Property Law Assn., Del. Bar Assn. (pres. 1999-2000). Office: NCC Courthouse 500 N King St Wilmington DE 19801-3734 Office Phone: 302-255-0509. Business E-Mail: donald.parsons@state.de.us.

**PARSONS, DONALD JAMES,** retired bishop; b. Phila., Mar. 28, 1922; s. Earl and Helen (Drabble) P.; m. Mary Russell, Sept. 17, 1955; children—Mary, Rebecca, Bradford. BA, Temple U., 1943; MDiv, Phila. Div. Sch., 1946, ThD, 1951, DD (hon.), 1964; postgrad., U Nottingham, Eng., 1968; DCL, Nashotah House, wiS., 1973. Ordained priest Episcopal Ch., 1946, consecrated bishop, 1973; curate Immanual Ch., Wilmington, Del., 1946-49; rector St. Peter's Ch., Smyrna, Del., 1949-50; prof. N.T. Nashotah House, 1950-73, pres., dean, 1963-73, Ramsey prof. ascetical theology, 2000—; bishop Diocese of Quincy, Ill., 1973-88. Author: A Life-time Road to God, 1966, In Time with Jesus, 1973, Holy Eucharist: Rite Two, 1976. Episcopalian. Home: 6901 N Galena Rd Apt 111 Peoria IL 61614-3158

**PARSONS, EDWIN SPENCER,** clergyman, educator; b. Brockton, Mass., Feb. 16, 1919; s. Edwin Webber and Ethel Faunce (Marsh) P.; m. Eleanor Millard, Nov. 3, 1944; children: William Spencer, Ellen, James Millard, Bradford Delano. AB, Denison U., 1941, D.D., 1967; B.D., Andover Newton Theol. Sch., 1945; D.D., Kalamazoo Coll., 1966; L.H.D., Chgo. Coll. Osteo. Medicine, 1978. Ordained to ministry Am. Baptist Ch., 1944; asst. minister First Bapt. Ch., Newton Centre, Mass., 1945-47; exec. dir. Bapt. Student Found., Inc., Cambridge, Mass., 1947-59; pastor Hyde Park Union Ch., Chgo., 1959-65; assoc. prof. ethics U. Chgo. Div. Sch., 1965-78, prof. 1978-81; dir. ministerial field ednr., 1977-79; asst. to dean, 1981-88; dean Rockefeller Meml. Chapel, 1965-79; v.p., dir. New Eng. office Health Resources Ltd., Boston, Mass., No., 1979-89; rect. Cons. dept. ch. and soc. Am. Bapt. Chs. of Mass., 1979-86, also editor Mass. Bapt. News, 1983-85; chmn. strategy and action com., bd. dirs. Mass. Coun. Chs., 1983-85; adj. prof. Andover Newton Theol. Sch., 1981-85 Author: The Christian Yes or No, 1964; contbr. chapters to books. Pres. Coun. Hyde Park-Kenwood Chs. and Synagogues, 1963; chmn. Abortion Rights Assn. Ill., 1974-79; founder, chmn. Ill. Religious Coalition for Abortion Rights, 1975, Ill. Clergy Consultation Svcs. on Problem Pregnancies, Chgo. Clergy Consultation Svcs., 1969-73; bd. dirs., chmn. clergy adv. com. Planned Parenthood Assn., Chgo., 1977-79; bd. dirs. Hyde Park YMCA, Facing History and Ourselves Nat. Found., 1983-87; bd. govs. Internat. House, Chgo., 1969-79; trustee Packard Manse (Mass.), Bapt. Theol. Union, U. Chgo., 1960-70, 81-96, hon. trustee, 1996—; pres., bd. mgrs. Ministers and Missionaries Benefit Bd., 1975-81; mem. policy coun. Religious Coalition for Abortion Rights of Mass., 1980-86; sec., treas. Bolton Inst. for Sustainable Future, 1983-87; mem. gen. bd., mem. exec. com., mem. commn. on Christian unity Am. Bapt. Chs., 1963-72, 74-81; bd. dirs. Planned Parenthood League of Mass., 1984-92. Democrat. Baptist. Home: 65 Briarwood Cir Apt 410 Worcester MA 01606-1254

**PARSONS, ERIC E.,** financial company executive; Degree, Lewis & Clark Coll., Northwestern U. V.p. Standard Ins. Co., pres. mortgage and real estate subs.; sr. v.p., CFO StanCorp Fin. Group/Standard Ins. Co., Portland, Oreg.; chmn., pres., CEO StanCorp Fin. Group. Trustee Oreg. Zoo Found.; bd. dirs. Portland Opera; mem. Metro Bus. Adv. Coun.; mem. Portland Mayor's Bus. Roundtable. Fellow Life Office mgmt. Inst. Office: StanCorp Fin Group Inc 1100 SW 6th Ave Portland OR 97204*

**PARSONS, ESTELLE,** actress, director, theater producer; b. Lynn, Mass., Nov. 20, 1927; d. Eben and Elinor (Mattson) P.; m. Richard Gehman, Dec. 19, 1953 (div. Aug. 1958); children: Martha and Abbie (twins); m. Peter L. Zimroth, Jan. 2, 1983; 1 child, Abraham. BA in Polit. Sci., Conn. Coll. Women, 1949; student, Boston U. Law Sch., 1949-50; DFA (hon.), Conn. Coll., 2005. Stage appearances include Happy Hunting, 1957, Whoop Up, 1958, Beg, Borrow or Steal, 1960, Threepenny Opera, 1960, Mrs. Dally Has a Lover, 1962, Ready When You Are C.B, 1964, Malcolm, 1965, Seven Descents of Myrtle, 1968, And Miss Reardon Drinks a Little, 1971, Mert and Phil, 1974, The Norman Conquests, 1975-76, Ladies of the Alamo, 1977, Miss Margarida's Way, 1977-78, The Pirates of Penzance, 1981, The Shadow Box, 1994; adapted, dir., performer Orgasmo Adulto Escapes from the Zoo, 1983, The Unguided Missile, Baba Goya, 1989, Shimada, 1992, Grace & Glorie, 1996, The Last of the Thorntons, 2000-01, Morning's At Seven, 2002, The Bay at Nice, 2004, Harold & Maude, 2005, Sister Mozart, 2005; film appearances include Bonnie and Clyde, 1966 (Acad. award), Rachel, Rachel, 1967, I Never Sang for My Father, 1969, Dick Tracy, 1990, Boys On The Side, 1995, Looking for Richard, 1996, That Darn Cat, 1997; TV appearances include Roseanne, 1990—, NBC Today, 1951-56; artistic dir. NY Shakespeare Festival Players, 1986, Actors' Studio, 1997-2003; dir. (Broadway play) Salome, the Reading, 2003. Recipient Theatre World award, 1962-63, Obie award, 1964, Motion Picture Acad. Arts and Scis. award, 1967, Medal of Honor, Conn. Coll., 1969; named to Theatre Hall of Fame, 2004. Home: 924 West End Ave Apt T5 New York NY 10025-3543 *It's in attempting all, that one succeeds.*

**PARSONS, GARY M.,** broadcast executive; m. Kathy. B in Engring.. Clemson U.; MBA, U. So. Carolina, 1978. With Bellsouth; prin. Telecom USA, 1984—90; with MCI Comm. Corp., 1990—96, CEO, MCImetro Inc., exec. v.p. telecommunications; joined Motient Corp., 1996, CEO, pres.,

chmn., 1998—2002; chmn., CEO Am. Mobile Satellite Ventures LP; CEO XM Satellite Radio, chmn., 1997—. Bd. dirs. Sorrento Networks Corp. Office: XM Satellite Radio 1500 Eckington Pl NE Washington DC 20002 Office Phone: 202-380-4000. Office Fax: 202-380-4500.*

**PARSONS, IRENE ADELAIDE,** management consultant; b. North Wilkesboro, N.C. d. Everett T. and Martha (Minton) P. BS in Bus. Edn. and Adminstrn., U. N.C., 1941, LLD (hon.), 1967; MS in Pub. Adminstrn. George Washington U., 1965. Tchr. Roanoke Rapids (N.C.) High Sch., 1941-42; rep. U.S. Civil Svc. Commn., 1942-43; with VA, 1946-74, asst. adminstr. vets. affairs, dir. personnel, dir. equal employment opportunity, 1965-74; mgmt. cons., 1974—. Exec. com. Pres.'s Study Group Careers for Women. Served to lt. USCGR, 1943-46. Recipient Fed. Woman's Outstanding Achievement award, 1966, Silver Helmet award Amvets, 1971, Career Svc. award Nat. Civil Svc. League, 1972, Disting. Alumni Achievement award George Washington U., 1973; named to Brevard Coll. Hall of Fame, 1984 Mem. Assn. Fed. Woman's Award Recipients (chmn. 1972-76) Address: PO Box 2046 North Wilkesboro NC 28659-2046

**PARSONS, JEFFREY ROBINSON,** anthropologist, educator; b. Washington, Oct. 9, 1939; s. Merton Stanley and Elisabeth (Oldenburg) P.; m. Mary Thomson Hrones, Apr. 27, 1968; 1 child, Apphia Hrones. BS, Pa. State U., 1961; PhD, U. Mich., 1966. Asst. prof. anthropology U. Mich., Ann Arbor, 1966-71, assoc. prof., 1971-76, prof., 1976—2006, dir. mus. anthropology, 1983-86, emeritus prof. 2006 . Vis. prof. Universidad Nacional Autonoma de Mexico, 1987; vis. prof. Universidad Buenos Aires, 1994, Univ. Nac de Catamarca, Argentina, 1996, Univ. Nac de Tucuman, Argentina, 1996, Univ. Mayor de San Andres, Bolivia, 1996. Author: Prehistoric Settlement Patterns in the Texcoco Region, Mexico, 1971; (with William T. Sanders and Robert Santley) The Basin of Mexico: The Cultural Ecology of a Civilization, 1979; (with E. Brumfiel) Prehispanic Settlement Patterns in the Southern Valley of Mexico, 1982; (with M. Parsons) Chinampa Agriculture and Aztec Urbanization in the Valley of Mexico, 1985; (with Mary H. Parsons) Maguey Utilization in Highland Central Mexico, 1990; The Production and Consumption of Salt During Postclassic Times in the Valley of Mexico, 1994; (with E. Brumfiel and M. Hodge) The Developmental Implications of Earlier Dates for Early Aztec in the Basin of Mexico, 1996; (with C. Hastings and R. Matos) Rebuilding the State in Highland Peru, 1997; A Regional Perspective on Inca Impact in the Sierra Central, Peru, 1998; (with C. Hastings and R. Matos) Prehispanic Settlement Patterns in the Upper Mantaro-Tarma Drainage, Peru, 2000; The Last Saltmakers of Nexquipayac, Mexico, 2001, The Last Pescadores of Chimalhuacan, Mexico, 2006; (with Luis Morett) Recursos aquaticos en la subsistancia Azteca, 2004, The Last Pescadores of Chimalhuacan, Mxico, 2006. Rsch. grantee NSF, 1967, 70, 72-73, 75-76, 81, Nat. Geog. Soc., 1984, 86, 88, 2003. Mem. Am. Anthrop. Assn. (Alfred V. Kidder award 1998), Soc. Am. Archaeology, AAAS, Inst. Andean Rsch., Inst. Andean Studies, Sociedad Mexicana de Antropologia, Sociedad Argentina de Antropologia. Office: Museum of Anthropology U Mich Ann Arbor MI 48109 Business E-Mail: jpar@umich.edu.

**PARSONS, JOHN THOREN,** manufacturing executive; b. Detroit, Oct. 11, 1913; s. Carl Berger and Edith Charlotte (Thorén) Parson; m. Elizabeth Mae Shaw, Apr. 20, 1940; children: Carl A, John T. II, Robert S., Grant W., David C., Meredith W. Student, Wayne U., 1934; D of Engring. (hon.), U. Mich., 1988; LLD (hon.), Lake Superior State U., 1997. With Parsons Corp., Detroit & Traverse City, Mich., 1928-68, owner Traverse City, Mich., 1954-68, pres., 1956-68, Parsons Co., France, 1959-68; pres., owner The John T. Parsons Corp., Traverse City, Mich., 1968—. Invited lectr., Japan, Germany, Brazil. Recipient Nat. Medal of Tech., U.S. Dept. Commerce, 1985, Jules Marie Jacquard award, AIM Tech., 1968, Disting. Service award, Nat. Tooling and Machining Assn., Citation Soc. Am. Value Engrs., inductee Inventors Hall of Fame, 1993. Fellow: Soc. Mfg. Engrs. (charter, internat. dir. 1992—93, citation 1975); mem.: Detroit Athletic Club. Democrat. Lutheran. Achievements include invention of products and mfg. processes. Avocations: music, reading. Home: 6936 Mission Rdg Traverse City MI 49686-6125

**PARSONS, LEONARD JON,** marketing educator, consultant; b. Pitts., Sept. 1, 1942; s. Leonard J. and Marion Jane (Williams) P.; m. Julia Grieve, Jan. 23, 1965; children: Lorelei, Leonard Jon Jr. BSChemE, MIT, 1964; MS in Indsl. Adminstrn., Purdue U., 1965, PhD in Indsl. Adminstrn., 1968. Asst. prof. Ind. U., Bloomington, 1968-70; assoc. prof. Claremont (Calif.) Grad. Sch., 1970-77; prof. marketing Ga. Inst. Tech., 1977—. Vis. scholar MIT, Cambridge, fall 1973; Fulbright-Hays sr. scholar Cath. U. Leuven, Belgium, spring 1977; vis. prof. INSEAD, France, fall 1984, Norwegian Sch. Mktg., Oslo, fall 1989, UCLA, spring 1990, Advt. Edn. Found., Anheuser Busch, St. Louis, summer 1993, CREER/FUCAM, Belgium, Fall 1995; mem. rsch. and test devel. com. Grad. Mgmt. Admissions Coun., 1988-90. Author: Using Microcomputers in Marketing, 1986; co-author: Marketing Management, 7th edit., 2000, Market Response Models, 2d edit., 2001, others; edtl. bd. Jour. Mktg. Rsch., 1970-80, 83-85, Jour. Bus. Rsch., 1973-79, Jour. Mktg., 1978-80; assoc. editor: Decision Scis., 1976-79; mktg. dept. editor: Mgmt. Sci., 1980-82; contbr. numerous chpts. to books, articles to profl. jours. Recipient first prize rsch. design contest Am. Mktg. Assn., 1971-72. Mem. Am. Mktg. Assn. (mem. adv. bd. mktg. rsch. spl. interest group 1998), Am. Statis. Assn. (chmn. stats. in mktg. sect. 1995), European Mktg. Acad. (mem. exec. com. 1981-84), Theta Delta Chi, Beta Gamma Sigma, Phi Kappa Phi. Office: Ga Inst Tech Coll Mgmt Atlanta GA 30308-0520 Office Phone: 404-894-4381. E-mail: len.parsons@mgt.gatech.edu.

**PARSONS, MARCIA PHILLIPS,** judge; Bankruptcy judge U.S. Bankruptcy Ct. (Tenn. ea. dist.), 6th circuit, Greeneville, 1993—. Office: US Courthouse Ste 321 220 W Depot St Greeneville TN 37743

**PARSONS, MICHAEL J.,** health facility administrator; BS in Acctg., U. New Orleans; MBA, Pepperdine U. Former sr. v.p., divisional CFO, v.p. fin. Nat. Med. Enterprises (now Tenet); former CFO Ctrl. Group, Columbia/HCA; former COO/CFO Pacific Group; exec. v.p., COO Triad Hosps., Inc., Plano, Tex. Mem.: Fedn. Am. Hosps. (bd. govs.). Office: Triad Hosps 5800 Tennyson Pky Plano TX 75024

**PARSONS, RICHARD DEAN,** communications executive; b. NYC, Apr. 4, 1948; s. Lorenzo Locklair and Isabelle (Judd) Parsons; m. Laura Ann Bush, Aug. 30, 1968; children: Gregory, Leslie, Rebecca. Student, U. Hawaii, 1968; JD, U. Ala. Law Sch., 1971; LLD (hon.), Adelphi U., 1990, Medgar Evers Coll., NYC, 1991; LHD (hon.), U. Hawaii, 2003. Bar: NY 1972. Asst. counsel to gov. State of NY, Albany, 1971-73, 1st asst. counsel to gov., 1973-74; dep. counsel to v.p. Office of V.P., Washington, 1975; gen. counsel, assoc. dir. domestic coun. White House, Washington, 1975-77; ptnr. Patterson, Belknap, Webb & Tyler, NYC, 1979—88; pres., COO Dime Savs. Bank NY, NYC, 1988-90, chmn., CEO, 1990-94; dir. Time Warner, NYC, 1991—, pres., 1995—99; co-COO AOL Time Warner, Inc., NYC, 1999—2002; CEO Time Warner Inc., NYC, 2002—, chmn., 2003—. Bd. dirs. Citigroup, Estee Lauder, Fed. Nat. Mortgage Assn., Philip Morris Co.; trustee, Rockefeller Bros. Found. Mem. Presdl. Drug Task Force; mayor-elect transition coun., head, 1993; chmn. Wildcat Svc. Orgn., NYC Econ. Devel. Corp.; bd. dir. NY Zool. Soc., Am. TV & Comm. Inc., Colonial Williamsburg Found., Com. to Encourage Corp. Philanthropy, Mus. Modern Art; trustee Howard U., Met. Mus. Art. Named one of Most Influential Black Americans, Ebony mag., 2006; recipient Disting. Alumnus award, U. Hawaii, 2003. Apollo Theatre Found. (chmn.). Office: Time Warner Inc 75 Rockefeller Plz New York NY 10019-6990*

**PARSONS, RICHARD HUGO,** lawyer; b. Okla., June 9, 1936; s. Alfred Richard and Veronica Cecilia (Hugo) Parsons; m. Catherine Ann Logan; children: Karen Ann (Parsons) Voss, Anne Logan (Parsons) Muren, Alfred Richard Parsons II. BA, Bradley U., Peoria Ill., 1958; JD, Wash. & Lee, Lexington, Va., 1961; Cert., Harvard Law Sch. Bar: Ill., DC. Asst. sec. Chgo. Title and Trust, 1961—68; pvt. practice Peoria, Ill., 1968—; fed. pub. defender Ctrl. Dist. of Ill., Peoria, 1995—. Commr./trial judge Ill. Ct. of Claims, Springfield, Ill., 1975—95; pres. Ill. Assn. of Criminal Def. Lawyers,

1994, Clarence Darrow Inn of the Am. Inns of Ct., Peoria, Ill.; chmn. ABA Criminal Justice Sect. Amicus Curiae Com., 2000—03; dir. Peoria County Bar Assn., Peoria, Ill. Author: Possible Issues for Review in Criminal Appeals, 2d edit., Warrants and Motions to Suppress: Inst. CLE Fed. Criminal Practice; editor: (newsletter) The Back Bencher. Founder, pres., grand marshall City of Peoria St. Patrick's Day Parade, Peoria, Ill., 1981; del. Dem. Nat. Conv., 1972; pres. Ancient Order of Hibernians, Peoria, Ill., 1981; precinct committeeman Dem. Precinct Committeeman, Peoria, Ill.; lector Sacred Heart Ch., Peoria. Mem.: Ill. Assn. Criminal Def. Lawyers (pres. 1994—95, Lawyer of the Yr. 2000), Nat. Assn. Criminal Def. Lawyers (life), KC (3d degree knight), Union League Club Chgo., Mt. Hawley Country Club, Sigma Phi Epsilon. Democrat. Avocations: tennis, golf, literature, crossword puzzles. Office: Federal Public Defender 401 Main Street - Suite 1500 Peoria IL 61602 E-mail: richard_parsons@fd.org.

**PARSONS, TOM,** geophysicist, researcher; b. Newport Beach, Calif., Nov. 2, 1962; s. Edward and Betty Parsons; m. Korina De Bruyne, Aug. 3, 1985; children: Sophie, Willem. BS in Applied Geophysics, UCLA, 1987; PhD, Stanford U., Calif., 1988—92. Fellow NRC, Menlo Park, Calif., 1992—94; rsch. geophysicist U.S. Geol. Survey, Menlo Park, 1994—. Contbr. more than 50 articles to profl. jours. and pubs. Fellow, NRC, 1992. Fellow: Geol. Soc. Am.; mem.: AAAS, Tsunami Soc., Seismol. Soc. Am., Am. Geophys. Union. Achievements include research in earthquake and volcano interactions; quantitative models of Earth deformation; Earth structure from seismic tomography. Office: US Geological Survey MS-999 345 Middlefield Rd Menlo Park CA 94025 Office Phone: 650-329-5074.

**PARSONS, VINSON ADAIR,** retired computer company executive; b. Frankfort, Ky., Oct. 22, 1932; s. Richard Adair and Nina (Mefford) P.; m. Elizabeth Ann Peltier, June 2, 1956. AS, Mitchell Coll., 1959; BS, U. Conn., 1960; Advanced Mgmt. Program cert., Harvard U., 1985. Auditor, Price Waterhouse & Co. (C.P.A.s), Hartford, Conn., 1960-65; controller Pervel Industries Inc., Plainfield, Conn., 1965-70; v.p., controller Akzo Am. Inc., Asheville, NC, 1970-71, 73-83, v.p., chief fin. officer, 1983-86, System Software Assocs. Inc., Chgo., 1986-89, also bd. dirs.; ret., 1990. Bd. dirs. Am. Tape Co., BRIntec Co., Control Tech. Corp. Elected commr. Town of Weaverville Bd. Commrs., 1994-2000. With USN, 1953-57. Mem. Am. Mgmt. Assn., Fin. Execs. Inst., Inst. Mgmt. Accts. (pres. local chpt. 1969-70) Clubs: Asheville Country; University (N.Y.C.); Reems Creek Golf. Home and Office: 15 Preston Ct Weaverville NC 28787-8907

**PARSONS, WILLIAM JONATHAN,** cardiologist; b. Apr. 3, 1955; married; 3 children. BA, Dartmouth Coll., 1977, MD, 1980. Diplomate Am. Bd. Internal Medicine, Am. Bd. Cardiovascular Diseases, Am. Bd. Nuclear Cardiology, Nat. Bd. Echocardiography. Resident in internal medicine Strong Meml. Hosp. U. Rochester (N.Y.), 1983-85; cardiology fellow Duke U. Med. Ctr., Durham, 1985-88, asst. prof., 1988-91; asst. prof. medicine Southwestern Med. Ctr. U. Tex., Dallas, 1991-93; attending cardiologist Baylor U. Med. Ctr., Dallas, 1993—2001, Rex Hosp., Raleigh, NC, 2001—. Contbr. articles to profl. jours. Gen. med. officer USPHS-IHS, 1981-83. Fellow Am. Coll. Physicians, Am. Coll. Cardiology, Am. Soc. Echocardiography. Office: Carolina Cardiology Cons 3324 Six Forks Rd Raleigh NC 27609 Office Phone: 919-781-7772. Personal E-mail: wjpdnp@aol.com.

**PARSONT, MINA RAINÈS-LAMBÉ,** retired literature educator; b. Paris, Apr. 11, 1935; came to U.S., Jan. 1950; d. Léon and Anna (Lentzner) Rainès-Lambé; m. Michael Allen Parsont, July 4, 1959; children: Marc Sheldon, Todd Jamie. AA, Sacramento City Coll., 1954; BA with honors, U. Calif., Berkeley, 1956; postgrad., La Sorbonne, Paris, 1958; MAT in French, Colo. State U., 1966; postgrad., U. Md., 1975. Cert. secondary tchr., Md., Calif. Tchr. Spanish Sacramento Sr. High Sch., 1956-57; asst. English Ecole de Jeunes Filles, Suresnes, France, 1958; tchr. French Beverly Hills (Calif.) Elem. Sch., 1962-63; teaching asst., instr. Colo. State U., 1963-66; tchr. French, Spanish Montgomery County (Md.) Pub. Schs., 1971-95; ret., 1995. Tchr. adult edn., Albany, Calif. and L.A., 1960-61, Montgomery County, 1972—; tutor French, 1955—. French Govt. scholar, 1987—; recipient Thanks to Tchrs. award Sta. WJLA-TV, Washington, 1991; named Chevalier, Ordre des Palmes Académiques, 1997. Mem. Am. Assn. French tchrs., Md. Fgn. Lang. Assn. (past bd. dirs.), Greater Washington Assn. Fgn. Lang. Tchrs. (Disting. Fgn. Lang. Educator award 1989), Na'amat Achievements include Co-developer Let's Talk Cards for fgn. lang. students. Avocations: travel, reading, theater, singing. Personal E-mail: minarmikep@aol.com.

**PART, HOWARD MITCHELL,** dean; b. NYC, Apr. 26, 1949; m. Kristine Kunesh-Part. BS, Ohio U.; MD, Ohio State U., 1982. Cert. Am. Bd. Internal Medicine. Intern Ohio State U. Hospitals, Columbus, 1982—83, resident in internal medicine, 1983—85; voluntary faculty mem. Wright State U. Sch. Medicine, Dayton, Ohio, 1986—88, mem. faculty, 1988—, chief of gen. medicine consult svc., dir. internal medicine residency program Dayton VA Med. Ctr., assoc. dean faculty and clin. affairs, 1995—98, acting dean, 1998—99, dean, 1999—. Recipient Dean's Award for Excellence in Med. Edn., Wright State U. Sch. Medicine, 1992, Disting. Teaching award, 1996, Master Teacher of Medicine award, Am. Coll. of Physicians, 2000. Fellow: Am. Coll. Physicians (Gov.'s Award - Ohio Chpt.); mem.: Am. Bd. of Internal Medicine. Office: 115 Med Scis Bldg Wright State U 3640 Colonel Glenn Hwy Dayton OH 45435-0001 Office Phone: 937-775-3010. Office Fax: 937-775-2211.

**PARTAIN, CLARENCE LEON,** radiologist, nuclear medicine physician, educator, health facility administrator; b. Memphis, July 12, 1940; s. Archie Leon and Vergie (Young) P.; m. Judith Stafford, Jan., 1964; children: David Blane, Teri Ellyn, Amy Leigh. BSNE, U. Tenn., 1963; MSNE, Purdue U., 1965, PhD in Nuc. Engring., 1967; MD, Washington U., St. Louis, 1975. Diplomate Am. Bd. Nuc. Medicine, Am. Bd. Radiology; registered profl. engr., Mo. Asst. prof. nuc. engring. U. Mo.-Columbia, 1968-71, assoc. prof., 1971-75; resident NC Meml. Hosp., Chapel Hill, 1975-79; assoc. prof. radiology U. NC-Chapel Hill, 1978-79; assoc. prof. Vanderbilt U., Nashville, 1980-85, prof. radiology and biomed. engring., 1985—, vice chmn. radiology 1989-92, dir. nuc. medicine, 1981-85, dir. magnetic resonance imaging, 1983-92, chmn. radiology, radiologist in chief, 1992-2000, dir. Ctr. for Imaging Rsch., 2000—; cons. NIH, Bethesda, Md., 1980—; Carol D. and Henry P. Pendegrass prof. radiology and radiol. scis. Vanderbilt U., 1997—. Author: Nuclear Magnetic Resonance (NMR) Imaging, 1983, NMR Imaging: Clinical Utility and Correlation, 1984, Thyroid and Parathyroid Imaging, 1986, Magnetic Resonance Imaging, 2d edit., 1988, Correlative Image: Nuclear Medicine, Magnetic Resonance, Computer Tomography, Ultrasound, 1988; editl. bd. Acad. Radiology, Magnetic Resonance Imaging, Jour. Magnetic Resonance Imaging, Jour. Nuclear Medicine; editor-in-chief Jour. of Magnetic Resonance Imaging. Scientific adv. coun. Whitaker Found. AEC Spl. fellow, 1964-66; grantee Nat. Inst. Neurosci., Communicative Diseases and Stroke, 1977-78 Fellow Am. Coll. Nuc. Physicians, Am. Coll. Radiology, Soc. Magnetic Resonance Imaging (bd. dirs.), Internat. Soc. of Magnetic Resonance in Medicine, Accreditation Coun. for Grad. Med. Edn.; Residency Rev. Com. Nuc. Medicine; mem. AMA, IEEE, Radiol. Soc. N.Am. (chair rsch. devel. com., trustees, R&E Found.), Assn. Univ. Radiologists (exec. com.), Radiology Rsch. Alliance (pres.), Soc. Nuc. Medicine (trustee, Benedict Casson lectr. 1981), Am. Roentgen Ray Soc. (exec. coun.), Soc. Magnetic Resonance in Medicine (trustee), Internat. Soc. Magnetic Resonance in Medicine (governance coun., bd. dirs.), Soc. Chmn. Acad. Radiology Depts. (bd. dirs.), Am. Bd. Radiology (examiner in nuc. medicine, Disting. Svc. award), Sigma Phi Epsilon. Baptist. Home: 5485 Pinewood Rd Franklin TN 37064-9235 Office: Vanderbilt U Med Ctr Dept Radiology RM RR-1223 MCN Nashville TN 37232-0001

**PARTAN, DANIEL GORDON,** retired lawyer; b. Gardner, Mass., Aug. 2, 1933; s. Toivo Antero and Lempi Sivia (Adamson) P.; m. Doris Liepmann, June 8, 1957; children: Andrew Stewart, Matthew Alexander, Sarah Ruth, Iliana Marai, Juan Carlos. AB, Cornell U., 1955; LLB, Harvard U., 1958, LLM, 1961. Bar: Mass. 1959. Rsch. assoc. Harvard Law Sch., 1961, Rule of Law Ctr., Duke U. Law Sch., 1962-65; assoc. prof. U. N.D., 1964-65; assoc.

prof. law Boston U., 1965-68, prof., 1968—, prof. London Inst., 2003—. NAFTA dispute settlement roster and binat. dispute panel U.S.-Can. Free Trade Agreement; dispute settlement panel roster World Trade Orgn.; sr. specialist roster U.S. Fulbright Commn.; cons. Dept. State, UN Devel. Program, Am. Acad. Arts and Sci.; pres., chmn. Bd. dirs. UN Assn. Greater Boston, 1969-71, 76-77; chmn. Brookline Selectmen's Com. on Harvard Energy Plant, 1976—; vis. scholar Harvard Law Sch., 1977-78; vis. fellow Cambridge (Eng.) U., 1972; vis. prof. Peking U., Beijing, 2000, 05; Fulbright prof. Tsinghua U. Law Sch., Beijing, 2003; vis. prof. Xiamen U., China, 2006. Author: Population in the United Nations System, 1973, Documentary Study of the Politicization of UNESCO, 2 vols., 1975, The International Law Process, 1992, Documents Supplement to the International Law Process, 1999; co-author: Legal Problems of International Administration, 1968, The United States and the International Labor Organization, 1980; co-editor: Corporate Disclosure of Environmental Risks: U.S. and European Law, 1990; contbr. chpts. to books, articles to profl. jours. Mem. ABA (amicus brief com. sect. internat. law and practice), Bretton Woods Com., Commn. to Study the Orgn. Peace, Am. Law Inst., Acad. Coun. UN System, Am. Soc. Internat. Law, Internat. Law Assn., European Communities Studies Assn., UN Assn. Coalition for a Strong UN, Trade Law Consultative Group, Boston Area Tchrs. Internat. Law (convenor). Office: 765 Commonwealth Ave Boston MA 02215-1401 Business E-mail: partan@bu.edu.

**PARTANEN, CARL RICHARD,** biology professor; b. Portland, Oreg., Nov. 23, 1921; s. Emil and Ellen (Engstrom) P.; m. Jane Nelson, June 24, 1961; children: Karen, Kirsten, Richard (dec.). Student, Multnomah Jr. Coll. 1946-48; BA, Lewis and Clark Coll., 1950; MA, Harvard, 1951, PhD, 1954. Am. Cancer Soc. postdoctoral research fellow Columbia, 1954-55, Harvard, 1955-57; research assoc. Childrens Cancer Research Found., Boston, 1957-61; asso. prof. biology U. Pitts., 1961-64, prof. biology, 1964-86, chmn. biology, 1964-70, prof. emeritus, 1987—; Research fellow U. Edinburgh, Scotland, 1971-72, U. Nottingham, Eng., 1978-79. Contbr. articles to profl. jours. Served with AUS, 1942-45, ETO. Recipient Distinguished Achievement award Lewis and Clark Coll., 1968 Mem. AAAS, Bot. Soc. Am., Soc. for Devel. Biology, Soc. for In Vitro Biology. Home: 1112 Farragut St Pittsburgh PA 15206-1746 Office: U Pitts Dept Biol Scis Pittsburgh PA 15260 Business E-Mail: cpartanen@comcast.net.

**PARTEN, PRISCILLA M.,** medical and psychiatric social worker, educator; b. Lowell, Mass., Dec. 7, 1944; d. Ralph Bailey and Margaret Lillian (McDonagh) Newton; m. Samuel L. Parten, June 27, 1965; children: Delora Parten Power, Edward Bailey, Ethan Rogers. BA, Northeastern U., 1968; MSW, Adelphi U., Burlington, Vt., 1987. Lic. ind. clin. social worker, Mass., NH, LCSW, Maine; bd. cert. diplomate NASW. Family support coord. Easter Seal Early Intervention, Derry, NH, 1988-91; med. and psychiat. social worker Salem (NH) Vis. Nurses, 1992-96; home sch. coord. Timberlane Regional Sch. Dist., Plaistow, NH, 1992—; dir. Priscilla M. Parten, MSW, ACSW, BCD, Londonderry, NH, 1992—. Spkr., author, presenter in field, interviewed on Nat. Pub. TV. Bd. dirs. Norwich U. Parents' Assn., 1st v.p., 1999—2001. Recipient commendation Pres.'s Com. on Mental Retardation, 1968. Mem. NASW, Nutfield Exch. Club (bd. dirs. 1994-96). Democrat. Congregationalist. Avocations: skiing, photography, crocheting, gardening, snorkeling. Office: 50 Nashua Rd Ste 214 Londonderry NH 03053-3444 E-mail: senatchie@hotmail.com.

**PARTENHEIMER, ROBERT CHAPIN,** emergency physician; b. Springfield, Mass., Feb. 12, 1923; s. Joseph Everad and Leila Ursula (Parker) P.; m. Marion Claire Hill, June 23, 1949 (div. Feb. 1971); children: Barbara Haislip, Robert Hill, Richard Chapin; m. Carol Griffiths, Jan. 1991. BA, Amherst Coll., 1945; MD, Cornell U., 1947. Rotating intern Orange (N.J.) Meml. Hosp., 1947-48; intern in medicine U. Hosp., N.Y.C., 1948-49; resident in internal medicine USPHS, Boston, 1950-52; pvt. practice Summit, NJ, 1954-71; emergency physician Raritan Bay Med. Ctr., Perth Amboy, NJ, 1971-77, 84-90, St. Cloud (Fla.) Hosp., 1997-99, Columbia HCA Rauterson Hosp., Okeechobee, Fla., 1992-96. Lt. comdr. USPHS, 1949-54. Em. N.J. Med. Soc., Union County Med. Soc. Methodist. Avocations: golf, boating, fishing, skiing. Home: 5213 Indian Bend Ln Fort Pierce FL 34951 Office Phone: 772-475-3220. Personal E-mail: cparte5210@aol.com.

**PARTH, FRANK R.,** consulting company executive, educator; b. Eichendorf, Germany, Apr. 26, 1949; came to U.S., 1952. s. Frank and Erna (Framelsberger) P.; m. Jane Hoppe, Dec. 27, 1974 (div. Jan. 1985); children: Katherine, Frank. BS in Physics, Creighton U., 1972; MS in Physics, U. Wyo., 1978; MS in Sys. Mgmt., U. So. Calif., L.A., 1986; MBA, Peter Drucker Inst., 2000. Design engr. Tex. Instruments, Dallas, 1978-81; asst. tech. dir. Martin-Marietta Space Sys., Long Beach, Calif., 1981-92; pres. InterVolve Mgmt. Sys., Mission Viejo, Calif., 1993-95; dir. sys. engring. Experian, Orange, Calif., 1995-97; mgr. Deloitte & Touche, Santa Ana, Calif., 1997-98; practice mgr. Keane, Inc., Long Beach, 1998-99; v.p. devel. Overstock Market (e-commerce), 2000—01; pres. Project Auditors, LLC, 2001—. Faculty U. So. Calif. Inst. Safety and Sys. Mgmt., L.A., 1993-97, U. Calif. Irvine, 1996—, Claremont Grad. U., 2000—; spkr. in field. Author, contbr. articles to profl. jours. Bd. dirs. Orange County (Calif.) Search and Rescue, 1989-2002, OC Project Mgmt. Inst., 1996-2004 v.p. membership 2003, v.p. profl. devel., 2004; constitutional rev. officer Mensa, 1993—. Mem. Internat. Coun. Sys. Engring., Mensa Internat. (pres. Orange County chpt. 1993, constn. rev. officer, 1993—), Project Mgmt. Inst. (Spkr.'s award 1998). Avocations: sailing, skiing, wine. Home: 21901 Palanca Mission Viejo CA 92692-1012 Office: PO Box 80688 Rancho Santa Margarita CA 92688-0688 Office Phone: 800-545-1340. Business E-Mail: Fparth@projectauditors.com.

**PARTHASARATHY, VINOD,** manufacturing engineer, consultant; b. Bombay, Aug. 17, 1979; arrived in U.S., 2001; s. Gopalan and Vasantha Parthasarathy. B in Engring. (hon.), U. E. London, 2000; MBA, Harvard U., 2005. Project engr. Ford Motor Co., London, 1999, Dormer Tools, Sheffield, England, 1999—2001; product engr. Freudenberg-Nok, Laconia, NH, 2001—04, sys. mgr., 2005—. Mng. ptnr. Digitized Artisan, Perth, Australia, 2005—. Contbr. articles to profl. jours. Vol. Red Cross, London, 1997—2000, Rep. Party, Concord, 2004—. Recipient Six Sigma Black Belt award, Freudenberg-Nok, 2005. Mem.: IEEE (chartered). Republican. Hinduism. Achievements include patents for drill detection transducer. Avocations: skydiving, writing, travel, surfing. Home: 68 Blueberry Ln Apt 18 Laconia NH 03246 Office: Freudenberg-Nok 51 Growtth Rd Laconia NH 03246 Office Phone: 603-527-6431. E-mail: iamvinny@hotmail.com.

**PARTHEMORE, JACQUELINE GAIL,** internist, educator, hospital administrator; b. Harrisburg, Pa., Dec. 21, 1940; d. Philip Mark and Emily (Buvit) Parthemore; m. Alan Morton Blank, Jan. 7, 1967; children: Stephen Eliot, Laura Elise. BA, Wellesley Coll., 1962; MD, Cornell U., 1966. Diplomate Am. Bd. Internal Medicine. Resident in internal medicine N.Y. Hosp./Cornell U., 1966-69; fellow in endocrinology Scripps Clinic and Rsch. Found., La Jolla, Calif., 1969-72; rsch. ednl. assoc. VA Hosp., San Diego, 1974-78; staff physician VA San Diego Health Care Sys., 1978-79, asst. chief, med. svc., 1979-83, acting chief, med. svc., 1980-81, chief of staff, 1984—; asst. prof. medicine U. Calif. Sch. Medicine, San Diego, 1974-80, assoc. prof. medicine, 1980-85, prof. medicine, assoc. dean, 1985—. Mem. nat. rsch. resources coun. NIH, Bethesda, Md., 1990—94. Contbr. chapters to books, articles to profl. jours. Mem. adv. bd. San Diego Opera, 1993—2006; mem. Roundtable and Channel 10 Focus Group, San Diego Millennium Project, 1999; v.p. bd. dirs. San Diego stri. Med. Rsch. Found., 1989—. Recipient Bullock's 1st Annual Portfolio award, 1985, Caring for San Diego Pres.'s Coun. Woman of Yr. award, 1985, YWCA Tribute to Women in Industry award, 1987, San Diego Women Who Mean Bus. award, 1999, Excellence in Leadership award Am. Hosp. Assn., 2002, Local Legend award AMWA/Nat. Libr. Medicine, 2005. Fellow ACP (v.p. gov. 2005-, mem. edn. com. 2006-); Am. Assn. Clin. Endocrinologists; mem. Endocrine Soc., Nat. Assn. VA Chiefs Staff/Physician Execs. (pres. 1989-91), Assn. Am. Med. Colls. (chief med. officer steering group 2006-), Wellesley Coll. Alumnae Assn. (1st v.p. 1992-95), San Diego Wellesley Club (pres. 1997-99), San Diego Herb Soc. (co-pres. 2003-04).

Avocations: gardening, reading, sailing, cooking, travel. Office: VA San Diego Healthcare Sys 3350 La Jolla Village Dr San Diego CA 92161-0002 Office Phone: 858-552-7419. Business E-Mail: jparthemore@ucsd.edu.

**PARTIDA, GILBERT A.,** lawyer; b. Nogales, Ariz., July 27, 1962; s. Enrique Gilberto and Mary Lou (Flores) P.; m. Soncee Ray Brown, July 30, 1992. BA with distinction, U. Ariz., 1984; JD cum laude, Pepperdine U., 1987; LLD (hon.), Calif. Western Sch Law, San Diego, 1993. V.p., bd. mem. Partida Brokerage, Inc., Nogales, 1983-91; law clk. Office of Ariz. Atty. Gen., Tucson, 1985; assoc. Gray, Cary, Ames & Frye, San Diego, 1986-89, sr. assoc., 1990-92, chmn. Mex. Practice Group, 1992; pres. Greater San Diego C. of C., 1993-98; pres., CEO Price Smart, San Diego, 1998—. Corp. counsel San Diego Incubator Corp., 1990—. Contbr. articles to profl. jours. Mem. United Way Latino Future Scan Com., 1990; mentor Puente, 1991; leadership tng. mentor Chicano Fedn., 1992; dinner com. Young at Art, 1991; mem. Children's Initiative, 1993, Superbowl Task Force, 1993, San Diego Dialogue, 1993; hon. mem. Sister City, 1993, LEAD, 1993; hon. chair Easter Seals Telethon, 1994; vice chmn. Border Trade Alliance, 1989-91; mem. nat. gala com. HDI Ednl. Svcs., 1990; Calif. state del. U.S.-Mexico Border Govs.' Conf., 1990, 92; exec. com. San Diego Conv. and Visitors Bur. Mem. San Diego County Hispanic C. of C. (chmn. 1991, pres. 1990-91, v.p. 1989-90, internat. com. chair 1989-90, sec. 1989, founding bd. mem. 1989), Consejo Nacional de Maquiladoras, Calif. Hispanic C. of C. (state conv. joint venture com. 1991, spl. projects chair 1991), San Diego/Tijuana Sister Cities Soc. (adv. coun. 1993—), San Diego County Bar Assn. (U.S./Mexico liaison com.), ABA (U.S./Mexico bar liaison com.), Hispanic Alliance for Free Trade, Rotary Club San Diego. Avocations: tennis, running, creative writing.

**PARTIE, DAVID JOHN,** language educator; b. Detroit, Mich., Apr. 14, 1944; s. William Richey and Arlene Esther Partie; m. Janice Sue Stanage, June 14, 1975; 1 child, Elizabeth Catherine. BA, U. of Redlands, 1966; postgrad., U. Heidelberg, Germany, 1967—68; MA, UCLA, 1971; MDiv, Talbot Theol. Sem., 1978; MA, U. of So. Calif., 1982, PhD, 1988. C.C. Instr. Credential in German Calif. Cmty. Colleges, 1974, Cert. of Completion, World Travel Counselor Tng. Program Automobile Club of So. Calif., 1981, Apollo Travel Services Tng. Cert. United Airlines, 1982, Qualification Cert. as an ESL Tchr. for Speakers of Japanese Japanese Cross Cultural Ctr./ LA, Calif., 1984, sys. direct access tng. program cert. Ea. Airlines, 88. Tchg. asst. in German UCLA, 1968—70; instr. in German, French, Spanish and English LA Bapt. Coll., Newhall, Calif., 1969—73; instr. in German Santa Monica City Coll., 1974—77; instr. in German and French Biola Coll., La Mirada, Calif., 1974—78; instr. in French and Spanish Baymonte H.S., Santa Cruz, Calif., 1978—79; tchg. asst. in freshman writing U. of So. Calif., 1979—82; tour counselor/world travel agt. Automobile Club of So. Calif., LA, 1979—82; account exec. Agnew Tech-Tran, Woodland Hills, Calif., 1982—84; instr. in ESL and German Berlitz Sch. of Langs., Pasadena, 1984—85; prof. English and modern langs. Liberty U., Lynchburg, Va., 1985—; adj. prof. English Ctrl. Va. C.C., Lynchburg, 1998—. Chmn. dept. of modern langs. Liberty U., 1985—93; mem. numerous coms. including most recently; mem., adv. bd. for the ctr. for global ministries Liberty U., 2001—, moderator of the faculty senate, 2002—03, chair, faculty senate exec. com., poetry editor Lamplight, 2003—, mem. pres.' com. on faculty devel. and welfare, 2004—, mem. grad. com. dept. English, 2004—; presenter in field. Author: The Poet's Domain; actor: (films) The Gathering, 1998; guest poet: TV series All the Arts, 1996, Joe Campbell Show, 1991; actor: (plays) U. Redlands, 1963—66, Cmty. Theater, Coll. Theater (outstanding contbn. to theater at Sweet Briar Coll., 1999, 2000), Morgan Theatre, 1967, Biola Coll., 1976, U. So. Calif., 1980, Lynchburg Fine Arts Ctr., 1990—2004, Sweet Briar Coll., 1999—2000; contbr. poems to mags. and jours. (Hon. Mention, Poet's Choice Award, vol. 13 of The Poet's Domain, 1997), acad. papers presented at numerous conf. Roving reader Lynchburg Pub. Schools, 1995—96; tchr. of creative writing Lynchburg Parks and Recreation Dept., 1995—95; forensics judge Va. Orgn. of German Students, Lynchburg, 1997—97; crisis counselor Centinella Valley Hotline, 1977—97, Suicide Prevention Ctr., L.A., 1985, Life Aid, 1988—89; mem. com. readers judging poems Maier Mus. of Art, 2005; mem. Lynchburg Rep. City Com., Lynchburg, 1988—2000; del. to state polit. conventions Rep. Party, Richmond, Va., 1988—96; legis. liaison to Va. state del. Joyce Crouch Va. Soc. for Human Life, Lynchburg, 1991—92; mem., mission selection com. Heritage Bapt. Ch., Lynchburg, 1991—98, 2002—04; student poetry contest judge Poetry Soc. of Va., Williamsburg, 1996—96. Recipient William Ward Bass award, Talbot Theol. Seminary, 1978, First Pl. In The Serious Poem Category, Lynchburg Poetry Festival, 1987, 1991, 1994, 2000, Karma Deane Ogden Prize for Poetry, Poetry Soc. of Va., 1991, Brodie Herndon Meml. Prize for Poetry, 1997, Carleton Drewry Meml. Prize for Poetry, 2000; Walter Loewy fellow for Grad. Study Abroad, U. of Heidelberg, 1967-68, Chancellor's Tchg. fellow, UCLA, 1966—70. Mem.: Poetry Soc. of Va. (assoc.; regional v.p. 2002—), Assn. for the Interdisciplinary Study of the Arts (assoc.), F. Scott Fitzgerald Soc. (assoc.), MLA (assoc.), Alpha Mu Gamma (life). Avocations: travel, athletics, church work, drama, book collecting. Office: Liberty U 1971 University Blvd Lynchburg VA 24502-2269 Office Phone: 434-582-2439. Business E-Mail: djpartie@liberty.edu.

**PARTIN, STEPHEN ANDREW,** music educator; b. Baxley, Ga., Dec. 25, 1962; s. Homer and Eddie T. Partin; 1 child, Tyler Keith. BMusEd, Valdosta State U., Ga., 1985; MMusEd, U. Nev., Las Vegas, 1995; AAS in Computer Info. Sys., South Ga. Tech. Coll., Cordele, 2004. Cert. tchr. PBT5 Ga., 1985. Self-employed profl. musician, Douglas, Ga., 1981—88; band dir. Jeff Davis County Schs., Hazlehurst, 1988—92; dir. bands Las Vegas (Nev.) Parochial Schs., 1992—95; band dir. Crisp County Schs., Cordele, Ga., 1995—. Composer and song writer. Scoutmaster Boy Scouts of Am., Cordele, Ga., 1995—2001. Recipient Eagle Scout, 1980. Mem.: Music Educators Nat. Conf., Ga. Music Educators Assn. Office: Crisp County Mid Sch 1116 East 24th Ave Cordele GA 31015 Office Phone: 229-276-3460.

**PARTLETT, DAVID F.,** dean, law educator; b. 1947; LLB, Sydney U., 1970; LLM, Mich. U., 1972, 74; SJD, U. Va., 1980. Bar: New South Wales 1971, Australian Cap. Terr. 1978. Vis. asst. prof. U. Ala., 1972-73; legis. officer Australia Atty. Gen.'s Office, 1974—75; dir, rsch. Australian Law Reform Commn., 1975—78; lectr. Australian Nat. U., 1978-80, sr. lectr., 1980-87, assoc. dean, 1982—85; vis. prof. Vanderbilt U., Nashville, 1987-88, prof. law, 1988-2000, acting dean, 1996-97; v.p., dean, prof. Sch. Law Washington & Lee U., Lexington, Va., 2000—. Sparkman Dist. vis. prof. Ala. U., 1986-87. Office: Washington & Lee U Sydney Lewis Hall Lexington VA 24450

**PARTNOY, RONALD ALLEN,** lawyer; b. Norwalk, Conn., Dec. 23, 1933; s. Maurice and Ethel Marguerite (Roselle) P.; m. Diane Catherine Keenan, Sept. 18, 1965. BA, Yale U., 1956; LL.B., Harvard U., 1961; LL.M., Boston U., 1965. Bar: Mass. 1962, Conn. 1966. Atty. Liberty Mut. Ins. Co., Boston, 1961-65; assoc. counsel Remington Arms Co., Bridgeport, Conn., 1965-70, gen. counsel, 1970-85, sec.; sr. counsel E.I. du Pont de Nemours & Co., Wilmington, Del., 1985-95. Served to capt. USNR, 1956-85. Mem.: ABA, Naval Res. Assn. (nat. exec. com. 1981—85, 1997—99, nat. v.p. 1997—99, nat. exec. com. 2001—03, nat. vp. 2001—03, 3d dist. pres.), U.S. Navy League (pres. Bridgeport coun. 1975—77, Conn. pres. 1977—80, v.p. Empire region 1980—85, nat. dir.); Am. Judicature Soc., Sporting Arms and Ammunition Mfrs. Inst. (chmn. legis. and legal affairs com. 1971—86), Assn. of Yale Alumni (del. 1997—2000), Yale Club of N.Y.C., Harvard Club of Phila., Harvard Club of Boston, Chancery Club. Home: 616 Bayard Rd Kennett Square PA 19348-2504

**PARTON, DOLLY REBECCA,** singer, composer, actress; b. Sevier County, Tenn., Jan. 19, 1946; d. Robert Lee and Avie Lee (Owens) P.; m. Carl Dean, May 30, 1966. Country music singer, rec. artist, composer, actress, radio and TV personality. Entrepreneur, owner entertainment park Dollywood, established 1985. Radio appearances include Grand Ole Opry, WSM Radio, Nashville, Cass Walker program, Knoxville; TV appearances include Porter Wagoner Show, from 1967, Cass Walker program, Bill Anderson Show, Wilburn Bros. Show, Barbara Mandrell Show; rec. artist, Mercury, Monument, RCA, CBS record cos.; albums include Here You Come Again (Grammy award 1978), Real Love, 1985, Just the Way I Am, 1986, Portrait, 1986, Think About Love, 1986, Trio (with Emmylou Harris, Linda Ronstadt) (Grammy award 1988), 1987, Heartbreaker, Great Balls of Fire, Rainbow, 1988, White Limozeen, 1989, Home for Christmas, 1990, Eagle When She Flies, 1991, Slow Dancing with the Moon, 1993 (Grammy nomination, Best Country Vocal Collaboration for Romeo (with Tanya Tucker, Billy Ray Cyrus, Kathy Mattea, Pam Tillis, & Mary-Chapin Carpenter), (with Tammy Wynette and Loretta Lynn) Honky Tonk Angels, 1994, The Essential Dolly Parton, 1995, Just the Way I Am, 1996, Super Hits, 1996, (with others) I Will Always Love You & Other Greatest Hits, 1996, Hungry Again, 1998, Trio II, 1998, Grass is Blue, 1999 (Grammy award for best bluegrass album), Best of the Best-Porter & Doll, 1999, Halos and Horns, 2002, For God and Country, 2003, Makin' Believe, 2003; appears on song "Creepin' In" with Norah Jones, 2004; composer numerous songs including Nine to Five (Grammy award 1981, Acad. award nominee and Golden Globe award nominee 1981); Film appearances include Nine to Five, 1980, The Best Little Whorehouse in Texas, 1982, Rhinestone, 1984, Steel Magnolias, 1989, Straight Talk, 1991; (TV films) A Smoky Mountain Christmas, 1986, Wild Texas Wind, 1991, Unlikely Angel, 1996, Blue Valley Songbird, 1999; (TV series) Heavens to Betsy, 1994, Mindin My Own Business, 1996; Author: Dolly, 1994. Recipient (with Porter Wagoner) Vocal Group of Yr. award, 1968, Vocal Duo of Yr. award All Country Music Assn., 1970, 71, Nashville Metronome award, 1979, Am. Music award for best duo performance (with Kenny Rogers), 1984, Grammy awards for best female country vocalist, 1978, 81, for best country song, 1981, for best country vocal performance with group, 1987, People's Choice award, 1980, 88, Nat. Medal of Arts Nat. Endowment for the Arts, 2005, Kennedy Ctr. Honor, John F. Kennedy Center for Performing Arts, 2006; co-recipient (with Emmylou Harris and Linda Ronstadt) Acad. Country Music award for album of the yr., 1987, (with Brad Paisley) Most Inspiring Video of Yr. for When I Get Where I'm Going, CMT Awards (Country Music TV), 2006, Video of Yr. and Vocal Event of Yr., Acad. Country Music award, 2006; named Female Vocalist of Yr., 1975, 76, Country Star of Yr., Sullivan Prodns., 1977, Entertainer of Yr., Country Music Assn., 1978, Female Vocalist of Yr., Acad. Country Music, 1980; Dolly Parton Day proclaimed, Sevier County, Tenn., designated Oct. 7, 1967, Los Angeles, Sept. 20, 1979; named to Small Town of Am. Hall of Fame, 1988, East Tenn. Hall of Fame, 1988. Address: RCA 6 W 57th St New York NY 10019-3901 Office: Dollywood Co 1020 Dollywood Ln Pigeon Forge TN 37863-4101*

**PARTRIDGE, BRUCE JAMES**, lawyer, educator, writer; b. Syracuse, NY, June 4, 1926; arrived in Can., 1969; s. Bert James and Lida Marion (Rice) P.; m. Mary Janice Smith, June 13, 1948 (dec. 1986); children: Heather Leigh, Eric James, Brian Lloyd, Bonnie Joyce; m. May S. Archer, May 28, 1988; stepchildren: Sheila Archer, Laurel Archer. AB cum laude, Oberlin Coll., Ohio, 1946; LLB, Blackstone Coll., Chgo., 1950, JD, 1952; LLB, U. B.C. 1974. Bar: B.C. 1976, N.W.T. 1980. Rsch. physicist Am. Gas Assn., Cleve., 1946-48; bus. mgr. Cazenovia (N.Y.) Coll., 1948—51; bus. mgr., purchasing agt., asst. treas. Rochester Inst. Tech., NY, 1953—58; bus. administr. Baldwin-Wallace Coll., Berea, Ohio, 1951-53; v.p. bus. and mgmt. U. Del., Newark, 1958-63; v.p. adminstrn. Johns Hopkins U., Balt., 1963-69; pres. U. Victoria, B.C., Can., 1969-72; assoc. Clark, Wilson & Co., Vancouver, B.C., Can., 1975-78; successively solicitor, mng. solicitor, gen. solicitor, v.p. law and gen. counsel, sec. Cominco Ltd., Vancouver, 1978-88; exec. dir. Baker & McKenzie, Hong Kong, 1988-90; v.p. Pacific Creations, Inc., 1990-92; faculty Camosun Coll., 1992-99. Author: Management in Canada: The Competitive Challenges, 2000; co-author: College and University Business Administration, 1968; chmn. editl. com. Purchasing for Higher Education, 1962; contbr. numerous articles to profl. jours. Chmn. commn. on adminstrv. affairs Am. Coun. on Edn., Washington, 1966-69; mem. Pres.'s Com. on Employment of Handicapped, Washington, 1967-69; mem. adv. coun. Ctr. for Resource Studies, Queen's U., 1983-88; bd. dirs. L'Arche in the Americas, 1984-88; mem. adv. coun. Westwater Rsch. Ctr., U. B.C., 1982-88. Mem. Assn. Can. Gen. Counsel, Def. Rsch. Inst. (product liability com.), Am. Inst. Parliamentarians, Nat. Assn. Parliamentarians. Unitarian Universalist. Business E-Mail: brucepart@telus.net.

**PARTRIDGE, LOREN WAYNE**, art historian, educator; b. Raton, N.Mex., Apr. 11, 1936; s. Don F. and Ruth (Isaacson) P.; widowed; children: Wendy, Amy; married. BA in English Lit., Yale U., 1958; cert. in L.Am. lit., U. Buenos Aires, 1959; diploma in Russian, U.S. Army Lang. Sch., Monterey, Calif., 1961; MA in Fine Arts, Harvard U., 1965, PhD in Fine Arts, 1969. Tchg. fellow Harvard U., Cambridge, Mass., 1964-66; lectr. U. Calif., Berkeley, 1968, acting asst. prof., 1969-70, asst. prof., 1970-76, assoc. prof., 1976-80, prof., 1980—, chmn. Dept. Art History, 1978—87, 1990—93, 1999, chmn. Dept. Art Practice, 2002—03, chmn. history of art history Am. Acad. in Rome, 1985; reviewer Art Bull, 1972, 78, 80, 83, Renaissance Quar., 1984, 87, 90, 99, Design Book Rev., 1987, Master Drawings, 1987, Am. Hist. Rev., 1993, Apollo, 1996. Author: John Galen Howard and the Berkeley Campus: Beaux-Arts Architecture in the Athens of the West, 1978, Caprarola, Palazzo Farnese, 1988, (with Randolph Starn) A Renaissance Likeness: Art and Culture in Raphael's Julius II, 1980, (with Randolph Starn) Arts of Power: Three Halls of State in Italy 1300-1600, 1992, The Art of Renaissance Rome, 1400-1600, 1996, Michelangelo: The Sistine Chapel Ceiling, Rome, 1996, Michelangelo Last Judgement: A Glorious Restoration, 1997; contbr. author: Ency. of Italian Renaissance, 1981, Internat. Dictionary Art and Artists, 1990, Dictionary of Art, 1996; contbr. articles to profl. jours. With U.S. Army, 1960-63. Scholar Yale U., 1955-58, Harvard U., 1964-66; Fulbright fellow, 1958-59, 75, Am. Acad. in Rome fellow, 1966-68, Kress fellow Inst. for Advanced Studies, 1974-75, U. Calif., 1972, 77, 82, 85, 93-94, 99-2000, 2003-04, Guggenheim fellow, 1981-92; grantee Kress Found., 1968-69, 71-72, Calif. Hum. grantee, 1988-89. Office: U Calif Dept Art History 6020 416 Doe Libr Berkeley CA 94720-6020 Office Phone: 510-643-6301. Business E-Mail: lpart@berkeley.edu.

**PARTRIDGE, MARK VAN BUREN**, lawyer, educator, mediator, writer; b. Rochester, Minn., Oct. 16, 1954; s. John V.B. and Constance (Brainerd) P.; m. Mary Roberta Moffitt, Apr. 30, 1983; children: Caitlin, Lindsay, Christopher. BA, U. Nebr., 1978; JD, Harvard U., 1981. Bar: Ill. 1981, U.S. Dist. Ct. (no. dist.) Ill. 1981, U.S. Dist. Ct. (ea. dist.) Mich. 1983, U.S. Ct. Appeals (1st. cir) 2003, U.S. Ct. Appeals (4th cir.) 1986, U.S. Ct. Appeals (5th cir.), 1992, U.S. Ct. Appeals (5th cir.) 1993, U.S. Ct. Appeals (3rd cir.) 1998. Assoc. Pattishall, McAuliffe, Newbury, Hilliard & Geraldson, LLP, Chgo., 1981-88, ptnr., 1988—, exec. com., 2003—. Adj. prof. John Marshall Law Sch., Chgo., 1987—; arbitrator Cook County Mandatory Arbitration Program, 1989-2003; v.p. Harvard Legal Aid Bur., 1980-81; mediator no. dist. Ill. Voluntary Mediation Program, 1997—; panelist World Intellectual Property Orgn., Domain Name Dispute Resolution Svc., 1999—; neutral Nat. Arbitration Forum, Intellectual Property Mediation and Arbitration Panel, 2004—; mediator Internat. Trademark Assn. Panel of Neutrals, 2005—; bd. adv. N.W. Law Sch., Jour. Tech. and Intellectual Property. Author: Guilding Rights Trademarks, Copyright and the Internet, iUniverse, 2003; contbr. articles to profl. jours.; mem. editl. bd. The Trademark Reporter, 1994-97; adv. bd. IP Litigator, 1995—. Vol. Chgo. Vol. Legal Svcs., 1983—. Fellow Am. Intellectual Property Law Assn. (com. chmn. 1989-91, 96-98, bd. dirs. 1998-2001); mem. ABA (com. chmn. 1989-91, 94-99, rep. 2006—), Internat. Trademark Assn. (com. vice chmn. 1996), World Intellectual Property Orgn. (experts panel internet domain name process 1998-99), Intellectual Property Law Assn. Chgo. (com. chmn. 1993-96), Brand Names Ednl. Found. (moot ct. regional chmn. 1994-96, nat. vice-chmn. 1997-98, nat. chmn. 1998-99), Nat. Spkrs. Assn. (Ill. chpt. pres.-elect 2006), Legal Club (v.p. 1998, pres. 1999), Lawyers Club Chgo. (pres. 2000, bd. dirs. 2000-01), Execs. Club, Union League Club, Harvard Club Chgo., Bagatelle Club. Avocations: writing, music, genealogy, travel, internet. Office: Pattishall McAuliffe Newbury Hilliard & Geraldson LLP 311 S Wacker Dr Ste 5000 Chicago IL 60606-6631 Office Phone: 312-554-7922. Business E-Mail: mpartridge@pattishall.com.

**PARTRIDGE, SHARON SUE**, secondary school educator; b. Girard, Kans., Dec. 22, 1943; d. Frank Darrel and Eda Luella (Hashagen) Bever; children: Joel Matthew, Joy Elaine, Julie Ann. BS Home Econs. Edn., Pittsburg State

U., Kans., 1965. Middle sch. tchr. United Sch. Dist. 445, Coffeyville, Kans., 1965—66, substitute tchr., 1966, secondary tchr., 1987—. Tchr. coord. Head Start, Coffevillle, Kans.; edn. supr. Head Start SEK-CAP, Girard, Kans. Mem.: PEO, Kans. Assn. Tchrs. of Family and Consumer Scis. Avocations: bowling, gardening, golf, quilting. Home: 1319 W Sixth St Coffeyville KS 67337 Office: Field Kindley Meml HS 8th and Roosevelt Coffeyville KS 67337 Office Phone: 620-252-6410. E-mail: partridgecs@cvilleschools.com.

**PARTRIDGE, WILLIAM FRANKLIN, JR.**, lawyer; b. Newberry, S.C., July 16, 1945; s. William F. and Clara (Eskridge) P.; m. Ilene S. Stewart, Aug. 16, 1969; children: Allison, William F. BA in History, The Citadel, 1967; JD, U. S.C., 1970. Bar: S.C. 1970, U.S. Ct. Claims 1971, U.S. Ct. Mil. Appeals 1971, U.S. Tax Ct. 1971, U.S. Supreme Ct. 1973, U.S. Dist. Ct. S.C. 1980. Instr. internat. law Chapman Coll., 1973-74; pub. issue com. S.C. Bar, 1982-83. Lt. Col. USAFR. Mem. Newberry Bar Assn. (pres. 1982-83), Palmetto Club, County of Newberry Club, Cotillion Club, Assn. Citadel Mens Club, Masons, Phi Delta Phi. Democrat. Methodist. Home: 2029 Harrington St Newberry SC 29108-3055 Office: 1201 Boyce St Newberry SC 29108-2705 Office Phone: 803-276-5968.

**PARTRIDGE, WILLIAM J.**, military officer, government agency administrator; b. Saugerties, N.Y. Grad., U.S. Mil. Acad., 1975; MS in Space Systems Engring., Naval Postgrad. Sch. Commd. 2d lt. U.S. Army, 1975, advanced through grades to col.; comdr. 2d Bn., 2d Aviation Regiment, 2d Infantry Divsn., Republic of Korea; battery fire direction control officer, battery exec. officer 1-15th Field Artillery, Ft. Carson; flight platoon leader, ops. officer 62d Aviation Co., Germany; co. comdr., brigade exec. officer 4th Aviation Brigade, Ft. Lewis, Wash.; plans officer U.S. Space Command; brigade exec. officer 4th Aviation Brigade, 4th Infantry Divsn., Ft. Carson; dep. chief of staff for ops. Army Space Command; chief current ops. divsn. Hqrs. U.S. Space Command, Peterson AFB, Colo.; comdr. Army Space Forces U.S. Army Space and Missile Def. Command, Colorado Springs, Colo., 2000—. Decorated Army Meritorious medal with 3 oak leaf clusters, Army Commendation medal with 1 oak leaf cluster, Army Achievement medal with 1 oak leaf cluster.

**PARTRIDGE, III, W. F.**, lawyer, defender; b. Newberry, SC, Nov. 2, 1975; s. W. Frank and Ilene Stewart Partridge; m. Meredith Allen Nock, June 24, 2000; 1 child, Nancy Stewart Partridge. BSc, The Citadel, Charleston, SC, 1998; JD, Appalachian U., Grundy, Va., 2002. Bar: SC, (US Tax Ct.), (US Ct. Fed. Claims), (US Ct. Appeals (4th cir.)); pvt. pilot FAA. Jud. law clk., Greenwood, SC, 2002—03; asst. atty. gen. SC Atty. Gen.'s Office, Columbia, SC, 2003—05; ptnr. Partridge Law Firm, Newberry, SC, 2005—. Asst. pub. defender Newberry Pub. Defender Corp., SC, 2005—. Mem.: Newberry Bar Assn., US Ct. Fed. Claims Bar Assn., SC Trial Lawyers, SC Bar Assn., Assn. Citadel Men, Masons. Republican. Avocations: flying, sailing, skeet shooting. Home: 1229 Walnut St Newberry SC 29108 Office: Partridge Law Firm 1201 Boyce St PO Box 1054 Newberry SC 29108 Office Phone: 803-276-6227. Office Fax: 803-276-9994. E-mail: troup@partridgelawfirm.com.

**PARUK, JAMES DAVID**, biology professor; s. Walter Adam and Phyllis Paruk; m. Stefania Strzalkowska, Oct. 27, 1997; children: Olivia, Emily. BS in Biology, Lake Superior State U., Sault Ste. Marie, Mich., 1984; MS in Biology, Northern Ill. U., DeKalb, Ill., 1987; PhD in Biology, Idaho State U., Pocatello, 1999. Field instr. Yosemite Inst., Calif., 1988—93; instr. U. Calif. Extension, Santa Cruz, Calif., 1993—95; prof. Feather River Coll., Quincy, Calif., 1999—2004; assoc. prof. Northland Coll., Ashland, Wis., 2004—. Bd. mem. Laerwatch, Ashland, Wis., 2004—, Biodiversity Rsch. Inst., Cocham, Maine, 1999—2005. Author: Sierra Nevada Tree Identifier, 1997 (runner up Nat. Park Assn. best book award, 1978). Named Tchr. of Yr., Feather River Coll., 2001, 2003. Mem.: Nat. Assn Biology Tchrs. Avocations: tennis, bicycling, birdwatching. Office: Northland Coll 1411 Ellis Ave Ashland WI 54806 Office Phone: 715-682-1325.

**PARVEEN, SALINA**, microbiologist, educator; b. Dhaka, Bangladesh, July 2, 1962; arrived in U.S., 1993; d. Abdul Jalil and Abeda Khanam; m. Mohammad Ali, Mar. 9, 1990; children: Sakib Mohammad Adnan, Adib Mohammad Adnan. B.Sc, Dhaka U., Bangladesh, 1985, M.Sc, 1988; PhD, U.Fla., Gainesville, 1997. Vis. scientist USDA, Agrl. Rsch. Svc., Dover, Del., 2001—02; asst. prof. U. of Md. Ea. Shore, Princess Anne, Md., 2002—. Contbr. articles to profl. jours. Recipient Chancellor award, Govt. of Bangladesh, 1987, Book award, Dhaka U., Bangladesh, 1987, Outstanding New Faculty award, Sch. Agrl. and Nat. Scis., U. Md. Ea. Shore, 2004, Sch. Agrl. and Natural Scis., U. Md. Ea. Shore; grantee USDA/CSREES, 1999, 2003. Mem.: Inst. of Food Technologists, Internat. Assn. for Food Protection, Am. Soc. for Microbiology. Achievements include development of method for detecting sources of fecal pollution. Avocations: reading, waching favorite show in tv, travel. Office: Univ Maryland Ea Shore 2112 Ctr for Food Sci & Tech Princess Anne MD 21853 Office Phone: 410-651-8339. Office Fax: 410-651-8498. E-mail: sparveen@umes.edu.

**PARVIS, PETER P.**, lawyer; b. NYC, Aug. 10, 1945; BA with honors, U. Md., 1968, JD with honors, 1977. Bar: Md. 1977. Ptnr., health care, pharm. Venable LLP (formerly Venable, Baetjer and Howard), Balt. Mem. ABA, Md. State Bar Assn., Bar Assn. Balt. City, Am.Health Lawyers Assn., Order of Coif. Office: Venable LLP Ste 2100 1800 Mercantile Bank & Trust Bldg 2 Hopkins Plz Baltimore MD 21201-2982 Office Phone: 410-244-7644. Office Fax: 410-244-7742. Business E-Mail: ppparvis@venable.com.

**PARZEN, STANLEY JULIUS**, lawyer; b. N.Y.C., Feb. 6, 1952; BA, Earlham Coll., 1973; LLB cum laude, Harvard U., 1976. Bar: Ill. 1970, U.S. Dist. Ct. (no. dist.) Ill. 1970, U.S. Dist. Ct. (no. dist.) Calif. 1989, U.s. Dist. Ct. (we. dist.) Mich. 1995, U.S. Ct. Appeals (7th cir.) 1981, U.S. Ct. Appeals (8th cir.) 1983, U.S. Ct. Appeals (5th cir.) 1992, U.S. Ct. appeals (D.C. cir.) 1992, U.S. Ct. Appeals (2d cir.) 1990, U.S. Ct. Appeals (9th cir.) 1996, U.S. Ct. Appeals (6th cir.) 2003. Law clk. to judge U.S. Ct. Appeals (7th cir.), 1976-77; ptnr. Mayer, Brown Rowed Maw LLP, Chgo. Mem. Phi Beta Kappa. Office: Mayer Brown Rowe Maw LLP 71 S Wacker Dr Chicago IL 60603-4637 Office Phone: 312-701-7326. E-mail: sparzen@mayerbrownrowe.com.

**PASACHOFF, JAY MYRON**, astronomer, educator; b. NYC, July 1, 1943; s. Samuel S. and Anne (Traub) P.; m. Naomi Schwartz, Mar. 31, 1974; children: Eloise Hilary, Deborah Donna. AB, Harvard U., 1963, AM (NSF fellow), 1965, PhD (NSF fellow, N.Y. State Regents fellow for advanced grad. study), 1969. Rsch. physicist Air Force Cambridge Rsch. Labs., Bedford, Mass., 1968-69; Menzel rsch. fellow Harvard Coll. Obs., Cambridge, Mass., 1969-70; rsch. fellow Hale Obs., Carnegie Instn., Washington, and Calif. Inst. Tech., Pasadena, 1970-72; from asst. prof., dir. Hopkins Obs. to prof. Williams Coll., Williamstown, Mass., 1972—84, Field Meml. prof. of astronomy, 1984—, chmn. astronomy dept., 1972—77, 1991—92, 1997—2001, 2004—. Adj. asst. prof. astronomy U. Mass., Amherst, 1975-77; adj. assoc. prof., 1977-83, adj. prof., 1986-90; vis. colleague and vis. assoc. prof. astronomy Inst. for Astronomy, U. Hawaii, 1980-81; vis. scientist Inst. d'Astrophysique, Paris, 1988; mem. Inst. Advanced Study, Princeton, 1989-90, Harvard-Smithsonian Ctr. for Astrophysics, 1993-94, 2001-02; total and other solar eclipse expdn. leader numerous locations, Pluto, Charon and Triton occultation expeditions, 1997—, transit of Venus expedition, 2004; guest investigator NASA, 1975-79, 1999-2000, 2004—; lectr. in field. Author: Contemporary Astronomy, 1977, 4th edit., 1989, Astronomy Now, 1978, Astronomy: From Earth to the Universe, 1979, 6th edit., 2002, A Brief View of Astronomy, 1986, First Guide to Astronomy, 1988, First Guide to the Solar System, 1990, Journey Through the Universe, 1992; co-author: (with Marc L. Kutner, Naomi Pasachoff) Student Study Guide to Contemporary Astronomy, 1977, (with Kutner, Pasachoff and N.P. Kutner) Student Study Guide to Astronomy Now, 1978; (with M.L. Kutner) University Astronomy, 1978, Invitation to Physics, 1981; (with N. Pasachoff, T. Cooney) Physical Science, 1983, 2d edit., 1990, Earth Science, 1983, 2d edit., 1990; (with D.H. Menzel) A Field Guide to the Stars and Planets, 4th edit., 2000; (with R.

Wolfson) Physics, 1987, 3rd edit., 1999 (Extended with Modern Physics, 1989, 3rd edit. 1999), (with N. Pasachoff, R.W. Clark, M.H. Westermann) Physical Science Today, 1987; (with N. Pasachoff and others) Discover Science, 7 vols., 1989; (with Michael Covington) Cambridge Eclipse Photography Guide, 1993; (with Len Holder and James DeFranza) Calculus, 1994, Single Variable Calculus, 1994, Multivariable Calculus, 1995; (with Edward Cheng, Patrick Osmer and Hyron Spinrad) The Farthest Things in the Universe, 1994; editor (with J. Percy) The Teaching of Astronomy, 1990, (with Leon Golub) The Solar Corona, 1997, rev. edit., 1998, (with Roberta J. M. Olson) Fire in the Sky: Comets and Meteors, the Decisive Centuries, 1998, rev. edit., 1999, Science Explorer: Astronomy, 1998, rev. edit., 2004, Sound and Light, 1999, (with J. Percy) Teaching and Learning Astronomy: Effective Strategies for Educators Worldwide, 2005; (with Alex Filippenko) The Cosmos: Astronomy at the New Millennium, 2000, 2d edit., 2003, The Complete Idiot's Guide to the Sun, 2003; assoc. editor: Jour. Irreproducible Results, 1972-94, Annals of Improbable Rsch., 1994—; abstractor from Am. jours. for Solar Physics, 1968-78; cons. editor McGraw-Hill Ency. Sci. and Tech., 1983—; co-editor-in-chief (with S.P. Parker), McGraw-Hill Ency. of Astronomy, 1993; cons. Random House Dictionary, 1983-86, Nat. Geographic Atlas, 5th edit., 1981, 6th edit., 1990; phys. sci. com. World Book Ency., 1989-95, cons., 1996—; contbr. articles to profl. jours. Recipient bronze medal Nikon Photo Contest Internat., 1971, photograph aboard NASA Voyagers, 1977, Dudley award Dudley Obs., 1985; grantee NSF, 1973-75, 79-83, 88—2002, Nat. Geog. Soc., 1973-86, 91—2001, 2004—, Rsch. Corp., 1973-78, 82-88, 2001, Getty Found., 1994-95, NASA, 1999-2000, 2004—. Fellow AAAS (chair sect. D 1987-88, 97-98), Royal Astron. Soc., Am. Phys. Soc. (mem.-at-large thrs. forum edn. 1995-98), Internat. Planetarium Soc.; mem. AAUP (chpt. pres. 1977-80), Internat. Astron. Union (U.S. nat. rep. Commn. tchg. astronomy 1976-2000, chair eclipse working group 1991—, rep. com. tchg. sci. internat. coun. sci. unions 1991-93, v.p. com. on edn. and devel. 2000-2003, pres. 2003—, US nat. liaison commn. on edn. and devel., 2000—), Am. Astron. Soc. (astronomy edn. adv. bd. 1990-97, astronomy news com. 1991-96, rep. to AAAS 2004—, Edn. prize 2003), Astron. Soc. Pacific, Union Radio Sci., Am. Assn. Physics Tchrs. (astronomy com. 1983-87), Sigma Xi (chpt. pres. 1973-74, 95—, nat. lectr. 1993-97), Phi Beta Kappa. Home: 111 Park Street Williamstown MA 01267-2116 Office: Williams Coll Hopkins Obs 33 Lab Campus Dr Williamstown MA 01267-2565 E-mail: jay.m.pasachoff@williams.edu.

**PASACHOFF, NAOMI**, writer; b. N.Y.C., Jan. 27, 1947; d. Isaac and Anna (Jacobson) Schwartz; m. Jay M. Pasachoff, Mar. 31, 1974; children: Eloise Hilary, Deborah Donna. AB magna cum laude, Harvard U., 1968; AM, Columbia U., 1969; PhD, Brandeis U., 1974. Editorial asst. Houghton Mifflin Co., Boston, 1970-71; with Berkshire Community Coll., Pittsfield, Mass., 1974; vis. asst. prof. Skidmore Coll., 1974-77, Rensselaer Polytech. Inst., Troy, N.Y., 1977-78; freelancer Williamstown, Mass., 1978—. Lectr. Williams Coll., 2005. Author: Playwrights, Preachers, and Politicians, 1975, Basic Judaism for Young People: Torah, 1986, Basic Judaism for Young People: Israel, 1986, Basic Judaism for Young People: God, 1987, Great Jewish Thinkers: Their Lives and Work, 1992, (with Robert Littman) Jewish History in 100 Nutshells, 1995, A Topical Bible, 1996, Links in the Chain: Shapers of the Jewish Tradition, 1997, (with Robert Littman)A Concise History of the Jewish People, 2005, (with others) Physical Science, 1983, 90, Earth Science, 1983, 90, Physical Science Today, 1987, Discover Science, 1989, Marie Curie and the Science of Radioactivity, 1996, Alexander Graham Bell: Making Connections, 1996, Frances Perkins: Champion of the New Deal, 1999, Niels Bohr: Physicist and Humanitarian, 2003, Linus Pauling: Advancing Science, Advocating Peace, 2004, Ernest Rutherford: Father of Nuclear Science, 2005, Barbara McClintock: Genius of Genetics, 2006; contbr. articles to Ency. Britannica Yearbook of Sci. and Future, World Book. Home and Office: 111 Pk St Williamstown MA 01267-2116

**PASAHOW, LYNN HAROLD**, lawyer; b. Ft. Eustiss, Va., Mar. 13, 1947; s. Samuel and Cecelia (Newman) P.; m. Leslie Aileen Cobb, June 11, 1969; 1 child, Michael Alexander. AB, Stanford U., 1969; JD, U. Calif., Berkeley, 1972. Bar: Calif. 1972, U.S. Ct. Appeals (9th cir.) 1972, U.S. Dist. Ct. (no. dist.) Calif. 1973, U.S. Dist. Ct. (ctrl. dist.) Calif. 1974, U.S. Supreme Ct. 1976, U.S. Dist. Ct. (ea. dist.) Calif. 1977, U.S. Ct. Appeals (fed. cir.) 1990. Law clk. judge U.S. Dist. Ct. (no. dist.) Calif., San Francisco, 1972—73; with McCutchen, Doyle, Brown & Enersen, Palo Alto, Calif., 1973—2001, San Francisco, 1973—2001; ptnr. Fenwick & West LLP, Mountain View, Calif., 2001—. Bd. dirs. Bay Area Biosci. Ctr., Boalt Hall Alumni Assn.; mem. adv. bd. Berkeley Ctr. for Law and Tech., 1998—. Author: Pretrial and Settlement Conferences in Federal Court, 1983; co-author: Civil Discovery and Mandatory Disclosure: A Guide to Effective Practice, 1994; contbr. articles to profl. jours. Mem. ABA, Calif. Bar Assn. Democrat. Office: Fenwick & West LLP Silicon Valley Ctr 801 California St Mountain View CA 94041 Office Phone: 650-335-7225. Business E-Mail: lpasahow@fenwick.com. *Notable cases include: Amazon.com v. BarnesandNoble.com, duPont vs. Cetus, PCR patent litigation, Elan Pharmaceutical transgenic mouse litigation, Iomega Zip Disk litigation, nicotine patch patent litigation, University of California & Vysis v. Oncor FISH litigation.*

**PASCAL, AMY BETH**, film company executive; b. LA, Mar. 1958; d. Tony and Barbara Pascal; m. Bernard Weinraub, Aug. 9, 1997; 1 adopted child, Anthony. BA in Internat. Rels., UCLA. With Kestral Films; v.p. prodn. 20th Century Fox, 1986—87, Columbia Pictures, 1987—89, exec. v.p. prodn., 1987—94; pres. prodn. Turner Pictures, 1994—96; pres. Columbia Pictures, Culver City, Calif., 1996-99, chmn., 1999—2002; vice chmn. Sony Pictures Entertainment, Culver City, Calif., 2002—06, co-chmn., 2006—; chmn. Sony Pictures Entertainment Motion Picture Group, Culver City, Calif., 2003—. Bd. trustees Kund Corp. Bd. trustees AFI; mem. UCLA Sch. Theater, Film & Television. Named one of 100 Most Powerful Women in Entertainment, Hollywood Reporter, 2004—05, 100 Most Powerful Women, Forbes mag., 2005—06, 50 Most Powerful People in Hollywood, Premiere mag., 2004—06. Office: Sony Pictures Entertainment 10202 Washington Blvd Culver City CA 90232*

**PASCAL, C(ECIL) BENNETT**, classics educator; b. Chgo., May 4, 1926; s. Jack and Goldie (Zeff) P.; m. Ilene Joy Shulman, Feb. 1, 1959; 1 child, Keith Irwin. BA, UCLA, 1949, MA, 1950, Harvard U., 1953, PhD, 1956. Instr. U. Ill., Champaign, 1955-56, Cornell U., Ithaca, NY, 1957-60; asst. prof., then assoc. prof. U. Oreg., Eugene, 1960-75, prof. classics, 1975-96, prof. emeritus, 1996—; head dept., various years - 1965-85. Author: Cults of Cisalpine Gaul, 1964; contbr. articles to profl. jours. Active Eugene Bicycle Com., 1971-83. Wwith USN, 1944-46. Traveling fellow, Italy, Harvard U., 1956-57, Fulbright-Hays fellow, Rome, 1967-68. Mem. Am. Philol. Assn., Classical Assn. Pacific N.W. (pres. 1965-66), AAUP, Archeol. Inst. of Am. (past pres., sec. Eugene Soc.) Democrat. Jewish. Avocations: skiing, fly fishing, novel writing. Home: 330 Fulvue Dr Eugene OR 97405-2788 Office: U Oreg Dept Classics Eugene OR 97403 Business E-Mail: cbpasc@uoregon.edu.

**PASCAL, ROGER**, lawyer; b. Chgo., Mar. 16, 1941; s. Samuel A. and Harriet E. (Hartman) P.; m. Martha Hecht, June 16, 1963; children: Deborah, Diane, David AB with distinction, U. Mich, 1962; JD cum laude, Harvard U., 1965. Bar: Ill. 1965, U.S. Dist. Ct. (no. dist.) Ill. 1965, U.S. Ct. Appeals (7th cir.) 1969, U.S. Supreme Ct. 1976, Wis. 1985, U.S. Ct. Appeals (2d, 6th, 9th and 10th cirs.) 1986. Assoc. Schiff Hardin LLP, Chgo., 1965-71, ptnr., 1972—. Adj. prof. law Northwestern U. Law Sch., 1994—; bd. dirs. Evanston Cmty. Defender. Bd. dirs., mem. exec. com. Chgo. Law Enforcement Study Group, 1975-80, pres., 1978-80; pres. Harvard Law Soc. Ill., 1976-78; bd. dirs. ACLU of Ill., 1984—, gen. counsel, 1986—. Recipient Roger Baldwin Lifetime Achievement award, 2003. Fellow Am. Bar Found.; mem. ABA (antitrust, intellectual property, and litigation sects.),Pub. Interest Law Initiative (bd. dirs. 1989—, v.p. 1995-97, pres. 1997-98), Fund for Justice (v.p., bd. dirs. 1986-97), Chgo. Coun. Lawyers (bd. dirs. 1970-74, 80-84, 2004—), Chgo. Legal Assistance Found. (bd. dirs. 1985-88), Chgo. Bar Found.(recipient Edward Lewis II Pro Bono Svc. award, 2003), Univ. Club, Met. Club, Phi Beta Kappa. Office: Schiff Hardin LLP 6600 Sears Tower Chicago IL 60606

**PASCAL, TRACEY MICHELE,** software engineer, director; d. Harold Saunders and Dinah Lee Pascal. BBA, Tex. Tech U., Lubbock, 1986. Lic. nursing home adminstr. Tex., 1986. Adminstr. ARA Living Ctrs., Weatherford, Tex., 1986—87, Beverly Enterprises, Van, Tex., 1987—88; CFO Carter Nursing Homes, Inc, Corsicana, Tex., 1988—90; sr. software engr./tech. lead Sprint, Irving, Tex., 1990—. Employee trainer and mentor Sprint, Irving, Tex., 2002—06. Author: (manual) Sprint Operatons for Offshore Employees, (training manual) How to Complete and Fix Production Codes, (flash cards) Sprint History Past and Present; contbr. articles to profl. jours. Mem.: NSDAR, Project Mgmt. Inst., Am. Acad. Med. Adminstrs., Golden Key, Pi Beta Phi. Office: Sprint/Nextel 1300 East Rochelle Blvd Irving TX 75062 Office Phone: 972-536-6628. Personal E-mail: valinese@aol.com.

**PASCALE, DANIEL RICHARD,** lawyer; b. Racine, Wis., Mar. 22, 1940; s. Domenic and Fannie Colette (Julian) P.; m. Mary Sara McDonald, June 28, 1986; 1 child, Alexander. AB cum laude, Harvard U., 1962; JD, U. Chgo., 1965. Bar: Ill. 1966, U.S. Ct. Appeals (7th cir.) 1967, U.S. Dist. Ct. (no. dist.) Ill. 1969, U.S. Supreme Ct. 1972. Asst. corp. counsel City of Chgo., 1966-72, chief appellate atty., 1972-79, 1st dep. corp. counsel, 1979-84; assoc. Rudnick & Wolfe, Chgo., 1984-87; ptnr., 1987-90; judge Circuit Ct. of Cook County, Ill., 1990-94, 96-98; adminstrv. dir. Adminstrv. Office of Ill. Cts., Chgo., 1995-96; sr. corp. atty. Dean Foods Co., 1999—2002; instr. Northeastern Ill. U., 2004—. Counsel to the chmn. com. on fin. Chgo. City Coun., 2005—. Bd. dirs. DeKoven Found., Racine, 1986—, The Church Home/Montgomery Pl., 1998—; adv. bd. Art Resources in Teaching, Chgo., 1987-94; v.p. Episcopal Homes Mgmt., Inc., Milw., 1988-94. Mem. Fed. Bar Assn., Ill. Bar Assn., Chgo. Bar Assn., English-Speaking Union. Independent. Episcopalian.

**PASCARELLA, HENRY WILLIAM,** lawyer; b. New Haven, Conn., Aug. 15, 1933; s. John Manlio and Mary (Iannotti) P.; m. Tessa Peruzzi, Jan. 28, 1967; children: Averardo, Leonora, Cassandra. BS in Econs., U. Pa., 1955; LLB, Yale U., 1958. Bar: Conn. 1958, U.S. Supreme Ct. 1963. Ptnr. Badger, Fisher, Cohen & Barnett and predecessors, Greenwich, Conn., 1959-73; sr. counsel to Taylor Cooper & Alcorn, Greenwich, Conn., 1978—2005. Pres., dir. The Timber Trails Corp. Sherman, Conn.; dir. Nine West Group Inc., 1995-99. Author column, theater critic Greenwich Times, 1964-67. Dir. Planned Parenthood League of Conn., Greenwich coun. Boy Scouts Am., 1990-96. Served to lt. (j.g.) USCG, 1959. Mem ABA, Greenwich Bar Assn. (pres. 1967), Conn. Bar Assn., Yale Club (N.Y.C.), Belle Haven Club (Greenwich). Home: 675 Steamboat Rd Greenwich CT 06830-7140 E-mail: henry@pascarellalaw.com.

**PASCARELLA, PERRY JAMES,** editor, writer; b. Bradford, Pa., Apr. 11, 1934; s. James and Lucille Margaret (Monti) P.; m. Carol Ruth Taylor, May 4, 1957; children: Cynthia, Elizabeth. AB, Kenyon Coll., 1956; Coll. William and Mary, William and Mary Coll., 1957; postgrad., George Washington U., 1958. Credit reporter Dun & Bradstreet, Cleve., 1956, 60; from asst. editor to mng. editor Steel mag., Cleve., 1961-69; mng. editor Industry Week mag., Cleve., 1970-71, exec. editor, 1971-86, editor-in-chief, 1986-89; v.p. editorial Penton Pub. Inc., 1989-96. Lectr. in field. Author: Technology-Fire in a Dark World, 1979, Humanagement in the Future Corporation, 1981, The New Achievers, 1984, The Purpose-Driven Organization, 1989, The Ten Commandments of the Workplace, 1996, Leveraging People and Profit, 1998, Christ-Centered Leadership, 1999; co-author: Optimistic Outlooks, 1982, Creating a Global Agenda, 1984, Leadership in a New Era, 1994, The New Bottom Line, 1996. Lt. comdr. USNR, 1957-60. Recipient Disting. Service award Kenyon Coll., 1975, 81, Am. Bus. Press Crain award, 1992; Carnegie scholar, 1952-56 Mem. World Future Soc., U. Akron Inst. for Future Studies (bd. advisors). Presbyterian (elder). Home: 694 Coronado Cir Avon Lake OH 44012

**PASCH, ALAN,** philosopher, educator; b. Cleve., Dec. 1, 1925; s. P. Jerome and Esther (Broverman) P.; m. Eleanor Kudlich Berna, Dec. 27, 1950; 1 child, Rachel. BA, U. Mich., 1949; MA, New Sch. Social Research, 1952; PhD, Princeton U., 1955; Bamford fellow, 1955-56. Instr. philosophy Ohio State U., 1956-59, asst. prof., 1959-60; assoc. prof. philosophy U. Md., College Park, 1960-67, prof., 1967-97, prof. emeritus, 1997—. Author: Experience and the Analytic, 1958; also articles, revs. Served with AUS, 1944-46, PTO. Mem. Am. Philos. Assn. (exec. dir. 1969-72, sec.-treas. Eastern div. 1965-68), Metaphys. Soc. Am., Washington Philosophy Club (pres. 1978-79), Washington Rare Book Group. Office: Dept Philosophy Univ Md College Park MD 20742 Business E-Mail: pasch@umd.edu.

**PASCHALL, LEE MCQUERTER,** retired communications executive; b. Sterling, Colo., Jan. 21, 1922; s. Lee McQuerter and Agnes (Woldridge) P.; m. Bonnie Jean Edwards, Oct. 24, 1942; children: Patricia Ann Grillos, Stephen Lee, David Edward. BA, U. Ala., 1957; MA, George Washington U., 1964. Served with U.S. Army, 1940-46; communications engr. Colo. Air N.G., Denver, 1946-51; commd. maj. U.S. Air Force, 1951, advanced through grades to lt. gen., 1974, ret., 1978; ind. cons. Springfield, Va., 1978-81; pres., chief exec. officer Am. Satellite Co., Rockville, Md., 1981-84, chmn., 1984-85. Dir. Gen. Data Comm. Industries. Contbr. numerous articles to profl. publs. Mem. com. rev. nat. communications system initiatives NRC, 1982-88. Decorated Legion of Merit with oak leaf cluster; decorated disting. service medals; recipient Eascon IEEE, 1979 Mem. Armed Forces Comms.-Electronics Assn. (chpt. pres., nat. bd. dirs. Disting. Svc.), Air Force Assn., Phi Beta Kappa. Mem. Christian Ch. (Disciples Of Christ). Home and Office: 1513 Hampton Hills Cir Mc Lean VA 22101-6018 Personal E-mail: lmpaschall@prodigy.net.

**PASCHE, BORIS CLAUDE ROGER,** physician; b. Lausanne, Vaud, Switzerland, Aug. 5, 1961; came to U.S., 1989; Rene Charles Edouard and Marina (Guidetti) P. MD, Karolinska Inst., Stockholm, 1986, U. Lausanne, Switzerland, 1987; PhD, Karolinska Inst., Stockholm, 1989. Cert. diplomate, Am. Bd. of Internal Med. 1994, diplomate, Am. Bd. of Medical Oncology 1997, diplomate, Am. Bd. of Hematology 1999, lic. New York State Med. Lic. 1995, Illinois Med. Lic. 2001. Clin. trial dir. Symtonic S.A., Renens, Switzerland, 1983-86, chief sci. officer, 1986—; pres. Symtonic U.S., N.Y.C., 1992-96; rsch. fellow in cardiovascular medicine Harvard Med. Sch., Boston, 1989-92; intern in medicine N.Y. Hosp. Meml. Sloan-Kettering Cancer Ctr., Cornell U. Med. Ctr., N.Y. C., 1992-93, resident in medicine N.Y. Hosp., N.Y.C., 1993-94; fellow in hematology-oncology Meml. Sloan-Kettering Cancer Ctr., N.Y.C., 1994—2000; att. phys. Northwestern Meml. Hosp., Chgo., 2001—; dir. Northwestern U. Cancer Genetics prog., 2002—. Asst. in medicine Clinique Bon Port, Montreux, Switzerland, 1988—2000; asst. physician Meml. Sloan-Kettering Cancer Ctr., Cornell U. Med. Ctr., N.Y.C. 1993—2000; asst. prof. medicine Feinberg Sch. Medicine. Northwestern U., 2000—05, assoc. prof. medicine, 2006— Inventor (with others): chimeric molecule with plaminogen activator activity and affinity for atherosclerotic plaques, method and system for applying low energy emission therapy; author: (books) Non-thrombogenic Properties of Artificial and Biological surfaces, Medecine Homeopathique Moderne; contbg. editor to Jour. Am. Med. Assn., contbr. articles to profl. jours and chpt. to book. With Swiss Med. Corps., 1980. Recipient Swiss Academic Soc. fellowship, 1983, Lausanne Academic Soc. Rsch. fellowship, 1984-86, Swedish Bd. for Tech. Devel. Rsch. fellowship, 1986-89; Physician Scientist award Nat. Cancer Inst.; Ohio State Human Cancer Genetics Program Commemorative medal, 2005. Mem. AAAS, AMA, Nat. Inst. Electromed. Info., Bioelectromagnetics Soc., European Bioelectromagnetics Soc., Internat. Soc. on Thrombosis and Haemostasis (Young Scientist Merit award 1989, Young Investigator Merit award 1991) Am. Soc. Hematology, Am. Soc. Clinical Oncology, Am. Assn. Cancer Research, Am. Soc. Human Genetics, Am. Heart Assn. (clin. cardiology coun., arteriosclerosis coun.), Am. Fedn. for Clin. Rsch. (Trainee Investigator award 1992), Fellow of the Am. Coll. Physicians (assoc.), mem. Cancer Genetics Panel of the National Comprehensive Cancer Network Avocations: skiing, windsurfing, classical music, fine arts. Home: 415 East North Water St Apt 1406 Chicago IL 60611 Office: Robert H Lurie Comprehensive Cancer Center Northwestern U Feinberg Sch of Med,676 N St Clair Street Suite 880 Chicago IL 60611 Business E-Mail: b-pasche@northwestern.edu.

**PASCHETTO, JOHN J.,** lawyer; b. Long Branch, N.J., Sept. 18, 1959; s. Edward and Elizabeth McCue Paschetto; m. Katherine Anne Dobrosky, Feb. 20, 1982. BA, Rutgers U., 1981; MA, U. Del., 1988; JD, Harvard U., 1998. Bar: Del. 1998, U.S. Dist. Ct. Del. 1999. Prnt. Young Conaway Stargatt & Taylor, LLP, Wilmington, Del., 1998—. Contbr. chapters to books. Mem.: ABA, Del. State Bar Assn., Harvard Law Sch. Assn. Del. (treas. 1998—). Office: Young Conaway Stargatt & Taylor LLP 1000 West St Wilmington DE 19801 Office Phone: 302-571-6608. Business E-Mail: jpaschetto@ycst.com.

**PASCHKE, JERRY BRYAN,** lawyer; b. Palmdale, Calif., Aug. 6, 1965; s. Donald Joseph and Diana Marie (Scott) P.; m. Randa Holewa 2000; children Lucy J., Adam J. BS, St. John's U., Collegeville, Minn., 1988; JD, Hamline U., 1991. Bar: Minn. 1991, Army Ct. Mil. Rev. 1992, U.S. Magistrates Ct. 1993. Commd. 2d lt. U.S. Army, 1988, advanced through grades to capt., 1992; post judge advocate U.S. Army-Sierra Army Depot, Herlong, Calif., 1992—94; brigade trial counsel U.S. Army-Camp Stanley, Uijongbu, Republic of Korea, 1994—95; legal instr. U.S. Army-Ft. Huachuca, Sierra Vista, Ariz., 1995—97, chief criminal law, 1997—98, mil. magistrate, 1995—97; acct. Accts.-On-Call, Mpls., 1998—2000; adminstrv. law officer USAR, Ft. Snelling, Minn., 1998—2004; staff acct. Best Buy, 2000—02; major USAR, Ft. Snelling, Minn., 2000—; instr. Rasmussen Coll., Mankato, Minn., 2004—; ROTC instr. Minn. State U., Mankato, 2004—. Mem. landlord-tenant hotline Minn. Pub. Interest Rsch. Group, Mpls., 1989; advisor DeMolay, Reno, 1992-94, football, basketball official Mankato Area Official's Assn., 2003-05; treas. Medford Civic Club, 2003—. Decorated Army Commendation medal, 3 Meritorious Svc. medals, Army Achievement medal. Mem. Order St. Barbara, Medford Area Rec Com. Avocations: hiking, chess, travel. Home: 15 6th St SE Medford MN 55049-7000 E-mail: medfordref@yahoo.com

**PASCHOUD, FRANÇOIS,** classicist, educator; b. Jan. 11, 1938; s. Maurice Paschoud and Nelly (Suter) Pascound; m. Anne-Marie Chene, July 24, 1978; children: Jerôme, Ubain. Lic. Letters, U. Lausanne, Switzerland, 1960, LittD, 1967. Mem. Swiss Inst., Rome, 1962—64; Wissenschaftlicher Mitarbeiter Thesaurus linguae Latinae, Munich, 1965—67; prof. extraordinarius, ordinarius U. Geneva, 1969—74, 1974—2004, hon. prof., 2004—; vis. mem. Inst. for Advanced Study Princeton (NJ) U., 1976—77, 1983—84. Author: Roma aeterna, 1967; translator: Commentary of Zosimus I, 1971, II 1 and II 2, 1979, III 1, 1986, III 2, 1989, Historia Agusta V 1, 1996, V 2, 2001. Mem.: Groupe Romand des Etudes Grecques et Latines (pres. 1978—81), Fondation Hardt pour l'étude de l'antiquité Vandoeuvres Geneve (pres. 1996—2003), Soc. Latin Studies Paris, Internat. Fedn. of Socs. of Classical Studies (sec. gen. 1974—2004), Real Academia Barcelona (corr.). E-mail: zosime@bluewin.ch.

**PASCIUTO, JOSEPH DORIA,** priest; b. Bklyn., June 27, 1945; s. Carmine Michael Pasciuto, Rose Marie (Doria) Pasciuto. BA, St. John's U., 1968, MBA, 1981; MDiv, Immaculate Conception Sem., Huntington, N.Y., 1991; MA in Theology, Immaculate Conception Sem., 1999; theol. studies, Pontifical N.Am. Coll., Vatican City, 2003. Ordination Roman Cath. Diocese Bklyn., 1991. CFO Local 371 AFSCME, N.Y.C., 1981—84; mgr. pers./labor rels Child Welfare Adminstrn., N.Y.C., 1984—87; vicar Our Lady Help of Christians, Bklyn., 1991—99, Our Lady of Hope, Queens, NY, 1999—2000, St. Brendan, Bklyn., 2000—03; adminstr. Holy Cross Roman Cath. Ch., Bklyn., 2003—. Chaplain Boy Scouts Am., Bklyn., 2000—, Internat. Firefighters Assn., N.Y.C., 2001. Mem.: KC (chaplain 1995—, 4th degree L.I. Assembly 2001), Montauk Club. Democrat. Avocations: music, reading, cooking. Home: 451 Abingdon Ave Staten Island NY 10308

**PASCO, HANSELL MERRILL,** retired lawyer; b. Thomasville, Ga., Oct. 7, 1915; s. John and Katherine (Merrill) P.; m. Williamine Carrington Lancaster, June 28, 1941; children: Hansell Merrill, Dabney, Robert, Elizabeth, Carrington. BA, Va. Mil. Inst., 1937; LL.B., U. Va., 1940. Bar: Va. bar 1939. Ptnr. Hunton & Williams, Richmond, Va., 1948-81; sr. counsel, 1981—2005, mng. partner, 1968-76; ret., 2005. Chmn. State Counsel Higher Edn. for Va., 1978-80; trustee Protestant Episcopal Sem., Alexandria, Va., 1980-85. Served with U.S. Army as observe officer, first asst. sec. war dept.gen. staff, sec., 1940-45.

**PASCOE, B. LYNN,** ambassador; b. Mo., 1943; m. Diane Pascoe; 2 children. BA, U. Kans.; MA, Columbia U. Spl. asst. to dep. sec. state US Dept. State, dep. exec. sec., Am. dep. chief of mission Beijing China, principal dep. asst. sec. East Asian and Pacific Bur.; dir. Am. Inst. Taiwan, Taipei, 1993—96; US spl. negotiator for Nagorno-Karabakh & regional conflicts, US co-chair for Orgn. for Security & Cooperation in Europe's Minsk Group US Dept. State, 1997—98, US amb. to Malaysia Kuala Lampur, 1999—2001; dep. asst. sec. Bur. European and Eurasian Affairs Washington, 2001—04, US amb. to Indonesia Jakarta, 2004—. Fluent in Mandarin Chinese.

**PASCOE, PATRICIA HILL,** former state legislator; b. Sparta, Wis., June 1, 1935; d. Fred Kirk and Edith (Kilpatrick) Hill; m. D. Monte Pascoe, Aug. 3, 1957; children: Sarah, Edward, William. BA, U. Colo., 1957; MA, U. Denver, 1968, PhD, 1982. Tchr. Sequoia Union H.S. Dist., Redwood City, Calif. and Hayward (Calif.) Union H.S. Dist., 1957-60; instr. Met. State Coll., Denver, 1969-75, Denver U., 1975-77, 81, rsch. asst. bd. edn., 1981-82; tchr. Kent Denver Country Day Sch., Englewood, Colo., 1982-84; freelance writer Denver, 1985—; mem. Colo. Senate, Dist. 32, Denver, 1989—93, Colo. Senate, Dist. 34, Denver, 1995—2003; chair minority caucus Colo. Senate, Denver, 1996-2000, chair policy and planning com., 2001, chair edn. com., 2002. Commr. Edn. Commn. of the States, Denver, 1975-82, 01-05. Contbr. articles to numerous publs. and jours. Bd. dirs. Samaritan House, 1990-94, Cystic Fibrosis Found., 1989-93, chmn. legis. com.; pres. East HS Parent Tchr. and Student Assn., Denver, 1984-85; mem. Moore Budget Adv. Com., Denver, 1966-72; legis. chmn. alumni bd. U. Colo., Boulder, 1987-89; del. Dem. Nat. Conv., San Francisco, 1984, NYC, 1992; mem. Denver Woman's Press Club, 1986—, pres., 2005-06, Colo. Arts Coalition, 1988-97, Conflict Ctr. Bd., 2003-05; bd. dirs. Opera Colo., 1996-02; mem. bd. ACLU Colo. Mem. Soc. Profl. Journalists, Common Cause (bd. dirs. Denver chpt. 1986-88), Lions Club (dir. 2003-05), Phi Beta Kappa. Democrat. Presbyterian.

**PASCRELL, WILLIAM J., JR.,** congressman; b. Paterson, NJ, Jan. 25, 1937; s. William J. Sr. and Roffie (Loffredo) Pascrell; m. Elsie Marie Botto; children: William III, David, Glenn. BA in Journalism, Fordham U., NY, 1959, MA in Philos., 1961; postgraduate student, Fairleigh Dickinson U. Tchr. Jr. HS, Clifton, NJ, 1962, Paramus HS, NJ, 1962-67; adj. prof. Fairleigh Dickinson U., Madison, NJ, 1964—69; ophthalmic technician Seymour Pollack Opticians, 1968—74; adult sch. tchr. Dwight Morrow HS, Englewood, NJ, 1969-70; dir. Dept. Pub. Works, Paterson, NJ, 1974-77, Dept. Policy, Planning and Devel., Paterson, NJ, 1979—87; mem. Paterson Planning Bd., NJ, 1975—77; pres. Bd. Edn., Paterson, NJ, 1979—82; mem. NJ Gen. Assembly, 1987—90; mayor Paterson, NJ, 1990—96; mem. US Congress from 8th NJ dist., 1997—. Co-chair Congl. Brain Injury Task Force US Congress; mem. transp. and infrastructure com., mem. homeland security com., ranking minority mem. emergency preparedness, sci. and tech. subcommittee. Bd. dirs. Passaic County Cmty. Coll., 1973-79, Boys Club, 1975-; campaign coord. Robert A. Roe for Gov., NJ, 1977; regional coord. James Florio for Gov., Hudson County, NJ, 1981; active County Chairmen for Sen. Frank Lautenberg, NJ, 1982; chmn. Passaic County Democrats, NJ, 1982-1990. Enlisted U.S. Army, 1961—62, sgt. USAR, 1962—67. Named Man of Yr., Mother Cabrini Soc., 1979, Fedn. Italian Socs., 1981, Unico Passaic County, 1982, Am. Legion John Raad Post, 1983, Passaic County Young Democrats, 1983; recipient Congl. Recognition award, Internat. Assn. Fire Fighters, 2001. Mem.: Pat Mone Assn., Charles Alfano Assn., Riverside Vets., KC, Fordham U. Alumni Assn., Am. Cancer Soc., Italian-Am. Fedn., Paterson Taxpayers Assn., Elks. Democrat. Roman Catholic. Office: US Ho Reps 2464 Rayburn Ho Office Bldg Washington DC 20515-3008 Office Phone: 202-225-5751.*

**PASCUAL, CARLOS,** ambassador; BA in Internat. Rels., Stanford U., 1980; MA in Pub. Policy, Harvard U., 1982. With USAID, South Africa, Mozambique, Washington, project devel. officer Sudan, 1983—92, dir., Office of Program Analysius and Coordinatoin for New Ind. States Task Force, 1994—94, dep. asst. adminstr. for Europe and New Ind. States, 1994—95; dir. for Russian, Ukrainian and Eurasian Affairs Nat. Security Coun., 1995—98, spl. asst. to Pres., sr. dir. for Russia, 1998—2000; U.S. amb. to Ukraine, 2000—03; coordinator for U.S. assistance to Europe and Eurasia U.S. Dept. State, 2003—. Office: Dept State Bureau European Eurasian Affairs 2201 C Street NW Washington DC 20520

**PASCUAL, MERCEDES,** biology professor; PhD in Joint Program, Woods Hole Oceanographic Inst. and MIT, 1995. Asst. prof. ecology and evolutionary biology U. Mich., 2001—. Mem. Ctr. for the Study of Complex Systems U. Mich. Named one of 50 Most Important Women in Sci., Discover mag., 2002; Alexander Hollaender Disting. Postdoctoral Fellow, U.S. Dept. of Energy, Centennial Fellowship, Global and Complex Systems from the James S. McDonnell Found. Office: U Mich Kraus 2045 Ann Arbor MI 48109-1048

**PASCUCCI, MARISA JONELL,** curator, art historian; b. Cleve., July 13, 1974; BA, Am. U., Washington, D.C., 1996; MA, Case Western Res. U., Cleve., Ohio, 1999. Instr. edn. and pub. programs Cleve. Mus. Art, 1999—99; coord. exhibitions and programs The Sculpture Ctr., Cleve., 2000; membership coord. Artists Archives We. Res., Cleve., 2000; assoc. curator collections and exhibitions Montgomery (Ala.) Mus. Fine Arts, 2001—05; sr. curator Everson Mus. Art, Syracuse, NY, 2005—. Grantee, Mus. Loan Network, 2004—06. Mem.: Coll. Art Assn., Am. Assn. Mus., Assn. Art Mus. Curators. Office: Everson Museum of Art 401 Harrison Street Syracuse NY 13202 Office Phone: 315-474-6064. Office Fax: 315-474-6943. Business E-Mail: mpascucci@everson.org.

**PASETTI, LOUIS OSCAR,** retired dentist; b. Tampa, Fla., Dec. 27, 1916; s. Joseph G. and Carmen (Gonzalez) P.; m. Mary Mendez, Jan. 11, 1942; children: Louis M., Arleen Pasetti Mariotti. BS, U. Fla., 1937; DDS, Emory U., 1941; postgrad., U. Pa., 1978. Capt. U.S. Army, 1942—46; dentist pvt. practice Tampa, Fla., 1947—2002; ret., 2002. Past. pres. Tampa Civitan Club, 1953; past lt. gov. Civitan Clubs of Tampa, 1962; past dep. gov. Civitan Internat., Fla., 1964; fin. officer Am. Legion Post 248. Named Fla. Dentist of the Yr., Fla. Acad. Gen. Dentistry, 1983; recipient meritorious Svc. award Fla. Acad. Gen. Dentistry, 1989, Disting. Svc. award, 1985. Fellow Acad. Gen. Dentistry (lifetime achievement award 2004), Am. Coll. Dentists, Internat. Coll. Dentists, Acad. Dentistry Internat.; mem. ADA, Fla. Dental Assn., Fla. Acad. Gen. Dentistry (pres. 1981, Lifetime Achievement award 1996, mem. emeritus 2002), Tampa Bay Acad. Gen. Dentistry (pres. 1977-78), Elks, Round Table of Civic Clubs of Tampa (sec. 1953), Palma Ceia Golf and Country Club. Democrat. Roman Catholic. Avocations: photography, orchid culture. Home: 10023 Hampton Pl Tampa FL 33618-4227

**PASHGIAN, MARGARET HELEN,** artist; b. Pasadena, Calif., Nov. 7, 1934; d. Aram John and Margaret (Howell) P. BA, Pomona Coll., 1956; student, Columbia U., 1957; MA in Fine Arts, Boston Univ., 1958. Art instr. Harvard-Newton Program Occidental Coll., 1977-78; artist in residence Calif. Inst. Tech., 1970-71. Grants panelist Calif. Arts Coun., Sacramento, 1993. One-woman shows include Rex Evans Gallery, L.A., 1965, 67, Occidental Coll., 1967, Kornblee Gallery, N.Y.C., 1969-72, U. Calif., Irvine, 1975, U. Calif. Santa Barbara, 1976, Stella Polaries Gallery, L.A., 1981-82, Kaufman Galleries, Houston, 1982, Modernism Gallery, San Francisco, 1983, Works Gallery, Long Beach, Costa Mesa, Calif., 1982-90, Malka Gallery, L.A., 1997; exhibited in group shows at Pasadena Art Mus. 1965, Carson Pirie Scott, Chgo., 1965, Calif. Palace of Legion of Honor, San Francisco, 1967, Esther Bear Gallery, Santa Barbara, 1967, 69, Lytton Ctr. of the Visual Arts, L.A., 1968, Salt Lake Art Inst., Salt Lake City, 1968, Mus. Contemporary Crafts, 1969, Second Flint (Mich.) Invitational, 1969, Milw. Art Ctr., 1969, U.S.I.S. Mus., N.Y.C., Mus. Contemporary Art, Chgo., 1970, Studio Merconi, Milan, 1970, Calif. Inst. Tech., Baxter Art Galley, 1971, 1980, Calif. Innovations, Palm Springs Dessert Mus., 1981, Calif. Internat. Arts Found. Mus. Modern Art, Paris, 1982, L.A. Artists in Seoul, Donsangbang Gallery, 1982, An Artistic Conversation, 1931-82, Poland, USA, Ulster Mus., Belfast, Ireland, 1983, Madison (Wis.) Art Ctr., 1994, Calif. State U., Fullerton, 1995, Oakland (Calif.) Mus., 1995, Molly Barnes Gallery, L.A., Calif., 2000, Pasadena (Calif.) Mus. Calif. Art, 2002; represented in pub. collections at River Forest (Ill.) State Bank, Atlantic Richfield Co., Dallas, Frederic Weisman Collection, L.A., Security Pacific Bank, L.A., Singapore, Andrew Dickson White Mus. Art, Cornell U., Ithaca, N.Y., L.A. County Mus. Art, Santa Barbara Art Mus., Laguna Beach Mus. Art, Portland (Oreg.) Art Mus. Trustee, Pomona Coll, Claremont, Calif., 1987—; parade judge Tournament of Roses Centennial Parade, Pasadena, 1987; bd. dirs. LA Master Chorale, 1992—, Ojai Music Festival, 2004— NEA grantee, 1986. Home: 731 S Grand Ave Pasadena CA 91105-2424

**PASIC, RESAD,** medical educator; b. Sarajevo, Bosnia-Herzegovina, June 26, 1951; s. Hamid and Advija Pasic; m. Djenita Muzurovic, Nov. 5, 1959. MD, U. of Sarajevo, 1975. Assoc. prof. U. of Louisville, 1999—. Editor (with others): (med. textbook) A Practical Manual of Laparoscopy: A Clinical Cookbook, 2002, A Practical Manual of Hysteroscopy and Endometrial Ablation: A Clinical Cookbook, 2004. Mem.: Am. Assn. Gynecol. Laparoscopists (bd. mem. 2004—06). Home: 2411 Newburg RD Louisville KY 40205 Office: U Louisville Dept Ob-Gyn Louisville KY 40202 Office Phone: 502-561-7465. Office Fax: 502-561-8684. Business E-Mail: paya@louisville.edu.

**PASICH, KIRK ALAN,** lawyer; b. La Jolla, Calif., May 26, 1955; s. Chris Nick and Iva Mae (Tormey) P.; m. Pamela Mary Woods, July 30, 1983; children: Christopher Thomas, Kelly Elizabeth, Connor Woods. BA in Polit. Sci., UCLA, 1977; JD, Loyola Law Sch., L.A., 1980. Bar: Calif. 1980, U.S. Dist. Ct. (no., so., ea. and cen. dists.) Calif. 1981, Mich. (ea. dist.) 1997, Tex. (ea. dist.) 2001, U.S. Ct. Appeals (9th cir.) 1981, U.S. Ct. Appeals (1st cir.) 1992. Assoc. Paul, Hastings, Janofsky & Walker, LA, 1980-88, ptnr., 1988-89, Troop Steuber Pasich Reddick & Tobey, LLP, 1989-2000, Howrey Simon Arnold & White LLP, 2001—03, Pasich & Kornfeld LLP, 2003—05, Dickstein Shapiro LLP, 2005—. Author: Casualty and Liability Insurance, 1990, 2000, 03; co-author: Officers and Directors: Liabilities and Protections, 1996, 2000, 03, The Year 2000 and Beyond: Liability and Insurance for Computer Code Problems, 2000; contbg. editor: West's California Litigation Forms: Civil Procedure Before Trial, 2000; co-author, co-editor: ABA Manual for Complex Insurance Coverage Litigation, 1999, 2000, 04; entertainment law columnist, ins. law columnist L.A. and San Francisco Daily Jour., 1989—; contbr. articles to profl. jours. Active bd. dirs. Nat. Acad. Jazz, L.A., 1988-89, chmn. bd. dirs. Woody Herman Found., L.A., 1989-92, Constnl. Rights Found., 2000; active L.A. City Atty's. Task Force for Econ. Recovery, 1992-93. Named to Calif's. Legal Dream Team as 1 of state's top 25 litigators, Calif. Law Bus., 1992; named one of the nation's top 45 lawyers under age 45, The Am. Lawyer, 1995, market leader for policyholder representation in California, Chambers Guide to Leading Bus. Lawyers 2003-04; named one of 500 Leading Lawyers in Am., Lawdragon, 2005. Mem. ABA (mem. Task Force on Complex Insurance Coverage Litigation), Risk & Insurance Mgmt. Soc., Def. Rsch. Inst. Office: 10866 Wilshire Blvd Ste 300 Los Angeles CA 90024 Office Phone: 310-441-8461. Business E-Mail: PasichK@dsmo.com.

**PASIERB, STEPHEN JOHN,** advertising executive, marketing professional; b. Ramsey, N.J., Oct. 9, 1962; s. Stephen Anthony and Leila Joy (Gommoll) P.; m. Wendy Ann Wiethorn, June 11, 1988. BS in Criminology, Ind. U., Ind., Pa., 1984, MEd (with honors), 1986. On-air personality Sta. WCLG, Morgantown, W.Va., 1981-83, Sta. WWVU, 1981-83, Sta. WGLU, Johnstown, Pa., 1983-85; ops. dir. Sta. WIUP, Ind., Pa., 1984-86; account exec. Sta. WLTJ, Pitts., 1986; dir. media svcs. GNVC Comm., Pitts., 1986-87; acct. mgr. mus. Sta. Freed & Assocs., Balt., 1987-91; mgr. media comm. Md. Gov.'s office, Towson, 1991-93; from sr. v.p., dep. dir. to pres., chief exec. Partnership for a Drug-Free Am., N.Y.C., 1993—. Adv. bd. mem. Sta.

WMAR-TV, Balt., 1994-96. Mktg. vol. Balt. Coalition Against Drugs, 1993-95; media vol. D.C. Cmty./Coalition Against Drugs. Recipient Markee awards Nat. Assn. Addictions Comm., Seattle, 1992, award of excellence Internat. Assn. Bus. Communicators, Balt., 1993, Discovery Health Channel Med. Honors, 2004; named to Advt. Hall of Fame, Am. Advt. Fedn., 2003. Mem. Advt. Assn. Balt. (sec. 1987—), Balt. Area Soaring Soc. (bd. dirs. 1991—, pres. 1992, newsletter editor 1993-97). Avocations: sailplanes, soaring, wine collecting, racquetball. Office: Partnership For A Drug-Free Am 405 Lexington Ave Rm 1601 New York NY 10174 Office Phone: 212-922-1560. Office Fax: 212-922-1570.*

**PASIK-DUNCAN, BOZENNA JANINA,** mathematics professor, researcher; b. Radom, Warsaw, Poland, June 30, 1947; d. Janina and Antoni Pasik; m. Tyrone Edward Duncan, May 21, 1983; 1 child, Dominique Duncan. MS, Warsaw U., 1970, PhD, 1978, D, 1986. Asst. prof. Warsaw Sch. Econ., 1970—84; instr. U. Kans., Lawrence, 1984—87, asst. prof., 1987—89, assoc. prof., 1989—93, prof. math., 1993—. Lectr. Warsaw Tech. U., 1973—75. Contbr. scientific papers to profl. jours. Membeer of the bd. of governors IEEE Control Systems Soc., Piscataway, NJ, 1996—2002. Recipient Excellence in Rsch. and Tchg., Ministry of Higher Edn. and Sci., 1975; fellow, IREX, 1982—83; Rsch. grant, NSF, 1987—. Mem.: AAUW, IEEE (v.p. 1999, bd. govs. 1996, medal 2000, Dist. Mem. award 2000, fellow 2001), Internat. Stats. Inst., Soc. Indsl. and Applied Math., Bernoulli Soc., Am. Math. Soc., Polish Math. Soc., Assn. Women in Math. (L. Hay award 2004), Math. Assn. Am. Achievements include research in stochastic adaptive control of continous time systems. Avocations: travel, music, poetry. Home: 1208 Schwarz Rd Lawrence KS 66049 Office: Univ Kans Dept Math Lawrence KS 66045 Office Phone: 785-864-5162. Office Fax: 785-864-5255. Business E-mail: bozenna@math.ku.edu.

**PASINETTI, PIER MARIA,** author; b. Venice, Italy, June 24, 1913; came to U.S., 1946, naturalized, 1952; s. Carlo and Maria (Ciardi) P. Dottore in Lettere, U. Padua, Italy, 1935; PhD in Comparative Lit., Yale U., 1949. Fellow La. State U., 1935-36, U. Calif. at Berkeley, 1936-37; lectr. U. Stockholm, 1942-46; prof. Italian and comparative lit. UCLA, 1949—. Author: L'ira di Dio, 1942, Venetian Red, 1960, The Smile on the Face of the Lion, 1965, From the Academy Bridge, 1970, Suddenly Tomorrow, 1971, Dall' Estrema America, 1975, Il Centro, 1979, Dorsoduro, 1983, Life for Art's Sake: Studies in the Literary Myth of the Romantic Artist, 1985, Melodramma, 1993, Piccole Veneziane Complicate, 1996, Astolfo, 1999; also articles, revs. Recipient Fiction award Nat. Inst. Arts and Letters, 1965, Prix Écureuil Li. Etrangère, 1996. Mem. Authors Guild. Clubs: Elizabethan Yale. Office: 1259 Dorsoduro Venice Italy 30123

**PASK, SCOTT,** set designer; Grad., Yale Sch. Drama. Broadway: Cabaret, 1998, Urinetown (Lucille Lortel nom.), 2001, Amour, 2002, Take Me Out, 2003, Little Shop of Horrors (Touring Broadway award, best prodn. design, 2005), La Cage aux Folles, 2004, Pillowman, (Tony award, best scenic design, 2005), Sweet Charity, 2005, The Wedding Singer, 2006, Fame Becomes Me, 2006, The Lieutenant of Inishmore, 2006; in London: On an Average Day, Tales from Hollywood, Albert Herring, Pillowman; also appeared at Almeida Theatre, Royal Nat. Theatre, Donmar Warehouse, Opera North, Atlantic Theater Co., The Pub. Theatre, Roundabout Theatre, Yale Rep., South Coast Rep., Ctr. Stage, Williamstown, NY Theatre Workshop, Classic Stage Co., Playwrights Horizons, Chgo. Opera Theater, Bklyn. Acad. Music. Recipient Lucille Lortel award, 1999, Henry Hewes award, Am. Theater Wing, 1999, Bessie award, 2001. Office: 4 Times Sq #15 New York NY 10036-6518*

**PASKACH, DAVID M.,** lawyer, food products executive; BS in Acctg., Iowa State U., 1980; JD, U. Ill., 1983. Bar: Iowa 1983, Ill. 1983, Minn. 1989. Atty., Iowa; corp. atty. Schwan Food, Marshall, Minn., 1989—93, sr. atty., 1993—97, gen. counsel, 1997, v.p. adminstrn., exec. v.p., gen. counsel, sec., 1997—2004; pres. Schwan's Venture Group, Marshall, 2005—. Lt. col. USAFR, ret. Office: Schwan Food 115 W College Dr Marshall MN 56258

**PASKIN, MICHAEL A.,** lawyer; b. Phila., Jan. 23, 1970; BA cum laude, Univ. Pa., 1992; JD, Fordham Univ., 1995. Bar: NY 1996. Law clk., Hon. Paul J. Kelly, Jr. US Ct. of Appeals, 10th Cir.; assoc. Cravath Swaine & Moore LLP, NYC, 1996—2003, ptnr., litig., 2003—. Assoc. editor Fordham Law Rev. Office: Cravath Swaine & Moore LLP Worldwide Plz 825 Eighth Ave New York NY 10019-7475 Office Phone: 212-474-1760. Office Fax: 212-474-3700. Business E-Mail: mpaskin@cravath.com.

**PASKINS, JANET LYNN,** psychology professor, educational consultant; d. Melvin L. and Cherryl Nadine Cannon; married, Mar. 21, 1986; children: Derek Ryan Nevins, Deren Ross Nevins. EdB, Ball State U., Muncie, Ind., 1970, MEd, 1972, MA in Counseling Psychology, 1983; postgrad., U. S. Fla., Tampa, 2000—. Pvt. practice psychotherapist, Anderson, Ind., 1983—84, Clearwater, Fla., 1984—98; coord. workplace devel. and placement ctr. coord. PHCC, New Port Richey, Fla., 1995—99; prof. psychology and sociology Pasco Hernando CC, Brooksville, Fla., 1999—. Cons. Internet Sch. Connection, Tampa, Fla., 1998—. Bus. devel. bd., New Port Richey, Fla., 1996—2000. Recipient Excellence in Curriculum and Instruction award, Fla. Assn. CC, 1998, Exemplary Initiatives award, Nat. Coun. Instl. Adminstrs., 1999, Sylva Thompson Leadership award, 1999, Nat. Tech. Prep award, 1999, Workforce Devel. award, Rotary, 2000; Curriculum Devel. grantee, Dept. of Edn., 1996. Mem.: APA (assoc.). Avocations: travel, tennis.

**PASKMAN, ANDREA,** dance specialist; d. Martin Paskman and Jane Sand; m. Anthony Cavoto, Oct. 13, 1973. BS, Temple U., Phila., 1972. Editl. rsch. asst. TV Guide mag., Radnor, Pa., 1972—79; copy editor Panorama mag., Radnor, Pa., 1980—81; co. mgr. Ballet Klov, Phila. 1990—91, assoc. dir. Dancery. Whig of Prussia, Pa., 1984—; assoc. editor Wyeth-Ayerst Labs., Radnor, Pa., 1993—96; quality liaison ptnr. Astra Pharms., Wayne, Pa., 1996—99; promotional regulatory affairs field assoc. dir. AstraZeneca, Wayne, Pa., 1999—2004, compliance and ethics leader, 2004—. (miniseries-broadcast on cbs) George Washington: The Founding of a Nation, (play) The Cherry Orchard, The Three Sisters, director (dance program) From Minuet to Cakewalk; author (presenter): (series of lectures) Hollywood and Historical Dance; (historical dance) guest choreographer for various organizations including Early Music Department of University of Pennsylvania, teacher (special workshops) for institutions including Swarthmore and Bryn Mawr Colleges, director (programs) covering various historical periods for museums, schs. Achievements include appearance on Jeopardy!; appearance on theme float of nationally broadcast We The People parade to celebrate Bicentennial of Constitution (1987). Business E-mail: andreapaskman@astrazeneca.com.

**PASNICU, CORNEL,** mathematician, educator; b. Bucharest, Romania, Sept. 6, 1953; arrived in U.S., 1992; s. Tanasa Pasnicu, Xenia Adina Pasnicu; m. Adina Melania Truta; 1 child, Nastasia Laura. BA, U. Bucharest, 1976, MS, 1977, PhD. Rsch. fellow INCREST (IMAR), Bucharest, Romania, 1980—91; vis. scholar U. Copenhagen, 1991—91; vis. assoc. prof. U. Toronto, Ont., Canada, 1992—92; assoc. prof. U. P.R., San Juan, 1992—97, full prof., 1997—. Mem. operator algebras/operator theory panel NSF, Arlington, Va., 2002. Contbr. articles to profl. jours. Recipient S. Stoilov prize, Romanian Acad., 1988; grantee, NSF, 1994—96, 1996—2000, 2001—, Army Rsch. Office, 2000—. Mem.: Am. Math. Soc. Avocations: reading, music, sports. Home: L12 Calle 15 San Juan PR 00926 Office Phone: 787-764-0000 4679. Business E-Mail: cpasnic@uprac.upr.clu.edu.

**PASQUALETTI, MARTIN J.,** geography educator; b. San Francisco, Feb. 5, 1945; s. Phyllis Laverne (Johnson) P.; m. Jennifer Smith, Sept. 5, 1967 (dec. July 1970); m. Mari Anne Williams, May 27, 1972; 1 child, Erika Britt. BA, U. Calif., Berkeley, 1967; MA, La. State U., 1969; PhD, U. Calif., Riverside, 1977. Instr. Crafton Hills Coll., Yucaipa, Calif., 1973—75; cons. Albert A. Webb Assocs., Riverside, Calif., 1974—77; prof. Ariz. State U., Tempe, 1977—; co-founder OnPoint Sys., Inc. Cons. EcoGroup, Tempe,

1990—93; prin. Energy Planning Cons., Tempe, 1990—96. Editor: Nuclear Energy, 1984, Nuclear Decommissioning, 1990, The Evolving Landscape, 1997; contbr. articles on energy to jours. Pres. Rural/Geneva Neighborhood Assn., Tempe, 1990—92; chmn. Bd. Adjustment, Tempe, 1996—2001; mem. Ariz. Solar Energy Adv. Coun., Phoenix, 2001—04, Ariz. Geographic Names, Phoenix, bd. dirs. Ariz. Solar Ctr., Phoenix, 1998—. With U.S. Army, 1968—74. Rsch. grantee Ariz. State U., 1983, NSF, Dept. Energy, Ariz. Energy Office. Mem. Assn. Am. Geographers (sec., treas. energy splty. group 1979-82, chmn. 1982-84, 96—). Democrat. Presbyterian. Avocations: tennis, photography, travel. Office: ArizState U Dept Geography Tempe AZ 85287-0104 Business E-Mail: pasqualetti@asu.edu.

**PASQUALONI, PAUL,** former college football coach; b. Aug. 8, 1949; BS in Health and Phys. Edn., Pa. State U., 1972; MS, So. Conn. State U. Asst. football coach Cheshire High Sch., So. Conn. U., 1976-80, def. coord.; head football coach/athletic dir. Western Conn. State U., 1981-86; coach linebackers Syracuse (N.Y.) U., 1987-91; head football coach Syracuse U., 1991—2004. Named Winningest 1st Yr. Coach, Syracuse U., 1991.

**PASQUERRELI, SHAWNA,** forensic specialist; b. NH, Oct. 15, 1970; BSc, Ea. Ky. U., 1989. Cert. in forensic sci. Investigations Unit, NH. Trainer Crime Rsch. Unit, NH, 1992—96; forensic scientist NH Investigation Site, 1996—2004, Meriks Sci. Truth, Bedford, NH, 2004—. Lutheran. Achievements include research in making scientific crime investigations more efficient with better computer technology; better organization on scientific databases; DNA and pinpointing crime rampant in certain populations. Office: Meriks Sci Truth 7 Colby Ct Bedford NH 03110-6427

**PASQUIER, JOËL,** music educator; b. Montmorency, France, Sept. 25, 1943; arrived in Can., 1967; s. Jean and Raymonde (Gourdin) P.; m. Anne Vachon, Nov. 28, 1970; 1 child, Ariane. Grad. in piano and chamber music, Conservatoire Nat. Superieur de Musique, Paris, 1962. Prof. Conservatoire de Musique de St. Germain-en-Laye, France, 1964-65; grad. asst. Sch. Music, Ind. U., Bloomington, 1965-67; tchr. piano U. Laval, Quebec, Canada, 1967—2003, dir., 1988-91. Recording artist ATMA Records. Appeared as solo pianist concert halls, radio, TV, with chamber and symphony orchs. in France, U.S., Can., The Netherlands. English schular Ind. U., 1965. Mem. Que. Yacht Club. Personal E-mail: orion_556@hotmail.com.

**PASRICHA, ATUL,** automotive executive; B, U. Delhi; MBA, U. Va. Dir. pension funding Gen. Motors, NY, 1994—95, dir. bus. devel., 1995—96, regional treas. Asia-Pacific ops. Singapore, 1996—98; asst. treas. Delphi Corp., Troy, Mich., 1998—2000, acting gen. dir. fin. electronics and mobile comm. sector, 2000—01, exec. dir. new markets unit, 2001—02, v.p. mergers acquisitions new markets, 2002—. Recipient Deal of Yr., Project Fin. Mag., 1998. Office: Delphi Corp World Headquarters 5725 Delphi Dr Troy MI 48098-2815

**PASS, CHARLOTTE LOUISE,** literature educator, consultant; b. Oneonta, Ala., Sept. 2, 1966; d. James Arnold and Betty Jo Pass. Cert. English Edn. Ala., 1998, ESL Ala., 2005. Acad. tutor, supr. U. Ala. Athletic Dept., Tuscaloosa, 1986—93; English/journalism tchr. Tuscaloosa Acad., 1989—91; grad. tchg. asst. U. Ala., Tuscaloosa, 1988—91, grad. instr., 2002—; English/music appreciation tchr. Hillcrest HS, Tuscaloosa, 1998—2001; home sch. tchr. Victory Christian Sch., Tuscaloosa, 2002—04. Literacy cons. Eastwood Mid. Sch., Ala., 2003—; presenter and cons. in field. Mem.: Am. Assn. Applied Linguistics (assoc.), Am. Ednl. Rsch. Assn. (assoc.), Mid-South Ednl. Ednl. Rsch. Assn. (assoc.), Tchrs. of English to Speakers of Other Languages (assoc.), Internat. Reading Assn. (assoc.), Nat. Reading Conf. (assoc.), Nat. Coun. Tchrs. of English (assoc.), Assn. Tchr. Educators (assoc.), ASCD (assoc.), Ala. Reading Assn. (assoc.), Ala. Coun. Tchrs. of English (assoc.), ASPCA, Amnesty Internat., Peta, Nat. Humane Soc., Phi Delta Kappa (assoc.), Phi Kappa Phi (life). Independent. Episcopal. Avocations: reading, piano, singing. Home: 1022 Fairfax Dr Tuscaloosa AL 35406 Office: Univ Ala PO Box 870232 204 Graves Hall Tuscaloosa AL 35487 Office Phone: 205-758-7567.

**PASSAGE, DAVID,** diplomat; b. Charlotte, N.C., June 16, 1942; s. John T. and Virginia (Beam) P. BA in Internat. Rels., U. Denver, 1964; MS in Internat. Econs., Georgetown U., 1966; student, Nat. War Coll., Ft. McNair, Washington, 1981-82. With U.S. Dept. State, 1966-99; politico-mil. affairs officer U.S. Embassy, London, 1966; pacification program analyst U.S. Mil. Command, Saigon, Vietnam, 1968; with U.S. State Dept. Ops. Ctr., 1970; officer Secretariat Staff, 1971; special asst. to Asst. Sec. State Politico-Mil. Affairs, 1972-74; pol. officer Quito, Ecuador, 1974-76; spl. asst. to Sec. of State Henry Kissinger U.S. State Dept., Washington, 1976; polit. counselor Am. Embassy, Canberra, Australia, 1977-79; dir. Press Office and Assoc.; 1979; from. dep. to acting spokesman U.S. Dept. State, dep. dir. So. African Affairs, 1982-84; dep. chief mission/charge d'affairs U.S. Embassy, 1984-86; dir. Office Regional Affairs Africa Bur., 1986; dir. for Africa, Nat. Security Coun. The White House, Washington, 1989; U.S. amb. to Botswana, 1990-93; polit. adviser to U.S. Spl. Opers. Command MacDill AFB, Fla., 1993-96; dir. Andean affairs Dept. State, Washington, 1996-99; ret., 1999—. Lectr. Nat. War Coll., John F. Kennedy Spl. Warfare Ctr., USAF Spl. Ops. Sch., Armed Forces Staff Coll., others. Contbr. chpt.: Managing Contemporary Conflict, 1996, The U.S. and Colombia, 2000; contbr. articles to profl. jours. Recipient Chuong My Boi Tinh medal (Vietnam), Sec. of State Career chievement Medal, State Dept. Superior Hon. Awd.; Gen. James Doolittle Educator of Yr. Awd., U.S. Air Force Def. Disting. Civilian Svc. medal Dept. Def.; Centennial scholar U. Denver. Avocation: environment and conservation. Home: 2416 Chain Bridge Rd NW Washington DC 20016-3304

**PASSAIC, JOSEPH G.,** lawyer; b. Newark, Aug. 23, 1953; BA, Pa. State Univ., 1975; JD, Widener Univ., 1979. Bar: Pa. 1979, DC 1985. Atty. Office of Gen. Counsel, FDIC, Washington, 1979—82, sr. atty., 1982—83; ptnr., Securities, Tech. Law, Banking practices, mem. mgmt. com. Patton Boggs LLP, Washington. Adj. prof. Georgetown Univ. Sch. Bus.; mem. editl. bd. Banking Law Report. Co-author: Banking Law in the U.S. Office: Patton Boggs LLP 2550 M St NW Washington DC 20037-1350 Office Phone: 202-457-6104. Office Fax: 202-457-6315. Business E-Mail: jpassaic@pattonboggs.com.

**PASSANO, E. MAGRUDER, JR.,** management consultant; b. Balt., Oct. 2, 1942; s. Edward M. and Mildred P. (Nelson) P.; m. Helen C. Marikle, Sept. 4, 1971; children: Catherine, Tammy, Sarah. BS, Johns Hopkins U., 1967, MA, 1969. With Waverly Inc., Balt., 1965-98, salesman, 1970-73, v.p., 1973-75, v.p. adminstrn., sec., 1975-90, vice chmn., sec., 1990-98; pres., CEO One Waverly LLC, Balt., 1998—. Chmn. Passano Found., Balt., 1982—; pres. Am. Lung Assn., Md., 1982-84; mem. exec. com. Vol. Coun. Equal Opportunity, Balt., 1978-2002, chmn., 1995-2002; bd. dirs. Combined Health Appeal Am., 1994-97; pres. (CHA) Combined Health Agys., Md., 1985-87, chmn. exec. com., 1987-95; pres. 12:30 Club Balt., 1981-83; mem. exec. com. Balt. City Life Mus., 1982-93, v.p. 1987-93; trustee emeritus, 1993-98; mem. adv. coun. Johns Hopkins U. Sch. Profl. Studies in Bus. and Edn., 1984—, exec. chair alumni chpt., 1986-89, chair edn. cmty. devel. iniative, 1995—2006; mem. Md. Gov.'s Commn. on High Blood Pressure and Related Cardiovascular Risk Factors, 1986-2002; bd. govs. Md. New Directions, Inc., 1987-94; bd. dirs., mem. exec. com. YMCA Ctrl. Md., 1988-96; treas., bd. dirs., chmn. edn. com. Pride of Balt., 1990—; bd. dirs. Ind. Coll. Fund Md., 1994—; mem. bd. visitors Towson State U., 1994—2006, chmn. 1997-2001, Sch. Medicine U. Md., 1995—; mem. planning com., bd. vis. Md. Bus. Responsive Govt., 1994-2002. With USN, 1963-65. Recipient Prince Hall Bicentennial award Masons, 1975; citations Mayor of Balt., 1976, City of Balt., 1977, Vol. of Yr. award for outstanding svc. to CICHA, 1984-85, Presdl. award for outstanding svc. to Am. Lung Assn. Md., 1985, Outstanding Vol., 1988, Disting. Svc. award Soc. Profl. Journalists, 1987, Outstanding Svc. award Am. Heart Assn., 1988, Outstanding Vol. Svc. award Balt. Assn. Retarded Citizens, 1990, Vol. of Yr./Outstanding Leadership and Dedication award Combined Health Agys., 1991-92, Outstanding Family of the Century,

Am. Lung Assn. Md., 2003, Outstanding Bd. Mem., Ind. Coll. Fund Md., 2004. Mem. Purchasing Mgmt. Assn. Md. (chmn. com. 1968-70), Balt. Jaycees (v.p. 1974-76, internat. senator 1975), Greater Balt. Minority Purchasing Coun. (Svc. award 1978), Soc. Colonial Wars (chpt. gov. 1989-91), Johns Hopkins U. Alumni Assn. (pres. Balt. 1984-86, Univ. Heritage award 1987). Democrat. Episcopalian. Home: 3925 Linkwood Rd Baltimore MD 21210-3001 Office: One Waverly LLC 1122 Kenilworth Dr Ste 115 Towson MD 21204-2142 E-mail: macpassano@verizon.net.

**PASSANO, WILLIAM M., III,** publishing executive; BS, Roanoke Coll.; MS, Columbia U. Bd. mem., past chmn. Mt. Washington Pediatric Hosp., Balt.; with Williams & Wilkins; CEO, bd. mem. SCP Comms., Inc., N.Y.C., 2001—. Office: SCP Comms 134 W 29th St New York NY 10001

**PASSANTINO, BENJAMIN ARTHUR,** marketing executive; b. Bklyn., Feb. 26, 1956; s. Anthony Frank and Ann Marie (Ruggerio) Passantino. Mgr. pub. rels. AT&T, NYC, mgr. mktg. comm. and new techs.; pres. B. Arthur Comm., Morristown, NJ, 1984-89; sr. v.p. bus. devel. IMEDIA Creative Corp. Mktg., Morristown, 1989-94, also dir.; mng. ptnr., CEO, Tribeca Global, Inc., Hackettstown, NJ; dir. media and comm. onProject.com, Morristown, NJ, 2000—01; pres. Avid Records, Inc., NYC, 2002—; COO Avid Listener, Inc., NYC, 2002—. Bd. dir. Dieknowlogist, Inc., N.Y.C., One World Botanicals, Inc., Red Bank, N.J., Lasercomb Am., Inc., N.Y.C., The Perfect Supply Co., Inc., N.Y.C., Imedia, Morristown, Medicines Global. Co-author: One with the Flame, NFL Quarterbacks; contbr. articles to mags. Bd. dir. Am. Cancer Soc., Morristown, Jr. Achievement, Basking Ridge, NJ; mem. Washington Twp. (Morris County) Planning Bd., chairperson econ. devel. com.; trustee Drakestown United Meth. Ch. Mem. IEEE, Internat. Assn. Bus. Communicators, Am. Mktg. Assn., Bus. Profls. of Advt. Assn., Conf. Bd. Office: 375 Mt Prospect Ave Ste 7BE Newark NJ 07104 Office Phone: 201-456-6500. E-mail: bap@avidrecords.com.

**PASSARO, PAUL CHARLES,** real estate company executive; b. Ridgewood, N.J., June 6, 1967; s. Richard Paul and Barbara (Brown) Passaro; m. Kristi-Anne Tolo, June 25, 1994; children: Peter James, Anne Marie, Charles Andrew. BA in History cum laude, Williams Coll., Williamstown, Mass., 1989; MBA, U. N.C., 1993. Mcpl. bond trader and salesman Roosevelt & Cross, Inc., N.Y.C., 1989—91; v.p. The Fraser Co., Hilton Head, SC, 1992—94; CFO Pine Needles and Mid Pines Resorts, Southern Pines, NC, 1994—2003; COO EastWest Ptnrs. Club Mgmt., Chapel Hill, NC, 2003—05. Bd. dirs. small bus. adv. bd. N.C. Citizens for Bus. and Industry, Raleigh, 1999—2002; v.p. The Toppers, N.Y.C., 1991; founder Habitat for Humanity Charity Golf Classic, Chapel Hill, 1992—2004; mem. fin. com. Trinity Sch., Durham and Chapel Hill, 1999—2002; bd. dirs. Leadership N.C., 1999—; mem. audit com. N.C. Rep. Party, Raleigh, 1999—2003, chmn., 2003—03; alt. del. 2004 Rep. Nat. Conv.; elder Christ Cmty. Ch., Chapel Hill, 1994—. Mem.: Christmas Fore Moore (treas. 1997—2003, Charity Golf Tourney), Theodore Roosevelt Assn. Republican. Avocations: bible study, golf, reading history, bird hunting. E-mail: pcpassaro@yahoo.com.

**PASSCHIER, SANDRA,** geologist, educator; m. Wobbe Frans Koning. BSc, MSc, U. Amsterdam, 1994; PhD, Ohio State U., Columbus, 2000. Rsch. geologist TNO-Netherlands Geol. Survey, Utrecht, 2001—05; asst. prof. Montclair State U., NJ, 2005—. Sci. team mem. Cape Roberts project NSF Office of Polar Programs, Washington, 1997—98; sci. team mem. leg 188 Ocean Drilling Program, College Station, Tex., 2000; steering com. mem. Sci. Com. Antarctic Rsch.-Antarctic Climate Evolution, 2005—. Author: Orbitally Induced Oscillations in the East Antarctic Ice Sheet: Direct Evidence from the Cape Roberts Drilling Project; contbr. articles to profl. jours. Recipient Antarctic Svc. medal, NSF, 2000. Mem.: Soc. Sedimentary Geology, Internat. Assn. Sedimentologists, Geol. Soc. Am. Office: Montclair State Univ 1 Normal Ave Montclair NJ 07043 Office Phone: 973-655-3185.

**PASSEY, GEORGE EDWARD,** psychologist, educator; b. Stratford, Conn., Sept. 28, 1920; s. Henry Richard and Elizabeth (Angus) P.; m. Algie Aldridge Ashe, Nov. 18, 1950; children: Richard Ashe, Elizabeth Aldridge, Mary Louise. BS, Springfield Coll., 1942; MA, Clark U., 1947; PhD, Tulane U., 1950. Asst. prof. U. Ala., Tuscaloosa, 1952-55, assoc. prof., 1955-56, 57-59, prof., 1959-63, prof. psychology, chmn. div. social and behavioral scis. Birmingham, 1967-73, prof. engring., 1969-84, Disting. Service prof. psychology, 1984-85, Disting Service prof. emeritus, 1985—; dean U. Ala. (Sch. Social and Behavioral Scis.), 1973-84. Research scientist Lockheed Ga. Co., Marietta, Ga., 1956-57, 63-65, cons., 1965-67; prof. Ga. Inst. Tech., 1965-67 Served with USNR, 1942-46, PTO; with USAF, 1951-52. Fellow Am. Psychol. Assn.; mem. So. Soc. for Philosophy and Psychology, Southeastern Psychol. Assn., Ala. Psychol. Assn., Pine Harbor Golf and Racquet Club, Sigma Xi. Home: 7341 Skyline Dr Pell City AL 35128-6936 E-mail: gpassey@centurytel.net. *Whatever success I have enjoyed ought to be attributed to the attempt I have made to carry out the admonitions of my parents to make choices only after having appraised the alternatives in terms of their consequences, to weigh ethical considerations above all others, never to demand of others what one is unwilling to give of himself, and to work untiringly for those causes to which one is committed.*

**PASSLOF, PAT,** artist, educator; b. Brunswick, Ga. m. Milton Resnick. Student Queen's Coll., 1946—48; student, Black Mountain Coll., 1948, Willem de Kooning, 1948—50; BFA, Cranbrook Coll., 1951. Prof. art Coll. of Staten Island, CUNY, 1972—. One woman shows at Elizabeth Harris Gallery, 1993, 96, 98, 2000, 02, 05. Fellow John Simon Guggenheim Meml Found., 1999-2000; recipient award of Mui for painting, Am. Acad. of Arts and Letters, 2000, Purchase award Hassam, Speicher, Betts and Symons Fund of the Am. Acad., 2000, award for achievement in the arts Coun. on Arts and Humanities for S.I., 2001, Edwin P. Palmer award, Nat. Acad. at 181st Ann. Invitational Exhbn., 2006. Address: c/o Elizabeth Harris Gallery 529 W 20th St 6E New York NY 10011

**PASSON, RICHARD HENRY,** retired academic administrator, language educator; b. Hazleton, Pa., Aug. 18, 1939; s. Henry Richard and Grace Miriam (Bernstein) P.; m. Margaret Rose Ferdinand, Aug. 14, 1965; children— Michael, Rebecca, Christopher. BA (Bishop Hafey scholar), King's Coll., Pa., 1961; MA, U. Notre Dame, 1963, PhD (NDEA fellow), 1965. From instr. to prof. English U. Scranton, 1964-73, chmn. English dept., 1970-73, fgn. student adviser, 1965-67; dean Coll. Arts and Scis., Creighton U., Omaha, 1973-77; acad. v.p. St. Joseph's U., Phila., 1977-84; provost U. Scranton, Pa., 1984-2000, prof. English Pa., 2000—02, Pa., 2004—; interim acad. v.p. St. Joseph's U., Phila., 2002—04. Contbr. articles profl. jours. Recipient grant Nat. Assn. Fgn. Students, 1966 Mem. MLA, Am. Assn. Higher Edn., Am. Assn. Acad. Deans, Nat. Coun. Tchrs. English. Democrat. Roman Catholic. Office: U Scranton 402 Brennan Hall Scranton PA 18510 Office Phone: 570-941-4327. Business E-Mail: passonr1@scranton.edu.

**PASSTY, JEANETTE NYDA,** literature and language professor, writer; b. L.A., Jan. 19, 1947; d. Walter Isaac and Mollie Sarah Nyda; m. Gregory Bohdan Passty, June 18, 1976; 1 child, Benjamin. AA, L.A. Valley Coll., 1966; BA, UCLA, 1968; MA, U. So. Calif., 1974, PhD, 1982. Cert. c.c. instr. Calif. Tchg. asst., lectr., assoc. dir. freshman English program U. So. Calif., 1971—78; lectr. English dept. U. Tex., Austin, 1983—85; vis. asst. prof., adj. assoc. prof. Tex. Luth. U., Seguin, 1983, 1985—87; from instr. to asst. prof. St. Philip's Coll., San Antonio, Calif., 1988—92, assoc. prof., 1992—. Lectr. UCLA, U. Tex. Austin, Western Mich. U., U. Louisville, Salisbury State U., Morehead State U., Tex. Tech. U., U. Wales, Bangor; humanities book reviewer CHOICE (ALA Jour.), 1985—86; manuscript reviewer Fairleigh Dickinson U. Press, 1991—; editl. cons. CONNECTIONS: Online Distance Learning Faculty Forum, 2002—. Author: Eros and Androgyny: The Legacy of Rose Macaulay, 1988, The Lion Tells Her Story: A Biography of the Honorable N.P. Brooks Hinton, 1998, Bringing Denis Home: The Hero from Hope, Kansas, 2001; annotator: Alice Crawford's Paradise Pursued, 1995; contbr. articles to encyclopedia and profl. jours.; guest Sta. KSPL Radio in Touch With, 1989; appearance Sta. KENS-TV, 1992; Channel 12 Morehead,

KY, 1998; CNN, 1995, Roadside (entr'acte with G.S. Bailey), 2000. Mem. Nat. Abortion Rights Action League, Tex. Abortion Rights Action League, Greenpeace, Environ. Def. Fund, The Nature Conservancy, NOW, Sierra Club, Handgun Control Inc., Orgn. Internat. Conf. on the Holocaust, San Antonio, 2000. Recipient Elizabeth K. Pleasants Tchg. award, U. So. Calif., 1974, letters of appreciation, Lord Bonham-Carter, 1987, HRH Princess Margaret, 1989—90, Oustanding Acad. Book award, ALA, 1989, Women Honoring Women award, Am. Assn. Women in C.C.s, 1997, Katherine Anne Porter Lit. prize, 1999, NISOD Internat. Conf. on Tchg. and Leadership Excellence Award, 2003, St. Philip's Coll. Tchg. Excellence award, 2003—04; Vierling Kersey scholar, L.A. Valley Coll., 1964—66, NEH grantee, Tex. Luth. U., 1986. Mem. AAUW, MLA, Nat. Coun. Tchrs. English, South Ctrl. Soc. 18th Century Studies, Victorians Inst., Virginia Woolf Soc. Avocations: Tae Kwon Do, travel. Office: St Phillips College Bookstore Tbc 951 County Road 769 Devine TX 78016-4422 Office Phone: 210-531-3373. Business E-mail: jpassty@accd.edu.

**PASSWATER, BARBARA GAYHART,** real estate broker; b. Phila., July 10, 1945; d. Clarence Leonard and Margaret Jamison; m. Richard Albert Passwater, June 2, 1964; children: Richard Alan, Michael Eric. AA, Goldey-Beacom Coll., 1963; BA, Salisbury State U., 1981. Notary pub., Md. Sec. DuPont, Wilmington, Del., 1963-65, Nuclear-Chgo., Silver Spring, Md., 1965-67; office mgr. Montgomery County Sch. System, Wheaton, Md., 1977-79; adminstrv. asst. Solgar Nutritional Rsch. Ctr., Berlin, Md., 1979-94, asst. to v.p. R&D, 1995—2001; assoc. broker Prudential-Groff Realty, Berlin, Md., 1983-87, ReMax, Inc., Berlin, Md., 1987-88; broker, mgr., developers rep. River Run Sales Ctr., Berlin, Md., 1988-96; broker Solgar Realty LLC, Berlin, Md., 1997—98, CAMBR Realty LLC, Berlin, 1998—. Treas. Ocean Pines (Md.) Vol. Fire Dept. Aux., 1981—84, emergency med. tech., 1983—95, life mem., 1996—; sec. Ocean Pines Fire Dept., 1990—95; mem. Citizens Rev. Bd., Snow Hill, Md., 1984—; state bd. del. Child Protection Sys.; bd. dirs. Worcester Gold, 2002—; mem. Worcester County Panel on Child Abuse and Neglect, 2002—; Worcester County organizer Rainbows, 2003—; mem. com. Worcester County YMCA, 2005; Sunday sch. tchr. Cmty. Ch. of Ocean Pines, 1999—2005, co-chair nuture and edn. com., 2001—05. Recipient Woman of the Yr., Worcester County Commn. for Women, 2006. Mem. Coastal Assn. of Realtors of Md., Inc., Worchester County Women's Commn. (Woman Yr., 2006), Beta Sigma Phi, Phi Kappa Phi. Avocations: photography, golf. Office: CAMBR Realty LLC 11017 Manklin Meadows Ln Berlin MD 21811-9340 Office Phone: 410-208-9006. Business E-mail: cambr@dmv.com.

**PASSWATER, RICHARD ALBERT,** biochemist, author; b. Wilmington, Del., Oct. 13, 1937; s. Stanley Leroy and Mabel Rosetta (King) P.; m. Barbara Sarah Gayhart, June 2, 1964; children: Richard Alan, Michael Eric. BS, U. Del., 1959; PhD, Bernadean U., 1976. Cert. firefighter. Supr. instrumental analysis lab. Allied Chem. Corp., Marcus Hook, Pa., 1959-64; tech. svcs. rep. F&M Sci. Corp., Avondale, Pa., 1965; dir. applications lab. Am. Instrument Co., Silver Spring, Md., 1965-77; dir. Am. Gen. Enterprises, Minn.; former daily broadcaster Sta. WMCA, N.Y.C., 1980-88, Sta. WRNG, Atlanta, 1982-85; rsch. dir. Solgar Nutritional Rsch. Ctr., Berlin, Md., 1978—. Corp. v.p. Solgar Co., Inc.; mem. health. edn., rsch. coun. adv. bd. ICCC, NGO, UN, 2003—; chmn. Worcester County Emergency Planning Com., 1995-96; bd. dirs. Worcester Meml. Hosp., Atlantic Gen. Hosp., River Run Assn.; pres. 1989-92, Subaqueous Exploration and Archeology Inc.; apptd. Md. State One Md. Com. and the Eastern Shore Econ. Task Force, Md. Gov. Glendenning, 1999, 2000. Author: Guide to Fluorescence Literature, vol. 1, 1967, vol. 2, 1970, vol. 3, 1974, Supernutrition, 1975, Supernutrition for Health Hearts, 1977, Super Calorie, Carbohydrate Counter, 1978, Cancer and Its Nutritional Therapies, 1978, 83, 93, The Easy No-Flab Diet, 1979, Selenium as Food and Medicine, 1980, The Slendernow Diet, 1982, (with Dr. E. Cranton), Trace Elements, Hair Analysis and Nutrition, 1983, The New Supernutrition, 1991, The Longevity Factor, 1993, Cancer Prevention and Nutritional Therapy, 1993, (with Ben Friedrich and Hans Kugler) Heart Health, 1994, Pycnogenol: The Super Protector Nutrient, 1994, Lipoic Acid: The Metabolic Antioxidant, 1995, numerous others; contbg. author: Fire Protection Guide to Hazardous Materials, 1991; editor Fluorescence News, 1966-77, Jour. Applied Health Scis., 1982-83; mem. editl. bd. Nutritional Perspectives, 1978-96, The Body Forum, 1979-80, Jour. Holistic Medicine, 1981-88, VIM Newsletter, 1979—99; contbg. Firehouse Mag., 1980-84, Jour. Applied Nutritrion; contbr. over 400 health articles to profl. jours.; co-editor booklet series Your Good Health; sci. adv. and columnist Whole Foods mag.; patentee in field. Bd. dirs. Sci. Documentation Ctr., Dunfermline, Eng.; Am. Found. Firefighter Health and Safety; chief Ocean Pines Vol. Fire Dept., 1984-93; active Emergency Med. Tech.; adviser Nat. Inst. Nutrition Edn.; past adv. bd. Stephen Decatur High Sch., Worcester County Dept. Edn. Cubmaster, 1975-79. Named Citizen of Yr. Ocean Pines, Md., 1987; recipient 5th Ann. Achievement award, 1989, VFW Cert. of Commendation, 1988, Industry award Nat. Inst. Nutritional Edn., 1991, Pres.'s award Nat. Nutritional Foods Assn., 1999, James Lind Scientific Achievement award, 2004, James Peter Zarger Free Press award, 2004; named to Delmarva Fireman's Hall of Fame, 1993. Fellow Internat. Acad. Preventive Medicine, Am. Inst. Chemists; mem. ASTM, AAAS, Am. Chem. Soc., Gerontology Soc., Am. Geriatric Soc., Am. Aging Assn. Internat. Found. Preventive Medicine (v.p.), Internat. Union Pure and Applied Chemistry, Royal Soc. Chemistry (London), Internat. Acad. Holistic Health and Medicine, Capital Chem. Soc., Nutrition Today Soc., Am. Acad. Applid Health Sci. (pres., bd. dirs.), Internat. Found. Preventive Medicine (v.p., dir.), Inst. Nutritional Rsch., N.Y. Acad. Scis., Nat. Fire Protection Assn. (cert. firefighter level III, com. on properties of hazardous chemicals), Pi Kappa Alpha. Office: 11017 Manklin Meadows Ln Berlin MD 21811-9340 E-mail: solgar@dmv.com.

**PASSY, CHARLES,** writer; b. N.Y.C., Jan. 9, 1964; s. Victor and Beverly (Green) P.; m. Leslie M. Olsen, Dec. 15, 1989; two children: Jacob E., Emma F. BA, Columbia U., 1985. Assoc. Jay K. Hoffman and Assocs., N.Y.C., 1983-87; sr. editor, mng. editor Ovation Mag., N.Y.C., 1988-89; editor Classical Mag., N.Y.C., 1989-91; editor-in-chief Musical Am. Pub., N.Y.C., 1991-92; staff writer The Palm Beach Post, West Palm Beach, Fla., 1992—. Announcer, prod. WNYC FM, N.Y., 1984-85; entertainment stringer N.Y. Newsday, 1987-92. Author (with others): New Voices: Selected University and College Prize Winning Poems, 1989, The New Grove Dictionary of Jazz, 1988, The New Grove Dictionary of American Music, 1986, The New Grove Dictionary of Music and Musicians, 2d edit., 2001; editor: The Letters of Virgil Thomson, 1988; contbr. numerous articles to publs. in field, columns in newspapers. Recipient Poetry award Acad. Am. Poets Columbia U., 1985, Criticism awards Soc. Profl. Journalists, 1995, 97, 99, 2001, 03, 05, Fla. Press Club, 1993, 2004, Fla. Soc. Newspaper Editors, 1993, 2001, Cox Newspapers, 2001, Am. Assn. Sunday and Feature Editors, 2002, 05, award Mo. Lifestyle Journalism, 2005; fellow Knight Ctr. for Specialized Journalism, 1993. Home: 180 Bent Tree Dr Palm Beach Gardens FL 33418-3597 Office: Palm Beach Newspapers Inc 2751 S Dixie Hwy West Palm Beach FL 33405-1298 Office Phone: 561-820-4589. Personal E-mail: chazpbg@aol.com. Business E-mail: charles_passy@pbpost.com.

**PASTAN, IRA HARRY,** medical researcher; b. Winthrop, Mass., June 1, 1931; s. Jacob and Miriam (Ceder) P.; m. Linda Olenik, June 14, 1953; children— Stephen, Peter, Rachel BS, Tufts U., 1953, MD, 1957. Med. house officer Yale U. New Haven Hosp., 1957-59; clin. assoc. Nat. Inst. Arthritis and Metabolic Disease, NIH, Bethesda, Md., 1959-61, sr. investigator sect. on endocrine biochemistry, clin. endocrinology br., 1963-69; postdoctoral fellow Lab. of Cellular Physiology Nat Heart and Lung Inst. NIH, Bethesda, Md., 1961-62; head molecular biology sect. endocrinology br. Nat. Cancer Inst., NIH, Bethesda, Md., 1969-70, chief lab. molecular biology, 1970—. Author: An Atlas of Immunofluorescence, 1985; author: Endocytosis, 1985; contbr. articles to profl. jours. Recipient Van Meter prize Am. Thyroid Assn. 1971, Superior Service award Dept. HEW and NIH, 1973, Meritorious Service medal USPHS, NIH, Nat. Cancer Inst., 1983, Disting. Service medal, 1985 Mem. AAAS, Am. Soc. Clin. Investigation, Am. Soc. Biol. Chemists, Am. Soc. for Microbiology, Am. Soc. for Cell Biology, Peripatetic Club, Nat. Acad. Scis., Clin. Immunology Soc., Am. Assn. Physicians, Am. Acad. Arts

and Scis., Molecular Medicine Soc., Alpha Omega Alpha. Office: Ctr Cancer Rsch Lab Molecular Biology 37 Convent Dr Bldg 37 Rm 5106 Bethesda MD 20892 Office Phone: 301-496-4797. Office Fax: 301-402-1344. E-mail: pastani@mail.nih.gov.*

**PASTAN, LINDA OLENIK,** poet; b. NYC, May 27, 1932; d. Jacob L. and Bess (Schwartz) Olenik; m. Ira Pastan, 1953; children: Stephen, Peter, Rachel. BA, Radcliffe Coll., 1954; MLS, Simmons Coll., 1955; MA, Brandeis U., 1957. Author: (poetry) A Perfect Circle of Sun, 1971, On the Way to the Zoo, 1975, Aspects of Eve, 1975, The Five Stages of Grief, 1978 (Alice Fay di Castagnola award Poetry Soc. Am. 1978), Setting the Table, 1980, Waiting for My Life, 1981, PM/AM: New and Selected Poems, 1982 (Am. Book award nomination 1982), A Fraction of Darkness: Poems, 1985, The Imperfect Paradise, 1988, Heroes in Disguise, 1991, An Early Afterlife, 1995, Carnival Evening: New and Selected Poems, 1968-98 (nat. Book award nomination 1998), The Last Uncle, 2002, Queen of a Rainy Country, 2006. Recipient Dylan Thomas Poetry award Mademoiselle, 1958, Virginia Faulkner award Prarie Schooner, 1992, Charity Randall citation Internat. Poetry Forum, 1996, Ruth Lilly Poetry prize, 2003; NEA fellow; grantee Md. Arts Coun.; poet laureate of Md., 1991-95. Jewish. Office: 11710 Beall Mountain Rd Potomac MD 20854-1105 Personal E-mail: lpastan@att.net.

**PASTER, HOWARD G.,** public relations and public affairs company executive; b. NYC, Dec. 23, 1944; BA with honors, Alfred U., 1966; MS in Journalism, Columbia U., 1967. Legis. dir. UAW, 1977-80; exec. v.p. Timmons & Co., 1980-92; asst. to pres. and dir. Office Legis. Affairs White House, Washington, 1993; chmn., CEO Hill and Knowlton, Inc., N.Y.C., 1994—2002; exec. v.p. WPP Group, N.Y.C., 2002—. Office: WPP Group 125 Park Ave 4th Fl New York NY 10017-5529

**PASTERNACK, DAVID,** chef; Ptnr., exec. chef Esca, N.Y.C. Office: Esca 402 W 43d St New York NY 10036-6322

**PASTERNACK, ROBERT FRANCIS,** chemistry professor; b. NYC, Sept. 20, 1936; 2 children. BA, Cornell U., 1957, PhD in Chemistry, 1962. Research assoc. in chemistry U. Ill., Champaign, 1962-63; from asst. to prof. chemistry Ithaca Coll., NY, 1963-66, Charles A. Dana Endowed prof. chemistry NY, 1976-82; Edmund Allen prof. chemistry Swarthmore Coll., Pa., 1984—. Invited speaker seminars, colls., univs., nat., internat. meetings, confs. including Bioinorganic Chem., Italy, Portugal, Gordon Rsch. Confs., Spanish Royal Soc. Chem., many others; lectr. series Nankai U., China, U. Messina, Italy; mem. adv. com. Rsch. Corp.; mem. sci. & art com. Franklin Inst.; co-organizer, chmn. workshop on rsch. at undergrad. instn. NSF, mem. undergrad. curriculm chem.; vis. prof., vis. rschr. U Messina, U. Paris, Nakai, Rome, King's Coll., London, Fritz Haber Inst., Berlin, Doshisha U., Kyoto; co-developer A Unified Lab. Program; initiator, chmn. C.P. Snow Lectr. Series. Author, co-author more than 100 sci. publs. Mem. com. on sci. and the arts Franklin Inst., 1992-98. Grantee NSF, 1965-66, 69-72, 77-78, 83-84, 86-94, 95-03, Petroleum Rsch. Fund, 1967-74, 86-88, NIH, 1971-82, 85-89, 2001-05, Monsanto Corp., 1986-92, Rsch. Corp., 1974-75, 78-79, 84-85, Danforth Assocs., 1978-84, Camille and Henry Dreyfus Found., 1981, 95, NATO, 1979, 88-89, 95-96; recipient Camille and Henry Dreyfus Tchg./Scholar award, 1987-89, NSF Manpower Improvement award, King's Coll., U. London, 1977-78, Commemorative medal for sci. contbns. U. Catania, 1994, Excellence in Tchg. award, Am. Chem. Soc., Phila. Section, 2005, Conspicuous Sci. Achievement Through Rsch. award, Am. Chem. Soc., 2005; NSF sci. faculty fellow U. Rome, 1968-70. Mem. AAAS, Am. Inst. Chemists (Hon. Scroll award 1998), Am. Chem. Soc. (award for rsch. at an undergrad. instn. 2001, Excellence award 2005, award conspicuous sci. achievement through rsch. 2005), NY Acad. Sci., Sigma Xi. Office: Swarthmore Coll Dept Chemistry Swarthmore PA 19081 Office Phone: 610-328-8559. Business E-mail: rpaster1@swarthmore.edu.

**PASTERNACK, ROBERT HARRY,** former federal agency administrator; b. Bklyn., Nov. 30, 1949; s. William and Lillian Ruth (Levine) P.; m. Jeanelle Livingston, Apr. 10, 1980; children: Shayla, Rachel. BA, U. South Fla., 1970; MA, N.Mex. Highlands U., 1972; PhD, U. N.Mex., 1980. Dir. Eddy County Drug Abuse Program, Carlsbad, N.Mex., 1972-73; adminstrv. intern U.S. Office Edn., Washington, 1975-76; exec. dir. Villa Santa maria, Cedar Crest, N.Mex., 1976-78; clin. dir. Ranchos Treatment Ctr., Taos, N.Mex., 1978-79; sch. psychologist N.Mex. Boys Sch., Springer, 1980—, supt., 1991; pres. Ensenar Health svcs., Inc., Taos, 1980—; CEO Casa de Corazon, Taos, N.Mex., 1994-98; state dir. spl. edn. N.Mex. State Dept. Edn., Santa Fe, 1998—2001; asst. sec. spl. edn. & rehab. services US Dept. Edn., Washington, 2001—03; v.p. edn. services Maximus Inc., 2004—. Instr. N.Mex. Highlands U., Las Vegas, 1980—, U. N.Mex., Albuquerque, 1980—; cons. N.Mex. Youth Authority, Santa Fe, 1988—, N.Mex. Detox Disabilities Bur., Santa Fe, 1986—, various sch. dists.; state dir. spl. edn., N.Mex., 1998—. Author: Growing Up: The First Five Years, 1986; contbr. articles to profl. publs. Pres., bd. dirs. Children's Lobby, N.Mex., 1978, N.Mex. Spl. Olympics, 1986-88, Child-Rite, Inc., Taos, 1990; mem. Gov.'s Mental Health Task Force, Albuquerque, 1988—. mem: N.Mex. Coun. on Crime and Delinquency, Nat. Alliance Mentally Ill, Correctional Edn. Assn., Nat. Assn. Sch. Psychologists. Avocations: tennis, racquetball, skiing, cooking. Office: Maximus Inc 11419 Sunset Hills Rd Reston VA 20190

**PASTERNACK, STEFAN ALAN,** psychiatrist, psychoanalyst; b. Jersey City, Nov. 5, 1939; BA, Cornell U., 1961; MD, Georgetown U., 1965. Diplomate in psychiatry Am. Bd. Neurology and Psychiatry; lic. physician, D.C., Md. Resident in psychiatry U. Cin. Gen. Hosp., 1966-69; psychiat. cons. North Cmty. Mental Health Ctr., Washington, 1971-97; asst. prof. psychiatry Georgetown U. Sch. Medicine, Washington, 1971-79, assoc. clin. prof. psychiatry, 1979-86, clin. prof. psychiatry, 1986—, co-dir. advanced studies prog. in psychiatry/psychoanalysis, 1995—. Pvt. practice psychiatry and psychoanalysis, Washington, 1978—. Editor: Violence and Victims, 1975; contbr. articles to profl. jours. Bd. dirs. Nat. Capital Med. Found., Washington, 1973-76, Forum for Psychoanalytic Study of Film, Washington, 1989—. Lt. comdr. USN, 1969-71. Fellow: Am. Psychiat. Assn. (life); mem.: Washington Psychiat. Soc. (mem. coun. 1987—99), Am. Psychoanalytic Assn., Cosmos Club. Avocations: motorboating and yachting, piano, writing. Home: 6924 Balboa Island Ct Delray Beach FL 33446-5641 Office: 4800 N Federal Hwy Ste E-102 Boca Raton FL 33431 Office Phone: 561-706-9584. Personal E-mail: sp39@aol.com.

**PASTERNAK, N. ALFRED,** lawyer, accountant; b. Washington, Mar. 16, 1936; s. Alfred and Minna (Wolf) P. AB, Colgate U., 1957; MBA, Columbia U., 1959; JD, George Washington U., 1965. Bar: Md. 1965, U.S. Dist. Ct. D.C. 1965, U.S. Tax Ct. 1965, U.S. Supreme Ct. 1968; CPA, D.C., Md. Acct. GAO, Washington, 1959-60, Touche, Ross & Co., Washington, 1960-61; atty. SEC, Washington, 1965-66; ptnr. Pasternak, Kaufmann & Glosser, Washington and Bethesda, Md., 1966-78, King & Nordlinger, Washington and Bethesda, 1979-80, Goldberg, Thompson, Pasternak & Sickles, Bethesda, 1981-90, Pasternak & Fidis, P.C., Bethesda, 1991—. Fellow Am. Coll. Trust and Estate Counsel; mem. ABA (real property, probate and trust law and taxation sects.), Nat. Assn. Estate Planning Couns. (accredidated estate planner), Md. Bar Assn. (chmn. sect. taxation 1985-86, Tax Excellence award 2004). Office: 7735 Old Georgetown Rd Ste 1100 Bethesda MD 20814-6183 Office Phone: 301-656-8850. Fax: 301-656-3053. E-mail: napasternak@pasternakfidis.com.

**PASTIN, MARK JOSEPH,** health science association administrator, educator; b. Ellwood City, Pa., July 6, 1949; s. Joseph and Patricia Jean (Camenite) Pastin; m. Joanne Marie Reagle, May 30, 1970 (div. Mar. 1982); m. Carrie Patricia Class, Dec. 22, 1984 (div. June 1990); m. Christina M. Brecto, June 15, 1991. BA summa cum laude, U. Pitts., 1970; MA, Harvard U., 1972, PhD, 1973. Asst. prof. Ind. U., Bloomington, 1973-78, assoc. prof., 1978-80; founder, pres. Compliance Resource Group, Inc., 1983—; chmn., CEO, pres. Coun. Ethical Orgns., Alexandria, Va., 1986—; prof. mgmt., dir. Ariz. State U., Tempe, 1988-92, prof. emeritus, 1996—; chair Health Ethics

Trust, 1995—. Mem. adv. bd. Aberdeen Holdings, San Diego, 1988-90; dir. Learned Nicholson, Ltd., 1990-91; bd. Japan Am. Soc. Phoenix, Found. for Ethical Orgns.; cons. GTE, Interim Healthcare, 1997-2000, U.S. Dept. Edn., 2002, Tex. Instruments, MicroAge Computers, Med-Tronic, Blood Sys., Inc., Opus Corp., GTE, NyNex, Am. Express Bank, Kaiko Bussan Co., Japan, Arex Co., Japan, Century Audit Co., U.S. Dept. Edn., Japan, Scottsdale Meml. Hosp., Consanti Found., Lincoln Electric Co., Tenet Healthcare, The Williams Co.; vis. faculty Harvard U., 1980; invited presenter Australian Inst. Mgmt., Nippon Tel. & Tel., Hong Kong Commn. Against Corruption, 1984, Young Pres.'s Orgn. Internat. U., 1990, Nat. Assn. Indsl. & Office Parks, 1990, ABA, 1991, Govt. of Brazil, 1991. Author: Hard Problems of Management, 1986 (Book of Yr. Armed Forces Mil. Comtrs. 1986, Japanese edit. 1994), Power by Association, 1991, The Hotline Handbook, 1996, Planning Forum, 1992; editor: Public-Private Sector Ethics, 1979; mem. editl. bd. Report on Medicare Compliance; pub. Pastin Report on Best Compliance Practices, 1998—, Guerin Lect. on Philanthropy, 1996. Founding bd. mem. Tempe Leadership, 1985-89; bd. mem. Ctr. for Behavioral Health, Phoenix, 1986-89, Tempe YMCA, 1986—, Valley Leadership Alumni Assn., 1989-92; mem. Clean Air Com., Phoenix, 1987-90. Nat. Sci. Found. fellow, Cambridge, Mass., 1971-73; Nat. Endowment for the Humanities fellow, 1975; Exxon Edn. Found. grant, 1982-83. Mem.: Found. Ethical Orgns. (chmn. 1988, pres.), Am. Soc. Assn. Execs. (invited presenter 1987—97), Mt. Vernon Country Club, Harvard Club D.C., Phi Beta Kappa, Golden Key. Avocations: golf, running. Office: 214 S Payne St Alexandria VA 22314-3530 Home: 7205 Regent Dr Alexandria VA 22307-2044 Office Phone: 703-683-7916. Personal E-mail: councile@aol.com.

**PASTOOR, ROBERTUS ANTONIUS,** academic administrator; b. Maastricht, The Netherlands, Jan. 6, 1953; arrived in U.S., 1961; s. Johannes Pastoor and Maria Van der Pas; m. Ann Marie Lynch, June 8, 1985; children: Thomas Lynch-Pastoor, Tully Lynch-Pastoor, Marijka Lynch-Pastoor. BS in History and Edn., Mount St. Mary's Coll., Emmitsburg, Md., 1976; MEd in Counseling, McDaniel Coll., Westminster, Md., 1979; EdD in Ednl. Leadership, U. Mont., Missoula, 2003. Asst. dean of students Mount St. Mary's Coll., Emmitsburg, Md., 1979—81, assoc. dean of students, 1981—83, dean of students, 1983—87, v.p. student affairs, 1987—95; v.p. student life Carroll Coll., Helena, Mont., 1985—2002; v.p. student affairs U. San Diego, 2002—05; pres. St. John's Cath. Prep, Frederick, Md., 2005—. Chair, bd. dirs. St Johns Lit Inst. at Prospect Hall, Frederick, Md., 1977—79; pres., bd. dirs. ASACCU, 1998—2003. Vol. Project Concern, Inc., Vienna, Va., 1968—71. Mem.: Assn. Student Affairs at Cath. Colls., ACPA, NASPA. Democrat. Roman Catholic. Avocations: tennis, music, reading. Office: St Johns Cath Prep 889 Butterfly Ln Frederick MD 21703 Home: 7022 Summerfield Dr Frederick MD 21702 Office Phone: 301-662-4210.

**PASTOR, EDWARD,** congressman; b. Claypool, Ariz., June 28, 1943; m. Verma Mendez; children: Yvonne, Laura. BA in chemistry, Ariz. State U., 1966, JD, 1974. Former chem. teacher N. High Sch.; former dep. dir. Guadalupe Org., Inc.; mem. Maricopa County Bd. Suprs., Phoenix, 1976-91, U.S. Congress from 4th Ariz. dist. (formerly 2nd), Washington, 1991—; mem. appropriations com., steering & policy com. Mem. Arts Caucus, Biotechnology Caucus, Border Caucus, Congressional Caucus on Women's Issues, Congressional Children's Caucus. Democrat. Office: US Ho Reps 2465 Rayburn Ho Office Bldg Washington DC 20515-0304

**PASTOR, STEPHEN DANIEL,** chemistry professor, researcher, consultant; b. New Brunswick, NJ, Feb. 15, 1947; s. Stephen and Irene (Bors) P.; m. Joan Ordemann, Apr. 3, 1971 (div. 1979); 1 child, Melanie; m. Joanne Behrens, July 13, 1985 (div. 1990). BA in Chemistry, Rutgers U., 1969, MS in Chemistry, 1978, PhD in Chemistry, 1983. Chemist Nat. Starch and Chem. Corp., Bridgewater, NJ, 1972—79; rsch. group leader CIBA-Geigy Corp., Ardsley, NY, 1979—84, rsch. mgr., 1985—87; group leader Ctrl. Rsch. Labs. CIBA-Geigy Ag, Basel, Switzerland, 1987—89, rsch. fellow Ardsley, 1989—90, rsch. mgr., 1990—97, sr. rsch. fellow, 1997—2003; cons. Mayhill, N.Mex., 2003—. Asst. adj. prof. Pace U., Pleasantville, NY, 1984—, assoc. adj. prof., 1989-93, adj. prof., 1994—. Contbr. articles to profl. jours. 1st lt. U.S. Army, 1969—71, Vietnam. Sr. Rsch. Fellow, Ciba Specialty Chemicals Corp., 1998—2003. Mem.: Am. Chem. Soc. (Westchester sect. Disting. Scientist award 1977). Achievements include research on organophosphorous and organosulfur chemistry, conformational analysis, germanium chemistry, organometallic chemistry, asymmetric synthesis, homogeneous catalysis, hypercoordinated compounds. Home: PO Box 195 Mayhill NM 88339-0195 E-mail: astro3d@pvtnetworks.net.

**PASTORE, WILLIAM M.,** insurance company executive; BS in Bus., L.I. U., MBA. Various positions Citibank, N.Y.C., divsn. exec. Nat. Servicing. Orgn.; sr. v.p. CIGNA HealthCare, Phila., 1995, pres., 1999—2002; COO Monster Worldwide Inc., Maynard, Mass., 2002—06, pres., COO, 2006—. Office: Monster Worldwide Inc 5 Clock Tower Pl Maynard MA 01754*

**PASTOREK, PAUL G.,** lawyer; Undergrad., Loyola U., 1976; JD, Loyola U. Sch. Law, 1979. Former ptnr. Adams and Reese, New Orleans; gen. counsel NASA, Washington, 2002—04; ptnr., spl. bus. svcs. Adams & Reese, LLP, New Orleans, 2004—. Served La. State Bd. Elem. and Secondary Edn., 1996—2004, pres., 2000—04; mem. various state bds. and commns. Chair, coun. exec. com. New Orleans Regional C. of C. area.

**PASTORES, GREGORY MCCARTHY,** pediatrician, medical geneticist, researcher; b. Bklyn., Sept. 4, 1959; s. Jovito Camara and Annie Harrington (McCarthy) P. BS in Biology, U. St. Thomas, 1979, MD, 1983. Diplomate Am. Bd. Pediat., Am. Bd. Med. Genetics in Clin. Genetics and Clin. Molecular Genetics. Resident in pediat. Mt. Sinai Med. Ctr., N.Y.C., 1986-89; fellow med. genetics Mayo Clinic Found., Rochester, Minn., 1989-91; fellow med. and molecular genetics Mt. Sinai Sch. Medicine, N.Y.C., 1991-92, instr. pediatrics, genetics, 1992-93, asst. prof. human genetics and pediatrics, 1993-97; asst. prof. neurology and pediatrics NYU Sch. Medicine, N.Y.C., 1997—2004, assoc. prof. neurology and pediatrics, 2004—. Roman Catholic. Home: 215 W 90th St Apt 6G New York NY 10024-1224 Office: NYU at Rivergate 493 E 34th St 2d Fl New York NY 10016 Office Phone: 212-263-8344. Business E-mail: gregory.pastores@med.nyu.edu.

**PASTORES, STEPHEN M.,** internist; b. NYC, Sept. 5, 1958; s. Jovito Camara and Annie McCarthy Pastores; m. Maria Teresa Desancho; children: Steven Michael, Monica Cristina. MD, Lyceum Northwestern Coll. Medicine, Philippines, 1982. Diplomate Am. Bd. Internal Medicine, Am. Bd. Pulmonary Disease, Am. Bd. Critical Care Medicine. Resident Met. Hosp. Ctr., 1989; attending critical care physician Montefiore Med. Ctr., Bronx, NY, 1993—96; dir. emergency svcs. Dept. VA Med. Ctr., Bronx, 1996—99, asst. dir. surg. ICU, 1996—99; assoc. attending critical care physician Meml. Sloan-Kettering Cancer Ctr., N.Y.C., 1999—, dir. critical care rsch. and critical care fellowship program; assoc. prof. medicine, anesthesiology Weill Med. Coll. Cornell U., N.Y.C., 2001—. Editor: (book) ICU Bedside Technology, 2000; contbr. articles to profl. jours. Fellow: ACP (2000-Present), Am. Coll. of Critical Care Medicine, Am. Coll. Chest Physicians (1997-Present). Office: Meml Sloan-Kettering Cancer Ctr 1275 York Ave M-210C New York NY 10021 Business E-mail: pastores@mskcc.org.

**PASTRANA, RONALD RAY,** Biblical theology professor, psychotherapist, retired public school system administrator; b. NYC, Sept. 5, 1939; s. Anthony and Mildred Pastrana; m. Josephine Pastrana; children: Christine, Therese. BA in History/Sci. Edn., Queens Coll., 1963; advanced sci. cert., Pace U., 1964-68; MS in Counseling Edn., St. John's U., 1967; diploma, U.S Acad. of Health Sci., 1975, U.S. Army Command and Gen. Staff Coll., 1979; D Ministry, Sch. Bible Theology Sem., 1996, ThD, 2000. Ordained min. Pentecostal Assemblies of God of Am.; diplomate Am. Bd. of Psychotherapy; cert. life support sys. in internat. space NOAA, NASA. Tchr. sci. Marie Curie Jr. HS, Bayside, NY, 1963-68; guidance counselor Half Hollow Hills HS, Dix Hills, NY, 1969-71, Walt Whitman HS, Huntington Station, NY, 1968-69, coord. occupational svcs., 1971-74; guidance coord. Dutchess County Bd.

Coop. Ednl. Svcs. Tech. Edn. Ctr., Poughkeepsie, NY, 1974-86; asst. prin., supr. sci. and math. Career and Tech. Inst. and Tech. Shop Programs, Poughkeepsie, 1986-96; asst. dir. Reach Out Sch. of Ministry, Hyde Park, NY, 1996—; prof. Bibl. theology Sch. Bible Theology Sem., San Jacinto, Calif., 1999—. Ednl. cons. N.Y. State Edn. Dept., Albany, 1975-83, Armed Forces Vocat. Testing Group, Dept. of Def., Washington, 1975-77; cert. educator Lunar Edn. Project, NASA, 1986-87, Asteroids, Lunar Rocks, Meteorites Edn. Projects, 1999—; earth and space sci. cons., 1998; pub. Reach Out Ministries. Author: Career Guidance in the Classroom, 1974, A Curriculum Guide to the Study of the Seven Dispensations and Eight Covenants, 1996, Dispensational Theology, 1997, Pentecostal Doctrine and Theology, 1998, Student Guide to the Seven Dispensations and Eignt Covenants, 1999, The Greek Fathers of the Early Christian Church, 2000, The Latin Fathers of the Early Christian Church, 2000, The Reformers of the Christian Church, 2001, Reach Out Ministries. Lt. col. USAR, ret. 1992. NSF Sci. Geology, Biochemistry, Biology, Genetics, Cell Physiology, Physics, Astronomy and Advanced Biol. Lab. Techniques Study grantee, 1964-68, grantee NASA and Nat. Ocean: and Atmos. Adminstrn., 1999; recipient Recognition award oustanding cultural and hist. achievement Town of Hyde Pk., 1987, Recognition award oustanding performance guidance and counseling Dutchess County Counseling Assn., 1990, Dutchess Counselor of Yr. award Dutchess County Counseling Assn., 1995, Commemorative Recognition award NASA Space Project and Jason Space Project Wappingers Ctrl. Sch. Dist., 2001, NASA medallion NASA Hdqrs., Washington, 2005, Founder and Recognition award outstanding svc. Students and Faculty Career and Tech. Inst., 2005; decorated Joint Svc. Commendation medal, Army achievement medal, Selective Svc. Meritorious medal, Army Res. Components Achievement medal, Nat. Def. Svc. medal, NY State medal Meritorious Svc., Meritorious Svc. award for civilian svc. USN, 2000. Mem. Am. Counselors Assn., Am. Mental Health Counselors Assn., Nat. Career Devel. Assn., Am. Assn. Christian Counselors, Am. Psychotherapy Assn., Planetary Soc., Nat. Space Soc., NY Acad. Scis., NY State Assn. Counseling and Devel., Sch. Adminstrs. Assn. NY State, Dutchess County Counseling Assn. (exec. bd. 1989-96), Sci. Tchrs. Assn. NY State, Phi Delta Kappa. Avocations: rock and mineral collecting, exercise, canoeing, hiking. Home: 24 Meadow Dr Red Hook NY 12571-1200

**PASTRANA, TRAVIS,** professional trick bike rider; b. Annapolis, Md., Oct. 8, 1983; Profl. dirt bike rider, 1998—. Actor: (films) Travis and the Nitro Circus, Travis and the Nitro Circus II, Global Addiction, Revelation 199. Achievements include winning Nat. Dual Slalom Mt. Bike, 1998; Double Gold Medalist at Summer Gravity Games, 1999; Nat. 125 Champ Rookie Yr., 2000; AMA Rookie Yr., 2000; being youngest rider ever to represent US for Moto-Cross De Nations, 2000; being East West SX Season Shootout Champion, 2000; first Place Daytona Supercross, St. Louis Supercross, Gold Medal X Games, 2000, 2001, 2006.*

**PASTUCH, BORIS MAX See MAX, BUDDY**

**PASTULA, LEAH LYNN,** mental health services professional; d. Wendy Jo Haworth and Richard Joseph Pastula. BS, U. Tenn., 1994; MA, Mid. Tenn. State U., 1998; DD (hon.), Universal Life Ch., 1999. Psychol. intern Cmty. Devel. Svcs., Martin, 1994, Tenn. Prison Women, Nashville, 1996—97; crisis response specialist, triage supr., hosp. liaison Centerstone Cmty. Mental Health Centers, Inc., Nashville, 1999—2000; crisis response specialist Vol. Behavioral Health Care Sys., Murfreesboro, Tenn., 2002—. Recipient 1st Pl. 7th Ann. U.S. Open, Tae Kwon Do Championship, 1993, Gold and Silver medal, Tae Kwon Do Championship, U.S. Nat. 1994. Mem.: APA, So. Poverty Law Ctr., Psi Chi (sec. U. Tenn. Martin chpt. 1993—94), Phi Kappa Phi, Pinnacle (life). Achievements include research in determining decision making power and relationship satisfaction among heterosexual married, heterosexual cohabiting, and lesbian cohabiting couples. Avocations: guitar, sports, computers, video games.

**PASUKINIS, CHERYL RENEE,** elementary school educator; b. Danville, Pa., Feb. 10, 1960; d. William Wayde and Janet Marie (Thomas) Beishline; m. William Albert Pasukinis, Dec. 14, 1985; children: William Beishline, Joseph Albert, Benjamin Thomas, Stanislaus Edward. BS in Elem. Edn., Bloomsburg U., Pa., 1983, MEd, 1985. Cert. reading specialist Bloomsburg U., profl. tchg. cert. Bloomsburg U., cert. tutor Laubach Literacy Action. Title I reading specialist So. Columbia Sch. Dist., Catawissa, Pa., 1983—84; remedial reading specialist, math instr., gifted instr. Cen. Susquehanna Intermediate Unit, Montandon, Pa., 1985; title I reading, remedial reading specialist Milton Area Sch. Dist., Pa., 1985—2003, lang. arts instr. 6th grade mid. sch., 2003—04; title I reading, Reading is Fundamental coord. Berwick Area Sch. Dist., Pa., 2004—. Fed. programs monitor Pa. Dept. Edn.'s Divsn. of Fed. Programs, Harrisburg, 1988—94; cooperating tchr. for grad. assts. and student tchrs. Milton Area Sch. Dist.; tchr. edn. course rev. com. Pa. Power and Light, Berwick; mem. instrnl. support team Milton Area Sch. Dist., 1996—2004, tchr. trainer, 1996—2004, peer coaching mentor model; mem. reading conf. planning com. Bloomsburg U.; mem. parent and child planning com. Bloomsburg U. and Cen. Susquehanna Intermediat Unit #16, Bloomsburg; intergenerational program coord. Milton Elem. Sch., 1999—2004; ARC cmty. project coord. Milton Area Sch. Dist., 2003—04; mem. planning com. Columbia County Early Childhood Conf., 2006. Mem. elem. by-laws com. Benton Elem. Parent Tchr. Assn.; asst. coach Am. Youth Soccer Orgn., Benton; actor Bloomsburg U. Cmty. Theater Group, soloist; stake seminar supr. Ch. of Jesus Christ of Latter-Day Saints, Ch. Ednl. Sys., Williamsport, Pa., 2005—06; stake primary 1st counselor Ch. of Jesus Christ of Latter-Day Saints, Williamsport, 1998—2005, primary 1st counselor Berwick Ward, music chairperson, dir. Berwick Ward choir. Recipient music scholarship, Bloomsburg U., Preschooler R.E.A.D.Y. Kits grant, Berwick Health and Wellness Found., Vocal Music award, Benton Area Sch. Dist. Chorus, Gift of Time Tribute award, Am. Family Inst., 1996, 1997. Mem.: Pa. State Edn. Assn. (assoc.), Berwick Area Edn. Assn. (assoc.), Pa. Assn. of Fed. Programs Coords. (life), Women's Relief Soc. (life). Home: 439 State Rte 239 Benton PA 17814 Office: Berwick Area Sch Dist 500 Line St Berwick PA 18603 Office Phone: 570-759-6400 3558. Office Fax: 570-759-6439. Business E-Mail: cpasukinis@berwicksd.org

**PASUPULETI, VENUMADHAV,** information technology executive; b. Hyderabad, India, Mar. 24, 1969; s. Srinivas Rao and Rama Kumari P.; m. Marilyn L. Miller, May 7, 1992; 1 child, Teja. Grad., Bur. of Data Processing Sys., Hyderabad, 1985; student, Wright State U., 1988-92. Info. tech. cons., 1984-93; mgr. Info. Horizons, Parsippany, NJ, 1993-95; exec. v.p. Globe Tech. Exch., Dayton, Ohio, 1995; COB/CEO Megasoft, Dayton, 1995—. Pres. Indian Student Assn. Wright State U., Dayton, 1989-92; vol. India Literacy Project, Dayton, 1990-95, Ohio India Project, Dayton, 1990-95, Project Outreach, Dayton, 1999—, Day of Caring, Dayton, 1990-95. Mem. IEEE, South Ctrl. Ohio Minority Bus. Coun. (coun. mem. 2000—), Assn. for Computing Machinery, Math. Assn. of Am. Office: Megasoft PO Box 20271 Dayton OH 45420-0271 Office Phone: 937-212-0679. Business E-Mail: ceo@megasoft.us.

**PASURKA, CARL A., JR.,** economist; b. Elgin, IL, Sept. 15, 1953; s. Carl A. Pasurka, Sr., Lorraine Pasurka. AA, Harper Jr. Coll., Palatine, Ill., 1973; BS, No. Ill. U., 1975; MS, PhD, U. Ill., 1981. Vis. asst. prof. econs. So. Ill. U., Carbondale, 1981—85, vis. asst. prof. dept. fin., 1983; asst. prof. dept. econs. Loyola U., Chgo., 1985—92; economist U.S. EPA, Washington, 1992—. V.p. Chgo. Energy Economists 1988—89, press., 1989—90, bd. advisors, 1999—91; adj. prof. Sch. Pub. Policy George Mason U., 2005. Assoc. editor: Jour. Environ. Econs. and Mgmt., 1994—96; contbr. chapters to books, articles to profl. jours. Grantee, U.S. EPA, 1991—92. Mem.: Am. Internat. Input-Output Assn., Productivity Analysis Rsch. Network, Assn. Environ. and Resource Economists, Am. Econs. Assn. Home: 320 23rd St S Apt 623 Arlington VA 22202-3806 Office: EPA 1301 Constitution Ave NW Washington DC Office Phone: 202-566-2275. Business E-Mail: PASURKA.CARL@EPA.GOV.

**PASVOLSKY, RICHARD LLOYD,** retired parks, recreation, and environment educator; b. Englewood, N.J., Feb. 16, 1924; s. Valentine and Ellen Isabel (Stoughton) P.; m. Jo Jane Evans, June 16, 1968. BEd, Panzer Coll., 1950; MA in Edn., NYU, 1955; D in Recreation, Ind. U., 1973. Asst. supt. recreation City of Rutland, Vt., 1951-53; supt. recreation City of Montpelier, Vt., 1953-55; dir. parks and recreation Twp. of Parsippany-Troy Hills, NJ, 1955-62; asst. prof. outdoor and environ. edn. NJ State Sch. Conservation, Branchville, NJ, 1962-71; assoc. prof. edn. Ramapo Coll. NJ, Mahwah, NJ, 1972-84, coach archery 1973-84; adj. prof. Kean Univ., Union, NJ, 1985—2003; ret., 2003. Instr. archery, dir. dance and recreation World Archery Ctr., Pomfret, Conn., 1964-92; dir. NJ State Coll. divsn. Nat. Archery Assn., 1978-84. Advisor to choreographer, cons. prodn. office closing ceremonies Statue of Liberty Centennial Celebration, 1986; rec. artist: Square Dances, 1961, 91, mag. articles, 1954-66; columnist Lines About Squares, 1983—. Instr. dance camp staff Lloyd Shaw Found., 1981—, bd. dirs., 1982-88; bd. trustees Sussex County Sr. Legal Resources Ctr., 1992-94. With U.S. Army, 1943-46, ETO. Recipient Alumni award Panzer Coll. NJ, 1979, Spl. Alumni award, 1987; named to Ramapo Coll. Athletic Hall of Fame, 1993, Lakewood (NJ) HS Hall of Fame, 1998. Mem. AAHPERD (Recreator of Yr. Ea. Dist. 1977), NJ Alliance Health, Phys. Edn., Recreation and Dance, Callers Coun. NJ, Callerlab, North NJ Sq. Dance Callers Assn. (pres. 1960-1963), Phi Delta Kappa. Avocations: calling square dances, ballroom dancing, skiing, golf, tennis. Home: 31 Newton Ave Branchville NJ 07826-4203

**PATAKI, ANDREW,** bishop; b. Palmerton, Pa., Aug. 30, 1927; Student, St. Vincent Coll., St. Procopious Coll., Lisle, Ill., Sts. Cyril and Methodius, Byzantine Cath. Sem., Grigorian U., Rome. Ordained priest Roman Cath. Ch., 1952. Apptd. aux. bishop of Passaic, N.J. Byzantine Cath. Diocese, 1983; bishop of Parma (Ohio) Diocese of Passaic, NJ, 1984—96, bishop NJ, 1996—. Home: 445 Lackawanna Ave West Paterson NJ 07424-2969

**PATAKI, GEORGE E.,** governor; b. Peekskill, NY, June 24, 1945; m. Elizabeth (Libby) Rowland; children: Emily, Teddy, Allison, George Owen. BA, Yale U., 1967; JD, Columbia U. Sch. Law, 1970. Mayor City of Peekskill, NY, 1981—84; elected mem. State Assembly, N.Y., 1985-92, State Senate, NY, 1993—95; assoc. Law Firm of Dewey, Ballantine, Bushby, Palmer & Wood, 1970-74; ptnr. Law Firm Plunckett & Jaffe, P.C., N.Y.C., White Plains, Albany and Peekskill, 1974-89; co-proprietor Pataki Farm, Peekskill, N.Y.; gov. State of NY, 1995—. Advanceman Friends of Rockefeller Team, 1970; upstate campaign coord. Com. to Elect Gov. Wilson, 1974; mem. Peekskill Rep. City Com., 1974—, chmn. 1977-83; mem. N.Y. State Rep. Com., 1980-85. Republican. Address: Office of the Gov Exec Chambers/State Capitol Albany NY 12224 Office Phone: 518-474-8390, 518-474-7516.*

**PATAKY, PAUL ERIC,** ophthalmologist; b. Phila., May 19, 1945; s. Andrew and Helen (Koffler) P.; m. Aimee Janet Margoles, June 13, 1971; Meryl Corinne, Lisa Ann. BS, Trinity Coll., 1966; MD, Pa. State U., 1971. Diplomate Am. Bd. Ophthalmology. Resident ophthalmology Mass. Eye and Ear Infirmary, Boston, 1972-76; asst. in ophthalmology Harvard Med. Sch., Boston, 1976-79; ophthalmologist Dedham (Mass.) Med. Assocs., 1976-79, Paul E. Pataky M.D. P.A., Boynton Beach, Fla., 1979—. Chmn. dept. surgery Bethesda Meml. Hosp., Boynton Beach, 1988-89; pres. med. staff, 1990-91, chmn. credentials chmn., 1992-93, chmn. surg. care com., 1993-97. Named One of Am.'s Top Ophthalmologists 2004-05, Consumer Rsch. Coun. Am., 2004. Fellow: Am. Acad. Ophthalmology; mem.: AMA, Pan-Am. Assn. Ophthalmology. Avocations: travel, fine art. Office: 2623 S Seacrest Blvd Ste 102 Boynton Beach FL 33435-7531 Office Phone: 561-734-5056.

**PATANKAR, RAVINDRA,** research scientist, educator; PhD, Pa. State U., 1999. Asst. prof. Mich. Technol. U., Houghton, 2001—04; sr. scientist Intelligent Automation, Rockville, Md., 2004—. Adj. prof. Mich. technol. U., Houghton, 2004—. Guest editor: International Jour. Vehicle Autonomous Systems; contbr. articles to profl. jours. Mem.: IEEE. Achievements include patents in field; first to state-space model of fatigue crack growth; research in steering control; fatigue modeling.

**PATCH, LISA E.,** health services director, nurse; b. Macomb, Ill., Jan. 19, 1967; d. Lyle Marlin Swearingen and Mildred Fern Swearingen-Engel; m. Allan Trent Patch, May 25, 1986; children: Breckon Nicole, Brighton Ellen, Brooklyn Leigh. AA in Nursing, N.Mex., 1997; BS, Western Ill. U., 1989. Intern Dona Ana Pub. Health, Las Cruces, N.Mex., 1990—97; pediatric registered nurse Mem. Med. Ctr., Las Cruces, 1997—2000; dir. health svcs Alamogordo Pub. Schs., Alamogordo, N.Mex., 1999—; registered nurse Dr. Paul's Family Practice, 2000. Adv. bd. N.Mex. State U., Alamogordo, N.Mex., 2002—; preceptor, 2005. Mem. Otero Path, Alamogordo, N.Mex., 2000—03, Otero County Health Coalition, Alamogordo, 2000—, Leadership Alamogordo, 2004; youth leader Wesley United Meth. Ch., Alamogordo, 2004—. Mem.: N.Mex. Sch. Nurse Assn. (exec. bd. mem. 2000—), Am. Sch. Health Assn., Nat. Assn. Sch. Nursing, Sigma Theta Tau. Avocation: travel. Office: Alamogordo Pub Schs 1211 Hawaii Ave Alamogordo NM 88310

**PATCH, PETER C.,** psychologist; b. Boston, Feb. 23, 1965; s. Charles George Patch and Mary Frances Petersen. BA, U. Vt., 1987; MA, U. of the Pacific, 1990; D in Psychology, Calif. Sch. Profl. Psychology, 2000. Lic. psychologist Mass., 2002, RI, 2003, cert. Nat. Bd. Behavior Analysts, 2001. Psychological trainee at various orgs., 1987—90, 1997—99; intern US Penitentiary, Atlanta, 1999—2000, Augusta Neuropsychology Ctr., Ga., 1999—2000; mental health specialist San Joaquin County Mental Health Svcs., Stockton, 1987—89; relief, on-call counselor Carefilll Homes, Stockton, 1988—89, com; Channel Manor, Stockton, 1989—90; outpatient therapist Kitsap Mental Health Svcs., Bremerton, Wash., 1991—92, mental health profl., 1991—92; specialist psychiatric evaluation Inmate Mgmt. Svcs., Seattle, 1992—95; specialist behavior Cipani and Assocs., Visalia, Calif. 1996—99; psychologist Judge Rotenberg Edn. Ctr., Canton, Mass., 2000—02; psychotherapist Bayview Assocs/South Shore Mental Health, Plymouth, 2002—03; psychologist Northeast Health Svcs., Taunton, 2002—03, Psychol. Ctrs. of RI, Middletown, 2002—04, Providence VA Med. Ctr., 2004; exec. dir. Northeast Behavioral Assocs., Attleboro, Mass., 2002—; supr. field experience Simmons Coll., Boston, 2003—; pvt. practice Attleboro, Mass., 2003—. Cons. and presenter in field; vis. lectr. dept. psychology U. Mass., Dartmouth, 2001—; mem. peer rev. com. Mass. Dept. Mental Retardation, 2004—. Dep. editor: Humanity and Society, Jour. Assn. Humanist Sociology, 1996—98, Jour. Forensic Psychology Practice, 1998—99; contbr. articles to profl. jours., chapters to books. Mem.: APA, Blackstone Valley Assn. Behavior Analysis (pres. 2005—), RI Psychol. Assn., Mass. Psychol. Assn., Greater Boston Assn. Behavior Analysis, Assn. Advancement Behavior Therapy, Assn. Behavior Analysis, APA Divsn. 25. Office Phone: 781-929-0553. Business E-Mail: pcpatch@northeastbehavioral.com.

**PATCHEN, KELLY A.,** elementary school educator; b. Cleve., Dec. 20, 1970; d. Dennis Malcher and Beverly Fick; m. Michael C. Patchen, Nov. 22, 1997; children: Blake, Ryan. BA, Alverna Coll., Reading, Pa., 1992; MEd, Seattle U., 1998. Cert. curriculum and instrn. specialist Wash., reading specialist Wash., early childhood specialist N.C. Tchr. Balt. City Pub. Schs., 1992—93; tchr. and wedding coord. Villa Acad. Seattle, 1993—2002; tchr. Cabarrus County Sch., Concord, NC, 2004—05; 0lead tchr. Carolina Internat. Sch., Harrisburg, NC, 2005—06, asst. prin. elem. edn., 2006—. Vol. Literacy Coun.; active ch. youth group. Named Tchr. of Yr., Balt. City Pub. Schs., 1992—93, Student Tchr. of Yr., Alverna Coll., 1992. Mem.: ASCD, Nat. Assn. Edn. of Young Children, Internat. Reading Assn. Avocations: scrapbooks, crafts, sports. Office: Carolina Internat Sch 8810 Hickory Ridge Rd Harrisburg NC 28075

**PATCHETT, ANN,** writer; b. LA, 1963; BA, Sarah Lawrence College. Writer-in-residence Allegheny Coll., 1989; vis. asst. prof. Murray State U., 1992. Author: (novels) The Patron Saint of Liars, 1992 (James A. Michener/ Copernicus award for a book in progress, 1990, TV movie, 1997),

Taft (also screenplay), 1994 (Janet Heidinger Kafka prize for the best work of fiction, 1994), The Magician's Assistant, 1997 (Nashville Banner Tennessee Writer of the Year Award), Bel Canto, 2001 (PEN/Faulkner prize, 2002), (non-fiction) Truth & Beauty, 2004 (Heartland Prize for Non-Fiction, Chgo. Tribune, Book Sense Honor Book for adult non-fiction, 2005); contbr. articles The New York Times Magazine, Chicago Tribune, Boston Globe, Vogue, GQ, Elle, Gourmet. Fellow Bunting Fellowship, Mary Ingrahm Bunting Institute at Radcliffe College, 1993, Guggenheim, 1994; grantee Residential fellowship, Fine Arts Work Ctr., Provincetown, Mass., 1990. Mailing: c/o HarperCollins Publishers 10 East 53rd Street New York NY 10022

**PATCHETT, ARTHUR ALLAN,** medicinal chemist, pharmaceutical executive; b. Middletown, N.Y., May 28, 1929; s. Arthur Allan and Anna Gertrude (Vossler) P.; m. Lois Rhoda Mc Neil, Aug. 18, 1962; Thomas John, Steven Edward. BA, Princeton U., 1951; PhD, Harvard U., 1955; DSc (hon.), Bloomfield Coll., 2001. Rsch. chemist NIH, Bethesda, Md., 1955-57; rsch. chemist Merck Rsch. Labs., Rahway, NJ, 1957-62, dir. synthetic chem. rsch., 1962-69, sr. dir. synthetic chem. rsch., 1969-71, sr. dir. new lead discovery, 1971-76, exec. dir. new lead discovery, 1976-88, v.p. exploratory chemistry, 1988-95, v.p. medicinal chemistry, 1995-2000, cons., 2000—. Contbr. over 170 papers to profl. jours., sci. confs. Named to, N.J. Inventors Hall of Fame, N.J. Inst. Tech., 1990; recipient Discoverers award, Pharm. Mfrs. Assn., 1992, Smissman Bristol-Myers Squibb award, 2001. Fellow AAAS; mem. Am. Chem. Soc. (chmn. div. medicinal chemistry 1971, E.B. Hershberg Important Discoveries in Medicinally Active Substances award 1993, Alfred Burger award in medicinal chemistry 2002). Achievements include 180 U.S. patents (co-holder); co-inventor antihypertensive drug Vasotec; key contbr. to discovery of cholesterol lowering drug Mevacor.

**PATCHIN, REBECCA J.,** anesthesiologist, educator, administrator; b. Detroit, Dec. 8, 1949; d. Robert Ira and Doris J. (Hubert) P.; m. Carl W. Anderson, 1988. ASN, Pacific Union Coll., 1969; BSN, Walla Walla Coll., 1971; MD, Loma Linda U., 1989. Diplomate in anesthesiology and pain mgmt. Am. Bd. Anesthesiology. Resident in internalmedicine Loma Linda U. Med. Ctr., Calif., 1989-90, resident in anesthesiology Calif., 1990-93, fellow in pain mgmt. dept. anesthesiology Calif., 1993-94, asst. prof. anesthesiology, 1994—; assoc. med. dir. Ctr. for Pain Mgmt., Loma Linda, 1995—. Presenter in field. Contbr. abstracts to profl. jours. Mem. AMA (mem. credentials com. 1986—, mem. awards com. bd. trustees 1988-89, del. ho. of dels. 1990—, mem. reference com. 1994—, chair coun. on med. edn. 2002-03, trustee 2003-, Internat. Anesthesiology Rsch. Soc., Internat. Assn. for Study of Pain, Am. Soc. Anesthesiology, Am. Pain Soc., Am. Soc. Regional Anesthesia, Am. Acad. Pain Medicine, Calif. Soc. Anesthesiology (del. resident component 1991-93, mem. com. on young physicians 1994—96, chair com. on young physicians 1996—), Calif. Med. Assn. (mem. reference com. 1988, trustee 1991-93, mem. com. on health professions and licensure 1992—, chair com. on health professions and licensure 1993-96, mem. coun. on legislation 1995-96, chair coun. on legislation 2000—), So. Calif. Cancer Pain Initiative, Riverside County Med. Assn. (sec.-treas 2002, pres. 2004), San Bernardino County Med. Soc. Office Phone: 951-413-0200.*

**PATE, JOHN GILLIS, JR.,** financial consultant, educator; b. Chattanooga, Jan. 27, 1928; s. John Gillis Pate and Iona Estelle (Bowman) Pate Ketchman; m. Daphne Mae Davis, Feb. 8, 1946; children: John Gillis III, Daphne Iona, Donna Gay. Student, U. Tampa, 1947-48; AA with highest honors, U. Fla., 1950; BS cum laude, Fla. State U., 1953, MS, 1958; PhD, Columbia U., 1968. CPA, S.C. Mgr. Grocery Concession, Albany, Ga., 1944-45, Variety Store, Panama City, Fla., 1946-47; asst. to CPA Standard Brands, Inc., Birmingham, Ala., 1951-53; acctg. supervisory trainee Birmingham, Ala., 1953-54; grad. asst. Fla. State U., Tallahassee, 1957-58; asst. to CPA Pensacola, Fla., 1956-58; CPA, 1958; asst. prof. U. Ga., Athens, 1958-60; lectr. Columbia U., N.Y.C., 1961-64; asst. prof. Bernard M. Baruch Coll. of CUNY, 1963-69; prof. acctg. U. Tex.-El Paso, 1969-85, U. S.C., Spartanburg, 1988-93. Cons. resource person fin. and human resources Charles Lea Ctr., Spartanburg, 1988—, dir. Internal Audit and Spl. Projects, 1994-2002. Author: Index C.P.A. Exams and Unofficial Answers, 1974-81; co-author: Accounting Trends and Techniques, 1967-88, Index to Accounting and Auditing Services, 1971; contbr. articles to ann. profl. publs. Tither, Coronado Bapt. Ch., El Paso 1969-86, Buck Creek Bapt. Ch., Spartanburg, 1987—; cons. Alderman of El Paso, 1982, County Councilman of Spartanburg, 1991-98. With l.t. j.g. USN, 1955-56. Columbia U. fellow, 1960; Earhart Found. fellow, 1960, Am. Acctg. Assn. fellow, 1960, Found fellow, 1961-62; recipient Haskins and Sells award, 1960. Mem. AICPA (cons. 1961-88), Am. Acctg. Assn., Moose, Masons, Shriners, Beta Alpha Psi, Beta Alpha Chi. Republican. Home: 12006 Aspen Ln Stafford TX 77477-1679

**PATE, LISA M.,** transportation services executive, lawyer; b. 1969; m. Hank Pate; children: Riley, Bealie, Casey. BS, Northwestern U.; JD, Cornell U. Bar: Tenn. 1996. Assoc. Witt, Gaither & Whitaker, PC, Chattanooga, 1996—2002, named shareholder, 2002; now gen. counsel US Xpress Enterprises, Inc., Chattanooga. Office: US Xpress Enterprises Inc 4080 Jenkins Rd Chattanooga TN 37421 Office Phone: 423-510-3000. Office Fax: 423-510-3318.

**PATE, MICHAEL LYNN,** lawyer; b. Ft. Worth, Tex., July 9, 1951; s. J.B. and Mary Anna (Hable) P.; m. Barbara Ann Linch, May 28, 1977. AA, Schreiner Coll., 1971; BS, Tex. Wesleyan Coll., 1973; JD, U. Tex., 1975. Bar: Tex. 1976, DC 1983, US Tax Ct. 1986, US Supreme Ct. 1987. Adminstrv. asst. to Senator Sherman, counsel natural resources com, Tex. Senate, 1976-77; adminstrv. asst. to Lt. Gov. Bill Hobby, Austin, Tex., 1977-79; legis. asst. Senator Bentsen, Washington, 1979-81, legis. dir., 1981-86; ptnr., head Washington office Bracewell & Giuliani LLP, Washington, 1986—. Trustee Schreiner U. Mem. ABA, Tex. Bar Assn., DC Bar Assn. Democrat. Methodist. Avocations: basketball, tennis, golf. Office: Bracewell & Giuliani LLP 2000 K St NW Ste 500 Washington DC 20006-1872 Office Phone: 202-828-5841. Business E-Mail: michael.pate@bracewellgiuliani.com.

**PATE, PAUL DANNY,** mayor; b. Ottumwa, Iowa, May 1, 1958; s. Paul Devern and Velma Marie (McConnell) P.; m. Jane Ann Wacker, July 15, 1978; children: Jennifer Ann, Paul Daniel III, Amber Lynn. AA in Bus., Kirkwood Coll., 1978; cert. fin. mgmt. program, U. Pa., 1990. Exec. dir. Jr. Achievement, Cedar Rapids, Iowa, 1978-82; pres. PM Systems Corp., Cedar Rapids 1982—; senator Iowa State Senate, Des Moines, 1989-93; Sec. of State State of Iowa, 1994-98; mayor City of Cedar Rapids, 2002—. Chmn. Iowa Young Reps., Des Moines, 1989-93. Recipient Guardian Small Bus. award Nat. Fedn. Independent Bus., 1990; named Young Entrepreneur of Yr. U.S. Small Bus. Adminstrn., Iowa, 1988, Alumnus of Yr. Kirkwood Coll., Cedar Rapids, 1990. Republican. Methodist. Avocation: water-skiing. Home: 6801 Bowman Ln NE Cedar Rapids Ia 52402-1575 Office: Pm Pate Asphalt 3285 3rd Ave Marion IA 52302-3928

**PATE, R. HEWITT (ROBERT HEWITT PATE III),** lawyer, former federal agency administrator; b. Ft. Sill, Okla., June 14, 1962; s. Robert and Ellen Pate; m. Lindsey Haines, Aug. 2, 1986; children: Elizabeth, Ellen. BA, U. NC, 1984; JD, U. Va., 1987. Bar: Va. 1989, DC 2000, bar: Brussels 2006. Law clk. for Hon. J. Harvie Wilkinson, US Ct. Appeals (4th cir.), Charlottesville, Va., 1987—88; law clk. for Justice Lewis F. Powell, Jr., US Supreme Ct., Washington, 1988—89, law clk. for Justice Anthony M. Kennedy, 1989—90; assoc. Hunton & Williams, Richmond, Va., 1990—95, ptnr., 1995—2000, 2005—; dep. asst. atty. gen., antitrust divsn. U.S. Dept. Justice, Washington, 2001—03, asst. atty. gen., 2003—05. Mem. Commn. on Future of Higher Edn. in Va., Richmond, 1994—95, Governor's Commn. on Self-Determination and Federalism, Richmond, 1994—96; Ewald disting. vis. prof. U. Va. Sch. Law, Charlottesville, Va., 1999; chmn. competition com. working party 3 Orgn. for Econ. Cooperation and Devel., Paris, 2003—05; chair internat. working group U.S. Atty. General's Task Force on Intellectual Property, Washington, 2004—04. Contbr. numerous articles to legal jours. Gen. counsel Children's Mus. Richmond, 1996—2000. Recipient Alumni Award for Academic Excellence, U. Va. Sch. Law, 1987, Roger and Madeline

Traynor prize, 1987. Mem.: ABA, Fourth Circuit Jud. Conf., The Federalist Soc., Raven Soc., Farmington Country Club, The Met. Club, Country Club Va., Omicron Delta Kappa. Republican. Episcopalian. Office Phone: 202-955-1921. E-mail: hpate@hunton.com.

**PATE, ROBERT HEWITT, JR.,** counselor educator; b. Abingdon, Va., Apr. 5, 1938; s. Robert Hewitt and Esther Frances (Kirk) P.; m. Ellen O'Neal Pope, Dec. 11, 1960; children: Robert Hewitt III, Mary Ellen Pate Barton. AB, Davidson Coll., 1960; MEd, U. Va., 1965; PhD, U. N.C., 1968. Lic. prof. counselor, Va. Marketer Sinclair Refining Co., Abingdon, Va., 1960-61, 63-64; counselor St. Andrews Presbyn. Coll., Laurinburg, NC, 1965-66; prof. edn., William Clay Parrish Jr. prof. edn. U. Va., Charlottesville, 1968—; interim dean, 1994-95, assoc. dean, 1995—. Mem. adj. faculty Fed. Exec. Inst., Charlottesville, 1978—. Author: Being A Counselor, 1983. 1st lt. U.S. Army 1961-63. Mem. ACA, Va. Counselors Assn. (pres. 1983-84), Nat. Bd. Cert. Counselors (chair 1996-97), Raven Soc. Avocation: reading. Home: 552 Dryden Pl Charlottesville VA 22903-4666 Office: Curry Sch Dean's Office 405 Emmet St S PO Box 400260 Charlottesville VA 22904-4260

**PATE, WILLIAM,** telecommunications industry executive; Grad. in Journalism, Ga. State U., grad. in Comm. Pub. rels. specialist Goodwill Industries, ARC; prodr. advt. and mktg. programs S.E. Dairy Assn.; with Knapp Inc., Atlanta; supr. domestic and internat. advt. and pub. rels. MCI; v.p. advt. and Pacific rels. BellSouth Corp., Atlanta, 1997—. Chmn. Atlanta Conv. and Visitors Bur., The Chick-Fil-A Peach Bowl; mem. bd. trustees Ga. State U.; bd. dirs. Alliance Theatre Co., The Ad Coun. Recipient Ad Campaign of Yr. for Gramercy Press campaign, Advt. Age mag., Campaign of Yr. award for Chatsford, Am. Mktg. Assn. Mem.: Pub. Rels. Soc. Am., Assn. Nat. Advertisers, Am. Advt. Fedn.

**PATE, WILLIAM PATRICK,** city manager; b. Duplin County, NC, July 30, 1962; s. William Atlas and Bonny Lou (O'Leary) P.; m. Sandra Martin, Aug. 17, 1985; children: William Glenn, Andrew Patrick. BA in Polit. Sci. and Religion, U. N.C., 1984, MPA, 1986. Budget and evaluation analyst intern City of Winston-Salem, NC, 1985-86, budget and evaluation analyst NC, 1986-87, lead budget and evaluation analyst NC, 1987; budget and risk mgr. City of Greensboro, NC, 1987-90, budget and evaluation dir. NC, 1990-99; asst. city mgr. City of High Point, NC, 1999—. Inst. of Govt. intern N.C. Office Coastal Mgmt., Raleigh, N.C., 1984; rsch. asst. U. N.C., Chapel Hill, 1984-85. Mem. Chmns. Soc. United Way of High Point, 1998—; mem. Leadership Greensboro, 1993-99, Leadership High Point, 2000—; elder, clk. session Faith Presbyn. Ch., Greensboro; mem. Salem Presbyn. World Ministries Cluster, 1997-99; chair staff parish rels. team Covenant Ch., 2005—. Recipient Disting. Svc. award Alpha Phi Omega, 1984. Mem. Internat. City Mgrs. Assn., Am. Soc. Pub. Adminstrn. (pres. Piedmont Triad chpt. 1994), Gov. Fin. Officers Assn. U.S. and Can. (exec. bd. 1998-2004, nat. com. on govtl. budgeting and mgmt. 1993-98, nat. com. on debt and fiscal policy 1998-2001, pres. 2002-03, Disting. Budget Presentation award reviewer, Disting. Budget Presentation award 1992-98), N.C. Local Govt. Budget Assn. (bd. dirs. 1990-92, 95, 1st v.p 1992-93, pres. 1993-94), N.C. City/County Mgrs. Assn., U. N.C. MPA Alumni Assn. (program chmn. 1992, pres-elect 1993, pres. 1994, Scholarship award 1985), U. N.C. Gen. Alumni Assn. (bd. dirs. 1994-95), Kiwanis Club (v.p. 2006—). Methodist. Home: 4509 Calabria Ct High Point NC 27265-9595 Office: City of High Point PO Box 230 High Point NC 27261-0230 E-mail: pat.pate@highpointnc.gov.

**PATÉ-CORNELL, MARIE-ELISABETH LUCIENNE,** finance educator, engineering educator; b. Dakar, Senegal, Aug. 17, 1948; arrived in U.S., 1971; d. Edouard Pierre Lucien and Madeleine (Tournissa) Paté; m. C. Allin Cornell, Jan. 3, 1981; children: Phillip Cornell, Ariane Cornell. Eng. Degree, Inst. Polytechnique de Grenoble, France, 1971; MS in Ops. Rsch., Stanford U., 1972, PhD in Engring.-Econ. Systems, 1978. Asst. prof. in civil engring. MIT, 1978-81; asst. prof. indsl. engring. Stanford (Calif.) U., 1981-84, assoc. prof. indsl. engring., 1984-91; indsl. engring., 1991—, chmn. dept. indsl. engring., 1997-99, chmn. dept. mgmt. sci. and engring., 2000—. Cons. SRI Internat., 1993, Electric Power Rsch. Inst., 1995, Atty. Gen. of N.Mex., 1995, Swiss Re, 2002, Boeing, 2003—; mem. adv. coun. NASA, 1995-98; mem. Marine Bd. NRC, 1995—97; mem. Army Sci. Bd., 1995—97, Air Force Sci. Bd., 1998—2002, Calif. Coun. on Sci. and Tech., 2000—, Pres.'s Adv. Bd. on Fgn. Intelligence, 2001—04; chmn. bd. advisors Naval-Postgrad. Sch., 2004—. Contbr. numerous articles to profl. jours. Numerous rsch. grants. Mem.: Nat. Acad. Engring. (councilor 2001—), Inst. for Mgmt. Scis., Ops. Rsch. Soc. Am., Soc. for Risk Analysis (councilor 1985—86, pres. 1995). Avocations: tennis, swimming, chess, music. Home: 110 Coquito Way Menlo Park CA 94028-7402 Office: Stanford U Dept Mgmt Sci and Engring Stanford CA 94305 E-mail: mep@leland.stanford.edu.

**PATEL, AJAY,** dean; m. Aparna Patel; 2 children. BS, St. Joseph's Coll., India; MBA, U. Balt.; PhD, U. Ga. Faculty appointments U. Mo., Bentley Coll.; faculty mem. Babcock Grad. Sch. Mgmt., Wake Forest U., 1993, Babcock rsch. prof. fin., 2001—, interim dean, 2003—04, dean, 2004—. Office: Babcock Grad Sch Mgmt Wake Forest Univ PO Box 7659 Winston Salem NC 27109-7659 Office Phone: 336-758-5419. E-mail: ajay.patel@mba.wfu.edu.

**PATEL, CHANDRA KUMAR NARANBHAI,** communications executive, educator, entrepreneur, researcher; b. Baramati, India, July 2, 1938; came to U.S., 1958, naturalized, 1967; s. Naranbhai Chaturbhai and Maniben P.; m. Shela Dixit, Aug. 20, 1961; children: Neela, Meena. BS in Engring., Poona U., 1958; MS, Stanford U., 1959, PhD, 1961. Mem. tech. staff Bell Telephone Labs., Murray Hill, NJ, 1961-93, head infrared physics and electronics rsch. dept., 1967-70, dir. electronics rsch. dept., 1970-76, dir. phys. rsch. lab., 1976-81, exec. dir. rsch. physics and acad. affairs div., 1981-87, exec. dir. rsch., materials sci., engring. and acad. affairs div., 1987-93, trustee Aerospace Corp., LA, 1979-88; vice chancellor rsch. UCLA, 1993-2000, prof. dept. physics and astronomy dept. chemistry, 2000—, prof. dept. elec. engring., 2000—; chmn., CEO Pranalytica, Inc, Santa Monica, Calif., 2001—. Mem. governing bd. NRC, 1990-91; bd. dirs. Newport Corp.; chmn. bd. Calif. Accuwave Corp., 1994-98; founder, chmn. bd. Pranalytica, Inc., Santa Monica, Calif.; co-founder Photuris, Inc. Contbr. articles to tech. jours. Chmn. Calif. Biomed. Found., 1994-2000; mem. exec. bd. Calif. Healthcare Inst., 1995-2000; mem. LA Regional Tech. Alliance, 1997-2003. Recipient Ballantine medal Franklin Inst., 1968, Nat. Sci. medal 1996, Coblentz award Am. Chem. Soc., 1974, Honor award Assn. Indians in Am., 1975, Founders prize Tex. Instruments Found., 1978, award N.Y. sect. Soc. Applied Spectroscopy, 1982, Schawlow medal Laser Inst. Am., 1984, Thomas Alva Edison Sci. award N.J. Gov., 1987, William T. Ennor Manufacturing Technology award ASME, 1995, Nat. Medal of Sci., 1996. Fellow AAAS, IEEE (Lamme medal 1976, medal of honor 1989, Millennium medal 2000), Am. Acad. Arts and Scis., Am. Phys. Soc. (coun. 1987-91, exec. com. 1987-90, George E. Pake prize 1988, pres. 1995), Optical Soc. Am. (Adolph Lomb medal 1966, Townes medal 1982, Ives medal 1989, Lifetime Achievement award Def. and Security Symposium 2006), Indian Nat. Sci. Acad. (fng.); mem. NAS (coun. 1988-91, exec. com. 1989-91), NAE (Zworykin award 1976), Def. and Security Symposium (Lifetime Achievement award 2006), Gynecol. Laser Surgery Soc. (hon.), Am. Soc. for Laser Medicine and Surgery (hon.). Third World Acad. Scis. (assoc.), Calif. Biomed. Found. (pres. 1994-00), Calif. Healthcare Inst. (exec. com. 1995-00), Fedn. Am. Scientists (bd. dirs. 2002-),Sigma Xi (pres. 1994-96). Achievements include invention of many lasers including the Carbon Dioxide laser. Office: Pranalytica Inc 1101 Colorado Ave Santa Monica CA 90401 Business E-Mail: patel@pranalytica.com.

**PATEL, HOMI BURJOR,** apparel executive; b. Bombay, June 28, 1949; s. Burjor Ratan and Roshen Burjor (Marfatia) P.; married; children: Neville H., Cyrus H., Natasha K. BS in Stats., U. Bombay, 1973; MBA in Fin. and Mktg., Columbia U., 1975. Exec. asst. to pres. Corbin Ltd., N.Y.C., 1976, dir. mktg., 1978; with subs. Hartmarx Corp., Chgo., 1979—; v.p., gen. mgr. Fashionaire Apparel Inc., Chgo., 1979-81; exec. v.p. Austin Reed of Regent St., Chgo., 1981-82, M. Wile and Co., Buffalo, 1982-84; pres., chief exec. officer M. Wile & Co., Johnny Carson Apparel, Intercontinental Apparel, Buffalo, 1984—; group exec. v.p. Hartmarx Mens Apparel Group Corp., Buffalo, 1987-91, chmn., ceo Chgo., 1991-92; pres., COO Hartmarx Corp., Chgo., 1992—, bd. dirs., 1994—2001, CEO, 2002—. Mem. Clothing Mfrs. Assn. Am. (bd. dirs. 1984—, chief labor negotiator for U.S. tailored clothing industry). Univ. Club N.Y., Chgo. Club. Office: Hartmarx Corp 101 N Wacker Dr Fl 23 Chicago IL 60606-1718

**PATEL, KEYUR,** medical educator; MB, U. of Southampton, Eng., 1989. Asst. prof. in medicine Duke U. Med. Ctr., Durham, NC, 2003—. Contbr. articles to profl. jours. Recipient Dame Sheila Sherlock award in Clin. and Translational Rsch., AASLD, 2004. Fellow: Royal Australasian Coll. of Physicians; mem.: Am. Assn. for Study of Liver Diseases, Am. Gastroent. Assn. Office: Duke Clinical Research Institute 2400 Pratt St Durham NC 27705 Office Phone: 919-668-7186.

**PATEL, KIRAN,** manufacturing executive; BEE; MBA, U. Tenn. CPA. With Cummins Inc., 1974—2000; CFO iMotors, 2000; exec. v.p. Solectron Corp., Milpitas, Calif., 2001—, CFO, 2001—. CFO iMotors, 2000. Mem.: Fin. Exec. Inst., Tenn. Soc. CPAs, Am. Inst. CPAs. Office: Solectron Corp 777 Gibraltar Dr Milpitas CA 95035

**PATEL, MANU V.,** physics educator; b. Jhalod, India, Jan. 4, 1934; arrived in US, 1965; s. Valabhai L. and Revaben V. Patel; m. Shashikala Patel, Sept. 27, 1940; children: Sanna M., Rupa M. BS in Physics, Gujarat U., India, 1955, EdB, 1958; MEd, M.S. U., Gujarat, 1960; MS in Physics, U. Conn., Storrs, 1970; PhD in Atomic Physics, U. Conn., 1975. Cert. tchr. Va. Tchr., asst. prin. various schs., Gujarat, 1955—64; tchr. sci. and math. Ballston Spa Ctrl. Schs., NY, 1965—66; asst. prof. Coll. Edn., Gujarat, 1967—68; grad. asst. U. Conn., Storrs, 1968—75; physics tchr. Alexandria City Schs., Va., 1976—. Test ctr. supr. Ednl. Testing Svc., Coll. Bd., Princeton, NJ, 1982—; mem. advanced placement test devel. com., 1988—92. Author: AP Exam Tests and Solution Manual, 1994; author: (in Gujarati) Inspirational Thoughts for Poor Students, 2006. Organizer Sohna-Rupa Charity Trusst, Jhalad, India, 1999—. Recipient honors, Alexandria Sch. Bd., City Coun., Va. State Ho. and Senate, Minority Tchg. award, RCA, 1987, Tchg. award, NSF, 1987, Excellence in Tchg. award, Alexandria C. of C., 1998; Fulbright scholar, 1965. Mem.: NEA, Va. Edn. Assn. Avocations: travel, gardening. Home: 6153-A Edsall Rd Alexandria VA 22304 Office: TC Williams HS Alexandria VA 22302 Office Phone: 703-824-6800. E-mail: mpatel@acps.k12.va.us.

**PATEL, MARILYN HALL,** judge; b. Amsterdam, NY, Sept. 2, 1938; d. Lloyd Manning and Nina J. (Thorpe) Hall; m. Magan C. Patel, Sept. 2, 1966; children: Brian, Gian. BA, Wheaton Coll., 1959; JD, Fordham U., 1963. Bar: N.Y. 1963, Calif. 1970. Immigration atty. Benson & Morris, Esq., N.Y.C., 1962-64; sole practice N.Y.C., 1964-67; atty. U.S. Immigration and Naturalization svc., San Francisco, 1967-71; sole practive San Francisco, 1971-76; judge Alameda County Mcpl. Ct., Oakland, Calif., 1976-80, U.S. Dist. Ct. (no. dist.) Calif., San Francisco, 1980—; now chief judge U.S. Dist. Ct. for No. Dist. Calif., San Francisco, 1998—. Adj. prof. law Hastings Coll. of Law, San Francisco, 1974-76 Author: Immigration and Nationality Law, 1974; also numerous articles Mem. bd. visitors Fordham U. Sch. Law. Mem. ABA (litigation sect., jud. adminstrn. sect.), ACLU (former bd. dirs.), NOW (former bd. dirs.), Am. law Inst., Am. Judicature Soc. (bd. dirs.), Calif Conf. Judges, Nat. Assn. Women Judges (founding mem.). Internat. Inst. (bd. dirs.), Advs. for Women (co-founder), Assn. Bus. Trial Lawyers (bd. dirs.). Democrat. Avocations: piano, travel. Office: US Dist Ct PO Box 36060 450 Golden Gate Ave Ste 36052 San Francisco CA 94102-3482

**PATEL, MULCHAND SHAMBHUBHAI,** biochemist, researcher; b. Sipor, India, Sept. 9, 1939; came to U.S., 1965; s. Shambhubhai J. and Puriben (Patel) P.; m. Kankuben M. Patel; children: Sumitra, Yashomati, Mayank. BS, Gujarat U., 1961; MS, U. Baroda, India, 1964; PhD, U. Ill., 1968. Asst. prof. pediat. rsch. Sch. Medicine Temple U., Phila., 1970-72, rsch. asst. prof. medicine, 1972-75, rsch. assst. prof. biochemistry, 1970-75, rsch. assoc. prof. biochem. medicine, 1975-78; assoc. prof. biochemistry Sch. Medicine Case Western Res. U., Cleve., 1978-86, prof., 1986-93; prof., chmn. biochemistry SUNY, Buffalo, 1993-98, assoc. dean biomed. rsch. edn., 1999—, 1999—2004, disting. prof., 2004—. Mem. NIH biochem. study sect. 2, 1984-88; mem. editl. bd. Jour. Biol. Chem., 1991-97, 99-2004, 06-. Contbr. articles to profl. jours. Recipient gold medal in biochemistry U. Baroda, 1973, Fulbright Rsch. Scholar award to India, 1987; prin. investigator, rsch. grantee NIH. Mem. Am. Soc. for Biochemistry and Molecular Biology, Am. Soc. Nutritional Scis. Office: SUNY-Dept Biochemistry Sch Medicine 140 Farber Hall 3435 Main St Buffalo NY 14214-3001 Business E-Mail: mspatel@buffalo.edu.

**PATEL, NARESH PRATAP,** medical educator, physician, consultant; b. Oct. 26, 1969; married. BA in Biology and Govt., Cornell U., 1991; MD, Baylor Coll. Medicne, 1995. Diplomate Am. Bd. Neurol. Surgery, lic. medicine and surgery N.Y., physician and surgeon Calif.; cert. BCLS, ACLS, advanced pneumatic instrumentation, microvascular surgery, med. lic. Ariz., lic. Drug Enforcement Agy. Intern in surgery Mt. Sinai Hosp., N.Y.C., 1995—96, resident in neurosurgery, 1996—2001; intra-residency complex spine fellowship UCLA Med. Ctr./Cedars Sinai Med. Ctr., L.A., 2000—01; clin. instr. Mayo Med. Sch., 2001—02, asst. prof. neurosurgery, 2003—, clin. cons., 2002—. Sr. assoc. cons. Mayo Clinic, 2001—; mem. CME com. Mayo Clinic Scottsdale, 2002—; presenter in field. Contbr. articles to profl. jours., chapters to books. Recipient Pi Kappa Phi Scholar award. Mem.: AMA (Physician Recognition award), World Spine Soc., N.Am. Spine Soc. (CME com. 2002—), Am. Assn. Neurol. Surgeons, Congress Neurol. Surgeons, Ariz. Med. Assn. Office: Mayo Clinic-Scottsdale 13400 E Shea Blvd Scottsdale AZ 85259 Business E-Mail: patel.naresh@mayo.edu.

**PATEL, NICK C.,** pharmacy professor, psychiatry professor; b. Houston, Tex., June 25, 1974; s. Chandu A. and Sharda C. Patel; m. Brooke R. Rennels, Feb. 9, 2003. BS, Tex. A&M U., College Station, 1995; PharmD, U. Tex., Austin, 2001; PhD, U. of Tex., Austin, 2004. Lic. pharmacist Tex., Ohio. Asst. prof. pharmacy and psychiatry U. Cin., 2004—. Achievements include research in Child and Adolescent Psychiatry, Adult Psychiatry. Office: U Cin PO Box 670004 3225 Eden Ave Cincinnati OH 45267-0004 Office Phone: 513-558-6093. Office Fax: 513-558-0731. E-mail: nick.patel@uc.edu.

**PATEL, SUNIT,** telecommunications industry executive; Treas. MFS Comm., Inc., 1994—97, MCI WorldCom, 1997—2000; CFO, co-founder Looking Glass Networks, Inc., 2000—03; group v.p., CFO Level 3 Comm., Inc., Broomfield, Colo., 2003—. Office: Level 3 Comm 1025 Eldorado Blvd Broomfield CO 80021

**PATEL, UPTAL DINESH,** nephrologist, researcher; BA, U. Calif. San Diego, 1993; MD, U. Calif. San Francisco, 1997. Diplomate Am. Bd. Internal Medicine, 2001, Diplomate, Subspecialty in Nephrology Am. Bd. Internal Medicine, 2005, Diplomate Am. Bd. Pediat., 2001, Diplomate, Subspecialty in Pediat. Nephrology Am. Bd. Pediat., 2005. Robert Wood Johnson clin. scholar U. Mich., Ann Arbor, 2003—05; asst. prof. medicine and pediat. Duke U., Sch. Medicine, Durham, NC, 2005—. Office Phone: 919-668-8008.

**PATEL, VINOD MOTIBHAI,** accountant; b. Kilosha, Tanzania, Mar. 1, 1944; came to U.S., 1971; s. Motibhai R. and Lalitaben M. (Lalitaben C.) P.; m. Surekha J. Patel, Dec. 6, 1969; children: Chirag, Roshni. BComm., U. Baroda, India, 1964. Chartered acct., India; CPA, Md. Acct. Dalal, Desai & Kumana, Bombay, 1964-70, Bellman, Atlas & Co., London, 1970-71, Garbelman, Winslow & Co., Upper Marlboro, Md., 1971-79; prin. Vinod M. Patel, CPA, Jacksonville, Fla., 1979—. Mem. AICPA, Md. Assn. CPA's, Inst. Chartered Accts. India. Hindu. Home and Office: 11262 Saint Augustine Rd Jacksonville FL 32257-1142 Office Phone: 904-899-9000.

**PATEL, VIRENDRA CHATURBHAI,** mechanical engineer, educator; b. Mombasa, Kenya, Nov. 9, 1938; arrived in U.S., 1969, naturalized, 1975; s. Chaturbhai S. and Kantaben N. (Rai) Patel; m. Manjula Patel, May 29, 1966; children: Sanjay, Bindiya. BSc with honors, Imperial Coll., London, 1962; PhD, Cambridge U., Eng., 1965; Doctor honoris causa, Tech. U. Civil Engring., Bucharest, Romania, 1994. Sr. asst. in rsch. Cambridge U., 1965-69; vis. prof. Indian Inst. Tech., Kharagpur, 1966; cons. Lockheed Ga. Co., Marietta, 1969-70; from mem. faculty to disting. prof. U. Iowa, Iowa City, 1971—90, disting. prof., 1990—, Edwin B. Green chair in hydraulics, 2000—; research engr. Iowa Inst. Hydraulic Rsch., 1971—, dir., 1994—2004, hon. prof. Dharamsinh Desai Inst. Tech., 2002—, dir. Ctr. Computer Aided Design, 2003—05. Mem. Iowa Gov. Sci. Adv. Coun., 1977—83; mem. resistance com. Internat. Towing Tank Conf., 1978—87; vis. prof. U. Karlsruhe, Germany, 1980—81, Ecole National Superieure de Mechanique, Nantes, France, 1984, Nantes, 96; jubilee prof. Chalmers Inst. Tech., Goteborg, Sweden, 1988; dir. Ctr. for Computer Aided Design, 2003—; cons. in field. Author: (book) Three Dimensional Turbulent Boundary Layers, 1972; contbr. articles to profl. jours.; assoc. editor: AIAA Jour., 1987—90. Recipient Sr. Scientist award, Alexander von Humboldt Found., 1980, 1993. Fellow: ASME (Fluids Engring. award 1997), AIAA (assoc.); mem.: Soc. Naval Archtl. Marine Engrs., Am. Soc. Engring. Edn., Pi Tau Sigma, Sigma Xi. Home: 60 Kennedy Pkwy Iowa City IA 52246-2780 Office: IIHR Hyrdo-science and Engring U Iowa 302 Hydraulics Laboratory Iowa City IA 52242-1585 Business E-Mail: v-c-patel@uiowa.edu.

**PATENAUDE, PAMELA HUGHES,** federal agency administrator; BA, St. Anselm Coll., 1983; MA, So. NH U. Liaison, spl. asst. to dep. asst. sec. for multifamily housing The White House, Washington, exec. asst. to dep. undersec. field coord.; v.p. Manor Homes Builders, Inc., Bedford, NH, 1988—96; mktg. and training dir. NH Small Bus. Ctr.; state dir. and dep. chief of staff Office of U.S. Senator Bob Smith; asst. dep. sec. field policy & mgmt. US Dept. Housing & Urban Devel., Washington; asst. sec. for community planning & devel., 2005—. Former chmn. Bedford Housing Adv. Com.; held leadership positions in various profl. and civic organizations. Office: 451 Seventh St SW Rm 7100 Mall Code D Washington DC 20410 Office Phone: 202-708-2690. Office Fax: 202-708-3336.

**PATERAKIS, ANGELA GREGORY,** art educator, consultant, writer; b. Oak Park, Ill., June 1, 1932; d. Kostas and Sophia (Spiliotou) Gregory; m. George A. Paterakis, July 31, 1958. B.A.E., Sch. of Art Inst. Chgo., 1954; M.A., U. Ill., 1955; art therapy cert., 1985. Tchr. jr. high sch., Oak Park, Ill., 1955-60; prof. emerita art edn. and art therapy Sch. of Art Inst. Chgo., 1961—; mem. arts advocacy groups, Ill. Author numerous articles, pamphlets on art edn.; pres. Ill. Alliance for Arts Edn.; bd. dirs. Hellenic Mus. and Cultrual Ctr., Chgo., 1990—. mem. Ill. Arts Adv. Com., 1989-91. Recipient Svc. Recognition award Ill. Alliance for Arts Edn., 1985; U. Ill. fellow, 1954-55. Mem. NEA (life), Nat. Art Edn. Assn., Ill. Art Edn. Assn. (named Outstanding Art Educator 1981, Disting. mem., 2000). Office: Sch of the Art Inst Chgo 37 South Wabash Ave Chicago IL 60603-3103

**PATERIK, FRANCES SUE,** secondary school educator, actress; b. Bloomington, Ill., Feb. 10, 1953; d. Francis LaVerne and Magaline Wilken. Student, Am. Cons. Music, Chgo., 1976—78, N.W. Ind. Opera Co., 1980, Hinsdale Opera Co., Ill., 1981; BA, MA, Western Ill. U., 1984. Tchg. asst. Western Ill. U., Macomb, 1982—84; music tchr. Cardinal Cmty. Schs., Eldon, Iowa, 1985—89, Johnston (Iowa) Cmty. Schs., 1990—94; music/performing arts tchr. Colfax (Iowa)-Mingo Cmty. Schs., 1995—2002, Merrill Middle Sch., Des Moines, 2002—. Dir. handbell choir 1st Christian Ch., Des Moines, 1996—2000; soprano soloist Des Moines Concert Singers, 1999—, Des Moines Choral Soc., 2002—; alto sect. leader St. John's Luth. Ch., 2004—. Actress: (various comedic roles) Ingersoll Dinner Theatre; Playhouse; Drama Workshop; Stage West; actress (various comedic roles) Ankeny Cmty. Theatre, St. John's Luth. Ch. Mem.: Des Moines Choral Soc., Iowa Choral Dirs. Assn., Am. Choral Dirs. Assn., Music Educators Nat. Conf., Nat. Wildlife Fedn., Sierra Club. Democrat. Avocations: gardening, dance. Office: Des Moines Pub Schs Des Moines IA 50312 Business E-Mail: f.paterik@mchsi.com.

**PATERNO, JOE (JOSEPH VINCENT PATERNO),** college football coach; b. Bklyn., Dec. 21, 1926; s. Angelo Lafayette and Florence (de LaSalle) P.; m. Suzanne Pohland, May 12, 1962; children: Diana Lynne, Mary Kathryn, David, Joseph Vincent, George Scott. BA, Brown U., 1950, LL.D., 1975. Asst. football coach Pa. State U. Nittany Lions, 1950-66, head coach, 1966—. Author (with Bernard Asbell): The Paterno Principle, 1989; Paterno: By the Book, 1989. Served with AUS, 1945-46. Named Coach of Yr. Walter Camp Football Found., 1972, 2005, Coach of Yr. Washington Touchdown Club, 1973, 86, Coach of Yr. Football Writers Assn. Am.,1968, 78, 82, 86, 2005; won Nat. Championship, 1982, 86; named Sports Illustrated's 1986 Sportsman of the Yr; elected into Coll. Football Hall of Fame, 2006. Mem. Am. Football Coaches Assn. (dir., Coach of Yr. awards 1968, 78, 82, 86). Ranked 4th in All-Time Divsn. IA Coaching Victories, 1st among active coaches. Office: Pa State U Lasch Football Bldg University Park PA 16802-7101

**PATERSON, BASIL ALEXANDER,** lawyer; b. NYC, Apr. 27, 1926; s. Leonard J. and Evangeline (Rondon) P.; m. Portia Hairston, 1953; children: Daniel, David. BS, St. John's Coll., 1948; JD, St. John's U., 1951. Bar: N.Y. 1952. Ptnr. Paterson, Michael, Dinkins and Jones, N.Y.C., 1956—77, Meyer, Suozzi, English & Klein, P.C., Mineola, NY, 1983—; mem. N.Y. State Senate, 1965-70; dep. mayor for labor rels. City of N.Y., 1978; sec. of state State of N.Y., 1979-82. Pres. Inst. Mediation and Conflict Resolution, 1971-77; chmn. 2d Jud. Screening Com., 1985-95; assoc. chmn. N.Y. State Sentencing Guidelines Com.; commr. Port Authority N.Y. and N.J., 1989-95; mem. commn. to promote confidence in judicial elections, 2003-. Bd. dirs. St. Benedict's Day Nursery, 1999—; vice chmn. Dem. Nat. Com., 1972-78, mem., 1972-78; chmn. KeySpan Found., 2003—. Recipient Eagleton Inst. Politics award, Disting. Svc. award Guardians Assn. N.Y. Police Dept., City Club N.Y. award, Black Expo award, Excellence medal St. John's U., Kibbe award CUNY. Roman Catholic. Office: Meyer Suozzi English Klein Pc PO Box 803 Mineola NY 11501-0803

**PATERSON, DAVID ALEXANDER,** state legislator; b. Bklyn., May 20, 1954; s. Basil and Portia (Hairston) P.; m. Michelle Paige; 1 child, Alexander Basil; 1 stepchild, Ashley Dennis. BA, Columbia U., N.Y.C., 1977; JD, Hofstra U., 1983. Mediator Inst. Mediation and Conflict Resolution, NYC, 1975; legal asst. Mcpl. Credit Union, NYC, 1976-78; asst. grants officer Bronx (NY) Community Coll., 1981; dir. Housing Preservation Dept. Fair Housing Office, 1982; asst. criminal law Queens (NY) Dist. Atty.'s Office, 1983-85; senator NY State Senate, 1985-98, minority leader, 1985—2002, minority leader, 2002—. Bd. dirs. Mil-Gar Home Care Service, NY; mem. adv. coun. Lower Manhattan Devel. Corp. Contbr. articles to profl. jours. Fundraising chmn. George McGoverns Presdl. Campaign, N.Y., 1972, Herman Badillo's Mayoral Campaign, N.Y., 1973, Black Citizens for Fair Media, N.Y., 1976, Manhattan Borough Pres. David Dinkins, N.Y., 1985; mem. Martin Luther King Dem. Club, N.Y., 1977—, Jewish Guild for the Blind, N.Y., 1986; mem. bd. trustees Am. Found. for Blind; bd. dirs. Achilles Track Club; mem. fed. steering com. African Burial Ground. Recipient Cmty. Svc. award N.H. Hairston Clan, 1984, Achievement award Courtsman A.A., Inc., 1986, Spl. award Profl. Archaeologists N.Y.C., 1993, Migel award Am. Found. for Blind, 1996; named Senator of Yr., N.Y. State NOW, 1989. Mem. NAACP (bd. dirs. Mid-Manhattan br. 1981—), N.Y. State Bar Assn. on Minorities, Macon B, Allen Black Bar Assn., Met. Com. of 100 (legal advisor 1979—). Avocations: basketball, theater, baseball, history. Office: NY State Senate 907 Legis Office Bldg Albany NY 12247 also: Adam Clayton Powell State Office Bldg Ste 912 163 W 125th St New York NY 10027-4404 also: Ste 1930 250 Broadway New York NY 10007 E-mail: paterson@senate.state.ny.us.*

**PATERSON, DAVID J.,** paper company executive; b. Washington, Aug. 15, 1954; BS, Cornell U., 1976; MBA, U. Mich., 1978. Mktg. analyst Continental Forest Industries, 1978—79; supr. fibre supply, 1979—80; shift foreman, 1980—82, mgr. quality control, 1982—83; sales mgr. containerboard S.W. Forest Industries, 1983—87; export sales mgr. containerboard Ga.-Pacific

Corp., Atlanta, 1987—88, dir. export pulp sales, 1988—92, dir. pulp sales & mktg., 1992—94, v.p. sales & mktg. pulp & bleached bd., 1994—95, v.p. market pulp and recycling ops., 1995—96, v.p. market pulp, 1996—2000, v.p. electronic commerce, 2000, sr. v.p. comm. papers, 2000—01, pres. paper, 2001, pres. paper & bleached bd., 2001, exec. v.p. pulp & paperboard, 2001—03, exec. v.p., pres. bldg. products, 2003—06; pres., CEO Bowater Inc., Greenville, SC, 2006—. Bd. mem. Rsch. Atlanta, Inc.; mem. ISAC12 U.S. Dept. Commerce. Mem.: Japan-Am. Soc. Ga. Office: Bowater Inc 55 E Camperdown Way Greenville SC 29601*

**PATERSON, DAVID LESLIE,** epidemiologist; arrived in U.S., 1997; s. Brian and Robin Paterson; m. Susan Mary Bellamy, Sept. 22, 1990; children: Matthew David, Alexander John. MB, BS, U. Queensland, Brisbane, 1988. Med. resident Princess Alexandra Hosp., Brisbane, 1989—92; infectious diseases registrar Royal Brisbane Hosp., Brisbane, 1993—95; infectious disease physician Sullivan, Nicolaides and Ptnrs., Brisbane, 1996; vis. rschr. U. Pitts. Med. Ctr., Pitts., 1997—99, dir. antibiotic mgmt. program, assoc. prof. dept. medicine, 2001—; dir. infectious diseases U. Pitts. Med. Ctr. - Italy/ISMETT (Inst. Mediterraneo per Trapiant e ad alta Specializzione), Palermo, Italy, 1999—2001; chief transplant infectious diseases U. Pitts. Med. Ctr., 2003—. Contbr. articles to profl. jours. Fellow: Royal Coll. Pathologists Australasian, Royal Australasian Coll. Physicians; mem.: Am. Soc. Microbiology (Merck Irving S. Sigal Meml. award for significant rsch. in microbiology and infectious diseases 2000). Office: Univ Pitts Med Ctr Falk Clini 3601 5th Ave Pittsburgh PA 15213 Business E-mail: patersond@msx.dept-med.pitt.edu.

**PATERSON, EVA,** legal association director, educator; b. 1949; BA, Northwestern U.; JD, Boalt Hall Sch. Law, U. Calif., Berkeley. Bar: 1975. Assoc. Legal Aid Soc. Alameda County; staff mem. Lawyers' Com. Civil Rights, 1977—90, exec. dir., 1990—2003; exec. dir., founder Equal Justice Soc., 2003—. Adj. prof. U. San Francisco Sch. Law, Hastings Sch. Law. Co-founder A Safe Place, Oakland, Calif., Calif. Coalition Civil Rights, chair; v.p. ACLU Nat. Bd.; chair Equal Rights Advocates. Named one of Top 25 Lawyers, San Francisco Chronicle, 2002; recipient Fay Stender award, Calif. Women Lawyers, Woman Yr. award, Black Leadership Forum, Earl Warren Civil Liberties award, ACLU No. Calif., Alumni award Merit, Northwestern U. Mem.: San Francisco Bar Assn. (chair). Achievements include first African Am. pres. student govt. at Northwestern U. Office: Equal Justice Soc 220 Sansome St 14th Fl San Francisco CA 94104 Office Phone: 415-288-8700.

**PATERSON, HATTIE P,** philanthropist; b. Grand Rapids, Mich., Sept. 14, 1944; d. Arthur L Tyler and Lura B Henson. BSc, Davenport U. Realtor, 1984; founder, marketer Mich. Utility and Co. Payment Sys., LLC, 1999. Founder Crime, Inc., 1971—. Home: P O Box 1654 Grand Rapids MI 49501

**PATERSON, KATHERINE WOMELDORF,** writer; b. Huaiyin, China, Oct. 31, 1932; came to U.S., 1940; d. George Raymond and Mary Elizabeth (Goetchius) Womeldorf; m. John Barstow Paterson, July 14, 1962; children: Elizabeth Polin, John Barstow, David Lord, Mary Katherine Nah-he-sah-pe-che-a. AB, King Coll., Bristol, Tenn., 1954; post grad., Kobe Sch. Japanese Lang., 1957-60; MA, Presbyn. Sch. Christian Edn., 1957; MRE, Union Theol. Sem., 1962; LittD. (hon.), King Coll., Bristol, Tenn., 1978; LHD (hon.), Otterbein Coll., 1979; LittD (hon.), St. Mary's of the Woods, 1981; LittD, Washington and Lee U., 1982; LittD (hon.), U. Md., 1982, Shenandoah Coll., 1982; LHD, Washington and Lee U., 1982; LHD (hon.), Norwich U., 1990, Mount St. Vincent U., Halifax, N.S., Can., 1994; LittD, Hope Coll., 1997; DLitt (hon.), Prebyn Coll., 2002. Tchr. Lovettsville Elem. Sch., Va., 1954-55; missionary Presbyn. Ch., Japan, 1957-61; master sacred studies and English Pennington Sch. for Boys, NJ, 1963-65. Author: The Sign of the Chrysanthemum, 1973, Of Nightingales That Weep, 1974, The Master Puppeteer, 1976, Bridge to Terabithia, 1977, The Great Gilly Hopkins, 1978, Angels and Other Strangers, 1979, Jacob Have I Loved, 1980, Rebels of the Heavenly Kingdom, 1983, Come Sing, Jimmy Jo, 1985, (with John Paterson) Consider the Lilies, 1986, Park's Quest, 1988, The Tale of the Mandarin Ducks, 1990, The Smallest Cow in the World, 1991, Lyddie, 1991, The King's Equal, 1992, Who Am I?, 1992, Flip-Flop Girl, 1994, A Midnight Clear: Stories for the Christmas Season, 1995, A Sense of Wonder, 1995, The Angel and the Donkey, 1996, Jip: His Story, 1996, Marvin's Best Christmas Present Ever, 1997, (with John Paterson) Images of God, 1998, Parzival, 1998, Celia and the Sweet, Sweet Water, 1998, Preacher's Boy, 1999, The Wide-Awake Princess, 2000, The Field of the Dogs, 2001, Marvin One Too Many, 2001, The Invisible Child, 2002, The Same Stuff as Stars, 2002, (with John Paterson) Blueberries for the Queen, 2004, Bread & Roses, Too, 2006; translator: The Crane Wife, 1981, The Tongue-Cut Sparrow, 1987. US nominee for Hans Christian Andersen award, 1979, 89, 97, 98; recipient Nat. Book award, 1977, 79, Newbery medal, 1978, 91, Newbery honor, 1979, New Eng. Book award New Eng. Booksellers Assn., 1982, Union medal Union Theol. Sem., 1992, Scott O'Dell award for hist. fiction, 1997, May Hill Arbuthnot Lectr. award, 1997, Lion award NY Pub. Libr., 1998, Literary Light award Boston Pub. Libr., 2000, Living Legend award Libr. of Congress, 2000, Jefferson cup Va. Libr. Assn., 2000, Vt. Gov.'s award for excellence in arts, 2001, Astrid Lindgren Meml. award Swedish Govt., 2006. Mem. Authors Guild, Children's Book Guild Washington. Democrat. Office: Clarion Books 215 Park Ave S New York NY 10003-1603

**PATERSON, RICHARD DENIS,** corporate financial executive; b. Ottawa, Ont., Can., Oct. 13, 1942; m. Antoinette Paterson; children: Christopher, Russell, Kathlyn, Victoria, Connor. B in Commerce, Concordia U., Montreal, Que., Can., 1964. Auditor Coopers & Lybrand, Montreal, 1964-67; acct. Genstar Corp., Montreal, 1967-69; dir. fin. and adminstrn. Indussa Corp. (subs. Genstar Corp.), N.Y.C., 1969-73; v.p.: comptroller Genstar Corp. Montreal and San Francisco, 1973 83; CFO San Francisco, 1983-87; exec. v.p. Genstar Investment Corp., San Francisco, 1987-95; mng. dir. Genstar Capital LP, San Francisco, 1996—. Bd. dirs. Installs Inc.; Am. Pacific Enterprises, Inc., Altra Indsl. Motion, Inc., Propex Fabrics, Inc., Woods Equipment Co., North Am. Constrn. Group., Inc.; chmn. Andros Inc. Mem. Order Chartered Accts. Que. Office: Genstar Capital LP Four Embarcadero Ctr Ste 1900 San Francisco CA 94111-4191 E-mail: rpaterson@gencap.com.

**PATERSON, ROBERT E.,** retail executive; b. Kearny, N.J., Nov. 30, 1926; s. Robert McKinley and Ethel Paterson; m. Eileen Josephine Connolly; children: Carol, Joan, Robert, Richard, Donald, Jeffrey. MBA, Columbia U., 1971. Sr. v.p. fin., treas. The Sperry & Hutchinson Co., Inc., N.Y.C., 1952-87, also bd. dirs. Mem. Nat. Assn. Accts., 1954-89, east. treas., 1985-88; bd. dirs. Govt. Obligations Fund, 1986-87. Elected mem. Borough Coun., 1991-98, 2002-04, coun. pres., 1995-98, 2002. Served with U.S. Army, 1944-45, PTO.

**PATHAK, DOROTHY RYBACZYK,** epidemiologist, researcher; b. Dlugosiodlo, Warsaw, Poland, Nov. 26, 1947; d. Henryk M. and Anna Bobowska Rybaczyk; m. Pramod K. Pathak, Dec. 6, 1969; children: Bogdan A., Leszek A., Anna D. PhD, U. of N.Mex, 1975; MS, Harvard Sch. of Pub. Health, 1983. Asst. prof. U. of N.Mex, Albuquerque, 1975—86, assoc. prof., 1986—94; vis. asst. prof. Harvard Med. Sch., Boston, 1982—83; vis. scholar Stanford U., Calif., 1988—88; assoc. prof. Mich. State U., E. Lansing, 1995—98, prof., 1998—; vis. scholar Harvard Sch. of Pub. Health, Boston, 2001—02. Author: (editl.) Cancer Causes and Control, (article) Am. Jour. of Epidemiology, Internat. Jour. of Cancer. Mem. Zdrowie Plus Inc. NFP-Breast Cancer Survivors Club, Chgo. Grantee Breast Cancer in Women of Polish Ancestry, Nat. Cancer Inst., 1997—, Improved Follow-up of Breast Abnormalities Through Comprehensive Breast Care in Women 40 Years and Older, Dept. of Def., 1998—2001, Breast Cancer: Gene-Diet Interactions in Polish Women, Nat. Cancer Inst., 2002—. Mem.: Am. Statis. Assn., Soc. for Epidemiologic Rsch. Home: 3947 Belding Ct Okemos MI 48864 Office: Mich State Univ 4660 S Hagadorn Rd East Lansing MI 48824

**PATHAK, SANJEEV,** psychiatrist, researcher; b. Shimla, Himachal Pradesh, India; MD, All India Inst. Med. Sci., 1993. Diplomate Am. Bd. of Psychiatry and Neurology. Resident in psychiatry U. Cin., 1996—99, fellowship in child and adolescent psychiatry, 1999—2001; asst. prof. psychiatry and neurology Cin. Children's Hosp., U. Cin. Coll. Medicine, Cin., 2001—. Contbr. articles to profl. jours. Achievements include research in pediatric mood disorders. Office: Cin Children's Hosp 3333 Burnet Ave D-3014 Cincinnati OH 45229 Office Phone: 513-636-4788. E-mail: sanjeev-pathak@cchmc.org.

**PATIENT, WILLIAM F.,** chemicals executive; V.p. sales and mktg. Borg-Warner Chemicals, v.p. mfg.; pres. Borg-Warner Chemicals Europe; sr. v.p. BF Goodrich Company, pres. Geon Vinyl divsn.; CEO Geon (now PolyOne Corp.), 1993—99; chmn. PolyOne Corp., 2003—06, lead dir., 2006—. Bd. dir. Navistar Internat. Corp. Bd. dir. Wash. U.; chmn. of bd. Cleve. State U. Found. Office: 33587 Walker RD Avon Lake OH 44012-1145*

**PATINKIN, MANDY,** actor, singer; b. Chgo., Nov. 30, 1952; s. Lester and Doris (Sinton) P.; m. Kathryn Grody, June 15, 1980; children: Isaac, Gideon. Student, U. Kans., 1970-72, Juilliard Sch. Drama, 1972-74; NC Sch. of Arts. Actor N.Y. Shakespeare Festival, 1975-81; plays include Hotspur in Henry IV, Part 1, Hudson Guild, N.Y.C., Rebel Women, Hamlet, Leave it to Beaver is Dead, Savages; (Broadway) Evita (Tony award 1980), Shadow Box, Sunday in the Park with George, 1984, The Knife, 1987, The Winter's Tale, 1989, Mandy Patinkin in Concert: Dress Casual, 1989, The Secret Garden, 1991, Man of La Mancha, 1996, Forbidden Broadway, 1999, The Wild Party, 2000; (films) The Big Fix, 1978, Last Embrace, 1979, French Postcards, 1980, Night of the Juggler, 1980, Ragtime, 1981, Yentl, 1983, Daniel, 1983, Maxie, 1985, The Princess Bride, 1987, The House on Carroll Street, 1988, Alien Nation, 1988, Dick Tracy, 1990, The Doctor, 1991, True Colors, 1991, The Music of Chance, 1993, Life with Mikey, 1993, Squanto: A Warrior's Tale, 1994, Men with Guns, 1997, Lulu on the Bridge, 1998, The Adventures of Elmo in Grouchland, 1999, Piñero, 2001, Choking Man, 2006, (voice) Everyone's Hero, 2006; (TV appearances): That Thing on ABC, That Second Thing on ABC, Taxi, Midnight Special, (TV series) Chicago Hope, 1994-95, 1999-2000 (Emmy award, 1995), Dead Like Me, 2003-04, Criminal Minds, 2005-; TV movies include Charleston, 1979, Sunday in the Park with George, 1986, Broken Glass, 1996, The Hunchback, 1997, Strange Justice, 1999, NTSB: The Crash of Flight 323, 2004; albums: Mandy Patinkin, 1984, Sunday in the Park with George, 1986, Dress Casual, 1990, Oscar and Steve, 1995, Experiment, 1994, Mamaloshen, 1998, Kidults, 2001. Recipient Music Achievement award Drama League, 1989. Mem. AFTRA, Screen Actors Guild, Actors Equity Assn. Office: United Talent Agy care Adam Isaacs 9560 Wilshire Blvd Ste 500 Beverly Hills CA 90212-2427 also: care Dodger Touring Ltd 501 Broadway Ste 2015 New York NY 10036*

**PATINKIN, TERRY ALLAN,** physician; b. Oak Park, Ill., Feb. 1, 1950; s. Lester D. and Marcella Jaqueline (Steynburg) P.; m. Sandra Lee Friedman, Apr. 21, 1985; children: Jonathan, Zachary. BS, U. Ill., 1971; MD, U. Calif., San Francisco, 1975; MPH in Health Care Mgmt., Harvard U., 1996. Diplomate Am. Bd. Emergency Medicine, Am. Bd. Family Medicine; cert. physician exec. Intern, resident in family practice U. Calif. Med. Francisco/Natividad Med. Ctr., Salinas, Calif., 1975-78, assoc. dir. family medicine residency program, 1978-90; dir. emergency dept. Natividad Med. Ctr., Salinas, 1985-91. dir. continuing med. edn., 1978-91, dir. undergrad. edn., 1978-90, emergency physician, 1979-91, Sturdy Meml. Hosp., Attleboro, Mass., 1991-94; dir. chmn. emergency dept. Roger Williams Hosp., Providence, 1994-99, Landmark Med. Ctr., Woonsocket, RI, 2000—02; med. dir. urgent care East Boston Neighborhood Health Ctr., 2002—. Asst. clin. prof. U. Calif. San Francisco, 1981-88, assoc. clin. prof., 1988-91; clin. asst. prof. Stanford U., 1990-93; asst. clin. prof. Brown U., Providence, 1995—, Boston U., 1999—. Fellow Am. Coll. Emergency Physicians; mem. Am. Coll. Physician Execs., Mass. Coll. Emergency Physicians, Mass. Med. Soc. U. Ill. Alumni Assn. (life), U. Calif. San Francisco Alumni Faculty Assn. Office: 10 Gove St East Boston MA 02128 Office Phone: 617-568-4639. Business E-Mail: patinkit@ebnhc.org.

**PATINO, DOUGLAS XAVIER,** government agency administrator, academic administrator; b. Calexico, Calif., Apr. 11, 1939; s. Jose Luis and Maria Teresa (Seymour) P.; m. Barbel Wilma Hoyer, Aug. 13, 1970; 1 child, Viktor Xavier. AA, Imperial Valley Coll., 1960; BA, Calif. State U., San Diego, 1962, MA, 1966; PhD, U.S. Internat. U., 1972. Deputy dir. Sacramento Concilio, Inc., Calif., 1968-69; v.p. student affairs U. So. Colo., Pueblo, 1973-75; dep. dir. for planning and rev. svc. br. to dir. Calif. Employment Devel. Dept., dir.; sec. Calif. Health & Welfare Agy., 1975-83; dir. Ariz. Dept. of Econ. Security, Phoenix, 1983-87; pres., chief exec. officer Marin Community Found., Larkspur, Calif., 1987-91; pres. New Partnership Found. and Patino Group, San Rafael, Calif., 1991; vice chancellor and pres. Calif. State U. Sys., Long Beach, 1991—2002; prof. social welfare Calif. State U., L.A., 1998—. Commr. W.T. Grand Found., 1986—88, Enterprize for the Ams., Washington, 1994—; trustee C.S. Mott Found., Flint, Mich., 1995—; Calif. Wellness Found., Woodland Hills, 1997—; bd. dirs. Marguerite Casey Found., Companide Found., 2003—, Assn. of Block Found. Exec., 2002—; chair, treas. Hispanics in Philanthropy, 1993—. Mem. Sec. of U.S. Dept. of Labor Task Force, Ariz., 1985-86, Staff Adv. Com. of the Human Resource Com., Nat. Gov. Assn., Washington, 1983-86; bd. dirs. Calif. Pauahi, Santa Cruz, Calif., 1985-95, No. Calif. Grantmakers, 1990-91, Ariz. Assn. Bus., 1984; chair U.S. Savs. Bond Dr. for State of Calif., 1982; trustee Nat. Hispanic U., Oakland, Calif., 1987-90, Hispanic Community Fund, San Francisco, 1989-95, bd. dirs. Calif. Sch. Profl. Psychology, 1989-94, Coun. on Found., Washington, 1990-96, Found. Ctr. N.Y., 1993; pres. Calif. State U. Found. Recipient The Monty Disting. Alumni award San Diego State U., 1997, Simon Bolivar award for cmty. leadership award Hispanic Cmty. Found. and Bay Area United Way 1996, Aztec award Human Devel. Corp., 1991, Leadership award Nat. Concilors of Am. and United Way of Bay Area, 1990, Disting. Performance award, Nat. Alliance of Bus., Washington, 1985, Superior Svc. Mgmt. award, Am. Soc. Pub. Adminstrn., 1985, Humanitarian award, Los Padrinos, Inc., 1981, Small and Minority Bus. award for the State of Calif. 1982, Disting. Alumni award, Calif. Jr. Community Coll. Assn., Sacramento, 1982, Silver Spur award, Nat. Fedn. of Charros in Guadalajaro, Jalisco, Mex., 1974, Calif. Community Svc. award, Former Gov. Ronald Reagan, Sacramento, 1973; named to 100 Most Influential Hispanics, Hispanic Bus., 1995, 97. Mem. Am. Pub. Welfare Assn. (bd. dirs., Leadership award 1987), Rotary, 1987-93. Office: The Patino Group Sacramento CA 95822

**PATINO-BRANDFON, SYLVIA,** retired psychologist; d. Alfonso and Zenobia Moeller Patino; children: Andrea, Thea. AB in English, U. N.Mex., 1956; MS in English, Wis. U., 1958; student, Tavistock Inst., London, 1970—71; MA in Child Study, Tufts U., 1975; PhD in Psychology, Boston Coll., 1980; student in Psychopharmacology, Internat. Coll. Prescribing Psychologist, 1995—97. Lic. psychologist Mass., 1981. Intern psychotherapy Judge Baker Guidance Ctr., Boston, 1972—74; intern McLean Hosp., Belmont, Mass., 1979—80, post doctoral fellow, 1980—81; pvt. practice Quincy and Taunton, Mass., 1982—99; ret., 1999. Spkr. in field. Author: (newsletter) ADHD and Other Behavior Problems, 1994—98. Mem. com. superior cts. Ariz. Supreme Ct., 2004—, mem. jud. performance rev. commn., 2004—, bd. overseeing reporters, 2004. Fellow: APA (life).

**PATKI, KIRAN C.,** pharmacologist, researcher; s. Chandrakant S. and Prabhavati C. Patki; m. Leena K. Patki, Nov. 20, 2003. MBBS, Grant Med. Coll., Bombay, India, 1994; MD, Seth GS Med. Coll., Bombay, 1997. Resident med. officer Seth GS Med. Coll., Bombay, 1994—97; sr. clinician Pfizer Internat. Clin. Rsch. Group, 1997—2001; fellow clin. investigations Harvard-MIT, Boston, 2001—03; fellow clin. pharmacology Tufts U. Sch. of Medicine, 2001—. Recipient Troika award best rsch. paper presentation, Indian Pharm. Soc. (Gujrat chpt.), 1996; scholar, Govt. of Maharashtra, India, 1988—94. Mem.: Am. Coll. Clin. Pharmacology, Am. Soc. Clin. Pharmacology and Therapeutics. Achievements include research in clin. pharmacology; identification of potential effects of polymorphisms; other factors in explaining the variability associated with CYP3A metabolism. Personal E-mail: kirancp@yahoo.com.

**PATLA, JOHN MICHAEL,** protective services official; s. John and Florence Steigel Patla; m. Linda Kay Pratt, June 23, 1973; children: Paige Ellen Patla Carroll, Derek John. BS in Bus., U. Colo., 1967; MPA, U. Ariz., 1980. Cert. drug recognition expert Internat. Assn. Chiefs of Police, fraud specialist Assn. of Cert. Fraud Specialists. Police officer Tucson Police Dept., 1971—77, police sgt., 1977—. Bd. dirs. (past chmn.) crime victim compensation fund Pima County Atty.'s Office, Tucson, 1998—; com. mem. criminal justice adv. com. Pima County C.C., Tucson, 1994—; com. mem. (past chmn.) blood-alcohol com. Ariz. Dept. Health Svcs., Phoenix, 1983—98. 1st lt. U.S. Army, 1967—70. Recipient Copper Letter, City of Tucson, 1996, Chief of Police Citation of Excellence, Tucson Police Dept., 2004. Mem.: Tucson Police Officers Assn., Ariz. Homicide Investigators Assn., Internat. Assn. Fin. Crimes Investigators, FOP. Office: Tucson Police Dept 270 S Stone Ave Tucson AZ 85701

**PATMOS, ADRIAN EDWARD,** retired dean; b. Paterson, NJ, June 29, 1914; s. Adrian and Myra (Van Splinter) P.; m. Pearl Van Den Heuvel, Apr. 25, 1942; children: Adrian Edward III, Bruce Douglas. BA magna cum laude, NYU, 1935, MA, 1936; LLD, Wittenberg U., 1996; postgrad., Am. U., 1936—37. Asst. prof. econs. Wittenberg U., 1938-47, assoc. prof., head dept., 1947-50, prof. econs., 1950—, head dept., 1950-64, dir. mngt. devel. program, 1952-79, eve. sessions, 1952-78; dean Wittenberg U. (Sch. Community Edn.), 1955-79, prof. and dean emeritus, 1979—. Jr. accountant Del. Plant Corp., Curtiss-Wright Corp., 1943; vis. instr. Ohio Wesleyan U., 1944; spl. field rep. NLRB, 1946; vis. lectr. econs. N.Y.U., 1946-48; vis. prof. econs. USAF Inst. Tech., 1949-50; cons. Clark C.C., 1982-84, Urbana U., 1983-94. Mem. Springfield City Firemen's Pension Bd., 1948-53; mem. Springfield City Planning Bd., 1953-58; chmn. Clark County Health Facilities Planning Com., 1965-66, City commr., Springfield, Ohio, 1958-62, mayor, 1960-62; Trustee United Way, Springfield and Clark County, 1960-74; trustee Clark Tech. Coll., 1965-78, chmn., 1969-71, trustee emeritus, 2004—; trustee Springfield Cmty. Hosp., 1975-84, Elderly United, 1979-92. Recipient Wittenberg award for meritorious svc. to univ., 1964, Silver Knight award Nat. Mgmt. Assn., Sta. WIZE award for outstanding cmty. svc., Cmty. Svc. award C. of C., 1979, award of distinction Bd. of Realtors, Outstanding Svc. in Cmty. Labor-Mgmt. Relationships award Fed. Mediation Svc., citation as one of Ohio's foremost educators Ohio Senate, Medal of Honor for leadership in liberal arts edn., 1987; named Jr. Achievement Hall of Fame laureate, 1996; NYU Penfield fellow, 1937-38. Mem. Ohio Coll. Assn. (pres. adult edn. sect. 1959-60), Am. Econs. Assn., Kiwanis (Disting. Svc. to Cmty. award), Phi Beta Kappa, Phi Gamma Delta, Blue Key. Baptist.

**PATMOS, MARCIA,** apparel designer; Grad. in Apparel Design, Rhode Island Sch. of Design. Designer, NYC, 1991—; co-owner, designer (with Tina Lutz) Lutz & Patmos, NYC, 2000—. Work featured in Vogue, Elle, Cosmopolitan, Town & Country, WWD, Glamour, NY Mag., NY Times, Marie Claire; work shown in Cooper Hewitt Museum, Pasadena Museum of Calif. Arts, Royal Museum of Scotland, San Francisco Modern Museum of Art. Office: Lutz & Patmos Ste 406 425 W 13th St New York NY 10014*

**PATNAUDE, WILLIAM EUGENE,** architect; b. Sanger, Calif., Sept. 24, 1937; s. Eugene Joseph Patnaude and Vera Mae (Giles) Patnaude Fagan; m. Mary Esther Simerly, Aug. 22, 1971 (div. 1987); children: Nathaniel, Matthew BArch, U. Calif., Berkeley, 1961; postgrad., Calif. State U., Fresno, 1968-72. Registered arch., Calif., Wash., Idaho, Nev., Colo., Utah, Ariz., Mont., Ind., Nebr., Ohio, N.Y., N.J. Draftsman, arch. Robert Stevens Assoc., Santa Cruz, Calif., 1963-66; arch. Llewelyn Davies, Weeks & Ptnrs., London, 1966, Allen Y. Lew, Fresno, Calif., 1967-69, assoc., 1969-74; v.p., arch. Lew & Patnaude, Inc., Fresno, 1974-84, pres., 1985—. Instr. Calif. State U., Fresno, 1968-81 Constn. arbitrator Am. Arbitration Assn., 1976-96; chair ctrl. area plan citizen's adv. com. City of Fresno, 1991-93, chair gen. plan update com., 1994-97; bd. dirs. Fresno Arts Ctr., 1971-74, Fresno County Alliance for the Arts, 1986-88, 91-94. With USNR, 1961-63. Recipient Merit award Calif. Hist. Preservation Conf., Orange County, 1983, Excellence award Woodwork Inst. Calif., 1982, Recognition cert. City Fresno, 2004, Calif. State Assembly commendation City Fresno, 2004. Fellow AIA (nat. dir. 1983-85, pres. Calif. Coun. 1982, San Joaquin chpt. 1978, Awards of Excellence, 1972-95); mem. Constrn. Specifications Inst. (pres. Fresno chpt. 1977). Democrat. Avocations: photography, fine wines. Home: 4190 N Van Ness Blvd Fresno CA 93704-4213 Office: Lew & Patnaude Inc 1050 S St Fresno CA 93721-1497 Office Phone: 559-486-8150. Business E-mail: billp@csufresno.edu.

**PATNER, ANDREW,** writer, art critic; Attended, U. Chgo., U. Wis., Madison. Lectr. and tchr. in Chgo. and Eastern Europe. Former editor, staff writer Chicago Magazine; staff reporter Wall Street Journal; former art critic. program host, prodr. WBEZ-FM, critic-at-large, interviewer WFMT Fine Art Radio, contbr. Chicago Sun-Times, 1991—, contbg. editor Art & Antiques, The Art Newspaper (London), The New Yorker, German GEO, Jewish Forward, New Art Examiner, Die Opernwelt, The Christian Science Monitor, High Performance, and other publs.; author: I.F. Stone: A Portrait, 1988; editor: Alternative Futures: Challenging Designs for Arts Philanthropy, 1995; dir.: "Democratic Vistas: Towards a New American Arts Policy", Columbia Coll. Chgo. sponsored by John D. and Catherine T. MacArthur Found. Recipient Peter Lisagor award. Mem.: The Cliff Dwellers, Assn. of Literary Scholars and Critics, Chgo. Art Critic Assn., Arts Club Chgo. (co-chair, interarts coun.). Address: 2175 W Leland Chicago IL 60625 E-mail: renrap@aol.com.

**PATON, JOHN GLENN,** voice educator; b. New Castle, Pa., Feb. 21, 1934, s. John Felor and Margaret Elinor (Hensley) Paton; m. Marion Anderson, Dec. 19, 1961 (div. 1987); 1 child, Andrew Werner; m. Joan Marsha Thompson, Jan. 17, 1987. MusB, Cin. Conservatory Music, 1955; MusM Lit., Eastman Sch. Music, 1960. Instr. U. Wis., Madison, 1961—68; prof. U. Colo., Boulder, 1968—89; lectr. U. So. Calif., LA, 1989—. Editor: (song anthologies) 26 Italian Songs and Arias, 1991, Gateway to German Lieder, 2000, Gateway to Italian Art Songs, 2004. D-Liberal. Home: 16823 McKeever St Granada Hills CA 91344 E-mail: paton@usc.edu.

**PATON WALSH, JILL,** writer; b. London, Apr. 29, 1937; d. John Llewelyn and Patricia (Dubern) Buss; m. Antony Edmund Paton Walsh, Aug. 5, 1961; Children: Edmund, Margaret, Clare. Author: Hengest's Tale, 1966, The Dolphin Crossing, 1967, Fireweed, 1969, (World Book Festival award 1970), Wordhoard, 1969, Goldengrove 1972, Farewell Great Kanga, 1972, Toolmaker, 1973, The Dawnstone, 1973, The Emperor's Winding Sheet, 1974 (Whitbread prize 1974), The Huffler, 1975, The Island Sunrise: Prehistoric Culture in the British Isles, 1975, Unleaving, 1976 (Boston Globe, Horn Book award 1976), Children of the Fox: Crossing to Salamis, 1977, The Walls of Athens, 1978, Persian Gold, 1978, A Chance Child, 1978, The Green Book, 1981, Babylon, 1982, Parcell of Patterns, 1983 (Universe prize 1984), Lost and Found, 1984, Gaffer Samson's Luck, 1984 (Smarties Grand prix 1984), Lapsing, 1985, A School for Lovers, 1989, Birdy and the Ghosties, 1990, "Grace", 1991, Matthew and the Sea Singers, 1992, When Grandma Came, 1992, The Wydham Case, 1993, Knowledge of Angels, 1994, A Piece of Justice, 1995, Connie Came to Play, 1995, Thomas and the Tinners, 1995, The Serpentine Cave, 1997, When I Was Little Like You, 1997, (with Dorothy L. Sayers) Thrones, Dominations, 1998, A Desert in Bohemia, 2000, (with Dorothy L. Sayers) A Presumption of Death, 2002, Debts of Dinosaur, 2006. Fellow Royal Soc. of Lit. (CBE award 1996). Address: care David Higham Assocs 5-8 Lower John St Golden Sq London W1R 3PE England

**PATOSKI, MARGARET NANCY,** historian, educator; b. Ellis County, Tex., Dec. 24, 1929; d. Bob Milton and Clara Clementine (Graham) Pearson; m. Victor Albert Patoski, July 23, 1960; children: Christina Victoria, Nicholas Joseph. BA magna cum laude, Tex. Christian U., 1968, MA, 1970, PhD, 1973. Asst. prof. history East Tex. State U., Commerce, 1973-77, Tex. Wesleyan U., Ft. Worth, 1977-83, assoc. prof. history, 1983-89, prof. history, 1989—2002; prof. emerita history, 2002—. Translator, annotator: Reminiscences of My Father, Peter A. Stolypin, 1970, The Career of a Tsarist Officer, 1975, Stolypin: Russia's Last Great Reformer, 1986, Boris Savinkov: Portrait of a

Terrorist, 1987; contbr. numerous articles, revs. to profl. pubs. Dem. precinct chair Tarrant County, Ft. Worth, 1980-95; bd. dirs. Pleasant Valley Hist. Cemetery, Cedar Hill, Tex., 1983—, Humane Soc. North Tex., Ft. Worth, 1985-91. Mem. Am. Assn. Advancement of Slavic Studies, Am. History Assn., World History Assn., Western Social Sci. Assn. (pres. 1981-82, Outstanding Svc. award 1984), Rocky Mountain Slavic Studies Assn. (pres. 1980-81), Southwestern Slavic Studies Assn. (pres. 1978-79). Episcopalian. Home: 4325 Lovell Ave Fort Worth TX 76107-5412 Personal E-mail: patoskim@earthlink.net.

**PATRIC, JASON,** actor; b. June 17, 1966; s. Jason and Linda Gleason Miller. Actor: (films) include The Lost Boys, 1987, The Beast, 1988, After Dark, My Sweet, 1990, Denial Loon, 1991, Rush, 1991, Geronimo-An American Legend, 1993, The Journey of August King, 1995, Sleepers, 1996, Incognito, 1997, Speed 2, 1997, Friends and Neighbors, 1998, 3 Days of Rain, 2000, Narc, 2002, The Alamo, 2004;(TV movies) Toughlove, 1985. Office: United Talent Agy care David Schiff 9560 Wilshire Blvd Ste 500 Beverly Hills CA 90212-2427

**PATRICELLI, GAIL LISA,** biology professor; d. Ernest Edward and Joyce Anne Patricelli. MS, U. Md., College Park, 2000, PhD, 2002. Postdoctoral fellow bioinformatics Cornell U., Ithaca, NY, 2002—04; asst. prof. U. Calif., Davis, 2004—. Office: Univ California Davis 2320 Storer Hall One Shields Ave Davis CA 95616 Office Phone: 530-754-8310.

**PATRICK, BRENDA JEAN,** educational consultant; b. Dallas, Aug. 24, 1955; d. Gene Everett and Peggy Rose Patrick; 1 child, Michael Everett. BS in Elem. Edn., Tex. A&M U., Commerce, 1981, MS, 1984, postgrad., 1989—. Cert. Tex. Edn. Agy. Tchr. Garland Ind. Sch. Dist., 1982-87, acad. coach, 1983-86; with Austin Acad. for Excellence, 1987-88; program coord., master cons. Region 10 Edn. Svc. Ctr., 1988—. Coord. Tchr. Expectation Student Achievement; trainer Devel. Capable People; trainer of trainers Profl. Devel. and Appraisal Sys.; developer, presenter workshops and seminars in field. Author: Better Teaching, Texas Secretary. Past bd. dirs. Dallas Arboretum's Fan Club; mem. adv. bd. Tex. Edn. Support Staff Assn. Recipient Tex. History Tchr. award Daus. of Republic of Tex., Am. History Tchr. award DAR; named Vol. with a Heart, YWCA. Mem. Tex. PTA (hon. life), Tex. Staff Devel. Coun., Phi Delta Kappa. Office Phone: 214-693-2411. Personal E-mail: bjp@brendajeanpatrick.com.

**PATRICK, CHARLES WILLIAM, JR.,** lawyer; b. Monroe, NC, Oct. 9, 1954; s. Charles William and Louise (Nisbet) P.; m. Celeste Hunt, June 5, 1976; children: Laura Elizabeth, Charles William III. BA magna cum laude, Furman U., 1976; JD, U. SC, 1979. Bar: S.C. 1979, U.S. Dist. Ct. S.C. 1981, U.S. Ct. Appeals (11th cir.) 1981, U.S. Ct. Appeals (10th cir.) 1983, U.S. Ct. Appeals (4th cir.) 1986. Law clk. to presiding judge 9th Cir. Ct. State of S.C. Charleston, 1979—80; assoc. Ness, Motley, Loadholt, Richardson and Poole and predecessor firm Blatt and Fales, Charleston, 1980—2002, 1980—84, ptnr., 1984—2002, Richardson, Patrick, Westbrook & Brickman, LLC, Charleston, 2002—. Exec. editor S.C. Law Review, 1978; contbr. articles to profl. jours. Mem. ABA, Assn. Trial Lawyers Am., S.C. Assn. Trial Lawyers, Trial Lawyers for Pub. Justice, Phi Beta Kappa. Democrat. Presbyterian. Avocations: boating, skiing, jogging. Home: 38 Church St Charleston SC 29401-2742 Office: Richardson Patrick Westbrook & Brickman LLC PO Box 879 174 East Bay St Charleston SC 29402-0879 Office Phone: 843-727-6500. Business E-Mail: cpatrick@rpwb.com.

**PATRICK, CONNIE L.,** federal official; m. John Patrick; 4 children. BA in Criminal Justice, U. Ctrl. Fla.; Grad., FBI Nat. Acad., Fla. Criminal Justice Exec. Inst., Fed. Exec. Inst. Dep. Sheriff's Office Brevard County, 1976—81; various positions including spl. agent, spl. agent supr., asst. spl. agent in charge of Tampa reg. ops. bur., dir. Fla. Criminal Justice Inst. Fla. Dept. Law Enforcement, 1981—95, dir. divsn. human resources & training, 1995—96; dir. gen. training Fed. Law Enforcement Training Ctr., 1996—98, assoc. dir. planning & resources, 1998—2001, assoc. dir. planning & workforce devel., 2001—02, dir., 2002—. Recipient Presdl. Meritorious Rank award, 2001. Office: Fed Law Enforcement Training Ctr 1131 Chapel Crossing Rd Brunswick GA 31524

**PATRICK, CRAIG,** former professional hockey team executive; b. Detroit, May 20, 1946; s. Lynn P.; m. Sue Patrick; children— Erin, Taylor, Ryan, CJ. MBA, U. Denver. Hockey player Calif. Golden Seals, 1971-74, St. Louis Blues, 1974-75, Kansas City Scouts, 1975-76, World Hockey Assn., Minn., 1976-77, Washington Capitals, 1977-79; v.p., gen. mgr. NY Rangers, NYC, 1981-86; dir. athletics and recreation Univ. Denver, 1987-89; gen. mgr., exec. v.p. Pitts. Penguins, 1989—2006. Named Exec. of Yr., The Sporting News, 1998, 1999; named to US Hockey Hall of Fame, 1996; recipient Lester Patrick Trophy, 2000. Achievements include being capt., US Nat. Team, World Championships, Moscow, 1979; asst. mgr. and asst. coach US Olympic Hockey Team, 1980.*

**PATRICK, DANICA SUE,** race car driver; b. Beloit, Wis., Mar. 25, 1982; d. T.J. and Bev Patrick; m. Paul Hospenthal, Nov. 19, 2005. With Team Rahal Letterman, 2002—; debut Formula Vauxhall Winter Series, England, 1998, Toronto, Canada, 2002; made her IndyCar Series debut Toyota Indy 300, 2005; signed with Andretti Green Racing, 2006. Co-author (with Laura Morton): Danica: Crossing the Line, 2006. Recipient numerous World Karting Assn. titles including National Points titles in WKA Manufactus Cup, 1994, 96, five Grand Lakes Sprint Series titles and Midwest Spring Series titles, 1996, Grand National championship and Summer National Championship, 1997; Gorsline Scholarship award, 2001 Won 39 of 49 feature karting races, 1996; finished 9th in Formula Vauxhall Championship, Eng., 1991, 2d in Formula Ford Festival (highest finish for an American), 2000, 4th in first appearance in the Indianapolis 500, 2005; became the first female to post a top three result in Atlantic Series, Monterrey, Mex., 2003; first female driver to win pole position in Toyota Atlantic, Portland, 2004.

**PATRICK, DEVAL LAURDINE,** lawyer; b. Chgo., July 31, 1956; s. Laurdine Kenneth and Emily Mae (Wintersmith) P.; m. Diane Louise Bemus, May 5, 1984; children: Sarah Baker, Katherine Wintersmith. AB cum laude, Harvard Coll., 1978, JD, 1982; JD (hon.). Dist. Columbia Law Sch., 1994, Morris Brown Coll., 1996, Curry Coll., 1997, Clark U., 1999, New Eng. Sch. of Law, 1999, Suffolk U., 2000, Northeastern U., 2002. Bar: Calif. 1983, Mass. 1987, U.S. Dist. Ct. Mass. 1987, U.S. Dist. Ct. (cen. dist.) Calif. 1983, U.S. Ct. Appeals (1st and 5th cirs.) 1984, U.S. Ct. Appeals (9th and 11th cirs.) 1984, U.S. Supreme Ct. 1988. Law clk. to Hon. Stephen Reinhardt U.S. Ct. Appeals (9th cir.), L.A., 1982-83; asst. counsel NAACP Legal Def. Fund, N.Y.C., 1983-86; ptnr. Hill & Barlow, Boston, 1986-94; asst. atty. gen. civil rights divsn. U.S. Dept. Justice, Washington, 1994-97; ptnr. Day, Berry & Howard, Boston, 1997-99; v.p., gen. counsel Texaco Inc., White Plains, NY, 1999-2001; exec. v.p., gen. counsel The Coca-Cola Co., Atlanta, 2001—04, corp. sec., 2002—04. Herman Phleger disting. vis. prof. Stanford Law Sch. 1997; lectr. Boston Coll. Sch. Law, 1997, Harvard Law Sch. 1998; mem. various corp. bd. dirs.; bd. overseers Harvard U., 1998—2003; dir. UAL Corp., 1997-2001, Reebok Internat. Ltd., 2001-05, Coca-Cola Enterprises Inc., 2001-04, ACC Capital Holdings (Ameriquest), 2004-06 Dir., mem. exec. com., chmn. New Eng. steering com. NAACP Legal Def. and Edn. Fund., Inc., 1991-94, vice chmn. Mass. Jud. Nominating Coun., 1991-93; trustee mem. exec. com. Milton Acad., 1985-97; overseer WGBH, 1993-94; trustee Nathan Cummings Found., 1998-2000, Ford Found., 2000-05 Recipient George Leisure award Harvard Law Sch., 1981; Rockefeller Traveling fellow, 1978. Mem. ABA (numerous bds. and coms.), Mass. Bar Assn., Mass. Black Lawyers Assn., Boston Bar Assn. (coun. mem. 1993), Harvard Alumni Assn. (dir. 1993-96). Avocations: squash, cooking, gardening.

**PATRICK, DONALD LEE,** sociologist, educator; b. Eugene, Oreg., Sept. 23, 1944; s. Lawrence Leonard and Marie Esther (Bell) P.; m. Shirley Anne Alexander Beresford, May 31, 1980; children: Alistair Lawrence Beresford, Mira Yvonne Bell. AB with distinction, Northwestern U., 1966; MSPH,

Columbia U., 1968, PhD, 1972. Rsch. assoc. U. Calif., San Diego, 1970-72; lectr. Yale U., New Haven, 1972-76; sr. lectr. U. London, 1976-82; assoc. prof. U. N.C., Chapel Hill, 1982-87; prof. and dir. social and behavioral scis. program U. Wash., Seattle, 1987—. Adj. prof. sociology, U. Wash., 1988—; dept. rehab. medicine, 1987—. Author: Health Status and Health Policy, 1993; editor: Sociology as Applied to Medicine, 1976, Disablement in Community, 1989. Mem. APHA (mem. coun. 1993-96), Spina Bifida Assn. Am. (chair profl. adv. bd. 1990-93, Pres.' award 1995), Internat. Soc. for Quality of Life Rsch. (pres. 1994-96, Pres. award 2001), Inst. Medicine. Democrat. Unitarian Universalist. Avocations: gardening, music, travel. Home: 5427 43rd Ave W Seattle WA 98199-1061 Office: U Wash PO Box 357660 Seattle WA 98195-7660

**PATRICK, H. HUNTER,** retired judge; b. Gasville, Ark., Aug. 19, 1939; s. H. Hunter Sr. and Nelle Frances (Robinson) P.; m. Charlotte Anne Wilson, July 9, 1966; children: Michael Hunter, Colleen Annette. BA, U. Wyo., 1961, JD, 1966. Bar: Wyo. 1966, U.S. Dist. Ct. Wyo. 1966, Colo. 1967, U.S. Supreme Ct. 1975. Mcpl. judge City of Powell (Wyo.), 1967-68; sole practice law Powell, 1966-88; atty. City of Powell, 1969-88; justice of the peace County of Park, Wyo., 1971-88; bus. law instr. Northwest C.C., Powell, 1968-98; dist. judge State of Wyo. 5th Jud. Dist., 1988—2006; drug ct. judge Park County, Wyo., 2001—06; ret., 2006. Mem. Wyo. Dist. Judges Conf., sec.-treas., 1993-94, vice chair, 1994-95, chair, 1995-96. Editor: Bench Book for Judges of Courts of Limited Jurisdiction in the State of Wyoming, 1980-90. Dir. cts. Wyo. Girls State, Powell, 1982-85, 89-99, 2005—; elder, deacon, moderator of deacons Powell Presbyn. Ch., 1997; mem. Wyo. Commn. Jud. Conduct & Ethics, 1997-2003; judge, chair mgmt. com. Park County Drug Ct., 2001—. Recipient Wyo. Crime Victim Compensation Commn. Judicial award, 1995, Wyo. Criminal Justice Assn. Svc. award, 2005. Fellow Am. Bar Found. (life), Wyo. Jud. Adv. Coun.; mem. ABA (Wyo. state del. to ho. of dels. 1994-2001, Wyo. del. jud. adminstrn. divsn., exec. com. nat. conf. trial ct. judges representing Wyo., Colo., Kans., Nebr., N.Mex. 1996-2000, Wyo. Bar Assn. (Cmty. Svc. award 1999, Am. Pub. Svc. award 1999), Colo. Bar Assn., Park County Bar Assn. (sec. 1969-70, pres. 1970-71), Wyo. Assn. Cts. Ltd. Jurisdiction (pres. 1973-80), Wyo. Dist. Judges Conf. (chair 1996), Am. Judicature Soc. (mem. jud. adv. coun.). Avocations: photography, travel, fishing, reading, writing. Home: PO Box 941 Powell WY 82435-0941 Personal E-mail: hpatrick2778@msn.com.

**PATRICK, HEATHER R.,** chemistry professor; BS in Engring., Princeton U., NJ, 1993; PhD, Ga. Inst. Tech., Atlanta, 2000. Asst. prof. chemistry Oxford Coll. Emory U., Ga., 2000—. Office: Oxford College of Emory University 100 Hamill St Oxford GA 30054 Office Phone: 770-784-8396.

**PATRICK, HUGH TALBOT,** economist, educator; b. Goldsboro, NC, Feb. 22, 1930; s. Talbot and Paula (Miller) P.; children: Stephen, Matthew, Catherine. BA, Yale U., 1951; MA in Far Eastern Studies, U. Mich., 1955, MA in Econs., 1957, PhD in Econs., 1960; MA (hon.), Yale U., 1968; PhD (hon.), Lingnan U., 2000. Econ. analyst U.S. Govt., 1951-52; lectr. econs. U. Mich., 1958-60; asst. prof. econs. Yale U., New Haven, 1960-64, assoc. prof., 1964-68, prof. Far Eastern econs., 1968-84; dir. Yale U. Econ. Growth Ctr., 1976-79, 80-83; R.D. Calkins prof. internat. bus. Columbia U., N.Y.C., 1984—2001, prof. emeritus, 2001—. Vis. prof. U. Bombay, 1961-62; mem. Japan-U.S. Econ. Rels. Group, 1978-81, U.S. Com. for Pacific Econ. Coop.; dir. Ctr. on Japanese Econ. and Bus., Columbia U., 1986—. Editor: Japanese Industrialization and Its Social Consequences, 1976, Japanese High Technology Industries-Lessons and Limitations of Industrial Policy, 1986; contbr. chpt. and co-editor (with Henry Rosovsky): Asia's New Giant-How the Japanese Economy Works, 1976, (with Masahiko Aoki): The Japanese Main Bank System: Its Relevance for Developing and Transforming Economies, 1994, (with Takatoshi Ito and David Weinstein) Reviving Japan's Economy: Problems and Prescriptions, 2005; co-editor (with Larry Meissner): Pacific Basin Industries in Distress: Structural Adjustment and Trade Policy in Nine Industrialized Economies, 1991 (Masayoshi Ohira Meml. prize 1992), (with Yung Chul Park) The Financial Development of Japan, Korea and Taiwan: Growth, Repression and Liberalization, 1994, (with Takeo Hoshi) Crisis and Change in the Japanese Financial System, 2000. Ford Found. fellow 1957-58; grantee Am. Coun. Learned Socs., 1962; Guggenheim fellow, 1964-65; Fulbright rsch. prof., 1964-65; Fulbright-Hays NDEA fellow, 1968-69; Assn. Asian Studies Disting. lectr., 1977. Mem. Japan Soc. (dir. 1973-79, 81-2000), Social Sci. Rsch. Coun. (dir., chmn. 1985-88), Pacific Trade and Devel. Confs. (chmn.). Democrat. Office: Columbia U 320 Uris Hall 3022 Broadway New York NY 10027-6945 Office Phone: 212-854-3497. Business E-Mail: htp1@columbia.edu.

**PATRICK, JAMES DUVALL, JR.,** lawyer; b. Griffin, Ga., Dec. 28, 1947; s. James Duvall and Marion Wilson P. BS in Indsl. Mgmt., Ga. Inst. Tech., 1970; JD, U. Ga., 1973. Bar: Ga. 1973, U.S. Dist. Ct. (mid. dist.) Ga. 1973, U.S. Dist. Ct. (so. dist.) Ga. 1983, U.S. Ct. Appeals (5th cir.) 1974, U.S. Ct. Appeals (11th cir.) 1981, U.S. Tax Ct. 1985, U.S. Supreme Ct. Assoc. Cartledge, Cartledge & Posey, Columbus, Ga., 1973-74; ptnr. Falkenstrom Hawkins & Patrick, Columbus, 1975, Falkenstrom & Patrick, Columbus, 1975-77; sole practice Columbus, 1977—. Instr. bus. law Chattahoochee Valley C.C., Phenix City, Ala., 1975-77; instr. paralegal course Columbus Coll., 1979, 84; del. U.S./China Joint Session on Trade, Investment, and Econ. Law, Beijing, 1987, Moscow Conf. on Law and Bilateral Econ. Rels., Moscow, 1990; U.S. del. U.S./Cuba Law Initiative, Havana, 2000. Mem. Hist. Columbus Found., Mayor's Comn. for the Handicapped, 1987-88; local organizer, worker Joe Frank Harris for Gov. Campaign, Columbus, 1982; bd. dirs. Columbus Symphony Orch., 1988-94. Fellow Am. Bar Found.; mem. ATLA, ABA (fellow found.), Am. Judicature Soc., State Bar Ga., Fed. Bar Assn., Ga. Trial Lawyers Assn., Columbus Lawyers Club, Columbus Kappa Alpha Alumni Assn. (sec.), Civitan (bd. dirs. 1975-77), Country Club of Columbus, Georgian Club (Atlanta), Buckhead Club, Chattahoochee River Club, Phi Delta Phi, Kappa Alpha. Methodist. Office: PO Box 2745 Columbus GA 31902-2745

**PATRICK, JOHN JOSEPH,** social sciences educator; b. East Chicago, Ind., Apr. 14, 1935; s. John W. and Elizabeth (Lazar) P.; m. Patricia Grant, Aug. 17, 1963; children— Rebecca, Barbara AB. Dartmouth Coll., 1957; Ed.D., Ind. U., 1969. Social studies tchr. Roosevelt High Sch., East Chicago, 1957-62; social studies tchr. Lab. High Sch., U. Chgo., 1962-65; research assoc. Sch. Edn., Ind. U., Bloomington, 1965-69, asst. prof., 1969-74, assoc. prof., 1974-77, prof. edn., 1977—2004, prof. emeritus edn., 2004—, dir. social studies devel. ctr., 1986—2004, dir. ERIC clearinghouse for social studies, social sci. edn., 1986—2003. Bd. dirs. Biol. Scis. Curriculum Study, 1980-83; ednl. cons. Author: Progress of the Afro-American, 1968, The Young Voter, 1974; (with L. Ehman, Howard Mehlinger) Toward Effective Instruction in Secondary Social Studies, 1974, Lessons on the Northwest Ordinance, 1987; (with R. Remy) Civics for Americans, 1980, rev. edit. 1986; (with Mehlinger) American Political Behavior, 1972, rev. edit. 1980; (with C. Keller) Lessons on the Federalist Papers, 1987; America Past and Present, 1983; (with Carol Berkin) History of the American Nation, 1984, rev. edit., 1987; Lessons on the Constitution, 1985, James Madison and the Federalist Papers, 1990, How to Teach the Bill of Rights, 1991, Ideas of the Founders on Constitutional Government: Resources for Teachers of History and Government, 1991, Young Oxford Companion to the Supreme Court of the United States, 1994, Founding the Republic: A Documentary History, 1995, (with Gerald Long) Constitutional Debates on Freedom of Religion: A Documentary History, 1999, (with Richard M. Pious and Donald A. Ritchie) The Oxford Essential Guide to the U.S. Government, 2000, The Bill of Rights: A History in Documents, 2002, Understanding Democracy, 2006, (with Kermit L. Hall) The Pursuit of Justice: Supreme Court Decisions That Shaped America, 2006. Bd. dirs. Law W. Soc. Found., 1984-88, Social Sci. Edn. consortium, 1984—; mem. Gov.'s Task Force on Citizenship Edn., Ind., 1982-87; active Ind. Commn. on Bicentennial of U.S. Constn., 1986-92; bd. dirs. Coun. for the Advancement of Citizenship, Nat. History Edn. Network, 1994-96; mem. Natr. Coun. for History Standards, 1991-94. Recipient John W. Ryan award

for disting. svc. in internat. programs and studies, Ind. U., 2002, Civic Edn. award, Ind. State Bar Assn., 2005. Mem. ASCD, Nat. Coun. Social Studies, Social Sci. Edn. Consortium (v.p. 1985-87), Coun. for Basic Edn., Am. Polit. Sci. Assn., Am. Hist. Assn., Orgn. Am. Historians, Ind. State Bar Assn. (recipient Civic Edn. award 2005), Phi Delta Kappa. Home: 1209 E University St Bloomington IN 47401-5045 Office: Ind U 2805 E 10th St Bloomington IN 47408-2601 Business E-Mail: patrick@indiana.edu.

**PATRICK, MICHELE MARY,** government official; b. Phila., Apr. 18, 1963; d. George Robert and Mary Elizabeth (Pristic) P. BA with honors in Econs., La Salle U., 1985; M in Govt. Adminstrn., U. Pa., 1990. Intern Phila. Water Dept., 1987; intern, asst. to exec. dir. Global Interdependence Ctr., Phila., 1988-89; intern, asst. to dep. dir. Phila. Fin. Dept., 1989, asst. to fin. dir., 1990; asst. mng. dir. City of Phila., 1990-91, 93-96; speechwriter to U.S. Senator Frank R. Lautenberg, 1996-97; speechwriter to Hon. Donna Shalala U.S. Sec. Health and Human Svcs., 1997—. Speaker in field. Author: Haunted Prague; co-author: sect. of Municipal Dept. Handbook; trivia writer Merit Inds., Bensalem, Pa., 1993-95; monthly columnist Global Stamp News, 1994-96. Recipient Fulbright fellowship, U.K., Bd. Fgn. Scholarships, Washington, 1985, Nat. Resource fellowship, Pacific-Asian Mgmt. Inst., U. Hawaii, 1984, Lindback award, La Salle U., Phila., 1985, Pa. Forensic Assn., State Championships, 1982, 83, 85, Nat. Forensic Assn. Nat. championship, 1985, Meyerson fellowship, U. Pa., Phila., 1987, Pres. Classroom scholarship, Pres. Classroom for Young Ams., Washington, 1982, James and Helen Hovorka scholarship, Coun. Higher Edn., Brookfield, Ill., 1982, 83, 84. Mem. Amnesty Internat., Am. Friends of Czech Republic, Fulbright Alumni Assn., Omicron Delta Epsilon. Avocations: historical travel, classical music, british and russian studies.

**PATRICK, PAUL,** emergency physician; b. Kingston, Jamaica, Mar. 22, 1975; arrived in U.S., 1989; s. Jennifer Jurianna Moore. BA, U. Rochester, 1998, MD, 2004. Psychiatric technician Strong Behavioral Health, Rochester, NY, 1998—99; med. resident Strong Meml. Hosp., Rochester, 1999—, intern, 2004—. Med. liaison Charles Drew Pre-Health/Pre-Med. Assn., Rochester, 2002—04. Big brother Baden St. Settlement, Rochester, 1998. Traveling scholar, Am. Psychiat. Assn., 2002. Mem.: Am. Coll. Emergency Physicians, Emergency Medicine Residents Assn. Avocations: photography, motorcycling, disc jockey. Home: 1545 Mount Hope Ave Rochester NY 14620 Office: Dept Emergency Medicine 601 Elmwood Ave Rochester NY 14642 Office Phone: 585-273-4124. Office Fax: 585-473-3516. Business E-Mail: paul_patrick@urmc.rochester.edu.

**PATRICK, RICHARD M.,** professional hockey team executive; b. Victoria, B.C., Can., Oct. 20, 1946; married; 3 children. Student, Dartmouth Coll., Am. U. Washington. Exec. v.p. Washington Capitals Hockey Team, Landover, Md.; now pres, gov. Washington Capitals, 1992—. Office: Washington Capitals MCI Center 601 F St NW Washington DC 20004-1605

**PATRICK, ROBERT,** playwright; b. Kilgore, Tex., Sept. 27, 1937; s. Robert and Beulah (Goodson) O'Connor. Author numerous plays produced off-off Broadway, off-Broadway, Broadway, also abroad including Robert Patrick's Cheep Theatricks (23 plays), 1972, Simultaneous Transmissions, 1973, Play-By-Play, 1975, The Golden Circle, 1975, Kennedy's Children, 1975, Let Me Tell It To You, Dr. Paroo, 1976, One Man, One Woman (6 plays), 1978, T-Shirts, 1979, Mutual Benefit Life, 1980, Mercy Drop and Other Plays (5 plays), 1980, My Cup Ranneth Over, 1984, Big Sweet, 1985, Untold Decades (7 plays), 1988, Drowned Out, 1990, Connie, 1991, Michaelangelo's Models, 1994, Bread Alone, 1994, The Trial of Socrates, 1994, Evan on Earth, 1995, Hollywood at Sunset, 2004, Pouf Positive (CD), 1996; author: (novels) Temple Slave, 1986, Echo, 1990, (book on CD) Film Moi, 2003, (films) Resident Alien, 1990, The O Boys Documentary, 1999; teleplays include: High Tide, 1994, Robin's Hoods, 1995, Ghost Story, 1997, (essay) Film Moi, 1999, Caffe Cino Picture Pages, 2006; contbr. poems, articles, stories to profl. jours. Rockefeller grantee, 1974, N.Y. State CAPS grantee, 1975; recipient Show Bus. Best Playwright award 1968-69, Glasgow Citizens' Theatre Best World Playwright award, 1974, Omni-Act One award, 1975, Robbie award, 1976, Founders award Internat. Thespians Soc., 1980, Blue is for Boys weekends in Manhattan, 1983, 86, Lifetime Achievement award for Gay Playwriting Robert Chesley Found., 1996. Home: 1837 N Alexandria Ave Apt 211 Los Angeles CA 90027-4068 Office Phone: 323-661-4737. E-mail: rbrtptrck@aol.com. *No object or action has any meaning except that given to it by a writer. Writers create the consciousness of humanity, which in turn creates our world. Writers write the world.*

**PATRICK, RUTH (MRS. RUTH HODGE VAN DUSEN),** botany educator, curator; b. Topeka; d. Frank and Myrtle (Jetmore) Patrick; m. Charles (IV) Hodge, July 10, 1931; 1 child, Charles (V). BS, Coker Coll., 1929; MS, U. Va., 1931, PhD, 1934; LLD (hon.), Coker Coll., 1971; LHD (hon.), Chestnut Hill Coll, 1974; DSc (hon.), Beaver Coll., 1970, PMC Colls., 1971, Phila. Coll. Pharmacy and Sci., 1973, Wilkes Coll., 1974, Cedar Crest Coll., 1974, U. New Haven, 1975, Hood Coll., 1975, Med. Coll. Pa., 1975, Drexel U., 1975, Swarthmore Coll., 1975, Bucknell U., 1976, Rensselaer Poly. Inst., 1976, St. Lawrence U., 1978, U. Mass., 1980, Princeton U., 1980, Lehigh U., 1983, U. Pa., 1984, Temple U., 1985, Emory U., 1986, Wake Forest U., 1986, U. S.C., 1989, Clemson, 1989, Glassboro State Coll., 1992. Assoc. curator microscopy dept. Acad. Natural Scis., Phila., 1939-47; curator Leidy Micros. Soc., 1937-47, curator limnology dept., 1947—, chmn. limnology dept., 1947-73; occupant Francis Boyer Research Chair Acad. Natural Scis., Phila., 1973—, chmn. bd. trustees, 1973-76, hon. chmn. bd. trustees, 1976—; lectr. U. Pa., 1950-70, adj. prof., 1970—; guest Fellow of Saybrook Yale, 1975. Participant Am. Philos Soc. limnology expdn. to Mexico, 1947; leader Catherwood Found. expdn. to Peru and Brazil, 1955; del. gen. assembly Internat. Union Biol. Scis., Bergen, Norway, 1947; bd. dirs. E.I. Du Pont, Pa. Power and Light Co.; chmn. algae com. Smithsonian Oceanographic Sorting Ctr., 1963—68; mem. panel on water blooms Pres. Sci. Adv. Com., 1966; mem. panel on water resources and water pollution Gov.'s Sci. Adv. Com., 1966; mem. nat. tech. adv. com. on water quality requirements for fish and other aquatic life and wildlife Dept. Interior, 1967—64; mem. citizen's adv. coun. Pa. Dept. Environ. Resources, 1971—73; mem. hazardous materials adv. com. EPA, 1971—74, exec. adv. com., 1974—79; chmn. com.'s panel on ecology, 1974—76; mem. Pa. Gov.'s Sci. Adv. Coun., 1972; mem. exec. adv. com. nat. power survey FPC, 1972—75; mem. coun. Smithsonian Instn., 1973—; mem. Phila. Adv. Coun., 1973—76; mem. energy R&D adv. coun. Pres.s Emergy Policy Office, 1973—74; mem. adv. coun. Renewable Nat. Resources Found., 1973—76, Electric Power Rsch. Found., 1973—77; mem. adv. com. for rsch. NSF, 1973—74; mem. gen. adv. com. ERDA, 1975—77; mem. adv. bd. Sec. Energy, 1975—89; mem. com. on human resources NRC, 1975—76; trustee Biological Abstracts, 1974—76; mem. adv. coun. dept. biology Princeton U., 1975—80; mem. com. on sci. and arts Franklin Inst., 1978—; mem. univ. coun. Yale Sch. Forestry and Environ. Studies, 1978—80; mem. sci. adv. coun. World Wildlife Fund-US, 1978—80; trustee Aquarium Soc., Phila., 1951—58, Henry Found.; bd. dirs. Wissahickon Valley Watershed Assn.; bd. govs. Nature Conservancy; bd. mgrs. Wistar Inst. Anatomy and Biology. Author: (series of volumes) Rivers of the United States Vol. 1, 1994, Rivers of the United States Vol. 2, 1997, Chemical and Physical Characteristics Vol. 3, 1995, Rivers of Atlantic and Eastern Gulf Drainage Vol. 4, The Mississipi River and Major Tributaries; co-author (with C.W. Reimer): Diatoms of the United States Vol. 1, 1966, Vol. II, Part 1, 1975; co-author: (with others) (books) Ground Water Contamination in the United States, 1983, 2nd edit.; co-author: (with others) (book) Surface Water Quality: Have the Laws Been Successful?, 1992; mem. editorial bd.with C.W. Reimer: sci. jours. Science, 1974—76, mem. editorial bd.: sci. jours. American Naturalist; contbr. articles over 150 to profl. jours. Recipient Disting. Dau. of Pa. award, 1952, Richard Hopper Day Meml. medal, Acad. Nat. Scis., 1969, Gimbel Phila. award, 1969, Gold medal, YWCA, 1970, Lewis L. Dollinger Pure Environment award, Franklin inst., 1970, Pa. award for excellence in sci. and tech., 1970, Eminent Ecologist award, Ecol Soc. Am., 1972, Phila. award, 1973, Gold medal, Pa. State Fish and Game Protective Assn., 1974, Internat. John and Alice Tyler Ecology award, 1975, Gold medas, Phila. Soc. for Promoting Agr., 1975, Pub. Svc. award, U.S.

Dept. Interior, 1975, Iben award, Am. Water Resources Assn., 1976, Outstanding Alumna award, Coker Coll., 1977, Francis K. Hutchinson medal, Garden Club of Am., 1977, Golden medal, Royal Zool. Soc. Antwerp, 1978, Green World award, N.Y. Bot. Garden, 1979, Hugo Black award, U. Ala., 1979, Sci award, Gov. Pa., 1988, Founders award, Soc. Environ. Toxicology and Chemistry, 1982, Environ. Regeneration award, Rene DuBois Ctr. 1985, Disting. Citizen award, Pa., 1989, Excellence award, N. Am. Benthological Soc., 1993, Benjamin Frankln medal, Am. Philosophical Soc., 1993, U.S. medal of svc., Pres. Bill Clinton, 1996, Nat. medal for sci., 1997, Nat. Wetlands award, 2000, Sci. Edn. Ctr. named in her honor, U. S. C., 1989. Fellow: AAAS (com. environ. alternatives 1973—74); mem.: Internat. Phycol. Soc., Am. Inst. Biol. Scis., Ecol. Soc. Am., Am. Soc. Naturalists (pres. 1975—76), Am. Soc. Limnology and Oceanography (Lifetime Achievement award 1996), Am. Soc. Plant Taxonomy, Internat. Soc. Plant Taxonomists, Internat. Limnological Soc., Phycol Soc. Am. (pres. 1954), Bot. Soc. Am. (mem. Darbarker prize com. 1956, Merit award 1971), Am. Acad. Arts and Scis., Assn. Metro. Sewage Agys. (Environ. award 1995), Am. Philos. Soc. (Benjamin Franklin Outstanding Sci. Achievement award 1993), Nat. Acad. Engring. (com.environ. engr. study explicit criteria for power plant siting 1973), Nat. Acad. Scis. (chmn. panel com. on pollution 1966, mem.environ. measures panel com. remote sensing earth resources survey 1973—74, mem. nominating com. 1973—75, mem. com. sci. and public policy 1973—77), Water Pollution Control Fedn. (hon.), Soc. Study Evolution, Sigma Xi. Presbyterian. Office: Acad Natural Scis 19th at Benjamin Franklin Pkwy Philadelphia PA 19103 Office Phone: 215-299-1098. Business E-Mail: Patrick@acnatsci.org.

**PATRICK, STEPHEN C.,** consumer products company executive; Joined Colgate-Palmolive Co., N.Y.C., 1982, CFO, 1996—. V.p. Fin. Acctg. Found.; bd. dirs. Arrow Electronics, 2003—. Office: Colgate-Palmolive Co 300 Park Ave New York NY 10022-7499

**PATRICK, SUSAN D.,** federal agency administrator; B in English, Colo. Coll.; M in Comm. Mgmt., U. So. Calif. Dir. distance learning campus Old Dominion U.; coord. Digital State Survey 2002 State of Ariz.; dep. dir. Office Edn. Tech. US Dept. Edn., Washington, dir. Office Edn. Tech., 2004—. Office: US Dept Edn Rm FB6-7E208 400 Maryland Ave SW Washington DC 20202 Office Phone: 202-205-4274. E-mail: susan.patrick@ed.gov.

**PATRICK, THOMAS M.,** gas utility company executive; BA, Wash. State Univ., 1969, JD, Univ. Chgo., 1973. Atty. Peoples Energy Corp., Chgo., 1976—89, v.p., dep. gen. counsel, 1989—91, v.p. regulatory affairs & gas supply, 1991—96, exec. v.p., 1996—98, pres., COO, 1998—2002, chmn., pres., CEO, 2002—06. Bd. dir. Aegis, Am. Gas Assn.; trustee Gas Tech. Inst. Bd. mem. Children's Mem. Hosp., Chgo. Urban League, Adler Planetarium, Chgo., Big Shoulders. Mem.: Ill. Bus. Roundtable, Executives Club Chgo., Econ. Club Chgo., Comml. Club Chgo. (mem. civic com.). Office: Peoples Energy Corp 130 E Randolph Dr 24th Fl Chicago IL 60601-6207

**PATRICK, VICTOR PHILLIP,** lawyer; b. Lake Forest, Ill., Jan. 7, 1958; s. Rodger Ralph Patrick and Phyllis Elaine Bachler; m. Elizabeth Fletcher, Aug. 9, 1985; children: Kathryn Elaine, Stephen James, Diane Elizabeth, Marie Christine, Thomas Grant, John Wallace, Daniel Victor, Emily Frances. AB in Politics magna cum laude, Princeton U., 1982; JD cum laude, Harvard U., 1985. Bar: DC 1986, NY 1986, U.S. Ct. Appeals (10th cir.) 1986. Law clk. U.S. Ct. Appeals 10th Cir., Denver, 1985-86; assoc. Cleary, Gottlieb, Steen & Hamilton, Washington, 1986-88, 92-94, Brussels, 1988—91; from asst. gen. counsel to v.p., sec. and dep. gen. counsel Honeywell Internat. Inc. (formerly AlliedSignal Inc.), Morristown, NJ, 1994—97, 1999—2002, Torrance, Calif., 1997—99; sr. v.p., gen. counsel, sec. Walter Industries, Inc., Tampa, Fla., 2002—06, vice chmn., gen. counsel, 2006—. Mem. ABA, Tampa Fla. Stake (pres.). Republican. Lds Ch. Business E-Mail: vpatrick@walterind.com.

**PATRIKIS, ERNEST T.,** lawyer; b. Lynn, Mass., Dec. 1, 1943; s. Theodore A. and Ethel (Stasinopolous) Patrikis; m. Emily Herrick Trueblood, Mar. 18, 1972. BA, U. Mass., 1965; JD, Cornell U., 1968. Bar: N.Y. 1969. Exec. v.p., gen. counsel Fed. Res. Bank N.Y., NYC, 1968—95, 1st v.p., 1995—98; spl. adv. to chmn. Am. Internat. Group Inc., NYC, 1998—2000, sr. v.p., gen. coun., 1998—2006; ptnr. Pillsbury Winthrop Shaw Pittman LLP, NYC, 2006—, head fin. svc. & regulatory practice, 2006—. Dep. gen. counsel Fed. Open Market Com., 1988—95; bd. dirs. Atlantic Legal Found. Contbr. articles to legal jours. Fellow: Fgn. Policy Assn.; mem. ABA (subcom. gen. banking matters 1986), Internat. Swaps and Derivatives Assn.9 (dir. 1999—), Coun. Fgn. Rels., N.Y. State Bar Assn. (banking law com. 1986—, chmn. com. internat. banking, securities and fin. transaction 1987—91, vice chmn. internat. practice sect. 1991—2003, derivatives and structured products com. 2006—), Assn. of Bar of City of N.Y. (banking law com. 1982—84, futures regulations com. 1986—89, banking law com. 1990—, ins. com. 2000—03, corp. law com. 2003, Joint Yr. 2000 Coun., European law com. 2000—06). Office: Pillsbury Winthrop Shaw Pittman LLP 1540 Broadway New York NY 10036 Office Phone: 212-858-1317. E-mail: erniepatrikis@yahoo.com.

**PATRINOS, ARISTIDES,** environmental scientist, federal agency administrator; b. July 18, 1947; Diploma in Mech. Engring. & Electrical Engring., Nat. Tech. U., Athens, 1970, PhD (hon.), 2001; PhD in Mech. Engring. and Astronautical Scis., Northwestern U., 1975. Asst. prof. mechanical & aerospace sciences U. Rochester, 1975—76; rsch. scientist Engring. Tech. Div., Oak Ridge Nat. Lab., 1976—80, Dept. Applied Scis., Brookhaven Nat. Lab. 1980—88; staff mem. EPA, Nat. Acid Deposition Assessment Program Washington, 1984—88; dir. Environ. Sciences Divsn. Office of Biological & Environ. Rsch., US Dept. Energy, 1991—93; acting assoc. dir. Biological & Environ. Rsch. Office of Biological & Environ. Rsch., US Dept. Energy, 1993—95; assoc. dir. Office of Biological & Environ. Rsch., US Dept. Energy, 1995—. Ex-offico mem. Nat. Cancer Adv. Bd., NIH. Contbr. articles to profl. jours. Recipient Sec.'s Gold Award, US Dept. Energy, 2001, 2003. Fellow: Am. Meteorological Soc.; mem.: AAAS, ASME, Nat. Tech. Soc. Greece, Am. Geophysical Union. Office: Office Biological and Environ Rsch US Dept Energy 19901 Germantown Rd Germantown MD 20874-1207 also: SC-23 / Germantown Bldg 1000 Independence Ave SW Washington DC 20585-1290 Office Phone: 301-903-3251. Office Fax: 301-903-5051. E-mail: ari.patrinos@science.doe.gov.

**PATRON, JUNE EILEEN,** former government official; b. N.Y.C., May 15; d. Irving B. and Mollie Patron. BA in Govt. with honors, Clark U., Worcester, Mass., 1965; MA, Am. U., 1967. With U.S. Dept. Labor, 1966-95, dir. Black Lung benefits program, 1976-79, asst. adminstr. pension and welfare benefit programs, 1979-84, assoc. dir. pension and welfare benefit programs, 1984-88, dir. program svcs., 1988-95; ret., 1995. Mem. Sr. Exec. Svc.; ind. contractor, mgmt. cons., 1997-2003. Vol. alumni admissions program Clark U., 1998—. Van Ness Neighborhood Network, 2003—. Recipient various awards dept. Labor. Mem. Nat. Assn. Ret. Fed. Employees, Sr. Execs. Assn. Home: 3001 Veazey Ter NW Washington DC 20008-5454 E-mail: jpdcny@aol.com.

**PATRON, SUSAN HALL,** librarian, writer; b. San Gabriel, Calif., Mar. 18, 1948; d. George Thomas and Rubye Denver Hall; m. René Albert Patron, July 27, 1969. BA, Pitzer Coll., 1969; MLS, Immaculate Heart Coll., 1972. Children's libr. LA Pub. Libr., 1972-79, sr. children's libr., 1980—. Reviewer Sch. Libr. Jour., 1980-90, Pubs. Weekly, 1986-91, The Five Owls, 1987-95. Author: (with Christopher Weiman) Marbled Papers, 1979, Burgoo Stew, 1991, Five Bad Boys, Billy Que, and the Dustdobbin, 1992, Maybe Yes, Maybe No, Maybe Maybe, 1993 (ALA Notable Book 1994), Bobbin Dustdobbin, 1993, Dark Cloud Strong Breeze, 1994, The Higher Power of Lucky, 2006. Mem. ALA (Caldecott award com. 1988, Laura Ingalls Wilder award com. 2001), PEN (mem. West Lit. awards jury 1997, 2006), Calif. Libr. Assn. (Patricia Beatty award com. 1987-89, 91-92), Internat. Bd. on Books for Young Children, Soc. Children's Book Writers and Illustrators, So. Calif.

Coun. on Lit. for Children and Young People (awards com. 1985), Authors Guild, Friends of Children and Lit. (mem. award com. 1984). Office: LA Pub Libr Childrens Svcs 630 W 5th St Los Angeles CA 90071-2002

**PATRYSHEV, VLAD,** application developer; b. Arkhangelsk, Russia, July 19, 1951; arrived in U.S., 1998; m. Julia Nicole Feld, Mar. 1, 1996; children: Asy, Stepan. Masters Degree, Leningrad U., Russia, 1973. Engr. Leningrad Metal Works, 1974—78; project lead SPKB BA, Leningrad, 1978—90; founder, dept. dir. Forth-Info, Leningrad, 1988—91; owner SWAP, St. Petersburg, Russia, 1991—95; engr., project lead Tangram, St. Petersburg, 1995—97; engr. Borland, Scotts Valley, Calif., 1998—2005, Google, Mountain View, Calif., 2005—. Author: (stories) Times, Places, Tales, (software library) My Java Tools. Mem.: Silicon Valley Pattern Group, Mensa. Achievements include patents pending for method of playing board games on two-dimensional manifolds. Home: 277 Esteban Way San Jose CA 95119

**PATSICOSTAS, SUSAN JOANNA,** mental health services professional, psychotherapist; d. Gordon Howard and Melba Christine Williams; m. Nicholas Patsicostas, May 31, 1970 (div.); children: Thanos Nicholas, William Nicholas, Anthony Nicholas. AA, Ctrl. Fla. C.C., 1989; BA, Stetson U., 1991; MS in Mental Health Counseling, Nova Southeastern U., 1997. Lic. profl. counselor La., mental health counselor Fla., cert. parent trainer Boys and Girls Town, 2001, anger mgmt. and domestic violence counselor 2003. Psychotherapist Lake County Boys Ranch, Ocala, Fla., 1996—2000; clin. dir. Right Choice, LLC, Opelousas, La., 2001—02; owner, dir. New Way Mental Health Resources, LLC, Ville Platte, La. Ct. apptd. adv. for foster children Guardian Ad Litem Program, Ocala, 1993—98. Recipient Above and Beyond award, Guardian Ad Litem Program, 1996. Mem.: Am. Counseling Assn., Assn. Play Therapy (licentiate), Psi Beta, Phi Theta Kappa. Office: New Way Mental Health Resources LLC 1769 West Main St Ville Platte LA 70586 Office Phone: 337-363-3703. Office Fax: 337-363-4008. E-mail: susantexas10@aol.com.

**PATTEN, BERNARD MICHAEL,** neurologist, writer, educator; b. N.Y.C., Mar. 23, 1941; children: Allegra, Craig. AB summa cum laude, Columbia Coll., 1962; MD, Columbia U., 1966. Med. intern N.Y. Hosp. Cornell Med. Ctr., N.Y.C., 1966-67; resident neurologist Columbia Presbyn. Med. Ctr., N.Y.C., 1967-69, chief resident neurologist, 1969-70; assoc. prof. neurology Baylor Coll. Medicine, Houston, 1973-95; ret., 1995. Asst. chief med. neurology NIH, Bethesda, Md., 1970-73; mem. med. bd. Nat. Myasthenia Gravis Found., 1973—, Nat. AmyoTrophic Lateral Sclerosis Found., 1982—, Nat. Myositis Assn., 1995—; invited faculty Rice U., 1999—; faculty Women's INst. Houston. Author: One or Two Things I Remember About Her, 1999, Tristan and Iseult: Modern Version, 2000, Investment Pearls for Modern Times Expressed in Meter and in Rhymes, 2000, The Great Cotzias, 2001, Ascent to Heaven, 2001, Quia Imperfectum, 2001, Truth, Knowledge or Bull: How to Tell the Difference, 2004, The Blood of a Million Christs, 2004; contbr. more than 200 articles to profl. jours. With USPHS, 1970-73. Rsch. grantee NIH, pvt. founds., nat. health orgns. Fellow ACP, Royal Coll. Physicians, Tex. Neurol. Soc. Achievements include discoverer (with others) L-Dopa for Parkinson's disease; pioneered use of immune suppression for myasthenia gravis, diagnosis and treatment of medical and neurologcal complications of breast implants. Home: 1019 Baronridge Dr Seabrook TX 77586-4001 Office Phone: 713-252-1306. Personal E-mail: DADPATTEN@aol.com.

**PATTEN, BETSEY LELAND,** state legislator; b. Newton, Mass., Apr. 26, 1945; m. Richard C. Patten; 1 child. Student, Kings Coll. With publ. dept. Raytheon Co., 1978—84; rec. sec. Planning and Zoning Bds. of Moultonborough, 1985—91; state rep. N.H. Ho. Reps., chmn. mcpl. and county govt. com. Chmn. Joint Legis. Com. on Adminstrv. Rules, Assessing Standards Bd., Carroll County Rep. Com., 1996—. Home: 46 Patten Hill Rd Moultonborough NH 03254 Office Phone: 603-271-3317. E-mail: rcpatten@worldpath.net.

**PATTEN, CHARLES ANTHONY,** management consultant, retired manufacturing company executive, writer, publisher; b. Allentown, Pa., May 12, 1920; s. Charles Henerie and Mae (Doyle) P.; m. Kathleen Marie Breene, Jan. 6, 1951 (dec. 1999); children: Charles Anthony Jr., Amy Elizabeth Goddard, Nancy Kathleen Hansen. BSM.E., Lehigh U., 1942. With Joy Mfg. Co., 1947-63, works mgr., 1956-63; v.p. mfg. White Motor Corp., 1963-68, Colt Industries, 1968-69; With Dravo Corp., Pitts., 1942-47, 69-85, gen. mgr. engring. works div., 1970-71, corp. v.p., gen. mgr. engring. works div., 1971-75, corp. group v.p., chief exec. officer Dravo Mfg. Group, 1975-81, corp. sr. v.p., mem. corp. policy com., chief exec. officer Dravo Mfg. Group, 1981-83, corp. sr. v.p., asst. to pres. and chief exec. officer, mem. exec. com., 1984-85; pres. C.A. Patten Enterprises, 1985—. Bd. dirs., v.p. Dravo (Can.) Ltd., 1975-85; dir. pres. Dravo-Dravo Co. Ltd., 1974-79; dir. Dravo Mfg. (Can.) Ltd., 1975-83, Tru Weld Grating Inc., 1983-85; v.p. Dravo Internat., Inc., 1974-85; adv. com. Nat. Mgmt. Assn., 1973-85; chief devel. officer Western Pa. Model RR. Mus., 2001-, corp. mem., Am. Mgmt. Assn., 1954-85 Seminar spkr. in field, contbr. publs. Trustee Ohio Valley Gen. Hosp., McKees Rocks, Pa., 1975-82, Marietta (Ohio) Coll., 1979-89, emeritus trustee 1989—; bd. dirs. Vocat. Rehab. Ctr. of Allegheny County, 1972-79, Jr. Achievement of S.W. Pa., 1975-80, Sherwood Oaks Residents Assn., 2003—. Recipient Silver Knight of Mgmt. award Nat. Mgmt. Assn., 1976. Mem. ASME, Neville Island Mfrs. Assn. (pres. 1975-85), Am. Arbitration Assn. (panel of arbitrators, 1989-95), Shipyard Steering Com. of Am. Waterways Operators, Inland Waterways Am. Bur. of Ships. Republican. Roman Catholic. Home and Office: 304 Norman Dr Cranbury Township PA 10066-1133 Office Phone: 724-776-8204. *The successful manager is a time-oriented goal setter. Without waiting for others to ask, envisions things that should happen and thinks through possible paths to reach the goals. When the goals are reached, is quick to laud and praise people for their accomplishments.*

**PATTEN, DUNCAN THEUNISSEN,** ecologist educator; b. Detroit, Oct. 13, 1934; s. Marc T. and Doris (Miller) P.; m. Eva Chittenden, July 27, 1957; children: Michael, Marc, Robin, Scott. BA, Amherst Coll., 1956; MS, U. Mass., Amherst, 1959; PhD, Duke U., 1962. Asst. prof. ecology Va. Poly. Inst., Blacksburg, 1962-65, Ariz. State U., Tempe, 1965-67, assoc. prof., 1967-73, prof., 1973-95, prof. emeritus, 1995—, dir. ctr. environ. studies, 1980-95. Rsch. prof. Mont. State U., 1995—. Contbr. articles to profl. jours. Fellow AAAS, Ariz.-Nev. Acad. Sci.; mem. Ecol. Soc. Am. (bus. mgr. 1979-95), Brit. Ecol. Soc., Soc. Range Mgmt., Am. Inst. Biol. Scis., Soc. Wetland Scientists (pres. 1996-97), Am. Water Resource Assn., Am. Geophys. Union, Sigma Xi Office: Mont State U Land Resources and Environ Scis Box 173120 Bozeman MT 59717-3120 Office Phone: 406-994-2784. Personal E-mail: dtpatten@starband.net. Business E-Mail: dtpatten@montana.edu.

**PATTEN, LANNY RAY,** gas industry executive; b. St. Joseph, Mo., July 31, 1934; s. E.L. and Sarah Catherine (Langner) P.; m. Ann Rogers Hall, Oct. 26, 1957; children: David, John, Jeffrey, Mark. BS in Engring., Iowa State U., 1956; AMP, Harvard U., 1976. Net sr. v.p. gases and equipment Air Products and Chems., Inc., Allentown, Pa., 1990-91; founder, pres, COO Airgas Inc., Radnor, Pa., 1990-91; founder, pres. CylServ, Inc., West Conshohocken, Pa., 1992—. Chmn. Lehigh U. Parents Assn., Bethlehem, Pa., 1977—90. Officer USAF, 1957—60. Recipient PACE award for Engring. Achievement Iowa State U. 1990, Friend of Lehigh award, 1991. Mem.: PASSAR (pres. 2005—), SAR (chpt. pres. 2006—), Allentown C. of C. (exec. bd. dirs. 1978—82), Internat. Oxygen Mfg. Assn., Compressed Gas Assn. (exec. bd. dirs. 1977—91), Pa. Soc. SR (bd. dirs.), Union League of Phila., Phila. Country Club, Kappa Sigma (Alumni Hall of Fame). Republican. Episcopalian. Avocations: baseball, golf, reading. Home: 1306 Club House Rd Gladwyne PA 19035-1006

**PATTEN, ROBERT LOWRY,** language educator; b. Oklahoma City, Apr. 26, 1939; s. Charles H. and Helen (Lowry) P.; m. Faith L. Harris, June 12, 1960 (div. 1974); children: Jocelyn S., Christina S. BA, Swarthmore Coll., 1960; MA, Princeton U., 1963, PhD, 1965. Lectr. Bryn Mawr (Pa.) Coll.,

1964-66, asst. prof. English, 1966-69; asst. prof. Rice U., Houston, 1969-71, assoc. prof., 1971-76, prof. English, 1976-96, chair, dept. of English, 1991-92, master Grad. House, 1992-95, Lynette S. Autrey prof. humanities, 1996—. Pres. PEN S.W., Houston, 1989—92. Author: Charles Dickens and His Publishers, 1978, George Cruikshank's Life, Times and Art, vol. 1, 1992, vol. 2, 1996 (best biography of the decade Guardian); editor: (book by Charles Dickens) Pickwick Papers, 1972, George Cruikshank: A Revaluation, 1974, 2d edit., 1992, (with John O. Jordan) Literature in the Marketplace, 1995, (with John Bourn) Palgrave Advances in Charles Dickens Studies, 2005; editor SEL: Studies in English Lit., 1978-84, 90—. Bd. dirs. Cultural Arts Coun., Houston, 1979-80, Tex. Com. for the Humanities, 1979-80; pres., bd. dirs. Houston Ctr. for the Humanities, 1976-84. NEH fellow, 1968-69, 77-78, 87-88; Guggenheim fellow, 1980-81; Nat. Humanities Ctr. fellow, 1987-88; Nat. Gallery of Art Assoc., 1988-89. Mem. AAUP, MLA, PEN Am. Ctr., Dickens Fellowship, Dickens Soc., Soc. for the History of Authorship, Reading and Pub. bd. dirs. 1992-2003, treas. 1997-2003, v.p. 2003-05, pres. 2005—), Coun. Editors of Learned Jours., Phi Beta Kappa (pres. Beta chpt. Tex. 1991-94, 97-2002, bd. dirs. Houston chpt. 1997—2000, adv. dir. 2000-03, senator 2002-03, Couper scholar, 2004—). Episcopalian. Avocations: travel, classical music. Office: Rice U Dept English MS 30 PO Box 1892 Houston TX 77251-1892 Office Phone: 713-348-4697. Business E-Mail: patten@rice.edu.

**PATTEN, RONALD JAMES,** university dean; b. Iron Mountain, Mich., July 17, 1935; s. Rudolph Joseph and Cecelia (Fuse) Pataconi; m. Shirley Ann Bierman, Sept. 5, 1959; children: Christine Marie, Cheryl Ann, Charlene Denise. BA, Mich. State U., 1957, MA, 1959; PhD, U. Ala., 1963. Acct. Price Waterhouse & Co., Detroit, 1958; instr. No. Ill. U., 1959-60; asst. prof. U. Colo., 1963-65; assoc. prof. Va. Poly. Inst. and State U., 1965-67, prof., 1967-73, head dept. accounting, 1966-73; dir. research Financial Accounting Standards Bd., Conn., 1973-74; dean Sch. Bus. Adminstrn., U. Conn., Storrs, 1974-88; chief of party-Eastern Caribbean Arthur D. Little Internat., 1988-89; dean Coll. Commerce and Kellstadt Grad. Sch. Bus. De Paul U., Chgo., 1989-99; dean Ritsumeikan Asia Pacific U. Grad. Sch. Mgmt., Beppu, Japan, 2003—06. Individual investors adv. com. NY Stock Exch., 1993—98; cons. in field. Contbr. chapters to books, articles to profl. jours. Bd. dirs. U.S. com. UNICEF, Chgo., 1996—99. Recipient Nat. Quartermaster award Nat. Quartermaster, Assn., 1956; Earhart Found. fellow, 1962-63. Mem. AICPA, Am. Acctg. Assn., Inst. Mgmt. Accts., Acad. Internat. Bus. (Internat. Dean of Yr. award 1987), Internat. Assn. for Acctg. Edn. and Rsch., Ill. Coun. Econ. Edn. (Chgo., trustee 1989—, chmn. bd. trustees 1997-2000), Pacioli Soc., Internat. Trade and Fin. Assn., dir. 1998-2000, West Towns Chorus, Heidelberg Club Internat., Scabbard and Blade, Golden Key, Beta Gamma Sigma (mem. bd. govs. 1975-90, nat. sec.-treas. 1980-82, nat. v.p. 1982-84, nat. pres. 1984-86), Beta Alpha Psi (bd. dirs. 1992-94), Delta Sigma Pi, World Assn. for Case Method Rsch. and Application, Adv Bd., 1998-, Phi Kappa Phi, Delta Mu Delta. Avocations: hiking, softball, golf, travel, singing. Home: 334 N Montclair Ave Glen Ellyn IL 60137-5253 Business E-Mail: rpatten@depaul.edu.

**PATTEN, THOMAS HENRY, JR.,** finance educator, personnel director; b. Cambridge, Mass., Mar. 24, 1929; s. Thomas Henry and Lydia Mildred (Lindgren) Patten; m. Rosalie Medina, May 23, 2002. AB, Brown U., 1953; MS, Cornell U., 1955, PhD, 1959. Dir. program planning Ford Motor Co., Dearborn, Mich., 1957-65; prof. mgmt. and sociology U. Detroit, 1965-67; prof. orgnl. behavior and personnel mgmt. Sch. Labor and Indsl. Relations, Mich. State U., E. Lansing, 1967-84; prof. mgmt. and human resources Calif. State Poly. U., Pomona, 1984—2003, prof. emeritus, 2003—. Cons. in field. Author: The Foreman: The Forgotten Man of Management, 1968, Manpower Planning and the Development of Human Resources, 1971, OD-Emerging Dimensions and Concepts, 1973, A Bibliography of Compensation Planning and Administration, 1960-1974, 2d rev. edit., 1981, 3d rev. edit., 1987, Pay: Employee Compensation and Incentive Plans, 1977, Classics of Personnel Management, 1979, Organizational Development Through Teambuilding, 1981, A Manager's Guide to Performance Appraisal, 1982, Fair Pay: The Managerial Challenge of Comparable Job Worth and Job Evaluation, 1988, Exercises for Developing Human Resources Management Skills, 1996. With USMC, 1946—51. Mem. ASTD (chmn. orgn. devel. div. 1972), Indsl. Rels. Rsch. Assn. (chpt. pres. 1970-71), Am. Sociol. Assn., Internat. Pers. Mgmt. Assn., Internat. Indsl. Rels. Assn., Inst. Applied Behavioral Sci., Am. Compensation Assn. Office: Calif State Poly U Dept Mgmt & Human Resources 3801 W Temple Ave Pomona CA 91768-2557 Home: 407 Mossy Ct Lincoln CA 95648-8158 *Human values come first.*

**PATTEN, VALERIE LYNN,** lawyer; b. L.A., Apr. 8, 1950; d. Russell Carl and Donna D. Patten; 1 child, Elizabeth Nicole Wood. AB, Stanford U., 1972; MFA, San Jose State U., 1981; JD, Georgetown U., 1992. Bar: Calif. 1992. Legal intern Washington Area Lawyers for the Arts, 1990—90; law clk. Garfinkle & Assocs., Washington, 1990—92; staff atty. Legal Advocates for Children and Youth, San Jose, Calif., 1992—93; assoc. atty. Law Offices of Robert L. Hoover, San Jose, 1994—96; pvt. practice Law Offices of Valerie L. Patten, Palo Alto, Calif., 1996—. Freelance writer Bay Area (Calif.) Art Publ., 1980—84; writer arts & entertainment Palo Alto (Calif.) Weekly, 1982—84; instr. art dept. U. Mont., Missoula, 1984—84; lectr. continuing edn. art dept. legal issues for artists San Jose State U., Calif., 1993; referral atty., lectr. Calif. Lawyers for the Arts, San Francisco, 1993—; asst. prof. art dept. San Francisco State U., 1994—95; atty. mem. Graphic Artists Guild, 1997—; presenter, continuing edn. seminar on custody and visitation in Calif. Nat. Bus. Inst., Eau Claire, Wis., 2003, Eau Claire, 06. One-woman shows include DeSaisset Mus., Pro Arts Gallery, Oakland, Henry Art Gallery, Seattle, exhibited in group show at Am. Acad. and Inst Arts and Letters, N.Y. (selected for Hassam and Speicher fund Purchase Exhbn., 1983). Pro tem judge Superior Ct. Santa Clara County, San Jose, 1999—; property divsn. mediator, 1998—2001; pro bono panel mem. Santa Clara County Bar Assn. Law Found., San Jose, 1993—; vol. tchr. Prisoners' Info. Svcs., Palo Alto, 1977—84; vol. atty. Pro Bono Project, San Jose, 2002—; bd. mem., sec. Young Audiences San Jose, 1998—2001; bd. mem. DanceVisions, Palo Alto, 1993—. Recipient Am. Jurisprudence award, Lawyers Coop. Pub., 1991; Charles Warren Kendrick Meml. scholar, Stanford U., 1968—72. Mem.: San Mateo County Bar Assn. (family law sect. 2003—), Calif. State Bar Assn., ABA (family law sect. 1992—), Santa Clara County Bar Assn. (family law sect. com. 1995—), State Bar Calif. Episcopalian. Avocations: painting, art history, hiking. Home: 1528 Rosita Rd Pacifica CA 94044 Office: Law Offices Valerie L Patten Ste 7 744 San Antonio Rd Palo Alto CA 94303 Office Phone: 650-855-9570. E-mail: valpatten@prodigy.net.

**PATTENAUDE, RICHARD LOUIS,** university administrator; b. Seattle, Feb. 22, 1946; s. Joseph Arthur and Alice June (Vrooman) P.; m. Michele Arlen Stevenson, May 31, 1975; children: Lauren, Lisa, Dylan, Joshua. BA with honors in Econs., San Jose State U., 1968; PhD in Polit. Sci., U. Colo., 1974. Asst./assoc. prof. Drake U., Des Moines, 1974-80, assoc. dean liberal arts, 1976-80; asst. v.p. acad. affairs SUNY-Binghamton, 1980-82, assoc. v.p., 1982-86; v.p. acad. affairs prof. polit. sci. Ctrl. Conn. State U., New Britain, 1986-91; pres., prof. polit. sci. U. So. Maine, Portland, 1991—. Cons. in field; panelist, presenter various nat. higher edn. meetings. Contbr. numerous articles to profl. jours., chpts. to books in field. Commr. Occupational and Licensing Commn., Iowa, 1978-80; mem. Gov.'s Com. Efficiency, 1979; mem. adv. coun. planning dept. City of Binghamton, 1984-1986; bd. dirs. Broome County United Way, 1985, Greater Hartford Red Cross, 1991-93, Mercy Hosp., Portland, 1992-94, Portland Symphony Orch., Maine Devel. Found., 1991-97, Maine Sci. & Tech. Found., 1992-98, Portland Mus. Art, 1993-99, Pmt. Symphony 1998-, Maine Med. Ctr., 2002-, Inst. Civic Leadership, 1992-94, Greater Portland United Way, Maine Med. Ctr., 2002-. With U.S. Army, 1969-71, Vietnam. Fanny W. Ames scholar, 1965; Title II fellow, 1970. Mem. Assn. Insti. Rsch. and Planning Officers (v.p. 1983-84, pres. 1984-85), Am. Assn. State Colls. and Univs. (state rep. 1995—, bd. dirs. 1999—2003), Council Adv. of C. Office: U So Maine Office of Pres 707 Law Building 96 Falmouth St Portland ME 04103-9300 Address: U So Maine PO Box 9300 Portland ME 04104-9300 Office Phone: 207-780-4480. Business E-Mail: pattenau@usm.maine.edu.

**PATTERSON, ANNE WOODS (ANNE BREVARD WOODS PATTERSON),** federal agency administrator, former ambassador; b. Ft. Smith, Ark., 1949; m. David R. Patterson; children: Edward, Andrew. BA in Econs., Wellesley Coll.; postgrad., U. N.C. With U.S. Fgn. Svc., 1973—, econ. officer Ecuador, 1974-77, desk officer Nicaragua, analyst for Ctrl. Am., trade specialist Can., econ. counselor Riyadh, Saudi Arabia, 1984-88, polit. counselor U.S. Mission to UN Geneva, dir. Office of Andean Affairs, 1991-93, dep. asst. sec. for Ctrl. Am. and the Caribbean, 1993-95, prin. dep. asst. sec. for inter-Am. affairs, 1995—97, US amb. to El Salvador San Salvador, 1997-2000, US amb. to Colombia Bogota, 2000—03; dep. permanent US rep. UN, NY, 2004—05, acting permanent US rep., 2005; dep. insp. gen. US Dept. State, Washington, 2003—04, asst. sec., Bur. Internat. Narcotics and Law Enforcement Affairs, 2005—. Recipient Superior Honor award, US Dept. of State, 1981, 88 Meritorious Honor award, 1977, 83, Presdl. award, 1993; Order of the Congress, Congress of Colombia, Order of Boyaca, Govt. Colombia, Order of Jose Matias Delgado, Govt. El Salvador. Office: US Dept State 2201 C St NW Rm 7333 Washington DC 20520 Office Phone: 202-647-8464. Office Fax: 202-736-4885. Business E-Mail: pattersonaw2@state.gov, pattersonz@state.gov.

**PATTERSON, BEVERLY ANN GROSS,** not-for-profit fundraiser, consultant, social services administrator, writer; b. Pauls Valley, Okla., Aug. 5, 1938; d. Wilburn G. Jack and Mildred E. (Steward) Gross; m. Kenneth Dean Patterson, June 18, 1960 (div. 1976); children: Tracy Dean Patterson, Nancy Ann Patterson-McArthur, Beverly Jeanne Patterson-Wertman; life ptnr. Molly A. Kretz, 1999. AA, Modesto (Calif.) Jr. Coll., 1958; BA in Social Sci., Fresno (Calif.) State U., 1960; M in Community Counseling, Coll. Idaho; postgrad., Stanislaus State Coll., Turlock, Calif., U. Idaho, Boise (Idaho) State U. Cert. secondary tchr., Calif., Idaho, lic. real estate agt., Idaho. Secondary tchr., Ceres and Modesto Calif., Payette and Weiser Idaho, Ontario Oreg., 1960-67; dir. vol. svcs. mental retardation and child devel. State of Idaho, 1967-70, cons. dir. vol. svcs. health and welfare, 1970-72; dir. Ret. Sr. Vol. Program, Boise, 1972-74; exec. dir. Idaho Nurses Assn., 1974-76; community svcs. adminstr. City of Davis, Calif., 1976-78; dir. devel. and fundraising Mercy Med. Ctr., Nampa, Idaho, 1978-85; exec. dir. St. Alphonsus Med. Ctr. Found., Boise, 1985-87; dir. devel. and gift planning Idaho Youth Ranch, Boise, 1989-94; fund devel. cons. Mercy Housing, Nampa, Idaho, 1994-96, Pratt Ranch Boys Home, Emmett, Idaho, 1994-96, Northwest Childrens Home, Lewiston, Idaho, 1994-96, Idaho Spl. Olympics, Boise, 1994-95, Idaho Found. for Parks and Lands, Boise, 1994-95, St. Vincent de Paul, Inc., Boise, 1995-96, Nampa Shelter Found., Inc., 1994-95, Turning Point Inc., Nampa, 1994-95, Port of Hope Treatment Ctr. Inc., Boise, 1994-97, Idaho Theater for Youth, Inc., Boise, 1995-96, Boise Tennis Coalition, Inc., 1995-2000, El Ada Cmty. Action Ctr., Boise, 1995, Hemophilia Found. Idaho, 1995-96, Boise YWCA, 1996, Marsing (Idaho) Sch. Dist., 1996-98. Founder Fellowship Christian Adult Singles, Boise, 1974; cons., exec. dir. Boise Hotline, 1988-90; co-dir. ACOA workshop leader Child Within Concepts, Inc., Boise, 1987—; cons. coord. Rural Hosp. Edn. Consortium, 1988; cons. hosp. fund devel. and cmty. resources Gritman Meml. Hosp., Moscow, Idaho, 1987-88; cons., conf. coord. State of Idaho, 1987-88; counsel Adult Children of Alcoholics, 1991; pres. Nonprofit Solutions, Inc., Boise, 1995—; co-dir. Child Within Concepts, Inc., Meridian, 1996—; cmty. resource devel. specialist Idaho Dept. Health and Welfare, 1997-2000, United Way Portland, 2000; chmn., pres. Creative Solutions P.A., 2000—; grant writing cons. sch. dist. # 3JT, Oreg., Tillamook Sch. Dist., Oreg., Banks Sch. dist., Oreg., North West Regional Ednl. Svcs. Dist., Oreg. Author poetry; contbr. articles to profl. jours. Coord. Idaho Golf Angels Open Pro-Am Tournament, Boise, 1997; founding exec. v.p. Coll. Fund for Students Surviving Cancer, 1993-96; bd. dirs. Arthritis Found., Idaho, 1984-86, Idaho Mental Health Assn., 1978-97; founder Ctrl. Vol. Bur., Boise, 1971. Named Idaho Statesman Disting. Citizen, 1985. Mem. Nat. Assn. for Hosp. Devel. (accredited, treas. 1980, accreditation chmn. 1984-86, conf. chmn. 1982, 85), Assn. Healthcare in Philanthropy (accredited), Nat. Soc. Fund Raising Execs., Idaho Devel. Network, Choices in Giving, Inc. Avocations: golf, woodworking. Address: 9451 N Polk Ave Portland OR 97203-1630

**PATTERSON, CARLY,** Olympic athlete; b. Baton Rouge, Feb. 4, 1988; d. Ricky and Natalie. Mem. TOPS Nat. Team, 1996, 1997, U.S. Nat. Gymnastics Team, 2000—; gymnast Team USA, Athens Olympic Games, 2004. Achievements include member of US World Championships Gold medal team, 2003; winning silver medal, all-around, World Championships, 2003; won Visa Am. Cup Championship by winning all four events, 2004; winning gold medal, all-around, Athens Olympic games, 2004; member of US Women's Silver medal Gymnastics team, Athens Olympic games, 2004. Office: c/o USOC One Olympic Plz Colorado Springs CO 80909

**PATTERSON, CHARLES DAROLD,** librarian, educator; b. Wahpeton, N.D., Aug. 8, 1928; s. Charles Irwin and Inez Fern (Slagg) P. BSc, Bemidji State U., 1950; MA, U. Minn., 1956; MusM, W.Va. U., 1964; advanced cert., U. Pitts., 1968, PhD, 1971. Tchr. music Fargo (N.D.) Pub. Schs., 1950; jr. reference libr. U. Minn. Librs., 1954-55; head libr. Bemidji (Minn.) State U., 1955-58; dir. librs., asst. prof. Glenville (W.Va.) State Coll., 1958-62; asst. prof. W.Va. U., 1962-66; instr. Grad. Sch. Libr. and Info. Scis. U. Pitts., 1966-71, asst. prof., 1971-72; assoc. prof. Sch. Libr. and Info. Sci. La. State U., Baton Rouge, 1972-78, prof., 1978-93, prof. emeritus, 1993—. Del. La. Gov.'s Conf. on Libr. and Info. Svcs., 1978. Author: Analysis of Library of Congress Music Subject Headings, 1971, JEL Cumulative Index, 1979, supplement, 1982, (with D.G. Davis) ARBA Guide to Library Science Literature, 1987, Letters from the Far East, 2003; editor W.Va. Libraries, 1963-66; mem. editl. bd. Jour. of Edn. for Librarianship, 1975-79, editor, 1980-84; editor Jour. Edn. for Libr. and Info. Sci., 1984-88; asst. editor Reference Svcs. Rev., 1986-93; contbr. articles to profl. jours. Served with U.S. Army, 1950-52. Recipient La. State U. Faculty Excellence award, 1984 Mem. ALA (chmn. scholarship jury 1972-73, award 1989, Disting. Mem. medal 2005), W.Va. Libr. Assn. (chmn. coll. and univ. libr. sect. 1960-61, exec. bd. 1960-61, 64-66), Assn. Coll. and Rsch. Librs. (pres. Tri-state chpt. 1972), Assn. Am. Libr. Schs. (exec. bd. 1980-88), La. Libr. Assn., Southeastern Libr. Assn., AAUP (pres. chpt. 1985-86), Am. Guild Organists (dean chpt. 1985-86), Pitts. Bibliophiles, Univ. Chamber Music Soc. (pres., dir. 1979-80), La. Sinfonietta (exec. bd. 1994—), Beta Phi Mu (dir.-at-large 1982-85). Methodist. Home: 1480 Kenmore Ave Baton Rouge LA 70808-1130 also: Birchmont Beach Bemidji MN 56601 Office: La State U Sch Libr And Info Sci Baton Rouge LA 70803-0001 *When one is confident in his own mind that he has, with given abilities, done his very best, then perhaps he has paid for his niche in eternity.*

**PATTERSON, COLLIS DELANO,** secondary school educator; b. Balt., Aug. 29, 1950; s. William Phillip Patterson and Lucille Mimi Patterson-Wheeler. BS, Towson U., 1973; MEd, Loyola Coll., Balt., 1988. Cert. tchr. grades 5-12 Md. State Dept. Edn. Tchr. Balt. City Schs., 1973—. Instr. Sojourner-Douglass Coll., Balt., 1990—92. Editor: Dr. Samuel L. Banks Speaks, 1995. Vol. Am. Friends, Balt., 1978—. Grantee Geography grant, Md. Geog. Alliance, Balt., 1988, Tchg. grant, NEH, Washington, 1990. Mem.: Third World Coalition (rep. 1995—98, Honor award 1997), Am. Friends Svc. Com. (clk. 1978—). Democrat. African Methodist. Avocations: gardening, collecting.

**PATTERSON, DAVID,** music educator; b. Oskaloosa, Iowa, July 14, 1950; s. Lloyd Morse and Patricia Barbara Patterson; m. Carolyn Jeanne Adolphs, Mar. 28, 1981; children: Sean Erie Patterson (deceased), Scott David. MusB in Edn., Drake U., Des Moines, Iowa, 1972; student, U. Iowa, Iowa City, Iowa, Clarke Coll., Dubuque, Iowa, Vandercook Coll. Music, Chgo., Ill. Tchr. orch. Thomas Jefferson Jr. H.S., Dubuque, 1972—75, Ottumwa H.S., Iowa, 1975—77, Stephen Hempstead H.S., Dubuque, 1978—. Founder, dir. English Handbell Choirs St. Luke's United Meth. Ch., Dubuque, 1978—; prin. cellist Dubuque Symphony Orch., 1986—91; cellist Dubuque String Quartet, 1978—, Telemann Trio, Dubuque, Iowa, 1972—75, SE Iowa Symphony, Ottumwa, Iowa, 1975—77; prin. cellist Des Moines Chamber Orch., Des Moines, 1971—71; cellist Des Moines Symphony, 1970—71; prin. cellist

---

Loras Coll. Choir Orch., Dubuque, 1977—93, Dubuque Chorale Orch., 1977—; adj. instr. U. Dubuque, 1978, Clarke Coll., Dubuque, 1980—83. Troop leader Boy Scouts Am., Dubuque, 1972—81. Named Outstanding Educator, N.E. Iowa C.C., 2003; named to, Outstanding Young Men of Am., 1980; recipient Vigil Honor award, Orcer of Arrow Boy Scouts of Am., 1978. Mem.: Iowa Music Educators Assn., Music Educators Nat. Conf., Iowa String Tchrs. Assn., Am. String Tchrs. Assn. Office: Stephen Hempstead High School 3715 Pennsylvania Avenue Dubuque IA 52002-3792 Office Phone: 563-552-5294.

**PATTERSON, DAVID ANDREW,** computer scientist, educator, consultant; b. Evergreen Park, Ill., Nov. 16, 1947; s. David Dwight and Lucie Jeanette (Ekstrom) P.; m. Linda Ann Crandall, Sept. 4, 1967; children: David Adam, Michael Andrew. BS in Math., UCLA, 1969, MS in Computer Sci., 1970, PhD, 1976. Mem. tech. staff Hughes Aircraft Co., L.A., 1972-76, Thinking Machines Corp., Cambridge, Mass., 1979; prof. computer sci. divsn. U. Calif., Berkeley, 1977—, chmn., 1990-93, E.H. and M.E. Pardee chair computer sci., 1992—. Cons. Sun Microsystems, Inc., Mountain View, Calif., 1984—. Author: A Taste of Smalltalk, 1986, Computing Unbound, 1989, Computer Architecture: A Quantative Approach, 2nd edit., 1996, Computer Organization & Design: The Hardware/Software Interface, 2nd edit., 1998. Recipient Disting. Teaching award, U. Calif., Berkeley, 1982, Diane S. McEntyre award for Excellence in Teaching, 1998, Outstanding Alumnus award UCLA Computer Sci. Dept. Fellow IEEE (undergrad. tchg. award 1996, tech. achievement award 1995, co-recipient Reynold B. Johnson Info. Storage award, John Von Neumann medal 2000, James H. Mulligan Edn. medal, 2000), Assn. Computer Machinery (Karl V. Karlstrom Outstanding Educator award, 1991, co-recipient, Sigmod Test of Time award 1998), Computer Soc., Am. Acad. Arts & Sciences; mem. NAE, Computing Rsch. Assn. (bd. dirs. Washington 1991—, chair 1993-97), Spl. Interest Group on Computer Architecture of Assn. Computer Machinery (bd. dirs. 1987-90, chair 1993-95, Pres. 2005-), NAS (mem. Computer Sci. and Telecommunications Bd.). Avocations: biking, soccer, weightlifting, body surfing, mountain biking, surfing. Office: U Calif Computer Sci Computer Sci Divsn 1776 635 Soda Hall Berkeley CA 94720-1776 Office Phone: 510-642-6587. Office Fax: 510-643-7352. Business E-Mail: patterson@cs.berkeley.edu.*

**PATTERSON, DEB,** women's college basketball coach; Grad., Rockford Coll., 1979. Asst. coach, recruiting coord. No. Ill. U., 1986-91; asst. coach So. Ill. U., 1991-92; top asst. coach, recruiting coord. Vanderbilt U., 1992-96; head coach Kans. State U., 1996—. Asst. coach 1997 World U. Games; women's sr. nat. team asst. coach USA Invitational Tournament of Champions, 1997. Named Women's Coll. Basketball Coach of the Yr. Kans. Basketball Coaches Assn., 1997, Coach of Yr. Ill. H.S. Assn., 1985, Conf. Coach of Yr., 1985, 86. Office: Kansas State U 1800 College Ave Manhattan KS 66502-3308 Fax: 785-532-6093.

**PATTERSON, DENNIS JOSEPH,** management consultant; b. Honolulu, Apr. 13, 1948; s. Joseph John and Dorothy Elizabeth (Snajkowski) P.; divorced; children: Valerie Jean, Christina Elizabeth. BA, Elmhurst Coll., Ill., 1970; MA, George Washington U., 1973. Asst. dir. Vancouver (B.C.) Gen. Hosp., 1973-76, dir., 1975-76; v.p. Shaugnessy Hosp., Vancouver, 1976-79; pres. Westcare, Vancouver, 1979-84; mgr. Ernst & Whinney, Chgo., 1984-86, sr. mgr., 1986-88, ptnr., 1988-93; pres. FHP Internat. Cons. Group, Inc., Fountain Valley, Calif., 1993-95; ptnr. KPMG Peat Marwick, 1996-97; sr. cons. Hay Group, 1997-98; chmn., CEO IMC Rsch. Inst. (now Healthcare Net); ptnr. Wellspring Ptnrs. Author: Indexing Managed Care, 1997; contbr. articles to profl. jours. Fin. mgr. Electoral Action Movement, Vancouver, 1978; trustee George Washington U., 1992-96, Calif. Sch. Profl. Psychology, 1993-96, Alliant U., 1999-2003, Elmhurst Coll., 2006—. Mem. Royal Vancouver Yacht Club, Union League Chgo., Chgo. Yacht Club, Phi Gamma Mu. Republican. Anglican. Avocations: sailboat racing, golf. Office Phone: 312-327-3020. E-mail: djp@wp-ltd.com.

**PATTERSON, DONALD EUGENE,** research scientist; b. El Paso, Tex., Feb. 7, 1958; s. Donald M. Patterson and Beverly Lee (Viles) McElroy; m. Mary Jane Ingram, May 6, 1989. BS, U. Tex., 1982, MS, 1984; MA, Rice U., 1987, PhD, 1989. Rsch. scientist Rice U., Houston, 1989-91; sr. rsch. scientist Houston Advanced Rsch. Ctr., The Woodlands, Tex., 1993, TSA, Inc., The Woodlands, 1991-95; sr. scientist SI Diamond Tech. Inc., Houston, 1991-95, dir. R & D, 1995-96; edn. supr. ITT Tech. Inst., Houston, 1996-97; prin. scientist Sys. & Processes Engring. Corp., Austin, Tex., 1997-98; founder, sr. v.p. product devel. Extreme Devices, Inc., Austin, 1998—2003; sr. scientist Nanohmics, Inc., Austin, 2004—. Contbr. articles to profl. jours. Recipient Harry B. Weiser award, Rice U., 1988; Grad. fellow, 1984, VFW Voice Democracy scholar, 1974, Davis and Bertha Green scholar, 1982, Grad. scholar, U. Tex. El Paso, 1983. Mem.: SID, AAAS, Am. Chem. Soc., Sigma Xi, Phi Kappa Phi. Achievements include patents in field. Home: 4728 Interlachen La Austin TX 78747 Office: Nanohmics Inc 6201 E Olfort St 400 Austin TX 78741 Office Phone: 512-389-9990. Business E-Mail: dpatterson@nanohmics.com.

**PATTERSON, DOUGLAS MACLENNAN,** finance educator; b. Jan. 16, 1945; s. Thomas and Ruth (MacLennan) P.; m. Sara Louise Lucas; children: Cara Beth, John Douglas BSEE, U. Wis., 1968, MBA, 1972, PhD, 1978. Elec. engr. Westinghouse Electric, Balt., 1968—71; asst. prof. U. Mich., Ann Arbor, 1976—80, Va. Tech., Blacksburg, 1980—86, assoc. prof., 1986—98, prof., 1998—. Vis. prof. U. Calif., Santa Barbara, 1989; vis. scholar U. Tex., Austin, 1994; participant Fin. Time Series Conf., Isaac Newton Inst. Math. Scis., Cambridge, Eng., 1998; dir. PhD program fin. Va. Tech., 1991-95; presenter, spkr. in field Co-author: A Nonlinear Times Series Workshop: A Tool Kit for Detecting and Identifying Nonlinear Serial Dependence; contbr. articles to profl. jours Mem. ad hoc com. Detroit Area Hosp. Assn., 1978-79 Recipient Tchg. Excellence award Va. Tech., 1983; U. Mich. fellow, 1979; USN grantee, 1984, 85, 90 Mem. Am. Fin. Assn., Am. Econ. Assn., Fin. Mgmt. Assn., Beta Gamma Sigma Methodist. Home: 702 Crestwood Dr Blacksburg VA 24060-6006 Office: Va Poly Inst Dept Finance 0221 Blacksburg VA 24061 Business E-Mail: findoc@vt.edu.

**PATTERSON, EDWIN,** minister; b. Andalusia, Ala., Sept. 6, 1921; s. Walter Levi and Kate Edline (Aughtman) P.; m. Margaret Alice Hall, May 14, 1966. Degree, Brennan Bus. Sch., 1940; postgrad., Samford U., 1950-57. Ordained to ministry So. Bapt. Conv., 1947. Pastor various chs., Ala., 1947—; including Hopewell Bapt. Ch., 1949-67, Harmony Bapt. Ch., Andalusia, 1967-80, Searight Bapt. Ch., Dozier, Ala., 1980—; acct. C.G. Tomberlin, M.D., Andalusia, 1985—. Mem. bd. regents Liberty U., Lynchburg, Va. Home: 407 Lakeview Dr Andalusia AL 36420-3542 Office: PO Box 486 Andalusia AL 36420-1209 *In Him, we live and move and have our being. Therefore, my heart's desire is to honor Christ in all things, for He is the way, the truth, and the life.*

**PATTERSON, ELAINE WILCOX,** art educator; b. Newburg, N.Y., Nov. 16, 1948; d. William Thomas and Julia B. Wilcox; m. Russell Saunders Patterson, Dec. 23, 1974; children: John Russell, Heath Tyler. BA English Art, Delta State Univ., 1970. Cert. Nat. Bd. Cert. Tchr. 2004. Mutal funds liaison Merrill Lynch, Memphis, 1969—71; flight attendant Delta Airlines, Memphis, 1971—74; adminstr. asst. Pikeville Coll./Tcr. Corps, Pikeville, Ky., 1974—79; art tchr. East Jr. High, Gaffney, SC, 1981—86, W.C. Friday Jr. High, Dallas, NC, 1986—93; missionary Honduras Bapt. Med. Dental Mission, Tegucigalpa, Honduras, 1992—99; tchr. Forestview H. S., Gastonia, NC, 1999—. Presenter NC Art Educators Assn. 2002, 03, 04. Exhibitions include various local and state level, 1999—. Sun. sch. tchr. East Bapt. Ch., Gastonia, NC, 1999—, choir mem., 1999—, banner ministry dir., 1999—. Named Outstanding Young Woman of the Year Tr, W.C. Friday Jr. High, 1992. So. Bapt. Office: Forestview H S 5545 Union Rd Gastonia NC 28056

**PATTERSON, ELIZABETH JOHNSTON,** retired congresswoman; b. Columbia, SC, Nov. 18, 1939; d. Olin DeWitt and Gladys (Atkinson) Johnston; m. Dwight Fleming Patterson, Jr., Apr. 15, 1967; children: Dwight

---

Fleming, Olin DeWitt, Catherine Leigh. BA, Columbia Coll., 1961; postgrad. in polit. sci., U. S.C., 1961, 62, 64; LLD (hon.), Columbia Coll., 1987; D Pub. Svc. (hon.), Converse Coll., 1989, M in Liberal Arts, 1999; LLD (hon.), Wofford Coll., 1999. Pub. affairs officer Peace Corps, Washington, 1962-64, VISTA, OEO, Washington, 1965-66; D Pub. Svc. Head Start and VISTA, OEO, Columbia, 1966-67; tri-county dir. Head Start, Piedmont Community Actions, Spartanburg, SC, 1967-68; mem. Spartanburg County Coun., 1975-76, S.C. State Senate, 1979-86, 100th-102nd Congresses from 4th S.C. dist., 1987-93; dir. continuing edn., converse II program Converse Coll., 1993—2003; ret. Adj. prof. Spartanburg Meth. Coll., 1993—2001. Trustee Wofford Coll., 1978—90, Columbia Coll., 1991—2003, Spartanburg Meth. Coll., 2004—; pres. Spartanburg Dem. Women, 1968; v.p. Spartanburg County Dem. party, 1968—70, sec., 1970—75, pres., 2004—; bd. dirs. S.C. Ind. Colls. and Univs., 1995—99, Charles Lea Ctr., 1978, Spartanburg Coun. on Aging; chmn., bd. dirs. Bethlehem Cmty. Ctr., 1998—. Mem.: Bus. and Profl. Women's Club, Alpha Kappa Gamma. Democrat. Methodist. E-mail: lizjpatterson@charter.net.

**PATTERSON, EUGENE CORBETT,** retired editor, publishing executive; b. Valdosta, Ga., Oct. 15, 1923; s. William C. and Annabel (Corbett) P.; m. Mary Sue Carter, Aug. 19, 1950; 1 child, Mary Patterson Fausch. Student, North Ga. Coll., Dahlonega, 1940-42; AB in Journalism, U. Ga., 1943; LL.D., Tusculum Coll., 1965, Harvard U., 1969, Duke U., 1978, Stetson U., 1984, Ind. U., 1990; Litt.D., Emory U., 1966, Oglethorpe Coll., 1966, Tuskegee U., 1966, Roanoke Coll., 1968, Mercer U., 1968, Eckerd Coll., 1977, U. South Fla., 1986, Dillard U., 1992, Colby Coll., 1994, North Ga. Coll. & State U., 1999. Reporter Temple (Tex.) Daily Telegram and Macon (Ga.) Telegraph, 1947-48; mgr. for S.C. United Press, 1948-49, N.Y. night bur. mgr. N.Y.C., 1949-53, mgr. London bur., also chief corr. U.K., 1953-56; v.p., exec. editor Atlanta Journal-Constitution, 1956-60; editor Atlanta Constitution, 1960-68; mng. editor Washington Post, 1968-71; prof. polit. sci. Duke U., 1971-72; editor, pres. St. Petersburg (Fla.) Times, 1972-84, chmn., chief exec. officer, 1978-88, editor emeritus, 1988—; editor, pres. Congl. Quar., Washington, 1972-86, chmn., chief exec. officer, 1978-88. Chmn. bd., chief exec. officer Fla. Trend mag., 1980-88, Ga. Trend mag., 1984-88, Ariz. Trend mag., 1986-88, Governing mag., 1987-88, Modern Graphic Arts, Inc., 1978-88, Poynter Inst. Media Studies, 1978-88, Poynter Fund, 1978-88. Author: The Changing South of Gene Patterson, 2002. Vice chmn. U.S. Civil Rights Commn., 1964-68; mem. Pulitzer Prize Bd., 1973-84; trustee ASNE Found., 1981-84, U. Ga. Found., 1982-88, North Ga. Coll. Found., 1991-93, Am. Press Inst., Reston, Va., 1983-88, Duke U., 1988-94, Fla. Bar Found., 1992-93. LeRoy Collins Ctr. for Pub. Policy, 1990-93. Decorated Silver Star, Bronze Star with oak leaf cluster in 10th Armored Divsn., Gen. Patton's 3rd Army; recipient Pulitzer prize for editl. writing Columbia U., 1967, William Allen White Nat. Citation award U. Kans., 1980, Elijah Parish Lovejoy award Colby Coll., 1994; inducted into Fla. Newspaper Hall of Fame Fla. Press Assn., 1997. Fellow Soc. Profl. Journalists; mem. Am. Soc. Newspaper Editors (pres. 1977-78), St. Petersburg Yacht Club. Home: Snell Isle 1967 Brightwaters Blvd NE Saint Petersburg FL 33704-3007 E-mail: Ecp1015@aol.com.

**PATTERSON, GARY,** college football coach; b. Larned, Kans., Feb. 13, 1960; m. Kelsey Patterson; children: Josh, Cade, Blake. BS in Phys. Edn., Kans. State, 1983; MEd, Tenn. Tech., 1984. Grad. asst. Kans. State, 1982; linebackers coach Tenn. Tech., 1983—84, Univ. Calif.-Davis, 1986, Pitts. State, Kans., 1988; defensive coord. Cal Lutheran, 1987, Sonoma State, Calif., 1989—91; secondary coach Utah State, 1992—94, Navy, 1995; defensive coord., safeties coach New Mexico, 1996—97, TCU, 1998—2000, head football coach, 2000—. Office: TCU Athletics PO Box 297600 Fort Worth TX 76129*

**PATTERSON, GILBERT EARL,** bishop; b. Humboldt, Tenn., Sept. 22, 1939; s. W. A. and Mary Patterson; m. Louise Patterson. Studied at, Detroit Bible Inst., LeMoyne Owen Coll.; ThD (hon.), Oral Roberts U. Ordained elder Ch. of God, 1958. Co-pastor Holy Temple Ch. of God in Christ, Memphis, 1962; founder, pastor Temple of Deliverance, Cathedral of the Bountiful Blessings, Memphis, 1975—; presiding bishop Church Of God In Christ, Inc. Pres. Charles H. Mason Bible Coll. of Tenn. Fourth Jurisdiction, Memphis. Author: Here Comes The Judge, 2002; pub. Bountiful Blessings Mag., contbg. writer Spirit Filled Life Bible. Named one of Most Influential Black Americans, Ebony mag., 2006. Office: Temple of Deliverance 369 G E Patterson Ave Memphis TN 38126*

**PATTERSON, HOWARD YATES,** academic athletics administrator; b. Boston, Aug. 22, 1950; s. Charles F. and Dorothy M. (Smith) P.; m. Cathi Dawn Cuba, Dec. 27, 1987; children: Jori, MacKenzie, Coleman. BS, Springfield (Mass.) Coll., 1973; MS, Midwestern State U., 1975; PhD, U. North Tex., 1995. Instr., coach soccer Midwestern State U., Wichita Falls, Tex., 1973-89; dir. athletics U. Incarnate Word, San Antonio, 1990—2001; dir. athletics, dean student affairs U. Tex., Tyler, 2001, asst. v.p. student affairs and external rels., 2001—. Office: Phone: 903-566-7350. Business E-Mail: hpatterson@uttyler.edu.

**PATTERSON, HUBERT CLIFTON,** physician; b. Durham, N.C., Nov. 25, 1948; s. Hubert Clifton and Elizabeth Fox Patterson; m. Laura Lynn Zelaites, Sept. 21, 1975; 1 child, Meggie Carol. MD, U. N.C., Chapel Hill, 1974. Diplomate Am. Acad. ENT, Head and Neck Surgery, 1980. Asst. prof. U. Wash. Sch. Medicine, Seattle, 1980—83; pvt. practice Raleigh (N.C.) ENT Assoc., 1983—. Col. U.S. Army, 1975—99. Decorated Bronze Star US Army. Fellow: Amer. Acad. ENT. Office Phone: 919-787-7171.

**PATTERSON, JAMES BRENDAN, JR.,** writer, former advertising executive; b. Newburgh, N.Y., Mar. 22, 1947; s. Charles H. and Isabelle (Morris) P. BA, Manhattan Coll., 1969; MA, Vanderbilt U., 1970. With J. Walter Thompson Co., N.Y.C., 1971—96; chmn. J. Walter Thompson U.S., 1990—96. Author: (children's books) santaKid, 2004, Maximum Ride: The Angel Experiment, 2005, (novels) The Thomas Berryman Number, 1976 (Edgar Allen Poe award Mystery Writers Am.), Season of the Machete, 1977, The Jericho Commandment, 1979, Virgin, 1980, Black Market, 1986, The Midnight Club, 1989, Along Came a Spider, 1993, Kiss the Girls, 1995, Hide and Seek, 1995, Jack and Jill, 1996, Miracle on the 17th green, 1996, See How They Run, 1997, Cat and Mouse, 1997, When the Wind Blows, 1998, Pop! Goes the Weasel, 1999, Black Friday, 2000, Cradle and All, 2000, Roses are Red, 2000, 1st to Die, 2001, Suzanne's Diary for Nicholas, 2001, Violets are Blue, 2001, 2nd Chance, 2002, The Beach House, 2002, Four Blind Mice, 2002, The Jester, 2003, The Lake House, 2003, The Big Bad Wolf, 2003, Sam's Letters To Jennifer, 2004 (Publishers Weekly Bestseller), London Bridges, 2004, Honeymoon, 2005 (NY Times Bestseller); co-author (with Maxine Paetro) 4th of July, 2005 (Publishers Weekly Bestseller); author Lifeguard, 2005, The 5th Horsemen, 2006, Judge & Jury, 2006. Recipient 6 Clio awards, 1983; recipient Effie awards, 1983. Mem. Phi Beta Kappa. Mailing: c/o Author Mail Little, Brown and Co 1271 Ave of the Americas New York NY 10020*

**PATTERSON, JAMES E.,** economist, author, speaker; b. Ft. Belvoir, Va., Jan. 1, 1955; s. James G. and Helen L. Patterson; m. Sheryl Rene Alexander; children: James H., Alexandra Baker. BS, Auburn U., 1978, MS in Econs., 1980. Recipient Bd. Agrl. Econs., Auburn, Ala., 1978—80; sys. analyst Ind. Employment Security Divsn., Indpls., 1981—84; economist /statistician U.S. Dept. of Commerce, Washington, 1984—87; economist USDA, Washington, 1987—92, diplomat/fgn. svc. officer, 1992—98; freelance writer Washington, 1999—. Prof. Grad. Sch., USDA, Washington, 1989—91; adj. prof. No. Va. C.C., Woodbridge, 1987; instr./ cons. Fairfax County Adult Edn. Dept., Fairfax, Va., 1985—87. Author: (newspaper column) Washington Scene, 1995; contbr. articles to mags. Mem. Rep. Nat. Com.; mem. precinct com. Marion County Rep. Party, Indpls., 1982—83. Named to Outstanding Young Men of Am., 1989; recipient Spl. Svc. award, U.S. Dept. Commerce, 1986, Productivity award, 1987, Performance award, 1989, Presdl. Point of Light, USDA, 1992, certs. from. Mem.: Alpha Zeta (sec., treas., VP 1988—92). Republican. Episcopal. Achievements include being profiled in

New York Times, Wall Street Journal, The Washington Times and The Foreign Service Journal, others. Avocations: coin collecting/numismatics, reading, golf, tennis, horseback riding.

**PATTERSON, JAMES RANDOLPH,** physician; b. Lancaster, Pa., Jan. 30, 1942; m. Linda Lewis Patterson, Nov. 22, 1969. AB, U. Pa., 1964; MD, Columbia U., 1968. Diplomate Nat. Bd. Med. Examiners, Am. Bd. Internal Medicine, Subsplty. of Pulmonary Disease. Pulmonary and critical care specialist The Oreg. Clinic, Portland, 1975—; clin. prof. medicine Oreg. Health Scis. U., Portland, 1978—. Mem. Am. Bd. Internal Medicine, Phila., 1995—, sec.-treas., 2002—; trustee Collins Med. Trust, Portland, Oreg., 1992—, chair subsplty. bd. pulmonary disease, 1998-2002. Contbr. numerous articles to profl. jours. Recipient Class of 1964 award U. Pa., Van Loan award Am. Lung Assn. Oreg., 1990, Meritorious Achievement award Oreg. Health Scis. U., 1991; named Class Pres. Coll. Physicians and Surgeons of Columbia U., 1968, Tchr. of Yr. Providence Med. Ctr., Portland, Oreg., 1976, Internist of Yr., 1983, Best Doctors in Am., 1992—; Consumers Guide to Top Doctors, 2002-. Mem. AMA, Am. Thoracic Soc., Am. Coll. Chest Physicians, Oreg. Lung Assn., North Pacific Soc. of Internal Medicine, Pacific Interurban Clin. Club, Multnomah County Med. Soc., Oreg. Med. Assn., Oreg. Soc. Critical Care Medicine. Office: The Oregon Clinic 507 NE 47th Ave Ste 103 Portland OR 97213-2236 Office Phone: 503-215-2300. Business E-Mail: jpatterson@orclinic.com.

**PATTERSON, JAN EVANS,** epidemiologist, educator; b. Ft. Worth, May 13, 1956; d. C. Wayne and Zona (Horn) Evans; m. Thomas F. Patterson, June 22, 1985 BA, Hardin Simmons U., 1978; MD, U. Tex., 1982. Diplomate Am. Bd. Internal Medicine, Am. Bd. Infectious Diseases. Asst. prof. medicine and lab. medicine Yale U. Sch. Medicine, New Haven, 1988-92; assoc. prof. medicine and pathology Health Sci. Ctr. U. Tex., San Antonio, 1993—99, prof. medicine and pathology, assoc. chair of medicine, 1999—2005, prof. medicine and pathology, vice chair medicine, 2005—; chief med. svc. Audie Murphy Vets. Hosp., 2004—. Hosp. epidemiologist Univ. Health Sys., San Antonio, 1993-2005, Audie Murphy Meml. Vets. Hosp., San Antonio, 1993-95, S. Tex. Vets. Healthcare System, San Antonio and Kerrville, 1995-2005. Contbr. articles to profl. jours. Fellow ACP, Infectious Disease Soc. Am.; mem. Soc. Hosp. Epidemiologists, Am. Soc. Tropical Medicine and Hygiene, Exec. Leadership in Academic Medicine, Alpha Omega Alpha. Office: Health Sci Ctr U Tex Divsn Infectious Diseases 7703 Floyd Curl Dr San Antonio TX 78284-6200

**PATTERSON, JEFFREY A.,** real estate company executive; Sr. fin. analyst Real Estate Investment Group Met. Life Ins. Co.; exec. v.p. The Prime Group, Inc., 1989—97; from exec. v.p. to pres. Prime Group Realty Trust, Chgo., 1997—2003, pres., 2003—, chief investment officer, 1997—. Mem.: Nat. Assn. Real Estate Investment Trusts, Urban Land Inst. (assoc.). Office: Prime Group Realty Trust 77 West Wacker Dr Ste 3900 Chicago IL 60601

**PATTERSON, JOHN DE LA ROCHE, JR.,** lawyer; b. Schenectady, N.Y., July 8, 1941; s. John de la Roche Sr. and Jane C. (Clay) P.; m. Michele F. Demarest, Nov. 28, 1987; children: Daniel C., Sara R., Amy C. BA, Johns Hopkins U., 1963; LLB, Harvard U., 1966. Bar: Mass. 1968. Vol. Peace Corps, Chad, 1966-67; assoc. Foley Hoag LLP, Boston, 1967-73, ptnr., 1974—, mem. exec com., 1989-97. Chmn. Kodaly Ctr. Am. Inc., Newton, Mass., 1977-87. Mem. ABA, Boston Bar Assn. Democrat. Avocations: sailing, tennis, travel, reading. Office: Foley Hoag LLP 155 Seaport Blvd Boston MA 02210- Office Phone: 617-832-1144. E-mail: jpatterson@FoleyHoag.com.

**PATTERSON, KENNETH,** nurse; b. Milledgeville, Ga., Dec. 14, 1968; s. William Thomas and Dotsie Mae Patterson; m. Daphne Marie Wise; children: Alexander, Kendra, DeAmber, Lucas, Ryan. Diploma in practical nursing, Macon Tech. Inst., 2003; BA in criminal justice, Mercer U., 2005. Lic. LPN. LPN, charge nurse Ctrl. State Hosp., Milledgeville, Ga., 1993—96, Macon Manor Nursing Rehab, Macon, Ga., 1996—99; resident care coord. Bel Arbor Nursing Ctr., Macon, Ga., 2000—02; intake coord. Regency Hosp. Co., Macon, 2004—05; dir. admissions Macon Manor Nursing Rehab, Macon, Ga., 2005—. Cons. Tri State Health Corp., Macon, Ga., 2005—. Bd. mem. Family Counseling Ctr., Macon, Ga., 2005—; vol. Vista Care Hospice, Macon, Ga., 2005—; co-coord. Mentor Leadership Program, Ballard Mid. Macon, Ga., 2001—02. Mem.: NAACP Mercer Chapter. Republican. Bapt. Avocation: youth mentoring. Home: 2858 Hwy 49 W Haddock GA 31033 Office: Macon Manor Nursing and Rehab 4373 Houston Ave Macon GA 31206 Office Phone: 478-784-1500. Office Fax: 478-784-1528. E-mail: pdaphne2@aol.com.

**PATTERSON, LYN,** director; d. Arthur Payne Whiteway and Joyce Walker; m. Hugh F. Cooper, May 30, 1981; children: Erin Elizabeth, Christopher Scott, Spencer Nicholas. BS. U. Okla., Norman, Okla., 1980, MS, 1987. Tchr. phys. edn. Norman Pub. Schs., 1987—89; coach swimming Norman H.S., 1989—2004, Norman North H.S., 1998—2004; resident camp dir. Camp Classen YMCA, Davis, Okla., 2004—, dir. outdoor schs. Camp Classen, 2004—. Named Tchr. of Yr., Dist. Fraust, 1991, Phys. Edn. Tchr. of Yr., Okla., 1993, Coach of Yr., Norman Pub. Schs., 2003. Avocations: kayaking, backpacking, painting, swimming. Home: 211 Crest Ct Norman OK 73071 Office: Camp Classen YMCA Rt 1 Box 47 Davis OK 73030

**PATTERSON, MARLENE (NONE),** secondary school educator; d. Mahratta Hazel and Oliver Jack Sansing (Stepfather), James Chauna Cox, m. Frank Nesbitt Patterson, Sept. 29, 1965; children: Gregory Thomas, Craig Henry, Jeffrey Shane, Frank Nesbitt Patterson III. BS, Limestone Coll., Gaffney, S.C., 1983. Tchr. sci. and social studies Cherokee Coounty Sch. Dist. # 1, Gaffney, SC, 1984—. Mem.: Nat. Tchrs. Orgn. (assoc.).

**PATTERSON, NEAL L.,** information systems company executive; BS in Fin., Okla. State U., MBA. Sys. cons.; mgr. Arthur Andersen & Co., Kansas City, Mo.; co-founder, CEO, chmn. bd. dirs. Cerner Corp., Kansas City, Mo., 1979—. Trustee Midwest Rsch. Inst.; mem. steering com. Coun. Growing Cos. Named Entrepreneur of Yr., Ernst & Young, 1991. Mem. Health Execs. Network. Office: Cerner Corp 2800 Rockcreek Pkwy Ste 601 Kansas City MO 64117-2521

**PATTERSON, OSCAR, III,** academic administrator; b. July 25, 1945; s. Oscar Jr. and Frances (Killian) P.; m. Kathy E. Gibson, June 6, 1966 (div. Apr. 1979); 1 child, Elizabeth Anne Patterson Cassel; m. Julie Ann Holmes, Dec. 28, 1990. BA, Pfeiffer U., 1967; MFA, U. Ga., 1973; PhD, U. Tenn., 1982. Asst. prof. architecture and fine arts Auburn (Ala.) U., 1972-75; chairperson BFA in Theatre program Western Carolina U., Cullowhee, N.C., 1975-79; dir. telecom. U. N.C., Pembroke, 1984—98; chair comm. and visual arts U. North Fla., Jacksonville, 1998—. Juvenile probation officer Cleveland Ct. Sys., Shelby, N.C., 1967-68; gen. mgr. news dir. WNCP-TV, N.C., 1984-98. Contbr. articles to profl. jours.; host pub. tv program, 1989-98. U.S. Army, 1968-75, Vietnam. Mem. AEJMC, Soc. Profl. Journalists, Phi Kappa Phi. Republican. Avocations: historical reenactment, beach exploration. Home: 248 Patrick Mill Cir Ponte Vedra Beach FL 32082-4013 Business E-Mail: opatters@unf.edu.

**PATTERSON, PAIGE,** church administrator, former seminary president; b. Tex., 1942; s. T.A. Patterson; m. Dorothy Jean Kelley; 2 children. BA, Hardin-Simmons U., Abilene, Tex.; ThD in Theology, ThD in Theology, New Orleans Sem. Ordained to ministry Bapt. Ch. Min. various chs.; pres. Criswell Coll., Dallas, 1975-92, Southeastern Bapt. Theol. Sem., Wake Forest, N.C., 1992-98, So. Bapt. Conv., So. Ea. Bapt. Sem., Nashville, 1998—2003, Southwestern Bapt. Theol. Sem., Fort Worth, Tex., 2003—. Office: Southwestern Bapt Theol Sem 2001 W Seminary Dr PO Box 22040 Fort Worth TX 76122-0040

**PATTERSON, PEYTON R.,** bank executive; b. Weisbaden, Germany; m. Thomas Patterson; 1 child. Degree in Polit. Sci., European Inst. Study, 1977; AB in Polit. Sci., Kenyon Coll., 1978; MBA in Mktg., George Washington U., 1983. From asst. v.p. group product mgr. retail deposit products to v.p. Corestates Fin. Corp., Phila., 1983—85, v.p., 1985—89; from v.p. group product mgr. to sr. v.p. Chemical Banking Corp., NYC, 1989—90, sr. v.p., 1990—95; sr. v.p., dir. nat. fin. svcs. group Chase Manhattan Bank, NYC, 1995—96; exec. v.p., gen. mgr. consumer fin. svcs. Dime Bank Corp., NYC, 1996—2001; chmn., pres., CEO New Haven Savings Bank (now NewAlliance Bancshares, Inc.), 2002—. Co-chmn. Greater N.Y. March of Dimes; mem. Regional Leadership Coun., Arts Coun. Greater New Haven; bd. dirs. United Way. Named One of 25 Most Powerful Women in Banking, US Banker mag., 2003, 2004, 2005; Rockefeller fellow, 2000—01, Henry Crown fellow, Aspen Inst. Office: NewAlliance Bancshares 195 Church St New Haven CT 06510*

**PATTERSON, P(ICKENS) ANDREW,** lawyer; b. Cotton Plant, Ark., Aug. 1, 1944; s. Pickens Andrew and Willie Mae (Miller) P.; m. Gloria Neltine Peebles, Nov. 25, 1967; children: Pickens Andrew, Staci Elizabeth. B.A., Fisk U., 1965; J.D., Harvard U., 1968. Bar: Ga. 1969, N.C. 1978, U.S. Dist. Ct. (no. dist.) Ga. 1969, U.S. Dist. Ct. (mid. dist.) N.C. 1978, U.S. Ct. Appeals (11th cir.) 1983. Vice pres. Urban East Housing Consl. Atlanta, 1968-69; mng. atty. Atlanta Legal Aid, 1968-70; sr. ptnr. Patterson, Parks, Jackson & Howell, Atlanta, 1970-77; atty. adviser HUD, Greensboro, N.C., 1977-81; exec. v.p. Arrington, Patterson & Thomas, P.C., Atlanta, 1982—; ptnr. Thomas, Kennedy, Sampson & Patterson, 1985—. Pres. Atlanta Legal Aid Soc., 1976, Central Carolina Legal Services, Greensboro, 1980; chair State Bd. Bar Examiners. Co-author pamphlet. Mem. Atlanta Charter Study Commn., 1972; bd. dirs. Louisville Presbyn. Theol. Sem., 1983—86. Recipient Key to City Atlanta, 1972, plaque awards Atlanta Legal Aid Soc., 1977, Central Carolina Legal Services, 1981, Cert. of Spl. Achievement, Office of Gen. Counsel, HUD, 1980. Mem. Nat. Bar Assn., State Bar Ga., N.C. Bar Assn., Atlanta Bar Assn., Gate City Bar Assn., Alpha Phi Alpha, Sigma Pi Phi. Democrat. Methodist. Home: 3905 Somerled Trl Atlanta GA 30349-2035 Office: 3355 Main St College Park GA 30331 Office Phone: 404-688-4503. Business E-Mail: pa.patterson@tksp.com.

**PATTERSON, RICHARD NORTH,** writer, lawyer; b. Berkeley, Calif., Feb. 22, 1947; s. Richard Wallace and Marjorie Frances (North) P.; children: Shannon Heath, Brooke North, Katherine Amber, Adam Chandler, Chase Kenyon. BA History, Ohio Wesleyan U., 1968; JD, Case Western Reserve, 1971. Bar: Ohio, 1971, D.C., 1973, Ala., 1975, Calif., 1984. Asst. atty. gen. State of Ohio, 1971-73; with divsn. enforcement SEC, Washington, 1973-75, San Francisco, Calif., 1878-81; assoc. atty. Berkowitz, Lefkovits & Patrick, Birmingham, Ala., 1975-77, ptnr., 1978; assoc. McCutchen, Doyle, Brown & Enerson, San Francisco, Calif., 1985-87, ptnr., 1987-93, of counsel, 1993-94. Author: The Lasko Tangent, 1979, The Outside Man, 1981, Escape the Night, 1983, Private Screening, 1985, Degree of Guilt, 1993, Eyes of a Child, 1995, The Final Judgement, 1995, Silent Witness, 1997, No Safe Place, 1998, Dark Lady, 1999, Protect and Defend, 2000, Balance of Power, 2003, Conviction, 2005. Bd. dirs. Common Cause. Named Man of Yr., WWRAP, 2001; recipient Edgar Allan Poe award for best 1st novel, Mystery Writers Am., 1979, Grand Prix de Literateur Policiere, 1995, Pres.'s award for Disting. Alumni, Case Western Res. U., 1997, Maggie award, Planned Parenthood, 2001.

**PATTERSON, ROBERT EDWARD,** lawyer; b. LA, Sept. 14, 1942; s. Ellis Elwood and Helen (Hjelte) Patterson; m. Christina Balboni Patterson, Oct. 2, 1971; 1 child, Victor Ellis. BA, UCLA, 1964; JD, Stanford U., 1972, grad. bus. exec. program, 1986. Bar: Calif. 1972. Sr. counsel Squire Sanders & Dempsey LLP, Palo Alto, Calif., 1972—. Bd. dirs. Peninsula Equity Ptnrs., Ctr. Pvt. Equity, Amos Tuck Sch., Dartmouth Coll., Sumida Corp., Synzyme Techs., LLC, Calif. State Pks. Found., Acuity Ventures, EARN Corp., Inst. Tech. Innovation-Energy, Scotland, Calif. Airlines, Greater China Project Stanford Project Regions Innovation and Entrepreneurship. Bd. dirs. John Ernest Found. Lt. comdr. USN, 1964—69. Vis. scholar, Amos Tuck Sch. Dartmouth Coll., 1998. Mem.: Bohemian Club, Menlo Circus Club, Palo Alto Club, Band of Angels. Democrat. Office: Squire Sanders & Dempsey LLP 600 Hansen Way Ste 100 Palo Alto CA 94304-1043 Office Phone: 650-856-6500. Business E-Mail: rpatterson@ssd.com.

**PATTERSON, ROBERT PORTER, JR.,** federal judge; b. NYC, July 11, 1923; s. Robert Porter and Margaret (Winchester) P.; m. Bevin C. Daly, Sept. 15, 1956; children: Anne, Robert, Margaret, Paul, Katherine. AB, Harvard U., 1947; LLB, Columbia U., 1950. Bar: N.Y. 1951, D.C. 1966. Law clk. Donovan, Leisure, Newton & Lumbard, N.Y.C., 1950-51; asst. counsel N.Y. State Crime Commn. Waterfront Investigation, 1952-53; asst. U.S. atty. Chief of Narcotics Prosecutions and Investigations, 1953-56; assoc. counsel Senate Banking and Currency Com., 1954; assoc. Patterson, Belknap, Webb & Tyler, N.Y.C., 1956-60, ptnr., 1960-88; judge U.S. Dist. Ct. (So. Dist.), NY, 1988—98, sr. judge NY, 1998—. Counsel to minority select com. pursuant to house resolution no. 1, Washington, 1967; mem. Senator's Jud. Screening Panel, 1974-88, Gov.'s Jud. Screening Panel, 1975-82, Gov.'s Sentencing Com., 1978-79. Contbr. articles to profl. jours. Chmn. Wm. T. Grant Found., 1974-94, Prisoners' Legal Services N.Y., 1976-88; dir. Legal Aid Soc. 1961-88, pres., 1967-71; chmn. Nat. Citizens for Eisenhower, 1959-60, Scranton for Pres., N.Y. State, 1964; bd. mgrs. Havens Relief Fund Soc., 1994—, Millbrook Sch., 1966-78, Vera Inst. Justice, 1981-99. New Sch. for Social Rsch. 1986-94, George C. Marshall Found., 1987-93; mem. exec. com. Lawyers Com. for Civil Rights Under Law, 1968-88; mem. Goldman Panel for Attica Disturbance, 1972, Temporary Commn. on State Ct. System, 1971-73, Rockefeller U. Council, 1986-88, exec. com. N.Y. Vietnam Vets. Meml. Commn., 1982-85, Mayor's Police Adv. Com., 1985-87. Served to capt. USAAF, 1942-46. Decorated D.F.C. with cluster, Air medal with clusters. Mem. ABA (ho. of dels. 1976-80), N.Y. State Bar Assn. (pres. 1978-79), Assn. Bar City N.Y. (v.p. 1974-75), N.Y. County Lawyers Assn., Am. Law Inst., Am. Judicature Soc. (bd. dirs. 1979). Republican. Episcopalian. Home: Fair Oaks Farm 1657 Route 9D Cold Spring NY 10516-3543 Office: US Dist Ct So Dist NY US Court House 500 Pearl St New York NY 10007-1316

**PATTERSON, RONALD PAUL,** publishing executive, educator, minister; b. Ashland, Ohio, Dec. 4, 1941; s. Donald Edward and Mildred (Niswender) P.; m. Marlene Pfahler, Sept. 1, 1962; children: Paul Edward, Mark Loren. BA, Malone Coll., 1963; MDiv, United Theol. Sem., Dayton, Ohio, 1967; MA, Syracuse U., 1970; DD, Cen. Meth. Coll., 1988. Ordained to ministry United Methodist Ch., 1967. Editor youth publs. Otterbein Press, Dayton, 1964-68; assoc. editor The Upper Room, Nashville, 1970-74; editor Word Books, Waco, Tex., 1974-77; editorial dir. Abingdon Press, Nashville, 1977-88; book editor United Meth. Ch. Pub. House, 1977-88, v.p., 1984-88, sr. editor Ch. Resources, 1988-92; pub., CEO UMR Comm., Inc., Dallas, 1992—. V.p. Religious Pub. Rels. Coun. Nashville, 1970-74; jr. coll. instr. creative writing, Waco; leader writers' workshops Author: (with others) The Kyle Rote Story, 1975; editor: Come On, Let's Pray, 1972; compiler: The Coming of Easter, 1973; founding editor Alive Now! devotional publ.; editorial dir. Quar. Rev., 1980-87; contbr. articles to mags. Tchr. Tenn. State Prison, Nashville, 1984-88; mem. exec. bd. Perkins Sch. Theology, 1996—; charter mem. Perkins Circle. Recipient George Washington Honor medal Nat. Freedom Found., Valley Forge, Pa., 1960, Paul M. Hinkhouse award Religious Pub. Rels. Coun., N.Y.C., 1973; named Communicator of Yr., Dallas/Ft. Worth chpt. Religion Comm. Coun., 2004; named one of Outstanding Young Men Am., 1972. Mem. Am. Acad. Religion, Religion Pub. Group, Christian Publs. Assn., Southeastern Pubs. Assn. (exec. com. 1985-88), Pubs. Assn. of South (treas.), Evang. Christian Pubs. Assn. (bd. dirs. 1987-88), Protestant Ch.-owned Pubs. Assn. (bd. dirs., chmn. biennial planning com. 1999—), Internat. Pubs. Assn. World Meth. Coun., Hogan Quality Roundtable (Dallas), CEO Inst., Dallas Press, Rotary. Democrat. Methodist. Avocations: bicycling, refinishing furniture, golf.

**PATTERSON, RONALD R(OY),** management consultant; b. Baton Rouge, Mar. 4, 1942; BS, U. Houston, 1965; MS, Trinity U., San Antonio, 1973. Asst. adminstr. U. Tex. Med. Br., Galveston, 1972-75; asst. v.p. Hosp. Affiliates Internat., Nashville, 1975-81; chief oper. officer Affiliated Hosp. Systems, Houston, 1981-82; sr. v.p. Republic Health Corp., Dallas, 1982-88; pres. Miller Patterson Inc., Plano, Tex., 1988-89; ind. healthcare mgmt. cons. Plano, 1989-90; sr. v.p. Harris Meth. Health System, Ft. Worth, 1990-91; exec. v.p., COO Champion Healthcare Corp., Houston, 1991-96; exec. v.p., pres. healthcare ops. Paracelsus Healthcare Corp., Houston, 1996-99; pres. R. Patterson Assocs., 1999—. Bd. dirs. Tarrant County Hosp. Dist., 2002—05, sec., 2002—05; bd. chair Metrowest Health Plan, 2002—04, Tex. Health Facilities Devel. Corp., 2002—05. Fellow Am. Coll. Healthcare Execs. (life); Tex. Hosp. Assn. (vice-chmn. multi-hosp. constituency 1987), Fedn. Am. Health Sys. (bd. govs. 1996-99, bd. dirs., sec. 1997-99). Office: R Patterson Assocs PO Box 489 Jacksboro TX 76458 Office Phone: 817-692-5132.

**PATTERSON, SALLY JANE,** communications executive, consultant; b. Ontario, Calif., May 28, 1948; d. James Lowell and Barbara Verle (Griffin) Swain; 1 child, Robert Elias Sandoval. BA, Calif. State U., Fullerton, 1970, MA, 1974. Adminstrv. asst. Congressman Jerry Patterson, U.S. House of Reps., Washington, 1978-81; v.p. Pub. Response Assocs., Washington, 1981-87, Hamilton & Staff, Washington, 1987-90; v.p. pub. affairs Planned Parenthood Fedn. of Am., N.Y.C., 1990-93; internat. cons. Mgmt. Sys. Internat., Washington, 1993—; v.p. Wagner & Assocs. Pub. Affairs Cons., Inc., NYC, Washington, 1994-99; pres. Radiant Comms. Inc., 2000—. Cons. Nat. Dem. Inst., Washington, 1994—. Author: Supporting Democracy in The Newly Independent States of The Former Soviet Union, 1994, Women in Government Relations: 20 Years of Vision, Leadership, Education and Networking, 1995, Pursuing a Paradox: Public Attitudes vs. Public Action on Campaign Finance Reform, How does Congress Approach Population and Family Planning Issues?, 1999, Generating Bazz Strategic Communication for Nonprofit Boards, 2005. Trainer Nat. Women's Campaign Fund; bd. dirs Round House Theatre, 2004—. Recipient Gold Key award PR Soc. Am., 1992; named one of 74 Women Shaping Am. Politics, Campaigns and Elections, 1993. Mem. NARAL, Women in Govt. Rels., Inc. (disting. mem., chair leader found. 1985-87, v.p. 1987-88, pres. 1988-89), Coun. Excellence in Govt. (prin.), NARAL Found. (bd. 1993-2005, chair 2001-2004, found. bd. 2001—). Democrat. Episcopalian. Office: Radiant Comms Inc 2121 K St NW Ste 800 Washington DC 20037-1829

**PATTERSON, SAMUEL C.,** retired political science professor; b. Omaha, Nov. 29, 1931; s. Robert Foster and Garnet Marie (Jorgensen) P.; m. Suzanne Louise Dean, June 21, 1956; children: Polly Ann, Dean Foster, Grier Edmund. BA, U. S.D., 1953; MS, U. Wis., 1956, PhD, 1959. Asst. prof. polit. sci. Okla. State U., Stillwater, 1959-61; asst. prof. U. Iowa, Iowa City, 1961-64, assoc. prof., 1964-67, prof., 1967-85, Roy J. Carver prof., 1985-86; prof. Ohio State U., Columbus, 1986-98, prof. emeritus, 1998—; ret., 1998. Vis. prof. U. Wis., 1962, U. Okla., 1968-78. U. Essex, Colchester, Eng., 1969-70, U. S.D., 2001. Author: (with others) Representatives and Represented, 1975, A More Perfect Union, 4th edit., 1989; co-author: The Legislative Process in the United States, 4th edit., 1986, Comparing Legislatures, 1979; editor: American Legislative Behavior, 1968; co-editor: Comparative Legislative Behavior: Frontiers of Research, 1972, Handbook of Legislative Research, 1985, Political Leadership in Democratic Societies, 1991, Parliaments in the Modern World, 1994, Great Theatre: The American Congress in the 1990s, 1998, Senates: Bicameralism in the Contemporary World, 1999; editor Am. Jour. Polit. Sci., 1970-73; co-editor Legis. Studies Quar., 1981-85; mng. editor Am. Polit. Sci. Rev., 1985-91. Served with U.S. Army, 1953-55 Recipient Disting. Scholar award Ohio State U., 1990; fellow social Sci. Rsch. Coun., 1961, 67, Guggenheim, 1984-85; vis. fellow Brookings Instn., 1984-85, Ctr. Advanced Study in Behavioral Scis., 1993-94; Fulbright Bologna chair, 1995. Mem. Internat. Polit. Sci. Assn., Am. Polit. Sci. Assn. (Frank J. Goodnow award, 2000), Midwest Polit. Sci. Assn. (pres. 1980-81), Phi Beta Kappa, Phi Kappa Phi, Pi Sigma Alpha. Personal E-Mail: patpat851@earthlink.net.

**PATTERSON, STEVE,** professional basketball team executive; b. Beaver Dam, Wis., Sept. 21, 1957; BBA with honors, U. Tex., 1980, JD, 1984. Bar: Tex. 1984. Gen. mgr., profl. basketball team counsel Houston Rockets, 1984-89, profl. basketball mktg. exec. group ticket sales, mgr., bus. ops. exec., gen. mgr., 1989-94; pres. profl. hockey team Houston Aeros, 1994-97; pres. Arena Oper. Co., Houston, 1995-99; exec. v.p. Houston NFL Holdings, 1997—2003; pres. Portland Trail Blazers, 2003—. Exec. v.p. Houston Texans Office: Portland Trail Blazers Ste 200 One Center Ct Portland OR 97227 E-mail: steve.patterson@blazers.com.

**PATTERSON, W. MORGAN,** college president; b. New Orleans, Oct. 1, 1925; s. E. Palmer and Jess Margaret (Wood) P.; m. Ernestine Mouth, June 10, 1948; children: W. Morgan II, Jay North BA, Stetson U., 1950, D.D. (hon.), 1979; M.Div., New Orleans Baptist Theol. Sem., 1953, Th.D., 1956; postdoctoral, Oxford U., 1965-66, 72-73. Prof. ch. history New Orleans Bapt. Theol. Sem., 1956-59; prof. ch. history, David T. Porter prof. ch. history, dir. grad. studies So. Baptist Theol. Sem., Louisville, 1959-76; dean acad. affairs Golden Gate Bapt. Theol. Sem., Mill Valley, Calif., 1976-84; pres. Georgetown Coll., Ky., 1984-91; asst. to pres. Coll. of Ozarks, Mo., 1994—. Vis. prof. Midwestern Bapt. Theol. Sem., Kansas City, Mo., La. Coll., Pineville, 1991—92, Golden Gate Bapt. Theol. Sem., Mill Valley, Calif., 1992—94, 1997, 2003—05, Okla. Bapt. U., 1997, Fla. Bapt. Theol. Coll., 1998—99, New Orleans Bapt. Sem., 1995—96, 1999—2000; vis scholar Campbell ville U. Ky., 2000-03, Ky., 2006, Chmn. Hist. commn. So. Bapt. Conv., Nashville, 1969—72; honored guest 2d Vatican Coun., Rome, 1965. Author: Baptist Successionism: A Critical View, 1969; co-editor: Professor in the Pulpit, 1963; contbr., editor: Ency. Southern Baptists; book rev. editor Review and Expositor, 1965-70 Served as flight officer USAF, 1943-46 Recipient Disting. Alumnus award Stetson U., 1992, Disting. Svc. award for outstanding contbn. to Bapt. history Hist. Commn., So. Bapt. Conv., 1993; Am. Assn. Theol. Schs. fellow, 1965-66. Mem. Am. Soc. Ch. History, So. Bapt. Hist. Soc. (pres. 1979-80), William H. Whitsitt Bapt. Heritage Soc., Conf. on Faith and History, Commn. on Bapt. Heritage of Bapt. World Alliance. Avocations: travel, stamp collecting/philately, collecting books. Home: 7 Pierce Dr Novato CA 94947-4450

**PATTERSON, WILLIAM BROWN,** dean, history professor; b. Charlotte, N.C., Apr. 8, 1930; s. William Brown and Eleanor Selden (Miller) P.; m. Evelyn Byrd Hawkins, Nov. 27, 1959; children: William Brown Patterson, Evelyn Byrd Donatelli, Lucy Patterson Murray, Emily Patterson Higgs. BA, U. South, 1952; MA, Harvard U., 1954, PhD, 1966, cert. ednl. mgmt., 1982; BA, Oxford U., Eng., 1955; MA, Oxford (Eng.) U., 1959; MDiv, Episc. Div. Sch., Cambridge, Mass., 1958. Ordained to ministry Episcopal Ch. as deacon, 1958, as priest, 1959. Asst. prof. history Davidson (N.C.) Coll., 1963-66, assoc. prof., 1966-76, prof. history, 1976-80, U. of South, Sewanee, Tenn., 1980—2005, dean Coll. Arts and Scis., 1980-91; Francis S. Houghteling prof. hist., 2005. Author: (with others) Discord, Dialogue, and Concord, 1977, This Sacred History: Anglican Reflections for John Booty, 1990, King James VI and I and the Reunion of Christendom, 1997; mem. bd. editors St. Luke's Jour. Theology, Sewanee, 1982-90; contbr. numerous articles to profl. jours. Trustee U. South, 1968-71; mem. internat. adv. com. U. Buckingham, Eng., 1977-93; pres. So. Coll. and Univ. Union; organizer Associated Colls. of South, 1988-89. Danforth Found. grad. fellow, 1952, Mellon Appalachian fellow U. Va., 1992-93, rsch. fellow NEH, 1967, Folger Shakespeare Libr., Washington, 1975, Inst. for Rsch. in Humanities, U. Wis., Madison, 1976, Newberry Libr., Chgo., 1979; Rhodes scholar, 1953. Mem. Am. Hist. Assn., Am. Soc. Ch. History (Albert C. Outler prize for best book in ecumenical ch. history 1999), N.Am. Conf. on Brit. Studies, Eccles. History Soc. Eng., Royal Hist. Soc. Eng., So. Hist. Assn., Soc. for Values in Higher Edn., Episcopal Div. Sch. Alumni/ae Assn. (mem. exec. com. 1984-87), Phi Beta Kappa, Beta Theta Pi. Avocations: gardening, tennis. Home: 195 N Carolina Ave Sewanee TN 37375-2040 Office: U of South Dept History 735 University Ave Sewanee TN 37383-0001 Business E-Mail: bpatters@sewanee.edu.

**PATTERSON, WILLIAM S.,** lawyer; b. Kings Mountain, N.C., July 16, 1947; BA, Wake Forest U., 1969; JD with honors, U. N.C., 1973. Bar: N.C. 1973. Staff atty. interpretive divsn. Office Chief Counsel U.S. Dept. Treasury, 1973-75, staff atty. tax ct. litigation divsn., 1975-77; mng. ptnr., bus. practice group Hunton & Williams LLP, Raleigh, N.C. Office: Hunton & Williams 1 Hanover Sq Ste 1400 421 Fayetteville St Mall Raleigh NC 27601 Office Phone: 919-899-3022. Office Fax: 919-833-6352. Business E-Mail: bpatterson@hunton.com.

**PATTILLO, GARY A.,** beverage distribution executive; b. Newport Beach, Calif., Dec. 11, 1969; s. J. Lee Pattillo and Janice E. Beach; m. Charlene E. Pattillo, June 26, 1999; children: Naliyah R. children: Alex L., Kyla N. BS in Criminal Justice Adminstrn., San Diego State U., 1993. Account mgr. Mesa Distbg. Co., Inc., San Diego, 1999—2005, dist. mgr., 2005—. Recipient Top Sales award, Mesa Distbg. Co., 2001, 2002. Mem.: Am. Mensa. Green Party. Avocations: home Internet business, travel, computers, Kakuro puzzles.

**PATTILLO, MANNING MASON, JR.,** academic administrator; b. Charlottesville, Va., Oct. 11, 1919; s. Manning Mason and Margaret (Camblos) P.; m. Martha A. Crawford, June 8, 1946 (dec.); children: Manning Mason III (dec.), Martha Crawford, John Landrum. Student, Johns Hopkins U., 1937-38; BA with highest honors, U. of South, 1941, DCL, 1993; student, U. Calif. at Berkeley, 1941-42; AM, U. Chgo., 1947, PhD, 1949; LLD, LeMoyne Coll., 1967, St. John's U., 1968, Oglethorpe U., 1994; LHD, U. Detroit, 1968, Coll. New Rochelle, 1967, Park Coll., 1973; LittD, St. Norbert Coll., 1967. From instr. to assoc. prof. higher edn. U. Chgo., 1949-56; assoc. dir. Lilly Endowment, Inc., Indpls., 1956-60, exec. dir. for edn., 1961-62; dir. Danforth commn. on ch. colls. and univs., 1962-66; assoc. dir. The Danforth Found., 1964-66, v.p., 1966-67; pres. The Found. Center, NYC, 1967-71; adj. prof. NYU, 1968-71; dir. spl. projects U. Rochester, 1972-75; pres. Oglethorpe U., Atlanta, 1975-88, hon. chancellor, 1988—. Cons. in field; tech. asst., then assoc. sec. commn. on colls. and univs. North Ctrl. Assn. Colls. and Secondary Schs., 1948-56; cons. USAF Acad., 1952, Phillips Exeter Acad., 1974; chmn. IBM Incentive awards com., 1970-75; adv. com. Brookings Instn., 1970-71; vis. prof. Inst. Higher Edn., U. Ga., 1988-90; bd. dirs. Fidelity Nat. Bank. Author: (with D.M. Mackenzie) Church Sponsored Higher Education in the United States, 1966; (with D.M. Mackenzie) Eight Hundred Colleges Face the Future, 1965, Private Higher Education in the United States, 1990, The Episcopal Church: Diagnosis and Reform, 1989; contbr. articles to profl. jours. Mem. pres.'s adv. coun. Wellesley Coll., 1969-72; trustee Seabury Press, Japan Internat. Christian U., 1970-72, Le Moyne Coll., 1970-83, Sacred Heart U., 1968-75, U. of South, 1984-88, St. Martin's Episc. Sch.; bd. dirs., interim pres., chmn. Atlanta Coll. Art, 1984-95, Howard Sch.; trustee Greater Rochester Cmty. Found., 1973-75, pres., 1975; trustee, chmn. Nat. Coun. on Philanthropy, 1968-80; trustee, chmn. bd. trustees Park Coll., 1967-74; bd. visitors Evangeline Booth Coll., 1997—; provost St. Mary's Coll. of Md., 1975; bd. visitors Kanuga Confs., Inc.; pres., life trustee Ga. Found. for Ind. Colls., 1977—; chmn. Univ. Center in Ga., 1978-79; pres. Assn. Pvt. Colls. and Univs. of Ga., 1980-81; trustee, chmn. Ga. Spl. Olympics; trustee, mem. exec. com. Nat. Assn. Ind. Colls. and Univs., Ind. Coll. Funds of Am., 1982-86; co-dir. Coll. Cons. Network, So. Assn. Colls. and Schs., 1988-96; mem. De Kalb County Cmty. Rels. Commn.; chmn. De Kalb Cmty. Coun. on the Aging; mem. commn. on colls. and steering com. on revision accrediting procedures So. Assn. Colls. and Schs.; vice-chmn bd. and life trustee, Woodruff Arts Ctr.; mem. adv. coun. ARC. With AUS, 1942-46. Mem.: English Speaking Union (dir., pres. br., nat. bd. dirs.), Guild of Scholars (nat. Assn. Ind. Schs. (bd. dirs.), Nat. Assn. Scholars, Country Day Sch. Headmasters Assn. US (hon.), DeKalb C. of C. (dir., chmn.), Atlanta Hist. Soc., St. Andrew's Soc., High Mus. Art, Am. Alphacar Coun. (chmn Atlanta chpt.), Phi Beta Kappa Assn. of Atlanta (pres., chmn., fellow nat. soc.), Kappa Sigma, Omicron Delta Kappa. Episcopalian (vestryman, sr. warden, mem. cathedral chpt., diocesan council, standing com.). Clubs: Century (NYC); Commerce, Capital City. Lodge: Rotary.

**PATTIS, S. WILLIAM,** publishing executive; b. Chgo., July 3, 1925; s. William Robert and Rose (Quint) P.; m. Bette Z. Levin, July 16, 1950; children: Mark Robert, Robin Quint Himovitz. BS, U. Ill., 1949; postgrad., Northwestern U., 1949-50. Exec. v.p., pub. United Bus. Publs., 1949-59; chmn., CEO 3M/Pattis, 1959-88; pres. NTC Pub. Group, Lincolnwood, Ill., 1961-96, Next Chapter Holdings, L.P., Highland Park, Ill., 1996—; dir. P-B Comm.; Winnetka, Ill., 1978-98; vice-chmn. Profl. Media Group, Norwalk, Conn., 1999—. Bd. dirs. 1st Colonial/Highwood; mem. book and libr. com. USIA, Washington, 1986—89, chmn., 1989—93; mem. exec. com. Pub. Hall of Fame, 1987—2000; chmn. U.S.-USSR Bilateral Media Confs., Washington and Moscow, 1990—91. Author: Opportunities in Advertising Careers, 1984, 1988, 1995, Opportunities in Magazine Publishing Careers, 1992, 2001, VGM Career Planing, 1988, Careers in Advertising, 1996, 2d edit, 2002, 3d edit., 2003, 4th edit., 2004; co-author: Opportunities in Publishing Careers, 1995, 2001. Mem. Pres.'s Coun. Youth Opportunity, 1968-70; bd. dirs. Photography Youth Found., 1968-70, Expt. in Internat. Living, 1970, Inst. Human Creativity, 1983—, Fund for Am.'s Libraries, 1996-99; vice chmn. bd. dirs. Annenberg Ctr. for Health Scis., 1991—, vice chmn., 1996-99; trustee Eisenhower Med. Ctr., Rancho Mirage, Calif., 1989—, exec. com. mem., 1996—, chmn. investment com., 2000-03; trustee Am. Coun. Tchrs. Russian, 1992-96; bd. dirs. Nat. Security Edn. Act, Washington, 1993-94, Knapp Sch. Entrepreneurship, Ill. Inst. Tech., 2005—; bd. dirs. resource bd. Coll Comm. U. Ill., 2006—; lord of manor, Kirkbride, Eng., 1989—. Recipient Human Rels. award Am. Jewish Com., 1971, Paul Simon award Ctrl. States Conf. on Tchg. Fgn. Langs., 1992. Mem. Standard Club (Chgo.), Club Internat. (Chgo.), Northmoor Country Club (Highland Park, Ill.), Tamarisk Country Club (Rancho Mirage). Office: Next Chpt Holdings Port Clinton Sq 600 Central Ave Highland Park IL 60035-3211 Home (Winter): 70843 Tamarisk La Rancho Mirage CA 92270 Office Phone: 847-432-8700. Business E-Mail: bpattis@nextchapterholdings.com.

**PATTON, ALTON DEWITT,** electrical engineering consultant; b. Corpus Christi, Tex., Feb. 1, 1935; s. Alton G. and Civilia Louise (Taylor) P.; m. Nancy Jo Elder, Mar. 1, 1959; children: Elizabeth, Carolyn. BEE, U. Tex., 1957; MEE, U. Pitts., 1961; PhD in Elec. Engring., Tex. A&M U., 1972. Registered profl. engr., Tex.; diplomate Am. Bd. Forensic Engring. and Tech. Engr. Westinghouse Electric Corp., Pitts., 1957-65; prof. elec. engring. dept. Tex. A&M U., College Station, 1965-79, 82-2000, head elec. engring. dept., 1992-96, Brockett prof., 1986, Dresser prof., 1987, dir. Electric Power Inst., 1976-79, 85-92, prof. emeritus, 2005—; rsch. fellow Tex. Engrng. Expt. Sta., College Station, 1985, dir. Ctr. for Space Power, 1987-92; pres. Associated Power Analysts Inc., College Station, 1973—. Mem. panel for assessment of NIST Elec. and Electronics Engring. Lab., 1995-2000, NRS. Contbr. articles to elec. engring. jours. Fellow IEEE (life, tech. com., Prize Paper award 1975, 94, Richard Harold Kaufmann award 2000); mem. NSPE. Republican. Presbyterian. Avocations: fishing, hunting, photography, stamp and coin collecting. Home: 8411 Spring Crk College Station TX 77845-4608 Office: Associated Power Analysts Inc 303 Anderson St College Station TX 77840-3114 Office Phone: 979-696-0010. Business E-Mail: adpatton@tca.net. E-mail: adewittpatton@msn.com.

**PATTON, ANTWAN ANDRE (BIG BOI),** vocalist; b. Savannah, Ga., Feb. 1, 1975; children: Jordan Alexus, Bamboo. Performer Outkast, 1992—. Singer: (albums) Southernplayalisticadillacmuzik, 1994, ATLiens, 1996, Aquemini, 1998, Stankonia, 2000 (Grammy awards: Best Rap Album, 2001, Best Rap Performance By A Duo Or Group for song "Ms Jackson", 2001), Big Boi and Dre Present...Outkast, 2001 (Grammy award: (with Killer Mike) Best Rap Performance By A Duo Or Group for song "The Whole World", 2002), Speakerboxxx/The Love Below, 2003 (Grammy awards: Album Of The Yr., 2003, Best Urban/Alternative Performance for song "Hey Ya!", 2003, Best Rap Album, 2003, Am. Music Awards Favorite Album-Rap/Hip-Hop, 2004), Idlewild, 2006; actor: (films) ATL, 2006, Idlewild, 2006. Recipient Best New Rap Group of Yr., Source award, 1995, Favorite Band, Duo or Group-Pop or Rock, Am. Music Awards, 2004, Favorite Band, Duo or Group-Rap/Hip-Hop, 2004, Duo/Group Artist of Yr., Billboard Music Awards, 2004, Billboard 200 Duo/Group Album Artist of Yr., 2004, Hot 100

Duo/Group of Yr., 2004, R&B/Hip-Hop Duo/Group of Yr., 2004, Digital Track of Yr., 2004. Office: Arista Records Inc 1540 Broadway New York NY 10036-4074 Address: Arista Records Inc 8750 Wilshire Blvd Beverly Hills CA 90211-2713*

**PATTON, BRUCE M.,** law educator, management consultant; b. Terre Haute, Ind., Oct. 14, 1956; s. William Eugene and Carol Ann P.; m. Diana McLain Smith, Oct. 21, 1994. AB, Harvard U., 1977, JD, 1984. Bar: Mass. Co-founder, assoc. dir. Harvard Negotiation Project, Cambridge, Mass., 1979-84, dep. dir., 1984—; co-founder, assoc. dir. Program on Negotiation at Harvard Law Sch., Cambridge, Mass., 1983—2002; co-founder, ptnr. Vantage Partners, LLC, Cambridge, 1997—. Co-founder, prin. Conflict Mgmt. Inc., Cambridge, 1984—; co-founder, dir. Conflict Mgmt. Group, Cambridge, 1984-2000; Thaddeus R. Beal lectr. Harvard Law Sch., Cambridge, 1985-99. Co-author: The Mainstream of Alegbra and Trigonometry, 2d edit., 1980, Getting To Yes, 2d edit., 1991, Difficult Conversations, 1999; contbr. articles to profl. jours. Fellow: Coll. of Trial Mediators (hon.). Avocations: squash, hiking, tennis. Office: Harvard Negotiation Project Pound Hall 524 Harvard Law Sch Cambridge MA 02138 also: Vantage Ptnrs Brighton Landing W Ste 350 10 Guest St Boston MA 02135 Office Phone: 617-354-6090. E-mail: bpatton@post.harvard.edu.

**PATTON, CARL ELLIOTT,** physicist, educator; b. San Antonio, Sept. 14, 1941; s. Carl Elliott and Geraldine Barnett (Perry) Patton. BS, MIT, 1963; MS, Calif. Inst. Tech., 1964, PhD, 1967. Sr. scientist Raytheon Co., Waltham, Mass., 1967-71; assoc. prof. physics Colo. State U., Ft. Collins, 1971-75, prof., 1975—. IEEE Magnetics Soc. Disting. lectr., 1993, sec.-treas. 2003-04, v.p. 2005—. Editor-in-chief IEEE Transactions on Magnetics, 1987-91. Recipient Lifetime Achievement award, Magnetics Soc., 2003. Fellow IEEE (Third Millenium medal 2000), Am. Phys. Soc. (chair topical group on magnetism and its applications 1998-99). Office: Colo State Univ Dept Physics Fort Collins CO 80523-0001

**PATTON, CARL VERNON,** academic administrator, educator; b. Coral Gables, Fla., Oct. 22, 1944; s. Carl V. and Helen Eleanor (Benkert) Patton; m. Gretchen West, July 29, 1967. BS in Cmty. Planning, U. Cin., 1967; MS in Urban Planning, U. Ill.-Urbana, 1969, MS in Pub. Adminstrn., 1970; MS in Pub. Policy, U. Calif.-Berkeley, 1975, PhD in Pub. Policy, 1976. From instr. to prof. U. Ill., 1968—83, dir. Bur. of Urban and Regional Planning Rsch., 1977—79, prof., chmn. dept., 1979—83; prof., dean Sch. Architecture and Urban Planning U. Wis., Milw. 1983—89; v.p. acad. affairs, prof. polit. sci., geography and urban planning U. Toledo, 1989—92; pres. Ga. State U., Atlanta, 1992—. Author: Academia in Transition, 1979; co-author: The Metropolitan Midwest, 1985; co-author: (with David Sawicki) Basic Methods of Policy Analysis and Planning, 1986, rev. 2d edit., 1993 Chinese translations, 2001, 2002; co-author: (with Kathleen Reed) Guide to Graduate Education in Urban and Regional Planning, 1986, 1988; editor: Spontaneous Shelter: International Perspectives and Prospects, 1988; co-editor (with G. William Page): Quick Answers to Quantitative Problems: A Pocket Primer, 1991; assoc. editor: Jour. of Planning Edn. and Rsch., 1983—87, editl. bd.: Habitat International, 1993—99, Intertrade and Investment (formerly Atlanta Internat. Mag.), 1993—2000; contbr. articles to profl. jours. Chmn. Cmty. Devel. Commn., Urbana, 1978—82; mem. Civic Design Ctr., Milw. 1983—87, City of Milw. Art Commn., 1988—89; mem. Toledo Vision, 1989—92, City of Toledo Bd. Cmty. Rels., 1990—92, Ga. Rsch. Alliance, Atlanta Convention and Vis. Bur., 1995—2005, Woodruff Art Ctr., 1996—2006, Fox Theatre, Ga. Coun. on Econ. Edn., Atlanta Neighborhood Devel. Partnership; chair Centennial Olympic Park Area Inc., 1998—2000, Ctrl. Atlanta Progress, 2000—03, Grady (Hosp.) Healthcare, Inc., 1998—2000, Atlanta Reg. Coun. for Higher Edn., 1998—; fellow U. Ill. Ctr. for Advanced Studies, 1973—74; bd. dirs., chair The Atlanta Downtown Partnership, 1997—2000. Fellow, NIMH, 1973—75. Fellow: Am. Inst. Cert. Planners; mem.: Met. Atlanta C. of C., Assn. Collegiate Schs. of Planning (v.p. 1985—87, pres. 1989—91), Am. Planning Assn. Avocations: racquetball, gardening, travel. Home: 250 Park Ave West NW # 908 Atlanta GA 30313 Office: Ga State U PO Box 3999 Atlanta GA 30302-3999 Office Phone: 404-651-2560. Business E-Mail: cpatton@gsu.edu.

**PATTON, DIANA LEE WILKOC,** artist, educator, illustrator; b. New Rochelle, N.Y., June 28, 1940; d. August E. and Meta Diane (Neuburg) Wilkoc; m. Gardner C. Patton, Aug. 10, 1963; children: Michael, Talryn, Shawn. AB cum laude, Brown U., 1962; postgrad., Pan-Am. Art Inst., 1962-63. Svc. mgr. Lord and Taylor, N.Y.C., 1962-63; tchr. adult edn., Mountain Lakes, NJ, 1972-74, Somerville, NJ, 1978-82, Jointure for Cmty. Adult Edn., 1982—. Artist in watercolors, pen and ink and acrylics; creator jewelry; card designer; instr. in field; developer art appreciation courses for children and adults; toymaker, 1973-76. Exhibited N.E. U.S., Perth, Australia, 1977, spl. bicentennial exhibit, Trenton, NJ, 1976, Rutgers U., 1980, Brookdale Coll., 1982, Camden County Coll., 9186, Moris County Coll., 1988, Bergen Mus. Arts and Scis., 1987-88, 90-91, Princeton Med. Ctr., 1993-94, 96, Madison Gallery-Morristown Music, 2001, 03, 05, Salmagundi Club, NYC, 2002, Gallery Capital Health Mercer, 2005; one-woman show SAA Pluckemin Galleries, 1998; represented in pvt. and pub. collections in U.S., Australia, N.Z., Germany, Luxembourg, Japan, Eng.; designer ofcl. poster N.J. Festival Ballooning, 1990, Arc Challenge Races, 1993-94. Recipient Bronze medal in watercolor Nat. Mystic (Conn.) Outdoor Art Festival, 1977, Mayor's purchase prize Franklin Twp., 1976, Tri-State Watercolor award Somerset County Coll., 1978, Best in Show award Raritan Valley Art Assn., 1978, 94, award Garden State Watercolor Soc., 1979, 84-85, 1st, 2d and Best in Show award Somerset and Westfield Art Assns. shows, 1st place for profl. watercolor Plainfield Tri-State Arts Festival, 1983, 85, 87, 96, 2001, N.E. Art Festival, Caldwell Coll., 1990, 95, Tewksbury award, 1990, 2d place in watercolor Internat. Miniature Art Show, Washington, 1983, Best in Show and Grumbacher award Caldwell State show, 1984, 1st place Carrier Clinic Tri-State, 1984, Grumbacher Bronze award, 1984, Grumbacher silver award, 1985, 88, 94, watercolor award Artists League Ctrl. NJ Show, Cornelious Lowe Mus., 1986, Winsor-Newton award Am. Artists Proleague, 1987, Robert Simmons award, 1989, Basking Ridge Environ. Ctr. award, 1994, Best in Show award NJ State Juried, Piscataway, 1988, 2d place NJ Miniature Art Soc., 1989, 1st Pro award Raritan Valley, 1992-93, 1st mixed media award Basking Ridge Environ. Ctr., 1994, award Essex Watercolor Club, 1999, Grumbacher Gold award Essex Watercolor Club, 2000, 1st Pro award Bridgewater Arts, 2001, 03; artist-in-residence graduate Middlesex Librs., 1983-92, watercolor demonstrator, 1983—; TV appearances State of Arts-N.J., 1986, Midday (spl. art shows), 1986, TKR, 1995; Elisha Benjamin scholar Brown U., 1960. Mem. Garden State Watercolor Soc. (writer, editor 1994—), Miniature Art Soc., Washington, N.J. Watercolor Soc., AAUW (life, various offices 1963-73), Art Assn. Raritan Valley (pres. 1980-82, writer, editor newsletter 1993—), Art Assn. Somerset, Art Assn. North Haven (Maine), Essex Watercolor Club, Am. Artists Profl. League, Bee Sharps Square Dance Club. Presbyterian. Home: 497 Stony Brook Dr Bridgewater NJ 08807-1945 E-mail: diana@dianapatton.com.

**PATTON, GREGORY KENNETH,** management educator; b. Sheridan, Wyo., Dec. 20, 1960; s. Philip Kenneth and Martha Jane Patton; children: Christopher Kenneth, Gentina Leigh. BA, Northwestern Coll., Orange City, Iowa, 1984; MBA, U.S.D., Vermillion, 1993; PhD, U. Iowa, Iowa City, 2002. Rsch. asst. bus. rsch. bur. U.S.D., Vermillion, 1992—93; instr. econs. Buena Vista Coll., Storm Lake, Iowa, 1993—95; grad. tchg./rsch. asst. U. Iowa, Iowa City, 1995—2000; asst. prof. mgmt. U. N.D., Grand Forks, 2000—. Retail store mgmt. Duckwall-ALCO Stores, Inc., Abilene, Kans., 1984—92; adj. instr. Northwestern Coll., Orange City, Iowa, 1993—95, Western Iowa Tech.-CC, Sioux City, Iowa, 1994—95. Contbr. articles to profl. jours. Second v.p. Kiwanis, Alliance, Nebr., 1992—95; com. mem. parish health ministries Bethel Luth. Ch., Grand Forks, ND, 2004. Named Vol. of Yr., YMCA of Alliance, Nebr., 1992; recipient Superior Instrn. and Noteworthy Devotion to the Advancement of Students, Quo Vadis Chpt. of Mortar Bd., 2003; Rsch. grantee, Small Bus. Devel. Ctr. ND, 2003—04. Mem.: APA, Soc. for Indsl. and Orgnl. Psychology, Acad. of Mgmt. (assoc. Scholarly Achievement award

(Human Resources divsn.) 2002), Beta Gamma Sigma. Avocations: running, architecture. Office: Univ ND Box 8377 Grand Forks ND 58202 Office Phone: 701-777-3632. E-mail: gregory_patton@und.nodak.edu.

**PATTON, JACK THOMAS,** family practice physician; b. Rogers, Ark., Feb. 18, 1941; s. Jack Marcus and Jewell Selah (Pense) P.; m. Lynette Anne Carr, Sept. 2, 1960; children: Robert, John, Mark, Christopher. BA in History, Calif. State U., Long Beach, 1963; MA in History, Calif. State U., Fresno, 1993; MD in Medicine, U. So. Calif., 1967; MA in Bibl. Studies, Mennonite Brethren Bib. Sem., Fresno, Calif., 1980. Cert. Bd. Med. Examiners, Calif., Hawaii. Intern Tripler Army Med. Ctr., Honolulu, 1967-68; resident in gen. practice Walson Army Hosp., Ft. Dix, NJ, 1968-70; med. supt. Nazarene Hosp., Papua New Guinea, 1973-80; chmn. family practice dept. Sharp Rees-Stealy, San Diego, 1981-86; chmn. occupational medicine Kaiser Permanent, Fresno, 1986-87; assoc. med. dir. Sharp Rees-Stealy, San Diego, 1987-92; med. dir. Summer Inst. Linguistics, Papua New Guinea, 1993-94; with family practice dept. Sharp Rees-Stealy Med. Group, San Diego, 1994-97, Northwest Med. Group, Fresno, Calif., 1997—; chmn. dept. family practice St. Agnes Med. Ctr., 2002—05. Family practice residency liaison Tripler Army Med. Ctr., Honolulu, 1972-73; chief medicine, dep. commr. Schofield Army Med. Clinics, Wahiawa, Hawaii, 1970-72; lectr. Calif. State U., Fresno, 1978-79, Pt. Loma Nazarene Coll., 1982-85, San Jose Christian Coll., 1997-2003; v.p. Patton Industries, Inc., 2005—. Mem. med. sch. support Salerni Collegium, U. So. Calif. Sch. Medicine, 1967-85; lectr. Ch.-Mission Inst., Mennonite Brethren Bib. Sem., 1984-92; sec. S.E. Asian task force Mennonite Brethren Ch. Fresno, 1990-93. Maj. U.S. Army, 1966-73. Mackenzie scholar U. So. Calif. Sch. Medicine, 1966-67; decorated Meritorious Svc. medal. Fellow Am. Acad. Family Physicians; mem. Am. Bd. Family Practice (diplomate), Calif. Acad. Family Physicians, Royal Soc. Medicine (assoc., London). Avocations: history, travel, hiking. Home: 1566 S Adler Ave Fresno CA 93727-5101 Office: 4770 W Herndon Ave Fresno CA 93722-8401 Office Phone: 559-271-6308.

**PATTON, JAMES RICHARD, JR.,** lawyer; b. Durham, N.C., Oct. 27, 1928; s. James Ralph and Bertha (Moye) P.; m. Mary Margot Maughan, Dec. 29, 1950; children: James Macon, Lindsay Fairfield. AB cum laude, U. N.C., 1948; postgrad., Yale U., 1948; JD, Harvard U., 1951. Bar: D.C. bar 1951, U.S. Supreme Ct. 1963. Attache of Embassy; spl. asst. to Am. ambassador to Indochina, 1952-54; with Office Nat. Estimates, Washington, 1954-55; atty. Covington & Burling, Washington, 1956-61; founding ptnr., chmn. exec. com. Patton Boggs, LLP, Washington, 1962—. Lectr. internat. law Cornell Law Sch., 1963-64, U.S. Army Command and Gen. Staff Coll., 1967-68; Mem. Nat. Security Forum, U.S. Air War Coll., 1965, Nat. Strategy Seminar, U.S. Army War Coll., 1967-70, Global Strategy Discussions, U.S. Naval War Coll., 1968, Def. Orientation Conf., 1972; mem. Com. of 100 on Fed. City, Washington; mem. adv. council on nat. security and internat. affairs Nat. Republican Com., 1977-81; bd. dirs. Security Nat. Bank (Wash.), Signet, N.A., Madeira Sch., Greenway, Va., 1975-81, Lawyers Com. for Civil Rights Under Law, Washington, Legal Aid Soc. Washington; mem. Industry Policy Adv. Com. for Trade Policy Matters, 1984-87; mem. nat. adv. bd. Ackland Art Mus. U. N.C., 1987—; chmn. exec. com. Anderson Ranch Arts Ctr., 2002-05. Adv. coun. mem. Johns Hopkins U. Sch. Advanced Internat. Studies, 1989-92; nat. bd. dirs. Aspen Mus., 1987-90; nat. coun. mem. Whitney Mus., 1992—; bd. dirs., exec. com. Nat. Mus. Natural History, Smithsonian, 1992—; bd. dirs. Smithsonian Nat. Bd., 1999-2002; trustee Aspen Music Festival and Sch., 1993-2003; chmn. Ariz. astronomy Bd. U. Ariz., 2003—; mdm. dean's bd. Coll. Sci., 2004—; chmn. Patton Boggs Found., 2000—. Fellow U.N.C. Wilson Library, 1996—. Mem. ABA (past com. chmn.), Inter-Am. Bar Assn. (past del.), Internat. Law Assn. (past com. chmn.), Am. Soc. Internat. Law (treas., exec. coun.), Washington Inst. Fgn. Affairs, Nat. Gallery (collectors com. 1988-91), Gerrard Soc., Met. Club (Washington), Phi Beta Kappa, Alpha Epsilon Delta.

**PATTON, JODY,** management company executive; With Pacific Northwest Ballet; pres., CEO Vulcan, Inc., Seattle; pres. Vulcan Prodns. Vice-chair First & Goal, Inc.; exec. dir. Experience Music Project, Seattle; co-founder Sci. Fiction Mus. and Hall of Fame, Seattle; bd. dir. Charter Comm. Exec. prodr.: The Blues. Exec. dir. Paul G. Allen Family Found.; bd. dir. U. Wash. Found., Internat. Glass Mus., Oreg. Shakespeare Festival, Theatre Comm. Group. Office: Vulcan Inc 505 Fifth Ave S Ste 900 Seattle WA 98104 Office Phone: 206-342-2000. Office Fax: 206-342-3000.

**PATTON, JOSEPH DONALD, JR.,** management consultant; b. Washington, Pa., Jan. 4, 1938; s. Joseph Donald and Priscilla Ann (Johnson) P.; m. Susan Oertel, June 3, 1967; children: Jennifer Ann, Joseph Donald III (dec.). BS in Phys. Scis. and Math. Edn., Pa. State U., 1959; MBA in Mktg., U. Rochester, N.Y., 1970. Registered profl. quality engr., Calif.; cert. profl. logistician; cert. quality engr.; cert. reliability engr. Tchr. Aschaffenburg (W.Germany) Am. Sch., 1963-64; with Xerox Corp., Rochester, 1964-75, mgr. field engring., 1975-93; CEO Patton Cons., Inc., Rochester, NY, 1993—Hilton Head, SC, 1993—. Chmn., Mgmt. Metrics Svcs., Inc., 1996-2001; mem. adj. faculty Rochester Inst. Tech., SUNY, Geneseo. Author 8 textbooks; contbr. over 200 articles to profl. jours. Capt. U.S. Army, 1959-63. Recipient Leadership and Svc. award Pa. State U. Coll. Edn., 1999. Fellow Am. Soc. Quality Control (reliability and maintainablity tech. award 1982), Soc. Logistics Engrs. (Sole Armitage medal 1980, 82, 97); mem. Instrument Soc. Am. (sr.), Assn. Field Svc. Mgrs. (publs. award 1981, Pres.'s Club 2005), Nat. Assn. Svc. Mgrs. (life cert. svc. exec.). Republican. Presbyterian (elder). Office: Patton Consultants Inc 36 Blue Heron Pt Hilton Head Island SC 29926-1209 Office Phone: 843-384-6232. Personal E-mail: JDPatton@aol.com.

**PATTON, JUNE ODESSA,** writer, consultant, educator, researcher; d. Joe Edward Patton and Nancy Odessa Britt. BA, Roosevelt U., Chgo., MS in Tchg.; PhD, postgrad., U. Chgo. Tchg. asst. U. Chgo.; rsch. assoc. U. Chgo.; vis. lectr. Governors State U., University Park, Ill.; instr. Roosevelt U., Chgo.; instr. Lab. H.S. U. Chgo., testing asst., rsch. assoc.; program officer Nat. Endowment for Humanities, Washington; prof. Governors State U. University Park, Ill. Midwestern regional dir. Assn. Black Women Historians, Washington, acting-nat. membership chairperson; program chair 75th ann. meeting Assn. for Study of African Am. Life and History, Washington; treas. and nat. membership chair Assn. of Black Women Historians, Washington; adv. reviewer Jour. African Am. History, Washington, mem. editl. bd.; exec. coun. Assn. for Study of African Am. Life and History, Washington; treas. Women's Edn. Network, Chgo.; cons. in field. Contbr. biographical American National Biography, biographical Encyclopedia of African-American Educators, biographical Black Women in the United States: An Historical Encyclopedia, educational Harcourt Brace Jovanovich Resource Guide for Multicultural Classroom; author: (book review) History of Education Quarterly; contbr. book The Closing Door: Conservative Policy and Black Opportunity; author: (documentary essay) The Journal of Negro History; contbr. articles to profl. jours. Charles Hubbard Judd centennial planning com. U. Chgo., 1975—78; rschr. and del. US-Africa Partnership for Bldg. Stronger Communities, Albany, NY, 1999—2003; com. mem., Katherine Dunham golden anniversary tribute festival Inst. for Intercultural Comm., Chgo.; bd. dirs. Catalyst for Youth, Chgo., 1973—78; cons. and spkr. Chgo. Humanities Festival, 1999—2002, DuSable Mus., Chgo., 1987—2002, Harold Wash. Libr. Reading Group, Chgo., 1999—2002; cons. and judge Chgo. Metro History Fair, Chicago, Ill., 1982—91; cons. and spkr. Ill. Humanities Coun., Chgo., 1984—91; bd. dirs. African Am. Geneal. Soc. of Chgo., 1979—89; bd. dirs., George E. Kent Meml. and Scholarship Fund U. Chgo., 1982—87; com. mem. Women's com. for 1992 Chgo. World's Fair, 1990—91; planning com., Ill. and Chgo. Salute to Katherine Dunhamgo State of Ill. and City of Chgo., 1982—83; planning com. City of Chgo.'s women's history week City of Chgo., 1982—83; advisor Chgo. Film Symposium, 1975—78. Recipient Achievement award, NAACP, 1980, Chairman's Cert. of Appreciation, Nat. Endowment for Humanities, 1993, Faculty Excellence award, Govs. State U. 1997 and 2000, Students Cert. of Appreciation, 1997 and 1998; scholarship, State of Ill., 1965-1967, Roosevelt U. Grad. Grant-in-Aid, Roosevelt U., 1967-1968, PhD assistantship, U. Ill., 1968-69; 1969-70 (unable to accept),

Ednl. fellowship, U. Chgo., 1970-71, Contingency grant, 1972, Ford Found. fellowship, The Ford Found., 1972, Nat. Dissertation Yr. Fellow, Ford Found., 1974-75; 1975-1976, Carter G. Woodson Disting. Scholar-In-Residence, Assn. for Study of African Am. Life and History, 1991—94, Adminstrv. fellowship, State of Ill., 1991-1992 (unable to accept), Profl. Devel. grant, Govs. State U. Alumni Assn., 2001. Mem.: So. Hist. Assn. (life), Orgn. of Am. Historians (life), Assn. of Black Women Historians (life; treas. and nat. membership chair 1993—95), Assn. for Study of African Am. Life and History (life; exec. coun. 1993—2000, 2005—). Avocations: tennis, white water rafting, bicycling, travel, golf. Office: Govs State Univ 1 University Pky University Park IL 60466-3165 Office Phone: 708-534-4574. Business E-Mail: j-patton@govst.edu.

**PATTON, LAURIE LOUISE,** religious studies educator, writer; b. Boston, Mass., Nov. 14, 1961; d. Anthony Seavey and Christine Card Patton. BA, Harvard U, Cambridge, Mass, 1983; MA, U of Chgo., Chgo., Ill, 1985, PhD, 1991. Asst. prof. Bard Coll., Annandale, 1991—96, Emory U., Atlanta, 1996—98, assoc. prof., 1998—2003, full prof., 2003, chair dept. religion, 1999—, Winship Disting. Rsch. prof., 2003—. Fellowship selection com. Am Coun. of Learned Societies, New York, NY, 2000—02; academic adv. bd. Carlos Mus., Atlanta, 2000—; mem. exec. bd. Am. Soc. Study of Religion, 2001—; academic task force Am. Acad. Religion, Atlanta, 2003—. Editor: Authority, Anxiety Canon; Myth & Method; Jewels of Authority; Notes from a Mandala; author: Myth as argument (DeGruyter Press), 1996, Bringing the Gods to Mind, 2003, Fires Goal: Poems from a Hindu Year; translator: The Bhagavad Gita, 2004. Exec. bd. Atlanta Interfaith Alliance, Atlanta, 2001—04; edn. com. Ahavath Achim Synagogue, Atlanta, 2002—. Grantee rsch., Am. Inst. of Indian Studies/Pure, India, 1992, Nat. Endowment for the Humanities/Pure, India, 1995, Fulbright, Jerusalem, 1999, Fulbright, India, 2004. Fellow: Am. Coun. Learned Socs., Gustafson Seminar (dir. 1999—2002); mem.: South Asia/Am. Acad. Religion (secretary 1998—2001), Humanities Coun. (chair 2000—03). Democrat. Judaism. Avocations: embroidery, photography. Office: Emory Univ Dept of Religion 537 Kilgo Circle Atlanta GA 30322-0001

**PATTON, RICHARD WESTON,** retired mortgage company executive; b. Evanston, Ill., Sept. 26, 1931; s. Robert Ferry and Sue Buckley P.; m. Lynda A. Kruse, Feb. 2, 1971; 1 child, Robert Weston BA, Amherst Coll., 1954. Sales engr. Thermo Fax Sales Corp., Chgo., 1958-60; account exec. Nat. Mortgage Investors, Inc., Chgo., 1960-61, sales mgr. Pasadena, Calif., 1962-66, asst. v.p., 1966-67, v.p., 1967-69, exec. v.p., 1969-73, pres., chief exec. officer, dir., 1973-84, vice-chmn. bd., 1984-90; pres. Richard W. Patton Enterprises, Pasadena, 1990—2004; ret., 2005. Pres., chmn. exec. com., dir. Ocean Park Restaurant Corp., Santa Monica, Calif., 1977-88; dir. Cenfed Bank, Cenfed Fin. Corp. Bd. dirs. Pasadena Boys' Club, 1963-66, Opera Assocs., 1984-90; mem. steering com. Amherst Coll. Capital Fund Drive, 1963-66; mem. citizens adv. com. L.A. County Sheriffs Dept. 1st Lt. USMCR, 1955-58. Mem. Amherst Coll. Alumni Assn. (bd. dirs. 1963—2001, pres. 1977-79, 86-89), Kroenstadt Ski Club (past pres.). Office: Rich W Patton Enterprises 3644 San Pasqual St Pasadena CA 91107-5419

**PATTON, SHARON F.,** museum director; BA, Roosevelt U., 1966; MA, U. Ill., 1969; PhD in Art History, Northwestern U., 1980. Mem. faculty U. Houston, 1976—79, U. Md., 1979—85; dir. art galleries Montclair State Coll., NJ, 1986—87; chief curator Studio Mus., N.Y.C., 1988—91; assoc. prof. art history U. Mich., Ann Arbor, 1991—98, dir. Ctr. for Arfoamerican and African Studies, 1996—98; dir. Allen Meml. Art Mus. Oberlin Coll., 1998—2003; mem. adv. bd. Nat. Mus. African Art, Washington, 2000—, dir., 2003—. Author: Memory and the Metaphor, the Art of Romare Bearden, 1991, African-American Art, 1998 (Choice Outstanding Book of Yr. award); contbr. articles to publs. in field. Mem. Rapid Transit Pub. Art Commn., Cleve., ArtTable, Cleve.; mem. visual arts jury Cleve. Arts Prize, 2000—02; mem. African Am. adv. coun. and Acquisition adv. com. Cleve. Art Mus. Mem.: ArtTable, Assn. Art Mus. Dirs., Am. Assn. Museums. Office: Nat Mus African Art Smithsonian Instn MRC 708 PO Box 37012 Washington DC 20013-7012

**PATTON, STUART,** biochemist, educator; b. Ebenezer, NY, Nov. 2, 1920; s. George and Ina (Neeper) P.; m. Colleen Cecelia Lavelle, May 17, 1945; children—John, Richard, Gail, Thomas, Mary Catherine, Patricia, Joseph. BS, Pa. State U., 1943; MS, Ohio State U., 1947, PhD, 1948. Chemist Borden Co., 1943-44; rsch. fellow Ohio State U.: Columbus, 1946-48; faculty Pa. State U., University Park, 1949-80, prof., 1959-80, Evan Pugh rsch. prof. agr., 1966-80; adj. prof. neuroscis. Sch. Medicine U. Calif., San Diego, 1981—99; ret., 1990. Vis. scientist Scripps Instn. Oceanography; cons. in field. Author: (with Robert Jenness) Principles of Dairy Chemistry, 1959; (with Robert G. Jensen) Biomedical Aspects of Lactation, 1975; Milk: Its Remarkable Contribution to Human Health and Well-Being, 2004. Lt. (j.g.) USNR, 1944-46. Recipient Borden award chemistry milk Am. Chem. Soc., 1957, Agrl. and Food Chemistry award, 1975, Alexander von Humboldt Sr. scientist award, 1981, Macy-Gyorgy award Internat. Soc. for Rsch. on Human Milk and Lactation, 1997, Distinguished Alumnus award, Pa. State U., 2002, Distinguished Svc. award Am. Dairy Sci. Assn., 1999, fellow Pa. State Alumni Assn., 2001. Fellow Am. Dairy Sci. Assn.; mem. Am. Chem. Soc., Am. Soc. Biochemistry and Molecular Biology, Am. Soc. Cell Biology. Home and Office: 6208 Avenida Cresta La Jolla CA 92037-6510 E-mail: spatton@ucsd.edu.

**PATTON, THOMAS EARL,** lawyer; b. Nov. 25, 1940; s. Thomas E. and Alice F. (Rodarmel) P.; m. Patricia Mann, Aug. 12, 1965 (dec.); m. Barbara Wood, Sept. 21, 1974; 1 child, David Earl AB, Cath. U. Am., 1962, JD summa cum laude, 1965. Bar: N Y 1966, D.C. 1966, Va. 1981. Assoc. Sullivan & Cromwell, N.Y.C., 1965-69; mem. Williams Connolly & Califano, Washington, 1970-75; asst. gen. counsel U.S. Dept. Energy, Washington, 1977-78; ptnr. Schnader, Harrison, Segal & Lewis, Washington, 1979-94. Disting. lectr. Cath. U. Am., 1979-90, 95—, bd. regents; nat. arbitrator Am. Arbitration Assn.; bd. dirs. Elcotel, Inc., IXI, Inc., Vanguard Found. Author: Securities Litigation, 1989, Federal Procedure Casebook, 1990; contbr. articles to profl. jours.; editor in chief Cath. U. Am. Law Rev. Mem. Washington World Affairs Coun., 1980—. Mem. ABA, D.C. Bar (founder and chair litigation sect.), Cosmos Club. Roman Catholic. Office: Tighe Patton Armstrong Teasdale 1747 Pennsylvania Ave NW Washington DC 20006-4688

**PATTON, THOMAS JAMES,** marketing executive, sales executive; b. Cleve., Nov. 2, 1948; s. Michael Anthony and Delores (Bammerlin) Patton; m. Thomasina Bernadette Cavallaro, Aug. 9, 1969; children: Thomasina, Thera V. A in Transp., Cleve. State U., 1971, BA in Mktg., 1973; BA, SUNY, Empire State, 1994. CLU; ChFC; registered health underwriter; registered employee benefit cons. Ins. salesman Manulife, Cleve., 1972-75, Mass. Mut., Cleve., 1976-80, Patton Ins. assn., Avon Lake, Ohio, 1976—; ins. cons. Diversified Benefit Plans, Inc., Avon Lake, 1978-93, dir. sales and mktg., 1993—; pres. commerce Benefits Group, Inc. and Ins. Mktg. Group, Inc., 1995; prin. Cmty. Health Ptnrs., Ltd., Ill., 1994. Pres. Commerce Benefits Group, Inc.; cons. Regional Sch. Consortium, Lorain County, Ohio, 1986—, County of Lorain, 1984—, City of Lorain, 1986—, County of Lorain, 1984—, City of Lorain, 1984—; prin. Cmty. Health Ptnrs. Ltd.; bd. Italian Cultural Found.; founder 1-888 Ohiocomp w/c MCO-Ohio, 1997; co-founder VocRehabOne, Inc., w/c Vocat. Rehab. Co. Pres. Lake Erie Retail Assn., Cleve., 1970-71; mem. Lorain County Dem. Ctrl. Com., Avon Lake, Ohio, 1986—; mem. com. Cleve. Leukemia Soc., 1985; bd. dirs. Villa Serena Sr. Housing, St. Francis Soc., Italian Cultural Found.; bd. trustees Found. Am. Coll., Bryn Mawr, Pa., 2002—. Mem. Nat. Assn. Life Underwriters, Profl. Ins. Agts. Assn., Cert. Profl. Ins. Agts. Soc., Soc. Benefit Plan Adminstrn., Lorain County Life Underwriters, Irish Heritage, Order Italian Sons and Daus., Profl. Assn. Dive Instrs./Nat. Assn. Underwater Instrs. (SCUBA diving instr.). Roman Catholic. Avocations: fishing, skin and scuba diving, photography. Office: Commerce Group PO Box 900 Elyria OH 44036-0900 Office Phone: 440-930-7500 ext. 203. Business E-Mail: tompatton@thecommercegroup.com.

**PATTON-NEWELL, JANET LAVELLE,** minister; b. Sharon, Pa., Jan. 15, 1965; d. Henry Elbert and Flora Lee Newby; m. Derrick Lamount Newell, June 17, 2000; children: Flora Evette Harris, Kellen Dauntae Newby, Kent Michael Patton, Kaston Moneke Patton, Grace Newell. Diploma in Bible studies, Full Bible Inst. Farrell, Pa., 2002; HHD, diploma in biblical studies, NCI Bible Coll. and Sch. Prophets, 2005; cert., Cambria County Prison Tng. Acad., Pa. Certificate of Congratulations New and Living Way Apostolic Ch. of Jesus Christ, 2003, Certificate of Appreciation ACTS Anointed Call To Singleness, 1999, Wind in the Word Outreach Ministry, 2002, Wind in the Word Outreach Ministry, 2003, Wind in the Word Outreach Ministry, 2004, lic. ordained World Missions Ministerial Assn., minister Ranha Outreach Internat. Orders clk. Mercer County Domestic Rels., (Child Support Bur.), Mercer, Pa., 1996—98; youth and young adult activities coord. Americorp Vista, (Mercer County Housing Authority), Sharon, Pa., 1998—99; evangelist New and Living Way Apostolic Ch. of Jesus Christ, Farrell, Pa., 1998—2000; overseer Paramount Ctr. for Learning, Farrell, Pa.; pastor Rivers Living Water Outreach Ministry, Farrell, Pa., 2000—01, Wind in the Word Outreach Ministry, Farrell, Pa., 2001—. Correction officer Mercer County Prison. Author: (self help) You are a Woman of Excellence, 2001, You are a Man of Excellence, 2001, Our Weapons are not Carnal, 2001; The Three Dimensions of the Prophetic, 2005. Mem. E.R.A.S.E. Anti Drug Coalition, Farrell, 1999, Wheels To Work, (Prince of Peace), Farrell, Pa., 1999; dir. New and Living Way Edn. Dept., Farrell, 1998—2000, Wind in the Word Outreach Ministry Edn. Dept., Farrell, 2001—05; mem. Walking in Black History, Erie, Pa., 1999. E-5 U.S. Army, 1987—2001, Fort Bragg, N. Carolina and Ansbach, Germany. Mem.: Women In Truth Fellowship, Women Speakers, Prophetic Women, Women N Power. Democrat. Apostolic. Avocations: computers, writing. Office: Wind in the Word Outreach Ministry 947 Hamilton Ave Farrell PA 16121 Office Phone: 724-734-1904. Business E-Mail: dr.janetl.newell@windintheword.com.

**PATTY, CLAIBOURNE WATKINS, JR.,** lawyer; b. Cleve., Feb. 19, 1934; s. Claibourne Watkins and Eleanor (Todd) P.; m. Barbara Benton, May 4, 1968; children— Claibourne Watkins III, William Jordan. BA, U. of South, 1955; JD, U. Ark., 1961. Bar: Ark. 1961. Law clk. U.S. dist. judge, Ft. Smith, 1961-63; pvt. practice Little Rock, 1963-68; asst. ins. commr. State of Ark., 1968-69; trust officer Union Nat. Bank of Little Rock, 1969-77; asst. dean U. Ark. Sch. Law, Little Rock; also exec. dir. Ark. Inst. for Continuing Legal Edn., 1977-86; law clk. 2d Div. Chancery Ct., Pulaski County, 1986-89; of counsel Gruber Law Firm, North Little Rock, 1989-2001; prin. Patty Law Firm, North Little Rock, 2001—. Lectr. law Ark. Sch. Law, 1965; bd. dirs., chmn. Pulaski County Legal Aid Bur., 1966—69; mem. com. on civil practice Ark. Supreme Ct., 1998—2004. Bd. dirs., pres. Family Svc. Agy. of Ctrl. Ark., 1976—81, 1986—93, 1999—2004, Good Shepherd Ecumenical Retirement Ctr., 1975—2002; mem. Ark. adv. com. U.S. Commn. on Civil Rights, 1985—89; bd. dirs. Am. Diabetes Assn., Ark. Affil., 1996—2005, Ark. Gerontol. Soc., 1996—. With AUS, 1955—57. Mem.: Phi Alpha Delta, Beta Theta Pi. Office: Patty Law Firm 315 N Broadway St North Little Rock AR 72114-5379 Office Phone: 501-375-5061. Personal E-mail: clairgpm@swbell.net.

**PATTY, PATRICIA KAE,** music educator; d. Raymond W. Brown and Mary Ann Allen; m. Samuel C. Patty, Aug. 3, 1974; children: Jacob, Arianne, Daniel, Julianne. B Music Edn., Okla. Bapt. U., Shawnee, 1974. Cert. tchr. Tex. Music tchr. Sequoyah Elem. Sch., Shawnee, 1974—76, Foster Elem. Sch., Arlington, Tex., 1976—77; presch. dir., music tchr. Happy Day Skelly Dr. Bapt., Tulsa, 1984—89; kindergarten-12th grade choral dir. Tulsa Christian Sch., 1989—91, Emmanuel Christian Sch., Tulsa, 1991—92, Wright Christian Acad., Tulsa, 1992—99; choral dir., guitar instr. Frank Seale Mid. Sch., Midlothian, Tex., 1994—. Sec. Christian Women Am., Topeka, 1980. Mem.: Tex. Choral Dirs. Assn., Tex. Music Educators Assn. Baptist. Office: Frank Seale Mid Sch 700 George Hopper Rd Midlothian TX 76065

**PATTYN, SUE,** publishing executive; b. Sept. 1, 1958; Pub. (directory) HIV/AIDS Resources, 1994—2001. Mem.: Guides for Living LLC. Office: PO Box 1104 Longmont CO 80502-1104 Home: 8921 Judson St Westminster CO 80031 Office Phone: 303-702-1254.

**PATULOT, JUN J. R.,** insurance company executive; b. Manila, Oct. 30, 1947; came to U.S., 1975; s. Silvino M. and Sotera P. Patulot; m. Connie Castro, Sept. 2, 1950; children: Patrick, Aires. BS in Fgn. Svc., Lyceum of Philippines, Manila, 1968; postgrad. in Law, San Sebastian Coll., Manila, 1972; postgrad. in Mgmt. and Supervision, Seattle C.C., 1980. Fgn. svc. staff officer Ministry of Fgn. Affairs, Manila, 1970-74, Philippine Consulate Gen., Seattle, 1975-84; spl. supr. Gt. Am. Res. Ins. Co., Seattle, 1985-87; exec. sales dir. Surety Life Ins. Co., Seattle, 1987-91; mng. gen. agt. N.W. Life Assurance of Am., Belligham, Wash., 1991—, Conseco Life Ins. and Investing Brokerage, Carmel, Wash., 2001—. Pvt. practice ins. brokerage, Seattle, 1987—. Recipient Nat. Sales Achievement award Nat. Assn. Life Underwriters, Nat Quality award Life Ins. Mktg. and Rsch. Assn. Mem. Million Dollar Round Table. Home: 11813 SE 75th Pl Newcastle WA 98056-1768 also: 11813 SE 75th Pl Newcastle WA 98056-1768 E-mail: junpatulot@hotmail.com.

**PATURIS, E(MMANUEL) MICHAEL,** lawyer; b. Akron, Ohio; s. Michael George and Sophia (Manos) P.; m. Mary Ann Toompas, Febr. 28, 1965. BS, U. N.C., 1954, JD with honors, 1959. Bar: N.C. 1959, D.C. 1969, Va. 1973; CPA. Acct., Charlotte and Wilmington, N.C., 1960-63; assoc. Poyner, Geraghty, Hartsfield & Townsend, Raleigh, N.C., 1963-64; atty. advisor Chief Counsel's Office, Washington, 1964-66, sr. trial atty. Richmond, Va., 1966-69; ptnr. Reasoner, Davis & Vinson, Washington, 1969-70, sole practitioner Alexandria, 1978—. Acctg. lectr. U. N.C., Chapel Hill, 1959-60; acctg., econs. lectr. N.C. State U., Raleigh, 1963-64; business law lectr. George Mason U., Fairfax County, Va., 1978-79. Mem. bd. editors U. N.C. Law Rev. With U.S. Army, 1954-56. Recipient U. N.C. Law Sch. Block award, 1959. Mem.: Washington Golf and Country Club, Beta Gamma Sigma, Phi Beta Kappa. Home: 6326 Stoneham Ln Mc Lean VA 22101-2345 Office: Law Offices of E Michael Paturis 431 N Lee St Alexandria VA 22314-2301 Office Phone: 703-836-2501.

**PATWARDHAN, AMIT,** research scientist; b. Mumbai, Maharashtra, India, July 17, 1973; s. Shubhanan Damodar and Shubhada Shubhanan Patwardhan; m. Anagha Amit Bhate, June 27, 2003; 1 child, Siddhant Amit. BTech in Chem. Engring., with honors, Indian Inst. Tech., Kharagpur, India, 1995; MS in Mining Engring., So. Ill. U., Carbondale, 1998, MBA, 2002. Rschr. So. Ill. U., Carbondale, 1998—2003, scientist, 2001—. Presenter lectrs. on coal prep.; chair several internat. confs. in mining, coal processing, and combustion byproducts utilization areas. Author: (rsch. poster exhbn.) An In-Plant Evaluation of Altair Jig for Fine Coal Cleaning; contbr. articles to profl. jours. (Editors Choice award, 2001, Outstanding Grad. Student award, 1998, Hon. Mention award, 2001). Recipient grants in field. Mem.: Indian Inst. of Chem. Engrs., Soc. of Mining Engineers (mem. nat. coal prep. com. 2003—), Am. Mensa. Achievements include research in energy production and utilization; development of new wettability procedure for coal dust supression; New technologies for enhancing coal quality; design of beneficial use coal combustion by-products applications. Office: So Ill Univ 1230 Lincoln Dr Carbondale IL 62901-6603 Office Phone: 618-534-8454. Business E-Mail: pamit@siu.edu.

**PATWARDHAN, MEENAL B.,** pathologist, researcher; arrived in U.S., 1997; d. Madhukar Bhalchandra and Sheila Madhukar Nisal; m. Bhalchandra H. Patwardhan, June 6, 1996; children: Devdutta Sanjay Warhadpande, Shantanu Sanjay Warhadpande. MBBS, Govt Med. Coll. Nagpur, India, 1980; MD in Pathology, Govt Med. Coll., India, 1984; MA in Human Svcs. Adminstrn., U. Kans., 2001. Lic. pathologist Maharashtra, India, 1984. Lectr. pathology Govt Med. Coll., Nagpur, Maharashtra, India, 1984—92, tech. dir. blood bank, 1993—95, assoc. prof. of pathology, 1992—99; dir. ops. Evidence-based Practice Ctr. Duke U., Durham, NC, 2004—, asst. prof. medicine Med. Ctr., 2004; sr. fellow Vets. Affairs - Health Svcs. Rsch.,

Durham, 2004—. Cons. in field. Recipient HAMMIG award, U. Kans. Mem.: Internat. Assn. Health Tech. Assn., Am. Coll. Healthcare Execs., Am. Heart Assn., Acad. Health, Soc. Med. Decision Making. Office Phone: 919-286-3399.

**PATZ, EDWARD FRANK,** retired lawyer; b. Balt., Aug. 25, 1932; s. Maurice A. and Violet (Furman) P.; m. Betty Seldner Levi, Nov. 18, 1956; children— Evelyn Anne, Edward Frank, Thomas L. BS, U. Md., 1954, LLB, 1959. Bar: Md. 1959, U.S. Dist. Ct. Md. 1959, U.S. Ct. Appeals (4th cir.) 1959, U.S. Supreme Ct. 1980. Ptnr. Weinberg and Green and predecessor firms (now merged into Saul Ewing), Balt., 1959—97; ret., 1997. Bd. dirs. Jewish Family and Children's Service, 1965-71; regional bd. dirs. NCCJ; pres. Suburban Club Balt. County, 1977-79; bd. trustees, exec. com. Flagler Ecumenical Social Svcs. Ctr., Inc., 1999-2002. Mem.: Hammock Dunes Club. Home: 39 Island Estates Pkwy Palm Coast FL 32137-2203

**PAUKA, KIRSTIN,** theater educator, director; b. Mannheim, Germany, Aug. 22, 1963; d. Johann and Dagmar Pauka. PhD, U. Hawaii, 1995. Assoc. prof. U. Hawaii, Honolulu, 1997—. Dir.: (plays) Indonesian Randai Theatre; musician: Kenny Endo Taiko Ensemble; author: Theatre and Martial Arts in West Sumatra: Randai and Silek of the Minangkabau; editor: Oxford Ency. on Theatre and Perrforming Arts. Grantee, German Academic Exch. Svc., 2003, Henry-Luce-Found., 1992, Peace Edn. Orgn., 1992, 1995, Asian Studies Devel. Program, 1998, US-Indonesia Soc., 2002, NRC, 2004—05; scholar, German Ministry Sci. and Rsch., 1988, German Academic Exch. Svc., 1993, AAUW, 1994. Fellow: Assn. Asian Performance (officer 2004, conf. coord. 2004). Achievements include first English language indepth research on Sumatran Randai theatre; first staging of English language Randai theatre in the U.S. Office: University of Hawaii 1770 East West Road Honolulu HI 96822

**PAUKEN, THOMAS WEIR,** venture capital executive, mediator; b. Victoria, Tex., Jan. 11, 1944; s. Thomas N. and Patricia (Weir) P.; m. Ida Ayala; children: Thomas II, Michelle, Angela, Elizabeth, Daniel, Victoria, Monica. AB in Polit. Sci., Georgetown U., 1965, postgrad., 1966-67; JD, So. Meth. U., 1973. Bar: Tex., 1975. White House staff asst., dep. dir. White Ho. fellows, Washington, 1970-71; pvt. practice atty. Dallas, 1974-80; dir. ACTION, Washington, 1981-85; pres. Sta. KRZI-Radio, Waco, Tex., 1985-86; v.p., corp. counsel Garvon, Inc., Dallas, 1986-91; pres. TWP, Inc., Dallas, 1991—. Bd. dirs. TOR Minerals, Inc. Author: The Thirty Years War - The Politics of the 60s Generation, 1994. Mem. Reagan transition team Counsel's Office, Washington, 1980-81; Tex. Rep. State chmn., 1994-97. 1st Lt. U.S. Army, 1967-70, Vietnam. Recipient Drug Edn. Leadership award PRIDE, 1985, Dir.'s award U.S. Office of Personnel Mgmt., 1985; Weaver fellow 1965. Mem. State Bar Tex. Roman Catholic. Avocation: reading. Office Phone: 214-378-9340. Business E-Mail: twpauken@sbcglobal.net.

**PAUL, ALIDA RUTH,** arts and crafts educator; b. San Antonio, May 30, 1953; d. Richard Irving and Anne Louise (Holman) Paul. B.S. in Edn., Southwest Tex. State U., 1975; M.Ed., U. Houston, 1984. Cert. tchr., Tex. Tchr. art and crafts Houston Ind. Sch. Dist., 1975—. Republican. Episcopalian. Home: 16830 Grampin Dr Houston TX 77084-1945

**PAUL, ANDREW MITCHELL,** investment advisor; b. NYC, Feb. 10, 1956; s. John William and Bobba Lorraine (Ice) P.; m. Margaret Rae Batchelor, Sept. 19, 1987. BA, Cornell U., 1978; MBA, Harvard U., 1983. Mktg. rep. IBM Corp., NYC, 1978-81; assoc. Hambrecht & Quist Venture Capital Co., San Francisco, 1983-84; gen. ptnr. Welsh, Carson, Anderson & Stowe, NYC, 1984—2000; chmn. Enhancee Capital Ptnrs.; mng. gen. ptnr. Enhanced Equity Fund. Mem. Nat. Venture Capital Assn., NY Venture Capital Assn., Bronxville Field Club, Siwanoy Country Club, Roaring Fork Club, Aspen., Blind Brook Country Club, Commanderie de Bordeaux, Chevaliers du Tastevin. Avocations: golf, skiing, biking, travel. Home: 283 Pondfield Rd Bronxville NY 10708-4936 Office: Enhanced Capital Partners 350 Park Ave 24th Fl New York NY 10022

**PAUL, ANDREW ROBERT,** defense and legislative consultant; b. N.Y.C., Aug. 14, 1938; s. Andrew B. and Maria (Filotas) P.; m. Britt-Marie Hagelbrant, Feb. 6, 1988. AB in French, Dartmouth Coll., 1960; MS in Fgn. Svc., Georgetown U., 1967. Dir. govt. rels. Motorola, Inc., Washington, 1968-75, Paramount Communications, Washington, 1975-90; sr. v.p. Satellite Broadcasting and Communications Assn., Alexandria, Va., 1990—2001; def. and legis. cons. Mem. GATT adv. com. on Intellectual Property, Washington, 1988-94; mem. adv. com. MS in Fgn. Svc. program Georgetown U., Washington, 1981-2004. Presdl. campaign advance man Rep. Nat. Com., 1964; pres. chpt. XI Spl. Forces Assn., Washington, 1981-82; chmn. Alternative House Crisis Intervention Ctr., Vienna, Va., 1983-84. Capt. U.S. Army, 1960-65. Roman Catholic. Home: 1013 Heather Hill Ct Mc Lean VA 22101-2024

**PAUL, ARA GARO,** university dean; b. New Castle, Pa., Mar. 1, 1929; s. John Hagop and Mary (Injejikian) P.; m. Shirley Elaine Waterman, Dec. 21, 1962; children: John Bartlett, Richard Goyan. BS in Pharmacy, Idaho State U., 1950; MS, U. Conn., 1953, PhD in Pharmacognosy, 1956. Cons. plant physiology Argonne (Ill.) Nat. Lab., 1955; asst. prof. pharmacognosy Butler U., Indpls., 1956-57; faculty U. Mich., Ann Arbor, 1957—, prof. pharmacognosy, 1969—; dean U. Mich. Coll. Pharmacy, 1975-96; dean emeritus, Hans W. Vahlteich prof. pharmacognosy, 2001—04. Vis. prof. microbiology Tokyo U., 1965-66; mem. vis. chemistry faculty U. Calif., Berkeley, 1972-73; del. U.S. Pharmacopeial Conv., 1980-90, a scholar in residence Am. Assn. Colls. Pharmacy, 1996; bd. grants Am. Found. Pharm. Edn., 1997—, chmn., 1999, co-chmn. endowment com., 2002—, bd. dirs., 2003—; mem. organizing com. Millennial World Congress Pharm. Scis., 1996-2000; mem. FIP Found., 2000—05, chmn. bd. trustees, 2001—05. Contbr. articles to profl. jours. Recipient Outstanding Tchr. award Coll. Pharmacy, U. Mich., 1969, Outstanding Alumnus award Idaho State U., 1976, Profl. Achievement award Coll. Pharmacy, Idaho State U., 1990; G. Pfeiffer Meml. fellow Am. Found. Pharm. Edn., 1965-66, Disting. Svc. Profile award Am. Found Pharm. Edn., 1992; fellow Eli Lily Found., 1951-53, Am. Found. Pharm. Edn.; 1954-56, NIH, 1972-73. Fellow AAAS; mem. Am. Pharm. Assn., Am. Soc. Pharmacognosy, Acad. Pharm. Scis., Am. Assn. Colls. Pharmacy, Am. Assn. Pharm. Scientists, Phi Lambda Upsilon, Sigma Xi, Phi Delta Chi, Phi Sigma Kappa, Rho Chi. Home: 1415 Brooklyn Ave Ann Arbor MI 48104-4496 Office: U Mich Coll Pharmacy Ann Arbor MI 48109-1065 Office Phone: 734-763-4267. E-mail: arapaul@umich.edu.

**PAUL, ARTHUR,** artist, illustrator, graphics designer, design consultant; b. Chgo., Jan. 18, 1925; m. Beatrice Miller, Dec. 24, 1949 (div. 1973); children: William Warren, Fredric; m. Suzanne Seed, Mar. 8, 1975; 1 stepdaughter, Nina. Student, Inst. Design, 1947-51. Vice-pres., art dir. HMH Pub. Co., Playboy, Chgo., 1953-82; also sr. art dir., corp. art dir. Playboy mag.; pres. Art Paul Design; freelance artist Chgo., 1984—. Lectr. in field. Freelance illustrator, designer, 1951-53; designer 1st issue: Playboy mag. 1953, Playboy Rabbit symbol, 1953; one-man shows include Etc. Gallery, 1949, 500D Gallery, 1965, U. Ill., 1965, Visual Identity Chgo., 1991, Chgo. Cultural Ctr. 1997-98; organizer, exhibitor: travelling exhbn. Beyond Illustration-The Art of Playboy; museums, Europe, Asia, U.S., 1971-73, Can., 1976-77; author: Vision-Art Paul, 1983, Art of Playboy, 1986, Sex Appeal, 2000; designer PBS-TV title Sence of Humor for humorous feature film presentations on American Playhouse; prodn. design cons. (PBS-TV movie) Who Am I This Time?; featured in Contemporary Master Works, 1991, Print mag., 2000, Graphis mag., 2004, Picturing Text, 2004. Trustee Chgo. Mus. Contemporary Art, 1970-86; apptd. trustee by Gov. of Ill. to Ill. Summer Sch. of Arts, 1987—. With USAAF, 1943-46. Recipient numerous art awards, including Outstanding Achievement in Trademark Design for Playboy Mag. award Soc. Typographic Arts, 1970, Gold medal for exhbn. Beyond Illustration City of Milan, 1971, Polycube award Art Dirs. Club Phila., 1975, Art Direction Mag. award, 1975, Top Midwest Mktg. award Playboy TV Subscription Ad, 1979, 82, Gold medal for Chgo. Film Festival poster Art Dirs. Club N.Y., 1980,

Profl. Achievement award IIT Inst. Design Alumni Assn., 1983, Herb Lubecin Lifetime Achievement award Soc. Publ. Designers, 2006; Art Inst. scholar, 1943; named to Art Dirs. Hall of Fame, 1986. Mem. Alliance Graphique Internat. *Design is more than a sense of order for me. It is beauty and common sense. To draw, to paint and to look at art is in the fabric of my life. I enjoy working with ideas and seeing them develop into a reality, after which I am fortunate enough to learn whether they have performed as intended.*

**PAUL, BESSIE MARGRETTE,** retired weaher forecaster; b. Absher, Mont., June 24, 1926; d. Fredrick Ernest Bergman and Margrette Marie Daly; m. Theodore Eugene Paul, Dec. 1, 1949 (dec. 1964); 1 child, Barbara Marie. AS, Eastern Montana Coll., 1988; BSBA in bus. adminstrn., Eastern Mont. Coll., 1992. Weather observer, map plotter US Weather Bur., Billings, Mont., 1944—53, map plotter San Francisco, 1955—56; forecaster Nat. Oceanic and Atmospheric Adminstrn., 1956—81; ret., 1981. Mem.: AAUW, Order of Eastern Star, Nat. Assn. Active and Ret. Fed. Employee. Avocations: cooking, baking, gardening, exercise, reading. Home: 2425 Ave B Billings MT 59102

**PAUL, CHRIS,** professional basketball player; b. Winston-Salem, NC, May 6, 1985; Attended, Wake Forrest Univ., NC, 2002—05. Guard New Orleans Hornets, 2005—. Recipient ACC Rookie Yr., 2003—04, ACC Player Yr. award, 2004—05, Best Breakthrough, Espy award, 2006. Achievements include Rookie Yr. honors with nearly unanimous vote for top ten league ratings in assists, steals, top rookie ratings in points, steals, assists, 2005-2006. Office: New Orleans/Oklahoma City Hornets Ste 1850 Olahoma Tower 210 Park Ave Oklahoma City OK 73102*

**PAUL, DEBAJYOTI,** geologist, educator; s. Anil Kumar and Kananbala Paul; m. Rumjhum Arora, Dec. 16, 2005. PhD in Geology, Cornell U., 2002. Postdoctoral fellow Max-Planck-Institut fur Chemie, Mainz, Germany, 2002—04; asst. prof. U. Tex., San Antonio, 2004—. Reviewer: Jour. Geochemistry, Geophysics, Geosystems, Jour. Geophysical Rsch., NSF. Recipient Gold medal for securing 1st position in MSc in Geology, Andhra U., India, 1994, Faculty Rsch. award, U. Tex. at San Antonio, 2005; Long fellow, Cornell U., 1998—99, Grad. Rsch. Assistantship, NSF, 2001—02, Alexander von Humboldt Rsch. fellow, Alexander von Humboldt Found., Germany, 2004. Mem.: Alexander von Humboldt Assn. Am., Geol. Soc. Am., Am. Geophys. Union, Geochemical Soc. Office: University of Texas at San Antonio 6900 N Loop 1604 W San Antonio TX 78249 Office Phone: 12104585751. Office Fax: 210-458-4469. Business E-Mail: debajyoti.paul@utsa.edu.

**PAUL, EVE W.,** retired lawyer; b. N.Y.C., June 16, 1930; d. Leo I. and Tamara (Sogolow) Weinschenker; m. Robert D. Paul, Apr. 9, 1952; children: Jeremy Ralph, Sarah Elizabeth. BA, Cornell U., 1950; JD, Columbia U., 1952. Bar: N.Y. 1952, Conn. 1960, U.S. Ct. Appeals (2nd cir.) 1975, U.S. Supreme Ct. 1977. Assoc. Botein, Hays, Sklar & Herzberg, N.Y.C., 1952-54; pvt. practice Stamford, Conn., 1960-70; staff atty. Legal Aid Soc., N.Y.C., 1970-71; assoc. Greenbaum, Wolff & Ernst, N.Y.C., 1972-78; v.p. legal affairs Planned Parenthood Fedn. Am., N.Y.C., 1979—91, v.p., gen. counsel 1991—2003; ret., 2003. Bd. dirs. Ctr. Advancement of Women, Inc. Contbr. articles to profl. jours Trustee Cornell U. Ithaca, N.Y., 1979-84; mem. Stamford (Conn.) Planning Bd., 1967-70; bd. dirs. Stamford LWV, 1960-62. Harlan Fiske Stone scholar Columbia Law Sch., 1952. Mem.: ABA, Fairfield County Bar Assn., Assn. Bar of City of N.Y., Conn. Bar Assn., Phi Kappa Phi, Phi Beta Kappa. Personal E-mail: evewpaul@aol.com. *The ability to plan the number and timing of my children has made it possible for me to enjoy career, marriage and family.*

**PAUL, GARY WAYNE,** music educator; b. Tulsa, July 15, 1954; s. Bill and Ellen Ada Paul; m. Bonnie Jean McIntosh, May 22, 1981; children: Jeanette Ellen, Marisa Nicole. BA in Edn., East Ctrl. U., 1977. Dir. bands Joliet H.S., Mont., 1987—88, Yale H.S., Okla., 1988—91, Hominy H.S., 1991—93, Wetumka H.S., 1993—96, Pocola H.S., 1996—99, Chelsea H.S., 1999—2003, Inola H.S., 2003—. Chair Mid-East Honor Band, Glenpool, Okla., 2000; adjudicator Northeastern A&M Coll. Contest, Miami, 1992; mem. staff ARk. Tech. U. Band Camp, Russellville, 1996—99. Mem. Tulsa Cmty. Band, 2001—. Mem.: Music Edn. Nat. Conf., Okla. Music Educators Assn., Okla. Bandmasters Assn. Democrat. Avocations: tennis, golf, camping. Home: 107 E 9th Pl S Claremore OK 74017 Office: Inola High Sch Inola OK 74036 Office Phone: 918-543-3122. Personal E-mail: bdpaul@olp.net. E-mail: gpaul3@cox.net.

**PAUL, GERALD D.,** electronics executive; D in Physics, Tech. U. Munich. Asst. to mgr. capacitor plant Draloric Electronic GmbH, Selb, Germany, 1978; from prodn. mgr. to mng. dir. Vishay Intertechnology, Malvern, Pa., 1987-94, pres. electronic components Europe, 1994-96, COO, 1996—, pres. 1998—, CEO, 2004—. Office: Vishay Intertechnology 63 Lincoln Hwy Malvern PA 19355*

**PAUL, GORDON LEE,** behavioral scientist, psychologist; b. Marshalltown, Iowa, Sept. 2, 1935; s. Leon Dale and Ione Hickman (Perry) P.; m. Joan Marie Wyatt, Dec. 24, 1954; children: Dennis Leon, Dana Lee, Joni Lynn. Student, Marshalltown Community Coll., 1953-54, San Diego City Coll., 1955-57; BA, U. Iowa, 1960; MA, U. Ill., 1962, PhD, 1964. Social sci. analyst VA Hosp., Danville, Ill., 1962; counseling psychologist U. Ill., Urbana, 1963; clin. psychologist VA Hosp., Palo Alto, Calif., 1964-65; pvt. practice clin. psychology, 1964-65; asst. prof. psychology U. Ill., Champaign-Urbana, 1965-67, assoc. prof., 1967-70, prof., 1970-80; Cullen disting. prof. psychology U. Houston, 1980—; pvt. practice psychology Champaign, 1965-80, Houston, 1980—. Psychotherapy rsch. cons., Palo Alto, 1964-65; cons. Ill. Dept. Mental Health, 1965-73, 78-82, NIMH, 1968-78; adviser Ont. (Can.) Mental Health Found., 1968-69, NSF, 1968-69, Can. Coun., 1969-75, VA, 1972, 80—, APA, 1970—, UCLA/VA Med. Ctr./Camarillo Schizophrenia Rsch. Ctr., 1978-93, Alliance for Mentally Ill, 1980—. Author: Insight vs. Desensitization in Psychotherapy, An Experiment in Anxiety Reduction, 1966, Anxiety and Clinical Problems, 1973, Psychosocial Treatment of Chronic Mental Patients, 1977, Assessment in Residential Treatment Settings, Part 1, 1986, Observational Assessment Instrumentation for Service and Research, Part 2, 1987, Part 3, 1988; mem. editl. bd. Behavior Therapy, 1969-75, Behavior Therapy and Exptl. Psychiatry, 1969—, Schizophrenia Bull., 1971-99, Jour. Abnormal Psychology, 1972-76, Jour. Residential Treatment, 1983—96, Jour. Psychopathology and Behavioral Assessment, 1985—; cons. editor Jour. Applied Behavior Analysis, 1966-77, 81—, Psychol. Bull., 1967—, Jour. Abnormal Psychology 1970-72, 76—, Psychosomatic Medicine, 1971-77, Psychophysiology, 1971—77, Archives Gen. Psychiatry, 1973-74, Behavior Therapy, 1976-87, Profl. Psychologist, 1977-87, Hosp. Cmty. Psychiatry, 1980—, Biobehavioral Revs., 1980-84, Jour. Cmty. Psychology, 1983, Am. Psychologist, 1983—, Brit. Jour. Clin. Psychology, 1985-87, Jour. Nervous and Mental Disease, 1992, Current Directions in Psychol. Sci., 1992—; contbr. articles to profl. jours. Served with USN, 1954-58. Recipient Creative Talent award Am. Inst. Rsch., 1964, Teaching award U. Ill., 1968, 75; rsch. award Mental Health Assn., 1985; listed one of 327 Best Mental Health Experts in Nation Good Housekeeping, 1994; NIMH fellow, 1963-64. Fellow APA (corr. com. 1965-70, pres. sect. III div. 12 1972-73, exec. coun. div. 12 1974-77, Disting. Scientist award sect. III, div. 12 1977, Disting. Sci. Contbns. to Clin. Psychology award Soc. Clin. Psychology divsn. 12 1999), Am. Psychol. Soc., Assn. Clin. Psychosocial Rsch., Am. Assn. Applied and Preventive Psychology; mem. Midwestern Psychol. Assn., Tex. Psychol. Assn., Houston Psychol. Assn., Assn. for Advancement Psychology, Phi Beta Kappa, Chi Gamma Iota. Achievements include being subject of NIMH sci. report monograph, 1981: Treating and Assessing the Chronically Mentally Ill: The Pioneering Research of Gordon L. Paul. Home: 6239 S Braeswood Blvd Houston TX 77096-3715 Office: U. Houston Dept Psychology 126 Heyne Bldg Houston TX 77204-5022 Office Phone: 713-743-8564. E-mail: gpaul@uh.edu.

**PAUL, HERBERT MORTON,** lawyer, accountant, educator; b. NYC; s. Julius and Gussie Paul; m. Judith Paul; children: Leslie Beth, Andrea Lynn. BBA, Baruch Coll.; MBA, LLM, NYU; JD, Harvard U. Ptnr. Touche Ross & Co. (predecessor Deloitte Touche), N.Y.C., assoc. nat. dir. tax, dir. fin counseling; mng. ptnr. Herbert Paul, P.C., N.Y.C., 1983—. Prof. taxation, trustee NYU. Author: Ordinary and Necessary Expenses; editor: Taxation of Banks; adv. tax editor The Practical Acct.; mem. adv. bd. Financial and Estate Planning, Tax Shelter Insider, Financial Planning Strategist, Tax Shelter Litigation Report; bd. dirs. Partnership Strategist, The Business Strategist; cons. Profl. Practice Mgmt. Mag.; mem. panel The Hot Line; advisor The Partnership Letter, The Wealth Formula; cons. The Insider's Report for Physicians; mem. tax bd. Business Profit Digest; cons. editor physician's Tax Advisor; bd. fin. cons. Tax Strategies for Physicians; tax and bus. advisor Prentice Hall; contbg. editor. Jour. of Accountancy; mem. editl. bd. Family Bus. Advisor. Trustee NYU, mem. bd. overseers Grad. Sch. Bus.; mem. com. on trusts and estates Rockefeller U.; trustee Alvin Alley Am. Dance Theatre, Assoc. Y's of N.Y.; mem. accts. divsn. Fedn. Philanthropies; mem. adv. bd. Family Bus. Advisor. Mem. ABA, Inst. Fed. Taxation (adv. com. chmn.), Internat. Inst. on Tax and Bus. Planning (adv. bd.), Assn. Bar City N.Y., NYU Tax Soc. (pres.), Bur. Nat. Affairs-Tax Mgmt. (adv. com. on exec. compensation), Am. Inst. CPAs (com. on corp. taxation), Tax Study Group, N.Y. County Lawyers Assn., N.Y. State Soc. CPAs Dir. (chmn. tax div. com. on fed. taxation, gen. tax com., furtherance com., com. on rels. with IRS, bd. dirs.), Nat. Assn. Accts., Assn. of Bar of City of N.Y., Accts. Club of Am., Pension Club, Nat. Assn. Estate Planners (bd. dirs.), N.Y. Estate Planning Coun. (bd. dirs.), N.Y. C. of C. (tax com.), Grad. Sch. Bus. of NYU Alumni Assn. (pres.), NYU Alumni Assn. (pres.), Wall St. Club, City Athletic Club (N.Y.C.), Inwood Country Club. Office: Herbert Paul PC 450 7th Ave Ste 3000 New York NY 10123 Office Phone: 212-752-3700.

**PAUL, JAMES CAVERLY NEWLIN,** law educator, retired dean; b. Chestnut Hill, Pa., Apr. 30, 1926; s. William Allen Butler and Adelaide Sims (Newlin) P.; m. Margaret Morris Clausen, June 25, 1948; children: Nicholas Newlin, Martha Morris, Adelaide Sims. BA, Princeton U., 1948; JD, U. Pa., 1951. Bar: Pa. bar 1952. Legal sec. to Chief Justice U.S., 1951-53; asst. prof. U. N.C., 1953-55; asst. dir. Inst. Govt., U. N.C., 1953-55; prof. law, dir. Inst. Legal Research, U. Pa., 1955-63; prof. law, dean and founder of faculty of law Haile Selassie U., Ethiopia, 1962—67, v.p. acad. affairs, 1967-69; exec. v.p. Ednl. and World Affairs, N.Y.C., 1969-70; dean Sch. Law, Rutgers U., Newark, 1970-74; prof. law, 1970-96, Newhouse scholar in law, 1984-88, William J. Brennan prof., 1988-96; exec. sec., trustee Internat. Ctr. for Law in Devel., N.Y.C., 1974—. Founding mem., sec.-treas. Internat. Third World Legal Studies Assn., N.Y.C., 1980—96; adj. prof. Columbia U., 1973—95; cons. US Peace Corps 1961—62, Constl. Commn. Transitional Govt. of Ethiopia, 1992—95, UN Devel. Programme, 1994—96, 2005; commr. Internat. Eritrean-Ethiopian Claims commn., The Hague, 2001—; chmn. Fund for Assistance to Legal Edn. in Ethiopia and Eritrea, 2006—. Author: Rift in the Democracy, 1951, (with others) Federal Censorship, 1961, Ethiopian Constitutional Development, 1969, Lawyers in the Third World, 1981, The International Context of Rural Poverty in the Third World, 1986, Incorporating Human Rights into the World Summit for Social Development, 1995; editor-in-chief U. Pa. Law Rev., 1950-51. Candidate for U.S. Congress from 9th Dist. Pa., 1958; del. Dem. Nat. Conv., 1960. Served with USNR (Amphibious forces), 1943-46, PTO. Recipient Spl. medal for distinguished service to the devel. of law and univ. edn. in Ethiopia, Emperor Haile Sellassie 1st, 1969; Eisenhower Exch. fellow, Africa, 1960. Mem. ABA, N.J. Bar Assn., Pa. Bar Assn., Am. Soc. Internat. Law, Internat. Third World Legal Studies Assn. (sec.-treas. 1980-96), Orgn. Am. Historians, Am. Law and History Assn., Order of Coif, Princeton Club (N.Y.C.). Home: 1352 Chancellor Pt Trappe MD 21673-1540 *My life in law and teaching about law gives satisfaction because it enables me to direct my energies towards thinking about social justice, individual dignity, and the possibilities of attaining more of the conditions enabling these ideals. But that satisfaction is tempered by constant realization of my own frailties and the failure everywhere of people, particularly those most fortunately endowed, to be guided by principled thinking.*

**PAUL, JAMES WILLIAM,** lawyer; b. Davenport, Iowa, May 3, 1945; s. Walter Henry and Margaret Helene (Hillers) P.; m. Sandra Kay Schmid, June 15, 1968; children: James William, Joseph Hillers. BA, Valparaiso U., 1967; JD, U. Chgo., 1970. Bar: N.Y. 1971, U.S. Ct. Appeals (2d cir.) 1971, U.S. Dist. Ct. (so. and ea. dists.) N.Y. 1972, U.S. Supreme Ct. 1977, U.S. Ct. Appeals (6th cir.) 1981, Ind. 1982, U.S. Dist. Ct. (no. dist.) Ind. 1982, U.S. Claims Ct. 1989, U.S. Dist. Ct. (ea. dist.) Mich. 1989, U.S. Ct. Appeals (fed. cir.) 1991. Assoc. Rogers & Wells, N.Y.C., 1970-78, ptnr., 1978—; ptnr., gen. counsel Clifford Chance US LLP, N.Y.C., 2000—. Officer Musica Sacra, Inc., 1972—81. Bd. dirs. Turtle Bay Music Sch., Am. Lauth. Publicity Bur., Wartburg Found., chmn. bd., 2004—06. Recipient Disting. Alumnus award, Valparaiso U., 1994. Mem. ABA (antitrust sect. ins. com.), Assn. Bar City N.Y. (com. legal and judl. ethics, com. on civil ct., com. profl. discipline), Fed. Bar Coun. Democrat. Home: 360 E 72nd St Apt A-710 New York NY 10021-4755 also: 5 Curtis Dr Sherman CT 06784-1507 Office: Clifford Chance US LLP 31 W 52nd St New York NY 10019-6131 Office Phone: 212-878-8227. Business E-Mail: james.paul@cliffordchance.com.

**PAUL, JERALD S.,** federal agency administrator, former state representative, lawyer; BS, Maine Maritime Acad.; MS, U. Fla.; JD, Stetson U. Nuclear engr. E.I. Hatch Nuclear Plant; ptnr. McKinley, Ittersagen, Gunderson and Berntsson, PA; mem. Fla. Ho. of Reps.; prin. dep. adminstr. Nat. Nuclear Security Adminstrn., US Dept. Energy, Washington, 2004—. Office: US Dept Energy Forestall Bldg 1000 Independence Ave SW, Rm 7A-04 Washington DC 20585-1290*

**PAUL, JOHN CHARLES,** lawyer; b. Norwalk, Conn., Mar. 3, 1954; s. John Andrew and Alberta (Miserendino) P. AB, Brown U., 1976; JD, Case Western Res. U., 1979. Bar: Ohio 1979, DC 1981, US.Patent and Trademark Office 1981, US Ct. Appeals (DC Cir.) 1981, US Ct. Appeals (Fed. Cir.) 1982, US Dist. Ct. DC 1982, US Supreme Ct. 1983. Patent examiner U.S. Patent and Trademark Office, Arlington, Va., 1980-81; assoc. Bacon & Thomas, Arlington, 1981-84, Finnegan, Henderson, Farabow, Garrett & Dunner LLP, Washington, 1984-91, ptnr., 1991—, leader, Intellectual Property Mgmt. Sect. Adj. faculty Cath. U. Law Sch., 1999—2003. Mem. ABA (young lawyers div. vice chmn. patent, trademark, copyright law com. 1989-90), Fed. Bar Assn. (young lawyers div., bd. dirs. 1982-85), DC Bar Assn. (young lawyers sect., exec. coun. 1987-90), Licensing Execs. Soc. (trustee 2005—). Office: Finnegan Henderson Farabow Garrett & Dunner LLP 901 New York Ave NW Washington DC 20001-3315 Office Phone: 202-408-4109. Office Fax: 202-408-4400. Business E-Mail: john.paul@finnegan.com.

**PAUL, KENNETH,** newspaper editor; b. NYC, June 7, 1948; s. Samuel D. and Rose (Markoff) P.; m. Sevara Jeleva, Dec. 5, 1993; 1 child, Kathryn Hannah. BA in English, Dartmouth Coll., Hanover, N.H., 1969; apl. diploma in social studies, Oxford (Eng.) U., 1973. Tchr. Concord HS, NH, 1969-71; dep. European editor LA Times/Washington Post News Svc., London, 1972-73; reporter, news editor Riverside Press Enterprise, Calif., 1973-76; specialists editor, copy editor, asst. nat. and day nat. editor Newsday, NY, 1976—87; mng. editor NY Observer, NYC, 1987-91; editor The Litchfield County Times, New Milford, Conn., 2002, Housatonic Pubs., New Milford, 2001—02; editor-in-chief Manhattan Media, NYC, 2002—04; day editor The NY Sun, NYC, 2004—05; staff editor New York Times, 2005—. Business E-Mail: kenpaul@nytimes.com.

**PAUL, LAURENCE M.,** editor; BA, Drake U., Des Moines, IA. Asst. mng. editor Des Moines Register; with NY Times, 1989—98; dep. editor NY Times News Svc., 1998—99; exec. editor, 1999—; NY Times Syndication Sales Corp., 2000—. Office: NY Times News Svc 9th Fl 229 W 43rd St New York NY 10036 also: NY Times Syndication Sales Corp 14th Fl 122 E 42nd St New York NY 10168 Office Phone: 212-556-4149. Office Fax: 212-556-3535, 212-499-3382. E-mail: lmpaul@nytimes.com.*

**PAUL, LES,** entertainer; b. Waukesha, Wis., June 9, 1915; s. George and Evelyn (Stutz) Polfuss; m. Mary Ford; children: Lester, Gene, Colleen, Robert, Mary. Student pub. schs., Waukesha. Appeared on numerous radio programs throughout Midwest, in 1920's and 1930's, formed Les Paul Trio, 1936—37, and appeared with Fred Waring, N.Y.C., appeared on first television broadcast with an orch. from NBC, N.Y.C., 1939; mus. dir: WJJD and WIND, 1941; appeared with Mary Ford on own television show, Mahwah, N.J., 1953—57; host Edison 100th Anniversary of invention of phonograph at Edison Home, West Orange, N.J. 1977, numerous TV, club appearances especially Fat Tuesday's, N.Y.C. recs. include Lover and Brazil, 1948, Nola, 1949, Goofus, 1950, Tennessee Waltz, 1950, Little Rock Getaway, 1950, Mockin' Bird Hill, 1951, Just One More Chance, 1951, Walkin' and Whistlin' Blues, 1951, How High The Moon, 1951 (Hall of Fame award 1979), Smoke Rings, 1952, The World's Waiting For The Sunrise, 1952, Tiger Rag, 1953, Meet Mr. Callaghan, 1953, Jazz Me Blues, 1952, Vaya Con Dios, 1954, Chester and Lester, 1976 (Grammy award), Guitar Monsters, 1977 (Grammy nominee), The Legend and the Legacy, 1991, The Best of the Capitol Masters with Mary Ford, 1992, The Guitar Artistry of Les Paul, Greatest Hits!, 1994. Served with Armed Forces Radio Service, World War II. Named to Grammy Hall of Fame Les Paul and Mary Ford, 1977, Rock 'N' Roll Hall of Fame, 1988, Wis. Performing Artists Hall of Fame, 1990, Nat. Inventors Hall of Fame, 2005; recipient Grammy Achievement award for contbns. to rec., musical instruments industry. Mem.: SAG, ASCAP, AFTRA, Am. Fedn. Musicians, Audio Engring. Soc. Achievements include consultant, Gibson Guitar Corp., Nashville; invention of multi-track tape recorder; first 8-track tape recorder; sound-on-sound recording; design of Les Paul electric solid body guitars. Address: Columbia Records Sony Music Entertainment 550 Madison Ave Fl 24 New York NY 10022-3211 *To be successful requires hard work, determination, a positive attitude, believing in one's self, a God given talent and luck.*

**PAUL, NORMAN LEO,** psychiatrist, educator; b. Buffalo, July 5, 1926; s. Samuel Joseph and Tannie (Goncharsky) P.; m. Betty Ann Byfield, June 6, 1951 (dec. May 1994); children: Marilyn, David Alexander; m. Janet Athos, Aug. 16, 2002. MD, U. Buffalo, 1948. Fellow pharmacology U. Cin. Coll. Medicine, Ohio, 1949-50; resident psychiatry Mass. Mental Health Ctr., Boston, 1952-55; fellow child psychiatry James Jackson Putnam Children's Ctr., Boston, 1957-58; Mass. Gen. Hosp., Boston, 1958-59; chief psychiatrist Day Hosp. Mass. Mental Health Ctr., Boston, 1960-64; dir. conjoint family therapy Boston State Hosp., 1964-65, cons. in family psychiatry, 1965-70; assoc. clin. prof. dept. neurology Boston U. Sch. Medicine, 1977—. Cons. Mental Health Ctr., Alaska Native Hosp., Anchorage, 1967-68; cons. family psychiatry Boston VA Hosp., 1967-71, Mass. Soc. for the Prevention of Cruelty to Children, Boston, 1993—; vis. family therapist St. George's Med. Sch., London, 1996-97; lectr. in psychiatry Harvard Med. Sch., Boston, 1976-2003; faculty assoc. Mgmt. Analysis Corp., Cambridge, Mass., 1979-82; presenter Internat. Conf. on Telemedicine and Telecare, London, 1996 Family therapist: (tv documentary) PBS-Trouble in the Family, 1965 (George Foster Peabody award 1965); co-author A Marital Puzzle, 1977, 86, German edit., 1987, French edit., 1995, Chinese edit., 1997, contbr. articles to profl. jours. Consultant to Repeal Abortion Laws, Boston, 1965-70; chair Audio Unit of Child Devel. and Mass Media, White House Conf. on Children and Youth, Washington, 1970; bd. trustees Cambridge (Mass.) Coll., 1977-89; bd. dirs. Let's Face It, 1990—, Ctr. for Family Connections, 1998—2002. Capt. USAF, 1950-52. Recipient Edward A. Strecker, M.D. award for young psychiatrist of yr., 1966, Cert. of Merit, Mass. Coun. on Family Life, Boston, 1967, Cert. of Commendation, Mass. Assn. for Mental Health, Boston, 1967, Disting. Achievement award Soc. for Family Therapy and Rsch., Boston, 1973, Lifetime Achievement award Mass. Assn. for Marriage and Family Therapy, 1998, Disting. Svc. award Physician Health Svcs., 1998. Fellow Royal Soc. Medicine, Am. Psychiat. Assn. (life); mem. Am. Assn. Marriage and Family Therapy (bd. dirs. 1983-86), Am. Family Therapy Assn. (v.p. 1982-83, Disting. Contbn. award 1984), Assn. for Rsch. in Nervous and Mental Disorders, Group for the Advancement Psychiatry (chair com. on the family 1982-84). Avocations: study of codes, travel. Office: 394 Lowell St Ste 6 Lexington MA 02420-2549 Office Phone: 781-863-5800. Personal E-mail: nlpaul@aol.com.

**PAUL, OGLESBY,** cardiologist, educator; b. Villanova, Pa., May 3, 1916; s. Oglesby and Laura Little (Wilson) P.; m. Marguerite Black, May 29, 1943 (dec. Jan. 1979); children: Rodman, Marguerite; m. Jean Lithgow, Jan. 17, 1981. AB, Harvard Coll., 1938; MD, Harvard Med. Sch., 1942. Intern Mass. Gen. Hosp., Boston, 1942-43, resident, 1946-48; prof. medicine Northwestern U., Evanston, Ill., 1963-77; sr. physician emeritus Brigham & Womens Hosp., Boston, 1977—; prof. medicine emeritus Harvard Med. Sch., Boston, 1977—. V.p. health scis. Northwestern U., Evanston, 1974-75; dir. admissions Harvard Med. Sch., Boston, 1977-82. Author: Take Heart, 1986, The Caring Physician, 1991. Pres. Am. Heart Assn., Dallas, 1960-61. Lt. USNR. Home: 10 Longwood Dr Apt 322 Westwood MA 02090-1142 Office: Harvard Med Sch Countway Libr 10 Shattuck St Boston MA 02115-6011 E-mail: oleypaul@aol.com.

**PAUL, PETER,** science administrator; PhD in Exptl. Nuclear Physics, U. Freiburg, 1959. Prof. dept. physics Stony Brook U., 1960—92, disting. svc. prof. dept. physics, 1992—98, cheif physics dept., 1986—90, 1996—98; dep. dir. sci. & tech. Brookhaven Nat. Lab., NY, 1998—. Contbr. articles to profl. jours. Fellow: Am. Phys. Soc. (Alexander von Humboldt Sr. Scientist award 1983). Office: Brookhaven Nat Lab PO Box 50000 Upton NY 11973

**PAUL, RICHARD WRIGHT,** lawyer; b. Washington, May 23, 1953; s. Robert Henry Jr. and Betty (Carey) P.; m. Paula Ann Coolsaet, July 25, 1981; children: Richard Haven, Timothy Carey, Brian Davis. AB magna cum laude, Dartmouth Coll., 1975; JD, Boston Coll., 1978. Bar: Mich. 1978, U.S. Dist. Ct. (ea. dist.) Mich. 1978, U.S. Ct. Appeals (6th cir.) 1982, U.S. Supreme Ct. 1989, U.S. Dist. Ct. (we. dist.) Mich. 1991. Assoc. Dickinson, Wright, Moon, Van Dusen & Freeman, Detroit, 1978-85, ptnr., 1985—. Case evaluator Wayne County Cir. Ct., Oakland County Cir. Ct.; mediator Mich. State Ct. Adminstrv. Office. Co-author, Barbarians At The Gate: Daubert Two Years Later, 1995; contbr. articles to profl. publs. Trustee Bloomfield Village Assn., Birmingham, Mich., 2001-04, sec., 2003-04, bd. dirs; mem. Little League, Birmingham, 2000—, treasurer 2005-. Mem. ABA, State Bar of Mich. (trans. litig. sect. 1998-99, sec. litig. sect. 1999-2000, chmn. elect litig. sect. 2000-01, chairperson litigation sect. 2001-02, mem. representative assembly 2004—), Def. Rsch. Inst., Detroit Met. Bar Assn., Mich. Def. Trial Counsel, Dartmouth Lawyers Assn., Oakland County Bar Assn., Assn. Def. Trial Counsel, Alumni Coun. Dartmouth Coll., Dartmouth Detroit Club (pres. 1980—). Avocations: tennis, bicycling. Office Phone: 248-433-7200. Business E-Mail: rpaul@dickinsonwright.com.

**PAUL, ROBERT ARTHUR,** steel company executive; b. NYC, Oct. 28, 1937; s. Isadore and Ruth (Goldstein) P.; m. Donna Rae Berkman, July 29, 1962; children: Laurence Edward, Stephen Eric, Karen Rachel. AB, Cornell U., 1959; JD, Harvard U., 1962, MBA, 1964. With Ampco-Pitts. Corp. (formerly Screw & Bolt Corp. Am.), N.Y.C., v.p., 1969-71, treas., 1973-79, exec. v.p., 1972-79, pres., COO, 1979-94, pres., CEO, 1994—2004, dir., 1969—, chmn., CEO, 2004—. Pres. bd. dirs. Louis Berkman Co.; bd. dirs. ECHO Real Estate Svs.; gen. ptnr. Romar Trading Co.; instr. Grad. Sch. Indsl. Adminstrn. Carnegie Mellon U., 1966-69; trustee emeritus Cornell U. Trustee H.L. and Louis Berkman Found., U. Pitts. Med. Ctr. Svs., Jewish Healthcare Found., U. Pitts.; trustee, pres. Fair Oaks Found. Mem. ABA, Mass. Bar Assn., Harvard Club (NY), Concordia Club, Pitts. Athletic Club, Duquesne Club, Williams Country Club, Laurel Valley Golf Club, Fox Chapel Golf Club. Republican. Jewish. Office: Ampco-Pitts Corp 600 Grant St Pittsburgh PA 15219-2702 Office Phone: 412-456-4400. Personal E-mail: rpaul@ampcopgh.com.

**PAUL, ROBERT CAREY,** lawyer; b. Washington, May 7, 1950; s. Robert Henry and Betty Jane (Casey) Paul. AB, Dartmouth Coll., 1972; JD, Georgetown U., 1978. Assoc. Milbank, Tweed, Hadley & McCloy, N.Y.C., 1978—85; ptnr. Dechert Price & Rhoads, N.Y.C., 1986—89, Kelley Drye &

Warren, Brussels, 1989—93; counsel Rockefeller & Co., Inc., N.Y.C., 1995—2003; cons. N.Y.C., 2003—05; corp. coun. Rockefeller Group Internat., Inc., NYC, 2005—; v.p., corp. coun. Rockefeller Group Technology Solutions, Inc., 2005—; corp. counsel Rockefeller Group Internat., Inc., N.Y.C., 2005—; corp. counsel Rockefeller Group Tech. Solutions, Inc., N.Y.C., 2005—. Editor-in-chief Real Property Probate and Trust Jour., 2001—06. Mem.: ABA (real property, probate and trust law sect. coun. 2006—). Home: 310 E 46th St Apt 19E New York NY 10017-3029 Office: 1221 Ave of the Americas New York NY 10020 Office Phone: 212-282-2650. Business E-Mail: rpaul@rockgrp.com.

**PAUL, ROLAND ARTHUR,** lawyer; b. Memphis, Jan. 19, 1937; s. Rol and Hattye (Mincer) P.; m. Barbara Schlesinger, June 10, 1962; children: Deborah Lynn, Arthur Eliot. BA summa cum laude, Yale U., 1958; LL.B. magna cum laude, Harvard U., 1961. Bar: N.Y. 1962, Mich. 1978, Conn. 1989. Law clk. to judge U.S. Ct. Appeals, 1961-62; fgn. affairs officer, spl. asst. to gen. counsel Dept. Def., 1962-64; assoc. firm Cravath, Swaine & Moore, N.Y.C., 1964-69; counsel fgn. relations subcom. security commitments U.S. Senate, 1969-71; assoc. firm Simpson Thacher Bartlett, N.Y.C., 1971-73; v.p., gen. counsel Howmet Corp., Greenwich, Conn., 1976-2000, Howmet Internat. Inc., 1997-2000; v.p., gen. counsel, dir. Pechiney Corp., Greenwich, Conn., 1984-95; counsel Day, Berry & Howard, Stamford, Conn., 2000—03, Ivey, Barnum & O'Mara, Greenwich, 2003—. Author: American Military Commitments Abroad. Mem. ABA, Coun. Fgn. Rels. Home: 8 Ellery Ln Westport CT 06880-5202 Office: 170 Mason St Greenwich CT 06832 Office Phone: 203-862-7740.

**PAUL, RONALD ERNEST,** congressman; b. Pitts., Aug. 20, 1935; m. Carol Paul; 5 children. BA, Gettysburg Coll., Pa., 1957; MD, Duke U. Med. Ctr., Durham, NC, 1961. Intern, resident Henry Ford Hosp., Detroit, 1961, 1962; ob-gyn. tng. U. Pitts., 1965—68; physician pvt. practice, Brazoria County, Tex., 1968; mem. US Congress from 14th Tex. dist., 1976—77, 1979—85, 1997—, mem. internat. rels. com., mem. joint econ. com., mem. fin. svcs. com., vice chmn. oversight and investigations subcommittee. Author: Challenge to Liberty, The Case for Gold, A Republic: If You Can Keep It. Flight surgeon USAF, 1963—65, flight surgeon US Air N.G., 1965—68. Recipient Taxpayer's Best Friend award Nat. Taxpayers Union, Mises Inst. Groseclose Prize and Leadership award, Leadership award Coalition for Peace Through Strength, Disting. Svc. award Am. Constl. Action, Torch Freedom award Young Conservatives Tex., Guardian Freedom award Young Am. Freedom. Republican. Office Phone: 202-225-2831.*

**PAUL, RONALD NEALE,** management consultant; b. Chgo., July 22, 1934; s. David Edward and Frances (Kusel) P.; m. Nona Maria Moore, Dec. 27, 1964 (div. Oct. 1981); children: Lisa, Karen, Brenda; m. Georgeann Elizabeth Lapkoff, Apr. 10, 1982. BS in Indsl. Engring., Northwestern U., 1957, MBA, 1958. Asst. to pres. Victor Comptometer Co., Chgo., 1958-64; cons. Corplan, Chgo., 1964-66; pres. Technomic Inc., Chgo., 1966—. Mng. ptnr. L/P Ptnrs., Chgo., 1978-84; bd. dirs. Summit Restaurants, Salt Lake City, 1990-96. Co-author: The 101 Best Performing Companies in America, 1986, Winning the Chain Restaurant Game, 1994. Mem. Am. Mktg. Assn., Am. Mgmt. Assn., Planners Forum, Pres.'s Assn., Product Devel. Mgmt. Assn., Beta Gamma Sigma. Avocations: reading, racquetball. Office: Technomic Inc 300 S Riverside Plz Ste 1940 Chicago IL 60606-6613 Office Phone: 312-876-0004. Business E-Mail: rpaul@technomic.com.

**PAUL, STEPHEN HOWARD,** lawyer; b. Indpls., June 28, 1947; s. Alfred and Sophia (Nahmias) P.; m. Deborah Lynn Dorman, Jan. 22, 1969; children: Gabriel, Jonathan. AB, Ind. U., 1969, JD, 1972. Bar: Ind. 1972, U.S. Dist. Ct. (so. dist.) Ind. 1972. Assoc. Baker & Daniels, Indpls., 1972-78, ptnr., 1979—, chmn. mgmt. com., 2004. Mem. bd. visitors Ind. U. Sch. Law, Bloomington. Editor in chief Ind. U. Law Jour., 1971. Pres. Belle Meade Neighborhood Assn., Indpls., 1974-78; v.p., counsel Brentwood Neighborhood Assn., Carmel, Ind., 1985-88, pres., 1988-91. Mem. ABA (state and local tax com. 1985—, sports and entertainment law com.), Am. Property Tax Counsel (founding mem.), Ind. State Bar Assn., Order of Coif. Office: Baker & Daniels 300 N Meridian St Ste 2700 Indianapolis IN 46204-1782 Office Phone: 317-237-0300. Business E-Mail: stephen.paul@bakerd.com.

**PAUL, T. V.,** social sciences educator; b. Kottayam, India, Nov. 10, 1956; m. Rachel Paul, Dec. 30, 1984; children: Kavya, Leah. PhD, UCLA, 1991. Asst. prof. McGill U., Montreal, Que., Canada, 1991—95, assoc. prof., 1995—2000, prof., 2000—02, James McGill prof. internat. rels., 2003—. Vis. scholar Harvard U. Cambridge, Mass., 1997—98; vis. prof. Naval Postgrad. Sch., Monterey, Calif., 2002—03; sr. vis. assoc. Ctr. for Nonproliferation Studies, MIIS, Monterey, 2002—03; dir. Rsch. Group in Internat. Security, Montreal, 2000—02. Author: Assymetric Conflicts: War Initiation by Weaker Powers, 1994, Power versus Prudence: Why Nations Forgo Nuclear Weapons, 2000 (Outstanding Academic Title, Choice Mag., 2001), India in the World Order: Searching for Major Power Status, 2003; editor: The Absolute Weapon Revisited: Nuclear Arms and the Emerging International Order, 1998, International Order and the Future of World Politics, 1999, The Nation-State in Question, 2003, Balance of Power: Theory and Practice in the 21st Century, 2004, The India-Pakistan Conflict: An Enduring Rivalry, 2005. Named a Popular Prof., MacLean's Mag. Guide to Can. Univs., 2005; recipient Peace Scholar award, US Inst. for Peace, 1989; grantee, Rockefeller Found., 1993—96, SSHRC, 1994—2004, Que. Provincial Granting Agy., 1997—. Mem.: Am. Polit. Sci. Assn., Brit. Internat. Studies Assn., Internat. Studies Assn. Office: McGill U 855 Sherbrooke St W Montreal PQ Canada H3A 2T7

**PAUL, THOMAS FRANK,** lawyer; b. Aberdeen, Wash., Sept. 23, 1925; s. Thomas and Loretta (Onstead) P.; m. Dolores Marion Zauge, Apr. 1, 1950; children: Pamela, Peggy, Thomas Frank. BS in Psychology, Wash. State U., 1951; JD, U. Wash., 1957. Bar: Wash. 1958, U.S. Dist. Ct. (no. and so. dist.) Wash. 1958, U.S. Ct. Appeals (9th cir.) 1958, U.S. Supreme Ct. 1970, Oreg. 2004, Alaska 2004. Ptnr., shareholder, pres. LeGros, Buchanan & Paul, Seattle, 1958—. Lectr. on admiralty and maritime law; bd. advisors U. San Francisco Law Jour., 1996—2002; mem. mediation and arbitration panel U.S. Dist. Ct. Seattle. Mem. bd. adv. U. San Francisco Law Jour., 1996—2002. Named one of Best Lawyers in Am., 2005—06. Mem.: ATLA (chmn. com. on admiralty and maritime litig. 1982—86), Fed. Bar Assn., Am. Judicature Soc., Asia Pacific Lawyers Assn., Am. Arbitration Assn., Transp. Lawyers Assn., Wash. Def. Trial Lawyers, Def. Rsch. Inst., Wash. State Trial Lawyers Assn., Maritime Law Assn. U.S.A., Million Dollar Advocates Forum, Propeller Club. Republican. Home: 1323 Willard Ave W Seattle WA 98119-3460 Office: LeGros Buchanan & Paul 701 5th Ave Ste 2500 Seattle WA 98104-7051 Office Phone: 206-623-4990. Business E-Mail: tpaul@legros.com.

**PAUL, VIVEK,** information technology executive; b. India; B in Engring., BITS, Pilani, India; MBA, U. Mass. With PepsiCo Inc., 1982—85, Bain & Co., Boston, 1985—89, GE, 1989—99; vice chmn., CEO Wipro, 1999—. Mem. adv. bd. Stanford U. Radiology Dept. Vol., bd. mem. local chpt. Jr. Achievement. Mem.: Calif. C. of C. (bd. mem., vice chmn. tech. com.), Silicon Valley Indus Entrepreneurs Orgn. (charter). Avocations: swimming, running, bridge.

**PAUL, WILLIAM,** physicist, researcher; b. Deskford, Scotland, Mar. 31, 1926; came to U.S., 1952; s. William and Jean (Watson) P.; m. Barbara Anderson Forbes, Mar. 28, 1952; children: David, Fiona. MA, Aberdeen U., Scotland, 1946; PhD, Aberdeen U., 1951; A.M. (hon.), Harvard U., 1960; D Honoris Causa, Paris, 1994. Asst. lectr., then lectr. Aberdeen U., 1946-52; mem. faculty Harvard U., 1953—; Gordon McKay prof. applied physics, 1963-91, Mallinckrodt prof. applied physics, 1991—2000, prof. physics, 1980-2000, Mallinckrodt rsch. prof. applied physics, 2000—04, rsch. prof. physics, 2000—04, Mallinckrodt prof. applied physics emeritus, prof. physics emeritus, 2004—. Professeur associé U. Paris, 1966-67; cons. solid state physics, 1954—; Ripon Coll., Calcutta, 1984 Author: Handbook on Semiconductors: Band Theory and Transport Properties, 1982; co-editor: Solids

Under Pressure, 1963, Amorphous and Liquid Semiconductors, 1980, Physics of Semiconductor Materials and Applications, 1986, High Pressure in Semiconductor Physics, Vols. 1 and 2, 1998. Carnegie fellow, 1952-53; Guggenheim fellow, 1959-60; Humboldt awardee, 1990; fellow Clare Hall Cambridge U., 1974-75. Fellow Am. Phys. Soc., Brit. Inst. Physics, N.Y. Acad. Scis., Royal Soc. Edinburgh Home: 57 Dartmouth Ct Bedford MA 01730 Office: Harvard U Pierce Hall Cambridge MA 02138 Business E-Mail: paul@deas.harvard.edu.

**PAUL, WILLIAM DEWITT, JR.,** retired art educator, photographer, videographer, museum director; b. Wadley, Ga., Sept. 26, 1934; s. William DeWitt and Sonoma Elizabeth (Tinley) Paul; m. Dorothy Hefling Paul, Sept. 2, 1962; children: Sarah Elizabeth, Barbara Susan, Dorothy Ann. Student, Emory U., summer 1952, U. Rome, summer 1953, Ga. State Univ., Atlanta, 1953—; B.F.A. Atlanta Art Inst., 1955; AB, U. Ga., 1958, M.F.A., 1959. Instr. art and art history Park Coll., Parkville, Mo., 1960-61; dir. exhbns., instr. art history Kansas City Art Inst., 1959-64, curator study collections, asst. prof. 1964-65; coordinator basic courses dept. art, asst. prof. art U. Ga., Athens, 1965-67; curator Ga. Mus. Art, assoc. prof. art, 1967-69, dir., asso. prof., 1969-80, prof., 1997—2002, gen. Sandy Beaver tchr. prof., 2000—02, prof. emeritus, 2002—. Lectr. Boston, L.A., New Orleans, San Antonio, Memphis, Birmingham; chmn. visual arts rev. panel Ga. Council for Arts and Humanities, 1976-77; v.p. Arts Festival Atlanta, 1982, 84, 85, trustee, 1982-93; guest artist Arts Festival Atlanta, 1987; mem. parents council Randolph-Macon Woman's Coll., Lynchburg, Va., 1986-87. Exhibited in one man shows at Ga. Mus. Art, 1959, Atlanta Art Assn., 1959, Unitarian Gallery, Kansas City, 1960, Palmer Gallery, Kansas City, 1965, Heath Gallery, Atlanta, 1976, Hunter Mus. Art, Chattanooga, 1976, Forum Gallery, NYC, 1977, Madison, Ga., Morgan Cultural Ctr., 1980, Columbus, Ga., Mus. Arts and Scis., 1980, Macon, Ga., Mus. Arts and Sci., 1980, Banks Haley Gallery, Albany, Ga., 1980, Augusta Richmond County, Ga., Mus., 1980, Heath Gallery 1982, Moon Gallery, Berry Coll., Rome, Ga., 1983, Bathhouse Gallery, Atlanta, 1987, MIA Gallery, Seattle, 1988, Valencia CC, Orlando, Fla., 1991, Gasperi Gallery, New Orleans, 1993, Contemporary Arts Ctr., New Orleans, 1994, Lyndon House Art Ctr., Athens, Ga., 2005, Averitt Art Ctr., Statesboro, Ga., 2006; numerous site-specific installations, 1986-97; exhibited group shows, New Arts Gallery, Atlanta, 1961, Kansas City Art Inst., 1960-64, Park Coll., 1960, Mulvane Art Ctr., Topeka, 1965, Palazzo Venezia, Rome, 1984, Elaine Benson Gallery, Bridgehampton, LI, NY, 1986, Dulin Gallery Art, Knoxville, Tenn., 1986, 1987 Atlanta Biennale, Nexus Contemporary Art Ctr., Atlanta, Valencia CC, Orlando, 1988, Greg Kucera Gallery, Seattle, 1992, King Plow Arts Ctr., Atlanta, 1994, Leslie-Lohman Found., NYC, 1995, Mus. Fine Arts, Tallahassee, 1996, Art Ctr., Miami Beach, Fla., 1997, Lebanon Valley Coll., Annville, Pa., 1998, others; represented in permanent collections Gen. Mills, Inc., Mpls., Hallmark Cards, Kansas City, Little Rock Arts Ctr., Ga. Mus. Art, U. Ga., The Kinsey Inst., Ind. U., Calif. State U., Tom of Finland Found. Ford Found. faculty enrichment grantee, 1978; recipient numerous awards for paintings. Mem. Am. Fedn. Arts (trustee 1969-81), Coll. Art Assn., Am. Assn. Museums (coun. 1981), Lovis Corinth Meml. Found., Ga. Alliance Arts Edn. (dir. 1975-77), Phi Kappa Phi. Home: 150 Bar H Ct Athens GA 30605-4702 Office: 4900 Barnett Shoals Rd Athens GA 30605 Office Phone: 706-613-2312. Business E-Mail: bpaul@uga.edu.

**PAUL, WILLIAM ERWIN,** immunologist, researcher; b. Bklyn., June 12, 1936; s. Jack and Sylvia (Gleicher) Paul; m. Marilyn Heller, Dec. 25, 1958; children: Jonathan M. Carmel, Matthew E. BA summa cum laude, Bklyn. Coll., 1956; MD cum laude, SUNY, Bklyn., 1960, DSc (hon.), 1991; PhD (hon.), Hebrew U., Jerusalem, 2003, Med. U. Cluj-Napoca, Romania, 2003; Laurea hon. causa, U. Rome, 2005. Intern, asst. resident Mass. Meml. Hosp., Boston, 1960—62; clin. assoc. Nat. Cancer Inst., NIH, Bethesda, Md., 1962—64; post doctoral fellow, instr. NYU Sch. Medicine, NYC, 1964—68; sr. investigator lab. immunology Nat. Inst. Allergy and Infectious Diseases, NIH, Bethesda, Md., 1968—70, chief lab. immunology, 1970—; dir. office of AIDS rsch. NIH, Bethesda, Md., assoc. dir. AIDS rsch., 1994—97. Chmn. selection com. Irene Diamond Fund Professorship in Immunology; Sackler sr. prof. Tel Aviv U., Israel; adj. prof. U. Pa., 2002—; chair sci. adv. bd. Lupus Rsch. Inst. Adv. editor Jour. Exptl. Medicine, 1974—2006; editor: Ann. Rev. Immunology, Volumes 1-25, 1983—; Fundamental Immunology, 1st - 6th edits., 1984—; Immunity, 2003—06; assoc. editor Cell, 1985—96, transmitting editor Internat. Immunology, 1989—96, corr. editor Procs. Royal Soc. Series B, 1989—93, mem. editl. bd. Molecular Biology of Cell, 1990—93; contbg. editor: Procs. NAS U.S.A., 1992—94; mem. editl. bd. Procs. NAS U.S.A., 2004—; contbr. numerous articles to sci. journals. Mem. sci. adv. bd. Trudeau Inst. With USPHS, 1962—64, with USPHS, 1975—96. Recipient Founders' prize, Tex. Instruments Found., 1979, Alumni medal, SUNY Downstate Med. Ctr., 1981, Disting. Svc. medal, USPHS, 1985, Life Sci. Award, 3M, 1988, Tovi Comet - Wallerstein prize, CAIR Inst., Bar Ilan U., 1992, 6th ann. Excellence Award in Immunologic Rsch., Duke U., 1993, Alumni Honors, Bklyn. Coll., 1994, Abbott Labs. Award in Clin. and Diagnostic Immunology, Am. Acad. Microbiology, 1998, Lifetime Achievement award, Am. Assn. Immunologists, 2002, Sci. Achievement in award, The Irvington Inst., 2002. Fellow: Am. Acad. Arts and Sci.; mem.: NAS, Am Assn. Immunologists (pres. 1986—87, Lifetime Achievement award 2002), Assn. Am. Physicians, Scandinavian Soc. Immunology (hon.), Am. Soc. Clin. Investigation (pres. 1980—81), Inst. Medicine NAS. Office: NIH Bldg 10 Rm 11n311 Bethesda MD 20892-1982 Office Phone: 301-496-5046. Business E-Mail: wpaul@niaid.nih.gov.

**PAUL, WILLIAM GEORGE,** lawyer; b. Pauls Valley, Okla., Nov. 25, 1930; s. Homer and Helen (Lafferty) P.; m. Barbara Elaine Brite, Sept. 27, 1963; children: George Lynn, Alison Elise, Laura Elaine, William Stephen. BA, U. Okla., 1952, LL.B., 1956. Bar: Okla. Bar 1956. Pvt. practice law, Norman, 1956; ptnr. Oklahoma City, 1957-84; with Crowe & Dunlevy, 1962-84, 96—; sr. v.p., gen. counsel Phillips Petroleum Co., Bartlesville, Okla., 1984-95; ptnr. Crowe & Dunlevy, Oklahoma City, 1996—. Assoc. prof. law Oklahoma City U., 1964-68; adv. bd. Martindale Hubbell, 1990—. Author: (with Earl Sneed) Vernon's Oklahoma Practice, 1965. Bd. dirs. Nat. Ctr. for State Cts., 1993-99, Am. Bar Endowment, 1986—, Bank 2, 2005—; trustee Nat. Constitution Ctr., 2000—. 1st lt. USMCR, 1952-54. Named Outstanding Young Man Oklahoma City, 1965, Outstanding Young Oklahoman, 1966, Okla. Hall of Fame, 2003. Fellow Am. Bar Found. (chmn. 1991), Am. Coll. Trial Lawyers; mem. ABA (bd. govs. 1995—, pres. 1999), Okla. Bar Assn. (pres. 1976), Oklahoma County Bar Assn. (past pres.), Okla Lottery Commn., Nat. Conf. Bar Pres. (pres. 1986), U. Okla. Alumni Assn. (pres. 1973), Order of Coif, Phi Beta Kappa, Phi Delta Phi, Delta Sigma Rho. Democrat. Presbyterian. Home: 13017 Burnt Oak Rd Oklahoma City OK 73120-8919 Office: Crowe & Dunlevy 20 N Broadway Ave Ste 1800 Oklahoma City OK 73102-8273 Office Phone: 405-239-6676.

**PAUL, WILLIAM GERALD,** educational psychologist; b. Phila., Nov. 27, 1948; s. Walter Michael and Sylvia (Schultz) P. BA in Psychology, Temple U., 1971, MEd in Sch. Psychology, 1972, PhD in Ednl. Psychology, 1978; postgrad., NYU, 1972-73. Rsch. assoc., statistician Family Ct., 1972; teaching asst. Temple U., Phila., 1976-78; testing and evaluation specialist Sch. Dist. Hamilton Twp., Hamilton Square, N.J., 1979—. Part-time rsch. evaluator Child Psychiatry Ctr. St. Christopher's Hosp. for Children, Phila., 1979-82. Mem. Am. Psychol. Assn., Am. Ednl. Rsch. Assn., Nat. Assn. Test Dirs., N.J. Prins. and Suprs. Assn. Home: 1448 Windsor Park Ln Havertown PA 19083-2706 Office: Hamilton Twp Sch Dist 90 Park Ave Hamilton NJ 08690-2024 Office Phone: 609-631-4100 3003. E-mail: wpaul@hamilton.K12.nj.us.

**PAUL, WILLIAM MCCANN,** lawyer; b. Cambridge, Mass., Feb. 9, 1951; s. Kenneth William and Mary Jean (Lamson) P.; m. Janet Anne Forest, Feb. 25, 1984; children: Emily L'Engle, Andrew Angwin, Elizabeth Seton. Student, U. Freiburg, Fed. Republic of Germany, 1971-72; BA, Johns Hopkins U., 1973; JD, U. Mich., 1977. Bar: D.C. 1978, U.S. Dist. Ct. D.C. 1978, U.S. Ct. Claims 1984, U.S. Ct. Appeals (4th cir.) 1980, U.S. Ct. Appeals (fed. cir.) 1983, U.S. Tax Ct. 1990. Law clk. to judge U.S. Ct. Appeals (5th cir.), Austin, Tex., 1977-78; assoc. Covington & Burling, Washington,

1978-87, ptnr., 1987-88, 89—; dep. tax legis. counsel U.S. Treasury Dept., 1988-89. Mem. ABA (asst. sec. tax sect. 1995-97, sec. 1997-99, coun. mem. 1999-2002, vice chair govt. rels. 2005—), D.C. Bar Assn., Am. Law Inst., Am. Coll. Tax Counsel, Order of Coif. Presbyterian. Home: 5604 Chevy Chase Pkwy NW Washington DC 20015-2520 Office: Covington & Burling PO Box 7566 1201 Pennsylvania Ave NW Washington DC 20004-2401 E-mail: wpaul@cov.com.

**PAULDINE, DAVID J.,** marketing executive, educator; b. Cortland, N.Y., May 25, 1957; s. William A. and Diana J. Pauldine; m. Maria C. Diaz de Rivera, Dec. 10, 1988. BA in Communication Arts, U. Dayton, 1979; postgrad., DePaul U. Nat. field trainer Bell and Howell Corp., Chgo., 1980-82, mgr. new student program, 1982-84, dir. sales and admissions, 1984-88; inst. dir./operation Bryant and Stratoon Corp., Buffalo, 1988-89; asst. v.p. mktg. and admissions Edn. Mgmt. Corp., Pitts., 1989-90, sr. v.p. mktg., 1998—99, exec. v.p., 1999—2000, pres. The Art Insts., 2000—05, exec. v.p., chief mktg. officer, 2003—05; pres. Art Inst. Seattle, 1990—93; exec. v.p. mktg. and recruiting DeVry Inst., 2005—. Bd. dirs., adv. com. State Bd. Vocat. Edn., Washington; lobbyist Art Insts. Internat., Seattle, Olympia and Washington, 1990—. Author and presenter in field. Point capt. Skills 2000 Coalition, Seattle, 1991; bd. dirs. Port of Seattle, Pier 66 Condominium Assn. Mem. Washington Fedn. Pvt. Vocat. Schs. (pres.-elect, bd. dirs., chmn. community rels. com. 1991—), Greater Seattle C. of C., Japanese Am. Soc., Downtown Seattle Assn. Roman Catholic. Avocations: travel, foreign languages, jazz, softball, golf. Office: DeVry Inc One Tower Lane Oakbrook Terrace IL 60181*

**PAULEY, BRUCE FREDERICK,** history professor; b. Lincoln, Nebr., Nov. 4, 1937; s. Carroll Righter and Blanche Marie (Hulsebus) P.; m. Marianne Barbara Utz, Dec. 21, 1963; children: Mark Allan, Glenn Hamilton. BA, Grinnell Coll., 1959; MA, U. Nebr., 1961; PhD, U. Rochester, 1966. Instr. history Coll. of Wooster (Ohio), 1964-65, U. Nebr., Lincoln, 1965-66; asst. prof. history U. Wyo., Laramie, 1966-71; from assoc. prof. to prof. history U. Ctrl. Fla., Orlando, 1971—, chmn. faculty senate, 1978-79. Vis. prof. history U. Nebr., Lincoln, 2002; cons., expert witness war crimes divsn. Can. Justice Dept., 1998-99. Author: The Habsburg Legacy, 1867-1939, 1972, Hahnenschwanz und Hakenkreuz: Steirischer Heimatschutz und österreichischer Nationalsozialismus, 1918-1934, 1972, Hitler and the Forgotten Nazis: A History of Austrian National Socialism, 1981, Der Weg in den Nationalsozialismus: Ursprünge und Entwicklung in Österreich, 1988, From Prejudice to Persecution: A History of Austrian Anti-Semitism, 1992 (Charles Smith prize So. Hist. Assn. best book European history, 1992, best book Austrian studies Austrian Cultural Inst., 1993), Eine Geschichte des österreichischen Anti-semitismus: Von der Ausgrenzung zur Auslöschung, 1993, Hitler, Stalin and Mussolini: Totalitarianism in the Twentieth Century, 1997, 2d edit., 2003. Chmn. parents' adv. com. Oviedo (Fla.) High Sch., 1981-82. Named Disting. Alumnus, U. Nebr., Lincoln, 1996; Fulbright fellow, 1963-64, rsch. fellow NEH, 1972, 87, Lifetime Achievement award, U. Nebr., Lincoln, 2005. Mem.: Soc. Austrian and Habsburg Historians, German Studies Assn. (exec. com. 1986—89), Am. Hist. Assn. Avocations: traveling to historical sites, photography, golf. Office: U Ctrl Fla Orlando FL 32816-1350 Office Phone: 407-823-5501. Business E-Mail: bpauley@pegasus.cc.ucf.edu.

**PAULEY, EDWARD E.,** museum administrator; b. Huntington, W.Va. BFA, Marshall U.; MFA in painting, Ohio U. Dir. edn. Huntington Mus. Art, W.Va.; exec. dir. Black Mountain-Swannanoa Ctr. for Arts, NC, Cultural Ctr. Fine Arts, Parkersburg, W.Va.; pres., CEO Plains Art Mus., Fargo, ND, 2003—. Tchr. Marshall U., Huntington, U. NC, Asheville. Office: Plains Art Mus 704 1st Ave N Fargo ND 58102 E-mail: epauley@plainsart.org.

**PAULEY, JAMES LEROY, JR.,** retired lawyer; b. Mason City, Iowa, Dec. 6, 1916; s. James Leroy and Clara May (Lampson) Pauley; m. Viola Jennie Lemker; children: James Donald (Don), Richard (Dick) Joseph. BA, U. Iowa, 1938, JD, 1940. Bar: Iowa 1940. Sole practitioner law, Scranton, Iowa, 1940—42; spl. agt. Fed. Bur. Investigation, Washington, 1942—43, N.Y.C., 1943—45, Louisville, 1945; practitioner law Pauley, Horak & Mumma, Jefferson and Scranton, Iowa, 1946—82; ret., 1982. Dir., v.p. Security Nat. Bank, Jefferson, Scranton, Iowa, 1955—95. Actor: (mag. articles) U.S. Specialist, 1973—90; author: (mag. articles) Iowa Postal History Soc. Bull., 2003. Mem.: Am. Diabetes Assn., Internat. Carnival Glass Assn., Inc., Univ. Iowa Alumni Assn., Iowa State Hist. Soc., Iowa Postal History Soc., Am. Philatelic Soc., U.S. Stamp Soc., Trans-Miss. Philatelic Soc., ABA, Iowa State Bar Assn., 16th Judicial Dist. Bar Assn. (pres. 1940—70), Greene County Bar Assn. (pres. 1940—) Lions Club (pres., zone chmn. 1947—). Republican. Congregational. Avocations: genealogy, antique collector, stamp collecting/philately. Home: 300 Edgewood Ave Jefferson IA 50129

**PAULEY, JANE,** newscaster, journalist; b. Indpls., Oct. 31, 1950; m. Gary Trudeau; 3 children. BA in Polit. Sci, Ind. U., 1971; D of Journalism (hon.), DePauw U., 1978. Reporter Sta. WISH-TV, Indpls., 1972—75; co-anchor WMAQ-TV News, Chgo., 1975—76, The Today Show, NBC, N.Y.C., 1976—90; from co-anchor to corr. NBC News, N.Y.C., 1976—; prin. writer, reporter NBC Nightly News, 1980—82, substitute anchor, 1990—2003; co-anchor Early Today, NBC, 1982—83; prin. corr. Real Life With Jane Pauley, NBC, 1991; co-anchor Dateline NBC, N.Y.C., 1992—99, prin. anchor, 1990—2003; anchor Time & Again MSNBC, 1999—2003; host The Jane Pauley Show, 2004—05. Author: Skywriting: A Life Out of the Blue, 2004 (Publishers Weekly Bestseller). Mem. adv. bd. Childrens Health Fund, Internat. Coun. Freedom From Hunger, bd. dirs. Pub. Edn. Needs Civic Involvement in Learning. Named Broadcaster of Yr., Internat. Radio and TV Soc., 1986, Best in Bus., Washington Journalism Rev., 1990; named to Broadcasting and Cable Hall of Fame; recipient Emmy award, Edward R. Murrow award, Gabriel award, Nancy Susan Reynolds award, Maggie award, Humanitas award, Commendation award, Am. Women in Radio and TV, Gracie Allen award, Clarion award, Assn. for Women in Comm., Wilbur award, Religious Pub. Rels. Coun., Salute to Excellence award, Nat. Assn. Black Journalists, Leonard Zeidenberg First Amendment award, Radio TV News Dirs. Found., Paul White award, NTNDA. Fellow: Soc. for Profl. Journalists (hon. chair Jane Pauley task force on mass comm. edn.).

**PAULEY, MARLENE JOAN,** musician, conductor; b. Anoka, Minn., July 30, 1954; d. Maynard Charles and Marjorie May Pauley; m. Glen Robert Lacher, May 26, 1990; 1 child, Elsa Pauley Lacher. BA, St. Olaf Coll., Northfield, Minn., 1976; MusM, Mich. State U., 1979. Clarinet instr. Crane Sch. Music, Potsdam, NY, 1979—80, Ark. State U., Jonesboro, 1980—81; clarinetist St. Paul Chamber Orch., 1982—2002, condr., 1999—; cond. condr. St. Paul Chamber Orch. Family and Edn. Concerts, 1999—. Clarinetist Grand Teton Music Festival, Jackson, Wyo., 1989—. Artistic dir. Greater Twin Cities Youth Symphonies, Mpls., 2004. Avocations: cooking, bicycling, hiking. Home: 5700 Duncan Ln Edina MN 55436

**PAULEY, MICHAEL WETZEL,** director, school psychologist; b. Madison, W.Va., Nov. 25, 1951; s. Wilmer and Mary (Meadows) Pauley; m. Julia Ann Pauley, Nov. 30, 1974; children: Matthew David, Benjamin Alexander. BA, Concord U., 1973; MA, Marshall U., Huntington, W.Va., 1978; EdS, Radford U., Va., 1986. Tchr. McDowell County Schs., 1973—74, Monroe County Schs., Peterstown, W.Va., 1974—80; spl. edn. specialist Mercer County Schs., Princeton, 1980—85; sch. psychologist Wyoming County Schs., Pineville, 1985—86, Summers County Schs., Hinton, 1986—87, Raleigh County Schs., Beckley, 1987—97, sch. psychologist, coord. spl. edn., 1997—99; asst. dir. spl. edn. Mercer County Schs., 1999—. Mem. Princeton-Glenwood Civitans, 2000—, Carnegie Hall, Lewisburg, 2002—; mem. alumni Concord U. Athens, Radford U.; soccer coach, coord. Monroe County Spl. Olympics, 1977—79. Mem.: W.Va. Assn. Sch. Psychologists, Nat. Assn. Sch. Psychologists. Democrat. Baptist. Avocations: hiking, travel, reading, gardening. Home: 1609 Honaker Ave Princeton WV 24740 Office: Mercer County Schs 1403 Honaker Ave Princeton WV 24740 Business E-Mail: mwpauley@access.k12.wv.us. E-mail: a_pauley4@hotmail.com.

**PAULEY, SHIRLEY STEWART,** religious organization executive; b. Boston, Sept. 13, 1938; d. Charles Norris and Nellie Consuelo (Yorke) Stewart; m. Edward Haven Pauley, May 29, 1964; children: David Stewart, Deborah Jeanne. BA, Gordon Coll., 1960; postgrad., Ariz. State U., 1961, Boston U., 1963. Sec./receptionist Atwell Co., Boston, summer 1956; sec., typist Kelley Girl, Boston, 1956-60; asst. office mgr. Radiator Chem. Corp., Scottsdale, Ariz., 1960-62; sec., clerical worker GM, Westwood, Mass., 1962-64; v.p. Truth Alive Ministries, Dallas, 1995—. Spkr. At Large, Boston, 1956-60; Sunday sch. tchr. Blaney Meml. Bapt. Ch., Boston, 1956-60; choir dir. Sherwood Bapt. Ch., Phoenix, 1961-62, co-youth dir., 1961; co-youth dir. Blaney Meml. Ch., Boston, 1964-66; messenger Bapt. Gen. Conv. Tex., Ft. Worth, 1996; leader bible study Prestonwood Bapt. Ch., Dallas, 2006—; v.p. Truth Alive Ministries, 1996—. Republican. Avocations: photography, reading, music. Office: Truth Alive Ministries PO Box 794945 Dallas TX 75379-4945

**PAULEY, STANLEY FRANK,** manufacturing executive; b. Winnipeg, Man., Can., Sept. 19, 1927; came to U.S., 1954, naturalized, 1961; s. Daniel and Anna (Tache) P.; m. Dorothy Ann Ruppel, Aug. 21, 1949; children: Katharine Ann, Lorna Jane. B.E.E., U. Man., 1949. With Canadian Industries Ltd., Kingston, Ont., 1949-53, sr. engring. asst., 1952-53; controls designer Standard Machine and Tool Co. Ltd., Windsor, Ont., 1953-54; prodn. supt. E.R. Carpenter Co., Richmond, Va., 1954-57, pres., 1957-83, chmn., CEO, 1983-94; chmn., CEO, Carpenter Co. (formerly E.R. Carpenter Co.), Richmond, 1994—, also bd. dirs. Bd. dirs. Carpenter Co. of Can., Carpenter de Mexico, Carpenter Plc., Carpenter S.A., Carpenter Gmbh. Trustee Va. Mus. Found. Mem. Commonwealth Club, Country Club of Va. Republican. Presbyterian. Home: 314 St Davids Ln Richmond VA 23221-3708 Office: Carpenter Co 5016 Monument Ave Richmond VA 23230-3620 E-mail: Stan.Pauley@carpenter.com.

**PAULHUS, NORMAN GERARD, JR.,** aerospace engineer; b. Washington, May 19, 1950; s. Norman Gerard and Kathryn Frances (Schwartz) P. BS Aerospace Engring. with high honors, U. Md., 1970; graduate (hon.), USCG Chief Petty Officers' Acad., 2003. Transp. intern U.S. Dept. Transp., Washington, 1970-71, aerospace engr. Office of Sec., 1971-72, gen. engr., 1972-82, dep. dir. Office Tech. and Planing Assistance, 1982-87, program devel. officer Rsch. and Tech., 1987-91, sr. tech. advisor Office Rsch. and Tech. Transfer, 1991—2002; transp. specialist Fed. Highway Adminstrn., 2002—05. Editor: (with D. McKelvey and D. Ewing) Procs. of 4th Nat. Conf. Rural Pub. Transp., 1979, Technology Sharing, 1979, (with A. Brecher, R. Stevens and others) Effective Global Transportation in the Twenty-First Century, 1999; contbr. articles to profl. jours. Recipient Sec.'s award U.S. Dept. Transp., 1974, Meritorious Achievement award, 1979, Spl. Achievement award, 1984, Superior Achievement award, 1989, Cert. Appreciation, Coun. Stat Govts., 1990, Way to Go award Dept. Transp., 1991, Cert. Appreciation, USCG Commandant, 1991, Sec.'s Find Good and Praise It award, 1999, Exemplary Achievemnt (Eagle) award, 2000, Commandant's Pub. Svc. medal USCG, 2002; named hon. chief petty officer, 2003. Mem. AAAS, Nat. Space Inst., U.S. Naval Inst., Navy League U.S., Planetary Soc., Inst. Noetic Scis., Am. Assn. State Hwys. and Transp. Ofcls. (Meritorious Pub. Svc. Citation, 2004), Tau Beta Pi, Sigma Gamma Tau, Phi Kappa Phi. Roman Catholic. Home: 18816 Muncaster Rd Rockville MD 20855-1430 Personal E-mail: otterx@erols.com. Business E-Mail: norman.paulhus@fhwa.dot.gov.

**PAULHUS, THOMAS A.,** social studies educator; b. Paterson, N.J., Oct. 8, 1953; s. Albert Richard and Shelby Ann Paulhus; m. Mary C. Fedigan, Aug. 28, 1988 (div. 1996). BA, Heidelberg Coll., Tiffin, Ohio, 1975; MA, Seton Hall U., 2002. Cert. tchr. social studies, N.J. Cons. The Triad Group, Boston, 1984-90, Toma Assocs., Little Falls, N.J., 1990—; tchr. Blessed Sacrament, Paterson, N.J., 1999—, asst. prin., 2002—. Mem.: Kappa Delta Pi. Democrat. Roman Catholic. Avocation: golf. Home: 275 6th Ave NW Paterson NJ 07524 Office Phone: 973-278-8787. E-mail: tpaulhusgr6@hotmail.com.

**PAULIKAS, GEORGE ALGIS,** retired physicist; b. Pagegiai, Lithuania, May 14, 1936; came to U.S., 1949, naturalized, 1955; s. George and Olga (Pacas) P.; m. Joan Marie Gross, Sept. 7, 1957; 1 child, Nancy Marie. BS in Engring. Physics, U. Ill., Chgo. and Urbana, 1957, MS (univ. fellow 1957-58), 1958; PhD in Physics (NSF fellow 1958-61), U. Calif., Berkeley, 1961. With Aerospace Corp., El Segundo, Calif., 1961-98; ret., head space particles and field projects, 1968, dir. space scis. lab., 1968-81, v.p. labs., 1981-85, sr. v.p. devel., 1985-89, sr. v.p. programs, 1989-94, exec. v.p., 1992-98. Mem. various ad hoc coms. NAS, 1970—, ann.; mem. adv. coun. geophysics U. Calif., 1973—75, exec. com space scis. lab., 1978—81; mem. sci. adv. bd. USAF, 1975—82, 1991—95; mem. def. space tech. com. NRC, 1987—92; mem. NAS/NRC Space Studies Bd., 1999—2006, vice chair, 2003—06; cons. in field. Author papers in field; asso. editor: Jour. Geophys. Research, 1972-75. Trustee Calif. Sci. Ctr., 1994-2000, Boy Scouts Am., L.A., 1996-2000. Recipient Aerospace Corp. Trustees Disting. Achievement award, 1980, Meritorious Civilian Svc. award USAF, 1982, 95, U. Ill. Alumni Disting. Engring. award, 1992, Nat. Reconnaissance Office Gold Medal, 1998; named U. Ill. (Navy Pier) Hall of Fame, 1996. Fellow AIAA (chmn. tech. com. space sci. and astronomy 1976-77), Am. Phys. Soc.; mem. Am. Geophys. Union, Sigma Xi. Home: 1537 Addison Rd Palos Verdes Estates CA 90274 Office Phone: 310-336-7076. E-mail: george.a.paulikas@aero.org.

**PAULIS, BRIAN E.,** conductor, composer; b. Cleve., Ohio, Oct. 31, 1961; s. Edward George and Colleen Gahagen Paulis; m. Deborah Gail Anderson, Aug. 18, 1990; children: Thomas Edward, James Jonathan, Lauren Gail. MusB, Baldwin-Wallace Coll., 1985; MusM, New Eng. Conservatory of Music, 1988; PhD, Kent State U., 1996. Music dir. Bethany United Ch. of Christ, Cuyahoga Falls, Ohio, 1990—94; choral arranging instr. U. Akron, Ohio, 1995; music theory, composition instr. Kent State U., Ohio, 1991—95; dir. music First Congl. Ch. of Hudson, Ohio, 1994—2000, First United Meth. Ch., Cuyahoga Falls, Ohio, 2000—. Artistic dir., founder Sacred Music Series at First Congl., Hudson, Ohio, 1995—2000; artistic dir. Arts Series at First UMC, Cuyahoga Falls, Ohio, 2000—. Dir. Epworth Youth Tour Choir, Cuyahoga Falls, Ohio, 2000—06. Mem.: Am. Choral Directors Assn. Avocations: golf, travel. Office: First United Meth Ch 245 Portage Trail Cuyahoga Falls OH 44221 Office Phone: 330-923-5241. Office Fax: 330-923-5241. E-mail: bepaulis@firstchurchcf.org.

**PAULISON, R. DAVID (ROBERT DAVID PAULISON),** federal agency administrator; b. Miami, 1947; m. Kathy Paulison. BA, Fla. Atlantic U.; postgrad., Harvard U. Rescue firefighter, lt., battalion comdr., dist. chief ops., divsn. chief, asst. chief, deputy dir. Miami-Dade Fire Rescue Dept., chief, 1992—2001; adminstr. US Fire Adminstrn. US Dept. Homeland Security, Emmitsburg, Md., 2001—, dir. preparedness divsn. Emergency Preparedness & Response Directorate (FEMA) Washington, 2003—05, acting under sec. of emergency preparedness & response, 2005—06, acting under sec. for Fed. Emergency Mgmt. (FEMA dir.), 2005—06; under sec. for Fed. Emergency Mgmt. (FEMA dir.) US Dept Homeland Security, Washington, 2006—. Pres. Internat. Assn. Fire Chiefs, 1996—97. Named Fire Chief of the Year, State of Fla., 1993; named to The Miami-Dade Community Coll. Hall of Fame; recipient Motorola Mason Lankford Fire Svc. Leadership award, Congl. Fire Svc. Inst., 2004, Leroy Collins Disting. Alumni award. Office: FEMA US Dept Homeland Security Fed Ctr Plz 500 C St SW Rm 828 Washington DC 20472*

**PAULISSEN, JAMES PETER,** retired pediatrician, county official; b. Chgo., Aug. 14, 1928; s. Joseph Edward and Louise Catherine (Muno) P.; m. Lorraine Antoinette Polly, Sept. 11, 1954; children: Linda, Steven, Mark, Daniel. Student, Loyola U., 1946-49, MD cum laude, 1953; MPH, Johns Hopkins U., 1966. Diplomate Am. Bd. Pediat. Intern Milw. County Hosp., 1953-54; resident Milw. Children's Hosp., 1957-58; practice medicine specializing in pediats. Wauwatosa Children's Clinic, Wis., 1959-65; pediat. fellow Johns Hopkins U., 1965—66; chief Bur. Maternal and Child Health Ill. Dept. Pub. Health, Springfield, 1966-70, chief Divsn. Family Health, 1970-

76; exec. dir. DuPage County Health Dept., Wheaton, Ill., 1976-93. Bd. dirs. mem. exec. com. Suburban Cook-DuPage Health Sys. Agy., Oak Park, Ill., 1976-82; bd. dirs., past pres. Comprehensive Health Coun. Met. Chgo., 1977-87; dir. Sr. Home Sharing, Inc., Wheaton, 1981-83; mem. Ill. Commn. on Children, 1971-85, vice chmn., 1983-85; chmn. Ill. Perinatal Adv. Com., 1981-84, mem., 1981-92; mem. Ill. Sch. Health Adv. Com., 1982-93, Gov.'s Adv. Coun. on Devel. Disabilities, 1973-76, Ill. Med. Determinations Bd., 1985-93; vice chmn. Ill. Pub. Health Advisors, 1988-91; mem. adv. bd. divsn. Svcs. Crippled Children U. Ill., 1986-94; trustee DuPage County Med. Found., 1976-82, 86-92, 1999-2006, treas. 2002-06; bd. dirs. DuPage Cmty. Clinic, 1993—, Cmty. Nursing Svc. of DuPage, 1993-99, vice chair, 1997-99; mem. cmty. health com. Ctrl. DuPage Health Sys., 1993-98; del. White House Conf. for Children, 1970. Capt. USAF, 1954-56. Recipient Dir.'s award for Sustained Excellence Ill. Dept. Pub. Health, 1988, Ill. Pediatrician of Yr. award, 1992, Humanitarian award DuPage County Health Planning Coun., 1994. Fellow Am. Acad. Pediats. (exec. com. Ill. chpt. 1978-81, sec. 1988-92), APHA, Am. Coll. Preventive Medicine; mem. Ill. Pub. Health Assn. (pres. 1977-78, Disting. Svc. award 1983), Ill. Assn. Maternal and Child Health (pres. 1975-76). Avocation: model building. Home: 28w660 Hawthorne Ln West Chicago IL 60185-2472

**PAULL, KATHARINE EVERHART,** language educator; b. Balt., Mar. 21, 1940; d. Edgar Shuman and Helen Elsenhans Everhart; children: Robert Christian, Julia Elizabeth. BA, Dickinson Coll., 1962; MA in Tchg., U. N.C., 1968. Cert. tchr. Calif., 1969. Tchr. Gar-Field H.S., Woodbridge, Va., 1962—63, Swansboro H.S., NC, 1964—65, Durham H.S., 1967—68, Sylmar H.S., Calif., 1969—2002; literacy coach UCLA/L.A. Unified Sch. Dist., 2002—. Presenter Calif. Writing Project, L.A., 1980—; dept. chair Sylmar H.S., 1974—85; mentor tchr. L.A. Unified Sshool Dist., 1990—97; mem. Calif. Assessment Program Writing Devel. Team, Berkeley, 1988—89; bd. mem. Southland Coun. Tchrs. English, L.A., 1990—92. Contbr. poetry to Wednesday, a poetry mag. Chair water com. Kagel Canyon Civic Assn., Calif., 1979—. Recipient H.S. English Tchr. Yr., LA City Tchrs. English, 1987. Mem.: ASCD, Am. Fedn. Tchrs., Calif. Assn. Tchrs. English. Democrat. Achievements include research in Teacher Researcher - UCLA; Chair - Conference of the Living Tree. Avocations: hiking, reading, writing, gardening, travel. Home: 12215 Park Trail Kagel Canyon CA 91342

**PAULL, MATTHEW H.,** food service executive; BA, U. Ill., M in Acctg. Ptnr. Ernst & Young; with McDonald's Corp., 1993—, v.p. corp. tax, sr. v.p. fin. Oak Brook, Ill., 1999—2001, exec. v.p., 2001—04, CFO, 2005—, sr. exec. v.p., 2004—. Adv. dir. bd. dirs. McDonalds Corp., 1999—2000, mem. chmns. coun., mem. Japan Bd., 2002—03; mem. adv. coun. Fed. Res. Bank, Chgo.; bd. dirs. Best Buy Co., Inc. Active Kohl Children's Mus., Chgo. Symphony Orch.; trustee Ravinia Festival Assn.; bd. mem. Loyola Ronald McDonald House. Office: McDonalds Corp McDonalds Plaza Oak Brook IL 60523*

**PAULL, RICHARD ALLEN,** geologist, educator; b. Madison, Wis., May 20, 1930; s. Ethra Harold and Martha (Schaller) P.; m. Rachel Kay Krebs, Mar. 6, 1954; children: Kay Marie, Lynn Ellen, Judith Ann. BS, U. Wis., 1952, MS, 1953, PhD, 1957. Party chief Pan Am. Petroleum Co., 1955-57; research group leader Jersey Prodn. Research Co., 1957-62; mem. faculty U. Wis.-Milw., 1962-97, chmn. dept. geol. scis., 1962-66, prof., 1966-97, prof. emeritus, 1997—. Cons. in field, 1966— Author books, papers in field. Co-exec. sec. NAGT/USGS/AASG-Coop. Summer Field Tng. Program, 1994-99. Served with USAF, 1953-55. Recipient Amoco Disting. Tchg. award, 1975 Fellow Geol. Soc. Am. (chmn. ann. meeting 1970, tech. program com. 1970, 77, membership com. 1977-80, chmn. 1980); mem. Am. Assn. Petroleum Geologists (chmn. sci. fair award com. 1980, membership com. 1981-87, vis. petroleum geologists com. 1982-87, pub. affairs com. 1982-85), Soc. Econ. Paleontologists and Mineralogists, Nat. Assn. Geology Tchrs. (v.p. 1976-77, pres. 1977-78), Am. Geol. Inst. (governing bd. 1977-79, sec. and exec. com. 1986-88. Home: 1657 W Canal Ct Littleton CO 80120-4515 Personal E-mail: rocdox@comcast.net.

**PAULOS, JOHN ALLEN,** mathematics educator, writer; b. Denver, July 4, 1945; s. Peter George and Helen (Sanavas) P.; m. Sheila Schwartz, Aug. 12, 1972; two children. PhD in Math., U. Wis., 1974. Prof. math. Temple U., Phila., 1973—. Spkr. in field; adj. prof. journalism Columbia U. Author: Mathematics & Honor, 1980, I Think Therefore I Laugh, 1985, Innumeracy, 1989, Beyond Numeracy, 1991, A Mathematician Reads the Newspaper, 1995 (100 Best Nonfiction Books of Century Random House Modern Libr.), Once Upon a Number, 1998 (Best Book of 1998, L.A. Times), A Mathematician Plays the Stock Market, 2004; columnist ABCNews.com, the Guardian; mem. editl. bd. Philadelphia Daily News; contbr. book reviews, columns in newspapers, sci. papers. Notable TV appearances include: The NewsHour with Jim Lehrer, 20/20, Larry King Live, Late Night with David Letterman. Recipient Pub. Understanding Sci. and Tech. award, AAAS, 2003. Fellow Com. Sci. Investigation of Claims of the Paranormal; mem. Math. Assn. Am., Assn. for Symbolic Logic, Authors' Guild. Office: Temple Univ Dept Math Philadelphia PA 19122 Business E-Mail: paulos@math.temple.edu.

**PAULOSE, RACHEL,** prosecutor; Grad., U. Minn. Litigator Dorsey & Whitney; US atty. dist. Minn. US Dept. Justice, 2006—. Bd. mem. Nat. Asian-Am. Bar Assn. Office: US Attys Ofice 600 US Courthouse 300 S Fourth St Minneapolis MN 55415*

**PAULSEN, BRIAN OLIVER,** art educator, artist; b. Seattle, Mar. 29, 1941; s. Edward and Sylvia Paulsen; m. Dianne C. Coulter, Sept. 1963; children: Geoffrey E., Erica L. Knudsvig. BA, U. Wash., 1963; MFA, Wash. State U., 1966. Asst. prof. Chico (Calif.) State Coll., 1966—71; sessional instr. U. Calgary, Canada, 1971—73; prof. U. ND, Grand Forks, 1973—, Chester Fritz disting. prof., 1990. Vis. artist 12 venues; juror nat. art exhbns. 86 one-man shows, more than 1000 group exhbns., more than 200 invitational exhibits. Artist fellowship award, Nat. Endowment Arts, Washington, 1981—82. Mem.: Nat. Acad. Design. Avocations: photography, biking. Business E-Mail: brian_paulsen@und.nodak.edu.

**PAULSEN, FRANK ROBERT,** college dean emeritus; b. Logan, Utah, July 5, 1922; s. Frank and Ella (Ownby) P.; m. Marye Lucile Harris, July 31, 1942; 1 son, Robert Keith; m. Lydia Ransier Lowry, Nov. 1, 1969. BS, Utah State U., 1947, MS, U. Utah, 1948, Ed.D., 1956, Kellogg Found. postdoctoral fellow, U. Oreg., 1958; Carnegie Found. postdoctoral fellow, U. Mich., 1959-60. High sch. prin., Mt. Emmons, Utah, 1948-51; supt. schs. Cokeville, Wyo., 1951-55; from asst. prof. to assoc. prof. edn. U. Utah, 1955-61; prof. edn., dean Sch. Edn. U. Conn., 1961-64; dean Coll. Edn. U. Ariz., Tucson, 1964-84, dean emeritus, prof. emeritus higher edn., 1984—. Scholar-in-residence Fed. Exec. Inst., Charlottesville, Va., 1970; Disting. prof. edn. U. Bridgeport, summer 1972; dir. Am. Capital Growth Fund, Am. Series Portfolio Stock Co., Houston, Am. Gen. Equity Fund, Am. Capital Bond Fund, Am. Capital Convertible Securities Fund, Am. Capital Exch. Fund, Am. Series Portfolio Co., Am. Capital Income Trust; exec. com. New Eng. Coun. Advancement Sch. Adminstrn., 1960-64; trustee Common Sense Trust Co., Houston. Author: The Administration of Public Education in Utah, 1958, Contemporary Issues in American Education, 1966, American Education: Challenges and Images, 1967, Changing Dimensions in International Education, 1968, Higher Education: Dimensions and Directions, 1969, also numerous articles. Trustee Joint Council Econ. Edn., 1962-70; v.p., dir. Southwestern Coop. Ednl. Lab., 1965-67; dir. chmn. Nat. League for Nursing, 1967-69, mem. com. on perspectives, 1966-72; dir., chmn. exec. com. ERIC Clearinghouse on Tchr. Edn., 1968-70; dir. Tucson Mental Health Center, 1968-70. Served with AUS, 1942-46, PTO. Mem. Aerospace Med. Assn., Am. Assn. Sch. Adminstrs., Am. Acad. Polit. and Social Sci., Utah Acad. Letters, Arts and Scis., Ariz. Acad., Am. Assn. Colls. Tchrs. Edn. (Conn. liaison officer 1962-64, mem. studies com. 1962-68, dir.), Ariz. Assn. Colls. Tchr. Edn. (pres. 1972-80), AAAS, Am. Ednl. Research Assn., Kappa Delta Pi, Pi Sigma Alpha, Pi Gamma Mu., Phi Delta Kappa. Lodges: Rotary.

**PAULSEN, SERENUS GLEN,** architect, educator; b. Spooner, Wis., July 27, 1917; s. Serenus Justin and Edna Anne (Dalton) P.; m. Virginia C. Habel, Jan. 26, 1944; children: Thomas J., Nancy Lee (Mrs. John Marshall). Student, U. Ill., 1938-42; B.Arch. cum laude, U. Pa., 1947; Diploma in Architecture and City Planning, Royal Acad. Art, Stockholm, 1948. With Carroll, Grisdale and Van Alan (Architects), Phila., 1946-47, Eero Saarinen & Assos., Bloomfield Hills, Mich., 1949-51, 53-57; chief designer Reisner & Urbahn (Architects), N.Y.C., 1951-52; archtl. coordinator Knoll Assos., N.Y.C., 1952-53; prin. Glen Paulsen Assos., Birmingham, Mich., 1958-69; prin., v.p. Tarapata-MacMahon-Paulsen Assos., Inc. (Architects), Bloomfield Hills, 1969-77; pres. Cranbrook Acad. Art, head dept. architecture, 1966-70; prof., chmn. Masters Program in Architecture U. Mich., 1976-78, Emil Lorch prof. architecture, 1982-85, prof. emeritus, 1985—. Mem. Nat. Com. on Urban Planning and Design, 1971-72; archtl. commn. U. Wash., Seattle, 1968-76 (Recipient 3d prize Bi-Nat. Competition for Design Rainbow Center Plaza, Niagara Falls, N.Y. 1972). Gov. emeritus Cranbrook Acad. Art. Served with C.E. USAAF, 1942-46. Fellow AIA (honor awards Detroit chpt. for Shapero Hall of Pharmacy 1965, Our Shepherd Lutheran Ch. 1966, Ford Life Sci. Bldg. 1967, Birney Elementary Sch., Detroit 1971, Fed. Bldg., Ann Arbor, Mich. 1978, gold medal for 1980 Detroit chpt.); mem. Mich. Soc. Architects, (Robert F. Hastings award 1985). Home: 1101 Silver Maples Dr Chelsea MI 48118-1187

**PAULSEN, VIVIAN,** editor; b. Salt Lake City, May 10, 1942; d. Paul Herman and Martha Oline (Blattmann) P. BA, Brigham Young U., 1964, postgrad., 1965, U. Grenoble, France, 1966. Cert. tchr., Utah. Tchr. French Granite Sch. Dist., Salt Lake City, 1966-67; assoc. editor New Era mag., Salt Lake City, 1970-82; mng. editor Friend mag., Salt Lake City, 1982—. Am. Field Service scholar, 1959; grad. fellow Brigham Young U., 1964-66 Republican. Mem. Ch. of Jesus Christ of Latter-day Saints Office: The Friend 50 E North Temple # F23 Salt Lake City UT 84150-0002

**PAULSON, BELDEN HENRY,** political scientist, educator; s. Henry Thomas and Evelina (Belden) P.; m. Louise D. Hill, Jan. 9, 1954; children: Eric, Steven AB, Oberlin Coll., 1950; MA, U. Chgo., 1955, PhD, 1962. With Italian svc. mission, Naples, 1950-53; organizer Homeless European Land Program, Sardinia, 1957—59; with UN High Commn. Refugees, Rome, 1960—61; mem. faculty U. Wis., Milw., 1962—; prof. polit. sci. U. Wis. ext., 1969—; founder and chmn. Ctr. Urban Cmty. Devel., 1967—90; co-founder and pres. High Wind Assn. for Modeling Cmty. for Sustainable Living, 1980—; pres. Plymouth Inst., 1995—98. Hon. rsch. prof. Internat. Tech. and Economy Inst, Inst. for Sci. of Scis., Shanghai, China, 1990—; mem. edn. task force Pres.'s Coun. on Sustainable Devel., 1995-98; co-founder Global Learning Ctr., 1998-2004 Author: The Searchers, 1966; also articles Served with USNR, 1945-46 Findhorn Found. fellow; grantee Social Sci. Rsch. Coun., 1967-68; recipient Lifetime Disting. Achievement award Oberlin Coll., 2004 Mem.: World Future Soc. Home: W7122 County Rd U Plymouth WI 53073-4538 Office: U Wis Dept Urban Cmty Devel 161 W Wisconsin Ave Fl 6 Milwaukee WI 53203-2602 Office Phone: 414-227-3270. E-mail: paulson@dotnet.com.

**PAULSON, BERNARD ARTHUR,** oil industry executive, consultant; b. Lakeview, Mich., July 12, 1928; s. Arthur Bernard and Genevieve Talbard (Bushley) P.; m. Joan Lee Curtiss, Dec. 4, 1954; children: James, Joseph (dec.), Ann, Thomas (dec.), Bernadette, Patricia, Steven. BS in Chem. Engring., Mich. State U.-East Lansing, 1949. Registered prof. engr., Tex. Process engr. Mid-West Refineries Inc., Alma, Mich., 1949-57; plant mgr. Kerr-McGee Corp., Cleve. and Wynnewood, Okla., 1957-66; v.p. Coastal States Petrochemical, Corpus Christi, Tex., 1966-71, Koch Industries Inc., St. Paul and Wichita, 1971-88, cons. Corpus Christi, Tex., 1988-94; pres. Koch Refining Co., Wichita, 1981-88; chmn. The Automation Group Inc.; chmn., CEO The Inspection Group Inc. CEO Tor Minerals Internat., 1997, also bd. dirs; dir. Orion Refining Corp., 1999—. Chmn., pres. Cleve. Area Hosp. Corp., 1962; bd. dirs. Ada Wilson Hosp. Found., Driscoll Hosp. Found., Coastal Bend Cmty. Found.; pres. Corpus Christ Bd. Trade; commr. Port of Corpus Christi Authority, vice chmn., 1997. 1st lt. USAF, 1955-57. Recipient Claud R. Erickson Disting. Alumnus award Mich. State U., 1994. Mem. AIChE (fuels and petrochem. award 1989), Nat. Petroleum Refiners Assn., Refining Am. Petroleum Inst., Wichita Area C. of C. (bd. dirs.), Bd. Trade, Corpus Christi Town Club (bd. dirs.), Elks. Home and Office: Tor Minerals 3 Ocean Park Dr Corpus Christi TX 78404-1600

**PAULSON, DAVID FREEMAN, JR.,** lawyer; b. Durham, NC, Sept. 16, 1964; s. David Freeman and Patricia Baker Paulson; m. Mary Beth Hansgen, May 29, 1993; children: Grier, Freeman. BA, Duke U., Durham, 1987; JD, MBA, Wake Forest U., Winston-Salem, NC, 1991. Bar: NC 1991. Assoc. Murchison, Guthrie et al, Charlotte, NC, 1991—92; ptnr. Murchison & Paulson, PLLC, Charlotte, 1992—95, Smith Helms Mulliss & Moore, LLP, Charlotte, 1995—2002, Helms Mulliss & Wicker, PLLC, Raleigh, NC, 2002—. Bd. dirs. Durham Nativity Sch., 2002—; trustee U. NC Ctr. Pub. TV, Research Triangle Park, 2004—, U. NC Ctr. Pub. TV Found., Research Triangle Park, 2004—. Mem.: NC Bar Assn. Office: Helms Mulliss & Wicker PLLC 2600 Two Hannover Sq Raleigh NC 27601

**PAULSON, DONALD ROBERT,** chemistry professor; b. Oak Park, Ill., Sept. 6, 1943; s. Robert Smith and Florence Teresa (Beese) P.; m. Elizabeth Anne Goodwin, Aug. 20, 1966; children: Matthew, Andrew. BA, Monmouth Coll., 1965; PhD, Ind. U., 1968. Asst. prof. chemistry Calif. State U., Los Angeles, 1970-74, assoc. prof., 1974-78, prof., 1979—, chmn. dept., 1982-90. Vis. prof. U. B.C., Vancouver, Can., 1977-78, U. Sussex, Brighton, Eng., 1984-85. Author: Alicyclic Chemistry, 1976; contbr. articles to profl. jours. Named Outstanding Prof., Calif. State U., Los Angeles, 1978, 84, 96. Mem. Am. Chem. Soc., Chem. Soc. (London), InterAm. Photochem. Soc., Nat. Assn. Sci. Tchrs., Sigma Xi. Democrat. Episcopalian. Avocations: photography, hiking, soccer. Home: 497 E California Blvd Apt 203 Pasadena CA 91106-3789 Office: Calif State U Dept Chemistry 5151 State University Dr Los Angeles CA 90032-4226 Office Phone: 323-343-2332. Business E-Mail: dpaulso@calstatela.edu.

**PAULSON, GWEN O. GAMPEL,** government relations consultant, life and leadership coach; b. Detroit, Mar. 16, 1947; d. Maurice V. and Lilyan Victor; div.; children: Jill Susan, Mindy Beth; m. Jerome A. Paulson, July 2, 1989. BA, Mich. State U., 1966; MA, Wayne State U., 1974; postgrad., U. Mich., 1981; cert. in Leadership Coaching, Georgetown U., 2005. Lectr. Oakland U. Mich., 1979—80, U. Mich., Ann Arbor, 1981; legis. asst. U.S. Rep. Pete Stark, Washington, 1982—85; mem. profl. staff, ways and means health subcom. U.S. Ho. of Reps., Washington, 1985—89; v.p. for health Capitol Assocs., Washington, 1989—90; pres. Congl. Cons., Washington, 1990—2005, Coaching and Cons. LLC, 2005—. Author: Women and the Structure of Society, 1984. Edward S. Beck fellow U. Mich., Ann Arbor, 1978-79; Rackham Dissertation grant U. Mich., Ann Arbor, 1980. Mem. Coun. for Excellence Govt., Bus. and Profl. Women, Fedn. Am. (co-chair 1999-2001), Internat. Coaching Fedn., Phi Alpha Theta, Tau Sigma Avocations: collecting contemporary glass, travel, history, politics, reading. Office: Coaching and Consulting LLC 1113 N Howard St Alexandria VA 22304-1627 Office Phone: 703-461-7683. Personal E-mail: gwencc@comcast.net.

**PAULSON, HANK (HENRY MERRITT PAULSON JR.),** secretary of the treasury, former diversified financial services company executive; b. Palm Beach, Fla., Mar. 28, 1946; s. Henry Merritt and Marianna (Gallaeur) P.; m. Wendy Judge, Sept. 6, 1969; children: Henry Merritt III, Amanda Clark. BA in English, Dartmouth Coll., 1968; MBA, Harvard U., 1970. Staff asst. to the asst. sec. def. (comptroller) US Dept. Def., Washington, 1970-72; staff asst. to Pres. Domestic Policy Coun. The White House, Washington, 1972-73; assoc. Goldman Sachs & Co., Chgo., 1974-77, v.p., 1977-82, ptnr. investment banking dept., 1982—, ptnr. in charge investment banking Midwest region, 1984-90, mgmt. com. co-head investment banking div., vice chmn., COO NYC, 1994—98, co-CEO, 1998—99; chmn., CEO The Goldman Sachs Group, Inc., NYC, 1999—2006; sec. US Dept. Treasury, Washington, 2006—. Mem. exec. com. NYC Investment Fund. Mem. adv. bd. J.L. Kellogg

Grad. Sch. of Mgmt., Northwestern U.; chmn. adv. bd. Tsinghua U. Sch. Econs. and Mgmt.; mem. governing bd. Indian Sch. Mgmt., chmn. The Nature Conservancy NCAA Scholar Athlete, 1967; named to 1st team All-Ivy, All New Eng., All-East; New Eng. Football Coaches' Selection as Outstanding Coll. Lineman, Div. I, New England, 1967 Mem. The Commercial Club (Chgo.), The Econ. Club (Chgo.), Chgo. Club, Phi Beta Kappa; bd. dirs. Peregrine Fund Inc. Republican. Mem. Christian Science Ch. Avocations: skiing, fishing, canoeing, tennis. Office: US Dept Treasury 1500 Pennsylvania Ave NW Rm 3330 Washington DC 20220*

PAULSON, JAMES MARVIN, retired engineering educator; b. Wausau, Wis., Jan. 1, 1923; s. Gustav Victor and Susanna (Dracy) P.; m. Marjorie Beulah Burton, May 11, 1946; children— Vicki Rae, Michael James. BS in Civil Engring, The Citadel, 1947; MS in Civil Engring, Ill. Inst. Tech., 1949; PhD, U. Mich., 1958. Registered profl. engr., Mich. Draftsman Wausau Iron Works, 1946; engr. Charles Whitney Cons. Engr., Milw., 1948-49; faculty Wayne State U., Detroit, 1949—, prof., 1961-85, chmn. dept. civil engring., 1967-72, assoc. dean Coll. Engring., 1973-83, prof. emeritus, 1985—; ret., 1985. V.p. Civil Engrs., Inc., 1954—; cons. in field. Served with AUS, 1943; Served with USMCR, 1943-46. Mem. ASCE (life), Mich. Soc. Profl. Engrs. (life), Am. Soc. for Engring. Edn., Sigma Xi, Tau Beta Pi, Chi Epsilon. Presbyterian. Home: PO Box 23 Greenbush MI 48738-0023

PAULSON, JEROME AVROM, pediatrician; b. Balt., July 31, 1949; s. Robert R. and Edna (Brenner) P.; m. Susan Miller, 1973 (div. 1986); m. Gwen Victor Gampel, July 2, 1989. BS in Biochemistry, U. Md., 1971; MD, Duke U., 1974. Diplomate Am. Bd. Med. Examiners. Resident in pediatrics Johns Hopkins Hosp., Balt., 1974-76, Sinai Hosp., Balt., 1976-77, fellow in ambulatory pediatrics, 1977-78; asst. prof. pediatrics Case Western Res. U., Cleve., 1978-86; dir. sci. rsch. and pub. policy devel. Joseph P. Kennedy Jr. Found., Washington, 1986-87; dir. pediatrics Regional Inst. for Children and Adolescents, Rockville, Md., 1987-89; clin. assoc. prof. pediatrics Georgetown U., Washington, 1987—; exec. dir. Research!America, Alexandria, Va., 1989-90; assoc. prof. medicine (formerly healthcare scis.) George Washington U., Washington, 1990—2002, assoc. prof. pediats., 1991—, fellow Ctr. Health Policy Rsch., 1991—98, assoc. prof. prevention and cmty. health, 1997—, assoc. rsch. prof. environ. and occupl. health, 2003—; co-dir. Mid-Atlantic Ctr. for Children's Health and the Environment George Washington U. Med. Ctr., 2000—. Mem. conf. on methodology and std. definitions for childhood injury rsch. Nat. Inst. Children & Human Devel., 1989; health adv. com. Congressman James Moran, 8th Congl. Dist., Va., 1992—94; mem. benefits working group Nat. Drinking Water Adv. Coun. EPA, 1989—99; adv. Health Pages, 1994—97; spl. asst. to dir. Nat. Ctr. for Environ. Health, Ctrs. for Disease Control, Washington, 1999—2001; Soros advocacy fellow Children's Environ. Health Network, 2000—02; bd. dirs. Crative Glass Ctr. Am. Author: Pediatrics: Review for New National Boards, 2000; contbr. articles to profl. jours., chpts. to books. Profl. adv. bd. Nat. Safety Town Ctr., Cleve., 1981-85; bd. dirs., pres. James Renwick Alliance, Washington, 1986-93, 95-98; bd. dirs. Jewish Social Svcs. Agy Greater Washington, 2002—, chmn. No. Va. com., 2002— Recipient Cert. for Ednl. and Pub. Policy Activity, Ohio State Senate/Ho. of Reps., 1985; Robert Wood Johnson Health Policy fellow, 1985-86, Soros Advocacy fellowship 2000-02. Fellow Am. Acad. Pediatrics; mem. Ambulatory Pediatric Assn. Jewish. Avocation: collecting contemporary american crafts. Office: CP & A Foggy Bottom 2141 K St NW # 401 Washington DC 20037-1866 Office Phone: 202-833-4543. Business E-Mail: jpaulson@cnmc.org.

PAULSON, KENNETH ALAN, editor; b. Chgo., Dec. 3, 1953; s. Knut Norman and Helen Elizabeth (Beardsley) P.; m. Peggy Jean Foot, June 12, 1976; children: Carrie Ann, David. BA in Journalism, U. Mo., 1975; JD, U. Ill., 1978. Bar: Ill., 1978, Fla. 1979. Reporter, bur. chief Fort Myers News-Press, Fla., 1978—80; metro editor to mng. editor Courier-News, Bridgewater, NJ, 1980—84; founding staff member USA Today, McLean, Va., 1982; editor Green Bay Press-Gazette, Wis., 1985—86; spl. asst./chief of staff to chmn. Gannett Co., 1986—88; exec. editor Florida Today, Brevard County, 1988—92; exec. editor, v.p. news Gannett Suburban Newspapers, White Plains, NY, 1992—96; exec. dir. 1st Amendment Ctr. Vanderbilt U., Nashville, 1997—2004; sr. v.p. Freedom Forum, Arlington, Va., 1997—2004; editor USA Today, McLean, Va., 2004—, USAToday.com. Adj. prof. Vanderbilt U. Law Sch.; host TV show Speaking Freely; trustee Freedom Forum Bd. Office: USA Today 7950 Jones Branch Dr Mc Lean VA 22108*

PAULSON, LORETTA NANCY, psychoanalyst; b. L.A., Nov. 5, 1943; d. Frank Morris and Rose (Kaufman) Fargo; m. Maurice Krasnow; 1 child, Kira. BA, U. So. Calif., 1966; MS in Social Work, Columbia U., N.Y.C., 1969; cert. psychoanalyst, C.G. Jung Inst., N.Y.C. LCSW; lic. clin. social worker, N.Y., Conn., N.J. Pvt. practice psychoanalysis, N.Y.C., 1976—; Past vice chmn. CGJ Inst. Tng. Bd. Mem. NASW (diplomate in clin. social work), Internat. Assn. for Analytical Psychology (past del., bd. dirs.), N.Y. Assn. for Analytic Psychology (past pres., past chair program com.). Conn. Soc. Clin. Social Work (com. on psychoanalysis), C.G. Jung Inst. Address: 334 W 86th St Apt 1A New York NY 10024-3130 Office Phone: 212-595-4111. E-mail: lnp222@aol.com.

PAULSON, PAUL JOSEPH, advertising executive; b. White Plains, NY, Sept. 25, 1932; s. Paul and Ann (Loughlin) P.; m. Kathryn P. Keeler, June 30, 1962; children: Thomas, Mark, Kathryn, John, Clifford. BSBA, Ohio State U., 1954; MBA, U. Pa., 1959. With Compton Advt. Inc., N.Y.C., 1959-78, mgmt. supr., 1965-78, sr. v.p., 1968-78, also dir.; pres., dir Doyle Dane Bernbach Inc., N.Y.C., 1978-83; pres., chief exec. officer Isidore & Paulson, Inc., N.Y.C., 1983-93; chmn., pres., CEO Paulson & Co. Mktg. Svcs., Greenwich, 1993—. Chmn. Mktg. Exec. Networking Group, 2000—03; mem. Ohio State U. Alumni Adv. Coun., 1982—; pres coun. mem. Ohio State U., 1993—. Author: Fundamentals of Consumer Goods Marketing, 1966. Chmn. Christmas for Underprivileged Children, N.Y.C., 1963—. Served to lt. (j.g.) USNR, 1955-58, MTO, ETO. Mem. Wharton Grad. Bus. Sch. Alumni Assn. (N.Y.C. club 1963-65, dir. 1972—), Ohio State U. Alumni Assn., Wharton Grad. Bus. Sch., Milbrook Owners Assn. (pres.). Clubs: N.Y. (dir.), Milbrook, Sigma Chi. Roman Catholic. Home: 45 W Brother Dr Greenwich CT 06830-6726 Office Phone: 203-629-3347. Personal E-mail: pjpmrktg@verizon.net, pjpmrktg@ortonline.net. E-mail: pjpmrktg@aol.com.

PAULSON, PETER JOHN, librarian, publishing executive; b. N.Y.C., Jan. 30, 1928; s. Peter John and Lillian Agnes Elaine (Neuman) P.; m. Josephine C. Bowen, Dec. 5, 1953 (dec. June 2002); children: David (dec. Apr. 1997), Debora. B.Social Scis. cum laude, CCNY, 1949; MA in History, Columbia, 1950; MA in L.S. SUNY, Albany, 1955. Library asst. N.Y. State Library, Albany, 1952-55, head, gift and exchange sect., 1955-65, head catalog sect., 1965-66, prin. librarian tech. services, 1966-71, dir., 1972-85; exec. dir. OCLC Forest Press, 1985-98. Adj. asst. prof. Library sci. State U. N.Y. at Albany, 1960-71; Adv. com. Ohio Coll. Library Center, 1970-71; adv. council to pub. printer depository libraries, 1972-77, chmn., 1975-77; com. for depository library service N.Y. State, 1960-70, chairperson, 1960-70; bd. dirs. Capital Dist. Libr. Coun., Nat. Info. Standards Orgn., N.E. Document Conservation Ctr. Mem. ALA (chmn. com. on legislation 1980-82, pres. state library assn. sect. 1982-83), N.Y. Library Assn. (pres. 1975), Hudson-Mohawk Library Assn. (v.p. 1964), SUNY-OCLC Network (governing bd. 1980-82), Phi Beta Kappa. Home: 24 Tillinghast Ave Albany NY 12204-2312 Office Phone: 518-465-3103.

PAULSON, RAYMOND ARNOLD, engineering executive; b. Eagle Rock, Calif., Dec. 29, 1921; s. Arnold Edwin and Clara (Martin) P.; m. Beverly Doris, Sept. 21, 1941; children: Larry, Jerry, Celeste. JD, Calif. Coll. Law, 1966; postgrad., Citrus Coll., Nat. U., U. S.C. Law instr. US Armed Forces Inst.; dir., mgr. nat maj. mfr., prodr. first tactical army missile The Corporal, 1959; sales mgr., asst. dir. So. Calif. Credit Bur.; engr. designer radiation and chem. evaluation test labs. USAF; dir.; mgr. electro-mech. bus.; founder Calif. Coll. Law; pres. chmn. bd. Paulson Internat. Corp., 1971-90, ret., hon. chmn., 1990—; pres World Trust Agy. (div. Paulson Devel. Corp.); founder Paulson Products Co.; sole proprietor Paulson Co.; established pvt. trust Paulson

Trust; established Guatemala Pvt. Sector Country Trust Fund. Devel., instr. exec. leadership tng. program dept. adult edn. Baldwin Pk. Schs.; founder Paulson Zero Emission Energy Rsch. Found. and lab. Talent locator and stage mgr. "I Love Lucy Show"; designer, assoc. dir. World Internat. Air and Space Show, 1995, Sky Harbor and McCarron Airports, Phenix. World Air and Space Tours; assoc. designer thermal battery and developer 1st semi-perpetual electric vehicle; pioneered color telecasting; 1st color stage mgr. with Carlton Winkler-Ed Wynn on Union Pacific show Sta. CBS-TV; joint originator USMC Christmas program for underprivileged kids Toys for Tots; surveyor, designer congress-approved US Canal, Brownsville, Tex., Nat. City, San Diego; designer Direct Fly by Wire Flight Control Sys.; mfr. 1st all composite single engine bullet proof two place jet spacecraft in world Mach 3 Plus; designer, developer VAC-PAC All Purpose Shipping Container for ship, rail and truck; designer, prodr. semi-perpetual self-contained charging sys. for electric vehicle battery sources, containers and vehicles too way sea level water way; designed concept for congress-approved Gulfo-Pacific Canal, Mex.; designer-mfr. pacemaker cs. for MedTronics Leadership tng. dir. Boy Scouts Am., Monte Vista dist.; founding mem. Air-Space Mus. Smithsonian Instn., 1994. B-29 radar navaigator pilot USAAF, 1944—45, WWII, Hiroshima Atomic Bombing and Nagaski. Decorated Air Medal and Battle Stars with presdl. citation; recipient Merit award, div. rsch. and sci. guidance L.A. County Supt. Schs. Mem. TV Acad. Arts and Sci. (co-originator, life assoc. mem.). Office: Paulson Co Internat World Trust Agy PO Box 4369 Covina CA 91723-4369 Office Phone: 626-332-4346. Office Fax: 626-332-4346.

PAULSON, RONALD HOWARD, language educator, humanities educator; b. Bottineau, N.D., May 27, 1930; s. Howard Clarence and Ethel (Tvete) P.; m. Barbara Lee Appleton, May 25, 1957 (div. 1982); children: Andrew Meredith, Melissa Katherine. BA, Yale U., 1952, PhD, 1958. Instr. U. Ill., 1958-59, from asst. to assoc. prof., 1959-63; prof. English Rice U., Houston, 1963-67, Johns Hopkins U., Balt., 1967-75, chmn. dept., 1968-75, Andrew W. Mellon prof. humanities, 1973-75, Mayer prof. humanities, 1984—2005, chmn. dept., 1985-91; prof. English Yale U., New Haven, 1975-84, Thomas E. Donnelly prof., 1980-84, Ward Phillips lectr., 1978, Alexander lectr., 1979, Brown and Haley lectr., 1979, Hodges lectr., 1980. Author: Theme and Structure in Swift's Tale of a Tub, 1960, Fielding, 1962, Hogarth's Graphic Works, 1965, rev. edits., 1970, 89, Fictions of Satire, 1967, Satire and the Novel, 1967, (with Thomas F. Lockwood) Fielding: The Critical Heritage, 1969, Satire: Modern Essays in Criticism, 1971, Hogarth: His Life, Art and Times, 1971, Rowlandson: A New Interpretation, 1972, Emblem and Expression: Meaning in Eighteenth Century English Art, 1975, The Art of Hogarth, 1975, Popular and Polite Art in the Age of Hogarth and Fielding, 1979, Literary Landscape: Turner and Constable, 1982, Book and Painting: Shakespeare, Milton and the Bible, 1983, Representations of Revolution, 1983, Breaking and Remaking, 1989, Figure and Abstraction in Contemporary Painting, 1990, Hogarth Vol. 1: The Making of the Modern Moral Subject, 1991, Hogarth Vol. 2: High Art and Low, 1991, Hogarth Vol. 3: Art and Politics, 1993, The Beautiful, Novel, and Strange: Aesthetics and Heterodoxy, 1996, Don Quixote in England: The Aesthetics of Laughter, 1998; editor: The Analysis of Beauty, 1997, The Life of Henry Fielding: A Critical Biography, 2000, Hogarth's Harlot: Sacred Parody in Enlightenment England, 2003; mem. editl. bd.: English Lit. History, 1967-2005, sr. editor, 1985-2002. 1st fellow AUS, 1952-54. Sterling fellow 1957-85, Guggenheim fellow 1965-66, 1986-87, NEH fellow 1977-78. Fellow Am. Acad. Arts and Scis.; mem. Am. Soc. for 18th Century Studies (pres. 1986-87). Home: 2722 Saint Paul St Baltimore MD 21218-4332 Office: Johns Hopkins U Dept English Baltimore MD 21218

PAULSON JR., HENRY MERRITT See PAULSON, HANK

PAULSTON, CHRISTINA BRATT, linguistics educator; b. Stockholm, Dec. 30, 1932; arrived in US, 1951; d. Lennart and Elsa Bratt; m. Rolland G. Paulston, July 26, 1963; children: Christopher-Rolland, Ian Rollandsson. BA, Carleton Coll., 1953; MA in English and Comparative Lit., U. Minn., 1955; Ed.D., Columbia U., 1966. Cert. tchr., Minn. Tchr. Clara City and Pine Island High Schs., Minn., 1955-60, Am. Sch. of Tangier, Morocco, 1960-62, Katrineholm Allmanna Laroverk, Katrineholm, Sweden, 1962-63, East Asian Library, Columbia U., N.Y.C., 1963-64; asst. instr. Tchrs. Coll., Columbia U., 1964-66; instr. U. Punjab, Chandigarh, India, summer 1966, Pontificia Universidad Catolica Del Peru, Lima, 1966-67; cons. Instituto Linguistico de Verano, Lima, 1967-68; asst. prof. linguistics U. Pitts., 1969-75, prof., 1975-99, prof. emerita, tchg. pro bono, 1999—, asst. dir. English Lang. Inst., 1969-70, dir. English Lang. Inst., 1970-97, acting dir. Lang. Acquistion Inst., fall 1971, acting chmn. dept. gen. linguistics, 1974-75, chmn., 1975-89. Apptd. internat. advisor in sociolinguistics to Summer Inst. of Linguistics, 1997. Author numerous books and articles on linguistics. Recipient research award Am. Ednl. Research Assn., 1980; Fulbright-Hays grantee, Uruguay, 1985. Mem. Assn. Tchrs. English to Speakers of Other Langs. (2d v.p., conv., chmn. 1972, exec. com. 1973-75, rsch. com. 1973-75, 78-80, chmn. 1973-75, 1st v.p. 1975, pres. 1976), Linguistics Soc. Am. (com. linguistics and pub. interest 1973-77), Internat. Assn. Tchrs. of English as a Fgn. Lang., Am. Coun. on Tchg. of Fgn. Langs., MLA (exec. com. lang. and soc. 1975-76), Ctr. Applied Linguistics (trustee 1976-81, exec. com. 1980, publs. com. 1981, rsch. com. 1981). Democrat. Episcopalian. Office: U Pitts Linguistics Pittsburgh PA 15260 Office Phone: 412-624-5900.

PAULU, FRANCES BROWN, retired international center administrator; b. Hastings, Minn., June 22, 1920; d. Thomas Andrew and Florence Ida (Tuttle) Brown; m. Burton Paulu, June 29, 1942; children: Sarah Leith Paulu Boittin, Nancy Jean Paulu Hyde, Thomas Brown BA magna cum laude, U. Minn., 1940. Case worker Family Welfare Assn., Mpls., 1943—45; interviewer County Health and Welfare Coun., Mpls., 1963; sch. social worker Project Head Start, Mpls., 1966; program dir. Minn. Internat. Ctr., Mpls., 1970—72, exec. dir., 1972—89; mem. tourism adv. com. City of Mpls., 1976—83; mem. adv. coun. Minn. World Trade Ctr., 1984—86. Pres. UN Rally, 1970—72; chmn. Mpls. Charter Commn., 1972—74; dir. Minn. World Trade Week, 1977—81; del. Nat. Coun. World Affairs, Taipei-Manila, 1988; coord. Voices from Around the World, 1996—2000; bd. dirs. Urban Coalition of Mpls., 1967—70; sec. Becketwood Coop., 2001—04; mgmt. team Minn. Awareness Project, 1982—89; participant Intercultural Comm. Project Japan, 1974; dir. Elder Learning Inst., 1995—2000. Fellow, U. Minn. Sch. Social Work, 1942—44; DeWitt Jennings Payne scholar, 1939—40. Mem.: LWV (pres. Mpls. chpt. 1967—69), Nat. Coun. Internat. Visitors (mem. exec. com. 1975—81, sec. 1976—77, v.p. 1977—78, leader fact-finding team N. Africa, Mid. East, India 1978, conf. chair 1989), Alliance Française (bd. dirs. 1991—94), People to People Internat. (Disting. Membership award 1987), UN Assn. Minn. (mem. adv. coun. 1979—92, sec. 1994—96, mem. adv. coun. 1996—2004), U. Minn. Women's Club (pres. 1992—94), Phi Beta Kappa, Lambda Alpha Psi, Alpha Omicron Pi. Home: 4300 W River Pkwy Apt 444 Minneapolis MN 55406-3681 E-mail: paulu005@umn.edu.

PAULUS, MICHAEL JOHN, government official, economist, bank executive; b. Port Washington, Wis., Feb. 18, 1957; s. John Peter and Elizabeth Jane (Streff) P.; m. Christine H. Kwon, Apr. 29, 2000; children: Alexandra, Veronica. BA, U. Wis. Milw., 1980 (cum laude); M.A. in Internat. Affairs, Columbia U., 1982. Economist Fed. Res. Bank, N.Y.C., 1982—85, sr. fgn. exch. trader, 1985—87, dep. chief fgn. exch. trader, spl. asst., 1987—88, mgr., chief fgn. exch. trader, 1988—90; v.p. capital markets group 1st Nat. Bank Chgo., 1990—92; v.p. treasury dept. Dresdner Bank, N.Y.C., 1992—94; v.p., mgr. instnl. mktg. desk Bank of Am., N.Y.C., 1994—97, v.p., mgr. sales and mktg., 1997—98, prin., mgr. mktg. and bus. devel. U.S. Fgn. Exch., 1998—2000; dep. asst. sec. for fed. fin. U.S. Dept. Treasury, Washington, 2000—01; mng. dir. head of U.K. investor sales, fgn. exch., global rates and currencies Citigroup, London, 2001—05, mng. dir., head pub. sector group Asia, Central, Hong Kong, 2005—. Fgn. Student scholar U. Freiburg, 1979; Sch. of Internat. Affairs fellow Columbia U., 1980-81, Internat. fellow Columbia U., 1981; recipient U.S. Dept. Treasury exceptional Svc. award, 2001. Mem. Mortar Bd., Phi Beta Kappa, Phi Kappa Phi. Roman Catholic.

Avocations: sports, history. Address: Apt 23-A The Summit 41-C Stubbs Rd Wanchai Hong Kong Fax: 852-2868-8911. Office Phone: 852-2868-7608. E-mail: michaeljpaulus@yahoo.com, michael.paulus@citigroup.com.

PAULY, EVELYN MAY ROCKWELL, physician, educator, dermatologist; b. Cin., May 5, 1924; d. George Edmond and Ruby Arvilla (Cleveland) R.; m. May 30, 1952 (dec. Nov. 1967); children: George G., Evan F., Thomas A., Florence T. AB, Western Coll., 1944; MD, U. Mich., 1948; cert. in acctg., Ind. U.-Purdue U., Ft. Wayne, 1989. Diplomate Am. Bd. Dermatology. Rsch. asst. bacteriology dept. U. Mich., Ann Arbor, 1946—47; intern Cin. Gen. Hosp., 1948-49, resident, 1949-52; pvt. practice Milford, Ohio, 1952-56; rsch. assoc. Kettering Lab., Cin., 1952-56; instr. dermatology Sch. Medicine U. Cin., 1952-56; cons. dermatology VA Hosp., Ft. Wayne, Ind., 1960-65; staff physician, specialist Ft. Wayne State Rehab. Ctr., 1965-87. Contbr. articles to profl. jours. Treas. AIDS Task Force, Ft. Wayne, 1990-92. Mem. Ind. Med. Soc., Ft. Wayne Med. Soc., Ind. CPA Soc. Republican. Home: 2304 Springfield Ave Fort Wayne IN 46805-1544 Personal E-mail: empauly@yahoo.com.

PAULY, JOHN EDWARD, retired anatomist; b. Elgin, Ill., Sept. 17, 1927; s. Edward John and Gladys (Myhre) P.; m. Margaret Mary Oberle, Sept. 3, 1949; children: Stephen John (dec.), Kathleen, Kathleen Anne, Mark Edward; m. Dola S. Thompson, Jan. 7, 2006. BS, Northwestern U., 1950; MS, Loyola U., Chgo., 1952, PhD, 1955. Grad. asst. gross anatomy Stritch Sch. Medicine, Loyola U., 1953-54, rsch. asst. anatomy Chgo. Med. Sch., 1952-54, rsch. instr., 1954-55, instr. in gross anatomy, 1955-57, assoc. in gross anatomy, 1957-59, asst. prof. anatomy, 1959-63, asst. to pres., 1960-62; assoc. prof. anatomy Tulane U. Sch. Medicine, 1963-67; prof., head dept. anatomy U. Ark. for Med. Scis., Little Rock, 1967-83, prof., head dept. physiology and biophysics, 1978-80, vice chancellor for acad. affairs and sponsored rsch., 1983-92, assoc. dean Grad. Sch., 1983-92, prof. anatomy, 1992-95, prof. emeritus, 1995—. Flight instr. Ctrl. Flying Svc., Little Rock, 1997—2002; tech. adviser Ency. Brit. Films, 1956; mem. safety and occupl. health study sect. Nat. Inst. Occupl. Safety and Health, Ctr. for Disease Control, 1975—79; vis. prof. faculty medicine Kuwait U., 1993, 94; vis. prof. anatomy U. Nev., 1996; chief of staff Ark. wing Civil Air Patrol, 2002—05. Author: (with Hans Elias) Human Microanatomy, 1960, 3d edit. 1966, (with Elias and E. Robert Burns) Histology and Human Microanatomy, 1978; editor: (with Lawrence E. Scheving and Franz Halberg) Chronobiology, 1974, (with Heinz von Mayersbach and Lawrence E. Scheving) Biological Rhythms in Structure and Function, 1981, The American Association of Anatomists, 1888-1987. Essays on the History of Anatomy in America and a Report on the Membership-Past and Present, 1987, (with Lawrence E. Scheving) Advances in Chronobiology, 1987, (with Dora K. Hayes and Russel J. Reiter) Chronobiology: Its Role in Clinical Medicine, General Biology and Agriculture, 1990; editor Am. Jour. Anatomy, 1980-92; co-mng. editor Advances in Anatomy, Embryology and Cell Biology, 1980-95; mem. adv. editl. bd. Internat. Jour. Chronobiology, 1973-83; contbr. articles to profl. jours. Chief of staff, mission pilot, instr. pilot and check pilot Ark. Wing Civil Air Patrol, 2002—05. With USNR, 1945—47. Recipient merit certificates AMA, 1953, 59; Bronze award Ill. Med. Soc., 1959; Lederle Med. Faculty award, 1966 Fellow AAAS; mem. Am. Assn. Anatomists (sec.-treas. 1972-80, pres. 1982-83, Centennial award 1987, Henry Gray award 1995), So. Soc. Anatomists (pres. 1971-72), Assn. Anatomy Chmn. (sec.-treas. 1969-71), Am. Physiol. Soc., Internat. Soc. Chronobiology, Pan-Am. Assn. Anatomy, Internat. Soc. Electrophysiol. Kinesiology, Internat. Soc. Steriology, Consejo Nacional de Profesores de Ciencias Morfologicas (hon.), Sigma Xi, Sigma Alpha Epsilon. Roman Catholic. Office Phone: 501-376-1729. Personal E-mail: flydoc1@comcast.net.

PAUP, MARTIN ARNOLD, securities investor, real estate investor; b. Seattle, Aug. 30, 1930; s. Clarence Jacob and Emaline Ethel (Lodestein) P.; m. Mary Jean Iske, Apr. 4, 1959; children: Barbara Ann Paup Soriano, Jennifer Marie, Elizabeth Paup-Byrnes. BS, U. Wash., 1952. Indsl. engr. Boeing Airplane Co., Seattle, 1954—60; owner Coopers Unfinished Furniture, Seattle, 1960—63; claims rep. Unigard Ins., Seattle, 1963—66; asst. benefits mgr. Equitable Life Assurance, Seattle, 1966—85; owner Paup Ventures, Seattle, 1974—, Paup Investment Co., Seattle, 1963—, Ella Paup Properties, Seattle, 1963—. Bd. dirs. Denny Regrade Property Owners' Assn., Seattle, Denny Regrade Bus. Assn., Seattle, First Ave. Assn., Seattle. Grantee, Seattle Dept. Cmty. Devel., 1980. Mem. Greenwood C. of C., Seattle Opera Guild. Democrat. Roman Catholic. Avocations: opera, travel, literature, history. Office Phone: 206-443-1548.

PAUPP, TERRENCE EDWARD, researcher; b. Joliet, Ill., Aug. 10, 1952; s. Edward Theodore and Mary Alice (Combs) P. BA in Social Scis., San Diego State U., 1974; ThM, Luth. Sch. Theology, 1978; JD, U. San Diego, 1990. Instr. philosophy San Diego City Coll., 1986-88, Southwestern Coll., Chula Vista, Calif., 1980-83; law clerk Sch. Law U. San Diego, 1987-88; law clerk Office of Atty. Gen., San Diego, 1988-89; rsch. assoc. Frank & Milchen, San Diego, 1989, Dougherty & Hildre, San Diego, 1990-95; sr. rsch.-assoc. Inst. for Ctrl. and Ea. European Studies, San Diego State U., 1996-98; sr. policy analyst Nuc. Age Peace Found., Santa Barbara, Calif., 2001—. Cons. Cmty. Reinvestment Act, San Diego, 1993-95; sr. rsch. assoc. Inst. Ctrl. and Ea. European Studies San Diego State U., 1994-95; adj. faculty in criminal justice and polit. sci. Nat. U.; cons., contbr. Inst. for Policy Studies, Washington, Interhemispheric Resource Ctr., N.Mex., The Ctr. of Concer, Washington, Global Exch., San Francisco. Author: Achieveing Inclusionary Governance: Advancing Peace and Devt. Iqument in First and Third World Nations, 2000; contbr. articles to newspapers. Appointed National Chancellor of the USA Internat. Assn. of Educators for World Peace, 2001; cons. Neighborhood House 5th Ave., 1994—95, PBS Frontline documentary The Nicotine Wars, 1994, Bethel Baptist Ch., 1994—95. Mem. ATLA, N.Y. Acad. Scis. Democrat. Lutheran. Avocation: tennis. Home: 10597 Porto Ct San Diego CA 92124-2015 E-mail: tpaupp@aol.com.

PAUSTIAN, PAUL ROBERT, library director; b. Kansas City, Mo., July 29, 1949; s. Paul Louis and Marguerite (Semstead) P.; m. Elisabeth Wilma Kalbach, June 12, 1971; children: Nathan Adam, Megan Elisabeth, Lauren Ingrid. BA, U. Mo., 1971; MA, U. Kans., 1975; postgrad., U. Toronto, 1977-78; MA, U. Mo., 1979. Libr. asst. U. Mo. Librs., Kansas City, Mo., 1972-73, 75-76, Columbia, Mo., 1978-79; asst. instr. U. Kans., Lawrence, 1973-75, grad. rsch. asst., 1976-77; asst. dir. Kansas City (Kans.) Pub. Libr., 1979; collections libr. U. Mo., Kansas City, 1979-82, asst. dir. librs., 1982-84; dir. libr. Wilkes Coll., Wilkes-Barre, Pa., 1984-88; dir. librs. U. S.D., Vermillion, 1988-91; dir. libr. Lebanon Valley Coll., Annville, Pa., 1991—. Contbr. articles to profl. jours. Mem. Twp. Planning Commn., North Lebanon (Pa.) Twp., 1992-94. Mem. ALA, Assn. Coll. and Rsch. Librs. (bd. dirs. Delaware Valley chpt. 1986-88, 93-99, chair bylaws com., 1996-2001, others), PALINET (fin. com. 1999-2001, chair spl. com. on bylaws 2001-04, trustee 2001-04, exec. com. 2002-04), Beta Phi Mu. Home: 821 Calico Ct Lebanon PA 17046-8254 Office: Lebanon Valley Coll Library Annville PA 17003

PAVALKO, ROBERT A., II, music educator; b. Youngstown, Ohio, May 6, 1979; s. Robert A and Judy A Pavalko; m. Susan M Reese, July 6, 2002. MusB in Edn., Youngstown State U., 2001, MS in Edn., 2006. Music K-12 Ohio Dept. of Edn., 2001, Pa. Dept. of Edn., 2003. Pvt. music tchr., Boardman, Ohio, 1997—; music tchr. St. Luke Sch., Boardman, Ohio, 2001—02, Kent City Sch. Dist., Ohio, 2002—03, Beaver Area Sch. Dist., Pa., 2003—04; quantum leaps coach Youth Employability Solutions, Inc., Youngstown, Ohio, 2004—05; music tchr. Lakeview (Ohio) Local Sch. Dist. 2005—. Scholar, First Cath. Slovak Ladies Assn., 2004, Youngstown State U., 2005—06. Mem.: NEA, Orgn. Am. Kodaly Educators, Ohio Edn. Assn., Ohio Music Educators Assn., Music Educators Nat. Conf., Golden Key, Omicron Delta Kappa (life), Order of Omega (life; pres. 2000—01), Sigma Phi Epsilon (life). R-Consevative. Roman Catholic. Avocation: music. Home: 670 Cathy Ann Dr Boardman OH 44512

**PAVALON, EUGENE IRVING,** lawyer; b. Chgo., Jan. 5, 1933; m. Lois M. Frenzel, Jan. 15, 1961; children: Betsy, Bruce, Lynn. BSL, Northwestern U., 1954, JD, 1956. Bar: Ill. 1956. Sr. ptnr. Pavalon, Gifford, Laatsch & Marino, Chgo., 1970—. Adj. prof. Northwestern U. Sch. Law; mem. com. on discovery rules Ill. Supreme Ct., 1981—; lectr., mem. faculty various law schs. Author: Human Rights and Health Care Law, 1980, Your Medical Rights, 1990; contbr. articles to profl. jours., chpts. in books. Mem. bd. overseers Inst. Civil Justice, Rand Corp., 1993-99; mem. vis. com. Northwestern U. Law Sch., 1990-96. Capt. USAF, 1956-59. Fellow Am. Coll. Trial Lawyers, Internat. Soc. Barristers, Internat. Acad. Trial Lawyers, Am. Bd. Trial Advs., Inner Cir. Advs., Roscoe Pound Found. (life mem., pres. 1988-90); mem. ABA, Chgo. Bar Assn. (bd. mgrs. 1978-79), Ill. Bar Assn., Ill. State Bar Assn., Ill. Trial Lawyers Assn. (pres. 1980-81, Lifetime Achievement award 1996), Trial Lawyers for Pub. Justice (founding mem., v.p. 1991-92, pres.-elect 1992-93, pres. 1993-94, Champion of Justice award 2000), ATLA (parliamentarian 1983-84, sec. 1984-85, v.p. 1985-86, pres.-elect 1986-87, pres. 1987, pres., bd. trustees 2003-05, Champion of Justice award 2003), Am. Bd. Profl. Liability Attys. (diplomate), Laureate, Ill. Acad. Lawyers, Chgo. Athletic Assn., Std. Club. Home: 1540 N Lake Shore Dr Chicago IL 60610-6684 Office: Pavalon Gifford et al 2 N La Salle St Chicago IL 60602-3702 Office Phone: 312-419-7400. Business E-Mail: pavalon@pglmlaw.com.

**PAVARINI, PETER ALFRED,** lawyer; b. N.Y.C., Feb. 21, 1952; s. Alfred S. and Anne M. (Pertusi) Pavarini; m. Colleen A. Wulf, Apr. 12, 1980. BA summa cum laude, SUNY-Albany, 1973; JD, Boston Coll., 1977. Bar: Mass. 1977, D.C. 1979, Ohio 1981. Aide N.Y. State Office of Gen. Svcs., Albany, 1973—74; rsch. asst. Boston Coll., 1975—76; intern Office of Mass. Atty. Gen., Boston, 1976—77; atty. HHS, Washington, 1977—81; assoc. Murphey Young & Smith, Columbus, 1981—85, ptnr., 1986—88, Squire, Sanders & Dempsey, Columbus, 1988—90. Lectr. Capital U. Law Sch., 1993—95, Fisher Sch. Bus., 2004—; chmn. adv. bd. Ohio Health Law Insider; editor-in-chief Health Law Jour. of Ohio, 1989—95. Editor: U.S. Health Care Law and Rules. Trustee Friends of the Homeless, 1991—94, Goodwill Columbus, 2003—. Recipient Congressman's medal of Merit, 1970, Gen. Counsel's award, HEW, 1979. Fellow: Am. Acad. Hosp. Attys.; mem.: ABA (Health Law sect.), Ohio Bar Assn. (chmn. 1991—93), Am. Health Lawyers Assn. (bd. dirs.). Avocations: music, skiing, bicycling, songwriting. Office Phone: 614-462-5016. Business E-Mail: peter.pavarini@szd.com.

**PAVAROTTI, LUCIANO,** lyric tenor; b. Modena, Italy, Oct. 12, 1935; s. Fernando and Adele (Venturi) Pavarotti; m. Adua Veroni, Sept. 30, 1961 (separated 1996); children: Lorenza, Cristina, Giuliana; m. Nicoletta Mantovani, Dec. 13, 2003; 1 child, Alice. Diploma magistrale, Istituto Magistrale Carlo Sigonio, 1955; studied with Arrigo Pola, studied with Ettore Campogalliani, degree. Formerly tchr. elem. schs.; salesman ins. Singer: (Operas) (debut) as Rodolfo in La Bohème, 1961, (roles) Edgardo in debut Lucia di Lammermoor, 1963, the Duke in debut Rigoletto, 1961, Rodolfo in La Bohème, 1963, Tonio in debut The Daughter of the Regiment, 1966, (appeared) Lucia di Lammermoor, 1965, (Am. debut) Miami, Fla., 1965; performer (numerous): European performances including Italy, Vienna Staatsoper, Paris; performer: with San Francisco Opera, 1967; singer: (Operas) (debut) Met. Opera, 1968; appeared (Operas) The Daughter of the Regiment, Met. Opera, 1971, Elisir d'Amore, 1973, La Bohème, Chgo. Opera, 1973, La Favorita, San Francisco Opera, 1973, Il Trovatore, 1975, Bellini I Puritani, Met. Opera, 1976, Ponchielli La Gioconda, San Francisco Opera, 1979, Aida, 1981, Mozart, Idomeneo, Met. Opera, 1982, Verdi, Ernani, Met. Opera, 1983, Tosca, Met. Opera, 1995, numerous internat. performances La Scala, Milan, Hamburg, Teatro Colon, Buenos Aires, Australian Opera, Sydney, concert series of Am. and internat. cities Carnegie Hall, 1973, Buenos Aires, Moscow, Beijing, Hong Kong, Tokyo, including arena concerts Madison Square Garden, 1984, and major cities in America, Europe, South America, performance in Central Park, NY, 1993, appeared (films) Yes, Giorgio, 1983, established Opera Co. Philadelphia/Luciano Pavarotti Vocal Competition, 1980, rec. artist (albums) Winner Concorso Internationale, Reggio Emilia, 1961, O Solo Mio, 1979, Mamma, 1984, Passione, 1985, Tutto Pavarotti, 1989, The Essential Pavarotti, 1990, Carreras, Domingo, Pavarotti in Concert, 1990, Amore, 1992, Ti Amo Puccini's Greatest Love Songs, 1993, Pavarotti and Friends, 1993, Pavarotti Plus-Deluxe Edit., 1995, The Three Tenors in Concert, 1994, Pavarotti and Friends 2, 1995, Pavarotti Plus, 1997, Pavarotti Greatest Hits: The Ultimate Collection, 1998, The Three Tenors in Paris, 1998, Arias & Duets Freni Pavarotti, 1998, Donizetti Arias, 1998, Notte d'Amore, 1998, Verdi Arias-La donna é mobile, 1999, I tre tenor L'album di Natale, 2000, The Three Tenors Arias, 2000, Quarant' anni per la Lirica, 2001, Live Recital, 2001, Nessundorma Arias & Duets, 2001, Amore: The Essential Romantic Collection, 2001, The Pavarotti Edit., 2001, Luciano Pavarotti-The Singers, 2002, The Best of the Three Tenors, 2002, Ti Adoro, 2003, The Millenium Collection: The Three Tenors, 2005, appeared (PBS TV spl. TV series) (with Placido Domingo & Jose Carreras) The Three Tenors, 1994; performer: Three Tenors Tour, Worldwide Farewell Celebration Tour, 2004—. Established teaching facility for young singing students, Mondena, Italy; created annual charity concert, Pavarotti & Friends, 1993—; UN Messenger for Peace. Named Artist of Yr. Gramophone, 1992; named to Italian Am. Hall of Fame in Music, Nat. Italian Am. Found., 2004; recipient Grammy award, Best Classical Vocal Soloist Performance for Luciano Pavarotti-Hits From Lincoln Ctr., 1978, Grammy award, Best Classical Vocal Soloist Performance for O Solo Mio-Favorite Neapolitan Songs, 1979, Grammy award, Best Classical Vocal Soloist Performance, Live From Lincoln Ctr.-Sutherland/Horne/Pavarotti, 1981, Grammy award, Best Classical Vocal Soloist Performance for Luciano Pavarotti In Concert, 1988, Grammy award, Best Classical Vocal Performance for Carreras, Domingo, Pavarotti in Concert, 1990, Commendatore Cross and Grand Official Cross for services to the Italian Republic, Nansen award, UN High Commissioner for Refugees, 2001, World Social award, Pres. Gorbachev, Vienna, 2001, John F. Kennedy Ctr. Honor award, 2001, Eisenhower Medallion, People to People Internat., 2004, Freedom of the City of London, Corp. of London, 2005, Red Cross award for Services to Humanity, 2005. Achievements include performance at opening ceremonies of Winter Olympics, Torino, 2006. Office: care Herbert Breslin 119 W 57th St New York NY 10019-2303*

**PAVEL, RADU,** mechanical engineer, researcher; PhD, U. Toledo, 2003. Rsch. asst. U. Toledo, 2000—03; machining/grinding rsch. engr. TechSolve, Inc., Cin., 2004—. Office Phone: 513-948-2060. Personal E-Mail: radpav513@aol.com.

**PAVELICH, DANIEL L.,** retired account and tax management consulting executive; CEO BDO Seidman LLP, Chgo.; ret., 1999. Office: BDO Seidman LLP Two Prudential Plaza 130 E Randolph St Fl 2800 Chicago IL 60601-6300

**PAVELICH, JUDITH,** secondary school educator; b. Bklyn., July 10, 1924; d. Abraham and Anna (Chaikin) Goldstein; m. Martin Pavelich, Dec. 5, 1948; children: Alyce, Susan, Sharon. BA, Moravian Coll., 1954; MA, Lehigh U. 1961; postgrad., Pa. State U., Mainland Inst., Marywood Coll. Tchr. spl. edn., Bethlehem, Pa., 1961—62; counselor Northampton Area Jr. H.S., Pa., 1962—. Coord., sec. Big Bros. and Sisters Northampton area; mem. cataract support group, treas. Israel Cancer Rsch. Fund; bd. dirs. Lehigh Social Svc. Exch.; vol. Lehigh Valley Ecumenical Soup Kitchen; vol. coord. Reibman for Congress Campaign, Reibman for Judge Campaign; campaign coord. Alan Black for Judge; aide leisure group B'rith Sholom Synagogue; mem. friendship cir. Jewish Cmty. Ctr. With WAVES USNR, 1943—48. Mem.: NEA, Am. Sch. Assn., Pa. Sch. Counselors Assn. (unit rep.), Lehigh Valley Guidance Assn. (sec.), Pa. Educators Assn., Northampton Area Educators Assn., Pa. Pers. and Guidance Assn., Am. Pers. and Guidance Assn. Home: 2235 W Highland St Allentown PA 18104-3631

**PAVELKA, ELAINE BLANCHE,** mathematics professor; b. Chgo. d. Frank Joseph and Mildred Bohumila (Seidl) P. BA, MS, Northwestern U.; PhD, U. Ill. With Northwestern U. Aerial Measurements lab., Evanston, Ill.; tchr. Leyden Cmty. H.S., Franklin Park, Ill.; prof. math. Morton Coll., Cicero, Ill.

Invited prof. Internat. Congress on Math. Edn., Karlsruhe, Germany, 1976. RecipientSci. Talent award Westinghouse Electric Co. Mem. Am. Edn. Rsch. Assn., Am. Math. Assn. 2-Yr. Colls., Am. Math. Soc., Assn. Women in Math., Can. Soc. History and Philosophy of Math., Ill. Coun. Tchrs. Math., Ill. Math. Assn. C.C., Math. Assn. Am. Am. Math. Action Group, Ga. Ctr. Study and Tchg. and Learning Math., Nat. Coun. Tchrs. Math., Sch. Sci. and Math. Assn., Northwestern U. Alumni Assn., U. Ill. Alumni Assn., Am. Mensa Ltd., Intertel, Sigma Delta Epsilon, Pi Mu Epsilon. Home: PO Box 7312 Westchester IL 60154-7312

**PAVER, ROBERT L.,** lawyer; b. May 1956; BA, U. Fla.; JD, Stetson College Law. Adj. law prof. Stetson U., 1985—; atty. Holland & Knight, St. Petersburg, Fla.; gen. counsel, corp. sec. Jabil Circuit Inc., St. Petersburg, Fla., 1997—. Office: Jabil Curcuit Inc 10560 9th St N Saint Petersburg FL 33716 Home: 200 Central Ave Apt 502 Saint Petersburg FL 33701-3326 Office Phone: 727-577-9749. Office Fax: 727-579-8529.

**PAVIET-HARTMANN, PATRICIA,** chemist, researcher; b. Cormeilles, France, June 8, 1964; came to U.S., 1997; d. Roland Jean and Josette Juliette (Camus) Paviet; m. Thomas Hartmann, Apr. 27, 1996; 1 child, Josephine Caroline. BS, U. Nice, France, 1986, MS, 1988; PhD Chemistry, U. Paris XI, 1992. Rsch. scientist Commissariat a l'Energie Atomique, Cadarache, France, 1990—92; postdoctoral fellow Lawrence Livermore Nat. Lab., Calif., 1992—93; mem. staff Forschungszentrum, Karlsruhe, Germany, 1993—97, Los Alamos Nat. Lab., 1997—2003, project leader in actinide chemistry, 2000—03; sr. scientist adv. MOX Project, Areva NP, Inc., Charlotte, NC, 2003—. Contbr. articles to profl. jours.; patentee in field. Mem. Am. Chem. Soc., Am. Nuclear Soc. Roman Catholic. Avocations: painting, piano, languages (french, english, german, italian, spanish). Home: 6738 Thornton Oaks Ct Charlotte NC 28270 Office: Areva NP Inc 128 S Tryon FC12A Charlotte NC 28202 Office Phone: 803-502-1889. Business E-Mail: Patricia.PavietHartmann@areva.com.

**PAVILACK, JOANN CLEMENTS,** history professor; b. Phoenix, June 8, 1966; d. Lawrence Lee Pavilack and Carol Ann McGrew Pavilack. BA cum laude, Harvard Coll., 1989; MA, Fla. Internat. U., 1993; PhD, Duke U., 2003. Vis. asst. prof. U. Miss., Oxford, 2003—04; asst. prof. U. Mont., Missoula, 2004—. Mem.: Latin Am. Studies Assn., Am. Hist. Assn. Office: Univ Mont History Dept Missoula MT 59812-6264

**PAVIN, COREY ALLEN,** professional golfer; b. Oxnard, Calif., Nov. 16, 1959; Mem. US Team Ryder Cup, 1991, 1993, 1996, Presidents Cup, 1994, 1996. Achievements include winning PGA Tour events including the Houston Coca-Cola Classic, 1984, Colonial Nat. Invitation Tournament, 1985, Hawaiian Open, 1986, 87, Greater Milw. Open, 1986, Bob Hope Chrysler Classic, 1987, 91, Tex. Open, 1988; winner, PGA Tour events including the Bell South Atlanta Golf Classic, 1991, Honda Classic, 1992, LA Open, 1994, Nissan Open, 1995, US Open, 1995, Mastercard Colonial, 1996, US Bank Championship, 2006; set a PGA Tour nine-hole record score of 26 at the US Bank Championship, 2006; finished number 1 on the PGA Tour money list, 1991. Address: c/o PGA TOUR 112 PGA TOUR Blvd Ponte Vedra Beach FL 32082*

**PAVLATH, ATTILA ENDRE,** chemist, researcher; b. Budapest, Hungary, Mar. 11, 1930; came to U.S., 1958; s. Eugene Rudolph and Yolanda Elizabeth (Hortobagyi) P.; m. Katalin Wappel, July 27, 1951; children: George, Grace. Diploma in chem. engring., Tech. U., Budapest, 1952; D in Chemistry, Hungarian Acad. of Sci., Budapest, 1955. Asst. prof. Tech. U., Budapest, 1952-56; group leader Cen. Chem. Rsch. Inst., Budapest, 1954-56; rsch. fellow McGill U., Montreal, Can., 1957-58; sr. group leader Stauffer Chem. Co., Richmond, Calif., 1958-67; project leader Western regional rsch. ctr. USDA, Albany, Calif., 1967-78, rsch. leader Western regional rsch. ctr., 1979—. Author three books; contbr. articles to profl. jours; patentee in field. Fellow Am. Inst. Chemists (councilor 1985-95, dir. 1993-95); mem. Am. Chem. Soc. (councilor 1973-90, dir. 1991-99, pres.-elect 2000, pres. 2001, immediate past pres. 2002), Royal Chem. Soc. Great Britain, Internat. Union of Pure and Applied Chemistry, German Chem. Soc., Hungarian Chem. Soc. Avocations: flying, bridge, tennis, ping pong/table tennis, computers. Office: USDA Western Regional Rsch Ctr 800 Buchanan St Berkeley CA 94710-1105 Office Phone: 510-559-5620. Business E-Mail: apavlath@pw.usda.gov.

**PAVLEY, FRAN J.,** state representative; b. LA, Nov. 11, 1948; m. Andy Pavley; children: Jennifer, David. BA, Calif. State U., Fresno, 1970; MA, Calif. State U., 1985. Cert. tchr. Calif. Tchr., 28 yrs.; mem. Calif. Assembly, 2000—. Founder Agoura Hills Disaster Response Team, 1987; mem. adv. com. Santa Monica Mountains Conservancy, 1990—; mem. Coastal Commn., State of Calif., 1995—2000; mem. coun., mayor Agoura Hills, Calif., 1982—97. Democrat. Office: PO Box 942849 Rm 3120 Sacramento CA 95814 Address: 6355 Topanga Canyon Blvd Ste 205 Woodland Hills CA 91367-2108 Office Phone: 916-319-2041.

**PAVLICK, JOHN J., JR.,** lawyer; b. Wurzburg, Germany, Mar. 30, 1948; BS, US Military Acad., 1970; JD, Univ. Pa., 1978. Bar: Pa. 1978, US Supreme Ct. 1982, US Ct. Fed. Claims 1989, DC 1991. Ptnr., govt. contracts, regulatory law and compliance Venable LLP, Washington. Contbr. articles profl. journals. To lt. col. U.S. Army, 1970—90, ret. Mem.: ABA, Nat. Contract Mgmt. Assn., Fed. Bar Assn., Phi Kappa Phi. Office: Venable LLP 575 Seventh St NW Washington DC 20004 Office Phone: 202-344-4894. Office Fax: 202-344-8300. Business E-Mail: jpavlick@venable.com.

**PAVLICK, PAMELA KAY,** nurse, consultant; b. Topeka, Aug. 16, 1944; d. Cy Pavlick and June Lucille Dull. Diploma in nursing, St. Luke's Hosp., Kansas City, Mo., 1966; BA in Psychology magna cum laude, U. North Fla., 1982, MS in Health Adminstrn. summa cum laude, 1987. RN, Mo., Ill., Fla.; cert. ins. rehab. specialist; lic. rehab. provider, Fla., Ga. Clin. instr. St. Luke's Hosp., Kansas City, 1966—70; instr. lic. practical nursing Springfield (Ill.) Sch. Bd., 1970—72; nursing supr. Jacksonville Beach (Fla.) Hosp., 1972—74; pub. health nurse State of Fla., Ocala, 1974—76; dir. nursing Upjohn Health Care, Jacksonville, Fla., 1976—77, mem. adv. com.; med. rep. Travelers Ins. Co., Jacksonville, 1977—84; rehab. cons. Aetna Life & Casualty, Jacksonville, 1985—, rep. nurse cons. adv. coun., 1988—90. Mem. ANA., Am. Assn. Rehab. Nurses, Nat. Assn. Rehab. Providers, Phi Kappa Phi. Republican. Episcopalian. Avocation: boating. Home: 14023 Tontine Rd Jacksonville FL 32225-2025 Office: Aetna Life & Casualty PO Box 2200 Jacksonville FL 32203-2200 E-mail: pampavlick@peoplepc.com.

**PAVLIK, WILLIAM BRUCE,** psychologist, educator; b. Cleve., Feb. 29, 1932; s. William Frank and Mary (Maco) P.; m. Mary Katherine Findley, May 22, 1979; children by previous marriage: William James, Heather Ann, Russell Matthew, James Clark; 1 child, Amelia Katherine. BS, Western Res. U., 1953; MA, Ohio State U., 1955, PhD, 1956. Asst. prof. psychology Western Mich. U., 1956-60; asst. prof., then assoc. prof. Rutgers U., 1960-68; prof. psychology Va. Poly. Inst. and State U., 1968-77, chmn. dept., 1968-72; prof. psychology U. Ga., Athens, 1977-94; ret., head dept., 1977-84. Author articles in field. Mem. Eastern Psychol. Assn., Southeastern Psychol. Assn. (pres. 1985-86), Psychonomic Soc. Home: 2509 Heidi Loop Flagstaff AZ 86004-1843

**PAVLOVSKIS-PETIT, ZOJA,** literature and language professor; b. Daugavpils, Latvia, Apr. 30, 1936; d. Prokopijs and Klaudija Pavlovskis; m. Thomas Arthur Petit (dec.). BA, Bryn Mawr Coll., Pa., 1958; MA, Cornell U., Ithaca, N.Y., 1959, PhD, 1962. From instr. to prof. of comparative lit. and classics SUNY (now known as Binghamton U.), Binghamton, NY, 1962—. Author: Man in an Artificial Landscape, 1973, The Praise of Folly: Structure and Irony, 1983; contbr. articles to profl. jours. Avocations: hiking, gardening, poetry, art. Office: Binghamton Univ Dept Comparative Lit Binghamton NY 13902-6000 E-mail: zppetit@binghamton.edu.

**PAVONY, WILLIAM H.,** retail executive, consultant; b. Bklyn., Mar. 1, 1940; s. Harry and Mollie (Leibel) Pavony; m. Geraldine Rice, June 10, 1961; 1 child, Sheryl. BBA cum laude, Hofstra U., 1960. CPA, NY, Tex. Mgr. Arthur Andersen & Co. Inc., N.Y.C., 1960-73; group sr. v.p. Purolator Svcs. Inc., New Hyde Park, NY, 1973-75; v.p., contr. Purolator Inc., Piscataway, NJ, 1975-78; sr. v.p. Zale Corp., Dallas, 1978-85; v.p. fin., chief fin. officer Alexander's Inc., N.Y.C., 1985-88, exec. v.p., chief fin officer, 1988-89; exec. v.p. adminstr. The Kobacker Co., Columbus, Ohio, 1989-93; also bd. dirs.; exec. v.p. Arthur Rutenberg Homes, Clearwater, Fla., 1993-94; CFO Color Tile, Inc., Ft. Worth, 1994-95; pres. Pavony Assocs., Corona Del Mar, Calif., 1995-99, Newport Coast, Calif., 1999, 2001—; exec. bus. cons. The Netplex Group, Newport Coast, Calif., 1999-2001; pres. Pavony Assocs., Newport Coast, 2001—. Treas., bd. dirs. Tex. Vis. Nurses Assn., Dallas, 1984-85. Mem AICPA, Fin. Execs. Internat. (past bd. dirs. North Tex. chpt., sec. Columbus chpts.), N.Y. Soc. CPAs, Inst. Mgmt. Accts. Home: 5 Adriana Newport Coast CA 92657-1224 Office Phone: 949-497-8026. Personal E-mail: Bpavony@aol.com.

**PAVUK, MARIAN,** epidemiologist, researcher; b. Presov, Slovak Republic; MD in Gen. Medicine, Komenskeho U. Coll. Medicine, Bratislava, Slovakia, 1989—95; MS in Preventive Medicine & Environ. Health, U. Iowa, Iowa City, 1996—98, PhD in Epidemiology, 1998—2000. Lic. doctor Slovakia, 1995. Postdoctoral fellowship dept. toxicology Inst. Preventive & Clin. Medicine, Bratislava, 1995—95; rsch. assoc. dept. preventive medicine & environ. health U. Iowa Coll. Medicine, 1996—2000; project dir. dept. epidemiology U. Iowa Coll. Pub. Health, 1998—2000; assoc. faculty, postdoctoral fellow U. Tex. Sch. Pub. Health, Dallas, 2001—03; lead epidemiologist, biostatistician SpecPro Inc., San Antonio, 2005—03, sci. dir. Air Force Health Study, 2005—. Cons. legal firms, Binghampton, NY, 2002—03, Mayo Clinic, Rochester, Minn., 2003—05, Def. Threat Response Agy., 2004—05. Contbr. articles to profl. jours., scientific papers, chapters to books. Grantee Marie Curie Individual Fellowship, European Commn., 2003—04; scholar Fogarty Internat. Fellowship, NIH, 1996—2000; Marie Curie Individual Fellowship, 2003—05, grant, NIEHS, 1998—99, 1999—2000, Slovak Min. Environment, 1998—99, Fogarty Internat. Ctr., 1999—2000, USAF Dept. Def., 2001—02, European Commn., Framework Five, 2001—04, Exxon Mobil, 2002—03, Marie Curie Individual Fellowship, Def. Threat Response Agy., 2004—05. Mem.: APHA, Internat. Soc. Exposure Analysis, Intenat. Soc. Environ. Epidemiology, Am. Assn. Cancer Rsch. Office: SpecPro Inc 12500 San Pedro Ave Ste 670 San Antonio TX 78216 Business E-Mail: mpavuk@specpro-inc.com.

**PAWL, RONALD PHILLIP,** neurosurgery educator; b. Chgo., July 26, 1935; s. Phillip Joseph and Ruby Helen (Graham) P.; m. Mary M. Rohner, July 11, 1959; children: Mary, Linda, Diane, Julie, Matthew, Michael. BS in Biology, Loyola U., Chgo., 1957, MD, 1961. Diplomate Am. Bd. Neurol. Surgery, Am. Bd. Pain Med. Intern Resurrection Hosp., 1961-62; resident in gen. surgery and orthopedics Hines VA Hosp., 1962-63; resident in neurology and neurosurgery U. Ill., Chgo., 1963-66, asst. prof. neurosurgery, 1968-73; asst. chief neurosurgery Tripler Army Med. Ctr., Honolulu, 1966-68; assoc. prof. neurosurgery U. Ill., Chgo., 1973—; dir. pain treatment ctr. Lake Forest (Ill.) Hosp., 1978—. Pres. Am. Bd. Pain Medicine, 1995, residency rev. com. chmn., 1997-2002, appeals com. 2001-. Author: Chronic Pain Primer, 1979; editor Seminars in Neurology, 1989; editor Clin. Jour. Pain, 1988—, Surg. Neurology, 1994—, Clin. Rev. of Pain, 1997-2002, Current Rev. of Pain, 1995-2001; contbr. articles to profl. jours. Capt. U.S. Army, 1966—68. Named Physician of Yr., Ill. Masonic Med. Ctr., Chgo., 1973. Mem. Ctrl. Neurosurg. Soc. (pres. 1979), Midwest Pain Soc. (pres. 1986), Am. Acad. Pain Medicine (treas. 1990), Ill. Neurosurg. Soc. (pres. 1982), Chgo. Neirological Soc. (pres. 1980). Roman Catholic. Avocations: anthropology, archaeology. Office: 900 N Westmoreland Rd Lake Forest IL 60045-1674 Office Phone: 847-535-6132. E-mail: ron@pawl.com.

**PAWLAK, ROMAN MACIEJ,** education educator; s. Regina and Zygmunt Pawlak. MS, Andrews U., Mich., 2001; PhD, U. So. Miss., 2003. Registered Dietitian Am. Dietetic Assn., 2002. Asst. prof. nutrition and dietetics East Carolina U., Greenville, NC, 2003—06. Mem.: Soc. Nutrition Edn. (assoc.). Office: East Carolina Univ E 5th St Greenville NC 27858 Office Phone: 252-328-4274.

**PAWLENTY, TIMOTHY J.,** governor; b. South St. Paul, Minn., Nov. 27, 1960; m. Mary Elizabeth Anderson, 1987; 1 child. BA, JD, U. Minn. Chmn. Eagan Planning Commn., 1988-89; mem. Minn. Ho. of Reps. St. Paul, 1993—2002; gov. State of Minn., St. Paul, 2003—. Active Eagan city coun., 1990-92. Fannie Gilbertson Coll. scholar. Republican. Office: Office of the Gov 130 State Capitol 75 Rev Dr Martin Luther King Jr Blvd Saint Paul MN 55155 Office Phone: 651-296-3391. Office Fax: 651-296-2089. E-mail: tim.pawlenty@state.mn.us.*

**PAWLEY, RAY L.,** retired zoological park administrator, curator; b. Midland, Mich., Nov. 7, 1935; s. John Richard and Alice Marie (Skelton) P.; m. Ethel Marie Condon, Feb. 19, 1955 (div. 1974); children: Ray Allyn, Shanna Sue, Cynthia Ann, Dawn Marie, Brandon Earl, Dareen Joy; m. Hedda P. Saltz, Mar. 16, 1997. Student, Mich. State U., 1954—57. Asst. curator, lectr. Black Hills Reptile Gardens, Rapid City, SD, 1952—53; owner, adminstr. Reptile Exhibit, St. Ignace, Mich., 1957—59; animal coord. Don Meier Prodns. Marlin Perkin's Wild Kingdom, Chgo. 1961—62; zoologist Lincoln Park Zool. Gardens, Chgo., 1961—64; curator Brookfield Zoo, Ill., 1964—97; ret., 1997. Formerly assoc. dept. zoology Field Mus. Natural History, Chgo.; internat. zoo and conservation cons., Russia, Latvia, Mex., Kenya, China, Ecuador, Galapagos Islands; past instr. herpetology Field Mus., Coll. of DuPage, Triton Coll.; assoc. zoologist Moscow Zool. Pk., Russia; info. resource for fed. and state wildlife agys.; lectr., cons. in field. Contbr. over 100 articles to profl. jours. and popular mags.; co-creator money bench Chgo. Children's Mus. Past v.p. Ill. Endangered Species Protection Bd., Springfield; liaison Endangered Species Tech. Adv. Com., Springfield. Mem. Am. Zoo Assn. (3 Outstanding Svc. awards), Chgo. Acad. Scis. (life), Chgo. Herpetological Soc. (life), Mensa. Achievements include development of several new live animal exibit concepts; discovery and documentation of parthenogenisis in snakes; research in fossil urolite identification; rattlesnake hibernation physiology; discovery and documentation of Goliath frog calls. Avocations: hiking, archaeology, art, paleontology. Home and Office: PO Box 12 Hondo NM 88336 Business E-Mail: raypawley@pvtnetworks.net.

**PAWLICZKO, GEORGE IHOR,** academic administrator; b. Rochester, N.Y., Oct. 26, 1950; s. Roman and Irene Olha (Zubryckyj) P.; m. Ann Maria Lencyk, June 10, 1978. BA, St. John Fisher Coll., 1972; MA, Fordham U., 1974, MBA, 1986, PhD, 1989. Admissions counselor Fordham U., Bronx, N.Y., 1977-78, asst. dean Grad. Sch. of Bus. N.Y.C., 1978-81; asst. to pres., dir. mgmt. info. systems Marymount Coll., Tarrytown, N.Y., 1981-82; exec. dir. N.Y. Inst. Credit, N.Y.C., 1982-94; The Global Inst. Fin. and Banking (formerly Am. Inst. Banking Greater N.Y.), N.Y.C., 1994—. Trustee St. Andrew's Ch., Hamptonburgh, N.Y. 1986-2002; bd. trustees St. Basil Coll., Stamford, Conn., 2006-. Mem. Shevchenko Scientific Soc., Beta Gamma Sigma, Phi Alpha Theta. Office: The Global Inst Fin and Banking 80 Maiden Ln New York NY 10038-4811 Office Phone: 212-480-3200.

**PAWLITSCHEK, DONALD PAUL,** management consultant; b. Heron Lake, Minn., Aug. 5, 1941; s. Paul P. and Marion (Erickson) Pawlitschek; m. Korrine Kunerth, Oct. 9, 1965; children: Andrew, Jennifer, Heidi, Sarah, Benjamin. Student, Southwest Tech. Inst., 1960, Mankato State Coll., 1965—66. Farmer, Heron Lake, 1967—73; pres. Dundee Steel, Inc., 1973—75, Alpha Prime, Inc., Heron Lake, 1975—80, Prime Ventures, Inc., Lake Crystal, Minn., 1980—. Bd. dirs. Am. Search and Referral Co. With U.S. Army, 1960. Mem.: Am. Entrepreneurs Assn., Nat. Assn. Fin. Cons., Elks, Am. Legion. Conservative. Roman Catholic. Achievements include patents for livestock flooring. Home and Office: Prime Ventures Inc 1801 499th Ave Lake Crystal MN 56055-9700

**PAWLOSKI, MICHAEL W.,** marketing professional; BS in Sociology, U. Wis., 1985; MBA, Lake Forest Grad. Sch. Mgmt., 1995. Mkt. rsch. assoc. Econs. Rsch. Assocs., 1985—87; mktg. auditor Bus. Pub. Audit of Circulation (BPA), Inc., 1987—88; account exec. Pub/Data, Inc., 1988—92; sr. account exec. Experian, 1992—94; mktg. officer, product mgr. Bankone, 1994—95, asst. v.p., sr. product mgr., 1995—96, v.p., mgr. database mktg., 1997—99; mgr. info. mgmt. Southern Co., Atlanta, 1999—2000, product mgr. new products and svcs., 2001—03, mgr. residential sales and mktg., 2003—04, brand mgr. SoCoGAS, 2004—. Home: 2796 Ashburn Ln Atlanta GA 30341

**PAXON, L. WILLIAM,** former congressman; b. Buffalo, Apr. 29, 1954; s. Leon W. and Mary P. (Sellers) P.; m. Susan Molinari, July 3, 1994; children: Susan Ruby, Katherine Mary. BA, Canisius Coll., 1977. Mem. Erie County Legis., N.Y., 1978-82, N.Y. State Assembly, 1983-89, 101st-105th Congresses from 31st (now 27th) N.Y. dist., 1989-98; chair Nat. Rep. Congrl. Com.; mem. com. on commerce; sr. advisor Akin, Gump, Strauss, Hauer & Feld, Washington, 1999—. Roman Catholic. Office: Akin Gump Strauss Hauer & Feld Ste 400 1333 New Hampshire Ave NW Washington DC 20036-1564

**PAXTON, BILL,** actor, film director; b. Ft. Worth, May 17, 1955; s. John Lane and Mary Lou (Gray) P; m. Louise Newbury, 1987, children: James, Lydia Student, NYU; studies with Stella Adler, Vincent Chase. Actor: (films) Crazy Mama, 1975, Stripes, 1981, Taking Tiger MOuntain, 1983, The Lords of Discipline, 1983, Night Warning, 1983, Streets of Fire, 1984, Mortuary, 1983, Impulse, 1983, Terminator, 1984, Weird Science, 1985, Commando, 1985, Aliens, 1985 (Saturn award Acad. of Sci. Fiction, Fantasy and Horror Films 1986), Near Dark, 1986, Pass the Ammo, 1987, Slipstream, 1989, Next of Kin, 1989, Back to Back, 1990, Brain Dead, 1990, The Last of the Finest, 1990, Navy Seals, 1990, Predator 2, 1990, The Dark Backward, 1991, One False Move, 1992, The Vagrant, 1992, Trespass, 1992, Future Shock, 1993, Indian Summer, 1993, Boxing Helena, 1993, Tombstone, 1993, True Lies, 1994, Apollo 13, 1995, Twister, 1995, Evening Star, 1996, The Last Supper, 1996, Titanic, 1997, A Simple Plan, 1998, Mighty Joe Young, 1998, U-571, 2000, Vertical Limit, 2000, Spy Kids 2: Island of Lost Dreams, 2002, Resistance, 2003, Spy Kids 3-D: Game Over, 2003, Ghosts of the Abyss, 2003, Club Dread, 2004, Thunderbirds, 2004, Haven, 2004; actor, dir. (films) Fraility, 2001, dir. only, The Greatest Game Ever Played, 2005; actor, prodr. (films) Traveler, 1997; actor, dir., prodr., writer, (theatrical short) Fish Heads, 1982 (Spl. Award Melbourne Film Festival 1982); actor (TV movies) Deadly Lessons, 1983, An Early Frost, 1985, Frank and Jesse, 1994, A Bright Shining Lie, 1998; actor (TV mini-series) The Atlanta Child Murders, 1985, Fresno, 1986; actor (TV series) The Six O'Clock Follies, 1980, Big Love, 2006-; (TV appearances) The Hitch-Hiker, 1986, Miami Vice, 1986, Tales From the Crypt, 1993, Frasier (voice only), 2003; (theatrical short) Fish Heads, 1982 (Spl. Award Melbourne Film Festival 1982); prodr., co-author (theatrical short) Scoop, 1983. Mem. Screen Actors Guild. Office: c/o Endeavor Agency 9601 Wilshire Blvd, 3rd Fl Beverly Hills CA 90212*

**PAXTON, GARY L.,** Auto rental company executive; Positions with Dollar Rent a Car, 1968—72, v.p. ops., 1972—74, v.p. properties, 1974—82, v.p. properties & facilities, 1982—86, sr. v.p. ops. & properties, 1986—90, pres., 1990—2002; pres., COO corp. ops. Dollar Thrifty Automotive Group, Inc., Tulsa, Okla., 2002—03, pres., CEO, 2003—. Office: Dollar Thrifty Automotive Group 5330 E 31st St Tulsa OK 74135 Office Phone: 918-665-3930.*

**PAXTON, GLENN GILBERT,** composer; b. Chgo., Dec. 7, 1931; s. Glenn G. and Florence A. (Nosek) P.; m. Leslie H. Davis, Dec. 8, 1962; children: Alexandra, Eben. BA, Princeton U., 1953. Freelance composer Broadway, opera, TV and film, 1959—. Composer: (theater prodns.) First Impressions, 1959, The Adventures of Friar Tuck, 1983 (Pulitzer prize nomination 1984), W.R. and Daisy, 2003, (opera) Monticello, 2000, (film) When the Legends Die, 1972, (concert pieces) Four Character Pieces for Piano, 1962, Sara's Diary, 9/11, 2003, The Evening Sing, 1981, (TV movies) Charlie and the Great Balloon Chase, 1981, Vital Signs, 1986, Dark Night of the Scarecrow, 1981, Isobel's Choice, 1981, The Two Worlds of Jenny Logan, 1979, The Clone Master, 1978, (TV shows) Amazing Stories, 1986, Willa Cather's America, 1976, Andy Rooney Takes Off, 1983, An American Christmas: Words and Music, 1971, The Hill Country: Lyndon Johnson's Texas, 1967, The Stately Ghosts of England, 1968, Barry Goldwater's Arizona, 1968, New World Visions, 1984, The American Image, 1969, others; (TV Special) Which Mother Is Mine, (1980 Emmy nominee) (multi-media) Walking Home, 1991; (CD) Prairie Indigo, 1995. Served to lt. (j.g.) USCG, 1953-56. Mem. ASCAP, Dramatists Guild, Am. Music Ctr., Am. Fedn. Musicians. Home and Office: 230A Saddle Ln Ojai CA 93023-4204 Office Phone: 805-640-9449. Personal E-mail: gpaxton@alumni.princeton.edu.

**PAXTON, JAY LEE,** lawyer; b. Ft. Worth, Dec. 24, 1947; s. Carl C. Paxton and Mildred F. (Fawver) Shepherd; m. Carolyn P. Paxton, June 21, 1969; 1 child, Laura. BA, U. Calif., Berkeley, 1970, JD, 1973. Bar: Calif. 1973. Spl. asst. to chancellor U. Calif., 1973-74; ptnr. Bianchi, Paxton, Engel, Keegin & Sherwood, San Rafael, Calif., 1974-90; mem., mng. dir. Ellman, Burke, Hoffman & Johnson, San Francisco, 1990—. Bd. dirs., v.p. Internat. House, U. Calif., Berkeley, 1974—; mem. exec. com. Ctr. Real Estate and Urban Econs.; trustee U. Calif. Berkeley Found., Marin Cmty. Found.; mem., chair San Francisco Dist. Coun., Urban Land Inst., 1976-; bd. dirs. Bay Area Coun. Mem. ABA, Calif. Bar Assn., Urban Land Inst., Lambda Alpha. Office: Ellman Burke Hoffman Johnson 601 California St Ste 1900 San Francisco CA 94108-2824

**PAXTON, JOHN RAY,** management educator; b. Denver; BEd, Northeastern State Coll., Okla., 1973; MBA, Okla. U., 1977; PhD, U. Nebr., Lincoln, 1988. Prof. Wayne (Nebr.) State Coll., 1992—. Contbr. articles to profl. journ. Louder Bngs Acom Aru, 1987—95. With USN, 1966—70. Mem.: State Coll. Educators Assn. (bd. dirs. 2004—). Office: Wayne State Coll 1111 Main St Wayne NE 68787

**PAXTON, ROBERT OWEN,** historian, educator; b. Lexington, Va., June 15, 1932; s. Matthew W. and Nell B. (Owen) P.; m. Sarah Plimpton, Dec. 9, 1983 BA, Washington and Lee U., 1954, LittD (hon.), 1974; BA, Oxford U., Eng., 1956, MA, 1961; PhD, Harvard U., 1963; DHL (hon.), SUNY, Stony Brook, 1994; DL (hon.), U. Caen, France, 1994; DL (hon.), U. Lyon, France, 2003. Instr. history U. Calif., Berkeley, 1961-63, asst. prof., 1963-67; asso. prof. SUNY, Stony Brook, 1967-69; prof. history Columbia U., 1969—, chmn. dept., 1980-82, dir. Inst. on West Europe, 1991-95. Author: Parades and Politics at Vichy, 1966, Vichy France: Old Guard and New Order, 1940-44, 1972, 2d edit., 2001, Europe in the Twentieth Century, 1975, 4th edit., 2001, French Peasant Fascism, 1997, Anatomy of Fascism, 2004; co-author: Vichy France and the Jews, 1981, 2d edit., 1995; co-editor: De Gaulle and the U.S., 1995. Served with USNR, 1956-58. Decorated comdr. Ordre National des Arts and des Lettres (France), officer Ordre Nat. du Mérite (France); recipient Scholarly Distinction award Am. Hist. Soc., 1998; Rhodes scholar, 1954-56; Am. Coun. Learned Socs. fellow, 1974-75; Rockefeller Found. fellow, 1978-79; German Marshall Fund fellow, 1986. Fellow Am. Acad. Arts and Letters; mem. Am. Philos. Soc., Linnaean Soc. NY (pres. 1978-80), Century Assn. Home: 460 Riverside Dr Apt 72 New York NY 10027-6801 Office: Columbia U Dept History New York NY 10027 Business E-Mail: rop1@columbia.edu.

**PAYACK, PAUL J.J.,** marketing professional, writer; b. Morristown, NJ, Jan. 3, 1950; BA in Comparative Lit., Harvard U., 1974, cert. advanced study in fine arts, 1983. Actor to pres., asst. dir. admissions Newbury Coll., Boston, 1975-78; tech. writer Digital Equipment Corp., Maynard, Mass., 1978-79, Wang Labs., Lowell, Mass., 1980-82; mktg. mgr., sales promotion Apollo Computer Inc. (now Hewlett-Packard Workstations), Chelmsford, Mass., 1982-87; corp. dir. mktg. Unisys Corp., Blue Bell, Pa., 1987-90; v.p., global comm. A.C. Nielsen, Unit of Dun & Bradstreet, Northbrook, Ill., 1990-93; dir., worldwide network mktg. Network Systems Corp., Mpls., 1994-95; v.p. corp. mktg. Intersolv, Rockville, Md., 1995-96; sr. v.p. strategic mktg. Intelliguard Software, Dublin, Calif., 1997; v.p. worldwide mktg. Legato

Sys., Mountainview, Calif., 1998-99; pres., wordman yourDictionary.com, Paoli, Pa., 2000—; v.p. Alacritus Software, 2002—05; pres Global Lang. Monitor, San Diego, 2003—. Cons., lectr. San Diego U., Babson Coll. GM/Hughes, Fed. Res. Bank of NY, Shandwick, Bunting's Window TV show, Bus. Week's Digital Economy, CIO conf.; adj. prof. Babson Coll., Harvard U., Mass State Coll. U. Tex. Author: A Ripple in Entropy, 1973, The Star-Tales Cycle (Solstice 1-3), 1979, Children of the Mind, 1984; (short stories) Mythomania, 1978, Shortest Tomas, 1980, A Plague of Darkness, or the Unseen and the Unseeable, 2003; Anatomical Plates, 1989, The Wind Turbine Studies, 2000, The Pacific Plates, 1999, The Paris Plates, 1999, The End of Empire, 1999, The Perspective Series, 1986, The Land of Orth, 1977, Unexpected Twist Series, 1976, The Book of Hours, 1986, The Idea Mine, a Brief Note on Metafiction, 2000; (play) Worlds to Shatter, Shattered Worlds, 2003, Conversations with the Wordman, and Other Words on Words, 2004; contr. articles to profl. jours. Office: #103 11184 Vista Sorrento Pkwy San Diego CA 92130 Office Phone: 925-367-7557. E-mail: pjjp@post.harvard.edu.

**PAYACK, PETER,** poet, writer, artist, educator; b. Mortistown, N.J., Jan. 3, 1950; s. Peter Paul and Florence (Marcello) P.; m. Monica Elizabeth Hynes, June 5, 1981; children: Michael, Peter Paul. BA, Cath. U. Am., 1972; postgrad., Harvard U., 1992-94. Asst. prof. Berklee Coll. Music, Boston, 1997—. Adj. vis. lectr. U. Mass., Lowell, 1987—; founder, pres. Speculative Poetics, Cambridge, Mass., 1976—; contbg. editor Creative Computing, Morristown, N.J., 1977-87; artist-in-residence MIT, Cambridge, 1982, 84, 86; mem. art adv. com. Internat. Space Sta., NASA. Author: (poetry and prose poems) No Free Will in Tomatoes, 1988, Blanket Knowledge, 1997, The Zen of America, 2002; contbt. poems, prose poems and short stories to more than 1000 publs. including The Paris Rev., The N.Y. Times, Asimov's Sci. Fiction Rev., Readers Digest, Boston Globe, Cornell Rev., also textbooks and anthologies; inventor, innovator. Recipient The Rhysling award Sci. Fiction Poetry Assn., 1979, Commendation, State of Mass., 1985, Commendation, City of Cambridge, 1995, 96, 98, 98, Youth Sports award Galluccio Assocs., 1998. Avocations: running (23 marathons), ancient and zen philosophy, metrology, collecting antiquities, coaching h.s. sports. Home: 65 Highland Ave Cambridge MA 02139-1039 Office: 64 Highland Ave Cambridge MA 02139 Office Phone: 617-512-9196. Personal E-mail: payack@aol.com.

**PAYARD, FRANCOIS,** food service executive; b. Nice, France; With Au Nid de Friandises, Riviera, France; pastry chef La Tour d'Argent, Paris, 1988; pastry chef under Alain Senderens Lucas Carton, 1989; pastry chef Le Bernardin, N.Y.C., 1990; pastry chef with chef Daniel Boulud Restaurant Daniel, 1993; pastry chef, owner Payard, N.Y.C., 1997—. Named Pastry Chef of Yr., James Beard Assn., 1995, Bon Appétit Food & Entertainment Awards, 1998, Isignia of Chevalier de l'ordre du mente agricole, French Govt., 2004. Office: Payard 1032 Lexington Ave New York NY 10021 Office Phone: 212-717-5252. E-mail: francois@payard.com.

**PAYMENT, KENNETH ARNOLD,** lawyer; b. Aug. 6, 1941; s. Arnold F. and Eleanor J. (Kinsey) Payment; m. Jane A. Conrad, Aug. 16, 1996; children: Simone, Elise, Ryan. BS, Union Coll., 1963; LLB, Cornell U., 1966. Bar: NY 66, U.S. Dist. Ct. (we. dist.) NY 67, U.S. Ct. Appeals (2d cir.) 68, U.S. Supreme Ct. 89. Assoc. Wiser, Shaw, Freeman, Van Graafeiland, Harter & Secrest, Rochester, 1966—75; ptnr. Harter, Secrest & Emery, Rochester, 1975—. Instr. Rochester Inst. Tech., 1969, U. Rochester, 1970, Cornell U. Law Sch., Ithaca, NY, 1971—72. Mem.: ABA, Best Lawyers in Am. (bus. litigation 1989—, antitrust 2003), Rochester C. of C., Monroe County Bar Assn. (trustee), NY State Bar Assn. (chmn. constrn. and suretyship divsn. 1978), Cornell Club. Home: 268 Harmon Rd Churchville NY 14428-9518 Office: Harter Secrest & Emery 1600 Bausch & Lomb Place Rochester NY 14604-2006 Office Phone: 585-231-1227.

**PAYMER, DAVID,** actor; b. Oceanside, Long Island, NY, Aug. 30, 1954; m. Liz Georges, 1988; 1 child. Attended, Lee Srasberg Theater Inst., Profl. Performing Arts Sch., Mich. U. Actor (Broadway plays) Grease; (films) The In-Laws, 1979, Airplane II: The Sequel, 1982, Irreconcilable Differences, 1984, Perfect, 1985, Love Mary, 1985, Pleasures, 1986, Howard the Duck, 1986, No Way Out, 1987, No Holds Barred, 1989, Crazy People, 1990, City Slickers, 1991, Mr. Saturday Night, 1992, Heart and Souls, 1993, Searching For Bobby Fischer, 1993, City Slickers II: The Legend of Curly's Gold, 1994, Quiz Show, 1994, Get Shorty, 1995, The American President, 1995, Nixon, 1995, City Hall, 1996, Carpool, 1996, Unforgettable, 1996, Amistad, 1997, (voice) The Long Way Home, 1997, The Sixth Man, 1997, Gang Related, 1997, Payback, 1998, Mighty Joe Young, 1998, Lazarus and the Hurricane, 1999, Enemies of Laughter, 1999, Payback, 1999, Chill Factor, 1999, Mumford, 1999, Bait, 2000, Bounce, 2000, State and Main, 2000, The Burial Society, 2002, Alex & Emma, 2003, In Good Company, 2004, Checking Out, 2004, Marilyn Hotchkiss' Ballroom Dancing and Charm School, 2005; (TV films) Grace Kelly, 1983, The Absent-Minded Professor, 1988, Sky High, 1990, Sunset Beat, 1990, Cagney & Lacey: The Return, 1994, Cagney & Lacey: Together Again, 1995, Crime of the Century, 1996, Dash and Lilly, 1999, For Love of Country: The Arturo Sandoval Story, 2000, From Where I Sit, 2000, RFK, 2002, Capital City, 2004; (TV series) The Commish, 1991-92, Line of Fire, 2003-04; actor, dir. (films) Candor City Hospital, 2003; dir. (TV series) Everwood, 2002-; TV appearances include Barney Miller, 1980, Lou Grant, 1980, The Greatest American Hero, 1981, Hart to Hart, 1981, Fame, 1982, Taxi, 1982, The Jeffersons, 1983, Hill Street Blues, 1984, Cagney & Lacey, 1984, 85, 87, Family Ties, 1985, Cheers, 1985, 86, 21 Jump Street, 1987, St. Elsewhere, 1988, Who's the Boss?, 1988, Matlock, 1989, L.A. Law, 1990, Murphy Brown, 1990, 91, Jake and the Fatman, 1991, The Wild Thornberrys, 1998, (voice) Justice League, 2002, Without a Trace, 2002, Jack & Bobby, 2004. Office: Susan Smith & Assocs 121 N San Vicente Blvd Beverly Hills CA 90211-2303

**PAYN, CLYDE FRANCIS,** technology company executive; b. Auckland, New Zealand, Jan. 17, 1952; came to U.S., 1973; s. Phillip Francis and Ngaire Eunice P.; m. Betsy Ann Dannels, June 17, 1978; children: Tamara, Brittany, Erik. Cert., Auckland Inst. Tech., 1971; MBA, Vanderbilt U., 1980. Tech. mgr. Carborundum (N.Z.) Ltd., Auckland, 1968-73; mem. product application tech. staff Carborundum Co., Niagara Falls, NY, 1973-78; mgr. product mktg. Universal Abrasives, Phila., 1978-80; bus. mgr., catalyst advocate Johnson Matthey, Inc., Phila., 1980-84; pres. Catalyst Cons., Inc., Phila., 1984—2004; CEO Catalyst Group, Phila., 1988—. Pres. Hideaway Hill Civic Assn., Maple Glen, Pa., 1988, 89. Mem. AIChE, Am. Chem. Soc., Catalysis Soc., Comml. Devel. Assn., Chem. Mktg. Rsch. Assn., Polymer Mfg. Engrs. Assn. Achievements include development of new process technology, catalyst and product development for petroleum, petrochemical, chemical, polymer, pharmaceutical, fine chemical and environ. industries. Office: The Catalyst Group Inc PO Box 637 Spring House PA 19477-0637 Office Phone: 215-628-4447. Office Fax: 215-628-2267. Business E-Mail: cfp@catalystgrp.com

**PAYNE, ALEXANDER,** film director, writer; b. Omaha, Nebr., Feb. 10, 1961; m. Sandra Oh, Jan. 1, 2003. BA in history and Spanish lit., Stanford U., 1984; MFA in filmmaking, UCLA, 1990; LHD (hon.), U. Nebr., 2004. Prodr., writer, dir.; (films) The Passion of Martin, 1991; dir., writer Citizen Ruth, 1996; dir., writer (screenplay) Election, 1999; About Schmidt, 2002 (Golden Globe award for best screenplay (with Jim Taylor), 2003); Sideways, 2004 (Golden Globe award for best adapted screenplay, 2005, Writers Guild award for best adapted screenplay, 2005, Academy award for best adapted screenplay, 2005); writer Jurassic Park III, 2001; exec. prodr.: (films) The Assassination of Richard Nixon, 2004. Office: Twentieth Century Fox Twentieth Century House 31-32 Soho Sq London W1D 3AP England

**PAYNE, BARBARA ANN,** artist, educator; b. Marionville, Mo., Jan. 14, 1938; d. Lewis Michel and Velma Etta Rapp; m. Kenneth L. Payne, Nov. 25, 1956 (dec.); children: Kevin James, Kendra Lynne, Keli Song. AA, Fort Scott Cmty. Jr. Coll., Kans., 1965—67; BS in Kans. State Coll., Pittsburg, 1967—69. Tchr. Dept. Def. Schs., Yokosuka, Japan, 1969—72, Seoul, Republic of Korea, 1972—74, Spangdahlem, Germany, 1974—75, Bitburg,

Germany, 1975—76, Doddea, ret. Contbr. articles to profl. jours.; one-woman shows include Galerie Fasanenstrasse 71, Berlin, 1983, Am. Embassy Club, Bonn, Germany, 1986, Mobau Wittemann, Aegidienberg, Germany, 1986, Spar-und Darlenhskasse, Aegidienberg, 1987, Stadtbücherei (City Libr.), Bonn-Dottendorf, Germany, 1988, Mehrzweckhalle, Unterpleichfeld, Germany, 1989, 1990, 1991, 1992, 1993, 1994, 1995, 1996, 2001, Kultur Stüble, Höchberg, Germany, 1991, 1992, Hotel Rebstock, Würzburg, Germany, 1993, Firme Volk, Am Markt, 1994, Farewell to Europe exhbn. Erps Kwerps, Brussels, 2002, exhibited in group shows at Berlin Am. Art Guild, West Berlin, Germany and Berlin Am. Cmtys. inside West Berlin, 1977—83, Bildungscentrum des Deutschen Beamtenbundes, Königswinter, Germany, 1986, Akademie Führungskraefte Deutsche Post, Bad Honnef, Germany, 1987, Alte Kirche, Waldbüttelbrunn, Germany, 1990, 1993. Mem. Berlin Am. Art Guild, 1977—83, pres., 1981—82. Mem.: Nat. Mus. Women in the Arts. Avocations: piano, antiques, poetry, art.

**PAYNE, BILLY (WILLIAM PORTER PAYNE),** real estate lawyer, sports association executive; b. Athens, Ga. m. Martha Payne. BA in polit. sci., U. Ga.; JD, U. Ga. Joseph Henry Lumpkin Sch. of Law; D (hon.), U. SC, Emory U., Mercer U., Oglethorpe U., Presbyn. Coll., U. Ga. Comml. real estate atty. in pvt. practice; dir. Healtheon/WebMD, Premiere Technols.; vice chmn. NationsBank, Bank of Am.; head Atlanta Com. for the Olympic Games 1996, 1992; ptnr. Gleacher Ptnrs.; chmn. August Nat. Golf Club and The Masters, 2006—. Founding mem. Ga. State Games; adv. bd. Nat. Distbg. Co.; chmn. Centennial Investment Properties; bd. dirs. Crown Crafts, Atlanta C. of C., Commerce Club, Convex Grp., Atlanta Falcons, ILD Telecom., Lincoln Financial Grp. (was Jefferson-Pilot Corpn.), Cousins Properties, Anheuser-Busch, 1997—; head The Masters media com., 2000—06; pres., CEO Ga. Amateur Athletic Found. Trustee U. Ga. Found.; mem. State of Ga. Internat. Edn. Task Force; bd. deacons, ruling elder St. Luke's Presbyn. Ch. Recipient Nat. Sports Marketeer of Yr., Washington, DC Touchdown Club, 1990, Presdl. citation, Morehouse Coll., 1996, Theodore Roosevelt award, NCAA, 1997, Olympic Order in Gold, Internat. Olympic Com., Disting. Svc. award, Martin Luther King, Jr. Ctr. for Non-violent Social Change, Cmty. Svc. Governor's award for Unique and Outstanding Vol. Svc. Mem.: ABA. Achievements include induction to Ga. Sports Hall of Fame, 1996. Office: US Olympic Com 1750 E Boulder St Colorado Springs CO 80909-5724*

**PAYNE, DANIEL HAROLD (HAROLD PAYNE),** real estate developer, small business owner; b. Caddo Mills, Tex., Feb. 12, 1921; s. Flavy Malone and Sally Ella Payne; m. Wanda Louise Lyday, Aug. 3, 1941; 1 child, Kyle Steven. At, Tex. A&M, Commerce, 1940—41; grad., Tex. Real Estate Sch., Dallas, 1971. Sales J.C. Penney, Greenville, Tex., 1940—41, A&P Grocery, Greenville, 1940—41; office and credit mgr. Firestone Tire Co., Ft. Worth, 1941—42; office mgr. Guy F. Atkinson Co., Denison, 1942—43; co-owner Payne Bros. Super Markets, 1945—55; owner Payne's Famous Furniture Village, Caddo Mills, Tex., 1955—90, Payne Magnavox Ctr., Garland, Tex., 1960—61, Harold Payne Land Sales & Devel., Caddo Mills, Tex., 1970—. Adv. bd. Tex. Retail Grocery Assn., Dallas, 1951—55; bd. mem. State Nat. Bank, Caddo Mills, 1972—99; adv. mem. Tex. Retail Furniture Assn., Dallas, 1967—88. Contbr. articles to trade periodicals. Pres. Lions Club Internat., Caddo Mills, Tex., 1955—56; treas. Hunt County Fair Bd., Greenville, 1966—, publicity chmn., 1966—87; public spkr. civic, military and ch. groups in Tex. and Okla., 1963—83; elder Faith Bible Ch., Caddo Mills, Tex.; bd. mem. and publicity chmn. Sky Ranch Christian Youth Camp, Van, 1962—63; founding mem. 390th Bomb Group Meml. Mus., Tucson. 2d lt. USAF, 1942—45. Recipient Advt. award, Tex. Furniture Assn., 1969, Nat. Sales award, Nat. Furniture Assn., 1976, numerous manufacturers' sales awards. Mem.: Hunt County Freedom Forum (chmn. 1957—63, chmn. of bd. 1959—81), Masons (32 degree 1973). Republican. Avocations: youth work, civic activities, church, scouting, athletics.

**PAYNE, DAVID EMER,** university administrator; b. Salt Lake City, Mar. 29, 1944; s. John W. and Sara (Harris) P.; m. Grettle Haglund, Nov. 17, 1973; children: Sara, John, Samuel, Daniel, James, David. BS, Brigham Young U., Provo, Utah, 1968; MS, U. N.C., 1970, PhD, 1972. Asst. prof. U. Iowa, Iowa City, 1972-76; assoc. prof. U. ND., Grand Forks, 1976-80, prof., 1980-81; fellow Am. Coun. Edn., New Orleans, 1981-82; dean social sci. S.E. Mo. State U., Cape Girardeau, 1982-88; v.p. acad. affairs Sangamon State U., Springfield, Ill., 1988-89, Emporia (Kans.) State U., 1989-96, Sam Houston State U., Huntsville, Tex., 1997—. Vis. prof. U. Iceland, Reykjavik, 1974-75. Contbr. articles to profl. jours. Dist. commr. Boy Scouts Am. Am. Coun. Edn. fellow, 1981-82, Bush Found. sr. fellow, 1982. Mem. Coun. Fellows Am. Coun. Edn., Am. Sociol. Assn., C. of C., Renaissance Group (exec. bd. dirs.), Alliance of Univs. for Democracy (exec. bd. dirs., v.p.), Rotary, Sigma Xi. Mem. Lds Ch. Office: Sam Houston State U Huntsville TX 77340 Home: 4 Rushing Oak Ct Huntsville TX 77320 Office Phone: 936-294-1001. Business E-Mail: payne@shsu.edu.

**PAYNE, DEBORAH ANNE,** retired medical company officer; b. Norristown, Pa., Sept. 22, 1952; d. Kenneth Nathan Moser and Joan (Reese) Dewhurst; m. Randall Barry Payne, Mar. 8, 1975 (div.). AA, Northeastern Christian Jr. Coll., 1972; B in Music Edn., Va. Commonwealth U., 1979. Driver, social asst. Children's Aid Soc., Norristown, Pa., 1972—73; mgr. Boddie-Noell Enterprises, Richmond, Va., 1979—79; retail food saleswoman Hardee's Food Systems, Inc., Phila., 1979—81; supr., with tech. tng. and testing depts. Cardiac Datacorp., Phila., 1981—95; tng. supr. Raytel Cardiac Svcs., Forest Hills, NY 1995—98, supr. tech. support Huddonneld, NJ, 1990—2000, ret., 2000. Mem. NAFE, Delta Omicron (pres. Alpha Xi chpt. 1978-79, pres. Epsilon province 1980-85, chmn. Eastern Pa. alumni 1986-88, Star award 1979), Am. Soc. Profl. and Exec. Women. Democrat. Avocations: music, sports. Home: Park Ter Apts 8040 Rowland Ave Apt A14 Philadelphia PA 19136 Personal E-Mail: d.a.payne@att.net.

**PAYNE, DONALD MILFORD,** congressman; b. Newark, July 16, 1934; 3 children. BA in Social Studies, Seton Hall U., NJ, 1957; grad. student, Springfield Coll., Mass.; D (hon.), Chgo. State U., Drew U., Essex County Coll., William Paterson U. Educator Newark Pub. Schs.; exec. Prudential Ins. Co.; v.p. Urban Data Systems, Inc.; mem. Essex County Bd. Chosen Freeholders, 1972—78, Newark Mcpl. Coun., 1982—88, US Congress from 10th NJ dist., 1989—. Mem. Dem. steering com. US Congress, mem. Dem. leadership; mem. internat. rels. com., ranking minority mem. Africa, global human rights and internat. ops. subcommittee, mem Dem. whip orgn. Nat. pres. YMCA, 1970—73, chmn. world refugee and rehab. com., 1973—81; bd. dirs. Nat. Endowment Democracy, TransAfrica, Discovery Channel Global Edn. Fund, Congl. Award Found., Boys and Girls Club Newark, Newark Day Ctr., Fighting Back Initiative, Newark YMCA. Named one of Most Influential Black Ams., Ebony mag., 2006; recipient Leadership award, Hudson County Urban League, NJ, 2003, Visionaries for Africa award, Africa Soc., 2004, Humanitarian Svc. award, Africare, 2004, Bishop John T. Walker Disting. Humanitarian Svc. award, 2004. Mem.: NAACP (life). Democrat. Baptist. Office: US Ho Reps 2209 Rayburn Ho Office Bldg Washington DC 20515-0001 Office Phone: 202-225-3436.*

**PAYNE, ELTON CURTIS, JR.,** adult education educator; b. Beaumont, Tex., Mar. 12, 1969; s. Elton Curtis and Annie Pearl Payne; m. Nitashia Renita Tennarse, Apr. 3, 2001; children: Elton Curtis, Aubren Nichille. BA, Prairie View A&M, Tex., 1992. Occupl. tng. dir. SE Tex. Regional Planning Commn., Port Arthur, Tex., 1992—97; program dir. Lamar U., Beaumont, Tex., 1997—. Pres. Bay Area Cmty. Devel. Corp., Baytown, Tex., 2004—. Mem.: Tex. Assn. Cmty. Svc. and Continuing Edn. (Excellence award 2003), Assn. Continuing Higher Edn. (minority affairs com., Minority Affairs award 2004), Meridian Estates Homeowners Assn. (pres.), Omega Psi Phi (intake com. mem. 1994—95). Progressive. Home and Office: Po Box 10008 Beaumont TX 77710 Office Phone: 409-880-1983. Personal E-mail: payneec@hal.lamar.edu.

**PAYNE, FRANCES ANNE,** literature educator, researcher; b. Harrisonburg, Va., Aug. 28, 1932; d. Charles Franklin and Willie (Tarvin) P. BA, B.Mus., Shorter Coll., 1953; MA, Yale U., 1954, PhD, 1960. adj. fellow St. Anne's Coll., Oxford Eng. Instr. Conn. Coll., New London, 1955-56, U. Buffalo, 1958-60, lectr., 1960, asst. prof., 1960-67; assoc. prof. SUNY, Buffalo, 1967-75, prof. English and medieval lit., 1975—. Adj. fellow St. Anne's Coll., Oxford, Eng., 1966—. Author: King Alfred and Boethius, 1968; Chaucer and Menippean Satire, 1981. Contbr. articles to scholarly publs. AAUW fellow, Oxford, 1966-67; Research Found. grantee SUNY Central, Oxford, 1967, 68, 71, 72; recipient Julian Park award SUNY-Buffalo, 1979. Mem. Medieval Acad. Am., New Chaucer Soc., Internat. Soc. Anglo-Saxonists, Pi Kappa Lambda Office: SUNY-Buffalo 306 Clemens Hall Buffalo NY 14260-4600 Office Phone: 716-645-2575. Business E-Mail: fapayne@buffalo.edu.

**PAYNE, FRED J.,** epidemiologist, educator; b. Grand Forks, N.D., Oct. 14, 1922; s. Fred J. and Olive (Johnson) P.; m. Dorothy J. Peck, Dec. 20, 1948; children: Chris Ann Payne Graebner, Roy S. William F., Thomas A. BS, U. Pitts., 1948, MD, 1949; MPH, U. Calif., Berkeley, 1958. Diplomate Am. Bd. Preventive Medicine. Intern St. Joseph's Hosp., Pitts., 1949-50; resident Charity hosp., New Orleans, 1952-53; med. epidemiologist Ctr. Disease Control, Atlanta, 1953-60; prof. tropical medicine Med. Ctr. La. State U., New Orleans, 1961—66, dir. Internat. Ctr. for Med. Rsch. and Tng. Costa Rica, 1963—66; exec. sec. 3d Nat. Conf. on Pub. Health Tng., Washington, 1966-67; epidemiologist Nat. Nutrition Survey, Bethesda, Md., 1967-68; chief pub. health professions br. NIH, Bethesda, 1971-74; med. officer, sr. rsch. epidemiologist Nat. Inst. Allergy and Infectious Diseases, 1974-78; asst. health dir. Fairfax County (Va.) Health Dept., 1978-94; dir. HIV/AIDS case mgmt. program, 1988-94; cons. epidemiologist, 1994—; med. advisor Ams. for Sound AIDS Policy, 1996—; Childrens AIDS Fund, 1997—. Clin. prof. La. State U., 1966-76; cons. NIH, 1979-81; leader WHO diarrheal disease adv. team, 1960. Contbr. articles to profl. jours. Served with AUS, 1942-46, 49-52. Decorated Combat Medic Badge. Fellow Am. Coll. Preventive Medicine, Am. Coll. Epidemiology; mem. AAAS, AMA, Am. Soc. Microbiology, Internat. Epidemiology Assn., Soc. Epidemiol. Rsch., USPHS Commd. Officers Assn., Sigma Xi. Office: PO Box 16433 Washington DC 20041 Office Phone: 703-433-1640. Personal E-Mail: fdpayne6@email.msn.com. Business E-Mail: jjiyd@ibm.net.

**PAYNE, GARELD GENE,** vocal music educator, medical transcriptionist; b. Colony, Okla., Aug. 27, 1931; s. Eugene A. and Agnes D. (Chastain) P.; children: Gareld, S. Raymond, Lynn Dita, Jana Lee. MusB, Oklahoma City U., 1965; MusM in Edn., North Tex. State U. (name change to U. North Tex.), 1969; ednl. specialist, Pitts. State U., 1989; EdD, Okla. State U., 2003. Ind. organist, pianist numerous nightclubs, nationwide, 1956-64; instr. vocal, instrumental music Muenster (Tex.) Ind. Sch. Dist., 1965-69; tchr. vocal music Dallas Ind. Sch. Dist., 1966-74, Carrizo Springs (Tex.) Ind. Sch. Dist., 1976-79, Coffeyville (Kans.) Unified Sch. Dist., 1979-91; tchr. elem. vocal music Oklahoma City Pub. Schs., 1996—. Rec. artist (album) Evening With Gareld, 1984; composer publ. anthems. With USAF, 1950—53. Scholar Oklahoma City U., 1949. Mem. Am. Fedn. Musicians, NEA, Am. Orff-Schulwerk Assn., Am. Recorder Soc., Am. Theater Organ Soc., Am. Guild Organist Orgns. of Am. Kodaly Educators, Phi Mu Alpha Sinfonia Frat., Phi Delta Kappa. Republican. Methodist. Avocations: astrology, oil and water color painting, cooking, reading, computers. Home: 3643 NW 15th St Oklahoma City OK 73107-4423 Personal E-Mail: pgareld_osu@brightok.net.

**PAYNE, GEORGE FREDERICK,** academic administrator; b. Summerville, SC, Jan. 29, 1941; s. Fred N. and Lota (Griffith) Payne; m. Kay Martin, June 23, 1963; children: John F., Mark C., Janet E. Student, Ga. Inst. Tech., 1959-60, U.S. Naval Acad., 1960-62; BS, U. S.C., 1963, MA, 1966; MRE, Luth. Theol. Sem., 1968; postgrad., U. Ga., 1969-71; LLD (hon.), Lincoln Meml. U., 1988. Cert. fund raising exec. 2000. From instr. to asst. prof. Ga. So. Coll., Statesboro, 1966-78; dir. admission Brewton-Parker Coll., Mt. Vernon, Ga., 1978-80; v.p. devel. North Greenville Coll., Tigerville, SC, 1980-86; pres. Limestone Coll., Gaffney, SC, 1986-91, dir. various grants, 1976-91; spl. agt., registered rep. Prudential Fin. Svcs., 1991-92; dir. ITT Tech. Inst., Greenville, SC, 1992-95; exec. dir. Inst. Adv. Greenville Tech. Coll./ Greenville Tech. Found., 1996—, GTF McAlister LLC, 2003—, GTF Student Housing LLC, 2004—. Author: (book) An Introduction to the Principles of Geography: Facts, Skills, Concepts, and Models, 1973; contbr. articles to profl. jours. Active Leadership Greer, SC, 1980—81, regent, 1982—84; active AACTion Consortium, 1980—82, Leadership Greenville, 1982—83; bd. dirs. Greenville County unit Am. Cancer Soc., 1985—86; advisor Cherokee County Arts Coun., 1986—91; trustee Rolling Green Village Continuing Care Ret. Cmty., 1996—2006, sec., 1998, 2003; trustee Baptist Found. S.C., 2001—05, Oakwood Sch., Va., 2002—; bd. mem. Greenville Redevel. Authority, 2005—, chair adminstrn. com., 2006. With USN, 1960—62. Recipient Disting. Svc. award, Brewton-Parker Coll., 1980, North Greenville Coll., 1986. Mem.: Coun. Advancement Support Edn. (Circle of Excellence award for ednl. fund-raising 2001, 2004), Assn. Fund-Raising Profls. (cert. fund-raising exec.), Greater Greer C. of C. (bd. dirs. 1981—84), Rotary. Baptist. Avocation: reading. Office: Greenville Tech Coll McAlister Ste B-12 225 S Pleasantburg Dr Greenville SC 29607 Office Phone: 864-250-8514. Business E-Mail: Fred.Payne@GvlTec.edu.

**PAYNE, GLORIA MARQUETTE,** business educator; b. Elkins, W.Va., Dec. 21, 1923; d. Anthony and Roselyn Marquette; m. Carl Wesley Payne, Mar. 6, 1950; 1 child, Mary Debra Payne Moore. BA, Davis and Elkins Coll., MHL (hon.), MA, W.Va. U.; PhD, U. Pitts., 1975; postgrad., NYU Fashion Inst. Tech. Cert. designed appearance cons. Sec. Equitable Ins. Co., Elkins, 1943-44; tchr., dept. head Spencer (W.Va.) H.S., 1944-45; prof. bus. Davis & Elkins Coll., Elkins, 1945-93; image cons. Elkins, 1988-93; bus. cons., 1970-93; mgr. Elkins Wallpaper Shop, 1945-65; owner Merle Norman Cosmetic Studio, Elkins, 1950-56. Dir. tchr. workshops W.Va. U., Marshall U., State Dept. Edn., Charleston, W.Va., summers; dir. machine shorthand workshops for tchrs. throughout the U.S.; dir. designer appearance World Modeling Assn., N.Y.C., 1989—; instr. modeling Davis & Elkins Coll., 1980-93. Author: A Methods Class is Interesting and Challenging, 1970, The Oak or the Pumpkin; mem. editl. bd. Nat. Assn. of Business Teachers Edn. Pub., 1993, 94; contbr. articles to profl. jours. Chair Bi-Centennial, City of Elkins; dir. Elkins Fair, City of Elkins; pres. St Brendans Parish; judge Mountain State Forest Festival Parades, 1988-2004; rep. Region I at Dallas Nat. Conv., 1994 (one of five nat. finalists); div. chair bus., econs., and tourism. Recipient Outstanding Prof. award Sears-Roebuck Co., Lois Latham award for Excellence in Tchg., Cmty. Svc. award Elkins C. of C., 1992, Outstanding Educator award BPW, 1997, W.Va. Bus. Edn. Assn., W.Va. Vocat. Assn., 1994, 97, Region I award for Outstanding Vocat.Educator, Outstanding Collegiate Tchr. Bus. award, 1997, award of merit Assn. Career and Tech. Edn., 2003-04, Outstanding Prof. of Region award, 2003, 04, 05, Humanitarian award Odd Fellows Lodge, 2004; 1st recipient James S. McDonnell Found. Fully Endowed Acad. Chair in Bus. and Econs.; named Educator of Yr., W.Va. Women's Club, Outstanding Educator AAUW, Randolph County C. of C. Citizen of Yr., 1998, Disting. Citizen, Gov. W.Va., W.Va. Women in Bus. Champion, Small Bus. Assn., 2005. Mem. Am. Bus. Writers Assn., W.Va. Edn. Assn. (past pres., Outstanding Prof., Outstanding Svc. award, Outstanding Bus. Educator award), Tri-State Bus. Assn. (historian, outstanding svc. award, Tchr.-Educator of the South award 1991), World Modeling Assn. (v.p. 1988-95, modeling award 1989), Designed Appearance U.S. (dir. 1990-98), W.Va. Bus. Edn. Assn. (award 1977, 85, 94, 97), Bus. and Profl. Women's Orgn., W.Va. C. of C., The Fashion Club (advisor), Beta Sigma Phi (advisor), Beta Alpha Beta (advisor), Pi Beta Phi, Phi Delta Lambda (advisor). Democrat. Roman Catholic. Avocations: flower arranging, modeling. Home: 301 Davis St Elkins WV 26241-4030 Office: Davis & Elkins Coll 100 Sycamore St Elkins WV 26241-3996

**PAYNE, HARRY MORSE, JR.,** architect; b. Norwood, Mass., Nov. 3, 1922; s. Harry Morse and Edna May (Beardsley) P.; m. Helen Marion Beasley, Aug. 29, 1946; children: Harry Morse, Thomas Beasley, Amelia Morse. Student, Boston Archtl. Center, 1946—49, MIT, 1949—50. Draftsman William G.

Upham, Norwood, 1946-47; designer William Riseman Assos., Boston, 1947-49, Harry J. Korslund, Norwood, 1949-51, William Hoskins Brown, Boston, 1951-52; designer, prin. dir. The Architects Collaborative, Cambridge, Mass., 1952-86, pres., 1975-77, emeritus, 1986—, Boston Archtl. Center, 1963-65, 71-73; asst. prof. Harvard U. Grad. Sch. Design, 1954-63. Prin. works include U.S. Embassy, Athens, Greece, U. Baghdad, Iraq, Temple Israel, Boston, Quincy Sch., Boston, Nauset Regional H.S., Cape Cod, Mass.; author: The Survey System of the Old Colony, 1985, Name Change--Paine to Payne, 1992, Cape Cod Land Strategy, 1994, New England 17th Century Land Strategy, 1997, America's Stonehenge As Architecture, 1998, Payne Paine Family—England and Cape Cod, 1999, The Ordering of Towns: Massachusetts Bay Colony 17th Century Land Strategy, 2002. Served with USN, 1943-46. Recipient Cascieri Lectureship in Humanities medal, Boston Archtl. Ctr., 2002. Fellow AIA; mem. Soc. Archtl. Historians, N.E. Antiquities Rsch. Assn., Boston Soc. Architects, Mass. State Assn. Architects, New Eng. Hist. and Geneal. Soc., The Colonial Soc. Mass., Mass. Soc. Genealogists (pres. 1986-88), Lincoln Hist. Soc. (pres. 1990-92). Home: 303 Winthrop Terr Bedford MA 01730

**PAYNE, HOWARD JAMES,** retired insurance company executive; b. Des Moines, Iowa, Oct. 22, 1940; s. James W. and Wilma F. (Kever) P.; m. Mary J. Kellam, June 8, 1963; children: Scott D., Steven M. MBA, U. Iowa, 1986. CPCU, assoc. in underwriting, assoc. in mgmt. Underwiter Allied Ins. Co., Des Moines, 1963-70, br. underwriting mgr. Phoenix, 1973-75, asst. br. mgr. Santa Rosa, Calif., 1975-77; casualty underwriting mgr. Am. States Ins. Co., Indpls., 1970-73; asst. v.p. underwriting Lumberman's Mut. Ins. Co., Mansfield, Ohio, 1977-80; asst. v.p., underwriting mgr. Hastings (Mich.) Mutual Ins. Co., 1980-82; v.p. underwriting John Deere Ins. Co., Moline, Ill., 1982-86, v.p., regional mgr., 1986-90; v.p. credit ins. mgr. John Deere Ins. Co, Des Moines, 1990-93; v.p., spl. program mgr. John Deere Transp., Brookfield, Wis., 1993-99. Ins. instr. Am. States Ins. Co., Indpls., 1971-73, CPCU chpt., Phoenix, 1973-75; ins. instr., adviser C.C. Mansfield, Ohio, 1978-80; pres. Am. States Credit Union, Indpls., 1973. Mem.: CPCU Soc. Republican. Avocations: tennis, exercise, reading. Home: 12 Spring River Ln Cherokee Village AR 72529

**PAYNE, JAMES ERICK,** lawyer; b. Port Arthur, Tex., Mar. 3, 1968; s. James Caleb and Jessie Bee (Hudson) Payne; m. Tracie Yvonne Wilson, July 22, 1995; children: James Caleb II, Joshua Christian, Taryn Jordan. BS, U. Houston, 1989, JD, 1993. Bar: Tex. 1993, U.S. Dist. Ct. (so. dist.) Tex. 1993, U.S. Dist. Ct. (ea. dist.) Tex. 1996, U.S. Ct. Appeals (5th cir.) 1997, U.S. Supreme Ct. 1998, bd. cert. personal injury lawyer; bd. cert. civil trial law: Nat. Bd. Trial Advocacy. Legis. asst. Congressman William Lehman, Washington, 1989; assoc. Vinson & Elkins, Houston, 1993-95; Provost & Umphrey, LLP, Beaumont, Tex., 1995—. Mem. Cmty. Adv. Com., Beaumont, 1996—97, Bapt. Healthcare Found., Beaumont, 1996—97. Mem.: ATLA, Tex. Super Lawyer Million Dollar Advocates Forum, Coll. of the State Bar of Tex., Jefferson County Bar Assn., Port Arthur Bar Assn. (sec. 1995—96, v.p. 1996—97), Tex. Trial Lawyers Assn. (bd. dirs. 2001—), Alpha Phi Alpha. Democrat. Baptist. Avocations: golf, bowling. Office: Provost and Umphrey Law Firm 490 Park St Beaumont TX 77701-2900 Office Phone: 409-835-6000. Business E-Mail: jpayne@provostumphrey.com.

**PAYNE, JEFFERY E.,** software quality management company executive; BS in Computer Sci., Allegheny Coll.; MS in Computer Sci., Coll. William and Mary. Co-founder, pres., CEO Cigital, Inc., Dulles, Va., 1992—, also bd. dir. Lectr. in field. Published more than 30 papers. Mem. Loudoun County Environ. Mem.: IEEE Computer Soc. (co-founder, No. Va. Chpt.), Assn. for Computing Machinery (ACM) (past nat. lectr.). Office: Cigital Inc 21351 Ridgetop Cir Ste 400 Dulles VA 20166-6503 Office Phone: 703-404-9293. Office Fax: 703-404-9295. Business E-Mail: jepayn@cigital.com.

**PAYNE, JOHN ROSS,** archivist, educator, library and information scientist, educator; b. Clarksville, Tex., Dec. 4, 1941; BA, Tex. Christian U., 1963; MLS, North Tex. State U., 1967. Successively acting dir., asst. to dir., assoc. libr. for acquisitions, assoc. libr. for ops., rsch. assoc. Harry Ransom Humanities Rsch. Ctr. U. Tex., Austin, 1969—85, prof. Grad. Sch. Libr. and Info. Sci., 1988—89, 1991—92, tchr. course in rare books and lit. manuscripts; dir. Payne Assocs., 1979—. Author: A Bibliography of W. H. Hudson, 1977, Modern British Fiction: An Exhibit, 1972; co-author: (with Elizabeth Johnson) Katherine Mansfield: An Exhibit, 1973, (with Adrian Goldstone) A Bibliographical Catalogue of John Steinbeck, 1975; contbr. articles to profl. jours. Lilly Fellow Ind. U., 1967-68. Mem. ALA, Am. Soc. Appraisers (state dep. dir.), Appraisers Assn. Am., Soc. Am. Archivists (hon., speaker at Atlanta meeting 1988), Manuscripts Soc., Tex. Libr. Assn., Tex. State Hist. Assn., Book Club of Tex., Tex. and Southwestern Collectors' Assn., Grolier Club. Address: 2309 Camino Alto Austin TX 78746-2404 Office Phone: 512-328-4535. Business E-Mail: payne@payne-associates.com.

**PAYNE, LADELL,** retired academic administrator; b. Birmingham, Ala., Dec. 6, 1933; s. Clyde Ladell and Martha Gerusia (McBrayer) P.; m. Mary Jean Taylor, Aug. 23, 1954; children: Lisa, Jennifer BA with honors, Samford U., 1955; MA in English, La. State U., 1956; PhD in English, Stanford U., 1966; LittD, Samford U., 1996; DHL, Randolph-Macon Coll., 1998. From instr. to prof. English, chmn. dept. lit. and presdl. asst. Claremont McKenna Coll., Calif., 1960-79; pres. Randolph-Macon Coll., Ashland, Va., 1979-97, prof. emeritus, 1997—, pres. emeritus, 1998—. Fulbright lectr. U. Vienna, Austria, 1971-72; nat. cons. Ctr. for Study So. Culture, U. Miss., Oxford, 1980—; adminstrv. assoc. Am. Coun. on Edn., Washington, 1979, mem. nat. panel, commn. on women in higher edn., 1981-97; founding mem. pres.'s commn. Nat. Collegiate Athletic Assn., 1984-97. Author: Thomas Wolfe, 1969, Black Novelists and the Southern Literary Tradition, 1981; contbr. articles on William Faulkner, Robert Penn Warren, Thomas Wolfe, and Ellen Glasgow to profl. jours. Mem. Va. bd. edn. NCCJ, 1980-92, chmn. Va. region, Richmond, 1982-85; trustee, mem. exec. com. The Collegiate Schs., Richmond, 1986-89; bd. dirs. Music in the Mountains, Nevada City, Calif. 2000-02. NEH fellow, 1973. Mem. Nat. Assn. Ind. Colls. and Univs. (bd. dirs. 1990-93), Coun. on Postsecondary Accreditation (bd. dirs. 1991-93), Pi Kappa Phi, Phi Beta Kappa. Methodist. Avocation: classical music.

**PAYNE, MARY LIBBY,** retired judge; b. Gulfport, Miss., Mar. 27, 1932; d. Reece O. and Emily Augusta (Cook) Bickerstaff; m. Bobby R. Payne; children: Reece Allen, Glenn Russell. Student, Miss. U. for Women, 1950-52; BA in Polit. Sci. with distinction, U. Miss., 1954, LLB, 1955. Bar: Miss. 1955. Ptnr. Bickerstaff & Bickerstaff, Gulfport, 1955-56; sec. Guaranty Title Co., Jackson, Miss., 1957; assoc. Henley, Jones, & Henley, Jackson, Miss., 1958-61; freelance rschr. Pearl, Miss., 1961-63; solo practitioner Brandon, Miss., 1963-68; exec. dir. Miss. Judiciary Commn., Jackson, 1968-70; chief drafting & rsch. Miss. Ho. Reps., Jackson, 1970-72; asst. atty. gen. State Atty. Gen. Office, Jackson, 1972-75; founding dean, assoc. prof. Sch. Law Miss. Coll., Jackson, 1975-78, prof., 1978-94, scholar in residence, prof. emerita, 2003—; judge Miss. Ct. Appeals, Jackson, 1995—2001; ret., 2001. Mem. bd. disting. alumnae Miss. U. Women, 1988—2000. Contbr. articles to profl. jours. Founder, bd. dirs. Christian Conciliation Svc., Jackson, 1983-93; bd. dirs. Exchange Club's Child Abuse Prevention Ctr. of Jackson, 1999-2001; counsel Christian Action Com. Rankin Bapt. Assn., Pearl, 1968-92; advisor Covenant Ministerial Fellowship, 1995-2002. Named Miss. Coll. Lawyer of Yr., Miss. Coll. Sch. Law Alumni Assn., 1998, Outstanding Woman Lawyer, Miss. Women Lawyers Assn., 1999, Susie Blue Buchanan award, Women in Profession Com. of Miss. Bar, 2000; recipient Book of Golden Deeds award, Pearl Exch. Club, 1989, Excellence medallion, Miss. U. Women, 1990, Woman of Yr. award, Miss. Assn. Women Higher Edn., 1989, Power of One award, Miss. Govs. Conf., 1996, Disting. Jurist award, Miss. Class, 2004, Lifetime Achievement aware, Miss. Bar, 2005. Fellow Am. Bar Found.; mem. Miss. Bar Found., Christian Legal Svc. (nat. bd. dirs. 1992-2001, Skeeter Ellis Svc. to Law Students award 1999, Lifetime Achievement award 2002). Baptist. Avocations: public speaking, travel, needlepoint, sewing, reading.

**PAYNE, MICHAEL DAVID,** English language educator; b. Dallas, Jan. 17, 1941; s. Fred G. Payne and Jocie Marie (Kirkham) Lundberg; children: Jeffrey, Jennifer, Albert, Edward. Student, U. Calif.-Berkeley, 1958-59, 61; BA, So. Oreg. Coll., 1962; PhD, U. Oreg., 1969. Tchr. English, Medford (Oreg.) Sr. High Sch., 1962-63; instr. English, U. Oreg., Eugene, 1963-69; asst. prof. to prof. English, Bucknell U., Lewisburg, Pa., 1969—, chmn. dept. history, 1980-82, chmn. dept. English, 1982-88, 92-94, chair faculty, 2000—04, Presdl. prof., 1982-86, John P. Crozer prof. English lit. 1986—2006; dir. Bucknell Univ. Press, 1972-76; assoc. editor Bucknell Rev., 1970-85, editor, 1985-88. Author: Irony in Shakespeare's Roman Plays, 1974, Reading Theory, 1993, Reading Knowledge, 1997; editor: Contemporary Essays on Style, 1969, Shakespeare: Contemporary Critical Approaches, 1979, Text, Interpretation, Theory, 1985, Self, Sign and Symbol, 1986, Perspective, 1986, Criticism, History and Intertextuality, 1987, New Interpretations of American Literature, 1987, The Senses of Stanley Cavell, 1988, Dictionary of Cultural and Critical Theory, 1996, Renaissance Literature: An Anthology, 2003, Life.after.theory, 2003, The Greenblatt Reader, 2005; gen. editor Bucknell Lectures in Lit. Theory, 1990-95. Recipient Lindback award for disting. teaching, 1976, Disting. Svc. award CEA, 1988, Profl. Achievement award, 1993; Folger Shakespeare Libr. fellow, 1973, NEH fellow, 1974, Bucknell Alumni fellow, 1978-79. Mem.: MLA, Children's Lit. Assn., Coll. English Assn., Inst. Romance Studies (U. London), Johnson Soc. London, Phi Beta Kappa (hon.). Home: 24 S Water St Lewisburg PA 17837-1562 Office Phone: 570-577-3020. E-mail: payne@bucknell.edu.

**PAYNE, PAULINE MARIA,** retired medical/surgical nurse; b. St. Louis, May 12, 1925; d. Elder and Lucille Miller Brown; m. Wardell Clark Payne, Sept. 30, 1950 (dec. Nov. 1962); children: Sandra Michele, William Michael. Diploma, Phillips Hosp. Sch. Nursing, 1947. RN Mo., 1947. Staff nurse Homer G. Phillips Hosp., St. Louis, 1947—49, clin. instr. med. ward, 1949—52; staff nurse Cochran VA Hosp., 1954—72; ret., 1972. Chmn. Rev. John & Regina Nance Meml. Scholar Fund, St. Louis, 1986—96. Recipient Cmty. Svc. award, ARC, St. Louis, 1981. Mem.: ANA, Black Nurses Assn. Greater St. Louis (treas. 1985—89), Nat. Black Nurses Assn. Baptist. Avocations: art, reading. Home: 5866 Julian Ave Saint Louis MO 63112

**PAYNE, ROGER LEE,** geographer; b. Winston-Salem, N.C., Oct. 26, 1946; s. Irvin Lee and Gladys Odel (Binkley) P.; m. Sara Lucinda Parker, Aug. 16, 1970 (div. Feb. 1992); 1 child, Jennifer Nicole; m. Anne F. Remen, June 11, 1995. BA, East Carolina U., 1969, MA, 1972. Geographer, chief geog. names U.S. Geol. Survey, Reston, Va., 1974—2006; instr. geography and history Pan Am. Inst./U.S. Geog. Survey, 1989—; exec. sec. U.S. Bd. Names, U.S. Geol. Survey. Washington, 1990—2006, emeritus, 2006—. Instr. East Caroline U., Greenville, N.C., 1969-71, George Washington U., Washington, 1977-90, George Mason U., Fairfax, Va., 1979-83, 1998—2003, Benjamin Franklin U., Washington, 1985-87, Old Dominion U., 2005—; del. UN, N.Y.C., 1987—2006, instr., 1995—; mem. scientist exch. Geol. Survey, Beijing, 1989; instr. Nat. Black Colls., Howard U., 1985; book reviewer AAAS, 1975—; mem. Antarctica Sci. Field Program, 1999-2000; cons. in field. Author: Urban Development in South Africa, 1972, Place Names of Outer Banks, 1985, Manuals on Auto Names, 1987, 89, 97; coord., editor: (book series) National Gazetter U.S., 1982—; contbr. articles to profl. jours. Chmn. E. Carolina Blood Dr., Greenville, 1969. Lt. USAF, 1970-72. Recipient Guy Buzzard award Gamma Theta Upsilon, 1970; Superior Svc. award Geol. Survey, 1988, Outstanding Achievement award, 1985, 86, 88, 97, 2004. Fellow Explorers Club; mem. Assn. Am. Geographers (various coms. 1969-95, pres. mid-Atlantic divsn. 1981-82, treas., sec.), Am. Name Soc. (pres. 1989), Am. Nat. Std. Inst. (rep. 1986—), Cosmos Club (cons. manuscript reviewer). Achievements include Mount Payne, Antarctica, named in his honor. Avocation: hiking. Home: 1462 Gleasons Landing Dr Saint Helena Island SC 29920 Office: US Geol Survey 523 National Ctr 12201 Sunrise Valley Dr Reston VA 20192-0523 Business E-Mail: rpayne@usgs.gov.

**PAYNE, ROGER SEARLE,** zoologist, researcher, science administrator, conservationist; b. NYC, Jan. 29, 1935; m. Katy Boynton, 1960 (div. 1985); children: John, Holly, Laura Sam; m. Lisa Harrow, Aug. 18, 1991. AB in Animal Behavior, Harvard U., 1957; PhD, Cornell U., 1961. Rsch. zoologist Inst. for Rsch. in Animal Behavior N.Y. Zool. Inst., N.Y.C., 1968-71; asst. prof. biology Rockefeller U., N.Y.C., 1968-71; founder, pres. Ocean Alliance, Lincoln, Mass., 1971—. Author: Among Whales, 1995; host (TV documentary) In the Company of Whales, 1992 (series) Ocean Planet, 1994-95; co-writer, co-dir. (film) Whales, 1995. Co-recipient Albert Schweitzer medal Animal Welfare Inst., 1980; recipient Joseph Wood Krutch medal Humane Soc. U.S., 1989, Lyndhurst prize Lyndhurst Found.; 1984; genius grantee John D. and Catherine T. MacArthur Found., 1984, Global 500 award UN, 1988; knighted, Netherlands, 1977. Home: 2141 Biscuit Hl South Woodstock VT 05071-9530 Office: Ocean Alliance 191 Weston Rd Lincoln MA 01773-4516 E-Mail: rpayne@oceanalliance.org.

**PAYNE, RONALD DEAN, II,** music educator, director; s. Ron and Johanna Smetena Payne; m. Linda Marie Wirzbicki, Jan. 1, 2005. MusB, Appalachian State U., Boone, 2004. Cert. music edn. K-12 NC Dept. Pub. Instrn., 2004. Dir. music Topsail HS, Hampstead, NC, 2005; dir. bands Alexander Ctrl. HS, Taylorsville, NC, 2005—. Ch. pianist New Salem Presbyn. Ch., Stony Point, NC, 2006—. Mem.: Music Educators Nat. Conf., Nat. Band Assn., NC Assn. of Educators, NC Bandmasters Assn. (webmaster 2005), Kappa Delta Pi, Kappa Kappa Psi (chpt. pres. 2003—04, sec. 2005). Office: Alexander Ctrl HS 241 School Dr Taylorsville NC 28681 Office Phone: 828-632-9090. Business E-Mail: ron_payne@alexander.k12.nc.us.

**PAYNE, ROY A.,** poet; b. Excelsior Springs, Mo., Mar. 7, 1916; s. Alvin and Laura Frances (Jones) Payne; m. Letha Payne (dec. Feb. 19, 1997); children: DeAnn June(dec.), Linda Cathy. Grad. H.S., Excelsior Springs, 1934. Clk. U.S. Post Office, Excelsior Springs, 1938—49, 1st supt. mails, 1949, asst. postmaster, 1950—70. Author: Rainbow In Your Tear, numerous poems. With U.S. Army, 1944—46, ETO. Recipient awards, Internat. Soc. Poets, Famous Poets Soc. Democrat. Home: 518 NW Shamrock Ave Apt 127 Lees Summit MO 64081-1174 E-mail: homedukecrimson@yahoo.com.

**PAYNE, ROY JULIA (Peck) P.;** lawyer; b. New Orleans, Aug. 30, 1952; s. Fred J. and Dorothy Julia (Peck) P.; m. Laureen Fuller, Sept. 8, 1973; children: Julie Elizabeth, Kelly Kathryn, Alex Steven, Michael Lawrence. BA with distinction, U. Va., 1974; JD, La. State U., 1977; LLM, Harvard U., 1980. Bar: La. 1977, U.S. Dist. Ct. (we. dist.) La. 1980, U.S. Ct. Appeals (5th cir.) 1980, U.S. Supreme Ct. 1983. Law clk. to judge U.S. Dist. Ct., Shreveport, La., 1977-79; assoc. Blanchard, Walker, O'Quin & Roberts, Shreveport, 1980-83, ptnr., 1984-87; U.S. Magistrate judge We. Dist. La., Shreveport, 1987—2005; pvt. practice Shreveport, 2005—. Instr. New Eng. Sch. Law, Boston, 1979-80. Contbr. articles to profl. jours. Chmn. Northwest La. Legal Svcs. Assn., Shreveport, 1984-85; pres. Shreveport Bar Found., 2003—. Mem. 5th Cir. Bar Assn., 5th Cir. Jud. Coun. (magistrate judges com. 1992-2000), La. State Bar Assn. (editl. bd. Forum jour., 1983-87, legal aid com.), Fed. Magistrate Judges Assn. (circuit dir. 2003-05), Shreveport Bar Assn., La. Assn. Def. Counsel (bd. dirs. 1987), Harry V. Booth Am. Inn of Ct. (pres. elect 1994-95, pres. 1996-98), Order of Coif, Phi Kappa Phi, Phi Delta Phi. Republican. Methodist. Home: 12494 Harts Island Rd Shreveport LA 71115-8505 Office: 2800 Youree Dr Ste 120 Shreveport LA 71104 Office Phone: 318-865-8680. E-mail: royspayne@gmail.com.

**PAYNE, SEPTEMBER ANNE,** music educator; arrived in U.S., 1982; d. Donald George and Jeanette Chalfont Payne. MusB, U. We. Ontario, 1978; MusM, Boston U., 1987; MusD, Rice U., 1996. Prof. flute South and North Shore Conservatories Music, Boston, 1984—93; prof. flute, dir. winds Houston (Tex.) Conservatory Music, 1993—97; prof. Grossmont Coll., San Diego, 2001—, Mesa Coll., San Diego, 2002—. Exec. dir. Pilgrim Fine Arts Acad., Houston, 1987—88; lectr. Houston (Tex.) C.C., 1990—97; adj. prof. San Diego (Calif.) State U., 1996—; condr. Civic Youth Orch., San Diego, 2000—04; condr. flute choir Calif. Inst. Music, 2004—, dir. Dept. Winds and Brass, 2004—. Author: Canadian Flute Music - Analysis, 1986, Catalogue of

Canadian Flute Music, 1986. Recipient Master Class award, James Galway Competition, 1999. Mem.: Nat. Flute Assn., Marcel Moyse Soc. (sec. 2003), Kappa Kappa Psi, Mu Phi Epsilon. Avocations: figure skating, backpacking, sailing, bicycling, painting. Office: San Diego State U Sch Music and Dance 5500 Campanile Rd San Diego CA 92182

**PAYNE, SIDNEY STEWART,** retired archbishop; b. Fogo, Nfld., Can., June 6, 1932; m. Selma Carlson, 1962; children: Carla Ann, Christopher Stewart, Robert Clement, Angela Marie Louise. BA, Meml. U., St. John's, Nfld., 1958; lic. of theology, Queen's Coll. St. John's, 1958; BDiv, Gen. Synod, 1968; DDiv (hon.), King's Coll., Halifax, N.S., Can., 1981. Ordained priest Anglican Ch., 1958, bishop, 1978, archbishop, 1990. Deacon Mission of Happy Valley, Goose Bay, Labrador, Nfld., Canada, 1957-65; rector Parish of Bay Roberts, Nfld., Canada, 1965-70, Parish of St. Anthony, 1970-78; bishop Diocese of Western Nfld., 1978-90, archbishop of Western Nfld. and Met. Eccles. Province of Can., 1990-97; ret., 1997. Pres. Diocesan Synod, chmn. exec. com., mem. ex-officio diocesan coms.; pres. Provincial Synod, Provincial Coun.; chair Provincial House of Bishops; mem. long range planning com., ministry com., mem. nat. exec. coun. Partners in World Mission, Stewardship and Fin. Devel. Com.; mem. Anglican/Roman Cath. Bishops' Dialogue, Can.; active Provincial and Nat. House of Bishops. Mem. Internat. Grenfell Assn. (past bd. dirs.). Anglican. Avocations: reading, walking, gardening, cross country skiing. Home: PO Box 2255 R R 1 Stn Main Corner Brook NL Canada A2H 2N2 E-mail: sspayne@nf.sympatico.ca.

**PAYNE, STANLEY E.,** mathematics professor; b. Chgo., Sept. 26, 1939; s. Don Ivan Payne and Agnes Eileen Craven - Payne; life ptnr. Angelika Adamic; m. Shirley Ann Ellison, Aug. 22, 1961 (div. Sept. 26, 1983); children: Tanya Marie Ker, Rahn Kenneth, Brian Curtis, Brett Ivan. MS in Math., Fla. State U., Tallahassee, 1963, PhD in Math., 1966. Prof. math. Miami U., Oxford, Ohio, 1966—84, U. Colo., Health Sci. Ctr., Denver, 1984—. Contbr. articles to profl. jours. Mem.: Inst. Combinatorics and Its Applications, Am. Math. Soc. (life). Achievements include discovery of new examples of ovals and generalised quadrangles. Office: U Colo at Denver CB 170 POBox 173364 Denver CO 80217-3364 Office Phone: 303-556-8443. Office Fax: 303-556-8550. Business E-Mail: stanpayne@mac.com.

**PAYNE, STEVEN M.,** musician, director; b. Dorchester, Dorset, United Kingdom, Oct. 3, 1973; s. Mark John and Diane Marion Payne; m. Ena Cathleen Murphy. MusM, Ind. U., Bloomington, 1995—98. Exec. dir. Pacific Symphony Youth Orch., Santa Ana, Calif., 2003—; advt. & promotions mgr. Dayton Philharm. Orch., Ohio. Grantee Fulbright award, 1995—96. Mem.: Am. Symphony Orch. League. Office: Pacific Symphony Youth Orchestra 3631 S Harbor Blvd Ste 100 Santa Ana CA 92704 Office Fax: 714-755-5799.

**PAYNE, TIMOTHY D.,** information technology executive; b. Oct. 25, 1958; BS, Univ. Calif., Santa Barbara, 1981. Pres., CEO Openware Technologies Inc., 1994—97; pres., COO Modis Inc., 1997—2000; pres., CEO MPS (Modis Profl. Services) Group Inc., Jacksonville, Fla., 2001—. Bd. dir. ITFlorida.com Inc. Office: MPS Group Inc 1 Independent Dr Jacksonville FL 32202*

**PAYNE, TYSON ELLIOTT, JR.,** retired insurance executive; b. Dallas, May 25, 1927; s. Tyson Elliott and Winnie Claris (Denman) P.; m. Billie Jane Spears, Aug. 28, 1948; children: David Tyson, Sally Jane. B.J., U. Tex., 1949. CLU, ChFC. Sports editor Lufkin (Tex.) News, 1949-51, Tyler (Tex.) Courier Times, 1951-53; with Am. Nat. Ins. Co., Galveston, Tex., 1953-88, v.p. health ins. ops. St. Louis, 1965-1970, v.p. mktg. Galveston, 1970-86; pvt. practice ins. agt. Austin, Tex., 1987-88; exec. v. p., dir. Sch. of Ins. & Fin. Svcs. at U. Houston, 1988-92; ret., 1992. Elder Presbyn. Ch. With USNR, 1945-46. Home: 8110 Cardin Dr Austin TX 78759-8704 Personal E-mail: tpaynejr@sbcglobal.net, tpaynejr1927@sbcglobal.net.

**PAYRI, JOEL,** pharmaceutical marketing executive; b. Sidi-Bel-Abbes, Algeria, Nov. 29, 1961; s. Rene and Marie P. DVM, Nat. Vet. Sch., Toulouse, France, 1985, diploma of anatomo-pathology, 1988; diploma of med. stats., U. Paris VI, 1989; MBA, INSEAD, Fontainebleau, France, 1991. Pvt. vet. practice, St. Gaudens, France, 1985-86; study dir. Searle Rsch. and Devel., Sophia Antipolis, France, 1986-87; head exptl. cardiology Rhone Poulenc Sante, Vitry sur Seine, France, 1988-90; mktg. mgr. Pharmuka-Rhone Poulenc, Paris, 1991-92; worldwide product mgr. Taxotere Rhone Poulenc Rorer, Paris, 1992-96; internat. mktg. dir. GlaxoSmithkline, London, 1996—2001; v.p. internat. Biogen Idec, Paris, 2001—06, Johnson & Johnson, 2006—. Surg. asst. Nat. Vet. Sch., Toulouse, 1984-85; press. new mgmt. team Rhone Poulenc Sante, Paris, 1989-91; interviewer INSEAD MBA cands. Biogen Idec, Paris, 1995-2006. Author: Telemetry and Gastric pH Measurements, 1985 (gold medal 1985); contbr. to websites and pubs. for Internat. Herpes Alliance. Capt. French Army, 1987-90, Paris. Grantee Ministry Agr., 1985. Mem. Am. Social Health Assn., Infectious Disease Soc. Am. Home: La petite Ourse Anse de Maldorme Bouches du Rhone 13007 Marseilles France Office: Johnson and Johnson 1 rue Camille Desmoulins 92787 Paris France Fax: 33-147-217535. Business E-Mail: jpayri@jnjfr.jnj.com.

**PAYSON, MARTIN F.,** lawyer; b. Bklyn., Dec. 25, 1940; m. Rhoda Shapiro, Oct. 8, 1961; children: Jacqueline, Marla. BBA, CCNY, 1961; JD, Bklyn. Law Sch., 1966. Bar: N.Y. 1967, Pa. 1989, U.S. Ct. Appeals (1st cir.) 1971, U.S. Ct. Appeals (2d and 3d cirs.) 1968, U.S. Ct. Appeals (4th cir.) 1969, U.S. Supreme Ct. 1970. Gen. ptnr. Jackson Lewis L.L.P. (formerly Jackson, Lewis, Schnitzler & Krupman), White Plains, NY, 1967—. Lectr. in field. Contbr. articles to various publs. With U.S. Army, 1961-62. Mem. N.Y. State Bar Assn. (labor and employee rels. sects.), Soc. for Human Resource Mgmt. Avocations: photography, bicycling, model railroading, gardening Office: Jackson Lewis LLP One N Broadway White Plains NY 10601 Office Phone: 914-328-0404. Business E-Mail: paysonm@jacksonlewis.com.

**PAYTON, CYDNEY,** museum director, curator; Owner Cydney Payton Artfolio, 1985—90; co-owner Payton-Rule Gallery, 1990—92; dir. Boulder Mus. Contemporary Art, Colo., 1992—2000; dir., curator Mus. Contemporary Art/Denver, 2001—. Office: Mus Contemporary Art/Denver 1275 19th St Denver CO 80202 Office Phone: 303-298-7554.

**PAYTON, DONNA S.,** minister; b. Norfolk, Va., Nov. 26, 1956; d. Everet and Joycelyn Payton; children: Salatheial Payton-Moodie, Sherene Payton-Moodie. B of Theology, United Christian Coll., Goldsboro, NC, 1997, D (hon.) of Div., 1997; M in Bibl. Studies, Jacksonville Sch. Theology, Fla., 2000, PhD in Clin. Christian Psychology, 2000. Dir. Mercy Ministries Inc, Norfolk, Va., 1988—; sr. evangelist, missionary Joe Martin Ministries, 1993—95; sr. pastor, overseer In His Presence Deliverance Ministries Internat., 2006—. Mem. Norfolk Civic League, 1987—2006. Home Fax: 757-282-5920. Personal E-mail: dr.donnapayton@inhispresencedeliveranceministri.

**PAYTON, GARY DWAYNE,** professional basketball player; b. Oakland, Calif., July 23, 1968; m. Monique Payton; children: Raquel, Gary Dwayne, Julian. Grad., Oreg. State U., 1990. Drafted NBA, 1990; guard Seattle Supersonics, 1990—2003, Milwaukee Bucks, 2003, L.A. Lakers, 2003—04, Boston Celtics, 2004—05, Miami Heat, 2005—. Author: (novels) Confidence Counts, 1999. Founder Gary Payton Foundation, 1996—. Named NBA All-Star, 1994—98, 2000—01, NBA Defensive Player of the Year, 1996; named to All-Am. 1st team, The Sporting News, 1990, NBA All-Def. 1st team, 1994—2001, All-NBA 1st team, 1998, 2000, All-NBA 2nd team, 1995—97, 1999; recipient Gold Medal, Atlanta Olympic Games, 1996, Sydney Olympic Games, 2000. Office: Miami Heat Am Airlines Arena 601 Biscyane Blvd Miami FL 33132*

**PAYTON, JOHN,** lawyer; b. Dec. 27, 1946; BA, Pomona Coll., 1973; JD, Harvard U., 1977. Bar: Calif. 1977, DC 1979. Law clk. to Hon. Cecil F. Poole U.S. Dist. Ct., Northern Dist. Calif.; corp. counsel D.C., 1991—94; ptnr., complex comml., civil rights Wilmer, Cutler & Pickering, Washington, head,

litig. dept., 1998—2000. Vis. prof. Harvard Law Sch., Georgetown Law Ctr. Comments editor Harvard Civil Rights, Civil Liberties Law Review. Named one of Am.'s Top Black Lawyers, Black Enterprise mag., 2003, Top Lawyers in DC, Washingtonian mag., 2004. Fellow: Am. Bar Found.; mem.: ABA (mem. House of Delegates 2000—02, mem. sec. on individual rights and responsibilities, mem. commn. of immigration policy), DC Pub. Defender Svc. (vice chair), Internat. Human Rights Law Group, Nat. Lawyers' Com. for Civil Rights Under Law (bd. mem., co-chair), Washington Lawyers' Com. for Civil Rights and Urban Affairs (bd. mem., co-chair), Am. Law Inst., DC Bar (pres. 2001—02). Office: Wilmer Cutler Pickering Hale and Dorr LLP 2445 M St NW Washington DC 20037 Office Phone: 202-663-6325. E-mail: john.payton@wilmerhale.com.

**PAYTON, MARK EDWARD,** statistician, educator; b. Sioux City, Iowa, Sept. 2, 1964; s. Homer Bill and Naomi Ruth Payton; m. Deanna Gail Corley, Mar. 7, 1992; children: Riley Jacob, Mackenzie Leigh. BS in Edn., S.W. Mo. State U., 1986; MS, Okla. State U., 1988, PhD, 1991. Asst. prof. dept. stats. Okla. State U., Stillwater, 1991—96, assoc. prof., 1996—2001, prof., 2001—, assoc. dean Grad. Coll., 2006—. Presenter in field. Mem. editl. bd.: BioScience, 2001—04; contbr. articles to profl. jours. Fellow: Am. Statis. Assn. (chpt. pres. 1992—93), Royal Statis. Soc.; mem.: Centennial Rotary Club, Mu Sigma Rho (nat. pres. 1997—2000). Office: Okla State Univ Dept Stats MSCS 301 Stillwater OK 74078 Office Fax: 405-744-3533.

**PAYTON, PAUL MAX,** application developer; b. San Francisco, Aug. 31, 1961; s. Gertrude Lychenheim; m. Patricia Fgan, Dec. 27, 2003. AS summa cum laude, Coll. San Mateo, Calif., 1980; BS magna cum laude, San Francisco State U., 1982. Cassoc. engr. Lockheed Martin, Palo Alto, Calif., 1982—84, sci. programmer, 1984—85, sr. sci. programmer, 1985—86, sci. programmer analyst, 1986—90, sci. programming specialist, 1990—96, staff engr., 1996—99, cons. software engr., 1999—2002, prin. software engr., 2002—. Lectr. in field. Contbr. articles to profl. jours.; Represented in permanent collections ARC, Amnesty Internat., N.Y.C., Space Imaging Inc., Thornton, Colo., numerous pvt. collections, Calif.; contbr. poetry to profl. jours. Mem.: Mensa (life), San Francisco State U. Alumni Assn., Alpha Gamma Sigma (life). Achievements include patents in field. Avocations: creative writing, poetry, mathematical research, algorithmic art. Home: PO Box 194391 San Francisco CA 94119-4391 Office: Lockheed Martin Missiles and Space Advanced Technology Ctr 3170 Porter Dr Org H1-42 Bldg 255 Palo Alto CA 94304

**PAYTON, ROBERT See PROUD, ROBERT**

**PAYTON, SALLYANNE,** law educator; b. 1943; BA, Stanford U., 1964, LLB, 1968. Bar: Calif. 1969, DC 1969. Staff asst. to Pres. of U.S. White House Domestic Coun., Washington, 1971-73; chief counsel urban mass transp. adminstrn. U.S. Dept. Transp., Washington, 1973-76; assoc. prof. U. Mich. Law Sch., Ann Arbor, 1976-85, prof., 1985—; William W. Cook Prof. Law. Trustee Stanford U., 1972-82; mem. Adminstrn. Conf. U.S., 1980—; bd. dirs. Roosevelt Ctr. Am. Policy Studies, 1982—. Fellow: Nat. Acad. of Pub. Adminstrn. Office: U Mich Law Sch 336 Hutchins Hall 625 S State St Ann Arbor MI 48109-1215 Office Phone: 734-763-0220. Office Fax: 734-763-9375. E-mail: spayton@umich.edu.

**PAYTON, SEAN,** professional football coach; b. San Mateo, Calif., Dec. 29, 1963; BS in Comm., Univ. Ea. Ill., 1987. Offensive coach San Diego State U., 1988—89, running backs coach, 1992—93; offensive coach Ind. State U., 1990—91; quarterbacks coach, offensive coord. U. Miami (OH), 1994—95; quarterbacks coach U. Ill., 1996, Phila. Eagles, 1997—98, NY Giants, 1999—2000, offensive coord., 2000—03; quarterbacks coach Dallas Cowboys, 2003, asst. head coach, offensive coord., 2004—05; head coach New Orleans Saints, 2006—. Named to U. Ea. Ill. Hall of Fame, 2000. Office: New Orleans Saints 5800 Airline Dr Metairie LA 70003*

**PAYTON, SUE C.,** civilian military employee; BS, Ea. Ill. U.; MS, U. So. Calif.; grad. exec. program, Goizueta Bus. Sch. Emory U., 1998. Sr. site systems integration mgr. Martin Marietta, 1989—94; v.p. bus. devel. Lockheed Martin Corp., 1994—96; v.p. applied tech. ImageLinks, Inc.; dir. Nat. Ctr. Applied Tech.; acting dir. def. rsch. and engring. US Dept. Def., Washington, dep. under sec. (advanced systems & concepts), 2001—06; asst. sec. acquisition USAF US Dept Def., Washington, 2006—. Office: USAF 1060 Air Force Pentagon Rm 4E964 SAF/AQ Washington DC 20330-1060 Office Phone: 703-697-6446. Office Fax: 703-693-6400. E-mail: sue.payton@osd.mil.*

**PAYTON, THOMAS WILLIAM,** finance company executive; b. Toronto, Ont., Can., Sept. 7, 1946; With Can. Imperial Bank of Commerce, Toronto; dir. Bramalea Ltd., Toronto, 1981-82, v.p., 1982-88, sr. v.p., 1988-90, sr. v.p., treas., 1991-93; dir. Cadillac Fairview, Inc., 1994-95; pres. Sunnybrook Properties Inc., 1997-2000, DelLyn Advisors Inc., 1993—. v.p. Hawthorne Realty Advisors Inc., 2003—. Personal E-mail: dellynadvinc@aol.com.

**PAYTON-WRIGHT, PAMELA,** actress; b. Pitts., Nov. 1, 1941; d. Gordon Edgar and Eleanor Ruth (McKinley) Payton Wright; m. David Arthur Butler, May 8, 1978 (div. 1989); 1 child, Oliver Dickon Hedley. Grad., St. Mary's Jr. Coll., 1961; BA, Birmingham So. Coll., 1963; postgrad., Royal Acad. Dramatic Arts, London, 1963-65. Actress (Broadway plays) The Show-Off, 1968, Exit the King, 1968, The Cherry Orchard, 1968, Jimmy Shine, 1969, The Crucible, 1972, Mourning Becomes Electra, 1972, All Over Town, 1975, The Glass Menagerie, 1976, Romeo and Juliet, 1977, A Streetcar Named Desire, 1988, Night of the Iguana, 1988, Ah Wilderness, 1988—90, Something Unspoken, 1995, Long Day's Journey Into Night, 2003, (off-Broadway) The Effect of Gamma Rays on Man-In-The-Wood Marigolds, 1970—71, Jesse and the Bandit Queen, 1975, The Seagull, 1980, Don Juan, 1982, Hamlet, 1982, Mrs. Warren's Profession, 1992, The Replacement, 1995, Richard III, 'Til the Rapture Comes, 1998, What You Get and What You Expect, 2000, Fifth of July, 2003, Duet, 2004, The Day Emily Married, 2004, Indian Blood, 2006, (plays) Skin of Our Teeth, 1972, Aimee, 1973, Othello, Troilus and Cressida, As You Like It, 1976, Lunch Girls, 1977, Summerfolk, 1978, The Greeks, 1982, The Misanthrope, 1982, Tobacco Road, 1984, Passion, 1984—85, Cat on a Hot Tin Roof, 1985, Little Eyolf, 1985, On the Verge, 1986, Our Town, 1987, The Road to Mecca, 1990, Picnic, 1991, The Way of the World, 1991, Quartermaine's Terms, 1993, Misalliance, 1993, Six Degrees of Separation, 1993, Ghosts, 1994, Sea Gull, 1994, The Rivals, 1996, Touch of the Poet, 1996, Glass Menagerie, 1997, Voir Dire, 1997, She Stoops to Conquer, 1997, Blithe Spirit, 1998, Transit of Venus, 1998, Sweet Bird of Youth, 1999, A Fair Country, 2000, Philadelphia Story, 2001, Seascape, 2002, Outward Bound, 2002, Hay Fever, 2005, Equus, 2005, The Learned Ladies of Park Avenue, (films) At the Dark End of the Street, 1980, Going in Style, 1981, Starlight, 1985, My Little Girl, 1985, Ironweed, 1987, The Freshman, 1989, In Dreams, 1999, Saving Face, 2004. Nominee Emmy, 1972, Lucille Lortel, 2003; recipient Fulbright award, 1963, Spl. medal, Edmund Gray prize for high comedy, Herbert Beerbohm Tree citation, Royal Acad. Dramatic Art, 1963—65, Obie award, 1970, 1975, 1976, Clarence Derwent award, Variety Critics' Poll citation, 1970, Drama Desk award, 1972, Best Actress citation, Dallas Theater Critics' Forum, 1994, Balt., 1997, Dean Goodman award, 1999, Joseph Jefferson award, 1996; Fox Grant fellow, 1999. Mem.: Screen Actors Guild, AFTRA, Actors Equity Assn. Episcopalian. Office: Bauman & Assocs 250 W 57th St New York NY 10019-3741

**PAZ, GEORGE,** health products executive; b. St. Louis, Aug. 27, 1955; s. Geronimo and Collen May (Hart) P.; m. Georgene Marie Wade, July 27, 1974; children: Stacy, Kelly, Rebecca. BSBA, U. Mo., St. Louis, 1982. CPA, Mo. Jr. acct. Gen. Am., St. Louis, 1980-82, sr. acct., 1982-83, acctg. adminstr., 1983-85, tax planning analyst, 1985-87, dir. tax planning, 1987—; ptnr. Coopers & Lybrand, 1988—93, 1996—98; exec. v.p. & CFO Life Partners Group, 1993—95; sr. v.p. & CFO Express Scripts Inc., St. Louis, 1998—2003, pres., 2003—, CEO, 2004—. Bd. dirs. Gen. Am. Employees Fed. Credit Union, 1985—. Fellow Life Office Mgmt. Assn.; mem. Am. Inst.

CPA's, Mo. Soc. CPA's, Pharm. Care Mgmt. Assn. Lutheran. Avocations: golf, running, softball. Office: Express Scripts Inc 13900 Riverport Dr Maryland Heights MO 63043 Home: 587 Tennyson Dr Wheaton IL 60187-7604*

**PAZ, HAROLD LOUIS,** hospital administrator, internist, educator; b. NYC, Jan. 3, 1955; BA in Biology and Psychology, U. Rochester, 1977, MD, 1982; MS in Life Sci. Engring., Tufts U., 1979. Diplomate subspecialty in pulmonary medicine Am. Bd. Internal Medicine. Intern in internal medicine Northwestern U. Med. Ctr., Chgo., 1982—83, resident in internal medicine, 1983—85, chief med. resident, 1985—86; instr. clin. medicine Northwestern U., Chgo., 1985—86; fellow in pulmonary and critical care Johns Hopkins U., Balt., 1986—88, fellow in environ. health scis., 1986—88; asst. prof. medicine Hahnemann U., Phila., 1988—92, asst. prof. anesthesia, 1989—92, assoc. dean grad. med. edn., 1992—94, assoc. prof. medicine, 1992—94, dir. med. ICU, 1988—94, assoc. hosp. med. dir., 1992—94, dir. Center for Clin. Outcomes, 1992—94; med. dir., assoc. dean for clin. affairs U. Medicine and Dentistry N.J. Robert Wood Johnson Med. Sch., New Brunswick, 1994—95, assoc. prof. medicine, 1994—2003, dean, 1995—2006; CEO U. Medicine and Dentistry N.J. Robert Wood Johnson U. Med. Group, New Brunswick, 1995—2006; prof. medicine U. Medicine and Dentistry N.J. Robert Wood Johnson Med. Sch., New Brunswick, 2003—06; CEO Penn State Milton S. Hershey Medical Ctr. and Penn State Coll. of Medicine, 2006—. Editor: Jour. Undergrad. Rsch., 1976, Med. Staff News newsletter, 1992—94; cons.: Annals Internal Medicine, Clin. Immunology and Immunopathology, Chest, Intensive Care Medicine, Physician Execs., N.Y. State Med. Jour., mem. editl. bd.: Jour. Disease Mgmt. and Clin. Outcomes, 1996—, Chest, 1998—2003. Named to Gold Humanism Honor Soc., 2005; recipient Disting. Svc. award, Motolinsky Rsch. Found., 1998, Cmty. Leaders of Distinction award, County C. of C., 1999, Sir William Oster Humanitarian award, 2005; Eudowood fellow, Johns Hopkins U., 1987—88, U. Rochester scholar, 1979. Fellow: ACP, Am. Coll. Chest Physicians; mem.: AMA, Laennec Soc. (pres. 1994—95), Philip Drinker Soc. for Critical Care (pres. 1992—94), Am. Thoracic Soc. Office: Penn State Hershey Med Ctr 500 University Dr Hershey PA 17033 Office Phone: 717-531-8323.

**PAZANDAK, CAROL HENDRICKSON,** liberal arts educator; b. Mpls. d. Norman Everard and Ruth (Buckley) Hendrickson; m. Bruce B. Pazandak (dec. 1986); children: David, Bradford, Chris, Eric, Paul, Ann; m. Joseph P. O'Shaughnessy, May 1991 (dec. Feb. 2000). PhD, U. Minn., 1970. Asst. dir. admissions U. Minn., Mpls., 1970-72, asst. dean liberal arts, 1972-79, asst. to pres., 1979-85, office of internat. edn., acting dir., 1985-87, asst. prof. to assoc. to prof. liberal arts, 1970-96, prof. emerita, 1996—; instr. Hollrad-Pers. Consulting, Reykjavik, Iceland, 1999—. Vis. prof. U. Iceland, Reykjavik, 1984, periods in 1983, 86-99; vis. rsch. prof. U. Oulu, Finland, 1993; exec. sec. Minn.-Iceland Adv. Com., U. Minn., 1984—; cons. U. Iceland, 1983-98; co-chair Reunion of Sisters-Minn. and Finland Confs., 1986-98; sec. Icelandic Assn. of Minn., 1995-97. Editor: Improving Undergraduate Education in Large Universities, 1989. Past pres. Minn. Mrs. Jaycees, Mpls. Mrs. Jaycees; formerly bd. govs. St. John's Preparatory Sch., Collegeville, Minn.; former bd. trustees Coll. of St. Teresa, Winona, Minn. Recipient Partnership award for contbn. to advancing shared interests of Iceland and Am., 1994, Recognition award U. Iceland, 2002, Recognition award yrs. collaboration Iceland and U. Minn., 2002; named to Order of the Falcon, Govt. of Iceland, 1990, Coll. Liberal Arts Alumna Notable Achievement, 1995, Pres.'s Club, U. Minn., 1996. Mem. APA, Waikoloa Village Outdoor Cir. Home: 4505 Harry's Ln Dallas TX 75229 Office: U Minn N 218 Elliott Hall 75 E River Rd Minneapolis MN 55455-0280 E-mail: carolpz@umn.edu.

**PAZNOKAS, LYNDA SYLVIA,** elementary school educator; b. Portland, Oreg., Feb. 19, 1950; d. Marley Elmo and Undine Sylvia (Crockard) Sims. BA, Wash. State U., 1972; MS, Portland State U., 1975; EdD, Oreg. State U., 1984. Cert. tchr. Oreg. Tchr. 5th grade, outdoor sch. specialist Clover Park Sch. Dist. 400, Tacoma, 1971-72; tchr. 6th grade, outdoor sch. specialist Hillsboro (Oreg.) elem. Dist. 7, 1972-78, Bend (Oreg.)-La Pine Sch. Dist., 1978-82, elem. curriculum specialist, 1983-85, tchr. 4th grade gifted and talented, 1985-90; grad. teaching asst. Oreg. State U., Corvallis, 1982-84; asst. prof., assoc. prof. No. Ariz. U., 1990-99, chair instnl. leadership, 1997-98; Boeing disting. prof. sci. edn. Wash. State U., Pullman, 1999—. Ednl. cons., tchr. workshops, 1973—; presenter workshop Soviet-Am. Joint Conf., Moscow State U., 1991, Meeting of Children's Culture Promoters, Guadalajara, Mex., 1994, internat. conf. Sci., Tech. and Math. Edn. for Human Devel., UNESCO, Panaji, India, 2001, Nishinomiya Joint Rsch. Conf., Japan, 2001, internat. workshop Promoting Sci. and Tech. Literacy Through Sci. Toys & Out-of-Sch. Sci. Activities, Pattaya, Thailand, 2005, others; faculty Ariz. Journey Schs. for Math. and Sci. Tchg. Improvement; coord. Odyssey of the Mind competition, Bend, 1985-89, tchr. mentor program for 1st yr. tchrs., Beaverton, Oreg., 1982-83; reviewer Sci. Books and Films AAAS, 1992—; presenter Social Edn. Assn. of Australia, 1997, Nat. State Tchrs. of Yr., Guam, 2005; steering com. Wash. LASER (Leadership and Assistance for Sci. Edn. Reform), 2002—, mem. sci. drafting team sci. curriculum instrnl. frameworks; mem. Nat. Ecol. Obs. Network Design Consortium. Author: Pathways of America: Lewis and Clark, 1993, Pathways of America: The Oregon Trail, 1993, Pathways of America: The California Gold Rush Trail, 1994, Pathways of America: The Santa Fe Trail, 1995, Fifty States, 1997, U.S. Presidents, 1997, U.S. Map Skills, 1997, Human body, 1998, National Parks and Other Park Service Sites, 1999, Our National Parks, 1999, Pathways of America: The California Mission Trail, 2000, Circling the World: Festivals and Celebrations, 2000, Endangered Species, 2001; mem. adv. bd. (jour.) Sci. and Children; contbr. articles to profl. jours.; reviewer Turkish Jour. Sci. Edn. Vol., leader, bd. dirs Girl Scouts U.S., 1997—, Elder First Presbyn. Ch., Bend, 1980—; vol. hist. interpretation High Desert Mus., Bend, 1987-91; docent Mus. No. Ariz.; pres. bd. dirs. The Arboretum at Flagstaff; former sec. and v.p. bd. dirs. Palouse Discovery Sci. Ctr. (pres. bd. dirs.); past pres. Arboretum bd.; mem. Ptnrs. Achieving Leadership in Sci., Wash., D.C., Leadership and Assistance for Sci. Edn. Reform, Wash., D.C. Recipient Excellence in Teaching award Bend Found., 1985-86, 86-87; named Tchr. Yr. Oreg. Dept. Edn., 1982, Higher Edn. Tchr. Yr., Wash. Sci. Tchrs. Assn. (WSTA), 2003; Celebration Teaching grantee Geraldine Rockefeller Dodge Found., 1989, 90, 91, 92, 93, 94, 95, EPA grantee, 1997-99, Eisenhower Math and Sci. Edn. Act grantee, 1997, 99, Grand Canyon Assn. grantee, 1996, 97, 98; commd. Ky. Col., 1993. Mem. NEA, Internat. Coun. Assns. Sci. Edn. (chair pre-secondary and informal sci. edn. of the exec. com. 2004—, editor Stepping Into Sci. Internat. Quar. jour. 2004—, jour/ advisor), Nat. Coun. Tchrs. Math., NSTA (past mem. nat. supervision com., internat. com.), Nat. Sci. Tchrs. Assn. of Yr. (nat. pres. 1988-90), Nat. Assn. Rsch. in Sci. Tchg., Oreg. Coun. Tchrs. Math. (bd. dirs. 1981-82), Oreg. Coun. Tchrs. English (bd. dirs. 1981-82), Ariz. Reading Assn. (bd. dirs.), Nat. Coun. for Social Studies, Coun. for Elem. Sci. Internat. (bd. dirs. 1995-98, 99—2003, chair informal edn. com.), Internat. Reading Assn., Oreg.-Calif. Trails Assn., Nat. Sci. Edn. Leadership Assn., Assn. for Sci. Tchr. Edn., Nat. Assn. for Rsch. in Sci. Tchg., Assn. for Sci. Edn., Wash. Sci. Tchrs. Assn. (higher edn. rep. bd. dirs. 2004—), N.W. Oreg.-Calif. Trails Assn., Lewis and Clark Trail Heritage Found., PEO (past corr. sec.), Delta Kappa Gamma (1st v.p.), Phi Delta Kappa (found. rep. 1991-92, v.p. programs 1992-93, historian 1993-94, v.p. membership 1994-95), Golden Key Hon., Pi Lambda Theta, Phi Kappa Phi, Kappa Delta Pi (chpt. counselor, mem. spkrs. bur., nat. Web com., sci. specialist), others. Avocations: cross country skiing, photography, hiking, researching immigrant trails, gardening. Home: 101 Enman-Kincaid Rd Pullman WA 99163

**PAZOUR, DON,** publishing executive; Pres. Miller Freeman, Inc., San Francisco. CEO Access Intelligence, LLC. Office: c/o Miller Freeman Inc 600 Harrison San Francisco CA 94107-1387

**PAZOURECK, REBECCA KIEFFER,** food sciences professor; b. Washington, Oct. 3, 1945; d. William Lewis and Marguerite Louise Kieffer; children: Joseph B. III, Leslie Rebecca Pazoureck-Wise. BS, Madison Coll., Harrisonburg, Va., 1967; MS, U. Okla., Norman, 1980; PhD, Okla. State U., Stillwater, 1986. Registered dietitian Am. Dietetic Assn. Dietitian USAF,

Riverside, Calif., 1967—70; prof. Cameron U., Lawton, Okla., 1979—2006. Bd. dirs. J. Roy Dunning Children's Shelter, Lawton, Okla., 1983—97. 1st lt. USAF, 1969—70. Named Prof. of Yr., Cameron U., 1988—89; recipient Hackler award, 2000—01. Mem.: Okla. Assn. Family and Consumer Scis. (found. treas. 2000—06, Profl. award 2004), Delta Kappa Gamma (treas. 2004—06). Office: Cameron Univ 2800 W Gore Blvd Lawton OK 73505 Office Phone: 580-581-2363.

**PEA, ROY,** education educator; BA in Philosophy and Psychology, Mich. State U., 1974; DPhil Oxon. in Developmental Psychology, Oxford U., Eng., 1978. NIMH postdoctoral fellow psycholinguistics Rockefeller U., 1978—79; asst. prof. psychology Clark U., 1979—81; assoc. dir. Ctr. for Children and Tech., Bank St. Coll. Edn., 1984—86, sr. rsch. scientist, 1981—86, Inst. for Rsch. on Learning, 1988—91; John Evans prof. edn. an dlearning scis. Northwestern U., 1991—96, dean Sch. Edn. and Social Policy, 1992—96; dir. Ctr. for Tech. in Learning SRI Internat., 1996—2001; prof. edn. and learning scis. Stanford (Calif.) U., 2001—. Co-founder Teachscape, 1999, bd. dirs.; established. dir. Stanford Ctr. for Innovations in Learning. Office: Stanford U Sch Edn 485 Lasuen Mall Stanford CA 94305-3096

**PEABODY, ARLENE L. HOWLAND BAYAR,** retired enterostomal therapy nurse; b. Deposit, NY, June 26, 1931; d. Burt and Olive (Oralls) Howland; m. Atilla C. Bayar, Dec. 8, 1956 (div.); m. Norman R. Peabody, Feb. 1, 1975 (dec.); children: Tildy Anne Bayar Sparrow, Carol A. Digilio; m. Robert A. Ehlers, Feb. 15, 2003. Diploma, Ridley's Sec. Sch., Binghamton, N.Y., 1949, Binghamton Sch. Practical Nursing, 1970, Harrisburg Hosp. Sch. Enterostomal Therapy, Pa., 1971; AAS, Empire State Coll., Saratoga Springs, N.Y., 1985; BS in Edn., SUNY, Oneonta, 1990. RN, N.Y.; cert. therapeutic touch practitioner, natural force healing practitioner, enterostomal nurse. Sec. pres.'s office Cornell U., Ithaca, NY, 1949—55; exec. sec. Rudolph Lang, Office Execs. Assn. N.Y. and Prestige Expositions Inc., N.Y.C., 1955—69; enterostomal therapy nurse M.I. Bassett Hosp., Cooperstown, NY, 1972—89; pvt. practice enterostomal therapy nurse Oneonta, NY, 1989—2002. Spkr. in field. Vol. Am. Cancer Soc., 1972-2002, Catskill Area Hospice, 1990-02, Glimmerglass Opera, 1975-2002; bd. dirs. Del. Heritage Inc., 1996-2002; trustee Unitarian Universalist Soc.; active Storytelling Ctr. of Oneonta, Oneonta Concert Assn., Oneonta Contradance. Mem. AARP (bd. dirs. 1986-2002), N.Y. State Hist. Assn., Delaware County Hist. Soc., Wound Ostomy and Continence Nurses Soc., United Ostomy Assn. (N.Y. state field svcs. rep.), Order Ea. Star. Avocations: heirloom quilting, traditional folk music, coutourier clothing, costuming, dance. Home: 13511 Pebblebrook Dr Houston TX 77079-6023

**PEACE, H. W., II,** small business owner, retired oil industry executive; b. Clinton, Okla., May 21, 1935; s. Herman Wilbern and Bernice (Mitchell) P.; m. Norma June Williams; children: Hugh William, Susannah Lee. BS in Geology, U. Okla., 1959, MS in Geology, 1964; postgrad., U. S.W. La., 1968. Jr. geologist Union Oil Co. Calif., Houston, 1964-65, area geologist Lafayette, La., 1965-70, geologist dist. exploration Oklahoma City, 1970-77, mgr. Rocky Mountain exploration Casper, Wyo., 1977-80; mgr. divsn. exploration Cotton Petroleum Corp., Tulsa, 1980-83; v.p. exploration Hadson Petroleum Corp., Oklahoma City, 1983-85, exec. v.p., COO, 1985-88, also bd. dirs.; exec. v.p., COO Mosswood Oil and Gas Co., Oklahoma City, 1985-88, Anadarko Supply Co., Oklahoma City, 1986-88, also bd. dirs.; mng. ptnr. EXAD, Oklahoma City, 1988-91, owner, 2006—; pres., CEO, dir. Panhandle Royalty Co., Oklahoma City, 1991—2006; pres., CEO Wood Oil Co. subs. Panhandle Royalty Co., 2001—06. Mgmt. com. PLC Energy Data, LLC, 1994—2001; bd. dirs. OIL Law Recs. Corp. Dir. sch. geology adv. com. U. Okla., Norman, 1984—, vice chmn. 1988-89, chmn. 1989-90, exec. com. 1990—. Lt. USN 1959-63, capt. USNR, 1963-82, ret. list 1995. Mem. Am. Assn. Petroleum Geology (rep. del. or alt. 1984—), Soc. Exploration Geophysicists, Soc. Econ. Paleontologists and Mineralogists, Petroleum Assn. Wyo. (v.p. 1979-80), Tulsa Geol. Soc., Oklahoma City Geol. Soc. (chmn. profl. affairs 1976-77), Naval Res. Assn., Cherokee Hills Homeowners Assn. (pres. 1971-73), Fieldstone Homeowners Assn. (pres. 1983), Navy League, Okla. Corp. Commn. (mem. royalty adv. com. 1998—), Rotary Club Republican. Avocations: golf, swimming, hiking. Office: EXAD Bradley Sq Ste 22 2932 NW 122d St Oklahoma City OK 73120

**PEACH, PAUL E.,** physician, health facility administrator; b. Owensboro, Ky., June 2, 1943; s. Elbert B. and Ermal M. (Bennett) P. Student, So. Meth. U., 1961-63; BS, Ind. U., 1965, JD, 1969; student, U. New Orleans, 1977-79; MD, La. State U., 1983. Bar: Ind., 1970; diplomate Am. Bd. Phys. Medicine and Rehab. Atty. pvt. practice, Indpls., 1970-72; staff atty La. Dept. Health & Human Svcs., New Orleans, 1972-77; resident La. State U. Charity Hosp., New Orleans, 1983-84, Wadsworth VA Hosp., Cedars-Sinai Hosp., L.A., 1984-86; med. dir. Roosvelt Warm Springs (Ga.) Inst. for Rehab., 1986-97, Palmyra Post-Polio Clinic, Albany, Ga., 1997—; med. dir. rehab. medicine Palmyra HCA Hosp., 2003—; med. dir. Palmyra Rehab. Ctr., 2004—. Pvt. practice atty., New Orleans, 1972-77; clin. assoc. prof. Ctr. for Rehab. Medicine Emory U., Atlanta, 1987—. Author: (with others) Late Effects of Poliomyelitis, 1991, Effect of Compliance in Treatment Outcomes in Patients with Post-Polio Syndrome, 1991. Fellow Am. Acad. Phys. Medicine and Rehab.; mem. Med. Assn. Ga., Tri-County Med. Assn. Ga. (pres. 1990-91, 93-96), Ga. Soc. Phys. Medicine and Rehab. (pres. 1989-90, 95-96), Am. Acad. Electrodiagnostic Medicine (assoc.), Am. Hosp. Assn. (governing bd. 1988-91, del. rehab. sect. 1990), So. Soc. Physical Medicine & Rehab. (pres. 2001—). Avocations: photography, music. Home: 1230 Rawson Dr Albany GA 31701-1852 Office: 810 13th Ave Ste 105 Albany GA 31701-1333 Office Phone: 229-446-8960.

**PEACH, ROBERT WESTLY,** retired small business owner, engineer; b. Balt., May 5, 1921; s. Eggelston Westly Peach and Ola English; m. Margaret Jean McClure, July 11, 1998 (dec.); children: John, Helen. AB, Ctrl. High, Phila., 1937; BSE, Univ. Mich., Ann Arbor, 1944, MSE, 1949. Registered profl. engr., Conn., 1958, Md., 1963. Engr. Toledo Shipbuilding, 1942; jr. engr. Bethlem Steel, Quincy, Mass., 1944—46; engr. Rocket Motors, Inc., Dover, NJ, 1950—52, Electric Boat Co., 1952—62; engring. mgr. Md. Drydock, Balt., 1962—67; engring. supr. Westinghouse Electric, Annapolis, 1967—73; owner R.W. Peach Engring. Assoc., Arnold, Md., 1973—90. Contbr. scientific papers. Mem. investment com. Ann Arundel Cmty. Coll., Arnold, 2005; founder, chmn., advisor, Chesapeake Sailing Yacht Symposium. Sgt. U.S. Army, 1946—47, Korea. Recipient Bill Zimme, Univ. Mich., 2002. Mem.: Marine Tech. Soc., Am. Soc. Naval Engr., Soc. Naval Arch. and Marine Engrs. Achievements include invention of 1974, 76. Avocations: sailing, swimming.

**PEACOCK, A(LVIN) WARD,** textile company executive; b. Durham, N.C., June 17, 1929; s. Erle Ewart and Vera Louise (Ward) P.; m. Barbara Sheppard White, July 2, 1955; children: Alvin Ward, Stephen White, Nancy Lay. BS in Commerce, U. N.C., 1950; MBA, Harvard U., 1952. Asst. to v.p. Erwin Mills, Inc., Durham, 1953-55, sec., 1957-62, sec.-treas., 1962-64; v.p. Dixie Yarns, Inc., Chattanooga, 1964-76, sr. v.p., 1976-81, Springs Industries, Fort Mill, SC, 1981-86, exec. v.p., 1986-92. Bd. dirs. Palmetto Seed Capital Corp.; regional dir. First Wachovia Corp., Charlotte, N.C., 1988-92. Trustee Holston Conf. Colls., Tenn., 1968-79, Sci. Mus. Charlotte, 1990-94; bd. dirs. Chattanooga Meml. Hosp., 1973-91, Charlotte Symphony, 1990-94, Greater Carolinas chpt. ARC, 1988-94; dir. Allied Arts Fund, 1978-81, Metrolina Food Bank, 1994-2003; mem. Chattanooga Wastewater Regulation Bd., 1978-81. 1st lt. USAF, 1955-57. Mem. Tenn. Mfrs. Assn. (chmn. bd. dirs. 1980-81), Chattanooga Mfrs. Assn. (pres. 1968-69), Am. Textile Mfrs. Inst. Univ. Club, River Hills Club, Phi Beta Kappa, Alpha Kappa Psi, Sigma Nu. Republican. Methodist. Home: 6618 Seton House Ln Charlotte NC 28277-4520

**PEACOCK, ERLE EWART, JR.,** surgeon, lawyer, educator; b. Durham, N.C., Sept. 10, 1926; s. Erle Ewart and Vera Louise (Ward) P.; m. Mary Louise Lowrey, Apr. 17, 1954; children: James Lowrey, Susan Louise, Virginia Gayle. Cert. in Medicine, U. N.C., 1947, BS, 1950, JD, 1999; MD, Harvard U., 1949. Bar: N.C. 1993. Intern, asst. resident surgery Roosevelt

Hosp., N.Y.C., 1949-51; from asst. resident gen. surgery U. N.C. Hosps., Chapel Hill, 1953-54, chief resident gen. surgery, 1954-55; resident in plastic surgery Barnes Hosp., St. Louis, 1955-56; mem. faculty dept. surgery U. N.C., Chapel Hill, 1956-69, prof. surgery, head divsn. plastic surgery, 1965-69; prof., chmn. dept. surgery U. Ariz., Tucson, 1969-77; prof. surgery Tulane U., New Orleans, 1977-82; pvt. practice surgery Chapel Hill, 1982-93; vis. prof. surgery U. Va., Charlottesville, 1988-97; clin. prof. surgery U.N.C., Chapel Hill, 1996—. Chief hand surgery Valley Forge Army Hosp., Phoenixville, Pa., 1951-53. Author: Wound Repair, 1977, 3d edit., 1982; assoc. editor: Am. Jour. Surgery, 1967—, Surgery Yearbook, 1970-89, Plastic and Reconstructive Surgery, 1972-78; asst. editor: Surg. Rsch., 1970-76. Served with U.S. Navy, 1945-46; served to capt. M.C. U.S. Army, 1951-53. Recipient Yandell medal Louisville Surg. Soc., 1972, McGraw medal Detroit Surg. Soc., 1973, Disting. Svc. award U. N.C., 1979, Jacob Markowitz award Acad. Surg. Rsch., 1993, Lifetime Achievement award Wound Healing Soc., 1994. Mem. AAAS, ACS, ABA, Womack Sur. Soc. (pres. 1979-80), Soc. U. Surgeons (treas. 1965-68), Plastic Surgery Rsch. Coun. (pres. 1966), Am. Surg. Assn., Am. Bd. Plastic Surgery (pres. 1976), Am. Bd. Gen. Surgery, Am. Assn. Plastic Surgeons (Clinician of Yr. 1985), Am. Soc. Surgery Hand, Internat. Soc. Surgeons, So. Surg. Assn., Am. Coll. Legal Medicine, Rotary, Alpha Omega Alpha. Republican. Methodist. Home and Office: 645 Rock Creek Rd Chapel Hill NC 27514-6714 E-mail: eepeacockmd@aol.com.

**PEACOCK, LAMAR BATTS,** retired physician; b. Albany, Ga., Sept. 21, 1920; s. Herbert A. and Helen Marian (LeVan) P.; m. Jane Bonner, June 7, 1947; children: Helen Lee Wade, Linda Jane Gossage, Lamar Bonner BA, Emory U., 1941; MD, Med. Coll. Ga., 1946. Diplomate: Am. Bd. Internal Medicine. Intern U. Hosp., Augusta, 1946—47, resident, 1947—48, 1948—50; fellow internal medicine U. Va. Hosp., Charlottesville, 1948—49; practice medicine specializing in internal medicine and allergy Atlanta, 1950—91. Mem. staff St. Joseph's Hosp., Crawford Long Hosp., Piedmont Hosp., Grady Meml. Hosp., Hughes Spalding Pavilion, Northside Hosp., All Atlanta, Cobb Gen. Hosp., Austell, Ga., Douglasville (Ga.) Hosp.; instr. internal medicine Ga. Bapt. Hosp., Atlanta, 1950-58, chief medicine, 1958-72; mem. faculty Emory U. Sch. Medicine, Atlanta, 1950—, asst. clin. prof. medicine, 1962—; instr. internal medicine Sch. Dentistry, 1958— Chief med. br., health svcs. Atlanta Met. Area Civil Def., 1960-63; mem. Ga. Pub. Health Assn., 1967-69, Ga. Bd. Health, 1966-72, Ga. Vocat. Rehab. Coun., 1973—; pres. trustees Med. Coll. Ga. Found., 1963 Recipient Physicians Physician award, MCG, 1984. Fellow ACP, Am. Coll. Allergy, Asthma and Immunology (nat. pres. 1972-73), Am. Acad. Allergy, Asthma and Immunology; mem. AMA, Am. Heart Assn., Ga. Heart Assn., Am. Soc. Internal Medicine, Ga. Soc. Internal Medicine, 5th Dist. Med. Soc., Ga. Thoracic Soc., Med. Assn. Atlanta (prs. 1965), Med. Assn. Ga. (1st v.p. 1966-67), Southeastern Allergy Assn. (pres. 1963-64), So. Med. Assn., Cherokee Town and Country Club Episcopalian. Home: 3120 Verdun Dr NW Atlanta GA 30305-1940 Personal E-mail: strutjbp@webtv.net.

**PEACOCK, MARCUS C.,** federal agency administrator; b. 1960; BS, U. So. Calif.; MS, Harvard U. Registered profl. engr., DC. Line supr., indsl. engr. R.R. Donnelly & Sons, LA, 1982—84; various positions including dep. chief nat. resources br. U.S. Office Mgmt. and Budget, Office Adminstrn. and Regulatory Affairs, 1986—90; divsn. mgr. environ. policy analysis and forecasting Jellinek, Schwartz & Connolly, Inc., 1990—95; subcom. staff mem. of water resources and environ. subcom.of ho. com. on transp. and infrastructure U.S. Ho. of Reps., 1995—98, staff dir. oversight and emergency response subcom. of com. on transp. and infrastructure 1999—2001; assoc. dir. nat. resource programs, Office Mgmt. & Budget Exec. Office of the Pres., 2001—05; dep. adminstr. EPA, 2005—. Mem.: AAAS, Inst. Indsl. Engrs. (sr.). Office: EPA Ariel Rios Fed Bldg 1200 Pennsylvania Ave NW Rm 3000 Washington DC 20460 Office Phone: 202-564-4711. Office Fax: 202-501-1450.

**PEACOCK, MARILYN CLAIRE,** primary school educator; b. Harvey, Ill., Aug. 2, 1952; d. Carmen Anthony and Helen Elaine (Welch) R. AA with high honors, Thornton C.C., 1972; BS in Edn. with high honors, Ill. State U., 1974; MEd, Nat.-Louis U., 1990. Cert. K-9, Ill. Tchr. kindergarten Primary Acad. Ctr., Markham, Ill., 1976-91, tchr. K-3, 1991—. Ill. State scholar, 1969. Mem. Ill. Edn. Assn. (assn. rep. 1976-88), Kappa Delta Pi, Phi Theta Kappa. Republican. Avocations: music, travel. Home: 2447 Clyde St Homewood IL 60430-3103 Office: Acad Ctr 3055 W 163rd St Markham IL 60426-5626 Personal E-mail: mcrpeacock@hotmail.com.

**PEACOCK, MARY WILLA,** magazine editor, consultant; b. Evanston, Ill., Oct. 23, 1942; d. William Gilbert and Mary Willa (Young) P. BA, Vassar Coll., 1964. Assoc. lit. editor Harper's Bazaar mag., N.Y.C., 1964-69; staff editor Innovation mag., N.Y.C., 1969-70; editor in chief, co-founder Rags mag., N.Y.C., San Francisco, 1970-71; co-founder, features editor Ms. mag., N.Y.C., 1971-77; pub., press Rags mag., N.Y.C., 1977-80; sr. editor Village Voice, N.Y.C., 1980-85, style editor, 1985-89; editor-in-chief Model mag., N.Y.C., 1989—, editorial cons., 1991—; fashion dir. Lear's Mag., N.Y.C., 1992-93; dep. editor In Style Mag., 1993-94, Mirabella mag., 1994-95; cons., 1995—2006. Internat. editor InStyle; writer and cons. in field.

**PEACOCK, MOLLY,** poet, educator; b. June 30, 1947; d. Edward Frank and Pauline Ruth (Wright) P. BA magna cum laude, Harpur Coll., Binghamton, N.Y., 1969; MA with hons., Johns Hopkins U., 1977. Adminstr., lectr. in english SUNY, Binghamton, 1970-76; instr. english Friends Sem., N.Y.C., 1981-92; poet-in-residence Bucknell U., 1993-94, Cathedral St. John the Divine, 2000—04; mem. grad. faculty Spalding U., 2001—. Author: And Live Apart, 1980, Raw Heaven, 1984, Take Heart, 1989, Original Love, 1995, Paradise, Piece by Piece, 1998, How To Read a Poem and Start A Poetry Circle, 1999, The Private I: Privacy in A Public World, 2001, Cornucopia: New and Selected Poems, 2002, The Shimmering Verge: A One-Woman Show in Poems, 2003; contbg. writer House and Garden mag., 1996-2001; contbr. poems to The New Yorker, The New Republic, The Nation, articles to O, the Oprah Mag., Elle, N.Y. Mag. Named Elliston poet U. Cin., 2006; Danforth Found. fellow, 1970, Yaddo fellow, 1980, 82, 89, Ingram Merrill Found. fellow 1981, 86, Lila Wallace/Woodrow Wilson fellow 1994, 95, 96, 2001; grantee Creative Artists Pub. Svc. Program, 1977, N.Y. Found. for Arts, 1985, NEA, 1991; Regents scholar U. Calif., Riverside, 1998. Mem. PEN, Poetry Soc. Am. (governing bd. 1988—, pres. emeritus). Home: 109 Front St E #1041 Toronto ON M5A 4P7 Canada Office Phone: 212-677-3535. E-mail: molly@mollypeacock.com

**PEACOCK, PENNE KORTH,** ambassador; b. Hattiesburg, Miss., Nov. 3, 1942; m. Fritz-Alan Korth, Dec. 15, 1965 (div. 1997); children: Fritz-Alan Jr., Maria Korth Chieffalo, James Frederick; m. Andrew Peacock, Sept. 21, 2002. Student, U. Tex., 1960—64. Sr. Washington assoc., client liaison and rep. trust and estate div. Sotheby's, 1986-89; amb. to Mauritius, Port Louis, 1989-92; pres. Firestone and Korth Ltd., Washington, 1993-97; commr. US Adv. Commn. Pub. Diplomacy, 1997—. Bd. dir. Chevy Chase Bank, 1993—; rep. Sotheby's Internat., 1997—; adv. com. Sydney (Australia) Cancer Ctr., 2003—. Sr. advisor Ptnrs. in Performance Internat., 2005—; co-chmn. Am. Bicentennial Presdl. Inauguration, Washington, 1988—99; mem. adv. bd. Washington Ballet, 2002—; mem. adv. com. Sydney Cancer Ctr.; bd. dirs. Hillwood Mus. and Gardens; counselor Meridian Internat. Ctr.; bd. dirs. Coun. of Am. Ambs., 1994—. Mem.: Assn. for Diplomatic Studies and Tng. (bd. dir. 1996—2002). Office: 11 Gladswood Gardens Double Bay 2028 NSW Australia

**PEAK, HOWARD W.,** former mayor; b. Tokyo, Dec. 31, 1948; m. Margie Bratten. BA in History, U. Tex., 1974, MA in Urban Studies/Environ. Mgmt., 1975. Councilman City of San Antonio, 1993-97, mayor, 1997—99. Owner Land Devel. Svcs.; instr. urban adminstrn. grad. program Trinity U.; former instr. land use planning Southwest Tex. State U.; former v.p. Trans Tex. Interests, Inc.; former mem. planning dept. City of San Antonio. Bd. dirs. Alamo Area Coun. Govts.; chmn. transp. steering com. Met. Planning Orgn.; mem. mcpl. solid waste adv. coun. Tex. Natural Resources Conservation Commn.; mem. standing coms. water, annexation, airport noise abatement,

city/county, state initiatives, ethics, military, policy & planning, joint land use study, planning commn. San Antonio City Coun.; past chmn., mem. planning commn. City of San Antonio; former vice chmn. bd. govtl. affairs North San Antonio C. of C.; former mem. airport noise abatement adv. com. City of San Antonio, water consolidation study task force; past mem. resource/technical team Greater San Antonio Area Citizens Com. on Water; former mem. steering com. South Bexar County Water Project. Formerly with U.S. Army. Recipient Merit award Tex. chpt. Am. Inst. Planners, 1978. Mem. Am. Planning Assn. (Merit award Tex. chpt. 1984, Pres.'s award 1996, Dir.'s award San Antonio sect.), Tex. Soc. Architects (hon.). Avocations: classic car restoration, long-distance running. Home: 238 Medford Dr San Antonio TX 78209-6429

**PEALE, RUTH STAFFORD (MRS. NORMAN VINCENT PEALE),** not-for-profit executive; b. Fonda, Iowa, Sept. 10, 1906; d. Frank Burton and Anna Loretta (Crosby) Stafford; m. Norman Vincent Peale, June 20, 1930; children: Margaret Ann (Mrs. Paul F. Everett), John Stafford, Elizabeth Ruth (Mrs. John M. Allen). AB, Syracuse U., 1928, LLD, 1953; LittD, Hope Coll., 1962; LHD (hon.), Judson Coll., 1988. Tchr. math. Cen. High Sch., Syracuse, NY, 1928—30; nat. pres. women's bd. domestic missions Ref. Ch. Am., 1936-46; sec. Protestant Film Commn., 1946-51; chmn. Am. Mother's Com., 1948-49; pres., editor-in-chief, gen. sec., CEO, chmn. bd. trustees, chmn. emeritus Guideposts Peale Ctr. Christian Living, 1940—; nat. pres. bd. domestic missions Ref. Ch. in Am., 1955-56; mem. bd. N. Am. Missions, 1963-69, pres., 1967-69; mem. gen. program coun. Ref. Ch. in Am., 1968—; mem. com. of 24 for merger Ref. Ch. in Am. and Presbyn. Ch. U.S., 1966-69; v.p. Protestant Council NYC, NYC, 1964-66; co-founder, pub. Guideposts, NYC, 1945—, pres., 1985-92, chmn. bd., 1999—2003, chmn. emeritus, 2003—; pres. Fleming H. Revell, Tarrytown, NY, 1985-92. Appeared on: (nat. TV program) What's Your Trouble, 1952—68; author: I Married a Minister, 1942, The Adventure of Being a Wife, 1971, Secrets of Staying in Love, 1984, A Lifetime of Positive Thinking, 2001; founder, pub. (with Dr. Peale) Guidepost mag., 1945—, co-subject with husband (film) One Man's Way, 1963. Named N.Y. State Mother of Yr., 1963, Disting. Woman of Yr., Nat. Art Assn., Religious Heritage Am. Ch. Woman of Yr., 1969, Woman of Yr., AAUW, 2000; recipient Cum Laude award Syracuse U. Alumni Assn. N.Y., 1965, Honor Iowans award Buena Vista Coll., 1966, Am. Mother's com. award for religion, 1970, Disting. Svc. award Coun. Chs., N.Y.C., 1973, Disting. Citizen award Champlain Coll., 1976, Disting. Svc. to Cmty. and Nation award Gen. Fedn. Women's Clubs, 1977, Horatio Alger award, 1977, Religious Heritage award, 1979, joint medallion with husband Soc. for Family of Man, 1981, Soc. Family of Man award, 1981, Alderson-Broaddus award, 1982, Marriage Achievement award Bride's mag., 1984, Gold Angel award Religion in Media, 1987, Adela Rogers St. John Roundtable award, 1987, Disting. Achievement award Am. Aging, 1987, Paul Harris award N.Y. Rotary, 1989, Leader's award Arthritis Found. Dutchess County, 1992, Dave Thomas Well Done! award, 1994, Norman Vincent Peale award for positive thinking, 1994, Master of Influence award, 1995, The Leadership award Worldwide Leadership Coun., 1998, Cert. for Disting. Svc., N.Y. State Fedn. Women's Clubs, 1999, Light award CANDL Found., 2000, Woman of Distinction awd RCA Women, 2001. Mem. Blanton-Peale Inst. (bd. exec. com.), Am. Bible Soc. (trustee 1948-93, hon. trustee 1993—, bd. dirs.), Nat. Bible Assn. (bd. dirs.), United Bible Soc., Interch. Ctr. (bd. dirs. 1957-92, chmn. 1982-90), Nat. Coun. Chs. (v.p. 1952-54, gen. bd.; treas. gen. dept. United Ch. Women, vice chmn. broadcasting and film commn. 1951-55, program chmn. gen. assembly 1966), N.Y. Fedn. Women's Clubs (chmn. religion 1951-53, 57-58), Home Missions Coun. N.A. (nat. pres. 1942-44, nat. chmn. migrant com. 1948-51), Internat. Platform Orgn. (bd. govs. 1994-2000), Cmty. Action Network (adv. bd. 1998—), Wainwright House (hon. trustee, advisor 2001), PEO, Sorosis (pres. 1953-56, hon. pres.), Alpha Phi (Frances W. Willard award 1976). Republican. Office: Guideposts 66 E Main St Pawling NY 12564-1409 Office Phone: 845-855-5000. Business E-mail: rpeale@guideposts.org.

**PEALE, STANTON JERROLD,** physics educator; b. Indpls., Jan. 23, 1937; s. Robert Frederick and Edith May (Murphy) P.; m. Priscilla Laing Cobb; June 25, 1960; children: Robert Edwin, Douglas Andrew. BSE, Purdue U., 1959; MS in Engring. Physics, Cornell U., 1962, PhD in Engring. Physics, 1965. Research asst. Cornell U., Ithaca, N.Y., 1962-64, research assoc., 1964-65; asst. research geophysicist, asst. prof. astronomy UCLA, 1965-68; asst. prof. physics U. Calif., Santa Barbara, 1968-70, assoc. prof., 1970-76, prof., 1976-94, prof. emeritus, rsch. prof., 1994—. Mem. com. lunar and planetary exploration NAS-NRC, Washington, 1980-84, lunar and planetary geosci. rev. panel, 1979-80, 86-89, 94-96, Planetary Sys. Sci. Working Group, 1988-93, Lunar and Planetary Sci. Coun., 1984-87, mem. com. astronomy and astrophysics, 1997—; lunar sci. adv. group NASA-JPL, Pasadena, Calif., 1970-72; mem. Keck time allocation com. NASA, 1996-98. Assoc. editor: Jour. Geophys. Research, 1987; contbr. articles to profl. jours. Recipient Exceptional Scientific Achievement medal NASA, 1980, James Craig Watson award Nat. Acad. Scis., 1982; vis. fellowships U. Colo., Boulder, 1972-73, 1979-80. Fellow AAAS (Newcomb Cleveland prize 1979); Am. Geophys. Union; mem. Am. Astron. Soc. (divsns. planet sci. and dynamic astronomy, Dirk Brouwer award 1992, chair dynamical astronomy 1999-2000), Internat. Astron. Union. Avocation: gardening. Office: U Calif Santa Barbara Dept Physics Santa Barbara CA 93106

**PEAPPLES, GEORGE ALAN,** retired automotive executive; b. Benton Harbor, Mich., Nov. 6, 1940; s. Arthur L. and Kathleen C. (Peters) Peapples; m. Rebecca Dean Sowers, June 27, 1962; children: Lucia Christine, Sarah Bouton. BA in Econs., U. Mich., 1962, MBA in Fin., 1963. Fin. analyst GM Corp., Detroit, 1964-68, fin. analyst treas. office NYC, 1968—72, dir. capital analysis and investment, 1972—73, asst. divsn. comptr. Delco Moraine divsn. Dayton, Ohio, 1973-75, asst. treas. bank rels. Detroit, 1975-77, asst. comptr., 1980-82; v.p., fin. mgr. GM Can. Ltd., Oshawa, Ont., 1982-84; group dir. strategic bus. planning Chevrolet-Pontiac-Can. group GM Corp., Warren, Mich., 1984-86; v.p. GM Corp., pres., gen. mgr. GM Can. Ltd., Oshawa, 1986-94; v.p. pub. policy GM Corp., Washington, 1994-99; ret. 2000; asst. sec. of Navy US Dept. Def., 1977-80. Bd. dirs. The Ark. Recipient Disting. Pub. Svc. award, Washington, 1980. Personal E-mail: gapeapples@aol.com.

**PEAR, CHARLES E., JR.,** lawyer; b. Macon, Ga., June 18, 1950; s. Charles Edward and Barbara Jane P.; m. Linda Sue King; children: Jennifer Sue, Charles Edward III, Stephanie Sue. BA, U. Hawaii, 1972 with honors; JD, U. Calif., Berkeley, 1975. Bar: Hawaii 1976, Fla. 1977, Colo. 1994, U.S. Ct. of Appeals (9th cir.). Assoc. Rush, Moore, Craven, Sutton, Morry & Beh, Honolulu, 1976-77, of counsel, 1987-90; assoc., ptnr. Carlsmith & Dwyer, Honolulu, 1977-82; ptnr. Burke, Sakai, McPheeters, Bordner & Gilardy, Honolulu, 1983-87; vis. prof. law and computers U. British Columbia, 1990-93; of counsel Holland & Hart, Denver, 1993-96; counsel, ptnr. McCorriston, Miller, Mukai, MacKinnon, Honolulu, 1996—. Mem. Hawaii Real Estate Commn. com. on condominium and resort real estate legis., 1978-79; spl. counsel to consumer protection com. Hawaii State Ho. of Reps., 1981-82; chair real property and fin. svcs. sect. Hawaii State Bar Assn., ABA. Editor-in-chief Hawaii Conveyance Manual II, 1987; editor Hawaii Commercial Real Estate Manual, 1988; bd. editors Hawaii Inst. of Continuing Legal Edn.; co-author: Nat. Assn. of Real Estate Licensing Law Officials and Nat. Timesharing Coun. Model Timesharing Act, 1981-82; contbg. author: Winning With Computers, 1992, Hawaii Real Estate Manual, 1997; lectr. in field, 1991—. Mem. ABA.

**PEARCE, ALAN S.,** lawyer; BS, Lehigh U., 1963; LLB, NYU, 1966. Bar: NY 1966. Ptnr., mem. oper. group Bryan Cave LLP, NYC. Office: Bryan Cave LLP 1290 Ave of the Americas New York NY 10104 Office Phone: 212-541-2111. E-mail: aspearce@bryancave.com.

**PEARCE, CAROLE ANN,** poet; d. Franklin Richard Markham and Mary Priscilla Jensen; m. Ronald Kent Chirrick, July 12, 1958 (div. 1964); children: Kenneth Scott Chirrick, Ronda Lee Buhler; m. Edwin Garth Pearce, Nov. 26, 1966; 1 child, Edwin Ryan. Degree in bus., Salt Lake Trade Tech. Coll., 1965; AS, Salt Lake C.C., 1998. Lic. real estate assoc. Utah. Real estate assoc. Utah

Dept. Bus. Regulation, Salt Lake City, 1976—80. Writer, editor fed. women's coord. U.S. Geol. Survey, Salt Lake City, 1989—94, equal employment opportunities officer, 1993. Contbr. poetry to Great Poems of the Western World, 1990, The Fountain of Peace, 2000, Nature's Gentle Kiss, 2003. Mem.: Dixie Newcomers of St. George (corr.), Acad. Am. Poets, Internat. Soc. Poetry (corr. Poet of Merit 2000, 2002, 2003, 2004). Avocations: swimming, dance, reading. Home and Office: 1831 Lazy River Dr Saint George UT 84790-4420 E-mail: lazypearce@aol.com.

**PEARCE, DONALD JOSLIN**, retired librarian; b. Southampton, Eng., May 31, 1924; came to U.S., 1949, naturalized, 1952; s. Alfred Ernest and Constance May (Jeffrey) P.; m. June Inez Bond, Dec. 7, 1946; children—Kristin, Kim. Student, Sch. Oriental and African Studies, U. London, 1942-43; AB, George Washington U., 1953; MS in L.S, Cath. U. Am., 1954. Part-time library asst. U.S. Dept. Agr., 1949-54; student asst. George Washington U., 1950-53; circulation librarian Denison U., 1954-56; staff Ohio State U. Library, 1956-59, asst. acquisition librarian, 1958-59; head librarian, asst. prof. U. N.D., 1959-69, chief bibliographer, 1969-73, asst. dir. libraries, 1973-75, asst. prof. Oriental philosophy, 1969-75; library dir., asst. prof. philosophy U. Minn., Duluth, 1975-88, ret., 1988. Chmn. staff orgn. round table Ohio Library Assn., 1958-59 Served with Brit. Army, 1943-47. Mem. ALA, N.D. Library Assn. (pres. 1965-67), Minn. Library Assn. (sec. 1978-80, v.p. 1985, pres. 1986), Assn. Coll. Reference Librarians, Mountain Plains Library Assn. (v.p. 1968-69), Buddhist Assn., Phi Beta Kappa, Beta Phi Mu. Home: 70 E St Marie St Apt 127 Duluth MN 55803 Personal E-mail: dpearce2310@inbox.com.

**PEARCE, DRUE**, federal official, former state legislator; b. Fairfield, Ill., Apr. 2, 1951; d. H. Phil and Julia Detroy (Bannister) P.; m. Michael F.G. Williams; 1 child, Tate Hanna Pearce-Williams. BA in Biol. Scis., Ind. U., 1973; MPA, Harvard U., 1984; cert. exec. program Darden Sch. Bus., U. Va., 1989. Tech. illustr., Clark County, Ind., 1973-74; curator of edn. Louisville Zoo, 1974—76; dir. Summerscene, Louisville, 1976—77; asst. v.p., br. mgr. Alaska Nat. Bank of the North, 1977-82; legis. aide to Rep. John Ringstad Alaska Ho. of Reps., Juneau, 1983, mem., 1984-88, minority whip, 1987—88; mem. Alaska Senate, 1989—2001, chmn. com. oil and gas, mem. exec. com. energy coun., 1989-90, chmn. com. labor and commerce, mem. exec. coms. western state conf., coun. state govts., energy coun., 1991-92, co-chmn. senate fin., chmn. energy coun., vice chmn. com. energy, nat. coun. state govts., 1993-94, mem. select com. legis. ethics and legis. coun., pres. senate, mem. exec. com. energy coun., vice chmn. senate coms. resources and rules, 1995-96, co-chmn. com. senate fin., mem. exec. com. energy coun., vice chmn. com. senate judiciary, 1997—98; sr. adv. to sec. for Alaska affairs US Dept. Interior, 2001—; fed. coord. for Alaskan Natural Gas Transp. Projects Fed. Energy Regulatory Commn., 2006—. Senate pres., 1995-96, 1999-2000, senate rules chmn., 2001; ptnr. Cloverland N., Anchorage, 1993—; resources cons. Arctic Slope Regional Corp., Anchorage, 1987-91, 95-96; sr. adv. Sec. Interior for Alaska Affairs, 2001-. Former bd. dirs. Alaska Women's Aid in Crisis, Anchorage Econ. Devel. Coun., Alaska Aerospace Devel. Corp., Alaska Spl. Olympics, Gov.'s Bd. Mem. DAR, Commonwealth North, Resource Devel. Coun., Alaska Miners Assn., Alaska Fedn. Rep. Women, Aircraft Owners & Pilots Assn., U.S. Trotting Assn. Republican. Office: Office of the Secretary Dept of the Interior 1849 C St NW MS 6020 Washington DC 20240

**PEARCE, ELIZABETH NIEWOEHNER**, endocrinologist, researcher; arrived in U.S., 1968; d. Dennis Erwin and Catherine Beattie Niewoehner; m. Richard A. Pearce, May 24, 1997; children: Alexander, Ian. BA, Harvard U., Cambridge, Mass., 1990; student, Bryn Mawr Coll., 1991—92; MD, Harvard U., 1997; MSc in Epidemiology, Boston U., Mass., 2004. Diplomate internal medicine, endocrinology, diabetes and metabolism. Intern internal medicine Beth Israel Deaconess Med. Ctr., Boston, 1997—98, resident internal medicine, 1998—2000; from fellow in endocrinology to asst. prof. medicine Med. Ctr. Boston (Mass.) U., 2000—04, asst. prof. medicine Med. Ctr., 2004—. Contbr. chapters to books, articles to profl. jours. Recipient K-23 Mentored Career award, NIH, 2003; grantee Pfizer Scholars in Endocrine, 2002. Mem.: Mass. Med. Soc., Am. Thyroid Assn., Endocrine Soc. Avocation: singing. Office: Boston Med Ctr Evans 201 88 E Newton St Boston MA 02118 Office Phone: 617-414-1348. Business E-Mail: elizabeth.pearce@bmc.org.

**PEARCE, HARRY JONATHAN**, lawyer, manufacturing executive; b. Bismarck, ND, Aug. 20, 1942; s. William R. and Jean Katherine (Murray) P.; m. Katherine B. Bruk, June 19, 1967; children: Shannon Pearce Baker, Susan J., Harry M. BS, USAF Acad., Colorado Springs, Colo., 1964; JD, Northwestern U., 1967; Degree in Engring. (hon.), Rose-Hulman Inst. Tech., 1997; LLD (hon.), Northwestern U., 1998. Bar: N.D. 1967, Mich. 1986. Mcpl. judge City of Bismarck, 1970-76, U.S. magistrate, 1970-76, police commr., 1976-80; sr. ptnr. Pearce & Durick, Bismarck, 1970-85; assoc. gen. counsel GM, Detroit, 1985-87, v.p., gen. counsel, 1987-92, exec. v.p., gen. counsel, 1992-94, exec. v.p., 1994-95, vice chmn., 1996—2001; chmn. Hughes Electronics, El Segundo, Calif., 2001—03; non exec. chmn. Nortel Networks Corp., Brampton, Ont., 2005—. Bd. dirs. GM Corp., Hughes Electronics Corp., GM Acceptance Corp., Delphi Automotive Sys. Corp., Alliance of Automobile Mfrs. of Am., Marriott Internat. Inc., Nortel Networks Corp., Econ. Strategy Inst., Theodore Roosevelt Medora Found., MDU Resources Group, Inc., Nat. Def. U. Found.; founding mem. minority counsel demonstration program Commn. on Opportunities for Minorities in the Profession, ABA; chmn. The Sabre Soc., USAF Acad.; trustee Howard U., U.S. Coun. for Internat. Bus., New Detroit, Inc.; The Mentor's Group Forum for U.S.-European Union Legal Edn. Affairs, The Conf. Bd., Network of Employers for Traffic Safety's Leadership Coun., Pres.'s Coun. on Sustainable Devel., World Bus. Coun. for Sustainable Devel., World Economic Forum Coun. Innovative Leaders in Globalization. Capt. USAF, 1964-70. Named Michiganian of Yr., The Detroit News, 1997; Hardy scholar Northwestern U., Chgo., 1964-67, recipient Alumni Merit award, 1991. Fellow Am. Coll. Trial Lawyers, Internat. Soc. Barristers; mem. Am. Law Inst. Avocations: amateur radio, woodworking, sailing. Office: Bowman and Brooke LLP 50 W Big Beaver Rd Ste 600 Troy MI 48084*

**PEARCE, JOHN Y.**, lawyer; b. New Orleans, Mar. 26, 1948; s. John Young II and Marina (Harris) P.; m. Marjorie Pamela Doyle, May 22, 1971 (div.); children: Andrea Elizabeth, Roger Wellington; m. Julia Evans Reed, May 10, 2003. BA, La. State U., 1973, JD, 1976. Bar: La. 1977, U.S. Dist. Ct. (ea., mid. and we. dists.) La., U.S. Ct. Claims, U.S. Ct. Appeals (5th and 11th cirs.), U.S. Supreme Ct. 2003. Assoc. Doyle, Smith & Doyle, New Orleans, 1977-79, ptnr., 1979-80, mng. ptnr., 1980-84; ptnr. Montgomery, Barnett, New Orleans, 1984—2003, mng. ptnr., 2003—. Pres. New Orleans Legal Assistance Corp., 1999—2002, S.E. La. Legal Svcs. Corp., 2002—04. Sgt. U.S. Army, 1969—71. Mem.: ABA (ho. of dels. 1998—2003), New Orleans Bar Assn. (pres. 1997—98, exec. com.), La. Bar Assn. (chmn. mineral law sect. 1994—95). Presbyterian. Office: Montgomery Barnett 3300 Energy Ctr New Orleans LA 70163 Office Phone: 504-585-3200. Business E-Mail: jpearce@monbar.com.

**PEARCE, LISA ANNE**, composer, musician; With Coronet Rec. Co., Columbus, Ohio, 1985—94; composer Tunes 4 U/ MLIYH, Mango, Fla., 2000—. Music tchr. MLIYH/ Tunes 4 U, Coral Springs, Fla., 2000—; Shamesheen Beth Hillel, Coral Springs, Fla., 2002—03. Recipient USO Talent Show award, USO, 1985; grantee Music scholarship, Sunshine Lady Found., 2004-2007. Mem.: The Highlander Club (v.p. Mango, Fla.). Office Phone: 866-456-8742. Personal E-mail: lisanne5@hotmail.com.

**PEARCE, PAUL FRANCIS**, retired electronics executive, aerospace engineer; b. Boston, Sept. 17, 1928; s. George Hamilton and Marie Louise (Duval) P.; m. Gilda Troisi, Apr. 11, 1953; children: Janet, Theresa, Diane. BSEE (Edwards scholar), MIT, 1950; MS, Mass. Inst. Tech., L.A., 1952; postgrad. (Hughes fellow), U. Calif., Los Angeles, 1957-58, U. So., Calif., 1958-59,

Inst. Mgmt. Northwestern U., 1966. Project engr. Trans-Sonics, Inc., Burlington, Mass., 1952-55; sect. head application engring., strategic systems Hughes Aircraft Co., Culver City, Calif., 1955-59; with Lockheed Electronics Co., Plainfield, NJ, 1959-67, gen. mgr. div. mil. systems, 1964-65, v.p., gen. mgr., 1965-67; v.p., div. mgr. Tele-Dynamics div. AMBAC Industries, Inc., Ft. Washington, Pa, 1967-74; group v.p. comml. and aerospace electronics group AMBAC Industries, Inc., Carle Place, NY, 1973-80; pres. James G. Biddle Co., Blue Bell, Pa., 1980-93, ret. Bd. dirs. AVO Internat. Ltd., 1987-91. Mem. Armed Forces Communications and Electronics Assn. (pres. 1969-71), Inst. Nav., Delaware Valley Mfrs. Assn. (sr. vice chmn. 1987-89, chmn. 1990-92—), Greater Phila. C. of C., Ft. Washington Indsl. Park Mgmt. Assn. (gov. 1973-74), Sigma Xi. Clubs: Mfrs'. Golf and Country (Oreland, Pa.) (handicap chmn. 1987-90), St. David's Golf Club (Wayne, Pa.). E-mail: pfpearce@att.net.

**PEARCE, RICHARD LEE**, lawyer; b. Racine, Wis., Apr. 11, 1959; s. John Wallace and Betty Jane Pearce; m. Cynthia Davis, June 11, 1983; 1 child, Melissa Lauren. BS in Chemistry, U. S.C., 1981, JD, 1984. Bar: S.C. 1984, U.S. Dist. Ct. S.C. 1985, U.S. Ct. Appeals (4th cir.) 1985. Law clk. to resident cir. judge Edward B. Cottingham, 1984-85; assoc. Fox, Zier, Burkhalter & Verenes, Aiken, S.C., 1985-86; ptnr. Toole & Toole, Aiken, 1986-96; asst. pub. svcs. dir., legis. liaison S.C. Bar, 1996-98; city solicitor, staff atty. City of Aiken, 1998—. Instr. Am. Banking Inst., Nat. Advocacy Ctr., Nat. Dist. Attys. Assn.; guest lectr., adj. instr. U. SC, Aiken, pro bono divsn. law sch. non lawyers, IMLA program; legal advisor Bd. Zoning Appeals, Hist. Preservation Commn., Neighborhoods Com., Tourism Bd., Arts Commn., City Dept. Dirs., Bldg. Code Bd. Appeals, Pks. Commn.; bd. dirs. Leadership Aiken County Class of 2003, 03-; Hitchcock Health Svcs., 2004-05; adv. bd. Soc. Prevention of Cruelty to Aminals, 2000-01; mem. spl. commn. on domestic violence, SC Atty. Gen.; mem. US Dept. Justice Operation Cease Fire. Emcee Sch. Bd. Acad. Tournament, Aiken, 1986; bd. dirs. Tri-Devel. Ctr., Aiken, 1985—86; spl. events com. Downtown Aiken Devel. Corp.; fundraising com. Am. Cancer Soc., 1985—2000, Am Heart Assn., 2000—01; legal advisor Children's Place, Inc.; judge mock trial h.s. competition, 1991—96; trustee Aiken, Barnwell, Bamberg and Edgefield Libr. Sys.; organizer, coord. Lladriadod Wales exchange program Aiken Youth C.; active Ptnrs. in Friendship, Sister Cities, Orvieto Italy and Schoalhaven, Australia, Mex./SC Govt. Study Exch. Seminars, Internat. Youth Exch., Groundhog Day Job Shadowing, Tech-Prep Career Advisor. Mem.: SC Solicitors Assn., Nat. Coll. Dist. Attys., Nat. Dist. Attys. Assn., Internat. Mcpl. Lawyers Assn., Aiken C. of C. (legal liaison 1986), Aiken County Bar Assn. (pres. 1990—92), SC Bar Assn. (ho. of dels. 1989—95, pro bono program 1989—97, resolution of fee disputes bd., lawyers' fund for client protection, task force on justice for all, ethics adv. com., unauthorized practice law com., co-editor Legis. Update, editor Ethics Adv. Opinion summaries, coord. annual jud. evaluation, sec. vice-chmn. govtl. law sect.), Leadership Aiken County (disting. grad. 2003, bd. dirs. 2003—), Hitchcock Woods Axe Club, Rotary Internat. (pres.-elect 1994—95, bd. dirs. 1994—96, pres 1995—96, group study exch. coord., active numerous projects, various offices exchange programs, chmn. internat. group study exch. hosting teams, team leader group study exch. with France 2006, Paul Harris fellow, Sustaining Paul Harris fellow), Omicron Delta Kappa. Presbyterian (vice-chair bd. deacons 1999-2000, chair 2001-02). Avocations: antique phonographs/records, grilling and barbecuing, outdoor activities, historical research, bicycling. Office: City of Aiken PO Box 1177 Aiken SC 29802-1177 Office Phone: 803-642-7658. Business E-Mail: rpearce@aiken.net.

**PEARCE, RONALD**, retired cosmetic company executive; b. Apr. 29, 1920; s. Fernley Charles and Medora Kate (Lissenden) P.; m. Olive Stacey, Apr. 4, 1942; children: David Fernley, Jane Ryding Robertson. Cambridge matriculation, Lindisfarne Coll., Ruabon, North Wales, U.K., 1937. Chief cashier Westminster Bank, Croydon, Eng., 1947-48; comml. officer Brit. Consulate, Dallas, 1949-52; v.p. World Gift Co., Dallas, 1953-63, Nelson Electronics, Dallas, 1963-68; stockbroker Walston & Co., Dallas, 1968-73; dir. purchasing Mary Kay Cosmetics, Inc., Dallas, 1973-85; pres. Global Water Techs., Inc., 1992-95; chmn. bd. Alpha Aqua, 1996—, Concha Holdings LTD, 2002—. Chmn. bd. Dallas Lighthouse for the Blind, 1987. Flight lt. RAF, 1940-46. Republican. Episcopalian. Home: 5455 La Sierra Dr Apt 1014 Dallas TX 75231

**PEARCE, STEPHEN FERRON**, music educator; b. Opp, Ala., Apr. 13, 1959; s. Raymond Ferron and Joan Dale Pearce; 1 child, William Benjamin. BA in Music, Troy State U., Ala., 1981, MA in Music, 1987. Dir. band Early County Bd. Edn., Blakely, Ga., 1981—82, Kinston H.S., Ala., 1982—84, McKenzie H.S., 1984—85, Foley H.S., 1985—88; police officer Gulf Shores Police Dept., 1988—95; dir. mktg., cmty. edn. Allied Health Options, Inc., Mobile, 1995—98; dir. band Foley Mid. Sch., 1998—. Musician: (performances) Northwest Fla. Symphony. Squadron comdr. USAF Aux., Foley, 2004—06. Recipient Commander's Commendation, USAF Aux., 2006. Mem.: Music Educator's Nat. Conf. Liberal. Achievements include research in Affect of Listening to Music on Spatial-Temporal Reasoning. Avocations: aviation, motorcycling, travel. Home: 608 North Pine Foley AL 36535 Office: Foley Middle School 201 North Pine Street Foley AL 36535 Office Phone: 251-943-1255.

**PEARCE, STEVE (STEVAN E. PEARCE)**, congressman; b. Lamesa, Tex., Aug. 24, 1947; m. Cynthia Pearce. BBA in Econs., N.Mex. State U., Las Cruces, 1970; MBA, Ea. N.Mex. U., Portales, 1991. Owner-operator crop dusting flying svc., Blytheville, Ark., 1975—78; chief pilot, check pilot Marshall Aviation, 1978—81; chief pilot RUNCO, Inc.; co-owner, operator Lea Fishing Tools, Inc., 1989—2002; mem. N.Mex. State Ho., Reps., 1997—2000, chmn. Rep. Com.; mem. US Congress from 2nd N.Mex. dist., 2003—. Mem. homeland security com. US Congress, mem. energy com., mem. resources com. Pilot USAF, 1970—76, Philippines. Decorated DFC, Air medal; co-recipient VIVA award, Assn. Commerce and Industry, 2001; named Outstanding Legislator, N.Mex. Tech. Showcase. Republican. Baptist. Office: US Ho Reps 1607 Longworth Ho Office Bldg Washington DC 20515-3102 Office Phone: 202-225-2365.*

**PEARL, JAMES HILDRED**, lawyer; b. Laredo, Tex., July 9, 1937; s. James H. Pearl and Maxine E. (Allen) Whittington; m. Kay C. Wood, May 10, 1986. BS, US Mil. Acad., 1960; JD, St. Mary's U., San Antonio, 1969. Bar: Tex. 1969, U.S. Dist. Ct. (we. dist.) Tex., U.S. Ct. Appeals (5th cir.), U.S. Supreme Ct. Tech. rep. E.I. duPont, 1965-67; assoc. Lieck, Leick & Leon, San Antonio, 1969-71, Baskin, Casseb, Leon, Rodgers & Robertson, San Antonio, 1971-74; mem. firm Casseb & Pearl, Inc., San Antonio, 1974—. Ptnr. CSPC, San Antonio, 1974—; sec. San Marcos (Tex.) Pontiac-GMC Truck, 1990-97; sec. Hill Country Enterprises, Kerrville, Tex., 1991-97; mng. ptnr. Pearl Ltd., 1992—. Hon. life mem. Alcoholic Rehab. Ctr., San Antonio, 1978—. Capt. U.S. Army, 1960-65. Mem. State Bar Tex. (cert. civil trial law, cert. family law), Tex. Acad. Family Law Specialists, Sons of Republic of Tex., West Point Soc. South Tex. (dir.). Democrat. Episcopalian. Avocation: farming. Office: Casseb & Pearl Inc 127 E Travis St San Antonio TX 78205-1613

**PEARL, JUDEA**, computer scientist, educator; b. Tel-Aviv, Sept. 4, 1936; U.S. citizen; m. Ruth Pearl; 3 children. BSc, Israel Inst. Tech., 1960; MSc, Newark Coll. Engring., 1961; PhD in Elec. Engring., Poly. Inst. Bklyn., 1965. Rsch. engr. Dental Sch., NYU, 1960-61; mem. tech. staff RCA Rsch. Labs., 1961-65; dir. advanced memory devices Electronic Memories, Inc., Calif., 1966-69; prof. Sch. of Engring./Dept. Computer Scis. UCLA, 1969—; co-founder, pres. Daniel Pearl Found., 2002—. Intern. Newark Coll. Engring., 1961; cons. Rand Corp., 1972, Integrated Sci. Corp., 1975, Hughes Aircraft 1989. Author: Heuristics, 1984, Probabilistic Reasoning in Intelligent Systems, 1988, Casuality: Models, Reasoning, Inference, 2000. Recipient: Outstanding Achievement award RCA Labs., 1965, Rsch. Excellence award, IJCAI, 1999; co-recipient: Purpose prize, Civic Ventures, 2006. Fellow IEEE, ACM, Am. Assn. Artificial Intelligence (Classical Paper award 2000, Lakatos award 2001), Acad. Engring. (Allen Newell award, 2003), Nat. Acad. Engring.; corr. mem. Spanish Acad. Engring. Office: UCLA Dept Computer Sci 4532 Boelter Hl Los Angeles CA 90095-0001*

**PEARL, LAURENCE DICKSON**, retired federal government executive; b. Phila., Mar. 2, 1934; s. Simon and Dorothy (Lichtig) P.; m. Ruth Switzer, Dec. 22, 1959 (div. Apr. 1972); children: Natasha, Lisa Talbott, Thomas Simon; m. Anne Womeldorf, Dec. 20, 1972. AB, Antioch Coll., 1955; postgrad., Harvard U., 1955-56; LLB, Yale U., 1959. Bar: D.C. 1959, U.S. Supreme Ct. 1983. Assoc. Trammell, Rand & Nathan, Washington, 1960-61; rsch. assoc. George Washington U., Washington, 1961; atty., advisor HUD, Washington, 1961-67, exec. asst. to gen. counsel, 1967-69, spl. asst. to asst. sec. for equal opportunity, 1969-72, dir. program standards and data analysis, 1972-74, dir. program compliance, 1974-86, dir. program standards and evaluation, 1986-98; ret., 1998. Pres. Capitol Hill Restoration Soc., Washington, 1990-92. Ford Found. fellow, 1955-56. Mem. Am. Bar Assn., Sr. Execs. Assn. (pres. HUD chpt. 1990-91). Avocations: music, gardening, cross country skiing.

**PEARL, MARY CORLISS**, wildlife conservationist; b. NYC, July 5, 1950; d. George Carleton and Margaret Lyon (Scheuer) Pearl; m. Don Jay Melnick, Oct. 3, 1981; children: Meredith, Seth. BA, Yale U., 1972, MPhil, 1976, PhD, 1982; DSc (hon.), Marist Coll., 2006. Dir. corp. devel. World Wildlife Fund, NYC, 1983-85, head NY office, 1984-85; adminstr. conservation progs. Wildlife Conservation Soc., NYC, 1985-87, asst. dir., 1988—; exec. dir., pres. Wildlife Trust (formerly Wildlife Preservation Trust Internat.); vis. scholar dept. biol. sci. Stanford U., 1987-88; assoc. dir. Ctr. Environ. Rsch. and Conservation Columbia U. Co-founder Consortium for Conservation Medicine, 1997; adj. rschr. Columbia U., N.Y.C.; cons. UNDP. Editl. adv. Wildlife Conservation mag., 1988; editor. Conservation for the 21st Century, 1989, Conservation Medicine: Ecosystem Health in Practice, 2002; co-editor: Conservation for the 21st Century; columnist Discover Magazine, 2006—; contbr. articles to profl. jour. Founding mem. Cons. in Higher Edn. Group of the Rainforest Alliance, NYC, 1988; trustee Gomez Found., NYC, 1985—; founder Calvin Hill Daycare Ctr., New Haven, 1970. Recipient David Lapham award, Yale U., 1971. Mem.: AAAS, Am. Soc. Primatologists, Internat. Primatological Soc., AAUW, Ecohealth Soc., Soc. for Conservation Biology (vice pres. 1990—93), Internat. Union for Conservation of Nature (primate specialist group species survival commn.), Internat. Women's Forum, Cosmos Club. Avocations: squash, birdwatching, reading, history. Office: Wildlife Trust 460 West 34th St 17th Floor New York NY 10001 Office Phone: 212-380-4460. Personal E-mail: pearl@wildlife.com. E-mail: pearl@wildlifetrust.org.

**PEARL, NANCY LINN**, librarian; b. Detroit, Jan. 12, 1945; d. Sidney and Anne Linn; m. Joseph Harold Pearl; children: Eily Raman, Katie. Grad., U. Mich., 1965, MLS, 1967. Head collection devel. Tulsa City County Libr., Okla.; exec. dir. Washington Ctr. Book Seattle Pub. Lib., 1993—2004. Author: Now Read This: A Guide to Mainstream Fiction, 1978-1998, 1999, Now Read This II: A Guide to Mainstream Fiction, 1990-2001, 2002, Book Lust: Recommended Reading for Every Mood, Moment and Reason, 2003, More Book Lust: Recommended Reading for Every Mood, Moment and Reason, 2005. Named Fiction Reviewer of Yr., Libr. Jour. Magazine, 1998; recipient Open Book award, Pacific Northwest Writer's Conf., 1997, Allie Beth Martin award, Pub. Libr. Assn., 2001, Humanities Washington award, 2003, Ontario Library Assn. Media and Communications award, 2004, Louis Shores Greenwood Publishing award for Reviews, ALA, 2004, Women's Nat. Book Assn. award, 2004—05, Louis Shores Greenwood Publishing award for Reviews, ALA, 2004—05. Achievements include the shushing librarian action figure based on likeness. Office: Sasquatch Books 119 S Main Suite 400 Seattle WA 98104

**PEARLMAN, JERRY KENT**, electronics company executive; b. Des Moines, Mar. 27, 1939; s. Leo R. Pearlman; married; children: Gregory, Neal. BA cum laude, Princeton U., 1960; MBA, Harvard U., 1962. With Ford Motor Co., 1962-70; v.p. fin. Behring Corp., 1970-71; from contr. to chmn. Zenith Electronics Corp., Glenview, Ill., 1971-95. Bd. dirs. Smurfit-Stone Container Corp, Ryerson-Tull Corp., Nanophase Techs., Evanston Northwestern Healthcare. Bd. dirs. Northwestern U. Office: 21 Linden Ave Wilmette IL 60091-2837 E-mail: jpearl@northwestern.edu.

**PEARLMAN, LOUIS JAY**, aviation executive, entertainment company executive; b. Flushing, N.Y., June 19, 1954; s. Herman and Reenie (Nevler) P. BA, Queens Coll., 1976; MBA, Century U., 1980; Degree in Sales Mgmt., SUNY, Buffalo, 1980; PhD in Bus. Adminstrn., Century U., 1983. Pres. Commuter Helicopter Corp., N.Y.C., 1974-75; COO Trans Continental Airlines, Inc., N.Y.C., 1975—, Trans Continental Records, Orlando, Fla., 1991—; chmn. Trans Continental Talent, Inc., 2002—. Gen. mgr. U.S. Westdeutsche Luftwerdung GmbH, N.Y.C., 1976-85; chmn., pres., CEO Airship Internat. Ltd., N.Y.C., 1982—; bd. dirs., 1985—; pres., CEO Trans Continental Records, Inc., 1992—; pres. Backstreet Boys, Inc., 1993-99; chmn. Natural Prodns. LLC, 2001-; CEO Chippendales, Inc., 1996-2000, Entertainment Internat. Ltd., 1997—, Planet Airways Inc. (PHC Holdings), 1998—, bd. dirs.; cons. Queens Coll., CUNY, 1977—. Author: Survey and Analysis of the Airline Industry, 1983; song writer. Active Mitchell-Linden Civic Assn., Flushing, 1980-82, Kissimmee (Fla.) Mcpl. Airport, 1985—. Recipient Govs. award NARAS, 2000. Mem. U.S. Power Squadron, Wings Club (disting, recipient Lighter-than-Air award 1987), Lighter-than-Air Soc. (hon.), Young Entrepreneurs Am. Young Millionaires Club, Internat. Air Transport Assn., Blimp Port U.S.A. (pres. 1987—), Friar's Club (N.Y.C.). Avocations: flying, helicopters and blimps, swimming, bowling, music, boating. Office: Trans Continental Cos Inc Trans Continental Bldg 127 W Church St Ste 350 Orlando FL 32801 Office Phone: 407-345-0004,

**PEARLMAN, PETER STEVEN**, lawyer; b. Orange, NJ, June 11, 1946; s. Jack Kitchener and Tiela Josephine (Fine) P.; m. Joan Perlmutter, June 19, 1969; children: Heather, Christopher, Megan. BA, U. Ill., 1967; JD, Seton Hall U., 1970. Bar: N.J. 1970, U.S. Dist. Ct. N.J. 1970, U.S. Dist. Ct. (so. dist.) N.Y. 2003, U.S. Dist. Ct. S.D., 2003, U.S. Dist. Ct. N.Y., 2003, U.S. Tax Ct. 1973, U.S. Supreme Ct. 1974, U.S. Ct. Appeals (2d cir.) 1981, U.S. Ct. Appeals (3d cir.) 1983, U.S. Ct. Appeals (7th cir.) 1985, U.S. Ct. Appeals (D.C. cir.) 1998, U.S. Ct. Appeals (4th cir.) 1999, U.S. Ct. Claims 2000; cert. civil trial atty., 1982. Assoc. Cohn & Lifland, Esquires, Saddle Brook, N.J., 1970-72; ptnr. Cohn, Lifland, Pearlman, Herrmann & Knopf, Saddle Brook, 1972—. Lectr. Nat. Inst. Trial Advocacy, Hempstead, N.Y., 1988—; active trial advocacy program Widener Law Sch.; adj. faculty mem. trial advocacy program Hofstra Law Sch.; master C. Willard Heckel Inn of Ct.; guest lectr. appellate advocacy Roger Williams Law Sch., 1995—; mem. panel arbitrators Am. Arbitration Assn.; lectr. for Inst. Continuing Legal Edn. for State of N.J. Mem. ABA, NJ Bar Assn., Fed. Bar Assn. of N.J. (trustee). Home: 9 Harvey Dr Short Hills NJ 07078-1122 Office: Cohn Lifland Pearlman Herrmann & Knopf 1 Park 80 Plz W Ste 4 Saddle Brook NJ 07663-5808 Office Phone: 201-845-9600. Business E-Mail: psp@njlawfirm.com.

**PEARLMAN, RONALD ALAN**, lawyer, educator; b. Hamilton, Ohio, July 10, 1940; AB with honors, Northwestern U., 1962, JD cum laude, 1965; LL.M. in Taxation, Georgetown U., 1967. Bar: D.C. 1971, U.S. Tax Ct. 1969, U.S. Supreme Ct. 1968. Atty. office chief counsel IRS, Washington, 1965—69; assoc. Thompson & Mitchell, St. Louis, 1969—70, ptnr., 1970—83; dep. asst. sec. for tax policy Dept. Treasury, Washington, 1983—84, asst. sec. tax policy, 1984—85; ptnr. Bryan, Cave, McPheeters & McRoberts (now Bryan Cave), St. Louis, 1986-88; chief of staff joint com. on taxation U.S. Congress, Washington, 1988—90; ptnr. Covington & Burling, Washington, 1991—2000; prof. Georgetown U. Law Ctr., Washington, 1999—. Ind. trustee Eaton Vance Mut. Funds, 2003—; vis. prof. Georgetown U. Law Ctr., Washington, 1998, Harvard U. Law Sch., Cambridge, Mass., 2002; adj. prof. Sch. Law Wash. U., St. Louis, 1972—83; vis. instr. Sch. Law U. Va., Charlottesville, 1995—98; mem. BNA Tax Mgmt. Adv. Bd., 1986—88, 1993—; participant seminars. Mem. bd. editors Northwestern U. Law Rev.; contbr. articles to various publs. Trustee Am. Tax Policy Inst., 1998—, pres., 2003—04. Fellow Am. Coll. Tax Counsel; mem. ABA (vice chair govt. rels. 1997-99, chair govt. rels. com. 1996-97, mem. coun., tax sect. 1986-88), Am. Law Inst. (tax adv. group, cons. pass-through entities project and tax integration project), Order of Coif. Office: Georgetown U Law Ctr 600 New Jersey Ave NW Washington DC 20001-2022 Office Phone: 202-662-9882. Business E-Mail: pearlman@law.georgetown.edu.

**PEARLMAN, SAMUEL SEGEL**, lawyer, educator; b. Pitts., May 28, 1942; s. Merle Maurice and Bernice Florence (Segel) P.; m. Cathy Schwartz, Aug. 16, 1964; children: Leah P. Kraner, Caren E. AB, U. Pa., 1963, LLB magna cum laude, 1966. Bar: Pa. 1966, Ohio 1967, U.S. Ct. Appeals (3d cir.) 1967. Law clk. U.S. Dist. Ct. for Ea. Dist. Pa., Phila., 1966-67; assoc. Burke, Haber & Berick, Cleve., 1967-72, prin., 1973-86, Berick, Pearlman & Mills, Cleve., 1986-99; ptnr. Squire, Sanders & Dempsey L.L.P., Cleve., 2000—. Lectr. law Case Western Res. U. Sch. Law, 1978-82; mem. registration com. Ohio Div. Securities, 1979-89; adv. dir. Midland Title Security, Inc.; trustee Realty ReFund Trust, N.Y. Stock Exch., 1990-98. Author: Cases, Forms and Materials for Modern Real Estate Transactions, 1978, 82. Mem. ABA, Ohio Bar Assn., Greater Cleve. Bar Assn. (chmn. securities law sect. 1985-86), Order of Coif. Republican. Jewish. Office: Squire Sanders & Dempsey 4900 Key Tower 127 Public Sq Ste 4900 Cleveland OH 44114-1304 Office Phone: 216-479-8500, 216-479-8025. Business E-Mail: spearlman@ssd.com.

**PEARLMAN, STEVEN JAY**, otolaryngologist, educator, surgeon; b. NYC, 1956; BA in biology, Brandeis U., 1978; MD, Mt. Sinai Sch. of Medicine, 1982. Cert. Am. Bd. Otolaryngology-Head and Neck Surgery, 1987, Am. Bd. Facial Plastic and Reconstructive Surgery. Resident gen. surgery Mt. Sinai Med. Ctr., NYC, 1982-83, resident otolaryngology-head and neck surgery, 1983-87; fellow facial plastic surgery St. Luke's Roosevelt Hosp., NYC, 1987-88, otolaryngologist, assoc. dir., head and neck surgery, now dir., facial plastic surg. divsn.; attending surgeon Lenox Hill Hosp., NY, Manhattan Eye Ear and Throat Hosp., NY. Asst. prof. clin. otolaryngology, Columbia U. Hosp. Ctr. of Physicians and Surgeons; tchr. facial plastic surgery, Columbia U. Med. Sch. and NY Eye and Ear Infirmary. Contbr. to numerous medical and sci. publs., to chpts. in books.; appeared on nat. and local television talk and news programs (including CNN, WABC, Eyewitness News, Good Day NY, The Food Network, Fox-Channel 5, Montel Williams Show, and performed "live" face lift on CNBC's "The Real Story".). Pro bono surgeon Face to Face; pro bono facial reconstructive surgeon Nat. Domestic Violence Project. Mem. AMA, Am. Acad. Otolaryngology-Head and Neck Surgeons, Am. Acad. Facial Plastic and Reconstructive Surgery (past eastern region v.p. and nat. com. chmn.) NY State Med. Soc., NY Facial Plastic Surgery Soc. (founding pres. 1993-). Office: 521 Park Ave New York NY 10021-8140 Office Phone: 212-262-4444, 212-223-8300. Office Fax: 212-644-8655, 212-523-6364.

**PEARLSTEIN, PHILIP**, artist; b. Pitts., May 24, 1924; s. David and Libbie (Kalser) Pearlstein; m. Dorothy Cantor, Aug. 20, 1950; children: William, Julia, Ellen. BFA, Carnegie Inst. Tech., 1949; MA, NYU, 1955. Instr. Pratt Inst., 1959-63; vis. critic Yale U., 1962-63; from asst. prof. to prof. art dept. Bklyn. Coll., 1963-88, disting. prof. emeritus; pres. Am. Acad. Arts Letters, 2003—. Exhibited in group shows at Carnegie Internat., 1955, 1964, 1967, Whitney Mus. Am. Art, 1955—56, 1958, 1962, 1965, 1967, 1970, 1972—74, 1979, 1991, U. Mich. Mus., 1965, U. Ill., 1965, 1967—68, Providence Art Club, 1965, Corcoran Gallery, 1967, Vassar Coll., 1968, Milw. Art, 1969, Pa. Acad. Fine Arts, 1971—72, Indpls. Mus. Art, 1972, Galerie Lowenadler, Stockholm, Sweden, 1973, Nat. Acad. Arts, Letter, NYC, 1973 (award, 1973), Yale U., 1973—74, Hofstra U., 1973, Helsinki Mus. Art, Finland, 1974, Art Inst. Chgo., 1974, Cleve. Mus. Art, 1974, US Dept. Interior, 1976, Wildenstein Gallery, NYC, 1976, Tokashima Art Mus., Japan, 1992, exhibitions include retrospective U. Tex., Austin, 1974, Finch Coll., 1974, Cranbrook Acad. Art, Mich., 1974, Miami Art, 1975, Kalamazoo Inst. Arts, Tampa Bay Art, Tampa, Fla., 1975, Grand Rapids Art Mus., Mich., 1975, Notre Dame U., 1975, exhibitions include Bicentennial, Am., 1976, exhibitions include retrospective Chryler Mus., 1980, Philbrook Art, 1980, San Antonio Mus., 1981, Akron Art Mus., 1981, Honolulu Acad. Art, 1994, exhibitions include Fahnemann Galerie, Berlin, 2003, Michael Hass, Zurich, 2004, Haas and Fuchs, Berlin, 2004, Robert Miller Gallery, NY, 2004, Betty Cunningham Gallery, 2005, Represented in permanent collections Columbus Mus., Ga., Phila. Mus. Art, San Antonio Mus. Assn., Pa. State U., Whitney Mus., Mus. Modern Art, NY, Met. Mus. Art, Bklyn Mus., Carnegie Mus., Syracuse U., James A. Michener Found., Hirshhorn Mus., Corcoran Gallery, Art Inst. Chgo., Milw. Art Ctr., Ludwig Collection, Aachen, Germany, Sydney and Frances Lewis Found., Richmond, Va., Cleve. Mus. Art, Milw. Mus. Grantee, NAD, 1983; Fulbright fellow, Italy, 1958—59, Guggenheim fellow, 1971—72, Nat. Endowment Arts grantee, 1968. Mem.: Am. Acad. Arts, Letters. (pres. 2003—06, grantee 1992).*

**PEARLSTEIN, SEYMOUR**, artist; b. Bklyn., Oct. 14, 1923; s. Morris Lazarus and Anna (Bassiur) P.; m. Toby Tessie Rubinstein, Mar. 21, 1943; children: Judith Helene, Lawrence Jonathan. Cert., Pratt Inst., Bklyn., 1950, Art Students League N.Y., 1954; student of Jack Potter. Owner, illustrator, designer Sy Pearlstein Advt. Art Studio, N.Y.C., 1946-71; artist-painter rep. by Far Gallery, N.Y.C., 1969-81; prof. N.Y.C. Tech. Coll., CUNY, Bklyn., 1971-94, prof. emeritus, 1994—, chmn. art and advt. design dept., 1988-93. One-man shows Silvermine Guild of Artists, New Canaan, Conn., 1973, Far Gallery, 1973, 75, 78, Klitgord Ctr., N.Y.C., C.C., 1974, De Mers Gallery, Hilton Head, S.C., 1975, Adelphi U., Garden City, N.Y., 1979, Grace Gallery, N.Y.C. Tech. Coll., 1992; group shows A.M. Sachs Gallery, N.Y.C., 1971, Springfield (Mo.) Art Mus., 1971, Am. Acad. Arts and Letters, N.Y.C., 1975, 76, 77, NAD, N.Y.C., 1986, 87, 89, 91, 92, Butler Inst. Art, Ohio, 1975, Ball State U., Queens Mus., N.Y.C., 1978, 81, Dept. State Art in Embassies Program, N.Y. Hist. Soc., 1981, Colo. Heritage Mus., Denver, 1981, 82, 86, Am. Watercolor Soc., N.Y.C., Ingber Gallery, N.Y.C., 1985, Audubon Artists, N.Y.C., 1990, 92, 97, Allied Artists Am., N.Y.C., 1991, 95, 2002, Nat. Arts Club, N.Y.C., 1989, Grace Gallery, N.Y.C. Tech. Coll., CUNY, 1999, 2000, others; represented in permanent collections Mus. N.Mex., Santa Fe, Mint Mus. Art, Charlotte, N.C., NAD, N.Y.C., Fine Arts Gallery, San Diego, Adelphi U., Queens Mus., N.Y.C., Munson-Williams-Proctor Inst., Utica, N.Y., N.Y.C. Tech. Coll., Bklyn. Served with AUS, 1942-46. Recipient Gold medal Nat. Acad. Design, 1969, Hassam Fund Purchase award Am. Acad. Arts and Letters, 1969, 77, Gold medal of honor Nat. Arts Club, 1970, Ranger Fund Purchase award NAD, 1971, 82, Gold medal Soc. Illustrators, 1972, Nat. Inst.-Am. Acad. Arts and Letters grant, 1975 Mem. NAD (sec. coun.) 1980-84, W.H. Leavin prize 1985), Am. Watercolor Soc. (bd. dirs. 1979-80, Watercolor U.S.A. award 1971), Art Students League of N.Y. (life), Allied Artists Am. (bd. dirs. 1976-79, E. Lowe award 1969, gold medal 1980, George Tweed Meml. award 1989, 92), Audubon Artists (bd. dirs. 1986-89, 91-93, Grumbacher award 1971, Fabri medal 1980), Alliance Figurative Artists (c0chmn. 1976-77), Profl. Staff Congress. Home: 52 Dartmouth St Forest Hills NY 11375-5142 Office: NYC Tech Coll AD Dept CUNY 300 Jay St Brooklyn NY 11201-1909 E-mail: spearlstein@nyc.rr.com.

**PEARLSTINE, NORMAN**, communications consultant, former editor; b. Phila., Oct. 4, 1942; s. Raymond and Gladys (Cohen) Pearlstine. BA, Haverford Coll., 1964; LLB, U. Pa., 1967. Staff reporter Wall Street Jour., Dallas, 1968—73, Detroit, 1968—73, LA, 1968—73, Tokyo bur. chief, 1973—76; mng. editor Asian Wall Street Jour., Hong Kong, 1976—78; exec. editor Forbes Mag., LA, 1978—80; nat. news editor Wall Street Jour., NYC, 1980—82; editor, pub. Wall Street Jour./Europe, Brussels, 1982—83; mng. editor, v.p. Wall Street Jour., NYC, 1983—91, exec. editor, 1991—92; press., CEO Friday Holdings, L.P., NYC, 1993—94; editor-in-chief Time Inc., NYC, 1995—2005; sr. adv. Time Warner Inc., NYC, 2006, The Carlyle Group, NYC, 2006—. Pres. Atsuko Chiba Found.; bd. councilors USC Annenberg Sch. Comm.; pres. adv. bd. Neiman Found. at Harvard U.; mem. adv. bd. CUNY Grad. Sch. Journalism, Arthur F. Burns Fellowship Program; bd. mem. The Carnegie Corp., The Arthur F. Burns Fellowship Program; bd. dirs. Com. to Protect Journalists, 2004—; trustee NY Hist. Soc., 1985—2005, chmn., 1989—93; pres. Am. Acad. in Berlin, 2006—. Named to Mag. Editors Hall of Fame, 2005; recipient Editor of Yr. award, Nat. Press Found., 1989, Lifetime Achievement award, ASME, 2005, Loeb Lifetime Achievement

award for disting. bus. and fin. journalism, 2000. Mem.: ABA, Am. Acad. Arts and Scis., Japan Soc., Coun. Fgn. Rels., D.C. Bar Assn., Tribeca Film Inst. (bd. dirs.). Office: The Carlyle Group 520 Madison Ave New York NY 10022

**PEARSALL, GEORGE WILBUR**, materials scientist, educator, mechanical engineer, consultant; b. Brentwood, NY, July 13, 1933; s. Milo Dickerson and Margaret Elizabeth (White) P.; m. Patricia Louise Stevens, Oct. 11, 1962. B. Metall. Engring., Rensselaer Poly. Inst., 1955; Sc.D. (Am. Soc. Metals fellow), MIT, 1961. Registered profl. engr., NC. Rsch. engr. Dow Chem. Co., Midland, Mich., 1955-57; rsch. asst. MIT, 1959-60, asst. prof. metallurgy, 1960-64; assoc. prof. mech. engring. Duke U., 1964-66, prof., 1966-81, prof. mech. engring. and materials sci., 1981—2001, prof. pub. policy studies, 1982—2001, acting dean Sch. Engring., 1969-71, dean, 1971-74, 82-83, prof. emeritus, 2001—. Trustee Triangle Univ. Ctr. for Advanced Studies, 1976-92, chmn. exec. com., 1983-88; dir. Duke-IBM Product Safety Inst., 1979-90. Author: (with W.G. Moffatt and J. Wulff) The Structure and Properties of Materials, 1964; mem. editl. bd. Jour. Products Liability, 1977-92, Jour. Products and Toxics Liability, 1993-96, Proceedings of the IEEE, 1994-96; contbr. articles to profl. jour. Served with AUS, 1957. Mem. ASME (Triodyne Safety Award 2001), Am. Soc. Metals (life), Phi Lambda Upsilon, Tau Beta Pi, Pi Tau Sigma. Home: 2941 Welcome Dr Durham NC 27705-5555 Office Phone: 919-660-5344. Business E-Mail: pearsall@duke.edu.

**PEARSALL, GLENN LINCOLN**, brokerage house executive; b. Huntington, NY, June 19, 1949; s. Alan W. and Jean (Doubrava) Pearsall; m. Carol Ann Ciesla, June 19, 1971; children: Adam, Heather. BA in English, SUNY, Oswego, 1971; cert. in investment mgmt. analyst, U. Pa., 1994. V.p. Pearsall Realty Inc., Wevertown, NY, 1975-85; investment exec. E. F. Hutton, Glens Falls, NY, 1985-87; fin. cons. Shearson, Lehman, Hutton, Glens Falls, Saratoga, NY, 1987-90; fin. advisor UBS (formerly PaineWebber), Glens Falls, 1990—, br. mgr., 1990—2002, divisional v.p., 1994—. Daily stock market reporter Stas. WLPW-FM, WIRD-AM, Lake Placid, 1985—90, Sta. WKBE-FM, Glens Falls, 1992—95, Sta. WWSC-AM, 1995, Sta. WCKM-FM, 1995—2002; fin. commentator TV 8 Monday Night News, Glens Falls, 1988—2002; mem. 1991 stock pickers coun. Capital Dist. Bus. Rev., Albany, NY, 1991. Fin. columnist: several weekly newspapers, 1988—. Bd. dirs. Adirondack coun. Girl Scouts U.S., fund-raising chmn., 1990; bd. dirs., v.p. Lake George Opera Festival; bd. dirs. Adirondack Ensemble, 1997—, v.p., 1999, chair fin. com., 1998—, pres., 2000—01; co-founder, pres. Glenn and Carol Pearsall Adirondack Found.; trustee Town of Johnsburg Libr. Found., 2001—, pres., 2003—, Libr. Found., Johnsburg; trustee Adirondack Cmty. Trust, 2006—; mem. Assemblyman Glenn Harris legis. adv. coun. Assembly Dist. 109 N.Y. State, 1985—90; pres. bd. dirs. North Creek (N.Y.) C. of C., 1978—86; trustee Adirondack Mus. Blue Moutain Lake, 2001—, chmn. personnel com., 2005—; trustee, pres. Johnsburg Pub. Libr. Endowment, 2002—; trustee Adirondack Cmty. Trust, 2006—; mem. Cornell Coop. Ext. Adv. Coun., 1982—91; bd. dirs. Warren County Coop. Ext., pres., 1985, 1986, Adirondack Civil War Round Table, 1997—99. Mem.: Investment Mgmt. Cons. Assn. Republican. Avocations: white water canoeing, skiing, fishing, reading. Office: UBS One Broad St Pla Glens Falls NY 12801 Office Phone: 800-526-3763. Business E-Mail: glenn.pearsall@ubs.com.

**PEARSALL, GLORIA W.**, retired elementary school educator; d. Fred D. and Pearl M. Williams; m. Freeman Pearsall, Dec. 23, 1958 (dec.); children: Everard F., Corinna D., Heaven-Leigh Rapture. BS, Fayetteville State U., 1954; MEd, Pa. State U., 1958. Tchr. Chinquipin (N.C.) Elem. Sch., 1954—55, P.W. Moore Elem. Sch., Farson, NC, 1955—62, Carver H.S., Mt. Olive, NC, 1964—66, Warsaw (N.C.) Elem. Sch., 1966—93, ret., 1993. Deaconess St. Stephens Amez Ch., Warsaw, 1978; treas. Ministry Kindness, Warsaw, 1963, trustee bd., 1963; compassion worker Bessie Williams Ever Ready Ch., Warsaw, 1970—99. Mem.: NEA, Nat. Assn. Advancement Colored People, N.C. Assn. Edn.

**PEARSALL, OTIS PRATT**, retired lawyer; b. Bklyn., Apr. 25, 1932; s. Willard Hall and Marilla Houghton (Pratt) P.; m. Nancy Jeanne Boden, July 7, 1956; 1 child, Melissa Mather BA, Yale U., 1953, LL.B., 1956. Assoc. Hughes, Hubbard, Blair & Reed, N.Y.C., 1956-59, 60-63; asst. U.S. atty. U.S. Atty.'s Office So. Dist. N.Y., N.Y.C., 1959-60; ptnr. Hughes Hubbard & Reed, N.Y.C., 1964-91, Arnold & Porter, N.Y.C., 1991—2002; ret. Mem. Art Commn. of the City of N.Y., 2001—; dir. Bridgehampton (N.Y.) Assocs., Inc., 1973—, pres., 2004—. Bd. dirs. Mcpl. Art Soc. N.Y., N.Y.C., 1967-74, v.p., 1973-74; trustee Soc. for Preservation of L.I. Antiquities, Setauket, N.Y., 1969-77, Bklyn. Mus., 1986-92, 93—, mem. adv. bd., 1992-93; bd. dirs. L.I. Hist. Soc., Bklyn., 1971-82; mem. historic city com., N.Y.C., 1987-88, commr. art commn., 2001—; trustee The Green-Wood Cemetery, Bklyn., 1992—; dir. N.Y. Preservation Archive Project, 2003-. Recipient Green Star award Environ. Action Coalition, Inc., 1989, Landmark Lion award N.Y. Hist. Dists. Coun., 1993, Lucy G. Moses Preservation Leadership award, NY Landmarks Conservancy, 2000. Fellow Am. Coll. Trial Lawyers; mem. Bklyn. Heights Assn. (gov., adv. com. 1960-), mem. ABA, Bridgehampton Club (pres. 1989-91), India House Club, Calif. Club, Univ. Club, Phi Beta Kappa. Republican. Congregationalist. Avocation: historic building restoration. Home: 157 Willow St Brooklyn NY 11201-2201

**PEARSALL, PAUL**, psychologist, educator; b. Detroit, Mar. 3, 1942; s. Frank and Carol Pearsall; m. Celest Malinowski, May 30, 1963; children: Roger, Scott. BA, U. Mich., Dearborn, 1964; PhD, Wayne State U., Detroit, 1968; postgrad., Harvard Sch. Medicine, Boston, 1975. Lic. psychologist Mich. Chief Problems of Daily Living Clinic, Sinai Hosp. Detroit, 1969—71; prof. psychology Henry Ford CC, Dearborn, 1968—98; adj. assoc. prof. dept. psychiatry and neuroscience Wayne State U. Sch. Medicine, 1972—77; dir. or profl. edn. Kinsey Inst. for Study of Sex and Reproduction, Bloomington, 1978—79; dir. behavioral medicine Beaumnt Hosp., Southfield, Mich., 1990—91; adj. clin. prof. dept. of nursing U. Hawaii at Manoa, Honolulu, 1998—. Bd. directors Hawaii State Consortium Integrative Health Care, Honolulu, 2000—; mem. clin. adv. bd. Waimanalo Health Ctr. Hawaiian Culture Healing Program, Waimanalo, Hawaii; lectr. in field. Author: Super Immunity, The Beethoven Factor, A Healing Intimacy, Partners in Pleasure, The Last Self-Help Book You'll Ever Need, The Power of the Family, Super Marital Sex, Super Joy, Miracle in Maui, The Pleasure Prescription, Toxic Success, The Heart's Code, The Beethoven Factor, Wishing Well. Mem. Kuhai Halau O Kawaikapuokalani Pa Olapa Kahiko, Honolulu, 1987—2006. Named Trail Blazer in Medicine, Scripps Med. Ctr. for Integrative Medicine; recipient Rush Gold medal, Am. Psychiat. Assn., 1974. Mem.: APA, Phi Kappa Phi. Achievements include research in heart transplant recipients receiving characteristics of their donor. Avocation: Hawaiian culture. Office: Ho'ala Hou PO Box 26356 Honolulu HI 96825 Office Phone: 808-395-9641. Office Fax: 808-396-0043. Business E-Mail: info@paulpearsall.com.

**PEARSALL, SAMUEL HAFF, III**, ecologist, geographer, foundation administrator; b. Nashville, Sept. 3, 1949; s. Sam H. Jr. and Margaret Isabelle (Ikard) P.; m. Patricia Davenport, July 1973 (div. 1978); 1 child, Rachel Claire; m. Linda Louise Parrish, Sept. 4, 1982; 1 child, Paul Samuel. BS, U. Tenn., 1942; M of Prof. Studies, Cornell U., 1982; PhD, U. Hawaii, 1993. Exec. dir. Coastal Resources Ctr., Bar Harbor, Maine, 1975-77; program dir. Natural Areas and Natural Heritage Survey Tenn. Dept. Conservation, Nashville, 1978-81, dir. Ecol. Svcs. divsn., 1982-85; dir. Pacific Sci. The Nature Conservancy, Honolulu, 1989-91, dir. sci. and stewardship Durham, NC, 1992-99, dir. sci. and Roanoke River Project, 2000—. Adj. faculty U. NC, 1993—, Nicholas Sch. Environment Duke U., 1999—, founder Pacific Sci. program Nature Conservancy, 1989, founding mem. conservation com., 1994-96, Ecoregions working group, 1996-97; mem. So. Blue Ridge Ecoregional Planning Team, 1996-97; leader Mid-Atlantic Coastal Plain Ecoregional Planning Team, 1997—; founding mem. Ga.-Pacific/Nature Conservancy Roanoke Ecosys. Partnership, 1995-97; sci. and tech. adv. com. Albemarle-Pamlico Nat. Estuari Program, 2004-05. Author: Terrestrial Coastal Environments and Tourism in Western Samoa, 1993, Managing for Future Change on the Albemarle Sound, 2005, Adapting Coastal Lowlands to Rising Seas, 2005; (with others) Wildlife Conservation Evaluation Methods in U.S., 1985; contbr. articles to profl. jours. Bd. dirs. Tenn. Environ. Coun.,

Nashville, 1980-85, Natural Areas Assn., Rockford, Ill., 1984-87, Bend, Oreg., 97-2000, treas., 1999-2000; counselor Conservation Trust for N.C., 1993-98; founder Tenn. Protection Planning Com.; student fellow East-West Ctr., 1985-90. Recipient Hodgson award Assn. Am. Geographers, 1988, Wiens award U. Hawaii, 1993, Conservation by Design award Nature Conservancy, 2003. Achievements include research in nature conservation, adaptive ecosystem management and landscape ecology in Western Samoa and North Carolina, coastal climate change and sea level rise in North Carolina; co-author FERC Lic. Settlement among Dominion Generation, Inc. and stakeholders at Lake Gaston and Roanoke Rapids dams. Home: 1307 Chaney Rd Raleigh NC 27606-2736 Office: Nature Conservancy Ste 209/One University Pl 4705 University Dr Durham NC 27707 Office Phone: 919-403-8558. Business E-Mail: sampearsall@tnc.org.

**PEARSE, WARREN HARLAND**, obstetrician, gynecologist, medical association administrator; b. Detroit, Sept. 28, 1927; s. Harry Albridge and Frances (Wressell) P.; m. Jacqueline Anne Langan, June 15, 1950; children: Kathryn, Susan, Laurie, Martha. BS, Mich. State U., 1948; M.B., MD, Northwestern U., 1951. Intern. Univ. Hosp., Ann Arbor, Mich., 1950-51; resident obstetrics and gynecology, 1951-53, 55-56; practice medicine specializing obstetrics and gynecology Detroit, 1956-58; mem. faculty U. Nebr. Med. Ctr., Omaha, 1959-71, Found. prof., chmn. dept. obstetrics and gynecology, 1962-71, asst. dean. Univ. Med. Coll. Va., Richmond, Va., 1971-75; exec. dir. Am. Coll. Obstetrics and Gynecology, 1975-93; cons., 1993—; editor Women's Health Issues, Washington, 1993—. Chmn. rsch. adv. group Maternal Child Health Svc., Health Sci. Mental Health Adminstrn., HEW, 1967—; cons. family planning Office Econ. Opportunity, 1970—. Author: (with V.L. Seltzer) Primary Health Care for Women, 1999—; contbr. chpts., articles tech. lit. Served from 1st lt. to capt. AUS, 1953-55. Mem. Am. Coll. Obstetrics and Gynecology (dist. sec., treas. 1964-68, vice chmn. 1968-71), Am. Gynecology Soc., Soc. Gynecology Investigation, Assn. Profs. Gynecology and Obstetrics (sec., treas. 1969—), Alpha Omega Alpha. Office: American College of Obs & Gyns 409 12th St SW Washington DC 20024-2125 Home: #5005 10450 Lottsford Rd Bowie MD 20721-3301 Office Phone: 202-863-2454.

**PEARSON, BROOKS C.**, geography educator, consultant; b. Murfreesboro, Tenn., Mar. 12, 1970; s. Larry Paul and Nancy June Pearson; m. April W. Willis, Nov. 28, 1992; children: Fletcher James, Meredith Ansley, Stewart William. BS, Mid. Tenn. State U., Murfreesboro, 1992; MA, Kans. State U., Manhattan, 1995; PhD, Ind. U., Bloomington, 1999. Asst. prof. geography State U. of West Ga., Carrollton, 1999—2005, U. Ctrl. Ark., Conway, 2005—. Contbr. articles to profl. jours., chapters to books. Grantee Technologies, US Dept Edn./Ark. Dept Higher Edn., 2006—. Mem.: Assn. Am. Geographers (dir. energy and environment splty. group 2000—06, Transp. Geography Splty. Group Dissertation award 2000). Achievements include development of techniques to quantify accuracy in historical maps; comparison of accuracy in historical maps of the Shenandoah Valley during the American Civil War. Office: U Ctrl Ark 201 Donaghey Ave Conway AR 72035 Office Phone: 501-450-5581. Office Fax: 501-450-5185. Business E-Mail: bpearson@uca.edu.

**PEARSON, CHARLES THOMAS, JR.**, lawyer, director; b. Fayetteville, Ark., Oct. 14, 1929; s. Charles Thomas and Doris (Pinkerton) P.; m. Wyma Lee Hampton, Sept. 9, 1988; children: Linda Sue, John Paddock. BS, U. Ark., 1953, JD, 1954; postgrad., U.S. Naval Postgrad. Sch., 1959; A.M., Boston U., 1963. Bar: Ark. bar 1954. Practice in, Fayetteville, 1963—. Dir. officer N.W. Comms., Inc., Dixieland Devel., Inc., Jonlin Investments, Inc., World Wide Travel Svc., Inc., Oklania Farms, Inc., N.W. Arl. Land & Devel., Inc., Garden Plaza Inns, Inc. Word Data, Inc., M.P.C. Farms, Inc., Fayetteville Enterprises, Inc., NWA Devel.Co., Delta Comm., Inc.; past. dir., organizer N.W. Nat. Bank. Adviser Explorer Scouts, 1968—; past pres. Washington County Draft Bd.; past pres. bd. Salvation Army. Served to comdr. Judge Adv. Gen. Corps USNR, 1955-63. Mem. ABA, Ark. Bar Assn., Washington County Bar Assn., Judge Advs. Assn., N.W. Ark. Ret. Officers Assn. (past pres.), Methodist Men (past pres.), U. Ark. Alumni Assn. (past dir.), Sigma Chi (past pres. N.W. Ark. alumni, past. chmn. house corp.), Alpha Kappa Psi, Phi Eta Sigma, Delta Theta Phi. Clubs: Mason (32 deg., K.T., Shriner), Moose, Elk, Lion, Metropolitan. Republican. Methodist. Office: 9 N College Ave Fayetteville AR 72701-5301 Office Phone: 479-521-2252. Business E-Mail: tpesq@cox.net.

**PEARSON, DANIEL R.**, federal official; m. Cindy Pearson; 2 children. BS in Agrl. Econ., MS in Agrl. Econ., U. Minn. Farmer, Ogilvie, Minn., 1979—80; agrl. legis. asst. to Senator Rudy Boschwitz US Senate, 1981—87; policy analyst Pub. Affairs Dept., 1987—98; asst. v.p., pub. affairs Cargill, Inc., 1998—2003; commr. US Internat. Trade Comm., Washington, 2003—. Office: US Internat Trade Comm 500 E St SW Washington DC 20436 Office Phone: 202-205-2000.*

**PEARSON, DEBORAH FAYE**, newscaster; b. Dothan, Ala., June 27, 1962; d. Lueretha Elaine Maynor; 1 child, Cameron Denzel. Student, Ala. State U., Montgomery, 1985. FCC radio comm. cert. Ala. News dir. Sta. WJJN-FM/WAGF-AM, Dothan, Ala., 1991—92; news anchor/reporter Sta. WOOF-TV, Dothan, 1992—. Named Best News Anchor, Ala. AP Broadcasters Assn., Best News Reporter; recipient Best Feature News Story, Best Public Affairs or Documentary, Best Regularly Scheduled Newscast. Mem.: E.L.E.T.E. Profls. - Dothan Assn. Womens Clubs. Office: WOOF Inc 2518 Columbia Hwy Dothan AL 36301 Office Phone: 334-792-1149. Personal E-mail: igtnws4u@yahoo.com.

**PEARSON, GERALD LEON**, food products executive; b. Mpls., June 24, 1925; s. Perry and Lillian (Peterson) P.; m. Beverly Mary Schultz, Nov. 10, 1946; children: Steven, Perry, Liecia. Treas. Trimont Packing Co., 1946-52; v.p. Spencer Foods, Iowa, 1952-68, pres., chief exec. officer Iowa, 1969-80, chmn. bd., chief exec. officer Iowa, 1972-80; chmn. Beef Specialists of Iowa Inc., 1983-94. Bd. dirs. Graffaloy, Inc.; chmn., CEO World Champions of Golf Inc.; owner Brooks Golf Club, Okoboji, Iowa. Pres. Pearson Art Found.; bd. dirs. Bethany Coll., Lindsborg; commr. Nat. Mus. Am. Art-Smithsonian Instn., 1995-99; founder Internat. Ctr. for Jazz Found. With USN, 1943-46. Mem. Swedish Royal Roundtable, Swedish Council Am. (bd. dirs.). Office: Brooks Golf Club PO Box 948 Okoboji IA 51355-0948 Home: 5209 Lake Shore Dr Okoboji IA 51355-2597 Office Phone: 712-332-7873. E-mail: bud.pearson@worldnet.att.net, bpearson@iowaone.net.

**PEARSON, HENRY CLYDE**, retired judge; b. Ocoonita Lee County, Va., Mar. 12, 1925; s. Henry James and Nancy Elizabeth (Seals) P.; m. Jean Calton, July 26, 1956; children: Elizabeth, Frances, Timothy Clyde. Student, Union Coll., 1947-49; LLB, U. Richmond, 1952. Bar: Va. 1952, U.S. Ct. Appeals (4th cir.) 1957, U.S. Supreme Ct. 1958. Sole practice, Jonesville, Va., 1952-56; asst. U.S. atty. Western Dist. Va., Roanoke, 1956-61; ptnr. Hopkins, Pearson & Engleby, Roanoke, 1961—70; so. states presdl. campaign mgr. Nelson A. Rockefeller, 1964; judge U.S. Bankruptcy Ct. Western Dist. Va., Roanoke, 1970-98; ret., 1998. Adv. com. fed. rules bankruptcy procedure; mem. Va. Ho. of Reps., 1954-56, Va. Senate, 1968-70; Republican nominee Gov. of Va., 1961. Editl. bd. Am. Survey Bankruptcy Law, 1979. With USN, 1943—46, PTO. Mem. Va. State Bar, ABA, Va. Trial Lawyers Assn., Amer. Trial Lawyers Am., Am. Judicature Soc., Am. Judges Assn., Fed. Bar Assn., Delta Theta Phi, Tribune Jefferson Senate, Am. Legion, VFW, Masons, Shriners. Methodist. Office: 1910 Mcvitty Rd Salem VA 24153-7406

**PEARSON, JENNIE SUE**, retired government administrator; b. Washington, Jan. 26, 1928; d. Orville Louis and Jennie (Rogers) Ganbin; m. Eugene Ryder Pearson, Feb. 3, 1945 (div. 1955); 1 child, Ronald Eugene. AA, Frederick (Md.) C.C., 1987. Title examiner Md. Motor Vehicle Adminstrn., Glen Burnie, 1970-74, title advisor, 1975-80, title supr., 1980-84, asst. br. mgr., 1984-91; ret., 1991. Pres. Rebekah Assembly Md., 1968-69, Internat. Assn. Rebekah Assemblies, Winston-Salem, N.C., 1973-74; v.p. Citizens

Nursing Home Aux. Vols., 1997-98, pres., 1999—; vice chmn. bd. dirs. Md. Odd Fellows Home, 1991-92; mem. Srs. and Law Enforcement Together Coun.-Frederick City Police Dept; mem. adv. bd. Inst. Learning in Retirement Frederick Cmty. Coll., bd. dirs.; trustee Schuyler Colfax Mus., Winston Salem, N.C.; bd. dirs. Frederick C.C. Found., Inc., Md. Sr. Citizens Hall Fame, 2003; mem. vol. Frederick Ret. Srs. Vol. Program, 2003; mem. Tng. for Future Disasters, Ret. Srs. Vol. Program. Recipient Outstanding Alumni award for significant contbns. Coll. Mission and Alumni Assn., 1991, 98, Meritorious Jewel Rebekah Assembly of Md. Outstanding Svc. in Fraternal Order and Cmty., Vol. of Month, Frederick Sr. Mag.; inductee Md. Sr. Citizens Hall of Fame, Inc. Mem. AARP (pres. Frederick chpt. 1997-99, Andrus award pin for vol. cmty. svc. 2003), Frederick C.C. Alumni Assn. (pres. 1991-98), Montgomery County Agrl. Ctr., Inc. (life), Frederick County Commn. for Women, Rebekah Lodge (past noble grand mem. 1997-98, Meritorious Jewel award 2000), Frederick Woman's Civic Club, Inc. (mem. com. 1992-2003, 1st v.p. 2003), Md. Sr. Citizens Hall of Fame, Inc. (bd. dirs. 2003), 1902 Club, Ret. Srs. Vol. Program. Republican. Methodist. Avocations: volunteer work, travel, ice skating, walking.

**PEARSON, JIM BERRY, JR.,** human resources specialist; b. Wichita Falls, Tex., Sept. 25, 1948; s. Jim Berry and June Louise (Young) P.; m. Cynthia Ann Medlin, Nov. 9, 1985 (div. Jan. 1999). Cert. mediator. Community organizer VISTA, Pitts., 1969-71; youth dir. East Liberty YMCA, Pitts., 1971-72; aide, therapist technician Austin (Tex.) State Sch., 1972-80; labor organizer Comm. Workers Am., Austin 1980-90; employee resource officer Austin State Hosp., 1990-96, human resource dir. Capital Area State-Operated Cmty. MHMR Svcs., Austin, 1996-97; human resources dir. Bluebonnet Trails Cmty. Mental Health/Mental Retardation Ctr, Round Rock, Tex., 1997-2001; employee rels. specialist Tex. Dept. Mental Health and Mental Retardation, Austin, 2001—03, Tex. Health and Human Svcs. Commn., Austin, 2003—05; dir. tng. and competency devel. Austin State Hosp., 2005—. Exec. bd. rep. Communications Workers Am./Tex. State Employees Union, Austin, 1987-90; trustee Austin Cen. Labor Coun. AFL-CIO, Austin, 1983-84. Vol. AFL-CIO Polit. Action Com., 1980—; del. founding conv. Labor Party, 1996. Recipient Vols. in Politics award Nat. ALF-CIO, Washington, 1984, Peacemaker award Travis County Dispute Resolution Ctr., 1993. Mem. Comm. Workers Am./Tex. State Employees Union Local 6186 (founding mem.). Avocation: pre-colombian archaeology. Home: 1118 Mclain St Taylor TX 76574-2343 Office: Austin State Hosp 4110 Guadalupe St Austin TX 78751 Office Phone: 512-419-2305. Personal E-mail: dzul@texas.net. Business E-Mail: jimb.pearson@dshs.state.tx.us.

**PEARSON, JOHN YEARDLEY, JR.,** lawyer; b. Norfolk, Va., July 23, 1942; BA, Washington & Lee U., 1964; JD, U. Va., 1971. Bar: Va. 1971. Atty. Willcox & Savage P.C., Norfolk. Mem editl. bd.: Va. Law Rev., 1969—71. Fellow Am. Coll. Trial Lawyers; mem. ABA (litig. sect.), Internat. Assn. Def. Counsel, Order of Coif. Office: Willcox & Savage PC 1800 Bank of America Ctr Norfolk VA 23510-2197 Office Phone: 757-628-5503. Business E-Mail: jpearson@wilsav.com.

**PEARSON, KEVIN,** health facility administrator; Pres. Med-Index (divsn. Medicode Inc.); CFO Medicode Inc., COO; sr. mgr. Ernst & Young, San Francisco; CEO health intelligence divsn. Ingenix, Unitedhealth Group, Inc., Minnetonka, Minn., 1990—2003, CEO, 2003—. Office: Unitedhealth Group Ctr 9900 Bren Rd E Minnetonka MN 55343

**PEARSON, LARRY LESTER,** journalism educator; b. Sioux Falls, S.D., Sept. 27, 1942; s. Lester Loren and Lois Ursula (Cochran) P.; m. Alice Marie Simons, Sept. 15, 1979; children: Gregory Eric, Hillary Yvette, Andrew Todd. BA cum laude, U. Minn., 1964, PhD, 1990; MA, U. Wis., 1969. Newsman UPI, Mpls., 1962-63; newsman Daily American, Rome, 1964-65; instr. Journalism Sch., U. Wis., 1965-67; with Mpls. Tribune, 1967-85, wire editor, 1970-72, news editor, 1972-82, Mpls. Star & Tribune, 1982; with Anchorage Daily News, 1996—. Asst. prof. U. Alaska, Anchorage, 1985-92, assoc. prof., 1992-99, dir. Ctr. for Info. Tech., 1990-92; spl. cons. to Alaska Ho. Com. on Telecomm., 1985-90; propr. Online Design, 1995—. Home: 2410 E 16th Ave Anchorage AK 99508-2906 Personal E-mail: design@alaska.net.

**PEARSON, LEE O.,** real estate investment trust executive; B in economics, U. Tex., Austin. Positions at Johnson Space Ctr., NASA, Houston, TRW Inc., Continental Airlines, Texas Instruments, AT&T, Title USA Ins., SCI, Hines Interest; dir. info. tech. Weingarten Realty Investors, Houston, 2002—03, v.p. info. tech., 2003—. Served U.S. Army, Vietnam War. Named one of Premier 100 IT Leaders, Computerworld, 2005. Office: Weingarten Realty Investors PO Box 924133 2600 Citadel Plaza Dr Houston TX 77292-4133 Office Phone: 713-866-6000. Office Fax: 713-866-6049.*

**PEARSON, LOUISE S.,** lawyer; b. 1955; BS in Chemistry, U. Wash.; MS in Chemistry, U. Tex.; JD, U. Houston. Bar: 1984. Pvt. practice Kirkland & Ellis, Vinson & Elkins; with Baxter Internat., 1991—2000; v.p., gen. counsel, sec. Dade Behring, Inc., Deerfield, Ill., 2000—. Mem.: ABA. Office: Dade Behring Inc 1717 Deerfield Rd Deerfield IL 60015 Office Phone: 847-267-5300.

**PEARSON, MICHAEL P.,** lawyer; b. Houston, June 9, 1953; BA, U. Tex., 1975, JD, 1978. Bar: Tex. 1978, U.S. Ct. Appeals (5th cir.) 1981. Atty. Jackson & Walker L.L.P., Houston, 1978—; ptnr. Jackson Walker LLP, Houston, 1984—. Assoc. editor: Tex. Law Rev., 1977-78; contbr. articles to profl. jours. Mem. ABA (litig. sect.), Bar Assn., Phi Beta Kappa, Phi Kappa Phi. Office: Jackson Walker LLP 1401 McKinney St #1900 Houston TX 77010-1900 Office Phone: 713-752-4311. E-mail: mpearson@jw.com.

**PEARSON, NATHAN WILLIAMS,** communications executive, investment executive; b. Sewickley, Pa., Aug. 1, 1951; s. Nathan Williams Sr. and Kathleen Patricia (McMurtry) P.; m. Jane Ruth Wallace, Oct. 12, 1985; children: Nathan McMurtry, Howe Quinn, Henry Wallace. BA and MA in Music, Conn. Wesleyan U., 1974; MBA, Columbia U., 1982. Pvt. practice cons., N.Y.C. and Washington, 1974-82; with McKinsey & Co., N.Y.C. and L.A., 1982-88; exec. v.p., chief fin. officer, mng. prin., sec., treas. Broadcasting Ptnrs., Inc., N.Y.C., 1988-95; chmn. Broadcasting Ptnrs., L.L.C., Rye, NY, 1995—; pres., CEO and chmn. RadioWave.com Inc., Chgo., 1999—2001; mng. dir. Manursing Group, Rye, NY, 2002—. Vice chmn. No. Light Comms., Reykjavik, 1995-2003; mng. dir. Commonwealth Holdings, Inc., N.Y.C., 1996-99; operating affiliate McCown DeLeeuw & Co., N.Y.C., 1997-99; ptnr. Windale Group, 2004-2006, 1105 Media Inc., 2006—; bd. dirs. Archway Broadcasting Group, Las Vegas TV Ptnrs., LLC, IPS Holdings, LLC. Author: 'Goin' to Kansas City,' 1987; producer LP records, TV and radio programs; contbr. articles to profl. jours. Sec., bd. dirs. CityLore, Inc., N.Y.C., 1986—; pres., 1990-92; pres. Young Audiences/N.Y., 1995-96; bd. dirs. Young Audiences, 1986—, Young Audiences, Inc., 1995—, Rye Nature Ctr., 2004—, Broadcom, 2005—. Mem. Soc. for Ethnomusicology, Am. Folklore Soc., Wadawanuck Club, Nat. Assn. Broadcasting, Manursing Island Club, Hillsboro Club, Rolling Rock Club, Beta Gamma Sigma. Avocations: boardsailing, river running, hiking. Home: 3 Holly Ln Rye NY 10580-3953 Office: Broadcasting Ptnrs Rye NY 10580 Office Phone: 914-643-3278. E-mail: bpearson@manurnsllc.com, bill-pearson@prodigy.net.

**PEARSON, NELS KENNETH,** retired manufacturing executive; b. Algonquin, Illinois, May 2, 1918; s. Nels Pehr and Anna (Frye) P.; m. Louise Mary Houston (Lenox), June 28, 1941 (dec. Dec. 1996); children: Lorine Marie Pearson Walters, Karla Jean; m. Ethel Jane Pearson, July 26, 1997. High Sch. grad. Assembly line foreman Oak Mfg. Co., Crystal Lake, Ill., 1935—43; served in U.S. Army, 1943—46; apprentice tool and die maker Oak Mfg. Co., Crystal Lake, Ill., 1946—50; co-founder, pres. Wauconda Tool and Engring. Co., Algonquin, Ill., 1950—86; co-founder, treas. Kenmode Tool and Engring. Co., Inc., Algonquin, 1960—72; founder, owner Kar-Lor Enterprises, Crystal Lake, 1986—. Avocation: restoring, showing and travelling in antique

automobiles 1911 thru 1927. Home: 125 Dole Ave Crystal Lake IL 60014-5837 Office: 910 Pyott Rd Crystal Lake IL 60014 Office Phone: 815-455-0959. Personal E-mail: eandk27@aol.com.

**PEARSON, P. DAVID,** dean; BA, U. Calif., Berkeley, 1963. Dean Coll. Edn. U. Ill., Urbana-Champaign, co-dir. Ctr. for Study of Reading; John. A. Hannah Disting. prof. edn. Mich. State U., co-dir. Ctr. for Study of Reading; dean Grad. Sch. Edn. U. Calif., Berkeley, 2001—. Recipient Oscar Causey Award, Nat. Reading Conf., 1989, William S. Gray Citation of Merit, 1990. Mem.: Phi Beta Kappa. Office: Grad Sch Edn 1501 Tolman Hall #1670 Berkeley CA 94720-1670 Office Phone: 510-642-3726. Office Fax: 510-643-8904. E-mail: ppearson@socrates.berkeley.edu.

**PEARSON, PAUL DAVID,** lawyer, arbitrator, mediator; b. Boston, Jan. 22, 1940; s. Bernard J. and Ruth (Bayla) Horblit; m. Carol A. Munschauer; children: David Todd, Lisa Kari, Grant M. BA, Bucknell U., 1961; LLB, U. Pa., 1964. Bar: Mass. 1966, N.Y. 1987. Staff atty., tech. assoc. lab. cmty. psychiatry dept. Med. Sch. Harvard U., Boston, 1966—68; assoc. Snyder Tepper & Berlin, Boston, 1969—71, ptnr., 1971—77; ptnr., chmn. family law dept. Hill & Barlow, 1977—87; ptnr. chmn. family law dept. Hodgson, Russ, LLP, Buffalo, 1987—96; of counsel Sullivan Oliverio & Gioia, Buffalo, 1996—2000; with Law Offices Kevin A. Ricotta, 2006—. Lectr. Mass. CLE, New Eng. Law Inst., dept. psychiatry SUNY Sch. Medicine, Buffalo, 1989—; instr. law and mental health Boston Psychoanalytic Soc. and Inst., 1975-87; lectr. law, mental health, alternative dispute resolution Contbr. articles to profl. jour. and interdisciplinary publs Founding mem Alliance for Dispute Resolution, 1996, Buffalo Collaborative Law Coun., 2002; bd. dir. Jewish Cmty. Ctr. Greater Buffalo, 1991-96, Am. Jewish Com. Buffalo, pres., 1995-97, nat. bd. govs., 1997—; bd. dir. Arts Coun. Buffalo and Erie County, 1992-99; legal coord. Parent Edn. and Custody Effectiveness program N.Y. 8th jud. dist.; pres., trustee, legal counsel Wayland (Mass.) Townhouse; trustee Family Counseling Svc. (region West); mem., chmn., clk. Wayland Zoning Bd. Appeals, 1970-80; v.p., counsel Arts Wayland Found., 1982-87; vis. fellow Woodrow Wilson Found., 1985-87, Mass. Gov. Spl. Commn. on Divorce, 1985-87. Capt. Mil. Police Corps USAR. Fellow Am. Acad. Matrimonial Lawyers (cert., pres., bd. mgr. Massj; mem. ABA (chair ADR family com.), Mass. Bar Assn. (chmn. family law sect.), Assn. Conflict Resolution (advanced practitioner), N.Y. State Coun. on Divorce Mediation, Assn. Family and Conciliation Ct., Boston Bar Assn. (family law com., legis. chmn.), N.Y. Bar Assn. (family law com., ADR com.), Erie County Bar Assn. (chair ADR com. 1992-96, family law com., judiciary com.) Home: 605 Lebrun Rd Amherst NY 14226-4232 Office: 1100 Main Place Tower 350 Main St Buffalo NY 14202-3711 Office Phone: 716-854-6424. Office Fax: 716-854-6425.

**PEARSON, PAUL HOLDING,** insurance company executive; b. Worcester, Mass., Feb. 14, 1940; s. Malcolm D. and Myra L. (Holding) P.; m. Judith N. Howe, July 13, 1958 (div. June 1974); children: Scott D., Todd E.; m. Anne Beck, July 26, 1974. BA in Bus. and Econs., U. Maine, 1961. C.L.U., 1971. Jr. life underwriter State Mut. Am., Worcester, 1961-63, life underwriter, 1963-67, sr. life underwriter, 1967-69; dir. life underwriting Security Mut. Life Ins. Co., Binghamton, NY, 1969, 2d v.p. underwriting, 1970, v.p., 1971-75, sr. v.p. ins. services div., 1975-79, exec. v.p., 1979-81, pres., 1981-96, chief exec. officer, 1987-97; chmn. Security Mutual Life Ins. Co. of N.Y., Binghamton, 1996-97. Chmn., CEO, bd. dirs. SML Properties corp., Binghamton, Security Equity Life Ins. Co., Binghamton, 1987-93; vice chmn. Generalife, 1997-99. Trustee, treas. Lourdes Meml. Hosp., Binghamton, 1978-92; mem. SUNY Found., Binghamton, 1982-89; trustee, chmn. fin. com. Elmira Coll., 1983-87; bd. dirs. Broome C.C. Found., 1982-91, pres. 1985-86; pres. New Industries for Broome, Binghamton, 1985-95, N.Y. State Bus. Devel. Coun., 1987-96; bd. dirs. Valley Devel. Found., 1987-91, Bus. Coun. N.Y., 1988-97, Am. Coun. Life Ins., 1990-96; bd. dirs., treas. Fiddlesticks C.C., 2002-05. Mem. Assn. for Advanced Life Underwriting, Nat. Assn. Life Underwriters, Broome County C. of C. (bd. dirs. 1980-88, chmn. 1986), Binghamton C/C Live Wire Club, Fiddlesticks Country Club (bd. dirs., treas. 2002-05). Office Phone: 239-768-0162. Personal E-mail: phapearson@aol.com.

**PEARSON, REBECCA E.,** lawyer; b. Balt., Jan. 14, 1964; AB, Duke Univ., 1985; JD, Univ. NC, Chapel Hill, 1989; LLM in Govt. Procurement with highest honors, George Washington Univ., 1996. Bar: Fla. 1989, DC 2000. Assoc. Venable LLP, Washington, ptnr., govt. contract litig., 2004—. Articles editor NC Jour. Internat. Law and Comml. Regulation, 1988—89, student editor-in-chief ABA Public Contract Law Jour., 1995—96; contbr. articles to profl. journals. With USAF, 1989—99. Mem.: ABA. Office: Venable LLP 575 Seventh St NW Washington DC 20004 Office Phone: 202-344-8183. Office Fax: 202-344-8300. Business E-Mail: repearson@venable.com.

**PEARSON, RICHARD JOSEPH,** archaeologist, educator; b. Kitchener, Ont., Can., May 2, 1938; s. John Cecil and Henrietta Anne (Wallwin) P.; m. Kazue Miyazaki, Dec. 12, 1964; 1 child, Sarina Riye. BA in Anthropology with honours, U. Toronto, 1960; PhD, Yale U., 1966. Asst. prof., then assoc. prof. archaeology U. Hawaii, 1966-71; mem. faculty U. B.C., Vancouver, 1971-2000. Conf. chmn. Internat. Jomon Conf., 2003. Author: The Archaeology of the Ryukyu Islands, 1969, Higashi Ajia no Nodai Shakai to Kokogaku, 1984, Windows on the Japanese Past, Studies in Archaeology and Prehistory, 1986, Ancient Japan, 1992; contbr. articles to profl. jours. Guggenheim fellow.

**PEARSON, ROBERT LAWRENCE,** executive recruiter; b. Chgo., Apr. 19, 1939; s. Jonas Peter and Caroline Margaret (Reilly) P.; m. Norma Eloise Dale, April 27, 1963; children: Jill C., Keith D. BSEE, Mich. State U., 1961; MS magna cum laude, MIT, 1963. Cons. McKinsey and Co., Inc., Chgo., 1964-68; v.p. Raymond James and Assoc., St. Petersburg, Fla., 1968-70; pres. Pearson Wade and Co., Inc., Ft. Lauderdale, Fla., 1970-71, Pearson, Inc., Racine, Wis., 1971-81; exec. dir. Russell Reynolds Assoc., Inc., Dallas, 1981-83; mng. dir. Lamalie Assoc., Inc., Dallas, 1984-89, chmn., 1989-94; pres. Lamalie Amrop Internat., Dallas, 1994-98, chmn., CEO, 1994—99; CEO Pearson Ptnrs. Internat., Inc., 1999—; mem., bd. dirs. Tatum CFO Inc., 1999—2003; mem. bd. dirs. Pentagon Techs. Inc., 2000—, Baird Capital Ptnrs. Inc., 2000—. Mem. fund raising com. Dallas Mus. of Art, 1983-85; mem. Dallas Mus. Natural History, 1985—, bd. dirs. 1980-90; mem. YMCA, Dallas; patron Ronald McDonald House of Dallas; speech writer Gov.'s Campaign, Chgo., 1968. Contbr. articles to profl. jours. Mem. MIT Enterprise Forum, Dallas C. of C., Phi Delta Theta (pres. 1959-61), Tower Club (Dallas), MIT (Dallas, pres. 1993-96), Gilda's Club North Tex. (founding sponsor), Dallas Nat. Golf Club, Broadmoor Golf Club. Episcopalian. Avocations: squash, jogging, deep sea fishing, hunting, marathon running. Office: Pearson Ptnrs Internat Inc Ste 1200 8080 N Central Expy Dallas TX 75206 Home: Apt 9D 3510 Turtle Creek Blvd Dallas TX 75219 Office Phone: 214-292-4130. Business E-Mail: rpear@pearsonpartners.intl.com.

**PEARSON, ROGER,** organization executive; b. London, Aug. 21, 1927; s. Edwin and Beatrice May (Woodbine) P.; m. Marion Primrose Simms, June 3, 1959; children: Edwin, Sigrid, Emma, Rupert BS with honors, U. London, 1951, MS, 1954, PhD, 1969. Chmn. Pakistan Tea Assn., 1963-64; mng. dir. Octavius Steel & Co. of Pakistan Ltd., Chittagong, East Pakistan, 1959-65; chmn. Plummer Bros., Ltd., Chittagong, East Pakistan, 1959-65, Chittagong Warehouses, Ltd., Chittagong, East Pakistan, 1959-65; chmn. dept. sociology and anthropology Queens Coll., Charlotte, NC, 1970-71; chmn. dept. anthropology U. So. Miss., Hattiesburg, 1971-74; dean acad. affairs, dir. research Mont. Coll. Mineral Sci. Tech., Butte, 1974-75; exec. dir. Council for Econ. and Social Studies, Washington, 1975—. Author: Eastern Interlude, 1954, Introduction to Anthropology, 1978, Anthropological Glossary, 1985, Race, Intelligence and Bias in Academe, 1991, Shockley on Eugenics and Race, 1992, Heredity and Humanity, 1996, Cultural Anthropology, 2002; editor: Ecology and Evolution, 1982, (jour.) Social Polit. and Econ. Studies, 1976—. Trustee, Benjamin Franklin U., Washington, 1984-87. Served to Brit. Indian Army, 1945-48. Office: Coun Econ and Social Studies 1133 13th St NW Washington DC 20005-4203

**PEARSON, ROGER LEE,** library director; b. Galesburg, Ill., Dec. 7, 1940; s. Clifford Emmanuel and Lillian Louise (Fisher) P. BA, Knox Coll., 1963; MA in Sociology, U. Nebr.-Omaha, 1968; MA in Library Sci., Rosary Coll., 1974. Vol. U.S. Peace Corps, Brazil, 1964-66; extension service supr. Brown County Libr., Green Bay, Wis., 1974-75; system adminstr. Nicolet Libr. System, Green Bay, 1976-77; exec. dir. South Central Libr. System, Madison, Wis., 1977-81; dir. Corpus Christi Pub. Librs., Tex., 1981-84, Naperville (Ill.) Pub. Librs., 1984-95, Sonoma County Libr., Santa Rosa, Calif., 1996-2001; interim dir. Spokane (Wash.) Pub. Libr., 2001; interim libr. dir. Coll. of Marin, Kentfield, Calif., 2002; interim dist. libr. Dixon (Calif.) Pub. Libr., 2002—03; interim dir. Kans. City (Mo.) Pub. Libr., 2004—05, Sonoma County Libr., Santa Rosa, 2005, Berkeley Pub. Libr., Calif., 2006. Lectr. Grad. Sch. Libr. and Info. Sci., Dominican U., River Forest, Ill., 1991-95. Mem. ALA, Train Riders Assn. Calif., Calif. Libr. Assn., Wine Libr. Assocs. Sonoma County. Avocations: power walking, travel research, train travel. Home: 1451 Country Manor Dr Santa Rosa CA 95401

**PEARSON, RONALD DALE,** retail food stores corporation executive; b. Des Moines, 1940; married. BS in Bus. Adminstrn., Drake U., 1962. With Hy-Vee Food Stores, Inc. (name changed to Hy-Vee, Inc. in 1996), Chariton, Iowa, 1962—; pres. Hy-Vee, Inc., Chariton, Iowa, 1983—, chmn., pres., & CEO, 1989—2001, chmn., CEO, COO West Des Moines, Iowa, 2001—. Dir. Beverage Mfrs., Inc., Civic Ctr. Cts., Inc.; chmn. Food Marketing Inst. Found., Washington. Bd. dir. Keep Iowa Beautiful Inc., Greater Des Moines Partnership. Office: Hy-Vee Inc 5820 Westown Pkwy West Des Moines IA 50266-8223*

**PEARSON, ROY LAING,** business administration educator; b. Victoria, Hong Kong, Oct. 18, 1939; s. Roy Ross and Martha Ann L.; m. Louise Elliott Johns, June 11, 1960; 1 child, Cynthia Laing. BS in Commerce, U. Va., 1961, PhD in Econs., 1968. Asst. prof. U. Ark. Sch. Bus. Adminstrn., Fayetteville, 1964-68; assoc. prof. Centenary Coll. La., Shreveport, 1968-71; assoc. prof. bus. adminstrn. Coll. William and Mary, Williamsburg, Va., 1971-76, prof. bus. adminstrn., 1976-87, dir. Bur. Bus. Rsch., 1985-98, Chancellor prof. bus. adminstrn., 1987—2005, prof. emeritus, 2005. V.p. Wessex Group, Inc., Williamsburg, Va., 1979—; sec.-treas. McKinley land Co., Inc., Williamsburg, 1969-2001. Editor, author: (newsletter) Virginia Business Report, Virginia Outlook, 1984-99. Bd. dirs. Williamsburg Community Hosp., 1985-90; gov.'s adv. bd. economists Commonwealth of Va., Richmond, 1984-98, 2002-; mem. trust fund adv. com. Va. Employment Comm., 1984—. NSF fellow, 1963. Mem. Va. Assn. Economists (pres. 1990-91, bd. dirs. 1985-91, disting. fellow 1998), Assn. for Univ. Bus. and Econ. Rsch. (bd. dirs. 1991-92, v.p. 1992-94, pres. 1994-95, hon. mem. 1999—), Nat. Assn. Bus. Economists, Internat. Inst. Forecasters (bd. dirs. 2001-2004), Nat. Bus. and Economics Soc. (v.p. 2004-), Richmond Assn. Bus. Economists, Nat. Economists Club. Avocations: scuba diving, underwater photography, science fiction. Home and Office: 4400 Chickasaw Ct Williamsburg VA 23188-8020 Business E-Mail: roy.pearson@mason.wm.edu.

**PEARSON, SCOTT ROBERTS,** retired economics professor; b. Madison, Wis., Mar. 13, 1938; s. Carlyle Roberts and Edith Hope (Smith) P.; m. Sandra Carol Anderson, Sept. 12, 1962; children: Sarah Roberts, Elizabeth Hovden. BS, U. Wis., Madison, 1961; MA, Johns Hopkins U., 1965; PhD, Harvard U., 1969. Asst. prof. Stanford U., Calif., 1968-74, assoc. prof., 1974-80; assoc. dir. Food Rsch. Inst., 1977-84, dir., 1992-96, prof. food econs., 1980—2002; ret., 2002. Cons. AID, World Bank, Washington, 1965—; staff economist Commn. Internat. Trade, Washington, 1970-71. Author: Petroleum and the Nigerian Economy, 1970; (with others) Commodity Exports and African Economic Development, 1974, (with others) Rice in West Africa, Policy and Economics, 1981, (with others) Food Policy Analysis, 1983, (with others) The Cassava Economy of Java, 1984, (with others) Portuguese Agriculture in Transition, 1987, (with Eric Monke) The Policy Analysis Matrix, 1989, (with others) Rice Policy in Indonesia, 1991, (with others) Structural Change and Small-Farm Agriculture in Northwest Portugal, 1993, (with others) Agricultural Policy in Kenya, 1995, (with others) Small Farm Agriculture in Southern Europe, 1998, (with others) Applications of the Policy Analysis Matrix in Indonesian Agriculture, 2004. Mem. Am. Agrl. Econs. Assn., Am. Econ. Assn. Home: 691 Mirada Ave Stanford CA 94305-8477 E-mail: pearson@stanford.edu.

**PEARSON, SELA,** poet, speaker; b. Bklyn., Aug. 10, 1952; d. Thomas Turner and Thelma (Brown) Razor; children: Nassar (dec.), Anwar, Jonathan BS, St. Joseph's Coll., Bklyn., 1988; MBA in Healthcare Mgmt., U. Phoenix, 2006. LPN. Psychiat., pediat. nurse Syosset Hosp., NY, 1974—78; sales agent Combined Life Ins. Co. N.Y., Albany, 1978—80; med., surg. nurse Bapt. Med. Ctr., Bklyn., 1980—86; nurse counselor Riker's Island Prison Hosp., Queens, NY, 1986—88; clinic nurse St. Christopher Ottilie, Queens, 1988—90; mgr. intensive case AIDS Ctr. Queens County, 1990—92; quality assurance, utilization rev. nurse Vanderbilt U. Med. Ctr., Nashville, 1992—94; program dir. Boys and Girls Club, Franklin, Tenn., 1994—95; spkr., writer, nurse Akanke Creations, Brentwood, Tenn., 1996—; ind. health contractor Clayton County Crisis Unit, 1997—98; nurse Phoenix Program FHC of Nashville, 1998—99; nurse Murci Homes, 1999—. Cons. Murphy Alternative Ctr., Nashville, 1996, Serendipity House, Nashville, 1996, Family and Ednl. Adv. Assocs., Inc., Nashville, 1996, Growing In Grace Leadership Sch., Nashville, 1996; storyteller, presenter poetry recitals; ind. contractor Crisis Group Home, Riverdale, Ga.; faculty mem. Antara Ctr., 2004. Author: New York Poetry Foundation Anthology, 1986, Beyond the Stars, 1995 (Editors Choice 1995), Sela's Sounds of Silence, 1995, A Soulful Journey, 2000; performer (video) A Soulful Journey, 1995, The Magic of Poet, 1996, Our Voices, 1996; author numerous poems; contbr. articles to profl. jours., mags Vol. Williamson County Libr., Franklin, 1995—, Boys and Girls Club, Franklin, 1996—, TPAC, bd. dirs. Nashville Peace Action, 1996—; mem. New Gospel Singers Choir, 1995—; storytelling del. to South Africa People to People Amb. Programs, invited Women in Soc. rep., Egypt, 2000—; mem. Coun. for the Written Word. Recipient Vol. Svc. award Berkshire Nursing Ctr., West Babylon, N.Y. 1977, Mayor's award for svc. in cmty. in arts, 2001; inclucson of poem Faith to Wm. Kings Regl. Art Ctr., 1999, Cmty. Svc. award Edith Taylor Langster, Ho. of Reps., 54th Dist., 2003. Mem. Nat. Spkrs. Assn., Brentwood Early Risers Toastmasters (v.p. membership 1996—various awards), Tenn. Writers Alliance, Harpeth Storytelling Group, Nat. Storytelling Assn., Internat. Soc. Poets (Poets Choice award 1995, Internat. Poet of Merit award 1995), Tenn. Writers Group Franklin, Tenn. Assn. Perpetuation Preservation Storytelling, Ga. Writers Group, Creative Artists Tenn., Tenn. Spkrs. Assn., Women Vision Enhancing Network (cert., dir. pub. rels.), Cherokee Wolf Clan (tribal coun.). Avocations: piano playing, travel, reading. Address: PO Box 111341 Nashville TN 37222-1341 Office Phone: 615-365-3187. Business E-Mail: sela@akankecreations.com.

**PEARSON, STEVEN ROBERT,** artist, art educator; b. Gloversville, NY, Apr. 7, 1968; s. Carl Ivan and Kathleen Ellen Pearson; m. Jessica L. Monaco, June 4, 2004. AA, Fulton-Montgomery C.C., Johnstown, NY, 1992; BS, Coll. St. Rose, Albany, NY, 1994; MFA, Md. Inst. Coll. Art, 1997. Adj. prof. Coll. St. Rose, Albany, NY, 1997—2001, Schenectady (NY) County C.C., 1998; asst. prof. Iowa State U., Ames, 2001—02, lectr. 2002—03; asst. prof. McDaniel Coll., Westminster, Md., 2004—, co-dir. Rice Gallery, 2005—. Asst. coord. foundations design Iowa State U., Ames, 2003; juror student exhbn. Lehman Coll., Bronx, NY, 2005; outside reviewer faculty devel. grants CUNY, NYC. Exhibition, DCAC, Washngton, exhibition, McDaniel Coll., Robert A. Peck Gallery, Ctrl. Wyo. Coll., Riverton, New Visions Gallery Inc., Marshfield, Wis. (Best in Show, 2003), Octagon Ctr. for Arts, Ames, Iowa (Best in Show, 2002). Petty officer USN, 1986—92, VA. Recipient Richard and Rebecca Evans Art award, Fulton-Montgomery C.C., 1992; scholar, Md. Inst. Coll. Art, 1995, 1996; Artists grantee, Vt. Studio Ctr., 2003, 2006, Faculty Devel. grantee, McDaniel Coll., 2004. Mem.: Foundations in Art-Theory and Edn., Coll. Art Assn., Phi Theta Kappa, Alpha Sigma Lambda. Democrat. Office: McDaniel Coll 2 College Hill Westminster MD 21157 Office Phone: 410-857-2770. Home Fax: 410-386-4657; Office Fax: 410-386-0512. Business E-Mail: spearson@mcdaniel.edu.

**PEARSON, THOMAS ARTHUR,** epidemiologist, educator; b. Berlin, Wis., Oct. 21, 1950; married; 2 children. BA, Johns Hopkins U., 1973, MD, MPH, Johns Hopkins U., 1976, PhD in Epidemiology, 1983; MA (hon.), U. Umeå, 2002. Fellow in cardiology Johns Hopkins Sch. Medicine, Balt., 1983-85, from asst. to assoc. prof. medicine, epidemiology, 1983-88; prof. epidemiology Columbia U., 1988-97, prof. medicine, 1995-97, prof. medicine, Jane Forbes Clark chair in health rsch. N.Y.C., 1995-97; dir. Mary Imogene Bassett Rsch. Inst., 1988-97; Kaiser prof., chair Sch. Medicine U. Rochester, N.Y., 1997—, sr. assoc. dean for clin. rsch., 2002—. Mem. clin. applications and prevention commn. NIH, 1987—91, chmn., 1990; dir. Rochester Prevention Rsch. Ctr., 2004—; bd. dirs. World Heart Fedn. Co-editor: Scandinavian Jour. Pub. Health, 2000—. Mem. ACP, Am. Heart Assn. (nat. rsch. com. 1987-92, coun. epidemiology 1987—, vice chmn. 1994-95, chmn. 1996-98), Am. Fedn. Clin. Rsch., Am. Coll. Epidemiology, Am. Coll. Preventive Medicine, Am. Coll. Cardiology (prevention com.), Soc. Epidemiol. Rsch. (rsch. prize 1978). Achievements include research in the etiology and pathogenesis of atherosclerosis. Office: U Rochester Sch Medicine Dept Cmty Preventive Med 601 Elmwood Ave Rochester NY 14642-0001 Office Phone: 585-275-2191.

**PEARSON, THOMAS SPENCER,** academic administrator; b. Rockville Center, N.Y., Sept. 19, 1949; s. Donn Spencer and June Leonora Pearson; m. Susan Louise Frankus, July 24, 1971; children: Timothy Spencer, Mark Thomas. BA in History (magna cum laude), Santa Clara U., 1971; MA in Russian History, U. N.C., Chapel Hill, 1973, PhD in Russian History, 1977. Asst. prof. history Auburn (Ala.) U., 1977—78, Monmouth Coll., West Long Branch, NJ, 1978—81, asst. prof., chair of history, 1981—85, assoc. prof., chair of history, 1985—92, acting provost, assoc. prof. history, 1992—94, provost, v.p. acad. affairs, prof. history, 1994—. Co-chair Two River Film Festival Bd. Dirs., West Long Branch, NJ, 2003—. Author: (book) Russian Officialdom in Crisis: Autocracy and Local Self-Government, 1861-1900, 1989, 2004. Sec. bd. trustees Rumson (N.J.) County Day Sch., 1990—92, v.p. bd. trustees, 1992—95; vice chair bd. trustees ECI Sch. for Children, Eatontown, NJ, 2001—. Grantee Fellowship to Russia, Internat. Rsch. and Exch. Bd., 1975—76. Mem.: Am. Assn. for Advancement of Slavic Studies. Roman Catholic. Avocations: film collector, tropical fish collector. Home: 184 Chatham Ave Oakhurst NJ 07755 Office: Monmouth Univ Provost's Office 400 Cedar Ave West Long Branch NJ 07764 Office Phone: 732-571-3405. E-mail: pearson@monmouth.edu.

**PEARSON, W. ROBERT (WILLIAM ROBERT PEARSON),** former federal agency administrator, former ambassador; b. Bells, Tenn., June 28, 1943; s. Marion Robert and Louise (Wilson) P.; m. Margaret Coplin, June 20, 1975; 1 child, Matthew. BA, Vanderbilt U., 1965; LLB, U.Va., 1968. Vice consul U.S. Consulate Gen., Auckland, New Zealand, 1976-78; staff asst./Conf. Asia Bur. US Dept. State, Washington, 1978-79, Chinese lang. tng. officer Washington and Taiwan, 1979-81; polit. officer US Embassy, Beijing, 1981-83; dep. dir. Ops. Ctr. US Dept. State, Washington, 1983-85; dep. exec. sec. NSC, Washington, 1985-87; dept. asst. sec. gen. NATO, Brussels, 1987-90; dep. exec. sec. US Dept. State, Washington, 1990-91, exec. sec., 1991—93; dep. permanent rep. to US mission NATO, 1993—97; dep. chief mission US Embassy, France, 1997—2000; US amb. to Turkey US Dept. State, Ankara, 2000—03, dir. gen. US Fgn. Svc. Washington, 2003—06, dir. human resources, 2003—06. Mem. Internat. Inst. of Strategic Studies.

**PEARSON, WALTER DONALD,** editor, columnist; b. Pittsfield, Mass., Feb. 5, 1916; s. Edgar C. and Edna (Scott) P.; divorced; children: Florence, Donald, Sharon; m. Elsa Swanson (dec.); 1 child, Richard Scott. Student, Dartmouth Coll., 1941-43. Advt. salesman, 1935-41; securities broker Charles A. Day Co., Boston, 1947-55; founder, owner, mgr. First New Eng. Securities Co., Inc., Southbridge, Mass., 1955-71; now owner, editor Pearson Investment Letter, Dover, Fla.; ptnr. Pearson Capital Inc.; fin. columnist World Intelligence Rev., CDL Report, Nationalist Times; free-lance columnist various publications; fin. advisor, investment mgr. Author: Investing for the Millions, 1990, Bridge Made Easy, 1995 With inf. U.S. Army, 1943-45, ETO. Decorated Bronze star, Croix de Guerre (France), Combat Infantry badge. Home: 1628 White Arrow Dr Dover FL 33527-5741 Office Phone: 813-659-2560. Personal E-mail: PearsonCap@aol.com.

**PEARSON-KING, LYNN,** music educator, director; d. Ricky and Jo Ann Pearson; m. Brian King, May 19, 2001; children: Jackson King, Madison Nelson King. BM, Appalachian State U., Boone, NC, 1995. Cert. tchr. Ga., 2001. Orch. dir. Forest Pk. Mid. Sch., Ga., 2001—04; dir. bands Henderson Mid. Sch., Chamblee, Ga., 2004—. Pvt. music tchr., Atlanta, 1995—. Mem.: Ga. Music Educators Assn., Nat. Music Educators Assn. Home: 3346 Woodrow Way NE Atlanta GA 30319 Office: Henderson Mid Sch 2830 Henderson Mill Rd Chamblee GA 30341 Office Phone: 678-874-2902. Personal E-mail: karen_lynn_king@fc.dekalb.k12.ga.us.

**PEART, SANDRA JOAN,** economics professor, researcher; b. Stratford, Canada, Apr. 4, 1959; d. Donald MacLean and Beverley Joan Peart; m. Craig Warren Heinicke, June 4, 1988; children: Nathan Casey Heinicke-Peart, Matthew Warren Heinicke-Peart. BA, U. Toronto, Ont., Can., 1982, PhD, 1989. Asst. prof. Coll. William and Mary, Williamsburg, Va., 1989—91; prof. econs. Baldwin-Wallace Coll., Berea, Ohio, 1991—. Vis. scholar Ctr. Study of Pub. Choice George Mason U., Fairfax, Va., 2004—05, dir. Summer Inst. Ctr. Study of Pub. Choice, 2004—. Co-author (with David Levy): The Vanity of the Philosopher: From Equality to Hierarchy in Post-Classical Economics, 2005; contrb. articles to profl. jours. Fellow, Am. Coun. Edn., 2005—06. Mem.: History Econs. Soc. (exec. com. 2000—05, pres.-elect 2006—, Best Dissertation award 1990). Achievements include research in the transition from egalitarian thinking to notions of race and hierarchy in economics; the role of sympathy in economics and social science; the role of the expert in social science. Office: Baldwin Wallace College 275 Eastland Rd Berea OH 44017 Office Phone: 440-826-2120. Office Fax: 440-826-3835. Personal E-mail: sandrajpeart@gmail.com. Business E-mail: speart@bw.edu.

**PEASE, DAVID GORDON,** artist, educator; b. Bloomington, Ill., June 2, 1932; s. Gordon A. and June (Stephens) P.; m. Julie Jensen, Mar. 29, 1956; children: Lisa Kay, Kerry Susan. BS, U. Wis., 1954, MS, 1955, M.F.A., 1958. Instr. audio visual ctr. Mich. State U., 1958-60; mem. faculty Tyler Sch. Art, Temple U., Phila., 1960-83, prof., 1970-83, chmn. painting dept., 1968-77, dean, 1977-83; prof. of painting Yale U. Sch. Art, New Haven, 1983-2000, Street prof., dean emeritus, 2000—, dean, 1983-96. Dir. grad. studies/painting, 1997-2000. Vis. faculty mem. Yale U. Summer Sch. Music and Art, 1970-72, Ohio State U., spring 2001. One-man shows include Baylor U., 1972, U. Wis., 1972, Pa. Acad. Fine Arts, 1977, Terry Dintenfass Inc., N.Y.C., 1969, 71, 76, Phila. Art Alliance, 1961, 70, Vassar Coll., 1999, Ohio State U., 2001; group exhbns. include Carnegie Internat., Pitts., 1961, Corcoran Biennial, Washington, 1961, 63, Whitney Annual, N.Y.C., 1963; represented in permanent collections Whitney Mus. Am. Art, Phila. Mus. Art, Pa. Acad. Fine Arts, Des Moines Art Center, Pa. State U., U. Wis., Temple U., Hallmark Cards Inc., Columbia Pictures, Yale U. Art Gallery, others. Trustee Louis Comfort Tiffany Found., 1988-97, 98—; bd. trustees Lyme Acad. Coll. Fine Arts, 1999—. With U.S. Army, 1955-57. Recipient William A. Clark award Corcoran Biennial, 1963, Lindbeck Found. Disting. Teaching award, 1968, Disting. Alumni award U. Wis., 1991; Guggenheim Found. fellow, 1965-66; Tiffany Found. grantee, 1975-76 Mem. Assn. Ind. Colls. Art and Design (trustee 1992-96). Home: 95 Thankful Stow Rd Guilford CT 06437-2529 Personal E-mail: david.pease@yale.edu.

**PEASE, EDWARD A.,** former congressman; b. Terre Haute, Ind., May 22, 1951; BA with distinction, Ind. U., 1973, JD cum laude, 1977; past postgrad. in English, Ind. State U. Past city atty. City of Brazil, Ind.; past gen. counsel Ind. State U., v.p. univ. advancement, 1993; past ptnr. Thomas Thomas & Pease; senator Ind. Gen. Assembly, 1980-92, past chmn. senate jud. com., past chmn. Ind. commn. trial cts., past chmn. Ind. code revision commn.; mem. U.S. Congress from 7th Ind. dist. 1997—2001 mem. jud. com., mem. transp. and infrastructure com. Past mem. adv. coun. on nat. coun. Boy Scouts Am., chmn. coun. Nat. Order of Arrow. Recipient

numerous awards Boy Scouts Am. Mem. Nat. interfraternity Conf. (past nat. pres.), Pi Kappa Alpha (nat. dir. alumni affairs, chpt. advisor, nat. pres.). Republican. Office Phone: 703-621-2797.

**PEASE, ROBIN A.,** performing company executive, actress; d. Royce Hollis and Pearl Agnes Pease; m. Thomas J. Kerr, Sept. 1, 1986; children: Sarah Pease-Kerr, Daniel Pease-Kerr. BFA, Boston Conservatory, 1977; MFA, Case Western U., Cleve., 1986. Instr. Notre Dame Coll. Ohio, South Euclid, 1986—88; artist-in-residence Laurel Sch., Shaker Heights, Ohio, 1986—88; dir., vis. prof., advisor Hiram (Ohio) Coll., 1988—90; dir. theater & dance Hawken Sch., Gates Mills, Ohio, 1990—96; founding artistic dir. Kulture Kids, Cleve., 1996—. Theater assessor Project Start ID, Columbus, Ohio, N.Y.C., 2002—04; presenter in field. Author, actress: (plays) America, Many Crayons One Box; Vision Quest; Lamp Beside the Golden Door; The Great Law of Peace, 1999; author, dir. Pocahontas on Trial, 2000; author, actress Escuchar y no Hables, 2002. Co-sponsor, performer Aurora (Ohio) Pow-Wow, 2003—; actor Wallpaper Project Auglaize County, Ohio, 2003—04; mistress ceremonies Dobama Theater, Ohio, 2004—05; dir. Now Let Me Fly Washburn U., 2004. Recipient Young Audiences Sunshine award, 2005, Healing Spaces Excellence in Citizenship award, 2005. Office: Kulture Kids 2163 Lee Rd Ste 104 Cleveland Heights OH 44118

**PEASE, RON DEAN,** artist; b. Palo Alto, Calif., Sept. 12, 1949; s. Doyce Chapman and Amelia Martha (Kukay) P.; m. Dawn Anne Schmidt, Oct. 27, 1987. Student, Cabrillo Coll., 1971-72, U. Calif., Santa Cruz, 1973-74. Artist, mem. Center Street Gallery, Santa Cruz, 1980-82. Co-founder, owner West Chaco Gallery, Aztec, N.Mex., 1994-98, co-juror Nat. Print & Drawings Exhbn., 1996, 97; vis. artist, guest spkr. Kans. State U., Manhattan, 2001, Pitts. (Kans.) State U., 2004. One man shows include Ti Bldg., Santa Cruz, 1980, Valencia Coll., Orlando, Fla., 1997, Kans. State U., Manhattan, 2001, Pitts. State U., 2004; exhibited in group shows at U. Calif., Santa Cruz, 1990, Sacramento Fine Arts Ctr., 1992, Bradley U., Peoria, Ill., 1993, Okla. State U., 1993, Coll. William and Mary, Va., 1994, Del Mar (Tex.) Coll., 1994, West Chaco Gallery, Aztec, N.Mex., 1996, San Juan (N.Mex.) Coll., 1996, Columbia (Mo.) Coll., 1998, Md. Fedn. of Arts, 1998, St. John's U., N.Y.C. 1998, Austin Peay Sate U., Clarksville, Tenn., 2001. De Mille scholar Pastel Soc.-West Coast, Sacramento, Calif., 1992; recipient Purchase award Austin Peay State U., Clarksville, Tenn., 2001, Purchase/Merit award Bradley U., Peoria, Ill., 1993. Mem. N.Y. Artist's Equity Assn.

**PEASE, WILLIAM HENRY,** history professor; b. Winchendon, Mass., Aug. 31, 1924; s. Clarence Albert Grover and Arline Greenlee (Brooks) Pease; m. Jane Hanna Pease, June 9, 1950. BA, Williams Coll. Williamstown, Mass., 1947; MA, U. Wis., Madison, Wis., 1948; PhD, U. Rochester, Rochester, N.Y., 1955. Tchr. Mt. Hermon Sch., Mass., 1948—51; instr. to assoc. prof. Rensselaer Polytechnic Inst., Troy, NY, 1955—64; vis. prof. Case Inst. of Tech., Cleve., 1957—58; fulbright lectr. Internat. People's Coll. Elsinore, Denmark, 1961—62; assoc. prof. Univ. Calgary, Canada, 1964—66; from assoc. prof. to prof. U. Maine, Orono, 1966—88; assoc. in history Coll. Charleston, SC, 1988—. Fulbright lectr. Univ. Genoa, Italy, 1985; referee faculty rsch. grants, history CUNY, 1975, Can. Govt., Ottawa, Canada, 1986. Author (with Jane H. Pease): Black Utopia, 1963, Bound With Them in Chains, 1972, They Who Would Be Free, 1974, The Web of Progress, 1985 (New Eng. Hist. Soc. prize, 1986, Soc. for Historians of Early Am. Republic prize, 1986), Ladies, Women, and Wenches, 1990, James Louis Petigru, 1995, A Family of Women, 1999 (Julia Cherry Spruill award, 2000), The Roman Years of a South Carolina Artist, 2003; contrb. articles to profl. jour. Recipient Pres. Rsch. Achievement award, U. Maine, Orono, 1977; Rsch. grantee, Am. Coun. of Learned Societies, 1965, Am. Philos. Soc., 1966, 2003, Nat. Endowment for the Humanities, 1980—82, Nat. Sci. Found., 1981—82, Archie K. Davis fellow, 1991. Mem.: S.C. Hist. Soc., Southern Hist. Assn., Orgn. of Am. Historians, Am. Hist. Assn., Soc. for Historians of the Early Am. Republic. Home: 750 Weaver Dairy Rd Apt 222 Chapel Hill NC 27514-1467

**PEASE-PRETTY ON TOP, JANINE B.,** community college administrator; b. Nespelam, Wash., Sept. 17, 1949; d. Benjamin and Margery Louise (Jordan) Pease; m. Sam Vernon Windy Boy, July 30, 1975 (div. Jan. 1983); children: Rosella L. Windy Boy, Sam Vernon Windy Boy; m. John Joseph Pretty On Top, Sept. 15, 1991. BA in Sociology, Anthropology, Ctrl. Wash. U., 1970; MEd, Mont. State U., 1987, EdD, 1994; HHD (hon.), Hood Coll., 1990; LLD (hon.), Gonzaga U., 1991; DHL (hon.), Teikyo/Marycrest U., 1992; EdD (hon.), Whitman Coll., 1993; HHD (hon.), Rocky Mountain Coll., 1998. Dep. dir. Wash. State Youth Commn., Olympia, 1971; tutor student svcs. Big Bend C.C., Moses Lake, Wash., 1971-72, upward bound dir., 1972-75; women's counselor Navajo C.C., Many Farms, Ariz., 1972; dir. adult & continuing edn. Crow Ctrl. Edn. Commn., Crow Agy., Mont., 1975-79; ednl. coms. Box Elder, Mont., 1979-81; dir. Indian career svc. Ea. Mont. Coll., Billings, 1981-82; pres. Little Big Horn Coll., Crow Agency, 1982—; with Rocky Mountain Coll., Billings, Mont. Exec. com. Am. Indian Higher Ednl. Consortium, Washington, 1983—; bd. dirs. Am. Indian Coll. Fund, N.Y.C., 1988—; sec. Indian Nations at Risk U.S. Dept. Edn., Washington, 1990-91, collaborator task force, 1990-91; 2d vice chmn. Nat. Adv. Coun. Indian Edn., Washington, 1994—. Chmn. Bighorn County Dem. Ctrl. Com., Hardin, Mont., 1983-88; mem. coun. First Crow Indian Bapt. Ch., 1989—; bd. dirs. Ctr. for Rocky Mountain West, 1998—; chmn. Mont. State Reappt. an Distructing Commn., 1999—. MacArthur fellow John D. & Catharine MacArthur Found., 1994. Mem. Nat. Indian Edn. Assn. (Indian educator of yr. 1990), Mont. Assn. Chs. (bd. dirs. 1997—), Crow Tribe Nighthawk Dance Soc.

**PEASLEE, JAMES M.,** lawyer; b. Scranton, Pa., Sept. 1, 1952; s. Robert Victor and Jean (Mark) P. BA, MA, Yale U., 1973; JD, Harvard U., 1976; LLM in Taxation, NYU, 1979. Bar: N.Y. 1977. Assoc. Cleary, Gottlieb, Steen & Hamilton LLP, NYC, 1976—84, ptnr., 1984—. Office: Cleary Gottlieb Steen & Hamilton LLP 43d Fl 1 Liberty Plz Fl 43D New York NY 10006-1404

**PEAT, RANDALL DEAN,** military analyst, retired military officer; b. Chgo., July 6, 1935; s. Thomas R. and Lulu M. (Ray) P.; m. Joyce Enid Hunter, Sept. 15, 1956; children: Brian James, Sondra Lee Peat Gadell BS in Journalism, Medill Sch. Journalism Northwestern U., Evanston, Ill., 1956, MS in Journalism Mgmt., 1957. Commd. officer U.S. Air Force, 1957, advanced through ranks to maj. gen.; pilot, instr. Strategic Air Command, Westover AFB and Clinton-Sherman, Okla., 1958-66; asst. air attache Am. Embassy, Djakarta, Indonesia, 1967; pilot Pacific Command Airborne Command Post, Hickam AFB, Hawaii, 1968-70; staff officer 7th Air Force, Saigon, Vietnam, 1971, Hdqrs. U.S. Air Force, Pentagon, DC, 1972-75, SHAPE, Belgium, 1976-79, Hdqrs. U.S. Air Force, Pentagon, DC, 1980-81; dep. dir. plans Office Joint Chief of Staff, Pentagon, DC, 1982-84; asst. chief of staff ops. Supreme Hdqrs. Allied Powers Europe, Belgium, 1984-87; chief of staff Strategic Air Command, Offutt AFB, Nebr., 1987-89; v.p. R&D Assocs., Europe, 1989—2002. Decorated Air medal, Bronze Star, Meritorious Service medal, Def. Superior Service medal, Def. Disting. Service medal; Republic of Vietnam Cross of Gallantry with Palm, Republic of Vietnam Campaign medal Mem. Daedalians (vice flight capt. 1976), Air Force Assn., Pi Alpha Mu Avocations: cooking, hiking, painting, british mystery writers. Home: 28 Likely Rd Santa Fe NM 87508

**PEAY, J.H. BINFORD, III,** retired army officer; b. Richmond, Va., May 10, 1940; m. Pamela Jane Pritchett; children: James, Ryan. BS, Va. Mil. Inst., 1962; MA, George Washington U., 1975; grad., U.S. Army Command and Gen. Staff Coll., U.S. Army War Coll. Commd. 2d Lt. U.S. Army, 1962, advanced through grades to gen., 1993, ret., 1997, commd. gen., 101st Airborne Divsn., 1989—91, vice chief staff Washington, 1993; comdr. in chief U.S. Ctrl. Command, MacDill AFB, Fla., 1994-97; ret., 1997; chmn. bd. Allied Def. Group, 2001—; supt. Va. Mil. Inst., 2003—. Served in Viet Nam, 1967-68, 71-72, Desert Storm, 1991. Decorated Def. D.S.M., Silver Star,

Legion of Merit with oak leaf cluster, Army D.S.M. with three oak leaf clusters, Def. D.S.S.M., Purple Heart, Bronze Star medal with three oak leaf clusters. Home: 412 VMI Parade Lexington VA 24450-2115 Office Phone: 540-464-7311.

**PECA, MICHAEL,** professional hockey player; b. Toronto, Ont., Can., Mar. 26, 1974; Center Vancouver Canucks, 1993—95, Buffalo Sabres, 1995—2000, NY Islanders, 2001—05, Edmonton Oilers, 2005—06, Toronto Maple Leafs, 2006—. Mem. Team Can., Olympic Games, Salt Lake City, 2002. Recipient Frank J. Selke Trophy, 1997, 2002. Achievements include mem. Gold medal Can. Hockey team, World Jr. Championships, 1994; mem. Gold medal Can. Hockey team, Salt Lake City Olympic Games, 2002. Office: Toronto Maple Leafs Air Canada Ctr 40 Bay St Ste 300 Toronto ON Canada*

**PECANO, DONALD CARL,** automotive manufacturing executive; b. L.A., Dec. 2, 1948; s. Domenick Lawrence and Carlotta Noble (Martello) P.; m. Sandra Ann Tuminello, Apr. 26, 1969; children: Julia Ann, Melissa Ann, Donald Carl. BS in Acctg, Pa. State U., 1970; MBA in Mktg., Youngstown State U., 1981. CPA, Pa.; cert. mgmt. acct., cert. fin. mgr. Contr. Atlas Guard Svc. subs. SERVISCO, East Orange, NJ, 1974-76; asst. to pres. SERVISCO, Hillside, NJ, 1976-77; v.p. fin. Columbus Svcs., Inc. subs. SERVISCO, New Castle, Pa., 1977-82; dir. fin. East Mfg. Corp. and subs. cos., 1982-88, v.p. fin. and adminstrn., 1988-99, also mem. exec. com., exec. v.p., CFO, 1999—; v.p. fin. Intermodal Techs. Inc., 1991—. Bd. dirs. Intermodal Techs. Inc. Weatherhead fellow Case Western Res. U., 1995. Republican. Roman Catholic. Office: 1871 State Route 44 Randolph OH 44265 *Placing the best interests of the company ahead of your own is ultimately in your own best interest.*

**PECHUKAS, DIANA GISOLFI** See GISOLFI, DIANA

**PECHUKAS, PHILIP,** chemistry professor; b. Akron, Ohio, Oct. 30, 1942; s. Alphonse and Evelyn (Grebenak) P.; children: Rolf Birkhoff, Maria Berenson, Sarah Landau, Fiona Veronese, Amy Hayes. BS, Yale U., 1963; PhD, U. Chgo., 1966. Asst. prof. chemistry Columbia U., N.Y.C., 1967-72, assoc. prof., 1972-78, prof., 1978—, chmn. dept. chemistry, 1984-87. Contbr. articles to profl. jours. Fellow Nat. Bur. Standards, 1966-67, Alfred P. Sloan Found., 1970-74, J.S. Guggenheim Found., 1975, Haverford Coll., 1985; Rockefeller Found. resident fellow Bellagio Study Ctr., 2000. Fellow AAAS, Am. Phys. Soc.; mem. Am. Chem. Soc. (chmn. theoretical chemistry subdivision 1985-86), Humboldt Sen. Scientist, 1993-94. Office: Columbia Univ Dept Chemistry 3000 Broadway New York NY 10027-6941 Business E-Mail: pechukas@chem.columbia.edu.

**PECHURA, CONSTANCE MARY,** foundation administrator; BS, Va. Commonwealth U., 1980; PhD, Uniformed Svcs. U. Health Scis, 1987. Lab. asst. dept. pharmacology Med. Coll. Va., Richmond, 1977-79, rsch. asst. dept. surgery, divsn. neurosurgery, 1979-81; staff fellow NIH-NINDS, 1987-88; sr. program officer Inst. Medicine, Washington, 1989-98, dir. divsn. neurosci. & behavioral health, 1994-98; sr. program officer Robert Wood Johnson Found., Princeton, NJ, 1998—. Contbr. chpts. to books and articles to profl. jours. Bd. dirs., trainer, counselor Richmond Hotline, 1975-78; dir., counselor Rape Crisis Outreach, Richmond, 1976-78; mem., chair bd. dirs. Student Pugwash, Washington, 1995-2000. Office: Robert Wood Johnson Found PO Box 2316 Rte 1 and College Rd E Princeton NJ 08543-2316

**PECK, ABRAHAM,** editor, writer, educator, media consultant; b. NYC, Jan. 18, 1945; s. Jacob and Lottie (Bell) Peckolick; m. Suzanne Wexler, Mar. 19, 1977; children: Douglas Benjamin, Robert Wexler. BA, NYU, 1965; postgrad., CUNY, 1965-67; cert. in advanced exec. program, Northwestern U., 1997. Engaged in cmty. organizing and tutoring, 1962-64; with N.Y.C. Welfare Dept., 1965-67; free-lance writer, 1967—; writer, organizer Chgo. Action Youth Internat. Party, 1968; editor Chgo. Seed, 1968-70; treas. Seed Pub., Inc., 1968-70; mem. coordinating com. Underground Press Syndicate, 1969; assoc. editor Rolling Stone mag., San Francisco, 1975-76, contbg. editor, 1976-2001; cons. various mags., 1984—; ednl. cons. Asian Sources Media Group, Hong Kong, Manila, 1989-97; editl. co-auditor Advanstar Comm., 1999—; strategic content cons. Putman Media, 2003—04; lectr. BPAWW seminars PRC, 2003—; feature writer Chgo. Daily News, 1977-78; with features dept. Chgo. Sun-Times, 1978-81; from asst. prof. to prof. Medill Sch. Journalism Northwestern U., Evanston, Ill., 1981—2001, Theodore R. & Annie Laurie Sills prof. journalism, 2001—06, dir. mag. programs Media Mgmt. Ctr., 2002—; contbg. editor Satisfaction Mag., 2005—. Editor, co-founder Sidetracks, alt. newspaper supplement, Chgo. Daily News, 1977—78; critic at large Sta. WBBM, 1979—82; mem. exec. com. mag. divsn. Assn. Edn. Journalism and Mass Communication, 1987—89, 1992—96, 2003—04, pres., 1994—95; mem. adv. bd. Academe mag., AAUP, 1990—2000, Heartland Jour., 1990—2002, Technos, 1992—, Chgo. chpt. Asian Am. Journalists Assn., 2002—; chair ethics subcom. Am. Bus. Media, 2002. Editor: (book) Dancing Madness, 1976; author: Uncovering the Sixties: The Life and Times of the Underground Press, 1985, 1991; consulting editor, contbr.: The Sixties, 1977, contbr.: The Eighties: A Look Back, 1979, Voices From the Underground, 1993. With U.S. Army, 1967. Named to Chgo. Journalism Hall of Fame, 2006; recipient Mag. Divsn. Educator of Yr., Assn. Edn. Journalism and Mass Comm., 2003—04. Office: Northwestern U Medill Sch Journalism 1845 Sheridan Rd Evanston IL 60208-0815 Office Phone: 847-491-2068. Business E-Mail: a-peck@northwestern.edu.

**PECK, ANDREW,** psychologist, educator; PhD, Pa. State U., University Park. Lectr. Pa. State U., University Park, 1998—. Office: The Pennsylvania State University 423 Moore Bldg University Park PA 16802 Office Phone: 814-865-1838.

**PECK, ANDREW JAY,** federal judge; b. 1953; AB, Cornell U., 1974; JD, Duke U., 1977. Bar: N.Y. 1978, U.S. Dist. Ct. (so. dist.) N.Y., U.S. Ct. Appeals (2d thru 11th cirs.), U.S. Supreme Ct. Law clk. to Hon. Paul Roney, U.S. Ct. Appeals for 5th Circuit, St. Petersburg, Fla., 1977-78; from assoc. to counsel Paul, Weiss, Rifkind, Wharton & Garrison, NYC, 1978-95; magistrate judge US Dist. Ct. (So. Dist.) NY, NYC, 1995—, chief magistrate judge, 2004—05. Adj. prof. Cardozo Law Sch., 2003—. Editor Duke Law Jour., 1976-77. Mem. ABA, N.Y. State Bar Found., Fed. Magistrate Judges Assn., Mystery Writers Am. Inc. (bd. dirs.), Order of Coif. Office: Daniel P Moynihan US Courthouse Rm 1370 500 Pearl St New York NY 10007-1312 Office Phone: 212-805-0036. Office Fax: 212-805-7933.

**PECK, ARTHUR JOHN, JR.,** retired manufacturing executive, lawyer; b. Trenton, NJ, Mar. 2, 1940; s. Arthur John and Mary Ellen (Kelly) P.; m. Susan Williams Lodge, July 18, 1970; children: David A., Margaret E. BA in Hist., Yale U., 1962; LLB, Washington & Lee U., 1968. Admissions officer Lawrenceville Sch., NJ, 1962-65; atty. Shearman & Sterling, N.Y.C., 1968-72; asst., assoc. counsel Corning (N.Y.), Inc., 1972-81, asst. sec., 1981—88, sec., v.p., 1988—2000, sr. v.p., 2000-01; ret., 2001. Sec. Teddington Co., Ltd., 1989-2001, Corning Inc. Found. 1981-01 Corning Europe, Inc., 1989-97, Corning Inc., 1988-2001, Corning Internat. Corp., 1991-2001; dir. asst. sec. Corning Inc. Fgn. Sales Corp., 1992-01 Corning Enterprises, Inc., 1974-97; asst. sec. Market St. Restoration Corp., 1974-01, Corning Mus. of Glass, 1981-98 sec., 1998-2001; trustee Rockwell Mus., sec. 1983-01, v.p., 2001—; trustee, sec. Corning Classic Charities, Inc., 1977-; bd. dirs. Guthrie Healthcare Sys., vice chmn., 2005-; bd. dirs. Guthrie Health; trustee Elmira-Corning Cmty. Found., 2005-. E-mail: jpeck@stny.rr.com.

**PECK, CAROLYN,** basketball coach; b. Jefferson City, Tenn. BA in Comm., Vanderbilt U., 1988. Mktg. cons., Nashville; salesperson; profl. basketball player Nippondenso Corp., Japan, 1991-93; asst. coach U. Tenn., U. Ky., 1995-96, Purdue U., West Lafayette, Ind., 1996-97, coach, 1997-98; head coach, gen. mgr. Orlando (Fla.) Miracle, 1999—2001; head coach Univ. of Fla., 2002—. Asst. coach USA Jones Cup team, 1997. Named AP Coach of the Yr., 1999, IKON/WBCA Div. I Nat. Coach of the Yr., 1999, Big 10 Coach of the Yr., 1999. Office: U Fla Women's Basketball PO Box 14485 Gainesville FL 32604

**PECK, CHARLES EDWARD,** retired construction and mortgage executive; b. Newark, Dec. 1, 1925; s. Hubert Raymond and Helen (White) P.; m. Delphine Murphy, Oct. 15, 1949; children: Margaret Peck Iovino, Charles Edward, Katherine Peck Koustmer, Perry Anne Peck Flanagan. Grad., Phillips Acad., 1943; student, MIT, 1944; BS, U. Pa., 1949; PhD in Pub. Svc. (hon.), Univ. Md. Univ. Coll., 1995. With Owens-Corning Fiberglas Corp., 1949-81, from sales mgr. home bldg. products to exec. v.p. Toledo, 1975-81; co-chmn. The Ryland Group, Columbia, Md., 1981-82, chmn., CEO, 1982-91; dir. The Delaware Group of Funds, 1991-2000; sec. Enterprise Homes, Inc., 1992-2000, New Homes by Enterprise, Inc., 2000-01. Statutory vis. com. U.S. Nat. Bur. Standards, 1972-77; adv. com. Fed. Nat. Mortgage Assn., 1977-78, 85-86; vis. com. MIT-Harvard Joint Ctr. for Urban Studies; chmn. Prodrs. Adv. Forum, 1977-81; mem. nat. adv. bd. Way Sta., 2004—. Vis. com. Harvard U. Grad. Sch. Design, 1981-86; chmn. Howard County United Way Campaign, Md., 1987; chmn. Cmty. Partnerships, 1991-94; bd. dirs. Nat. Inst. for Urban Wildlife, 1986-90, United Way Ctrl. Md., 1987-91, Howard County Gen. Hosp., 1988-94, NAHB Rsch. Found., 1989-92, Alliance to End Childhood Lead Poisoning, 1990-93, Meml. Hosp. Found., 2004—; co-chair psychiatry adv. bd. Johns Hopkins Med. Instns., 2005—; mem. adv. bd. U. Md. Engring. Sch., 1990-2003, Continuing Edn. Johns Hopkins U., 1988-91; policy adv. bd. Harvard Joint Ctr. Housing Studies, 1984-94; chancellor's adv. com. U. Md. Sys., 1988-2001, chmn., 1988-99; chmn. Univ. Md. Found., 1990-94, bd. dirs., 1990—; bd. visitors U. Md. Ctr. Environ. Sci., 2001—; exec. fellow Kennedy Sch., Harvard U., 1990-92; chmn. Affordable Housing Initiative, Columbia, Md., 1990-92; bd. overseers U. Md., College Park, 1994-97; bd. visitors Sch. Law U. Md., Balt., 1996-2004; vis. com. U. Md. Univ. Coll., 1997—; bd. dirs. Ctr. for Grant Devel., 1994-98, Victory '94 com. Md. State Rep. party, chmn. election inquiry funding com., 1994-95; chmn. Children of Separation and Divorce Ctr., 1995-2000; pres. adv. coun. Washington Coll., Chestertown, Md., 1997-2005, chmn., 2000-05; mem. Commn. on Future, Howard C.C. bd. visitors, 1999-2002; mem. Howard County Delta Project; pres. Peck Family Found., 1992—; co-chmn. Smart Growth Forum, 2001; bd. dirs. Columbia Festival of Arts, Md., 1988-91, 2002-03; active Marylanders for Coll. Opportunity, 2005—. Mem. U.S.C. of C. (bd. dirs. 1975-81), Ohio C. of C. (bd. dirs. 1975-81), Depression and Related Affective Disorders Assn. (pres. 1986-89, bd. dirs. 1986-2000, hon. pres. 1993-94), Ctr. Club, Phi Gamma Delta. Home and Office: 6855 Pea Neck Rd Saint Michaels MD 21663-2725 Personal E-mail: tpeck123@toad.net.

**PECK, DOUGLAS CATON,** dean, educator; b. Sturgis, Mich., Feb. 12, 1945; s. Herman Darwin and Volga Marceille Peck; m. Anna Kay Abraham, Aug. 23, 1969. BSChemE, Tri-State U., Angola, Ind., 1967; BA, U. Akron, 1972, MA, 1979, MS in Edn., 1997, PhD, 1993; grad., Ohio Statewide Leadership Acad. Cert. computing profl. Inst. for Certification of Computing Profls., 1990. R & d mgmt. trainee The Goodyear Tire & Rubber Co., Akron, Ohio, 1967—68, staff compunder, tire devel. divsn., 1968—70, programmer/analyst, product performance and field engring., 1972—74, engring. analyst, task force on radial passenger tire uniformity, 1974—80, systems analyst, tire devel. info. systems, 1980—82, systems analyst, tech. computer ops., 1982—91, sr. program designer, computer tng., computer applications analyst, exec. compensation and succession planning, 1996—97; tech. services engr., plant 2 tire prodn. The U. of Akron, Akron, Ohio, 1970—72, vis. asst. prof. of sociology, 1998—2000, adj. asst. prof. of sociology, 2000—01; dir. - evening, weekend and summer programs Ashland U., Ashland, Ohio, 2001—03; dean - gen. studies and pub. svc. technologies Stark State Coll. of Tech., Canton, Ohio, 1993—. Cons. on statis. analysis, data utilization, and orgnl. analysis. Exhibition, Oculis Sinistris; author: (book review) The Journal of Higher Education (Shaping the College Curriculum: Academic Plans in Action), musician university band and summer concert band; drawings, Old and Young / Noble and Commonplace - Portraits in Color Pencil, sculptures in steel and plaster, Sharp and Pointy / Soft and Rounded, metalworking, Metamorphosis: Ancient, Early Scientific and Advanced Scientific Views of Matter; contbr. articles and papers to jours., confs. Team mem. Summit Edn. Initiative, Akron, Ohio, 2000; mem. - career tech. adv. com.: career paths for the tchg. profession Perry H.S., Massillon, Ohio; judge Canton Artists' League, Canton, Ohio; pres. Hampton Ridge Homeowners' Assn., Akron, Ohio; adv. bd. Akron Chpt. of the Arthritis Found., Akron, Ohio, 1994—98, Dept. Chem. and Bioprocess Engring., Tri-State U., Angola, Ind.; trustee Tau Kappa Epsilon, Beta-Rho Chpt., Akron, Ohio, The Arthritis Found. of NE Ohio, Cleveland, Ohio, 1989—95; grant reader - fund for the improvement of postsec. edn. US Dept. of Edn.; grant reviewer (small bus. innovation program) NSF; peer reviewer Social Sci. Computer Rev. - NC State U., NC; merit reviewer (course, curriculum, and lab. improvement program) The NSF, Washington; co-chair, social sci. transfer and articulation guide project Ohio Bd. of Regents, Columbus, Ohio, 2004—05; steering com. mem. Stark County Coll. Tech Prep Consortium, Canton, Ohio; mem. - tchr. acad. adv. com. Wash. H.S., Massillon, Ohio; facilitator ARC - Akron Chpt., Akron, Ohio; area dir. coord. for united way campaign The Goodyear Tire & Rubber Co.; vol. Home at Last Animal Rescue, Akron, Ohio, 1998—2004. Recipient Cert. of Faculty Appreciation, Interfraternity Coun./Panhellenic Coun., The U. of Akron; scholar Trustees' scholar, Bd. of Trustees, Tri-State U., 1967. Mem.: Am. Tech. Edn. Assn., Am. Conf. of Academic Deans (assoc.), Kappa Delta Pi, Phi Alpha Theta, Alpha Kappa Delta, Omicron Delta Kappa, Golden Key (hon.). Avocations: playing saxophone and flute, reading. Home: 370 Goodhue Dr Akron OH 44313 Office: Stark State College of Tech 6200 Frank Ave NW Canton OH 44720-7299 Office Phone: 330-966-5457. Office Fax: 330-494-0571. Personal E-mail: dpeck1@neo.rr.com. Business E-mail: dpeck@starkstate.edu.

**PECK, DOUGLAS EDWARD,** lawyer; b. Bloomington, Ill., Apr. 15, 1961; s. Richard Ray and Sarah Josephine (Wilhoit) P.; m. Martha Elaine Jones. BA, U.N.C., 1983, JD, 1986. Bar: N.C. 1986, Tenn. 1987, U.S. Dist. Ct. (ea. dist.) Tenn. 1987, U.S. Ct. Appeals (6th crct.) 1991, U.S. Tax Ct. 1990 Shareholder Shumacker Witt Gaither & Whitaker, P.C. Chattanooga, 1986— Editor N.C. Law Rev., 1985-86. Office: Shumacker Witt Gaither & Whitaker PC 736 Market St Ste 1100 Chattanooga TN 37402 Office Phone: 423-425-7000. E-mail: dpeck@swgwlaw.com.

**PECK, EDWARD LIONEL,** retired foreign service officer, corporate executive; b. LA, Mar. 6, 1929; s. Alexander George and Rae (Lee) P.; m. Heather Dianne Hicks-Beach, Jan. 20, 1957 (div. July 1971); m. Ann Day Slevin, May 5, 1974; children: Heather Anne, Brian Michael, Thomas William, Julia Katherine BS, UCLA, 1956; MBA, George Washington U., 1973. Joined Fgn. Service Dept. State, Washington, 1957, intelligence specialist, 1968-71, spl. asst., 1971-74; econ. counselor U.S. Embassy, Cairo, 1974-77; chief of mission U.S. Interests Sect., Baghdad, Iraq, 1977-80; dir. Office of Egyptian affairs Washington, 1980-82; ambassador U.S. Embassy, Nouakchott, Mauritania, 1983—85; dep. dir. cabinet task force combating terrorism White Ho., 1985-86; dir. Office of Career Transition, 1986-88; ret., 1989; pres. Fgn. Svcs. Internat., 1989—; exec. sec. Am. Acad. Diplomacy, 1989-92. Trainer, lectr., cons. on fgn. affairs, internat. bus., 1990—; dir. polit. tradecraft program Nat. Fgn. Affairs Tng. Ctr., Arlington, Va., 1991-96; sr. assoc. Global Bus. Access Ltd., Washington, 1991—; Woodrow Wilson vis. fellow, 1993—. Bd. dirs. Am. for Middle East Understanding, 1999—; chmn. Coun. for the Nat. Interest Found., 2001-03. Served to capt. U.S. Army, 1946-49, 50-52 Recipient Meritorious Honor award Dept. State, 1967, 73, 77, 79, Superior Honor award Dept. State, 1974, 88, Wilbur J. Carr award, 1989; Rivkin award Am. Fgn. Svc. Assn., 1973 Home and Office: 106 Grafton St Bethesda MD 20815-3426 Office Phone: 301-652-8318. Personal E-mail: peckfsi@erols.com.

**PECK, ERNEST JAMES, JR.,** academic administrator; b. Port Arthur, Tex., July 26, 1941; s. Ernest James and Karlton Maudean (Luttrell) P.; children: David Karl, John Walter, Michael R. Peck. BA in Biology with honors, Rice U., 1963, PhD in Biochemistry, 1966. Rsch. assoc. Purdue U., West Lafayette, Ind., 1966-68, asst. prof., 1968-73, Baylor Coll. Medicine, Houston, 1973-74, assoc. prof., 1974-80, prof., 1980-82; prof., chmn. biochemistry Sch. Med. Sci., U. Ark., Little Rock, 1982-89; dean sci. and math. U. Nev., Las Vegas, 1989-95; vice chancellor acad. affairs U. Nebr., Omaha, 1995-98; exec. dir. Coun. Colls. of Arts and Scis., rsch. prof. Ariz. State U., Tempe, 1998—. Adj.

prof. U. Ark., Pine Bluff, 1986-88; program dir. NSF, Washington, 1988-89; mem. editl. bd. Jour. Neurosci. Rsch., N.Y.C., 1982-92. Co-author: Female Sex Steroids, 1979, Brain Peptides, 1979. Recipient Rsch. Career award NIH, Nat. Inst. of Child Health and Human Devel., 1975-80; NIH fellow, 1964-66. Fellow AAAS; mem. Am. Chem. Soc., Am. Soc. Biochemistry and Molecular Biology, Endocrine Soc., Sigma Xi. Avocations: fishing, hunting. Office: Ariz State U Coun Coll Arts Scis PO Box 873108 Tempe AZ 85287-3108 Office Phone: 480-727-6064. Business E-Mail: epeck@asu.edu.

**PECK, FRED NEIL,** economist, educator; b. Bklyn., Oct. 17, 1945; s. Abraham Lincoln and Beatrice (Pikholtz) P.; m. Jean Claire Ginsberg, Aug. 14, 1971; children: Ron Evan, Jordan Shefer, Ethan David. BA, Binghamton (NY) U., 1966; MA, SUNY, Albany, 1969; PhM, NYU, 1984; PhD, Pacific Western U., 1984; MS in Edn., Coll. New Rochelle, 1993. Lectr. SUNY, Albany, 1969-70; research asst. N.Y. State Legislature, Albany, 1970; sales and research staff Pan Am. Trade Devel. Corp., N.Y.C., 1971; v.p., economist The First Boston Corp., N.Y.C., 1971-88; mng. dir. Sharpe's Capital Mkt. Assocs. Inc., N.Y.C., 1988-89; pres., chief economist Hillcrest Econs. Group, N.Y.C., 1989-93; dir. edn. The Ednl. Advantage, Inc., New City, N.Y., 1990-95; dir Robert F. Kennedy Acad., N.Y. Dept. Edn., 1998—. Adj. prof. Hofstra U., Hempstead, NY, 1975, Mercy Coll., 2004-06, Touro Coll., 2004—; lectr. NYU, 1982; faculty New Sch. Social Rsch., N.Y.C., 1974-94; coord. ednl. tech. N.Y.C. Bd. Edn., 1990-98. Author; editor: Handbook of Securities of U.S. Government, 1972-86. Mem. ASCD, Am. Econ. Assn., Ea. Econ. Assn., Econometric Soc., Nat. Assn. Bus. Economists, Am. Statis. Assn., Coun. Exceptional Children, Doctorate Assn. of N.Y. Educators, Beta Gamma Sigma (hon. soc.), Phi Delta Kappa. Lodges: Knights Pythias, Knights Khorassan. Democrat. Jewish. Office: Robert F Kennedy Sch 110 East 88th St New York NY 10128 Personal E-mail: docfnp@bigfoot.com. E-mail: fpeck@schools.nyc.gov. *March in one place long enough and eventually you will wind up leading the parade of progress...No one grows old. When you tire of learning, of experiencing new things you are old.*

**PECK, GARNET EDWARD,** pharmacist, educator; b. Windsor, Ont., Can., Feb. 4, 1930; s. William Crozier and Dorothy (Marentette) P.; m. Mary Ellen Hoffman, Aug. 24, 1957; children: Monique Elizabeth, Denise Anne, Philip Warren, John Edward. BS in Pharmacy with Distinction, Ohio No. U., 1957; MS in Indsl. Pharmacy, Purdue U., 1959, PhD, 1962. Sr. scientist Mead Johnson Research Center, 1962-65, group leader, 1965-67; assoc. prof. indsl. and phys. pharmacy Purdue U., West Lafayette, 1967—73, prof., 1973—2003, dir. indsl. pharmacy lab., 1975—, assoc. dept. head, 1989-96, prof. emeritus, 2003—. Cons. in field; Contbr. articles to profl. jours. Mem. West Lafayette Mayor's Advisory Com. on Community Devel., 1973-; mem. West Lafayette Citizen's Safety Com., 1974-81; mem. West Lafayette Park Bd., 1981-, pres., 1983-96. Served with U.S. Army, 1951-53. Recipient Lederle Faculty award Purdue U., 1976 Fellow APHA, AAAS, Am. Inst. Chem., Am. Assn. Pharm. Scientists; mem. Am. Chem. Soc., Acad. Rsch. and Sci. (Sidney Riegelman award 1994), Am. Assn. Colls. Pharmacy, Cath. Acad. Sci. (founding mem.), KC, Knight of Holy Sepulchre, Sigma Xi, Rho Chi, Phi Lambda Upsilon, Phi Kappa Phi, Phi Sigma Lambda, Phi Lambda Sigma. Roman Catholic. Office: Purdue U Sch Pharmacy & Pharm Scis Dept Industrial & Physical Pharm West Lafayette IN 47907 Office Phone: 765-494-1400. Business E-Mail: gepeck@pharmacy.purdue.edu.

**PECK, H. DANIEL,** literature educator; b. Milw., July 15, 1940; s. Henry Edward and Carmen (Barbulesco) P.; m. Patricia B. Wallace, Apr. 3, 1982; 1 child, Jennifer Peck; stepchildren: Christopher Wallace, Matthew Wallace BA, Ohio Wesleyan U., 1962; MA, U. Iowa, 1971, PhD, 1974. Asst. prof. to assoc. prof. U. Calif., Santa Barbara, 1972—80; assoc. prof. Vassar Coll., Poughkeepsie, NY, 1980—83, prof. lit., 1983—. Dir. Am. culture program Vassar Coll., Poughkeepsie, 1989—92, John Guy Vassar chair, 1999—, founding dir. environ. studies program, 2000—03; dir. NEH Summer Insts. for Coll. and Univ. Faculty, 1993, 97. Author: Thoreau's Morning Work, 1990, A World by Itself: The Pastoral Moment in Cooper's Fiction, 1977; editor: The Green American Tradition, 1989, New Essays on the Last of the Mohicans, 1992, World's Classics edit. Fenimore Cooper's Deerslayer, 1993, A Year in Thoreau's Journal: 1851, 1993, Thoreau's A Week on the Concord and Merrimack Rivers, 1998, Mark Twain's The Adventures of Tom Sawyer, 2003; contbr. Columbia Lit. History of the U.S., 1988, Health Anthology of Am. Lit., 1996—; mem. editl. bd. Hudson River Valley Rev., 2006— Fellow Am. Coun. Learned Socs., 1977-78, NEH, 1984, 94, Georgia O'Keeffe Mus. Rsch. Ctr., 2002; grantee Mellon Found., 2006— Mem. MLA (chmn. divsn. 19th Century Am. Lit. 1986), Am. Studies Assn., New Eng. Am. Studies Assn. (coun. 1991-93), Assoc. for Study Lit. of Environ. (editl. bd., 1995—), John Burroughs Assoc. (bd. dir. 1994-2001) Home: 26 Sunrise Ln Poughkeepsie NY 12603-4213 Office: Vassar Coll Box 226 Poughkeepsie NY 12604-0226 Office Phone: 845-437-5662. E-mail: peckd@vassar.edu.

**PECK, LOUIS MOSES,** editor; b. NYC, Apr. 16, 1951; s. Seymour and Susan (Lustig) P.; m. Nancy Jean Schwerzler, Sept. 5, 1987. BA in Am. History, Brown U., 1973. Govt. and politics reporter Frankfort (Ind.) Times, 1974-76, Poughkeepsie (N.Y.) Jour., 1976-78; regional corr. Gannett News Svc., Washington, 1978-82; congl. and polit. corr., 1983-87; editor Campaigns and Elections, Washington, 1988-89; freelance writer editor Washington, 1989-91; editor Congress Daily, Washington, 1991—; editor-in-chief Nat. Jour.'s Tech. Daily, 2000—. Vis. instr. Medill Sch. Journalism, Northwestern U., Washington, 1988, 90. Editorial cons.: Reform and Reality: The Financing of State and Local Campaigns, 1990, Financing Politics: Money, Elections and Political Reform, 1991. Mem. Washington Ind. Writers. Office: Nat Jour 600 New Hampshire Ave NW Washington DC 20037 Business E-Mail: lpeck@nationaljournal.com.

**PECK, MALCOLM CAMERON,** educational exchange specialist; b. Boston, Apr. 4, 1939; s. Wilfred Cameron and Ruth Lorriaux (Murdoch) P.; m. Adelaida Boquilon Ravelo, Dec. 30, 1972; 1 child, John Cameron. AB, Harvard U., 1961, AM, 1966; MA, Tufts U., 1963, MALD, 1964, PhD, 1970. Instr. U. Chattanooga (now U. Tenn.), 1967-68; postdoctoral fellow Harvard U., Cambridge, Mass., 1969-70; asst. to the pres., dir. programs Middle East Inst., Washington, 1970-81; Arabian peninsula affairs analyst U.S. Dept. State, Washington, 1981-83; program officer Meridian Internat. Ctr., Washington, 1984-2000, sr. program officer, 2000—04; ret., 2004. Pres., bd. dirs. nat. com. to Honor the 14th Centennial of Islam, Washington, 1979-83. Author: The United Arab Emirates: A Venture in Unity, 1986, Historical Dictionary of the Gulf Arab States, 1997; contbr. articles to profl. jours. Sec. Ch. of the Holy City, 1998-2005. NDFL fellowship U.S. Govt., 1964-65; postdoctoral fellowship Harvard U., 1969-70. Mem. Middle East Studies Assn., Middle East Inst. (resident fellow 1983), Philippine Arts, Letters, and Media Coun. (sec. 1995-2005, pres. 2005—), Soc. for Gulf Arab Studies (co-founder, sec. 1987-2002). Democrat. Avocations: bicycling, music, reading. Home: 3118 1st St N Arlington VA 22201-1033 Office Phone: 202-939-5581. Personal E-mail: aandmpeck@comcast.net. E-mail: mpeck@meridian.org.

**PECK, MARYLY VANLEER,** retired academic administrator, chemical engineer; b. Washington, June 29, 1930; d. Blake Ragsdale and Ella Lillian (Wall) VanLeer; m. Jordan B. Peck, Jr., June 15, 1951; children: Jordan B. III, Blake VanLeer, James Tarleton VanLeer, Virginia Ellaine.; m. 2d, Walter G. Ebert, Sept. 3, 1983 (dec. June 1990); m. 3d Edwin L. Carey, Apr. 13, 1991. Student, Ga. Inst. Tech., 1948, 55-58, Duke U., 1947-48; B.Ch.E., Vanderbilt U., 1951; MSE., U. Fla., 1955, PhD, 1963. Chem. engr. Naval Research Lab., Washington, 1951-52; chem. engr. Med. Field Research Lab., Camp LeJeune, NC, 1952; asso. research and instr. U. Fla., Gainesville, 1953-55; chem. engr., research asso. Ga. Tech. Expt. Sta., Atlanta, 1956-58; lectr. Ga. State Coll., Atlanta, 1957-58; lectr. math. East Carolina Extension, Camp Lejeune, 1959; sr. research engr. Rocketdyne div. N.Am. Aviation Co., 1961-63; self-employed as lectr., 1963; assoc. prof. Campbell Coll., Buie's Creek, NC, 1963-66, prof., 1966; acad. dir. St. John's Episcopal Sch., Upper Tumon, Guam, 1966-68; chmn., prof. phys. scis. U. Guam, Agana, 1968-73, dean Coll. Bus. and Applied Tech., 1973-74, dean Community Career Coll., 1974-77; pres. Cochise Coll., Douglas, Ariz., 1977-78; systems planning

analyst Urban Pathfinders, Inc., Balt., 1978-79; dean undergrad. studies U. Md. Univ. Coll., College Park, 1979-82; pres. Polk Community Coll., Winter Haven, Fla., 1982-97, pres. emeritus, 1997—; headmaster All Saints' Acad., 1997-99. Cons. in field. Founder, pres. Guam Acad. Found., 1972-77; bd. dirs. Cochise Coll. Found., 1977-78; charter bd. dirs. Turnaround Inc., 1987-91, chmn. 1990-93; bd. dirs. United Way Ctrl. Fla., 1986-95, vice-chmn., 1992, chair elect, 1993, chmn. 1994; founding mem. Prince George's Ednl. TV Cable Coalition; mem. Prince George's Cable TV Ednl. Adv. Group, 1980-82, Polk County Coun. Econ. Edn., 1982; sec. Polk C.C. Found., 1982-97; mem. Polk County Coord. Coun. Vocat. Edn., 1983-87, PRIDE Adv. Coun.; vice-chmn. Fla. Job Tng. Coord. Coun., 1983-87, Fla. Edn. Fund Bd., 1988-93; active Girls Inc. Bd., 1992—, pres., 2000-2001, hon. mem., 2005; trustee All Sts.'s Acad. 1994-2002; trustee Vanguard Sch., 2001—06, mem. Fdn. Bd., 2001—06; bd. dirs. Theater Winter Haven, 2000—, chair, 2002-03. Named Disting. Alumnus U. Fla., 1992, Woman of Distinction Girls Scouts U.S.A., 1994, Woman of Distinction, 1997; fellow NSF, 1961-63; recipient She Knows Where She's Going award Girls Inc. of Winter Haven, 1995, Cmty. Svc. award Jr. League Winter Haven, 2002, Boy Scout Disting. Citizen award Lake Region Dist. Gulf Ridge Coun. Am., 2005, NDAR Cmty. Svc. award, 2005. Fellow Soc. Women Engrs. (nat. v.p. 1962-63); mem. AAUW, AIChE, DAR (Cmty. Svc. award 2005), Am. Chem. Soc., NSPE, Am. Assn. for Higher Edn., Am. Assn. Cmty. and Jr. Colls., Am. Assn. Univ. Adminstrs., Rotary (sec. 1999-2000, pres.-elect 2003-04, centennial pres. 2004-), Sigma Xi, Tau Beta Pi, Chi Omicron Gamma, Phi Kappa Phi, Delta Kappa Gamma. Episcopalian. Home: 5390 Woodland Lakes Dr 206 Palm Beach Gardens FL 33418-3959 E-mail: marylypeck@bellsouth.net.

**PECK, PAUL LACHLAN,** minister; b. Glens Falls, NY, Sept. 11, 1928; s. Paul Lee and Caroline Jeannette (Stanton) Peck; children: Paul Barrett, Kathryn Elizabeth, Gretchen, Kole W. BS, U. Conn., 1952; ThD, Bernadean U., 1976; MEd, Westfield State Coll., 1983. Ordained to ministry Truth Ctr., 1972. With Proctor and Gamble Co., Watertown, NY, 1956-60; dir. deferred giving programs Syracuse (N.Y.) U., 1960-68, v.p., 1968-70, Fairleigh-Dickinson U., NJ, 1970-71, Manhattan Coll., Bronx, NY, 1971-73; founder, pastor Arete' Truth Ctr., San Diego, 1975—. Author: Footsteps Along the Path, 1978, Inherit the Kingdom, 1978, Milestones of the Way, 1978, Freeway to Health, 1980, Freeway to Work and Wealth, 1981, Freeway to Human Love, 1982, Freeway to Personal Growth, 1982, Your Dreams Count, 1990, Heroic Love Poems, 1990, Worth The Room: An Autobiography of Survival and Service, 2005 Bd. dirs. Girl Scouts U.S.A., Syracuse, 1967-70; trustee, bd. dirs. Erickson Ednl. Found., 1970-75; vol. chaplain Auburn (N.Y.) State Prison, 1967-68; mem. chaplains' coun. Syracuse U., 1960-70; co-founder suicide and drug abuse prevention program Syracuse U., 1968-71, Fairleigh-Dickinson U., 1970-71, Manhattan Coll., 1971-75. Staff sgt. USNG, 1947-50. Mem. Internat. New Thought Alliance, SAR, Rotary, Knights of Malta (svc. award 1973), Masons, Shriners, Spiritual Frontiers Fellowship. Avocations: golf, book collecting.

**PECK, RALPH BRAZELTON,** civil engineering educator, consultant; b. Winnipeg, Man., Can., June 23, 1912; (parents Am. citizens); s. Orwin K. and Ethel Indie (Huyck) Peck; m. Marjorie Elizabeth Truby, June 14, 1937; children: Nancy Jeanne Peck Young, James Leroy. D in Civil Engring., Rensselaer Poly. Inst., 1937; postgrad., Harvard U., 1938; D Eng. (hon.), Rensselaer Poly. Inst., 1974; DSc (hon.), Laval U., 1987. Registered Ill., structural engr., Ill., civil engr., Calif. Structural detailer Am. Bridge Co., Ambridge, Pa., 1937; asst. subway engr. City of Chgo., 1939—43; chief engr. testing Holabird & Root, Scioto Ordnance Plant, Marion, Ohio, 1943; research asst. prof. soil mechanics U. Ill., Champaign-Urbana, 1943—48, research prof. found. engring., 1948—57, prof. found. engring., 1957—74, prof. emeritus, 1974—. Cons. in field. Author (with K. Terzaghi and G. Mesri): Soil Mechanics in Engineering Practice, 1948, 3rd edit., 1996; author: (with T.H. Thornburn and W.E. Hanson) Foundation Engineering, 1953, 2d edit., 1973, Judgment in Geotechnical Engineering: The Professional Legacy of Ralph B. Peck, 1984; contbr. articles to profl. jours. Named to Hall of Fame, Rensselaer Poly. Inst., 1998; recipient Disting. Civilian Svc. award, Dept. of Army, 1973, Moles Non-mem. award, 1973, Nat. Medal Sci., Pres. Gerald Ford, 1974, Golden Beaver award, 1983, Disting. Svc. award, Deep Founds Inst., 1984, Merit award, Am. Cons. Engrs. Coun., 1988, John F. Parmer award, 2004. Fellow: Geol. Soc. Am. (sr.); mem.: NSPE (award 1972), ASCE (hon.; nat. dir. 1962—65, Norman medal 1944, Wellington prize 1965, Terzaghi award 1969, Washington award 1976, Pres.'s award 1986, John Fritz medal 1987, Rickey medal 1988, Geo-Inst. award 2000, Outstanding Projects and Leaders award 2001), NAE, Can. Geotech. Soc. (Spl. award 2002), Internat. Soc. Soil Mechanics and Geotech. Engring. (pres. 1969—73), Am. Acad. Arts and Scis., Mexican Soc. Soil Mechanics (hon.), Japanese Soc. Soil Mechanics (hon.), Southeast Asian Soc. Soil Mechanics (hon.), Phi Kappa Phi, Tau Beta Pi, Chi Epsilon, Sigma Xi. Home: 1101 Warm Sands Dr SE Albuquerque NM 87123-4328

**PECK, ROBERT A.,** publishing executive, state legislator; b. Riverton, Wyo., Oct. 7, 1924; s. LeRoy E. and Elvira Eugenia (Sostrom) P.; m. Cordelia S. Peck, Oct. 5, 1949 (dec. Feb. 1996); children: Christopher, George, Steven. BA, U. Wyo., 1949. Pub. The Riverton Ranger, 1949—; mem. Wyo. Senate, Dist. 26, Cheyenne, 1991—. Pres. Central Wyo. Coll. Bd., Riverton, 1966-81; sec. CWC Found., Riverton, 1968—. Staff sgt. U.S. Army, 1943-46, ETO. Mem. Soc. Profl. Journalists, Masons, Phi Beta Kappa. Republican. Methodist. Office: The Riverton Ranger 421 E Main PO Box 993 Riverton WY 82501-0993 Office Phone: 307-856-2244. E-mail: bpeck@wyoming.com, ranger@wyoming.com.

**PECK, ROBERT MCCRACKEN,** naturalist, historian, writer; b. Phila., Dec. 15, 1952; s. Frederick William Gunster and Matilda (McCracken) P. BA in Art History, Princeton U., 1974; MA, U. Del., 1976. Dir. Pocono Lake (Pa.) Preserve Nature Ctr., 1971, 72; asst. to dir. Natural History Mus. Acad. Natural Scis., Phila., 1976-77, spl. asst. to pres., 1977-82, acting v.p. Nat. History Mus., 1982-83, fellow, 1983—, curator Art and Artifacts, 2000—, editor sci. publs., 2001—03; sr. fellow, libr., 2003—; tech. dir. Bartram Heritage Study U.S. Dept. Interior and Bartram Trail Conf., Atlanta and Montgomery, Ala., 1977-78. Cons. BBC, Eng., 1987-92; bd. dirs. Phila. Conservationists, Natural Lands Trust, Phila., Libr. Co. of Phila., Phila. City Inst.; mng. editor Frontiers, 1979-82, editor Proceedings of The Acad. of Natural Scis., 2001-04; fellow in field. Author: A Celebration of Birds: The Life and Art of Louis Agassiz Fuertes, 1982, Headhunters and Hummingbirds: An Expedition Into Ecuador, 1987, Wild Birds of America: The Art of Basil Ede, 1991, Land of the Eagle: A Natural History of North America, 1991, German edit., 1992; author: (with others) John James Audubon in the West: The Last Expedition, 2000, William Bartram's Travels, 1980, John Cassin's Illustrations of the Birds of California, Texas, Oregon, British and Russian America, 1991; author: (forward) The Birds of America by John James Audubon, 1985; editor: Bartram Heritage Report, 1978; author: (with others), editor: Philadelphia Wildfowl Exposition Catalog, 1979; contbr. chpts. to books, articles to mags. and newspapers including The New York Times. Recipient Richard Hopper Day Meml. award Acad. Natural Scis. of Phila., 1991, Wyck-Strickland award for contbns. to cultural life of Phila., 2003; Eleanor Garvey fellow in printing and graphic arts Houghton Libr., Harvard U., 1995; Yale Ctr. for Brit. Art fellow, 1997. Fellow Royal Geog. Soc., Explorers Club (various coms. 1983—, Explorers award 1988); mem. Soc. History of Natural History, Sigma Xi. Achievements include discovery of new species of frog, Eleutherodactylus pecki; research in orthoptera indigenous to the Caribbean; status of invasive African Desert Locust in the West Indies; the Orinoco River and its tributaries, botanical, entomological, ichthyological, herpetological and malacological specimens for the Smithsonian Institution and the Academy of Natural Sciences; participation in expeditions which discovered several new species of fish in Guyana Shield, Venezuela; discovery of several new species of amphibians and insects; current projects include biological and cultural research in Mongolia, the natural history illustrations of Edward Lear; research in 19th century exploration. Office: Acad Natural Scis 1900 Benjamin Franklin Pkwy Philadelphia PA 19103-1195 Office Phone: 215-299-1138. Business E-Mail: peck@acnatsci.org.

**PECK, ROBERT STEPHEN,** lawyer, educator; b. Bklyn., Dec. 11, 1953; s. Irwin and Edith Rose (Welt) P.; m. Terre Garcia; 1 child, Zachary Madison. BA in Polit. Sci., George Washington U., 1975; JD, Cleve.-Marshall Law Sch., 1978; postgrad., NYU, 1978; LLM, Yale U., 1990. Bar: N.Y. 1979, U.S. Dist. Ct. (so. and ea. dists.) N.Y. 1979, D.C. 1989, U.S. Ct. Appeals (9th and 11th cirs.) 2004, U.S. Ct. Appeals (2d cir.) 2006, U.S. Supreme Ct. 2002. Congl. aide U.S. Ho. of Reps., Washington, 1972-74; divsn. dir. Automated Correspondence, Washington, 1974-75; law clk. to presiding justice Cleve. Mcpl. Ct., 1976; editor Matthew Bender & Co., N.Y.C., 1977-78; legal dir. Pub. Edn. Assn., N.Y.C., 1978-82; staff dir. ABA, Chgo., 1982-87, Washington, 1987-89; jud. fellow U.S. Supreme Ct., 1990-91; legis. counsel ACLU, 1991-95; adj. prof. Am. U., Washington, 1991—, George Washington U., Washington, 2000—; dir. legal affairs Assn. Trial Lawyers Am., 1995-98, sr. dir. legal affairs, 1998—2003; pres. Ctr. for Constl. Litigation, 2001—. Legal advisor Freedom to Read Found., Chgo., 1986-2002, exec. com. bd. trustees, 1987-90, 93-97, pres., 1988-90, v.p., trustee, 1993-97; bd. dirs. Nat. Constl. Ctr., 1990-93; bd. overseers RAND Inst. Civil Justice, 2001—; mem. lawyers com. Nat. Ctr. for State Cts., 2002—, bd. dirs., 2005—; lectr. on constl. law, legal ethics. Author: We the People, 1987, The Bill of Rights and the Politics of Interpretation, 1991, Libraries, the First Amendment and Cyberspace, 1999; co-author: Speaking and Writing Truth, 1985; editor: Understanding the Law, 1983, Blessings of Liberty, 1986, To Govern A Changing Society, 1990; contbr. numerous articles on constl. law to law revs. Mem. N.Y. State Edn. Adv. Bd., Albany, N.Y., 1979-81; bd. dirs. Nat. Com. on Pub. Edn. and Religious Liberty, 1995-97, Ams. for Religious Liberty, 1995-2000, Citizens for Constitution, 1997—; nat. chair Lawyers for Librs., 1996-2002; chair legal adv. com. Nat. Ctr. for Sci. Edn., 1996-2000; mem. first amendment adv. coun. Media Inst., 1996—. NEH grantee 1983, 85. Mem.: ABA (chmn. pub. election law com. 1983—85, 1987—90, vice chmn. access to justice com. 1997—98, program chmn. consumer and personal rights litigation com. 1997—2000, chmn. 1998—99, chmn. first amendment com. 1999—2005, chmn. appellate adv. com. 2001—02, chmn. com. Am. Law Inst. and Uniform Laws 2002—03, spl. advisor Commn. on 21st Century Judiciary 2002—03, mem. governing coun. tort, trial and ins. law sect. 2003—, chmn. 20/20 vision task force 2004—, mem. Commn. Am. Jury 2005—, chmn. task force disaster relief 2005—), U.S. Supreme Ct. Fellows Alumni Assn. (pres. 2004—06). Democrat. Jewish. Avocations: tennis, music, travel. Office: Ctr for Constl Litigation 1050 31st St NW Washington DC 20007-4499 Office Phone: 202-944-2874. Business E-Mail: robert.peck@cclfirm.com.

**PECK, SUSAN NELL,** pediatric nurse; b. Dayton, Ohio, July 21, 1951; d. D. Bradley and Helen Louise (DePree) P. BSN, Northeastern U., Boston, 1974; MSN, U. Va., 1981. Cert. registered nurse practitioner. Sr. staff nurse Tufts-New Eng. Med. Ctr., Boston, 1974-79; staff nurse U. Va. Med. Ctr., Charlottesville, 1980-81, grad. teaching asst., 1980-81; clin. nurse specialist in gastroenterology The Children's Hosp. of Phila., 1981—. V.p. nurse profl. edn. Delaware Valley chpt. Crohn's and Colitis Found. Am., Phila., 1992—. Contbr. articles to profl. jours.; author videotape: Facts From Your Friends, 1991. Bd. dirs. Phila. chpt. Am. Liver Found., 1988—. Named Woman of the Yr., Crohn's and Colitis Found. of Am., 1995, Nurse Profl. of Yr., Am. Liver Found., 1997; inducted into Northeastern U. Nursing Hall of Fame, 1998. Mem. ANA, Nat. Assn. Pediatric Nurse Practitioners and Assocs., Soc. Gastroenterology Nurses and Assocs. (editl. bd. 1986-92), Assn. Pediatric Gastroenterology and Nutrition Nurses (founder, sec.-treas. 1989-94, sec. 1994-95, treas. 1996), Sigma Theta Tau. Avocations: travel, reading. Office: Childrens Hosp of Phila 34th And Civic Center Blvd Philadelphia PA 19104

**PECK, WILLIAM ARNO,** internist, educator, dean, academic administrator; b. New Britain, Conn., Sept. 28, 1933; m. Patricia Hearn, July 10, 1982; children by previous marriage: Catherine, Edward Pershall, David Nathaniel; stepchildren: Andrea, Elizabeth, Katherine. AB, Harvard U., 1955; MD, U. Rochester, N.Y., 1960; DSc (hon.), U. Rochester, 2000. Intern, then resident in internal medicine Barnes Hosp., St. Louis, 1960-62; fellow in metabolism Washington U. Sch. Medicine, St. Louis, 1963; mem. faculty U. Rochester Med. Sch., 1965-76, prof. medicine and biochemistry, 1973-76, head divsn. endocrinology and metabolism, 1969-76; John E. and Adaline Simon prof. medicine, co-chmn. dept. medicine Washington U. Sch. Medicine, St. Louis, 1976-89; physician in chief Jewish Hosp., St. Louis, 1976-89; prof. medicine and exec. vice chancellor med. affairs, dean sch. medicine, pres. univ. med. ctr. Washington U. St. Louis, 1989—2003, Wolff disting. prof., dean emeritus and dir. ctr. for health policy, 2003—. Chmn. endocrinology and metabolism adv. com. FDA, 1976-78; chmn. genetic medicine study sect. NIH, 1979-81; chmn. Gordon Conf. Chemistry, Physiology and Structure of Bones and Teeth, 1977, Consensus Devel. Conf. on Osteoporosis, NIH, 1984; co-chmn. Workshop on Future Directions in Osteoporosis, 1987; chmn. Spl. Topic Conf. on Osteoporosis, U.S. FDA, 1987; bd. dirs. Angelica Corp., Allied Healthcare Products, Rsch! Am., St. Louis Regional Chamber and Growth Assn., TIAA-CREF Trust Co. Editor Bone and Mineral Rsch. Annns., 1982-88. Pres. Nat. Osteoporosis Found., 1985-90. Served as med. officer USPHS, 1963-65. Paul Harris fellow Rotary Found., 2001; recipient Lederle Med. Faculty award, 1967, Career Program award NIH, 1970-75, Commr.'s Spl. citation FDA, 1988, Humanitarian award Arthritis Found. Ea. Mo., 1995, Crohn's and Colitis Fedn. Am., 1999, Founders award Nat. Osteoporosis Found., 1996, Huntington Disease Soc. Am. award, 2002, Juvenile Diabetes Rsch. Found. Lifetime Achievement award, 2003, Internat. Brotherhood award Bikur Cholim Hosp., Jerusalem, 2003, Nat. Children's Cancer Soc. Legacy award, Disting. Svc. award Washington U. Sch. Medicine, Lifetime Achievement award health care. Fellow AAAS, ACP; mem. Internat. Bone & Mineral Soc., Royal Soc. Medicine, Am. Assn. Clin. Endocrinologists, Am. Geriatrics Soc., Am. Soc. Biochemistry & Molecular Biophysics, Am. Soc. Bone and Mineral Rsch. (councilor 1978-81, pres.-elect 1982-83, pres. 1983-84), Am. Soc. Clin. Investigation, Am. Soc. Internal Medicine, Assn. Am. Med. Colls. (coun. deans adminstrv. bd. 1992—, chmn. 1996-97, chair elect 1997-98, chair 1998—, immediate past chair 1999), Assn. Am. Physicians, Endocrine Soc., Orthopaedic Rsch. Soc., Soc. Med. Adminstrs., St. Louis Metro. Med. Soc., St. Louis Soc. Internal Medicine (pres. 1986), Inst. Medicine Nat. Acad. Sci., Washington U. Health Adminstrn. Program Alumni Assn. (hon.), Research! Am. (vice chair 1999—), Pi Theta Epsilon (hon.), Sigma Xi, Alpha Omega Alpha (bd. dirs 1992-95). Home: 32 Huntleigh Downs Saint Louis MO 63131 Office: Washington U Sch Medicine #1 Brookings Dr Box 1133 Saint Louis MO 63130

**PECK, WILLIAM HENRY,** curator, archaeologist, educator, art historian, writer; b. Savannah, Ga., Oct. 2, 1932; s. William Henry Peck and Mildred (Bass) Peck Tuten; m. Ann Amelia Keller, Feb. 2, 1957 (dec. 1965); children: Alice Ann, Sarah Louise; m. Elsie Holmes, July 8, 1967; 1 child, William Henry IV. Student, Ohio State U., 1950-53; BFA, Wayne State U., 1960, MA, 1961. Jr. curator Detroit Inst. Arts, 1960-62, asst. curator, 1962-64, assoc. curator, 1964-68, curator ancient art, 1968—2004, acting chief curator, 1984-88, sr. curator, 1988—2004; lectr. art history Coll. Creative Studies, 2004—. Lectr. art history Cranbrook Acad. Art, Bloomfield Hills, Mich., 1963-65; vis. lectr. U. Mich., Ann Arbor, 1970, U. Mich., Dearborn, 2005—; adj. prof. art history Wayne State U., Detroit, 1966—; excavations in Egypt, Mendes, 1964-66, Precinct of Mut, Karnak, 1978—; adj. faculty art history Coll. Creative Studies, Detroit, 2004—, U. Mich., Dearborn, 2005—; sessional instr. U. Windsor, Ont., 2006. Author: Drawings from Ancient Egypt, 1978, The Detroit Institute of Arts: A Brief History, 1991, Splendors of Ancient Egypt, 1978; co-author: Ancient Egypt: Discovering its Splendors, 1978, Mummies, Diseases and Ancient Cultures, 1980, Arts and Humanities Through the Ages: Ancient Greece and Rome, 2005; contbr. articles to profl. publs. With U.S. Army, 1953-55. Recipient award in the arts Wayne State U., 1985; Ford Motor Co. travel grantee, 1962; Am. Rsch. Ctr. Egypt fellow, 1971; Smithsonian Instn. travel grantee, 1975. Mem. Archaeol. Inst. Am., Am. Rsch. Ctr. Egypt, Internat. Assn. Egyptologists, Soc. Study Egyptian Antiquities, Assn. Study Travel in Egypt and the Near East, Am. Assn. Mus., Oriental Inst.-U. Chgo. Democrat. Episcopalian. Avocations: oragami, early music performance, collecting T.E. Lawrence material. Office: 1901 Orleans Detroit MI 48207-2718 Personal E-mail: whpeck@yahoo.com.

**PECKENPAUGH, DONALD HUGH,** psychologist, consultant, writer; b. East Chicago, Ind., Aug. 11, 1928; s. George Martin and Thelma Mentia P.; m. Mary Frances Dreesen, Sept. 2, 1950; children: Ann Dreesen, Eve Louise. PhB, U. Chgo., 1948, AM, 1954, PhD, 1968. Lic. psychologist, Ill., Ind., Minn. Author: A School System's Role in Social Renewal, 1966, A Comprehensive Concept for Vocational Educational Facilities, 1967, Partners in Education, 1967, Exemplary Programs in Multi-Cultural Education, 1974, Population and You, 1975, Moral Education, 1976, The Public School as Moral Authority, 1977, Psychoeducational Evaluation, 1984. Nat. Inst. Mental Health fellow, 1965-67. Mem. Am. Psychol. Assn., Am. Assn. Sch. Adminstrs. (life), Phi Delta Kappa. Office: 3 Brook Ln Palos Park IL 60464-1289 E-mail: donpeckenpaugh@att.net.

**PECKENPAUGH, ROBERT EARL,** investment advisor; b. Potomac, Ill., July 17, 1926; s. Hilery and Zella (Stodgel) P.; m. Margaret J. Dixon, Sept. 21, 1945; children: Nancy Lynn, Carol Sue, David Robert, Daniel Mark, Jeanne Beth, Douglas John. Student, Ind. U., 1946—47; BS, Northwestern U., 1949, MBA with distinction, 1952. Chartered fin. analyst. With First Nat. Bank Chgo., 1949—52; pres. Security Suprs., Inc., Chgo., 1952—73; v.p. Chgo. Title & Trust Co., 1973—77; pres. Hotchkiss & Peckenpaugh, Inc., Chgo., 1977—84; v.p. Morgan Stanley Asset Mgmt. Inc., Chgo., 1984—86, Morgan Stanley & Co., Inc., Chgo., 1986—91; pres. Peckenpaugh Asset Mgmt. Inc., Chgo., 1991—. Chmn., Evang. Covenant Ch. of Hinsdale, Ill., 1981-84. Served with USNR, 1944-46. Mem. Investment Analyst Soc. Chgo. (pres. 1963-64), Mid-Day Club, Hinsdale Golf Club. Home: 429 S County Line Rd Hinsdale IL 60521-4724 Office: Peckenpaugh Asset Mgmt 429 S County Line Rd Hinsdale IL 60521-4724

**PECKER, DAVID J.,** magazine publishing company executive; b. N.Y.C., Sept. 24, 1951; m. Karen Balan, Oct. 31, 1987. BBA, postgrad., Pace U. CPA, N.Y. Sr. auditor Price Waterhouse & Co.; mgr. fin. reporting Diamandis Communications, Inc., N.Y.C., 1979; dir. fin. reporting, dir. acctg., asst. contr., 1983; COO, CFO, exec. v.p. pub. Hachette Mags., Inc., N.Y.C., 1990-91, pres., COO, 1991-92, pres. and CEO, 1992-99; chmn., CEO Am. Media Inc., 1999—, pres., CEO, COO Lake Worth, Fla., 1999—. Mem. Fashion Group's Internat. Adv. Bd., The N.Y. City Partnership Com.; mem. bd. dirs. The Madison Square Boys & Girls Club. Bd. dirs. Pace U., N.Y.C., Drug Enforcement Agents Found., 1995—. Mem. Am. Mgmt. Assn. Office: Am Media Inc 600 East Coast Ave Lake Worth FL 33464-0001

**PECKHAM, DONALD,** computer company executive; b. Aberdeen, S.D., Feb. 8, 1932; s. Donald Seth and Crystal (Maytum) P.; m. Jeanette G. Mackenzie, June 20, 1967 (div. Jan. 1980); children: Dean, Deanna Jean. BSEE, U. Wash., 1957; MSEE, Calif. Inst. Tech., 1958. Engr. Hughes Aircraft Co., Culver City, Calif., 1957-60; sr. engr. Nortronics divsn. Northrup Corp., Hawthorne, Calif., 1960-61, rsch. scientist Nortronics divsn., 1965-67, tech. dir. Aircraft divsn., 1985-92; v.p. Digitek Corp., Inglewood, Calif., 1961-63, v.p., gen. mgr. L.A., 1963-65; mem. staff Decade Computer Corp., Huntington Beach, 1967-71; mgr. software Pertec Computer Corp., Santa Ana, Calif., 1971-81; mgr. software tools CXC Corp., Irvine, Calif., 1981-85; instr. U. So. Calif., 1960-61; pres. Modern Computer, Carlsbad, Calif., 1992-2001, Modern.net, Oceanside, Calif., 2001—. With USN, 1950-54. Mem. IEEE, Assn. Computing Machinery, Tau Beta Pi. Home and Office: Unit 85 3890 Vista Campana S Oceanside CA 92057-8160

**PECKHAM, ELLEN,** artist, poet; b. Rochester, N.Y., Sept. 28, 1938; d. Walter Fredrick and Florence Albertina (Schmanke) Stoepel; m. Anson Wheeler Peckham, Sept. 10, 1976 Exhibitions include Atelier A/E Enterprises, N.Y.C., 1994—, Instituto Cultural Peruano Norteamericano, Peru, 1997—, Art Internat., N.Y.C., 1998, Boston Printmakers, 1999—, Katonah Mus., N.Y., 1999—, Collage/Assemblage Soc., N.Y.C., 2000—02, Brand Libr. and Art Ctr., Glendale, Calif., 2001—, Springfield Art Mus., Mo., 2001, Stocker Ctr., Elyria, Ohio, 2001, U. Richmond, Va., 2002, N.W. Arts Coun./Ill. Arts Coun., Woodstock, 2002, Sothebeys, N.Y.C., 2002, Pacific States Biennial, Hilo, Hawaii, 2002, No. Ariz. U., Flagstaff, 2002, Multisensory Hera Gallery, Warwick, R.I., 2003, Warwick, 2004, Solarplate Traveling Exhibits, NY, Mass., Va., Maine, Conn., 2003, 2004, 2005, Zimmerli Mus., Rutgers U., N.J., 2004, Robert Blackburn Printmaking Workshop, N.Y., 2004, Taller Boricua, 2005, N.Y. Soc. Etchers, 2005, Gualala Arts Ctr., Calif., 2006, Bright Hills Art Ctr., N.Y., 2006; author numerous poems. Avocations: gardening, theater. Office Phone: 212-620-8103.

**PECKHAM, EUGENE ELIOT,** judge, lawyer; b. Stamford, Conn., Aug. 11, 1940; s. Joseph E. and Margaret (Nabors) P.; m. Judith Alice Chamberlain, Dec. 19, 1964; children: Margaret, Joseph, Elizabeth. BA with honors, Wesleyan U., Middletown, Conn., 1962; JD, Harvard U., 1965. Bar: N.Y. 1965, Fla. 1981, U.S. Tax Ct. 1974, U.S. Ct. Appeals (2d cir.) 1975, U.S. Dist. Ct. (no. dist.) N.Y. 1965. Assoc. Hinman, Howard & Kattell, Binghamton, N.Y., 1965-72, ptnr., 1972-2000; surrogate judge Broome County, N.Y., 2001—; acting justice N.Y. Supreme Ct. (6th jud. dist.), 2003—. Instr. Broome C.C., Binghamton, 1968-69, Am. Coll. Life Underwriters, Bryn Mawr, Pa., 1969-70, Am. Coll. Property and Casualty Underwriters, Bryn Mawr, 1970-71; adj. lectr. SUNY, Binghamton, 1972-77, adj. asst. prof., 1977-81, adj. assoc. prof., 1981-87, adj. prof. acctg., 1987—2003; vis. lectr. Cornell U., Ithaca, N.Y., 1978, adj. prof., 1984. Author: Warren's Heaton Surrogate's Courts, Federal and New York Estate Taxes, vol., revised, 1988, 89, Bender's Federal Tax Service " Income Taxation of Estates & Trusts", 1989; mem. bd. editors Warren's Heaton on Surrogate Courts, 2001-; contbr. articles to profl. jours. Peace Corps vol. tchr. Santa Maria U., Arequipa, Peru, 1966-67, treas. Joint Legis. Adv. Com. on Estates, Powers and Trusts Law and The Surrogates Ct. Procedure Act, 1990—; pres. Binghamton Girls Club, N.Y., 1974-76, bd. dirs., 1970-77; chmn. bd. Binghamton Boys and Girls Club, 1977, trustee, 1987-2000, chmn. bd. trustees, 1990-2005; bd. dirs. A. Lindsay and Olive B. O'Connor Found., 1982—, Dr. G. Clifford and Florence B. Decker Found., 1984-2001; bd. dirs. Comty. Found. South Ctrl. N.Y., 1996-2002; mem. trust fund. com. Broome County United Way, N.Y., 1979-94; pres. SUNY Found., Binghamton, 1977-79, bd. dirs., 1975-82; bd. dirs. Estate Planning Coun. So. Tier, 1983-87, treas., 1983, sec., 1984, v.p., 1985, pres., 1986; bd. dirs. Samaritan Counselling Ctr. So. Tier, Inc., 1982-87, v.p., 1986, pres., 1987; co-chmn. sta. WSKG-TV auction, 1983; treas. Roberson Ctr. Arts & Scis., 1980, bd. dirs., 1977-80, 87-95; bd. dirs. Twin Tier Home Health, Inc., 1990-97, v.p., 1991-93, pres., 1993-95; chmn. Broome County Cmty. Ambassador Project, 1970-71; mem. Broome Bd. Ethics, 1985-89, chair, 1999-2000; mem. Broome County Arena Bd., 1987-89; deacon 1st Presbyn. Ch., Binghamton, 1971-74, moderator, 1974, elder, 1975-78, 87-90, trustee, 1980-83, 92-95; exec. com. Broome County Rep. Com., 1980-83, 96-2000, co-chmn. fin. com., 1982-83, vice chmn., 1996-2000; pres. Broome County Young Rep. Club, 1969-70. Recipient SUNY-Binghamton Alumni Recognition award, 1984. Fellow Am. Coll. Trust and Estate Coun.; mem. N.Y. State Bar Assn. (exec. com. trusts and estates sect. 1980-84, 86-92, treas. 1986, sec. 1987, chmn. elect 1988, chmn. 1989, tax sect. 1972-2000, chmn. spl. commn. on alt. sources funding legal svcs. 1976-78, action unit 6 1984-86, ethics com. 1993-82, bd. editors N.Y. State Bar Jour. 1998—; v.p. 1999-2002, ho. dels. 1990-94, 95-2002), Fedn. Bar Assns. 6th Jud. Dist. (pres. 1984-85), Broome County Bar Assn. (chmn. prepaid legal ins. com. 1976-80, ethics com. 1981-87, chmn. jud. rating com. 1988-90). Home: 1 Stonecrest Ct Binghamton NY 13903 Office: Broome County Surrogate Ct PO Box 1766 Binghamton NY 13902-1766 Office Phone: 607-778-2118.

**PECKHAM, JOHN MUNROE, III,** investment executive, author, lecturer; b. Abington, Mass., July 25, 1931; s. John Munroe and Mildred P.; m. Ann M. Murphy, Apr. 30, 1995; children: Lisa, Holly, John M. IV. AB, Tufts U., 1955; postgrad., Columbia U., 1955-56. Pres. Peckham Boston Adv. Co., 1964—; pres., chmn. Boston Hall Corp., Boston, 1987—; pres. Boston Hall Pub. Co., 1988—; founder, exec. dir. Real Estate Cyberspace Soc., 1996—. Founder Realtors Concerned for Realtors, Chgo., 1986—; mem. bd. advisors Kids Stop, Boston, 1988-89; bd. dirs. Am. Fedn. for Children and Youth, L.A., 1988-89. Lt. comdr. USN, 1956-62. Mem. Nat. Assn. Realtors (v.p.), Realtors Nat. Mktg. Inst. (v.p. 1988), Internat. Fedn. Realtors, Inst. Real Estate Mgmt.,

Ten Club (pres. Boston chpt. 1974-79), Friends of Bill W. Republican. Baptist. Avocations: bicycling, swimming, cribbage, speaking, reading. Office: Real Estate Cyberspace Soc 4 Longfellow Pl Ste 2003 Boston MA 02114-2817

**PECKHAM, THOMAS ELWOOD,** lawyer; b. Arlington, Mass., Apr. 25, 1947; s. Alford S. and Janet (Gates) P.; m. Ellen A. Petersen, July 16, 1964; children: Samuel, Anne, Tavish, Duncan. BA, Brown U., 1969; JD, Boston U., 1972, LLM, 1976. Bar: Mass. 1972, U.S. Ct. Claims, U.S. Tax Ct. 1979, U.S. Supreme Ct. 1979, U.S. Dist. Ct. Mass., U.S. Ct. Appeals (1st cir.) 1982. Assoc. Goodwin, Procter & Hoar, Boston, 1976-83; ptnr. Segal, Moran, Feinberg, Peckham & Lobel, Boston, 1983-85; mng. ptnr. Peckham, Lobel, Casey, Prince & Tye LLP, Boston, 1985-99; ptnr. Bingham McCutchen LLP, Boston, 1999—, chmn. estate planning practice group. Contbr. articles to profl. publ. including Fun & Games with Split Interest Gifts, ALI-ABA Jour., others; lectr. in field. Adv. bd. Janet Gates Peckham Scholarship Fund; pres. Friends of the Marblehead (Mass.) Pub. Schs. Inc., 1994-97, mem. adv. bd., 1997—. Fellow Am. Coll. Trust and Estate Counsel; mem. ABA, Mass Bar Assns., Boston Bar Assn., Boston Estate Planning Coun., Boston Probate and Trust Forum. Office: Bingham McCutchen LLP 150 Federal St Boston MA 02110 Office Phone: 617-951-8954. Office Fax: 617-345-5094. Business E-Mail: tom.peckham@bingham.com.

**PECKOL, JAMES KENNETH,** consulting engineer; b. Cleve., Oct. 24, 1944; s. William John and Elinor Elizabeth (Bustard) P.; children: Erin, Robyn. BS Engring., Case Inst. Tech., 1966; MSEE, U. Wash., 1975, PhDEE, 1985. Cons. GE, Raytheon, Ling Temco Vought, RCA, Boeing Co., 1966-72; sr. staff engr. indsl. products bus. unit John Fluke Mfg. Co., Seattle, 1972-83, sr. staff engr. automated systems bus. unit, 1983-86, sr. staff engr. MR&D Bus. unit, 1986-93; founder Oxford Cons., Edmonds, Wash., 1987—. Affiliate asst. prof. elec. engring., affiliate asst. prof. dept. computers and software sys. U. Wash., Seattle, 1984-87, 95—, prof. dept. elec. engring., 1997—; sr. lectr., assoc. prof. dept. elec. engring. U. Aberdeen, Scotland, 1987; lectr. dept. math. and sci. Shoreline C.C., Seattle, 1989—; lectr. dept. computer sci. Edmonds (Wash.) C.C., 1992—; assoc. prof. dept. engring./computer sci. U. Nantes, Frances, 1993, 96; mem. computer sci. and elec. engring. curriculum adv. bd. Wash. State U., 1990—; lectr. various confs. and univs. Contbr. articles to profl. jours.; patentee in field. Mem. IEEE, Am. Assn. Artificial Intelligence, Assn. Computing Machinery, Tau Beta Pi. Home and Office: Oxford Cons Ltd 859 14th St SW Edmonds WA 98020-6611

**PECKOLICK, ALAN,** painter, graphics designer, photographer; b. NYC, Oct. 3, 1940; s. Charles and Belle (Binenbaum) P.; m. Jessica Margot Weber, June 3, 1984. AAS, Pratt Inst., Bklyn., 1968. Art dir. McCann-Erickson, 1964-68; graphic designer Herb Lubalin, 1968-72; v.p., creative dir. Lubalin, Smith, Carnase, Inc., N.Y.C., 1972-74, LCS & P Design Group, Inc., N.Y.C., 1974-76; pres. Lubalin Peckolick Assoc., N.Y.C., 1976-81, Pushpin, Lubalin, Peckolick, N.Y.C., 1981-86, Peckolick and Ptnrs., N.Y.C., 1986-89; design dir. Addison Design Cons., N.Y.C., 1989-91; chmn. Peckolick Inc., N.Y.C., 1991—; painter, 2000—. Bd. advisors Designworld mag., Victoria, Australia, 1983—, Herb Lubalin Study Ctr., N.Y.C.; lectr. Pratt Inst., Parsons Sch. Design, Sch. Visual Arts, also various orgns. Co-author, designer Herb Lubalin Graphic Designer, 1986; exhibitions include Sony Gallery, Tokyo, 1989, one-man shows include Gallery 468, N.Y.C., 2000, Agora Gallery, 2002, Lucky St. Gallery, Key West, Fla., 2001, 2003, 2004, Salamagundi Club Invitational, 2002, Gallery 468, N.Y.C., 2002, Agora Gallery, 2003, Photo Dist. Gallery, 2004, Fales Libr. at NYU, 2005, Cosa Gallery, London, 2004, Atlantic Gallery, N.Y.C., 2006, Hermes Gallery, 2006. Bd. dirs. Glaucoma Found., 1993, Whale Conservation Inst., 1994. Recipient awards AIGA, Art Directors Club awards. Mem. N.Y. Art Dirs. Club (6 gold medals, over 50 awards), N.Y. Type Dirs. Club (bd. dirs.), Alliance Graphique Internationale, Art Dirs.Club Bergen (Norway) (hon.). Avocations: sculpting, collecting art and prints, cooking, travel, photography. Home: 30 E 10th St New York NY 10003-6202 E-mail: alanart@verizon.net.

**PECORA, ANDREW LOUIS,** hematologist, oncologist; b. Newark, 1957; B magna cum laude, Seton Hall U.; MD, U. Medicine and Dentistry NJ 1983. Diplomate Am. Bd. Internal Medicine, Am. Bd. Hematology, Am. Bd. Med. Oncology. Intern NY Hosp.-Cornell Med. Ctr., NYC, 1983—84, resident in internal medicine, 1984—86; fellow in hematology and oncology Meml. Sloan Kettering Cancer Ctr., NYC; asst. dir. adult stem cell/bone marrow transplantation program Hackensack U. Med. Ctr., NJ, 1990—93, chief, program dir., 1993—, dir. stem cell collection and storage svc., 1993—, chmn., 1999—, chmn., dir. Cancer Ctr., 2001—. Clin. asst. hematology/oncology Hackensack U. Med. Ctr.; prof. medicine U. Medicine and Dentistry NJ Med. Sch. Named one of Top Drs. in N.Y. Metro Area, Castle Connolly, Top Drs. 2003, N.J. Monthly Mag. Office: The Cancer Ctr Hackensack U Med Ctr 20 Prospect Ave Ste 400 Hackensack NJ 07601-1962

**PEDACE, ROBERTO L.,** economics professor; BA in Econs., Calif. State U., San Bernardino, 1993; PhD in Econs., U. Calif., Riverside, 1999. Lectr. Scripps Coll., Claremont, Calif., 1998—99; economist U.S. Census Bur., Washington, 1999—2000; asst. prof. U. Redlands, Calif., 2001—05, assoc. prof., 2005—, chair dept. econs. 2005—06. Vis. asst. prof. Claremont McKenna Coll., Claremont, 2000—01. Contbr. articles to profl. jours., chapters to books. Grantee, John Randolph Haynes and Dora Haynes Found., 2005. Mem.: Western Econ. Assn. Internat., Latin Am. Studies Assn., Assn. Instl. Thought, Am. Econ. Assn. Office: University of Redlands 1200 East Colton Avenue Redlands CA 92373 Office Phone: 909-748-8569. Office Fax: 909-748-6294. E-mail: roberto_pedace@redlands.edu.

**PEDDABOINA, VENKATAIAH,** botanist, researcher; b. Warangal, India, May 5, 1970; s. Balaiah and Uppalamma Peddaboina; m. Kavitha Peddaboina, Mar. 23, 2000; children: Karthik, Vaishnavi. BS, MS in Botany, Kakatiya U., Andhra Pradesh, India; BEd, Osmania U., Andhra Pradesh, India; PhD, Kakatiya U., Andhra Pradesh, India. Asst. prof. Kakatiya U., Andhra Pradesh, India, 1997—. Home: # 2-11-424 Vidyanagarapuri Hanamkonda Warangal 506009 India Office: Kakatiya Univ Dept Botany Warangal 506009 India Office Phone: +01 9866272536. Office Fax: 2438800. E-mail: peddaboina@hotmail.com.

**PEDDICORD, ROLAND DALE,** lawyer; b. Van Meter, Iowa, Mar. 29, 1936; s. Clifford Elwood and Juanitas Irene (Brittain) P.; m. Teri Linn O'Dell; children: Erin Sue, Robert Sean. BSBA with honors, Drake U., 1961, JD with honors, 1962. Bar: Iowa 1962; cert. civil trial specialist Nat. Bd. Trial Advs.; cert. mediator Am. Acad. ADR Attys., 2000. Asst. atty. gen. State of Iowa, 1962-63; assoc. Steward, Crouch & Hopkins, Des Moines, 1962-65; ptnr. Peddicord, Wharton, Spencer & Hook, Des Moines, 1965—. Lectr. in law Drake U., 1962-68; lectr. law Coll. Osteo. Medicine, Des Moines, 1965-72. Editor and chief Drake Law Rev., 1961-62 Past mem. nat. bd. dirs., nat. coun. YMCA of U.S.A., past vice chmn. nat. bd.; bd. dirs., past chmn. Greater Des Moines YMCA, 1984-57. Mem. ABA, ATLA, Iowa Bar Assn., Polk County Bar Assn., Iowa Trial Lawyers Assn., Iowa Acad. Trial Lawyers, Am. Bd. Trial Advs. (mem. nat. bd., past pres. Iowa chpt.), Am. Acad. ADR Attys. (past pres.). Republican. Methodist. Office: 405 6th Ave Ste 700 Des Moines IA 50309-2415 also: Peddicord Wharton Spencer & Hook LLP PO Box 9130 Des Moines IA 50306-9130 Office Phone: 515-243-2100 ext. 515. Business E-Mail: dale.peddicord@peddicord-law.com.

**PEDEN, KEITH J.,** human resources specialist; b. Mich., May 1950; BA, Western Mich. U.; MA, Ea. Mich. U. Human resources staff Honeywell, Prime Computer; dir. worldwide compensation, benefits and human resources info. systems Lotus Devel. Corp.; v.p., head human resources Alexander & Alexander Consulting, Boston; dir. benefits, compensation, human resources mgmt. systems Raytheon Co., Lexington, Mass., 1993—97, v.p., dep. dir. human resources initiatives, 1997—2001, sr. v.p. human resources, 2001—

**PEDERSEN, CAROLYN HANFORD,** artist; b. Syracuse, NY, Dec. 12, 1942; d. George Warner and Kathryn (Fox) Hanford; m. Thomas Keith Pedersen, Aug. 15, 1964; children: Thomas Scott, Kirsten Heidi. BS in Edn., Syracuse U., 1964, BS in Audio. and Speech Pathology, 1964. Tchr. watercolor Rockland Ctr. for Arts, West Nyack, NY, 1987-92; adj. prof. watercolor Coll. of New Rochelle, NY, 1990—; represented by Piermont Fine Arts Gallery, NY; adj. prof. watercolor Seton Hall U., 1997—2000. Founding mem. Piermont (NY) Fine Arts Gallery, 1993—. Exhibited in group shows at Springfield (Mo.) Mus., Allied Artist, NYC, Audubon Artists, Mus. Fine Arts, Springfield, Mass., Neville Mus., Green Bay, Wis., Patterson (NJ) Mus., Watercolor West Riverside (Calif.) Mus., Bergen Mus., NJ, others; represented in permanent collections at Mus. Galleries of Hebrew Home for Aged, Riverdale, NYC, Rockland County, New City, NY, Legis. Chambers Art in Pub. Places, G.C. Hanford Mfg. Co., Syracuse, NY, Minigrip Corp., others; included in Splash America's Best Contemporary Watercolorists, 1991, 2000, The Best of Watercolor, 1995, Floral Inspirations, 1997, The Artistic Touch, 1999. Juror for local, regional and nat. art orgns.; demonstrator watercolors to various orgns.; pres., bd. dirs. Art and Craft Assn. Rockland, 1975-85; exhbn. com. Rockland Ctr. for Arts, West Nyack, 1988-91. Recipient Traveling Exhbn. award Am. Watercolor Soc., 1984, Dimauro Com. award Acad. Artists Assn., 1985, William Kowalsky Meml. award Adirondack Nat. Exhbn., 1985, The Best of Watercolor, 1995. Fellow Am. Artists Profl. League; mem. Nat. Watercolor Soc., Nat. Assn. Women Artists, N.E. Watercolor Soc. (membership chmn. 1989-91, President's award 1990), Artists Equity, Audubon Artists (Alice Melrose Meml. award 1989), Catherine Lorillard Wolfe Art Club (asst. treas. 1990-92, Katherine Lovell award 1985, 90).

**PEDERSEN, DARHL MAX,** psychology professor; b. Orem, Utah, Oct. 12, 1935; s. Max Barlow and Edith (Aiken) P.; 1 child, Clark. BS, Brigham Young U., 1957, MS, 1958; PhD, U. Ill., 1962. From asst. prof. psychology to prof. Brigham Young U., Provo, Utah, 1962—71, prof., 1971—, chmn. Dept. Psychology, 1967—77. Postdoctoral assoc. Ames Research Ctr., NASA, Moffett Field, Calif., 1969-70. Author: Psychological Tests and Measurements, 1965, Essentials for Understanding Statistics, 1978, Environmental Psychology, 1978, Learning Statistics, 1988; contbr. over 100 papers to profl. jours. V.p. Provo Coun. Boy Scouts Am., 1978-81, coun. commr., 1981-86. NSF fellow, 1962; recipient Creative Talent award Am. Inst. Rsch., 1962. Mem. Soc. for Sci. Study of Religion, Sigma Xi (ann. lecture 1973), Phi Kappa Phi, Psi Chi. Republican. Mem. Lds Ch. Avocation: outdoor activities. Home: 1815 N 1550 E Provo UT 84604-5709 Office: Brigham Young U 1090 SWKT Provo UT 84602 Office Phone: 801-422-6364. Business E-Mail: darhl_pedersen@byu.edu.

**PEDERSEN, DARLENE DELCOURT,** publishing executive, writer, psychotherapist; b. Westbrook, ME; 1 child, Jorgen David. BSN, U. Conn., 1967; postgrad., U. B.C., 1974-75; MSN, U. Penn., 1996—97. RN bd. cert. clinical specialist, advanced practice registered nurse, bd. cert. in adult psychiatric and mental health nursing. Am. Nurses Credentialing Ctr. Various nursing positions, psychiat. cmty. health, 1967-79; assoc. editor JB Lippincott Co., Phila., 1979-84; sr. acquisition editor WB Saunders Co., Phila., 1984-88, v.p., editor in chief, 1988-91, sr. v.p., editorial dir. books divsn., liaison to London office, 1991-95; domestic and internat. pub. cons. Phila., 1995—; psychotherapist pvt. practice, 1997—. Team leader Northwestern Human Svcs. Delaware County, 1998—99; dir. PsychOptions, 2000—; v.p. content ops. MedCases, Phila., 2000—03; exec. editor Thomson Physicians World, 2003—04; mng. editor FA Davis Co., Phila., 2004—. Author: Canadian Nurse, 1976, PsychNotes, 2005 (Book of Yr. award Am. Jour. Nursing, 2005); contbg. editor: (book) Basic Nursing Skills, 1977; acquisition editor: book Saunders Manual of Medical Practice, Comprehensive Cytopathology. Mem.: ANA, Internat. Soc. Traumatic Stress Studies, U.S. Dressage Fedn., Inc., Am. Orthopsychiat. Assn., Internat. Platform Assn., Assn. Profl. Comm. Cons., Manuscript Soc., Forum Exec. Women, Internat. Soc. Psychiat. Mental Health Nurses, Med. Mktg. Assn., Assn. Am. Pubs., Med. Mktg. Assn., Am. Med. Writers Assn., Am. Med. Pubs. Assn., Am. Psychiat. Nurses Assn., Am. Group Psychotherapy Assn., Emily's List, U. Club Penn., Sigma Theta Tau (Xi chpt.). Avocations: autograph and art collection, travel, music, reading, movies. Office: FA Davis Co 1915 Arch St Philadelphia PA 19103 Office Phone: 215-568-2074. Business E-Mail: ddp@fadavis.com.

**PEDERSEN, JAMIE D.,** lawyer; b. Puyallup, Wash., Sept. 9, 1968; s. Douglas Kirk and Audrey Mary (Draheim) P. BA summa cum laude, Yale U., 1990, JD, 1994. Bar: Wash. 1994. Law clk. Hon. Stephen F. Williams US Ct. Appeals, DC Cir.; ptnr. Preston Gates & Ellis LLP, Seattle; co-chair nat. bd. dirs Lambda Legal Defense & Edn. Fund, Inc. Outside gen. counsel McKinstry Co., Pacific Med. Ctr., Parametrix, Inc. Pres. Yale Russian Chorus, New Haven, 1992-94. Recipient Charles G. Albom prize Yale Law Sch., 1994; Nat. Merit scholar, 1986. Mem. Phi Beta Kappa. Democrat. Lutheran. Avocations: swimming, flute. Office: Preston Gates & Ellis LLP Ste 2900 925 Fourth Ave Seattle WA 98104-1158 Office Phone: 206-370-7987. Office Fax: 206-370-6152. E-mail: jamiep@prestongates.com.

**PEDERSEN, JEANNINE LYNN,** curator; d. Dean and Linda Pedersen. Bachelor's degree, Marquette U., 1996; Master's degree, Ea. Ill. U., 1998. Rsch. asst. Old World Wis., Eagle, Wis., 1996; hist. archivist Consol. Comm., Inc., Matoon, Ill., 1996—97; collections asst. Tempe (Ariz.) Hist. Mus., 1997—98; hist. cons. Lake County Pub. Adminstr. and Guardian's Office, Waukegan, 1998; curator Catalina Island Mus., Avalon, Calif., 1998—. Author: (book) Catalina by Sea: A Transportation History, Catalina Island, The Art of Catalina Clay Products; editor: The Casino; author: (newspaper column) I Was Wondering; exhbn., Catalina Steamers: In All the World No Trip Like This (Cert. of Commendation, Am. Assn. for State and Local History, 2001); contbr. articles to profl. pubs. Recipient Conservation and Mus. Exhbn. scholarship, Calif. Assn. of Mus., 2002. Mem. Hist. Admstrn. Program Assn. (chair nominating com. 2002—03), Am. Assn. for State and Local History (Calif. state chair for am. awards program 2000—04), Am. Assn. of Mus. (assoc.; bd. mem.-at-large 2004—06), Pi Gamma Mu (life), Phi Alpha Theta (life). Office: Catalina Island Mus PO Box 366 1 Casino Way Avalon CA 90704 Office Phone: 310-510-2414.

**PEDERSEN, JON ERLE,** education educator, dean; b. Fremont, Nebr., July 15, 1960; s. Earl and Virginia Pedersen; m. Conni Marie Tebo, Sept. 4, 1982; 1 child, Kailee Marie. BS, U. Nebr., 1982, MEd, 1988, PhD, 1990. Sci. tchr. Southeast HS, Lincoln, Nebr., 1984—88; prof. U. Ark., Fayetteville, 1990—95; prof., assoc. dean East Carolina U., Greenville, NC, 1995—2000, U. Okla., Norman, 2000—. Author (with A.O. Digby): Cooperative Learning: Theory and Practice, 1995; author: (with S. Totten) Social Issues and Community Service/Service Learning at the Middle Level, 1996, Researching and Teaching Social Issues: The Personal Stories and Pedagogical Efforts of Professors of Education, 2005; author: Stiquito for Beginners: An Introduction to Robotics-Teacher's Guide, 2000; contbr. articles to profl. jours., chapters to books. Named Outstanding Young Educator, 1986; recipient Outstanding Rsch. and Scholarship award, U. Okla. Coll. Edn., 2003; grantee, Carnegie Corp., 1991, Winthrop Rockefeller Found., 1992, NSF, 1993, Ark. Dept. Higher Edn. Eisenhower Funds, 1994, 1995, Thomas W. Rivers Endowment Fund, 1996, Eisenhower Title II Funds, 1997, US-Japan Found., Tokyo, 1999, EPSCOR, 2005, Okla. MSP, 2005; Foundn. for the Mid South Faculty fellow, 1998. Mem.: Nat. Assn. Sci. and Tech. Soc., Am. Edn. Rsch. Assn., Internat. Coun. for Assns of Sci. Educators (sect. editor 1998—2006), Assn. Sch. Sci. and Math., Assn. for Edn. of Tchrs. in Sci. (exec. sec. 1997—2003, bd. dirs 2005—), Nat. Sci. Tchrs. Assn., Nat. Assn. Rschrs. in Sci. Tchg., Rotary (study group to S.Am. 1987, bd. dirs.), Phi Beta Delta (pres. local chpt. 1997—99). Office: U Okla 820 Van Vleet Oval Norman OK 73019 Office Phone: 405-325-1081.

**PEDERSEN, KAREN SUE,** electrical engineer; b. Indianola, Iowa, Apr. 27, 1942; d. Donald Cecil and Dorothy Darlene (Frazier) Kading; m. Wendell Dean Pedersen, May 6, 1961; children: Debra Ann Pedersen Schwickerath, Michael Dean. BA in Math., Grand View Coll., Des Moines, 1975; BSEE, Iowa State U., 2007; MBA in Econ., Bentley Coll., Waltham, Mass., 1989. Registered profl. engr., Iowa, Mass., Ill. Engr. Iowa Power & Light Co., Des Moines, 1978—80, rate engr., 1980—84; sr. rsch. engr. Boston Edison Co., Boston, 1984—87, sr. engr., 1987—94, prin. rsch. analyst, 1994—98; sr. engr. MidAmerican Energy Co., Davenport, Iowa, 1998—2006; prin. Pedersen Power Solutions, Davenport, 2006—. Ops. chmn. Old South Ch., Boston, 1989-98. Recipient Disting. Svc. award, Iowa Engring. Soc., 2004. Mem. IEEE (chmn. Iowa ctrl. sect. 1983-84, sec. Iowa-Ill. sect. 2003), NSPE (v.p. 1999-2000, v.p. North Ctrl. region 2001-03, Outstanding Svc. award), Mass. Soc. Profl. Engrs. (pres. 1992-93), Eta Kappa Nu. Republican. Congregationalist. Avocations: golf, gardening. Office: Pedersen Power Solutions 2520 Hayes St Davenport IA 52803 Office Phone: 563-340-2139. Personal E-mail: kspedersen@mchsi.com. Business E-Mail: kspedersen@midamerican.com.

**PEDERSEN, KEITH ERNEST,** music educator; b. Innisfail, Can., Sept. 12, 1960; arrived in US, 1989; s. S. Rudolf Pedersen and Lucille A. Pedersen-Navy; m. Bettina Jane Tate, July 21, 1984; children: Kai Jordan Tate, Soren Christian Tate. BA in Music Edn., NW Nazarene U., Nampa, Idaho, 1983; MusM, Temple U., 1991; D of Musical Arts, U. Ill., 1997. Music tchr. Lindsay Thurber Comprehensive HS, Red Deer, Alta., Canada, 1983—89; music dir., condr. Vermilion Festival Chorus, Danville, Ill., 1991—96; assoc. dir. Danville Symphony Orch., 1993—94; choir dir. Univ. Pl. Christian Ch., Champaign, Ill., 1994—97; choir master Episcopal Ch. of the Transfiguration, Arcadia, Calif., 1997—98; prof. Point Loma Nazarene U., San Diego, 1998—; dir. of choral ministries La Jolla (Calif.) Presbyn. Ch., 2001—. Guest condr. Pacific Acad. of Eccliastical Music, San Diego, 2003—04. Mem.: Nat. Assn. Ch. Musicians (bd. dirs. San Diego chpt.), Am. Choral Dirs. Assn. Avocations: bicycling, reading. Business E-Mail: kpederse@ptloma.edu.

**PEDERSEN, KNUD GEORGE,** retired economics professor, academic administrator; b. Three Creeks, Alta., Can., June 13, 1931; s. Hjalmar Neilsen and Anna (Jensen) P.; m. Joan Elaine Vanderwarker, Aug. 15, 1953 (dec. 1988); children: Greg, Lisa; m. Penny Ann Jones, Dec. 31, 1988. Diploma in Edn., Provincial Normal U., 1952; BA, U. B.C., 1959; MA, U. Wash., 1964; PhD, U. Chgo., 1969; LLD (hon.), McMaster U., 1996; DLitt (hon.), Emily Carr Inst. of Art and Design, 2003; LLD (hon.), Simon Fraser U., 2003, U. No. B.C., 2005. Asst. prof. econs. of edn. U. Toronto; asst. prof. econs. of edn., assoc. dir. U. Chgo., 1970-72; dean, assoc. prof., then prof. U. Victoria, B.C., 1972-75, acad. v.p., prof., 1975-79; pres., vice-chancellor, prof. Simon Fraser U., Vancouver, B.C., 1979-83, U. B.C., Vancouver, 1983-85; pres., vice-chancellor U. Western Ont., London, Can., 1985-94, prof. econs. of edn., 1985-96; interim pres. U. No. B.C., 1995; founding pres., vice-chancellor Royal Roads U., 1995-96; chancellor U. No. B.C., 1998—2004; vice chmn. bd. govs. Emily Carr Inst. Art and Design, 2004—05, chmn. bd. govs., 2005—. Bd. dirs. Assn. Univs. and Colls., Canada, 1979—84, chmn., Canada, 1989—91; bd. dirs. Vancouver Bd. Trade, 1983—85; pres. Can. Club Vancouver, 1983—84; mem. coun. trustees Inst. for Rsch. on Pub. Policy, Ottawa, Ont., Canada, 1983—89; chmn. Coun. Ont. Univs., 1989—91. Author: The Itinerant Schoolmaster, 1972; contbr. chpts. to books, numerous articles to profl. jours. Chmn. B.C. (Can.) Region Can. Cystic Fibrosis Found.; mem. Min. Advanced Edn. Adv. Com. Decorated officer Order of Can., Order of Ont., Order of B.C.; recipient 125th Anniversary of Confedn. of Can. medal, Queen's Jubilee medal; fellow Ford Found., 1965-68, Can. Coll. Tchrs., 1977, Royal Soc. for Encouragement of Arts, 1984; also 11 major scholarships. Mem. Semiahmoo Golf and Country Club, Loomis Trail Golf and Country Club. Avocations: golf, fishing, gardening, cooking, art. Personal E-mail: pedersen@sfu.ca.

**PEDERSEN, LEE G.,** chemistry professor; b. Oklahoma City, June 15, 1938; s. Leonard Melnot Pedersen and Naomi Shinn; m. Barbara L. Pedersen; children: Lars, Kurt. B in Chemistry, U. Tulsa, 1961; PhD in Chemistry, U. Ark., 1965. From asst. prof. to prof. chemistry U. N.C., Chapel Hill, 1967—, now M.A. Smith prof. chemistry. Cons. NIEHS, Research Triangle Park, N.C., 1985—. Author: Problems in Quantum Chemistry and Physics, 1974. NSF fellow, Columbia U., N.Y.C., 1965-66, NIH fellow Harvard U., Boston, 1966-67. Office: Dept Chemistry U NC Chapel Hill CB 3290 Chapel Hill NC 27599 Office Phone: 919-962-1578.

**PEDERSEN, PAUL BODHOLDT,** psychologist, educator; b. Ringsted, Iowa, May 19, 1936; BA in History and Philosophy, U. Minn., 1958, MA in Am. Studies, 1959; ThM, Luth. Sch. Theology, Chgo., 1962; MA in Edn. Psychology, U. Minn., 1966; PhD in Asian Studies, Claremont (Calif.) Grad. Sch., 1968. Asst. prof. dept. psychoednl. studies, psychologist U. Minn., Mpls., 1971-75; sr. fellow Culture Learning Inst. East-West Ctr., Honolulu, 1975-76, sr. fellow coord., 1975-76; assoc. prof. dept. psychoednl. studies, psychologist U. Minn., 1975-79, higher edn. coord., 1976-77; sr. fellow Culture Learning Inst. East-West Ctr., 1979-81; prof., chmn. dept. counselor edn. Syracuse (N.Y.) U., 1982-90, prof. edn. dept. counseling and human svcs., 1989—95, adj. prof. dept. internat. rels., 1993—95, prof. emeritus, 2000—; prof. counseling edn. U. Ala., Birmingham, 1996-2001. Vis. lectr. Nommensen U., Medan, Sumatra, Indonesia, 1962—65, U. Malaya, 1969—71; vis. prof. dept. psychology U. Hawaii, 1978—81, 2000—; spkr. in field. Author numerous books, chpts. in books, articles to profl. jours.; mem. editl. bd. Am. Jour. Multicultural Counseling and Devel.; editl. advisor Jour. Profl. Psychology, Jour. Simulation and Games, Internat. Jour. Intercultural Rels. Sr. Fulbright fellow Nat. Taiwan U., Taipei, 1999-2000. Mem. APA, Am. Assn. Counseling and Devel. Internat. (mem. rels. com., editl. bd. Jour. Counseling and Devel., editor Internationally Speaking newsletter, mentor media com.), Internat. Assn. for Cross Cultural Psychology, Internat. Coun. Psychologists, Soc. Intercultural Tng. and Rsch. (exec. com., program chairperson 1977, chairperson Pacific Coun. 1977, pres. 1978-80, editl. bd. Jour. Intercultural Rels.). Home: 1550 Ala Moana Blvd Apt 1306 Honolulu HI 96814-4221 Office Phone: 808-589-2662.

**PEDERSEN, PAUL MARK,** sportswriter, educator, columnist; b. Stratton, Nebr., Sept. 21, 1970; s. Harold Clifford and Cassandra Sue Pedersen; m. Jennifer Lynn Estes, May 31, 1991; children: Hallie Susannah, Zack Paul, Brock Victor, Carlie Elizabeth. AA in Bibl. Studies, Hobe Sound Bible Coll., Hobe Sound, Fla, 1990; BSBA, Palm Beach Atlantic U., West Palm Beach, Fla., 1992; MA in History, U. Ctrl. Fla., Orlando, 1993; MA in Bus. Comm. and Pub. Rels., Emerson Coll., Boston, 1997; PhD in Sport Mgmt., Fla. St. U., Tallahassee, 2000. Lic. FCC Broadcasting Fed. Comm. Comm./Washington, 1993. Sportswriter, agate clk. Palm Beach Post, West Palm Beach, Fla., 1996—98, sports corr., 1998—2002; comm. instr. Palm Beach Atlantic U., 1997—98, asst. prof. sport mgmt., 2003—05; grad. tchg., rsch. asst. Fla. State U., Tallahassee, 1988—2000, sport mgmt. instr., 2001—01; asst. prof. sport mgmt. Bowling Green State U., Ohio, 2001—03; assoc. prof. sport com. Ind. U., Bloomington, 2005—. Presider Fla. AAHPERD Conf., Orlando, 2000; book rev. editor Academic Athletic Jour., 2001—03; sports bus. columnist Treasure Coast Bus. Jour., Stuart, 2003—05; mem. editl. bd. Internat. Jour. Sport Mgmt., 2004—, Internat. Jour. Sport Mgmt. and Mktg., 2005—; pres., founder Premier Sports Cons., LLC, 2004—. Author: Build It and They Will Come: Arrival of the Tampa Bay Devil Rays, 1997, Bobby Bowden: Win by Win, 2003; editor: Sport and Law Press, 2004; contbr. articles to profl. jour. Recipient Outstanding BS Grad., Palm Beach Atlantic U., 1992. Mem.: North Am. Soc. for Sport Mgmt., Fla. Alliance for Health, Phys. Education, Recreation, and Dance (pres.-sport 2004—05), Phi Kappa Phi, Phi Alpha Theta. Office: Ind U 1025 E 7th St HPER 170 Bloomington IN 47405 Office Phone: 812-855-4066.

**PEDERSEN, PEDIE,** physiology educator; b. Milan, Tenn., Apr. 12, 1948; d. E.E. and Bettye M. Pedersen. BA, Rhodes Coll., 1970; MS, U. Ala., 1972; BS, U. New Orleans, 1977; PhD, Tulane U., 1986. Tchr. biology Holy Name Sch. and Chapelle H.S., New Orleans, 1978-81; vis. instr., postdoctoral fellow Tulane U., New Orleans, 1986-87; asst. prof. physiology Delgado C.C., New Orleans, 1987-91, assoc. prof., 1991—. Author: Human Anatomy and Physiology: Lecture Outlines and Self Tests I and II, 1995. Mem. Human Anatomy and Physiology Soc., Sweet Adelines, Sigma Xi. Office Phone: 504-483-4426.

**PEDERSEN, PEER,** lawyer; BS, U. Ill., 1947, JD, 1948. Bar: Ill. 1949. Assoc. Arrington & Healy; founding ptnr. Pedersen & Houpt, 1957—. Bd. dirs. Delray Farms, Inc., Fla. Office Property Co., Inc., Home Access Health Corp., Martin Brower Co., River East Devel., Spraying Systems Co., Tempel Steel Co., Tennis Corp. Am. Pres. Robert R. McCormick Boys and Girls Club; bd. dirs. Boys and Girls Club Chgo., Children's Meml. Hosp., Children's Meml. Found., Rehabilitation Inst. Chgo., Lyric Opera Chgo. Served USN, WWII. Mem.: ABA, Ill. State Bar Assn., Chgo. Bar Assn., Law Club. Office: Pedersen & Houpt 161 N Clark Ste 3100 Chicago IL 60601-3242

**PEDERSEN, RICHARD FOOTE,** diplomat, academic administrator; b. Miami, Ariz., Feb. 21, 1925; s. Ralph Martin and Gertrude May (Foote) P.; m. Nelda Newell Napier, May 9, 1953; children: Paige Elizabeth, Jonathan Foote, Kendra Gayle. BA summa cum laude, Coll. of Pacific, 1946; MA, Stanford U., 1947; PhD, Harvard U., 1950; LLD (hon.), George Williams Coll., 1964, U. of Pacific, 1966; DHL (hon.), Am. U., Cairo, 1997. Teaching fellow, tutor Harvard U., Cambridge, Mass., 1949-50; with UN econ. and social affairs Dept. State, Washington, 1950-53; adviser econ. and social affairs U.S. Mission to UN, N.Y.C., 1953—55, adviser polit. and security affairs, 1956-59, sr. advisor polit. and security affairs, 1959-64, minister, counselor, 1964-66, ambassador, sr. adviser to U.S. rep., 1966-67; ambassador, dep. U.S. rep. UN Security Coun., N.Y.C., 1967—69; counselor Dept. State, 1969-73; ambassador to Hungary, 1973-75; sr. v.p. internat. U.S. Trust Co., 1975-78; pres. Am. U., Cairo, 1978-90; dir. internat. programs Calif. Poly Pomona U., 1990-95. Mem. adv. bd. Nat. Coun. U.S.-Arab Rels., 1985—; trustee Consortium for Internat. Devel., 1990—95; mem. adv. bd. Ctr. Near Eastern Studies UCLA, 1996—99; adv. bd. Sch. Internat. Studies, U. Pacific, 1997—. Mem. Nat. Coun. YMCAs, 1961-73; bd. dirs. Ctr. for Civic Edn., 1995—; Physicians for Peace, 1988-90; mem. Fulbright bd., Egypt, 1980-82, adv. bd. Fulbright Cultural Enrichment Program, So. Calif., 1991—2001. With AUS, 1943-45 ETO. Recipient Sumner Peace prize Harvard U., 1950, Outstanding Alumnus award U. Pacific, 1962, Order of Sacred Treasure, Gold and Silver Star, Govt. of Japan, 1987; named One of 10 Outstanding Young Men, U.S. Jr. C. of C., 1956; awarded Order of Scis. and Arts, first class Govt. of Egypt, 1990. Mem. Coun. Fgn. Rels., Am. Soc. Internat. Law, L.A. World Affairs Coun., Am. Fgn. Svc. Assn., Mid. East Inst., Oriental Inst., UN Assn. Am., Internat. Assn. Univ. Pres., Pacific Coun. Internat. Policy, Asia Soc. Clubs: Harvard (N.Y.); Cosmos (Washington). Democrat. Congregationalist. Avocations: swimming, tennis, egyptology, local history. Home: 2503 N Mountain Ave Claremont CA 91711-1545 E-mail: rfpdrsn@earthlink.net.

**PEDERSEN, WESLEY NIELS M.,** public relations and public affairs counselor; b. South Sioux City, Nebr., July 10, 1922; s. Peder Westergaard and Marie Gertrude (Sorensen) P.; m. Angeline Kathryn Vavra, Oct. 17, 1948; 1 son, Eric Wesley. Student, Tri-State Coll., Sioux City, Iowa, 1940-41; BA summa cum laude, Upper Iowa U.; postgrad. in Russian, George Washington U., 1958—59. Editor, writer Sioux City Jour., 1941-50; corr. N.Y. Times, Life, Time, Fortune, 1948-50; editor Dept. State, 1950—52, fgn. svc. officer Hong Kong, 1960-63; fgn. affairs columnist, roving corr., counselor summit meetings and fgn. ministers confs. USIA, 1952—60, chief, worldwide spl. publs. and graphics programs, 1963-69; chief Office Spl. Projects, Washington, 1969-78, Office Spl. Projects, Internat. Comm. Agy. 1978-79; v.p. Fraser Assocs., pub. rels., Washington, 1979-80; dir. comm. and pub. rels. Pub. Affairs Coun., Washington, 1980—2006; prin. Wes Pedersen Comms., 2006—. Lectr. creative comm. Upper Iowa U., 1975; chmn., Europe, Ambassadorial Internat. Affairs Seminar, Fgn. Svc. Inst., 1975; lectr. internat. pub. rels. Pub. Rels. Inst., Am. U., 1976; lectr. bus. and mgmt. divsn. NYU, 1976-78; cons. pub. rels., editl. and design; del. founding sessions 1st Amendment Congress, Phila. and Williamsburg, Va., 1980, exec. com., 1980. Columnist: (as Paul L. Ford) The World Today, 1952-60; (as Benjamin E. West) Behind the Curtain, 1952-60; White House Report, 1966-69 (as Wesley Pedersen), Washington Report-Pub. Rels. Jour., 1980-85; author: Mr. President: Lyndon B. Johnson, 1964, Legacy of a President, 1964, Journey to the Pacific, 1965, Mr. President: Richard M. Nixon, 1969, American Heroes of Asian Wars, 1969; co-author: Effective Government Public Affairs, 1981; editor: The Imam's Story, 1961, Escape at Midnight and Other Stories (Pearl S. Buck), 1962, Exodus From China (Harry Redl), 1962, Macao, 1962, The Dividing Line (Arturo Gonzalez), 1962, China's Men of Letters (K.E. Priestley), 1963, Children of China (Pearl S. Buck and Margaret Wylie), 1963, Destination the Moon (William Howard), 1964, Man on the Moon, 1964, Nine From Little Rock, 1964, To the Moon and Beyond, 1965, Bounty From the Land, 1965, Workers Paradise Lost (Eugene Lyons), 1967, The Americans and the Arts (Howard Taubman), 1969, The Dance in America (Agnes de Mille), 1969, Getting the Most From Grassroots Public Affairs Programs, 1980, Computer Applications in Public Affairs, 1984, Cost-Effective Management for Today's Public Affairs, 1984, Making Community Relations Pay Off: Tools and Strategies, 1988, Winning at the Grassroots: How to Succeed in the Legislative Arena by Mobilizing Employees and Other Allies, 1989, Leveraging State Government Relations, 1990, Managing the Business-Employee PAC, 1992, Adding Value to the Public Affairs Function, 1994, Winning at the Grassroots (with Tony Kramer), 2000, Managing the Corporate Political Action Committee, 2001; Pub. Affairs Rev. Mag., 1980-86, 2000, 01, 02, 03, 04, 05, Impact newsletter on nat. and internat. pub. affairs, 1980—2006; contbr. to The Commissar, 1972, Informing the People: A Public Affairs Handbook, 1981, The Practice of Public Relations, 1984, 2d edit., 2003; mem. editl. bd. Pub. Rels. Quar., 1975—, Washington editor, Pub. Rels. Quar., 1998—, Fgn. Svc. Jour., 1975-81; mem. editl. adv. bd. Pub. Rels. News, 1991-98, contbg. editor Pub. Affairs News Mag., London, 2004—; author scripts Uncle Walter's Doghouse radio show, 1938; contbr. articles to profl. jours. Founding chmn. bd. dirs. Nat. Inst. for Govt. Pub. Info. Rsch., Am. U., 1977-80. Served with USAAF, 1943-46. Recipient 3 awards A.P. Mng. Editors Assn., Iowa, 1948-49, Meritorious Svc. award USIA, 1963, Superior Svc. award USIA, 1964, Presdl. commendation, Iowa, 70, 1st prize Fed. Editors Assn., 1970, 74-75, Agy. Dir.'s citation USIA, 1965, 74, 78, Soc. Tech. Comm., 1974-76, Gold award Internat. Newsletter Conf., 1982, Silver award, 1985, Eddi award for design excellence Editor's Workshop, 1983, Gold Circle award Am. Soc. Assn. Execs., 1983-89, 97-2000, Ten Cool award Am. Soc. Assn. Execs., 2001, Editors' Forum award, 1988-90, 94-96, Assn. Trends award 1989-2005, Lifetime Great Assn. Communicator award, Assn. Trends, 1999, Best of Century Comm. award, Assn. Trends, 2001, spl. citation Assn. Trends, 2001, Silver award 2004, 05, Gold award, 2004, Excellence award, 2006, Grand prize Internat. Ann. Report Conf., 1989, Gold award 1997, Comm. Concepts awards, 1989-2006, Grand Comm. Concepts awards, 1992, 95, 2000, 02, 04, 05, 06, MerComm awards, 1990-2000, Nat. Media Conf. award, 1989, 90, Internat. Acad. Comm. Arts and Scis. award, 1994-98, 2000, Grand prize, 1995, awards Printing and Graphic Assn., 1987, 91, 96-97, 2000, Excell award Soc. of Nat. Assn. Publishers, 2000, Judges' award 2000; named Most Outstanding Info. Officer in Exec. Br. Govt. Info. Orgn., 1975, Ky. Col. and Adm. Nebr. Navy, 1984; inducted into PRSA Hall of Fame Nat. Capital Divsn., 2005. Mem. DAV, Am. Fgn. Svc. Assn., Am. Legion, Internat. Assn. Bus. Communicators (Communicator of Yr. Washington chpt. 1978, various awards 1973, 76-78, 84, 90, 94-2004, Winners' Circle awards dist. III 1996-2003), Nat. Assn. Govt. Communicators (pres. 1978-79, Communicator of Yr. 1977, Disting. Svc. award 1978), Pub. Rels. Soc. Am. (mem. Counselor's Acad. 1980—, chmn. 1st Amendment task force 1980-81, co-recipient Thoth award 1980-81, 94, twin Thoth awards 1995-97, 2003, Thoth awards 1998-2003, Bronze Anvil award 2000, named to Hall of Fame 2005), Am. Soc. Profl. Communicators (Colonial award 2002, Masters award 2004), World Affairs Coun., Soc. Profl. Journalists, The Acad. Polit. Sci., Fgn. Svc. Club, Nat. Press Club, Overseas Press Club. Episcopalian. Office: Wes Pedersen Comms and Pub Rels 4701 Willard Ave Ste 1007 Chevy Chase MD 20815-4622 Office Phone: 301-718-9191. Personal E-mail: wesped@comcast.net, editorwes@hotmail.com. *Keenness of mind and an abundance of luck, it is said, are the key ingredients of personal success. The truth be told, however, I've performed only one act of brilliance in my lifetime: the selection of my parents. But I've had an enormous amount of good fortune, a fact manifestly clear to anyone who has ever met my wife, my son and my granddaughters. They, thank goodness, chose me.*

**PEDERSEN, WILLIAM FRANCIS,** lawyer; b. NYC, Apr. 4, 1943; s. William F. and Priscilla S. (Auchincloss) P.; m. Ellen L. Frost, Feb. 2, 1974; children: Mark Francis, Claire Ellen. BA, Harvard U., 1965, LLB, 1968. Bar: Mass. 1969, D.C. 1978. Assoc. Ropes & Gray, Boston, 1969-72; staff atty. EPA, Washington, 1972-75; dep. gen. counsel, then assoc. gen. counsel, 1976-85; staff counsel Senate Com. on Govt. Ops., Washington, 1975-76; lectr. Harvard Law Sch., 1985-86; of counsel Perkins Coie, Washington, 1987—89, ptnr., 1989-94, Shaw, Pittman, Potts & Trowbridge, Washington, 1994-2001; pvt. practice Washington, 2001—. Vis. prof. Law Sch., U. Mich., 1997-98. Contbr. articles to profl. jours. Mem. ABA (standing com. on environ. law 1987-89). Republican. Episcopalian. Office: William F Pedersen PLLC Ste 1350 1615 L St NW Washington DC 20036 Office Phone: 202-296-8884. Business E-Mail: bill.pedersen@billpedersen.com.

**PEDERSON, DONALD OTIS,** academic administrator, physicist, educator; s. Otis A. and Dorothy Rose Pederson; m. Kathryn Elizabeth Werner; children: Julie Renée, Michael Andrew. BS, Tex. Tech U., Lubbock, 1965—66; PhD, Rice U., Houston, 1966—71. Robert A. Welch Found. postdoctoral fellow, part-time physics instr. Tex. Tech U., Lubbock, 1971—72; asst. prof. physics U. Ark., Fayetteville, 1972—78, assoc. prof. physics, 1978—84, prof. physics, 1984—, chmn. dept. physics, 1978—83, assoc. dean fulbright coll., 1983—85, acting chief academic officer, 1985—86, vice-chancellor academic affairs, 1986—98, vice chancellor fin. & adminstrn., 1998—. Mem., officer Ark. Sci. & Tech. Authority, Little Rock, 1988—97. Contbr. articles to profl. jours. Mem.: Am. Assn. Physics Tchrs. (nat. rep. 1975—79), Am. Phys. Soc., Sigma Pi Sigma, Sigma Xi. Avocations: running, genealogy. Office Phone: 479-575-5828.

**PEDERSON, GORDON ROY,** state legislator, retired military officer; b. Gayville, S.D. Aug. 8, 1927; s. Roy E. and Gladys F. (Masker) P.; m. Betty L. Ballard, Mar. 8, 1955; children: James D., Carol A. Pederson Niemann, Nancy G. Pederson Holub, Gary W. Student, Yankton Coll., 1948-50, Fla. State U., 1963; advanced course, Infantry Sch., 1958-59. Drafted U.S. Army, 1945-47, commd. 2nd lt., 1952, advanced through grades to lt. col., 1967, served CONUS World War II, platoon leader 17th infantry regiment, 7th infantry divsn. Korea, 1953-54, served Korean War, 1950-54, rifle co. commdr. 10th mountain divsn. Germany, 1955-58, instr., dir. instrn. U.S. Army Jungle Warfare Tng. Ctr. Ft. Sherman, Canal Zone, 1961-63, comdr. post, 1963-64, 1st brig., 1st infantry divsn. Vietnam, 1965—66, dir. tng. hdqs. G3, Ft. Leonard Wood, 1966—68; advisor Ministry of Nat. Def., Rep. China on Taiwan, 1969-70; retired U.S. Army, 1970; operator Elkton Ho. Post, 1971—78; rep. S.D. Ho. Reps., Pierre, 1977-99, 2001—; operator Dairy Queen, Wall, SD, 1990-95. Chmn. transp. com. S.D. Ho. Reps., 1979-93, vice chair state affairs com., 1996-98, vice chair commerce com., 1998, chmn. budget audit com., 2001-2002, chmn. transp. com., 2002—. Del. S.D. Rep. Conv., 1974-78, 80, 82, 84, 86, 88, 90, 92, 94, 96, 98, 2000, 02, 04, Nat. Rep. Conv., 1976, 80, 84, 88, 92, 96, 2000, 04; bd. dirs. Legis. Rsch. Coun., 1988, 90, 92, 96, 98, 2001-02, 05-06. Decorated Bronze Star, Medal of Merit, U.S. Presdl. Unit Citation, Rep. Korea Presdl. Unit Citation, Rep. Vietnam Presdl. Unit Citation, Combat Infantry Badge with Star, Legion of Merit, Air Medal with 2 Oak Leaf Clusters, Army Accomodation medal with 2 oak leaf clusters, Cross of Gallantry with Palm, Republic Vietnam. Mem. VFW, DAV, Am. Legion, Retired Officers Assn., Wall C. of C., Internat. Lions Club, Sons of Norway. Lutheran. Home: PO Box 312 116 W 7th St Wall SD 57790 Office: SD Ho of Reps State Capitol Bldg Pierre SD 57501 Office Phone: 605-279-2610. Fax: 605-279-2609. Business E-Mail: bpers@gwtc.net, rep.gordonpederson@state.ussd.

**PEDERSON, JOHN MARTIN,** education educator; b. Lanigan, Saskatchewan, Can., Nov. 23, 1969; s. Lee Denise Pederson and Marjorie Christine Benson Pederson. BA, Concordia Coll., 1992; MA, U. N.D., 1994; PhD, U. Nebr., 1998. Asst. prof. Mayville State U., ND, 1998—2004, assoc. prof., 2004—. V.p., faculty rep. to Acad. Affairs Coun. N.D. U. Sys., 2003—04, pres. coun. coll. faculties, 2004—05, faculty advisor, state bd. of higher edn., 2005—. Coun. mem. Mayville Luth. Ch., ND, 2005; synod coun. mem. Ea. ND Synod of the Evang. Luth. Ch. in Am., Fargo, 2005. Mem.: Sons of Norway (v.p. 2005). Lutheran. Home: 114 6th Ave SE Mayville ND 58257 Office: Mayville State Univ 330 Third St NE Mayville ND 58257

**PEDERSON, PATRICIA VELDE,** education educator, consultant; BS, SD State U., 1979; MA, U. Minn., 1987, PhD, 1998. Tchr. Am. Sch. of Kuwait, 1979—81; instr. Am. Cmty. Sch., Abu Dhabi, United Arab Emirates, 1981—83; social studies tchr. Am. Embassy Sch., New Delhi, 1983—85; lead social studies tchr. Khartoum Am. Sch., Sudan, 1987—90; lead tchr. Am. Embassy Sch., 1990—94; sr. dir. Harcourt Assessment, San Antonio, 1998—2005; asst. prof. edn. Am. U. of Beirut, 2005—. Editor (content editor): (achievement test) Metropolitan Achievement Tests; contbr. articles to profl. jours. Mem.: ASCD, NCSS Internat. Assembly, NCSS Coll. and U. Faculty Assn., Nat. Coun. for the Social Studies, Am. Ednl. Rsch. Assn. Avocations: jogging, reading, travel. Office: Am Univ of Beirut PO Box 11-0236 Beirut 56433 Lebanon Office Phone: 961-1-350-000-3116. Home Fax: 961-1-744-461; Office Fax: 961-1-744-461. Business E-Mail: pp02@aub.edu.lb.

**PEDERSON, SALLY,** lieutenant governor; b. Muscatine, Iowa, Jan. 13, 1951; d. Gerald and Wineva Pederson; m. James A. Autry, Feb. 6, 1982; children: Rick, Jim Jr., Ronald. Grad., Iowa State U., 1973. With Meredith Corp., 1973-84; sr. food editor Better Homes & Gardens mag.; lt. gov. State of Iowa, Des Moines, 1999—. Pres. Polk County Health Svcs.; bast bd. trustees Nat. Alliance for Autism Rsch.; bd. trustees Autism Soc. Iowa; founding pres. The Homestead Living and Learning Ctr. for Adults with Autism; past cmty. bd. svcs. includes Des Moines Cmty. Playhouse, Very Spl. Arts Iowa, YWCA Aliber Child Care Ctr., YMCA Ctr. Br.; named rep. Heartland AEA Autism Steering Com.; mem. Iowa State Spl. Edn. Adv. Bd; bd. dirs. Blank Children's Hosp., Mid-Iowa Health Found.; gov.'s appointee State Spl. Edn. Adv. Panel. Democrat. Office: Office of Lt Governor Rm 9 State Capitol Bldg Des Moines IA 50319-0001 Office Phone: 515-281-0225. Office Fax: 515-281-6611.*

**PEDERSON, TONY WELDON,** newspaper editor; b. Waco, Tex., Oct. 27, 1950; s. Lloyd Moody and Ida Frances (Walker) P.; m. Julianne Kennedy, Mar. 21, 1974 BA, Baylor U., 1973; MA, Ohio State U., 1976. Sports writer Waco (Tex.) Tribune, Tex., 1970-73; sports writer Houston Chronicle, 1974-75, copy editor, 1976-80, sports editor, 1980-83, mng. editor, 1983-99; exec. editor and sr. v.p. Houston Chromicle, 2000—. Adj. faculty U. Houston, 1977-79 Mem. Houston Com. Fgn. Rels. Mem. Nat. AP Mng. Editors Assn.; Tex. AP Mng. Editors Assn. Methodist. Avocations: golf, reading. Office: Houston Chronicle Pub Co 801 Texas St Houston TX 77002-2996

**PEDERSON, WILLIAM CHRISTOPHER,** plastic surgeon; b. Texas City, Tex., July 15, 1952; s. Alton Curtis and Lucy Vernor (Windham) P.; m. Cynthia Lea Anderson, June 17, 1978; children: Liv, Anton, Candice. BA, U. Tex., 1974, MD, 1978. Hand fellow U. Louisville, 1984; rsch. fellow Duke U. Med. Ctr., Durham, N.C., 1985; microsurgery rsch. fellow St. Vincent's Hosp., Melbourne, 1986; asst. prof. plastic surgery Duke U. Med. Ctr., Durham, 1087-89; chief of plastic surgery U. Tex. Health Sci. Ctr., San Antonio, 1989—. Contbr. articles to profl. jours. Bd. dirs. C.E. Homeowner's Assn., San Antonio, 1990—. Fellow ACS (assoc.); mem. Am. Soc. Plastic and Reconstructive Surgery, Am. Assn. Hand Surgery, Am. Soc. Reconstructive Microsurgery.

**PEDESCLEAUX-MUCKLE, GAIL,** retired business analyst, writer, artist; b. Cleve., June 20, 1949; d. Alfonso Pedescleaux and Belle Pinkard Pedescleaux; m. Kirk Muckle, Oct. 24, 1997; 1 stepchild, Christopher Corey Muckle. BA in English Lit., Ctrl. Mich. U., 1971. Acct. asst. Travelers Ins. Co., Southfield, Mich., 1972—79, underwriter Garden City, NY, 1979—81, Commerce and Industry, N.Y.C., 1981—83; sr. underwriter Firemans' Fund, N.Y.C., 1983—85; bus. analyst Am. Internat. Group, N.Y.C., 1985—94, sr. quality assurance analyst Livingston, NJ, 1994—2000, sr. bus. analyst

Parsippany, NJ, 2000—04; ret., 2004. Cons. in field; patient rep. JFK Family Practice, 2005—. Author: (anthology) America at the Millennium, 2000 (Editor's Choice, 2000), Poetry's Elite: The Best Poets of 2000, 2001 (Editor's Choice, 2001), Throwing Stardust, 2003 (Editor's Choice, 2003), Celebrating Poetry, 2003, Theatre of the Mind, 2003, The Best Poems and Poets of 2003, 2003, Colours of the Heart, 2004, Twilight Musings, 2005 (Editors Choice award, 2005). Mem. DAV: Comdr.'s Club, 1993—, Nat. Multiple Sclerosis Soc., 1994—, Nat. Trust, 1993—, Am. Mus. Natural History, 1996, Nat. Civil Rights Mus., 2002, So. Poverty Law Ctr., 2002, Susan G. Komen Breast Cancer Found., 2003; patient rep. JFK Family Medicine, 2005; decorating cons. Jazzercise, 2005—. Mem.: Acad. Am. Poets, Edison Arts Soc., N.Y.C. Ballet Guild, Nat. Mus. Women in the Arts, Met. Mus. Art. Avocations: jazzercise, photography, writing, theater, writing children's stories and poetry. Home: 54 Rainford Rd Edison NJ 08820-2903 Personal E-mail: pedymuck@msn.com.

**PEDIGO, PAUL F.,** lawyer; b. Chattanooga, Tenn., Oct. 22, 1954; BA in English, Vanderbilt Univ., 1976, BS in Chem. Engring., 1980; JD, Loyola Univ., 1985. Bar: Ill. 1986, NC 1988, registered: US Patent and Trademark Off. 1984. Ptnr., leader, Chem. and Pharm.Patent Solicitation Group Alston & Bird LLP, Charlotte, NC. Mem.: Am. Intellectual Property Law Assn., Carolinas Patent, Trademark and Copyright Law Assn. Office: Alston & Bird LLP Ste 4000 Bank of Am Plz 101 S Tryon St Charlotte NC 28280-4000 Office Phone: 704-444-1021. Office Fax: 704-444-1111. Business E-Mail: ppedigo@alston.com.

**PEDINI, EGLE DAMIJONAITIS,** radiologist; b. Kaunas, Lithuania, July 22, 1943; d. Vytautas and Elena Damijonaitis; m. Kenneth Pedini, June 4, 1966; children: David Durand, Julian Adam. BA cum laude, Boston U., 1967, MD, 1967. Diplomate Am. Bd. Radiology. Intern St. Elizabeth's Hosp., Brighton, Mass., 1967—68; resident in radiology Boston City Hosp., 1968—71; radiologist St. John's Hosp., Lowell, Mass., 1972, Chelmsford X-Ray, Mass., 1979—80, Amesbury Hosp./Amesbury Health Ctr., Mass., 1973—98, New Eng. Meml. Hosp./Boston Regional Med. Ctr., Stoneham, Mass., 1973—98, Anna Jacques Hosp., Newburyport, Mass., 1973—98. Ptnr. NE Radiology Assocs., Brockton, Mass., 1980-98; chief radiology Anna Jacques Hosp., Newburyport, Mass., 1984, Amesbury Hosp., 1988, 89, 90. Founder, bd. dirs. Andover Sch. Montessori, Mass., 1974-79; parent ann. fundraising com. Phillips Exeter (N.H.), 1985, 86, 87. Mem. Am. Coll. Radiology, Mass. Radiol. Soc., New Eng. Roentgen Ray Soc., Stonehorse Yacht Club, Chatham Women's Club, Garden Club Harwich.

**PEDINI, KENNETH,** radiologist; b. Hartford, Conn., Mar. 19, 1940; s. Daniel Victor and Elizabeth Catherine Pedini; m. Egle Damijonaitis; children: David D., Julian A. AB in Philosophy, Trinity Coll., 1962; MD, Boston U., 1966. Diplomate Nat. Bd. Med. Examiners, Am. Bd. Radiology. Resident in radiology Boston City Hosp., 1967—70, chief resident in radiology, 1969—70, jr. staff radiologist, 1970—71, U. Hosp., Boston, 1970—71; ptnr. Shawsheen Radiology, Andover, Mass., 1971—98; sr. radiologist Lawrence Gen. Hosp., Mass., 1971—, dir. radiology, 1976—87; sr. radiologist Melrose-Wakefield Hosp., Mass., 1971—99, chief radiologist, 1993—97, emeritus staff, 1999; pres. L & M Radiology Inc, Andover, Mass., 1994—98. Bd. trustees Lawrence Gen. Hosp., 1984-89, fin. com., 1986-03. Mem. Townwide Water Quality Mgmt. Task Force, 2001—, Class XI, Greater Naples Leadership, Inc., 2006; trustee Lawrence Gen. Hosp. Health Enterprises, Inc., 1990—93; mem. fin. com. Lawrence Gen. Regional Health Sys., 1996—2003; mem. alumni adv. com. Trinity Coll., 1995; co-founder Andover Sch. Montessori, 1975—. Fellow Am. Coll. Radiology (councilor 1979-81); mem. New Eng. Roentgen Ray Soc., Mass. Radiol. Soc. (pres. 1985-86, pres.-elect 1984-85, v.p. 1983-84, exec. com. 1977-87), Mass. Med. Soc., Stonehorse Yacht Club, Algonquin Club. Personal E-mail: wychview@comcast.net.

**PEDLEY, JOHN GRIFFITHS,** archaeologist, educator; b. Burnley, Eng., July 19, 1931; arrived in U.S., 1959, naturalized, 1963; s. George and Anne (Whitaker) Pedley; m. Mary Grace Sponberg, Aug. 30, 1969. BA, Cambridge U., Eng., 1953, MA, 1959; postgrad. (Norton fellow), Am. Sch. Classical Studies, Greece, 1963-64; PhD, Harvard U., 1965. Loeb rsch. fellow in classical archaeology Harvard U., Cambridge, Mass., 1969-70; asst. prof. classical archaeology and Greek U. Mich., Ann Arbor, 1965-68, assoc. prof., 1968-74, acting chmn. dept. classical studies, 1971-72, 75-76; dir. Kelsey Mus. Archaeology, 1973-86, prof., 1974—2002, prof. emeritus, 2002—. Guest scholar J. Paul Getty Mus.; mem. staff excavations, Sardis, Turkey, 1962—64, Pylos, Greece, 1964; co-dir. excavations, Apollonia, Libya, 1966—68; field dir. Corpus Ancient Mosaics, Tunisia, 1972—73; co-prin. investigator excavations, Paestum, North Africa, 1975—79; dir. excavations, Paestum, Italy, 1982—85, Paestum, 1993, Paestum, 95; vis. scholar UCLA, 1989; resident in archaeology Am. Acad., Rome, 1990. Author: (book) Sardis in the Age of Croesus, 1968, Sardis in the Age of Croesus, reprint, 1999, Ancient Literary Sources on Sardis, 1972, Greek Sculpture of the Archaic Period: The Island Workshops, 1976, Paestum: Greeks and Romans in Southern Italy, 1990, Greek Art and Archaeology, 1992, Greek Art and Archaeology, 3d edit., 2002, Sanctuaries and the Sacred in the Ancient Greek World, 2005; co-author: Apollonia, the Port of Cyrene, 1977, The Sanctuary of Santa Venera at Paestum, Vol. 1, 1993, Corpus des Mosaiques de Tunisie, Vol. III, 1996; editor: New Light on Ancient Carthage, 1980; co-editor: Studies Presented to GMA Hanfmann, 1971. Fellow Am. Coun. Learned Socs., 1972—73, NEH, 1986; grantee, Am. Philol. Soc., 1979, Nat. Endowment Arts Mus., 1974, 1977, 1979, 1980, NEH, 1967, 1975, 1983, 1984. Home: 1720 Morton Ave Ann Arbor MI 48104-4522 Office: Dept Classical Studies Univ Mich Ann Arbor MI 48109 E-mail: jpedley@umich.edu.

**PEDLEY, LAWRENCE LINDSAY,** lawyer; b. Hopkinsville, Ky., May 27, 1932; s. Gracean McGoodwin and Elizabeth (Lindsay) Pedley; m. Ellen Mack, Oct. 9, 1957 (div. 1981); children: Lawrence Lindsay Jr., David M., Joan Elizabeth; m. Jill Flick, 1981 (div. 1991); 1 child, Jill Katharine; m. Wanda Polk, Feb. 3, 1995. BA, The Citadel, S.C., 1955; JD, Yale U., 1959. Bar: Ky. 1959, Fla. 1980, U.S. Dist. Ct. Ky. 1959, U.S. Ct. Appeals (6th cir.), 1975, U.S. Supreme Ct. 1981. Prin. atty. Ky. Dept. of Hwys., Frankfort, 1960; v.p. Nat. Industries, Louisville, 1964-66; gen. counsel, v.p., dir. Life Ins. Co. Ky., Louisville, 1966-69; ptnr. Goldberg & Pedley, Louisville, 1970-80, Pedley, Zielke, Gordinier and Pence, Louisville, 1980—. Owner Exec. Express, Louisville, 1969—80. Capt. JAGC, 1967. Mem. ABA, Ky. Bar Assn., Fla. Bar Assn., Filson Club, Harmony Landing Country Club, Pendennis Club. Office: Pedley Zielke Gordinier and Pence 2000 Meidinger Tower 462 S 4th Ave Louisville KY 40202-2512 Office Phone: 502-589-4600.

**PEDLEY, TIMOTHY ASBURY, IV,** neurologist, educator, researcher; b. Phoenix, Aug. 31, 1943; s. Timothy Asbury Pedley III and Mary Adele (Newcomer) Melis; m. Barbara S. Koppel, Mar. 17, 1984. BA, Pomona Coll., 1965; MD, Yale U., 1969. Cert. neurology, electroencephalography, clin. neurophysiology; diplomate Am. Bd. Psychiatry and Neurology. Intern Stanford U. Hosp., 1969-70, resident in neurology, 1970—73, postdoctoral fellow, 1973-75; asst. prof. neurology Stanford U., 1975-79; from assoc. prof. neurology to prof., vice chmn. Columbia U., 1979-98, Henry and Lucy Moses prof., chmn. neurology, 1998—; neurologist-in-chief Columbia U. Med. Ctr., N.Y.C., 1998—. Dir. comprehensive epilepsy ctr. Columbia U. Med. Ctr., 1983-97. profl. adv. bd. Epilepsy Found Am., 1984-98, chmn. profl. adv. bd., 1985-87, pres. bd. dirs., 1991-93, chmn. 1993-95. mem. rev. com. NIH Nat. Inst. Neurol. and Chronic Diseases and Strokes, 1985-89, chmn., 1988-89; various adv. coms. NIH/NINDS, 1990-98; vis. fellow in exptl. neurology Inst. Psychiatry, London, 1978-79; mem. merit rev. bd. neurobiology rsch., VA, 1992-96. chmn., 1995-96; vis. prof. various univs., U.S. and abroad. Editor-in-chief: Epilepsia, 1993—2001; contbr. articles to profl. jours. Fellow AAAS, N.Y. Acad. Medicine; Recipient various honors and awards. Fellow Am. Acad. Neurology (sec. bd. trustees 2003—), Am. Electroencephalographic Soc. (pres. 1989-90, bd. dirs 1981-85), Royal Soc. Medicine; mem. Am. Neurol. Assn. (coun. 1992-94, treas. 1995-98, first v.p. 2003-04, pres.-elect 2005-), Am. Epilepsy Soc. (treas. 1980-83, pres. 1991-92), Soc. Neurosci., Internat. League Against Epilepsy (exec. com. 1994-02), Vidonian

Club, Yale Club, N.Y. Med. Surg. Soc., Shenorock Shore Club, Alpha Omega Alpha. Office: The Neurological Inst 710 W 168th St New York NY 10032-2603 Office Fax: 212-305-6978. Business E-Mail: tap2@columbia.edu.

**PEDOWITZ, MARK,** broadcast executive; b. Bklyn., 1953; m. Carolyn Martin. BA in history, Rockford Coll.; JD, John Marshall Law Sch. Atty. MCA Inc., 1979—80; v.p. bus. affairs Reeves Entertainment Group/Alan Landsburg Prodns., 1980—85; v.p. bus. affairs, gen. counsel Landsburg Co., 1985—87; sr. v.p. bus. affairs & adminstrn. MGM/UA TV Prodn. Group, 1987—91; sr. v.p. bus. affairs & contracts ABC Entertainment; sr. v.p. bus. affairs ABC Entertainment TV Group Walt Disney Co., exec. v.p. bus. affairs & adminstrn., ABC Entertainment TV Group, 1998—, pres. Touchstone TV Burbank, Calif., 2004—. Mem.: Hollywood Radio and TV Soc. (past mem. exec. bd.), Acad. TV Arts and Scis. (found bd. dirs., past mem. exec. bd.). Office: Touchstone TV 500 S Buena Vista St Burbank CA 91521

**PEDROSA, VERONICA,** journalist; b. Manila, Philippines; d. Carmen Navarro Pedrosa; m. Mark Phillips; children: Gabriel, Isabel. Grad., Cambridge U. Television reporter, presenter, prodr. ABS-CBN, Manila; reporter BBC World Television, BBC World Svc. Radio, London; news anchor CNN Internat., Atlanta, news anchor Asia, 2000—05, co-anchor World News Asia; news anchor Al Jazeera Internat., Kuala Lumpar, Malaysia, 2005—. Named Best News Anchor, Asian Television Awards, 2004. Mailing: c/o Al Jazeera International PO Box 23127 Doha Qatar*

**PEDROTTI, LENO STEPHANO,** physics professor; b. Zeigler, Ill., May 21, 1927; s. Celeste Louis and Dolores (Galeaz) P.; m. Wilma Jean Sullivan, June 23, 1951; children—Daro Stephano, Michael Louis, Sandra Maria, Laura Jean, Catherine Ann, Leno Matthew, Mary Ann, John Owen. BS in Edn, Ill. State U., 1949; MS in Physics, U. Ill., 1951; PhD, U. Cin., 1961. Teaching asst. U. Ill., Urbana, 1949-51; prof. physics, chmn. dept. Air Force Inst. Tech., Wright-Patterson AFB, Ohio, 1951-82, prof. emeritus, 1982—; cons., editor Ctr. Occupational Rsch. & Devel., Waco, Tex., 1975-82, sr. v.p., 1982—. Presenter in field, 1982—; author, editor, lectr. laser and electro-optics Engring. Tech., Inc., Waco, 1978—; mem. indsl. adv. com. laser electro-optics program Cin. Tech. Coll., 1981-82; tech. cons. Univ. Eye Surgeons, Inc., Ohio State U., 1979-82; mem. exec. com. joint svcs. optical program Optical Scis. Ctr., U. Ariz., 1975-82. Author: Principles of Technology, 1986, Introduction to Optics, 1987, rev. edit., 1992, Applied Mathematics, 1988, Optics and Vision, 1998; contbg. author Technical Prep Associate Degree: A Win/Win Experience, 1991, The Science Technology, Society Movement, 1993; contbr. articles to profl. jours. Fellow Faculty fellow, NSF, 1959. Fellow Optical Soc. Am.; mem. Am. Nuclear Soc., Am. Phys. Soc. (vice chmn. then chmn. Ohio sect. 1974-76), Laser Inst. Am. (bd. dirs. 1974-84), Am. Assn. Physics Tchrs., Am. Soc. Engring. Edn., Am. Vocat. Assn. (Outstanding Mem. award 1988 vocat. instrnl. materials affiliate Ednl. Exhibitor Assn.-SHIP citation for outstanding commitment to vocat.-tech. edn. 1994), Nat. Coun. Tchrs. Math., Sigma Xi, Tau Beta Pi (Outstanding Tchr. award 1961, 62, 63, 68), Sigma Pi Sigma. Home: 11006 Trailwood Dr Waco TX 76712-3131 Office: CORD 601 Lake Air Dr Waco TX 76710-5841 Office Phone: 254-741-8392. Business E-Mail: Pedrotti@cord.org.

**PEDROW, BRENDA M.,** language educator; b. NYC, Aug. 31, 1942; d. Howard and Stella Stevenson; m. Donald P Pedrow, Aug. 25, 1962; 1 child, Brian D; 1 child, Bradley D. BA in history, Millersville U., 1980. Tutor Millersville U., Millersville, Pa., 1978—80; tchr. Adult Sch. for Cuban Refugees, Lebanon, Pa., 1980, Linden Hall Sch. for Girls, Lititz, Pa., 1981—82; tutor Conestoga Valley Sch. Dist., Lancaster, Pa., 1984—87; tchr. Lancaster Sch., 1985; ESL tchr. Am. Home Life Internat., Lancaster, Pa., 1989; tchr. Manheim Twp. Sch. Dist., Lancaster, 1986—2000. Bd. mem. Lancaster Lit. Coun., 1980—86. Rschr. Interfaith Rels. Lancaster County Human Rels. Commn., 1972; org. fundraiser Lancaster Cmy. Action Program, 1976; founder First Internat. Club, Manheim Twp. H.S. Recipient Cert. Appreciation, Adult Edn. Cuban Refugees, 1980, Exceptional Svc. award, Boy Scouts Am., 1971, Cmty. Svc. award, Cmty. Action Program, 1980. Mem.: Pa. Assn. Sch. Retirees, Nat. Edn. Assn. Avocations: exercise, travel, reading. Home: 6121 Geneva Dr East Petersburg PA 17520

**PEDUZZI, CLAUDIA CLAIRE,** elementary school educator; b. Westerly, RI, Apr. 10, 1952; d. Everett Orlando and Claire Eve Peduzzi. BA, U. RI, 1974; MEd, RI Coll., 1991, MEd, 1993. Reading specialist, cons. East Providence (RI) Sch. Dist., 1990—93, Chariho Sch. Dist., Wood River Junction, RI, 1993—. Mem.: RI Reading Assn., Internat. Reading Assn. Avocations: reading, gardening, walking, cooking, sewing. Business E-Mail: Claudia.Peduzzi@chariho.k12.ri.us.

**PEEBLES, ALLENE KAY,** manufactured housing company executive; b. Waukegan, Ill., Feb. 9, 1938; d. Allan Laverne and Kathryn Bernice (McGill) Sedlmayr; m. William Ross Peebles, July 9, 1960; children: Ross William, Robb Allan, Raymond John, Renda Kay (Mrs. Christopher Sivak). BS with high honors, U. Wis., 1960, MS, 1967; grad., Realtors Inst., 1968. Cert. home economist. Tchr. Horicon (Wis.) High Sch., 1960-61, Oconomowoc (Wis.) High Sch., 1961-67; freelance writer, 1967-70; v.p. Luxury Homes, Inc., Watertown, Wis., 1970-93, Land Devel. Plus Devel. Inc., Watertown, 1970—; co-developer Hidden Meadows Condominium Community, Watertown, 1976-96; ptnr. W and A Elderly Housing Ltd. Partnership, Watertown, 1988—; pres. Housing Am., Inc., Watertown, 1991—2003. Gen. ptnr. Sunrise Housing Ltd., 1990—; builder new and rehab low-income housing, 1983-2003 Active Wis. Gov.'s Conf. on Family, 1980, long range planning team, 1996—2003; dist. membership chmn. Boy Scouts Am., 1984—90; chmn. Ams. Abroad Am. Field Svc., Oconomowoc, 1982—87; del. Wis. Rep. Conv., 1997—; chmn. adminstrv. bd. United Meth. Ch., Oconomowoc, 1974—77, 1996—99, lay leader, 2000—03, pres. United Meth. Women, 2002—06, chmn. family ministry Wis. Conf., del. Wis. conf., 2000—03. Recipient Dist. award of Merit Potawatomi Area coun. Boy Scouts Am., 1986; named Woman of Yr., United Meth. Women, 2003. Mem.: AAUW (pres. Oconomowoc br. 1981—83, pres. Oconomowoc 1983—85, officer's bd. 1984—93, fin. advisor 1995—2002), NAFE, Wis. Assn. Family and Consumer Scis. (state bd. 1999—, state housing chmn. 2000—02), Met. Builders Assn. Greater Milw., Internat. Fedn. Home Economists (USA internat. del. 1997—), Wis. Manufactured Housing Assn. (bd. dirs. 1979—90, chmn. bd. 1985—88, Mem. of Yr. award 1986), Wis. Builders Assn., Waukesha Bd. Realtors, Wis. Assn. Realtors, Am. Assn. Family and Consumer Scis., Nat. Assn. Realtors, Wis. Home Economists in Bus. (state chmn. 1987—88, internat. rep. 1998—2000, Home Economist in Bus. of Yr. 1987), Internat. Profl. and Bus. Women, Nat. Assn. Home Builders, Nat. Home Economists in Bus. (internat. com. 1985—87, regional U.S. advisor 1990—92), Wis. Home Econs. Assn. (parliamentarian 1984—99), Am. Home Econs. Assn., Phi Lambda Theta, Kappa Omicron Nu, Phi Upsilon Omicron, Phi Kappa Phi. Republican. Avocation: writing. Home: 37788 Mapleton Rd Oconomowoc WI 53066

**PEEBLES, CHRISTOPHER SPALDING,** anthropologist, educator, academic administrator; b. Clearwater, Fla., May 26, 1939; s. Frederick Thomas and Corinne deGarmendia (Stephens) P.; m. Laura Ann Wisen, Oct. 6, 1993. AB, U. Chgo., 1963; PhD, U. Calif., Santa Barbara, 1974. Asst. prof. U. Windsor, Ont., Canada, 1970-74; asst. curator U. Mich., Ann Arbor, 1974-81; prof. prehistory U. Amsterdam, Netherlands, 1981-82; prof. Ind. U., Bloomington, 1983—, dean acad. computing, assoc. v.p., 1992—. Author: Excavations at Moundville, 1974, Representations in Archaeology, 1992 With USAF, 1956-60. Mem. Cosmos Club. Avocation: flying. Office: Ind U Glenn A Black Lab 423 N Fess Bloomington IN 47408-3800 Office Phone: 812-855-9544. Business E-Mail: peebles@indiana.edu.

**PEEBLES, E(MORY) B(USH), III,** lawyer; b. Hattiesburg, Miss., May 3, 1943; s. E.B. Jr. and Lee (Baldwin) P.; m. Celeste H. Hodges; children: E.B. IV, Catharine Celeste, Thomas Hill. BA, Vanderbilt U., 1965; JD, U. Ala., 1967. Bar: Ala. 1967, U.S. Dist. Ct. (so. dist.) Ala., U.S. Ct. Appeals (5th and 11th cirs.), U.S. Supreme Ct. Assoc. Armbrecht, Jackson, DeMouy, Mobile,

Ala., 1967-72, ptnr., 1972—. Bd. dirs. South Ala. area bd. Am. South Bank. Mem. Ala. Securities Commn., 1989-93; chmn. sports com. Mobile Area C. of C., 1988-90; bd. dirs. Am.'s Jr. Miss Orgn., Mobile, 1983-90; active Mobile area coun. Boy Scouts Am., 1979—; mem. Sr. Bowl Com., Mobile, 1978—; chmn. trustees Nat. Maritime Mus. of the Gulf of Mexico; trustee United Way, Mobile, 2003—. bd. dirs. Mobile Area Conv. and Visitors Bur., 2003—. Mem. ABA (chmn. fin. svcs. com., tort and ins. practice sect. 1989-90, comml. fin. svcs. com. bus. law sect. 1984—), Ala. Bar Assn., Maritime Law Assn. U.S., Southea. Admiralty Law Inst., Internat. Bar Assn., Am. Soc. Internat. Law, Inter-Am. Bar Assn., Ala. Law Inst. (mem. governing coun. 1975—, corp. law com., letters of credit com.), Mobile Touchdown Club (pres. 1987-88), Mobile Area C. of C. (bd. dirs. 2000—). Office: 1300 Riverview Plz Mobile AL 36602

**PEEBLES, PEYTON ZIMMERMANN, JR.,** electrical engineer, educator; b. Columbus, Ga., Sept. 10, 1934; s. Peyton Zimmermann Peebles Sr. and Maida Erlene Dials; m. Barbara Ann Suydam, Sept. 6, 1969; children: Peyton Zimmermann III, Edward Arlen. BSEE, Evansville Coll., 1957; MSEE, Drexel Inst., 1963; PhD, U. Pa., 1967. Design engr. RCA, Moorestown, NJ, 1958-64, systems engr., 1966-69; prof. U. Tenn., Knoxville, 1969-75, 76-81; vis. prof. U. Hawaii, Honolulu, 1975-76; prof. U. Fla., Gainesville, 1981-84, 90-96, assoc. chmn., 1984-90, prof. emeritus, 1996—. Cons. in field. Author: Communication System Principles, 1976, Probability, Random Variables and Random Signal Principles, 1980, 4th edit., 2001, Digital Communication Systems, 1987; prin. author: Principles of Electrical Engineering, 1991, Radar Principles, 1998; contbr. articles to profl. jours.; patentee in field. Capt. USAFR, 1957-61. David Sarnoff fellow, 1964-66. Fellow IEEE (life); mem Sigma Xi, Eta Kappa Nu, Tau Beta Pi, Sigma Pi Sigma, Phi Beta Chi. Methodist. Avocations: fishing, painting, woodworking. Business E-Mail: ppeeb@ece.ufl.edu.

**PEEK, JEFFREY M.,** corporate financial executive; BA in Internat. Affairs, Princeton U., 1969; MBA, Harvard Bus. Sch., 1972. With Merrill Lynch, 1983—2002; exec. v.p. Merrill Lynch & Co., Inc., 1997—2001; pres. Merrill Lynch Investment Managers, 1997—2001; vice chmn. Credit Suisse First Boston LLC, 2002—03; pres., COO CIT Group Inc., Livingston, NJ, 2003—04, pres., CEO 2004—05, chmn. CEO, 2005—. Treas. NYC Ballet; chmn. advisory coun. Bendheim Ctr. for Fin.; bd. dirs. CIT Group, Travelers Property Casual Corp., Freddie Mac, 2005—, NJ Performing Arts Ctr.; bd. trustees Teachers Coll, Columbia U. Office: CIT Group 1 CIT Dr Livingston NJ 07039*

**PEEL, HARRIS,** retired small business owner; b. Decatur, Ill., Nov. 14, 1923; s. Wilbur David Peel and Ruth Harris; m. Margaret Backus, Oct. 11, 1946 (dec. Nov. 1990); children: Susan Harris, Jane Peel Fuller, David Harris. BS, Columbia U., 1950; MS, George Washington U., 1967. Editor War Dept., Frankfurt, Germany, 1946; writer Holiday Mag., Europe, 1947-48; fgn. svc. officer U.S. Dept. State and USIA, various locations, 1950-74; owner Peel Gallery Fine Art, Danby VT, Mar., 1976—2005. Author: (book) History of 254th Infantry Regiment, 1945. Advisor on psychol. warfare U.S. Army and USN, Ft. Bragg, N.C., 1971-74. Cpl. U.S. Army, 1943-45. Decorated Bronze star with oak leaf cluster U.S. Army, 1945, Disting. Civilian Svc. medal U.S. Army; 4-yr. scholar Chgo. Tribune, 1941. Mem. Vt. Assn. Galleries (pres. 1978-98), Overseas Press Club. Avocation: astronomy. Home: 1 Peel Rd Danby VT 05739 Office: Peel Gallery Peel Rd Danby VT 05739 E-mail: hpeel@vermontel.net.

**PEEL, MARK,** chef, restaurant owner; b. Calif. children: Vanessa, Benjamin, Oliver. Student, Calif. Poly. U. Former apprentice Ma Maison, L.A.; former mem. staff La Tour d'Argents, Moulin de Mougins; former sous chef Michael's, Santa Monica, Calif.; former mem. staff Chez Panisse, Berkeley, Calif.; head chef Spago, Hollywood, Calif., 1985—89; co-owner, chef Campanile, L.A., 1989—. Author (with Nancy Silverton): Mark Peel and Nancy Silverton at Home. Two Chefs Cook for Family and Friends, The Food of Campanile. Nominee Best Am. Chef, Calif., James Beard Found., 1990, 1995, 1996; named Restaurateur of Yr., So. Calif. Restaurant Writers, 1995; named one of Best New Chefs, Food & Wine Mag., 1989; recipient Best Am. Chef, Calif., James Beard Found., 2001, 2002, 2004. Office: Campanile 624 S La Brea Ave Los Angeles CA 90036

**PEELE, KATHERINE N.,** architect; BArch (summa cum laude), NC State U., 1988. With Boney, PLLC, Raleigh, NC, 1988—, dir. Raleigh office, 1992—, COO, 2002—. Sch. constrn. support com. Wake County Pub. Sch. Sys. Fellow: AIA (pres. 2000, chair com. arch. edn. 2001, adv. bd. nat. com. arch. edn.); mem.: NC Ednl. Facility Planners (pres. 1999). Office: 5511 Capital Ctr Dr Ste 105 Raleigh NC 27606 Office Phone: 919-851-9393. E-mail: knp@booneyarchitects.com.

**PEELE, ROGER,** hospital administrator; b. Elizabeth City, N.C., Dec. 24, 1930; s. Joseph Emmett and Catherine (Groves) P.; m. Diana Egan, June 15, 1963 (dec.); children: Amy, Rodney, Holly; m. Gail Nelson Oct. 15, 1992. AB, U. N.C., 1955; MD, U. Tenn., 1960. Cert. adminstrv. psychiatry, 1970 cert. forensic psychiatry, 1982. Intern St. Elizabeths Hosp., Washington, 1960-61, resident in psychiatry, 1961-64, tng. officer, 1964-67, chief of service William A. White div., 1967-69; dir. Area D Community Mental Health Center, 1969-73, asst. supt., 1974-75, 77-79, acting supt., 1975-77, chmn. dept. psychiatry, 1979-95. Clin. prof. George Washington U., 1979—; asst. dir. NIMH, 1978-79; chief clin. officer D.C. Commn. on Mental Health, 1987-91; med. dir. Northern Va. Mental Health Ctr., 1996-98; attending George Washington U., 1998-2001; chief psychiatrist Montgomery County, Md. Contbr. articles on clin., forensic and adminstrv. issues in Am. psychiatry to profl. jours. Served with USAF, 1950-53. Superior Service award IIEW 1967. Fellow Am. Coll. Psychiatry, Am. Psychiat. Assn. (speaker 1986-87, Adminstr. of Yr. 1989); mem. AMA, D.C. Med. Soc., Am. Assn. Psychiat. Adminstrs. (past pres.), Group for Advancement Psychiatry, Med. Soc. St. Elizabeth's Hosp. (past pres.), Fed. Physicians Assn. (past pres.). Episcopalian. Home: 413 King Farm Blvd Apt 401 Rockville MD 20850 Office Phone: 240-777-3351. Personal E-mail: RogerPeele@aol.com. *A key to effective treatment is not to allow the seductiveness of logic to narrow one's observations.*

**PEELER, BOB,** lieutenant governor; b. Gaffney, South Carolina, 1952; s. Smith and Sally (Bratton) P.; m. Bett (Carter); children: Caroline, Robert, Jr. V.p. Peeler's Milk Now Peeler Bros. Dairy, Cattle Co.; former chmn. Cherokee County Sch. Bd., S.C. State Bd. Edn.; lt. gov. State of S.C., 1995—. Founding mem. Advancement Bd. Coll. Commerce, Clemson Univ. Mem. S.C. Dairy Assn. (past pres.),;Cherokee County C. of C. (past pres.); Sertoma Internat. (life); Rotary (Gaffney chpt.); Masons; York Rite. Republican. Methodist.

**PEELER, STUART THORNE,** gas industry executive, consultant; b. Los Angeles, Oct. 28, 1929; s. Joseph David and Elizabeth Fiske (Boggess) P.; m. Sylvia Frances Townley, Nov. 5, 1985. BA, Stanford U., 1950, JD, 1953. Bar: Calif. 1953. Ptnr. Musick, Peeler & Garrett, L.A., 1958-73; with Santa Fe Pacific Corp., Orange, Calif., 1973-81, v.p., sec., assoc. gen. counsel, 1973-74, sr. v.p., gen. counsel, dir., 1975-81; vice-chmn. bd., chmn. exec. com. Supron Energy Corp., 1978-82; chmn. bd., CEO Statex Petroleum, Inc., 1982-89; chmn., pres., CEO Polymargo Prodn. Co., Tucson, 1989—. Bd. dirs. Chieftain Internat. Inc. Trustee J. Paul Getty Trust, 1963-99; mem. U.S. Tuna Team, 1957-67, capt.; mem. Served with U.S. Army, 1953-55. Decorated Army Commendation medal. Mem. AIME, State Bar Calif., Am. Judicature Soc., Theta Chi, Phi Delta Phi, Skyline Country Club. Republican. Congregationalist. Office: PO Box 35852 Tucson AZ 85740-5852 Office Phone: 520-575-0709. Office Fax: 520-544-0632.

**PEELER, WILLIAM JAMES,** lawyer; b. Highland Park, Mich., Nov. 27, 1927; s. Herb and Beulah (Wells) P.; m. Nancy Jean Bradley, Dec. 26, 1949; children: Nannette Peeler Bradley, Jeana Peeler Hosch, Jacqueline Peeler Safstrom. LLB, Cumberland U., 1952. Bar: Tenn. 1952. Ptnr. Porch, Peeler,

---

Williams & Thomason, Waverly, Tenn., 1952—. Mem. Tenn. Ho. of Reps., 1959-63; majority leader Tenn. Senate, 1967-75; trustee emeritus Cumberland U., Lebanon, Tenn., 1985—. Fellow Am. Coll. Trial Lawyers, Tenn. Bar Found.; mem. Am. Judicature Soc., ABA, Tenn. Bar Assn., Humphreys County Bar Assn., Masons (32 deg.), Shriners, Elks, Cumberland Club, City Club. Democrat. Mem. Ch. of Christ. Home: 2351 Ogden Rd Waverly TN 37185 Office: Porch Peeler Williams & Thomason 102 S Court Sq Waverly TN 37185-2198

**PEEPLES, JAMES THOMAS,** computer engineer, musician; b. Texarkana, Tex., Dec. 24, 1965; s. Pearl Josefine Peeples; m. Shannon Marie Wyatt, Oct. 10, 2000. AS in Electronics. Musician: (Irish traditional music) Irish Flute and Whistle in Session. Mem.: Mensa. Home: 24 Meadowbrook Conway AR 72032 Office: Acxiom Corp 301 Industrial Blvd Conway AR 72032 Office Phone: 501-336-1000. E-mail: james.peeples@acxiom.com.

**PEEPLES, THELMA J.,** elementary school educator; Recipient award N.Y.C. Dept. Edn., 1993. Office: 8201 Rockaway Blvd Ozone Park NY 11416-1200

**PEEPLES, WILLIAM DEWEY, JR.,** mathematics professor; b. Bessemer, Ala., Apr. 19, 1928; s. William Dewey and Thelma Jeannette (Chastain) P.; m. Katie Ray Blackerby, Aug. 30, 1956; children: Mary Jeannette, William Dewey III, Gerald Lewis, Stephen Ray. BS, Samford U., 1947; MS, U. Wis., 1949; PhD, U. Ga., 1951. Rsch. mathematician Ballistics Rsch. Lab., Aberdeen, Md., summer 1951; mem. faculty Samford U., Birmingham, Ala., 1951-56, prof. math., 1959-95, head dept., 1967-95; prof. emeritus, 1995; mem. faculty Auburn U., 1956-59. Cons. Hayes Internat. Corp. Co-author: Modern Mathematics for Business Students, 1969, Finite Mathematics, 1974, Modern Mathematics with Applications to Business and the Social Sciences, 4th edit, 1986, Finite Mathematics with Applications to Business and the Social Sciences, 1981, 2d edit., 1987; Contbr. articles to profl. publs. Served to 1st lt. AUS, 1954-56. Mem. Am. Math. Soc., Math. Assn. Am., Nat. Council Tchrs. Math., Ala. Coll. Tchrs. Math. (pres. 1969), Sigma Xi, Pi Mu Epsilon, Phi Kappa Phi (pres. 1977), Lambda Chi Alpha. Baptist (deacon, chmn. 1986). Club: Mason (Shriner). Home: 419 Poinciana Dr Birmingham AL 35209-4129 E-mail: wdpeeples@peoplepc.com.

**PEER, DIANA KAY,** principal; d. Onial Claud and Doris Collier Wortham; m. Steven G. Peer, Sept. 22, 1973; children: Kathryn, Debora, Aaron. Ba. Hendrix Coll., 1976; MEd., Ark. 1990; EdS, Ark. Tech. U., 2004. Choral dir. Darby Jr. High, Ft. Smith, Ark., 1976—82; libr. media specialist Sophia Meyer Sch., Van Buren, Ark., 1985—87, Parkview Sch., Van Buren, Ark., 1987—98, prin. 1998—; choral dir. Heritage U., Van Buren, Ark., 1982—2005; adj. prof. Ark. Tech. U., Russellville, 2005—. Commr. Mcpl. Auditorium Commn., Van Vuren, Ark., 2000—02. Named Prin. of Yr., PTA City Coun., Van Buren, 2001, Master Prin., Ark. Leadership Acad., 2001, 2005, 2006. Mem.: ASCD (bd. dirs. 2005—), Ark. Assn. Elem. Prins. (finalist Prin. of Yr. 2004, 2005), Nat. Assn. Elem. Prins. Avocations: reading, travel, music. Office: Parkview Elem 605 Parkview St Van Buren AR 72956 E-mail: dpeer@ubsd.us.

**PEER, LARRY HOWARD,** literature educator; b. Ogden, Utah, Jan. 2, 1942; s. Howard Harvey and Edna Celina (Baron) P.; m. Janet Priday; 9 children. BA, Brigham Young U., 1963, MA, 1965; PhD, U. Md., 1969. From asst. to assoc. prof. U. Ga., Athens, 1968-73; assoc. prof. Brigham Young U., Provo, Utah, 1975-78, prof., 1978—. Acting head dept. comparative lit. U. Ga., Athens, 1973-74, Brigham Young U., Provo, 1978-81; pres. Western Regional Honors Coun., 1978-79; exec. dir. Am. Conf. on Romanticism, 1992—. Author: Beyond Haworth, 1984, The Reasonable Romantic, 1986, The Romantic Manifesto, 1988. Mem. MLA, Am. Comparative Lit. Assn. (exec. officer 1988-94), Am. Soc. for Aesthetics, Rocky Mountain Soc. for Aesthetics (pres. 1986-87), Internat. Byron Soc., Internat. Brontë Soc. Mem. Lds Ch. Avocation: travel. Office: Brigham Young U Comparative Lit Dept Provo UT 84602

**PEERCE, MARJORIE J.,** lawyer; b. New York, NY, Mar. 16, 1958; d. Stuart Bernard and Barbara Toni Peerce; m. Mark L. Fuerst, Mar. 2, 1986; children: Benjamin Fuerst, Sarah Fuerst. BA, Tufts U., 1976—80; JD, Georgetown U. Law Ctr., 1980—83. Bar: N.Y. 1984, (so. and ea. dist.) N.Y. 1985, D.C. 1985, US Ct. Appeals: (2nd cir.) N.Y. 1989. Law clk. to Hon. Vincent Broderick US Dist. Ct., New York, NY, 1983—85; assoc. Stillman & Friedman, P.C., New York, NY, 1986—90, ptnr., 1991—. Sec. NY Coun. of Def. Lawyers, New York, NY, 2000—02, v.p., 2002—04, pres., 2005—; editor-in-chief Fed. Bar Coun. News, N.Y., 2002—; chairperson criminal law com. Assn. of the Bar, New York, NY, 2004—. V.p., bd. of trustees Bklyn Heights Montessori Sch., Bklyn., 2003. Mem.: NY Coun. of Def. Lawyers (bd. dirs. 2000—). Home: 30 Butler St Brooklyn NY 11231 Office: Stillman & Friedman PC 425 Park Ave New York NY 10022 Office Fax: 212-223-1942. E-mail: mpeerce@stillmanfriedman.com.

**PEERMAN, DEAN GORDON,** magazine editor; b. Mattoon, Ill., Apr. 25, 1931; s. Staley Jacob and Irene (Monen) P. BS with highest distinction, Northwestern U., 1953; postgrad., Cornell U., 1953-54; B.D., Yale, 1959; D.D., Kalamazoo Coll., 1967. With Christian Century Found., 1959—; copy editor Christian Century mag., 1959-61, assoc. editor, 1961-64, mng. editor, 1964-81, exec. editor, 1981-85, sr. editor, 1985-98, contbg. editor, 1998—. Author: (with M.E. Marty) Pen-ultimates, 1963, (with Marty, L.M. Delloff, J.M. Wall) A Century of The Century, 1987; editor: Frontline Theology, 1967; co-editor: (with Marty) New Theology 1-10, 1964-73, A Handbook of Christian Theologians, 1965, enlarged edit., 1984, (with Alan Geyer) Theological Crossings, 1971; contbg. author: Chile: Under Military Rule, 1974; editor, contbr. Faithful Witness, 2002. Active Chgo. cmty. theater groups. Recipient award for distinction in lay ministry within the church Yale Div. Sch., 1995. Mem. ACLU, Fellowship of Reconciliation, Amnesty Internat., Chgo. Religious Leadership Network on Latin Am., Phi Beta Kappa. Democrat. Baptist. Office: Christian Century Mag 104 S Michigan Ave Ste 700 Chicago IL 60603-5901 Office Phone: 312-263-7510 x236. E-mail: dpeerman@christiancentury.org.

**PEET, AMANDA,** actress; b. NYC, Jan. 11, 1972; d. Charles and Penny Peet. BA in History, Columbia U., 1994. Actor: (TV series) Central Park West, 1995—96, (guest appearance) Law & Order, 1995, The Single Guy, 1996, Spin City, 1997, Seinfeld, 1997, Jack & Jill, 1999, Partners, 1999; (TV films) Ellen Foster, 1997, Date Squad, 2001; (films) Animal Room, 1995, She's the One, 1996, One Fine Day, 1996, Virginity, 1996, Grind, 1997, Touch Me, 1997, Sax and Violins, 1997, 1999, 1998, Southie, 1998, Playing by Heart, 1998, Origin of the Species, 1998, Simply Irresistible, 1999, Jump, 1999, Two Ninas, 1999, Body Shots, 1999, Isn't She Great?, 2000, The Whole Nine Yards, 2000, Takedown, 2000, Whipped, 2000, Saving Silverman, 2001, High Crimes, 2002, Changing Lanes, 2002, Igby Goes Down, 2002, Whatever We Do, 2003, Identity, 2003, Something's Gotta Give, 2003, The Whole Ten Yards, 2004, Melinda and Melinda, 2004, A Lot Like Love, 2005, Syriana, 2005, The Martian Child, 2005; (plays) Whale Music, Winter Lies, 27 Sketches: Fear and Misery in the Third Reich, The Country Club, This Is How It Goes, 2005, Escape: 6 Ways to Get Away, 2005, Barefoot in the Park, 2006. Office: The Gersh Agy Ste 201 232 N Canon Dr Beverly Hills CA 90210*

**PEET, CHARLES D, JR.,** lawyer; b. N.Y.C., Sept. 3, 1935; s. Charles D and Margaret Louise (Sherman) P.; children: Alisa, Amanda. BA, Yale U., 1957; JD, Harvard U., 1960. Bar: N.Y. 1962. Assoc. Milbank, Tweed, Hadley & McCloy, N.Y.C., 1960-68, ptnr., 1969-98; of counsel Freshfields Bruckhaus Deringer LLP (and predecessor firm), N.Y.C., 1998—. Mem. Assn. Bar N.Y.C. Office: Freshfields Bruckhaus Deringer LLP 520 Madison Ave Fl 34 New York NY 10022-4213 Office Phone: 212-277-4000. E-mail: charles.peet@freshfields.com.

---

**PEET, PHYLLIS IRENE,** women's studies educator; b. Winnipeg, Man., Can., Mar. 3, 1943; came to the U.S., 1948; d. Harold Parsons and Gladys Mae (Riley) Harrison; m. Thomas Peter Richman, June 14, 1963 (div. 1969); m. Charles Francis Peet, Sept. 9, 1972. BA in Art, Calif. State U., Northridge, 1972; MA in Art History, U. Calif., L.A., 1976, PhD in Art History, 1987. Sec. L.A. County Supr. Kenneth Hahn, 1960-68; assoc. in art history L.A. County Mus. Art, 1974-75; asst. dir., curator Grunwald Ctr. for the Graphic Arts, U. Calif., L.A., 1975-78; Am. art scholar High Mus. Art, Atlanta, 1984-90; instr. women's studies Monterey (Calif.) Peninsula Coll., 1989—; instr. women's programs/women's studies, 1989—. Dirs.' adv. com. The Art Mus. of Santa Cruz County, 1981-84, 89-94; vis. lectr. Calif. State U., Fresno, 1984; program coord. conf. Inst. for Hist. Study, San Francisco, 1987; lectr. bd. studies in art U. Calif. Santa Cruz, 1991-95. Author, co-curator, editor, compiler: (book and exhbn.) The American Personality: The Artist Illustrator of Life in the United States, 1860-1930, 1976; author, curator: (book and exhbn.) American Women of the Etching Revival, 1988; co-author: American Paintings in the High Museum of Art, 1994; contbr. articles to profl. jours. including Am. Nat. Biography, Fitzroy Dict. of Women Artists, 1997, Dict. Literary Biography, 1998. Vol., activist Dem. Party, L.A., 1960-66, Peace and Freedom Party, L.A., 1967-71; vol. Dem. Party Candidates, Santa Cruz, Calif., 1979-96, Santa Cruz Action Network, 1980-85; mem. nominating com. Girl Scouts of Am., Monterey Bay, 1991-93. Rockefeller Found. fellow UCLA, 1978-80, Dickson grantee U. Calif. LA, 1981-82; recipient Women Helping Women award Soroptimists, Monterey and Carmel, Calif., 1991, 95, Allen Griffin for Excellence in Edn. award Cmty. Found. Monterey County, 1993, Quality of Life award Econ. Devel. Corp., Monterey, 1994, Excellence in Edn. aard Monterey Peninsula Coll. Found., 2004, 05, 06; named Tchr. of Yr., Tchrs. of Tomorrow, 2004, Academic Excellence award Monterey Peninsula Coll. Found., 2004, 2005. Mem.: NAACP, ACLU, AAUW, NOW, Nat. Mus. Women in the Arts (founding mem.), Coll. Art Assn., UN Assn., Western Assn. Women Historians, Inst. for Hist. Study, Nat. Women's Studies Assn., Planned Parenthood, Monterey Bay Women's Caucus for Art (founder, bd. dirs. 1988—93), Women's Internat. League for Peace and Freedom. Avocations: print collecting, photography. Office: Womens Programs Monterey Peninsula Coll 980 Fremont St Monterey CA 93940-4704 Office Phone: 831-646-4276. Business E-Mail: ppeet@mpc.edu. E-mail: ppeet@aol.com.

**PEETZ, KAREN B.,** bank executive; married; 2 children. BS, Penn State. U.; MS, Johns Hopkins U. Various client services, sales, credit and risk mgmt. positions JP Morgan Chase (formerly Chase Manhattan Bank and Chemical Bank); sales mgr. global trust services then head global client mgmt. Chase Manhattan Bank, NYC, sr. v.p., bus. mgr. global trust services London; sr. v.p., divsn. head domestic corp. trust bus. Bank of NY, 1998, head global payments services group, haed corp. trust, 2003, sr. exec. v.p., 2006—. Mem. Women's Leadership Initiative Penn State U.; bd. trustees Brooklyn Acad. Music; steering com. Women United in Philanthropy United Way NYC. Mem.: Women's Bond Club. Office: Bank of NY One Wall St 10th Fl New York NY 10286*

**PEFANIS, HARRY N.,** oil industry executive; b. Buffalo, 1957; Grad., U. Okla., 1979. Exec. v.p. Plains All American Pipeline LP, Houston, 1998, pres., COO, 1999—. Office: Plains All American Pipline LP 333 Clay St Ste 1600 Houston TX 77002*

**PEFLEY, NORMAN GORDON,** bank executive; b. Eugene, Oreg., Dec. 15, 1955; s. Gordon Vergne Pefley and Jean Pefley (Lee) Hawley; m. Emma Ginete Lacuesta, July 5, 1986. BA, U. Calif., Davis, 1977; MA, Johns Hopkins U., 1979; MBA, U. Chgo., 1981; MA, Golden Gate U., 2001. CFA, CPHQ. Rsch. analyst Chgo. Bd. Options Exch., 1981-83; sr. fin. analyst Bank of Am., San Francisco, 1983-89, v.p., 1989-99. Referee Jour. Futures Markets, N.Y.C., 1984-87. Mem.: ASTD, Nat. Assn. Healthcare Quality, The Security Analysts of San Francisco, Internat. Soc. Performance Improvement, CFA Inst., Toastmasters Internat., Omicron Delta Epsilon, Delta Phi Alpha, Phi Beta Kappa. Avocation: languages.

**PEGALIS, STEVEN E.,** lawyer; b. NYC, Apr. 12, 1942; BA, Queens Coll. of City NY, 1962; LLB, NY Law Sch., 1965, JD, 1979. Bar: NY 1966, Pa. 1992, admitted to practice: US Ct. Appeals (2nd Cir.) 1969, US Dist. Ct. (Ea. Dist.) NY 1969. Adj. prof., med. malpractice NY Law Sch. Author: American Law of Medical Malpractice (3d edit.). Bd. dir. NY Law Sch.; bd. editors Cancer Litig. (NY Law Jour. Publishing Co.). Fellow: Roscoe Pound Found.; mem.: ABA ("Experts Analyze Brain Damaged Baby Cases," Nat. CLE Program Adv. Com.), Am. Soc. Law and Medicine, Am. Coll. Medicine (Assoc. in Law), Assn. Trial Lawyers Am., NY State Trial Lawyers Assn., Nassau County Bar Assn., Queens County Bar Assn., Assn. Bar City NY. Office: Pegalis & Erickson 1 Hollow Ln Ste 107 New Hyde Park NY 11042 Office Phone: 516-684-2900. Office Fax: 516-684-2939.

**PEGELS, C. CARL,** management consultant, educator; b. Barendrecht, Holland, The Netherlands, Feb. 26, 1933; came to U.S., 1962, naturalized, 1968; s. Bertus and Adriana Maria (Denotter) P.; children: Janice Joy, Kevin Carl. BS in Mech. Engring., Detroit Inst. Tech., 1961; MS, Purdue U., 1963, PhD in Mgmt., 1966. Prodn. engr. Ford Motor, Windsor, Can., 1955-62; instr. Purdue U., W. Lafayette, Ind., 1962-66; prof. SUNY, Buffalo, 1966—, v.p. Ctr. Mgmt. Sys., Buffalo, 1978—91. Author: Basic for Business, 1973, Health Care & Elderly, 1980, Japan vs The West, 1984, Q.C. in Health Care, 1985, Decision Support Systems for Production and Operations Management, 1986, Management and Industry in China, 1987, Strategic Management for Hospitals and Health Care Corporations, 1987, Health Care and the Older Citizen, 1988, Decision Support Systems for Management Science/Operations Research 1989, Strategic Information Systems, 1993, Total Quality management, 1995, Strategies and Tools for the Learning Company, 1998, Proven Solutions for Reducing Health Care Costs, 2003; Proven Solutions for Improving Supply Chain Management, 2005. Krannert fellow, 1966; Krannert scholar Purdue U., 1963. Mem. Acad. of Mgmt., Prodn. and Ops. Mgmt. Soc., Am. Inst. Decision Scis. Avocation: running. Home: 150 Arielle Ct Apt D Buffalo NY 14221-1969 Office: Sch of Mgmt SUNY at Buffalo Buffalo NY 14260-0001 Personal E-mail: cpegels@yahoo.com. Business E-Mail: cpegels@buffalo.edu.

**PEGIS, ANTON GEORGE,** retired language educator; b. Milw., Feb. 21, 1920; s. George Anton and Eugenia (Stathas) Pegis; m. Harriet Louise Stevens, June 1, 1949; children: Stefani Elizabeth, Penelope Eugenia. AB, We. State Coll. Colo., 1949; MA, Denver U., 1951, PhD, 1956. Jr. engr. North Shore Gas Co., Waukegan, Ill., 1946—47; instr. Ft. Lewis Coll., 1952—53; process control technician Gates Rubber Co., Denver, 1953—54; prof. English Colo. Sch. Mines, Golden, 1954—82, asst. to pres., 1964—68, v.p. devel., 1968—73, v.p. external affairs, 1973—74, prof. emeritus, 1982—. Cons. Office Mineral Reports U.S. Bur. Mines, Washington, CSC, San Francisco, 1974—94, Regional Tng. Ctr. Office Pers. Mgmt., Denver, 1983. Author: Social Theory in the Novels of Ford Madox Ford, 1956, An Intensive Course in English for Foreign Engineering Students, 1957, Humanism and the Practical Order, 1964, Excellence and the Odyssean Philosophy, 1965, Platonism in the Renaissance Lyric, 1965, Education for Leadership, 1966, Totality in Engineering Education, 1968, Course Recommendations for the Resource Engineer, 1968, Encroachment of Competing Land Uses on Mineral Development, 1976. Chmn. United Way Fund; sec. Colo. Sch. Mines Found.; pres. Roland Valley Civic Assn., 1974—75. With U.S. Army, 1940—46, maj. AUS Ret. Named Disting. Sgt., 121st Field Arty. Rgt., 1988, Outstanding Prof., Tau Beta Pi, 1963, Hon. Col., 115th Engring. Rgt., 1988; recipient Outstanding Prof. award, Colo. Sch. Mines, 1976, Amoco Found. awards. Mem.: MLA, Am. Soc. Engring. Edn. (chmn. Rocky Mountain sect.), Am. Alumni Coun. (chmn. dist. VII 1971—72), Golden C of C. (pres. 1968), Blue Key, Kappa Psi Omega, Theta Chi. Home: 415 Scenic Ct Golden CO 80401-2533

**PEGRAM, JOHN BRAXTON,** lawyer; b. Yeadon, Pa., June 29, 1938; s. William Bement and Marjorie (Rainey) P.; m. Patricia Jane Narbeth; Aug. 21, 1965; children: Catherine, Stephen. AB in Physics, Columbia U., 1960; LLB,

NYU, 1965. Bar: N.Y. 1965, U.S. Dist. Ct. (ea. and so. dists.) N.Y. 1967, U.S. Supreme Ct. 1971. Engr. Fairchild Camera and Instrument Corp., Clifton, N.J. 1960-66; assoc. Davis Hoxie Faithfull and Hapgood, LLP, N.Y.C., 1966-71; ptnr. Davis Hoxie Faithfull and Hapgood, N.Y.C., 1972-95; prin. Fish & Richardson P.C., N.Y.C., 1995—2002; sr. counsel, 2003—. Mem. intellectual property litig. adv. com. U.S. Dist. Ct. for the Dist. Del., 1994-96; mem. neutral evaluation and mediation panels U.S. Dist. Ct. for the Eastern Dist. of N.Y., 1994-97; mem. mediation panel U.S. Dist. Ct. for the So. Dist. N.Y., 1994-97. Editor The Trademark Reporter jour., 1984-86, mem. editl. adv. bd., 1986—; contbr. articles to profl. jours. Fellow Am. Bar Found. (life), Am. Intellectual Property Law Assn. (chmn. fed. practice and procedure com. 1974-76, chmn. unauthorized practice com. 1977-79, chmn. trade secrets com. 1992-94, mem. Japan practice com. 1992—, mem. editl. bd. Quar. Jour., 1994-95, chmn. fed. litig. com. 1995-97, chmn. internat. com. 1998-00, bd. dirs. 2000-03, mem. amicus com. 2003—, mem. spl. com. legis. strategies 2003-05, mem. proprofl. responsibility com. 2005—); mem. IEEE, ABA (chmn. antitrust law sect. com. on patents, trademarks and know how 1986-89, mem. legal econs. sect., bus. law sect., chmn. intellectual property law divsn. IV 1995-96), Am. Phys. Soc. (life), Fed. Bar Coun., Fed. Cir. Bar Assn., N.Y. State Bar Assn., Assn. Bar City of N.Y., NY Intellectual Property Law Assn. (sec. 1981-84, dir. 1984-86, pres. 1989-90), US Bar-European Patent Office Liaison Coun. (del. 2003-), Japan Patent Office Liaison Coun. (del. 1990—), Am. Judicature Soc., Internat. Intellectual Property Soc., Internat. Patent and Trademark Assn. (coun. of AIPPI), Internat. Trademark Assn. (bd. dirs. 1985-87, fin. com 1987-95, pub. com. 1997-98). Office: Fish & Richardson PC Citigroup Ctr 153 E 53rd St 52d Fl New York NY 10022-4611 Office Phone: 212-765-5070.

**PEHRSON, GORDON OSCAR, JR.,** lawyer, venture capitalist; b. San Antonio, Feb. 18, 1943; s. Gordon Oscar and Frances (Burns) Pehrson; m. Janice Sue Hagedorn, May 17, 1969; children: Christopher Wells, Ashley Stewart; m. Sharon Ann McNellage, Jan. 1, 1983; m. Maria Terresa Sitvin Basso del Pont, Mar. 25, 1997. AB, Coll. William and Mary, 1964; JD cum laude, U. Mich., 1967; postgrad., U. London, 1967-68. Bar: Ill. 1968, DC 1969, US Ct. Claims 1968, US Ct. Mil. Appeals 1968, US Ct. Appeals (DC cir.) 1976, US Supreme Ct. 1976, US Ct. Appeals (3d and 5th cirs.) 1979, US Ct. Appeals (fed. cir.) 1982, US Tax Ct. 1990. Assoc. Sutherland, Asbill & Brennan, Washington, 1970-75, ptnr., 1975—97; sr. tax and corp. ptnr. Hopkins & Sutter, Washington, 1997—2000; founder, mng. ptnr. Potomac Capital LLP, Washington, 2000—. Adj. prof. law Georgetown U., Washington, 1977—81; vis. prof. law Coll. Ins., NYC, 1997—98; founder, bd. advisors The Inst. Tax Rev., 1986—. Contbr. articles on tax law to profl. jours.; editor The Tax Rev., 1986-94. Trustee U.S. Supreme Ct. Hist. Soc., 1993—, Food for Christmas Found., 1992-94; bd. advisors Hartford Inst. Ins. Taxation, 1993—, U.S. Humane Soc., 1994-96, Coll. William and Mary Sch. Bus., 1995-99. Fellow in internat. law U. Mich., 1967 Master: ABA (co-chair investment, fin. and taxation, com. sect. torts and ins. practice 1994—96, chair tax procedure com.sect. adminstrv. law and regulatory practice 1994—); mem.: FBA, Am. Law Inst., DC Bar Assn., Fed. Cir. Bar Assn. (chair tax appeals com. 1994—96), Knickerbocker Club (NYC), Econ. Club Washington, Met. Club (Washington), Nat. Press Club (Washington), Order of Coif. Episcopalian. Home: Apt 1176 198 Halpine Rd Rockville MD 20852 Address: Ave Libertador 2602 6A Buenos Aires Argentina Office Phone: 301-984-4202. E-mail: gopehrson@netzero.com.

**PEI, I.M. (IEOH MING PEI),** architect; b. Canton, China, Apr. 26, 1917; arrived in U.S., 1935, naturalized, 1954; s. Tsu Yee Pei and Lien Kwun Chwong; m. Eileen Loo, June 20, 1942; children: Ting Chung, Chien Chung, Li Chung, Liane. BArch, MIT, 1940; MArch, Harvard U., 1946; DFA (hon.), U. Pa., 1970, Rensselaer Poly. Inst., 1978, Carnegie Mellon U., 1980, U. Mass., 1980, Brown U., 1980, NYU, 1980, Dartmouth Coll., 1991, Northeastern U.; LLD, Chinese U., Hong Kong, 1970, Pace U.; LHD, Columbia U., 1980, U. Colo., 1982, U. Rochester, 1982, U. Hong Kong, 1990, Am. U., Paris, 1990. Practice architecture, N.Y.C., 1939—42; asst. prof. Harvard Grad. Sch. Design, 1945—48; dir. archtl. divsn. Webb & Knapp, Inc., 1948—55; with Pei Cobb Freed & Partners (formerly I.M. Pei & Ptnrs., I.M. Pei & Assocs.), N.Y.C., 1955—96; now ind. arch. N.Y.C., 1996—. Prin. works include Mile High Ctr., Denver, Nat. Ctr. Atmospheric Rsch., Boulder, Colo., planning projects include, S.W. Washington Redevelopment Plan, prin. works include Dallas City Hall, John Fitzgerald Kennedy Libr., Boston, Can. Imperial Bank Commerce Complex, Toronto, Overseas Chinese Banking Corp. Ctr., Singapore, Dreyfus Chemistry Bldg., MIT, East-West Ctr. U. Hawaii, Honolulu, Mellon Art Ctr. and Choate Rosemary Hall Sci. Ctr., Wallingford, Conn., Univ. Plz., NYU, Johnson Mus. Art Cornell U., Ithaca, N.Y., Washington Sq. East, Phila., Everson Mus. Art, Syracuse, N.Y., Nat. Gallery Art, East Bldg., Washington, Wilmington Tower, Raffles City, Singapore, West Wing Mus. Fine Arts, Boston, expansion and modernization of Louvre Mus., Paris, Morton H. Meyerson Symphony Ctr., Dallas, MIT Arts and Media Ctr., Jacob K. Javits Conv. Ctr., N.Y.C., Fragrant Hill Hotel, Beijing, Tex. Commerce Tower, Houston, Bank of China, Hong Kong, Creative Artists Agy., Beverly Hills, Calif., Guggenheim Pavilion, Mount Sinai Med. Ctr., N.Y.C., Rock n' Roll Hall of Fame and Mus., Cleve., Mus. Modern Art, Athens, Greece, Miho Mus. of Art, Shiga, Japan, Bilbao (Spain) Estuary Project, Four Seasons Hotel, N.Y.C., others, planning projects include, S.W. Washington Redevelopment Plan, Govt. Ctr. Redevelopment Plan, Boston, Oklahoma City Downtown Redevelopment Plan, Bedford Stuyvesant Super Block, Bklyn., master plan Columbia U. Mem. Nat. Def. Rsch. Com., Princeton, NJ, 1943—45, Nat. Coun. Humanities, 1966—70, Nat. Coun. on Arts, 1981—84. Recipient Thomas Jefferson Meml. medal for Architecture, 1976, gold medal for architecture, Am. Acad. Arts and Letters, 1979, Nat. Arts Club Gold medal of honor, 1981, Mayor's award of Honor for Art and Culture, N.Y.C., 1981, La Grande Medaille D'or L'Académie d'Architecture, 1981, Pritzker Architecture prize, 1983, Medal of Liberty, 1986, Medal of French Legion of Honor, 1988, Nat. Medal of Art, 1988, Praemium Imperiale, Japan Art Assn., 1989, UCLA Gold medal, 1990, Colbert Found. first award for excellence, 1991, Excellence 2000 award, 1991, Freedom medal, 1993, Legion of Honor, France, 2006; fellow MIT traveling, 1940, Wheelwright, Harvard U., 1951. Fellow: AIA (Medal of Honor N.Y. chpt. 1963, Gold Medal 1979), ASID (hon.); mem.: NAD, Urban Design Coun., Royal Inst. Brit. Architects, Am. Acad. and Inst. Arts and Letters (chancellor 1998—), Am. Acad. Arts and Scis., Nat. Inst. Arts and Letters (Arnold Brunner award 1961).*

**PEIPERL, ADAM,** sculptor, photographer; b. Sosnowiec, Poland, June 4, 1935; arrived in US, 1953, naturalized, 1958; s. Jacob and Fanny (Alster) P.; m. Martha Rose Dorf, June 15, 1958; children: Maury, Laurence, Linda. Grad., Cours Complementaire Gen, Paris, 1952; BS in Chemistry, George Washington U., 1957; postgrad., Pa. State U., 1959. Cons. in Russian sci. lit. Libr. Congress, Washington, 1959-61, 66-67; chemist Nat. Bur. Standards, Washington, 1961-63; sci. translator Am. Inst. Physics, NYC, 1973-94, Plenum Pub., 1993-98. One-man shows include Balt. Mus. Art, 1969, Pa. Acad. Fine Arts, 1969, Marlborough Gerson Gallery, NYC, 1969, Smithsonian Mus. History and Tech., 1972, Phila. Art Alliance, 1978; group shows include Washington Gallery Modern Art, 1968, Corcoran Gallery Art, 1968, Kent State U., McKay Art Inst., San Antonio, 1969, NASA Manned Spacecraft, Houston, 1970-71, Nat. Mus. Am. Art, 1972-82, Meml. Art Gallery, U. Rochester, 1978, Foster Harmon Galleries Am. Art, Sarasota, Fla., 1982-83, Artworks Gallery, Santa Barbara, Calif., 1989, Art of the Sixties, Fred Jones Jr. Mus. of Art, U. Okla., 2002, Radicals and Conservatives: Abstraction 1945 to the Present, Pa. Acad. Fine Arts, 2004; represented in permanent collections Kreeger Mus., Pa. Acad. Fine Arts, Mus. Boijmans-Van Beuningen, Hirshhorn Mus. and Sculpture Garden; with choreographer Denise Vale collaboration involving projections of sculpture video, U. Okla., 2003. Home: 1135 Loxford Ter Silver Spring MD 20901-1130 E-mail: digitall@comcast.net.

**PEIPERT, JAMES RAYMOND,** journalist; b. Alton, Ill., Nov. 15, 1942; s. Lawrence George and Virginia Pauline (Sieve) Peipert; m. Mary Ellen Finney, Aug. 1, 1970; children: Benjamin, Matthew, Thomas. BA, So. Ill. U., 1965. Reporter, editor AP, Chgo., 1965-68, N.Y.C., 1968-70, corr. Moscow, 1970-

74, London, 1974-80, news editor Johannesburg, 1980-81, East Africa bur. chief Nairobi, Kenya, 1981-86; nat.-fgn. editor Ft. Worth Star-Telegram, 1986-2001, mem. editl. bd., 2001—. With US Army, 1965—67. Roman Catholic. Avocations: bicycling, maintaining 1967 Mustang, reading. Office: Ft Worth Star Telegram PO Box 1870 Fort Worth TX 76101-1870 Office Phone: 817-390-7753. Business E-Mail: jpeipert@star-telegram.com.

**PEIRCE, CAROLE,** elementary school educator; b. Oshkosh, Wis., June 11, 1943; d. Charles J. and Bernadette (Graf) P.; m. Jack McDowell, Nov. 18, 1982. BS, U. Wis., Oshkosh, 1965; MA, U. Wis., Madison, 1966. Instr. U. Wis. Ctr. System, Marinette & Fond Du Lac, 1966-70, Concordia Coll., Milw., 1970-71; tchr. of French Behavioral Rsch. Labs., Palo Alto, Calif., 1971-73; elem. tchr. Nido De Aguilas Internat. Sch., Santiago, Chile; elem. bilingual tchr. Alum Rock Sch. Dist., San Jose, Calif., 1978-87; elem. tchr. Huntsville (Ark.) Sch. Dist., 1987-95; French, Spanish, and ESL tchr. Huntsville (Ark.) H.S., 1995-2000. Presenter Bay Area Sch. Dists. Calif., 1984-87, Springdale Tchrs. Co-op, Little Rock, Arkadelphia, Ark., Dallas, Albuquerque, St. Paul, Dominican Republic; tchr., cons. Nat. Geog. Soc., 1990-96. Author Social Studies Review Article 1985. Grantee Environ. Edn. State of Calif., 1986, NSTA to Internat. Geographical Congress, Washington, 1992, NASA Ednl. Workshop for Elem. Sci. Tchrs., 1993; Christa McAuliffe fellow, 1993-94; recipient Nat. Disting. Teaching award Nat. Achievement Coun. Geographic Edn., 1993. Mem. NEA, Nat. Coun. for Social Studies, Nat. Coun. for Geog. Edn., Ark. Geog. Alliance (newsletter editor, Geography Tchr. of Yr., 1993-94), Ozark Soc. Avocations: global studies, geography, outdooring, travel. Home: 2046 Madison 8325 Hindsville AR 72738-9727

**PEIRCE, KAREN PATRICIA,** education educator; b. Providence, July 12, 1971; d. Raymond Fales and Patricia Kay Peirce. ABH, Rollins Coll., Winter Park, Fla., 1993; MA, Carnegie Mellon U., Pitts., 1997; PhD, U. Ariz., Tucson, 2006. Peer writing cons. Rollins Coll. Writing Ctr., Winter Park, Fla., 1990—93; Fulbright English tchg. asst. Korean Am. Edn. Commn., Ulsan, 1993—94; pub. rels. asst. Embassy of the Republic of Korea, Washington, 1995—96; rsch. asst. Carnegie Mellon U., Pitts., 1996—97; English instr. The Sawyer Sch., Warwick, RI, 1997—98; upper divsn. English tchr. Berkeley Prep. Sch., Tampa, Fla., 1998—2001; grad. assoc. tchg. U. Ariz., Tucson, 2001—06; asst. prof. English US Mil. Acad., West Point, NY, 2006—. Mem.: MLA, Rhetoric Soc. Am., Internat. Writing Ctr. Assn., Conf. on Coll. Composition and Comm., Nat. Coun. Tchrs. English. Home: 281 Hudson St Ste 2 Cornwall On Hudson NY 12520-1039

**PEIRCE, NEAL R.,** journalist; b. Phila., Jan. 5, 1932; s. J. Trevor and Miriam deS. (Litchfield) P.; m. Barbara von dem Bach-Zelewski, Apr. 18, 1959; children: Celia, Andrea, Trevor. BA, Princeton U., 1954; postgrad., Harvard U., 1957-58. Polit. editor Congl. Quar., 1960-69; co-founder, contbg. editor Nat. Jour., Washington, 1969-97. Cons. and commentator elections CBS News, 1962, 67-76, NBC News, 1964-66; lectr. in field; syndicated newspaper columnist Washington Post Writers Group; chmn. The Citistates Group; mem. faculty Salzburg (Austria) Seminar, 1980, 84, 97; 1st Weinberg prof. Princeton U.'s Woodrow Wilson Sch. Pub. and Internat. Affairs, 1992. Author: The People's President, 1968, 2d edit., 1981, The Megastates of America, 1972, The Pacific States of America, 1972, The Mountain States of America, 1972, The Great Plains States America, 1973, The Deep South States of America, 1974, The Border South States, 1975, The New England States, 1976, The Mid-Atlantic States of America, 1977, The Great Lakes States of America, 1980, The Book of America: Inside Fifty States Today, 1983, Citistates: How Urban America Can Prosper in A Competitive World, 1993, Breakthroughs: Recreating The American City, 1993; Corrective Capitalism, 1987; editor Peirce Report series on 24 regions' Citistate futures starting with Phoenix Republic and Gazette, 1987, including New England Futures Project, 2005-06. Founder, chmn. S.W. Neighborhood Assembly, Washington, 1963-65; mem. exec. com. Nat. Civic League, 1990-95; trustee German Marshall Fund U.S., 1987-97. With CIC, U.S. Army, 1954-57. Fellow Woodrow Wilson Internat. Center Scholars, 1971-74 Fellow Nat. Acad. Pub. Adminstrn.; mem. Newfound Lake Region Assn. (v.p. 1989-92), Phi Beta Kappa. Episcopalian. Home and office: 610 G St SW Washington DC 20024-2440 Business E-Mail: npeirce@citistates.com.

**PEIRIS, SUHITHI MAHESICA,** chemist, researcher; b. Colombo, Sri Lanka, Nov. 23, 1965; d. Suran A. and Marguerite M. Peiris; m. Brett M. Goodman, Apr. 28, 2001. BS with honors, U. Mich., 1991; PhD in Inorganic Chemistry, U. Chgo., 1996. Postdoctoral fellow U. Chgo., 1996-97; staff scientist Nova Rsch. Inc., Alexandria, Va., 1997-98; rsch. chemist Naval Rsch. Lab., Washington, 1998-2000, Naval Surface Warfare Ctr., Indian Head, Md., 2000—. Contbr. articles to profl. jours. Sci. fair judge, Washington, 1999, Indian Head, 2000. Recipient Outstanding Young Scientist award, Gordon Rsch. Conf., 2000. Mem. Am. Chem. Soc. Avocations: swimming, reading. Business E-Mail: suhithi.peiris@navy.mil.

**PEIRSOL, AARON,** Olympic athlete; b. Irvine, Calif., July 23, 1983; s. Tim Hartig and Wela Peirsol. Student, U. Texas. Swimmer U.S. Olympic Team, Sydney Olympic games, 2000, U.S. Olympic Team, Athens Olympic games, 2004. Named NCAA Swimmer of the Yr., 2003. Silver medal, 200m backstroke, Sydney Olympic games, 2000, Gold medal, 200m backstroke, World Championships, 2001, Gold Medal, 100m, 200m backstroke, 400m relay, Pan American games, 2002, Gold Medal, 100m backstroke, 200m backstroke, 4x100m medaly relay, Athens Olympic Games, 2004, Holds world record in the 200m backstroke (long and short course meters), mem. Gold Medal U.S. 400m medley relay team, World Championships, 2003, Gold Medal, 200m backstroke World Championships, 2003, Youngest American (age 15) to break two minutes in 200m backstroke.

**PEISCH, ALICE HANLON,** state legislator; BA, Smith Coll.; JD, Suffolk U. Law Sch. Town clerk Wellesley, 2000—03; state rep. Mass. House, 2003—. Bd. overseers Newton-Wellesley Hosp., 1996—; mem. League of Women Voters of Wellesley, 1986—; bd. mem. Senior Living, Inc., 2001—; mem. Wellesley Svc. League, 1988—; bd. dirs. Wellesley Edn. Found., 1999—2005, adv. bd., 2005—. Democrat. Office: Rm 26 State House Boston MA 02133 Office Phone: 617-722-2080. E-mail: Rep.AlicePeisch@hou.state.ma.us.

**PEITHMAN, ROSCOE EDWARD,** physicist, educator; b. Hoyleton, Ill., Feb. 26, 1913; s. Edward Henry Peithman and Sarah Jane Smith; m. Laura Jane Davenport, Apr. 3, 1936 (dec. Oct. 13, 1987); children: Ann Davenport, Stephen Edward. BS, So. Ill. U., 1935; MS, U. of Ill., 1939; EdD, Oreg. State U., Arcata, Calif., 1946—77, chmn. divsn. of phys. scis., 1960—69, dean Sch. Scis., 1969—70, emeritus prof. of physics, 1977—. Academic senator Calif. State U. Sys., Calif., 1963—66. Lt. comdr. USNR, 1942—73. Fellow: Am. Men and Women of Sci. (life); mem.: Am. Assn. of Physics Tchrs. Avocation: amateur radio. Home: 2704 Sunny Grove Ave Mckinleyville CA 95519-7912 Personal E-mail: W6BME@cox.net.

**PEITZ, TODD ADAM,** music educator; b. Dayton, Ohio, Oct. 14, 1976; s. Richard M. and Mary Ann Peitz. B of Edn., U. Toledo. Dir. bands Arlington Local Schs., Arlington, Ohio, 2003—04, Port Clinton City Schs., 2004—. Mem.: Ohio Music Edn. Assn. (pres. elect - dist. II 2005—), Kappa Kappa Psi, Conservative. Roman Catholic. Home: 3236 N Utility Dr Apt 1 Port Clinton OH 43452 Office: Port Clinton City Schs 821 S Jefferson St Port Clinton OH 43452 Office Phone: 419-734-2147. Business E-Mail: tpeitz@pccsd.net.

**PEIXOTO NETO, JOSE ULYSSES,** internist, researcher; b. Crato, Ceará, Brazil, Aug. 29, 1930; s. Adérito de Aquino Silva and Adelite Alencar Peixoto; m. Maria Isolda Teles Cartaxo, May 23, 1958; children: Jose Ulysses Peixoto Filho, Eunice Ulysséia Peixoto Maia, Jorge André Cartaxo Peixoto. 1st degree, State Coll. Goias, Brazil, 1942; postgrad., 1942-49; 2d degree, St. John Coll., Fortaleza, Brazil, 1949; postgrad., Fed. U., Recife, Brazil, 1955; Laurel, Cearense Med. Ctr., 1994. Med. resident St. Michael Hosp., Rio de

Janeiro, 1956; intern St. Anthony Hosp., Iguatú, Ceará, 1957; founder Social Providence, Crato, Ceará, 1958-64; attendent St. Frances Hosp., Crato, 1958-69; founder St. Michael Hosp., Crato, 1967-93, pres., dir., 1983-93, internist, researcher, 1993—; founder Faculty of Law, Crato, 1977-78. Lectr. faculty of medicine The Fed. U. of Ceará, 1976—. Recipient Good Svc. award Lyons Club, 1992, Laurel Cearense Med. Ctr., 1994, Cert. Merit Health Care Profls. Juazeiro North Profl. Health Assn., 1998, Gold Medal of Profl. Merit, Ceara Estate Regional Coun. Medicine, 1999, Plaque of profl. merit Cariri sect. Coun. of Ceara, 2002, Diploma of Ethical Profl. Merit Fed. Medicine Coun., 2006, Jubilee of Gold, Diploma of Fifty Yrs. as Med. Doctor, Medice Meml. Pernam Buco, 2006. Fellow Brazilian Med. Assn. (specialist); mem. AAAS, ACP, Brazilian Soc. Clin. Medicine (specialist), NY Acad. Sci. Roman Catholic. Avocations: reading, walking, movies, farming. Office Phone: (088) 3521 1217.

**PEJAKOVIC, DUSAN,** physicist; b. Belgrade, Serbia-Monteneg (Yugoslavia), Oct. 13, 1969; s. Bosiljka and Aleksandar Pejakovic; life ptnr. Jelena Batinic. BS in physics, U. of Belgrade, 1994; MS in physics, Ohio State U., 2000, PhD in physics, 2001. Postdoctoral rschr. Dept. Physics, Ohio State U. Columbus, 2001—02; postdoctoral fellow Molecular Physics Lab., SRI Internat., Menlo Pk., Calif., 2002—05. Rsch. physicist, 2005—. Recipient Innovation in Rsch. award, SRI Internat.; Presdl. fellowship, Ohio State U., 2001, U. Fellowship, 1996—97. Mem.: Am. Geophys. Union, Am. Phys. Soc. Achievements include discovery of first organic-based optically tunable magnet; research in polymeric and organic-based magnets; light-induced magnetic effects; kinetics and collisional energy transfer in electronically excited oxygen molecules for airglow modeling. Avocations: tennis, travel. Office: SRI Internat 333 Ravenswood Ave Menlo Park CA 94025 Office Phone: 650-859-5129. E-mail: dusan.pejakovic@sri.com.

**PEKARSKY, MELVIN HIRSCH,** artist; b. Chgo., Sept. 18, 1934; s. Abe and Inda (Levin) P. Student, Sch. of Art Inst., Chgo., 1951-52; BA, Northwestern U., 1955, MA, 1956. Faculty Northwestern U., 1955-56; faculty Kendall Coll., 1960-67, chmn. art dept., 1965-67; asst. dean Sch. Visual Arts, N.Y.C., 1967-68, assoc. dean, 1968-69; grad. faculty NYU, 1970-71; assoc. prof. art SUNY, Stony Brook, 1975-84, prof. art, 1984—, chmn. dept., 1977-78, 84-89, dir. MFA and studio programs, 1990—2003. Chmn. SUNY, 2005—. One-man shows include Gimpel and Weitzenhoffer, N.Y.C., 1974, Lehigh U., 1975, Ball State U. Gallery, Muncie, Ind., 1975, G.W. Einstein Co., Inc., N.Y.C., 1975, 77, 78, 80, 81, 82, 84, 86, 88, 91, 95, 97, Hull Gallery, Washington, 1978, Centro Colombo-Americano, Bogotá, Colombia, 1980, 112 Greene St. Gallery, N.Y.C., 1980, 82, Marianne Deson Gallery, Chgo., 1987, Butler Inst. Am. Art, Youngstown, Ohio, 1990, The Mus. at Stony Brook, 1993, Nev. Mus. Art, Reno, 2001, Nielsen Gallery, Boston, 2002-03; group shows include Chgo. Art Inst., 1966, Whitney Mus., N.Y.C., 1971, Bklyn. Mus., 1974, Cleve. Mus., 1978, Cooper-Hewitt Mus., 1971, Mus. Modern Art Corp., Lending and Adv. Svc. Exhbns., Kuznetsky-Most Galleries, Moscow, 1989, NAD, N.Y.C., 1990, Fogg Mus. Art/Harvard U., 2000, 06, Am. Acad. and Arts and Letters, N.Y.C., 2001, Nielsen Gallery, Boston, 2001, 02, 03, 04, 05, public murals commns., Houston and Crosby Sts., N.Y.C., 1972, Lafayette and Bleecker Sts., N.Y.C., 1969; represented in permanent collections, Cleve. Mus., Fogg Mus. Art, Harvard U., Indpls. Mus., Nev. Museum of Art, Roswell Mus. Art, N.Mex., Westinghouse Corp., Corcoran Gallery Art, Yale U., Notre Dame U., AT&T, Chase Manhattan Bank, other pub. and corp. collections, also pvt. collections Founding mem., v.p., bd. dirs. City Walls, 1969-77. Served with Combat Engrs. AUS, 1957-59. Recipient grants in public art through City Walls Kaplan Fund, 1969, City Walls Bernhard Found., 1971, City Walls N.Y. State Council on Arts, 1970, City Walls Nat. Endowment for the Arts, 1971 Mem. Coll. Art Assn., Pub. Art Fund. Home: PO Box 1575 Stony Brook NY 11790-0875 Office: SUNY Art Dept Stony Brook NY 11794-5400 Office Phone: 631-689-9586. Personal E-mail: pekarsky@aol.com. Business E-Mail: mpekarsky@ms.cc.sunysb.edu.

**PEKER, ELYA ABEL,** artist; b. Moscow, June 15, 1937; came to U.S. 1972; s. Aba Z. and Frieda I. (Warshavsky) P.; m. Katrina Friedman, May 19, 1977; 1 child, Benjamin E. Diploma of Artist for Theater Decoration, Art Inst., Moscow, 1956. Comml. artist, N.Y.C., 1972-88. One-man shows include Nakhamkin Fine Art Gallery, N.Y.C., 1980-85; exhibited in group shows in Basel, Switzerland, Hong Kong, others; represented in permanent collections of Kennedy-Onassis family, Emil Wolf, Frank L'Angella, Campbell family, Benjamin family, others; contemporary flower and still-life poster series published 1991, reproductions published worldwide. Mem. Am. Biog. Inst. (dep. gov., order internat. ambs., Gold Record Achievement 1995, 20th Century Achievement award 1995, Internat. Cultural Diploma Honor 1996), Internat. Platform Assn., Licensing Industry Merchandiser's Assn. Home: 1610 E 19th St # 297-196 Brooklyn NY 11229

**PELACCIO, ZAKARY,** chef; Grad., U. VT, French Culinary Inst. Cook Seri Melayu, Kuala Lumpur, Malaysia, Westin Hotel, Chiang Mai, Thailand, The French Laundry, Daniel, Chickenbone Café, Brooklyn; owner, mgr. wired-kitchen.com; mgr., purchasing agt. Myriad Restaurant Grp.; script writer, field prodr. Dining Around, Food Network; exec. chef 5 Ninth, NYC, Fatty Crab, NYC. Adv. bd. Heritage Foods USA. Named one of NYC's Rising Stars, StarChefs.com, 2006. Mem.: Slow Food. Office: 5 Ninth 5 9th Ave New York NY 10014 Office Phone: 212-929-9460.*

**PÉLADEAU, MARIUS BEAUDOIN,** art historian, historian, consultant, retired museum director; b. Boston, Jan. 27, 1935; s. Marius and Lucienne (Beaudoin) P.; m. Mildred L. Cole, Feb. 26, 1972. BA cum laude, St. Michael's Coll., 1956; MS, Boston U., 1957; MA, Georgetown U., 1962. Assoc. editor Public Utilities Fortnightly, Washington, 1962-66; adminstrv. asst., press sec. to U.S. Congressman J. P. Vigorito, Washington, 1967-72; dir. Maine League Hist. Socs. and Mus.'s, Monmouth, 1972-76, William A. Farnsworth Library and Art Mus., Rockland, Maine, 1976-87; gen. mgr. The Theater at Monmouth, Maine, 1989; cons. in field, 1990—. Author: The Verse of Royall Tyler, 1968, The Prose of Royall Tyler, 1972, Chansonetta: The Life and Photographs of Chansonetta Stanely Emmons, 1858-1937, 1977, Charles Daniel Hubbard, 1876-1951: American Impressionist, 1996, John Francis Sprague: Chronicler of Maine History, 1998, Burnished Rows of Steel: The Role of Vermont Troops at the Battle of Gettysburg, July 1-3 1963, 2002, Willie Went to War: Willie Johnston, Drummer, 3rd Vermont Volunteers and Youngest Medal of Honor Recipient, 2005. Trustee Mus. Glass and Ceramics, 1983-2003; guest curator L.C. Bates Mus., Hinckley, Maine, 1993-2000; v.p. Readfield Historical Soc., 2005-. Fellow Co. Mil. Historians; mem. Vt. Hist. Soc. Democrat. Roman Catholic. Office Phone: 207-685-4537. Personal E-mail: peladeau@gwi.net.

**PELAVIN, SOL HERBERT,** research company executive; b. Detroit, Dec. 16, 1941; s. Norman J. and Alice A. Pelavin; m. Diane Christine Blakemore, Aug. 14, 1966; 2 children. BA in Math., U. Chgo., 1965, MAT in Math., 1969; MS in Stats., Stanford U., 1974, PhD candidate in mathematical models of edn. research, 1975. Tchr. pub. schs., 1965-70. teaching rsch. asst. Stanford (Calif.) U., 1972-74; cons. Rand Corp., Santa Monica, Calif., 1975; policy analyst SRI Internat., Menlo Park, Calif., 1975-78; exec. officer NTS Research Corp., Durham, N.C., 1978-82; pres. Pelavin Assocs., Inc., Washington, 1982-94; exec. v.p., COO Am. Inst. Rsch., 1994-2001, pres., CEO, 2001-; dir. Data Analysis and Tech. Support Ctr., Washington, 1989-93, Policy Analysis Support Ctr., Washington, 1993—; expert witness to U.S. Congress, 1977, 79, Cabinet briefing 1983; cons. Frank, Bernstein, Conway and Goldman, Balt., 1980-81; dir. Ednl. Analysis Ctr., Washington, 1982-85. Author: (with P. Barker) A Study of the Generalizability of the Results of Standardized Achievement Tests, 1976, (with J.L. David) Research on the Effectiveness of Compensatory Education Programs: A Reanalysis of Data, 1977, (with others) Federal Expenditures for the Education of Children and Youth With Special Needs, 1981, (with D.C. Pelavin) An Evaluation of the Fund for the Improvement of Postsecondary Education, 1981, 83, (with others) Evaluation of the Commodity Supplemental Food Program, 1982, An Evaluation of the Bilingual Education Evaluation, Dissemination and Assessment Centers, 1984, A Study of a Year-Round School Program, 1978, Teacher

Preparation: A Review of State Certification Requirements, 1984, Analysis of the National Availability of Mathematics and Science Teachers, 1983, Minority Participation in Higher Education, 1988, Changing the Odds, 1990, others; contbr. articles to profl. jours. NSF fellow U. Chgo., 1968-69; Cuneo fellow Stanford U., 1973. Mem. Am. Ednl. Research Assn., Am. Psychol. Assn. Democrat. Jewish. Office: American Inst Rsch 1000 Thomas Jefferson Washington DC 20007-3500 Office Phone: 202-342-5000. Business E-mail: spelavin@air.org.

**PELCYGER, ELAINE,** school psychologist; b. Jersey City, N.J., Apr. 13, 1939; d. Maurice C. and Bessie (Schneider) Morley; m. Iran Pelcyger, June 4, 1956; children: Stuart Lawrence, Gwynne Ellice, Wayne Farrol. BA magna cum laude, L.I. U., 1983; MS, St. John's U., Flushing, N.Y., 1985. Cert. sch. psychologist N.Y., N.Y.C., nat. cert. sch. psychologist, group psychotherapist, N.Y. Sch. psychologist N.Y.C. Bd. Edn., 1985—2006; trauma and loss sch. specialist; ret., 2006. Mem. Nat. Assn. Sch. Psychologists, Am. Group Psychotherapists, N.Y. Assn. Sch. Psychologists, Psi Chi. Avocations: handicrafts, reading, old time radio. Office Phone: 718-329-8039. E-mail: epelcyger@nyc.boe.net.

**PELFREY, D. PATTON,** lawyer; b. Ky., 1941; BA, Calif. State U., L.A., 1963; JD, U. Louisville, 1968. Bar: Ky. 1968. Trial atty. region 9 NLRB, Cin., 1968-72; mem. Frost Brown Todd LLC, Louisville, 1972—. Prof. labor law sch. law U. Louisville. Fellow Coll. Labor and Emloyment Lawyers; mem. ABA (sect. labor and employment law), Ky. Bar Assn. (labor sect.), Louisville Bar Assn. (mem. labor com. 1983—), Delta Theta Phi. Office: Frost Brown Todd LLC 400 W Market St Ste 3200 Louisville KY 40202-3363 Office Phone: 502-589-5400. E-mail: ppelfrey@fbtlaw.com.

**PELHAM, ANN,** publishing executive, department chairman; BA, Duke Univ., 1974. Reporter The News & Observer, Raleigh, NC, Congl. Quarterly, Washington, Governing Mag.; reporter through exec. editor Legal Times, Washington, 1988—96, assoc. pub., 1996—98, publisher, 1998—; v.p. Duke U. Alumni Assn., 2004—; chmn. Duke Student Pub. Co., 2003—. Editor: The Chronicle (Duke Univ. newspaper). Office: Legal Times Ste 800 1730 M St NW Washington DC 20036 Office Phone: 202-457-0686. Office Fax: 202-457-0718.

**PELHAM, JUDITH,** health system administrator; b. Bristol, Conn., July 23, 1945; d. Marvin Curtis and Muriel (Chodos) Pelham; m. Jon N. Coffee, Dec. 30, 1992; children: Rachel Welch, Molly, Edward. BA, Smith Coll., 1967; MPA, Harvard U., 1975. Various govt. postions, 1968-72; prin. analyst Urban Systems, Cambridge, Mass., 1972-73; dir. devel. and planning Roxbury Dental and Med. Group, Boston, 1975-76; asst. to dir. for gen. medicine and ambulatory care Peter B. Brigham Hosp., Boston, 1976-77, asst. dir. ambulatory care, 1977-79; asst. v.p. Brigham and Women's Hosp., Boston, 1980-81; dir. planning and mktg. Seton Med. Ctr., Austin, Tex., 1980-82, pres., 1982-92, CEO, 1987-92; pres., CEO Daughters of Charity Health Svcs., Austin, 1987-92, Mercy Health Svcs., Farmington Hills, Mich., 1993—2000, Trinity Health (merger of Mercy Health Svcs. and Holy Cross Health Sys.), Novi, Mich., 2000—04, pres. emeritus, 2005—. Bd. dirs. Amgen, 1995—, Cath. CEO Healthcare Connection, 1998—2004; cons. Robert W. Johnson Found., 1979—80; mem. mgmt. bd. Inst. for Diversity in Health Mgmt., 1994—97; chair Coalition for Non-Profit Healthcare, 1997—2000, exec. com., 1997—2002; mem. Healthcare Rsch. and Devel. Inst., 1998—2005, bd., 2003—05; mem. adv. bd. RAND Health Compare Strategic Policy, 2005—; mem. strategic adv. bd. Shattuck Hammond, 2005—; mem. strategic adv. com. for comprehensive assessment of reform efforts RAND Corp., 2006—. Contbr. articles to profl. jours. Trustee A. Shivers Radiation Therapy Ctr., Austin, 1982—92, Marywood Maternity and Adoption Agy., 1982—86; bd. dirs. Quality of Life Found., Austin, 1985, Austin Rape Crisis Ctr., adv. bd. mem., 1986—88; bd. dirs., trustee League House, 1992—93, Seton Fund, 1982—93, Greater Detroit Area Health Coun.; mem. Gov.'s Job Tng. Coordinating Coun., 1983—85; mem. adv. coun. U. Tex. Social Work Found., 1983—85; charter mem. Leadership Tex., Austin, 1983—93. Named one of Detroit's 100 Most Influential Women, Crain's Detroit Bus., 1997, 2002; recipient Leadership award, YWCA Austin, 1986, CEO IT Achievement award, Modern Healthcare, Healthcare Info. Mgmt. Sys. Soc., 2004. Fellow: Am. Hosp. Assn., Am. Coll. Healthcare Execs. (bd. dirs. 1987—95); mem.: Cath. Health Assn. (sec., treas. 1982—95, com. on govt. rels. 1984—91, chair fin. com. 1992—95, bd. dirs. 1987—95), Tex. Coll. Health Facilities (bd. dirs. 1985—89, pres. 1988), Austin Area Rsch. Orgn., Tex. Hosp. Assn. (various couns. 1982—87). Home (Winter): 9939 E Celtic Dr Scottsdale AZ 85260

**PELHAM, TOM,** commissioner; Commr. fin. and mgmt. dept. Vt. State Fin. and Mgmt. Dept., Montpelier, 2000—. Office: Vt State Fin and Mgmt Dept Pavilion Office Bldg 109 State St Montpelier VT 05609-0001

**PELKEY, LAWRENCE MICHAEL,** school psychologist; b. Oswego, N.Y., Sept. 24, 1964; s. Richard David and Elizabeth Anne Pelkey. BA, SUNY, Oswego, 2001, MS, 2004. Nat. cert. sch. psychologist. Asst. coord. disability svcs. office SUNY, Oswego, 2001—03; sch. psychologist Syracuse (N.Y.) City Sch. Dist., 2003—04, Canastota (N.Y.) Cen. Sch. Dist., 2003—04, Cayuga-Onondaga Bd. Coop. Edn. Svcs., Auburn, NY, 2004—. Team coord. sch.-based intervention Cayuga-Onondaga Bd. Coop. Edn. Svcs., Auburn, 2004—; sch. bd. intervention team coord. Syracuse City Sch. Dist., 2003—04. Vol. pet visitor VA Hosp., Syracuse, 2002—; Babe Ruth coaching asst. North Syracuse Youth Baseball; umpire Cen. Sq. Youth Softball. Recipient William G. McGarvey award for Outstanding Sr. in Psychology, Oswego State U., 2000, presdl. scholarship, SUNY Oswego, 2002, Donald Snygg Grad. award, 2003. Mem.: N.Y. Assn. Sch. Psychologists, Nat. Assn. Sch. Psychologists, Psi Chi, Phi Kappa Phi. Avocations: sewing, camping, motorcycle, hiking. Home: 6057 B East Taft Rd Syracuse NY 13212 Office: Cayuga Onondaga Bd Coop Edn Svcs 5980 South St Rd Auburn NY 13021 E-mail: limpelkey@hotmail.com.

**PELL, ARTHUR ROBERT,** human resources specialist, consultant, writer; b. NYC, Jan. 22, 1920; s. Harry and Rae (Meyers) P.; m. Erica Frost, May 19, 1946; children— Douglas, Hilary. AB, NYU, 1939, MA, 1944; PhD, Calif. Coast U., 1977; diploma, Cornell U., 1943. Personnel dir. Eagle-Electric Mfg. Co., Long Island City, N.Y., 1946-50, North Atlantic Constructors, N.Y.C., 1950-53; v.p. Harper Assos., Inc., N.Y.C., 1953-75; cons. Human Resources Mgmt., Hempstead, N.Y., 1975—. Adj. assoc. prof. mgmt. NYU Sch. Continuing Edn., 1962-84, St. John's U. Coll. Bus. Adminstrn., 1971-76; lectr. Baruch Sch. Bus. and Pub. Adminstrn. Coll. City N.Y., 1948-67. Author: (with W.B. Patterson) Fire Officer's Guide to Leadership, rev. edit., 1963, Placing Salesmen, 1963, Placing Executives, 1964, Police Leadership, 1967, How to Get the Job You Want After 40, 1967, Recruiting and Selecting Personnel, 1969, (with M. Harper) Starting and Managing an Employment Agency, 1970, Recruiting, Training and Motivating Volunteer Workers, 1972, Be a Better Employment Interviewer, 1972, rev. edits., 1978, 86, 94, The College Graduate Guide to Job Finding, 1973; (with Wilma Rogalin) Women's Guide to Executive Positions, 1975; (with Albert Furbay) College Student's Guide to Career Planning, 1975; (with Dale Carnegie Assocs.) Managing Through People, 1975, rev. edits., 1978, 1987, Choosing a College Major: Business, 1978, Enrich Your Life: The Dale Carnegie Way, 1979, The Part Time Job Book, 1984, Making the Most of Medicare, 1987, rev. edit., 1990; (with George Sadek) Resumes for Engineers, 1982, Resumes for Computer Professionals, 1984, How to Sell Yourself on an Interview, 1982, The Job Finder's Kit, 1989, Getting the Most from Your People, 1990, Diagnosing Your Doctor, 1991, The Supervisor's Infobank, 1994, The Complete Idiot's Guide to Managing People, 1995, 3d edit., 2003, The Pocket Idiot's Guide to One Minute Management, 1999, The Complete Idiot's Guide to Team Building, 1999, The Complete Idiot's Guide to Recruiting The Right Stuff, 2000, The Complete's Idiot Guide to Human Resources Management, 2001, (with Franklin C. Ashley) Embracing Excellence, 2001; editl. cons. for revision Dale Carnegie's How to Win Friends and Influence People, 1981;

author syndicated feature The Human Side; contbr. articles to profl. jours. With AUS, 1942-46. Home and Office: 400 High Point Dr Apt 101 Hartsdale NY 10530-1125 Office Phone: 914-949-1382. Personal E-mail: arpell22@optonline.net.

**PELL, CLAIBORNE,** former senator; b. NYC, Nov. 22, 1918; s. Herbert Claiborne and Matilda (Bigelow) P.; m. Nuala O'Donnell, Dec. 1944; children: Herbert Claiborne III, Christopher T. Hartford, Nuala Dallas Yates, Julia L.W. Student, St. George's Sch., Newport, R.I.; AB cum laude, Princeton U., 1940; AM, Columbia U., 1946; 51 hon. degrees. Enlisted USCGR, 1941; served as seaman, ensign North Atlantic sea duty, Africa, Italy; hospitalized to U.S., 1944; instr. Navy Sch. Mil. Govt., Princeton, 1944-45; capt. USCGR; ret.; on loan to State Dept. at San Francisco Conf., 1945, State Dept., 1945-46, U.S. embassy, Czechoslovakia, 1946-47; established consulate gen. Bratislava, Czechoslovakia, 1947-48; vice consul Genoa, Italy, 1949; assigned State Dept., 1950-52; v.p., dir. Internat. Rescue Com.; senator from R.I., 1961-96; U.S. del. to UN, 97—. Ranking minority mem. Fgn. Rels. Com., Labor and Human Resources Subcom. on Edn., Arts, and Humanities; mem. Rules and Adminstrn. Com., Joint Com. on Libr. and Congl. Intern Program, Senate Dem. Policy Com.; U.S. del. Internat. Maritime Consultative Orgn., London, 1959, 25th Gen. Assembly, 1970; disting. vis. prof. Salve Regina U., Newport, R.I., 1997—. Author: Megalopolis Unbound, 1966, (with Harold L. Goodwin) Challenge of the Seven Seas, 1966, Power and Policy, 1972. Hon. bd. dirs. World Affairs Council R.I.; trustee St. George's Sch.; trustee emeritus Brown U.; Cons. Democratic Nat. Com., 1953-60; exec. asst. to chmn. R.I. State Dem. Com., 1952-54; chmn. R.I. Dem. Fund drive, 1952, Dem. nat. registration, chmn., 1956, co-chmn., 1962; chief delegation tally clk. Dem. Nat. Conv., 1956, 60, 64, 68. Decorated knight Crown of Italy, Grand Cross Order of Merit Italy, Red Cross of Merit Portugal, Legion of Honor France, comdr. Order of Phoenix Greece, Grand Cross Order of Merit Liechtenstein, Grand Cross Order of Christ Portugal, Order of Henry the Navigator, Portugal, Grand Cross Order of N. Star Sweden, Grand Cross of Merit Knights of Malta, Grand Officer of Merit Luxembourg, Grand Comdr. Lebanon; recipient Caritas Elizabeth medal Cardinal Franz Koenig, Grand decoration of honor in silver with sash Austria, Gold medal of St. Barnabas (Cyprus), recipient Pres.'s Fellow award R.I. Sch. Design, medal Nat. Order of Cedar, Hugo Grotius Commemorative medal The Netherlands, recipient Harold W. McGraw, Jr. Prize in Education, McGraw-Hill, 1988. Mem. Soc. Cin. Clubs: Hope (Providence); Knickerbocker (N.Y.C.); Racquet and Tennis (N.Y.C.), Brook (N.Y.C.); Metropolitan (Washington); Travellers (Paris); Reading Room (Newport); White's (London). Democrat. Episcopalian. *I have a seven word definition of my job and of my life: "Translate ideas into events, and help people.".*

**PELL, JONATHAN LAURENCE,** performing company executive; b. Memphis, Oct. 20, 1949; s. Burton Marshall and Eleanor (Leopold) P. BA, U. So. Calif., 1971. Interior designer Gene Morse Assocs., Wichita, Kans., 1971-77; mgr. Internat. Artists Mgmt., N.Y.C., 1977-79, Robert Lombardo Assocs., N.Y.C., 1979-80; TV producer Sta. WNET, N.Y.C., 1980-83; dir. publicity John Curry Skating Co., N.Y.C., 1983; prodr. Jerome Kern Centennary Gala Town Hall, N.Y.C., 1984; dir. artistic administration The Dallas Opera, 1984—. Vocal competition judge Met. Opera Nat. Coun. Auditions, Pavarotti Competition, Bidu Sayao Internat. Competition, Brazil, George London Awards, Ctr. for Contemporary Opera, Jensen Found. Competition, Dallas Opera Guild, Denver Lyric Opera Guild, Ft. Worth Opera, Marguerite McCammon Competition, San Antonio Opera Guild, Richard Tucker Award, others; tchr. master classes for young singers Opera Am., Nat. Opera Assn., Can. Opera Co., S.W. Chpt. NATS, Performing Arts Assistance Corp., U. North Tex., Internat. Sch. Performing Arts, Amarillo Opera, So. Meth. U.; host Dallas Opera Radio Hour, WRR, 1994—97, Inside the Dallas Opera, WRR, 2004—; advisor singer svcs. com. Opera Am.; lectr. on opera Crystal Cruises. Bd. dirs., chmn. nat. auditions com., mem. award selection com. Richard Tucker Music Found.; mem. adv. bd. Awards Recognizing Individual Artistry; advisor to singer svcs. com. Opera Am. Office: Dallas Opera Campbell Ctr I LBI-11 8350 N Central Expy Ste 210 Dallas TX 75206-1601 Office Phone: 214-443-1043.

**PELL, SIDNEY,** epidemiologist; b. NYC, Dec. 13, 1922; m. Lola May, July 2, 1950. MBA, CCNY, 1952; PhD, U. Pitts., 1956. Biostatistician E.I. Du Pont de Nemours and Co., Wilmington, Del., 1955-76, mgr. epidemiology sect., 1976-82, sr. cons., 1982-85; epidemiology cons. Wilmington, 1985—. Epidemiology cons. Del. Divsn. Pub. Health, Dover, 1986-95. Contbr. articles to New Eng. Jour. Medicine, Jour. Occupational Medicine, Jour. AMA. With U.S. Army, 1943-45, ETO. Recipient Merit in Authorship Hon. Mention, Inds. Med. Assn., 1959. Fellow Am. Coll. Epidemiology, Am. Heart Assn., Am. Pub. Health Assn., Delta Omega. Home: 1416 Emory Rd Wilmington DE 19803-5120 E-mail: pell104@aol.com.

**PELL, TERENCE J.,** legal association administrator; BA, Haverford Coll., 1976; JD, Cornell Law Sch., 1981; PhD, U. Notre Dame, 1996. Atty. Arent, Fox, Kintner, Plotkin & Kahn; dep. asst. sec. for civil rights U.S. Dept. Edn., 1985—88; gen. counsel, chief of staff Office of Nat. Drug Control Policy; sr. counsel Ctr for Individual Rights, Washington, 1997—2000, pres., 2000—. Office: Ctr for Individual Rights 1233 20th St NW Ste 300 Washington DC 20036

**PELLA, MILTON ORVILLE,** science educator; b. Wilmot, Wis., Feb. 13, 1914; s. Charles August and Ida Marie (Pagel) P.; m. Germaine Marie Reich, Dec. 9, 1944. B.E., Milw. State Tchrs Coll. 1935, M.S., 1940, PhD, 1948. 1chr. sci. and math. Wyler Mil. Acad., 1937-38; tchr. elementary sch. Delavan Pub. Schs., 1938-39; tchr. sci. U. Wis. High Sch., 1939-42; prof. sci. edn. U. Wis., Madison, 1946-80, prof. emeritus, 1980—; With Fgn. Ednl. Service, 1959—81. Author: Physical Science for Progress, 3d edit, 1970, Science Horizons— The Biological World, (with Branley and Urban), 1965-70. Served with AUS, 1942-46. Fellow AAAS; mem. Ctrl. Assn. Sci. and Math. (pres. 1955), Nat. Assn. for Rsch. in Sci. Tchg. (pres. 1966), Nat. Sci. Tchrs. Assn. (dir. 1950, 60), Masons. Home: 6175 Mineral Point Rd Rm 328 Madison WI 53705

**PELLEGRINI, CLAUDIO,** physicist, educator; b. Rome, May 9, 1935; arrived in U.S., 1978; s. Edmondo and Margherita (Sabatini) Pellegrini; m. Maria Grazia Tomassetti, Dec. 27, 1961; children: Luca, Matteo, Flavia. Laurea, U. Rome, 1958, libera docenza, 1965. Physicist Frascati (Italy) Nat. Lab., 1959-63, physicist, group leader, 1963-76, divsn. head, 1976-78; sr. scientist Brookhaven Nat. Lab., Upton, 1978-89, assoc. chmn. Nat. Synchrotron Light Source, 1985-89; disting. prof. UCLA, 1989—, chmn. dept. physics & astronomy, 2001—04. Mem. high energy physics adv. panel Dept. Energy, 1992—. Editor: (book) High Power Laser and Applications, 1978, Laser Handbook: Free Electron Laser, 1991. Recipient Internat. Free Electron Laser prize, 2000; fellow, Fulbright Found., 1997. Fellow: Am. Phys. Soc. (chair particle beam divsn. 1988—89, R.R. Wilson prize 2000). Achievements include discovery of head-tail effect; research in particle accelerators and colliders; free electron lasers and high brightness electron beams; theory of high gain, self-amplified spontaneous emission for x-ray free electron laser. Office: UCLA Los Angeles CA 90024-1547 Office Phone: 310-206-1677.

**PELLEGRINI, JOHN B.,** lawyer; b. Leominster, Mass., Jan. 1, 1942; AB cum laude, Boston Coll., 1963; LLB, Columbia U., 1966; LLM in Internat. Law, NYU, 1973. Bar: NY 1970, US Ct. Internat. Trade 1971. Atty. US Customs Svc., 1970-73; J.C. Penny Co. Inc.; ptnr. Kaplan & Pellegrini, NYC, Baskin & Steingut, NYC; joined Ross & Hardies, NYC, 1985; now co-mng. ptnr. NYC office McGuireWoods LLP. Mem. ABA (internat. trade com., internat. law sect. 1976—), Customs and Internat. Trade Bar Assn. (adminstrv. practice com. 1981-84, bd. dirs. 1984-88). Office: McGuireWoods LLP 7th Fl 1345 Ave of the Americas New York NY 10105-0106 Office Phone: 212-548-7020. Office Fax: 212-715-2301. Business E-mail: jpellegrini@mcguirewoods.com.

**PELLEGRINO, EDMUND DANIEL,** internist, educator, retired academic administrator; b. Newark, June 22, 1920; s. Michael J. and Marie (Catone) Pellegrino; m. Clementine Coakley, Nov. 17, 1944; children: Thomas, Virginia, Michael, Andrea, Alice, Leah. BS, St. John's U., 1941, DSc (hon.), 1971; MD, NYU, 1944; 39 hon. degrees. Diplomate Am. Bd. Internal Medicine. Intern Bellevue Hosp., N.Y.C., 1944—45, asst. resident medicine, 1948—49; resident medicine Goldwater Meml. Hosp., N.Y.C., 1945—46; fellow medicine NYU, 1949—50; supervising Tb physician Homer Folks Hosp., Oneonta, NY, 1950—53; dir. internal medicine Hunterdon Med. Center, Flemington, NJ, 1953—59, med. dir., 1955—59; prof., chmn. dept. medicine U. Ky. Med. Center, 1959—66; prof. medicine SUNY, Stony Brook, 1966—72, v.p. for health scis., dir. Health Scis. Center, 1968—73, dean Sch. Medicine, 1968—72; v.p. health affairs U. Tenn. System; chancellor U. Tenn. Med. Units, Memphis, 1973—75; prof. med. Yale U., New Haven, 1975—78; pres. Yale-New Haven Med. Center, 1975—78, Cath. U. Am., Washington, 1978—82, prof. philosophy and biology, 1978—82; John Carroll prof. medicine and med. ethics Georgetown U., Washington, 1982—; dir. Kennedy Inst. Ethics, Washington, 1983—88; dir. Ctr. for Advanced Study Ethics Georgetown U., Washington, 1988—94, dir. Ctr. for Clin. Bioethics, 1991—, acting chief Divsn. Gen. Internal Medicine, 1993—94, chief Gen. Internal Medicine, 1995. Founding editor: Jour. Medicine and Philosophy, 1983—. Chmn. Pres.'s Coun. on Bioethics, 2005—. With USAF, 1946—48. Master: ACP; fellow: N.Y. Acad. Medicine; mem.: Inst. Medicine NAS, AMA, Am. Clin. and Climatol. Assn., Assn. Am. Physicians. Office: Georgetown U Ctr for Clin Bioethics Washington DC 20007 Office Phone: 202-687-5397, 202-296-5754.

**PELLEGRINO, PETER,** surgeon; b. Camden, N.J., July 7, 1934; s. Peter and Alice (Alchin) P.; m. Barbara Ann Holdon, June 18, 1960; children: Peter Scott, Kathleen Ann, Lisa Marie. AB in Psychology, Franklin-Marshall Sch., 1956; MD, Hahnemann Med. Coll., 1960. Diplomate Am. Bd. Surgery. Intern, Hahnemann Hosp., Phila., 1960-61, surg. resident, 1961-62, surg. resident, 1965-67, 68, attending surgeon, 1969—; chief dept. surgery Kessler Hosp., Hammonton, N.J., 1969—. Served to capt., U.S. Army, 1962-65. Fellow ACS; mem. Am. Acad. Proctology, Soc. Abdominal Surgeons, AMA, N.J. Med. Soc., Hahnemann Alumni Assn. (1st v.p. 1984). Republican. Office Phone: 609-561-8150.

**PELLEGROM, DANIEL EARL,** health and development executive; b. Three Rivers, Mich., May 29, 1944; s. Francis Robert and Regina Elizabeth (Valentine) P.; m. Sally Margaret Stukenbroeker, Nov. 30, 1968; children: Daniel Jr., Benjamin, Sara. BA, Western Mich. U., 1966; MDiv, Union Theol. Seminary, 1969. Ordained to ministry, Presbyn. Ch., 1970. Dir. coll. programs Planned Parenthood Fedn., N.Y.C., 1969-71; exec. dir. Memphis Planned Parenthood, 1971-75, Md. Planned Parenthood, Balt., 1975-85; pres. Pathfinder Internat., Watertown, Mass., 1985—. Mem. Gov.'s conf. on children and youth State of Md., Balt., 1978-80; assoc. Sch. Hygiene and Pub. Health Johns Hopkins U., Balt., 1984-85; pres. bd. mgrs. Brush Found., Cleve.; bd. dirs. InterAction, WAshington, World Neighbors, Oklahoma City, Planned Parenthood League of Mass., Boston. Recipient Leadership award Greater Balt. Com., 1983-84, UN Population award Pathfinder Internat., 1996, Internat. award Nat. Family Planning and Reproductive Health Assn., 1997, Friendship award Pathfinder Internat. Govt. Vietnam, 2005. Mem. APHA. Democrat. Avocations: baseball, travel, hiking. Home: 48 Bound Brook Rd Newton MA 02461-2036 Office: Pathfinder Internat 9 Galen St Ste 217 Watertown MA 02472-4523 E-mail: dpellegrom@pathfind.org.

**PELLETIER, ANDREW JOHN,** music educator; b. Lewiston, Maine, Sept. 8, 1973; s. Paul Leo Pelletier and Lucille Priscilla Caron; m. Christina Marie Laberge, June 5, 1994. MusB in Performance, U. So. Maine, 1995; MusM, U. So. Calif., 1998, MusD, 2001. Adj. prof. horn Dept. Music Moor (Calif.) Pk. Coll., 2001—04; asst. prof. horn Coll. Musical Arts Bowling Green (Ohio) State U., 2005—. Vis. asst. prof. horn Coll. Musical Arts Bowling Green (Ohio) State U., 2004—05. Musician: American Horn Competition (First prize U. Divsn., 1997, Grand prize, 1997, First prize Profl. Divsn., 2001), Santa Barbara (Calif.) Syphony Orch., 2002—, (films) Lethal Weapon IV, The X-Men, Frequency, other TV and Film work. Named Oustanding Graduate, U. So. Calif., Flora L. Thornton Sch. Music, 1998; recipient, 2001, Robert Marstellar Meml. Brass award, 2001, Ronald F. Cole Disting. Alumni award, U. So. Maine Sch. Music, 2002; Jon Hawkins Meml. scholarship. Mem.: Hist. Brass Soc., Brit. Horn Soc., Internat. Horn Soc. Democrat. Episc. Achievements include research in natural horn construction at the Bate Collection of Musical Instruments at the University of Oxford, England. Research resulted in new designs of natural and Baroque horns. Avocations: reading, cooking, travel, history, calligraphy. Office: Bowling Green State University College of Musical Arts-1058 MMAC Bowling Green OH 43403 Office Phone: 419-372-2321. Office Fax: 419-372-2938. E-mail: pandrew@bgnet.bgsu.edu.

**PELLETIER, ARTHUR JOSEPH,** state legislator, data processing executive, educator; b. Dec. 13, 1946; s. Joseph Telesphor and Elsie Jane (Dillon) Pelletier; m. Marsha Lynn Mingle, May 19, 1973; 1 child, John. Diploma, N.H. Vocat. Tech. Inst., 1966; BA, Kans. State U., 1970, MS, 1972. Asst. to dir. Kans. State U. Divsn. Contbg. Edn., Manhattan, 1971-74; tchr. drafting Portsmouth (N.H.) HS, 1974-86; tchr. computer programming McIntosh Coll., Dover, NH, 1982-84; assoc. prof. N.H. Vocat.-Tech. Coll., Stratham, 1986-87; kitchen designer Area Kitchen Ctr., Portsmouth, 1987; mem. N.H. Ho. of Reps., 1993—2004; asst. to archivist Berwick Acad., South Berwick, Maine, 2005—. Mem. legis. sci., tech. and energy com. N.H. Ho. of Reps., 1993—96, 2003—04, mem. legis. edn. com., 1997—2000; co-founder N.H. Coalition Edn.; mem. Dover Ready to Learn Task Force, 1995—2001; mem. evaluation and rev. com. Dover Scho.; mem. curriculum com., 1997—2001; bd. advs. Hub Family Support Ctr., 1996—97. Mem. Partnership Healthier Cmty., 1995—97, Ams. Non-Smoker's Rights, 1996—; chmn. Friends Dover Libr., 2004—. Avocations: radio-controlled model aircraft, tennis, photography. Home: 94 Back River Rd Dover NH 03820-4411

**PELLETIER, JOHN B., JR.,** mathematics professor, consultant; s. John B. and Doris B. Pelletier; m. Judi B. Pelletier, June 12, 1971; children: Jennifer Ann, Sara D. BS, Castleton State U., Vt., 1973, MAE, 1978. Middle sch. math. tchr. Rockingham Sch. Dist., Bellows Falls, Vt., 1973—2003, math coord. grades 5-8, 2003—04; math. tchr. Leland & Grey Unified H.S., Townshend, Vt., 2004—05, SAU 29 Keene H.S., 2005—. Network math leader Vt. Dept. Edn., Montpelier, 2001—04, per-diem cons., 2003—04. Recipient Sportsmanship award, Vt. Soccer Ofcls. Orgn., 1999. Mem.: KC (grand knight 753 2001—04, 4th degree color guard 2000—). Roman Catholic. Avocations: fly fishing, fishing, bus driving, coaching. Home: 3 Overpass Rd Chester VT 05143 Office: Keene HS Arch St Keene NH

**PELLETIER, LOUIS CONRAD,** surgeon, educator, health facility administrator; b. Montreal, Que., Can., Mar. 15, 1940; s. Conrad L. and Lucienne (Rochette) P.; m. Louise Montpetit, June 26, 1965; children: Conrad R., Marie-Helene. BA, Brébeuf Coll., Montreal, 1959; MD, U. Montreal, 1964, MBA, 1996. Resident in cardiovascular and thoracic surgery U. Montreal, 1964-70, chmn. dept. surgery, 1986-94; rsch. asst. Mayo Clin. Found., Rochester, Minn., 1970-72; mem. dept. surgery Maisonneuve-Rosemont Hosp., Montreal, 1972-76, Sacré-Coeur Hosp., Montreal, 1972-80, Montreal Heart Inst., 1979—2000, head dept. surgery, 1979-87; dir. rsch. Ctr. Sacré-Coeur Hosp., 1998—2002; pres. Cardianove, Inc., 1998—; dir. med. affairs Sacré-Coeur hosp., 2000—02; cons. in health adminstrn. and mgmt. of emergency wards, 2002—. Contbr. articles to profl. jours. Mem. adminstrv. bd. College Stanislas, Montreal, 1979-86, Que. Heart Found., 1980-84, regional healthcare bd., 1991-92, Hotel-Dieu Hosp., 1993-95. Recipient Young Investigator's award Am. Coll. Cardiology, 1972; Med. Rsch. Coun. Can. scholar U. Montreal, 1973-78. Fellow Royal Coll. Physicians and Surgeons Can.; mem. ACS, Association des Medecins de Langue Francaise du Canada, Can. Med. Assn., Royal Coll. Can., Assn. Cardiovascular and Thoracic Surgery Que., Can. Cardiovascular Soc., Montreal Cardiac Soc., Clin. Rsch. Club Que., Soc. Thoracic Surgeons, Can. Assn. Clin. Surgeons, Sociedad de Cardiocirujanos, Coun. on Cardiovasular Surgery, Am. Heart

Assn., Internat. Soc. for Heart Transplantation, Can. Soc. Cardiovascular and Thoracic Surgeons, Am. Assn. Thoracic Surgery, Am. Surgical Assn. Roman Catholic. Avocations: skiing, bicycling.

**PELLETIER, MARSHA LYNN**, secondary school educator, poet; b. Mt. Pleasant, Mich., July 29, 1950; d. Eugene Russell and Mary Ellen (Edde) Mingle; m. Arthur Joseph Pelletier, May 19, 1973; 1 child, John Frederick. BS in Home Econs. and Edn., Kans. State U., 1971, MS in Edn. Guidance and Counseling, 1972. Lic. real estate broker N.H. Conf. coord., guidance counselor Kans. State U., Manhattan, 1971-73; tchr. home econs. Franklin (Mass.) HS, 1974, Exeter (N.H.) HS, 1974-75, Barrington (N.H.) Mid. Sch., 1975-81, Pentucket Regional Jr. HS, West Newbury, Mass., 1981-82; realtor assoc. Century 21 Ocean and Norword Realty, Portsmouth, NH, 1983-86; tchr. interior design, cons. U. N.H., Durham, 1986-87; tchr. family and consumer sci. Dover (N.H.) Mid. Sch., 1983—2001; tchr. Dover HS, 2001—; mem. legis. adminstrn. com. N.H. Ho. of Reps., Concord, 1992—94, 1996—2002; ind. real estate broker Dover, 1986-2000. Bd. dirs. N.H. State Profl. Bd. Stds., 1999—2004; assessor Nat. Bd. Profl. Tchg. Stds., 2001; tchr. assessor Nat. Tchrs. Bd. Cert., 2002—. Author: (poems) Portsmouth Unabridge: New Poems for an Old City, 2002, Arriving at the Crossroads, 2003, Exeter, New Hampshire: Where the River Meets the Tide, 2005; costume dir. & designer: Guys and Dolls, 2004; actress (hist. dramatization) Factory on Fire. Bd. dirs. Dover Adult Learning Ctr., 1995—98; mem. Health Task Force, Dover, Concord, 1993—94, Cornerstone Dancers, Dover Friends of Pub. Libr., 1996—, bd. supt. adv. com., 2001—06, poetry judge, 2003—; bd. principal's adv. com., 2004—; mem. faculty coun. Dover H.S., 2004—; trustee St. John's Meth. Ch., 1995—97. Named to Nat. Honor Roll for Outstanding Am. Tchrs., 2006; recipient Best Poets award, Internat. Soc. Poetry, 2000, 2001, 2002, 2004. Mem.: NEA (local pres., negotiator, v.p., membership chair, mem. leadership exec. com., bldg. rep. 1979—, N.H. del. to nat. conv.), Seacoast Writers Assn., Nat. Coalition Consumer Econ., Alpha Delta Kappa (v.p., historian, altruistic chmn. 1984—89). Democrat. Avocations: gardening, aerobics, poetry, sewing, cooking. Home: 94 Back River Rd Dover NH 03820-4411

**PELLETIER, SHO-MEI**, musician, educator; b. Tucson, July 25, 1952; d. Harold W. and Mary Pelletier; m. Dwight E. Shambley, Aug. 12, 1979; children: Aaron Joshua Pelletier-Shambley, Alexis Jessica Pelletier-Shambley. Student, No. Ariz. U., 1965—66, Ariz. State U., 1965—66; MusB in Violin, Ind. U., 1974; student with, Josef Gingold, 1970—75, Ivan Galamian, 1969—75, Sally Thomas, 1969, Sydney Harth, 1967, Angel Reyes, 1968, Dr. Frank Spinosa, 1965—70, Dr. Harold W. Pelletier, 1966. Asst. prin. violinist Dallas Symphony Orch., assoc. prin. violinist, 1993—, solo violinist, 1993, 1995; assoc. prin. violinist Santa Fe Opera, Santa Fe, 1973—98; prin. violinist Dallas Chamber Orch., 1975—92, Dallas Bach Soc., 1975—95. Mem. youth ens. svc. quintet Dallas Symphony Orch., 1978—, charter tchr. Young Strings Minority Scholarship program, 1988; part-time tchr. Booker T. Washington Arts Magnet HS, Dallas, 1982—85. Musician (solo violinist): Sun Valley Music Festival, 1966—67, Interlochen, 1968, Meadowmount, 1969, Walden Ensemble, 1975—, New Arensky Piano Trio, 1975—, Anton A Piano Trio, 1975—, Kodaly Duo, 1975—, Voices Change Ensemble, 1975—; Haydn's Double Concerto for Violin & Harpsichord, 1993, The Arensky Violin Concerto in Am. with Dallas Symphony Orchestra as Violin Concerto Soloist, 1995; author: (book) The Simple Dictionary for Classical Musicians, 2000. Charter mem. Nat. Mus. Women Art, Washington; mem. Klanwatch So. Poverty Law Ctr. Named concertmaster, Ariz. All-State Orch., 1968, 1969, Outstanding Young Women of Am., 1982; recipient awards, Plano Art Soc., 1980—, Richardson Art Soc., 1980—. Mem.: Phi Beta Kappa. Avocations: painting, drawing, photography. Home: 9648 Whitehurst Dr Dallas TX 75243 Office: Dallas Symphony Orch 2301 Flora St Dallas TX 75201-2497 Office Phone: 214-871-4000. Personal E-mail: dwightshambley@sbcglobal.net.

**PELLETT, JON MICHAEL**, lawyer; b. Orlando, Fla., Nov. 16, 1961; s. Milton Francis and Jean Ellen (Avery) P.; m. Karen Walker, July 21, 1984 (div. Sept. 1990). BS in Biology, U. Ctrl. Fla., Orlando, 1984. BS in Stats., 1985; JD, Fla. State U., 1993. Bar: Fla. 1995. Legal trainee Dept. Bus. and Profl. Regulation, Tallahassee, 1993-95; staff atty. Agy. for Health Care Adminstrn., Tallahassee, 1995-96; assoc. Freeman, Hunter & Malloy, Tampa, Fla., 1996-2000, Barr, Murman, Tonelli et al, Tampa, 2000—. Vol. guardian ad litem Guardian ad Litem Program, Tallahassee, 1991-95; mem. Coun. for Licensure Enforcement and Regulation, 2003—; bd. dirs. Suncoast Healthcare Execs., Tampa, Fla. Bd. dirs. Friends of Arboretum, Orlando, 1998—2003, Sun Coast Healthcare Execs., Tampa, Fla., 2004—; treas. Mem. ABA, ATLA, Hillsborough County Bar Assn. Avocations: racquetball, beach volleyball. Office: Barr Murman Tonelli Et Al 201 E Kennedy Blvd Ste 1750 Tampa FL 33602-5829 Office Phone: 813-223-3951.

**PELLI, CESAR**, architect; b. Tucumn, Argentina, Oct. 12, 1926; arrived in U.S., 1952, naturalized, 1964; s. Victor V. and Teresa S. Pelli; children: Denis G., Rafael A. BArch cum laude, U. Tucuman, 1949; MS in Architecture, U. Ill., 1954. Assoc. firm Eero Saarinen & Assocs., 1954-64, Daniel. Mann, Johnson & Mendenhall, 1964-68, Gruen Assocs. Inc., L.A., 1968-77, Pelli Clarke Pelli Arch., New Haven, 1977—; dean Sch. Architecture, Yale U., New Haven, 1977-84. Works include Pacific Design Ctr. and Expansion, LA (Honor award So. Calif. chpt. AIA 1976), US Embassy, Tokyo, Mus. Modern Art Expansion, NYC, World Fin. Ctr. and Winter Garden, NYC (Bard award 1992), Cleve. Clinic (Honor award AIA 1986), Herring Hall, Rice U., Houston (Honor award AIA 1986), Carnegie Hall Tower, NYC (Honor award AIA 1994, Design award AIA/Conn. 1991), Boyer Ctr. Molecular Medicine Yale U. (Design award AIA/Conn. 1991), Bank of Am. Corp. Ctr., Charlotte, NTT Corp. Hdqrs., Tokyo (Design award AIA/Conn. 1997), Terminal B/C Washington Nat. Airport (Design award AIA/Conn. 1998, NE Design award 1999, Design for Transp. award 2000), Aronoff Ctr. for the Arts, Cin. (USITT Honor award 1996, Design award AIA/CIN 1996, Design award AIA/Conn. 1997), Petronas Towers, Kuala Lumpur, Malaysia (Design award AIA/Conn. 1999, NE Design award 2000, Honor award AIA 2000), Frances Lehman Loeb Art Ctr. Vassar Coll., Poughkeepsie, N.Y. (Design award AIA/Conn. 1996), Internat. Fin. Ctr., Hong Kong, Nat. Mus. of Art, Osaka, Japan, Miami Performing Arts Ctr., Fla., Mpls. Ctrl. Libr. Bank of Okla. Ctr., Tulsa, Conn. Ctr. for Sci. and Exploration, Hartford, One Beacon Ct., NY, Winnipeg Airport Terminal, Nat. Children's Mus., Wash., DC; editor Yale Seminars on Architecture, 1981-82; author Observations for Young Architects, 1999 Fellow AIA (Firm award 1989, named to top ten list of living Am. archs. 1991, Gold medal 1995, Aga Khan award, 2004); mem. NAD (Arnold M. Brunner Meml. prize 1978), Am. Acad. Arts and Letters (academician), Internat. Acad. Architecture (academician). Office: Pelli Clarke Pelli Arch 1056 Chapel St New Haven CT 06510-2402

**PELLITTERI, JOHN STEVEN**, psychologist, psychotherapist, educator; b. Bklyn., Feb. 19, 1964; s. Horace Mario and Lorraine (LoNano) Pellitteri; m. Leda Sabio, June 21; children: Alexander Rafael, Maya Paloma. BS in Music Edn., NYU, 1985, MA in Music Therapy, 1988; MEd in Psychol. Counseling, Columbia U., 1993; PhD in Counseling Psychology, NYU, 1999. Lic. psychologist N.Y., 2000, cert. sch. counselor N.Y., 1998, lic. music educator N.Y., 1985, cert. music therapist Am. Music Therapy Assn., 1988, martial arts instr. 1985-96. Music tchr. Leif Ericson Day Sch., Bklyn., 1986—87; crisis counselor Postgrad. Ctr. for Mental Health, N.Y.C., 1986—89; music therapist Northside Ctr. for Child Devel., N.Y.C., 1987—91; sch. counselor Archdiocese Drug Prevention Program, Bronx, NY, 1991—93; clin. supr. and music therapist Heartsong Music Therapy Program, Bronxville, NY, 1993—2000; pvt. psychotherapy practice Bklyn., 2000—. Program dir. Queens Coll. City U N.Y., Flushing, NY, 2000—, asst. prof. Queens Coll., 1998—2005, assoc. prof., 2005—; cons. Bay Ridge Prep. Sch., Bklyn., 2000—02; mem. adv. bd. N.Y.C. Bd. Edn., 2001—03; bd. dir. Heartsong Music/Art Therapy Program, 2000—05. Lead editor Emotionally Intelligent School Counseling, 2006; contbr. articles to profl. jours. Recipient Student Rschr. award, NYU, 1994; scholar, 1983—85. Mem.: Am. Psychol. Assn., World Martial Arts Assn. Avocations: martial arts, music, marathon running. Office: Queens College City Univ NY 65 30 Kissena Blvd Flushing NY 11367 Office Phone: 718-997-5246.

**PELOFSKY, JOEL**, lawyer; b. June 23, 1937; s. Louis J. and Naomi (Hecht) Pelofsky; m. Brenda L. Greenblatt, June 19, 1960; children: Mark, Lisa, Carl. AB, Harvard U., 1959; LLB, Harvard Law Sch., 1962. Bar: Mo. 62, U.S. Dist. Ct. (we. dist.) Mo. 62, U.S. Ct. Appeals (8th cir.) 68, U.S. Ct. Appeals (10th cir.) 70. Law clk. to judge U.S. Dist. Ct. (we. dist.) Mo., 1962—63; mem. Miniace & Pelofsky, Kansas City, Mo., 1965—80; asst. pros. atty. Jackson County, Mo., 1967—71; mem. Kansas City (Mo.) City Coun., 1971—79; judge U.S. Bankruptcy Ct. Western Dist. Mo., Kansas City, 1980—85; ptnr. Shughart, Thomson & Kilroy P.C., Kansas City, 1986—95; U.S. Trustee Ark., Mo., Nebr., 1995—2003; of counsel Spencer, Fane, Britt and Browne, LLP, Kansas City, Mo., 2003—. Intermittent lectr. in law U. Mo. Bd. dirs., mem. exec. com. Truman Med. Ctr., Kansas City, Mo., pres. bd., 1988—90, chmn. bd., 1990—92; pres. trustee JVS, 2000—04; mem. Kansas City (Mo.) Sch. Bd., 2002—. Lt. U.S. Army, 1963—65. Mem.: ABA, Am. Coll. Bankruptcy, Kansas City Met. Bar Assn., Mo. Bar. Office: 1000 Walnut Ste 1400 Kansas City MO 64106-2140 Office Phone: 816-292-8189. E-mail: jpelofsky@spencerfane.com.

**PELOQUIN, LORI JEANNE**, clinical psychologist; b. Milw., Sept. 21, 1957; d. Wayne Joseph Peloquin and Jeanne Audrey (Ehlers) Driessen; m. Allen Theodore Retzlaff Jr., May 5, 1990; children: Austin Miles Retzlaff, Landry Quinn Retzlaff. Student, U. Wis., Eau Claire, 1975-76; BA summa cum laude, U. Minn., 1978; MA, U. Rochester, 1982, PhD, 1985. Lic. psychologist N.Y., cert. trained psychologist Interdisciplinary Council on Developmental and Learning Disasters, 2004. Teaching asst. U. Rochester, N.Y., 1981-83, instr. psychology N.Y., 1984; co-dir. Early Intervention Specialist Tng. Program Strong Ctr. for Devel. Disabilities Rochester Sch. Medicine, 1992-94; instr. depts. pediatrics and psychiatry (psychology) U. Rochester Sch. Medicine and Dentistry, N.Y., 1984-93; sr. clin. instr. dept. pediatrics and psychiatry, 1993—; pvt. practice Rochester, 1985—. Cons. Rochester Children's Nursery and Bd. Coop. Ednl. Svcs., 1986-90, Hillside Children's Ctr., Rochester, 1985-87, Roosevelt Children's Ctr., 2003—, Bright Start Pediat. Svcs., 2003—, Devel. Evaluation Clinic, Syracuse, 2005—; cons. bd. Cooperative Ednl. Svcs. #2, 2002-04; planning coord. Crisis Intervention Program, Rochester, 1985-86; mem. steering com. Early Childhood Intervention Coun. Monroe County, 1989-90; tng. faculty Interdisciplinary Coun. on Devel. and Learning Disorders, 2001-; mem. regional adv. group Western N.Y. Regional Ctr. of N.Y. Autism Network, 1998-2000. Contbr. chpts. to books, articles to profl. publs. Mem. Monroe County Autism Guidelines Com., 1999-2001; cert. Interdisciplinary Coun. Devel. and Learning Disorders, 2004, mem. parents steering com., 1998-2004, editor regional networks sect., 1998-2004. Mem. APA, Rochester Area Assn. Clin. Psychologists (v.p. 1987-89, pres. 1989-90, exec. com. 1990-91, ann. banquet com. chair 1991), Genesee Valley Psychol. Assn. (program com. 1991-93, Outstanding Psychologist of Yr. 2001), Coalition for Svcs. to Parents with Devel. Disabilities (com. chmn. 1985-90, coord. 1988-90), N.Y. State Psychol. Assn., Mental Health Assn., Phi Beta Kappa. Presbyterian. Avocations: cooking, yoga. Office: 2541 Monroe AveSte B4 Rochester NY 14618-3123 Office Phone: 585-697-0944. E-mail: peloquin@frontiernet.net.

**PELOSI, HAYDEE**, sculptor; b. Buenos Aires, Nov. 27, 1942; d. Oriondo Pelosi and Maria Ester Repp; m. Donald G. Pullum, Nov. 10, 2000. A, N.Y. U., 1963; B, SICC, 1972; student, Am. U., Cairo, 1975; D (hon.), Belgeano U., Buenos Aires, 1983. Interpreter Associated Press, N.Y., 1960—62; street artist N.Y.C., 1960—69; corr. Tankian Pub., N.Y.C., 1976—82; sculptor, 1987—. Author: How to Create in Clay, 2001. Mem.: Debary Art League (dir. programs 2003—, v.p. 1999—2002), Phi Theta Kappa. Democrat. Unitarian. Avocations: reading, tennis, painting. Office: Debary Art League 37 Keeble Ave Debary FL 32713

**PELOSI, NANCY PATRICIA**, congresswoman; b. Balt., Mar. 26, 1940; d. Thomas J. D'Alesandro Jr.; m. Paul Pelosi; children: Nancy Corinne, Christine, Jacqueline, Paul, Alexandra. AB in Polit. Sci., Trinity Coll., 1962. Chair No. Calif. Dem. Party, 1977—81; chmn. Calif. State Dem. Com., 1981—83; committeewoman Dem. Nat. Com., 1976, 1980, 1984; fin. chmn. Dem. Senatorial Campaign Com., 1987; mem. US Congress from 5th Calif. dist., 1987-93, US Congress from 8th Calif. dist., 1993—; minority whip, 2002; minority leader, 2002—; mem. appropriations com., intelligence com.; vice chmn. Dem. Nat. Conv., 1996, co-chmn., 2004. Pub. Svc. award, Fedn. of Am. Societies for Experimental Biology, 1997, Congl. Svc. award, InterAction (Am. Coun. for Voluntary Internat. Action), 1999, Alan Cranston Peace award, Global Security Inst., 2003, Cesar E. Chavez Legacy award, Cesar E. Chavez Found., 2003, Nat. Legis. award, League of United Latin Am. Citizensm 2004, One of 100 Most Powerful Women in World, Forbes Mag., 2005. Democrat. Office: US Ho Reps 2371 Rayburn Ho Office Bldg Washington DC 20515-0508*

**PELOSO, JOHN FRANCIS XAVIER**, lawyer; b. NYC, Oct. 7, 1934; s. Rocco C. and Victoria P.; m. Elizabeth Byrne Peloso, Oct. 7, 1961; children: Alycia, John, Matthew. BA, Fordham U., 1956, LLB, 1960. Bar: N.Y. 1960, U.S. Dist. Ct. (so. dist.) N.Y. 1962, U.S. Ct. Appeals (2nd cir.) 1967, U.S. Supreme Ct. 1968. Law clk. to judge U.S. Dist. Ct. (so. dist.) N.Y., 1960-61; asst. U.S. Atty. U.S. Atty.'s Office, N.Y., 1961-65; assoc. Carter Ledyard & Milburn, N.Y., 1965-70; chief trial counsel NYRO-SEC, N.Y., 1970-75; ptnr. to chmn. Sage Gray Todd & Sims, N.Y., 1975-87; ptnr. to mng. ptnr. Morgan, Lewis & Bockius, LLP, N.Y.C., 1987-95, 95-99, sr. counsel, 2000—. Adj. prof. law Fordham Law Sch., 2000—; spkr. in field. Contbr. articles to profl. jours. Capt. inf. USAR, 1956-64. Mem. ABA (sect. corp., banking and bus. law, com. fed. regulation securities 1975—, com. bus. and corp. litig., chair subcom. securities litig. 1993-99, litig. co-chmn. com. securities 1983-87, com. on liaison with jud. 1987-88, coun. 1989-91, co-chmn. com. trial evidence 1994-95, co-chmn. task force on the ind. lawyer 1995-99), Assn. Bar of City of N.Y. (arbitration com. 1970-73, fed. legis. com. 1975-78, fed. cts. com. 1982-86), Nat. Assn. Securities Dealers (nat. panel arbitrators 1975—, nat. arbitration com. 1982-85, fixed income com. 2005—), CPR Inst. for Dispute Resolution (Disting. Neutral). Office: Morgan Lewis & Bockius LLP 101 Park Ave Fl 44 New York NY 10178-0060 Office Phone: 212-309-6240. Business E-Mail: jpeloso@morganlewis.com.

**PELOSO, PAUL MICHAEL**, medical educator; b. Hamilton, Ont., Can., Jan. 10, 1958; s. Dino F and Donna Marie Peloso; m. Marie Lise Riley, Oct. 5, 1960; children: Nicholas John, Oliver Michael. BA, McMaster U., 1981, BSc, 1980; MSc, U. Toronto, 1994; MD, U. Calgary, 1985. Diplomate Am. Bd. Internal Medicine. Prof. internal medicine U. Saskatoon, Canada, 1994—2000; med. cons. VA Hosp., Iowa City, 2001—; assoc. prof. internal medicine U. Iowa Health Care, 2001—; adj. prof. epidemiology U. Iowa, 2003—. Sci. secreatrivate WHO Task Force on Mild Traumatic Head Injury, Edmonton, Alta., Canada, 1998—. Contbr. articles to profl. jours. Recipient Rsch. award, Pan Am. League Against Rheumatism, 1998; grantee Multi Ctr. Osteoarthritis Trial, NIH, 2001-2005, Aerobic Exercise vs. Stretching and Strengthening vs. Edn. in Osteoarthritis of the Hip, Can. Arthritis Soc., 1998-2000; Rsch. scholar, Inst. for Work and Health, 1993-1994, Arthritis Soc. Rsch. scholar, Can. Arthritis Soc., 1992-1993, Arthritis Soc. Clin. fellow, 1990-1991. Fellow: Royal Coll. of Physicians and Surgeons of Can.; mem.: ACP-ASIM, Ctrl. Soc. for Clin. Rsch., Osteoarthritis Rsch. Soc., Can. Rheumatology Assn., Am. Pain Soc., Am. Coll. of Rheumatology. Avocations: coaching youth hockey, ice hockey. Office: U Iowa Health Care Room E 330 GH 200 Hawkins Dr Iowa City IA 52242 Home: 4533 Via Rio Thousand Oaks CA 91320-6850 E-mail: paul-peloso@uiowa.edu.

**PELSTER, WILLIAM CHARLES**, lawyer; b. St. Louis, May 11, 1942; s. William R. and Marie C. (Graefe) P.; m. Terry C. Cuthbertson, Aug. 9, 1969. BA, Oberlin Coll., 1964; JD, U. Mich., 1967. Bar: Mo. 1967, N.Y. 1968, US Dist. Ct. (so. dist.) N.Y. 1968, U.S. Ct. Appeals (2d cir.) 1968, U.S. Supreme Ct. 1972. Law clk. to judge Lenord P. Moore U.S. Ct. Appeals (2d cir.), N.Y.C., 1967-68; assoc. Donovan, Leisure, Newton & Irvine, N.Y.C., 1968-75; ptnr. Skadden, Arps, Slate, Meagher & Flom, LLP, N.Y.C., 1976—. Trustee Cancer Care Inc. N.Y.C., 1975—. Mem. ABA, Assn. of Bar of N.Y. Office: Skadden Arps Slate Meagher & Flom LLP 4 Times Sq Fl 24 New York NY 10036-6595 E-mail: wpelster@skadden.com.

**PELTO, GRETEL H.**, nutritional anthropologist, educator; b. Mpls., May 6, 1940; d. Isaac L. and Deana (Harris) Hoffman; m. Pertti J. Pelto, July 27, 1968 (div. Dec. 1995); children: Jonathan, Dunja, Ari; m. Jean-Pierre Habicht, June 13, 1997. Student, Bennington Coll., Vt., 1957—60; BA, U. Minn., Mpls., 1963, MA, 1967, PhD, 1970; DSc (hon.), U. Helsinki, 1996. Clin. assoc. U. Conn. Sch. Medicine, Farmington, 1970-74; asst. prof. anthropology U. Conn., Storrs, 1974-77, prof. nutritional scis., 1977-92; scientist, child health divsn. WHO, Geneva, 1992-98; prof. nutritional scis. Cornell U., Ithaca, NY, 1998—. Mem. adv. bd. divsn. diarrheal disease control WHO, 1987-92; mem. adv. bd. subcom. on maternal and infant nutrition NAS, Washington, 1980-83; cons. UN U., Washington and Tokyo, 1985, Population Coun., NYC, 1980-82. Co-author: Anthropological Research, 1978, Community Assessment of Natural Food rces of Vitamin A; co-editor: Nutritional Anthropology, 2000; symposium editor: Jour. Nutrition, 2006; mem. editl. bd. Ecology of Food and Nutrition, Maternal and Child Nutrition, Human Orgn. Bd. dirs. Parent-Child Rsch. Ctr. for Eastern Conn., 1974-79; mem. task force Hartford Area Health Edn. Ctr., Conn., 1980-82; mem. adv. com. Travelers Ctr. on Aging, Hartford, 1988-89. Fulbright grantee, 1984; hon. rsch. fellow U. Birmingham, Eng., 1994-97; U.S. AID rsch. grantee, Mex., 1982-87. Fellow Soc. for Applied Anthropology, Am. Soc. for Nutrition (mem. long range planning com. 2001-05, coun. mem. 2004-05, councilor 2004—06, symposium editor 2006); mem. Soc. for Internat. Nutritional Rsch. (bd. dirs. 1989-92), Coun. on Nutritional Anthropology (pres. 1982-84, v.p. 1998-2000), Soc. for Med. Anthropology (bd. dirs. 1980-82). Avocations: photography, cooking. Home: 129 Eastlake Rd Ithaca NY 14850-9700 Office: Cornell U Div Nutritional Sci MVR 3M1 Ithaca NY 14853 Office Phone: 607-255-6277. Business E-Mail: gp32@cornell.edu.

**PELTON, ERIK MICHAEL**, lawyer; b. Boston, Nov. 12, 1972; s. Stephen Ira and Irene (Fromberg) Pelton; m. Rebecca D. Tax, Oct. 11, 2003; 1 child, Elijah I. BA, Boston U., 1994; JD, Cath. U. Am., 1997. Bar: NJ 1999. Trademark examiner US Patent and Trademark Office, Arlington, Va., 1997—99; pvt. practice Arlington, 1999—. Bd. dirs. Clarendon Alliance, Arlington, 2004—05. Named one of Top 20 Trademark Filers, Nameprotect's Trademark Insider, 2004. Office: PO Box 100637 Arlington VA 22210 Office Phone: 703-525-8009.

**PELTON, JAMES RODGER**, librarian; b. St. Louis, Mar. 21, 1945; s. Norman C. and Leona V. (Schulte) P.; m. Sandra Lee Birdsell, Mar. 29, 1969; children: Joni Lee, Vicki Sue. BA, U. Mo., 1967, MLS, 1969. Br. libr. Scenic Regional Libr., Union, Mo., 1968-71; adminstr. Daniel Boone Regional Libr. - Columbia Ctr., Columbia, Mo., 1971-78; cons. La. State Libr., Baton Rouge, 1978-80; dir. Shreve Meml. Libr., Shreveport, La., 1980-. Mem. ALA, La. Libr. Assn. Home: 3201 Old Mooringsport Rd Shreveport LA 71107-3926 Office: 424 Texas St Shreveport LA 71101-3522 Office Phone: 318-226-5870. Business E-Mail: jpelton@shreve-lib.org.

**PELTON, M. LEE**, academic administrator; B magna cum laude, Wichita U., 1974; D, Harvard U., 1984. Tchg. fellow, English instr. Harvard U., 1980—86; sr. tutor Winthrop Ho., 1986; dean of student to dean of coll. Colgate U., 1986—91; dean of coll., adj. prof. Dartmouth Coll., 1991—98; pres. Willamette U., 1998—. Mem. bd. Oregon Ind. Coll. Fund, 1998—, Oregon Ind. Coll. Assn., 1998—; bd. overseers Harvard U., 2000; mem. Commn. on Minorities in Higher Edn., 2000—02. Mem.: Governor's Commn. on Financing Higher Edn. (Ore.), President's Coun. of Nat. Collegiate Athletic Assn. (Div. III), Nat. Assn. of Ind. Colleges and Universities (com. on policy analysis and pub. rels. 2000—03), Am. Coun. on Edn., Am. Assn. of Higher Edn. Office: Willamette U 900 State St Salem OR 97301

**PELTON, MARGARET MARIE MILLER**, retired art educator, academic administrator, artist; b. Charlotte, NC, Nov. 5, 1934; d. William Andrew Miller and Helen Cook Miller Margolin; m. Donald Wesley Pelton Jr.; children: Donald W. III, Charles F. BS, U. Miami, 1956; MS, Fla. State U., 1957; EdD in Coll. Adminstrn., Southeastern Nova U., 1979. Art tchr. Miami Dade Pub. Sch., Fla., 1957—70; art instr. Kendall Campus, Miami-Dade Coll., Fla., 1970—79, dept. chair, 1971—79, assoc. dean humanities, Rank prof., 1979—86; founder, vice provost New world Sch. Arts, 1987—96; ret., 1996. Bd. mem. Fla. Very Spl. ART, 1986—96; founder Louis Wolfsou II Fla. Moving Image Archive, Miami, 1986—96, pres., 1986—, v.p., 1996—. Exhibitions include Miami Water Color Soc., Spring Exhbn., 1999, 2001, 2002, 2003 (Outstanding award), Miami Water Color Soc., Fall Exhbn., 2001 (Peoples Choice award), Macon County Fair, Franklin, NC, 2000, Watercolor Soc. NC, Western Regional Show, Asheville, 2001, Watercolor Soc. NC, New Bern, 2003, Macon County Fair, Franklin, NC, 2001, Bet Breira Gallery, 2002 (First award), Fla. Profl. Art Guild, 2003 (Second award), Bascon Louise Gallery, Highlands, NC, 2003, Art League Highlands, 2003, one-woman shows include Kendall Campus Gallery, Miami-Dade Cmty. Coll., 2002, 45 other exhbns. Mem. Dade Commn. Status of Women, Fla., 1983—86; bd. mem. Dade Heritage Trust, Fla., 1995—2001. Recipient Fla. Art Educator of Yr. award, Fla. Art Edn. Assn., 1989. Mem.: DAR, Miami Watercolor Soc. (trustee), Macon County Art Assn., NC Watercolor Soc., Fla. Watercolor Soc., United Daus. Confederacy. Republican. Presbyterian. Home (Winter): 11725 SW 82nd Rd Miami FL 33156-5104

**PELTON, RUSSELL GILBERT**, retired lawyer; b. Monticello, N.Y., July 23, 1914; s. William and May (Morgan) P.; m. Marion Gosart, Dec. 14, 1940; children: William, Marjorie, Marilyn Pelton Barringer. BS, Syracuse U., 1935; JD, George Washington U., 1944. Bar: D.C. 1944, N.Y. 1947, U.S. Supreme Ct. 1948, U.S. Dist. Ct. N.Y. 1947; U.S. Dist. Ct. (fed. dist.). Ptnr. Darby & Darby, N.Y.C., 1944-56; sr. v.p. N.Am. Philips Corp., N.Y.C., 1956-75; exec. v.p. U.S. Philips Corp., N.Y.C., 1968-75; of counsel Rogers, Hoge & Hills, N.Y.C., 1976-78; organizer, mgr. Patent Law Office in U.S. Siemens of Germany, White Plains, NY, 1979—83; ret., 1983. Officer, dir. Tech. Container Corp., N.Y.C., 1977-95; former dir. Ferroscube Corp., Savgerties, N.Y., Polyseal Corp., N.Y.C.; lectr. Practising Law Inst., 1953-69; arbitrator, mediator Am. Arbitration Assn., 1953—. Patentee in field. V.p. Siwanoy coun. Boy Scouts Am., 1948-53; v.p. Rye Neck Bd. Edn., Mamaroneck, N.Y., 1952-62; mem. Zoning Bd. Appeals, 1966-70; town justice, 1970-85; trustee Syracuse U., 1967-73. Served with Signal Corps, U.S. Army, 1941-45. Mem. ABA, Am. Patent Law Assn. (past chmn. antitrust com.), N.Y. State Bar Assn. (ethics com., Iola com.), N.Y. Patent Law Assn. (past bd. govs.), State Magistrates Assn., County Magistrates Assn. (treas., v.p., pres.), Westchester County Bar Assn. (dir., chmn. ethics com., alternative dispute resolution com.), Assn. Bar City N.Y. (patent com.), IEEE, Am. Radio Relay League, Aircraft Owners and Pilots Assn., Wings Club, Cloud Club, Winged Foot Golf Club, Waccabuc Country Club, Masons, Elks. Home: 3 Oxford Rd Larchmont NY 10538-1428

**PELTON, RUSSELL MEREDITH**, lawyer; b. Chgo. May 14, 1938; BA, DePauw U., 1960; JD, U. Chgo., 1963. Bar: Ill. 1963, U.S. Supreme Ct. 1979. Assoc. Peterson, Ross, Schloerb & Seidel, Chgo., 1966-72, ptnr., 1972-90. Oppenheimer, Wolff & Donnelly, Chgo., 1990-2000, Chgo. mng. ptnr., 1992-95, 98-2000; ptnr. Ross & Hardies, Chgo., 2000—03, McGuireWoods LLP, Chgo., 2003—. Co-founder, gen. counsel Chgo. Opportunities Industrialization Ctr., 1969—83; gen. counsel Delta Dental Plan Ill., 1979—96, Am. Assn. Neurol. Surgeons, 1996—. Pres. Wilmette Jaycees, 1970; chmn. Wilmette Sch. Bd. Caucus, 1970-71; Wilmette Dist. 39 Bd. Edn., 1972-80; bd. dirs. Wilmette United Way, 1980-86, campaign chmn., 1983-85, pres., 1985-86; Wilmette Zoning Bd. Appeals, 1989-2000, chmn., 1990-2000. Served to capt. USAF, 1963-66. Mem.: ABA, Soc. Trial Lawyers, Chgo. Bar Assn., Ill. Bar Assn., Ill. State Dental Soc. (hon.), Plaza Club (chair 2003—). Office: McGuireWoods LLP 77 W Wacker Dr Ste 4100 Chicago IL 60601-1815 Office Phone: 312-750-8652. Business E-Mail: rpelton@mcguirewoods.com.

**PELTON, VIRGINIA LUE**, small business owner; b. Utica, Kans., Apr. 15, 1928; d. Forrest Selby and Nellie (Simmons) Meier; m. Theodore Trower King Jr., Oct. 27, 1956 (div.); m. Harold Marcel Pelton, July 11, 1970; children: Mary Virginia Joyner, Diana Jean. Student, Kans. State U., 1946-47, Ft. Hays U., 1947-48, Washington U., St. Louis, 1950-51. Instr. Patricia

Stevens Modeling Sch., Kansas City, Mo., 1948-50; model various cos., Calif. and N.Y., 1951-53; fashion cons. Giorgio, Beverly Hills, Calif., 1967-68, Charles Gallay, Beverly Hills, 1975-77, Dorso's, Beverly Hills, 1977-79; buyer, mgr. giftware Slavick's, Laguna Hills, Calif., 1980-83; owner P.J. Secretarial Svcs., Laguna Hills, 1980—; v.p. H.P. Fin. Inc., Laguna Hills, 1983—. Editor Profl. Network newsletter, 1980—. Sec. Leukemia Soc. Am., Santa Ana, 1985—; mem. Laguna Beach Art Mus., 1986—. Mem. Profl. Network Assn. (sec. 1986-96), Market Plus The Consumer Network, Saddleback C. of C., Laguna Hills Club, Kappa Delta. Republican. Methodist. Avocations: gourmet cooking, sewing. Home: 24942 Georgia Sue Laguna Beach CA 92653-4323

**PELTON, WALTER EUGENE,** information technology executive, mathematician, physicist; s. Clarence Elijah and Mary Hartman Pelton; children: Denel Renee' Pugh, Steven James. Student, Calif. Inst. Tech., 1957—60. Rsch. engr. autonetics divsn. N.Am. Rockwell, Anaheim, Calif., 1961—63; tech. specialist Filtors, Inc., Port Washington, NY, 1963—64; head circuits dept. Whittaker Controls, North Hollywood, Calif., 1964—65; owner, mgr., tech. cons. C.E.I. Co., Canoga Park, Calif., 1965—67; design specialist, exec. staff Am. Data Systems, Canoga Park, 1967—69; owner, mgr., tech. cons. Gen. Consulting, Corona, Calif., 1970—80, Dallas, 1981—86; software engr. Ilex Systems, Inc., Milpitas, Calif., 1995; head R&D Hand Held Products, Inc., Charlotte, NC, 1987—94; sr. RF design engr. GRE Am., Belmont, Calif., 1996; sr. design engr. analog and digital integrated circuits Sierra Rsch. and Tech., Mountain View, Calif., 1996—98; PhD advisor Northwestern Poly. U., Fremont, Calif., 1998—2000; CEO Agnitio Techs., Inc., Fremont, 2000—; pres. Faster Fourier Transforms, Inc., Fremont, 2000—. Cons. in field. Mem.: Am. Math. Assn. Achievements include patents for Low Power Optical Sensing and Decoding of Data; Sample Integrated Fourier Transform; invention of Rotational Fourier Transform; Special Case Processing Paradigm; Modern Switching Power Supply; development of Integrated Circuit with Jack Kilby et al; Multilayer Printed Circuit Team Physicist; First Solid-State Boiler Controller for Ship; Deep Space Low-Power Data Theory; research in Sliding Aperture Fourier Transform. Personal E-mail: walter@alumni.caltech.edu.

**PELTZ, CISSIE JEAN,** art gallery director, cartoonist; d. Morton Dunbar Liebshutz and Myrtle Jewel Friedman; m. Richard Walter Peltz, Jan. 1, 1953 (dec. Feb. 21, 1975); 1 child, David Lee. BA, U. Chgo., 1947. Freelance cartoonist Milw. Jour., 1975—77, Chgo. Tribune, 1948—68, Today's Health, Chgo., 1959—71, Cosmopolitan mag., N.Y.C. 1950—85, Look Mag., N.Y.C., 1950—85, N.Y. Times, N.Y.C., 1950—85, Saturday Rev., N.Y.C. 1950—85, Chgo. Mag., 1950—85, Great Books Found., Chgo., 1950—85; owner, dir. Peltz Gallery, Milw., 1989—. Illustrator: book Everyday Speech, 1949, Laugh Your Way to Work, 1977, illustrator: booklets, advt. filmstrips. Named Communicator of Yr., Univ. Chgo., 1963. Mem.: Milw. Art Mus. Contemporary Art Soc., Mil. Art Mus. Print Forum (v.p., pres. 1987—89, bd. dirs. 1989—2002), Milw. Art Dealers Assn. Democrat. Avocations: collecting art, theater, movies. Office: Peltz Gallery 1119 E Knapp St Milwaukee WI 53202 Office Phone: 414-223-4278.

**PELTZ, NELSON,** manufacturing executive; b. NYC, June 24, 1942; s. Maurice Herbert and Claire (Wechsler) P.; m. Claudia Peltz; children by previous marriage: Andrew, Brooke. MBA, U. Pa., 1962. With A. Peltz & Sons, Inc., NYC, 1963-70; pres. chief exec. officer APS Food Systems, Inc., NYC, 1970-72, Flagstaff Corp., NYC, 1972-78, Coffee-Mat Corp. (merged with Flagstaff Corp. 1976), Kenilworth, NJ, 1975-76; formerly chmn. bd., chief exec. officer Trafalgar Industries, Inc., NYC; chmn. bd., CEO Triangle Industries, Inc. (now Trian Group Ltd. Partnership), NYC, 1983—88, also bd. dirs.; chmn. bd., CEO Avery Inc. (now Trian Group Ltd. Partnership), 1989—93, Triarc, 1993—. Chmn. bd. NPM Group, Inc.; bd. dirs., Encore Capital Group, Inc., 2003-; gen. ptnr. Brook Fund. Trustee U.S. Olympic Ski Team, 1975—. Named one of Forbes Richest Americans, 2006. Mem. Young Pres.'s Orgn., Madison Sq. Garden Club, Old Oaks Country Club, City Athletic Club. Office: Triarc Group 280 Park Ave New York NY 10017*

**PELTZ, PAULETTE BEATRICE,** corporate lawyer; b. Bklyn., May 30, 1954; BA, SUNY, Binghamton, 1976; JD, Am. U., 1979. Bar: D.C. 1980, Va. 1982, Md. 1986. Atty. U.S. EPA, Washington, 1979-83; assoc. Mahn, Franklin & Goldenberg, Washington, 1983-85, Deso, Greenberg & Thomas, P.C., Washington, 1985-87; corp. gen. counsel Western Devel. Corp., Washington, 1987-91; v.p. and corp. gen. counsel Mills Corp., 1992-94; sr. v.p., gen. counsel Charter Oak Ptnrs., 1994—2004; asst. division. counsel Charles E. Smith Real Estate divsn. Vornado Realty Trust, Arlington, Va., 2004—. Personal E-mail: ppeltz@vno.com.

**PELTZ, RUBY,** elementary school educator; b. Youngstown, Ohio, Apr. 22, 1949; d. Peter and Dorothy Raseta Hrelec; m. Kenneth L. Peltz, May 22, 1971; children: Kenneth L. Jr., David A. BS in Edn., Youngstown State U., 1971, MS in Edn., 1975. Educator Campbell (Ohio) City Schs., 1971—. Co-chmn. Bond Issue Com., Campbell, 1999; exec. mem. Campbell Acad. Assn., 1995—, pres. 2002-; memtor Campbell Schs., 1999—. Recipient Outstanding Educator, Indsl. Info. Inst. for Edn., Inc., 2002. Mem. NEA, Ohio Edn. Assn., Ea. Ohio Coun. Tchrs. Math., Campbell City Fest. Com., Campbell Edn. Assn. (blg. rep. 1981-89), Delta Kappa Gamma Democrat. Avocations: reading, kick boxing, skiing, gardening. Home: 71 Creed Cir Campbell OH 44405-1256 Office: Campbell E&M Sch 2002 Community Cir Campbell OH 44405 E-mail: camp_rxp@access.k12.org.

**PELTZER, DOUGLAS LEA,** manufacturing executive, b. Clinton, Iowa, July 2, 1938; s. Albert and Mary Ardelle (Messer) P.; m. Nancy Jane Strickler, Dec. 22, 1959; children: Katharine, Eric, Kimberly. BA, Knox Coll., 1960; MS, N.Mex. State U., 1964; MBA, U. Phoenix, 1990. Rsch. engr. Advanced Computer Lab., GE, Sunnyvale, Calif., 1964—67; engr. large scale integrated circuit R&D Lab., Fairchild Camera & Instrument, Palo Alto, Calif., 1967—70, bipolar memory divsn. Mountain View, Calif., 1970—83, dir. tech., 1977—83; v.p. tech. ops. Trilogy Sys. Corp., Cupertino, Calif., 1983—85; pres. Tactical Fabs, Inc., Cupertino, 1985—89; v.p. process devel. Chips and Techs. Inc., Cupertino, 1988—92; pres., CEO Camlan, Inc., San Jose, Calif., 1992—94; staff Chip Express, Santa Clara, Calif., 1998; prin. Corp. Tech. Devel., Santa Clara, 1994—2004, Ft. Lauderdale, Fla., 2001—. NSF fellow, 1962-63; recipient Sherman Fairchild award for tech. excellence, 1980, Semiconductor Equipment and Materials Inst. award, 1988; Inventor of Yr. award Peninsula Patent Law Assn., 1982. Mem. IEEE, Sigma Pi Sigma. Achievements include patents in field. Home: 340 San Marco Dr Fort Lauderdale FL 33301

**PELTZMAN, SAM,** economics professor; b. Bklyn., Jan. 24, 1940; s. Benjamin Raphael and Ceil (Heller) P.; m. Nancy Virginia Bradney, Sept. 7, 1952; children: Shira Malka, Talya Rose. BBA, CCNY, 1960; PhD, U. Chgo., 1965. Prof. econs. UCLA, 1964-73; sr. staff economist Coun. Econ. Advisers, Washington, 1970-71; prof. econs. grad. sch. bus. U. Chgo., 1973-87, Sears, Roebuck prof., 1987-2001, dir. George J. Stigler Ctr. Study of Economy and the State, 1992—2005, Ralph and Dorothy Keller disting. svc. prof., 2001—05, Ralph and Dorothy Keller prof. emeritus, 2005—. Vis. fellow Inst. for Advanced Study Hebrew U., Jerusalem, 1978; dir. CMP Industries LLC, 1995—; mem. coun. acad. advisers Am. Enterprise Inst., 1995—. Author: Political Participation and Government Regulation, 1998; co-author: Public Policy Toward Mergers, 1967; editor Jour. Law and Econs.; contbr. articles to profl. jours. Mem. Am. Econ. Assn., Mt. Pelerin Soc. Jewish. Office: U Chgo Grad Sch Bus 5807 S Woodlawn Ave Chicago IL 60637-1620 Office Phone: 773-702-7457. Business E-Mail: s-peltzman@uchicago.edu.

**PELUSO, JOHN,** lawyer; b. 1947; BA in English, St. John's U.; MBA in Mktg., Bernard Baruch Coll. (CUNY); JD, St. John's U. Law Sch. Bar: N.Y. 1987. Mgr. advt. & sales promotion Guardian Life Ins. Co. of Am., 1974—83, legal asst., 1983—87, asst. counsel, 1987—89, counsel, 1989—96, second v.p., ins. ops. counsel, 1994—96, v.p. & assoc. gen. counsel, 1996—97, v.p. & gen. counsel, 1997—. Mem. ABA. Office: Guardian Life Ins Co of Am 7 Hanover Sq New York NY 10004-2616

**PELUSO, MICHELLE,** Internet company executive; b. Middletown, NY; B. in Finance and Multinational Mgmt., U. of Pa. Wharton Sch. Bus.; M. in Economics, Phil. and Politics, Pembroke Coll., Oxford U. Mgmt. cons., case leader Boston Consulting Group, NYC, 1995—98; White House Fellow, sr. advisor to sec. of labor, 1998—99; founder, CEO Site59.com (acquired by Travelocity), NYC, 1999—2002; sr. v.p. product strategy and distribution Travelocity, 2002, COO, 2003, pres., CEO, 2003—. Founder A New Generation for Peace. Named Technol. Person of the Year, Travel Agent mag., 2001; named to Fast 50, Fast Co. mag., 2004; recipient Thoroun scholarship, Ernst and Young Entrepreneur of the Year award, 2002. Office: Travelocity 3150 Sabre Dr Southlake TX 76092

**PELYPENKO, ELIZABETH,** lawyer; b. Chgo., Dec. 17, 1961; d. Mykola and Lydia Pelypenko; m. Arthur Italo, May 31, 1997; 1 child, Valentino Italo. BA Polit. Sci., Northwestern U., Evanston, Ill., 1984; JD, U.Ga., Athens, Ga., 1988. Atty. Pelypenko Law Firm, P.C., Atlanta, 1992—. Lectr. in field. Editor: Calendar Call mag., Verdict mag.; contbr. articles to profl. jours. Named a Ga. Super Lawyer, Atlanta Mag., 2005; named Pre-eminent Lawyer, Martindale-Hubbell Registry, 2005—06. Fellow: Melvin Belli Soc.; mem.: ABA, MENSA, ATLA, So. Trial Lawyers Assn., Roscoe Pound Inst., State Bar of Ga., Ga. Trial Lawyers Assn. (chair CLE com. 2004—), Million Dollar Advocates Forum, Ga. Assn. for Women Lawyers, Athletic Club NE Fencing, Lawyers Club of Atlanta. Independent. Avocation: fencing. Office: Pelypenko Law Firm PC 100 Galleria Pkwy Ste 1320 Atlanta GA 30339 Office Phone: 770-937-0800. Business E-Mail: ep@pelypenkolawfirm.com.

**PELZ, CAROLINE DUNCOMBE,** retired educational administrator; b. White Plains, NY., Dec. 20, 1918; d. David Sanford and Helena (Ebert) Duncombe; m. Edward Joseph Pelz, July 11, 1942; children: Caroline Pelz Elbow, Margaret L. (dec.), Patricia Pelz Hart, Sanford M. AB, Barnard Coll., 1940. Adjustments supr. R.H. Macy & Co., N.Y.C., 1940-42; admissions interviewer Barnard Coll., 1960-63; alumni sec. Allen-Stevenson Sch., N.Y.C., 1967-70, admissions asst., 1969-70; adminstrv. asst. Ednl. Records Bur., N.Y.C., 1970-72; dir. admissions Grace Ch. Sch., N.Y.C., 1972-87; ret. Trustee Barnard Coll., 1963-67. Recipient Columbia U. Alumni Fedn. medal, 1991, Litetime Alumnae Svc. Recognition award, Barnard Coll., 2005. Mem. Barnard Coll. Alumnae Assn. (pres. 1963-66). Republican. Episcopalian. Home: PO Box 395 Berlin NY 12022-0395

**PELZ, ROBERT LEON,** lawyer; b. NYC, Nov. 18, 1918; s. Leon S. and Fanny M. (Berk) P.; m. Mary Jane Gips, Feb. 11, 1949; children: Kathryn Louise, Robert Leon Jr. AB, Columbia U., 1939, JD, 1942. Bar: N.Y. 1942. Since practiced in, N.Y.C.; ptnr. Hess Segall Guterman Pelz Steiner & Barovick, 1953-86, Loeb and Loeb, N.Y.C., 1986-2000. Life trustee, former v.p. Fedn. Jewish Philanthropies; bd. dirs., former chmn. bd. dirs. Fedn. Jewish Philanthropies Svc. Corp.; past trustee Coll. Pharm. Scis. Columbia U.; former chmn. bd. trustees Am. Jewish Com. AUS, WWII. Office: Loeb and Loeb 345 Park Ave Fl 18 New York NY 10154-1895

**PEMBERTON, ALAN A.,** lawyer; b. Nov. 4, 1952; BA with honors, U. Chgo., 1974; MA in English Lit., U. Mich., 1977, JD cum laude, 1981. Ptnr. Covington & Burling, Washington, coord. Govt. Contracts Practice Group, vice chmn. pub. svc. com. Adj. prof. law Georgetown U. Law Ctr., Washington. Co-author: Obtaining Adequate Compensation for Delay, 1999, 2d edit., 2005. Bd. dirs. Indigent Civil Litig. Fund, Inc., DC Prisoners Legal Services Project, Inc. Mem.: US Dist. Ct. DC (pro se litig. com.). Office: Covington & Burling 1201 Pennsylvania Ave NW Washington DC 20004-2401 Office Phone: 202-662-5642. Office Fax: 202-662-6291. Business E-Mail: apemberton@cov.com.

**PEMBERTON, BRADLEY POWELL,** lawyer; b. Ft. Scott, Kans., June 15, 1952; s. Howard Duane and Juanita Lucille (Powell) P.; m. Kathleen Frances Querrey, May 22, 1976 (div. Feb. 1984); m. Lori Scott, June 18, 1994. BSBA, U. Mo., Columbia, 1974; JD, U. Mo., Kansas City, 1977. Bar: Mo. 1977, U.S. Dist. Ct. (we. dist.) Mo. 1981, U.S. Tax Ct. 1981; CPA, Mo. Tax acct. Alexander Grant & Co., Kansas City, Mo., 1977-79; shareholder Polsinelli Shalton Welte Suelthaws, Kansas City, 1979—; also bd. dirs. Kansas City Active Vol. Atty. Project, Kansas City, 1984—; bd. dirs. Synergy House Inc., Kansas City, 1985-88, Youth Vol. Corps of Am., 1991—, March of Dimes, 1995—. Mem. ABA, Internat. Entrepreneurs Coun. (bd. dirs.), Mo. Bar Assn., Kansas City Bar Assn., AICPAs, Mo. Soc. CPAs, Kansas City C. of C. Avocations: tennis, golf, private aviation. Home: 5806 W 131st St Shawnee Mission KS 66209-3639 Office: Polsinelli Shalton Welte Suelthaus 700 W 47th St Ste 1000 Kansas City MO 64112-1805 Office Phone: 816-753-1000. Business E-Mail: bpemberton@pswslaw.com.

**PEMBERTON, WILLIAM BERTRAM, II,** lawyer; b. Nashville, Tenn., Nov. 11, 1949; s. William Bertram and Martha Carolyn (Hutsell) P.; m. Sue Zan Williams, June 9, 1973 (div. Sept. 1987); children: Jennifer Leigh, William Bertram III, Charles Williams; m. Martha Louise Lewis, Nov. 5, 1988. BS, U. Tenn., 1971, JD, 1974; MBA, Millsaps Coll., 1990. Bar: Tenn. 1974, Miss. 1977, U.S. Dist. ct. (so. dist.) Miss. 1987. Land mgr. R.E. Williams Oil & Gas Co., Jackson, Miss., 1975-83; assoc. Smith, Clement, Rudolph & Pemberton, Nashville, 1984; ind. landman, Jackson, 1985-91; ptnr. Pemberton & Williams, Jackson, 1992; sole practice Jackson, 1992—; 2d lt. U.S. Army, 1974-75. Mem. ABA, ATLA, Miss. Trial Lawyers Assn., Miss. Bar, Beta Gamma Sigma. Republican. Episcopalian. Avocations: golf, bridge, sailing. Office: Atty at Law 612 Towne Ctr Blvd Ridgeland MS 39157 Office Phone: 601-956-3227. Business E-Mail: pembertn@bellsouth.net.

**PEÑA, AMADO MAURILIO, JR.,** artist, curator, lecturer; b. Laredo, Tex., Oct. 1, 1943; s. Amado Maurilio and Maria Baldomera (Arambula) P.; children: Marcos, Jose Luis, Amado Maurilio III. BA, Tex. A&I U., 1965, MA in Art, 1971. Tchr. Laredo Ind. Sch. Dist., 1965-70, Tex. A&I U., Kingsville, 1970-72, Crystal City Ind. Sch. Dist., Tex., 1972-74, Austin Ind. Sch. Dist., Tex., 1974-80; resident artist El Taller, Inc., Austin, 1985—. One man shows include Squash Blossom, Denver, 1985, Lincoln Sq. Gallery, Arlington, Tex., 1985, Galeria Capistrano, San Juan Capistrano, Calif., 1985, Andrews Gallery, Albuquerque, N.Mex., 1985, Joy Tash Gallery, Scottsdale, Ariz., 1985, Byrne-Getz Gallery, Aspen, Colo., 1985, Parke Gallery, Vail, Colo., 1985, Am. West Gallery, Chgo., 1985, Adagio Gallery, Palm Springs, Calif., 1985, Houshang's Gallery, Dallas, 1985, Mus. Native Am. Art, Spokane, Wash., 1985, El Taller, Taos, N.Mex., 1985, Austin, 1985, Kauffman Gallery, Houston, 1985, now Peña Studio Gallery, Santa Fe, N.Mex.; represented in permanent collection: Palacio del Gobernador, Baja California, Mex., Hist. Creative Arts Ctr., Lufkin, Tex., Mus. Nuevo Santander, Laredo, Smithsonian Inst., Washington, Whitney Mus., San Antonio, Tex., also corp., univs., and pvt. collections. Commd. by civic and arts orgns. for fund-raising events and spl. presentations. Avocations: purchasing quarter horses; horseback riding. Office: Peña Studio Gallery 235 Don Gaspar Santa Fe NM 87501 Office Phone: 505-820-2286. Business E-Mail: penastudios@earthlink.net.

**PENA, ANTONIO FRANCISCO (TONY PENA),** professional athletics coach; b. Monte Cristy, Dominican Republic, June 4, 1957; m. Amaris Pena; children: Tony, Jennifer Amaris. Profl. baseball player Pitts. Pirates, Nat. League, 1980-86, St. Louis Cardinals, 1986-89, Boston Red Sox, 1989—93, Cleveland Indians, 1994—97; mgr. Astros AAA farm club, New Orleans, 1997—2001, Kansas City Royals, 2002—05; first base coach NY Yankees, 2005—. AL Mgr. of the Year, 2003. Player Major League All-Star Game, 1982, 84; winner Gold Glove. Office: New York Yankees 161st St and River Ave Bronx NY 10451*

**PEÑA, ELIZABETH,** actress; b. Elizabeth, NJ, Sept. 23, 1961; d. Mario Peña and Margarita Toirac; married; 2 children. Grad., Sch. Performing Arts. Actor: (plays) Rome and Juliet, Antigone, Blood Wedding, Night of the Assassins, Italian-American Reconciliation, Cinderella, Act One and Only; (films) El Super, 1979, Times Square, 1980, They All Laughed, 1981, Crossover Dreams, 1984, Down and Out in Beverly Hills, 1985, La Bamba, 1986, Batteries Not Included, 1987, Vibes, 1988, Blue Steel, 1989, Jacob's Ladder, 1990, The Waterdance, 1991, Across the Moon, 1992, Free Willy II, 1994, Dead Funny, 1995, Lone Star, 1996 (Independent Spirit award, 1996, Bravo award, 1996), The Pass, 1997, Strangeland, 1997, Rush Hour, 1998, Seven Girlfriends, 1999, Imposter, 2000, Tortilla Soup, 2001 (ALMA award, 2001), Ten Tiny Love Stories, 2001, Zig-Zag, 2001, Keep Your Distance, 2003, Sueño, 2003, How the Garcia Girls Spend Their Summer, 2003, Down in the Valley, 2004, (voice) The Incredibles, 2004, Keep Your Distance, 2005, Transamerica, 2005, Sueño, 2005; (TV films) Fugitive Among Us, 1992, It Came From Outer Space II, Contagious, 1996, Dead Man's Gun, 1997, Aldrich Ames: America Betrayed, 1998, Border Line, 1999, Hollywood Dead Moms Society, 2003, Suburban Madness, 2004; (TV miniseries) Drug War: The Camarena Story, The Invaders; (TV series) Saturday Night Live, Hillstreet Blues, Cagney and Lacey, Dellaventura, I Married Dora, 1987—88, Shannon's Deal, Tough Cookies, Resurrection Blvd., 2000—02, Boston Public, 2003, C.S.I. Miami, 2003, (voice) Maya and Miguel, 2004; dir.: (plays) Celebrando La Diferencia, 1992; (films) The Brothers Garcia, 2002; (TV series) Resurrection Blvd., 2002. Mem.: AFTRA, SAG, Dirs. Guild Am., Actors' Equity Assn. Office: Paradigm care Joel Rudnick 10100 Santa Monica Blvd Fl 25 Los Angeles CA 90067-4003*

**PENA, GUILLERMO ENRIQUE,** lawyer; b. Miami Beach, Fla., Aug. 16, 1963; s. Gustavo A. and Rosa Amelia (LeRiverend) P.; m. Jacqueline Torre, Sept. 11, 1993, children: Jade Allison, Allison Lee. BBA, Austin Peay State U., Clarksville, Tenn., 1988; JD, Fla. State U., 1991. Bar: Fla. 1991, U.S. Dist. Ct. (no. and so. dists.) Fla. 1991, U.S. Ct. Appeals (11th cir.) 1991, U.S. Supreme Ct. 1996; cert. in criminal trial law Criminal Trial Law Found., Middle Dist. of Fla., 1998, Dist. of Utah, 1999, Western Dist. of Tex., 1998. Assoc. Boehm, Brown, Rigdon & Seacrest, P.A., Tallahassee, 1990-92, Raia & Preira, Miami Beach, Fla., 1992-95, Jeffrey S. Weiner, P.A., Miami, Fla., 1995-96; pvt. practice Miami, 1996—. Guest judge U. Miami Sch. Law-Moot Ct. Camp, 1996—99; adj. prof., bus. law U. Miami. Young pres. Mt. Sinai Hosp., Miami Beach. Fla. Sgt. U.S. Army, 1984—86. Recipient Recognition award Legal Svcs. Greater Miami, 1996, Pro Bono Svc. award Dade County Bar Assn., Miami, 1995, Young Pres. Mt. Sinai Hosp., 1999. Mem. ABA (criminal justice sect.), Cuban Am. Bar Assn. (Pro Bono Project 1996), Nat. Assn. Criminal Def. Lawyers, Am. Judicature Soc., Am. Inns of Ct. (barrister), Fla. Assn. Criminal Def. Lawyers, Fla. Bar (cert. as specialist in criminal law), Young Pres. Club. Office: 444 Brickell Ave Ste 51 Miami FL 33131-2407 Office Phone: 305-377-1119. E-mail: gepena@yahoo.com.

**PEÑA, JUAN JOSÉ,** interpreter; b. Hagerman, N.Mex., Dec. 13, 1945; s. Rosa Peña; m. Petra Cervantes, Dec. 22, 1974 (div. 1982); children: Federico Ezequiel, Margarita María Blea. BA, N.Mex. Highlands U., 1968, MA, 1972, postgrad. With Albert Garcia Gen. Contre., Las Vegas, N.Mex., 1955-67; tchg. asst. N.Mex. Highlands U., Las Vegas, Nev., 1971-72, prof. Spanish, Chicano studies, 1972-78; teaching asst. U. N.Mex., Albuquerque, 1978-79; attendant N.Mex. State Mental Hosp., Las Vegas, Nev., 1982-83; staff and supervisory interpreter US Dist. Ct. N.Mex., Albuquerque, N.Mex., 1983—. Head Raza Unida del to PLO in Lebanon, 1981, head negotiator with Iranians for release of 2 Chicanos and 1 Indian; supr ct. interpreters and reporters sect. US Dist. Ct. N.Mex.; co-chmn. Cuatro-Centennial Com., Inc.; mem. exec. com. N.Mex. Human Rights Coalition. Author collection of poetry: Angustias y Remembranzas; contbr. articles to profl. jour.; author play: Canto a La Raza, 1978. Pres. Dads Against Discrimination, Albuquerque, 1993—; chmn. bd. trustees No. N.Mex. Legal Svcs., Las Vegas 1972-81; mem. exec. com. Ind. Socialist Parties of Latin Am.; exec. commn. N.Mex. Human Rights Coalition; vice chmn. Barelas Cmty. Devel. Corp.; Barelas rep. Hist. Neighborhoods Alliance; mem. cmty. coun. on equity Albuquerque Pub. Sch.; mem. N.Mex. Cmty. Loan Fund; bd. dir. Albuquerque Downtown Action Team, N.Mex. Land Grant Forum; mem. textbook rev. committee N.Mex. Dept. Edn., mem. bilingual edn. adv. coun.; commr. N.Mex. Textbook Selection Commn., 2001—; nat. sec. Am. GI Forum of US, 2000-01, 2003-2004; v.p. Cmty. Enrichment Svc. Orgn., Inc.; bd. trustees, Nat. Hispanic Cultural Ctr. N.Mex., 2003—; vice chmn., Hispano Round Table N.Mex., 1999-2003, chmn. 2003-2004; v.p. Cmty. Enrichment Svcs. Orgn., Inc.; bd. dir., bd. trustees Nat. Hispanic Cultural Ctr. N.Mex., v.p. 2005-06, U. N. Mex. Coll. Edu. Advancement Coun.; mem. adv. com. U. N.Mex Coll. Edn.; nat. sec. Am. GI Forum, 2003-, chmn. N. Mex. Voter Registration Project; chmn. Hispanic Round Table N.Mex., 2004-05. Decorated Bronze Star; recipient Human Rights award City of Albuquerque Human Rights Bd., N.Mex. State Coun. Profile of Courage award Vietnam Vets. Am., 1995, N.Mex. Nat. Guard Cinco de Mayo award, 1995, Hispanics for U N.Mex. Achievement award, 1999, Human Rights award Albuquerque Human Rights Bd., 2000. Bd. dir. Albuquerque Downtown Action Team; mem. N.Mex. Translator and Interpreters Assn. (pres. 1984-86), Nat. Assn. Judiciary Interpreters (sec. 1986-88), Nat. Partido Raza Unida (pres. 1976-81), N.Mex. Partido Raza Unida (pres. 1972-75, 77-78), Vietnam Vets. Am. (vice chmn. chpt. 1993—), Vietnam Vets. N.Mex.; Am. GI Forum (Albuquerque chpt. 1 comdr. 1993—, vice comdr. 1997-98, sec.), N.Mex. GI Forum (comdr. 1996), Univ. of N.Mex. Sch. of Ed. Adv. comm. mem., Nat. Assn. Chicano Studies (founding mem.), N.Mex. Chicano Studies Assn. (pres. 1972-78), Hispanic Round Table of N.Mex. (chmn. 1995, 98), Barelas Neighborhood Assn. (pres.), Hist. Neighborhoods Assn., Barelas Cmty. Devel. Corp. (rep.), Phi Sigma Iota. Democrat. Roman Catholic. Avocations: weightlifting, swimming, ice skating, hiking, camping. Home: 1115 9th St SW Albuquerque NM 87102-4027 Office: US Dist Ct Dist NMex 333 Lomas Blvd NW Albuquerque NM 87102-2272 Office Phone: 505-242-8085. E-mail: jpena71@comcast.net, jjp3000@aol.com.

**PEÑA, MARY ANNE,** language educator; d. Michael Leonard and Norma Elaine (Kolb) Mahoney; m. Leonidas Peña, Sept. 24, 1977; children: Leo, Alicia. Diploma Nursing, Albert Einstein Sch. Nursing, 1976; BSN, U. Pa., Phila., 1980; tchr. cert. edn., Prairie View A&M, Tex., 2000. Staff nurse surg. Albert Einstein Med. Ctr., Phila., 1976—81; tchr. ESL Inst. Domingo Americano, Santa Domingo, 1981—82; nurse Am. Embassy Santo Domingo, Dominican Republic, 1982—91; Dept. Pub. Health, Brenham, Tex., 1992—93; tchr. asst. Brenham I.S.D., 1995—97, bilingual tchr., 1997—. Sec. Brenham U. Women, 1993—; v.p., 1993—, pres., 1993—; bd. mem. Brenham Young Life, 2003—. Named Tchr. of Yr., Brenham Mid. Sch., 2000—01; recipient Meritorious Honor award, Am. Embassy, Santo Domingo, 1986, 1989, 1990. Mem.: Nat. Coun. English Tchrs., Tchrs. of ESL Learners, Internat. Reading Assn. Republican. Baptist. Avocations: reading, aerobics, cross stitch. Office Phone: 979-277-6585.

**PEÑA, MICHAEL ANTHONY,** actor; b. Chgo., 1976; Actor: (films) Running Free, 1994, My Fellow Americans, 1996, Boogie Boy, 1998, La Cucaracha, 1998, Bellyfruit, 1999, Gone in Sixty Seconds, 2000, United States of Leland, 2003, Love Object, 2003, The Calcium Kid, 2004, Crash, 2004 (ALMA award for Outstanding Actor in a motion picture, 2006), Million Dollar Baby, 2004, (TV movies) Semper Fi, 2001, Walkout, 2006, Fifty Pills, 2006, World Trade Center, 2006, (TV appearances) The Sentinel, 1998, Moesha, 1998, Profiler, 1999, Felicity, 1999, The District, 2000, Roswell, 2001, Men, Women and Dogs, 2001, American Family, 2002, Andy Richter Controls the Universe, 2002, Twilight Zone, 2003, ER, 2003, NYPD Blue, 1997, 2004, CSI, 2005, The Shield, 2005. Mailing: c/o Innovative Artists Talent & Lit Agy 1505 Tenth St Santa Monica CA 90401*

**PENA, RAYMUNDO JOSEPH,** bishop; b. Corpus Christi, Tex., Feb. 19, 1934; s. Cosme A. and Elisa (Ramon) P. DD, Assumption Sem., San Antonio, 1957. Ordained priest Roman Cat. Ch., 1957. Assist. pastor St. Peter's Ch., Laredo, Tex., 1957—60, St. Joseph's-Our Lady of Fatima, Alamo, Tex., 1960—63, Sacred Heart, Mathis, Tex., 1963—67, Christ the King and Our Lady of Pillar Parishes, Corpus Christi, 1967—69; pastor Our Lady of Guadalupe Parish, Corpus Christi, 1969—; v.p. Corpus Christi Diocesan Senate of Priests, 1970—76; aux. bishop San Antonio 1976—80; bishop El Paso, 1980—95, Brownsville, Tex., 1995—. Mem. secretariat Prep. Synod of

Bishops for Am., 1996—97; Synodal Father Synod of Bishops for Am., 1995. Mem.: U.S. Conf. Cath. Bishops (chmn. bishops' com. for Hispanic affairs 1987—90, bishops' com. for ch. in L.Am. 1994—97, 2000). Roman Catholic. Home: 741 Bowie Alamo TX 78516 Office: PO Box 2279 Brownsville TX 78522-2279 Office Phone: 956-542-2501. Business E-Mail: rjpena@cdob.org.

**PENA, RICHARD,** lawyer; b. San Antonio, Feb. 13, 1948; s. Merced and Rebecca (Trejo) P.; m. Carolyn Sarah Malley, May 25, 1979; 1 stepchild, Jason Charles Schubert. BA, U. Tex., 1970, JD, 1976. Bar: Tex. 1976, Colo. 1986. Pvt. practice, Austin, Tex., 1976—. Instr. bus. law St. Edwards U., Austin, 1983, Austin C.C., 1981-82; broker Tex. Real Estate Commn., 1980—; sports editor Austin Light, 1982. Bd. dirs. Ctr. for Battered Women, 1979-82, Austin Assn. Retarded Citizens, 1980-82; chmn. Austin Travis County Mental Health/Mental Retardation Pub. Responsibility Com., 1979-84; chmn. pvt. facilities monitoring com. Austin Assn. Retarded Citizens, 1981; bd. dirs. Boys Club of Austin, 1987-88; chair Homeless Task Force Austin, 1999—. Named one of Outstanding Young Men of Am., 1982. Fellow Tex. Bar Found. (sustaining life; trustee 1994, sec., treas. 1994, vice-chmn. 1995, chmn. 1996); mem. ABA (ho. dels., nominating com. 1998—, immigration bono com. 2000—, chair 2004—, vice chair credentials com. 2001, state del. 2002), Am. Bar Found. (bd. dirs. 2003-04, fellows officer 2003-04, chair 2004-05), Nat. Conf. Bar Pres. (exec. com. 2001-03), State Bar Tex. (bd. dirs. Dist. 9 1991-94, exec. com. 1992—, chmn. minority representation com. 1991-92, chair James Watson Inn 1997-98, pres. 1998-99, chmn. profl. devel. com. 1991-92, policy manual com. 1993, fed. jud. appts. com. 1984-86, opportunities for minorities in the profession com. 1990-91, mem. advt. rev. com., pres.-elect 1997, pres. 1998-99), Travis County Bar Assn. (trustee lawyer referral svc. 1984-85, bd. dirs. 1986-88, sec. 1988, pres. 1990-91, chmn. jud. screening com. 1987, chmn. 1988-89, ins. com. 1988, 89, chmn. law day banquet com. 1988-89, lawyer referrel svc. com. 1983-84, trustee 1984-86, membership com. 1989), Capitol Area Mex. Am. Lawyers (pres. 1985, Outstanding Hispanic Lawyer Austin 1989), Legal Aid Soc. Ctrl. Tex. (bd. dirs. 1984), Austin Young Lawyers Assn., Tex. Trial Lawyers Assn., Austin C. of C. (Leadership Austin 1985-86). Democrat. Office: 2028 E Ben White #220 Austin TX 78741 Office Phone: 512-327-6884. Personal E-mail: richard@rpena73.com.

**PENACHIO, ANTHONY JOSEPH, JR.,** psychotherapist, hypnotherapist, behavioral therapist; b. Stamford, Conn., Apr. 3, 1953; 1 child, Ariana. Cert. in psychotherapy, Am. Sch. Med. Hynotherapy, 1978; DD, Aquarian Ch. of Jesus, 1978; PSD, Neotharian Sch. of Philosophy, 1980. Cert. clin. registered med. hypnotherapist, psychotherapist, behavioral therapist, biomed. electronics, personal and bus. coach, psychophysiologist, personal coach; ordained counseling min. Aquarian Ch.; diplomate Am. Psychotherapy Assn. Counseling min., exec. dir. Inst. Clin. Tricotomy, Stamford, 1978—. Author, emotional investment profiler Wall St., corp. and govt.; lectr., radio and cable TV talk show seminar presenter. Contbr. articles profl. jour., corp. and govt. Mem. Am. Coun. Hypnotherapist-Psychotherapist (bd. examiners), NY Acad. Sci. (lectr.). E-mail: hypnosis@ict.com.

**PENBERTHY, STANLEY JOSIAH, JR.,** publisher; b. Des Moines, Sept. 3, 1921; s. Stanley Josiah and Beatrice Ann (Voith) P.; m. Dorothea Oehmke, July 7, 1945; 1 child, Robert Bruce. Student, Drake U., 1940—43. Engaged in broadcasting WJR, Detroit, 1941—56; freelance radio, TV, motion picture, actor, narrator, 1956—95. V.p. Fed. I-D Equipment Corp., Dearborn, Mich., 1951-62; pres. Publishers, Inc., Detroit, 1976-99. Author, prodr., narrator nat. radio series These Were Our Presidents, 1975; contbr. Mich. Sesquicentennial hist. articles; author: Living Under Cover, Episodes of Life and other Relatives, Cottage Industry, The Photographs of William A. Roeser: A Talent Unfulfilled, From the Golden Tower of the Fisher Building. Past mem. bd. dirs. Sleeping Bear Dunes Citizens Coun., Traverse City, Mich., 1968-72, Cass Park Area Devel. Corp., City of Detroit, 1989; pres. Heritage Village Condominium Assn.; trustee Detroit Masonic Temple Assn.; mem. Founders Soc. Detroit Inst. Arts. Mem. AFTRA (past dir.), Adcraft Club Detroit, Detroit Execs. Assn. (dir.), Am. Film Inst., Detroit Prodrs. Assn., Broadcast Pioneers, Screen Actors Guild, Masons (33rd degree), Alpha Tau Omega (past alumni pres.). Home: 35560 Heritage Ln Farmington MI 48335-3136

**PENCE, HOBERT LEE,** physician; b. Campton, Ky., July 14, 1941; s. Bruce Elmer and Elva (Banks) P.; m. Marsha Lee Sweet, June 29, 1962; children: Robert, Ryan, Stefanie. BS, Ohio State U., Columbus, 1963, MD, 1968. Residency Walter Reed Gen. Hosp., Washington, 1969-71, fellowship in allergy and clin. immunology, 1971-73; pvt. practice ent. practice, Louisville, 1975—. Asst. clin. prof. medicine U. Louisville, 1976-81, assoc. clin. prof. medicine, 1981—; assoc. clin. prof. Pediat. U. Louisville, 1995—. Contbr. articles to profl. jours. V.p Jefferson County Med. Soc., Louisville, 1984-86; pres. Greater Louisville Allergy Soc., 1990-92. Major U.S. Army, 1969-75. Fellow ACP, Am. Acad. Allergy Asthma and Immunology, Am. Coll. Allergy and Immunology; mem. Southeastern Allergy Assn. (1st v.p., pres. elect, pres. 1996). Avocations: golf, tennis, reading. Office: Kentuckiana Allergy 9113 Leesgate Rd Louisville KY 40222-5003 Office Phone: 502-426-1621.

**PENCE, IRA WILSON, JR.,** engineering executive, researcher; b. Pontiac, Mich., June 18, 1939; s. Ira Wilson and Fern Elizabeth (Fraser) P.; m. JoAnna Springer, Sept. 5, 1959; children: Ira W. III, Teresa Ann, Deidre Lynn. BS, U. Mich., 1962, MSEE, 1964, PhD, 1970. Rsch. engr. Willow Run Labs., Ypsilanti, Mich., 1960-67, Dow Lab., Ann Arbor, Mich., 1967-70, GE, Schenectady, NY, 1970-80, engring. mgr. Charlottesville, Va., 1980-83; v.p engring. Unimation, Inc., Danbury, Conn., 1983-87; dir. MHRC Ga. Inst Tech., Atlanta, 1987-97, dir., pres. Intelligent Integrated Info. Sys., 1999—. Cons. Superior Motor, Hartford, 1987—89; bd. dirs. Wesley Found.; mem. adv. coun. Westinghouse, Pitts., 1983—87; treas. Wesley Comm. Ctrs., Inc., 1999—2003; exec. pres. Intelligent Integrated Info. Sys., 1999—; dir. 21iii.com, 2000—05. Editor: Progress in Material Handling and Logistics, 1988; Material Handling for 90's, 1990. Trustee United Meth. Ch., 1988—, Camp Wesley, Inc. 1998— (treas. 2003-). Recipient New Product of Yr. award Innovation Today, 1985. Mem. IEEE (sr., sect. chmn. 1978), ASME (Materials Handling Engring. divsn. chair 1994). Republican. Methodist. Avocations: cabinet making, golf. Office Phone: 770-435-3183. Office Fax: 770-435-0493. Business E-Mail: ipence@isye.gatech.edu.

**PENCE, JEAN VIRGINIA (JEAN PENCE),** retired real estate broker; d. William Roscoe and Sophie Cottrell; m. Robert Albert Pence, June 14, 1947; children: Marjorie Pence Tuinstra, Robert J. Grad., Realtors Inst., Ill. Assn. Realtors. Cert. in real estate Central YMCA Coll., 1976. Sales assoc. William Knight Co., Realtors, LaGrange, Ill., 1962—70, sales mgr., 1970—76; pres. Pence & Co., Realtors, LaGrange, 1976—86; freelance writer Sun City Center, Fla., 1999—. Chmn. LaGrange Go-Getters Com. Channel 11 WTTG, Chgo., 1973—74. Author: (genealogy) The Cottrell Adventure With the Wright Connection, (novel) The Apprentice Angel, short stories. Sec. bd. deacons St. Andrew Presbyn. Ch., Sun City Center, 2003—05. Mem.: DAR (vice regent Clearwater chpt. 1984—86), Women's Coun. Realtors (pres. West suburban chpt. 1979—81), DuPage Bd. Realtors, LaGrange Bd. Realtors (sec.-treas. 1973—75, dir. multiple listing service 1978, chmn. profl. standards com. 1985—86), Nat. Assn. Realtors, Coterie (pres. 1982—83), LaGrange Park Woman's (sec. 1967—68), Pierre Chastain Family Assn. (press chmn. 1998—2001).

**PENCE, LINDA LEE,** lawyer; b. Indpls., Dec. 24, 1949; d. Woodrow Wilson and Patsy Mae (Kelley) P. BA in Polit. Sci., Ind. U., 1971, JD, 1974. Bar: Ind. 1974, DC 1982, US Dist. Ct. (no., so. dist. Ind.), US Ct. Appeals (4th, 7th, 9th, 10th, Fed. cir.), US Supreme Ct. Trial atty., chief U.S. Dept. Justice, Washington, 1974-83; assoc. Akin, Gump, Strauss, Hauer & Feld, Washington, 1983-84; ptnr. Spriggs, Bode & Hollingsworth, Washington, 1985-86, Johnson Smith Pence Densborn Wright & Heath, Washington, 1994; dir., ptnr., bus. litig., white collar criminal def. practices Sommer Barnard, Indianapolis. Bd. dir. Indianapolis Symphony Orch.; mem. & past pres. bd. vis. Ind. Univ. Sch. Law; founding mem. & past pres. Ind. Fed. Cmty.

**PENCE, MICHAEL RICHARD,** congressman; b. Columbus, Ind., June 7, 1959; m. Karen; 3 children. Grad., Hanover Coll., 1981; JD, Ind. U. Sch. Law, 1986. Atty., 1986—91; pres. Ind. Policy Rev. Found., 1991; mem. US Congress from 2nd Ind. dist., 2001—. mem. judiciary com., internat. relations com., agr. com., chmn. Ho. Rep. Study Com., 2004—. Host (radio shows) The Mike Pence Show, 1992—99. Republican. Office: US Ho Reps 426 Cannon Ho Office Bldg Washington DC 20515-1406 Office Phone: 202-225-3021. Office Fax: 202-225-3382.*

**PENCE, ROBERT DUDLEY,** biomedical researcher, consultant, hospital administrator; b. Hillsboro, Ohio, June 16, 1928; s. Glenn Roush and Mildred (Wright) P. BA cum laude, Miami U., Oxford, Ohio, 1950; postgrad., U. Montpellier, France, 1950-51. Mktg. rep. Tex. Petroleum Co., West Africa, 1956-58; mgr. lab. and office svcs. Sloan-Kettering Inst. for Cancer Rsch., N.Y.C., 1958-68; bus. mgr., cancer rsch. inst. New Eng. Deaconess Hosp., Boston, 1968-72, adminstr. Shields Warren Radiation Lab., 1970-78, asst. dir., 1972-86, adminstrv. dir., cancer rsch. inst., 1974-88, adminstrv. dir. Shields Warren Radiation Lab., 1978-88, dir. div. of rsch., 1986-88, cons., 1988—. Field liaison fellow ACS, Chgo., 1987-88. Pres. Am. Cancer Soc., Brookline, Mass. Served to lt. (j.g.) USN, 1951-55. Fulbright scholar, Montpellier, 1950. Mem. Assn. Community Cancer Ctrs. (del.), Internat. Union Against Cancer (U.S. standing com.), Assn. Am. Cancer Insts., Soc. Rsch. Adminstrs. (charter), Nat. Coun. Univ. Rsch. Adminstrs., Nat. Tumor Registrars Assn. (advisor 1980—), Tumor Registrars Assn. New Eng. (bd. dirs. 1975—), Phi Beta Kappa. Home: 30 Driftwood Cir Norwood MA 02062-5505

**PENCE, STEPHEN BEVILLE,** lieutenant governor; b. Dec. 22, 1953; m. Ruth Ann Cox; 5 children. BS, Ea. Ky. U., 1976, MBA, 1978; JD, U. Ky., 1981; PhD (hon.), Eastern Ky. U., 2004. Asst. atty. gen. State of Ky., 1981—82; assoc. Taustine and Post, 1987—88, Borowitz and Goldsmith, 1988—90; ptnr. Sheffer and Hoffman, 1995—96, Pedley, Zielke, Gordinier and Pence, Louisville, 1996—2001; U.S. Atty. We. Dist. Ky U.S. Dept. Justice, 2001—03; lt. gov Commonwealth of Ky., 2003—. JAG Corps U.S. Army, 1982—87. Recipient Ky Bar Assn.'s Outstanding Lawyer award, 1995. Republican. Office: Office Lt Governor 700 Capitol Ave Ste 142 Frankfort KY 40601 Office Phone: 502-564-2611. Office Fax: 502-564-2849.*

**PENCIL, FAITH ANN,** music educator; b. Springfield, Ohio, Aug. 16, 1951; d. Robert and Ruth Pencil. BA, Anderson (Ind.) U., 1973; MA, Ohio State U., 1990. Cert. tchr. Ohio. Music tchr. Albion (Ohio) City Schs., 1977—78; music/elem. tchr. Springfield (Ohio) Christian Schs., 1979—99; music instr. Clark State C.C., Springfield, 2000—; asst. prof. music Urbana (Ohio) U., 2001—. Handbell dir. Maiden Ln. Ch. of God, Springfield, 1985—. Chmn. bd. dirs. Christian Edu-Care, Springfield, 1980—. Mem.: ACDA (assoc.), Music Educators Nat. Conf (assoc.). Home: 1038 Maiden Ln Springfield OH 45504 Office: Urbana U 579 College Way Urbana OH 43978 Office Phone: 937-484-1246. E-mail: fpencil@urbana.edu.

**PENDELL, ZHANNA I.,** music educator; b. Baranovichi, Belarus, Oct. 4, 1974; d. Ivan and Valentina Maysyuk; m. Perry Pendell, July 3, 2005. Bachelor's in Performance, Boston Conservatory of Music, 1997; Master of Music Edn. in Percussion Performance, Boston U., 2000. Choral dir., tchr. gen. music Bartlett Mid. Sch. Lowell Pub. Schs., Mass., 2000—02; tchr. elem. music Harvard-Kent Sch. Boston Pub. Schs., 2002—03; choral dir. K-12 music Schroon Lake Ctrl. Sch., NY, 2003—. Musician: Vt. Mozart Festival, 1998—, Glens Falls Symphony/City Orch., —. Mem.: Pi Kappa Lambda. Office: Schroon Lake Ctrl Sch 1125 US Rt 9 Schroon Lake NY 12870

**PENDER, MARTHA HELEN,** retired singer; b. Abilene, Tex., Nov. 8, 1927; d. Herman Arthur and Mary (Paxton) Pender. MusB, North Tex. State U., 1949; MusM, U. Tex., 1970; pvt. studies, Rome, 1950—67. Voice tchr. Ind U., 1967—68. Tex.-Tech U., Lubbock, 1968—73. Soprano with faculty quartet Tex. Tech U., 1970—73. Opera debut: Cavalleria, 1953, soprano: Lady MacBeth, 1964, Rome, Turin, Naples, 1955—67. Organizer reopening Paramount Theater, Abilene, Tex., 1981, organizer concert series, 1981—83. Recipient art award, Abilene Cultural Affairs Coun., 1989, Disting. Svc. award, Harmony Club, 2002. Mem.: Nat. Assn. Tchrs. Singing (life), Abilene Opera Assn. (pres.), Alpha Psi Omega (life), Alpha Iota (life). Republican. Baptist. Home: 1209 Musken Rd Apt H Abilene TX 79601

**PENDER, NANCY,** newscaster; b. Concord, Calif., 1960; BBus in mktg. with honors, Sacramento State U. Freelance reporter, LA and San Francisco; dep. press sec. Calif. Assembly Spkr. Willie J. Brown, Jr.; with KCRL-TV, Reno, Orange County Newschannel, Calif., KMST-TV, Monterey, KJEO-TV, Fresno, KCOY-TV, Santa Maria; morning news anchor KUSI-TV, San Diego; weekend news anchor and reporter WFLD-TV, Chgo., 1997—. Office: WFLD-TV 205 N Mich Ave Chicago IL 60601

**PENDERGRAFT, JANICE GAYLE,** volunteer; b. San Antonio, Mar. 9, 1950; d. Janice Gayle and John Joseph Pendergraft (Stepfather); m. Pete E. Kraus, Nov. 3, 1973 (dec. Aug. 3, 1987); 1 child, Heather Kraus; m. John Joseph Pendergraft, June 18, 1988. Cert. dental asst., L.A. Coll. Med. and Dental Assts., San Bernardino, Calif., 1969. Cert. dental asst. Vol. M.A.D.D., San Bernardino, 1995—, Ronald McDonald House, Loma Linda, Calif., 1998—. Author poetry. Active Yucaipa Edn. Bd., Calif., 1980—98. Recipient several poetry awards, 1998—2002. Office: Ronald Mcdonald House Barton Rd Loma Linda CA 92353

**PENDERGRASS, HENRY PANCOAST,** radiologist, nuclear medicine physician; b. Bryn Mawr, Pa., Jan. 29, 1925; s. Eugene Percival and Rebecca (Barker) P.; m. Carol Lowe Dodson, Aug. 27, 1960 (dec. Aug. 1993); children: Sharon (dec. Aug. 1993), Lisa (dec. Aug. 1993), Deborah, Margaret; m. Carol Minster Roberts, Oct. 2, 1994. Student, U.S. Naval Acad., 1944-46; AB, Princeton U., 1948; MD, U. Pa., 1952; MPH, Harvard U., 1969. Diplomate Am. Bd. Radiology, Am. Bd. Nuc. Medicine. Intern Pa. Hosp., 1952—53; resident Hosp. U. Pa., 1953—56; mem. staff and faculty U. Pa. Med. Sch. and Univ. Hosp., Phila., 1956—58, U. Pa. Med. Sch. & U. Hosp., 1960—61; clin. asst. in neuroradiology Inst. Neurology Queen Sq., London, 1959-60; mem. staff and faculty Harvard U. Med. Sch. and Mass. Gen. Hosp., Boston, 1958-59, 61-76; prof. radiology Vanderbilt U. Sch. Medicine, Nashville, 1976-95, prof. emeritus, 1995—, vice chmn., 1976-89; adj. prof. radiology U. Pa. Sch. Medicine, Phila., 1996—. Mem. editorial bd. Am. Family Physician, 1980-94, Jour. Digital Imaging, 1987-96; contbr. chpts. to books, articles to med. jours. Mem. cancer control rev. com. Nat. Cancer Inst., 1975-79; Bd. dirs. state and local div. Am. Cancer Soc., 1976-85; mem. Project Hope Med. Mission, Peru, 1962; trustee Harpeth Hall Sch., Nashville, 1983-88. With U.S. Army, USN, 1943-46. Am. Cancer Soc. grantee, 1956-57; Nat. Cancer Inst. grantee, 1957-58; Nat. Inst. Neurol. Disease and Blindness grantee, 1959-60; Nat. Inst. Gen. Med. Scis. grantee, 1968-69. Fellow: AMA (sect. coun. on radiology 1979—99, chair 1997-99, sect. on med. schs. 1979—99, sec. 1986—97, mem. ho. of dels. 1986—99, specialty and svc. sect. 1986—99, grad. med. edn. adv. com. 1994—97, chair 1996, Gold medal 1994), Tenn. Radiol. Soc. (exec. com. 1984—88, pres.-elect then pres. 1985—86, Disting. Svc. award 1993), Soc. Magnetic Resonance in Medicine, Soc. Thoracic Imaging, Mid. Tenn. Radiol. Soc. (pres. 1984—85), Tenn. Med. Assn., Am. Soc. Emergency Radiology, Radiol. Soc. N.Am. (bd. dir. 1972—77, chmn. 1975—76, pres.-elect then pres. 1977—78, appointee to AMA ho. dels. 1986—97, sec.-treas. 1988—90, trustee RSNA rsch. and edn. found., Gold medal 1984), Nashville Acad. Medicine (chmn. com. on ethics 1981—82), Mass. Med. Soc. (counselor 1968—76), Mass. Radiol. Soc. (v.p.

1967—68, 1975—76, sec.-treas. 1985—94), Assn. U. Radiologists, Ea. Radiol. Soc. (sci. program chmn. 1964, pres. 1968—72, trustee 1968—72), Coun. on Med. Specialty Socs., Brit. Inst. Radiology, Am. Roentgen Ray Soc., Am. Coll. Radiology (coun. steering com. 1968—73, bd. chancellors 1977—81, appointee to AMA ho. of dels. 1997—99, coun., Gold medal 2002); mem.: Cap & Gown Club (Princeton, NJ), Merion Golf Club, Belle Meade Country Club, Merion Cricket Club, Amateur Ski Club NY, Delta Psi, Sigma Xi. Home: 1400 Waverly Rd Villa 25 Gladwyne PA 19035-1273

**PENDERGRASS, TEDDY (THEODORE D. PENDERGRASS),** musician; b. Phila., Mar. 26, 1950; m. Karin Michelle Still, June 20, 1987; children: Tisha, Ladonna, Teddy. Student major schs. Drummer for various groups, 1966-69; Singer, lead singer Harold Melvin & Blue Notes, 1969-75; solo artist, 1975—; pres. Teddy Bear Enterprises, Phila. Squire, Memphis. Albums include: Life Is a Song Worth Singing, 1978, Teddy, 1979, T.P., 1980, Live Coast to Coast, 1980, It's Time for Teddy, 1981, Teddy Pendergrass, 1982, This One's For You, 1982, Heaven Only Knows, 1983, Greatest Hits, 1984, Love Language, 1984, Workin' It Back, 1985, Joy, 1988, Truly Blessed, 1991, A Little More Magic, 1993, You & I, 1997, Greatest Hits, 1998, This Christmas, 1998, (with Harold Melvin & The Blue Notes) Teddy Live Coast to Coast, 1994. Recipient civic and pub. service awards-, Image award NAACP, 1973, 80, Black Achievement award Ebony Mag., 1979, award outstanding mus. contbn. Afro-Am. Hist. Mus., 1983, award of merit City of Detroit, 12 gold and 7 platinum albums; recipity Keys to Cities, Lakeland (Fla.), Detroit, Savannah (Ga.), Memphis; named New Artist of 1977 for Top Pop Album Billboard Mag.

**PENDLETON, AUSTIN,** actor, theater director; b. Warren, Ohio, Mar. 27, 1940; m. Katina Commings; 1 child, Audrey Christine. BA, Yale U., 1961. Apprentice Williamstown Theatre Festival, Mass., 1957—58; actor & dir. Steppenwolf Co., 1970; artistic dir. Circle Repertory Co., NYC, 1995—. Actor: (plays) Oh Dad, Poor Dad, Momma's Hung You in the Closet and I'm Feeling So Sad, 1962, Fiddler on the Roof, 1964, Hail Scrawdyke, 1966 (Clarnece Derwent award), The Little Foxes, 1967, The Last Sweet Days of Isaac, 1970 (Obie award, Drama Critic's Poll award), An American Millionaire, 1974, The Sorrows of Frederick, 1976, The Three Sisters, 1977, Julius Caesar, 1978, Waiting for Godot, 1979, Doubles, 1985, Booth, Uncle Bob, Orson's Shadow, 2001, 2005; dir.: Shelter, 1973, Little Egolf, 1974, Benita Cereno, 1976, The Runner Stumbles, 1976, After the Fall, 1980; (TV films) Say Goodnight Gracie, 1979; actor: Alice in Wonderland, 1983, Lethal Innocence, 1991, Four Eyes and Six-Guns, 1992, Don't Drink the Water, 1994, Long Island Fever, 1995; (films) Skidoo, 1968, Catch-22, 1970, What's Up, Doc?, 1972, Every Little Crook and Nanny, 1972, The Thief Who Came to Dinner, 1973, The Muppet Movie, 1979, Starting Over, 1979, Simon, 1980, First Family, 1980, Off Beat, 1986, Short Circuit, 1986, Mr. & Mrs. Bridge, 1990, The Ballad of the Sad Cafe, 1991, True Identity, 1991, My Cousin Vinny, 1992, My Boyfriend's Back, 1993, Mr. Nanny, 1993, Guarding Tess, 1994, Two Much, 1995, Sgt. Bilko, 1996, The Proprietor, 1996, The Associate, 1996, The Mirror Has Two Faces, 1996, Amistad, 1997, Brokendown Love Story, 1999, Joe the King, 1999, Fast Food, Fast Women, 2000, A Beautiful Mind, 2001, (voice) Finding Nemo, 2003, Uptown Girls, 2003, Christmas with the Kranks, 2004, Dirty Work, 2005. Office: care Coleman/Rosenberg 210 E 58th St New York NY 10022-2030

**PENDLETON, FLORENCE HOWARD,** shadow senator; b. Columbus, Ga., Jan. 1928; d. John Milton and Elease Brooks Howard; m. Oscar Henry Pendleton, 1943; children: Oscar Henry Jr., Howard Thompson. BS, Howard U., 1949, MS, 1957. Tchr. Columbus Pub. Sch., Ga., 1951—55; instr. Morgan State Coll., Balt., 1957—58; tchr. DC Pub. Schs., Washington, 1958—70, asst. prin., 1970—80, prin., 1980—93; ret., 1993; chmn. Ward Five Dem. Com., Washington, 1979—82; mem. DC Dem. State Party, Washington, 1979—90; DC shadow senator to U.S. Congress, 1995—. Alt. delegate Dem. Nat. Convention, NYC, 1980; commr. Ward Five C07 Advisory Neighborhood Com. Clerk Berean Baptist Ch., 1965—94, clerk emeritus, 1994—. Named Disting. Citizen, Washington, 1980, Outstanding Cmty. Leader Ward Five, Berean Baptist Ch., 1981. Mem.: South St. And Affiliate Streets Block Club (pres. 1975—), Bloomingdale's Civic Assn. (admin. 1978—80), Ctr. City Cmty. Corp. (mem. chmn. exec. com. 1976—79). Democrat. Office: 441 Fourth St NW Ste 10518 Washington DC 20001 Office Phone: 202-727-8099. Office Fax: 202-483-6301.*

**PENDLETON, MARY CATHERINE,** retired foreign service officer; b. Louisville, June 15, 1940; d. Joseph S. and Katherine R. (Toebbe) Pendleton. BA, Spalding Coll., 1962; MA, Ind. U., 1969; cert., Nat. Def. U., 1990; D (hon.), U. N. Testemitanu, Moldova, 1994. Cert. secondary tchr. Ky. Tchr. Presentation Acad., Louisville, 1962-66; vol. Peace Corps, Tunis, Tunisia, 1966-68; employment counselor Ky. Dept. for Human Resources, Louisville, 1969-75; gen. svcs. Am. Embassy, Khartoum, Sudan, 1975-77, counsular officer Manila, 1978-79, adminstrv. officer Bangui, Central African Republic, 1979-82, Lusaka, Zambia, 1982-84; post mgmt. officer Dept. of State Bur. European and Can. Affairs, Washington, 1984-87; adminstrv. counselor Am. Embassy, Bucharest, Romania, 1987-89; dir. adminstrv. tng. divsn. Fgn. Svc. Inst., Arlington, Va., 1990-92; ambassador Am. Embassy, Chisinau, Moldova, 1992-95, adminstrv. counselor Brussels, 1995-98; consul gen. U.S. Consulate Gen., Montreal, 1998-2001; mgmt. counselor Am. Embassy, Cairo, 2001—04; diplomat in residence U. Memphis, 2004—05; ret., 2005. Bd. dirs. Cairo Am. Coll., 2001—04, Am. Sch. Bucharest, 1987—89. Named to. Hon. Order Ky. Cols., 1988. Democrat. Roman Catholic. Avocation: volunteer activities. Home: 1946 N Cleveland St Arlington VA 22201 Personal E-mail: pendletonmc@gmail.com.

**PENDLETON, MILES STEVENS, JR.,** diplomat; b. Montclair, NJ, Mar. 22, 1939; s. Miles Stevens and Lucille (Bond) P.; m. Elisabeth Morgan, Aug. 13, 1967; children: Constance Morrow, Nathaniel Palmer. BA magna cum laude, Yale U., 1961; MPA, Harvard U., 1967; diploma, War Coll., 1980. Tchr. Ghana Secondary Sch., Koforidua, 1962-63; Adisadel Coll., Cape Coast, Ghana, 1963-64; vice consul Am. Embassy, Tel Aviv, 1968-70, polit. and econ. officer Bujumbura, Burundi, 1970-72; watch officer Ops. Ctr. Dept. State, Washington, 1972-73, staff officer Secretariat Staff, 1973-74, spl. asst. to Dep. Sec. of State Office Dep. Sec., 1974-76, dep. dir. Office of No. European Affairs, 1980-82, dir. Office of Israel and Arab-Israel Affairs, 1982-83, exec. asst. to under sec. of state for polit. affairs, 1983-85, dir. Office of Ecology and Terrestrial Conservation, 1995-97; polit. officer U.S. Mission to NATO, Brussels, 1976-79; min.-counselor for polit. affairs Am. Embassy, London, 1985-89, min., counselor for polit. affairs Paris, 1989-93; prof. strategy Indsl. Coll. Armed Forces Nat. Def. U., Washington, 1993-95. Mem. Am. Fgn. Svc. Assn., North Haven (Maine) Yacht Club, Met. Club (Washington), Phi Beta Kappa. Avocations: sailing, travel. Home: 3410 Lowell St NW Washington DC 20016-5023 Office Phone: 202-363-2601. E-mail: milespendleton@hotmail.com.

**PENDLETON, MOSES ROBERT ANDREW,** dancer, choreographer; b. St. Johnsbury, Vt., Mar. 28, 1949; s. Nelson Augustus and Mary Elizabeth (Patchel) P. BA, Dartmouth Coll., 1971. Co-founder, dir. dancer, choreographer Pilobolus Dance Theater, Washington, 1971—; founder, artistic dir. Momix Dance Theater, Washington, 1980—. Tchr., artist-in-residence at univs throughout U.S., 1997; tchr., condr. workshops. Choreographer, dancer numerous works including Pilobolus, 1971, Anendrom, 1972, Walklyndon, 1972, Ocellus, 1972, Ciona, 1973, Monkshood's Farewell, 1974, Untitled, 1975, Eve of Samhain, 1977, Alraune, 1975, Lost in Fauna, 1976, Shizen, 1977, Bonsai, 1978, Day Two, 1981, Elva, 1987, Debut C, 1988, Accordion, 1989, Fantasy on a Variation on a Theme, 1989; choreographer Am. premiere of Jean Cocteau's Les Marie de la tour Eiffel, 1988; actor, dancer: (film) Pilobolus and Joan, 1974; choreographer: Erik Satie Festival, Paris Opera, 1978, The Elatesse for Romania Gymnastic Federation, Opus Cactus, 1999; co-choreographer: Molly's Not Dead, 1978; choreographer: (for Pilobolus Dance Theater) Day Two 1981, Stabat Mater, 1985, Carmina Burana Side II, 1985; Joffrey Ballet Relache, 1980, Closing Ceremonies 1980 Winter Olympics, Berlin Opera Tutuguri, 1981, Moses Pendleton Presents Moses Pendleton, 1982, Ballet de Nancy, France, Pulcinella, 1985, (for Momix

Dance Theater) E.C., 1982, Skiva, 1984, Kiss Off Spiderwoman, 1986, Spawning, 1986, Venus Envy, 1986, Medusa, 1986, Preface to Preview, 1986, excerpts from Gifts from the Sea, 1986, (opera for Spoleto Festival) Platee, 1987, White Widow, 1990, Passion, 1991, Table Talk, 1992, Baseball, 1995, Jonas et Latude, 1995, Orbit, 1996, Tvv, 1996, Sputnik, 1997; created show Centennial Fiat in Torino, Italy, 1999. Recipient Edinburgh Fringe Festival Scotman's award, 1973, Berlin Critic's prize, 1975, Gov.'s award Conn. Commn. on Arts, 1998, Positano Choreography award, 1999; Nat. Endowment for Arts grantee, 1975-76; Guggenheim fellow in choreography, 1977. Democrat. Office: Momix PO Box 1035 Washington Depot CT 06793-0035

**PENDLETON, ROBERT GRUBB,** pharmacologist; b. Kansas City, Mo., Apr. 24, 1939; AA, Kansas City Jr. Coll., 1959; AB in Chemistry, U. Mo., 1961; PhD in Pharmacology, U. Kans., 1966. Sr. scientist SmithKline and French, Phila., 1966-67, assoc. sr. investigator, 1967-69, sr. investigator, 1969-74, asst. dir., 1974-79, assoc. dir., 1977-80, dir. pharmacology, 1980-81; dir. gastroenterology Merck, West Point, Pa., 1981-86; dir. biology Rorer Ctrl. Rsch., King of Prussia, Pa., 1986-90; dir. pharmacology Sepracor, Marlborough, Mass., 1991-96; lectr. pharmacology Thomas Jefferson U., 1991—; assoc. prof. Temple U., Phila., 1993—. Lab. sci. cons. Office Surgeon Gen., U.S. Army, Washington, 1989-96, Ft. Detrick, Md., 1996-99. *Achievements include the discovery of the prototype dopamine-1 receptor agonist SK&F 38393, which led to the antihypertensive medicine fenoldopam (CORLOPAM); long active antagonists of histamine-2 receptors including famotidine (PEPCID), and the chiral bronchodilator, R-albuterol (XOPENEX). Other discoveries include inhibitors of adrenaline biosynthesis, antidepressant drugs that also inhibit gastric acid secretion through a CNS action. New approaches to treat ischemia by increasing the release of oxygen from red blood cells and that the critical role of the hormone CCK in the gut is to contract the gall bladder. Current research involves the use of fruit flies containing a human gene to discover new treatments for Parkinson's disease.* Col. U.S. Army. Decorated Legion of Merit. Mem.: Soc. Armed Forces Med. Lab. Scientist, Am. Chem. Soc., Am. Soc. Pharmacology and Exptl. Therapeutics. Achievements include patents for dopamine receptor agonists; PNMT inhibitors; discovery of new drugs to activate dopamine reactors in CNS and kidney; new drugs to inhibit epinephrine biosynthesis in adrenal gland and CNS; new drugs to block histamine receptors insurmountably including Pepcid; tricyclic antidepressants act in CNS to decrease gastric acid secretion; role of CCK in gut; research in pharmacology of chiral molecules including Xopenex and in transgenic models of Parkinson's disease and neurodevelopment. Avocation: ballroom dancing. Home and Office: 1312 Sumneytown Pike Lower Gwynedd PA 19002-1303 Office Phone: 215-654-5022. Personal E-mail: robertpendleton@comcast.net.

**PENDLEY, DONALD LEE,** association executive; b. Jersey City, Nov. 5, 1950; s. Donald L. and Loretta M. (Purcell) P.; m. Donna Lynn Meade, Oct. 14, 1984; 1 child, Katelyn. BA, Montclair State Coll., 1972; MA, Syracuse U., 1974. Reporter/rewriter The Herald-News, Passaic, N.J., 1969-72; reporter The Dispatch, Union City, N.J., 1973; writer Keep America Beautiful, Inc., N.Y.C., 1974-75, comm. dir., 1976-78, v.p. comm. program devel., 1979-84; sr. v.p. comm. Greater Newark C. of C., 1985-86; dir. pub. rels. Internat. Coun. Shopping Ctrs., N.Y.C., 1987-92; exec. dir. N.J. Hospice and Palliative Care Orgn., Scotch Plains, N.J., 1993-97, pres., 1997—. Creator, dir. theatre composer series William Carlos Williams Ctr., 1987-91; creator, dir. SRO Cabaret Series, 1991-99. Pres. State Repertory Opera, South Orange, N.J., 1985-88, 92-99, Ars Musica Chorale, Englewood, N.J., 1979-81; mem. steering com. Coun. of States, 1999—2003, chmn. 2000—03; bd. dirs. Nat. Hospice Orgn., 2000—03; pres. Cmty. Health Charities of NJ, 2003—; Recipient Award of Excellence Am. C. of C. Execs. 1986, Gold Key awards, Pub. Rels. News, 1982, 86. Mem. PRSA (accredited, sec.-treas. assn. sect. 1989-90, vice-chmn. assn. sect. 1990-91, chmn. 1991-92), Am. Soc. Assn. Execs. (cert., Gold Circle award 1988, comm. sect. coun. 1994-96, dean Sch. Pub. Rels. 1998-2000), Am. Mensa, Ltd. (nat. devel. officer 1985-89, 96-2003, regional tng. officer 1989-93), Intertel. Avocations: music, photography. Home: 32 Hamilton Rd Glen Ridge NJ 07028-1109 Business E-Mail: don@njhospice.org.

**PENDLEY, WILLIAM TYLER,** military officer, educator; b. Paris, Ky., June 21, 1936; s. Louis Tyler and Virginia Lorene (Poplin) P.; m. Anne Carroll Cooke, Dec. 13, 1958; children: Stephen Tyler, Robert Randolph, Lisa Carroll, Leslie Brooks. BS in Engring., U.S. Naval Acad., 1958; MA, Am. U., Washington, 1965. Commd. ensign USN, 1958, advanced through grades to rear adm., 1983; comdg. officer Patrol Squadron 45, Jacksonville, Fla., 1975-76; ops. officer Patrol Wing 11, U.S. Atlantic Fleet, Jacksonville, 1976-78, comdr., 1979-81; exec. sec. for joint chief of staff matters Chief Naval Ops., Washington, 1978-79, planner for joint chief of staff matters, 1981-82, dir. plans policy and strategy divsn., 1985-86; exec. asst. to comdr. in chief U.S. Pacific Fleet, Pearl Harbor, Hawaii, 1982-83; comdr. patrol wings U.S. Atlantic Fleet, Brunswick, Maine, 1983-85; commdr. Naval Forces Korea, Seoul, 1986-89; sr. mem. UN Mil. Armistice Commn., 1986-89; dir. strategic plans and policy USCINCPAC, Camp H. M. Smith, Hawaii, 1989-91; dep. asst. sec. def. for East Asia and Pacific affairs Dept. Def., Washington, 1992-93; prof. internat. rels. Air War Coll., Maxwell AFB, Ala., 1993-98. Lectr. and cons., 1998—; fellow Georgetown U. Leadership Seminar, Washington, 1985. Co-author: Nuclear Coexistence, 1994; contbr. articles to profl. jours. Decorated Def. D.S.M. with oak leaf cluster, Legion of Merit with 4 gold stars; named hon. Ky. col., 1975; recipient Def. medal for disting. pub. svc., 1993. Mem. Phi Kappa Phi, Pi Gamma Mu. Methodist. Avocations: golf, travel. Home: 10 Walden Ln Bluffton SC 29909 Office Phone: 843-589-9080. E-mail: pendleyw@yahoo.com.

**PENDYALA, RAMARAO,** chemist, educator; b. Guntur, Andhra Pradesh, India, Aug. 1, 1964; s. Hanumaiah and Ramadyalu m. Sri Latha Devi Miriampalli; children: Chandra Jvss, Sindhura Rupa. BS, Andhra U., Waltair, India, 1984, M of Pharmacy, 1991; B of Pharmacy, Gulbarga U., India, 1988; PhD, Osmania U., Hyderabad, India, 1998. Registered pharmacist. Exec. R&D NATCO Pharma Ltd., Hyderabad, 1998—99, scientist R&D, 1999—2001, dep. mgr. R&D, 2001—02, mgr. R&D, 2004—. scientist Eminent Svcs. Corp., Frederick, Md., 2004—. Rsch. guide for PhD Jawaharlal Nehru Tech. U., Hyderabad, 1999—; dissertation guide for MPharm Annamalai U., India, 2000—03; examiner Gulbarga U., India, 1991—96; lectr. in pharmacy Vutkoor Laxmaiah, India, 1991—94. Contbr. articles to profl. jours., 20 rsch. papers in various internat. and nat. jours. Ency. Pharm. Tech. Social worker Nat. Cadet Course, Guntur, 1982—84. Sr. rsch. fellow, Coun. Sci. and Indsl. Rsch., 1994. Fellow: Instn. Chemists; mem.: Indian Pharm. Assn. (life; mem. sci. com. 2000). Achievements include 12 patents, India and abroad. Avocations: chess, reading, music. Office Phone: 301-524-2105. E-mail: Pendyala_ramarao@hotmail.com, drraep@yahoo.com.

**PENFIELD, PAUL LIVINGSTONE, JR.,** electrical engineering educator; b. Detroit, May 28, 1933; s. Paul Livingstone and Charlotte Wentworth (Gilman) P.; m. Martha Elise Dieterle, Aug. 24, 1956 (dec. Apr. 1988); children: David Wesley, Patricia Jane, Michael Baldwin; m. Barbara Jean Buehrig Lory, July 22, 1989. BA, Amherst Coll., 1955; ScD, MIT, 1960. Asst. prof. elec. engring. MIT, Cambridge, 1960-64, assoc. prof., 1964-69, prof., 1969—2005, head dept. elec. engring. and computer sci., 1989-99. Author: Frequency-Power Formulas, 1960, MARTHA User's Manual, 1971; co-author: Varactor Applications, 1962, Electrodynamics of Moving Media, 1967, Tellegen's Theorem and Electrical Networks, 1970. Sr. postdoctoral fellow NSF, 1966-67. Fellow IEEE (chmn. Boston sect. 1971-72, Darlington award 1985, Centennial medal 1984, Golden Jubilee award 1999); mem. Nat. Acad. Engring., Am. Phys. Soc., Assn. for Computing Machinery, Audio Engring. Soc., Sigma Xi. Avocation: field identification of ferns and fern hybrids. Office: MIT Dept EECS Cambridge MA 02139

**PENG, FENG,** environmentalist; b. Shenyang, China, Sept. 15, 1966; d. Qingshu Peng and Zhaogui Zhu; m. Lingsen Zhang; children: Yuanqi Zhang, Alysa Xinqi Zhang. BS, Nanjing U., China, 1987, MS, 1990; PhD in Environ. Sci. and Forestry, SUNY, 2002. Engr. Jiangsu Pesticide Rsch. Inst., Nanjing, 1990—96; sr. rsch. scientist Upstate Freshwater Inst., Syracuse, 2003—.

Contbr. articles to profl. jours. Recipient Postgrad. award, Am. Inst. Chemists, 2001. Achievements include research in analytical technique for characterizing aquatic particles for turbidity controls and related fate study of particles and toxins in drinking water systems and other aquatic systems; development of comprehensive light scattering models and advanced capabilities of remote sensing. Office: Upstate Freshwater Inst PO Box 506 Syracuse NY 13214 Office Phone: 315-431-4962.

**PENG, JUNHUA,** molecular biologist; b. Sichuan, China, Sept. 4, 1962; BS in Agronomy, Sichuan Agrl. U., China, 1983, MS in Plant Genetics & Breeding, 1986; PhD in Molecular Biology/Plant Genomics (scholar 1996-2000), U. Haifa, Israel, 2001. Asst. scientist Crop Inst. Sichuan Acad. Agrl. Scis., Chengdu, China, 1986—92, rsch. assoc. prof., 1992—94; assoc. prof. dept. agronomy Guangdong Ocean U., China, 1994—96; sr. rsch. assoc. dept. soil and crop scis. Colo. State U., Ft. Collins, Colo., 2000—05, asst. prof., 2005—. Co-author: Crop Breeding, 1996, Crop Breeding Research, 1994; reviewer numerous jour. manuscripts; contbr. over 80 articles to profl. jours. Grantee, Fin. Ministry Israel, 1997; scholar, Israel-China Friendship Soc., 1998, China Friendship Soc., 1999; vis. scholar, Govt. of Japan, 1989; EMBO Short Term fellow, Germany, 1998. Mem.: AAAS, Genetics Soc. Am., China Crop Sci. Soc., Internat. Genetics Soc., China Genetics Soc., Soc. Advancement Breeding Rsch. Asia and Oceania, Israelis Soc. Plant Sci. and Plant Molecular Biology. Achievements include research in plant genomics; molecular marker techniques; genomic mapping; bioinformatics; QTL analysis; quantitative genetics and biostatistics; plant breeding. Office: Colo State U Dept Soil and Crop Scis Fort Collins CO 80523-1170 Office Phone: 970-491-5335.

**PENG, LIANG-CHUAN,** mechanical engineer; b. Taiwan, Feb. 6, 1936; came to U.S., 1965, naturalized, 1973; s. Mu-Sui and Wang-Su (Yang) P.; m. Wen-Fong Kao, Nov. 18, 1962; children: Tsen-Loong, Tsen-Hsin, Lina, Linda. Diploma, Taipei Inst. Tech., 1960; MS, Kans. State U., 1967. Registered profl. engr., Tex., Calif. Project engr. Taiwan Power Co., 1965—66; asst. engr. Carlson & Sweatt, N.Y.C., 1966—67, Pioneer Engrs., Chgo., 1967—68; mech. engr. Bechtel, San Francisco, 1969—71; sr. specialist Nuc. Svcs. Co., San Jose, Calif., 1971—75; sr. engr. Brown & Root, Houston, 1975; stress engr. Foster Wheeler, Houston, 1976; staff engr. AAA Technologists, Houston, 1977; prin. engr. M.W. Kellogg, Houston, 1978—82; pres., owner Peng Engring., Houston, 1982—. Instr. U. Houston; condr. piping tech. seminars. Developer: (computer programs) SIMFLEX. Chmn. South Bay Area Formosan Assn., 1974, No. Calif. Formosan Fedn., 1975. Mem. ASME, NSPE. Buddhist. Home: 3010 Manila Ln Houston TX 77043-1312 Business E-Mail: lcpeng@pipestress.com.

**PENG, STANFORD LEE-YU,** physician; s. Syd and Felicia Peng; m. Andrea Jeanne Gerth, Sept. 8, 2001; children: Avery, Charlotte. PhD, Yale U., New Haven, Conn., 1991—96, MD, 1991—97. Cert. in internal medicine ACP, 2000, in rheumatology ACP, 2002, diplomate Am. Bd. Internal Medicine, Am. Bd. Rheumatology. Interin in internal medicine Hosp. U. Pa., Phila., 1997—98, resident in internal medicine, 1998—99; rsch. assoc. immunology and infectious diseases Harvard U. Sch. Pub. Health, Boston, 2002; clin. rsch. fellow in rheumatology Brigham and Women's Hosp., Boston, 1999—2002; asst. prof. Wash. U. Sch. Medicine, St. Louis, 2002—. Group leader Roche, Palo Alto, 2005—, dir. arthritis rsch., 2005—. Named Keck Disting. Young Scholar, 2005; recipient Arthritis Investigator, Arthritis Found., 2003. Mem.: Am. Assn. Immunologists, Am. Coll. Rheumatology. Office: 3431 Hillview Ave M/S R7-101 Palo Alto CA 94304 Office Phone: 314-747-3609, 650-855-5649. Business E-Mail: stanford.peng@roche.com.

**PENG, ZHONG-REN,** education educator; PhD, Portland State U., 1994. Assoc. prof. U. Wis., Milw., 2001—05, prof., 2005—. Dir. Ctr. for Advanced Spatial Info. Rsch. U. Wis., Milw., 2003—. Author: Internet GIS: Distributed Geographic Information Services for the Internet and Wireless Networks, 2003; contbr. articles to profl. jours. Recipient Excellence in Rsch. award, U. Wis. Found., 2002. Mem.: Soc. Chinese Am. Professors and Scientists (v.p., bd. dirs. 2006), Transp. Rsch. Bd., Am. Planning Assn., Urban and Regional Info. Systems Assn. (bd. dirs. 2005—), Inst. Transp. Engrs. (life). Office: U Wis SARUP PO Box 413 Milwaukee WI 53201-0413 Office Phone: 1-414-229-5887.

**PENG CHEN, HSIU-HUI,** music educator; b. Kaosiung, Taiwan, Jan. 12, 1957; arrived in U.S., 1993; d. San-Jen Chen and Jin-Ju Shi; m. Chin-Yuan Perng, Sept. 13, 1981; children: Wei Perng, Powell Perng. BA, Nat. Cheng-Chi U., Taiwan, 1979. Pvt. piano tchr., Taipei, Taiwan, 1975—83; choir dir., piano accompanist Acctg. Dept. Cheng-Chi U., Taipei, 1976—78; piano tchr. Palo Alto, Calif., 1984—89; pvt. piano tchr. Ann Arbor (Mich.) Piano Tchr. Guild, 1994—. Mem.: Am. Coll. Musicians, Mich. Music Tchrs. Assn., Nat. Guild Piano Tchrs., Music Tchrs. Nat. Assn. (chmn. Students Achievement Test Day N.E. Ctr. Sr. Finals 2003—). Home: 2515 Whitetail Run Ct Ann Arbor MI 48105

**PENGRA, R. RENE,** lawyer; b. 1967; BA, U. Wyo., 1988; JD, NYU, 1993. Bar: Ill. 1995, N.Y. 2000. Law clk. to hon. David B. Sentelle U.S. Ct. Appeals, D.C. Cir., 1993; with Sidley Austin Brown & Wood, Chgo., 1993—, ptnr., 2002—. Office: Sidley Austin Brown and Wood Bank One Plz 10 S Dearborn St Chicago IL 60603

**PENHOET, EDWARD,** foundation administrator, former biochemicals company executive, former dean; b. Oakland, Calif., Dec. 11, 1940; AB in Biology, Stanford U., 1963; PhD in Biochem., U. Wash., 1968. Prof. biochem. U. Calif., Berkeley, 1971—81; co-founder, CEO Chiron Corp., 1981—98; dean Sch. Pub. Health U. Calif., Berkeley, 1998—2002; dean emeritus, 2002—; sr. dir. Sci. & Higher Education Gordon and Betty Moore Found., 2002—04, pres., 2004—. Bd. dirs., sr. adv. to CEO Chiron Corp. Recipient Outstanding Philanthropist award, Assn. of Fundraising Professionals, No. Calif. Entrepreneur of the Yr. award, Ernst & Young and Inc. Mag. Mem.: Am. Soc. of Biological Chemists, Nat. Acad. of Sci., Inst. Medicine. Office: Gordon and Betty Moore Found Presidio of San Francisco PO Box 29910 San Francisco CA 94129 also: Chiron Corp 4560 Horton St Emeryville CA 94608-2900*

**PENICK, ANGELA LUCAS,** elementary school educator; b. Roanoke Rapids, N.C., Sept. 7, 1950; d. George Alexander and Carrie Louise (Hinson) Lucas; m. Charles Inglesby Penick, Jr. (div.); 1 child, Carrie Hayes. AA, Marjorie Hebster Jr. Coll., Washington, 1970; BA in Edn., U. N.C., Chapel Hill, 1972. Cert. tchr. phys. edn., health, presch. handicap. Accounts payable clk. Boddie-Noell Ent., Rocky Mount, NC, 1973—75; tchr. Rocky Mount City Schs., 1975—80; admissions counselor N.C. Wesleyan Coll., 1980—81; dropout counselor Nash C.C., 1981—85; social worker Britthaven Nursing Home, Nags Head, 1988—89; early childhood interventionist Halifax County Mental Health Ctr., Poanoke Rapids, 1989—99, Edgecombe-Nash Mental Health Ctr., Rocky Mount, 1989—99; tchr. Nash-Rocky Mount Schs., 1999—. Chmn. Good Shepherd Day Sch., Rocky Mount, 2000—02; mem. Tar River Orch. & Chorus, Rocky Mount, 2004—05; vol. Episc. Ch. Women, Am. Cancer Soc., March of Dimes; leader Bible Study Fellowship, Rocky Mount, 2004—05; mem. vestry Ch. of the Good Shepherd, Rocky Mount, 1999—2002, mem. search com., 2003—04, mem. youth coun.; bd. dirs., sec. My Sister's House, Rocky Mount, SC, 1995—98. Mem.: Women's Tennis League, U.S. Tennis Assn., Benvenue Country Club. Republican. Episcopalian. Avocations: tennis, gardening, drawing, weight training, jogging. Home: 605 S Taylor St Rocky Mount NC 27803 Office: Nash-Rocky Mount Schools 930 Eastern Ave Nashville NC 27856 Office Phone: 252-937-5622. E-mail: anjo950@aol.com.

**PENICK, ANN CLARISSE,** minister, counselor; b. Woodstock, Ill., Feb. 17, 1951; d. Preston Edwin and Marjorie Jane Yeoman; m. John William Schoenberger (div.); m. James Lal Penick, Jr., Aug. 9, 1986; stepchildren: Michael Andrew, Katherine Leona. BA in History, No. Ill. U., DeKalb, 1977; MA in History, Loyola U., Chgo., 1987; MA in Counseling, U. Ala.,

Birmingham, 1995. Cert. minister Diocese Birmingham, Ala., 1993; lic. counselor S.C., 1997, cert. Nat. Bd. Certified Counselors, 1999, lic. mental health counselor Mass., 2006. Substitute tchr. Regina Dominican H.S., Wilmette, Ill., 1987—88; adj. faculty Birmingham (Ala.) So. Coll., 1988—91; tchr. theology John Carroll Cath. H.S., Birmingham, 1993—94; chaplain intern Bon Secours St. Francis Hosp., Charleston, 1996—97; minister Cath. Campus Diocese Charleston, Coll. of Charleston, SC, 1997—2000; pastoral assoc. St. Ann U. Parish, Archdiocese Boston, 2000—02, assoc. cath. chaplain Tufts U., 2002—. Adj. faculty Nat. U., Chgo., 1988; coord. sexual abuse awareness Archdiocese Boston, 2002—, facilitator marriage preparation, 2002—. Contbr. articles to profl. jours. Aid worker Polish Refugee Camp, Vienna, 1982; spokesperson Nat. Night Out, Charleston, 1996; vol. Dem. Nat. Com., Boston, 2004; vol. pastoral counselor Hospice Charleston, 1995—98. Named Advisor of Yr., Emerson Coll., 2001. Mem.: Assn. for Spiritual, Ethical and Religious Values in Counseling, Mass. Mental Health Counselors Assn., Cath. Campus Ministry Assn., Am. Counseling Assn. (bd. dir. 2001—04, Svc. award 2004). Democrat. Roman Cath. Avocations: dance, guitar, singing. Home: 5 Walden Mews Cambridge MA 02140 Office: Tufts Cath Chaplaincy Goddard Chapel 3 on the Green Medford MA 02155 Personal E-mail: annpenick@hotmail.com.

**PENICK, ELIZABETH C.,** psychologist; b. New Orleans, July 17, 1934; d. Rawley M. Penick and Marie G. Sells. BA, Newcomb Coll., 1957; MS, Tulane U., 1960; PhD, Washington U., St. Louis, 1975. Diplomate clin. psychology Am. Bd. Profl. Psychology. Prof. dept. psychiatry Kans. U. Med. Ctr., Kansas City, 1980—, dir. divsn. psychology. Rsch. grantee Nat. Assn. Alcohol Abuse and Alcoholism, Washington, 1980-97. Mem. APA, Kans. Psychol. Assn. (dir.). Home: 12231 Charlotte Kansas City MO 64146 Office: Kans U Med Ctr Dept Psychiatry 3901 Rainbow Blvd Kansas City KS 66160 E-mail: epenick@kumc.edu.

**PENICK, JOHN E.,** education educator; b. Langley, Va., Jan. 2, 1944; s. Edgar Cohen and Bessie (Beene) P.; m. Nell Inman, July 23, 1966; children: Lucas T., Megan J. Penick. BS, U. Miami, 1966, MA, 1969; PhD, Fla. State U., 1973. Sci. dept. head Miami (Fla.) Jackson High Sch., 1967-70; instr. Miami-Dade Community Coll., 1968, Fla. State U., Tallahassee, Fla., 1970-73; dir. tchr. edn. Loyola U., Chgo., 1973-75; prof. U. Iowa, Iowa City, 1975-97, head Sci. Edn. Ctr., 1982, 89-93; prof., head dept. math., sci. and tech. edn. N.C. State U., Raleigh, 1998—. Editor: (monograph series) Focus on Excellence, 1983—89; author: Biology: A Community Context, 2003; contbr. numerous articles to profl. jours. Named Disting. Alumnus Fla. State U., 1987; recipient Burlington No. award for outstanding career achievement U. Iowa, 1992; Fulbright fellow USIA, Portugal, 1985. Fellow Iowa Acad. Sci.; mem. NSTA (bd. dir. 1986-88, pres. 2003, Ohaus awards), Nat. Assn. for Rsch. in Sci. Tchg. (assoc. editor 1979-84), Coun. Sci. Soc. Prs. (sec. 1991-92, treas. 2003-04), Nat. Assn. Biology Tchrs. (pres. 1989, hon. mem. award, 2004), Assn. Sci. Tchr. Educators (pres. 2002, Outstanding Paper 1978, Outstanding Sci. Educator 1987, Outstanding Mentor 1997), Sigma Xi, Esilon Pi Tau (Dist. Svc. Citation, 2003). Office: NC State U 326 Poe Hl Raleigh NC 27695-7801

**PENIKETT, TONY,** mediator, negotiator, writer, political organization worker; b. Nov. 14, 1945; s. Erik John Keith and Sarah Ann (Colwell) P.; m. Lula Mary Johns, 1974 (div. 1997); children—John Tahmoh, Sarah Lahlil, Stephanie Sahyun Exec. asst. to nat. leader New Dem. Party, Ottawa, Ont., Canada, 1975-76, nat. pres., 1981-85, fed. councillor, 1973—, leader Whitehorse, Y.T., Canada, 1980—, campaign mgr. N.W.T., Canada, 1972; alderman City of Whitehorse, Y.T., Canada, 1977-79; elected mem. Yukon Legis. Assembly, 1978-95, opposition leader Y.T., Canada, 1982-85, 92-95, elected premier Yukon Terr., 1985-92; sr. policy advisor Govt. of Sask., 1995-97; dep. min. negotiations Ministry of Fin. and Corp. Rels., Govt. of B.C., Victoria, 1997-2000; dep. min. labor Ministry of Fin., Govt. of B.C., Victoria, 2000—01; propr. Tony Penikett Negotiations Inc., Vancouver, B.C., Canada, 2001—. Author (film): The Mad Trapper, 1972, La Patrouille Perdue, 1974, Breaking Trail, 2004. Office: Tony Penikett Negotiations Inc 550 Beatty St Unit 7-8 Vancouver BC Canada V6B 2L3 Office Phone: 604-724-6720. Personal E-mail: tony_penikett@telus.net. Business E-Mail: tony_penikett@sfu.cn.

**PENISTEN, GARY DEAN,** entrepreneur; b. Lincoln, Nebr., May 14, 1931; s. Martin C. and Jayne (O'Dell) P.; m. Nancy Margaret Golding, June 3, 1951; children: Kris D., Janet L., Carol E., Noel M. BS in Bus. Adminstrn., U. Nebr., Omaha, 1953; LLD (hon.), Concordia Coll., 1993. With Gen. Electric Co., 1953-74, mgr. group fin. ops. power generation group N.Y.C., 1973-74; asst. sec. navy fin. mgmt., 1974-77; sr. v.p. fin., chief fin. officer, dir. Sterling Drug Inc., N.Y.C., 1977-89; sr. v.p. fin., health group Eastman Kodak Co., N.Y.C., 1989-90. Chmn. bd. dirs. Acme United Corp. Mem. corp. adv. bd. U. Nebr. Coll. Bus., Omaha. Recipient Disting. Public Service award Navy Dept., 1977; Alumni Achievement citation U. Nebr., Omaha, 1975. Mem. Fin. Execs. Inst., Navy League of U.S., Army and Navy Club (Washington), Rotary, Union League (N.Y.), Ft. Lauderdale (Fla.) Country Club, White Eagle Golf Club (Naperville). Republican. Unitarian Universalist. Home and Office: 1409 Aberdeen Ct Naperville IL 60564-9787 Office Phone: 630-978-7093. Personal E-mail: asnfm@aol.com.

**PENLAND, JAMES GRANVILLE,** psychologist; b. Dallas, Mar. 1, 1951; s. James Marr and Katherine (Lindsley) P.; m. Michelle Elizabeth Stahl, Aug. 13, 1977; children: Abraham Christopher, Simon Peter, Zachary James. BA summa cum laude, McMaster Coll., 1977, MA, U. N.D., 1979, PhD, 1981. Instr. U. N.D., Grand Forks, 1978-83, statistician, 1981-84, psychologist, 1984-85; rsch. psychologist USDA, Agrl. Rsch. Svc., Grand Forks, 1985—. Adj. prof. U. N.D., 1984—; mem. panel on micronutrients Food and Nutrition Bd. Inst. of Medicine, 2002—; cons. Mil. Nutrition Rsch.; cons. in field. Mem. editl. bd. Nutritional Neurosci.; contbr. articles to profl. jours. Met. State Coll. scholar, 1977. Mem. APA, Am. Inst. Nutrition, Midwestern Psychol. Assn., N.D. Acad. Sci., Am. Statis. Assn., Sigma Xi. Home: 1804 S 36th St Grand Forks ND 58201-5740 Office: USDA Agrl Rsch Svc GFHNRC Box 9034 2420 2nd Ave N Grand Forks ND 58202-9034 E-mail: jpenland@gfhnrc.ars.usda.gov.

**PENLAND, JOHN THOMAS,** retired import/export and development company executive; b. Guntersville, Ala., Mar. 31, 1930; s. James B. and Kathleen (Bolding) P.; m. Carolyn Joyce White, May 30, 1961; children—Jeffrey K., Mark A., Michael J. BA, George Washington U., 1957. Vice pres., dir. Rouse, Brewer, Becker & Bryant, Inc., Washington, 1957-63; staff mem. SEC, Washington, 1963-67; pres., dir. INA Trading Corp., Phila., 1968-69; v.p. INA Security Corp., Phila., 1967-69; from v.p. to pres. Shareholders Mgmt. Co., L.A., 1969—75; v.p. Shareholders Capital Corp., L.A., 1972-73; v.p., dir. several mut. funds managed by Shareholders Mgmt. Co., 1970-75; pres., chmn. CEO, HMO Internat. and its subs., L.A., 1975; founder, pres., chmn. Pendlar Corp., Atlanta, 1977-97; chmn., pres. Bella Vista Developers, Inc., Albuquerque, 1977-98; chmn. CompuComp Corp., Atlanta, 1977-81; chmn., pres. Fran Stef Corp., N.Y.C., 1982-89; pres., chmn. Engineered Products Corp., Dandridge, Tenn., 1983-90; founder, chmn., CEO Am. Accessories Corp., Covington, Ga., 1983-98; founder, chmn. Chamisa Properties, Inc., Albuquerque, 1988-94, Glorieux Ltd., Atlanta, 1988-96, Ga. Ptnrs. Ltd., Covington, 1988-94, Premier Trading Internat., Inc., Atlanta, 1989—98, Chamisa Enterprises, Inc., Covington, 1988-96; founder, mng. ptnr. Ft. Hill Ptnrs., Knoxville, Tenn., 1990-93; chmn. Einson Freeman & Detroy Corp., Fair Lawn, NJ, 1978-83; founder, dir., pres. West Point Contract Packaging, Inc., Martinsville, Va., 1991-98; founder, mng. ptnr. Harbor View, Ltd., Fernandina Beach, Fla., 1992-94; founder, chmn. West Point Tech. Assembly, Inc., Winston-Salem, N.C., 1993—2002; dir., pres. BKP Industries, Inc., Monroe, Ga., 1995-97. With U.S. Army, 1948—55. Republican. Episcopalian. Home: PO Box 549 Social Circle GA 30025-0549 Personal E-Mail: cjpenland@bellsouth.net.

**PENLEY, JULIE ANNE,** psychologist, educator; d. John and Marcheta Isabelle Dietzen; m. Howard Lawson Penley. PhD, U. Tex., 2001. Tchg. asst. U. Tex., El Paso, 1995—96, rsch. asst., 1996—2001; instr. Dona Ana C.C., Sunland Park, N.Mex., 1999; part-time instr. El Paso C.C., 2000—02, asst. prof., 2002—; evaluation coord. U. Tex., El Paso, 2001—02. Mem.: APA, Am. Assn. Women in Cmty. Colls. Lutheran. Office: El Paso Community Coll PO Box 20500 El Paso TX 79998-0500 Office Phone: 915-831-3210. Business E-mail: jpenley@epcc.edu.

**PENLEY, LARRY EDWARD,** academic administrator, finance educator; b. Bristol, Va., Feb. 9, 1949; s. William Edward and June (Caudill) P.; m. Yolanda Elva Sanchez, Nov. 25, 1977; children: Jonathan Andrew, Josephine Anna. BA, Wake Forest U., 1971, MA, 1972; PhD, U. Ga., 1976. Vis. prof. ITESM, Monterey, Mexico, 1977, Universidad de Carobobo, Valencia, Venezuela, 1978; assoc. dean U. Tex., San Antonio, 1980-85; prof., chmn. dept. Ariz. State U., Tempe, 1985—90, dean Coll. Bus., 1990—2003; pres. Colo. State U., 2003—; chancellor Colo. State U. Sys., 2003—. Contbr. articles to profl. jours. Mem. NCAA Task Force on Future of Athletics, Nat. Western Stock Show and Rodeo, Citizen of West Com.; mem. adv. counsel Group Ecole Superieure De Commerce de Toulouse, 1997; chmn. Assn. Advance Collegiate Sch. of Bus., 2000—01; bd. mem. dir. Greater Phoenix Econ. Coun., 1993—2003. Recipient Frank C. Carr Founders award, IN-ROADS, 1997, Disting. Svc. award, Greater Phoenix Econ. Coun., 2002. Mem.: Assn. Advance Collegiate Schs. of Bus. (chmn. 2001—02), Rocky Mountain Bd., Inst. Internat. Edn., Mountain States Employers Coun. Bd., Greater Denver Metro Chamber Bd., Acad. Mgmt. (chmn. divsn. program 1986), Mountain West Conf. Bd., Inst. of Tech. Bd., Colo. Concern. Roman Catholic. Home: 3001 Hearthstone Dr Fort Collins CO 80528-9171 Office: Colo State U Office of the Pres Fort Collins CO 80523-0100 Office Phone: 970-491-6211. E-mail: presofc@lamar.colostate.edu.

**PENLEY, VIRGINIA LONG,** social worker; b. Statesville, N.C., July 3, 1955; d. Robert Long and Mary Joyce Broussard; m. Jeffrey Michael Penley. AA, Mitchell C.C., 1975; BA in Social Work, Greensboro Coll., 1977. LCSW; cert. Dir. Vol. Svcs. Social worker Moses H. Cone Hosp., Greensboro, 1987—94; dir. vol. svcs. and patient rels. Women's Hosp. Greensboro, NC, 1994—. Mem.: NASW (Piedmont rep. 1991—92), N.C. Soc. Dirs. Vol. Svcs. (chair publicity 2000—, corr. sec., edn. co-chair 1997—99), N.C. Zoologica. Presbyterian. Avocations: travel, antiques, reading. Office: Women's Hosp Greensboro 801 Green Valley Rd Greensboro NC 27408 Office Phone: 336-832-6586. Business E-mail: ginger.penley@mosescone.com.

**PENLIDIS, ALEXANDER,** chemical engineering professor; b. Kozani, Greece, Feb. 12, 1957; Diploma in engring., U. Thessaloniki, 1980; PhD in Chem. Engring., McMaster U., 1986. Rsch. assoc. Polymer Prodn. Techs., McMaster Inst., Canada, 1985-86; from asst. prof. to assoc. prof. chem. engring. U. Waterloo, Ont., Canada, 1986-90, assoc. prof., 1990-95, prof., 1995—, assoc. dir. Inst. Polymer Rsch. Ont., Canada, 1990-95, dir. Ont., 1995—, assoc. dean rsch. & grad. studies faculty engring. Ont., Cameroon, 1998—2004. Can. Rsch. chmn. in poly. engring., 2002—; cons. in field. Founding co-editor Polymer Reaction Engring. Jour., 1990-2003. Fellow Chem. Inst. Can., Can. Acad. Engring.; mem. AIChE, Am. Chem. Soc., Can. Soc. Chem. Engring. Office: Univ Waterloo Inst Polymer Rsch Chem Engring Dept Waterloo ON Canada N2L 3G1 Office Phone: 519-888-4567 x 6634. Business E-mail: penlidis@uwaterloo.ca.

**PENN, AUDREY S.,** federal agency administrator; BA, Swarthmore Coll., Pa., 1956; MD, Columbia U., NYC, 1960. Intern, asst. resident Bronx Mcpl. Hosp. Ctr., Albert Einstein Coll. Medicine, 1960—62; asst. resident in neurology, Neurol. Inst. Columbia Presbyn. Med. Ctr., NYC, 1962—64, neurologist; asst. and instr. in neurology Coll. Physicians and Surgeons, Columbia U., NYC, 1964—67, assoc. prof. neurology, 1973—82, assoc. prof. to prof. neurology, 1973—95; dep. dir. Nat. Inst. Neurol. Disorders and Stroke, NIH, 1995—, acting dir., 1998, 2001—03. Bd. dirs. Am. Bd. Psychiatry and Neurology, 1975—82, exec. com, 1981—82; mem. immuno-logical soc. study sect. NIH, 1982—86; mem. rev. panel for rsch. tng. fellowships Howard Hughes Med. Inst., 1989—91, chair rev. panel, 1992—94; mem. nat. adv. neurol. disorders and stroke coun. NIH, 1992—95. Mem.: AAAS, Assn. Rsch. in Nervous and Mental Disease, Harvey Soc., Am. Acad. Neurology, Am. Neurol. Assn. (pres. 1994). Office: Nat Inst Neurol Disorders & Stroke Bldg 31 8A52 31 Center Dr Bethesda MD 20892-2540 Office Phone: 301-496-3167.

**PENN, BUDDIE J.,** civilian military employee; BS, Purdue U.; MS, George Washington U. Cert. Aerospace Safety U. So. Calif., Nat. Security for Sr. Officials Harvard U. Former naval aviator; EA-6B pilot, 1972; held various leadership assignments including nuclear exec. officer/commdg. officer VAQ 33; battalion officer U.S. Naval Acad.; air officer USS Am.; spl. asst. to Chief of Naval Ops.; commdg. officer NAS N. Island, Calif.; dep. dir. Navy Office Tech. Transfer and Security Assistance; dir. internat. bus. Loral Fed. Sys., 1995—98; with Naval Electronics and Surveillance Sys. Dept. of Navy, 1998, dir. indsl. base assessments, 2001—05, asst. sec. installations & environ., 2005—.

**PENN, J. B.,** economist; b. Lynn, Ark., Dec. 18, 1944; s. Jacob Bernard and Virginia Lucille (Martin) P.; m. Martha Ann Brannon (div.); children: Penny Alane, Kristin J. Rens. BS, Ark. State U., 1965; MS, La. State U., Baton Rouge, 1967; PhD, Purdue U., 1973. Rsch. economist ERS/USDA, Baton Rouge, W. Lafayette, Ind., Raleigh, N.C., 1967-75, leader policy group Washington, 1975-76; mem. sr. staff Pres.'s Coun. Econ. Advisers, Washington, 1977-78; dep. adminstr. for econs. ERS/USDA, Washington, 1979-81; pres. Econ. Perspectives, Inc., Washington, 1981-88; sr. v.p. Sparks Commodities, Inc., Washington, 1988—2001; under secy. for farm & foreign agr. svcs USDA, 2001—06; chief economist Deere & Co., Moline, Ill., 2006—. Co-author: (textbook) Agriculture and Food Policy, 3d edit., 1995. Mem. adv. bd. Ctr. for Nat. Policy, Washington, 1990; bd. dirs. Found. for Devel. of Polish Agr., Warsaw, 1990, Farm Found., 1995. Mem. Am. Agrl. Econs. Assn., Am. Econs. Assn. Office: Deere & Co 1 John Deere Rd Moline IL 61265-8098*

**PENN, LEE,** information scientist, consultant, journalist; b. Midland, Tex., Jan. 19, 1953; s. Rhesa and Dorothy Penn. BA, Harvard U., 1976; MBA, MPH, U. Calif., Berkeley, 1986. Freelance journalist Oregon mag. and others, Portland, 1975-79, San Francisco, 1998—; rsch. asst. Kaiser Permanente Ctr. for Health Rsch., Portland, 1979-83; sys. planner Alta Bates Corp., Berkeley, 1985—86; sr. fin. analyst St. Mary's Hosp., San Francisco, 1987; mgr. assoc., cons. JDA/SAIC, San Francisco, 1992-96; prin. Penn Cons., San Francisco, 1988—. Adj. faculty, Golden Gate U., San Francisco, 1990-98 Author: False Dawn: The United Religions Initiative, Globalism, and the Quest for a One-world Religion, 2005; contbr. articles to profl. jours. and mags. including Jour. Ambulatory Care Mgmt., chpts. to books Vestryman, thmn. fin. com., mem. search coms. Episcopal Parish St. John the Evangelist, San Francisco, 1989-94 Edgar F. Kaiser Sr. fellow U. Calif., 1983-84, Regents fellow, 1984-85 Mem. IEEE Computer Soc., Soc. Profls. in Healthcare, Am. Coll. Health Care Execs., Phi Beta Kappa. Office: 1470 Sand Hill Rd # 301 Palo Alto CA 94304-2030 E-mail: leepenn@aol.com.

**PENN, SEAN,** actor; b. Burbank, Calif., Aug. 17, 1960; s. Leo and Eileen (Ryan) P.; m. Madonna Louise Ciccone, Aug. 16, 1985 (div. Jan. 10, 1989); m. Robin Wright Penn, April 27, 1996; 2 children: Dylan Frances, Hopper Jack. Actor: (plays) Heartland, 1981, Slab Boys, 1983, Hurlyburly, 1988; (films) Taps, 1981, Fast Times at Ridgemont High, 1982, Summerspell, 1983, Bad Boys, 1983, Crackers, 1984, Racing with the Moon, 1984, The Falcon and the Snowman, 1985, At Close Range, 1986, Shanghai Surprise, 1986, Color Blue, 1988, Colors, 1988, Judgment in Berlin, 1988, Casualties of War, 1989, We're No Angels, 1989, State of Grace, 1990, Carlito's Way, 1993, Dead Man Walking, 1995 (Golden Globe award nominee for best actor, 1995, Best Actor award Berlin Film Festival, 1996, Acad. award nominee for best actor, 1996), The Game, 1997, U Turn, 1997, Hugo Pool, 1997, The Thin Red

Line, 1998, Hurly Burly, 1998, As I Lay Dying, 1998, Up at the Villa, 2000, Before Night Falls, 2000, The Weight of Water, 2000, I Am Sam, 2001, It's All About Love, 2003, Mystic River, 2003, (Golden Globe for best dramatic actor, 2004, Acad. Award for best actor, 2004, Golden Satellite award, 2004, London Critics Circle Film awards, 2004, Screen Actors Guild Award nomination for best actor, 2004), 21 Grams, 2003, The Assassination of Richard Nixon, 2004, The Interpreter, 2005, All the King's Men, 2006; actor, prodr.: Loved, 1997; actor, exec. prodr.: She's So Lovely, 1997; dir., writer: The Indian Runner, 1991; dir., prodr., writer: The Crossing Guard, 1995; dir., prodr.: The Pledge, 2001; actor (TV movies) Hellinger's Law, 1981, The Killing of Randy Webster, 1981. Recipient John Steinbeck award, San Francisco Chronicle, 2004. Office: Ste 2500 2049 Century Park E Los Angeles CA 90067-3127*

**PENN, STANLEY WILLIAM,** journalist; b. NYC, Jan. 12, 1928; s. Murray and Lillian (Richman) P.; m. Esther Aronson, July 12, 1952; children— Michael, Laurel. Student, Bklyn. Coll., 1945-47; B. Journalism, U. Mo. 1949. With Wall St. Jour., 1952-90; investigative reporter N.Y. bur., 1957-90. (Co-recipient Pulitzer prize for nat. reporting 1967). Home: 380 Riverside Dr New York NY 10025-1858 Personal E-mail: estan380@hotmail.com.

**PENN, VERNITA LYNN,** government agency administrator; d. Welborne L. and Bonita L. Richmond; m. Ray C. Penn, Mar. 21, 1992 (div. Oct. 1994); 1 child, Courtney James. BA, Langston U., 1980; MA, U. Okla., 1992. Lic. tchr. Okla., cert. mediator. Instr. COPE Inc., Oklahoma City, 1998—99; inventory mgmt. specialist Tinker AFB, Midwest City, Okla., 1999—. Bd. dirs. Credit Advisors Am., Midwest City. Mem. Ambs. Concert Choir, Oklahoma City, 1999—, Oklahoma City Beautiful, 2001—. Mem.: Okla. Assocs. Black Journalist, Tinker Mgmt. Assn., Okla. Acad. Mediators and Arbitrators, Nat. Assn. Female Execs., Okla. Bar Assn. (assoc.), Tinker Officers Club, Alpha Kappa Alpha (Silver Soror award 2002). Democrat. Baptist. Avocations: singing, dance, writing, opera, symphony. Home: PO Box 14871 Oklahoma City OK 73113 Office: Tinker AFB 3001 Staff Dr Tinker Afb OK 73145 Office Phone: 405-736-4481. E-mail: vernitavernita@netscape.net.

**PENN, ZACHARY OWEN,** screenwriter; b. N.Y.C., Mar. 23, 1968; s. Arthur Steven and Marilyn (Spicehandler) P. BA, Wesleyan U., 1990. Writer: (films) Last Action Hero, 1993, Inspector Gadget, 1999, Behind Enemy Lines, 2001, X2, 2003, Suspect Zero, 2004, Elektra, 2005, X-Men: The Last Stand, 2006; writer, prodr.: (TV series) Ozzy & Drix, 2002-03; writer, prodr., dir.: (films) Incident at Loch Ness, 2004; actor: (films) Star Maps, 1997, Chuck & Buck, 2000; actor, writer: (films) PCU, 1994; actor, prodr.: (films) Osmosis Jones, 2001. Mem. Writers Guild of Am. Avocations: creative writing, basketball, tennis.*

**PENNAMPED, BRUCE MICHAEL,** lawyer; b. Kearney, Nebr., July 16, 1948; s. Matthew Paul and Betty Fern (Harper) P.; m. Victoria A. Crull, May 13, 1972 (div. Dec. 1980); 1 child, Katheryn A.; m. Melissa J. Barth, July 22, 1985. BS in Mgmt., Ind. U., 1970, JD, 1972. Bar: Ind. 1972, U.S. Dist. Ct. (no. and so. dists.) Ind. 1972, U.S. Ct. Appeals (7th cir.) 1978; cert. family law specialist. Assoc. Rocap Rocap Reese & Young, Indpls., 1972-76; pvt. practice Indpls., 1976-78, 88-91; ptnr. Forbes & Pennamped, Indpls., 1978-88, Lowe Gray Steele & Hoffman, Indpls., 1991-96, Lowe Gray Steele & Darko, Indpls., 1996—2001, Pennamped & Assocs., Indpls., 2001—. Chair and panelist Ind. Continuing Legal Edn. Forum; mem. Ind. Child Custody and Support Adv. Commn. Contbr. articles to profl. jours. Majority atty. Ind. Ho. of Reps., Indpls. Cpl. USMCR, 1967-69. Fellow Am. Acad. Matrimonial Lawyers, Ind. Family Law Specialist Bd. (co-chair). Home: 9662 Decatur Dr Indianapolis IN 46256-9654 Office: Pennamped & Associates 3925 River crossing Pky Ste 280 Indianapolis IN 46240 Office Phone: 317-815-9736. Business E-Mail: bruce@pennamped-associates.com.

**PENNARDT, ANDRE M.,** emergency physician; b. Munich, Sept. 26, 1965; s. Werner Friedrich and Ingrid Ria P. BA, U. Rochester, 1987; MD, SUNY, Syracuse, 1991. Diplomate Nat. Bd. Med. Examiners, Am. Bd. Emergency Medicine. Intern in surgery Walter Reed Army Med. Ctr., Washington, 1991-92; battalion surgeon 5th Spl. Forces Group, Ft. Campbell, Ky., 1992-94; resident in emergency medicine Brooke Army Med. Ctr., Ft. Sam Houston, Tex., 1994-97; staff emergency physician Womack Army Med. Ctr., Ft. Bragg, N.C., 1997—. Disaster dir. Womack Army Med. ctr., 1997—, chief emergency med. svcs., 1998—; clin. instr. Joint Mil. Med. Ctrs., San Antonio, 1997—. Instr. life support Am. Heart Assn., San Antonio, 1994-97. Maj. U.S. Army. Mem. Am. Coll. Emergency Physicians, Am. Acad. Emergency Medicine, Assn. Mil. Surgeons U.S., Soc. Acad. Emergency Medicine, Nat. Assn. EMS Physicians, Aerospace Med. Assn., Nat. Assn. Search and Rescue. Avocations: scuba diving, climbing, wilderness medicine, rafting, hiking.

**PENNEKAMP, PETER HENK,** public radio executive, arts administrator; b. Berkeley, Calif., Mar. 19, 1952; s. Alfred and Marianne (Hochenheimer) P.; m. Linda Strickland, June 10, 1979; children: Paul, Sean. BA summa cum laude, Humboldt State U., 1974. Dir. CenterArts Humboldt State U., Arcata, Calif., 1976-87; dir. InterArts program Nat. Endowment for the Arts, Washington, 1987-89; v.p. cultural programming & program svcs. Nat. Pub. Radio, Washington, 1989—92; exec. dir. Humboldt Area Found., 1993—. Grant panelist Rockefeller Found., N.Y.C., 1989, 90, Ford Found., N.Y.C. 1990; keynote speaker Pub. Libr. Assn. Ann. Conf., Chgo., 1990; mem. steering com. Cultural Grounding Confs., N.Y.C., 1989-91; radio fund policy advisor Corp. for Pub. Broadcasting, Washington, 1990, 91; co-convener Working Group on a New Am. Sensibility, 1990—; seminar presenter Gov's. Arts Awards, Harrisburg, Pa., 1991; presenter arts summit Calif. Inst. of the Arts, Valencia, 1991; bd. dirs. Calif. Endowment. Recipient Disting. Svc. award Nat. Endowment for the Arts, Washington, 1989; named one of 15 Who Made a Difference by Mag. of Pub. Broadcasting, Washington, 1990. Office: Humboldt Area Found 373 Indianola Rd Bayside CA 95524*

**PENNELL, DANIEL MARK,** researcher; b. Valparaiso, Ind., July 14, 1971; s. Lawrence Foster Pennell and Nancy Lea Rogan. BA, Ind. U., Bloomington, Ind., 1989—93, MA, 1997—99, MLS, 1999—2001. Bibliographer for Russian, east European, and Germanic studies U. of Pitts., Pitts., 2001—; asst. slavic bibliographer Ind. U., Bloomington, Ind., 1996—2001; program mgr. for edn. US Peace Corps., Saratov, Russia, 1995—96. Asst. dir. Inst. for the Study of Russian Edn., Bloomington, Ind., 1996—98; reviews editor Slavic and East European Info. Resources, Pitts., 2003—, Balkan Academic News, Pitts., East European Politics and Societies, 2004—. Author: (article) New Approaches to Balkan History, (annotated bibliography) Romanian Studies: An Annotated Guide to Bibliographies, Encyclopedias, and Handbooks. Fellow Fgn. Lang. Area Studies Fellowship, Ind. U., 1997-2000. Mem.: Southeastern European Studies Assn., Soc. for Romanian Studies, Am. Libr. Assoication, Am. Assn. for the Advancement of Slavic Studies, Phi Beta Kappa. Achievements include development of Slavic, East European, and Germanic Studies Research Collections; research in Modern Russian and Eastern European History. Office: University of Pittsburgh 3960 Forbes Avenue G-20X Hillman Library Pittsburgh PA 15260 Home: 1517 S Negley Ave Pittsburgh PA 15217 Office Phone: 412-648-7791. Personal E-mail: pennell@pitt.edu.

**PENNELL, DANNY JOE,** social worker; b. Aug. 31, 1945; s. Donald Louis and Lela Geneva (Murray) P.; m. Janis Evelyn Reynolds, Dec. 26, 1984; children: Joel, Jason, Jaime, Chad, Colter. BA, U. Ill., 1970, MSW, 1972. Social worker Dept. Child and Family Svcs., Danville, Ill., 1971-72, social worker supr. Rockford, Ill., 1972-74; instr. Rockford Coll., 1977-78; pres., CEO Goldie B. Floberg Ctr., Rockton, Ill., 1974—. Exec. dir. Found. Ft. Lewis Coll., Durango, Colo., 1986-87; bd. dirs. Winnebago County Child Protection Assn., Rockford, 1974-76; bd. dirs., mem. legis. affairs com., chmn. mental health devel. disabilities com., spl. edn. com. Child Care Assn. Ill., Springfield, Ill., 1980—; mem. child welfare adv. com. Ill. Dept. Children and Family Services; mem. devel. disabilities adv. com. Dept. Mental Health, mem. children's svcs. subcom.; cons. in field. Bd. dirs., v.p. H.O.P.E. Found., 2001—. Grantee Ill. Dept. Children and Family Svcs., 1970-72. Mem. Nat.

Soc. Fund Raising Execs. (bd. dirs., sec. 1984-85, v.p. 1986-87), Nat. Soc. Fund Raising Dirs. (pres. bd. dirs. 1988, v.p. 1987, v.p. 1986, bd. mem. various coms. 1984, 85), Am. Assn. Mental Deficiency, Nat. Assn. Retarded Citizens, Coordinating Council for Handicapped Children, Nat. Assn. Devel. Disabilities Mgrs., Roscoe C. of C. (bd. dirs. 2000—). Home: 12080 N Ledges Dr Roscoe IL 61073-9600 Office: Goldie B Floberg Ctr PO Box 346 Rockton IL 61072-0346 Personal E-mail: dpenn58@aol.com.

**PENNELL, WILLIAM BROOKE,** lawyer; b. Mineral Ridge, Ohio, Oct. 28, 1935; s. George Albert and Katherine Nancy (McMeen) P. AB, Harvard U., 1957; LLB cum laude, U. Pa., 1961; m. Peggy Polsky, June 17, 1958; children: Katherine, Thomas Brooke. Bar: NY 1963, US Dist. Ct. (so. dist.) NY 1964, US Dist. Ct. (ea. dist.) NY 1964, US Ct. Appeals (2d cir.) 1966, US Ct. Claims 1966, US Tax Ct. 1967, US Supreme Ct. 1967. Clk. US Dist. Ct., (so. dist.) NY, NYC, 1961-62; assoc. Shearman & Sterling, NYC, 1962-71, ptnr., 1971-91. Recent case editor U. Pa. Law Rev., 1960-61. Bd. dirs. Bklyn. Heights Assn., 1964-74, pres., 1969-71; chmn. bd. Willoughby House Settlement, 1972-95. Served with US Army, 1957. Fellow Salzburg Seminar Am. Studies, 1965. Mem. Rembrandt Club. Home and Office: PO Box 249 Canaan NY 12029-0249

**PENNELLO, GENE ANTHONY,** statistician; b. Huntsville, Ala., Nov. 23, 1962; s. Julian Joseph and Beatrice Pennello; m. Chung-Chin Sun, Sept. 18, 1993; children: Julian, Chelsie. BS in Computer Sci. & Math., U. Calif., Davis., 1985, BS in Statis., 1985, MS in Statis., 1989; PhD in Statis., Oreg. State U., 1993. Math. statis. Food and Drug Adminstrn., Rockville, Md., 1998—. Lectr. George Washington U., 1996-97. Author: Atlas of Cancer Mortality: 1950-1994, 1999; contbr. articles to profl. jours. Postdoctoral fellow Nat. Cancer Inst., Bethesda, Md., 1994-98. Mem. Am. Statis. Assn. Republican. Roman Catholic. Avocations: origami, tennis. Office: Food & Drug Adminstrn 1350 Piccard Dr Rockville MD 20850 E-mail: gxp@cdrh.fda.gov.

**PENNER, KEITH,** former Canadian government official; b. Sask., Can., May 1, 1933; BA, U. Alberta, Can., 1955; MDiv, Toronto U., 1959; MEd, U. Ottawa, Can., 1971. Secondary sch. tchr., Dryden, Ont., Canada, 1961-68; mem. parliament Cochrane-Superior, Ont., 1968-88; mem. Can. Transp. Agy., Ottawa, 1988—2003; pres. dispute resolution Keith Penner & Assocs., Ottawa, 2003—. Past parliamentary sec. to Min. of State Sci. and Tech., past parliamentary sec. to Min. of Indian Affairs and No. Devel., past chmn. Standing Com. on Indian Affairs and No. Devel.; vis. fellow Sch. of Polit. Sci., Queen's U., 1987-88; chmn. Chartered Inst. Logistics and Transport, N.Am., 2004. Fellow: Chartered Inst. Logistics and Transport (chmn. 2004—); mem.: Lic. Appeal Tribunal Ont. Office: Ottawa ON Canada Office Phone: 613-828-3067. E-mail: keith.penner@disputeres.ca, keith.penner@rogers.ca.

**PENNER, STANFORD SOL,** director; b. Unna, Germany, July 5, 1921; arrived in U.S., 1936, naturalized, 1943; s. Heinrich and Regina (Saal) P.; m. Beverly Preston, Dec. 28, 1942; children: Merilynn Jean, Robert Clark. BS, Union Coll., 1942; MS, U. Wis., 1943, PhD, 1946; Dr. rer. nat. (hon.), Technische Hochschule Aachen, Germany, 1981. Rsch. assoc. Allegany Ballistics Lab., Cumberland, Md., 1944-45; rsch. scientist Standard Oil Devel. Co., Esso Labs., Linden, NJ, 1946; sr. rsch. engr. Jet Propulsion Lab., Pasadena, Calif., 1947-50; mem. faculty Calif. Inst. Tech., 1950-63, prof. divsn. engring., jet propulsion, 1957-63; dir. rsch. and engring. divsn. Inst. Def. Analyses, Washington, 1962-64; prof. engring. physics, chmn. dept. aerospace and mech. engring. U. Calif., San Diego, 1964-68, vice chancellor for acad. affairs, 1968-69, dir. Inst. for Pure and Applied Phys. Scis., 1968-71, dir. Energy Ctr., 1973-91. Bd. dirs. Optodyne Corp.; U.S. mem. adv. group aero. rsch. and devel. NATO, 1952-68, chmn. combustion and propulsion panel, 1958-60; mem. adv. com. engring. scis. USAF-Office Sci. Rsch., 1961-65; mem. subcom. on combustion NACA, 1954-58; mem. rsch. adv. com. on air-breathing engines NASA, 1962-64; mem. com. on gas dynamics and edn. Internat. Acad. Astronautics, 1969-80; nat. lectr. Sigma Xi, 1977-79; chmn. fossil energy rsch. working group Dept. Energy, 1978-82, chmn. advanced fuel cell commercialization working group, 1993-95; mem. assembly engring. NAE, 1978-82; chmn. NAS-NRC U.S. Nat. Com. IIASA, 1978-82; mem. commn. engring. tech. sys. NRC, 1982-84; spl. guest Internat. Coal Sci. Confs., 1983, 85, 87, 89, 91; mentor Def. Sci. Studies Group, 1985-93; chmn. studies mcpl. waste incineration NSF, 1988-89, Calif. Coun. Sci. Tech., 1992; pub. info. com. Nat. Acad. Engring., 1994-98, Ind. Commn. on Environ. Edn., 1995-97, Environ. Literacy Coun., 1998-2005; sci. adv. bd., San Diego County, 1997-, chair, 2004-. Author: Chemical Reactions in Flow Systems, 1955, Chemistry Problems in Jet Propulsion, 1957, Quantitative Molecular Spectroscopy and Gas Emissivities, 1959, Chemical Rocket Propulsion and Combustion Research, 1962, Thermodynamics, 1968, Radiation and Reentry, 1968; sr. author: Energy, Vol. I (Demands, Resources, Impact, Technology and Policy), 1974, 81, Energy, Vol. II (Non-nuclear Energy Technologies), 1975, 77, 84, Energy, Vol. III (Nuclear Energy and Energy Policies), 1976; editor: Chemistry of Propellants, 1960, Advanced Propulsion Techniques, 1961, Detonations and Two-Phase Flow, 1962, Combustion and Propulsion, 1963, Advances in Tactical Rocket Propulsion, 1968, In Situ Shale Oil Recovery, 1975, New Sources of Oil and Gas, 1982, Coal Combustion and Applications, 1984, Advanced Fuel Cells, 1986, Coal Gasification: Direct Applications and Syntheses of Chemicals and Fuels, 1987, CO2 Emissions and Climate Change, 1991, Commercialization of Fuel Cells, 1995, Advanced Nuclear Techs., 1998; assoc. editor Jour. Chem. Physics, 1953-56; founding editor Jour. Quantitative Spectroscopy and Radiative Transfer, 1960-92, Jour. Def. Rsch., 1963-67, Energy (The Internat. Jour.), 1975-98; sect. editor Energy and Power Systems, Ency. Phys. Sci. and Tech., 1998-2002. Recipient spl. award People-to-People Program, pub. svc. award U. Calif., San Diego, N. Manson medal Internat. Colloquia on Gasdynamics of Explosions and Reactive Systems, 1979, internat. Columbus award Internat. Inst. Comm., Genoa, Italy, 1981, disting. assoc. award U.S. Dept. Energy, 1990, Edward Teller award for def. of freedom, 1997, Rockwell medal, 2003. Fellow Am. Phys. Soc., Optical Soc. Am., AAAS, N.Y. Acad. Scis., AIAA 1964-66, past chmn. com., G. Edward Pendray award 1975, Thermophysics award 1983, Energy Systems award 1983), Am. Acad. Arts and Scis.; mem. Nat. Acad. Engring., Internat. Acad. Astronautics, World Level Hall of Fame for Engring., Sci. and Tech., Am. Chem. Soc., Sigma Xi. Home: 5912 Avenida Chamnez La Jolla CA 92037-7402 Office: U Calif San Diego 9500 Gilman Dr La Jolla CA 92093-0411 Office Phone: 858-534-4284. Business E-Mail: spenner@ucsd.edu.

**PENNEY, ALEXANDRA,** magazine editor-in-chief, writer; b. May 23, 1939; married; 1 child. Grad., Smith Coll.; MA, Hunter Coll., 1977. Editor health and beauty Glamour mag.; editor at large Bantam Doubleday; editor-in-chief Self mag., 1989. Author: How to Make Love to a Man, 1981, Great Sex, 1985, How to Keep Your Man Monogamous, 1989; co-author (with Howard Kaminsky): Magic Words: A Collection of Workplace Wisdom for Spectacular Results on the Job, 2004, Magic Words at Work, 2004; contbr. (articles) to N.Y. Times Mag., Vogue, others.

**PENNEY, BETH,** language educator, editor, writer; b. Carmel, Calif., Feb. 7, 1955; d. William Carroll Penney and Raylynn Thyrza (Crabbe) Moore. BA in Journalism and English, Calif. State U., Fresno, 1978, MA in English Lit., 1985. Mng. editor Paul Kagan Assoc., Inc., Carmel, Calif., 1980-89; tech. writer Computer Svcs. Corp., Monterey, Calif., 1989-90; publs. mgr. Data Rsch. Assoc., Inc., Monterey, 1990-98; English faculty Monterey (Calif.) Peninsula Coll., 1990—, chmn. English dept., 2005—. Feature writer, reviewer Carmel Pine Cone, 1994—97. Newsletter editor Monterey Peninsula Dickens Fellowship, Pacific Grove, Calif., 1991—. Pres. Pacific Grove (Calif.) Feast of Lanterns, 1995-2000, Friends of the Dickens Project, 1995-2000; founder, hon. sec. Monterey Peninsula Dickens Fellowship, 1991—. Mem. Pacific Grove C. of C. Democrat. Avocations: reading, needlecrafts, collecting depression glass. Home: PO Box 604 Pacific Grove CA 93950-0604 Office Phone: 831-646-4159.

**PENNEY, CHARLES RAND,** lawyer, civic worker; b. Buffalo, July 26, 1923; s. Charles Patterson and Gretchen (Rand) P. BA, Yale U., 1945; JD, U. Va., 1951; DFA (hon.), SUNY, 1995. Bar: Md. 1952, NY 1958, U.S. Supreme Ct. 1958. Law sec. to US Dist. Ct. Judge W.C. Coleman, Balt., 1951-52; dir. devel. office Children's Hosp., Buffalo, 1952-54; sales mgr. Amherst Mfg. Corp., Williamsville, NY, 1954—56, Delevan Electronics Corp., East Aurora, NY; mem. firm Penney & Penney, Buffalo, 1958-61; pvt. practice Niagara County, NY, 1961—. Numerous contemporary art collection exhbns. include Mus. Modern Art, NYC, 1962, Whitney Mus. Am. Art, NYC, 1963, 79, 80, Burchfield-Penney Art Ctr., 1973, 92-2003, Meml. Art Gallery, Rochester, 1976, 78, 83, 88, U. Iowa, 1978, Columbus (Ohio) Gallery Fine Arts, 1976, 78. Hon. life trustee Burchfield-Penney Art Ctr.; adv. bd. Found. Study of Arts and Crafts Movement at Roycroft; hon. bd. dirs. Buffalo-Lille/France Assn. Inc. 2d lt. U.S. Army, 1943-46. Recipient Pres.'s Disting. Svc. award Buffalo State Coll., 1991, Disting. Svc. to Culture award Coll. Arts and Scis., SUNY, Potsdam, 1983; named Disting. fellow Cultural Studies of the Burchfield-Penney Art Ctr., 1994, Outstanding Individual Philanthropist, Nat. Soc. Fund Raising Execs. Western NY, 1996, Individual Patron of the Arts award Buffalo and Erie County Arts Coun. and Buffalo of C., 1997, Citation for Outstanding Achievements and Svc. to Lockport Cmty., NY State Assembly, 1997; awarded Key to City of Lockport, 1997; inductee Lockport Hist. Walk of Fame, 1999. Fellow The Explorers Club; mem. AARP, YWCA Niagra (life), Albright-Knox Art Gallery Buffalo (life), Buffalo Mus. Sci. (Life), Buffalo and Erie County Hist. Soc. (life, Red Jacket award 2000), Niagara County Hist. Soc. (life), Old Ft. Niagara (life), Buffalo Soc. Artists (hon. trustee), Hist. Lockport (life), Landmark Soc. Western NY (life), Am. Ceramic Cir., Hist. Lewiston (life), Friends of U. Rochester Librs. (life) Meml. Art Gallery U. Rochester (hon. bd. mgrs., hon. life), Winslow Homer Soc. of Dirs. Cir. (hon. life), Smithsonian Instn. (benefactors cir.), Rochester Hist. Soc. (life), Am. Hist. Print Collectors Soc. (life), Burchfield Homestead Soc. (hon. life), Charles E. Burchfield Nature and Art Ctr., Archives Am. Art, Mark Twain Soc. (hon.), U. Rochester's Pres.'s Soc. (hon. life), U. Iowa's Pres.'s Club (hon. life), Va. Law Found., Nat. Geog. Soc. (life), World's Fair Collectors Soc., Hist. Soc. of Tonawandas (life), Pres.'s Cir. Buffalo State Coll. (hon. life), Buffalo State Alumni Assn. (life), Yale Sailing Assocs., Yale Glee Club Assocs., Peanut Pals, Grolier Club, Pan Am. Expo Collectors Soc., Buffalo Indsl. Heritage Com., Roycrofters-at-Large Assn. (life), Arctic Cir. Club, Order of the Alaska Walrus, Automobile Club (Lockport), Niagara County Antiques Club (hon.), Rochester Art Club (hon. life), Fine Arts Mus. San Francisco (patron), De Young & Legion of Honor Museums (patron), Chi Psi, Phi Alpha Delta. Office: 538 Bewley Building Lockport NY 14094-2944 Office Phone: 716-433-2524. Personal E-mail: charliepenney@aol.com. *I have tried to strive for excellence in whatever I undertake, be it small or large. What success I may have achieved has required initiative, imagination, and dedication to the task at hand. Satisfaction comes from the hard work that leads to an objective. In all that I do I adhere to the Golden Rule and to fairness, honesty, and understanding in human relationships. I try to maintain a sense of humor at all times. And I enjoy living in a small community because it is from such areas that the strength of America comes.*

**PENNEY, GEOFF,** finance company executive; b. England; m. Linda Penney; children: Neill, Daniel, Leslie. BA, St. John's Coll., PhD in organic chemistry. Sr. v.p. mng. dir. Bankers Trust Co., NY and London; sr. v.p. Fidelity Investments, Boston; head of fin. products and internat. tech. Charles Schwab, 1997—96, exec. v.p., 1998—, CIO, 2001—. Mem. exec. com. Charles Schwab Corp.; bd. dirs. Keynote Systems.

**PENNEY, NANCY SANFORD,** retired special education educator; b. East Liverpool, Ohio, July 7, 1934; d. Ralph Lewis and Ruth Allis (Peterson) Sanford; m. David Paul Penney, June 2, 1956; children: D. Jeffrey, Lauri Penney Salverda. AB, Eastern Nazarene Coll., Wollaston Park, Mass., 1956; MA, U. Rochester, 1976; Cert. in Advanced Study in Administrn., SUNY, 1988. Rsch. tech. Boston U., 1956-58, United Fruit Co., Norwood, Mass., 1958-61; tchr. Monroe County Bd. Coop. Edn. Svcs., Fairport, NY, 1968—82, instrn. specialist, 1982—95; dir. instructional resource ctr. Monroe County Bs. Coop. Edn. Svcs., 1993—95; ret., 1995. E-mail: nespny@aol.com.

**PENNEY, SHERRY HOOD,** academic administrator, consultant; b. Marlette, Mich., Sept. 4, 1937; d. Terrance and B. Jean (Stoutenburg) Hood; m. Carl Murray Penney, July 8, 1961 (div. 1978); children: Michael Murray, Jeffrey Hood; m. James Duane Livingston, Mar. 30, 1985. BA, Albion Coll., 1959; MA, U. Mich., 1961; PhD, SUNY, Albany, 1972; LLD (hon.), Albion Coll., 1989; degree (hon.), Quincy Coll., 1999. Vis. asst. prof. Union Coll., Schenectady, NY, 1972-73; assoc. higher edn. NY State Edn. Dept., Albany, 1973-76; assoc. provost Yale U., New Haven, 1976-82; vice chancellor acad. programs, policy and planning SUNY System, Albany, 1982-88; acting pres. SUNY, Plattsburgh, 1986-87; chancellor U. Mass., Boston, 1988-95; pres. U. Mass. Sys., Boston, 1995; chancellor U. Mass. Boston, 1996-2000, endowed prof., 2001—. Chmn., bd. dirs. Nat. Higher Edn. Mgmt. Sys., Boulder, Colo., 1985-87; mem. commn. on higher edn. New Eng. Assn. Schs. and Colls., Boston, 1979-82, Mid. States Assn. Schs. and Colls., Phila., 1986-88; mem. commn. on women Am. Coun. Edn., Washington, 1979-81, commn. on govt. rels., 1990-94; bd. dirs. NSTAR, 1990—, Carnegie Found. for Advancement of Teaching, 1994-2002. Author: Patrician in Politics, 1974; co-author (with James D. Livingston) A Very Dangerous Woman: Martha Wright and Women's Rights, 2004; editor: Women and Management in Higher Education, 1975; contbr. articles to profl. jours. Nat. adv. com. Nat. Initiative for Women in Higher Edn., 2001—05; mem. Internat. Trade Task Force, 1994—96; mem. exec. com. Challenge to Leadership, 1988, chair, 1995—98; bd. dirs. HERS, 1992—, Mary Baker Eddy Libr., Boston, 2001—; trustee Berkeley Div. Sch., Yale U., 1978—82, John F. Kennedy Libr. Found., 1980—2001, bd. dirs. Albany Symphony Orch., 1982—88, U. Mass. Found., 1988—2000, Mcpl. Rsch. Bur., Boston, 1990—2001, New Eng. Coun., 1990—2000, Greater Boston C. of C., 1989—2002, Met. Affairs Coalition, chair, 1999—2001; bd. trustees New Eng. Aquarium, 1990—2004; bd. dirs. Greater Boston One to One Leadership Coun., 1990—2000, NASULGC Commn. Urban Affairs, 1990—2000, The Ednl. Resource Inst., chair, 1996—; bd. dirs. The Environ. Bus. Coun., 1991—97; bd. visitors WEIU, 2002—06. Recipient Disting. Alumna award Albion Coll., 1978, Disting. Citizen award for racial harmony Black/White Boston, 1994, Am. Coun. on Edn./Nat. Identification Program award, Mass., Leadership award, 1995, New Eng. Women's Leadership award, 1996, Pinnacle award for Lifetime Achievement Greater Boston C. of C., 1998, Abigail Adams award Mass. Women's Polit. Caucus, 2003. Mem. Orgn. Am. Historians, St. Botolph Club, Comml. Club (Boston). Unitarian Universalist. Office: U Mass Boston 100 Morrissey Blvd Boston MA 02125-3300

**PENNIMAN, NICHOLAS,** editor; Editor TomPaine.com. Office: Institute for America's Future Suite 205 1025 Connecticut Ave NW Washington DC 20036

**PENNIMAN, NICHOLAS GRIFFITH, IV,** retired newspaper publisher; b. Balt., Mar. 7, 1938; s. Nicholas Griffith Penniman III and Esther Cox Lony (Wight) Keeney; m. Linda Jane Simmons, Feb. 4, 1967; children: Rebecca Helmle, Nicholas G. V. AB, Princeton U., 1960; MA, Washington U., 1999. Asst. bus. mgr. Ill. State Jour. Register, Springfield, 1964-69, bus. mgr., 1969-75; asst. gen. mgr. St. Louis Post-Dispatch, 1975-84, gen. mgr., 1984-86, pub., 1986-99; sr. v.p. newspapers ops. Pulitzer Pub. Co., 1986-99; pres., CEO Pulitzer Comm. Newspapers Inc., 1997-99; chmn. bd. Penniman & Browne, Inc., Balt., 2001—. Chmn. Downtown St. Louis, Inc., 1988-90, Mo. Health and Ednl. Facilities Adminstrn., 1982-85, Ill. State Fair Bd., Springfield, 1973-75, Forest Pks. Forever, 1991-93, Pks. and Open Space Task Force St. Louis 2004, 1996-00, St. Louis Sports Com., 1992-93, Gateway Pks. and Trls. 2004, 1999-04; pres. Caring Found. Children, 1988-91; trustee St. Louis Country Day Sch., 1983-86, Nat. Recreation Found., 2003—, Merc. Libr. St. Louis, 1997-00; bd. dirs. Mo. Coalition for the Environment, 1997-00, Randall Rsch. Ctr., Pineland, Fla., 2001—, Friends of Rookery Bay, 2004—; chmn. bd. Am. Rivers, 2004—, Conservancy of S.W. Fla., 2004—;

mem. Collier County (Fla.) Environ. Adv. Coun., 2005—. With U.S. Army, 1962—67. Mem.: Elkridge Club, Noonday Club (pres. 1994), Grey Oaks Country Club. Home: 611 Portside Dr Naples FL 34103-4118 E-mail: ngpiv@aol.com.

**PENNIMAN, RICHARD WAYNE See LITTLE RICHARD**

**PENNIMAN, W. DAVID,** information scientist, educator, management consultant; b. St. Louis, Dec. 19, 1937; s. William Leon and Laura Mae (Van Winkle) P.; m. Charlotte Ann Meder, Mar. 17, 1973; children: Kara, Rachel, John; 1 child by previous marriage, Jessica. BS in ME, U. Ill., 1960, MS in Journalism, Communications, 1962; PhD in Communication Theory, Ohio State U., 1975. Registered profl. engr., Ohio. Assoc. dir. engring. publs. U. Ill. Coll. Engring., Urbana, 1965-66; rsch. scientist info. systems Battelle Columbus Labs., Columbus, Ohio, 1966-69, assoc. mgr. info. systems, 1969-77; rsch. scholar Internat. Inst. Applied Systems Analysis, Laxenburg, Austria, 1977; mgr. rsch. Online Computer Library Ctr., Dublin, Ohio, 1978-79, dir. software devel., 1979-82, v.p. planning and rsch., 1982-84; dir. libraries and info. systems AT&T Bell Labs., Murray Hill, NJ, 1984-90, dir. info. svcs. group, 1990-91; pres. Coun. on Libr. Resources, Inc., Washington, 1991-95; dir. Ctr. for Info. Studies, 1995-99; prof. sch. of info. Scis. Univ. Tenn., 1995-99; private cons., 1999—2001; prof. informatics U. Buffalo, Buffalo, 2001—, dean sch. informatics, 2001—06. Chmn. Engring. Info. Inc., N.Y.C., 1983-91; governing com. Forest Press Inc., Albany, N.Y., 1985-88; adv. com. info. sci. Rutgers U., 1982-91. Author numerous book chpts. and articles in profl. jours. Advisor United Way, Columbus, 1981-83. Served with U.S. Army, 1963-65. Named Tech. Person of Yr., Columbus Tech. Coun., 1982, U.S. Del. to Internat. Inst. for Applied Systems Analysis, 1977. Fellow AAAS; mem. IEEE (sr.), Am. Soc. Info. Sci. (pres. 1988-89), Assn. for Computing Machinery. Avocations: antique automobiles, hiking. Office: U Buffalo Sch of Informatics Buffalo NY 14260 Office Phone: 716-645-6481 x 1176. Business E-mail: penniman@buffalo.edu.

**PENNINGER, FRIEDA ELAINE,** retired literature educator; b. Marion, NC, Apr. 11, 1927; d. Fred Hoyle and Lena Frances (Young) Penninger. AB, U. N.C., Greensboro, 1948; MA, Duke U., 1950, PhD, 1961. Copywriter Sta. WSJS, Winston-Salem, NC, 1948-49; asst. prof. English Flora Macdonald Coll., Red Springs, NC, 1950-51; tchr. English Barnwell, SC, 1951-52, Brunswick, Ga., 1952-53; instr. English U. Tenn., Knoxville, 1953-56; instr., asst. prof. Woman's Coll., U. N.C., Greensboro, 1956-58, 60-63; asst. prof., assoc. prof. U. Richmond (Va.), 1963-71; chair. dept. English Westhampton Coll., Richmond, 1971-78; prof. English U. Richmond, 1971-91, Bostwick prof. English, 1987-91, ret., 1991. Author: William Caxton, 1979, Chaucer's "Troilus and Criseyde" and "The Knight's Tale": Fictions Used, 1993, (novel) Look at Them, 1990; compiler, editor: English Drama to 1660, 1976; editor: Festschrift for Prof. Marguerite Roberts, 1976. Fellow Southeastern Inst. of Mediaeval and Renaissance Studies, 1965, 67, 69. Mem.: Friends of The Libr. U. NC Greensboro (bd. dirs. 2005—). Democrat. Presbyterian. Home: 2701 Camden Rd Greensboro NC 27403-1438

**PENNINGER, SAMUEL A., JR.,** consumer products company executive; Founder Serologicals Corp., Atlanta, 1971, pres., 1983-93, chmn. bd. dirs., 1993—. Mem. Am. Blood Resource Assn. (past bd. dirs.), Am. Assn. Blood Banks. Office: Serologicals Corp 5655 Spalding Dr Norcross GA 30092-2504

**PENNINGTON, AUBREY EL,** director; s. Elhanan and Rosie Mae Pennington; m. Kathy Lee Alstott, Dec. 28, 1985; children: Zachary El, Tyler Ray. BS, Campbellsville U., 1993; MA, Western Ky. U., 1999; Rank I, Union Coll., 2002. Cert. provisional secondary tchr. Ky. Dept. Edn., 1994, curriculum cons. Ky. Dept. Edn., 2005. History/social studies tchr. Casey Co. Pub. Schs., Liberty, Ky., 1993—99; region six social studies cons. Ky. Dept. Edn., Corbin, 2000—03; curriculum specialist Pulaski Co. Pub. Schs., Somerset, Ky., 2003—. Program cons. Am. Legacies Fed. History Grant, Frankfort, Ky., 2003—; mid. sch. social studies textbook editor McGraw-Hill Publishers, Inc., Englewood, NJ, 2005; vol. hist. interpreter Stones River Nat. Battlefield Pk., Murfreesboro, Tenn., 2006—; vol. oral historian U. Tex. Tech: Vietnam Oral History Project, Austin, 2005—. Mem.: Ky. Assn. Soc. Studies Admnstrs. (assoc.), Assn. Supr. for Curriculum Devel. (assoc.), Ky. Assn. Tchrs. of History (assoc.), Ky. Coun. for Social Studies (assoc.), Nat. History in Edn. Assn. (assoc.), Am. Hist. Assn. (assoc.), Ky. Hist. Soc. (assoc.). Avocations: local historical research, photography, hiking. Office: Pulaski County Public Schools 500 University Dr Somerset KY 42502 Office Phone: 606-679-1123. Personal E-mail: history2234@yahoo.com.

**PENNINGTON, BEVERLY MELCHER,** financial services company executive; b. Vermillion, SD, Feb. 8, 1931; d. Cecil Lloyd and Phyllis Cecelia (Walz) M.; m. Glen D., Sept. 1, 1965 (dec. Aug. 1989); 1 child, Terri Lynn. BS, U. S.D., Vermillion, 1952. Enrolled agt. cert. IRS 1989. Sec. budget dept. Bur. of Indian Affairs, Aberdeen, S.D., 1952-53, pvt. sec., 1953-54, U.S. P.H.S. Indian Health, Aberdeen, 1954-55; adminstr. asst. U.S. Pub. Health Svc., Anchorage, 1955-58, U.S. Pub. Health, Dental Pub. Health, Washington, 1958-61; grant adminstr. Dental Pub. Health, Washington, 1961-65; co-owner Penn Mel Marina, Platte, S.D, 1965-74, Pennington Tax Service, Platte, 1974-86, owner, 1986-93; pres., CEO White Tiger Fin. Svc., Inc., Platte, 1994—. Contbr. articles to profl. jours. Mem. Platte Women's Club, sec., 1965-68, pres., 1968-70, 89-91; mem. Libr. Bd. Svc., 1982-85, treas., 1995—. Fellow Am. Soc. Tax Profls. (sec. 1989-91, 2d v.p. 1995, 1st v.p. 1996, pres. 1997); mem. NAFE, Platte C. of C. (v.p. 1989, pres. 1990), Lyric Theatre Mus. Soc. (pres. 1988-92, v.p. 2005—), U.S. C. of C., Washington Dakota Cen. Com. Republican. Presbyterian. Avocations: collecting jewelry, reading, dress designing, gourmet cooking. Office: White Tiger Fin Svc Inc 420 Main St Platte SD 57369 Office Phone: 605-337-2600 Business E-Mail: whitetigerfinancial@inbox.com.

**PENNINGTON, CLAUDIA,** museum director; Dir. Key West Mus. Art & Hist., Fla., 2000—. Office: Key West Mus Art & Hist 281 Front St Key West FL 33040

**PENNINGTON, JOHN ROBERT,** biology educator, department chairman; b. East Cleveland, Ohio, May 7, 1950; s. William E. and Frances S. Pennington; m. Heather A. Pennington, May 29, 1993; children: Nathan, Michael, Gabrielle. AA, Lakeland C.C., Kirtland, Ohio, 1976; BS in Edn. magna cum laude, Lake Erie Coll., Painesville, Ohio, 1978. Cert. tchr. biology; sci., grades 7-12 Ohio. Sci. tchr. Willowick Jr. High, Ohio, 1978—82; biology tchr. Willoughby South High, Ohio, 1983—, chair sci. dept., 2001—. Staff sgt. USAF, 1971—75. Recipient Vietnam Svc. medal, USAF, 1973, Adell Knight Tchr. Excellence award, 2003, Tchr. Excellence award, Berlin Family Found., 2003. Avocations: travel, camping, nature photography. Home: 30214 Mildred St Willowick OH 44095 Office: Willoughby South HS 5900 Shankland Blvd Willoughby OH 44094 Office Phone: 440-975-3648. E-mail: hjpenn@adelphia.net.

**PENNINGTON, KAREN HARDER,** lawyer; b. Amarillo, Tex., June 7, 1956; d. Alvin L. and Rosemary Herskowitz Harder; BS in Biology, W. Tex. State U., 1977; JD, U. Tex., 1986. Bar: Calif. 1986, Tex. 1998, US Patent and Trademark Office 1993, Hopi Tribal Ct. 1993. Assoc. atty. Thelen, Marrin, Johnson & Bridges, L.A., 1986—89, Quinn, Emanuel & Urquhart, L.A., 1989—91, Crosby, Heafey, Roach & May, L.A., 1991—92; atty. Law Office of Karen H. Pennington, Long Beach, Calif., 1993—97, Cath. Charities Immigration Counseling Svcs., Dallas, 1998—2000; immigration atty. Law Office of Karen H. Pennington, Dallas, 2000—. Recipient cover story, Sept. 9 issue, Tex. Lawyer mag., 2002. Mem.: Dallas Bar Assn., LA County Bar Assn., Tex. Bar Assn., Calif. Bar Assn., Am. Immigration Lawyers Assn., North Tex. Coalition Just Peace, United For Peace and Justice, Dallas Peace Ctr. Roman Catholic. Achievements include representation of post-Sept. 11 immigration/national security detainees both before the courts and in FBI interrogations. Office: Law Office of Karen H Pennington Ste 110 701 Commerce St Dallas TX 75202 Office Phone: 214-741-7711. Office Fax: 214-741-7733. Business E-mail: penningtonlaw@yahoo.com.

**PENNINGTON, RICHARD J.,** police chief; m. Renee Pennington; 1 child. BA, American U.; MA, U. Dist. Columbia. Asst. police chief Met. Police Dept., Washington, 1993—94; chief of police New Orleans Police Dept., 1994—2002, Atlanta Police Dept., 2002—. Named an Most Influential Black Americans, Ebony mag., 2006. Mem.: Nat. Orgn. of Black Law Enforcement Execs. (NOBLE) (v.p., pres., immediate past pres. 2006). Office: Atlanta Police Dept 675 Ponce De Leon Ave Atlanta GA 30308*

**PENNINGTON, ROBERT EDGAR,** music educator; b. West Line, Mo., Nov. 27, 1931; s. William Ray Pennington, Edna Marie Johnson. BMus, Northwestern U., 1953, M in Music, 1955, DMus, 1966. Instr. Howard Coll., Birmingham, Ala., 1955—56; prof. piano Drury Coll., Springfield, Mo., 1959—65, West Chester (Pa.) U., West Chester, 1966—. Mem.: Mo. Music Tchrs. Assn. (editor notes 1962—63), Music Tchrs. Nat. Assn., Pi Kappa Lambda. Avocation: Travel. Office: West Chester Univ West Chester PA 19383 Home: 121 W Miner St #2W West Chester PA 19382-3238 Office Phone: 610-436-2640. Office Fax: 610-436-2873. Business E-Mail: rpennington@wcupa.edu.

**PENNINGTON, WILLIAM MARK,** sportswriter; b. Hartford, Conn., Dec. 12, 1956; s. Albert William and Lillian Anne (Lewis) P.; m. Joyce Hand, July 14, 1990; children: Anne D'Amour, Elise Holly, John Taylor. BS, Boston U., 1978. Reporter The Bristol Press, Bristol, Conn., 1976-77, The Associated Press, Boston, 1977, The Providence Jour.-Bull., Providence, 1977-79, The Stamford Advocate, Stamford, Conn., 1979-84, The Record, Hackensack, NJ, 1984-89, syndicated columnist, sr. writer, 1989-97; reporter The New York Times, 1997—. Author: The Winning Spirit, 1991, The Heisman, 2004; contbg. author: (book) Best Sports Stories, 1983, 85, 87, 94. Recipient Best Story award Associated Press Sports Editors, 1985, 89, 91, 93, 96, Best Columnist award, 1983, 89, 95, 96, 2004; Best Story award, 1999. Mem. Baseball Writers Assn. of Am., Boston U. Football Alumni Assn., New England Hist. Genealogical Soc. Roman Catholic. Office: The NY Times 229 W 43rd St New York NY 10036-3959 Office Phone: 212-556-7371.*

**PENNISI, LIZ,** women's health nurse; b. Bklyn., Nov. 20, 1953; d. Alexander and Marjorie (Soviero) Perillo; children: Stephen, Scott, Greg. Diploma, Beth Israel Sch. Nursing, N.Y.C., 1974. RN, N.Y.; cert. ambulatory women's health nurse. Staff nurse Montefiore Hosp., Bronx, NY, 1974-75; mem. staff Beth Israel Med. Ctr., N.Y.C., 1975-77; office nurse Martin Kurman, M.D., N.Y.C., 1977-80, Adam Romoff, M.D. and Suzanne Yale, M.D., P.C., 1984—. Mem. AWHONN. Avocations: tennis, horseback riding, reading. Office: Drs Romoff and Yale 768 Park Ave New York NY 10021-4153 E-mail: lizpennisi@hotmail.com.

**PENNISTEN, JOHN WILLIAM,** computer scientist, actuary, linguist; b. Buffalo, Jan. 25, 1939; s. George William and Lucy Josephine (Gates) P. AB in Math. and Chemistry with honors, Hamilton Coll., 1960; postgrad., Harvard U., 1960-61, U.S. Army Lang. Sch., 1962-63; MS in Computer Sci. with honors, NY Inst. Tech., 1987. Cert. Application Developer IBM, 2006; in Taxation NYU, 1982, in Asian Langs. NYU, 1992, in Profl. Banking Am. Inst. Banking, Am. Bankers Assn., 1988. Actuarial asst. New Eng. Mut. Life Ins. Co., Boston, 1965-66; asst. actuary Mass. Gen. Life Ins. Co., Boston, 1966-68; actuarial assoc. John Hancock Mut. Life Ins. Co., Boston, 1968-71; asst. actuary George B. Buck Cons. Actuaries, Inc., NYC, 1971-75, Martin E. Segal Co., NYC, 1975-80; actuary Laiken Siegel Co., NYC, 1980; cons. Bklyn., 1981—; timesharing and database analyst banklink corp. cash mgmt. div. Chem. Bank NYC, 1983-85; programmer analyst Empire Blue Cross and Blue Shield, NYC, 1986-88, Mt. Sinai Med. Ctr., NYC, 1988-89, French Am. Banking Corp. (subs. Banque National de Paris), NYC, 1989; sr. programmer analyst Dean Witter Reynolds, Inc., NYC, 1989-92; computer specialist for software NYC Dept. Fin., 1992—97, computer specialist, 2003—; sr. cons. Pinkerton Computer Cons., Inc., NYC, 1997-99; tech. officer J.P. Morgan Chase Co., NYC, 1999—2003. Enrolled actuary U.S. Fed. Pension Legis. Bklyn., 1976—. Contbr. articles to profl. jours. With US Army, 1961-64. Fellow: Soc. Actuaries; mem.: IEEE Computer Soc., MLA, AAAS, Harvard Grad. Soc., Am. Friends of Covent Garden, Bklyn. Heights Assn., Nat. Ry. Hist. Soc., Am. Chem. Soc., Math. Assn. Am., Nat. Model R.R. Assn. (life), Ry. and Locomotive Hist. Soc. (life), Am. Math. Soc., Assn. Computational Linguistics, Linguistic Soc. Am., Am. Assn. Artificial Intelligence, Assn. Computing Machinery, Met. Opera Guild, Nat. Rep. Club Capitol Hill, Am. Legion, Phi Beta Kappa. Republican. Presbyterian. Home: 135 Willow St Brooklyn NY 11201-2255 Office: NYC Dept Fin 345 Adams St 12th Fl Brooklyn NY 11201 Business E-Mail: pennistenj@finance.nyc.gov.

**PENNOCK, PEGGY ANN,** secondary school educator; b. Detroit, Nov. 16, 1947; d. Roy James Griffin and Ada Louise (Newby) Cain; m. Arthur Kirkland Jr., Feb. 24, 1973 (div. Apr. 1980); 1 child, Julian Arthur; m. David Pennock, July 20, 1991. BA, Wayne State U., 1970; MA, NYU, 1976; cert. Edn. Specialist, Wayne State U., 1987. Cert. elem. tchr., Mich. Tchr. Lessenger Jr. H.S., Detroit, 1970-73, New Hyde Park (N.Y.) Meml. H.S., 1973-75; adj. lectr. La Guardia C.C., L.I., N.Y., 1976-77; tchr. Southfield (Mich.) H.S., 1977-81, St. Theresa-Visitation Sch., Detroit, 1981-82; adj. lectr. Lawrence Tech. U., Southfield, 1982-83; dir. alternative edn. program Ferndale (Mich.) H.S., 1985-86, tchr., coord., 1984—. Spkr. Nat. Alliance for Bus., Chgo., 1987, Nat. Coun. of Negro Women, Detroit, 1987; adj. lectr. Oakland C.C., 1998; author, founder at-risk programs and peer counseling programs; textbook cons., Ferndale H.S., English dept. coord., 2002—. Author numerous poems. Vol. United Negro Coll. Fund., 1977—83; hosted German Exch. student, 1991; participated tchr. exchange programs Scotland, Germany, 1990—98; hosted tchrs. from Germany, Belgium, Brazil and Denmark, 1993—2004; lay reader Old Mariners' Ch., Detroit, 1981—; trustee Old Mariners' Ch, Detroit, 2001—. Recipient Outstanding Tchr. award, Southfield HS, 1981, Tchr. of Yr. award, Ferndale H.S., 2004. Mem. NEA, Nat. Coun. Tchrs. English, Delta Sigma Theta. Republican. Anglican Catholic. Avocations: travel, ballroom dancing. Office: Ferndale High Sch 881 Pinecrest Dr Ferndale MI 48220-2386 Office Phone: 248-548-8600. Personal E-mail: peggystarz@aol.com. Business E-Mail: ppennock@ferndaleschools.org.

**PENNOYER, ROBERT M.,** lawyer; b. N.Y.C., Apr. 9, 1925; BA, Harvard U., 1946; LL.B., Columbia U., 1950. Bar: N.Y. 1951, U.S. Supreme Ct. 1971. Asst. US atty. criminal divsn. (so. dist.) NY US Dept. Justice, 1953-55; asst. to gen. counsel US Dept. Def., Washington, 1955-57, spl. asst. to asst. sec. for internat. security affairs, 1957-58; ptnr. Patterson, Belknap, Webb & Tyler, N.Y.C., 1962-95, of counsel, 1995—. Trustee Carnegie Instn., Washington, 1968-79, John Merck Fund, 1982—, Mrs. Giles Whiting Found., 1970—2000, Met. Mus. Art, 1966—, Pierpont Morgan Libr., 1969—, Columbia U., 1982-88, Boyce Thompson Inst. for Plant Rsch., Cornell U., 1974-97, Inst. Democracy Studies, 1999-2002. Lt. (j.g.) USNR, PTO, 1944-46. Recipient Lifetime Achievement award, Am. Lawyer mag., 2006. Mem. ABA, N.Y. State Bar Assn., Assn. Bar City N.Y., Century Assn. Office: Patterson Belknap Webb & Tyler Rm 2200 1133 Ave of the Americas New York NY 10036-6731 Office Phone: 212-336-2700. Business E-Mail: rmpennoyer@pbwt.com.

**PENNY, BRAD,** professional baseball player; b. Blackwell, Okla., May 24, 1978; Pitcher Fla. Marlins, 2004—, Los Angeles Dodgers, 2004—. Achievements include starting pitcher Nat. League MLB All-Star Game, 2006; pitching two career complete game shut-outs, 2001, 2002. Office: Los Angeles 1000 Elysian Park Ave Los Angeles CA 90012-1199*

**PENNY, ROGER PRATT,** retired management consultant; b. Buffalo, July 13, 1936; s. George Albert and Louise (Mings) P.; m. Judith Stevens, Aug. 25, 1957; children: David, Sarah, Julia. BA in Adminstrv. Engring., Union Coll. 1958; grad., Wharton Bus. Sch., 1993. From supt. to pres. Bethlehem Steel Corp., Lackawanna, NY, 1958—91, pres., 1991—99, vice chmn., 1999—2000, ret. 2000. Mem. United Way, Buffalo, 1960-82; chmn. campaign United Way Porter County, Valparaiso, Ind., 1986; mem. Orchard Park Town Bd., 1970-82; mem. adv. bd. Purdue U., West Lafayette, Ind., 1985-86,

Bus. Sch., Valparaiso U., 1986; bd. dirs. Minsi Trails coun. Boy Scouts Am., Lehigh Valley, Pa., 1988—, pres., 1996; trustee St. Luke's Hosp., 1998-2001. Mem. Am. Iron and Steel Inst., Assn. Iron and Steel Engrs., Valparaiso C. of C. (dir. 1985-86), Orchard Park C. of C., Buffalo C. of C., Sand Creek Club (pres. 1983-86), Buffalo Soccer Club (pres., sec. 1960-75), Saucon Valley Country Club, Wynstone Golf Club. Republican. Episcopalian. Office Phone: 847-756-4211.

**PENROD, MARIAN PENUEL,** personnel consultant, retired school librarian; b. Statesville, Tenn., May 11, 1930; d. Hayden L. Penuel and Zoie L. Cunningham; m. William T. Penrod, Jr., June 8, 1954 (div. Oct. 1979); children: Cheryl Anne Penrod Puryear, Paula Wynn, Laura Lynn Penrod Moseng. BS, Middle Tenn. State Coll., 1952; M of Religious Edn., So. Bapt. Theol. Sem., Louisville, 1955; EdM, U. Miami, 1958. Cert. specialist in pastoral care Pastoral Counseling Ctrs. Tenn., Inc., 2002. Tchr. Parma (Mich.) Elem., 1953—54, Dunbar (Ky.) Elem., 1955—57, West Jackson (Tenn.) Bapt., 1965—66; tchr. libr. Madison County, Jackson, 1967—69; tchr. Dyer County, Dyersburg, Tenn., 1969—70; sch. libr. Murfreesboro (Tenn.) City Schs., 1972—98; ind. wellness cons. Nikken, Inc., 1998—. Baptist. Avocations: reading, writing, travel, continued education. Office Phone: 615-893-7398.

**PENROSE, CHARLES, JR.,** professional society administrator; b. Phila., Oct. 9, 1921; s. Charles and Beatrice (d,Este) P.; m. Ann Lucille Cantwell, Apr. 17, 1943; children: James, Thomas, John. Grad., Episcopal Acad., Overbrook, Pa., 1940. Exec. sec. Newcomen Soc. N.Am. (N.A.), Phila., 1946-48; dist. sales mgr. Fitchburg Paper Co., Mass., 1948-50, 52-53; from sales mgr. to v.p. sales A.M. Collins Mfg. Co., Phila., 1953-55; sales mgr. A.M. Collins divsn. Internat. Paper Co., N.Y.C., 1955; asst. to sales mgr. fine paper and bleached bd. divsn., 1956-57; sr. v.p., CEO Newcomen Soc. in N.Am., Downingtown, Pa., 1957-61, also bd. dirs.; pres., CEO Newcomen Soc. U.S., 1961-87, chmn., 1987-89, chmn. emeritus, 1989—; sr. v.p. N. Am. Newcomen Soc., London, 1957-89, hon. v.p., 1989—. Pres., CEO Newcomen publs. in N. Am., Inc., 1958-61, trustee, 1948-61; pres., dir. Rocaton, Inc., Darien, Conn., 1960-61. Author: They Live on a Rock in the Sea The Isles of Shoals in Colonial Days, 1957. Sec., asst. treas. Chester County Investment Fund Assn., Phila., 1959-64; v.p. Brit. Am. Ednl. Found., Inc., N.Y.C., 1968-70, pres., 1970-75, trustee, 1968-81; trustee Stanley Mus., Kingfield, Maine, 1995-2000; sec. Stanley Mus., Maine, 1996-98, 1999-2000, trustee. Capt. USAAF, 1940-46, PTO; capt. U.S. Army, 1950-2. Mem. Most Venerable Order Hospice of St. John of Jerusalem (London). Mem. Newcomen Soc. U.S., Newcomen Soc. London, Royal Soc. Arts (Benjamin Franklin fellow 1980), Pilgrims of U.S., First Troop Phila. City Calvary (hon.), Nat. Inst. Social Scis., Soc. Am. Historians, Marine Hist. Assn., N.H. Hist. Soc., Mt. Washington Obs., Sandwich (N.H.) Hist. Soc. (trustee 1992-94, v.p. 1994-98), Chi Psi Omicron. Clubs: Tokeneke (Darien); Tamworth Outing (N.H.); Wonalancet Outdoors (N.H.). Republican. Presbyterian. also: 11 Mansfield Ave Darien CT 06820-4714 Home: 81 Mansfield Ave Darien CT 06820 Office Phone: 203-655-4504.

**PENROSE, CYNTHIA C.,** retired health care consultant; b. Manila, Philippines, Nov. 24, 1939; d. Douglas Lee Lipscomb Cordiner and Jane (Sturgeon) Edises; m. Douglas Francis Penrose, July 11, 1959 (div. 1981); children: Vicki Flores, Lee Douglas; m. Alan Harrison Magazine, Aug. 30, 1984. BA, U. Calif., Berkeley, 1963; MBA, U. Santa Clara, 1977. LCSW. V.p., dir. employment Resource Ctr. for Women, Palo Alto, Calif., 1973-78; bus. planner Raychem Corp., Menlo Park, Calif., 1979; adminstrv. mgr. Electric Power Rsch. Inst., Palo Alto, 1979-83; sr. ptnr. MB Assocs., Washington, 1983-88; dir. ops. Utility Data Inst., Washington, 1984-85, Randmark, Inc., 1986-87; coord. market devel. for Mid-Atlantic states Kaiser Found. Health Plan, Washington, 1987-88, asst. to assoc. regional mgr., 1988-94; market planner MetraHealth, Vienna, Va., 1995; exec. staff asst. United HealthCare, Vienna, 1995, dir. strategic planning, splty. cos., 1996-97; dir. spl. projects MetraComp subs. United HealthCare, Vienna, 1995, v.p. regulatory affairs and compliance, 1997-99; ptnr. Penrose Mag. LLC, 2000—01; ret., 2001. Bd. dirs., treas. Unique Enterprises, Washington, 1985-87; sec. Wesley Property Mgmt. Co., 1987-89; bd. dirs. Wesley Housing Devel. Corp., 1988-89. Chair vol. com. Habitat for Humanity, No. Va., 2002—03, bd. dirs., 2003—, chair Restore adv. com., 2003—05, v.p., mem. exec. com., 2005—; mem. Affirmative Action Adv. Com., Palo Alto, 1975—76; bd. dirs., sec. Am. Hospice Found., 1995—97, treas., 1998—2000; bd. dirs. Nat. Inst. for Med. Options, 1999—2001; bd. dirs., v.p. LWV, Berkeley and Palo Alto, 1966—73; chmn. program adv. com. Resource Ctr. for Women, Palo Alto, 1980—83; bd. dirs. HFHNV, 2003—. Mem. Peninsula Profl. Women's Network (v.p. 1981-82), U. Calif. Alumni Assn., AAUW (Bicentennial br. sec. 1986-88), Capitol Area Soc. Healthcare Planning and Mktg., Nat. Capital Healthcare Execs., LWV. Democrat. Episcopalian. Avocations: swimming, nutrition and health, reading. Home and Office: 322 S Fayette St Alexandria VA 22314-5903 E-mail: ccpenrose@comcast.net.

**PENSABENE, JUDITH K.,** lawyer; b. 1945; BA, U. Mo., Kansas City; postgrad., U. Houston; JD, U. Tulsa, 1975. Bar: Okla. 1975, D.C. 1978. Assoc. Holliman Langholz Runnels & Dowart, Tulsa, 1974—78; cons. environ. issues, 1980—89; sr. minority counsel Com. Energy & Natural Resources, U.S. Senate, 1990—95; v.p. & counsel Constellation Energy Group, Washington, 1995—2002; dep. chief counsel Com. Energy & Natural Resources, U.S. Senate, 2002—03, chief counsel, 2003—. Articles editor: U. Tulsa Law Jour. Mem.: Phi Delta Phi, Order of Curule (chair). Office: Committee on Energy and Natural Resources Room 364 Senate Dirksen Office Building Washington DC 20510-6150 Office Phone: 202-224-4971.

**PENSADO, OSVALDO,** research scientist; b. Xalapa, Veracruz, Mex., May 31, 1971; s. Faustino Pensado and Ana María Rodríguez; m. Esperanza Ortiz-Pensado; children: Diego children: Edna. BS in Physics and Math., U. de las Américas, 1994; PhD in Engring. Sci., Pa. State U., 1998. Asst. prof. Univ. Veracruzana, Xalapa, Mexico, 1995; rsch. asst. Pa. State Univ. Univ. Pk., 1995; rsch. engr. Southwest Rsch. Inst., San Antonio, 1999—2002, sr. rsch. scientist, 2002—. Contbr. rsch. articles to sci. jours. Mem.: Materials Rsch. Soc., Electrochem. Soc. Avocation: playing soccer and tennis. Office: S W Rsch Inst 6220 Culebra Rd San Antonio TX 78238 Business E-Mail: opensado@swri.org.

**PENSE, ALAN WIGGINS,** metallurgical engineer, academic administrator; b. Sharon, Conn., Feb. 3, 1934; s. Arthur Wilton and May Beatrice (Wiggins) P.; m. Muriel Drews Taylor, June 28, 1958; children: Daniel Alan, Steven Taylor, Christine Muriel. B.Metall. Engring., Cornell U., 1957; MS, Lehigh U., 1959, PhD, 1962. Research asst. Lehigh U., Bethlehem, Pa., 1957-59, instr., 1960-62, asst. prof., 1962-65, assoc. prof., 1965-71, prof., 1971-96, chmn. dept. metallurgy and materials engring., 1977-83, assoc. dean Coll. Engring. and Applied Scis., 1984-88, dean, 1988-90, v.p., provost, 1990-96, prof. emeritus, 1996—. Mem. bd. dirs. Advanced Tech. for Large Structural Systems NSF, 1986-89; cons. adv. com. on reactor safeguards NRC, 1965-86; rsch. engr., 1997—; cons. Lehigh U., 1997—. Author: (with D. Henkel) Structure and Properties of Engineering Materials, 5th edit, 2001; also articles. Recipient Robinson award Lehigh U., 1965, Stabler award, 1972, Hillman award 1997, Materials Sci. and Engring. Disting. Alumni award, 2002; Danforth fellow, 1974-86. Fellow Am. Soc. Metals, Am. Welding Soc. (William Sprarragan award 1963, Adams Membership award 1966, Jennings award 1970, Adams lectr. 1980, William Hobart medal 1982, Plummer lectr. 1995); mem. ASTM, Am. Soc. Engring. Edn. (Western Elec. award 1986), Internat. Inst. Welding, Nat. Acad. Engring. Republican. Evang. Congregationalist (bd. trustees Lynhurst Dr Bethlehem PA 18017-3940 Office: The ATLSS Rsch Ctr 117 Atlss Dr Bethlehem PA 18015-4728 Office Phone: 610-758-6104 Business E-Mail: awp0@lehigh.edu. *Achievement of significant goals in our life must be balanced by the quality of that life itself, for what we are is as important as what we do.*

**PENSHORN, JOHN S.,** health facility administrator; Stock analyst Piper Jaffray; dir. Capital Markets Comm. and Strategy UnitedHealth Grp., Minnetonka, Minn., 1998—, sr. v.p. Office: UnitedHealth Grp 9900 Bren Rd E Minnetonka MN 55343

**PENSKAR, MARK HOWARD,** lawyer; b. Detroit, Mar. 4, 1953; s. Sol Leonard and Frances (Rosenthal) P.; m. Carol Ann Stewart, Aug. 7, 1977; children: David, Rebecca. BA, U. Mich., 1974, M in Pub. Policy, 1975, JD cum laude, 1977. Bar: Calif. 1977, U.S. Dist. Ct. (ea. and ctrl. dists.) Calif. 1977, U.S. Dist. Ct. (so. dist.) Calif. 1977, U.S. Dist. Ct. (no. dist.) Calif. 1988, U.S. Ct. Appeals (9th cir.) 1987, U.S. Tax Ct. 1993. Assoc. Pillsbury, Madison and Sutro, San Francisco, 1977-84, ptnr., 1985-96; sr. bus. litig. atty. Pacific Gas and Electric Co., San Francisco, 1996—, dir. and sect. head comml. and employment sect., 2006—. Mediator Superior Ct. early settlement program, San Francisco; mediator and early neutral evaluator U.S. Dist. Ct. Alternative Dispute Resolution Program; bd. dirs. Legal Aid Soc. of San Francisco Employment Law Ctr. Mem. ABA, San Francisco Bar Assn., Commonwealth Club, Phi Gamma Delta (past pres. Bay Area grad. chpt.). Avocations: camping, golf, wine collecting, fishing. Home: 29 E Altarinda Dr Orinda CA 94563-2415 Office: Pacific Gas & Electric Co Law Dept B30A PO Box 7442 San Francisco CA 94120-7442 E-mail: MHP5@pge.com.

**PENTIUK, RANDALL ALAN,** lawyer; b. Garden City, Mich., Mar. 15, 1955; s. Eugene Otto and Marjorie Bernice (Baynes) P.; children: Amanda Rene, Kristen Lynne, Stephanie Joyce; m. Cynthia Marie West, July 29, 1999; 1 child, Katheryn Alexandra. BSBA, Wayne State U., 1976; JD magna cum laude, Detroit Coll. Law, 1981. Bar: Mich. 1981, U.S. Dist. Ct. (ea. dist.) Mich. 1981, U.S. Ct. Appeals (6th cir.) 1984, U.S. Supreme Ct. 1984, D.C. 1985. Rsch. atty. Mich. Ct. Appeals, Detroit, 1981; ptnr. Logan, Huchla, Wycoff & Pentiuk and predecessor Logan, Huchla & Wycoff, P.C., Riverview, Mich., 1981-84, ptnr.-89, Pentiuk, Miller & Waterman, P.C., 1989-93, Pentiuk, Couvreur & Kobiljak, 1993—; atty. City of Riverview, Mich.; corp. counsel City of Melvindale, Mich. Contbr. to profl. jours. Mem. Trenton Planning Commn., Mich., 1982-92, chmn. 1985-87. Down River Rep. Club, Trenton, 1983-85; exec. com. 16th Dist. Rep. Party Mich., 1989-91; pres. Rutherford Inst. Mich., 1987-89; bd. dirs. Detroit City Rescue Mission, chmn., 1992—; bd. dirs. Promise Village, chmn., 1996-97. Mich. Consol. Gas scholar Detroit Coll. Law, 1978, Burton scholar, 1979, Alumni scholar, 1980. Mem. ABA, State Bar Mich., Comml. Law League Am., Fed. Bar Assn., Nat. Inst. Mcpl. Legal Officers (com. federalism, sect. zoning and planning law), Nat. Assn. Housing Coops (bd. dirs.), Midwest Assn. Housing Coops. (bd. dirs.), Mich. Assn. Mcpl. Attys., Christian Legal Soc. Baptist. Home: 20460 Coachwood Cir Riverview MI 48192-7910 Office: 2915 Biddle Ste 200 Wyandotte MI 48192 Office Phone: 734-281-7100. Business E-Mail: rpentiuk@pck-law.com. E-mail: kuitnep@aol.com.

**PENTKOWSKI, RAYMOND J.,** principal; Former supt. Battenkill (Vt.) Valley Supervisory Union, Addison-Rutland (Vt.) Supervisory Union; formerly prin. Ludlow (Vt.) Elem. Sch.; prin. Poultney (Vt.) Elem. Sch. Named state finalist Nat. Supt. of Yr. award, 1989. Office: PoultneyElem Sch Poultney VT 05764 Office Phone: 802-287-5212. Business E-Mail: ray.pentkowski@rswsu.org.

**PENWELL, REBECCA ANN,** science educator; b. Dayton, Ohio; d. Harold Russell Penwell, Jr. and Karen Ann Penwell. BS, Allegheny Coll., 1996; MS, Fla. Internat. U., 1999; MEd, U. Fla., 2001, PhD, 2003. Asst. prof. Brenau U., Gainesville, Ga., 2003—. Content specialist Ga. Profl. Stds. Commn., Atlanta, 2003—04. Contbr. articles to profl. jours. Mem.: NSTA, Am. Ednl. Rsch. Assn., Ga. Acad. Sci. Avocations: scuba diving, snorkeling, reading. Office Phone: 770-534-6218. Business E-Mail: rpenwell@brenau.edu.

**PENZIAS, ARNO ALLAN,** astrophysicist, research scientist, information scientist; b. Munich, Apr. 26, 1933; arrived in U.S., 1940, naturalized, 1946; s. Karl and Justine (Eisenreich) Penzias; m. Sherry Chamove Levit, Aug. 2, 1996; children: David Simon, Mindy Gail, Laurie Shifra. BS in Physics, CCNY, 1954; MA in Physics, Columbia U., 1958, PhD in Physics, 1962; DHC (hon.), Observatoire de Paris, 1976; ScD (hon.), Rutgers U., 1979, Wilkes Coll., 1979, CCNY, 1979, Yeshiva U., 1979, Bar Ilan U., 1983, Monmouth Coll., 1984, Technion-Israel Inst. Tech., 1986, U. Pitts., 1986, Ball State U., 1986, Kean Coll., 1986, U. Pa., 1992, Ohio State U., 1988, Iona Coll., 1988, Drew U., 1989, Lafayette Coll., 1990, Columbia U., 1990, George Washington U., 1992, Rensselaer Univ., 1992, U. Pa., 1992, Bloomfield Coll., 1994, Rankin Tech. U., 1997, Hebrew Union Coll., 1997, Oxford U., 2002. Mem. tech. staff Bell Labs., Holmdel, NJ, 1961—72, head radiophysics rsch. dept., 1972—76, dir. radio research lab., 1976—79, exec. dir. rsch., communications scis. div., 1979—81, v.p. rsch., 1981—85; v.p., chief scientist Lucent Technologies, 1995—98; sr. tech. adv., 1998—2000; venture ptnr. New Enterprise Assocs., 1997—. Bd. dirs. Alien Tech. Corp.; sr. advisor New Enterprise Assocs., 1997—98; adj. prof. earth and scis. SUNY, Stony Brook, 1974—84, Univ. Disting. lectr., 1990; lectr. dept. astrophys. Scis. Princeton U., 1967—72, vis. prof., 1972—85; rsch. assoc. Harvard Coll. Obs., 1968—80; Edison lectr. U.S. Naval Rsch. Lab., 1979; Kompfner lectr. Stanford U., 1979; Gamow lectr. U. Colo., 1980; Jansky lectr. Nat. Radio Astronomy Obs.1983, 1983; Michelson Meml. lectr., 85; Grace Adams Tanner lectr., 87; Klopsteg lectr. Northwestern U., 1987; grad. faculties alumni Columbia U., 1987—89; Regents' lectr. U. Calif., Berkeley, 1990; Lee Kuan Yew Disting. vis. Nat. U. Singapore, 1991; mem. astronomy adv. panel NSF, 1978—79, mem. indsl. panel on sci. and tech., 1982—92, disting. lectr., 1987; affiliate Max-Planck Inst. for Radioastronomy, 1978—85; chmn. Fachbeirat, 1981—83; rschr. in astrophysics, info. tech., its applications and impacts; bd. dirs. Konarko Techs., 2004—. Patentee auction-based selection of telecom. carriers, participant tracking in conference call, computer-based transportation system, fraud prevention in calling cards, identifying telephone extensions in residence environment, double-encrypted identity verification sys.; author: Ideas and Information Managing in a High-Tech World, 1989, Harmony-Business, Technology and Life After Paperwork, 1995; editl. bd. Ann. Rev. Astronomy and Astrophysics, 1974—78, AT&T Bell Labs. Tech. Jour., 1978—84, chmn., 1981—84, assoc editor Astrophys. Jour., 1978—82, contbr. over 100 articles to tech. jours. Bd. overseers U. Pa. Sch. Engring. and Applied Sci., 1983—86; mem. vis. com. Calif. Inst. Tech., 1977—77; mem. Com. Concerned Scientists, 1975—, vice chmn., 1976; mem. adv. bd. Union of Couns. for Soviet Jews, 1983—95; bd. dirs. Coun. on Competitiveness, 1989—92; bd. trustees Trenton U.J. State Coll., 1977—79. With U.S. Army, 1954—56. Named to N.J. Lit. Hall of Fame, 1991; recipient Herschel medal, Royal Astron. Soc., 1977, Nobel prize in Physics, 1978, Townsend Harris medal, CCNY, 1979, Newman award, 1983, Joseph Handleman prize in the scis., 1983, Grad. Faculties Alumni award, Columbia U., 1984, Achievement in Sci. award, Big Bros. Inc., N.Y.C., 1985, Priestly award, Dickinson Coll., 1989, Pender award, U. Pa., 1992, N.J. Sci. and Tech. medal, 1996, Internat. Eng. Cons. Fell. award, 1997, Indsl. Rsch. Inst. medal, 1998. Mem.: AAAS, NAS (Henry Draper medal 1977), IEEE (hon.), NAE, World Acad. Arts and Sci., Internat. Astron. Union, Am. Phys. Soc. (Gage prize 1990), Am. Astron. Soc. Office: New Enterprises Assocs 2490 Sand Hill Rd Menlo Park CA 94025-6940*

**PENZIEN, JOSEPH,** structural engineering educator; b. Philip, SD, Nov. 27, 1924; s. John Chris and Ella (Stebbins) P.; m. Jeanne Ellen Hunson, Apr. 29, 1950 (dec. 1985); children: Robert Joseph, Karen Estelle, Donna Marie, Charlene May; m. Mi-jung Park, June 16, 1988. Student, Coll. Idaho, 1942—43; BS, U. Wash., 1945; ScD, MIT, 1950. Staff Sandia Corp., 1950—51; sr. structures engr. Consol. Vultee Aircraft Corp., Fort Worth, 1951—53; asst. prof. U. Calif. at Berkeley, 1953—57, assoc prof., 1957—62, prof. structural engring., 1962—88, prof. emeritus, 1988—; dir. Earthquake Engring. Rsch. Ctr., 1968—73, 1977—80. Cons. engring. firms; chief tech. adv. Internat. Inst. of Seismology and Earthquake Engring., Tokyo, Japan, 1964-65; chmn. bd. Ea. Internat. Engrs., Inc., 1980-90, Internat. Civil Engring. Cons., Inc., 1990—. NATO Sr. Sci. fellow, 1969. Fellow ASCE. Mechanics; hon. mem. ASCE (Walter Huber Rsch. award, Alfred M. Freudenthal medal, Nathan M. Newmark medal, Ernest E. Howard award), Earthquake Engring. Rsch. Inst. (hon., Hausner medal), IAEE (hon.), EERI

(Alfred E. Alquist award, Dist. Lectr. 2000); mem. Am. Concrete Inst., Structural Engrs. Assn. Calif., Seismol. Soc. Am., Nat. Acad. Engring. Home: 800 Solana Dr Lafayette CA 94549-5004 Office: Int Civil Engr Cons Inc 1995 University Ave Berkeley CA 94704 Office Phone: 510-841-7328. Business E-Mail: penzien@icec.com.

**PEON, ROBERTO,** telecommunications industry executive; b. Mexico City, Mex. BA in Bus. Adminstrn., Ctrl. Coll.; postgrad. Drake U. Mktg. dir. Contel Cellular, Inc.; product mgmt. InteCom, Inc.; v.p. L.Am. Bellsouth Internat.; pres. ops. Bellsouth Internat., CEO BCP Telecomm., Brazil, 1997—2000; chief mktg. officer Bellsouth Corp., Atlanta, 2000—. Mem. telecomm. adv. bd. Compaq; mem. adv. bd. MedShare Internat. Co-chmn. Ams. Gateway Strategy, Atlanta; bd. dirs. Ga. Dept. Trade and Tourism.

**PEOPLES, ALICE LEIGH,** not-for-profit executive; married; 4 children. Nat. v.p. Jack & Jill of Am., Inc., nat. pres., 2005—. Named one of Most Influential Black Americans, Ebony mag., 2006. Office: Jack & Jill of Am, Inc PO Box 970284 Ypsilanti MI 48197 also: 1930 17th St NW Washington DC 20009 Office Phone: 734-487-7725. Office Fax: 734-487-1596. E-mail: np@jackandjillinc.org.*

**PEOPLES, GERALD C.,** college president; m. Verjanis Andrews; children: Takiyah Jamila, Nicholas Antoine. BS in Sociology, Grambling State U., MS in Guidance and Counseling; D in Higher Edn., Kans. State U. Vicechancellor for student affairs So. Univ. and A&M Coll., Baton Rouge; dean of student life, coord. alumni affairs, others Grambling State U., La.; spl. asst. La. State Supt. of Edn., Baton Rouge; pres. So. Univ., New Orleans, 1997—2000. Former city councilman, City of Grambling; bd. dirs. New Orleans Job Initiatives, New Orleans Technology Coun., Greater New Orleans Edn. Found., Urban League, Boy Scouts of Am., Entergy New Orleans, Inc. Office: 6400 Press Dr New Orleans LA 70126-1009

**PEOPLES, JOHN ARTHUR, JR.,** former university president, consultant; b. Starkville, Miss., Aug. 26, 1926; s. John Arthur and Maggie Rose (Peoples) P.; m. Mary E. Galloway, July 13, 1951; children: Kathleen, Mark Adam. BS, Jackson State U., 1950; MA, U. Chgo., 1951, PhD, 1961. Tchr. math. Froebel Sch., Gary, Ind., 1951-58; asst. prin. Lincoln Sch., Gary, 1958-62; prin. Banneker Sch., Gary, 1962-64; asst. to pres. Jackson (Miss.) State U., 1964-66, v.p., 1966-67, pres., 1967-84; Trustees disting. prof. Univs. Ctr. of Jackson, 1984-85; asst. to pres. SUNY, Binghamton, 1965-66; cons. in higher edn., 1985—. Lectr. summers numerous univs. and colls. Contbr. articles to profl. jours. Active Boy Scouts Am.; bd. govs. So. Regional Edn. Bd.; bd. visitors Air U.; adv. com. U.S. Army Command and Gen. Staff Coll.; mem. Commn. Excellence Am. Assn. State Colls. and Univs.; bd. commrs. Jackson Airport Authority. Served with USMCR, 1944-47. Recipient Disting. Am. award Nat. Football Found., Presdl. citation, Lifetime Achievement award Nat. Black Coll. Alumni Found., 1993—; named to Southwestern Athletic Hall of Fame. Mem. Am. Council Edn. (chmn. dir. 1975), Am. Assn. Higher Edn. (dir. 1971-74), NEA, Miss. Tchrs. Assn., Jackson C. of C. (econ. council), Alpha Kappa Mu, Phi Kappa Phi, Phi Delta Kappa, Omega Psi Phi (Man of Year, Sigma Omega chpt. 1966), Sigma Pi Phi. Lodges: Masons (33 deg.).

**PEOPLES, JOHNNY RAY,** music educator; b. West Plains, Mo., Sept. 24, 1964; s. James and Brenda Peoples; life ptnr. Steve Downey; children: Adam Miles, Nathaniel Ronald, Logan Scott, Abbey Christine. MusB in Edn., Ark. State U., 1987, MusM in Edn., 1988. Choral dir. Forrest City H.S.; music educator Mt. View (Mo.) Birch Tree Schs., 1989—90; choral dir. Westminster Presbyn. Ch., Des Moines, 1991—93, Valley H.S., West Des Moines, 1992—93, Marked Tree (Ark.) Schs., 1994—95; music educator Nettleton Schs., Jonesboro, Ark., 1995—99, Plainview (Ark.) Rover Schs., 1999—2000; choral dir. East Jr. H.S., West Memphis, Ark., 2001—. Organist Cornerstone United Meth. Ch., Jonesboro, Ark., 1995—2001; music dir. First United Meth. Ch., West Memphis, 2001—03; asst. conductor Memphis Vocal Arts Ensemble, 2004—; tenor soloist St. John's United Meth. Ch., Memphis, 2004—. Recipient Outstanding Young Men in Am. award, 1999, Nat. Multicultural Honors Choir, Am. Choral Dirs. Assn., 2001, State, Reg. Finalist, Nat. Assn. Tchrs. of Singing, 1988. Mem.: Ark. Choral Dirs. Assn., Am. Choral Dir. Assn. D-Liberal. Meth. Home: 87 N Highland Memphis TN 38111 Office: East Jr H S 1151 Goodwin Ave West Memphis AR 72301-2714 Personal E-mail: choirman41@hotmail.com.

**PEPE, FRANK A.,** cell and developmental biology educator; b. Schenectady, May 22, 1931; s. Rocco and Margherita (Ruggiero) P. BS, Union Coll., 1953; PhD, Yale U., 1957. Instr. anatomy U. Pa., Phila., 1957-60, assoc. in anatomy, 1960-63, asst. prof., 1963-65, assoc. prof., 1965-70, prof., 1970-92, chmn. dept. anatomy, 1977-90, prof. cell. and devel. biology, 1992-96, emeritus prof., 1996—. Editor: Motility in Cell Function, 1979. Recipient Rsch. Career Devel. award USPHS, 1968-73, Raymond C. Truex Disting. Lecture award Hahneman U., 1988. Fellow AAAS; mem. Am. Assn. Anatomists, Am. Chem. Soc., Biophys. Soc., Microscopy Soc. Am., Sigma Xi. Home: 4614 Pine St Philadelphia PA 19143-1808 E-mail: fpepe@mail.med.upenn.edu.

**PEPER, CHRISTIAN BAIRD,** lawyer; b. St. Louis, Dec. 5, 1910; s. Clarence F. and Christine (Baird) Peper; m. Ethel C. Kingsland, June 5, 1935 (dec. Sept. 1995); children: Catherine K. Peper Larson(dec.), Anne Peper Perkins, Christian B.; m. Barbara C. Pleiter, Jan. 25, 1996. AB cum laude, Harvard U., 1932; LLB, Washington U., 1935; LLM, Yale U., 1937. Bar: Mo. 1934. Pvt. practice, St. Louis; of counsel Blackwell Sanders Peper Martin LLP, St. Louis. Instr. Washington U. Law Sch., St. Louis, 1943—61; ptnr. A. G. Edwards & Sons, 1945—67; pres. St. Charles Gas Corp., 1953—72; bd. dirs. El Dorado Paper Bag Mfg. Co., Inc. Editor: (book) An Historian's Conscience: The Correspondence of Arnold J. Toynbee and Columba Cary-Elwes, 1986. Mem. vis. com. Harvard Div. Sch., 1964—70. Sterling fellow, Yale U., 1936. Mem.: ABA, East India Club (London), St. Louis Bar Assn., Mo. Bar Assn., Harvard Club, Noonday Club, Univ. Club, Order of Coif, Phi Delta Phi. Roman Catholic. Home: 1454 S Mason Rd Saint Louis MO 63131-1211 Office: Blackwell Sanders Peper Martin LLP 720 Olive St Saint Louis MO 63101-2338 Office Phone: 314-345-6000. Business E-Mail: cpeper@blackwellsanders.com.

**PEPER, GEORGE FREDERICK,** writer, retired publishing executive; b. Nyack, NY, Jan. 25, 1950; s. Gerhard Wilhelm and Doris Elene (Bargfrede) Peper; m. Elizabeth Marshall White, May 20, 1978; children: Timothy William, Christopher Scott. BA in English and Comparative Lit., Princeton U., 1972; postgrad., Yale U., 1973. Assoc. editor Winchester Press, NYC, 1973—75; communications dir. Met. Golf Assn., NYC, 1976; assoc. editor, exec. editor Golf Mag., NYC, 1976—78, editor, 1979—90, editor-in-chief, 1990—2002, editor-at large, 2002—; editl. dir. Golf Mag. Properties, NYC, 1992—2002, sr. v.p., bus. devel. Grey Town Golf LLC, Pebble Beach, CA; Fife, Scotland. Author: Scrambling Golf, 1977, Golf's Supershots, 1982, Masters Tournament Anns., 1983—, The PGA Championship 1919-1984, The PGA Championship, 1985, Golf Courses of the PGA Tour, 1986, 1994, Grand Slam Golf, 1991, Golfwatching: A Viewer's Guide to World Golf, 1995, The Story of Golf, 1999, The 500 World's Greatest Golf Holes, 2000, Playing Partners, 2003, The Secret of Golf, 2005, Two Years in St. Andrews, 2006; co-author: Shark Attack: Greg Norman's Guide to Aggressive Golf, 1988, Greg Norman's Instant Lessons, 1993, Golf Mags. Complete Book of Golf Instructions, 1997, Cinderella Story, My Life in Golf, 1999; scriptwriter: Jack Nicklaus-The Year in Golf, 1994; Official U.S. Open Video, 1994—97, Official PGA Championship Video, 1994—98; editor: Golf in America: The First 100 Yrs., 1988, Shinnecock Hills Golf Club, 1981—92, Official U.S. Sr. Golf Video, 1998. Nominee for Emmy award Best Original Script for The Story of Golf, 1999; recipient Time's Mirror Chmns. award, 1997. Mem.: Am. Soc. Mag. Editors, Turnberry Golf Club (Scotland), Royal and Ancient Golf Club of St. Andrews (Scotland), Met Golf Writers Assn.,

Nat. Golf Found. (bd. dirs. 1996—), Golf Writers Assn. Am. (bd. dirs. 1996—98), Local Lomond Golf Club (Scotland), Sleepy Hollow Country Club. Office: Grey Town Golf LLC 4117 Sunridge Rd Pebble Beach CA 93953 Home: Scotland*

**PÉPIN, JACQUES G.**, chef; b. Bourg-en-Bresse, France, Dec. 1935; arrived in U.S., 1959; m. Gloria Pépin. MA in 18th Century French Lit., Columbia U., 1972. Personal chef to three French heads of state, including Charles de Gaulle, 1956—58; employee Le Pavillon restaurant, NYC; dir. of rsch. and new devel. Howard Johnson Co.; dean French Culinary Inst., NYC. Adj. faculty mem. Boston U.; Founder Am. Inst. of Wine and Food; mem. Nat. Assn. of Cooking Profls.; bd. trustees James Beard Found. Former columnist New York Times, columnist Food & Wine mag., Host with daughter (PBS TV series) Jacques Pépin's Kitchen: Cooking with Claudine, 1998, Jacques Pépin's Kitchen: Encore with Claudine, 1998, Host with Julia Child, Julia and Jacques Cooking at Home (James Beard Found. award for Best Nat. Cooking Show, 2001; Daytime Emmy award, 2001); author: (cookbooks) La Technique, 1976, La Methode, 1979, Jacques Pépin Celebrates (James Beard award, 2002), 2001, Jacques Pépin's Complete Techniques, 2001, The Apprentice: My Life in the Kitchen, 2003, Jacques Pépin's Fast Food My Way, 2004. Recipient Chevalier de L'Ordre du Mérite Agricole, France, 1992, Chevalier de L'Ordre des Arts et des Lettres, 1997, Disting. Alumni, Columbia Univ. Sch. of General Studies, Lifetime Achievement award, The James Beard Found., 2005. Avocation: painting.*

**PEPONIS, HAROLD ARTHUR**, insurance agent, portfolio manager; b. Chgo., Dec. 12, 1928; s. Arthur Harold and Ethel (Karambis) P.; m. Toula H. (Preketes), Mar. 1, 1952 (dec. Dec. 1984); one child, Arthur Harold II; m. Aphrodite E. (Stavros), May 26, 1990. BS, Loyola U., Chgo., 1950, postgrad., 1991. Treas. Plaza Cleaners and Dyers, Inc., Chgo., 1950—58; owner Exch. Cleaners, Chgo., 1958—63, Park West Plaza Cleaners, Chgo., 1963—69; ins. agt. Aetna Life and Casualty, Lisle, Ill., 1969—2006; ind. broker Registered Rep., Evanston, Ill., 1995—; ptnr. lecture series, author. Images of Orthodoxy; instr. religion Plato Acad., Chgo., 1998—99. Pres. Tesera Assoc., Evanston, Ill., 1973-2000; dir. Faith Net, Inc., 2003-. Mem. editl. bd. Christianity and Arts mag., 1996-98; columnist Coyote Chronicle Newsletter, 2003-. Pres. parish coun. United Greek Orthodox Ch. of Chgo., 1963—64, Annunciation Cathedral, 1991—92, 1994; archon Order of St. Andrew, Greek Orthodox Ch., state comdr., 1994—2001, regional comdr., 2001—; mem. Greek Orthodox Archdiocesan Coun., 1998—; sec. Metroplis Coun. Greek Orthodox Metroplis of Chgo., 2004—. Recipient Medal of St. Paul, Greek Orthodox Archdiocese, 1999. Mem. Pan Arcadian Fedn. Am. (nat. pres. Chgo. 1963-64), Du Page Life Underwriters Assn., 2626 North Lakeview Condominium Assn. (bd. dirs. 2004-05, sec. bd. dirs. 2005-06, v.p. bd. dirs., 2006-, lectr. Chgo. neighborhood tours 1998—). Home: 2626 N Lakeview Apt 2503 Chicago IL 60614-1821 Office: 2626 No Lakeview Ste 806 Chicago IL 60614 Business E-Mail: hapeonis26@aol.com.

**PEPONIS, JOHN**, architect, educator; b. Athens, Greece, June 21, 1955; s. Anastassios Peponis and Mavra Kanaris; m. Evlabia Periklaki, Oct. 15, 1957; children: Elpida, Mavra Maria. BS in Architecture, U. Coll., London, 1976, MS in Architecture, 1977, PhD in Architecture, 1983. Assoc. prof. Ga. Inst. Tech., Atlanta, 1989—2003, prof., 2003—. Author: (book) Chorographies - Descriptions of Space (in Greek); editor: Contemporary Industrial Buildings in Greece, Proceedings, 3rd International Conference on Space Syntax; contbr. articles to profl. jours., chapters to books; mem. editl. bd. Jour. Arch., Environ. and Planning (B): Planning and Design. With Greek Mil., 1984—85. Grantee, Minsitry Energy, Industry and Rsch., Greece, 1986—88, NSF, 2000—01, GSA, 2002—04, Steelcase Corp., 2004—05. Office: Georgia Inst Tech 247 Fourth St Atlanta GA 30332-0155 Office Phone: + 1 404 894 7667. Business E-Mail: john.peponis@coa.gatech.edu.

**PEPOY, MARYA ALEXANDRA**, healthcare educator, coach; b. Johnstown, Pa., Apr. 10, 1957; d. Stephen Joseph and Gladys Ann (Margo) P. BS in Health and Phys. Edn., Slippery Rock U., 1979, MEd in Curriculum Devel. in Phys. Edn. Tchr. Forest Hills Jr. High Sch., Sidman, Pa., 1979-83, Sacred Heart Elem. Sch., Pinellas Park, Fla., 1984, Chamberlain High Sch., Tampa, Fla., 1984-86; tchr., athletic trainer, coach Conemaugh Twp. High Sch., Davidsville, Pa., 1986—. Intramural organizer, 1979-83; instr. Nautilus Fitness Ctr., 1980-82. Vol. soccer coach Am. Youth Soccer Orgn., 1987-89; vol. coach Spl. Olympics, 1981-83. Named Coach of the Yr., State of Fla., 1985. Mem. NEA, AAHPERD, Pa. State Assn. Health, Phys. Edn., Recreation and Dance, Pa. State Edn. Assn. Nat. Strength and Conditioning Assn., Delta Zeta (pres. 1977-78). Roman Catholic. Avocations: all sports, jogging, weightlifting. Home: PO Box 253 Saint Michael PA 15951-0253 Office: Conemaugh Twp High Sch W Campus Ave Davidsville PA 15928 Office Phone: 814-479-4014.

**PEPPAS, NICHOLAS ATHANASSIOU**, chemical and biomedical engineering educator, consultant; b. Athens, Greece, Aug. 25, 1948; s. Athanassios Nikolaou Peppas and Alice Petrou Rousopoulou; m. Lisa Brannon, Aug. 10, 1988; children: Katherine, Alexander. Diploma in Engring., Nat. Tech. U., Athens, 1971; ScD, MIT, 1973; D honoris causa, U. Parma, Italy, 1999, U. Ghent, Belgium, 1999, U. Athens, 2000. Asst. prof. chem. engring. Purdue U., West Lafayette, Ind., 1976-78, assoc. prof., 1978-81, prof., 1981—2002, Showalter Disting. prof. of chem. and biomed. engring., 1993—2002; prof. chem. engring. U. Tex., Austin, 2003—, prof. biomed. engring., 2003, prof. pharmaceutics, 2003—, Fletcher S. Pratt disting. prof., 2003—. Vis. prof. U. Geneva, 1982-83, Calif. Inst. Tech., Pasadena, 1983, U. Paris, 1986, Hoshi U., Japan, 1994, Hebrew U., Jerusalem, 1994, U. Naples, 1995, Free U. Berlin, 2001, Complutense U. Madrid, 2001; adj. prof. U. Parma, Italy, 1987; cons. in field; mem. adv. bd. several cos. Author: Biomaterials, 1982, Hydrogels in Medicine and Pharmacy, 1987, One Hundred Years of Chemical Engineering, 1989, Pulsatile Drug Delivery, 1993, Biopolymers, 1993, Superabsorbent Polymers, 1994, Biomaterials for Drug and Cell Delivery, 1994, Polymer/Inorganic Interfaces, 1995, Physicochemical and Cellular Foundations of Biomaterials, 2004; contbr. over 900 articles and over 300 abstracts to jours. Active Austin Symphony Orch., Transfiguration Orthodox Ch. Austin. Recipient APV medal, Herbert McCoy award Purdue U., 2000. Fellow: AIChE (chem. materials divsn. 1988—90, dir. bioengring. divsn. 1994—97, bd. dirs. 1999—2002, Materials Engring. Sci. award 1984, Bioengring. award 1994, Best Paper award 1994, William Walker award 2006), Am. Phys. Soc., Italian Soc. Medicine and Scis., Soc. Biomaterials (pres.-elect 2002, pres. 2003—04, Founders award 2005), Am. Phys. Soc., Am. Inst. Med. Biol. Engrs., Am. Assn. Pharm. Scientists (Rsch. Achievements Pharm. Tech. award 1999, Dale Wurster award 2002); mem.: NAE, French Acad. Pharmacy, Biomed. Engring. Soc. (Best Rsch. award 2002), Polymer Pioneer, Am. Soc. Engring. Edn. (AT&T award 1982, Curtis McGraw award 1988, G. Westinghouse award 1992), Soc. Biomaterials (Clemson award 1992), Controlled Release Soc. (pres. 1987—88, Founders award 1991, Eurand award 2002), N.Y. Acad. Sci., Am. Chem. Soc. (Newsmaker of Yr. award 2002), Sigma Xi. Avocations: linguistics, opera, rare maps, classical record collecting, wine collecting. Office: U Tex Dept Chem Engring Austin TX 78712 Office Phone: 512-471-6644. Business E-Mail: peppas@che.utexas.edu.

**PEPPEL, MICHAEL E.**, computer company executive; BA, U. Notre Dame. Money desk mgr. Edward J. DeBartolo Corp., 1987-90; dir., CFO Diversified Data Products, Inc., 1990-96; v.p., CFO Miami Computer Supply Corp., Dayton, Ohio, 1996—.

**PEPPER, ALLAN MICHAEL**, lawyer; b. Bklyn, July 5, 1943; s. Julius and Jeanette (Lasovsky) P.; m. Barbara Benjamin, Aug. 30, 1964; children—Leslie Anne, Joshua Benjamin, Adam Richard, Robert Benjamin BA summa cum laude, Brandeis U., 1967; LL.B. magna cum laude, Harvard U., 1967. Bar: N.Y. 1968, U.S. Dist. Ct. (so. and ea. dists.) N.Y. 1968, U.S. Ct. Appeals (2d cir.) 1968, U.S. Supreme Ct. 1988. Law clk. U.S. Ct. Appeals for 2d Circuit, NYC, 1967-68; assoc. Kaye, Scholer, Fierman, Hays & Handler LLP, NYC, 1968-74; ptnr. Kaye, Scholer LLP, NYC, 1975—. Lectr. in field. Exec. com., assoc. nat. chmn. Brandeis U. Alumni Fund, 1979-82, nat. chmn.

1982-85, chmn. 25th reunion gift com., 1989, devel. com., trustee, 1982-85, pres., councillor, 1980—, 35th reunion gift com., 1999; trustee Brandeis U., 1985-95, sec., 1992-93, budget and fin. com., 1988-95, chmn. com. strategic plan, 1990-91, acad. affairs com., 1985-92, student life and phys. facilities com., 1985-89, vice-chmn. ad hoc by-laws com., 1988-89, long range planning com., 1989-91, chmn. audit com., 1991-95, exec. com., 1990-91; bd. dir. Styles Brook Homeowners Assn., 1990—, exec. com., 1994—, 2d v.p., 2002—; mem. nominating com. Edgemont Sch. Bd., 1992-93; trustee Edgemont Sch. Found., 1994—2002, 2003-; 30th reunion gift com. Harvard Law Sch., 1996-97, class agt., 1998-2001; mem. bd. edn. Edgemont Union Free Dist., Scarsdale, NY, 2006—. Recipient Henry Jones-Golda Meier Bnai Brith Youth Services award, 1986, LI Press Valedictory medal, 1960; Felix Frankfurter scholar Harvard U. Law Sch., 1964-65; Louis D. Brandeis hon. scholar Brandeis U., 1964 Mem. ABA, Assn. Bar City N.Y. (law firm mgmt. com. 1987-91, litig. com, 1998-2001), N.Y. State Bar Assn. (comml. and fed. litig. sect., com. on discovery 1993-97, 2004—), Brandeis U. Alumni Assn. (exec. com. 1982-87, alumni giving strategic planning com., 1992, Alumni Svc. award 1988), Phi Beta Kappa (LI Alumni award 1960), B'nai B'rith (pres. Henry Jones Lodge 1982-84, Westchester-Putnam coun. 1982-85, bd. gov. dist. 1, 1985-86). Democrat. Jewish. Office: Kaye Scholer 425 Park Ave New York NY 10022-3506 Office Phone: 212-836-8665. E-mail: apepper@kayescholer.com.

**PEPPER, BARRY**, actor; b. Campbell River, BC, Can., Apr. 4, 1970; m. Cindy Pepper, Nov. 1997; 1 child. Actor: (films) Urban Safari, 1996, Firestorm, 1998, Saving Private Ryan, 1998, Enemy of the State, 1998, The Green Milc, 1999, Battlefield Earth: A Saga of the Year 3000, 2000, We All Fall Down, 2000, Knockaround Guys, 2001, We Were Soldiers, 2002, 25th Hour, 2002, Mr. Ripley's Return, 2004, Ripley Under Ground, 2005, The Three Burials of Melquiades Estrada, 2005; (TV films) A Killer Among Friends, 1992, Johnny's Girl, 1995, Titanic, 1996, 61*, 2001, others; actor, exec. prodr.: (films) The Snow Walker, 2003; actor, co-exec. prodr: (TV films) 3: The Dale Earnhardt Story, 2004. Office: c/o 9100 Wilshire Blvd W Tower 6th Fl Beverly Hills CA 90212*

**PEPPER, DAVID M.**, physicist, educator, writer; b. LA, Mar. 9, 1949; s. Harold and Edith Pepper; m. Denise Danyelle Pepper, Mar. 19, 1992. BS in Physics summa cum laude, UCLA, 1971; MS in Applied Physics, Calif. Inst. Tech., 1974, PhD in Applied Physics, 1980. Mem. tech. staff Hughes Rsch. Labs., Malibu, Calif., 1973—87, sr. staff physicist, 1987—91, head nonlinear and electro-optic devices sect., 1989—91, sr. scientist, 1991—94; sr. rsch. scientist HRL Labs. (formerly Hughes Rsch. Labs.), Malibu, 1994—2004; owner, rsch. scientist Malibu Sci., 2004—. Adj. prof. math. and physics Pepperdine U., Malibu, 1981—); adv. panel NSF, Washington, 1997; panel advanced signal processing U. Va., 1999; mem. Def. Sci. Rsch. Coun., U.S. Govt., Washington, 1999; presenter in field Author: Scientific American, 1986, 2d edit., 1990; co-author: Optical Phase Conjugation, 1983, Laser Handbook, Vol. 4, 1985, Optical Phase Conjugation, 1995, Spatial Light Modulator Technology, 1995, CRC Handbook of Laser Science and Technology, 1995; contbr. articles to profl. jours. Mem. Sons and Daughters of 1939 Club, 2d Generation of Martyrs Meml., Mus. Holocaust Recipient Rudolf Kingslake award Soc. Photo-Optical Instrumentation Engrs., 1982, Publ. of Yr. award Hughes Rsch. Lab., 1986, Patent award HRL Labs., 1997-2004; NSF trainee Calif. Inst. Tech., 1971; Howard Hughes fellow Hughes Aircraft Co., 1973-80 Fellow Optical Soc. Am. (conf. chair 1996-2001, adv. bd. topical conf. on nonlinear optics, Hawaii 1996, 98, 2000, invited tutorial meeting laser ultrasound 2001, Top 10 cited Paper award); mem. AAAS, IEEE (guest editor, assoc. editor, program com. US CLEO laser conf. 1997-2001, 2005, instr. laser tech. 1994-2000, invited tutorial laser tech. 2001, European CLEO laser conf. program com. 2003), SPIE (guest editor, conf. co-chmn. 1998-2000), N.Y. Acad. Scis., Am. Phys. Soc., Laser Inst. Am., Internat. Coun. Sci. Unions (com. sci. and tech. in developing countries), Sigma Xi (v.p. 1986-87, chpt. pres. 1987-88, 90-92), Sigma Pi Sigma Jewish. Achievements include 41 patents in field; patents pending in field. Avocations: classical music, travel, sports, astronomy. Office: Malibu Scientific P O Box 126 Malibu CA 90265-0126 Personal E-mail: dmpepper@charter.net. *Personal philosophy: We all have a profound, meaningful purpose and mission in life—the challenge is to identify, appreciate, realize and embrace our dreams and goals.*

**PEPPER, JEFFREY MACKENZIE**, publishing executive; b. Dallas, June 11, 1957; s. Doris Jane (Mackenzie) P.; m. Christy Dale Pepper, Nov. 5, 2004; children: Katherine McRaven, Anne Mackenzie. BA, Coll. Wooster, 1979. Sales rep. Acad. Press, N.Y.C., 1979-82; program editor Addison-Wesley Pub. Co., Reading, Mass., 1982-83, acquisitions editor, 1983-86; sr. editor Osborne McGraw-Hill, Berkeley, Calif., 1986-90, editor-in-chief, 1990-95; v.p., editl. dir. Acad. Press Profl., Chestnut Hill, Mass., 1995-97; v.p., editor-in-chief computer books Prentice Hall PTR, Upper Saddle River, NJ, 1997-98, v.p., pub., 1999—2005; exec. editor O'Reilly Media, Inc., 2005—. Contbr. articles to profl. jours. Avocations: storytelling, computers, gardening. Home: 5331 Burriss Ct Southport NC 28461

**PEPPER, JOHN ENNIS, JR.**, former consumer products company executive, historical museum executive; b. Pottsville, Pa., Aug. 2, 1938; s. John Ennis Sr. and Irma Elizabeth (O'Connor) P.; m. Frances Graham Garber, Sept. 9, 1967; children: John, David, Douglas, Susan BA, Yale U., 1960; PhD (hon.), Mt. St. Joseph Coll., St. Petersburg U. Russia, Xavier U. Staff asst. Procter & Gamble Co., Cin., 1963-64, asst. brand mgr., 1964-66, brand mgr., 1966-68, copy supr., 1968-69, brand promotion mgr., 1969-72, advt. mgr. bar soap and household cleaning products divsn., 1972-74, gen. mgr. Italy subs., 1974-77, divsn. mgr. internat., 1977-78, v.p. packaged soap and detergent divsn., 1978-80, group v.p. bar soap and household cleaning products divsn., 1980-81, group v.p. Europe, 1981-84, exec. v.p. U.S. bus., 1984-86, pres. U.S. Bus., 1986-90, pres. internat. bus., 1990-95, chmn., CEO, 1995-99, chmn., 1999—2002, mem. exec. com. of bd., 2000—03; v.p. fin. & adminstrn. Yale U., New Haven, 2004—05. Bd. dirs. Xerox Corp. 1990-2005, Motorola, Inc., 1994-2005, Boston Scientific Corp., 1999-2001, The Walt Disney Co., 2006—. Chmn. U.S. Advisory Com. for Trade Policy and Negotiations; group chmn. Cin. United Appeal Campaign, 1980; bd. trustees Xavier U., 1985-89, mem. exec. com., 1989; trustee Cin. Coun. World Affairs, Cin. Art Mus., Ctr. Strategic & Internat. Studies, Christ Ch. Endowment Fund; fellow Yale Corp.; gen. chmn. United Way Campaign, 1994; mem. Gov.'s Edn. and Bus. Advisory Group, State of Ohio; mem. adv. coun. Yale Sch. Mgmt.; mem. schs. com. Cin. Bus. Com.; co-chmn., mem. exec. com. Cin. Youth Collaborative; mem. Total Quality Leadership steering com.; mem., bd. dirs. United Negro Coll. Fund; former v.p. Am. C. of C., Brussels, Belgium (1981-84); former mem. Cin. Symphony Bd. (1979-81), Cin. Art Mus; bd. mem. Population Services Internat.; honorary co-chair, Nat. Underground Railroad Freedom Ctr, CEO 2006—. Served to lt. USN, 1960—63. Mem. Am. Soc. Corp. Execs., Grocery Mfrs. Am., Nat. Alliance Businessmen (chmn. communication com.), Partnership for a Drug-Free Am., Soap and Detergent Assn. (bd. dirs.), The Bus. Coun., Bus. Roundtable, Yale Club, Queen City Club, Commonwealth Club, Comml. Club (former pres.). Office: Nat Underground Railroad Freedom Ctr 50 E Freedom Way Cincinnati OH 45202*

**PEPPER, JOLINE ROMANO**, psychologist, educator; b. Malden, Mass., Nov. 4, 1971; d. Leo Richard and Geraldine Kathleen Romano; m. Eric Edward Pepper; 1 child, Erica Jade. BA, Merrimack Coll., 1993; MS, U. Mass., 1996. Sch. psychologist North Reading (Mass.) Pub. Schs., 1996—. Adj. faculty mem. Western New Eng. Coll., Mass., 1999—. Recipient Allen J. Ash award, Nat. Honor Soc. in Psychology. Mem.: Nat. Assn. Sch. Psychologists, Psi Chi. Avocation: exercise. Personal E-mail: jpepper@comcast.net.

**PEPPER, JONATHON L.**, media executive; b. Dearborn, Mich., Aug. 23, 1955; s. Joseph Daniel and Norma (McIntyre) P.; m. Diane Sharon Garelis, May 12, 1984; children: Jonathon Jay, Lauren Claire, Scott Joseph. BA, Mich. State U., 1977. Copywriter Detroit Free Press, 1977-84, reporter, 1984-87; nat. corr. Detroit News, 1987-91, bus. columnist, 1991-2000; host talk show

Sta. WXYT, 1995-96; assoc. bus. editor Detroit News, 1997-2000; pres. Small Times Media LLC, Ann Arbor, Mich., 2000—. Mem. Writers Guild Am., The Fairlane Club (vice chmn.). E-mail: jonpepper@ardesta.com.

**PEPPER, PAMELA POE**, psychologist; b. Erwin, NC, Feb. 21, 1953; d. Thomas Wesley Poe, Jr. and Norma Jean (Ferrell) Poe; m. Eugene Vance Pepper, Jr., May 15, 1976; children: Katherine McIver, Anna Faison. BA in Psychology & English, Salem Coll., 1975; MA in Counseling, U. NC, 1980; PhD in Sch. Psychology, U. NC-Chapell Hill, 1992. Lic. psychologist NC, health svcs. provider, psychologist NC, registered electroencephalography tech. Duke U., cert. provider psychol. svcs. traumatic brain injured students NC Dept. Public Instruction. Postdoctoral fellow in neuropsychology Wake Forest U., Bowman Gray Sch. Med., Winston-Salem, NC, 1993—95; rsch. technologist electroencephalography Epilepsy Rsch. Ctr., Va. Med. Ctr., Durham, NC, 1975—76; clin. assoc. biological psychiatry, program dir. electrophysiological tech. Duke U., Durham, 1978—81; mgr. staff edn. & devel. Durham Regional Med. Ctr., 1982—88; postdoctoral fellow in neurology, divsn. neuropsychology Wake Forest U. Bapt. Med. Ctr., Bowman Gray Sch. Medicine, 1993—95; adj. asst. prof. grad. studies edn. Salem Coll., Winston-Salem, 1994; clin. neuropsychologist Salem Psychiatric Assocs., P.A., Winston-Salem, 1995—97; clin. neuropsychologist, found. ptnr. Tri-Care, P.A., Winston-Salem, 1997—2003; clin. neuropsychologist Pepper Neuropsychol. Consulting., PLLC, Winston-Salem, 2004—. Spkr. in field. Bd. advisors quality assurance Qual Choice Behavioral Health, Winston-Salem, 1996—2001; mem. Jr. League Durham, 1975; pres. Durham/Chapel Hill Salem Coll. Alumnae Assn., 1975—76; bd. dirs. So. Soc. Electroencephalographic Technologists, Atlanta, 1980—81, Mental Health Assn. Forsyth County, Winston-Salem, 2000—02. Recipient Order of Scorpion, Salem Coll., 1973—75. Mem.: APA Clin. Neuropsychology Divsn., APA, Internat. Neuropsychol. Soc., Brain Injury Assn. NC (spkrs. bureau 1998—). Democrat. Presbyterian. Avocations: reading, writing, gardening, rock collecting, birdwatching. Office Phone: 336-409-4705. Business E-Mail: drpampepper@aol.com.

**PEPPERS, JERRY P.**, lawyer; b. Cleve., Mar. 8, 1946; s. Jerry P. and Katherine M. Peppers; m. Sue E. Schafer, June 14, 1969; children: Amy E., Erica K., Christina A., Michele S. BBA, Ohio U., 1968; JD, Duke U., 1971. Bar: N.Y. 1972, U.S. Dist. Ct. (so. dist.) N.Y. 1972, U.S. Ct. Appeals (2nd cir.) 1972. Assoc. Pillsbury Winthrop Shaw Pittman LLP, NYC, 1971-81, ptnr., 1982—; co-chair Mergers and Acquisitions Group, 2006—. Mem. N.Am. pension com. The Morgan Crucible Co., Windsor, England. Editor (booklet): Outline of Mergers and Acquisitions in the United States, 15th edit., 2003. Trustee emeritus, mem.alternative investment com. Ohio Univ. Found., Athens, 1991—; trustee Scarsdale Youth Soccer Club, Inc.; bd. dirs. Atheneum Venture Fund, Athens, 1996—; com. mem. Fields for Kids. Mem.: ABA, Soc. Automotive Engrs., Assn. Bar City NY, Internat. Bar Assn., India House, Fox Meadow Tennis Club (Scarsdale, NY). Avocation: coaching soccer. Office: Pillsbury Winthrop Shaw Pittman LLP 1540 Broadway New York NY 10036-4039 Office Phone: 212-858-1205. Business E-Mail: jerry.peppers@pillsburylaw.com.

**PEPPERS, JULIUS**, professional football player; b. Wilson, NC, Jan. 18, 1980; BA in Afro-Am. Studies, U.N.C., Chapel Hill, 2002. Defensive end Carolina Panthers, 2002—. Named to Freshman All-Am. Team, Sporting News, 1999, NFC Pro Bowl Team, 2005; recipient NFL Def. Rookie Yr., 2002—03, Lombardi award for Nations Top Lineman, NCAA, 2001. Office: Carolina Panthers 800 So Mint St Charlotte NC 28202*

**PEPPET, RUSSELL FREDERICK**, accountant; b. Chgo., Oct. 3, 1939; s. George Russell and Elizabeth (Foster) P.; m. Rosemary Meyer, June 18, 1960 (dec. 2000); children—Cynthia, Jeffrey, Scott; m. Sandra S. Wharton, Feb. 2, 2002. BS in Math, Mich. State U., 1960; MBA, Northwestern U., 1963. C.P.A., Ill., Minn. Cons. Peat, Marwick, Mitchell & Co., Chgo., 1961-68, head mgmt. cons. dept. Mpls., 1968-72, partner, 1969-88; sr. cons. partner for Continental Europe, Paris, 1972-78, partner-in-charge mgmt. cons. dept., N.Y. office, 1978-81, vice chmn. mgmt. cons., 1981-86; mng. ptnr. San Jose Bus. Unit, 1986-88; v.p. internat. devel. Towers Perrin, N.Y.C., 1989-90; vice-chmn. Quirk Carson Peppet Inc., N.Y.C., 1990-98; prin. Churchill Capital Inc., N.Y.C., 1999—2001; ptnr. Park Ave. Equity Ptnrs., 2005—. With U.S. Army, 1962-64. Mem. AICPA, Country Club of Darien (Conn.). Home and Office: 5 Topping Ln Norwalk CT 06854-3418

**PEPYNE, EDWARD WALTER**, lawyer, educator, psychologist; b. Springfield, Mass., Dec. 27, 1925; s. Walter Henry and Frances A. (Carroll) P.; m. Carol Jean Dutcher, Aug. 2, 1958; children—Deborah, Edward, Jr., Susan, Byron, Shari, Randy, David, Allison, Jennifer, Jaymie Page. BA, Am. Internat. Coll., 1948; MS, U. Mass., 1951, Ed.D., 1968; postgrad., NYU, 1952-55; prof. diploma, U. Conn., 1964; JD, Western New Eng. Coll., 1978. Bar: Mass. 1978, U.S. Supreme Ct. 1981, Vt. 2004. Prin. tchr. Gilbertville Grammar Sch., Hardwick, Mass., 1948-49; sch. counselor West Springfield High Sch., Mass., 1949-53; instr. NYU, 1953-54; supt. schs. New Shoreham, RI, 1954-56; asst. prof. edn. Mich. State U., 1956-58; sch. psychologist, guidance dir. Pub. Sch. System, East Long, Mass., 1958-62; lectr. Westfield State Coll., 1961-65; dir. pupil services Chicopee Pub. Sch., 1965-68; assoc. prof. counselor edn. U. Hartford, West Hartford, Mass., 1968-71, prof., 1971-85, dir. Inst. Coll. Counselors Minority and Low Income Students, 1971-72, dir. Div. Human Services, 1972-77; cons. Aetna Life & Casualty Co., Hartford, 1962-75; hearing officer Conn. State Bd. Edn., 1980-99; cons. dir. Sinapi Assocs., 1959-78; pvt. practice, Derby, Vt., 1978—. Co-author: Better Driving, 1958; assoc. editor: Highway Safety and Driver Education, 1954; chmn. editorial com.: Man and the Motor Car, 5th edit., 1954; contbr. numerous articles to profl. jours. Chief Welfare Svcs. Civil Def., Levittown, N.Y., 1953-54; chmn. Ashfield Planning Bd., Mass., 1979-83; moderator Town of Ashfield, 1980-81, town counsel, Charlemont, Mass., 1983-84; mem. jud. nominating coun. Western Regional Com., 1993-99; mem. Mohawk Regional Sch. Com., 1999-2000. Mem. ABA, APA, Mass. Bar Assn., Vt. Bar Assn., Mass. Acad. Trial Attys., Am. Pers. and Guidance Assn., New Eng. Pers. and Guidance Assn. (bd. dirs.), New Eng. Ednl. Rsch. Orgn. (pres. 1971), Am. Assn. Sch. Adminstrs., Am. Ednl. Rsch. Assn., Mt. Tom Amateur Radio Assn., Franklin County Amateur Radio Club, Elks, Kiwanis (pres. 1988-89, lt. gov. div. 12, 1991-92), Masons (master 1994-96), Shriners, Phi Delta Kappa. Home: 1585 Pine Hill Rd Newport VT 05855-9830 Personal E-mail: pepyne@earthlink.net.

**PERADOTTO, JOHN JOSEPH**, retired classics educator, editor; b. Ottawa, Ill., May 11, 1933; s. John Joseph and Mary Louise (Giacometti) P.; m. Noreen Doran, Aug. 29, 1959 (div. 1982); m. Marlene Rosen, Aug. 29, 1992; children: Erin, Monica, Noreen, Nicole. BA, St. Louis U., 1957, MA, 1958; PhD, Northwestern U., 1963. Instr. classics and English Western Wash. U., Bellingham, 1960-61; instr. Georgetown U., 1961-63, asst. prof. classics, 1963-66, SUNY, Buffalo, 1966-69, asso. prof., 1969-73; prof., chmn. classics U. Tex., Austin, 1973-74; prof. classics SUNY-Buffalo, 1974-2000, Andrew V.V. Raymond prof. classics, 1984-99, Disting. tchg. prof., 1990-2000, Disting. tchg. prof. emeritus, 2000—, chmn. dept., 1974-77, dean div. undergrad. edn., 1978-82. Benedict Disting. vis. prof. Carleton Coll., 2003; Martin lectr. Oberlin Coll., 1987; dir. summer seminar for coll. tchrs. NEH, 1976, for secondary sch. tchrs., 1984; vis. scholar winter quarters U. Calif., San Diego, 2000—. Author: Classical Mythology: An Annotated Bibliographical Survey, 1973, Man in the Middle Voice: Name and Narration in the Odyssey, 1990, also articles and revs.; founding assoc. editor: Arethusa, editor-in-chief:, 1974—95, mem. bd. editors: SUNY Press, 1978—81; editor: SUNY Press Classical Series, 1981—2000, Classical Literature and Contemporary Literary Analysis, 1977, Women in the Ancient World, 1978, 1983, Studies in Latin Literature, 1984, Under the Text; co-editor: Marxism and the Classics, 1986, Herodotus and the Invention of History, 1987, Gonimos: Neoplatonic and Byzantine Studies Presented to L.G.

Westerlink at 75, 1988, The Challenge of Black Athena, 1989, Pastoral Revisions, 1990, Reconsidering Ovid's Fasti, 1992, Bakhtin and Classical Studies, 1993, Rethinking the Classical Canon, 1994, Horace: 2000 Years, 1995, The New Simonides, 1996, The Iliad and its Contexts, 1997. Fellow Center for Hellenic Studies, 1972-73; recipient Chancellor's award for teaching excellence State U. N.Y., 1975, Disting. Retiring Editor award Coun. of Editors of Learned Jours., 1995. Mem. Am. Philol. Assn. (dir. 1974-77, pres. 1990), Classical Assn. Atlantic States (exec. com 1976-78). Office: Dept Classics State U Ny Buffalo NY 14261-0011 Office Phone: 716-645-2154 ext. 115. Business E-Mail: peradott@buffalo.edu.

**PERALTA, EVERETT FIGUEROA,** social sciences educator; b. Hermosillo, Sonora, Mex., May 20, 1954; came to U.S., 1958; s. Everado Grijalva and Dora (Figueroa) P. BS, SUNY, Albany, 1985. Resident dir. Ariz. State U., Tempe, 1979-82; coord. leadership devel. program U. Bridgeport, Conn., 1982-85; dir. Grad. Student Assn. Ariz. State U., Tempe, 1985-87; vice-chmn. Ariz. State Bd. Econ. Planning and Devel., Phoenix, 1987-88; sr. mgmt. cons. Crystal Resources, Tempe, 1988—94; tchr. Creighton Elem. Sch. Dist., 1995—97; tchr., substitute prin. Maricopa County Regional Schs., 1997—2001; prof. edn. Am. Indian Coll., 2001—, chmn. Dept. Edn., 2005—. Exec. dir. Coun. Family Concerns and Resources, 1993—95; prof. Cochise C.C., 1990—94, We. Internat. U., 2005—; presenter in field; cons. in field. Author: College Study Skills, 1992, Organizational Development and Leadership Skills, 1985. Bd. dirs. Rural Schs. Project, Willcox, 1972-73, Cochise County Learning Adv. Coun., Bisbee, Ariz., 1991-1994; election bd. clk. City of Willcox, 1992; mem. commn. Tempe City Transp. Commn., 1989; precinct committeeman, dep. registrar Rep. Cen. Com., Maricopa County, Ariz., 1983. Recipient Leadership award Omicron Delta Kappa; named one of Outstanding Young Men Am. Mem. UN Assn. (state treas., bd. dirs. Conn. chpt. 1984-85), Ctr. for Study of Presidency, K.C. (3d degree knight), Theta Kappa Epsilon. Avocations: reading, writing, politics, public speaking, woodwork and carpentry. Home: 10020 North 15th Avenue Phoenix AZ 85021 Office Phone: 602-944-3335.

**PERALTA, PEDRO,** mechanical engineer, educator, consultant; m. Jessenia Ortiz, Sept. 13, 1997. BSME, Univ. Simon Bolivar, Caracas, Venezuela, 1989; MSME, U. Pa., 1994, PhD in Materials Sci., 1996. Postdoctoral fellow Los Alamos (N.Mex.) Nat. Lab., 1996—98, vis. scientist, 1999—; asst. prof. Ariz. State U., Tempe, 1998—2004, assoc. prof., 2004—. Grantee, NSF, 2000—05. Mem.: ASME (Orr Award 2005), Minerals, Metals and Materials Soc. Office: Ariz State U Engrint Ctr G-Wing Rm 346 Tempe AZ 85287-6106 Office Phone: 480-965-2849.

**PERALTA-VIDEA, JOSE R.,** environmental scientist, researcher; b. Pueblo Nuevo, Nicaragua; MS, Tropical Agrl. Rsch. & Higher Edn. Ctr., Costa Rica, 1978; PhD, Postgraduate Coll., Mex., 1986, U. of Tex. at El Paso, 2002. Cert. Agronomist Nat. Sch. of Agrl., Managua, Nicaragua, 1975. Rschr. coffee program Ministry of Agr., Managua, Nicaragua, 1974—76; leader cocoa program Ctrl. Bank of Nicaragua, Managua, 1978—79; sub-leader agrl. rsch. Agrl. Devel. Ministry, Managua, Nicaragua, 1979—82; prof., rschr. grad. coll., plant breeding dept. "Hermanos Escobar" Agricltrural Sch., Ciudad Juarez, Mexico; HS prin. Monterey Inst. of Tech., Ciudad Juarez, Mexico, 1992—95; assoc. prof. Monterrey Inst. of Tech., Ciudad Juarez, Mexico, 1995—99; rsch. asst. U. of Tex. at El Paso, 1999—2001, rsch. specialist, 2001—. Recipient Best H.S. full prof., Monterrey Inst. of Tech., 1993, 1997, Outstanding Doctoral Student award, U. of Tex. at El Paso, 2002; grantee, U.S. Dept. of Energy, 2003—05, SW Ctr. For Environ. Rsch. and Policy, 2005—06, Stanford Synchrotron Radiation Lab. (Ssrl), 2005—. Mem.: Soc. for Advancement of Chicanos and Native Ams. in Sci. (assoc.), Am. Chem. Soc. (assoc.). Achievements include patents for Production of gold and silver nanoparticles by living plants; research in uptake and translocation of inorganic elements within the transport system of vascular plants exposed to excess heavy metals; use of growth factors and chelating agents to enhance the metal translocation from the roots to the leaves and the effects produced on the whole-plant element accumulation. Office: Univ of Texas at El Paso 500 West Univ Ave El Paso TX 79968 Office Phone: 915-747-8998. Business E-Mail: jperalta@utep.edu.

**PERCIVAL, MEGHAN JEANNE,** secondary school educator; d. Catherine Anne Pervical. BA, Cath. U. Am., Washington, 1998; MEd, U. Va., Charlottesville, 2001. Tchr. McLean HS, Va., 1998—. Named Tchr. of Yr., McLean HS, McLean C. of C., 2005; recipient Freeman award, Va. Assn. Journalism Tchrs. and Advisors, 2005. Mem.: Columbia Scholastic Press Assn., Nat. Scholastic Press Assn., Nat. Coun. Social Studies. Office: Arlington HS 1633 Davidson Rd Mc Lean VA 22101

**PERCIVAL, NORA LOURIE,** writer, retired editor; b. Samara, Samara Province, Russia, Oct. 14, 1914; arrived in U.S., 1922; d. Adolph and Adalia (Olga) Eliasberg Gund; m. Herman Gund, 1936 (dec. 1939); 1 child, Peter Herman Gund; m. James Percival, 1943 (dec. 1984); children: Elizabeth, Julia (Jill) Wynns, Laurie Oates, Nora James. BA, Barnard Coll., 1936. Dir. of alumnae affairs Barnard Coll., N.Y.C., 1969—73; editor periodicals Am. Mgmt. Assn., N.Y.C., 1961—69. Counselor to women workers Sperry Gyroscope Co., Lake Success, NY, 1942—45. Author: Weather of the Heart, 2003 (Memoir of the Yr., HCW, 2003), Silver Pages on the Lawn, 2004 (Biography of the Yr., HCW, 2005). Mem.: High Country Writers, Sr. Scholars (life). Avocations: reading, gardening, travel, music. Personal E-mail: noralp@goboone.net.

**PERCUS, JEROME KENNETH,** physicist, researcher; b. NYC, June 21, 1926; s. Philip M. and Gertrude B. (Schweiger) P.; m. Ora Engelberg, May 20, 1965; children: Orin, Allon. BSE.E., Columbia U., 1947, MA, 1948, PhD, 1954. Instr. elec. engring. Columbia U., N.Y.C., 1952-54; asst. prof. Stevens Inst. Tech., Hoboken, NJ, 1955-58; assoc. prof. NYU, N.Y.C., 1958-65, prof. physics, 1965—. Dir. Nat. Biomed. Research Found. Author: (book) Many-Body Problem, 1963, Kinetic Theory and Statistical Mechanics, 1969, Combinatorial Methods, 1971, Combinatorial Methods in Developmental Biology, 1977, Mathematical Methods in Developmental Biology, 1978, Mathematical Methods in Enzymology, 1984, Lectures on the Mathematics of Immunology, 1986, Mathematics of Genome Analysis, 2001; editor: (Jours.) Pattern Recognition, Jour. Statis. Physics. With USN, 1944-46. Recipient Pregel Chemistry Physics award N.Y. Acad. Scis., 1975, Joel Henry Hildebrand award in the Theoretical and Exptl. Chemistry of Liquids, Am. Chem. Soc., 1993, Pattern Rec. Soc. award, 1992. Fellow AAAS, Am. Phys. Soc.; mem. Am. Math. Soc., Sigma Xi. Office: NYU 251 Mercer St New York NY 10012-1110 Business E-Mail: percus@cims.nyu.edu.

**PERCY, HELEN SYLVIA,** physician; b. Atlanta, May 7, 1923; d. George L. and Sophia (Toulchin) P.; 1 child, Valentina Stewart-Annor. BS, U. San Francisco, 1951; MD, Med. Coll. Pa., 1958. Diplomate Am. Bd. Family Practice. Intern Harbor Gen. Hosp., Torrance, Calif., 1958-59, resident, 1959; physician Maui Med. Group, Lahaina, Hawaii, 1968—; asst. prof. medicine U. Hawaii, Honolulu, 1977—2000. Adv. bd. Maui Community Health Ctr., 1986-89; v.p. Maui AIDS Found., 1986-89. Mem. AMA, Maui County Med. Soc. (councilor 1988—), Hawaii Med. Assn. (Maui councilor). Democrat. Buddhist. Avocation: dance. Office: Maui Med Group 130 Prison St Lahaina HI 96761-1247 Office Phone: 808-661-0051.

**PERCY, LEE EDWARD,** motion picture film editor; b. Kalamazoo, Feb. 10, 1953; s. Richard Noyes and Helen Louise (Sheffield) P. Student, Goodman Sch., Chgo., 1971, Juilliard Sch., 1972; AB, U. Calif., Santa Cruz, 1977. Radio news reporter McGovern Campaign, Chgo., 1972; cons. Kjos Pub. Co., Chgo., 1973-74; dir. VisArt, Ltd., San Francisco 1977; ind. film editor L.A., 1978—. Editor: (films) Re-Animator, 1984, Kiss of the Spiderwoman, 1985 (Acad. award Best Actor), Slam Dance, 1987, Checking Out, 1988, Blue Steel, 1989, Reversal of Fortune, 1990 (Acad. award Best Actor), Year of the Gun, 1991, Single White Female, 1992, Against the Wall, 1993 (Eddie award, 1995, nominated for Cable ACE award), Corrina, Corrina, 1994, Kiss of Death, 1995, Before and After, 1996, Desperate Measures, 1997, "54", 1998,

Boys Don't Cry, 1999 (Acad. award Best Actress), The Center of the World, 2001, Lift, 2001, The Believer, 2001 (winner Sundance Film Festival), Our Lady of the Assassins (La Virgen de los Sicarrios), 2001, Murder by Numbers, 2002, Maria Full of Grace, 2003 (Sundance Film Festival Audience award, Best Actress at Venice Film Festival), A Home at the End of the World, 2004, A Love Song for Bobby Long, 2004, The Ice Harvest, 2005, Mrs. Harris, 2006, Wind Chill, 2006. Mem. Am. Cinema Editors, Acad. of Motion Picture Arts and Scis., Motion Picture Editor's Guild.

**PERDEW, JOHN PAUL,** physics professor; b. Cumberland, Md., Aug. 30, 1943; BS, Gettysburg Coll., 1965; PhD, Cornell U., 1971. Postdoctoral fellow U. Toronto, 1971-74, Rutgers U., New Brunswick, NJ, 1974-77; prof. physics Tulane U., New Orleans, 1977—, chair physics dept., 1991—94, 2001—03. Vis. scientist Nordita, Copenhagen, Argonne Nat. Lab., ETH Zurich, ITP Santa Barbara, Naval Rsch. Lab., Washington, Rice U.; invited lectr. numerous internat. confs. Contbr. more than 200 sci. articles to profl. jours. NSF Rsch. grantee, 1978—, Petroleum Rsch. Fund grantee 1998-2000; recipient Tulane LAS award for excellence in rsch., 1990. Fellow Am. Phys. Soc.; mem. Am. Chem. Soc., Am. Assn. Physics Tchrs., Internat. Acad. Quantum Molecular Sci., Phi Beta Kappa. Office: Tulane U Dept Physics New Orleans LA 70118 Business E-Mail: perdew@tulane.edu.

**PERDIGÓ, LUISA MARINA,** foreign language and literature educator; b. Havana, Cuba, Dec. 25, 1947; came to U.S. 1962; d. Mario and Hortensia Dolores (Alvarez) P. AB, CUNY, 1971, MA, 1974, PhD, 1981; MA, Columbia U., 1987. LPN, 2005; cert. translator English/Spanish Am. Translators Assn., ins. and coding specialist. Asst. prof. Spanish, asst. dean St. Thomas Aquinas Coll., Sparkill, NY, 1982-87; asst. prof. Spanish and French CUNY, La Guardia, 1987-88, asst. prof. Spanish, City Coll., 1988-89; asst. prof. Spanish St. Peter's Coll., Jersey City, 1989-91; asst. prof. Spanish and French Clarion U., Pa.: 1992-94, Rockland Coll. SUNY, 1995-96, Mercy Coll., 1998—. Author: La Estética de Octavio Paz, 1975, The Origins of Vicente Huidobro's Creacionismo (1911-1916) and its Evolution (1917-47), 1994, The Lyrics of the Troubadour Perdigon, 2002, (poetry) Desde el Hudson/From the Hudson, 1993, Huellas/Footprints, 1997, America at the Millenium, 2000, The Best Poems and Poets of 2002, Theatre of the Mind, 2003; author numerous poems; contbr. articles to profl. jours. Participant seminar in poetry, NEH, U. Kans., 1991; Rsch. fellow Orgn. Am. States, Chile, 1981; grantee CUNY, 1975; scholar Columbia U., 1982-84. Mem. MLA, Clarion Hist. Soc., Circulo de Cultura Panamericano, Sigma Delta Pi, Pi Delta Phi.

**PERDIKIS, GALEN,** plastic surgeon; MB BCh, U. Witwatersrand, South Africa, 1988. Asst. prof. dept. plastic surgery Mayo Clinic, Jacksonville, Fla., 2001—. Contbr. articles to profl. jours. Recipient Trubshaw prize, Coll. of Medicine, South Africa, 1993, Golden Apple, Student Body, Creighton U., 1999; Herbert Davis scholarship, Creighton U., 1999. Fellow: ACS; mem.: Southeastern Soc. of Plastic and Reconstructive Surgeons, Greater Jacksonville Soc. of Plastic Surgeons, Am. Soc. of Plastic Surgery, Alpha Omega Alpha. Office: Mayo Clinic 4500 San Pablo Rd Jacksonville FL 32224 Office Phone: 904-953-2073.

**PERDIKOU, KIM,** information technology executive; BSc. Comp. Sci. and Operational Rsch., Paisley U., Scotland; MA Info. Systems, Pace U. Dir. Network Svcs. Knight Ridder; VP, CIO Women.com Networks, Inc., 1999—2000; CIO Juniper Networks, Inc., Calif., 2000—. Office: Juniper Networks Inc 1194 N Mathilda Ave Sunnyvale CA 94089

**PERDUE, BEVERLY EAVES,** lieutenant governor, geriatric consultant; b. Grundy, Va., Jan. 14, 1948; d. Alfred P. and Irene E. (Morefield) (dec.) Moore; m. Robert W. Eaves, Jr.; children: Garrett, Emmett. BA, U. Ky., 1969; MEd, U. Fla., 1974, PhD, 1976. Pvt. lectr., writer, cons., 1980-86; pres. The Perdue Co., New Bern, N.C., 1985—; rep. N.C. State Gen. Assembly, Raleigh, 1986-90; senator N.C. Gen. Assembly, Raleigh, 1990-2001; lt. gov. State of N.C., 2001—. Bd. dirs. Nations Bank, New Bern. Bd. dirs. N.C. United Way, Greensboro, 1990-92; exec. mem. N.C. Dem. Party, Raleigh, 1989—; mem. N.C. travel bd. Nat. Conf. State Legislators. Named Outstanding Legislator, N.C. Aging Network, 1989, 92, 100 to Watch, Dem. Leadership Coun. 2003; Toll fellow Nat. Conf. State Legislators, Lexington, Ky., 1992. Mem. Nat. Coun. on Aging, Bus. and Profl. Women, Rotary. Democrat. Episcopalian. Office: Office of Lt Governor 310 N Blount Blvd 20301 Raleigh NC 27699-0401 Office Fax: 919-733-7350, 919-733-6595. E-mail: bperdue@ncmail.net.*

**PERDUE, DAVID A., JR.,** finance company executive, consultant; b. Macon, Ga., Dec. 10, 1949; s. David A. Sr. and Gervaise (Wynn) P.; m. Bonnie Dunn Perdue, Aug. 26, 1972; children: David A. III, Blake R. BS, Ga. Inst. Tech., 1972, M in Ops. Rsch., 1975. Registered securities principal; cert. fin. planner; cert. mgmt. cons. Staff cons. Kurt Salmon Assocs., NYC, 1972-75, ptnr., 1976—83; v.p. Profl. Planning Assocs., Atlanta, 1983-86, Paul R. Ray and Co., Atlanta, 1986-87; pres. Wester Holding Co., Atlanta, 1987—92; senior v.p. ops. Sara Lee Corp., Hong Kong, China, 1992—94; senior v.p. Haggar Inc., 1994—98; senior v.p. Global Supply Chain Reebok Intern. Ltd., 1998—99, exec. v.p. Global Oper. Units, Reebok Brand, 1999—2001, exec. v.p Global Supply Chain, 2001—02, pres., CEO Reebok Brand, 2001—02; chmn., CEO Pillowtex Corp., 2002—03, Dollar General, 2003—. Mem. investor liaison com. Mortgage Banking Assn., Atlanta, 1989—; bd. dirs. Carl R. Young Sr. Trust, Johnson City, Tenn., Alliant Energy Corp., Ga. Tech. Adv. Bd. Mem. Ga. Coun. on Youth, Atlanta, 1972, Atlanta Care Adv. Bd., 1983-85, Atlanta Athletic Club House Com., 1988—. Mem. Mortgage Banking Assn., Inst. Cert. Fin. Planners, Inst. Mgmt. Cons. Atlanta Athletic Club. Republican. Baptist. Avocations: tennis, golf, sailing, reading. Office: Westar Holding Co PO Box 720132 Atlanta GA 30358-2132*

**PERDUE, GEORGE (SONNY PERDUE),** governor, former state legislator; b. Perry, Ga., Dec. 20, 1946; s. Ervin and Ophie Perdue; m. Mary (Ruff); children: Leigh, Lara, Jim, Dan. PhD in Vet. Medicine, U. Ga. Mem. Ga. Senate (dist. 18), Atlanta, 1990—2002; pres. pro tem; mem. appropriations, ethics, rules, reapportionment coms.; also fin. and pub. utilities, health and human svcs. coms.; former chmn. higher edn., def. conversion com.; co-chair joint commn. legis. info. mgmt.; gov. State of Ga., Atlanta, 2003—. Capt. USAF, 1971-74, Vietnam. Democrat. Baptist. Office: Office of the Gov 203 State Capitol Atlanta GA 30334 Office Phone: 404-656-1776.*

**PERDUE, JAMES A. (JIM PERDUE),** food products executive; b. 1949; BS, Wake Forest U., 1973; MA in Marine Biology, Southeastern Mass. U., 1976; PhD in Fisheries, U. Wash., 1983. With U. Md., Cambridge, 1976-78; chmn. bd. Perdue Transp., Inc., Salisbury, Md., 1983—, Perdue Farms Inc., 1983—, CEO, 1991—. Dir. Nat. Chicken Coun. Office: Perdue Farms Inc 31149 Old Ocean City Rd Salisbury MD 21804 Office Phone: 410-543-3743. Office Fax: 410-543-3874. E-mail: jim.perdue@perdue.com.*

**PERDUE, JOHN D.,** state official; b. Manila, W.Va. s. Glenn and Mary Perdue. BS in Agriculture, W.Va. U., 1972. Mem. W.Va. Assn. State Treas. (pres. 2005), W.Va. Forestry Assn., Alpha Gamma Rho, Alpha Tau Alpha. Office: WVa State Treasurers Office 1900 Kanawha Blvd Capital Complex Bldg 1 Rm E-145 Charleston WV 25305 Office Phone: 304-558-5000. Business E-Mail: john.perdue@wvsto.com

**PERDUNN, RICHARD FRANCIS,** management consultant; b. Trenton, N.J., Dec. 12, 1915; s. Francis R. and Edith (Nogle) P.; m. Eugenia E. Morel, June 7, 1941; 1 child, Justine Reneau; m. Doris D. Andrus, Jan. 30, 1993. BS, Lehigh U., 1939; postgrad. student, U. Pitts., 1939-40, Johns Hopkins, 1941-42. With U.S. Steel Co., also Glenn L. Martin, 1939-43, supt. machine and assembly, 1941-43; partner Nelson & Perdunn (engrs. and cons., also); v.p. Penco Corp., 1947-49; with Merck & Co., 1949-54, mgr. adminstrn., 1951-54; with Stevenson, Jordan & Harrison (mgmt. engrs.), N.Y.C., 1954-68, exec. v.p., 1962-64, pres. 1964-68; pres., chief exec. officer Bachman-Jacks, Inc., Reading, Pa., 1968-71; sr. v.p. Golightly Internat., N.Y.C., from

1971, also dir. Chmn. Perdunn Assocs., Inc., 1979—; dir. West Point & Annapolis Text Book Pub. Co., 1948—, Indsl. Edn. Films Inc., 1966—, Eldun Corp., 1964—, Security Nat. Bank, Newark, 1964—, Suburban Life Ins. Co., 1966—, Mainstem Inc., 1965—, Greenhouse Decor Inc., 1961—, Neuwirth Mut. Fund Inc., 1975—; Lectr. on finance and mfg. in, U.S., Can., Eng., Sweden. Assoc. editor: Systems and Procedures Quar, 1948-51; Contbr. articles to profl. publs. Bd. dirs. Inst. Better Confs., Internat. Inst. Bus. Devel., Inst. Urban Affairs, People Care, Inc.; dir. finance Assn. Help for Retarded Children. Served with USAAF, 1942-47. Mem. N.Y.C. C. of C., Council Econ. Devel., Am. Mgmt. Assn., AIM (pres.'s council), Newcomen Soc. N.Am., Systems and Procedures Assn. Am., Soc. Advanced Mgmt. Died May 27, 2006.

**PEREHUDOFF, REBECCA,** artist; arrived in U.S., 1989; BA, LLB, U. Sask.; MA in Art Therapy, U. Ill. One-woman shows include Gallery One, Toronto, 1990, Buschlen-Mowatt Gallery, Vancouver, B.C., 1990, Robertson Gallery, Ottawa, Ont., 1991, 1992, Elca London Gallery, Montreal, 1992, Newzones Gallery Contemporary Art, Calgary, 1996, 1998, SXU Gallery, St.-Xavier U., Chgo., 1997, Fine Arts Gallery, 2000, Art Placement Gallelry, 2005, exhibited in group shows at Buschlen-Mowatt Gallery, Vancouver, 1992, Can. Coun. Art Bank, Montreal, 1992, Buschlen-Mowatt Gallery Artists, Singapore, 1992, Newzones Gallery Contemporary Art, Calgary, 1994, 1995, Gallery One, Toronto, 1996, Tamara Backdrop Studios, Chgo., 1998, pub., pvt., and corp. collections. Mem.: Am. Art Therapy Assn. Office Phone: 708-415-3692. E-mail: rminton2005@sbcglobal.net.

**PEREIRA, FRED A(LFRED),** medical researcher; PhD, U. Manitoba, 1993. Instr. Baylor Coll. Medicine, Houston, 1998—99, asst. prof., 1999—. Recipient Shannon award, NIH-Nat. Inst. Deafness Comm. Disorders, 2000; grantee, Nat. Inst. Deafness Comm. Disorders, 2001—. Mem.: AAAS (assoc.), Nat. Inst. Deafness Comm. Disorders-NIH, Fedn. Am. Socs. Exptl. Biology (assoc.), Am. Rsch. Otorhinolaryngology (assoc.), Soc. Devel. Biology (assoc.), Endocrine Soc. (assoc.). Achievements include research in orphan nuclear receptors in hearing. Office Phone: 713-798-6933. Office Fax: 713-798-1610. E-mail: fpereira@bcm.tmc.edu.

**PEREIRA, HOFFMANN URQUIZA,** music educator; s. Sabino Andrade Pereira and Terezinha Urquiza Andrade; m. Thelma Soares Silva, July 31, 1999. B Música Sacra, Seminário Teológico Batista Norte Brasil, Recife, 1990; Licenciatura em Música, U. Fed. Pernambuco, Recife, 1992; MusM, La. State U., 1997, D Musical Arts, 2006. Asst. prof. music, dir. choral activities Hiwassee Coll., Madisonville, Tenn., 2001—, coord. music dept., 2003—. Mem.: Coll. Music Soc., Am. Choral Dirs. Assn. Office: Hiwassee Coll 225 Hiwassee College Dr Madisonville TN 37354 Office Phone: 423-442-2001 1867. Business E-Mail: pereirhu@hiwassee.edu.

**PEREIRA, JOHN WILLIAM MILLER,** theater educator; s. John Pereira and Madeline Miller. BA, Queens Coll., Flushing, NY, 1975; MA, CUNY, NYC, 1979, MPhil, 1982, PhD, 1986. Adj. assoc. prof. drama, theatre and dance Queens Coll., Flushing, 1978—; asst. prof./adj. assoc. prof. dept. theatre and dance Nassau C.C., Garden City, NY, 1989—. Coord. PhD Alumni Assn. CUNY, NYC, 1980—; cons. CUNY-TV, NYC, 1985—, McGraw-Hill Pub. Co., NYC, 1993—2003, Nat. Com. on Am. Fgn. Policy, NYC, 1993—2002, Am. Theatre Wing, NYC, 2004—05; contbg. writer Theater Week Mag., NYC, 1986—88; manuscript reviewer St. Martin's Press, NYC, 1999; external examiner PhD dissertation James Cook U., Townsville, Australia, 2001. Author: Opening Nights: 25 Years of the Manhattan Theatre Club; dir.: (plays) Twelfth Night, 1987, A Midsummer Night's Dream, 1989, What the Butler Saw, 1990, It's Only a Play, 1999, Three Viewings, The Long Weekend, Art, Office Hours, Say Goodnight, Gracie, Luv, Album, Sylvia; actor: The Imaginary Invalid, 1991, The Palace of the Dead, 1995, Dr. Faustus, 1996; co-editor: (jour.) Nonprofit and Voluntary Sector Quarterly; contbr. articles to profl. jours. Mem.: PhD Alumni Assn. CUNY (bd. dirs.). Office: Nassau Community College One Education Dr Garden City NY 11530-6793 Office Phone: 516-572-8069. Business E-Mail: pereirj@ncc.edu.

**PEREL, DAVID,** editor; Sports editor Washington Post; editor-in-chief Nat. Enquirer, 1986—2005, 2006—; pres. AMI Books, 2005—; editor-in-chief Looking Good Now mag., 2005; exec. v.p. & editl. dir. Globe, 2005, Nat. Examiner, 2005, Sun, 2005, Weekly World News, 2005. Co-author: Freak! Inside the Twisted World of Michael Jackson, 2003, Bat Boy Lives! The Weekly World News Guide to Politics, Culture, Celebrities, Alien Abductions, and the Mutant Freaks That Shape Our World, 2005. Office: National Enquirer 1000 American Media Way Boca Raton FL 33464-1000*

**PEREL, JAMES MAURICE,** pharmacology and psychiatry educator, researcher; b. Buenos Aires, Mar. 30, 1933; came to U.S., 1947, naturalized, 1954; s. Aria and Bella (Silverberg) P.; m. July 18, 1959 (div. 1971); 1 child, Allan B.; m. Audrey Feldman, Apr. 9, 1972; children: Alissa A., Stephen M. BS, CUNY, 1956; MS, NYU, 1961, PhD, 1964. Nuclear chemist N.Y. Naval Shipyard Lab., Bklyn., 1956-58; assoc. rsch. scientist NYU, Goldwater Meml. Hosp., 1964-67; asst. prof. medicine and chemistry Emory U., Atlanta, 1967-70; asst. prof. psychiatry, pharmacology Columbia U. Coll. Physicians and Surgeons, NYC, 1970-76; assoc. prof. clin. pharmacology, chief psychiat. rsch. NY State Psychiat. Inst., NYC, 1976-80; chief clin. pharmacology VA Med. Ctr. Highland Drive, Pitts., 1979-83; prof. psychiatry U. Pitts. Sch. Medicine, 1980—2001, acting chmn. dept. pharmacology, 1985-88, prof. pharmacology, 1980—, prof. emeritus psychiatry, 2001—; dir. clin. pharmacology Western Psychiat. Inst. and Clinic, Pitts., 1980—; prof. grad. neurosci., 1988—; postdoctoral fellow in clin. pharmacology NIH, 1964-67, NYU. Lectr. chemistry CUNY, 1963-67; assoc. rsch. scientist NY State Psychiat. Inst., 1970-76; cons., mem. grant-awarding study sects. NIH, NIMH. Mem. editorial bd. Psychopharmacology, Neuropsychobiology, Therapeutic Drug Monitoring, Focus on Schizophrenia and Bipolar Disorders, Applied PHarmacokinetics and Pharmacodynamics, 4th edit.; contbr. over 400 articles to sci. jours., chpts. to books. Named Psychopharmacologist of Yr., U. Toronto, 1993; named to Honor Roll, Century of Therapeutics and Sci. 1900-2000, Am. Soc. Clin. Pharmacology and Therapeutics; recipient Founders Day award, NYU, 1974, Julius Koch Meml. award, Rho Chi, 1983; predoctoral fellow, NSF, 1955—60, numerous rsch. grants, including NIH, NIMH, Founds. Fund for Rsch. in Psychiatry, pharm. cos., pvt. founds. Fellow: Am. Inst. Chemists; mem.: Soc. Biol. Psychiatry, Internat. Assn. Therapeutic Drug Monitoring and Clin. Toxicology (com. chair), Am. Chem. Soc., Am. Soc. Pharmacology and Exptl. Therapeutics, Am. Soc. Clin. Pharmacology and Therapeutics (sect. chair), Sigma Xi. Jewish. Achievements include discovery of several widely-used pharmacotherapeutic agents. Office: U Pitts Sch Medicine 3811 Ohara St Pittsburgh PA 15213-2593 Office Phone: 412-246-6600. Business E-Mail: pereljm@upmc.edu, pereljm@pitt.edu.

**PERELLA, JOSEPH ROBERT,** investment banker; b. Newark, Sept. 20, 1941; s. Dominic A. and Amy Gralnick, Jan. 20 1974 BS, Lehigh U., 1964; MBA, Harvard U., 1972. C.P.A., N.Y. Pub. acct. Haskins & Sells, NYC, 1964-70; cons. Internat. Bank for Reconstruction & Devel., Washington, 1971; assoc. The First Boston Corp., NYC, 1972-74, asst. v.p., 1974-75, v.p., 1975-78, mng. dir., 1978-88; chmn. Wasserstein, Perella & Co., NYC, 1988—2001; head, investment banking div. Morgan Stanley & Co., Inc., NYC, 1997—2000, chmn., instl. securities, 2000—05; co-founder Perella Weinberg Partners, NYC, 2006—. Trustee Lehigh U. Office: Perella Weinberg Partners 767 Fifth Ave New York NY 10153 Office Phone: 212-287-3200. Office Fax: 212-287-3201.*

**PERELMAN, JEFFREY E.,** real estate company executive; BA with hon., Univ. Ill.; JD, Ill. Inst. Tech. Chgo. Kent Coll. Law. Former owner, mgr. Commodities Brokerage Firm; with Sterling Real Estate Ptnrs., Chgo., 1996—, now prin. Named one of TOP 200 Art Collectors ARTnews Mag., 2006. Avocation: collecting art. Office: Sterling Real Estate Ptnrs Ste 600 1033 Skokie Blvd Northbrook IL 60062*

**PERELMAN, RONALD OWEN,** consumer products company executive; b. Greensboro, NC, Jan. 1, 1943; s. Raymond and Ruth (Caplan) P.; m. Faith Golding, 1965 (div. 1983), 4 children; m. Claudia Cohen, Jan. 11, 1985 (div. 1994), 1 child, Sammantha; m. Patricia Duff, Dec. 20, 1995 (div. Sept. 10, 1998), 1 child, Caleigh Sophia; m. Ellen Barkin, June 28, 2000 (separated. Jan. 19, 2006) BA, U. Pa., 1964; MBA, Wharton Sch. Fin., 1966. With Belmont Industries Inc., 1966-78; chmn., chief exec. officer, dir. MacAndrews & Forbes Holdings Inc., Wilmington, Del., 1983—; chmn., chief exec. officer MacAndrews & Forbes Group Inc. (subs.), NYC, 1978—; chmn., chief exec. officer, dir. Revlon Group Inc. (subs. MacAndrews & Forbes Group Inc.), NYC, 1985—, Revlon Inc. (subs.), NYC, 1985—; also chmn. Nat. Health Labs. Inc., La Jolla, Calif., 1985—, Andrews Group Inc., La Jolla, 1985—; pres. bd. of trustees Solomon R. Guggenheim Mus., La Jolla, 1995—. Named one of Top 200 Collectors, ARTnews Mag., 2004, Forbes Richest Americans, 2006. Jewish. Achievements include being named one of World's Richest People by Forbes in 1999, 2000, 01, 02, 03, 04. Avocation: Collecting Contemporary Art. also: Solomark Guggenheim Mus 1071 5th Ave New York NY 10128-0173 Office: Revlon Consumer Products Corp 466 Lexington Ave Fl 13 New York NY 10017-3227

**PERENCHIO, ANDREW JERROLD,** film and television executive; b. Fresno, Calif., Dec. 20, 1930; s. Andrew Joseph and Dorothea (Harvey) P.; m. Robin Green, July 16, 1954 (div.); children: Candace L., Catherine M., John Gardner; m. Jacquelyn Claire, Nov. 14, 1969 (div.); m. Margaret McHugh, 1987. BS, UCLA, 1954. V.p. Music Corp. Am., 1958-62, Gen. Artists Corp., 1962-64; pres., owner theatrical agy. Chartwell Artists, Ltd., LA, from 1964; chmn. bd. Tandem Prodns., Inc. and TAT Communications Co., LA, 1973-83; pres., CEO Embassy Pictures, LA, 1983—85; pres. Chartwell Partnerships Group, LA; chmn., CEO Univision Communications, 1992—. Promoter Muhammad Ali-Joe Frazier heavyweight fight, 1971, Bobby Riggs-Billie Jean King tennis match, 1973. Served to 1st lt. USAF, 1954-57. Named one of Richest Americans, Forbes Mag., 1999—, World's Richest People, 2001—. Mem.: Bel-Air Country Club (LA); Westchester Country Club, NY; Friars Club, NYC. Office: Univision Communications 1999 Ave Of Stars Ste 3050 Los Angeles CA 90067-4611*

**PERERA, LAWRENCE THACHER,** lawyer; b. Boston, June 23, 1935; s. Guido R. and Faith (Phillips) P.; m. Elizabeth A. Wentworth, July 5, 1961; children: Alice V. Perera Lucey, Caroline F. Perera Barry, Lucy E.Perera Adams, Lawrence Thacher, Jr. BA, Harvard U., 1957, LL.B., 1961. Bar: Mass. 1961, U.S. Supreme Ct. 1973. Clk. Judge R. Ammi Cutter, Mass. Supreme Jud. Ct., Boston, 1961-62; assoc. Palmer & Dodge, Boston, 1962-69, ptnr., 1969-74; judge Middlesex County Probate Ct., East Cambridge, Mass., 1974-79; ptnr. Hemenway & Barnes, Boston, 1979—. Mem. nat. coun. Hon. Nat. Jud. Coll., Reno, prof., pres. Mass. CLE, Inc., 1988-90; trustee Mass. Investors Trust, 1981—; trustee, vice chmn. Boston Found., 1981-1996. Chmn. Boston Fin. Commn., 1969-71; overseer Boston Lyric Opera; chmn. bd. overseers Boston Opera Assn.; chmn. Back Bay Archtl. Commn., 1966-72; trustee emeritus Sta. WGBH Ednl. Found.; Boston Athenaeum, Wang Ctr. Performing Arts, Social Law Libr. Fellow Am. Acad. Matrimonial Lawyers, Am. Coll. Trust and Estate Counsel; mem. ABA, Am. Bar Found., Am. Law Inst., Mass. Bar Assn., Mass. Bar Found., Boston Bar Assn., Boston Bar Found. Home: 18 Marlborough St Boston MA 02116-2101 Office: 60 State St Boston MA 02109-1800

**PERERA, UNIL A.G.,** physics educator, researcher; b. Colombo, Sri Lanka, Nov. 12, 1956; came to U.S., 1982; s. Weymen and Daya (Daluwatta) P.; m. Shrima Y. Samaranayake, July 1, 1983; children: Nuwan, Nirosha. BS in Physics, U. Colombo, 1981; MS, U. Pitts., 1983, PhD, 1987. Asst. lectr. U. Colombo, 1981-82; tchg. asst. U. Pitts., 1982-83, rsch. asst., 1983-87, rsch. assoc., 1987-88, rsch. asst. prof., 1988-92; asst. prof. physics Ga. State U., Atlanta, 1992-95, assoc. prof., 1995-2001, prof., 2001—, grad. dir. physics, 1995—, dir. IRML, 1995—. Lectr. Nat. Rsch. Coun., Ottawa, Ont., Can., 1990, Indiana U. Pa., 1991, Calif. Inst. Tech., 1995, AAAS, Colombo, 1995, Emory U. Atlanta, 1995, U. Colombo, 1997, U. Peradeniya, Sri Lanka, 1997, Tech. U., Vienna, Austria, 1997, U. Linz, Austria, 1997, U. Ill., Chgo., 1998, U. Turkey, Istanbul, 1998, UCLA, 1998, CRL, Tokyo, 1998, Nat. U. Singapore, 1999, Inst. Fund Studies, Sri Lanka, 1999, Inst. for Physics of Microstructure, Nizhny Novogorod, Russia, 2000. Editor: Handbook of Thin Film Devices; contbr. more than 100 articles to profl. jours.; patentee in field. Mentor McNair Program, Atlanta, 1994-97. Grantee NASA, 1997—, NSF, 1990—, Ga. State U., 1992—, others. Fellow Am. Phys. Soc.; mem. IEEE (sr.), Soc. Photo Instrumentation Engrs. Buddhist. Office: Ga State U Dept Physics 29 Peachtree Center Ave NE Atlanta GA 30303-2515 Office Phone: 404-651-3221. Business E-Mail: uperera@gsu.edu.

**PERES, EDWARD M.,** preventive medicine physician, educator; b. Detroit, Aug. 11, 1968; s. Edward and Sally Peres; m. Michelle R. Walker, Nov. 20, 1993; children: Cameron A., Kyle. MD, Ross U., Dominica, 1996. Medical MI, 1997. Bone marrow transplant Karmanos Cancer Ctr., Detroit, 2003—, staff Detoirt, 2003—06. Dir. cord blood bank Karmanos, Detroit, 2004—06. Dir. cord blood program Karmanos, Detoirt, 2004—06; dir. NMDP, Detoirt, 2004—06. Mem.: ASBMT (assoc.). Jewish. Office: Karmanos Cancer Ctr 4100 John R Detroit MI 48201 Office Phone: 3134-576-8711. Business E-Mail: perese@karmanos.org.

**PERES, FRANK J.,** healthcare administrator; b. Havanna, Cuba, Oct. 4, 1943; arrived in U.S., 1962; s. Julian N. and Silvia N. (Hernandez) P.; m. Carmen Rosario Perez, Apr. 10, 1966; children: Shelley, Vanessa, Karen. BS, Columbia Union Coll., 1970; M in Health Care Adminstrn., George Washington U., 1974. Exec. v.p. Christ Hosp., Jersey City, 1974-79; exec. dir. Bella Vista Hosp., Mayaquez, PR, 1979-85, Caribe Hosp. Affiliates, Bayamon, PR, 1985-88; pres. Atlantic Adventist Health care, Stoneham, Mass., 1988-94, Cmty. Hosps. of Ea. Middlesex, Stoneham, 1992-94, New England Meml. Hosp., Stoneham, 1988-94; pres., CEO Kettering (Ohio) Med. Ctr., 1994—. Pres. State Health Facilities Com., Mayaquez, 1985-90; bd. dirs. New Am. Hosp. Assn. Co-author: The Conference Board, 1995; contbr. articles to profl. jours. Trustee Hospice of Dayton, Ohio, 1995-96, Dayton Ballet, 1995-96; bd. dirs. Ohio Quality Cardiac Care Found., Columbus, 1996. Recipient Presdl. Citation for Sustained Bus. Leadership Atlantic Union Coll., 1993; named one of Top 10 Latino Leaders LatinoLeaders mag., 2004 Fellow Am. Coll. of Healthcare Execs., Am. Hosp. Assn., Kettering Coll. of Med. Arts (bd. dirs. 1994-96), Greater Dayton Area Hosp. Assn. (bd. dirs. 1994-96), Dayton Area C. of C. (trustee 1996), PPS State Hosp. Assn. (bd. dirs., v.p., chmn. 1985-88) Office: Kettering Med Ctr 3535 Southern Blvd Kettering OH 45429-1221*

**PERES, JUDITH MAY,** journalist; b. Chgo., June 30, 1946; d. Leonard H. and Eleanor (Seltzer) Zurakov; m. Michael Peres, June 27, 1972; children: Dana, Avital. BA, U. Ill., 1967; M Studies in Law, Yale U., 1997. Acct. exec. Daniel J. Edelman Inc., Chgo., 1967-68; copy editor Jerusalem (Israel) Post, 1968-71, news editor, 1971-75, chief night editor, 1975-80, editor, style book, 1978-80; copy editor Chgo. Tribune, 1980-82, rewriter, 1982-84, assoc. fgn. editor, 1984-90, nat. editor, 1990-95, nat./fgn. editor, 1995-96, specialist writer, 1997—; Yale Law fellow, 1996-97. Recipient Media award, U. Mich., 2000, award, Soc. Women's Health Rsch., 2004. Office: Chicago Tribune 435 N Michigan Ave Chicago IL 60611-4066 Office Phone: 312-222-4330. Business E-Mail: jperes@tribune.com.

**PERESMAN, JOEL,** foundation administrator; b. 1957; Grad., U. Tex. With William Morrisy Agy.; co-founder Internat. Talent Group; exec. v.p. Madison Sq. Garden, 1995—2004; COO Clear Channel Entertainment, NYC, 2004—06; CEO Rock and Roll Hall of Fame Found., 2006—. Office: Rock and Roll Hall of Fame Found 1290 Avenue of the Americas New York NY 10104*

**PERETSMAN, NANCY B.,** investment banker; b. Worcester, Mass., Mar. 27, 1954; d. George Peretsman and Norma (Burofsky) O'Haire; m. Robert Scully, Sept. 17, 1988. AB with hons., Princeton U., 1976; MPPM, Yale, 1979. V.p. Blyth, Eastman, Dillon & Co., NYC, 1979—83; dir., head of media

group Salomon Bros., NYC, 1983—95; exec. v.p., mng. dir. Allen & Co., NYC, 1995—. Bd. mem. Charter Comm., Inc. Charter trustee Princeton U., 1976. Named one of 50 Women to Watch, Wall St. Jour., 2005. Office: Allen & Co Inc 711 5th Ave New York NY 10022*

**PERETTI, PETER ORAL,** psychology professor, researcher; s. Peter Charles and Estelle Agnes (Janas) Peretti; children: Robert Peter, Kathryn June. BA, Lake Forest Coll., 1962; MA in Sociology, Roosevelt U., 1964, MA in Psychology, 1967; PhD in Psychology, Walden U., 1974. Prof. Purdue North Ctrl. U., Westville, Ind., 1964—66, Ill. Benedictine Coll., Lisle, 1966—69, North Park Coll., Chgo., 1969—72, City Coll. Chgo., 1972—. Author: 8 books, numerous poems, jour. articles. Recipient Regional and All City Science Fair Judge awards, 1974—, Golden Apple award for Tchg., 2002. Mem.: Assn. Supervision and Curriculum Devel., Assn. Rsch. Animal Behavior, Criterion Bar Assn., Internat. Soc. Poets (Disting. Mem. award, Found. Laureate award 2005), The Hounds, Field Mus. (life), Chgo. Acad. Scis. (life), Mystery Writers Am., Hugo's Companions, Caxton Club, Phi Theta Kappa (hon.). Avocations: book clubs, bicycling, jogging.

**PERETZ, MARTIN,** publishing executive, educator; b. NYC, July 30, 1939; s. Julius and Ellen (Weberman) P.; m. Anne Labouisse, June 16, 1967; children— David, Anne Elise, Jesse, Evgenia. BA, Brandeis U., 1959; MA, Harvard U., 1965, PhD, 1966; DHL (hon.), Bard Coll., 1982; DLL (hon.), Coe Coll., 1983; PhD (hon.), Hebrew U., Jerusalem, 1987; DLL (hon.), Long Island Univ, 1988, Brandeis Univ, 1989, Hebrew Coll, 1990, Chgo. Theol. Sem., 1994. Instr. Harvard, 1965-68, asst. prof., 1968-72, lectr. social studies, 1972—; master Cabot House, 1972-75; chmn. editorial bd. New Republic mag., 1974-75; editor-in-chief New Republic, 1975—, chmn., 1998—. Bd chm Digital Learning Group; dir. Dreyfus Money Market Instruments, Dreyfus A Bonds, Dreyfus Instl. Money Market Fund, Dreyfus Balanced Fund, Dreyfus Global bond Fund, Dreyfus Growth and Income Fund, Dreyfus Internat. Funds, Dreyfus Variable Investment Fund and Premier Equity Funds. Bd. govs. Hebrew U. Jerusalem; hon. chmn. Jerusalem Found.; dir. Leukosite; trustee Ctr. for Blood Rsch., Harvard Med. Sch.; co-chmn. THEStreet, Inc. Woodrow Wilson fellow, 1959-61; recipient medal excellence in journalism U. Mo. Sch. Journalism, 1982 Democrat. Jewish. Office: New Republic Ste 700 1331 H St NW Washington DC 20005

**PEREYRA-SUAREZ, CHARLES ALBERT,** lawyer; b. Paysandu, Uruguay, Sept. 7, 1947; arrived in U.S., 1954, naturalized, 1962; s. Hector and Esther (Enriquez-Sarano) Pereyra-Suarez; m. Susan H. Cross, Dec. 30, 1983. BA in History magna cum laude, Pacific Union Coll., 1970; postgrad., UCLA, 1970-71; JD, U. Calif., Berkeley, 1975. Bar: Calif. 1975, DC 1980. Staff atty. Western Ctr. Law and Poverty, Inc., LA, 1976; trial atty. civil rights divsn. U.S. Dept. Justice, Washington, 1976—79, asst. U.S. atty., criminal divsn. LA, 1979—82; sr. litig. assoc. Gibson, Dunn & Crutcher, LA, 1982—84; pvt. practice LA, 1984—86, 1998—; ptnr. McKenna & Cuneo, LA, 1986—95, Davis Wright Tremaine, LA, 1995—98. Democrat. Avocations: tennis, jogging, travel. Office Phone: 213-623-5923. Business E-Mail: cpereyra@cpslawfirm.com.

**PEREZ, ANNIE RIVERA,** elementary school educator; d. Francisco Bontugan and Isabel Rivera Perez. BA in elem. edn., U. of Guam, 1975; MEd, U. Portland, 1994. Cert. Profl. II Elem.K-5, P.E. K-6 Guam Pub. Sch. Sys., 2005. Elem. tchr. Guam Pub. Sch. Sys., Hagatna, Guana Island, 1975—2000; elem. tchr. 5th grade San Vicente Cath. Sch., Barrigada, 2001—. Coord. elem. divsn. administrv. team San Vicente Cath. Sch., Barrigada, 2001—. Commr. Chamorro Land Trust, Hagatna, Guam, 2004—06. Mem.: Internat. Reading Assn. (assoc.). Roman Catholic. Home: PO Box 7521 Guam Tamuning 96931 Guana Island Office: San Vicente Cath School 196 Bejong Guam Barrigada 96913 Guana Island Office Phone: 671-735-4240. Personal E-mail: arp@guam.net.

**PEREZ, ANTONIO M.,** imaging company executive; b. Spain; BSEE, Madrid U. Corp. v.p., mem. exec. coun., pres. consumer bus. Hewlett-Packard Co., pres., CEO inkjet imaging bus., 1995—99; pres., CEO Gemplus Internat., 2000—01; pres., COO Eastman Kodak Co., Rochester, NY, 2003—05, CEO, 2005—, chmn., 2006—. Bd. dirs. Eastman Kodak Co., Freescale Semicondr., Inc; mem. Internat. Consultative Conf. on Future Econ. Devel. of Guangdong Province, China. Trustee George Eastman House. Named one of 50 Most Important Hispanics in Tech. & Bus., Hispanic Engr. & Info. Tech. mag., 2005. Mem.: Bus. Roundtable, Bus. Coun. Office: Eastman Kodak Co 343 State St Rochester NY 14650

**PEREZ, DAWN MARIE,** elementary school educator; b. Bayshore, N.Y., Aug. 2, 1969; d. Michael James and Diane Marie Tehan; m. Daniel Adam Perez, Apr. 11, 1998. B in Elem. Edn., Oneonta State Coll., 1991; M in Spl. Edn., Dowling Coll., 1997. Tchr. 4th grade PS 98, Douglaston, NY, 1993—99; tchr. Westhampton Beach Elem. Sch., NY, 1999—. Episcopalian. Avocations: jogging, reading, music, movies. Home: 28 Beechwood Dr Manorville NY 11949 Office: Westhampton Beach Sch Dist 379 Mill Rd Westhampton Beach NY 11978 Office Phone: 631-288-3800.

**PEREZ, EDDIE A.,** mayor; b. Corozal, PR, 1957; arrived in U.S.; 1969; m. Maria Perez, 2 children. AAS in Liberal Arts, Capital Cmty. Coll.; BA in Econs., Trinity Coll. Assoc. v.p. cmty. and govt. rels. Trinity Coll.; mayor City of Hartford, Hartford, Conn., 2002—. Exec. dir., chmn. Southside Instns. Neighborhood Alliance, Inc. (SINA); vol. VISTA, 1978; founder, dir. ONE/CHANE, Inc., North Hartford, dir. program M.A.S.H (Make Something Happen), Urban League Greater Hartford, Conn. Puerto Rican Forum; former commr. Met. Dist.; established teen pregnancy program Breaking the Cycle; MetroHartford Regional Econ. Alliance. Office: 550 Main St Hartford CT 06103

**PEREZ, EDITH R.,** lawyer; BA, U. Calif., Davis, 1976; JD, U. Calif., Berkeley, 1980. Bar: Calif. 1982. Vis. atty. Sergio Augusto Malta Advogados, Rio de Janeiro, Pablo Martinez Cano y Asociados, Mexico City; with Latham & Watkins, L.A., 1984—. Mem. adv. com. on women in svcs. U.S. Dept. Def.; mem. bd. dirs. Hugh O'Brian Youth Leadership Found., Nat. Conf. Christians and Jews, Cmty. Enhancement Corp., Mex.-Am. Legal Def. and Ednl. Fund, ARC, Latino Mus. History, Art and Culture; bd. regents Loyola Marymount U.; mem. adv. coun. on equal opportunity to CEO of So. Calif. Edison; mem. Calif. Gov.'s Task Force on Diversity and Outreach. V.p. L.A. Bd. Recreation and Pks. Commrs., 1994—95; pres. L.A. Bd. Police Commrs., 1997—99; mem. bd. dirs. Nat. Recreation Found., Ctr. for Study of L.A., Loyola Marymount U., Oakwood Sch. Named one of 25 Up-and-Coming Attys. Who Are Making a Difference in Calif., L.A. Daily Jour., 1994, 100 Most Influential Hispanics in U.S., Hispanic Bus. Mag., 1996; recipient Bringing Up Daughters Differently award, NOW Legal Def. and Edn. Fund, 1996, Redesigning Policing award, Nat. Ctr. for Women and Policing, 1997, Cmty. Commitment award, Calif. Latino Civil Rights Network, 1998, Women of Achievement award, Anti-Defamation League, 1998, Legal Svcs. award, Mex.-Am. Legal Def. and Ednl. Fund., 1998, Twice a Citizen award, L.A. Police Res. Found., 1999. Mem.: ABA, Mex. Am. Bar Assn., L.A. County Bar Assn., Calif. State Bar Assn. Office: Latham and Watkins LLP 633 W Fifth St Ste 4000 Los Angeles CA 90071

**PEREZ, JORGE M.,** real estate developer; b. Argentina; arrived in U.S., 1968; M in urban planning, Univ. Mich. Chmn., CEO Related Group of Fla., Miami, 1979—. Bd. dir. Regions Fin. Corp. Past. mem. Dem. Nat. Com.; trustee Univ. Miami; vice chmn. Miami Dade Cultural Affairs Council; dir. Miami Film Festival, Miami Downtown Develop. Authority. Named one of 25 Most Influential Hispanics, Time Mag., 2005, Forbes' Richest Americans, 2006. Democrat. Avocations: art collecting, especially Latin Am. contemporary art, tennis. Office: Related Group of Florida 2828 Coral Way Miami FL 33145*

**PEREZ, JOSE RAFAEL, JR.,** lawyer; b. Victoria de las Tunas, Oriente, Cuba, May 14, 1955; s. Jose Rafael Perez and Yolanda Ramona Sosa; m. Joan Anne Terp, Dec. 9, 1984; children: Alexander Rafael, Gabriella Susanna. BA in History, St. Mary's U., San Antonio, 1977, MA in History, 1980; JD, Tex. So. U., 1985. Cert.: Tex. Bd. Legal Specialization (immigration and nationality law) 1993, bar: Tex. Shareholder Quan, Burdette & Perez, PC, Houston, 1986—. Spkr. in field; consular liaison with U.S. consulate Tex. Am. Immigration Lawyers Assn., Ciudad Juarez, Mexico, 1997—99. Pres. Immigration Counseling Ctr., Houston, 1996—. Mem.: Am. Immigration Assn. (spkr.). Avocations: reading, exercise. Home: 6111 Riverview Way Houston TX Office: Quan Burdette and Perez PC 5177 Richmond Ave Ste 800 Houston TX 77056 Office Phone: 713-625-9231. E-mail: jperez@quanlaw.com.

**PEREZ, JOSEPHINE,** psychiatrist, educator; b. Tijuana, Mex., Feb. 10, 1941; came to the U.S., 1960, U.S. citizenship, 1968. BS in Biology, U. Santiago de Compostela, Spain, 1971, MD, 1975. Nuc. medicine technician, EEG technician, supr. Electrographic Labs., Encino, Calif., 1963—69; clerkships in internal medicine, gen. surgery, otorhinolaryngology, dermatology and venereology Gen. Hosp. of Galicia, Spain, 1972-75; resident in gen. psychiatry U. Miami, Jackson Meml. Hosp. and VA Hosp., Miami, Fla., 1976-78; practice medicine specializing in psychiatry, marital and family therapy, individual psychotherapy Miami, 1979—. Emergency room physician Miami Dade Hosp., 1975; attending psychiatrist Jackson Meml. Hosp., 1979—, asst. dir. adolescent psychiat. unit, 1979-83; mem. clin. faculty U. Miami Sch. Medicine, 1979—, clin. instr. psychiatry, 1979—. Mem. AMA (Physicians' Recognition award 1980, 83, 86, 89, 98, 2000, 01, 05), Am. Assn. for Marital and Family Therapy (cert. clin. mem., treas. 1982-84, pres.-elect 1985-87, pres. 1987-89), Am. Psychiat. Assn., Am. Med. Women's Assn., Assn. Women Psychiatrists, Fla. Psychiat. Soc., South Dade Women Physicians Assn. Office: 420 S Dixie Hwy Ste 4A Coral Gables FL 33146-2228 Office Phone: 305-666-7766.

**PEREZ, LEYANEE C.,** nutritionist, consultant; b. Habana, Cuba, Dec. 7, 1966; d. Andres and Teresa Perez; m. Guillermo Jose Cuevas, Mar. 9, 1996; 1 child, Fernando J. Cuevas. AA, Miami Dade C.C., 1989; BS, Fla. Internat. U., 1992. Cert. RDLD Am. Dietetic Assn. Nutritional specialist NutriSystem, Miami, 1990—92; cons. dietitian Med. Offices Miami Lakes, Miami, 1992—95; clin. dietitian Cedars Med. Ctr., Miami, 1993—95, Hialeah Hosp., Miami, 1995—96; cons. dietitian and corp. mem. Nutrition & Wellness Consultants, Miami, 1995—99; regional cons. to chief clin. cons. Integrated Health Svcs., Miami, 1996—2001; owner, mgr. dietician The Floridian Day Spa Salon & Nutritional Inst., Miami, 2001—. Author: The Ultimate Diet - A Journey into the new Millennium. Mem.: Am. Fedn. Astrologers, Am. Dietetic Assn. R-Conservative. Avocations: reading, writing, astrology. Office: The Floridian Day Spa 7160 W 20th Ave Ste M 133 Hialeah FL 33016

**PEREZ, LOUIS ANTHONY,** radiologist; b. NYC, June 11, 1939; s. Salvatore Lawrence and Valvadina Rose (Ruscillo) P.; divorced, 1988; children: Lisa, Gregg, Nicole; m. Patricia Ann McVey, May 19, 1990; 1 child, Kelsey. BEE, Manhattan Coll., 1962; MD, SUNY, Bklyn., 1966. Diplomate Am. Bd. Radiology (oral examiner), Am. Bd. Nuclear Medicine. Chief nuclear medicine Misericordia Hosp., Bronx, 1973-75; cons. Manhattan Coll., Radiology Inst., Riverdale, N.Y., 1974-81; chief nuclear medicine Norwalk (Conn.) Hosp., 1975-82; dir. radiology Lawrence Hosp., Bronxville, NY, 1982—2004; asst. clin. prof. radiology Columbia U. Coll. Physicians and Surgeons, N.Y.C., 1995—. Contbr. articles to profl. jours., chpts. to books. Lt. comdr. USN, 1963-77. Grantee, Am. Cancer Soc., 1968-70, USPHS, 1974-75. Fellow Am. Coll. Radiology; mem. Soc. Nuc. Medicine (trustee 1985-89, 92—, chmn. sci. subcom. 1988—, chpt. pres. 1982), NY State Med. Soc. Republican. Roman Catholic. Office: Northeast Radiology No Westchester Hosp Ctr 400 E Main St Mount Kisco NY 10549 Office Phone: 914-666-1898.

**PEREZ, PAUL IGNATIUS,** prosecutor, lawyer; b. Cuba, 1955; Bachelor, Jacksonville U.; Master, U. Fla.; grad. in Law, George Washington U. Assoc. Smith & Hulsey, P.A., Jacksonville, 1985—88; ptnr. Mahoney, Adams, & Criser P.A., Jacksonville, 1988—89, 1992—94, Booth, Arnold & Perez P.A., Jacksonville, Fla., 1994—2002; US atty. (mid. dist.) Fla. US Dept. Justice, Jacksonville, Fla., 1988—92, 2002—; chmn. US Attys Office Mid Dist 400 N Tampa St Ste 3200 Tampa FL 33602 Office Phone: 813-274-6000.*

**PEREZ, SYLVIA,** newscaster, reporter; married; 2 children. B, U. Okla. Sch. of Journalism. Reporter KRPC-TV, Houston, Denver, Lawton, Okla.; weekend anchor and reporter WLS-TV, Chgo., 1989—, med. reporter, anchor 11am news. TV journalist with prodr. Holly Grisham HealthBeat, WLS-TV (Silver Dome award, 2001), TV journalist with prodr. Christine Tressel Desktop Doctors (Peter Lisagor award, 2002). Office: WLS-TV 190 N State St Chicago IL 60601

**PEREZ, WILLIAM D.,** retail executive; b. Akron, Ohio, 1947; m. Catherine A. Perez; 2 children. BA in Govt., Cornell U., 1969; BIM, American Grad. Sch. of Internat. Mgmt., 1970. Joined Johnson Wax SC Johnson & Son, Inc., 1970, gen. mgr. Spanish Johnson, v.p., regional dir. Americas, v.p. home care bus., exec. v.p. N. American consumer products, pres., COO worldwide consumer products Racine, Wis., 1993-97, pres., CEO, 1997—2004; pres., CEO, bd. dir. Nike Inc., 2004—06. Bd. dirs. May Dept. Stores Co., 1998—2004, Kellogg Co., 1999—, Hallmark Cards, Inc. Mem. Cornell U. Council; advisory bd. Racine Youth Leadership Acad.; bd. dirs. Sustainable Racine. Recipient Out & Equal Champion for Workplace Equality award, Out & Equal Workplace Advocates, 2002. Mem.: Grocery Manufacturers of Am (bd. dirs.). Achievements include 11 marathons. Avocation: running.*

**PEREZ-CRUET, JORGE,** psychiatrist; b. Santurce, P.R., Oct. 15, 1931; s. Jose Maria Perez-Vicente and Emilia Cruet-Burgos; m. Anyes Heimendinger, Oct. 4, 1958; children: Antonio, Mick, Graciela, Isabelle. BS magna cum laude, U. P.R., 1953, MD, 1957; diploma in psychiatry, McGill U., Montreal, Que., Can.. 1976. Diplomate Am. Bd. Geriat. Psychiatry, Am. Bd. Psychiatry and Neurology, Nat. Bd. Med. Examiners, lic. Can. Coun. Med. Examiners, Med. Coun. Can., cert. in quality assurance, CHPQ HQCB, specialist in psychiatry RCPC, eligible Am. Bd. Psychiatry and Neurology, re-cert. in geriatric psychiatry Am. Bd. Psychiatry and Neurology, 2001. Rotating intern Michael Reese Hosp., Chgo., 1957-58; fellow in psychiatry Johns Hopkins U. Med. Sch., 1958-60, instr., then asst. prof. Psychiatry, 1962-73; psychiatrist neurophysiology and psychosomatic lab. Walter Reed Army Inst. Rsch., Washington, 1960-62, cons., 1963-65; rsch. assoc. lab. chem. pharmacology NHI, NIH, Bethesda, Md., 1969-71; med. dir. USPHS adult psychiatry sect. lab. clin. sci. NIMH, Bethesda, 1971-73; psychiatry resident diploma course in psychiatry McGill U. Sch. Medicine, Montreal Gen. Hosp., 1973-76, Montreal Children's Hosp., 1975; prof. psychiatry, chief psychopharmacology lab. U. Mo.-Mo. Inst. Psychiatry, St. Louis, 1976—78; chief psychiatry svc. San Juan (P.R.) VA Hosp., pharmacy and therapeutic com., 1978—2004; prof. psychiatry U. P.R. Med. Sch., 1978-92, U. Okla. Health Sci. Ctr., 1992—2004, Okla. City VA Med. Ctr., 1992—2004; pvt. practice. Spl. cons. NASA, Moffettfield, Calif., 1963-65; cons. divsn. narcotic addition and drug abuse NIDA, 1972-73; drug adv. com. FDA/NIDA, 1976-80, pharmacy and therapeutic com., 1992—; local organizer Internat. Coll. Neuropsychiatry, San Juan, P.R., 1986, CINP, 1986; spl. advisor mental health P.R. Senate, P.R. sec. health, 1989; prin. investigator NASA biosatellite project JH Sch. Med., 1963-65.; staff sr. psychiatrist and supt.psychiatry ward, VA Med. Ctr., Oklahoma City, 1992-1995, sr. staff psychiatrist and physician substance abuse clinic, 1995-2004, med. dir. opioid treatment program, 2001-2004. Editor: Catholic Physicians Guild Archiocese of Okla., 1997-98. Mem. Rep. Nat. Com., 1995; mem. Eisenhower Commn., 2001. Capt. M.C. USAR, 1960-62; sr. surgeon USPHS, 1969-71, med. dir. 1971-73. Recipient Coronas award, 1957, Ruiz-Arnau award, 1957, Diaz-Garcia award 1957, Geigy award, 1975, 74, AMA Recognition award 1971, 76, 81, Horner's award 1975, 76, Pavlovian award, 1978, Recognition cert. VA Svc. awards and commendations, 1980-98, Senate of P.R. 1986, Cert. of Merit Gov. of P.R., 1986, Cert. Recognition, Sec. Health, San Juan, Puerto Rico, Appreciation plaque Fifth World Congress of IRMA, Manila, Philippines, Eisenhower Commn., 1995. Fellow APA (Disting., life), Interam. Coll. Physicians and Surgeons, Royal Coll. Physicians and Surgeons Can. (sr., cert.), Am. Psychiat Assn. (Disting., life); mem. AAAS, Am. Coll. Med. Quality (bd. dirs. 2004), Am. Physiol. Soc., Am. Coll. Psychiatrists, Pavlovian Soc., Am. Fedn. Clin. Rsch., Am. Fedn. Med. Rsch., Am. Assn. Geriat. Psychiatry, Am. Geriat. Soc., Am. Coll. Preventive Medicine, Am. Soc. Clin. Pharmacology and Therapeutics, Am. Soc. Pharmacology and Exptl. Therapeutics, Am. Soc. Addiction Medicine (cert.), Am. Acad. Addiction Psychiatry (dir. Area VIII, 2002-), Soc. Neurosci., Nat. Assn. Healthcare Quality (mem. editl. bd. Jour. Health Quality, 2005), Internat. Soc. Rsch. Aggression, Okla. Psychiat. Assn., Am. Soc. Clin. Psychopharmacology, Menninger Found., Charles F. Menninger Soc., Okla. Assn. Health Care Quality, Alumni, UPR Sch. Med., Johns Hopkins Med. Surg. Inst., N.Y. Acad. Scis., NIH Alumni (life), McGill, Okla. Hist. Soc.(life). Republican. Roman Catholic. Avocations: painting, writing. Home: 3304 Rosewood Ln Oklahoma City OK 73120-5604 Office Phone: 405-834-3001. E-mail: jperezcrue@aol.com.

PEREZ-CRUET, MICK (MIGUELANGELO) JORGE, neurosurgeon, educator; b. Washington, May 3, 1961; s. Jorge Fortunato and Anyes Lilly Perez-Cruet; m. Donna Jeanne Roggenbuck, July 9, 1994; children: Kristin Magdalene, Joshua Michael, Rachel Elizabeth, David Gabriel. BA, Grinell Coll., 1983; MSc in Chemistry, U. South Fla., 1986; MD, Tufts U., 1991. Commd. 2d lt. USAF, 1987, advanced through grades to maj., 1997, ret., 2001; intern surg. svc. Baylor Coll. Medicine, Houston, 1991-92, resident in neurosurgery, 1992-97; attending neurosurgery, v. chmn. Wilford Hall Med. Ctr., San Antonio, 1997—2001; spinal fellow Rush U./CINN, Chgo., 2001—02; asst. prof., dir. minimally invasive spine surgery Rush U., Chgo., 2002—03; assoc. dir. Inst. Minimally Invasive Spine Surgery Mich. Head and Spine Inst., 2003—; assoc. prof. Oakland Univ.; dir. minimally invasive spine surgery Providence Med. Ctr., 2003—, dir. spine fellowship program, 2004—. Prin. investigator clin. trials; presenter in field; appointee Coun. State Neurosurg. Socs., 1997, chmn. young physicians com., chmn. workforce com., corr. sec., publs. com.; mem. sci. adv. bd. Neospine; founding surgeon US Spine CNS Publs. Com., 2002—; dir. socioecon. peer rev. articles AANS Bull. Editor: (textbooks) Outpatient Spinal Surgery, An Anatomical Approach to Minimally Invasive Spine Surgery, (DVD) AANS Minimally Invasive Spine Techniques; asst. editor: AANS Bull. Com.; contbr. chapters to books, articles to profl. jours. Chmn. class reunion Tufts Sch. Medicine, 1995-96; dir. class fund Grinnell Coll., 1999—. Air Force Health Professions scholar, 1987—91. Mem. AMA, ACS, AAAS, Congress Neurol. Surgeons, Am. Assn. Neurol. Surgeons (dir. spine courses, editor-in-chief AANS Bull. Socioecon. Jour. 2005—), Mich. Med. Soc., Mich. Assn. Neurol. Surgeons (treas., pres. 2006-), Sigma Xi (grantee 1985). Achievements include invention of spine instrumentation. Avocations: hunting, fishing, scuba diving, archery, poetry. Office: Mich Head and Spine Inst 22250 Providence Dr Ste 300 Southfield MI 48075 Office Phone: 248-440-2162. E-mail: perezcruet@yahoo.com.

PEREZ DE ALONSO, MARCELA, human resources specialist, information technology executive; b. Chile; Grad., Cath. U., Chile. Various sr. level positions in human resources and ops. Citigroup, global consumer head human resources, 1996—99; divsn. head Citigroup North L.Am. Consumer Bank, 1999—2004; exec. v.p. human resources and workforce devel. Hewlett-Packard Co., Palo Alto, Calif., 2004—. Mem. adv. bd. Marshall Bus. Sch. U. So. Calif.; spkr. in field; bd. dirs. Catalyst, NYC, Hewlett-Packard Co. Fin. Svcs. Mem. adv. bd. U. So. Calif. Marshall Bus. Sch.; bd. mem. Next Door Solutions to Domestic Violence. Named Corp. Exec. of Yr., Hispanic-Net, 2005; named one of 50 Most Important Hispanics in Tech. and Bus., Hispanic Engr. & Info. Tech. mag. Office: Hewlett Packard Co 3000 Hanover St Palo Alto CA 94304

PEREZ DE LA MESA, MANUEL JOSE, swimming pool company executive; b. Havana, Cuba, Mar. 20, 1957; came to the U.S., 1961; s. Manuel Adolfo Oscar and Olga Marta (Cuervo) Perez de la Mesa; m. Ana Lidia Vidal, June 19, 1982; children: Rosario, Manuel, Cristina. BBA in Fin., Fla. Internat. U., 1977; MBA in Controllership, St. John's U., 1980. Fin. analyst Latin Am. Sea-Land Svc., Inc., Ft. Lauderdale, Fla., 1977-79; sr. fin. analyst Edison, N.J., 1979-80, regional contr. Latin Am. Ft. Lauderdale, 1980-82; ops. auditor IBM, San Jose, Calif., 1982-85, advisory pricing staff Bethesda, Md., 1985-87; asst. corp. contr. Del Monte Fresh Produce Inc., Coral Gables, Fla., 1987-88, v.p. fin. and ops. Latin Am. San Jose, Costa Rica, 1988-90, v.p. ops. S.Am. Santiago, Chile, 1990-91, v.p. planning and devel. Coral Gables, 1991-94; v.p, fin. and ops. Gemaire Distbrs. Inc., Deerfield Beach, Fla., 1994-96; v.p. ops. Watsco, Inc., Miami, Fla., 1996—99; press. and COO SCP Pool Corp., Covington, La., 1999—2001, pres., CEO, 2001—. Chmn. Agribusiness, Caribbean/Latin Am. Action, Washington, 1991-93; dir., investment banking consulting Latin Fin. Inc., N.Y.C., Miami, Mexico City, 1993—. Mem. Inst. Mngmt. Acctg. Avocations: sports, investment analysis, family. Home: 15885 W Prestwick Pl Miami Lakes FL 33014-6523*

PÉREZ-DÍAZ, VÍCTOR MIGUEL, sociology educator; b. Madrid, Dec. 8, 1938; s. Miguel Pérez-Poyo and Victoria Díaz-Alonso; m. Marina González Olivares, Apr. 2, 1938. PhD in Sociology, Harvard U., 1976, Complutense U., Madrid, 1978, PhD in Law, 1978. Fellow Inst. Advanced Study, Princeton U., 1976-77; rsch. dir. INI Found., Madrid, 1977-80, FIES Found., Madrid, 1980-86; founding dir. Ctr. Social Sci. Juan March Inst., Madrid, 1987-92; dir. rsch. ctr. Analistas Socio-Políticos, 1993; prof. sociology Complutense U., Madrid, 1978—. Vis. prof. MIT, Cambridge, 1988-89, U. Calif., LaJolla, 1987-93, Harvard U., Cambridge, 1992-93, Inst. for Advanced Study, Princeton, 1975-76, Inst. nat. des Scis. & Politiques, Paris, 1994-95; mem. adv. com. PRISA, Madrid, 1991, Spanish Min. Health, 1996, New Sch. for Social Rsch., N.Y., 1999, Hans Seper vis. prof., 1999; mem. adv. com., prof. King Juan Carlos Ctr., NYU, 2000; mem. adv. bd. REPSOL, Madrid, 1993. Author: State, Bureaucracy and Civil Society, 1978, Castilian Peasants, 1992, The Return of Civil Society, 1993, Spanish Democracy, 1996, Public Sphere and Civil Society, 1997, Spain at the Crossroads, 1999, La lezione spagnola, 2003. Mem. Commn. on Unemployment Spanish Govt., Madrid, 1987-88, Study Group on Social Policy: European Communities Brussels, 1991-93; com. mem. Social Sci. Rsch. Coun., N.Y., 1983-89; mem. Nat. Com. Rules Ethical Behavior, 1997-2000, Prize Libre Empresa, 2002, Fund Rafael del Pino. Mem. Acadmia Europaea, Am. Acad. Arts and Scis. (fgn. hon. mem.). Home: Comandante Fortea 3 28008 Madrid Spain Office: Analistas Socio-Políticos Gabinete de Estudios c/Quintana, 24-5 dcha 28008 Madrid Spain Office Phone: 34 91 5414746. Personal E-mail: asp@ctv.es.

PEREZ-FIRMAT, GUSTAVO FRANCISCO, writer, language educator; b. Havana, Cuba, Mar. 7, 1950; came to U.S., 1960; s. Gustavo Perez and Luz Maria Firmat; m. Rosa Perelmuter, Aug. 12, 1973 (div. 1990); children: David, Miriam; m. Mary Anne Adamson, Feb. 8, 1991. AB, MA, U. Miami, 1973; PhD, U. Mich., 1979. Instructor, dept. Romance studies Duke U., Durham, NC, 1978—79, asst. prof., 1979—83, assoc. prof., 1983—88, prof., 1988—99, 1988-89; David Feinson prof. in Humanities Columbia Univ. NYC, 1999—. Author: Idle Fictions, 1982, Literature and Liminality, 1986, Carolina Cuban, 1986, The Cuban Condition, 1989, Equivocaciones, 1989; editor: Do the Americas Have a Common Literature?, 1991. Fellow Am. Coun. Learned Socs., 1981, Guggenheim Found., 1986; sr. fellow NEH, 1985. Fellow: Am. Acad. Arts & Sci. Mem. MLA, Am. Assn. Tchrs. Spanish and Portuguese, Am. Studies Assn., Phi Beta Kappa. Office: Dept Spanish & Portuguese Columbia Univ New York NY 10027 E-mail: gpf@columbia.edu.

PEREZ - GOMEZ, ADA IRIS, law educator; b. Carolina, PR, Jan. 5, 1975; d. Luis Enrique Perez - Figueroa and Ada Iris Gomez - Romero. BA in Criminal Justice and Criminal Investigation cum laude, Interamerican U. PR Met. Campus, San Juan, 1995. MA in Criminal Justice, 1997; JD, Pontifical Cath. U. PR Sch. Law, Ponce, 2001. Investigator Women's Advocate's Office, San Juan, PR, 1993—94, Patients Advocate's Office, 2004—; prof. Puerto Rico East U., Carolina, 2005—. Master: Profls. Criminal Justice Assn.; mem.: PR Notary Assn., Phi Alpha Delta.

PEREZ-LUNA, VICTOR HUGO, chemical engineer, educator; researcher; b. U.S., 1989; s. Braulio Perez-Valdivia and Carolina Luna-Gomez; m. Esther Romo-Ortiz, Aug. 25, 1989; children: Victor Hugo Perez-Romo, Pablo Alfonso Perez-Romo. BS in Chem. Engring., U. Guadalajara, 1987, MSc in Chem. Engring., 1989; PhD in Chem. Engring., U. Wash., 1995. Design engr. Swecomex, Gudalajara, Mexico, 1987; grad. rsch. asst. U. Guadalajara, 1988—89, U. Wash., Seattle, 1989—95; rsch. asst. prof. The U. N.Mex, Albuquerque, 1996—96, vis. rsch. instr., 1997—2000; asst. prof. Ill. Inst. Tech., Chgo., 2000—. Recipient Student Rsch. award, Soc. Biomaterials, 1994; grantee, Office Naval Rsch. 2003—04, 2004—05, 2005—. Mem.: Am. Vacuum Soc., Am. Chem. Soc. Achievements include patents pending for fluorescence and FRET based assays for biomolecules on beads; research in biomaterials, biosensors, hydrogels, surface chemistry, nanotechnology. Office: Illinois Institute of Technology 10 West 33rd Street Chicago IL 60616 Office Phone: 312-567-3963.

PÉREZ-MONFORTI, JESSICA L., social sciences educator, researcher; b. Islip, NY, Feb. 6, 1976; d. Steven K. and Maryann Monforti. BS, Fla. State U.; MA, PhD, Ohio State U. Rsch. asst. FSU Survey Rsch. Lab, Tallahasse, Fla., 1995—97; intern Dept. of Edn. Legis. and Cabinet Affairs, Tallahasse, Fla., 1995—97; instr. Ohio State U., 1999—2001; adj. instr. U. of South Fla., Tampa, 2001; asst. prof. Mercer U., Macon, Ga., 2001—. Mem. family selection com. Habitat Humanity, Columbus, Ohio, 1997—2000; founder, adv. Hispanic and Latin Am. Student Union, Macon, Ga., 2001—. Recipient hon. mention, Ford Found., 1998, GSARA award, Ohio State U., 1999; grantee, So. Scholarship Found., 1996. Mem.: Western Polit. Sci. Assn., So. Polit. Sci. Assn., Midwest Polit. Sci. Assn., Am. Polit. Sci. Assn., Nat. Assn. of Black Polit. Scientists, Alpha Psi Lambda (v.p. 1998—99).

PEREZ-NIEVES, ROBERTO, plastic surgeon, educator; b. Areribo, PR, Nov. 15, 1963; children: Benjamin Reinier, Roberto C., Mia M. BS, Internat. U., 1987. Commd. humanitarian surg. missions US Army South, Honduras, 2002, advanced through grades to lt. col., 2005, humanitarian surgical missions Paraguay, 2004, Dominican Republic, 2005; subject matter expert US Army Med. Sch., San Antonio, 2003—05; asst. prof. U. Tex., San Antonio, 2004—05. Decorated Commendation medal US Army. Fellow: ACS; mem.: Am. Soc. Plastic Surgery. Avocations: scuba diving, parachuting, running, skiing, dance. Office: PO Box 388 Mercedita PR 00715-0388 Office Phone: 787-840-1114.

PÉREZ-RIVERA, FRANCISCO (FRANK RIVERA), writer; b. Vertientes, Cuba, Oct. 3, 1938; came to U.S., 1968, naturalized, 1974; s. Francisco Daniel Pérez and María Eloísa Rivera. BA, Camagüey Coll., Cuba, 1955; MA in Romance Langs., U. Munich, 1967. Newsman, script writer Bavarian Radio, Munich, 1964-68; newsman AP, N.Y.C., 1968-92, arts and entertainment editor, 1992—2006, ret., 2006; dir. Spanish programs for lang. labs., 1987. *Francisco Pérez-Rivera single-handedly created the arts and entertainment section of the AP's Latin American Desk in New York. Since he was named as the first entertainment editor ever of that desk in 1992, his work gave the AP's Spanish Service an unusually high profile in the cultural field. He retired from the AP in February, 2006. Of his fiction, professor Carol Wasserman writes: "The dominant elements of (his) stories are the consistency of style and the versatility of the genre. Behind each word we can trace an unrelenting course towards a revelation that is always cunning and often hair-raising." As a fiction writer, his byline is Frank Rivera.* Author: (poetry) Constructions, 1979; (novel) Bells Over the Prairies, 1986, 2d edit., 2004; (short stories) Cuban Short Stories, 1992; (short stories) Varadero and Other Cuban Short Stories, 1998; co-author: Introduction to Spanish Literature, 1982; short stories in the anthologies New Cuban Storytellers (in Spanish), 1961, Cuba: Nouvelles et contes d'aujourd'hui, 1985, Narrative and Liberty: Cuban Tales of the Dispersion, 1996, Prosa moderna del mundo hispánico, 1997; author, narrator audio books The Golden Age of Spanish Literature, 2002. Grantee German Academic Exchange Svc., Munich, 1961-67; fellow Cintas Found., N.Y., 1980; 1st prize short story Círculo de Escritores y Poetas Latinoamericanos, N.Y., 1997, Internat. Short Story award Círculo de Cultura Panamericano, N.J., 1997. Home: 212 E 77th St Apt 1G New York NY 10021-2111 Personal E-mail: fprivera@yahoo.com.

PEREZ-STRUMOLO, LYSANDRA MARIE, psychologist, educator; d. Jose A. Perez-Llavona and Jeannette M. Perez; m. David Strumolo, Mar. 7, 1992; children: David G., Alyna M., Olivia E. BA in Psychology and Philosophy, Rutgers U., 1992; PhD in Clin. Psychology, Farileigh Dickinson U., 2000. Psychologist Eric J. Feldman Child and Family Devel. Ctr., Newark, 1994—2001; adj. prof. William Paterson U., Wayne, NJ, 2000—02; asst. prof. Ramapo Coll., Mahwah, NJ, 2002—. Mem.: APA, NJ Psychol. Assn., Latino Psychol. Assn. NJ (pres. 2006). Office: Ramapo Coll NJU 505 Ramapo Valley Rd Mahwah NJ 07430

PERFETTI, ROBERT NICKOLAS, educational consultant; b. Staples, Minn., Jan. 8, 1937; s. Nickolas Albert and Lila Bertha (Beurge) P. BS, St. Cloud State U., 1960; postgrad., Bemidji State U., 1961-62, Calif. State U., L.A., 1964-68, Pepperdine U., 1967-68; MA, La Verne U., 1970; postgrad., U. So. Calif., 1972-73, Point Loma U., Pasadena, Calif., 1974-75; EdD, Pacific States U., 1975. Cert. admistr., counselor, secondary, community coll., jr. high sch., adult, and elem. edn. Calif. Prin. Richmond (Minn.) Pub. Schs., 1960-62; elem. tchr. Sebeka (Minn.) Sch. Dist., 1962-63; team leader lang. arts, social sci. and summer sch. Rowland Unified Sch. Dist., Rowland Heights, Calif., 1965-76, coord. math. lab., 1976-79, secondary counselor, 1979-81, coord. work experience edn., career edn. and career ctr., 1981-95, home ind. study coord., ednl. cons., 1992-95; mental health counselor St. Gabriel's Hosp., Little Falls, Minn., 1999. Coord. Gender Equity, 1980-95, Job Tng. Partnership Act, 1980-95; advisor Nat. Tech. Honor Soc., 1991-95; alumni dir. Sacred Heart Sch., Staples. Editor: (profl. newspaper) Reaction, Officer parish coun. Our Lady of the Assumption Ch., Claremont, Calif., chmn. edn. com.; chmn. PTA, Rowland Heights; rep. fed. project, Rowland Heights; scoutmaster, chmn. troop com. Boy Scouts Am. Recipient Svc. Commendation Rowland Unified Sch. Dist., 1978; named L.A. County Tchr. of Yr. Calif. State Dept. Edn., 1975, Outstanding Secondary Educator of Am., 1974, Giano Tchr. of Yr. Giano Intermediate Sch., 1973, Tchr. of Yr. Rowland Unified Sch. Dist., 1974. Mem. NEA (life), Calif. Tchrs. Assn., Assn. Rowland Educators (v.p.), Calif. Assn. Work Experience Educators (Alpha chpt. v.p.), Alpha Phi Omega (pres.), Pi Delta Epsilon (pres.), KC (3d degree). Roman Catholic. Avocations: water sports, travel, research, writing. Home: 200 4th St SE Little Falls MN 56345-3116 E-mail: perfetti7@msn.com.

PERGER, DONNA SPAGNOLI, retired secondary school mathematics educator; b. Portsmouth, Va., Apr. 24, 1951; d. Delmo John and Lurline M. (Smith) Spagnoli; m. Steve John Perger Jr., June 9, 1980; 1 stepchild, Stephanie Lee. BS in Secondary Edn., Old Dominion U., 1973. Tchr. math. Manor H.S., Portsmouth, Va., 1973—74, Bettie Williams Sch., Virginia Beach, Va., 1974—78, Virginia Beach Jr. H.S., 1978—80, Queens Lake Sch., York County, Va., 1980—2003, chair dept. math. Lead tchr. VQUEST. Art work published in Stampers Sampler, Somerset Studio and Gallery mags. Elder Olive Br. Christian Ch. Named Mid. Sch. Tchr. of Yr. Daily Press Newspaper, Newport News, 1993. Avocations: paper embossing (repousse), needlecrafts, sewing, gardening.

PERHACH, JAMES LAWRENCE, pharmaceutical executive; s. James Lawrence and Elizabeth Louise (Hoffman) P.; m. Judith Irene Selter, Apr. 15, 1967; children: Laura Anne, Amy Elizabeth. BS, U. Dayton, 1966; MS, U. Pitts., 1969, PhD, 1971. Sr. scientist dept. pharmacology Mead Johnson Rsch. Ctr., divsn. Bristol Myers, 1971—74, sr. investigator dept. biol. rsch., 1974—76, sr. rsch. assoc. dept. biol. rsch., 1976—77, sr. rsch. assoc. dept. pathology and toxicology, 1977—78, prin. rsch. assoc. dept. pathology and toxicology, 1978—80; from dir. pharmacology to dir. biol. rsch. to dir. clin. investigation Wallace Labs. Divsn. Carter-Wallace, Inc., Cranbury, NJ, 1980—87, v.p. clin. pharmacology and pharmacokinetics, 1987—2001; sr. dir. clin. pharmacology Purdue Pharma, L.P., 2001—04; sr. dir. CNS Therapeutic Area Forest Rsch. Inst. 2004—05, exec. dir. clin. devel., 2005—.

Adj. asst. prof. dept. pharmacy practice and adminstrn. Ernest Mario Coll. Pharmacy Rutgers U., 1993—; adv. bd. clin. rsch. ctr. U. Medicine and Dentistry NJ Robert Wood Johnson Med. Sch., 1995-2003; drug utilization rev. coun. State of NJ, 1983-2003, med. pharmacologist, 1983; sec., 1984, chmn., 1985-87. Fellow: Am. Coll. Clin. Pharmacology; mem.: Am. Soc. Pharmacology and Exptl. Therapeutics, Am. Coll. Clin. Pharmacology, Drug Info. Assn., Am. Soc. Clin. Pharmacology and Therapeutics. Achievements include research in drug discovery, elucidation of mechanism of action and safety evaluation of new therapeutic agents. Office: Forest Rsch Inst Harbor Side Fin Ctr Plaza V Jersey City NJ 07311 Office Phone: 201-427-8465. Business E-Mail: james.perhach@frx.com.

PERHACS, MARYLOUISE HELEN, musician, educator; b. Teaneck, N.J., June 15, 1944; d. John Andrew and Helen Audrey (Hosage) P.; m. Robert Theodore Sirinek, Jan. 27, 1968 (div. Jan. 1975). Student, Ithaca (N.Y.) Coll., 1962-64; BS, Juilliard Sch., 1967, MS, 1968; postgrad., Hunter Coll., 1976, St. Peter's Coll., Jersey City, N.J., 1977. Cert. music tchr., N.Y., N.J. Instr. Carnegie Hall, N.Y.C., 1966-69; program developer, coord., instr. urban edn. program Newburgh (N.Y.) Pub. Sch. System, 1968-69; adj. prof. dept. edn. St. Peter's Coll., Jersey City, 1976-92; tchr. brass instruments Indian Hills High Sch., Oakland, NJ, 1976; tchr. Jersey City Pub. Schs., 1976-77, N.Y.C. Pub. Sch., Bronx, 1980-84; pvt. tchr. Cliffside Park, NJ, 1976—; vocal music tchr. East Rutherford, NJ, 1990; tchr. music Bergen County Spl. Svcs. Sch. Dist., 1990-91; tchr. gen. music Little Ferry (N.J.) Pub. Schs., 1991-92; tchr. mid. sch. instrumental Paramus (N.J.) Pub. Schs., 1993-94; tchr. vocal music West New York (N.J.) Pub. Schs., 1995—. Tchr. music summer enrichment program, West New York, NJ, 1999-2000; tchr. summer instrumental music program Park Ridge (NJ) HS, 1995-96, Waldwick Concert Band, 2003-04; singer, trumpeter Norwegian Caribbean Lines, 1981-82, Jimmy Dorsey Band, Paris and London, 1974; lectr. in field. Singer with Original PDQ Bach Okay Chorale, 1966, Live from Carnegie Hall Recordings, 1970, St. Louis Mcpl. Opera, 1970, Ed Sullivan Show, 1970; singer, dancer, actress (Broadway shows) Promises, Promises, 1969-71, Sugar, 1971-72, Lysistrata, 1972; trumpeter (Broadway shows) Jesus Christ Superstar, 1973, Debbie!, 1976, Sarava!, 1979, Fiddler on the Roof, Lincoln Ctr., 1981, Sophisticated Ladies, 1982; writer, host series on women in music Columbia Cable/United Artists, 1984; recordings: Carnegie Hall Live, Avery Fisher Hall, Lincoln Ctr. Cons. to cadette troop Girl Scouts U.S., Jersey City, 1967-68, Bergen County N.J. Coun., 1995—. Mem. NEA, AFTRA, Actors Equity Assn., Am. Fedn. Musicians (mem. theatre com. local 802 N.Y.C. 1972—, chmn. 1973), Music Educators Nat. Conf., N.J. Music Educators Assn., N.J. Sch. Music Assn., N.J. Edn. Assn., Internat. Women's Brass Guild (charter mem.), Internat. Trumpet Guild, Mu Phi Epsilon. Democrat. Episcopalian. Avocations: cats, cake decorating, food sculpting, horticulture, sewing. Home and Office: 23 Crescent Ave Cliffside Park NJ 07010-3003

PERHAM, ROY GATES, III, industrial psychologist; b. Hackensack, N.J., Apr. 22, 1958; s. Roy Gates Jr. and Titania Joan (Robbitts) P. BA with honors, Bates Coll., 1980; MS, Stevens Inst. Tech., 1982, PhD, 1989. Intern Sen. Edmund S. Muskie, Washington, 1978; psychometrician Lab. Psychol. Studies Stevens Inst. Tech., Hoboken, NJ, 1981-83, instr., 1985, adj. asst. prof., 1990—, Fairleigh Dickinson U., Rutherford, NJ, 1986; sr. assoc. AAI Orgnl. Performance Cons., Florham Park, NJ, 1990-94; assessment projects mgr. Tech. Employee Selection and Tng. Inc., Hasbrouck Heights, NJ, 1995—. WordStar coord. NY Computer Soc., NYC, 1985-88. Chmn. Juvenile Conf. Com., Hasbrouck Heights and Wood-Ridge, NJ, 1985-95; mem. NJ State Juvenile Delinquency Commn., Trenton, NJ, 1988-91; county exec.'s rep. Bergen County Youth Svcs. Commn., 1990-2002, chair, 1994-96; chair Bergen County Task Force on Youth Violence, 1993-95; asst. Bergen County Exec. for Juvenile Justice, NJ, 1999—2002; mem. NJ Gov's. Juvenile Justice and Delinquency Prevention Com., 2001—. Named Citizen of Yr., Lions Club of Hasbrouck Heights, NJ, 1988. Mem. APA, Am. Psychol. Soc., Met. NY Assn. for Applied Psychology, NJ Property Owners Assn., Soc. for Indsl./Orgnl. Psychology, Inc., Phi Beta Kappa, Psi Chi. Home: 269 Raymond St Hasbrouck Heights NJ 07604-1723 Office: Technical Employee Selection & Tng Inc The Profl Bldg 248 Blvd Hasbrouck Heights NJ 07604 E-mail: Rperham@compuserve.com.

PERIARD, DOUGLAS DEE, social studies educator; b. Saginaw, Mich., Aug. 28, 1963; s. William Edward and Dorothy Ann Periard; m. Anne Marie Periard, June 19, 1999; children: Grace Marie, Hugh Douglas. BS in Edn., Ctrl. Mich. U., 1986, MA in Edn. Adminstrn., 1993. Tchr. Kaleva Norman Dickson Sch., Brethren, Mich., 1987—89, Suttons Bay Pub. Sch., 1993—. Mem. Suttons Bay Planning Commn., 2004—. Named Baseball Dist. Coach of Yr., MHSBLA, 1998, 2003. Democrat. Roman Catholic. Home: 688 S Herman Rd Suttons Bay MI 49682 Office: Suttons Bay Schs Suttons Bay MI 49682

PERIASWAMY, PADMINI, materials scientist, researcher; d. Periaswamy Nanjappa and Amirthavalli Periaswamy. BS in Applied Scis., PSG Coll. Tech., Coimbatore, 1988, MS in Materials Sci., 1990; PhD, Indian Inst. Sci., Bangalore, India, 1996. Postdoctoral rschr. Technische Universitaet, Dresden, Germany, 1997—98; asst. rsch. engr. U. Calif., Santa Barbara, 1998—2000; postdoctoral rschr. U. Ala., Tuscaloosa, 2000—01, asst. rsch. engr., 2001—02, assoc. rsch. engr., 2002—. Contbr. articles to profl. jours. Grantee, Dept. of Energy Exptl. Program to Stimulate Competitive Rsch., 2003—06, Office of Naval Rsch., 2003—06; Humboldt Rsch. fellow, Humboldt Found., Germany, 1997—98. Mem.: IEEE, Materials Rsch. Soc., Am. Phys. Soc. Achievements include research in field. Avocations: travel, music, tennis, reading. Office: U Alabama 317 Houser Hall Tuscaloosa AL 35487 Office Phone: 205-348-1685. Home Fax: 205-348-1685; Office Fax: 205-348-1685. Business E-Mail: padmini@bama.ua.edu.

PERIBERE, JEROME L., agricultural products executive; M in Bus. Econs. and Fin., Inst. D'Etudes Politiques, Paris. With Dow Chem. Co., 1977—, regional mktg. mgr. Ea. Europe, 1982—85, regional mgr. Mid. East and Africa, 1985—88, dir. European agr. bus., 1988—89, comml. dir. agr. bus. Europe, 1989—93, global comml. dir. Indpls., 1993—97, corp. strategy leader Dow AgroSciences, 1997—98, global leader Weed Mgmt. Global Bus. Unit European Trade area, 1998—2002, global leader agr. chems., 2002—04, pres., CEO Dow AgroSciences, 2004—, mem. Office of the Chief Exec., 2006—. Mem. bd. BioCrossroads. Named a Power Player in Life Sci. and Tech., Indpls. Bus. Jour., 2005. Office: Dow AgroSciences LLC 9330 Zionsville Rd Indianapolis IN 46268

PERICAK-VANCE, MARGARET A., health facility administrator; b. Buffalo, June 28, 1951; m. Jeff Pericak-Vance; 1 child. PhD in Med. Genetics, Ind. U., 1978. Dir. Ctr. Human Genetics Duke U. Med. Ctr., Durham, NC, James B. Duke prof. medicine, chief, med. genetics sect. Co-recipient McKnight Memory & Brain Disorders award, 2001; named to Century Club: 100 People to Watch as We Move to the Next Millennium, Newsweek Mag., 1997; recipient Louis D. scientific prize, Inst. France Acad. Sci., 2001. Mem. Inst. Medicine, Am. Coll. Med. Genetics (founding fellow). Office: Duke U Med Ctr Ctr for Human Genetics Box 3445 Durham NC 27710*

PERICH, TERRY MILLER, retired secondary school educator; b. Greensburg, Pa., Sept. 22, 1948; s. Miller and Eleanor Ann (Schmuck) P.; m. Kathleen Ann Ferrari, July 26, 1975. BA in Elem. Edn., Edinboro U., 1970; elem. cert., Pa. State U., 1973; Masters equivalency degree, U. Pitts., 1994; postgrad., Carlow Coll., 1994. Trained student assistance profl., Pa.; cert. tchr. elem. edn. Tchr. sci. and math., Penn Trafford Schs., Harrison City, Pa., 1970—2003; v.p. Jeannette Area Hist. Soc., 2003—06. Mentor, tchr. Tchr. Enhancement Inst. St. Vincent Coll., Latrobe, Pa.; selected tchr. Watershed Restoration St. Vincent Coll. Latrobe. Author: Image of America, 2005; co-author: Postcard History, 2005, Postcard History Series. County committeeman Dem. Party, Penn Twp., Pa., 1987—; lion tamer Bushy Run Lions Club, Claridge, Pa., 1993—; sch. v.p. 1995, 2d v.p. 1996, 1st v.p. 1997—. Recipient Commendation, Pres.-elect Clinton, Student Assistance Program award for working with students at risk St. Vincent Coll. Prevention Projects, 1991. Mem. NEA, ASCD, PACE, Nat. Sci. Tchrs. Assn., Pa. Tchrs. Edn.

Assn., Pa. Sci. Tchrs. Assn., Westmoreland County Assn. Student Assistance Profls. (bd. dirs. 1992-94, mem. Westmoreland county student assistance team 1995-96, 96-97), Penn Trafford Edn. Assn. (exec. bd. dirs. 1990-91). Roman Catholic. Avocations: travel, education. Home: 13 Rizzi Dr Irwin PA 15642-8902 Office Phone: 724-205-1983. E-mail: middie22@aol.com.

**PERICH, THOMAS J.,** lawyer; b. Galveston, Tex., 1945; BS, Georgetown U., 1967; MA with honors, in Economics, U. Tex., 1971, JD with honors, 1975. Bar: Tex. 1976, admitted to practice: US Ct. Appeals (5th Cir.), bar: US Ct. Appeals (11th Cir.). Ptnr. Dept. Bus. Transactions Andrews & Kurth LLP, Houston, mem. policy com. Mem. Tex. Law Rev., 1974—75. Mem.: Tex. Assn. Bank Counsel, Houston Comml. Lawyer Forum, Houston Bar Assn., State Bar Tex., ABA, Order of Coif. Avocation: languages. Office: Andrews Kurth LLP 600 Travis St Ste 4200 Houston TX 77002-3090 Office Phone: 713-220-4268. Office Fax: 713-238-7175. Personal E-mail: tperich@akllp.com. Business E-Mail: tperich@andrewskurth.com.

**PERILLO, SALVATORE J.,** lawyer; b. Apr. 25, 1945; m. Elizabeth E. Perillo. BS, SUNY Albany; JD, Woodrow Wilson College Law. Gen. counsel Mohawk Industries, Calhoun, Ga. Office: Mohawk Industries 160 S Industrial Blvd Calhoun GA 30701 Home: 406 Elkhorn Cv Woodstock GA 30189-7170 Office Phone: 706-629-7721. Office Fax: 706-624-3825.

**PERIN, NOEL I.,** neurosurgeon; arrived in US, 1984; s. Rajes Perinpanaya-gam; m. Frances J. Baker, Nov. 30, 1985; children: Christopher D., Michelle N. MD, U. Colombo, Sri Lanka, 1973. Cert. neurosurgery Am. Assn. Neurol. Surgeons, 1994. Neurosurgeon, gen surgeon Middlesex Hosp., London, 1986—90; spine fellowship NYU Med. Ctr., 1991; dir. trauma U. Cin., 1991—94; dir. spinal neurosurgery Mt. Sinai Med. Ctr., N.Y.C., NY, 1994—2001; dir. spine and minimally invasive spinal surgery St. Luke's-Roosevelt Hosp. Ctr., N.Y.C., 2001—. Clin. assoc. prof. Roosevelt Hosp. Ctr., N.Y.C. Co-author: Thorascopic Spinal Surgery, 1999. Fellow: ACS (assoc.), Royal Coll. Surgeons Edinburgh. Achievements include research in pharmacological treatment in spinal cord injury. Avocations: golf, tennis, travel. Office: Roosevelt Hosp Ctr Ste 5G 80 1000 10th Ave New York NY 10019 Office Phone: 212-523-6720. Office Fax: 212-523-6115. E-mail: nperin@slrhc.org.

**PERINGIAN, LYNDA ANN,** dietician, writer; d. Mike and Clara A. Peringian. BS in Dietetics, U. Detroit, 1974; MS in Foods and Nutrition, Wayne State U., Detroit, 1976. Registered dietitian, cert. personnel cons. Clin. dietitian North Oakland Gen. Hosp.; chief dietitian Drs. Hosp., Detroit; dir. Healthcare divsn. Roth Young, Detroit, 1977—88; pres. Peringian & Assoc., Dryden, Mich., 1988—. Author: Healthcare Textbook, 1989, THE MIRACLE ROSES - A True Story, 2005. Vol. Birmingham (Mich.) Cmty. House. Avocations: sports, piano, cooking, reading, gardening.

**PERINO, DANA MARIE,** federal official; m. Peter McMahon. BA in Mass Comm., U. So. Calif., 1994; postgrad., U. Ill. Staff asst. for Rep. Scott McInnis US Congress, Washington, press sec. to Rep. Dan Schaefer; spokesperson US Dept. Justice; dir. comm. White House Coun. on Environ. Quality; spl. asst. to pres., dep. press sec. The White House, dep. asst. to Pres., dep. press sec., 2006—. Office: The White House 1600 Pennsylvania Ave NW Washington DC 20500*

**PERIQUITO, PAULO F.M.O.,** manufacturing executive; Formerly with ITT Data Svcs., São Paulo, Brazil; contr. manufactured product divsn. Alcoa, 1983—84, from gen. mgr. to dir. distbn. bus. unit, 1984—88, dir. all bus. units, 1988—89, CFO Latin Am., bd. dirs. Mex., 1989—91, v.p. corp. planning, human resources and quality, CEO Grupo Aluminio subs., 1991—94, exec. v.p., bd. dirs. Latin Am., 1994—96; exec. v.p., pres. Latin Am. Whirlpool Corp. Office: Whirlpool Corp 2000 N M-63 Benton Harbor MI 49022

**PERISIC, IGOR,** engineer; s. Miodrag and Dubravka Perisic. Dipl. Ing., Swiss Fed. Inst. of Tech., Lausanne, 1991; PhD, Harvard U., Cambridge, MA, 2000. Chief scientist Entopia Inc., Redwood Shores, Calif., 2000—05; cto Healthline Networks, Inc., San Francisco 2005—. Chmn. adv. bd. Entopia Inc., Redwood Shores, Calif., 2005—; vis. scholar Stanford U., Calif. 2005—; adv. bd. mem. Plazes.com, Berlin, 2005—. Grant, Swiss Nat. Sci., 1995—96, NSF, 1996, NIH, 1995—97. Mem.: IEEE, AAAS, Assn. for Computing Machinery, Soc. for Indsl. and Applied Math., Am. Statis. Assn. Achievements include patents for system and method for perosnalized information retrieval based on user expertise; patents pending for system and method for a dynamic content driven rendering of social networks; system and method for the harmonizing of content relevancy accross structured and unstructured data. Office: Healthline Networks Inc 660 third St San Francisco CA 94107 Personal E-mail: igor.perisic@post.harvard.edu.

**PERITO, ROBERT MICHAEL,** political scientist; b. Denver, June 27, 1942; s. Michael and Alice Perito; m. Patricia Perito, Sept. 30, 1967 (dec. Jan. 2003); children: Robert, Samantha. BA, U. Denver, 1964; MA, George Mason U., Fairfax, Va., 2000. Vol. U.S. Peace Corps, Nigeria, 1965—67; fgn. svc. officer Dept. State, Washington, 1967—95; dir. ICITAP, Dept. Justice, Washington, 1996—2001; sr. fellow U.S. Inst. Peace, Washington, 2001—. Diplomat in residence SIS, Am. U., Washington, 2003—; adj. prof. George Mason U., Fairfax, 1998—2003; vis. lectr. Princeton U., NJ, 2003. Author: Where is the Lone Ranger: The Search for Post-Conflict Security, 2003, American Experience with Police in Peace Operations, 2002; contbr. articles to profl. jours. Recipient Pres.'s Meritorious Honor award, USG, 1992, Avocations: hiking, running. Home: 311 Oak Knoll Terr Rockville MD 20850 Office: US Inst of Peace 1200 17th St NW Washington DC 20076

**PERKEL, ROBERT SIMON,** photojournalist, educator; b. Jersey City, Apr. 23, 1925; s. Louis Leo and Flora Sonia (Levin) Perkel. BS, NYU, 1948; MS, Barry U., 1964; postgrad., Columbia U. Owner, operator Gulfstream Color Labs., Miami Beach, Fla., 1955-61; graphics instr. Dade County Pub. Schs., 1962-66; freelance photojournalist, 1967—. Rep. News Events Photo Svc., Ft. Lauderdale, Fla.; instr. photography Broward CC, 1982—92; rep. Patch Comm., Titusville, Fla., 1985—88; pub. Biograph/Comm., North Miami Beach, Fla., 1987—90. Contbr. photos stories and photographs to numerous mags. and indsl. trade publs.; exhibitions include Met. Mus. and Art Ctr., Coral Gables, Fla., Mus. Fine Arts, Boston. Former publicity dir. Coun. Internat. Visitors Greater Miami. With U.S. Army, 1943—46, ETO. Recipient Cmty. Spirit award, Zonta Club Greater Miami, 1980, Found. medal, Nat. Press Photographers Found., 2000. Mem.: VFW (life), DAV (life; trustee Jack Schwartz chpt., past comdr. Miami Beach-Surfside chpt., nat. citation for disting. svc. 1969, nat. svc. plaque 2000), Covenant Soc., Guardian Soc., Nielsen Media Rsch., Nat. Press Photographers Assn. (life), Barry U. Alumni Assn., Steamship Hist. Soc. Am. Found. (life; S.E. Fla. chpt.), NYU Alumni Fedn. (Leadership award for 1982-1983 fund campaign), World Ocean and Cruise Liner Soc., Silver Leader, Commander's Club, Am. Legion, Order of the Flame, Alpha Mu Gamma. Home: 3619 NE 207th St Apt 2107 Aventura FL 33180-3805

**PERKIEL, MITCHEL H.,** lawyer; b. NYC, Oct. 26, 1949; s. Frank and Ella Perkiel; m. Lois E. Perkiel, June 24, 1984; children: Joshua L., Alexa Kim, Griffin. BA, SUNY, Stony Brook, 1971; JD, New York Law Sch., 1974. Bar: N.Y. 1975, U.S. Dist. Ct. (so. and ea. dists.) N.Y. 1975, U.S. Ct. Appeals (2d cir.) 1975, Conn. 1988, Utah 1999. Law clk. to presiding justice N.Y. County Civil Ct., 1975; assoc. Levin & Weintraub & Crames, NYC, 1975-80, ptnr., 1980-90, Kaye, Scholer, Fierman, Hayes & Handler, NYC, 1990—2001, Jenkens & Gilchrist, Parker Chapin, 2001—05, Troutman Sanders LLP, 2005—. Notes and comments editor New York Law Rev., 1973-74. With USAR, 1969-73. Mem. ABA, Assn. of Bar of City of N.Y., Am. Bankruptcy Inst., Turnaround Mgmt. Assn. (dir.). Office Phone: 212-704-6016. Business E-Mail: mitchel.perkiel@troutmansanders.com.

**PERKINS, ANTHONY B.,** editor-in-chief, writer, educator; b. Dec. 6, 1957; Student, U. Calif., Davis, Calif. V.p. bus. devel. Silicon Valley Bank; founder, CEO Upside Pub. Co.; founder, CEO, editor-in-chief Red Herring Comms., 1993—2003; founder Always On, Woodside, Calif., 2003—, editor-in-chief, 2003—. Commentator CNN Fin. Network Digital Jam show, CNN, CNBC, ZDTV's News programs, Silicon Spin, European Bus. News; spkr. in field. Contbr. guest columns for various industry pubs.; co-author: The Internet Bubble. Founding chmn. Churchill Club, Palo Alto, Calif.; mem. bd. dirs. Am. Entrepreneurs Econ. Growth, Wash. Named one of the top ten tech./bus. journalists, Mktg. Computers mag.

**PERKINS, BRADFORD,** historian, educator; b. Rochester, NY, Mar. 6, 1925; s. Dexter and Wilma (Lord) P.; m. Nancy Nash Tucker, June 18, 1949 (dec.); children: Dexter III, Matthew Edward, Martha Nash. James Bradford (dec.). AB, Harvard U., 1946, PhD, 1952. From instr. to asso. prof. history U. Calif. at, Los Angeles, 1952-62; prof. history U. Mich., 1962-97, chmn. dept., 1971-72, 80-81, prof. emeritus, 1997—. Commonwealth Fund lectr. Univ. Coll., London, Eng., 1964; vis. prof. history Brandeis U., 1970, Ecole des Hautes Etudes en Sciences Sociales, Paris, 1983; Albert Shaw lectr. Johns Hopkins U., 1979; mem. council Inst. Early Am. History and Culture, 1968-71; program dir. Nat. Endowment for Humanities Fellowships in Residence for Coll. Tchrs., 1974-75 Author: The First Rapprochement: England and the United States, 1795-1805, 1955, Youthful America, 1960, Prologue to War: England and the United States, 1805-1812, 1961, Causes of the War of 1812, 1962, Castlereagh and Adams: England and the United States, 1812-1823, 1964, The Great Rapprochement: England and the United States, 1895-1914, 1968, The Creation of a Republican Empire, 1993. Served with AUS, 1943-45, ETO. Decorated Bronze Star; Recipient Bancroft prize, 1965, Disting. Faculty award U. Mich., 1986; Warren fellow, 1969-70; Faculty Rsch. fellow Social Sci. Rsch. Council, 1957-60; Guggenheim fellow, 1962-63 Mem. Am. Hist. Assn., Soc. Am. Historians, Orgn. Am. Historians (coun. 1969-72), Soc. Historians Am. Fgn. Rels. (coun. 1967-72, pres. 1974, Graebner award 1992), Mass. Hist. Soc., Am. Antiquarian Soc. Home: 827 Asa Gray Dr # 458 Ann Arbor MI 48105 Business E-Mail: bperkins@umich.edu.

**PERKINS, CHARLES, III,** newspaper and website editor; b. Brockton, Mass., July 25, 1952; s. Charles II and Barbara Perkins; m. Linda C. Burroughs, Jan. 4, 1985. BA, Dartmouth Coll., 1975. Editor Journal-Opinion, Bradford, Vt., 1977-78; reporter, editor The Union Leader and N.H. Sunday News, Manchester, 1978-81; Sunday editor N.H. Sunday News, Manchester, 1981-84; mng. editor The Union Leader and N.H. Sunday News, Manchester, 1984-92, exec. editor, 1992—; v.p. editl. N.H. Union Leader and UnionLeader.com, Manchester, 2000—. Recipient Andrzeja Drawicza award, Pres. Poland, 2005. Office: PO Box 9555 Manchester NH 03108-9555

**PERKINS, CHARLES THEODORE,** real estate developer, consultant; b. Houston, Aug. 16, 1967; s. Charles Abraham and Mary Margaret Perkins. Attended, St. John's Coll., Santa Fe, 1985-86; AB in Psychology, AB in French, Washington U., St. Louis, 1989; MBA, Institut Superieur Des Affaires/Groupe HEC Paris, 1994; postgrad. The Wharton Sch., U. Pa., 1994-95. Lic. broker, N.Y. Asset mgr. A. David Schwarz, III, Inc., Houston, 1989-93; pres. CTP Interests, Inc., Houston, 1991—; projet mgr. Washington Sq. Ptnrs., N.Y., 1995—, The Arete Group, N.Y., 1995—; mng. dir. Plymouth Ptnrs. Ltd., 1997—. Broker's lic. Tex. Real Estate Commn., Austin, 1991—. Dir. Washington Crew Classic Regata, St. Louis, 1989; founding coach Rice U. Crew, Houston, 1990; lic. judge referee U.S. Rowing Assn., 1991—, level I coach, 1991—. Recipient Prix De L'excellence BDE, Groupe HEC-ISA, Paris, 1994. Mem. The Penn Club of N.Y., N.Y. Sports Club, Mensa. Episcopalian.

**PERKINS, CHERYL A.,** paper company executive; b. Aug. 1960; m. Mark D. Perkins; 2 children. BS in Chemistry, Ga. Inst. Tech., 1983, M in Polymers, Chemical Engring. Dept., 1989. With Smith-Kline Laboratories, Atlanta; researcher Kimberly-Clark Corp., Roswell, Ga., 1984—87, with nonwovens tech. and product develop. grp., 1987—94, rsch. mgr., absorbent tech. Neenah, Wis., 1994—96, dir., absorbent tech., 1996, dir., feminine care R&D, 1996, v.p., global feminine care R&D, 1999—2000, v.p., sr. tech. officer, 2000—01, chief technical officer, 2001—02, v.p., chief innovation officer Tex., 2002—. Mem. adv. com. Inst. Paper Chemistry Rsch., Atlanta; mem. external adv. bd. for textile and fiber engring. Ga. Inst. Tech.; spkr. in field. Bd. dir. Fox Cities Children's Mus., Appleton, Wis. Named Outstanding Young Engring. Alumni, Ga. Inst. Tech., 2000; named one of 25 Masters of Innovation, BusinessWeek. Achievements include patents in field.*

**PERKINS, DWIGHT HEALD,** economics professor; b. Chgo., Oct. 20, 1934; s. Lawrence Bradford and Margery (Blair) P.; m. Julie Rate, June 15, 1957; children: Lucy Fitch, Dwight Edward, Caleb Blair. BA, Cornell U., 1956; AM, Harvard U., 1961, PhD, 1964. From instr. to assoc. prof. Harvard U., Cambridge, Mass., 1963-69 prof. econs., 1969-81, assoc. dir. East Asian Rsch. Ctr., 1973-77, chmn. dept. econs., 1977-80, H.H. Burbank prof. polit. economy, 1981—, dir. Asia Ctr., 2002—05; dir. Harvard Inst. Internat. Devel., Cambridge, 1980-95. Trustee China Med. Bd., 1995—2004, chair, 2000—04; cons. permanent subcom. on investigations U.S. Senate, 1974-80; H.M. Jackson vis. prof. Chinese studies U. Wash., 1985, Phi Beta Kappa lectr. 1992-93; Faculty Stanford seminar, 1996; lectr. Fulbright tchg. policy program, Vietnam, 1997-2004; mem. Internat. Adv. Group to Prime Min. of Papua, New Guinea, 1991-92, 2000-02; cons. Korea Devel. Inst., 1972-80, Govt. Malaysia, 1968-69, 2005. Author: (with M. Halperin) Communist China and Arms Control, 1965, Agricultural Development in China, 1368-1968, 1969, Market Control and Planning in Communist China, 1966, China's Modern Economy in Historical Perspective, 1975, (with L.S. Mason and others) The Economic Modernization of Korea, 1980, (with S. Yusuf) Rural Development in China, 1984, (with M. Gillis and others) Economics of Development, 1983, 5th edit., 2001; editor: China's Modern Economy in Historical Perspective, 1975, (with R. Roemer) Reforming Economic Systems in Developing Countries, 1991, (with J. Stern and others) Industrialization and the State: The Korean Heavy and Chemical Industry Drive, 1995; (with others) Assisting Development in a Changing World, 1997, Industrialization and the State: The Changing Role of the Taiwan Government in the Economy, 1945-1998, 2001, Innovative East Asia: The Future of Growth, 2003. Vis. com. Far Ea. studies U. Chgo., 1973-77; bd. govs. East-West Ctr., Honolulu, 1979-82; comoderator Aspen Inst. Seminar on Korea, Colo., 1980-83. Lt. (j.g.) USNR, 1956-58. Fgn. Area Tng. fellow, Ford Found., NY, 1958—62, NSF Sci. Faculty fellow, Tokyo, 1968—69. Mem. Am. Philos. Soc., Assn. Asian Studies, Assn. Comparative Econ. Systems (pres. 1999-2000), Am. Econ. Assn., Phi Beta Kappa. Home: 64 Pinehurst Rd Belmont MA 02478-1504 Office: Harvard Univ Dept Econs Cambridge MA 02138-5781 Business E-Mail: dwight_perkins@harvard.edu.

**PERKINS, EDWARD A., JR.,** elementary school educator; s. Edward A. and Shirley A. Perkins; 1 child, Krista. BS, Wayland Bapt. U., Plainview, Tex., 1981; MBA, East Tex. A&M, 1983; MS, Tex. Tech. U., 2004. Tchr. Eaton County Ind. Sch. Dist., Odessa, Tex., 1996—2000, Lubbock Ind. Sch. Dist., Tex., 2000—05, 2006—, Frisco Ind. Sch. Dist., Tex., 2005—06. Meteorol. observer US Army, 1974—77. Named Tchr. of Yr., Staked Plains Coun. for the Social Studies, Lubbock, 2005. Mem.: ASCD, Nat. Coun. for the Social Studies, Sierra Club. Avocations: hiking, camping.

**PERKINS, FRANK OVERTON,** academic administrator, marine biologist; b. Fork Union, Va., Feb. 14, 1938; s. Frank Otie and Mary Ella Perkins; m. Beverly Anne Weeks. BA, U. Va., 1960; MS, Fla. State U., Tallahassee, 1962, PhD, 1966. Marine scientist Va. Inst. Marine Sci., Coll. William and Mary, Gloucester Point, 1966-69, sr. marine scientist, 1969-77, asst. dir., 1977-81, dir., dean Sch. Marine Sci., 1981-91, prof. marine sci., 1991-97; asst. v.p. rsch. and grad. edn. U. Hawaii, Honolulu, 1997—. Baptist. Home: 7519 Olowalu Pl Honolulu HI 96825-2950 Office: U Hawaii 223 Crawford Hall Honolulu HI 96822 Office Phone: 808-956-6635. E-mail: fperkins@hawaii.edu.

**PERKINS, GEORGE,** writer, educator; b. Lowell, Mass., Aug. 16, 1930; s. George Burton Perkins and Gladys Beatrice Jones; m. Barbara Miller Perkins, May 9, 1964; children: Laura, Suzanne, Alison. AB, Tufts U., 1953; MA, Duke U., 1954; PhD, Cornell U., 1960. Instr. Wash. U., St. Louis, 1957—60; asst. prof. Baldwin-Wallace Coll., Berea, Ohio, 1960—63, Fairleigh Dickinson U., Rutherford, NJ, 1963—66; lectr. U. Edinburgh, Scotland, 1966—67; prof. Ea. Mich. U., Ypsilanti, 1967—2001. Author, editor: The American Tradition in Literature, The Reader's Encyclopedia of American Literature, others. Fellow Inst. for Advanced Studies in the Humanities, U. Edinburgh, 1981; Sr. Fulbright scholar Australia Coun. for Internat. Exch. of Scholars, 1989. Avocations: travel, tennis, literature, basketball. Home: 1316 King George Blvd Ann Arbor MI 48108-3212 Personal E-mail: george.perkins@emich.edu.

**PERKINS, GEORGE BRANT,** lawyer; b. Searcy, Ark., Apr. 16, 1964; s. H. George and Marion H. Perkins. BS, Ark. State U., 1985; MS in Accountancy, U. Miss., 1986, JD, 1989. CPA Ark. Assoc./ptnr. Womuck Landa Phelps McNeill and McDaniel, Jonesboro, Ark., 1989—97; owner, ptnr. Perkins Law Firm, Jonesboro, 1997—. Fin. com. S.W. Ch. of Christ, 2002—06; bd. dirs., pres. ARC/Craighead County, Jonesboro; bd. dirs. Girl Scouts U.S., Jonesboro, 2000—06, Better Life Counseling Ctr., Jonesboro, 2003—06. Mem.: ABA, Craighead County Bar Assn., Ark. Bar Assn. (bd. dirs. young lawyers sect., ho. of dels.). Church Of Christ. Avocations: hunting, fishing. Office: The Perkins Law Firm 624 S Main St #101 Jonesboro AR 72403

**PERKINS, HOMER GUY,** manufacturing executive; b. New Haven, Oct. 23, 1916; s. Frank W. and Emily (Oesting) P.; m. Dorothy C. Stock, Jan. 24, 1942; children: Maribeth Perkins Grant, Homer Guy Jr., Hazel Mary Perkins Adolphson, Dorothy Catherine, Caroline Anne, Faith Elizabeth Perkins Crotteau, Ruth Emily Perkins Sico. BA in Internat. Rels., Yale U., 1938; LLD (hon.), Westfield (Mass.) State Coll., 1977. With Enesco Group, Inc. (formerly Stanhome, Inc.), Westfield, 1939—, v.p., 1965-66, exec. v.p., 1966-70, pres., CEO, 1970-78, chmn., 1978-81. Treas. Stanley Park of Westfield, 1949-2005; pres. Citizens Scholarship Found., Easthampton, Mass., 1966-67, Easthampton Cmty. Chest, 1960-61; chmn. fin. com., bd. dirs. Western Mass. coun. Girl Scouts U.S., 1966-69; mem. devel. com. Clarke Sch. Deaf, Northampton, 1965-68; mem. fin. com. Town of Easthampton, 1962-70, chmn. fin. com., 1967-68; dir. Frank Stanley Beveridge Found., Westfield, 1956-95, pres., 1966-87; trustee Cooley Dickinson Hosp., Northampton, 1963-70, 84-92, chmn. bd. trustees, 1989-91; pres. bd. trustees Northampton Sch. for Girls, 1964-73; bd. dirs. Porter Phelps Huntington Found., Hadley, Mass., 1960-92, Guild of Holy Child, Westfield, 1969-76; mem. bd. overseers Williston Acad., Easthampton, 1961-64, Old Sturbridge (Mass.) Village, 1970-76; v.p. bd. trustees Williston-Northampton Sch., 1970-75, pres., 1975-78; dir. The Lathrop Communities, 2000, chair fin. com., 2001, pres. bd. dirs., 2005. With USAAF, 1942-46. Mem. Direct Selling Assn. (chmn. 1975, bd. dirs., mem. Hall of Fame), Paperweight Collectors Assn. (pres. 1991-95), Lions (past pres. Easthampton club). Home: 112 Bassett Brook Dr Easthampton MA 01027-1096

**PERKINS, HUEL DAVIS,** retired academic administrator; b. Baton Rouge, La., Dec. 27, 1924; s. John Earl Perkins, Sr. and Velma Davis Perkins; m. Thelma Ovella Smith; 1 child, Huel Alfred. BS, So. U., Baton Rouge, La, 1947; MusM, Northwestern U., 1951, PhD, 1958; LHD (hon.), La. State Univ., 2005. Dean coll. of arts & humanities So. U., Baton Rouge, 1968—78; from asst. vice chancellor for academic affairs to spl. asst. to chancellor La. State U., Baton Rouge, 1980—98, spl. asst. to the chancellor, 1998—2005. Vis. faculty Havard U., Boston, 1968; chmn. alpha phi alpha edn. found. Alpha Phi Alpha Frat., Balt., 1986—92; nat. chmn. scholars selection com. Coca Cola Found., Atlanta, 1996; invited participant Caribbean-American Scholars Exch. Program, Port-au-Prince, Haiti, 1974; mem. Pres. Clinton's Commn. on Black Coll. and U., Washington, 1994—96. Composer: (musical composition) Southern U. Fight Song, 1953, (songs) Alpha Phi Alpha Sweetheart Song, 1974; book reviewer: Black World Mag., 1973. Pres. Capital Area United Way; torch bearer U.S. Olympics, Baton Rouge, 1995. Named one of 100 Most Influential African Americans, Ebony Mag., 1995; recipient Brotherhood Award, Nat. Conf. of Christian and Jews, 1986, 100 Most Influential African Americans, Ebony Mag., 1994; fellow Humanities fellowship, Nat. Endowment for the Humanities, 1972, Huel D. Perkins Doctoral fellowship, La. State U., 1995; grantee Tchr. grant, Danforth Found., 1957. Mem.: Am. Soc. of Composers, Authors and P:ub., Omicron Delta Kappa, Pi Kappa Lambda, Sigma Pi Phi (grand sire archon 1992—94), Alpha Phi Alpha (chmn. edn. found. 1986—92). Democrat. Baptist. Avocations: tennis, reading, opera. Home: 1923 79th Avenue Baton Rouge LA 70807 Personal E-mail: hperk@cox.net.

**PERKINS, JACK EDWIN,** lawyer; b. Portola, Calif., May 25, 1943; s. Charles James and Vira Almena (Wing) P.; m. Barbara Kay Nielson, Jan, 18, 1969; children: Jill Christy, Keith Anne. BA, San Jose State Coll., 1966; JD, Hastings Coll. Law, 1972. Bar: Calif. 1972, D.C. 1989. From asst. U.S. atty. to dir. ops. bd. immigration appeals Exec. Office Immigration Rev. Dept. Justice, San Francisco, 1973—2004; dir. ops. bd. immigration appeals Exec. Office Immigration Rev., 2004—. Served to capt. USMC, 1966-69, Vietnam. Recipient John Marshall award Dept. Justice, 1986. Avocations: tennis, jogging, racquetball. Office: Exec Office Immigration Rev 5107 Leesburg Pike Ste 2519 Falls Church VA 22041-2400

**PERKINS, JIM C.,** automotive executive; V.p. Hendrick Automotive Group, Charlotte, NC, 1996—97, CEO, pres., 1997—. Office: C/O Hendrick Automotive Group 6000 Monroe Rd Ste 100 Charlotte NC 28212-6178

**PERKINS, JOHN ALLEN,** lawyer; b. New Bedford, Mass., Sept. 13, 1919; s. Ralph Chamberlain and Louise Bartlett (Allen) P.; m. Lydia Bullard Cobb, Sept. 9, 1944; children: John A., Susan W., Robert C., William B. AB, Harvard U., 1940, LL.B. 1943. Bar: Mass. Of counsel Edwards Angell Palmer & Dodge LLP, Boston; clk. Social Law Library, 1961-83; grad. researcher Univ. Coll., Oxford U. 1978. Bd. dirs. Greater Boston Legal Services, Inc., 1972-91. Author: The Prudent Peace— Law as Foreign Policy, 1981; contbr. articles to profl. jours. Mem. Dedham (Mass.) Sch. Com., 1959-65, chmn., 1963-65, town counsel, Dedham, 1971-72. Mem. Am. Law Inst., Am. Coll. Trust and Estate Counsel, Mass. Bar Assn. (dir. 1973-75), Internat. Acad. Estate and Trust Law (exec. coun. 1990-94), Boston Bar Assn. (council 1972-75, v.p. 1981-82, pres. 1982-84). Home: 100 Newbury Court Ste 610 Concord MA 01742-5835 Office: Edwards Angell Palmer & Dodge LLP 111 Huntington Ave at Prudential Ctr Boston MA 02199-7613

**PERKINS, LAWRENCE BRADFORD, JR.,** architect; b. Chgo., Jan. 13, 1943; s. Lawrence Bradford and Margery Isabella (Blair) P.; m. Phyllis Barbara Friedman, Sept. 11, 1966; children: Rachael Naomi, Judith Eve, Rebecca Abigail. BA, Cornell U., 1967; MBA, Stanford U., 1969; BArch, CCNY, 1976. Registered architect, N.Y., Conn., Md., Ohio, Ill., Conn., Pa., Mass., Ill., N.J., Ga., Fla., Mo., Ariz., Tex. Pres. Perkins Eastman Archs., N.Y.C., 1983—. Omnidata Svcs., N.Y.C., 1971-73; mng. prtnr. Llewelyn-Davies Assocs., N.Y.C., 1973-77, Perkins & Will, N.Y.C., 1977-81; ptnr. Attia & Perkins, N.Y.C., 1981-83. Author: Design of K-12 Schools; contbr. .hpts. to books and articles to profl.jours. Bd. dirs. Castle Gallery Coll. New Rochelle, N.Y., 1985—, Settlement Housing Fund, N.Y.C., 1991—, Helen Keller Internat. N.Y.C., 1993—, various other Scarsdale village bds. and coms.; chmn. bd. Hudson Planning Group. Fellow AIA (mem. various coms.), Am. Inst. Cert. Planners, Cornell U. Coun., Expiston Assn. (pres. 1993-96). Home: 4 Rectory Ln Scarsdale NY 10583-4314 Office: Perkins Eastman Archs 115 5th Ave New York NY 10003-1004

**PERKINS, LEEMAN LLOYD,** music educator, musicologist; b. Salina, Utah, Mar. 27, 1932; s. Milton Lloyd and Ida Margaret (Johnson) P.; m. Marianne Suzanne Contesse, Nov. 14, 1956; children: Eric Raymond, Bruce Philippe, Marc Christian (dec.), Patrick Thierry. BFA, U. Utah, 1954; PhD, Yale U., 1965. Instr. Boston U., 1964, Yale U., 1964-67, asst. prof., 1967-71, dir. undergraduate studies in music history, 1969-70; assoc. prof. music history, coord. for musicology U. Tex., Austin, 1971-75, grad. adv. for musicology, 1976; prof. music Columbia U., N.Y.C., 1976—2003, prof. emeritus, 2003—, chmn. dept music, 1985-90. Instr. advanced seminar in Medieval History, Smith Coll., 1968; vis. assoc. prof. music Columbia U., 1975; vis. prof. Boston U., 1978; dir. NEH Summer Seminar, 1977. Editor: Johannes Lheritier Opera Omnia, 1969, (with Howard Garey) The Mellon Chansonnier, 1979, Music in the Age of the Renaissance, 1999; gen. editor: Masters and Monuments of Renaissance Music, 1978—. Chmn. grad. musicology com., Columbia U., 1980-84, 1993-96, 97-2001. Sgt., 7th Army Symphony, U.S. Army, 1957-59. Recipient James Morris Whiton Fund award Yale U., 1965, The Otto Kinkeldey award Am. Musicological Soc., 1980, la Médaille de la Ville de Tours, 1997; Trumbull Coll. fellow Yale U., 1966-71, Lewis-Farmington fellow Yale U., 1962-63, Morse fellow Yale U., 1967-68, Am. Coun. Learned Soc. fellow, 1973-74, NEH fellow, 1979, 1984-85, French Archival Scis. fellow Newberry Libr. Center for Renaissance Studies, 1991; Martha Baird Rockefeller grantee, 1963-64, Paul Mellon Found. grantee, 1972, Am. Coun. Learned Soc., 1972, 82, U. Tex. grantee, 1975, Mem. Am. Musicological Soc. (chmn. program com. 1979, bd. dirs. 1980-81, adv. bd., 1985-86, chmn. ad hoc sub com., 1985-86, exec. com. delegate, 1989-92, mem. fellowship com. 1995-98), Internat. Musicological Soc., The Renaissance Soc. of Am., Phi Beta Kappa, Phi Kappa Phi. Mem. Lds Ch. Business E-mail: LLP1@columbia.edu.

**PERKINS, LUCIAN**, photographer; Grad., U. Tex. Intern The Washington Post, 1979, now staff photographer. Founder InterFoto (U.S./Russian photography orgn.). Author: (photography book) Runway Madness, 1998. Named Newspaper Photographer of Yr., Pictures of Yr. competition, 1993; recipient Pulitzer prize for explanatory journalism, 1995, Pulitzer prize for feature photography, 2000, Photo of Yr. award, World Press, 1996. Office: The Washington Post 1150 15th St NW Washington DC 20071-0002

**PERKINS, MARK L.**, university chancellor; b. Richmond, Va., Oct. 13, 1948; m. Carolyn J. Snider; children: Patricia, Diana. BA in Psychology, St. Andrews Presbyn. Coll., 1972; MA, U. Ga., 1974, PhD in Psychometrics and Stats., 1976. With divsn. of pers. Gov.'s Office Commonwealth of Va., 1972-73; rsch. assoc., instr. U. Ga., Athens, 1973-76; various positions Old Dominion U., Norfolk, Va., 1976-86, exec. asst. to pres. for policy and planning, assoc. prof., 1981-82, assoc. exec. v.p., prof., 1982-86; v.p. for adminstrn., prof. Calif. State U., Stanislaus, Turlock, 1986-91, exec. v.p., prof., 1991-94; chancellor, prof. U. Wis., Green Bay, 1994—. Environ. mgmt. cons., 1990-95. Contbr. articles to profl. jours. Trustee Green Bay Symphony, 1995—; bd. dirs. Downtown Green Bay, Inc., 1996—, Weidner Ctr. Presents Inc., 1994—; trustee Calif. State U. Stanislaus Found., 1986-94, treas., 1986-94; mem. adv. coun. St. Vincent Hosp., 1994—. Named to Outstanding Young Men of Am., 1984. Mem. APA, Am. Ednl. Rsch. Assn., Am. Assn. for Higher Edn., Am. Assn. State Colls. and Univs., Soc. for Coll. and Univ. Planning, Green Bay Area C. of C./Ptnrs. in Edn. (exec. bd. 1996—), Green Bay Downtown Rotary Club, Phi Eta Sigma, Phi Kappa Phi, Kappa Delta Pi, Phi Delta Kappa. Avocations: running, racquetball, music. Office: 3000 Cabarrus Dr Greensboro NC 27282

**PERKINS, NANCY JANE**, industrial designer; b. Phila., Nov. 5, 1949; d. Gordon Osborne and Martha Elizabeth (Keichline) P. Student, Ohio U., 1967—68; BFA, U. Ill., 1972. Indsl. designer Emerson Bednar Assocs., Evanston, Ill., 1972-74; Deschamps Mills Assos., Bartlett, Ill., 1974-75; dir. graphic design Cameo Container Corp., Chgo., 1975-76; indsl. design cons. Sears Roebuck & Co., Chgo., 1977-88; cons. indsl. design, 1988—, Lectr. CUNY, 1995; founder Perkins Design Ltd., Anna Wagner Keichline Gallery, Bellefonte, Pa.; adj. prof. grad. design seminar U. Ill. Chgo., 1982, 88, 91, 93, adj. instr. undergrad. design, 1984, 88, 91, 93; adj. instr. Ill. Inst. Tech., 1987, 91; vis. assoc. prof. Carnegie-Mellon U., 1991; juror annual design rev. Indsl. Design mag., 1986; mem. tech. rev. com. Ben Franklin Partnerships, 1991—; keynote spkr. several major U.S. design groups; spkr. Design in Am. symposium, Nagoya, Japan, 1989. Contbg. author: Design and Feminism, 1999; featured in Bard Grad. Ctrs.' Exhibit, NYC, 2000; contbr. articles to profl. jours.; patents in field. Co-leader Cadette troop DuPage County coun. Girl Scouts US, 1978-79. Recipient Outstanding Alumni award U. Ill. Alumni Jour., 1981, Goldsmith award, 1992; profiled in Indsl. Design mag., 1986, Feminine Ingenuity (by Anne L. Macdonald), 1992, Dun & Bradstreet Reports, 1993; profiled The Phila. Inquirer Mag., 1994; featured in Chgo. Athenaeum "33 plus 20", 1993, Pratt Manhattan Gallery, NYC, 1994. Fellow Indsl. Designers Soc. Am. (treas. Chgo. chpt. 1977-79, vice chmn. 1979-80, chmn. 1981, mem. dist. membership com. 1982, mem. ann. conf. com. 1983, mem. publs. com. 1985, bd. dir.-at-large 1987-88, v.p. Midwest dist. 1989-90, nat. sec.-treas. 1991-92, del. Internat. Coun. of the Socs. Indsl. Design 1989, dist. conf. speaker Mideast, 1993, Midwest, 2000, co-founder women's sect. 1992). Office Phone: 888-223-5211. Personal E-mail: njperkins@earthlink.net.

**PERKINS, NANCY LEEDS**, lawyer; b. Washington, June 19, 1956; d. Roswell Burchard and Joan (Titcomb) P. AB, Harvard U., 1979, M in Pub. Policy, 1987, JD, 1987. Bar: Pa. 1988, D.C. 1989, U.S. Dist. Ct. D.C. 1990. Jud. clk. U.S. Dist. Ct. (ea. dist.) N.Y., Bklyn., 1987—88; counsel Arnold & Porter, Washington, 1988—. Contbr. articles to profl. jours. Recipient Pro Bono svc. award Internat. Human Rights Law Group, 1990. Democrat. Avocation: tennis. Office: Arnold & Porter 555 12th St NW Washington DC 20004-1206 Office Phone: 202-942-5065. Business E-mail: nancy_perkins@aporter.com.

**PERKINS, RAYMOND LAMONT**, retired government official; b. New Rochelle, N.Y., Apr. 8, 1924; s. Raymond Lamont and Dorothy Marie (Porter) P.; m. Margaret Johnson, Aug. 25, 1946; children: Deborah, Doriane, Amy. AB, U. Denver, 1946, LLB, 1948. Bar: Colo. Pvt. practice, Springfield, Colo. 1949-54; fgn. svc. officer Dept. State, various locations, 1954-86; ret., 1986. Lmem. Fgn. Svc. Grievance Bd., Washington, 1990-2000. Contbr. articles to profl. jours. County atty. Baca County, Colo. 1949-54, dep. dist. atty., 1949-52. Capt. USAR. Mem. Kiwanis. Methodist. E-mail: rperkpeg@aol.com.

**PERKINS, RICHARD D(ALE)**, protective services official, state legislator; b. Boulder City, Nev., Nov. 15, 1961; s. Daniel Kenneth and Shirley Joan (Williams) P.; m. Terri Perkins, Feb. 24, 1989; children: Nicole, Stephanie, Brian, Ashley, Rikki. BA in Criminal Justice and Political Science, U. Nev., Las Vegas, 1979—; grad., FBI Nat. Acad., 1995. Police officer Henderson (Nev.) Police Dept., 1984-91, sgt., 1991-95, capt., 1995—2001, deputy police chief, 2001—; state assemblyman Nev. Legis., Carson City, 1993—, majority floor leader, 1996—2001, spkr. of assembly, 2001—. Mem. adv. bd. McCaw Sch., Henderson, 1996—; mem. Nev. Sentencing Adv. Commn., 1995-97, Indsl. Adv. Panel, Henderson, 1996; v.p. Henderson Dem. Club, 1992—; mem. chmn.'s coun. Big Bros.-Big Sisters; bd. dirs. Safe House Domestic Violence Shelter; mem. adv. bd. Nev. Ptnrs. against ALS. Recipient Meritorious award Clark County Dist. Atty., 1991, Silver State Citizen award Nev. Atty. Gen., 1991, Freshman Legislator of Yr. award Nev. Conf. Police/Sheriffs, 1993, Excellence award Nev. Trial Lawyers, 1995, Counc. of State Govmts. Toll Fell., 1997, Amer. Swiss Found. Young Political Leader, 1997, Leadership Las Vegas Grad., 1998. Avocations: competitive sports, travel, reading, hunting, fishing. Office: Henderson Police Dept 223 Lead St Henderson NV 89015-7328 Home: 328 Fife St Henderson NV 89015-2700 Office Phone: 775-684-8503.

**PERKINS, ROBERT EDWARD**, retired secondary school educator; b. Hartford, Conn., Mar. 22, 1939; s. Alfred Warren and Montez Ordell (Rideout) P.; m. Jane Richmond Dickey; children: Ann, Margaret. BA, Harvard Coll., 1961; MA, U. Maine, 1964. M of French Deerfield (Mass.) Acad., 1968—94; tchr. French Flint Hill Sch., Oakton, Va., 1990—2004; ret., 2004. Organist, choir dir. South Congl. Ch., Amherst, Mass., 1966—80, 1st Ch. Deerfield, Mass., 1980—90; organist Little Falls Presbyn. Ch., Arlington, Va., 1991—2005; ret., 2005. Pres. PTO Old Deerfield (Mass.) Grammar Sch., 1972; treas., bd. dirs. Pioneer Valley Symphony, Greenfield, Mass., 1975—85; pres. Ballet Arts Regional Rep. Ensemble, Greenfield, 1978—82.

---

Lt. comdr. USNR, 1961—63. Mem.: Am. Guild Organists (treas. Nova 1998—2001). Democrat. Home: 404 Lennox Rd W Palm Harbor FL 34683 Personal E-mail: vaorganguy@aol.com.

**PERKINS, ROGER ALLAN**, lawyer; b. Port Chester, N.Y., Mar. 4, 1943; s. Francis Newton and Winifred Marcella (Smith) P.; m. Katherine Louise Howard, Nov. 10, 1984; children: Marshall, Morgan, Matthew, Justin, Ashley. BA, Pa. State U., 1965; postgrad., U. Ill., 1965-66; JD with honors, George Washington U., 1969. Bar: Md. 1969, Mass. 1975. Trial atty. Nationwide Ins. Co., Annapolis, Md., 1969-72; assoc. Arnold, Beauchemin & Huber, PA, Balt., 1973; from assoc. to ptnr. Goodman & Bloom, PA, Annapolis, 1973-76; ptnr. Luff and Perkins, Annapolis, 1976-78; pvt. practice Annapolis, 1978—. Temp. adminstrv. hearing officer Anne Arundel County, 1984—; asst. city atty., Annapolis, 1980-82; atty. Bd. Appeals of City of Annapolis, 1986-2003, 2005—; mem. Appellate Jud. Nominating Commn., 1995—. Editl. adv. bd. Daily Record, 1996-97. Mem. Gov.'s Task Force on Family Law, 1991-94; adv. coun. on family legal need of low income persons MLSC, 1991; coach youth sports. Fellow Am. Acad. Matrimonial Lawyers, Am. Bar Found., Md. Bar Found. (bd. dirs. 1992-95); mem. ABA (ho. dels. 1991-93, 94-96, standing com. on solo and small firm practitioners 1993-97, chair 1996-97), Md. State Bar Assn. (pres. 1992-93, treas. 1988-91, bd. govs. 1985-87, chair membership com. 2002-04, chair spl. com. on lawyer profl. responsibility 1994-95, family and juvenile law sect. coun. 1983-89, chair 1987-88), Anne Arundel County Bar Assn. (pres. 1984-85). Home: 503 Bay Hills Dr Arnold MD 21012-2001 Office: The Courtyards 133 Defense Hwy Ste 202 Annapolis MD 21401-8907 Office Phone: 410-266-3558. E-mail: roger@perkinslaw.com.

**PERKINS, ROSWELL BURCHARD**, lawyer; b. Boston, May 21, 1926; AB cum laude, Harvard U., 1945. LLB cum laude, 1949; LLD, Bates Coll. 1988. Bar: Mass. 1949, N.Y. 1949. Assoc. Debevoise, Plimpton & McLean, N.Y.C., 1949-53; ptnr. Debevoise & Plimpton and predecessor firm, N.Y.C., 1957-96; of counsel, head rep. office Debevoise & Plimpton LLC, Moscow, 1997-01. Asst. sec. U.S. Dept. HEW, 1954-56; counsel to Gov. Nelson A. Rockefeller State of N.Y., 1959; asst. counsel spl. subcom. Senate Commerce Com. to investigate organized crime in interstate commerce, 1950; chmn. N.Y.C. Mayor's Task Force on Transp. Reorgn., 1966; mem. Pres.'s Adv. Panel on Pers. Interchange, 1968, chmn. adv. com. Medicare Adminstrn. Contracting, Subcontracting HEW, 1973-74; dir. Fiduciary Trust Co., N.Y., 1963-2000; trustee Bowery Savs. Bank, 1975-82; mem. legal com. to bd. dirs. N.Y. Stock Exch., 1995-2000. Editor Harvard Law Rev., 1948-49. Mem. N.Y. Lawyers Com. Civil Rights, 1970-73; mem. nat. exec. com., 1973-1980, co-chmn. 1973-75; mem. adv. coun. Woodrow Wilson Sch. Pub. and Internat. Affairs, Princeton U., 1967-69; bd. dirs. The Commonwealth Fund, 1974-97, Sch. Am. Ballet, 1974-85, chmn. bd. 1976-80; dir., sec. N.Y. Urban Coalition, 1967-74; trustee Pomfret Sch., 1961-76; The Brearley Sch., 1969-75; dir. Salzburg Seminar Am. Studies, 1970-80; mem. overseers vis. com. Kennedy Sch. Govt., Harvard U., 1971-77, Harvard and Radcliffe Colls., 1958-64, 1971-77, Davis Ctr. for Russian and Eurasian Studies, 2000-05 Recipient Spl. Merit citation Am. Judicature Soc., 1989, Harvard Law Sch. Assn. award, 1994, 50 Yr. award Fellows of ABA, 2002. Mem. ABA (commn. on law and economy, 1975-79, mem. ho. of dels. 1983-93), N.Y. State Bar Assn., Assn. of the Bar of the City of N.Y. (chmn. spl. com. on fed. conflict of interest laws 1958-60). Harvard Alumni Assn. (pres. 1970-71), Am. Law Inst. (mem. coun. 1969, pres. 1980-93, chmn. coun. 1993—), Am. Arbitration Assn. (bd. dirs. 1966-71), Russian Inst. Dirs. (mem. expert coun. 2002-), Ind. Dirs. Assn. (mem. adv. com. Russia 2002-). Home: 1120 5th Ave New York NY 10128-0144 Office: Debevoise & Plimpton 919 3rd Ave 46th Fl New York NY 10022-3916 Office Phone: 212-909-6421. Business E-Mail: rbperkins@debevoise.com.

**PERKINS, SANDRA LAIRD**, biology educator; b. Ancon, Canal Zone, Panama, Dec. 20, 1949; d. Duncan, Jr. and Harriett Uphoff Laird; m. James Stuart Perkins, Aug. 5, 1972; children: Laird Stuart, Duncan Peirce. BS, U. Ill., Urbana-Champaign, 1972; MS. So. Ill. U., Edwardsville, 2002. Antibiotic & vitamin analysis technician dept. ag. analytical svcs. Tex. A&M U., College Station, 1973; mt(ascp) Howard Meml. Hosp. Lab., Biloxi, Miss., 1975—77, USAF Hosp. Lab., RAF Lakenheath, England, 1983—84; biology tchr. Triad HS, Troy, Ill., 1991—; adj. prof. St. Louis U., 2005—. Sponsor Triad HS Saturday Scholars, Troy, 1991—, Triad HS Envirothon, Troy, 1995—, Triad HS Sci. Club, Troy, 1995—2001, Triad HS WYSE, Troy, 2005—; presenter in field. Recipient ROSE award, Triad CUSD #2, 1998, Excellence in Tchg. award, SIUE, 1999—2000, award of Excellence, Ill. Math and Sci. Acad., 2004; Summer Rsch. Tchr. fellow, Am. Pysiological Soc., 2001. Mem.: NEA, Ill. Edn. Assn. (bldg. rep. 1996—98), Ill. Sci. Tchrs. Assn. (key leader 2004—06), Nat. Assn. Biology Tchrs., Am. Soc. Clin. Pathologists (assoc. Mt(Ascp). Avocations: flora & fauna appreciator, reading, birdwatching. Office: Triad HS 703 E Hwy 40 Troy IL 62294 Office Phone: 618-667-8851.

**PERKINS, SUSAN LAMMONDS**, art educator; b. Rockingham, N.C., 1957; d. Bobby Gene and Phyllis Ann Lammonds; m. Robert Eugene Perkins, Dec. 24, 1979. AA, Sandhills C.C., 1978; BSc, U. N.C., Pembroke, N.C., 1981; MEd. U. N.C., 1990. Cert. art tchr. Nat. Bd., 2003. Art tchr. Richmond Sr. H.S., Rockingham, NC, 1986—. Bd. dirs. Arts Richmond, Rockingham; chmn. Richmond County Art Educators, Rockingham, 1999—. Named Tchr. of Yr., Richmond Sr. H.S., 2005. Mem.: N.C. Educators Assn., Nat. Art Edn. Assn., Rockingham (N.C.) Woman's Civic Club (pres. 2000—03, bd. dir. 2000—03), Rockingham (N.C.) Intermediate (pres. 1997—2000), Rockingham (N.C.) Jr. Women's Club (life; various positions 1981—97). Avocations: gardening, painting, designing jewelry. Home: 323 Marshall Ave Rockingham NC 28379 Office: Richmond Sr High School PO Box 1748 Rockingham NC 28380-1748 Office Phone: 910-997-9812. E-mail: rperkins13@carolina.rr.com.

**PERKINS, TOM (THOMAS JAMES PERKINS)**, venture capital company executive; b. Oak Park, Ill., Jan. 7, 1932; s. Harry H. and Elizabeth Perkins; m. Gerd Thune-Ellefsen, Dec. 9, 1961 (dec.); children: Tor Kristian, Elizabeth Siri; m. Danielle Steel, 1998 (div. 1999). BSEE, MIT, 1953; MBA, Harvard U., 1957. Founder Univ. Lab. (merged with Spectra Physics in 1960's); gen. mgr. computer div. Hewlett Packard Co., Cupertino, Calif., 1965-70, dir. corp. devel., 1970-72; co-founder, gen. partner Kleiner & Perkins, San Francisco, 1972-80; sr. ptnr. Kleiner Perkins Caufield & Byers, San Francisco, 1980—; chmn. bd. Tandem Computers, Inc., Cupertino, Calif. 1974—97. Founder, chmn. Genentech; bd. dirs. Spectra Physics., Symantec, Corning Glass Works, Collagen Corp., LSI Logic Corp., Hybritech Inc., Econics Corp., Vitalink Communications Corp., News Corp., Iolon, Philips Electronics NV, Compaq Computer, Hewlett Packard Co., 2002-04, 2005-06; chmn. Acuson, Tandem Computers. Author: Classic Supercharged Sports Cars, 1984, Sex and the Single Zillionaire, 2006. Trustee San Francisco Ballet, 1980—. Mem. Nat. Venture Capital Assn. (chmn. 1981-82, pres. 1980-81) Clubs: N.Y. Yacht, Links, Am. Bugatti (pres. 1983—). Office: Kleiner Perkins Caufield & Byers 2750 Sand Hill Rd Menlo Park CA 94025*

**PERKINS, WILLIAM CLINTON**, manufacturing executive; b. Decatur, Ill., Mar. 7, 1920; s. Glen Rupert and Frances Lola (Clinton) P.; m. Eunice Cagle, Sept. 7, 1939 (div. 1954); stepchildren: William Rea Cagle, Howard Christy Cagle; 1 child, Clinton Colcord; m. Lillian Wuollet, Sept. 7, 1955 (div. 1965); m. Shirley Thomas, Oct. 24, 1969. BS Mil. Sci. and Meteorology, U. Md., 1954; MS in Bus. and Pub. Adminstrn., Sussex Coll., Eng., 1973. Commd. USAF, 1943—73, advanced through grades to col.; with Ship Sys. divsn. Litton Ind., Culver City, Calif., 1973—75; dir. material Hughes Aircraft Co., Tehran, Iran, 1974—78; mgr. internat. sv. Northrop Corp., Dhahran, Saudi Arabia, 1979—81; dir. materiel CRS, Riyadh, Saudi Arabia, 1981—83; head major subcontracts Lear Ziegler Corp., Santa Monica, Calif., 1984—88; pres., chmn. bd., CEO Snowtech, Inc., L.A., 1984—. Bd. dirs. Ice Village Ctrs., Inc., L.A., Forefront Industries, Maywood, Calif. Bd. dirs. World Children's Transplant Fund, L.A., 1987-95; mem. Mayor's Space Adv. Com., L.A., 1970-74; mem. Aerospace Hist. Com., Aerospace Mus., L.A., 1988-, Mus. of Flying, 1998—. Mem. AIAA (sec. chmn. 1970), Ret. Officers Assn. (pres. 1992-95), Military Officers Assn. of Am. (chpt. pres. 2003-2005),

---

Soc. for Non-destructive Testing (program chmn. 1973), Aerospace Hist. Soc., Am. Soc. Quality Control, Am. Meterol. Soc., Sigma Alpha Epsilon (alumni chpt. pres. 1974-76). Avocations: golf, scuba diving, sailing, flying, gardening. Home: 8027 Hollywood Blvd Los Angeles CA 90046-2510 Personal E-mail: snowtech@pacbell.net.

**PERKINS, WILLIAM CLYDE**, business educator; b. Lebanon, Ind., Aug. 2, 1938; s. Clyde Philip and Dorothy May (Finch) P.; m. Phyllis Louise Swinford, June 18, 1960; children: Bonnie Michele, Betsy Anne Hawkins, Jeffrey William. BS in Civil Engring., Rose Polytech. Inst., 1960; MBA, Ind. U., 1962, DBA, 1966. Instr. U.S. Mil. Acad., West Point, N.Y., 1964-65, asst. prof., 1965-66, Ind. U., Bloomington, 1966-69, assoc. prof., 1969-74, prof., 1974—2003, prof. emeritus, 2003—. Author: Managing Information Technology, 1991, 94, 99, 2002, 2005, FORTRAN for Business Students, 1981, Computers and Information Systems, 1973. Capt. U.S. Army, 1964-66. Fellow Decision Scis. Inst. (treas. 1984-86, v.p. 1982-84, pres. 1992-93, disting. svc. award 1988), Midwest Decision Scis. Inst. (pres. 1984-85, 25 yr. disting. svc. award 1994); mem. Assn. for Info. Sys. Mem. United Ch. of Christ. Avocations: hiking, travel, reading. Home: 4308 E Cambridge Dr Bloomington IN 47408-3109 Office: Ind U Kelley Sch Bus Bloomington IN 47405 Business E-Mail: perkinsw@indiana.edu.

**PERKINS, WILLIAM H., JR.**, retired finance company executive; b. Rushville, Ill., Aug. 4, 1921; s. William H. and Sarah Elizabeth (Logsdon) P.; m. Eileen Nelson, Jan. 14, 1949; 1 child, Gary Douglas. Student, Ill. Coll. Pres. Howlett-Perkins Assos., Chgo. Mem. Ill. AEC, 1963-84, sec., 1970-84; apptd. by Pres. to adv. bd. Nat. Armed Forces Mus., Smithsonian Instn., 1964-82. Sgt.-at-arms Democratic Nat. Conv., 1952, 56, del.-at-large, 1964, 68, 72; spl. asst. to chmn. Dem. Nat. Com., 1960; mem. Presdl. Inaugural Com., 1961, 65, 69, 73. With U.S. Army, 1944-46 Mem. Ill. Ins. Fedn. (pres. 1965-84), Ill. C. of C. (chmn. legis. com. 1971), Chgo. Assn. Commerce and Industry (legis. com., Raoul Wallenberg Humanitarian award 1993), Sangamo Club, Masons, Shriners. Methodist. Home: 726 Community Dr La Grange Park IL 60526-1555

**PERKINS- BANAS, MELISSA VERONICA**, psychologist; b. New London, Conn., Oct. 28, 1970; d. Roy Dennis and Marian Dana Perkins; m. Joseph Paul Banas, July 3, 1999. BA, U. RI, 1992; MA, U. Hartford, 1995, MS, 1996; PsyD, Yeshiva U., 2004. Cert. Psychologist 1999. Sch. psychologist Norwich Pub. Schools, Norwich, Conn., 1999—2003; psychologist Plainfield Pub. Schools, Plainfield, Conn., 2003—. Post- doctoral neuropsychology fellowship Fielding Inst., NYC, 2004—. Sponsored athlete Adidas Woodbridge Racing Team, Woodbridge, Conn., 2000—02. Recipient Conn. Distance Runner of the Yr., Hi Tek Racing Team, 2001; Cecilia Rothenberg scholarship, Yeshiva U., 2002—03. Mem.: Assn. Advancement of Applied Sport Psychology, Conn. Assn. Sch. Psychologists, NASP, Am. Psychology Assn. (Divsn. 40, clin. neuropsychology), Psi Chi Nat. Honor Soc. Psychology. Roman Catholic. Home: 58 Lake St Norwich CT 06360 Office: Plainfield Pub Sch 35 Church St Moosup CT 06354 Office Phone: 860-334-0103. Personal E-mail: jpbanas01@snet.net. Business E-mail: perkinsbanasm@plainfieldschools.org.

**PERKINS-MUNN, TIFFANY SABRENA**, psychologist, researcher; b. Colorado Springs, Colo., Sept. 12, 1969; d. Gladstone Perkins and Gail Synovia Baldwin; m. Vincent C. Munn, Dec. 28, 1998. BA, Georgetown U., 1991; MA, CUNY, 1998, PhD, 2002. Assoc. rsch. scientist Inst. for Basic Rsch. in Developmental Disabilities, S.I., NY, 1997—2001; dir. rsch. practices Mktg. Metrics, Paramus, NJ, 2001—. Cons. Rockefeller Found., 2001—. Co-author: (book) Keeping the Struggle Alive, 2002; contbr. articles to profl. jours. Recipient rsch. fellowship, Inst. for Basic Rsch., 1997—2001. Mem.: Am. Statis. Assn., Am. Psychol. Assn. Avocations: writing, racquetball, interior design. Home: 246 6th Ave Roselle NJ 07203-2044 Office: Mktg Metrics 305 Rte 175 Paramus NJ Office Phone: 212-762-2366. Personal E-mail: tiffola@aol.com.

**PERKINSON, ROBERT RONALD**, psychologist, consultant; b. Richmond, Va., Aug. 8, 1945; s. Gordon Archibald and Sarah (Haskins) P.; m. Elizabeth Godfrey Fly, July 27, 1968 (div. 1984); children: Robert Reps, Nyshie Page, Shane William; m. Angela Kaufman, Sept. 20, 1991. BS, Colo. State U., 1968; MS, Ea. Wash. State U., 1970; PhD, Utah State U., 1974. Lic. psychologist, S.D.; cert. chem. dependency counselor level III, S.D.; nat. cert. gambling counselor; nat. cert. alcohol and drug counselor; lic. marriage and family counselor, S.D. Juvenile ct. psychologist, Cedar City, Utah, 1971-72; psychologist in pvt. practice Jackson, Wyo., 1974-83; dir. psychol. svcs. Western Wyo. Mental Health Assn., Jackson, 1977-78, psychologist, 1983—; psychologist, clin. dir. Keystone Treatment Ctr., 1988—. Cons. in field; chief psychologist Grand Teton Nat. Pk., Teton County Sheriff's Office and Police Dept. Copyrights: The Yellowstone Park Game, The Good Health Game, The Grizzly Control Team, Communication from God, Chemical Dependency Counseling, The Mystics, God Talks CD, Peace Will Come CD, The Treatment of Pathological Gambling: A Step By Step Approach. Author: Chemical Dependency Counseling: A Practical Guide, 1997, The Chemical Dependency Treatment Planner, 1998, God Talks to You, 2000, The Addiction Treatment Planner, 2001, 2006, Chemical Dependency Counseling: A Practical Guide, 2d edit., 2002, The Alcoholism and Drug Abuse Patient Workbook, 2003, The Gambling Addiction Patient Workbook, 2003, Treating Alcoholism: Helping Your Clients Find the Road to Recovery, 2004; contbr. articles to profl. jours. Mem. APA, S.D. Psychol. Assn., S.D. Chem. Dependency Assn., Biofeedback Soc. Am. (sec. bd. dirs. Wyo. br.), Wyo. Bd. Psychologist Examiners (pres. 1997, bd. dirs. S.D. coun. problem gambling), Nat. Registere of Health Svc. Providers in Psychology. Address: PO Box 159 Canton SD 57013-0159 Personal E-mail: perk@iw.net.

**PERKO, FRANCIS MICHAEL**, church administrator, researcher; b. Chgo., Nov. 6, 1946; s. Frank and Mary (Potochnik) P. BA, MA, Boston Coll., Chestnut Hill, Mass., 1970; MDiv, Loyola U., Chgo., 1975; MA, Stanford U., Calif., 1976, PhD, 1981. Prof. Loyola U., Chgo., 1981—2005; canon to the ordinary Diocese of the Rio Grande, Albuquerque, 2006—. Adj. asst. prof., Xavier U., Cin. Author: American and Catholic: A Popular History, 1989, To Enlighten the Rising Generation, 1988, A Time to Favor Zion, 1987. Scholar Stanford U., U. London, Ecumenical Inst., Jerusalem; fellow U. Chgo. Mem. Internat. Soc. Edn. Biography (past pres.), Midwest Hist. Edn. Soc. (past pres.), AERA.

**PERKOVIC, ROBERT BRANKO**, retired international management consultant; b. Belgrade, Yugoslavia, Aug. 27, 1925; came to U.S., 1958, naturalized, 1961; s. Slavoljub and Ruza (Pantelic) P.; m. Jacquelyn Lee Lipscomb, Dec. 14, 1957; children: Bonnie Kathryn, Jennifer Lee. MS in Econs, U. Belgrade, 1954; B.F.T., Am. Grad. Sch. Internat. Mgmt., 1960; grad. Stanford exec. program, Stanford U., 1970. Auditor Gen. Foods Corp., White Plains, NY, 1960-62, controller Mexico City, 1962-64; dir. planning Monsanto Co., Barcelona, 1964-67, dir. fin. Europe, Brussels, 1967-70, dir. fin. planning-internat. St. Louis, 1970-71, asst. treas., 1971-72, Brussels, 1972-74; corp. treas. Fiat-Allis Inc. & BV, Deerfield, Ill., 1974-78; v.p., treas. TRW Inc., Cleve., 1978-88; pres. RBP Internat. Cons., Cleve., 1988—. Former dir. U.S. Bus. Coun. for Southeastern Europe, Inc. Active Cleve. Commn. on Fgn. Relations. Inc. Served with Yugoslavian Army, 1944-47. Mem. Fin. Execs. Inst., Cleve. Treas. Club (past bd. dirs., pres.), Latin Am. Bus. Assn. (co-founder), Mayfield Village (Ohio) Racquet Club. Office: RBP Internat Cons 26 Pepper Creek Dr Cleveland OH 44124-5248

**PERKOWSKI, JAN LOUIS**, language, literature and folklore educator; b. Perth Amboy, N.J., Dec. 29, 1936; m. Liliana Asenova Daskalova, May 24, 1989. AB magna cum laude, Harvard U., 1959, AM, 1960, PhD, 1965. Asst. prof. U. Calif. Santa Barbara, 1964-65; assoc. prof. U. Tex., Austin, 1965-74; prof. U. Va., Charlottesville, 1974—. Author: A Kashubian Idiolect in U.S., 1969, Vampires, Dwarves & Witches Among the Ontario Kashubs, 1972, Vampires of the Slavs, 1976, Gusle & Ganga Among the Hercegovinians of Toronto, 1978, The Darkling-A Treatise on Slavic Vampirism, 1989, Vampire

Lore, 2006; contbr. over 65 articles to profl. jours. Grantee, fellow Ford Found., Harvard U., Kościuszko Found., U. Tex., Am. Philos. Soc., Nat. Mus. Man, U. Va., NEH, Kennan Inst., I.R.E.X., Fulbright, others. Mem. Am. Assn. for the Advancement of Slavic Studies, Am. Assn. Tchrs. of Slavic and East European Langs., Am. Assn. S.E. European Studies, Bulgarian Studies Assn. Office: U Va Dept Slavic Langs & Lits PO Box 400783 Charlottesville VA 22904 Office Phone: 434-924-3548.

**PERL, HAROLD,** neonatologist, pediatrician; b. July 24, 1950; m. Esther Jayde Strauss, June 18, 1972; children: Ari, Sharona, Gil, Doniel. BA, Yeshiva Coll., 1972; MD, Albert Einstein Coll Medicine, 1975. Diplomate Am. Bd. Pediatrics, cert. in neonatal and perinatal medicine. Intern, resident Montefiore Hosp. and Med. Ctr., NYC, 1975-78; dir. neonatology Hackensack (NJ) U. Med. Ctr., 1991—2005; co-dir. SIDS Ctr. NJ; pres. Gateway-N.W. Consortium NJ, 2005—. Mem. biomed. ethics com. Hackensack U. Med. Ctr., 1985—. Mem. health profls. adv. com. March of Dimes, No. N.J., 1982-97. Office Phone: 201-996-5362. E-mail: hperl@humed.com.

**PERL, MARTIN LEWIS,** physicist, educator, chemical engineer; b. NYC, June 24, 1927; children: Jed, Anne, Matthew, Joseph. B in Chem. Engring., Poly. Inst. Bklyn., 1948; PhD, Columbia U., 1955; ScD (hon.), U. Chgo., 1990. Chem. engr. Gen. Electric Co., 1948—50; asst. prof. physics U. Mich., 1955—58, assoc. prof., 1958—63; prof. Stanford U., 1963—. Author: High Energy Hadron Physics, 1975, Reflections on Experimental Science, 1996; contbr. articles on high energy physics and on relation of sci. to soc. to profl. jours. With U.S. Mcht. Marine, 1944—45, with U.S. Army, 1946—47. Recipient Wolf prize in physics, World Found., Israel, 1982, Nobel prize in physics, 1995. Fellow: Am. Phys. Soc.; mem.: NAS, Am. Acad. Arts and Scis. Home: 3737 El Centro Ave Palo Alto CA 94306-2642 Office Phone: 650-926-2652. Business E-Mail: martin@slac.stanford.edu.

**PERL, PETER,** editor; b. 1951; With Washington Post, 1981—; staff writer Washington Post Mag., 1996—2004; dir. training & career devel. Washington Post, 2004—06, asst. mng. editor, 2006—. Mem. exec. coun. Washington-Baltimore Newspaper Guild, 2001—; prof. journalism Georgetown U., Washington, Poynter Inst., St. Petersburg, Fla. Recipient over 35 journalism awards. Office: Washington Post 1150 15th St NW Washington DC 20007-0070 Office Phone: 202-334-6000.*

**PERLBERG, JULES MARTIN,** lawyer; b. Chgo., Jan. 28, 1931; s. Maurice and Louise Mae (Schonberger) P.; m. Dora Ann Morris, Dec. 22, 1968; children: Julia, Michael. BBA with high distinction, U. Mich., 1952, JD with high distinction, 1957. Bar: Ill. 1958, D.C. 1964; C.P.A., Ill. Acct. Arthur Andersen & Co., Chgo., 1954-55; faculty U. Mich. Law Sch., Ann Arbor, 1957-58; assoc. Sidley & Austin and predecessor firm, Chgo., 1958-65, ptnr., 1966-98, sr. counsel, 1998—. Mem. Glencoe (Ill.) Bd. Edn., 1980-87, pres., 1985-86; bd. dirs. Juvenile Diabetes Found., Chgo., 1981-2001, v.p. 1983-85, treas., 1988-90, 96-98; exec. bd. Am. Jewish Com., Chgo., 1978-88, v.p., 1981-83; trustee New Trier Twp. Schs., 1987-91, pres., 1989-91; class co-chairperson parents com. Duke U., 1992-94. 1st lt. U.S. Army, 1952-54. Recipient Gold medal Ill. Soc. C.P.A.s, 1955 Mem. ABA, Chgo. Bar Assn., Lawyers Club, Mid-Day Club (Chgo.), Std. Club. Clubs: Legal, Law; Mid-Day (Chgo.); Standard. Home: 568 Westley Rd Glencoe IL 60022-1071 Personal E-mail: djperlberg@com.net.

**PERLE, EUGENE GABRIEL,** lawyer; b. NYC, Dec. 21, 1922; s. Philip and Simme (Meschenberg) P.; m. Ellen Carlotta Kraus, Nov. 26, 1953 (dec. 1964); 1 child, Elizabeth Anne Perle; m. Ruth Friedberg Lerner, May 23, 1972 (div. 1977); m. Patricia Fitzpatrick Sinnott, Jan. 24, 1981. BA, Queens Coll., 1943; JD, Yale U., 1949. Bar: NY 1950, Conn. 1995. Assoc. Cravath, Swaine & Moore, NYC, 1949-53; asst. counsel NY State Moreland Commn. Investigation Harness Racing, NYC, 1953-54; assoc. Gordon, Brady, Caffrey & Keller, NYC, 1954-56; assoc. gen. atty. Time Inc., NYC, 1956-66, pub. counsel, 1966-73, v.p. law, 1973-80, corp. v.p. law, 1980-85; counsel Proskauer & Rose, NYC, 1985-92, Chapman & Fennell, 1992-94; mem. Ohlandt, Greeley, Ruggiero & Perle, Stamford, Conn., 1995-97, sr. counsel, 1998—. Co-author: Perle & Williams Publishing Law, 1988-2004; mem. editl. bd. Yale Law Jour., 1948-49; mem. adv. bd. Bur. Nat. Affairs Patent, Trademark and Copyright Jour., 1972-86; contbr. to Bull. Copyright Soc. USA. Trustee Baron deHirsch Fund, 1959-87, hon. trustee, 1988—; commr. Nat. Commn. New Technol. Uses Copyrighted Works, 1975-78; bd. dirs. NY Sch. Circus Arts, Inc., 1979-87, Am. Arbitration Assn., 1979-84; justice of peace City of Norwalk, Conn., 1960-63. Lt. USNR, 1943-46. Mem. ABA (chmn. copyright divsn. 1970-71, 86-87, chmn. com. copyright new tech. 1971-73, chmn. com. econs. profession 1976, coun. patent, trademark copyright sect. 1979-83, governing bd. forum com. comms. law 1979-85, chmn. related fields future devels. divsn. forum com. entertainment sports industries 1979), Copyright Soc. USA (trustee 1962-64, 69-70, 71-74, pres. 1976-78, hon. trustee 1978—), US Trademark Assn. (bd. dirs. 1969-72, 74-77, v.p. 1972-73), Assn. Bar City NY, Sunningdale Country Club, Century Assn., Banyan Golf Club of Palm Beach. Democrat. Office: Ohlandt Greeley Ruggiero & Perle One Landmark Sq Stamford CT 06901 Office Phone: 203-327-4500. E-mail: egperle@ix.netcom.com, egperle@ogrp.com.

**PERLE, GEORGE,** composer; b. Bayonne, N.J., May 6, 1915; s. Joseph and Mary (Sanders) Perlman; m. Laura Slobe, 1940; m. Barbara Philips, Aug. 11, 1958 (dec.); children: Kathy, Annette; 1 stepchild, Max Massey; m. Shirley Gabis Rhoads, June 6, 1982; stepchildren: Paul Rhoads, Daisy Rhoads. MusB, DePaul U. 1938; MusM, Am. Conservatory of Music, 1942; PhD, NYU, 1956. Faculty U. Louisville, 1949-57, U. Calif., Davis, 1957-61, Juilliard Sch. Music, 1963, Yale U., 1965-66, U. So. Calif., summer 1965, Tanglewood, summers 1967, 80, 87; from asst. prof. to prof. CUNY, 1961-85, prof. emeritus, 1985—; composer in residence San Francisco Symphony, 1989-91. Vis. Birge-Cary prof. music SUNY, Buffalo, 1971-72; vis. prof. U. Pa., 1976, 80, Columbia U., 1979, 83; vis. Ernest Bloch prof. music U. Calif., Berkeley, 1989; vis. disting. prof. music NYU, N.Y.C., 1994. Author: Serial Composition and Atonality 1962, 6th edit., 1991, Twelve-Tone Tonality, 1977, 2d edit., 1996, The Operas of Alban Berg, vol. 1, 1980, vol. 2, 1985, The Listening Composer, 1990, The Right Notes, 1995, Style and Idea in the Lyric Suite of Alban Berg, 1995, 2d edit., 2001; contbr. articles in Am., fgn. mus. jours.; composer: Pantomime, Interlude and Fugue, 1937, Little Suite for Piano, 1939, Two Rilke Songs, 1941, Sonata for Solo Viola, 1942, Three Sonatas for Clarinet, 1943, Piano Piece, 1945, Hebrew Melodies for Cello, 1945, Lyric Piece for Cello and Piano, 1946, Six Preludes for Piano, 1946, Sonata for Solo Cello, 1947, Solemn Procession for Band, 1947, Sonata for Piano, 1950, Three Inventions for Piano, 1957, Quintet for Strings, 1958, Wind Quintet I, 1959, Sonata I for Solo Violin, 1959, Wind Quintet II, 1960, Fifth String Quartet, 1960-67, Three Movements for Orchestra, 1960, Monody I for flute, 1960, Music for The Birds of Aristophanes, 1961, Monody II for double bass 1962, Serenade I for Viola and Chamber Ensemble, 1962, Three Inventions for Bassoon, 1962, Sonata II for Solo Violin, 1963, Short Sonata for Piano, 1964, Solo Partita for Violin and Viola, 1965, Six Bagatelles for Orch., 1965, Concerto for Cello and Orch., 1966, Wind Quintet III, 1967, Serenade II for Chamber Ensemble, 1968, Toccata for Piano, 1969, Suite in C for Piano, 1970, Fantasy-Variations for Piano, 1971, Sonata Quasi una Fantasia for Clarinet and Piano, 1972, Seventh String Quartet, 1973, Songs of Praise and Lamentation for chorus and orch. 1974, Six Etudes for Piano, 1976, 13 Dickinson Songs, 1978, Concertino for Piano, Winds, and Timpani, 1979, A Short Symphony, 1980, Ballade for Piano, 1981, Sonata a quattro, 1982, Serenade III for Piano and Chamber Ensemble, 1983, Six New Etudes for Piano, 1984, Wind Quintet IV, 1984, Sonata for Cello and Piano, 1985, Sonatina I for Piano, 1986, Sonata a cinque, 1986, Dance Fantasy for Orch., 1986, Lyric Intermezzo for fifteen players, 1987, Lyric Intermezzo for piano, 1987, New Fanfares for brass ensemble, 1987, Sinfonietta, 1987, Windows of Order for string quartet, 1988, Sextet for winds and piano, 1988, Concerto for Piano and Orch., 1990, Sinfonietta II, 1990, Concerto No. 2 for Piano and Orch., 1992, Adagio for Orch., 1992, Transcendental Modulations (commd. for 150 anniversary N.Y. Philharmonic), 1993, Phantasyplay for Piano, 1994, Duos for French horn and string quartet, 1995, Six Celebratory Inventions for Piano, 1995, Critical Moments

for Six Players, 1996, Chansons Cachées for Piano, 1997, Musical Offerings for Piano (left hand alone), 1998, Brief Encounters for string quartet, 1998, Nine Bagatelles for Piano, 1999, Critical Moments (2) for Six Players, 2001, Triptych for Solo Violin and Piano, 2003, Bassoon Music for Solo Bassoon, 2004, Lyric Suite, Universal, 2005, The Operas of Alban Berg, 2005 (Otto Kinkeldey award); writer, editor: Preface of Berg's Lyric Suite, 2005. Served with AUS, 1943-46, ETO, PTO. Recipient award Nat. Inst. Arts and Letters, 1977, Pulitzer prize, 1986; Guggenheim fellow, 1966-67, 74-75, MacArthur fellow, 1986; grantee Am. Council Learned Socs., 1968-69, NEA, 1978-79, 85. Fellow Am. Acad. Arts and Scis.; mem. Am. Musicol. Soc., ASCAP (Deems Taylor award 1973, 78, 81), Am. Acad. Arts and Letters. Personal E-mail: gxperle@aol.com.

**PERLE, RICHARD NORMAN,** former federal agency administrator; b. NYC, Sept. 16, 1941; s. Jack Harold and Martha Gloria Perle; m. Leslie Joan Barr, July 31, 1977; 1 child, Jonathan. BA, U. So. Calif.: 1964; postgrad. in econs., U. London, 1962-63; MA, Princeton U., 1967. Prof. staff mem. subcom. nat. security Senate Com. on Govt. Ops., Washington, 1970-72; profl. staff mem. to Senator Henry M. Jackson committee on armed services U.S. Senate, Washington, 1969-80; asst. sec. internat. security policy US Dept. Def., Washington, 1981-87; resident fellow Am. Enterprise Inst. for Pub. Policy Rsch., Washington, 1987—. Mem. Def. Policy Bd., 1987—2004, chmn., 2001—03; co-founder Project for the New Am. Century. Prodr.: (TV miniseries) The Gulf Crisis: The Road to War, 1992; author: (non-fiction) Hard Line, 1992; author: (with David Frum) An End to Evil: How to Win the War on Terror, 2004; editor: Reshaping Western Security, 1991. Office: Am Enterprise Inst Pub Policy Rsch 1150 17th St NW Washington DC 20036-4603 E-mail: rperle@aei.org.

**PERLEGOS, GEORGE,** electronics executive; b. Greece; BS Electrical Engring., 1972. With American Microsystems; design engr. Intel, 1974—81; co-founder, v.p. tech. Seeq Technology, 1981—84; founder, pres., CEO, chmn. Atmel Corp., San Jose, 1984—2006, bd. dirs., 1984—. Achievements include inventing EEPROM technology, the basic technology for flash memory. Office: Atmel Inc 2325 Orchard Pkwy San Jose CA 95131-1034*

**PERLER, BRUCE ALAN,** surgeon; b. New Bedford, Mass., Mar. 12, 1950; s. J. Leonard and Muriel Marcia (Katzman) P.; children: Mason, Rachel. AB in Zoology summa cum laude, Duke U., 1972, MD, 1976; MBA, Johns Hopkins U., 2004. Diplomate Am. Bd. Gen. Surgery, cert. spl. qualificatons in gen. vascular surgery; lic. physician, Mass., Md. Surg. intern Mass. Gen. Hosp., Boston, 1976-77, surg. resident, 1977-81, clin. and rsch. fellow in vascular surgery, 1981-82; clin. fellow surgery Harvard Med. Sch., 1977-82; asst. prof. surgery Johns Hopkins U. Sch. Medicine, Balt., 1982-88, assoc. prof., 1988—97, prof., 1997—; asst. surgery Mass. Gen. Hosp., Boston, 1981-82; dir. noninvasive lab., mem. med. bd., vice-chmn. med. staff com. Johns Hopkins Hosp., Balt., 1982—, chief divsn. vascular surgery, 2002—, attending vascular surgeon, 1982—, med. dir. intermediate care unit, 1989-91, mem. med. bd., 1995—99; Julius H. Jacobson II prof. Johns Hopkins U. Sch. Medicine, Balt., 2002—; Cons. vascular surgery Johns Hopkins Bayview Med. Ctr., Balt., 1982—; circulatory system devices panel Ctr. Devices and Radiologic Health, FDA, Washington, 1989—, Rsch. Adv. Group, VA, Washington, 1993—; mem. diagnostic and therapeutic tech. assessment panel AMA, 1991; lectr. throughout U.S. and Can. Mem. editl. bd. Jour. Vascular Surgery, asst. editor, assoc. editor, 2006—; editl. bd. Jour. Vascular Endovascular Surgery, Annals of Vascular Surgery; contbr. articles to profl. jours., chpts. to books. Rsch. grantee NIH, 1986-87, 92-94. Mem. ACS, Am. Surg. Assn., Soc. Vascular Surgery (bd. dirs.), So. Assn. Vascular Surgery (program com. 1992-95, exec. coun. 2004—), Ea. Vascular Soc. (membership com. 1991-94, sec. 2001-, pres. 2004-), Soc. Univ. Surgeons, Assn. Acad. Surgery, Chesapeake Vascular Soc. (pres. 1992-93), Balt. Acad. Surgery, Duke Med. Alumni Assn., Phi Beta Kappa. Office: Johns Hopkins Hosp - Harvey 611 Dept Surgery 600 N Wolfe St Dept Surgery Baltimore MD 21287-8611 Office Phone: 410-955-2618.

**PERLESS, ELLEN,** advertising executive; b. NYC, Sept. 9, 1941; d. Joseph B. and Bertha (Messinger) Kaplan; m. Robert L. Perless, July 2, 1965. Student, Smith Coll., 1958-59; BA, Bard Coll., 1962. Copywriter Doyle, Dane Bernbach, N.Y.C., 1964-70, Young & Rubicam, N.Y.C., 1970-74, creative supr., 1974-76, v.p., creative supr., 1977, v.p., assoc. creative dir., 1978, sr. v.p., assoc. creative dir., 1979-84; v.p., assoc. creative dir. Leber Katz Ptnrs., 1984-85, sr. v.p., creative dir., 1986-87; sr. v.p., sr. creative dir. Foote Cone & Belding, N.Y.C., 1987-93, sr. v.p., group creative dir., 1994—2002; sr. v.p., sr. creative dir. Euro RSCG Life Becker, N.Y.C., 2003—04; creative cons. pvt. practice Greenwich, Conn., 2004—. Author: numerous poems. Recipient Clio awards, Andy awards, awards Art Dirs. Club N.Y., N.Y. Festivals, One Club. Home: 37 Langhorne Ln Greenwich CT 06831-2611 E-mail: ellen@perless.com.

**PERLESS, ROBERT L.,** sculptor; b. NYC, Apr. 23, 1938; s. Meyer and Ethel (Glassman) Perless; m. Ellen R. Kaplan, July 2, 1965. Student, U. Miami, Fla., 1955-59. One-man shows include Bodley Gallery, N.Y.C., 1968, 1970, Galerie Simonne Stern, New Orleans, 1969, Bernard Danenberg Gallery, N.Y.C., 1970—72, Bonino Gallery, 1976, exhibited in group shows at Bodley Gallery, 1970, Whitney Mus., 1970, Forum Gallery, N.Y.C., 1975, Bonino Gallery, 1975, Houston Gallery, Aldrich Mus., Ridgefield, Conn., 1978, 1987, 1994, 1997—98, Taft Mus., Cin., 1980, Stamford (Conn.) Mus., 1989, Bruce Mus., Greenwich, Conn., 1989, 2001, André Emmerich's Top Gallant Farm, 1991—96, Greenwich Art Soc., 2000, Sculpture Now, Stockbridge, Mass., 2003, Art Omi Internat. Arts Ctr., NY, 2004—06, Represented in permanent collections Whitney Mus., Aldrich Mus., Chrysler Mus., Norfolk, Va., Okla. Art Ctr., Oklahoma City, Phoenix Art Mus. Stamford Mus., Benton Mus., Storrs, Conn., Bard Coll., Annandale-on-Hudson, N.Y., Bucknell U., Lewisburgh, Pa., City of Corpus Christi, Tex., City of Palm Desert, Calif., Syracuse Hancock Internat. Airport, Miami U., Oxford, Ohio, Rusk Inst., NYC, Salt Lake C.C., Town of Port Chester, NY, U. Conn., Storrs, U. No. Iowa, Cedar Falls, Utah Valley State Coll., Heber City, others. Mem.: Sculptors Guild. Address: 37 Langhorne Ln Greenwich CT 06831-2611 Office Phone: 203-869-0710. E-mail: robert@perless.com.

**PERLGUT, MARK RALPH,** public relations executive; b. New Brunswick, NJ, Oct. 4, 1942; s. Louis Eliot and Mildred Ruth (Shapiro) P.; m. Phyllis Norma Hershon, May 21, 1946; children: Lauren, Andrew. AB in History, Rutgers U., 1964; MS in Journalism, Columbia U., 1965. Investigative reporter Atlantic City (N.J.) Press, 1965-67; nat. and local reporter N.Y. Times, 1967-72; assoc. editor McGraw-Hill Inc., 1973-77; dir. new ventures Instnl. Investor, Inc., 1977-78; editl. mgr., personal speechwriter Donald T. Regan Merrill Lynch & Co., Inc., 1978-80; sr. policy writer N.Y. Stock Exch., Inc., 1980-82; v.p. dir. policy comms. Chem. Bank, 1982-84, v.p., dep. head of corp. comms. divsn., 1984-85; pres. Mark Perlgut Pub. Rels., 1985-87; v.p., editorial dir., account group supr. Fin. Rels. Bd., Inc., 1987-90; pres. Perlgut Pub. Rels., Inc., 1990-96, Investor Rels. Co. N.Y., 1992-96; sr. v.p., mng. dir. investor rels. divsn. Lobsenz Stevens, Inc., 1996-99; exec. prin., mng. dir., investor rels. Publicis Dialog, N.Y.C., 1999—2001; mng. dir. Stern & Co. Comm., N.Y.C., 2001—02; pres. Perlgut Group Comms., N.Y.C., 2002—. Author: Electricity Across the Border: The U.S.-Canadian Experience, 1978. Chmn. Fair Harbor (N.Y.) Community Assn., 1980-82. Recipient 1st pl. award Fin. World Ann. Report Competition, 1st pl. award ARC awards Ann. Report Competition, 1989. Mem. Nat. Investor Rels. Inst. Office: 230 W 41st St New York NY 10036 Business E-Mail: mark@perlgutgroup.com.

**PERLICK, RICHARD ALLAN,** steel company executive; b. Chgo., June 23, 1947; s. Allan Arthur and Lorraine Perlick; m. Sharon Behrendt, Mar. 29, 1969; children: Jill Sharon, Timothy Richard, David Matthew. BS in Metall. Engring., Mich. Tech. U., 1969. Corrosion engr. CarTech Specialty Steel Corp., Reading, Pa., 1969-71; nondestructive test engr. Union, NJ, 1971-75; quality control sr. engr. heavy products AlTech Specialty Steel Corp., Watervliet, NY, 1975-78, gen. supt. bar finish Dunkirk, NY, 1978-79, gen. supt. metallurgist rod mill, 1979-86, mgr. product metallurgy, 1986-87, wire mill supt., 1987-89, sr. product metallurgist, 1989-90; gen. mgr. Techalloy

Co.-Union (Ill.) Wire Plant, 1990-94; dir. corp. metall. svcs. Techalloy Co., Inc., Union, Ill., 1994-96, v.p. metallurgy, process and quality depts., 1997—. Pub. spkr. and trainer on metallurgy of stainless steel; expert in field. Author, co-patentee in field; contbr. articles on stainless steel wire products to profl. jours. Cubmaster, scoutmaster Boy Scouts Am., Fredonia, N.Y., 1982-90; mem. ch. choir St. Paul Luth., Dunkirk, 1980-82. Recipient Pres.'s Scoutmaster's award Boy Scouts Am., 1988. Mem. AIChE, ASTM, Nat. Assn. Corrosion Engrs., Indsl. Forming and Fasterner Inst., Am. Soc. for Materials, Wire Assn. Internat., Am. Soc. Surface Finishing, Soc. Automotive Engrs., Kiwanis. Republican. Avocations: vegetable gardening, woodworking, fishing, golf, camping. Home: 1758 Woodhaven Dr Crystal Lake IL 60014-1940 Office: Techalloy Co Olson And Jefferson St Union IL 60180 Office Phone: 815-923-2131 x143. Business E-Mail: rperlick@techalloy.com.

**PERLIN, ALEXANDR,** oceanographer; b. St. Petersburg, Russia, May 15, 1969; m. Natalie Krochavkevich, Oct. 2, 1991 (div.); children: Michael, Daniel; life ptnr. Anna Kelbert. MSc (hon.), Russian State Hydrometeorol. U., St. Petersburg, 1993; PhD, Tel-Aviv U., 2000. Rsch. assoc. in phys. oceanography Coll. of Oceanic and Atmospheric Sci., Oreg. State U., Corvallis, 2000—. Contbr. articles to profl. jours. Office: COAS/Oreg State U 104 COAS Admin Bldg Corvallis OR 97331-5503 Office Phone: 541-231-2319.

**PERLIN, ARTHUR SAUL,** chemistry professor; b. Sydney, N.S., Can., July 7, 1923; s. Benjamin and Eva (Gaum) P.; m. Ruth Laurel Freedman, Nov. 18, 1950; children: Anna, Louise, Deborah, Myra, David BSc, McGill U., Can., 1944, MSc, 1946, PhD, 1949. Rsch. officer Nat. Rsch. Council Can., Ottawa, Ont., Can., 1948-67; E.B. Eddy prof. chemistry McGill U., Montreal, Que., Can., 1967-91, prof. chemistry emeritus, 1991—; rsch. scientist Pulp and Paper Rsch. Inst. Can., Montreal, Que., 1967—. Contbr. articles to profl. jours., chpts. to books; patentee in field Fellow Royal Soc. Can., Chem. Inst. Can.; mem. Am. Chem. Soc. (C.S. Hudson award 1979) Office: McGill U Dept Chemistry Montreal PQ Canada H3A 2K6 Office Phone: 514-398-6188.

**PERLIN, BERNARD,** artist; b. Richmond, Va., Nov. 21, 1918; Student, New Sch. of Design, 1936—37, Art Students League, 1936—37. Illustrator Life Mag., Fortune Mag.; instr. Wooster Cmty. Art Ctr., Danbury, Conn., 1967—69. Represented in permanent collections US Post Off., Tate Gallery, London, Nat. Collection Fine Art, Smithsonian Inst., Mus. Modern Art & Whitney Mus. Am. Art, NYC, Va. Mus. Fine Art. Recipient Nat. Inst. Arts & Letters award, 1964; grantee Koscuiszko Found. award, Poland, Fulbright Fellow, 1950, John Simon Guggenheim Fellow, 1954—55, 1959. Mem.: NAD (assoc. 1957—94, academician 1994—).

**PERLIN, JONATHAN BRIAN,** health services company executive, former federal agency administrator; b. 1961; s. Seymour Perlin; m. Donna Perlin; 1 child, Benjamin. MS in Health Adminstrn., Va. Commonwealth U., Ph.D in Pharmacology & Toxicology. Med. dir. quality improvement Med. Coll. Va. Hosps. Va. Commonwealth U., assoc. dir. internal medicine residency tng. prog.; chief quality and performance officer US Dept. Veterans Affairs, Washington, 1999—2002, dep. under sec. health, 2002—04, acting chief rsch. & devel. officer, 2003—04, acting under sec. for health, 2004—05, under sec. for health, 2005—06; sr. v.p. quality, chief med. officer HCA Inc., Nashville, 2006—. Contbr. articles to profl. jours. Fellow: ACP. Office: HCA Inc One Park Plz Nashville TN 37203*

**PERLIN, SEYMOUR,** psychiatrist, educator; b. Passaic, N.J., Sept. 27, 1925; s. Samuel and Fanny (Horowitz) P.; m. Ruth Joan Rudolph, Aug. 21, 1958; children: Jonathan Brian, Steven Michael, Jeremy Francis. Student, Johns Hopkins U., 1943-44; BA summa cum laude, Princeton U., 1946; MD, Columbia U., 1950; grad., Washington Psychoanalytic Inst. Diplomate Am. Bd. Psychiatry and Neurology. Intern Univ. Hosp., Ann Arbor, Mich., 1951-52; resident N.Y. State Psychiat. Inst., 1950-51, 53-54, Manhattan State Hosp., 1952; practice medicine specializing in psychiatry and psychoanalysis Bethesda, Md., 1954-59, Stanford, Calif., 1959-60, N.Y.C., 1960-63, Balt., 1964-72, Bethesda, 1974—; chief div. psychiatry Montefiore Hosp., 1960-63; dir. clin. care and tng. Henry Phipps Psychiat. Clinic, Johns Hopkins Hosp., 1964-72; sr. research scholar Ctr. for Bioethics, Kennedy Inst., Georgetown U., Washington, 1974-78; clin. prof. psychiatry UCLA Sch. Medicine, 1973-74, George Washington U. Sch. Medicine, 1974-76, prof. to prof. emeritus, 1977-97, 97—; also dir. residency tng., 1977-93; lectr. psychiatry Columbia U., 1963-64; assoc. prof. psychiatry Johns Hopkins Sch. Medicine, 1964-65, prof., 1966-72; dep. chmn. dept. psychiatry and behavioral scis., 1969-72; program dir. Fellowship Program in Suicidology, 1967-72; adv. council Univ. health services Princeton, 1970-82. Vis. fellow Princeton U., 1973, Oxford U., 1974; Joseph P. Kennedy fellow medicine, law and ethics, 1974-75; chief sect. psychiatry Lab. Clin. Sci., NIMH, 1955-59, mem. clin. program-project com., 1967-70; fellow Ctr. Advanced Study in Behavioral Scis., 1959-60; chmn. mental health study sect. B, div. research grants NIH, 1964-66; cons. Community Mental Health Services, Md. Dept. Mental Hygiene, 1964-72; chmn. bd. dirs. Youth Suicide Nat. Ctr., 1985-87. Cons. editor: Jour. Suicide and Life Threatening Behavior, 1970-89; editorial bd.: Johns Hopkins Med. Jour., 1970-72; editor: Handbook for the Study of Suicide; co-editor: Ethical Issues in Death and Dying; contbr. numerous articles to med. jours. Served with USNR, 1944-46, with USPHS, 1954-58. Recipient Meirhoff award in pathology, 1950, Bicentennial Silver medal for achievement in psychiatry, 1967, both Coll. Phys. and Surg. Columbia. Fellow Am. Psychiat. Assn. (named Disting. Life fellow 2003); mem. Am. Coll. Psychiatry, Washington Psychoanalytic Soc., Med. Soc. D.C., Washington Psychiat. Soc., Am. Assn. Suicidology (pres. 1969-70, Dublin award 1978, ann. lectureship in suicidology in his name George Washington U. 1995), Phi Beta Kappa. Home and Office: 5125 Westbard Ave Bethesda MD 20816-1413 Office Phone: 301-229-5330.

**PERLINGIERI, ILYA SANDRA,** art history scholar, writer; b. N.Y.C. d. Nathaniel Gordon and Dr. Naomi Miller Coval-Apel; children: Blake Andrew, Chemynne Alida. BA, U. Mo., 1966; MA, San Diego State U., 1982; PhD, Columbia Pacific U., 1999. Cert. life C.C. credential, Calif. Dir. Ilya Sandra Perlingieri Sewing and Design Sch., San Diego and Miami, Fla., 1973-92; asst. prof., chmn. dept. fashion design Marist Coll., Poughkeepsie, N.Y., 1984-85; mem. faculty Fashion Inst. Design, San Diego, 1986-87, L.A., 1999—2000. Adj. prof. San Diego State U., 1989-92; dir. Textile Arts and Conservation Ctr., San Diego, 1979-83; guest lectr. Met. Mus. Art, N.Y.C., Nat. Gallery, London, Art Inst. Chgo., Los Angeles County Mus. Art, Nat. Gallery, Washington, NYU, Yale U., others; guest PBS-TV, Sta. NPR, NBC-TV, BBC, London. Author: Sofonisba Anguissola: The First Great Woman Artist of the Renaissance, 1992 (transl. into French 1992), The Uterine Crisis, 2003; contbg. editor Threads mag.; contbr. numerous articles on costume and art history to profl. jours. and mags. Dir. edn. Nomad Mus. Tribal Art, Portland, 1999-2001. Recipient award Prague Quadriennale, 1979, Gildred Found., 1980, Samuel H. Kress Found., 1989, 99; French Fgn. Ministry Lecture grantee, 1995, grantee The Thanks be to Grandmother Winifred Found., 2001. Mem. Renaissance Soc. Am., Costume Soc. Am. (charter), Royal Horticultural Soc. (London), Victoria and Albert Mus., Met. Mus. Art, Huntington Libr. and Art Collections, Early Modern Women (charter), Am. Herbalists Guild, Am. Bot. Coun. Avocations: playing classical piano, lyric soprano, organic gardening, needlecrafts, gourmet cooking.

**PERLIS, DONALD M.,** artist; b. NYC, July 29, 1941; s. Herman and Sylvia M. (Marks) P.; m. Theresa Brown, June 9, 1968. Student, Art Students League, 1961, Sch. Visual Arts, N.Y.C., 1965, Skowhegan Sch., 1965. One-man show Sindin Gallery, N.Y.C., 1994, 95, Walter Wickiser Gallery, N.Y.C., 1996-97, Claudia Carr Gallery, N.Y.C., 1999; exhibited in group shows Whitney Mus., N.Y.C., Graham Gallery, 1971, 75, Sindin Galleries, 1993, 95, Charas-Elbohio, 1993; represented by Denise Bibro Gallery, N.Y.C.; documentary film on artist produced by Time Capsule Films, 1993; author: (monograph) Allegories of Love, 1995. Mem. NAD. Home: 110 Duane St #5R New York NY 10007

**PERLIS, MICHAEL FREDRICK,** lawyer; b. N.Y.C., June 3, 1947; s. Leo and Betty F. (Gantz) P.; children: Amy Hannah, David Matthew, William Garrison, Grace Joanne; m. Colleen M. DeLee, Sept. 8, 2003; children: William G., Grace J. BS in Fgn. Svc., Georgetown U., 1968, JD, 1971. Bar: D.C. 1971, N.Y. 1993, U.S. Dist. Ct. D.C. 1971, U.S. Ct. Appeals 1971, D.C. Ct. Appeals 1971, Calif. 1980, U.S. Dist. Ct. (no. dist.) Calif. 1980, U.S. Dist. Ct. (cen. dist.) Calif. 1985, U.S. Ct. Appeals (9th cir.) 1980, U.S. Supreme Ct. 1980, N.Y. 1993. Law clerk D.C. Ct. Appeals, Washington, 1971-72; asst. corp. counsel D.C., Washington, 1972-74; counsel U.S. SEC, div. enforcement, Washington, 1974-75, br. chief, 1975-77, asst. dir., 1977-80; ptnr. Pettit & Martin, San Francisco, 1980-89, ptnr., fedl. securities law litig., Stroock & Stroock & Lavan, L.A., 1989—, mem. operating exec. com.; adj. prof. Cath. U. Am., 1979-80. Mem. ABA (co-chmn. subcom. securities and commodities litigation 1982-83), D.C. Bar Assn., Calif. State Bar Assn. Office: Stroock & Stroock & Lavan 2029 Century Park E Ste 1800 Los Angeles CA 90067-3086 Office Phone: 310-556-5821. Business E-Mail: mperlis@stroock.com.

**PERLIS, MICHAEL STEVEN,** magazine publisher; b. Feb. 12, 1953; s. Sanford and Vivian (Lee) P.; m. Marilyn Dunlap, May 5, 1979; children: Morgan, Steve. BA in Psychology, Syracuse U., 1976. Mktg. dir. Bretton Woods (N.H.) Resort, 1976-78; exec. dir. Mt. Washington Valley C. of C., North Conway, N.H., 1978-80; pub. N.H. Profiles mag., N.Eng. Guide Rumford Nat. Graphics, Concord, N.H., 1980-81; v.p., pub. New Eng. Pubs., Camden, Maine, 1981-82, pres., 1982-84; pub. spls. Rodale Press, Inc., Emmaus, Pa., 1984-85, pub. Runners World mag., 1985-86, group pub., 1986-87; pres. Internat. Data Group, Peterborough, N.H., 1987-89; sr. v.p., pub. Playboy Enterprises, Chicago, 1989-90, sr. v.p., pres. - pub. group, 1990-92, exec. v.p., pres. - pub. group, 1992-94; pub. GQ Mag., 1994—96; COO, pres. TVSM Inc., N.Y.C., 1996—98; pres., CEO Ziff Davis Pub. 1998—2000; mng. ptnr. Softbank Capital Ptnrs., N.Y.C., 1998—. Mem. Mag. Pubs. Am., Young Pres. Org. Office: Softbank Capital Ptnrs 461 5th Ave 15th Fl New York NY 10017

**PERLIS, ROBERT VINCENT,** mathematician, educator; s. Sam and Esther Perlis; m. Susan Holz, Apr. 2, 1982; children: Alexander Russell, Rachel Samantha, David Joseph. PhD, MIT, Cambridge, Mass., 1972. Cecil Taylor alumni prof. La. State U., Baton Rouge, 2006—. Co-author: (book) A Survey of Trace Forms of Algebraic Number Fields. Scoutmaster Troop 7, Boy Scouts Am., Baton Rouge, 1987—96. Recipient Faculty Excellence award, La. State U. Alumni Assn., 1996, Disting. Faculty Tchg. award, La. State U. Found., 2002, TAF Honors Coll. Undergrad. Tchg. award, La. State U. Honors Coll., 2004; Woodrow Wilson fellow, Purdue U., 1968. Mem.: Math. Assn. Am., Am. Math. Soc. Achievements include research in witt rings, dedekind zeta functions, and trace forms of algebraic number fields. Office Phone: 225-578-1673.

**PERLIS, SHARON A.,** lawyer; b. New Orleans; d. Rogers I. and Dorothy Perlis. BA in French, Principia Coll., 1967; JD, Tulane U., 1970. Officer, dir. Perlis, Inc., New Orleans, 1973—2003; pres. SILREP Internat. Co., Metairie, 1984—; officer, dir. Internat. Auto. Svcs., Inc., New Orleans, 1985-89; prin. Perlis & Assocs., Metairie, 1985—2005; pres. Sharon A. Perlis P.C., 1981—2005. Legal counsel La. Ins. Rating Commn., 1980-84; adminstrv. law judge State of La., 1980-84, mem. Econ. Devel. Adv. Coun., 1982-84; exec. com. small bus. coun. Bd. of Trade, 1987-89, chmn. small bus. coun., 1988, exec. com. East Jefferson coun., 1989-96; dir. World Trade Ctr., 1985-2005, vice chmn. internat. bus. com.; dir. New Orleans br. Fed. Res. Bank of Atlanta, 1982-88, chmn., 1984, 86, 88; dir. Metairie Bank & Trust, 1997-2005; bd. of commr. Port of New Orleans, 1992-96, vice chmn., 1995, chmn. bd., 1996; del. U.S. Def. Dept.'s Joint Civilian Orientation Conf., 1997; adj. prof. A.B. Freeman Sch. Bus., Tulane U.; mem. Coun. for a Better La.; mediator U.S. Postal Svc., Econ. Devel. Commn.; mem. La. Econ. Devel. Commn., Inst. Women in Govt., Nichols State U.; mem. internat. adv. bd. A.J. Butts Sch. Bus., Loyola U. Mem. human rels. commn. City of New Orleans, 1992-93, Commn. To Reorganize City Govt., Leadership La., 2001; mem. exec. bd. La. Coun. Econ. Edn., 1986-89, Pvt. Enterprise Edn. Found., 1986-89; state del. White House Conf. on Small Bus., La. rep. internat. trade issues, 1986; dir. Metro YMCA, 1990-97; exec. com. agy. rels. United Way, 1987-90; mem. exec. com. Jr. Achievement Project Bus., 1987; vice chmn. La. Dist. Export Coun.; bd. dirs. Bur. Govtl. Rsch.; bd. dirs. La. Internat. Trade Commn.; mem. adv. bd. Internat. Program for Non-profit Leadership; mem. Econ. Devel. Commn., State of La.; mem. New Orleans Leadership Inst.; vice chmn. bus.-higher edn. coun. U. New Orleans; trustee New Orleans Pub. TV Found.; mem. New Orleans Pub. R.R. Commn.; mem. Jefferson Econ Devel. Commn.; commr. New Orleans Pub. Belt RR. Recipient Achiever's award Woman Bus. owners Assn., 1994, Jefferson Econ. Devel. Commn. award, 1994, Advocacy of Yr. award Small Bus. Adminstrn., 1988, 89, Iberville award New Orleans Pub. Group, 1996, Women of the Yr. award New Orleans Pub. Group, 2000, Patty Strong award Jefferson-25, 2000; named Young Leadership Coun. Role Model, 2001. Fellow Loyla Inst. of Politics, U. New Orleans Govt. Leadership Inst.; mem. ABA, Bankers Assn., Am. Arbitration Assn. (arbitrator/mediator), Jefferson Bar Assn., Orleans Bar Assn., Federal Bar Assn., Adv. Coun. Federalist Soc., La. Estate Planning Coun., La. Bar Assn., Gov.'s Commn. on Internat. Trade Devel., New Orleans Regional C. of C. (bd. dirs. 1990-2001), New Orleans Regional Leadership Inst., New Orleans Area Polit. Action Coun. (pres.), Leadership La., Greater New Orleans Found., New Orleans Estate Planning Coun. Avocations: reading, sailing, tennis. Office: Perlis & Assocs 6069 Magazine St New Orleans LA 70118-6006

**PERLMAN, BARRY STEVEN,** sociologist, educator; b. Bklyn., Aug. 25, 1944; s. Aubrey and Grace Perlman; m. Joan Paul Perlman, Apr. 29, 1984; children: Adam, Ryan. AA, Queensborough C.C., 1964; BA, Queens Coll., CUNY, 1966; postgrad., Adelphi U., 1966—68, Temple U., 1968—71. Lectr. Chestnut Hill Coll., Phila., 1968—69, LaSalle U., Phila., 1968—70; instr. Temple U., Phila., 1968—71; assoc. prof. C.C. Phila., Phila., 1971—, chmn. Dept. Social Scis., 1983—89. Chmn. coms. C.C. Phila., 1973—; reviewer articles various publs.; presenter and session chair profl. meetings and confs. Contbr. articles to profl. jours. Founding mem. Am. Cancer Rsch. Ctr., 1978; key communicator Bensalem Twp. Schs., Pa., 1976—79. Recipient Outstanding Contbn. award, Human Svcs. Careers Student Assn., 1990; fellow, NIMH. Mem.: Human Svcs. Career Assn., Am. Sociol. Assn., Am. Fedn. Tchrs., Nat. Social Sci. Assn. Jewish. Office: Community College Phila 1700 Spring Garden St Philadelphia PA 19130 Office Phone: 215-751-8560.

**PERLMAN, BARRY STUART,** electrical engineer, researcher; b. Bklyn., Dec. 5, 1939; s. Harold Wallace and Jane (Cohen) P.; m. Carolyn Amelia Francis; 1 child, David Matthew. BEE, CCNY, 1961; MSEE, Poly. U. N.Y., 1964; PhD in Electrophysics, Poly. Inst. N.Y., 1973. Mem. tech. staff, comms. lab. RCA Corp., N.Y.C., 1961-68; mem. tech. staff RCA Labs., Princeton, NJ, 1968-81, mgr. microwave rsch. lab., 1981-86, head design automation rsch. 1986-88; chief microwave photonic devices br. Electronics and Power Source Directorate, Army Rsch. Lab., Ft. Monmouth, NJ, 1988-95; dir. electronics divsn. Phys. Scis. Directorate, Army Rsch. Lab., Ft. Monmouth, 1995-96; chief RF and electronics divsn. Sensor and Electron Devices Directorate, Army Rsch. Lab., Ft. Monmouth and Adelphi, Md., 1996-97; R&D Engring. Ctr. staff Comm.-Electronics Command, Ft. Monmouth, 1997-98, chief applied comm., 1998-99; assoc. dir. prin. scientist Intel and Info Directorate, 1999—2003; assoc. dir. DARPA liaison office RDEC Hdqrs., 2002—03; assoc. dir. CERDEC, RDECOM, 2003—. Pres., mem. bd. dirs. INTEREX, Los Altos, Calif., 1981—83; rep. adv. group on electron devices, chmn. subpanel on RF Components Office of Undersec. of Def., chmn. Computational Electronics and Nanoelectronics tech. area HPCMO, 1995—2005, program mgr. modeling and simulation Electronic Battlefield Environ. Portfolio, 2000—2005, chmn. Darpa working group, program mgr., agt. Nanomechanical Array Signal Processors, MTO; sys. study team, modeling/simulation team for FCS comms. DARPA, agt. Intelligent RF Front End Program and tech. Agile Efficient Microsystems Program, 1999—2002; NASA/JPL adv. com. for SATCOM sys. on a chip U. Mich.; tech. adv. bds. UCLA; ind. adv. bd. Computer Applications to Electromagnetics Edn. NSF and U. Utah, 1990—94; mem. ind. adv. bd. Computer Applications to

Electromagnetics Edn. MIMICAD Ctr., U. Colo., 1989—95; adv. bd. Elec. Engring./WAMI U. So. Fla.; ind. adv. bd. Wireless Commns. NJ Inst. Tech., U. Hawaii, Manoa, 2003—; Ctr. prof. microwave/lightwave engring. Drexel U., Phila., 1992—; computational tech. area leader, adv. panel CTAAP; advisor NJ Nanotech. Consortium; mem. R&D Coun. N.J.; agt. Tech. for Eff. Agile Microsys., 2002—. Editor: Advances in Microwaves, 1974; mem. editl. bd. Wiley Jour. MW.MMW CAD, 1992—; contbr. articles to profl. jours.; patentee in field. Bd. dirs. YMCA, Princeton, 1975-78; pres. Home Owners Assn., E. Windsor, N.J., 1976-78; instr. Am. Heart Assn., N.J., 1978-82; chief rescue squad, E. Windsor, 1978-82. Fellow: IEEE (life; admission and advancement com. 1987—, tech. program chair Sarnoff Symposium 1999—2002); mem.: Comm., Antennas & Propagation, Automated RF Techniques Group (treas. 1984—88, v.p. 1990—91), Cirs. and Sys., Ultrasonics, Ferroelectrics and Frequency Control, Microwave Theory and Tech. Soc. of IEEE (IMS tech. program com. 1980—, editl. bd. chmn. CAD com. MTT-1 1985—92, MTT adcom. 1990—94, chmn. Instersoc. Liaison 1995—97, MTT adcom. 2002—, chmn. meetings and symposia com. 2002—04, chmn. membership svcs. com., repcom tech. adv. bd. 2005—). Avocations: woodworking, photography, pistol/rifle target competition, gardening, gourmet cooking. Office: Army Comm-Electronics Ctr RDEC Hdqrs AMSRD CER TSP Bldg 2700 Fort Monmouth NJ 07703-5000 Office Phone: 732-427-4883. Personal E-mail: bperlman@comcast.net. Business E-Mail: barry.perlman@us.army.mil.

**PERLMAN, BURTON,** judge; b. Dec. 17, 1924; s. Phillip and Minnie Perlman; m. Alice Weihl, May 20, 1956; children: Elizabeth, Sarah, Nancy, Daniel. BE, Yale U., 1945, ME, 1947; LLB, U. Mich., 1952. Bar: Ohio 1959, N.Y. 1953, Conn. 1952, U.S. Dist. Ct. (so. and ea. dists.) N.Y. 1954, U.S. Dist. Ct. (so. dist.) Ohio 1959, U.S. Ct. Appeals (2d cir.) 1953, U.S. Ct. Appeals (6th cir.) 1959. Assoc. Armand Lackenbach, N.Y., N.Y., 1952—58; pvt. practice Cin., 1958—61; assoc. Paxton and Seasongood, Cin., 1961—67; ptnr. Schmidt, Effton, Josselson and Weber, Cin., 1968—71; U.S. magistrate U.S. Dist. Ct. (so. dist.) Ohio, 1971—76, U.S. bankruptcy judge, 1976—. With U.S. Army, 1944—46. Mem.: ABA, Cin. Bar Assn., Am. Judicature Soc., Fed. Bar Assn. Office: US Bankruptcy Ct Atrium 2 8th Fl 221 E 4th St Cincinnati OH 45202-4124

**PERLMAN, DAVID,** journalist; b. Balt., Dec. 30, 1918; s. Jess and Sara Perlman; m. Anne Salz, Oct. 15, 1941 (dec. 2002); children: Katherine, Eric, Thomas. AB, Columbia U., 1939, MS, 1940. Reporter Bismarck Capital, ND, 1940, San Francisco Chronicle, 1940—41, reporter, sci. editor, 1977-79, assoc. editor, sci. editor, 1979—; reporter New York Herald Tribune, Paris, NYC, 1945-49; European corr. Colliers mag. and New York Post, 1949-51. Regents prof. human biology U. Calif., San Francisco, 1974; vis. lectr. China Assn. Sci. and Tech., Beijing, Chengdu, Shanghai; sci. writer-in-residence U. Wis., 1989. Contbr. articles to mag. Founding dir. Squaw Valley (Calif.) Cmty. Writers; bd. dirs. Alan Guttmacher Inst., 1990—99; trustee Scientists Inst. Pub. Info., 1986—94; chmn. pub. svc. award com. Nat. Sci. Bd., 1998—2001. With inf. USAAF, 1941—45. Recipient Atomic Indsl. Forum award, 1975, Sci. Writing award, AAAS, Exploratorium award, 1977, Ralph Coates Roe medal, ASME, 1978, Margaret Sanger Cmty. Svc. award, 1981, Fellows' medal, Calif. Acad. Scis., 1984, Career Achievement award, Soc. Profl. Journalists, 1989, Glenn T. Seaborg award, Internat. Platform Assn., 1993, Sustained Achievement award for sci. journalism, Am. Geophys. Union, 1997, medal, U. Calif., San Francisco, 2000, Journalism award, Columbia U., 2000, award for disting. med. reporting, San Francisco Med. Soc., 2000, Grady-Stack award for sci. journalism, Am. Chem. Soc., 2001, John Wesley Powell award, U.S. Geol. Survey, 2004; Poynter Inst. fellow, Yale U., 1984, Carnegie Corp. fellow, Stanford U., 1987. Fellow: Calif. Acad. Scis.; mem.: AAAS (adv. bd. Science-81-86 mag., mem. com. Pub. Understanding Sci. 1985—90), Astron. Soc. Pacific (bd. dirs. 1976—78), Nat. Assn. Sci. Writers (pres. 1970—71, Disting. Sci. Journalism award 1994), Coun. Advancement Sci. Writing (pres. 1976—80), Sigma Xi. Office: San Francisco Chronicle 901 Mission St San Francisco CA 94103-2905 Business E-Mail: dperlman@sfchronicle.com.

**PERLMAN, HARVEY STUART,** academic administrator; b. Lincoln, Nebr., Jan. 17, 1942; s. Floyd Ted and Rosalyn (Lashinsky) P.; m. Susan G. Unthank, Aug. 27, 1966; children: Anne, Amy. BA, U. Nebr., 1963, JD, 1966. Bar: Nebr. 1966, Va. 1980. Teaching fellow U. Chgo. Law Sch., 1966-67; mem. faculty U. Nebr. Sch. Law, 1967-74, prof., 1972-74; prof. law U. Va., Charlottesville, 1974-83; dean law sch. U. Nebr., Lincoln, 1983—98, interim sr. vice chancellor, 1995—96, interim chancellor, 2000—01, chancellor, 2001—; exec. dir. Nebr. Commn. on Law Enforcement. Author: (with Edmund Kitch) Legal Regulation of the Competitive Process, 1972, 79, 86; asso. editor: Jour. Law and Human Behavior, 1974-86. Named Ida Beam Distinguished Vis. Prof. Law, U. Iowa, 1981-86. Mem. Am. Bar Assn., Nebr. Bar Assn., Law-Psychology Assn., Am. Law Inst. Office: U Nebr Office of the Chancellor 201 ADM UNL Lincoln NE 68588 E-mail: hperlman1@unl.edu.*

**PERLMAN, ITZHAK,** violinist; b. Tel Aviv, Aug. 31, 1945; arrived in U.S., 1958; s. Chaim and Shoshana P.; m. Toby Lynn Friedlander, 1967; children: Noah, Navah, Miriam, Leora, Ariella. Student, Tel Aviv Acad. Music; studied with Ivan Galamian & Dorothy DeLay, Juilliard Sch.; student, Meadowmount Sch. Music.; degree in music (hon.), Tufts U., 1986; degree (hon.) Harvard U., Yale U., Brandeis U., Roosevelt U., Yeshiva U., Hebrew U. Appeared with numerous orchs. including N.Y. Philharm., Cleve. Orch., Phila. Orch., Nat. Symphony Orch., Berlin Philharm., English Chamber Orch., London Symphony, London Philharm., Royal Philharm., BBC Orch., Vienna Philharm., Israel Philharm.; founder Perlman Music Program, N.Y., 1998—; prin. guest condr. Detroit Symphony, 2001—; participant numerous music festivals including Ravinia Festival, Tanglewood Music Festival, Aspen Music Festival, Israel Festival, Wolf Trap Summer Festival; recital tours U.S., Can., S.Am., Europe, Israel, Australia, Far East; recorded for Angel, London, RCA Victor, DG, Telarc, Teldec, Sony. Albums include Vivaldi: The Four Seasons, 1977 (Grammy award best classical performance 1977), Beethoven: Sonatas For Violin And Piano, 1978 (Grammy award best chamber music performance 1978), Brahms: Concerto For Violin In D, 1978 (Grammy award best classical album 1978), The Spanish Album, 1980 (Grammy award best classical performance 1980), Brahms: Violin And Cello Concerto In A Minor, 1980 (Grammy award best classical performance 1980), Berg: Violin Concerto/Stravinsky: Violin Concerto In D, 1980 (Grammy award best classical performance 1980), Music For Two Violins, 1980 (Grammy award best chamber music performance 1980), Isaac Stern: 60th Anniversary Celebration, 1981 (Grammy award best engineered recording 1981, Grammy award best classical album 1981), Tchaikovsky: Piano Trio In A Minor, 1981 (Grammy award best chamber music performance 1981), Elgar: Violin Concerto In B Minor, 1982 (Grammy award best classical performance 1982), Chausson: Violin Concerto, 1984, An Isaac Stern Vivaldi Gala, 1985, Beethoven: The Complete Piano Trios, 1987 (Grammy award best chamber music performance 1987), Bach: Double Concerto, 1987, Mozart Violin Concertos Nos.1 & 2, 1987 (Grammy award best classical performance 1987), Paganini & Giuliani: Duos for Violin and Guitar, 1987, The Italian Album, 1989, Brahms: The 3 Violin Sonatas, 1990 (Grammy award best small ensemble performance 1990), Dvorák In Prague: A Celebration, 1994, Bach: Violin Concertos, 1995, The American Album: Works Of Bernstein, Barber, Foss, 1995 (Grammy award best instrumental soloist performance with orch. 1995), Cinema Serenade, 1997, John Williams Greatest Hits 1969-1999 Cinema Serenade 2, 1999, Classic Yo-Yo, 2001, Classic Perlman: Rhapsody, 2002; appeared in PBS documentary Fiddling for the Future, 1998 (Emmy award outstanding cultural music-dance program 1999); TV specials Perlman in Russia, 1992 (Emmy award outstanding classical program 1992), Itzhak Perlman: In The Fiddler's House, 1996 (Emmy award outstanding cultural music-dance program 1996). Founder Perlman Music Program, 1995. Recipient Leventritt prize, 1964, Medal of Liberty, 1986, Nat. Medal of Arts, 2000, Kennedy Ctr. Honor, 2003; named Musician of Yr., Musical Am. 1981; inductee Am. Classical Music Hall of Fame, 2001. Address: IMG Artists 825 7th Ave New York NY 10019-6014*

**PERLMAN, JERALD LEE,** lawyer; b. Baton Rouge, Feb. 25, 1947; s. Ralph Robert and Carol Mayer (Herzberg) P.; m. Francine Evonne McKelvey, May 8, 1984; children: Louise, Lee, Kevin. BA, Washington & Lee U., 1969; JD, La. State U., 1972. Bar: La. 1972, Tex. 1994, U.S. Dist. Ct. (we. dist.) La. 1972, U.S. Dist. Ct. (ea. and we. dists.) Ark. 1991, U.S. Ct. Appeals (5th cir.) 1977, U.S. Supreme Ct. 1990. Assoc. Blanchard, Walker, O'Quin & Roberts, Shreveport, La., 1972-76, ptnr., 1976-83, Walker, Tooke, Perlman & Lyons, Shreveport, 1983-94; regional office chief litigation divsn. La. Dept. Justice, Shreveport, 1994—. Assoc. editor La. State U. Law Rev., 1971-72. Bd. dirs. Broadmoor Southside YMCA, Shreveport, 1984-88, vice chmn., 1986, chmn., 1987; bd. dirs. Shreveport Met. YMCA, 1987, N.W. La. chpt. ACLU, 1987-93, N.W. La. Ctr. for Families, 2005—. Capt. USAR, 1972 Named to La. State U. Law Ctr. Hall of Fame. Mem. La. Bar Assn. (com. on uniform court rules 1998-2002), Shreveport Bar Assn., La. Assn. Def. Counsel (bd. dirs. 1979-81), Order of Coif, Phi Beta Kappa, Omicron Delta Kappa. Jewish. Avocations: tennis, reading. Office: La Dept Justice Litigation Divsn 330 Marshall St Ste 777 Shreveport LA 71101-3016 Office Phone: 318-676-5711. E-mail: perlmanj@ag.state.la.us

**PERLMAN, JON ARTHUR,** plastic surgeon; b. N.Y.C., Dec. 17, 1948; Bachelor, Lafayette Coll.; MD, Cornell U., 1973. Diplomate Am. Bd. Plastic Surgery, cert. Am. Bd. Surgery. Intern Mass. Gen. Hosp., Boston, 1973—74, resident in surgery, 1974—78; resident in plastic surgery UCLA Med. Ctr., 1978—80; pvt. practice plastic surgery Beverly Hills, Calif., 1980—. Attending plastic surgery Cedars-Sinai Med. Ctr., L.A.; chief divsn. plastic surgery Brotman Med. Ctr., 1985—; asst. clin. prof. plastic surgery UCLA Med. Ctr.; featured plastic surgeon ABC's Extreme Makeover. Fellow: Am. Coll. Surgeons; mem.: L.A. Soc. Plastic Surgeons, Calif. Soc. Plastic Surgeons, Am. Soc. Plastic Surgeons, Am. Soc. Aesthetic Plastic Surgeons. Office: 414 N Camden Dr 8th Fl Beverly Hills CA 90210 Office Fax: 310-275-5079.

**PERLMAN, LAWRENCE,** retired information technology executive; BA, Carleton Coll., 1960; JD, Harvard U., 1963. Bar: Minn. 1963. Law. clk. for fed. judge, 1963; assoc., ptnr. Fredrikson & Byron, Mpls., 1964-75; gen. counsel, exec. v.p. U.S. pacing ops. Medtronic, Inc., Mpls., 1975-78; sr. ptnr. Oppenheimer, Wolff & Donnelly, Mpls., 1978-80; exec. Control Data Corp. (now Ceridian Corp.), 1980—2000, CEO, 1990—92, chmn., CEO, 1992—2000; ret., 2000. Dir., chmn. Seagate Tech., 1989-2000; bd. dirs. Carlson Cos., Inc., The Valspar Corp.; chmn. Arbitron Inc.; trustee Carleton Coll. Bd. dirs. Walker Art Ctr.; regent Univ. of Minn., 1993-95; chmn. 21st Century Workforce Commn., 1999-2000. Address: 818 W 46th St 201 Minneapolis MN 55419

**PERLMAN, MARK,** economist, educator; b. Madison, Wis., Dec. 23, 1923; s. Selig and Eva (Shaber) P.; m. Naomi Gertrude Waxman, June 7, 1953; 1 child, Abigail Ruth Williams. BA in Econs., MA in Econs., U. Wis., 1947; PhD in Econs., Columbia U., 1950. Asst. prof. U. Hawaii, 1951—52, Cornell U., 1952—55; from asst. to assoc. prof. Johns Hopkins U., 1955—63; prof. econs. U. Pitts., 1963—68, prof. history, 1964—94, chmn. dept. econs., 1965—70, prof. econs. of pub. health, 1976—94, univ. prof. econs., 1968—93, univ. prof. econs. emeritus, 1994—. Survey team for Brazilian pub. health rsch. sys. Johns Hopkins U., 1960, med. manpower survey team, 1962—64, vis. prof. Sch. Hygiene and Pub. Health, 1963—64; vis. fellow Clare Hall U. Cambridge, 1976—77, ofcl. visitor faculty econs. and polit. sci., 1976—77; adj. scholar Am. Enterprise Inst., 1980—, co-organizer program on Am.-European trade in 1990s, 1988—90; mem. Princeton Inst. for Advanced Study, 1981—82; Österreichischer Länderbank Joseph Schumpeter prof. Technische U., Vienna, 1982; disting. scholars' program selectee NAS-Chinese Acad. Social Sci., 1983; internat. com. social sci. documentation UNESCO, 1987—95, exec. com., 1993—94; vis. prof. U. Augsburg, 1992, U. Chemnitz, 1993; mem. jury Rechtenwald Prize, Nuremburg, Germany, 1993—2004. Author: Judges in Industry: A Study of Labor Arbitration in Australia, 1954, Labor Union Theories in America: Background and Development, 1958, 2d edit., 1976, The Machinists: A New Study in American Trade Unionism, 1961, Democracy in the I.A.M., 1962; author: (with T.D. Baker) Health Manpower in a Developing Economy, 1967; author: The Character of Economic Thought, Economic Characters, & Economic Institution: Selected Essays by Mark Perlman, 1996; author: (with Charles R. McCann Jr.) Pillars of Economic Understanding: Ideas and Traditions, 1998, Pillars of Economic Understanding: Factors and Markets, 2000; author: Editing Economics: Essays in Honour of Mark Perlman, 2001; editor: Human Resources in the Urban Economy, 1963; editor: (with Reuben E. Slesinger and Asher Isaacs) Contemporary Economics and Selected Readings, 1967; author (with Benjamin Chinitz and Charles Levin): Spatial, Regional, and Population Economics: Essays in Honor of Edgar M. Hoover, 1972; editor (with Norval Morris): Law and Crime: Essays in Honor of Sir John Barry, 1972; editor: Economics of Health and Medical Care, 1974, The Organization and Retrieval of Economic Knowledge, 1977; editor: (with Gordon K. MacLeod) Health Care Capital: Competition and Control, 1978; editor: (with J. van der Gaag) Health, Economics, and Health Economics, 1981; editor: (with Klaus Weiermair) Studies in Economic Rationality: X-Efficency Examined and Extolled, 1990; editor: (with Arnold Heertje) Evolving Technology and Market Structure: Studies in Schumpeterian Economics, 1990; editor: (with Claude Barfield) Capital Markets and Trade: The United States Faces a United Europe, 1991; editor: (with Norman J. Ornstein) Political Power and Social Change: The United States Faces a United Europe, 1991; editor: (with Claude Barfield) Industry, Services, and Agriculture: The U.S. Faces a United Europe, 1991; editor: (with Frederic M. Scherer) Entrepreneurship, Technological Innovation, and Economic Growth: Studies in the Schumpeterian Tradition, 1992; editor: (with Yuichi Shionoya) Innovation in Technology, Industries, and Institutions: Studies in Schumpeterian Perspectives, 1994, Schumpeter in the History of Ideas, 1994; editor: (with Kenneth Arrow, Enrico Colombatto, and Christian Schmidt) The Rational Foundations of Economic Behaviour, 1996; editor: (with Ernst Helmstädter) Behavioral Norms, Technological Progress, and Economic Dynamics: Studies in Schumpeterian Economics, 1996; editor: (with Francisco Louca) Is Economics an Evolutionary Science?, 2000; founding, cons. editor Portfolio on Internat. Econ. Perspectives, 1972—74, founding mng. editor Jour. Econ. Lit., 1968—81, founding mng. co-editor Jour. Evolutionary Econs., 1989—96, corr. editor Revue d'Economie Politique, 1990—; series editor: Cambridge Surveys of Economic Lit., 1977—94; series editor Cambridge Surveys of Economic Institutions and Policies, 1991—95, Great Economists of the World, 1990—95, gen. editor Joseph A. Schumpeter Intellectual Soc., 1986—94, mem. editl. bd. Indsl. and Labor Rels. Rev., 1953—95; contbr. articles to profl. jours. With U.S. Army, 1943—46. Social Sci. Rsch. Coun. pre-doctoral fellow, 1949—50, Ford Found. fellow, 1962—63, Sr. Fulbright lectr., Melbourne U., 1968, resident scholar, Rockefeller Found. Ctr., Villa Serbelloni, Bellagio, Italy, 1983, issue in honor of Mark Perlman, Jour. Evolutionary Econs., 2004. Fellow: European History Econs. Soc. (hon.), History Econs. Soc. (hon.; v.p. 1978, pres. elect, program chair 1983—84, pres. 1984—85); mem.: J.A. Schumpeter Gesellschaft (editor 1986—96), Verein fuer Sozial-Politik, Ausschuss fuer Dogmengeschichte, Royal Econ. Soc., Am. Econ. Assn. (founding and mng. editor Jour. Econ. Lit. 1968—81), European Assn. History Econ. Thought Soc. (hon.), Phi Beta Kappa. Jewish. Home: 302 Fox Chapel Rd Apt 414 Pittsburgh PA 15238-2337 Office Phone: 412-784-1374. Business E-Mail: mperlman@pitt.edu.

**PERLMAN, MATTHEW SAUL,** lawyer; b. Washington, Aug. 30, 1936; s. Jacob and Helene (Aronson) P.; m. Julia Gertrude Hawks, June 22, 1966; children— Penelope Leah, Deborah Jane, Sarah Louise, Jacob Henry AB, Brown U., 1957; LLB, Harvard U., 1960. Bar: D.C. 1960, Md. 1960, U.S. Supreme Ct. 1965. Atty. Air Force Gen. Counsel's Office, Washington, 1960-65; mem. Armed Services Bd. of Contract Appeals, Washington, 1965-67; gen. counsel Pres.' Commn. on Postal Orgn., Washington, 1967; asst. gen. counsel Dept. Transp., Washington, 1967-69; ptnr. Arent, Fox PLLC, Washington, 1969—2001, arbitrator, 2002—. Mem. Pres. Reagan's Transition Team for GSA, Washington, 1980-81; mem. adv. bd. Fed. Contracts Report, Washington, 1970-97; overseas corr. Internat. Constn. Law Rev., London, 1983—. Contbr. articles to profl. jours. Pres. Civic Assn. River Falls, Potomac, Md., 1975-77; mem. Montgomery County Md. Citizens Adv.

Commn. for Rock Run AWT Plant, 1979-85. Served to capt. USAF, 1960-63 Mem. ABA (pub. contracts sect.), Fed. Bar Assn., Cosmos Club. Republican. Jewish. Home: 10517 Stable Ln Potomac MD 20854-3867 Office: Arent Fox PLLC 1050 Connecticut Ave NW Ste 500 Washington DC 20036-5303 Office Phone: 202-857-6279. Personal E-mail: mspjgp@comcast.net. Business E-Mail: perlmann@arentfox.com.

**PERLMAN, RHEA,** actress; b. Bklyn., Mar. 31, 1948; d. Philip Perlman; m. Danny DeVito, Jan. 28, 1982; children: Gracie Fan, Lucy Chet, Jake. Grad. in Drama, Hunter Coll. Co-founder (with Danny DeVito) Colonades Theatre Lab., NYC, Jersey Films. Stage appearances include What! And Leave Bloomingdales?, The Last Night of the Ballyhoo, The Tale of the Allergist's Wife, 2002; TV movies include I Want to Keep My Baby!, 1976, Stalk the Wild Child, 1976, Intimate Strangers, 1977, Having Babies II, 1977, Mary Jane Harper Cried Last Night, 1977, Like Normal People, 1979, Drop Out Father, 1982, The Ratings Game (cable), 1984, Dangerous Affection, 1987, A Family Again, 1987, To Grandmothers House We Go, 1992, A Place To Be Loved, 1993, Houdini, 1998, In the Doghouse, 1999, A Tail of Two Bunnies, 2000, Secret Cutting, 2000; TV series include Cheers, 1982-1993; motion pictures include Love Child, 1982, My Little Pony (voice) 1986, Enid is Sleeping, 1990, Ted and Venus, 1991, Class Act, 1992, There Goes The Neighborhood, 1992, Canadian Bacon, 1995, Sunset Park, 1996, Matilda, 1996, Carpool, 1996, H-E Double Hockey Sticks, 1999; prodr. Pearl, 1996; guest appearances Taxi, 1979, 1980, 1981, 1982, Angie, 1979, St. Elsewhere, 1982, Blossom, 1991, The Simpsons, 1991, Union Square, 1997, Almost Perfect, 1995; author (children's books): Born to Drive, 2006, Canyon Catastrophe, 2006. Recipient Emmy award for Outstanding Supporting Actress in a Comedy Series, 1984, 85, 86, 89, Am. Comedy award for funniest supporting female-TV. Jewish. Office: Creative Artists Agy c/o Jonathan Ruiz 9830 Wilshire Blvd Beverly Hills CA 90212-1804*

**PERLMUTH, WILLIAM ALAN,** lawyer; b. NYC, Nov. 21, 1929; s. Charles and Roe (Schneider) P.; m. Loretta Kaufman, Mar. 14, 1951; children: Carolyn, Diane. AB, Wilkes Coll., 1951; LLB, Columbia U., 1953. Bar: N.Y. 1954. Assoc. Cravath, Swaine & Moore, N.Y.C., 1955-61; ptnr. Stroock & Stroock & Lavan, N.Y.C., 1962—. Editor Columbia U. Law Rev., 1952-53. Trustee Aeroflex Found., N.Y.C., 1965—, Harkness Found. for Dance, N.Y.C., 1976—, Wilkes U., Wilkes-Barre, Pa., 1980—, Hosp. for Joint Diseases Orthopaedic Inst., N.Y.C., 1980—, Weininger Found., 1985—, NYU Hosps. Ctr., 1994—2005, City Ctr. 55th St. Theater Found., 1995—, Sch. Am. Ballet, 1997—, Bklyn. Acad. Music, 2004—; chmn. bd. trustees Hosp. for Joint Diseases Orthopaedic Inst., 1994—. Mem. N.Y. State Bar Assn., Assn. of Bar of City of N.Y. Jewish. Home: 880 5th Ave New York NY 10021-4951 Office: Stroock & Stroock & Lavan 180 Maiden Ln Fl 34 New York NY 10038-4982 Office Phone: 212-806-5860. Business E-Mail: bperlmuth@stroock.com.

**PERLMUTTER, ALVIN HOWARD,** television and film producer; b. Poughkeepsie, N.Y., Mar. 24, 1928; s. Fred and Jennie (Albert) P.; children: James F., Stephen H., Tom W. Student, Colgate U., 1945-47; BA, Syracuse U., 1949. Dir. pub. affairs Sta. WNBC, also Sta. WNBC-TV, N.Y.C., 1957-59; program mgr. Sta. WNBC-TV, 1959-61; exec. producer Nat. Ednl. TV, 1961—; v.p. news documentaries NBC, from 1975; pres. Alvin H. Perlmutter Inc., N.Y.C.; instr. TV news and pub. affairs NYU, 1957, Fairleigh Dickinson U., 1962; pres., CEO, Sunrise Media LLC, N.Y.C., 1997—. Cons. John and Mary Markle Found., Pub. Agenda Found.; chmn. Dore Schary Awards for film and TV, Anti-Defamation League. Producer: series Assignment America; Great American Dream Machine, Consumer Reports Presents, Money Matters, Cover Story, Black Journal; various spl. programs including: Native Land, The Primal Mind, Adam Smith's Money World series, Family Computing series, Priceless Treasures of Dresden, The Perpetual People Puzzle; exec. producer: Report From Philadelphia, The Secret Government, The Power of Myth, Muslims (PBS spl. documentary). Chair Dore Schary awards, Anti-Defamation League; bd. dirs. N.Y. Open Ctr., Citizens for Ind. Pub. Broadcasting, Rockland Ctr. for the Arts. 1st lt. AUS, 1950-53; mem. adv. bd. CUNY TV. Recipient various citations and awards including 6 Emmy awards, Peabody award, Robert Kennedy award. Mem. Acad. TV Arts and Scis. (gov. N.Y. chpt., nat. trustee, chmn. awards com. 1968), Assn. Pub. TV Producers (chmn. 1969) Clubs: Overseas Press (N.Y.C.), University, Coffee House, The Econ. Club of N.Y.C., N.Y. Athletic Club. Home: 200 Central Park South New York NY 10019 Office: 45 W 45th St New York NY 10036-4602

**PERLMUTTER, BARBARA S.,** retired advertising executive; b. Hartford, Conn., Oct. 7, 1941; d. Leon and Ethel (Zinman) Sondik; m. Louis Perlmutter, Dec. 11, 1966; children: Kermit, Eric. BA, Smith Coll., 1963; MA in History, Columbia U., 1965; MBA, NYU, 1979. Analyst Celanese Internat. Co., N.Y.C., 1965-69; sr. econ. analyst Nat. Econ. Rsch. Assoc., White Plains, N.Y., 1979-85; dir. pub. affairs Marsh & McLennan Companies, Inc., N.Y.C., 1985-88, v.p. pub. affairs, 1988-99, sr. v.p. pub. affairs, 1999—2006. Avocations: aerobics, reading, tennis.

**PERLMUTTER, DAVID H.,** physician, educator; b. Bklyn., May 11, 1952; s. Herman Arthur and Ruth (Jacobs) P.; m. Barbara Ann Cohlan, Feb. 7, 1981; children: Andrew, Lisa. BA, U. Rochester, 1974; MD, St. Louis U., 1978. Intern then resident in pediatrics U. Pa. Sch. Medicine, Phila., 1978-81; fellow in pediatric gastroenterology Harvard U. Sch. Medicine, Boston, 1981-84, instr. pediatrics, 1983-85, asst. prof. pediatrics, 1985-86; Donald Strominger prof. of pediatrics Washington U. Sch. Medicine, St. Louis, 1986-89, prof. cell biology, physiology, 1989—. Editor: Pediatric Rsch., 1990—; editl. bd. Gastroenterology, 1990—; dir. divsn. gastrology and nutrition and pediatrics; contbr. articles to profl. jours. Recipient Established Investigator award Am. Heart Assn., 1987, Rosh. Scholar award Am. Gastroent. Assn., 1985, RJR Nabisco Co., 1986. Mem. Soc. Pediatric Rsch. (coun. rep. 1990—), Am. Soc. Cell Biology, Am. Soc. Clin. Investigation.

**PERLMUTTER, DIANE F.,** marketing executive; b. N.Y.C., Aug. 31, 1945; d. Bert H. and Frances (Smith) P. Student, NYU Grad. Sch. of Bus., 1969—70; BA in English, Miami U., Oxford, Ohio, 1967. Writer sales promotion Equitable Life Assurance, N.Y.C., 1967-68; bus. administr. de Garmo, Inc., N.Y.C., 1968-69, asst. account exec., 1969-70, account exec., 1970-74, v.p., account supr., 1974-76; mgr. corp. advt. Avon Products, Inc., N.Y.C., 1976-79, dir. comm. Latin Am., Spain, Can., 1979-80, dir. brochures, 1980-81, dir. category merchandising, 1981-82, group dir. motivational comm., 1982-83, group dir. sales promotion, 1983-84, v.p. sales promotion, 1984, v.p. internat. bus. devel., 1984-85, area v.p. Latin Am., 1985, v.p. advt. and campaign mktg., 1985-87, v.p. U.S. operational planning, 1987; cons. N.Y.C., 1987-88; sr. v.p. Burson-Marsteller, N.Y.C., 1988-90, exec. v.p., mng. dir. consumer products, 1991-93, bd. dirs., 1992—98, co-chief oper. officer, 1993-94, chief oper. officer, 1994-96, chmn. mktg. practice/U.S., 1996-98; vice chmn., CEO Cohn & Wolfe, N.Y.C., 1998—2000; CEO Gilda's Club Worldwide, 2001—05, bd. dirs., 2002—; prin. Oxford Hall Assocs., 2003—. Chair ann. meeting Direct Selling Assn., Washington, 1982; v.p. Nat. Home Fashions League, N.Y.C., 1975—76; adj. instr. SUNY/ Fashion Inst. Tech., 1992—; vice chmn. Columbia-Greene Hosp. Found., 2000—; vice chmn., bd. dirs. Olana Partnership, 2000—03; bd. dirs. Double L.P. Industries, Inc. Bd. dirs. Hudson Opera House, 2002—. Named to YWCA Acad. Women Achievers, 1996. Mem.: Women in Comm., Advt. Women of N.Y., Pub. Rels. Soc. Am., Women's Econ. Round Table (bd. dirs. 1998—2000), Miami U. Alumni Assn. (pres., chair 1986), The Women's Forum (bd. dirs. 1998—2000, pres. 2002—04), YMCA of Greater N.Y. (bd. dirs. 1996—2003), Publicity Club N.Y. (bd. dirs. 1994—96). Personal E-mail: dianefperlmutter@yahoo.com.

**PERLMUTTER, LOUIS,** investment banker, lawyer; b. Cambridge, Mass., Oct. 3, 1934; s. Kermit H and Rachel P (Ehrlich) Perlmutter; m. Barbara Patricia Sondik, Dec. 11, 1966; children: Kermit, Eric. BA, Brandeis U., 1956, LHD (hon.), 1995; JD, U. Mich., 1959. Bar: Mass 1959, NY 1961. Law practice, N.Y.C., 1960-65; asst. to pres. New Eng. Industries, N.Y.C., 1965-67; pres. Octagon Assocs., N.Y.C., 1967-75; sr. v.p. White Weld,

N.Y.C., 1975-78; mgn. dir. Merrill Lynch, White, Weld, N.Y.C., 1978; exec. mng. dir. Lazard Freres & Co. LLC, N.Y.C., 1978-99, ltd. mng. dir., 2000—05; sr. adv. Corp. Ptnrs., 2005—. Contbr. articles to profl jours. Bd. dirs. Charles H. Revson Found.; chmn. Transatlantic Inst.; bd. dirs., treas. World Fedn. UNA; chmn. bd. trustees Brandeis U., Waltham, Mass., 1988—95, Am. Jewish Congress, N.Y.C., 1988—94; bd. dirs., chmn. exec. com. UN Assn. USA, 1993—96; com. visitors U. Mich. Law Sch.; bd. fellows Harvard Med. Sch.; adv. bd. Fgn. Affairs, Medis Techs.; mem. coun. fgn. rels., adminstrv. coun. Blaustein Inst. Advancement Human Rights; bd. dirs. Harvard Med. Internat. Recipient Human Rels. award, Am. Jewish Com., 1995, Pub. Svc. award, Phoenix H.S., 1999, tribute dinner, Israel Policy Forum, 2001, honoree, World Fedn. UN Assn., 2003. Home: 39 E 79th St New York NY 10021-0216 Office: Lazard 30 Rockefeller Plz New York NY 10112-5900

**PERLMUTTER, SAUL,** astrophysicist, educator; AB in Physics (magna cum laude), Harvard U., 1981; PhD in Physics, U. Calif. Berkeley, 1986. Postdoctoral rschr. Space Sci. Lab., Lawrence Berkeley Nat. Lab., 1987—88; sr. staff scientist, astrophysicist Lawrence Berkeley Nat. Lab.; prof., physics dept. U. Calif. Berkeley, 2004—. Leader Internat. Supernova Cosmology Project, 1998—. Contbr. articles to profl. jours., to Sky and Telescope mag.; guest appearances Pub. Broadcasting Sys., BBC documentaries on astronomy and cosmology. Co-recipient Shaw prize in Astronomy, Shaw Found., Hong Kong, 2006; named Scientist of Yr., Calif., 2003; recipient Henri Chretien award, Am. Astronomical Soc., 1996, Breakthrough of Yr. award, Science Mag., 1998, E.O. Lawrence award in Physics, Dept. Energy, 2002, John Scott award, 2005, Padua prize, 2005, Feltrinelli Internat. prize, Phys. and Math. Scis., Lincei Acad., Rome, 2006. Achievements include discovery of the universe's accelerating expansion using supernovae as "standard candles" to measure the cosmic expansion rate. Office: Lawrence Berkeley Lab 50-232 Univ Calif 392 LeConte Berkeley CA 94720 Office Phone: 510-486-5203, 510-642-3596. Office Fax: 510-486-5401. Business E-Mail: saul@lbl.gov.*

**PERLOFF, CAREY,** performing company executive, theater director, playwright; children: Lexie, Nicholas. BA in classics and comparative lit., Stanford U., 1980. Artistic dir. Classic Stage Co., N.Y.C., 1986—92; faculty Tisch School of the Arts N.Y.U., 1986—92; artistic dir. Am. Conservatory Theater Found., San Francisco, 1992—. Playwright, dir.: The Colossus of Rhodes, 2001. Recipient Obie award for Artistic Excellence, The Village Voice, 1988; Fulbright Fellow, Oxford, 1981. Mem.: Phi Beta Kappa. Office: Am Conservatory Theater Found 30 Grant Ave San Francisco CA 94108-5800

**PERLOFF, MARJORIE GABRIELLE,** literature educator; b. Vienna, Sept. 28, 1931; arrived in U.S., 1998; d. Maximilian and Ilse (Schueller) Mintz; m. Joseph K. Perloff, July 31, 1953; children: Nancy Lynn, Carey Elizabeth. AB, Barnard Coll., 1953; MA, Cath. U., 1956, PhD, 1965. Asst. prof. English and comparative lit. Cath. U., Washington, 1966-68, assoc. prof., 1969-71, U. Md., 1971-73, prof., 1973-76; Florence R. Scott prof. English U. So. Calif., LA, 1976—; prof. English and comparative lit. Stanford (Calif.) U., 1986—, Sadie Dernham prof. humanities, 1990—, prof. emerita, 2000. Vis. prof. U. Utah, 2002; scholar-in-residence U. So. Calif., 2004—. Author: Rhyme and Meaning in the Poetry of Yeats, 1970, The Poetic Art of Robert Lowell, 1973, Frank O'Hara, Poet Among Painters, 1977, 2nd edit., 1998, The Poetics of Indeterminacy: Rimbaud to Cage, 1981, 2d edit., 1999, The Dance of the Intellect: Studies in the Poetry of the Pound Tradition, 1985, 2d edit., 1996, The Futurist Moment: Avant-Garde, Avant-Guerre and the Language of Rupture, 1986, 2d edit., 2003, Poetic License: Essays in Modern and Postmodern Lyric, 1990, Radical Artifice: Writing Poetry in the Age of Media, 1991, Wittgenstein's Ladder: Poetic Language and the Strangeness of the Ordinary, 1996, Frank O'Hara, 2d edit., 1998, Poetry On and Off the Page: Essays for Emergent Occasions, 1998, Twenty-first Century Modernism, 2001, The Vienna Paradox, 2004, Differentials, 2004; editor: Postmodern Genres, 1990; co-editor: John Cage: Composed in America, 1994; contbg. editor: Columbia Literary History of the U.S., 1987; contbr. preface to Contemporary Poets, 1980, A John Cage Reader, 1983. Guggenheim fellow, 1981-82, NEA fellow, 1985; Phi Beta Kappa scholar, 1994-95. Fellow Am. Acad. Arts and Scis.; mem. MLA (exec. coun. 1977-81, Am. lit. sect. 1993—, 1st v.p. 2005, pres. 2006), Comparative Lit. Assn. (pres. 1993-94, mem. adv. bd. Libr. of Am.), Lit. Studies Acad. Home: 1467 Amalfi Dr Pacific Palisades CA 90272-2752 Personal E-mail: mperloff@earthlink.net.

**PERLOFF, ROBERT,** psychologist, educator; b. Phila., Feb. 3, 1921; s. Myer and Elizabeth (Sherman) P.; m. Evelyn Potechin, Sept. 22, 1946; children: Richard Mark, Linda Sue, Judith Kay. AB, Temple U., 1949; MA, Ohio State U., 1949, PhD, 1951; DSc (hon.), Oreg. Grad. Sch. Profl. Psychology, 1984; DLitt (hon.), Calif. Sch. Profl. Psychology, 1985. Diplomate Am. Bd. Profl. Psychology. Instr. edn. Antioch Coll., 1950—51; with pers. rsch. br. Dept. Army, 1951—55, chief statis. rsch. and cons. unit., 1953—55; dir. R & D Sci. Rsch. Assocs., Inc., Chgo., 1955—59; vis. lectr. Chgo. Tchrs. Coll., 1955—56; mem. faculty Purdue U., 1958—59, prof. psychology, 1964—69; 1961field assessment officer univ. Peace Corps Chile III project, 1962; Disting. Svc. prof. bus. adminstrn. and psychology U. Pitts. Joseph M. Katz Grad. Sch. Bus., 1969—90, Disting. Svc. prof. emeritus, 1991—; dir. rsch. programs U. Pitts. Grad. Sch. Bus., 1969—77; dir. Consumer Panel, 1980—83. Bd. dirs. Book Ctr.; adv. com. assessment exptl. manpower R & D labs. NAS, 1972-74, mem. rsch. rev. com. NIMH, 1976-80, Stress and Families rsch. project, 1976-79; cons. in field. Contbr. articles to profl. jours.; editor Indsl. Psychologist, 1963-65, Evaluator Intervention: Pros and Cons; book rev. editor Personnel Psychology, 1952-55; co-editor: Values, Ethics and Standards Sourcebook, 1979, Improving Evaluations; bd. consulting editors Jour. Applied Psychology; bd. advs. Archives History Am. Psychology, Psychol. Svc. Plus., Recorded Psychol. Jours.; guest editor Am. Psychologist, 1972, Edn. and Urban Soc., 1977, Profl. Psychology, 1977; adv. editor Contemporary Psychology, 1994—. Bd. dirs., v.p. Sr. Citizens Svc. Corp., Calif. Sch. Profl. Psychology; bd. dirs. Greater Pitts. chpt. ACLU, sec., 1997-98; chmn. nat. adv. com. Inst. Govt. and Pub. Affairs, U. Ill., 1986-89, sec. nat. adv. com., 1997—; mem. adv. com. Cornell Inst. for Rsch. on Children, 2002—. Decorated Bronze Star; named in his honor, Robert Perloff Grad. Rsch. Assistantship in Inst. Govt. and Pub. Affairs, U. Ill., 1990, in his honor, Robert Perloff Career Achievement award, Knowledge Utilization Soc., 1991; recipient Legacy award, Greater Pitts. Psychol. Assn., 2001, Hist. Preservation award, City of Pitts., 2002. Fellow: APA (mem.-at-large exec. com. divsn. consumer psychology 1964—67, coun. reps. 1965—68, pres. divsn. 1967—68, chmn. sci. affairs com., divsn. consumer psychology 1968—69, edn. and tng. bd. 1969—72, mem.-at-large exec. com. divsn. consumer psychology 1970—71, coun. reps. 1972—74, dir. 1974—82, chmn. fin. com., treas. 1975—84, chmn. investment com. 1977—82, pres. 1985, adv. bd., bd. sci. affairs 1994—96, task force intelligence and Intelligence Tests, author column Std. Deviations in jour., pres. address selected as one of 50 over 50 yrs.), AAAS, Ea. Psychol. Assn. (dir. 1977—80, pres. 1980—81); mem.: Coun. of Sci. Soc. (found. alumnus pres. 1998—), Knowledge Utilization Soc. (pres. 1993—95), Soc. Psychologists in Mgmt. (pres. 1993—94, Disting. Contbn. to Psychology Mgmt. award 1989), Am. Evaluation Assn. (pres. 1977—78), Am. Psychol. Found. (v.p. 1988—89, pres. 1990—92, trustee 1995—98, Lifetime Achievement in Psychology Gold Medal award 2000), Assn. for Consumer Rsch. (chmn. 1970—71), Pa. Psychol. Assn. (Disting. Svc. award 1985), Internat. Assn. Applied Psychology, Am. Psychol. Soc., Phi Beta Kappa, Psi Chi, Beta Gamma Sigma, Sigma Xi (pres. U. Pitts. chpt. 1989—91). Student St James St Pittsburgh PA 15232-2112 Office Phone: 414-648-1554. Personal E-mail: rperloff@katz.pitt.edu. Experiment. Innovate responsibly. Take risks judiciously. Do not shrink from new ventures for fear of failure. No one is immune from adversity. The hallmark of a successful achieving person is his or her ability to snap back after misfortune, and to benefit from and not be immobilized by failure.

**PERLOW, GILBERT JEROME,** retired physicist, retired editor; b. N.Y.C., Feb. 10, 1916; s. David and Esther (German) P.; m. Mina Rea Jones (dec. April 2004). AB, Cornell U., 1936, MA, 1937; PhD, U. Chgo., 1940. Instr.

physics U. Minn., Mpls., 1940-41; physicist Naval Ordnance Lab., Washington, 1941-42, Naval Rsch. Lab., Washington, 1942-52; rsch. assoc. physics dept. U. Minn., Mpls., 1952-53; assoc. physicist Argonne (Ill.) Nat. Lab., 1953-57, sr. physicist, 1957—; editor Jour. Applied Physics Am. Inst. Physics/Argonne Nat. Lab., 1970-73, editor Applied Physics Letters, 1970-90, consulting editor Applied Physics Letters, 1990-2000; ret., 2000. Vis. assoc. prof. physics U. Wash., Seattle, 1957; vis. prof. German univs., Munich, Berlin; exch. physicist AERE Harwell, Berkshire, Eng., 1961. Contbr. over 70 articles to profl. jours., also chpts. to books; author numerous U.S. patents. Recipient Alexander von Humboldt award Alexander von Humboldt Found., Tech. U. Munich, 1972. Fellow Am. Phys. Soc.; mem. Chgo. Corinthian Yacht Club (life mem., commodore 1974). Avocations: sailing, woodworking, painting. Home: 4919 Northcott Ave Downers Grove IL 60515-3434 Office: Argonne Nat Lab Physics Divsn 9700 Cass Ave Argonne IL 60439-4803

**PERLSTEIN, ITAY,** research scientist; b. Tel Aviv, July 24, 1969; s. Abraham and Nitza Perlstein; m. Merav Yonit Eilat, Oct. 13, 1996; children: Abigail Tova, Odelia Rebecca. PhD, Hebrew U., 2000. Pharmacist Ministry of Health, Israel, 1995. Animal technician, rsch. asst. Hebrew U. of Jerusalem, 1991—94, mgr. telemetry sys. devel. team, 1995—96, bioequivalence studies, 1997—99; rsch. fellow, cardiology dept. Children's Hosp. of Phila., 2001—03; clin. PK modeling and simulations GlaxoSmithKline, King of Prussia, Pa., 2004—. Instr. (undergraduate students) Hebrew U. of Jerusalem, 1996—2000. Contbr. articles to profl. jours. Recipient Joseph Rapaport Found. prize for distinction in the rsch. field of pharmacy, Hebrew U. Jerusalem, 1999; Postdoctoral fellow, Am. Heart Assn., 2001—03. Achievements include development of controlled release medicated devices for gene therapy; controlled gene therapy model for arrhythmia; pharmacokinetic/pharmacodynamic (PK/PD) models for CNS and population PK/PD Models for cardiovascular acting drugs. Home: 330 Monroe St Philadelphia PA 19147 Office: GlaxoSmithKline 709 Swedeland Rd PO Box 1539 King Of Prussia PA 19406 Business E-Mail: itay.2.perlstein@gsk.com.

**PERLSTEIN, WILLIAM JAMES,** lawyer; b. NYC, Feb. 7, 1950; s. Justin Sol and Jane (Goldberg) P.; m. Teresa Catherine Lotito, Dec. 20, 1970; children: David, Jonathan. Student, London Sch. Econs., 1969-70; BA summa cum laude, Union Coll., 1971; JD, Yale U., 1974. Bar: Conn. 1974, D.C. 1976, U.S. Dist. Ct. D.C. 1977, U.S. Ct. Appeals (D.C. cir.) 1978, U.S. Supreme Ct. 1993, N.Y. 2000. Law clk. to judge Marvin Frankel U.S. Dist. Ct., N.Y.C., 1974-75; assoc. Wilmer, Cutler & Pickering, Washington, 1975-82, ptnr., 1982—2004, mem. mgmt. com., 1995—2004, chmn., 1998—2004; co-mng. ptnr. & co-chmn. mgmt. com. Wilmer Cutler Pickering Hale & Dorr, Washington, 2004—. Mng. editor Yale Law Jour., 1973-74; contbg. author The Workout Game, 1987. Dir. Neighborhood Legal Svcs. program. Mem.: Am. Bar Found., Am. Coll. Bankruptcy (gen. counsel), Am. Law Inst., Am. Bankruptcy Inst. (chmn. legis. com. 1986—89, bd. dirs. 1989—93, 1997—2002), ABA (bus. bankruptcy com 1983—, v.chmn. executory contracts subcom. of bus. bankruptcy com. 1988—90, bankruptcy cts. subcom. 1990—97, chmn. legislation subcom. 1997—), Phi Beta Kappa. Jewish. Office: Wilmer Cutler Pickering Hale & Dorr 2445 M St NW Washington DC 20037 Office Phone: 202-663-6274. Office Fax: 202-663-6363. Business E-Mail: william.perlstein@wilmerhale.com.

**PERNA, MARIE IMMACULATE,** retired physical education educator; b. Middletown, NY, Sept. 23, 1942; d. Ralph and Caroline Margaret (Cosco) D'Onofrio; m. Donald Perna, July 31, 1965; children: Donna, Debbie, Anne. BS in Health and Phys. Edn., Ithaca Coll., NY, 1964. Tchr. various organs., 1965—80; weight control specialist Weight Watchers and Weight Control, 1980—2001; coord. Accessible RI, 2001—. Self help group leader Nat. Multiple Sclerosis Soc. Author: Dare To Dream, 2001. Team capt. Multiple Sclerosis Walk, 1998—; moderator Nat. Listserve Sel-help Group Leaders, 2002—; mem. NM3S L.I. Class Leadership program, Transp. Work Group; coord. 3d edit. Accessible RI; mem. Transp. Work Group; catechist Roman Cath. Initiation Adults, 1997—2000; tchr. HS religious edn., 1994—98; transp. workgroup Rhodes to Indendence, 2005. Mem.: Nat. Multiple Sclerosis Soc. (gov. rels. com. (Long Island chpt.) 1999—2001, Achievement award 2000, 2003). Avocations: golf, bridge, movies. Home: 425 Meshanticut Valley Pkwy #305 Cranston RI 02920 Personal E-mail: marieperna@cox.net.

**PERNA, MICHAEL LEWIS,** language educator; b. Hampton, Va., Oct. 3, 1941; s. Michael Archangel and Rita M. (Kocher) Perna. AB, Wash. Coll., Chestertown, Md., 1963; MA, Duke U., PhD, 1977. Spanish tchr. St. Mary's County Schs., Chaptico, Md., 1964—68; instr. Spanish U. N.C., Chapel Hill, 1968—70, Duke U., Durham, NC, 1970—73; acting asst. prof. U. Va., Charlottesville, 1973—76; Spanish tchr. The Tandem Sch., Charlottesville, 1977—78; asst. prof. Spanish U. Maine, Orono, 1978; assoc. prof. Romance langs. Hunter Coll., N.Y.C., 1979—. Editor, contbr.: Twentieth-Century Spanish Poets, 1991; Dictionary of Literary Themes and Motifs, 1988; contbr. articles pub. to profl. jour. Mem., activist Harlem Peacemakers, N.Y.C., 1986—96; chair South Africa com. Ch. of Heavenly Rest, N.Y.C., 1987—92; mem., activist Episcopal Peace Fellowship, Chgo., 1981—. Recipient Summer Rsch. Stipend, U. Va., 1976; grantee Hunter Coll. grant award: Presdl. Initiatives in Tchg. and Learning, 2003—04; scholar, Md. State Senate, 1959—63. Mem.: Renaissance Soc. Am., Soc. Spanish and Portuguese Hist. Studies, Am. Assn. Tchrs. Spanish and Portuguese, Northeast Modern Lang. Assn. (exec. dir. 1988—90). Episcopalian. Avocations: camping, music, sailing. Home: 161 E 91 St New York NY 10128 Office: Hunter Coll Dept Romance Lange 605 Park Ave New York NY 10021 Office Phone: 212 772 5106. Business E-Mail: mperna@hunter.cuny.edu.

**PERNICIARO, CHARLES VINCENT,** dermatologist, educator, entrepreneur; b. New Orleans, June 15, 1957; s. Ernest Gabriel and Phereby Sheppard Perniciaro; children: Jamie Lynn, Kelly Gabrielle. BS, U. La., Lafayette, 1979; MD, La. State U., New Orleans, 1983. Diplomate Am. Bd. Dermatology, Am. Bd. Dermatology and Pathology. Staff physician Ochsner Clin. of Baton Rouge, La., 1987-90; sr. assoc. cons. and staff dermatologist Mayo Clinic, Jacksonville, Fla., 1990-93, cons., staff dermatologist and dermatopathologist, 1993-99; pvt. practice dermatology Brunswick, Ga., 1999—, Neptune Beach, Fla., 1999—2006, Ponte Vedra Beach, Fla., 2006—. Pres., CEO Holiday Lighting Concepts, Inc., 1996-2000; lectr., presenter in field; adj. clin. assoc. prof. pathology U. Fla. Shands Jacksonville Med. Ctr., 1999-2001; dir. dermatopathology Bernhardt Labs., Jacksonville, Fla., 2001—. Contbr. articles to profl. jours. Founder, bd. dirs. S.W. La. Skin Cancer Found., 1987. Recipient Outstanding Paper award Noah Worcester Dermatol. Soc., 1993, First Place Poster award 17th Internat. Colloquium Dermatopathology, 1996; named one of Best Doctors, 2000-06, How to Find the Best Fla. Doctors, 2000, Am. Top Physicians, 2003-05. Fellow: Am. Soc. Dermatopathology (chmn. membership com.), Am. Acad. Dermatology (com. on preventive dermatology 1988—90, task force on dermatologic oncology 1990—93, environ. coun. 1994—96, adv. coun. 1995—2001, abd. 2006—); mem.: So. Med. Assn. (vice chair sect. dermatology 1995—96, chair-elect 2001—06, Resident-in-Tng. award 1994), Fla. Soc. Dermatology (bd. dirs. 1998—2006, chmn. membership com. 1999—2002, v.p. 2002—03, pres. 2003—04), Jacksonville Dermatology Soc. (sec.-treas. 1995, pres. 1996, webmaster 2003—04), Lions (charter, bd. dirs. Ponte Vedra Beach 1997—98). Avocations: tennis, computers. Home: 514 Midway St Neptune Beach FL 32266 Office: Brunswick Dermatology Clinic 3008 E Park Ave Brunswick GA 31520-4241

**PERNICK, MARTIN STEVEN,** history professor; b. NYC, June 2, 1948; s. Louis W. and Florence P. (Goldberg) P. m. Marie R. Deveney, July 8, 1983; 1 child, Benjamin William. BA, Brandeis U., 1968; MA, Columbia U., 1969, PhD, 1979. Lectr. Coll. Medicine Pa. State U., Hershey, 1972-79; from asst. prof. to prof. U. Mich., Ann Arbor, 1979—. Vis. lectr. Harvard U., Cambridge, Mass., 1975-76; creator, dir. Hist. Health Film Collection, Ann Arbor, 1986—. Author: A Calculus of Suffering, 1985, The Black Stork, 1996;

contbr. chpt. to Death: Beyond Whole-Brain Criteria, 1988. Nat. Libr. Medicine fellow, 1984-85, NEH fellow, 1985-88. Mem. Am. Assn. History Medicine (exec. coun. 1992-95). Office: U Mich Dept History Ann Arbor MI 48109-1003

**PERNOT, GUILLERMO,** chef, restaurant owner; Chef de cuisine Treetops Restaurant, Phila., Vega Grill; exec. chef, co-owner Pasión!, Phila., 1998—. Author: Ceviche, 2001 (Best Single Subject Cookbook award, 2001). Named Chef to Watch, Phila. Mag., 1998, Chef of Yr., Esquire Mag., 1999, Best Chef Mid-Atlantic, 2001; named one of Best New Chefs, Food & Wine Mag., 1998, 10 Rising Stars, Restaurant Hospitality, 1998; recipient James Beard award, 2001. Office: Pasion! 211 S 15th St Philadelphia PA 19102-3804 Office Phone: 215-875-9895. Personal E-mail: lgpernot@aol.com.

**PERNOTTO, JAMES ANGELO,** artist; b. Youngstown, Ohio, Oct. 20, 1950; s. Luke Andrew Pernotto and Elizabeth Marie Hallahan. BFA, Ohio State U., Columbus, 1973; MFA, U. Wis., Madison, 1975. Dir. Art on Thompson, NYC, 1996—98, Pacifico Fine Art, NYC, 1998—2002. Exhibitions include The Butler Inst. of Am. Art, The Alternative Mus., NYC, McDonough Mus. Art, SPACES, Cleve., Ctr. for Book Arts, NYC, Madison Ctr. of Contemporary Art, Agnes Gund Gallery at OAC. Internat. Studio Program fellow, Inst. Art and Urban Resources, PS1, 1987, Visual Artist fellow in painting, Ohio Arts Coun., 1993, The Arts Mid-West /NEA, 1994. Mem.: Am. Museums. Home and Office: 27 Federal Plz W Youngstown OH 44503 Office Phone: 917-407-7769. E-mail: jamespernotto.com.

**PERONE, ANTHONY THOMAS, III,** language educator; b. Mount Vernon, N.Y., Jan. 29, 1972; s. Magdalena Louise Perone. AB magna cum laude, Cornell U., 1994; student, SUNY, 1998—2000; MEd, U. Ill., 2005. Tchr. English Berlitz Internat., White Plains, N.Y. 1991—95; instr. English EF Internat., Tarrytown, N.Y., 1995—97; specialist youth outreach Family Info. and Referral Svc. Teams, Inc., White Plains, NY, 2000—01; adult and family literacy educator team leader U. Ill., Chgo., 2001—. Outreach counselor Split Pillow NFP, Chgo., 2004—; intern Chgo. (Ill.) Improv Festival, 2002; mgr. program Youth Outreach Svcs., Chgo., 2001—02; adj. lectr. East-West U., Chgo., 2001; workshop leader in field. Actor: (plays) So Long, Miss America; contbr. articles to profl. jours. Vol. edn. and tng. com. Gay Lesbian and Straight Edn. Network, Chgo., 2001—02; vol. N.Y. Presbyn. Hosp., White Plains, NY, 1998—99. Recipient Tchr. Recognition award, Humboldt Pk. YMCA Head Start, 2004. Mem.: Am. Ednl. Rschr. Assn., Ill. Tchrs. English to Spkrs. Other Langs., Tchrs. English to Spkrs. Other Langs. Achievements include research in the role of improvisation and play in language learning for adults. Avocations: swimming, hiking, reading, music, movies. Office: University Illinois at Chicago 1645 N California Avenue Room 302B Chicago IL 60647 Office Phone: 773-489-8944. Business E-Mail: aperone@uic.edu.

**PEROT, ROSS (H. ROSS PEROT, HENRY ROSS PEROT),** real estate company executive, investment company executive, data processing executive; b. Texarkana, Tex., June 27, 1930; s. Gabriel Ross and Lulu May Perot; m. Margot Birmingham, 1956; children: Ross Jr., Nancy, Suzanne, Carolyn, Katherine. Ed., US Naval Acad., 1949—53. Data processing salesman IBM Corp., 1957-62; founder Electronic Data Systems Corp., Dallas, 1962-84, sold to GM, 1984, chmn., CEO, also dir., to 1986; founder The Perot Group, Dallas, 1986—, Perot Systems Corp., Washington, 1988—, bd. mem. Dallas, 1988—94, Plano, 1997—, chmn. Dallas, 1988—92, Plano, 2000—04, chmn. emeritus, 2004—. Ind. candidate US Presdl. Election, 1992, Reform Party candidate, 96. Author (books) United We Stand: How We Can Take Back Our Country, 1992, Not for Sale at Any Price: How We Can Save America for Our Children, 1993, Intensive Care: We Must Save Medicare and Medicaid Now, 1995, Preparing Our Country for the 21st Century, 1995, Ross Perot: My Life & the Principles for Success, 1996; co-author (with Pat Choate) Save Your Job, Save Our Country: Why NAFTA Must Be Stopped-Now!, 1993, (with Senator Paul Simon) The Dollar Crisis: A Blueprint to Help Rebuild the American Dream, 1996. Served with USN, 1953-57. Recipient Winston Churchill Award, 1986, Internat. Disting. Entrepreneur Award, U. Man., 1988, Raoul Wallenberg Award, Jefferson Award, Patrick Henry Award, Nat. Bus. Hall of Fame Award, Sarnoff Award, Eisenhower Award, Smithsonian Computerworld Award, Horatio Alger Award.; named one of Forbes' Richest Americans, 2006 Named one of World's Richest People by Forbes in 1999, 2000, 01, 02, 03, 04. Office: Perot Systems Corp 2300 W Plano Pkwy Plano TX 75075 also: Perot Family Trust PO Box 269014 Plano TX 75026-9014

**PEROT, ROSS, JR., (HENRY ROSS PEROT JR.),** real estate developer, professional sports team executive; b. Arlington, Tex. m. Sarah Fullinwider, 1984. BBA, Vanderbilt U., 1981. With Petrus Oil Co., Okla., 1981-83; mng. ptnr. The Perot Group, 1983—; owner Hillwood Devel., Dallas, 1988—; majority owner Dallas Mavericks basketball, 1996—2000; pres., CEO Perot Systems, Dallas, 2000—04, chmn., 2004—. Exec. com. Prince of Wales Bus. Leaders' Forum, Winston Churchill Found. Pilot, USAFR, 1983-1991. Achievements include completing first flight around the world in a helicopter. Office: Perot Systems 2300 W Plano Pkwy Plano TX 75075

**PEROTTI, ROSE NORMA,** lawyer; b. St. Louis, Aug. 10, 1930; d. Joseph and Dorothy Mary (Roleski) Perotti. BA, Fontbonne Coll., St. Louis, 1952; JD, St. Louis U., 1957. Bar: Mo. 1958. Trademark attr. Sutherland, Polster & Taylor, St. Louis, 1958-63, Sutherland Law Office, 1964-70, Monsanto Co., St. Louis, 1971-85, sr. trademark atty., 1985-91, assoc. trademark counsel, 1991-94, trademark counsel, 1994-96, Polster, Lieder, Woodruff & Lucchesi, 1996—. Honored with dedication of faculty office in her honor, St. Louis U. Sch. Law, 1980. Mem. ABA, Mo. Bar, Bar Assn. Met. St. Louis, Am. Judicature Soc., Friends St. Louis Art Mus., Mo. Bot. Garden. Office: Polster Lieder Woodruff & Lucchesi 12412 Powers Court Dr Ste 200 Saint Louis MO 63131-3615 Office Phone: 314-238-2400. Business E-Mail: rperotti@patpro.com.

**PEROULIS, DIMITRIOS,** engineering educator, consultant; s. Emilios and Katerina Peroulis. BSc in Elec. Engring. and Computer Sci., Nat. Tech. U. Athens, Greece, 1993—98; MS in Elec. Engring., U. Mich., Ann Arbor, 1998—99, PhD, 2000—03. Asst. prof., elec. and computer engring. Purdue U., West Lafayette, Ind., 2003—. Contbr. articles to profl. jours. Mem.: IEEE. Achievements include patents pending for reconfigurable slot antennas for VHF/UHF applications. Avocations: travel, chess, ballroom dancing. Office: Purdue Univ 465 Northwestern Ave EE Bldg West Lafayette IN 47906 Office Phone: 765-494-3491. Office Fax: 765-494-4371. E-mail: dperouli@purdue.edu.

**PERREAULT, WILLIAM DANIEL, JR.,** business administration educator; b. N.Y.C., Apr. 7, 1948; s. William Daniel Sr. and Barbara Louise (Peckham) P.; m. Pamela Pittard, May 27, 1972; children: Suzanne Elizabeth, William Daniel III. BS, U. N.C., 1970, PhD, 1973. Asst. prof. U. Ga., Athens, 1973-76, U. N.C., Chapel Hill, 1976-79, assoc. prof., 1979-81, prof., 1981-83, Hanes prof., 1983-88. Vis. prof. Stanford (Calif.) U., 1986-87, assoc. dean, 1988-92. Kenan prof., 1988—; vis. prof. Cambridge (Eng.) U., 1997. Co-author: Essentials Marketing, 2003, The Marketing Game, 2001, Basic Marketing, 2005; editor: Jour. Mktg. Rsch., 1982-85; contbr. articles to profl. jours. Chmn. adv. com. Bur. Census, Washington, 1982—86. Mem. Am. Mktg. Assn. (v.p. 1986, 95, bd. dirs. 1986-89, 94-95, Odell award 1985, Disting. Educator award 1997, Churchill award 1997), Acad. Mktg. Sci. (Outstanding Edn. award 1995), Decision Scis. Inst. (coun. 1977), Assn. Dir. Consumer Rsch. Conf. (chmn. 1976—), Mktg. Sci. Inst. (trustee 1989-94), Phi Beta Kappa. Republican. Presbyterian. Office: U NC CB 3490 Mccoll Bldg Chapel Hill NC 27599-3490 Business E-Mail: bill.perreault@unc.edu.

**PERRENOD, DOUGLAS ARTHUR,** aerospace engineer, astronaut, aerospace scientist; b. Sept. 13, 1947; s. George Edward and Eunice Lillian (Cohn) P. Student, Fla. Inst. Tech., 1968-72; BA in Interdisciplinary Sci., U. South Fla., 1973; postgrad., Calif. State U., 1982—; grad. engr. mgmt. Cert. program, Calif. Inst. Tech., 1987; bioenvironmental engr., USAF Sch. Aerospace Medicine, 1992. Cert. glider flight instr. FAA; cert. sci. rsch. diver

Am. Acad. Underwater Scis. Engr. trainee NASA Kennedy Space Ctr., Fla., 1969-73; quality control engr. Pelletech Corp., Fontana, Calif., 1976-77; electronics specialist Gen. Telephone Co., San Bernardino, Calif., 1977-79; aerospace and project engr. Rockwell Internat., Downey, Calif., 1979-85, Lockheed Corp., Ontario, Calif., 1986-87, Lockheed Engring. Mgmt. Svc. Co., 1987, Eagle Engring., 1988—89, Eagle Tech. Svcs., 1989—92; program mgr., scientist for advanced sci. and tech. rsch. USAF-NASA, 2000—. Aviation cons., owner-founder Flight Unltd., Long Beach, Calif.; rsch.-flight test pilot; mission pilot, project engr. Flight Level 500 High Altitude Soaring Project Astronauts of Soaring; dep. dir. Tex. EquuSearch, 2001—. Developed concept for and co-authored unprecedented Inter-agency agreement between USAF and NASA for exchange of advanced environmental technology, 1994; designer telescope mount for 1st astronomy obs. Fla. Inst. Tech., 1969. Vol. mem. Orange County Human Svcs. Agy., 1981-86; active Big Bros. of Am., 1978. Lt. col. USAFR, 1994. Recipient Amelia Earhart award CAP, 1968, Manned Flight Awareness Apollo 11 medallion NASA, 1971, 1st Shuttle Flight Achievement award NASA, 1981, Aerospace Maintenance Officer of Yr. award USAFR, 1979, Symons Wave Meml. award, 1988, Hon. Aquanaut award Aquarius Undersea Rsch. Ctr., 2001, 1st prize Great Annual Fish Count Digital Photo Contest, 2002; named to Engr. Honor Roll, Rockwell Internat., 1982, 83, 85. Mem. AIAA, Assn. Mil. Surgeons U.S., Res. Officers Assn., Officers Assn., Air Force Assn., Soc. Flight Test Engrs., Assoc. Glider Soc. of So. Calif., Long Beach Navy Aero. Club.

**PERRET, GARY WILLIAM,** priest, educator; b. Sioux City, Iowa, May 20, 1947; s. William Joseph and Geraldine Marie (Maurice) Perret. BA in Secondary Edn., U. Ariz., Tucson, 1970; ThM, St.Mary's U., San Antonio, Tex, 1991. Asst. pastor St, Albert the Great, Compton, Calif., 1976—77; asst. pastor St. Joseph, Granite City, Ill., 1977—78; dir. vocations Misssionaries of Holy Family, Overland, Mo., 1978—82; pastor St. Joseph, Granite City, 1982—86; dir. adult religious edn. Our Lady of Guadalupe, Seguin, Tex., 1986—92, St. Joseph Parish, Donna, Tex., 1993—96, Brownsville (Tex.) Diocese, 1993—96. Dir. R.C.I.A. Various Parishes, San Antonio, 1986—92; instr. sacred scriptures Parishes and Diocese, Tex. Valley, 1993—96. Mem.: KC. Home: 3601 E Seneca Tucson AZ 85716

**PERRET, GERARD ANTHONY, JR.,** orthodontist; b. New Orleans, Feb. 13, 1959; s. Gerard A. and Marie M. (Gamino) P.; m. Catherine J. McMahon, 1996; 1 child, Caroline Marie. BS in Chemistry, La. State U., 1981; DDS, La. State U., 1986, cert. orthodontics, 1989. Diplomate Am. Bd. Orthodontists. Clin. asst. prof. La. State U. Sch. Dentistry, New Orleans, 1986-87; pvt. practice dentistry Lakeside Dental Group, Metairie, La., 1986-87; pvt. practice orthodontics Jacksonville, Fla., 1989-91, Tampa, Fla., 1991—; founder, pres. Orthogap, Inc., Tampa, 1993—, Resdent Realty, Inc., 2001—. Patentee in field. Active mem. New Tampa Cmty. Coun.; chmn. New Tampa Rotary Found., Inc., 2003—04. Mem. ADA, Am. Assn. Orthodontists, Fla. Assn. Orthodontists, Hillsborough County Dental Soc., Hillsborough County Dental Rsch. Clinic, So. Assn. Orthodontists, Rotary (pres. New Tampa chpt. 1997-98), Omicron Kappa Upsilon. Avocations: sailing, fishing, music, golf. Home: 16014 Penwood Dr Tampa FL 33647-1137 US: 15283 Amberly Dr Tampa FL 33647 Office Phone: 813-977-2828.

**PERRETTA, MICHAEL A.,** lawyer; b. Carlstadt, N.Y., July 4, 1921; s. John and Lucy Perretta; children: Andrea, Deborah. BA, State Univ. Albany, N.Y.; LLD, Albany Law Sch. Town justice Town Lenox, Madison County, town atty.; vill. justice Canastota, Madison County, sch. atty. Rep. chmn. Town Lenox, Madison County. Sgt. USAF, 1943—46. Avocation: travel.

**PERRICONE, CHARLES,** former state legislator; b. Oct. 10, 1960; Student, Kalamazoo Coll., Western Mich. U.; DPS (hon.), W. Mich. U. Rep. Mich. State Dist. 61, 1995—2001; spkr. of the house Lansing, 1999—2001; pres., CEO New Era Consulting. Vice chair tax policy com.; mem. corrections com., house oversight and ethics com., legis. coun.; asst. Rep. leader. Recipient Champion of Commerce, Mich. Chamber of Commerce, Guardian of Small Business, Nat. Fed. of Ind. Bus. Republican.

**PERRICONE, NICHOLAS V.,** dermatologist; b. New Haven, Conn., June 23, 1948; BA, U. New Haven, 1970; MD, Mich. State U., East Lansing, 1982. Diplomate Am. Bd. of Dermatology, 1996. Intern in pediat. Yale U. Sch. Medicine, New Haven, 1982—83; resident in dermatology Henry Ford Med. Ctr., Detroit, 1983—86; chmn. Internat. Symposium on Aging Skin, Conn., 1997—; physician Dermatology and Dermatol. Surgery, Meriden, Conn., 1986—2002; chief of dermatology State Vet.'s Hosp., Rocky Hill, Conn., 1987—95; clin. instr. of dermatology Yale U. Med. Sch., New Haven, 1988—97, asst. clin. prof. of dermatology, 1997—2002; adj. prof. Coll. of Human Medicine, Mich. State U., East Lansing, 2002—. Author: (non-fiction book) The Perricone Prescription, 2002 (NY Times #1 Bestseller, 2002), (chapter in textbook) The Basic Principles and Practice of Anti-Aging Medicine and Age Management for the Aesthetic Surgeon and Physician, (non-fiction book) The Perricone Prescription Personal Journal, 2003, The Wrinkle Cure, 2002 (NY Times #1 Bestseller, 2002), The Perricone Promise, 2004; contbg. editor: Jour. Geriatric Dermatology, 1997—, mem. editl. bd.: Archives of Gerontology and Geriatrics, 2000—; contbr. articles to profl. jours. Specialist level 4 Army Mil. Police, 1970—76. Recipient Eli Whitney award, Conn. Intellectual Property Law Assn., 2001, Norman E Clark, Sr. Lecture award, Am. Coll. for Advancement in Medicine, Crystal Communicator award, PBS, 2001, Annenberg Cir., Dermatology Found., 2001. Fellow: Internat. Soc. of Tropical Dermatology, Am. Bd. of Dermatology, N.Y. Acad. Scis., Am. Coll. of Nutrition; mem.: AAAS, Soc. of Investigative Dermatology, New Haven County Med. Assn., Conn. State Med. Soc., Am. Acad. of Dermatology, Conn. Dermatology & Dermatologic Surgery Soc., Assn. of Am. Physicians and Surgeons, Oxygen Soc., Nutrition Rsch. Acad. Achievements include patents for Treatment of Rosacea using Lipoic Acid; Treatment of skin damage using polyenylphosphatidylcholine; Stabilized ascorbyl compositions; Treatment of scar tissue using lipoic acid; Topical administration of catecholamines and related compounds to subcutaneous muscle tissue using percutaneous penetration enhancers; Razor comfort strip with alpha hydroxy acid additive; Lipoic Acid In Topical Compositons; Topical compositions and methods for treatment of skin damage and aging using catecholamines and related compounds; Method and compositions for topical application of ascorbic acid fatty acid esters for treatment and/or prevention of skin damage; Method and compositions for treatment and/or prevention of skin damage and aging; Method and compositions for topical application to the skin of tocotrienols for prevention and/or treatment of skin damage; Treatment of Skin Damage using Olive Oil Polyphenols; Method for treating and prevention of sunburn and sunburn damage to the skin; Method and compositions for topical application to the skin for prevention and/or treatment of radiation-induced skin damage; Method for the topical treatment of psoriasis; Method for the topical treatment and prevention of pseudofolliculitis barbae; Skin Whiteners containing Hydroxytetronic Acid; Electronic Muscle Stimulator Glove; Electronic Muscle Stimulator Finger Tip Triplet; Electronic Stimulator Finger Tip; Treatment of Acne using Lipoic Acid; Topical Scar Treatments using Alkanolamines; Treatment of Skin Damage using Conjugated Linoleic Acid and Ascorbyl Fatty Acid Esters. Office: NV Perricone MD Ltd 639 Research Pkwy Meriden CT 06450 Office Phone: 203-379-0726. Office Fax: 203-379-0817.

**PERRIN, CHARLES R.,** light manufacturing executive; b. 1945; BA in History, Trinity Coll., 1967; MBA, Columbia U., 1969. With Gen. Foods Corp., 1969-73; various mgmt. positions with Chesebrough-Pond's, Inc., 1973-85; with Duracell Inc., Bethel, Conn., 1985—; v.p., pres. Duracell N.Am. Duracell Internat. Inc., 1988—, pres., COO internat. devel. markets, 1992—; chmn. The Warnaco Group. Office: The Warnaco Group 501 7th Ave New York NY 10018

**PERRIN, EDWARD BURTON,** biomedical researcher, public health educator; b. Greensboro, Vt., Sept. 19, 1931; s. J. Newton and Dorothy E. (Willey) P.; m. Carol Anne Hendricks, Aug. 18, 1956; children: Jenifer, Scott. BA, Middlebury Coll., 1953; student in Stats., Edinburgh U., Scotland, 1953—54; MA in Math. Stats., Columbia U., 1956; PhD, Stanford U., 1961.

Asst. prof. dept. biostats. U. Pitts., 1959-62; asst. prof. dept. preventive medicine U. Wash., Seattle, 1962-65, assoc. prof., 1965-69, prof., 1969-70, prof., chmn. dept. biostats., 1970-72, prof. dept. health svcs., adj. prof. dept. biostats., 1975-98, chmn. dept., 1983-94, prof. emeritus, 1999—; hon. prof. West China U. of Med. Scis., Szechwan, China, 1988-98; overseas fellow Churchill Coll., Cambridge U., 1991-92; sr. scientist Seattle Vets. Affairs Med. Ctr., 1994—2001. Biometrician VA Co-op Study on Treatment of Esophageal Varices, 1961—73; sr. cons. biostatistics Wash., Alaska regional med. programs, 1967—72; mem. epidemiology & disease control study sect. NIH. 1969—73; clin. profl. dept. cmty. medicine and internat. health Sch. Medicine, Georgetown U., Washington, 1972—75; dep. dir. Nat. Ctr. Health Stats. HEW, 1972—73, dir., 1973—75; rsch. scientist Health Care Study Ctr. Battelle Human Affairs Rsch. Ctr., Seattle, 1975—76, dir., 1976—78, Health & Population Study Ctr. Battelle Human Affairs Rsch. Ctr., 1978—83; chmn. health svcs. rsch. study sect. HEW, 1976—79; chmn. health svcs. R & D field program rev. panel VA, 1988—91; chmn. health svcs. info steering com. State of Wash., 1993—94; mem. nat. adv. coun. Agy. for Health Care Policy & Rsch. Dept. HHS U.S. Govt., 1994—97; mem. com. on nat. stats. NRC, NAS, 1994—2000; chmn. sci. adv. com. Med. Outcomes Trust, 1994—99; mem. report rev. com. NAS, 2005—. Contbr. articles on biostats., health svcs. and population studies to profl. publs.; mem. editl. bd.: Jour. Family Practice, 1978-90, Pub. Health Nursing, 1992-98. Mem. tech. bd. Milbank Meml. Fund, 1974-76, Health Svcs. and Outcomes Rsch. Methodology, 1999-04. Recipient Outstanding Svc. citation HEW, 1975; Fulbright scholar 1953-54. Fellow AAAS, APHA (Spiegelman Health Stats. award 1970, program devel. bd. 1971, chmn. stats. sect. 1978-80, governing coun. 1983-85, stats. sect. recognition award 1989), Am. Statis. Assn. (mem. adv. com. to divsn. statis. policy 1975-77); mem. Assn. Health Svcs. Rsch. (pres. 1994-95, bd. dirs. 1991-2000), Inst. Medicine of NAS (chmn. membership com. 1984-86, mem. bd. on health care svcs. 1987-96, forum health stats. 1994-95, chmn. com. on clin. evaluation 1990-93), Biometrics Soc. (pres. Western N.Am. Region 1971), Sigma Xi, Phi Beta Kappa. Home: 4900 NE 39th St Seattle WA 98105-5209 Office: U Wash Dept Health Svcs PO Box 358852 Seattle WA 98195-8852 Office Phone: 206-524-9410. E-mail: perrin@u.washington.edu.

**PERRIN, MICHAEL WARREN,** lawyer; b. Cameron, Tex., Nov. 10, 1946; s. Frank W. and Mary Ann (Green) P.; m. Melinda Elizabeth Hill, Aug. 9, 1969; children: Elizabeth, Carter, Hunter. BS, U. Tex., Austin, 1969, JD, 1971. Bar: Tex. 1972, U.S. Dist. Ct. (no., ea., we. and so. dists.) Tex., U.S. Ct. Appeals (5th and 11th cirs.), U.S. Supreme Ct. Assoc. Vinson & Elkins, Houston, 1972-73; assoc. Fisher, Roch & Gallagher, Houston, 1973-76; ptnr. Fisher, Gallagher, Perrin & Lewis, Houston, 1976-91; sole practice Houston, 1991-96; ptnr. King & Spalding, Houston, 1996—. Fellow Am. Coll. Trial Lawyers, Internat. Acad. Trial Lawyers, Internat. Soc. Barristers; mem. Am. Bd. Trial Advocates, Am. Bar Found., Houston Young Lawyers Assn. (sec. 1974-75), Tex. Young Lawyers Assn. (dir. 1976-78, chmn. bd. 1978-79), Houston Trial Lawyers Assn. (pres. 1987-88), Tex. Trial Lawyers Assn. (pres. 1989-90), Tex. Bar Found. (Houston chpt.), U. Tex. Devel. bd. Methodist.

**PERRIN, ROBERT,** writer, consultant; b. Ann Arbor, Mich., Aug. 21, 1925; m. Barbara J. Groom, June 25, 1949; children: Stephen, Jennifer Perrin Hummel. BS, U. Minn., 1945. Reporter United Press Assn., Detroit, 1948-49, Detroit Free Press, 1949-55; adminstrv. asst. U.S. Senate, Washington, 1955-66; asst. dir. U.S. Office Econ. Opportunity, Washington, 1966-68, dep. dir., 1968-70; v.p. Mich. State U., East Lansing, 1970-79; vice-chancellor SUNY System, Albany, 1979-85; exec. v.p. Tchrs. Ins. and Annuity Assn.-Coll. Retirement Equities Fund, N.Y.C., 1987-92; cons. Dept. State, 1993-94. Author: Piggy's Luck and More Tales of Grilolog, 1998, Keeping in Practice, 2001; contbr. articles to mags., newspapers. Mem. U.S.-Mex. Commn. on Border Devel., Washington, 1967-68. Lt. USNR, 1943-46, PTO. Fellow Reid Found., 1954; Pulitzer prize nominee Detroit Free Press, 1956. Home: 2435 Emerald Lake Dr East Lansing MI 48823-7256

**PERRINE, RICHARD LEROY,** environmental engineer, educator; b. Mountain View, Calif., May 15, 1924; s. George Alexander and Marie (Axelson) P.; m. Barbara Jean Gale, Apr. 12, 1945; children: Cynthia Gale, Jeffrey Richard. AB, San Jose State Coll., 1949; MS, Stanford U., 1950, PhD in Chemistry, 1953. Cert. environ. profl., 1987. Research chemist Calif. Research Corp., La Habra, 1953-59; assoc. prof. UCLA, 1959-63, prof. engring. and applied sci., 1963-92, prof. emeritus, 1992—, chmn. environ. sci. and engring., 1971-82; prin. Aspen Environ. Group, 1990-93. V.p. Sage Resources, 1988-91; cons. environ. sci. and engring., energy resources, flow in porous media; mem. Los Angeles County Energy Commn., 1973-81; mem. adv. council South Coast Air Quality Mgmt. Dist., 1977-82; mem. air conservation com. Los Angeles County Lung Assn., 1970-84; mem. adv. com. energy div. Oak Ridge Nat. Lab., 1987-90; mem. policy bd. William D. Ruckelshaus Inst. Environ. and Natural Resources U. Wyo., 1994-2004. Editor in chief The Environ. Profl., 1985-90. Served with AUS, 1943-46. Recipient Outstanding Engr. Merit award in environ. engring. Inst. Advancement Engring., 1975; ACT-SO award in field of chemistry West Coast region NAACP, 1984. Fellow AAAS; mem. Am. Chem. Soc., Soc. Petroleum Engrs., Am. Inst. Chem. Engrs., Can. Inst. Mining and Metallurgy, N.Am. Assn. Environ. Edn., Nat. Assn. Environ. Profls. (cert.), Air and Waste Mgmt. Assn., Assn. Environ. Engring. and Sci. Profs., Sierra Club, Wilderness Soc., Audubon Soc., Sigma Xi, Tau Beta Pi, Phi Lambda Upsilon. Home: 22611 Kittridge St West Hills CA 91307-3609 Office: Univ Calif Engring Bldg I Rm 3066D Los Angeles CA 90095-0001 E-mail: rperrine@ucla.edu.

**PERRINEAU, HAROLD,** actor; b. Bklyn., Aug. 7, 1963; s. Harold Williams; m. Brittany Perrineau; 1 child, Aurora. Studied, Shenandoah Conservatory. Actor: (films) Shakedown, 1988, King of NY, 1990, Smoke, 1995, Flirt, 1995, Blood and Wine, 1996, The Edge, 1997, Come To, 1998, Lulu On The Bridge, 1998, The Tempest, 1998, A Day in Black and White, 1998, The Best Man, 1999, Woman on Top, 2000, Overnight Sensation, 2000, Someone Like You, 2001, Prison Song, 2001, On Line, 2002, The Matrix Reloaded, 2003; (TV series) Fame, 1982, Oz, 1997, Lost, 2004 (Outstanding Performance by an Ensemble in a Drama Series, Screen Actors Guild award, 2006). Office: c/o ABC Inc 77 W 66th St New York NY 10023-6298*

**PERRIS, TERRENCE GEORGE,** lawyer; b. L.A., Oct. 18, 1947; s. Theodore John Grivas and Penny (Sfakianos) Perris. BA magna cum laude, U. Toledo, 1969; JD summa cum laude, U. Mich., 1972. Bar: Ohio 1972, U.S. Tax Ct. 1982, U.S. Ct. Fed. Claims 1983, U.S. Supreme Ct. 1983. Law clk. to judge U.S. Ct. Appeals (2d cir.), N.Y.C., 1972-73; law clk. to Justice Potter Stewart U.S. Supreme Ct., Washington, 1973-74; assoc. Squire, Sanders & Dempsey LLP, Cleve., 1974-80; ptnr., taxation practice group Squire, Sanders & Dempsey, Cleve., 1980—. V.p., trustee SS&D Found., Cleve., 1984—; nat. coord. Taxation Practice Area, 1987—, mgmt. com., 1996—2000; chmn. Cleve. Tax Inst., 1993; vis. prof. law U. Mich., 1996; adj. prof. Case Western Res. U., Cleve., 2001—; lectr. in field. Vis. com. U. Mich. Law Sch., 1986—. Capt. U.S. Army, 1974. Mem.: ABA, Tax. Club Cleve., Supreme Ct. Hist. Soc., Cleve. Bar Assn., Ohio Bar Assn. (subchtp. C of internal revenue code task force), Pres.'s Club, Union Club Cleve., Club Cleve., U. Mich. Club Cleve., Order of Coif, Phi Kappa Phi. Republican. Eastern Orthodox. Avocation: landscape gardening. Office: Squire Sanders & Dempsey LLP 4900 Key Tower 127 Public Sq Cleveland OH 44114-1216 Office Phone: 216-479-8647. Office Fax: 216-479-8780. E-mail: tperris@ssd.com.

**PERRITT, HENRY HARDY, JR.,** law educator; b. Little Rock, Dec. 30, 1944; s. Henry Hardy and Margaret Frances (Floyd) P. SB in Engring., MIT, 1966, SM in Mgmt., 1970; JD, Georgetown U., 1975. Bar: Va. 1976, Pa. 1977, D.C. 1981, Md. 1995, Ill. 1998, U.S. Supreme Ct. 1981, U.S. Ct. Appeals (3d cir.) 1979, U.S. Ct. Appeals (2d cir.) 1979, U.S. Ct. Appeals (4th cir.) 1983. Sr. sales planner Lockheed Corp., Marietta, Ga., 1968-71; exec. sec. Cost of Living Coun., Washington, 1972-75; legis. analyst U.S. Dept. Commerce, 1971-72; mem. staff White House, Washington, 1975; dep. undersec. U.S. Dept. Labor, Washington, 1975-76; gen. counsel labor Conrail, Phila., 1976-81; prof. law Villanova U., Phila., 1981—97, dir. Villanova Ctr. for Info. Law and Policy, 1992-99, dir. Project Bosnia, 1996-99; dean Kent Coll. of Law, Chgo., 1997—2002, prof. law, 1997—. Cons. atty. Morgan,

Lewis & Bockius, Washington, 1981-90; Conrail, 1981-90; vice chmn. Coal Commn., U.S. Sec. of Labor, 1990; mem. computer sci. and telecom. bd. Nat. Rsch. Coun., Coun. Fgn. Rels.; bd. dirs. Chgo. (Ill.) Coun. Fgn. Rels. Author: Employee Dismissal Law and Practice, 1984, 4th edit., 1997, Labor Injunctions, 1986, How to Practice Law with Computers, 1988, Employee Benefits Claims Law and Practice, 1989, Workplace Torts Rights and Liabilities, 1990, Americans with Disabilities Act Handbook, 1990, 3d edit., 1998, Trade Secrets: A Practitioner's Guide, 1994, Law and The Information Superhighway, 1996, 2d edit., 2001; contbr. articles to profl. jours. Dem. nominee for U.S. Congress 10th Dist. Ill., 2002. Mem. ABA (chmn. com. on R.R. and airline labor law 1983-86, chmn. com. on regulatory initiatives and info. tech., adminstrv. law sect., co-vice chmn. dispute resolution com., adminstrv. law sect. 1987-90, sec. labor and employment sect. 2000-01), Assn. Am. Law Schs. (chmn. sect. on law and computers 1991), Econ. Club. Democrat. Office Phone: 312-906-5098. E-mail: hperritt@kentlaw.edu.

**PERRON, EDWARD ADRIAN,** lawyer; b. Washington, Jan. 19, 1954; s. Edward Joseph and Irene (Lum) P.; m. Julie Corman, June 29, 1980; children: Kelly Elizabeth, Christopher Edward. BA in Economics and East Asian Studies, Harvard U., 1975, JD, 1979. Bar: Calif. 1979, U.S. Dist. Ct. (ctrl. dist.) Calif. 1979, U.S. Ct. Appeals (9th cir.) 1980, D.C. 1995, N.Y. 1996. Assoc. Lillick & McHose, Los Angeles, 1979-85, ptnr., 1985-90; ptnr., mem. exec. com., chair office mgmt. com. Pillsbury Madison & Sutro, Los Angeles, 1991—, vice chmn., ptnr. compensation com., 1996, chmn., ptnr. compensation com., 1997—98; (Pillsbury Madison & Sutro merged with Winthrop, Stimson, Putnam, 2001); ptnr., mem. mng. bd. & ptnr. compensation com. Pillsbury Winthrop LLP, Los Angeles, 2001—; (Pillsbury Winthrop LLP merged with Shaw Pittman LLP, 2005); ptnr., corp. & securities dept., mem. mng. bd. & ptnr. compensation com. Pillsbury Winthrop Shaw Pittman LLP, Los Angeles, 2005—. Mem. exec. adv. bd. Japan Am. Cmty. & Cultural Ctr., L.A., 1990—. Los Angeles Econ. Devel. Corp. 2004-; dir. Asian Pacific-Am. Legal Ctr., L.A., 1990—. Mem. Japan Am. Soc. So. Calif. (gen. counsel, dir. 1985—), Japan Bus. Assn. So. Calif., ABA, Calif. Bar Assn., Los Angeles County Bar Assn. Office: Pillsbury Winthrop Shaw Pittman LLP 725 S Figueroa St Los Angeles CA 90017-5524 Office Phone: 213-488-7352. Office Fax: 213-629-1033. Business E-Mail: edward.perron@pillsburylaw.com.

**PERRONE, NICHOLAS,** engineering company executive; b. NYC, Apr. 30, 1930; B. Aero. Engring., Poly. Inst. Bklyn., 1951, MS, 1953, PhD, 1958. Research asst., then assoc. applied mechanics Bklyn. Poly. Inst., 1951-58; asst. prof., then assoc. prof. Pratt Inst., 1958-62; sr. scientist Structural Mechanics br. Office Naval Research, Washington, 1962-67, acting head dept., 1967-68, dir. program, 1968-69, 71-82; pres. CASA Gifts Inc., 1983-85; dep. to pres. Advanced Tech. and Research Inc., 1986-87; pres. Perrone Forensic Cons. Inc., 1987—. Lectr. civil engring. Cath U. Am., 1962-64, adj. prof., 1965-91; spl. research fellow NIH, Georgetown U., 1969-70; participant numerous workshops, confs., symposia; lectr. in field. Contbg. author: Biodynamics, 1980; editor or co-editor numerous monographs; editorial adv. bd.: Advances in Engring. Software, Computers and Structures, Engineering Fracture, Pressure Vessels and Piping; contbr. numerous articles to profl. jours. Fellow AAAS, ASME, Am. Acad. Mechanics; mem. ASCE, AIAA, N.Y. Acad. Sci., Am. Soc. Engring. Edn., Soc. Automotive Engrs., Soc. Mfg. Engrs. Address: 8 Cherry Ln Newtown Square PA 19073-3949 Office Phone: 610-325-4447. E-mail: nicholasperrone@comcast.net.

**PERROT, PAUL NORMAN,** museum director; b. Paris, July 28, 1926; came to U.S., 1946, naturalized, 1954; s. Paul and K. Norman (Derr) P.; m. Joanne Stovall, Oct. 23, 1954; children—Paul Latham, Chantal Marie Claire, Jeannine, Robert. Student, Ecole du Louvre, 1945-46, N.Y. U. Inst. Fine Arts, 1946-52. Asst. The Cloisters, Met. Mus. Art, 1948-52; asst. to dir. Corning (N.Y.) Mus. Glass, 1952-54, asst. dir. mus., 1954-60, dir., 1960-72; editor Jour. Glass Studies, 1959-72; asst. sec. for mus. programs Smithsonian Instn., Washington, 1972-84; dir. Va. Mus. Fine Arts, 1984-91, Santa Barbara Mus. Art, 1991-94, mus. cons., 1995—. Lectr. glass history, aesthetics, museology; past v.p. Internat. Coun. Mus. Found.; past pres. N.E. Conf. Mus.; past pres. Internat. Centre for Study of Preservation and Restoration of Cultural Property, Rome, mem. coun., 1974-88. Author: Three Great Centuries of Venetian Glass, 1958, also numerous articles on various hist. and archael. subjects. Former trustee Winterthur Mus.; former trustee, treas. Mus. Computer Network; former mem. Internat. Cons. Com. for the Preservation of Moenjodaro; former chmn. adv. com. World Monuments Fund; former chmn. vis. com. Getty Conservation Inst. Mem. Am. Assn. Mus. (past v.p., coun. 1967-78), N.Y. State Assn. Mus. (past pres.), Internat. Assn. History Glass (past v.p.) Corning Friends of Library (past pres.), So. Tier Library System (past pres.). E-mail: paulnperrot@comcast.net.

**PERROTTA, ANTONIO,** trust company executive; arrived in U.S., 1993; BS in Engring., Mil. Inst. Engring., Rio de Janeiro, 1981; BS in Econs., Rio de Janeiro State U., 1982; MS in Computer Sci., Mil. Inst. Engring., Rio de Janeiro, 1985. Sr. tech. mgr. Bamerindus Bank, Rio de Janeiro, Rio de Janeiro, 1981—93; sr. mgr. Price Waterhouse, NYC, 1993—95; v.p. J.P.Morgan, NYC, 1995—2003; chief tech. officer Bessemer Trust, Woodbridge, NJ, 2003—.

**PERRUCCI, ROBERT,** sociologist, educator; b. N.Y.C., Nov. 11, 1931; s. Dominic and Inez (Mucci) P.; m. Carolyn Land Cummings, Aug. 4, 1965; children: Mark Robert, Celeste Ann, Christopher Robert, Alicca Cummings, Martin Cummings. BS, SUNY, Cortland, 1958; MS (Social Sci. Research Council fellow), Purdue U., 1962. Asst. prof. sociology Purdue U., West Lafayette, Ind., 1962-65, assoc. prof., 1965-67, prof., 1967—, head dept., 1978-87. Vis. Simon prof. U. Manchester (Eng.), 1968-69; bd. dirs. Ind. Center on Law and Poverty, 1973-76 Author: Sociology, 1983, Circle of Madness, 1974, Divided Loyalties, 1980, The Triple Revolution, 1971, Profession Without Community, 1968, The Engineers and the Social System, 1968, Mental Patients and Social Networks, 1982, Plant Closings: International Context and Local Consequences, 1988, Networks of Power, 1989, Japanese Auto Transplants in the Heartland: Corporatism and Community, 1994, The New Class Society, 1999, Science Under Siege?, 2000, The New Class Society: Goodbye American Dream, 2003; editor: The American Sociologist, 1982—84, Social Problems, 1993-96, Contemporary Sociology, 2000-2005; contbr. articles to profl. jours. Served in USMC, 1951-53. Recipient grants, NSF, 1966—68, 1976—78, NIMH, 1969—72, Sloan Found., 2002—05. Mem. Am. Sociol. Assn., Soc. Study Social Problems (dir. 1980-83, v.p. 1996-97, pres. 1999—), N. Central Sociol. Assn. (pres. 1973-74) Home: 305 Leslie Ave West Lafayette IN 47906-2411 Office: Dept Sociology Purdue U West Lafayette IN 47907

**PERRY, ANNE MARIE LITCHFIELD,** secondary school educator; b. LaJunta, Colo., June 20, 1943; d. Robert Silas and Anne (Kennedy) Hovey, Robert Latta Litchfield (Stepfather); m. Franklin Haile Perry, Dec. 21, 1968; children: Kristina Marie, Tad Kennedy. BE, Drake U., 1966; MA, U. Tex., 1969; PhD, Tex. A&M U., 1977. Grade sch. tchr., San Antonio, 1966—67, Austin, 1967—68; rsch. assoc. R&D Ctr., U. Tex., Austin, 1968; grad. asst., instr. Tex. A&M U., 1969—70; kindergarten tchr., 1970—72; instr. U. St. Thomas, 1973—74; spl. edn. tchr., supr. Cypress, Cypress-Fairbanks Ind. Sch. Dist., Houston, 1974—77; supr. gifted/talented, bilingual, English lang. devel. programs, 1977—80; mem. adj. faculty U. Houston, 1979—80; lower sch. dir. curriculum and ednl. resources Kinkaid Sch., Houston, 1980—85, dir. young writers workshops, 1985—; tchr., chair lang. arts dept. Klein Intermediate Sch. Dist., Tex., 1986—2001. Vis. asst. prof. Tex. A&M U., 1988—89; cons. in field. Author (photographer): Riders Ready, 1985; author: Teacher Guide and Student Packet for Frindle, 2002, Just Like Always, 2005; editor: Travels in Mexico and California, 1988, Bluebonnet Books-Activities for 1996, Lonestar Books-Activities for 1993-1994 and 1994-1995. Named Tchr. of Yr., Hancock Elem. Sch., 1975. Mem.: NEA,

Harley Owners Group-Branzos de Dios, Soc. of Children's Book Writers and Illustrators, Tex. State Tchrs. Assn., Run for the Wall. Methodist. Home: 10965 Clyde Acord Rd Franklin TX 77856-5821 Personal E-mail: aperry@flash.net.

**PERRY, BARRY W.,** manufacturing executive; b. South Dartmouth, Mass., May 1946; s. Antone and Adelaide Perry; m. Janice G. Perry; 3 children. BS in plastics engring., U. Mass., 1968. With GE; group v.p., gen. mgr. latex specialty polymers divsn. Rhone-Poulenc, 1991—93; group v.p., gen. mgr. pigments and additives group Engelhard Corp., 1993—97, pres., 1997—2001, CEO, 1997—, chmn., 2001—. Bd. dirs. Arrow Electronics Inc., Cookson Group PLC, 2002—. Mem. corp. coun. Conservation Fund. Avocations: antique weapons, bicycling, walking. Office: 101 Wood Ave Iselin NJ 08830*

**PERRY, CHARLES OWEN,** sculptor; b. Helena, Mont., Oct. 18, 1929; s. Owen Hindmarch and Margaret Carroll (Bache) P.; m. Sheila Alicia Henry, June 22, 1962; children— Paul, Carlo, Daniela, Patrick, Marco. Student, Columbia U., 1953; M.Arch., Yale U., 1958. Architect Skidmore Owings & Merrill, San Francisco, 1958-64, Prix de Rome Architecture, 1964-66. Sculptor-in-residence Dartmouth Coll., 1973. One-man shows include Hansen Gallery, San Francisco, 1964, Waddell Gallery, N.Y.C., 1967, 70, Dartmouth Coll., 1973, Arts Club, Chgo., 1973, Auguste st-Gaudens Mus., N.H.; exhibited in group shows at Whitney Mus., 1964, 66, Spoleto Festival, 1967, Venice Biennale, 1970, Quadrienalle di Arte de Roma, 1977, Katonah Gallery N Y; represented in permanent collections at Mus. Modern Art, N.Y.C., Art Inst. Chgo., San Francisco Mus. Art, U. Ind. Mus. Art, Dartmouth Coll., U. Mich., Nat. Air and Space Mus., IBM, Charlotte, N.C., Hyatt Regency, San Francisco, Fed. Res. Bank, Mpls., Barnett Plaza, Tampa, Lincoln Ctr., Dallas, Shell Oil Bldg., Melbourne, Australia, GE Hdqrs., Fairfield, Conn., Bushnell Park, Hartford, Conn., Crystal City, Arlington, Va., Zeimu U., Tokyo, Kokubu Civic Ctr., Japan; patentee in furniture design field. Served with U.S. Army, 1951-53. Decorated Bronze star, Am. Iron & Steel Inst Citation for Excellende in Fine Art, 1969, 1971, Prix de Rome in Arch., 1964, Best of Show Nat. Acad. Design award sculpture, 1987, Product Design award, Inst. Bus. Designers, 1992, Internat Design Expo., Canada, 1990, 1998. Fellow Am. Acad. Rome, Nat. Acad. Design; mem. Century Assn. (N.Y.C.), Internat. Sculpture Ctr. Roman Catholic. Studio: 3 Raymond St Norwalk CT 06854-3107 Personal E-mail: coperry@aol.com. Business E-Mail: charles@charlesperry.com.

**PERRY, CHRIS NICHOLAS,** retired advertising executive; b. Pitts., Dec. 25, 1945; s. Nicholas and Georgia (Demas) P.; Kathleen Clarke, June 19, 1971; children: Damien, Adam, Dana. BA, U. Pitts., 1968. With Youngstown (Ohio) Steel, 1968-70; creative supr. Ketchum Communications, Pitts., 1970-74; pres., creative dir. Hedding, Perry, Davis Inc., Charlotte, N.C., 1974-76; v.p., creative dir. Fahlgren & Swink Advt., Marion, Ohio, 1976-79, Meldrum and Fewsmith Communications, Inc., Cleve., 1979-82, sr. v.p. creative services, 1982-85, exec. v.p. creative services, 1985-86, pres., chief operating officer, 1986-87, chmn., chief exec. officer, creative dir., 1987-98, also bd. dirs. Mem. bd. disting. judges and advisors The N.Y. Festivals, 1988—. Recipient numerous awards for creative excellence. Mem. Am. Assn. Advt. Agys. (sec.-treas. cen. region 1990-91, chmn. 1992-93), Cleve. Advt. Club, Cleve. Soc. Communicating Arts (pres. 1985-87, Disting. Communicator award 1991), The Hermit Club, Columbia Hills Country Club, The Union Club, Firestone Country Club.

**PERRY, CONSTANCE KARIN,** philosopher, educator; b. Huntington, N.Y., May 15, 1965; d. John Isaac Green, Patricia Karen and adopted d. Richard Harry Ihlenburg; m. Kevin J. Perry, Aug. 19, 1990; 1 child, Duncan Ethan. BA in Health and Sociology, U. Rochester, Rochester, N.Y., 1987; MA in Philosophy, U. Buffalo, Amherst, N.Y., 1989, PhD in Philosophy, 1994. Asst. prof. Sch. Humanities and Health Scis. Hahnemann U., Phila., 1994—2000; assoc. prof. Coll. Nursing and Health Professions Drexel U., Phila., 2000—. Co-chmn. hosp. ethics com. Hahnemann U., 2003—. Contbr. chapters to books, articles to profl. jours. Recipient Tchg. Recognition azward, Drexel U. Dept. Ob-gyn., 2002; scholar, U. Buffalo, 1987—90. Mem.: Internat. Network Feminist Approaches to Bioethics, Ethics Network Del. Valley Region, Am. Soc. Bioethics and Humanities, Am. Philos. Assn., Alpha Eta. Office: Drexel University 1505 Race St MS 503 Philadelphia PA 19102 Office Phone: 215-762-7857. Office Fax: 215-762-8429. Business E-Mail: cp28@drexel.edu.

**PERRY, CYNTHIA SHEPARD,** federal agency administrator; Grad., Ind. State U.; EdD, U. Mass. Chief edn. and human resources Africa Bus. USAID, 1982—86; ambassador Sierra Leone, 1986—89, Burundi, 1990—93; dir. internat. investment adv. svcs. FCA Corp., Houston, 1996—2001; U.S. dir. African Devel. Bank, Abidjan, Cote d'Ivoire, 2001—. N. counsel gen., Senegal. Office: African Devel Bank 01 BP 1387 Abidjan 01 Cote d'Ivoire

**PERRY, DALE LYNN,** chemist; b. Greenville, Tex., May 12, 1947; s. Francis Leon and Violet (Inabinette) P. BS, Midwestern U., 1969; MS, Lamar U., 1972; PhD, U. Houston, 1974. NSF fellow dept. chemistry Rice U., Houston, 1976-77; Miller Research fellow dept. chemistry U. Calif.-Berkeley, 1977-79; prin. investigator solid state chemistry and spectroscopy Lawrence Berkeley Lab. U. Calif., 1979—, sr. scientist, 1987—. Lectr. Ana G. Mendez Ednl. Found., 1988; rsch. mem. G.T. Seaborg Inst. for Transactinium Sci. Author, editor: Instrumental Surface Analysis of Geologic Materials, 1990, Applications of Analytical Techniques to the Characterization of Materials, 1992, Applications of Synchrotron Radiation Techniques to Materials Science, 1993, II, 1995, III, 1996, IV, 1998, V, 2001, VI, 2002, Handbook of Inorganic Compounds, 1995, Materials Synthesis and Characterization, 1997; contbr. articles to profl. jours. Named Outstanding Mentor for Undergrad. Rsch., U.S. Dept. Energy, 2002. Fellow AAAS, Royal Soc. Chemistry (London); mem. Am. Chem. Soc. (chmn. materials chemistry and engring. subdivsn., indsl. and engring. chemistry divsn., 1992-96), Soc. Applied Spectroscopy, Coblentz Soc., Materials Rsch. Soc. (corp. participation com. 1991-96), Sigma Xi (nat. rsch. award 1974). Office: U Calif Lawrence Berkeley Nat Lab Mail Stop 70A 1150 Berkeley CA 94720-0001

**PERRY, DONNA SUE,** special education educator; d. Lionel Earl and Alberta L. Turner; m. Lafe Leon Perry, Aug. 8, 1973; children: Micah Jennifer, Brent Michael. BS in Elem. Edn., Southeast Mo. State U., 1976; MA in Edn., Ball State U., 1982. Tchr. spl. edn. Switzerland County Schs., Vevay, Ind., 1976—77; tchr. learning disabled elem. edn. North Newton Schs., Morocco, 1977—79; tchr. high sch. spl. edn. South Ripley High Sch., Versailles, 1979—. Mem. adv. com. Reading Stds. Bd., Indpls., 2002. Active Dabney Bapt. Ch., Holton, Ind., 1979—. Mem.: NEA, Ind. State Tchrs. Assn., Coun. Exceptional Children, Delta Kappa Gamma. Home: 354 N Main Versailles IN 47042 Office: South Ripley Sch Corp Versailles IN 47042

**PERRY, DOUGLAS,** opera singer; B.M., Wittenberg U.; MA, Ball State U. Made debut as Don Basilio in Marriage of Figaro, with N.Y.C. Opera; appeared as King Kaspar in: Amahl and the Night Visitors; appeared as Timothy in: Help! Help! The Globolinks; appeared as Guillot in: Manon; Dancing Master and Brighella in: Ariadne auf Naxos; Met. Opera debut as scientist/first mate in: The Voyage (Philip Glass); European debut with Netherlands Opera as Mahatma Gandhi in Satyagraha (Philip Glass); appeared as analyst in A Quiet Place (Bernstein), La Scala and Vienna Stadtsoper, as Sailor 1, Scientist 3, Traveler 2 world premier Corvo Bronco, Teatro Camõ, Lisbon, Portugal, Teatro Real, Madrid; featured soloist on tours and recs. with Gregg Smith Singers and Camerata Singers; performed with Sante Fe Opera, also performed with Ft. Worth Opera, Chatauqua Opera, N.Y.C. Opera, Opera Co. of Boston, Houston Grand Opera, Balt. Opera., Miami Opera, Chgo. Lyric Opera, Seattle Opera, San Francisco Opera, Opera Co. Phila.; recs. include Satyagraha, Songs from Liquid Days, A Quiet Place, Mother of Us All. Address: 170 W End Ave New York NY 10023-5401 Office: Pinnacle Arts Mgmt 889 9th Ave Ste 1 New York NY 10019-0999

**PERRY, DOUGLAS SKIP DALE,** music educator; b. Charleston, W.Va., Apr. 13, 1951; s. Orville Wright and Bertha Marie Perry; m. Kimberley Ann Fink, Aug. 6, 1977; children: Matthew Ryan, Benjamin Tyler. BA Music Edn., U. Charleston, 1973. Cardio-pulmonary technician Charleston Area Med. Ctr. - Meml. Divsn., Charleston, W.Va.; 1973—75; band dir. Kanawha County Pub. Schs., Charleston, 1976—81; ednl. sales rep. Mack and Dave's, Charleston, 1981—84, N.C.'s Music World, Charleston, 1984—86; ad specialty sales rep. Bob Morrison Specialty Products Co., Cross Lanes, W.Va., 1986—87; music educator Orange County Pub. Schs., Orlando, Fla., 1987—. Chmn., clinician, conductor Orange County Mid. Sch. Jazz Honors Band, 1996. Music educator (jazz ensemble) Midwest Clinic: Am Internat. Conf., Chgo., 2005. Named Tchr. of Month, Walker Mid. Sch., 1989, Tchr. of Yr., 1991, Tchr. of Month, Piedmont Lakes Mid. Sch., 2001, 2005. Mem.: Music Educators Nat. Conf. (assoc.), Internat. Assn. Jazz Educators (assoc.), Nat. Band Assn. (assoc. Outstanding Performance award 2005), Fla. Bandmasters Assn. (assoc.), Phi Beta Mu. Home: 16508 Magnolia Terr Montverde FL 34756 Personal E-mail: perryspromo@cs.com.

**PERRY, E. LYNN,** lawyer; b. Tucson, Mar. 23, 1949; d. Eldon G. Perry and Doris E. (Wismer) Noonan BA, U. Ariz., 1970; JD, Loyola U., 1976. Bar: Ill. 1977, US Dist. Ct. (no. dist.) Ill. 1977, NY 1980, US Dist. Ct. (so. and ea. dists.) NY, Calif. 1980, US Dist. Ct. (no., ea. and cen. dists.) Calif., US Ct. Appeals (9th cir.), US Supreme Ct. Flight attendant Pan American World Airways, N.Y.C. and L.A., 1971-75; asst. state's atty. Cook County State's Atty., Chgo., 1977-79; assoc. Kass, Goodkind, Wechsler & Labaton, N.Y.C., 1980-81; assoc. counsel MasterCard Internat., Inc., N.Y.C., 1981-84; assoc. Townsend and Townsend and Crew, San Francisco, 1984-89, ptnr., 1989—2002, Thelen Reid & Priest, 2002—06, Perry IP Group, Greenbrae, Calif., 2006—. Adj. prof. U. Calif. Hastings Coll. Law, 2005—; spkr. in field. Scholar U. Ariz., Tucson, 1970, Loyola U., L.A., 1976. Mem. ABA (Governing Com. Forum Franchising 1991-93), Internat. Trademark Assn. (editl. bd. Trademark Reporter 1985—, profl. writing competition judge 1988-2005, panel of neutrals 2003—), Calif. State Bar (trademarks chair 1990-91, Exec. Com. Intellectual Property Sect. 1991-94), San Francisco Intellectual Property Law Assn. (program chair 1987-88). Avocations: tennis, yoga, skiing. Office: Perry IP Group Ste 100 100 Drake's Landing Dr Greenbrae CA 94904

**PERRY, GEORGE,** neuroscientist, educator; s. George Richard and Mary Arlene (George) P.; m. Paloma Aguilar, May 21, 1983; children: Anne, Elizabeth. AA in Liberal Arts, Allan Hancock Coll., Santa Maria, Calif., 1973; BA in Zoology with hons., U. Calif., Santa Barbara, 1974; PhD in Marine Biology, U. Calif., San Diego, 1979. Postdoctoral fellow Baylor Coll. Medicine, Houston, 1979-82; from asst. prof. to prof. pathology Case Western Res. U., Cleve., 1982-94, prof., 1994—, interim chair dept. 2001—05; prof. chemistry and biochemistry U. Alaska, Fairbanks, 2001—06; dean Coll. of Scis. U. Tex., San Antonio, 2006—. Tchg. asst. U. Calif., San Diego, 1977, Stanford U., 1978—79; memory task force on Alzheimer's disease Ohio Gov., 1987, 90; mem. sci. adv. bd. Familial Alzheimer's Disease Rsch. Found., 1988—; mem., chair neurology scis. study sect. NIH, Bethesda, Md., 1989—95; cons. Nymox, Inc., Panacea Pharms., Inc., Prion Devel. Labs., Voyager, Takada Pharm., Alzheimer Rsch. Disease and Regeneration Forum; mem. Faculty of 1000 Biology, Neurobiology Sect., 2004—; spkr. in field; mem. numerous rev. bds. nationally/internationally. Author: The Neuronal Cytoskeleton, 1992, numerous publs. in field; co-author: Frontiers in Biosciences, 2002, Neurosignals, 2002, Brain Pathology, 2004, Microscopy Rsch. & Technique, 2005, Internat. Jour. Exptl. Pathology, 2005; assoc. editor Am. Jour. Pathology, 1994-2000; sr. assoc. editor Microscopy Rsch. and Technique; mem. editl. bd. Am. Jour. Pathology, 1992—, Alzheimer Disease and Associated Disorders, 1994—, Alzheimer's Disease Rev., 1995-98, Jour. Alzheimer's Disease, 1997—, Jour. Exptl. Neurol., 1997-99, Molecular Chem. Neuropathology, 1997-99, Jour. Neural Transmission, 1998-2003, Investigational Drugs Jour., 1998—, Brain Pathology, 1999—, Jour. Molecular Neurosci., 1999-2001, Antioxidant and Redox Signaling, 2000-2002, Research Signpost, 2000, Lab. Investment, 2000—, Brain Rsch., 2002—, Current Medicinal Chemistry, 2002—, Neurobiology of Lipids, 2003—, Jour. Biomed. Biotechnique, 2002—, Pathology, 2003—, Pharm. Devel. Regime, 2003—, Med. Chemistry Rev.-Online, 2003—, Current Alzheimer Rsch., 2003—, NeuroSignals, 2003-05, Disease Markers, 2003—, Neurobiology Disease, 2004—, Lett Drug Design Discovery, 2004—; reviewer Acta Neuropathol., Alan Liss Publ. Co., Am. Jour. Pathol., Ann Neurol, others; contbr. articles to Exptl. Cell Rsch., Jour Cell Biology, Devel. Biology, Brain Rsch., Am. Jour. Pathology, Jour. Neurosci., European Jour. Cell Biology, Nature, Annals Neurology, Lancet, Acta Neuropathology, Jour. Neurochemistry, Neurosci. Letters, Neuroreport, Med. Hypotheses, Nature Medicine, Neurodegeneration, Sci., others. Pres. Serra Club, 1995-97. Tng. corps. USAR, 1972—74, U. Calif. Santa Barbara. Recipient Bausch and Lomb medal, 1971, Rsch. Career Devel. award, NIH, 1988—93, Career Devel. award, 1988, Temple award, Alzheimer's Assn., 1999, Disting. Am. Portuguese Ancestry award, Portuguese-Am. Hist. Found., Inc., 2001, Mensch Alzheimer's Assn., 2004; fellow, Kennecott Copper, 1974-75, Muscular Dystrophy Assn., 1980—82, Philip Morris, USA, 2004—; grantee, NIH, 1985—, Am. Health Assistance Found., 1988—90, 1997—99, Alzheimer's Assn., 1989—90, 1998—2002, 2004—, United Mitochondrial Disease Fund, 2000—02. Fellow AAAS; mem. AAUP (exec. com. 1996—2006, membership chair 1996-98, v.p. 1998-99, pres. 1999—2006), Am. Soc. Cell Biology, Electron Microscopy Soc. N.E. Ohio (treas. 1986-88, trustee 1988-90, pres. 1990-91), Soc. Neurosci., Am. Assn. Neuropathologists (awards com. 1992-93, 95-2002, chmn. 2001-02, internat. congress neuropathology concilator 1995-2000, sec. treas. 2003—), Am. Soc. Investigative Pathology (program com. 1998-2001), Am. Soc. Neurochemistry, U.S. and Can. Acad. of Pathology, Hispanic Med. Assn. (com. on status of Portuguese in medicine and sci.), Soc. for Neurosci., Sigma Xi (pres. chpt. 2004-06). Democrat. Roman Catholic. Avocation: genealogy. Office: U Tex San Antonio Coll Scis 6900 North Loop 1604 W San Antonio TX 78249-0661 Business E-Mail: george.perry@case.edu.

**PERRY, GEORGE LEWIS,** research economist, consultant; b. N.Y.C., Jan. 23, 1934; s. Lewis G. and Helen L.P.; m. Jean Marion West, 1956; children: Elizabeth, Lewis G., George A.; m. 2d, Dina Needleman, 1987. BS, MIT, 1954, PhD, 1961. Editor Brookings Papers on Econ. Activity, 1970—; columnist L.A. Times, 1981-93. Bd. dirs. State Farm Mut. Automobile Ins. Co., Bloomington, Ill., Dreyfus Mut. Funds, N.Y.C.; co-dir. Brookings Panel Econ. Activity. Author: Unemployment, Money Wage Rates and Inflation, 1966, Curing Chronic Inflation, 1978, Economic Events, Ideas and Policies, 2000; contbr. articles to profl. jours. With USAF, 1955—57. Mem. Am. Econs. Assn. Office: Brookings Instn 1775 Massachusetts Ave NW Washington DC 20036-2103 E-mail: gperry@brookings.edu.

**PERRY, GEORGE WILLIAMSON,** lawyer; b. Cleve., Dec. 4, 1926; s. George William and Melda Patricia (Arther-Holt) P. BA in Econs., Yale U., 1949; JD, U. Va., 1953, D.C. 1958, U.S. Supreme Ct. 1958, U.S. Ct. Appeals (D.C. cir.) 1959. Atty. U.S. Dept. Justice, Washington, 1954-56; assoc. Roberts and McInnis, Washington, 1957-59; atty. assoc. counsel Com. on Interstate Fgn. Commerce, U.S. Ho. Reps., Washington, 1960-65; atty., advisor ICC, Washington, 1965-68; assoc. dir. Amtrak, Yale U., New Haven, 1968-70; trust officer The No. Trust Co., Chgo., 1970-71; dir. tax rsch. Pan Am. World Airways, N.Y.C., 1973-75; hearing officer Indsl. Commn. Ohio, Cleve., 1978-81; sole practice Cleve., 1981—. With U.S. Army, 1945-46. Mem. Soc. Cin. in State of Conn., Ancient and Hon. Artillery Co. (mem. Boston-hereditary), Phi Delta Phi, Chi Delta. Home: 1801 E 12th St Cleveland OH 44114-3541 E-mail: gperryxyz@yahoo.com.

**PERRY, GEORGE WILSON,** oil and gas company executive; b. Pampa, Tex., July 18, 1929; s. Frank M. and Ruth (Ingersoll) P.; m. Patricia Carberry Bowen, 1950; children: Sally Jett Perry Pemrick, Susan Jeanne Perry Bynder-Schrier, Virginia Anne Perry Haynie, Tobe Jackson Perry. BS in Petroleum Engring., U. Tulsa, 1952. Registered profl. engr., Tex. Engr.

Stanolind Oil & Gas Co., Oklahoma City, 1952—53, Parker Drilling Co., Tulsa, 1953—54, Holm Drilling Co., Tulsa, 1954—55; drilling engr. Mobil Oil, Victoria, Tex., 1955—61, engr. Lake Charles, La., 1955—61, Paris, 1961—68; ops. mgr. Anaco, Venezuela, 1968—72, NYC, 1972—73, Tehran, Iran, 1973—74, Stavanger, Norway, 1974—78, New Orleans, 1978—79; exec. v.p. Loffland Bros. Co., Tulsa, 1979—89; pres., CEO Gas Well Properties, Inc., Dallas, 1989—. Mem. Delta Tau Delta. Avocation: astronomy. Office: Gas Well Properties Inc PO Box 795302 5995 Summerside Dr Dallas TX 75379

**PERRY, GREGORY J.,** museum director; BA, U. Ill., Urbana-Champaign, 1982; JD, DePaul U., 1990; MA in modern art hist., theory and criticism, Sch. of Art Inst. Chgo., 2003. Assoc. Robert W. Smith & Assocs., Ill., Hillside, and Fein and Seeskin, Ill.; assoc. dir. Attn Ernst Inst. Chgo.; assoc. dir. Jane Voorhees Zimmerli Art Mus., Rutgers U., NJ, 2000—02, acting dir., 2002, dir., 2003—. Office: Rutgers U Jane Voorhees Zimmerli Mus 71 Hamilton St New Brunswick NJ 08901

**PERRY, HAROLD OTTO,** dermatologist; b. Rochester, Minn., Nov. 18, 1921; s. Oliver and Hedwig Clara (Tornow) P.; m. Loraine Thelma Moehnke, Aug. 27, 1944; children: Preston, Oliver, Ann, John. AA, Rochester Jr. Coll., 1942; BS, U. Minn., 1944, MB, 1946, MD, 1947; MS, Mayo Grad. Sch. Medicine, 1953. Diplomate Am. Bd. Dermatology with spl. competence in dermatopathology. Intern Naval Hosp., Oakland, Calif., 1946-47; resident in dermatology Mayo Grad. Sch. Medicine, 1949-52; practice medicine specializing in dermatology Rochester, 1953-86; mem. staff Mayo Clinic, 1953-86, mem. emeritus staff, 1987—; instr., asst. prof., assoc. prof. Mayo Med. Sch., 1953-86, prof., 1978-83, Robert H. Kieckhefer prof. dermatology, 1978-83, head dept. dermatology, 1975-83, emeritus prof. dermatology, 1987—. Civilian cons. dermatology to surgeon gen. USAF, 1973-84. Contbr. articles to med. jours. and, chpts. to books. With USNR, 1943-45, 46-49. Inducted into Rochester (Minn.) C.C. Alumni Hall of Fame, 1993; recipient Disting. Alumnus award Mayo Found., 1995. Mem. AMA, Am. Acad. Dermatology (pres. 1981, Sulzberger internat. lectr. 1986, Gold Medal for visionary leadership 1998), Am. Dermatol. Assn. (bd. dirs. 1985-89, pres. 1989-90), Am. Bd. Dermatology (bd. dirs. 1979-90, v.p. 1989, pres. 1990), Noah Worcester Dermatol. Soc. (pres. 1969), Minn. Dermatol. Soc. (pres. 1967), Chgo. Dermatol. Soc., Internat. Soc. Tropical Dermatology, Minn. Med. Assn.; hon. mem. French Dermatol. Soc., Spanish Acad. Dermatology, Brazilian Dermatol. Soc., Ga. Dermatol. Soc., Iowa Dermatol. Soc., Korean Dermatol. Soc., Bolivar Soc. Dermatology, Jacksonville Dermatol. Soc., N.Am. Clin. Dermatol. Soc., Pacific Dermatol. Assn. Office: Mayo Clinic Emeritus Staff Ctr 10th Fl Plummer Bldg Ctr Rochester MN 55905-0001

**PERRY, HELEN,** medical/surgical nurse, secondary school educator; b. Birmingham, Ala., Mar. 4, 1927; d. Van Mary Ellenol (Thornton) Curry; m. Charlie Pitts, May 1960 (div.); 1 child, Charlenia Pitts; m. George Perry (dec. 1989); children: Hattie Mae(dec.), George Jr., Bishop, Jose Sr. Student, LaSalle Extension U., Chgo., 1968, Georgetown U., 1979; Doctorate/Mayanuis Mosaic Soc., Duke Univ., San Antonio, 1979. Cert. paramedic, of completion Ptnrs. in Health Sheperd Ctr. Am. South Side, 2006; LPN. Tchr. Wenona HS City Bd. Edn., Birmingham, 1977—2005, supply tchr., 2005—. Notary pub., Ala., 1975—; home health nurse U. Ala. Birmingham Hosp., 1988—; math. and reading tutor Princeton Elem. Sch. 2004. Trustee Nat. Crime Watch, 1989; mem. adv. bd. Am. Security Coun., Va., Washington, 1969—91; mem. Coalition for Desert Storm; others; vol. ARC, Birmingham, 1970—; mem. crime watch Ala. Police, Washington, 1989; mem. Hall of Fame Pres. Task Force, Washington, 1983—91, Image Devel. Adv. Bd.; nominee Nat. Rep. Com., Washington, 1991, 1992; selected VIP guest del. Rep. Nat. Conv., Houston, 1992; life mem. Rep. Presdl. Task Force, Washington, 1992; mem. Jefferson Com., 2001; mem. adv. bd. Nat. Congl. Com., Washington; mem. fin. com. fundraiser Middleton for Congress Campaign, 1994, Dist. # 59 Bd. Reps.; mem. exec. com. Jefferson County Rep., chairperson legis. dist. 52; chair Harriet Tubman Rep. Com.; del. Commonwealth of Ky. So. Rep. Leadership Conf., 2000; min. Greater Emmanuel Temple Holiness Ch., Birmingham, 1957—; ordained elder, vice champion mother bd.; mem. Nat. Law Enforcement Assn., 1989. Nominee Presdl. Election Registry, Rep. Presdl. Task Force, 1992; named Good Samaritan, Law Envforcement Officers; recipient award, Ala. Sheriff Assn., 1989, Navy League, 1989—91, cert. of appreciation, Pres. Congl. Task Force, 1990, Rep. Nat. Com., 1994, Diamond award, U.S.A. Serve Am., 1992, Rep. Presdl. award, Legion of Merit, 1994, Royal Proclamation, Royal Highness Kevin, Prince Regent of Hutt River Province, 1994, Royal Ceremonial jewel, Svc. award, Ala. Bd. Nursing, Outstanding Sr. Citizen's cert. of recognition. Mem.: Ala. Nurses Assn., Nat. Assn. Unknown Players, Nat. Rep. Women Assn., LaSalle Ext. U. Alumni (life). Avocations: singing, writing, reading, gardening. Home: 2021 10th Ave S Apt 513 Birmingham AL 35205-2716

**PERRY, I. CHET,** petroleum company executive; b. Phila., Jan. 18, 1943; s. Irving Chester Sr. and Erma Jackson (McNeil) P.; m. Eve Evenson Perry; 1 child, London Schade. BA in Psychology, Bus., Lake Forest Coll., 1965. Lic. real estate broker, Ill. Sr. mgmt. trainee British Overseas Airways Corp., London, 1968—69; owner Itec Internat. Ltd., Barrington, Ill., 1970—, Itec Refining & Mktg. Co., Ltd., Barrington, 1970—, CEO, mng. dir., 1986—. I.t. U.S. Army, 1965-68, Vietnam. Decorated Bronze Star, Purple Heart. Mem. Am. Petroleum Inst., European Petrochem. Assn., Barrington Bd. Realtors (bd. dirs. 1974-78), Forest Grove Club, Barrington Tennis Club. Republican. Mem. Soc. Of Friends. Avocations: tennis, photography. Home: 3 Porter School Rd Barrington IL 60010 Office Phone: 847-304-4700. Business E-Mail: chetperry@itecref.com.

**PERRY, J. WARREN,** health facility administrator, educator; b. Richmond, Ind., Oct. 25, 1921; s. Charles Thomas and Zona M. (Ohler) Perry. BA, DePauw U., 1944; postgrad., Harvard U., 1948—49; MA, Northwestern U., 1952, PhD, 1955; DSc (hon.), D'Youville Coll., 1990, Med. Coll. Ohio, 1996, DePauw U., 1998. Instr. St. John's Mil. Acad., Delafield, Wis., 1944—47; counselor, asst. prof. psychology U. Ill.-Chgo., 1953—56; dir. prosthetic-orthotic edn., assoc. prof. orthopaedic surgery Northwestern U. Med. Sch., 1957—61; lectr. psychology U. Chgo., 1957—61; asst. chief div. tng. Vocat. Rehab. Adminstrn., HEW, 1961—64, dep. asst. commr. research and tng., 1964—66; prof. health scis. adminstrn. SUNY-Buffalo, 1966—95, founding dean Sch. Health Related Professions, 1966—77, dean and prof. emeritus 1985—. Mary E. Switzer Meml. lectr., Dallas, 1977, Lexington, 91; mem. Task Force for Legislation for Allied Health Professions, 1966—67; com. edn. allied health professions and svcs., coun. med. edn. AMA, 1968—73; nat. adv. com. Am. Dietetic Assn., 1970—75, chmn., 1972—75; nat. rev. com., regional med. programs HEW, 1969—72; mem.steering com. on manpower policy for primary care bd. health promotion and disease prevention Inst. of Medicine-NAS, 1981—83, sr. advisor com. to study role allied health, com. to study med. manpower in VA, 1988—91; spl. med. adv. com. VA, 1974—77; mem. task force on manpower for prevention Fogarty Internat. Inst., NIH, 1975—76; mem. acad. planning com. Mass. Gen. Hosp. Founding editor Jour. Allied Health, 1972—78, editor emeritus, 1985—; contbr. articles to profl. jours. Mem. Legacy Soc.; charter mem. Cmty. Found. for Greater Buffalo, 1998—; patron of the arts Coun. of Buffalo and Erie County, 2000; bd. dirs., dir. opera edn. Lyric Opera Guild, Chgo., 1957—61; chmn. acad. divsn. dr., coun. trustees Buffalo Philharm. Orch., 1987—93; bd. dirs. Goodwill Industries, Buffalo, 1969—76; trustee Cmty. Music Sch. Buffalo, 1977—80; adv. bd., v.p. Sisters of Charity Hosp., Buffalo, 1969—87, pres., 1986—87; bd. visitors U. Pitts., 1977—80; coun. trustees D'youville Coll., Buffalo, 1978—88, trustee emeritus, 1989—95; bd. dirs. Am. Lung Assn. Western N.Y., 1975—92, pres., 1983; bd. dirs. ARC, Buffalo, Artpark State Performing Arts Ctr., Lewiston, NY, 1986—96, Am. Lung Assn. N.Y.State, 1981—85, exec. com., 1989—92; chmn. N.Y. State Coalition Smoking or Health, Albany, NY, 1987—91; trustee Theodore Roosevelt Inaugural Site Found., 1987, pres., 1991—94; bd. advisors Buffalo Coun. on World Affairs, 1987—89; trustee Buffalo Opera Co., 1989—94, chmn. opera adv. coun., 1995—97. Named Outstanding Individual Philanthropist, Nat. Soc. Fundraising Execs. Western N.Y., 1992, Ky. Col., 1969, Nebr. Admn., 1964, Man of the Yr., Opera Found. Buffalo, Inc., 2000, J.

Warren Perry Disting. Author award in his honor, Jour. Allied Health, Perry Scholarship in his honor, U. Buffalo Found., J. Warren Perry Outstanding Vol. Leadership award in his honor, Western N.Y. chpt. ALA, J. Warren Perry Meml. lectr. in his honor, SUNY, Buffalo, Buffalo Philharmonic Chorus, 2003; recipient Sustained Superior Svc. award, HEW, 1965, Disting. Svc. award, Am. Orthotics-Prosthetics Assn., 1966, Buffalo Opera Co., 1995, Chancellor's award for adminstrv. svc., SUNY, 1977, 1st Allied Health Leadership award, 1988, Disting. Author award, Jour. Allied Health, 1978, Cert. of Merit, AMA, 1979, Pres. Cir. Pin, Buffalo State Coll., 1993, 50th Anniversary Alumni citation, De Pauw U., 1994, Outstanding Svc. award, Theodore Roosevelt Inaugural Site Found., 1994, Theodore Roosevelt Exemplary Citizenship award, 1997, Brotherhood/Sisterhood award in health, NCCJ Western N.Y., 1995, Christmas Seal Hall of Fame award, ALA N.Y. State, 1995, Disting. Citizenship award, Mayor of Buffalo, 1995, Patron of the Arts award, Arts Coun. of Buffalo and Erie County, 2000, Alumni Achievement award, SUNY-Buffalo, 2000, Wisdom award of honor, 1999, Humanitarian award, Coordinated Care Assn. Buffalo, 2002, Clara Barton award, ARC (Greater Buffalo chpt.), 2004; fellow Wisdom Hall of Fame fellow, Wisdom Soc., 1999; Perry Lecture Hall, D'Youville Coll. named in his honor, 2004. Fellow: Assn. Schs. of Allied Health Professions (pres. 1969—70, Cert. of Merit 1977, Pres.'s award 1978, Honors of Soc. award 1984); mem.: Nat. Rehab. Assn., Am. Pers. and Guidance Assn., Am. Dietetics Assn. (hon.), APA, Phi Beta Kappa, Delta Tau Delta, Phi Delta Kappa (pres. 1955). Home: 705 Renaissance Dr Apt 208 Williamsville NY 14221

**PERRY, JACQUELIN,** orthopedist, surgeon; b. Denver, May 31, 1918; d. John F. and Tirzah (Kuruptkat) P. BE, U. Calif., LA, 1940; MD, U. Calif., San Francisco, 1950; DSc (hon.), U. So. Calif., 1996. Intern Children's Hosp., San Francisco, 1950-57; resident in orthop. surgery U. Calif., San Francisco, 1951-55; orthop. surgeon Rancho Los Amigos Hosp., Downey, Calif., 1955—, chief stroke svc., 1972-75; chief pathokinesiology Rancho Los Amigos Med. Ctr., 1961—; mem. faculty U. Calif. Med. Sch., San Francisco, 1966—, clin. prof., 1973—; mem. faculty U. So. Calif. Med. Sch., 1969—, prof. orthop. surgery, 1972—, dir. polio and gait clinic, 1972—. Disting. lectr. for hosp. for spl. surgery and Cornell U. Med. Coll., NYC, 1977-78; Packard Meml. lectr. U. Colo. Med. Sch., 1970; Osgood lectr. Harvard Med. Sch., 1978; Summer lectr., Portland, 1977; Shands lectr.; cons. USAF; guest spkr. symposia; cons. Biomechanics Lab. Centinela Hosp., 1979—. Served as phys. therapist U.S. Army, 1941-46. Recipient Disting. Svc. award Assn. Rehab. Facilities, 1981, Pres.'s award, 1984, Isabelle and Lenard Goldensen award for tech. United Cerebral Palsy Assn., 1981, Jow Dowling award, 1985, Profl. Achievement award UCLA, 1988, Milton Cohen award Nat. Assn. Rehab., 1993, Tribute Pres. award Ruth Jackson Orthop. Soc., 2004; named Woman of Yr. for Medicine in So. Calif. LA Times, 1959, Alumnus of Yr. U. Calif. Med. Sch., 1980, Physician of Yr. Calif. Employment Devel. Dept., 1994; Jacquelin Perry Neuro Trauma Inst. Rancho Clin. Bldg. named in her honor, 1996. Mem. AMA, Am. Acad. Orthop. Surgeons (Kappa Beta award for rsch. 1977, orthop. rsch. svc., 1976), Am. Orthop. Assn. (Shands lectr. 1988), Western Orthop. Assn., Calif. Med. Soc., LA County Med. Soc., Am. Phys. Therapy Assn. (hon. Golden Pen award 1965), Am. Acad. Orthotists and Prosthetists (hon.), Scoliosis Rsch. Soc., LeRoy Abbott Soc., Am. Acad. Cerebral Palsy, Gait & Clin. Movement Analysis Soc. (mem. emeritus, Lifetime Achievement award 2000), Orthop. Rsch. Soc. (Shands award 1998, 99). Home: 12319 Brock Ave Downey CA 90242-3503 Office: Rancho Los Amigos Med Ctr 7601 Imperial Hwy Downey CA 90242-3456 Office Phone: 562-401-7177. E-mail: pklab@larei.org.

**PERRY, JAMES ALFRED,** environmental scientist, consultant, science educator, academic administrator; b. Dallas, Sept. 27, 1945; BA in Fisheries, Colo. State U., 1968; MA, Western State Coll., 1973; PhD, Idaho State U. 1981. Sr. water quality specialist Idaho Div. Environ., Pocatello, 1974-82; area mgr. Centrac Assocs., Salt Lake City, 1982; H.T. Morse disting. prof. water quality U. Minn., 1982—, head dept. fisheries, wildlife, conservation biol., 2000—06, dir. natural resources policy and mgmt., 1985—2002, spl. asst. to dean grad. sch., 1996-2000; dep. dir. AID-funded Environ. Tng. Project for Ctrl. and Ea. Europe, 1992-96. Vis. scholar Oxford U., Green Coll., England, 1990—91; cons. in field. Author: Water Quality Management of a Natural Resource, 1996, Ecosystem Management for Central and Eastern Europe, 2001; editor: Jour. Natural Resources and Life Scis. Edn. 1996—2004; mem. editl. bd. Mitigation and Adaptation Strategies for Global Change. Charter mem. Leadership Devel. Acad., Lakewood, Minn., 1988; bd. dirs. Minn. Ctr. for Environ. Advocacy, 1995-2006, vice chmn., 2005. Fellow Pres.'s Academic Leadership Initiative, 2003-05; recipient Richard C. Newman Art of Tchg. award, 1998, Morse-Alumni award, 1999, Outstanding Svc. award U. Minn., 2001, Ctr. Integrative Study Work award interdisciplinary tchg. of writing, 2003, Juror Brock Internat. Edn. prize, 2006; ACOP/ESCOP nat. leadership fellow, 1995-96, CIC acad. leadership fellow, 2000-01, Gordon L. Starr Leadership award, 2003-05. Fellow: Am. Inst. Fish Resource Biology; mem.: Nat. Assn. Univ. Fish and Wildlife Programs (sec./treas.), The Soc. for Conservation Biology, The Wildlife Soc., Am. Fisheries Soc., N.Am. Benthol. Soc. (exec. bd. Albuquerque 1990—91), Internat. Soc. Theoretical and Applied Limnology, Internat. Water Resources Assn., Am. Water Resources Assn., Minn. Acad. Scis. (bd. dirs. 1987-90), Gamma Sigma Delta (merit award 2001), Xi Sigma Pi, Sigma Xi. Office: U Minn Dept Fisheries Wildlife and Conservation Biology 204 Hodson Hall 1980 Folwell Ave Saint Paul MN 55108-1037 Office Phone: 612-625-4717. Business E-Mail: jperry@umn.edu.

**PERRY, JAMES BENN,** casino and hotel executive; b. New Castle, Pa., Jan. 15, 1950; s. Samuel Wesley Jr. and Grace Elizabeth (Brumbaugh) P.; m. Cathy Ann Jackson, Dec. 27, 1982; children: James Benn Jr., Lauren Elizabeth, Julie Ann. BA in History, Ohio Wesleyan U., 1972; postgrad., Ariz. State U., 1975-76; student, Tulane U., 1968-70. CPA, N.J. Internal auditor Ramada Inns, Phoenix, 1976-78, regional controller, 1978-79, v.p., contr., 1985-87; asst. controller Tropicana Hotel & Casino, Las Vegas, Nev., 1979-80, controller Atlantic City, 1980-82, v.p. fin., 1982-85, sr. v.p. casino ops., 1987-89; exec. v.p./asst., gen. mgr. ops. TropWorld Casino and Entertainment Resort, Atlantic City, 1989-92, pres., gen. mgr. 1992—96; pres. Hospitality Group, Keating Bldg. Group, 1996—97, Argosy Gaming Co., Alton, Ill., 1997—2002, CEO, 1997—2003, also bd. dir., 2000—; CEO Trump Entertainment Resorts, Inc., 2005—. Mem. AICPA, N.J. Soc. CPAs (chmn. gaming conf. com. 1985-86). Avocation: golf. Office: Trump Entertainment Resorts Inc 1000 Boardwalk Atlantic City NJ 08401 Office Phone: 609-449-6515. Office Fax: 609-449-6586.

**PERRY, JAMES FREDERIC,** philosophy educator, writer; b. Washington, Jan. 21, 1936; s. Albert Walter and Helene Anna Maria (Neumeyer) P.; m. Sandra Jean Huizing, Feb. 18, 1957 (div. May 1972); children: Sandra Elaine, James Frederic Jr., Bartholomew; m. Roberta Schofield, June 6, 1984. Student, Princeton U., 1953-56, Marietta (Ohio) Coll., 1958-60; BA with honors in Philosophy, Ind. U., 1962, PhD in Philosophy of Edn., 1972. NDEA fellow in philosophy U. N.C., 1962—65; instr. N.C. State U., Raleigh, 1965-66; Univ. fellow Ind. U., 1971, adj. lectr. Bloomington, 1972-75; prof. philosophy Hillsborough C.C., Tampa, Fla., 1975-77, 2005—, honors prof. philosophy, 1997—2005. Adj. prof. U. South Fla., 2000—, adj. honors prof., 2006—. Author: Random, Routine, Reflective, 1989; contbr. articles to profl. jours. Precinct committeeman Dem. Party, Tampa, Fla., 1988—2004. Mem. AAUP (pres. Fla. conf. 1986-89, chair com. "A" on acad. freedom 1989-2002), C.C. Humanities Assn. (so. divsn. exec. bd. 1981-89), Am. Philos. Assn., Fla. Philos. Assn. (pres. 2004—), Internat. Soc. Philos. Enquiry, Internat. Congress for Critical Thinking and Moral Critiques (founding mem. S.E. coun. 1991), World Congress Philosophy (Boston 1998, Istanbul 2003), Princeton Alumni Assn. of Fla. Suncoast (sec. 1983-86, pres. 1986-95), Mensa, Authors Guild, Textbook and Acad. Authors Assn. Avocations: travel, genealogy. Office: Hillsborough C C PO Box 10561 Tampa FL 33679-0561 Office Phone: 813-253-7357. Business E-Mail: jperry@hccfl.edu.

**PERRY, JAMES MICHAEL,** museum administrator, historian; b. Washington, Jan. 30, 1960; s. Gillmore Milton and Pauline Downer (Hagood) P.; m. Mary Claire Fellows, May 26, 1982; 1 child, Elizabeth Anne. BA in History,

Roanoke Coll., 1982; cert. in mus. studies, Coll. of William and Mary, 1984, MA in History, 1984. Hist. area svcs. coord. Colonial Williamsburg (Va.) Found., 1984-90; park ranger Nat. Park Svc. (White House, Clara Barton Nat. Hist. Site), Washington and Glen Echo, Md., 1990-91; vis. programs coord. Supreme Ct. of U.S., Washington, 1991—. Author: Colonial Williamsburg: A Guide for the Handicapped, 1983, Colonial Williamsburg: A Guide for Deaf and Hearing Impaired Visitors, 1984; editor: The Visitor's Companion, 1986; contbr. articles to profl. jours. Vol. disaster svcs. ARC, Washington, 1987—; v.p. Williamsburg Vol. Fire Dept., 1988-90; EMT Bethesda (Md.) Chevy Chase Rescue Squad, 1990—. Mem. Am. Assn. for State and Local History, Am. Assn. Mus., Hist. Soc. Washington, Manuscript Soc., Md. Hist. Soc., Blue Key Soc., Phi Alpha Theta, Pi Gamma Mu. Office: Supreme Ct US One 1st St NE Washington DC 20543

**PERRY, JEAN,** elementary school educator; Spl. Edn./Elem., Bridgewater State Coll., Mass., 1977—80; M of Spl Edn., Framingham State Coll., Mass., 1998—2000. Elem. Edn. tchr. Mass. Dept. Edn., 1980. Tchr. Burlington Pub. Schs., Mass., 1991—2006. Bd. mem. Burlington HSA, 2003—06. Mem.: ASCD (assoc.).

**PERRY, JEAN LOUISE,** retired dean, academic administrator; b. Richland, Wash., May 13, 1950; d. Russell S. and Sue W. Perry. BS, Miami U., Oxford, Ohio, 1972; MS, U. Ill., Urbana, 1973, PhD, 1976. Cons. added. placement office U. Ill., 1973-75; adminstrv. intern Coll. Applied Life Studies, 1975-76, asst. dean, 1976-77, assoc. dean, 1978-81, asst. prof. dept. phys. edn., 1976-81; assoc. prof. phys. edn. San Francisco State U., 1981-84, prof., 1984-90, chair, 1981-90; dean Coll. Human and Cmty. Scis. U. Nev., Reno, 1990—2006, spl. asst. to pres. for athletics academics and compliance, 2006—. Named to Excellent Tchr. List, U. Ill., 1973—79. Mem.: AAHPERD (fellow rsch. consortium, pres. 1988—89), Nat. Assn. Girls and Women in Sports (guide coord., pres.), Nat. Assn. Phys. Edn. in Higher Edn., Am. Ednl. Rsch. Assn., Am. Assn. Higher Edn., Phi Delta Kappa, Delta Psi Kappa. Home: 3713 Ranchview Ct Reno NV 89509-7437 Office: U Nev Legacy Hal/ 232 Reno NV 89557-0001 Office Phone: 775-784-3505.

**PERRY, JOSIE LYNN,** social studies educator; b. Elkton, Md., Dec. 20; d. Jimmie Dean Able Sr. and Ella Jo Able; m. Thomas Melton Perry III, July 8, 2000; children: Keegan Thomas, Kaitlin Grace. BA in History and Secondary Edn., Salisbury U., Md., 1999; MEd in Sch. Counseling, Wilmington Coll., New Castle, Del., 2002. Cert. Nat. Bd. Profl. Tchg. Stds. Tchr. North East (Md.) H.S., 1999—2005. Mem.: NEA, Nat. Coun. Social Studies. Office: North East High Sch 300 Irishtown RD North East MD 21901 Office Phone: 410-996-6200. Office Fax: 410-996-6264. Business E-Mail: jperry@ccps.org.

**PERRY, JOYCE FITZWILLIAM,** secondary school educator; b. San Francisco, Aug. 12, 1946; d. Leo Matthew and Mildred E. (McBain) Fitzwilliam; m. Robert James Perry, June 21, 1969 (div. Apr. 1980); children: Dominic Matthew, Alex Michael. BA, Gonzaga U., 1968; M in Counseling, U. Phoenix, 1995. Cert. tchr., nat. cert. counselor, Ariz. Middle sch. lang. arts and social studies tchr. Frank Ode Jr. High, Bellevue, Wash., 1969-72, Greenway Middle Sch., Phoenix, 1979-82, Sunrise Middle Sch., Scottsdale, Ariz., 1982—2002, Mountain Trail Middle Sch., Phoenix, 2002—06; CEO Ednl. Alternatives, Phoenix, 2006—. Mem. evaluation team North Ctrl. Schs. Accreditation, Ariz., 1988-90. Author: Seasons of the Heart, 1982. Named Middle Level Educator of Yr., Ctrl. Ariz. Middle Level Assn., 1994. Mem. ACA, Phi Delta Kappa.

**PERRY, KENNETH WALTER,** retired integrated oil company executive; b. Shamrock, Tex., Feb. 24, 1932; s. Charles Bowman and Sunshine Virginia (Grady) P.; m. Mary Dean Sudderth; children: Mary Martha Ernst, Kathryn Virginia. BSME, U. Okla., 1954. Sales engr. Mid-Continent Oil Well Supply Co., 1954-55; with Cosden Oil & Chem. Co., Big Spring, Tex., from 1957, jr. engr., 1957-59, project engr., 1959-60, chem. salesman, 1960-64, chem. products mgr., 1964-65, mktg. mgr., then v.p. mktg., 1965-69, v.p. chems., 1969-72, sr. v.p., 1972-76, pres., from 1976; group v.p. Am. Petrofina, Inc., Dallas, 1976-85, sr. v.p., 1985—89, pres., CEO, 1989, vice chmn., bd. dirs., 1989-92; CEO Nimir Petroleum Co. Ltd., Dallas, 1992-96; ret., 1992. CEO United Commerce Bank, Highland Village, Tex., 1990—91. Mem. bd. govs. Dallas Symphony Orch., 1987-93; bd. dirs. Dallas Coun. World Affairs, 1980; mem. engring. com. U. Okla. Aerospace, Nuclear, 1982; bd. dirs. Colo. Mcpl. Water Dist., 1972; bd. visitors Coll. Engring., U. Okla., 1990—. 1st lt. USASC, 1955-57. Mem. Am. Petroleum Inst. (bd. dirs. 1986-90), Nat. Petroleum Coun., Nat. Petroleum Refiners Assn. (chmn. petrochem. com. 1984-87), Ctr. Strategic and Internat. Studies, 25-Yr. Clubs, Petroleum Industry Club, Petrochem. Industry Club, Northwood Club, Dallas Petroleum Club.

**PERRY, KENNETH WILBUR,** finance educator; b. Lawrenceburg, Ky., May 21, 1919; s. Ollie Townsend and Minnie (Monroe) P.; m. Shirley Jane Kimball, Sept. 5, 1942; 1 dau., Constance June (Mrs. Linden Warfel). BS, Eastern Ky. U., 1942; MS, Ohio U., 1949; PhD, U. Ill., 1953; LL.D., Eastern Ky. U., 1983. C.P.A., Ill. Instr. Berea Coll., 1949-50, U. Ky., summer 1950; teaching asst. U. Ill. at Champaign, 1950-53, asst. prof. accounting, 1953-55, asso. prof., 1955-58, prof., 1958—, Alexander Grant prof., 1975—. Vis. prof. Northeastern U., summer 1966, Parsons Coll., 1966-67, Fla. A. and M. U., fall 1971; Carman G. Blough prof. U. Va., fall 1975; dir. Illini Pub. Co. Author: Accounting: An Introduction, 1701, Passing the C.P.A. Examination, 1964, (with N. Bedford and A. Wyatt) Advanced Accounting, 1960; contbg. author: Complete Guide to a Profitable Accounting Practice, 1965, C.P.A. Review Manual, 1971; Editor: The Ill. C.P.A, 1968-70; contbg. editor: Accountants' Cost Handbook, 1960. Served to maj. AUS, 1942-46; col. Res. ret. Named outstanding alumnus Eastern Ky. U., 1969 Mem. Am. Accounting Assn. (v.p. 1963, Outstanding Educator award 1974), Am. Inst. C.P.A.'s, Am. Statis. Assn., Nat. Assn. Accountants (dir. 1969-71). Ill. Soc. C.P.A.s (chair in accountancy), Beta Alpha Psi, Beta Gamma Sigma (Distinguished scholar 1977-78), Omicron Delta Kappa. Methodist. Home: 2314 Fields South Dr Champaign IL 61822-9302 Office: Commerce W U Ill Champaign IL 61822

**PERRY, LOUIS BARNES,** retired insurance company executive; b. LA, Mar. 4, 1918; s. Louis Henry and Julia (Stoddard) P.; m. Genevieve Patterson, Feb. 8, 1942; children: Robert Barnes, Barbara Ann, Donna Lou. BA, UCLA, 1938, MA, 1940, PhD, 1950; fellow in econs., Yale U., 1941; LL.D., Pacific U., 1964; L.H.D., Whitman Coll., 1967, Linfield Coll., 1981; D.C.S., Willamette U., 1977. Teaching asst. UCLA, 1940-41, research teaching asst., 1946-47; faculty Pomona Coll., 1947-59, asst. to pres., 1955-57, prof. econs., 1957-59; pres. Whitman Coll., Walla Walla, Wash., 1959-67; v.p., treas. Standard Ins. Co., Portland, Oreg., 1967-68, exec. v.p., 1968-71, pres., 1972-83, chmn., 1983-85, also bd. dirs. Investment counselor, broker Wagenseller & Durst, L.A., 1951-59; rsch. coord. So. Calif. Rsch. Coun., 1952-54; cons. Carnegie Survey Bus. Edn., 1957-58. Author: (with others) Our Needy Aged, 1954, A History of the Los Angeles Labor Movement, 1963; Contbr. (with others) articles to profl. jours. Mem. Oreg. Bd. Higher Edn., 1975-87, pres., 1975-80. Served to maj. AUS, World War II; lt. col. Res. Mem. Am. Coll. Life Underwriters (trustee 1972-81), Rotary, Phi Beta Kappa, Beta Gamma Sigma, Phi Delta Kappa, Pi Gamma Mu, Alpha Gamma Omega, Artus. Methodist. Home: 1585 Gray Lynn Dr Walla Walla WA 99362-9282 *In looking back over the years, an unspoken and oftentime subliminal guiding principle has been to reach beyond one's realistic grasp. This concept coupled with an interest in treating others as one would like to be treated has made it possible to react to new challenges. Successfully meeting the latter has provided a varied career in a number of different fields of activity.*

**PERRY, LUKE (COY LUTHER PERRY III),** actor; b. Fredericktown, Ohio, Oct. 11, 1966; s. Coy Luther Sr. and Ann Perry; m. Minnie Sharp, Nov. 18, 1993 (div.); children: Jack, Sophie. Actor: (TV series) Loving, 1987—88, Another World, 1988—89, Beverly Hills, 90210, 1990—95, 1998—2000; dir. episodes Fortune Cookie and Laying Pipe (TV series) Beverly Hills, 90210, 1999; actor: (TV series) Windfall, 2006—, (voice) The Simpsons, 1989, Pepper Ann, 1997, Spin City, 1996, Johnson County War, 2002, (voice): (TV miniseries) Mortal Kombat: The Animated Series, 1995, The Incredible Hulk, 1996, Robin Cook's Invasion, 1997, Supernova, 2005; (TV films) Riot, 1997, Invasion, 1997, Indiscreet, 1998, The Last Buckaroo, 2000, The Triangle, 2001, Johnson County War, 2002, Descent, 2005, (voice) The Night of the Headless Horseman, 1999, (also prodr.) Jeremiah, 2002—04.; (films) Scorchers, 1991, Terminal Bliss, 1992, Buffy the Vampire Slayer, 1992, The Webbers, 1993, For Our Children, 1993, 8 Seconds, 1994, Vacanze di Natale 95, 1995, Normal Life, 1996, American Strays, 1996, The Fifth Element, 1997, Lifebreath, 1997, Last Breath, 1998, Storm, 1998, The Florentine, 1999, The Heist, 1999, Blue Light Special, 1999, Attention Shoppers, 2000, The Enemy, 2001, Dirt, 2001, Luxury of Love, 2001, Fogbound, 2002, Down the Barrel, 2003, Dishdogz, 2005, (Broadway performance) Rocky Horror Picture Show, 2001; performer: (stage adaption) When Harry Met Sally, 2004; actor: (TV guest appearances) Parker Lewis Can't Lose, 1992, The Simpsons, 1993, Biker Mice From Mars, 1994, 1995, Spin City, 1997, Family Guy, 2000, Oz, 2001—02, Night Visions, 2001, Pet Star, 2003, Clone High, 2003, Will & Grace, 2005, What I Like About You, 2005.*

**PERRY, MALCOLM BLYTHE,** biologist, researcher; b. Birkenhead, Cheshire, Eng., Apr. 26, 1930; s. Cyril A. and Hilda P. (Blythe) Perry; m. Eileen M. Perry, Aug. 10, 1956 (dec. Nov. 1981); children: Sara Jane, Judith Anne; m. Philomena C. Kingsley, July 25, 2001. B.Sc., U. Bristol, Eng., 1953; PhD, U. Bristol, 1956, D.Sc., 1969. Banting rsch. fellow Queen's U., Kingston, Ont., Canada, 1955, asst. prof., 1956-60, R.S. McLaughlin research prof., 1960-62; sr. reschr. officer Nat. Rsch. Coun., Ottawa, 1962—81, prin. rsch. officer, 1981—. Scientist U. Cambridge, Eng., 1969, U. Paris, 1979; prof. U. Ottawa, 1982 Contbr. articles to profl. jours. Fellow Royal Soc. Can., Royal Inst. Chemistry, mem. Can. Soc. Microbiology (award 1991), Am. Soc. Microbiology, Internat. Endotoxin Soc. (award 2002). Home: 769 Hemlock Rd Ottawa ON Canada K1K 0K6 Office: NRC 100 Sussex Dr Ottawa ON Canada K1A 0R6 Business E-Mail: malcolm.perry@nrc-cnrs.gc.ca.

**PERRY, MARGARET,** librarian, writer; b. Cin., Nov. 15, 1933; d. Rufus Patterson and Elizabeth Munford (Anthony) P. AB, Western Mich. U., 1954; Cert. d'etudes Francaises, U. Paris, 1956; MSLS, Cath. U. Am., 1959. Young adult and reference libr. N.Y. Pub. Libr., N.Y.C., 1954-55, 57-58; libr. U.S. Army, France and Germany, 1959-63, 64-67; chief circulation U.S. Mil. Libr., West Point, NY, 1967-70; head edn. libr. U.S. Army Nuclear, NY, 1970-75, asst. prof. NY, 1973-75, assoc. prof. NY, 1975-82, asst. dir. librs. for reader svcs. NY, 1975-82, acting dir. librs. NY, 1976-77, 80; univ. libr. Valparaiso U., Ind., 1982-93; ret., 1993. Mem. Task Force on Coop. Edn., Rochester, 1972; freelance writer Mich. Land Use Inst., 1995-01. Author: A Bio-bibliography of Countee P. Cullen, 1903-1946, 1971, Silence to the Drums: A Survey of the Literature of the Harlem Renaissance, 1976, The Harlem Renaissance, 1982, The Short Fiction of Rudolph Fisher, 1987; also numerous short stories; contbr. articles to profl. jours. and children's mags. Bd. dirs. Urban League, 1978-80 Recipient 1st prize short story contest Armed Forces Writers League, 1966; 2d prize Frances Steloff Fiction prze, 1968, 1st prize short story Arts Alive, 1990, 2d prize short story Willow Rev., 1990; seminar scholar Schloss Leopoldskron, Salzburg, Austria, 1956, 3d prize short story West Shore C.C., Scottville, Mich., 1995. Mem. ALA. Democrat. Roman Catholic. Avocations: violin and viola, collecting book marks, gardening, reading, travel. Home: 8 Muriel St Ithaca NY 14850 Office Phone: 607-257-3997. Personal E-mail: mperry515@yahoo.com.

**PERRY, MATTHEW,** actor; b. Williamstown, Mass., Aug. 19, 1969; Actor Friends, 1994—2004. Appeared on TV series including Boys Will Be Boys, Sydney, Growing Pains; TV movies include Dance 'Til Dawn, 1988, Call Me Anna, 1990, Deadly Relations, 1993, Parallel Lives, 1994, The Ron Clark Story, 2006; films include A Night in the Life of Jimmy Reardon, 1988, She's Out of Control, 1989, Getting In, 1994, Fools Rush In, 1997, Edwards and Hunt: The First American Road Trip, 1997, Almost Heroes, 1998, Three to Tango, 1999, The Whole Nine Yards, 2000, Serving Sarah, 2002, The Whole Ten Yards, 2004; film writer: Imagining Emily, 1999; TV guest appearances include Silver Spoons, 1982, Family Ties, 1982, Charles in Charge, 1984, The Tracey Ullman Show, 1987, Highway to Heaven, 1984, Empty Nest, 1988, Who's The Boss, 1984, Beverly Hills, 90210, 1990, Dream On, 1990, The John Larroquette Show, 1993, Caroline in the City, 1995; theater debut Sexual Perversity in London, 2003.*

**PERRY, SIR MICHAEL (SIR MICHAEL SYDNEY PERRY),** industrialist; b. Eastbourne, Sussex, Eng., Feb. 26, 1934; s. Sydney Albert and Jessie Kate (Brooker) P.; m. Joan Mary Stallard, Oct. 18, 1958; children: Carolyn Clare, Deborah Anne, Andrew John William. MA, St. John's Coll., Oxford, U.K., 1957. From mem. staff to chmn. Unilever PLC, London, 1957—92, chmn., 1992—96, Dunlop Slazenger Group Ltd., London, 1996—2001, Centrica PLC, London, 1997—2004; v.p. Liverpool Sch. Tropical Medicine, England, 2001—. Non-exec. dir. Bass Plc, London; chmn. Japan Trade Group, London, 1985-98; dep. chmn. Bass PLC, 1991-2001; non exec. dir. Marks & Spencer Ltd., 1996-2001; chmn. Shakespeare Globe Trust, 1993, chmn.; v.p., then pres. Liverpool (Eng.) Sch. Tropical Medicine, 1993-2001; non exec. dir. Brit. Gas, 1992, 1997; mem. supervisory bd. Royal Ahold, 1997-2004; pres. Mktg. Coun.; chmn. faculty bd. Oxford U., 2001-. Decorated Knight Bachelor; decorated comdr. Brit. Empire, knight grand cross Brit. Empire; award GBE double knighthood, 2002. Mem. Oriental Club. Avocations: golf, music.

**PERRY, MICHAEL C.,** theatre publisher, educator; b. Denver, Nov. 20, 1953; s. Maurice L. and Maryann Jane (Champlin) P.; m. Sharon Yvonne Ronson, June 26, 1981; children: Jessica, Janalyn, Joelle, Jon-Christopher. BA, Brigham Young U., 1982. Cert. tchr., Utah. Technician Osmond Studios, Orem, Utah, 1977-84; educator Pleasant Grove (Utah) H.S., 1986-87, Spanish Trak (Utah) H.S. 1988—2000, prof. Encore Performance Pub., Orem, 1979—. Author, composer (musical play) Tom Sawyer, 1987; composer (musical play) Turn the Gas Back On, 1989, Onstage, 1992; editor (scene books) For Teens and Child Actors, 1992. Recipient Best of West award Rocky Mountain Pub. Broadcasting, 1977, Emmy award Acad. of TV, 1977. Mem. Am. Soc. Composers, Authors and Pubs., Am. Alliance for Theatre and Edn. (Disting Play award 1995), Ednl. Theatre Assn., Christians In Theatre Arts, Utah Theatre Assn., Rocky Mountain Theatre Assn. Office Phone: 801-282-8159. E-mail: encoreplay@aol.com.

**PERRY, MICHAEL CLINTON,** internist, educator, academic administrator; b. Wyandotte, Mich., Jan. 27, 1945; s. Clarence Clinton and Hilda Grace (Wigginton) P.; m. Nancy Ann Kaluzny, June 22, 1968; children: Rebecca Carolyn, Katherine Grace. BA, Wayne State U., 1966, MD, 1970; MS in Medicine, U. Minn., 1975. Diplomate Am. Bd. Internal Medicine, Am. Bd. Hematology, Am. Bd. Oncology. Intern in internal medicine Mayo Grad. Sch. Medicine, Rochester, Minn., 1970-71, resident, 1971-72, fellow, 1972-75; instr. Mayo Med. Sch., Rochester, 1974-75; asst. prof. U. Mo., Columbia, 1975-80, assoc. prof., 1980-85, prof., 1985—, chmn. dept. medicine, 1983-91, sr. assoc. dean, 1991-94, Nellie A Smith chair oncology, dir. div. hematology/oncology, 1994—. Prin. investigator Cancer and Leukemia Group B, Nat. Cancer Inst., Chgo., 1982-84, 1987-90. Author, co-author 30 book chpts.; editor: Toxicity of Chemotherapy, 1984, The Chemotherapy Source Book, 1992, 96, 2001, Comprehensive Textbook of Thoracic Oncology, 1996; contbr. articles to profl. jours. Recipient Faculty Alumni award U. Mo., Columbia, 1985, Disting. Alumnus award Wayne State U., 1995, Disting. Oncologist of Yr. award So. Assn. Oncology, 2000. Fellow ACP; mem. Am. Soc. Hematology, Am. Soc. Clin. Oncology, Cen. Soc. Clin. Research, Am. Soc. Internal Medicine (Young Internist of Yr. 1981), Sigma Xi, Alpha Omega Alpha. Home: 1112 Pheasant Run Columbia MO 65201-6254 Office: U Mo-Columbia 516 Ellis Fischel Cancer Ctr 115 Business Loop 70 W Columbia MO 65203-3244 E-mail: perrym@health.missouri.edu.

**PERRY, MICHAEL W.,** bank executive; BBA with honors, Calif. State U., Sacramento. CPA. With Commerce Security Bank, 1987—92, sr. exec. v.p. Mortgage Banking Divsn.; joined IndyMac, 1993, COO, 1993—97, pres., 1997—99, bd. dirs., 1997—; vice chmn. bd. IndyMac & IndyMac Bank FSB, 2000—03, chmn. bd., 2003—, CEO. Bd. trustees, mem. acad. affairs com.

Mayfield Jr. Sch.; bd. dirs. YMCA of Pasadena. Named LA Bus. Jour. Hall of Fame; recipient Fin. Industry Leader of Yr. award, LA Bus. Jour., 2002, Entrepreneur of Yr., fin. services, LA Ernst & Young, 2002. Mem.: Young Presidents' Org. (San Gabriel chpt.), Calif. Soc. CPAs, Am. Inst. CPAs. Office: IndyMac Bank 155 North Lake Ave Pasadena CA 91101 E-mail: michael.perry@indymac.com.*

**PERRY, NADINE MARGARET,** retired art educator, artist; b. Cleve., Nov. 9, 1925; d. Andor Elec and Luella Lee Literaty; m. Charles Frederick Perry (div.); children: Barbara Elise Morgan, David Lowell, Richard Dean. AB in Art and Biology, U. Mich., Ann Arbor, 1948; M in Art Edn., U. Toledo, Ohio, 1977; student, Rangemark Chen Chi Jean Dobie Workshop, Bar Harbor, Maine. Cert. tchr. art grades 7-12 Ohio. Wax mushroom maker Cleve. Mus. Natural History, 1940—44; life painter Natural History Mus., Ann Arbor, 1947—49; tchr. art 8th grade Willow Run Schs., Mich., 1948—50; tchr. art grades 8-12 Grand River Acad., Austinberg, Ohio, 1965—67; tchr. art grades 6-12 Maumee Schs., Ohio, 1969—92; ret., 1992. Spkr. Ohio Art Edn. Assn.; art club sponsor Maumee Schs., fire prevention art chair. Chmn. Lupine Project Funton County East for County Commr., 2006; precinct chair Swan Creek East I, 2005—06; mem. Nat. and State Dem. Party; bd. mem. Fulton County Dem. Women, 2005—06. Democrat. Protestant. Home: 5908 County Rd Two Swanton OH 43558

**PERRY, NANCY,** foundation administrator; m. Ken Perry; 1 child, Brad. BS in Elem. Edn., U. Kans. Kindergarten tchr. Avondale East Elem. Sch.; host local Romper Room TV program; variety/talk show host; pres., CEO United Way of Greater Topeka. Mem. fin. and outreach coms., mem. altar guild Grace Episcopal Cathedral. Mem.: Rotary Club. Office: United Way of Greater Topeka 1315 SW Arrowhead Rd Topeka KS 66604

**PERRY, NANCY BLAND,** accountant; b. Houston, Miss., Aug. 17, 1955; d. Charles Edward Bland, Minnie Lou Bland; 1 child, Cheryl Elizabeth Crisco; m. Paul D Perry. BS in Edn. with distinction, Miss. Coll., 1975, cert. acctg., 1988. CPA Miss. CPA, acct. various CPA firms, Jackson, Miss., 1983—89; pvt. practice CPA Clinton, Miss., 1989—91; sr. acct. Chem. First Inc., Jackson, 1991—2003; asst. v.p. acctg. Denmiss Corp., 2003—. Bd. dirs., various offices Girl Scouts U.S. Mid. Miss., Jackson, 1992—; team mem. Leadership Clinton, 1997—98; bd. dirs., various positions Clinton Pub. Sch. Dist. PTA, 1988—96; bd. dirs., sec. treas. ChemFirst Found., Inc., Jackson, 1996—2002; trustee Clinton Pub. Sch. Dist., 1998—; bd. dirs. Clinton Jr. Miss, 1997—2004; trustee Frances Rushton Meml. Scholarship Trust, 1998—, chair, 2001—. Nominee GIVE, Gov. of Miss., 1995; named Parent of the Yr., Clinton Pub. Sch. Dist., 1995; recipient Metro Jackson's Finest award, Cystic Fibrosis Foundation, 1999, Thanks Badge, Girl Scouts U.S. Mid. Miss., 1995. Mem.: AICPA, Miss. Soc. CPAs, Am. Soc. Women Accts. (bd. dirs., various positions 1996—2001), Jr. Aux. Clinton (bd. dirs., treas. 1996—2000, trustee Francecs Rushton Meml. Scholarship Trust 1999—, chair 2001—), Clinton C. of C. Ch. Of Christ. Business E-Mail: nperry@denkmann-ms.com.

**PERRY, NANCY ESTELLE,** psychologist; b. Pitts., Oct. 30, 1934; d. Simon Warren and Estelle Cecelia (Zaluski) Reichard; children: Scott, Karen, Elaine. BS, Ohio State U., 1956, MA in Psychology, 1969, PhD in Psychology, 1973. Nurse various locations, 1956-63; psychologist Pub. Schs., Columbus, Ohio, 1970-72; human devel. specialist Madison County (Ohio) Schs., 1972-75; pvt. practice clin. psychology; cons. psychology Worthington, Ohio, 1975-80; tchr. U. Wis. Sch. Nursing, Milw., 1980-88, Milw. Devel. Ctr., 1980-83; pvt. practice Assoc. Mental Health Svcs., 1983-87, Glendale Clinic for Stress Mgmt. and Mental Health Clinics, 1987-98, Cambridge Group, 1999—; pvt. practice life transitions therapy Milw. and Santa Fe, 1999—. Mem. faculty Wis. Profl. Schs.; adj. faculty U. Wis., Milw. Ohio Dept. Edn. grantee, 1973-76. Bd. dirs. Youth Shelters & Family Svcs., Santa Fe. EPDA fellow Ohio State U., 1973; Ohio Dept. Edn. grantee, 1973-76. Fellow Internat. Soc. Study of Dissociation (sec.-treas. 1995-98), Wis. Psychol. Assn.; mem. APA, Am. Soc. Clin. Hypnosis, Am. Assn. Marriage and Family Therapists. Office: 355 E Palace Ave Santa Fe NM 87501 Home: 47 Avenida Frijoles Santa Fe NM 87507-3431 Office Phone: 505-955-1995. Personal E-mail: nperry1034@comcast.net.

**PERRY, RALPH BARTON, III,** lawyer; b. NYC, Mar. 17, 1936; s. Ralph Barton Jr. and Harriet Armington (Seeley) P.; m. Mary Elizabeth Colburn, Sept. 2, 1961; children: Katherine Suzanne, Daniel Berenson. AB, Harvard U., 1958; LLB, Stanford U., 1963. Bar: Calif. 1964. Assoc. and mem. Keatinge & Sterling, L.A., 1963—68; mem. firm Graven Perry Block Brody & Qualls, L.A., 1968—. Bd. dirs. Planning and Conservation League, 1968-2005, PLC Found., 2005—, Coalition for Clean Air, 1970—, pres. 1972-80, 85-88. Served with U.S. Army, 1956-58. Mem. ABA (ho. of dels. 1975-95), State Bar Calif., L.A. County Bar Assn., Lawyers Club L.A. County (gov. 1968-82), Nat. and Internat. Wildlife Fedns., Sierra Club, L.A. Athletic Club. Home: 296 Redwood Dr Pasadena CA 91105-1339 Office: Graven Perry 523 W 6th St Ste 723 Los Angeles CA 90014-1223 Office Phone: 213-680-9770. Personal E-mail: rbp3@earthlink.net.

**PERRY, RICHARD C.,** financier; b. 1955; m. Lisa Perry. BA, Wharton Sch. U. Pa., 1977; MBA, NYU. Equity trader Goldman, Sachs & Co., 1977—88; founder, chmn., CEO Perry Capital LLC, 1988—. Chmn. bd. FTD Corp.; dir. Radio & Records, Inc. Bd. trustees Facing History and Ourselves, Allen-Stevenson Sch., Milton Academy, Harlem Children's Zone; mem. Wharton Undergrad Exec. bd.

**PERRY, RICK,** governor; b. Paint Creek, Tex. Mar. 4, 1950; m. Anita Thigpen, children: Griffin, Sydney. B.Animal Sci., A&M U., 1972. Farmer/rancher; mem. Tex. Ho. of Reps., 1985-90, mem. appropriations and calendars com.; commr. of agr. State of Tex., 1991-98, lt. gov. Austin, 1999-2000, gov., 2000—. Active Boy Scouts Am. Capt. USAF, 1972-77 Named One of the Most Effective Legislators, Dallas Morning News, 1989. Mem. Am. Legion. Republican. Methodist. Office: Office of Governor 1100 San Jacinto PO Box 12428 Austin TX 78711 Office Fax: 512-463-5571.*

**PERRY, ROBERT FRANCIS,** lawyer; b. SI, Dec. 28, 1957; s. William J. and Marian P. Perry. B of Engring., Manhattan Coll., Riverdale, NY, 1979; MBA, Seton Hall U., South Orange, NJ, 1983; JD, Seton Hall Law Sch., Newark, NJ, 1989. Application engr. Worthington Pump Corp., East Orange, 1980—81; product mgr. Alfa-Laval, Inc., Ft. Lee, NJ, 1981—89; ptnr. Kenyon & Kenyon, NYC, 1989—2004, King & Spalding LLP, 2004—. Mem.: ABA, Am. Intellectual Property Law Assn., NJ Patent Law Assn., NY Intellectual Property Law Assn., NJ State Bar Assn. Home: 38 Enclosure Dr Morganville NJ 07751 Office: King & Spalding LLP 1185 Ave of Americas New York NY 10036 Office Phone: 212-827-4350. Home Fax: 732-970-0049; Office Fax: 212-556-2222. Personal E-mail: robertperry@optonline.net. E-mail: rperry@kslaw.com.

**PERRY, ROBERT MICHAEL,** lawyer, consultant, rancher; s. John Robert and Katherine Marie Perry. BA in History, St. Mary's U., San Antonio, 1959, JD, 1959; LLM, Georgetown U., Washington, 1964; diploma, U.S. Army Arty. and Missile Sch., Ft. Sill, Okla., 1959, JAG Sch. U. Va., Charlottesville, 1962, U.S. Army Command and Gen. Staff Course, 1978. Bar: Tex. 1961, US Supreme Ct., US Ct. Appeals (2d cir.), US Ct. Appeals (3d cir.), US Ct. Appeals (4th cir.), US Ct. Appeals (5th cir.), US Ct. Appeals (7th cir.), US Ct. Appeals (9th cir.), US Ct. Appeals (10th cir.), US Ct. Appeals (DC cir.), US Ct. Mil. Appeals, US Ct. Claims, US Tax Ct. Served to col. US Army, 1959—94, legal officer 1st armored divsn. Ft. Hood, Tex., 1959—61; staff officer JAG Dept. of Army, Washington, 1961—64; trial atty. Land and Natural Resources Divsn. Dept. of Justice, 1964—69; trial counsel Exxon Co. USA, Houston, 1969—80; gen. counsel and adminstr. enforcement US EPA, Washington, 1981—83; legal cons. San Antonio, Washington and Garrison, NY, 1983—. Mobilization designee US Army, Washington, 1964—94; chmn. Oil and Gas Industry Litigation Com. Trans Alaskan Pipeline, Alaska Native Claims and Offshore Oil and Gas Leasing Litigation, Houston, Washington

and Anchorage, 1971—80; co-chmn US Army Environ. Orgn. Study Com., Washington, 1984—94. Co-author: Fed. Condemnation Handbook 3 vols., 1964—69; editor-in-chief: US Dept. Justice Land and Natural Resources Divsn. Jour., 1967—68, The Forum (Fed. Bar Assn. DC), 1967—68; contbr. articles to govt. jours. Pres. and CEO Perry-Gething Found., San Antonio and Garrison, NY, 1975—; event pres. San Antonio Fiesta Commn., 1978—; pres. and CEO Frontier Times Mus., Bandera, 2001—. Decorated Legion of Merit, Commendation medal with oak leaf cluster US Army; recipient Spl. Achievement award, Adminstr. US EPA, 1982. Mem.: Tex. and Southwestern Cattle Raisers Assn., Tex. Bar Assn. Avocation: raising rare Jacob sheep and hybrid cattle. Home: Perrymount Ranch PO Box 531 Bandera TX 78003 Office: Perry-Gething Found PO Box 830233 San Antonio TX 78283-0233 Office Phone: 210-227-9498.

**PERRY, STEPHEN A.,** museum administrator, former federal agency administrator; b. Ohio, 1945; m. Sondra Perry; 5 children. B in Acctg., U. Akron; M in Mgmt., Stanford U.; attended, U. Mich. Exec. Develop. program. Various acctg. positions including dir. acctg., dir. purchasing, sr. v.p. Timken Co., Canton, 1964, v.p. human resources, purchasing and communications, 1993—97, sr. v.p., 1997—2001; dir. Dept. Adminstrv. Services State of Ohio, 1991—93; adminstr. US Gen. Services Adminstrn., Washington, 2001—05; pres., exec. dir. Pro Football Hall of Fame, Canton, Ohio, 2006—. Chmn. Human Resources Coun. of the Mfrs. Alliance for Productivity and Innovation; served on Human Resources Policy Com. Steering Group, Nat. Assn. of Mfrs.; bd. dir. Labor Policy Assn. Chmn. Canton Scholar Fund, Stark County Dist. Libr. Bd., United Way Campaign Ctrl. Stark County, 1996, Jr. Achievement, 1999, Leadership Stark County Selection Com., mem. Ohio Bd. Regents, 1993—2002; bd. trustees Canton Urban League, 1968—83, Profl. Football Hall of Fame, 1993—2001; gen. chmn. Profl. Football Hall of Fame Festival, 1999; bd. trustees Timken Mercy Med. Ctr., 1984—91; mem. Walsh U. Adv. Bd., 1987—91; served on the Mgmt. Improvement Commn. appointed by Ohio Gov. Bob Taft. Named Man of Yr., Canton Christian Hall of Fame, 2000; recipient Disting. Svc. award, Jaycees, 1977, Pres. Social Responsibility award, Kent State U., 1995, Disting. Alumni award, Kent State U., Stark Campus Alumni Coun., 1996, Dr. Frank L. Simonetti Disting. Bus. Alumnus award, U. Akron, Coll. Bus. Alumni Assn., 1999, Disting. Alumni award, Trimken High Sch. Alumni Assn., 1999, U. Akron, 2001. Office: Pro Football Hall of Fame 2121 George Halas Dr NW Canton OH 44708*

**PERRY, STEPHEN R.,** law educator; b. 1952; BA, U. Toronto, 1975, BPhil, 1977, LLB, 1981; DPhil, Oxford U., 1988. Law clk. Supreme Ct. of Can., Ottawa, 1983—84; asst. prof. McGill U., Montreal, Canada, 1985—86; assoc. prof., 1991—96; prof. U. Pa. Law Sch., 1996—97, John J. O'Brien prof. law, 1997—2003, dir. Inst. Law & Philosophy, 2001—03; prof. philosophy U. Pa., 1997—2003; Fiorello La Guardia prof. law NYU Sch. Law, 2003—. Vis. prof. U. San Diego Law Sch., 1994, NYU Sch. Law, 1999—2000. Mem.: Am. Law Inst. Office: NYU Sch Law Vanderbilt Hall Rm 504 40 Washington Sq S New York NY 10012-1099 Office Phone: 212-998-6753. E-mail: perrys@juris.law.nyu.edu.

**PERRY, TROY D.,** minister, religious organization administrator; divorced; 2 children; m. Phillip Ray De Blieck, July 16, 2003. Student, Midwest Bible Sch., 1959; D in Ministry (hon.), Samaritan Coll., L.A., 1982; D in Human Svcs., Sierra U., Santa Monica, Calif., 1985; DDiv (hon.), Episcopal Div. Sch., Cambridge, Mass., 2003. Former pastor Ch. of God of Prophecy, Santa Ana, Calif.; founder, moderator Universal Fellowship Met. Cmty. Chs., L.A. Rep. Met. Community Chs. and gay and lesbian rights movement numerous TV shows including 60 Minutes, Phil Donahue, The Mike Douglas Show; author: The Lord is My Shepherd and Knows I'm Gay, Don't Be Afraid Anymore, 1991, (video) God, Gays and The Gospel: This is Our Story; contbg. editor Is Gay Good? Mem. Los Angeles County Commn. Human Rels.; del. 1st White House Conf. on AIDS, 1993; del. 1st White House Conf. on Hate Crimes, 1997; trustee Chgo. Theol. Sem., 2002—. Recipient Humanitarian award Gay Press Assn., Equality award Human Rights Campaign, 1996. Mem. Universal Fellowship Mcc Office: Universal Fellowship Mcc PO Box 691728 West Hollywood CA 90069-9728 Office Phone: 310-360-8640 ext. 211. E-mail: revtroyperry@mccchurch.org.

**PERRY, TYLER,** playwright, actor, theater director, theater producer; b. New Orleans, Sept. 13, 1969; Author: (plays) I Know I've Been Changed, I Can Do Bad All By Myself, 2000, Why Did I Get Married, Meet the Browns, 2004; auth. & actor (plays) Diary of a Mad Black Woman, 2001, auth., actor & dir. Madea's Family Reunion, 2002, Madea's Class Reunion-The Class That Had No Class, 2003, Madea Goes to Jail, 2005, co-auth. (with Bishop T. D. Jakes), dir. & prodr. Woman, Thou Art Loosed, 1999, Behind Closed Doors, 2001; author: (books) Don't Make a Black Woman Take Off Her Earrings, 2006. Named one of Most Influential Black Americans, Ebony mag., 2006.*

**PERRY, WALTER LEO,** information scientist, operations research specialist; m. Stella Claire Pepin, July 23, 1960; children: Stephanie Lynne Berlin, Geoffrey Scott, Jodie Lee VanDuren, Christopher Jerome, Kimberly Claire. AB in math. and econ., Northeastern U., 1958; MBA, Tulane U. Grad. Sch. of Bus., 1969—71; MS in ops. rsch., Tulane U. Sch. of Engring., 1969—71; PhD, George Mason U. Sch. of Info. Tech. and Engring., 1985—91. Sr. info. scientist RAND, Washington, 1984—; adj. prof. George Mason U., Fairfax, Va., 1984—99; adj. prof.lectr. George Wash. Grad. Sch. of Elec. Engring. and Computer Sci., 1992—; exch. scientist Centre for Defence Analysis, West Byfleet, England, 1994—96. Adj. prof., sch. of mgmt. George Mason U., Fairfax, Va., 1997; asst. prof. math. US Mil. Acad., West Point, NY, 1978—81. Author: (book) Disjointed War: Military Operations in Kosovo, 1999, Exploring Information Superiority: A Methodology for Measuring the Quality of Information and its Impact on Shared Awareness, Measures of Effectiveness for the Information-Age Army, Disjointed War: Military Operations in Kosovo, 1999, Response to Warning: Decisionmaking on Strategic Force Readiness, Operational Control of Republic of Korea (ROK) and US Forces in Korea: Issues and Requirements, Measures of Effectiveness for the Information-Age Navy, Measures of Effectiveness for the Information-Age Army; contbr. articles to profl. jours. Lt. col. U.S. Army, 1964—84, US and Overseas. Recipient Knox award for Def. Acquisition, Dept. of Def., 1975. Mem.: Inst. of Elec. and Electronic Engineers (corr.), Math. Assn. of Am. (corr.), Mil. Ops. Rsch. Soc. (corr.), Armed Forces Comm. and Electronics Assn. (assoc.). Roman Catholic. Avocations: church choir, woodworking, antiquarian book collecting, amateur art. Office: Rand 1200 South Hayes St Arlington VA 22202

**PERRY, WILLIAM BRIAN,** colorectal surgeon; b. Natchitoches, La., Dec. 18, 1963; s. William Nathaniel and Joyce Hargis Perry; m. Holly Christine Hundemer, June 27, 1987; children: Katherine Mitchell, Patrick William, Austin Joseph. BS, La. State U., 1986; MD, Duke U., 1990. Lic. colon and rectal surgery Am. Bd. of Colon and Rectal Surgery, gen. surgery Am Bd. of Surgery, Tex. State Bd. of Med. Examiners. Chief of colorectal surgery Wilford Hall Med. Ctr., Lackland AFB, Tex. 1997—2006, gen. surgery residency program dir. 2002—. Cons. to USAF surgeon gen. for colorectal surgery USAF Med. Corps, Bolling AFB, DC, 1997—2004; chief med. ops., chief of staff 4407th Med. Group, Prince Sultan Air Base, Saudi Arabia, 1998; chief trauma surgeon 332d Expeditionary Med. Group, Balad Air Base/LSA Anaconda, Iraq, 2005. Contbr. articles to med. jours. and texts. Lt. col. USAF, 1990—2006. Decorated Commendation Medal USAF. Fellow: ACS, Am. Soc. of Colon and Rectal Surgeons; mem.: VFW, Soc. of Air Force Clin. Surgeons (pres. 2004—06), Delta Tau Delta (treas. 1983—84). Office: 859 Msgs/Mcsg 2200 Bergquist Dr Lackland Afb TX 78236-5300 Office Phone: 210-292-5906. E-mail: william.perry@lackland.af.mil.

**PERRY, WILLIAM JAMES,** education educator, former secretary of defense; b. Vandergrift, Pa., Oct. 11, 1927; s. Edward Martin and Mabelle Estelle (Dunlap) Perry; m. Leonilla Green, Dec. 29, 1947; children: David, William, Rebecca, Robin, Mark. BS in Math., Stanford U., 1949, MS, 1950; PhD, Pa. State U., 1957. Instr. math. Pa. State U., 1951—54; sr. mathematician HRB-Singer Co., State College, Pa., 1952—54; dir. electronic def. labs.

GTE Sylvania Co., Mountain View, Calif., 1954—64; founder & pres. ESL, Inc., Sunnyvale, Calif., 1964—77; tech. cons. US Dept. Def., Washington, 1967—77, under sec. for research & engring., 1977—81; mng. dir. Hambrecht & Quist (investment bankers), San Francisco, 1981—85; chmn. Tech. Strategies & Alliances, Menlo Park, Calif., 1985—93; prof., co-dir. Ctr. for Internat. Security and Arms Control Stanford U., 1989—93; dep. sec. US Dept. Def., Washington, 1993—94, sec., 1994—97; prof. mgmt. sci. and engring. Stanford (Calif.) U., 1997—, sr. fellow, Hoover Inst. 1997—, co-dir., Preventive Defense Project, 1997—; chmn. Global Tech. Ptnrs. With U.S. Army, 1946—47. Recipient Def. Disting. Svc. medal, U.S. Govt., 1980, 1981, Achievement medal, Am. Electronics Assn., 1980, Forrestal medal, 1994, Henry Stimson medal, 1994, Arthur Bueche medal, NAE, 1996, Eisenhower award, 1996, Presdl. Medal Freedom, 1997, Outstanding Civilian Svc. medals, U.S. Army, 1997, USN, 1997, USAF, 1997, USCG, 1997, NASA, 1981, Def. Intelligence Agy., 1997; sr. fellow, Freeman Spogli Inst. Internat. Studies, Stanford U., 1997—. Mem.: bd. dirs., Anteon Internat. Corp. Office: Stanford U CISAC Encina Hall Stanford CA 94305 Office Phone: 650-725-6501. Office Fax: 650-725-0920.

**PERRY, WILLIAM JOSEPH,** food processing company executive; b. Sacramento, Calif., Nov. 4, 1930; s. Joseph Nasciemeto and Jennie (Nunez) P.; m. Beverly Ann Styles, Dec. 9, 1956 (div. May 1981); children: Katherine, Bill Jr., Kathleen, Barbara; m. Leslie Z. Blumberg, June 30, 1986. BS, U. Calif., Berkeley, 1953; MBA, U. So. Calif., 1995. Quality control supr. Stokely Van Camp, Oakland, Calif., 1953-54; plant mgr. Safeway Stores, Brookside div., Grandview, Wash., 1954-61, Gallo Winery, Modesto, Calif., 1961-62; gen. mgr. Bocca Bella Olive Assoc., Wallace, Calif., 1962-65; v.p. Early Calif. Ind., L.A., 1965-74, Fairmont Foods, Santa Ana, Calif., 1974-75; pres. Cal Agra Ind., Stockton, Calif., 1975-76; exec. v.p. Food Brokers Internat., L.A., 1976—; pres., co-owner G.F.F., Inc., L.A., 1981—. Dir. G.F.F., Inc., L.A., 1981—; Food Brokers, Inc., L.A., 1976—, Cozad & Assoc. Ad Agy., Encino, Calif., 1985-87. Wrestling com., dir. protocol, L.A. Olympic Com., 1981-84; dir. Nat. Kidney Cancer Assn., 1999. Mem. Nat. Food Brokers Assn., Assn. of Dressings and Sauces, Product Mktg. Assn., Nat. Single Svc. Assn., Am. Chem. Soc., Calif. League Food Processors (dir. 1997), U. Calif. Alumni Assn., U. So. Calif. Alumni Assn., L.A. Athletic Club. Republican. Roman Catholic. Avocations: tennis, photography, bicycling, amateur sports associations. Home: 3700 Brigantine Cir Thousand Oaks CA 91361-3816 Office: 145 N Willow City Of Industry CA 91746-2118

**PERRY-BÖTTINGER, LYNNE VALENCIA,** interventional cardiologist; b. Washington, June 1, 1961; d. Levi V. and Eula F. Perry; m. Erwin Paul Böttinger, Nov. 26, 1994; 2 children. AB cum laude, Harvard-Radcliffe U., 1982; MD cum laude, Yale U., 1986. Resident in internal medicine Yale-New Haven Hosp., 1986-89, chief med. resident, 1989-90; fellow in cardiology Johns Hopkins Hosp., Balt., 1990-94; instr. medicine Georgetown Univ. Hosp., Washington, 1996-97; asst. prof. medicine Albert Einstein Coll. Medicine, Bronx, 1997-2000; interventional cardiologist N.Y. Hosp. Queens, Flushing, NY, 2000—, Columbia-Presbyn. Hosp., 2002—; clin. asst. prof. medicine Cornell U. Weill Med. Coll.; asst. dir. cardiac cath lab., interventional cardiologist N.Y. Hosp., Queens; asst. prof. clin. medicine Columbia U. Fellow: Am. Coll. Cardiology. Democrat. Roman Catholic. Office: 140A Lockwood Ave New Rochelle NY 10801- Office Phone: 914-576-7577. Personal E-mail: dr.perry-bottinger@savehearts.com.

**PERSAD, ANAND BHOPRAJ,** entomologist; b. Doon and Sumatee Persad. BS, U. West Indies, 1992, PhD, 2001. Asst. lectr. U. WI, St. Augustine, Trinidad and Tobago, 2000—01; rsch. entomologist U. Fla., Gainesville, 2001—04. Regional tech. advisor Davey Inst., Kent, Ohio, 2004—. Contbr. rsch. articles in field. Mem.: Entomol. Soc. of Am. Achievements include discovery of initiation and propagation of parasitoid colonies. Office Phone: 330-673-9511.

**PERSAD, CHADEE,** information technology manager; b. Rio Claro, Trinidad and Tobago; s. Chandrika and Indardaye Persad; m. Tara Gopaul, Aug. 4, 1974; children: Govind, Geeta. BSME, U. West Indies, 1974; MSME, City U., London; PhD, U. Tex. at Austin, 1983. Rsch. assoc. U. Materials Sci., U. Tex., 1984—90; rsch. scientist U. Tex., Austin, Tex., 1990—2000; sr. rsch. scientist U. Tex. Inst for Advanced Technology, Austin, Tex., 2001—; faculty, dept. mech. engring. U. West Indies. Vis. faculty U. Netherlands, Antilles, Currcao, 1983—84. Author: (technical publications) Performance of Advanced Materials (US State Dept.) for contributions to the ISTC, 1996). Grantee Multidisciplinary - Friction and Wear Scis., Office of Naval Rsch., 2004-2007. Mem.: ASME. Achievements include research in high performance materials for sliding electrical contacts. Avocation: travel. Office Phone: 512-232-4492.

**PERSANS, PETER DAVID,** physics educator, researcher; b. N.Y.C., Mar. 25, 1953; BS in Physics, Poly. Inst. N.Y., 1975; SM in Physics, U. Chgo., 1977, PhD in Physics, 1982. Rsch. scientist Exxon Corp. Rsch., NJ, 1981; asst. prof. physics Rensselaer Poly. Inst., Troy, NY, 1986-89, assoc. prof., 1989—98, prof., 1998—. Contbr. more than 150 articles to sci. and tech. jours. Mem. Materials Rsch. Soc., Am. Phys. Soc. Home: Rensselaer Poly Inst Physics Dept Troy NY 12180 Office Phone: 518-276-2934. E-mail: persap@rpi.edu.

**PERSAUD, TRIVEDI VIDHYA NANDAN,** anatomy educator, researcher, consultant; b. Port Mourant, Berbice, Guyana, Feb. 19, 1940; arrived in Canada, 1972; s. Ram Nandan and Deen (Raggy) P.; m. Gisela Gerda Zehden, Jan. 29, 1966; children: Indrani Uta and Sunita Heidi (twins), Rainer Narendra. MD, Rostock U., Germany, 1965, DSc, 1974; PhD in Anatomy, U. West Indies, Kingston, Jamaica, 1970. Intern, Berlin, Germany, 1965-66; govtl. med. officer Guyana, 1966-67; lectr., sr. lectr. anatomy dept. U. West Indies, 1967-72; assoc. prof. anatomy dept. U. Man., Winnipeg, 1972-75, prof., 1975—, prof. ob-gyn., reproductive scis., 1979-99, prof. emeritus, 1999—, prof. pediatrics and child health, 1989—, prof., chmn./head dept. human anatomy & cell sci., 1977-93, dir. Teratology Rsch. Lab., 1977-93. Cons. in teratology, Children's Centre, Winnipeg, 1973—; mem. sci. staff Health Scis. Centre, Winnipeg, 1973—. Author, editor 22 med. textbooks, including: Early History of Human Anatomy: From Antiquity to the Beginning of the Modern Era, 1984, (with others) Basic Concepts in Teratology, 1985, Environmental Causes of Human Birth Defects, 1991, History of Human Anatomy: The Post-Vesalian Era, 1997, (with K.L. Moore) The Developing Human, 7th edit., 2003, Before We Are Born, 6th edit., 2003; rev. Medical Embryology, 6th edit., 2003; contbr. numerous chpts. to books, over 200 articles to profl. jours. Recipient Carveth Jr. Scientist award Can. Assn. Pathologists, 1974, Albert Einstein Centennial medal German Acad. Scis., 1975, Dr. & Mrs. H.H. Saunderson award U. Manitoba, 1985, 12th Raymond Truex Disting. Lectureship award Hahnemann U., 1990, Queen Elizabeth II Golden Jubilee medal Govt. Can., 2003. Fellow Royal Coll. Pathologists of London; mem. Can. Assn. Anatomists (pres. 1981-83, J.C.B. Grant award 1991), Am. Assn. Anatomists, Teratology Soc., European Teratology Soc. Office: U Man Dept Anatomy & Cell Sci 730 William Ave Winnipeg MB Canada R3E OW3 Office Phone: 204-789-3333. Business E-mail: persaud@ms.umanitoba.ca.

**PERSAVICH, WARREN DALE,** diversified manufacturing company executive; b. Cleve., Dec. 15, 1952; s. Nick and Sophie (Makris) P.; m. Anita Geraldine Zeleznik, Oct. 12, 1974; children: Nicholas, Katherine. BBA, Kent State U., 1975. CPA, Ohio. Staff acct. Price Water House, Cleve., 1975-76; asst. contr. Banner Industries Inc., Cleve., 1976-79, contr., 1979-86, treas., 1986-88, v.p., treas., 1988-90; sr. v.p., chief fin. officer Banner Aerospace Inc., 1990-98, v.p., chief oper. officer, 1998-99; pres. Banner Aerospace Distbn. Group, 2000—. Pres. aerospace divsn. The Fairchild Corp., McLean, Va. Mem. AICPA, Ohio Soc. CPAs. Republican. Office: The Fairchild Corp Ste 1400 1750 Tysons Blvd Mc Lean VA 22102

**PERSCHBACHER, PETER WESLEY,** environmental science educator, research scientist; b. Davenport, Iowa, Nov. 15, 1946; s. Wesley Adolph and Margaret Pohly P.; m. Virginia Brady, Feb. 14, 1986. BS, U. Mich., 1968; MS, Auburn U., 1975; PhD, Tex. A&M U., 1985. Rsch. assoc. U. N.C. Inst. Marine Sci., Morehead City, N.C., 1975-79; grad. rsch. asst. Tex. A&M U., Baytown, 1980-85; Aquaculture Trainer-Peace Corps Rsch. Planning Inst., Ft. Pierce, Fla., 1983; aquaculture biologist Caribbean Marine Rsch. Ctr., Lee Stocking Island, Bahamas, 1985; aquaculture advisor Harza Engring. Internat., Mymensingh, Bangladesh, 1986-87; rsch. biologist Agrl. Rsch. Svc., USDA, Tishomingo, Okla., 1989-93; assoc. prof. U. Ark., Pine Bluff, 1993—. Cons. KTAADIN, Newton, Mass., Norwegian Govt., Trondheim, Norway; affiliate faculty NASA; presenter in field Author: Recirculation-Aeration Bibliography for Aquaculture, 1993; editor, contbg. author: Small Scale Aquaculture, 2003; contbg. author: Third National Reservoir Symposium, 1997, Am. Chem. Soc. symposium in Agr., 2002, Third World Fisheries Congress, Beijing, 2000; contbr. article to N.Am. Jour. Aquaculture (named to top ten papers of 1998), others. Chair Clean and Beautiful Commn. Bd., Pine Bluff, 2000; active Natural Harmony Task Force, Pine Bluff, 1996—98; organizer Environ. Fair Grace Episcopal Ch., Pine Bluff, 1997, 1999, 2001, 2003, 2005; organizer waste mgmt. and splty. animal prodn. workshop U. Ark., 1999, chair rural life conf., 2003. Grantee Mgmt. of Environmentally-Derived Off-Flavors in Warmwater, USDA, Stoneville, Miss., 1995-2000, USDA-CSRS, 1999-2004. Mem. Am. Fisheries Soc., Am. Inst. Fisheries Rsch. Biologists, World Aquaculture Soc. (chair small-scale aquaculture spl. session 2002), Asian Fisheries Soc., Sigma Xi, Xi Sigma Pi, Gamma Sigma Delta. Democrat. Episcopalian. Avocations: native orchids, palms. Office Phone: 870-575-8145. Business E-mail: pperschbacher@uaex.edu.

**PERSCHBACHER, REX ROBERT,** dean, law educator; b. Chgo., Aug. 31, 1946; s. Robert Ray and Nancy Ellen (Beach) P.; children: Julie Ann, Nancy Beatrice. AB in Philosophy, Stanford U., 1968; JD, U. Calif., Berkeley, 1972. Bar: Calif. 1972, U.S. Dist. Ct. (no. dist.) Calif. 1973, U.S. Dist. Ct. (so. dist.) Calif. 1979, U.S. Ct. Appeals (9th cir.) 1980, U.S. Dist. ct. (ea. dist.) Calif. 1985. Law clk. to judge U.S. Dist. Ct. (no. dist.) Calif., San Francisco, 1973-74; asst. prof. law U. Tex., Austin, 1974-75; assoc. Heller, Ehrman, White & McAuliffe, San Francisco, 1975-78; asst. prof. law U. San Diego, 1978-79, assoc. prof. law, 1980-81; mem. faculty Inst. on Internat. and Comparative Law, London, 1984—88; acting prof. law U. Calif., Davis, 1981-85, prof., 1988—, assoc. dean, 1993-98, dean Law Sch., 1998—. Dir. clin. edn. Univ. Calif., Davis, 1981-93, acad. senate, law sch. rep., 1989-91; vis. prof. law Univ. Santa Clara (Calif.), summer 1986. Co-author: California Civil Procedure and Practice, 1996, California Legal Ethics, 5th edit., 2005, Problems in Legal Ethics, 7th edit., 2005, Cases and Materials on Civil Procedure, 5th edit., 2005; The United States Legal system-An Introduction, 2002; contbr. articles to legal jours. Bd. dirs. Legal Svcs. of No. Calif., 1990-96. Mem. ABA (Section of Legal Edn. and Admissions to Bar, Accreditation Com., 2000-), Calif. Bar Assn., Am. Assn. Law Schs., Inn of Ct. Democrat. Avocation: travel. Office: UC Davis Sch Law Dean Office 400 Mrak Hall Dr Davis CA 95616 Office Phone: 530-752-0243. E-mail: rrperschbacher@ucdavis.edu.

**PERSCHETZ, ARTHUR DRIBAN,** lawyer; b. Ossining, N.Y., May 17, 1943; s. S. Philip and Rose Lucy (Driban) P.; m. Lois Marsha Winebaum, May 13, 1971; children: Emily Karen, Rachel Carrie. BA, Syracuse U., 1965, JD, 1967. Bar: N.Y. 1969, U.S. Dist. Ct. (so. dist.) N.Y. 1971, U.S. Dist. Ct. (ea. dist.) 1972, U.S. Supreme Ct. 1981. Counsel Royal Indemnity Co., N.Y.C., 1970-73, 1973-83, asst. corp. sec., 1978—, asst. v.p., 1983-86, asst. gen. counsel, 1985—, v.p. legal Charlotte, N.C., 1986-91, also bd. dirs., corporate sec., 1991; sr. v.p., gen. coun. Maryland Casualty Co., Balt., 1991. Mem. Saltaire Citizens Adv. Com., N.Y., 1976; trustee Inc. Village of Saltaire, 1977-78; chmn. citizens oversight com. for cable TV to Charlotte City Counsel, 1987-90; bd. dirs. Mercy Hosp. Found., United Family Svcs., Charlotte, 1988-90, 829 Park Ave. Corp., N.Y.C., 1977-86, pres., 1978-86; bd. dirs. Foxcroft Assn., Mint Mus., v.p., 1991; bd. dirs. Magic Me, vice chair bd. dirs., 1992-95. Capt. U.S. Army, 1967-68, Vietnam. Mem. ABA, N.Y. State Bar Assn., N.Y. County Bar Assn., N.C. County Counsel Assn., N.C. State Bar Assn., Mecklenburg County Bar Assn., Nat. Assn. Ins. Commrs. (various coms.). Avocations: tennis, music, wine collecting. Office: Maryland Casualty Co 10900 Keswick Rd Baltimore MD 21211-2296 Home: 1711 Lancaster St Baltimore MD 21231-3412

**PERSCHETZ, MARTIN L.,** lawyer; b. Bklyn., Sept. 15, 1952; s. Louis and Edith (Sandhaus) Perschetz; m. Babs D. Hanfling, Mar. 23, 1980; children: Monica, Keith, Evan. BA, U. Mich., 1974; JD, SUNY, Buffalo, 1977. Bar: NY 1978, US Dist. Ct. (So. Dist.) NY 1978, US Dist. Ct. (Ea. Dist.) NY 1979, US Ct. Appeals (2nd Cir.) 1984, US Dist. Ct. (No. Dist.) NY 1989, US Dist. Ct. Colo. 1998, US Dist. Ct. (Ea. Dist.) Mich. 2003, US Ct. Appeals (6th Cir.) 2003. Assoc. Obermaier, Morvillo & Abramowitz, N.Y.C., 1977—80; asst. U.S. atty. So. Dist. N.Y., N.Y.C., 1980—86, chief major crimes unit, 1985—86; chief counsel N.Y.C. Spl. Commn. to Investigate City Contracts, N.Y.C., 1986; dep. commr. N.Y.C. Dept. Investigation, N.Y.C., 1986; spl. counsel Schulte, Roth & Zabel, N.Y.C., 1986—87; ptnr. Schulte, Roth & Zabel, LLP, N.Y.C., 1988—. Contbr. articles to profl. jour.; spkr. in field. Recipient Joseph Halpern award, Buffalo Law Rev., 1977. Mem.: NY Coun. Def. Lawyers, NYS Bar Assn., ABA. Office: Schulte Roth & Zabel LLP 919 Third Ave New York NY 10022-4774 Office Phone: 212-756-2247. E-mail: martin.perschetz@srz.com.

**PERSELL, CAROLINE HODGES,** sociologist, educator, author, researcher, consultant; b. Ft. Wayne, Ind., Jan. 16, 1941; d. Albert Randolph and Katherine (Rogers) Hodges; m. Charles Bowen Persell III, June 17, 1967; children: Patricia Emily, Stephen David. BA, Swarthmore Coll., 1962; MA, Columbia U., 1967, PhD, 1971. Sr. assoc., then nat. coord. Nat. Scholarship Svc. and Fund for Negro Students, N.Y.C., 1962-66; project dir. Bur. Applied Social Rsch., N.Y.C., 1968-71; asst. prof. NYU, 1971-76, assoc. prof., 1976-86, prof., 1986—; dir. grad. studies dept. sociology, 1984-87, chair dept. sociology, 1987-93, Robin Williams Disting. lectr., 1993-94. Author: Education and Inequality, 1977, Understanding Society, 1984, 3d edit., 1990; author: (with Cookson) Preparing for Power, 1985, Making Sense of Society, 1992; author: (with Maisel) How Sampling Works, 1996; assoc. editor: Tchg. Sociology, 1983—85, Sociology of Edn., 1991—95, Gender & Society, 1992—95; contbr. articles to profl. jours. Carnegie scholar Advancement of Tchg., 2000-01; grantee Fund for Improvement of Postsecondary Edn., 1989-92, NSF Equipment Fund, 1993-96; recipient Faculty Devel. award NSF, 1978-79, Women Educators' Rsch. award, 1978. Mem.: Sociologists for Women in Soc., Ea. Sociol. Soc. (pres. 1995—96), Am. Ednl. Rsch. Assn., Am. Sociol. Assn. (chair sect. 1983—84, chmn. publs. com. 1987—89, chair sect. 1988—89, v.p. 2004—05). Avocations: violin, gardening, opera, sports. Office: NYU Dept Sociology 269 Mercer St New York NY 10003-6633 Office Phone: 212-998-8350. Business E-mail: chp1@nyu.edu.

**PERSELLIN, ROBERT HAROLD,** physician; b. Fargo, N.D., July 3, 1930; s. James Harry and Bessie (Hoffman) P.; m. Bonnie Feibleman, June 27, 1957 (dec. 1983); children: Kathleen, Jamie; m. Diane Cummings, June 14, 1986. BS, Northwestern U., 1952, MD, 1956, MS, 1959. Diplomate: Am. Bd. Internal Medicine, Am. Bd. Rheumatology. Intern Charity Hosp., New Orleans, 1956-57; resident in internal medicine Northwestern U. Med. Center, 1957-60; fellow in rheumatology Southwestern Med. Sch., 1962-64; asst. prof. medicine U. Oreg. Med. Sch., 1964-68; prof. medicine, head div. rheumatology U. Tex. Health Sci. Ctr., San Antonio, 1968—81, prof. family practice, 1993—2003. Cons. rheumatology VA Hosps., U.S. Army, Internat. Med. Corps, Kosovo and Republic of Moldova; vis. prof. rheumatology Kingstown Med. Coll.; vis. scholar Corpus Christi Coll., Cambridge U., 1979-80; vis. scientist Strangeways Rsch. Lab., Cambridge. Contbr chpts. to books, articles to profl. jours. Bd. dirs. San Antonio Chamber Music Soc., 1970-75, 80-96, pres., 1983-85; bd. dirs. Friends of Strings, 1972-75, San Antonio Bot. Soc., 1985-87; Dem. precinct committeeman Washington County, Oreg., 1966-68. Served to capt. M.C. U.S. Army, 1960-62. Fellow ACP, Am. Coll. Rheumatology (exec. com. mem.); mem. Arthritis Found. (chmn. med. and sci. com. South Ctrl. Tex. chpt.), Heberden Soc., Am. Fedn.

Clin. Rsch., So. Soc. Clin. Investigation, Tex. Rheumatism Assn. (pres.), Nat. Soc. Clin. Rheumatology, Mex. Rheumatology Soc. (hon.). Office: 635 E Olmos Dr San Antonio TX 78212-2504

**PERSHAN, RICHARD HENRY,** lawyer; b. NYC, Jan. 4, 1930; s. Benjamin and Sadie (Aronowsky) P.; m. Kathryn Schaefler, June 11, 1952; children: Lee S., Richard H. Jr., Pamela P. Hochman, Julia B. BA, Yale U., 1951, LLB, 1956. Bar: N.Y. 1956, U.S. Supreme Ct.1969. Assoc. Davis, Polk & Wardwell, N.Y.C., 1956-60; ptnr. Finch & Schaefler, N.Y.C., 1960-85, LeBoeuf, Lamb, Greene & MacRae, N.Y.C., 1986-94, of counsel, 1995—. Counsel Mcpl. Art Soc., N.Y.C., 1965-70, Fine Arts Fedn., N.Y.C., 1975-80. Served to 1st It. USAF. Fellow Am. Coll. Trust and Estate Counsel (author, editor, articles and studies 1960—); mem. Assn. of Bar of City of N.Y., Yale Club (N.Y.C.), N.Y. Croquet Club. Democrat. Avocations: croquet, fitness. Home: 1435 Lexington Ave New York NY 10128-1630 Office: LeBoeuf Lamb Greene & MacRae 125 W 55th St New York NY 10019-5389 Office Phone: 212-424-8523. Personal E-mail: rpershan@yahoo.com. Business E-mail: rpershan@llgm.com.

**PERSHING, ROBERT GEORGE,** retired telecommunications industry executive; b. Battle Creek, Mich., Aug. 10, 1941; s. James Arthur and Beulah Francis P.; m. Diana Kay Prill, Sept. 16, 1961 (div. Jan. 1989); children: Carolyn, Robert; m. Charlene Jean Reed Wallis, Mar. 18, 1989 (div. Dec. 1995); m. Luz F. Villalon Dreisbach, July 23, 2006. BSEE, Tri-State Coll. 1961. Comm. engr. Am. Elec. Power, Ind., N.Y. and Ohio, 1961-69; design supr. Wescom, Inc., Ill., 1969-74; dir. engring. Tellabs, Inc., Lisle, Ill., 1974-78; pres., CEO Teltrend, Inc., St. Charles, Ill., 1979-89, chmn. bd., 1979-88; CEO DKP Prodns., Inc., St. Charles, Ill., 1986-89; exec. cons. Teltrend, St. Charles, Ill., 1979-93; asst. treas. Magnekopy, inc., Villa Park, Ill. Bd. dirs. TI Investors, Inc.; advisor entrepreneural studies U. Ill.; engring. cons. Recipient Chgo. Area Small Bus. award, 1986., INC 500 awards, 1987, 88. Mem. IEEE. Office: PO Box 3377 Show Low AZ 85902 Office Phone: 928-537-8952. E-mail: rpershing@frontiernet.net.

**PERSICO, JOSEPH EDWARD,** writer, historian; b. Gloversville, N.Y., July 19, 1930; s. Thomas Louis and Blanche (Perrone) P.; m. Sylvia La Vista, May 23, 1959; children: Vanya, Andrea. BA, SUNY-Albany, 1952, PhD (hon.), 1996; postgrad., Columbia U., 1955. Writer on staff of gov. N.Y. State, Albany, 1955-59; commd. fgn. service officer USIA, 1959, served in Buenos Aires, Rio de Janeiro, 1959-62; speechwriter Commr. N.Y. State Health Dept., Albany, 1963-66; chief speechwriter for gov. N.Y. State, Albany, 1966-74; speechwriter for Vice Pres. Nelson Rockefeller The White House, Washington, 1975-77. Commr. Am. Battle Monuments Commn. Author: My Enemy My Brother: Men and Days of Gettysburg, 1977, (novel) The Spiderweb, 1979, Piercing the Reich: The Penetration of Nazi Germany by American Secret Agents During World War II, 1979, The Imperial Rockefeller: A Biography of Nelson A. Rockefeller, 1982, Edward R. Murrow: An American Original, 1988, Casey: William J. Casey, From the OSS to the CIA, 1990, Nuremberg: Infamy on Trial, 1994, Roosevelt's Secret War: FDR and World War II Espionage, 2001, Eleventh Month, Eleventh Day, Eleventh Hour: Armistice Day, 1918: World War I and Its Violent Climax, 2004; co-author: Colin Powell: My American Journey, 1995. Served to It. (j.g.) USN, 1952-55. Recipient Disting. Alumnus award SUNY-Albany, 1982 Mem.: Coun. Fgn. Rels., Authors Guild, Inc.

**PERSING, JOHN ARTHUR,** surgeon; b. Burlington, Vt., Apr. 16, 1948; s. Raymond Maurice and Natalie (Vespucci) P.; m. Susan Powers Light, June 22, 1971; children: Sarah Merriman, John Scott. BA cum laude, U. Vt., 1970, MD, 1974; MA (hon.), Yale U., 1992. Diplomate Am. Bd. Plastic and Reconstructive Surgery, Am. Bd. Neurol. Surgeons. Resident gen. surgery Hosp. of U. Ariz., Tuscon, 1974-76; resident neurol. surgery Hosp. of U. Va., Charlottesville, 1976-82, resident plastic surgery, 1982-84, dir. cranial base surgery, 1988-92, vice chmn. dept. of plastic surgery, 1988-92, chief divsn. of craniofacial surgery, 1988-92; asst. prof. plastic and neurosurgery U. Va., Charlottesville, 1984-87, assoc. prof. of plastic and neurosurgery, 1987-89, prof. plastic and neurosurgery, 1989-92; prof. plastic surgery and neurosurgery Yale U. Sch. of Medicine, New Haven, Conn., 1992—, chief sect. of plastic surgery, 1992—; fellow Trumbull Coll. Yale U., New Haven, 1994—. Editor: Clinics in Plastic Surgery, July, 1995; co-editor Jour. of Craniofacial Surgery, 1992—, Scientific Foundations and Surgical Treatment for Craniosynostosis, 1989, Neurosurgery Clinics of North America, July, 1991; assoc. editor Plastic and Reconstructive Surgery, 1997-2005. Recipient Donald D. Matson award Am. Assn. of Neurol. Surgeons, 1981. Mem. Am. Assn. Pediatric Plastic Surgeons (pres. 1995-97), Am. Assn. Plastic Surgeons (membership com. 1994-95), Am. Soc. Plastic and Reconstructive Surgeons (coms.), Am. Cleft Palate-Craniofacial Assn. (coms.), Am. Soc. Maxillofacial Surgeons (coms., v.p. 2000-01,pres. 2002-03, Bernd Speissl award 1991, Maxillofacial Surgeons Found. Rsch. award 1992), Plastic Surgery Edn. Found. (sec. 2005-), Assn. Acad. Chmn. of Plastic Surgery (plastic surgery residency tng. evaluation com. 1993, chair issues com. 1994, v.p. 2002-03, pres. 2004-05), Northeastern Soc. Plastic Surgeons (program com. 1995), Plastic Surgery Rsch. Coun. (program com. 1991-94), Am. Bd. Plastic Surgery (chmn. 2005). Office: Yale Plastic Surgery 330 Cedar St # 2 New Haven CT 06510-8041 Office Phone: 203-785-2570. Business E-mail: john.persing@yale.edu.

**PERSINGER, DEL LOUIS,** pharmaceutical company executive; b. Whiting, Iowa, Aug. 2, 1949; s. Ardell L. and Doris L. Persinger; m. Mary L. Tabor, Sept. 16, 1984; children: Christopher, Benjamin Hammerschlag, Sarah Hammerschlag. BSChemE with distinction, Iowa State U., 1971, MS in Journalism and Mass. Comm., 1975; MBA in Fin., Am. U., 1990. Refinery process engr. Exxon Co., Baton Rouge, 1971-73; environtl. and pub. affairs mgr. Am. Petroleum Inst., Washington, 1975-89, sr. assoc. refining, 1989-92, dep. dir. mfg., distbn. and mktg., 1992-94, dir. mgmt. and budget, 1994-96; v.p. fin. ops. Pharm. Rsch. and Mfrs. of Am., Washington, 1996—2006, sr. v.p., CFO, 2006—; pres., CEO PhRMA Found., Washington, 1999—. Trustee, past pres. Bethesda Jewish Congregation, 1992—2000. Mem. Fin. Execs. Inst., Am. Soc. of Assn. Execs., Am. Found. for Pharm. Edn. (bd. dirs. 1999—), Phi Kappa Phi, Tau Beta Pi, Omega Chi Epsilon. Office: Pharm Rsch and Mfrs of Am Ste 300 950 F St NW Washington DC 20004

**PERSKY, MARLA SUSAN,** lawyer; b. Pitts., Feb. 15, 1956; d. Bernard and Elaine (Matus) P.; m. Craig Heberton IV, May 20, 1984. BS, Northwestern U., 1977; JD, Washington U., St. Louis, 1982. Bar: Ill. 1982. Asst. dir. med. records Chgo. Lake Shore Hosp., 1978; sales/mktg. rep. Colgate-Palmolive Co., Chgo., 1978-79; mem. Lurie Sklar & Simon, Chgo., 1982-86; corp. counsel Baxter Healthcare Corp., Deerfield, Ill., 1986-91; lead litigation counsel Baxter Internat. Inc., 1991-94; assoc. gen. counsel Baxter Healthcare Corp., Deerfield, 1994—98, dep. gen. counsel, 1998—2004, acting gen. counsel, corp. sec., 2004—. Dir. Cytyc Corp. Sr. editor Urban Law Ann. 1981-82; contbr. articles to profl. jours. Mem. Chgo. Bar Assn., Ill. Bar Assn. (writing contest award 1983), ABA (vice chmn. medicine and law com. 1984-86), Am. Soc. Law and Medicine, Am. Acad. Hosp. Attys. Democrat. Office: Baxter Internat Inc One Baxter Pkwy Deerfield IL 60015-5281

**PERSLIDEN, JAN R. G.,** physicist; b. Norrkoping, Sweden, July 13, 1950; s. Rune E.B. and Ruth E.M. (Roxne) P.; m. Lena K. Åman, Aug. 1, 1976; children: Sara, Hanna, Mikael, Persliden. PhD, Linkoping U., 1986. Rsch. asst. dept. radiation physics U. Linkoping, 1976-82; med. physicist Univ. Hosp., Linköping, Sweden, 1982-88, prin. med. physicist, 1988-99, assoc. prof., 1993, prof., 2002—. Cons. med. physicist Norrkoping Hosp., Motala Hosp., Sweden, 1994-99; head med. physics dept. U. Hosp., Örebro, Sweden, 1999-. Contbr. articles to profl. jours. Mem. Swedish Soc. of Radiation Physics (bd. dirs. 1994-2001, pres. 1999-2001), Swedish Electrotech. Commn. Standardization: church activities, cross country skiing. Office: Dept Radiation Physics Univ Hosp 701 85 Örebro Sweden Office Phone: +46 19 602 1000. Personal E-mail: Jan.Persliden@orebroll.se.

**PERSOFF, NEHEMIAH,** actor, artist; b. Jerusalem, Aug. 2, 1919; came to U.S., 1929; s. Samuel and Puah (Holman) P.; m. Thia Persov; children: Jeffrey Jonathan, Dan Deckel, Perry Erez, Dahlia. Student, Hebrew Tech. Inst., N.Y.C., 1934-37. Ind. stage, screen and TV actor, 1945—. Actor: (Broadway prodns.) Sundown Beach, Galileo, Richard the 3d, King Lear, Peer Gynt, Peter Pan, Reclining Figure, Flahooly, Montserrat, Tiger at the Gate, Only in America, (local, regional prodns.) Fiddler on the Roof, Man of La Mancha, Oliver, I'm Not Rappaport, 1988, Death of a Salesman (Stratford, Ont.), Two, Drinking America, Rosebloom, Dybbuk (Best Actor L.A. Critics 1975), Glass Menagerie (Israeli prodn.), Volpone, Of Mice and Men, (films) In Search of the Real Jesus, The Harder They Fall, The Wrong Man, This Angry Age, Men in War, Some Like It Hot, Al Capone, Green Mansions, The Commancheros, The Greatest Story Ever Told, Voyage of the Damned, Yentl, The Hook, The Last Temptation of Christ, Twins, numerous TV shows including For Whom the Bell Tolls (Sylvania award for best supporting actor 1958), The Big Knife, Alfred Hitchcock Presents, Rawhide, Twilight Zone, The Untouchables, The Wild, Wild West, I Spy, Gunsmoke, Police Story, Columbo, Barney Miller, Six Million Dollar Man, Delta House, Littlest Hobo, Magnum P.I., Hotel, Adderly; (TV miniseries) The French Atlantic; (one-man show) Aleichem Sholem-Sholem-Alecheim, 1971 (L.A. Critics award, San Francisco Critics Circle award 1979); paintings exhibited at George Krevsky Fine Arts, San Francisco, Seago Gallery, Cambria, Calif. With U.S. Army, 1942—45. Jewish. E-mail: thiap@thegrid.net.

**PERSON, CURTIS S., JR.,** state legislator, lawyer; b. Nov. 27, 1934; married; 6 children. BS, Memphis State U., 1956; LLB, U. Miss., 1959. Chief legal officer Juvenile Ct. Memphis and Shelby County; former mem. Tenn. Ho. Reps.; mem. Tenn. Senate, 1968—, Senate Rep. whip, 1973-76, minority caucus chmn., 1976-82. Chmn. Senate Judiciary com. 95th-104th Gen. Assemblies. Pres. Memphis-Shelby County Mental Health Assn., 1969-73, Handicapped Inc., 1972-74; chmn. Memphis Commn. Drug Abuse, 1970-71; charter pres. Memphis State Tiger Rebounders; past trustee Memphis State U.; exec. committeeman St. Jude's Memphis Open Golf Classic; co-chmn. Shelby County Legis. Del., 1973-74, vice chmn., 1970, 75, 76, 85-88; chmn. Shelby Rep. Del., 1977, 83-84; mem. adv. bd. Jr. League Memphis, 1995-98; vice chmn. Select Com. Children and Youth, 1997-2002, ex officio Senate Mem., Juvenile Justice Reform Commn., 1998. Named Memphis and Tenn. Outstanding Young Man of Yr., Jaycees, 1969, Outstanding Legis. of Yr., Govt. Leader Against Drunk Driving, Tenn. MADD, 1988, Legis. of Yr., Tenn. Alcohol and Drug Assn., 1988, Legislator of Yr. Tenn. Juvenile Svcs. Yr., 2001; recipient Liberty Bell Freedom award Memphis/Shelby County Bar Assn., 1969, Tenn. Adv. of Yr. Handicapped Children, 1978, Outstanding Svc. Children award Tenn Coun. Juvenile Ct. Judges, 1981, Pres.' Svc. award Tenn. Juvenile Ct. Svcs. Assn., 1981, Americanism award Memphis Civitan Club, 1986, Disting. Svc. award County Ofcls. Assn. Tenn., 1989, Cmty. Svc. award Tenn. Med. Assn., 1989, Eagle award Eagle Forum, 1994, Bill Bates Legis. award United Tenn. League, 1994, Champion for Children award Tenn. Assn. Child Care, 1995, Outstanding Legis. award County Ofcls. Assn. Tenn., 1996, Tenn. Juvenile Svcs. Assn. Pres. Svc. award, 1997, Tenn. Trial Lawyers Assn. Legis. of Yr. award, 1997, Shelby County Rep. Party Chmn. of Yr. award, 1999, Am. Lung Assn. Tenn. Legis. of Yr. award, 1999, Tenn. Task Force Against Domestic Violence Outstanding Legis. of Yr. award, 1999, Tenn. Dispensing Opticians Assn. Legis. of Yr. award, 2000, award Tenn. Juvenile Ct. Svcs. Assn., 2001, Spl. Honor Elvis Presley Meml. Martial Arts Hall of Fame, 2002, Lifetime Achievement award Defenders of Freedom, 2002, Animal Advocacy award Metro Animal Svcs., 2002, Legislator of Yr. award Tenn. Trial Lawyers Assn., 2003; named Legislator of Yr. Tenn. Devel. Dists., 2003, Hon. Fellow and Legislator of Yr., Opticians Assn. Am., 2003, Legislative Leadership award, Tenn. Cable Telecommunications Assn., 2003-2004, Friend of the Family award Tenn. Home Edn. Assn., 2004, Humane Legislator award Humane Soc. U.S., 2004, Thomas B. Murphy Longevity of Svc. award Southern Legislative Conf., 2004, Legislator of Yr., Animal Control Assn. of Tenn., 2004, award of appreciation Tenn. Silica Justice Coalition, 2006; named Champion Tenn. Disability Coalition, 2003-04, Outstanding Legislator, Co. Ofcls. Assn. Tenn., 2004. Office: War Meml Bldg Rm 308 Nashville TN 37243 Office Phone: 615-741-2419. E-mail: sen.curtis.person@legislature.state.tn.us.

**PERSON, EVERT BERTIL,** retired newspaper and radio executive; b. Berkeley, Calif., Apr. 6, 1914; s. Emil P. and Elida (Swanson) P.; m. Ruth Finley, Jan. 26, 1944 (dec. May 1985); m. 2d, Norma Joan Betz, Mar. 12, 1986. Student, U. Calif., Berkeley, 1937; LHD, Calif. State Univs., 1983, Sonoma State U., 1993. Co-publisher, sec.-treas. Press Democrat Pub. Co., Santa Rosa, Calif., 1945-72 editor, 1972-73, pres., pub., editor-in-chief, 1973-85; sec.-treas. Finley Broadcasting Co., Santa Rosa, 1945-72, pres., 1972-89, Kawana Pubs., 1975-85; pub. Healdsburg Tribune, 1975-85; prin. Evert B. Person Investments, Santa Rosa, 1985—. Pres. Person Properties Co., Santa Rosa, 1945-70; v.p. Finley Ranch & Land Co., Santa Rosa, 1947-72, pres., 1972-79; pres. Baker Pub. Co., Oreg., 1957-67, Sebastopol (Calif.) Times, 1978-81, Russian River News, Guerneville, Calif., 1978-81; pres. publ. Kawana Pubs., 1978-85; mem. nominating com. AP, 1982-84, mem. auditing com., 1984-85 Bd. dirs Empire Coll., Santa Rosa, 1972-98, Sonoma County Taxpayers Assn., 1966-69, San Francisco Spring Opera Assn., 1974-79; bd. dirs. San Francisco Opera, 1986-95, v.p., 1988-95; pres. Calif. Newspaperboy Found., 1957-58; chmn. Santa Rosa Civic Arts Commn., 1961-62; pres. Santa Rosa Sonoma County Symphony Assn., 1966-68, Luther Burbank Meml. Found., 1979, Santa Rosa Symphony Found., 1967-77; adv. bd. Santa Rosa Salvation Army, 1959-67; commodore 12th Coast Guard Dist. Aux., 1969-70; trustee Desert Mus.; Palm Springs, 1987-92, v.p. Nat. Bd. Canine Companions, Inc., 1989-92. Decorated Knight of the Holy Sepulchre. Mem. Calif. Newspaper Pubs. Assn. (pres. 1981-82), Internat. Newspaper Fin. Execs. (pres. 1961-62), Bohemian Club, Sonoma County Press Club, Santa Rosa Golf and Country Club, The Springs Club, Santa Rosa Rotary (past pres.), Masons (33 degree, Legion of Merit), Shriners. Roman Catholic. Home: 775 White Oak Dr Santa Rosa CA 95409-6155 Office: The Oaks 1400 N Dutton Ave Ste 12 Santa Rosa CA 95401-4644

**PERSON, PHILIP,** biomedical consultant, biochemist, dentist; b. N.Y.C., Aug. 6, 1919; s. Barney and Lena (Spindel) P.; m. Bertha Paula Kaufman, Mar. 14, 1953; children: Sarah, Naomi, Matthew. BS, CUNY, 1940; DDS, NYU, 1946; MS, Rutgers U., 1951, PhD, 1952. Lic. dentist. Chief dental research lab. VA Med. Ctr., Bklyn., 1954-86; vis. prof. biochemistry Boston U. Sch. Grad. Dentistry, 1964-74; sr. vis. investigator systematics-ecology Marine Biol. Lab., Woods Hole, Mass., 1966-72; spl. research fellow (NIH) Inst. for Muscle Research, Woods Hole, 1967-68; adj. prof. oral biology Columbia U. Sch. Dental and Oral Surgery, N.Y.C., 1969-73; adj. prof. biochemistry and periodontics NYU Coll. Dentistry, N.Y.C., 1977—; dir. oral health studies Research Testing Labs., Little Neck, N.Y., 1986—; biomed. cons. Little Neck, 1986—. Mem. NIH Dental Study Sect., Bethesda, Md., 1963-66; cons. NIDR, NIAMD (NIH), Bethesda, 1963-80, Radiation and Solid State Lab., NYU, N.Y.C., 1965-68, dental health, marine biology WHO, Geneva, 1967-68, Coun. on Dental Therapeutics, ADA, Chgo., 1984-89. Editor: Metabolism of Oral Tissues, 1962, Biology of the Mouth, 1968. Investigator Biocore, Mission of Apollo 17, NASA, Ames Research Ctr., Moffet Field, Calif., 1973. Capt. USAR, 1952-54. Fellow AAAS, Am. Inst. Chemists, N.Y. Acad. Sci., The Harvey Soc. Office: 13787 75th Rd Flushing NY 11367-2815

**PERSONIUS, KEVIN T.,** financial analyst; b. N.J., Oct. 1971; s. Thomas C. and Dorothy A. Personius; m. Christina Personius, Aug. 0, 1998; 1 child, Allison. BS in Accountancy, Villanova U., Pa., 1989—93, MBA, 1996—99. Fin. analyst Westinghouse, Horseheads, NY, 1993—95; sr acct. CertainTeed Corp., Valley Forge, Pa., 1995—98; fin. supr. Bird Corp., Norwood, 1998—2000; sr fin. analyst CertainTeed Corp. Valley Forge 2000—02, six sigma black belt, 2002—04; sr fin. analyst Exelon Corp., Plymouth Meeting, 2004—. Mem.: MENSA (assoc.). Republican. Roman Catholic. Avocations: softball, basketball. Office: Exelon Corp 680 Ridge Pike Plymouth Meeting PA 19462 Office Phone: 610-941-1666.

**PERSONS, JOHN WADE,** lawyer; b. Fitchburg, Mass., Dec. 6, 1953; s. Roger W. and Marjorie L. (Boudreau) P.; m. Marjorie L. Smith, July 18, 1980; children: Katherine A., Elizabeth W. BA in History magna cum laude, U. Conn., 1975, MA, 1977; JD, Albany Law Sch., 1980. Bar: N.Y. 1981, U.S. Dist. Ct. (no. dist.) N.Y. 1981, U.S. Dist. Ct. (ea. dist.) N.Y. 1985. From law clk. to assoc. Cade & Saunders, Albany, NY, 1978—84; legal rschr., writing instr. Albany Law Sch., 1979—80; assoc. Glynn and Mercep, Stony Brook, NY, 1984—86; ptnr. Glynn, Mercep and Persons, Stony Brook, NY, 1987—91; assoc. Faruolo, Caputi, Weintraub & Neary, Huntington, NY, 1991—96; from assoc. to ptnr. Grey & Grey, LLP, Farmingdale, NY, 1996—2003; assoc. Montfort, Healy, McGuire and Salley, Garden City, NY, 2004—. Law guardian Albany County Family Ct., 1984. Mem. N.Y. State Bar Assn. (ins. sect., negligence and compensation law sect.), Suffolk County Bar Assn. (ins. negligence and compensation), Killington Sch. for Instrs; Clubs: Stony Brook Yacht. Democrat. Home: 53 Cedar St Stony Brook NY 11790-1732 Office: Montfort Healy McGuire & Salley PO Box 7677 1140 Franklin Ave Garden City NY 11530-7677 Office Phone: 516-747-4082. Business E-Mail: john_persons@mhms-law.com.

**PERSONS, W. RAY,** lawyer, educator; b. Talbottan, Ga., July 22, 1953; s. William and Frances (Crowell) P.; m. Wendy-Joy Mottley, Sept. 24, 1977; children: Conrad Ashley, April Maureen. BS cum laude, Armstrong State Coll., 1975; JD, Ohio State U., 1978. Bar: Ga. 1979, U.S. Dist. Ct. (so. dist.) Ga. 1980, U.S. Dist. Ct. (no. dist.) Ga. 1986, U.S. Ct. Appeals (11th cir.) 1986. Assoc. Troutman, Sanders, Lockerman & Ashmore, Atlanta, 1978-79; atty. Nat. Labor Rels. Bd., Atlanta, 1980-82; legis. counsel U.S Ho. Reps., Washington, 1983-86; atty. Mack & Bernstein, Atlanta, 1986-87; ptnr. Arrington & Hollowell, Atlanta, 1987-95, Swift, Currie, McGhee & Hiers, Atlanta, 1995-99, Hunton and Williams, Atlanta, 1999—2001, King & Spalding, Atlanta, 2001—. Adj. prof. litigation Ga. State U., Atlanta, 1989—; spl. asst. atty. gen. State of Ga., Atlanta, 1988—. Master Am. Inns of Ct. (Lamar chpt.); fellow Am. Coll. Trial Lawyers; mem. ABA, Internat. Soc. Barristers, Am. Bd. Trial Advocates, State Bar Ga., Atlanta Bar Assn., Lawyers Club of Atlanta. Roman Catholic. Office: King & Spalding LLP 191 Peachtree St NE Atlanta GA 30303-1763 Office Phone: 404-572-2494. E-mail: rpersons@kslaw.com.

**PERSSON, ERLAND KARL,** electrical engineer, engineering executive; b. Soderala, Sweden, Oct. 9, 1923; arrived in U.S., 1949, naturalized, 1953; m. Elaine Darm; children: Ann Monn, Eric. BSEE, U. Minn., 1955. Registered profl. engr., Minn. Prin. engr. Gen. Mills, Mpls., 1956-61; v.p. engring. Electro-Craft Corp., Hopkins, Minn., 1961-72, v.p. R & D, 1972-83, sr. v.p., chief tech. officer, 1983-86; pres. Erland Persson Co., Mpls., 1987—. Contbr. articles to profl., chapters to books. Mem. mech. engring. adv. com. U. Minn.; bd. dirs. Minn. High Tech. Coun., 1984—86, mem., 1987. Fellow: IEEE (life; mem. indsl. drives com.), Audio Engring. Soc. (life; founder midwest chpt. 1974); mem.: Eta Kappa Nu. Achievements include patents in field. Office: 216 Janalyn Cir Minneapolis MN 55416-3321 Office Phone: 763-377-1663. Business E-Mail: persso002@tc.umn.edu.

**PERTH, ROD,** network entertainment executive; b. LA; s. Milford Robert Martinson and Phyllis (Hove) Perth; m. Jill Sunderland, Apr. 27, 1974; children: Chelseah, Lauren, Eric. BS in Mgmt., San Jose State U., 1966. V.p., gen. mgr. spot sales CBS TV, N.Y.C., 1974—86; v.p., station mgr. WBBM-TV, Chgo., 1986—89; sr. v.p. late night non-network programming CBS-TV, L.A., 1989—94; pres. entertainment USA Network, L.A., 1994—95; pres. HRTS, L.A., 1995—99, Jim Henson T.V.; programming dir. USA Network. Account exec. KNXT, L.A., 1968—71; ea. mgr. spot sales CBS, N.Y.C., 1971—74, dir. midwest spot sales, Chgo., 1974—76; dir. sales KMOX-TV, St. Louis, 1976—79; bd. dirs. HRTS. Contbr. L.E.A.R.N. program, L.A., 1995, Alliance for Children, L.A., 1996; bd. mem. State St. Coun., Chgo., 1988. Lt. j.g. USN, 1968—74. Named Man of Yr., Alliance for Children, L.A., 1996. Mem.: Hollywood (Calif.) Radio and TV Soc. (pres. 1995—). Avocations: skiing, motorcycling, photography. Office: Jim Henson Television 1416 N Labrea Ave Hollywood CA 90068

**PERTHOU, ALISON CHANDLER,** interior designer; b. Bremerton, Wash., July 22, 1945; d. Benson and Elizabeth (Holdsworth) Chandler; m. A. V. Perthou, III, Sept. 9, 1967 (div. Dec. 1977); children: Peter T. R., Stewart A. C. BFA, Cornish Coll. Arts, 1972. Pres. Alison Perthou Interior Design, Seattle, 1972—; Optima Design, Inc., Seattle, 1986-89; treas. Framejoist Corp., Bellevue, Wash., 1973-90; pres. Classics: Interior Design and Constrn., Inc., 1988—; Gemini Holdings LLC, 2004—. Cons. bldg. and interiors com. Children's Hosp., Seattle, 1976—; guest lectr. U. Wash., Seattle, 1980—81. Mem. procurement com. Patrons N.W. Cultural and Charitable Orgn., 1985—, mem. antiques com., 1991—; trustee Cornish Coll. Arts, Seattle, 1973—80, sec. exec. com., 1975—77. Mem.: Am. Soc. Interior Design, Sunset Club, Seattle Tennis Club (mem. house and grounds com. 1974—75). Office: 563 Lake Washington Blvd E Seattle WA 98112-4226 Office Phone: 206-322-7909. Office Fax: 206-322-2335.

**PERTSCHUK, LOUIS PHILIP,** pathologist, consultant; b. London, July 4, 1925; s. Isaac M. and Rose Pertschuk; m. Andrea Roberts, June 28, 1985; children: Eric, Shawn, Brandy. AB, NYU, 1946; DO, Phila. Coll. Osteo. Medicine, 1950. Diplomate Am. Bd. Pathology. Instr. Downstate Med. Ctr./SUNY, Bklyn., 1974-75, asst. prof., 1975-79, assoc. prof., 1979-86, prof., 1986—. Cons. Corning (N.Y.) Glass Works, 1982-86, Zeus Sci. Co., 1982-94, Abbott Labs., 1982-92, Lifecodes Corp., 1989-93, Oncor, Inc., Gaithersburg, Md., 1994-96, Internat. Bioimmune Sys., Great Neck, N.Y., 1994-96, DiaGnos, Sav Rames, Calif., 1990 99. Author: Immunocytochemistry for Steroid Receptors, 1990; editor: Localization of Putative Steroid Receptors, 1985. Served with U.S. Army, 1943-46. NCI/NIH grantee, 1979, 82, 85, 92. Fellow Coll. Am. Pathologists, Am. Soc. Clin. Pathologists; mem. AAAS, Am. Assn. Pathologists, Internat. Acad. Pathology, N.Y. Acad. Sci., Histochem. Soc. Achievements include identification of steroid hormone binding sites in human neoplasms by histochemical and immunohistological techniques. Office: SUNY Health Sci Ctr at Bklyn 450 Clarkson Ave # 25 Brooklyn NY 11203-2056

**PERUSHEK, DIANE,** university librarian; BA, Lake Erie Coll.; MLS, U. Mich.; MA in Asian Studies, Columbia U. Curator Wason Collection, Cornell U., Gest Oriental Libr.; dean collection svcs. U. Hawaii; bus. libr. for collection mgmt. Northwestern U.; univ. libr. U. Hawaii at Manoa Libr., 2001—. Office: U Hawaii at Manoa Libr 2550 McCarthy Mall Honolulu HI 96822 Office Phone: 808-956-7205. Office Fax: 808-956-5968. E-mail: perushek@hawaii.edu.*

**PERUZZO, ALBERT LOUIS,** actuary, accountant; b. Chgo., Dec. 27, 1951; s. Anthony L. and Annette Peruzzo. BS Math., No. Ill. U., 1973, BS Accountancy, 1974, MBA, 1975. CPA Ill.; CLU 2003; chartered fin. cons. 2005. Auditor Deloittes CPA, Chgo., 1976—79; valuation analyst IV CNA Ins., Chgo., 1979—89, mgr. valuation compliance, 1989—92, valuation analyst, 1992—97, asst. actuary, 1998—2000, actuarial dir., 2000—02, actuarial cons. dir., 2002—04, Valley Forge Life Ins., 2004—05. Treas., bd. dirs. Dignity/Chgo., 1982-84, Integrity/Chgo., 1988-93; dep. vol. Voter's Registrar Bd. Elections, Chgo., 1984-86; bd. dirs. Colonial Condo, 1990-99 Fellow Conf. Cons. Actuaries, Soc. Actuaries (edn. and exam. com. 1998-99), Life Mgmt. Inst. (with distinction); mem. AICPA (exam hon. mention 1975),

Am. Acad. Actuaries (participant valuation task force 1998-99), Ill. CPA Soc. (Silver medal 1975), Beta Gamma Sigma (life charter Chgo. chpt.), Mensa (life), ACLU Democrat. Roman Catholic.

**PERWO, GEORGE EDWARD,** music educator; b. Turnersville, NJ, June 6, 1979; s. George Gardner Perwo; life ptnr. Brendan Francis Healy. MusB in Music Edn. Piano/Voice, The Coll. of NJ, Ewing, 2002. Organist Ctrl. Bapt. Ch., Ewing, 2000—02; choir dir., organist Kirkpatrick Meml. Presbyn. Ch., Ringoes, NJ, 2002—04; elem. music educator South Brunswick Schs., Kendall Park, NJ, 2002—04; piano/trombone studio tchr. Westminster Conservatory of Music, Princeton, NJ, 2004—06; dir. music and worship St. Paul's United Meth. Ch., Ocean Grove, NJ, 2004—. Dir. Ctrl. Jersey Brass Ensemble, Ocean Grove, 2002—, St. Paul's Oratorio Choir, Ocean Grove, 2004—. Mem.: Monmouth County Arts Assn., Royal Sch. of Ch. Music in Am., Organ Hist. Soc., Am. Choral Dirs. Assn., Am. Guild Organists. Home: 512 7th Ave Apt 2 Asbury Park NJ 07712 Office: St Paul's United Meth Ch 80 Embury Ave Ocean Grove NJ 07756 Office Phone: 732-775-1125 ext 16. Office Fax: 732-775-4540. Personal E-mail: perwo2@yahoo.com. E-mail: nperwo@oceangrovechurch.com.

**PERZ, ERVA KAY,** retired elementary school educator; b. Canton, Ohio, May 23, 1936; d. Paul and Erma Louella (Hert) Wenger; m. Thomas E. Perz; children: Michael (dec.), David, Doug, Kathy, Thomas Jr., Dann. BS, Kent State U., Ohio, 1964, MA, 1980. Tchr. Canton City Schs., Ohio, 1956-58, 67-70; 5th grade tchr. Brunswick City Schs., Ohio, 1971—97; ret., 1997. Bd. dirs. Christian Centre Sch, Parma, Ohio, S.W. Christian High Sch., Parma. Mem. Delta Kappa Gamma.

**PERZ, SALLY,** academic administrator, former state legislator; m. Joseph Perz; children: Allison, Julie, Melanie, Andrea, Brian. BA, Siena Heights. Ohio State rep. Dist. 52, 1993; mgmt. cons. Perz, Inc., 1996—; exec. dir. U. Toledo. Active Boy Scouts Am. Recipient Carlson Counyt Mktg. award, 1984-93, Women of Achievement award, 1993. Mem. Toledo Club, Toledo C. of C., Toledo Rotary, Toledo Sisters Cities (exec. bd.). Home: 3245 River Rd Toledo OH 43614-4218 Office: U Toledo 2801 W Bancroft St Toledo OH 43606-3328

**PERZEK, PHILIP JOHN,** lawyer; b. Chgo., Sept. 25, 1960; s. Thomas John and Dorothy (Malis) P.; m. Gayle Karon Scott, Aug. 17, 1985; 1 child, Rachel Karon. BS, No. Ill. U., 1982; JD, Northwestern U., 1986. Bar: Ill. 1986, U.S. Dist. Ct. (no. dist.) Ill. 1986. Law clk. to Hon. Nicholas J. Bua U.S. Dist. Ct. (no. dist.) Ill., Chgo., 1986-88; ptnr. Latham & Watkins LLP, Chgo., 1988—. Mem. Ill. State Bar Assn., Nat. Comml. Fin. Assn. Home: 207 W 8th St Hinsdale IL 60521-4448 Office: Latham & Watkins 5800 Sears Tower Chicago IL 60606 Office Phone: 312-876-7699. Business E-Mail: Philip.Perzek@lw.com.

**PESCATORE-SHIREY, HOPE JEAN,** middle school reading educator; b. Hollywood, Fla., Sept. 12, 1966; d. Earle Milton Sr. and Faith Lucille Pescatore. BS, Nova U., 1987, MS, 1990. Cert. tchr., Fla. Tchr. 1st, 2d and 3d grades Sunland Park Elem. Sch., Ft. Lauderdale, Fla., 1987—92; tchr. reading Omni Mid. Sch., Boca Raton, Fla., 1992—99; tchr. reading I, II, III Lake Worth H.S., Fla., 1999—2001; reading coach Okeeheelee Cmty. Mid. Sch., Greenacres, Fla., 2001—. Facilitator Regional League Mid. Sch. Conf., 2003, 04, Fla. Online Reading Devel., 2002—; prof. Fla. OnLine Reading Devel., 2002—; spkr. in field; trainer in field. Acad. scholar Nova U., Success grantee Citibank, 1995; named Greenacres Tchr. of Yr. Wal-Mart, 2005 Mem. Internat. Reading Assn. (session trainer 1995). E-mail: shirey@palmbeach.k12.fl.us.

**PESCH, ELLEN P.,** lawyer; BA, Barat Coll., 1986; JD, John Marshall Law Sch., 1989; LLM, DePaul U., 1991. Bar: Ill. 1989, U.S. Dist. Ct. (no. dist.) Ill. With Sidley Austin Brown & Wood, Chgo., 1989—, ptnr., 2001—. Mem.: ABA, Internat. Swaps and Derivatives Assn., Stable Value Investment Assn. Office: Sidley Austin Brown and Wood Bank One Plz 10 S Dearborn St Chicago IL 60603

**PESCI, JOE,** actor; b. Newark, N.J., Feb. 9, 1943; m. Martha Haro (div.); m. Garrett Warren; 1 child, Tiffany. Film appearances include Death Collector, 1976, Raging Bull, 1980, I'm Dancing as Fast as I Can, 1982, Easy Money, 1983, Dear Mr. Wonderful, 1983, Eureka, 1983, Once Upon a Time in America, 1984, Tutti Dentro, 1984, Man On Fire, 1987, Moonwalker, 1988, Backtrack, 1988, Lethal Weapon II, 1989, Goodfellas (Acad. award Best Supporting Actor, 1991, D.W. Griffith Award, 1990), Home Alone, 1990, The Super, 1991, JFK, 1991, Lethal Weapon III, 1992, Home Alone II, 1992, The Public Eye, 1992, My Cousin Vinny, 1992, A Bronx Tale, 1993, With Honors, 1994, Jimmy Hollywood, 1994, Casino, 1995, Gone Fishin, 1997, 8 Heads in a Duffel Bag, 1997, Lethal Weapon 4, 1998; appeared in TV series Half Nelson, 1985.

**PESEC, DAVID JOHN,** data systems executive; b. Cleve., Apr. 19, 1956; s. Rudolph J. and Martha C. (Kessler) P. BS, Cleve. State U., 1988; MBA, U. Phoenix, 1999; PhD, Trinity Coll., 2000. Pvt. practice cons., Cleve., 1976—78; programmer Champion Svc. Corp., Cleve., 1978; sr. sys. programmer United Tel. of Ohio, Mansfield, 1978—89; dir. devel. Broderick Data Sys., Mansfield, 1989—97; prin. cons. Keane, Inc., Independence, Ohio, 1997—2000; pres. Pesec Creative Mgmt., Inc., Mansfield, 2000—. Adj. prof. Ashland U. 2001—. Am. Intercontinental U., 2001. 1 bd. dirs. Park Av Pets., Inc. Bd. dirs. ARC, Mansfield, 1989—, Mansfield Emergency Svc., 1986; assoc. pastor Cornerstone Grace Brethren Ch., 1995—; life mem. Rep. Nat. com., 1991—, Rep. Senatorial Inner Circle, 1991—. Recipient Senatorial medal of freedom, 1996. Mem. Am. Mgmt. Assn., Assn. Computing Machinery, Intercity Radio Club (pres. 1987-90), NRA, Gideons (v.p. 1992), Profl. Photographers. Republican. Mem. Grace Brethren Ch. Avocations: flying, auto racing. Office: Pesec Creative Mgmt Inc 1633 Hickory Ln Mansfield OH 44905-2945 Office Phone: 419-589-7418. Business E-Mail: dpesec@peseccreativemanagement.com.

**PESERIK, JAMES E.,** electrical engineer, consultant, safety engineer, computer engineer; b. Beloit, Wis., Sept. 30, 1945; s. Edward J. and G. Lucille Peserik; m. Elaine L. Peserik, May 6, 1972. BSEE, U. Wis., 1968; MS, St. Joseph's U., 1990. Registered profl. engr., registered profl. land surveyor; cert. fire and explosion investigator, cert. fire investigation instr.; diplomate Am. Coll. Forensic Examiners. Development and instrumentation engr. Square D Co., Milw., 1968-71; product engr. I-T-E Imperial Corp., Ardmore, Pa., 1971-72; project engr. Harris-Intertype Corp., Easton, Pa., 1972-74; elec. engr. Day & Zimmerman, Inc., Phila., 1974-76; sr. elec. engr. S.T. Hudson Engrs., Inc., Phila., 1980-81; pvt. practice James E. Peserik Assoc., Coopersburg, Pa., 1976—. Mem. adv. coun. Swenson Skills Ctr., Phila., 1990—95; lectr. in field. Contbr. articles to profl. jours. Treas. Salford-Fraconia Joint Parks Commn., Montgomery County, Pa., 1980-83. Mem. IEEE (sec. indsl. applications group Phila. chpt. 1980, chmn. 1981, chmn. Lehigh Valley computer sect. 1999—), NSPE, Pa. Soc. Profl. Engrs., Del. Assn. Profl. Engrs. (external affairs com. 1995—), Nat. Fire Protection Assn., Internat. Assn. Arson Investigators, Nat. Assn. Fire Investigators. Office: PO Box 181 Coopersburg PA 18036-0181 Office Phone: 215-234-8901. E-mail: jepeserik@enter.net.

**PESHKIN, MURRAY,** physicist; b. Bklyn., May 17, 1925; s. Jacob and Bella Ruth (Zuckerman) P.; m. Frances Julie Ehrlich, June 12, 1955; children—Michael, Sharon, Joel. BA, Cornell U., 1947, PhD, 1951. Instr., then asst. prof. physics Northwestern U., 1951-59; physicist, then sr. scientist Argonne (Ill.) Nat. Lab., 1959—, assoc. dir. physics div., 1972-83. Fellow Weizmann Inst. Sci., Rehovoth, Israel, 1959-60, 68-69. Served with AUS, 1944-46. Home: 838 Parkside Ave Elmhurst IL 60126-4813 Office: Argonne Natl Lab Argonne IL 60439 Business E-Mail: peshkin@anl.gov.

**PESHKIN, SAMUEL DAVID,** lawyer; b. Des Moines, Oct. 6, 1925; s. Louis and Mary (Grund) P.; m. Shirley R. Isenberg, Aug. 17, 1947; children: Lawrence Allen, Linda Ann. BA, State U. Iowa, 1948, JD, 1951. Bar: Iowa 1951. Ptnr. Bridges & Peshkin, Des Moines, 1953-66, Peshkin & Robinson, Des Moines, 1966-82. Mem. Iowa Bd. Law Examiners, 1970—. Bd. dir. State U. Iowa Found., 1957—, Old Gold Devel. Fund, 1956—, Sch. Religion U. Iowa, 1966—. Fellow Am. Bar Found., Internat. Soc. Barristers; mem. ABA (chmn. standing com. membership 1959—, ho. of dels. 1968—, bd. govs. 1973—), Iowa Bar Assn. (bd. govs. 1958—, pres. jr. bar sect. 1958-59, award of merit 1974), Inter-Am. Bar Assn. Internat. Bar Assn., Am. Judicature Soc., State U. Iowa Alumni Assn. (dir., pres. 1957) Office Phone: 480-607-3136.

**PESIN, ELLA MICHELE,** journalist, public relations executive; b. North Bergen, N.J., Aug. 29, 1956; d. Edward and Helene Sylvia (Rattner) P. BA, Sarah Lawrence Coll., 1978. Press rep. CBS-TV News and Entertainment, N.Y.C., 1978-80; publicist Newsweek Mag., N.Y.C., 1980-81; freelance journalist N.Y.C., 1982-85; publicist Universal Studios MCA Inc., L.A., 1982-83; with publicity and mktg. NBC-TV News, N.Y.C., 1985-86; media exec. Burson Marsteller Pub. Rels., N.Y.C., 1986-87; prin. Pesin Pub. Rels., 1987—. Contbg. editor Cable Age mag., TV Radio Age mag., Advt. Forum, Facts Figures & Film, Advt. Compliance Svc.; syndicated newspaper columnist. Active Israel Bonds/United Jewish Appeal, N.Y.C., Rudolph Giuliani for N.Y.C. Mayor campaign. Mem. Pub. Rels. Soc. Am., Women in Comm., Publicity Club N.Y., Healthcare Pub. Rels. and Mktg. Soc. Avocations: photography, sculpture, modern dance, tennis, skiing. Home and Office: 1483 3rd Ave Apt 22C New York NY 10028 E-mail: eem75p@aol.com.

**PESKOV, VLADIMIR DMITRIEVICH,** physicist, consultant, physics professor; b. Karaganda, Russia, Jan. 30, 1947; s. Dmitri S. and Olga D. (Petrova) Peskov; m. Tatiana R. Zabotina, May 3, 1973; children: Dmitri, Tatiana. MS in Physics, Phys. and Tech. Inst., Moscow, 1971; PhD in Physics, USSR Acad. Sci., Moscow, 1976, DSc, 1981. Rschr. Inst. Phys. Problems, Moscow, 1971-76, sr. rschr., 1976-97, leading scientist, 1981-97, prof., 1998—2005; chief scientist Inst. Applied Mechanics, Russian Acad. Sci., 1997—2000; assoc. scientist European Ctr. Nuc. Rsch., Geneva, 1986-92; application physicist II Fermi Nat. Accelerator Lab., Batavia, Ill., 1992-95; invited prof. Coimbra U., Portugal, 1995-98; NRC sr. rsch. assoc. Marshall Space Ctr., Huntsville, Ala., 1995-98; guest prof. Royal Inst. Tech., 1998—2004; prof. Leonard de Vinci U., Paris, 2004—06; chief scientist Inst. Chemical Physics, Russian Acad. Sci., 2005—; assoc. scientist CERN, Geneva, 2006—. Mem. adv. bd. numerous internat. confs.; mem. org. com. Internat. Conf. Imaging, Stockholm, 2000, Stockholm, 03; mem. neutron time flight experiment European Orgn. Nuc. Rsch. Contbr. articles to profl. jours.; inventor (exhibitions) INNOVACT, Reims, France, 2004. Participant Internat. Meeting Chem. Disarmament, Rome, 1989, Forum di Amore, Italy, 1991, Internat. Meeting Our Nature, 1991. Recipient prize of World Fedn. Scientists, World Lab./Italian Physics Soc., 1993—2002. Mem.: Italian Phys. Soc., Am. Phys. Soc. Achievements include discovery of plasma instability, connected to accumulation of excited atoms and molecules, a flux-induced breakdown, cathode excitation effect; invention of device for magnetic field measurement of landing spacecraft, position sensitive gas scintillating detector; detectors and methods for radiation measurement and med. imaging (some demonstrated at INNOVACT); patents in field. Office: CERN PH Div 23 Geneva Switzerland Office Phone: 41227674643. Business E-Mail: vladimir.peskov@cern.ch.

**PESLIER, ANNE H.,** geochemist; Postdoctoral fellow Smithsonian Instn., 1999—2000; rsch. scientist U. of Houston, 2001—. Contbr. scientific papers to peer-reviewed jours. Mem.: Am. Geophys. Union. Achievements include research in High-Temperature Geochemistry. Office: Univ Houston TcSUH HSC Bldg 202 Houston TX 77204

**PESMEN, SANDRA (MRS. HAROLD WILLIAM PESMEN),** editor, educator; b. Chgo., Mar. 26, 1931; d. Benjamin S. and Emma (Lipschutz) Zuckerman; m. Harold W. Pesmen, Aug. 16, 1952; children: Bethann, Curtis. BS, U. Ill., 1952. Reporter Radio and Community News Service, Chgo., 1952-53; wire editor Champaign-Urbana (Ill.) Courier, 1953; reporter, feature writer Lerner Chgo. N. Side Newspapers, 1953-55; stringer corr. Wayne (Mich.) Eagle, 1958-61; reporter, feature writer Chgo. Daily News, 1968-78; features editor Crain's Chgo. Business mag., 1978-89; corp. features editor Crain Communications, Inc., 1989-95; tchr. feature writing Northwestern U. Evening Sch., 1972-81. Author: Writing for the Media, 1983, Dr. Job's Complete Career Guide, 1995; editor: Career News Service; author syndicated column Dr. Job, 1985—. Recipient Golden Key award Ill. Mental Health Dept., 1966, 71, award Inst. Psychoanalysis, 1971, Penny Mo. award, 1978, Stick o'Type award Chgo. Newspaper Guild, 1978, award AP, 1975, Peter Lisagor award Soc. Profl. Journalists, 1991; inductee Chgo. Journalism Hall of Fame, 1997. Home: 2811 Fern Ave Northbrook IL 60062-5809

**PESNER, CAROLE MANISHIN,** art gallery owner; b. Boston, Aug. 5, 1937; m. Robert Pesner (dec. 1983); children: Ben, Jonah; m. Martin Cherkasky, 1995 (dec. 1997). BA, Smith Coll., 1959. Asst. dir. Kraushaar Galleries, Inc., N.Y.C., 1959-86, dir., 1986-90, pres., 1991—. Author, editor publs., catalogues in field. Mem. Art Dealers Assn. Am., Internat. Fine Print Dealers Assn. Office: Kraushaar Galleries Inc 724 5th Ave New York NY 10019-4106 Office Phone: 212-307-5730. Business E-Mail: info@kraushaargalleries.com.

**PESNER, STEVEN M.,** lawyer; b. Suffern, NY, Oct. 27, 1945; BA with distinction, U. Va., 1967; JD, NYU, 1971. Bar: NY 1972; US Ct. Appeals NY (2d cir. 1973, 3d cir. 1981, 9th cir. 1982); US Dist. Ct. NY (so. and ea. dist. 1973, no. dist. 1986); US Supreme Ct. 1976. Asst. village atty. Village of Tarrytown, 1975-77, Village of Dobbs Ferry, 1975-76; ptnr. Anderson, Kill, Olick & Oshinsky, P.C., NYC, 1974—94; ptnr., lead of litig. practice and mem. mgmt. com. Akin Gump Strauss Hauer & Feld LLP, NYC, 1994—. Lectr. N.Y. Inst. Credit, 1978, U. Va., The Colgate Darden Grad. Sch. Bus. Adm., 1983—, PLI 1989—; mem. panel of arbitrators Am. Arbitration Assn. Mem. ABA (sect. on antitrust law), Assn. of Bar of City of NY, NY State Bar Assn., NY County Lawyer's Assn. (com. on bankruptcy, 1974-79), Am. Arbitration Assn. (panel of arbitrators). Office: Akin Gump Strauss et al 590 Madison Ave New York NY 10022-2524 Office Phone: 212-872-1070. Office Fax: 212-872-1002. Business E-Mail: spesner@akingump.com.

**PESOLA, GENE RAYMOND,** physician; b. Hancock, Mich, Oct. 21, 1952; s. Raymond Lloyd and Helen Eleanor Pesola; m. Helen Rostata, Jan. 5, 1991; children: Gene Richard, Glen Raymond, Gary Roger. BS in Biology magna cum laude, Mich. Technol. U., Houghton, 1974; MD, Wayne State U., 1979; MPH in Biostats. magna cum laude, Columbia U., 1998. Diplomate Am. Bd. Internal Medicine, also sub-bds. pulmonary medicine and critical care medicine; cert. BCLS, ACLS, ATLS, PALS. Intern Harlem Hosp., NYC, 1979-80; resident U. Tenn. Affiliated Hosps., Memphis, 1980-82; fellow in pulmonary medicine Mt. Sinai Hosp. and Affiliates, NYC, 1982-84; fellow in critical care medicine Meml. Sloan-Kettering Cancer Ctr., NYC, 1984-85, rsch. fellow, 1985-87; asst. prof. medicine and anesthesia Albert Einstein U., Bronx, NY, 1988-89; attending physician Mt. Vernon Emergency Room, NY, 1989-90; rschr. cell/molecular pharmacology and exptl. therapeutics Med. U. SC, Charleston, 1991-94; attending physician critical care and emergency medicine N.Y. Cmty. Hosp., Bklyn., 1989—; attending physician dept. emergency medicine St. Vincent's Hosp., NYC, 1994—2000; asst. prof. emergency medicine NY Med. Coll., 1995-2000, assoc. prof. emergency medicine, 2000; assoc. attending physician Divsn. Pulmonary and Critical Care Medicine, Harlem Hosp./Columbia U., NYC, 2001—; assoc. clin. prof. medicine Columbia U., NYC, 2001—; co-prin. investigator ACRN, NYC, 2001—04. Mem. editl. bd. Academic Emergency Medicine, 2002—, assoc. editor, 2006—; Internet Jour. Asthma, Allergy and Immunology, 2002—; contbr. chapters to books, numerous articles to profl. jours.; reviewer numerous jours. including CHEST, Catheterization and Cardiovasc. Interventions, Annals of Emergency Medicine, The Lancet, Academic Emergency

Medicine. Grantee Am. Fedn. Clin. Rsch., 1992; Pharm. Mfr. Found. fellow, 1992-94; named one of Am. Top Physicians, Consumer's Rsch. Coun., 2004-05; named Tchr. of Yr. Dept. Medicine, Harlem Hosp., 2006.

**PESOLA, WILLIAM ERNEST,** restaurant management executive; b. Marquette, Mich., Mar. 2, 1945; s. Ernest Ensio and Janice Mary (LeDuc) P.; m. Kathleen Mary Deschaine, July 9, 1966; children: Christie Lynn, Laurie Anne. BS, No. Mich. U., 1968, MS, 1971. Route driver Coca Cola Co., Marquette, 1963-68; tchr. Gwinn (Mich.) Schs., 1968-73, pub. Sch. News, 1969; pres. Pesola Mgmt., Marquette, 1974—; Humboldt Ridge, Marquette, 1977—; treas. Elite Bar, Inc., Marquette, 1978—; v.p., dir. Marquette Cablevison, 1981-85; pres. Upper Peninsula Big Boy, Marquette, 1990—. Cons. cable TV, 1985—, Bresnan Comm., 1984—. Pres. Gwinn Edn. Assn., 1975-77; regional pres. Upper Peninsula Edn. Assn., 1977-78; mem. Marquette City Commn., 1977-81. Mem. NEA, Marquette Econ. Club, Mich. Edn. Assn., Marquette C. of C. (Exemplary Citizen award 1990), Rotary. Roman Catholic. Home: 1026 N Front St Marquette MI 49855-3514 Office Phone: 906-228-7200. Personal E-mail: bepesola@chartermi.net.

**PESSAH, ISAAC NESS,** pharmacology and toxicology educator; b. Cairo, Feb. 14, 1955; s. Ness Isaac and Esther (Gohar) P.; m. Beatrice Ann Boffen, Mar. 30, 1983. BS, Cornell U., 1977; MS, U. Md., Catonsville, 1981; PhD, U. Md., 1983. Postdoctoral fellow Pesticide Chemistry & Toxicology Lab. U. Calif., Berkeley, 1984-85, rsch. specialist in biochemistry, 1985-87, asst. prof. Davis, 1988-93, assoc. prof., 1993—. Mem. exec. com. Grad. Group in Pharmacol. & Toxicology, Davis, 1989—, Grad. Group in Neuroscis., Davis, 1993—. Contbr. numerous sci. articles to profl. jours. Recipient 1st award NIH, 1988, Grant-in-Aid, Calif. affiliate Am. Heart Assn. Mem. AAAS, Am. Assn. for Pharmacology and Exptl. Therapeutics, Am. Chem. Soc., Biophys. Soc. Jewish. Avocations: scuba diving, hiking, long distance cycling. Home: 3104 Oyster Bay Ave Davis CA 95616-2639 Office: U Calif Dept Molecular Bioscis 2147 Haring Hall Davis CA 95616

**PESSIN, JEFFREY E.,** physiology educator; b. N.Y.C., Jan. 2, 1953; s. Al Pessin; m. Rene Debra Bronner, June 23, 1975; children: Jacob, Lauren, Melanie. BA in Chemistry, MA in Chemistry, CUNY, 1975; PhD in Biochemistry, U. Ill., 1980; postgrad., U. Mass., 1980. Grad. rsch. asst. U. Ill., Urbana, 1975-80; asst. prof. physiology U. Iowa, Iowa City, 1983-88, assoc. prof., 1988-91, prof., 1991—, assoc. dir. Diabetes and Endocrinology Rsch. Ctr., 1991—. Contbr. articles to Molecular and Cellular Biology, Endocrinology. Basil O'Connor rsch. scholar March of Dimes Birth Defects Found., 1987-90; grantee NIH, 1988-93. Mem. AAAS, NIH (mem. metabolism study sect. 1989-93), Am. Chem. Soc., Am. Diabetes Assn. (R & D award 1985-87, rsch. award 1995), Sigma Xi. Office: U Iowa Dept Physiology and Biophysics Bowman Sci Bldg 5-530 Iowa City IA 52242 Home: 51 Woodchuck Hollow Ct Port Jefferson NY 11777-2093

**PESTA, BEN W., II,** lawyer, writer; b. Hagerstown, Md., Oct. 15, 1948; s. Ben W. Pesta and Irene (Kirkpatrick) Ethel; m. Monique Raphel High, Dec. 7, 1987; 1 stepchild, Nathalie Carroll. AB, UCLA, 1969; JD, U. Calif., Berkeley (Boalt Hall), 1972. Bar: US Supreme Ct., US Ct. Appeals, 9th Appellate Cir., US Dist. Cts. Central and Eastern Dist. Calif., Eastern Dist. Wis., Dist. Ariz., all Calif. Cts. Assoc. editor Esquire Mag., 1972—74; instr. grad. profl. writing program U. So. Calif., 1980—82; assoc. pub. Weider Health & Fitness, Woodland Hills, Calif., 1984—90; pvt. practice law LA, 1990—. Freelance writer. Contbr. articles and reviews to Esquire, Playboy, Rolling Stone, Crawdaddy, Sport, TV Guide, Cosmopolitan, Self, LA Style mags., etc., LA Times, LA Daily News, LA Weekly, and profl. jours. Capt. USAF, 1973, 438th MAW. Mem.: ACLU, Authors Guild, Calif. Pub. Defenders Assn., Calif. Atty. for Criminal Justice, Nat. Assn. Criminal Def. Lawyers, Fed. Bar Assn., LA County Bar Assn., State Bar Calif. Office: 1901 Ave of the Stars Ste 390 Los Angeles CA 90067 Office Phone: 310-201-0666. E-mail: pestalaw@aol.com.

**PESTANA, CARLOS,** surgeon, retired dean, educator; b. Tacoronte, Tenerife, Canary Islands, Spain, June 10, 1936; came to U.S., 1968, naturalized, 1973; s. Francisco and Blanca (Suarez) P.; m. Myrna Lorena Serrato, Aug. 25, 1966; children— Becky Elizabeth, George Byron. BS, Nat. U. Mex., 1952, MD, 1959; PhD in Surgery, U. Minn., 1965. Intern St. Mary of Nazareth Hosp., Chgo., 1959-60; resident Mayo Clinic, Rochester, Minn., 1961-65; surgeon Hosp. 20 de Noviembre Mexico City; asst. prof. surgery Nat. U. Mex., 1966-67, U. Tex. Med. Sch. at San Antonio, 1968-70, asso. prof., 1970-74, prof., 1974—, asso. dean for acad. devel., 1971-73, asso. dean for student affairs, 1973-86, assoc. dean acad. affairs, 1986-97, clin. prof. surgery, 1998-2000, prof. emeritus, 2000—. Recipient Edward John Noble Found. award, 1965, Piper Prof. award Minnie Stevens Piper Founds., 1972, Nat. Golden Apple award Am. Med. Student Assn., 1999. Mem. Alpha Omega Alpha (Robert J. Glaser Disting. Tchr. award 1997). Home: 10123 N Manton Ln San Antonio TX 78213-1932 Office: 7703 Floyd Curl Dr San Antonio TX 78284-6200

**PESTELLO, FRED P.,** academic administrator; BA in Sociology, John Carroll U.; MA in Sociology, PhD in Sociology, U. Akron. Joined U. Dayton, Ohio, 1984, prof. sociology, assoc. dean, 1997—2001, v.p. for ednl. affairs and provost, 2001—. Office: Office of the Provost Univ Dayton 300 College Park St Marys Hall 212 Dayton OH 45469-1634

**PESTILLO, PETER JOHN,** auto parts company executive, lawyer; b. Bristol, Conn., Mar. 22, 1938; s. Peter and Ruth (Hayes) P.; m. BettyAnn Barraclough, Aug. 29, 1959; children: Kathleen, Karen, Kerry. BSS, Fairfield U., Conn., 1960; LLB, Georgetown U., 1963. Bar: D.C. 1964. Mgr. union relations planning Gen. Electric Co., N.Y.C., 1968-74; v.p. employee relations B.F. Goodrich Co., Akron, Ohio, 1974-80; v.p. labor relations Ford Motor Co., Dearborn, Mich., 1980-85, v.p. employee relations, 1985-86, v.p. employee and external affairs, 1986—90, v.p. corp. rels. and diversified businesses, 1990—93, exec. v.p. corp. rels., 1993, vice chmn., chief of staff; chmn. Visteon Corp., Dearborn, 2000—, CEO, 2000—04. Mem. adv. bd. United Found., Detroit. Mem. Am. Arbitration Assn. (dir.), U.S. C. of C. (labor relation com.), D.C. Bar, Bus. Roundtable, Labor Policy Assn., Nat. Assn. Mfgrs., UBA. Office: Visteon Corp 17000 Rotunda Corp Dearborn MI 48120

**PESTOVA, EKATERINA,** scientist; b. Moscow, Sept. 27, 1966; life ptnr. Peter Ferro; 1 child, Anna. BS in Biology, Moscow U., 1988, MS in Microbiology, 1991; PhD, U. Ill., Chgo., 1997. Sr. application scientist Motorola, Northbrook, Ill., 1999—2001; adj. asst. adjunct pathology Northwestern U. Med. Sch., Chgo., 2000—04; sr. scientist Abbott Molecular, Inc. divsn. Abbott Labs., Des Plaines, Ill., 2001—. Mem.: Am. Soc. Microbiology (Sustaining Mem. Student Travel grantee 1998), Am. Soc. Human Genetics, Phi Kappa Phi. Achievements include patents for single nucleotide polymorphism biochip analysis; research in competence for genetic transformation in streptococcus pneumoniae, elements of the quorum-sensing pathway; discovery of energetic metabolism of gram-positive methylotrophic bacteria utilizing methanol, novel methanol dehydrogenase. Office: Abbott Molecular Inc 1300 E Touhy Ave 1D Des Plaines IL 60018

**PESZKE, MICHAEL ALFRED,** psychiatrist, writer; b. Deblin, Poland, Dec. 19, 1932; arrived in U.S., 1956; s. Alfred Bartlomiej and Eugenia Halina (Grebocka) Peszke; m. Alice Margaret Sherman, Sept. 20, 1958; children: Michele Halina Olender, Michael Alexander. BA, Trinity Coll., Dublin, Ireland, 1956; MB, BCh, BAO, Dublin U., 1956. Cert. Bd. cert. psychiatrist. Staff psychiatrist Yale Student Health Svc., New Haven, 1961-64; asst. prof. sch. medicine U. Chgo., 1964-68; cons. psychiatrist Wesleyan U., Middletown, Conn., 1968-70; asst. prof. Sch. Medicine U. Conn., Farmington, 1970-73, assoc. prof., 1973-80, prof. psychiatry, 1980-90; clin. prof. U. Md. Sch. Medicine, Balt., 1991-99; chief Psychiatry Svc. Perry Point (Md.) VA Med. Ctr., 1990-98, co-coord. R&D, 1998-99. Dir. psychiat. clin. svcs. John Dempsey Hosp. U. Conn. Health Ctr., Farmington, 1983—87; chief VA Med. Ctr., Newington, Conn., 1987—90; ind. rschr., 1999—; chmn. adv. com. to

the endowed chair of Polish and Polish Am. studies Ctrl. Conn. State U., 2001—; advisor Am. Polish Adv. Coun. Author: Involuntary Treatment of the Mentally Ill: The Problem of Autonomy, 1975, Battle for Warsaw, 1939-44, 1995, Poland's Navy: 1918-1945, 1999; co-author (edited by L.A. Pervin, L.R. Reik, W. Dalrymple): The College Drop-out and the Utilization of Talent, 1966; co-author: (edited by J. Zusman, E. Bertsch) The Future of Psychiatric State Hospitals, 1975; co-author: The Polish Underground Army, The Western Allies and the Failure of Strategic Unity in World War II, 2005; contbr.; book reviewer U. Chgo. Law Rev., 1968, Conn. Law Rev., 1976, Am. Jour. Psychiatry, 1976—99. Advisor Am. Polish Adv. Coun., 2003—. Fellow: APA (life; disting.); mem.: Polish Inst. Arts and Scis. Am., Inc., Am. Coll. Psychiatrists, Royal United Svc. Inst. (London), Soc. for Mil. History, Stonington Harbor Yacht Club.

**PETAK, WILLIAM JOHN,** systems management educator; b. Johnstown, Pa., June 23, 1932; s. Val Andrew and Lola Agatha (Boroski) P.; m. Ramona Janet Cayuela, Dec. 28, 1957; children: Elizabeth Ann Petak-Aaron, William Matthew, Michael David. BS in Mech. Engring., U. Pitts., 1956; MBA, U. So. Calif., 1963, DPA, 1969. Engr. Northrop Corp., Hawthorne, Calif., 1956-59; test engr. Wyle Labs., El Segundo, Calif., 1959-63; we. regional mgr. Instrument div. Budd Co., Phoenixville, Pa., 1963-69; v.p., dir. J.H. Wiggins Co., Redondo Beach, Calif., 1969-81; prof. systems mgmt. U. So. Calif., LA, 1982-98, exec. dir. Inst. Safety and Sys. Mgmt., 1987-98, prof. policy, planning and devel., 1998—2005, emeritus prof., 2005—. Mem. earthquake mitigation com. Nat. Com. on Property Ins., Boston, 1990-92; mem. com. on natural disasters NRC, Washington, 1985-91, mem. U.S. nat. com. for the decade for natural disaster reduction, 1989-92. Co-author: Natural Hazard Risk Assessment and Public Policy, 1982, Politics and Economics of Earthquake Hazard Reduction, 1986, Disabled Persons and Earthquake Hazards, 1988; editor spl. issue Pub. Adminstrn. Rev., 1985. Commr. County of Los Angeles, 1994—; mem. policy bd. So. Calif. Earthquake Prep. Project, L.A., 1986-92; trustee Marymount Coll., Palos Verdes, Calif., 1974—. Sgt. U.S. Army, 1950-52. Mem. Soc. for Risk Analysis, Earthquake Engring. Rsch. Inst., Am. Soc. for Pub. Adminstrn., Sigma Xi. Republican. Roman Catholic. Avocations: skiing, fishing, hiking. Office: U So Calif MC 0626 Sch Policy Planning & Devel Los Angeles CA 90089-0001 Office Phone: 310-377-3872. Business E-Mail: petak@usc.edu.

**PETCHESKY, ROSALIND POLLACK,** political scientist, educator, social sciences educator; b. Bay City, Tex., Aug. 16, 1942; BA, Smith Coll., 1964; MA, Columbia U., 1966, PhD, 1974. Prof., polit. sci. and women's studies, Hunter Coll. CUNY, 1987—, head, women's studies program, Hunter Coll., 1987—91. Bd. dirs. Women's Environ. and Develop. Orgn., 2000—. Author: The Individual's Rights and the International Organization, 1966, Abortion and Women's Choice: The State, Sexuality and Reproductive Freedom, 1984 (Joan Kelly Meml. prize Am. Hist. Assn., 1984), Abortion and Women's Choice: The State, Sexuality and Reproductive Freedom, 2d edit., 1990; co-editor: Negotiating Reproductive Rights: Women's Perspectives Across Countries and Cultures, 1998; serves governing bd. Jour. Reproductive Matters. Founder, first internat. coord. Internat. Reproductive Rights Rsch. Action Group. Fellow, MacArthur Found., 1995. Office: CUNY Hunter Coll Dept Polit Sci Hunter West 1726 695 Park Ave New York NY 10021-5024 Office Phone: 212-772-5500, 212-772-5682. E-mail: rpetches@igc.org.

**PETCHKIS, ANTHONY JAMES,** artist; b. New Haven, May 3, 1955; s. Anthony Joseph Petchkis and Jacqueline Marie McGann; m. Dennis Ray Haywood, Sept. 1, 2004. BFA, Paier Sch. Art, Hamden, Conn., 1977. Continuous exhibit, Newbury Fine Arts, Boston, 1984—, Erlich Gallery, Marblehead, Mass., 2003—, A Z Fine Arts, Wellesley Hills, Mass., 2005—, exhibitions include Mass. Coll. Art Benefit Auction, Boston, 1993—, LynnArts, Inc., Lynn, Mass., 2004, Anton Fine Arts Gallery, Wakefield, Mass., 2004, artSPACE@16, Malden, Mass., 2004, Art Attack, Somerville, Mass., 2005, Buttonwoods Mus., Haverhill, Mass., 2005—. Recipient Spl. Merit award, Artrom Gallery, 2004, Silver Medal award of merit, Eurogallery Live Art, 2005—06. Mem.: Conn. Pastel Soc. (signature), NW Pastel Soc., Pastel Painters Soc. Cape Cod, Vt. Pastel Soc., Pastel Soc. Am. (assoc.). Achievements include being the subject of an article in Pastel Journal. Home: 53 Eastern Ave Lynn MA 01902 Office: AJP Fine Art 53 Eastern Ave Lynn MA 01902 Office Phone: 781-842-3091. Office Fax: 253-541-2724. E-mail: info@ajpfineart.com.

**PETE, ERIC E.,** writer, claims representative; b. Seattle, Oct. 1, 1968; s. Earl Joseph Pete and Edna Mae Bushnell; m. Marsha Bluin; 1 child, Chelsea. BS, McNeese State U., 1993. Assoc. in mgmt., assoc. in claims, sr. claims law assoc. Claim rep. State Farm Cos., 1994—; owner E-fect Pub., Houston, 2000—. Author: (novels) Real for Me, 2000, Someone's In the Kitchen, 2002, Gets No Love, 2004, Don't Get It Twisted, 2005, Lady Sings the Cruels, 2006. With U.S. Army, 1987—89. Mem.: Toastmasters Internat., Delta Sigma Pi. Avocations: reading, travel, dance, weightlifting, art. Office: PO Box 670562 Houston TX 77267-0562 Home: 3139 Crossout Cr Spring TX 77373 Business E-Mail: heyeric@att.net.

**PETER, PHILLIPS SMITH,** lawyer; b. Washington, Jan. 24, 1932; s. Edward Compston and Anita Phillips (Smith) P.; m. Jania Jayne Hutchins, Apr. 8, 1961; children: Phillips Smith Peter Jr., Jania Jayne Hutchins Stone. BA, U. Va., 1954, JD, 1959. Bar: Calif. 1959. Assoc. McCutchen, Doyle, Brown, Enerson, San Francisco, 1959-63; with GE (and subs.), various locations, 1963-94, v.p. govtl. rels., 1980-94; counsel, head govt. rels. dept. Reed Smith Shaw & McClay, Washington, 1994—. Chmn. bd. govs. Bryce Harlow Found., 1990-92, bd. dirs. Mem. editl. bd. Va. Law Rev., 1957-59. Trustee Howard U., 1981—89; bd. dirs., exec. com. Nat. Bank of Washington, 1981—86; v.p. Fed. City Coun., Washington, 1979—85; bd. dirs. Carlton, 1987—90, 1995—98, pres., 1995—96. Mem. Calif. Bar Assn., Order of Coif, Wee Burn Club, Ea. Yacht Club, Farmington Country Club, Landmark Club, Congl. Country Club, Georgetown Club, Chevy Chase Club, Carlton Club (bd. dirs. 1990-98), Coral Beach and Tennis Club, Johns Island Club, The Windsor Club, Omicron Delta Kappa. Episcopalian. Home: 10805 Tara Rd Potomac MD 20854-1341 Address: Johns Island 1000 Beach Rd 690 Ocean Rd & 10656 Eton Way Windsor Vero Beach FL 32963-3429 Office Phone: 202-414-9258. Business E-Mail: ppeter@reedsmith.com.

**PETER, RICHARD ECTOR,** zoology educator, dean; b. Medicine Hat, Alta., Can., Mar. 7, 1943; s. Arthur E. and Josephine (Wrobleski) P.; m. Leona L. Booth, Dec. 27, 1965; children: Jason E., Matthew T.B. BSc with honors, U. Atla., 1965; PhD, U. Wash., 1969. Postdoctoral fellow U. Bristol, Eng., 1969-70; asst. prof. U. Alta., Edmonton, 1971-74, assoc. prof., 1974-79, prof., 1979—, chmn. dept. zoology, 1983—92, dean of sci., 1992—2002; v.p. Alta. Rsch. Coun., 2002—04; CEO, Inst. for Food and Agrl. Scis. Alta., 2005; dir. Bamfield Marine Scis. Ctr., 2006—. Contbr. over 300 papers to sci. publs. Recipient Outstanding Leadership in Alberta Sci. award Alberta Sci. and Tech. Leadership Awards Found., 1998, Excellence in Mentoring award U. Alberta, 2002; named Disting. Biologist, Can. Coun. Univ. Biology Chairmen. Fellow AAAS, Royal Soc. Can.; mem. Can. Soc. Zoology (pres. 1991-92), Endocrine Soc., Internat. Soc. Neuroendocrinology, Can. Coun. of Univ. Biology Chmn. (pres. 1986-87), Internat. Fedn. Comparative Endocrinol. Socs. (pres. 1989-93, Pickford medal 1985), Canadian Conf. of Deans of Sci., 1995-96 (pres.), Western Can. Univs. Marine Scis. Soc. (pres. 2001-02). Office Phone: 780-492-5685. Business E-Mail: dick.peter@ualberta.ca.

**PETERA, ANNE PAPPAS,** state official; b. Richmond, Va., Feb. 13, 1950; d. Evangel Thomas and Margaret Theresa (McGuire) Pappas; m. Ronald Petera, Sept. 15, 1968; 1 child, Paul Evangel. BS, Va. Commonwealth U., 1980; grad., Realtors Inst. Br. officer Cent. Fidelity Bank, Richmond, 1972-79; asst. v.p. Signet Bank, Richmond, 1979-85; sales assoc. Hermitage Realty, Richmond, 1985-92; assoc. broker Napier Old Colony, Richmond, 1992-95, Bowers, Nelms & Fonville & Jefferson-Jones, Richmond, 1995-96; chair Va. Dept. Alcoholic Beverage Control, 1996-97; sec. Commonwealth of Va.,

1998–2002; chief of staff to Atty. Gen. of Va., 2002—. Mem. faculty Richmond Assn. Realtors Sch. Real Estate, 1991-96; bd. visitors Va. Commonwealth U., 2001-04, vice rector, 2003-04. Vice-chmn. Hanover (Va.) County Rep. Com., 1990-92, chmn., 1992-94; chmn. 1st Congl. Dist., Rep. Party Va., Richmond, 1994-98, budget dir., 1996-98, treas. 1998-2001; mem. Rep. Nat. Com., 2001—. Named Disting. Achiever, Richmond Assn. Realtors, 1986, 87, 89, 90, 91, 92, 93, 94. Mem. Nat. Alcohol Beverage Control Assn. (dir. 1996-98), Nat. Assn. Realtors, Nat. Assn. Bank Women. Republican. Roman Catholic. Avocations: golf, reading, travel. Office: Office of the Atty Gen 900 E Main St Richmond VA 23219-2725 E-mail: annepetera@aol.com.

**PETERAF, MARGARET ANN,** strategic management and organization educator; d. Stephen Peteraf and Wanda Romanska; m. Paul Jacob Wolfson, Aug. 4, 1984; children: Jesse Peteraf Wolfson, Sarah Peteraf. MA, Yale U., New Haven, Conn., 1981, MPhil, 1982, PhD in Econs., 1987. Asst. prof. Kellogg Sch., Northwestern U., Evanston, Ill., 1987—94, vis. asst. prof., rsch. assoc., 1994—96; assoc. prof. U. Minn., Mpls., 1996—2000, Tuck Sch., Dartmouth U., Hanover, NH, 2000—05; prof. strategic mgmt. and orgn. Tuck. Sch. Bus., Dartmouth U., Hanover, 2005—. Assoc. prof. U. of Minn. Minneapolis, Minn., 1996—2000, Tuck Sch. at Dartmouth, Hanover, NH, 2000—05; prof. of strategic mgmt. and orgn. Tuck Sch. of Bus. at Dartmouth, Hanover, NH, 2005—. Author: (book) Dynamic Capabilities: Understanding Strategic Change in Organizations; contbr. articles to profl. jours. (SMJ Best Paper prize, 1999). Recipient Strathcona Fellowship for Transp. Studies, Yale U., 1982—83, Yale U. grad. fellowships in econs., 1979—83; fellow Rsch. Fellowship Eno Found. for Transp., Yale U., 1985. Mem.: Acad. Mgmt. (program chair bus. policy and strategy divsn. 2002—03, divsn. chair bus. policy and strategy divsn. 2004—05), Strategic Mgmt. Soc. (chair competitive strategy interest group 2003—05). Office: Dartmouth U Tuck Sch Bus 100 Tuck Hall Hanover NH 03755 Office Phone: 603-646-1944.

**PETERLE, TONY JOHN,** zoologist, educator; b. Cleve., July 7, 1925; s. Anton and Anna (Katic) P.; m. Thelma Josephine Coleman, July 30, 1949; children: Ann Faulkner, Tony Scott. BS, Utah State U., 1949; MS, U. Mich., 1950, PhD (univ. scholar), 1954; Fulbright scholar, U. Aberdeen, Scotland, 1954-55; postgrad., Oak Ridge Inst. Nuclear Studies, 1961. With Niederhauser Lumber Co., 1947—49, Macfarland Tree Svc., 1949—51; rsch. biologist Mich. Dept. Conservation, 1951—54; asst. dir. Rose Lake Expt. Sta., 1955—59; leader Ohio Coop. Wildlife Rsch. unit U.S. Fish and Wildlife Svc., Dept. Interior, 1959—63; asso. prof., then prof. zoology Ohio State U., Columbus, 1959—89, prof. emeritus, 1989, chmn. faculty population and environ. biology, 1968—69, chmn. dept. zoology, 1969—81, dir. program in environ. biology, 1970—71; liaison officer Internat. Union Game Biologists, 1965—93; chmn. internat. affairs com., mem. com., ecotoxicology coorganizer XIII Internat. Congress Game Biology, 1979—80; propr. The Iron Works, 1989—. Pvt. cons., 1989—; mem. com. rev. EPA pesticide decision making Nat. Acad. Scis.-NRC; mem. vis. scientists program Am. Inst. Biol. Scis.-ERDA, 1971-77; mem. com. pesticides Nat. Acad. Scis., com. on emerging trends in agr. and effects on fish and wildlife; mem. ecology com. of sci. adv. council EPA, 1979-87; mem. research units coordinating com. Ohio Coop. Wildlife and Fisheries, 1963-89; vis. scientist EPA, Corvallis, 1987. Author: Wildlife Toxicology, 1991; editor: Jour. of Wildlife Mgmt., 1969-70, 84-85, 2020 Vision Meeting the Fish and Wildlife Conservation Challenges of the 21st Century, 1992. Served with AUS, 1943-46. Named Internat. Scientists of Yr., 2002. Fellow AAAS, Am. Inst. Biol. Scis., Ohio Acad. Sci.; mem. Wildlife Disease Assn., Wildlife Soc. (regional rep. 1962-67, v.p. 1968, pres. 1972, Leopold award 1990, hon. mem. 1990, Profl. award of merit North Ctrl. sect. 1993), Nat. Audubon Soc. (bd. dirs. 1985-87), Ecol. Soc., INTECOL-NSF panel U.S.-Japan Program, Xi Sigma Pi, Phi Kappa Phi. Home: 4072 Klondike Rd Delaware OH 43015-9513 Office: Ohio State U Dept Ecology Evolution and Organismal Bi 1735 Neil Ave Columbus OH 43210-1220

**PETERMAN, DONNA COLE,** communications executive; b. St. Louis, Nov. 9, 1947; d. William H. Cole and Helen A. Morris; m. John A. Peterman, Feb. 7, 1970. BA in Journalism, U. Mo., 1969; MBA, U. Chgo., 1984. Mgr. employee comm. Sears Merchandise Group, Chgo., 1975-80; affairs and mktg. comm. Seraco Real Estate, Chgo., 1980-82; dir. corp. comm. Sears, Roebuck and Co., Chgo., 1982-85; sr. v.p., dir. corp. comm. Dean Witter Fin. Svcs. Group, N.Y., 1985-88; sr. v.p., mng. dir. Hill and Knowlton, Inc., Chgo., 1988-94; exec. v.p. N.Y.C., 1994-96; sr. v.p., dir. corp. comm. Paine Webber Group, Inc., N.Y.C., 1996-2000; mng. dir., regional head comms. and mktg. The Americas, UBS Americas Inc., 2000—03; sr. v.p., dir. corp. comm. PNC Fin. Svcs. Group Inc., 2003—. Media chair DeKalb County Comm., Ga., 1975; media dir. Mo. Atty. Gen., 1971, Rep. Govs. Conf., 1974; copywriter Govt. of Mo., 1971. Chmn. bd. trustees Securities Industry Found. for Investor Edn. Mem. Pub. Rels. Soc. Am., Arthur Page Soc., Pub. Rels. Seminar, Edgewood Country Club, Palmetto Pines Country Club, The Wise Men. Republican. Roman Catholic. Avocations: tennis, golf, sailing, skiing, bridge. Office: The PNC Fin Svcs Group Inc 1 PNC Plaza 249 5th Ave Pittsburgh PA 15222-2707

**PETERMANN, HANS JÜRGEN,** research scientist; b. Vienna, Feb. 2, 1942; MA in German, Calif. State U., 1971; PhD in Physics, 2d Phys. Inst., Vienna, Austria, 1976; PhD in Botany (hon.), Bot. Inst., Berlin, Germany, 1980. Prof. phys. scis. Coll. of Desert, Palm Desert, Calif.; rsch. scientist Palm Springs, Calif., 1991—. Chmn., sr. v.p. Galaxy Energy Sys., Inc. Author: The Esoteric Sciences Vol. 1, 2d edit., 2001, The Esoteric Curiosities of Plant Kingdom Vol. 1, 2d edit., 2003, The Esoteric Sciences Vol. 2, 2003, Gravitation, Matter and Space Travel, 3d edit., 2006. With U.S. Army, 1963—66. Achievements include development of magnetic generator-motor; advanced turbine-generator-motor; patents in field. Avocations: hiking, tennis, scuba diving, mountain climbing, swimming. Office: PO Box 4513 Palm Springs CA 92263-4513 Office Phone: 760-778-4254.

**PETERS, ALAN,** anatomy educator; b. Nottingham, Eng., Dec. 6, 1929; came to U.S., 1966; s. Robert and Mabel (Woplington) P.; m. Verona Muriel Shipman, Sept. 30, 1955; children: Ann Verona, Sally Elizabeth, Susan Clare. BSc, Bristol U., Eng., 1951, PhD, 1954. Lectr. anatomy Edinburgh (Scotland) U., 1958-66; vis. lectr. Harvard, 1963-64; prof., chmn. dept. anatomy and neurobiology Boston U., 1966-98, Waterhouse prof., 1998—. Anatomy com. Nat. Bd. Med. Examiners, 1971-75; mem. neurology B Study sect. NIH, 1975-79, chmn., 1978-79; affiliate scientist Yerkes Regional Primate Rsch. Ctr., 1984—. Author (with S.L. Palay and H. deF Webster): The Fine Structure of the Nervous System, 1970, The Fine Structure of the Nervous System, 3rd edit., 1991; author: Myelination, 1970; mem. editl. bd.: Anat. Record, 1972—81, Jour. Comparative Neurology, 1981—97, Neurocytology, 1972—89, 1993—, Cerebral Cortex, 1990—2005, Studies of Brain Function, Anat. and Embryology, 1989—92; editor (with E.G. Jones): (book series) Cerebral Cortex, 1984—2000; exec. prodr.(with R. Payne): Cat Visual Cortex, 2001; contbr. articles to profl. jours. Served to 2d lt. Royal Army Med. Corps, 1955-57. Recipient Henry Gray award, 1998, Sanford L. Palay award Jour. Comparative Neurology, 2004; grantee NIH, 1986. Mem. Anat. Soc. Gt. Britain and Ireland (Symington prize anatomy 1962, overseas mem. coun. 1969), Assn. Anatomy Chmn. (pres. 1976-77), Am. Anat. Assn. (exec. com. 1986-90, pres. 1992-93, Henry Gray award 1998), Am. Soc. Cell Biology, Soc. Neuroscis., Internat. Primatological Soc., Cajal Club (Harman lectr. 1990, Cortical Discoverer award 1991). Home: 16 High Rock Cir Waltham MA 02451-2207 Office: Boston U Sch Medicine Dept Anatomy and Neurobiology 80 E Concord St Roxbury MA 02118-2307 Office Phone: 617-638-4235.

**PETERS, BARBARA WATERMAN,** artist, educator; b. Topeka, Nov. 3, 1944; d. L.E. Clifton Bailey and Gertrude Minnie McFarland; m. John Herman Waterman, Dec. 21, 1965 (div. Dec. 1985); m. Larry Dean Peters, May 30, 1986. BFA, Washburn U., 1973; MFA, Kans. State U., 1998. Adj. instr. Washburn U., Topeka, 1985—88, adj. asst. prof., 1989—96, 1999—2001; grad. tchg. asst. Kans. State U., Manhattan, 1997—19, temporary asst. prof., 2004—, asst. prof. painting, 2004—05. Mus. specialist ednl.

svcs. Mulvane Art Mus., Topeka, 1987; faculty advisor Washburn Art Students Assn., Topeka, 1994-96; guest curator Water Marks exhbn. Mulvane Art Mus., Topeka, 1995-96; exhbn. juror in field; spkr., reviewer in field. One-woman shows include Bedyk Gallery, Kansas City, Mo., 1983, 88, Collective Art Gallery, Topeka, 1988-90, 96-97, 1999-2000, 2002-2004, 2006, Yost Gallery-Highland (Kans.) C.C., 1989, 95, Art Craft Gallery, Denver, 1994-95, 97, Fourth St. Gallery, Kansas City, 1997, Michael Cross Gallery, Kansas City, 1999-2000, Wichita Ctr. Arts, 2001, Kanas Artist Gallery, Mulvane Art Mus., 2002; group shows include Holman Art Gallery-Trenton State Coll., 1979, N.Mex. Art League, Albuquerque, 1980, Nat. Soc. Painters, N.Y., 1980 (Michael Engle Meml. award), Ball State U. Art Gallery, Muncie, Ind., 1981, Portsmouth (Va.) Cmty. Ctr., 1982, Nelson-Atkins Mus., Kansas City, 1982, Owensboro (Ky.) Mus. Fine Art, 1982 (award), Joslyn Art Mus., Omaha, 1988, others, Women's Conf., Beijing, 1995, Jan Weiner Gallery, Kansas City, 1995, The Columbian Art Gallery, Wamego, Kans., 1997, 2002, Topeka and Shawnee County Pub. Libr., 1997, 2002, 05, Strecker Gallery, Manhattan, Kans., 1999-2000, Cedar Rapids (Iowa) Mus. Art, 1997, Wichita Ctr. for the Arts, 2000, 02, Birger Sandzen Gallery, Lindsborg, Kans., 2001, 2006, U. Kans. Art and Design Gallery, 2002, Strecker-Nelson Gallery, Manhattan, Kans., 2002, 05, 06, Mulvane Art Mus., Topeka, 2003, Emporia Art Ctr., Kans., 2003, Gallery of Framewoods, Topeka, 2004, 05, Kemper Gallery, Kans. State U., 2005, Ctrl. Mo. State U., 2006, Nat. League Am. PEN Women, 2006, Foundry Art Centre, St. Charles, Mo., 2006 (award), Kans./Mo. Artists, Carter Art Ctr., Kansas City, Mo., 2006; visual artist Andrew J. and Georgia Neese Gray Theatre, Washburn U., 1999—; contbr. articles to profl. jours. Vol. art gallery Topeka and Shawnee County Pub. Libr. 1986—; panelist Kans. Arts Commn., Kans. Presswomen, 1990—, N.E. Kans. Music Tchrs. Assn./Topeka Music Tchrs. Assn., 2004; mem. ad hoc com. Kans. Arts Commn., 2002—04, mem. fellowship selection panel, 2004, mem. arts in edn. grants selection panel, 2006; mem. ad hoc com. Topeka Cmty. Found., 2002—03; bd. dirs. Arts Coun. Topeka, 2002—. Recipient Outstanding Achievement award, Am. Inst. Banking, Topeka, 1977, assistantship in lithography, Kans. Arts Commn., 1981, Woman of Distinction in the Arts award, Kaw Valley Girl Scouts, Topeka, 1996, Artist's Residency award, The Raymer Soc., 2001—04, Cert. of Recognition Outstanding Contributions, State Kans., 2003. Mem.: Kemper Mus. Contemporary Art, Am. Arts Action Fund, Nat. League Am. PEN Women, Birger Sandzén Meml. Gallery, Am. Craft Coun., Manhattan Arts Ctr., Assn. Cmty. Arts Agys. of Kans. (bd. dir. 2004—06, sec.-treas. 2006—), Lawrence Art Ctr., The Collective (charter, treas. 1987—89, v.p 1990—94, 1999—2000, newsletter editor 2000—, pres. 2001—06), Mulvane Art Mus., St. Louis Artists Guild, Kansas City Artists Coalition, Chgo. Artists' Coalition, Nat. Mus. Women in the Arts, Raymer Soc. (bd. dir.), Kans. Authors' Club (conv. workshop presenter 2004, selection com. J. Donald Coffin award 2004—05, v.p. dist. 1 2005—, pres. dist. 1 2006), Kans. Citizens for Arts, Libr. Friends of Art Topeka and Shawnee County Pub. Libr., Friends of Art Bd. Beach Mus. Art (collections com. 1997—), Catharine Lorillard Wolfe Art Club (assoc.). Avocations: reading, writing, travel. Home: 2223 SW Knollwood Dr Topeka KS 66611-1623 E-mail: barbara.r.peters@att.net.

**PETERS, BERNADETTE (BERNADETTE LAZZARA),** actress; b. Queens, N.Y., Feb. 28, 1948; d. Peter and Marguerite (Maltese) Lazzara; m. Michael Wittenberg, July 20, 1996 (dec. Sept. 26, 2005). Student, Quintano Sch. for Young Profls., N.Y. 2d. actress, entertainer, 1957—. Appeared on TV series All's Fair, 1976-77; frequent guest appearances on TV; (films) The Longest Yard, 1974, Silent Movie, 1976, Vigilant Force, 1976, W.C. Fields and Me, 1976, Silent Movie, 1976, The Jerk, 1979, Heartbeeps, 1981, Tulips, 1981, Pennies from Heaven, 1981 (Golden Globe award best actress), Annie, 1982, Slaves of New York, 1989, Pink Cadillac, 1989, Impromptu, 1991, Alice, 1990, Anastasia (voice), 1997, Cinderella, 1997, Snow Days, 1999, Prince Charming, 2001, Bobbie's Girl, 2002, A Few Good Years, 2002, It Runs in the Family, 2003; (TV movies) Cinderella, ABC-TV, 1997, Holiday in Your Heart, 1997; (stage appearances) This is Google, 1957, The Most Happy Fella, 1959, Gypsy, 1961, Curly McDimple, 1967, Johnny No-Trump, 1967, George M!, 1968 (Theatre World award, 1968), Dames at Sea, 1968 (Drama Desk award, 1968), La Strada, 1969, On the Town, 1971, Tartuffe, 1972, Mack and Mabel, 1974, Sally and Marsha, 1982, Sunday in the Park with George, 1983-85 (Tony nom., 1983), Song and Dance, 1985-86 (Drama League award best actress, 1985, Tony award best actress, 1986, Drama Desk award best actress, 1986), Into the Woods, 1987, The Goodbye Girl, 1992-93, Annie Get Your Gun 1998-1999 (Tony award best actress, 1999, Outer Critics Circle award best actress, 1999, Drama Desk award best actress, 1999), Gypsy, 2003; TV mini-series The Odyssey, 1997; rec. artist: (MCA Records) Bernadette Peters, 1980, Now Playing, 1981; CD's include I'll Be Your Baby Tonight, Angel Records, 1996 (Grammy nomination), Sondheim Etc: Bernadette Peters Live at Carnegie Hall, Angel Records, 1997 (Grammy nom.), solo concert Radio City Music Hall, 2002. Founder Ann. Broadway Barks fundraiser. Recipient Hasty Pudding Theatrical award, 1987 Woman of Yr. award, Sara Siddons Actress of Yr. award, 1993-94, Actors Fund medal for artistic achievement, 1999, NYC Parks Citizen award, 2006; named Woman of Yr., Police Athletic League, 1999; named to Theatre Hall of Fame. Office: William Morris Agency c/o Jeff Hunter 1325 Ave of the Americas 15th Fl New York NY 10019*

**PETERS, CAROL ANN,** secondary school educator; b. Ashtabula, Ohio, Feb. 12, 1946; d. Leonard Jay and Anniece Edna Hawkins; m. Robert Lewis Peters, June 12, 1971; children: Brian Jay, Sharon Lynne. BS in Edn., Kent State U., 1968; ESL cert., U. Houston, 1990; postgrad., S.W. Tex. State U., 1999—, Cert. secondary edn. Tex. Tchr. Fairport (Ohio) Exp Village Sch. Dist., 1968—71; substitute tchr. Spring Branch Ind. Sch. Dist., Houston, 1972—74, tchr., 1987—93; substitute tchr. San Marcos (Tex.) Ind. Sch. Dist., 1993—94; tchr. Wackenhut Corrections Corp., Lockhart Tex, 1994—96; tutor, mem. Village School, Maxwell, Tex., 1998—; tchr. cons. Nat. Evaluation Sys., Inc., Austin, Tex., 2000—. Mem. San Marcos H.S. campus improvement team San Marcos Cons. Ind. Sch. Dist., 1999—2002, mem. facilities task force, 2000—02. Troop leader, svc. unit officer Girl Scouts USA, Houston, 1981—93; organizer Ann. Promise Youth Summit City of San Marcos, Tex., 1998—99, youth commr., 1998—. Mem.: NEA, TESOL, Internat. Dyslexia Assn., San Marcos Area and Hispanic C. of C. (edn. com.), Tex. PTA (life), Lions Internat. (youth outreach chair). Roman Catholic. Avocations: bridge, playing piano and organ, camping, landscaping, writing. Home: 36 Mill St Maxwell TX 78656 Office: Village Sensei 36 Mill St Maxwell TX 78656

**PETERS, CAROL ANN DUDYCHA,** counselor; b. Ripon, Wis., Dec. 23, 1938; d. George John and Martha (Malek) Dudycha; m. Milton Eugene Peters, Aug. 27, 1960 AB, Wittenberg U., 1960, MEd, 1963; leadership devel. cert., Ctr. for Creative Leadership, Greensboro, N.C., 1986; postgrad., U. Toledo, 1973—97, U. Findlay, 1997—99. Lic. profl. counselor, Ohio; nat. cert. counselor, nat. cert. career counselor Nat. Bd. Cert. Counselors, Inc.; cert. basic critical incident stress mgmt. Internat. Critical Incident Stress Found., 1999. Tchr. Springfield City Schs., Ohio, 1960—62, Mad River-Green Local Schs., Springfield, 1962—63; counselor Napoleon Area Schs., Ohio, 1963—70, Findlay City Schs., Ohio, 1970—2000; field counselor Career Relocation Corp. Am., Armonk, 1992—95, 1998—99; sr. lectr. U. Findlay, 1999—2002. Cons., prin. Peters and Findlay, 1979—; leader Creative Edn. Found., Buffalo, 1980-91, colleague, Hadley, Mass., 1985—; founder adult. corp. Career Info. Bur. Hancock County, 1974 Pres. Big Bros./Big Sisters Hancock County, 1982-83; bd. dirs. Citizens Opposing Drug Abuse, Findlay, 1982-2005; advisor, leader Hancock Addictions Prevention for Youth, 1985-91; edn. com. Hancock County Cmty. Devel. Found., 1990-93, Findlay/Hancock County Am. 2000 New Sch. Design Team, 1991-92; mem. Hancock County Crisis Response Team, 1991-97, 99—; assets/needs assessment com. United Way, 1997-98; mem. Findlay Juvenile Diversion Task Force, 1997-98; mem. City of Findlay Mayor's Cmty. Issues Visioning Com., 2004-05 Named One of Outstanding Young Women Am., 1967, Outstanding Woman in Edn., Bus. and Profl. Women, 1983; recipient Outstanding Citizenship award The Lincoln Ctr., Findlay, 1989; Meritorious Svc. award Big Bros./Big Sisters Hancock County, 1988 Mem. ACA, AAUW, NEA (life), Nat. Career Devel. Assn., Ohio Ret. Tchrs. Assn. (life), Ohio

Counseling Assn., Findlay-Hancock County C. of C. (sec. edn. com. 1984-90), Ohio Career Devel. Assn., Black Studies and Libr. Assn. (trustee 2005—, sec. bd. trustees 2006—) Lutheran. Avocations: flower arranging, cooking.

**PETERS, CHARLES H.R.,** lawyer; BS magna cum laude, Miami U., 1982; JD cum laude, Northwestern U., 1986. Bar: Ill. 1986, U.S. Dist. Ct. No. Ill. 1986, U.S. Ct. Appeals 7th cir. 1992, U.S. Supreme Ct. 2001. Ptnr. Schiff Hardin, Chgo. Mem.: ABA, Chgo. Council Lawyers. Office: Schiff Hardin 6600 Sears Tower Chicago IL 60606-6473

**PETERS, CHARLES WILLIAM,** nuclear energy industry executive; b. Pierceton, Ind., Dec. 9, 1927; s. Charles Frederick and Zelda May (Line) Peters; m. Katharine Louise Schuman, May 29, 1953; 1 child, Susan Kay; m. Patricia Ann Miles, Jan. 2, 1981; stepchildren: Bruce Miles Merkle, Leslie Ann Merkle Sanaie, Philip Frank Merkle, William Macneil Merkle. AB, Ind. U., 1950; postgrad., U. Md., 1952-54. Supervisory rsch. physicist Naval Rsch. Lab., Washington, 1950—71; physicist EPA, Washington, 1971—76; mgr. advanced sys. EATON-Consol. Controls Corp., Springfield, Va., 1976—89; v.p. Nuc. Diagnostic Sys., Inc., Springfield, Va., 1989—92; cons. Am. Tech. Inst., Tucson, 1993—. With U.S. Army, 1945—47. Mem.: AAAS, IEEE, Am. Phys. Soc. Home and Office: 5235 N Whispering Hills Ln Tucson AZ 85704-2510

**PETERS, CONNIE JANE,** librarian, media specialist; b. Decatur, Ill., Oct. 21, 1949; d. Sylvester Thomas and Kathryn Harriet (Wittig) Peters. BA in History, Millikin U., 1971; MA in History, Sangamon State U., 1972; MS in Libr. Sci., Ea. Ill. U., 1973, Edn. Specialist degree in Inst. Media, 1985; Basic Cert. in Electronics, Richland C.C., 1992. Cert. elem.and secondary tchr. Ill. Grad. asst. Ea. Ill. U., Charleston, Ill., 1972—73; instr. media ctr. libr. Decatur Pub. Schs., 1974—76; libr. St. Teresa H.S., Decatur, 1976—77; media specialist Thomas Jefferson Mid. Sch., Decatur, 1978, Cerro Gordo Unit Schs., Ill., 1980—81, St. Teresa H.S., Decatur, 1982—92; instrnl. media specialist Stephen Decatur H.S., Decatur, 1995—2000; tchr. social studies MacArthur H.S., Decatur, 2000—01, Mound Mid. Sch., Decatur, 2001—04; libr. Eisenhower H.S., Decatur, 2004—. Mem. NEA, Ill. Edn. Assn., Decatur Edn. Assn., bd. dirs., secondary dir., membership com.), Ill. Assn. for Ednl. Comms. and Tech., Ill. Sch. Libr. and Media Assn., Ill. Computing Educators, Ill. State Hist. Soc., Foursquare Gospel. Pentecostal. Avocations: photography, stamp collecting/philately, coin collecting/numismatics, web page design. Office Phone: 217-424-3104. Personal E-mail: conniepeters@juno.com. E-mail: cpeters@dps61.org.

**PETERS, DAVID ALLEN,** mechanical engineering educator, consultant; b. East St. Louis, Ill., Jan. 31, 1947; s. Bernell Louis and Marian Louise (Blum) P.; children: Michael H., Laura A., Nathan C. BS in Applied Mechanics, Washington U., St. Louis, 1969, MS in Applied Mechanics, 1970; PhD in Aeros. and Astronautics, Stanford U., 1974. Assoc. engr. McDonnell Astronautics, 1969-70; rsch. scientist Army Aeronautics Lab., 1970-74; asst. prof. Washington U., 1975-77, assoc. prof., 1977-80, prof. mech. engring., 1980-85, chmn. dept., 1982-85; prof. aerospace engring. Ga. Inst Tech., Atlanta, 1985-91; dir. NASA Space Grant Consortium Ga. Inst. Tech., Atlanta, 1989-91; dir. Ctr. for Computational Mechanics Washington U., 1992—, prof. dept. mech. engring. St. Louis, 1991—, chmn. dept. mech. engring., 1997—, McDonnell Douglas prof. engring., 1999. Contbr. 150 articles to profl. jours. Recipient sci. contbn. award NASA, 1975, 76. Fellow AIAA, ASME, Am. Acad. Mechanics, Am. Helicopter Soc. (jour. editor 1987-90); mem. Am. Soc. for Engring. Edn., Internat. Assn. for Computational Mechanics (charter), Tau Sigma (gold medal 1978). Baptist. Home: 7629 Balson Ave Saint Louis MO 63130-2150 Office: Wash U Dept Mech Engr Campus Box 1185 Saint Louis MO 63130 Office Phone: 314-935-4337. Business E-Mail: dap@me.wustl.edu.

**PETERS, DENNIS GAIL,** chemist; b. L.A., Apr. 17, 1937; s. Samuel and Phyllis Dorothy (Pope) P. BS cum laude, Calif. Inst. Tech., 1958; PhD, Harvard U., 1962. Mem. faculty Ind. U., 1962—, prof. chemistry, 1974—, Herman T. Briscoe prof., 1975—. Co-author textbooks, contbr. articles to profl. jours. Woodrow Wilson fellow, 1958-59; NIH predoctoral fellow, 1959-62; vis. fellow Japan Soc. for Promotion Sci., 1980; recipient Ulysses G. Weatherly award disting. teaching Ind. U., 1969, Disting. Teaching award Coll. Arts and Scis. Grad. Alumni Assn. Ind. U., 1984, Nat. Catalyst award for Disting. Teaching Chem. Mfrs. Assn., 1988, Henry B. Linford award The Electrochem. Soc., 2002; grantee NSF. Fellow Ind. Acad. Sci., Am. Inst. Chemists; mem. ACS (grantee, Div. of Analytical Chemistry award for excellence in teaching 1990, James Flack Norris award 2001). Home: 1401 S Nancy St Bloomington IN 47401-6051 Office: Dept Chemistry Ind U Bloomington IN 47405 Office Phone: 812-855-9671. Business E-Mail: peters@indiana.edu.

**PETERS, DOUGLAS ALAN,** risk management consultant; b. Portsmouth, Va., Oct. 4, 1968; s. Terrance Gene and Pamela (Haffner) P. BA in Philosophy, Va. Poly. Inst. and State U., 1992; BSN summa cum laude, James Madison U., 1995; JD, U. Md., Balt., 2003. RN Md.; cert. case mgr., legal nurse cons. Photojournalist CVNI/The Greene County Record, Stanardsville, Va., 1992; nursing asst. Rockingham Meml. Hosp., Harrisonburg, Va., 1993-95; clin. nurse Bapt. Hosp., Pensacola, Fla., 1995-96; nurse mgr. quality assurance Escambia County Jail Infirmary, Pensacola, 1996-97; case mgr./U.R. Total Health Care, Balt., 1997-98; case mgr. Blue Cross/Blue Shield of Md., Balt., 1998-2000, appeals analyst, 2000—01, sr. appeals analyst, 2001—04; jud. law clk. 23d Jud. Cir., W.Va., 2004—05. Legal cons. CareFirst, 2005, Blue Cross Blue Shield, 2005 Vol. templer unit Rockingham Meml. Hosp., 1994-95; vol. Tourette Syndrome Assn., 1996-2000, Alley Cat Allies. Mem.: ABA (health law sect.), Am. Soc. Healthcare Risk Mgmt., Am. Assn. Nurse Attys., Montgomery County Med. Res. Corps, Am. Assn. Legal Nurse Cons., Md. State Bar Assn., Montgomery County Bar Assn., Alley Cat Allies, Phi Alpha Delta, Sigma Theta Tau, Alpha Chi Sigma. Avocations: Civil War history, darts, photography. Office Phone: 301-639-4776. E-mail: dapeters2004@yahoo.com.

**PETERS, DOUGLAS SCOTT,** health care executive; b. Columbus, Ohio, Nov. 2, 1943; s. Edward Alvin and Jane (Appleman) P.; m. Karen Ann Jones, June 19, 1965; children: Brian Edward, Laura Kathleen. BS, Ohio State U., 1965; MHA with distinction, U. Mich., 1967. Assoc. dir. U. Mich. Hosp., Ann Arbor, 1969-74; dir. U. Nebr. Hosps. and Clinics, Omaha, 1974-77; exec. dir. Henry Ford Hosp., Detroit, 1977-83, pres. ceo, 1983-91; v.p. Henry Ford Healthcare Corp., Detroit, 1983-87; pres. ceo Main Line Health, 1991—. Cons. PanAm. Health Orgn., Washington, 1971-73; asst. prof. dept. med. and ednl. adminstrn. U. Nebr., 1974-77. Bd. dirs. New Detroit, Inc., 1985—; co-chmn. Multiple Sclerosis Testimonial Dinner, Detroit, 1985; big bro. Big Bros./Big Sisters, Omaha, 1975. Served to lt. USNR, 1967-69. Fellow Am. Coll. Healthcare Execs. (regent 1984); mem. Young Pres. Orgn., Mich Hosp. Assn. (bd. dirs.), Frontiers in Health Services Mgmt. (mem. editorial bd. 1983), mem. The Pennsylvania Soc, Amer. Hosp. Assoc. Regency Policy Bd, Foster G. McGaw Prize Review Panel, AHA, 1989-; Katahdin Medical and Philosophical Soc., 1992-; Amer. Healthcare Sys. Risk Purchasing Grp, 1993-; Amer. Healthcare Sys. Insur. Assoc., 1993-; bd of dirs: Healthshare Inc., 1988-; Amer. Healthcare Sys., 1991-; The Philadelphia Contributionship, 1992-; Amer. Red Cross, 1992-; First Fidelity Bank, 1994-; Radnor Education Found., 1994-; Amer. Heart Assoc., 1995. Republican. Office: Main Line Health 130 S Bryn Mawr Ave Bryn Mawr PA 19010-3121

**PETERS, EDWARD MURRAY,** history professor; b. New Haven; BA, Yale U., 1963, MA, 1965, PhD, 1967. Instr. English and history Quinnipiac Coll., Hamden, Conn., 1964-67; asst. prof. history U. Calif., San Diego, 1967-68, U. Pa., Phila., 1968-70, assoc. prof., 1970-76; Henry Charles Lea prof. history, 1981—; curator Henry Charles Lea Library, 1968—; vis. prof. Cath. U. Leuven, Belgium, 1992, 2004. Vis. prof. history Yale U., 1998, 2001-02. Author: The Shadow King, 1970; author: (with A.C. Kors) Witchcraft in Europe, 1100-1750, 1972, 2d edit., 2000; author: Europe: The World of the

Middle Ages, 1977, The Magician, The Witch and The Law, 1978, Europe and the Middle Ages, 1983, 4th edit., 2003, Torture, 1985, expanded edit., 1996, Inquisition, 1988, Limits of Thought and Power in Medieval Europe, 2001, (TV series) The World of the Middle Ages, 1974, The World Around the Revolution, 1977, also articles, revs. and introductions; editor, transl. (series) The Middle Ages, 1970—95, (with Jeanne Krochalis) The World of Piers Plowman, 1975; editor: Heresy and Authority in Medieval Europe, 1980. Served with AUS, 1956-59. Woodrow Wilson fellow, 1963-64, dissertation fellow, 1966-67, hon. Sterling fellow, 1966-67, ACLS fellow, 1981-82, Guggenheim fellow, 1988-89. Fellow Medieval Acad. Am., Royal Hist. Soc.; mem. Am. Hist. Assn., Medieval Acad. Am., Am. Soc. Legal History, Maiestas, Iuris Canonici Medii Aevi Consociatio, Soc. Jean Bodin, Dante Soc. Am., Renaissance Soc. Am. Office: U Pa Dept History Philadelphia PA 19104-6228 E-mail: empeters@sas.upenn.edu.

**PETERS, ELIZABETH,** media organization director; Degree in film, U. Tex. Dir. Austin (Tex.) Film Soc., 1995—98; exec. dir. Assn. Ind. Video and Filmmakers, Inc., N.Y.C., 1999—; pub. The Ind. Film & Video Monthly, 1999—. Tchr. prodn. classes. Prodr., dir. Women's Action Coalition, asst. editor (documentary) The Maine Coast, (feature film) Office Space. Office: Assn Ind Video & Filmmakers Inc 304 Hudson St 6th Fl N New York NY 10013 Business E-mail: elizabeth@aivf.org.

**PETERS, ELLEN ASH,** retired judge; b. Berlin, Mar. 21, 1930; arrived in U.S., 1939, naturalized, 1947; d. Ernest Edward and Hildegard (Simon) Ash; m. Phillip I. Blumberg; children: David Bryan, James Douglas, Julie Haden Dreisch. BA with honors, Swarthmore Coll., 1951, LLD (hon.), 1983; LLB cum laude, Yale L., 1954, MA (hon.), 1964, LLD (hon.), 1985. U. Hartford, 1983, Georgetown U., 1984, Conn. Coll., 1985, N.Y. Law Sch., 1985; HLD (hon.), St. Joseph Coll., 1986; LLD (hon.), Colgate U., 1986, Trinity Coll., 1987, Bates Coll., 1987, Wesleyan U., 1987, DePaul U., 1988; HLD (hon.), Albertus Magnus Coll., 1990; LLD (hon.), U. Conn., 1992, U. Rochester, 1994, Detroit Mercy Coll. Law, 2001. Bar: Conn. 1957. Law clk. to judge U.S. Circuit Ct., 1954-55; assoc. in law U. Calif., Berkeley, 1955-56; prof. law Yale U., New Haven, 1956-78, adj. prof., 1978-84; assoc. justice Conn. Supreme Ct., Hartford, 1978-84, chief justice, 1984-96; ret., 1996. Judge trial referee Appellate Ct., Hartford, Conn., 2000—. Author: Commercial Transactions: Cases, Texts, and Problems, 1971, Negotiable Instruments Primer, 1974; contr. articles to profl. jours. Bd. dirs. Nat. Ctr. State Cts., 1992—96, chmn., 1994; bd. mgrs. Swarthmore Coll., 1970—81; trustee Yale-New Haven Hosp., 1981—86, Yale Corp., 1986—92; mem. conf. Chief Justices, 1984—, pres., 1994; hon. chmn. U.S. Constl. Bicentennial Comm., 1986—91; mem. Conn. Permanent Commn. on Status of Women, 1973—74, Conn. Bd. Pardons, 1978—87, Conn. Law Revision Commn., 1978—84; bd. dirs. Hartford Found., 1997—2002. Named Laura A. Johnson Woman of the Yr., Hartford Coll., 1996; recipient Ella Grasso award, 1982, Jud. award, Conn. Trial Lawyers Assn., 1982, citation of merit, Yale Law Sch., 1983, Pioneer Woman award, Hartford Coll. Women, 1988, Disting. Svc. award, U. Conn. Law Sch. Alumni Assn., 1993, Raymond E. Baldwin Pub. Svc. award, Quinnipiac Coll. Law Sch., 1995, Disting. Svc. award, Conn. Law Tribune, 1996, Nat. Ctr. State Cts., 1996. Mem.: ABA, Am. Philos. Coun., Am. Acad. Arts and Scis., Am. Law Inst. (coun.), Conn. Bar Assn. (Jud. award 1992, Spl. award 1996). Office: Appellate Ct 75 Elm St Hartford CT 06106-4431 Office Fax: 860-713-2216.

**PETERS, EVELYN JOAN,** artist; b. Anchorage, Alaska, Mar. 25, 1927; d. Algernon Sidney Jones and R. Lee (Bartholf) Jones-Lange; m. Curtis Gordon Chezem, Sept. 29, 1945 (div. Oct. 1956); children: Joanne Lee Chezem, David Gordon Chezem; m. Frederick William Peters Jr., May 30, 1958. Student, U. Oreg., 1945-50, Oreg. State Coll., 1955-56. Pvt. sec. Pub. Svc. Commn., Las Vegas, Nev., 1957-58; tech. sec. Los Alamos (N.Mex.) Nat. Lab., 1958-70; sr. sec. EG&G, Los Alamos, 1970-71. Chmn. bd. dirs. Buchanan Arts and Crafts, Inc., Buchanan Dam, Tex., 1980, 86. One-woman shows include Frame Corner Gallery, Farmington, 1996, San Juan Coll., 1998, invitational retrospective St. Francis Newman Ctr., Silver City, N.Mex., 1994, exhibited in group shows at Inn of Loretto, Santa Fe, 1982, Capital Rotunda, Austin, Tex., 1983, Golub Gallery, Steamboat Springs, Colo., 1985, Cowtown Invitational, Ft. Worth, 1987, Safari Park Hotel, Nairobi, Kenya, 1990 (Artistic Expressions award, 1990, Gold medal, 1990), St. John's Coll., Cambridge, Eng., 1992 (Bronze medal, 1992), Western N.Mex. U., Silver City, 1993, Sixth Bear River Western Hist. Art Exhbn., Craig, Colo., 1994, Fed. Hall Mus., N.Y.C., 1994, 1997, Ann. COGAP Exhbn., Governor's Island, N.Y., 1994 (George Gray award, 1993), Apples, Aspen and Art, Cedaredge, Colo., 1995 (Most Popular Painting), Western and Wildlife Art Show, Estes Park, Colo., 1995, Sheraton-on-the-Park Hotel, Sydney, Australia, 1995, Colo. Indian Market, Denver, 1995, Art Concepts Gallery, Tacoma, Wash., 1997, Keble Coll., Oxford, Eng., 1997, Sunwest Bank, Farmington, 1997, Rotunda Canon Office Bldg., U.S. Ho. of Reps., Washington, 1997, Alpine Holiday, Ouray, Colo., 1997, 1999, 2000, Durham (Eng.) Art Gallery, 2000, Arts for the Parks, 2000, Williamson Gallery & Mus., Wirral, Eng., 2004, Represented in permanent collections Aviation Heritage Mus., Anchorage, Daystar Found., Oklahoma City, Eleanor Bliss Ctr. Arts, Steamboat Springs, Marble Falls Depot Mus., Mus. N.W. Colo., Craig, Nat. Gallery Rural Art, Bonner Springs, Kans., Pioneer and R.R. Mus., Temple, Tex., San Juan Coll., Farmington, N.Mex., USCG, art, numerous mags., books, calendars and catalogs. Pres. Highland Arts Guild, Marble Falls, Tex., 1977, 90, 2d v.p., 1989; sec. Highland Lakes Arts Coun., Marble Falls, 1986. Recipient Marine Safety award Olin-Matheson, 1968, cert. of appreciation USCG Aux., 1969, 70, 1st and award award Kiwanis Art Competition, Granbury, Tex., 1983, 2d Pl. award Tex. Women Western Artists Show, Cresson, Tex., 1983, 2d and 3d pl. awards Llano Rodeo Art Show, 1986, 1st pl. award 9th Nat. Small Painting Western Show, 1987, 1st and purchase award Gt. Am. Art Competition, 1988, Most Popular Painter award 3d Ann. Invitational Art Show, Waco, Tex., 1988, Best of Show award Bear Valley Hist. Art Show, Craig, 1989, Best of Show, 1st Watercolor, 1st Oil, 1st Sculpture, Highland Lakes Arts Competition, Kingsland, Tex., 1991, Internat. Woman of Yr. in art Internat. Biog. Ctr., 1991-92, Most Popular Painting award Western Colo. Ctr. for Arts, 1996, Purchase award NWNMAC, Farmington, 1997, Purchase award Ouray Coll. 39th Ann. Art Exhibit, 1999, choice award 8th Ann. Nat. Christian Art Show, San Juan Coll., Farmington, N.Mex., 2000, Top 200 Arts for the Parks, 2000, 1st pl. Gateway Regional Art Show, Farmington, N.Mex., 2000, Internat. Peace prize United Cultural Conf., 2003, award NAPA exhbn. Williamson Art Gallery and Mus., Birkhead, Eng., 2004, numerous others Mem. N.W. N.Mex. Arts Coun., Nat. Acrylic Painters Assn. (bd. dirs. 2001-04, invitation cover award 5th Internat. Open Exhibit 2000), World Found. of Successful Women (charter mem.), Internat. Soc. Acrylic Artists (signature mem., bd dirs 2005—, Nat. Oil and Acrylic Painters Assn., Nat. Soc. Painters in Casein and Acrylic (assoc.), Digital Fine Art Soc. N.Mex., Am. Biog. Inst. Rsch. Assn. (life, dep. gov. 1989, Gold Cup 1993, Medal of Honor 1992, Woman of Yr. 1994, 95), World Inst. of Achievement (life, Excellence as Painter award 1988), N.W. N.Mex. Arts Coun. (acting exec. dir. 1998-2003, Internat. Peace prize United Cultural Conv. 2003), Rio Rancho Art Assn. (charter, bd. dirs. 2004—), Rio Grande Art Assn Avocations: gardening, photography, reading, travel. Office Phone: 505-892-2324. Personal E-mail: petersart@sprynet.com.

**PETERS, FREDERICK WHITTEN,** lawyer; b. Omaha, Aug. 20, 1946; s. Jordan Holt and Elizabeth (O'Bryant) P.; children: Mary Irvin, Elizabeth Holt, Margaret Etheridge. BA magna cum laude, Harvard U., 1968; MS with distinction, London Sch. Econs., 1973; JD magna cum laude, Harvard U., 1976. Bar: D.C. 1978, U.S. Dist. Ct. D.C. 1978, U.S. Dist. Ct. Md., 1994, U.S. Ct. Appeals (3d and D.C. cirs.) 1979, U.S. Ct. Claims 1981, U.S. Ct. Appeals (11th cir.) 1986, U.S. Ct. Mil. Appeals 1993. Law clk. to Hon. J. Skelly Wright U.S. Ct. Appeals (D.C. cir.), Washington, 1976-77; law clk. to justice William J. Brennan U.S. Supreme Ct., Washington, 1977-78; assoc Williams & Connolly, Washington, 1978-84, ptnr., 1984-95, 2001—; prin. dep. gen. counsel Dept. of Defense, 1995-97, undersec., acting sec. USAF, 1997-99, sec. USAF, 1999-2001; ptnr. Williams & Connolly LLP, Washington, 2001—. Legal ethics com. DC Bar, 1988-94, chmn. rules rev. com., 1991-96; rules com. US Ct. Mil. Appeals, 1993-95. Pres. Harvard Law Rev., 1975-76. Bd.

dirs. Cleveland Park Hist. Soc., Washington, 1986-91, 2001-02, Washington Area Lawyers for the Arts, 1987-93, Air Force Enlisted Found., 2001—, Air Force Aid Soc., 2002—; adv. com. on streamlining procurement laws DOD, 1991-93, vice chmn. adv. com. on future of US aerospace industry, 2001-2002. Lt. USNR, 1969-72. Fellow Am. Bar Found.; mem. ABA. Democrat. Episcopalian. Avocations: sailing, computer science, golf. Home: 735 S Union St Alexandria VA 22314-3889 Office: Williams & Connolly 725 12th St NW Washington DC 20005 Office Phone: 202-434-5440. E-mail: wpeters@wc.com.

**PETERS, GEOFFREY WRIGHT,** lawyer, fundraising executive; b. Wilmington, Del., Oct. 30, 1945; s. William Ernest and Ann Miller Peters; m. Cecile Felicia Dziekonski, Aug. 26, 1967; children: Gregory Kent, Jessica Mohr. AB, Northwestern U., 1967; MA, JD, U. Denver, 1972. Bar: Colo. 1972, Nebr. 1972, Va. 1978, Minn. 1980, U.S. Supreme Ct. 1980. Sole practice, Denver, 1972; prof. law Creighton U., Omaha, 1972-78; dep. dir. Nat. Ctr. State Cts., Williamsburg, Va., 1978-80; pres., dean law William Mitchell Coll. Law, St. Paul, 1980-83; exec. v.p., gen. counsel Minn. Protective Life Ins. Co., Eden Prairie, 1983—86; v.p. ops. Garvey Industries, Wichita, 1986—90; pres. Corp. Investment Internat. (Garvey subs.), Phoenix, 1988-89, Firm One, Inc., Phoenix, 1988-89; chmn. Mid-Am. World Trade Ctr., Wichita, Kans., 1986—91; pres. Pres.'s Coll., 1989—91; exec. v.p. Amortibanc (Garvey subs.), 1989—91; pvt. practice Vienna, Va., 1991—; pres., mng. dir. Creative Dir. Mktg. Internat., Crofton, Md., 1995—2001; pres. Creative Direct Response, 2001—. Cons. Nat. Wiretap Commn., Washington, 1973—74; adj. prof. law William & Mary-Marshall Wythe Sch. Law, Williamsburg, 1978—80; gen. counsel Am. Charities Reasonable Fundraising Regulation, Vienna, 1995—; chmn., dir. Coun. Govt. Reform, Arlington, Va., 1992—2002; spkr. in field. Pres. Vigurie Co., Falls Ch., Va., 1990—91. With U.S. Army, 1969—71, West Point, NY. Decorated Army Commendation medal U.S. Army; named one of 50 Most Influential Persons in Nonprofit Sector, The Nonprofit Times, 2005; recipient Pub. Svc. award, DMA Nonprofit Fedn.; grantee prin. investigator more than 20 various grant funded projects, 1972-1980. Fellow: Am. Bar Found.; mem.: Minn. Bar Assn. (bd. govs. 1980—83). Achievements include first to create an international direct response fundraising agency operating in 15 countries. Avocations: flight instructing, commercial piloting, scuba diving, travel. Office: Am Charities for Reasonable Fundraising Regulation 9112 Tetterton Ave Vienna VA 22182 also: Creative Direct Response 1670 Village Green Crofton MD 21114 Office Phone: 703-938-1809. Office Fax: 703-938-2207. Personal E-mail: gpeters@gpeters.net. E-mail: gpeters@cd-nfl.com.

**PETERS, GORDON BENES,** retired musician; b. Oak Park, Ill., Jan. 4, 1931; s. Arthur George and Julia Anne (Benes) P.; children: Rénee Kemper, Erica Kemper. Student, Northwestern U., 1949-50; studied with Pierre Monteux, 1952—63; MusB, Eastman Sch. Music, 1956, MusM, 1962. Founder, dir. Marimba Masters, 1954—59; percussionist Rochester (NY) Philharm. Orch., 1954—59; prin. percussionist, asst. timpanist Grant Park Symphony Orch., Chgo., 1954—58; mem. faculty Rochester Bd. Edn., 1956-57, Geneseo State Tchrs. Coll., 1957-58; acting prin. percussionist Rochester Philharm., NY, 1958-59; prin. percussionist and assoc. prin. timpanist Chgo. Symphony Orch., 1959—2001; condr., administr. Civic Orch. Chgo., 1966-87; condr. Elmhurst Symphony Orch., 1968-73. Instr. percussion instruments Northwestern U., 1963-68, lectr., 1991; guest condr. Bangor Symphony, Maine, 1993; lectr. Winthrop U., SC, 1996. Author, pub. Treatise on Percussion, 1962, rev., 1975 as The Drummer: Man, 1975, rev., 2003 (CD); arranger-pub. Marimba Ensemble arrangements; composer-pub.: Swords of Moda-Ling; editor: percussion column Instrumentalist mag, 1963-69; contbr. articles to profl. jours. Bd. dirs. Pierre Monteux Sch., Hancock, Maine, 1965-95. With US Mil. Acad. Band, 1950-53. Recipient Pierre Monteux Disciple Conducting award, 1962, Prin. Timpani chair named GBP, Chgo. Youth Symphony Orch., 2000. Mem. Percussive Arts Soc. (pres. 1964-67, bd. dirs. Hall of Fame 2004), Am. Symphony Orch. League, Condrs. Guild (treas., exec. com. 1979-82, 86-90), Japan Xylophone Assn., Phi Mu Alpha Sinfonia (life). Home (Winter): 824 Hinman Ave Evanston IL 60202-5906 Home (Summer): PO Box 403 Hancock ME 04640-0403

**PETERS, GRETCHEN J.,** artist, educator; b. Grand Island, Nebr., Aug. 31, 1949; d. Maynard Gene and Margaret Louise Schudel; m. William C. Peters, Aug. 4, 1973. BFA in Edn., U. Nebr. 1971; MS summa cum laude, Chadron State Coll., 1991. Tchr. Central City (Nebr.) Schs., 1971—73, Gering (Nebr.) Pub. Schs., 1973—; artist, 1971—; faculty Prairie Visions Arts Coun., Omaha, 1988—99. One-man shows include Gov.'s Mansion Exhbn. Selection, 2003, W. Nebr. Arts Ctr., 2004, exhibited in group shows at Carnegie Art Ctr. Alliance, 2004, Represented in permanent collections Nebr. Mus. Art, Kearney. Mem. various coms. Oreg. Trail Days, Gering, 1978—; bd. dirs. Nebr. Arts Coun., Omaha, 1994—2000, Nebraskans for Arts, Omaha, 2004—; mem. adv. bd. Theatre West, Scotts Bluff, Nebr., 1996—2005, Nebr. Endowment Arts, Omaha, 2000—; trustee Nebr. State Hist. Soc., Lincoln, 1997—2000; mem. Nebr. Supreme Ct. Chief Justice Appointment Commn., Lincoln, 1998—2002, Hist. Midwest Theater, Scotts Bluff, 2003—. Recipient 1st prize Nebr. Statewide Arboretum Bot. Print Competition, 2006. Mem.: NEA, Gering Edn. Assn. (mem. polit. action com. 1973—, mem. negotiations team 1990, liaison legis. candidate rev. 1992—2005), Nebr. State Edn. Assn., Nebr. Art Educators Alliance (bd. dirs. 2003—05), Pi Lambda Theta. Democrat. Avocation: art. Home and Studio: 1850 Bonanza St Gering NE 69341

**PETERS, HENRY AUGUSTUS,** neurologist; b. Oconomowoc, Wis., Dec. 21, 1920; s. Henry Augustus and Emma N. P.; m. Jean McWilliams, 1950; children—Henry, Kurt, Eric, Mark. BA, MD, U. Wis. Prof. dept. neurology and rehab. medicine U. Wis. Med. Sch., Madison, emeritus prof., 1996—. Mem. med. adv. bd. Muscular Dystrophy Assn. Served to lt. M.C. U.S. Navy. Fellow A.C.P.; mem. Wis. Med. Assn., Am. Acad. Neurology, Am. Psychiatric Assn. Clubs: Rotary. Office: 600 Highland Ave Madison WI 53792-0001 Office Phone: 608-233-1568. Business E-mail: hapeters@hosp.wisc.edu.

**PETERS, HOWARD NEVIN,** foreign language educator; b. Hazleton, Pa., June 29, 1938; s. Howard Eugene and Verna P.; m. Judith Anne Griessel, Aug. 24, 1963; children: Elisabeth Anne, Nevin Edward. BA, Gettysburg Coll., 1960; PhD, U. Colo., 1965. Asst. prof. fgn. langs. Valparaiso (Ind.) U., 1965-69, assoc. prof., 1969-75, dir. grad. divus., 1967-70, acting dean Coll. Arts and Scis., 1970-71, assoc. dean Coll. Arts and Scis., 1971-74, dean Coll. Arts and Scis., 1974-81, prof. fgn. langs., 1975—, prof. emeritus fgn. langs. and lits., chair dept. fgn. langs. and lits., 1994—95, prof. emeritus fgn. langs. and lits., 1995—. Author (poetry) Espejo De Son, 1997. NDEA fellow, 1960-63 Mem. Midwest MLA, Phi Beta Kappa, Sigma Delta Pi, Phi Sigma Iota. Lutheran. Home: 860 N Cr 500 E Valparaiso IN 46383 Office: Meier Hall Rm 113 Valparaiso U Valparaiso IN 46383 Business E-mail: Howard.Peters@valpo.edu.

**PETERS, JAMES C.,** retail executive; Various operating positions Office Depot, 1994—97; exec. v.p. US Stores, 1997—99; pres. US Retail Staples, 1998—2000; pres., COO Ross Stores, Newark, Calif., 2000—; also. bd. dirs. Office: Ross Stores Inc 4440 Rosewood Dr Pleasanton CA 94588-3050

**PETERS, JEAN KOH,** law educator; AB, Radcliffe Coll., 1979; JD, Harvard U., 1982. Bar: NY 1983, Conn. 1989. Law clk. to Hon. William P. Gray US Dist. Ct., LA, 1982—83; staff atty. Juvenile Rights Div., Legal Aid Soc. NY, 1983—85; asst. clin. prof., assoc. dir. Child Advocacy Clinic, Columbia U., 1986—89; assoc. clin. prof. Yale U., New Haven, 1989—93, clin. prof., 1993—. Contbr. Representing Children in Child Protective Proceedings: Ethical & Practical Dimensions, 2001; contbr. articles to law jours. Office: Yale Law Sch PO Box 208215 New Haven CT 06520 E-mail: jean.peters@yale.edu.

**PETERS, JOANNA EILENE,** music educator; d. Lawrence Edward and Anna Ruth Robinson; m. Gary W. Peters, July 8, 2000. MusB, Shenandoah U., 2000. Lic. tchr. Va. Music tchr. Taunton (Mass.) Pub. Schs., 2000—01,

Mullein Hill Christian Acad., Lakeville, Mass., 2001—02; mid. sch. choral dir. Culpeper (Va.) Pub. Schs., 2002—04; h.s. choral dir. Spotsylvania (Va.) Pub. Schs., 2004—. Vol. Potter League Animal Shelter, Newport, RI, 2002; pianist Good Hope Bapt. Ch., Spotsylvania, 2003—05. Named Student Tchr. of Yr., Shenandoah Conservatory, 2000. Mem.: Am. Choral Dirs. Assn., Music Educators Nat. Conf. Office: Spotsylvania HS 6975 Courthouse Rd Spotsylvania VA 22553

**PETERS, JOHN DOUGLAS,** lawyer, artist; b. Dover, NH, Jan. 23, 1948; s. John Philip Peters, Helen Irene Hurst; m. Christine K. Consales, June 23, 1973. BA, U. NH, 1971; JD, U. Toledo, 1975. Exec. dir. PSRO 4th Ohio Area PSR Coun., Toledo, 1974—75; shareholder Charfoos & Christensen, P.C., Detroit, 1975—. Legal dir. Mich. Med. Schs. Coun. of Deans, Ann Arbor, 1978—80; lectr. law U. Toledo, 1978—88; assoc. prof. Sch. Medicine Wayne State U., Detroit, 1978—; cons. Georgetown U. Inst. for Health Policy, Washington, 1989, Office of Tech. Assessment, Washington, 1992—96, Robert Wood Johnson Found., Washington, 1994—98. Author: The Law of Medical Practice in Michigan, 1981, Anesthesiology and the Law, 1983, Obstetrics/Gynecology and the Law, 1984, The Law of Medical Practice in Pennsylvania and New Jersey, 1984, Detroit: Freight Cars Before Automobiles, 2005, Social Security Disability Claims, 2006; editor: Legal and Ethical Aspects of Treating Terminally Ill Patients, 1982; contbr. articles to profl. jours. Bd. dirs. Am. Lung Assn., Detroit, 1978—83, Vis. Nurse Assn., Detroit, 1987—96, Preservation Wayne, 1992—. Avocations: Persian textiles, folk art, collecting and studying antiquities. Office: Charfoos and Christensen PC 5510 Woodward Ave Detroit MI 48202 Office Phone: 313-875-8080.

**PETERS, JUANITA TEAL,** music educator; b. Dallas, Aug. 4, 1929; d. William Mosely and Vashti Elizabeth Teal; m. Dale Hugh Peters, June 4, 1960; children: Derek, Todd. MB, North Tex. State Coll., 1951; postgrad., U. Minn., 1952—53, Royal Acad. Music, London, 1956—57. Instr. Southeastern Okla. State U., Durant, 1967—79; lectr. U. North Tex., Denton, 1974—. Soloist: Dallas Symphony, Corpus Christi Symphony, Abilene Symphony, Wichita Falls Symphony, Ft. Worth Opera. Recipient G.B. Dealey award, Dallas Symphony, 1954, Wallace award, Wichita Falls Symphony, 1954, 1959. Home: 2818 Glenwood Denton TX 76209 Office: Univ North Tex Denton TX 76203 E-mail: jpeters@music.unt.edu.

**PETERS, JULIE ANNE,** writer; b. Jamestown, N.YU., Jan. 16, 1952; BA, Colo. Women's Coll. Rsch. asst., computer programmer Tracom Corp., Denver, 1975—84; computer sys. designer Electronic Data Sys., 1985—88; ednl. asst. Jefferson County Sch. Dist., Lakewood, Colo., 1990—94; writer, 1994—. Author: The Stinky Sneakers Contest, 1992, Risky Friends, 1993, B.J.'s Billion-Dollar Bet, 1994, How Do You Spell G-E-E-K?, 1996, Revenge of the Snob Squad, 1998, Romance of the Snob Squad, 1999, Love Me, Love My Broccoli, 1999, Define Normal, 2000, A Snitch in the Snob Squad, 2001, Keeping You a Secret, 2002, Luna: A Novel, 2004 (Nat. Book Award finalist, 2004). Recipient Top Hand Award, Colo. Authors' League. Address: 14 Twilight Dr Lakewood CO 80215 E-mail: juliepeters@juno.com.

**PETERS, LEO FRANCIS,** environmental engineer; b. Melrose, Mass., Aug. 14, 1937; s. Joseph Leander and Mary Gertrude (Phalen) Peters; m. Joan Catherine Anderson, May 20, 1961; children: Elizabeth M., Susan J., Carolyn A., Jennifer L. BSCE, Northeastern U., Boston, 1960, MSCE, 1966; postgrad., Harvard U., 1989. Registered profl. engr., Mass., N.H., diplomate, Am. Acad. Environ. Engrs. Jr. engr. N.Y. Dept. Transp., Albany, 1960-61; chief engr. John M. Cashman, Weymouth, Mass., 1961-62; project engr. Metcalf & Eddy, Inc., Boston, 1962-65, Weston & Sampson Boston, 1965-67, assoc., 1967-70, prin., 1970-76; exec. v.p. Weston & Sampson Engrs., Inc., Boston, 1976-82, pres., CEO Wakefield and Peabody, Mass., 1982-99, chmn., 1999—2002, chmn. emeritus, 2002—. Treas. Engring. Ctr., 1991—93; mem. corp. Northeastern U., Boston, 1992—, dir. nat. coun., 1993—; treas. Engring Ctr. Edn. Trust, 1992—94, chmn., 1994—1995. Clk., mem. Melrose (Mass.) Planning Bd., 1969—91; mem. Conservation Commn., 2003—06, Design Selection Bd. Commonwealth of Mass., 2004—; bd. dir. Environ. Bus. Coun. New Eng., 1997—2002. Named Outstanding Civil Engr., Northeastern U. Civil Engring. Alumni, Young Engr. of the Yr., Mass. Soc. Profl. Engrs., Disting. Engring. Alumnus, Northeastern U., 2005; recipient Environ. Merit award, Environ. Bus. Coun. New Eng., Leadership award, Engring. Ctr., 2001. Fellow: Am. Coun. Engring. Cos. (v.p. 1995—96, v.p. 1996—97, pres. 1999—2000); mem.: ASCE (life), Boston Soc. Civil Engrs. (hon. life), New Eng. Water Works Assn. (hon. life) (pres. 1989—90), Am. Coun. Engring. Couns. New Eng. (pres. 1990—91), Water Environ. Fedn., Am. Pub. Works Assn., Am. Water Works Assn. Roman Catholic. Home: 187 E Emerson St Melrose MA 02176-3534 Office: Weston & Sampson Engrs Inc 5 Centennial Dr Peabody MA 01960-7985 E-mail: leopeters@comcast.net.

**PETERS, LEON, JR.,** engineering educator; b. Columbus, Ohio, May 28, 1923; s. Leon P. and Ethel (Howland) Pierce; m. Mabel Marie Johnson, June 6, 1953; children: Amy T. Peters Thomas, Melinda A. Peters Todaro, Maria C. Cohee, Patricia D., Lee A., Roberta J. Peters Camenruca, Karen E. Peters Ellingson. BSE.E., Ohio State U., 1950, MS, 1954, PhD, 1959. Asst. prof. elec. engring. Ohio State U., Columbus, 1959-63, assoc. prof., 1963-67, prof., 1967-93, prof. emeritus, 1993—; assoc. dept. chmn. for rsch. Columbus, 1990-92, dir. electro sci. lab., 1983-94. Contbr. articles to profl. jours. Served to 2d lt. U.S. Army, 1942-46, ETO. Fellow: IEEE. Home: 2087 Ellington Rd Columbus OH 43221-4138 Office: Ohio State U Electrosci Lab 1320 Kinnear Rd Columbus OH 43321-1156 Office Phone: 614-292-6153. Business E-Mail: peters.6@osu.edu.

**PETERS, LEONARD K.,** environmental scientist; BS, MS, PhD, U. Pitts. Joined U. Ky., 1974, asst. prof. chem. engring. to v.p. rsch. and grad. studies; rschr. Alcoa Rsch. Labs., Cleve. State U.; with Va. Tech., 1993—2003, mgr. rsch. and grad edn. programs, sr. exec. rsch. divsn.; dir. Pacific NW Nat. Lab. operated by Battelle U.S. Dept. Energy, 2003—; sr. v.p. Battelle, 2003—. Mem. adv. bd. Wash. State U. Coll. Engring. and Architecture; bd. dirs. Heritage Coll., VITEX Sys., Inc., Wash. Tech. Alliance, Wash. Roundtable, Wash. State U. Rsch. Found., Tri Cities Devel. Coun.; chmn. bd., pres. Va. Tech. Intellectual Properties, Inc.; chmn. rsch. com. Va. Rsch. and Tech. Adv. Commn. Adv. bd. Jr. Achievement Greater Tri-Cities; bd. dirs. United Way Benton and Franklin Counties; Tri-Cities Indsl. Devel. Coun. Recipient Recognition award for contributions to Sci. and Tech., Nat. Sci. Found., 1990. Mem.: AIChE, Oreg. Coun. Knowledge and Econ. Devel., Am. Soc. Engring. Edn., Am. Assn. Aerosol Rsch., Air and Waste Mgmt. Assn., Sigma XI. Office: Pacific NW Nat Lab PO Box 999 Richland WA 99352

**PETERS, LEROY RICHARD,** materials management consulting company executive; b. Milw., June 26, 1943; s. LeRoy Edwin and Eleanor Hedwig (Bensing) Peters; m. Barbara Jean Hackney, Nov. 18, 1964 (div. July 1970); 1 child, Neal; m. Nancy Elizabeth Till, July 17, 1971; children: Richard, Brenda, Eric, Linda. BS, U. Wis., 1966; Grad., U.S. Army/Command and Gen. Staff Coll., Ft. Leavenworth, Kans., 1977. Cert. fellow in prodn. and inventory mgmt. Inventory supr. Bucyrus Erie, Erie, Pa. and Pocatello, Idaho, ach3-76; inventory mgr. Am. Microsystems, Pocatello, 1976-78; prodn. mgr. Worthington Compressor, Buffalo, 1978-80; mfg. mgr. St. Regis WPM Div., Denver, 1980-82; materials mgr. Robinson Brick Co., Denver, 1982-86; prodn. mgr. Merritt Equipment Co., Denver, 1986-89; instructional designer Martin Marietta, Denver, 1989-90; sr. cons. J.D. Edwards, Denver, 1990-93; sr. cons. mgr. AMX Internat., 1993-97; v.p. The Thompson Group, 1997-98; CEO, Enterprise Resource Mgmt., Inc., 1998—. Editorial cond.: Aerospace and Defense Dictionary, 1990; contbr. articles to profl. jours. Scoutmaster Boy Scouts Am., Denver, 1989, cubmaster, 1988, outdoor chmn., Denver, 1990; dist. capt. Adams County Colo. Reps., Denver, 1986. Col. U.S. Army, 1966-94, Vietnam, Desert Storm. Decorated Legion of Merit, Bronze Star, Meritorious Svc. medal, Army Commendation medal. Fellow Am. Prodn. and Inventory Control Soc. (bd. dirs. region VI 1990—, pres. Colo. chpt. 1989-90); mem. Am. Def. Preparedness Assn., Moose. Lutheran. Avocations: fishing, reading, music, photography, geology.

**PETERS, LINDA S.,** musician, educator; b. Erie, Pa., Aug. 13, 1952; d. Willard and Della Amale Smith; m. Rocky Grant Peters, Apr. 25, 1997; 1 child, Patrick Harold Allyn. MusB and Tchr. Certification, Mansfield State Coll., 1974; MS Music, Mansfield U., 1989. Cert. nat. certified tchr. music Music Tchrs. Nat. Assn. Tchr. vocal music Wyalusing Area Elem. Schs., Pa., 1975—77; instr. piano 171 Cedar Arts Ctr., Corning, NY, 1978—80, 171 Cedar Art Ctr., 2004—; freelance accompanist Sayre, Pa., 1978—94; head tchr. preschool Barclay Sch., Towanda, Pa., 1983—86; instr. piano Fletcher's Pianos and Organs, Horseheads, NY, 1989—2000; dir. music Big Flats First Presbyn. Ch., 1993—. Accompanist/adjudicator N.Y. State Sch. Music Assn. Festivals, Elmira, 2000—. Musician: (audio tape) Ivory Treasures; musician: (pianist) (audio cd) Classics & Jazz. Session elder Big Flats First Presbyn. Ch., 2002—. Mem.: Music Tchrs. Nat. Assn., N.Y. State Music Tchrs. Assn. Achievements include Winner/Penn State Ragtime Piano Competition; Accompanist at the National Federation of Music Clubs National Convention; Established Fletcher's Showcase of Music Piano Competition, now in its 10th year. Avocations: running, watercolor painting, jewelry designing. Office: 171 Cedar Arts Ctr Studio G Corning NY 14830 Personal E-mail: fingers8@infoblvd.net.

**PETERS, MARY E.,** former federal agency administrator; m. Terry Peters; 3 children. BA, U. Phoenix; attended govt. program for state & local govt., Harvard U. With Ariz. Dept. Transp., 1983—98, dir., 1998—2001; adminstr. Fed. Highway Adminstrn., US Dept. Transp., Washington, 2001—05; nat. dir. for transp. policy, cons. HDR, Inc., Phoenix, 2006—; nominee for sec. US Dept. Transp., Washington, 2006. Past bd. dirs. Project Challenge, Nat. Guard; past chair adv. bd. Hwy. Expansion Loan Program; mem. Gt. Ariz. Develop. Authority; past mem Growing Smarter Commn. Named Women of Yr., Women's Transp. Seminar, 2004; named one of Most Influential Person in Ariz. Transp., Ariz. Bus. Jour.; recipient George S. Bartlett award, 2005. Mem.: We. Assn. State Hwy. Transp. Officials, Am. Assn. State Hwy. Officials (past chair standing com. on planning, assest mgmt. task force, reauthorization steering com. 2001). Office: HDR Inc Ste 350 & Ste 250 3200 E Camelback Rd Phoenix AZ 85018-2311*

**PETERS, MERCEDES,** psychotherapist; b. N.Y.C. BS, L.I. U., 1945; MS, U. Conn., 1953; tng. in psychotherapy, Am. Inst. Psychotherapy, 1960-70; PhD in Psychoanalysis, Union Inst., 1989. Cert. in psychoanalysis. Sr. psychotherapist Cmty. Guidance Svc., 1960-75; staff affiliate Postgrad. Ctr. for Mental Health, 1974-76; pvt. practice psychoanalysis and psychotherapy, Bklyn., 1961—; tchr., supr. psychoanalytic psychotherapy at various psychotherapeutic tng. ctrs., 1975—; cons. to advanced tng. program Jewish Bd. Family and Children's Svcs., 2000—. Contbr. articles to profl. jours. Past bd. dirs. Brookwood Child Care Assn. Fellow: Am. Orthopsychiat. Assn.; mem.: NASW, LWV, NAACP, Postgrad. Psychoanalytic Soc., Nat. Assn. Advancement Psychoanalysis (past bd. dirs., chair UN com.). Wednesday Club. Office: 142 Joralemon St Brooklyn NY 11201-4709 Office Phone: 718-875-9874.

**PETERS, MILTON EUGENE,** educational psychologist; b. Anderson, Ind., July 22, 1938; s. Olen A. and Dorothy LaVerne (Lambert) P.; m. Carol Ann Dudycha, Aug. 27, 1960. BA, Wittenberg U., 1960; M in Div., Hamma Sch. Theology, 1963; MA, Bowling Green State U., 1965; PhD, U. Toledo, 1975. Lic. psychologist, Ohio. Pastor Luth. Ch. Am., 1966-69; instr. psychology Defiance (Ohio) Coll., 1969-70, Bluffton (Ohio) Coll., 1970-72; tchr., rsch. asst. U. Toledo, 1973-75, prof., 1975-76; dir. instl. rsch., asst. prof. psychology U. Findlay, Ohio, 1976-85, assoc. prof. psychology, 1985-89, prof., 1989—. Cons., lectr. in field; ednl. rschr. Contbr. articles to profl. and religious jours. Mem. APA, Am. Assn. Univ. Prof. (pres. U. Findlay), Midwestern Psychol. Assn., Creative Edn. Found. (colleague), Findlay Beacon Club, Fostoria Power Squadron. Home: 1130 Country Club Dr Findlay OH 45840-6342 Office: 1000 N Main St Findlay OH 45840-3653 Office Phone: 419-434-4523. Business E-Mail: peters@findlay.edu.

**PETERS, MORGAN JAMES,** language educator, social studies educator, actor, writer, film director; s. Randolph G., Sr. and Shirley Peters; 1 child, Morgan James. BA, Boston U., 1991, MS, 1993; MFA, Goddard Coll., Plainfield, Vt., 2006. Cert. theatre arts edn. New African Co., Mass. Artistic dir. Oversoul Theatre Collective, Mashpee, Mass., 1994; playwright-in-residence New African Co., Boston; artist-in-residence The Point CDC/ Live From The Edge Theatre, Bronx, 2001—03; asst. prof. U. Mass., North Dartmouth, 2003—; filmmaker-in-residence Sta. WGBH, Boston, 2005—06. Filmmaker Midnight Groove Multimedia, New Bedford, Mass., 1992—; grant writer Union Lodge #4, F&AM, New Bedford, 2004—. Author: (plays) OM! A Street Corner Griot's Comedy (Outstanding New Playwright, 2003), Working Things Out, Look At My Shorts (Outstanding New Playwright, 2003), (novels) Where The Black Squirrels Roam; co-writer, dir., editor: (films) About A Bridge (WGBH Residency, 2005); songwriter, record prodr.: Morning Rock Records, 2000—. Mem. Mashpee (Mass.) Wampanoag Indian Tribal Coun., co-chair edn. com., 2000; grand lodge historian com. Prince Hall Grand Lodge Mass., Boston, 2005; dir. fine arts Native Am. Acad., Chapel Hill, NC. Media Arts fellow, New Eng. Broadcasting Assn., 1992, 1993, Ira Aldridge fellow, New African Co., 1997, 1998, 1999, Alice Childress fellow, Harlem Theatre Co., 2000, Fine Arts grantee, Martin Luther King Jr. Soc. Cape Cod, 1993, 1994. Mem.: AUDELCO, Black Writer's Guild, Masons (jr. warden 2004), Alpha Phi Alpha. Avocations: travel, swimming, camping, reading, gardening. Office: U Mass 285 Old Westport Rd North Dartmouth MA 02747 Office Phone: 508-999-9304. Office Fax: 508-999-9235. Business E-Mail: mpeters@umassd.edu.

**PETERS, RALPH EDGAR,** architectural firm executive, engineering executive; b. Harrisburg, Pa., Feb. 20, 1923; s George Edward and Ruthanne Maria (Mihenci) P.; m. Roberta Jane Shaffer, June 12, 1948; children: Sheila Jane, Gail Marie, Ralph Jr., Bret Edward. Student, U. Pa., 1942; BA in Bus. Adminstrn., Pa. State U., 1948. From payroll supt. to asst. budget supr. Pa. State U., 1948-52; chief acct., pers. officer Haller, Raymond & Brown, State College, Pa., 1952-54; from contr. to CEO and chmn. bd. Benatec Assocs., Inc. (formerly Berger Assocs., Inc.), Camp Hill, Pa., 1954—. Chmn. bd. advisors Pa. State U., Harrisburg, 1979—; chmn. bd. dirs. Holy Spirit Hosp., Camp Hill, 1982—; past pres. Tri-County United Way, Harrisburg, 1978—; chmn. Pvt. Industry Coun., Harrisburg, 1982-87. With U.S. Army, 1943-45, ETO, 1952-53, Korea. Recipient Comty. Svc. award Salvation Army, 1980, Disting. Pennsylvanian award Greater Phila. C. of C., 1981, Catalyst award Capital Region Econ. Devel., 1992, James Skelly award for exceptional svcs. to the hwy. program Associated Constructors of Pa., 1993, Alexis de Tocqueville Humanitarian award United Way, 1999; named Transp. Adv. of Yr., Pa. Hwy. Info. Assn., 1994; finalist Ctrl. Pa. Entrepreneur of Yr., 1996; Paul Harris fellow Rotary Internat., 1997. Mem. Pa. C. of C. (bd. dirs., transp. com. 1972-90), Harrisburg Area C. of C. (pres., chmn. 1979-83), Ams. for Competitive Enterprise Sys. (pres. 1981-83), Cumberland County Transp. Authority, Susquehanna Valley Regional Airport Authority, Lions, Masons, Pa. Jaycees (pres. 1955-56, nat. v.p. 1956-57), Delta Sigma Pi. Lutheran. Office: Benatec Assocs Inc 200 Airport Rd New Cumberland PA 17070-2467 Office Phone: 717-901-7055. Business E-Mail: rpeters@benatec.com.

**PETERS, RALPH FREW,** investment banker; b. Mineola, N.Y., Mar. 21, 1929; s. Ralph and Helen Louise (Frew) P.; m. Ann Marie Haberski, Dec. 31, 1997; children from previous marriages: Louise Frew, Jean Reid, Ralph Frew, Melvyn T., Richard Clayton. BA, Princeton U., 1951; postgrad., Rutgers U., 1962. With Corn Exchange Bank & Trust Co., 1947-52; chmn. bd., dir. Discount Corp. N.Y., N.Y.C., 1955-93. Bd. dirs. Van Eck Funds. Served with USNR, 1948-55. Mem. Anglers Club, Leash Club, North Woods Club. Episcopalian.

**PETERS, RAYMOND ANDREW,** music educator; b. Lakewood, NJ, June 9, 1969; s. Raymond H. Peters and Martha Campbell. M of Music Tchg., Oberlin Coll., Ohio, 1992. Tchr. gen. music Wilson Elem. Sch., Imperial, Pa., 1993—. Orch. dir. West Allegheny H.S., Imperial, 1998—. Musician:

(freelance clarinet/saxophone) Stage 62 Theatre; Various High Schools. Mem.: Music Educator's Nat. Conf., Phi Beta Kappa. Office: West Allegheny Sch Dist PO Box 55 Imperial PA 15126 Office Phone: 724-695-3300. E-mail: apeters@westallegheny.k12.pa.us.

**PETERS, RAYMOND EUGENE,** historian, writer; b. New Haven, Conn., Aug. 24, 1933; s. Raymond and Doris Winthrop (Smith) P.; m. Millie Mather, July 14, 1978 (div. Nov. 1983); life ptnr. Mamie L. Romero, 1986—. Student, San Diego City Coll., 1956-61; cert., Lumbleau Real Estate Sch., 1973, Southwestern Coll., Chula Vista, Calif., 1980. Cert. quality assurance engr., Southwestern Coll., 1980. Founder, pub. Silhouette Pub. Co., San Diego, 1960-75; co-founder, news dir. Sta. XEGM, San Diego, 1964-68; news dir. Sta. XERB, Tijuana, Mex., 1973-74; founder, chief exec. officer New World Airways, Inc., San Diego, 1968-77; co-founder, exec. vice chmn. bd. San Cal Rail, Inc.-San Diego Trolley, San Diego, 1974-77; founder, pres., CEO Ansonia Sta., micro systems, San Diego, 1986—. Cons. on multimedia and electronic commerce sys., 1995—; co-founder, dir. S.E. Cmty. Theatre, San Diego, 1960-68; commr. New World Aviation Acad., Otay Mesa, Calif., 1971-77; co-founder New World Internat. Trade and Commerce Commn., Inc., 1991-94, New World Airways Inc, 1968-77 Author: Profiles in Black American History, 1971, Black Americans in Aviation, 1975, Eagles Don't Cry, 1988, Forgotten Renaissance, African American History, 2005, Diss-Function, The Self Genocide of Negro's in America, 2005; founder, pub., editor Oceanside Lighthouse, 1958-60, San Diego Herald Dispatch, 1959-60 Co-founder, bd. dirs. San Diego County Econ. Opportunity Commn., 1964-67; co-founder Edn. Cultural Complex, San Diego, 1966-75; co-founder, exec. dir. S.E. Anti-Poverty Planning Coun., Inc., 1964-67; mem, U.S. Rep Senatorial Inner Circle Com., Washington, 1990—; mayoral candidate, city of San Diego, 1986; mem. bus. adv. bd. Value Add Reseller, 1995; ambassador Sycuan Casino and Singing Hills Golf Resort, 2000-05 With U.S. Army, 1950—53, Korea. Decorated (2) Bronze Svc. stars, UN medal; recipient Pres. of Korea award medal. Mem. Am. Soc. Quality Control, Nat. City C. of C., Afro-Am. Micro Sys. Soc. (exec. dir. 1987—), Negro Airmen Internat. (Calif. pres. 1970-75, nat. v.p. 1975-77), Tuskegee Airmen (charter, bd. dirs. Benjamin O. Davis San Diego chpt. 1995—), Internat. Platform Assn., U.S. C. of C., Greater San Diego Minority C. of C. (bd. dirs. 1974—, past chmn. bd.), Masons (most worshipful grand master, supreme coun.), Shriners (Al Kadosh Disting. Cmty. Svc. award 1975). Republican. Methodist. Achievements include being first African American to co-found a jet powered transcontinental airline that set a national safety record. Avocations: creative writing, golf, world history, public speaking. Home: Meadowbrook Estates # 245 8301 Mission Gorge Rd Santee CA 92071-3500 Personal E-mail: ansonia@cox.net.

**PETERS, RICHARD SPENCER,** musician; b. San Antonio, Feb. 2, 1951; s. Alva Spencer and Lucy Alma Peters; m. Nellie Julia Cruz, June 16, 1990; children: Matthew, Brittany. BA in Music and Edn., U. So. Miss., Hattiesburg, MS, 1973; MA in Music and Edn., Miss. Coll., Clinton, 1984. Band dir. Mt. Olive Attendance, Miss., 1973—75; band dir./supr. Brookhaven H.S., Miss., 1975—78; head band dir. Mendenhall H.S., Miss., 1978—85, Newton City Schools, Miss., 1985—87; asst. band dir. Mission Ind. Sch. Dist. Ctr., Tex., 1987—91, McAllen Ind. Sch. Dist., Tex., 1991—92; dist. music coord. East Ctrl. Ind. Sch. Dist., San Antonio, 1992—. Mem. adv. bd. US Achievement Acad., Huntsville, Ala., 1980—85, Salvation Army, McAllen, 1989—91. Contbg. editor: Bandworld Mag. Vol. Salvation Army, San Antonio, Tex., 1992; choir mem. Cornerstone Ch., 1996. Named to Outstanding Young Men of Am., 1987; recipient Outstanding Educator, 1985. Mem.: Tex. Music Adminstrs. Conf., Nat. Fedn. Interscholastic Music Assn., Detroit Concert Band Assn., Percy Grainger Soc., Assn. Tex. Profl. Educators, Nat. Band Assn., Tex. Bandmasters Assn., Tex. Music Educators Assn. Home: 715 Arch Stone San Antonio TX 78258

**PETERS, ROBERT K.,** dean, newscaster, newswriter, journalist; b. Tyler, Tex., June 2, 1941; s. Robert K. and Ruth Bailey Peters; m. Judy D. Loden, Feb. 23, 1980; children: Jonathan W., Anne E. AA, Tyler Jr. Coll., 1961—; BA, Tex. Christian U., 1962; M in History, Stephen F. Austin State Coll., 1964; PhD, U. Tex., 1977. Staff writer, weather, and sci. Tyler Courier Times Telegraph, 1962—; newsreader weather KTBB Radio Sta., Tyler, 1962—; dean univ. studoes Tyler Jr. Coll., 1966—; observer, sta. keeper Nat. Weather Svc., Tyler, 1992—. Dir. bd. dirs. Horizon, Tyler, 1977—; trustee Tyler Mus. Art, 1999—. Author: Texas from Annexation to Succession: 1846-1861, 1977, Practicing Texas Politics, Instructor Resource Manual, 1994, 1995, 1997, 1998, 2000, 2001, 2003. Mem. Tex. Coun. Workforce and Econ. Competitiveness, Austin, 1999—2003, N.E. Tex. State Sub-Commrs. Revision, Austin, 1973—74, Tex. Commn. Blind Bd., Austin, 1985—91, 1999—2004, Tex. Coun. Disabilities, Austin, 1990—91, City of Tyler Rev. Bd., 1990—94, Tex. Planning Coun. Disabilities, Austin, 1991—93. Recipient Piper Prof. award, Piper Found., San Antonio, 1993, Nat. Weather Svc. Cooperating Observer award, Nat. Weather Svc., Shreveport, La., 2002. Mem.: Tex. State Hist. Soc., So. Hist. Soc., Orgn. Am. History, Am. Hist. Soc. Republican. Episcopalian. Avocations: reading, cooking. Home: 3813 Brookwood Tyler TX 75701 Office: Tyler Jr Coll 1400 E 5th St Tyler TX 75711 Fax: 903-510-2708. E-mail: rpet@tjc.edu.

**PETERS, ROBERT WAYNE,** small business owner; b. LaPorte, Ind., Jan. 2, 1950; s. Harry Carl and Dorothy May (Fischer) P.; m. Frances Kay Cooley, Aug. 21, 1971; children: Carolyn Marie, Angela Lynn. BA, Purdue U., 1972. CLU. Mgr. pension adminstrn. Gen. Life Ins. Corp., Milw., 1973-75; dir. qualified plan devel. Cen. Life Assurance Co., Des Moines, 1976-84; v.p individual ops. First Farwest Ins. Co., Portland, Oreg., 1984-90; pres. CAF Enterprises, Inc., Portland, 1990—. Lectr. in field. Contbr. articles to profl. jours. Mem. N.W. Vintage Thunderbird (v.p. 1988, pres. 1989-90, exec. bd. 1991, sec. 1992-93 97-2002, treas. 1995-96 mt annual 2000), N.W. Car Collectors Assn. (treas. 2002-06) Avocations: reading, vintage thunderbirds. Office: CAF Enterprises Inc PO Box 1529 Tualatin OR 97062-1529 Personal E-mail: bob@tbirdsanctuary.com.

**PETERS, ROBERT WOOLSEY,** retired architect; b. Mpls., Mar. 24, 1935; s. John Eugene and Adelaide Elizabeth (Woolsey) P. BArch., U. Minn., 1958; MArch., Yale U., 1964. Registered architect, N.Mex. Participating assoc. Skidmore Owings & Merrill, Chgo., 1961-74; dir. design Schaefer & Assocs., Wichita, Kans., 1975-76; ptnr. Addy & Peters, Albuquerque, 1979-82; owner, sole proprietor Robert W. Peters AIA Architect, 1982—2004, ret., 2004. Exhibited work Centre Georges Pompidou, Paris, 1980, U. Art Mus., Albuquerque, 1982, 92, Albuquerque Mus., 1988; contbr. articles to Century Mag., Progressive Architecture, House & Garden, House Beautiful, also others. Recipient honor awards N.Mex. Soc. Architects, 1980-83, 86, 87, 92, HUD, 1980; 5th Nat. Passive Solar Conf., Amherst, Mass., 1981. Fellow AIA; mem. Contemporary Art Soc. N.Mex. (bd. dirs., pres.), N.Mex. Arch. Found. (pres. 2004-), Yale N.Mex. Democrat. Roman Catholic.

**PETERS, ROBERTA,** soprano; b. NYC, May 4, 1930; d. Sol and Ruth (Hirsch) Peters; m. Bertram Fields, Apr. 10, 1955; children: Paul, Bruce. Litt.D., Elmira Coll., 1967; Mus. D., Ithaca Coll., 1968, Colby Coll., 1980; L.H.D., Westminster Coll., 1974, Lehigh U., 1977; D.F.A., St. John's U., 1982; LittD, Coll. New Rochelle, 1989; MusD, U. R.I., 1992, Fla. Atlantic U., 1997. Author: Debut at the Met; singer: (Operas) Met. Opera debut as Zerlina in Don Giovanni, 1950, recorded numerous operas, (appeared motion pictures including) Tonight We Sing, 1996, frequent appearances radio and TV, (stage appearances include) The King and I, 1973, Bittersweet, Merry Widow, The Sound of Music, Royal Opera House, Vienna State Opera, Munich Opera, West Berlin Opera, Salzburg Festival, The White House, debuts at festivals in Vienna and Munich, premiered Ani M'amin, Carnegie Hall, 1973, concert tours in U.S., Soviet Union, Scandinavian countries, Israel, China, Japan, Taiwan, South Korea, (debut) Kirov Opera, sang at Bolshoi Opera (1st Am. recipient Bolshoi medal). Trustee, bd. dirs Carnegie Hall; trustee Ithaca Coll.; dir. Met. Opera Guild; chmn. Nat. Inst. Music Theater, 1991—; apptd. by Pres. Bush to Nat. Coun. Arts, 1991; overseer Colby Coll., Bklyn. Coll. Performing Arts Ctr.; past chair Nat. Cystic Fibrosis Found.; active Israel Bonds, AIDS rsch. Named Woman of Yr., Fedn. Women's Clubs, 1964;

recipient honored spl. ceremony on 35th anniversary with Met. Opera Co., 1985, Nat. Medal of Arts, Pres. Clinton, 1998. Avocation: tennis. Office: ICM Artists Ltd 40 W 57th St Fl 16 New York NY 10019-4098 *I believe that life is a series of just one darn thing after another. If we can learn that, we can expect, meet, and solve our problems.*

**PETERS, SARAH WHITAKER,** art historian, writer; b. Kenosha, Wis., Aug. 17, 1924; d. Robert Burbank and Margaret Jebb (Allen) Whitaker; m. Arthur King Peters, Oct. 21, 1943; children: Robert Bruce, Margaret Allen, Michael Whitaker. BA, Sarah Lawrence Coll., 1954; MA, Columbia U., 1966; student, L'Ecole du Louvre, Paris, 1967-68; diplome, Ecole des Trois Gourmandes, Paris, 1968; PhD, CUNY, 1987. Freelance critic Art in Am., N.Y.C. Lectr.-in-residence Garrison Forest Sch., Owings Mills, Md.; adj. asst. prof. art history C.W. Post, U. L.I.; lectr. Bronxville (N.Y.) Adult Sch. Internat. Mus. Photography, 1979, Tufts U., 1979, Madison (Wis.) Art Ctr., 1984, Meml. Art Gallery, Rochester, N.Y., 1988, 91, Caramoor Mus., Katonah, N.Y., 1988, Yale U. Art Gallery, New Haven, Conn., 1989, The Cosmopolitan Club, N.Y.C., 1977, 91, Sarah Lawrence Coll., Bronxville, 1992, The Phillips Collection, Washington, 1993, Mpls. Inst. Arts, 1993, Whitney Mus. Am. Art, Champion, 1994, U. Wis., Parkside, 1994, Nat. Mus. Wildlife Art, Jackson Hole, Wyo., 1995, The Georgia O'Keeffe Mus., Santa Fe, 1997, Bronxville Pub. Libr., 1998, Weatherspoon Art Mus., Greensboro, NC, 2003, Amon Carter Mus., Ft. Worth, 2003, Vassar Coll., 2003, Pa. Acad. Fine Arts, Phila., 2004. Author: Becoming O'Keeffe: The Early Years, 1991, 2d edit., 2001, Pattern of the Past: A Kenosha Memoir, 2001; contbr. essays to Portraits of American Women, 1991, The Dictionary of Art, 1996, Frames of Reference; Works from the Whitney Museum of American Art, 1999, American Art Review, 2003, Georgia O'Keeffe: Color and Conservation, 2006, N.Mex. Hist. Rev., 2006, Seeing American: Painting and Sculpture, 2006; TV appearances include: BBC, London, The Late Show, 1993, A&E Network Biography series on Georgia O'Keeffe, 2004; radio interview: Art Today, Australia Broadcasting Corp., 1999; contbr. articles to profl. jours. Mem. Coll. Art Assn., Bronxville Field Club, The Cosmopolitan Club. Avocations: horseback riding, rock climbing, tennis, cooking. Home: 14 Village Ln Bronxville NY 10708-4806

**PETERS, THOMAS,** foundation administrator; BA, San Francisco State U., 1966; PhD, U. Minn., 1973. Various positions including assoc. dir. of health Dept. of Public Health, San Francisco, 1974—90; dir. Health and Human Services, Marin County, 1991—98; pres., CEO Marin Community Found., 1998—. Mem. Cmty. Leadership Team Council on Foundations; bd. mem. Cmty. Foundations of Am., League of Calif. Cmty. Foundations; fellow NIH, 1968—71. Office: Marin Cmty Found 5 Hamilton Landing Novato CA 94949*

**PETERS, THOMAS J,** management consultant, writer; b. Baltimore, 1942; m. Susan Peters; 2 children. BCE, MCE, Cornell U.; MBA, PhD, Stanford U.; degree (hon.), U. San. Fran., Rhodes Coll., State U. Mgmt., Moscow, 2004. Sr. drug abuse adv. White House, 1973—74; with McKinsey & Co., 1974—81, ptnr., 1979—81; founder Tom Peters Group, Palo Alto, Calif., 1981—. Co-author (with Robert H. Waterman Jr.): In Search of Excellence: Lessons in America's Best-Run Companies, 1982 (Named one of Top Three Business Books of the Century, 1999); co-author: (with Nancy Austin) A Passion for Excellence: The Leadership Difference, 1985; author: Thriving on Chaos: Handbook for a Management Revolution, 1987, Liberation Management: Necessary Disorganization for the Nanosecond Nineties, 1992, The Pursuit of Wow! Every Person's Guide to Topsy-Turvy Times, 1994, The Tom Peters Seminar: Crazy Times Call for Crazy Organizations, 1994, The Circle of Innovation: You Can't Shrink Your Way to Greatness, 1997, The Brand You 50: Or: Fifty Ways to Transform Yourself from an Employee into a Brand That Shouts Distinction, Commitment, and Passion!, 1999, Re-Imagine! Business Excellence in a Disruptive Age, 2003. Navy Seabee USN, 1966—70, Vietnam. Named Second in Top 50 Business Intellectuals, Accenture's Inst. for Strategic Change, 2002. Fellow: Soc. Quality and Participation, Internat. Customer Svc. Assn., World Productivity Assn., Internat. Acad. Mgmt. Office: Tom Peters Company 101 Commerce Blvd Loveland OH 45140

**PETERS, TROY CLARK,** conductor, composer; b. Greenock, Scotland, Mar. 19, 1969; s. Melvin Troy Peters and Allerton Ann Madden; m. Anne Conaway, June 13, 1998; 1 child, Sophie Grace. MusB, Curtis Inst. Music, 1991; MA, U. Pa., 1995. Asst. condr. Phila. Youth Orch., 1991—95; artistic dir. Perpetuum Mobile, 1991—92, Pacific Chamber Soloists, Tacoma, 1993—97; music dir. Vt. Youth Orch., Colchester, 1995—; orch. condr. Middlebury Coll., 2004—. Pres. Vt. ASTA with NSOA, Colchester, 2005—. Composer: (orchestral work) Between Hills Briefly Green, (cantata) Quis ut Deus; arranger (cd) Trey Anastasio, Trey Anastasio: Seis de Mayo; composer: (opera) A Quarreling Pair. Recipient Adventurous Programming award, ASCAP, 1999, 2000, 2001, 2003. Home: 103 Granite Creek Rd Colchester VT 05446 Office: Vt Youth Orch 223 Ethan Allen Ave Colchester VT 05446 Office Phone: 802-655-5030. Office Fax: 802-655-5034. Personal E-mail: troy@vyo.org.

**PETERS, WILLIAM,** writer, film producer, film director; b. San Francisco, July 30, 1921; s. William Ernest and Dorothy Louise (Wright) P.; m. Mercy Ann Miller, Oct. 12, 1942 (div. 1968); children: Suzanne Peters Payne, Geoffrey Wright, Jennifer Peters Johnson, Gretchen Peters; m. Helene Louise Yager White, May 31, 1987. BS, Northwestern U., 1947. Account exec. pub. relations J. Walter Thompson Co., Chgo., 1947-51; mem. fiction staff Ladies' Home Jour., 1951-52; article editor Woman's Home Companion, N.Y.C., 1952-53; freelance writer, Pelham, NY, 1953-62; producer CBS Reports, CBS News, N.Y.C. 1967-66, freelance writer, film dir. and TV producer/exec. producer N.Y.C., 1966-82; dir. Yale U. Films New Haven, 1982-89; freelance writer, film dir., TV producer/exec. producer Guilford, Conn., 1990—. Author: American Memorial Hospital--Reims, France: A History, 1955, Passport to Friendship--The Story of the Experiment in International Living, 1957, The Southern Temper, 1959; author: (with Mrs. Medgar Evers) For Us, The Living, 1967; author: A Class Divided, 1971, A More Perfect Union, 1987, A Class Divided: Then and Now, 1987; prodr., writer, dir. (CBS Reports documentaries) Mississippi and the 15th Amendment, 1962, Storm Over the Supreme Court, Parts II and III, 1963 (George F. Peabody award, Golden Gavel award ABA), The Priest and the Politician, 1963, Filibuster--Birth Struggle of a Law, 1964, Segregation: Northern-Style, 1964, co-prodr. After Ten Years: The Court and the Schools, 1964 (Nat. Sch. Bell award NEA), (ABC News documentaries) Africa (East Africa), 1967 (Peabody award, NATAS award), Southern Accents--Northern Ghettos, 1967 (nominee for writing achievement Writers Guild Am.), The Eye of the Storm, 1970 (George Foster Peabody award, Cine Golden Eagle award, Cath. Broadcasters Assn. Gabriel award, Am. Film Festival Blue Ribbon, Saturday Rev. TV award, hon. mention Monte Carlo TV Festival, Nat. Media awards of the Am. Psychol. Found.), An Echo of Anger, 1976, Suddenly an Eagle, 1976, Death of a Family (Writers Guild Am. award), A Bond of Iron, 1982, A Class Divided, 1985 (Emmy award, Sidney Hillman award, Cine Golden Eagle award); others, prodr., dir.; writer Bill Moyer's Jour. (PBS), S.C. Edel. TV Network; exec. prodr.: Boswell's London Journal, 1984; contbr. over 80 articles to mags., jours. Co-founder North Shore Citizens Com., 1946, bd. dirs., 1946-51; co-founder Pelham Com. Human Relations, 1963, vice chmn., 1963-65, chmn., 1965-66. Served to capt., pilot USAAF, 1942-45, ETO. Decorated D.F.C. Air medal with 2 oak leaf clusters; recipient Benjamin Franklin mag. award, 1954, Peabody TV award, 1963, 1970, 1976, Golden Gavel award, ABA, 1963, Sch. Bell award, NEA, 1964, Emmy award, Sidney Hillman award, 1985, Lincoln Univ. awards (2), Howard Blakeslee award, Am. Heart Assn., Intergroup Rels. award, Adelphi chpt. B'nai B'rith women and Anti-Defamation League of Phila. award. Mem. Dirs. Guild Am., Writers Guild Am. Democrat. Home: 3108 Long Hill Rd Guilford CT 06437-3619 Office Phone: 203-457-1744.

**PETERS, WILLIAM P.,** oncologist, educator, science administrator, dean; b. Buffalo, Aug. 26, 1950; m. Elizabeth Zentai; children: Emily, Abigail, James. BS, BS, BA, Pa. State U., 1972; MPhil, PhD, Columbia U., 1976, MD,

1978; postgrad., Harvard U., 1984; MBA, Duke U., 1990. Diplomate Am. Bd. Internal Medicine, Am. Bd. Med. Oncology. Prof. medicine Duke U. Med. Ctr., Durham, N.C., 1993-95, assoc. dir. for clin. ops. Duke Comprehensive Cancer Ctr., 1994-95, dir. bone marrow transplant program, 1984-95; pres., CEO, Mich. Cancer Found., Detroit, 1995—2001; pres., dir., CEO Karmanos Cancer Inst., Detroit, 1995—2001; assoc. dean for cancer programs Wayne State U., Detroit, 1995—2001, prof. oncology, medicine, surgery and radiation oncology, 1995—; disting. chair of oncology Wayne State U., Detroit, 2002—; pres., dir., CEO CETAID, Karamanos Cancer Inst., 2001—; pres. Inst. for Strategic Analysis and Innovation, Detroit Med. Ctr., 2001—. Sr. v.p. for cancer svcs. Detroit Med. Ctr., 1995-2001.

**PETERSEN, ANNE C. (CHERYL PETERSEN),** foundation administrator, educator; b. Little Falls, Minn., Sept. 11, 1944; d. Franklin Hanks and Rhoda Pauline (Sandwick) Studley; m. Douglas Lee Petersen, Dec. 27, 1967; children: Christine Anne, Benjamin Bradfield. BA, U. Chgo., 1966, MS, 1972, PhD, 1973. Asst. prof., rsch. assoc. Dept. Psychiatry U. Chgo., 1972-80, assoc. prof., rsch. assoc., 1980-82; prof. human devel., head Dept. Individual and Family Studies Pa. State U., University Park, 1982-87, dean Coll. Health and Human Devel., 1987-92, prof. health and human devel., 1987-92; dean grad. sch., v.p. for rsch. throughout state U. Minn., Mpls., 1992-94, prof. adolescent devel. and pediatrics, 1992-96; dep. dir., COO NSF, Arlington, Va., 1994-96; sr. v.p. programs W.K. Kellogg Found., 1996—. Vis. prof., fellow Coll. Edn., R&D Psychology, Roosevelt U., Chgo., 1973-74; cons. Ctr. for Health Adminstrn. Studies U. Chgo., 1976-78, Ctr. for New Schs., Chgo., 1974-78, Robert Wood Johnson Found. Mathtech, Inc., 1987-89; coord. clin. rsch. tng. program Michael Reese Hosp. and Med. Ctr., Chgo., 1976-80, dir. Lab. for Study of Adolescence, 1975-82; faculty Ill. Sch. for Profl. Psychology, 1978-79; statis. cons. Coll. Nursing U. Ill. Med. Ctr., 1975-83; assoc. dir. health program MacArthur Found., 1980-82, also cons. health program, 1982-88; chair sr. adv. bd. NIMH, 1987-88; nat. adv. mental health coun. NIH, 1997—; trustee Nat. Inst. Statis. Scis., 1998—. Author: Sex Related Differences in Cognition Functioning: Developmental Issues, 1979, Promoting Adolescent Health: A Dialog on Research and Practice, 1982, Firls at Puberty: Biological and psychosocial Perspectives, 1983, Brain Maturation and Cognitive Development: Comparative and Cross Cultural Perspectives, 1991, Narrowing the Margins: Adolescent Unemployment and the lack of a social role, 1991, Grofit: A Fortran Program for the Estimation of Parameters of a Human Growth Curve, 1972, Girls at Puberty: Biological and Psychosocial Perspectives, 1983, Adolescence and Youth: Psychological Development in a Changing World, 1984, Youth Unemployment and Society, 1994, Transitions Through Adolescence: Interpersonal Domains and Context, 1996; reviewer Jour. Youth and Adolescence, 1975-80, Devel. Psychology, 1979—, Sci., 1979—, Jour. Edn. Psychology, 1979—, Child Devel., 1980—, Jour. Edn. Measurement, 1980, Ednl. Rschr., 1980, Am. Ednl. Rsch. Jour., 1981—, Jour. Mental Imagery, 1982-92, Sex Roles, 1984—; cons. editor Psychology of Women Quar., 1978-82, assoc. editor, 1983-86; adv. editor Contemporary Psychology, 1985-86; mem. editl. bd. various profl. jours.; contbr. chpts. to books and articles to profl. jours. Bd. overseers Lewis Coll., Ill. Inst. Tech., 1980-82; mem. adv. bd. longitudinal data archive project Murray Ctr., Radcliffe Coll., 1985-91, mem. sci. adv. bd., 1983-91 Fellow: APA (chmn. task force on reproductive freedom 1979—81, program chmn. 1981—82, chmn. task force on long range planning 1986—89, pres. divsn. 7 1992—93), AAAS; mem. NAS (nat. forum on future children and their families 1987—91, chmn. panel on child abuse and neglect 1991—93, mem. forum on adolescence Inst. of Medicine 1997—2000, chair bd. on behavioral, cognitive and sensory scis. 1997—), Soc. for Rsch. on Adolescence (pres. 1990—92, past pres. 1992—94, chmn. nominations com. 1992—94), Acad. Europaea, Psychometric Soc., Behavior Genetics Assn., Assn. Women in Sci. (bd. dirs. 1996—2000), Am. Ednl. Rsch. Assn. (various offices), Internat. Soc. for the Study of Behavioral Devel. (coun. mem. 1995—, pres.-elect 2002—), Inst. for Medicine. Home: 3715 Blackberry Ln Kalamazoo MI 49008-3333 E-mail: globalphilliance@yahoo.com.

**PETERSEN, ARNE JOAQUIN,** chemist; b. L.A., Jan. 27, 1932; s. Hans Maria Theodore and Astrid Marie (Pedersen) Petersen; m. Sandra Joyce Sharp, Aug. 12, 1961; children: Christina Lynn, Kurt Arne. AA, Compton Coll., 1957; BS, Calif. State U. Long Beach, 1959; BA, U. Calif. Irvine, 1975. Lic. comml. pilot. Chemist, scientist Beckman Instruments, Inc., Fullerton, Calif., 1959—62, engr., scientist, 1962—65, project, sr. project engr., 1965—72; project/program mgr. clin. divsn. Beckman Clin. Ops., Fullerton/Brea, 1974—80; ops. mgr. Graphic Controls Corp., Irvine, 1980—82; engr./mgr. R&D Carle Instruments Chromatography, Anaheim, Calif., 1982—84; mgr. ops. Magnaflux/X-Ray Devel., L.A., 1984—85; dir. R&D, new products Am. Chem. Sys., Irvine, 1985—86; rsch. assoc. U. Calif., Irvine, 1987—88; ind. cons., contractor, sales real estate investment, 1989—. Career guidance counselor U. Calif., Irvine, 1976; co-founder Cak, Inc., 2001. Contbr. articles and sci. papers in field to profl. jours. Exec. svc. A.I.D. Internat. Exec. Svc. Corps, Egypt, 1993—94; vol. F.I.S.H., Costa Mesa, Newport Beach, Calif.; basketball coach Boys-Girls Club, Newport Beach, 1975—78; baseball coach Newport Beach Parks, 1975—78; adv. com. Newport/Costa Mesa Sch. Bd., 1974—75. Mem.: AAAS, AMA, Am. Chem. Soc., Biomed. Engring. Soc., U. Calif. Univ. Club (bd. dirs.), Chi Gamma Iota (pres. Compton Coll. chpt. 1956), Kappa Sigma (founder Calif. State U. Long Beach chpt.). Achievements include patents in field. Avocations: flying, photography, travel, bridge, surfing. Personal E-mail: AJPetersen@earthlink.net.

**PETERSEN, BARRY REX,** news correspondent; b. Norfolk, Va., Jan. 14, 1949; s. Kermit and Mavis Lucille (Sutton) P.; m. Sandra H. Petersen, June 7, 1971 (div. Dec. 1984); children: Emily Jensine, Juliette Rose; m. Jan Chorlton, Feb. 14, 1985. BS in Journalism, Northwestern U., 1970, MS in Journalism, 1972. Sports columnist Sidney (Mont.) Herald, 1964-66; city hall reporter Arlington Heights (Ill.) Day, 1968-69; columnist, copy editor Chgo. Today, 1970-71; pub. Daily Northwestern, Evanston, Ill., 1970-71; reporter Milw. (Wis.) Jour., 1971-72; investigative reporter Sta. WITI-TV, Milw., 1972-74; reporter, anchor Sta. WCCO-TV, Mpls., 1974-78; corr. CBS News, L.A., 1978-81, San Francisco, 1981-85, Tokyo, 1986-88, Moscow, 1988-90, London, 1991-95, Tokyo, 1995—. Pres. AFRTA, Milw., 1973-74; Josephine B. and Newton N. Minow vis. prof. in communications Northwestern U., Evanston, Ill., 1991. Recipient Investigative Reporting award Wis. Press Assn., 1973, Nat. Emmy award, 1994, 97, World gold medal radio breaking news N.Y. Festivals, 1999, Edward R. Murrow award, 2004. Mem. Fgn. Corrs. Club Japan, Fgn. Club of China. Lutheran. Avocations: sailing, travel, international real estate. also: CBS News 5-3-6 Akasaka Minato-ku Tokyo 107 Japan Office Phone: 212-975-3019. Business E-Mail: bp3@cbsnews.com.

**PETERSEN, BENTON LAURITZ,** paralegal; b. Salt Lake City, Jan. 1, 1942; s. Lauritz George and Arleane (Curtis) P.; m. Sharon Donnette Higgins, Sept. 20, 1974 (div. Aug. 9, 1989); children: Grant Lauritz, Tashya Eileen, Nicholas Robert, Katrina Arleane. AA, Weber State Coll., 1966, BA, BA, Weber State Coll., 1968; M of Liberal Studies, U. Okla., 1980; diploma, Nat. Radio Inst. Paralegal Sch., 1991; JD, Monticello U., 1999. Registered paralegal. Announcer/news dir. KWHO Radio, Salt Lake City, 1968-70, KDXU Radio, St. George, Utah, 1970-73, KSOP Radio, Salt Lake City, 1973-76; case worker/counselor Salvation Army, Midland, Tex., 1976-84; announcer/news dir. KBRS Radio, Springdale, Ark., 1984-86; case worker/counselor Office of Human Concern, Rogers, Ark., 1986-88; announcer KAZM Radio, Sedona, Ariz., 1988-91; paralegal Benton L. Petersen, Manti, Utah, 1991—. Cons. Sanpete County Srs., Manti, 1992—. Award judge Manti City Beautification, 1992-96; treas. Manti Destiny Com., 1993-98; tourism com. Sanpete County Econ. Devel., Ephraim, Utah, 1993-96. Served with U.S. Army N.G., 1959-66. Mem.: Nat. Assn. Attys. in Fact (past pres.), Am. Assn. Individual Investors. Mem. Lds Ch. Avocation: reading. Home: 470 E 120 N Manti UT 84642-1164 Office Phone: 435-835-8689. E-mail: bpfreedom@hotmail.com.

**PETERSEN, CATHERINE HOLLAND,** lawyer; b. Norman, Okla., Apr. 24, 1951; d. John Hays and Helen Ann (Turner) Holland; m. James Frederick Petersen, June 26, 1973 (div.); children: T. Kyle, Lindsay Diane; m. Lester E.R. Doty, Apr. 17, 2004. BA, Hastings Coll., 1973; JD, Okla. U., 1976. Bar: Okla. 1976, U.S. Dist. Ct. (we. dist.) Okla. 1978. Legal intern, police legal advisor City of Norman, 1974-76; sole practice Norman, 1976-81; ptnr. Williams Petersen & Denny, Norman, 1981-82; pres. Petersen Assocs., Inc., Norman, 1982—2004; ptnr. Petersen, Henson & Meadows, PC, Norman, 2004—. Adj. prof. Oklahoma City U. Coll. Law, 1982, U. Okla. Law Ctr., 1987; instr. continuing legal edn. U. Okla. Law Ctr., Norman, 1977, 79, 81, 83, 84, 86, 89-95; instr. Okla. Bar Assn., ABA, Am. Acad. Matrimonial Lawyers. Bd. dirs. United Way, Norman, 1978-84, pres., 1981; bd. dirs. Women's Resource Ctr., Norman, 1975-77, 82-84; mem. Jr. League, Norman, 1980-83, Norman Hosp. Ayx., 1982-84; trustee 1st Presbyn. Ch., 1986-87. Named among Outstanding Okla. Women of 1980s, Women's Polit. Caucus, 1980, Outstanding Young Women of Am., 1981, 83. Fellow Am. Acad. Matrimonial Lawyers (pres. Okla. chpt. 1990-91, bd. govs. 1991-95); mem. ABA (family law sect., faculty Family Law Inst. 1993—), Cleveland County Bar Assn., Okla. Bar Assn. (chmn. family law sect. 1987-88), Phi Delta Phi. Republican. Home: 4716 Sundance Ct Norman OK 73072-3900 Office: PO Box 1243 314 E Comanche St Norman OK 73069-6009 Office Phone: 405-329-3307.

**PETERSEN, DAVID L.,** lawyer; AA, Concordia Jr. Coll., Milw., 1963; BA, Concordia Sr. Coll., Ft. Wayne, Ind., 1965; JD, Valparaiso U., Ind., 1968. Bar: Wis. 1968, U.S. Dist. Ct. (ea. dist.) Wis. 1969, U.S. Ct. Appeals (7th cir.) 1972, U.S. Supreme Ct. 1988, Fla. 1989. Ptnr. Quarles & Brady, Milw. and Naples, Fla., 1968—. Author: Wisconsin Condominium Law, 1988, 98, 2003; editor Valparaiso U. Law Rev., 1967-68; contbr. articles to profl. jours. Mem. Greater Milw. Com. Cmty. Devel., 1983; bd. dirs. Goals for Greater Milw. 2000, 1982, Broward Com. of 100; mem. nat. adv. bd. Nat. Ctr. for Missing and Exploited Children, Washington, Adam Walsh Children's Fund, Palm Beach, Fla.; dir. Boys and Girls Club Collier County. Lt. col., instr. pilot USAF/Wis. Air N.G., 1970-90. Mem. ABA, Wis. Bar Assn., Milw. Bar Assn., Fla Bar Assn., Broward County Bar Assn., Palm Beach County Bar Assn., Collier County Bar Assn., Am. Coll. Real Estate Lawyers, Milw. Yacht Club, Palm Beach Yacht Club. Office: Quarles & Brady LLP 1395 Panther Ln Naples FL 34109 also: Quarles & Brady LLP 411 E Wisconsin Ave Ste 2550 Milwaukee WI 53202-4409 Office Phone: 239-434-4959.

**PETERSEN, DAVID M.,** electrical engineer; b. Athens, Ga., May 2, 1964; s. David Muir and Okie Lee Petersen; m. Sharon Faye Culberson, May 17, 1991; children: Sela Olivia, Cady Alyssa. BSEE, U. Tenn., 1987. Distbn. engr. City of Oak Ridge, Tenn., 1988—93; supr. elec. engring. Decatur (Ala.) Utilities, 1993—98; supr. elec. distbn. Solutia, Decatur, 1998—2004; plant elec. engr. GAF Materials Corp., Nashville, 2004—06. Elec. cons. Fowler Engring., Decatur, 1993—; bd. dirs. Assoc. Valley Industries, 2005. Vol. United Way, Decatur, 1993—98, loaned exec., 1998—2000, bd. dirs., 2000—04. Mem.: IEEE. Republican. Presbyterian. Avocations: fishing, scuba diving, water-skiing, hiking, softball. Office: Air Liquide 200 Chastain Ctr Blvd Ste 295 Kennesaw GA 30144

**PETERSEN, DONALD SONDERGAARD,** lawyer; b. Pontiac, Ill., May 14, 1929; s. Clarence Marius and Esther (Sondergaard) P.; m. Alice Thorup, June 5, 1954; children: Stephen, Susan Petersen Schuh, Sally Petersen Riordan. Student, Grand View Coll., 1946—48; BA, Augustana Coll., Rock Island, Ill., 1951; JD, Northwestern U., 1956. Bar: Ill. 1957. Assoc. Norman & Billick and predecessors, Chgo., 1956-64, ptnr., 1965-78; counsel Sidley & Austin, Chgo., 1978-80, ptnr., 1980-93, ret., 1993. Pres. Chgo. Exhibitors Corp., Chgo., 1972-85. Bd. dirs. Mount Olive Cemetery Co. Inc., Chgo., 1972-90; bd. dirs. Augustana Hosp., 1983-87, The Danish Home, 1976—; bd. dirs. Luth. Gen. Hosp., Park Ridge, Ill., 1968-2005, chmn., 1979-81, 89-91; bd. dirs. Luth. Gen. Health System and predecessors, Park Ridge, 1980-95, chmn., 1980-81, 83-85; bd. dirs., chmn. Parkside Health Mgmt. Corp., Parkside Home Health Svcs., 1985-88. With U.S. Army, 1951-53. Mem. Chgo. Bar Assn., Ill. State Bar Assn. Clubs: Union League (Chgo.). Home: 241 N Aldine Ave Park Ridge IL 60068-3009 Office: 9th Fl One S Dearborn St Chicago IL 60603 Office Phone: 312-853-7232.

**PETERSEN, DOROTHY VIRGINIA,** investment company executive; b. Milw., Sept. 22, 1929; d. Carl Arndt and Loretta Louise Laura (Bremer) Scherer; m. Glenn Charles Petersen, Aug. 27, 1949; children: Dr. Vicki Lynn Abbott, Larry Dean, Dr. Rick Randall. BS magna cum laude, U. Wis.-Parkside, 1975. Repair dept. clk. Eastman Kodak Co., Milw., 1946—47; sec. First Wis. Trust Co., Milw., 1947—49; head sec. art edn. dept. U. Wis., Madison, 1949—50; sec. and asst. Red Star Yeast Co., Milw., 1950—51; exec. sec. Boy Scouts Am., Milw., 1963—65, Applied Power, Pewaukee, Wis., 1965—67; sec., treas. Westshore Muffler Shops, Milw., 1983—2002; asst. sec. and treas. Fastrack, Inc., Mequon, Wis., 2002—. Paintings (Honorable Mention, Wis. Art Show, Twin Lakes, 1976). Head fund drive Town of Greenfield ARC, 1956, helper fund drive, 1955, helper fund, 1957—59; leader Girl Scouts Am., Wauwatosa, Wis., 1960—61; cub pack sec. Boy Scouts Am., Wauwatosa, 1962—63; children's class tchr. Baha'i World Faith, Greenfield, Milw., Burlington, 1959—72, spkr. Milw., Burlington, 1970—99. Mem.: Order Ea. Star (Wauwatosa chpt. #219). Baha'i Avocations: day trading, genealogy, reading, photography, miniature poodles. Home: 7907 W Willowbrook Dr 115N Mequon WI 53097 Personal E-mail: dvpetersen29@hotmail.com.

**PETERSEN, JAMES L.,** lawyer; b. Bloomington, Ill., Feb. 3, 1947; s. Eugene and Cathryn Theresa (Hemmele) P.; m. Helen Louise Moser, Nov. 20, 1971; children: Christine Louise, Margaret Theresa. BA, Ill. State U., 1970; MA, U. Ill., Springfield, 1973; JD magna cum laude, Ind. U., 1976. Bar; Ind. 1976, Fla. 1980, U.S. Dist. Cts. (no. and so. Ind.), U.S. Ct. Appeals (7th cir.), U.S. Supreme Ct. Admissions officer U. Ill., Springfield, 1970-71, asst. to v.p., 1971-72, registrar, 1972-73; assoc. Ice Miller, Indpls., 1976-83, ptnr., 1983—. Pres. United Cerebral Palsy of Ctrl. Ind., 1981-83, pres. Found., 1988-90, Stanley K. Lacy Leadership Series participant. Mem. ABA, Fla. Bar Assn., Ind. Bar Assn., Am. Coll. Trial Lawyers, Intl. Franchise Assn. (bd. mem. Symposium Organizing Cmte., 2003-04), Defense Trial Coun. Ind. (past co-chair, Prods. Liability Cmte; elected 1997 Diplomat), The Business Council, Inc., Ill. State U. Alumni Assn. (pres. 1990-92), Ind. U. Law Alumni Assn. (bd. dirs. 1992—, pres. 1998-99), Ind. U. Bd. Visitors 1998-99, Order of Coif. Home: 11827 Sea Star Dr Indianapolis IN 46256-9400 Office: Ice Miller LLP PO Box 82001 One American Sq Indianapolis IN 46282 Office Phone: 317-236-2308.

**PETERSEN, JEAN SNYDER,** educational association administrator; b. NYC, Oct. 16, 1931; d. Peter Eugene and Helyn Brownell (Parker) Snyder; m. Elton Reed Petersen, Sept. 16, 1954; children— Bruce Brownell, Craig Reed. Student, N.Y. U., 1949-51; degree fgn. banking, Am. Inst. Banking, 1952. Fgn. credit investigator Chase Nat. Bank Hdqrs., N.Y.C., 1952-56; nat. exec. dir. Assn. Children and Adults with Learning Disabilities (name changed to Learning Disabilities Assn. of Am.), Pitts., 1972—. Mem. exec. com., treas. Jr. League, Pitts.; bd. dirs. Found. for Children with Learning Disabilities, N.Y.C., Children's Hosp., Pitts., Music for Mt. Lebanon, Vocat. Rehab. Ctr., Pitts.; bd. dirs., v.p., mem. exec. com. Assn. Retarded Citizens Pa.; ptnr. UN Internat. Yr. of Disabled; ruling elder Presbyn. Ch.Assn. Retarded Citizens Pa.; mem. exec. com. Pat Buckley Moss Nat. Children's Charity Found; chmn. bd. dirs. Masonic Learning Ctrs. for Children. Recipient Sustainers award Jr. League, 1977, Recognition award, 1975, Pres.'s award, 1978. Mem. AAUW, Meeting Planners Internat. (treas.), Am. Soc. Assn. Execs. Republican. Presbyterian. Home: 343 Shadowlawn Ave Pittsburgh PA 15216-1239 Office: 4156 Library Rd Pittsburgh PA 15234-1349 Fax: (412) 5634537.

**PETERSEN, JOHN D.,** academic administrator; m. Carol Petersen; 2 children. BS in Chemistry, UCLA, 1970; PhD in Inorganic Chemistry, U. Calif., Santa Barbara, 1975. Asst. prof. chemistry Kans. State U., 1975—80; head dept. chemistry, assoc. dean rsch. Coll. Scis. Clemson (S.C.) U.,

1980—93; prof. chemistry, dean Coll. Sci. Wayne State U., 1994—2000; provost, exec. v.p. univ. affairs U. Conn., Storrs, 2000—04; pres. U. Tenn., Knoxville, Tenn., 2004—. Mem.: Nat. Assn. State Univ. and Land Grant Coll. (exec. com. for chief academic officers), Coun. Chem. Rsch., Am. Chem. Soc. Office: U Tenn Office of Pres 800 Andy Holt Tower Knoxville TN 37996-0180 Office Phone: 865-974-2241. Office Fax: 865-974-3753.*

**PETERSEN, LISA RAE,** elementary school educator; b. Crosby, N.D., Dec. 2, 1972; d. Allan and Marlys Ekness; m. Steven James Petersen, Aug. 2, 2003; children: Jesse, Shawn, Andrew. BA, Concordia Coll., Moorhead, Minn., 1995. Elem. tchr.; literacy coach White Pine County Schs., Ely, Nev., 1995—. Sci. fair coord. DEN Elem., Ely, Nev., 1997—2006. Pres. White Pine Ladies Golf Assn., Ely, Nev., 1997—99. Mem.: Internat. Reading Assn. Republican. Lutheran. Avocations: motherhood, camping, reading, fishing. Home: 1118 Ave K Ely NV 89301 Office: DEN Elem 1001 Eleventh St E Ely NV 89301 Office Phone: 775-289-4846. E-mail: lspetersen1014@sbcglobal.net.

**PETERSEN, MARTIN EUGENE,** curator; b. Grafton, Iowa, Apr. 21, 1931; s. Martin S. and Martha Dorothea (Paulsen) P. AA, Mason City Jr. Coll., Iowa; BA, State U. Iowa, 1951, MA, 1957; postgrad., The Hague (Netherlands), 1964. Curator San Diego Mus. Art, 1957-96; advisor Olaf Wieghorst Mus., El Cajon, Calif., 1996—. Extension instr. U. Calif., 1958, lectr., 1960 Author art catalogues, books, articles in field. Served with AUS, 1952-54. Mem. So. Calif. Art Historians. Achievements include specialist in early southern California art. Home: 2003 Bayview Heights Dr Spc 138 San Diego CA 92105-5537

**PETERSEN, MARTIN ROSS,** public affairs executive; b. Bakersfield, Calif., Aug. 14, 1944; s. Peter Arthur and Valerie A. (Swink) P.; m. Geri Gottuso, Nov. 12, 1987; children: Kaitlin Jean, Alexander Ross. BA in Govt., Calif. State U., Sacramento, 1969. Asst. dir. govtl. affairs Calif. State U. and Colls., Sacramento, 1967-72; adminstr. divsn. consumer svcs. Calif. Dept. Consumer Affairs, Sacramento, 1972-75; dir. Office External Liaison The White House Office Consumer Affairs, Washington, 1975-77, 83-85; pres. Knauer & Assocs., Inc., Washington, 1977-83; dir. corp. pub. affairs and N.J. ops. adminstrn. Playtex Products, Inc., Allendale, 1985—. Exec. v.p. Trade Net, Washington, 1981-85; chmn. Washington Legis. Group, 1984-85; mem. bd. govs. Ramapo (N.J.) State Coll., 2001—. Editor: Auto Imports, 1979; founding editor Customer Relationship Mgmt., 1980-82. Pub. mem. Voluntary Effort To Contain Health Care Costs in Am., Chgo., 1977-80; sec. subcom. on consumer affairs Rep. Nat. Com., Washington, 1979-80; mem. transition team and inaugural com. Reagan-Bush White House, Washington, 1981; v.p. Nat. Coalition for Consumer Edn., Washington, 1981-91; v.p. Oakland (N.J.) Rep. Club, 1990, 2001; councilman Borough of Oakland, 1991-2002; author, vol. in pub. svc. Consumer Product Safety Commn., 1977. With USAF, 1962-66. Mem. Soc. Consumer Affairs Profls. in Bus. (nat. bd. dirs. 1979-83, 98—2002, exec. com. 1980-83, 99—2002, pres. D.C. chpt. 1977-78, Outstanding Leader of Yr. award 1985), Am. League Lobbyists, Govt. Affairs Profls. (N.Y.C.), Am. Soc. Quality, Internat. Facility Mgmt. Assn., Internat. Bus. Comm. Assn. Home: 10 Wichita Path Oakland NJ 07436-3818 Office: Playtex Products Inc 75 Commerce Dr Allendale NJ 07401-1600 E-mail: martin.petersen@usa.net.

**PETERSEN, ROBERT ALLEN,** pediatric ophthalmologist; b. NYC, Dec. 30, 1933; s. Harold Marinus and Elinor Louise (Buckley) P.; m. Veronica Margiana Stinnes, Dec. 22, 1956; children: Anne, Catherine, John. BS, Queens Coll., CUNY, 1955; MD, Columbia U., 1959, DrMedSc, 1964. Diplomate Am. Bd. Ophthalmology. Med. resident Presbyn. Hosp., N.Y.C., 1959-61; USPHS postdoctoral fellow Columbia U. Coll. Physicians and Surgeons, N.Y.C., 1961-62; USPHS preclin. trainee Howe Lab. of Ophthalmology, MEEI, Boston, 1962-63; resident in ophthalmology Mass. Eye and Ear Infirmary, Boston, 1963-66; instr. in ophthalmology to asst. prof. Harvard Med. Sch., Boston, 1970—; assoc. in Ophthalmology to sr. assoc. Children's Hosp., Boston, 1966—. Contbr. articles to profl. jours. Cons., vision task force Mass. Dept. Pub. Health, 1981-85. Major U.S. Army, 1967-69, South Vietnam. Various rsch. grants NIH, 1961-63, 94—. Fellow Am. Acad. Ophthalmology, Am. Acad. Pediatrics; mem. Am. Assn. for Pediatric Ophthalmology and Strabismus (bd. dirs. 1974-76, edn. com. 1987-93, Costenbader Lectureship com. 1993-96, 97-2000, chair 1995-96, 99-2000, chair site selection com. 1995-97), New Eng. Ophthal. Soc. Mem. Soc. Of Friends. Achievements include rsch. on the genetics of reinoblastoma; first to describe optic nerve hypoplasia in the children of diabetic mothers; to describe eye findings in a variety of systemic anomalies. Office: Children's Hosp 300 Longwood Ave Boston MA 02115-5737 E-mail: robert.petersen@childrens.harvard.edu.

**PETERSEN, ROBERT E.,** magazine publishing executive; b. LA, Sept. 10, 1926; s. Einar and Bertha (Putera) P.; m. Margie McNally, Jan. 26, 1963. Founder Petersen Pub. Co. (pubs. Hot Rod, Motor Trend, Car Craft, Motorcyclist, Photog., Skin Diver, Teen, Hunting, Guns & Ammo, Circle Track, Dirt Rider, Los Angeles, 1948-2000; owner, chmn. bd. Petersen Properties, L.A., 1996—; owner Petersen Aviation, Van Nuys, Calif., 1996—. Co-founder benefactor Petersen Automotive Mus., L.A. Mem. Los Angeles Library Commn., 1963-64; Bd. dirs. Boys Club Am., past pres. Hollywood br.; bd. dirs. Thalians; founder Petersen Automotive Mus., L.A. Served with USAF. Mem.: So. Calif Safari, Confrerie de la Chaine des Rotisseurs, Chevaliers du Tastevin. Office: Petersen Properties 6420 Wilshire Blvd Los Angeles CA 90048-5502

**PETERSEN, ROLAND,** artist, printmaker; b. Endelavé, Horsens, Denmark, 1926; came to US, 1928; m. Caryl Ritter, Mar. 4, 2003; children from previous marriage: Dana Mark, Maura Brooke, Julien Conrad, Karena Caia. BA, U. Calif., Berkeley, 1949, MA, 1950; postgrad., Han Hofmann's Sch. Fine Arts, 1950-51, S.W. Hayter's Atelier 17, Paris, 1950, 63, 70, Islington Studio, London, 1976, The Print Workshop, 1980. Tchr. State Coll. Wash., Pullman, 1952-56; faculty U. Calif., Davis, 1956-91, prof. art, 1991; ret., 1991. Exhibited one-man shows: Oakland At Mus., 1954, Calif. Palace Legion of Honor, San Francisco, 1961, Gump's Gallery, San Francisco, 1962, Staempfli Gallery, N.Y.C., 1963, 65, 67, Adele Bednarz Gallery, Los Angeles, 1966, 69, 70, 72, 73, 75, 76, Crocker Art Gallery, Sacramento, 1965, de Young Mus., San Francisco, 1968, La Jolla Mus., 1971, Phoenix Mus., 1972, Santa Barbara Mus., 1973, USIS sponsored touring one-man exhbn., Turkey, U. Reading, Eng., 1977, 80, U. Calif., Davis, 1978, 92, Brubaker Gallery, Sarasota, Fla., 1979, Rorick Gallery, San Francisco, 1981, 82, 83, 84, 85, Himovitz-Salomon Gallery, Sacramento, 1987-88, 91, Vanderwoude Tananbaum Gallery, N.Y.C., 1987-89, Harcourts Gallery, San Francisco, 1989, 91, 93, U. Calif., Davis, 1992, Maxwell Galleries, San Francisco, 1995, Endelave (Denmark) Mus., 1996, John Natsoulas Gallery, Davis, Calif., 1998, Hackett-Freedman Gallery, San Francisco, 2002, 2004; group shows include Calif. Palace Legion of Honor, San Francisco Art Inst., 1962, Mus. Art, Carnegie Inst., Pitts., 1964, Obelisk Gallery, Washington, John Herron Art Inst., Indpls., 1964, Pa. Acad. Fine Arts, Phila., Crocker Art Gallery, Sacramento, 1965, 81, Art Inst. Chgo., 1965, Va. Mus. Fine Arts, Richmond, 1966, U. Ariz. Art Gallery, Tucson, 1967, Am. Cultural Center, Paris, 1971, Nat. Gallery, Washington, 1972, Otis Art Inst. Gallery, Los Angeles, 1974, Auerbach Fine Art Gallery, London, 1977, U. Wis., Madison, 1977, Bklyn. Mus., 1978, U. Ill., 1978, U. Nev., Las Vegas, 1980, Brubaker Gallery, Sarasota, Fla., 1983, U.S.A. World Print Council, San Francisco, Nat. Mus., Singapore, Nat. Gallery, Bangkok; Thailand, Amerika Haus, Berlin, Malmo Konsthall, Sweden, Museo Carrillo Gil, Mexico City, all 1984-86, Crocker Art Mus., 1991, Fresno Met. Mus., 1992, Hall of Pictures, Uman, Russia, 1992, Calif. State U., L.A., 1992, San Bernardino, 1993 Pence Gallery, Davis, Calif., 1993, Artists Contemporary Gallery, Sacramento, 1994, Andre Milan Gallery, Sao Paulo, Brazil, 1995; represented in permanent collections: de Young Mus., San Francisco, San Francisco Mus. Modern Art, Va. Mus. Fine Arts, Richmond, Mus. Modern Art, N.Y.C., Phila. Mus. Art, Whitney Mus. Am. Art, Phoenix Mus., Santa Barbara Mus., Musée Municipal, Brest, France, Smithsonian Instn. Nat. Collection Fine Arts & Archives of Am. Art, Hirschorn Coll., Washington, San Jose Mus. Art, Calif., others. With USN, 1944-46, PTO. Guggenheim fellow, 1963, U. Calif. creative arts fellow, 1967,

70, 77; Fulbright grant, 1970. Mem. AAUP, San Francisco Art Assn., Calif. Soc. Printmakers. Home: 1148 Crespi Dr Pacifica CA 94044-3539 Office: Hackett Freedman Gallery 250 Sutter St Fl 4 San Francisco CA 94108 Office Phone: 415-362-7152.

**PETERSEN, ULRICH,** geology educator; b. Negritos, Peru, Dec. 1, 1927; s. Georg and Harriet (Bluhme) P.; m. Edith Martensen, Apr. 27, 1952 (dec. Aug. 1978); children: Erich, Armin (dec.), Heidi.; m. Eileen Bourque, June 19, 1982. Mining Engr., Escuela Nacional de Ingenieros, Lima, Peru, 1954; MA, Harvard U., 1955, PhD, 1963. Geologist Instituto Geológico del Peru and Instituto Nacional de Investigación y Fomento Mineros, 1946-51; geologist Cerro de Pasco Corp., Peru, 1951-54, asst. chief geologist, 1956-57, chief geologist, 1958-63; lectr. Harvard, 1963-66; assoc. prof. Harvard U., 1966-69, prof. mining geology, 1969-81, Harry C. Dudley prof. econ. geology, 1981-95; cons. geologist, 1963—; prof. emeritus, 1996—. Named comendador de la orden al Merito por Servicios Distinguidos Peru, 1968; recipient A. von Humboldt rsch. award, 1992-93, 2003-04, diploma de honor Ingeniero del Año Soc. de Ingenieros del Peru, 1996, Honor al Mérioto, Colegio de Ingenieros del Peru, 2000, Antorcha de Habich, U. Nacional de Ingenieria del Peru, 2005. Mem. Soc. Econ. Geologists (pres. 1988-89), Geol. Soc. Am., Soc. Geologica del Peru (hon.) Home: 414 Marsh St Belmont MA 02478-1109 Office: 20 Oxford St Cambridge MA 02138-2902 E-mail: ulrichp@aol.com.

**PETERSEN, WOLFGANG,** film director; b. Emden, Germany, Mar. 14, 1941; m. Maria Dow, Apr. 5, 1970 (div. 1980); m. Maria Petersen; 2 children. Asst. state dir. Ernst Deutsch Theatre, Hamburg, Fed. Republic Germany. Dir.: (films) Eine-der Andere, 1967, Ich nicht, 1969, I Will Kill You, 1971, One or the Other of Us, 1973, Jeremy Mine, 1985, (TV) Tatort-Blechschaden, 1971, Tatort-Strandgut, 1972, Anna und Toto, 1972, Van der Valk und die Reichen, 1973, Smog, 1973 (Prix Futura award 1975), Tatort-Jagdrevier, 1973, Tatort-Nachtfrost, 1974, Aufs Kreuz gelegt, 1974, Stellenweise Glatteis, 1975, Stadt im Tal, 1975, For Your Love Only, 1976, Hans im Glück, 1976, Black and White Like Day and Night, 1978; dir., writer: (TV) Vier gegen die Bank, 1976, Planübung, 1977, Das Boot, 1981, (films) The Consequence, 1977, Das Boot (Acad. award nomination Best Adapted Screenplay 1981), NeverEnding Story, 1984; dir., prodr.: In the Line of Fire, 1993, Outbreak, 1995, Air Force One, 1997, The Perfect Storm, 2000, Troy, 2004, Poseidon, 2006; dir., writer, prodr.: Shattered, 1991; prodr.: Bicentennial Man, 1999, exec. prodr.: Red Corner, 1997, Instinct, 1999, (TV) The Agency, 2001, Avenger, 2006. Office: Creative Artists Agy care Rand Halston 9830 Wilshire Blvd Beverly Hills CA 90212-1804

**PETERSEN-FREY, ROLAND,** manufacturing executive; b. Hamburg, Germany, Aug. 17, 1937; arrived in U.S. 1958; s. Georg and Erna (Coltzau) Petersen-Frey; m. Pamela Susan Mobley, Feb. 2, 1993; children: Martin, Anya, Daniel. BA in Fin., CUNY, 1967, MA in Fin., 1970. Asst. v.p. Mfrs. Hanover, N.Y.C., 1961-70; v.p. gen. mgr. Rusch Inc., N.Y.C., 1970-75; CEO, chmn. bd. dirs. Inmed Corp., Atlanta, 1975-89; chmn. bd. dirs. Burrellco, Inc., Atlanta, 1989-90; pres., chmn., CEO A4, Inc., Atlanta, 1997—; pres., CEO The Ga. Contractor LLC. Bd. dirs. Albert Int; chmn. bd. dirs. A4, Inc; mng. ptnr. Bunter Holdings Ltd, Atlanta, chmn. bd. dirs.; bd. dirs. Albert Holdings USA, Inc., Canton, Ga., v.p.; chmn. TGC Pub., LLC. With U.S. Army, 1959—61. Fellow: Inst Dirs. Republican. Avocations: tennis, hiking, swimming. Office Phone: 770-521-8877. Business E-Mail: r.frey@a4inc.com.

**PETERSON, ANDREW JAMES,** physician, military officer; b. State College, Pa., Sept. 15, 1977; s. Donald Lee and Sandra K. Peterson. BS in Biology, Mansfield U., Pa., 1996—2000; PhD in Osteopathic Medicine, W.Va. Sch. Osteopathic Medicine, Lewisburg, 2000—04. Internship internal medicine USAF, Biloxi, Miss., 2004—05; resident internal medicine US Navy, Bethesda, Md., 2005—. Capt. USAF, 2000—, Bethesda. Mem.: Am. Geriatrics Assn., Am. Osteopathic Assn., Am. College Physicians.

**PETERSON, ANN SULLIVAN,** physician, consultant; b. Rhinebeck, NY, Oct. 11, 1928; AB, Cornell U., 1950, MD, 1954; MS, MIT, 1980. Diplomate Am. Bd. Internal Medicine. Intern Cornell Med. Divsn.-Bellevue Hosp., NYC, 1954—55, resident, 1955—57; fellow in medicine and physiology Meml.-Sloan Kettering Cancer Ctr., Cornell Med. Coll., NYC, 1957—60; instr. medicine Georgetown U. Sch. Medicine, Washington, 1962—65, asst. prof., 1965—69, asst. dir. clin. rsch. unit, 1962—69; assoc. prof. medicine U. Ill., Chgo., 1969—72, asst. dean. 1969—71, assoc. dean, 1971—72; assoc. prof. medicine, assoc. dean Coll. Physicians and Surgeons, Columbia U., NYC, 1972—80, Cornell U. Med. Coll., NYC, 1980—83; assoc. dir. divsn. med. edn. AMA, Chgo., 1983—86, dir. div. grad. med. edn, 1986—89, v.p. mgmt. cons. corp., 1989—93; ind. cons. Chgo., 1993—2005. Contbr. articles to med. jours. Mem. bd. regents Uniformed Svcs. U. of Health Scis., 1984—90. John and Mary R. Markle scholar, 1965—70, Alfred P. Sloan fellow, MIT, 1979—80. Fellow: ACP; mem.: Mortar Bd., Alpha Omega Alpha, Alpha Epsilon Delta.

**PETERSON, ANNE ELIZABETH WALLACE,** music educator, composer; b. Aurora, Ill., June 17, 1949; d. Vernon Ammon and Marjorie Lois (Loudon) Wallace; m. Thomas Leonard Peterson (dec. 1990); m. Tim Allen Gasser, Feb. 27, 1993. Attended, Macphail Sch. Music, 1964—67, San Francisco Conservatory Music, 1974—77, U. Edinburgh, 1979, Baroque Performance Inst., 1992; studied with Martha Ivory, 1970, studied with Charlene Brendler, 1978; BA in English and Music, U. Minn., 1971; MA in Music, Lone Mountain Coll., 1978; studied harpsichord, with Laurette Goldberg, 1974—78; studied harpsichord with Peter Williams. Cert. in Tech. Writing De Anza Coll., Cupertino, Calif., 1981. Music tchr. Pillsbury-Waite Cultural Arts Ctr., Mpls., 1971—72, Music Schs., Sunnyvale, Calif., 1991—; tech. writer, editor, rschr. SRI Internat., Menlo Park, Calif., 1973—90, Music tchr. Cmty. Sch Music and Arts, Mountain View, Calif., 1973—78, Mountain View, 1979—2001; harpsichord performer No. Calif. Renaissance Faire, 1979—85, Minn. Renaissance Festival, 1982; mem. Soc. Tech. Communication, 1979—90, conv. spkr. 1983; keyboard gen. music instr. Boys' and Girls' Club, Redwood City, Calif., 1990—92; pvt. piano and harpsichord tchr., Redwood City, 1980—; musician, Palo Alto. San Francisco, Calif.; conf. workshop presenter in field. Author: (book) Harpsichord Tuning: An Easy Start, 1978, (book, CD) Follow the Rainbow, 2003; musician (harpsichordist): (albums) Then, 1997, Harpsichord at Hampstead, 1999, Starpirations, 2000; musician: Good Company (with Tudor Rose Ensemble), 1997; musician: (harpsichordist) Come and Adore! (Christmas-variety) Starpirations, 1999; musician: (harpsichordist, ensemblist, vocalist) Elizabeth Gambarini, 2000. Mem.: Music Tchrs. Assn. (Appreciation award 2000), Music Tchrs. Assn. Calif. (program chair 2000—01), Toastmasters Internat. (Achievement award 1989), Phi Beta (pres. Pi Lambda chpt. 1993—95, program chair 1974—85, 2002—03, Grad. Grant-In Aid award, Marie Logan award 1979, Nat. Historian award 2004). Office Phone: 650-365-5375. Personal E-mail: awpgmusic@yahoo.com.

**PETERSON, ARTHUR LAVERNE,** foundation administrator; b. Glyndon, Minn., June 27, 1926; s. John M. and Hilda C. (Moline) P.; m. Connie Lucille Harr, June 14, 1952 (dec. July 26, 2002); children: Jon Martin, Rebecca Ruth, Donna Harr, Ingrid Bliss; m. Mary Kinum, Sept. 12, 2003. AB, Yale U., 1947; MSPA, U. So. Calif., 1949; postgrad., U. Chgo., 1949-50; PhD, U. Minn., 1962; LLD, Lebanon Valley Coll., 1988. Mem. Wis. State Legislature, 1951-55; from instr. to asst. prof. polit. sci. U. Wis., Eau Claire, 1954-60; assoc. prof. to prof. polit. sci. Ohio Wesleyan U., Delaware, 1961-65, 70-80; pres. Am. Grad. Sch. Internat. Mgmt., Phoenix, 1966-70; dean spl. programs Eckerd Coll., St. Petersburg, Fla., 1980-84, dir. Acad. Sr. Profls., 1987-94; pres. Lebanon Valley Coll., Annville, Pa., 1984-87; pres., CEO Ctr. for the Study of the Presidency, 1997-99; Scott prof. leadership Rocky Mountain Coll., Billings, Mont., 1999—2002; mem. Mont. Ho. Reps., 2001—; pres. Thomas Wathen Found. Acad.; Riverside, Calif., 2002—. Bd. dirs. Arnold Industries; asst. to chmn. Rep. Nat. Com., Washington, 1960-61; founding dir. Ctr. Internat. Bus., L.A., 1969-70; cons. Novin Inst. Polit. Affairs, Tehran, Iran, 1973; exec. dir. Fla. Assn. Colls. and Univs., 1988—. Author: McCarthyism: Ideology and Foundations, 1962; co-author: Electing the President,

1968; contbr. articles to profl. jours. Chmn. Ohio Civil Rights Commn., 1963-65; dep. chmn. Republican Nat. Com., 1965-66; mem. Ohio Ethics Commn., 1976-80. Capt. USMC, 1951-52, Korea Citizenship Clearing House Nat. Faculty fellow, 1960; recipient citation for excellence Sigma Phi Epsilon, 1977, Marshall award Ohio Wesleyan Students, 1979. Mem. Am. Polit. Sci. Assn., Am. Judicature Soc. (dir. 1975—), Soc. Polit. Enquiries (pres. 1985—), Acad. Polit. Sci., Rotary, Masons, Pi Sigma Alpha (dir. 1972—), Phi Mu Alpha Sinfonia, Omicron Delta Kappa Republican. Mem. United Ch. of Christ. Avocations: sailing, flying, music. Home: 26555 Chambers Ave Sun City CA 92586-2132 Office: Wathen Found 4130 Minner Ave Riverside CA 92509 E-mail: apeter333@aol.com. *Give the most you can give, of what you are and what you believe, both talent and treasure - where you are - now!*.

**PETERSON, BARBARA ANN BENNETT,** history professor, television personality; b. Portland, Oreg., Sept. 6, 1942; d. George and Hope Bennett; m. Frank Lynn Peterson, July 1, 1967. BA, BS, Oreg. State U., 1964; MA, Stanford U., 1965; PhD, U. Hawaii, 1978; PhD (hon.), London Inst. Applied Rsch., 1991, Australian Inst. Coordinated R, 1995. From prof. history to prof. emeritus U. Hawaii, 1967—95, prof. emeritus, 1995—; prof. history Oreg. State U., 2000—03. Prof. Asian history and European colonial history and world problems Chapman Coll. World Campus Afloat Semester At Sea, 1974, European overseas exploration, expansion and colonialism U. Colo., Boulder, 1978, Modern China, Modern East Asia, The West in the World U. Pitts., 1999; assoc. prof. U. Hawaii-Manoa Coll. Continuing Edn., 1981; Fulbright prof. history Wuhan (China) U., 1988-89; Fulbright rsch. prof. Sophia U., Japan, 1967; rsch. assoc. Bishop Mus., 1995-98; lectr. Capital Spkrs., Washington, 1987—; prof. world civilization Hawaii State Ednl. Channel, U. Hawaii Sys., 1993-97; adj. fellow East-West Ctr., Honolulu, 1998-99; prof. history U. Pitts. Semester at Sea, fall 1999; adj. prof. Hawaii Pacific U.; adj. fellow East-West Ctr., Hawaii, 1998-99. Co-author: A Woman's Place is in the History Books, Her Story: A Curriculum Guide for American History Teachers, 1980; author: America in British Eyes, 1988, John Bull's Eye on America, 1995, Sarah Childress Polk, First Lady of Tennessee and Washington, 2002 (nominated for Pulitzer prize 2003), Avery O. Craven award 2003, Merle Curti award 2003, Albert J. Beveridge award 2003), Emalani, 2003; editor: Notable Women of Hawaii, 1984, (with W. Solheim) The Pacific Region, 1990, 91, American History: 17th, 18th and 19th Centuries, 1993, America: 19th and 20th Centuries, 1993, Notable Women of China, 2000 (nominated for Pulitzer prize 2001), Hawaii in the World, 2000; assoc. editor Am. Nat. Biography, 1998 (Dartmouth medal); contbr. articles to profl. publs. Participant People-to-People Program, Eng., 1964, Expt. in Internat. Living Program, Nigeria, 1966; chmn. 1st Nat. Women's History Week, Hawaii, 1982; pres. Bishop Mus. Coun., 1993-94; active mem. Hawaii Commn. on Status of Women; fundraiser local mus. and children's activities. Fulbright scholar, Japan, 1967, sr. tchg. Fulbright scholar, China, 1988-89; NEH-Woodrow Wilson fellow Princeton U., 1980; recipient state proclamations Gov. of Hawaii, 1982, City of Honolulu and Hawaii State Legis., 1982, Outstanding Tchr. of Yr. award Wuhan (China), U., 1988, Woman of Yr. award, 1991; inducted into the Women's Hall of Fame, Seneca Falls, N.Y., 1991; co-champion Hawaii State Husband and Wife Mixed Doubles Tennis Championship, 1985. Fellow: World Lit. Acad. (Eng.); mem.: AAUW, Am. Studies Assn. (Hawaii chpt. pres. 1984—85), Women in Acad. Adminstrn., Hawaii Found. History and Humanities (mem. editl. bd. 1972—73), Fulbright Assn. (founding pres. Hawaii chpt. 1984—88, mem. nat. steering com. chairwomen ann. conf. 1990, pres. 1998—99), Am. Hist. Assn. (mem. numerous coms., nominated Albert J. Beveridge award 2003), Maison Internat. des Intellectuals, Phi Kappa Phi, Pi Beta Phi (mem. mortar bd.). Avocations: writing, cooking, fund raising for charity and children's organizations and museums, gardening, travel. Address: Oreg State U History Dept 306 Milam Hall Corvallis OR 97331 E-mail: fandbpeterson@aol.com.

**PETERSON, BART,** mayor; b. June 15, 1958; m. Amy Minick; 1 child, Meg. Grad., Purdue U., 1980; JD, U. Mich., 1983. Atty. Ice Miller Donadio & Ryan, Indpls.; from exec. asst. for environ. affairs to chief of staff Ind. Gov. Evan Bayh, 1989-95; pres. and co-founder Precedent Cos., 1995; mayor City Indpls., 2000—03, 2003—. Bd. mem. Ind. Nature Conservancy, Regenstrief Found. Office: 2501 City-County Bldg 200 E Washington St Indianapolis IN 46204-3307 Office Phone: 317-327-4622, 317-327-3601. Office Fax: 317-327-3980. E-mail: mayor@indygov.org.*

**PETERSON, BRUCE D.,** lawyer; b. Chgo., Nov. 1956; BA, North Park Coll., 1978; JD, U. Notre Dame Law Sch., 1982. Fgn. svc. officer US State Dept., Washington, 1982; ptnr. Hunton & Williams, Washington, 1988—2002; sr. v.p., gen. counsel DTE Energy Co., Detroit, 2002—. Mem. legal com. Am. Gas Assn., Edison Electric Inst. Bd. dirs. Detroit Symphony Orch.; trustee Cranbrook Ednl. Cmty.; bd. govs. Cranbrook Inst. Sci. Office: DTE Energy Co 2000 2nd Ave Detroit MI 48226-1279

**PETERSON, CARL ERIC,** metal products executive, banker; b. Wareham, Mass., Apr. 8, 1944; m. Frances Harkness, Sept. 7, 1966; children: Robin, Alec Harkness. BA, Brown U., 1966; MA, U. Pa., 1971. With R.I. Hosp. Trust Nat. Bank, Providence, 1971-82; with Engelhard Corp., Iselin, NJ, 1982-85, Dryvit System, Inc., West Warwick, RI, 1986, Gerald Metals, Inc., Stamford, Conn., 1987—2002. Mem. corp. Woods Hole Oceanographic Instn., 1981—92, 2004—, trustee, 2005—; pres. Woods Hole Oceanographic Inst. Assocs., 2005—. With USN, 1967—. Mem.: NY Yacht Club.

**PETERSON, CHARLES HAYES,** lawyer; b. St. Louis, May 8, 1938; s. Edmund Herbert and Dorothy Marie (Brennan) P.; m. Auli Irene Ahonen, Nov. 28, 1981; children: Mika, Charles, Michael, Katja. BS, U.S. Naval Acad., 1960; MBA, Stanford U., 1971, JD, 1974. Commd. midshipman USN, 1956, advanced through grades to capt., resigned, 1969 with USNR, 1969-89, ret., 1990; counsel Gen. Electric, San Jose, Calif., 1973-79; divsn. counsel Syracuse, NY, 1980-83; v.p. COGEMA, Inc., Washington, 1983-87; pres. NUEXCO Trading Co., Washington, 1987-95; of counsel Morgan, Lewis & Bockius, LLP, 1995—2001; ptnr. Pillsbury Winthrop Shaw Pittman, Washington, 2001—. Recipient Meritorious Service medal State of Calif., 1986. Mem. Calif. and Washington Bar Assns. Lutheran. Office: Pillsbury Winthrop Shaw Pittman 2300 N Street NW Washington DC 20037 Office Phone: 202-663-8083. Office Fax: 202-663-8007.

**PETERSON, CHARLES MARQUIS,** medical educator; b. NYC, Mar. 8, 1943; s. Charles William and Elisabeth (Marquis) P.; m. Karen Pielop, Dec. 26, 1996; children: Caroline, Elisabeth, Christopher. BA in cum laude, Carleton Coll., 1965; MD, Columbia Coll., 1969; MBA, U. Calif., Irvine, 2000. Intern Harlem Hosp., N.Y.C., 1969-70, resident, 1970-73, chief resident, 1972-73; guest investigator, asst. physician Rockefeller U., N.Y.C., 1971-73, assoc. physician, 1973-78, asst. prof., 1973-78, assoc. prof., 1978-84; clin. prof. medicine U. So. Calif., L.A., 1985-98; program dir. blood diseases program Nat. Heart, Lung and Blood Inst., NIH, Bethesda, Md., 1998—. Vis. clin. fellow Columbia Coll. Physicians and Surgeons, 1970-73; asst. vis. physician Harlem Hosp., 1973-84; cons. pediatrics Cornell U. Med. Ctr., 1975-84; assoc. attending medicine Beth Israel Med. Ctr., 1976-84; lectr. Mt. Sinai Sch. Medicine, 1977—; adj. assoc. prof. dept. medicine Cornell U. Med. Ctr., 980-84; assoc. attending physician dept. medicine N.Y. Hosp., 1980-84; attending physician in medicine Cottage Hosp., Santa Barbara, Calif., 1984-98; clin. rsch., med. dir. Sansum Med. Rsch. Found., 1984-96, sr. scientist, 1997-98; dir. diabetes Endocrine Clinic, Santa Barbara County, 1989-98; CEO, Sansum Med. Rsch. Found., 1995-96; program dir. Blood Diseases Program Nat. Heart Lung Blood Inst., NIH, 1998-2000, acting dir. and dir. divsn. blood diseases and resorces, 2000—. Author: Self Monitoring of Blood Glucose: A Physician's Guide, 1981, Take Charge of Your Diabetes, 1982, Diabetes Management in the 80's, 1982; co-author: The Diabetes Self-Care Method, 1990, A Touch of Diabetes, 1991, Vivere con il Diabete, 1992, and many others; mem. editorial bd. Diabetes Care, 1980-84, Diabetes in the News, 1985—, Diabetes News Bureau, 1985—, Diabetes Profl., editor-in-chief, 1988-91, Diabetic Nephropathy/Jour. of Diabetic Complications, 1982-91; contbr. numerous articles to Prensa Medica, Jour. Lab. and Clin. Medicine, New England Jour. Medicine, Annals of Internal Medicine, Archives of Neurology, Blood, Jour. Nat. Med. Assn., Am. Jour. Obstetrics

and Gynecology, many others. Mem. med. adv. bd. Cooley's Anemia Vols., 1975-84; bd. mem. Diabetes Control Found., 1980-88; dir. Diabetes Self Care Program, 1978-84, med. dir., 1981-84; bd. mem. Leake and Watts, 1978-84, Gifts for Life, 1986-89; bd. dirs. Sports Tng. Inst., 1984-86, others. Fellow ACP; mem. AAAS, Am. Chem. Soc., Am. Diabetes Assn., Am. Fedn. Clin. Rsch., Am. Med. Writers Assn., Am. Soc. Clin. Investigation, Am. Soc. Hematology, Am. Soc. Pharmacology and Experimental Therapeutics, Coun. Biology Editors, Diabetes and Pregnancy Study Group West (founder), N.Y. Acad. Scis., Rsch. Soc. Alcoholsim, Soc. Experimental Medicine and Biology, Am. Med. Writers Assn., Am. Diabetes Assn. (founding bd. mem. Santa Barbara chpt. 1988-98, pres. 1991-92), Sigma Xi. Office: 6701 Rockledge Dr # 7950 Bethesda MD 20817-1813 E-mail: petersoC@nhlbi.nih.gov.

**PETERSON, CLARK C.,** announcer, writer, poet, speaker; b. Pine City, Minn., Dec. 27, 1947; s. Carl A. and Bernice C. Peterson. AA, U. Minn., 1967, B Econs., 1969; AA in Bible, Grace Bible Coll., 1993, PhD in Biblical Studies, 2003, Grace Bible Coll., Morrisville, NC, 2004. Announcer Sta. KOLM/KWWK Radio, Rochester, Minn., 1974-84; pub. affairs specialist U.S. Army, Fort Sill, 1985—86, Oklahoma City, 1986—97; announcer, writer Power Zone Wresting Fedn., Oklahoma City, 1992-97; corr. Pro Wrestling Illustrated Mag., 1992-97; announcer, writer New Mid-South Wrestling Fedn., Oklahoma City, 1998—2002, Mid-South Wrestling Alliance, 2002—06; corr. The Wrestling Tribune, 1993—2004; host weekly pro wrestling radio talk show "The Three Count" aired throughout one-half of continental U.S., 2001. Parade announcer Mora's (Minn.) Centennial, 1983; announcer Richards-Gebaur AFB Open House, Kansas City, Mo., 1973, Nat. Drum and Bugle Corps Contest, Stillwater, Minn., early 1980's; announcer, entertainment Rochester's (Minn.) 125th Anniversary, 1983; announcer, writer, entertainment, flags & decorations Korn & Klover Karnival, Hinckley, Minn., 1973-87, 90-91, 2005-06; judge Miss Teen Minn. Pageant, St. Paul, 1984. Author: The Great Hinckley Fire, 1978, Blasted Unto a Pile of Rubble, 1995, Blasted Unto a Pile of Rubble, Surviving the Oklahoma City bombing and its controversies, 2006, The Devouring Rages of Fire, the two most terrifying forest fires in North American History, 2006; co-author: In Their Name, 1995, We Will Never Forget, 1996, Forever Changed, 1998; contbg. author: Wrestling Title Histories, 2000. Mem., survivor Apr. 19, 1995 Oklahoma City Bombing, Family and Survivors United, 1995—; bd. dirs. Grace Bible Coll., Morrisville, NC, 2002—; Served with USAF, 1970-74. Recipient Best Coverage of a Local Story in the U.S., AP, 1978, Civil Svc. Achievement medal U.S. Army, 1997, 14 New Idea/Suggestion awards (one of the highest numbers in U.S. Civil Svc.), 1997; co-recipient Best Advt. and Pub. Affairs Office U.S. Army Recruiting Command, 1989; named #2 Broadcast Journalist of Yr.-Civilian U.S. Army Training and Doctrine Command, 1985, among 25 winners Turner Broadcasting's Nationwide Wrestling Announcing Contest, 1992; inducted into Profl. Wrestling's Wall of Fame, 1998; scholarship Grace Bible Coll., 2003. Avocations: outdoor Christmas lighting displays, state, territorial, and city flag collections, coin collecting/numismatics.

**PETERSON, COLLIN C.,** congressman; b. Fargo, ND, June 29, 1944; children: Sean, Jason, Elliott. BA in Bus. Adminstrn. and Acctg., Moorhead State U., 1966. CPA Minn. Senator State of Minn., 1976-86; mem. US Congress from 7th Minn. dist., 1991—; mem. agrl. com., subcoms. gen. farm commodities, specialty crops and natural resources, livestock, environ. credit and rural devel.; mem. permanent select Com. Intelligence, 2001—; mem. govt. ops. com., chmn. subcom. employment housing and aviation; mem. resource conservation com., rsch. and forestry subcom., livestock, dairy and poultry subcom., govt. reform and oversight com.; nat. econ. growth com., nat. resources and regulatory affairs com.-ranking minority mem., vet. affairs com. With U.S. Army N.G., 1963-69. Mem. Am. Legion, Ducks Unltd., Elks, Sportsmen's Club, Rural Caucus, Mainstream Forum, Cormorant Lakes Sportsmen Club, Congl. Sportsman's Caucus, Mainstream Forum, Congl. Rural Caucus. Democrat. Office: US Ho Reps 2159 Rayburn Ho Office Bldg Washington DC 20515-2307 also: Lake Ave Plaza Bldg Ste 107 714 Lake Ave Detroit Lakes MN 56501

**PETERSON, COURTLAND HARRY,** law educator; b. Denver, June 28, 1930; s. Harry James and Courtney (Caple) P.; m. Susan Schwab, Gisvold, Jan. 28, 1966; children: Brooke, Linda, Patrick. BA, U. Colo., 1951, LLB, 1953; MCL, U. Chgo., 1959; JD, U. Freiburg, Germany, 1964. Bar: Colo. 1953. Mem. faculty U. Colo. Law Sch., 1959—, prof., 1963—, dean, 1974-79, Nicholas Rosenbaum prof., 1991-94, Nicholas Doman prof. emeritus, 1995—. Vis. prof. UCLA Law Sch., Max Planck Inst., Hamburg, Germany, 1969-70, U. Tex. Law Sch., Austin, 1973-74, Summer Program, Tulane U., Rodos, Greece, 1993, Summer Program, La. State U., Aix-en-Provence, France, 1996; bd. dirs. Continuing Legal Edn. in Colo., 1974-77. Author: Die Anerkennung Auslaendischer Urteile, 1964; Translator: (Bauer) An Introduction to German Law, 1964. Served to 1st lt. USAF, 1954-56. Fgn. Law fellow U. Chgo., 1957-59; Ford Found. Law Faculty fellow, 1964; Alexander von Humboldt Stiftung fellow, 1969-70. Mem. ABA, Colo. Bar Assn. (bd. govs. 1974-79), Boulder County Bar Assn., Soc. Comparative Law (dir., bd. editors, treas. 1978-89, hon. pres. 1996-98), Internat. Acad. Comparative Law, Am. Law Inst., Boulder County Bar Found. (trustee 1995-2000), U. Colo. Ret. Faculty Assn. (pres. 1998-2000). Home: 4135 Caddo Pky Boulder CO 80303 Office: U Colo Law Sch Boulder CO 80309-0001 Personal E-mail: courtpeterson@comcast.net.

**PETERSON, DAVID FREDERICK,** retired government agency administrator; b. Washington, Apr. 4, 1937; s. Victor Henry and Alice Augusta (Vogle) P.; m. Laurie A. Cadigan, June 11, 1988. AB, Harvard U., 1959; LLB, Cornell U., 1962. Bar: D.C. 1969. With Metromedia Inc., N.Y.C. and Los Angeles, 1963—70; exec. dir. consumer info. ctr. GSA, Washington, 1970—76, dir. consumer affairs, 1976—82, assoc. archivist for mgmt. Nat. Archives and Records Service, 1982—83; asst. archivist for Fed. Records Ctrs. Nat. Archives and Records Adminstrn., Washington, 1983—96; asst. archivist Presdl. Librs., 1996—2001; ret., 2001. Served with U.S. Army, 1963 Home: 2730 NE Sewalls Landing Ln Jensen Beach FL 34957

**PETERSON, DAVID LARS,** music educator; b. Mpls., Apr. 12, 1943; s. Paul Edward Peterson, Sr. and Signe Christine (Huser) Peterson; m. Roberta Jean Schmidt, Aug. 14, 1965; children: Scott David, Lance Eric. BS in Music Edn., U. Minn., Duluth, 1965; MusM, U. Minn., 1970. Dir. bands Utley Jr. HS, Flint, Mich., 1965—67, Ainsworth HS, Flint, 1968—69; fellow in tchg. U. Mich., Ann Arbor, 1969—70; dir. bands Anoka-Hennepin Schs., Minn., 1970—. Adjudicator music Minn. State HS League, Twin Cities, 1972—; performer various brass groups Minn. Symphonic Winds, Edinta, 1982—; co-founder, performer Lake Wobegon Brass Band, Anoka, 1992—. Recipient Stanbury State award, Am. Sch. Band Dirs. Assn., 1972. Mem.: Nat. and Minn. Edn. Assns., Am. Fedn. Musicians, Minn. Music Educators Assn., Music Educators Nat. Conf. Avocations: walking, bicycling, travel.

**PETERSON, DAVID MAURICE,** retired physiologist; b. Woodward, Okla., July 3, 1940; s. Maurice Llewellyn and Katharine Anne (Jones) P.; m. Margaret Ingegerd Sundberg, June 18, 1965; children: Mark David, Elise Marie. BS, U. Calif., Davis, 1962; MS, U. Ill., 1964; PhD, Harvard U. 1968. Rsch. biologist Allied Chem. Corp., Morristown, NJ, 1970-71; plant physiologist U.S. Dept. Agr.-Agrl. Rsch. Svc., Madison, Wis., 1971—2004; from asst. prof. to prof. U. Wis., Madison, 1971—2004, ret., 2004. Capt. U.S. Army, 1968-70. Capt. U.S. Army, 1968—70. Fellow AAAS; mem. Am. Soc. Plant Biologists (editorial bd. 1984-86), Am. Assn. Cereal Chemists (assoc. editor 1988-91), Crop Sci. Soc. Am. (assoc. editor 1975-78).

**PETERSON, DAVID ROBERT,** lawyer, former Canadian government official; b. Toronto, Can., Dec. 28, 1943; s. Clarence and Laura Marie (Scott) P.; m. Shelley Peterson, Jan. 16, 1974; children: Benjamin David, Chloe Matthews, Adam Drake Scott BA, U. Western Ont., 1964; LLB, U. Toronto, 1967; LLD (hon.), U. Ottawa, Am. U. of Caribbean, U. Tel Aviv, U. Toronto. Bar: Ont. 1969, Queens counsel 1981. Chmn. Peterson Co. Ltd., 1969-75, Cambridge Acceptance Corp., 1969-75; M.P. Ont. Parliament,

Canada, 1975—; leader Ont. Liberal Party, 1982; premier Province of Ont., 1985-90; chmn. Cassels Brock & Blackwell LLP, Toronto, 1991—. Bd. dirs. Rogers Comms., Inc., Inscape, Industrielle-Alliance Life Assurance Co., BNP Paribas (Can.), others; founding chmn. Chpts. Inc., Cassels-Pouiliot Noriega. Leader of the ofcl. opposition party, Liberal Party, Ont., 1982-85; dir. Legal Svcs., Yorkville; mem. Kidney Found. Can., Ont., Cystic Fibrosis Found. Fellow McLaughlin Coll., 1985; appointed Knight of Order of Legion of Honor, Govt. France, 1994; recipient Ordre de la Pléiade, Internat. Assembly French-Speaking Parliamentarians, 1995. Mem. Law Soc. U.C., Young Pres. Orgn., London O. of C., London Hunt Country Club, London Racquets Club, Can. Club, Toronto Raptors Basketball Club Inc. (founding chmn.). Mem. United Ch. Of Christ. Avocations: theater, riding, jogging, skiing, tennis. Office: Cassels Brock Blackwell LLP 40 King St W Ste 2100 Toronto ON Canada M5H 3C2 E-mail: dpeterson@casselsbrock.com

PETERSON, DAWN MICHELLE, entrepreneur, writer; b. Rochester, Minn., Oct. 28, 1962; d. Kenneth Eugene and Lois Ann Silker; m. Bud Lamont Peterson, Feb. 14, 1981; children: Jacquline Ann Peterson, Holly Marie Schill, Cassie Jan Wilson. Student, Internet Svcs. Corp. Continuing Bus. Edn., 1985—2005, Legacy Bus. Group Bus. Edn., 2005—. Mgr. of fine dining restaurant and pvt. club Hilton Hotels, Ogden, Utah, 1983—85; pres. B & D Enterprise, Layton, Utah, 1985—; dir. of internat. divsn. Wilson Enterprises, Inc., Ogden, 1991—98; pres. Emma's Daycare, Layton, 2002—, D. S. Peterson Lit. Co., Layton, 2004—. Directorship, Brazilian divsn. Wilson Enterprises, Inc., Ogden, Utah, 1993—95, directorship, Turkish divsn. 1994—96, directorship, Ctrl. Am. divsn., 1994—96, directorship, Polish divsn., 1993—96, directorship, UK divsn., 1993—98, directorship, German divsn., 1993—98, directorship, Mex. divsn., 1993—98, directorship, Austra- lian divsn., 1994—98; US overseer Wilson Enterprises, Inc. and World Wide Dvsn., 1993—98, seminar spkr., 1993—; sr. bus. cons. Victory Devel., Guadalajara, Mexico, 1998—; com. mem. for internet services corp. India launch team Internet Services Corp./Wilson Enterprises, Inc., 1998; organizer and key note spkr. Germany's Women in Bus. Conf., 1996. Author: (novels) Code Breakers; author: (also actor and dir.) (plays) The Tale of the Pigs with the Folders on Their Heads, Barn Yard Animals (Sch. Creativity award, 1970), Laverne and Shirley go into Business; author/speaker (audio presentation) Empowering Women Business Owners, It's an Amazing Trip. Mem. Women In Bus., Ogden, Utah, 1983—85, Ogden C. of C., 1983—85, Rep. Nat. Com., 1987—2005; del. Utah Rep. Party, 1986. Recipient All Around Title, Buckaroo Rodeo, 1974, 1976, Appaloosa Horsemen's Assn., 1980, Endurance Champion, Utah Endurace Racing Assn., 1980, Lake Powell Fesitval of Lights Parade, Lake Powell Festival Com., 2002, 5th in Top 25 Producers, Quixtar Corp., 2002. Mem.: Ind. Bus. Owners Assn. (assoc.). R-Consevative. Christian. Avocations: travel, writing, reading. Office Phone: 801-510-9336. Personal E-mail: bpeterson5673@msn.com.

PETERSON, DELAINE CHARLES, lawyer, bank executive; b. Villisca, Iowa, July 28, 1936; s. Reuben Merrill and Margaret Helena (Sederquist) P.; m. Marcia Joan Hitchcock, Aug. 18, 1962; children: Robert, Paul, Janet BBA, U. Iowa, 1963, JD, 1966. Bar: Iowa 1966. Asst. trust officer Security Nat. Bank, Sioux City, Iowa, 1966—73, mgr. trust dept., 1974—82, sr. v.p., 1983—92, sr. v.p., chief trust officer, 1992—2001; assoc. atty. Corbett Anderson Law Firm, Sioux City, 2001—. Bd. dirs. Siouxland Easter Seals, Sioux City, 1983-91, St. Luke's Health Sys., Inc., 1987-2000, chmn. 1989-91; bd. dirs. St. Luke's Regional Med. Ctr., chmn. 1988-89; bd. dirs. St. Luke's Coll. Nursing and Health Scis., 1991-2000, chmn., 1991-93; trustee Prairie Gold coun. Boy Scouts Am., 1987—, pres., 1989-92; mem. Iowa Coll. Found., 1975-85; com. mem. Morningside Coll. Found., 1989-95 Mem.: ABA, Iowa Bar Assn., Woodbury Bar Assn., Iowa Trust Assn. (pres. 1978), Rotary (pres. 1984), Masons (past master 1988). Republican. Methodist. Office: Corbett Anderson Law Firm 423 Sixth St Ste 400 Sioux City IA 51101

PETERSON, DONALD KENT, telecommunications industry executive; b. Worcester, Mass., Aug. 13, 1949; s. John Ludwig and Ruth Ingeborg (Anderson) P.; m. Maureen Mack, Aug. 27, 1976; children: Janine Marie, Daniel Thomas. BS in Mech. Engring., Worcester Poly. Inst., 1971; MBA, Dartmouth Coll., 1973. CLU; chartered fin. analyst. Investment analyst State Mut. Life Assurance Co. Am., Worcester, 1973-76; cash and credit mgr. No. Telecom, Nashville, 1976-78, asst. treas., 1978-80, Mississauga, Ont., 1980- 81, controller, 1981-83, v.p. fin. Nashville, 1983-85, v.p. ops., 1985-86, sr. v.p. fin., CFO Mississanga, Ont., 1986—87, pres. Nortel Communications Sys. Inc., 1994—95; CFO Communication Svc. Group AT&T, 1995—96; exec. v.p., CFO Lucent Technologies, 1996—2000, CEO enterprise networks group, 2000; pres. & CEO Avaya Inc., Basking Ridge, NJ, 2000—02, chmn. & CEO, 2002—06, chmn., 2006. Bd. dir. Reynolds & Reynolds & Co., 1998—2005. Mem. Coun. on Fgn. Relations, World Economic Forum; trustee Teachers Ins. & Annuity Assn. Am., Com. for Economic Development; chmn. bd. trustees Worcester Polytech. Inst.; bd. overseers Amos Tuck Sch. Bus. Adminstrn. Dartmouth Coll. Recipient Washburn Achievement award, Worcester Poly. Inst., 1986. Mem.: Fin. Execs. Forum of Conf. Bd., Fin. Execs. Inst. Lutheran. Avocation: woodworking. Office: Avaya Inc 211 Mt Airy Rd Basking Ridge NJ 07920*

PETERSON, DONALD ROBERT, editor, vintage automobile consultant; b. Sandstone, Minn., Apr. 1, 1929; s. Martin Theodore and Margaret Mildred (Dezell) P.; m. Lois Taylor, Dec. 31, 1951 (div. 1975); children: Wyatt A., Winston B., Whitney C. (dec.), Westley D., Webster E.; m. Edie Tannenbaum, Aug. 31, 1975; 1 child, Ryan Kerry. Student, U. Minn., Mpls., 1947—50; BS, Gustavus Adolphus Coll., St. Peter, Minn., 1952. Asst. underwriter Prudential Ins. Co. Am., Mpls., 1953—64; chief health underwriter North Ctrl. Life, St. Paul, 1964—66; pres. 1st State Bank Murdock, Minn., 1967—73, EDON, Inc., Roswell, Ga., 1974—; editor Car Collector mag., Roswell, 1977—91, editor emeritus, 1992—; v.p., dir. Classic Pub. Inc., Atlanta, 1979—97. Contbr. chpt. to book. Councilman, City of Murdock, 1968-72, mayor, 1972-74; del. State Republican Conv., 1970-72; treas. Swift County Rep. Com., 1970-73. Served with U.S. Navy, 1946-47. Recipient citation for disting. service Classic Car Club Am., 1965, Hemmings Motor News Hobby Hero Award, 2002. Mem. Internat. Soc. Philos. Enquiry, Swift County Bankers Assn. (pres. 1970-73), Soc. Automotive Historians, Am. Legion, Mensa (pres. Ga. chpt. 1976-78), Classic Car Club Am. (chpt. pres. 1959, 60, 63, nat. bd. dirs. 1978-81, 97-2005), Rolls-Royce Owners Club, Antique Automobile Club, Vet. Motor Car Club Am., Packard Club, Cadillac-La Salle Club, Lincoln and Continental Owner's Club, Horseless Carriage Club Am. Republican. Avocations: automobile collecting, travel. Home: 1400 Lake Ridge Ct Roswell GA 30076-2869 Office Phone: 770-993-5622.

PETERSON, DONALD ROBERT, psychologist, educator, academic ad- ministrator; b. Pillager, Minn., Sept. 10, 1923; s. Frank Gordon and Ruth (Friedland) P.; m. Jane Hole, Feb. 10, 1952 (div.); children: Wendy, Jeffrey, Roger, Lisa; m. Jane Snyder Salmon, Dec. 21, 1974. BA, U. Minn., 1948, MA, 1950, PhD, 1952. Mem. faculty U. Ill., Urbana, 1952-75, prof. clin. psychology, 1963-75, head div. clin. psychology, 1963-70, dir. Psychol. Clinic, 1961-70, dir. D. Psychology program, 1970-75; dean Grad. Sch. Applied and Profl. Psychology Rutgers U., New Brunswick, 1975-89. Pres. Nat. Coun. Schs. of Profl. Psychology, 1981-83. Author: The Clinical Study of Social Behavior, 1968, reissued with new intro., 2004, Educating Profes- sional Psychologists, 1997, Twelve Years of Correspondence with Paul Meehl, 2005; co-author: Close Relationships, 1983, reissued with new intro., 2002; also articles; editor Jour. Abnormal Psychology, 1970-72. With AUS, 1943-46. Mem. N.J. Psychol. Assn., Am. Psychol. Assn. (awards for disting. contbns. to practice of psychology 1983, disting. contbns. to edn. and tng. 1989) Office: Rutgers U Grad Sch Applied & Profl Psychology Piscataway NJ 08854-8085 E-mail: drpeters@rci.rutgers.edu.

PETERSON, DONN NEAL, forensic engineer, engineering company ex- ecutive; b. Northwood, ND, Jan. 1, 1942; s. Emil H. and Dorothy (Neal) Peterson; m. Lorna Jean Kappedal, July 8, 1962 (div. July 1966); m. Donna Sue Butts Daiker, Aug. 26, 1967; children: Barbara Daiker, Elizabeth Plamondon, Phoebe, Phaedra Howard, Rosalind Ward. BSME, U. N.D., 1963; MSME, U. Minn., 1972. Registered profl. engr., cert. forensic engr., Internat.

Inst. Forensic Engring. Scis. Advanced engring. courses student GE, Even- dale, Ohio, 1963-66; systems engr. GE Aircraft Engine Group, Evendale, Ohio, 1963-70; prin. Donn N. Peterson & Assocs., Mpls., 1971-74; pres. Donn N. Peterson & Assocs., Inc., Mpls., 1974-85, Peterson Engring., Inc., Mpls., 1985—. Instr. GE Edn. Program, 1968—69; presenter State Bd. Registration, Mpls., 1980; seminar leader Minn. Fedn. Engring. Socs., Mpls., 1990—91; spkr., expert witness in field. Del. Minn. 6th Dist. Rep. Convs., Brooklyn Park, 1982. Fellow: Nat. Acad. Forensic Engrs. (v.p. 1996, sr. v.p. 1997—98), Am. Acad. Forensic Scis. (sect. chmn. 1989—90, Founders award 1991); mem.: NSPE, ASME (state chmn. 1979—80, Young Engr. of the Yr. 1976), Internat. Inst. Forensic Engring. Scis., Internat. Inst. Forensic Engring. Sci. (pres. 2004—), Profl. Engrs. Pvt. Practice (state pres. 1987—88, Svc. award 1988), Soc. Automotive Engrs., Brooklyn Park C. of C. (city hwy. 610 corridor com. 1992—94), Rotary (Brooklyn Park chpt. sec. 1990—93, v.p. 1993—94, pres.-elect 1994—95, pres. 1995—96, Svc. award 1992, 2005). Lutheran. Achievements include development of mathematical models to simulate jet engine transient performance and wave dynamics in gas flow; computer simulations for vehicle and occupant dynamics during collisions. Office: PO Box 664 Brainerd MN 56401-0664 Office Phone: 218-765-3556. Personal E-mail: donnnpeterson@aol.com.

PETERSON, DONNA RAE, gerontologist; b. Wichita, Kans., Aug. 29, 1948; d. Raymond Houston and Edna Brooks (Waddell) Hobbs; m. William E. Peterson, Nov. 7, 1993; 1 child, Shauna Layne Heath. Student, Wichita State U., 1968—70; BS in Mgmt., N.W. Christian Coll., 1996, MA in Interdisciplinary Studies Gerontology, 2000. Adminstrv. asst. postgrad. edn. Med. Sch. U. Kans., Wichita, 1974—80; activity coord. continuing med. edn. Wesley Med. Ctr., Wichita, 1980—84; mgr. support svcs. 9th dist. Farm Credit Svcs., Wichita, 1984—88; mgr. sales and mktg. Amb. Travel, Eugene, Oreg., 1988—93; dir. mktg. Peterson Design Devel., Eugene, 1993—95; pres. Davinci Designs, Eugene, 1996—2000; owner 24 Half Dynamics, 2000—; dir. Alzheimer's program Sunwest Mgmt., Inc., 2002—04; adult/elder spe- cialist, life coach United Behavioral Health, 2004—. Cons. Jr. League Wichita, 1983, Plancon, Inc., Martinsville, NJ, 1987-88, Changing Creatively, 1997; continuing edn. instr. Lane C.C., 2000—; mem. adv. bd. Lane C.C. Ctr. for Leisure and Learning, 2000—. Mem. Wichita Conv. and Visitors Bur., 1987; mem. events com. Wichita Festivals, Inc., 1987; mem. Eugene Conv. and Visitors Bur., 1988—; mem. Eugene Airport Commn., 1991—, chmn., 1992-93; bd. dirs. Campus Life, chmn., 1993-94; mem. steering com. Eugene Celebration, 1991-94, Oreg. Women Bus. Owners Conf., 1997; bd. pres. Of Coun. for Bus. Edn., 1999-2000. Mem. AAUW, Am. Mktg. Assn. (pres. S.W. chpt. 1991—, pres. 1992-94, bd. dirs.), Soc. Travel Agt. in Govt., adminstry. Mgmt. Soc., Forum for Exec. Bus. Women, Gt. Plains Bus. Adminstrn. Group, Assn. Travel Exec., Eugene C. of C. (bus. devel. com. 1990-91), The Gerontol. Soc. Am. (student campus rep. 1999), Alzheimers Assn. (Oreg. chpt., edn. com., 2002—), Eugene High Ground Assn. (chmn.), Delta Gamma Alumni Assn. Republican. Avocations: decorating, writing, skiing, water- skiing, camping. Home: 1460 Olive St Apt 32 Eugene OR 97401-3991 Office Phone: 541-520-2567. Personal E-mail: gerovision@comcast.net.

PETERSON, DOROTHY HAWKINS, artist, educator; b. Albuquerque, Mar. 14, 1932; d. Ernest Lee and Ethel Dawn (Allen) Hawkins; m. John W. Peterson, July 9, 1954; children: John Richard, Dorothy Anne. BS in Edn., U. N.Mex., Albuquerque, 1953; MA, U. Nex., 1979. Freelance artist, 1960—; educator, instr. Carlsbad (N.Mex.) Ind. Elem. Sch. Dist., 1953-54; instr. Charleston (S.C.) County Schs., 1955-56; instr. in painting Midland (Tex.) Coll., 1971-76, Roswell (N.Mex.) Mus. Schs., 1981-83, 91—; instr. in art history Ea. N.Mex. U., Roswell, 1989—2000; instr. painting N.Mex. Mil. Inst., Roswell, 1992—94. Bd. dirs. N.Mex. Arts Commn., Santa Fe; cons. Casa de Amigos Craft Guild, Midland, Tex., 1971-73. One woman shows include Art Inst., Permian Basin, Odessa, Tex., 1994. Tutor Roswell Literacy Coun., 1988-89; bd. dirs. N.Mex. Arts & Crafts Fair, Albuquerque, 1983-85. Named Best of Show, Mus. of the S.W., 1967, 69; recipient Top award, 1973, 75, Juror award N.Mex. Arts & Crafts Fair, 1986, 1st pl. award Profl. Watercolor N.Mex. State Fair, 1988; Talens-d' Arches award, Tex. Watercolor Soc., 1998; Bd. Dirs. award, San Diego Watercolor Soc., 1998, N. Mex. Watercolor Soc., 1998. Mem. Nat. Watercolor Soc. (San Diego Watercolor Soc. award 1988), N.Mex. Watercolor Soc. (2d pl. award 1981, 1st pl. award state fair 1988, Grumbacher award 1993, Wingspread award 1994, 1st pl. award 1995, 1st, 3rd and Graham award 1997, Best of Show 2001, Best of Show 2004, Masterworks award N.Mex. Tricentennial 2005, 3d pl. award 2006, 1st pl. Masterworks, 2006). Office: Dorothy Peterson Studio PO Box 915 Roswell NM 88202-0915 Personal E-mail: dhpeterson@dfn.com.

PETERSON, DOUGLAS PETE (PETE PETERSON), former ambassa- dor, retired congressman; b. Omaha, June 26, 1935; m. Carlotta Ann Neal (dec.); children: Michael, Paula, Douglas (dec.); m. Vi Peterson. Grad., Nat. War Coll., 1975; BA, U. Tampa, 1976; postgrad., U. Ctrl. Mich., 1977. Commd. USAF, 1954, advanced through grades to col., ret., 1980; exec. CRT Computers, 1984-90; mem. faculty Fla. State U., 1985-90; mem. US Congress from 2nd Fla. Dist., 1991-96; mem. appropriation com.-energy and water, agrl.; US amb. to Vietnam US Dept. State, Hanoi, 1997—2001; pres. Peterson Internat., Inc., 2001—. Founder, CEO The Alliance for Safe Children. Prisoner of war, Vietnam. Mem.: VFW, Am. Acad. Diplomacy, Coun. Am. Ambs., Am. Legion. Roman Catholic. Office: 27 Bowen St Camberwell VIC 3124 Australia Office Phone: 66-2-655-4811. E-mail: petevi@bigpond.net.au.

PETERSON, E. ANNE, former federal agency administrator; married; 3 children. MD. Mayo Med. Sch.; MPH, Emory U. Cert. bd. cert. gen. preventive medicine and pub. health, lic. Va., Ga., Minn., Zimbabwe. Resident Emory U.; commr. health State of Va., 1998—2001; asst. adminstr. bur. global health USAID, Washington, 2001—04. Cmty. devel., pub. health tng. and AIDS prevention, Kenya, Zimbabwe.

PETERSON, EDWARD ADRIAN, lawyer; b. St. Louis, May 19, 1941; s. Adrian J. and Virginia (Hamlin) P.; m. Catherine Frances Younghouse, Dec. 17, 1960; children: Kristin, Kendra, BSBA, Washington U., St. Louis, 1963; LLB, So. Methodist U., 1966. Bar: Tex. 1966, U.S. Dist. Ct. (no. and so. dists.) Tex. Instr. bus. law and acctg. Midwestern U., Wichita Falls, Tex., 1966-67; assoc. Schenk & Swebrooks, Wichita Falls, 1966-67, Newman & Pickering, Dallas, 1967-72; ptnr. Moore & Peterson, Dallas, 1972-89, Winstead Sechrest & Minick P.C., Dallas, 1989—. Spkr. in field. Contbr. articles to legal jours. Bd. dirs. Leukemia Soc., 1970-71, North Tex. Commn., 1992-96, South Dallas/Fair Park Trust Fund, 1992, Tex. Ch. Extension Fund, Tex. Dist., Tex. Dist. Luth. Ch. Mo. Synod. Fellow Am. Coll. Mortgage Attys., Tex. Bar Found. (life), Dallas Bar Found., Coll. State Bar Tex.; mem. ABA, Am. Coll. Real Estate Lawyers (title ins. com., common interest com.), State Bar Tex., Tex. Coll. Real Estate Attys., Dallas Bar Assn., Phi Alpha Delta, Sigma Alpha Epsilon. Lutheran. Home: Ste 617 2808 McKinney Ave Dallas TX 75204-2562 also: 131 Hilton Head Island Dr Mabank TX 75147-9325 Office: Winstead Sechrest & Minick PC 5400 Renaissance Tower 1201 Elm St Dallas TX 75270-2199 Office Phone: 214-745-5642. Business E-Mail: epeterson@winstead.com

PETERSON, EDWIN J., retired judge, mediator, law educator; b. Gilman- ton, Wis., Mar. 30, 1930; s. Edwin A. and Leora Grace (Kitelinger) P.; m. Anna Chadwick, Feb. 7, 1971; children: Patricia, Andrew, Sherry. BS, U. Oreg., 1951, LLB, 1957. Bar: Oreg. 1957. Assoc. firm Tooze, Kerr, Peterson, Marshall & Shenker, Portland, Oreg., 1957-61, mem. firm, 1961-79; assoc. justice Supreme Ct. Oreg., Salem, 1979-83, 91-93, chief justice, 1983—91; ret., 1993; disting. jurist-in-residence, adj. instr. Willamette Coll. of Law, Salem, 1994—. Chmn. Supreme Ct. Task Force on Racial Issues, 1992-94, Oreg. Law Enforcement Contacts Policy and Data Review Com., 2005-; standing com. on fed. rules of practice and procedure, 1987-93; bd. dirs. Conf. Chief Justices 1985-87, 88-91; founder Understanding Racism Found., 1998, mem. Oreg. Joint Bench-Bar Commn. on Professionalism, 1996-, chair, 1996-97. Chmn. Portland Citizens Ct. Commn., 1968-70; vice-chmn. Young Rep. Fedn. Oreg., 1951; bd. visitors U. Oreg. Law Sch., 1978-83, 87-93, chmn. bd. visitors 1981-83; pres., bd. dirs. Understanding Racism Found.,

1999-2002. 1st lt. USAF, 1952-54. Mem. Oreg. State Bar (bd. examiners 1963-66, gov. 1973-76, vice chmn. profl. liability fund 1977-78), Multnomah County Bar Assn. (pres. 1972-73), Phi Alpha Delta, Lambda Chi Alpha. Episcopalian. Home: 3365 Sunridge Dr S Salem OR 97302-5950 Office: Willamette Univ Coll Law 245 Winter St SE Salem OR 97301-3916 Office Phone: 503-375-5399. Business E-mail: epeterso@willamette.edu.

PETERSON, ELIZABETH HOLLY, art association administrator; b. Nyack, N.Y., Dec. 30, 1967; d. John Lawrence and Holly Winifred Peterson; life ptnr. Jean Dolan, Sept. 18, 2004. BA in Studio Art, Wells Coll., Aurora, N.Y., 1989; MS in Theory, Criticism and History of Art, Design and Architecture, Pratt Inst., Bklyn., 1997; postgrad., NYU, 2003. Exhbn. coord., asst. to the dep. dir. The Mus. of Modern Art, N.Y.C., 1997—2004; dir. The Print Rsch. Found., Stamford, Conn., 2005—. Exhbn. coord. Masterworks from the Mus. Modern Art, Strangely Familiar: Approaches to Scale in the Collection of The Museum of Modern Art, Masterworks from MoMA, 1900-1955, project coord. CAFE/ETC. Recipient Cert. of Excellence award for Outstanding Merit, Pratt Inst., 1997, Distinction in the Spl. Field of Studio Art, Wells Coll., 1989. Mem.: Coll. Art Assn., Am. Assn. of Mus. Avocations: singing, painting, travel, yoga. Office: The Print Research Foundation 258 Atlantic St Stamford CT 06901 E-mail: epeterson@printresearch.org.

PETERSON, ERIC F., headmaster; m. Krista Peterson. BA, Dartmouth Coll.; JD, Northwestern U. Sch. of Law. Former asst. headmaster & English teacher & dir. upper sch. Forsyth Country Day Sch., Lewisville, NC; headmaster St. George's Sch., Middletown, RI, 2004—. Office: St George's Sch 372 Purgatory Rd Middletown RI 02842-5984

PETERSON, ERIK CHARLES, prosecutor; BA, Drake U., 1992; JD, Marquette U. Law Sch., 1995. Asst. dist. atty. Richland County, 1995-98; dist. atty. Iowa County, 1999—2006; US atty. (we. dist.) Wis. US Dept. Justice, Madison, 2006—. Office: US Atty PO Box 1585 Madison WI 53701

PETERSON, EVONNE STEWART, elementary school educator; d. Rich- ard Alan and Theresa Johnson Stewart; m. Kelvin Osborne Peterson (div.); 1 child, Chelsey Denise. BA in Art Edn., N.C. Ctrl. U., 1979; MA in Art Edn., Winthrop U., 1998; MEd in Reading, Lang., and Literacy, U. N.C., 2001; postgrad., Western Carolina U., 2006—. Cert. K-12 Reading Education Charlotte-Mecklenburg Schools, Charlotte, NC, 2001, K-12 Art Education Charlotte-Mecklenburg Schools, Charlotte, NC, 1991. Adminstrv. svcs. clk. Bachelor Enlisted Quarters, Rota, Spain, 1985—88; tour cons. Am. Airlines, Cary, NC, 1989—90; tchr. afterschool enrichment program Bruns Ave. Elem., Charlotte, 1991—92; tchr. art Lincoln Heights Elem., 1992—2004, tchr. Title I literacy, 2004—, Title I summer sch. site coord., lead tchr., 2005—. Sch. leadership team chair Lincoln Heights Elem., Charlotte, 2002—, tchr. adv. coun. rep., 2001—, mentor, 2000—, literacy/writing com., 2002—, key communicator, 2002—04, diversity facilitator, 2002—04; selected participant Tchg. Fellows Inst., White Oaks, Charlotte, 2005; presenter in field. Recipient Tchr. of Month award, Coca-Cola, 2003; grantee, World Affairs Coun., 1998, IMPACTII, 2000, Charlotte-Mecklenburg Schs., 2001. Mem.: N.C. Educators Assn. (corr.), Internat. Reading Assn. (corr.), Kappa Delta Pi, Phi Kappa Phi. Baptist. Avocations: aerobics/strength training, travel, reading, arts and crafts. Office: Lincoln Heights Elem Sch 1900 Newcastle St Charlotte NC 28216

PETERSON, FRED MCCRAE, retired librarian; b. Mpls., Dec. 29, 1936; BA, U. Minn., 1958, MS, 1960; PhD in L.S., Ind. U., 1974. Asst. to dir. Iowa State U. Library, 1961-64, head catalog dept., 1964-67, asst. dir. library, 1967-69, assoc. dir. library, 1969-70; with Catholic U. Am., Washington, 1970-82, asst. prof., assoc. chairperson, 1973-77, acting dir. libraries, 1977- 78, dir., 1978-82; univ. librarian Ill. State U., Normal, 1982-96, univ. libr. emeritus, 1996—. Mem. ALA, Ill. Libr. Assn. (past pes., Libr. of Yr. award 1994). Home: 32792 Via Malaga San Juan Capistrano CA 92675-4455 E-mail: fmpeterson@cox.net.

PETERSON, G. P. (BUD PETERSON), academic administrator; b. Prairie Village, Kans. BS in Mech. Engring. and Math., Kans. State U., 1975, MS in Engring., 1980; PhD, Tex. A&M U., 1985. Engring. prof. Tex. A&M U., College Station, 1981—2000; provost Rensselaer Poly. Inst., Troy, NY, 2000—06; chancellor U. Colo., Boulder, 2006—. Editor: Jour. Exptl. Thermal and Fluid Scis.; assoc. editor: ASME Jour. Heat Transfer, AIAA Jour. Thermophysics and Heat Transfer, Internat. Jour. Heat and Fluid Flow, Microscale Thermophysical Engring.; contbr. articles to profl. jours. Recipi- ent Best Paper award, AIAA, 1990, award for outstanding mgmt., NSF, 1994, Ralph James and the O. L. (Andy) Lewis awards, ASME, Dow Outstanding Young Faculty award, ASEE, Pi Tau Sigma Gustus L. Larson Meml. award, ASME, Thermophysics award, AIAA, Meml. award, ASME, Sustained Svc. award, AIAA; fellow, Tex. Engring. Expt. Sta., 1986, 1988; sr. fellow, 1989. Fellow: Am. Inst. of Aeronautics and Astronautics, Am. Soc. of Mech. Engrs.; mem.: Phi Kappa Phi, Sigma Xi, Tau Beta Pi, Pi Tau Sigma. Office: U Colo Office of Chancellor 17 UCB, Regent 301 Boulder CO 80309 Office Phone: 303-492-8908. E-mail: chanchat@spot.colorado.edu.*

PETERSON, GALE EUGENE, historian; b. Sioux Rapids, Iowa, May 23, 1944; s. George Edmund and Vergene Elizabeth (Wilson) P. BS, Iowa State U., 1965; MA, U. Md., 1968, PhD, 1973. Instr. dept. history U. Md., College Park, 1971-72, Cath. U. Am., Washington, 1972-73; prin. investigator Gregory Directory project Orgn. Am. Historians, Bloomington, Ind., 1973-75; instr. dept. history Purdue U., West Lafayette, Ind., 1975-76; dir. U.S. Newspaper Project, Orgn. Am. Historians, Bloomington, Ind., 1976-78; exec. dir. Cin. Hist. Soc., 1978-96, exec. dir. emeritus, 1996—; exec. dir. Ohio Humanities Coun., 1998—. Author: (with John T. Schlebecker) Living Historical Farms Handbook, 1970, Harry S Truman and the Independent Regulatory Commissions 1945-52, 1985. Mem. Cin. Bicentennial Commn., 1983-88. Mem. Orgn. Am. Historians (treas. 1993-2003), Am. Assn. State and Local History, Am. Hist. Assn., Am. Assn. Mus., Assn. Midwest Museums (v.p.-at-large 1993-95, exec. v.p. 1995-96, pres. 1996-98), Nat. Coun. on Pub. History (bd. dirs. 1992-95). Office: Ohio Humanities Coun Ste 1620 471 E Broad St Columbus OH 43215-3857 Office Phone: 614-461-7802. Personal E-mail: galep@one.net.

PETERSON, GARY ANDREW, agronomics researcher; b. Holdrege, Nebr., Apr. 30, 1940; s. Walter Andrew and Evelyn Christine (Johnson) P.; m. Jacquelyn Charlene Flick, June 18, 1965; children: Kerstin, Ingrid. BS, U. Nebr., 1963, MS, 1965; PhD, Iowa State U., 1967. Research assoc. agronomy Iowa State U., Ames, 1964-67; prof. U. Nebr., Lincoln, 1967-84; prof. soil and crop scis. Colo. State U., Ft. Collins, 1984—, head dept. soil and crop scis., 2003—. Assoc. editor AGronomy Jour., 1979-81, tech. editor, 1981-83, editor, 1984-89, editor-in-chief, 1991-96; contbr. articles to profl. jours. Fellow Am. Soc. Agronomy (Ciba-Geigy Agr. Achievement award 1974, Agronomic Achievement award-Soils 1990), Soil Sci. Soc. Am. (Applied Rsch. award 1987); mem. Soil Conservation Soc. Am. Avoca- tions: reading, hiking, skiing. Office: Colo State U Dept Soil Crop Scis Fort Collins CO 80523-0001 Office Phone: 970-491-6501. Business E-Mail: gary.peterson@colostate.edu.

PETERSON, GARY J, retail executive; Gen. mgr. WalMart, 1984—85; dir. of distbn. and transp. systems, 1985—88; sr. v.p. Carter, Hawley, Hale Stores, 1988—91; sr. v.p. of operation svcs. Thrifty Drug Stores, 1991—93; COO Southeast Frozen Foods, LP, 1993—96; exec. officer, COO Blockbuster Entertainment, 1996—2000; pres., COO OfficeMax, 2000—.

PETERSON, GEORGE EMANUEL, JR., retired lawyer; b. Mt. Vernon, N.Y., Mar. 8, 1931; s. George E. and Lydia Evelyn (Peterson) P.; m. Barbara Ritter, Aug. 30, 1957; children— Lisa Manvel, George Emanuel III. BA, Yale, 1953; LL.B., U. Va., 1958. Bar: N.Y. State 1959, Conn. 1974. Assoc. firm Reid & Priest, N.Y.C., 1958-68, ptnr. 1968-70; v.p., gen. counsel Insilco Corp., Meriden, Conn., 1970-72, v.p. fin. 1972-76, v.p., sec., 1976-79, v.p., gen. counsel, 1976-89; pvt. practice North Haven, Conn., 1989-90. Served to lt. USNR, 1953-55. Mem. ABA, N.Y. State Bar Assn., Conn. Bar Assn. Home: 225 Blue Trl Hamden CT 06518-1601

**PETERSON, GEORGE FOLKE,** retired insurance company executive, writer; b. Racine, Wis., June 4, 1926; s. George Edwin Peterson and Anna Zetterquist; m. Evelyn Marie Malcolm, Dec. 29, 1959. Student, Carthage Coll., 1945—48; BA, Ariz. State U., 1949. Mng. ptnr., co-pub. Opportunities Pub. Co., Racine, 1949—50; dir. mkt. rsch., dir. circulation Watson Publs., Chgo., 1955—58; circulation dir., rsch. mgr. Am. Aviation Pub. Co., Washington, 1958—62; editor, pub. Astrosci. News, Washington, 1962—64; mgmt. cons. Alexander Proudfoot Co., Chgo., 1964—66; field exec. Blue Cross of Fla., Inc., St. Petersburg, 1968—84; freelance writer Holiday, Fla., 1984—. Co-founder, CEO Inst. Cons. Engrs., Chgo., 1956—58; CFO Corp. Treas. Anchor Det. Co., Bristol, Va., 1962—64. Editor, pub.: Sci. Newsletter, 1964; author: Accounts Receivable Management, 1984; author: (as Lane Stevenson) (novel) To Las Vegas With Love, 2002, Searching for Krisztina, 2004. Bd. dirs. Health Sys. Agy., Fla., 1980—83; former mem. Fla. Health Sys. Agy. With Med. Corp U.S Army, 1950—52. Recipient Pub.'s Achievement award, Am. Aviation Pub. Co., 1960, Cert. of Recognition, Sec. of Def. William Cohen, 2000, Sec. of Def. Donald Rumsfeld, 2005. Mem.: NY Acad. Scis. Avocations: astronomy, cosmology, particle physics, string theory physics. Home and Office: 3538 Burntwood Ct Holiday FL 34691 Personal E-mail: pgeorge347@yahoo.com

**PETERSON, GERALD ALVIN,** physics professor; b. Chesterton, Ind., Apr. 12, 1931; s. Gustaf Albert and Esther Josephine (Carlson) P.; m. Doris Lee DeJonge, Dec. 22, 1953; children— Curtis Mark, Thomas Andrew, Anna Beth. BS, Purdue U., 1953, MS, 1955; PhD, Stanford U., 1962. Lectr. Yale U., New Haven, 1962-64; asst. prof., 1964—68; research scientist Inst. voor Kernphysisch Onderzoek, Amsterdam, 1967-68; assoc. prof. physics U. Mass., Amherst, 1968-73, prof., 1973-2000, prof. emeritus, 2000—. Vis. prof. U. Mainz, Fed. Republic Germany, 1975, Japan Soc. Promotion Sci., 1972, 89; U.S.-Israel Binat. Sci. Found. vis. prof. Tel Aviv U., 1983; cons. in field. Contbr. articles to profl. jours. Served with U.S. Army, 1955-57. NATO fellow, 1969, U.K. sr. rsch. fellow, 1970. Fellow Am. Phys. Soc. (chmn. New Eng. sect. 1996); mem. Sigma Xi. Congregationalist. Achievements include research in electron scattering; nuclear structure; energy and environmental problems. Home: 10 Old Briggs Rd Leverett MA 01054-9759 Office: U Mass Nuclear Physics Grad Rsch Ctr Amherst MA 01003 Office Phone: 413-545-2008. E-mail: peterson@physics.umass.edu.

**PETERSON, JAMES KENNETH,** manufacturing executive; b. Sioux City, Iowa, Oct. 17, 1934; s. David Winfield and Beulah Lillian (Johnson) P.; m. Nanette Kay Olin, Feb. 2, 1957; children: Kimberly, Kristin, David. BA in Econs, Mich. State U., 1956. R & D engr. Reynolds Metals Co., Richmond, Va., 1957-59, sales rep., 1959-61, dist. sales mgr., 1961-65, regional sales mgr., 1965-67, asst. to exec. v.p., 1968, mktg. dir., 1969-71; dir. nat. account sales The Continental Group, Stamford, Conn., 1971, gen. mgr. sales, 1972-73, div. gen. mgr., 1974-78, v.p., corp. officer, 1974-80, v.p., gen. mgr. global bus. devel., 1979; pres., COO Ludlow Corp., Needham, Mass., 1980-82, also bd. dirs.; pres., CEO, dir. Graphic Packaging Corp., Paoli, Pa., 1982-89; pres., CEO, Peterson Group, Easton, Md., 1989—. Bd. dirs. Jenard Co., Graphic Packaging Corp., South Chester Tube Co. Served to 1st lt. U.S. Army, 1957. Mem. Merion Golf Club, Merion Cricket Club, Talbot Country Club. Home: 27779 Waverly Rd Easton MD 21601-8121

**PETERSON, JAMES LINCOLN,** museum executive; b. Kewanee, Ill., Nov. 12, 1942; s. Reinold Gustav and Florence Josephine (Kjellgren) P.; m. M. Susan Pepin, Aug. 15, 1964; children: Hans C., Erika C. BA, Gustavus Adolphus Coll., 1964; PhD, U. Nebr., 1972. Sci. tchr. pub. schs., Ill. and Minn., 1964-68; research asst. U. Nebr., Lincoln, 1968-72; research assoc. U. Wis., Madison, 1972-74; staff ecologist Nat. Commn. Water Quality, Washington, 1974-75; v.p. research Acad. Nat. Scis., Phila., 1976-84, v.p. devel., 1982-84; pres. Sci. Mus. Minn., St. Paul, 1984—. Bd. dirs. Ea. Pa. chpt. Nature Conservancy, Phila., 1982-84, Downtown Coun., St. Paul, 1986-93, Keystone (Colo.) Ctr., 1989-93; mem. St. Paul Riverfront Commn., 1987-91; mem. adv. com. U. Minn. Coll. Biol. Scis., 1989-95. Mem. Assn. Sci. Mus. Dirs., Assn. Sci. and Tech. Ctrs. (pres. 1993-95), Sci. Mus. Exhibit Collaborative (pres. 1986-89), St. Paul C. of C. (bd. dirs. 1985-89), Informal Club.

**PETERSON, JAMES MICHAEL,** drama educator; b. Indianapolis, Ind., Sept. 17, 1966; s. Delane Rabuck and James Peterson; m. Angela D. Dobson, June 27, 1992; children: Ivan, Erik. M. Butler U., Indpls., 1996. Theatre/english educator Huntington Pk. H.S., Los Angeles, Calif., 1989—92; drama dir. Carmel H.S., Carmel, Ind., 1992—. Actor: (film) Saving Star Wars (Best Supporting Actor, 2005). Mem.: Ednl. Theatre Assn. Am. Alliance of Theatre Educators (state rep. 2000—06). Office: Carmel HS 520 E Main St Carmel IN 46032 Office Phone: 317-846-7721. Office Fax: 317-571-4066. E-mail: jpeterson@ccs.k12.in.us.

**PETERSON, JAMES ROBERT,** engineering psychologist; b. St. Paul, Apr. 16, 1932; s. Palmer Elliot and Helen Evelyn (Carlson) P.; m. Marianna J. Stockvig, June 26, 1954; 1 child, Anne Christine. BA in Psychology cum laude, U. Minn., 1954, MA in Exptl. Psychology, 1958; PhD in Engring. Psychology, U. Mich., 1965. Devel. engr. Honeywell Inc., 1961-65, sr. devel. engr., 1965-67, staff engr., 1967-90, sr. project staff engr., 1990-93, retired, 1993. Honeywell sponsor rep. Shuttle Student Involvement Program, 1982, 84. Contbr. articles to profl. jours. With USMC, 1954-57, USMCR, 1957-62. Mem. Human Factors and Ergonomics Soc. (life), Air & Space Mus. (charter), Smithsonian Inst., Masons, Am. Legion. Achievements include invention of Apollo translation hand controller; participation in development work in all U.S. Manned Space Programs (Mercury, Gemini, Apollo, Lunar Excursion Module, Manned Orbiting Laboratory, Space Shuttle and Space Sta.) as member/manager of associated human factors groups. Home: 3303 San Gabriel St Clearwater FL 33759-3341 Personal E-mail: bpeteputt@aol.com.

**PETERSON, JAMES SCOTT (JIM PETERSON),** Canadian government official; b. Ottawa, Can., 1941; married Heather Peterson. BA, LLB, U. We. Ont.; Diploma, L'Acad. de Droit Internat., The Hague and La Sorbonne; DCL, McGill U.; LLM, Columbia U. Mem. faculty of law U. Toronto, 1974-79; elected mem. of parliament Willowdale, 1980—; chair Cambridge Acceptance Corp. Ltd., 1984-87; chair standing com. on fin. Minister of State, Minister of Justice, 1993-97; sec. of state Internat. Fin. Instns., Ottawa, 1997—2002; min. internat. trade Govt. of Canada, Ottawa, 2003—. Legal counsel and cons. UN. Office: Office of the Min for Internat Trade 515S Ho of Commons Rm 359 West Block K1A 0A6 Ottawa ON Canada Office Phone: 613-992-7332. Business E-mail: james.peterson@international.gc.ca

**PETERSON, JOHN E.,** congressman; b. Titusville, Pa., Dec. 25, 1938; s. Axel Benjamin and Mary Elizabeth (Baker) Peterson; m. Saundra June Watson, 1968; children: Richard D., Florence Waychoff. Grad. from rural leadership prog., Pa. State U. Owner retail food market, Pleasantville, Pa., 1958-84; mem. City Coun., Pleasantville, Pa., 1969—77, Pa. State Ho. Reps., 1977-84, Pa. State Senate, 1984-96, US Congress from 5th Pa. dist., 1997—; mem. appropriations com., mem. resources com., co-chair Congl. Rural Caucus. Mem. Pub. Health and Welfare Com., now chmn.; active PENNVEST Bd., Pa. Hardwoods Devel. Coun.; sec. Ctr. Rural Pa. Mem. regional adv. coun. Pitts. Cancer Inst.; bd. advs. Foxview Manor, Inc.; mem. adv. bd. U. Pitts., Titusville and Bradford campuses; mem. adv. coun. Ind. U. of Pa. Culinary Sch.; active Pa. Trauma Ctr. Found., Venango County Indsl. Bd. Served in U.S. Army, 1957—63. Recipient John Heinz Meml. award; Presdl. Distinction medal U. Pitts. at Bradford, Recognition award Pa. Acad. Family Physicians, Appreciation award, Better Life award Pa. Health Care Assn., Guardian of Small Bus. award Nat. Fedn. Ind. Bus., Spl. Achievement award Pa. Bar Assn., Elected Officials award Pa. Home Health Assn., 1994, Congl. Partnership award Nat. Assn. Devel. Orgns.; named Senator of Yr. Jewish Coalition, Legislator of Yr., Pa. Assn. County Human Svc. Admnstrs., 1993,

Pa. Home Health Care Assn., 1993, Nat. Rural Health Assn., 2002, Policymaker of Yr. Assn. Career and Tech. Edn. Mem. Titusville Area C. of C., Pleasantville PTA, Lions. Republican. Methodist. Office: US Ho Reps 123 Cannon Ho Office Bldg Washington DC 20515-0001 Office Phone: 202-225-5121.*

**PETERSON, JOHN WILLARD,** composer, publishing executive; b. Lindsborg, Kans., Nov. 1, 1921; s. Peter Ephraim and Adlina Mary (Nelson) P.; m. Marie Alta Addis (Feb. 11, 1944); children: Sandra Lynn Peterson Catzere, Candace Kay Peterson Strader, Pamela Lee Peterson Cruse. Student, Moody Bible Inst., 1947-48; MusB, Am. Conservatory Music, 1952; MusD (hon.) John Brown U., 1967; DD (hon.), West Bapt. Sem., 1970; DFA (hon.), Grand Canyon U., 1979. Radio broadcaster Sta. WMBI, Chgo., 1950-55; editor in chief, pres. Singspiration, Inc., Grand Rapids, Mich., 1955-71, exec. composer Carefree, Ariz., 1977-83; pres. Good Life Prodns., Scottsdale, Ariz., 1977-83, John W. Peterson Music Co., Scottsdale, 1983-88. Bd. dirs. Gospel Films, Inc., Muskegon, Mich. Co-author: (autobiography) The Miracle Goes On, 1976; composer works include numerous cantatas, musicals, gospel songs, hymns and anthems. 1st lt. USAAF 1942-45, CBI. Decorated Air medal; recipient Sacred Music award Nat. Evang. Film Found., 1966, Music Achievement award Christian Artists, 1985; Honor Cert. Freedoms Found., 1975; winner Internat. Gospel Composition of Yr., Soc. European Stage, Authors and Composers, 1986, Ray DeVries Ch. Music award, 1996; inductee Gospel Music Hall of Fame, 1986. Mem. ASCAP, Hump Pilots Assn. Home: 11668 N 80th Pl Scottsdale AZ 85260-5650 Office Phone: 480-483-3306.

**PETERSON, JOSEPH F. H.,** military officer; b. Honolulu; BS in Econs., U. Santa Clara, 1972; MBA, Chaminade U.; grad., Army Command Gen. Staff Coll., Army War Coll. Commd. 2d lt. U.S. Army, 1972, advanced through grades to brig. gen.; early assignments incldue bn. motor officer, platoon leader then co. comdr., 9th infantry divsn., Ft. Lewis, Wash.; comdr. B co., 2d bn., 72d Armor 2d Infantry divsn., Korea; comptr. Army Staff, Office of Jt. Chiefs of Staff, Washington, 1980; inspector gen., bn. S-3, comdg. officer 1st bn., 64th Armor, Brigade S-3, 2d Brigade, 3d Infantry, Germany; adc to Supreme Allied Comdr. Comdr. in Chief U.S. European Command, Belgium, 1989-91; comdr. 2d bn., 35th Armor, 4th Infantry divsn. Ft. Carson, Colo., 1991-93; divsn. plans officer, ops. officer, 1996-98; comdr. 3d brigade Combat team 1st Armored divsn., Ft. Riley, Kans., 1996-98; dep. chief of staff for Resource mgmt. Tng. and Doctrine Command, U.S. Army, Ft. Monroe, Va., 1998-99; asst. divsn. comdr. for support 3d infantry divsn., Ft. Stewart, Ga., 1999—.

**PETERSON, KATHERINE H.,** federal agency administrator, former ambassador; b. Pasadena, CA; Student, Nat. War Coll.; BA, U. Calif., Santa Cruz. Mem. staff Foreign Svc., 1976, Bureau of African Affairs, Washington; deputy chief of mission Amer. Embassy, Windhoek, Namibia, 1993—96; U.S. ambassador to Lesotho U.S. Dept. State, Washington, 1998—2001; dir. Fgn. Service Inst., Washington, 2001—.

**PETERSON, KENNETH ALLEN, JR.,** lawyer; b. Chgo., Sept. 14, 1966; s. Kenneth Allen Peterson, Sr. and Marilyn Peterson; m. Alice Irene Bruen, Jan. 10, 1999; children: Alexander Louis, Randall Tyler, Cameron Edward, Kaitlyn Samantha Bilotta. BA, Purdue U., West Lafayette, Ind., 1984—88; Jurisprudence D, Ind. U., Bloomington, Ind., 1988—91. Bar: Ill. 1991. Assoc. Chapman & Cutler, Chgo., 1991—96; mem. Bell, Boyd & Lloyd, LLC, Chgo., 1996—. Chmn. Cub Scout Pack 173, Steger, Ill., 2005—06; mem. Kiwanis Internat., Steger, 2005—; dist. chmn. crossroads dist. Calumet Coun Boy Scouts Am., Munster, Ind., 2006—; chmn. Bd. Fire & Police Commrs. of Village of Steger, Ill., 2001—03; village trustee Village of Steger, 2003—, chmn. Econ. Devel. Com., 2004—. Recipient Eagle Scout award, Boy Scouts Am., 1980. Fellow: Am. Coll. Investment Coun.; mem.: Order of Coif, Order of Arrow (life). Lutheran. Home: 3134 Sandy Ridge Dr Steger IL 60475 Office: Bell Boyd & Lloyd LLC 70 W Madison St Ste 3100 Chicago IL 60602 Business E-mail: kpeterson@bellboyd.com.

**PETERSON, KENT WRIGHT,** physician; b. Portsmouth, Va., Apr. 16, 1943; s. Gerald Milton and Julia Elizabeth (Hoover) P.; children: Liesl Lynn, Owen Sonne. BA, U. N.C., Chapel Hill, 1964; MD, U. Pa., 1968. Diplomate Am. Bd. Preventive Medicine, Am. Bd. Occupl. Medicine. Intern U. Wis., 1968-69, resident, 1970-71; Robert Wood Johnson clin. scholar George Washington U., 1975-77; family physician E. Madison Clinic, Madison, Wis., 1969; chief med. officer policy devel. U.S. Cost of Living Council, Washington, 1973-74; assoc. dir. Assn. Univ. Programs in Health Adminstrn., Washington, 1974-77; exec. v.p. Am. Coll. Preventive Medicine, Washington, 1977-81; corp. mgr. preventive and environ. medicine IBM Corp., White Plains, NY, 1981-84; corp. med. dir. Am. Standard, N.Y.C., 1984-86; pres. Occupational Health Strategies, Charlottesville, Va., 1984—. Clin. asst. prof. Georgetown U. Sch. Medicine, 1979-85; clin. assoc. prof. NYU dept. environ. medicine, 1985-2004; rep. to Coun. Med. Specialty Socs., 1980-86; mem. Accreditation Coun. for Continuing Med. Edn., 1981-86; vice chmn. Med. Rev. Officer Cert. Coun., 1992—; v.p. Am. Bd. Ind. Med. Examiners, 1995-98; sr. v.p. Inst. for Health and Productivity Mgmt., 1997-02. Author of 8 books including Handbook of Occupational Health Informatics, 11th edit., 2000, SPM Handbook of Health Assessment Tools, 4th edit., 1999; contbr. numerous articles to profl. jours. and chpts. in books. Pres. Children of the Americas Found., 1979-84; treas. Alliance for Transforming the Lives of Children, 2000—; bd. dirs., Conserva Va., 1996-2000. Served to maj. M.C. U.S. Army, 1971-73. Fellow Am. Coll. Preventive Medicine, Am. Coll. Occupl. and Environ. medicine (pres. 1996-97); mem. APHA Metadore (pres. nom. 1904—), Rehabil. Soc., Soc. Prospective Medicine (officer), World Future Soc., Coun. for Liveable World, Va. Occupl. Medicine Assn. (pres. 1988-90). Home: 1314 Dunlora Dr Charlottesville VA 22901 Office: Occupational Health Strategies Inc 901 Preston Ave Ste 400 Charlottesville VA 22903-4491 Personal E-mail: kent@healthyself.com.

**PETERSON, KEVIN BRUCE,** newspaper editor, publishing executive; b. Kitchener, Ont., Can., Feb. 11, 1948; s. Bruce Russell and Marguerite Elizabeth (Hammond) P.; m. Constance Maureen Bailey, Feb. 11, 1975 (dec. May 1975); m. Sheila Helen O'Brien, Jan. 9, 1981 BA, U. Calgary, Alta., Can., 1968. Chief bus. editor Calgary Herald, 1972-75, city editor, 1976-77, news editor, 1977-78, bus. editor, 1978, mng. editor, 1978-86, editor, asst. pub., 1986-87, gen. mgr., 1987-88, pub., 1989-96; sr. counsel GPC Comms., 1999—. Pres. Canadian Univ. Press, Ottawa, Ont., Can., 1968-69; dir. New Directions for News. Harry Brittain Meml. fellow Commonwealth Press Union, London, 1979 Mem. Can. Mng. Editors (bd. dirs. 1983-87), Am. Soc. Newspaper Editors, Horsemen's Benevolent and Protective Assn., Alta. Legis. Press Gallery Assn. (v.p. 1971-76), Can. Daily Newspaper Assn. (bd. dirs. 1990-96, vice chmn., treas 1992, chmn. 1993-96), Alta. Theatre Projects (bd. dirs. 1996—, v.p. 1998—), Calgary Ctr. for Non-Profit Mgmt. (bd. dirs. 1998—), Calgary Petroleum Club, Ranchmen's Club, 100-t-1 Club, (Arcadia, Calif.) Avocations: thoroughbred horse racing, art collecting.

**PETERSON, KURT C.,** lawyer; b. Salem, NJ, Mar. 31, 1953; BA in economics & polit. sci., Stanford U., 1975; JD, U. Calif. Hastings Coll. Law, 1978. Bar: Calif. 1978, US Dist. Ct. No. Dist. Calif., US Dist Ct. Ctrl. Dist. Calif. Law clk. to Hon. Robert Kane Calif. Ct. Appeal 1st Dist., 1978; with Crosby Heafey Roach & May (combined with Reed Smith in 2003), 1978—2003, opened L.A. office & served as first mng. ptnr., 1990, opened Century City office, 1997, mng. ptnr., 2000—03; ptnr., mem. exec. com. Reed Smith LLP, 2003—. Contbr. ABA Profl. Liability Litig. Newsletter. Bd. trustees Ctr. for Law in the Pub. Interest; bd. dirs. Music Ctr. of LA County. Named Alumnus of Yr., Hastings Alumni Assn. Calif. Law Bus., 2001; named one of the top 25 lawyers under 45 in Calif., Calif. Law Bus., 1993. Mem.: ABA (vice chair litig. sect. legal malpractice subcom. 1989—92), Assn. Bus. Trial Lawyers, L.A. Bar Assn. Office: Reed Smith LLP 1901 Ave of the Stars, Ste 700 Los Angeles CA 90067-6078 Office Phone: 310-734-5201. Office Fax: 310-734-5299. Business E-mail: kpeterson@reedsmith.com.

**PETERSON, LANCE ROBERT,** physician; b. Mpls., Sept. 2, 1947; s. Alvin Robert and Norma Lorraine (Soderlin) P.; m. LoAnn Charlotte Liukonen, Aug. 24, 1968; children: Anja Kristine, Kari Elizabeth. BS, U. Minn., 1970, MD, 1972. Diplomate Am. Bd. Internal Medicine, Am. Bd. Infectious Diseases, Am. Bd. Med. Microbiology. Intern U. Minn., 1972—73, resident, 1973—75; med. dir. home care VA Med. Ctr., Mpls., 1975—77, staff infectious diseases, 1977—92; dir. microbiology Northwestern Meml. Hosp., Chgo., 1992—2002; dir. microbiology and infectious diseases rsch. Evanston Northwestern Healthcare, 2002—. Prof. medicine U. Minn., Mpls., 1990—92, prof. lab. medicine, 1990—92; prof. pathology and medicine Northwestern U., Chgo., 1992—; healthcare epidemiology Evanston Northwestern Healthcare, 2005—; chief microbiology VA Med. Ctr., Mpls., 1979—92, assoc. chief molecular biology, 1987—89; staff infectious diseases Northwestern Meml. Hosp., Chgo., 1992—2002, dir. prevention epicenter, 1999—2002. Co-editor: Diagnostic Microbiology, 9th edit.; editor: The Biologic and Clinical Basis of Infectious Diseases, 5th edit.; contbr. chpts. to books and articles to profl. jours. Pres. Greater Mpls. Day Care Assn., 1985-86; bd. dir. Chrty. Child Care Ctr., Mpls., 1986-89, VA Employees Child Care Ctr., Mpls., 1987-92, chair fundraising com., 1987-92. Grantee, VA Dept., 1978—88, Bayer, Inc., 1985—2006, R.W. Johnson Rsch. Instn., 1990—2004, Ctrs. Disease Control, 1999—2004, Wyeth, Inc., 2003—, Wash. Sq. Health Found., 2003—04, 2006—, Gene Ohm Scis., 2006—, others. Fellow: Ctrl. Soc. Clin. Rsch. (chair. infectious diseases sect. 1995—97), Am. Soc. Clin. Pathologists, Infectious Diseases Soc. Am. (regional bd. 1991—92, sec.-treas. Chgo. area 2003—), Am. Acad. Microbiology; mem.: Brit. Soc. Antimicrobial Chemotherapy, Am. Soc. Microbiology (BD Rsch. Clin. Microbiology award 2005). Avocations: travel, jogging, dining, gardening. Office: Evanston Northwestern Healthcare 2650 Ridge Ave Evanston IL 60201 Office Phone: 847-570-1637. Business E-mail: lpeterson@enh.org.

**PETERSON, LESLIE RAYMOND,** barrister; b. Viking, Alta., Oct. 6, 1923; s. Herman S. and Margaret (Karen) P.; m. Agnes Rose Hine, June 24, 1950; children: Raymond Erik, Karen Isabelle. Student, Camrose Luth. Coll., Alta., McGill. U., Can., London U.; LLB, U. B.C., Can., 1949; LLD (hon.), U. B.C., 1993; LLD, Simon Fraser U., Can., 1965; EdD, Notre Dame U., Nelson, Can., 1966; diploma tech. (hon.), B.C. Inst. Tech., 1994. Bar: B.C. 1949; called to Queens Counsel, 1960. Pvt. practice barrister, Vancouver, B.C., 1949-52; with Peterson & Anderson, 1952, Boughton & Co., 1953—55; mem. B.C. Legislature for Vancouver Centre, 1956—63, Vancouver-Little Mountain, 1966; min. of edn., 1956-68; min. of labour, 1960-71; atty. gen., 1968-72; bd. govs. U. B.C., Vancouver, 1979-83, chancellor, 1987-93. Bd. dirs. Can. Found. Econ. Edn., Inst. Corp. Dirs. Can., West Vancouver Found., Inst. for Pacific Ocean Sci. and Tech.; trustee Peter Wall Inst. for Advanced Studies; chmn. U.B.C. Found., 1990—96. Bd. dirs. Portland unit Shriners Hosp. for Children, 1994-96; past bd. dirs. Western Soc. of Rehab., YMCA, Victoria B.C.; past pres. Twenty Club; hon. mem. Vancouver Jr. C. of C.; former v.p. Normanna Old People's Home; founding mem. Convocation, Simon Fraser U. and U. Victoria; hon. dep. French Nat. Assembly, Paris; hon. commr. labor State of Okla.; gov. Downtown Vancouver Assn. With Can. Army, 1942-46, ETO. Recipient Disting. Alumnus award Camrose Luth. Coll., 1980. Fellow: Royal Soc. Arts; mem.: Internat. Assn. Govt. Lawyer Ofcls. (chmn. standing com., Can. mins. of edn. 1965—66), Law Soc. B.C., Vancouver Bar Assn., Wesbrook Soc. of U. B.C. (chmn. 1987), Union Club (Victoria), Terminal City Club (pres. 1991—92), Scandinavian Bus. Men's Club (past pres.), Order of Can., Venerable Order of Saint John (comdr.), Order of B.C., Freemason (potentate Gizeh Temple Shrine 1988), Order of St. Lazarus (knight comdr.). Avocations: skiing, golf, fishing, tennis. Home: 814 Highland West Vancouver BC Canada V7S 2G5 Office: Boughton Peterson Law Corp 595 Burrard St Ste 1000 PO Box 49290 Vancouver BC Canada V7X 1S8 Office Phone: 604-647-4156. Personal E-mail: lpeterson@bpya.com. Business E-mail: lpeterson@boughton.ca.

**PETERSON, LINDA H.,** English language educator; b. Saginaw, Mich., Oct. 11, 1948; BA in Lit. summa cum laude, Wheaton Coll., 1969; MA in English, U. R.I., 1973; PhD in English, Brown U., 1978; DHL, Quinnipiac U., 2004. From lectr. to assoc. prof. Yale U., New Haven, 1977-92, prof., 1992—; dir. undergrad. studies English, 1990-94, chair 1994-2000, acting chair, 2003, Niel Gray Jr. prof. of English, 2002—; dir. grad. studies, 2005—. Dir. Bass writing program Yale Coll., 1979-89, 90-2004; mem. various departmental and univ. coms. Yale U., 1977-; presenter in field. Author: Victorian Autobiography: The Tradition of Self-Interpretation, 1986, Traditions of Victorian Women's Autobiography: The Poetics and Politics of Life Writing, 1999; co-author: Writing Prose, 1989, A Struggle for Fame: Victorian Women Artists and Authors, 1994; co-editor: Wuthering Heights: A Case Study in Contemporary Criticism, 1992, 2d edit., 2003, The Norton Reader, 11th edit., 2004, Instructor's Guide to the Norton Reader, 2004; mem. editl. bd. Writing Program Adminstrn., 1983-85, Coll. Composition and Comm., 1986-88, Auto/Biography Studies, 1990—; Victorian Poetry, 2002—; contbr. articles to profl. jours. Resident fellow Branford Coll., 1979-87, Mellon fellow Whitney Humanities Ctr., 1984-85, fellow NEH, 1989-90, fellow Harry Ransom Humanities Rsch. Ctr., U. Tex., 1997; life fellow Clare Hall, Cambridge, Eng., 1998—. Mem. MLA (del. assembly 1984-86, mem. program com. 1986-89, mem. non-fiction divsn. com. 1988-92, mem. nominating com. 1993-94, mem. teaching of writing divsn. 1993-98, mem. Victorian lit. divsn. 2004-), Nat. Writing Program Adminstrs. (mem. cons.-evaluator program 1982-95, mem. exec. bd. 1982-84, 89-90, v.p 1985-86, pres. 1987-88), Nat. Coun. Tchrs. English (mem. CCCC nominating com. 1985, mem. coll. sect. com. 1987-90). Home: 53 Edgehill Rd New Haven CT 06511-1343 Office: Yale U Dept English PO Box 208302 New Haven CT 06520-8302 Office Phone: 203-432-2226. Business E-mail: linda.peterson@yale.edu.

**PETERSON, LINDA LOU,** special education educator; b. Bakersfield, Calif., Oct. 17, 1939; d. Wiley Karl and Chrystine Walker Peterson. AA, El Camino Coll., Gardena, Calif., 1959; BS, U. So. Calif., L.A., 1961; postgrad., San Jose State U., 1988—96. Chpt. 1 tchr. Mt. Pleasant Unified Sch. Dist., Calif., 1986—88; resource specialist in spl. edn. Hayward Unified Sch. Dist., Calif., 1988—. Advisor, dir. Russian Hill Neighbors Bd., San Francisco, 1993—, hospitality and raffle chmn. Named Merit Tchr., San Marino Unified Sch. Dist., 1967. Mem.: NEA (del. to conf. 2004), Hayward Edn. Assn.; Vintner's Club. Avocations: reading, exercise, fine dining, travel, jazz. Home: 1001 Pine St #1407 San Francisco CA 94109 Personal E-mail: l_peterson888@hotmail.com.

**PETERSON, LINDA S.,** lawyer; b. Grand Forks, ND, Mar. 15, 1952; BA summa cum laude, Yale U., 1973; JD, Yale U., 1977. Bar: N.D. 1977, D.C. 1978, U.S. Dist. Ct. D.C. 1979, U.S. Ct. Appeals (D.C. cir.) 1979, U.S. Ct. Appeals (3d cir.) 1982, Calif. 1986, U.S. Ct. Appeals (fed. cir.) 1986. Law clk. Ct. of Appeals for D.C., Washington, 1977-78; ptnr. Sidley & Austin, L.A., 1978—. Dep. counsel Webster Commn., 1992—. Mem. adj. faculty Southwestern U. Sch. Law, 1995. Recipient Dean Phillips Memorial Award, Vietnam Veterans of America. Mem. State Bar Calif. (rules of ct. com. 1987-90), L.A. County Bar Assn. (conf. dels. 1987-90, trustee 1998-99), Women Lawyers Assn. L.A. (bd. dirs. 1989-99, pres. 1998-99), Phi Beta Kappa. Office: Sidley Austin Brown & Wood LLP 555 W 5th St Ste 4000 Los Angeles CA 90013-3000

**PETERSON, LLOYD, JR.,** academic administrator, consultant; b. San Antonio, July 20, 1958; s. Lloyd Peterson, Sr. and Dorothy Garrett Phifer; m. Debra Gay Culbertson; 1 child, Jaela Culbertson Grayson. AB in Medieval Lit., Colo. State U., Fort Collins, 1976—80; MS in Applied Human Scis., 1980—82. Sr. admissions officer Yale U., New Haven, 1987—96; dir. admissions Vassar Coll., Poughkeepsie, NY, 1996—2000; v.p., edn. Coll. Coach, LLC, Boston, 2000—. Co-chmn. Black Admissions Officers, Ivy League and Sister Schs., Cambridge, Mass.; chair, minority rels. com. Colo. Coun. HS & Coll. Rels., Colorado Springs. Author: (book) College Admissions. Edn. cons. Horizons Initiative, Boston; pres. El Paso County Black Caucus, Colorado Springs, Colo.; chair, edn. com. Urban League, Pikes Peak Region, Colorado Springs, Colo. Recipient Best Writers Award, Mt. Holyoke Coll., Blue Key Award, City of Colo. Springs; scholar, Sachs Found. Mem.:

New Eng. Assn.Coll. Admissions Counseling, Nat. Assn. Coll. Admissions Counselors. Liberal. Avocations: cooking, writing, classical music, jazz. Office: Coll Coach LLC 233 Needham St Newton MA 02464 Office Phone: 617-527-4441. Office Fax: 617-527-8882. E-mail: volvolp@rcn.com.

**PETERSON, M. JEANNE,** historian, educator; b. Minn., Nov. 26, 1937; d. Clifford Woodrow and Mildred Amelia (Kukas) P.; divorced. BA, U. Calif., 1966, PhD, 1972. Lectr., asst., assoc. prof. Ind. U., Bloomington, 1971-87, prof. history, 1987—, chairperson dept. history, 1987—93, exec. assoc. dean Coll. Arts and Scis., 1993—99, acting chair gender studies dept., 1999—2000, prof. emerita history, found. prof. emerita gender studies, 2001—. Cons. Jour. Women's History, Bull. Hist. Medicine, U. Mich. Press, Butler U., Indpls., Harvard U. Press, Princeton U. Press, Columbia U. Press, Ind. U. Press, SUNY Press, Food and Foodways, Med. History, ACLS, Am. Hist. Rev., Victorian Studies, NEH, NIH, Can. Coun., U. Nebr., U. Iowa, Adam Matthew Ltd., Johns Hopkins U. Press. Author: The Medical Profession in Mid-Victorian London, 1978, Family, Love, and Work in the Lives of Victorian Gentlewomen, 1989; assoc. editor: Oxford Dictionary of National Biography; co-editor: Lizzie Borden: A Case Book of Family and Crime in the 1890s, 1980; contrb. articles to profl. jours. NEH fellow, 1978-79, Guggenheim Found. fellow, 1984-85, Inst. for Advanced Study fellow Ind. U., 1984-85. Mem. Am. Hist. Assn., Soc. for the Social History Medicine, N.Am. Conf. Brit. Studies, Am. Assn. History Medicine, N.Am. Victorian Studies Assn. Home: 1311 S Rechter Ct Bloomington IN 47401-6173 Office: Ind U Dept Gender Studies 742 Ballantine Rd Bloomington IN 47401-5022 Office Phone: 812-855-0101. E-mail: petersom@indiana.edu.

**PETERSON, MARISSA,** information technology executive; BS in mech. engring., Kettering U.; MBA, Harvard U. Mgmt. cons. Booz, Allen and Hamilton; previously held mktg., fin., and engring. positions Saturn Corp., Gen. Motors; dir. US mfg. Sun Microsystems, Santa Clara, Calif., 1993—95, v.p. worldwide ops., logistics, 1995—98, v.p. worldwide ops., 1998—99, exec. v.p. worldwide ops., 2000—02, exec. v.p. worldwide ops. and chief customer advocate, 2002—. Bd. dirs. Covisint, SuperValu. Bd. trustees Kettering U., Industry Advisory Coun., Alliance for Innovative Mfg., Stanford U.; bd. dirs. Lucille Packard Children's Hosp., Stanford. Named to Top 100 in Bus., SF Bus. Times; recipient Silicon Valley Tribute to Women and Industry, Mgmt. Achievement award, Kettering U. Office: Sun Microsystems Inc 4150 Network Cir Santa Clara CA 95054 Office Phone: 650-960-1300, 800-555-9786. Office Fax: 408-276-3804.

**PETERSON, MARJORIE,** former mayor; b. Chisholm, Minn., Aug. 16, 1924; d. Martin and Catherine Mihelick Champa; m. Andrew Levchak, July 6, 1946 (dec. Mar. 2, 1975); children: Carol, Andrea, Richard, Lisbeth; m. Walter C. Peterson, Sept. 25, 1976. Bookkeeper Ford Sales & Svc., Chisholm, Minn.; dental asst. Office of Dr. J.E. Hoffman, Chisholm, 1960—65; podiatrist asst. Office of Dr. Larson, Hibbing, Minn., 1967; divsn. sec. Fin. Programs, Hibbing, 1967—74; mem. city coun. City of Chisholm, 1977—85, 1989—95, ofcl., 1989—95, mayor, 1996—98. Mem. Pub. Utilities Bd., Chisholm. Contrb. poetry to anthologies. Pres. Range Assn. Sch. and City, Chisholm; bd. dirs. Chisholm-Hibbing Airport Authority, Hibbing, Minn., 1991—, mem. 1991—2001; v.p. bd. dirs. Mus. Mining, 2002; mem. Friends of Libr.; bd. dirs. League Minn. Cities, St. Paul, 1984. Recipient C.C. Ludwig award, League Minn. Cities, 1984, Silver award, World of Poetry, 1990, Golden Poet award, 1998, Famous Poet, Famous Poet Soc., 2000. Mem.: Moose. Democrat. Roman Catholic. Achievements include being first woman elected to City Council in Chisholm, and first woman elected as mayor. Avocations: reading, volunteer work, travel, cards. Home: 405 7th St NW Chisholm MN 55719

**PETERSON, MERRILL DANIEL,** historian, educator; b. Manhattan, Kans., Mar. 31, 1921; s. William Oscar and Alice Dwinell (Merrill) P.; m. Jean Hymphrey, May 24, 1944 (dec. Nov. 1995); children: Jeffrey Ward, Kent Merrill. Student, Kans. State U., 1939-41; AB, U. Kans., 1943; PhD in History of Am. Civilization, Harvard U., 1950. Teaching fellow Harvard U., Cambridge, Mass., 1948-49; instr., then asst. prof. history Brandeis U., Waltham, Mass., 1949-55; asst. prof., bicentennial preceptor Princeton U., N.J., 1955-58; mem. faculty Brandeis U., Waltham, Mass., 1958-62, dean students, 1960-62; Thomas Jefferson Found. prof. U. Va., Charlottesville, 1962-87, prof. emeritus, 1987—; chmn. dept. history, 1966-72, dean faculty Arts and Scis., 1981-85; Mary Ball Washington prof. Am. History University Coll., Dublin, Ireland, 1988-89; vol. Peace Corps, Armenia, 1997. Scholar in residence Bellagio Study Ctr., 1974; faculty Salzburg Seminar in Am. Studies, 1975; Lamar lectr. Mercer U., 1975; Fleming lectr. La. State U., 1980; lectr. at 20 European univs., 40 Am. colls. and univs. Author: The Jefferson Image in the American Mind, 1960 (Bancroft prize, Gold medal Thomas Jefferson Meml. Found.), Major Crises in American History, 2 vols., 1962, Democracy, Liberty and Property: The State Constitutional Convention Debates of the 1820s, 1966, Thomas Jefferson and the New Nation: A Biography, 1970, James Madison: A Biography in His Own Words, 1974, Adams and Jefferson: A Revolutionary Dialogue, 1976, Olive Branch and Sword: The Compromise of 1833, 1982, The Great Triumvirate: Webster, Clay and Calhoun, 1987; editor: Thomas Jefferson: A Historical Profile, 1996, The Portable Thomas Jefferson, 1975, Thomas Jefferson Writings, 1984, Thomas Jefferson: A Reference Biography, 1986, The Virginia Statute for Religious Freedom: Its Evolution and Consequences in American History, 1988, Visitors to Monticello, 1989, Lincoln in American Memory, 1994 (History finalist, Pulitzer prize, PBK Book award U. Va.), Coming of Age with the New Republic, 1938-1950, 1999, The John Brown Legend Revisited, 1859-2000, 2002, Starving Armenians: America and the Armenian Genocide. 1915-1930 and After, 2004. Bd. dirs. Thomas Jefferson Found.; chmn. Thomas Jefferson Commemoration Commn., 1993-94. Guggenheim fellow, 1962-63, Ctr. for Advanced Study in Behavioral Scis. fellow, 1968-69, NEH and Nat. Humanities Ctr. fellow, 1980-81; recipient 20th Anniversary award Va. Found. for Humanities, 1994, Nat. First Freedom award First Freedom Coun., 1997, Career Achievement award, 2005, Libr. Va. Fellow Am. Acad. Arts and Scis.; mem. Am. Hist. Assn., Am. Antiquarian Soc., Mass. Hist. Soc., Phi Beta Kappa. Home and Office: 250 Pantops Mountain Rd Apt 6 Charlottesville VA 22911-8600 Office Phone: 434-972-2346.

**PETERSON, MILLIE M.,** state senator; b. Merced, Calif., June 11, 1944; BS, U. Utah, 1979, MSW, 1984. Mem. Utah Senate Dist. 12, Salt Lake City, 1991—2002. Susa Young Gates award, UT. Mem. NASW. Democrat. Address: 7131 W 3800 S West Valley City UT 84128-3416 Office Phone: 801-566-4423. Personal E-mail: mpeter7131@aol.com.

**PETERSON, NAD A.,** retired lawyer; b. Mt. Pleasant, Utah, 1926; m. Martha Peterson, 1948 (dec. 2004). AB, George Washington U., 1950, JD, 1953. Bar: D.C. 1953, Calif. 1960, U.S. Supreme Ct. 1958. Law practice, Washington, 1953-60; sec., asst. gen. counsel Dart Industries, L.A., 1960-67; chief counsel Fluor Corp., 1967-73; gen. counsel, 1973-79, v.p. law, 1979-82, sr. v.p. law, 1983-84, sr. v.p., sec. Irvine, Calif., 1984-93; sr. v.p., gen. counsel San Diego Gas & Electric Co., 1993-95. With USNR, PTO, 1944-46. Mem. ABA, Calif. Bar Assn., Phi Delta Phi. Home: PO Box 9101 Rancho Santa Fe CA 92067-4101 E-mail: sanpete1@aol.com.

**PETERSON, NANCY,** special education educator; AS, Webster State Coll., 1963; BS in Elem. Edn. magna cum laude, Brigham Young U., 1964, MS in Ednl. Psychology, 1966, PhD in Ednl. Psychology, 1969. Instr. in tchr. edn. Brigham Young U., Provo, Utah, 1966-69; asst. prof. ednl. dept. spl. edn. U. Kans., Lawrence, 1969-74; dir. spl. edn. classes for handicapped children Clin. Tng. Ctr., 1969-89, project dir. head start tng., 1973-74, coord. edn. univ. affiliated facility Clin. Tng. Ctr., 1969-74, coord. pers. tng. programs in mental retardation, 1973-76, assoc. prof. edn.; 1974-88, project dir. pers. tng. programs, 1986-93, prof. assoc. dept. spl. edn., 1988—, dept. chair, 1994—. Rsch. sci. Bur. Child Rsch., U. Kans., 1969—; prin. investigator for Kans. U. Kans. Early Childhood Rsch. Inst., 1977-82; Matthew Guglielmo Endowed Chair, Charter Sch. Edn., Calif. State U., LA, 1998-2000; Mary Ann Alia

lectureship Charter Sch. Edn. Calif. State U. LA, 1999; prof. spl. edn. U. Kans., 2000—. Recipient J.E. Wallace Wallin award Internat. Coun. Exceptional Children, 1993. Office: U Kans Dept Spl Edn 521 Pearson Hall Lawrence KS 66045-3101

**PETERSON, NEAL N.,** lawyer; b. 1968; BA summa cum laude, St. Olaf Coll., 1990; JD, Cornell Univ., 1993. Bar: Conn. 1993, Minn. 1996. Assoc. health law dept. Murtha, Cullina, Richter and Pinney, 1993—96; assoc. Dorsey & Whitney LLP, Mpls., 1996—2000, ptnr., health care practice group, 2001—, head, health care practice group. Writer, lectr. in field. Named a Rising Star, Minn. Law & Politics Mag. Mem.: Minn. State Bar Assn. (governing coun., health sect.), Am. Health Lawyers Assn. Office: Dorsey & Whitney LLP Ste 1500 50 S Sixth St Minneapolis MN 55402-1498 Office Phone: 612-343-7943. Office Fax: 612-340-2868. Business E-mail: peterson.neal@dorsey.com.

**PETERSON, PAM M.,** museum director; b. Phila. Pa. d. Warren Allen and Bernice Straub Matthias; m. John W Peterson, Sept. 14, 1968; children: Matthew Park, Joanna Joohee. BA, Chatham Coll., 1964—68; MEd, Boston U., 1974; cert. for advanced studies, Harvard U. Fogg Ctr. for Conservation, 1983. Conservator of art Isabella Stewart Gardner Mus., Boston, 1970—76, U. Heidelberg, Germany, 1976—79; conservator of art intern Fogg Mus., Harvard U., 1983; conservator of art Peabody Essex Mus., Salem, Mass., 1982—98; dir. exhibits and edn. Marblehead Mus. and Hist. Soc., Marblehead, Mass., 1998—2003, mus. dir., 2003—. Mem. bd. dirs. Marblehead Arts Assn., 2001—03; commr. Essex Nat. Commn., 2000—03. Mem.: (book) J. O. J. Frost, 2003. Pres. Marblehead Middle Sch. Parents Council, 1995—96. Grant, Marblehead Mass. Cultural Coun., 2000, 2003. Mem.: New England Mus. Assn., Marblehead C. of C. Democrat. Episc. Avocations: painting, writing. Home: 45 Seaview Ave Marblehead MA 01945 Office: Marblehead Mus and Hist Soc 170 Washington St Marblehead MA 01945 Office Phone: 781-631-1768. Business E-mail: mmhspeterson@yahoo.com.

**PETERSON, PAMELA CARMELLE,** language educator; b. Bakersfield, Calif., Sept. 24, 1954; d. Bob Eugene and Carmelita Denyse (Coodey) York; m. Robert Leroy Peterson, Feb. 9, 1979; children: Aimee, Sara, Matthew, Hannah. AA, Bakersfield Coll., 1992; BA in History, Calif. State U. Bakersfield, 1994. Exec. adminstr. Kern Bldg. Materials, Bakersfield, 1973—95; prin. Rosewall Christian Acad., Bakersfield, 1994—; prin., tchr. Dynasty Christian Schs., Bakersfield, 1995—97; instr. ESL Calif. State U., Bakersfield, 1997—; instr. English Santa Barbara Bus. Coll., Calif., 1998—. Pres. bd. Dynasty Christian Schs., 1995; exec. sec. bd. dirs. Kern Bldg. Materials, 1983-95; adj. prof. English Bakersfield Coll., 2006. Mem. Assn. Christian Schs., Inc., Assn. Christian Sch. Adminstrs., Cherokee Nation, Phi Alpha Theta (sec. 1994-95, v.p. 1995-96). Avocations: history, reading, needlecrafts, gardening, baking. Home: 6309 Juniper Rd Lake Isabella CA 93240-2529 Office: Rosewall Christian Acad 7850 White Ln # E149 Bakersfield CA 93309-7689 Office Phone: 661-549-0098. E-mail: rcateach@aol.com.

**PETERSON, PENELOPE LORAINE,** dean, education educator; b. Moline, Ill., Nov. 25, 1949; d. Leroy P.; m. W. Patrick Dickson; children: Andrew, Joshua, Elissa. BS, Iowa State U., 1971; MS, PhD, Stanford U., 1976. Asst. prof. dept. ednl. psychology U. Wis., Madison, 1976-80, assoc. prof., 1980-81, prof. ednl. psychology, 1982-85, Sears-Bascom Prof., 1985-87; prof. ednl. psychology & tchr. edn. Mich. State U., East Lansing, 1987—91, co-dir. Inst. Rsch. on Teaching, 1987—97, co- dir. Elem. Subjects Ctr., 1987-92, co-dir. Ednl. Policy Practice Study, 1992—97; dean Northwestern U. Sch. Edn. & Social Policy, Evanston, Ill., 1997—, Eleanor R. Baldwin prof. edn., 1997—. Author chpts. to books; editor: Rev. Ednl. Rsch, 1984-90; contbr. articles to profl. jours. Recipient Palmer O. Johnson award Am. Edn. Rsch. Assn., 1980, Raymond B. Cattell Early Career award Am. Ednl. Rsch. Assn., 1986, Disting. Rsch. award Assn. Tchr. Edn., 1992. Fellow Am. Psychol. Soc. Office: Northwestern U Sch Edn & Social Policy Annenberg Hall Rm 252 2120 Campus Dr Evanston IL 60208 E-mail: p-peterson@northwestern.edu.

**PETERSON, PER A.,** health products executive; V.p. drug discovery R.W. Johnson Pharm. Rsch. Inst. Johnson & Johnson, 1994—98, grp. v.p. Pharm. Rsch. Inst., 1998, pres. Pharm. Rsch. Inst., 1998—2000, chmn. rsch. and devel. Pharms. Grp., 2000—, mem. exec. com., 2001—. Office: Johnson & Johnson 1 Johnson & Johnson Plz New Brunswick NJ 08933*

**PETERSON, PETER GEORGE,** investment company executive; b. Kearney, Nebr., June 5, 1926; s. George and Venetia P.; m. Sally H., May 1953 (div. 1979); children: John, Jim, David, Holly, Michael; m. Joan Ganz Cooney, Apr. 26, 1980. BS, Northwestern U., 1947; MBA, U.Chgo., 1951; PhD (hon.), Colgate U., George Washington U., Northwestern U., Georgetown U., U. Rochester, New School U., Southampton Coll. at L.I. Exec. v.p. Market Facts, Chgo., 1948-52; v.p. McCann Erickson, Chgo., 1952-58; pres. Bell and Howell, Chgo., 1961—63, exec. v.p., 1961—63, chmn., CEO, 1963-71; asst. to Pres. for internat. econ. affairs The White House, Washington, 1961-63; sec. US Dept. Commerce, Washington, 1972-73; CEO, chmn. bd. Lehman Bros. and Lehman Bros., Kuhn, Loeb, Inc., NYC, 1973-84; sr. chmn., co-founder The Blackstone Group, 1985—. Chmn. Fed. Res. Bank NY, 1999-2003; founding pres. The Concord Coalition co-chmn, The Conf. Bd. Comm. on Publ. Trust and Pvt. Enterprise. Author: Facing Up: How to Rescue the Economy from Crushing Debt and Restore the American Dream, 1993, Will America Grow Up Before it Grows Old: How the Coming Social Security Crisis Threatens You, Your Family, and Your Country, 1996, Gray Dawn: How the Coming Age Wave Will Transform America--and the World, 1999, Running on Empty: How the Democratic and Republican Parties Are Bankrupting Our Future and What Americans Can Do About It, 2004; editor: Readings in Market Organization and Price Policies; co-author: On Borrowed Time: How The Growth In Entitlement Spending Threatens America's Future, 1989. Founding mem. Bi-Partisan Budget Appeal; pres. The Concord Coalition; trustee Commn. for Econ. Devel., Mus. Modern Art, NYC; bd. dir. Pub. Agenda. Recipient Outstanding Service award Phoenix House, NYC, 1976, Stephen Wise award Am. Jewish Congress, 1981, U. Chgo. Alumni medal, 1983, Man of Vision award, 1994, Nebraskalander award, 1994, Harvard Bus. Sch. Leadership award, 2004, Coro N.Y. Leadership award, 2004; named to Pres. Clinton's Bi-Partisan Comm. on Entitlement Reform, 1994. Mem. Coun. on Fgn. Rels. (chmn. bd. 1985—), Inst. Internat. Econ. (chmn. bd 1980), Nat. Bur. Econ. Rsch. (trustee), Japan Soc., Blind Brook Club (Purchase, NY), Deepdale Club (Manhasset, NY), Maidstone Club (Easthampton, NY), Chgo. Club, River Club, Links, Augusta Nat. Club, Friar's Head Golf Club (Riverhead, NY), Burning Tree (Washington), Quail Valley Golf Club, Atlantic Club, Windsor Club; fellow Am. Acad. Arts & Sciences Republican. Home: 435 E 52nd St Apt 11G New York NY 10022-6445 Office: The Blackstone Group 345 Park Ave Ste 3101 New York NY 10154-0004 Office Phone: 212-583-5817.*

**PETERSON, RALPH RANDALL,** engineering executive; b. Hayti, Mo., Oct. 12, 1944; s. James Tony and Helen Irene (Webb) P.; m. Betty Shoemaker, Nov. 7, 1964; children: Jamie Marie Jeffrey, Jeffrey Scott. BSCE, Oreg. State U., 1969; MS in Environ. Engring., Stanford U., 1970; AMP in Bus., Harvard U., 1991. Registered profl. engr., Oreg., Wash., Colo. Engring. aide Johnson, Underkofler & Briggs, Boise, Idaho, 1962—63; surveyor Smith, Keyes, & Blakely, Caldwell, Idaho, 1963—64; with Chronic & Assocs., Boise, Idaho, 1964—65; various project devel. and dept. mng. roles CH2M Hill Cos., Corvallis, Oreg., 1965-78, v.p. in indsl. process divsn., 1978-87, sr. v.p., tech. dir. Denver, 1987-90, CEO, 1990—, also chmn. bd. Bd. dirs. Std. Ins. Co., Portland, Oreg.; bd. advisors Constrn. Industry Pres. Forum, Washington, 1994—; co-chair Nat. Congress Advancement of Minorities in Environ. Professions, Atlanta, 1993-94; industry co-chair tech. for sustainable future White House Office Sci. and Tech. Policy, 1995-96. Bd. dirs. Stapleton Devel. Corp., Denver, 1994—, Wetland Water Ctr., Denver, 1990—; corp. patron Smithsonian Instn. Corp. Patron. Recipient Colo. Gov.'s award for internat. trade devel., 1995. Mem. ASCE, Am. Water Works Assn., Water Environment

Fedn., Colo. Environ. Bus. Assn. (co-chair 1993—), Oreg. State U. Alumni Assn. (bd. dirs. 1992—). Avocations: skiing, camping, fishing, performing arts. Office: CH2M Hill 9191 S Jamaica St Englewood CO 80112*

**PETERSON, RANDALL THEODORE,** law educator, law librarian; b. Sioux City, Iowa, Aug. 27, 1944; s. Theodore Melvin and Ileann Grace (Wendrich) Peterson; m. Judith Ashcroft, Aug. 24, 1967; children: Kristin, Randall, Heidi, Travis, Robert, Quinn. Student, Dixie Coll., 1962—63; BS, Brigham Young U., Provo, Utah, 1968, MLS, 1974; JD, U. Utah, 1972. Asst. law libr. Brigham Young U., Provo, Utah, 1972—74, assoc. law libr., 1974—77; asst. prof. law and dir. libr. svcs. John Marshall Law Sch., Chgo., 1977—86, assoc. prof. law and dir. libr. svcs., 1986—90, assoc. prof. law, 1990—. Mem.: ABA. Mem. Lds Ch. Office: John Marshall Law Sch 315 S Plymouth Ct Chicago IL 60604-3968 Office Phone: 312-978-2372. E-mail: 7rtp@jmls.edu.

**PETERSON, RICHARD HERMANN,** retired history professor; b. Berkeley, Calif., Jan. 16, 1942; s. William Martin and Dorothy Jeane (Heyne) P.; m. Nora Ann Lorenzo, June 21, 1970; 1 child, Nina Elizabeth. AB, U. Calif., Berkeley, 1963; MA, San Francisco State U., 1966; PhD, U. Calif., Davis, 1971. Calif. community coll. teaching credential. Asst. prof. history Ind. U., Kokomo, 1971-76; instr. social studies Coll. of Redwoods, Ft. Bragg, Calif., 1976-78; assoc. prof. history San Diego State U., 1978-82, prof. history, 1982-96, prof. emeritus, 1996—; freelance writer, artist, 1996—. Author: Manifest Destiny in the Mines, 1975, The Bonanza Kings, 1977, 91, Bonanza Rich, 1991; book rev. editor Jour. of San Diego History, 1978-82, editl. cons., 1980-82; contbr. articles to profl. jours., book revs., websites, newspapers. Judge for papers Internat. History Fair, San Diego, Tijuana, Mex., 1983-88. Faculty Summer fellow Ind. U., 1975, 76, San Diego State U., 1980, Meritorious Performance and Prof. Promise award, 1989; rsch. grantee Sourisseau Acad., 1977, Am. Assn. State/Local History, 1988, 1st Pl. award in History Poetry Contest, Distant Frontier Press, 2001, 2d Pl. award Showcase Writers Contest, San Diego, 2002; named Golden Poet of Yr., World of Poetry, 1987-89. Mem. Mining History Assn., Calif. Hist. Soc., Western History Assn. Avocations: golf, gardening, poetry, travel. Home: 7956 Lake Adlon Dr San Diego CA 92119-3117 Office Phone: 619-464-7935.

**PETERSON, RICHARD WILLIAM,** retired judge, retired lawyer; b. Council Bluffs, Iowa, Sept. 29, 1925; s. Henry K. and Laura May (Robinson) Peterson; m. Patricia Mae Fox, Aug. 14, 1949; children: Katherine Ilene Peterson Sherbondy, Jon Eric, Timothy Richard. BA, U. Iowa, 1949, JD with distinction, 1951; postgrad., U. Nebr.-Omaha, 1972-80, 86. Bar: Iowa 1951, U.S. Dist. Ct. (so. dist.) Iowa 1951, U.S. Supreme Ct. 1991, U.S. Ct. Appeals (8th cir.) 1997. Pvt. practice law, Council Bluffs, 1951—; U.S. commr. U.S. Dist. Ct. (so. dist.) Iowa, 1958-70, U.S. magistrate judge, 1970—99. Nat. faculty Fed. Jud. Ctr., Washington, 1972—82; emeritus trustee Children's Sq., U.S.A., 1969—; verifying ofcl. Internat. Prisoner Transfer Treaties, Mexico City, 1977, La Paz, Bolivia, 1980—81, Lima, Peru, 1981. Author: The Court Moves West: A Study of the United States Court Decision of Appeals from the United States Circuit and District Court of Iowa, 1846-1882, 1988, West of the Nishnabotna: The Experience of Forty Years of a Part-Time Judicial Officer as United States Commissioner, Magistrate and Magistrate Judge, 1958-1998, 1998; author: (with George Mills) No One is Above the Law: The Story of Southern Iowa's Federal Court, 1994; contbr. articles to legal publs. Bd. dirs. Pottawattamie County chpt. ARC, Iowa, state fund chmn. Iowa, 1957—58; dist. chmn. Trailblazer dist. Boy Scouts Am., 1952—55; state chmn. Radio Free Europe, 1960—61; mem. exec. coun. Mid-Am. Ct., 1976—; pres. St. John Found., 1986; Sunday sch. tchr. St. John Luth. Ch., Council Bluffs, 1952—72, coun. mem., 1955—75. With U.S. Army, 1943—46. Decorated Purple Heart, Bronze Star; named Outstanding Young Man, Council Bluffs C. of C., 1959; recipient Jason award, Children's Sq., 2005. Fellow: Am. Bar Found. (life); mem.: ABA, Hist. Soc. U.S. Cts. 8th Jud. Cir. (pres. 1989—99, ct. historian U.S. Dist. Ct. S.D. and Iowa 2000—), Iowa Conf. Bar Assn. (pres. 1985—87), Fed. Magistrate Judges Assn. (pres. 1978—79), Inter-Am. Bar Assn., Fed. Bar Assn., Pottawattamie County Bar Assn. (pres. 1979—80), Iowa Bar Assn. (chmn. com. fed. practice 1978—80, probate and trust coun. and sect. 1997—), Am. Judicature Soc., Supreme Ct. Hist. Soc., Masons, Kiwanis, Omicron Delta Kappa, Delta Sigma Rho, Phi Delta Phi. Republican. Lutheran. Home: 1007 Arbor Ridge Cir Council Bluffs IA 51503-5000 Office: PO Box 248 25 Main Pl Ste 200 Council Bluffs IA 51503-0790

**PETERSON, ROBERT ALLEN,** marketing educator; b. N.Y.C., Mar. 25, 1944; s. Robert A. and Carrol D. (Collins) P.; m. Diane S. Femrite, June 18, 1966; children: Jeffrey, Jennifer, Matthew. BS, U. Minn., 1966, MS, 1968, PhD, 1970. Asst. prof. mktg. U. Tex., Austin, 1970-73, assoc. prof., 1973-77, prof., 1977—; John T. Stuart chair, 1985—, chmn. dept. mktg. adminstrn., 1983-85, assoc. dean for rsch., 2002—04; deputy dir. IC2 Inst. Prin. Group Seven Assocs., Austin Author: Marketing Research, 1982, 2d edit., 1988; co-author: Modern American Capitalism, 1990, Strategic Marketing, 10th edit., 2004; editor: Jour. Mktg. Rsch., 1985-88, Jour. Acad. Mktg. Sci., 1991-94; mem. editorial bd. Jour. Mktg., Internat. Mktg. Rev. Recipient rsch. award AMA, 1988, Charles Hurwitz fellow, 1983—. Fellow Southwestern Mktg. Assn. (pres. 1977-78), Am. Mktg. Assn. (v.p. 1980-81), Acad. Mktg. Sci. (bd. govs. 1982-86, chmn. 1994-98, pres. 2000-02), Am. Inst. Decision Scis. (dir. 1974-75). Lutheran. Office: Univ Texas Dept Mktg Austin TX 78712

**PETERSON, ROBERT AUSTIN,** retired manufacturing executive; b. Sioux City, Iowa, July 5, 1925; s. Austen W. and Marie (Mueller) P.; m. Carol May Hudy, May 17, 1952; children: Roberta, Richard., Bruce. BS, U. Minn., 1946, BBA, 1947. Credit mgr. New Holland Machine div. Sperry Rand Corp., Mpls., 1952-61; from credit mgr. to treas. Toro Co., Mpls., 1961-70, v.p., treas. internat. fin., 1970-83; v.p. fin., pres. Toro Credit Co., 1983-93. Chmn. Prior Lake Spring Lake Watershed Dist., 1970-80; chmn., bd. dirs. Prior Lake Bd. Edn., 1965-71; chmn. Scott County Republican Party, 1969-70; bd. dirs. Scott Carver Mental Health Center, 1969-73, Minn. Watershed Assn., 1972-76. Served to ensign USNR, 1943-46. Mem.: Prior Lake Yacht Club (bd. dirs.).

**PETERSON, ROBERT SCOTT,** electrical engineer; b. McKeesport, Pa., Mar. 24, 1930; s. William James and Emma Elizabeth (Scott) P.; m. Betty Louise Oleska, Aug. 11, 1962 (dec. 1995). BSEE, Pa. State U., 1952; MSEE, U. Pitts., 1961. Lic. profl. engr., Pa. Sr. application, design engr. Westinghouse Elec., Pitts., 1952-63, devel. engr. Buffalo, 1963-85, Pitts., 1985-89, AEG Automation Corp., Pitts., 1989-94; cons. engr. CDI-Ctrl. Corp., Pitts., 1994—. Holder 30 U.S. patents. Coach Midget Football League, McKeesport, 1953-55. With U.S. Army, 1955-57. Mem. IEEE, NY Acad. Scis., Assn. Iron Steel Engrs. Achievements include patents in field. Avocations: gardening, woodworking, painting, dance, sports. Home and Office: 719 Heathergate Dr Pittsburgh PA 15238-1000 Office Phone: 412-767-4690.

**PETERSON, ROBIN TUCKER,** marketing educator; b. Casper, Wyo., July 31, 1937; s. Walfred Arthur and Mary Lurene Peterson; m. Marjorie K. Greenwald, June 25, 1963; children: Timothy, Kimberly. BS, U. Wyo., 1959, MS in Bus., 1961; PhD, U. Wash., 1967. Mem. faculty Idaho State U., Pocatello, 1963-73; prof. mktg., head mktg. dept. St. Cloud Univ., Minn. State U., 1973-76, N.Mex. State U., Las Cruces, 1976—. Fulbright lectr. Yugoslavia, 1973; vis. scholar Ea. Mont. State Coll., 1985; Sunwest Fin. Svcs. Disting. Centennial prof. N.Mex. State U., 1991, 92; Norwest Disting. prof. N.Mex. State U., 1999, Wells Fargo Disting. prof., 2002; vis. lectr. Nirma Inst. Ahmedabad, India, 1999, Chiang Moi U., Thailand, 2000; Fulbright lectr. Kathmandu U., Nepal, 2001. Author: Marketing-A Contemporary Introduction, 1976, Forecasting, 1976, edit., 1983, Personal Selling, 1977, Marketing in Action, 1977, Lembook Marketing, 1984, Marketing: Concepts and Decision Making, 1987, Principles of Marketing, 1989, Argentina, 1990, Managing the Distributor Sales Network, 1990, Business Forecasting, 1992, Getting New Products to Market Rapidly, 1993, exec. editor Bus. Forecaster, 1993-94; editor Jour. Bus. and Entrepreneurship, 1994-98; contbr. articles to profl. publs. Served with USAR, 1962-63. Fellow Assn. Small Bus. Entrepreneurship; mem. Am. Mktg. Assn., Sales and Mktg. Execs. Internat.; Acad. Mktg. Sci. (pres. 1977-78, 80-82), Am. Arbitration Assn. (Outstanding Educators Am. award), S.W. Small Bus. Assn. (pres. 1983-84, Outstanding Mktg. Educators award, Outstanding Educator, Assn. of Small Bus., 2002), S.W. Mktg. Assn., Western Mktg. Educators, Las Cruces C. of C., Las Cruces Sales and Mktg. Club, Beta Gamma Sigma, Phi Kappa Psi, Alpha Kappa Psi, Alpha Mu Alpha. Republican. Presbyterian. Home: 4350 Diamondback Dr Las Cruces NM 88011-7539 Office: NMex State U PO Box 5280 Las Cruces NM 88003-5280 Office Phone: 505-646-3341. Business E-mail: ropeters@nmsu.edu.

**PETERSON, ROBYN GAYLE,** museum director; b. San Francisco, Jan. 17, 1958; BA, UCLA, 1979; MA, U. Wis., 1982, PhD, 1987. Goldsmith, 1974-80; collections acquisition asst. social studies bibliographer Meml. Libr./U. Wis., 1984-86; curator of collections The Rockwell Mus., Corning, N.Y., 1988-99; sr. dir. exhbns. and programs Turtle Bay Exploration Park, Redding, Calif., 1999–2006; exec. dir. Yellowstone Art Mus., Billings, Mont., 2006—. Author: American Frontier Photography, 1993, Edward Borein, 1997, Warp and Weft: Cross-cultural Exchange in Navajo Weavings, 1997, Transforming Trash: Bay Area Fiber Art, 2000, Second Nature: the Art of Michael Haykin, 2006; contbg. author: Allgemeines Künstlerlexikon, 1998—; editor/contbr.: Collector's Choice Review: Masterpieces of Glassmaking; Frederick Carder and the Steuben Glass Works, 1993, Brilliance in Glass: The Lost Wax Glass Sculpture of Frederick Carder, 1993, Journey to Justice: The Wintu People and the Salmon, 2002, The Other Side of the Looking Glass: The Glass Body and Its Metaphors, 2003, Bug-Eyed: Art, Culture, Insects, 2004; mng. editor: Frederick Carder and Steuben Glass: American Classics (Thomas P. Dimitroff), 1998; contbr. articles to profl. jours.; peer reviewer IMLS. Mem. Coll. Art Assn., Am. Assn. Mus. (peer reviewer accreditation). Office: Yellowstone Art Mus 401 N 27th St Billings MT 59101 Office Phone: 530-242-3142, 406-256-6804. Business E-mail: rpeterson@turtlebay.org. E-mail: director@artmuseum.org.

**PETERSON, ROGER,** community bank executive, retired international investment banker, retired manufacturing executive, retired air force officer; b. Chgo., June 7, 1929; s. Milton Albert and LaVergne Geraldine (Andelin) P.; m. Sally Ann Alder, Apr. 25, 1952; children: Bruce Roger, Dale Alder, Drew Alan. BS in Acctg., UCLA, 1955; MS in Mgmt., U. Colo., 1964; grad., Air Command and Staff Coll. Air U., Ala., 1965; grad. Exec. Program for Internat. and Nat. Security, J.F. Kennedy Sch. Govt., Harvard U., 1983. Joined USAF, 1955, advanced through grades to maj. gen., 1981, pilot, 1956-61, mgr. tactical missile site constrn., 1961; air officer comdg. 11th Cadet Squadron, Air Force Cadet Wing USAF Acad., 1961-64; asst. sec. Joint Chiefs of Staff and NSC matters for Hdqrs. Pentagon, 1965-68; transport pilot USAF, Vietnam, 1968, asst. chmn. U.S.-Japan Joint Com., Adminstrn. of Status of Forces Agreement, 1968-73, chief program cost, dir. budget, 1973-76, chief plans, comptroller of Air Force, 1976-78, dir. mgmt. analysis, 1978-79, dir. programs, asst. chief of staff for research and devel., 1979-81; asst. dir. plans, policies and programs Def. Logistics Agy., Alexandria, Va., 1981-82, dep. dir., 1982-83; asst. dep. chief staff for logistics and engring. Hdqrs. USAF, Washington, 1983-84; pres., chief exec. officer advanced tech. factory, 1984-85; strategic planner United Techs. Corp., 1985-88; v.p., chief oper. officer Sikorsky Support Svcs. Inc., 1988-90; exec. asst. to mng. ptnr. O'Connor & Assocs., 1990-92; mng. dir. global ops. and svcs. Swiss Bank Corp., Zurich, 1992-96, chief of staff Chgo., 1996-99, br. mgr. Chgo. N.Am. and S.Am., 1996-99; mng. dir. UBS A.G. (formerly Swiss Bank Corp.), NY, 1996-99, UBS AG, N.Y.C., 1999—2001; mng. dir. mktg. and strategic planning nmSouth Bank, Dothan, Ala., 2002—. Decorated D.S.M., Legion of Merit, Air medal with oak leaf cluster, Joint Service Commendation medal, Air Force Commendation medal with two oak leaf clusters Mem. Air Force Assn., Beta Gamma Sigma, Sigma Iota Epsilon Presbyterian. Achievements include designing and negotiating consolidation of U.S. Air Force bases in Tokyo, 1970-73; negotiating mil. and civil aviation agreement for return of Okinawa to Japan; created global bus. mgmt. system for Swiss Bank Corp. Home: 1602 Deerpath Rd Dothan AL 36303-2173 Office: SunSouth Bank 108 Jamestown Blvd Dothan AL 36302 Office Phone: 334-677-4411. Personal E-mail: sbcrogerp@aol.com. *Always with honor.*

**PETERSON, RONALD R.,** health service administrator; b. New Brunswick, NJ, 1948; m. Elizabeth Rooney; children: Joey, Susie. MA in Hosp. Adminstrn., Johns Hopkins U.; Balt., 1970. Adminstrv. resident Johns Hopkins U., Balt., 1973, adminstr. Henry Phipps Psychiatric Clinic, 1974, adminstr. cost improvement program, 1975, adminstr. Children's Ctr., 1978, adminstr. Balt. City Hosps., 1982, exec. v.p., COO Johns Hopkins Health Sys., 1995—, acting pres. Hopkins Hosp. and Health Sys., 1996, pres., John Hopkins Health Sys., 1997—. Mem. bus. adv. coun., Balt.; vol. ARC, United Way, Am. Heart Assn. Mem. Md. Hosp. Assn. (mem. exec. com.), Md. C. of C. Office: Johns Hopkins Hosp 600 N Wolfe St Baltimore MD 21287-0005 also: Johns Hopkins U 720 Rutland Ave Baltimore MD 21205-2109 Office Phone: 410-955-5000.*

**PETERSON, RONALD ROGER,** lawyer; b. Chgo., July 27, 1948; married; children: Elizabeth G., Ronald W. AB, Ripon, 1970; JD, U. Chgo., 1973. Bar: Ill. 1974, U.S. Dist. Ct. (no. dist.) Ill. 1974, U.S. Ct. Appeals (7th cir.) 1974, U.S. Dist. Ct. (ea. dist.) Wis. 1975, U.S. Dist. Ct. (no. dist.) Ind. 1978, U.S. Dist. Ct. (ctrl. dist.) Ill. 1980, U.S. Ct. Appeals (8th cir.) 1984, U.S. Ct. Appeals (6th cir.) 1990, U.S. Ct. Appeals (9th cir.) 1996, U.S. Dist. Ct. (we. dist.) Mich. 1999, U.S. Ct. Appeals (3d cir.) 2001, U.S. Dist. Ct. (ea. dist.) Mich. 2004. Commd. 2d lt. U.S. Army, 1968, advanced through grades to 1st lt., 1973, with mil. intelligence, 1968-78; ptnr. Jenner & Block, Chgo., 1974—. Mem.: ABA, Am. Coll. Bankruptcy Lawyers, Am. Bankruptcy Inst., Comml. Law League, Internat. Soc. Insolvency Practitioners, Chgo. Bar Assn., U.S. Supreme Ct. Hist. Soc. Avocation: skiing. Office: Jenner & Block 1 E Ibm Plz H 4000 Chicago IL 60611-7603 Office Phone: 312-923-2981. Business E-mail: rpeterson@jenner.com.

**PETERSON, RUSSELL WILBUR,** environmental services administrator, retired governor; b. Portage, Wis., Oct. 3, 1916; s. John Anton and Emma (Anthony) P.; m. E. Lillian Turner, June 30, 1937 (dec. Apr. 28, 1994); children: Russell Glen, Peter Jon, Kristin, Elin; m. June B. Jenkins, Oct. 21, 1995. BS, U. Wis., 1938, PhD, 1942, LLD (hon.), 1984; DSc (hon.), Williams Coll., 1975, Butler U., Springfield Coll., Stevens Inst. Tech., 1979, Gettysburg Coll., 1980, Alma Coll., 1981, Ohio State U., SUNY-Syracuse, Northland Coll., Fairleigh Dickinson U., 1981; LLD (hon.), Monmouth Coll., 1982, Salisbury State U., 1988; LHD, Meadville-Lombard Theol. Sch., 1992; DHL, Colby-Sawyer Coll., 2000; DSc (hon.), U. Del., 2006. With E. I. DuPont de Nemours & Co., Inc., 1942-69, rsch. dir. textile fibers dept., 1954-55, 56-59, merchandising mgr. textile fibers, 1955-56, dir. new products divsn. textile fibers, 1959-62, dir. R & D divsn. devel. dept., 1963-69; chmn. exec. com. Textile Research Inst., Princeton, NJ, 1959-61, chmn. bd. dirs., 1961-63, fellow, 1969; gov. State of Del., 1969—73; chmn. exec. com. Nat. Commn. Critical Choices for Am., 1973; chmn. U.S. Council on Environ. Quality, 1973-76; pres. Nat. Audubon Soc., 1979-85; mem. Nat. Commn. Critical Choices for Am., 1973-74; dir. Office Tech. Assessment, U.S. Congress, 1978-79. Pres. New Directions, 1976-77; regional v.p. Nat. Mcpl. League, 1968-78; chmn. Ed. Commn. States, 1970; chmn. com. nuclear energy and space tech. So. Govs. Conf. 1970-71; chmn. Nat. Adv. Commn. on Criminal Justice Standards and Goals, 1971-73; chmn. com. law enforcement, justice and pub. safety Nat. Govs. Conf., 1970-73; v.p. Council State Govts., 1970-71; chmn. adv. bd. Solar Energy Research Inst., 1979-83; vis. prof. Dartmouth Coll., 1985, Carleton Coll., 1986, U. Wis., Madison, 1987; chmn. Centennial Internat. Symposium, Nat. Geog. Soc., 1986-88. Author: Oral History, Russell W. Peterson, 1995, Rebel with a Conscience, 1999, Delaware Heritage Series, 1999, Patriots, Stand Up!, 2004, (CD) We Can Save the Earth, 2000; contbr. articles to profl. jours. Chmn. Del. River Basin Commn., 1971-72; founding chmn. Bio-Energy Coun., 1976-78; bd. dirs. World Wildlife Fund, 1976-82; Population Action Internat., 1973-97, Alliance to Save Energy, 1979-93, Global Tomorrow Coalition, 1981-91, chmn., 1981-87; regional councillor Internat. Union Conservation Nature and Natural Resources, 1981-88, v.p., 1984-88; mem. Pres.'s Commn. on Accident at

Three Mile Island, 1979; pres. Nat. Audubon Soc., 1979-85, Internat. Coun. Bird Preservation, 1982-90; chmn. Ctr. on Consequences of Nuclear War, 1983-87; vice-chmn. Better World Soc., 1985-90, pres., 1985-87; vis. com. John F. Kennedy Sch. Govt., 1979-85; Goodwill amb. UN Environ. Program, 1984-2002, world environ. prize com., 1989-2002; mem. Gov. Cuomo's Environ. Adv. Bd., 1985-94; adv. bd. Pace U. Sch. Law, 1988-98, Earth Island Inst., 1988-2002; chmn. bd. Earth Lobby, 1992-96; Gov.'s task force on rejuvenating Wilmington waterfront, 1992-95; exe. com. Del. Riverfront Devel. Corp., 1995—. Decorated Order of Golden Ark (The Netherlands); Disting. fellow U. Del., 2000; recipient Ann. award NCCJ, 1966, Gold medal World Wildlife Fund, 1971, Ann. award Comml. Devel. Assn., 1971, Gold Plate award Nat. Acad. Achievement, 1971, Audubon award Nat. Audubon Soc., 1977, Frances K. Hutchinson medal Garden Club Am., 1980, Spl. Recognition award Population Reference Bur., 1983, Robert Marshall award Wilderness Soc., 1984, Nat. Conservation medal DAR, 1989, Human and Civil Rights award Del. Human Rights Commn., 1989, Spl. Recognition award Del. State Human Rels. Commn., 1989, Environ. Law Inst. award, 1990, Dr. Martin Luther King, Jr. Citation, Mt. Joy Meth. Ch., 1991, Ann. award Am. Civil Liberties Found. Del., 1992, Lawrence Solid Waste award Assn. N.Am., 1993, Kiwanis Cmty. Svc. award, 1993, Lifetime Achievement award Global Tomorrow Coalition, 1994, Lifetime Achievement award League of Conservation Voters, 1995, Del. Nature Soc., 1997, Liberty Bell award Del. State Bar Assn., 1998, Green Century award Resource Renewal Inst., 1999, Spl. Recognition award Water Resources Assn., 2002, Presdl. medal Del. State U., 2003, Holmes Weatherly award Unitarian-Universalist Assn., 2004; Paul Harris fellow Rotary Internat., 2002; named Conservationist of Yr., Nat. Wildlife Fedn., 1972, Swedish-Am. of Yr., Vasa Order of Am. In Sweden, 1982, Lifetime Achievement award Creative Grandparenting, 1999, NAACP, 1999; Del. refuge named in his honor Russell W. Peterson Wildlife Refuge, 2000; bronze statue in his honor on Wilmington Waterfront, 2002. Fellow Am. Inst. Chemists (hon.), AAAS (past bd. dirs.); mem. Am. Ornithologists Union, Linnaean Soc., Fedn. Am. Scientists, Am. Chem. Soc. (Parsons award 1974), Del. Acad. Sci., U.S. Assn. for Club of Rome, Cosmos Club (Cert. of Appreciation 2001), Phi Beta Kappa, Sigma Xi (Proctor prize 1978), Phi Lambda Upsilon, Phi Kappa Phi. Unitarian Universalist. Address: 11 E Mozart Dr Wilmington DE 19807-1942

**PETERSON, RUTH D.,** sociologist; BA, Cleve. State Univ., 1969, MA, 1973; PhD, Univ. Wis.. Madison, 1993. Asst. prof. Univ. Iowa, 1982—85, Ohio State Univ., 1985—89, assoc. prof., 1989—96, prof., 1996—; dir. Criminal Justice Rsch. Ctr., Ohio State Univ., 1999—. Mem. editl. bd. Race and Society, 1998—2002. Co-editor: Crime and Inequality, 1995; editor (assoc.): Criminology, 1997—2000; contbr. articles to prof. jour. Fellow: Am. Soc. Criminology (v.p. 1999—2000, Herbert Bloch award 1995); mem.: Am. Sociol. Assn. Office: Ohio State University Sociology Department 300 Bricker Hall 190 N Oval Mall Columbus OH 43210

**PETERSON, SAMUEL RAY,** dermatologist, department chairman; b. Salt Lake City, Utah, July 12, 1966; s. Gerald Joseph and Christa Peterson; m. Sarah Devon Galland, Dec. 27, 1991; children: Zoe Anne, Ava Lynne, Samuel Galland, Madison Maxwell, Meg Rose. MD, U. Tex., Houston, 1998. Cert. assoc. in Mohs sugery Wis., 2003, Am. Bd. Dermatology, 2002. Chmn. dept. dermatology IHC Urban South Region, Provo, Utah, 2005—. Author: articles in field of dermatology in profl. jours. Fellow: Am. Coll. Mohs Micrograpic Surgery and Cutaneous Oncology (assoc., fellow 2003—); mem.: Alpha Omega Alpha. R-Consevative. Church Of Latter-Day Saints. Achievements include research in Surgical/Oncological Work. Avocations: horticulture, fishing. Home: 4366 N Sheffield Dr Provo UT 84604 Office: Central Utah Clinic 1055 N 500 West Provo UT 84604 Office Phone: 801-374-8999. Office Fax: 801-489-8063.

**PETERSON, STEPHEN JOSEPH,** internist; b. Bellerose, N.Y., Mar. 17, 1953; s. Robert Francis and Veronica Mae (Burns) P. BS in Biology, Fairfield U., Conn., 1975; MD, Cebu Drs. Coll. Medicine, Cebu City, The Philippines, 1982. Diplomate Am. Bd. Internal Medicine, 1985. Intern internal medicine Met. Hosp. Ctr. N.Y. Med. Coll., 1982—83, resident to chief resident internal medicine Valhalla, NY, 1983—86, dir. medicine clerkship, 1994—2003; assoc. program dir. Met. Hosp. Ctr., NYC, 1986—88; dep. dir. dept. medicine Lincoln Med. & Mental Health Ctr., Bronx 1988—93; attending physician Westchester Sq. Hosp Med. Ctr., Bronx, 1993—94; dir. internal medicine residency tng. program Westchester Med. Ctr., Valhalla, 1994—, chief gen. internal medicine, 1994—. Bd. dirs. St. Agnes Hosp., White Plains, NY, 1995—2003; asst. prof. medicine NY Med. Coll., 1986—96, assoc. prof. clin. medicine, 1996—99, adj. prof. pharmacology, 2001—; mem. med. edn. coms. N.Y. Med. Coll., Westchester Med. Ctr.; prof. clin. medicine NY Med. Coll., 1999—2006, vice-chmn. dept. medicine, 2002—06, exec. vice chair, 2006—; prof. medicine and pharmacology N.Y. Med. Coll., 2006—. Contbr. articles to profl. jours. Recipient Advisor award Med. Explorers Boy Scouts Am., 1986, 88. Mem. AMA, ACP (gov. Hudson Valley region 2004—), Clerkship Dirs. Internal Medicine, Assn. Program Dirs. Internal Medicine, Assoc. Chiefs Gen. Internal Medicine, Soc. Gen. Internal Medicine. Rep. Roman Cath. Avocations: singing, exercise. Office: NY Med Coll Munger Pavillion # 256 Valhalla NY 10595 Office Phone: 914-493-8370. Business E-Mail: stephen_peterson@nymc.edu.

**PETERSON, THOMAS W.,** engineering educator; b. Tucson, June 15, 1950; BS in Chem. Engring., Tufts U., 1972; MS in Chem. Engring., U. Ariz., 1973; PhD, Calif. Inst. Technology, Pasadena, 1977. From asst. prof. to prof., dean chem. engring. dept. U. Ariz., Tucson, 1977—; head dept. chem. and environ. engring., 1990—98, dean Coll. Engring. and Mines. Office: U Ariz Coll Engring Engring Bm 200 PO Box 210020 Tucson AZ 85721

**PETERSON, VICTOR LOWELL,** aerospace engineer, consultant; b. Saskatoon, Sask., Can., June 11, 1934; came to U.S., 1937; s. Edwin Galladet and Ruth Mildred (McKeeby) P.; m. Jacqueline Dianne Hubbard, Dec. 21, 1955; children: Linda Kay, Janet Gale, Victor Craig. BS in Aero. Engring., Oreg. State U.; 1956; MS in Aerospace Engring., Stanford U., 1964; MS in Mgmt., MIT, 1973. Rsch. scientist NASA-Ames Rsch. Ctr., Moffett Field, Calif., 1956-68, asst. chief hypersonic aerodyns., 1968-71, chief aerodyns. br., 1971-74, chief thermo and gas dynamics div., 1974-84, dir. aerophysics, 1984-90, dep. dir., 1990-94; pvt. mgmt. cons., 1994—. Mem. nat. adv. bd. U. Tenn. Space Inst., Tullahoma, 1984-94. Contbr. numerous articles to profl. jours. Treas. Woodland Acres Homeowners Assn., Los Altos, Calif., 1978—. Capt. USAF, 1957-60. Recipient medal for outstanding leadership NASA, 1982; Alfred P. Sloan fellow MIT, 1972-73. Fellow AIAA. Republican. Methodist. Achievements include development of numerical aerodynamic simulation system for aerospace, of method for reconstructing planetary atmosphere structure from accelerations of body entering atmosphere, of theory for motions of tumbling bodies entering planetary atmospheres. Home: 484 Aspen Way Los Altos CA 94024-7100 Personal E-mail: vicpeterson@comcast.net. *Achievements in life are maximized by creating visions of success and focussing relentlessly on successful accomplishment of intermediate objectives.*

**PETERSON, WALLACE CARROLL, SR.,** economics professor; b. Omaha, Mar. 28, 1921; s. Fred Nels and Grace (Brown) P.; m. Eunice V. Peterson, Aug. 16, 1944 (dec. Nov. 1985); children: Wallace Carroll Jr., Shelley Lorraine; m. Bonnie B. Watson, Nov. 11, 1988 (dec. Oct. 1996). Student, U. Omaha, 1939-40, U. Mo., 1940-42; BA in Econs. and European History, U. Nebr., 1947, MA in Econs. and European History, 1948, PhD in Econs. and European History, 1953; postgrad., Handelshochschule, St. Gallen, Switzerland, 1948-49, U. Minn., 1951, London Sch. Econs. and Polit. Sci., 1952. Lic. pilot. Reporter Lincoln (Nebr.) Jour., 1946; instr. econs. U. Nebr., Lincoln, 1951-54, asst. prof., 1954-57, assoc. prof., 1957-61, prof., 1962—, chmn. dept. econs., 1965-75, George Holmes prof. econs., 1966-92; George Holmes prof. econs. emeritus, 1992—; v.p. faculty senate U. Nebr. Lincoln, 1972-73, pres. faculty senate, 1973-74; S.J. Hall disting. vis. prof. U. Nev., Las Vegas, 1983-84. Author: The Welfare State in France, 1960, Elements of Economics, 1973, Our Overloaded Economy: Inflation, Unem-

ployment and the Crisis in American Capitalism, 1982, Market Power and the Economy, 1988, Transfer Spending, Taxes and the American Welfare State, 1991, Income, Employment and Economic Growth, 8th edit., 1996, Silent Depression: The Fate of the American Dream, 1994; co-author: (with F.R. Strobel) The Coming Class War: Power, Conflict and the Consequences of Middle Class Decline, 1998, The Social Security Primer: What Every Citizen Should Know, 1999, Pylon! The Omaha Air Races, 1931-1934, 2002. Mem. Nebr. Dem. Cen. Com., 1968-74, vice-chmn., chmn. Nebr. Polit. Accountability and Disclosure Commn., 1977-80; chmn. Nebr. Coun. Econ. Edn., 1976-77. Capt. USAAF, 1942-46. Recipient Champion Media award for Econ. Understanding, 1981; Fulbright fellow, 1957-58, 64-65; Mid-Am. State Univs. honor scholar, 1982-83. Mem. ACLU, AAUP (pres. Nebr. 1963-64, nat. coun.), Assn. for Evolutionary Econs. (pres. 1976, Veblen-Commons award 1991), Am. Econs. Assn., Midwest Econs. Assn. (pres. 1968-69), Mo. Valley Econ. Assn. (pres. 1989), Assn. Social Econs. (pres. 1992, Thomas F. Devine award 1995), Fedn. Am. Scientists, Antique Aircraft Assn., Aircraft Owners and Pilots Assn., Exptl. Aircraft Assn., Nat. Assn. R.R. Passengers. Office: U Nebr Dept Econs CBA Lincoln NE 68588-0489 E-mail: wcpeterson@mindspring.com.

**PETERSON, WALTER FRITIOF,** retired academic administrator; b. Idaho Falls, Idaho, July 15, 1920; s. Walter Fritiof and Florence (Danielson) P.; m. Barbara Mae Kempe, Jan. 13, 1946; children: Walter Fritiof III, Daniel John. BA, State U. Iowa, 1942, MA, 1948, PhD, 1951; HHD (hon.), Loras Coll., 1983; LHD (hon.), Clarke Coll., 1991; DHum (hon.), U. Dubuque, 1997. Asst. prof. history, chmn. dept. history Milw. Downer Coll., 1952-57, assoc. prof. history, chmn. social sci. div., 1957-64; assoc. prof. history Lawrence U., Appleton, Wis., 1964-67, prof. history, Alice G. Chapman libr., 1967-70; pres. U. Dubuque, 1970-90, chancellor, 1990—2000, chancellor emeritus, 2000. Regional tng. officer Peace Corps, 1965-68; cons. history Allis-Chalmers Mfg. Co., 1959-75, Secura Ins. Group, 1968-92, Wm. C. Brown Pub. Co., 1981-92, bd. dirs. Editor: Transactions of Wis. Acad. Scis., Arts and Letters, 1965-72, The Allis-Chalmers Corporation: An Industrial History, 1977, A History of Wm. C. Brown Cos., 1994, A History of Hawkeye Bancorporation, 1996. Advisor Templeton Prize for Progress in Religion, 1986-91; bd. dirs. Finley Hosp., pres., 1983-84; chmn. Finley Health Found., 1986-95, Finley Health Found. Hall of Fame, 2000; bd. dirs. Dubuque Symphony Orch., Dubuque Art Assn., Jr. Achievement, Nat. River Hall of Fame, 1984; chmn. Iowa Assn. Coll. and Univ. Pres., 1975-76; chmn. Iowa Coll. Found., 1982-83; chair Grand Opera House Found., 1998—. With USAAF, 1942-45, PTO. Recipient Dubuque 1st Citizen award, 1990, Disting. Civic Svc. award, 1991, Benjamin Franklin award Nat. Soc. Fundraising Execs., 1994, Paul Harris fellowship, Duduque Rotary Club, 1993; named to Dubuque Bus. Hall of Fame, 1990 Mem. Iowa Assn. Ind. Colls. and Univs. (chmn. 1988-89), Dubuque County Hist. Soc. (bd. dirs.), Dubuque Shooting Soc., Dubuque Golf and Country Club, Phi Alpha Theta, Kappa Delta Pi, Phi Delta Kappa, Dubuque Shooting Soc Office Phone: 563-556-4365.

**PETERSON, WAYNE HOWARD,** musician; b. Chgo., Apr. 19, 1959; s. Howard Gordon and Evelyn Elizabeth Peterson; 1 child, Robert Sterling. BA, Concordia Coll., River Forest, Ill., 1981; MM with distinction, Ind. U., Bloomington, 1987; DSM, Grad. Theol. Found., South Bend, Ind., 2004. Cert. tchr. Ill. Organist-choirmaster Trinity Episcopal Ch., Fort Wayne, Ind., 1987—; assoc. faculty Ind. U.-Purdue U., Fort Wayne, 1998—2003. Composer music arranging. Mem. Cmty. Arts Coun., Fort Wayne, 1987—90; interim dir. Opus 18, Fort Wayne; mem. Diocesan Liturgy and Music Commn., South Bend, 1987—2000; at large Cmty. Concerts of Greater Ft. Wayne, 1987—90; com. Wellspring Interfaith Social Svcs., Fort Wayne, 2003; therapeutic foster parent Specialized Alternatives for Families and Youth, Fort Wayne, 1999—2004; founder, dir. Trinity-East Side West Side Children's Choir, Fort Wayne, 2000. Recipient Child Advocacy award, Specialized Alternatives for Family and Youth, 2003. Fellow: Am. Guild Organists (assoc.; dean Ft. Wayne chpt. 1989—90, Choir Master 1994, ind. state dist. convener 2003); mem.: Am. Recorder Soc. (co-founder Ft. Wayne chpt.), Royal Sch. of Ch. Music, Assn. Anglican Musicians, Quest Club. Episcopalian. Avocations: skiing, golf, reading, travel. Office: Trinity Episcopal Ch 611 West Berry St Fort Wayne IN 46802 Office Phone: 260-423-1693 13.

**PETERSON, WILLIAM GEORGE,** lawyer; b. Minn., Sept. 30, 1944; s. Henry Gaufin and Grace Marie (Reker) P.; m. Ann Ophoven; children: Emily Marie, Elizabeth Ann B.A., U. Minn., 1966, J.D., U. Pitts., 1969. Bar: Minn. 1969, U.S. Dist. Ct. Minn. 1970, U.S. Ct. Appeals (8th cir.) 1976, U.S. Supreme Ct. 1976, Wis. 1983. Spl. asst. atty. gen. State of Minn., St. Paul, 1969-78; sole practice, Bloomington, Minn., 1978-80; ptnr. Peterson & Lange, Bloomington, 1980-81; owner Peterson & Assocs., Bloomington, 1981-97, Peterson Law Office, P.A., 1997—; instr. hotel and restaurant law Normandale C.C., Bloomington, 1981-87; referee Hennepin County Conciliation Ct., Mpls., 1982—; arbitrator ins. claims Am. Arbitration Assn., 1988-2005. Contbr. articles to profl. jours. Bd. dirs. Viking Coun. Boy Scouts Am., 1981-84, Minn. Valley YMCA; chmn. Hennepin County Ind. Republicans, Mpls., 1984-90; mem. Minn. Legislature, 1978-82, Bloomington City Merit Bd., 1983-96. Recipient Silver Beaver award Boy Scouts Am., 1981, Legis. Excellence award Minn. Legis. Evaluation Assembly, 1981. Mem. ABA, Minn. State Bar Assn., Minn. Trial Lawyers Assn. Roman Catholic. Home: 4103 Overlook Cir Minneapolis MN 55437-3540 Office: Law Office 3601 Minnesota Dr Ste 800 Minneapolis MN 55435 Office Phone: 952-921-5818. E-mail: petersonlaw@visi.com.

**PETH, HOWARD ALLEN,** law educator; b. Calif., Apr. 20, 1955; s. Howard Allen and Diane Marie (Munyan) P.; m. Gloria Gene Stockton, Aug. 9, 1997; children: Andrew Howard, Rachel Gloria. BA, U. Calif., San Diego, 1980; MD, U. Santiago, 1984; JD, U. Mo., 1991. Bar: Calif. 1993, U.S. Ct. Appeals (9th cir.) 1993, U.S. Ct. Claims, U.S. Ct. Appeals (fed. cir.) 1993, U.S. Dist. Ct. (so. dist.) Calif. 1993, U.S. Supreme Ct. 1997; diplomate Am. Bd. Internal Medicine, Be. Cert. Emergency Medicine; lic. physician, Calif., Mo., Wis.d. Asst. prof. U. So. Med. Medicine, Columbia, 1997—2005; ptnr. Lake Emergency Specialists, Osage Beach, Mo., 2005—. Fellow Am. Coll. Legal Medicine; mem. AMA, ABA (health law sect.), ACP, Am. Coll. Emergency Physicians. Republican. Episcopalian. Office: Lake Regional Hosp Dept Emergency Medicine 54 Hospital Dr Osage Beach MO 65065 Home: PO Box 357 Osage Beach MO 65065-0357 Office Phone: 573-434-2791. Personal E-mail: hpethmdjd@aol.com.

**PETHICK, CHRISTOPHER JOHN,** physicist; b. Horsham, Sussex, Eng., Feb. 22, 1942; s. Richard Hope and Norah Betty (Hill) P. BA, Magdalen Coll., Oxford U., Eng., 1962, DPhil, 1965. Fellow Magdalen Coll., Oxford U., 1965-70; research assoc. U. Ill., Urbana, 1966-68, research asst. prof., 1968-69, assoc. prof. physics, 1970-73, prof. physics, 1973-95, Nordita, Copenhagen, 1975—. A.P. Sloan research fellow, 1970-72. Fellow Am. Phys. Soc.; mem. European Phys. Soc. Office: Nordita Blegdamsvej 17 DK-2100 Copenhagen Denmark Office Phone: 45 35 32 52 26.

**PETIET, CAROLE ANNE,** psychologist; b. Newport News, Va., Mar. 1, 1952; d. Gaston Kaleski and Ann (Snyder) Pettit Johnson; m. Lawrence Phillip Bischoff III, Dec. 29, 1973 (div. 1979); m. Robert Jomax Brooks, May 4, 1984 (div. 1989); 1 child, Nicole; stepchildren: Gregory, Randall. BS in Nursing, Baylor U., 1975; MA, Calif. Sch. Profl. Psychology, Berkeley, 1980, PhD, 1982. RN Calif.; lic. psychologist Calif., Colo. Charge nurse Elizabeth Knutsson Hosp., Estes Park, Colo., 1975-76; nurse coordinator, staff nurse Alta Bates Hosp., Berkeley, Calif., 1976-83; pvt. practice psychotherapy, cons., sports psychology Berkeley, Calif., 1982—; tng./clin. cons., rsch. cons. Phoenix Recovery Ctrs., Alameda, Calif., 1983-88; staff psychologist Kaiser Permanente Med. Ctr., Vallejo, Calif., 1982-84. Sports psychology cons. Women's Ski Programs, Aspen, Colo., and B.C., Can., 1986-93; coord. women's studies splty., mem. faculty Rosebridge Grad. Sch., Walnut Creek, Calif., 1986-94; supvr., mem. adj. faculty CSPP, Berkeley/Alameda, 1986-89; intern Eden Youth and Family Svcs., Hayward, Calif., 1978-79, No. Calif. State Correctional Med. Facility, Vacaville, 1979-80, Kaiser Vallejo, 1980-81, Kaiser San Francisco, 1981-82; rschr. in field. Contbr. articles, presentations to profl. publs. Scholar Baylor Hosp. Women's Aux., 1974, Soroptimists, 1981; recipient Am. Coll. Scholarship, 1979. Mem. APA, Assn. Women in Psychology, World Fedn. Mental Health, NOW, Amnesty Internat. Democrat. Achievements include research on neuropsychological effects of altitude on women climbers. Office: 2340 Ward St Ste 105 Berkeley CA 94705-1146 Office Phone: 510-843-6760.

**PETILLO, JOHN J.,** former academic administrator, former priest; b. Montclair, NJ, Mar. 19, 1947; s. Gennaro and Geraldine (Illaria) Petillo; m. Sabina M. Porcaro; 1 child. Earned undergraduate degree, Seton Hall U., 1969, MA in Counseling, 1971; profl. diploma in counselor edn., Fordham U., 1973, PhD in Counseling and Personnel Services, 1976; M.Div. in Pastoral Theology, Darlington Sch. Theology, 1975; M.P.A., Rutgers U., 1977. Ordained priest Roman Catholic Ch., 1973; left priesthood in 1990. Asst. dir. office research and planning Archdiocese Newark, Roman Cath. Ch., 1975-77, chancellor for adminstrn., 1978-83; dep. dir. Cath. Community Services, NJ, 1976-78; asst. to pres. Seton Hall U., South Orange, NJ, 1978, chancellor, chief exec. officer, 1983-90, also mem. bd. trustees and bd. regents, 1983—; chancellor, chief exec. officer Immaculate Conception Sem., 1983; CEO for several insurance companies Tribus Companies, Care Advantage, Inc., Blue Cross and Blue Shield, NJ (also pres.), 1990—2001; pres., CEO Newark Alliance, 2001—04; chmn. bd. trustee U. Medicine and Dentistry NJ, 2003—, interim pres., 2004, pres., 2004—06. Mem. Archdiocesan Bd. Adminstrn. Mem. long range-strategic planning com. United Way Am.; bd. dirs. Blue Cross NJ, Nat. Soc. Prevention Blindness, Nat. Commn. on Coop. Edn., Found. Ednl. Alternatives, Ind. Coll. Fund NJ, NJ State Police Meml. Library and Mus. Assn., labor-higher edn. council Am. Council on Edn. and AFL-CIO, Commn. for Pub. Responsibility for Ednl. Success, Washington Ctr. NJ Scholarship Program, Statue of Liberty Centennial Commn. State NJ, NJ Performing Arts Ctr., St. Joseph's Health System, Wachovia Regional Found., Lincoln Educational Svcs.; chmn. bd. Essex County Coll. Found. Mem. Assn. Ind. Colls. and Univs. NJ (bd. dirs.) Office: The Univ Med Dentistry 65 Bergen St Newark NJ 07103 Office Phone: 973-972-4400. Business E-Mail: petillo@umdnj.edu.*

**PETILLON, LEE RITCHEY,** lawyer; b. Gary, Ind., May 6, 1929; s. Charles Ernest and Blanche Lurene (Mackay) Petillon; m. Mary Anne Keeton, Feb. 20, 1960; children: Andrew G., Joseph R. BBA, U. Minn., 1952; LLB, U. Calif., Berkeley, 1959. Bar: Calif. 1960, U.S. Dist. Ct. (so. dist.) Calif. 1960. V.p. Creative Investment Capital, Inc., L.A., 1969—70; corp. counsel Harvest Industries, L.A., Calif., 1970—71; v.p. gen. counsel, dir. Tech. Svcs. Corp., Santa Monica, Calif., 1971—78; ptnr. Petillon & Davidoff, L.A., 1978—92, Gipson Hoffman & Pancione, 1992—93; pvt. practice Torrance, Calif., 1993—94; ptnr. Petillon & Hansen, Torrance, Calif., 1994—2003, Petillon & Hiraide LLP, Torrance, 2004—. Co-author: R&D Partnerships, 2d edit., 1985, Representing Start-Up Companies, 1992, 13th edit., 2005; contbr. chapters to books. Chmn. Neighborhood Justice Ctr. Com., 1983-85, Middle Income Co., 1983085; active Calif. Senate Commn. on Corp. Governance, State Bar Calif. Task Force on Alternative Dispute Resolution, 1984-85; chmn. South Bay Sci. Found., Inc.; vice-chmn. Calif. Capital Access Forum, Inc.; dir., legal counsel ACE-Net.org, Inc. Recipient Cert. of Appreciation L.A. City Demonstration Agy., 1975, United Indian Devel. Assn., 1981, City of L.A. for Outstanding Vol. Svcs., 1984, Outstanding Vol. award Torrance C. of C., 2000, Small Bus. Adv. of Yr. award Torrance C. of C., 2001, Marvin Greene award Los Angeles County Bar Assn., 2005; named Small Bus. Adv. of Yr. Calif. C. of C., 2001. Mem.: ABA (venture capital and pvt. equity com.), Los Angeles County Bar Assn. (trustee 1984—85, alt. dispute resolution sect. 1992—94, bus. and corp. law sect. 2000—, chmn. law tech. sect., Griffin Bell Vol. Svc. award 1993), Los Angeles County Bar Found. (bd. dirs.), Calif. State Bar Assn. (pres., Pro Bono Svcs. award 1983). Avocations: backpacking, reading, music, painting. Home: 1636 Via Machado Palos Verdes Estates CA 90274-1930 Office: Petillon & Hiraide LLP 21515 Hawthorne Blvd Ste 1260 Torrance CA 90503-6503 Office Phone: 310-543-0500. Business E-Mail: lpetillon@corplawp-h.com.

**PETINGA, CHARLES MICHAEL,** transportation executive; b. Atlantic City, July 9, 1946; s. Thomas Joseph and Rose Marie (Merindino) P.; m. Velna Mae McVicker, June 7, 1969; children: Scott, Jeffery. BS in Geology, Geography, U. Wis., Superior, 1969. Ops. supr. Schneider Transport, Inc., Green Bay, Wis., 1973-74, prodn. mgr., 1974-76, safety dir., 1976-79; dir. safety Schneider Nat., Inc., Green Bay, Wis., 1979-82, dir. risk mgmt., 1982-87; gen. mgr. Petinga Candy Co., Atlantic City, 1987-89; sr. v.p., midwest practice leader Transp. Industry, Appleton, Wis., 1989-2000; exec. v.p. Smith Transport Inc., Roaring Spring, Pa., 2003—; prin. Transp. Assocs., Appleton, Wis., 2005—06; exec. dir. transp. HNI Risk Svcs., New Berlin, Wis., 2006—. Cons. local charitable groups, Green Bay, 1985-88; preactice leader freight/logistics Global Transp. Industry; adviser, cons. Small Bus. Execs., Green Bay, 1989; mem. worker compensation task force Wis. Motor Carriers, Madison, 1991; nat.-internat. spkr. at univs., bus. schs., vocat. schs. and high schs.; speaker to motor carrier assns., bd. directors, and industry mgmt. groups, nat. and state assns. Co. liaison Green Bay United Way, 1985, 86. With U.S. Army, 1971-73. Mem. Wis. Coun. Safety Suprs., Nat. Safety Mgmt. Soc., Wis. Motor Carriers Assn., Risk and Ins. Mgmt. Soc., Nat. Safety Coun., Am. Trucking Assn. Avocations: martial arts, physical fitness, weightlifting. Home: 842 Whisper Falls Ln Menasha WI 54952 Office: Smith Global Transp Group 59 Park Pl Appleton WI 54914-8230 Office Phone: 920-731-9224. Business E-Mail: cpetinga@new.rr.com.

**PETIT, EMMANUEL J.,** architecture educator; MArch, Swiss Fed. Inst. Tech., Zürich, 1998; PhD, Princeton U., NJ, 2006. Lectr., critic Yale U., New Haven, 2001—05, asst. prof., 2005—. Office: Yale U Sch Architecture 180 York St New Haven CT 06520 E-mail: emmanuel.petit@yale.edu.

**PETITAN, DEBRA ANN BURKE,** elementary school educator, counselor, design engineer, writer; b. Chgo., Mar. 12, 1932; d. James Marcellus and Susan Florence (Hines) Burke; m. Kenneth Charles Petitan, Aug. 9, 1952; 1 child, Susan Florence. AA, Wilson Jr. Coll., Chgo., 1951, N.Y. Inst. Photography, 1952; BS in Primary Edn., Chgo. State U., 1956, MS in Indsl. Edn., 1967; DSc in Applied Sci. and Tech., London Inst. Tech., 1971; postgrad., U. Wis., Bradley U., U. Calif., U. Ill.; grad., Inst. Children's Lit., West Redding, Conn., 1991; cert. in Childrens' Portraiture, North Light Art Sch., 1977. Tchr. Chgo. Bd. Edn., 1958-71, guidance counselor, 1976-84, now tchr., cons.; nat. dir. edn. Nation of Islam, 1971-75; design engr. Fed. Sign and Signal Corp., Chgo., 1975-76; CEO, owner Petitan's Creative Projects, Inc. Nat. adv. bd. Nat. Right to Work Orgn., 1976-85; cons. ednl. devel., 1978; computer libr. cons.; owner, CEO, Fayzah's Fin. Svcs., Instrm. Svcs. in Trading and Investing, Fayzah's Creative Projects, Inc.; ednl. cons. tech. analysis and chart reading stock market; participant summer writing festival U. Iowa, 1991. Photographer VISTA News, 1969-70; writer children's lit.; author curriculum introducing computer-aided design techniques in the pub. schs., 1975. Cmty. svc. rec. sec. 9600 Block Club; navigator, pub. rels. officer IL wing Squadron 8, capt. Civil Air Patrol, 1953—56; chmn. Career Women for Johnson/Humphrey, Chgo., 1965; dir. Christian edn. Trinity United Ch. Christ, Chgo., 1978—81, family counselor, 1978—81; organizer, leader family counseling ministry, lic. lay Eucharistic min. Episcopal Ch. St. Edmund, Chgo. Episc. Diocese, 1989. Named Woman of Yr. Iota Phi Lambda, 1978; recipient 250 Hr. medal Ground Observer Corps, 1952, 25 Yr. Service medal Chgo. Bd. Edn., 1987. Mem. Off-Campus Writer's Workshop (editor newsletter), Soc. of Children's Book Writers, Am. Contract Bridge League, Am. Bridge Assn. (sr. life master; rec. sec.), Children's Reading Roundtable, Green River Writers, Epsilon Pi Tau. Achievements include introduction of Computer Aided Design curriculum to field of educator. Office: Fayzah's Analytical Guidance Svc Chicago IL 60628 E-mail: drdap1@ameritech.net.

**PETITO, MARGARET L.,** foundation administrator; b. Dallas, Sept. 28, 1950; d. Jacob Charles and Eileen (Shank) Loehr; m. John Haven Petito, 1978 (div. 1984); children: John Christian Robert, David Nelson. BA, So. Meth. U., 1972; MA, Georgetown U., 2006. Mem. Action/Vista Program U.S. Govt., Middlesex, NY, 1972—74; dir., curator Oliver House Mus., Penn Yan, NY,

1975—77; staff asst. Williams & Jensen, P.C., Washington, 1986—89; dir. fed. rels. Chambers Devel. Co., Inc., 1989—92; dir. fed. affairs DSSI-U.S. Biotech., Washington, 1992—94; cons., dir. pub. affairs Embassy Ecuador, Govt. Ecuador, Washington, 1994—96; prin. Petito & Assocs., Washington, 1994—. Dir. external events Internat. Cancer Alliance, Bethesda, Md., 1996—97, Sch. of Bus., Georgetown U., Washington, 1998—99; pres., exec. dir. Friends of Rule of Law in Ecuador, Inc., 2001—. Spl. legis. advisor Drugwatch Internat., Chgo., 1993—; bd. dirs. Nyumbani Orphanage for Kenyan Children with AIDS, Washington, 1989—99; dir. Marshall Ho. Mus., Lambertville, NJ, 1980—82; founder, co-chair Forum for Environ., Washington, 1989—91; pres. Cultural Partnership of the Ams., Washington, 1999—. Mem.: Tex. State Soc. Roman Catholic. Avocations: squash, needlepoint, fishing. Home and Office: Friends of Rule of Law in Ecuador Inc 6008 34th Pl NW Washington DC 20015-1607 Office Phone: 202-537-1327. Business E-Mail: mlp3@starpower.net.

**PETITTO, LAURA-ANN,** cognitive neuroscience educator; b. N.Y.C. m. Kevin Dunbar; children: Eva-Molly Dunbar, Annafaye Dunbar, Maaraluisa Dunbar. PhD, EdD, Harvard U., 1984; MA (hon.), Dartmouth Coll. 2004. Rsch. project coord. and primary tchr. project nim chimpsky Columbia U., N.Y.C., 1973—76; staff lectr. N.Y. Soc. for the Deaf, N.Y.C., 1978—79; asst. prof. dept. psychology McGill U., Montreal, 1983—89, assoc. prof., dept psychology, 1989—99, prof. dept psychology, 1999—2001; prof. Dartmouth Coll.gy, Hanover, NH, 2001—; chmn., dir. cognitive neuroscience NIRS Brain Imaging lab. for lang. and child devel. Dartmouth Coll., 2001—. Rschr. in neurolinguistics lab. for am. sign lang.; The Salk Inst. for Biol. Studies, San Diego, 1980—85; rsch. scientist, McDonnell-pew ctr. for cognitive neuroscience Montreal Neurol. Inst., 1983—2001, rsch. scientist, 1983—2001; prof. of psychology and dir. of cognitive neuroscience lab. for lang., sign, & cognition McGill U., Montreal, Quebec, Canada, 1983—2001. Contbr. articles to profl. jours., chapters to books. Recipient Career Develop. award, Natural Sciences and Engring. Rsch. Coun. of Can., 1985—95, Young Psychologist award, APA, 1988, Outstanding Tchg. & Sci. Achievements award, Golden Key Nat. Hon. Soc., 1997, Pub. Achievement award, Boys Town Med. Ctr. /U. of Nebr., 1997, Justine and Yves Sergent Fund Internat. prize cognitive neurosci., 2004; fellow, The John D. and Catherine T. MacArthur Found., 1983—84, The John Simon Guggenheim Meml. Found., 1998; grantee, Social Sciences and Humanities Rsch. Coun. of Can., 1997—2000, 2000—03, The Spencer Found., 2000—03, Montreal Neurol. Inst., Brain Imaging Ctr., 2000—. Mem.: AAAS (mem.-at-large), Soc. Lang. Devel., Internat. Mind, Brain, Edn. Soc., Soc. Rsch. in Child Devel., Soc. Neuroscience, Can. Deafness Rsch. & Tng. Inst. Coop. Coun. (assoc.; exec. adv. com. mem. 1983—2003), Phi Beta Kappa (hon.). Office: Dartmouth Coll Dept Edn 110 Raven House Hanover NH 03755 E-mail: laura-ann.petitto@dartmouth.edu.

**PETKANICS, DONNA M.,** lawyer; BA, Northwestern U., 1980; JD, U. Calif., Boalt Hall Law Sch., 1985. Staff economist President Carter Administrn., Washington; with Wilson Sonsini Goodrich & Rosati, Palo Alto, Calif., 1985—, assoc. mng. ptnr., 1996—97, co-chmn., nominating com., 1997, 1998, mng. dir. - ops., ptnr., mem. exec. mgmt. com. & policy com. Office: Wilson Sonsini Goodrich & Rosati 650 Page Mill Rd Palo Alto CA 94304-1050 Office Phone: 650-493-9300. Office Fax: 650-493-6811. Business E-Mail: dpetkanics@wsgr.com.

**PETKOVIC, LUCIA M.,** research scientist; PhD, U. Nebr., Lincoln, 1999. Assoc. prof. Universidad Nacional San Juan, Argentina, 1999—2003; staff scientist Idaho Nat. Lab., Idaho Falls, 2003—. Mem.: AIChE, Am. Chem. Soc. Achievements include research in Heterogeneous Catalysis.

**PETLIN, IRVING,** artist; b. Chgo., 1934; BFA, Univ. Chgo.; MFA, Yale Univ. Art faculty Dartmouth Coll., UCLA, Haifa Univ., Art Inst., Chgo., Cooper Union. One-man shows include Cliffdweller Gallery, Chgo., 1956, Galerie du Dragon, Paris, 1960, 1962, 1963, 1964, 1968, Odyssia Gallery, NY, 1967, 1968, 1969, 1970, 1979, 1981, 1983, Galleria II Fante Di Spade, Rome, 1968, Galleria Bergamini, Milan, 1972, 1977, Marlborough Fine Art, London, 1982, Galerie Jean Briance, Paris, 1987, Elizabeth Franck Gallery, Knokke-le-Zoute, Belgium, 1990, Gallery 400, Univ. Chgo., 1990, Kent Fine Art, NYC, 1990, 1992, Galerie Krugier-Ditesheim Art Contemporain, Geneva, 1992, 1997, 2000, one-man shows include Weinstein Gallery, Mpls., 1997, Jan Krugier Gallery, NYC, 1998, Galleria Tega, Milan, 2001, exhibited in group shows at Americain Sect., Paris Biennial, 1961, Galerie Mathias Fels, Paris, 1962, Civic Mus., Bologna, 1965, Mus. Modern Art, Parais, 1966, Spertus Mus., Chgo., 1976, Am. Acad. Arts & Letters, NYC, 1981, Marlborough Fine Art, Tokyo, 1984, Cooper Union Sch. of Art, NYC, 1990, Whitney Mus. of Am. Art, 2000. Founder Artists and Writers Against the War in Vietnam. Grantee Cassandra Found., Guggenheim Fellowship.

**PETOSA, JASON JOSEPH,** publisher; b. Des Moines, Iowa, Apr. 26, 1939; s. Joseph John and Mildred Margaret (Cardamon) P.; m. Theodora Anne Doleski, Aug. 12, 1972; 1 son, Justin James. Student, Marquette U., 1957-59, St. Paul Sem., 1959-63, 65-67, Colegio Paolino Internationale, Rome, 1963-65. Asso. editor Cath. Home Mag., Chicago, Ohio, 1965-67, editor, 1968; dir. Alba House Communications, Canfield, 1968-71; with Office of Radio and TV, Diocese of Youngstown, Ohio, 1969-71; dir. pub. relations, instr. Alice Lloyd Coll., Pippa Passes, Ky., 1971-76; writer, cons. Bethesda, Ohio, 1976-79; pres., pub. Nat. Cath. Reporter, Kansas City, Mo., 1979-85; v.p., gen. mgr. Towsend-Kraft Pub. Co., Liberty, Mo., 1985-86; pres., pub. Steadfast Pub. Co., Kansas City, 1986—. Bd. dirs. David (Ky.) Sch., 1973-79; mem. Mayor's UN Day Com., Kansas City. Mem. Kansas City Direct Mktg. Assn., UN Assn. Dir. dirs. Met. Kansas City chpt., pres. 2000). Roman Catholic. Office: 19 W Linwood Blvd PO Box 410265 Kansas City MO 64141-0265 Office Phone: 816-561-4561.

**PETOUD, STÉPHANE,** chemistry professor, researcher; b. Lausanne, Vaud, Switzerland, Feb. 23, 1966; s. Jean-Claude and Simone Marcelle Petoud. MS in Chemistry, U. Lausanne, Switzerland, 1991, PhD in Scis., 1997. Cons. LJL Biosystems, Inc., Sunnyvale, Calif., 1999—2000; chief sci. officer Lumiphore Inc., Redwood City, Calif., 2001—02, founder, 2001—, chief sci. adviser, 2002—; prof. chemistry U. Pitts., 2002—. Grantee, NSF, 2004 - 2007; Postdoctoral Studies fellowship, Nat. Swiss Sci. Found., 1997 - 1998, Leenaards Found., 1999 - 2000, Novartis Stiftung, 1999 - 2000. Mem.: European Rare-Earth and Actinide Soc., Soc. of Biol. Inorganic Chemistry, New Swiss Chem. Soc., Am. Chem. Soc. Achievements include patents for Salicylamide-lanthanide complexes for use as luminescent markers; Phthalamide lanthanide complexes for use as luminescent markers; patents pending for Semiconductor Nanocrystals as Novel Antennae for Lanthanide Cations; research in design, synthesis, characterization and use of luminescent lanthanide complexes and nanomaterials. Development of applications that take advantage of their luminescence properties. Office: Univ Pitts Dept Chemistry 219 Parkman Ave Pittsburgh PA 15260 Office Phone: 412-624-8210. Business E-Mail: spetoud@pitt.edu.

**PETRACCHI, HELEN E.,** social worker, educator; m. Glenn S. Pawlak; children: Isaac J. Merritt, Elizabeth M. Merritt. BS in Social Work, Carroll Coll., Waukesha, Wis., 1978; MSSW, U. Wis., Madison, Wis., 1983, PhD, 1992. Cert. social worker Nat. Assn. Social Work, 1988. Counselor Ethan Allen Sch. Boys, Oconomowoc, Wis., 1977; social worker Oconomowoc Developmental Tng. Ctr., Inc., 1978—80; instr. Wis. Dept. Health and Social Svcs., Madison, Wis., 1982; tchg. asst. Sch. Social Work U. Wis. Madison, 1984—90, instr. social work U. Pitts., 1991—2002. Counselor pregnancy option Planned Parenthood, Madison, 1987—89; mem. rsch. coun. Office Provost U. Pitts., rschr. Ctr. Race and Social Problems, rschr. ctrl. R&D fund; rschr. Inst. Race and Ethnicity U. Wis. Vol. Three Rivers Cmty. Fund, Pitts., 1997—2000; mem. task force Allegheny County Young Fathers Working Group, Pitts., 1994—98; cons. Ctr. Creative Play, Inc., Pitts., 1998—2000; trustee ShadyLane Bd., Pitts., 2004; mem. adv. bd. C.C. Allegheny County, Pitts., 2002—. Mem.: NASW (treas. Pa. chpt. 1995—97, mem. adv. com.

continuing edn. Pa. chpt. 1993—95), ACSW. Office: University of Pittsburgh School of SW 4200 5th Ave 2117 CL Pittsburgh PA 15260 Office Phone: 412-624-6334. Office Fax: 412-624-6323. Business E-Mail: hpssw@pitt.edu.

**PETRAEUS, DAVID HOWELL,** career military officer; b. Cornwall, N.Y., Nov. 7, 1952; s. Sixtus and Miriam Sweet (Howell) P.; m. Hollister Knowlton, July 6, 1974; children: Anne, Stephen. BS, U.S. Mil. Acad., 1974; grad., U.S. Army Command and Gen. Staff Coll., Ft. Leavenworth, Kans., 1983; M in Pub. and Internat. Affairs, Princeton U., 1985, PhD, 1987. Commd. 2d lt. US Army, 1974, advanced through grades to lt. gen., 2004; platoon leader, adjutant 1-509th Inf. (Airborne), Vicenza, Italy, 1975—79; co. comdr., ops. officer, aide-de-camp 24th Inf. divsn., Ft. Stewart, Ga., 1979—87; asst. prof. internat. relations Dept. Social Scis., U.S. Mil. Acad., West Point, NY, 1985-87; mil. asst. to supreme allied comdr. Europe, 1987-88; bn. and brigade ops. officer 3rd infantry divsn. U.S. Army, 1988-89, asst. divsn. comdr. for operations, 82nd Airborne divsn., chief of staff, XVIII Airborne Corps. Ft. Bragg, NC, asst. chief of staff for military ops. Joint HQ Ctr., Allied Command Europe, 2001—02, comdr., 101st Airborne Divsn. Ft. Campbell, Ky., 2002—04, comdr. multinational security transition commd. Iraq, comdr. Combined Arms Ctr. Ft. Leavenworth, Kans., 2005—. Mem. NATO Tng. Mission, Iraq. Author: The American Military and the Lessons of Vietnam, 1987; contbr. to: Strategy, Democracy, and Vietnam, 1987; co-editor: NATO At Forty, 1989; contbr. articles to profl. jours. Decorated Disting. Svc. medal U.S. Army, Def. Disting. Svc. medal, Bronze Star with v, Meritorious Svc. medal NATO; recipient Golden award of the Iraqi Order of the Date Palm, 2005. Mem. Council on Fgn. Relations, Assn. U.S. Army, Phi Kappa Phi. Clubs: Army-Navy (Arlington, Va.). Presbyterian. Avocations: distance running, writing. Office: Army Combined Arms Ctr 415 Sherman Ave Fort Leavenworth KS 66027

**PETRAKIS, HARRY MARK,** author; b. St. Louis, June 5, 1923; s. Mark E. and Stella (Christoulakis) P.; m. Diane Perparos, Sept. 30, 1945; children: Mark, John, Dean. Student, U. Ill., 1940-41, LHD (hon.), 1971, Gov.'s State U., 1980, Hellenic Coll., 1984, Roosevelt U., 1987, Am. Coll. Greece, 2004. Freelance writer, tchr., lectr.; tchr. workshop classes in novel, short story; McGuffey vis. lectr. Ohio U., Athens, 1971; writer-in-residence Chgo. Pub. Library, 1976-77, Chgo. Bd. Edn., 1978-79; Kazantzakis Prof. San Francisco State U., 1992. Author: Lion at My Heart, 1959, The Odyssey of Kostas Volakis, 1963, Pericles on 31st Street, 1965 (nominated for Nat. Book award), The Founder's Touch: The Life of Paul Galvin of Motorola, 1965, A Dream of Kings, 1966 (Nat. Book award nomination), The Waves of Night, 1969, Stelmark: A Family Recollection, 1970, In the Land of Morning, 1973, The Hour of the Bell, 1976, A Petrakis Reader, 28 Stories, 1978, Nick the Greek, 1979, Days of Vengeance, 1983, Reflections on a Writer's Life and Work, 1983, Collected Stories, 1986, Ghost of the Sun, 1990, Tales of the Heart, 1999, Twilight of the Ice, 2003, The Orchards of Ithaca, 2004; writer (films) A Dream of Kings, 1969, Picture Windows, 1995; contbr. short stores to mags. including, Atlantic Monthly, Sat. Eve. Post, Harper's Bazaar, Country Beautiful. (Story included in Prize Stories, also O. Henry Award 1966). Recipient awards Friends of Am. Writers, Friends of Lit., Soc. Midland Authors, Carl Sandburg award, Ellis Island medal of honor, 1995, O'Henry award; named Kazantzakis chair in Modern Greek Studies San Francisco State U., 1992. Mem. Authors Guild, PEN, Writers Guild Am.-West. Address: Dune Acres 80 East Rd Chesterton IN 46304-1035 Personal E-mail: hmp801@comcast.net. *"...The older I become, the more clearly I see that there is a stunning purity in the writing of a book that I cannot achieve in my own life with its frailty and desperation. The work takes over with a life of its own. In those moments, I wouldn't trade writing with all its loneliness and sometimes with its pain, for any other profession in the world.*

**PETRAKIS, MYRON TITOS,** retired mechanical engineer; b. Chgo., Apr. 6, 1922; s. Titos Myron and Elpis Lagovardos Petrakis; m. Catherine Theresa Rinaldi, Sept. 20, 1952; children: Stephen Paul, Barbara Jean, Mary Ann. BSME, Ill. Inst. Tech., Chgo., 1951. Tool and dye maker Republic Flow Meters Co., Chgo., 1941—44; project engr. Gen. Am. Plastics, East Chicago, Ind., 1951—53; mgr. plastic molding Fed. Tool Corp., Lincolnwood, Ill., 1953—67; sales engr. Application Engring. Corp., Elk Grove, Ill., 1967—69; pres. B/P Plastic Equipment Co., Rosemont, Ill., 1969—91. Civil def. dir. Village of Norridge, Ill., 1964—66; commn. sec. Bd. of Fire and Police Commn., Norridge, 1959—; publicist Norridge H.S. Problems Com., 1957—59; historian Village of Norridge, 1996—. With USN, 1944—46. Recipient Sheriff's Sr. Medal of Honor, Cook County Sheriff, Chgo., 2003. Mem.: Soc. Plastic Engrs. (dir., chair edn. 1970—73), K.C. (4th deg.). Achievements include design of accessories for plastic injection molding. Avocations: photography, woodworking, stained glass, fishing. Home: 4437 N Ottawa Ave Norridge IL 60706 Office: Norridge Board of Fire and Police Commrs 4000 N Olcott Ave Norridge IL 60706

**PETRAKIS, NICHOLAS LOUIS,** epidemiologist, medical researcher, educator; b. San Francisco, Feb. 6, 1922; s. Louis Nicholas and Stamatina (Boosalis) P.; m. Patricia Elizabeth Kelly, June 24, 1947; children: Steven John, Susan Lynn, Sandra Kay. BA, Augustana Coll., 1943; BS in Medicine, U. S.D., 1944; MD, Washington U., St. Louis, 1946. Intern Mpls. Gen. Hosp., 1946-47; physician, researcher U.S. Naval Radiol. Def. Lab., San Francisco, 1947-49; resident physician Mpls. Gen. Hosp., 1949-50; sr. asst. surgeon Nat. Cancer Inst., USPHS, San Francisco, 1950-54; asst. research physician Cancer Research Inst., U. Calif., San Francisco, 1954-56; asst. prof. preventive medicine U. Calif. Sch. Medicine, San Francisco, 1956-60, assoc. prof., 1960-66, prof., 1966-91, chmn. dept. epidemiology and internat. health, 1978-88, prof. emeritus, 1991—; prof. epidemiology U. Calif. Sch. Pub. Health, Berkeley, 1981-91. Assoc. dir. G.W. Hooper Edn., U. Calif., San Francisco, 1970-74, acting dir., 1974-77, chmn. dept. epidemiology and internat. health, 1979-89; co-dir. Breast Screening Ctr. of No. Calif., Oakland, 1976-81; cons. Breast Cancer Task Force, Nat. Cancer Inst., Bethesda, Md., 1972-76; chmn. Biometry & Epidemiology Contract Rev. Com., Bethesda, 1977-81; mem. bd. sci. counselors, div. cancer etiology Nat. Cancer Inst., Bethesda, 1982-86; mem. scientific adv. com. Calif. State Tobacco-Related Disease Rsch. Program, 1991-93; cons. U. Crete Sch. Medicine, Heraklion, Greece, 1984; bd. dirs. No. Calif. Cancer Ctr., 1991. Contbr. over 130 rsch. papers on breast cancer, med. oncology and hematology. Eleanor Roosevelt Internat. Cancer fellow Am. Cancer Soc., Comitato Reserche Nucleari, Cassacia, Italy, 1962; U.S. Pub. Health Service Spl. fellow Galton Lab., U. London, 1969-70; recipient Alumni Achievement award Augustana Coll., Sioux Falls, S.D., 1979, Axion award Hellenic-Am. Profl. Soc. of Calif., San Francisco, 1984, Lewis C. Robbins award Soc. for Prospective Medicine, Indpls., 1985, Otto W. Sartorius, MD, award from Susan Love MD Breast Cancer Found., 2001. Mem. Am. Soc. Preventive Oncology (founding, pres. 1984-85, Disting. Achievement award 1992), Soc. for Prospective Medicine (founding), Am. Assn. Cancer Rsch., Am. Epidemiol. Soc., Am. Soc. Clin. Investigation, Am. Bd. Preventive Medicine (cert.). Home: 335 Juanita Way San Francisco CA 94127-1657 Office: U Calif Sch Medicine Dept Epidemiology & Biostats Box 0560 MU420W San Francisco CA 94143-0001 Personal E-mail: petrakis@ix.netcom.com.

**PETRALIA, RONALD SEBASTIAN,** entomologist, neurobiologist; b. Lawrence, Mass., Nov. 7, 1954; s. Samuel and Rosalie (Zanfagna) P. BS in Entomology summa cum laude, U. Mass., 1975; PhD in Entomology and Biology, Tex. A&M U., 1979. Rsch. assist. Tex. A&M U., College Station, 1975-79, rsch. assoc., 1979-80; asst. prof. biology St. Ambrose Coll., Davenport, Iowa, 1980-85; rsch. fellow dept. anatomy George Washington U., Washington, 1985-90; sr. staff fellow Nat. Inst. Deafness and Other Comm. Disorders, NIH, Bethesda, Md., 1991-97, staff scientist, 1997—. Presenter in field. Contbr. chpts. to books: Excitatory Amino Acids, 1992, The Mammalian Coclear Nuclei: Their Role in Neuroendocrine Function, 1996, The Ionotropic Glutamate Receptors, 1997, Ionotropic Glutamate Receptors in the CNS, 1999, Handbook of Chemical Neuroanatomy: Glutamate, 2000; contbr. articles to profl. jours. Mem. AAAS, Chesapeake Soc. Microscopy (coun. mem., newsletter editor, past pres.), Soc. Neurosci., Entomol. Soc. Am., Microscopy Soc. Am., Assn. Rsch. Otolaryngology, Cambridge

Entomol. Club, Sigma Xi. Roman Catholic. Home: 3 Pooks Hill Rd Apt 218 Bethesda MD 20814-5404 Office: NIDCD NIH Rm 50/4142 9000 Rockville Pike Bethesda MD 20892-8027 Business E-Mail: petralia@nidcd.nih.gov.

**PETRANEK, STEPHEN LYNN,** editor; b. Wash., Aug. 19, 1944; s. Chester J. and Mabel Oleta (Mercer) P.; m. Barbara Ergas, 1983. Student, U. Okla., 1962-63; BS, U. Md., 1970; postgrad., U. Mo., 1970-71. Editor-in-chief The Diamondback, U. Md., 1969-70; reporter Democrat and Chronicle, Rochester, NY, 1972, financial writer, 1972-73, asst. Sunday editor, 1973; editor Upstate mag., 1974—77; editor-in-chief Tropic Mag. The Miami Herald, 1977-78; dep. editor The Washington Post Mag., 1978-81, mng. editor, 1982-90; sr. editor LIFE mag., 1990-96; editor-in-chief This Old House mag., 1996—99, Discover mag., 1999—2006, editor-at-large, 2006—; editor-in-chief Weider History Mags., 2006—. Author: newspaper series Decline and Fall of Stirling Homex, 1972. Recipient John Hancock award for fin. writing, 1972, Bus. Journalism award U. Mo., 1973, Frank Tripp Newswriting award, 1973; finalist Nat. Mag. award, 1997, 2000, 03. Mem. Sigma Delta Chi, Kappa Tau Alpha, Omicron Delta Kappa, Pi Delta Epsilon. Mem. United Ch. of Christ. Home: 38545 John Wolford Rd Waterford VA 20197 Office: 741 Miller Dr SE Ste D-Z Leesburg VA 20175 Office Phone: 703-779-8389. Business E-Mail: spetranek@discover.com, steve@weiderhistorygroup.com.

**PETRASH, JEFFREY MICHAEL,** lawyer; b. Cleve., Dec. 14, 1948; s. Robert Anthony and Naomi Marjorie (Close) P.; 1 child, Michael Stewart. AB, U. Mich., 1969, JD, 1973. Bar: Mich. 1974, D.C. 1975, Md. 1997. Assoc. Dickinson, Wright, McKean, Cudlip & Moon, Detroit, 1973-75, Hamel, Park, McCabe & Saunders, Washington, 1975-78; from assoc. to ptnr. Dickinson, Wright, Washington, 1978-99, sr. counsel Am. Gas Assn., Washington, 2000—. Served to capt. U.S. Army, 1969—77. Mem. Soc. Barristers. Episcopalian. Avocation: sailing. Home: 6606 Hillandale Rd Bethesda MD 20815-6406 Office: 400 N Capitol St NW Washington DC 20001-1511 Office Phone: 202-824-7231. E-mail: jpetrash@aga.org.

**PETREE, SANDRA AILEY,** language educator; b. Shawnee, Okla., Mar. 1, 1945; d. Orva Ray Ailey and Gladys Iola Parker; m. Jerry Lee Johnson (div.); m. James H. Petree, Feb. 14, 1990 (dec.); children: Gonzalez, Lisa Smiley, Michael S., Theresa Ann, T. Benjamin. B.Gen.Studies, Ft. Hays State U., Hayes, Kans., 1990; MA in English, Ft. Hays State U., 1992; PhD in English, U. Ark., Fayetteville, 1999. Instr. English Fort Hays State U., 1992—94; asst. prof. English Northwestern Okla. State U., Alva, 2000—05, assoc. prof. English, fgn. land. and humanities, 2005—. Office mgr. dept. physics North Tex. State U., Denton, 1968—69; conf. presenter in field. Editor: Recollections of Past Days: The Autobiolgraphy of Patience Loader Rozsa, 2006; contbr. poetry to profl. jours. Mem. Ellis County Election Bd., Kans.; active various charitable orgns.; edn. counselor Stillwater Relief Soc. Fellow Vance and Mary Randolph fellow, U. Ark., 1998; grantee Rsch. grantee, Fulbright Coll. Arts and Scis., 1998. Mem.: AAUP, John Whitmer Hist. Assn., Mormon History Assn., Utah State Hist. Soc., Western Lit. Assn. Republican. Lds. Avocation: genealogy.

**PETREQUIN, HARRY JOSEPH, JR.,** foreign service officer; b. Ste. Genevieve, Mo., July 1, 1929; s. Harry Joseph and Crescentia Ellen (Bechter) P.; m. Katharine McDonnell Drouin, Oct. 7, 1980; children: John Andrew, Marc Christopher, Paul Nicholas. AB, Westminster Coll., 1950; B of Fgn. Trade, Am. Grad. Sch. Internat. Mgmt., 1954; postgrad., Johns Hopkins U., 1960; MA, Tufts U., 1970. Joined U.S. Fgn. Svc., 1955; assigned AID and predecessor agys., 1955—; dep. dir. S.E. Asia Regional Econ. Devel. Office, Thailand, 1970-74; U.S. coord. Senegal River Basin Authority, Dakar, 1975-76; dir. ASEAN and South Pacific Affairs, 1977-80; dir. program devel. and evaluation staff Bur. Internat. Orgn. Affairs State Dept., 1980-81; dep. dir. AID Mission, Morocco, 1981-85; coord. AID Sr. Mgmt. Course, 1985-86, Indsl. Coll. of the Armed Forces, 1986-87; faculty dept. nat. security policy Nat. War Coll., Washington, 1987-89; internat. devel. cons. Black Mountain, NC, 1989—. Adj. prof. polit. sci. Warren Wilson Coll., Swannanoa, NC, 1993-94; faculty U. NC Coll. Srs., 1995—. Lt. (j.g.) USCGR, 1951-53, Comdr. Ready Res., 1973. Recipient Superior Honor award AID, 1979, State Dept. Superior Honor award, 1981, Comdrs. award for Civilian Svc., Dept. of the Army, 1989. Mem. Soc. Internt. Devel., World Federalist Assn. (nat. bd. dirs.), Am. Fgn. Svc. Assn., UN Assn. U.S., Acad. Polit. Sci., Cousteau Soc., Common Cause, Nat. Noetic Scis., World Future Soc., Amnesty Internat., Coast Guard Combat Vets Assn., Greenpeace, Vets. for Peace, The Land Inst., Phi Alpha Theta. Office Phone: 828-669-8404.

**PETRI, THOMAS EVERT,** congressman; b. Marinette, Wis., May 28, 1940; s. Robert and Marian (Humleker) Petri; m. Anne Neal, Mar. 26, 1983; 1 child, Alexandra. BA in Govt., Harvard U., 1962, JD, 1965. Bar: Wis. 1965. Law clk. to US Judge James Doyle US Dist. Ct. (we. dist.) Wis., Madison, 1965-66; vol. Peace Corps, Somalia, 1966-67; aide White House, Washington, 1969-70; dir. crime and drug studies Pres.'s Nat. Adv. Coun. on Exec. Orgn., 1969; lawyer pvt. practice, Fond du Lac, Wis., 1970-79; mem. Wis. State Senate, Madison, 1973-79, US Congress from 6th Wis. dist., 1979—, vice chmn. edn. and the workforce com., vice chmn. transp. and infrastructure com., chmn. highways, transit and pipelines subcommittee. Editor: Nat. Indsl. Policy: Solution or Illusion, 1984. Republican. Lutheran. Avocations: reading, swimming, hiking, bicycling, skiing. Office: US Ho Reps 2462 Rayburn Ho Office Bldg Washington DC 20515-0001 Office Phone: 202-225-2476.*

**PETRICK, ALFRED, JR.,** economist, educator; b. Mt. Vernon, NY, Dec. 30, 1926; s. Alfred and Ruth (Updike) P.; m. Ruth Goodridge, Jan. 2, 1956; children: Elizabeth, Andrew Wayne. BS, BA, Columbia U., 1952, MS, 1962; MBA, Denver U., 1966; PhD, U. Colo., 1969. Registered profl. engr., Colo. Sales engr. Ingersoll Rand Co., N.Y.C., 1953-54; project engr. U.S. AEC, Grand Junction, Colo., 1954-57; mining engr. Reynolds Metals Co., Bauxite, Ark., 1957-61, Guyana, 1957-61; mineral economist U.S. Bur. Mines, Denver, 1963-70; Coulter prof. Colo. Sch. Mines, Golden, 1970-84, emeritus prof., 1984—; dir. Petrick Assocs., Evergreen, Colo., 1974—2004; ret., 2004. Author: Economics International Development, 1977, Economics of Minerals, 1980, Preparacion y Evaluacion, 1982. Mem. com. tech. aspects strategic materials Nat. Acad. Sci., Washington, 1973-76, mem. com. surface mining and reclamation, 1979. Served with USAF, 1945-47, PTO. Fulbright research scholar U. Otago, Dunedin, New Zealand, 1986; recipient Edn. award Instituto Para Funcionarios De Las Industrias Minera y Siderurgica, Mexico City, 1981; recipient Service award Office Tech. Assessment, U.S. Congress, 1981. Mem. AIME (chmn. council econs. 1977-78, Henry Krumb lectr. 1986, service award), Profl. Engrs. Colo. Presbyterian. Home: 5544 S Hatch Dr Evergreen CO 80439-7233 Office: Colo Sch Mines Golden CO 80401 Personal E-mail: peta33@comcast.net.

**PETRICK, ERNEST NICHOLAS,** mechanical engineer, researcher; b. Pa., Apr. 9, 1922; s. Aurelius and Anna (Kaschak) P.; m. Magdalene Simcoe, June 13, 1946; children: Deborah Petrick Healey, Katherine, Denise, Victoria Petrick Kropp. BS in Mech. Engring. Carnegie Inst. Tech., 1943; MS, Purdue U., 1948, PhD, 1955. Registered profl. engr., Mich. Faculty Purdue U., 1946-53; dir. heat transfer research Curtiss-Wright Corp., Woodridge, NJ, 1953-56; chief advanced propulsion systems Curtiss-Wright Research divsn., Quehanna, Pa., 1957-60; chief research engr. Kelsey-Hayes Co., Detroit, 1960-65; chief scientist, tech. dir. U.S. Army Tank-Automotive Command, Warren, Mich., 1965-82; chief scientist, dir. engring. labs. Gen. Dynamics, 1982-87; engring. cons., 1987—; panel mem. combat vehicles NATO, 1973-82; mem. adv. bd. on basic combustion research NSF, 1973; chmn. advanced transp. systems com. White House Energy Project, 1973; mem. adv. com. NSF-RANN research program Drexel U. Coll. Engring., 1976-78; mem. Army Sci. Bd., 1983-89; cons. Air Force Studies Bd. NRC, 1991-93, cons. Def. Sci. Bd., 1994-95; cons. NAS, 1997—99, 2001—03, Bd. Army Sci. and Tech. Rev. NAS Naval Studies Bd., 2003; adj. prof. engring. Wayne State U., Detroit, 1972-82, U. Mich., Ann Arbor, 1982-83. Contbr. articles on thermal, ground vehicles, propulsion and project mgmt. to profl. jours. Lt., chief engr. destroyer USNR, 1942—46, WWII. Recipient certificate of achievement U.S. Army, 1967, Outstanding Performance awards, 1970, 71, 76, 82, Outstanding Mech. Engring. award Purdue U., 1991; named Disting. Engring. Alumnus

Purdue U., 1966. Mem. Soc. Automotive Engrs. (nat. dir. 1978-80), Am. Def. Preparedness Assn. (chmn. land warfare survivability divsn. 1990-95, Silver medal 1992, Recognition award 1992), Assn. U.S. Army, Sigma Xi, Pi Tau Sigma. Home: 1540 Stonehaven Rd Ann Arbor MI 48104-4150 Office: ENP Cons 1540 Stonehaven Rd Ann Arbor MI 48104

**PETRICK, JOSEPH ANTHONY,** small business owner, management consultant, educator; b. Pueblo, Colo., Dec. 31, 1946; s. Joseph John and Hermina Emma Petrick; m. Kimberly Marie Weber, Sept. 22, 1984. BA in Philosophy, Colo. State U., 1968; PhD, Pa. State U., 1972; MBA, U. of Cin., 1990. Cert. Human Resources Certification Inst., Wash., D.C., 1993. Asst. prof. of philosophy Coll. of Charleston, SC, 1972—75; assoc. prof. and head of philosophy dept. No. Ky. U., Highland Heights, Ky., 1975—82; asst. dean So. Ohio Coll., Fairfield, Ohio, 1982—84; head Dept. off-Campus Bus. Wilmington (Ohio) Coll., 1984—87; prof. U. of Cin., 1987—89; prof. of mgmt. Wright State U., Dayton, Ohio, 1989—. Prin., owner Orgnl. Ethics Assocs., Cin., 1992—, Performance Leadership Assocs., Cin., 1996—, Integrity Capacity Assocs., Cin., 2002—; bd. dirs. Human Resources Cert. Inst. Author: Total Quality in Managing Human Resources, 1995, Total Quality and Organization Development, 1997, Management Ethics: Integrity at Work, 1997, Managing Project Quality, 2002. Baldrige quality award examiner U.S. Dept. of Commerce, Washington, 1998—2000; examiner Ohio Quality Award for Excellence, Dayton, Ohio, 1999—2000. Recipient Innovation in Bus. Edn. Group award, Midwestern Deans of U.S. Bus. Schs., 1998; fellow, Pa. State U., 1969—71, Woodrow Wilson Nat. Found., 1971—72, Malone Arabic Studies fellow, U.S. Arab Rels. Inst., 1995. Mem.: Acad. of Mgmt., Midwestern Soc. Human Resources and Indsl. Rels. (pres. 1996—97), U.S. Assn. Small Bus. and Entrepreneurship (v.p. individual entrepreneurship 1994—95), Am. Philos. Assn., Soc. Human Resource Mgmt., Sigma Iota Epsilon, Internat. Bus. Honor Soc. (pres. 2006), Beta Gamma Sigma. Democrat. Avocations: travel, reading, films, dance, golf. Home: 3505 Arborcrest Court Cincinnati OH 45236 Office: Wright State University 3640 Colonel Glenn Hwy Dayton OH 45435 Office Phone: 937-775-2428. E-mail: joseph.petrick@wright.edu.

**PETRICK, MICHAEL JOSEPH,** journalism educator; b. Antigo, Wis., Sept. 6, 1942; BS, U. Wis., Milw., 1965, MS, 1967; PhD, U. Wis., Madison, 1970. News editor Milw. South Times Star, 1966-67; disting. teaching fellow U. Wis., Madison, 1969-70; from asst. to assoc. prof. U. Md., College Park, 1970-78; copy editor Evening Star, Washington, 1974-75; chairperson dept. journalism Ctrl. Mich. U., Mt. Pleasant, 1978-84, prof., 1984-2000, prof. emeritus, 2000—. Writing and editing coach Ctrl. Mich. Newspapers, 1984-85; writing and reporting coach Greenville (Mich.) Daily News, 1997-99; chair bd. in control of student media Ctrl. Mich. U., 1997-99 Co-author: Using the Mass Media, 1975; contbr. articles to profl. jours Named to Ctrl. Mich. Jour. Hall of Fame, 2006. Mem. Md.-Del.-D.C. Press Assn. (chmn. freedom of info. com. 1972-73), Soc. Profl. Journalists (campus chpt. adviser 1970-99), Nat. Coun. Editl. Writers, Assn. for Edn. in Journalism and Mass Communication Office: PO Box 6 Mount Pleasant MI 48804-0006 E-mail: michael.petrick@cmich.edu.

**PETRICOFF, M. HOWARD,** lawyer, educator; b. Cin., Dec. 22, 1949; s. Herman and Neoma P.; m. Hanna Sue, Aug. 11, 1974; children: Nicholas, Eve. BS, Am. U., 1967-71; JD, U. Cin., 1971-74; M in Pub. Adminstrn., Harvard U., 1980-81. Bar: Ohio, U.S. Ct. Appeals (D.C. cir.) 1977, U.S. Ct. Appeals (10th cir.) 1985, U.S. Ct. Appeals (6th cir.) 1989, U.S. Supreme Ct. 1989. Asst. city law dir. City of Toledo (Ohio), 1975-77; asst. atty. gen. Ohio Atty. Gen. Office, Columbus, 1977-82; ptnr. Vorys, Sater, Seymour & Pease, Columbus, 1982—. Adj. prof. law Capital U. Law Sch., Columbus, 1991—. Contbr. articles to profl. jours. Reginald Heber Smith Found. fellow Washnigton, 1974-75. Mem. Ohio Bar Assn., Columbus Bar Assn., Ohio Oil and Gas Assn. Office: Vorys Sater Seymour & Pease PO Box 1008 52 E Gay St Columbus OH 43215-3161 Office Phone: 614-464-6400. Business E-Mail: mhpetricoff@ussp.com.

**PETRIDES, GEORGE ATHAN,** ecologist, educator; b. NYC, Aug. 1, 1916; s. George Athan and Grace Emeline (Ladd) P.; m. Miriam Clarissa Pasma, Nov. 30, 1940; children: George H., Olivia L., Lisa B. BS, George Washington U., 1938; MS, Cornell U., 1940; PhD, Ohio State U., 1948; postdoctoral fellow, U. Ga., 1963-64. Naturalist Nat. Park Service, Washington and Yosemite, Calif., 1938-43, Glacier Nat. Park, Mont., 1947, Mt. McKinley Nat. Park, Alaska, 1959; game technician W.Va. Conservation Commn., Charleston, 1941; instr. Am. U., 1942-43, Ohio State U., 1946-48; leader Tex. Coop. Wildlife Unit; assoc. prof. wildlife mgmt. Tex. A and M. Coll., 1948-50; assoc. prof. wildlife mgmt., zool. and African studies Mich. State U., 1950-58, prof., 1958—; research prof. U. Pretoria, S. Africa, 1965; vis. prof. U. Kiel, Germany, 1967; vis. prof. wildlife mgmt. Kanha Nat. Park, India, 1983; del. sci. confs. Warsaw, 1960, Nairobi and Salisbury, 1963, Sao Paulo, Aberdeen, 1965. Lucerne, 1966, Varanasi, India, Nairobi, 1967, Oxford, Eng., Paris, 1968, Durban, 1971, Mexico City, 1971, 73, Banff, 1972, Nairobi, Moscow, The Hague, 1974, Johannesburg, 1977, Sydney, 1978, Kuala Lumpur, 1979, Cairns, Australia, Mogadishu, Somalia, Peshawar, Pakistan, 1980. Participant NSF Expdn., Antarctic, 1972, FAO mission to, Afghanistan, 1972, World Bank mission to, Malaysia, 1975 Author: Field Guide to Trees and Shrubs, 1958, 2d edit., 1972, Field Guide to Eastern Trees, 1988, 98, Field Guide to Western Trees, 1992, 98, First Guide to Trees, 1993, Trees of the California Sierra Nevada, 1996, Trees of the Pacific Northwest, 1998, Trees of the Rocky Mountains and Intermountain West, 2000, Trees of the American Southwest, 2005; editor wildlife mgmt. terrestrial sect. Biol. Abstracts, 1947-72; contbr. articles to biol. publs. Served to lt. USNR, 1943-46. Fulbright research awards in E. Africa Nat. Parks Kenya, 1953-54; Fulbright research awards in E. Africa Nat. Parks Kenya, Uganda, 1970-71; N.Y. Zool. Soc. grantee Ethiopia, Sudan, 1957; N.Y. Zool. Soc. grantee Thailand, 1977; Mich. State U. grantee Nigeria, 1962; Mich. State U. grantee Zambia, 1966; Mich. State U. grantee Kenya, 1969; Mich. State U. grantee Africa, 1970, 71, 73, 81; Mich. State U. grantee Greece, 1974, 83; Mich. State U. grantee Iran, 1974; Mich. State U. grantee Botswana, 1977; Mich. State U. grantee Papua New Guinea, Thailand, 1979; Iran Dept. Environment grantee, 1977; Smithsonian Instn. grantee India and Nepal, 1967, 68, 75, 77, 83, 85; World Wildlife Fund grantee W. Africa, 1968 Mem. Am. Ornithologists Union, Am. Soc. Mammalogists, Wildlife Soc. (exec. sec. 1953), Wilderness Soc., Am. Comm. Internat. Wildlife Protection, Ecol. Soc., Fauna Preservation Soc., E. African Wildlife Soc., Internat. Union Conservation Nature, Zool. Soc. So. Africa, Sigma Xi. Presbyterian. Home: 4895 Barton Rd Williamston MI 48895-9305 Office: Mich State U Dept Botany East Lansing MI 48824 E-mail: petrides@msu.edu.

**PETRIE, BRUCE INGLIS,** lawyer; b. Washington, Nov. 8, 1926; s. Robert Inglis and Marion (Douglas) P.; m. Beverly Ann Stevens, Nov. 3, 1950 (dec. Oct. 1993); children: Laurie Ann Roche, Bruce Inglis, Karen Elizabeth Medsger. BBA, U. Cin., 1948, JD, 1950. Bar: Ohio 1950, U.S. Dist. Ct. (so. dist.) Ohio 1951, U.S. Ct. Appeals (6th cir.) 1960, U.S. Supreme Ct. Assoc. Kunkel & Kunkel, 1950-51, Graydon, Head & Ritchey, 1951-57, ptnr., 1957—. Exec. prodr. (sch. video) Classical Quest, 2000; author: How To Get the Most Out of Your Lawyer, 2002; contbr. articles to legal jours. Mem. bd. Charter Com. Greater Cin., 1952—; pres. Charter Rsch. Inst., 2000—03; mem. bd. mem. Indian Hill Exempted Village Sch. Dist., 1965—67, pres., 1967; mem. adv. bd. William A. Mitchell Ctr., 1969—86; mem. Green Areas adv. com. Village of Indian Hill, Ohio, 1969—80, chmn., 1976—80; mem. Ohio Ethics Com., 1974—75; founder Parents as Tchrs. Metro Housing Authority Commn., 1991—; a prin. advocate merit selection judges Ohio; trustee, mem. bd. Seven Hills Neighborhood Houses' Inst. for Learning in Retirement; mem. bd. Hamilton County Good Govt. League; organizer Late Gt. Lakes Book Distbn. project, global vol. tchr. China, 2003—06; elder, trustee, deacon Knox Presbyn. Ch.; bd. dirs. Murray Seasongood Good Govt. Fund, 1975—, chmn.; mem. bd. dirs. Nat. Civic League, Cin. Vol. Lawyers for Poor Found., Linton Music Series, Amernet Chamber Music Soc.; co-founder Sta. WGUC-FM; mem. WGUC-FM Cmty. Bd., 1974—76. Recipient Pres.'s award U. Cin., 1976, Disting. Alumnus award, 1995. Fellow: Am. Bar Found.; mem.: ABA, Ohio State Bar Assn. Found.

(Outstanding Rsch. in Law and Govt. award 1986, Charles P. Taft Civic Gumption award 1988, Ohio Bar medal 1988), Am. Law Inst., Nat. Civic League (coun. 1984—, Disting. Citizen award 1985), Am. Judicature Soc. (dir., Herbert Lincoln Harley award 1973), Cin. Bar Assn. (pres. 1981, Trustee's award 2000), Ohio Bar Assn., Cin. Country Club, Univ. Club, Cincinnatus Assn., Lit. Club, Order of Coif. Avocations: tennis, squash, woodworking, writing, horticulture, music. Home: 2787 Walsh Rd Cincinnati OH 45208-3428 Office: Graydon Head & Ritchey 1900 Fifth 3d Ctr 511 Walnut St Ste 1900 Cincinnati OH 45202-3157

**PETRIE, DONALD JOSEPH,** banker; b. NYC, Sept. 2, 1921; s. John and Elizabeth (Thomson) P.; m. Jane Adams, Aug. 27, 1949; children: R. Scott, Anne, Elizabeth, Douglas, Susan. BBA, Manhattan Coll., 1950. Personnel mgr. Otis Elevator Co., N.Y.C., 1951-59; personnel dir. Brown Bros. Harriman & Co., N.Y.C., 1959-68; exec. v.p. U.S Trust Co., N.Y.C., 1968-79; sr. v.p. Marine Midland Bank, N.Y.C., 1979-86, Drake Beam Morin Inc., N.Y.C., 1986-90; chmn., chief exec. officer Webster Corp., N.Y.C., 1990—. Lectr. Baruch Sch. Bus., Coll. City N.Y., 1955-58; pres., chmn. exec. and fin. coms., dir. Webster Apts., N.Y.C., 1973—; adj. prof. mgmt. Hofstra U., Hempstead, N.Y., 1986-93. Author: Explaining Pay Policy, 1969, Handling Employee Questions About Pay, 1976. Capt. USAAF, 1942-46. Mem. N.Y.C. Partnership and C. of C. (chmn. mgmt. edn. and adv. com. 1964-98). Home: 11 Fairview Ave Great Neck NY 11023-1462 Office: 419 W 34th St New York NY 10001-1596 Office Phone: 212-967-9000.

**PETRIE, FERDINAND RALPH,** illustrator, artist; b. Hackensack, N.J., Sept. 17, 1925; s. Archibald John and Bessie (Rutherford) P.; m. Phyllis L. Haddow, Oct. 19, 1951; children: Beth, David. Advt. cert., Parson's Sch. Design, N.Y.C., 1949; student, Art Students League, 1947-49, Famous Artists Course in Illustration, 1958-59. Illustrator J. Gans Assos., N.Y.C., 1950-69. Free lance illustrator, artist, 1969—, owner, Petrie Gallery, Rockport, Mass., 1971-95; represented in permanent collections, U.S. Supreme Ct., Smithsonian Instn., Washington, Indpls. Mus. Art; designer U.S. commemorative stamp design, 2 Zaire commemorative stamps, 1980, USN, USCG, The Salvation Army; Author: Drawing Landscapes in Pencil, 1979; illustrator: The Drawing Book, 1980, The Color Book, 1981, The Alkyd Book, 1982, The Watercolorists Guide to Painting Trees, 1983, The Watercolorists Guide to Painting Skies, 1984; The Watercolorists Guide to Painting Water, 1985, Painting Nature in Watercolor, 1990. Served with U.S. Maritime Service, 1943-46. Mem. Artists Fellowship, Rockport Art Assn., Am. Artists Profl. League, N.J. Watercolor Soc. Presbyterian. Address: 51 Vreeland Ave Rutherford NJ 07070-2227

**PETRIE, GREGORY STEVEN,** lawyer; b. Seattle, Feb. 25, 1951; s. George C. and Pauline P.; m. Margaret Fuhrman, Oct. 6, 1979; children: Kathryn Jean, Thomas George. AB in Polit. Sci and Econs., UCLA, 1973; JD, Boston U., 1976. Bar: Wash. 1976, U.S. Dist. Ct. (we. dist.) Wash. 1976. Adminstr. Action/Peace Corps, Washington, 1973, Fed. Power Commn., Washington, 1974; assoc. Oles Morrison et al, Seattle, 1976-80; ptnr. Schwabe Williamson Ferguson & Burdell, Seattle, 1981-94; mng. shareholder Krutch Lindell Bingham Jones & Petrie, Seattle, 1994—. Mem. Seattle-King County Bar Assn., Profl. Liability Architects and Engrs., Wash. Athletic Club. Avocations: woodworking, skiing. Office: Krutch Lindell Bingham Jones & Petrie 1420 Fifth Ave Ste 3150 Seattle WA 98101 Office Phone: 206-682-1505. Business E-Mail: gsp@krutchlindell.com.

**PETRIE, NANCY SUE YENSHAW,** music educator; b. Ferndale, Mich., June 26, 1953; d. George Adolph Yenshaw and Elizabeth Helen Johnson Yenshaw Allen; m. David LaVerne Petrie, May 18, 1984. BS in Edn., Ctrl. Mich. U., 1976; MS in Edn., Elmira Coll., NY, 1994. Cert. educator N.Y., 1994. Tchr. Ctrl. Lake Pub. Sch., Mich., 1976—79, Penn Yan Ctrl. Sch. Dist., NY, 1994—2006, Canandaigua City Sch. Dist., 2006—. Pvt. practice tchr. singing, Dundee, NY, 1990—. Composer (singer, music arranger): (songs) A Latin King, 1996. Dir. handbells Penn Yan (N.Y.) United Meth. Ch., 1988—2001, St. Thomas Episc. Ch., Bath, NY, 2003—04. Mem.: AAUW, NEA, N.Y. State Edn. Assn., Am. Choral Dirs. Assn., Kappa Delta Pi. Democrat. Avocations: handbell ringing, travel, reading.

**PETRIE, WILLIAM MARSHALL,** psychiatrist; b. Louisville, Oct. 19, 1946; s. Garner McReynolds and Claire (Samuels) P.; children: Christopher W., Ellen M., Shelley M.; m. Lori L. Molchin, Oct. 1, 1994. BA, Vanderbilt U., 1968, MD, 1972. Research psychiatrist NIMH, Rockville, Md., 1975-77; asst. prof. dept. psychiatry Vanderbilt Med. Ctr., Nashville, 1977-81, assoc. prof., 1981-82, assoc. clin. prof., 1982-87, clin. prof., 1992—; pvt. practice psychiatry Psychiat. Cons., P.C., Nashville, 1982—, pres., 1996—. Bd. dirs Psychiat. Solutions, Inc.; clin. instr. Georgetown U. Med. Ctr., 1975—77; cons. psychopharmacology rsch. br. NIMH, 1977—80; rschr. in geriatric psychopharmacology; med. dir. memory Study Ctr., 1987—; chmn. of psychiatry Parthenon Pavilion, 1994—96; bd. trustees Centennial Mutual Ctr., 1994—2000, vice-chmn. bd. trustees, 1998—2000; pres. Columbia Psychiat. Care Network, 1997—98, Psychiat. Cons., PC, 1999—2005. Mem. editorial bd. Gen. Hosp. Psychiatry, 1995—, Audio Digest Psychiatry, 1996-99; author numerous articles and book chpts. on psychopharmacology and geriatric psychiatry. Fellow Am. Psychiat. Assn. (disting. fellow, pres. mid. Tenn. dist. br. 1986-87); mem. AMA, Tenn. Med. Assn., Am. Assn. Geriatric Psychiatrists, Am. Coll. Psychiatrists, Tenn. Psychiat. Assn. (pres. 1999-2000). Democrat. Republican. Office: Psychiat Cons PC 310 25th Ave N Nashville TN 37203-1515 Office Phone: 615-250-6780. Business E-Mail: wpetrie@psychiatricconsultants.com.

**PETRIK, F. A.,** music educator; s. Frank P. Petrik and Anne R. Porter; m. Amanda F. Fleming, Aug. 15, 1998; children: Charles F., Cecelia A. BA in Music Edn., Mont. State U., Bozeman, 1999; MA in Ednl. Instrnl. Tech., Am. Intercontinental U., Alanta, Ga., 2004. Cert. tchr. Oreg., 1999. Band dir. Portland Pub. Schs., Oreg., 1999—2002, Mt. Angel Pub. Schools, Oreg. Musician Jazz Express Big Band, Portland, 2001—02, Keizer Cmty. Jazz Band, Keizer, Oreg. Vol. fire fighter Sourdough Fire Dept., Bozeman, 1994—95; youth adv. com. St. Paul Cath. Ch., Silverton, Oreg., 2005—06. Grantee Music Tech., Intel, 2001, New Music Instruments For Students, Mr. Holland's Opus Found., 2002. Mem.: Music Educator's Nat. Conf., Oreg. Music Educator's Assn. (licentiate). Conservative. Roman Catholic. Avocations: camping, soccer, fly fishing, mountain biking. Home: 216 N James St Silverton OR 97381 Office: Mt Angel Sch Dist 890 E Marquam St Mount Angel OR 97362 Office Phone: 503-845-6137. Personal E-mail: fmpetrik@msn.com. Business E-Mail: petrik_frank@mtangel.k12.or.us.

**PETRIK, MICHAEL THOMAS,** lawyer; b. Chgo., Jan. 13, 1957; s. Thomas J. and Bette J. (Sarich) P.; m. Susan Renée Prince, June 2, 1979; children: Michael Ray, Stephanie Renée. BS in Bus. Mgmt. and BA in Econs., Ea. Ill. U., 1979; JD, Duke U., 1983. Bar: Ga. 1983, U.S. Tax Ct. 1985. Assoc. Alston & Bird LLP, Atlanta, 1983—90, ptnr., 1991—, leader state and local tax group. Instr. constnl. law and tax, Atlanta Law Sch., 1984-92, state and local tax law, Ga. State U., 1992-98; edit. adv. bd. State Income Tax Alert, 1991—, Ga. corr. State Tax Notes, Arlington, Va., 1990-97, interstate tax rep., 1996—; tech. cons. Sales and Use Tax Alert, 1991-92. Contbr. articles to profl. jours. Mem. emergency intervention svc. coun. United Way, Atlanta, 1984-90, bd. dirs. 1995-04; mem. Met. Atlanta Mentors' Coun., 1992-95, One-to-one Atlanta Leadership Coun., 1993-96, St. Joseph's Mercy Found. Leadership Coun., 2005-; bd. adv. United Way 211, 1992-03, chair, chmn. St. Pius Catholic H.S., 2004-, Big Bros./Big Sisters, Atlanta, 2004-, United Way Cmty. Impact Coun., Atlanta, 2006-; vol. DeKalb, Atlanta, 1984-86; bd. dirs. Arrive Alive, Inc., Atlanta, 1987-91, Duke Law Alumni Assn., 2005-, Delta Sigma Phi Found., 2006-, Brother Rice HS, Chgo., 2006-; trustee Lawyers Comm. Civil Rights, 2001-, chair, Vasser Woolley Found., 2002-, Leadership Atlanta, 2001-, chair. MCK. Ga. Bar Assn. (state coun. 1983—), Atlanta Bar Assn., Federalist Soc., St. Thomas More Soc., Serra Internat., Commerce Club, Delta Mu Delta, Omicron Delta Epsilon. Roman Catholic.

Avocations: religion, literature, music. Office: Alston & Bird LLP 1201 W Peachtree St One Atlantic Ctr Atlanta GA 30309-3424 Office Phone: 404-881-7479. Office Fax: 404-881-7777. Business E-Mail: mike.petrik@alston.com.

**PETRILLO, LEONARD PHILIP,** lawyer, retired investment company executive; b. Toronto, Ont., Can., June 20, 1941; s. Philip and Bernice Petrillo; m. Linda née Hodgson; children: Larissa, Matthew, Stefanie, Ann-Marie, Karen. BSc, U. Toronto, 1964; LLB, Osgoode Hall Law Sch., Toronto, 1967. Bar: Ont. 1969. Ptnr. Robinson & Petrillo, 1969-79; corp. counsel Seel Enterprises Ltd., 1979-81; gen. counsel Toronto Stock Exch., 1981, v.p., gen. counsel, corp. sec., sec. to bd. dirs., 1984—2003; dir. OTG Fin. Inc., 2004—. Personal E-mail: leonard.petrillo@sympatico.ca.

**PETRINI, FABRIZIO,** computer scientist, researcher; b. Foligno, Italy, May 26, 1964; s. Mario DiGiacomo, June 22, 1997; 1 child, Alessandro DiGiacomo. Laurea in computer sci., U. Pisa, Italy, 1990, PhD in Computer Sci., 1997. Rsch. fellow Hewlett Packard Labs, Pisa, 1990-93, U. Oxford, U.K., 1999; mem. tech. staff Los Alamos (N.Mex.) Nat. Lab., 1999—2005; lab. fellow Applied Computer Sci. Group, Pacific N.W. Nat. Lab., Richland, Wash., 2006—. Grantee Enidata, 1990; Marie Curie fellowship European Cmty., 1997; recipient Excellence award Nat. Nuc. Security Agy., 2002, Def. Program award ASCI Q Integration Team, 2003. Mem. IEEE, Computer Soc. Office: Pacific Northwest Nat Lab Applied Computer Sci Group Richland WA 99352 Office Phone: 505-372-2874. Business E-Mail: fabrizio.petrini@pnl.gov.

**PETRINO, BOBBY,** college football coach; b. Helena, Mont. Mar. 10, 1961; m. Becky Schaff; children: Kelsey, Nick, Bobby, Katie. BS in Math, Phys. Edn., Carroll Univ., 1983. Quarterbacks coach Jacksonville Jaguars, 1999—2001; wide receiver, tight ends coach Weber State, 1987—88; offensive coord. Carroll Univ., 1985—86, Idaho Univ., 1989—91; quarterbacks coach Ariz. State, 1992—93; offensive coord. Nevada, 1994, Utah State, 1995—97, Louisville Univ., 1998, head coach, 2002—. Office: Athletics Dept Univ Louisville Louisville KY 40292 Office Phone: 502-852-7775. Business E-Mail: Bobby.Petrino@louisville.edu.*

**PETRINOVICH, LEWIS FRANKLIN,** psychologist, educator; b. Wallace, Idaho, June 12, 1930; s. John F. and Ollie (Steward) Petrinovich. BS, U. Idaho, 1952; PhD, U. Calif., Berkeley, 1962. Asst. prof. San Francisco State Coll., 1957-63; from assoc. to prof. SUNY, Stony Brook, 1963-68; prof. U. Calif., Riverside, 1968-91, chmn. psychology, 1968-71, 86-89, prof. emeritus, 1991—. Bd. dirs. Eastman Med. Products, Cymed Corp. Author: Understanding Research in Social Sciences, 1975, Introduction to Statistics, 1976, Human Evolution, Reproduction and Morality, 1995, Living and Dying Well, 1996, Darwinian Dominion: Animal Welfare and Human Interests, 1999, The Cannibal Within, 2000; editor: Behavioral Development, 1981, Habituation, Sensitization and Behavior, 1984; cons. editor Behavioral and Neural Biology, 1972-90, Jour. Physiol. and Comparative Psychology, 1980-82, Jour. Comparative Psychology, 1983-90. Bd. dirs. Friends of Big Band Jazz, 2001—. Fellow APA, Am. Psychol. Soc., Calif. Acad. Scis., Human Behavior and Evolution Soc., Western Psychol. Assn.; mem. Am. Ornithol. Union, Animal Behavior Soc., Sigma Xi Home: 415 Boynton Ave Berkeley CA 94707-1701 Office: U Calif Riverside Psychology Dept Riverside CA 92521-0001 Personal E-mail: lpetrin@aol.com.

**PETRO, JAMES MICHAEL,** state attorney general; b. Cleve., Oct. 25, 1948; s. William John and Lila Helen (Janca) P.; m. Nancy Ellen Bero, Dec. 16, 1972; children: John Bero, Corbin Marie. BA, Denison U., 1970; JD, Case Western Res., 1973. Bar: Ohio 1973, U.S. Dist. Ct. (no. dist.) Ohio 1974, U.S. Ct. Appeals (6th cir.), U.S. Supreme Ct. Spl. asst. U.S. senator W.B. Saxbe, Cleve., 1972-73; asst. pros. atty. Franklin County, Ohio, 1973-74; asst. dir. law City of Cleve., 1974; ptnr. Petro & Troia, Cleve., 1974-84; dir. govt. affairs Standard Oil Co., Cleve., 1984-86; ptnr. Petro, Rademaker, Matty & McClelland, Cleve., 1986-93, Buckingham, Doolittle & Burroughs, Cleve., 1993-95; auditor State of Ohio, 1995, atty. gen., 2003—. Mem. city coun. Rocky River, Ohio, 1977-79, dir. law, 1980; mem. Ohio Ho. of Reps., Columbus, 1981-84, 86-90; commr. Cuyahoga County, Ohio, 1991-95. Mem.: ABA, Ohio State Bar Assn., Cleve. Bar Assn. Republican. Methodist. Home: 1933 Lake Shore Dr Columbus OH 43204-4963 Office: 30 E Broad St Columbus OH 43266 Office Phone: 614-466-4320. Business E-Mail: jpetro@ag.state.oh.us.

**PETRO, LEE GEORGE,** lawyer; JD, Cath. U. Am., Washington, 1997. Atty. Pepper & Corazzini, LLP, Washington, 1997—99, Gardner, Carton & Douglas, Washington, 1999—2002; mem. Fletcher, Heald & Hildreth, PLC, Arlington, Va., 2002—. Editor: CommLaw Conspectus, Jour. Comm. Law and Policy. Trustee, asst. treas. FCBA Found., Washington, 2005—. Office: Fletcher Heald & Hildreth PLC 1300 N 17th St 11th Fl Arlington VA 22209 Office Phone: 703-812-0400. Business E-Mail: petro@fhhlaw.com.

**PETROCELLI, DANIEL M.,** lawyer; b. East Orange, NJ; m. Allison Petrocelli; 4 children. BS cum laude, U. Calif., Los Angeles, 1976; JD magna cum laude, Southwestern U., 1980. Bar: Calif. 1981, US Ct. Appeals (9th Cir.) 1981, US Dist. Ct. (Ctrl. and No. Districts. Calif.) 1981, US Supreme Ct. 1981, US Dist. Ct. (Dist. Colo.) 1998. Ptnr. (Century City office) O'Melveny & Myers LLP, LA, mem. policy com. Mem. The American Lawyer's Litigation Dept. of Yr.; nat. commentator on trials and other legal issues; spkr. to bus. groups, bar and judges associations, and citizen groups. Mem. Southwestern U. Law Review, 1978—79, editor-in-chief, 1979—80; author: Triumph of Justice: The Final Judgement on the Simpson Saga, 1998; contrb. articles to profl. jours. Named Litigator of Yr., Century City Bar Assn., honoree, Columbus Citizens Found., Alumnus of Yr., Southwestern U., Trial Lawyer of Yr., Malibu Bar Assn., San Diego Trial Lawyers Assn., So. Calif. Super Lawyer, LA Mag.; named one of Los Angeles' Top 50 Litigators, LA Bus. Jour., Lawyers of Yr., Calif. Lawyer. Mem.: Assn. of Bus. Trial Lawyers, State Bar Calif. (antitrust and unfair competition sects.), ABA (litigation sect. and corp. counsel com.), LA County Bar (antitrust and unfair competition sects.). Office: O'Melveny & Myers LLP 1999 Avenue of Stars 7th Fl Los Angeles CA 90067-6035 Office Phone: 310-246-6850. Office Fax: 310-246-6779. Business E-Mail: dpetrocelli@omm.com.

**PETROFF, LAURA R.,** lawyer; b. Cleve., July 7, 1955; BA, Denison U., 1977; JD, Vanderbilt U., 1980. Bar: Ill. 1980, U.S. Dist. Ct. Ill. (No. dist.) 1980, Calif. 1986, U.S. Dist. Ct. Calif. (Ctrl. So. and No. dist.) 1986, U.S. Ct. Appeals (9th cir.). Ptnr. Winston & Strawn LLP, L.A., 2000—, mng. ptnr. Chair, atty. compensation com. Winston & Strawn LLP, L.A., mem. exec. com., mem. diversity com. Gen. counsel PIHRA Found.; founding mem. Women Rainmakers Roundtable. Mem.: ABA (bd. dirs. pub. counsel law ctr.), State Bar Calif., L.A. County Bar Assn. (co-chair edn. com. 1989—91, mem. exec.com—1992). Office: Winston & Strawn LLP 333 S Grand Ave Los Angeles CA 90071-1543 Office Phone: 213-615-1736. Office Fax: 213-615-1750. E-mail: lpetroff@winston.com.

**PETRONE, JOHN R.,** retired music educator, composer; b. Youngstown, Ohio, Dec. 26, 1932; s. Angelo R. and Mary C. Petrone; m. Diane Rupple Petrone, Oct. 18, 1987; m. Margaret Adams Petrone, Apr. 12, 1958 (div. Feb. 20, 1986); children: Nicolette, Jennifer, John, Margaret, Michael, Susan. MusB, Youngstown Coll., 1958; MusM, Duquesne U., 1963; PhD in music composition, Conservatoire Musique La Lille, France, 1982. Cert. permanent tchg. cert. Ohio, 1980. Dir. music St. Mary's HS, Warren, Ohio, 1957—58; elem. music supr. Cath. Diocese of Youngstown (Ohio), 1958—60; music dir. Cardinal Mooney HS, Youngstown, Ohio, 1960—65; music dir., specialist Willoughby (Ohio) Eastlake Schs., 1965—84; ret. state of Ohio tchr., 1984; adj. faculty Ursuline Coll., Pepper Pike, Ohio, 1986—2005, ret., 2005. Composer (arranger and conductor): The Flight of Apollo Eleven, 1979; composer: (arranger, music dir.) Augustine, 1980, Mr. Jingeling, 1981, Care Bears, 1982; composer: NASA/Higbees Christmas show, 1983, (songs) Goin' Baroque, 1977, Haydn Seek, 1979, Disco-Tinued, 1979, Also Sprach What-

sisname. With spc. svcs. USAF, 1951—54, Korea. Recipient Outstanding Secondary Educator of Am., 1974, Martha Holden Jennings Scholar, 1975—76. Mem.: ASCAP, Am. Fedn. Musicians, Simfonia, Kappa Delta Pi, Phi Mu Alpha. Roman Catholic. Avocation: car racing. Home: 7325 Chardon Rd Kirtland OH 44094 Personal E-mail: J.R.Petrone@adelphia.net.

**PETRONE, WILLIAM FRANCIS,** pediatrician, microbiologist, corporate executive; b. Bklyn., Sept. 12, 1949; s. Arthur Carmen and Helen (Kenny) P.; m. Kathleen Anne Baron, Aug. 25, 1979; children: William Gaetano, Katherine Bridget, Jason Daniel. BA, U. Conn., 1972; MS, U. Mass., 1974; PhD, U. R.I., 1978; MD, U. South Ala., 1984. Diplomate Am. Bd. Pediatrics, Pediatric Emergency Medicine, Gen. Pediatrics. Sr. rsch. assoc. Coll. Medicine U. South Ala., Mobile, 1978-80; resident in pediat. Orlando (Fla.) Regional Med. Ctr., 1984-85, W.Va. Univ. Med. Ctr., 1985-87; emergency rm. physician, pediat. emergency svcs Mercy Hosp., Springfield, Mass., 1987—. Pres. Med. Simulation Software, Cmty. Pediat. Assoc. Contrb. articles on inflamation and white blood cell function to sci. jours. Fellow Am. Acad. Pediat., Am. Coll. Emergency Physicians; mem. AAAS, AMA, N.Y. Acad. Scis., Sigma Xi. Roman Catholic. Office: Mercy Hosp Emergency Unit PO Box 9012 Springfield MA 01102-9012

**PETRONELLA, MICHAEL A.,** publishing executive; b. NJ; BS in Acctg., Rider U., MBA. Joined as acct. Dow Jones & Co., 1974, sr, accountant, 1980—81, acctg. supr., 1981—84, acctg. mgr., 1984—88, budget dir., 1988—93, pres., Dow Jones Indexes/Ventures NYC, 1997—. Mem. supervisory bd. STOXX Ltd. Office: Dow Jones & Co 1 World Financial Ctr 200 Liberty St New York NY 10281

**PETROPOULOS, EVANGELOS,** former health institute director, educator, researcher; b. Athens, Greece, Jan. 14, 1935; arrived in U.S., 1965; s. Anastassios P. and Metaxia P. Petropoulos; m. Panayota E. Tzela, Nov. 12, 1964; children: Anna, Anastassios. MD, U. Athens, 1959, PhD in Exptl. Medicine, 1964; PhD in Endocrinology, U. Calif., San Francisco, 1970; MD (hon.), Med. U. Sofia, Bulgaria, 2003. Spl. NIH fellow U. Calif., San Francisco, 1968—73; attending physician in endocrinology Evangelinos Med. Ctr., Athens, 1973—75; prof., head dept. physiology U. Zimbabwe Med. Sch., Harare, 1975—82, prof., dean, 1982—85, prof. physiology, 1986—88; dir. Inst. Internat. Health, prof. physiology Mich. State U., E. Lansing, 1988—2002, dir., prof. emeritus, 2003—. Mem. com. regional office Africa WHO, Brazzaville, Republic of the Congo, 1982—85; mem. com. Commonwealth Secretariat, London, 1984—85; cons. African health policies World Bank, Washington, 1991. Contbr. articles and monographs to profl. jours. Lt. Med. Corp. Greek Air Force, 1960—63. Grantee, NIH, 1968, 1972, 1994, 1996, 1999, 2001; Internat. fellow in health, Kellogg Found., 1986—90. Mem.: NY Acad. Scis., Am. Physiol. Soc. Christian Orthodox. Achievements include research in etiology of Balkan endemic nephropathy in Bulgaria, Serbia and Romania. Avocations: classical music, church chanting, farming, underwater fishing, history of medicine. Home: 11 Nichols Ln Peabody MA 01960 Office: Inst Internat Health Mich State U B-301 W Fee Hall East Lansing MI 48824-1315

**PETROS, RAYMOND LOUIS, JR.,** lawyer; b. Pueblo, Colo., Sept. 19, 1950; BS, Colo. Coll., 1972; JD, U. Colo., 1975. Bar: Colo. 1975. Jud. clk. to Justice Paul V. Hodges Colo. Supreme Ct., Denver, 1975-77; assoc. Bermingham, White, Burke & Ipsen, Denver, 1977-78; from assoc. to ptnr. Hall & Evans, Denver, 1978-81; ptnr. Kirkland & Ellis, Denver, 1981-86; mem. Holme, Roberts & Owen, Denver, 1986-96, Petros & White, LLC, 1996—. Contbr. articles to profl. jours. Bd. dirs. Rocky Mountain Poison Control Found., Denver, 1988-94. Office: Petros & White LLC 730 Seventeenth St Ste 820 Denver CO 80202-3518

**PETROSKI, HENRY,** engineering educator, writer; b. NYC, Feb. 6, 1942; s. Henry Frank and Victoria Rose (Grygrowych) P.; m. Catherine Ann Groom, July 15, 1966; children: Karen Beth, Stephen James. B Mech. Engring., Manhattan Coll., 1963, DP (hon.), 2003; MS, U. Ill., 1964, PhD, 1968; DSc (hon.), Clarkson U., 1990; DHL (hon.), Trinity Coll., Hartford, Conn., 1997; DSc (hon.), Valparaiso U., 1999. Registered profl. engr., Tex.; chartered engr., Inst. of Engrs. of Ireland. Instr. U. Ill., Urbana, 1965-68; asst. prof. U. Tex., Austin, 1968-74; engr. Argonne (Ill.) Nat. Lab., 1975-80; assoc. prof. civil engring. Duke U., Durham, NC, 1980-87, prof., 1987-93, Aleksandar S. Vesic prof., 1993—, prof. history, 1995—, chmn. dept. civil and environ. engring., 1991-2000, dir. grad. studies, 1981-86. Author: To Engineer is Human, 1985, Beyond Engineering, 1986, The Pencil, 1990, The Evolution of Useful Things, 1992, Design Paradigms, 1994 (Best Book award in engring., Am. Assn. U. Presses, 1994), Engineers of Dreams, 1995, Invention by Design, 1996, Remaking the World, 1997, The Book on the Bookshelf, 1999, Paperboy, 2002, Small Things Considered, 2003, Pushing the Limits, 2004, Success Through Failure, 2006; writer, presenter: documentary To Engineer is Human, 1987, columnist: Am. Scientist, 1991—, ASEE Prism, 2000—. Fellow NEH, 1987-88, Nat. Humanities Ctr., 1987-88, Guggenheim fellow, 1990-91; recipient Outstanding Engring. Grad. award Manhattan Coll., 1992, Alumni award for disting. svc. Coll. Engring. U. Ill. at Urbana-Champaign, 1994, Washington award Western Soc. Engrs., 2006. Fellow ASCE (Civil Engring. History and Heritage award 1993), ASME (Ralph Coats Roe medal 1991), Am. Acad. Arts and Sci., Am. Philos. Soc., Inst. Engrs. Ireland, NAE, Soc. History Tech., The Moles (hon.), Sigma Xi, Tau Beta Pi. Office: Duke U Sch Engring Durham NC 27708-0287 Office Phone: 919-660-5203. Business E-Mail: petroski@duke.edu.

**PETROV, ALEXANDER ALEXANDROV,** research scientist, educator; b. Sofia, Bulgaria, Dec. 29, 1969; s. Alexander Simeonov Petrov and Olga Nikolova Petrova; m. Petya Ivanova Vakarelska-Petrova, Aug. 15, 1999; 1 child, Victoria Alexander Petrova. MSc, Sofia U., 1995; PhD, New Bulgarian U., 1998. Postdoctoral rschr. Carnegie Mellon U., Pitts., 1999—2001, U. Calif., Irvine, 2001—05, U. Colo., Boulder, 2005—06; asst. prof. Ohio State U., Columbus, 2006—. Author: articles in peer-reviewed jours. Mem.: Vision Scis. Soc., The Psychonomic Soc., Cognitive Sci. Soc. Avocation: Aikido. Office: 200B Lazenby Hall 1827 Neil Ave Columbus OH 43210 Office Phone: 614-292-1123. Personal E-mail: apetrov1969@alexpetrov.com.

**PETROV, ANDREI YURIEVICH,** mechanical engineer, researcher; s. Yuri Vasilievich Petrov and Tamara Ivanovna Petrova; m. Margarita Vladimirovna Semenova; 1 child, Dmitry Andreevich. MME, Tech. U., Moscow, 1985, PhD in Tech. Sci., 1997. Engr. ORGRES Co., Moscow, 1986—91; sr. rsch. scientist Moscow (Russia) Power Inst. Tech. U., 1991—2001; rsch. assoc. Oak Ridge (Tenn.) Nat. Lab., 2001—. Recipient Hon. Mention Tech. Poster award, Ann. Internat. Pitts. Coal Conf., 2002, Appreciation cert., U.S. Dept. Energy, 2002, 2003, 2004, 2005, 2006; grantee, Internat. Sci. Found., 1995. Mem.: ASME, Am. Soc. Heating, Refrigerating, and Air-Conditioning Engrs., Internat. Assn. Properties of Water and Steam (grantee 1997). Achievements include research in characterization and definition of real environment inside steam turbines. Personal E-mail: petran4444@yahoo.com.

**PETROV, IVAN,** physicist, materials scientist; b. Shumen, Bulgaria, Sept. 6, 1949; s. Georgi Petrov and Russanka Petrova; m. Vania Petrova, May 22, 1950; 1 child, Georgi. MSc in Physics, Sofia U., Bulgaria, 1974; PhD in Physics, Bulgarian Acad. Sci., Sofia, 1985. Rsch. prof. Bulgarian Acad. of Scis., Sofia, 1986—89; vis. prof. U. Ill., Urbana, 1989—91; vis. prof. surface engring. Sheffield Hallam U., Sheffield, England, 2000—; adj. prof. materials sci. U. Ill., Urbana, 1998—; prin. rsch. scientist Frederick Seitz Materials Rsch. Lab., 1998—. Dir. Ctr. for Microanalysis Materials, Urbana, 1998—. Contbr. over 180 rsch. articles in peer rev. jours. Recipient Dept. of Energy Sustained Excellence Rsch award, US Dept. Energy, 1996; fellow, Am. Vacuum Soc. Mem.: Microscopy Soc. Am., Materials Rsch. Soc. (symposium organizer). Office: U Ill 104 South Goodwin Ave Urbana IL 61801 Home Fax: 217-244-2278. Personal E-mail: petrov@uiuc.edu.

**PETROVIC, BOJAN,** nuclear engineer, educator; b. Zagreb, Croatia, 1955; arrived in U.S., 1991; s. Gajo and Asja Petrovic; m. Senka Petrovic, 1976; children: Nada, Sonja. BSc in Theoretical Math., U. Zagreb, Croatia, 1979; MSc in Nuc. Engring., U. Zagreb, Croatia, 1981; PhD in Nuc. Engring., 1995. Rsch. staff Rudjer Boskovic Inst., Zagreb, Croatia, 1979—91; rsch. asst. Pa. State U., U. Pk., 1992—95, rsch. faculty, 1995—99; sr. scientist Westinghouse Electric Co., Pitts., 1999—2004, prin. scientist, 2004—05, fellow scientist, 2005—. Participant expert/specialist confs. Internat. Atomic Energy Agy., Vienna, 1988—; assoc. dir. Penn State Transport Theory Group, U. Pk., Pa., 1995—99; cons. in field, 1997—99; chair tech. program com. Internat. Conf. Advances in Nuc. Fuel Mgmt. III, Hilton Head, SC, 2003; author-presenter internat. confs. and symposia; guest editor Nuclear Technology, 2005; reviewer profl. jours. and confs., 1996—. Mem. editl. adv. bd.: Nuc. Tech., 2006—. Fellow, Internat. Atomic Energy Agy., 1986—87. Mem.: ASME (session organizer and chair 2000—06), ASTM (mem. sci./tech. program com. 1996—), Am. Nuc. Soc., Am. Nuc. Soc. Engring. Edn. (mem. 19.10 stds. com. 1993—, reviewer 1996—, mem.exec. com. reactor physics divsn., co-recipient Best Paper Reactor Physics Divsn. 1993, co-recipient Best Paper Math. and Computation Divsn. 1995). Office: Sci & Tech Dept Westinghouse Electric Co 1344 Beulah Rd Pittsburgh PA 15235-5068

**PETROVIC, KIMBERLY ANN,** nursing researcher, nursing educator; d. Joseph Felix and Janet Marie Petrovic. B in Biology, Wheaton Coll., Ill., 1994; M in Sociology, N.Mex. State U., Las Cruces, 1998; MSN, Vanderbilt U., Nashville, 2000; postgrad., U. Conn., Storrs. RN Oreg., cert. gerontological nurse practitioner, Oreg. Grad. student rschr. Oreg. Health and Scis. U., Portland, 2000—02; unit mgr., supr. geriatrics Crestview, Portland, 2002—03; supr., weekend mgr. Harborside Healthcare, West Hartford, Conn., 2003—. Program dir. Ctr. on Aging and Human Devel. U. Conn., Storrs, 2003—05, instr. gerontology dept. human devel. and family studies, 2004—, instr., faculty mem. Sch. Nursing, 2005—; rsch. asst. Ctr. for Devel. Disabilities U. Conn. Health Ctr., Farmington, 2003—05; geriatrics rschr. Hartford Hosp., Conn., 2004—; rsch. mentor geriatric nursing, 2005—; presenter in field. Co-author (with others): Physician Attitudes and Practices on Providing Care To Individuals with Intellectual Disabilities: An Exploratory Study, 2004, Complementary and Alternative Medicine for Older Adults with Intellectual Disabilities, 2004; co-author: Respite Care Manual, 2005; author: Nursing Care Management of Older Adults with HIV/AIDS and Chronic Depression, 2006; guest editor: Jour. Conn. State Med. Soc., 2004, reviewer: Potential N.C.L.E.X. (Nursing) Questions, 2005—. Named to, Conn. Geriatric Edn. Consortium; recipient Nat. Rsch. Svc. award in geriatric nursing, NIH, 2000—02; rsch. fellow, U. Conn. Dept. Human Devel. and Family Studies, 2006, Pauline Toner grantee, U. Conn. Sch. Nursing, 2006. Mem.: Conn. Geriatrics Soc., Nat. Coun. on Family Rels., Gerontol. Soc. Am. (campus rep. U. Conn. 2003—04), Am. Geriatrics Soc., Sigma Theta Tau. Avocations: running, pilates, travel, windsurfing, writing. Office: Dept Human Devel and Family Studies Sch Nursing Univ Conn Storrs CT 06269

**PETROVICH, DOROTHY,** elementary school educator; b. N.J., July 14, 1931; d. Nicholas and Freida (Kleva) Frantin; m. Walter Petrovich, Aug. 22, 1954; children: David, Amy. BS, Jersey City State Tchrs. Coll., 1953. Cert. Newspaper Inst. of Am., 1949, The Inst. Children's Lit., 1996. Tchr. Bd. Edn., Middletown, NJ, 1953-54; substitute tchr. various schs., 1954-70; remedial math. tchr. Monmouth Beach (N.J.) Bd. Edn., 1970-72, 1st-4th grade tchr., 1972-91, ret., 1991. Editorial asst. to Socialist Republic, winner writing awards, cons. to editorial bd: internat. mag. Mem. ACLU, N.J. Edn. Assn., NEA, Monmouth Beach Edn. Assn. (sec.-treas.). Home: 165 S Manor Ct Wall NJ 07719-3658 E-mail: Dorpet247@aol.com.

**PETROW, GEORGE J.,** lawyer; b. 1953; BA cum laude, Univ. Neb., Lincoln, 1976; JD, Univ. Utah, 1979. Bar: Calif. 1979, Utah 1980, Conn. 1983, NY 1988. Law clk. Hon. Bruce S. Jenkins, US Dist. Ct., Dist. of Utah, 1980—81; ptnr., securitization and structured fin. Sidley Austin Brown & Wood LLP, NYC, 1997—, now mng. ptnr. NYC office, and mem. mgmt. and exec. committees. Exec. editor Utah Law Rev., 1978—79. Mem.: ABA. Office: Sidley Austin Brown & Wood LLP 787 Seventh Ave New York NY 10019 Office Phone: 212-839-8700. Office Fax: 212-839-5599. Business E-Mail: gpetrow@sidley.com.

**PETROWSKI, JOE,** oil industry executive; BA in Econ. and Govt., Harvard Univ., 1976. Former pres., CEO Louis Dreyfus Energy Co. No. Am.; former exec. pres. Duke Louis Dreyfus; former pres., CEO Consolidated Natural Gas Energy Svcs.; mng. dir. JHP Assoc., LLP; pres., CEO Gulf Oil Am., 2005—. Contbr. articles to numerous profl. jours. Office: Gulf Oil 99 Everett Ave Chelsea MA 02150*

**PETRU, SUZANNE MITTON,** retired health care finance executive; b. Shawano, Wis., Sept. 26, 1947; d. William Wallace and Gertrude Priscilla Mitton; m. W. James Petru, Jan. 2, 1987. BSBA, Northwestern U., 1970, MBA, 1971. CPA, Ill., Wis. Diplomate Am. Coll. Healthcare Execs. Sr. acct. Arthur Andersen & Co., Chgo., 1971-77; v.p. fin. Thorek Hosp. and Med. Ctr., Chgo., 1977-82; sec./treas. La Grange (Ill.) Meml. Health Sys., 1982-85; v.p. fin. La Grange Meml. Hosp., 1982-85; audit prin. Deloitte & Touche (formerly Touche Ross & Co.), Chgo., 1985-88; sr. v.p. fin., treas. SSM Health Care Sys., St. Louis, 1988-95; pres. healthcare divsn. Am. Home Assurance Co. (subs. Am. Internat. Group, Inc.), 1995-96; v.p., CFO, treas. Group Health Plan (subs. Coventry Corp.), 1996-98; v.p. Petru Enterprises, Petru Internat., 1998—; sr. v.p. fin., CFO Rockford (Ill.) Health Sys., 2000—05; ret., 2005. Mem. investment com. Sisters of Charity Healthcare Sys., Cin., 1993-96, mem. fin. com., 1994-96; mem. assoc. bd. La Grange Meml. Hosp., 1988-95; advisor Jr. Achievement, 1971-76. Fellow Healthcare Fin. Mgmt. Assn. (bd. dirs. 1989-91, principles and practices bd. 1992-95, nat. matrix 1985-86, 88-89, pres., pres.-elect, sec., bd. First Ill. chpt. 1979-80, compliance officers forum adv. coun. 1998—, Follmer Bronze award 1982, Reeves Silver award 1985, Muncie Gold award 1988, Alice V. Runyan chpt. 1988); mem. Fin. Execs. Inst., Country Club at Legends (adv. bd. 1991-93), St. Louis Club (house com. 1991-95). Republican. Presbyterian. Avocations: golf, travel. Personal E-mail: spetru@gboalliance.com.

**PETRUCCI-SAMIJA, MARIA,** chemist; PhD in Inorganic Chemistry, McGill U., 1999. Chemist Lumenon Innovative Lightwave Tech., 2000—02; chemist, leader photonics team DuPont Experimental Station, 2002—. Named one of Top 100 Young Innovators, MIT Tech. Review, 2004. Office: DuPont Experimental Station 1007 Market St Wilmington DE 19898

**PETRUS, ROBERT THOMAS,** internet business owner, investor; b. Manchester, Conn., 1957; s. John Joseph and Geraldine Petrus; m. Laura Lee Waggoner, Nov. 22, 1986; children: Elizabeth Ashley, Nicholas Kent. BA with honors, Trinity Coll., Hartford, Conn., 1979. Mgmt. intern Aetna Life & Casualty Co., Hartford, 1979-82, sr. administr. data processing ops., 1982-85, cons. Tech. Ctr., 1985-90; pres. Omoo Distbn. Corp., Mansfield, Conn., 1990—; v.p. Cogitore, Inc., 1990—. Author: Get Organized!, 1991. Chmn. Conn. Youth for Pres. Ford, l976; com. mem. Big Bros.-Big Sisters, Hartford, 1982-83; loaned exec. Greater Hartford United Way-Combined Health Appeals Campaign, 1985. Recipient ofcl. citation Conn. Ho. of Reps., 1985. Mem. Phi Beta Kappa, Pi Gamma Mu, Mu Alpha Theta. Republican. Avocations: photography, golf, skiing. Office: ODI-Omoo Distbn Inc 27 Wormwood Hill Rd Ste 101 Mansfield Center CT 06250-1135 Office Phone: 866-687-6857. E-mail: odi@ibocity.com.

**PETRUSKI, JENNIFER ANDREA,** speech and language pathologist; b. Kingston, NY, Jan. 28, 1968; d. Andrew Francis and Judith (Cruger) Petruski. BS, SUNY, Buffalo, 1990, MSEd in Speech-Language Pathology, 1992. Cert. tchr. speech-hearing handicapped N.Y., lic. speech-lang. pathology N.Y., cert. of clin. competence. Speech-lang. pathologist Kingston (N.Y.) City Schs., 1992—, student rev. team facilitator, 2002; clin. practicum supr. SUNY, New Paltz, 1996—. Cooperating tchr. SUNY, New Paltz, 1995—2004; ind. contr. speech svcs. Ulster County, 1997; cooperating tchr. Coll. St. Rose, 1997, 2004; summer sch. tchr. New Paltz Sch. Dist., 2002. Mem.: NY State

Speech-Lang. and Hearing Assn., Am. Speech and Hearing Assn. (Continuing Edn. award 2004, 2006), Speech and Hearing Assn. Hudson Valley (corr. sec. 1995—2001, newsletter editor 1995—2002, membership com. 1995—2002, treas. 1997, pres. 1999—2000, nominating com. 1999—2000, membership chmn. 2000—02, legis. chmn. 2000—04, website adminstr. 2001—, historian 2001—, continuing edn. adminstr. 2002, program com. 2003, newsletter com. 2003—04), Bd. Regional Assn. Presidents (membership chair 2000—02, pub. info. chair 2003—04, Disting. Svc. award 2005). Home: PO Box 88 Hurley NY 12443 E-mail: jpetruski@aol.com.

**PETRUZZELLI, JULIE A.,** lawyer; b. Glen Ridge, NJ, Apr. 18, 1957; BS in Chemistry/Biochemistry, Brown Univ., 1979; JD, Univ. Va., 1982. Bar: NY 1983, DC 1989, US Patent & Trademark Office. Ptnr., head, intellectual property and tech. divsn. Venable LLP, Washington. Mem.: ABA, NY Bar Assn., Women's Bar Assn. DC, NY Patent, Trademark, and Copyright Law Assn., Am. Intellectual Property Law Assn. Office: Venable LLP 575 Seventh St NW Washington DC 20004 Office Phone: 202-344-4010. Office Fax: 202-344-8300. Business E-Mail: japetruzzelli@venable.com.

**PETRUZZI, CHRISTOPHER ROBERT,** business educator, consultant; b. Peoria, Ill., July 28, 1951; s. Benjamin Robert and Mary Katherine (Urban) P.; m. Georgina Sailer, June 20, 1992; 1 child, Lillian Caroline. BA, Wabash Coll., 1972; MBA, U. Chgo., 1974; PhD, U. So. Calif., 1983. Lectr. bus. U. Wis., Milw., 1975-77; cons. H.C. Wainwright, Boston, 1978-79; lectr. U. So. Calif., 1978-81; prof. bus. U. Pa., Phila., 1981-82; prof. acctg. NYU, 1984-89, Calif. State U., Fullerton, 1989—. Pres. ECON Investment Software, San Clemente, Calif., 1987-2000; pres. Euronet Securities Corp., N.Y.C., 2000-2001, Smart Excution LLC, 2001-. Earhart fellow, 1972-73. U. Chgo. fellow, 1974-76. Libertarian. Christian. Office: Ste 302B 629 Camino de los Mares San Clemente CA 92673 Home: 1527 Via Tulipan San Clemente CA 92673 Personal E-mail: chris@smex.com.

**PETRY, ALICE HALL,** scholar, educator, writer; b. Hartford, Conn., July 8, 1951; d. James B. and Elizabeth K. Hall. BS with highest honors, U. Conn., 1973; MA, Conn. Coll., 1976; PhD, Brown U., 1979. Asst. prof. English RISD, Providence, 1980-86, assoc. prof., 1986-92, prof., 1992—, head dept. English, 1993-95; chair, prof. dept. English So. Ill. U., Edwardsville, 1995—2001. Lectr. ArtsAm. program USIA, Japan, 1991; vis. prof. U. Colo., Boulder, 1987. Author: Genius in His Way: The Art of Cable's Old Creole Days, 1988, Fitzgerald's Craft of Short Fiction: The Collected Stories, 1920-1935, 1991, Understanding Anne Tyler, 1990, Critical Essays on Anne Tyler, 1992, Critical Essays on Kate Chopin, 1996, On Harper Lee: Essays and Reflections, 2007. Am. Coun. Learned Socs. sr. postdoctoral fellow, 1987-88; Fulbright scholar, Brazil, 1985. Avocation: travel. Office: So Ill U Dept English Edwardsville IL 62026-1431 Office Phone: 618-692-2060. E-mail: apetry@siue.edu.

**PETRY, RUTH VIDRINE,** retired principal; b. Eunice, La., Jan. 20, 1947; d. Adea and Ruth Alice (Fox) Vidrine; m. Carson Clinton Petry, June 19, 1976. BA, La. Coll., 1971; MEd, McNeese State U., 1984. Cert. Tchr. La. Tchr. jr. h.s. Jefferson Davis Parish, Jennings, La., 1970—72; tchr. h.s. St. Tammany Parish, Mandeville, La., 1972—73; Jefferson Parish, Gretna, La., 1973—81; tchr. jr. h.s. Acadia Parish, Crowley, La., 1981—90; tchr. lang. arts Crowley Jr. H.S., 1981—90; master tchr. assessor La. State Dept. Edn., Lafayette, 1990—91; tchr. Crowley Mid. Sch., 1991—94, instrnl. asst., 1994—95; exec. dir. Assoc. Profl. Educators of La., Baton Rouge, 1995—96; asst. prin. Rayne H.S., La., 1996—2001, prin., 2001—04, ret., 2004. Writing assessment coord. Crowley Jr. H.S., 1984-85, mem. faculty insvc. team, 1986-89, chmn. spelling bee, 1983-90, 92-93, co-chmn. interim self study Crowley Jr. H.S. So. Assn., 1985-86; mem. state selection com. for La. Tech. of Yr., Students of Yr., 1992-93; mem. Tchr. Evaluation Revision Panels, I, III, IV, 1992-93, Prin.'s Evaluation State Com., 1993; adj. prof. edn. La. State U., Eunive, 2002-04; presenter workshops in field. Co-sponsor Nat. Jr. Hon. Soc., 1984-90; mem. La. Gov.-Elect's Edn. Transition Team, 1991-92; mem. La. Goals 2000 steering com. on sch. governance and accountability, 1994-95, mem. sch. fin. commn., 1999-2000. Named Crowley Jr. High Tchr. of Yr., 1985-86. Mem. Assn. Profl. Educators La. (pres. Acadia chpt. 1988-92, dist. VII state assn. bd., 1990-91, state pres.-elect 1991-92, state pres. 1992-94), La. Assn. Prins., La. Assn. for Retarded Citizens, Delta Kappa Gamma (chpt. pres. 1988-90, state leadership scholar 1993). Republican. Baptist. Avocations: music, reading, sewing. Home: 206 Bruce St Lafayette LA 70503-6102 Personal E-mail: ruthpetry@msn.com.

**PETRYSHYN, WOLODYMYR V.,** retired mathematician; b. Murovane, Ukraine, Jan. 22, 1929; arrived in U.S.A., 1950; s. Vasyl and Maria Petryshyn; BA, Columbia U., 1953, MS, 1954, PhD, 1961. Postdoc. fellow NYU, 1961—64; assoc. prof. math. U. Chgo., 1964—67; prof. math. Rutgers U., New Brunswick, NJ, 1967—96, ret., 1996. Dir. Math.-Physics Sect. Shevchenko Sci. Soc., N.Y.C. Author: Approximation-Solrability of Nonlinear Functional and Differential Equations, 1993, Generalized Topological Degree and Semilinear Equations, 1995, Development of Mathematical Sciences in Ukraine, 2004. Recipient M. Krylov award, Acad. Scis. Ukraine, 1992; grantee, NSF, 1964—94. Mem.: Ukrainian Acad. Sci. in Kiev. Achievements include first to establishing a new branch of mathematics, the A-proper mapping theory. Home: 10 Jackson Drive Cranford NJ 07016

**PETSEV, DIMITER NIKOLOV,** chemistry professor; b. Sofia, Bulgaria, Jan. 13, 1962; s. Nikolai Dimitrov Petsev and Ivanka Markova Petseva; m. Tatiana Angelova Tsvetanova, Jan. 28, 1963; children: Nikolai Dimitrov, Nia Dimitrova Petseva. PhD, U. Sofia, 1996. Postdoctoral rschr. dept. chemistry Purdue U., West Lafayette, Ind., 1996—98; sr. rsch. assoc. Ctr. Materials Rsch. UAH, Huntsville, Ala., 1998—2003; rsch. asst. prof. dept. ChNE U N.Mem. Albuquerque, 2003—03, asst. prof. dept. ChNE, 2005—. Mem.: Am. Chem. Soc. Office: Dept ChNE U NMex 209 Farris Engineering Ctr Albuquerque NM 87131 Office Phone: 505-277-3221. Office Fax: 505-277-5433. Business E-Mail: dimiter@unm.edu.

**PETSONK, EDWARD LEE,** pulmonologist, researcher; s. Edward M and Julia Leopold Petsonk; m. Susan R Brown, June 18, 1983; children: Samuel B, Ann E. AB in physics, Cornell U., 1965—69; MD, McGill U., 1969—73. Cert. Am. Bd. of Internal Medicine, 1978, pulmonary diseases subspecialty Am. Bd. of Internal Medicine, 1980. Med. officer U.S. Pub. Health Svc., Indian Health Svc., Parker, Ariz., 1974—76, Nat. Inst. for Occupl. Safety and Health, Morgantown, W.Va., 1979—81; asst./assoc. prof. W.Va. U. Sch. of Medicine, 1981—86; sr. med. officer Nat. Inst. for Occupl. Safety and Health, Morgantown, 1986—; adj. prof. of medicine W.Va. U. Sch. of Medicine, 1998—. Capt. U.S. Pub. Health Svc., 1974—. Fellow: Am. Coll. Physicians. Office: Niosh 1095 Willowdale Rd Morgantown WV 26505 Office Phone: 304-285-5754.

**PETT, JOHN LYMAN,** banker; b. Erie, Pa., Dec. 7, 1948; s. Peter Paul and Dorothy (Rhoades) P. BS, Gannon U., 1971; MBA, DePaul U., 1977; postgrad., Harvard Bus. Sch., 1989. Asst dir. acctg. and adminstrn. Constrn. Engring. div. Continental Can Co., Chgo., 1974-77; comml. v.p. and lending officer Mfrs. & Traders Trust Co., Buffalo, 1977-79, unit mgr. Mid. Market Lending, 1979-84, exec. v.p., chief credit officer, 1984—. Mem., cons. Erie County Fiscal Res. Com., Buffalo, 1984-86. Capt. USMC, 1971-74. Mem. Robert Morris Assocs., Am. Bankers Assocs., Wanakah Country Club (Hamburg, N.Y.). Republican. Roman Catholic. Avocations: golf, running, reading.

**PETTENGILL, GORDON H(EMENWAY),** physicist, researcher; b. Providence, Feb. 10, 1926; s. Rodney Gordon and Frances (Hemenway) P.; m. Pamela Anne Wolfenden, Oct. 28, 1967; children: Mark Robert, Rebecca Jane. BS, MIT, 1948; PhD, U. Calif., Berkeley, 1955. Staff mem. Lincoln Lab. MIT, Lexington, 1954-63, 65-68, prof. planetary physics, dept. earth, atmospheric and planetary scis. Cambridge, 1971—2001, dir. Ctr. Space Rsch., 1984-90; assoc. dir. Arecibo (P.R.) Obs., 1963-65, dir., 1968-71. Served with inf., Signal Corps AUS, 1944-46. Decorated Combat Inf. badge; recipient

Magellanic Premium, Am. Philos. Soc., 1994. Fellow Am. Geophys. Union (Whipple award 1995, Charles A. Whitten award 1997); mem. AAAS, Am. Phys. Soc., Am. Astron. Soc., Internat. Astron. Union, Internat. Radio Sci. Union, Nat. Acad. Sci., Am. Acad. Arts and Sci. Achievements include pioneering several techniques in radar astronomy for describing properties of planets and satellites; discovering 59-day rotational period of planet Mercury. Office: MIT 77 Massachusetts Ave Rm 37-582D Cambridge MA 02139-4307

**PETTERCHAK, JANICE A.,** writer; b. Springfield, Ill., Sept. 15, 1942; d. Emil H. and Vera C. (Einhoff) Stukenberg; m. John J. Petterchak, Oct. 5, 1963; children: John A., Julie Gilmour, James. AA, Springfield Coll., 1962; BS, Sangamon State U., 1972, MA, 1982. Supr. hist. markers Ill. State Hist. Soc., Springfield, 1973-74, asst. exec. dir., 1985-87; curator photographs Ill. State Hist. Libr., Springfield, 1974-79, assoc. editor, 1979-83, rep. local history svcs., 1983-85, libr. dir., 1987-95. Author: Mapping a Life's Journey: The Legacy of Andrew McNally III, 1995, Jack Brickhouse: A Voice for All Seasons, 1996, Taming the Upper Mississippi, 2000; To Share: The Heritage, Legend and Legacy of Nathan Cummings, 2000, Out To Sea Again: A Naval Armed Guard in World War II, 2002, Lone Scout: W.D. Boyce and American Boy Scouting, 2003, Where Eagles Soar: A Brief History of Community Banking in Illinois, 2004, Historic Illinois, 2005; editor: Illinois History: An Annotated Bibliography, 1995; assoc. editor Ill. Hist. Jour.; contbr. articles to profl. jours. Grantee NEH, 1987-95 Mem. Ill. State Hist. Soc., Sangamon County Hist. Soc. (bd. dirs. 1991-94, 99-2002, 04—, v.p. 1996-97, pres. 1995-96). Home: 11381 Mallard Dr Rochester IL 62563-8011 E-mail: petterchak@biogwriter.com.

**PETTERS, ROBERT M.,** education educator; BA, U. Del., Newark, 1972; MS, PhD, NC State U., Raleigh, 1976. Postdoctoral rschr. Yale U., New Haven, 1976—78; asst. prof. Pa. State U., University Park, Pa., 1978—83; assoc. prof. NC State U., Raleigh, 1983—90, prof., 1990—. Basil O'Connor Starter Rsch. grant, March of Dimes. Mem.: AAAS, Genetics Soc. Am., Am. Assn. for Animal Sci., Assn. for Rsch. in Vision and Ophthalmology, Internat. Embryo Transfer Soc. Achievements include invention of hexaparental mouse; development of culture medium for early stage pig embryos; research in produced rhodopsin transgenic pigs as a model of retinitis pigmentosa. Office: NC State Univ Dept Animal Sci Raleigh NC 27695-7621 Office Phone: 919-515-4021.

**PETTERSEN, KEVIN WILL,** investment company executive; b. Yonkers, N.Y., July 4, 1956; s. Kjell Will and Marilyn Ann (Stevens) Pettersen; m. Mary Elizabeth Murphy, Aug. 30, 1981; children: Kelly, Elizabeth, Erin. Diploma academia, Chaminade, Mineola, N.Y., 1974; BA in Econs., SUNY, Stony Brook, 1978. Buyer JC Penney Co., N.Y.C., 1979-82; nat. sales mgr. Randa Corp., Inc., N.Y.C., 1982-83; dir. sales Wemco, Inc., N.Y.C., 1983-86; mng. dir., sr. v.p. D.H. Blair & Co., Inc., N.Y.C., 1986-89; exec. v.p. Brean Murray, Foster Securities, Inc., N.Y.C., 1989-90; v.p., br. mgr., corp. officer A.G. Edwards and Sons, Inc., Glen Cove, N.Y., 1990—. Mem. pres. coun. A. G. Edwards, mem. Million Dollar Club, mem. chmn.'s coun., 1998; mem. exec. coun. Oppenheimer Funds Group. Active Oyster Bay Supr.'s Adv. Com. Crime, 1993—95; basketball coach girls team Cath. Youth Orgn., 1998—2006; del. Rep. Planning Com.; bd. dirs. Harbour Green L.I. Assn., 1990—94, pres., 1991. Recipient Outstanding Character award, Chaminade, 1974. Mem.: Chaminade Wall St. Assn., St. Rose of Lima Father's Guild, Soc. of the Friendly Sons of St. Patrick, Chaminade Torch Club, Green Harbour Beach Club (bd. dirs. 1994—98, treas. 1999). Republican. Roman Catholic. Avocations: golf, skiing, boating. Home: 85 Biltmore Blvd Massapequa NY 11758-8142 Office: AG Edwards and Sons Inc 51 Glen St Glen Cove NY 11542-2738 Office Phone: 516-656-5566. Business E-Mail: kevin.pettersen@agedwards.com.

**PETTERSEN, KJELL WILL,** securities trader, consultant; b. Oslo, June 19, 1927; came to U.S., 1946, naturalized, 1957; s. Jens Will and Ragna O. (Wickstrom) P.; m. Marilyn Ann Stevens, Aug. 16, 1952; children: Thomas W., Maureen, Kevin W., Maryann, Kathleen. Student, Zion Theol. Sch., 1945—49, N.Y. Inst. Finance, 1955—56. Mgr. A.M. Kidder & Co., N.Y.C., 1954-64; sr. v.p., sec., dir. Halle & Stieglitz, Fillor Bullard Co., Inc., 1964-73; sr. v.p., dir. mktg. Parrish Securities, Inc., N.Y.C., 1973-74; cons. Loeb, Rhoades & Co., N.Y.C., 1974-79; mng. dir. Prudential Securities, N.Y.C., 1979-89; pres. Arbitration Recovery Cons., Marco, Fla., 1992-93; vice chmn. Noddings Investment Group, Inc., Oakbrook Terrace, Ill., 1993-95; mem. City Coun., Marco Island, Fla., 1997—2002, chmn., 2001—02. Dir. Ski for Light Inc., Mpls., Creative Arts Rehab. Ctr. Inc., N.Y.C. Dem. candidate N.Y. State Assembly, Nassau County, 1962; past dir. Guadalupe Ctr., Marco YMCA; pres. Quest for Peace Internat.; co-chmn. Marco Island Celebration 2000. Mem. Nat. Assn. Security Dealers (bd. arbitrators), N.Y. C. of C., Norwegian-Am. C. of C. (dir. Guadalupe Ctr.), Scandinavian Found., Bankers Club of Am., Norwegian Club (N.Y.C.), Rotary. Home: 350 Rockhill Ct Marco Island FL 34145-3860 Personal E-mail: marcokjell@aol.com.

**PETTERSEN, THOMAS MORGAN,** accountant, corporate financial executive; b. Poughkeepsie, NY, Nov. 9, 1950; s. Olsen Thomas and Reva Frances (Palmer) P. BS, U. Albany, 1973. CPA NY. Sr. acct. Arthur Andersen and Co., N.Y.C., 1973-76; sr. ops. auditor Gulf and Western Inc., N.Y.C., 1977, fin. analyst, 1978; adminstr. auditing NBC, N.Y.C., 1979, mgr. auditing Burbank, Calif., 1980, dir. auditing, 1981-88, dir. acctg. systems and ops. analysis, 1988-90; v.p. fin. and adminstrn. Data Dimensions, Inc., Culver City, Calif., 1991-92; cons. Westwood One, Inc., Culver City, 1992-93; CFO Computer Image Sys., Inc., Torrance, Calif., 1993-97; dir. corp. fin. DeCrane Aircraft Holdings, Inc., El Segundo, Calif., 1997-2000; bus. cons., 2000—. Mem. AICPA, Fin. Execs. Internat. Republican. Roman Catholic. Avocations: sports, travel. Home: 217 1st Pl Manhattan Beach CA 90266 6502

**PETTEWAY, SAMUEL BRUCE,** college president; b. Fayetteville, N.C., July 18, 1924; s. Walter Bernard and Margaret Maysie (Cole) P.; m. Eleanor Glenn Sugg, Nov. 27, 1948; children: Margaret Petteway Small, Samuel Bruce. BS, N.C. State U., 1949, MEd, 1966, EdD, 1968. Gen. mgr. Homeowners Ins. and Realty Co., 1960-63; engring. tech. dept. chmn., dean occupational and transfer programs, dir. evening programs Lenoir County Community Coll., 1963-68; pres. Coll. of the Albemarle, Elizabeth City, NC, 1968-75, N.C. Wesleyan Coll., Rocky Mount, 1975-86; br. mgr. Sherwin Williams, 1953—60; first class radio engr. Radio WFTC-AM, 1949—53. Prof. Va. Poly. Inst. and State U., 1973-75, East Carolina U., 1994-99; pres. Philanthropic Cons., Inc., Raleigh, 1986-96; sec. Coll. Mgmt. Svcs., Inc., Raleigh, N.C., 1989; lic. amateur radio operator, 1992—. Pres. chpt. Am. Cancer Soc., 1960-61, Boys' Club Lenoir County, 1987-91, Westminster Homeowners assn., 1997; bd. dirs. Rocky Mount Coll., 1979-80, Triangle East, Inc., 1985-86, Cypress Glen Retirement Home, chmn. 1996; chmn. deferred giving com. N.C. Meth. Found., 1979-86; chmn. coun. on ministries 1st United Meth. Ch., Rocky Mount, 1980-81, Westminster United Meth., 1989-90, chmn. bd. trustees, 1994-99, chmn. adminstrv. bd., 2001-03; chmn. bd. trustees Art Edn. Found., 1980; mem. Nash County Bd. Health, 1985-86; bd. trustees United Meth. Retirement Homes, Inc., 1996-99; treas. Meth. Home for Children, 1997-2002. With USN, 1943—46, with USNR, 1946—51. Named Tar Heel of Week News and Observer, 1975, Today's Outstanding N.C. Citizen WNCT-TV, 1975; NSF fellow U. Ill., 1963 Mem. Nat. Assn. for Hosp. Devel., N.C. Assn. Colls. and Univs., N.C. Conf. United Meth. Ch. (chmn. bd. trustees 1979-97), Nat. Soc. Fund Raising Execs. (cert.), Rocky Mount C. of C. (bd. dirs. 1980-84), Rotary (scholarship com. dist. 7730 1995-2004), Phi Kappa Phi, Theta Alpha Phi. Clubs: Benvenue Country, Galaxy Social; Kinston Country. Lodges: Rotary (pres. 1980-81, bd. dirs. Kinston chpt. 1988-92). Republican. Office: 708 Westminster Ln Kinston NC 28501-2770 Personal E-mail: bpetteway@cox.net.

**PETTIBON, RAYMOND,** video artist; b. Tucson, June 10, 1957; BA, UCLA, 1977. One-man shows include Semaphore Gallery, NYC, 1986, Feature Gallery, NYC, 1989, 90, 93, Richard/Bennett Gallery, LA, 1990, 91, Robert Berman Gallery, LA, 1991, Galerie Rudiger Schottle, Munich, 1991, Massimo de Carlo Arte Contemprana, Milan, Italy, 1991, N.A.M.E. Gallery, Chgo., 1991, Feature Gallery, NYC, 1991, Galerie Marc Jancou, Zurich,

Switzerland, 1992, Galerie Metropol, Vienna, Austria, 1992, 94, Esther Schipper Galerie, Cologne, Germany, 1992, Matrix Gallery, U. Calif. Berkeley, 1992, Air de Paris, Nice, France, 1992, Univ. Galleries, Ill. State U., Normal, 1993, Regen Projects, LA, 1993, 95, 98, Jack Hanley Gallery, San Francisco, 1993, Galerie Beaumont, Luxembourg, 1994, Galeria Ramis Barquet, Garza, Mex., 1994, Ynglingagatan, Stockholm, Sweden, 1995, 14/16 Verneuil, Paris, 1995, Contemporary Fine Arts, Berlin, 1995, 98, Galeria Massimo De Carlo, Milan, 1995, Kunsthalle Bern, Switzerland, 1995, David Zwirner Gallery, NYC, 1995, 97, Tramway, Glasgow, Scotland, 1996, Taka Ishii Gallery, Tokyo, 1996, Meyer Kainer, Vienna, 1998, The Renaissance Soc., Chgo., 1998, The Drawing Ctr., NYC, 1999, Phila. Mus. Art, 1999, Galerie Meyer Kainer, Vienna, 1999; exhibited in group shows at Whitney Mus. Am. Art, NYC, 1997-98, 98-99, Sudwestdeutsche Landesbank, Stuttgart, Germany, 1997, Galerie Tanya Rumpff, Haarlem, The Netherlands, 1998, 11 Duke Street Ltd., London, 1998, The Parrish Art Mus., Southampton, NY, 1998, Laguna Art Mus., 1999, Austin Mus. Art, 1999, David Swirner, NY, 2000, Whitechapel Art Gallery, London, 2001, plots laid thick, MACBA, Barcelona, Spain, 2002, Am. Short Stories, Mus. Contemporary Art, North Miami, 2003, New Work, David Zwirner, NY 2004, Contemporary Fine Arts, Berlin, Germany, 2005, and others; group exhibitions include Richard Heller Gallery, Santa Monica, Calif., 1996, Whitney Biennial, Whitney Mus. Am. Art, 1998, 2004, Contemporary Arts Mus., Houston, 2001, Inst. Contemporary Art, London, 2002, State of the Art, The Surf Gallery, Laguna Beach, Calif., 2003, Michael Kohn Gallery, LA, 2003, Subway Series: The New York Yankees and the American Dream, Bronx Mus. Art, NY, 2004, Paper, Patricia Faure Gallery, Santa Monica, Calif., 2004. Recipient Awards Painting, Sculpture, Prinmaking, Photography, & Craft Media, Louis Comfort Tiffany Found., 1991, Wolfgang-Hahn-Prize, Ludwig Mus., Cologne, Germany, 2001, Buskbaum Award, Whitney Mus. Am. Art, 2004.

**PETTIBONE, DENNIS LYNN,** history professor; b. Takoma Park, Md., Aug. 6, 1941; s. Marion Mark and Ruth Leona (Nicholas) Pettibone; m. Carol Jean Nelson, June 12, 1966; children: Lori Lynn Pettibone Futcher, Teresa Jean Pettibone Strout. BA, La Sierra U., Riveside, Calif., 1962; MA, Loma Lima U., 1966; PhD, U. Calif., Riverside, 1979. Tchr. So. Calif. Conf. SDA, Glendale, 1962—64, Potomac Conf. SDA, Staunton, Va., 1966—68, Orangewood Acad., Garden Grove, Calif., 1968—72; instr. Atlantic Union Coll., South Lancaster, Mass., 1972—74; tchr. Potomac Conf. SDA, Staunton, Va., 1975—78, Rocky Mountain Conf. SDA, Denver, 1979—82; adj. prof. Columbia Coll., Aurora, Colo., 1980—88; prof. history So. Adventist U., Collegedale, Tenn., 1988—. Author: His Story in Our Time, 1997, Century of Challenge: The Story of Southern College, 1992. Mem.: Immigration and Ethnic History, Am. Soc. Ch. History, Am. Hist. Assn. Office: So Adventist U PO Box 370 Collegedale TN 37315 Office Phone: 423-236-2741.

**PETTIBONE, PETER JOHN,** lawyer; b. Schenectady, NY, Dec. 11, 1939; s. George Howard and Caryl Grey (Ketchum) P.; m. Jean Kellogg, Apr. 23, 1966; children: Stephen, Victoria. AB summa cum laude, Princeton U., 1961; JD, Harvard U., 1964; LLM, NYU, 1971. Bar: Pa. 1965, D.C. 1965, N.Y. 1968, U.S. Supreme Ct. 1974, Russia (fgn. legal cons.) 1995. Lectr. Heidelberg (Fed. Republic Germany) U., 1965-67; assoc. Cravath, Swaine & Moore, N.Y.C., 1967-74, Lord Day & Lord, Barrett Smith N.Y.C., 1974-76, ptnr. N.Y.C. and Washington, 1976-94, Patterson, Belknap, Webb & Tyler LLP, N.Y.C. and Moscow, 1994-99, Hogan & Hartson LLP, N.Y.C. and Moscow, 2000—. Pres. 1158 Fifth Ave. Corp., N.Y.C., 1991-94; pres. North Ferry Co., Shelter Island, N.Y., 1987-90; bd. dirs., vice-chmn. N.Y. State Facilities Devel. Corp., N.Y.C., 1983-89. Editor USSR Legal Materials, Columbia U., 1990-92. Trustee, treas. Hosp. Chaplaincy Inc., N.Y.C., 1980-86, Civitas, N.Y.C., 1984-92; mem. Coun. Fgn. Rels., 1993—; trustee Union Chapel, Shelter Island, N.Y., 1990—, CEC Internat. Ptnrs., 1996-2002; bd. dirs., vice chmn. Geonomics Inst., Middlebury, Vt., 1991-98; mem. vestry Ch. of Heavenly Rest, 1987-93; mem. Nat. Adv. Coun. Harriman Inst. Columbia U., 1996—; mem. Russia com. Episcopal Diocese of N.Y.; bd. dirs. Transatlantic Ptnrs. Against AIDS. Capt. U.S. Army, 1965-67, Heidelberg, Germany. Mem. ABA, Assn. Bar City NY (chmn. com. on CIS affairs 1991-94), US-USSR Trade and Econ. Coun. Inc. (US co-chmn. legal com. 1980-92), US-Russia Bus. Coun. (bd. dirs.), Soc. of Cin., Anglers Club NYC, NY Yacht Club, Shelter Island Yacht Club, Moscow Country Club, Amateur Ski Club NY (pres. 1980-82), Canterbury Choral Soc. (pres. 1983-84), Internat. Tax and Investment Ctr. (bd. dirs.), Phi Beta Kappa. Avocations: Home: 1158 5th Ave New York NY 10029-6917 also: 10 Wesley Ave Shelter Island Heights NY 11965 Office: Hogan & Hartson LLP 875 3rd Ave New York NY 10022 Office Phone: 212-918-3510. Business E-Mail: pjpettibone@hhlaw.com.

**PETTIGREW, CAROLYN LANDERS,** academic administrator, minister; b. Columbus, Ohio, Sept. 30, 1945; d. Wayman and Mary Gerldine (Lambert) Landers; m. Grady L. Pettigrew, Jr. Jan. 27, 1968; children: Dawn Karima, Grady Landers. BSc in Edn., Ohio State U., 1967; MDiv, Meth. Theol. Sch., Delaware, Ohio, 1987; postgrad., Washington Theol. Union, 1991—, United Theol. Sch., Dayton, Ohio. Ordained to ministry United Ch. of Christ, 1988; lic. speech and hearing therapist, Ohio. Youth min., dir. Christian edn. 1st Congl. Ch., Columbus, 1983-86; assoc. chaplain Grant Med. Ctr., Columbus, 1987-90; ednl. asst. to acad. dean for MA in alcohol and drug abuse ministry and continuing edn. Meth. Theol. Sch., 1990-94. Trustee United Ch. of Christ House, Chautauqua, N.Y., 1990—, Chautauqua Inst. Arts, 1990-99; chmn. new clergy orientation Met. Area Ch. Bd., Columbus, 1990-91, co-convenor drug abuse task force; sec., tchr. gifted children's program Ohio Wesleyan U.; speaker in field; faculty Ea. Union Bible Coll., 1998—; planning team U.S. Atty. Gen. Drug Abuse Task Force, 1990-94. Compiler, author: African American Spirituality: A Bibliography, 1991. Mem. women's bd. Martin Luther King Ch. for Performing Arts, Columbus, 1987—; mem. docent alumni group Columbus Mus. Arts; mem. women's agenda on human svcs. Ohio Gov.'s Task Force, Columbus, 1990—; mem. Chgo. Conf. Spiritual Renewal Task Force; exec. bd. United Ch. Christ, Cleve., 1997—. Recipient 11 Kudos, Grant Med. Ctr., 1987-90, Humanitarian award Columbus chpt. Alpha Kappa Alpha, 1990. Mem. Women's Theol. Group, Cen. S.E. Assn. United Ch. of Christ (chair dept. Christian edn. 1985-90), Jr. League Columbus, Zora Lit. Club (founder, convenor), Ladies of Lambda. Office: Meth Theol Sch Delaware OH 43015-0931 Home: 1780 Halleck Pl Columbus OH 43209-3224

**PETTIGREW, DAWN KARIMA,** writer; d. Grady L. Jr. and Carolyn (Landers) Pettigrew. BA, Harvard U., 1992; MFA, Ohio State U., 1996. Corr. News from Indian Country, Hayward, Wis., 1995—, Whispering Wind Mag., Folsom, La., 1998—; writer-in-residence Western Carolina U., Cullowhee, NC, 2002—. Author: (novels) The Way We Make Sense, 2002, The Marriage of Saints, 2006; co-author Children Learn What They Read, 2003; author: (CD) The Worship of Angels. 2006. Active The Northeasterns, Columbus, Ohio, 1996—, Assoc. Writing Programs, 2000—, Ladies Bapt. Assn., Cherokee, NC, 2001—. Mem.: Native Am.Music Assn., Wordcraft Cir. Native Writers and Storytellers, Native Writers Cir. of the Am., Native Am. Journalists Assn. Baptist. Avocations: beading, singing, travel.

**PETTIGREW, GRADY GIL LANDERS,** biology professor; b. Columbus, Ohio; s. Grady Lee Pettigrew and Carolyn Landers-Pettigrew. MS in Biology, Ctrl. Mo. State U., Warrensburg, 2000. Biology instr. Miami-Dade Coll., Fla., 2002—. Avocations: creative writing, travel, photography, birding, hiking. Office: Miami-Dade Coll InterAm Campus 627 SW 27th Ave Miami FL 33135 E-mail: gpettigr@mdc.edu.

**PETTIGREW, L. EUDORA,** retired academic administrator; b. Hopkinsville, Ky., Mar. 1, 1928; d. Warren Cicero and Corrye Lee (Newell) Williams; children: Peter W. Woodard, Jonathan R. (dec.). MusB, W.Va. State Coll., 1950; MA, Ohio So. Ill. U., 1964, PhD, 1966; PhD honoris causa. U. Pretoria, South Africa, 2002, Holy Family Coll., 2002, Western Conn. State U., 2004. Music/English instr. Swift Meml. Jr. Coll., Rogersville, Tenn. 1950-51; music instr., librarian Western Ky. Vocat. Sch., Paducah, 1951-52; music/English instr. Voorhees Coll., Denmark, SC, 1954-55; dir. music and recreation therapy W.Ky. State Psychiatric Hosp., Hopkinsville, 1956-61;

research fellow Rehab. Inst., So. Ill. U., Carbondale, 1961-63, instr., resident counselor, 1963-66, coordinator undergrad. ednl. psychology, 1963-66, acting chmn. ednl. psychology, tchr. corps instr., 1966; asst. prof. to assoc. prof. dept. psychology U. Bridgeport, Conn., 1966-70; prof., chmn. dept. urban and met. studies Coll. Urban Devel. Mich. State U., East Lansing, 1974-80; assoc. provost, prof. U. Del., Newark, 1981-86; pres. SUNY Coll. at Old Westbury, 1986-98. Cons. for rsch. and evaluation Hall Neighborhood House Day Care Tng. Project, Bridgeport, 1966-68, U.S. Ea. Regional Lab., Edn. Devel. Ctr., Newton, Mass., 1967-69; coordinator for edn. devel., 1968-69; cons. Bridgeport Public Schs. lang. devel. project, 1967-68, 70; Lansing Model Cities Agy., Day Care Program, 1971; U. Pitts., 1973, 74, Leadership Program, U. Mich. and Wayne State U., 1975, Wayne County Pub. Health Nurses Assn. 1976, Ill. State Bd. Edn., 1976-77; assoc. prof. U. Bridgeport, 1970, Ctr. for Urban Affairs and Coll. of Edn., Mich. State U., East Lansing, 1970-73; program devel. specialist Lansing Public Schs. Tchr. Corps program, 1971-73; coord. workshop Conflict Resolution The Woman's Role in Our World, 4th Internat. UN Conf. on Women, Beijing, China, 1995; lectr. in field; condr. workshops in field; guest spkr. Internat. Conf. on The New Role of Higher Edn. in the Context of an Ind. Palestinian State, An-Najah Nat. U., Nablus, Palestine, 1996. Tv/radio appearances on: Black Women in Edn, Channel 23, WKAR, East Lansing, 1973, Black Women and Equality, Channel 2, Detroit, 1974, Women and Careers, Channel 7, Detroit, 1974, Black Women and Work: Integration in Schools, WITL Radio, Lansing, 1974, others; editor: Universities and Their Role in World Peace, 2003; contbr. articles to profl. jours. Mem. exec. com. UN Non Govtl. Orgns. Dept. Public Info., 2004; mem. bd. YWCA, New Castle County, 2005-. Recipient Diana award Lansing YWCA, 1977, Outstanding Profl. Achievement award, 1987, award L.I. Ctr. for Bus. and Profl. Women, 1988, Educator of Yr. 100 Black Men of L.I., 1988, Black Women's Agenda award, 1988, Woman of Yr. Nassau/Suffolk Coun. of Adminstrv. Women in Edn., 1989, Disting. Ednl. Leadership award L.I. Women's Coun. for Equal Edn. Tng. and Employment, 1989, L.I. Disting. Leadership award L.I. Bus. News, 1990, Disting. Black Women in Edn. award Nat. Coun. Negro Women, 1991; named Outstanding Black Educator, NAACP, 1968, Oustanding Woman Educator, Mich. Women's Lawyers Assn. and Mich. Trial Lawyers Assn., 1975, Disting. Alumna, Nat. Assn. for Equal Opportunity in Higher Edn., 1990, Woman of Yr., Nassau County League of Women Voters, 1991, Disting. Alumna So. Ill. U., 1997, N.Y. State Senate resolution of commendation, 1998; Elected to Achievers Hall of Fame: Long Island Bus. and Profl. Women's Orgns., 2001 Mem. AAAS, Nat. Assn. Acad. Affairs Administrs., Internat. Assn. Univ. Pres. (exec. com., spl. adviser to pres.), Phi Delta Kappa.

**PETTIGREW, PIERRE S.,** Canadian government official; b. Quebec City, Can., Apr. 18, 1951; BA in Philosophy, U. Que., Trois-Rivières, 1972; M in Philosophy in Internat. Rels., Balliol Coll., Oxford, 1976. Dir. polit. com. NATO Assembly, Brussels, 1976-78; exec. asst. to the leader Que. Liberal Party, 1978-81; fgn. policy advisor Prime Min. Can., 1981-84; v.p. Samson Bélair Deloitte & Touche Internat., Montreal, 1985-95; co-chair First Nat. Forum on Can. Internat. Rels., 1994; min. internat. coop., min. responsible for La Francophonie Can. Ho. of Commons, 1996, min. human resources devel. Can., 1996-99, min. for internat. trade, 1999—2003; min. health, 2003—04; min. intergovernmental affairs, 2003—04; min. ofcl. languages, 2003—04; min. foreign affairs Canada, 2004—. Author: The New Politics of Confidence, 1999; contbr. articles to profl. jours. Office: House of Commons Rm 507 Confederation Bldg Ottawa ON Canada K1A 0A6 also: Foreign Affairs Canada 125 Sussex Dr Tower A Ottawa ON Canada KIA OG2

**PETTIGREW, RODERIC I.,** federal agency administrator, radiologist, researcher; BS in Physics cum laude, Morehouse Coll., 1972; MS in Nuc. Medicine and Engring., Rensselaer Poly. Inst., 1973; PhD in Applied Radiation Physics, MIT, 1977; MD, U. Miami, 1979. Intern and resident internal medicine Emory U.; resident nuc. medicine U. Calif. San Diego; clin. rsch. scientist Picker Internat.; Robert Wood Johnson Found. fellow Emory U., 1985; prof. radiology, medicine (cardiology) and bioengineering Emory U. Sch. Medicine, Atlanta, dir. Ctr. for MR Rsch.; dir. Nat. Inst. Biomedical Imaging and Bioengineering NIH, Bethesda, Md., 2002—. Named Most Disting. Alumnus, U. Miami, 1990; recipient Benjamin E. Mays Award, 1989; Merrill scholar, Morehouse Coll., Whitaker Harvard-MIT Health Sci. scholar, MIT. Fellow: Am. Inst. Med. and Biomedical Engring., Internat. Soc. Magnetic Resonance in Medicine, Am. Coll. Cardiology, Am. Heart Assn.; mem.: Phi Beta Kappa. Achievements include research in dynamic three-dimensional imaging of the heart using magnetic resonance; co-developer first computer software package specifically designed for cardiac imaging using MRI. Office: Nat Inst Biomedical Imaging and Bioengineering 6707 Democracy Blvd Bethesda MD 20892 Office Phone: 301-496-8859. Office Fax: 301-480-0679. E-mail: pettigrr@mail.nih.gov.*

**PETTIGREW, THOMAS FRASER,** social psychologist, educator; b. Richmond, Va., Mar. 14, 1931; s. Joseph Crane and Janet (Gibb) Pettigrew; m. Ann Hallman, Feb. 25, 1956; 1 child, Mark Fraser. AB in Psychology, U. Va., 1952; MA in Social Psychology, Harvard U., 1955, PhD, 1956; DHL (hon.), Governor's State U., 1979. Rsch. assoc. Inst. Social Rsch., U. Natal, Republic South Africa, 1956; asst. prof. psychology U. N.C., 1956-57; asst. prof. social psychology Harvard U., Cambridge, Mass., 1957-62, lectr., 1962-64, assoc. prof., 1964-68, prof., 1968-74, prof. social psychology and sociology, 1974-80; prof. social psychology U. Calif., Santa Cruz, 1980-94, rsch. prof. social psychology, 1994—; prof. social psychology U. Amsterdam, 1986-91. Adj. fellow Joint Ctr. Polit. and Econ. Studies, Washington, 1982—; adv. bd. women's studies program Princeton (N.J.) U., 1985-2001; vis. prof. West-faelishe Wilhelms-U., Germany, 1993, Philipps U., Germany, 2000, Schiller U., Germany, 2002; disting. vis. prof. Flinders U., Australia, 1997; sr. fellow Rsch. Inst. for the Comparative Study of Race and Ethnicity, Stanford U., 2001-02, mem. German govt. adv. com. Intercultural Conflicts and Social Integration, 2003-2006 Author: (with E.Q. Campbell) Christians in Racial Crisis: A Study of the Little Rock Ministry, 1959, A Profile of the Negro American, 1964, Racially Separate or Together?, 1971; (with Frederickson, Knobol, Glazer and Veda) Prejudice, 1982; (with Alston) Tom Bradley's Campaigns for Governor: The Dilemma of Race and Political Strategies, 1988, How to Think Like a Social Scientist, 1996; editor: Racial Discrimination in the United States, 1975, The Sociology of Race Relations: Reflection and Reform, 1980; (with C. Stephan & W. Stephan) The Future of Social Psychology: Defining the Relationship Between Sociology and Psychology, 1991; mem. editorial bd. Social Issues, 1954-59, Social Psychology Quarterly, 1977-80; assoc. editor Am. Sociol. Rev, 1963-65; adv. bd. Integrated Edn, 1963-84, Phylon, 1965-93, Edn. and Urban Society, 1968-90, Race, 1972-74, Ethnic and Racial Studies, 1978-95, Rev. of Personality and Social Psychology, 1980-85, Cmty. and Applied Social Psychology, 1989-2004, Individual and Politics, 1989-93, Jour. Ethnic and Migration Studies, 1994—, 21st Century Afro Rev., 1994—; contbr. articles to profl. jours. Chmn. Episcopal presiding Bishop's Adv. Com. on Race Relations, 1961-63; v.p. Episcopal Soc. Cultural and Racial Unity, 1962-63; mem. Mass. Gov.'s Adv. Com. on Civil Rights, 1962-64; social sci. cons. U.S. Commn. Civil Rights, 1966-71; mem. White House Task Force on Edn., 1967; mem. nat. task force on desegregation policies Edn. Commn. of States, 1977-79; trustee Ella Lyman Cabot Trust, Boston, 1977-79; Emerson Book Award com. United Chpts. Phi Beta Kappa, 1971-73; com. status black Ams. NRC, 1985-88. Guggenheim fellow, 1967-68, Sr. Scientist fellow NATO, 1974, Ctr. Advanced Study in Behavioral Scis. fellow, 1975-76, Sydney Spivack fellow Am. Sociol. Assn., 1978, Netherlands Inst. Advanced Study fellow, 1984-85, Bellagio (Italy) Study Ctr. resident fellow, Rockefeller Found., 1991; Fulbright New Century scholar, 2003-04; recipient Kurt Lewin Meml. award Soc. for Psychol. Study Social Issues, 1987, (with Martin) Gordon Allport Intergroup Rels. Rsch. prize, 1988, Faculty Rsch. award U. Calif., Santa Cruz, 1988, (with Tropp) Gordon Allport Intergroup Rels. Rsch. prize, 2003. Fellow APA (Weiss meml. lectr., 2003), Am. Sociol. Assn. (coun. 1979-82); mem. Soc. Psychol. Study Social Issues (coun. 1962-66, pres. 1967-68, Disting. Svc. award 1998), Soc. Exptl. Social Psychology (Disting. Scientist award 2002), European Assn. Social Psychology. Home: 524 Van Ness Ave Santa Cruz CA 95060-3556

**PETTIJOHN, FRED PHILLIPS,** retired publishing executive; b. Balt., May 11, 1917; s. Fred and Adelaide Josephine (Phillips) P.; m. Elaine Wilson, Dec. 7, 1946; children: Fred Phillips, Mark Clay. BAE, U. Fla., Gainesville, 1941. Sports editor Tallahassee Democrat, 1946-53; with Fort Lauderdale News, 1953-82, exec. editor, 1960-68, gen. mgr., 1968-77, editl. dir., from 1977; 1st v.p. Gore Newspapers Co., from 1960; now cons. Bd. dirs. Salvation Army, 1975-79, v.p., 1979; bd. dirs. Fla. Council 100, 1976-78. With AUS, 1943—45. Recipient Disting. Service award Fla. Press Assn., 1976, Disting. Alumnus award U. Fla., 1977; inducted into Fla. Newspaper Hall of Fame, 1990. Mem. Fla. Press Assn. (pres. 1963-64, 69-70), AP Mng. Editors (bd. dirs. 1964-66), So. Newspaper Pubs. Assn., Lauderdale Yacht Club, Tower Club, Sigma Delta Chi, Theta Chi. Democrat. Presbyterian. Home: 1564 Marion Ave Tallahassee FL 32303-5831

**PETTINELLA, EDWARD,** real estate company executive; Degree, State U., Geneseo; MBA, Syracuse U., NY. With Rochester (N.Y.) Cmty. Savings Bank, 1980—97; pres. N.Y. Divsn. Charter One Bank, 1997—2001; exec. v.p. Charter One Fin., Inc., 1997—2001, Home Properties, Rochester, 2001—04, CEO, 2004—. Bd. dir. Home Properties, State U. Geneseo, Geneseo Found.; bd. dir. Sch. Bus. Syracuse U. Bd. dir. United Way, Rochester, YMCA, Rochester. Office: Home Properties 850 Clinton Square Rochester NY 14604

**PETTINELLA, NICHOLAS ANTHONY,** corporate financial executive; b. Little Falls, NY, Sept. 9, 1942; s. Nicholas and Rose (Zuccaro) P.; m. Nancy C. Whitehouse, Oct. 28, 1978; children: Albert J., Michael A. BS, Bentley Coll., 1968; MBA, Babson Coll., 1975; postgrad., Harvard U., 1979, Stanford U., 1983. CPA. Mass. auditor Coopers & Lybrand, Boston, 1970-76; treas. Courier Corp., Lowell, Mass., 1976-80; controller corp. ops. Digital Equipment Corp., Maynard, Mass., 1980-81; dir. fin. Intermetrics, Inc., Burlington, Mass., 1981-83, sr. v.p. fin., chief fin. officer, treas., 1983-98; sr. v.p. fin., treas. Averstar, Inc., Burlington, 1999-2000; v.p., CFO IronBridge Networks, Inc., Lexington, Mass., 2000—01; CFO ideaLogix, Inc., Framingham, Mass., 2001—02, Accordare, Arlington, Mass., 2002—04; exec. v.p., CFO Harmony Line, Inc., Cambridge, Mass., 2004—. Bd. dirs. The Computer Mus., Boston, treas. 1988-98, bd. overseers 1997-99, Mus. Scis., Boston, 1999-2003. Chmn. fin. com. Town of Ashland, Mass., 1980-82. Served with U.S. Army, 1964-66. Mem. Fin. Execs. Inst., AICPA, Inst. Mgmt. Accts., Mass. Soc. CPAs, Treas. Club Boston, Pacioli Soc. Roman Catholic. Home: 141 South St Ashland MA 01721-2263

**PETTIS-ROBERSON, SHIRLEY MCCUMBER,** retired congresswoman; b. Mountain View, Calif. d. Harold Oliver and Dorothy Susan (O'Neil) McCumber; m. John J. McNulty (dec.); m. Jerry L. Pettis (dec. Feb. 1975); children: Peter Dwight Pettis, Deborah Pettis Moyer; m. Ben Roberson, Feb. 6, 1988. Student, Andrews U., Berrien Springs, Mich., 1942—43, student, 1945, U. Calif., Berkeley, 1944—45; PhD (hon.), Loma Linda U., Calif., 2002. Mgr. Audio-Digest Found., LA, Glendale, 1958—61; sec. treas. Pettis, Inc., Hollywood, Calif., 1958-68; mem. U.S. Congress, Calif., 1975—79. Pres. Women's Rsch. Edn. Inst., 1979—80; bd. dirs. Lumbermens Mut. Ins. Co., Kemper Corp., Am. Motors, Am. Mfg. Co. Mem. Former Mems. Congress, 1988—, Pres.'s Commn. Arms Control Disarmament, 1982—85, Commn. Presdl. Scholars, 1990—93; chair bd. Loma Linda U. Children's Hosp. Found.; trustee U. Redlands, Calif., 1980—83, Loma Linda U. Med. Ctr., Calif., 1990—95, bd. mem. Mem.: Morningside Country Club (Rancho Mirage, Calif.).

**PETTIT, DONALD P.,** retired career officer; b. Apr. 20, 1955; m. Carol Pettit; 1 child. BEd., U. Miami, 1974; MA in Counseling, Pepperdine U., 1978. Enlisted aircraft electronics technician, 31st tactical fighter wing USAF, Homestead Air Force Base, Fla., 1968—72, advanced through grades to brig. gen., 1999; student Minuteman Missile Combat Crew Tng. Prog., Vandenberg AFB, Calif., 1974; minuteman combat crew mem., dep. flight comdr., comdr., and wing sr. standardization evaluator, 341st Strategic Missile Wing Malmstrom AFB, Mont., 1974—78; minuteman ops. evaluator 3901st Strategic Missile Evaluation Squadron, Vandenberg AFB, Calif., 1978-81; air staff tng. officer Office of the Vice Chief of Staff Hdqrs., Washington, 1981-82; planner, dir. ICBM requirements Hdqrs. Strategic Air Command, Offutt AFB, Nebr., 1982-84; student Air Command and Staff Coll., Maxwell AFB, Ala., 1984—85; missile ops. staff officer, then exec. officer, dir. ops. Hdqrs. USAF, Washington, 1985-87; strategic policy planner, the exec. officer to vice dir. Joint Staff, Washington, 1987-89, strategic plans and policy dir., 1987-89; comdr. 68th Strategic Missile Squadron, Ellsworth AFB, SD, 1989-91; aide-de-camp, comdr. in chief Strategic Air Command, Offutt AFB, Nebr., 1991-92; sr. contr., ops. dir. Hdqrs. U.S. Strategic Command, Offutt AFB, 1992-93; comdr. 341st Missile Wing, Malmstrom AFB, Mont., 1993-94; student Air War Coll., Maxwell AFB, Ala., 1994—95; chief nuclear ops. divsn., Ops. Directorate, the Joint Staff, Washington, 1995-97; dep. dir. plans and programs Hdqrs. AF Space Command, Peterson AFB, Colo., 1997-99; comdr., 45th Space Wing, dir., Eastern Range, dep., dept. def. mgr. for Manned Space Flight Support Patrick AFB, Fla., 1999—2002; ret., 2002. Defense Superior Service medal, Defense Meritorious Service medal with oak leaf cluster, Meritorious Service medal with two oak leaf clusters, Joint Service Commendation medal, Air Force Commendation medal, Combat Readiness medal

**PETTIT, DONALD R.,** astronaut, flight engineer, researcher; b. Silverton, Oreg., Apr. 20, 1955; married; 2 children. BSChemE, Oreg. State U., 1978; PhD in Chemical Engring., U. Ariz., 1983. Staff scientist Los Alamos Nat. Lab., Los Alamos, N.Mex., 1984—96, mem. synthesis group, slated with assembling the technology to return to the moon and explore Mars, 1990, mem. Space Station Freedom Redesign Team, 1993; mission specialist, Lyndon B. Johnson Space Ctr. with technical duties in the Astronaut Office Computer Support Branch NASA, Houston, 1996—. Projects included: Reduced gravity fluid flow and materials processing experiments aboard the NASA KC-135 airplane, atmospheric spectroscopy measurements on noctolucent clouds seeded from sounding rocket payloads, volcano fumarole gas sampling on active volcanos, investigated problems in the detonation physics applied to weapons systems; completed first space flight as NASA ISS science officer and flight engineer aboard the International Space Station, Expedition-6 (launched in the STS-113 Space Shuttle Endeavour and returned to Earth on Soyuz TMA-1), Nov. 23, 2002 to May 3, 2003, logged over 161 days in space and 2 EVAs (spacewalks) totalling 13 hours and 17 minutes. During the 5 1/2 months aboard the ISS, the crew worked with numerous US and Russian science experiments. Office: NASA Lyndon B Johnson Space Ctr Houston TX 77058

**PETTIT, FREDERICK SIDNEY,** metallurgical engineering educator, department chairman; b. Wilkes Barre, Pa., Mar. 10, 1930; s. Edwin Humes and Edith Mae (Barnecut) P.; m. Lou-Jean Mary Corso, Aug. 30, 1958; children: Frederick N., Theodore E., John C., Charles A. B in Engring., Yale U., 1952, M in Engring., 1960, D in Engring., 1962. Jr. engr. Westinghouse Electric Corp., Pitts., 1952-54; engr. Avco-Lycoming, Stratford, Conn., 1957-58; postdoctoral student Max Planck Inst. Phys. Chemistry, Gottingen, Fed. Republic Germany, 1962-63; sr. staff scientist Pratt & Whitney Aircraft Co., East Hartford, Conn., 1963-79; prof. metall.-material engring. dept., chmn. U. Pitts., Pa., 1979-88, prof., 1988—2006, prof. emeritus, 2006—, Harry S Tack prof. materials engring., 1992—; mem. adv. bd. Jour. Oxidation of Metals, Plenum Press, N.Y., 1975—. 1st lt USMC, 1954-57. NSF fellow, 1962-63 Mem. Metall. Soc. (program dir. 1982-83), Electrochem. Soc. (sec.-treas. high temperature materials div. 1979-83), Am. Soc. Metals, Materials Rsch. Soc. Roman Catholic. Home: 201 Ennerdale Dr Pittsburgh PA 15237-4026 Office: U Pitts 848 Benedum Hall Pittsburgh PA 15261-2208 Business E-Mail: pettit@engr.pitt.edu.

**PETTIT, GEORGE ROBERT,** chemist, educator, cancer researcher; b. Long Branch, NJ, June 8, 1929; s. George Robert and Florence Elizabeth (Seymour) P.; m. Margaret Jean Benger, June 20, 1953; children: William Edward, Margaret Sharon, Robin Kathleen, Lynn Benger, George Robert III. BS, Wash. State U., 1952; MS, Wayne State U., 1954, PhD, 1956. Tchg. asst. Wash. State U., 1950-52, lecture demonstrator, 1952; rsch. chemist E.I.

duPont de Nemours and Co., 1953; grad. tchg. asst. Wayne State U., 1952-53, rsch. fellow, 1954-56; sr. rsch. chemist Norwich Eaton Pharms., Inc., 1956-57; asst. prof. chemistry U. Maine, 1957-61, assoc. prof. chemistry, 1961-65, prof. chemistry, 1965; vis. prof. chemistry Stanford U., 1965; prof. chemistry Ariz. State U., 1965—, chmn. organic chemistry divsn., 1966-68, disting. rsch. prof., 1978-79, Dalton prof. medicinal chemistry and rsch., 1986—, Regent's prof. chemistry Ctr. Cancer Rsch., 1990—. Vis. prof. So. African. Univs., 1978; dir. Cancer Rsch. Lab., 1974-75, 2005, Cancer Rsch. Inst., 1975—; co-dir. Ariz. Prostate Cancer Task Force, 2000—; lectr. various colls. and univs.; cons. in field. Contbr. articles to profl. jours. Mem. adv. bd. Wash. State U. Found., 1981—85. With Res. USAF, 1949—53. Recipient Alumni Achievement award, Wash. State U., 1984. Fellow: Am. Inst. Chemists (Pioneer award 1989, Ariz. Gov.'s Excellence award 1996); mem.: Am. Soc. Oncology, Am. Assn. Cancer Rsch., Am. Soc. Pharmacognosy (Rsch. Achievement award 1995), Chem. Soc. London, Am. Chem. Soc. (mem. awards com. 1968—71, Guenther award in chemistry of natural products 1998), Phi Lambda Upsilon, Sigma Xi. Office: Ariz State U Ctr Cancer Rsch Tempe AZ 85287-2404

**PETTIT, GHERY DEWITT,** retired veterinary medicine educator; b. Oakland, Calif., Sept. 6, 1926; s. Hermon DeWitt Pettit and Marion Esther (St. John) Menzies; m. Frances Marie Seitz, July 5, 1948; children: Ghery St. John, Paul Michael. BS in Animal Sci., U. Calif., Davis, 1948, BS in Vet. Sci., 1951, DVM, 1953. Charter diplomate Am. Coll. Vet. Surgeons. Asst. prof. vet. surgery U. Calif., Davis, 1953-61; prof. vet. surgery Wash. State U., Pullman, 1961-91, prof. emeritus, 1991—. Mem. Wash. State Vet. Bd. Govs., 1981—88, chmn., 1987; vis. fellow Sydney U., Australia, 1977. Author/editor: Intervertebral Disc Protrusion in the Dog, 1966; co-author: Centennial History of the Washington State University College of Veterinary Medicine, 1999; cons. editorial bd. Jour. Small Animal Practice, Eng., 1970-88; mem. editorial bd. Compendium on C.E., Lawrenceville, N.J., 1983-86, editoral rev. bd. Jour. Vet. Surgery, Phila., 1984-86, editor 1987-92; contbr. articles to profl. jours., chpts. to books. Elder Presbyn. Ch., Pullman, 1967—. With USN, 1944—46. Recipient Norden Disting. Tchr. award Wash. State U. Class 1971, Faculty of Yr. award Wash. State U. Student Com., 1985. Mem.: AVMA, Am. Coll. Vet. Surgeons (recorder 1970—77, pres., chmn. bd. dirs. 1978—80), Kiwanis Internat., Am. Legion, Phi Kappa Sigma (chpt. advisor 1981—, internat. 2d v.p. 1993—98, internat. pres. 1998—2000), Phi Zeta, Sigma Xi. Republican. Avocations: camping, sailing.

**PETTIT, GHERY ST. JOHN,** electronics engineer; b. Woodland, Calif., Apr. 6, 1952; s. Ghery DeWitt and Frances Marie (Seitz) P.; m. Marilyn Jo Van Hoose, July 28, 1973; children: Ghery Christopher, Heather Kathleen. BS in Electrical Engring., Wash. State U., 1975. Nuclear engr. Mare Island Naval Shipyard, Vallejo, 1975-76; electronics engr. Naval Electronic Systems Engring. Ctr., Vallejo, 1976-79; sr. engr. Martin Marietta Denver Aerospace, 1979-83; staff engr. Tandem Computers Inc., Santa Clara, Calif., 1983-90, mgr. electromagnetic capability Cupertino, Calif., 1990-91, electromagnetic compatibility lead engr., 1991-95; electromagnetic compatibility engr. Intel Corp., Hillsboro, Oreg., 1995-96, Dupont, Wash., 1996—. Mem. U.S. tech. adv. group subcom. I, Spl. Com. on Radio Frequency Interferences subcom. Internat. Electrotechnical Commn.; mem. CISPR SC I, WG2, WG3 and WG4. Asst. cubmaster Boy Scouts Am., San Jose, Calif., 1985-86, cubmaster, 1986-88, ast. scoutmaster, 1988-90, scoutmaster, 1990-93. Mem. IEEE (sr.), Nat. Rsch. Coun. (bd. assessment of NIST programs 1999—2005), EMC Soc. (bd. dirs. 1999-2004, 2006—, v.p. commn. svcs. 2003—), Electromagnetic Capability Soc. (sec.-treas. Littleton, Colo. chpt. 1983, sec. Santa Clara Valley chpt. 1985-87, vice chmn. 1987-89, chmn. 1989-91, sec. Santa Clara Valley sect. 1991-92, treas. 1992-93, vice chmn. 1993-94, chmn. 1994-95), IEEE Electromagetic Capability Soc. (chmn. Seattle chpt. 1997-2000). Republican. Presbyterian. Avocations: flying, amateur radio, sailing. Office: Intel Corp 2800 Center Dr Dupont WA 98327-9773 Business E-Mail: ghery.pettit@intel.com.

**PETTIT, JOHN DOUGLAS, JR.,** management educator; b. Alice, Tex, Aug. 19, 1940; s. John Douglas and Vivian Iola (Beaman) P.; m. Suzanne McLeod, Aug. 23, 1964; children: Melanie Ann Wilson, David Bryant. BBA, U. North Tex., 1962, MBA, 1964; PhD, La. State U., 1969. Instr. mgmt. Miss. State U., Starkville, Miss., 1964-65; grad. asst. La. State U., Baton Rouge, 1965-67, instr. mgmt., 1967-68; asst. prof. bus. Tex. Tech. U., Lubbock, Tex, 1968-69; assoc. prof. mgmt. U. North Tex., Denton, Tex., 1969-78, prof. mgmt., 1978-95; chair excellence in free enterprise Austin Peay State U., Clarksville, Tenn., 1995-96; interim chair and prof. dept. info. and decision scis. U. Tex., El Paso, Tex., 2000-2001, vis. prof. Dept. Mktg. and Mgmt., 2005—, interim chmn., 2005—06. Bd. dirs. Capital Instnl. Svcs., Dallas and N.Y.C., mem. audit com., 2003—; cons. various orgns., 1969—98; mgr., co-owner Pettit's Cleaners/Hatters, Alice, 1992—96; vis. prof. mgmt. Wichita (Kans.) State U., 1994—95; vis. prof. Ecole Superieure de Commerce et de Mgmt., Poitier and Tours, France, 2002—03, U. Kuopio, Finland, 2003—04. Kuopio, Finland, 2002, Co-author: Business Communication: Theory and Application, 7th edit. 1993, Report Writing for Business, 10th edit. 1998, Lesikar's Basic Business Communication, 8th edit. 1999; mem. editl. bd. Organl. Comm. Abstracts, 1980-85; mem. editl. bd. Jour. Bus. Comm., 1987-90, mng. editor, 1990-94. Mem. choir Trinity Presbyn. Ch., Denton, 1985-2006; docent, Bass Performance Hall. Ft. Worth, 2006, usher, 2006; trainer, Metroport Meals on Wheels, Argyle, Tex., 2002-, driver, 2002-; actor, singer Denton Cmty. Theater Summer Prodn., 1988-95. Recipient Master's Degree award Chgo. Bd. Trade, 1963. Fellow Assn. Bus. Comm. (pres., 1st v.p., exec. dir., 1990-94); mem. Southwestern Fedn. Adminstrv. Disciplines (pres., v.p.), Acad. Mgmt., Denton Country Club (bd. dirs.), Blue Key Nat. Hon. Fraternity, Beta Gamma Sigma (hon.), Phi Kappa Phi (hon.), Delta Sigma Pi. Presbyterian. Avocations: music, tennis. Home: 9122 David Fort Rd Argyle TX 76226-2953 Business E-Mail: jpettit@utep.edu.

**PETTIT, JOHN W.,** health facility administrator; b. Detroit, Mar. 6, 1942; s. John W. and Clara (Schartz) P.; m. Kathleen Endres, Aug. 8, 1970; children: Julie, Andrew, Michael. BBA, U. Notre Dame, 1964; MBA, Mich. State U., 1974. CPA, Mich.; CFP, 2001. Acct. Ernst & Ernst, Detroit, 1964-67; chief acct. Detroit Inst. Tech., Detroit, 1967-69; controller, dir. adminstrn. & fin. Mich. Cancer Found., Detroit, 1969-80; chief adminstrv. officer Dana-Farber Cancer Inst., Boston, 1980-94; exec. v.p., chief oper. officer John Wayne Cancer Inst., Santa Monica, Calif., 1995-97; fin. cons. L.A., 1998—. Grant reviewer Nat. Cancer Inst., Bethesda, Md., 1979-94. Pres. advanced mgmt. program Mich. State U., 1978-79; mem. adv. bd. Arthritis Found. So. Calif. chpt., 1999—2004; mem. Town Meeting, Wellesley, Mass., 1991-94. Mem.: AICPA, Fin. Planning Assn. Avocations: sailing, woodworking, photography, music. Office: 21031 Ventura Blvd Ste 705 Woodland Hills CA 91364 Office Phone: 818-226-3838. E-mail: jwpettit@yahoo.com.

**PETTIT, LAWRENCE KAY,** university president; b. Lewistown, Mont., May 2, 1937; s. George Edwin and Dorothy Bertha (Brown) P.; m. Sharon Lee Anderson, June 21, 1961 (div. Oct. 1976); children: Jennifer Anna, Matthew Anderson, Allison Carol, Edward McLean; m. Elizabeth DuBois Medley, July 11, 1980 (div. Dec. 1988). BA cum laude, U. Mont., 1959; AM, Washington U., St. Louis, 1962; PhD, U. Wis., 1965. Legis. asst. U.S. Senate, 1959-60, 62; asst. & assoc. prof. dept. polit. sci. Pa. State U., 1964-67; assoc. dir. fed. rels. Am. Council Edn., Washington, 1967-69; chmn. dept. polit. sci. Mont. State U., 1969-72; adminstrv. asst. to gov. State of Mont., 1973; chancellor Mont. Univ. System, Helena, 1973-79; pvt. practice ednl. cons. Mont. State U., 1969-72; adminstrv. asst. to gov. State of Mont., 1973; chancellor Mont. Univ. System, Helena, 1973-79; pvt. practice ednl. cons. Mont., 1979-81; dep. commr. for acad. affairs Tex. Coordinating Bd. for Higher Edn., 1981-83; chancellor Univ. System of South Tex., 1983-86; chancellor (now pres.) So. Ill. U., Carbondale, Edwardsville, 1986-91, Disting. vis. prof., 1992; pres. Indiana U. Pa., 1992—2003, ret., 2003. Mem. adv. bd. S & T Bancorp., 1997-2003; mem. regional adv. bd. Nat. City Bank, 1997-99; bd. dirs. Ind. Healthcare Group. Author: (with H. Albinski) European Political Processes, 2d edit. 1974, (with E. Keynes) Legislative Process in the U.S. Senate, 1969, (with S. Kirkpatrick) Social Psychology of Political Life, 1972, (with J. Goetz and S Thomas) Legislative Process in Montana, 1975; mem. editl. bd. Ednl. Record, 1985-88. Mem. adv. bd. Leadership Ctr. Ams. 1988-90, Ill. Coalition, 1989-92; dem. primary candidate for 2d dist. U.S. Ho. of Reps., Mont., 1980; mem. Ill. Gov.'s Com. on Sci. and Tech., 1986-90; bd. dirs. Tex. Guaranteed Student Loan Corp., 1985-86, Reschini Found., 2003—; chmn. Ill.-Niigata Commn. on Edn. and Econ. Devel., 1990-92; chair bd. dirs. Nat. Environ. Edn. and Tng. Ctr., 1994-04; mem. adv. bd. Princeton Rev., 2003-04. U. Wis. fellow 1962-63, Vilas fellow U. Wis., 1963-64. Mem. AAUP (pres. Mont. conf. 1971-72), Nat. Assn. Sys. Heads (pres. 1991), Am. Coun. on Edn. (chmn. leadership commn. 1989-90, sr. fellow 1991-92), Am. Assn. Higher Edn., Am. Assn. State Colls. and Univs. (Disting. Svc. award 1991), Newcomen Soc., Duquesne Club Pitts., World Affairs Coun. Pitts., Pa. Soc. (life), Ind. Country Club, Rotary (Paul Harris fellow), Ind. C. of C. (bd. dirs. 1992-03), Sigma Chi (Significant Sig award 1988), Phi Kappa Phi. Episcopalian. Home: 209 Saddlebrook Dr Indiana PA 15701 Office Phone: 724-388-2543. Business E-Mail: lpettit@auxmail.iup.edu.

**PETTITT, JAY S.,** architect, consultant; b. Redford, Mich., Jan. 6, 1926; s. Jay S. and Florence Marian (Newman) P.; m. Ruth Elizabeth Voigt, June 21, 1947; children—J. Stuart, Laura Ellen, Patricia Lynn, Carol Ann B.Arch., U. Mich., 1951. Registered architect, Mich. Draftsman Frank J. Stepnoski and Son, Fond du Lac, Wis., 1951; project architect Albert Kahn Assocs., Inc., Detroit, 1951-62, chief archtl. devel., 1962-67, v.p., 1967-88, dir. architecture, 1975-88; archtl. cons. Beulah, Mich., 1988—. Active Jr. Athletic Assn. Redford, Mich., 1959-63; com. mem. Detroit Boy Scouts Am., 1960-65; supr. Benzonia Twp. Served with U.S. Army. 1943-46, ETO. Fellow AIA; mem. Mich. Soc. Architects (pres. 1967), Am. Arbitration Assn., Am. Assn. Hosp. Planning, Engring. Soc. Detroit, U. Mich. Pres.' Club Avocations: sailing, skiing. Office Phone: 231-882-4040. Personal E-mail: jaypettitt@bignetnorth.net.

**PETTITTE, ANDREW EUGENE (ANDY PETTITTE),** professional baseball player; b. Baton Rouge, June 15, 1972; m. Laura Pettitte, Jan. 9, 1993; children: Joshua Blake, Jared, Lexy Grace. Student, San Jacinto Coll., Tex. Pitcher N.Y. Yankees, Bronx, 1995—2003, Houston Astros, 2004—. Coauthor (with Bob Reccord, Mark Tabb): (autobiography) Strike Zone: Targeting a Life of Integrity & Purity, 2005. Mem. World Series championship team, 1996, 1998, 1999, 2000; named to Am. League All Star team, 1996, 2001 Office: Houston Astros PO Box 288 Houston TX 77001-0288*

**PETTY, BRIAN E.,** speech pathology/audiology services professional, opera singer, voice educator; b. Clay Ctr., Kans., Feb. 21, 1970; s. Bruce Alan and Bonnie Claire (Brandenburg) Petty; life ptnr. Christopher Scott Leedy. MusB, Okla. State U., 1992; MA, Ohio State U., 1994, MA, 1999. Speech path., clin. fellow Hennepin County Med. Ctr., Mpls., 1999—2000; speech-lang. pathologist Courage Ctr., Mpls., 2000—02; clin. speech-lang. pathologist, voice specialist U. Wisc., 2002—. Nominee Grammy award (as mem. of the Warland singers) for best choral recording, 2003. Mem.: Voice and Alaryngeal Speech Subcommittee. Democrat. Meth. Office: Univ Wisc Dept Surgery G3/225 CSC 600 Highland Madison WI 53792

**PETTY, GEORGE OLIVER,** lawyer; b. LA, Mar. 31, 1939; s. Hugh Morton and May (Johnson) P.; m. Sandra Diane Kilpatrick, July 14, 1962; children: Ross Morton, Alison Lee, Christopher Henry. AB, U. Calif., Berkeley, 1961; LLB, U. Calif., 1964. Bar: Calif. 1965. Eng. and Wales 1986, U.S. Supreme Ct. 1976. Atty. Huovinen & White, Oakland, Calif., 1967-69; counsel Bechtel Power Corp., San Francisco, 1969-83; prin. counsel Bechtel Ltd., London, 1983-86; gen. counsel Sun-Diamond Growers of Calif., Pleasanton, Calif., 1987-95; pvt. practice, 1995—96; gen. counsel Tone Bros. Inc., 1997—. Capt. U.S. Army, 1965-67. Mem. Calif. State Bar Assn., Alameda County Bar Assn., Eng. and Wales Bar Assn., Bar Assn. for Commerce, Fin. & Industry (Eng.), Middle Temple Inn. Office: ABF NAm Holdings Inc 8 California St 600 San Francisco CA 94111 Office Phone: 415-477-2800. E-mail: gopetty@aol.com.

**PETTY, JAMES ALAN,** mathematics professor, consultant; b. Dublin, Ind., Dec. 27, 1954; s. Orris Delmar and Blanche Irene Petty; m. Soranee Holasuit, May 17, 1980; 1 child, Krissada Holasuit Petty; m. Christy Foley, Feb. 18, 2001. BS in Math. and Econs., Ball State U., 1977, MS in Math., 1978; PhD, Purdue U., 1994. Instr. math./statistics U. Md.-Asia, Andersen AFB, Guam, 1990-94; tchr. educator Western Ky. U., Bowling Green, 1994-95; asst. prof. math. Ind.-Purdue U., Ft. Wayne, 1995-97; asst. prof. U. Tenn., Martin, 1997-00. V.p. mktg. FPA Ednl. Consulting, Martin, 1995-00. Contbg. author: Epistecybernetics, 1997; contbr. articles to profl. jours. Mem. Math. Assn. Am., Nat. Coun. Tchrs. Math., Navy League U.S., Psychology Math. Edn.-N.Am., Tenn. Assn. Math. Educators, Phi Delta Kappa (program coord. N.W. Tenn. chpt. 1998-00). Republican. Office: U Tenn 240 J Gooch Hl Martin TN 38238-0001 E-mail: jpetty@utm.edu.

**PETTY, M. S. MARTY,** publisher; b. St. Louis, Mo., Dec. 17, 1952; married; 2 children. BA in Journalism, Univ. Mo., 1975; MS in Mgmt., Hartford Grad. Ctr. (Rensselaer), 1989. Asst. mng. editor Kansas City Star and Times; mng. editor Hartford (Conn.) Courant, 1983—89, dc. exec. editor, assoc. pub., 1989, sr. v.p., gen. mgr.; pub., CEO Hartford (Conn.) Courant, 1997—2000; pres. St. Petersburg (Fla.) Times, 2000—, pub., 2004—. Trustee Poynter Inst. for Media Studies, Tampa Bay Newspapers Inc.; juror Pulitzer Prize awards; pres. Soc. of Newspaper Design, 1985; bd. dir. Wm. Randolph Hearst Found. journalism bd., 1987—89. Trustee Congressional Quarterly, Governing Mag., Fla. Trend Mag. Named a Woman of Distinction, Girl Scouts of Suncoast Coun., 2004; named Bus. Woman of Yr., Women's Coun., St. Petersburg Area C. of C., 2005. Mem.: Nat. Assn. Minority Media Executives, Newspaper Assn. Am. (diversity bd.), Am. Press Inst. (adv. bd.), Florida Press Assn (bd. dir.) Office: St Petersburg Times 490 1st Ave S Saint Petersburg FL 33701

**PETTY, MARGE D.,** state senator; b. Ft. Wayne, Ind., Feb. 26, 1946; children: Brandon, Megan. BS, Tex. Christian U., 1968; MEd, Kans. U., 1978; JD, Washburn U. Sch. Law, 1990. Tchr., 1968-69; mgmt. consultant, 1981—94; health educator, 1978-81; mem. City Council of Topeka, 1985-89; dep. mayor Topeka, 1986; mem. Kans. Senate, 1989—2000; dir. pub. affairs and consumer protection Kans. Corp. Commn., 2000—. Mem. Topeka Metro. Ballet, Chamber of Commerce, Mulvane Art Ctr. Episcopalian. Home: PO Box 4327 Topeka KS 66604 Address: 1500 SW Arrowhead Rd Topeka KS 66604-4027

**PETTY, PRISCILLA HAYES,** columnist, television producer; b. Nashville, Aug. 22, 1940; d. Anderson Boyd and Margaret Louise Hayes; m. Gene Paul Petty, Jan. 10, 1961; children: Eric, Damon, Boyd. BA in English, Vanderbilt U., 1962; postgrad., Lang. Inst., Dartmouth Coll., 1965. Cert. tchr. Ohio. Tchr. English Cin. Suburban Pub. Schs., 1962-65, head dept. English, tchr., 1971-79; newspaper columnist Cin. Enquirer, 1978-89; also syndicated newspaper columnist Gannett News Svc., Washington, 1982-89. Cons. Arthur Andersen & Co., 1981-82; writer United Western Corp., 1982; exec. producer, on camera interviewer national TV documentary, 1992; commentator nat. bus. TV show, 1992; pres., owner, Petty Comns. Prodns., producer Total Quality Tng. Tapes. speaker W. Edwards Deming Seminars; cons. in field. Author: History of a Boardsman (oral history), 1979, Under a Lucky Star: The Story of Frederick A. Hauck, 1986, What's in It for You and the Firm: CEOs and Presidents Look at Community Involvement. Mem. Cin. Coun. World Affairs; chmn. Cin. Media-Bus. Exch., 1983; founder, pres., bd. trustees Cin. Oral History Found., 1984—. Named Outstanding Tchr., Project Teach, Ohio Edn. Assn., 1978; recipient WICI Great Lakes Regional Communicators' award; Pulitzer Prize nominee for Harvard U. Bus. Rev. article. Mem. Women in Comms. (Outstanding Communicator of Yr. 1985), Oral History Assn., Ky. Profl. Journalist, Wyo. Woman's Club. Home: 229 Oliver Rd Cincinnati OH 45215-2638

**PETTY, RICHARD,** retired race car driver; b. Level Cross, N.C., July 2, 1937; s. Lee and Elizabeth T. P.; m. Lynda Owens, 1958; children: Kyle, Sharon, Lisa, Rebecca. Auto racer, 35 years; ret., 1992; owner Car # 43.

Actor(voice): (films) Cars, 2006. Mem. Pres.'s Coun. Fitness and Sport. Recipient Myers Bros. award Nat. Motorsports Press Assn., 1961, 67, 71, Excellence award NASCAR, 1987; named Grand Nat. Rookie of Year, 1959: Most Popular Driver in Grand Nat., 1962, 64, 68, 70, 74, 75, 76, 77, 78; Martini & Rossi Am. Driver of Year, 1971; Driver of Year Nat. Motorsport Press Assn., 1974-75; Driver of Quarter Century, 1991; inducted into N.C. Athletic Hall of Fame, 1973. Mem. Nat. Assn. Stock Car Auto Racing (7 time champion; Winston Cup grand nat. champion 1964, 67, 71, 72, 74, 75, 79) Achievements include entered 1015 Grand Nat. Races, winner 200, 1958-86, with 55 Superspeedway wins; winner Daytona 500, 1964, 66, 71, 73, 74, 79, 81; 1000th career Winston Cup start June 15, 1986 at Mich. Internat. Speedway; 500th consecutive start on Aug. 21, 1988 in Champion Spark Plug 500. Address: Petty Enterprises Inc 311 Branson Mill Rd Randleman NC 27317-8008*

**PETTY, SCOTT, JR.,** rancher; b. San Antonio, Apr. 10, 1937; s. Olive Scott and Edwina (Harris) P.; m. Marie Louise James, June 10, 1959 (dec. Dec. 1981); children: Joan Louise Petty, Susan Harris Arnim, Scott James; m. Eleanor Oliver, Apr. 30, 1983; children: Tim A. Weed, Richard Oliver Weed. BS in Petroleum Engring., U. Tex., 1960, MS in Petroleum Engring., 1961. Profl. engr. Tex., La. Asst. to pres. Petty Geophys. Engring., 1961-63, v.p., 1963-65; pres., exec. officer Petty Labs., 1965-67; pres., dir. Petty Geophys. Engring., 1967-73; exec. v.p. Petty-Ray Geophys., 1973-74; cons. Geosource Internat., 1974-76; chmn. bd. C.H Guenther & Son, Inc., San Antonio, 1982—. Mem. chancellor's coun. U. Tex., Austin, devel. bd., San Antonio; bd. dirs. Tex. and Southwestern Cattle Raisers, Ft. Worth, Nat. Cattleman's Beef Assn. Mem. Am. Assn. Petroleum Geologists, Assn. Profl. Engrs., Geologists & Geophysicists of Alberta, Geophys. Soc. Houston, Soc. Exploration Geophysicists, Soc. Petroleum Engrs., South Tex. Geol. Soc., Tex. Soc. Profl. Engrs., Explorers Club. Republican. Episcopalian. Home: 202 La Jara Blvd San Antonio TX 78209-4444 Office: Petty Ranch Co 711 Navarro St Ste 235 San Antonio TX 78205-1710 Office Phone: 210-225-6571.

**PETTY, THOMAS LEE,** internist, educator; b. Boulder, Colo., Dec. 24, 1932; s. Roy Stone and Eleanor Marie (Kudrna) P.; m. Carol Lee Piepho, Aug. 7, 1954; children: Caryn, Thomas, John. BA, U. Colo., 1955, MD, 1958. Intern Phila. Gen. Hosp., 1958-59; resident U. Mich., 1959-60, U. Colo. Denver, 1960-62, pulmonary fellow, 1962-63, chief resident medicine, 1963-64, instr. medicine, 1962-64, asst. prof., 1964-68, assoc. prof., 1968-74, prof. medicine, 1974—; pres. Presbyn./St. Luke's Ctr. for Health Scis. Edn., 1989-95; practice medicine, specializing in internal medicine, pulmonary medicine Denver, 1962—; prof. medicine Rush Univ., 1992—. Cons. Kindred Hosp., 1991-. Author: For Those Who Live and Breathe, 1967, 2d edit., 1972, Intensive and Rehabilitative Respiratory Care, 1971, 3d edit., 1982, Chronic Obstructive Pulmonary Disease, 1978, 2d edit., 1985, Principles and Practice of Pulmonary Rehabilitation, 1993, Enjoying Life With COPD, 1995, 3d edit., others; contbr. articles to profl. jours. NIH and Found. grantee, 1966-88. Master ACP, Am. Coll. Chest Physicians (master, pres. 1982); mem. Assn. Am. Physicians, Assn. of Pulmonary Program Dirs. (founding pres. 1983-84, chmn. nat. lung health edn. program 1995—, co-chmn. 2000-04), Am. Bd. Internal Medicine (bd. govs. 1986-92), Am. Thoracic Soc. (Disting. Achievement award 1995), Phi Beta Kappa, Phi Delta Theta, Alpha Omega Alpha, Phi Rho Sigma (pres. 1976-78). Home: 1940 Grape St Denver CO 80220-1353 Office: 899 Logan St Ste 103 Denver CO 80203 Office Phone: 303-996-0868. Personal E-mail: tlpdoc@aol.com.

**PETTY, TOM (THOMAS EARL PETTY),** musician, composer; b. Gainesville, Fla., Oct. 20, 1950; s. Earl and Katherine Petty; m. Jane Benyo, 1974 (div. Sept. 9, 1996); children: Adria, Kim; m. Dana York, June 3, 2001. With band the Sundowners (1964) which later was called the Epics (1965-69) and Mudcrutch (1970-74), Gainesville, Fla.; songwriter, musician for Leon Russell, 1974—75; leader Tom Petty and the Heartbreakers, 1975—; toured the world with Bob Dylan, 1986; toured Am. with Georgia Satellites and Del Fuegos (Rock 'n' Roll Caravan tour), 1987. Albums: (with the Heartbreakers) Tom Petty and the Heartbreakers, 1976, You're Gonna Get It, 1978, Damn the Torpedoes, 1979, Hard Promises, 1981, Long After Dark, 1982, Southern Accents, 1985, Pack Up the Plantation-Live!, 1986, Let Me Up (I've Had Enough), 1987, Into the Great Wide Open, 1991 (Grammy nomination for Best Rock Performance by a Duo or Group with Vocal, 1992), Tom Petty and the Heartbreakers' Greatest Hits, 1993, Playback, 1995, She's The One (soundtrack), 1996, Echo, 1999 (Grammy nomination for Best Rock Album, 2000), Anthology: through the Years, 2000, The Last DJ, 2002, Live at the Olympic: The Last DJ and More, 2003; (with The Traveling Wilburys) Traveling Wilburys Vol. 1, 1989 (Grammy Award for Best Rock Performance by a Duo or Group with Vocal, 1990), Grammy nomination for Album of Yr., 1990), Traveling Wilburys Vol. 3, 1990; (solo albums) Full Moon Fever, 1989 (Grammy nomination for Album of Yr., 1990), Wildflowers, 1994 (Grammy nomination for Best Rock Album, 1996), Highway Companion, 2006; hit singles include Breakdown, 1978, Here Comes My Girl, 1979, Refugee, 1979, (duet with Stevie Nicks) Stop Dragging My Heart Around, 1981, The Waiting, 1981, You Got Lucky, 1982, Don't Come Around Here No More, 1985, Jammin' Me, 1987, Free Fallin', 1989, Running Down A Dream, 1989, I Won't Back Down, 1989, Into the Great Wide Open, Learning to Fly, 1991, Mary Jane's Last Dance, 1993, You Don't Know How It Feels, 1994, You Wreck Me, 1994, Walls, 1996, Free Girl Now, 1999, Swingin', 1999; Songs appear in films: Fast Times at Ridgemont High, 1982, Streets of Fire, 1984, The Silence of the Lambs, 1991, She's the One, 1996, Jerry Maguire, 1996; Actor (films) Made in Heaven, 1987, The Postman, 1997; (TV appearances) The Simpsons, 2002 (voice only), King of the Hill (voice only), 2005; host (radio show) Bried Treasure, 2005- Grammy nomination for Best Rock Performance by a Duo or Group with Vocal (with Stevie Nicks for Stop Draggin' My Heart Around) 1982, Grammy nomination for Best Rock Song (Learning to Fly), 1992, Grammy nomination for Best Rock Performance by a Duo or Group with Vocal (with Bob Dylan, Roger McGuinn, Neil Young, Eric Clapton, and George Harrison for My Back Pages), 1994, Grammy nomination for Best Rock Song (with the Heartbreakers for Room At The Top), 2000, Grammy Award for Best Male Rock Vocal Performance (for You Don't Know Hot It Feels), 1996, MTV Video Music Award for Best Male Video (with the Heartbreakers for Mary Jane's Last Dance), 1994, Video Vanguard Award, MTV Video Music Awards, 1994, MTV Video Music Award for Best Male Video (for You Don't Know How It Feels), 1995, Songwriter Award, ASCAP, 1990, Golden Note Award, ASCAP, 1996, Nat. Veteran's Foundation Special Award of Recognition, 1995, UCLA George & Ira Gershwin Award, 1996, Bill Graham Lifetime Achievement Award, CA Music Awards, 1998, Hollywood Walk of Fame Star (with the Heartbreakers), 1999, inducted, Rock & Roll Hall of Fame (with the Heartbreakers), 2002, Legend Award, Radio Music Awards, 2003, Century award, Billboard Music Awards, 2005. Office: Warner Bros Records 3300 Warner Blvd Burbank CA 91505-4694

**PETTY, WILLIE CLIFFORD,** musician, composer, educator; b. Eufaula, Ala., Sept. 24, 1967; s. Willie Edward and Arrie Pearl Petty; 1 child, LaKeyla Tarshay Jones-Petty. M in Music Edn. summa cum laude, Ala. State U., Montgomery, 1999; degree, Ala. State U., 1991. Cert. profl. educator Ala. Music educator, fine arts chmn. St. Jude HS, Montgomery, Ala., 1991—2000; pastoral musician, composer-in-residence Resurrection Cath. Missions, Montgomery, 1993—2005; composer, rec. artist World Libr. Publs., Franklin Park, Ill., 2002—. Composer: Come Magnify The Lord With Me, Glory To God, If Today You Hear His Voice, Have Mercy on Us for We Have Sinned, Mass of the Holy Spirit, Let the Children Come to Me, Everytime I Feel the Spirit; prodr.: (rec.) I Can Not Tell It All; singer: (rec.) Testify, Barbara Frost & Friends, (rec.) In Spirit and Truth. Mem. Montgomery AIDS Outreach, 1996—2004; mem. the Greater Montgomery AIDS Task Force, 2000; mem. Look Up Ministries, Dothan, Ala., 2000. Named Tchr. of Yr., Ala. Dem. Party, 1999—2000; named one of Outstanding Coll. Students of Am., 1986—91; named to Who's Who in Am. Colls. and Univs., 1986—91; scholar, Pressor Found., 1989—90. Mem.: Nat. Assn. Pastoral Musicians (assoc.), Ala. Vocal Assn. (assoc.), ASCAP (assoc.), Music Educators Nat. Conf. (assoc.), Phi Kappa Lambda, Alpha Kappa Mu, Phi Eta Sigma. Democrat. Roman Catholic. Avocation: Aikido. Home: 1941 Green Acres Ct

Montgomery AL 36106 Office: Resurrection Cath Missions 2815 Forbes Dr Montgomery AL 36110 Office Phone: 334-230-1916. Home Fax: 334-396-9965; Office Fax: 334-265-8081. Personal E-mail: wcliffordpetty@bellsouth.net. E-mail: cpetty@rcmsouth.org.

**PETZ, EDWIN V.,** real estate company executive, lawyer; b. Beatrice, Nebr., May 14, 1935; s. Virgil Leonard and Ruth Elenor (Thomsen) P.; m. Darlene Cross, May 17, 1958 (div. June 1964); 1 dau., Katherine J.; m. Anne Higgins, Dec. 3, 1964 (div. Sept. 1993); 1 son, W. Christopher; m. Louise Loosli, Jan. 9, 1997. BA, Principia Coll., Elsah, Ill., 1955; JD, Harvard U., 1958. Bar: N.Y. 1959, Mass. 1976. Assoc. Chadbourne, Parke, Whiteside & Wolff, N.Y.C., 1958-62; asst. assoc. counsel Martin Marietta Corp., Bethesda, Md., 1963-64, 1965-75; gen. atty. sec. Bunker-Ramo Corp., Oakbrook, Ill., 1964-65; assoc. gen. counsel United Brands Co., N.Y.C., 1975-82, v.p., gen. counsel, sec., 1982-84; sr. v.p., gen. counsel Milstein Properties Corp., 1985—2003; sr. v.p., gen counsel The Milstein Group Inc., 1992—; sr. v.p., gen. counsel Ogden CAP Properties, LLC, 2003—. Mem. ABA, Assn. of Bar of City N.Y. Clubs: University (N.Y.). Republican. Episcopalian. Office: Ogden CAP Properties LLC 390 Park Ave New York NY 10022

**PETZ, THOMAS JOSEPH,** internist; b. Detroit, Feb. 10, 1930; s. Arthur J. and Marie (McCarthy) P.; m. Catherine Crowe, June 13, 1959; children: Thomas Jr., William, David, John, Catherine. BS, U. Detroit, 1951; MD. Wayne State U., Detroit, 1955. Diplomate Am. Bd. Internal Medicine and Pulmonary Disease. Intern Harper Hosp., Detroit, 1955-56, resident, 1958-59, 60-62, U. Calif., San Francisco, 1959-60; clin. instr. Wayne State U., Detroit, 1962-72, assoc. prof., 1972-76, clin. assoc. prof., 1976-95, clin. prof., 1996-97, prof. emeritus, 1997—; pvt. practice pulmonary disease and internal medicine Detroit, 1962-72, St. Clair Shores, Mich., 1977-96; med.-legal cons. Northville, Mich., 1996—. Chief pulmonary Wayne State U., Detroit, 1974-76, Harper Hosp., Detroit, 1972-79; dir. med. intensive care unit Harper Hosp., Detroit, 1977-83; chmn. dept. medicine Bon Secours Hosp., Grosse Pointe, Mich., 1984-86; chmn. Gen. Motors human rsch. com., 1995. Bd. govs. Wayne State Sch. of Medicine Alumni Assn., Detroit, 1981-85. Fellow Detroit Acad. Medicine (pres. 1982-83), Am. Coll. Chest Physicians, Detroit Med. Acad.; mem. Am. Coll. Physicians, Found. of Southeast Mich., 1992- (pres.2006-), Detroit Med. Club. Republican. Roman Catholic. Avocations: golf, skiing.

**PETZAL, DAVID ELIAS,** editor, writer; b. NYC, Oct. 21, 1941; s. Henry and Aline Born (Bixer) P.; m. Arlene Anne Taylor, May 29, 1974. BA, Colgate U., 1963. Editor Maco Publs., N.Y.C., 1964—69; mng. editor Davis Publs., N.Y.C., 1969—70; features editor Hearst Publs., N.Y.C., 1970—72; mng. editor CBS Publs., N.Y.C., 1972—79, editor, 1979—83, exec. editor, 1983—2001, Field & Stream Mag., N.Y.C., 1983—2001, mng. editor, 2001—03, dep. editor, 2002—. Author: The .22 Rifle, 1972; editor: The Experts Book of the Shooting Sports, 1972, The Experts Book of Upland Game and Waterfowl Hunting, 1975, The Experts Book of Big-Game Hunting in North America, 1976, The Ency. of Sporting Firearms, 1991. Office: Time 4 Mags 10th Fl 2 Park Ave New York NY 10016-5602 Office Phone: 212-779-5287. Business E-Mail: david.petzal@time4.com.

**PETZOLD, CAROL STOKER,** state legislator; b. St. Louis, July 28; d. Harold William and Mabel Lucille (Wilson) Stoker; m. Walter John Petzold, June 27, 1959; children: Ann, Ruth, David. BS, Valparaiso U., 1959. Tchr. Parkwood Elem. Sch., Kensington, Md., 1960-62; legis. aide Md. Gen. Assembly, Annapolis, 1975-79; legis. asst. Montgomery County Bd. Edn., Rockville, Md., 1980; cmty. sch. coord. Parkland Jr. H.S., Rockville, 1981-87; mem. Md. Ho. of Dels., Annapolis, 1987—, mem. constl. and adminstrv. law com., 1987-93, mem. judiciary com., 1994—, chair subcom. on criminal justice, 2003—, vice chair Montgomery County del., 1995—, dep. majority whip, 1999—2002. Chair spl. com. drug and alcohol abuse Md. Ho. Dels., 1999—; mem. transp. planning bd. Nat. Capitol Region, 1989—; vice chmn. assembly on fed. issues Nat. Conf. State Legislatures, 1996-97, chair adv. com. on energy, 1997-99, chair energy and transp. com., 1998-99, pres. women's legis. network, 2004-05, chair transp. com., 2004-05. Editor Child Care Sampler, 1974, Stoker Family Cookbook, 1976. Pres. Montgomery Child Care Assn., 1976-78; mem. Md. State Scholarship Bd., 1978-87, chmn. 1985-87; chmn. Legis. Com. Montgomery County Commn. for Children and Youth, 1979-84; mem., v.p. Luth. Social Services Nat. Capitol Area, Washington, 1980-86; mem. exec. com. coun. Montgomery United Way, 1981-2000. Named Mother of Yr., March of Dimes, 2000; named one of Top 100 Md. Women, Daily Record, 2002, 2004; recipient Statewide award, Gov.'s Adv. Bd. on Homelessness, 1994, recognized for outstanding commitment to children, U.S. Dept. HEW, 1980, Award of Excellence, MADD, 2002, Disting. Legislator award, 2003, Impaired Driving Coalition, 2003, Legis. award, Md. Network Against Domestic Violence, 2003. Mem.: AAUW (honoree Kensington br. 1971, 2002, honoree Md. divsn. 1981), Women Legislators of Md. (hon. Women Legislators Caucus (chmn. exec. com. 2003—04), Women's Polit. Caucus (chmn. Montgomery County 1981—83). Democrat. Lutheran. Home: 14113 Chadwick Ln Rockville MD 20853-2103 Office Phone: 301-858-3001. Business E-Mail: Carol_Petzold@house.state.md.us.

**PEVEAR, ROBERTA CHARLOTTE,** retired state legislator; b. Bethel, Maine, July 4, 1930; d. Frank Albert Sr. and Thirza Estella (Hickford) Gibson; m. Edward Gordon Pevear, Aug. 21, 1971. Diploma in Comml. Art, Gould Acad., 1947. Sec. Wilner Wood Products, South Paris, Maine, 1947-50; sec. export dept. Whitaker Cable, North Kansas City, Mo., 1951-56; sec. br. and dist. Anheuser-Busch, Inc., Kansas City, Mo., 1957-59; legal sec. Johnson & Johnson, New Brunswick, NJ, 1960-65, St. John, Ronder & Bell, Kingston, NY 1966-67, adminstrv. asst. John Roebuck & Co., Overland Park, Kans., 1967-70, Exeter, NH, 1971-77; salesman Avon Products, Hampton Falls, NH, 1978-86; mem. ho. reps. State of N.H., 1979-88, ret., 1988. Commr. Rockingham Planning Commn., N.H., 1979-88. N.H. Planning Com., 1985-88; clk. Environment and Agrl. Com. N.H. Ho. Reps., 1983-88; del. mem. Rockingham County, 1979-88, exec. bd., 1984-88; chmn. Rockingham County Home, 1987-88. Civil Def. dir., Hampton Falls, NH, 1980—88. Recipient Community Citizen award Hampton Falls Grange, 1982, Seacoast Retired Sr. Service award, 1985. Mem. Nat. Order Women Legislators, N.H. Order of Women Legislators, DAR. Avocations: writing, genealogy, travel.

**PEVEC, ANTHONY EDWARD,** bishop; b. Cleve., Apr. 16, 1925; s. Anton and Frances Darovec P. MA, John Carroll U., Cleve., 1956; PhD, Western Res. U., Cleve., 1964. Ordained priest Roman Cath. Ch., 1950. Assoc. pastor St. Mary Church, Elyria, Ohio, 1950—52, St. Lawrence Ch., Cleve. 1952—53; rector-prin. Borromeo Sem. HS, Wickliffe, Ohio, 1953—75; adminstrv. bd. Nat. Cath. Edn. Assn., 1972—75; pastor St. Vitus Ch., Cleve., 1975—79; rector-pres. Borromeo Coll., Wickliffe, 1979—82; aux. bishop Diocese of Cleve., 1982—. Mem. v.p. Slovenian-Am. Heritage Found., Cleve., 1975—. Named Man of Yr., Fedn. Slovenian Nat. Homes, Cleve., 1985, Cath. Man of Yr., KC, 1998, Man of Yr., Pioneer Assn., 2001, Cathedral Latin Alumni Assn., 2003; named to Hall of Fame, St. Vitus Alumni Assn., 1989, Wickliffe Hall of Fame, 2000; recipient honoree, Heritage Found., Cleve., 1982, Alumni medal, John Carroll U., 2004. Mem.: KC (state chaplain 2003—05), Cath. Order Foresters (state chaplain 2000—04), U.S. Cath. Conf. (nat. adv. coun. 1996—97), Nat. Conf. Cath. Bishops (com. on vocations 1984—86, com. on pro-life activities 1990—92, com. on priestly formation 1993—95, com. on sci. and human values 1993—96). Democrat. Roman Catholic. Avocations: reading, music. Home and Office: Diocese of Cleveland 28700 Euclid Ave Wickliffe OH 44092-2527 Business E-Mail: bpaepevec@dioceseofcleveland.org. *Ultimately I must always remember that the Lord is totally in control of my life, no matter how complicated it may seem to be. I am here to do the Lord's will, and wherever I go I come to do His will.*

**PEW, JOHN GLENN, JR.,** lawyer; b. Dallas, Apr. 18, 1932; s. John Glenn Sr. and Roberta (Haughton) P. BA, U. Tex., 1954, LLB, 1955. Bar: Tex. 1955, U.S. Dist. Ct. (no. dist.) Tex. 1959, U.S. Supreme Ct. 1959, U.S. Ct. Appeals (5th cir.) 1961, U.S. Ct. Appeals (10th cir.) 1982. Ptnr. Jackson Walker LLP,

Dallas, 1964—. With USNR, 1955-58. Mem.: Order of Coif, Phi Beta Kappa. Republican. Presbyterian. Office: Jackson Walker LLP 901 Main St Ste 6000 Dallas TX 75202-3797 Office Phone: 214-953-6000. E-mail: jpew@jw.com.

**PEW, ROBERT ANDERSON,** retired real estate and equipment leasing corporation officer; b. Phila., Aug. 22, 1936; s. Arthur Edmund and Mary Elizabeth (Elliott) P.; children from previous marriage: Robert Anderson (dec.), James Cunningham, Glenn Edgar, Joan Elliott; m. Daria S. Decerio, June 19, 1993; 1 child, Richard Westerman. Student, Princeton U., 1954-56; BS, Temple U., 1959; MS in Mgmt. (Alfred P. Sloan fellow), MIT, 1970; LLD (hon.), Widener U., 1982; DPS (hon.), Temple U., 1983; LHD (hon.), Gettysburg Coll., 1984. Ops. asst. prodn. div. Sun Oil Co., Premont, Tex., 1959-60, ops. asst. prodn. div. Morgan City, La., auditor internal audit dept. Phila., 1960-65, staff asst. treasury dept., 1965-69, asst. to exec. v.p. corp. projects group, 1970-71, sec.-treas., mgr. financial control of products group, 1971-74, corp. sec., 1974-77; pres. Helios Capital Corp., 1977-96; CEO Radnor Corp., 1995-96; bd. dirs. Glenmede Corp., Phila., chmn., 1997—2004. Bd. dirs. Sun Co., Inc., Phila., Pew Charitable Trusts, Phila., Glenmede Trust Co. N.A., Phila. Trustee Children's Hosp., Phila., vice chmn., 1991—. Served Pa. Air N.G., 1956—59. Recipient R. Kelso Carter award Widener U., 1971 Mem. Aircraft Owners and Pilots Assn. (trustee, chmn. 1974-77, 85-2002, vice-chmn. 1979-85), Am. Hosp. Assn. (hon.), Coll. Physicians Phila., Union League Club, Harbor Club (pres. 1992-96), Phila. Aviation Country Club, Merion Cricket Club, N.E. Harbor Fleet, Seal Harbor Yacht Club. Republican. Presbyterian. Home: 916 Muirfield Rd Bryn Mawr PA 19010-1921 E-mail: dungarnem@aol.com.

**PEWITT, JAMES DUDLEY,** academic administrator; b. Franklin, Tenn., July 28, 1930; s. James Isaac and Eleanor (Dudley) P.; m. Betty Louise Hightower, Oct. 31, 1952; children: Ransom D., James P., Thomas E. Student, Vanderbilt U., 1948-51; MBA, MS, U.S.C., 1964, D in Bus. Adminstrn., 1967. Commd. lt. USAF, 1952, advanced through grades to col., 1969; AMC test pilot, 1958—62; spl. asst. for econ. analysis Office of Sec. of Air Force, 1967; exec. to asst. sec. Air Force for Fin. Mgmt. Nat. War Coll., 1971; asst. Da Nang Air Base, Vietnam, 1972; dep. comdr. for ops. Vietnam, 1972; vice comdr. Gunfighters, 1972; chief linebacker ops. Staff of Dir. of Ops., Vietnam, 1972; dir. mgmt. analysis USAF, 1973, ret., 1973; dir. grad. sch. bus. U. Ala., Birmingham, 1973-74, asst. v.p. ops. and planning, 1974-77, v.p. adminstrn., 1977-84, sr. v.p. adminstrn., 1984-90, Disting. prof., 1990—. Bd. dir. Birmingham Cable Communications, Allied Products Co. Mem. Birmingham Airport Authority, (bd. mem. chmn. bd. So. Mus. of Flight, 1993-2005; faculty rep. Sun Belt Conf., 1983-90, pres., 1989-90; mem. NCAA Coun., 1990-94. Decorated D.F.C. with 3 oak leaf clusters, Bronze Star, Legion of Merit with 2 oak leaf clusters, Air medal with 11 v-devices, 10 other awards and fgn. decorations; named to Ala, Aviation Hall of Fame, 2003. Mem. Birmingham C. of C. (bd. dirs. 1977-84, pres. 1983, chmn. 1984), Birmingham Country Club, Skull & Dagger, Phi Kappa Phi, Beta Gamma Sigma, Sigma Xi, Omicron Delta Kappa, Kappa Alpha, Order of Daedalians, Order of Quiet Birdmen. Avocations: flying, golf. E-mail: dpewitt@aol.com.

**PEYER, JOAN,** information technology executive; BA in Econs., MA in Econs., CUNY. V.p. mgmt. of internal controls Chase Manhattan Bank, 1984—90; v.p. Barnett BankCard Systems/Audit, 1990—95; dir. systems and svcs. Gelita USA, Inc., 1996—2003, v.p., chief info. officer, dir. IT/audit, 2003—. Home: 420 N Royal Troon Dakota Dunes SD 57049

**PEYREFITTE, ASHTON GEORGE, JR.,** meteorologist, educator; b. New Orleans, Oct. 5, 1942; s. Ashton Gonzalo Peyrefitte and Melba Catherine Parpal. BS, Fla. State U., Tallahassee, 1967, MS, 1969; PhD, U. Utah, Salt Lake City, 1986. Mem. faculty St. Aloysius H.S., New Orleans, 1964—65; rsch. asst. Fla. State U., Tallahassee, 1967—70; instr. U. Lowell, Mass., 1971—72, SUNY, Oneonta, 1972—80; assoc. instr. U. Utah, Salt Lake City, 1980—81; assoc. prof. meteorology Plymouth State U., NH, 1985—2000, faculty emeritus; asst. prof. meteorology Ctrl. Mich. U., Mt. Pleasant, 2000—. Contbr. articles to profl. jours. Named Outstanding Tchg. Asst., U. Utah, 1981; fellow, NSF, 1969. Mem.: Am. Meteorol. Soc. (banquet held in honor 2006). Office: Central Mich Univ Dept Geography 296A Dow Science Mount Pleasant MI 48859

**PEYROT GONZALEZ, MARCO A.,** secretary of the navy of Mexico; b. Mexico City, June 10, 1940; B in Geograph. Engring., Heroic Mil. Naval Sch., 1957; M in Mil. Adminstrn. in Nat. Security and Def., Nat. Def. Coll.; grad., Naval Superior Studies Ctr., Mex. Navy, 1977. Lt. of corvette Mexican Navy, advanced through grades to adm., cargo officer, 1st officer, comdr. several ships and naval fleets, comdr. Pacific Naval Forces, chief of staff and comdr. different naval regions, naval zones and naval sectors; high-command activities related to planning and decision-making for naval ops. and applied logistics Navy Gen. Staff, Commn. on Spl. Studies, Commn. on Laws and Regulations, Social Security Inst. Mexican Armed Forces; naval attaché Mexican Embassy, Italy and France, France; tchr. maths.; physics, ballistics, hygrography, artillery, electronics Heroic Mil. Naval Coll.; sec. of navy Govt. of Mex., 2000—. Instr. physics and math. and port engring. U. Veracruz; leader various confs.; spkr. in field. Contbr. articles on mil. adminstrn. in nat. security and def. Decorated Condecoracion al Merito Docente Naval. Office: Eje 2 Ote Tramo Heroica Escuela Naval # 861 04830 Mexico City Mexico

**PEYTON, ELIZABETH JOY,** writer, painter; b. Danbury, Conn., Dec. 20, 1965; d. Paul Leason and Elizabeth Ann (Gordon); m. Rirkrit Tiravanija, July 21, 1991. BA, Sch. Visual Arts, N.Y.C., 1987. Author: Live Forever, 1997, Craig, 1998; exhibitions include Art of Four Decades 1958-1998, San Francisco, Mus. Modern Art, 1998, Examining Pictures, Mus. Contemporary Art, Chgo., 1999, Remix: Contemporary art & pop, Tate Liverpool, 2002, Cher peintre- Peintures figuratives despuis l'ultime Picabia, Centre Pompidou, Paris, 2002, Inaugural Exhbn., Regen Project, LA, 2003, New Paintings, 2003, EDITION SPECIALE, Galerier Suzanner Tarasieve, Paris, 2003, Whitney Biennial, Whitney Mus. Am. Art, 2004. Avocations: swimming, surfing the internet. Office: Regen Projects 633 N Almont Dr West Hollywood CA 90069-5607

**PEYTON, JOHN,** mayor; b. July 28, 1964; m. Kathryn Pearson; 1 child, John Conner. Grad. Exec. Edn. Program, Harvard Bus. Sch.; BA, Mercer U., 1986. V.p. Gate Petroleum Co.. Fla.; mayor City of Jacksonville, Fla., 2003—. Past pres. Greenscape of Jacksonville, 1998—99; chmn. Jacksonville Symphony Assn.; mem. St. John's Episcopal Ch.; bd. mem. Jacksonville Transp. Authority, 1996—99, chmn., 1999—2003. Republican.*

**PEZICK, PATRICIA,** music educator; b. Upper Darby, Pa., Mar. 20, 1954; d. Robert Thomas Pezick and Gloria Jean Christie; m. Robert James McCarthy; children: Maura McCarthy, Colin McCarthy. BS in Music Edn., West Chester U., 1976; M in Music Edn., Temple U., 1981. Cert. Orff-Schulwerk levels I and II. Tchr. 8th grade music Phoenixville (Pa.) Sch. Dist., 1976—77; tchr. music William Penn Sch. Dist., Lansdowne, Pa., 1977—80; grad. asst. Temple U., Phila., 1980—81; dir. choral, tchr. gen. music, coord. music curriculum Germantown Acad., Ft. Washington, Pa., 1983—, dir. musical, 2002—03. Music prof. Chestnut Hill Coll., Phila., 1992; ch. organist in field. Edward R. Kast grantee, Germantown Acad., 1987, 1989, 2003, 2005. Mem.: Music Educators Nat. Conf., Am. Choral Dirs. Assn. Democrat. Roman Catholic. Avocations: reading, travel, exercise, musical theatre. Home: 883 Crestline Dr Blue Bell PA 19422 Office: 340 Morris Rd Fort Washington PA 19034 Office Phone: 215-646-3300 x233. Personal E-mail: patricia.pezick@germantownacademy.net.

**PEZZELLA, JERRY JAMES, JR.,** investment company executive, real estate company executive; b. Chesapeake, Va., Sept. 30, 1937; s. Jerry James Sr. and Mabel (Aydlett) P.; m. Carolyn Blades; children: James M., Stanley J. v.p. Va. Nat. Bank (now Bank of Am.), Norfolk, 1964-68; chmn. bd., pres. First Am. Investment Corp., First Ga. Investment Corp., Atlanta, 1968-74;

v.p. Great Am. Investment Corp., Atlanta, 1974-78; sr. exec. v.p., 1984-85; exec. v.p. Equity Fin. & Mgmt. Co., Chgo., 1978-99; pres., chmn. bd. First Capital Fin. Corp., Chgo., 1983-85; pres. GAFGI Holdings Inc., Chgo., 1983-98; chmn. bd. 1st Property Mgmt. Corp., 1990-92; dir. fin. officer, treas. Bear Paw Svc. Dist., 2002—. Bd. dirs. Great Am. Mgmt. and Investment, Inc., Chgo., Nat. Multi Housing Coun., 1992-94, mem. exec. com.; real estate cons., 1997—. Bd. dirs., exec. com. Nat. Multi-Housing Coun., 1991-93. Mem. Met. Club (Chgo.). Home: 1240 Village Rd Murphy NC 28906-1763

**PEZZULLO, RALPH MICHAEL,** writer, playwright; b. N.Y.C., Dec. 27, 1954; s. Lawrence Anthony Pezzullo and Josephine DeMattia; m. Alice Palmisano, Aug. 8, 1980 (div. Jan. 1994); children: John Lawrence, Michael Richard; m. Jessica Rae Pezzullo, May 19, 1994; children: Francesca Sophia, Alessandra Sabina. M in Pub. and Internat. Affairs, George Washington U., 1975. Grants specialist Nat. Endowment Arts, Washington, 1975—79. Author: At the Fall of Somoza, 1994, Eve Missing, 2003, Jawbreaker, 2005, Plunging Into Haiti, 2006, (plays) From Behind the Moon, 1984, The Tail of the Tiger, 1985, Eating the Shadow, 1990, Wilderness of Mirrors, 1994, Hide Mother in My Heart, 1996, Gauquin's Parrot, 1997, Spain, 1998, Stakes, 1999, Okeechobee Split, 2000, Murder Sketched Gently, 2000, (radio drama/series) The Life and Times of Swamp Fox, 1985. Recipient Spl. citation Kesselring award, 1986, award, Ctr. Theater, 1994, Screenwriting award, Writer's Guild Am. E. Found., 1987; Playwriting fellow, Jerome Found., 1997, 1998, 1999, 2001. Mem.: PEN USA, Pvt. Eye Writers Am., Mystery Writers Am., Author's League Am., Art Student's League, Dramatists Guild. Avocations: painting, sports. Home: 10055 Reevesbury Dr Beverly Hills CA 90210 E-mail: pezzullo@mindspring.com, ralph@ralphpezzullo.com.

**PEZZULO, JACQUELINE,** psychologist, researcher; b. N.Y.C., Aug. 10, 1966; d. John Gerald Johnson and Maria Lopez de Rivera; children: Matthew, John children: Matthew Isaiah Rivera. BS in Psychology, summa cum laude, SUNY, Albany, 1993, MS in Edn. Psychology and Stats., 1996, cert. of Advanced Study, 1996, D in Psychology, 2000. Cert. sch. psychology NY State Dept. of Edn., 1996, psychologist NY State Dept. of Edn., 2003. Cmty. mental health specialist St. Mary's Hosp., Amsterdam, NY, 1998—2000; sch. psychologist Chatham Ctrl. Sch. Dist., Chatham, NY, 2000—01; asst. dir. child and adolescent svcs. rsch. N.Y. State Office Mental Health, Albany, NY, 2001—. Cons. Inst. Cmty. Rsch., Hartford, Conn., 1996—97, VanGuard Comm., 2003—; rsch. cons. SUNY, Buffalo, 1994—96; behavioral health cons. Multiple Sch. Dists. in Urban and Rural Counties, Multiple, NY; presenter in field. Contbr. articles to profl. jours., chapters to books; author: Eliminating Barriers for Learning Social and Emotional Factors that Enhance Secondary Education. Adv. and adv. mem. Coalition of Latino Svc. Providers, Amsterdam, NY, 1998—2000; youth mentor Third Ref. Ch. of Am., Albany, NY, 1996—2000; presenter Am. Ednl. Rsch. Assn., San Francisco, 1995; adv. mem. Coordinated Children's Svcs. Intitiative, Amsterdam, NY, 1998—2000. Post-Doctoral Rsch. fellow, Ctr. for Info. Tech. and Evaluation Rsch., 2002—03, State Planning grantee, NIMH, 2003—, Challenge grantee, NY State Divsn. Criminal Justice, 2001—02. Mem.: Nat. Assn. Sch. Psychologists (assoc.), Soc. Rsch. in Child Devel. (assoc.), APA (assoc.), Golden Key, Phi Beta Kappa. Avocations: travel, gardening, dancing and music, theater, reading and writing. Office: NY State Office of Mental Health 44 Holland Ave Floor 6 Albany NY 12229

**PEZZUTO, JOHN MICHAEL,** dean, pharmacology educator; b. Hammonton, N.J., Aug. 29, 1950; s. Michael L. and Elizabeth (Brown) P.; m. Mimi Faith Rotstein, Aug. 29, 1986; 1 child, John-Henry Albert; 1 child from previous marriage, Jennifer Anne. AB, Rutgers U., 1973; PhD, Coll. Medicine & DentistryN.J., 1977. Postdoctoral assoc. MIT, Cambridge, 1977-79; instr. chemistry U. Va., Charlottesville, 1979-80; asst. prof. U. Ill.-Chgo., 1980-84, assoc. prof., 1984-91, prof., 1991—2002, Disting. Univ. prof., 2002; dean Purdue U., Coll. Pharmacy, Nursing and Health Scis., West Lafayette, Ind., 2002—06, prof. medicinal chemistry and molecular pharmacology, 2002—06; founding dean Coll. Pharmacy, U. Hawaii, Hilo, 2006—. Assoc. dir. U. Ill. Cancer Ctr, 1991-95, dep. dir., 2000-02; interim head dept. med. chemistry and pharmacognosy, U. Ill., Chgo., 1992-95, 2000-01, head, 2001-02; dir. program for collaborative rsch. in pharm. scis. U. Ill., Chgo., 1995-98; pres., co-founder Internat. Therapeutics Inc., River Forest, Ill., 1996—; assoc. dean for rsch. and grad. edn. U. Ill., Chgo., 1998-2002. Editor-in-chief Internat. Jour. Pharmacology, 1991-95, editor-in-chief Combinatory Chemistry and High Throughput Screening, 1996-97, Pharmaceutical Biology, 1997—; editor: Biotechnology and Pharmacy; contbr. articles to sci. jours. and books. NIH fellow, 1977-80, Rsch. fellow Alexander von Humboldt Found., 1990-91; NIH Rsch. Career Devel. awardee, 1984-89, grantee NAt. Cancer Inst., 1984—, Nat. Inst. Dental Rsch., 1984-85. Mem. AAAS, Am. Chem. Soc., Am. Soc. Pharmacognosy, Am. Assn. Cancer Rsch., N.Y. Acad. Scis., Am. Soc. Biol. Chemists. Office: Coll Pharmacy U Hawaii at Hilo 200 W Kawili St Hilo HI 96720-4091*

**PFAFF, JUDY,** artist; b. London, 1946. Student Wayne State U., 1965-66, So. Ill. U., 1968-69; B.F.A., Washington U.-St. Louis, 1971; postgrad. Yale U., 1970, M.F.A., 1973. Prof. arts, Columbia U., 1992-94, Milton Avery Disting. prof. art, Bard Coll., 1989, 91, 94- One-woman exhbns. include: Webb and Parsons Gallery, New Canaan, Conn., 1974, Artists Space N.Y., 1975, Theatre Gallery, U. So. Fla., Tampa, 1977, Los Angeles Contemporary Exhbn., 1978, Holly Solomon Gallery, N.Y., 1980, Daniel Weinberg Gallery, Los Angeles, 1984, Wacoal, Japan, 1985, Holly Solomon Gallery, 1986, Nat. Mus. Women in the Arts, Washington, 1989, Cleve. Ctr. for Contemporary Art., Cleve., 1990, Fabric Workshop, N.Y., 1991, Rotunda Gallery, N.Y., 1993; group exhbns. include: Whitney Mus. Am. Art, 1975, Hallwalls Gallery, Buffalo, 1976, Art Mus., U. Calif.-Santa Barbara, 1979, Neuberger Mus., SUNY-Purchase, 1979, Contemporary Arts Mus., Houston, 1980, Contemporary Arts Ctr., Cin., 1980, Mus. Modern Art, N.Y.C., 1984, Venice Biennale, 1984, Rotunda Gallery, Bklyn., 1984, Bklyn. Mus., 1985, WHitney Mus. Am. Art., N.Y., 1988, Internat. Art Projects, Asia, 1990, Mis. Modern Art., 1989, Inst. Contemporary Art, Phila., 1991, Cultural Space, N.Y., 1992, Henie-Onstad Art Ctr., Norway, 1992, Whitney Mus. Am. Art at Champion, Stamford, Conn., 1993, Drawing Ctr., N.Y., 1993; commd. work Spokane City Hall, 1984. Nat. Endowment Arts grantee, 1979; Named a Guggenheim fellow, 1983, MacArthur Fellow, 2004; Award of Merit Medal for Sculpture, Am. Acad. of Arts and Letters, 2002. Office: Bard Coll PO Box 5000 Annandale On Hudson NY 12504-5000 E-mail: pfaff@bard.edu.

**PFAFF, LAURA KING,** auction house executive; b. San Francisco; m. Rick Pfaff. BA in English, U. So. Calif., L.A., 1976. Acct. exec. The Pacific Group, San Francisco, 1986—90; pres. Laura King & Co., San Francisco, 1990—94; sr. v.p., regional dir. Christie's, San Francisco, 1994—2001; chmn. Bonhams & Butterfields, San Francisco, 2001—. Bd. mem. San Francisco Symphony, No. Calif. Cancer Ctr., Calif. Pacific Med. Ctr., Fort Mason Found.; former bd. mem. San Francisco C. of C. Office: Bonhams & Butterfields 220 San Bruno Ave San Francisco CA 94103 Office Phone: 415-861-7500.

**PFAFF, WILLIAM WALLACE,** medical educator; b. Rochester, N.Y., Aug. 14, 1930; s. Norman Joseph and Eleanor Blakesley (Wells) P.; m. Patricia Ann Clark; children: Nancy, Karen, Margaret, Mary Catherine. AB, Harvard U., 1952; MD, SUNY, 1956. Intern U. Chgo., 1956-58; sr. asst. surgeon NIH, Bethesda, Md., 1958-60; resident Stanford U. Med. Ctr., Palo Alto, Calif., 1960-65; asst. prof. U. Fla., Gainesville, 1965-68, assoc. prof., 1968-71, prof. surgery, 1971-95, prof. emeritus, adj. prof., 1995—, dir. organ transplant programs, 1971-95. Bd. dirs. United Network for Organ Sharing, Richmond, Va., pres. elect, 1997-98, pres., 1998-99; pres., chmn. Southeastern Organ Procurement Found., Richmond, 1973-95. Fellow Am. Coll. Surgeons; mem. Am. Surg. Assn., Am. Soc. Transplant Surgeons, So. Surg. Assn., Transplantation Soc., Alachua County Med. Soc. (pres. 1977-78). Home: 2445 NW 15th Pl Gainesville FL 32605-5148 Office: U Fla Dept Surgery PO Box 100286 Gainesville FL 32610-0286 Office Phone: 352-265-0606. Personal E-mail: puffer12@aol.com. Business E-mail: pfaff@surgery.ufl.edu.

**PFAFFENROTH, PETER ALBERT,** lawyer; b. Mineola, NY, Mar. 29, 1941; s. Albert and Genevieve Astrid (Anderson) P.; m. Sara Ann Beekey, June 26, 1966; children: Elizabeth Cartwright, Peter Cyrus, Catherine Genevieve. BS in Engring., Princeton U., 1963, Diploma in European Civilization, 1963; JD, U. Mich., 1966; LLM in Taxation, NYU, 1972, LLM in Corp., 1976, LLM in Internat. Law, 1998. Bar: N.J. 1966, U.S. Dist. Ct. (N.J. dist.) 1966. With Daimler-Benz, Stuttgart, Fed. Republic Germany, 1961, B.P. Benzin & Petroleum, Hamburg, Fed. Republic Germany, 1962, Office of Internat. Affairs, U.S. Treasury Dept., Washington, 1963, Office of Export Control, U.S. Commerce Dept., Washington, 1964, Commrs. Office, U.S. Patent Office, Washington, 1965; atty. McCarter & English, Newark, 1966-68, Kentz & Gilson, Esqs., Summit, NJ, 1968-69; corp. counsel Tex. Plastics, Maine Sugar Industries, Robbinsville, NJ, 1969-70; atty. c/o Lewis Stein, Esq., Netcong, NJ, 1970-71; pvt. practice Chester, NJ, 1971—. Avocations: antiques, foreign languages, travel, wine.

**PFALTZ, HUGO MENZEL, JR.,** lawyer; b. Newark, Sept. 23, 1931; s. Hugo M. and Mary E. (Horr) Pfaltz; m. Marilyn M. Muir, Sept. 29, 1956; children: Elizabeth W., William M., Robert L. BA, Hamilton Coll., 1953; JD, Harvard U., 1960; LLM, NYU, 1965. Bar: N.J. 1960, U.S. Dist. Ct. N.J. 1960, U.S. Supreme Ct. 1977. Assoc. McCarter & English, Newark, 1960—61, Bourne & Noll, Summit, NJ, 1961—74; sole practice Summit, 1974—82; ptnr. Pfaltz & Woller, 1983—. Mem. Battleship N.J. Commn., 1985—, NJ Law Revision Commn., 1986—2003. Assoc. editor N.J. Law Jour., 1966—2002, editor, 1984—86. Chmn. Summit Rep. City Com., 1966; mem. N.J. Constl. Conv., 1966, N.J. Assembly, 1968—72. Served to lt. USNR, 1953—62. Mem.: ABA, Summit Bar Assn., Union County Bar Assn., N.J. Bar Assn., Summit Tennis Club, Beacon Hill Club (Summit), Baltusrol Club (Springfield, N.J.), Univ. Club (Washington), Univ Club (N.Y.C.). Home: 118 Prospect St Summit NJ 07901-2472 Office: 382 Springfield Ave Summit NJ 07901-2707 Office Phone: 908-273-1974. Personal E-mail: hugopf@aol.com.

**PFARR, ALBERT D.,** sculptor, director; b. Huntington, NY, July 3, 1960; m. Julie A. Stevenson. MFA, Alfred U., 1990. Lectr. ceramics Wash. U., St. Louis, 1995—2005; dir. ops. Clay Art Ctr., Port Chester, NY, 2005—. Large-scale ceramic sculpture, Three Born, Reproductive Nature, Saturation, Solubility series. Personal E-mail: adpfarr@yahoo.com.

**PFAU, JAMES MICHAEL,** lawyer; b. Milw., Aug. 22, 1958; s. Raymond Aloysius and Patricia Ann (Foley) P.; children: Gretchen Canright, Anna Katharine. BS in Journalism with distinction, Northwestern U., 1979; JD magna cum laude, U. Mich., 1983. Bar: Minn. 1983, U.S. Dist. Ct. Minn. 1983. Ptnr. Faegre & Benson, Mpls., 1983—. Contbr. articles to profl. jours. Bd. dirs. St. Anthony Pk. Community Coun., St. Paul, 1989-92. Mem. Minn. State Bar Assn. Episcopalian. Home: 2140 Fairmount Ave Saint Paul MN 55105 Office: Faegre and Benson LLP 90 S 7th St Ste 2200 Minneapolis MN 55402-3901 Office Phone: 612-766-8616. E-mail: jpfau@faegre.com.

**PFAU, RICHARD ANTHONY,** university president; b. N.Y.C., Feb. 19, 1942; s. Hugo and Irene Beatrice P.; m. Nancy Ann DiPace, Sept. 12, 1964; children: Bradley Madison, Aleksandra Nicole. AB, Hamilton Coll., 1964; MA, U. Va., 1973, PhD, 1975. Systems analyst Equitable Life Ins. Co., N.Y.C., 1964-66; asst. prof. history Dickinson Coll., Carlisle, Pa., 1975-80; assoc. prof., assoc. dean U. Miami, Coral Gables, Fla., 1980-85; dean of faculty, provost Emory (Va.) and Henry Coll., 1985-93; pres. Ill. Coll., Jacksonville, Ill., 1993—2002, Averett U., Danville, Va., 2002—. Author: No Sacrifice Too Great: The Life of Lewis L. Strauss, 1985. Contbr. articles, book revs. to profl. publs. Vestryman St. Thomas Episc. Ch., Abingdon, Va., Epis. Ch. Epiphany, Denville, Va.; chmn., sec.-treas., exec. com., bd. dirs. Va. Found. for Humanities and Pub. Policy; mem. bd. trustees Carlisle Sch., Martinsville, Va.; mem. adv. bd. Salvation Army, Jacksonville, Ill. Capt. USAF, 1966-71. DuPont fellow, 1974-75; Hoover fellow, 1982. Mem. Danville Golf Club, Omicron Delta Kappa, Alpha Psi Omega, Pi Delta Epsilon. Home: 500 Hawthorne Drive Danville VA 24541 Office: Averett Univ Pres Office 420 West Main Street Danville VA 24541

**PFEFFER, CYNTHIA ROBERTA,** psychiatrist, educator; b. Newark, May 22, 1943; d. Edward I. and Ann Pfeffer. BA, Douglas Coll., 1964; MD, NYU, 1968. Assoc. dir. child psychiatry inpatient unit Albert Einstein Coll. Medicine, Bronx, NY, 1973-79; chief child psychiatry inpatient unit N.Y. Hosp. Cornell Med. Ctr., White Plains, NY, 1979-95; assoc. prof. clin. psychiatry Weill Med. Coll. Cornell U., N.Y.C., 1984—. Prof. psychiatry Cornell U. Med. Coll., 1989—; pres. N.Y. Coun. on Child and Adolescent Psychiatry, N.Y.C., 1989—; dir. childhood bereavement program Weill Med. Coll. Cornell U., 1999—. Author: The Suicidal Child, 1986, Difficult Moments in Child Psychotherapy, 1988; editor: Youth Suicide: Perspectives on Risk and Prevention, 1989, Intense Stress and Mental Disturbance in Children, 1996; co-editor: Neurologic Disorders: Developmental and Behavioral Sequelae for Child and Adolescent Psychiatric Clinics of North America. 1999. Recipient Erwin Stengel award Internat. Assn. Suicide Prevention, 1987, Wilford Hulse award N.Y. Coun. on Child & Adolescent Psychiatry, 1989, Sigmund Freud award Am. Soc. Psychoanalytic Physicians, 1994. Fellow Am. Psychiat. Assn., Am. Acad. Child and Adolescent Psychiatry (councillor-at-large 1989—, Norbert Rieger award 1988), Am. Psychopathological Assn.; mem. Am. Assn. Suicidology (pres. 1987, Young Contbrs. award 1981, 82). Office: NY Hosp Westchester Div 21 Bloomingdale Rd White Plains NY 10605-1504 also: 1100 Madison Ave New York NY 10028-0327 Office Phone: 914-997-5849, 212-717-2334. Business E-mail: cpfeffer@med.cornell.edu.

**PFEFFER, DAVID H.,** lawyer; b. NYC, Mar. 15, 1935; B. Chem. Engring., CCNY, 1956; JD, NYU, 1961, LL.M. in Trade Regulation, 1967. Bar: N.Y. 1961. With patent dept. U.S Rubber Co., Wayne, NJ, 1957-61; assoc. Watson, Leavenworth, Kelton & Taggart, N.Y.C., 1961-63, Morgan & Finnegan, LLP, N.Y.C., 1963-70, ptnr., 1971—. Village prosecutor Roslyn Harbor, N.Y., 1976-78, village justice, 1979-2003; panel of arbitrators Am. Arbitration Assn, Ctr. Dispute Resolution, NY Civil Ct., Nat. Arbitration Forum, CPI Inst. Dispute Resolution. Mem. ABA (litigation sect.), N.Y. State Bar Assn., Assn. Bar City N.Y. Am. Intellectual Property Law Assn. (com. alt. dispute resolution), N.Y. Intellectual Property Law Assn. (com. alt. dispute resolution), Order of Coif. Office: Morgan & Finnegan LLP 3 World Financial Ctr New York NY 10281-2101 Office Phone: 212-415-8700. E-mail: dpfeffer@morganfinnegan.com.

**PFEFFER, JEFFREY,** business educator; b. St. Louis, July 23, 1946; s. Newton Stuart and Shirlee (Krisman) P.; m. Kathleen Frances Fowler, July 23, 1986. BS, MS, Carnegie Mellon U., 1968; PhD, Stanford U., 1972. Tech. staff Rsch. Analysis Corp., McLean, Va., 1968-69; asst. prof. U. Ill., Champaign, 1971-73; from asst. prof. to assoc. prof. U. Calif., Berkeley, 1973-79; prof. Grad. Sch. Bus. Stanford (Calif.) U., 1979—. Dir. SonoSite, Inc., Audible Magic, Inc.; vis. prof. Harvard U. Sch. Bus., Boston, 1981-82, London Bus. Sch., 2005, IESE, Barcelona, 2006. Author: The External Control of Organizations, 1978, Organizational Design, 1978, Power in Organizations, 1981, Organizations and Organization Theory, 1982 (Terry Book award 1984), Managing with Power, 1992, Competitive Advantage Through People, 1994, New Directions for Organization Theory, 1997, The Human Equation, 1998, The Knowing-Doing Gap, 1999, Hidden Value, 2000, Hard Facts, Dnagerous Half-Truths, and Total Nonsense, 2006; monthly columnist (mag.) Bus. 2.0. Fellow Acad. Mgmt. (bd. govs. 1984-86, New Concept award 1979, Richard D. Irwin award for scholarly contbns. to mgmt. 1989); mem. Labor and Employment Rels. Assn. Jewish. Avocations: cooking, music. Home: 425 Moseley Rd Hillsborough CA 94010-6715 Office: Stanford U Grad Sch Bus Stanford CA 94305 Office Phone: 650-723-2915. E-mail: pfeffer_jeffrey@gsb.stanford.edu.

**PFEFFER, PHILIP ELLIOT,** biophysicist; b. NYC, Apr. 8, 1941; s. Charles and Della (Smith) P.; m. Judith Stashen, Dec. 22, 1962; children: Charles, Ari, Shira. AB, Hunter Coll., 1962; MS, Rutgers U., 1964, PhD, 1966. Rsch. asst. dept. chemistry Rutgers U., New Brunswick, NJ, 1964-66; rsch. fellow dept.

chemistry U. Chgo., 1966-68; rsch. scientist Ea. Regional Rsch. Ctr. USDA, Phila., 1968-88, rsch. leader Ea. Regional Rsch. Ctr., 1976-88, lead scientist Ea. Regional Rsch. Ctr., 1988—. Editor-at-large Marcel Dekker, N.Y.C., 1990—; adj. prof. dept. biosci. and biotech. Drexel U., Phila., 1996—; vis. prof. U. Bordeaux, France, 1998. Editor: Nuclear Magnetic Resonance in Agriculture, 1989, Nuclear Magnetic Resonance in Plant Biology, 1996; mem. editl. bd. Jour. Carbohydrate Chemistry, 1989—, Jour. Magnetic Resonance Analysis; contbr. articles to profl. jours. including Plant Physiology, Carbohydrate Rsch., Biochemica Acta, Biophysica, Jour. Magnetic Resonance. Recipient Bond award Am. Oil Chemists Soc., 1976, Fed. Svcs. award Phila. Fed. Assn., 1979, Science and Edn. award USDA, 1982; fellow Orgn. for Econ. Cooperation and Devel., 1989; Agrl. Rsch. Svc. rsch. fellow, 1989; vis. scientist grantee Centre d'Etudes Nucleaires de Grenoble, 1986, Oxford U., 1989; Nat. Rsch. Initiative grantee, 1997, 2002. Mem. AAAS, Internat. Soc. for Magnetic Resonance, Am. Chem. Soc. (Phila. sect. Scientist of Yr. 1982), Soc. for Applied Spectroscopy. Achievements include patents and publs. concerning use of alpha-anions; discovery of deuterium isotope shift NMR method for determining carbohydrate structures; development of P-31 NMR in vivo methodology for studying metal ion transport and C-13 NMR for studying plant/microbe interactions in nitrogen fixing plant nodules and symbiotic mycorrhizae. Office: USDA 600 E Mermaid Ln Wyndmoor PA 19038-8598

**PFEFFER, RICHARD LAWRENCE,** meteorology and geophysics educator; b. Bklyn., Nov. 26, 1930; s. Lester Robert and Anna (Newman) P.; m. Roslyn Ziegler, Aug. 30, 1953; children— Bruce, Lloyd, Scott, Glenn. BS cum laude, CCNY, 1952; MS, MIT, 1954, PhD, 1957. Research asst. MIT, 1952-55, guest lectr., 1956; atmospheric physicist Air Force Cambridge Research Center, Boston, 1955-59; sr. scientist Columbia U., 1959-61, lectr., 1961-62, asst. prof. geophysics, 1962-64; assoc. prof. meteorology Fla. State U., Tallahassee, 1964-67, prof. meteorology, 1967-96, disting. rsch. prof., 1997—, Carl-Gustav Rossby prof. meteorology, 1999—; dir. Geophys. Fluid Dynamics Inst., 1967-93. Cons. NASA, 1961-64, N.W. Ayer & Son, Inc., 1962, Ednl. Testing Service, Princeton, N.J., 1963, Voice of Am., 1963, Grolier, Inc., 1963, Naval Research Labs., 1971-76; Mem. Internat. Commn. for Dynamical Meteorology, 1972-76 Editor: Dynamics of Climate, 1960; Contbr. articles to profl. jours. Chmn. religious concern and social action com. Temple Israel, Tallahassee, 1971—72; bd. dirs. B'nai B'rith Anti-Defamation League, Tallahassee. Am. Meterol. Soc. (program chmn. ann. meeting 1963); mem. Am. Geophys. Union, N.Y. Acad. Scis. (chmn. planetary scis. sect. 1961-63), Sigma Xi, Chi Epsilon Pi, Sigma Alpha. Home: 9042 Shoal Creek Dr Tallahassee FL 32312 Office Phone: 850-644-5594. Business E-Mail: pfeffer@gfdi.fsu.edu.

**PFEFFER, ROBERT,** chemical engineer, academic administrator, educator; b. Vienna, Nov. 26, 1935; arrived in U.S., 1938, naturalized, 1944; s. Joseph and Gisela (Aberbach) P.; m. Marcia Borenstein, Dec. 24, 1960; children: Michael, Jacqueline. B in Chem. Engring., NYU, 1956, M in Chem. Engring., 1958, D in Engring. Sci., 1962. Mem. faculty CCNY, 1957-92, asst. prof. chem. engring., 1962-66, assoc. prof., 1966-71, prof., 1971-92, chmn. dept. chem. engring., 1973-87, Herbert Kayser prof., 1980-92, dean grad. studies and rsch., dep. provost, 1987-88, provost, v.p. acad. affairs, 1988-92; v.p. rsch. and grad. studies, prof. chem. engring. N.J. Inst. Tech., Newark, 1992-97, Disting. prof. chem. engring., 1997—. Vis. prof. Imperial Coll., London, 1969; Fulbright scholar Technion-Israel Inst. Tech., 1976-77; cons. in field. Contbr. articles to tech. publs. Fulbright Hays scholar, 1976-77; DuPont faculty fellow, 1962; NASA faculty fellow, 1964-65 Mem. AIChE (Particle Tech. Forum Nat. award 2000), Thomas Baron Nat. award 2000), Am. Soc. Engring. Edn., Sigma Xi, Tau Beta Pi, Phi Lambda Upsilon. Jewish. Office: NJIT University Heights Newark NJ 07102 Office Phone: 973-642-7496. Business E-Mail: pfeffer@njit.edu.

**PFEIFER, PAUL E.,** state supreme court justice; b. Bucyrus, Ohio, Oct. 15, 1942; m. Julia Pfeifer; 3 children. BA, Ohio State U., 1963, JD, 1966. Asst. atty. gen. State of Ohio, 1967-70; mem. Ohio Ho. of Reps., 1971-72; asst. prosecuting atty. Crawford County, 1973-76; mem. Ohio Senate, 1976-92, minority floor leader, 1983-84, asst. pres. pro-tempore, 1985-86; ptnr. Cory, Brown & Pfeifer, 1973-92; justice Ohio Supreme Ct., 1992—. Chmn. jud. com. Ohio Senate, 10 yrs. Mem. Grace United Meth. Ch., Bucyrus. Office: Supreme Court of Ohio 65 S Front St Columbus OH 43215-3431 Office Phone: 614-387-9020.*

**PFEIFER, TRACY M.,** plastic surgeon; b. Yonkers, NY, Dec. 20, 1960; d. Adrienne K and William A Pfeifer. BA, Rutgers U., 1982—84; MS, Calif. State U., Los Angeles, 1984—85; MD, U. of Medicine and Dentistry of NJ, 1987—91. Bd. cert. Am. Bd. of Plastic Surgery, 2001, Am. Bd. of Surgery, 1999. Plastic surgeon, pvt. practice Pfeifer Plastic Surgery, PLLC, NYC, 1999—. Fellow: Am. Coll. Surgeons; mem.: Am. Soc. Aesthetic Plastic Surgery, Am. Soc. Plastic Surgeons, NY Regional Soc. of Plastic Surgeons (exec. bd. mem. 2000—). Office: Pfeifer Plastic Surgery PLLC 565 Park Ave New York NY 10021 Office Phone: 212-860-0670. Office Fax: 212-593-8823. E-mail: tpfeifer@drpfeifer.com.

**PFEIFFER, ERIC ARMIN,** psychiatrist, gerontologist, writer; b. Rauental, Germany, Sept. 15, 1935; came to U.S., 1952; naturalized, 1957; s. Fritz and Emma (Saborowski) P.; m. Natasha Maria Emerson, Mar. 21, 1964; children: Eric Alexander, Michael David, Mark Armin. AB, Washington U., 1956, MD, 1960. Intern Albert Einstein Coll. Medicine, Bronx, NY, 1960-61; resident in psychiatry U. Rochester, NY, 1961-64; practice medicine specializing in psychiatry Durham, NC, 1966-76, Denver, 1976 78; asst. prof. Duke U., Durham, 1966-69, assoc. prof., 1969-72, prof., 1973-76, project dir., 1971-76, assoc. dir., 1974-76; dir. Davis Inst. Care and Study Aging, Denver, 1976-77; prof. psychiatry U. Colo., Denver, 1976-78; prof. psychiatry, chief div. geriatric psychiatry U. South Fla. Coll. Medicine, Tampa, 1978—; dir. Suncoast Gerontology Ctr., 1980—. Chief psychiatry svc. Tampa VA Med. Ctr., 1979-80; cons. in field; chmn. bd. Social Systems, Inc., 1975-76; chmn. com. on mental health and mental illness of elderly HEW, 1976-77. Author: Disordered Behavior, 1968, (with E.W. Busse) Behavior and Adaptation in Late Life, 1970, 3d edit., 1977, Successful Aging, 1974, Multidimensional Functional Assessment, 1977, Alzheimer's Disease, 1989. With USPHS, 1964-66. Markle Found. scholar acad. medicine, 1968-73; Eric Pfeiffer Chair in Alzheimer's Disease Rsch. named in his honor, U. S. Fla., 1985. Fellow Gerontol. Soc. (chmn. clin. medicine sect. 1975-76), Am. Psychiat. Assn.; mem. Am. Geriatrics Soc. (Allen Gold medal 1977), So. Psychiat. Soc., Phi Beta Kappa. Office: 12901 Bruce B Downs Blvd Tampa FL 33612-4742 Office Phone: 813-974-4355. E-mail: epfeiffe@hsc.usf.edu.

**PFEIFFER, GARY M.,** chemicals executive; b. Richmond, Va., Oct. 24, 1949; m. Lear Strange; 2 children. BA in Polit. Sci., Coll. William and Mary, MBA. From mem. staff to sr. v.p., CFO DuPont, Wilmington, Del., 1974-97, sr. v.p., CFO, 1997—. Office: DuPont 1007 Market St 8th Fl Wilmington DE 19898*

**PFEIFFER, GARY R.,** information technology manager; b. Pitts., Sept. 30, 1957; s. Richard J. and Virginia C. Pfeiffer. Plumbing foreman Lisk Plumbing and Heating, 1970—79; counter sales Nicklas Supply, 1979—82; supr. Hush Maintenance, 1982—83; dir. engring. and maintenance Passavant Hosp., 1983—95; application engr. Surface Engring., 1995—97; project mgr. Carmel Constrn., 1996—97; network build-out engr. Winstar Wireless, 1997—2000; constrn. mgr. Gen. Dynamics Corp., 2000—02; sr. cons. Tekmark Global Solutions, 2002—03; constrn. supr. Mid-West Nextel Build Gen. Dynamics, 2003; constrn. field inspector LCC Internat. Inc., 2003—06; utility warehouse person Adecco/US Liner, 2006—. Mem. adv. bd. Allegheny County Bur. Air Pollution, 1990—95, Environ. Info. Assn., 1993—95; zoning bd. ofcl. Economy Boro, 2004—05; presenter in field. Recipient Shining Star award, LCC Internat., 2004. Avocations: golf, gardening, movies. Office: Am Mare/US Liner 19 Leonberg Rd Cranberry Township PA

**PFEIFFER, JANE CAHILL,** former broadcasting company executive, consultant; b. Sept. 29, 1932; d. John Joseph and Helen (Reilly) Cahill; m. Ralph A. Pfeiffer, Jr., June 3, 1975. BA, U. Md., 1954; postgrad., Cath. U. Am., 1956—57; LHD (hon.), Pace Coll., 1978, U. Md., 1979; LHD (hon.), Manhattanville Coll., 1979, Amherst U., 1980, Babson Coll., 1981, U. Notre Dame, 1991; LHD (hon.), Bryant Coll., 1995, St. Thomas Aquinas Coll., 2006. With IBM Corp., Armonk, NY, 1955-76, sec. mgmt. rev. com., 1970, dir. comm., 1971, v.p. comm. and govt. rels., 1972-76; bus. cons., 1976-78; chmn. NBC, Inc., N.Y.C., 1978-80; bus. cons., 1980—. Trustee The Conf. Bd., 1991. Pres.'s adv. com. White House Fellows, 1966, Pres.'s Gen. Adv. Commn. on Arms Control and Disarmament, 1977-80, Pres.'s Commn. Mil. Compensation; trustee Rockefeller Found., U. Md., Carnegie Hall, 1981-1986, U. Notre Dame; bd. dirs. Catholic Univ. of Am., 1973-1978, Rockefeller Found., 1973-1985, White House Fellows, 1976-1981, Kettering Found., 1975-1979. Recipient Achievement award Kappa Kappa Gamma, 1974-80, Eleanor Roosevelt Humanitarian award NY League for Hard of Hearing, 1980, Disting. Alumna award U. Md., 1975, Humanitarian award NOW, 1980, Centennial Alumna medallion U. Md., 1988; White House fellow, Washington, 1966, Making Waves award, Greatest 50 Women in Radio and Television-AWRT, 2002. Mem. Coun. Fgn. Rels., Overseas Devel. Coun., Econ. of N.Y. Club. Office: C/O Jonathan L Smith Chesapeake Asset Mgmt LLC 1 Rockefeller Plz Rm 1210 New York NY 10020-2002 Home: Johns Island 1050 Beach Rd Apt 1G Vero Beach FL 32963-3413 Office Phone: 212-218-4044.

**PFEIFFER, MARGARET KOLODNY,** lawyer; b. Elkin, NC, Oct. 7, 1944; d. Isadore Harold and Mary Elizabeth Kolodny; m. Carl Frederick Pfeiffer II, Sept. 2, 1968. BA, Duke U., 1967; JD, Rutgers U., 1974. Bar: NJ 1974, NY 1976, DC 1981, US Supreme Ct. 1979. Law clk. to Hon. F.L. Van Dusen U.S. Ct. Appeals 3d cir., Phila., 1974-75; assoc. Sullivan & Cromwell, NYC and Washington, 1975-82, ptnr. antitrust, intellectual property, internat. trade and investment practice area, criminal def. and investigations, 1982—. Contbr. articles to profl. jours. Trustee Nat. Law Ctr. on Homelessness and Poverty; mem. bd. visitors Trinity Coll. of Duke U. Mem. ABA, Internat. Bar Assn., DC Bar Assn., NY State Bar Assn., Assn. of Bar of City of NY, Am. Soc. of Internat. Law. Avocations: gardening, reading, music. Office: Sullivan & Cromwell 1701 Pennsylvania Ave NW Washington DC 20006-5866 Office Phone: 202-956-7540. Business E-Mail: pfeifferm@sullcrom.com.

**PFEIFFER, MICHELLE,** actress; b. Santa Ana, Calif., Apr. 29, 1957; d. Dick and Donna P.; m. Peter Horton, 1981 (div. 1988); 1 adopted child, Claudia Rose; m. David Kelley, Nov. 13, 1993, 1 child. Student, Golden West Coll., Whitley Coll. Actress: (feature films) Falling in Love Again, 1980, Hollywood Knights, 1980, Charlie Chan and the Curse of the Dragon Queen, 1981, Grease II, 1982, Scarface, 1983, Ladyhawke, 1985, Into the Night, 1985, Sweet Liberty, 1986, Amazon Women on the Moon, 1987, Witches of Eastwick, 1987, Married to the Mob, 1988, Tequila Sunrise, 1988, Dangerous Liaisons, 1988 (Acad. award nominee for best supporting actress, 1989, BAFTA award, 1990), The Fabulous Baker Boys, 1989 (L.A. Film Critics Assn. award for best actress, 1989, D.W. Griffith award Nat. Bd. Rev., 1989, N.Y. Film Critics award, 1989, Nat. Soc. Film Critics award for best actress, 1990, Golden Globe award for best actress drama, 1990, Acad. award nominee for best actress, 1990), The Russia House, 1990, Frankie & Johnny, 1991, Love Field, 1992 (Acad. award nominee for best actress, 1993), Batman Returns, 1992, The Age of Innocence, 1993, Wolf, 1994, Dangerous Minds, 1995, Up Close and Personal, 1996, To Gillian on her 37th Birthday, 1996, One Fine Day, 1996, A Thousand acres, 1997, The Prince of Egypt (voice), 1998, The Story of Us, 1998, A Midsummer Night's Dream, 1999, Deep End of the Ocean, 1999, What Lies Beneath, 2000, I Am Sam, 2001, White Oleander, 2002, Sinbad: Legend of the Seven Seas (voice), 2003; (TV movies) The Solitary Man, 1979, Callie and Son, 1981, The Children Nobody Wanted, 1981, Splendor in the Grass, 1981, One Too Many, 1983, Tales from the Hollywood Hills: Natica Jackson, 1987, Power, Passion and Murder, 1987; (TV series) Delta House, 1979, B.A.D. Cats, 1980; prodr: (films) A Thousand Acres, 1997; exec. prodr.: (films) One Fine Day, 1996. Named Woman of the Yr., Harvard's Hasty Pudding Theater Club, 1995; recipient Crystal award, Women in Film, 1993.

**PFEIFFER, NORMAN,** architectural firm executive; b. Kirkland, Wash., 1940; married. Grad., U. Wash. Co-founder, ptnr. Hardy, Holzman, Pfeiffer Assocs. LLP, L.A., 1968—. Mem. Archtl. Commn. U. Wash., 1989—. Fellow: AIA. Office: HHPA Ste 430 811 W 7th St Los Angeles CA 90017

**PFEIFFER, PHILIP JOHN,** lawyer; b. Houston, Aug. 16, 1947; BS, Sam Houston State U., 1969; JD, So. Meth. U., 1972. Bar: Tex. 1972. Ptnr. Fulbright & Jaworski LLP, 1979—, former ptnr.-in-charge San Antonio office San Antonio. Editor-in-chief Employment Discrimination Law (Second Supplement to Lindemann and Grossman). Named a Tex. Super Lawyer, Tex. Monthly Mag., 2003, 2004, 2005. Mem. ABA, State Bar Tex., San Antonio Bar Assn., San Antonio Bar Found., Tex. Bar Found., Order of Coif, Phi Alpha Delta. Office: Fulbright & Jaworski LLP 300 Convent St Ste 2200 San Antonio TX 78205-3792 Office Phone: 210-270-7117. Office Fax: 210-270-7205. Business E-Mail: ppfeiffer@fulbright.com.

**PFEIFFER, PHYLLIS KRAMER,** publishing executive; b. NYC, Feb. 11, 1949; d. Jacob N. and Estelle G. Rosenbaum-Pfeiffer; m. Stephen M. Pfeiffer, Dec. 21, 1969; children: Andrew Kramer, Elise Kramer. BS, Cornell U., 1970; postgrad., U. San Diego, 1976-78. Instr. Miss Porter's Sch., Farmington, Conn., 1970; tchr. Dewey Jr. HS NYC Bd. Edn., 1970—73; rschr. Hunter Coll., NYC, 1971—72; account exec. La Jolla (Calif.) Light, 1973—75, advt. dir., 1975—77, gen. mgr., 1977-78, pub., 1978-87; exec. v.p. Harte Hanks So. Calif. Newspapers, 1985—87; gen mgr San Diego edit. L.A. Times, 1987—93, pres., pub. Martin Ind. Jour., Novato, Calif., 1993—2000; v.p. advt. and mktg. Contra Costa Times, 2000—04; sr. v.p. advt. San Francisco Chronicle, 2005—. Dir. comm. ctr. San Diego State U., 1980-93. Bd. dirs. La Jolla Cancer Rsch. Found., 1979-82, YMCA, San Diego Ballet, 1980, Dominican Coll., San Rafael, Calif, 1994—, Marin Theater Co., Alvarado Hosp., 1981-88, chmn. fin. com., 1986, sec. bd., 1986; co-chmn. Operation USS La Jolla, USN, 1980—; mem. mktg. com. United Way, 1979-81, chmn., 1983; trustee La Jollan's Inc., 1975-78, Nat. Pk. Trust, 2000-02, Dogs for the Blind, 2001-; mem. Conv. and Visitors Bur. Blue Ribbon Com. on Future, 1983; mem. resource panel Child Abuse Prevention Found., 1983—; bd. overseers U. Calif., San Diego; mem. violent crimes task force San Diego Police Dept.; dir. Guide Dogs for the Blind, Oakland Mus. Grantee N.Y. Bd. Edn., 1971-72; named Pub. of Yr., Gannet Co., Inc., 1995. Mem. Newspaper Assn. Am., Calif. Newspaper Pubs. Assn. (bd. dirs., exec. com.), Chancellor's Assn. U. Calif.-San Diego, Clairemont Club. Office: 250 The Uplands Berkeley CA 94705 Office Phone: 415-777-7272. E-mail: ppfeiffer@sfchronicle.com.

**PFEIFFER, SOPHIA DOUGLASS,** retired state legislator, lawyer; b. NYC, Aug. 10, 1918; d. Franklin Chamberlin and Sophie Douglass (White) Wells; m. Timothy Adams Pfeiffer, June 7, 1941; children: Timothy Franklin, Penelope Mesereau Keenan, Sophie Douglass. AB, Vassar Coll., 1939; JD, Northeastern U., 1975. Bar: R.I. 1975, U.S. Ct. Appeals (1st cir.) 1980, U.S. Supreme Ct. 1979. Editl. rschr. Time, Inc., NYC, 1940-41; writer Officer War Info., Washington, 1941-43, NYC, 1943-45; editl. staff Nat. Geog. Mag., Washington, 1958, 69-70; editor Turkish Jour. Pediatrics, Ankara, 1961-63; staff atty. R.I. Supreme Ct., Providence, 1975-76, chief staff atty., 1977-86; mem. Maine Ho. Reps., 1990-94; lectr. U. So. Maine, 1995. Bd. dirs. Death and Dying project. Contbr. in field. Chair bioethics study League Women Voters; pres. Karachi (Pakistan) Am. Sch., 1955-56; chair Brunswick Village Rev. Bd., 1986-89; trustee Brunswick Sewer Dist., 2000-05, bd. dirs. Coll. Guild, 2003—, ret., 2005. Home: 15 Franklin St Brunswick ME 04011-2101

**PFEIFFER, STEVEN BERNARD,** lawyer; b. Orange, NJ, Jan. 19, 1947; s. Bernard Victor and Elizabeth Sophia (Bissell) P.; m. Kristin Reagan, June 27, 1970; children: Victoria Pfeiffer Metz, Rachel Catherine, Emily Dorothea, Stephanie Kristin Bissell, Andrew Steven Bernard. BA in Govt., Wesleyan U.,

1969; BA in Jurisprudence, Oxford U., 1971, MA, 1983; MA in African Studies, U. London, 1973; JD, Yale U., 1976. Bar: N.J. 1976, D.C. 1978. Assoc. Fulbright & Jaworski, Houston, London, 1976—83, ptnr. London, Washington, 1983—, ptnr.-in-charge London, 1983—86, 1989—2002, head internat. dept., 1989—2003, ptnr.-in-charge Washington office, 1998—2002, chmn. exec. com., 2003—. Bd. dirs. The Africa Am. Inst., N.Y.C., Project HOPE, Washington, Barloworld Ltd., Johannesburg, Iridium Holdings LLC, Washington. Contbr. articles to profl. jours. Alumni-elected trustee Wesleyan U., Middletown, Conn., 1976-79, charter trustee, 1980-92, vice chmn. bd. trustees, 1986-87, chmn. bd. trustees, 1987-92, chmn. emeritus, 1992—; trustee St. Andrews Sch., Middletown, Del., 1995—. With USN, 1969, 72-74; asst. cinceur plans officer, Office of CNO, Washington, 1972-73; spl. asst. to Sec. of Navy, Washington, 1973-74. Rhodes scholar, 1969-72; Thomas Watson Travel fellow, The Watson Found., 1969. Mem. ABA, N.J. State Bar Assn., Am. Soc. Internat. Law, Internat. Bar Assn. (past chmn. sect. energy and natural resources law 1992-94). Naval Res. Assn., Internat. Inst. Strategic Studies (London), Coun. Fgn. Rels. N.Y. Avocations: tennis, history, fishing, books. Office: Fulbright & Jaworski LLP Market Sq 801 Pennsylvania Ave NW Washington DC 20004-2623 Office Phone: 202-662-4585. Office Fax: 202-662-4643. Business E-Mail: spfeiffer@fulbright.com.

**PFEIFFER, WILLIAM SANBORN,** education educator, writer; b. Akron, Ohio, July 29, 1947; s. Harold Arthur and Jean Sanborn Pfeiffer; m. Evelyn Hepp Pfeiffer, July 17, 1976; children: Zachary Paul, Kathryn Blaire. BA in English, Amherst Coll., 1969; MA in English, Kent State U., 1973, PhD in English, 1975. Dept. head Southern Poly State U., Marietta, Ga., 1989—97, assoc. dean, arts and sci., 2000, v.p. acad. affairs, 2001—03; founding provost Ramapo Coll., Mahwah, NJ, 2003—04, interim pres., 2004—05, provost, interim CIO, 2005—06; pres. Warren Wilson Coll., Asheville, NC, 2005—. Author: (book) Technical Communication: A Practical Approach, 2006; author: (with Steven B. Zwickel) Pocket Guide to Technical Presentations and Professional Speaking, 2006; author: Technical Writing: A Practical Approach, 2004; author: (with J. Boogerd) Pocket Guide to Technical Writing, 2004; author: Pocket Guide to Public Speaking, 2002; author: (with C.H. Keller Jr.) Proposal Writing: The Art of Friendly and Winning Persuasion, 2000; author: Proposal Writing: The Art of Friendly and Persuasion, 1989; contbr. articles to profl. jours. Avocations: jogging, hiking, travel, fly fishing. Home: 106 North Lane Swannanoa NC 28778 Office: Warren Wilson Coll PO Box 9000 Asheville NC 28815 Office Phone: 828-771-2070.

**PFEISTER, RAYMOND LYNN,** diversified financial services company executive; b. Cape Girardeau, Mo., May 31, 1946; s. Herman Joe and Imogene Elsie (Groseclose) P.; m. Susan Jane Selby, July 1, 1969; children: Joseph Robert, John Charles. BS, U. Ill., 1969, MBA, 1971; PhD, CUNY, 1978. Sales analyst Koppers Co., Magnolia, Ark., 1969-70; instr. bus. U. Ill., Urbana, 1971; spl. agt. Prudential Ins. Co. Am., Champaign, Ill., 1971, divsn. mgr. Balt., 1971-74, mktg. specialist, mgr. group pension Newark and NYC, 1974; account exec. Alexander & Alexander Inc., NYC, 1974-76, asst. v.p., 1976-78, v.p., 1978-80, Johnson & Higgins, NYC, 1980-83; founder, chmn. bd., CEO Pfeister Barter Inc., NY Reciprocal Trade Exch., 1979-87; founder, chmn., pres. Pfeister Corp., Wilmington, Del., 1977—; co-founder, pres., treas. Chattan Group, Ltd., NYC, 1983—; co-founder, pres., CEO Sheffield Assocs., Ltd., NYC, 1985—; co-owner Ceramic Design Ltd., Greenwich, Conn., 1987—2006; vice chmn. Fred Alger Mgmt., NYC, 2006—; chmn. bd. Pfeister Capital Mgmt., Bronxville, NY, 2006—; bd. dirs. U.S. Ceramic Tile Corp., Canton, Ohio, London Pacific Life Ins. Co., Calif.; lectr., cons. in field. Author: The Strategic Planning Process for Alexander & Alexander Services, Inc. and Subsidiaries, 1980; contbg. author: The Practice of Planning—Strategic, Administrative and Operational, 1981. Pres. Jr. Achievement, Denver, 1963-64; active boy Scouts Am., 1964—, United Fund, 1973. Mem. APA, Acad. Mgmt., Nat. Eagle Scout Assn., Soc. Am. Foresters, Forest Products Rsch. Soc., Nat. Life Underwriters Assn., Nat. MBA Assn., U. Ill. Alumni Assn. (life, v.p. 1974—), Siwanoy Country Club, Campfire Club Am., Union League Club, Sigma Iota Epsilon. Office Phone: 914-337-1877. E-mail: raypfiester@yahoo.com.

**PFENDER, EMIL,** mechanical engineering educator; b. Stuttgart, Germany, May 25, 1925; came to U.S., 1964, naturalized, 1969; s. Vinzenz and Anna Maria (Dreher) P.; m. Maria Katharina Staiger, Oct. 22, 1954; children: Roland, Norbert, Corinne. Student, U. Tuebingen, Germany, 1947-49; diploma in physics, U. Stuttgart, Germany, 1953, D Ing. in Elec. Engring., 1959. Assoc. prof. mech. engring. U. Minn., Mpls., 1964-67, prof., 1967—2000, prof. emeritus, 2000—. Contbr. articles to profl. jours.; patentee in field. Fellow: ASME; mem.: NAE. Home: 1947 Bidwell St Saint Paul MN 55118-4417 Office: U Minn Dept Mech Engring 111 Church St SE Minneapolis MN 55455-0150 Office Phone: 612-625-6012. Business E-Mail: pfender@tc.umn.edu.

**PFEUFFER, ROBERT JOHN,** musician; b. Cleve., Dec. 25, 1925; s. Henry Vincent and Elmo Alice (Burger) P.; m. Betty June Weller, Sept. 21, 1946; children— Barbara (Mrs. Steven Mosley), Jeanne, Susan, Catherine. B.Mus. in Edn., U. Mich., 1950, M.Mus. in Edn. 1951. Contrabassoonist, bassoonist Detroit Symphony Orch., 1951-61, Phila. Orch., 1962-91; instr. bassoon Wayne State U., 1957-61, New Sch. Music, Phila., 1969—; prin. bassoon Lynchburg Symphony, 1994—, Roanoke Opera, 1996—. Served with AUS, 1942-44. Mem. U.S. Power Squadron, Kappa Kappa Psi, Pi Mu Alpha. Roman Catholic. Home: 6 Sharp Ln Camden Wyoming DE 19934-4526

**PFIFFNER, JAMES PRICE,** political science professor; b. Stevens Point, Wis., June 24, 1946; s. James Sturtevant and Alice Price Pfiffner; m. Debra Ann Jones, Aug. 11, 1979; children: Megan Cyr, Katherine Courtney, Megan Mechan. BA in Polit. Sci., U. Wis., 1968, MA in Polit. Sci., 1972, PhD in Polit. Sci., 1975. Tchg. asst. U. Wis., Madison, 1971-74; rsch. fellow Brookings Inst., Washington, 1974-75; asst. prof. U. Calif., Riverside, 1975-78, Calif. State U., Fullerton, 1978-80, assoc. prof. polit. sci., 1980-84, John Brown Mason prof., 1983-84; spl. asst. to dir. Office Pers. Mgmt., Washington, 1980-81; assoc. prof. govt. and pub. policy George Mason U., Fairfax, Va., 1984-87, prof., 1987—, univ. prof., 2003—. Author: The President, the Budget, and Congress: Impoundment and the 1974 Budget Act, 1979, The Strategic Presidency: Hitting the Ground Running, 1988, 2d edit., 1996, The Modern Presidency, 1998, 4th edit., 2005, The Character Factor: How We Judge America's Presidents, 2004; editor: The President and Economic Policy, 1986, The Managerial Presidency, 1991, 2d edit., 1999, Governance and American Politics: Classic and Current Perspectives, 1995; co-editor: The Presidency in Transition, 1989, The Presidency and the Gulf War, 1993, Understanding the Presidency, 1997, 3d edit., 2005, The Future of Merit, 2000. With U.S. Army, 1969-70, Vietnam. Decorated Army Commendation medal for Valor, Vietnam/Cambodia, 1970; Brookings Instn. fellow, 1974-75, vis. scholar, 1983, 97; Nat. Assn. Sch. Pub. Affairs and Adminstrn. faculty fellow, 1980-81. Mem. Nat. Acad. Pub. Adminstrn., Cosmos Club. Office: George Mason U Sch Pub Policy 3C6 Fairfax VA 22030-4444 Office Phone: 703-993-1417. Business E-Mail: pfiffner@gmu.edu.

**PFIFFNER, PATRICK MEEHAN,** musician, educator; b. Stevens Point, Wis., Mar. 19, 1948; s. James Sturtevant and Alice Mary (Price) Pfiffner; m. Linda Sue Ridenour, Aug. 6, 1972; children: James Stanley, Jeffrey Allen. MusB, San Diego State U., 1976, MusM, 1977. Extra percussionist/timpanist San Diego Symphony, 1972—; percussionist Nederlander Orgn., San Diego, 1976—; resident drummer/percussionist/contractor Starlight Light Opera, San Diego, 1981—; extra percussionist/timpanist San Diego Opera, 1982—; prin. percussionist/timpanist San Diego Chamber Orch., 1985—; prof. music Point Loma Nazarene U., San Diego. Percussionist Sammy Davis, Bob Hope, George Burns, Mickey Rooney, Robert Goulet, Andre Bocelli, Johnny Mathis, Milton Berle, 1981—; dir. Grand Pacific Band, 1986—, Grossmont Coll. concert and jazz bands, 1979—86, Heartland Youth Orch., 1983—84. Author: The Ancestors of Patrick Meehan Pfiffner, 2002; contbr. articles to profl. issues; performer: (CD) Those Hollywood Marches, with Lalo Shifrin, 1990, Russian CD, San Diego Chamber Orch., 1989, French CD, 1991, Berlioz: Symphonie Fantastique, San Diego Symphony Orch., Malcolm Arnold CD, 1992, Magnification CD, Rock Group Yes, 2001, nat. tours

Broadway shows, including Beauty and the Beast, Hello Dolly, King and I, Ragtime, The Producers, Hairspray, others. Musician 2d class USN, 1967—71, USS Little Rock, Mediterranean Sea. Mem.: ASCAP, Percussive Arts Soc., Am. Fedn. Musicians Local 325. Avocations: long distance running, genealogy. Home: 13138 Beechtree St Lakeside CA 92040-3307 Office: Pt Loma Nazarene U 3900 Lomaland, Dr San Diego CA 92106 Personal E-mail: patpfiffner@cox.net.

**PFISTER, CLOYD HARRY,** former military officer, consultant; b. State College, Pa., Dec. 20, 1936; s. Rudolf John Pfister and June Ruth (Braun) Pfister Gray; m. Rita Askerc Kracht, Aug. 17, 1962 (div. Mar. 1982); m. Gail Williams, Apr. 24, 1982; children, Gabriele, Catherine, Michael, Romi, Eric Williams, Lori Williams. BA in Philosophy, Oberlin Coll., 1957; MA in Internat. Rels., Am. U., 1964, postgrad., 1964-67. Enlisted U.S. Army, 1957, advanced through grades to maj. gen., 1989; staff officer Nat. Security Agy., Fort Meade, Md., 1965-68; S3 (Ops.) 303d Radio Rsch. Bn., Plantation, Vietnam, 1968-69; instr. JFK Ctr. and Sch., Fort Bragg, N.C., 1969-72; politico-mil. officer, Office Dep. Chief of Staff for Ops. Hdqrs. Dept. Army, Washington, 1972-75; comdr. 307th U.S. Army Security Agy. Bn., VII U.S. Corps, Ludwigsburg, Fed. Republic Germany, 1975-77; asst. chief of staff intelligence 8th Mech. Inf. Div., Bad Kreuznach, Fed. Republic Germany, 1977-79; Mid. East staff officer, Internat. Security Affairs Office Sec. Def., The Pentagon, 1979-82; comdr. U.S. Army Field Sta., Berlin, 1982-84; chief of staff U.S. Army Intelligence Ctr. and Sch., Fort Huachuca, Ariz., 1984-85, dep. comdt., 1985-86; dir. intelligence (J2), Hdqrs., U.S. Cen. Command, MacDill AFB, Fla., 1986-88; dep. chief of staff intelligence Hdqrs., U.S. Army Europe and 7th Army, Heidelberg, Fed. Republic Germany, 1988-91; asst. dep. chief of staff Intelligence Hdqrs., Dept. Army, Pentagon, 1991-93. Cons. Def. Sci. Bd., 1994, Def. Airborne Reccon Office, 1994-97, Nat. Imagery and Mapping Agy., 1999-2001; chmn. Cmty. Adv. Coun. on Cancer, Inova, 2000—. Decorated Def. D.S.M., D.S.M. Def. Superior Svc. medal, Legion of Merit with two oak leaf clusters, Nat. Intelligence D.S.M.; Ehrenkreutz der Bundeswehr (gold) (Fed. Republic Germany); other awards. Mem. Internat. Inst. for Strategic Studies, Middle East Inst., Security Affairs Support Assn., Assn. U.S. Army, Armed Forces Communs. Electronics Assn.(intelligence non.). Nat. Correlation Working Group (bd. dirs.). Avocations: tennis, photography, gardening. Office: Tech Strategies & Alliances 5242 Lyngate Ct Burke VA 22015-1631

**PFISTER, DONALD HENRY,** biology professor; b. Kenton, Ohio, Feb. 17, 1945; s. William A. and Dorothy C. (Kurtz) P.; m. Cathleen C. Kennedy, July 1, 1971; children: Meghan, Brigid, Edith. AB, Miami U., Oxford, Ohio, 1967; PhD, Cornell U., 1971; AM (hon.), Harvard U., 1980. Asst. prof. biology U. P.R., Mayaguez, 1971-74; asst. prof. biology, asst. curator Farlow Herbarium Harvard U., Cambridge, Mass., 1974-77, assoc. prof. biology, assoc. curator Farlow Herbarium, 1977-80, prof. biology, curator Farlow Herbarium, 1980—, dir., Farlow Herbarium, 1983-95, dir. & curator, Farlow Herbarium, 1999—, Asa Gray prof. botany, 1984—. Vis. mycologist U. Copenhagen, 1978; vis. prof. field station U. Minn., Itasca, 1979; master Kirkland House Harvard U., 1982-00. Contbr. over 80 articles to profl. jours. Grantee NSF, 1973-75, 81-85, 85, Am. Philos. Soc., 1975-76, Whiting Found., 1986. Fellow AAAS, Linnean Soc. London; mem. Mycol. Soc. Am. (sec. 1988-91, v.p. 1993-94, pres.-elect 1994-95, pres. 1995-96), Am. Phytopath. Soc., Am. Microbiol. Soc., New Eng. Bot. Club, Sigma Xi. Office: Harvard U Herbarium 22 Divinity Ave Cambridge MA 02138

**PFISTER, MARC,** consumer products company executive, medical researcher; s. Erwin and Gertrud Pfister; m. Susanna Pfister, Sept. 9, 1999. BS, U. Berne, 1983, MD, 1988; diploma in pub. health, U. Basel, Switzerland, 1991; cert., U. Berne, 1998. Clin. fellow Hosp. Interlaken, Berne, 1992—94; rsch. fellow U. Hosp. Berne, 1994, med. officer, clin. fellow, 1995—99; clin. rsch. fellow U. Calif., San Francisco, 1999—2002; assoc. dir. Sanfoni Aventis Pharm., Bridgewater, NJ, 2002—04; head, dir. clin. rsch. Bristol-Myers-Squibb, Princeton, NJ, 2004—. Contbr. articles to profl. jours.; reviewer: to numerous jours. Founder, chair Modeling And Simulation Applications in Clin. Pharmatherapy Orgn. Fellow: Am. Coll. Clin. Pharm.; mem.: Am. Soc. Nephrology (1st prize 1998), Am. Soc. Hypertension. Achievements include design of disease new method for dialysis treatment; novel computer models for clinical research. Avocations: piano, jazz, classical music. Office: Bristol-Myers-Squibb Rsch Inst PO Box 4000 Rt 206 Princeton NJ 08540 Office Phone: 609-252-5322. Office Fax: 609-252-7822. E-mail: mpfistersf@cs.com.

**PFLANZE, OTTO PAUL,** history professor; b. Maryville, Tenn., Apr. 2, 1918; s. Otto Paul and Katrine (Mills) P.; m. Hertha Maria Haberlander, Feb. 20, 1951; children: Stephen, Charles, Katrine. BA, Maryville Coll., 1940; MA, Yale U., 1942, PhD, 1950. Historian Dept. State, 1948-49; instr. N.Y. U., 1950-51; asst. prof. U. Mass., 1952-58, U. Ill., 1958-61; prof. history U. Minn., 1961-76, Ind. U., 1977-86, emeritus, 1986; Stevenson Prof. of History Bard Coll., Annandale On Hudson, NY, 1987-92, emeritus, 1992. Chmn. Conf. Group Central European History, 1978; mem. exam. bd., grad. record exam Ednl. Testing Service, 1972-76; mem. Inst. Advanced Study, 1970-71, mem. Historisches Kolleg, Munich, 1980-81. Author: Bismarck and the Development of Germany: Vol. 1.-The Period of Unification, 1815-1871, 1963 (Biennal Book award Phi Alpha Theta), rev. edit., 1990, Vol. 2-The Period of Consolidation, 1871-1880, 1990, Vol. 3-The Period of Fortification, 1880-1898, 1990 (3 vols. collectively named Most Outstanding Book in History, Govt. & Polit. Sci. by Assn. Am. Pubs., 1991); translated as Bd. I-Bismarck, Der Reichsgründer, 1997, Bd II-Bismarck, Der Reichskanzler, 1998 (Einhard prize 1999); co-author: A History of the Western World: Modern Times, 3d edit, 1975; editor: Innenpolitische Probleme des Bismarck-Reiches, 1983; co-editor: Documents on German Foreign Policy, 1918-1945, Vols. I-III, 1949-50; editor Am. Hist. Rev., 1976-85; mem. editl. bd. Jour. Modern History, 1971-73, Central European History, 1972-74. Served to 1st lt. U.S. Army, 1942-46. Fulbright research fellow, 1955-57; fellow Am. Council Learned Socs., 1951-52; fellow Guggenheim Found., 1966-67; fellow Nat. Endowment Humanities, 1975-76; fellow Internat. Research and Exchanges Bd., 1976; fellow Thyssen Stiftung, Essen, 1986; recipient Humanities award McKnight Found., 1962. Mem. Am. Hist. Assn., German Studies Assn.

**PFLUM, BARBARA ANN,** retired allergist; b. Cin., Jan. 10, 1943; d. James Frederick and Betty Mae (Doherty) P.; m. Makram I. Gobrail, Oct. 20, 1973; children: Christina, James. BS, Coll. Mt. St. Vincent, 1967; MD, Georgetown U., 1971; MS, Coll. St. Joseph, 1993. Cons. Children's Med. Ctr., Dayton, Ohio, 1975—2006, dir. allergy clinic, 1983-89; dir. allergy divsn. Hopeland Splty. Clinic, Dayton, 1998-2000; ret., 2006. Fellow Am. Acad. Pediatrics, Am. Acad. Allergy and Immunology, Am. Coll. Allergy and Immunology; mem. Ohio Soc. Allergy and Immunology, Western Ohio Pediatric Soc. (pres. 1985-86) Roman Catholic. Office Phone: 937-293-8263. Personal E-mail: bapflum@hotmail.com.

**PFLUM, WILLIAM JOHN,** physician; b. NYC, July 30, 1924; s. Peter Arthur and Caroline (Schmidt) P.; m. Roseann Sarah Stubing, Oct. 13, 1956; children: Carol Jean, Jeanine, Suzanne, Denise, Peter. BS, Georgetown U., 1947; MD, Loyola U., Chgo., 1951. Diplomate Am. Bd. Allergy & Immunology. Intern St. Vincent's Hosp, N.Y.C., 1951-52; resident in internal medicine NYU div. Goldwater Meml. Hosp., N.Y.C., 1952-53; resident in allergy Inst. Allergy Roosevelt Hosp., N.Y.C., 1956; attending internist allergy & immunology Overlook Hosp., Summit, NJ, 1958—. Assoc. attending Inst. Allergy, Immunology and Infectious Diseases, Roosevelt Hosp., N.Y.C., 1957-92; pvt. practice medicine, specializing in allergy and immunology, Summit, 1957-92; ret., cons. in field. With USAAF, 1943—45, ETO. Decorated Purple Heart, air medal with two clusters, POW medal. Fellow Am. Acad. Allergy, Am. Coll. Allergists, Am. Assn. Clin. Immunology and Allergy; mem. Summit Med. Soc., Am. Assn. Clin. Immunology and Allergy (pres. Mid-Atlantic region 1975-76), Disabled Am. Vets., Mil. Order Purple Heart, Am. Ex-Prisoners of War, 8th Air Force Hist. Soc., World Marathon

Runners Assn., Robert A. Cooke Allergy Alumni Assn. Achievements include completion of 26 consecutive Boston Marathons, 1971-1996 with Am. Med. Athletic Assn. Home: 922 North Shore Dr NE Saint Petersburg FL 33701

**PFOUTS, RALPH WILLIAM,** economist, consultant; b. Atchison, Kans., Sept. 9, 1920; s. Ralph Ulysses and Alice (Oldham) P.; m. Jane Hoyer, Jan. 31, 1945 (dec. Nov. 1982); children: James William, Susan Jane Pfouts Portman, Thomas Robert (dec.), Elizabeth Ann Pfouts Klenowski; m. Lois Bateson, Dec. 21, 1984 (div.); m. Felicia Sprincenatu, 1993 (div.); m. June St. James, July 14, 2001 BA, U. Kans., 1942, MA, 1947; PhD, U. N.C., 1952. Rsch. asst., instr. econs. U. Kans., Lawrence, 1946—47; instr. U. N.C., Chapel Hill, 1947—50, lectr. econs., 1950—52, assoc. prof. econs., 1952—58, prof. econs., 1958—87; pvt. practice Chapel Hill, 1987—2005, Boise, Idaho, 2005—. Vis. prof. U. Leeds, 1983; vis. rsch. scholar Internat. Inst. for Applied Sys. Analysis, Laxenberg, Austria, 1983; prof. Ctrl. European U., Prague, 1991; chmn. grad. studies dept. econs. Sch. Bus. Adminstrn., Chapel Hill, 1957-62, chmn. dept. econs. Sch. Bus. Adminstrn., 1962-68 Author: Elementary Economics-A Mathematical Approach, 1972; editor: So. Econ. Jour, 1955-75; editor, contbr.: Techniques of Urban Economic Analysis, 1960, Essays in Economics and Econometrics, 1960; mem. editl. bd. Metroeconomica, 1961-80, Atlantic Econ. Jour, 1973—; contbr. articles to profl. jours Served as deck officer USNR, 1943-46 Social Sci. Rsch. Coun. fellow U. Cambridge, 1953-54; Ford Found. Faculty Rsch. fellow, 1962-63 Mem. AAAS, Am. Statis. Assn., N.C. Statis. Assn. (past pres.), Am. Econ. Assn., So. Econ. Assn. (past pres.), Atlantic Econ. Soc. (v.p. 1973-76, pres. 1977-78), Population Assn. Am., Econometric Soc., Math. Assn. Am., Phi Beta Kappa, Pi Sigma Alpha, Alpha Kappa Psi, Omicron Delta Epsilon Home and Office: 2308 W Norcrest Dr Boise ID 83705 Office Phone: 208-331-1234. Personal E-mail: rwpfouts@msn.com.

**PFUND, EDWARD THEODORE, JR.,** electronics company executive; b. Methuen, Mass., Dec. 10, 1923; s. Edward Theodore and Mary Elizabeth (Banning) P.; BS magna cum laude, Tufts Coll., 1950; postgrad U. So. Calif., 1950, Columbia U., 1953, U. Calif., L.A., 1956, 58; m. Marga Emmi Andre, Nov. 10, 1954 (div. 1978); children: Angela M., Gloria I., Edward Theodore III; m. Ann Lorenne Dille, Jan. 10, 1988 (div. 1990). Radio engr., WLAW, Lawrence-Boston, 1942-50; fgn. svc. staff officer Voice of Am., Tangier, Munich, 1950-54; project. engr. Crusade for Freedom, Munich, Ger., 1955; project mgr., materials specialist United Electrodynamics Inc., Pasadena, Calif., 1956-59; cons. H.I. Thompson Fiber Glass Co., L.A., Andrew Corp., Chgo., 1959, Satellite Broadcast Assocs., Encino, Calif., 1982, TRW Inc., Redondo Beach, Calif., 1994; teaching staff Pasadena City Coll. (Calif.) 1959: dir. engring., chief engr. Electronics Specialty Co., L.A. and Thomaston, Conn., 1959-61; with Hughes Aircraft Co., various locations, 1955, 61-89, mgr. Middle East programs, also Far East, Latin Am. and African market devel., L.A., 1971-89, dir. internat. programs devel., Hughes Comm. Internat., 1985-89; mng. dir. E.T. Satellite Assocs. Internat., Rolling Hills Estates, Calif., 1989; dir. programs devel. Asia-Pacific TRW Space and Tech. Group, Redondo Beach, Calif., 1990-93, Pacific Telecom. Coun., Honolulu, 1993—. With AUS, 1942-46. Mem. AIAA, Phi Beta Kappa, Sigma Pi Sigma. Contbr. articles to profl. jours. Home: 4431 Pacific Coast Hwy Apt L104 Torrance CA 90505-5672

**PHADKE, ARUN G.,** engineering educator; b. Gwalior, M.P., India, Aug. 27, 1938; came to U.S., 1959; s. Gajanan G. and Indira G. Phadke; m. Kusum K. Joglekar, Sept. 14, 1964; 1 child, Ajit B. BS, Agra U., India, 1959; B in Tech. with honors, Indian Inst. Tech., 1959; MS, Ill. Inst. Tech., 1961; PhD, U. Wis., 1964. Systems engr. Allis Chalmers, Milw., 1963-67; asst prof. elec. engr. dept. U. Wis., Madison, 1967-69; cons. engr. Am. Elec. Power Svc. Corp., N.Y.C., 1969-82; univ. disting. prof. Va. Poly Inst. & State U., Blacksburg, 1982—, 2000—. Cons. various electric utilities, equipment mfrs., 1980—. Co-author: Computer Relaying for Power Systems, 1988; patentee in field. Disting. Svc. citation, 1987, Centennial medal U. Wis., 1991. Fellow IEEE (chmn. power sys. relaying com., outstanding educator Power Engring. Soc. 1991, Millennium medal, Halperin award); mem. Edison Elec. Inst. (outstanding educator 1986), Conf. Internat. Grand Reseaux Electrique (intern working groups). Nat. Acad. Engring. Avocations: painting, tailoring. Office: Va Poly Inst & State U Elec Engring Dept 426 Whittemore Hall Blacksburg VA 24061-0111 E-mail: aphadke@vt.edu.

**PHAIR, JOSEPH BASCHON,** lawyer; b. NYC, Apr. 29, 1947; s. James Francis and Mary Elizabeth Phair; m. Bonnie Jean Hobbs, Sept. 04, 1971; children: Kelly I., Joseph B., Sean P. BA, U. San Francisco, 1970, JD, 1973. Bar: Calif., U.S. Dist. Ct. (no. dist.) Calif., U.S. Ct. Appeals (9th cir.). Assoc. Berry, Davis & McInerney, Oakland, Calif., 1974-76, Bronson, Bronson & McKinnon, San Francisco, 1976-79; staff atty. Varian Assocs., Inc., Palo Alto, Calif., 1979-83, corp. counsel, 1983-86, sr. corp. counsel, 1986-87, assoc. gen. counsel, 1987-90, v.p., gen. counsel, 1990-91, v.p., gen. counsel, sec., 1991-99; v.p. adminstrn., gen. counsel, sec. Varian Med. Sys., Inc., Palo Alto 1999—. Mem. devel. bd. St. Vincent de Paul Devel. Coun., San Francisco, 1992—. Mem. Bay Area Gen. Counsel, Silicon Valley Assn. Gen. Counsel, The Olympic Culb. Roman Catholic. Office: Varian Med Sys Inc M S V 250 3100 Hansen Way Palo Alto CA 94304-1030 Business E-mail: joseph.phair@varian.com.

**PHAIR, LIZ,** vocalist; b. Cin., Apr. 17, 1967; d. John and Nancy Phair; m. Jim Staskouskas, 1995 (div. 2001) 1 child, James Nicholas Staskouskas Diploma, Oberlin Coll., 1990. Freelance artist, 1990; singer, songwriter, 1992—. Albums include: Exile in Guyville (name Album of Yr. Village Voice), 1993, Whip-Smart, 1994, Whitechocolatespaceegg, 1998, Liz Phair, 2003, Everything to Me, 2005; Actor (films) Cherish, 2002, Seeing Other People, 2004; (TV appearances) America Dreams, 2004 Named Best New Female Vocalist Rolling Stone Critic's Poll. Office: Matador Records 625 Broadway New York NY 10012-2611*

**PHALEN, PATRICIA FRANCES,** media specialist, educator; b. Waterbury, Conn., Mar. 27, 1958; d. John Philip and Elizabeth McGowen Phalen. BA in Comm. and English, Boston Coll., 1980, MBA, 1983; PhD, Northwestern U., Evanston, Ill., 1996. Asst. prof. Ohio U., Athens, Ohio, 1996—98; assoc. prof. George Wash. U., Washington, 1998—. Instr. Inst. Media and Entertainment, N.Y., Act One Exec. Program, Hollywood, Calif. Co-author: Ratings Analysis: The Theory and Practice of Audience Research, The Mass Audience: Rediscovering the Dominant Model. Instr. Program for Academic and Leadership Skills, Washington, 2004—06; mem. bd. Youth Leadership Found., Washington, 1999—2003. Recipient Kenneth Harwood Outstanding Dissertation award, Northwestern U., 1997. Mem.: Internat. Assn. Media History, Broadcast Edn. Assn., Am. Polit. Sci. Assn. (assoc.). Roman Catholic. Home: 5115 Van Ness St NW Washington DC 20016-1919 Office: The George Washington University 805 21st St NW Suite 400 Washington DC 20052 Office Phone: 202-994-4016. Business E-Mail: phalen@gwu.edu.

**PHALEN, ROBERT FRANKLYNN,** environmental scientist; b. Fairview, Okla., Oct. 18, 1940; married, 1966; 2 children. B in Physics, San Diego State U., 1964, M in Physics, 1966; PhD in Biophysics, U. Rochester, 1971. Engring. aide advanced space systems dept. Gen. Dynamics/Astronautics, San Diego, 1962-63; asst. to radiation safety officer, lab. teaching asst. San Diego State U., 1964-66, instr. physics dept., 1966; mem. summer faculty biology dept. Rochester (N.Y.) Inst. Tech., 1970-72; rsch. assoc. aerosol physics dept. Lovelace Found. for Med. Edn. and Rsch., Albuquerque, 1972-74; from adj. asst. prof. to assoc. prof. in residence dept. community and environ. medicine U. Calif., Irvine, 1974-84, prof., dir. Air Pollution Health Effects Lab., 1985—; faculty Ctr. for Occupl. Environ. Health, 1985—. Editor Aerosol Sci. and Tech., mem. editl. bd., 2002-05; reviewer Am. Rev. Respiratory Disease, Applied Indsl. Hygiene, Bull. Math. Biology, Exptl. Lung Rsch., Jour. Toxicology and Environ. Health, Jour. Toxicology and Applied Pharmacology, Jour. Aerosol Sci., Sci. Toxicol. Scis.; reviewer, mem. editl. bd. Fundamental and Applied Toxicology, 1986-92, Inhalation Toxicology, 1988-04, Jour. Aerosol Medicine, 1988-98; mem. safety and occupl. health study sect. NIH, 1988-01, mem. spl. study sects., 1980, 81, chmn. spl. study sects., 1982-84, 87, 88, 92, mem. site visit teams, 1980-01;

mem. expert panel on sulfur oxides EPA, mem. inhalation toxicology divsn. peer rev. panel, 1982, session chmn., 1983, participant workshop on non-oncogenic lung disease, 1984, mem. grants rsch. sci. rev. panel on health rsch., EPA advisor, 1985-88, 93-98, 03; mem. com. animal models testing interventions against aerosol agts. Nat. Acad. Sci., 2005-06; mem. task group on respiratory tract kinetic model Nat. Coun. Radiation Protection, 1978-97; mem. adv. panel on asbestos APHA, 1978; chmn. atmospheric sampling com. Am. Coun. Govtl. Indsl. Hygienists, 1982-92; chmn. NIOSH spl. study sect., 1983; panelist workshop NHLBI, 1982; sci. advisor Prentice Day Sch., 1986-04; dir. four internat. confs. on health effects of particulate air pollution; dir. internat. conf. on inhaled aerosol doses. Author: Inhalation Studies: Foundations and Techniques, 1984, The Particulate Air Pollution Controversy, 2002, (with others) Advances in Air Sampling, 1988, Concepts in Inhalation Toxicology, 1989, Deposition, Retention and Dosimetry of Inhaled Radioactive Substances, 1997; editor: Methods in Inhalation Toxicology, 1997; contbr. numerous articles to profl. jours. Am. Legion scholar. Fellow Acad. Toxicol. Scis.; mem. Am. Assn. Aerosol Rsch. (charter, chmn. ann. meeting 1985), Am. Conf. Govtl. Indsl. Hygienists, Am. Indsl. Hygiene Assn. (jour. reviewer, chmn. ann. conf. 1981, 85, 86), Brit. Occupl. Hygiene Soc., Internat. Soc. Aerosols in Medicine, So. Calif. Acad. Scis., Soc. for Aerosol Rsch., Health Physics Soc., Internat. Hormesis Soc. (charter), Soc. Toxicology, Career Achievement award 2000). Achievements include research in nasal, tracheobronchial and pulmonary transport of inhaled deposited particles and effects of pollutant exposure on transport kinetcs, laboratory simulation and characterization of airborne environmental pollutants, respiratory tract deposition and clearance models for inhaled particles, including species comparisons and body size effects, behavior of highly-concentrated aerosols with respect to deposition in the respiratory tract. Office: U Calif Air Pollution Health Effects Lab Cmty & Environ Medicine Irvine CA 92697-1825 Business E-Mail: rfphalen@uci.edu.

**PHAM, CHINH H.,** lawyer; s. Cuong H. Pham and Chauha T. Dam; m. Laureen T. McVay, Jan. 8, 1994; children: Collin James Minh, Caraline Theresa Lan. BA, U. Calif., Berkeley, 1987; JD, U. San Francisco 1993. Bar: Calif. 1993, Mass. 1994, U.S. Patent and Trademark Office 1994. Atty. Bromberg & Sunstein LLP, Boston, 1994—98, Foley Hoag. LLP, Boston, 1998—2003; of counsel Greenberg Traurig, LLP, Boston, 2003—. Founder Nano Tech. & Bus. Forum, Boston, 2004—06. Named Super Lawyer, Law & Politics, 2004, 2005. Mem.: ABA, Asian Am. Lawyers Assn. Mass. (treas. 2002—04), Nat. Asian Pacific ABA, Boston (Mass.) Patent Law Assn., Boston (Mass.) Bar Assn. (co-chmn. 2004—06, mem. edn. com.), Am. Intellectual Property Law Assn., NanoBusiness Alliance, ASTM Internat. (sec. 2005—), U. Calif. Berkeley Alumni Club (exec. v.p. 1999—2001). Office: Greenberg Traurig LLP One International Place Boston MA 02110 Office Phone: 617-310-6000. Office Fax: 617-310-6001. Business E-Mail: phamc@gtlaw.com.

**PHAM, CHRISTOPHER HOANG,** electrical engineer, educator; s. Le Pham and Nhung Thi Hoang; m. Vivian Trang Nguyen; children: Christopher Jr. HuyVu, Ariel ThuyTien, Elise CatTien. MSEE, San Jose State U., 1995, BSEE, 1994; postgrad., U. Calif., Davis, 1998—2000. Tech. support Hewlett Packard, Mountain View, Calif., 1987—88, NovTek Inc., San Jose, 1989—90; assoc. design engr. Ancot Corp., Menlo Park, Calif., 1990—92; devel. engr. Quantrads Corp., Santa Clara, Calif., 1993—94; sofware devel. engr. Adaptec Inc., Milpitas, Calif., 1994—95; software devel. engr. Credence Systems Inc., Fremont, Calif., 1995—96; mem. of tech. staff SUN Microsystems Inc., Menlo Park, Calif., 1997—98; sr. software engr. Cisco Systems Inc., San Jose, Calif., 1998—2000, software mgr. I and II, 2000—01, engring. mgr. III, 2002—. Adj. prof. Evergreen Valley Coll., San Jose, 1998—2000, San Jose State U., 1995—. Contbr. articles to profl. jours. Pres.-elect VACETS, San Jose, 2006—, bd. dirs., 2006—. Recipient Asian Am. Engr. of the Yr. award, CIE-USA, 2005. Master: IEEE. R-Liberal. Achievements include patents for Patents in technologies. Avocations: travel, language art. Home: SJSU EE Dept One Washington Sq San Jose CA 95192-0084 Office: Cisco Systems Inc 170 West Tasman Dr San Jose CA 95134 Office Phone: 408-525-8047. Personal E-mail: phamc@email.sjsu.edu. Business E-Mail: chpham@cisco.com.

**PHAM, DAVID LAN,** secondary school educator, writer; b. Binh Chuan, Thudaumot, Vietnam, Feb. 1, 1940; s. Khoai Van Pham and Chuc Thi Le; m. Tam Thi Nguyen, Nov. 22, 1965; children: Albert, Elizabeth, Wellington, An, Victoria. BEd, Faculty of Pedagogy, Saigon Vietnam, 1963; BA in History, Faculty of Letters, Saigon Vietnam, 1965; M in Libr. Sci, Faculty of Pedagogy, Saigon Vietnam, 1973. Tchr., chief libr. Ly Thuong Kiet Comprehensive H.S., Hoc Mon, Gia Dinh, Vietnam, 1963—75; social svcs. coord. Cath. Social Svcs. Refugee Resettlement Program, Bayou La Batre, Ala., 1987—96. Advisor Binh Duong Bo De Sch., 1968—75; advisor Binh Duong Confedn, Vietnamienne du Travail, 1968—75; vis. Thailand for Libr. Sci. Observation, 1973; advisor, founder Mutual Assistance Assn., Bayou La Batre, Ala., 1988—89. Columnist Thoi Bao Daily, Saigon, Vietnam, 1963—64, columnist Point South, Mobile, Ala., 1991—94; columnist Binh Duong News, 2000— (award of apperciation, 2003); editor: (Bulletin) Bulletin Tin Viet, Dac San Que Huong, 1987—96; author: Two Hamlets in Nam Bo, 1999, Earthy Life, 2001, Vietnam History Dictionary, 2002, International Politico - Cultural Influences on Vietnam in the 20th Century, 2004. Gen. sec. Assn. Vietnamese Tchrs. of History and Geography, 1967—69, Viet. Libr. Assn. 1973—74; founder Tutorial Program, Bayou La Batre, Ala., 1992—96. Buddhist. Avocations: reading, travel, walking, writing, zen. Home: 1341 Leith Dr Toledo OH 43614 E-mail: davidlanpham@hotmail.com.

**PHAM, DUC,** entrepreneur, engineering executive, researcher; b. Hoi An, Quang Nam Da Nang, Vietnam, Nov. 17, 1970; arrived in U.S., 1992; s. De Ba Pham and Tu Thi Cam Nguyen; m. Hong Hieu Nguyen, May 26, 1998. BS, Calif. Poly. State U., San Luis Obispo, 1998; MS, San Jose State U., Calif., 1999; DEng, Santa Clara U., Calif., 2002. Project engr. Remec Inc., San Jose, 1999—2000; product mgr. Micro Lambda Wireless, Inc., Fremont, Calif., 2000—02; pres. and CEO Advanced Rsch. Labs, Inc., San Jose, 2002—05; founder and CEO Advanced Sci., Inc., 2005—. Cons. Gerson Lehrman Group, N.Y.C., 2001—, Avista Cons. Group, N.Y.C., 2002—. Mem.: N.Y. Acad. Sci. (hon.), Sigma Xi (hon.). Achievements include research in electronic/communication systems; self navigation vehicle; enhance vision system; nanotechnology. Avocations: golf, reading, travel. Office Phone: 408-691-7415, 408-660-7111. E-mail: dpham19@yahoo.com, phamducphd@yahoo.com.

**PHAM, KHANH DAI,** aerospace engineer, researcher; s. Viet Son Pham and Linh Kim Bang; m. Huong Dieu Nguyen, Dec. 18, 2003; 1 child, An Duy. D Elec. Engring., U. Notre Dame, 2004. Registered profl. engr., Nebr. Postdoctoral rschr. U. Notre Dame, Ind., 2003—04; aerospace and rsch. engr. Air Force Rsch. Lab., Kirtland AFB, N.Mex., 2004—. Recipient Best Paper Presentation award, IEEE, 2000, 2004; Arthur J. Schmidt Presdl. fellow, U. Notre Dame, 1998—2002, Ctr. Applied Math. Grad. Rsch. fellow, 2000, 2003. Mem.: ASME, AIAA, SPIE (program com. 2005), AAS (nat. chmn. 2005—06), Golden Key Nat. Honor Soc., Phi Theta Kappa, Eta Kappa Nu, Tau Beta Pi. Achievements include research in statisical control theory. Office: AF Rsch Lab 3550 Aberdeen Ave SE Kirtland Afb NM 87117 Office Phone: 505-846-4823. Office Fax: 505-846-7877. Business E-Mail: khanh.pham@kirtland.af.mil.

**PHAM, KINH DINH,** electrical engineer, educator, engineering executive; b. Saigon, Republic of Vietnam, Oct. 6, 1956; came to U.S., 1974; s. Nhuong D. (dec.) and Phuong T. (Tran) P.; m. Ngan-Lien T. Nguyen, May 27, 1985; children: Larissa, Galen. BS with honors, Portland State U., 1979, MSEE, Portland, 1982; postgrad. Portland State U., 1988-90. Registered profl. engr., Oreg., Calif., Ariz., Fla., Wash., Mass., Conn., R.I., Tex. Elec. engr. Irvington-Moore, Tigard, Oreg., 1979-80; Elcon Assocs., Inc., Beaverton, Oreg., 1980-87, from sr. elec. engr., assoc. ptnr., 1987-96, v.p., 1996—. Adj. prof. Portland (Oreg.) C.C., 1982-2003, George Fox U., 2005—; mem. adv. bd. Mass Transit System Compatibility, 1994. Co-author: FE/EIT Exam:

Electrical Engineering Review and Study Guide, 2000, Electrical Engineering Professional Engineer License Exam Review Handbook, 2001; pub.: Research and Education and Association, 2000; cons. tech. editor Rsch. and Edn. Assn., 1998—; contbr. articles to profl. jours. Recipient Cert. Appreciation, Am. Pub. Transit Assn. and Transit Industry, 1987. Sr. mem. IEEE, Industry Applications, Power Engring. and Vehicular Tech. Soc.; mem N.Y. Acad. Scis., Mass Transit Sys. Compatibility Adv. Bd, Eta Kappa Nu. Buddhist. Avocations: reading, travel, antiques, music. Office: Elcon Assocs Inc 12670 NW Barnes Rd Portland OR 97229-9001 Office Phone: 503-644-2490 x119. Personal E-mail: kinhpham@comcast.net. Business E-Mail: kpham@elconassoc.com.

**PHAM, LARA BACH-VIEN,** small business owner; b. Ba-Xuyen, Vietnam, Jan. 11, 1962; d. Thi Van and Huong Thi Nguyen; m. Thien Van Pham, Apr. 17, 1982; children: Minh-Thu, Sheena, Lisa, Jimmy. Diploma, Brand's Beauty Coll., Charlotte, NC, 1990. Lic. securities NASD, life and health ins., in property and liability, in real estate sales, real estate broker, loan officer, cosmetology tchr. Hair stylist, owner Hair Studio, Charlotte, 1990—; beauty cons. Beauti Control, Charlotte, 1990—93, 2001—; flower arranger Charlotte, 1995—; ptnr. Carolina Choice Realty, Charlotte, 2004—, Charlotte Nails Acad., 2004. Office Phone: 704-566-8966. E-mail: larabvpham@hotmail.com.

**PHAM, SI MAI,** cardiothoracic surgeon; b. Ninh Hoa, Khanh Hoa, Vietnam, Oct. 6, 1955; arrived in US, 1975; s. Tro Pham and Nhung Thi Mai; m. Marie Christine Pham, Sept. 9, 1987; children: Benjamin Bartley, Anthony Ninh, Vivienne Elisabeth, Victoria B.H. Student, U. Saigon, Sch. Pharmacy, Vietnam, 1973-75; BS in Chem. magna cum laude, Lebanon Valley Coll., Annville, Pa., 1979; MD, U. Pitts., 1983; D (hon.), U. Morón, 2002. Diplomate, surg. critical care Am. Bd. Surgery, Am. Bd. Thoracic Surgery. Intern, resident gen. surgery U. Pitts., 1983-86, rsch. fellow, cardiothoracic surgery, 1986-87, sr. and chief resident, gen. surgery, 1987-89, resident cardiothoracic surgery, 1989-92, asst. prof. surgery, Sch. of Medicine, 1992-97, dir. adult cardiac transplant program, Sch. of Medicine, 1993-97, assoc. dir. heart transplant and artificial heart program, 1997-98, dir. cardiothoracic transplant rsch., 1997-98; dir. extracorporeal membrane oxygenation svc. Presbyn. U. Hosp., Pitts., 1993-98; dir. cardiopulmonary transplantation and artifical heart program, divsn. cardiothoracic surgery U. Miami Sch. Medicine, 1998—; assoc. prof. surgery U. Miami Sch. Medicine, 1998—2002, prof., 2002—. Prof. surgery U. Miami Sch. Medicine, 2002—; reviewer various med. jours. Contbr. articles to profl. jours., chapters to books, scientific papers. Recipient Am. Chem. award, 1979, Radiology award U. Pitts., 1983, Dalsemer rsch. scholar award Am. Lung Assn., 1997-99; ACS Faculty fellowship award, 1994-96; grantee Children's Hosp. Pitts., 1987, Am. Heart Assn., 1987-89, 94-96, 96-99, Thoracic Surgery Found., 1996-97, 97-98, Am. Lung Assn., 1997—, Presbyn. U. Hosp., 1987-89, NIH, 1999—, Vietnamese Am. Med. Rsch. Found. sci. award, 2005. Fellow Am. Coll. Surgeons, Am. Heart Assoc. (cmty. bd. mem.); mem. Am. Soc. Artificial Internal Organs, Internat. Soc. Heart and Lung Transplantation, Soc. Critical Care Medicine, Am. Assn. Advancement of Sci., Am. Soc. Transplant Surgeons, Soc. Thoracic Surgeons, Am. Assn. Thoracic Surgery, Extracorporeal Life Support Organization, Assn. for Acad. Surgery, Phi Alpha Epsilon, Transplant Found. South Fla. (adv. bd. mem.). Avocations: reading, gardening. Home: 13250 SW 67th Ave Miami FL 33156-6929 Office: U Miami Sch Medicine Highland Profl bldg 1801 NW 9th Ave Ste 5th Fl Miami FL 33136 Office Phone: 305-355-5070. Business E-Mail: spham@med.miami.edu.

**PHAN, ANH-VU,** adult education educator, researcher; b. Saigon (Ho Chi Minh City), Vietnam, Aug. 16, 1959; s. Tinh Van Phan and Hao Thi Ly; m. Tran-Nam Phan, Jan. 4, 1995; children: Jerrick Dac-Huy children: Johann Anh-Huy. B in Mech. Engring., Ho Chi Minh City U. of Tech., Vietnam, 1977—82; DEA (MS equivalent), Institut Nat. Polytechnique de Grenoble, France, 1992—93; PhD, Ecole Polytechnique, U. of Montreal, Can., 1994—97. Asst. lectr., dept. mech. engring. Ho Chi Minh City U. of Tech., Vietnam, 1982—84, lectr., dept. mech. engring., 1984—92; consulting engr. RENAULT, Ho Chi Minh City, 1993—93; lectr., assoc. chair, dept. mech. engring. Ho Chi Minh City U. of Tech., Vietnam, 1993—94; post-doctoral rschr., dept. mech. engring. Ecole Polytechnique de Montreal, 1998—99; post-doctoral rsch. assoc. Computer Sci. and Math. Divsn., Oak Ridge Nat. Lab., Tenn., 1999—2001; rsch. staff mem. Computational Scis. and Engring. Divsn., Oak Ridge Nat. Lab., 2002; asst. prof. dept. mech. engring. U. South Ala., 2002—06, assoc. prof., dept. mech. engring., 2006—. Contbr. numerous articles in profl. jours. Recipient Ralph E. Powe Jr. Faculty award, Oak Ridge Associated Univs., 2004, Best Faculty Mem. award, U. South Ala. Coun. Internat. Students Orgn., 2004—05; grantee Bourse d'Excellence, Govt. of Que., 1994-1997, post-doctoral fellowship, Ecole Polytechnique de Montreal, 1998—99, Bourse de Stage, French Govt., 1992—93, post-doctoral rsch. assocs. fellowship, Oak Ridge Associated Universities, 1999—2001. Mem.: Am. Soc. for Engring. Edn., Internat. Assn. for Computational Mechanics, US Assn. for Computational Mechanics, Internat. Soc. of Structural and Multidisciplinary Optimization (assoc.). Achievements include research in Further development of the Boundary Contour Method for applications in Stress Analysis, Shape Optimization and Linear Fracture Mechanics; modeling the growth of nanostructures and the simulation of machining processes; invention of Development of a new crack tip element for Fracture Mechanics using the Boundary Element Methods. Office: U of South Alabama EGCB 212 307 University Blvd Mobile AL 36688-0002 E-mail: vphan@usouthal.edu.

**PHAN, K. LUAN DINH,** neuroscientist, psychiatrist; MD, U. Mich., Ann Arbor, 1998. Asst. prof. U. Chgo., 2004—. Office Phone: 773-834-5954.

**PHAN, LONG THANH,** structural engineer, researcher; b. Saigon, Vietnam, July 1, 1958; arrived in U.S., 1981; s. Tru Thanh Phan and Thanh Thi Dung, m. Trinh Thi Nguyen, Jan. 14, 1984; 1 child, Dexter Duy Viet Phan. BS in Civil Engring., PhuTho Poly. U., Saigon, 1980; MS in Civil Engring., Wash. U., 1984, PhD in Civil Engring., 1988. Registered profl. engr., Va., 1993. Rsch. structural engr. Nat. Inst. Stds. and Tech., Gaithersburg, Md., 1984—. Sr. mem. modelling and applications of mech. concrete properties at high temperatures com. Internat. Union Labs. and Experts in Constrn. Materials, Systems and Structures (RILEM), Paris, 1998—; chmn. fire protection structures com. Am. Concrete Inst., Ann Harbor, Mich., 1999—. Mem. ASCE (spl. 9-11 report) The Pentagon Building Performance Report. Basketball coach St. Ambrose Cath. Sch., Arlington, Va. Mem.: ASCE. Achievements include research in punching shear resistance of Arctic offshore structures; effect of fire on high-strength concrete structures; serving as expert team member evaluating performance of Pentagon structures following the September 11 attacks. Avocations: travel, reading, soccer, building/carpentry, coaching basketball.

**PHAN, PHILLIP HIN CHOI,** business educator, consultant; b. Singapore, Feb. 23, 1963; arrived in US, 1982; s. Bryan K. and Rosaline (Teo) Phan; m. Soo-Hoon Lee, Feb. 13, 1988. BBA with distinction, U. Hawaii, 1984; MBA, PhD, U. Wash., 1992. Cost contr. Westin Hotels & Resorts, Dallas and Singapore, 1984—88; assoc. prof. York U., Toronto, 1992—2000; cons. World Bank, 1998—2001, OECD, 1998—2000; Bruggeman prof. Rensselaer Poly. Inst., Troy, NY, 1998—. Asst. prof. CUNY, 1997; vis. prof. Nat. U. Singapore, 1998—2003, Singapore Mgmt. U., 2003—, Thammasat U., Thailand, 1997; Haniel Found. vis. prof. Humboldt U., Germany, 2004—05; ptnr. Core Competence Cons., Inc., Toronto, 1993—98; dir. Blood Trac Sys. Internat., Edmonton, 1996—98; mem. multi-nat. enterprises and investment com. Can. Coun. Internat. Bus., 1993—2000. Mem. editl. bd. Jour. Bus. Venturing, 1998—, Acad. Mgmt. Jour., 2002—, Jour. Fin. Stability, 2003—, Jour. Tech. Transfer, 2003—; co-editor: Asia Pacific Jour. Mgmt., 1999—2001. Named MBA Educator of the Yr., RPI, 2004; recipient Endowment Excellence award, Boeing Corp., 1992, Schulich Sch. Faculty Rsch. award, 1996; fellow, Am. Acad., 2006—; Rsch. grantee, Social Scis. and Humanities Rsch. Coun. Can., 1997, John Broadbent Rsch. Fund, 2000—, Kauffman Entrepenuer Found., 2002, Edna G. Benson fellow, 1992, Michael G. Foster fellow, 1992, George W. Tyler scholar, 1992. Mem.: Acad. Internat. Bus. (mem. senatorial com.), Inst. Mgmt. Scis., Acad. Mgmt. Republican. Avocations: reading,

bicycling, tennis, scuba diving. Office: Lally Sch M&T 110 8th St Troy NY 12180-3522 Home: 250 S President St # 900 Baltimore MD 21202 Office Phone: 518-276-2319. E-mail: pphan@rpi.edu.

**PHAN, RICHARD MAN,** chemist; b. Saigon, Vietnam, July 30, 1970; came to U.S., 1993; s. Hong Van Phan and Tan Thi Nguyen; m. Ha Ngan Phung. BS, U. Utah, 1998, PhD, 2003. Project scientist Battelle, Dugway, Utah, 2003—04; sr. scientist Geomet Techs., Dugway, 2004—. NIH fellow, 2000. Mem. Golden Key Nat. Honor Soc. Office: Dugway Proving Ground PO Box 247 Dugway UT 84022 Home: 716 Deer Hollow Rd Tooele UT 84074 Office Phone: 435-831-7332. E-mail: phanmr@yahoo.com.

**PHANSTIEL, HOWARD G.,** managed healthcare company executive; BA in Political Sci., Syracuse U., M in Pub. Adminstrn. Exec. budget officer Wis. Bureau of Planning and Budget; division chief, office of fiscal affairs Ill. Bureau of Budget; dir., office of mgmt. and budget, health care financing administration US Dept. of Health, Ed. and Welfare; exec./mgmt. Prudential Bache Internat. Bank/Securities, Marine Midland Banks, Sallie Mae; exec. v.p. fin./info. svcs. WellPoint Health Networks, Inc., Woodland Hills, Calif.; chmn., CEO ARV Assisted Living, Inc., Costa Mesa, Calif.; exec. v.p., CFO PacifiCare Health Sys., Inc., Calif., 2000, pres., CEO Calif., 2000—04, pres., CEO, chmn., 2004—06.*

**PHARES, ALAIN JOSEPH,** physicist, researcher; b. Beirut, Apr. 20, 1942; came to U.S., 1975, naturalized, 1982; s. Joseph Michel and Renee Cecile (Doummar) P.; m. Claude Tawa, July 27, 1968; children— Caroline, Denis, Pascal. BS in Engring., St. Joseph U., 1964; Docteur-es-Sciences, U. Paris, 1971; PhD, Harvard U., 1973. Research fellow Nat. Council Sci. Research, Lebanon, 1973-75; assoc. prof. Lebanese U., 1973-75; research fellow Internat. Centre Theoretical Physics, Trieste, Italy, 1974, Harvard U., 1975-76; vis. asst. prof. U. Mont., 1976-77; asst. prof. physics Villanova U., Pa., 1977-79, assoc. prof. Pa., 1979-82, prof. Pa., 1982—, chmn. dept. Pa., 1981-91, dir. secondary sci. div., 1981-94. Contbr. articles to profl. jours. Fellow, IAEA, 1974; grantee, NSF, 1991—98, PSC, 1991—, SDSC, 2002—03; French Govt, fellow, 1964—66. Mem. Am. Phys. Soc., Internat. Assn. Math. and Computers in Simulation, Sigma Xi Office: Villanova U Dept Physics Villanova PA 19085 Office Phone: 610-519-4889. Business E-Mail: alain.phares@villanova.edu.

**PHARES, E. JERRY,** retired psychology professor; b. Glendale, Ohio, July 21, 1928; s. Bruce and Gladys (West) P.; m. Betty L. Knost, Aug. 6, 1955; 1 dau., Lisa M. BA, U. Cin., 1951; MA, Ohio State U., 1953, PhD, 1955. Faculty Kans. State U., Manhattan, 1955—, prof. psychology, 1964-91, head dept., 1967-89, prof. emeritus, 1991—. Vis. assoc. prof. Ohio State U., Columbus, Ohio Wesleyan U., 1961-62 Author, co-author books.; Contbr. articles to profl. jours. Research grantee NIMH, 1960, 80; Research grantee NSF, 1964-76; Research grantee Population Council, 1971 Fellow Am. Psychol. Assn., Am. Psychol. Soc. Office: 2812 Nevada St Manhattan KS 66502-2330 E-mail: ephares@ksu.edu.*

**PHELAN, JOHN C.,** lawyer; b. NYC, Mar. 5, 1956; BA cum laude, Williams Coll., 1978; JD, Boston Univ., 1981. Bar: Mass. 1981, NY 1984. Ptnr., chmn. Real Estate Fin. practice group DLA Piper Rudnick Gray Cary, NYC. Faculty mem. NYU Real Estate Inst., 1989—93. Mem.: ABA, NY State Bar Assn. Office: DLA Piper Rudnick Gray Cary 1251 Ave of the Americas New York NY 10020-1104 Office Phone: 212-835-6140. Office Fax: 212-835-6001. Business E-Mail: john.phelan@dlapiper.com.

**PHELAN, MARILYN ELIZABETH,** law educator; b. Lubbock, Tex., July 12, 1938; m. Harold L. Phelan, Sept. 1, 1960; children: Pat, Scott, Kimberly. BA, Tex. Tech U., 1959, MBA, 1967. PhD, 1971; JD, U. Tex., 1972. Bar: Tex. 1961; CPA. Assoc. prof. Tex. Tech U., Lubbock, 1971-77, prof. law, 1977—, Paul Whitfield Horn prof. law, 1993—. Author: Law of Cultural Property, 1998, Nonprofit Enterprises--Corporations, Trusts, and Associations, 2000, Representing Tax Exempt Organizations, 2001, Museum Law., 2001, Nonprofit Organizations, 2003. Mem. ABA, AICPA, Nat. Conf. Commrs. Uniform State Laws, Am. Law Inst., State Bar Tex., Internat. Coun. Mus. (legal affairs com. mem.). Office: Tex Tech Univ Sch Law 18th & Hartford Sts Lubbock TX 79409 Office Phone: 806-742-3787 ext 251. Business E-Mail: marilyn.phelan@ttu.edu.

**PHELAN, MARTHA ARMSTRONG,** realtor; b. Shelby, Ohio, July 26, 1927; d. George Woodburn and Anna Louise (Wood) A.; m. Vincent Roche Phelan, Aug. 9, 1952 (dec. July 2000); children: Elizabeth Ann Riley, David Woodburn, Anne Louise. BA, Oberlin Coll., 1949; studied, Katherine Gibbs Secretarial Sch., 1950. Sec. U.S. Govt., Washington, 1950-52; adminstrv. officer Com. for Free Asia, N.Y.C., 1952-53; legal sec. Atty. V.R. Phelan, Shelby, Ohio, 1975-79; realtor Mattox Realtors, Mansfield, Ohio, 1976-93, Hancock Agy., Shelby, Ohio, 1993—. Precinct committeeman Rep. Orgn., Shelby, 1965—; poll worker Richland County Bd. Elections, Shelby, 1960—; mem. exec. com. Richland County Republicans, Mansfield, 1965—; mem. Kingwood Ctr. Gardens; elder Presbyn. Ch., mem. choir, pres. Presbyn. Women, 2002—. Mem. Nat. Assn. Realtors, Mansfield Bd. Realtors, Rotary, Shelby Garden Club (pres. 1997-99), Shelby Women's Club (sec. 1990-01), Presyn. Choir 45 yrs., ch. session 7 yrs., Pres. Presbyn. Women 20 yrs. Republican. Presbyterian. Avocations: gardening, reading, creative arts and crafts, swimming, music. Home: 26 Woodland Rd Shelby OH 44875

**PHELAN, RICHARD MAGRUDER,** mechanical engineer; b. Moberly, Mo., Sept. 20, 1921; s. Frederick William and Ethel Ray (Magruder) P.; m. Olive Bernice McIntosh, May 25, 1951; children— William James, Susan Ray Student, Moberly Jr. Coll., 1939-41: BS in Mech. Engring. U. Mo., Columbia, 1943; M.M.E., Cornell U., 1950; postgrad., U. Mich., 1956-57. Instr. Cornell U., 1947-50, asst. prof. mech. engring., 1950-56, assoc. prof., 1956-62, prof., 1962-87, prof. emeritus, 1988—. Author: Fundamentals of Mechanical Design, 1957, 3d rev. edit., 1970, Dynamics of Machinery, 1967, Automatic Control Systems, 1977. Served with USNR, 1943-46. Mem. ASME, Am. Soc. Engring. Edn., Soc. Exptl. Stress Analysis, Am. Gear Mfrs. Assn., AAUP, AAAS, N.Y. Acad. Scis., Soc. Exptl. Mechanics, Sigma Xi, Phi Kappa Phi, Pi Tau Sigma, Tau Beta Pi. Home: 4 Cornell Walk Ithaca NY 14850-6145 Office: Cornell U Upson Hall Ithaca NY 14853

**PHELAN, ROBIN ERIC,** lawyer; b. Steubenville, Ohio, Dec. 28, 1945; s. Edward John and Dorothy (Borkowski) P.; m. JoAnn Keach, June 27, 1970 (dec. May 18, 1994); children: Travis McCoy, Tiffany Marie, Trevor Monroe; m. Melinda Jo Ricketts, May 27, 1995; 1 child, Taezja Monet. BSBA, Ohio State U., 1967, JD, 1970. Bar: Tex. 1971, U.S. Ct. Appeals (5th cir.) 1981, U.S. Ct. Appeals (11th cir.) 1981, U.S. Ct. Appeals (6th cir.) 1986, U.S. Ct. Appeals (10th cir.) 1988, U.S. Supreme Ct. Ptnr. Haynes and Boone, Dallas, 1970—. Co-author: Bankruptcy Practice and Strategy, 1987, Cowans Bankruptcy Law and Practice, 1987, Annual Survey of Bankruptcy Law, 1988, Bankruptcy Litigation Manual; contbr. articles to profl. jours. Mem. ABA (chmn. insolvency and secured transactions com. internat. law sect.), Internat. Bar Assn., Internat. Insolvency Inst. (bd. dirs.), Am. Bankruptcy Inst. (dir., past pres.), Am. Coll. Bankruptcy, State Bar Tex. (chmn. bankruptcy law com. sect. bus. law 1989-91), Dallas Bar Assn. Roman Catholic. Avocation: athletics. Home: 4214 Woodfin Dr Dallas TX 75220-6416 Office Phone: 214-651-5612. Business E-Mail: robin.phelan@haynesboone.com.

**PHELAN, THOMAS,** clergyman, academic administrator, educator; b. Albany, N.Y., Apr. 11, 1925; s. Thomas William and Helen (Rausch) P. AB NY State Regents scholar 1942, President's medal 1945, Coll. Holy Cross, Worcester, Mass., 1945; S.T.L., Catholic U. Am., 1951; postgrad., Oxford U., Eng., 1958-59, 69-70. Ordained priest Roman Cath. Ch., 1951; pastor, tchr., adminstr. Diocese of Albany, 1951-58; resident Cath. chaplain Rensselaer Poly. Inst., Troy, NY, 1959-72, prof. history, 1972—; dean Sch. Humanities and Social Scis., 1972-95, inst. historian, inst. dean, sr. adviser to pres., 1995—. Chmn. architecture and bldg. commn. Diocese Albany, 1968-2003; cons. in field. Author: Hudson Mohawk Gateway, 1985, 2001, Achieving the

Impossible, 1995; author monographs, articles, revs. in field. Treas. The Rensselaer Newman Found., 1962-2002; pres. Hudson-Mohawk Indsl. Gateway, 1971-84, bd. dirs. exec. com. 1984—; mem. WMHT Ednl. Telecomm. Bd., 1966-77, 84-90, chmn. 1973-77; chmn. Troy Hist. Dist. and Landmarks Rev. Commn., 1975-86, chmn. hist. adv. com., 1987-2003; v.p. Preservation League N.Y. State, 1979-82, mem. trustees coun., 1982-87, 89—, pres. 1987-89; sec. and bd. dirs. Ptnrs. for Sacred Places, 1989—; bd. dirs. Hall of History Found., 1983-87; trustee Troy Pub. Libr., 1992—. With USN, 1943-46. Recipient Paul J. Hallinan award Nat. Newman Chaplains Assn., 1967, Ann. award Albany Arts League, 1977, Disting. Cmty. Svc. award Rensselaer Poly. Inst., 1979, Edward Fox Demers medal Alumni Assn. Rensselaer Poly. Inst., 1986, Disting. Svc. award Hudson-Mohawk Consortium of Colls. and Univs., 1988; named Acad. Laureate of the SUNY Found. at Albany, 1988; Danforth Found. fellow, 1969-70; grantee Homeland Found., 1958-59, Dorothy Thomas Found., 1969-70. Fellow Soc. Arts, Religion and Contemporary Culture; mem. Ch. Soc. Coll. Work (dir., exec. com. 1970—), Am. Conf. Acad. Deans, Liturgical Conf., Soc. Indsl. Archaeology, Assn. Internat. pour l'Etudes des Religions Prehistoriques et Ethnologiques, Cath. Campus Ministry Assn., Cath. Art Assn., Assn. for Religion and the Intellectual Life (bd. dirs. 1987—), Soc. History of Tech. Clubs: Ft. Orange, Troy Country; Squadron A (N.Y.C.). Home: 5 Whitman Ct Troy NY 12180-4732 Office: Rensselaer Poly Inst Troy NY 12180 Business E-Mail: phelan@rpi.edu. *Service and community building have motivated most of my business and personal actions. I received these values from my parents and from the church. I work to make positive contributions towards a world in which there is more justice and consequent hope of peace.*

**PHELIZON, JEAN FRANCOIS,** finance company executive; b. Paris, Apr. 28, 1946; s. Christian and Anne (Camuset) P.; m. Isabelle Delatour, July 3, 1971; children: Camille, Constance, Charlotte. MBA and MS, Paris U., 1970, PhD in Econ. Sci., 1975. Contr. Flat Glass div. St. Gobain, Paris, 1979; CFO St. Gobain Spain, Madrid, 1983-85; CFO paper wood div. St. Gobain, Paris, 1985-89; CEO, Lembacel, Lyon, France, 1988-89; CFO, Compagnie St. Gobain, Paris, 1989-2000, sr. v.p., 1998—; pres., CEO, Saint-Gobain Corp., 2000—; CEO, Certain Teed, 2000—04. Editor: Economica, 1970, 2d edit. 1977, 3d edit. 1985, 4th edit. 1998, also 1998, 99, 2001, 02, 03, Masson, 1981, 2d edit. 1984, Citic (China), 2003, 04. Dir. French-Am. C. of C., Nat. Assn. Mfrs. Decorated chevalier Order of Merit, Legion of Honor. Home: 1315 Wrenfield Way Villanova PA 19085 Office: SG Corp PO Box 860 750 E Swedesford Rd Valley Forge PA 19482 E-mail: jfp@sgcna.com.

**PHELPS, AMANDA C.,** materials scientist, researcher; b. Long Beach, Calif., Feb. 2, 1976; d. Robert J. and Carol L. Phelps. BS, Pepperdine U., 1998; MS, UCLA, 2005. Rsch. staff mem. HRL Labs., Malibu, Calif., 1998—; adj. prof. Pepperdine U., Malibu, 1999—. Mem.: Materials Rsch. Soc., Am. Chem. Soc., Golden Key Nat. Honor Soc., Gamma Phi Beta Alumni. Republican. Roman Catholic. Achievements include patents in field. Office: HRL Labs 3011 Malibu Canyon Malibu CA 90265 Office Phone: 310-317-5000.

**PHELPS, ARTHUR VAN RENSSELAER,** physicist, consultant; b. Dover, NH, July 20, 1923; s. George Osborne and Helen (Ketchum) P.; m. Gertrude Kanzius, July 21, 1956 (dec. Jan. 3, 2003); children: Wayne Edward, Joan Susan. ScD in Physics, MIT, 1951. Cons. physicist rsch. labs. Westinghouse Elec. Corp., Pittsburgh, 1951-70; sr. rsch. scientist Nat. Bur. Standards, Boulder, Colo., 1970-88; fellow Joint Inst. Lab. Astrophysics U. Colo., Boulder, 1970-88, adjoint fellow, 1988—, chmn., 1979-81. Chmn. Gordon Rsch. Conf., Plasma Chemistry, 1990. Recipient Silver Medal award Dept. Commerce, 1978. Fellow Am. Phys. Soc. (Will Allis prize 1990). Achievements include patent for Schulz-Phelps ionization gauge; research on electron and atomic collision processes involving low energy electrons, molecules, ions, metastable atoms and resonance radiation; on laser processes and modeling; on gaseous electronics. Office: U Colo JILA Campus Box 440 Boulder CO 80309-0440 Home: 1331 E Hecla Dr Unit 247 Louisville CO 80027-2341

**PHELPS, ASHTON, JR.,** newspaper publisher; b. New Orleans, Nov. 4, 1945; s. Ashton Sr. and Jane Cary (George) Phelps; m. Suzanne Dupuy Phelps; children: Cary Clifton, Mary Louise, Sanders. BA, Yale U., 1967; JD, Tulane U., 1970. Trainee Times-Picayune Pub. Corp., New Orleans, 1970—71, asst. to pub., 1971—79, pres., pub., 1979—97, pub., 1997—. Chmn. Audit Com. of Associated Press, 1986—90, mem. nominating com., 1996—2002; bd. dirs. Bur. Govtl. Rsch., New Orleans, 1973—89, Xavier U. La., New Orleans, 1974—82, Internat. House, New Orleans, 1981—83, Coun. for Better La., 1982—85, Ochsner Found. Hosp., New Orleans, 1982—, Pub. Affairs Rsch. Coun., New Orleans, 1982—85, 2000—, La. Children's Mus., New Orleans, 1983—90, Yale Alumni Assn. La., 1985, Newspaper Advt. Bur. Future of Advt. Com., 1986—89, Met. Area Com., New Orleans, UNCF, 2004—. Mem.: La. Press Assn. (bd. dirs. 1984—93, v.p. 1989—96, pres. 1991—92), So. Newspaper Pubs. Assn. (bd. dirs. 1982—85, found. bd. dirs. 1982—83, pres. 1990—91). Avocation: tennis. Office: The Times-Picayune 3800 Howard Ave New Orleans LA 70125-1429

**PHELPS, BARTON CHASE,** architect, educator; b. Bklyn., June 27, 1946; s. Julian Orville and Elizabeth Willis (Paull) P.; m. Karen Joy Simonson; 1 child, Charlotte Simonson Phelps. BA in Art with honors, Williams Coll., 1968; MArch, Yale U., 1973. Registered architect, Calif. With Colin St. John Wilson & Ptnrs., London, 1972-73, Frank O. Gehry and Assocs., Santa Monica, Calif., 1973-76, Charles Moore/Urban Innovations Group, L.A., 1976-78; dir. architecture Urban Innovations Group, L.A., 1990-84; prin. Barton Phelps & Assocs., L.A., 1984—; asst. prof. architecture Rice U. Sch. of Architecture, Houston, 1977-79; asst. dean Grad. Sch. Architecture and Urban Planning, UCLA, 1980-83; prof. architecture Sch. Arts and Architecture UCLA, 1979—2001. Faculty mem. Nat. Endowment Arts, Mayors Inst. for City Design, 1990, 92, 98. Author, editor Architecture California, 1988-92, mem. editl. bd., 1998; editor: Views From the River, 1998; mem. editl. bd. Archtl. Record, 1998-2000. Mem. design review com. U. Calif., Santa Barbara, Calif., 2000—06; jury mem. US Presdl. Design Awards, 2000, Nat. AIA Honor Awards, 2003; mem. mayor's advisory panel Cultural Affairs Commn., LA, 2001—06; mem. architectural advisory bd. for oversees bldg. ops. US State Dept., 2005—06; bd. dirs. U. Elem. Sch. UCLA, 2000—06. Fellow Graham Found. for Advanced Studies in the Fine Arts, 1989, 96, Nat. Endowment for the Arts, 1990, 98. Mem. AIA (Coll. of Fellows, chair nat. com. on design, design excellence program USGSA, recipient design awards for L.A. Pub. Libr., Los Feliz, Woodland Hills, Will & Ariel Durant Branch, Cabrillo Marine Aquarium, Royce Hall at UCLA, Arroyo House, Kranz House, Sinquefield Ho., North Range Clark Libr. UCLA, L.A. Dept. Water and Power Ctrl. Dist. Hdqrs., North Hollywood Pump Sta., East Bldg. Seeds U. Elem. Sch., UCLA, Inst. Honor for Collaborative Design, Games XXIII Olympiad L.A. 1984), L.A. Conservancy (bd. dirs.). Democrat. Home: 10256 Lelia Ln Los Angeles CA 90077-3141 Office: Barton Phelps & Assocs 5514 Wilshire Blvd Los Angeles CA 90036-3829 Office Phone: 323-934-8615. Personal E-mail: bpala@aol.com. Business E-Mail: bphelps@bpala.com.

**PHELPS, BONNIE NOREEN,** language educator, secondary school educator; d. Norton Robert and Joyce Madelaine Phelps. B, U. Colo., 1966; M, Rivier Coll., 1974. Cert. tchr. State of NH., 1974. Sr. English tchr. Nashua H.S. North, NH, 1966—. Running start faculty mem. NH. Cmty. Tech. Coll., Claremont, NH, 2000—; mem. faculty leadership com. High North Site Coun., 2005. Author: (poetry) The 14th (Illiand Lit. Presdl. Lit. award and hon. award, 1994), Hurricane Bonnie in POETRY'S ELITE Poetry.com, (poem) Sibilance (semifinalist N.Am. Open Poetry contest, 1993). Judge Yankee Pen Poetry Contest, Boston Writing Project in Nantucket, 2004; vol. Penguin Plunge Spl. Olympics, NH, 2005. Recipient Creative Comms. Poetic Achievement award, Nashua H.S. North, 1992. Mem.: Am. Fedn. Tchrs., Nat. Coun. Tchrs. English (assoc.), Poetry Soc. N.H. (corr.; sec. of round robins 1987—88). Independent. Avocations: reading, writing, research on alternative health. Office: Nashua High School North 10 Chuck Druding Drive Nashua NH 03063 Personal E-Mail: bnphelps@msn.com.

**PHELPS, CHARLES ELLIOTT,** economics professor, director; b. N.Y.C., Apr. 20, 1943; s. McKinnie L. and Carolyn (McCleery) P.; m. Dale L. King, Sept. 2, 1967; children: Darin, Teresa. BA in Math., Pomona Coll., 1965; MBA, U. Chgo., 1968, PhD, 1973. Economist RAND Corp., Santa Monica, Calif., 1973-84; prof. econs. U. Rochester, N.Y., 1984—, provost, 1994—. Cons. JUREcon, Inc., L.A., 1977-86; pvt. cons., Rochester, N.Y., 1986—. Author: Health Economics, 3d edit., 2002; also over 70 articles. Fellow Nat. Bur. for Econ. Rsch.; mem. Inst. Medicine, Am. Econ. Assn., Nat. Acad. Social Ins., Soc. for Med. Decision Making (trustee 1991-93), Assn. for Pub. Policy Analysis (sec. 1982-91). Avocations: photography, archery, astronomy, canoeing, woodworking. Office: Office of the Provost U Rochester 200 Wallis Hall Rochester NY 14627-0001

**PHELPS, CHRISTOPHER,** history professor; b. Andrews AFB, Md., Aug. 31, 1965; s. Charles D. and Margaret Dorsey Phelps; m. Carol E. Hollier, Aug. 24, 1994; children: Emma Eleanor Hollier, Nowell Hollier, Rosa Hollier. BA, Reed Coll., 1988; MA, U. Oreg., 1992; PhD, U. Rochester, 1995. Vis. asst. prof. Simon Fraser U., Burnaby, BC, Canada, 1995—96, U. Oreg., Eugene, 1996—97; editl. dir. Monthly Rev. Press, NYC, 1998—99; asst. prof. Ohio State U., Mansfield and Columbus, 1999—2003, assoc. prof., 2003—. Fulbright sr. lectr. U. Pecs, Hungary, 2000; Fulbright disting. chair in Am. studies and lit. U. Lodz, Poland, 2004—05. Author: Young Sidney Hook: Marxist and Pragmatist; editor and writer of introduction for new edit.: The Jungle (Upton Sinclair); editor and writer of introduction: Race and Revolution (Max Shachtman); contbr. articles to profl. jours. J. William Fulbright grantee, Coun. for Internat. Exch. of Scholars, 2000, 2004—05. Mem.: AAUP, Am. Studies Assn. (life), Am. Hist. Assn. (life), Orgn. Am. Historians (life). Office: Ohio State U 1680 University Dr Mansfield OH 44907 Office Phone: 419-755-4380.

**PHELPS, DANIEL CHRISTOPHER,** information scientist, researcher; b. Somerville, NJ, Oct. 7, 1969; s. Robert Scott Phelps and Eleanor Isabelle Jaeger, Ernest Jaeger (Stepfather); m. Gianna Lynne McDevitt, Sept. 2, 1992; children: Daniel Christopher Phelps, II, Katharine Amanda, John Robert. AS in Emergency Med. Svc., Tallahassee CC, 1990; BA in Spanish, Fla. State U., Tallahassee, 1997, MS in Info. Studies, 1998, PhD, 2005. Cert. paramedic Fla., 1989, respiratory therapist Fla., 1995. From tchg. asst. to mem. faculty Coll. Info. Fla. State U., Panama City, Fla., 1998—2002, mem. faculty Coll. Info., 2002—. V.p. Tallahassee Info. Sys. Security Assn., Tallahassee, 2003—04; rschr. Info. Tech. Process Inst., Eugene, Oreg., 2005—. Contbr. articles to profl. jours. Mem.: IEEE, Assn. Info. Sys., Assn. Computing Machinery. Office: Fla State U 4750 Collegiate Dr Panama City FL 32405 Office Phone: 850-522-2089. Office Fax: 850-872-7720. Business E-Mail: dphelps@ci.fsu.edu.

**PHELPS, DAVID DWAIN,** state agency administrator, former congressman; b. Eldorado, Ill., Oct. 26, 1947; m. Leslie Phelps; 4 children. BS, So. Ill. U. Mem. Ill. Ho. of Reps. from 118th dist., 1985-98; mem., 106th Congress from 19th Ill. dist., 1999—2003; mem. agr. com.; mem. small bus.; asst. sec. Ill. Dept. Transp., Springfield, Ill., 2003—. Mem. Transp. and Motor Vehicles, Appropriations I, Energy, Environ. and Natural Resources, Edn. Appropriations, Human Svcs., Elem. and Secondary Edn., Counties and Twp., Econ. Devel. Coms. Ill. Ho. of Reps., vice chmn. Coal Devel. and Mktg., Econ. and Urban Devel. Coms., chmn. Health Care Com. Democrat. Office: Ill Dept Transp 2300 S Dirksen Pkwy Rm 300 Springfield IL 62764

**PHELPS, DENNIS LANE,** minister, educator, author; b. Monroe, La., July 23, 1955; s. Vaughn Lavelle and Vestal (Humphreys) P.; m. Robbin Jean Loewer, May 27, 1979; children: Kristen Lane, David Loewer. BA, La. Coll., 1978; MDiv, New Orleans Bapt. Theol. Sem., 1981; PhD, Southwestern Bapt. Theol. Sem., 1990. Ordained to ministry Bapt. Ch., 1978; cert. interim sch. Coord. ch. ministries La. Moral and Civic Found., Baton Rouge, 1973-79; staff evangelist Dennis Phelps Evangelistic Ministries, 1979—; pastor Brownfields Bapt. Ch., Baton Rouge, 1981-82; grader/teaching fellow Southwestern Bapt. Theol. Sem., Ft. Worth, 1982-87; pastor St. Francis Village Protestant Fellowship, Crowley, Tex., 1986-88; assoc. prof. of preaching Bethel Theol. Sem., St. Paul, 1988-99; assoc. tchg. pastor, exec. adminstr. Severns Valley Ch., Elizabethtown, Ky., 1998—. V.p. Global Horizons, Inc., 1994—. Editor Jour. of Am. Acad. Ministry 1995-98. Mem. strategy coun. AD2000: Mission Twin Cities, 1994-98; chmn. resolutions com. Ky. Bapt. Conv., 2000-2001; bd. dirs. Youth Connection, Inc., 1997-1999; v.p. Hardin County Ministerial Assn., 2002, pres. 2002-2003; bd. dirs., Helping Hand of the Heartland, 2002—. Named Southwesterner of Yr., Minn.-Wis. S.W. Bapt. Theol. Sem. Alumni, 1994. Mem. Inst. Bibl. Rsch., Religious Speech Comm. Assn., Acad. Homiletics, Am. Assn. Religion, Soc. Bibl. Lit., Assn. Practical Theology, Am. Acad. Ministry (charter), Nat. Storytelling Assn., Evang. Homiletics Soc. (charter), Southwestern Bapt. Theol. Sem. Alumni Assn. (pres. Ky. chpt. 1999-2000). Office: Severns Valley Ch PO Box 130 Elizabethtown KY 42702-0130

**PHELPS, EDMUND STROTHER,** economics professor; b. Evanston, Ill., July 26, 1933; s. Edmund Strother and Florence Esther (Stone) P.; m. Viviana Regina Montdor, Oct. 1, 1974. BA, Amherst Coll., 1955, DLitt (hon.), 1985; MA, Yale U., 1956, PhD, 1959. Economist Rand Corp., Santa Monica, Calif., 1959-60; asst. prof. Yale U., Cowles Found., 1960-62, assoc. prof., 1963-66; vis. assoc. prof. M.I.T., 1962-63; prof. econs. U. Pa., Phila., 1966-71, Columbia U., 1971-78, 79-82, McVickar prof. polit. economy, 1982—; scholar Russell Sage Found., 1993-94; prof. NYU, 1978-79. Fellow Ctr. for Advanced Study in Behavioral Scis., 1969-70; sr. advisor Brookings Inst., 1976—; econ. advisor European Bank for Reconstrn. and Devel., 1991-94; mem. econ. policy panel Observatoire Francais des Conjonctures Economiques, 1991—. Author: numerous books including Golden Rules of Economic Growth, 1966, Microeconomic Foundations of Employment and Inflation Theory, 1970, Economic Justice, 1973, Studies in Macroeconomic Theory, Vol. I, 1979, Vol. II, 1980, Political Economy, 1985, The Slump in Europe, 1988, Structural Slumps, 1994, Rewarding Work, 1997. Recipient Kenan Enterprise award, William R. Kenan Charitable Trust, 1996; fellow Social Sci. Rsch. Coun., 1966; Guggenheim fellow, 1978. Fellow: AAAS, Econometric Soc., Am. Econ. Assn. (disting. exec. com. 1976—78, v.p. 1983); mem.: Nat. Acad. Scis., Phi Beta Kappa. Home: 45 E 89th St New York NY 10128-1251 Office: Columbia Univ Dept Economics Rm 1004 New York NY 10027*

**PHELPS, GERRY CHARLOTTE,** economist, minister; b. Norman, Okla., Oct. 15, 1931; d. George and Charlotte LeNoir (Yowell) P.; 1 child, Scott. BA, U. Tex., 1963, MA, 1984; MDiv, San Francisco Theol. Seminary, 1984. Cert. tchr., Calif. Lectr. in econs. U. Houston, 1966—69; pastor United Meth. Ch., Kelseyville, Calif., 1980—82; sr. pastor Bethany United Meth. Ch., Bakersfield, Calif., 1982—84; founding exec. dir. Bakersfield Homeless Ctr., 1982—84; pres., founding exec. dir. San Jose Family Shelter, Calif., 1985—92; pastor United Meth. Ch., Flatonia, Tex., 1993—97; founding exec. dir. CRISES, Austin, 1994—98, v.p. devel., 1998—99; pvt. practice cons. poverty issues, 1999—. Cons. in ch. growth, 2001—. Author: Nutrition for Better Living, 1999, Budgeting for Better Living, 1999; author: Out of the Iron Furnace, 2000, Up and Out: A Guide to True Compassion for the Poor, 2001. Mem. Task Force on the Homeless, San Jose, 1987, Santa Clara County, 1991. Recipient commendation Mayor of Bakersfield, 1984, Santa Clara County Bd. Suprs., 1992. Avocations: latin american studies, refugee assistance, homeless assistance, study of connections between economic and social problems. Personal E-mail: gphelps@austin.rr.com.

**PHELPS, JERRY SCOTT,** psychologist, educator; b. Lompoc, Calif., Mar. 31, 1964; s. Vernon Kelly and Virginia Mae Phelps; m. Jennifer Phelps, Aug. 25, 1989; children: Sara Z., Megan Kelly. BA, U. of Calif., Berkeley, 1986; MA, PhD, U. of Colo., 1995. Lic. psychologist Calif. Post-doctoral fellow San Diego VA Med. Ctr. Behavioral Medicine, La Jolla, Calif., 1995—98; staff psychologist San Diego VA Healthcare Sys., La Jolla, 1996—98; psychologist psychol. and counseling svcs. U. Calif-San Diego, La Jolla, 1998—, asst. clin. prof. psychiatry Sch. Medicine, 1999—2006, dir. Substance/Alcohol Feedback and Edn. Program, 2001—. Cons. Dept. of Edn.

Grant (Alcohol and Violence Prevention), La Jolla, 2001—, HIV Neurobehavioral Rsch. Ctr., La Jolla, 2001—05; trainer Continuing Edn. Seminars, L.A., 2005—. Contbr. articles to profl. jours. Recipient regents scholarship, U. of Calif., Berkeley, 1986. Mem.: APA, Motvational Interviewing Network of Trainers. Office: U Calif - San Diego CB 0509 9500 Gilman Dr La Jolla CA 92093-0509 Office Phone: 858-822-2614. Business E-Mail: jsphelps@ucsd.edu.

**PHELPS, JUDSON HEWETT,** health facility administrator, marketing professional; b. Evanston, Ill., Oct. 18, 1942; s. Sidney Norman and Mary Schuyler (Coons) Phelps; m. Barbara Ann Ray, Dec. 21, 1963; children: Wyeth Hewett, Christopher Ashley, Whitney Magee. BA, Williams Coll., 1964; MS, Springfield Coll., 1993. Lic. alchohol, drug counselor. Asst. brand mgr. Procter & Gamble Co., Cin., 1968—70; brand mgr. Memorex, Santa Clara, Calif., 1970—72; product mgr. Chesebrough Ponds Inc., Greenwich, Conn., 1972—76; v.p. mktg. L'Oreal subs. Cosmair Inc., NYC, 1976—77; v.p. sales Bio Products, Inc., Norwalk, Conn., 1978, exec. v.p., 1979, pres., 1980—86; corp. v.p. Ketchum & Co. parent co. Bio Products, Norwalk, 1982—86; mng. dir. Dameon Ptnrs. Inc., Wilton, Conn., 1987—88; pres. Theracom Corp., Rye, NY, 1988—89; v.p. Promotion Info. Bur., Norwalk, 1990; prin. Daniel Adams Co., Danbury, Conn., 1991—92; clin. coord., addictions therapist, counselor Ctr., Bridgeport, Conn., 1993—97; program dir. Gosnold-Thorne Counseling, Hyannis, 1998—. Adj. faculty Housatonic Cmty. Tech. Coll., Bridgeport, 1995—97. Family counselor Caregivers, Assn. Religious Communities, Danbury, Conn., 1975—79; leader, treas. Ridgefield Emmaus Teenage Christian Retreats, Conn., 1983—92; pres. Camp Dudley (YMCA) Alumni Assn., Westport, NY, 1974—79; chmn. Ridgefield Alcohol and Drug Use Commn., 1992—97. Lt. USNR, 1964—68. Home: 53 Gingerbread Ln Yarmouth Port MA 02675-1110 Office Phone: 508-375-6805.

**PHELPS, MICHAEL,** Olympic athlete; b. Balt., June 30, 1985; Mem. U.S. Men's Olympic Swim Team, Sydney, 2000, Athens, 2004, Team Speedo, 2001—. Hon. bd. mem. Pathfinders for Autism. Named Swimmer of the Yr., 2001, 2003, Am. Internat. Athlete of Yr., 2004. Achievements include holds World Record in 200m fly, 200m IM, 400m IM; holds American Records in 200m fly, free, 200m IM, 400m IM, 400m free, 800m free; only swimmer in history to set 5 world records in one international meet; became the youngest world record holder in modern history at age 15, Sydney Olympic games, 2000; being first male swimmer to break two world records in separate events in the same day; being a five time world champion with 21 national titles; winning gold medal, 200m IM, 400m IM, 100m butterfly, 200m butterfly, 4x200m free relay, 400m MR, Bronze medal, 200m free, 4x100m free, Athens Olympic games, 2004; tied World Record with 8 medals in single Olympic games, Athens, 2004. Office: USA Swimming 1 Olympic Plaza Colorado Springs CO 80909

**PHELPS, MICHAEL EDWARD,** biophysics professor; b. Cleve., Aug. 24, 1939; s. Earl E. and Regina Bridget (Hines) P.; m. Patricia Emory, May 15, 1969; children: Patrick, Kaitlin. BA in Chemistry and Math., Western Wash. State U., 1965; PhD in Chemistry, Washington U., St. Louis, 1970. Asst. prof. Washington U. Sch. Medicine and Engring., 1970-73, assoc. prof., 1973-75; assoc. prof. dept. radiology U. Pa., Phila., 1975-76; prof. radiological sciences UCLA, 1976—92, prof. biomathematics, 1980—, chief divsn. biophysics, 1981—84, Jennifer Jones Simon prof., 1983—86, Norton Simon prof., 1996—, chief div. nuclear medicine, 1984—92, dir. Crump Inst. for Biol. Imaging, 1989—, chmn. dept. molecular and med. pharmacology, 1992—, chief, divsn. nuclear medicine, dept. molecular and med. pharmacology, 1992—; assoc. dir. UCLA/DOE Lab. Structural Biology and Molecular Medicine, 1984—, chief, divsn. nuclear medicine, 1984—; dir. UCLA/DOE Inst. Molecular Medicine, 1989—2002. Mem. study sect. NIH, Bethesda, Md., 1974-78. Author: Reconstruction Tomography in Diagnostic Radiology and Nuclear Medicine, 1977, Physics in Nuclear Medicine, 1980, 1987, 2002, Principles of Tracer Kinetics, 1983; contbr. articles to profl. jours. Recipient Von Hevesy Found. award, 1975,George Von Hevesy prize Von Hevesy Found., Zurich, 1978, 82, Oldendorf award, Soc. for Computerized Tomography and Neurological Imaging, 1981, S. Weir Mitchell award, Am. Acad. of Neuology, 1981, Ernest O. Lawrence award US Dept. Energy, 1984, Spec. award for Individual Distinction, Am. Nuclear Soc., 1984, Landauer Mem. award, Am. Assn. for Physicists in Medicine, 1988, Robert J. and Claire Pasarow Found. award, 1992, Disting. Scientists award, Inst. for Clin. PET, 1995, Enrico Fermi Presdl. award, 1999, Charles F. Kettering prize, GM Cancer Rsch. Found., 2001; holder Norton Simon endowed chair, 1983-; named Disting. Alumnus Western Wash. State U., 1980 Fellow Am. Heart Assn.; mem. ACP (Richard and Hinda Rosenthal award 1987), Inst. Medicine NAS (elected), Nat. Acad. Scis. (elected 1999), Soc. Nuclear Medicine (Paul Aebersold award 1983, Ted Block Mem. award, 1989), Internat. Soc. Cerebral Blood Flow and Metabolism (Cert. Excellence award 1979), NY Acad. Scis. (Sarah L. Poiley award 1984), Soc. Neuroscis. Roman Catholic. Business E-Mail: mphelps@mednet.ucla.edu.*

**PHEMISTER, ROBERT DAVID,** veterinary medical educator; b. Framingham, Mass., July 15, 1936; s. Robert Irving and Georgia Nora Phemister; m. Ann Christine Lyon, June 14, 1960; children: Katherine, David, Susan. D.V.M., Cornell U., 1960; PhD, Colo. State U., Ft. Collins, 1967. Diplomate: Am. Coll. Vet. Pathologists. Research assoc. U. Calif., Davis, 1960-61, vis. rsch. pathologist, 1974-75; staff scientist Armed Forces Inst. Pathology, Washington, 1962-64; sect. leader to dir. collaborative radiol. health lab. Colo. State U., 1964-77; mem. faculty Coll. Vet. Medicine and Biomed. Scis., 1968-85, prof. vet. pathology, 1973-85, assoc. dean, 1976-77, dir. expt. sta., 1977-85, dean, 1977-85, interim acad. v.p. Univ., 1982, interim pres. Univ., 1983-84, spl. counselor to pres., 1984-85; vis. prof. Colo. State U., 1995-96; prof. vet. pathology Cornell U., 1985-99, dean and prof. emeritus, 1999—, dean Coll. Vet. Medicine, 1985-95. Cons. Mass. Vet. Sch., 1977-81; commr. Colo. Advanced Tech. Inst., 1983-84; mem. governing bd. N.Y. Sea Grant Inst., 1985-95, vice chmn., 1990-92; mem. vet. medicine adv. com. FDA, 1984-88; mem. joint coun. on food and agrl. scis. USDA, 1988-92, mem. exec. com., 1989-92; chmn. Zweig Meml. Fund for Equine Rsch., 1985-95; mem. adv. panel for vet. medicine Pew Health Professions Commn., 1991-93. Author papers in field. Served to comdr. USPHS, 1960-68. Recipient Charles A. Lory award and Disting. Univ. Leadership award Colo. State U., 1984, Disting. Practitioner award Nat. Acad. Practice, 1985, Regional Health Adminstr.'s award, 1985; named Honor Alumnus, Colo. State U., 1989. Mem. AVMA (coun. on edn. 1985-91, adv. bd. vet. specialities 1985-89), Assn. Am. Vet. Med. Colls. (pres. 1982-83), Colo. Vet. Med. Assn. (Disting. Svc. award 1985), N.Y. State Vet. Med. Soc. (Centennial award 1990), Sigma Xi, Phi Zeta, Phi Kappa Phi, Gamma Sigma Delta (Merit award for Adminstrn. 1995). Home: 3136 Rock Park Dr Fort Collins CO 80528

**PHIBBS, CLIFFORD MATTHEW,** surgeon, educator; b. Bemidji, Minn., Feb. 20, 1930; s. Clifford Matthew and Dorothy Jean (Wright) P.; m. Patricia Jean Palmer, June 27, 1953; children: Wayne Robert, Marc Stuart, Nancy Louise BS, Wash. State U., 1952; MD, U. Wash., 1955; MS, U. Minn., 1960. Diplomate Am. Bd. Surgery. Intern Ancker Hosp., St. Paul, 1955—56; resident in surgery U. Minn. Hosps., 1956—60; practice medicine specializing in surgery Oxboro Clinic, Mpls., 1962—, pres., 1985—; cons. to health risk mgmt. corps., 1994—. Mem. Children's Hosp. Ctr., Northwestern-Abbott Hosp., Fairview-Southdale Hosp., Fairview Ridges Hosp.; clin. asst. prof. U. Minn., Mpls., 1975-78, clin. assoc. prof. surgery, 1978—; med. dir. Minn. Protective Life Ins. Co. Contbr. articles to med. jours. Bd. dirs. Bloomington Bd. Edn., Minn., 1974—, treas., 1976, sec., 1977-78, chmn., 1981-83; mem. adv. com. jr. coll. study City of Bloomington, 1964-66, mem. community facilities com., 1966-67, advisor youth study commn., 1966-68; vice chmn. bd. Hillcrest Meth. Ch., 1970-71; mem. Bloomington Adv. and Rsch. Coun., 1969-71; bd. dirs. Bloomington Symphony Orch., 1996—, Wash. State U. Found., trustee, 1990—; dir. bd. mgmt. Minnesota Valley YMCA, 1970-75; bd. govrs. Mpls. Met. YMCA, 1970—; dir. Bloomington Heart-Health Found., 1989—, Martin Luther Manor, 1989; pres. Oxboro Clinics, 1985—; bd. dirs. Bloomington History Clock Tower Assn., 1990—; bd. dirs. Fairview Hosp. Clinic, 1994—, Bloomington Sister city Orgn., 1999—, Bloomington Cmty. Found., 1997-, Bloomington Health Adv. Bd., 2000-, MMA Minority

and Cross-Cult. Affairs Com., 2000-, Com. on Cult. Competence Minnesota Med. Assn., 1986. Capt. M.C., U.S. Army, 1960-62. Mem. ACS, AMA (Physician Recognition awards 1969, 73, 76, 79, 82, 85, 88, 91, 94), Assn. Surg. Edn., Royal Soc. Medicine, Am. Coll. Sports Medicine, Minn. Med. Assn. (del. 1991-94), Minn. Surg. Soc., Mpls. Surg. Soc., Hennepin County Med. Soc., Pan-Pacific Surg. Assn., Jaycees, Bloomington C. of C. (chmn. bd. 1984, chmn. 1985-86), Bloomington Adv. Bd. health, Bloomington Sister City Bd., Bloomington Cmty. Found. (bd. dirs. 1996-). Home: 9613 Upton Rd Minneapolis MN 55431-2454 Office: 600 W 98th St Minneapolis MN 55420-4773 E-mail: kphiibs@aol.com.

**PHILANDER, SAMUEL GEORGE HARKER,** oceanographer; b. Cape Town, South Africa, July 25, 1942; came to the U.S., 1963; s. Peter and Alice (Harker) P.; m. Hilda Teresa Storari, Sept. 16, 1967; 1 child, Rodrigo. BS, U. Cape Town, 1963; PhD, Harvard U., 1970. Sr. rsch. oceanographer GFDL/NOAA, Princeton, NJ, 1978-89; prof. geoscis. Princeton U., 1990—, chmn., 1994—, Knox Taylor prof. geosciences. Author: El Niño, La Niña and the Southern Oscillation, 1990, Is The Temperature Rising? The Uncertain Science of Global Warming, 1998, Our Affair with El Niño, 2004. Recipient Gold medal U.S. Dept. Commerce, 1985. Fellow Am. Meteorol. Soc. (Sverdrup Gold medal 1985), Am. Geophys. Union, Am. Acad. Arts and Scis.; mem. NAS. Office Phone: 609-258-5683. Business E-Mail: gphlder@princeton.edu.*

**PHILBIN, ANN,** art facility director; b. Boston, Mar. 21, 1952; d. Richard Moore and Ann Theresa (Muller) Philbin BA in art history, BFA in painting, U. NH, 1976; MA in mus. studies/arts adminstrn., NYU, 1982. Rschr. Frick Art Reference Libr., NYC, 1977-79; asst. to dir., program coord. Artists Space, NYC, 1979-80; asst. curatorial coord. The New Mus., NYC, 1980-81; curator Ian Woodner Family Collection, NYC, 1981-83; asst. dir. Grace Borgenicht Gallery, NYC, 1983-85; dir. Curt Marcus Gallery, NYC, 1985-88; account dir., dir. Art Against AIDS Livet Reichard Inc., NYC, 1988-90; dir. The Drawing Ctr., NYC, 1990—99, UCLA Hammer Museum, LA, 1999—. Bd. dirs. Elizabeth Streb, Ringside, NY, 1990, HIV Law Project, N.YC, 1993; founding mem. Women's Action Coalition, NYC, 1991. Recipient Best Monographic Mus. Show Nationally Award for exhibition Lee Bontecou: A Retrospective, Internat. Assn. Art Critics/USA, 2004. Address: UCLA Hammer Museum 10899 Wilshire Blvd at Westwood Blvd Los Angeles CA 90024*

**PHILBIN, REGIS (REGIS FRANCIS XAVIER PHILBIN),** television personality; b. NYC, Aug. 25, 1931; s. Frank and Florence P.; m. Kay Faylan, 1957 (div. 1968); children: Amy, Danny; m. Joy Senese, Mar. 1, 1970; children: Joanna, Jennifer. Student, U. Notre Dame. Hollywood stagehand, NBC page The Tonight Show; TV pioneer, news writer, newswriter, sportscaster. Co-host The Joey Bishop Show, 1967-69, host Sta. KABC A.M. L.A., 1975-83, Sta. WABC TV Morning Show, 1983-88 (with Kathy Lee Gifford in 1985); co-host (syndicated show) Live! With Regis and Kathie Lee, 1988-2000, Live! With Regis and Kelly, 2001—, exec. prodr., 2001—, Miss Am. Pageant, 1991, 92, 95; host, Who Wants to Be a Millionaire, 1999-2002; co-author: Cooking with Regis and Kathie Lee, 1993, Entertaining with Regis and Kathie Lee, 1994; host (TV show) America's Got Talent, 2006-; author: I'm Only One Man, 1995, Who Wants to Be Me?, 2003; TV appearances include The Danny Thomas Hour, 1968, Get Smart, 1968, The Big Valley, 1968, Rowan & Martin's Laugh-In, 1968, Love, American Style, 1969, 71, That Girl, 1970, The Silent Force, 1970, The Jimmy Stewart Show, 1972, The Neighbors, 1975, The San Pedro Beach Bums, 1977, CHiPs, 1978, Lucan, 1978, Fantasy Island, 1979, 83, Ryan's Hope, 1987, 1988, Mad About You, 1993, Seinfeld, 1994, The Larry Sanders Show, 1994, The Cosby Mysteries, 1995, Hope & Gloria, 1995, The Fresh Prince of Bel-Air, 1996, Life's Work, 1996, Spin City, 1997, 99, 2000, Diagnosis Murder, 1998, Caroline in the City, 1998, The Simpsons, 1998, Becker, 2001, One Life to Live, 2002, Hope and Faith, 2003, 2005, 2006 The Apprentice, 2004, Extreme Makeover: Home Edition, 2004, Less Than Perfect, 2005; TV Film appearances SST:Death Flight, 1977, Mad Bull, 1977, Mirror, Mirror, 1979, Perry Mason: The Case of the Telltale Talk Show Host, 1993; Film appearances include The Bad News Bears Go To Japan, 1978, The Emperor's New Clothes, 1993, The Man Who Loved Women, 1983, Night and the City, 1992, Dudley Do-Right, 1999, Little Nicky, 2000, People I Know, 2002, Cheaper by the Dozen, 2003, The Breakup Artist, 2004, Miss Congeniality 2: Armed and Fabulous, 2005; (voice roles) Happily Ever After: Fairy Tales for Every Child, 1995, Mother Goose: A Rappin' and Rhymin' Special, 1997, Hercules, 1998, Family Guy, 2002, Pinocchio, 2002, Lilo & Stitch: The Series, 2004; albums It's Time For Regis!, 1968, When You're Smiling, 2004; host Walt Disney World Very Merry Christmas Parade, 1991, 1992, Walt Disney World Christmas Day Parade, 2002-05, Walt Disney World Happy Easter Parade, 1992, New Year's Rockin' Eve 2005, Fox New Year's Eve Live 2006. Named Personality of Yr., TV Guide, 2001; named to Guinness Book of World Records for the most hours on camera, 2004, Acad. TV Arts & Sciences Hall of Fame, 2006; recipient Four Daytime Emmy awards, Broadcasting & Cable Lifetime Achievement award, Crystal Apple award for contributions to the NY TV industry, Mayor Rudolph Giuliani, Star on Hollywood Walk of Fame, 2003. Achievements include setting Guinness World Record in 2004 for Most Hours on Camera (15,188 hours). Office: Regis & Kelly 7 Lincoln Sq New York NY 10023-5900*

**PHILBRICK, DOUGLAS ROBERT,** principal, librarian, educator, mental health professional; b. St. Louis, Mar. 17, 1942; s. Robert Gilbert and Alice Hazel (LaRoche) P.; m. Lynda J. Harmon; children: Alma Robert, Amber, David, Mark, Holly, Amos, June. B of Pub. Address, Brigham Young U., 1969, MLS, 1972; MA in Secondary Adminstrn., No. State Coll., 1977; EdS, U. S.D., 1991. Cert. EMT, N.Mex.; cert. supt. specialty, edn. specialist U. S.D. Libr. dir. Inst. of Am. Indian Arts, Santa Fe, 1973, D.Q. Univ., Davis, Calif., 1973—74; tchr., libr. Lower Brule (S.D.) High Sch., 1974—75; prin. Crow Creek Sioux Tribe, Fort Thompson, SD, 1975, Bur. Indian Affairs, Lower Brule, 1975—76, Kinlichee, Ariz., 1977—79; edn. supt. Stewart, Nev., 1979—80, Sells, Ariz., 1980, Fort Thompson, SD, 1981—85, edn. specialist Phoenix, 1985—91, prin. Keam Canyon, Ariz., 1992—94; mental health tech/counselor, tchr. Indian Health Svc., Sacaton, Ariz., 1994—98, tchr. substance abuse, regular, and spl. edn. tchr., 1998—2006. Farmer/rancher, Chamberlain, S.D., 1956-61; chmn. curriculum com. Inst. Am. Indian Arts, Santa Fe, 1973; fed. intern Washington, 1971. Author adapted Libr. of Congress classification system for Indians, 1973, Bibliography of Indian Newspapers and Periodicals, 1974. Leader 4-H, Crow Creek Indian Reservation, 1956-61; scout master Boy Scouts Am., Chamberlain, 1984, Mesa, 1995-98. With USAF, 1961-64. Recipient scholarship, Libr. Adminstrn. Devel. Program, U. Md., 1972. Republican. Mem. Lds Ch. Home: 1014 E 8th Pl Mesa AZ 85203-5610 Office Phone: 888-431-4096. E-mail: ljhp1@juno.com.

**PHILBRICK, NATHANIEL,** writer; married; 2 children. BA, Brown Univ.; MA in Am. Lit., Duke Univ. Founding dir. Egan Inst. Maritime Studies, Nantucket, Mass., 1986—. Editor-in-chief Yaahting: A Parody, 1984; author: The Passionate Sailor, 1987, Away Off Shore: Nantucket Island and Its People 1602-1890, 1994, Abram's Eyes: The Native American Legend of Nantucket, 1998, Second Wind: A Sunfish Sailor's Odyssey, 1999, In the Heart of the Sea, 2000 (Nat. Book award for nonfiction, 2000), Sea of Glory, 2003 (Theodore and Franklin D. Roosevelt Naval History prize, 2003), Revenge of the Whale, 2003 (Boston Globe-Horn Book honor book), Mayflower, 2006; contbr. articles to Vanity Fair, NY Times Book Rev., Wall St. Jour., LA Times, Boston Globe. Named Nathaniel Bowditch Maritime Scholar of Yr., Am. Merchant Marine Mus., 2002; recipient Byrne Waterman award, Kendall Whaling Mus., 2001. Fellow: Soc. Am. Historians, Am. Antiquarian Soc., Mass. Hist. Soc., Nantucket Hist. Assn. Avocation: sailing. Office: Egan Inst Maritime Studies Coffin Sch 4 Winter St Nantucket MA 02554 Address: c/o Penguin Group USA Publicity 375 Hudson St New York NY 10014*

**PHILIP, PETER VAN NESS,** former trust company executive; b. N.Y.C., Feb. 23, 1925; s. Van Ness and Lilian (Davis) P.; m. Sabina FitzGibbon, May 3, 1952; children: William Van Ness, Thomas Winslow, Peter Sandys. AB,

Yale U., 1945W; MBA, NYU, 1950. With Price, Waterhouse & Co., N.Y.C., 1947-52; W.H. Morton & Co., Inc., N.Y.C., 1952-73; pres., CEO Equitable Securities, Morton & Co., Inc., 1970-73; sr. v.p., dir. White Weld & Co., Inc., N.Y.C., 1974-76; v.p. Morgan Guaranty Trust Co., N.Y.C., 1977-88, ret. With 86th inf. div. AUS, 1943-45. Decorated Purple Heart, Bronze Star. Mem.: Racquet and Tennis (N.Y.C.); Links; Yale (N.Y.C.), Downtown Assn. (N.Y.C.), Bond (N.Y.C.); Bedford ((N.Y.); Golf and Tennis; Ekwanok (Manchester, Vt.). Home: Box 395 740 Guard Hill Rd Bedford NY 10506-1042

**PHILIP, SUNNY KOIPURATHU,** municipal official; b. Ranny, Kerala, India, Sept. 3, 1957; came to U.S., 1983; s. Mathai Koipurathu and Sosamma (Ninan) P.; m. Achamma John; children: Sunny K. Jr., Christine. B in Commerce, U. Kerala, India, 1978; M in Commerce, U. Kerala, 1982. Controller St. Thomas Evang. Ch. Hdqtrs., Kerala, India, 1978-81; instr. Minerva Coll., Kerala, 1981-83; fin. dir. City of La Feria, Tex., 1983-91; exec. dir. La Feria Indsl. Devel. Corp., Tex., 1991-93; city mgr. City of La Feria, Tex., 1993—. Controller La Feria Indsl. Found. Corp., 1986—. Chmn. Cub Scouts Pack 47. Mem. Tex. City Mgrs. Assn.; Tex. Indsl. Devel. Coun., Tex. Assn. Assessing Officers, Govt. Fin. Officers Assn. Tex. Lodges: Lions (treas. La Feria club 1983—). Methodist. Avocations: fishing, travel, reading. Home: PO Box 671 La Feria TX 78559-0671 Office: City of La Feria 115 E Commercial Ave La Feria TX 78559-5002 E-mail: sunbest@aol.com.

**PHILIP, TOM,** reporter; married; 2 children. BA in Journalism, Northwestern Univ. Staff writer Sacramento Bee, 1992—97, assoc. editor, editl. bd. mem., 1997—. Recipient Best of West first place for deadline writing, 1992, Am. Assn. Univ. Prof. top prize, 1994, Calif. Newspaper Publishers Assn. Better Newspapers first place award for editl. comment, 2000, Harold Gilliam award for excellence in environ. reporting, Bay Inst. of San Francisco, 2001, Walker Stone award, Scripps Howard Found., 2004, Sigma Delta Chi award for editl. writing, 2004, Nat. Headliner award for editl. writing, 2004, Pulitzer Prize for editl. writing, 2005. Office: Sacramento Bee 2100 Q St Sacramento CA 95816 Office Phone: 916-321-1001.

**PHILIPP, ADAM LIEF KAKIMOTO,** lawyer; b. Honokaa, Hawaii, Oct. 19, 1969; s. Joan Alice Philipp; m. Masako Kakimoto Kakimoto, June 15, 1997; 1 child, Samantha. BA, Tufts U., 1991; JD, U. San Diego, 1995; postgrad., San Diego State U., 1995-98. Bar: Calif. 1995, U.S. Patent and Trademark Office. Pvt. practice, San Diego, 1995-98; assoc. Baker & McKenzie, San Diego, 1998—. Mem. ABA, Am. Intellectual Property Assn., San Diego Intellectual Property Assn., Phi Delta Phi. Avocations: scuba diving, photography, computer software development. Office: Baker & McKenzie 1101 W Broadway Fl 12 San Diego CA 92101-3336

**PHILIPP, KARLA ANN,** music educator, conductor, musician; b. Milw., Sept. 12, 1955; d. John William and Catherine Ann Philipp. MusB, U. Ariz., 1977; MusM, Memphis State U., 1979. Tchr. itinerant strings Memphis City Schs., 1979—; condr. youth string ensemble and youth sinfonia Memphis Youth Symphony, 1997—. Sect. bass player Tucson Symphony Orch., 1977—78, Memphis Symphony Orch., 1979—89; prin. bass Jackson Symphony Orch., 1989—; note reading tchr., condr. Am. Suzuki Inst., Stevens Point, Wis., 1993—2005; dir. orch. Intermountain Suzuki String Inst., Salt Lake City, 2001—04; notereading tchr., dir. orch. Suzuki Inst. U. Memphis, 2005—, dir. orch. Summer String Camp, 2006—. Mem. Integrity, Memphis, 2003—. Recipient award for tchr. excellence, Rotary Club, Memphis, 1998, Outstanding Tchr. award, Tenn. Gov.'s Sch. for Arts, 1991, 1994, 1995; grantee, Rotary Club, Memphi, 1991, 1997; Haldeman scholar, U. Ariz. Sch. Music, 1974—78. Mem.: Internat. Soc. Bassists, Suzuki Assn. of Ams., West Tenn. Sch. Band and Orch. Assn., Tenn. Music Educators Assn., Music Educators Nat. Conf., Am. String Tchrs. Assn. (west Tenn v.p. 1993—95), Am. Fedn. Musicians Local 71. Episcopalian. Avocations: reading, travel. Office: Ridgeway Mid Sch 6333 Quince Rd Memphis TN 38119 Office Phone: 901-416-1588. E-mail: philippbass@aol.com.

**PHILIPPE, PAUL,** chemist; b. Md., Jan. 5, 1960; m. Janie Philippe; children: Antonio, Angela Randall. BSc, Kean U., 1982, DSc, 1986. Cert. in lab. processing Chem. Labs., 1988. Lab. technician Epidemiology and Pharms., 1990—95; dir. The Drug Control Indsl. Corp., Mass., 1995—2000; chemist Background Labs., Mass., 2002—04; Meriks Chems. and Mixtures, Newton Centre, 2004—. Named Chemist of Yr., Chem. Ptnrs. mag., 2001; recipient Discovery award, Sci. Experimentation Bd., 2003. Mem.: Creative Ideas Assn., Soc. Lab Technicians and Chemists, Sci. and Discovery Assn., Phi Beta Kappa. Roman Catholic. Avocations: bowling, boxing. Office: Meriks Chems and Mixtures 831 Beacon St 195 Newton Center MA 02459-1840

**PHILIPPS, EDWARD WILLIAM,** former banker, real estate appraiser; b. N.Y.C., Dec. 19, 1938; s. Edward Charles and Eleanor Elizabeth (Eisenger) P.; m. Diane Rose DiCuffa, June 12, 1960; children: James Michael, Robert Christopher. Appraiser Dry Dock Savs., N.Y.C., 1956-70, Nat. Bank of West, White Plains, NY, 1970-72, Aires Real Estate, Yonkers, NY, 1972-74; sr. v.p. Am. Savs. Bank (merger Empire Savs. Bank), N.Y.C., 1974-92; self employed real estate appraiser Yonkers, 1992-93; sr. v.p., chief lending officer LaJolla (Conn.) Bank, 1993-99; cons., 1999—. Mem. mortgage Com. Cmty. Preservation Corp., N.Y.C., 1990-92. Mem. Am. Inst. Real Estate Appraisers, Homebuilders Assn. Fairfield County (bd. dirs.). Avocations: wood working, fishing. Home and Office: 261 Kimball Ave Yonkers NY 10704-3030 E-mail: ephilip@optonline.net.

**PHILIPPS, KINGA (SZPAKIEWICZ),** TV show host; b. Warsaw, Aug. 16, 1976; arrived in Okla., 1981; BS in Broadcast Journalism, Oklahoma State U. Host (TV series) E-Travelers, Travel Channel, Beauty Factor TV, Ready for the Weekend Movie, USA Network, 2004, Travel a la Mode, Feedback, Food Network, 2005—, Google Current, Current TV, 2005—; actor(appearances): (TV series) The West Wing, 2002, Cold Case, 2004, According to Jim, 2004; (TV miniseries) For the Love of Skype, 2006.; (films) Tomcats, 2001, Austin Powers: Goldmember, 2002, Torque, 2004, Leaving L.A., 2006; author: children's books. Office: Current TV LLC 118 King St San Francisco CA 94107*

**PHILIPPUS, AL A.,** former police chief; b. San Antonio, Mar. 18, 1951; m. Jeanne Theresa Philippus; children: Dawn Michelle, Jason Allen, Mary Lamm. A. in Law Enforcement, San Antonio Coll., 1977; BS in Criminal Justice magna cum laude, SW. Tex. State U., 1979; MS in Criminal Justice Mgmt./Adminstrn., Sam Houston State U., 1992, PhD in Criminal Justice Mgmt./Adminstrn., 1994. Patrol officer City of San Antonio Police Dept., 1975-81, detective homicide unit, 1981-84, sgt. patrol divsn., 1984-86, sgt. internal affairs, 1986-88, lt., dir. tech. and planning, 1988-89, capt., comdr. fiscal mgmt. and rsch. divs., 1989-94, dep. police chief, comdr. uniform divsn., 1994-95, chief of police, 1995—2001. Adj. prof. St. Mary's U., San Antonio, 1993—. Adv. bd. Police Found. Law Enforcement; law enforcement adv. bd. Alamo Area Coun. Govts.; mem. law enforcement coord. com. U.S. Western Dist. Tex.; bd. dirs. Tex. Ctr. for Legal Ethics and Professionalism. Sgt. USAF, 1969-73. Named Officer of the Yr., Greater San Antonio Builder's Assn., 1979, Optimist Club, 1993. Mem. Internat. City Mgmt. Assn., Nat. Assn. Rschrs. and Planners, Internat. Assn. Law Enforcement Planners, Internat. Assn. Chiefs of Police, Police Exec. Rsch. Found., Am. Pub. Welfare Assn., Assn. of Police Planning and Rsch. Officers, Combined Law Enforcement Assn. of Tex., San Antonio Police Officers Assn.

**PHILLIPS, JEREMY,** media company executive; b. London, Eng. Grad., U. NSW, Harvard U. Various media and telecom. positions McKinsey & Co.; bus. devel. mgr. PBL Online Pub. and Broadcasting Ltd., Australia, 1997; dep. chmn. corp. Ltd., Australia, 1999—2001; dir. strategic investments Citigroup; sr. v.p. office of the chmn. News Corp., N.Y.C., 2004—. Office: The News Corp Ltd 1211 Avenue of the Americas New York NY 10036

**PHILLABAUM, LESLIE ERVIN,** publisher; b. Cortland, N.Y., June 1, 1936; s. Vern Arthur and Beatrice Elizabeth (Butterfield) Phillabaum; m. Roberta Kimbrough Swarr, Mar. 17, 1962; children: Diane Melissa, Scott Christopher. BS, Pa. State U., 1958, MA, 1963. Editor Pa. State U. Press, 1961-63; editor-in-chief U. N.C. Press, 1963-70; assoc. dir., editor La. State U. Press, Baton Rouge, 1970-75, dir., 1975—2003, emeritus dir., 2003—. Served to 1st lt. U.S. Army, 1959—61. Mem.: Assn. Am. Univ. Presses (dir. 1978—80, 1983—86, pres. 1984—85), Acacia, Alpha Kappa Psi, Omicron Delta Kappa. Democrat. Home: 769 Castle Kirk Dr Baton Rouge LA 70808-6018

**PHILLIPE, CHESTER TOLLESON,** alcohol/drug abuse services professional, educator; b. Long Beach, Calif., Oct. 15, 1929; s. Chester Marion Phillipe and Ethyle Kent Theinhaus; m. Florence Marie Phillipe (dec. July 1998); children: Jeffrey, Patrick, Melissa, Andrew, Aimee. BA in Religion and Bus. Adminstrn., Calif. Bapt. Coll., 1972; MDiv, Golden Gate Bapt. Theol. Sem., 1975. Cert. alcohol and drug abuse counselor; coll. instr. Calif. Alcohol and drug abuse counselor Calif. Assn. Alcohol and Drug Abuse Counselors, Sacramento, 1981—; CEO Family Addictions Ctr. Treatment. Mem. faculty in human svcs. Porterville Coll. Author: (book) Church Under Fire, 1998; editor: (addiction manuals) Substance Abuse, A Physical Disease, 1998. Bd. dirs. Calif. Alcohol and Drug Commn. Edn. Programs, Sacramento. Sgt. Army Security Agy. U.S. Army, 1947—50. Grantee, Idaho Mental Health, 1981. Mem.: Calif. Assn. Alcohol and Drug Abuse Counselors (bd. dirs. 1980—, Excellent Svc. award 1991), Nat. Assn. Alcohol and Drug Abuse Counselors, Internat. Consortium Reciprocity Commn. Republican. Avocations: reading, fishing, travel. E-mail: chetp@psnw.com.

**PHILLIPPE, RYAN,** actor; b. Sept. 10, 1974; m. Reese Witherspoon; children: Ava Elizabeth, Deacon. Student, New Castle Bapt. Acad., 1992. Co-founder prodn. co. Actor: (TV series) One Life to Live, 1992, The Secrets of Lake Success, 1993; (films) Crimson Tide, 1995, White Squall, 1996, Nowhere, 1996, Little Boy Blue, 1997, I Saw What You Did Last Summer, 1997, 54, 1998, Playing by Heart, 1998, Cruel Intentions, 1999, The Way of the Gun, 2000, Antitrust, 2001, Gosford Park, 2001, Igby Goes Down, 2002, The I Inside, 2003, Crash, 2004 (recipient, Outstanding Performance by a Cast in a Motion Picture, 2006), Five Fingers, 2005, Chaos, 2005. Office: c/o William Morris Agy Attn: John Fogelman 151 El Camino Dr Beverly Hills CA 90212*

**PHILLIPS, ANTHONY FRANCIS,** lawyer; b. Hartford, Conn., May 18, 1937; s. Frank and Lena Phillips; m. Rosemary Karran McGowan, Jan. 28, 1967; children: Karran, Antonia, Justin. BA, U. Conn., 1959; JD, Cornell U., 1962. Bar: NY 1964, US Dist. Ct. (so. dist., ea. dist.) NY 1965, (ctrl. dist.) Calif. 1980, US Tax Ct. 1981, US Ct. Appeals (2nd cir.) 1967, (3d cir.) 1985, (4th cir.) 1983, (5th cir.) 1972, (7th cir.) 1987, (9th cir.) 1983, (10th cir.) 1983, US Supreme Ct. 1971. Assoc. Willkie, Farr & Gallagher, NYC, 1963-69, ptnr., 1969—. Mem. adv. com. Cornell U. Law Sch., 1994—. Fellow Am. Bar Found.; mem. ABA, NY State Bar Assn., NY County Bar Assn. (bd. dirs. 1989-95), Assn. of Bar of City of NY Home: 3 Elm Rock Rd Bronxville NY 10708-4202 Office: Willkie Farr & Gallagher 787 7th Ave Lbby 2 New York NY 10019-6018 Personal E-mail: anthonyfphillips@aol.com. Business E-Mail: aphillips@willkie.com.

**PHILLIPS, ANTHONY GEORGE,** neurobiology researcher; b. Barrow, Cumbria, Eng., Jan. 30, 1943; came to Can., 1953; s. George William and Mabel Lilian (Wood) P. BA, U. Western Ont., London, Can., 1966, MA, 1967, PhD, 1970. Asst. prof. psychobiology U. B.C., Vancouver, Canada, 1970-75, assoc. prof., 1975-80, prof., 1980—, head dept. psychology, 1994-99, prof. dept. psychiatry, 1999—, dir. U. B.C. Inst. Mental Health. Founder Quadra Logic Tech., Inc., Vancouver. Contbr. numerous papers to sci. jours. Chair inst. adv. bd. CIHR Inst. for Neurosci. Mental Health & Addiction; bd. dirs. Tibetian Refuge Aid Soc., 1980—; chmn. Can.-India Village Aid, Vancouver, 1981—86, 2003—05. Recipient Killam Rsch. prize Can. Coun., 1977, D.O. Hebb award Can. Psychol. Assn.; Steacie fellow Nat. Scis. and Engring. Rsch. Coun. Can., 1980. Fellow Royal Soc. Can.; mem. Soc. Neurosci., Can. Soc. for Neurosci., Can. Coll. Neuropsychopharmacology. Office: U BC Dept Psych 2255 Wesbrook Mall Vancouver BC Canada V6T 1Z4 Office Phone: 604-822-4624. Business E-Mail: aphillips@psych.ubc.ca.

**PHILLIPS, ARLENE MARIE,** retired secondary school educator; b. Lindsborg, Kans., May 14, 1936; d. Herbert Jeremiah and Florence Eleanor (Swenson) Watts; children: Kirk, Scott. BS, McPherson Coll., 1959; postgrad., Colo. State U., 1966—67. Tchr. home econs. Alexander (Kans). H.S., 1959—61; adult edn. tchr. Oberlin, Kans., 1964—65; tchr. home econs. Lincoln Jr. H.S., Ft. Collins, Colo., 1967—68, Blevins Jr. H.S., Ft. Collins, 1968—90, ret., 1990. Home: 1014 Sandstone Dr Jeffersonville IN 47130-8446

**PHILLIPS, AUDREY PATRICIA (PAT PHILLIPS),** secondary school educator; b. Smarrs, Ga., Jan. 24, 1938; d. Guy Watson and Mandy Elizabeth (Hudson) Meeks; m. Henry Arnold Phillips, June 25, 1961; children: Henry David, William Arnold. BS in Edn., Ga. State Coll. for Women, 1960; MEd, Ga. Coll. at Milledgeville, 1968; EdS, Ga. State U., 1978; EdD, U. Ga., 1992. Cert. tchr., Ga. Tchr. chemistry Griffin(Ga.)-Spalding Bd. Edn., 1960-96; ret., 1996. Adj. prof. Mercer U., 1992-2002. Contbg. author: Labs: Laboratory Assessment Builds Success, 1988. Grantee NSF, 1986-88, 92-93; recipient Regional Catalyst award Am. Chem. Soc., 1983, Nat. Catalyst award Am. Chem. Soc., 1983, Nat. Catalyst award Am. Chem. Soc. Mem. NEA, Nat. Sci, Tchrs. Assn., Ga. Edn. Assn. (del., dist. du.), Ga. Sci. Tchrs. Assn. (dist. officer), Griffin-Spalding Sci. Tchrs. (founding, various offices 1985—). Baptist. Home: 66 Green Acres Rd Griffin GA 30224-7931

**PHILLIPS, BARNET, IV,** lawyer; b. NYC, July 5, 1948; s. Barnet III and Isabelle (Auriema) P.; m. Sharon Walsted Packey, Jan. 2, 1981; children: Victoria Ilonka, Caroline Walsted. BA, Yale U., 1970; JD, Fordham U., 1973; LLM, NYU, 1977. Bar: NY 1974. Assoc. Hughes Hubbard & Reed, NYC, 1973—76, Skadden, Arps, Slate, Meagher & Flom, NYC, 1977—81, ptnr., 1981—. Adj. assoc. prof. Fordham U., NYC, 1987-88; articles editor The Tax Lawyer, 1989-91. Co-author: Structuring Corporate Acquisitions--Tax Aspects. Bd. dirs Student/Sponsor Partnership, NYC, 1990-95; bd. cons. Portsmouth Abbey Sch., RI, 1991-96, chmn., 1997-2002; bd. trustees Saint Thomas More, the Cath. Chapel & Ctr. Yale U., New Haven, Conn., 2004—. Republican. Avocations: skiing, opera, triathlons. Home: 6 Hycliff Rd Greenwich CT 06831-3223 Office: Skadden Arps Slate Meagher & Flom Four Times Square 42nd Flr New York NY 10036-6522 Office Phone: 212-735-2220. Business E-Mail: bphillip@skadden.com.

**PHILLIPS, BETTY LOU (ELIZABETH LOUISE PHILLIPS),** writer, interior designer; b. Cleve. d. Michael N. and Elizabeth D. (Materna) Suvak; m. John S. Phillips, Jan. 27, 1963 (div. Jan. 1981); children: Bruce, Bryce, Brian; m. John D.C. Roach, Aug. 28, 1982. BS, Syracuse U., 1962; postgrad. in English, Case We. Res. U., 1963—64. Cert. elem. and spl. edn. tchr., N.Y.; cert. interior designer, Calif. Tchr. pub. schs., Shaker Heights, Ohio, 1960—66. Sportswriter Cleve. Press, 1976-77; spl. features editor Pro Quarterback Mag., N.Y.C., 1976-79; bd. dirs. Cast Specialties Inc., Cleve. Author: Chris Evert: First Lady of Tennis, 1977, Picture Story of Dorothy Hamill, 1978 (ALA Booklist selection), American Quarter Horse, 1979, Earl Campbell: Houston Oiler Superstar, 1979, Picture Story of Nancy Lopez, 1980 (ALA Notable book), Go! Fight! Win! The NCA Guide for Cheerleaders, 1981 (ALA Booklist), Something for Nothing, 1981, Brush Up on Your Hair, 1981 (ALA Booklist), Texas.The Lone Star State, 1989, Provençal Interiors-French Country Style in America, 1998, French by Design, 2000, French Influences, 2001, Villa Décor: Decidedly French and Italian Style, 2002 (Foreword Mag. Best Non-Fiction Book, 2003), Unmistakably French, 2003, Emily Goes Wild, 2003 (Tex. Inst. Letters Best Children's Book, 2004), Secrets of French Design, 2004, The French Connection, 2005, Emily Works

Out, 2005, Emily's Manners, 2005; contbr. articles popular mags. Mem.: Am. Soc. Interior Designers (profl. mem., cert.), Soc. Children's Book Writers, Delta Delta Delta. Republican. Roman Catholic. Home: 4278 Bordeaux Ave Dallas TX 75205-3718

**PHILLIPS, CARL,** poet, educator; b. 1959; BA magna cum laude, Harvard U., 1981; MA in Latin and Classical Humanities, U. Mass., Amherst, 1983; MA in Creative Writing, Boston U., 1993. Latin tchr., 1983—91; asst. prof. English Washington U., St. Louis, 1993—95, assoc. prof., 1995—, dir. creative writing prog., 1996—98, 2000—02. Author: In the Blood, 1992 (Samuel French Morse Poetry Prize, 1992), Cortege, 1995 (Nat. Book Critics Cir. Award finalist, Lambda Lit. Award finalist), From the Devotions, 1998 (Nat. Book Award finalist), Pastoral, 2000 (Lambda Lit. Award), The Tether, 2001 (Kingsley Tufts Poetry Award), Rock Harbor, 2002, The Rest of Love: Poems, 2004 (Nat. Book Award finalist, 2004). Recipient Lit. Award, AAAL, Pushcart Prize, Acad. Am. Poets Prize; grantee Witter Bynner Found. Fellowship, Libr. Congress, 1997, Guggenheim Fellowship. Fellow: Am. Acad. Arts & Sci. Office: Washington U Campus Box 1122 One Brookings Dr Saint Louis MO 63130 Office Phone: 314-935-7133. E-mail: cphillips@wustl.edu.

**PHILLIPS, CARLY,** writer; b. Mount Vernon, NY, July 7, 1965; d. Leonard Robert and Arlene Weinberg; m. Phillip Drogin, Mar. 23, 1985; children: Jaclyn Lindsay, Jennifer Ashley. BA, Brandeis U., Waltham, MA, 1987; JD, Boston U, 1990. Bar: N.Y. 1991, Conn. 1991. Author: (novels) The Bachelor, 2002 (NY Times Bestseller List), Reading with Ripa Nationally Televised Bookclub, 2002), The Playboy, 2003 (NY Times Bestseller List, 2003), The Heartbreaker, 2004 (NY Times Extended Bestseller List), Summer Lovin', 2005 (NY Times Extended Bestseller List), Hot Number, 2005, Cross My Heart, 2006, Hot Item, 2006 (NY Times Extended Bestseller List). Mem.: Novelists, Inc., Romance Writers of Am. Office: PO Box 483 Purchase NY 10577 E-mail: carlyphillips@optonline.net.

**PHILLIPS, CAROLINE L.,** lab administrator; b. Washington, Oct. 7, 1955; d. Elinor and Frank duBose Phillips; m. Raymond L. Baumler, Oct. 1, 1983; 1 child, Irene Caroline Baumler. MS, Va. Commonwealth U., Richmond, 1981. Computer programmer/analyst Nat. Inst. Aging, Bethesda, Md., 1986—2000, info. tech. specialist data mgmt., 2001—. Vol. Sunday sch. tchr. Seven Locks Bapt. Ch., Potomac, Md., 2001—06; mem. Heritage Ctr. Children Christian Children's Fund, Richmond, Va., 2005—06. Named Sec.'s Employee of the Month, Nat. Inst. Aging, 1989, 1996; recipient NIA Group award for publ. of a resource data book, 1990, Pub. Health Svc. On-the-Spot award, NIH/Nat. Inst. Aging, 1992, 1998, 1999, NIH award of Merit, 1994. Mem.: Psi Chi. Achievements include development of specifications for database of neuropsychological tests for a large epidemiologic study in Iceland; data management for a large epidemiologic sstudy of elderly people in Italy. Avocations: drawing, painting, jogging, swimming, music. Office Phone: 301-496-1178.

**PHILLIPS, CARTER GLASGOW,** lawyer; b. Canton, Ohio, Sept. 11, 1952; s. Max Dean and Virginia Scott (Carter) P.; m. Sue Jane Henry, June 5, 1976; children: Jessica, Ryan. BA, Ohio State U., 1973; MA, Northwestern U., 1975, JD, 1977. Bar: Ill. 1977, D.C. 1979, U.S. Dist. Ct. (no. dist.) Ill., U.S. Dist. Ct. (D.C. dist.), U.S. Ct. Appeals (1st, 2d, 3d, 4th, 5th, 6th, 7th, 8th, 9th, 10th, 11th, D.C. and Fed. cirs.). Law clk. U.S. Ct. Appeals (7th cir.), Chgo., 1977—78; law clk. to chief Justice Warren E. Burger U.S. Supreme Ct., Washington, 1978—79; asst. prof. law U. Ill., Champaign, 1979—81; asst. solicitor gen. U.S. Dept. Justice, Washington, 1981—84; ptnr. Sidley & Austin, Washington, 1984—; mng. ptnr. DC office Sidley Austin Brown & Wood LLP, Washington, 1995—, and mem. mgmt. com. Chmn. dean's adv. bd. Northwestern U. Law Sch., 2002—04, mem. dean's adv. bd., 2002—; chmn. Fed. Cir. Adv. Coun., U.S. Ct. Appeals, 2003—05, mem., 2003—; pres., master Edward Coke Appellate Inn of Ct.; adj. prof. law Northwestern U. Law Sch., 2006—. Contbr. articles to profl. jours. Bd. trustees Supreme Ct. Hist. Soc.; bd. advs. Georgetown Univ. Law Ctr.'s Supreme Ct. Inst. Mem.: Am. Coll. Trial Lawyers, Am. Acad. Appellate Lawyers, Am. Law Inst. Republican. Episcopalian. Office: Sidley Austin LLP 1501 K St NW Fl 10 Washington DC 20005-3705 Office Phone: 202-736-8270. E-mail: cphillips@sidley.com.

**PHILLIPS, CARYL,** writer; b. St. Kitts, West Indies, Mar. 13, 1958; BA with honors, The Queen's Coll., Oxford, Eng., 1979; AM (hon.), Amherst (Mass.) Coll., 1995; DUniv (hon.), Leeds Metro. U., 1997; D (hon.), U. York, 2003; DLitt (hon.), U. Leeds, 2003; AM (hon.), Yale U., 2006. Writer in residence Factory Arts Ctr. Arts Coun. Great Britain, London, 1980-82; writer in residence U. Mysore, India, 1987, U. Stockholm, 1989; vis. writer Amherst Coll., 1990-92, writer in residence, 1992—98, co-dir. creative writing ctr., 1994-97, prof. English, writer-in-residence, 1994-98; prof. English, Henry R. Luce prof. migration and social order Barnard Coll., Columbia U., N.Y.C., 1998—2005, dir. Initiatives in the Humanities, 2003—05; prof. English Yale U., 2005—. Vis. lectr. U. Ghana, 1990, U. Poznan, 1991; vis. writer Humber Coll., 1992, 93; writer-in-residence Nat. Inst. Edn., Singapore, 1994; vis. prof. English NYU, 1993; vis. prof. humanities U. W.I., 1999—2000; mem. arts coun. Gt. Britain Drama Panel, 1982—85; mem. prodn. bd. Brit. Film Inst., 1985—88, Bush Theatre, 1985—89; mem. Caribbean Writer bd. U.S. V.I., 1989—; hon. sr. mem. U. Kent, 1988—; cons. editor Faber & Faber, Inc., 1992—94, Caribbean series editor, 1996—2000; participant, keynote spkr 12 ann. confs. German-speaking countries New Lits. in English, Giessen, Germany, 1989; resident writer Hull (Engl.) Internat. Lit. Festival, 1992; instr. writing Arvon Found., summers, 1983—; reader, lectr. in theatre. Author: The Final Passage, 1985 (Malcolm X prize for lit., 1985) A State of Indepndn ce, 1986, The European Tribe, 1987 (Martin Luther King Meml. prize, 1987), Higher Ground, 1989, Cambridge, 1991, Crossing the River, 1993 (James Tait Black meml. prize), The Nature of Blood, 1997, The Atlantic Sound, 2000, A New World Order: Selected Essays, 2001, A Distant Shore, 2003 (PEN/Faulkner Award for Fiction nominee, 2004, Commonwealth Writers prize, 2004, Hurston/Wright Legacy award finalist, Nat. Book Cir. Critics finalist in fiction), Dancing in the Dark, 2005; editor: Extravagant Strangers: A Literature of Belonging, 1997, The Right Set: A Tennis Anthology, 1999; author: (plays) Strange Fruit, 1980, Where There Is Darkness, 1982, The Shelter, 1983, (TV documentary screenplays) Welcome to Birmingham, 1983, The Hope and Glory, 1984, Lost in Music, 1984, The Record, 1985, Darker Than Blue: Curtis Mayfield, 1995, BBC Profile Spl. Caryl Phillips Interviews Chinua Achebe, 2003, South Bank Show: Caryl Phillips, ITV, 2003, (films) Playing Away, 1986, The Final Passage, 1996, The Mystic Masseur, 2001 (Mar Del Plata Film Festival Silver Ombu for Best Screenplay), (radio plays) The Wasted Years, 1984 (Best Radio Play of Yr. award BBC, 1984), Crossing the River, 1985, The Prince of Africa, 1987, Writing Fiction, 1991, A Kind of Home: James Baldwin in Paris, BBC Radio 4, 2004, Hotel Cristobel, 2005, (radio documentaries) St. Kitts (Pride of Place), 1983, Sport and the Black Community, 1984, No Complaints: James Baldwin at Sixty, 1985, Archive Hour: I Too am America BBC Radio, 2003; contbr. (documentary programs) Bookmark, 1984, Black on Black, London Weekend TV, 1983, others; contbr. articles to periodicals. Recipient Young Writer of Yr. award, London Sunday Times, 1992, award, Lannan Lit., 1994, Caribbean Am. Heritage award for outstanding contbn. to lit., 2004; fellow, Guggenheim, 1992, 50th Anniversary, 1998, Royal Soc. Lit., 2000; Mel and Lois Tukman fellow, N.Y. Pub. Libr. Ctr. for Scholars and Writers, 2003, hon. fellow, The Queen's Coll. Oxford, 2006. Address: care G Garrett AP Watt Ltd 20 John St London WC1N 2DR England Office: Yale U English Dept 315 Linsly Chittenden Hall 63 High St New Haven CT 06520 Business E-Mail: Ggarrett@apwatt.co.uk.

**PHILLIPS, CHANDLER ALLEN,** biomedical engineer; b. L.A., Dec. 21, 1942; s. Chandler A. and Ann P.; m. Jane Draper, Feb. 14, 1980. AB in Biol. Scis., Stanford U., 1965; MD, U. So. Calif., 1969; AB in Classical Langs., Wright State U., 1982; PhD (hon.), U. Human Studies, Las Vegas, 1985. Registered profl. engr., Ohio, Calif. Rsch. physician U. Dayton (Ohio), 1972-74; asst. prof. Wright State U., Dayton, 1975-79, assoc. prof. biomed. engring., 1979-84, prof. biomed. engring., 1984-91, prof. biomed. and human factors engring., 1991—99, prof. biomed. indsl. and human factors engring., 1999—. Author: Functional Electrical Rehabilitation, 1991, Human Factors Engineering, 2000; sr. editor: Mechanics of Skeletal and Cardiac Muscle, 1983, Effective Extremity Prostheses, 1989; regional editor Auto Medica, 1997—; mem. editl. bd. Jour. Biomechanics, 1984-87, Jour. Clin. Engring., 1984-98, Prosthetics-Orthotics Engring., 1995-98, Frontiers in Bioscience, 2003—. Capt. USAF, 1970-72. Fellow IEEE (Harry Rowe Mimno award 1984), Am. Inst. for Med. and Biol. Engring., Aerospace Med. Assn. (John Paul Stapp award 2002), Am. Acad. Neurologic Orthopedic Surgeons (hon.). Avocations: amateur radio, commercial-instrument pilot, fishing, classical philology. Office: Dept Biomed Indsl Human Factors Engring Wright State U Dayton OH 45435 Office Phone: 937-775-5044.

**PHILLIPS, CHARLES ALAN,** accounting firm executive; b. Cin., Aug. 12, 1939; s. Charles Stanley and Mary Lucile (Kirkpatrick) P. BS in Bus. Adminstrn., Northwestern U., 1960, MBA, 1961. Cert. systems profl. Investment adviser Continental Ill. Bank, Chgo., 1960-65; asst. to pres. A.S. Hansen, Chgo., 1965-67; investment adviser Francis I. du Pont, N.Y.C., 1967-70; prof. North Central Coll., Mansfield, Ohio, 1970-73; prin. Peat, Marwick, Mitchell (now KPMG Peat Marwick), Cleve., Tulsa, Houston, 1973-88. Presbyterian. Avocations: classical music, natural history, gardening.

**PHILLIPS, CHARLES E., JR.,** computer company executive; BS in Computer Sci., USAF Acad.; MBA in Fin., Hampton U.; JD, N.Y. Law Sch. CFA; bar: Ga., D.C. Prin. Morgan Stanley & Co., Inc., 1994—95, mng. dir., 1995—2003; exec. v.p. strategy, partnerships & bus. devel. Oracle Corp., Redwood City, Calif., 2003—04, pres., 2004—, co-pres. PeopleSoft Calif. 2004. Bd. dir. Oracle Corp., 2004—, Viacom Corp., Morgan Stanley, 2006—. Trustee N.Y. Law Sch., bd. dir. Jazz at Lincoln Ctr., NYC; trustee Joing Ctr. for Polit. and Econ. Studies, Washington. Capt. USMC. Named one of 50 Black Profls. on Wall Street, Black Enterprise Mag. Office: Oracle Corp 500 Oracle Pkwy Redwood City CA 94065*

**PHILLIPS, CHERYL,** reporter; Sports reporter Fort Worth Star-Telegram, Tex.; govt. reporter Great Falls Tribune, Mont.; computer-assisted reporting projects editor Detroit News; computer-assisted reporting editor USA Today; investigative reporter Seattle Times. Bd. dirs. Investigative Reporters & Editors, v.p., 2001—. Office: Seattle Times PO Box 70 Seattle WA 98111 Office Phone: 206-464-2111. Office Fax: 206-464-2261. E-mail: cphillips@seattletimes.com.*

**PHILLIPS, DANIEL ANTHONY,** trust company executive; b. Boston, Feb. 24, 1938; s. Lyman Waldo and Harriet Anthony (Carlow) P.; m. Diana Walcott, Aug. 18, 1962; children: Lisa Walcott Phillips Harrington, Bradford Lyman, Phillips. AB cum laude, Harvard U., 1960, MBA, 1963. From v.p. to dir. to mem. exec. com. Fiduciary Trust Co., Boston, 1963-92, exec. v.p., dir., trust com. sec., trust officer, 1992—, exec. v.p., dir., trust com., trust officer, 1993-94, pres., CEO, 1993—2002, chmn., 2002—. Dir., sec., treas. Ways To Work, 1998—. Bd. dirs. Family Svc. Am., chair fin. comm., 1993-95, treas., chair bd. dirs., 1995-97; bd. dirs., mem. exec. com. Am. Meml. Hosp., Reims, France, pres., 1988-98, treas., 2002—; bd. dirs. Family Found., N.Am., 1993-99, Lend A Hand Soc., bd. dirs., treas. Grimes-King Found. for the Elderly, Inc.; v.p., treas. Frederick E. Weber Charities Corp.; chair bd. dirs. Families Internat., Inc., 1997-99; founds. chair United Way Mass. Bay, 1996—, dir., 1998—, chair cmty. investments, 2000, vice chmn., bd. dirs., mem. exec. com.; trustee, French Libr. and Cultural Ctr., 2003—; overseer Cambridge Cmty. Found.; trustee Cambridge Homes. Staff sgt. USAR, 1960—66. Decorated chevalier Legion of Honor (France), 2002; recipient Grand medal of Reims Am. Meml. Hosp., 1998, Champagne Ardenne medal Am. Meml. Hosp., 1998. Mem. Boston Soc. Security Analysts, Harvard U. Alumni Assn. (1st v.p. 1996-97, pres. 1997-98, Harvard Alumni Assn. award 1995), Boston Econ. Club, Comml. Club. Office: Fiduciary Trust Co 175 Federal St Boston MA 02110-2210 Home: Po Box 381082 Cambridge MA 02238-1082 E-mail: DAPharvard@aol.com.

**PHILLIPS, DAVID L.,** diplomat, mediator, foundation executive; Exec. dir., Internat. Conflict Resolution Program Columbia U.; program dir. Internat. Peach Rsch. Inst., Oslo; dir. European Ctr. Common Ground; pres. Congl. Human Rights Found.; sr. adv. UN Secretariat Office Coord. Humanitarian Affairs, 2000; fgn. affairs expert, sr. adviser US Dept. State Bur. Near Eastern Affairs, 1999—2000; now vis. scholar, Ctr. Middle East Studies Harvard Univ.; dir. Program Conflict Prevention and Peace-bldg. Am. Univ. Ctr. Global Peace; analyst NBC News, BBC World News; sr. fellow, dep. dir. Ctr. Preventive Action Coun. Fgn. Rels., NYC, 2005—. Co-editor: Indonesia Commission: Peace and Progress in Papua, 2003; author: Unsilencing the Past: Track Two Diplomacy & Turkish-Armenian Reconciliation, 2005, Losing Iraq: Inside the Postwar Reconstruction Fiasco, 2005; contbr. articles to profl. jours. Office: Ctr Preventive Action Fgn Rels 58 E 68th St New York NY 10021 also: The Harold Pratt House 58 E 68th St New York NY 10021 Office Phone: 212-434-9495. Office Fax: 212-434-9832. Personal E-mail: daviddlpl@cs.com. Business E-Mail: dphillips@cfr.org.

**PHILLIPS, DAVID P.,** grocery company executive; CFO Publix Super Markets, Lakeland, Fla., 1999—, treas. Publix Super Markets PO Box 407 Lakeland FL 33802-0407 Office Phone: 863-688-1188.*

**PHILLIPS, DON,** investment research company executive; b. 1963; BA in engring., U. Tex., 1984; MA in lit., U. Chgo., 1986. Mutual fund analyst Morningstar Inc., 1986—95, pres., 1995—97, pres., CEO, 1997—2000, mng. dir., 2000—, editor Morningstar Mutual Funds. Named one of Most Influential People in Fin. Planning, Fin. Planning mag. and Investment Advisor mag., 2003, 10 Key Players in Industries, Registered Rep mag., 2002. Achievements include Morningstar's first mutual fund analyst; development of Morningstar Style Box and Morningstar Rating. Office: Morningstar Inc 225 W Wacker Dr Chicago IL 60606 Office Phone: 312-696-6000. Office Fax: 312-696-6001.

**PHILLIPS, DOROTHY KAY,** lawyer; BS, U.Pa.; MA, NYU; JD, Villanova Law Sch., 1978. Bar: Pa. 1978, NJ 1978, US Dist. Ct. (ea. dist.) Pa., US Dist. Ct. NJ, US Ct. Appeals (3d cir.), US Supreme Ct. Lectr. Marriage Coun. Phila., U. Pa., Hahnemann Med. Sch., Phila., 1970-75; atty. Adler, Barish, Daniels, Levin & Creskoff, Phila., 1978-79, Astor, Weiss & Newman, Phila., 1979-80; ptnr. Romisher & Phillips P.C., Phila., 1981-86; prin. Dorothy K. Phillips & Assocs., LLC, 1986—; judge Reimel Moot Ct. Competition, Villanova Law Sch., 1986—. Faculty Pa. Bar Inst., CLE Temple U. Sch. Law, 1987-89, Nat. Bus. Inst., lectr. 1998, 00, 01, 03, 04. Author: The Legal Intelligencer, The Phila. Lawyer, 1998; family law columnist: Pa. Law Weekly, 2005; contbr. articles to profl. jours. Named Super Lawyer Phila. mag., 2005; featured in Wall St. Jour., Phila. Inquirer, Phila. Bus. Jour., Harper's Bazaar, WPVI-ABC6, KYW-CBS3, WCAU-NBC10, FOX Phila., CN8. Mem.: ATLA, ABA, Lawyers Club, Montgomery County Bar Assn., Phila. Trial Lawyers Assn., Phila. Bar Assn. Custody Rules Drafting Com. (Supreme Ct. Pa., faculty), NJ State Bar Assn., Pa. Bar Assn., Pa. Trial Lawyers Assn. E-mail: dkp@dkphillipslaw.com.

**PHILLIPS, DOROTHY REID,** retired medical library technician; b. Hingham, Mass., Apr. 21, 1924; d. James Henry and Emma Louise (Davis) Reid; m. Earl Wendell Phillips, Apr. 22, 1944; children: Earl W., Jr., Betty Herrera, Carol Coe. Cert. Durham Vocat. Sch., 1952; BS in Comml. Edn., N.C. Central U., 1959; postgrad. U. Colo., 1969; M.Human Relations, Webster Coll., 1979; postgrad. Grad. Sch. Library Sci., U. Denver, 1983. Vocat. nurse Meml. Hosp., U. N.C., Chapel Hill, 1955-59; vol. work, Cairo, Egypt, 1965-67; library technician Base Library, Lowry AFB, Colo., 1960-65, Fitzsimons Med. Library, Aurora, Colo., 1976-93; ret. 1993; mem. Denver Mus. Natural History, Denver Art Mus., Mariners. Mem. AARP, NARFE, AAUW (chpt. community rep. 1982-83, state community rep. 1982-84, pres. Denver br. 1984-86), Altrusa Internat. (corr. sec. Denver 1982-83, bd. dirs. 1984-85, pres. Denver chpt. 1988), Friends of Library, Peace Links,

---

Colo. Coordinating Coun. of Womens Orgn., Inc. (pres. coun.), Colo. Library Assn., Council Library Technicians, Federally Employed Women, Delta Sigma Theta (corr. sec. Denver 1964-66), Women's Assn. of Peoples Presbyn. Ch., League of Women Voters, Denver Urban League. Democrat. Presbyterian. Home: 3085 Fairfax St Denver CO 80207-2714

**PHILLIPS, EARL NORFLEET, JR.,** diplomat, financial services executive; b. High Point, N.C., 1940; s. Earl Norfleet Phillips and Lillian Jordan; m. Sarah Boyle, Oct. 19, 1971; children: Courtney Dorsett, Jordan Norfleet. BSBA, U.N.C., 1962; MBA, Harvard U., 1965. Security analyst Wertheim & Co., N.Y.C., 1965-67; exec. v.p. Factors Inc., High Point, 1967-71, First Factors Corp., High Point, 1972-81, pres., 1982-98; chmn. GE Capital First Factors, High Point, 1998-2000; pres. Phillips Interests, 2000—; U.S. amb. to Eastern Caribbean, 2002—03. Bd. dirs. Oakdale Cotton Mills, N.C. Enterprise Corp., Culp Inc. Mem. nat. adv. coun. SBA, 1988—91; trustee High Point Regional Hosp., Asian Inst. Tech., Bangkok; former mem. Piedmont Triad Airport Authority; trustee U. N.C., Chapel Hill, 1983—91, chmn. bd., 1989—91, mem. endowment bd., 1985—2001; mem. U. N.C. Found., 1987—91; bd. govs. U. N.C. Sys., 1995—99; mem. N.C. Econ. Devel. Bd., Raleigh, 1984—91; bd. dirs. N.C. Citizens for Bus. and Industry, chmn., 1999—2000. Named Young Man of Yr., High Point Jaycees, 1971, High Point Citizen of Yr., 2000; named one of Five Outstanding Young Men, N.C. Jaycees, 1971; recipient Global Leadership award, Kenan-Flagler Bus. Sch., U. N.C., 2001. Disting. Alumnus award, U. N.C. Alumni Assn., 2002. Mem. Nat. Comml. Fin. Assn. (bd. dirs.), The Brook, High Point C.C. Club, String and Splinter Club, Linville Golf Club, Gorgons Head Lodge. Office: Phillips Interests Box 830 101 S Main St High Point NC 27261 Office Phone: 336-882-6431. E-mail: philphillips@northstate.net.

**PHILLIPS, EDWARD JOHN,** consulting firm executive; b. Phila., Sept. 8, 1940; s. Harold E. and Mary C. P.; m. Kathleen A. Everett, July 23, 1960; children: Elizabeth J., Edward J. B of Mech. Engring., Villanova U., 1973; MBA, Widener U., 1975. Registered profl. engr., Ill., Pa., Ohio; chartered engr., U.K. Tech. ops. mgr. Motorola, Inc., Franklin Park, Ill., 1976-81; v.p. engring. Rival Mfg. Co., Kansas City, Mo., 1981-82; prin., sr. cons. Richard Muther & Assocs., Kansas City, 1982-85; chmn. KANDE, Inc., Overland Park, Kans., 1983-86; pres., CEO Sims Cons. Group Inc., Lancaster, Ohio, 1986—; chmn. bd. dirs., pres. Sims Consulting Group, Lancaster, Ohio. Bd. dirs. KANDE, Inc., Wilmington, Del. Author: Manufacturing Plant Layout, 1997; contbr. articles to profl. jours. Recipient Profl. Achievement award, Villanova U., 2006. Mem. NSPE, ASME (chmn. material handling divsn. 1989-91, mem. internat. mgmt. com. 1997), MIMechE, Soc. Mfg. Engrs., Tau Beta Pi, Pi Tau Sigma. Office: Sims Cons Group Inc PO Box 968 Lancaster OH 43130-0968

**PHILLIPS, ELIZABETH JASON,** lawyer, state agency administrator; b. Boston, Sept. 3, 1936; d. Richard Eliot and Elizabeth Harding (McClure) Jason; m. William Morris Phillips, Jr., Mar. 2, 1991; children: Meredith Rowe, william Morris III, Eleanor Anne, Robert J., Lee B. Stewart. BA in History, U. Mass., 1958; MEd, U. Hartford, 1969; JD, Western New Eng. Coll., Springfield, Mass., 1977. Bar: Mass. 1977, U.S. Dist. Ct. Mass. 1978, Va. 1981, U.S. Dist. Ct. (ea. dist.) Va. 1981, U.S. Dist. Ct. DC 1981, U.S. Dist. Ct. (we. dist.) Va. 1982, U.S. Ct. Appeals (4th cir.) 1982, U.S. Supreme Ct. 1984. Ptnr. Thompson & Stewart, Ludlow, Mass., 1977-80; adminstr. Office Atty. Gen., Commonwealth of Va., Richmond, 1980-82, asst. atty. gen., 1982-84; dep. Commr. Indsl. Commn. Va., 1984-91; dep. commr., mgr. dispute resolution divsn. Va. Workers' Compensation Commn., Richmond, 1991—2001. Trustee Gloucester County Libr., 2002, sec.; Trustee Ludlow Hosp., 1979—80. Mem.: ABA, Va. Exec. Inst., Va. Assn. Adminstrv. Law Judges and Hearing Officers (pres-elect 1999), Va. Bar Assn., Richmond Bar Assn., Ludlow C. of C. (pres. 1980). Episcopalian. Home: Cedar Shade 3859 Raymond Walker Rd Hayes VA 23072-4620 Personal E-mail: ephil75441@aol.com.

**PHILLIPS, ERNIE HOWARD,** music educator; b. Gainesville, Ga., Apr. 5, 1957; s. Ernest Cecil and Charlotte (Inez) Phillips; m. Connie Harrison, June 5, 1982; children: Matthew, Ryan, Hamilton. MusB, U. Ga., 1979, M in Music Edn., 1981. Asst. band dir. East Hall HS, Gainesville, 1981—88; band dir., fine arts dept. head West Hall HS, Gainesville, 1988—. Guest honor band condr. U. Ga. Music Festival, 1998, Ga. Music Educators In-Svc. Conf., 1998; guest condr. U. Ga. Redcoat Band, 2001. Musician (prin. tubist): Gainesville Symphony Orch., 1982—, North Winds Symphonic Band, 1985—. Dir. Soc. Preservation and Encouragement Barber Shop Quartet Singing in Am., Gainesville, 1983—95; donor U. Ga. Scholarship Fund, Athens, 1993—; bass sect. mem. Lakewood Baptist Worship Choir, Gainesville, 1984—. Recipient Legion of Honor award, John Philip Sousa Found., 2001. Mem.: Ga. Music Educators Assn. (9th dist. instrumental chmn. 2005—), Nat. Band Assn., Music Educators Nat. Conf., U. Ga. Alumni Soc., Phi Beta Mu. Baptist. Home: 5024 Jay Creek Rd Oakwood GA 30566 Office: West Hall HS 5500 McEver Rd Oakwood GA 30566 Office Phone: 770-967-9826 ext 250. Business E-Mail: ernie.phillips@hallco.org.

**PHILLIPS, EUAN HYWEL,** publishing executive; b. Chipstead, Surrey, Eng., Mar. 31, 1928; s. Edgar Aneurin and Elsie Llewella (Davies) P.; m. Margaret June Savage, June 12, 1954; children: David John, Janet Margaret. BA, Emmanuel Coll., Cambridge, Eng., 1949, MA, 1965. Cost acct. J. Lyons & Co. Ltd., London, 1950-53; dispatch mgr. Pickerings Produce Canners Ltd., Manchester, Eng., 1953-56; mgmt. cons. P.A. Mgmt. Cons. Ltd., London, 1956-65; mng. dir. Unwin Bros. Ltd., Old Woking, England, 1965-73; univ. printer designate Cambridge U. Press, England, 1973-74, univ. printer, 1974-76; dir. Am. br. N.Y.C., 1977-82; exec. dir. Assn. Am. U. Presses, 1987-90. Gov. Guildford Sch. Art, 1966-69, Cambridge Coll. Arts and Tech., 1974-76; dir. East Asian History of Sci., Inc., 1978-81 Contbr. to scholarly pub. With Royal Navy, 1946-48. Mem. Brit. Printing Industries Fedn. (coun. 1966-73, pres. Home Counties Alliance 1970-71), Troupers Light Opera Co., Connestee Falls Golf Assn. (pres. 1996-97), Connestee Falls Property Owners Assn. (bd. dirs. 2001—04). Home: 2637 Connestee Trl Brevard NC 28712

**PHILLIPS, FREDERICK FALLEY,** architect; b. Evanston, Ill., June 18, 1946; s. David Cook and Katharine Scaife (Falley) P.; m. Gay Fraker, 1983 (div. 1993); m. Linda Gardner, 2002; children: Daniel Gardner, Alice Katharine. BA, Lake Forest Coll., 1969; MArch, U. Pa., 1973. Registered architect, Ill., Wis. Intern Harry Weese & Assocs., 1974, 75; architect pvt. practice, Chgo., 1976-81; pres. Frederick Phillips and Assocs., Chgo., 1981—. Bd. dirs. Landmarks Preservation Coun., 1981-85, Chgo. Acad. Sci., 1988-97, Friends of Ceuros de Escazu, Costa Rica, 1992-95, Project Rush Chgo., 2001—; mem. aux. bd. Chgo. Architecture Found., 1975-89. Recipient award Townhouse for Logan Sq. Competition, AIA and Econ. Redevel. Corp. Logan Sq., 1980, Gold medal award Willow St. Houses, Ill. Ind. Masonry Coun., 1981, Silver award for pvt. residence, 1989, Gold medal award pvt. residence, 1994, Three Record Houses awards Archtl. Record, 1990, 95, award 2d Compact House Design Competition, 1990, award of exellence for pvt. residence AIA/Nat. Concrete Masonry Assn., 1992, 98, award pvt. residence Am. Wood Coun., 1993, Honorable mention-Best in Am. Living award Profl. Builders Mag., 1995, Builder's Choice award pvt. residence, Builder Mag., 1996, Jury's Choice award pvt. residence Chgo. Athenaeum, 1996, 2001, Am. Architecture award Chgo. Athenaeum, 2001, Grand award Residential Architecture Mag., 2003, award Custom Builder Mag., 2003, award Am. Inst. Steel Construction, 2004. Fellow AIA (chmn. task group mfg. housing Nat. Com. Design 1994-96, mem. awards task group 1998-01, chmn. 2000-01, Disting. Bldg. award for Willow St. Houses, Chgo. chpt. 1982, for Pinewood Farm 1983, for Pvt. Residences 1990, 92, 98, for Tower House, 2001, Housing Com. award 2006); mem. Chgo. Archtl. Club, Racquet Club (bd. govs. 1983-89), Arts Club, Cliff Dwellers Club (bd. govs. 1985-88). Office: Frederick F Phillips & Assocs 1456 N Dayton St Ste 200 Chicago IL 60622-2636

---

**PHILLIPS, GENEVA FICKER,** academic editor; b. Staunton, Ill., Aug. 1, 1920; d. Arthur Edwin and Lillian Agnes (Woods) Ficker; m. James Emerson Phillips, Jr., June 6, 1955 (dec. 1979). BS in Journalism, U. Ill., 1942; MA in English Lit., UCLA, 1953. Copy desk Chgo. Jour. Commerce, 1942-43; editl. asst. patents Radio Rsch. Lab. Harvard U., Cambridge, Mass., 1943-45; asst. editor adminstrv. publs. U. Ill., Urbana, 1946-47; editl. asst. Quar. of Film, Radio and TV UCLA, 1952-53; mng. editor The Works of John Dryden, Dept. English UCLA, 1964—2002. Bus. Univ. Religious Conf., L.A., 1979—. UCLA teaching fellow, 1950-53, grad. fellow 1954-55. Mem. Assn. Acad. Women UCLA, Friends of Huntington Libr., Friends of UCLA Libr., Friends of Ctr. for Medieval and Renaissance Studies, Samuel Johnson Soc. So. Calif., Assocs. U. Calif. Press, Conf. Christianity and Lit., Soc. Mayflower Descendants. Lutheran. Home: 213 First Anita Dr Los Angeles CA 90049-3815 Office: UCLA Dept English 2225 Rolfe Hall Los Angeles CA 90024

**PHILLIPS, GERALD BAER,** internal medicine scientist, educator; b. Bethlehem, Pa., Mar. 20, 1925; s. Abel H. and Cecilia (Blum) P.; m. Maria Bonzi Lewis, July 15, 1970; children: Abigail, Elizabeth. AB, Princeton U., 1946; MD, Harvard U., 1948. Diplomate Am. Bd. Internal Medicine. Intern Presbyn. Hosp., N.Y.C., 1948-50; rsch. fellow Thorndike Meml. Lab., Med. Sch. Harvard U., Boston, 1950-53; vis. fellow biochemistry Columbia U. Coll. Physicians and Surgeons, N.Y.C., 1954-56, from assoc. in medicine to assoc. prof., 1956-73, prof., 1973—. Sr. attending physician St. Lukes-Roosevelt Hosp.; attending physician N.Y.-Presbyn. Hosp. Sr. asst. surgeon USPHS, 1952-54. Mem.: Am. Soc. for Biochemistry and Molecular Biology, Am. Soc. for Clin. Investigation, Alpha Omega Alpha. Home: 196 E 75th St New York NY 10021-3257 Office: 1000 10th Ave New York NY 10019-1147 E-mail: gbp1@columbia.edu. *I attribute any success I may have had to heredity and luck.*

**PHILLIPS, GLYNDA ANN,** editor; b. Riverside, Calif. d. Henry Grady and Patricia (Loflin) P. BA in English, Millsaps Coll., Jackson, Miss., 1977; MS in Comms., Miss. Coll., Clinton, 1996; postgrad., Inst. Children's Lit., 1998—2002. News editor The Magee (Miss.) Courier, 1981-84; editor Miss. Farm Country mag., Jackson, 1984—. Contbr. articles to profl. jours. Recipient first place personal column Nat. Fedn. Press Women, 1984, first place personal column Miss. Press Women's Assn., 1984, 1st Pl. award Miss. Press Women's Assn., 1984, Best Media Campaign award AFBF Info. Contest, 1996, Excellence and Pres.'s award AFBF Pub. Rels. and Info. Program, 2006.

**PHILLIPS, GRAHAM HOLMES,** retired advertising executive; b. London, Jan. 30, 1939; emigrated to U.S., 1965, naturalized, 1974; s. Leonard George and Mary Marjorie (Holmes) P.; m. Laurel Gilbert; 1 child, Debra Ann. Student, RAF Coll. Cranwell, 1957-58; MBA, London U., 1962. Mgmt. trainee Shell Internat. Petroleum, Ltd., London, 1957-59; aviation sales rep., 1960-63; aviation sales mgr. Shell Philippines, Inc., 1964; with Ogilvy & Mather (U.S.), N.Y.C., 1965—; account mgr., 1965-73, dep. mgr., account supr. Houston, 1970, v.p., 1971-72, sr. v.p., mgmt. supr., 1972-73; mng. dir. Ogilvy & Mather Inc., Amsterdam, 1973-75; former pres., then chief exec. officer Ogilvy & Mather (Can.) Ltd., Toronto, from 1975, former chmn., from 1979; dir. Ogilvy & Mather, 1978-82; former chief fin. officer Ogilvy & Mather Internat., from 1983; former exec. v.p. Ogilvy & Mather (U.S.), N.Y.C., from 1979, former gen. mgr., from 1980, former mng. dir., chief fin. officer, from 1981; former chmn., CEO Ogilvy & Mather Worldwide, 92; chmn. Burson-Marsteller, New York, from 1997—. Episcopalian. Office: Young and Rubican 285 Madison Ave New York NY 10017-6486

**PHILLIPS, GRETCHEN,** social worker; b. Erie, Pa., July 14, 1941; life ptnr. Beverly Campbell, June 10, 1989. BA, Mercyhurst Coll., 1966; MSW, Yeshiva U., 1972; postgrad., Advanced Ctr. Psychotherapy, 1972-73, Washington Sq. Inst., 1973-77. Diplomate clin. social work, LCSW NY. Psychiat. social worker, forensic social worker Creedmoor Psychiat. Ctr., Queens Village, NY, 1972-80; med. social worker Bellevue Hosp. Ctr., N.Y.C., 1980-83; intake probation officer N.Y.C. Probation, Family Ct. Bklyn., 1983—. Mem.: NASW. Home: 125 Radford St Apt 3C Yonkers NY 10705-3014 Office: Probation Intake Kings Family Ct 330 Jay St Brooklyn NY 11201-2804 Office Phone: 718-802-2609.

**PHILLIPS, HAROLD JOHN, III,** protective services official, consultant; b. Rochester, NY, Jan. 13, 1949; s. Harold John Jr. Phillips; m. Georgann Faulkner, Jan. 8, 1983; children: Tamara Lee, Sherri Ann Streb, Harold John IV, Nicole Marie, Ashley Dawn. Cert. fire protection tech., Monroe CC, Rochester, NY, 1989. Fire officer Ridge Rd. Fire Dist., Rochester, NY, 1968—2000, fire chief, exec. fire officer, 2000—. Pres. Pub. Safety Mgmt. Cons. Group, Rochester, 1990—. Mem.: Nat. Fire Protection Assn., Nat. Soc. Exec. Fire Officers, Internat. Assn. Fire Chiefs, NY State Assn. Fire Chiefs (com. chmn. 1985—), Greece C. of C. Home: 104 Pearson Ln Rochester NY 14612 Office: Ridge Road Fire Dist 1299 Long Pond Rd Rochester NY 14626 Office Phone: 585-453-1201. Home Fax: 585-225-0815; Office Fax: 585-227-4040. Personal E-mail: bphillips@publicsafetymngt.com. Business E-Mail: hphillips@rrfd.org.

**PHILLIPS, HARRY ROBERT,** language educator; b. Cambridge, Mass., Sept. 21, 1948; s. Michael and Harriette Becker Phillips. PhD, Wash. State U., 1994. Curator native plants NC Bot. Garden, Chapel Hill, 1975—86; instr. English Ctrl. Piedmont C.C., Charlotte, 1994—. Mediator Mecklenburg County Dispute Settlement Program, Charlotte, 1995—. Author: (propagation manual) Growing and Propagating Wild Flowers. Officer Charlotte Area Green Party, 2000—. Recipient Mediator of Yr., Mecklenburg County Dispute Settlement Program, 2005, Tchg. Excellence award, Ctrl. Piedmont C.C., 1996, Outstanding Tchr., Levine Campus, 2000, Merit award for Svc. to the Coll., 1998, 2002. Mem.: NC Conf. English Tchrs. (bd. dirs. 1995—98), Two Yr. Coll. English Assn.-Southeast (conf. program chair 1996—98), C.C. Humanities Assn. (conf. planning com. 2003—04), Nat. Coun. Tchrs. of English. Green Party. Avocation: gardening. Home: 7114 McWhorter Rd Waxhaw NC 28173 Office: Central Piedmont CC PO Box 35009 Charlotte NC 28235 Office Phone: 704-330-5012. Business E-Mail: harry.phillips@cpcc.edu.

**PHILLIPS, HARVEY G.,** musician, educator, performing arts educator; b. Aurora, Mo., Dec. 2, 1929; s. Jesse E. and Lottie A. (Chapman) P.; m. Carol A. Dorvel, Feb. 22, 1954; children: Jesse E., Harvey G., Thomas A. Student, U. Mo., 1947-48, Juilliard Sch. Music, 1950-54, Manhattan Sch. Music, 1956-58; MusD (hon.), New England Conservatory of Mu, 1971; HHD (hon.), U. Mo., Columbia, 1987. Founder, v.p. Mentor Music, Inc., N.Y.C., 1958—79; v.p. Wilder Music, Inc., N.Y.C., 1964-77, Magellan Music, Inc., N.Y.C., 1971—, Peaslee Music Inc., 1971—; established faculty position Aspen Sch. Music, summer 1962, U. Wis., summer 1963, Hartt Sch. Music, Hartford, Conn., 1962-64, Mannes Sch. Music, N.Y.C., 1964-65; exec. v.p. Orch. USA, N.Y.C., 1962-65; exec. v.p., pers. mgr. tubist Symphony of the Air N.Y.C., 1957-66; v.p. Brass Artists, Inc., N.Y.C., 1964—; adminstrv. asst. to Julius Bloom, Rutgers U., New Brunswick, N.J., 1966-67; v.p. fin. affairs New Eng. Conservatory of Music, Boston, 1967-71; mem. faculty Sch. Music, Ind. U., Bloomington, 1971-94, disting. prof. music, trustee, 1979, disting. prof. emeritus, 1994. Adv. bd. Am. Brass Chamber Music, Inc., 1971—; chmn. bd. Summit Brass/Keystone Brass Inst., 1985—92, Rafael Mendez Brass Inst., 1993—; cons. Margun Music, Inc., 1977—; bd. dirs. Summit Brass. Brass coach Festival at Sandpoint, Idaho, 1986-94; mem. faculty Joven Orch. Spain, 1987-94, Festival Casal Orch., San Juan, P.R., 1964-76; dir. 1st Internat. Tuba Symposium Workshop, 1973, Brass-Wind Music Studios, Carnegie Hall, N.Y.C., 1961-67; tubist, King Bros. Circus Band, 1947, Ringling Bros. & Barnum & Bailey Circus Band, 1948-50, N.Y.C. Ballet Orch., 1951-71, N.Y.C. Opera Orch., 1951-62, Voice of Firestone Orch., 1951-53, Sauter-Finegan Orch., 1952-53, Band of Am., 1952-54, NBC Opera Orch., 1956-65, Bell Tel. Hour Orch., 1956-66, Goldman Band, 1957-62; founding mem. N.Y. Brass Quintet, 1954-67; condr., co-prodr. Burke-Phillips All Star Concert Band, 1962-66; co-founder, tubist Matteson-Phillips Tubajazz Consort, 1976—; founding mem. TubaShop Quartet, 1996—; rec. artist Crest Records, 1958-78—; originator

Octubafest, TubaChristmas, Tubasantas, Tubajazz, TubaEaster, Tubacompany, Summertubafest; exec. editor Instrumentalist mag., 1986-96, bd. advisors, 1996—. Founder, pres. Harvey Phillips Found., Inc., N.Y.C., 1977—; bd. dirs. Mid-Am. Festival of the Arts, 1982-90, Bloomington Area Arts Coun., 1983-90; judge 1st Internt. tuba competition of CIEM Internat. Competition for Musical Performers, Geneva, 1991. Served with U.S. Army Field Band, 1955-56. Recipient Disting. Svc. to Music award Kappa Kappa Psi, 1978, Cmty. Svc. award City of Bloomington, 1978, Nat. Assn. Jazz Educators award, 1977, 78, Nat. Music Conf. award, 1977, T.U.B.A. award, 1978, MI Hummel The Tuba Player award, 1990, Disting. Achievement award Ednl. Press Assn. Am., 1991, Mentor Ideal award Assn. Concert Bands, 1994, Lifetime Achievement award United Music Instruments, 1995, Sudler award medal of the Order of Merit Sousa Found., 1995, Summit Brass Outstanding Svc. and Support Internat. Brassfest, 1995, Orpheus award Phi Mu Alpha Sinfonia, 1997; elected to Acad. Wind and Percussion Arts Nat. Band Assn., 1995; recipient Edwin Franko Goldman citation Am. Bandmasters Assn., 1996, Devel. of Mus. Artistry and Opportunities for Future Generations award Colonial Euphonium Tuba Inst., 1998, Lifetime Achievement award Rafael Mendez Brass Inst., 1998, Platinum Piston Lifetime Achievement award, U. Ga., 1999; Legion of Hon., Goldman Meml. Band, 2002; Harvey Phillips Day proclaimed New England Conservatory Music, 1971, Harvey Phillips Day proclaimed Marionville, Mo. Bicentennial, 1976, Harvey Phillips Weekend Gov. of Mo., 1982; named hon. mem. U.S. Army Band Pershings Own, 1984. Mem. Am. Fedn. Musicians, Tubists Universal Brotherhood Assn. (bd. advs. 1973—, pres. 1984-87, hon.), Hoagy Carmichael Jazz Soc. (founder, acting pres. 1983—), Tau Beta Sigma, Phi Mu Alpha Sinfonia (Orpheus award 1997), Kappa Gamma Psi. Home and Office: Tubaranch 4769 S Harrell Rd Bloomington IN 47401-9028 Office: Sch of Music Ind U Bloomington IN 47405 Business E-Mail: philliph@indiana.edu.
*The role of a performer and teacher is to give, to share skills and knowledge. My primary goal in life is to create new opportunities in the music profession, to develop, expand, and preserve the music arts.*

**PHILLIPS, HOWARD WILLIAM,** investment banker; b. N.Y.C., May 16, 1930; s. Louis and Helen (Klein) P.; children: Jan Davis, Richard Louis; m. Carol Napack, June 9, 1985. BA, Dartmouth Coll., 1951, MBA, 1952; JD, Harvard U., 1957. Bar: NY 1957. Assoc. Cahill, Gordon, Reindel & Ohl, N.Y.C., 1957-64; v.p., gen. counsel McCall Corp., N.Y.C., 1964-68; sr. v.p., 1968-69; prin. Oppenheimer & Co., N.Y.C., 1969-81; chmn. Holmes, Phillips & Co., N.Y.C., 1981-83; dir. corp. fin. D.H. Blair Investment Banking Corp., 1983-95. Bd. dirs. Pioneer Behavioral Health, Boston; pres. Asolo Theatre Co., Sarasota, Fla., 2004-. Served to lt. (j.g.) USNR, 1952-54. Mem. Easthampton (N.Y.) Tennis Club, Longboat Key Club (Sarasota), Sara Bay Country Club (Sarasota). Home: Box 2047 3 Cove Hollow Farm Rd East Hampton NY 11937 Office: 500 S Palm Ave Sarasota FL 34236 Office Phone: 941-365-1995.

**PHILLIPS, IAN M.,** physiologist, educator; b. London, July 30, 1938; arrived in US, 1967; s. Robert Leonard and Winifred Maud (Wheatley) Phillips; m. Blanca Aguiar, Nov. 29, 2004; m. Kate Phillips (div.). BSc with honors, U. Exeter, Eng., 1962; PhD, U. Birmingham, Eng., 1967, DSc, 1985. Vis. asst. prof. U. Mich., Ann Arbor, 1967—69; fellow Calif. Inst. Tech., Pasadena, 1969—70; prof. U. Iowa, Iowa City, 1970—80; chmn., prof. U. Fla., Gainesville, 1980—2003; v.p. rsch. U. South Fla., Tampa, 2003—06; rschr. prof. Keck Grad. Inst., Claremont, Calif., 2006—. Program dir. neuro. NSF, Washington, 1990; chmn. cardiovascular study sect. NIH, Washington, 1992—94. Editor: Regulation Peptides, 1990—2006, Gene Therapy, 2002, 3d edit., 2005; co-author: Principles of Hormone & Behavior, 2005; author: (plays) Rembrandt. Bd. dirs. Moffit Cancer Ctr., Tampa, Fla., 2003—06. Recipient Lucian award, McGill U., Can., 1989, Frank Annunzio award, 2002, Merit award, NIH, 1995—2006. Fellow: Am. Heart Assn. Achievements include discovery of brain peptides in hypertension; research in gene therapy for hypertension, stem cell rsch. on heart failure. Office: Keck Grad Inst 535 Watson Dr Claremont CA 91711

**PHILLIPS, JAMES CHARLES,** physicist, researcher; b. New Orleans, Mar. 9, 1933; s. William D. and Juanita (Hahn) P.; m. Joanna Vandenberg, Mar. 1, 1996. BA, U. Chgo., 1952, BS, 1953, MS, 1955, PhD, 1956. Mem. tech. staff Bell Labs., 1956-58; NSF fellow U. Calif. at Berkeley, 1958-59, Cambridge (Eng.) U., 1959-60; faculty U. Chgo., 1960-68, prof. physics, 1965-68; mem. tech. staff Bell Labs., 1968-96; cons. Bell Labs., Lucent Tech., 1996—. Sloan fellow, 1962-66; Guggenheim fellow, 1967. Fellow Am. Phys. Soc. (Buckley prize 1972), Minerals, Metals and Materials Soc. (William Hume-Rothery award 1992); mem. NAS. Home: 204 Springfield Ave Summit NJ 07901-3909

**PHILLIPS, JAMES D.,** retired diplomat; b. Peoria, Ill., Feb. 23, 1933; s. James D. and Ehila (Hardy) P.; m. Rosemary Leeds, Mar. 30, 1957 (div. Dec. 1981); children: Michael, Madolyn, Catherine; m. Lucie Gallistel, Jan. 7, 1984; stepchildren: Charles, David BA, Wichita State U., 1956, MA, 1957; cert., U. Vienna, Austria, 1956; postgrad., Cornell U., 1958-61. Joined fgn. svc. Dept. State, 1961; served at am. embassy Paris, before 1975; Am. Consulate Zaire, before 1975; Dept. State Washington, before 1975; dep. chief of mission am. Embassy, Luxembourg, 1975-78, charge d'affaires The Gambia, 1978—80; student Nat. War Coll., Washington, 1980-81; office dir. Dept. State, Washington, 1981-84; consul gen. Am. Consulate, Casablanca, Morocco, 1984-86; US Amb. to Burundi, 1986-90; US Amb. Republic of the Congo, 1990-93; diplomat in residence The Carter Ctr., Atlanta, 1993-94; ret., 1994; pres. Dan Phillips & Assoc., Arlington, Va., 1994—. Bd. dir. Gulf Resources, H M Salaam Found. Contbr. articles to profl. jours. Del. dic. June Goodall Inst., 1994-2000. Mem.: Chevy Chase Club. Avocations: golf, tennis, skiing. Home: 3607 Military Rd Arlington VA 22207-4829 Office: 1101 30th St NW Ste 200 Washington DC 20007-3769

**PHILLIPS, JAMES DICKSON, JR.,** retired federal judge; b. Scotland County, NC, Sept. 23, 1922; s. James Dickson and Helen (Shepherd) Phillips; m. Jean Duff Nunalee, July 16, 1960; children: Evelyn, James Dickson III, Elizabeth Duff, Ida Willis. BS cum laude, Davidson Coll., 1943; JD, U. N.C., 1948. Bar: N.C. 1948. Asst. dir. Inst. Govt., Chapel Hill, NC, 1948—49; ptnr. Phillips & McCoy, Laurinburg, NC, 1949—55, Sanford, Phillips, McCoy & Weaver, Fayetteville, NC, 1955—60; from asst. prof. to prof. law U. N.C., 1960—78, dean Sch. Law, 1964—74; judge US Ct. Appeals (4th Cir.), 1978—94, sr. judge, 1994—. Vice-chmn. N.C. Cts. Commn.; chmn. N.C. Bd. Ethics, 1977—78. With U.S. Army, 1943—46. Decorated Bronze Arrowhead, Bronze Star, Purple Heart; recipient John J. Parker Meml. award, Thomas Jefferson award, Disting. Alumnus award, U. N.C., 1993. Mem.: Am. Law Inst. Democrat. Presbyterian.

**PHILLIPS, JAMES EDGAR,** lawyer; b. N.Y.C., Aug. 30, 1947; s. Jack Louis Phillips and Jacqueline (Kasper) Ehrman; children: Zachary J., Mark H. BA, Boston U., 1971; JD, Case Western Reserve U., 1975. Bar: Ohio 1975, U.S. Supreme Ct. 1977, U.S. Dist. Ct. (so. dist.) 1978, U.S. Ct. Appeals (6th cir.) 1981, U.S. Dist. Ct. (no. dist.) 1982. Asst. prosecutor Franklin County Prosecutor Office, Columbus, Ohio, 1975-77, sr. asst. prosecutor, 1977-79; assoc. Vorys, Sater, Seymour & Pease, Columbus, 1979-84, ptnr., 1984—; spl. prosecutor State of Ohio, 1993—. Gen. counsel Nat. Fraternal Order of Police, Washington, 1987-2002, Conrail Police #1, U.S. Postal Police #2; mem. Bd. Profl. Law Enforcement Certification; pres. Ohio Ctr. for Law-Related Edn., 1985-95; mem. Wong Sun Soc., 1997—; adj. prof. Ohio State U. Moritz Sch. Law, 2005—. Author: Civil Recovery in Ohio, 1986, Collective Bargaining in the Pub. Sector, 1988; editor Bar Briefs; contbr. articles Jours., 1987-89. Bd. dirs. Schottenstein Stores Corp., 2002—. Fellow Ohio Bar Found.; Columbus Bar Found., Ohio Bar Assn. (chmn. com. law-related edn. 1982-86), Columbus Bar Assn., Sixth Cir. Jud. Conf. (life); Ohio Assn. Criminal Defense Lawyers (bd. dirs., treas.). Office: Vorys Sater Seymour & Pease PO Box 1008 52 E Gay St Columbus OH 43215-3161 Office Phone: 614-464-5610. Business E-Mail: phillips@vssp.com.

**PHILLIPS, JANET COLLEEN,** retired educational association administrator, editor; b. Pittsfield, Ill., Apr. 29, 1933; d. Roy Lynn and Catherine Amelia (Wills) Barker; m. David Lee Phillips, Feb 7, 1954; children— Clay Cullen, Sean Vincent. BS, U. Ill, 1954. Reporter Quincy (Ill.) Herald Whig, 1951, 52, soc. editor, 1953; editorial asst. Pub. Info. Office U. Ill.-Urbana, 1953-54, asst. editor libr., 1954-61; asst. editor Assn. for Libr. and Info. Sci. Edn., State College, Pa., 1960-61, mng. editor, 1961-89, exec. sec., 1970-89; adminstrv. dir. Interlibr. Delivery Svc. of Pa., 1990-99; ret. Mem. Palmer Mus. Arts, State Coll. Cmty. Theatre, Mt. Nittany Med. Ctr. Aux. Mem. Assn. for Libr. and Info. Sci. Edn., Embroiderer's Guild Am., Pa. State Blue Golf Course Club, Univ. Women's Club (Pa. State), Ctr. Hills Country Club, Am. Wine Soc., Cmty. Acad. Lifelong Learning, Delta Zeta. Presbyterian. Avocations: travel, golf, sewing, needlecraft. Home: 471 Park Ln State College PA 16803-3208 E-mail: janph2@aol.com.

**PHILLIPS, JANET K.,** music educator; b. Stillwater, Okla., Mar. 12, 1957; d. Charles Scottie McMillin and Alice Norma Burden; m. Steven Frank Phillips, Feb. 3, 1979; children: Kristin Lynn, Timothy Steven. AA, Muscatine C.C., 1977; BA, Marycrest Coll., Davenport, 1978; MA, U. Iowa, 1997. Adj. faculty Muscatine C.C., Iowa, 1980—96, dir. music activities, 1997—. Dir. music Muscatine Civic Chorale, 1995—. Bd. mem. Muscatine Symphony Orch., 2004—. Recipient Chancellor's award, Eastern Iowa C.C. Dist. Mem.: Am. Choral Dirs. Assn. Home: 2724 Birdie Dr Muscatine IA 52761-9711 Office: Muscatine CC 152 Colo St Muscatine IA 52761 Office Phone: 563-288-6038. Business E-Mail: jphillips@eicc.edu.

**PHILLIPS, JILL META,** writer, critic, astrologer; b. Detroit, Oct. 22, 1952; d. Leyson Kirk and Leona Anna (Rasmussen) P. Student pub. schs., Calif. Lit. counselor Book Builders, Charter Oak, Calif., 1966-77; pres. Moon Dance Astro Graphics, Covina, Calif., 1994—. Author: (with Leona Phillips) A Directory of American Film Scholars, 1975, The Good Morning Cookbook, 1976, G.B. Shaw: A Review of the Literature, 1976, T.E. Lawrence: Portrait of the Artist as Hero, 1977, The Archaeology of the Collective East, 1977, The Occult, 1977, D.H. Lawrence: A Review of the Literature and Biographies, 1978, Film Appreciation: A College Guide Book, 1979, Annus Mirabilis: Europe in the Dark and Middle Centuries, 1979, (with Leona Rasmussen Phillips) The Dark Frame: Occult Cinema, 1979, Misfit: The Films of Montgomery Clift, 1979, Butterflies in the Mind: A Précis of Dreams and Dreamers, 1980; The Rain Maiden: A Novel of History, 1987, Walford's Oak: A Novel, 1990, The Fate Weaver: A Novel in Two Centuries, 1991, Saturn Falls: A Novel of the Apocalypse, 1993, Birthday Secrets, 1998, Your Luck is in the Stars, 2000; columnist Dell Horoscope Mag., Astrology Your Daily Horoscope Mag., 1998—; contbr. book revs. to New Guard mag., 1974-76; contbr. numerous articles to profl. jours. including Dell Horoscope, Midnight Horoscope, Astrology-Your Daily Horoscope, Am. Astrology. Mem. Young Ams. for Freedom, Am. Conservative Union, Elmer Bernstein's Film Music Collection, Ghost Club London, Count Dracula Soc. Dracula Soc. London, Richard III Soc. Republican. Personal E-mail: queenofwands52@aol.com.

**PHILLIPS, JOHN A(TLAS), III,** geneticist, educator; b. Sanford, N.C., Jan. 24, 1944; s. John A. and Rachael (Sloan) P.; m. Gretchen Lynch, Aug. 1, 1965; children: Jennifer Allene, John Atlas IV, Charles Andrew, James William. Student, U. N.C., 1962-65; MD, Wake Forest U., 1969. Diplomate Am. Bd. Pediatrics, Am. Bd. Med. Genetics. Intern Children's Hosp. Med. Ctr., Boston, 1969-70, jr. resident, 1970-71, sr. resident, 1973-74, chief resident, 1974-75; asst. prof. Johns Hopkins U., Balt., 1978-82, assoc. prof., 1982-84; prof. pediatrics Vanderbilt U., Nashville, 1984—, prof. biochemistry, 1986—; David T. Karzon chair genetics, 1992—. Bd. sci. counselors Nat. Inst. Child Health, Washington, 1984-88; counsilor Ctr. Study Polymorphisme Humain, Paris, 1988—; mem. adv. com. Ctr. Reproductive Biology, Nashville, 1990-94; bd. dirs. March of Dimes Birth Defects Found., Nashville, 1986—; mem. adv. bd. Nat. Neurofibromatosis Found., Tenn., 1990—; mem. Tenn. Genetics Adv. Com., Nashville, 1984—. Contbr. to profl. publs. Lt. comdr. USNR, 1971-73. Recipient Sidney Farber award Children's Hosp., Boston, 1975, E Mead Johnson award Mead Johnson Co., 1984; Pediatric Postdoctoral fellow Johns Hopkins U. Sch. Medicine, 1975-77. Mem. Am. Soc. Clin. Investigation, Soc. Pediatric Rsch., Am. Coll. Med. Genetics (founding, bd. dirs. 1995—), Phi Beta Kappa, Alpha Omega Alpha. Achievements include discovery of cause of hemoglobin H disease in Black Americans; chromosomal location of multiple genes in humans; improved diagnoses of cystic fibrosis, hemophilia, inborn metabolic errors, familial neurodegenerative diseases, familial pulmonary hypertension, familial pulmonary fibrosis. Office: Vanderbilt U Sch Medicine Divsn Med Genetics DD 2205 Nashville TN 37232-0001 Office Phone: 615-322-7601.

**PHILLIPS, JOHN EDWARD,** zoologist, educator; b. Montréal, Que., Can., Dec. 20, 1934; s. William Charles and Violet Mildred (Lewis) P.; m. Eleanor Mae Richardson, Sept. 8, 1956; children: Heather Anne, Jayne Elizabeth, Jonathan David, Catherine Melinda, Wendy Susannah. BSc with honors, Dalhousie U., Halifax, N.S., 1956, MSc, 1957; PhD, Cambridge U., Eng., 1961. Asst. prof. Dalhousie U., Halifax, N.S., 1960-64; assoc. prof. U. B.C., Vancouver, Canada, 1964-71, prof., 1971—, head dept. zoology, 1991-96. Vis. rschr. Cambridge (Eng.) U., 1972, 76, 81; chair grant selection com. Nat. Rsch. Coun. Can., Ottawa, Ont., 1969-71; mem. coun. Nat. Sci. and Engring. Rsch. Coun., Ottawa, 1983-87. Mem. editorial bd.: Can. Jour. Zoology, 1971-75, Am. Jour. Physiology, 1978-93, Jour. Experimental Biology, 1981-85, Am. Zool., 1996-01; contbr. articles to profl. jours. Mem. grant selection com. Can. Cystic Fibrosis Found., Toronto, 1989-91; active Vancouver Bach Choir. Named to James chair St. Francis Xavier U., Antigonish, N.S., 1993; recipient Killam Rsch. prize U. B.C. Fellow Royal Soc. Can.; mem. Can. Soc. Zoologists (sec. 1972-76, v.p 1976-78, pres. 1979, Fry medal 2000), Am. Soc. Zoologists (exec. 1983-85, chair divsn. comp. physiol. biochemistry 1987-87). Avocations: music, singing. Home: 12908 22 B Ave White Rock BC Canada V4A 6Z3 Office: U BC Dept Zoology Vancouver BC Canada V6T 1Z4 E-mail: jephillips@telus.net.

**PHILLIPS, JOHN P(AUL),** retired neurosurgeon; b. Danville, Ark., Oct. 14, 1932; s. Brewer William Ashley and Wave Audrey (Page) P.; m. June Helen Dunbar, Dec. 14, 1963; children: Todd Eustace, Timothy John Colin, Tyler William Ashley. AB cum laude, Hendrix Coll., 1953; MD, U. Tenn., 1956. Diplomate Am. Bd. Neurol. Surgeons. Intern Charity Hosp. La., New Orleans, 1957; resident surgery U. Tenn. Hosps., 1958; resident neurol. surgery U. Tenn. Med. Units, 1958-62; practice medicine, specializing in neurol. surgery Salinas, Calif., 1962-93; ret., 1993. Chief of staff, chief of surgery Salinas Valley Meml. Hosp.; mem. staffs Community Hosp. Monterey Peninsula, U. Calif. Hosp., San Francisco; asst. clin. prof. U. Calif., 1962—. Commd. Ky. col. Mem. AMA, ACS, Internat. Coll. Surgery, Harvey Cushing Soc., Congress Neurol. Surgery, Western Neurosurg. Assn., San Francisco Neurol. Soc., Pan Pacific Surg. Assn., Stanford U. Faculty Club (emeritus), Alpha Omega Alpha, Phi Chi, Alpha Chi. Office Phone: 831-484-1253.

**PHILLIPS, JOHN R.,** lawyer; b. Leechburg, Pa., Dec. 15, 1942; BA, U. Notre Dame, 1966; JD, U. Calif., 1969. Bar: Calif. 1970, U.S. Supreme Ct. 1992, DC 1993, U.S. Dist. Ct. DC 1993. Assoc. O'Melveny & Myers, L.A.; ptnr. Phillips & Cohen, LLP, Washington. Co-founder, dir. Ctr. Law in the Pub. Interest, LA, 1971—88; mem. 9th cir. jud. conf., 1989—92; appointee Commn. White House Fellowships, 1997—2001; spkr. in field. Mem. bd. editors: Calif. Law Rev., 1968—69; contbr. articles to profl. jours. Office: Phillips & Cohen LLP 2000 Massachusetts Ave NW First Fl Washington DC 20036 Office Phone: 202-833-4567. Office Fax: 202-883-1815.

**PHILLIPS, JOHN ROBERT,** political scientist, educator; b. Henderson, Ky., Dec. 16, 1942; s. Leander Armstead and Ann Reid (Brown) P. Diploma, Lang. Inst., Chateauroux, France, 1966; BA, Centre Coll., Danville, Ky., 1969; MA, Western Ky. U., Bowling Green, 1973. Instr. Drury Coll., Springfield, Mo., 1971-73, Western Ky. U., Bowling Green, 1975-79; asst. prof. Thiel Coll., Greenville, Pa., 1979-83, scholar-in-residence, 1983-85; pvt. cons., 1985—; adj. prof. Lockyear Coll., Evansville, Ind., 1987-88, prof. adminstrv. and social scis., 1988-91, acad. dean, 1988-90, v.p. acad. affairs, dean coll., 1990-91, Helen Hoffman disting. svc. prof., 1990-91; exec. dir.

Henderson County Human Rels. Commn., 1991-93; dean acad. affairs, prof. political studies/govt. Springfield (Ill.) Coll., 1993-97, acting pres., 1996-97, provost, dean coll., 1997-98, prof. polit. and social scis., 1998—, Rose and H. Paul LaFata Endowed Chair for Disting. Tchg., 2003. Adj. prof. pub. adminstrn. Ind. State U., Terre Haute, 1991-92; field investigator on religion and culture in ancient city of Taxila, Pakistan, 1968, on indsl. pollution of hist. bldgs. and monuments, France, Italy, Austria, 1969; rschr. on nationalism, Scotland, 1972, 2002, on local Scottish govt. and urban deves., 1993; participant in internat. confs. on The Future of a Unitary Germany, 1991; mem. adv. coun. St. John's Hosp. Sch. Respiratory Therapy, 1993-97, Ursuline Acad Sch. Bd., v.p., 1995-97, pres., 1997-99, Cen. Ill. Fgn. Lang. and Internat. Studies Consortium, 1993—, chmn., 1994-96; cons.-evaluator Higher Learning Commn., North Ctrl. Assn. Colls. and Schs., 1999—. Mem. editl. bd.: Jour. Urban Affairs, 1985—89, book rev. editor: Pub. Voices, 2003, manuscript referee: Pub. Adminstrn. Rev., 1985—87, asst. editor: Pub. Voices, 2001—03; contbr. articles to profl. jours. Policy advisor Lt. Gov.'s Office, Frankfort, Ky., 1985-86; cons. Commn. on Ky.'s Future, Frankfort, 1985-87; mem. Bd. Cath. Edn., Diocese of Springfield, 1994-97; trustee Springfield Coll., 1996-97, commn. on human sexuality Episcopal Diocese of Springfield, 1997-98; bd. dirs. Liturgical Arts Festival of Springfield, 1998-2001. With USAF, 1963-68. Recipient Outstanding Tchg. in Polit. Sci. award, Am. Polit. Sci. Assn. and Pi Sigma Alpha, 2003, Most Inspirational Tchr. award, Western Ill. U., 2002. Mem. Am. Polit. Sci. Assn. (Leon Weaver Award com. 1990-93), Am. Soc. Pub. Adminstrn. (publs. com. 1984-88, 92-95), Urban Affairs Assn. (publs. com. 1985-89, nominating com. 1984-85, 88-89), Pi Sigma Alpha, Alpha Sigma Lambda. Democrat. Episcopalian. Home: 2605 Delaware Dr Springfield IL 62702-1213 Office: Springfield College L-106 Becker Libr 1500 N 5th St Springfield IL 62702-2643 Business E-Mail: jphillips@sci.edu.

**PHILLIPS, JOSEPH BRANTLEY, JR.,** lawyer; b. Greenville, SC, Dec. 5, 1931; BS in Bus. Adminstrn., U. S.C., 1954, JD, 1955. Bar: SC 1955. Assoc. Leatherwood, Walker, Todd & Mann, Greenville, 1958-63, ptnr., 1963—. Chmn. bd. deacons Presbyterian Ch., 1970-71, pres. Men of Ch., 1968-69, chmn. Christian Service Ctr., 1972-73; bd. dirs. Greenville Urban Ministry, 1978. Mem. ABA, S.C. Bar Assn., Greenville Bar Assn., Greenville Young Lawyers Club (pres. 1961-62), Lawyers Pilots Bar Assn., Kiwanis (pres. 1973). Clubs: Greenville Country (pres. 1977). Home: 207 Butler Springs Rd Greenville SC 29615-2261 Office: PO Box 87 Greenville SC 29602-0087

**PHILLIPS, JOSEPH DANIEL,** geophysicist, oceanographer; b. Woodbury, N.J., Sept. 11, 1938; s. Joseph Francis and Katherine Cecelia (Browne) P.; m. Gwendolyn Williams, 1961; children: Julia Kear, Stephanie Morgan, Joseph Williams. BA, Rutgers U., 1961; MS in Engring., Princeton U., 1963, MA, 1964, PhD, 1966. Engr. trainee Mobil Oil Co., N.Y.C., 1957, N.Y. Shipbuilding Corp., Camden, NJ, 1958-60; engr. mgmt. trainee N.J. Bell Tel. Co., Newark/Camden, NJ, 1961; rsch. asst. Princeton (N.J.) U., 1962-65; asst. scientist Woods Hole (Mass.) Oceanographic Inst., 1965-68, assoc. scientist, 1968-77; staff rsch. scientist MIT, Cambridge, 1977-79; sr. rsch. scientist U. Tex., Austin, 1978-96; chief scientist World Geoscience Corp., Houston, 1996-1999; chief scientist, dir. tech. svcs. Fugro Airborne Surveys, Houston, 1999-2000; chief scientist, dir. tech. svcs. Integrated Geophysics Corp., Houston, 2000. Cons. Mobil Oil Corp., Dallas, 1969, Exxon Corp., Houston, 1977, Bell Tel. Labs., Whippany/Murray Hill, N.J., 1976-78; vis. scholar U. Cambridge, Eng., 1974-75; adj. prof./instr. marine geophysics, seismics and geomagnetism, oceanography, acoustics and potential fields, faculty advisor MIT, Woods Hole Oceanographic Inst., U. Tex., 1968-96; cons. airborne/marine archeology Nat. Underwater and Marine Archeologic Agy., 1997, 98, 2003-. Contbr. articles to Jour. Geophys. Rsch. Sci., Geol. Soc. Am., Am. Petroleum Geologist, Ency. Brittanica. Fellow Explorers Club; mem. Am. Soc. Naval Engrs., Am. Geophys. Union, Soc. Exploration Geophysicists, AAAS, Marine Lodge, Phi Beta Kappa, Sigma Xi. Achievements include design of phase lock-in amplifiers for rock magnetometers; USN multi-beam sonar for seafloor geology; acoustically navigated vehicles for seafloor studies; vertical seismic profiling aboard deep ocean drilling project ships; aeromagnetic/electromagnetic detection of archeologic and groundwater salinity contamination sites, pipeline and wellhead surveying; multichannel acoustic seismo-acoustic reflection profile imaging of ocean watermasses; T-phase transmission studies; oceanic ridge and trench seismicity. Home: 3805 Gaines Ranch Austin TX 78735 Personal E-mail: joephillipsD@sbcglobal.net.

**PHILLIPS, JOSHUA PHILLIPS,** pediatrician; b. Cleveland, Miss., Aug. 6, 1976; s. Barbara Brown Oltremari and Jack Franklin Phillips. MD, U. Miss., Jackson, 2002. Resident U. Miss. Med. Ctr., Jackson, 2002—06, chief resident pediat., 2006—. Missionary to Kenya Pinelake Bapt. Ch., Brandon, Miss., 2006—06. Mem.: Am. Acad. Pediat. (assoc.), AMA (assoc.). R-Liberal. Baptist. Avocations: travel, running. Home: 104 Stonecastle Ct Brandon MS 39047 Office: Univ Miss Med Ctr 2500 North State St Jackson MS 39216 Office Phone: 601-984-1000. Personal E-mail: jfphillips@medicine.umsmed.edu.

**PHILLIPS, JOY LAMBERT,** lawyer, banker; b. Ft. Bragg, N.C., Sept. 25, 1955; d. Jurloew Lambert and Mary Carolyn (Gregory) Trivette; m. Frank Warren Phillips, May 10, 1975. AA, N.E. Miss. Jr. Coll., Booneville, 1974; BA, U. Miss., 1977, JD, 1980. Bar: Miss. 1980. Assoc. Daniel, Coker, Horton & Bell, P.A., Jackson, Miss., 1980-85; sr. v.p., asst. gen. counsel Deposit Guaranty Nat. Bank, Jackson, 1985—98; gen. counsel Hancock Bank, Gulfport, Miss., 1999—. Seminar speaker, 1990-91. Treas., Miss. Opera Guild, Jackson, 1990-97, mentor Miss. Coll. Sch. Law, Jackson, 1989-92. Mem. ABA, Miss. Bar Assn. (pres. 2005-06), Hinds County Bar Assn., Harrison County Bar Assn., Miss. Women Lawyers (pres. 1989-90), Jackson Young Lawyers, Kiwanis (dir. 1991-93, pres. 1966). Avocations: reading, walking, dogs, hiking. Home: PO Box 819 Gulfport MS 39502-0819 Office: Hancock Bank One Hancock Plz Gulfport MS 39501 Office Phone: 228-563-5755. E-mail: joy_phillips@hancockbank.com.

**PHILLIPS, JULIEANNE APPLESON,** history professor; b. Cleve., Jan. 15, 1952; d. Nick Appleson and Patricia Kepic (Appleson) Zajac; m. William Harold Phillips, July 2, 1977; children: Kristen Ann, Amy Lynn. AA, Cuyahoga C.C., Parma, Ohio, 1987; BA in History, Baldwin-Wallace Coll., Berea, Ohio, 1989; MA in History, Cleve. State U., 1990; PhD in Am. History, Case Western Res. U., 1996. Cert. secondary edn. history Ohio. Grant coord. Dayton-Tchg. Am. History, 2003—05; asst. prof. Urbana U., Ohio, 2005—. Author: (ency.) U.S. Aging Policy Interest Groups Institutional Profiles, (Web project) The History Place, (Web resource) Workshop for Teachers: Celebrating the 150th Anniversary of the Women's Rights Movement 1848-1998, (tchg. resource) Dayton Public Schools Social Studies Instructional Guide, (ency.) Encyclopedia of New England Culture, The Eleanor Roosevelt Encyclopedia, Organizing Black America, African American Women in the United States, The Historical Encyclopedia of World Slavery; contbr. articles and revs. to profl. jours. Judge Nat. Spelling Bee, Dayton, 2005, Nat. History Day, Cleve. 1986—2005; dir. Women Historians of Western Ohio, Dayton, 2000—05. Recipient Elizabeth S. Magee Doctoral fellowship, Case Western Res. U., 1990—95, U.S. Achievement Acad. All Am. scholarship, U.S. Achievement Acad., 1989, Nat. Collegiate Edn. award Nat. Collegiate Edn., 1989; fellow, Ohio Bd. of Regents, 1989—91. Mem.: Ohio Acad. of History (assoc.), Nat. Coun. for History Edn. (assoc.), Orgn. of Am. Historians (assoc.), Am. Hist. Assn. (assoc.). Office: Urbana Univ 579 College Way Urbana OH 43078 Office Phone: 937-484-1265. Business E-Mail: jphillips@urbana.edu.

**PHILLIPS, KAREN,** secondary school educator; Physical edn. tchr., adminstr. Walter D. Johnson Jr. H.S., Las Vegas, 1993-97; asst. prin. Lied Mid. Sch., Las Vegas, 1997-99; prin. Clifford J. Lawrence Jr. High Sch., 1999—. Recipient Middle Sch. Physical Edn. Tchr. of the Yr. Nat. Assn. for Sport and Physical Edn., 1993. Office: Clifford J Lawrence Jr High Sch 4410 S Juliano Rd Las Vegas NV 89147-8691

**PHILLIPS, KAREN A.,** urban planner; b. Ocilla, Ga. BA landscape architecture, Sch. Environ. Design U. Ga.; MA landscape architecture, Harvard U. Grad. Sch. Design, 1982. Urban planner, Atlanta, 1975—77; project mgr. econ. devel. dept. N.Y. State Urban Devel. Corp.; co-founder, pres., CEO Abyssinian Devel. Corp., N.Y.C., 1989—2002; mem. N.Y.C. Planning Commn., 2002—. Real estate analyst Port Authority of NY and NJ, 1982—87; adj. prof. Sch. Architecture and Environ. Studies, City Coll. N.Y., 1992; cmty. devel. fellow Milano Grad Sch., New Sch. U., 2002—03. Mem. Parks Coun., Atlanta, 1975—80, Preservation League of NY, Manhattan Coun. Boy Scouts Am.; apptd. design com. Martin Luther King., Jr. Nat. Monument Project; bd. NY Women's Found., 2003—; Mayor's rep. Studio Mus. of Harlem; mem. NY Women's Found. Fellow: Am. Soc. Landscape Arch. Office: NYC Dept City Planning 22 Reade St New York NY 10007-1216 Office Phone: 212-720-3516.

**PHILLIPS, KAREN BORLAUG,** economist, rail transportation executive; b. Long Beach, Calif., Oct. 1, 1956; d. Paul Vincent and Wilma Borlaug. Student, Cath. U. P.R., 1973-74; BA, BS, U. N.D., 1977; postgrad., George Washington U., 1978-80. Rsch. asst. rsch. and spl. programs adminstrn. U.S. Dept. Transp., Washington, 1977—78, economist, office of sec., 1978—82; profl. staff mem. (majority) Com. Commerce Sci., Transp. U.S. Senate, Washington, 1982—85, tax economist (minority) com. on fin., 1985—87, chief economist (majority) senate com. on fin., 1987—97; commr. Interstate Commerce Commn., Washington, 1988—94; v.p. legis. Assn. Am. Railroads, Washington, 1994—95, sr. v.p. policy, legis. and comm., 1995—98; pres. Policy & Advocacy Assocs., Alexandria, Va., 1998—2000; v.p. N. Am. pub. and govt. affairs Can. Nat. Ry. Co., Washington, 2000—. Contbr. articles to profl. jours. Recipient award for Meritorious Achievement, Sec. Transp., 1980, Spl. Achievement awards, 1978, 80, Outstanding Performance awards, 1978, 80, 81. Mem. Am. Econ. Assn., Women's Transp. Seminar (Woman of Yr. award 1994), Transp. Rsch. Forum, Assn. Transp. Law, Logistics and Policy, Tax Coalition, Can.-Am. Bus. Coun. (bd. dirs.), Blue Key, Phi Beta Kappa, Omicron Delta Epsilon. Republican. Luth. Office: Can Nat Rlwy Co Ste 500 601 Pennsylvania Ave NW Washington DC 20004 Office Phone: 202-347-7816. Personal E-mail: karen.phillips@cn.ca.

**PHILLIPS, KAREN DIANE,** surgeon; b. Dayton, Ohio, Jan. 11, 1968; d. Charles Joseph and Theresa Olwen Muscato; m. Ian Daniel Same, Sept. 24, 1999; children: Luke Daniel, Maya Charles. BS in Chemistry, Mary Washington U., Fredericksburg, Va., 1990; MD, Med. U. Ohio, Toledo, 1995. Diplomate Am. Bd. Surgery, 2001. Chief resident U. SC, Columbia, 1995—2000; intern, resident U. SC, Richland Meml. Hosp. and the Dorn Vets. Adminstrn. Hosp., 1996—2000; gen. surgeon Alamogordo Surg. Assocs., Alamogordo, N.Mex., 2001—04; So. Surg. Group, Lexington, SC, 2004—. Fellow: ACS; mem.: AMA, Soc. S.C. Surgeons, So. Med. Assn., Am. Soc. Breast Surgeons. Office: So Surg Group 2728 Sunset Blvd West Columbia SC 29169 Home: 1149 Katy Meadow Ct Fairborn OH 45324 Office Phone: 803-767-3816. Home Fax: 803-251-3382. Personal E-mail: kphillipsmd@hotmail.com.

**PHILLIPS, KATHLEEN GAY,** small business owner; b. Clarkston, Wash., Nov. 7, 1952; d. Cecil Martin Phillips and Nellie Florance Robertson; 1 child, John Cecil Dickeson-Phillips. Student, Lewis & Clark State Coll., 1973, Walla Walla C.C., 1990—91, Lewis & Clark State Coll., 1992; grad., H&R Tax Course, 2003. Cert. notary State of Idaho. Accounts clk. Lewis Clark State Coll., Lewiston, Idaho, 1975; co-founder Christina's Creations, Altus, Okla., 1982—, Funmates, Lewiston, 1982; dir. TK Springer, Inc., 1981; asst. mgr. Circle Drive Mobile Home Park, 1982—87. Surveyor Consumer Mail Panel, Palatine, Ill., 2000; restorer Gray Hut Apt. - Hist. Baughman House, Lewiston, 1993—99; rep. Western Modern Jewelry and Jewelry by Kathleen G. Phillips; history cons. Corps. Engrs. at Clarkston. With Medic Alert, 1979—; established Memory Walk & Safe Return, Alzheimer's Assn., 2005; worked with Gov. Kerathoun, Senator Craig, Senator Crapio, House of Rep. Helen Cheenawith, CL Otter. Pvt. U.S. Army, 1991, Gulf War, with USNR. Recipient Oldest Tree award, Pks. & Recreation Bd., 1999. Mem.: Idaho Hist. Soc., Lewiston C. of C., The Planetary Soc., Clan Donald U.S.A., Am. Legion, Order of Ea. Star (life), Pi Beta Lambda. Methodist. Avocations: needlecrafts, painting, reading, archaeology.

**PHILLIPS, KEITH WENDALL,** minister; b. Portland, Oreg., Oct. 21, 1946; s. Frank Clark and Velma Georgina (Black) P.; m. Mary Katherine Garland, July 16, 1973; children: Joshua, Paul, David. BA, UCLA, 1968; MDiv, Fuller Theology Sem., 1971, D. of Ministries, 1972; LHD (hon.), John Brown U., 1990; LHD (hon.), Sterling Coll., 2002. Dir. Youth For Christ Clubs, L.A., 1965-71; pres. World Impact, L.A., 1971—. Commencement speaker Tabor Coll., 1969, 91, John Brown U., 1990, Sterling Coll., 2002. Author: Everybody's Afraid in the Ghetto, 1973, They Dare to Love the Ghetto, The Making of a Disciple, 1981, No Quick Fix, 1985, Out of Ashes, 1996. Chmn. L.A. Mayor's Prayer Breakfast Com., 1985—; bd. dirs. Christian Cmty. Devel. Assn., 1992—; founder/coord. Crowns of Beauty Confs.; spkr. Promise Keeper. Named Disting. Staley lectr., 1969. Mem. Evangelistic Com. of Newark (pres. 1976—), World Impact of Can. (pres. 1978—), The Oaks (pres. 1985—), Faith Works (pres. 1987—) Baptist. Office: World Impact 2001 S Vermont Ave Los Angeles CA 90007-1279 *Our knowledge of God's Word outruns our obedience. The challenge for Christians is to live what we know.*

**PHILLIPS, KENNETH EDWARD,** history educator, writer; b. Elamville, Ala., Dec. 29, 1947; s. Counce A. and Alma Ruth Phillips; m. Veva Elaine Roberts, May 4, 1973; 1 child, Haley Leigh. AA, George C. Wallace State Cmty. Coll., 1978; BSc, Troy State U., 1979; MA, Auburn U., 1982, PhD, 1999. History instr. Gordon Jr. Coll., Barnesville, Ga., 1986—87, Martin Meth. Coll., Pulaski, Tenn., 1988—89; archivist hist. U.S. Army Missile Command, Redstone Arsenal, Ala., 1989—90; history instr. Auburn U., Ala., 1990—91, George C. Wallace State Cmty. Coll., Dothan, Ala., 1991—. Contbg. author: Encyclopedia of Alabama. Councilman Ariton City Coun., 1976—78. E5 USN, 1968—71. Recipient Malcolm C. McMillan History award, Auburn U., 1981, Colonel Dames award, 1984, Robert L. Partin award, 1986. Mem.: Ala. Hist. Assn., Southern Hist. Assn., Agrl. Hist. Assn. Democrat. Meth. Avocations: reading, writing, films. Office: Wallace Cmty Coll Wallace Hall 102 1141 Wallace Dr Dothan AL 36303

**PHILLIPS, KENNETH WAYNE,** music educator; b. Pensacola, Fla., Feb. 16, 1963; s. James F. and Jane K. Phillips; m. Elizabeth Gonzalez Phillips, June 22, 2003. MA, Pensacola Jr. Coll., Fla., 1984; BA in Ch. Music, U. Mobile, 1987; M in Music Edn., U. So. Miss., 1992; PhD in Music Edn., Temple U., 1997. Cert. tchr. Fla. Dept. of Edn., 2002. Music tchr. Escambia County Sch. Dist., Pensacola, Fla., 1990—92; tchg. asst. Temple U., Phila., 1993—97; vis. prof. of music edn. Western Ill. U., Macomb, Ill., 1997—98; assoc. prof. music edn. Palm Beach (Fla.) Atlantic U., 1998—. Singer: (DVD) Sarah Brightman, La Luna, 2001. Scholar, Temple U., 1993—96. Mem.: Soc. for Rsch. in Music Edn., Fla. Collegiate Music Educators Assn., Fla. Music Educators Assn., Music Educators Nat. Conf. Home: 333 Palmetto Street West Palm Beach FL 33405 Office: Palm Beach Atlantic University PO Box 24708 West Palm Beach FL 33416-4708 Office Phone: 561-803-2411. Business E-Mail: ken_phillips@pba.edu.

**PHILLIPS, LARRY ARTHUR,** artist; b. Syracuse, N.Y., Mar. 6, 1951; s. Arthur Foster and Vivian Phillips. Cork Gallery, Lincoln Ctr., N.Y.C., 1990. Mem.: Ward-Nasse Gallery, Intuit the Ctr. for Intuitive and Outsider Art, Christians in Visual Arts. Home: 709 S West St Apt 4 Syracuse NY 13202

**PHILLIPS, LARRY EDWARD,** lawyer; b. Pitts., July 5, 1942; s. Jack F. and Jean H. (Houghtelin) P.; m. Karla Ann Hennings, June 5, 1976; 1 son, Andrew H.; 1 stepson, John W. Dean IV. BA, Hamilton Coll., 1964; JD, U. Mich., 1967. Bar: Pa. 1967, Fla. 2004, US Dist. Ct. (we. dist.) Pa. 1967, US Tax Ct. 1969. Assoc. Buchanan Ingersoll PC, Pitts., 1967—73, shareholder, 1973. Mem. ABA (sect. taxation, com. on corp. tax and sect. real property, probate and trust law), Am. Coll. Tax Counsel, Pa. Bar Assn., Fla. Bar, Tax Mgmt. Inc.

(adv. bd.), Pitts. Tax Club, Allegheny County Bar Assn., Collier County Bar Assn., Duquesne Club. Republican. Presbyterian. Office: Buchanan Ingersoll PC One Oxford Ctr 301 Grant St Fl 20 Pittsburgh PA 15219-1410 Office Phone: 412-562-8846. E-mail: phillipsle@bipc.com.

**PHILLIPS, LAUGHLIN,** retired museum director, retired editor; b. Washington, Oct. 20, 1924; s. Duncan and Marjorie Grant (Acker) P.; m. Elizabeth Hood, 1956 (div. 1975); children: Duncan Vance, Elizabeth Laughlin; m. Jennifer Stats Cafritz, 1975. Student, Yale U., 1942-43; MA, U. Chgo., 1949. Fgn. svc. officer, 1949—64, Hanoi, Vietnam, 1950—53, Tehran, Iran, 1957—59; co-founder Washingtonian mag., 1965, editor, 1965-74, editor-in-chief, 1974-79; pres. Washington Mag., Inc., 1965-79; dir. Phillips Collection, 1972-92, chmn. bd., 1967—2002, chmn. emeritus, 2002—. Trustee Nat. Com. for an Effective Congress, 1966—; MacDowell Colony, 1977-79; bd. dirs. UN Assn. Am., 1997-2001. With AUS, 1943-46, PTO. Decorated Bronze Star; comendador Orden de Mayo al Mérito (Argentina); chevalier de l'Ordre de la Couronne (Belgium), knight's cross 1st class Order of Danebrog (Denmark); officier Arts et Lettres (France). Mem.: Rolling Rock Club (Ligonier, Pa.), Met. Club (Washington), Cosmos Club (Washington). Personal E-mail: locphil@aol.com.

**PHILLIPS, LAWRENCE H., II,** neurologist, educator; b. Clarksburg, W.Va., Dec. 30, 1947; m. Elayne K. Phillips, 1985; children: Joshua, Melanie. AB, Princeton U., 1970; MD, U. W.Va., 1974. Diplomate Am. Bd. Psychiatry and Neurology. Intern U. Wis. Hosps., Madison, 1974-75; resident in neurology Mayo Clinic, Rochester, Minn., 1975-78, rsch. fellow neurophysiology, 1978-79; instr. neurology Mayo Med. Sch./U. Minn., 1979-80; asst. prof. U. Va. Med. Ctr., Charlottesville, 1981-87, dir. electromyography lab., 1981—, assoc. prof., 1987-95; dir. neuromuscular ctr. Muscular Dystrophy Assn. Clinic, Charlottesville, 1983—; prof. U. Va. Med. Ctr., Charlottesville, 1995—, vice chair dept. neurology and T.R. Johns prof., 1995—. Mem. med. adv. com. Diabetes Rsch. and Tng. Ctr., U. Va., 1981-88; cons. neurologist Mayo Clinic, 1979-80, VA Hosp., Salem, 1983—; cons. panel AMA Diagnostic and Therapeutic Tech. Assessment, 1989—; arbitrator panel, 1990—; expert panel mem. NIH, 1991. Recipient Young Investigator Travel award Internat. Congress Electromyography, 1979. Mem. Am. Neurol. Assn., Am. Acad. Neurology, Am. Assn. Electrodiagnostic Medicine, Assn. Univ. Profs. Neurology, Sigma Xi. Office: U VA Neuromuscular Ctr Med Health Sys PO Box 800394 Charlottesville VA 22908-0001

**PHILLIPS, LEO HAROLD, JR.,** lawyer; b. Jan. 10, 1945; s. Leo Harold and Martha C. (Oberg) P.; m. Patricia Margaret Halcomb, Sept. 3, 1983. BA summa cum laude, Hillsdale Coll., 1967; MA, U. Mich., 1968, JD cum laude, 1973; LLM magna cum laude, Free U. of Brussels, 1974. Bar: Mich. 1974, N.Y. 1975, U.S. Supreme Ct. 1977, D.C. 1979. Fgn. lectr. Pusan Nat. U., Korea, 1969-70; assoc. Alexander & Green, N.Y.C., 1974-77; counsel Overseas Pvt. Investment Corp., Washington, 1977-80, sr. counsel, 1980-82, asst. gen. counsel, 1982-85; Manor Care, Inc., Gaithersburg, Md., 1985-91, asst. sec., 1988-99, assoc. gen. counsel, 1991-99, v.p., 1996-99. Vol. Peace Corps, Pusan, Korea, 1968-71; mem. program for sr. mgrs. in govt. Harvard U., Cambridge, Mass., 1982. Contbr. articles to legal jours. Chmn. legal affairs com. Essex Condominium Assn., Washington, 1979-81; mem. fin. com., cmty. leadership bd. Miami City Ballet, 2001—; deacon Chevy Chase Presbyn. Ch., Washington, 1984-87, moderator, 1985-87, supt.-ch. sch., elder, trustee, 1987-90, pres., 1988-90, mem. nominating com., 1995-96; trustee Independence Grove, 2006—. Recipient Alumni Achievement award Hillsdale Coll., 1980; Meritorious Honor award Overseas Pvt. Investment Corp., 1981, Superior Achievement award, 1984. Mem. ABA (internat. fin. transactions com., vice-chmn. com. internat. ins. Law), Am. Soc. Internat. Law (Jessup Internat. Law moot ct. judge semi-final rounds 1978-83, chair corp. counsel com. 1993-97), Internat. Law Assn. (Am. br.; com. sec. 1982), D.C. Bar, N.Y. State Bar Assn., Royal Asiatic Soc. (Korea br.), State Bar Mich., Washington Fgn. Law Soc. (sec.-treas. 1980-81, bd. dirs., program coord. 1981-82, v.p. 1982-83, pres.-elect 1983-84, pres. 1984-85, chmn. nominating com. 1986, 88), Washington Internat. Trade Assn. (bd. dirs. 1984-87), Assn. Bar City N.Y., Hillsdale Coll. Alumni Assn. (co-chmn. Washington area 1977-90), Univ. Club (N.Y.C.), Rotary (Delray Beach treas. 2003-2004, pres.-elect 2004-05, pres. 2005-06, asst. dist. gov. 2006-), Beach Property Owners Assn.(trustee 2006—).

**PHILLIPS, MARION GRUMMAN,** civic volunteer, writer; b. N.Y.C., Feb. 11, 1922; d. Leroy Randle and Rose Marion (Werther) Grumman; m. Ellis Laurimore Phillips, Jr., June 13, 1942; children: Valerie Rose (Mrs. Adrian Parsegian), Elise Marion (Mrs. Edward E. Watts III), Ellis Laurimore III, Kathryn Noel Phillips, Cynthia Louise (Mrs. Charles Prosser). Student, Mt. Holyoke Coll., 1940-42; BA, Adelphi U., 1981. Civic vol. Mary C. Wheeler Sch., 1964-68, Historic Ithaca, Inc., 1972-76, Ellis L. Phillips Found., 1960-91. Bd. dirs. North Shore Jr. League, 1960-61, 64-65, 68-69, Family Svc. Assn. Nassau County, 1963-69, Homemaker Svc. Assn. Nassau County, 1959, 61. Author: (light verse) A Foot in the Door, 1965, The Whale-Going, Going, Gone, 1977, Doctors Make Me Sick (So I Cured Myself of Arthritis), 1979; editor: (with Valerie Phillips Parsegian) Richard and Rhoda, Letters from the Civil War, 1982, Wooden Shoes the story of my Grandfather's Grandfather (F.M. Sisson), 1990, Irish Eyes, family hist. of McTarsneys and Sissons, 1990, The Log Chapel, A History of the Congregational Community Church, Rockwood, Maine, 1999; editor Jr. League Shore Lines, 1960-61, The Werthers in America-Four Generations and their Descendants, 1987; A B-Tour of Britain, 1986; contbr. articles on fund raising to mags. Mem. New Eng. Hist. Geneal. Soc., N.Y. Geneal. Biographical Soc., Hannah Adams Womens Club, PEO Sisterhood, Medfield Garden Club. Congregationalist. Address: 279 North St Medfield MA 02052-1211

**PHILLIPS, MARJORIE SHAW,** pharmacist, educator; b. Coral Gables, Fla. d. Howard Albert and Ricki Rose Shaw; m. William G. Phillips, Aug. 25, 1985. BS in Pharm., U. Fla., Gainesville, 1982, MS in Pharm., 1984. Pharmacy coord. medication safety and clin. rsch. Med. Coll. Ga. Health Sys., Augusta, Ga., 2004—; clin. prof. pharmacy practice U. Ga. Coll. Pharmacy, 2005—. Mem. safe medication use expert com. US Pharmacopeia, Rockville, Md., 2000—, vice chair safe medication use expert com., 2005—; vice chair human assurance com. Med. Coll. Ga., Augusta, 2001—, mem. human assurance com., 1992—, adj. asst. prof. dept. pharmacology, 2006—; pharmacist investigational drug svc. & med use improvement Med. Coll. Ga. Health Sys., 1991—2004, pharmacist, 1990—91; pharmacist quality assurance Meml. Hosp. Ormond Beach, Fla., 1985—90; pharmacy supr. fiscal affairs Shands Hosp., U. Fla., Gainesville, 1984—85. Contbr. articles to profl. jours., chapters to books. Recipient Forerunner award, Fla. Soc. Heath Sys. Pharmacists, 1988. Fellow: Am. Soc. Health-Sys. Pharmacists (chair ho. del. 2003—06, bd. dirs. 2002—06); mem.: Am. Soc. Cons. Pharmacists, Ga. Soc. Health-Sys. Pharmacists (pres. 1995—96, Pharmacist Yr. 1997). Office: Medical College of Georgia Health System Pharmacy 1120 Fifteenth Street BI-2101 Augusta GA 30912-5600 Office Phone: 706-721-0802. Business E-Mail: mphillip@mcg.edu.

**PHILLIPS, MATTHEW TODD,** history educator; b. Pitts., June 25, 1981; s. Henry Walter and Doreen Elaine Phillips; m. Sara Klingensmith, June 11, 2005. BA, Thiel Coll., Greenville, Pa., 2003; MA, Kent State U., Ohio, 2005. Tchg. asst. dept. history Kent State U., 2003—. Mem.: Soc. Historians Am. Fgn. Rels., Am. Hist. Assn., Alpha Chi, Phi Alpha Theta. Office: Dept History Kent State U 305 Bowman Hall PO Box 5190 Kent OH 44240

**PHILLIPS, MICHELLE GILLIAM,** actress, writer; b. Long Beach, Calif., June 4, 1944; d. Gardner Burnett and Joyce Leon (Poole) Gilliam; m. John Phillips, Dec. 31, 1962 (div. 1970); children: Gilliam Chynna Phillips, Austin D. Hines, Aron S. Wilson. Grad. high sch., Ft. Jones, Calif. Model Francis Gill Agy., N.Y.C., 1962-64; singer Mamas and Papas, 1965-69. Guest appearances in TV shows include VegaS, 1980, The Fall Guy, 1983, Santa Barbara, 1984, Murder, She Wrote, 1984, Scene of the Crime, 1985, Alfred Hitchcock Presents, 1985, T.J. Hooker, 1985, Star Trek: The Next Generation, 1988, Herman's Head, 1994, Diagnosis Murder, 1994, 99, Burke's Law, 1994, Lois & Clark: The New Adventures of Superman, 1995, Too Something,

1996, Beverly Hills, 90210, 1997, 98, Pauly, 1997, The Magnificent Seven, 1998, 99, 2000, The Love Boat: The Next Wave, 1998, Rude Awakening, 1999, Providence, 1999, Twice in a Lifetime, 2000; appeared in tv movies The Death Squad, 1974, The California Kid, 1974, The Useres, 1978, Moonlight, 1982, Murder Me, Murder You, 1983, Secrets of a Married Man, 1984, Covenant, 1985, Paint Me a Murder, 1985, Stark: Mirror Image, 1986, Assault and Matrimony, 1987, Mike Hammer: Murder Takes All, 1989, Trenchcoat in Paradise, 1989, Appearances, 1990, Rubdown, 1993, Rock 'n' Roll Revolution: The British Invade America, 1995, 919 Fifth Avenue, 1995, No One Would Tell, 1996, Pretty Poison, 1996, Sweetwater, 1999; appeared in feature films Monterey Pop, 1969, The Last Movie, 1971, Dillinger, 1973, Valentino, 1977, Bloodline, 1979, The Man with Bogart's Face, 1980, Savage Harvest, 1981, American Anthem, 1986, Let It Ride, 1989, Flashing on the Sixties: A Tribal Document, 1990, Scissors, 1991, Army of One, 1993, Anna Petrovic, You Rock!, 1998, Lost in the Pershing Point Hotel, 2000, TV series Aspen, 1977, The French Atlantic Affair, 1979, Hotel, 1983, Knots Landing, 1979, Second Chances, 1993, Malibu Shores, 1996, Knots Landing: Back to the Cul-de-Sac, 1997; author: California Dreamin', 1986, Monday Monday (Grammy award). Recipient medal of Honor for Stop War Toys Campaign Alliance for Survival, 1987, Soap Opera Awards for Best Villainess, 1990.

**PHILLIPS, OLIVER,** tropical forest ecologist, researcher; NERC Rsch. fellow U. Leeds, England, 1996-99, lectr., 1999—2003, reader in tropical ecology, 2003—06, prof. tropical ecology, 2006—; rsch. assoc. Mo. Bot. Garden, 1997—. Recipient Edmund H. Fulling award Soc. Econ. Botany, 1992. Mem. Soc. for Econ. Botany (mem. coun. 1996-99), Assn. Trop. Biology, Brit. Ecol. Soc. (Founder's Prize, 2004). Office: U Leeds Geography Sch Earth & Biosphere Inst Leeds LS2 9JT England Office Phone: 44 113 343 6832. Business E-Mail: o.phillips@leeds.ac.uk.

**PHILLIPS, PATRICIA JEANNE,** retired school system administrator; b. Amarillo, Tex., Jan. 13, 1935; d. William Macon and Mary Ann (Cawthon) Patrick; m. William Henry Phillips, June 22, 1962; 1 child, Mary Jeanne. BA, Millsaps Coll., 1954; MA, Vanderbilt/Peabody U., 1957; EdD, U. So. Miss., 1978. Tchr. Jackson (Miss.) Pub. Schs., 1954-73, prin., 1973-75, asst. prin., 1975-77; dir. ednl. program Eden Prairie (Minn.) # 272, 1977-80; dir. elem. edn. Meridian (Miss.) Pub. Schs., 1980-91, asst. supt. curriculum, 1991; ret., 1991. Prof. Miss. Coll., Clinton, 1977, Miss. State U., Meridian, 1981-2000; cons. in field. Co-author: (testing practice) Test Taking Tactics, 1987; contbr. articles to profl. jours. Pres. Meridian Symphony Orch., 1987, 2000—; v.p. Meridian Coun. Arts, 1986; bd. dirs. Meridian Art Mus. Named Boss of Yr., Meridian Secretarial Assn., 1985, Arts Educator of Yr., Meridian Coun. Arts, 1991; recipient Excellence award Pub. Edn. Form, 1993. Mem. ASCD, Miss. ASCD, Miss. Assn. Women (pres.), Rotary, Phi Kappa Alpha, Phi Delta Kappa (pres. 1986-87), Alpha Delta Kappa Gamma (pres. 1962, pres.-elect 2006), Kappa Delta Phi. Republican. Methodist. Achievements include development of tng. materials Best Practices, Brain Growth: Applications for the Classroom. Avocations: grant writing, computers, golf, heirlooms. Home: 8450 SE 168th Kittredge Loop The Villages FL 32162-2851 Personal E-mail: jeannephill@earthlink.net.

**PHILLIPS, PETER CHARLES BONEST,** economist, educator, researcher; b. Weymouth, Dorset, Eng., Mar. 23, 1948; came to U.S. 1980; s. Charles Bonest and Gladys Eileen (Lade) P.; m. Emily Dowdell Birdling, Feb. 10, 1971 (div. 1980); 1 child, Daniel Lade; m. Deborah Jane Blood, June 13, 1981; children: Justin Bonest, Lara Kimberley. BA, Auckland (New Zealand) U., 1969, MA, 1971; PhD, London U., 1974; MA (hon.), Yale U., 1979. Teaching fellow U. Auckland, 1969-70, jr. lectr., 1970-71; lectr. in econs. U. Essex, Colchester, Eng., 1972-76; prof. econs. U. Birmingham, Eng., 1976-79, Yale U., New Haven, Conn., 1979-85, Stanley Resor prof. econs., 1985-89, Sterling prof. econs., 1989—; Alumni disting. prof. econs. U. Auckland, 1991—; pres. Predicta Software Inc., Madison, Conn., 1994—. Vis. scholar Ecole Polytechnique, Paris, 1977; univ. vis. prof. Monash U., Melbourne, Australia, 1986; vis. prof. Inst. Advanced Studes, Vienna, Austria, 1989; disting. visitor London Sch. Econs., 1989. Editor Econometric Theory jour., 1985; joint editor Asia Pacific Economic Review, 1995—; contbr. over 180 articles, book revs., notes to profl. jours. Recipient award for promotion of sci. Japan Soc., 1983, New Zealand medal Sci. and Tech., 1998, Plura Scripsit, 1997, Plurima Scripsit Econometric Theory award, 2000, Nzier Qantas Economist of Yr., 2000; Commonwealth Grants Com. scholar, Eng., 1971, Guggenheim fellow, N.Y., 1984-85. Fellow Am. Acad. Arts & Scis., Royal Soc. New Zealand (hon.), Econometric Soc., Jour. Econometrics, Am. Statis. Soc.; mem. Inst. Math. Stats., Modsim Soc. (Biennial Medal, 2003). Avocations: running, building, poetry, reading, native plant restoration. Office: Cowles Found PO Box 208281 New Haven CT 06520-8281 Home: PO Box 208281 New Haven CT 06520-8281 E-mail: peter.phillips@yale.edu.

**PHILLIPS, PHILIP EDWARD,** English professor; b. Fayetteville, Ark., Feb. 7, 1969; s. Carl M. P. and Peggy Sue P.; m. Sharmila Patel; 1 child: Edward. BA, Belmont U., Nashville, 1990; Cert. Langue Français Moyen 1, U. Cath. de l'Ouest, Angers, France, 1989; MA, Vanderbilt U., Nashville, 1992, PhD, 1996. Tchg. fellow Vanderbilt U., Nashville, 1991-96, lectr. in English, 1996-97; upper sch. tchr. in English and French Battle Ground Acad., 1997—99; asst. prof. English Mid. Tenn. State U., 1999—2004, assoc. prof., dept. English, 2004—, dir. grad. admissions. Author: John Milton's Epic Invocations, 2000; co-editor: New Directions in Boethian Studies, 2006; contbr. articles to Medieval English Studies; contbr. revs. to EMLS, Byron Jour., Carmina Philosophiae, poems to Vanderbilt Rev. Mem. Medieval Acad., MLA, Milton Soc. Am., Internat. Boethius Soc. (rec. sec. 1995—, editor newsletter, 1995, co-editor Carmina Philosophiae 1996-), Heights Nat. Alumni Assn. (bd. dirs. 1990—), Poe Found., Poe Studies Assn. Democrat. Episcopalian. Avocations: Tae Kwon Do, music, travel. Home: PO Box 246 Franklin TN 37065-0246 Office: Middle Tenn State U Dept English Box 70 Murfreesboro TN 37132 Office Phone: 615-898-2699. Office Fax: 615-898-5098. Business E-Mail: pphillip@mtsu.edu.

**PHILLIPS, RENÉE,** writer; b. Freeport, NY; Student, Art Students League, 1979, Am. Art Sch., 1979, Fashion Inst. Tech., 1980, New Sch. for Social Rsch., 1980. Dir., founder Artopia, not-for-profit art orgn., N.Y.C., 1980-84; pub., editor-in-chief Manhattan Arts Internat., N.Y.C., 1983—2000; editor-in-chief www.Manhattan Arts.com. Juror Excellence in Arts Awards, 1988, N.Y. Lung Assn. Ann. Exhbn., 1990, Manhattan Arts Internat. Ann. Internat. Art Competition, 1992—; juror, co-curator Redefining Visionary Art, Doma Gallery, N.Y.C.; 1989; curator Synthesis of Painting and Sculpture exhbn. 1st Women's Bank, N.Y.C., 1984, Salute to Unbery internat. art exhbn., N.Y.C., 1986, HerStory exhbns., 1999-2005, Small Works, 2004-05, The Healing Power of Art, 2002-04; editor-in-chief www.ManhattanArts.com; curator I Love Manhattan, N.Y.C., 2003, The Healing Power of Art, N.Y.C., 2003-05; bd. dirs., v.p. Women's Studio Ctr., L.I., N.Y., 2003—; spkr., lectr. in field Author: The Complete Guide to New York Art Galleries, 1995-2006, Presentation Power Tools for Fine Artists, 1998, 2d edit., 2000, 3d edit., 2002, Success Now! for Artists: A Motivational Guide, 1998, 2d edit., 2003 Recipient award of merit Muscular Dystrophy Assn., 1986, award for outstanding contbns. to arts Mayor of N.Y.C., 1987. Mem. Internat. Assn. Art Critics, N.Y. Artists Equity (former bd. dirs.). Office: Manhattan Arts Internat 200 E 72nd St New York NY 10021-4537 Office Phone: 212-472-1660. Business E-Mail: info@ManhattanArts.com.

**PHILLIPS, RICHARD A.,** English educator; b. Chester, Pa., June 6, 1949; s. Albert Phillips and Florence (Dunn) P. BS, Cheyney (Pa.) U., 1971. Cert. tchr., Del. Tchr. Colonial Sch. Dist., New Castle, Del., 1971-87, 1991—2005, HighCroft Sch., Williamstown, Mass., 1988; exec. dir. Sylvan Learning Ctrs., Wilmington, Del., 1987-90; ret., 2005. Mem.: NEA, Del. State Edn. Assn., New Castle County Edn. Assn. (bd. dirs. 1991—2005, v.p. 1998—2005), Colonial Edn. Assn. (exec. com. 1971—84), Nat. Coun. Tchrs. English.

**PHILLIPS, ROBERT,** engineering educator, researcher; BS, U. Minn., 1986; PhD, Wash. U., 1989. Clark Millikan vis. asst. prof. Caltech, 1997—2000, prof. mech. engring. and applied physics, 2000—. Contbr. articles to profl. jour. Recipient Pioneer award, NIH, 2004. Achievements include research in exploring nanoscale mechanics in biol. systems; the way DNA binding proteins that control gene expression expert mechanical forces on DNA resulting in the formation of loops. Office: Calif Inst Tech MC 128-95 Office 221 Steele 1200 E Calif Blvd Pasadena CA 91125 Office Phone: 626-395-3374. Office Fax: 626-583-4963. Business E-Mail: phillips@aero.caltech.edu.

**PHILLIPS, ROBERT GLENN,** energy executive; b. Midland, Tex., Oct. 9, 1954; s. Glenn Sterling and Mary Ruth (McGee) P.; m. Shirley Jean Davanay, July 14, 1979; children: Brittany Kyle, Cameron Sterling, Christian Victoria, Courtland Price, Mallory Blair. AB, Tyler Jr. Coll., 1974; BBA, U. Tex., 1977; JD, S. Tex. Coll., 1981. Contract adminstr. Gulf Oil Co., Houston, 1977-78; with hydrocarbon sales Anadarko Prodn. Co., Houston, 1978-79; gas purchase rep. Tenn. Gas Transmission Co., Houston, 1979-80; gas supply mgr. Tex. Gas Corp., Houston, 1980-81; v.p., gen. mgr. Eastex Gas Transmission Co., Houston, 1981-83; pres., chmn. bd., CEO Eastex Energy Inc., Houston, 1983—95; pres. El Paso Field Svc. (merger with Enterprise Products Ptnr. LP), 1996—2004; CEO GulfTerra Energy Ptnr. LP, 1999—2004; chmn. bd. GulfTerra Energy Ptnr. LP (merger with Enterprise Products Ptnr. LP), 2002—04; pres. & COO Enterprise Products Ptnr. LP, Houston, 2004—05, pres. & CEO, 2005—. Mem. Nat. Gas Assn. Houston, Tex. Lyceum Assn., United Shareholder Assn. (chmn. Houston chpt. 1988—). Avocations: golf, hunting.*

**PHILLIPS, ROBERT L., JR.,** application developer, consultant; s. Bettye Phillips and Robert L. Phillips, Sr.; m. Sarah E. Bohler, June 21, 2003; children: Tyler Evan childless Brandon. BS in computer sci., Miss. Valley State U., 1988—92, Java cert Ga. 2000. Exec. dir., invoice presentation and enhancement H.O. Sys., Savannah, Ga., 2000—02; mgr., product devel. H.O. Software, Savannah, 1998—2000. Adv. cons. Savannah Tech, 2000—. Designer, developer (computer software) X-Solutions. Mem.: Alpha Phi Alpha (life). Avocations: travel, reading, sports. Office: VeriSign - VTS 222 W Oglethorpe Ave Savannah GA 31401 Office Phone: 912-527-4249. Personal E-mail: rphillipsjr1@comcast.net. E-mail: rphillips@verisign.com

**PHILLIPS, ROGER,** retired steel company executive; b. Ottawa, Ont., Can., Dec. 17, 1939; s. Norman William Frederick and Elizabeth (Marshall) P.; m. Katherine Ann Wilson, June 9, 1962; 1 child, Andrée Claire. BSc, McGill U., Montreal, Can., 1960. V.p. mill products Alcan Can. Products Ltd., Toronto, Ont., 1969-70, exec. v.p., 1971-75; pres. Alcan Smelters and Chems. Ltd., Montreal, Que., 1976-79; v.p. tech. Alcan Aluminium Ltd., Montreal, 1980-81; pres. Alcan Internat. Ltd., Montreal, 1980-81; pres., CEO IPSCO Inc., Regina, Sask., Canada, 1982—2001. Sr. mem. Conf. Bd., Inc., NY, 1987—2002; bd. dirs. Toronto Dominion Bank, Can. Pacific Rlwy., Imperial Oil Ltd.; hon. dir. IPSCO Inc.; dir. Inco Ltd., Cleveland-Cliffs Inc. Bd. dirs. Conf. Bd. of Can., 1984-87; chmn. Coun. for Can. Unity, 1987-88. Fellow Inst. of Physics U.K. (chartered physicist); mem. Can. Assn. Physicists, Am. Iron and Steel Inst. (bd. dirs. 1984-2001), Sask. C. of C. (bd. dirs. 1984-2001), Que. C. of C. (pres. 1981), Order of Can. (officer 1999), St. Denis Club, Univ. Club (Montreal). Home: 3220 Albert St Regina SK Canada S4S 3N9 Office: IPSCO Inc Armour Rd Regina SK Canada S4P 3C7 E-mail: rphillips@ipsco.com.

**PHILLIPS, RONALD EDWARD,** artist, sales executive; b. Clovis, N.Mex. Apr. 10, 1937; s. Rodney Vernon and Ethel Edna (Huff) Phillips; m. May Frances Willingham, Aug. 27, 1957 (div.); children: Rhonda Louise, Russell Kent, Teresa Gail; m. Janet Irene Johnsonbaugh Smith, July 4, 1972 (dec. Nov. 29, 1999); stepchildren: Steven, Gregg, Laura. Student, Ea. N.Mex. U., 1955-56, U. N.Mex., 1957, Famous Artist Schs., 1963-64, North Light Art Sch., 1989-90. Group merchandiser women's fashions J.C. Penney Inc., Albuquerque, 1957-64; chem. salesman Take Over Products, Clovis, 1964-65; with International Auto Leasing, Albuquerque, 1965; salesman Pennsalt Chems., N.Mex. div., Albuquerque, 1965-67; N.Mex. sales rep. W.W. Grainger Inc., Chgo., 1967-72; nfounder Pueblo Arts, Inc., Albuquerque, 1972—; mgr. Dairy Queen, Santa Rosa and Lovington, N.Mex., 1982-85; owner, mgr. Western Pit n Grill & Food Gallery, Lovington, 1985-88; owner Pueblo Arts Inc./Trailwest Gallery, Albuquerque, 1988—. Tchr. quick draw, continuous line drawing, 1990; artist, guide Pueblo Arts Inc. Trailwest Paintouts, Guide for Artists, 1990—; ind. sales cons. SWEPCO Bldg. Projects, 1993—96. Sketchbooks, Traveling Man's Old Town Sketchbook, 1990, The Shooting of Wyatt Earp, 1994, 75th Anniversary Sketchbook of Route 66, 2001; actor: (plays) You Can't Take It With You. Pres. Albuquerque Wildlife and Conservation, 1963—64; active Albuquerque Conf. & Vis. Bur., 1988—, Albuquerque Arts Alliance, 1994—95, Tourism Assoc. N.Mex., Albuquerque Film Commn. Mem.: Guild Albuquerque Artist Models (advisor, bd. dirs. 1994—98), Albuquerque Arts Alliance, Indian Arts and Crafts Assn. (ethics com. 1973—74), N.Mex. Art League (hon.; pres. 1964—65, instr., bd. arts after sch. project 1995—96). Republican. Avocation: art. Office: Pueblo Arts Inc Trailwest Gallery PO Box 12944 Albuquerque NM 87195 Office Phone: 505-877-1468. Personal E-mail: ronpuebloarts@juno.com.

**PHILLIPS, RONALD FRANK,** academic administrator; b. Houston, Nov. 25, 1934; s. Franklin Jackson and Maudie Ethel (Merrill) P.; m. Jamie Jo Bottoms, Apr. 5, 1957 (dec. Sept. 1996); children: Barbara Celeste Phillips Oliveira, Joel Jackson, Phil Edward. BS, Abilene Christian U., 1955; JD, U. Tex., 1965. Bar: Tex. 1965, Calif. 1972. Bldg. contractor Phillips Homes, Abilene, Tex., 1955-56; br. mgr. Phillips Weatherstripping Co., Midland and Austin, Tex., 1957-65; corp. staff atty. McWood Corp., Abilene, 1965-67; sole practice law Abilene, 1967-70; law Pepperdine U., Malibu, Calif., 1970—, dean Sch. Law, 1970-97, dean emeritus, 1997—, vice chancellor, 1995—. Mem. Nat. Conf. Commrs. on Uniform State Laws, 1988—2003. Deacon North A and Tenn. Ch. of Christ, Midland, 1959-62; deacon Highland Ch. of Christ, Abilene, 1963 /0t elder Malibu Ch. of Christ, 19/8-95; mgr., coach Little League Baseball, Abilene, Huntington Beach and Malibu, 1968-78, 90-95; coach Youth Soccer, Huntington Beach, Westlake Village and Malibu, 1972-80, 85-86, 91. Recipient Alumni citation Abilene Christian U., 1974 Fellow Am. Bar Found. (life); mem. ABA, State Bar Tex., State Bar Calif., Christian Legal Soc., L.A. Bar Assn., Assn. Am. Law Schs. (chmn. sect. on adminstrn. law schs. 1982, com. on cts. 1985-87), Am. Law Inst. Republican. Office: Pepperdine U 24255 Pacific Coast Hwy Malibu CA 90263-4951 Business E-Mail: ronald.phillips@pepperdine.edu.

**PHILLIPS, RONALD LEWIS,** plant geneticist, educator; b. Huntington County, Ind., Jan. 1, 1940; s. Philemon Lewis and Louise Alpha (Walker) P.; m. Judith Lee Lind, Aug. 19, 1962; children: Brett, Angela. BS in Crop Sci., Purdue U., 1961, MS in Plant Breeding and Genetics, 1963, Doctorate (hon.), 2000; PhD in Genetics, U. Minn., 1966; postgrad., Cornell U., 1966-67. Rsch. and tchg. asst. Purdue U., 1961-63; rsch. assist. U. Minn., St. Paul, 1962—66, rsch. assoc., 1967—68, asst. prof., 1968—72, assoc. prof., 1972—76, prof. genetics and plant breeding, 1976—93, Regents prof., 1993—, McKnight presdl. chair in genomics, 2000—. Vis. prof., Italy, 1981, Canada, 83, China, 86, Japan, 90, Morocco, 96; program dir. Competetive Rsch. Grants Office USDA, Washington, 1979, chief scientist, 1996—98, mem. advt grant panels, NSF, DOE; chmn. Gordon Conf. on Plant Cell and Tissue Culture, 1985; mem. sci. adv. coun. U. Calif. Plant Gene Expression Ctr., Berkeley, 1986—93, chair, 1992—95; program adv. com. Palm Oil Rsch. Inst. Malaysia, 1992—2001; non-resident fellow Noble Found., 2001—; sci. adv. bd. Donald Danforth Plant Sci. Ctr., St. Louis, 2000—; sci. liaison officer Internat. Rice Rsch. Inst. USAID, 2000—03, bd. trustees, 2004—; mem. adv. grant panels; dir. Plant Molecular Genetics Inst., 1991—94; trustee Biol. Stain Commn.; mem. Nat. Plant Genetic Resources Bd.; dir. Ctr. Microbial and Plant Genomics U. Minn., 2000—05. Co-editor: Cytogenetics, 1977, Molecular Genetic Modification of Eucaryotes, 1977, Molecular Biology of Plants, 1979, The Plant Seed: Development, Preservation and Germination, 1979, Genetic Improvement of Crops: Emergent Techniques, 1980, DNA-Based Markers in Plants, 1994, 2d edit., 2001; assoc. editor Genetics, 1978—81, Can. Jour. Genetics and Cytology and Genome, 1985—90, mem. editl. bd. Maydica, 1978—, In Vitro Cellular and Devel. Biology, 1988—92, Cell Culture and Somatic Cell Genetics of Plants, 1983—91, Jour. of the Oil

Palm, 1994—, Proc. NAS, 1996—98; contbr. chpts. to Maize Beeding and Genetics, 1978, Staining Procedures, 1981, Chromosome Structure and Function, 1987, Corn and Corn Improvement, 1988, Plant Transposable Elements, 1988, Chromosome Engring. in Plants, 1991, Maize Handbook, 1994, sci. articles to profl. jours. Mem. chmn. coun. on ministries, lay leader United Meth. Ch., 1968, dir. Project AgGrad, 1983—; Cub Scout Pack co-chmn. Boy Scouts Am., 1976-77; judge Minn. Regional and State Sci. Fair, 1970-80. Recipient Purdue Agrl. Alumni Achievement award, 1961, Purdue Disting. Agrl. Alumni award, 1993; NSF fellow, 1961; NIH fellow, 1966-67; recipient Northrup King Oustanding Faculty Performance award, 1985, DeKalb Genetics Crop Sci. Disting. Career award, 1997. Fellow: AAAS (chair sect. O, program com. 2003—); Crop Sci. Soc. Am. (awards com., divsn. chmn., bd. rep. 1988—91, pres.-elect 1998—99, pres. 1999—2000, past pres. 2000—01, Rsch. award 1988), Am. Soc. Agronomy (Caleb-Dorr award); mem.: NAS (chair sect. 62 1999—2002, nominating com. 2002), Am. Soc. Agronomy (award student sect.), Genetics Soc. Am., Sigma Xi, Alpha Zeta, Gamma Sigma Delta (award of merit 1994), Gamma Alpha (nat. treas.). Office: U Minn Dpt Agronomy-Plant Genetics Saint Paul MN 55108 Business E-Mail: phill005@umn.edu.

**PHILLIPS, RUTH AMELIA,** retired music educator, artist; b. Gunnison, Colo., Feb. 20, 1922; d. Singleton Harvey and Edna Eloise (Mooseman) Flannery; m. Albert Phillips Jr., Aug. 9, 1942; children: Carl David, Carla Ann. Student, Mesa Satte Coll., Grand Junction, Colo. Cert. music tchr. Colo. Pres., organizer Palisade (Colo.) Art Lovers, 1964—. Pvt. piano and voice tchr. Exhibitions include We. Colo. Ctr. Arts, Grand Junction, Apple Shed Gallery, Cedaredge, Colo., Edge of Cedars Art Gallery, Artist's Hue Art Gallery, Parachute, Colo., Ouray Co. Arts Assn., Ouray, Colo., Glenwood Springs (Colo.) Ctr. Arts, Palisade (Colo.) Meml. Bldg., Delta (Colo.) Fine Arts, Montrose (Colo.) Visual Arts Guild. Music dir. Palisade Christian Ch., 1967—2003. Mem.: Philanthropic Ednl. Org. (pres.). Avocations: singing, painting. Home: 2996 County Rd Grand Junction CO 81504

**PHILLIPS, RUTH ANN,** retired secondary school educator; b. Greensboro, NC, Nov. 26, 1948; d. Paul Frank and Agnes Elizabeth (Butler) P. AB, Elon Coll., 1971. Cert. health and phys. edn. tchr., N.C. Tchr. health and phys. edn., chmn. dept. Sellars-Gunn Jr. H.S., Burlington, NC, 1972-81, coach tennis, basketball, softball, 1973-81; tchr., coach varsity softball, chmn. health and phys. edn. Walter M. Williams Sr. H.S., Burlington, 1981—2001, ret., 2001. Named Tchr. of Yr., Sellars-Gunn Jr. High Sch., 1975, Secondary Phys. Edn. Tchr. of Yr., N.C., 1998, Eight Who Make A Difference, Homer Thompson Meml., 2001. Mem.: State Employees Assn. NC, N.C. Assn. Educators. Democrat. Methodist. Avocations: racquetball, softball. Home: 2027 S Mebane St Burlington NC 27215-7617

**PHILLIPS, RUTHANNE,** special education administrator; d. George and Margaret Ann Mitro. BA in Psychology, cum laude, Wittenberg U., Springfield, Ohio, 1979; MS in Spl. Edn., Calif. Luth. U., Thousand Oaks, 1983; MA in Ednl. Leadership, Calif. State U., LA, 2004. Multiple subjects tchg. credential Calif., learning handicapped specialist tchg. credential Calif., severely handicapped specialist tchg. credential Calif., resource specialist cert. of competence Calif., adminstrv. svcs. credential Calif., computers in edn. cert. Calif. Luth. Coll., child mental health specialist Calif. Luth. Coll. and Camarillo State Hosp., specially designed acad. instrn. in English Calif. Grad. student asst. Camarillo (Calif.) State Hosp. and Devel. Ctr., 1979—80, tchg. asst., 1980—81, spl. edn. tchr., 1981—96, Calif. Dept. of Youth Authority at Fred C. Nelles Sch., Whittier, Calif., 1996—97; spl. edn. resource specialist tchr. L.A. County Office of Edn.-Divsn. of Juvenile Cts. and Comty. Schs. at Pacific Lodge Boys Home, Woodland Hills, Calif., 1997—99; spl. edn. tchr. L.A. County Office Edn. Divsn. Spl. Edn. at High Desert Prin.'s Adminstrv. Unit, Palmdale, Calif., 1999—2000; spl. edn. program specialist Antelope Valley Spl. Edn. Local Plan Area, Palmdale, 2000—. Mem. Calif. Assn. Sys. of Pers. Devel. Adv. Coun., Sacramento, 2003—05, Calif. Svcs. Tech. Assistance and Tng. Region 11 Coordinating Coun., L.A., 2000—, sec., 2001—02, chairperson, 2002—04; mem. Antelope Valley Family Focus Resource and Empowerment Ctr. Adv. Bd., Palmdale, 2003—05, Chapman U., Antelope Valley Campus Adv. Bd., Palmdale, 2001—03, Pacific Lodge Sch. Site Coun., Woodland Hills, 1997—99. Mem. Friends of the Acton-Agua Dulce Libr., Acton, Calif., 2005—, Friends of Acton Park, Calif., 2005—; liturgy coord. St. Mary's Acton-Agua Dulce Mission, Acton, 2002—; historian, 2000—, lector, 2000—; religious edn. tchr. St. Mary's Acton-Aqua Dulce Mission, 2001—03; asst. religious edn. coord. St. Mary's Acton-Agua Dulce Mission, Acton, 2004—05; literacy tutor Camarillo, 1992—97, Acton and Palmdale, 2002—. Recipient Wittenberg Alumni scholarship, Wittenberg U., 1975—79. Mem.: ASCD, CEC, Internat. Reading Assn., L.A. County Adminstrs. of Spl. Edn., Assn. Calif. Sch. Adminstrs., Antelope Valley Astronomy Club, Psi Chi, Alpha Xi Delta (Zeta chpt. historian 1978—79). Democrat. Roman Catholic. Avocations: scrapbooking, cardmaking, reading, travel, collecting 1st editions by Stephen King and Dean Koontz. Office: Antelope Valley SELPA 39139 10th Street East Palmdale CA 93550 Office Phone: 661-274-4136.

**PHILLIPS, SIDNEY FREDERICK,** gastroenterologist, educator; b. Melbourne, Australia, Sept. 4, 1933; s. Clifford and Eileen Frances (Fitch) P.; m. Decima Honora Jones, Mar. 29, 1957; children: Penelope Jane, Nichola Margaret, David Sidney. M.B.BS, U. Melbourne, 1956, MD, 1961. Resident med. officer Royal Melbourne Hosp., 1957-61, asst. sub-dean clin. sch., 1961-62; research asso. Central Middlesex Hosp., London, 1962-63; rsch. assoc. Mayo Clinic, Rochester, Minn., 1963-66, cons. in gastroenterology, 1966-2000; prof. medicine Mayo Med. Sch., 1976-2000, prof. medicine emeritus, 2000—, dir. gastroenterology rsch. unit, 1977-94; program dir. Mayo Grad. Clin. Rsch. Ctr., 1974-87, dir. Mayo Digestive Diseases Core Ctr., 1984-90; Karl F. and Marjory Hasselman prof. rsch., 1994-2000. Editor: Digestive Diseases and Sciences, 1977-82, Gastroenterology International, 1990-95; sr. assoc. editor: Gastroenterology, 1991-96; contbr. chpts. to books, articles to profl. jours. Fellow ACP, Royal Coll. Physicians, Royal Australian Coll. Physicians; mem. Am. Motility Soc. (pres. 1994-96), Am. Soc. Clin. Investigation (emeritus), Gastroenterology Soc. Australia (hon.), Am. Gastroenterology Assn. Assn. Am. Physicians, Brit. Soc. Gastroenterology (hon.). Home: 1207 19th Ave NE Rochester MN 55906-4317 Office: St. Mary's Hosp Gastroenterology Unit 200 1st St SW Rochester MN 55905-0001 Personal E-Mail: DecimaSidney@aol.com.

**PHILLIPS, STACY D.,** lawyer; b. NYC, Sept. 5, 1958; d. Gerald F. and Francine Anne (Mentor) Phillips; m. Craig S. Bloomgarden, Apr. 21, 1985; 2 children. AB, Dartmouth Coll., 1980; JD, Columbia U., 1983. Cert.: Family Law Specialist, bar: Calif. 1984, US Dist. Ct. Ctrl. and So. Districts Calif., US Ct. Appeals 9th Cir. Law clk. to Hon. Edward Rafeedie US Dist. Ct., LA, 1983-84; assoc. Wyman, Bautzer, Rothman, Kuchel & Silbert, LA, 1984-85, Jaffe & Clemens, Beverly Hills, Calif., 1986—90; founding ptnr. Mannis & Phillips, LA, 1995—2000, Phillips Lerner & Lauzon LLP, LA, 2000—. Guest commentator various TV programs including Good Morning America, Hard Copy, Inside Edition; contbr. Divorce Mag., adv. bd.; bd. dirs. Legal Momentum (previously NOW Legal Def. and Edn. Fund); co-chair Calif. Leadership Coun. Bd. dirs. Vista del Mar Child and Family Services, Levitt & Quinn Family Law Ctr., Bnai Zion Found. Inc.; bd. trustees Alternative Living for the Aging. Named one of 50 Most Powerful Women in LA Law, LA Bus. Jour., 1998, Top 20 Attorneys Under 40 Years Old, LA Daily Jour., 1998, Top 50 Women Litigators in Calif., 2003; recipient Women of Action Award, Israel Cancer Rsch. Fund, 2000, Women of Achievement Award, Bnai Zion Found. Inc., 2001, Women Who Make a Difference Award, LA Bus. Jour., 2001, Patricia McClure Award, Asthma & Allergy Found. Am., 2001, Women of Achievement Award in Family Law and Mediation, Century City C. of C., 2001, 2002; grantee Policy Study Internship, Dartmouth U., 1978—78. Mem.: Beverly Hills Bar Assn. (mem. family law sect., mem. alternative dispute resolutions com.), LA Bar Assn. (mem. family law sect.), State Bar Calif. (mem. child custody and visitation com.), ABA (mem. family law sect.), Chancery Club of LA. Avocations: cooking, tennis. Office: Jaffe & Clemens 433 N Camden Dr 11th Fl Beverly Hills CA 90210

**PHILLIPS, STEVE,** computer company executive; arrived in U.S., 2001; BSEE with hons., Essex U. With Thorn EMI, 1984—96, Diageo, 1996—99; from v.p. info. tech. to sr. v.p., chief info. officer Gateway, Dublin, 1999—2003, sr. v.p. Poway, Calif., 2003—, chief info. officer, 2003—. Fellow: IEEE. Office: Gateway Inc 7565 Irvine Ctr Dr Irvine CA 92618-2930

**PHILLIPS, STONE,** television journalist; b. Texas City, Tex. married; 1 child. BA in Philosophy with honors, Yale Univ. Past prodr., reporter WXIA-TV, Atlanta; formerly with documentary unit Close-Up ABC News, assignment editor Washington, 1979—81, gen. assignment corr., 1982—86, corr. 20/20, 1986—92; prin. anchor Dateline NBC-TV, N.Y.C., 1992—; contbg. corr. MSNBC. Past remedial-reading tchr. Fulton County Juvenile Ct., Atlanta; substitute host Good Morning America, 1986; guest sports anchor World News Sunday, 1986; past substitute anchor NBC Nightly News, Today, Meet the Press. Named to Scholar Athlete Hall of Fame, Nat. Football Found.; recipient F. Gordon Brown award, Yale U., 1976, 3 Nat. Headliner awards for Outstanding Journalism, Overseas Press Club award, Nat. Assn. Black Journalists award, AMA award, Am. Psychol. Assn. award, B'nai B'rith award; NCAA Post-Grad. scholar. Office: NBC News-Dateline Rm 408 30 Rockefeller Plz New York NY 10112-0002

**PHILLIPS, SUSAN LESLIE,** writer; b. San Diego, May 3, 1954; d. Frederick Sherman Liepitz, Vera Mae Liepitz; m. Donald Lee Phillips; children: Adrienne, Wes. Writer, Long Beach, Calif., 1984—. Motivational spkr. Romance Writers Am., Orange, Calif., 1989—2001. Author (writing as Susan Phillips): (novels) Rapture's Legacy, 1989; author: (writing as Susan Leslie Liepitz) This Time Together, 1996; author: (writing as Susan Liepitz) That Wilder Man, 1997; author: (writing as Susan Leslie Liepitz) Mystic Memories, 1998; author: (writing as Gillian Doyle) Paranormal Suspense, 2005. Named Vol. of Yr., Orange County Chpt., Romance Writers Am., 1992; recipient Vera Kelleher award for Outstanding Svc., Long Beach Coun. Parent Participation Nursery Sch., 1983, Orange Blossom award for Outstanding Volunteerism, Orange County Chpt., Romance Writers Am., 1998, Daphne du Maurier award, 2003. Mem.: Writers' Guild Am., Am. Cetacean Soc. (chpt. sec. 2001—02), Romance Writers Am. (chpt. v.p. 1988—89, chpt. pres. 1989—90, chpt. v.p. 1992—93, chpt. treas. 2005—06), Long Beach Parent Participation Nursery Schs. Avocations: travel, interior decorating, landscape gardening, metaphysical studies. Business E-Mail: suephillips503@yahoo.com

**PHILLIPS, SUSAN MEREDITH,** academic administrator, economist; b. Richmond, Va., Dec. 23, 1944; d. William G. and Nancy (Meredith) Phillips. BA in Math., Agnes Scott Coll., 1967; MS in Fin. in Ins., La. State U., 1971, PhD in Fin. and Economics, 1973. Asst. prof. La. State U., 1973—74, U. Iowa, 1974—78; econ. fellow Directorate of Econ. and Policy Rsch., SEC, 1976—78; assoc. prof. fin. dept. U. Iowa, 1978—83, assoc. v.p. fin. & univ. services, 1979—81; commr. Commodity Futures Trading Commn., 1981—83, chmn., 1983—87; prof. fin. dept., v.p. fin. and univ. svcs. U. Iowa, Iowa City, 1987—91; bd. govs. Fed. Res. Sys., Washington, 1991—98; dean Sch. of Bus., prof. fin. dept. George Washington U., Washington, 1998—. Trustee Fin. Acctg. Found., Norwalk, 2006—; bd. dirs. Chgo. Bd. Options Exch., Nat. Futures Assn., Kroger Co., State Farm Mutual Auto. Co. Co-author (with J. Richard Zecher): The SEC and the Public Interest; contbr. articles to profl. jours. Fellow Brookings Econ. Policy fellow, 1976—77. Office: George Washington U Sch Bus Ste 660 2201 G St NW Washington DC 20052 Business E-Mail: gwsbdean@gwu.edu

**PHILLIPS, TARI,** professional basketball player; b. Mar. 6, 1969; Student, U. Ga.; grad., Ctrl. Fla. U., 1991. With Orlando Miracle Women's Basketball Team, Fla., 1999, N.Y. Liberty, N.Y.C., NY, 2000—; player USA Basketball Women's Nat. Team, 2002, 2004. Named Most Improved Player, WNBA, 2000; named to All-WNBA Second Team, 2002; recipient Gold Medal, World Championships, 2002. Office: New York Liberty 2 Penn Plz 14th Fl New York NY 10121

**PHILLIPS, TEDDY STEVE, SR.,** conductor, saxophone player, production company executive; b. Chgo., June 15, 1917; s. Steve and Kaliope Phillips; children: Jody, Teddy. Saxophone player with big bands, across country, 1940-45; staff musician Radio Sta. CBS, Chgo., 1944-45; condr. Teddy Phillips Orch., across country, 1945-55, 57-62; prin. Teddy Phillips Show, Sta WBKB-TV-ABC, Chgo., 1956-57; condr. Tedd Phillips and Orch. Ambassador Hotel, L.A., 1962-80, Flamingo Hotel, Las Vegas, 1962-80, Statler Hotels, Aragon Ballroom, Hilton Hotels, Chgo.; dir. Guy Lombardo Orch. and Royal Canadians, 1980—. Pres. P&M Prodns., Woodland Hills, Calif., 1976—, Heads Hallmark Ltd.; pres. Encore Records, Encore Mgmt. Ltd.; sec./treas. Internat. Country Music Fanfest '94, L.A. TV prodr. Great Concert in the Sky; record prodr.; writer Do the Camel Hump?, Wishin; writer, arranger, condr. on tour Great Concert in the Sky, 1986—; prodr., condr., writer Lion and the Turtle; pres. Nostalgic Records. With U.S. Army, 1940-41. Recipient Gould Tech. Achievement award, Spl. award Rotary, Medal of Honor Heart Found., cert. Optimists Club, Musicians Union, Masons. Greek Orthodox. Home and Office: PO Box 8328 Calabasas CA 91372-8328

**PHILLIPS, TERRY LEMOINE,** investment advisor; b. Washington, July 27, 1938; s. Clifford LeMoin and Dorothy Louise (Schuman) P.; m. Lynne Ann Bruce, Aug. 12, 1962; children: Susan Rae, Stephen Kirk. BS, Purdue U., 1964, MS, 1966. CPA Ind., pers. fin. specialist, Ind. Assoc. program leader, data processing Purdue U. Lab. Applications of Remote Sensing, West Lafayette, Ind., 1966-71, program leader, 1971-74, dep. dir., 1974-85; mgr. personal computer oper. Purdue U Computing Ctr., West Lafayette, 1986-92, adminstr. Continuing Edn. Ctr., West Lafayette, 1992-2000; investment advisor rep. Diesslin & Assocs., West Lafayette, 2000—. Cons. AID, Computer Scis. Corp. Scoutmaster, explorer advisor Boy Scouts Am., bd. dirs. Sagamore Coun.; sports coord. youth sports Battleground, Ind.; elder, deacon, trustee, treas. Presbyn. Ch.; bd. dirs. Tippecanoe chpt. Am. Diabetes Assn. With USN, 1956-59. Recipient Most Innovative Idea award Am. Diabetes Assn., 1987. Mem. IEEE (sr.), AICPA, Assn. Inst. for Certification of Computer Profls. (cert. in date practice), Assn. Computing Machinery, Data Processing Mgmt. Assn. (internat. dir., co-founder, v.p., pres., treas. Sagamore chpt., Individual Performance award 1983, 85, 88), Rotary (bd. dirs., treas.), Tau Beta Pi, Eta Kappa Nu. Office: Diesslin & Assocs 2639 Yeager Rd West Lafayette IN 47906 Home: 3711 Brixford Dr West Lafayette IN 47906-8705 Office Phone: 765-497-7744. E-mail: terry@diesslin.com, tl.phillips@insightbb.com

**PHILLIPS, THEODORE LOCKE,** radiologist, educator; b. Phila., June 4, 1933; s. Harry Webster and Margaret Amy (Locke) Phillips; m. Joan Cappello, June 23, 1956; children: Margaret, John, Sally. BSc, Dickinson Coll., 1955; MD, U. Pa., 1959. Intern Western Res. U., Cleve., 1960; resident in therapeutic radiology U. Calif., San Francisco, 1963, clin. instr., 1963—65, asst. prof. radiation oncology, 1965—68, assoc. prof., 1968—70, prof., 1970—, chmn. dept. radiation oncology, 1973—98. Rsch. radiobiologist U.S. Naval Radiologic Def. Lab., San Francisco, 1963—65; rsch. physician Lawrence Berkeley Lab. Contbr. numerous articles to profl. publs. With USNR, 1963—65. Grantee, Nat. Cancer Inst., 1970—99. Mem.: Inst. Medicine, No. Calif. Radiation Oncology Assn., Radium Soc., Radiation Rsch. Soc. (pres. 1977), Am. Coll. Radiology, Calif. Med. Assn., Am. Assn. Cancer Rsch., N.Am. Hyperthermia Soc. (pres. 1994), Radiol. Soc. N.Am., Am. Soc. Clin. Oncology, Am. Soc. Therapeutic Radiology and Oncology (pres. 1984), Alpha Omega Alpha, Phi Beta Kappa. Republican. Office: U Calif San Francisco Dept Radiation Oncology 1600 Divisidero St ste H1031 San Francisco CA 94143-1708

**PHILLIPS, THOMAS EDWORTH, JR.,** investment company executive, consultant; b. Danville, Va., July 7, 1944; s. Thomas Edworth Sr. and Jean (Worley) P.; m. Claudia Mitchell, July 23, 1966; children: Kelly Marie, Melissa Joyce. BS in Econs., Va. Tech., 1966; cert. in investments, N.Y. Inst. Fin., 1969; MS in Bus., Va. Commonwealth U., 1973; postgrad., U. Pa., 1989.

Cert. investment mgmt. analyst; registered investment adviser. Edn. coord. Prince William County Schs., Manassas, Va., 1966-67; investment broker Conrad and Co., Richmond, Va., 1967-68; investment exec. UBS Paine Webber, Inc., Richmond, 1968—, divisional v.p., 1980-99, sr. v.p. and prime cons., 2000—; registered prin. NY Stock Exch., Nat. Assn. Securities Dealers, 1987—. Access program nat. com. UBS Paine Webber, N.Y.C., Inc., 1989-90, mem. dir.'s coun., 1987-88, managed accounts nat. adv. bd., 1991-93; mem. mut. fund Nat. Assn. Coun., 1996—, pres.' council, 1997—; bd. dirs. Madison Group, Inc., Richmond, Meadowbrook Assocs., Inc., Richmond; speaker in field. Bd. dirs. Va. Non-Profit Housing Coalition, pres., 1992—; chmn. bd. deacons. Mt. Olivet Ch., Hanover, Va., 1984-85; trustee Hanover Acad., Ashland, Va., 1980-84; mem. alumni bd. Va. Commonwealth U., Richmond. Rotary Found. fellow, 1989. Mem. Investment Mgmt. Cons. Assn., Capital Soc., Melody Hills Property Owners Assn. (bd. dirs. 1980—), Va. Tech. Alumni Assn., Va. Commonwealth U. Alumni Assn., Rotary, Bull and Bear Club, Omicron Delta Epsilon. Avocations: horses, tennis, golf. Office: UBS PRIME Consulting Group 1021 E Cary St Ste 1800 Richmond VA 23219-4000 Home: 13464 Lakeview Pl Ashland VA 23005 Office Phone: 804-644-4111. Business E-Mail: tom.phillips@ubs.com.

**PHILLIPS, THOMAS J., JR.,** accountant, educator; b. Shreveport, La., May 8, 1954; s. Thomas J. and Elma S. Phillips; m. Myla D. Davis, Feb. 4, 1955; children: Trenton J., Tyler J. BS, U. La. Lafayette, 1975; MS, La. State U., Baton Rouge, 1977; PhD, Ga. State U., Atlanta, 1984. CPA La., 1979. Acct., cons., expert witness Various, Lafayette, Baton Rouge, Shreveport, and New Orleans, La., 1973–2006; instr. Acctg. Dept. Southeastern La. U., Hammond, 1979—80; tchg. fellow Ga. State U., 1980—81; asst. prof., assoc. prof. La. State U. Shreveport, 1984—87; asst. prof., assoc. prof., prof. La. Tech U., Ruston, 1987—95, dir. and KPMG prof., 1995—. Contbr. articles to academic and profl. jours. Recipient Outstanding Contbr. Award, Inst. Internal Auditors, 1988; fellow Ctrl. Bank Endowed Prof., La. Tech U., 1995—2000, KPMG Endowed Prof., 2000—. Mem.: AICPA, Inst. Mgmt. Accts. (Merit Cert. for Article 1993—94), Am. Acctg. Assn., Soc. La. CPA (pres. Shreveport chpt. 1991—92, Outstanding Educator award 1990). Mem. Ch. Of Christ. Avocations: travel, fishing. Office: La Tech U Railroad Ave 123 CAB Ruston LA 71272

**PHILLIPS, THOMAS JOHN,** lawyer; b. Mpls., Nov. 24, 1948; BA, U. Minn., 1970; JD, U. Utah, 1973; LLM in Taxation, NYU, 1974. Bar: Wis. 1974. Ptnr. Quarles & Brady, Milw., 1991—. Co-author: Wisconsin Limited Liability Company Forms and Practice Manual, 1999. Mem. ABA (corp. tax com. tax sect.), Wis. Bar Assn., Profl. Inst. Taxation, Mil. Tax Club, North Shore Country Club, Order of Coif. Avocations: gardening, golf, hockey, jogging, racquetball. Office: 411 E Wisconsin Ave Ste 2040 Milwaukee WI 53202-4497 Office Phone: 414-277-5831. Business E-Mail: tjp@quarles.com.

**PHILLIPS, THOMAS ROYAL,** lawyer, former state supreme court chief justice; b. Dallas, Oct. 23, 1949; s. George S. and Marguerite (Andrews) P.; m. Lyn Bracewell, June 26, 1982; 1 son, Daniel Austin Phillips; 1 stepson, Thomas R. Kirkham. BA, Baylor U., 1971; JD, Harvard U., 1974; LLD (hon.), Tex. Tech. U., 1997; DHL (hon.), St. Edwards U., 1998. Bar: Tex. 1974; cert. in civil trial law Tex. Bd. Legal Specialization. Briefing atty. Supreme Ct. Tex., Austin, 1974-75; assoc. Baker Botts LLP, Houston, 1975-81, ptnr. Austin, 2005—; judge 280th Dist. Ct., Houston, 1981-88; chief justice Supreme Ct. Tex., Austin, 1988—2004; Spurgeon E. Bell disting. vis. prof. South Tex. Coll. Law, Houston, 2004—05; disting. prof. Sch. Law So. Meth. U., Dallas, 2004. Com. on fed.-state rels. Jud. Conf. U.S., 1990-96, Conf. Chief Justice, 1988—, pres. 1997-98; chair Tex. Jud. Dists. Bd., 1988-2004; mem. Tex. Jud. Coun., 1988-2004, chair, 1998-2004; mem. State Judges Mass Tort Litig. Com., 1991-96, Carter-Baker Commn. Fed. Election Reform, 2005; bd. dirs. Elmo B. Hunter Citizens Ctr. for Jud. Selection, 1992-94, Ctr. Am. Internat. Law., South Tex. Coll. Law; chair Nat. Mass Tort Conf. Planning Com., 1993-94; jud. bd. commn. Instns. of Democracy, Annenberg Found., 2003-04; mem. major infractions com. Divsn. 1 NCAA, 2006—; bd. dirs. Inst. Jud. Adminstrn. Bd. adv. Ctr. for Pub. Policy Dispute Resolution, U. Tex. Law Sch., 1993—; planning com. Tex. Hist. Commn., 2005-; adv. dir. Austin Habitat for Humanity, 1993-96; bd. dirs. Bastrop County Hist. Soc., 2005-. Recipient Outstanding Young Lawyer award Houston Young Lawyers Assn., 1986, Outstanding Tex. Leader award John Ben Sheppard Pub. Leadership Forum, 1989, award of excellence in govt. Tex. C. of C., 1992, Disting. Svc. award Nat. Ctr. for State Cts., 1999, Rosewood Gavel award St. Mary's U. Sch. Law, 2002, Price Daniel award for disting. pub. svc. Baylor U., 2004, Champion Children award Dallas (Tex.) CASA, 2004, Professionalism in Law award Burton Found., 2004, Harry L. Carrico award for Judicial Innovation Nat. Ctr. for State Cts., 2005; named Appellate Judge of Yr., Tex. Assn. Civil Trial and Appellate Specialists, 1992-93, Disting. Alumnus, Baylor U., 1998. Mem. ABA (task force lawyers polit. contbns. 1997-98, com. on 21st Century judiciary, 2002-03), Am. Law Inst. (advisor Fed. Jud. Code Project 1996-2001), Nat. Ctr. for State Ctrs. (chair, bd. dirs. 1997-98), State Bar Tex. (chmn. pattern jury charges IV com. 1985-87, vice chmn. adminstrn. justice com. 1986-87), Am. Judicature Soc. (bd. dirs. 1989-95, 99-2005, exec. bd. 1995-96), Tex. Philol. Soc., Houston Philol. Soc., Houston Bar Assn., Travis County Bar Assn., Bastrop County Bar Assn., Order of Coif (hon.). Republican. Episcopalian. Office: Baker Botts LLP 1500 San Jacinto Ctr 98 San Jacinto Blvd Austin TX 78701 Office Phone: 512-322-2500. Personal E-Mail: cj@tomphillips.com. Business E-Mail: thomas.phillips@bakerbotts.com.

**PHILLIPS, THOMAS WADE,** judge, lawyer; b. Oneida, Tenn., July 6, 1943; s. W.T. and Lucille (Lewallen) P.; m. Dorothy Mills, Jan. 2, 1971; children: Lori Ann, Wade Thomas. BA, Berea (Ky.) Coll., 1965; JD, Vanderbilt U., 1969; LLM in Labor Law, George Washington U., 1978. Bar: Tenn. 1969, U.S. Supreme Ct. 1972, U.S. Ct. Appeals (6th cir.) 1980. Assoc., ptnr. Baker, Worthington, Crosley, Stansberry & Wolfe, Huntsville, Tenn., 1973—77; ptnr. Phillips & Williams, P.C., Oneida, Tenn., 1977—91; U.S. magistrate judge ea. dist., Tenn., 1991—2002, U.S. dist. judge Tenn., 2002—. County atty. Scott County, Huntsville, 1976-91; city atty. Town of Oneida, 1978-91. Capt. JAGC, U.S. Army, 1969-73. Mem. ABA, Tenn. Bar Assn. (ho. of dels. 1989-91), Scott County Bar Assn. Office: US District Court Howard H Baker Jr Courtho 800 Market St Knoxville TN 37902-2327

**PHILLIPS, TIKERA MONIQUE,** elementary school educator; d. Tina E. Phillips. MS in Elem. Edn., LI U., Brookville, NY, 1995–2004. Customer rels. coord. Cablevision/Lightpath, Jericho, NY, 2000—04; tchr. Allen Christian Sch., Jamaica, NY, 2004—. Tutor First Bapt. Ch. Westbury, NY, 1998—2005. Baptist.

**PHILLIPS, TODD,** film director, film producer; b. Bklyn., 1970; Attended, NYU. Director, prodr.: (films) Hated, 1994; Frat House, 1998; Bittersweet Motel, 2000; dir., writer, actor Road Trip, 2000; dir., prodr., writer, actor Old School, 2003; dir., writer Starsky & Hutch, 2004; exec. prodr.: All the King's Men, 2006; actor: (TV series) Public School, 2004. Office: 8439 Sunset Blvd 1st Fl Los Angeles CA 90069 Office Phone: 323-822-4300. E-mail: toodstf@aol.com.*

**PHILLIPS, VICKI L.,** school system administrator; b. Marion, Ind., Jan. 15, 1958; d. Denver Phillips and Vivian (Burnette) Fuqua. BS in Edn., Western Ky. U., 1980, MA in Psychology, 1987; doctoral student, U. Ky., 1988—; EdD in instrml. leadership, U. of Lincoln, Eng., 2002. Dir. devel. tng. dept. Panorama, Bowling Green, Ky., 1978—80; tchr. learning and behavior disorders Simpson County Bd. Edn., 1981—85; exceptional child cons. Ky. Dept. Edn. Office Edn. for Exceptional Children, 1986—90; chief exec. asst. to edn. commr. Ky. Dept. of Edn., 1986—93; dep. dir./chief of staff Nat. Alliance for Restructuring Edn., Wash., 2003—95; dir. Greater Phila. First Partnership for Reform; exec. dir. Children Achieving Challenge, 1995—98; supt. Sch. Dist. of Lancaster, 1998—2003; sec. of edn. Pa. Dept. Edn., Harrisburg, 2003—04; supt. Portland Pub. Schools, Oreg., 2004—. Mem. ASCD, Nat. Coun. for Exceptional Children, Coun. for Behavior

Disorders, Nat. Assn. for Sch. Psychologists, Ky. Assn. Sch. Adminstrs., Ky. Assn. for Psychology in the Schs., Ky. Assn. for Family-Based Svcs., Ky. Families for Family-Based Svcs., Ky. Families as Allies. Office: 501 N Dixon St Portland OR 97227-1804

**PHILLIPS, WALTER MILLS, III,** psychologist, educator; b. N.Y.C., Sept. 29, 1947; s. Walter Mills and Grace Mary (Mullen) P.; m. Anne Marie Boyle, July 3, 1971; children: Jonathan, Elizabeth. BS, Fordham U., 1970; MA, U. S.D., 1973, PhD, 1975. Lic. clin. psychologist, Conn.; diplomate Am. Coll. Forensic Examiners, Am. Bd. Disability Evaluators, Am. Bd. Disability Analysts; cert. sr. disability analyst. Adolescent resident counselor Hawthorne (N.Y.) Cedar Knolls Sch., 1970—71; NIMH tng. fellow, 1971—75; clin. psychology intern Inst. of Living, Hartford, Conn., 1974—75, clin. staff psychologist, 1975—79, sr. staff psychologist, 1977—82, asst. dir. dept. clin. psychology, 1980—82, dir. clin. psychology tng., 1980—82; co-dir. outpatient psychiatry U. Conn., Farmington, 1982—88; asst. prof. psychiatry, dir. psychiatry evaluation svc. U. Conn. Health Ctr., 1982—88, dir. Anxiety Rsch. and Treatment Ctr., 1985—88; pvt. practice psychotherapy Hartford, 1976—; dir. adolescent/young adult svc. Grandview Psychiat. Resource Ctr., Waterbury, Conn., 1988—90; dir. psychology Waterbury Hosp., 1990—98; pvt. practice clin. psychology Waterbury and Middlebury, Conn., 1990—. Asst. clin. prof. psychiatry Sch. Medicine Yale U., New Haven, Conn., 1988—; mem. psychology exec. com. Sch. Medicine Yale U., New Haven, 1990-98. Contbr. articles to profl. jours. Bd. dirs. Mem. APA, Am. Psychotherapy Assn. (diplomate), Conn. Psychol. Assn., Soc. Psychotherapy Rsch., Soc. Personality Assessment, Conn. Hosp. Assn. (chmn., dir. psychology conf. 1992-96), N.Y. Acad. Scis., Sigma Xi. Office: 415 Middlebury Rd Middlebury CT 06762 Office Phone: 203-758-8333. E-mail: phillips.walter@comcast.net.

**PHILLIPS, WALTER RAY,** law educator; b. Democrat, N.C., Mar. 19, 1932; s. Walter Yancey and Bonnie (Wilson) P.; m. Patricia Ann Jones, Aug. 28, 1954; children: Bonnie Ann, Rebecca Lee. AB, U. N.C., 1954; LL.B. Emory U., 1957, LL.M., 1962, JD, 1970; postgrad., Yale U., 1965-66. Bar: Ga. 1957, Fla. 1958, Tex. 1969, Mo. 2001, U.S. Supreme Ct. 1962. With firm Jones, Adams, Paine & Foster, West Palm Beach, Fla., 1957-58; law clk. to chief judge U.S. Dist. Ct., Atlanta, 1958-59; with firm Powell, Goldstein, Frazer & Murphy, Atlanta, 1959-60; bankruptcy judge U.S. Cts., Atlanta, 1960-64; prof. law U.N.D., 1964-65; teaching fellow Yale U., 1965-66; prof. law Fla. State U., 1966-68, Tex. Tech. U., 1968-71; Disting. vis. prof. law Baylor U., 1971; atty. Commn. on Bankruptcy Laws of U.S., Washington, 1971-72; dep. dir., adminstrv. officer, 1972-73; prof. Sch. Law, U. Ga., 1973-2000, assoc. dean, 1975-83, acting dean, 1976, Joseph Henry Lumpkin prof., 1977-94, also dir. univ's self. study, 1978, Herman E. Talmadge prof., 1994-2000. Chapman disting. vis. prof. law U. Okla., 1985-86; vis. prof. law U. Okla., 1990, U. Mo., Columbia, 1993, 94, 2001—; reporter Gov.'s Legislation for Ga., 1973; v.p., dir. Killearn Estates, Inc.; mem. Conf. on Consumer Fin. Law; prof. London Law Consortium, 1999. Author: Florida Law and Practice, 1960, Encyclopedia of Georgia Law, 1962, Seminar for Newly Appointed Referees in Bankruptcy, 1964, Damages: Cases and Materials, 1967, (with James William Moore) Debtors' and Creditors' Rights, Cases and Material, 1966, 5th edit., 1979, The Law of Debtor Relief, 1969, 2d edit., 1972, supplement, 1975, (with James William Moore) Rule 6, Moore's Federal Practice, 1969, Adjustment of Debts for Individuals, 1979, 2d edit., 1981, supplement, 1982, 84, 85, Liquidation Under the Bankruptcy Code, 3d edit., 1988, supplement, 1989, 90, 91, 92, 93, 94, Cases and Materials on Corporate Reorganization, 1983, 3d edit., 1986, 4th edit., 1988, 5th edit., 1990, 7th edit., 1996, 8th edit., 1998, Family Farmer and Adjustment of Individual Debts, 1987, supplement, 1988, 89, 90, 91, 92, 93, 94, A Primer of Chapters 12 and 13 of the Bankruptcy Code, 1995. Bd. dirs. Lubbock Day Nurseries, 1969, pres., 1970-71. Served with USAF, 1950. Mem. ATLA, ABA (consumer bankruptcy com. 1973—, chmn. 1986-90), Fed. Bar Assn., Fla. Bar Assn., Tex. Bar Assn., Western Circuit Bar Assn., Ga. Bar Assn. (vice chmn. publs. com. 1977-89, com. on profl. responsibility 1983—2002), Mo. Bar Assn., Am. Judicature Soc., Phi Alpha Delta (chief tribune) Baptist. Home: 3800 Wakefield Dr Columbia MO 65203-5630 Office Phone: 573-882-0270. Business E-Mail: phillipswr@missouri.edu.

**PHILLIPS, WANDA CHARITY,** secondary school educator, writer; b. Gettysburg, Pa., Apr. 1, 1947; d. Roy Homer and Frances Marie (White) Kuykendall; m. James E. Phillips; children: Jenny, Peter, Micah. BS in Secondary Edn., Shippensburg U., Pa., 1968; cert. elem. edn., Grand Canyon Coll., 1973; MA in Adminstrn., No. Ariz. U., Flagstaff, 1993. Tchr. Littlestown H.S., Pa., 1969, Phoenix Indian Sch., 1971-72, Peoria Sch. Dist., Ariz., 1973—99; author ISHA Enterprises, Inc., Scottsdale, Ariz., 1985—. Ednl. seminar presenter ISHA Enterprises, Scottsdale, Ariz., 1986—, Assn. Christian Sch. Internat., Calif., 1988—. Author: Easy Grammar, 1986, Daily Grams: Guided Review Aiding Mastery Skills, 1986, Daily Grams: Guided Review Aiding Mastery Skills for Grade 3, 2003, Grade 4, 2003, Grade 5, 2003, Easy Writing, 1991, Daily Grams: Guided Teaching and Review for Grades 2 and 3, 1992, Easy Grammar, Grades 5 and 6, 1994 (children's book) My Mother Doesn't Like to Cook, 1993, Easy Grammar Plus, 1995, Easy Grammar: Grades 4 and 5, 1996, Easy Grammar: Grades 3 and 4, 1998. Daily Grams: Grades 3, 4, 5, 6, and 7, 2002. Raspberry Cottage Tearoom Ministries. Mem.: Nat. Trust for Hist. Preservation, Paradise Valley Women's Club. Office: ISHA Enterprises Inc Easy Grammar Systems PO Box 25970 Scottsdale AZ 85255 Office Phone: 480-502-9454. E-mail: info@easygrammar.com.

**PHILLIPS, WARREN HENRY,** publishing executive; b. June 28, 1926; s. Abraham and Juliette (Rosenberg) P.; m. Barbara Anne Thomas, June 16, 1951; children: Lisa, Leslie, Nina. AB, Queens Coll., 1947, LHD (hon.), 1987; JD (hon.), U. Portland, 1973; LHD (hon.), Pace U., 1982, L.I. U., 1987. Copyreader Wall St. Jour., 1947-48, fgn. corr. Germany, 1949-50, chief London bur., 1950-51, fgn. editor, 1951-53, news editor, 1953-54, mng. editor Midwest edit., 1954-57, mng. editor, 1957-65, pub., 1975-88; exec. editor Dow Jones & Co., 1965-70, v.p., gen. mgr., 1970-71, exec. v.p., 1972, editl. dir., 1971-88, pres., 1972-79, CEO, 1975-90, also bd. dirs., past chmn., 1972-97; co-pub. Bridge Works Pub. Co., 1992—. Copyreader European edit. Stars and Stripes, 1945-46; past chmn. Am. Coun. Edn. for Journalism, 1971-73; mem. Pulitzer Prize Bd., 1977-87; adj. faculty Grad. Sch. Journalism, Columbia U., 1992, John F. Kennedy Sch. Govt., Harvard Univ., 1992. Author: (with Robert Keatley) China: Behind the Mask, 1973. Trustee Columbia U., 1980-93, trustee emeritus, 1993—; mem. vis. com. John F. Kennedy Sch. Govt., Harvard U., 1984-90, 92-97; corp. adv. bd. Queens Coll., 1986-90, found. bd. trustees, 1990-97, trustee emeritus, 1997—. Named one of 10 Outstanding Young Men in U.S., U.S. Jaycees, 1958; inductee Info. Industry Assn.'s Hall of Fame, 1984. Mem. Am. Newspaper Pubs. Assn. (bd. dirs. 1976-84), Am. Soc. Newspaper Editors (pres. 1975-76), Bridgehampton Club, River Club. Office: Bridge Works Publ PO Box 1798 Bridgehampton NY 11932-1798

**PHILLIPS, WILLIAM DANIEL,** physicist; b. Wilkes-Barre, Pa., Nov. 5, 1948; s. William Cornelius and Mary Catherine (Savine) Phillips. BS, Juniata Coll., Huntingdon, Pa., 1970; PhD, MIT, 1976. Rsch. asst. MIT, Cambridge, 1970—76, Chaim Weizmann fellow, 1976—78; physicist Nat. Inst. Standards and Tech., Gaithersburg, Md., 1978—90, group leader, 1990—95, fellow, 1995—. Vis. prof. Ecole Normale Superieure, Paris, 1989—90; disting. prof. physics U. Md., College Park, 1991—. Editor (author): Laser Manipulation of Atoms and Ions, 1992; contbr. articles to profl. jours. Co-recipient Nobel Prize for physics, 1997, Schawlow prize in laser sci., APS, 1998; named Outstanding Young Scientist, Md. Acad. Sci., 1982; recipient Sci. Achievement award, Wash. Acad. Scis., 1982, Silver medal, Dept. Commerce, 1983, Gold medal, U.S. Dept. Commerce, 1993, Albert A. Michelson medal, Franklin Inst., 1996, Gold medal, Pa. Soc., 1999. Fellow: Am. Acad. Arts and Scis., Optical Soc. Am., Am. Phys. Soc.; mem.: NAS, Pontifical Acad. Sci. (academician 2004), Soc. Physics Students, Sigma Xi. Achievements include demonstrated laser cooling of atomic beams; electromagnetic trapping of neutral atoms; discovery of sub-doppler laser cooling; produced submicrokelvin 3D kinetic temperatures. Office: Nat Inst Stds & Tech 216 B123 100 Bureau Dr Stop 8424 Gaithersburg MD 20899-0003 Office Phone: william.phillips@nist.gov.*

**PHILLIPS, WILLIAM E.,** advertising agency executive; b. Chgo., Jan. 7, 1930; s. William E. and Alice N. Phillips; children: Michael, Tom, Sarah; m. Barbara Smith, Nov. 27, 1997. BS, Cornell U., 1951; MBA, Northwestern U., 1955. Brand mgr. Procter & Gamble, Cin., 1955-59; with Ogilvy & Mather, N.Y.C., 1959-90; CEO Ogilvy Group, 1981-88; exec. in residence, prof. Johnson Grad. Sch. Mgmt. Cornell U., 1989-90. Bd. dirs. Gen. Housewares, Sun Glass Hut, Inc., Alliance Nat. Office Ctrs. Chmn. emeritus Outward Bound Internat.; chair Outdoor Edn., Cornell U., 1990—; co-chair Cayuga Soc. for Planned Giving at Cornell U.; trustee emeritus Cornell U.; trustee Internat. Tennis Hall of Fame, Newport, R.I., Florence Griswold Mus., Old Lyme, Conn., 1991—. Lt. (j.g.) USN, 1951-54, Korea/Pacific/Mediterranean. Recipient Disting. Svc. award, Singapore Outward Bound, 1997, Kurt Hahn award, Outward Bound, 1998, Rhodes Exemplary Alumni Svc. award, Cornell U., 2001. Mem. Old Lyme Country Club, Am. Alpine Club, Explorers Club, Cornell Club, Univ. Club, Naval Mil. Club (London), Achilles Club N.Y.C. (bd. dirs.). Home: 200 N Cove Rd Old Saybrook CT 06475-2537

**PHILLIPS, WILLIAM ROBERT,** physician; b. Wash., Apr. 26, 1950; BA, U. Wash., 1971, MD, MPH, U. Wash., 1975. Diplomate Nat. Bd. Med. Examiners, Am. Bd. Family Practice, Am. Bd. Preventive Medicine; lic. physician and surgeon, Wash. Resident family practice Providence Med. Ctr., Seattle, 1975-78; resident preventive medicine U. Wash. Sch. Pub. Health & Cmty. Medicine, Seattle, 1976-79; vis. prof. U. Auckland, New Zealand, 1979, U. Tasmania, Hobart, Australia, 1979, U. Zimbabwe, Harare, 1993; clin. prof. family medicine U. Wash., Seattle, 1994—. Chief staff Ballard Cmty. Hosp., Seattle, 1985, chief family practice, 1984. Sr. assoc. editor Annals of Family Medicine, 2001—; Contbr. articles to profl. jours. Bd. trustees Ballard Cmty. Hosp., Seattle, 1985. Recipient USPHS primary care policy fellowship, 1995; named Family Physician of the Yr. Wash. Acad. Family Physicians, 1990. Fellow Am. Acad. Family Physicians (Mead Johnson award 1976, Warner-Chilcott award 1979), Wash. Acad. Family Physicians (Family Physician of Yr. 1999), Am. Coll. Preventive Medicine; mem. N.Am. Primary Care Rsch. Group (pres., rsch. awards), Soc. Tchrs. of Family Medicine. Office: Univ Washington Dept Family Medicine Box 356390 Seattle WA 98195-6390

**PHILLIPS, WINFRED MARSHALL,** university administrator, mechanical engineer, educator, biomedical researcher; b. Richmond, Va., Oct. 7, 1940; s. Claude Marshall and Gladys Marian (Barden) P.; children: Stephen, Sean. BSME, Va. Poly. Inst., 1963; MA in Engring., U. Va., 1966, DSc, 1968. Mech. engr. U.S. Naval Weapons Lab., Dahlgren, Va., 1963; NSF trainee, tchg. and rsch. asst. dept. aerospace engring. U. Va., Charlottesville, 1963—67, rsch. scientist, 1966—67; asst. prof. dept. aerospace engring. Pa. State U., University Park, 1968-74, from assoc. prof. to prof., 1974—80, assoc. dean rsch. Coll. Engring., 1979—80; head Sch. Mech. Engring. Purdue U., West Lafayette, Ind., 1980-88; dean Coll. Engring. U. Fla., Gainesville, 1988-99, assoc. v.p. engring., 1989—99, v.p. rsch. and Don and Ruth Eckis prof. biomed. engring., 1999—. Bd. dir. Wachovia Bank, Gainesville; vis. prof. U. Paris, 1976—77; adv. com. Nimbus Corp., 1985—90, Hong Kong U. Sci. and Tech., 1990—93, AvMed Inc.; co-founder, v.p. CEO Inc., 1990—; acad. adv. coun. Indsl. Rsch. Inst., 1991—96; sci. adv. com. Electric Power Rsch. Inst., 1994—99; vice-chmn. Southeastern Coalition for Minorities in Engring., 1995—2000, chmn., 2001—04; internat. revs. for univs. in Saudi Arabia, Russia, Netherlands, Kuwait, Mexico, China, France Accreditation Bd. on Engring. and Tech., 1995—; chair coun., bd. dirs., mem. exec. com. Oak Ridge Associated Univs., 2002—05; mem. U.S. Pres.'s Commn. on Nat. Medal of Sci., 2003—. Sect. editor Am. Soc. Artificial Internal Organs Jour., 1985-99; contbr. over 175 articles to profl. jours., chpts. to books. Mem. Ind. Boiler and Pressure Vessel Code Bd., 1981—88; bd. dirs. Ctrl. Pa. Heart Assn., 1974—80, U. Fla. Found., 1989—91, 1995—2001. Named Disting. Hoosier Ind., 1987, Sagamore of the Wabash, 1988; recipient Career Rsch. award, NIH, 1974—78, NIH Surgery and Bioengring. Study sect., 1988—91, Fla. High Tech. and Industry Coun., 1990—94, Nat. Engring. award, Am. Assn. Engr. Socs., 2000, Linton Grinter award, 2000, Global Messenger award, Southeastern Consortium for Minorities in Engring., 2003. Fellow AAAS, AIAA, ASEE (vice chair 2001-02, chmn. bd. 2002—, Lamme award 2003), ASME (sr. v.p. edn. 1986-88, bd. dirs. 1995-2000, pres. 1998-99, Dedicated Svc. award 2001, Ralph Coates Roe medal 2005), NY Acad. Scis., Am. Astron. Soc., Am. Inst. Med. and Biol. Engring. (founding fellow, chair coll. fellows 1994-95, pres. 1996-97), Am. Soc. Engring. Edn. (past chmn. long range planning soc. awards 1990-92, chair chmn. engring. deans coun. 1991-93, chair 1993—, bd. dirs. 1994-98, 1st v.p. 1994-95, pres. 1996-97), Royal Soc. Arts, Biomed. Engring. Soc., Am. Soc. Artificial Internal Organs (trustee 1982-90, sec.-treas. 1986-87, pres. 1988-89, adv. bd. 1998—); mem. Nat. Assn. State Univs. and Land-Grant Colls. (com. quality of engring. edn.), Univ. Programs in Computer-Aided Engring., Design and Mfg. (bd. dirs. 1985-91), Am. Phys. Soc., Internat. Soc. Biotheology, Fla. Engring. Soc., Cosmos Club, Fla. Blue Key, Rotary (pres. Lafayette 1987-88), Sigma Xi, Phi Kappa Phi, Phi Tau Sigma, Sigma Gamma Tau, Tau Beta Pi (eminent engr.). Achievements include research in artificial heart pumps; reentry aerodynamics; blood rheology; modeling blood flow; fluid dynamics of artificial hearts; use of smooth blood contacting surface; prosthetic valve fluid dynamics; laser Doppler studies of unsteady biofluid dynamics. Home: 4140 NW 44th Ave Gainesville FL 32606-4518 Office: U Fla Rsch and Grad Programs 223 Grinter Hall Gainesville FL 32611 Office Phone: 352-392-9271. Business E-Mail: wphil@ufl.edu.

**PHILLIPS, WINIFRED PATRICIA,** radio producer, composer; b. Mobile, Ala., Apr. 13, 1972; d. Winifred Waldron Phillips. BA summa cum laude in Comms., Kean U., 1994. Composer, prodr., actress, writer Nat. Pub. Radio, Washington, 1992—2002; composer, prodr., actress, writer Radio Tales XM Satellite Radio Dramas, Washington, 2002—; owner music and audio prodn. co. Gens. Prodns.; composer Take Two Interactive, NYC, 2005—06. Composer Sony Computer Entertainment Am., Santa Monica, Calif., 2004. Composer, prodr., actress, writer (National Public Radio dramas) Generations Radio Theater Presents: Radio Tales, 1996—2002, (radio dramas) Radio Tales, XM Satellite Radio, 2002—, composer, prodr., actress (radio drama) The Odyssey Trilogy, 2003, Arabian Nights Trilogy, 2003, The Gift of the Magi, 1996, The Yellow Wallpaper, 1996, The Fall of the House of Usher, 1998, Sleepy Hollow, 1998, The Time Machine, 1999, Gulliver's Travels, 1999, The Mummy, 1999, The Island of Doctor Moreau, 2000, Dr. Jekyll and Mr. Hyde, 2000, Journey to the Center of the Earth, 2000, The Pit and the Pendulum, 2000, The Hunchback of Notre-Dame, 2001, Jason and The Argonauts, 2001, War of the Worlds, 2001, Phantom of the Opera, 2001, Beowulf, 2001, Twenty Thousand Leagues Under the Sea, 2001, The Invisible Man, 2001, The Lost World, 2002, composer, actress, author (radio musicals) Celtic Hero, 2000; composer, actress, author: radio musicals Lord of the Celts, 1998; author: (short stories) Breaking Point, 1991, Celtic Beauty for Sword and Sorceress 20 book anthology, 2003, (radio drama script) Light of Truth, 1985; composer: (video games) God of War, 2004, Charlie and the Chocolate Factory, 2005, The Da Vinci Code, 2006. Recipient GRACIE award for best nat./network drama series, Am. Women in Radio and TV, 2001, 2003, 2004, N.Y. Festivals award, Internat. Radio Festivals, 1997, AUDIE Honors award, Audio Pubs. Assn., 1999, GOLDEN REEL Merit award, Nat. Fedn. Cmty. Broadcasters, 2001, GRACIE award for outstanding achievement by an actress, Am. Women in Radio and TV, 1998, N.Y. Festivals award, Internat. Radio Festivals, 2001, N.Y. Festivals World medal, 2004, Outstanding Achievement in Original Music Composition for Videogame, Acad. Interactive Arts Sci., 2005, Best Original Score of Yr. awrd, Game Zone, 2005, Best Original Music award, Game Spot, 2005, Best Original Score award, IGN PS2, 2005, Music of Yr., Game Audio Network Guild, 2005, Best Interactive Score, 2005, Best Cinematic/Cut Scene Audio, 2005, Audio of Yr., 2005; grantee Endowment grantee, Wallace - Reader's Digest Funds, 1996—2002, NEA, 1996—2002, Durkin Hayes Publ., 1998. Mem.: SAG, BMI, NARAS, Game Audio Network Guild, Ind. Game Developers Assn., Am. Fedn. Musicians. Avocations: reading, Web design, computer art, travel. Business E-Mail: phillips@radiotales.com.

**PHILLIPS, ZAIGA ALKSNIS,** pediatrician; b. Riga, Latvia, Sept. 13, 1934; came to U.S., 1949; d. Adolfs and Alma (Ozols) Alksnis; (div. 1972); children: Albert L., Lisa K., Sintija. BS, U. Wash., 1956, MD, 1959. Fellow Colo. Med. Ctr., Denver, 1961-62; sch. physician Bellevue and Issaquah (Wash.) Sch. Dists., 1970-77; pvt. practice Bellevue, 1977—; staff pediatrician Overlake Med. Ctr., 1977—, Childrens Hosp. and Med. Ctr., Seattle, 1977—, Evergreen Med. Ctr., 1977—. Attending physician Allergy Clinic, Childrens Hosp., Seattle, 1988-2005; cons. and contact to pediatricians in Latvia, 1988—; team mem. to Latvia, Healing the Children Contact with Latvia, 1993-97; bd. mem. Bellevue's Stay in Sch. Program, 1994-97. Mem. Am. Latvian Assn., 1972—, Wash. Latvian Assn., Seattle, 1972—; pres. Latvian Sorority Gundega, Seattle, 1990-93; bd. dirs. Sister Cities Assn. Bellevue, 1992-98, Wash. Asthma Allergy Found. Am., 1992-99. Recipient Recognition award, City of Liepaja, 1995, Latvian Assn. Am., 2003, Recognition cross, Pres. of Latvia, 2005. Fellow Am. Acad. Pediat.; mem. Am. Latvian Physicians Assn. (bd. dirs. 1998—), Wash. State and Puget Sound Pediatric Assn. Office: Pediatric Assn 2700 Northup Way Bellevue WA 98004-1463 Office Phone: 425-827-4600. Business E-mail: zap@u.washington.edu.

**PHILLIPS-LESANE, FAY M.,** mental health professional; b. Petersburg, Va., Feb. 2, 1956; d. Orlando F. Phillips Sr., Mary E. Phillips. BSW cum laude, Va. State U., 1978; MSW summa cum laude, Howard U., 1981; postgrad., Am. Sch. Profl. Psychology, 1995. LCSW Va., LICSW D.C. Psychiat. social worker Ctrl. State Hosp., Petersburg, Va., 1978—79; mental health specialist Alexandria Cmty. Mental Health, Alexandria, Va., 1979—82; social worker supr., program dir. Luth. Social Svcs., Washington, 1982—88; clin. adminstr. Commn. on Mental Health, Washington, 1988—96; prevention specialist U. D.C., Washington, 1996—2000; pres., CEO Agape Mental Health, Woodbridge, Va., 1998—. Bd. dirs. U. D.C. Dept. Social Work, Christian Hope Child Care, Woodbridge; mem. adv. bd. Nat. Consortium for Am. Children; dir. Inst. Human Devel. Nat. Consortium for African Am. Children. Mem.: Alpha Kappa Alpha. Democrat. Avocations: music, sports, travel, art, bowling. Home: 13400 Forest Glen Rd Woodbridge VA 22191 Office: Agape Mental Health And Consulting Servi PO Box 4986 Woodbridge VA 22194-4986

**PHILLIPSON, DONALD E.,** lawyer; b. Denver, July 22, 1942; BS, Stanford U., 1964, JD, 1968; MS, U. Calif., Berkeley, 1965. Former mem. Davis, Graham & Stubbs, Denver; now cons., writer. Mem. Nat. Soccer Hall of Fame (adminstr.). Office: 14325 Braun Rd Golden CO 80401-1431 Office Phone: 303-279-1577.

**PHILLIS, JOHN WHITFIELD,** physiologist, educator; b. Port of Spain, Trinidad, Apr. 1, 1936; came to U.S., 1981; s. Ernest and Sarah Anne (Glover) P.; m. Pamela Julie Popple, 1958 (div. 1968); children: David, Simon, Susan; m. Shane Beverly Wright, Jan. 24, 1969. B in Vet. Sci., Sydney U., Australia, 1958, D in Vet. Sci., 1976; PhD, Australian Nat. U., 1961; DSc, Monash U., Australia, 1970. Sr. lectr. Monash U., 1963-69; vis. prof. Ind. U., Indpls., 1969; prof. physiology, assoc. dean sch. U. Man., Winnipeg, Canada, 1970-73; prof., chmn. dept. physiology U. Sask., Saskatoon, Canada, 1973-81, asst. dean sch., 1973-75; prof. physiology Wayne State U., Detroit, 1981—2004, prof. emeritus, 2004—, chmn. dept. physiology, 1981-97; courtesy prof. U. Fla., Gainsville, 2004—. Mem. scholarship and grants com. Can. Med. Rsch. Coun., Ottawa, Ont., 1973-79; rsch. prof., 1980; mem. sci. adv. bd. Dystonia Med. Rsch. Found., Beverly Hills, Calif., 1980-85, Curtis Rsch. Inst., Risingsun, Ohio, 1998-2000; mem. sci. adv. panel World Soc. for Protection of Animals, 1982-98; Wellcome vis. prof. Tulane U., 1986; mem. acad. scholars Wayne State U., 1995. Author: Pharmacology of Synapses, 1970; editor: Veterinary Physiology, 1976, Physiology and Pharmacology of Adenosine Derivatives, 1983, Adenosine and Adenine Nucleotides as Regulators of Cellular Function, 1991, The Regulation of Cerebral Blood Flow, 1993, Novel Therapies for CNS Injuries: Rationales and Results, 1996; editor Can. Jour. Physiology and Pharmacology, 1978-81, Progress in Neurobiology, 1973-97. Mem. grants com. Am. Heart Assn. of Mich., 1985-90, mem. rsch. coun., 1991-92, mem. rsch. forum com., 1991-96, chair, 1992-93; mem. Brain/Stroke Consortium Study Group, Am. Heart Assn., 1998. Wellcome fellow London, 1961-62; Can. Med. Rsch. Coun. grantee, 1970-81; NIH grantee, 1983-2000. Mem. Brit. Pharmacol. Soc., Am. Physiol. Soc., Soc. Neurosci., Internat. Brain Rsch. Orgn. Personal E-mail: jphillis@med.wayne.edu.

**PHILLIS, MARILYN HUGHEY,** artist; b. Kent, Ohio; d. Paul Jones and Helen Margaret (Miller) Hughey; m. Richard Waring Phillis, Mar. 19, 1949; children: Diane E., Hugh R., Randall W Student, Kent State U., 1945; BS, Ohio State U., 1949. Chemist Battelle Meml. Inst., Columbus, Ohio, 1949—53; illustrator periodical We. Res. Hist. Mag., Garrettsville, Ohio, 1974—79; illustrator book AAUW, Piqua, Ohio, 1976; instr. art Edison State C.C., Piqua, 1976; instr. watermedia Springfield Mus. Art, Ohio, 1976—84. Juror art exhbns. state and nat. art groups, 1980—; instr. painting state and nat. orgns., 1980—; lectr. art healing Wheeling Jesuit Coll., W.Va., 1994—96; founder, coord. Nat. Creativity Seminar, Stretching Boundaries for Creative People, 1993, 1995, 1997, 1999, 2002. Author: Watermedia Techniques for Releasing the Creative Spirit, 1992, (chpt.) Bridging Space and Time, 1998; contbr. The Art of Layering: Making Connections, 2004, articles and illustrations to profl. jours.; one-woman shows include Stifel Fine Art Ctr., Wheeling, Springfield Art Mus., Zanesville Art Ctr., Ohio, Ohio U., Lancaster, Ohio U. East St. Clairsville, Cleve. Inst. Music, Columbus Mus. Art, Cheekwood Mus. Art, Bot. Hall, Nashville, Idaho Falls Art Ctr., Monroe C.C., Mich., exhibitions include N.Y.C., Wheeling, Butler Mus. Am. Art, Youngstown, Ohio, Taiwan Art Edn. Inst., Taipei, 1994, Represented in permanent collections Ohio U., Lancaster and St. Clairsville, Springfield Mus. Art Heritage Hall mun., Taiwan ga. Art, Ohio Watercolor Soc., W.Va. Women Artists, U. Charleston, also corp. collections. Co-chmn. Cmty. Health and Humor Program, Wheeling, 1992 Recipient First awards Watercolor West, Riverside, Calif., 1990, Hudson Soc. award Nat. Collage Soc., 1995, Art Masters award Am. Artist Mag., 1996; elected to Hall of Fame, Kent, Ohio, 2000, Hall of Fame, Wheeling, 2000 Mem. Internat. Soc. Study of Subtle Energies and Energy Medicine (art cons. sci. jour. 1992—), art and healing workshop 1995), Am. Watercolor Soc. (dir. 1991-93, newsletter editor 1992—,chmn. Jury of Awards, 2003, Osborne award 1975), Soc. Layerists in Multi-Media (nat. v.p. 1988-93), Ohio Watercolor Soc. (sec. 1979-82, v.p. 1982-89, pres. 1990-96, dir. biennial creativity seminars 1993-95, 97, 99, 2002, Gold medal, Best of Show 1993), Nat. Watercolor Soc. (chmn. selection jury 2001), Internat. Noetic Sci., West Ohio Watercolor Soc. (pres. 1979-80, 2d award 1982), Allied Artists N.Y., W.Va. Watercolor Soc. (1st award 1993), Ky. Watercolor Soc., Ga. Watercolor Soc., So. Watercolor Soc. (pres. 1997-98, Silver award 1999) Avocations: hiking, reading, genealogy, music, travel. Home and Office: Phillis Studio 72 Stamm Cir Wheeling WV 26003-5549 E-mail: mhphillis@aol.com.

**PHILOGENE, BERNARD J. R.,** academic administrator, science educator; b. Beau-Bassin, Mauritius, May 4, 1940; came to Can., 1961; s. Raymond Pierre and Simone Marie (Ruffier) P.; m. Hélène Marie Lebreux, July 7, 1964; children: Simone, Catherine. BS, U. Montreal, 1964; MS, McGill U., 1966; PhD, U. Wis., 1970; DSc (hon.), Compiègne, 1995; DSc (hon.), U. de Pau, France, 2005. Rsch. officer Can. Forestry Svc., Que., 1966—70, rsch. scientist Que., 1970—71; asst. prof. U. B.C., Vancouver, 1971-74; asst. prof., assoc. prof., then prof. entomology U. Ottawa, Canada, 1974—2005, vice dean sci. and engring., 1982—85, dean faculty of sci., 1986—90, acad. vice rector, 1990—97, acting dean, 1985—86, prof. emeritus, 2005—; pres. Can. Consortium of Sci. Socs., 1992—94. Cons. OAS, Washington, 1979-80, Agence de Coop. Culture & Tech., Paris, 1982-83, Can. Internat. Devel. Agy., Ottawa, 1983-85, UN Environ. Program, Geneva, Switzerland, 1985-86, Internat. Devel. Research Ctr., Ottawa, 1985—. Mem. Ont. Pesticide Adv. Com., 1987-91. Decorated commandeur de l'Ordre des Palmes Académiques (France); knight of merit Order of St. John of Jerusalem. Fellow Entomol. Soc. Can. (bd. dirs. 1977-80); mem. Am. Inst. Biol. Scis., Entomol. Soc. Am., Can. Pest Mgmt. Soc., Assn. Can.-Française Advancement Sci. (bd. dirs.

1984-86), Internat. Soc. Chem. Ecology, Entomol. Soc. of Can. (Gold Medal 2000). Office: U Ottawa PO Box 450 30 Marie Curie St Ottawa ON Canada K1N 6N5 Office Phone: 613-562-5800. E-mail: bphilog@uottawa.ca.

**PHILP, RICHARD NILSON,** writer, editor, journalist; b. Plainfield, N.J., July 7, 1943; s. Lester Prery and Gladys Emma Linea (Nilson) P. BA in English and Theater cum laude, U. N.C., 1965; MA in Theater Lit. and Playwriting, Yale U., 1968. Lectr. in field. Author 8 plays, produced 1963-72; author: To Move, To Learn, 1973, Danseur: The Male in Ballet, 1977; editor and contbg. author: Memoirs of a Dancer: Shadows, Dreams, Memories, 1979, Alvin Ailey American Dance Theater, 1993; exec. editor: Dance Books subs. Dance Mag., 1984-93; founding bd. dirs. World Dance Alliance, 1993; chmn. Dance Mag. Prize for Reportage, Video Danse, 1992, 93; also numerous articles and dance/theater criticism; faculty summer Dance Festival, U. Wyo., 1995, 96, 97; mng. editor Dance Mag., 1970-88, editor-in-chief, 1989—; assoc. editor Critics Choice, 1969-70, After Dark, The Magazine of Entertainment, 1970-75; contbr. monthly column Kickoff, 1989—. Co-chmn. internat. adv. bd. Jackson (Miss.) Ballet Competition, 1989—; mem. selection com. ann. Astaire awards Dance Mag., 1989—; bd. dirs. Israel Dance Collection Libr., 1989—, Joffrey Ballet Sch., Video Danse, Paris; mem. adv. bd. Juilliard Sch.; vestryman Christ Ch., Episcopal, Hudson, N.Y., 1979-82, 94—, lic. lay reader, chalice-bearer, also bd. dirs. Lively Art; mem. bd. advisors Thomas Cole's Cedar Grove, 1999—. Recipient Spl. citation Soc. Illustrators, Bronze medal 28th Internat. Film and TV Fest, N.Y.C., 1985, Silver medal Chgo. Internat. Film Festival, 1985, TV Documentary Writing award Am. Film Festival, 1986, Nijinsky award, 1994. Mem. Greene County Hist. Soc., Catskill Writers Group (founder 1978), Devon (Eng.) Beekeepers Assn. Home: 166 Bridge St Catskill NY 12414-1404 also: The Towers Apt 22 33-15 80th St Jackson Heights NY 11372 Office: Dance Mag Inc 33 W 60th St New York NY 10023-7905

**PHILPOT, JOHN LEE,** retired physics professor; b. Kansas City, Mo., May 7, 1935; s. John L. and Millie Ann (Johnson) P.; m. Nancy J. Tucker, Nov. 22, 1956 (div. Jan. 1978); children: John Michael, Patricia Ann; m. Sharon Carol Wuckowitsch, May 15, 1982; 1 child Mellissa Phillips. AB, William Jewell Coll., 1957; MS, U. Ark., 1962, PhD, 1965. Prof. physics U. Mo., Kansas City, 1963-68, William Jewell Coll., Liberty, Mo., 1962—2000; ret., 2000. Thin film lab. Bendix Corp., Kansas City, 1963, 64. Contbr. articles to profl. jours. NDEA fellow, 1961-64. Mem. Am. Phys. Soc., Am Assn. Physics Tchrs., Mo. Acad. Sci. Baptist. Home: 349 Don Allen Rd Liberty MO 64068-9209

**PHILPOTT, HARRY MELVIN,** former university president; b. Bassett, Va., May 6, 1917; s. Benjamin Cabell and Daisy (Hundley) P.; m. Pauline Breck Moran, Sept. 15, 1943; children: Harry Melvin, Jean Todd, Benjamin Cabell II, Virginia Lee. AB, Washington and Lee U., 1938, LL.D., 1966; PhD, Yale U., 1947; D.D., Stetson U., 1960; LL.D., U. Fla., 1969, U. Ala., 1970; H.H.D., Samford U., 1978, Montevallo U., 1980, Auburn U., 1981. Ordained to ministry Bapt. Ch., 1942; dir. religious activities Washington and Lee U., 1938-40; prof. religion U. Fla., 1947-52, v.p., 1957-65; dean, head dept. religion and philosophy Stephens Coll., 1952-57; pres. Auburn U., 1965-80. Mem. Regional Edn. Bd., 1966-82, vice chmn., 1973-75; chmn. Ala. Edn. Study Commn., 1967-69; pres. Southeastern Conf., 1972-74. Served to 1st lt. Chaplains Corps., USNR, 1943-46. Mem. Nat. Assn. State Univs. and Land-Grant Colls. (chmn. council presidents 1972-73, exec. com. 1973-78, pres. 1976-77), Fla. Blue Key, Kappa Alpha, Omicron Delta Kappa, Kappa Delta Pi, Phi Kappa Phi, Phi Beta Kappa. Home: PO Box 3037 Auburn AL 36831-3037

**PHILPOTT, LARRY LA FAYETTE,** horn player; b. Alma, Ark., Apr. 5, 1937; s. Lester and Rena (Owens) P.; m. Elise Robichaud, Nov. 24, 1962 (div. June 1975); children: Daniel, Stacy; m. Anne Sokol, Feb. 14, 1984. BS, Ga. So. Coll., 1962; MusM, Butler U., 1972. Instr. in horn Butler U., De Pauw U.; dir. music Cedarcrest Sch., Marysville, Wash., 1991—; instr. horn Western Wash. U., Dept Music, Bellingham, 1995-98. Mem., N.C. Symphony, 1960, Savannah (Ga.) Symphony, L'Orchestre Symphonique de Quebec, Que., Can., 1962-64, prin. horn player, Indpls. Symphony Orch., 1964-89, Flagstaff Summer Festival, 1968-; artist in-residence Ind.-Purdue Indpls.; appeared with, Am. Shakespeare Theatre, summer 1965, Charlottetown Festival, summers 1967-68, Flagstaff Summer Festival, 1968-85, Marrowstone Music Festival, 1985—. Served with USN, 1956-60. Mem. Music Educators Nat. Conf., Am. Fedn. Musicians, Internat. Conf. Symphony and Opera Musicians, Internat. Horn Soc., Coll. Music Soc., Phi Mu Alpha Sinfonia. Home: 14925 63d Ave SE Snohomish WA 98296-5277 Personal E-mail: larryphilpott@hotmail.com.

**PHILSON, RICHARD MICHAEL,** academic administrator; b. Lakeland, Fla., Aug. 27, 1950; s. Glenn McRae and Jeane Baker Philson; children: Matthew Chou, Renee Yu. BA, Wash. U., St. Louis, 1972; MA, U. Wis., Madison, 1977, U. Hawaii, Honolulu, 1983; PhD, U. Mich., Ann Arbor, 1999. Trainer/prodr. ednl. media U. South Pacific, Suva, Fiji, 1977—79; rsch. intern East-West Ctr., Honolulu, 1981—83; English faculty Chiang Mai U., Thailand, 1983—84; English instr. Tunghai U., Taichung, Taiwan, 1984—86, Myongji U., Seoul, 1987—88; pres. Plumeria's of Hawaii, Honolulu, 1986—87; pub. info. officer U. Hawaii, Honolulu, 1988—90; recruiting/mktg. officer Edmonds C.C., Kobe, Japan, 1990—91; instr./eap coord. Minn. State U., Akita, Japan, 1991—95; rsch. asst. U. Mich., Ann Arbor, 1995—99; pres. Kanda Inst. of Fgn. Languages, Tokyo, 1999—2001; exec. dir., internat. edn. Wichita State U., Kans., 2001—. U. Hawaii working com. Govs. Congress on Hawaii's Internat. Role, Honolulu, 1988; organizing com. mem. Akita Internat. Fair, 1991—92; pres. Akita Faculty Assn. Minn. State U., 1993—95. Author: (handbook) Quality Standard Guidelines for Electronically Delivered Instruction, (booklet) Visions Toward the 21st Century; contbr. chapters to books, articles to profl. jours. Mem. Com. Fgn. Rels., 2003—, Global Learning Ctr., Wichita, 2003—. Mem.: Assn. Internat. Educators (subcom. info. mgmt. 2005—), Chinese-Am. Soc. Ann Arbor (bd. dirs. 1999—2000), Rotary Club (internat. com. planning mem. 1990). Independent. Avocations: tennis, travel, glass-blowing. Home: 2329 Addison Cir Wichita KS 67226 Personal E-mail: mikephilson@yahoo.com.

**PHIPARD, NANCY MIDWOOD,** retired special education educator, poet; b. Boston, Jan. 31, 1929; d. William Henry and Jean Estelle (Dubbs) McAdams; m. Kenneth E. Brown, June 17, 1949 (div.); children: Christopher M. Brown, Jennifer Progodich, Michael H. Brown, Jeffrey D. Brown; m. Arnold J. Midwood, Jr., July 2, 1980 (dec.); m. Harvey F. Phipard, Jan. 14, 1998 (dec.). Student, Mt. Holyoke Coll., 1946-48; BA, Wellesley Coll., 1973; MEd, Boston Coll., 1975. Dir. confs. and insvc. tng., chmn. bd. Mass. Assn. for Children with Learning Disabilities, Waltham and Framingham, 1969-75; chmn. core edn. teams, cons. to spl. programs, grant writer Needham (Mass.) Pub. Schs., 1974-79; ret., 1979; pres., feature writer S.D. Assocs., Inc., Wellesley, Mass., 1980-81; dir. pub. rels., women's career conf. Babson Coll., Wellesley, 1982. Mem. program evaluation team Mass. Dept. Edn., Quincy, 1978. Author (as Nancy Brown, with Louis Dickstein): Psychological Reports, 1974; author: (poems) Portraits of a Life, 1996, Fields of Gold, 1996, Ever-Flowing Stream, 1997, Best Poems of 1998, 2002, Colors of the Past, 2000, Echoes of Yesteryear, 2000, America at the Millennium, The Best Poems and Poets of the 20th Century, 2000, Memories of Tomorrow, 2000, Journey to Infinity, 2000, Theatre of the Mind, 2003 (The Best Poems and Poets of 2003, 2004, The Best Poems and Poets of 2004, 2005). Bd. dirs., fundraiser Hospice Palm Beach (Fla.) County S., 1993—97; bd. dirs. La Coquielle Villas, Inc., Manalapan, Fla., 1994—98; bd. dirs., chair cmty. rels. Lincoln Child Ctr., Oakland, Calif., 1983—85; docent Calif. Hist. Soc., San Francisco, 1982—87. Recipient Editor's Choice award, Internat. Libr. Poetry, 1996, 1998, 2000, 2003, The Best Poems and Poets of 2003, 2004, 2005. Mem.: Internat. Soc. Poets (disting. mem.), Phi Beta Kappa. Avocations: tennis, travel, duplicate bridge.

**PHIPPS, BENJAMIN KIMBALL, II,** lawyer; b. Boston, Jan. 16, 1933; s. Benjamin Kimball and Bertha Elizabeth (Forsyth) P.; m. Phyllis Jarrett Anderson, Jan. 10, 1962; children: Lisa Jarrett, Christina Caroline. BS in

Commerce, U. Va., 1955, LLB, 1958. Bar: Fla. 1964, U.S. Dist. Ct. (no. dist.) Fla., U.S. Claims Ct., U.S. Ct. Appeals (5th and 11th cirs.), U.S. Tax Ct.; cert. Inst. Profls. in Taxation, 2004. Pvt. practice, Tallahassee, 1965—. Counsel tax com. Fla. Ho. of Reps., 1966-72, counsel to spkr., 1973-74, mem. adv. com. fin. & tax com., 1983-84; mem. Legis. Task Force Taxpayers' Bill Rights, 1989-91; elected dir. Fla. Coun. Property Tax Lawyers, 2003 Contbr. articles to profl. jours.; columnist Tallahassee Democrat. Chmn. Hist. Tallahassee Preservation Bd., 1970-91; mem. Tallahassee Trust for Hist. Preservation, 1997—, treas., 1998—. Served to capt., U.S. Army, 1958-64. Mem. ABA (tax sect. state and local tax com.), Tallahassee Bar Assn., Fla. Bar Assn. (treas., vice chmn., chmn. tax sect. 1985-86, editl. bd. Fla. Bar Jour. News, chmn. 1975-76), Gov.'s Club, Univ. Ctr. Club, Cosmos Club, Exch. Club, Tiger Bay Club (dir.), Fla. Econ. Club, St. Andrews Soc. (pres. 1978-79), Sigma Alpha Epsilon, Phi Alpha Delta, Pi Delta Epsilon. Republican. Episcopalian. Office: PO Box 1351 Tallahassee FL 32302-1351 Office Phone: 850-222-7000. Business E-Mail: bkp@thephippsfirm.com.

**PHIPPS, JOHN RANDOLPH,** retired army officer; b. Kansas, Ill, May 16, 1919; s. Charles Winslow and Kelsey Ethel (Torrence) P.; m. Pauline M. Prunty, Feb. 8, 1946; children: Charles W., Kelsey J. Phipps-Selander. BS in Econs. with honors, U. Ill., 1941; M.P.A., Sangamon State U., 1976; A course, Command and Gen. Staff Coll., 1959, nuclear weapons employment course, 1962; course, U.S. Army War Coll., 1973, U.S. Nat. Def. U., 1978. Owner, operator chain shoe stores in, Ill., 1946-70; commd. 2d lt. F.A. U.S. Army, 1941, advanced through grades to capt., 1943; service in Philippines and Japan; discharged as maj., 1946; organizer, comdr. Co. E, 130th Inf., Ill.; N.G., Mattoon, 1947, comdg. officer 2d Bn., 130th Inf., 1951, lt. col. 2d Bn., 130th Inf., 1951; called to fed. service, 1952; adv. (29th Regt., 9th Republic of Korea Div.), 1952-53; comdr. officer 1st Bn., 130th Inf., Ill. N.G., 1954, col., 1959; comdg. officer 2d Brigade, 33d Div., 1963-67; asst. div. comdr. 33d Inf. Div., 1967, brig. gen., 1967; comdr. 33d Inf. Brigade, Chgo., 1967-70, Ill. Emergency Ops. Hdqrs., 1970, asst. adj. gen. Ill., 1970-77, acting adj. gen., 1977-78, adj. gen., 1978, promoted to maj. gen., 1978, now maj. gen. ret. Decorated Silver Star, Bronze Star, Disting. Service medal, Combat Infantry Badge, Army Disting. Service medal Ill., various Philippine and Korean decorations; State of Ill. Long and Honorable Service medal. Mem. VFW, Adj. Gens. Assn. U.S., N.G. Assn. U.S., N.G. Assn. Ill., Am. Legion, Amvets. Home: 100 Wabash Ave Mattoon IL 61938-4524

**PHIPPS, PATRICK MICHAEL,** plant pathology educator; b. New Martinsville, W. Va., Oct. 19, 1945; m. Janet Phipps, 1967; 1 child, James. BS, Fairmont State Coll., 1970; MS, Va. Polytech. Inst. & State U., 1972; PhD in Plant pathology, W. Va. U., 1974. Asst. prof. plant pathology N.C. State U., 1974-78; prof. plant pathology Tidewater Agrl. Rsch. and Ext. Ctr. Va. Polytech. Inst. and State U., 1989—. Recipient Excellent in Ext. award Am. Phytopathol. Soc., 1994, Dow AgroScis. award for excellence in edn., 1999, award for contbns. to peanut industry Am. Peanut Coun., 2000. Fellow: Am. Peanut Rsch. and Edn. Soc. (pres. 2005—06). Office: Tidewater Agrl Rsch & Ext Ctr 6321 Holland Rd Suffolk VA 23437-9588 E-mail: pmphipps@vt.edu.

**PHIPPS, PATSY DUNCAN,** retired auditor; b. New Bern, N.C., July 10, 1934; d. Lawrence C. and Pagie P. Duncan; m. Robert A. Phipps, Sept. 27, 1953 (div. Feb. 2, 1992); children: Kathryn Phipps Sublett, Patricia Phipps Bryant. Cert. in Acctg., U. N.C., Greensboro, 1953; postgrad., U. N.C., 1973; BAI in Auditing, U. Wis., 1986. Regional instr. First Citizens Bank, New Bern, 1976—78; br. mgr. First Citizens Bank & Trust Co., New Bern, 1974—76, supr. account svcs. and ops., 1963—74, v.p., regional audit supr., 1978—97; v.p. auditor So. Bank and Trust Co., Mt. Olive, NC, 1997—99. Cons. Millennia Cmty. Bank, Greenville, NC, 2000—04. Active Broad St.Disciples of Christ Ch. Mem.: Nat. Assn. Bank Women (sec. Ea. N.C. group sec. 1975—76, chmn. 1978—80), Inst. Internal Auditors, New Bern Bus. and Profl. Women's Club (treas. 1973-74, 3d v.p. 1974—75, treas. 1981—82), N.C. Bus. and Profl. Women's Assn. (trustee 1976—82), Nat. Assn. of Bus. and Profl. Women's Clubs. Home: 1105 Peach Tree Ln New Bern NC 28562-8327 Office: Vespect Consulting Co 1105 Peach Tree Ln New Bern NC 28562-8327 Personal E-mail: patsinfo@cox.net.

**PHIPPS, PETER A.,** psychology professor; b. Charlottesville, Va., Dec. 27, 1956; adopted s. John Akers and s. Pauline Chunn Phipps; m. Suzanne Petri, June 1, 1991; 1 child, Aidan Thomas. BSW, Va. Commonwealth U., 1982; MA, Marymount U., 1990; MS, Lehigh U., 1992; PhD, Saybrook Grad. Sch., San Francisco, 1999. Asst. prof. Sullivan County C.C., Loch Sheldrake, NY, 1999—2002; dept. head Dutchess C.C., Poughkeepsie, NY, 2002—. Psychologist, Burlington, NC, 1994—99 Com. mem. PTA, Poughkeepsie, 2005—06. Sgt. U.S. Army, 1975—79. Mem.: APA, Delta Epsilon Sigma. Democrat. Achievements include research in Developmental paths for psychotherapists; Health care in a rural county. Avocations: bicycling, reading, painting, hiking. Office: Dutchess C C 53 Pendell Rd Poughkeepsie NY 12601 Office Phone: 845-431-8341. Office Fax: 845-431-89921. E-mail: phipps@sunydutchess.edu.

**PHOCAS, GEORGE J.,** lawyer; b. N.Y.C., Dec. 1, 1927; m. Katrin Gorny, Feb. 26, 1966; 1 child, George Alexander. AB, U. Chgo., 1950, JD, 1953. Bar: N.Y. 1955, U.S. Supreme Ct. 1962. Assoc. Sullivan & Cromwell, N.Y.C., 1953-56; counsel Creole Petroleum Corp., Caracas, Venezuela, 1956-60; internat. negotiator Standard Oil Co. N.J. (Exxon), 1960-63; sr. ptnr. Casey, Lane & Mittendorf, London, 1963-72, counsel, 1972-76. Exec. v.p. Occidental Petroleum Corp., Los Angeles, 1972-74; adv., U.S. del. UN, ECAFE, Teheran, 1963 Trustee Assn. Naval Aviation, Washington, Owl's Head Aviation Mus., Maine; mem. vis. bd. U. Chgo. Law Sch.; bd. visitors U. Chgo. Law Sch Capt. Infantry U.S. Army Mem. ABA, Law Soc. London, Brit. Inst. Comparative Law, Am. Soc. Internat. Law, Assn. Bar City N.Y.; Clubs: Boodles (London), Met. (N.Y.C.). Home: 29 Duchess of Bedford Walk London W87 QH England Address: Burnt Island Spruce Head ME 04859

**PHOENIX, G. KEITH,** lawyer; b. Centralia, Ill., Aug. 13, 1946; BA in Liberal Arts, So. Ill. U., 1968; JD, St. Louis U., 1973. Bar: Mo. 74, U.S. Dist. Ct. (so. dist.) Ill. 75, U.S. Ct. Appeals (7th and 8th cirs.) 82. Assoc. Coburn, Croft & Shepherd & Putzell, St. Louis, 1974—79; sr. counsel, pres. Sandberg, Phoenix & von Gontard, St. Louis, 1979—. Legal cons. Am. Acad. Pedist. Contbr. articles on med./legal topics to profl. jours. Mem. bd. trustees St. Louis U., 2005—. 1st lt. U.S. Army, 1968—71, Vietnam. Decorated Bronze Star with cluster, Air medal with cluster, Vietnam medal; named one of Mo. and Kans. Civil Litig. Super Lawyers, 2005; named to Best Lawyers in Am., 2003, 2004, 2005, 2006. Mem.: Product Liability Adv. Coun., Am. Bd. Trial Advocacy (past pres.), Lawyer's Assn. (past pres.), U.S. Louis Bar Assn., Mo. Bar Assn., Ill. Bar Assn. (Named One of the Top Trial Lawyers in Am. 2002, 2003). Office: Sandberg Phoenix & von Gontard One City Centre 1500 Saint Louis MO 63101-1880 Office Phone: 314-231-3332. E-mail: kphoenix@spvg.com.

**PHOENIX, JOAQUIN RAPHAEL,** actor; b. San Juan, PR, Oct. 28, 1974; s. John Bottom and Arlyn Dunetz. Actor: (TV films) Backwards: The Riddle of Dyslexia, 1984, Kids Don't Tell, 1985, Secret Witness, 1988; (TV series) Morningstar/Eveningstar. 1986; (films) SpaceCamp, 1986, Russkies, 1987, Parenthood, 1989, Walking the Dog, 1991, To Die For, 1995, Inventing the Abbotts, 1997, U Turn, 1997, Return to Paradise, 1998, Clay Pigeons, 1998, 8MM, 1999, The Yards, 2000, Gladiator, 2000, Quills, 2000, Buffalo Soldiers, 2001, Signs, 2002, It's All About Love, 2003, (voice) Brother Bear, 2003, The Village, 2004, Ladder 49, 2004, Hotel Rwanda, 2004, Walk the Line, 2005 (Best Performance by an Actor in a Motion Picture-Musical or Comedy, Hollywood Fgn. Press Assn. (Golden Globe award), 2006). Office: Iris Burton Agy 1450 Belfast Dr Los Angeles CA 90069*

**PHUNG, NGUYEN DINH,** medical educator; b. Ninh Binh, Vietnam, Sept. 25, 1950; came to U.S., 1975; s. Thu Dinh Nguyen and Minh Tuyet Le; m. Thuy Thanh Tran, Sept. 25, 1974; children: The-Ngoc, Khoi-Nguyen, Thien Huong. MD, Saigon Med. Sch., 1973. Diplomate Am. Bd. Internal Medicine, Am. Bd. Allergy and Immunology. Clin. instr. medicine, staff physician U.

Okla. Health Scis. Ctr. & Vets. Hosp., Oklahoma City, 1982-84; clin. asst. prof. medicine U. Tex. Med. Sch., Houston, 1989—. Co-author: Practical Allergy & Immunology, 1983; contbr. articles to profl. jours. Mem. ACP, Am. Acad. Allergy and Immunology. Avocations: writing, music. Office: Allergy and Asthma Clinic 2905 Milam St Houston TX 77006-3609

**PI, EDMOND HSIN-TUNG,** psychiatry educator; MD, Cath. U. Coll. Medicine, 1972. Cert. Am. Bd. Psychiatry and Neurology. Chief resident U. Ky. Med. Ctr., Lexington, 1977-78; instr. psychiatry U. So. Calif. Sch. Medicine, L.A., 1978-80, asst. prof., 1980-83; assoc. prof. Med. Coll. Pa., Phila., 1983-85, U. So. Calif. Sch. Medicine, 1985-88, prof. clin. psychiatry, 1988—98; prof. Charles R. Drew U. Medicine and Sci., 1998—2003; clin. prof. psychiatry Sch. Medicine, UCLA, 1999—2005; prof. clin. psychiatry Sch. Medicine, U. So. Calif., 2005—. Asst. dir. psychopharmacology U. So. Calif. Sch. Medicine, 1978-80; instr. adult psychiat. clinic L.A. County and U. So. Calif. Med. Ctr., 1980-83; dir. adult psychiat. clinic Med. Coll. Pa., Phila., 1983-85; dir. Adult Psychiat. Inpatient Svcs., L.A. County and U. So. Calif. Med. Ctr., 1985-91; dir. Adult Psychiat. Outpatient Svcs., 1995-97; dir. transcultural psychiatry U. So. Calif. Sch. Medicine, 1991-98; med. dir. State of Calif. Dept. Mental Health, 1997-98; dir. Consultation and Liaison Svcs., L.A. County and U. So. Calif. Med. Ctr., 1998; exec. vice-chmn., assoc. ctr. dir. Augustus F. Hawkins Mental Health Ctr., Martin Luther King. Jr./Charles R. Drew U. Med. Ctr., 1998-2003; dir. psychiat. inpatient svc. Harbor/UCLA Med. Ctr., 2003-05; dir. psychiat. consultation and liaison svcs. L.A. (Calif.) County and U. So. Calif. Med. Ctr., 2005— Author: Reactions to Psychotropic Medications, 1987, (book chpts.) Transcultural Psychiatry, Clinical Psychopharmacology, 1985—; contbr. articles to profl. jours. Mem. Calif. Gov.'s Com. Employment of Disabled Persons, Sacramento, 1993—; bd. dirs. Chinese Bus. Assn., L.A., 1990—92, Com. of 100, N.Y.C., 1993—98, San Gabriel chpt. ARC, Calif., 1994—97, Mental Health Assn., L.A. County, Calif., 1995—97, 1998—2001. Vis. scholar Com. on Scholarly Comm. with People's Republic of China U.S. Nat. Acad. Scis., Washington, 1987-88; Treval fellow Am. Coll. Neuropsychopharmacology, 1982. Fellow Am. Psychiat. Assn. (chair com. Asian-Am. psychiatrists 1998-2000); Am. Soc. Social Psychiatry, Pacific Rim Coll. Psychiatry (treas. 1991-97), Am. Coll. Psychiatrists; mem. Soc. Study Psychiatry and Culture, Pacific Rim Assn. Clin. Pharmogenetics, Assn. Chinese Am. Psychiatrists (pres. 1995—). Avocations: photography, writing, travel, tennis, media communications. Office: LAC & USC Med Ctr Dept Psychiatry 2020 Zonal Ave IRD 13 Los Angeles CA 90033 Office Phone: 323-226-7975. Business E-Mail: ehpi@usc.edu.

**PIA, PAMELA CARMEL,** editor, director; d. Nunzie Peter and Theresa V. Pia; 1 child, Christopher M. BA, NYU, 1978; MBA, U. Bridgeport, 1987. Asst. program mgr. Easton Press, Norwalk, Conn., 1978—93; sr. editor Longmeadow Press, Stamford, Conn., 1993—95; editl. dir. Reader's Digest Young Families, Pleasantville, NY, 1995—. Editor: The Country Mouse and the City Mouse, 2003 (Silver award Soc. Illustrators, 2003), Pinocchio - A Tale of Honesty, 2004 (iParenting Media award, 2004), Lions (iParenting Media award), Bears (iParenting Media award). Recipient Proud Little Peacock iParenting Media award, 2004, Keep Trying Little Zebra iParenting Media award, 2004, Parenting Media award for Lions, 2005, Parenting Media award for Bears, 2005. Mem.: LWV. Democrat. Avocations: travel, photography, reading, music. Office: Readers Digest Young Families One Readers Digest Road Pleasantville NY 10570 Office Phone: 914-244-4872. Business E-Mail: pam_pia@rd.com.

**PIACENTINI, NICHOLAS A., JR.,** military officer; b. Sacramento, Calif. AA, Sacramento City Coll.; BS, Sacramento State Coll. Commd. USAR, 1970, advanced through grades to sgt. maj.; from drill sgt. to 1st sgt. for cos. B and D 3d Bn., 360th Regiment, 1st Brigade, 91st Divsn., Sacramento, 1970; command sgt. mjr. hq. 5th Bn., Lathrop, Calif.; command sgt. maj./commandant 91st Divsn. Leadership Drill Sgt. Sch., Dublin, Calif.; command sgt. maj. hq. 1st Brigade, Sacramento; command sgt. maj. 351st Civil Affairs Command, Mountain View, Calif., Army Res. Pers. Ctr., St. Louis, 1994—98, 3d Med. Command, Atlanta, 1998—2000, Fort McCoy, 2000—02, USAR Command, Ft. McPherson, Ga., 2002—. Decorated Meritorious Svc. medal with 4 oak leaf clusters, Army Commendation medal, Army Res. Components Achievement medal with 4 oak leaf clusters, Armed Forces Res. medal with silver hourglass device, many others; recipient Mil. Outstanding Vol. Svc. medal. Office: Army Reserve Command Hq Fort McPherson 1401 Deshler St, SW Fort Mcpherson GA 30330-1069

**PIAN, THEODORE HSUEH-HUANG,** engineering educator, consultant; b. Shanghai, Jan. 18, 1919; came to U.S., 1943; s. Chao-Hsin Shu-Cheng and Chih-Chuan (Yen) P.; m. Rulan Chao, Oct. 3, 1945; 1 child, Canta Chao-Po. B in Engring., Tsing Hua U., Kunming, China, 1940; MS, MIT, 1944, DSc, 1948; DSc (hon.), Beijing U. Aeros. and Astronautics, 1990; PhD (hon.), Shanghai U., 1991. Engr. Cen. Aircraft Mfg. Co., Loiwing, China, 1940-42, Chengtu Glider Mfg. Factory, 1942-43; tchg. asst. MIT, Cambridge, 1946-47, rsch. assoc., 1947-52, asst. prof., 1952-59, assoc. prof., 1959-66, prof., 1966-89, prof. emeritus, 1989—. Vis. assoc. Calif. Inst. Tech., Pasadena, 1965-66; vis. prof. U. Tokyo, 1974, Tech. U., Berlin, 1975; vis. chair prof. Nat. Tsing Hua U., Hsin Chu, Taiwan, 1990, Nat. Ctrl. U., ChungLi, Taiwan, 1992; hon. prof. Beijing U. Aero. and Astronautics, Beijing Inst. Tech., Southwestern Jaiotong U., Dalian U. Tech., Huazhong U. Sci. and Tech., Changsha Rwy. U., Ctrl.-South U. Tech., Hohai U., Nanjing U. of Aero. and Astronautics, Dalian Rwy. U., Shashi U. of Sci. and Tech. of China. Recipient von Karman Meml. prize TRE Corp., Beverly Hills, Calif., 1974. Fellow AAAS, AIAA (assoc. editor jour. 1973-75, Structures, Structural Dynamics and Materials award 1975), U.S. Assn. Computational Mechanics (founding mem.); mem. ASME (hon.), NAE, Academia Sinica Taiwan, Am. Soc. Engring. Edn., Internat. Assn. for Computational Mechanics (hon. mem. gen. coun.). Home and Office: 14 Brattle Cir Cambridge MA 02138-4625 Office Phone: 617-876-9036. Personal E-Mail: thhpian@aol.com.

**PIANALTO, SANDRA,** bank executive; b. Valli del Pasubio, Italy, Aug. 4, 1954; B in Economics, U. Akron, 1976; M in Economics, George Washington U., 1985; LHD (hon.), U. Akron, Baldwin-Wallace Coll., Kent State U., Ursuline Coll. Economist bd. govs. Fed. Reserve Sys.; staff mem. budget com. U.S. Ho. of Reps.; economist rsch. dept. Fed. Res. Bank Cleve., 1983—84, asst. v.p. pub. affairs, 1984—88, v.p., sec. bd. dirs., 1988—93, first v.p., COO, 1993—2003, pres., 2003—. Bd. dirs. Cleve. Found., Gr. Cleve. Partnership, U. Hosp. Health Sys., United Way Svcs. Cleve., Rock and Roll Hall of Fame and Mus., N.E. Ohio Coun. Higher Edn., Cath. Diocese Cleve. Found., Ohio Bus. Alliance for Higher Edn. and Economy. Office: Fed Reserve Bank Cleveland PO Box 6387 Cleveland OH 44101-1387*

**PIANKO, THEODORE A.,** lawyer; b. Dennville, NJ, Sept. 5, 1955; s. Theodore and Pasqualina (Liguori) Pianko; m. Beatriz Maria Olivera (div. Dec. 1985); m. Kathryn Anne Lindley, Feb. 18, 1990; children: Matthew James, Samuel Wahoo, Zoe Wahoo. BA, SUNY, 1975; JD, U. Mich., 1978. Bar: Mich. 1978, Ill. 1979, Calif. 1980. Atty. Ford Motor Co., Dearborn, Mich., 1978-83; assoc. Lillick McHose & Charles, L.A., 1980-83; ptnr. Sidley & Austin, L.A., 1983-94, Christie, Parker & Hale, Newport Beach, Calif., 1994—. Home: PMB 281 1533 Culver Dr Ste 340 Irvine CA 92604 Office Phone: 949-476-0757. Personal E-Mail: ted@pianko.com.

**PIANO, RENZO,** architect; b. Genoa, Italy, Sept. 14, 1937; m. Magda Arduino, 1962; m. Emilia Rossato, 1992; children: Carlo, Matteo, Lia, Giorgio Anthony. Dip.Arch., Poly. of Milan, 1964; PhD in Fine Arts (hon.), Pratt Inst., NY, 2002. Worked with Franco Albini, Milan, 1962-64, E. Piano, Genoa, 1964-65, Z.S. Makowsky, London, 1965-70; ptnr. Piano and Rogers Architects, London, Genoa, Paris and Genoa, 1970—, Piano and Rice, Genoa, Paris and London, 1977—93, Renzo Piano Building Workshop, Genoa, Paris and London, 1994—. Lectr. Poly. of Milan, 1965-68; vis. lectr. Columbia U., NYC, 1967, U. Pa., Phila., 1967, U. Bucharest, Romania, 1968, Poly. of Delft, Netherlands, 1969, Unesco, Paris, 1973, Oslo Sch. Architecture, 1976; prof. architecture Archtl. Assn., London, 1971, Poly. Cen. London, 1971, created with Harvard U., Architecture Workshop Found., 2001-. Prin. works

include Italian Industry Pavilion, Expo '70, Japan, 1970, Fitzroy St. Comml. Ctr., Cambridge, UK, 1970, B&B Italia Offices, Como, 1971, Universal Oil Products U.K. Head Office and UOP Fragrances Ltd. Lab., Tadworth, Surrey, 1972, Aston Martin Lagonda Ltd. Offices, Showroom, Restaurant, etc., London, 1973, PATScentre, Cambridge, 1975, Inst. de Recherche et de Coordination Acoustique, Paris, 1977, Centre Beaubourg, Paris, 1977, Kronenbourg factory, Strasbourg, 1978, Quartiere Il Rigo housing estate, Corciano, Perugia, Italy, 1978-82, Civic Ctr. and Libr., Loano, Savona, Italy, 1980, Nationalgalerie extensions & housing, West Berlin, 1981, De Menil Collection bldg., Houston, 1981-83, Bance Agricola Comml. bldg., Reggio Emilia, Italy, 1981-83, IBM travelling exhbn. extensions, 1982, Palazzo a Vela conversion, 1982, Centocelle/Torrespaccata Bus. Ctr., Rome, 1982, Banca Agricola Comml. in Modena, Italy, 1982, 5 Met. Rwy. Stas., Genoa, 1983, Il Prometeo music rsch. lab., Venice, 1984, Centre Georges Pompidou cinema extensions, Paris, 1984, Comml. Ctr. office bldgs., Naples, Italy, 1984, Kenya Energy Tech. Inst., Nairobi, 1984, Leisure Ctr., Cremona, Italy, 1984, Columbus Expedition 500th Anniversary designs, 1984-90, Office Bldg. for Lowara factory, Vicenza, Italy, 1985, Mus. for Menil Collection, Houston, 1986, Hdqs. for Light Metals Exptl. Inst., Novara, Italy, 1987, Nicola Football stadium, Bari, Italy, 1990, Bercy Comml. Ctr., Paris, 1990, IRCAM Extension, Paris, 1990, Cruise Ships for P&O, USA, 1990, Housing City of Paris, 1991, Thomson factories, Guyancourt, France, 1991, Underground stas. for Ansaldo, Genoa, Italy, 1991, Hdqrs. Credito Indsl. Sardo, Cagliari, Italy, 1992, Kansai Internat. Airport, Osaka, 1994, Lingotto Congress-Concert Hall, Turin, Italy, 1994, Renzo Piano Bldg. Workshop Office, Genoa, 1994, Cy Twombly Pavilion, Houston, 1995, Meridien Hotel at Lingotto and Bus. Ctr., Torino, Italy, 1995, Hdqs. Harbour Authorities, Genoa, 1995, Cinema, Offices, Contemporary Art Mus., Congress Ctr., Landscape, Cité Internat., Lyon, France, 1996, I Portici (Shopping St. at Lingotto), Turin, 1996, Ushibuka Bridge, Kumamoto, Japan, 1997, Mus. Sci. and Tech., Amsterdam, The Netherlands, 1997, Mus. Beyeler Found., Riehen, Basel, Switzerland, 1997, Mercedes Benz Design Ctr., Stuttgart, Germany, 1998, Lodi (Italy) Bank Hdqs., 1998, NY Times Bldg., NYC, 2000; Renovation and expansion of the Calif. Acad. Sciences, 2000, Morgan Pierpont Library, NYC, 2000, U. of Mich. Law Sch., 2002, Morgan Libr. and Mus., 2006, numerous others; exhbns. include Triennale, Milan, 1967, Archtl. Assn., London, 1970, Musée des Arts Decoratifs, Paris, 1973, IBM Travelling Exhbn. in Europe, 1986, Columbus Internat. Exposition, Aquarium and Congress Hall, Genoa, 1992, Out of the blue, Kunst-und Ausstellungshalle, Bonn, Germany, 1997, Out of the blue, Villa Pignatelli, Naples, Italy, 1997, Out of the blue, Gallery MA, Tokyo, 1998, Renzo Piano: The architect's studio, La. Mus. of Modern Art, Humlebaek Copenhagen, Denmark, 2003. Recipient 1st prize Place Beaubourg Competition, Paris, 1971, Auguste Perret prize Internat. Union Architects, 1978, Compasso d'Oro award, Milan, 1981, Arnold W. Brunner Memorial Prize in Architecture Am. Acad. of Arts and Letters, 1994, Erasmus prize, Netherlands, 1995, Art pirze Akademie Künste, Berlin, 1995, Premio Capo Circeo, 1996, Diploma European award for steel structures for elevated heliport structure at Lingotto (Italy), 1997, Pritzker Arch. prize, The White House, 1998, Wexner Prize, Wexner Ctr. for the Arts, 2001, Médaille D'Or, International Union of Architects, Berlin, 2002, Michelangelo Antonioni for the Arts, Rome Auditorium, Italy, 2002, Gold medal Italian Architecture, Milan, 2003, Bus. Cultural award, Italy-Am. C. of C., NY, 2003, McKim prize, Am. Acad. in Rome, 2005; decorated officer Nat. Order Legion of Honor (France), 2000; named one of 100 Most Influential People, Time Mag., 2006. Fellow: Am. Inst. Architects (hon.). Office: Atelier Piano 34 rue des Archives 75004 Paris France also: Studio Renzo Piano Via Rubens 29 16158 Genoa Italy E-mail: italy@rpbw.com, france@rpbw.com.*

**PIASSICK, JOEL BERNARD,** lawyer; b. Atlanta, June 2, 1940; s. Louis S. and Sarah (Freeman) P.; m. Karen Pevow, Aug. 11, 1963; children: Joan, Louis. BA in Polit. Sci., Tulane U., 1962; LLB, U. Va., 1965. Bar: Va. 1965, Ga. 1966, Colo. 1999. Ptnr. Smith, Gambrell & Russell, Atlanta, 1967-90, Kilpatrick Stockton LLP, Atlanta, 1990—. Fellow Am. Coll. Bankruptcy. Office: Kilpatrick Stockton LLP 1100 Peachtree St NE Ste 2800 Atlanta GA 30309-4530 E-mail: jpiassick@kilstock.com.

**PIATT, JACK BOYD,** manufacturing executive; b. Washington, Pa., Jan. 8, 1928; s. Harold Boyd and Violet Marie (Amos) P.; m. Thelma Jean Ritchie, Mar. 16, 1948 (div. 1974); children: Jack Boyd, Rod L., Rebecca, Regina; m. Kathleen Mary Shattuck, May 4, 1975. Student, Washington, Pa. Chmn. Millcraft Industries, Washington, Pa., 1928—. Bd. dirs. Pitts. br. Fed. Res. Bank Cleve. Pres., bd. dirs. Meadowcroft Found., Availa, Pa.; bd. dirs. Southeastern Found., Miami, Fla., 1983-84. Recipient Disting Svc. award Greater Washington Area Jaycees, 1980; named Tri-State Entrepreneur of Yr., Arthur Young and Inc. Mag., 1989. Mem. Am. Iron and Steel Inst., Eastern States Blast Furnace Assn., Assn. Iron and Steel Engrs., Duquesne Club (Pitts.). Republican. Home: PO Box 396 Meadow Lands PA 15347-0396 Office: Millcraft Industries Southpointe Plaza I 400 Southpointe Blvd Ste 400 Canonsburg PA 15317-8551

**PIATT, JESSICA ANN,** psychologist; b. Clarksville, Tenn., Nov. 8, 1974; Specialist degree in Sch. Psychology, Ea. Ky. U., 2004. Sch. psychologist Kenton County Sch. Dist., Ft. Wright, Ky., 2004—. Personal E-mail: Jestat@aol.com.

**PIAZZA, KRIS A.,** writer, editor; b. Buffalo, Nov. 8, 1967; d. Andrew Nicholas Piazza and Jean Ann Reeves. BA in Media Comm., Medaille Coll., 1992. Dir., thinkfirst injury prevention program Kaleida Health, Buffalo, 1996—2001, project mgr., 2001—03, sr. writer/editor, 2003—. Cons. The We Care Group, Buffalo, 2002—. Author: IMPACT; contbr. articles to profl. jours. Bd. mem. United Way Buffalo & Erie County, 2003—, Child Care Coalition Niagara Frontier, 2002—; adv. bd. for consumer directed personal asst. program People, Inc., 1999—2004; inspirational speaker life after spinal cord injury. Recipient Chair Yr. award, United Way Buffalo & Erie County, 2001, Vol. of Yr., YWCA, N.Y., 2002, 2002 Salt Lake City Torch Relay, 2002, Alumni Yr., Medaille Coll., 2002, Lifesavers award, Nat. Hwy. Traffic Safety Adminstrn., 2001, Ms. Wheelchair N.Y., 2001. Office: Kaleida Health Foundation 1260 Delaware Ave Buffalo NY 14209-2401 Office Phone: 716-843-7456. Home Fax: NA. Personal E-Mail: kp28f@aol.com. Business E-Mail: kpiazza@kaleidahealth.org.

**PIAZZA, MIKE (MICHAEL JOSEPH PIAZZA),** professional baseball player; b. Norristown, Pa., Sept. 4, 1968; m. Alicia Rickter, 2005. Student, Miami-Dade C.C. Catcher LA Dodgers, 1992—97, Fla. Marlins, 1998, NY Mets, 1998—2005, San Diego Padres, 2006—. Named Nat. League Rookie Player of Yr., Sporting News, 1993, Nat. League Rookie of Yr., Baseball Writers' Assn., 1993; named to Nat. League All-Star Team, 1993—2002, 2004, 2005, Slugger Team, Nat. League, 1993. Achievements include setting the Major League record for home runs by a catcher, 2004. Office: c/o San Diego Padres PO Box 122000 San Diego CA 92112-2000*

**PICADIO, ANTHONY PETER,** lawyer; b. Latrobe, Pa., Dec. 7, 1941; s. Peter J. and Elsie M. (Caldarelli) P.; m. Lynette Norton. BA, U. Pitts., 1965, JD, 1970. Bar: Pa. 1970, U.S. Dist. Ct. (we. dist.) Pa. 1970, U.S. Ct. Appeals (3d cir.) 1971, U.S. Supreme Ct. 1998. Asst. atty. gen. Dept. Environ. Protection Commonwealth Pa., 1970-72; ptnr. Reding, Blackstone, Rea & Sell, Pitts., 1972-75, Tucker, Arensberg, P.C., Pitts., 1975-85; founder, sr. ptnr. practice in bus. litigation and environ. law Picadio, Sneath, Miller & Norton, Pitts., 1985—. Mem.: Order of Coif. Picadio Sneath Miller & Norton PC US Steel Tower 600 Grant St Ste 4710 Pittsburgh PA 15219-2703 Office Phone: 412-288-4000. E-mail: picadio@psmn.com.

**PICARD, CECIL,** school system administrator; b. Maurice, La. m. Gaylen David; children: Tyron, Layne. BA in Upper Elem. Edn., Southwestern La. Inst.; MA in Adminstrn. and Supervision, Sam Houston Tchrs. Coll.; postgrad., La. State U.; HHD (hon.), McNeese State U., 1996. Cert. tchr. elem. edn., secondary edn., prin., city/parish supr., La. Tchr., coach Vermilion Parish Sch. System, 1959-66, h.s. prin., 1966-80; mem. La. Senate, 1979-96, chmn., mem. numerous coms.; mem. La. Ho. of Reps., 1976-79; supt. of edn. State of La., 1996—. Mem. Nat. Conf. of State Legislatures, La. Ednl. TV

Authority Bd., La. Ednl. Assessment Testing Commn., So. Regional Edn. Bd., Edn. Commn. of the States, La. Commn. on the Deaf. Bd. trustees Tchrs. Retirement System of La.; bd. dirs. La. Sch. for Math, Sci. and the Arts, Acadiana United Way; mem. St. Alphonse Cath. Ch.; mem. Acadian Heritage and Culture Found., Inc., La. Teenage Pregnancy Commn. Recipient Disting. Legislator award La. Assn. of Educators, 1986, Disting. Svc. award, 1989, Senator of Yr. award La. Fedn. of Tchrs., 1988, Friend of Edn. award, 1996, Legislator of Yr. award La. Assn. of Prins., 1994-95. Mem. La. Farm Bur. and Cattleman's Assn., Chamber of C., Jaycees, Kiwanis Club, La. H.S. Athletic Assn. (exec. com.). Office: Edn Dept PO Box 94064 Baton Rouge LA 70804-9064

**PICARD, LESLIE,** publishing executive; With Conde Nast, NYC, 1996—; ad mgr. Vanity Fair, NYC, 1996—98; adv. dir. Conde Nast corp. sales divsn., NYC, 1998—2001, v.p., 2001—04; v.p., pub. Bon Appetit, NYC, 2004—. Office: Bon Appetit Fl 15 4 Times Square New York NY 10036-6522

**PICASSO, PALOMA,** fashion designer; b. Paris, Apr. 19, 1949; d. Pable Picasso and Françoise Gilot; m. Rafael Lopez-Cambil, 1978. Student, U. Sorbonne, Paris; studied jewellry design and fabrication. Designer jewellery Yves St. Laurent, 1969, Zolotas, 1971; founder Paloma Picasso Botique, Paris, Japan, Hong Kong. Designed costumes and sets for L'Interprétation, 1975, Success, 1978; creations designed by her for Paloma Picasso brand include: jewellery for Tiffany & Co., 1980; fragrances Paloma Picasso, 1984, Minotaure, 1992; cosmetics for L'Oréal; women's accessories for Lopez-Camil Ltd., 1987; hosiery and eyewear for Carrera; bone china, crystal, silverware and tiles for Villeroy & Boch; home linens for Martex; fabrics and wallcoverings for Motif; appeared in film Immoral Tales, 1974. Office: Lopez-Cambil Ltd 37 W 57th St Fl 12 New York NY 10019-3411 also: Nourithe Serraf Martine Herbin 13 cité de Pusy 75017 Paris France*

**PICCARRETA, CARL ALAN,** lawyer; b. Rochester, NY, Feb. 25, 1955; s. Carl Anthony and Jennie E. (Belluscio) P.; m. Raquel Hernandez, Oct. 25, 1985 (div. 1988); m. Grace Honne Robles, Oct. 19, 1991. BA, U. Ariz., 1977; JD, U. Toledo, 1980. Bar: Ohio 1980, U.S. Dist. Ct. (no. dist.) Ohio 1981, Ariz. 1982, U.S. Dist. Ct. Ariz., 1985, U.S. Ct. Appeals (9th cir.) 1988. Atty. Advocates for Basic Legal Equality, Toledo, 1980-83, Pima County Pub. Defender's Office, Tucson, 1983-85, Pima County Atty.'s Office, Tucson, 1985-86, Piccarreta & Davis, P.C., Tucson, 1986—. Mem. Supreme Ct. Commn. on Jud. Performance Rev., 2003—. Bd. dirs. Tucson Metro Soccer League, 1992—, pres., 1994—, coord. Courts Are Us, 2004—, bd. dirs. Susan G. Komen Breast Cancer Found., So. Ariz., 2004-; mem. Tucson City Magistrate Merit Selection Com., 1996-00, vice chmn., 1998-99, chmn., 1999-00; vol. U. Ariz. Domestic Violence Law Clinic, 1998—. Howard U. fellow, 1980-82. Mem. ATLA, Pima County Bar Assn., Ariz. State Bar Assn. (trial practice sect., judicial performance rev. team mem. 1997—), Ariz. Trial Lawyers Assn., Fed. Bar Assn. (exec. coun. Tucson chpt. 2004-). Democrat. Roman Catholic. Avocations: soccer, scuba diving, skiing. Office: Piccarreta & Davis PC 145 S Sixth Ave Tucson AZ 85701-2007 Office Phone: 520-622-6900. E-mail: carlp@pd-law.com.

**PICCININI, ROBERT M. (BOB PICCININI),** grocery store chain executive; s. Mike Piccinini. Head, real estate dept. Save Mart Supermarkets, Modesto, Calif., 1971, pres., 1981, owner, 1985—, CEO, chmn. Former owner Fresno Giants. Mailing: Save Mart Supermarkets PO Box 4278 Modesto CA 95352-4278 Office: Save Mart Supermarkets 1800 Standiford Ave Modesto CA 95350*

**PICCININNO, ANTHONY RAY,** government administrative executive; b. Orange, N.J., Aug. 19, 1972; s. Michael Angelo and Dona Lee (Martin) Piccininno; m. Karen Veintimilla, July 25, 2003. AS, County Coll. of Morris, Randolph, N.J., 1994; BA, Rutgers U., 1997; grad. cert., U. of Oxford, Eng., 2000; postgrad., Georgetown U., 2001. Vol. income tax assistance, IRS; incident command sys. USCG, direct mktg. Montclair State U., cert. Leadership and Mgmt. Sch., USCG. Sales adminstr. Prestige Volvo, East Hanover, NJ, 1988—99; tech. materials analyst Volvo Cars of N.Am., Rockleigh, NJ, 1994—96; office adminstr. Harvard Coop. Soc., Cambridge, Mass., 1998—99; acctg. Bridgewater Volvo, Somerville, NJ, 1999—2000; svc. advisor Morristown (N.J.) BMW, 2000—01; adminstrv. exec. Exec. Office of the Pres., Washington, 2001—. Auxiliarist USCG Aux., 1999—. Decorated Nat. Def. Svc. medal USCG; recipient acad. scholarship, Harvard U., 2000, 1999. Conservative. Roman Catholic. Avocations: travel, reading. Office: Exec Office of the Pres NEOB 7002 725 17th St NW Washington DC 20503 Home: 38 Peach Tree Ave East Hanover NJ 07936-1560

**PICCININO, ROCCO MICHAEL,** librarian; b. Phila., Aug. 21, 1949; s. Rocco Anthony and Ida Marie (Minicozzi) P. BA in History magna cum laude, LaSalle Coll., 1971; postgrad., U. N.C., 1971—73; MSLS, Drexel U., 1981. Ednl. resources specialist C.C. of Phila., 1973-74; asst./assoc. libr. United Engrs. & Constructors Inc. (A Raytheon Co.) Libr., Phila., 1974-81, head libr. Boston, 1981-84; asst./assoc. dir. Wentworth Inst. of Tech. Libr., Boston, 1984-89; sci. libr. Smith Coll. Librs., Northampton, Mass., 1989-91, coord. br. libr. svcs., sci. libr., 1991—. Mem. ALA (Assn. Coll. Rsch. Librs. divsn. instruction sect. policy com. 2002-04, sci. and tech. sect. coun., co-chair coll. libr. discussion group 1998-02, forum for sci. and tech. libr. rsch. 2000-02, comparison of sci. and tech. com. 2002-04, conf. program planning com. 2003-05, nominating com. 2005—), Libr. Adminstrn. and Mgmt. Assn. (bldg. and equipment sect., bldgs. for coll. and univ. librs. com., 2000-02, sys. and svcs. sect. program com. 2004-06), Libr. and Info. Tech. Assn., Spl. Librs. Assn. (sci.-tech. divsn., Boston chpt. adv. coun. 1996-04, chair We. Outreach 1996-04, nominating com. 2004-05), IEEE (libr. adv. coun. 2002-03), Beta Phi Mu. Democrat. Roman Catholic. Avocations: travel, biking, reading, films. Home: 104 Woods Rd Northampton MA 01062-3507 Office: Smith Coll Young Sci Libr Northampton MA 01063-0001 Office Phone: 413-585-2951. Business E-Mail: rpiccini@email.smith.edu.

**PICCO, STEVEN JOSEPH,** lawyer; b. N.Y.C., Sept. 9, 1948; s. Carl and Constance (Speers) Picco; m. Ada T. Ryan, July 15, 1972; children: Christopher, Timothy, Kaitlin. BS, Rider Coll., 1970; JD, Seton Hall U., 1975. Bar: N.J. 1975, U.S. Dist. Ct. N.J. 1975, U.S. Ct. Appeals (3d cir.) 1975. Data processing programmer-sys. engring. N.J. Dept. Labor and Industry, Trenton, 1970—75; project specialist N.J. Dept. Environ. Protection, Trenton, 1975—76, dir. regulatory and govtl. affairs, 1976—78, acting dep. commr., 1979—80, asst. commr., 1979—81, N.J. Dept. Energy, Newark, 1978—79; ptnr. Greenstone & Sokol, Trenton, 1981—87, Picco Mack Herbert Kennedy Jaffe & Yoskin, Trenton, 1988—97, Reed Smith LLP, Princeton, NJ, 1997—, mng. ptnr. N.J. market. Bd. dirs. Mercer County C. of C., Robert Wood Johnson U. Hosp. at Hamilton; mem. N.J. Seed., Am. Heart Assn., Heritage Bd. Avocations: golf, reading, community volunteer work. Office: Reed Smith LLP Princeton Forrestal Village 136 Main St Ste 250 Princeton NJ 08540 Office Phone: 609-514-5970. Business E-Mail: spicco@reedsmith.com.

**PICHASKE, DAVID RICHARD,** language educator; b. Kenmore, N.Y., Sept. 2, 1943; s. Donald Richard Pichaske and Martha Theresa Schisa; m. Elaine Ezekian (div.); children: Stephen Geoffrey, Kristin Diane; m. Michelle Lynn Payne, Sept. 3, 1991. BA, Wittenberg U., 1965; MA, Ohio U., 1967, PhD, Ohio U., 1969. Asst. to assoc. prof. Bradley Polytech. Inst., Peoria, Ill., 1969—; assoc. to prof. S.W. Minn. State U., Marshall, 1980—. Sr. Fulbright lectr. U. Lodz, Poland, 1989—91, U. Latvia, Riga, 1996—97, Mongolian Nat. U., 2003. Author: Beowulf to Beatles: Approaches to Poetry, 1972, Writing Sense: A Handbook of Composition, 1975, A Generation in Motion: Popular Music and Culture in the Sixties, 1979, Chaucer's Literary Pilgrimage: Movement in the Canterbury Tales, 1977, Beowulf to Beatles and Beyond: The Varieites of Poetry, 1981, The Poetry of Rock, 1981, The Jubilee Diary: April 10, 1980-April 19, 1981, 1982, Visiting the Father and Other Poems, 1987, Late Harvest: Rural American Writing, 1992, Poland in Transition: 1989-91, 1994, Southwest Minnesota: The Land and the People, 2000, UBO3: A Season in Outer Mongolia, 2003, Hallelujah Anyway!, 2004, The Father Poems, 2005; co-author (with Joseph Amato and Richard Davies): A Place Called Home,

2003. Recipient Minn. Book award, Minn. Humanities Commn., 2003. Mem.: Jour. Popular Music and Soc. (adv. editor 1995—), Minn. Machinery Mus. (bd. dirs. 2003—). Office: Southwest Minn State Univ Marshall MN 56258 Home: 10489 810th Ave Granite Falls MN 56241-4024 Office Phone: 507-537-6463. Personal E-mail: pichasked@hotmail.com.

**PICHLER, JOSEPH ANTON,** food products executive; b. St. Louis, Oct. 3, 1939; s. Anton Dominick and Anita Marie (Hughes) Pichler; m. Susan Ellen Eyerly, Dec. 27, 1962; children: Gretchen, Christopher, Rebecca, Josh. BBA, U. Notre Dame, 1961; MBA, U. Chgo., 1963, PhD, 1966. Asst. prof. bus. U. Kans., 1964—68, assoc. prof., 1968—73, prof., 1973—80; dean U. Kans. Sch. Bus., 1974—80; exec. v.p. Dillon Cos. Inc., 1980—82, pres., 1982—86; exec. v.p. Kroger Co., Cin., 1985—86, pres., COO, 1986—90, CEO, 1990, CEO, 1990—2003, chmn., 2003—, also bd. dirs. Spl. asst. to asst. sec. for manpower U.S. Dept. Labor, 1968—70; chmn. Kans. Manpower Svcs. Coun., 1974—78; bd. dirs. Milacron Inc., Federated Dept. Stores, Inc., Catalyst. Author (with Joseph McGuire): The Poor and the Rich in America, 1969; co-author: Creativity and Innovation in Manpower Research and Action Programs, 1970, Contemporary Management: Issues and Viewpoints, 1973, Institutional Issues in Public Accounting, 1974, Co-Creation and Capitalism: John Paul II's Laborem Exercens, 1983; co-editor (contbg. author): Ethics, Free Enterprise, and Public Policy, 1978; contbr. articles to profl. jours. Nat. bd. dirs. Boys Hope, 1983—96; mem. Nat. Alliance of Bus. Bd., 1988—95, chmn., 1991—93; mem. fellow adv. com. Woodrow Wilson Found., 1990—93; mem. adv. bd. Salvation Army Sch. for Officers Tng., 1994—2000; bd. dirs. Cin. Opera, 1987—96, adv. mem., 1996—; bd. dirs. Tougaloo Coll., 1986—; mem. Cin. Bus. Com., 1991—, chmn., 1997—98. Named Disting. Alumnus U. Chgo., 1994; recipient Disting. Svc. award, Nat. Conf. Cmty. Justice, 2000, William Booth award, Salvation Army, 1998, Horatio Alger award, 1999, Hall of Fame, Greater Cin. and No. Ky. Bus., 2001; Woodrow Wilson fellow, Ford Found. fellow, Standard Oil Indsl. Rels. fellow, 1966. Mem.: Greater Cin. C. of C. (trustee), Catalyst Bd., Bus. Roundtable, Comml. Club of Cin., Queen City Club. Office: Kroger Co 1014 Vine St Cincinnati OH 45202-1100

**PICK, ANNE DANIELSON,** psychology professor; b. Sycamore, Ill., Jan. 1, 1938; d. Clifford and Marjorie Gilbert Danielson; m. Herbert L. Pick Jr., Dec. 28, 1961; children: Cynthia, Karen, Gretchen. BA, Smith Coll., 1959; PhD, Cornell U., 1963. Asst. prof. Macalester Coll., St. Paul, 1963—66; prof. U. Minn., Mpls., 1973—. Vis. lectr. Makarere U., Kamplala, Uganda, 1969—70; vis. prof. Katholieke U., Nijmegen, Netherlands, 1978, 81; dir. grad. studies U. Minn., 1996—. Co-author: An Ecological Approach to Perceptual Learning and Development, 2000; contbr. articles to profl. jours. Fellow, Ctr. Advanced Study, Stanford, Calif., 1972—73. Mem.: AAUP (pres. Minn. chpt. 1999—2001). Home: 2261 Folwell St Saint Paul MN 55108 Office: U Minn Inst Child Devel 51 E River Rd Minneapolis MN 55455 E-mail: annepick@umn.edu.

**PICK, JAMES BLOCK,** business professor, writer; b. Chgo., July 29, 1943; s. Grant Julius and Helen (Block) Pick. BA, Northwestern U., 1966; MS in Edn., No. Ill. U., 1969; PhD, U. Calif., Irvine, 1974. Cert. computer profl. Asst. rsch. statistician, lectr. Grad. Sch. Mgmt., U. Calif., Riverside, 1975-91, dir. computing 1984-91; co-dir. U.S.-Mex. Database Project, 1988-91; assoc. prof. mgmt. and bus., dir. info. mgmt. program U. Redlands, Calif., 1991-95, 99-01, prof. bus., 1995—, chair dept. mgmt. and bus., 1995-97, 98-99, chair faculty assembly Sch. Bus., 2001—04. Vis. prof. U. Iberoam., Mexico City, 1997, Mexico City, 2001; cons. internat. divsn. U.S. Census Bur., 1978; mem. Univ. Commons. Bd., 1982—86; mem. nat. curriculum task force IS, 1997; mem. U. Commn. Future Bus. Programs, 1998—2000; pres. Orange County chpt. Assn. Sys. Mgmt., 1978—79; mem. bd. govs. PCCLAS, Assn. Borderlands Studies, 1989—92, v.p., 2000—01, pres., 2002—; bd. profls. advisors demographic analysis U. Calif, Irvine, 2002—03; mem. exec. coun. Info. Resources Mgmt. Assn., 2003—; vis. rschr. Ctr. for Rsch. on Immigration, Population, and Pub. Policy U. Calif., Irvine, 2005. Author: Geothermal Energy Development, 1982, Computer Systems in Business, 1986, Atlas of Mexico, 1989, The Mexico Handbook, 1994, Mexico Megacity, 1997, Mexico and Mexico City in the World Economy, 2001, Geographic Systems in Business, 2004, Exploring the Urban Community: A GIS Approach, 2005; mem. editl. bd. Jour. Borderlands Studies, 1999—, Jour. Info. Tech. Cases and Applications, 2002—, condr. rsch. info. sys., population, environ. studies; contbr. articles to profl. jours. Trustee Newport Harbor Art Mus., 1981—87, 1988—96, Berkeley Art Mus. and Pacific Film Archives, 2003—; mem. acquisitions com. Newport Harbor Art Mus., 1987—91, v.p., 1991—96; trustee, chmn. collection com. Orange County Mus. Art, 1996—; mem. com. Block Mus., 1999—2001. Recipient Thunderbird award, Bus. Assn. L.Am. Studies, 1993, Outstanding Alumnus award, No. Ill. U., 2004; Ford Found. grantee, 1998—99, Sr. Fulbright scholar, 2001. Mem.: AAAS, Am. Assn. Geographers, Sociedad de Demografia Mexicana, Internat. Union Sci. Study Population, Population Assn. Am., Am. Statis. Assn., Am. Sociol. Assn., Assn. for Info. Systems, Assn. Computing Machinery, Standard Club (Chgo.). Office: U Redlands Sch Bus 1200 E Colton Ave Redlands CA 92374-3755

**PICK, RYAN THOMAS,** music educator; b. Alexandria, Va., Mar. 29, 1978; s. Gary Ryan and Lori Ann Pick; m. Darlene Loretta Stiles, Oct. 15, 2005. BA, Shenandoah Conservatory, 2003. Music tchr., 2004—; music dir. Epiphany Luth. Ch., Mount Vernon, Va., 2005—. Pvt. piano instr., Va., 2004—. Composer, performer, condr.: Psalm 23 (Bishop's Approval, 2002). Mem.: Music Educators Nat. Conf. Roman Catholic. Avocations: music, reading, cooking, card games, board games. Personal E-mail: ryanthomaspick@musician.org.

**PICKARD, JOHN BENEDICT,** language educator; b. Newton, Mass., Oct. 4, 1928; s. Greenleaf Whittier and Helen (Liston) P.; m. Margaret Suzanne Dederich, Nov. 24, 1956; children: Brigham, Ellen, Nathaniel, Thaddeus, John Samuel; m. Carol Jones Hutcheson, Nov. 22, 2003. BA, Holy Cross Coll., 1950; postgrad., Boston Coll., 1950-51; PhD, U. Wis., 1954. Instr. U. Calif. (Far East Extension), 1956; asst. prof. English Rice U., 1956-63; assoc. prof. U. Fla., Gainesville, 1963-68, prof., 1968—96; ret., 1996. Pres. Alachua Press, Inc., 1999—2003. Author: J.G. Whittier: an Introduction and Interpretation, 1961, Legends of New England by J.G. Whittier, 1965, Emily Dickinson, 1967, Memorabilia of J.G W., 1968, The Letters of John Greenleaf Whittier, 3 vols, 1975, Whittier and Whittierland, 1976, The Parkman Dexter Howe Library: Part IV, The John Greenleaf Whittier Collection, 1987; editor: Samuel Kipnis Film Collection, 1982, Historic Gainesville: A Tour Guide to the Past, 1990, rev., reprinted 1992, Florida's Eden: An Illustrated History of Alachua County, 1994, Historic Alachua County and Old Gainesville, 2002, Dudley Farm: A History of Florida Farm Life, 2003, A Partnership withthe Past: The Alachua County Historic Trust Story, 2004; editor Everhill Whittier Clubs Whittier Newsletter, 1966-87, 1996-04. V.p. Nat. Newman Orgn., 1962-63; bd. dirs. Hist. Gainesville, Inc., 1971-72, 86-90, v.p., 1987-88, editor newsletter, 1987-89, pres., 1988-89; bd. dirs. Matheson Hist. Ctr., 1989-2003, editor newsletter, 1991-98; bd. dirs. St. Augustine Sch. Religion, 1971-72; bd. dirs. Fla. Trail Assn., 1977-80, adv. bd., 1980-86; bd. dirs. Alachua County Hist. Soc., 1995-97, pres., 1997-99; trustee John Greenleaf Whittier Homestead, 1966-81, 1996-2004; pres. The Alachua Press, 1999-2003. Served with U.S. Army, 1954-56 Named Outstanding Tchr. Rice U., 1958; Am. Philos. Soc. grantee, 1962, 67, 69 Mem. MLA, South Cen. MLA, Fla. Coll. Tchrs., English, Am. Film Inst., Fla. Trail Assn., Fla. Trust for Hist. Preservation. Democrat. Roman Catholic. Home: 35 George Cir Maggie Valley NC 28751-7667 Personal E-mail: candben@sbcglobal.net.

**PICKARD, WILLIAM FRANK,** plastics company executive; b. LaGrange, Ga., Jan. 28, 1941; s. William H. and Victoria (Woodward) P. AS, Mott Community Coll., 1962; BS, Western Mich. U., 1964; MSW, U. Mich., 1965; PhD, Ohio State U., 1971; PhD in Bus. Adminstrn. (hon.), Cleary Coll., 1980. Dir. employment and edn. Urban League Cleve., 1965-67; exec. dir. NAACP, Cleve., 1967-69; assoc. dir. dept. urban studies Cleve. State U., 1971-72; assoc. prof. Wayne State U., Detroit, 1972-74; owner, operator McDonald's Restaurants, Detroit, 1971—; chmn., chief exec. officer Regal Plastics, Roseville, Mich., 1985—. Vis. lectr. Cleve. State U., U. Chgo., Hiram Coll.,

U. Toledo, U. Mich., Case Western Res. U., Ohio State U., Wayne County Community Coll., McDonald's Hamburger U.; participant mgmt. seminar Case Western Res. U., Greater Cleve. Associated Found. and Rockefeller Found., 1968; chmn. Gov.'s adv. com. on minority bus., pres. 1976; bd. dirs. First Nat. Nat. Bank, Mich. Nat. Bank Corp., Farmington Hills. Mem. Pres.-elect Ronald Regan's transition team to SBA; chmn. econ. devel. com. Nat. Black Rep. Council, 1978, bd. dirs. com. to elect Gov. Ronald Reagan Pres., 1980, chmn. congl. liaison com., 1982; chmn. Mich. Reps. Urban Campaign to elect Gov. Reagan Pres., 1980; vice chmn. Mich. Rep. State Com., 1981; bd. control Grand Valley State Coll., Allendale, Mich.; bd. dirs. Oakwood Hosp., Kirkwood Gen. Hosp., Detroit, Detroit Black Causes, Detroit Econ. Devel. Corp., 1977, Nat. Minority Purchasing Council, Washington, Detroit Urban League, vice chmn.; appointed by Pres. Ronald Regan, and confirmed by U.S. Senate Chmn. of African Devel. Found., 1983. Named one of Ten Outstanding Young Men Cleve., Jaycees, 1969; Alice W. Gault schlor, 1962-63; Nat. Urban League fellow, 1964. Mem. Booker T. Washington Bus. Assn., NAACP, Jaycees, Alpha Phi Alpha. Home: 335 Pine Ridge Dr Bloomfield Hills MI 48304-2140

**PICKEN, MARIA M. (MARIA M. MROZOWICZ-PICKEN),** pathologist; d. Jozef and Marianna Mrozowicz; m. Roger N. Picken, Dec. 19, 1978. MD, Med. Sch., Gdansk, Poland, 1972, PhD, 1978. Cert. anatomic and clin. pathology Am. Bd. Pathology, 1987, immunopathology Am. Bd. Pathology, 1988. Asst. prof. Loyola U. Med. Ctr., Maywood, Ill., 1988—94, assoc. prof., 1994—2000, prof., 2000—. Dir. Loyola U. Med. Ctr., Maywood, Ill., 1988—; mem. med. adv. bd. Nat. Kidney Found. Ill. Contbr. chapters to books, scientific papers to profl. jours. Mem.: U.S. and Canadian Acad. Pathology (amb. 2006—), Renal Pathology Soc. (councilor 2006—). Office: Loyola Univ Med Ctr Pathology Bldg 110 Rm 2242 2160 S First Ave Maywood IL 60153 Office Phone: 708-327-2607. Home Fax: 847-240-0467; Office Fax: 708-327-2620. E-mail: mpicken@lumc.edu.

**PICKENPAUGH, THOMAS EDWARD,** archaeologist, anthropologist; b. St. Clairsville, Ohio, Feb. 8, 1945; s. Douglas Giffin and Betty June (Brown) P. BA, Kent State U., 1970, MA, 1971; ABD, Cath. U., 1980. Anthropologist, instr. sociology and anthropology Wheeling Coll., W.Va., 1972-73; anthropologist, instr., asst. prof. anthropology Ohio U.-Ea., 1972-74, 78, archaeologist, asst. prof. anthropology St. Clairsville, 1986-95; mus. technician US Dept. Interior, Nat. Pk. Svc., Washington, 1983; mus. technican Nat. Mus. Natural History, Smithsonian Instn., Washington, 1984-87; mus. specialist, loan officer USN, Naval Hist. Ctr., Washington, 1987—. Dir. archaeol. excavations Brokaw Village Site, St. Clairsville, Ohio, 1972-74, 76-78, 82, 86-96, 98, mem. archaeol. staff Thunderbird Site, Front Royal, Va., Savannah River, Ga., SC, Richard B. Russell Dam Project, 1980, El Mirador Site, Guatemala, 1980, Louis Berger Internat. Project, Trenton, NJ, 1983-84, Sully Plantation, Loudon County, Va., 1984, Fells Point Project, Balt., 1984, exhibited rsch. on Symbols of Rank and Power, Ohio U. Eastern Art Gall., 1998, others. Author: Dominant Predators and Paramount Leaders: Symbols of Rank and Power in Traditional Cultures, 2005; rsch. exhibition: Martin Luther King Meml. Libr., 2003—04; contbr. articles to profl. jours. Rsch. grantee US Dept. Interior, Nat. Pk. Svc., 1978-79, Nat. Geog. Soc., 1992-93. Mem. AAAS, Am. Anthropol. Assns., Washington Assn. Profl. Anthropologists, Anthropol. Soc. Washington, Am. Assn. Museums, Internat. Platform Assn. Achievements include rsch. on prehistoric Am. Indians and the symbols of rank and power in traditional cultures, evidence for Late Archaic in uplands of eastern Ohio, geographical range of Hamilton Incurvate triangle in area. Home: # 201 12512 Village Square Ter Rockville MD 20852-1954 Office: Naval Hist Ctr Washington Navy Yard 805 Kidder Breeze SE Washington DC 20374-5060 Office Phone: 202-433-7886. Business E-Mail: thomas.pickenpaugh@navy.mil.

**PICKENS, ALEXANDER LEGRAND,** retired education educator; b. Waco, Tex., Aug. 30, 1921; s. Alex LeGrand and Elma L. (Johnson) P.; m. Frances M. Jenkins, Aug. 20, 1955. BA, So. Meth. U., 1950; MA, North Tex. U., Denton, 1952; EdD, Columbia U., 1959. Tchr. art public schs., Dallas, 1950-53, Elizabeth, N.J., 1953-54; instr. Coll. Architecture and Design U. Mich., 1954-59; assoc. prof. dept. art U. Ga., Athens, 1959-62; assoc. prof. Coll. Edn. U. Hawaii, Honolulu, 1962-68, prof. edn., 1969—2001, chmn. doctoral studies curriculum instrn. Coll. Edn., 1984-89, asst. to dean for alumni affairs coll. devel., 1989-01, ret., 2001, emeritus prof., 2002—. Dir. children's classes Ft. Worth Children's Mus., 1951-53; head art Nat. Music Camp, Interlochen, Mich., summers, 1957-58, U. Oreg., Portland, summers 1959-60, 62; cons. youth art activities Foremost Dairies, 1964-74; cons. art films United World Films, 1970-75; art edn. cons. Honolulu Paper Co., 1970-76, Kamehameha Sch., Bishop Estate, 1978-95. Exhibited ceramics, Wichita Internat. Exhbn., Syracuse (N.Y.) Nat. Exhbn., St. Louis Mus., Dallas Mus., San Antonio Mus., Detroit Art Inst., Hawaii Craftsmen, also others; editorial bd.: Arts and Activities mag, 1955-82; editor: U. Hawaii Edn. Perspectives, 1964-99; contbr. articles to profl. jours. Mem. adult com. Dallas County chpt. Jr. ARC, 1951-53; mem. exec. com. Dallas Crafts Guild, 1950-53; v.p., publicity chmn. U. Ga. Cmty. Concert Assn., 1960-62, program chmn. Gov.'s Commn. Observing 150 Yrs. Pub. Edn. in Hawaii, 1990-91; bd. dirs. Honolulu Theatre for Youth, 1998-2003; bd. dirs. Honolulu Symphony, 1989—; bd. dirs. Chamber Music Hawaii, 2003—. Served with USAAF. Recipient award merit Tex. State Fair, 1957, All-Am. award Ednl. Press Assn. Am., 1968, 70, 72, 75, 79, Regents' medal for tchg. U. Hawaii, 1989, Gov.'s Commn. Observance of 150 Yrs. Pub. Edn., 1990-91. Mem. AAUP, NEA, Internat. Soc. Edn., Nat. Art Edn. Assn., Coun. for Advancement and Support of Edn., Assn. Fundraising Profls., Nat. Planned Giving Coun., Hawaii Planned Giving Coun., Phi Delta Kappa, Kappa Delta Pi. Address: 1471 Kalaepohaku St Honolulu HI 96816-1804 Personal E-mail: apickens@hawaii.rr.com.

**PICKENS, BOONE (THOMAS BOONE PICKENS JR.),** oil industry executive; b. Holdenville, Okla., May 22, 1928; s. Thomas Boone Pickens and Grace Molonson; m. Lynn O'Brien, 1949 (div. 1971); 4 children; m. Beatrice Louise Carr, Apr. 21, 1972 (div.); 1 adopted child; m. Nelda Cain, 1999. BS in Geology, Okla. State U., 1951. Geologist Phillips Petroleum Co., 1951-54; consulting geologist, 1954-56; with Petroleum Exploration, Inc., 1956, Altair Oil & Gas Co.; chmn. bd., pres., dir. Mesa Petroleum Co., Inc., 1964-85; gen. ptnr., CEO Mesa Ltd. Partnership, 1985—96; founder BP Capital Mgmt., 1996—, Mesa Water, 1999—. Mem. Nat. Petroleum Council, 1970-; founder, chmn. United Shareholders Assn., Washington. Author: Boone, 1987, The Luckiest Guy in the World, 2000. Adviser Nat. Campaign for Drug Free Am. Named one of Forbes' Richest Americans, 2006. Office: BP Capital 8117 Preston Rd Ste 260 Dallas TX 75225*

**PICKENS, FRANCES JENKINS,** artist, educator; b. Dodd's, Tex., Feb. 26, 1927; d. John Morgan and Mary (Burton) Jenkins; m. Alexander Pickens, Aug. 20, 1955. BA, U. of North Tex., 1947, MA, 1954; MEd, U. Hawaii, 1976. Tchr. art public schs., Dallas, 1948-55, Dearborn, Mich., 1955-58, White Plains, N.Y., 1958-59, Athens, Ga., 1960-62; gallery lectr. Honolulu Acad. Arts, 1962—63; tchr. art Punahou Sch., Honolulu, 1963-65, The Kamehameha Schs., Honolulu, 1965-85; jewelry and metal artist Honolulu, 1963—. Instr. jewelry U. Hawaii, Honolulu, 1967, 75, 77. Exhibited works in shows at Mus. of Contemporary Crafts, N.Y., Schmuckmuseum, Germany, Renwick Gallery, Washington, Wichita Mus., Women in Design Internat., Mich. Influence, 1981, Materials Hard and Soft, United States Metal, Hawaii Craftsmen Ann., Artists of Hawaii, 1965— (Disting. Artist 1991), East-West Ctr. Gallery, 2003, retrospective Honolulu Acad. Arts, 2001, KDA Gallery, Honolulu, 2005; represented in permanent collection at Acad. of Arts, The Contemporary Mus., Honolulu, Hawaii State Art Mus., Renwick Gallery, Washington, Wichita Art Assn., Kans.; photographs of work included in Goldsmith's Jour., Jewelry, Contemporary Design and Technique, Jewelry/Metalwork Survey, The Metalsmith's Book of Boxes and Lockets; contbr. articles to Arts and Activities mag., Sch. Arts, Ornament mag. Chmn. state crafts State Fair Tex., Dallas, 1954; Crafts Symposium planning com. Hawaii State Found. Culture and Arts, Honolulu, 1968-69; workshop for instrs. U.S. Army Arts and Crafts, Ft. Shafter, 1975. Named Distinguished

Artist of Hawaii, Honolulu Acad. Arts, 1991. Mem. Soc. N.Am. Goldsmiths, Dallas Craft Guild, Hawai Craftsmen (charter, v.p., pres.), Renwick Alliance. Avocations: travel, jewelry, metalwork. Home: 1471 Kalaepohaku St Honolulu HI 96816-1804

**PICKENS, ROBERT BRUCE,** retired accountant; b. Uniontown, Pa., May 20, 1926; s. Joseph Abraham and Margaret Gertrude (Brown) P.; m. Mary Ellen Evans, Sept. 9, 1950; children: Laura Gail Martin, Rachel Diane Rosen, David Bruce. BS in Bus. Adminstrn, Waynesburg Coll., 1950. C.P.A., Pa., Ill., Ind. Vice pres. Home Bottle Gas Corp., Uniontown, 1950-51; jr. accountant to sr. accountant Tenney & Co., Uniontown, 1951-56; mgr. Hosp. Service Assn. Western Pa., Pitts., 1956-57; auditor U. Pitts., 1957-58; sr. accountant Eugene A. Conniff Co., Pitts., 1958-59; mgr. Sheppard & Co., Pitts., 1959-63; supr. Alexander Grant & Co., Chgo., 1963-65; asst. to treas. CTS Corp., Elkhart, Ind., 1965, gen. auditor, controller, chief acctg. officer, 1966-81; ret. 1981; self-employed as acct., 1981-86; sec., controller, chief acctg. officer SEA Group, Inc. and SEA-ILAN, Inc., 1987-88; pvt. cons., 1989—; ret., 1999. Mem. Bower Hill Civic League, 1956-62; active Boy Scouts Am., 1938-62. Served to cpl. USAAC, 1944-45; USAF Res., 1947-50. Mem. AICPA, Pa. Inst. CPAs, Ill. CPA Soc., Ind. CPA Soc. Republican. Presbyn. (elder, trustee 1959-61, treas. 1960-61). Home: 73 Rogers Rd Carmel IN 46032-1467

**PICKENS, SCHANICA LYNN,** homefinding supervisor, online educator; b. Far Rockaway, NY, Oct. 30, 1977; d. Joe Willie and Betty Pearl Pickens; life ptnr. Johnny Marvin Toussaint; 1 child, Kahmari Johnny Toussaint. BA, Oswego State U., NY, 1999; MSW, NYU, 2003. Homefinding specialist St. Christopher-Ottilie Svcs. for Children and Families, Freeport, NY, 1999—2001; program dir. Project Hope The New Direction, Inc., Queens Village, NY, 2000—02; tng., compliance, investigations coord. HeartShare Human Svcs., Bklyn., 2001—02, chairperson, 2001—02; homefinding supr. SCO Family Svcs., Bklyn., 2002—; online coll. instr. Axia Coll. Western Internat. U., Phoenix, 2006—. Behavior mgmt. cons., trainer People Places, Inc., NYC, 2005—, So. Queens Pk. Assn., Inc., Jamaica, NY, 2004—. Mem.: NASW (assoc.). Home: 834 Central Ave Far Rockaway NY 11691 Office: SCO Family Svcs 398 Grant Ave Brooklyn NY 11208 Office Phone: 718-827-8485. Personal E-mail: pickens25@aol.com. E-mail: spickens@sco.org.

**PICKENS, SCOTT E.,** lawyer; b. Rochester, NY, June 27, 1956; BS with distinction, Cornell Univ., 1978, JD cum laude, 1981. Bar: DC 1981, US Ct. of Fed. Claims, US Ct. Appeals (Fed. cir.). Law clk. Judge John H. Pratt, US Dist Ct., DC Dist., 1981—82; ptnr. Miller & Chevalier Chartered, Washington; ptnr., leader Govt. Contracts & Govt. Disputes practice Pillsbury Winthrop Shaw Pittman, Washington. Editor: Cornell Law Rev. Mem.: ABA (vice chmn. E-Commerce com.), Bd. of Contract Appeals Bar Assn., Nat. Contract Mgmt. Assn. Nat. Def. Indsl. Assn., Fed. Cir. Bar Assn., DC Bar Assn. Office: Scott E Pickens Of Pillsbury Winthrop 2300 N St Nw Washington DC 20037-1122 Office Phone: 202-775-9843. Office Fax: 202-833-8491. E-mail: scott.pickens@pillsburylaw.com.

**PICKER, RANDAL C.,** law educator; b. 1959; BA in Economics, U. Chgo., 1980, MA in Economics, 1982, JD, 1985. Bar: Ill. 1986, US Ct. Appeals 5th Cir., US Ct. Appeals 7th Cir. Law clk. to Hon. Richard Posner US Ct. Appeals 7th Cir., 1985—86; assoc. Sidley & Austin, Chgo., 1986—89, counsel, 1993—99; asst. prof. U. Chgo. Law Sch., 1989—93, prof., 1993—97, Paul and Theo Leffman prof. comml. law, 1998—, academic assoc. dean, 1994—96, dir. Olin Program in Law & Economics, 1999—2001. Commr. Nat. Conf. Commissioners on Uniform State Laws, 1991—; sr. fellow The Computation Inst. of U. Chgo. & Argonne Nat. Lab., 2000—. Co-author (with D. Baird & R. Gertner): Game Theory and the Law, 1994; co-author: (with D. Baird & T. Jackson) Security Interests in Personal Property: Cases, Problems and Materials, 2002. Mem.: ABA, Nat. Bankruptcy Conf., Am. Assn. Law Schools, Am. Bankruptcy Inst., Am. Law & Economics Assn. Office: U Chgo Law Sch 1111 E 60th St Chicago IL 60637 Office Phone: 773-702-0864. E-mail: r-picker@uchicago.edu.

**PICKERELL, JAMES HOWARD,** photojournalist; b. Dayton, Ohio, June 9, 1936; s. Howard and Frances (Harrison) P.; m. Mary Louise Fisher, June 26, 1965; children: Cheryl Elizabeth, Stacy Rae. Student, Ohio U., 1954-56; BA, UCLA, 1963. Comml. photographer, 1963—; ind. photographer Vietnam, 1963-67. Author: Vietnam in the Mud, 1966, Marketing Photography in the Digital Environment, 1994, Negotiating Stock Photo Prices, 5th edit., 2001; writer, pub.: newsletter Selling Stock. With USN, 1956-60. Mem. Nat. Press Photographers Assn. (1st Pl. Spot News award 1965), Am. Soc. Media Photographers (nat. bd. 1987-89), Profl. Photographers Assn., Beta Theta Pi. Address: 8104 Cindy Ln Bethesda MD 20817-6915 Office Phone: 301-251-0720. Personal E-mail: jim@chd.com.

**PICKERING, CHIP (CHARLES WILLIS PICKERING JR.),** congressman; b. Laurel, Ms., Aug. 10, 1963; m. Leisha Jane Prather; 5 children. BA in Bus. Adminstrn., U. Miss., 1986; MBA, Baylor U., Waco, Tex., 1989. Presdl. appointee USDA, 1989—90; legis. asst. Staff of US Senator Trent Lott, Miss., 1992—96; mem. US Congress from 3rd Miss. dist., 1997—. Co-chmn. Miss. for Bush, 2000, 04; vice chmn. energy and commerce com. US Congress, mem. agr. com., transp. and infrastructure com., sci. com., House Rep. Policy com., asst. majority whip. Republican. Office: US House of Reps 229 Cannon House Office Bldg Washington DC 20515-0001*

**PICKERING, JAMES HENRY, III,** academic administrator, educator; b. NYC, July 11, 1937; s. James H. and Anita (Felber) P.; m. Patricia Paterson, Aug. 18, 1962; children: David Scott, Susan Elizabeth. BA, Williams Coll., 1959; MA, Northwestern U., 1960, PhD, 1964. Instr. English Northwestern U., 1963-65; mem. faculty Mich. State U., East Lansing, 1965-81, prof. English, 1972-81, grad. and assoc. chmn. dept., 1968-75, dir. Honors Coll., 1975-81; dean Coll. Humanities and Fine Arts U. Houston, 1981-90, sr. v.p., provost, 1990-92, pres., 1992-95. Author: The Spy, 1971, The Harper Reader, 1971, Fiction 100, 1974, 78, 82, 85, 88, 92, 95, 98, 2001, 04, The World Turned Upside Down: Prose and Poetry of the American Revolution, 1975, The Spy Unmasked, 1975, The City in American Literature, 1977, Concise Companion to Literature, 1981, Literature, 1982, 86, 90, 94, 97, Mountaineering in Colorado, 1987, Wild Life on the Rockies, 1988, A Mountain Boyhood, 1988, The Spell of the Rockies, 1989, Purpose and Process, 1989, Poetry, 1990, In Beaver World, 1990, Rocky Mountain Wonderland, 1991, A Summer Vacation in the Parks and Mountains of Colorado, 1992, Fiction 50, 1993, Knocking Round the Rockies, 1994, Drama, 1994, Frederick Chapin's Colorado, 1995; This Blue Hollow: Estes Park, The Early Years, 1859-1915, 1999, Mr. Stanley of Estes Park, 2000, In the Vale of Elkanah, 2003, The Ways of the Mountains, 2003, Early Estes Park Historical Narratives, 4 vols., 2004, America's Switzerland: Estes Park and Rocky Mountain National Park, The Growth Years, 2005, Enos Mill's Colorado, 2005, Estes Park and Rocky Mountain National Park, Then and Now, 2006. Mem. Coll. English Assn. (pres. 1980-81), Phi Beta Kappa, Phi Kappa Phi, Omicron Delta Kappa. Office: U Houston Dept English Houston TX 77204-0001 Personal E-mail: jhpick@earthlink.net.

**PICKERING, THOMAS REEVE,** former aerospace transportation executive, former diplomat; b. Orange, NJ, Nov. 5, 1931; s. Hamilton R. and Sarah C. (Chasteney) P.; m. Alice J. Stover, Nov. 24, 1955; children: Timothy R., Margaret S. AB, Bowdoin Coll., 1953; MA, Fletcher Sch. Law and Diplomacy, 1954, U. Melbourne, Australia, 1956. Joined U.S. Fgn. Svc., 1959; fgn. affairs officer ACDA, 1961; polit. adviser U.S. del. 18 Nation Disarmament Conf., Geneva, 1962-64; consul Zanzibar, 1965-67; counselor of embassy, dep. chief mission Am. Embassy, Dar es Salaam, Tanzania, 1967-69; dep. dir. Bur. Politico-Mil. Affairs State Dept., 1969-73; spl. asst. to Sec. of State May 1973-74; exec. sec. State Dept., 1973-74; U.S. amb. to Jordan, 1974-78; asst. sec. for Bur. Oceans, Internat. Environ. and Sci. Affairs, Washington, 1978-81; U.S. amb. to Nigeria, 1981-83; U.S. amb. to El Salvador, 1983-85; U.S. amb. to Israel, 1985-88; U.S. permanent rep. to UN, 1989-92; U.S. amb.

to India, 1992-93; U.S. amb. to Russia, 1993-96; pres. Eurasia Found., 1996-97; undersec. of state for polit. affairs Dept. of State, Washington, 1997—2000; sr. v.p. internat. relations The Boeing Comp., 2001—06; ret., 2006. Served to lt. comdr. USNR, 1956-59. Mem. Council Fgn. Relations, Internat. Inst. Strategic Studies, Phi Beta Kappa. Business E-Mail: thomas.r.pickering@boeing.com.

**PICKETT, BETTY HORENSTEIN,** psychologist; b. Providence, Feb. 15, 1926; d. Isadore Samuel and Etta Lillian (Morrison) Horenstein; m. James McPherson Pickett, Mar. 10, 1952. AB magna cum laude, Brown U., 1945, ScM, 1947, PhD, 1949. Asst. prof. psychology U. Minn., Duluth, 1949-51; asst. prof. U. Nebr., 1951; lectr. U. Conn., 1952; profl. assoc. psychol. scis. Bio-Scis. Info. Exch., Smithsonian Instn., Washington, 1953-58; exec. sec. behavioral scis. study sect. exptl. psychology study sect. div. research grants NIH, Bethesda, Md., 1958-61; rsch. cons. to mental health unit HEW, Boston, 1962-63; exec. sec. rsch. career program NIMH, 1963-66, chief cognition and learning sect. div. extramural research program, 1966-68, dep. dir., 1968-74, dir. div. spl. mental health programs, 1974-75, acting dir. div. extramural rsch. program, 1975-77; assoc. dir. extramural and collaborative rsch. program Nat. Inst. Aging, 1977-79; dep. dir. Nat. Inst. Child Health and Human Devel., Bethesda, Md., 1979-81, acting dir., 1981-82, dir. Div. Rsch. Resources, 1982-88. Mem. health scientist administr. panel CSC Bd. Examiners, 1970—76, 1981—88; mem. coun. on grad. edn. Brown U. Grad. Sch., 1989—91. Contbr. articles to profl. jours. Mem. APA, Am. Psychol Soc., Psychonomic Soc., Assn. Women in Sci., AAAS, Phi Beta Kappa, Sigma Xi. Home: Morgan Bay Rd PO Box 198 Surry ME 04684-0198

**PICKETT, CECIL B.,** pharmaceutical executive; BS in Biology, Calif. State U., Hayward; PhD in Cell Biology, UCLA. Held various positions including rsch. fellow, biochemical regulation; assoc. dir. to dir., dept. molecular pharmacology & biochemistry Merck Rsch. Labs.; exec. dir., rsch. Merck Frosst Ctr. for Therapeutic Devel., Montreal, Canada, v.p.; joined advancing to exec. v.p. discovery rsch. Schering-Plough Rsch. Inst., Schering-Plough Corp., Kenilworth, NJ, 1993—2002, pres., 2002—, v. v.p., 2002—. Spkr. in field; mem. sci. bd. FDA; adv. com. to dir. NIH; nat. cancer policy bd. Inst. Medicine; disting. lectr. Jonsson Comprehensive Cancer Ctr., U. Calif., LA, 1995. Contbr. articles to profl. jours.; various editl bds.; med. jours. and rsch. orgns. Mem. vol. bd. dir. NJ Performing Arts Ctr. Named one of Leading Women and Minority Scientists, NJ Acad. Sciences, 2005; recipient Scholarly Achievement and Acad. Dist., UCLA Alumni Assn., 1976, Robert A. Scala award, Rutgers U. and Univ. Medicine and Dentistry NJ, 1993, CIIT Ctr. for Health Rsch. Founders' award, 2001; scholar Macy scholar, Marine Biol. Labs, 1978. Mem.: AAAS, Inst. Medicine, Am. Assn. Cancer Rsch., Am. Soc. Biochemistry and Molecular Biology, Am. Soc. Cell Biology. Office: Schering-Plough Rsch Inst 2000 Galloping Hill Rd Kenilworth NJ 07033*

**PICKETT, CECIL BRUCE,** cell biologist; b. Canton, Ill., Oct. 5, 1945; married; two children. BS, Calif. State U., 1971; PhD, UCLA, 1976. Fellow in cell biology UCLA, 1976-78; with Merck Sharp & Dohme Rsch. Labs., 1978—93; exec. v.p. discovery rsch. Schering-Plough Rsch. Inst., Kenilworth, NJ, 1993—2002, pres., 2002—; sr. v.p. Schering Corp., 2004—; pres. SPRI, 2004—. Macy scholar Marine Biol. Lab, Woods Hole, Mass., 1978; vis. asst. prof. Coll. Medicine Howard U., Washington, 1978-83; adj. assoc. prof. N.J. Sch. Medicine & Dentistry, 1985-88; assoc. prof. U. Montreal, 1989; adj. prof. McGill U., 1990; disting. lecturer, Jonsson Comprehensive Cancer Ctr., UCLA, 1995; mem. sci. adv. bd. FDA; member. mem. GM Adv. Council, Cancer Rsch. Found., 2004. Recipient Robert A. Scala Award and Lectureship in Toxicology, Rutgers U. & U. Medicine & Dentistry of NJ, 1993, Founders award, CIIT Centers for Health Research, 2001. Mem. AAAS, IOM, NAS, Am. Soc. Biochemistry & Molecular Biology, Am. Assn. Cancer Rsch., Am. Soc. Cell Biology, Am. Assn. Advancement Sci.; mem. adv. com. to dir. NIH. Office: Schering-Plough Rsch Inst 2015 Galloping Hill Rd Kenilworth NJ 07033-1300

**PICKETT, DONN PHILIP,** lawyer; b. Chgo., May 3, 1952; s. Philip Gordon and Gloria Joan (Hansen) P.; m. Janet Benson, Aug. 25, 1973; children: Jessica Kelly, William Benson. BA magna cum laude, Carleton Coll., Minn., 1973; JD, Yale U., 1976. Bar: Calif. 1976, U.S. Dist. Ct. (no. dist.) Calif. 1976, U.S. Dist. Ct. (ctrl. dist.) Calif. 1980, U.S. Dist. Ct. (ea. dist.) Calif. 1983, U.S. Ct. Appeals (9th cir.) Calif. 1979, U.S. Ct. Appeals (5th cir.) Tex. 1994, U.S. Supreme Ct. 1991, U.S. Dist. Ct. Ariz. 1997, U.S. Dist. Ct. Colo. 1997, U.S. Ct. Appeals (fed. cir.) 1997, U.S. Ct. Appeals (11th cir.) 1998. Assoc. McCutchen, Doyle, Brown & Enersen, San Francisco, 1976-83, ptnr., 1983—2002, chair, 2001—02; ptnr. Bingham McCutchen LLP, San Francisco, 2002—, vice chmn., 2002—. Mem. U.S. Dist. Ct. Civil Justice Reform Act adv. group, 1995-99; bd. dirs. Equal Justice Works, 2005—, Legal Aid Soc., San Francisco, 2006—. Bd. dirs. Bay Area Coun., 2003—. Mem. ABA (chmn. civil practice com. antitrust sect. 2001-04, vice chmn. trial practice com. 2004-), State Bar Calif. (com. on adminstrn. of justice 1988-91, vice chmn. 1992-93, chmn. 1993-94, legis. chmn. 1994-96), San Francisco Bar Assn. (judiciary com. 1988-92, exec. com. conf. of dels. 1993-96, 2000, bd. dirs. 1997-99), Phi Beta Kappa. Office: Bingham McCutchen LLP 3 Embarcadero Ctr San Francisco CA 94111 Office Phone: 415-393-2082. Business E-Mail: donn.pickett@bingham.com.

**PICKETT, JAMES V.,** food service executive; Chmn. Pickett Realty Advisors, Inc., Dublin, Ohio; pres., CEO of various companies generally known as Pickett Companies, 1969—; vice-chmn. Banc On Capital Corp., 1993—99; prin. Stonehedge Fin. Holding, Inc., 1999—2004. Bd. dir. Wendy's Internat., Inc., Dublin, 1982—2006, chmn. bd. dirs., 2006—. Mailing: Wendy's Internat Inc One Dave Thomas Blvd Dublin OH 43017*

**PICKETT, JUSTUS CUNNINGHAM,** medical association administrator; BA, W.Va. U., 1954, BS, 1956; MD, Med. Coll. Va., 1958. Diplomate Am. Bd. of Orthop. Surgery, 1967. Surg. intern Med. Coll. Va. Hosps., 1958—59, resident, 1959—62, chief resident in orthop., 1961—63; pres. Calif. Med. Assn., Sacramento, 1999—2000, chair bd. trustees, 2000—. Polit. cons. Calif. Med. Assn., Sacramento. Pres. Rotary Club of Napa, Calif. Col. USAF Res., 1982—93. Recipient MacClaggen award, Calif. Med. Assn., 2005. Fellow ACS, Am. Acad. of Orthop. Surgeons; mem.: Calif. Orthop. Assn., Western Orthop. Assn. Episcopalian. Office: JC Pickett MD Inc 3260 Beard Rd Napa CA 94558 Office Phone: 707-255-8877.

**PICKETT, OWEN BRADFORD,** lawyer, former congressman; b. Richmond, Va., Aug. 31, 1930; BS, Va. Poly. Inst., 1952; LLB, U. Richmond, 1955. CPA Va.; bar: Va. 1955, D.C. 1962. Pvt. practice, Virginia Beach, Va., 1964—86; mem. Va. Ho. of Dels., Richmond, 1972—86, US Congress from 2d Va. dist., Washington, 1987—2001; of counsel Troutman, Sanders, LLP, Virginia Beach, 2001—. Mem. resources com. Armed Svcs. Com.; chmn. Va. Dem. State Ctrl. Com., 1980—82. Mem.: D.C. Bar Assn., Va. Bar Assn. Office: Troutman Sanders LLP Ste 2000 222 Ctrl Pk Dr Virginia Beach VA 23462 Office Phone: 757-687-7525. Personal E-mail: obpickett@msn.com. Business E-mail: owen.pickett@troutmansanders.com.

**PICKETT, SANDRA,** information scientist; BS, U. Tex.; MA, U. Houston. Councilwoman City of Liberty, Tex., 1974—98, mayor pro tem, 1976—98; commr., chair Tex. State Libr. and Archives Commn., Austin, 1995—. Past chmn. Liberty County Hist. Commn.; past dir., pres. Preservation Tex.; mem. Nat. Mus. and Libr. Svcs. Bd., Washington, 2004—. Named Citizen of Yr. of C., 1981; recipient John Ben Shepperd Leadership award, Tex. Hist. Commn., 1993; Paul Harris fellow Rotary Internat., 1998. Mem.: Atascosito Hist. Soc. (pres.). Mailing: PO Box 19191 Liberty TX 77575 Office: Tex State Libr and Archives Commn PO Box 12927 Austin TX 78711

**PICKETT, STEPHEN ALAN,** hospital administrator; b. Ft. Wayne, Ala., Dec. 22, 1953; s. James Benjamin Pickett and Dorothy Jane (Howell) Pickett Fancher; m. Neil Annette Horsley, Mar. 5, 1977; children: Stefanie Leigh, Allison Marie. BBA, U. Montevallo, 1976; MPH, Tulane U., 1995. CPA, Ala.

Sr. acct. Ernst & Whinney, Birmingham, Ala., 1976-78; contr. East End Meml. Hosp., Birmingham, 1978, v.p. fin., 1979-84, W. Va. U. Hosps., Morgantown, 1985-87, exec. v.p., adminstr., 1987-91; adminstr., COO Tulane U. Hosp. and Clinic, New Orleans, 1991-95, CEO, 1995—2004; CFO, UAB Health System, Birmingham, Ala., 2004—. Bd. dirs. Met. Hosp. Coun., 1991—, Associated Hosp. Svcs., 1991—. Active sustaining mem. campaign BSA, 1978; mem. Jefferson County Rep. Exec. Com., Birmingham, 1982, First Bapt. Ch. New Orlean (fin. com. 1993—). Fellow Healthcare Fin. Mgmt. Assn.; mem. AICPA, Ala. Soc. CPAs, U. Montevallo Alumni Assn. (life), Alpha Tau Omega Alumni Assn., Rotary. Baptist. Office: Chief Fin Officer UAB Health Sys 500 22d St S Ste 408 Birmingham AL 35233 Office Phone: 205-975-5412. Business E-Mail: spickett@uabmc.edu.

**PICKETT, STEPHEN WESLEY,** academic administrator, consultant; b. Billings, Mont., May 27, 1956; s. Wesley William and Carol Ann (Bollum) P. BA, Houston Bapt. U., 1980; MS, U. North Tex., 1988. Cert. elem. tchr., rehab. counselor, Tex. Hosp. tchr. Houston Ind. Sch. Dist., 1981-85; asst. to assoc. dean of students U. North Tex., Denton, 1988-90, asst. coord. disabled student svcs., Office Student Devel., 1990-91, dir. Office Disability Accommodation, 1991—2001, univ. mentor/advisor, 1992—2001; dir. disability svcs. U. Oreg., Eugene, 2002—, assoc. dir. office of acd. advising, 2002—. Co-author: curriculum guide The Newspaper as a Student Communicator, 1982 (winner Exxon Found.'s Impact Two award for creative teaching). Chair Mayor's Com. on Employment of Persons with Disabilities, Denton, 1990; mem. coun.-at-large Sam Houston Area Coun. Boy Scouts Am., Houston, 1975—; grad. Denton C. of C. Leadership Program, 1992; pub. rels. chair leadership Denton Steering Com., 1993-94; mem. ad. bd. city of Denton Transit, 1990-2001; exec. bd. Svc. provision for Aging Needs, a United Way Agy., 1997-2001; mem. U. of North Tex. Adv. Bd. for ADA Access, 1992-2001, co-chair UNT ADA adv. com., 2000-01; mem. budget com. Denton County United Way, 1998-2001. Recipient Cmty. Svc. award U. North Tex., 1992, award for svcs. to persons with disabilities North Tex. Rehab. Assn., 1993, Disting. Alumnus award Houston Bapt. U., 1994, Outstanding Alumnus award Ctr. for Rehab. Studies, U. North Tex., 1995. Mem. Assn. Higher Edn. and Disability, Nat. Assn. Student Pers. Adminstrs., Tex. Assn. Coll. and Univ. Student Pers. Adminstrs. (chair multicultural com. 1994-95, v.p. 1995-96, co-chair endowment found. com. 1996-97), Tex. Assn. Higher Edn. and Disabilities (sec. 1998-99, conf. co-chair 1999). Presbyterian. Avocations: reading, travel, stamp collecting/philately. Office: U Oreg Disability Svc 164 Oregon Hall 5278 U Oreg Eugene OR 97403-5278 E-mail: stevewp@att.net.

**PICKHOLTZ, RAYMOND LEE,** electrical engineering educator, consultant; b. NYC, Apr. 12, 1932; s. Isidore and Rose (Turkish) P.; m. Eda Rebecca Mittler, June 30, 1957; children: Robin, Andrew, Julie. BEE, CUNY, 1954, MEE, 1958; PhD, Poly. U. N.Y., 1966. Research engr. RCA Labs., Princeton, NJ, 1954-57, ITT Labs., Nutley, NJ, 1957-61; assoc. prof. Poly. Inst. Bklyn., 1962-71; prof. elec. engring., chmn. dept George Washington U., Washington, 1977-80, prof., 1971—; pres. Telecommunication Assocs., Fairfax, Va., 1963—; cons. Inst. Def. Analyses, 1971-90, IBM Research, Yorktown Heights, NY, 1968-72; del. Union Radio Scientifique, Geneva, 1979—, vice chmn., 1987; del. NRC, Washington, 1980-83; cons. Motorola, CBC, NAB, USADR, Lucent, Verizon, 1996—. Vis. prof. U. Que., 1977; vis. scholar U. Calif., 1983; chmn. U.S. Nat. Commn. C, Union Radio Sci. Internat., 1990-92; mem. sci. and indsl. adv. bd. Telecom. Inst. Ont., Can. and Inst. Nacionale de La Recherches Scientique; vice chair, wireless panel World Tech. Evaluation Ctr. Editor: book series Computer Science Press, 1979—; IEEE Trans., 1975-80; editor-in-chief Jour. of Comms. and Networks, 2005—; author: Local Area and Multiple Access Networks, 1986; contbr. articles to profl. jours.; patentee in field. Recipient rsch. award RCA Labs., 1955; rsch. grantee Office of Naval Research, Washington, 1982, E-Systems, Falls Church, Va., 1983-96, MCI, Falls Church, Va., Instelsat, Washington, Nortel Networks, 1996—, DARPA, NSF, 1999—. Fellow IEEE (bd. govs. 1979-82, digital comm. com., Centennial medal 1984), AAAS, Washington Acad. Scis.; mem. IEEE Comm. Soc. (v.p. 1986-88, pres. 1990-92, Donald W. McLellan award, 1994, Erskine fellow New Zealand 1997, Third Millennium medal 2000, ACM MSWIN prize paper award, 1999, Best paper of 1999 in Jour. of Comms. and Networks, 2000, gen. chair, Infocom, Kobe, Japan 1997, gen. chair, ACM Mobicom Y2K, Boston, 2000), Math. Assn. Am., Cosmos Club, Sigma Xi, Eta Kappa Nu. Home: 3613 Glenbrook Rd Fairfax VA 22031-3210 Office: George Washington U Dept Elec Computer Engring Washington DC 20052-0001

**PICKLE, GEORGE EDWARD,** lawyer; b. New Orleans, Nov. 22, 1950; s. George E. Sr. and Virginia (Crowe) P.; m. Karen Lyle, Sept. 18, 1976; children: George E. III, Lauren M. Student, Rhodes Coll., 1968-70; BA, Millsaps Coll., 1972; JD, Georgetown U., 1975. Bar: Miss. 1975, U.S. Ct. Claims 1979, U.S. Tax Ct. 1979, U.S. Ct. Mil. Appeals 1979, U.S. Ct. Appeals (D.C. cir.) 1979, U.S. Supreme Ct. 1979, U.S. Dist. Ct. (so. dist.) Miss. 1980, U.S. Ct. Appeals (5th cir.) 1980, La. 1982, U.S. Dist. Ct. (ea. dist.) La. 1982, U.S. Dist. Ct. (mid. dist.) La. 1985, Tex. 1986., U.S. Dist. Ct. (so. dist.) Tex. 1986, U.S. Dist. Ct. (we. dist.) La. 1988. Law clk.to presiding justice U.S. Ct. Appeals (5th cir.), Askerman, Miss., 1975-76; assoc. Upshaw & Ladner, Jackson, Miss., 1980-82, Barham & Churchill, New Orleans, 1982-85; sr. atty. litigation, energy, environ., admiralty and products Shell Oil Co., Houston, 1985-96, assoc. general counsel, 1997—. Contbr. law rev., 1975; co-author, editor: Syllabus on Environmental Law, 1986. Bd. dirs. Tex. Civil Justice League, 1996—, Product Liability Advisory Coun., 1997—, chair operating Com. Civil Justice Reform Group, 1994—, Lawyers for Civil Justice Class Action Task Force, 2001-; sr. warden Episcopal Ch. of the Good Shepherd, Kingwood, Tex., 1991, dir. capital fund corp., 1988, lay eucharistic min., 1986-99; del. Tex. Senatorial and State Rep. convs., 1988-92; mem. exec. and vacancy coms. Rep. Party Harris County, 1990-96, chmn. precinct, 1990-96; mem. Georgetown U. Barristers Coun., 1973-75; referee N.W. Aquatic League, 1990-97; pres. Bear Br. Swim Team, 1991-93. Lt. cmdr. (head environ. litigation) USNR, 1976-79. Southwestern Scholar Rhodes Coll., Memphis, 1968. Mem. ABA (chmn. legis. jud. and govt. com. 2002-, vice chmn. young lawyers div. com. on environ. law, exec. editor Am. Criminal Law Rev. 1973-74, award for Profl. Merit 1976), Def. Rsch. Inst., Miss. Bar Assn. (elections com. 1982), La. Bar Assn., Tex. Bar Assn., Internat. Assn. Defence Coun. (vice chmn., sec. corp coun. 1991—), Alpha Tau Omega, Phi Alpha Theta, Omicron Delta Kappa, Pi Kappa Delta. Republican. Avocations: golf, water-skiing. Home: 3507 Tree Ln Humble TX 77339-2639 E-mail: ed.pickle@shell.com.

**PICKLE, JERRY RICHARD,** lawyer; b. Paris, Tex., Feb. 2, 1947; s. Joseph Rambert and Martha Marie (Biggers) P.; m. Helen Leigh Russell, May 3, 1975; children: Jonathan Russell, Stephen Richard (dec.), Sarah Elizabeth. BA in History, U. Houston, 1969, JD, 1971. Bar: Tex. 1972, U.S. Dist. Ct. (no. dist.) Tex. 1974. Mem. Luna, Ballard & Pickle, Garland, Tex., 1972-74; assoc. Hightower & Alexander, Dallas, 1974-76, Cuba & Johnson, Temple, Tex., 1976-77; sr. corp. counsel Scott & White Clinic, Temple, 1977—. Asst. prof. Tex. A&M U. Coll. of Medicine, Temple, 1986—. Contbr. articles to profl. jours. V.p. The Caring House, Temple, 1989; v.p. Tex. divsn. Am. Cancer Soc., Temple, 1976—77; adv. bd. R.R. & Pioneer Mus., Temple, 1982—84; hist. preservation bd. City of Temple, 1979—90; chmn. Bell County Hist. Commn., 1980—82; bd. dirs. Bell County Mus., 1992—96, Temple Coord. Child Care Coun., 1991—93, Sr. Citizens Activities Ctr., Temple 1993—94, pres., 1992—96; bd. dirs. Temple Cultural Activities Ctr., 1992—98, 2001—, pres., 1994—95; chair Heart o'Tex. Coun., Chisholm Trl. Dist., Boy Scouts Am., 1987—88; mem. U. N.C.-Chapel Hill Parents Coun., 2001—05; trustee Temple Ind. Sch. Dist., 2005—; dir. Tax Appraised Bd. Bell County, Tex., 2006—. Mem.: ABA, Temple C. of C. (bd. dirs. 1985-, 1988—90), Coun. Med. Group Practice Attys. (chair 2001—02), Am. Health Lawyers Assn. (chair tchg. hosp. and acad. med. ctrs. 1997—99), Bell-Lampasas-Mills Counties Young Lawyers Assn. (pres. 1980—81), Bell-Lampasas-Mills Counties Bar Assn. (bd. dirs. 1985—90, pres. 1988—89), State Bar Coll., Tex. Bar Found., Tex. Young Lawyers Assn., State Bar Tex. (health law sect. councilman 1980—84, chmn. 1983—84), Jaycees (chpt. dir. 1977—78),

Rotary (chpt. dir. 1981—85, 1986—87). Democrat. Episcopalian. Avocations: reading, golf, music. Office: Scott & White Clinic 2401 S 31st St Temple TX 76508-0001 Office Phone: 254-724-3001. Office Fax: 254-724-4501. Business E-Mail: jpickle@swmail.sw.org.

**PICKLE, ROBERT DOUGLAS,** lawyer, apparel executive; b. Knoxville, Tenn., May 22, 1937; s. Robert Lee and Beatrice Jewel (Douglas) P.; m. Rosemary Elaine Noser, May 9, 1964. AA summa cum laude, Schreiner Mil. Coll., Kerrville, Tex., 1957; BSBA magna cum laude, U. Tenn., 1959, JD, 1961; graduate (hon.), Nat. Def. U., 1979, US Army JAG Sch., US Army Logistics Mgmt. Sch.; graduate, US Army Inf. Sch., Army Command-Gen. Staff Coll. Bar: Tenn. 1961, Mo. 1964, U.S. Ct. Mil. Appeals 1962, U.S. Supreme Ct. 1970. Atty. Brown Shoe Co., Inc., St. Louis, 1963-69, asst. sec., atty., 1969-74, sec., gen. counsel, 1974-85; v.p., gen. counsel, corp. sec. Brown Shoe Co., Inc. (formerly Brown Group, Inc.), St. Louis, 1985—. Indiv. mobilization augmentee, asst. army judge adv. gen. civil law The Pentagon, Washington, 1984-89. Provisional judge Municipal Ct., Clayton, Mo., summer 1972; chmn. Clayton Region attys. sect.; profl. div. United Fund Greater St. Louis Campaign, 1972-73; team capt., 1974-78; chmn. City of Clayton Parks and Recreation Commn., 1985-87; liaison admissions officer, regional and state coordinator U.S. Mil. Acad., 1980—. Col. JAGC, U.S. Army, 1961-63. Decorated Meritorious Svc. medal; 1st U. Tenn. Law Coll. John W Green law scholar; recipient Cold War Recognition cert. Sec. Def. Fellow Harry S. Truman Meml. Library; mem. ABA, Tenn. Bar Assn., Mo. Bar Assn., St. Louis County Bar Assn., Bar Assn. Met. St. Louis, St. Louis Bar Found. (bd. dirs. 1979-81), Am. Corp. Counsel Assn., Am. Soc. Corp. Secs. (treas. St. Louis regional group 1976-77, sec. 1977-78, v.p. 1978-79, pres., mem. Quarter-Century Club 1979-80), U. Tenn. Gen. Alumni Assn. (pres., bd. dirs. St. Louis chpt. 1974-76, 80-84, bd. govs. 1982-89), U.S. Trademark Assn. (bd. dirs. 1978-82), Tenn. Soc. St. Louis (bd. dirs. 1980-88, treas., sec., v.p. 1984-87, pres. 1987-88), Smithsonian Nat. Assocs., World Affairs Coun. St. Louis, Inc., Am. Legion, University Club (v.p., sec. St. Louis chpt. 1976-81, bd. dirs. 1976-81), Stadium Club, West Point Soc. St. Louis (hon. mem., bd. dirs. 1992—), Conf. Bd. (coun. chief legal officers), Fontbonne Coll. Pres.'s Assocs. (O'Hara and Tower Socs), St. Louis U. Billiken Club, St. Louis U. DuBourg Soc. (hon. v.p.). Republican. Presbyterian. Avocations: reading, sports. Home: 214 Topton Way Saint Louis MO 63105-3638 Office: Brown Shoe Co Inc 8300 Maryland Ave Saint Louis MO 63105-3645 E-mail: rpickle@brownshoe.com.

**PICKREL, PAUL,** language educator; b. Gilson, Ill., Feb. 2, 1917; s. Clayton and Inez (Murphy) P. AB, Knox Coll., 1938; MA, Yale U., 1942, PhD, 1944. Instr. English Lafayette Coll., 1941-42; instr. Yale U., 1943-45, asst. prof., 1945-50, lectr. English, 1954-66, chmn. Scholar of House Program, 1959-60, 61-66; fellow Morse Coll., 1962-66; adviser John Hay fellows, 1959-66; vis. prof. English Smith Coll., Northampton, Mass., 1966-67, prof., 1967-87; prof. emeritus, 1987—; chmn. dept., 1972-75, 81-82. Author: (novel) The Moving Stairs, 1948; also essays on fiction, numerous book revs.; mng. editor: Yale Rev., 1949-66; chief book critic: Harper's mag., 1954-65. Mem. Aurelian Honor Soc., Elizabethan Club (New Haven), Faculty Club (Northampton), Phi Beta Kappa. Clubs: Elizabethan (New Haven), Faculty (Northampton); Yale (N.Y.C.).

**PICKTON, ROBERT (BOB) J.,** information technology executive; b. Akron, Ohio, July 14, 1947; BS, Miami Univ.; MBA, Pepperdine Univ. V.p. & chief info. officer EHS Healthcare, Oakbrook, Ill., Mose Cone Health Sys., Greensboro, NC; sr. v.p. & chief info. officer Baylor Health Care Sys., Dallas, 1995—. Charter mem. Coll. Healthcare Info. Mgmt. Exec.; founding mem. HLT Standards Group. Office: SVP & CIO Baylor Health Care Sys 3500 Gaston Ave Dallas TX 75246 Business E-Mail: bobp@baylorhealth.edu.*

**PICOT, PIERRE BERNARD,** artist, educator; b. Tours, France, Jan. 11, 1948; arrived in U.S., 1960; s. Pierre Theophile Picot and Ella Biegun; m. Nancy Riegelman (div.). MFA, Calif. Inst. of the Arts, Valencia, 1973. Vis. artist Claremont Grad. Sch., Calif., 1980, U. So. Calif., L.A., 1984—87; asst. prof. Art Ctr. Coll. of Design, Pasadena, 1984—. Works on paper, Armory Ctr. for the Arts, Pasadena, 2002—; exhibited in group shows at Elizabeth Leach Gallery, Portland, Oreg., 2002, Biennial at Enghien-les-Bains. France, 2004, Represented in permanent collections FRAC, Bretagne, Framce, Los Angeles County Mus. Art, L.A., Joel Wachs Gallery, N.Y.C. and L.A. Recipient award, NEA, 1987. Home: 3516 Crestmont Ave Los Angeles CA 90016

**PICOTTE, LEONARD FRANCIS,** naval officer; b. Calumet, Mich., Dec. 8, 1939; s. Irving René and Maria (Tamborino) P.; m. Sandra Lees Whiteley, July 14, 1984; children from previous marriage: Mary Elizabeth, Lance, Michael. BS in Econs. cum laude, U. No. Mich., 1963; MA in Polit. Sci., San Diego State U., 1975; grad. with distinction, Armed Forces Staff Coll., Norfolk, Va., 1976; M in Strategic Studies, Naval War Coll., Newport, R.I., 1985. Commd. ensign USN, 1963, advanced through grades to rear adm., 1991; comdg. officer USS Marathon, Vietnam, 1971-73; exec. officer USS Point Defiance, San Diego, 1976-78; exec. officer, officer in charge Surface Warfare Officers' Sch., Coronado, Calif., 1978-80; exec. officer Naval Sta., San Diego, 1980; comdg. officer USS Alamo, San Diego, 1980-82; surface warfare detailer Bur. Naval Pers., Washington, 1982-84; comdg. officer USS Duluth, San Diego, 1986-88; 1st comdg. officer USS Wasp, 1988-90; insp. gen. Comdr. in Chief, U.S. Atlantic Command, Comdr. in Chief, U.S. Atlantic Fleet, Norfolk, 1990-92; comdr. Amphibious Group Two, Norfolk, 1992-95; ret., 1995; v.p. expeditionary warfare programs Am. Sys. Corp., Chesapeake, Va., 1995-2006; pvt. practice Chesapeake, Va., 2006—. Decorated Legion of Merit (2); recipient Disting. Svc. medal. Mem. Surface Navy Assn., USS Wasp Assn. (hon.), Army and Navy Club, Town Point Club, Hampton Roads Coun. Navy League Republican. Roman Catholic. Avocations: jogging, hunting, reading, gardening, chess. Home: 119 Northgate Ln Suffolk VA 23434-4300 Address: Lighthouse Ln Calais ME 04619 Personal E-mail: lfpicotte@verizon.net.

**PICOULT, JODI,** writer; b. Long Island, NY; m. Tim Van Leer; 3 children. BA, Princeton Univ; MEd, Harvard Univ. Technical writer; textbook editor; English tchr. Author: (novels) Songs of the Humpback Whale, 1992, Harvesting the Heart, 1993, Picture Perfect, 1995, Mercy, 1996, The Pact, 1998, Keeping Faith, 1999, Plain Truth, 1999, Salem Falls, 2001, Perfect Match, 2002, Second Glance, 2003, My Sister's Keeper, 2004 (Publishers Weekly Bestseller, 2005), Vanishing Acts, 2005 (Publishers Weekly Bestseller, 2005), The Tenth Circle, 2006. Avocation: ice hockey. Office: PO Box 508 Etna NH 03750 Business E-Mail: jodi@jodipicoult.com.*

**PICOWER, WARREN MICHAEL,** editor; b. NYC, Aug. 21, 1934; s. Abraham and Nell (Bloom) P.; divorced; children: Jenny Emelia, Eve Julie. BA, Queens Coll., 1956; MA, New Sch. for Social Rsch., 1978; PsyD in Psychology, Heed U., L.A., 1982. Editorial asst. Newsweek mag., N.Y.C., 1956-59; assoc. editor Zimmerman Pub. Co., N.Y.C., 1961-63; assoc., mng. editor Fawcett Pubs., N.Y.C., 1963, 64-65; mng. editor Tuesday Publs., N.Y.C., 1965-67, exec. editor, v.p., 1967-73; sr. editor King Features Syndicate, N.Y.C., 1974-78; mng. editor Food & Wine Mag., N.Y.C. 1978-93; consulting editor Travel Holiday Mag., N.Y., 1993-94; mng. editor Zagat Survey restaurant and hotel guides, N.Y.C., 1994-97; sr. project editor Money Mag., N.Y.C., 1997-98. Cons. in field; awards judge James Beard Found. Contbr. articles to profl. jours. Mem. Am. Soc. Mag. Editors.

**PICRAUX, SAMUEL THOMAS,** physicist, researcher; b. St. Charles, Mo., Mar. 3, 1943; s. Samuel F. and Jeannette D. Picraux; m. Danice R. Kent, July 12, 1970; children: Jeanine, Laura, Samantha. BS in Elec. Engring., U. Mo., 1965; postgrad., Cambridge U., Eng. 1965-66; MS in Engring. Sci., Calif. Inst. Tech., 1967, PhD in Engring. Sci. and Physics, 1969. Mem. tech. staff Sandia Nat. Labs., Albuquerque, 1969-72, div. supr., 1972-86, dept. mgr., 1986-96, dir. 1996-2001; prof. materials engring., exec. dir. materials rsch. Ariz. State U., 2001—05; chief scientist Ctr. Integrated Nanotech., Los Alamos Nat. Lab., 2005—. Mem. solid state scis. com. NRC, 1996-98; vis. scientist dept. physics Aarhus U., Denmark, 1975; NATO lectr., 1979, 81, 83,

86.; NSF lectr. 1976, 81. Author: Materials Analysis by Ion Channeling, 1982; editor: Applications of Ion Beams to Metals, 1974, Metastable Materials Formation by Ion Implantation, 1982, Surface Alloying by Ion Electron and Laser Beams, 1986, Beam-Solid Interactions and Transient Processes, 1987; editor Nuclear Instruments and Methods International Jour. B, 1983-91; contbr. numerous articles to profl. jours. Recipient Ernest Orlando Lawrence Meml. award U.S. Dept. Energy, 1990, 3 Basic Energy Scis. Outstanding Rsch. awards U.S. Dept. Energy, 1985, 92, 94, Mo. Honor award disting. svc. in engring., 2006; Fulbright fellow, 1965-66. Fellow AAAS, Am. Phys. Soc. (chmn. materials physics divsn. 1990); mem. IEEE (sr.), Am. Vacuum Soc., Materials Rsch. Soc. (pres. 1993). Office: Los Alamos Nat Lab Ctr Integrated Nanotech MST-CINT MSK771 Los Alamos NM 87545 Office Phone: 505-665-8554. Business E-Mail: picraux@lanl.gov.

**PIDDOCK, JAMES ANTHONY,** actor; b. Rochester, Kent, Eng., Apr. 8, 1956; came to U.S., 1981; s. Charles Frederick and Celia Mary (O'Callahan) P. BA in English, London U., 1977. Dir., tchr. drama The Drama Studio, Berkeley, London, Calif., 1980-81. Actor: (films) Lethal Weapon 2, 1989, Multiplicity, 1996, Independence Day, 1996, Best in Show, 2000, Austin Powers: Goldmember, 2002, A Mighty Wind, 2003, Love for Rent, 2005, Garfield: A Tale of Two Kitties, 2006, (TV films) A Mom for Christmas, 1990, The Women of Windsor, 1992, Mermaid Chronicles Part 1: She Creature, 2001, (TV miniseries) From the Earth to the Moon, 1998; actor, writer: (films) Traces of Red, 1992; writer: (films) One Good Turn, 1996, The Man, 2005; co-prodr.: (films) A Different Loyalty, 2004; exec prodr.: (TV series) Too Much Sun, 2000; Broadway theater Noises Off, 1983 (N.Y. Drama Desk award), Present Laughter, 1982, Design for Living, 1985; off-Broadway The Box's Own Story 1983; theatre The Caretaker, 1988, How the Other Half Loves, 1988; TV guest appearances include The Tracey Ullman Show, 1987, Coach, 1990, 91, Murder She Wrote, 1993, Mad About You, 1994-96, Angel, 2000, Yes, Dear, 2001, Friends, 2001, The Drew Carey Show, 2002, ER, 2002, Crossing Jordan, 2003, Lost, 2005. Avocations: soccer, baseball. Office: Harry Gold Assocs 3500 W Olive Ave Ste 1400 Burbank CA 91505-4659*

**PIDERT, SANDY KRISTIN,** finance educator; d. Fred William and Barbara Chaderski Piderit; m. Scott A. Kovatch, Aug. 21, 1993; 1 child, Julia Piderit Kovatch. BA, Case Western Res. U., Cleve., 1991; PhD, U. Mich., Ann Arbor, 1999. Instr. U. Mich., Ann Arbor, 1996, Case Western Res. U., Cleve., 1998—99, asst. prof., 1999—2006. Treas. NEOBAN, Cleve., 2006—. Co-editor: Handbook of Women in Business Management, 2006. Mem.: Acad. Mgmt. (rep. at large). Office: Case Western Res Univ PBL 425-10900 Euclid Ave Cleveland OH 44106-7235

**PIDGEON, JOHN ANDERSON,** headmaster; b. Lawrence, Mass., Dec. 20, 1924; s. Alfred H. and Nora (Regan) P.; children: John Anderson, Regan S., Kelly; m. Barbara Hafer, May 1986. Grad., Phillips Acad., 1943; BA, Bowdoin Coll., 1949; Ed.D., Bethany Coll., 1973; D.Litt., Washington and Jefferson Coll., 1979. Instr. Latin, adminstrv. asst. to headmaster Deerfield Acad., 1949-57; headmaster Kiskiminetas Springs Sch., Saltsburg, Pa., 1957—2004. Dir. Saltburg Savs. & Trust. Trustee Winchester-Thurston Sch.; vol. swimming coach Ind. U., Pa. Served as ensign USNR, 1943-46. Mem. New Eng. Swimming Coaches Assn. (pres. 1956-57), Cum Laude Soc., Delta Upsilon. Home and Office: 157 Greenview Dr Indiana PA 15701 Office Phone: 724-349-2151.

**PIDGEON, LESLEA SHARON,** artist, writer; b. Dayton, Ohio, Jan. 5, 1940; d. Charles Henry and Lettie Kathleen (Myers) P. Student, Brenau Coll., 1958-59, Dayton Art Inst., 1959-63, George Washington U., 1970's, Wright State U., Dayton, 1977. Office worker, Dayton, 1958-69; clk.-typist U.S. Army, 1969-77; trainee signal U.S. Army Res., Wright-Patterson AFB, Ohio, 1977-78; clk.-typist VA, Dayton, 1977, Def. Electronics Supply Ctr., Kettering, Ohio, 1977-79; illustrator Aero. Sys. Ctr., Wright-Patterson AFB, 1979-84; clk.-typist Smithsonian Instn., Washington, 1984-88. Exhibited in group show Nat. Capitol Ceramic Assn., 1998 (3d pl. award); contbr. poetry to books, jours. Democrat. Avocations: videos, tapes, jewelry, photography

**PIDOT, WHITNEY DEAN,** lawyer; b. NYC, Mar. 2, 1944; s. George B. and Virginia (Ulrich) P.; m. Jeanne Stoddard, April 23, 1973; children: Whitney Dean Jr., Philip Martin, Seth Thayer. AB magna cum laude, Harvard U., 1966; JD, MBA, Columbia U., 1970. Bar: N.Y. 1971. Ptnr. Shearman & Sterling, NYC, 1970, global mng. ptnr., 1998—2002, mem. exec. goup, 1998—2003, Asia mng. ptnr., 2001—03, of counsel, 2004—; chair, CEO Goelet Co. LLC, 2004—. Mem. adv. bd. Barclays Bank N.Y., 1989-92, Molecular Tool, Inc. (biotech.) Balt., 1991-96, Equine Genetic Rsch. Ptnrs., Balt., 1991-95; trustee, vice chair Winthrop Univ. Hosp., Mineola, N.Y. Mayor, Village of Matinecock, Locust Valley, N.Y., 1977-92; vice chmn. North Shore Mayors Com., Long Island, N.Y., 1980-92; bd. dirs. Nassau County (N.Y.) Village Officials Assn., 1978-80; commr. Locust Valley Fire Dist., 1979-93. Mem. N.Y. Bar Assn., Piping Rock Club (pres. 1988-94), Union League N.Y.C., Phi Delta Phi. Republican. Home: Matinecock Farms PO Box 653 Locust Valley NY 11560 Office: Shearman & Sterling 599 Lexington Ave Ste C-2 New York NY 10022-6030 also: Goelet Co LLC 425 Park Ave New York NY 10022 Business E-Mail: wpidot@shearman.com.

**PIEDILATO, JANET,** psychologist; d. Filomeno and Jeanette G. Riche; m. Ignazio Piedilato, Sept. 7, 1970; children: Janette(dec.), Ignatius. BA, Notre Dame U., 1969; MS, Long Island U., 1971; PhD in Biology, N.Y. U., N.Y.C., 1976; studied, Sch. Herbal Medicine, 1996, Inst. Shamanic Studies, 1998; PhD in Psychology, Saybrook G.S., 1999; diploma in pastry chef, French Culinary Inst., N.Y., 2003. Tchg. fellow N.Y. U., N.Y.C., 1972—76; pvt. practice Staten Island, 1999—. Adj. lectr. Coll. S.I., 1975—77; rsch. asst. Pub. Health Hosp., 1981—83; faculty St. Ignatius U., 2001—; CEO Immaginal 2002—; dir. Temenos Retreat, NJ, 1994. Contbr. articles to profl. jours., chapters to books. Mem.: Am. Psychol. Assn. Avocations: mythology, culinary arts. Office: Immaginal 600 Forest Ave Staten Island NY 10310 Office Phone: 866-775-0546.

**PIEDT, DAVID LAWRENCE,** musician; b. Ft. Lauderdale, Fla., Nov. 28, 1979; s. Lawrence Thomas and Nancy Lee Piedt; m. Summer Dawn Bogart, Aug. 7, 2004. B of Music Edn., Miss. Coll., 2002; postgrad., Southwestern Bapt. Theol. Sem., 2004—. Assoc. music min. Pinelake Bapt. Ch., Brandon, Miss., 2002—04; profl. musician Fort Worth, 2004—. Condr./dir. various musical ensembles, 2002—. Conductor, director, singer: various symphonic, jazz/blues music. Presdl., Honors Leadership, Music scholar, Miss. Coll., 1998—2002. Mem.: Music Educator's Nat. Conf. (life), Miss. Coll. Republicans (hon.; v.p. 1999—2001), Alpha Lambda Delta (life), Phi Mu Alpha Sinfonia (life; v.p. 2000—02). Republican. Baptist. Avocations: music, flying, computers. Home: 4124 William Fleming Ct Apt F Fort Worth TX 76115 Personal E-Mail: psalter777@hotmail.com.

**PIEFER, GREGORY RICHARD,** information technology executive; b. Milw., July 11, 1976; s. Richard and Judith Piefer. BSEE, U. Wis., Madison, 1999, M in Nuc. Engring., 2004, PhD in Nuc. Engring., 2006. Pres. Phoenix Nuc. Labs LLC, Middleton, Wis., 2005—06; chief tech. officer Gillware Inc., Madison, 2004—. Recipient James W. Paukey award, U. Wis., Madison. Engring. Dept. 2004; fellow, NASA, 2003; grantee, 2006; Hilldale fellow, U. Wis., 1997—98. Mem.: Am. Nuc. Soc. Achievements include research in study of radioactivity and waste free nuclear energy. Home: 4201 Savannah Ct Middleton WI 53562 Office: Phoenix Nuclear Labs LLC 8123 Savannah Ct Middleton WI 53562 Office Phone: 608-826-4267. Business E-Mail: greg.piefer@phoenixnuclearlabs.com.

**PIEFER, THOMAS R.,** history educator; b. Auburn, Wash., Dec. 15, 1952; s. Raymond Andrew and Marion Piefer; m. Teresa Kay Willard, Dec. 26, 1971; children: Rebecca, Christina, Craig. BA in Edn., Ctrl. Wash. U., Ellensburg, 1987; MS in Edn., Walla Walla Coll., College Place, Wash., 1993, Antioch Coll., Seattle, Wash., 2003. Cert. lifeguard, advanced lifesaving. Tchr. Ctrl. Mid. Sch., Milton-Freewater, Oreg., 1987—2006, chair, social studies, 2004—06; tchr. Christian Edn. Trinity Bapt. Ch., Walla Walla, Wash.,

1987—2006; trainer in social studies, state of Oreg. Teach Tchrs. Author: (book) Helping Hispanic Parents Through the Education Maze. Mentor Oreg. Youth Guard, Milton-Freewater, Oreg.; youth worker Trinity Baptist Ch., Oreg., 1988—2006, vol., Awana, 1987—2006. With USAF, 1971—2002. Recipient Noncommissioned Officer of Quarter award, USAFR, 1973, 1975, 1985, 2006, Tchr. of Quarter award, Ctrl. Mid. Sch., Milton-Freewater, Oreg., 2003, 2004. Mem.: Milton-Freewater Edn. Assn., Walla Walla Hot Wheels Car Club. Avocations: jogging, camping, woodworking, teaching. Home: 84608 Eastside Rd Milton Freewater OR 97862 Office Phone: 541-938-5504. Personal E-Mail: piefert@neofast.net.

**PIEGARI, JAMES A.,** psychologist; b. Bklyn., Aug. 4, 1951; s. Vincent and Olympia Piegari. BS in Psychology, Georgetown U., 1972; MA in Clin. Psychology, St. John's U., 1975; MA in Psychology, Rutgers U., 1995, New Sch. Social Rsch., 1995; PhD in Psychology, Saybrook Grad. Sch. and Rsch. Ctr., 1999. Lic. psychologist NY, cert. sch. psychologist NY. Ops. rsch. analyst USPHS Hosp., S.I., NY, 1976—78; applied behavioral scis. specialist United Cerebral Palsy Assns. NY State, S.I., 1978—80, Terence Cardinal Cooke Health Care Ctr., NYC, 1980—2001, psychologist, 2002—; pvt. practice psychologist S.I., 2002—. Mem. publs. com. Flower Hosp., NYC, 1980—81; cons. Vietnamese refugee program Mission of Immaculate Virgin, Mt. Loretto, S.I., 1986—96; assoc. prof. Mercy Coll., Arthur Kill Correctional Facility, S.I., 1989—90; supt. provider psychol. svcs. NYC Dept. Edn., 2002—; cert. mediator S.I. Cmty. Dispute Resolution Ctr.; mem. alumni admissions program Georgetown U. Contbr. articles to profl. jour., chapters to books. Mem. health and hosps. com. NYC Cmty. Bd., S.I., NY, 1979—80; charter mem. Friends of South Beach Psychiat. Ctr., S.I., NY, 1980—81, bd. dirs., 1980—81, chmn. mental health symposium com., 1980—81; mem. appellate divsn. panel mental health profl. psychologist Supreme Ct., NY. Recipient Employee Recogition award, Terence Cardinal Cooke Health Care Ctr., 2001. Mem.: APA, NY State Psychol. Assn. Avocations: Civil War antiques, photography, travel, motorcycle touring. Home and Office: 7 Azalea Ct Staten Island NY 10309

**PIEHLER, BARBARA F.,** insurance company executive; BBA in acctg., U. Wis., Madison. Positions with Arthur Young & Co., Joseph Schlitz Brewing Co., Stroh Brewing Co.; joined contr.'s dept. Northwestern Mutual, 1983, named asst. contr., 1988, asst. to pres., 1990, v.p. corp. services, 1991, v.p. - asst. to pres., 1994, v.p. policy owner services, 1995, v.p. internet, v.p. info. services, 2001, sr. v.p., chief info. officer, 2002. Named one of Premier 100 IT Leaders, Computerworld, 2005. Office: Northwestern Mutual 720 E Wisconsin Ave Milwaukee WI 53202-4797 Office Phone: 414-271-1444.*

**PIEKARSKI, VICTOR J.,** lawyer; b. Lawrence, Mass., Feb. 20, 1950; BA cum laude, Boston Coll., 1971; MBA, U. Chgo., 1978; JD cum laude, Northwestern U., 1974. Bar: Ill. 1974, U.S. Ct. Appeals (7th cir.) 1977, U.S. Supreme Ct. 1978. Ptnr. Querrey & Harrow Ltd., Chgo., to 1997, O'Hagan, Smith and Amundsen, LLC, Chgo., 1997—. Mem. ABA, Def. Rsch. Inst. Office: O'Hagan Smith and Amundsen LLC 150 N Michigan Ave Ste 3300 Chicago IL 60601-7586 E-mail: vpiekarski@osalaw.com.

**PIEKARZ, FRANK JEFFREY,** music educator; s. Frank Raymond and Dorothy Ann Piekarz; m. Jodi Ann Rhodes; children: Elizabeth, Jeffrey, Emily. BS in Music Edn., U. Ill., 1994; MusM in Music Edn., No. Ill. U., 1999, postgrad., 2003—. Music tchr., math. tchr. Butler Jr. HS, Oakbrook, Ill., 1994—96, Downers Grove (Ill.) North and South High Schs., 1996—97; music tchr., dir. choirs Downers Grove North HS, 1997—. Vis. asst. prof. No. Ill. U. Sch. Music, DeKalb, 2006—. Mem.: ASCD, Am. Choral Dirs. Assn., Ill. Music Educators Assn. Office: North HS 4436 Main St Downers Grove IL 60515 Office Phone: 630-795-8085. E-mail: fpiekarz@csd99.org.

**PIEKNIK, REBECCA ANNE,** technologist, educator; b. Detroit, Sept. 30, 1960; AA in Allied Health, Baker Coll., 1998; BS in Health Svc. Adminstrn., Baker Coll. Flint, 2002; MS in Bioethics, Union U., 2005. Cert. surg. technologist, surg. asst. Clin. instr. Baker Coll. Flint, 1999—; cert. surg. technologist Pontiac Osteopathic Hosp., Mich., 2001—02; program dir. surg. tech. Oakland C.C./William Beaumont Hosp., 2002—. Office Phone: 248-898-7685.

**PIEL, EMIL J.,** retired engineering educator; b. Fairview, N.J., Apr. 17, 1918; s. Harry and Anna (Decker) P.; m. Elizabeth Mayer Lautenschlager, Apr. 7, 1945 (dec. July 1995); two children; m. Maybelle Rodgeres Buck, Sept. 15, 2001. BA, Montclair State U., 1940, MA, 1947; EdD, Rutgers U. 1960. Tchr. physics Ft. Lee H.S., NJ, 1940—41, 1945—48; airway traffic contr. FAA, Jacksonville, Fla., 1941—42; combat pilot USMC, South Pacific, 1942—45; tchr. physics Caldwell H.S., NJ, 1948—52; sci. dept. chair East Orange H.S., NJ, 1952—60; prin. West Essex H.S., North Caldwell, NJ, 1960—66; chair dept. sci. & technology SUNY, Stony Brook, 1966—87, prof. emeritus, 1987—. Co-author: The Man Made World, 1972, Technology: Handle with Care, 1978. Fellow AAAS; mem. Ret. Officers Assn. Home and Office: 459 Passaic Ave C300 West Caldwell NJ 07006 Personal E-Mail: jpiel8402@aol.com.

**PIELET, BRUCE WILLIAM,** obstetrician; b. Chgo., 1957; MD, Loyola U. 1981. Bd. cert. ob-gyn., bd. cert. maternal and fetal medicine. Resident ob-gyn. U. Chgo., 1981—85; fellow maternal fetal medicine Northwestern U., Chgo., 1985—87; physician Advocate Luth. Gen. Hosp., Park Ridge, Ill. Office: Luth Gen Hosp Ste 325 1875 Dempster St Park Ridge IL 60068-1127

**PIEN, GRACE,** medical educator; d. Shui-hsien and Arlene C. Pien. MD, Columbia U., NYC, 1994; MS, U. Pa., Phila., 2004. Asst. prof. medicine U. Pa. Sch. Medicine Phila. 2002. Office: Hospital Univ Pennsylvania 9 Maloney Bldg 3400 Spruce St Philadelphia PA 19104 Office Phone: 215-662-7772. Office Fax: 215-662-7749.

**PIEN, HOWARD,** pharmaceutical executive; b. 1958; BS, MIT; MBA, Carnegie Mellon U. With Abbott Laboratories, Merck; v.p. & dir. product mktg.-US SmithKline Beecham, 1992—93, v.p. & dir. new product devel.- US, 1991—92, v.p. & dir. mktg.-US, 1993—95, mng. dir. & sr. v.p.-UK, 1995—97, sr. v.p. & dir.-North Asia, 1997; pres. pharm. internat. Glaxo-SmithKline, 2001—03; CEO & dir. Chiron Corp., Emeryville, Calif., 2003—, chmn., 2004—. Office: Chiron Corp 4560 Horton St Emeryville CA 94608-2916*

**PIENE, CHLOE,** artist, filmmaker; b. Stamford, Conn., 1972; Exhibitions include Me & More, Kunstmuseum, Luzern, 2003, Whitney Biennial, Whitney Mus. Am. Art, NY, 2004, Spirit, Galerie Nathalie Obadia, Paris, 2004, Videodrome II, Bates Coll. Mus. Art, 2004, Boys Will Be Boys?, Mus. Contemporary Art, Denver, 2005, Getting Emotional, 2005, Mus. Contemporary Art, Denver, 2005, Chloe Piene Galleries Nathalie Obadia, Sandroni Rey Gallery, LA, Klemens Gasser and Tanja Grunert, NYC. Studio: 66 Washington Ave 3rd Fl Brooklyn NY 11205 Personal E-mail: cpstudio@verizon.net.

**PIENTA, AMY MEHRABAN,** sociologist, demographer; b. Buffalo, Aug. 31, 1968; d. Edward Frank and Florence Mary Pienta; m. Derek Andrew Mehraban, July 9, 1999; children: Abigail Layla Mehraban, Lucy Darya Mehraban. BA, SUNY, Buffalo, 1990, MA, 1992, PhD, 1996. Asst. prof. Wayne State U., Detroit, 1996—99, U. Fla. Gainesville, 1999—2003; acquisitions dir. ICPSR U. Mich., Ann Arbor, 2003—. Fellow postdoctoral Fellow, Nat. Inst. Aging, 1995—97. Mem.: Am. Sociol. Assn., Gerontol. Soc. Am., Population Assn. Am. Office: U Mich PO Box 1248 Ann Arbor MI 48106 Office Phone: 734-615-7957.

**PIEPER, CARL F.,** statistician, educator; b. Fort Pierce, Fla., Aug. 4, 1953; s. William H. and Agnes Jensen Pieper; m. Kathy M. Shipp, Oct. 7, 1999; 1 child, Ellen L. DPH, Columbia U., NYC, 1990. Asst. prof. Cornell Med. Ctr., NYC, 1991—92, Duke U. Med. Ctr., Durham, NC. Grantee, Nat. Inst. Drug Abuse, 2005—. Liberal. Achievements include research in methods for the

analysis of 24 hour ambulatory blood pressure monitoring data. Home: 3224 Chatham Church Rd Moncure NC 27559 Office: Duke University Medical Center Box 3003 Center on Aging DUMC Durham NC 27710 Office Phone: 919-660-7525. Office Fax: 919-684-8569. Personal E-mail: cpieper@mindspring.com. E-mail: carl.pieper@duke.edu.

**PIEPER, MICHAEL JOSEPH,** television producer, actor, talk show host; b. Detroit, July 12, 1958; s. Frank John Pieper and Marie Yolanda Dansereau; m. Barbara Marie Michalik (div. Feb. 1990); children: Melanie Lynn, Heather Irene. Student, Marygrove Coll., 1976—78, Specs Howard Sch. Broadcast Arts, 1988. Ordained min. Universal Life Ch., 2000. Owner, prodr. Quixote Video, Huntington Beach, Calif., 1981—. Actor (TV series) T-bone Playhouse, 1981—82, actor, co-prodr. comedy soap opera, Daze of Our Wives, 1982—85; performer: (TV series) game show, Out-patient Bonanza, 1984—85; actor: (radio series) Proceed With Caution, 1985—86; (TV films) Streetlevel, 1983, The Banana Republic, 1983; actor, co-prodr. (TV films) Bartolo's Cafe, 1984, The Paper, 1992, host, co-prodr. (talk show) Forum, 1983—85, host Detroit Metro Magazine, 1985, songwriter Feathersong, 1996; songwriter: Legacy, 2006. Mem.: Internat. Platform Assn. (life). Avocations: singing, painting, photography, metaphysics. Office: Quixote Video PO Box 502 16787 Beach Blvd Huntington Beach CA 92647-4848 Office Phone: 714-893-2720. Personal E-mail: angelfeather2001@gmail.com.

**PIEPER, PATRICIA RITA,** artist; b. Paterson, N.J., Jan. 28, 1923; d. Francis William and Barbara Margaret (Ludwig) Farabaugh; m. George F. Pieper, July 1, 1941 (dec. May 3, 1981); 1 child, Patricia Lynn; m. Russell W. Watson, Dec. 9, 1989. Student, Baron von Palm, 1937-39, Deal Conservatory, NJ, 1939, 40, Utah State U., 1950-52; student Baron von Palm, 1937—39, student Deal (N.J.) Conservatory, 1939—40, student Utah State U., 1950—52. One-woman shows include Charles Russell Mus., Great Falls, Mont., 1955, Fisher Gallery, Washington, 1966, Tampa City Libr., 1977-81, 83, 84, Ctr. Pl. Art Ctr., Brandon, Fla., 1985; exhibited in group shows Davidson Art Gallery, Middletown, Conn., 1968, Helena (Mont.) Hist. Mus., 1955, Dept. Commerce Alaska Statehood Show, 1959, Joslyn Mus., Omaha, 1961, Denver Mus. Natural History, 1955, St. Joseph's Hosp. Gallery, 1980, 82, 84-86; represented in pvt. collections. Pres. Bell Lake Assn., 1976-78, 79; mem. Pasco County (Fla.) Water Adv. Coun., 1976—, chmn., 1979-82, 83-84, 86-88, 92—; gov.'s appointee to S.W. Fla. Water Mgmt. Dist., Hillsborough River Basin Bd., 1981-82, 84-87, sec., 1988-91, vice chmn., 1992; active Save Our Rivers program, 1982-84, 85-86, 92—; ad hoc chmn., 1991-92; mem. adv. bd. Fla. Suncoast Expwy., 1988-90; pres. Bell Lake Assn., 1986, 87; mem. adv. bd. Tampa YMCA, 1979-80. Winner photog. competition Gen. Tel. Co. of Fla., 1979; recipient Outstanding Svc. award Bell Lake Assn., 1987, Meml. award Land O'Lake Bd. of Realtors, 1989, Appreciation award Southwest Fla. Water Mgmt. Dist., 1993, finalist, Awds. of Excellence, Photographers winner in top 100 out of 8,000 Nat. Wildlife Fedn. competition, 1986, 1st place photography MacDill AFB, 1991. Mem. VFW (life), Nat. League Am. Pen Women (v.p. Tampa 1976-78, Woman of Yr. award 1977-78), Tampa Art Mus., Ret. Officer's Wives Assn., Land O'Lakes C. of C. (bd. dirs. 1981-82, Outstanding Svc. award 1980), Fla. Geneal. Soc., West State Archaeol. Soc. (distaff mem.), Ret. Officer's Assn., Lutz Club, Land O'Lakes Women's Club, Moose. Home: 3304 E Derry Dr Sebastian FL 32958-8577 I believe that those of us born with the gift of creativity are truly blessed. It is our duty to make the most of, and be worthy of that gift. And if we work hard and sincerely apply ourselves a chosen few will become immortal through the beauty we leave behind for others to enjoy. As an artist and photographer I am truly blessed.

**PIEPGRAS, DAVID G.,** neurosurgeon, educator; b. Luverne, Minn., 1940; MD, U. Minn., 1965. Diplomate Am. Bd. Neurol. Surgery. Intern Mary Hitchcock Hosp., Hanover, Minn., 1965—66; resident in surgery Hennepin County Gen. Hosp., Mpls., 1969—70; resident in neurol. surgery Mayo Grad. Sch. Medicine, Rochester, 1970—74; staff St. Mary's Hosp., Rochester, 1974—, Rochester Meth. Hosp., 1974—; staff cons. dept. neurosurgery Mayo Clinic, Rochester, 1974—, prof. neurol. surgery. Bd. dirs. Am. Bd. Neurol. Surgery, 2002—. Fellow: ACS; mem.: AMA, Congress of Neurol. Surgeons, Am. Acad. Neurol. Surgeons. Office: Mayo Clinic Dept Neurol Surgery Rochester MN 55905-0001

**PIEPHO, LEE (EDWARD LEE PIEPHO),** humanities educator; b. Detroit, Jan. 10, 1942; s. Edward Ernest and Dolores Faye (Dowis) P.; m. Susan Brand, June 13, 1964. AB, Kenyon Coll., 1964; MA, Columbia U., 1966; PhD, U. Va., 1972. Instr. Sweet Briar Coll. Va., 1969—72, asst. prof., 1972—78, assoc. prof., 1978—83, prof., 1983—94, Shallenberger Brown prof., 1994—2006, rsch. prof., 2006—; dept. chmn., 2000—01, coord. European civilization program, 1986—89. Author: Holofernes' Mantuan, 2001; translator, editor: Adulescentia: The Eclogues of Mantuan, 1989; contbr. articles to profl. jours. Fellow, SIMRS, 1979, NEH, 1985, 1997; Dulin fellow, Folger Shakespeare Libr., 1989—90, Mednick fellow, 1996. Mem. Internat. Assn. for Neo-Latin Studies, Modern Lang. Assn. Am., Renaissance Soc. Am. Avocations: golf, tennis, scuba diving. Home: 137 Woodland Rd Sweet Briar VA 24595 Office: Sweet Briar Coll Dept English Sweet Briar VA 24595 Business E-Mail: lpiepho@sbc.edu.

**PIEPHO, ROBERT WALTER,** pharmacy educator, researcher; b. Chgo., July 31, 1942; s. Walter August and Irene Elizabeth (Huybrecht) Apfel; m. Mary Lee Wilson, Dec. 10, 1981. BS in Pharmacy, U. Ill.-Chgo., 1965; PhD in Pharmacology, Loyola U., Maywood, Ill., 1972. Registered pharmacist, Ill., Colo. Assoc. prof. U. Nebr. Med. Ctr., Omaha, 1970-78; prof. pharmacy, assoc. dean Sch. Pharmacy U. Colo., Denver, 1978-86; prof. pharmacol., dean U. Mo. Sch. Pharmacy, Kansas City, 1987—. Contbr. articles to profl. jours. chptr. to books. Phi Chi Club Midwest Homeowners Assn., Denver, 1980-82. Named Outstanding Tchr. U. Nebr. Coll. Pharmacy, 1975; recipient Arthur Hassan Colo. Pharmacal Assn., 1983, Excellence in Teaching U. Colo. Med. Sch., 1983 Fellow Am. Coll. Clin. Pharmacology (regent 1983-88, 91-96, pres. 1998-2000); mem. Am. Soc. Hosp. Pharmacists, Am. Soc. Pharmacology and Exptl. Therapeutics, Rho Chi Roman Catholic. Office: U Mo Sch Pharmacy 5005 Rockhill Rd Kansas City MO 64110-2239 Office Phone: 816-235-1609. Business E-Mail: piephor@umkc.edu.

**PIERANGELI, SILVIA SUSANA,** medical educator, consultant; b. Buenos Aires, Oct. 10, 1955; d. Hector Raul Pierangeli and Nelida Susana Vega de Pierangeli; m. Alvaro Schleh, Jan. 16, 2003; children: Maria Cecilia Miranda, Maria Eugenia Miranda. PhD, U. of Louisville, 1990. Lab. dir. Coll. of Am. Pathologists. Rsch. assoc. U. of Louisville, 1990—96; prof. Morehouse Sch. of Medicine, Atlanta, 1996—2006, U. Tex. Med. Br., 2006—. Tech. dir. Louisville APL Diagnostics, Inc, Doraville, Ga., 1993—. Contbr. scientific papers to profl. pubs. Recipient Fulbright scholarship, USIA, 1985—88. Mem.: Am. Coll. of Rheumatology. Achievements include research in Mechanisms of thrombosis induced by antiphospholipid antibodies in the antiphospholipid syndrome; discovery of better antigen for detection of antiphospholipid antibodies; development of better laboratory assay for diagnosis of antiphospholipid syndrome. Office Phone: 409-772-0222. Personal E-mail: pierans@aol.com. Business E-Mail: sspieran@utmb.edu.

**PIERARD, RICHARD VICTOR,** history educator; b. Chgo., May 29, 1934; s. John Perkins and Diana Florence (Russell) P.; m. Charlene Burdett, June 15, 1957; children: David, Cynthia. BA, Calif. State U., L.A., 1958, MA, 1959; PhD, U. Iowa, 1964. Prof. history Ind. State U., Terre Haute, 1964-2000, emeritus, 2000—. Vis. prof. Greenville (Ill.) Coll., 1972-73, Free Theol. Acad., Seeheim, Fed. Republic Germany, 1971, 78, Regent Coll., Vancouver, B.C., Can., 1975, Trinity Evang. Div. Sch., Deerfield, Ill., 1982, No. Bapt. Theol. Sem., Lombard, Ill., 1987, Fuller Theol. Sem., Pasadena, Calif., 1988, 91, Moscow Theol. Sem., 1997, 99, 2001, 2003, Gordon Coll., Wenham, Mass., 2000-2001; scholar-in-residence Gordon Coll., 2000—; Fulbright prof. U. Frankfurt, Fed. Republic Germany, 1984-85; Fulbright prof. U. Halle, German Dem. Republic 1989-90; pres. Greater Terre Haute Ch. Fedn. 1987-88; del. Lausanne II Congress on World Evang., Manila, Philippines, 1989; mem. Bapt. Heritage & Identity Study Commn., Bapt. World Alliance, 1990. Author: The Unequal Yoke: Evangelical Christianity and Political Conservatism, 1970, Bibliography on the Religious Right in America, 1986; co-author: Twilight of the Saints: Biblical Christianity and Civil Religion, 1978, Civil Religion and the Presidency, 1988, Two Kingdoms: The Church and Culture through the Ages, 1993, The Revolution of the Candles: Christians in the Revolution of the German Democratic Republic, 1996, The New Millennium Manual, 1999; contbr. articles to religious and hist. publs. Del. White House Conf. on Librs., Washington, 1979, Ind. Dem. Party Convention, Indpls., 1980, 88; precinct committeeman Dem. Party, Terre Haute, 1978-80, 90—; mem. Ind. Gov.'s Adv. Com. on Librs., 1980-81. With U.S. Army, 1954-56. Recipient Terre award for cmty. svc., Terre Haute, Ind., 1991; Fulbright scholar U. Hamburg (Fed. Republic Germany), 1962-63; rsch. fellow U. Aberdeen (Scotland), 1978; Chavanne scholar Baylor U., 1988. Mem. Conf. on Faith and History (sec.-treas. 1967—), Evang. Theol. Soc. (pres. 1985), Am. Hist. Assn., Am. Soc. Ch. History, Ind. Assn. Historians, Am. Soc. Missiology, Internat. Assn. Mission Studies, Soc. for Encouragement and Preservation of Barbershop Quartet Singing in Am., Am. Bapt. Hist. Soc. (bd. mgrs. 1993—). Democrat. Home: 11 Pine Rd Beverly MA 01915 Personal E-mail: charrichp@aol.com.

**PIERCE, ALLAN DALE,** engineering educator, researcher, editor; b. Clarinda, Iowa, Dec. 18, 1936; s. Franklin Dale and Ruth Pauline (Wright) P.; m. Penelope Claffey, Oct. 27, 1961; children: Jennifer Irene, Bradford Loren. BS, N.Mex. Coll. Agrl. and Mechanic Arts, 1957; PhD, MIT, 1962. Registered profl. engr., Mass. Staff rschr. Rand Corp., Santa Monica, Calif., 1961-63; sr. staff scientist Avco Corp., Wilmington, Mass., 1963-66; asst. prof. MIT, Cambridge, 1966-68, assoc. prof., 1968-73; prof. mech. engring. Ga. Inst. Tech., Atlanta, 1973-76, Regent's prof., 1976-88; Leonhard chair in engring. Pa. State U., University Park, 1988-93; chmn. dept aerospace and mech. engring. Boston U., 1993-99, prof., 1993—. Vis. prof. Max Planck Inst., Goettingen, Fed. Republic Germany, 1976-77; vis. scientist Woods Hole Oceanographic Inst., 2002-03, adj. scientist, 2003-; cons. in field. Author: Acoustics: An Introduction to Its Physical Principles and Applications, 1981; editor phys. acoustics monograph series, 1988-97; editor Jour. Computation Acoustics, 1992-99; contbr. articles to profl. jours. Recipient Sr. U.S. Scientist award Alexander von Humboldt Found., 1976, Cert. of Recognition Nat. Aeronautics and Space Adminstrn., 1984, Per Bruel Gold medal for noise control and acoustics ASME, 1995; NSF fellow, 1957-60, Shell Oil fellow, 1960-61, Faculty fellow U.S. Dept. Transp., 1979-80. Fellow Acoustical Soc. Am. (editor-in-chief 1999—, Silver medal 1991, Rossing prize in acoustics edn. 2004, Gold medal 2005), ASME (Rayleigh lectr. 1992, Per Bruel Gold medal 1995, chair Noise Control and Acoustics Divsn. 1999-2000); mem. IEEE, AIAA. Home: PO Box 339 East Sandwich MA 02537-0339 Office: Boston U Dept Aerospace & Mech Engring 110 Cummington St Boston MA 02215-2407 Business E-Mail: adp@bu.edu.

**PIERCE, CHARLES ELIOT, JR.,** library director, educator; b. Springfield, Mass., Dec. 25, 1941; s. C. Eliot and Dora Mason (Redway) P.; m. Barbara G. Hanson, Oct. 18, 1969; children: Sheila H., Charles Eliot III BA, Harvard U., 1964, MAT., 1966, PhD, 1970. Prof. English Vassar Coll., Poughkeepsie, NY, 1970-87; dir. Pierpont Morgan Library, N.Y.C., 1987—. Mem. vis. com. Vassar Coll. Art Gallery, Am. Trust for the Brit. Libr., Sherman Fairchild Found. Author: (literary criticism) The Religious Life of Samuel Johnson, 1983 Mem. Art Mus. Dirs., Johnsonians, Century Assn., Grolier Club, Walpole Soc., Knickerbocker Club. Republican. Home: 11 Clinton Corners Rd Salt Point NY 12578-2502 Office: Pierpont Morgan Libr 29 E 36th St New York NY 10016-3490 Office Phone: 212-590-0305. Business E-Mail: cpierce@morganlibrary.org.

**PIERCE, CHESTER MIDDLEBROOK,** retired psychiatrist, educator; b. Glen Cove, N.Y., Mar. 4, 1927; s. Samuel Riley and Hettie Elenor (Armstrong) P.; m. Jocelyn Patricia Blanchet, June 15, 1949; children: Diane Blanchet, Deirdre Anona. AB, Harvard U., 1948, MD, 1952; ScD (hon.), Westfield Coll., 1977, Tufts U., 1984; D in Engring. Tech. (hon.), Wentworth Inst. Tech., 1997. Instr. psychiatry U. Cin., 1957-60; asst. prof. psychiatry U. Okla., 1960-62, prof., 1965-69; prof. edn. and psychiatry Harvard U., 1969—; pres. Am. Bd. Psychiatry and Neurology, 1977-78; ret., 1997. Mem. Polar Rsch. Bd.; cons. USAF. Author publs. on sleep disturbances, media, polar medicine, sports medicine, racism; mem. editl. bds. Advisor Children's TV Workshop; chmn. Child Devel. Assn. Consortium; bd. dirs. Action Children's TV. With M.C. USNR, 1953-55. Fellow: Brit. Royal Coll. Psychiatrists (hon.), Royal Australian and New Zealand Coll. Psychiatrists (hon.); mem.: Am. Acad. Arts and Scis., Am. Orthopsychiat. Assn. (pres. 1983—84), Black Psychiatrists Am. (chmn.), Inst. Medicine of NAS. Democrat. Home: 17 Prince St Jamaica Plain MA 02130-2725 Office Phone: 617-495-4929.

**PIERCE, CONSTANCE LAUNDON,** artist, educator; b. Cleve., May 24, 1946; d. Richard H. and Patricia Leece Pierce; 1 child, Matthew Laundon Pierce Wohlgemuth. BFA, The Cleve. Inst. Art, 1973; MFA, Md. Inst. Coll. Art, 1975. Mem. faculty Interlochan Ctr. for the Arts, 1973—76, Lafayette Coll., Pa., 1977—81; artist-in-residence The Henry Luce III Ctr. Arts and Religion, Washington, 1990—93, Millsaps Coll., Jackson, Miss., 1994—96; mem. faculty Penland (N.C.) Sch. Fine Arts and Crafts, 1994—97; rsch. fellow Divinity Sch., Yale U., New Haven, 1997—2000; mem. faculty Nat. Summer Program, Cleve. Inst. Art, 2000—01; mem. faculty Campus on the Mall, Smithsonian Inst., Washington, 2002; prof. visual and performing arts St. Bonaventure U., NY, 2002—. Cons. in field. Represented in permanent collections Nat. Mus. Women in Arts, Washington, The Archive Am. Art Smithsonian Inst., Nat. Gallery Art Rare Book Libr., Yale Ctr. Brit. Art Sketchbook Archives, New Haven, Conn., NIH, Washington, one-woman shows include Dadian Gallery, Washington, D.C., 1993, Washington Printmakers Gallery, 1993, Gallery 475 Riverside, N.Y.C., 1994, Newman Gallery of Capitol Hill, Washington, 1995, Libr., Divinity Sch., Yale U., 1998, Regina A. Quick Ctr. Arts, Olean, N.Y., 2003, Henry Luce III Ctr. Arts and Religion, Washington, 2005, Haughton Coll., NY, 2006, exhibited in group shows at The Camden Arts Ctr., London, Eng., 1977, The May Show The Cleve. (Ohio) Mus. Art., 1985, The Corcoran Hemicycle Gallery, Washington, 1993, Montgomery Coll. Print Biennial, 1993, Nat. Mus. Women in Arts, 1994, Fairchild Gallery Georgetown U., 2000, Internat. Marian Rsch., Inst. Dayton U., Ohio, 2000, Foundry Gallery, Washington, 2005. Hoffberger fellow, 1975, Magi Endowment grant, Cath. U. Am., 1990—93, grant, Lilly Endowment, Inc., 2003, 2004, James Martine Endowment grants, 2003, 2005. Mem.: Am. Art Therapy Assn., So. Graphics Coun., Am. Print Alliance, Soc. Arts in Healthcare, Md. Printmakers Assn., Coll. Art Assn. Avocation: writing. Home: PO Box 144 Olean NY 14760-0144 Office: Vis and Perf Arts Faculty Regina A Quick Arts Ctr St Bonaventure Univ Saint Bonaventure NY 14778 Office Phone: 716-375-2696. Business E-Mail: cpierce@sbu.edu.

**PIERCE, DANIEL THORNTON,** physicist; b. LA, July 16, 1940; s. Daniel Gordon Pierce and Celia Francis Thornton Thayer; m. Barbara Harrison, Nov. 19, 1988; children: Jed, Maia, Stephen. BS, Stanford U., 1962, PhD in Applied Physics, 1970; MA, Wesleyan U., Middletown, Conn., 1966. NSF rsch. asst. materials sci. dept. Stanford U., 1961; lectr in physics U.S. Peace Corps, Kathmandu, Nepal, 1962-64; rsch. assoc. Wesleyan U., 1964-66, Stanford Electronics Lab., 1966-70, rsch. assoc., 1970-71; rsch. staff Solid State Physics Lab., Swiss Fed. Inst. Tech., 1971-75; physicist Nat. Inst. Standards and Tech. (formerly Nat. Bur Standards), Gaithersburg, Md., 1975—, fellow, 1994—. Contbr. chpts. to books, numerous articles to profl. jours. Trustee Unitarian Ch. of Rockville, Md.; 1994-96 Recipient IR-100 award R&D Mag., 1980, 85, Gold medal Dept. Commerce, 1987, William P. Schlichter award Nat. Inst. Standards and Tech., 1992. Fellow Am. Phys. Soc. (exec. com. Materials Physics Divsn. 1998-2001), Am. Vacuum Soc. (surface sci. exec. com. 1984-88, Gaede-Langmuir prize 1994). Achievements include patents for use of spin polarized electrons, absorbed current and low energy spin polarization detectors; development of scanning electron microscopy with polarization analysis. Office: Nat Inst Standards and Tech Mail Stop 8412 Bldg 216 Rm A223 Gaithersburg MD 20899-8412 Office Phone: 301-975-3711. Business E-Mail: daniel.pierce@nist.gov.

**PIERCE, DANNY PARCEL,** artist, educator; b. Woodlake, Calif., Sept. 10, 1920; s. Frank Lester and Letitia Frances (Parcel) P.; m. Julia Ann Rasmussen, July 19, 1943; children: Julia Ann, Mary L., Danny L., Duane Nels. Student, Art Ctr. Sch., L.A., 1939, Chouinards Art Inst., 1940-41, 46-47, Am. Art Sch., N.Y.C., 1947-48, Bklyn. Mus. Art Sch., 1950-53; BFA, U. Alaska, 1963. Instr. Hunter Coll., N.Y.C., 1952-53, Burnley Sch. Art, Seattle, 1954-58, Seattle U., 1956-59; publ. Red Door Studio Press, Kent, Wash., 1959—; artist-in-res. U. Alaska, College, 1959-63; asst. prof. U. Wisc., Milw., 1964; head art dept Cornish Sch. Allied Arts, Seattle, 1964-65; prof. art U. Wisc., Milw., 1965-84, prof. emeritus, 1984—. One-man shows include Contemporaries Gallery, N.Y.C., 1953, Handforth Gallery, Tacoma, Washington, 1958, U. Alaska, College, 1959, 63, 73, 74, Gonzaga U., Bradley Galleries, Milw., 1966, 68, 70, 72, 74, 76, 78-80, 82, Martin-Zambito Gallery, Seattle, 1997, 2002, Apple Blossom Time, 2000, Centennial Gallery, Kent, Wash., 2003, 04; father/son exhbn. 2002 Desert Images, Martin-Zambito Gallery, 1999; represented in permanent collections Bibliothèque Nationale, Paris, Mus. Modern Art, N.Y.C., Libr. Congress, Washington, Smithsonian Instn., Washington, Seattle Art Mus., U. Washington Henry Art Gallery, Bklyn. Mus., Princeton U., U. Alaska, U. So. Calif., William and Mary Coll., Oostduinkerke (Belgium) Nat. Fishing Mus., Nat. Mus. Sweden, Stockholm, Johnson Wax Found., Racine, Wisc., Gen. Mills Collection Art, Mpls., Huntington Libr., San Marino, Calif., various pvt. collections; pub. 27 ltd. edit. books, 1959-98. Recipient Best Oil Landscape award Conn. Acad. Fine Arts, Hartford, 1st Prize oil Kohler Gallery, Seattle, 1974, others; chosen one of twelve artists to represent State Wash. Expo 70, Osaka, Japan, rep. U.S. Internat. São Paulo Biannual Art Exhbn.; established archives at Golda Meier Libr., U. Wis.-Mils. Mem. Artist Equity Assn. (charter, pres. Seattle chpt. 1958), Am. Colorprint Soc., Internat. Arts and Letters (life). Office: Red Door Studio 404 Summit Ave N Kent WA 98030-4712

**PIERCE, DAVID,** information technology executive; With New World Pictures, New World Home Entertainment; sr. v.p. Columbia Tristar Home Video, 1989—94; exec. v.p., gen. mgr. Sony Wonder; pres., CEO Atari Inc., NYC, 2006—. Office: Atari Inc 417 Fifth Ave New York NY 10016-2204*

**PIERCE, DAVID HYDE,** actor; b. Albany, NY, Apr. 3, 1959; BA in theatre & English, Yale U., 1981. Appeared in plays Beyond Therapy, 1982, Holiday, 1982, Summer, 1983, That's It, Folks! 1983, Candida, 1984, The Seagull, 1984, The Grand Hysteric, 1984, The Three Zeks, 1984, Tartuffe, 1984, Donuts, 1985, Hamlet, 1986, The Author's Voice, 1987, The Maderati, 1987, Camille, 1987, The Cherry Orchard, 1988, Zero Positive, 1988, Much Ado About Nothing, 1988, The Heidi Chronicles, 1989, Elliot Loves, 1990, It's Only a Play, 1991, Monty Python's Spamalot, 2005, Curtains, 2006; films include Bright Lights, Big City, 1988, Crossing Delancey, 1988, Rocket Gibraltar, 1988, The Fisher King, 1991, Little Man Tate, 1991, Sleepless in Seattle, 1993, Addams Family Values, 1993, Wolf, 1994, Nixon, 1995, Hercules, 1998, A Bug's Life, 1998, Jackie's Back!, 1999, Mating Habits of the Earthbound Human, 1999, Isn't She Great, 2000, Chain of Fools, 2000, Wet, Hot, American Summer, 2001, Osmosis Jones, 2001; TV series include The Powers That Be, 1993, Frasier, 1993-2004 (seven Am. Comedy awards), Laud Weiner, 2001, Full Frontal, 2002, Treasure Planet (voice), 2002, Down with Love, 2003. Recipient Emmy award, 1995, 1998, 1999, 2004, SAG Award, 1996, 2000, Q Award 1994, 95, 96, 98, TV Guide award, 2000, TV Critics Assn. award 1997, 1998. Am. Comedy award 1995-2000.

**PIERCE, DIANE JEAN,** artist; b. Evanston, Ill., Apr. 9, 1952; d. Kenneth William and Marjorie J. (Hansen) P.; m. William Carry Reuling, Sept. 8, 1991 (div. July 1992). BFA in Drawing and Painting, U. Utah, 1976. Illustrator Ensign Mag., Salt Lake City, 1977-79, Scott Foresman & Co. Pubs., Glenview, Ill., 1980, Children's Press, Chgo., 1981-82; mansion artist Adnan-Khoshagi's Devereaux Mansion, Salt Lake City, 1984-87; illustrator Friend Mag./Era Mag., Salt Lake City, 1978-80; artist-painter Lido Gallery, Park City, Utah, 1990-93, Thomas Charles Gallery, Las Vegas, New., 1994, Art Dimensions Gallery, Hollywood, Calif., 1994-96, Meyer Gallery, Park City, Utah, 1996-98; with Don Huntsman Gallery, Aspen, Colo., 1999—2001; artist Winter Olympics, Park City, Utah, 2002. Apprentice photographer Reynel Salgado Mirando, 1980 Elections, Acapulco, Mexico, 1980; juror exhbn. com. Alliance Gallery, Salt Lake Art Ctr., 1984, 85, invitational artist, fundraiser for Town and Country magazine: Women in Need, N.Y., 1998. Exhibited in group shows at New Genre, 1985, 5 Star Auction Invitational, 1985, Springville Nat. Salon, 1985, Utah Women Artists, 1985, Chase Mansion Guthrie Artists Show, 1986, Guthrie Artists, 1986, NAD, 1986, Eccles Art Ctr., 1986, 1987, Women's Show, 1987, 1989, 1991, 1993, Park City Open Painting Competition, 1989—90, 1993, Mus. Art, Alliance Gallery, Chase Mansion, Salt Lake Art Ctr., Tivoli Gallery, Cliff Lodge Gallery, U. Utah Mus. Art, Devereaux Mansion, 1984—87, Utah divsn. Assn. Women Artists traveling show, 1989—90, 100 Yrs.-100 Women traveling show, N.Y.C., 1989—91, Springville Mus. Art, 1992, Nat. Assn. Women ann. nat. competition, 1993, Janet Dumbar Interiors, Sun Valley, Idaho, 1991—93, Lido Gallery, 1990—93, Elouises' Interiors, Park City, Utah, 1993—98, Thomas Charles Gallery, 1994, Art Dimensions Gallery, 1994—96, Springville Mus. Art nat. competition, Art Space, 1995, Gallery Stroll, 1995, Nat. Assn. Women Artists ann., Soho, N.Y., 1995, Nat. Assn. Women Artists, Athens, Greece, 1996, NAWA NY Soho Show, 1999, Springville Mus. Natl. 75th April Salon, 1999—2000, Soho Nat. Assn. Women Artists, 1999, Represented in permanent collections Salt Lake City, Profl. Figure Skaters Hdqs., Sun Valley, Springville Mus. Art, Moonie & O'Conner, Cin., Van Cott, Bagley, Cornwall & McCarthy, Salt Lake City, also pvt. collections; contbr. color plates Painting and Sculptors by Serdirect, Olphin, 1985, color plates in Visual Selling and Design by Mary Irish, 1990, articles to profl. jours. Recipient Art Dirs. award, Era Mag., 1979, Dirs. award, U. Utah Statewide Competition, Springville Mus. Fine Art, 1987, Best of Show, Eccles Statewide Competition, Ogden Utah, 1987, Best Traditional Painting, Nat. Assn. U. Women, Utah divsn., Ogden, 1989, Best of Show, Open Painting Exhbn., Kimball Art Ctr., Park City, Utah, 1989, 3rd pl. open painting competition, Kimball Art Ctr, Park City, 1990, Visual Merchandising & Design Mag. award, Designer Excellence, 1990, Best of Show open painting exhbn, Kimball Art Ctr., Park City, 1993, award of merit, Springville Mus. Fine Art, 1995; grantee, Artists Fellowship, Inc., N.Y.C., 1993. Mem. Nat. Assn. Women Artists (N.Y. chpt., Susan Kahn award 1987), Nat. Mus. Women in Arts. Home: PO Box 330 1605 South W Stookey Ln Rush Valley UT 84069

**PIERCE, DONALD SHELTON,** retired orthopedic surgeon, educator; b. Castine, Maine, May 21, 1930; s. Frederick Ernest and Jeannie (Emmet) P.; m. Janet Ten Broeck, Dec. 29, 1956; children: Donald Shelton, Stanton ten Broeck, Frederick Ernest, Jennifer Emmet. AB cum laude, Harvard U., 1953, MD, 1957. Diplomate Am. Bd. Spine Surgery, Am. Bd. Orthop. Surgery. Intern U. Hosp., Cleve., 1957-58, resident, 1958-62; rsch. assoc. biomechanics lab. U. Calif., San Francisco, 1962-64; practice medicine specializing in orthopedic surgery San Francisco, 1962-64; instr. orthopedic surgery U. Calif. Med. Sch., San Francisco, 1962-64, Harvard Med. Sch., 1964-66; clin. and rsch. assoc. J.P. Kennedy Jr. Meml. Hosp., Brighton, Mass., 1964-66; clin. assoc. in orthopedics Harvard Med. Sch., 1966-67, clin. asst. prof. orthopaedic surgery, 1979-87, clin. assoc. prof., 1987-2000; ret., 2000; sr. orthopedic surgeon Mass. Gen. Hosp., Boston. Chief dept. rehab. medicine Mass. Gen. Hosp., Boston, 1965-72, assoc. orthopedic surgeon, 1969—, vis. orthopedic surgeon, 1969—; lectr. dept. mech. engring. MIT, 1970-72. Co-author: Amputees and Their Prostheses, 1971; contbr. articles in field to profl. jours. Pres. Wellesley (Mass.) Friendly Aid Assn., 1965-67, dir., 1967-70; dir. Family Svc. Counseling Region West, Wellesley, 1965-67; mem. exec. com., task force chmn. Mass. Rehab. Planning Commn., 1966-68; pres. Maine Ret. Skippers Race, 2003-05; co-chmn. capital campaign com. Trinity Espic. Ch., Maine. With USAF, 1951-52. Fellow ACS, Am. Acad. Orthopedic Surgeons, Royal Soc. Health, Pan Am. Med. Assn., Soc. Internat. Chirurgerie, Ortopaedie et Traumatologie; mem. NAS (mem. skeletal com. 1966-68, mem. subcom. basic projects, mem. com. prosthetics R & D 1966-68), NRC (musculoskeletal com., mem. subcom. basic projects, mem. com. prosthetics

R & D), Othopedic Rsch. Soc., Am. Orthopaedic Assn., Cervical Spine Rsch. Soc. (pres. 1986), Fedn. Spine Assns. (pres. 1987), N.E. Med. Assn. (pres.). Personal E-mail: treetops1@comcast.net.

**PIERCE, FRANCIS CASIMIR,** civil engineer; b. Warren, RI, May 19, 1924; s. Frank J. and Eva (Soltys) Pierce; m. Helen Lynette Steinouer, Apr. 24, 1954; children: Paul F., Kenneth J., Nancy L., Karen H., Charles E. Student, U. Conn., 1943-44; BS, U. R.I., 1948; MS, Harvard U., 1950; postgrad., Northeastern U., 1951-52. Registered profl. engr. Conn., N.H., Mass., R.I., Vt.; registered profl. land surveyor R.I. Instr. civil engring. U. R.I., Kingston, 1948-49, U. Conn., Storrs, 1950-51; design engr. Praeger-Maguire & Ole Singstad, Boston, 1951-52; chief found. engr. C.A. Maguire & Assocs., Providence, 1952-59, assoc., 1959-69, v.p., 1969-72; sr. v.p. C.E. Maguire, Inc., 1972-76, officer-in-charge Honolulu office, 1976-78, exec. v.p., corp. dir. ops., 1975-87; dir. The Maguire Group, Inc., 1979—; gen. mgr. East Atlantic Casualty Co. Ltd., 1987-88; also dir. Pres. Magma, Inc., tech. ops. svc. co., 1986—88; lectr. found. engring. U. R.I., 1968—69, trustee, 1987—2002; 19mem. Coll. Engring. adv. coun., 1986—98; mem. U.S. com. Internat. Commn. on Large Dams; mem. register of expert witnesses in the constrn. industry ABA. Contbr. articles to profl. jours. Vice chmn. Planning Bd. East Providence, R.I., 1960-73; bd. dirs. R.I. Civic Chorale and Orch., 1986-90. With AUS, 1942-46. Decorated Bronze star, Combat Infantry badge, Presdl. Unit citation; named Acad. of Fellows, Am. Mil. Engr., 1996, Coll. Engring. Hall of Fame, U. R.I., 2000; recipient Commendation, Min. Pub. Works Rep. Venezuela, 1970, Geotech. award, ASCE sect. Boston Soc. Civil Engrs., 1979, USCG Meritorious Pub. Svc. award, 1987, Chester H. Kirk Disting. Engr. award, U. R.I. Coll. Engring., 1987. Fellow Soc. Am. Mil. Engrs., ASCE (life, chpt. past pres., dir.), NSPE (life); mem. Am. Arbitration Assn., R.I. Soc. Profl. Engrs. (nat. dir., engr. of yr. award 1973), ASTM, Am. Soc. Engring. Edn., Soc. Marine Engrs. and Naval Architects, Am. Soc. Planning Ofcls., Harvard Soc. Engrs., Scientists, Providence Engrs. Soc., R.I. Soc. Planning Agys (past pres.), U. R.I. Alumni Assn. (pres. and dir., S.W. Fla. Gators chpt. 2000-2002, Outstanding Svc. award 2002). Home: 36 Barney St Rumford RI 02916-1202 Office: 225 Foxborough Blvd Foxboro MA 02035-2854

**PIERCE, FRANK POWELL,** lawyer, judge; b. San Antonio, Dec. 28, 1953; s. Arnold Leigh and Marie Pierce; m. Ernestine Pierce; 4 children. BA in Polit. Sci., U. Houston, 1977; JD, Tex. So. U., 1980. Bar: Tex. 1980, U.S. Dist. Ct. (so. and we. dists.) Tex. 1982, U.S. Ct. Appeals (5th cir.) 1982, U.S. Supreme Ct. 1984. Atty. Bexar County Legal Aid, San Antonio, 1980-83; asst. city atty. City of San Antonio, 1983-87; judge County Ct. at Law No. 2, San Antonio, 1987—; asst. atty. gen., 1993—2001; judge Child Support Ct. 2, Harris County, 2001—. Mem. Bexar County Bail Bond Bd., 1987-88; mem. faculty St. Philip's Coll., part-time; adj. prof. South Tex. Coll. Law. Mem. speaker's bur. San Antonio Literacy Coun., 1988, mediation bd. Bexar County, 1989—; deacon Mt. Zion 1st Bapt. Ch., San Antonio; alumnus Leadership San Antonio; mem. minority recruitment task force Dental Sch., U. Tex. Health Sci. Ctr.; mem. Palmer Drug Abuse Bd., 1987—; bd. mgrs. Alamo br. YMCA, San Antonio; bd. dirs. Halfway House San Antonio, 1989; city councilman, San Antonio, 1991-93. Named Black Achiever in Govt., Iota Phi Lamda, 1984; recipient Citizen of Yr. award Omega Psi Phi, 1987, Man of Yr. award Mission Lodge, San Antonio, 1988. Mem. Tex. Bar Assn. Office: 49 San Jacinto Ste 304 Houston TX 77002

**PIERCE, HARVEY R.,** insurance company executive; m. Delores Pierce. Agt. Am. Family Ins. Group, 1963, exec. v.p. field ops., regional v.p., state dir., dist. sales mgr., pres., COO, 1990—99, chmn., CEO Madison, Wis., 1999—. Mem. adv. bd. U. Wis. Children's Hosp.; mem. Founders' Club S.W. Mo. State U. Ins. Chair. Mem.: Ins. Inst. Hwy. Safety (chmn. 2004—05), Property Casualty Insurers Assn. Am. (chmn. bd. govs. 2005). Office: Am Family Ins Group 6000 American Pky Madison WI 53783-0001 Office Phone: 608-249-2111.

**PIERCE, HILDA (HILDA HERTA HARMEL),** painter; b. Vienna; arrived in U.S., 1940; m. Herman J. Slutzky; 1 child, Diana Rubin Daly (dec.). Student, Art Inst. Chgo.; studied with Oskar Kokoschka, Salzburg, Austria. Art tchr. Highland Park (Ill.) Art Ctr., Sandburg Village Art Workshop, Chgo., Old Town Art Ctr., Chgo.; owner, operator Hilda Pierce Art Gallery, Laguna Beach, Calif., 1981-85. Guest lectr. maj. art mus. and art tours, Carribean cruises South America, Argentina, Brazil, France, Switzerland, Austria, Italy, Mex., San Diego, China, India, 1998—2002, Russian river cruise and major art mus., St. Petersburg, Moscow, 1994; lectr., Mexico, 1994—2006, U. Calif. Geisel Libr., San Diego, 2003; founder, chmn. Art Encounters, San Diego. One-woman shows include Fairweather Hardin Gallery, Chgo., Sherman Art Gallery, Marshall Field Gallery, exhibited in group shows at Old Orchard Art Festival, Skokie, Ill., Union League Club, Chgo., North Shore Art League, Winnetka, Ill., Art Inst. Chgo., Represented in permanent collections U. Calif. San Diego Art Libr., La Jolla, Carnival Cruise Lines megaliner M.S. Fantasy, megaliner M.S. Imagination, Rebecca and John Moores Cancer Ctr., U. Calif. San Diego, U. Calif. San Diego Geisel Libr.; featured (video) Survivors of the Shoa, Stephen Spielberg Found., 1996; contbr. articles to profl. jours. and newspapers. Recipient Outstanding Achievement in Art award, Chgo. Immigrants Svc. League, 1964. Office Phone: 858-558-7556. *An artist's most precious quality is curiosity. It has kept me young for many years, kept me searching, experimenting and never being complacent, in my life and my work.*

**PIERCE, JAMES CLARENCE,** surgeon, educator; b. Huron, S.D., Aug. 5, 1929; s. Henry Montraville and Carrie Bernice (Matson) P.; m. Carol Sue Wilson, 1967; children: Henry MacDonald, Richard Matson, Elizabeth Gail. BA, Carleton Coll., 1951; MD, Harvard U., 1955; MS, U. Minn., 1963, PhD in Surgery, 1966. Diplomate Am. Bd. Surgery. Surg. intern Peter Bent Brigham Hosp., Boston, 1955-56; surg. fellow U. Minn., 1959-66; instr. surgery Med. Coll. Va., Richmond, 1966, prof. surgery and microbiology, 1972-75; dir. Tissue Typing Lab., 1969-75; attending surgeon, dir. surg. research, dir. transplantation service St. Luke's Hosp. Center, N.Y.C., 1975-78; prof. surgery Columbia U., 1976, Ailsa Mellon Bruce prof. surgery, 1977-78; clin. prof. surgery Pa. State U. and, 1978-83; chmn. dept. surgery Geisinger Med. Center, Danville, Pa., 1979-90, chmn. emeritus, 1990—. Clin. prof. surgery Jefferson U., 1990—. Contbr. articles to profl. jours. Elder Presbyn. Ch. With M.C., USAF, 1957-59. NIH fellow, 1963-65; Royal Soc. Medicine Found. travelling fellow, 1971; James IV Assn. Surg. traveller, 1978 Mem. ACS (pres. Ctrl. Pa. chpt. 1981-82), Transplant Soc., Am. Soc. Transplant Surgeons, Ea. Surg. Soc., N.Y. Clin. Soc., Soc. Univ. Surgeons, Sigma Xi. Republican. Home: 1906 Red Ln Danville PA 17821-8415

**PIERCE, JENNIFER BUREK,** library and information scientist; d. Richard David and Ann J. Burek; m. Matthew Shawn Pierce, June 19, 1999. PhD, Ind. U., Bloomington, 1995—99. Ref. libr./alert editor NCEMCH Georgetown U., Arlington, Va., 1999—2000; adj. faculty SLIS Cath. U. Am., 2000—01; web handbook editor Agy. Healthcare Rsch. & Quality, Rockville, Md., 2002; asst. prof. SLIS Iupui, Indpls., 2002—05, U. Iowa, Iowa City, 2005—. Reviewer Libr. Jour., NYC, 2002—; grassroots report columnist Am. Libraries Mag. ALA, Chgo., 2003—; mem. editl. bd. Women's Studies in Comm., Orgn. Rsch. on Women & Comm., WSCA. Contbr. articles to profl. jours. Mem.: ALA, Assn. History Authorship, Reading & Pub., Am. Assn. History Medicine. Office: SLIS Univ Iowa 3076 Main Library Iowa City IA 52242-1420 Business E-Mail: jennifer-burek-pierce@uiowa.edu.

**PIERCE, JERRY EARL,** publishing executive; b. Hindsdale, Ill., Aug. 3, 1941; s. Earl and Adeline A. (Zaranski) P.; m. Carol Louise Martin, Aug. 15, 1964; children: Patricia, Barbara, Linda. Bradley. BS, U. Ill., 1964. With R.R. Donnelley & Sons, Chgo., 1964-70, Western Pub. Co., Racine, Wis., 1970—, nat. pubs. acct. exec., 1975—. Chair bd. Pierce Sale Co., Inc., Restaurant Equipment World, Inc., Heat Transfer Engring. Inc.; chmn. bd. Tech Industries & Millwork, Inc., 1989-93; pres. B.J. Installation Co., Inc., 1989-91, ROI World Equipment, 1993—; v.p., sec. Savers Clubs Am., Inc.; v.p. Pierce Aviation, 2000—; chmn. adv. bd. Greater Winter Park, Bankfirst Bank, Winter Park, Fla. Chmn. Leadership Trust of Nat. Fedn. Ind. Bus. 1st lt. U.S.

Army, 1968—70. Mem.: Nat. Bus. Aviation Assn., Food Equipment Distbrs. Assn. (bd. dirs. 1997—98), Food Svc. Cons. Soc., Fla. Restaurant Assn., Tiger Bay Club of Orlando, Cleve. Advt. Club, Interlachen Country Club (bd. dirs. Winter Pk., Fla.), Ctrl. Fla. Veterans Mem. Found. (bd. dirs.), Ctrl. Fla. Vets. Inc. (pres.). Republican. Episcopalian. Achievements include patents for refrigeration-to-water utility cost control system; invention of E-Commerce business model. Home: 2639 Ultra Vista Dr Maitland FL 32751 Office: 2413 N Forsyth Rd Orlando FL 32807-6455

**PIERCE, JOHN GERALD (JERRY PIERCE),** lawyer; b. Winter Haven, Fla., Jan. 12, 1937; s. Francis E. and Margaret (Butler) P.; m. Kathleen E., Dec. 1, 1989; children: Kathleen M. Cooke, Nancy A., John Gerald Jr., Michael J. BChemE, U. Fla., Gainesville, 1959, JD with honors, 1965. Bar: Fla. 1966, US Dist. Ct. (mid. dist.) Fla. 1966, US Ct. Appeals (11th cir.) 1983. Assoc. Anderson & Rush, Dean & Lowndes, Orlando, Fla., 1966—68, Arnold, Matheny & Eagen, Orlando, 1968—70; ptnr. Pierce, Lewis & Dolan, Orlando, 1970—74; pvt. practice Orlando, 1974—2002; prin., owner Pierce & Assocs. PL, Orlando, 2003—. Served to 1st lt. U.S. Army, 1959—65. Named Businessman of Yr., Nat. Rep. Congl. Com., 2004. Mem. ABA, Fla. Bar Assn., Orange County Bar Assn. Republican. Roman Catholic. Avocations: golf, boating, skiing. Home: 605 Fox Valley Dr Longwood FL 32779-2417 Office: 800 N Ferncreek Ave Orlando FL 32803-4127 Office Phone: 407-898-4848. Business E-Mail: jerry@johnpierce.com.

**PIERCE, JOHN RANDALL,** medical inspector, pediatrician; b. Nashville, May 9, 1947; MD, U. Tenn., 1971. Cert. Pediatrics, 1977, Neonatal-Perinatal Medicine, 1981. Chief Dept. Pediatrics, residency program dir. U.S. Army Med. Corps.; dep. comdr. clin. svcs., dir. med. edn. Walter Reed Army Med. Cu., cons. pediatrics US Surgeon Gen.; dep. med. inspector Veterans Health Adminstrn., US Dept. Veterans Affairs, Washington, 2002—04. med. inspector, 2004—. Asst. prof. pediatrics Uniformed Svcs. U. of Health Scis.; historian Walter Reed Soc. Co-author: Yellow Jack: How Yellow Fever Ravaged America and Walter Reed Discovered Its Deadly Secrets, 2005; contbr. articles to profl. jours. Col. med. corps U.S. Army. Decorated Legion of Merit, Meritorious Svc. Medal, Joint Svc. Commendation Medal, Army Commendation Medal, Army Achievement Medal, Order of Mil. Med. Merit Surgeon Gen. Fellow: Am. Acad. Pediatrics. Office: US Dept Vet Affairs Vets Health Adminstrn 810 Vermont Ave NW Washington DC 20420 Office Phone: 202-273-5400.*

**PIERCE, LAWRENCE WARREN,** retired federal judge; b. Phila., Dec. 31, 1924; s. Harold Ernest and Leora (Bellinger) Pierce; m. Wilma Taylor, 1948 (dec. May 1978); m. Cynthia Straker, July 8, 1979; children: Warren Wood, Michael Lawrence, Mark Taylor. BS, St. Joseph's V., Phila., 1948, DHL, 1967; JD, Fordham U., 1951, LLD, 1982, Fairfield U., 1972, Hamilton Coll., 1987, St. John's U., 1990. Bar: N.Y. 1951, U.S. Supreme Ct. 1968. Civil law practice, N.Y.C., 1951—61; asst. dist. atty. Kings County, N.Y., 1954—61; dep. police commr. N.Y.C., 1961—63; dir. N.Y. State Divsn. for Youth, Albany, 1963—66; chmn. N.Y. State Narcotic Addiction Control Commn., 1966—70; vis. prof. criminal justice SUNY, Albany, 1970—71; dist. judge U.S. Dist. Ct., So. Dist. N.Y., 1971—81; judge U.S. Ct. Appeals 2d Cir., 1981—95; ret., 1995. Dir. Cambodian ct. tng. project Internat. Human Rights Law Group, 1995. Past bd. dirs. CARE, Havens Fund Soc., Lincoln Hall for Boys, S-R and S.A.R., N.Y. chpts., Cath. Interracial Coun., Practising Law Inst. Mem.: ABA (com. on corr. svc. and facilities 1970—71, alt. observer U.S. Mission to UN 1988—90, site evaluation com., sec. legal action. 1996—98), Spl. Com. Army Confinement Facilties (Office of Sec. of Army 1970), Urban League, Nat. Bar Assn., Am. Law Inst., Coun. Fgn. Rels. Home: PO Box 2234 Sag Harbor NY 11963-0111

**PIERCE, LISA MARGARET,** telecommunications industry executive, marketing professional, educator; b. Nyack, NY, June 2, 1957; d. William and Elizabeth Pierce. BA with honors, Gordon Coll., Wenham, Mass., 1978; MBA, Atkinson Sch., Salem, Oreg., 1982. Campaign mgr. Carter/Mondale, Manchester, Mass., 1976; investigator Dept. Social Svcs., Nyack, 1977-78; paralegal Beverly, Mass., 1978-79; campaign mgr. Reagan Presdl. Primary, Rockland County, NY, 1980; cons. Sidereal, Portland, Oreg., 1981-82; performance analyst Dept. Social Svcs., Pomona, NY, 1982; market analyst Momentum Techs., Parsippany, NJ, 1983; cons. Booz Allen & Hamilton, Florham Park, NJ, 1984, Deloitte-Touche, Morristown, NJ, 1985; market rschr., forecaster AT&T, Bedminster, NJ, 1985-87, asst. pvt. line product mgr., 1987-89, Integrated Svcs. Digital Network product mgr., 1989-93; dir. Telecom. Rsch. Assocs., St. Marys, Kans., 1994-98; v.p., rsch. fellow Giga Info. Group/Forrester Rsch., Cambridge, Mass., 1998—. Panelist, contbr. TeleCom. Assn., San Diego and Seattle, Internat. Comm. Assn., Atlanta, Ea. Comm. Forum, NY, Nat. Engring. Consortium, Chgo., Super Comm., Soc. Telecom. Consultants, MPLS Forum, Mid Atlantic Venture Assn., GSA Fed. Telecom. Svc. Forums, VoiceCon, others; contbr. NY State ISDN/Internat User's Group; feature commentator AP Adio, Nat. Pub. Radio (All Things Considered and MarketWatch), Pub. Broadcasting Svc. Nightly Bus. Report, MSNBC, CNN and CNBC, Radio Wall Street, CBS Evening News Columnist Network World, 2001—02, Bus. Comm. Rev., 2002—. Named one of Top 10 Most Influential IT Analysts, Tech. Mktg. Mag., 2002, 2003; grantee in field. Mem.: IEEE. Personal E-Mail: lmpierce@att.net. Business E-Mail: lpierce@forrester.com.

**PIERCE, MARY,** professional tennis player; b. Montreal, Que., Can., Jan. 15, 1975; d. Jim and Yannick Pierce. Profl. Tennis Player, 1989—. Victories include Comeback Player of the Yr., 1997, Australian Open (singles), 1995, French Open (singles & doubles), 2000, Wimbledon (doubles), 2005; 17 WTA Career Singles Titles, 10 WTA Career Doubles Titles. Office: IMG Ctr 1360 E 9th St Ste 100 Cleveland OH 44114

**PIERCE, MARY E.,** retired elementary school educator, public relations consultant; b. Chgo. d. Henry Harris and Eva Irene (Hanes) P. BE, Chgo. Tchrs. Coll., 1944. One room sch. tchr. Will County, Monee, Ill.; tchr. 5th grade Peotone (Ill.) Sch. Dist.; tchr. elem. and jr. h.s. Steger (Ill.) Sch. Dist., chair lang. arts dept.; ret., 1979; chair sch. improvement plan; pub. rels. cons. Former cons. Steger Edn. Assn.; chmn. bd. dirs #194 Employee Credit Union, Steger, 1972-95. Village clk. Village of Richton Park, 1992—; pres. Friends of Libr., Richton Park, 1980-2005, v.p.; bd. dirs. So. Suburban Cancer Soc., Tinley Pk., Ill., 1994—, S.E. Chpt. Ill. Credit Union, Calumet City, Ill., 1994-95. Recipient Cmty. Svc. award Cook County Sheriff's Office, Chgo., Merit award S.E. chpt. Ill. Credit Union League. Mem. Delta Kappa Gamma Soc. (Lambda State Beta Beta chpt. treas. 1979-2003). Avocation: golf. Home: 22147 Karlov Ave Richton Park IL 60471-1227

**PIERCE, MICHAEL NORMAN,** internist; b. N.Y.C., May 1, 1955; s. Samuel and Ingeborg Pierce. BA in Biology, SUNY, Binghamton, 1977; MD, U. Vt., 1982. Diplomate Am. Bd. Internal Medicine. Intern, gen. surg. resident L.A. County/U. So. Calif. Med. Ctr., L.A., 1982—84; intern, resident in internal medicine Calif.-Pacific Med. Ctr., San Francisco, 1985—88; attending physician St. Francis Meml. Hosp., San Francisco, 1989—96, Montefiore Med. Ctr., East Elmhurst, NY, 1997—98, St. Barnabas Hosp./CHS/HHC, East Elmhurst, 1998—2001; asst. attending physician St. Luke's Roosevelt Hosp. Ctr., N.Y.C., 2002—05, assoc. attending physician NYC, 2005; dir. HIV medicine and internal medicine attending All Med Med. and Rehab. NY, 2006. Chair Spring conf. St. Luke's Roosevelt Hosp. Ctr., 2003; judge, mem. abstract rev. bd. for resident's poster competition N.Y. Downstate ACP-ASIM sci. meetings; asst. attending physician St. Luke's Roosevelt Hosp. Ctr., N.Y.C., 2002—04, mem. CME med. bd. com., 2002—05, key faculty, internal medicine residency program; asst. clin. prof. medicine Columbia U. Coll. Physicians and Surgeons, N.Y.C., 2002—05; active HIV mgmt. preceptorship program Johns Hopkins U. Sch. Medicine, Balt., 2001; mem. Infectious Disease Soc. Am., Infectious Disease Soc. Am. HIV Med. Assn.; HIV med. specialist State of N.Y. Mem. editl. bd. Johns Hopkins U. Sch. Medicine Advanced Studies in Medicine, 2002—. Recipient Physician's Recognition award, AMA, 1991—; Pharm. Mfrs. Assn. grantee, 1979. Fellow: ACP (com. on med. students 2001—), Soc. Gen. Internal

Medicine; mem.: AMA, N.Y. County Med. Soc., Med. Soc. State N.Y. (surveyor-reviewer hosp. CME programs 1998—, mem. com. on edn.). Office Phone: 718-292-0100. E-mail: mnpny@aol.com.

**PIERCE, MILDRED LOUISE,** librarian; b. Fulton County, Ga., Nov. 30, 1928; d. John Oliver Pierce and Florence Idella (Carr) Sansted; m. Harry Eugene Springer, Oct. 17, 1967; 1 child, Jesse Ladd. BS in Edn., SUNY, Geneseo, 1951; MA in Librarianship, U. Denver, 1955. Lic. Episcopalian lay reader, lay preacher. Libr. asst. SUNY, New Paltz, 1951; elem. libr. Hastings Pub. Schs., Hastings-on-the-Hudson, NY, 1951; libr. grad. student aide Denver Pub. Libr., 1954—55; children's bookmobile libr. Alexander Mitchell Pub. Libr., Aberdeen, SD, 1955—56; libr. Mineral County Sch. Dist., Hawthorne, Nev., 1956—64; adult edn. tchr. Clark County Sch. Dist., Las Vegas, Nev., 1964—65; tech. libr. RADSAFE, Reynolds Elec. and Engring. Co., Mercury, Nev., 1965—67; reference cons. Mother Lode Libr. Sys., Auburn, Calif., 1967—68; dir. Tech. Info. Svc., Hawthorne, 1976—; dep. gen. conv., commn. liturgy and music Domestic and Fgn. Missionary Soc. of Protestant in the Episcopal Ch. of U.S.A., 2003. Author: Nevada Rockfinder, 1970; columnist An Ounce of Prevention, 1973—75; editor: Wordwebs, 1979—81. Founder, trustee Walker-Wassuk Arts Alliance, Hawthorne, 1977; founder trustee Preservation Mineral County Courthouse and Flag Chowder and Marching Soc., 1982; pres. Desert Dance Arts Theater, 1989—; candidate Nev. Senate, 1976, Nev. Assembly, 1978, 1980. Mem.: NEA, ALA, States Assn., Am. Assn. Sch. Libr., Mineral County Tchrs. Assn., Nev. State Tchrs. Assn., Nev. Alliance for the Arts, Mineral County Coun. on Alcohol and Drug Abuse, Kappa Delta Pi. Republican. Episcopalian. Home: 674 I St PO Box 1721 Hawthorne NV 89415-1721 Office: Tech Info Svc PO Box 1721 Hawthorne NV 89415-1721 E-mail: tis@sisna.com

**PIERCE, MORTON ALLEN,** lawyer; b. Liberec, Czechoslovakia, June 25, 1948; m. Nancy Washor, Dec. 14, 1975 (dec.); children: Matthew J., Nicholas L. BA, Yale Coll., 1970; JD, U. Pa., 1974; postgrad., Oxford U., 1974-75. Bar: N.Y. 1975. Assoc. Reid & Priest, NYC, 1975-83, ptnr., 1983-86, Dewey Ballantine, NYC, 1986—, vice-chmn., 2002—03, co-chmn., 2003—05, chmn., 2005—. Mem. mgmt. com. 1988—, chmn. corp. dept., 1999—, chmn., mergers and acquisitions group, 1990—, mem. exec. com., 2001—. Contbr. articles to profl. jours. Mem. ABA (chmn. subcom. on internat. securities matters 1985-91, adv. com. to fed. regulation of securities com. 1991-2000, task force on rev. of the fed. securities law 1991-2000), Assn. of the Bar of the City of N.Y. (securities law com. 1988-91, chmn. subcom. on securities and exch. commn. enforcement matters 1990-91), Internat. Bar Assn. (com. on securities transactions), Legal Aid Soc. (bd. dirs.), Gordon A. Rich Found. (bd. dirs.). Home: 188 E 76th St New York NY 10021-2826 Office: Dewey Ballantine LLP 1301 Ave Of The Americas New York NY 10019-6022 Office Phone: 212-259-6640. Office Fax: 212-259-6333. Business E-Mail: mpierce@dbllp.com.

**PIERCE, NAOMI ELLEN,** biology professor, researcher; b. Denver, Oct. 19, 1954; d. Arthur Preble and Ruiko (Ishizaka) P; m. Andrew James Berry, Mar. 9, 1996; children: Kate Clark Berry, Megan Elizabeth Berry. BS, Yale U., 1976; PhD, Harvard U., k1983. Fulbright postdoctoral fellow Griffith U., Brisbane, Australia, 1983-84; rsch. lectr. Christ Ch., U. Oxford, Eng., 1984-86; asst. prof. Princeton U., N.J., 1986-91; Sydney A. and John H. Hessel prof. biology, curator lepidoptera Harvard U. and Harvard Mus. Comparative Zoology, Cambridge, Mass., 1991—. Contbr. articles to profl. jours. MacArthur Found. fellow, Chgo., 1988-93. Fellow Harvard Soc. of Fellows (sr.). Office: Harvard U 26 Oxford St Cambridge MA 02138-2902

**PIERCE, PATRICIA ANN,** university administrator; b. Harriman, Tenn., Feb. 13, 1949; d. Fred Ernest and Lela Nora (Jones) P.; m. Jacky Albert Goss, Sept. 21, 1991; children: Wesley Matthew Goss, James Michael Goss. BS, U. Tenn., 1973; cert., Bryn Mawr Coll., 1991. Cert. secondary edn. tchr., Tenn.; cert. diversity trainer. Field rep. Tenn. Human Rights Commn., Nashville, 1973-76, compliance dir., 1976-78; assoc. dir.Opportunity Devel. Ctr. Vanderbilt U., Nashville, 1978-81, dir., 1981—. Cons. Pierce Consulting, Nashville, 1985—; presenter in field. Contbr. articles to profl. jours. Chairperson Mayor's Adv. Com. for People with Disabilities, Nashville, 1988-89; pres. bd. dirs. League for Hearing Impaired, Nashville, 1994-95, Nashville YWCA, 1996-98; spkr. Nat. Intramural Recreation Sports Assn., Nashville, 1994; del. People to People Internat. Learning Disability Del., Beijing, 1995; nongovtl. rep. NGO Forum, 4th World Conf. on Women, Beijing, 1995; People to People Internat. del. to Cuba, 2003; active Gov. Adv. Com. on Equal Employment Opportunity, 1992-96; mem. Leadership Nashville, 2003; commr. Tenn. Human Rights Commn., 2005—; bd. dirs. Internat. Athena, 2004—. Recipient Jean Harris award Rotary 1998, Mary Jane Werthern award Vanderbilt 1997, Nashville ATHENA award, 2003; named to Leadership America 2000; inducted in Acad. of Women of Achievement, 2002. Mem.: Women in Higher Edn. in Tenn. (historian 1999—, pres.), CABLE Profl. Womens Networking Orgn. (pres. 1991—92, historian 2000—, Promote Women award 1993), Am. Coun. Edn. (state facilitator 1994—95, bd. mem. 1994—, mem. Tenn. planning com., Outstanding Contbns. cert. 1995), Internat. Assn. Higher Edn. and Disability (pres. 1988—89, Ronald Blosser Dedicated Svc. award 1989), Women's Polit. Caucus (v.p. 2001—02), Women in Numbers (bd. mem. 2000—, pres. 2003). Avocations: hiking, tennis, photography. Home: 954 Caney Creek Rd Harriman TN 37748 Office: Vanderbilt U VU Station B 351809 Nashville TN 37235-1809 E-mail: patricia.a.pierce@vanderbilt.edu.

**PIERCE, PAUL,** professional basketball player; b. Oct. 13, 1977; s. Lorraine Hosey. Degree in crime and deliquency studies, Kans. State U., 1999. Profl. basketball player Boston Celtics, 1998—. Named to All-Rookie First Team, 1999, Eastern Conf. All-Star Team, NBA, 2005—06. Avocation: music. Office: Boston Celtics 151 Merrimac St # 1 Boston MA 02114-4714*

**PIERCE, PHILIP SARGENT,** clinical psychologist; b. Medford, Mass., Aug. 25, 1941; s. Elmer Grandville and Pauline Dudley Pierce; m. Rae Foster, Oct. 10, 1967; children: Jennifer, Jessica, John, Jill. BA, U. Maine, 1963; MA, U. N.H., 1965; PhD, U. S.C., 1971. Lic. psychologist, Maine. Clin. psychologist Pineland Ctr., Pownal, Maine, 1965-77, Togus (Maine) Vets. Med. and Regional Office Ctr., 1977-83, sr. psychologist, 1983—, acting chief mental health svc., 2003. Vis. lectr. psychology U. So. Maine, Portland, 1971-72; asst. prof. psychology St. Joseph's Coll., North Windham, Maine, 1972-78, U. Maine, Augusta, 1977-78; clin. assoc. psychology U. Maine, Orono, 1981—; lectr. on psychology grad. program in sch. and health psychology U. New Eng., Biddeford Pool, Maine; adj. clin. faculty mem. Antioch New Eng. Grad. Sch., 1996-2000; cons., spkr., presenter in field; northeastern regional exam. coord. Am. Bd. Clin. Psychology, 1993-95, nat. credential rev. officer, 1995-97; mem. Am. Bd. Profl. Psychology, Inc. Contbr. numerous articles to profl. jours. Trustee Falmouth Congl. Ch., 1981-84, chmn. bd. trustees, 1983-84, sec. mem. giving and investments subcom., 1982-84, mem. Christian enlistment com., 1985-88, chmn., 1987-88, mem. nominations com., 1989-92, chmn. ch. coun., 1990-93, mem. bylaws com., 1994-97; bd. dirs. Falmouth Little League, 1984-90, coach, 1983-85, treas., 1984-90, umpire, 1983-93; bd. dirs. Maine Running Hall of Fame, 1994—, vice chmn., 1995-96, chmn., 2001-02; bd. dirs. Maine Sports Hall of Fame, 1994—2004, 1st v.p., 1995-2001, chmn. honors and selection com., 1996-2002, pres. 2001-02. With U.S. Army, 1966 Fellow APA (divsn. newsletter editor 1981-84, treas. 1981-82, pres. 1985-86, chmn. fellow com. 1990-96, coun. of reps. 1977-79, coun. liaison to Maine psychol. Assn. 1995-97, coun. reps. for Maine and Vt. 1998-2001, chmn. rural caucus), Maine Psychol. Assn. (newsletter editor 1971-74, mem. exec. bd. 1971-88, pres. 1975-77, chmn. ethics com. 1992-98, policy coun. 1992-2002), Am. Psychol. Soc., Acad. Clin. Psychology (bd. dirs. 1993-2002, v.p. 1998-2002); mem. AAAS, N.Y. Acad. Sci., mem. VA Lead Psychologists (chmn. geropsychology task force 1983-84, chmn. APA-VA interaction task force 1984-85), Soc. Maine Psychologists (chmn. continuing edn. com. 1990-92, 98-2000, pres. 1992-94, treas. 1994-98), Maine Soc. Forensic Psychologists, Maine Track Club (sec. 1985-86, v.p. 1986-87, pres. 1987-88, race dir. 1984—). Democrat. Avocation: long distance running. Home: 79 Waites Landing Rd Falmouth ME 04105 E-mail: philip.pierce@med.va.gov.

**PIERCE, PONCHITTA ANN,** TV host, television producer, journalist, writer, consultant; b. Chgo., Aug. 5, 1942; d. Alfred Leonard and Nora (Vincent) P. Student, Cambridge U., Eng., summer 1962; BA in Journalism cum laude, U. So. Calif., 1964; DHL, Franklin Pierce Coll., 1986. Asst. editor Ebony mag., 1964-65, assoc. editor, 1965-67; editor Ebony mag. (N.Y.C. office), 1967-68; chief N.Y.C. editl. bur. Johnson Pub. Co., 1967-68; corr. news divsn. CBS, N.Y.C., 1968-71; contbg. editor McCall's mag., 1971-77; editl. cons. Philps Stokes Fund, 1971-78; staff writer Reader's Digest, 1976-77, roving editor, 1977-80; co-prodr., host Today in New York, Sta. WNBC-TV, N.Y.C., 1982-87; freelance writer, TV broadcaster, media cons. Co-host Sunday WNBC-TV, 1973—77, The Prime of Your Life, 1977—80; author: Status of American Women Journalists on Magazines, 1968, History of the Phelps Stokes Fund 1911-1972; contbg. editor: Earth Times Monthly, 2002. Del. to WHO Conf., Geneva, 1973; bd. dirs. Morris-Jumel Mansion, Housing Enterprise for the Less Privileged, Third St. Music Sch. Settlement, Inner-City Scholarship Fund, Josephson Inst. Ethics, Marina del Rey, Sta. WNET-TV; active Columbia Presbyn. Health Scis. Adv. Coun.; bd. dirs. U. So. Calif. Ctr. on Pub. Diplomacy, Cuban Artists Fund Recipient Penney-Mo. mag. award excellence women's journalism, 1967; John Russwurm award NYC Urban League, 1968; AMITA Nat. Achievement award in comm., 1974 Mem. NATAS, Women in Comm. (Woman Behind the News award 1969, Nat. Headliner award 1970), Fgn. Policy Assn. (mem. bd. govs., bd. dirs.), Women's Fgn. Policy Group, Coun. on Fgn. Rels., Calif. Scholarship Fedn. (life), Econs. Club N.Y., Lotos Club, Nat. Honor Soc., Mortar Bd.

**PIERCE, RICHARD HARRY,** oceanographer; PhD in Chem. Oceanogra phy, U. R.I. 1973. Sr. scientist, dir. Ctr. for Eco-Toxicology, Mote Marine Lab., Sarasota, Fla. Office: Mote Marine Lab 1600 Ken Thompson Pkwy Sarasota FL 34236-1096 E-mail: rich@mote.org.

**PIERCE, RUDOLPH F.,** lawyer; b. Boston, Aug. 12, 1942; s. Fred D. and Edna M. (Owens) P.; m. Carneice T. Pierce, July 1, 1967; children: Kristen, Khari. BA, Hampton Inst., 1967; JD, Harvard U., 1970. Bar: Mass. 1970, DC 2002. Ptnr. Crane, Inker & Oteri, Boston, 1972-75, Keating, Perretta & Pierce, Boston, 1975-76; magistrate U.S. Dist. Ct. Mass., Boston, 1976-79; justice Mass. Superior Ct., Boston, 1979-85; ptnr. LeBoeuf, Lamb, Leiby & MacRae, Boston; dir., bus. & securities litig. Goulston & Storrs, Boston & Washington. Chmn. bd. dir. Nat. Inst. Trial Advocacy. Contbr. articles to profl. jours. Trustee Children's Hosp., Boston, 1986—, Inst. Healthcare Improvement; past chmn. New Eng. Aquarium. Fellow Am. Coll. Trial Lawyers; mem. Internat. Acad. Trial Lawyers, ABA, Mass. Bar Assn. (bd. dels.), Boston Bar Assn. (pres. 1989-90). Office: Goulston & Storrs 400 Atlantic Ave Boston MA 02110-3333 also: Goulston & Storrs Ste 1100 2001 K St NW Washington DC 20006 Office Phone: 617-574-4078, 202-721-1153. Office Fax: 617-574-7623. Business E-Mail: rpierce@goulstonstorrs.com.

**PIERCE, SHAYN,** biomedical engineer, educator; PhD in Biomedical Engring., U. Va., 2002. Asst. prof. biomedical engring. U. Va. Contbr. articles to profl. jours. Named one of Top 100 Young Innovators, MIT Tech. Review, 2004; recipient Rita Shaffer Young Investigator award, Biomedical Engring. Soc., 2004. Office: U Va Dept Biomedical Engring Box 800759 Health System Rm 2324 Charlottesville VA 22908

**PIERCE, SHELBY CRAWFORD,** oil industry executive, consultant; b. May 26, 1932; s. William Shelby and Iris Mae (Smith) Pierce; m. Marguerite Ann Grado, Apr. 2, 1954; children: Cynthia Dawn, Melissa Carol. BSEE, Lamar U., Beaumont, Tex., 1956; grad. program for sr. execs., MIT, 1980. With Amoco Oil Co., Texas City Refinery, 1956—, elec. engr., elec. foreman, area foreman, 1956—60, zone supt., gen. foreman, maintenance, 1961—67, oper. supt., 1967—69, coord. results mgmt., 1969—72; dir. results mgmt. Amoco Oil Co. Corp. Hdqs., Chgo., 1972-75; mgr. ops. Amoco Oil Co. Whiting (Ind.) Refinery, 1975—76, asst. refinery mgr., 1977-79; dir. crude replacement program Amoco Oil Co. Corp. Hdqs., Chgo., 1979-81, mgr. corp. refining and transp. engring., 1981—91, gen. mgr. engring. and constrn., 1992, v.p. internat. bus. devel., 1993-94, ret., 1994. Pres., dir. Amoco Eurasia Oil Co., Amoco Mex. Oil Co., Amoco India, Inc., Amoco Tech. Assistance Co., Trinidad; dir. Amoco Orient Oil Co.; v.p. Amoco Tech. Devel. Co., Latin Am., 1994; pres. Pierce Cons. Svc., 1995—; CEO, pres. Environ. Constrn. Co., 1996—98; mem. steering com. contractor safety U.S. Dept. Labor, 1989. Trustee Lamar U. Found., 1994—. Mem.: AIChE (mem. exec. bd. 1985—89, chmn. engring. constrn. contracting divsn. 1988, Divsn. Man of Yr. award 1995), N.W. Ind. Bus. Roundtable (organizer and user coun. chmn. 1986, chmn. exec. bd. 1986—87), The Bus. Roundtable (constrn. com., adv. bd., chmn. constrn. cost effectiveness task force 1992—94), Constrn. Industry Inst. (Bus. Roundtable coun., mem. strategic planning com. 1991—93), Flossmoor Country Club, Sigma Tau. Republican. Methodist. Home and office: 1715 Brookwood Dr Flossmoor IL 60422-1823 Office Phone: 708-798-4498. Office Fax: 708-957-4995. Business E-Mail: shelbypierce@msn.com.

**PIERCE, SUSAN RESNECK,** academic administrator, literature educator, consultant; b. Janesville, Wis., Feb. 6, 1943; d. Elliott Jack and Dory (Block) Resneck; m. Kenneth H. Pierce; 1 child, Alexandra Siegel. BA, Wellesley Coll., 1965; MA, U. Chgo., 1966; PhD, U. Wis., 1972. Lectr. U. Wis., Rock County, 1970-71; from asst. prof. to prof. English Ithaca (N.Y.) Coll., 1973-82, chmn. dept., 1976-79; program officer Nat. Endowment for Humanities, 1982-83, asst. dir., 1983-84; dean Henry Kendall Coll. Arts and Scis. U. Tulsa, 1984-90; v.p. acad. affairs prof. English Lewis and Clark Coll., Portland, Oreg., 1990-92; pres. U. Puget Sound, Tacoma, 1992—2003, Boca Raton Comty. Hosp. Found., 2004—05; v.p. practice, 2005—. Vis. assoc. prof. Princeton (N.J.) U., 1979; bd. dirs. Janet Flson Scholarship Fund, 1989-1990, Tulsa Edn. Fund, Phillips Petroleum Scholarship Fund, 1985-90, Okla. Math. & Sci. High Sch., 1984-90, Hillcrest Med. Ctr., 1988-90, Portland Opera, 1990-92, St. Joseph's Hosp., 1992—, Seattle Symphony, 1993—; cons. U. Oreg., 1985, Drury Coll., Springfield, Mo., 1986; mem. Middle States and N. Cen. Accreditation Bds.; mem. adv. com. Fed. Women's Program, NEH, 1982-83; participant Summit Meeting on Higher Edn., Dept. Edn., Washington, 1985; speaker, participant numerous ednl. meetings, sems., commencements; chair Frederick Ness Book Award Com. Assn. Am. Colls., 1986; mem. award selection com. Dana Found., 1986, 87; mem. Acad. Affairs Council, Univ. Senate, dir. tchr. edn., chmn. adv. group for tchr. preparation, ex-officio mem. all Coll. Arts and Scis. coms. and Faculty Council on Internat. Studies, all U. Tulsa; bd. dirs. Am. Conf. Acad. Deans; bd. trustees Hillcrest Med. Ctr.; participant Aspen Inst. Md. 1999, Annapolis Group Media Roundtable, 1996, Harvard Seminar, 1992; former bd. dirs. Assn. Am. Colls. and Univs., 1989-92, Am. Conf. of Academic Deans, 1988-91, Am. Assn. Colls., 1989-92. Author: The Moral of the Story, 1982, also numerous essays, jour. articles, book sects., book revs.; co-editor: Approaches to Teaching "Invisible Man"; reader profl. jours. Mem. Bd. dirs. Arts and Humanities Coun., Tulsa, 1984-90, Mizener Pk., 2004—; trustee Hillcrest Hosp., Tulsa, 1986-90; mem. cultural series com., community rels. com. Jewish Fedn., Tulsa, 1986-90; bd. dirs. Tulsa chpt. NCCJ, 1986-90, Kemper Mus. 1996—, Seattle Symphony, 1993-96, St. Joseph Hosp., 1992-93, Portland Opera, 1990-92. Recipient Best Essay award Arix. Quar., 1979, Excellence in Teaching award N.Y. State Edn. Council, 1982, Superior Group Service award NEH, 1984, other teaching awards; Dana scholar, Ithaca Coll., 1980-81; Dana Research fellow, Ithaca Coll., 82-83; grantee Inst. for Ednl. Affairs, 1980, Ford Found., 1987, NEH, 1989. Mem. MLA (subcom. on job market 1973-74), South Ctrl. MLA, NIH (subcom. on college drinking), Assn. Governing Bds. (coun. of pres.), Nat. Inst. on Alcohol Abuse (presl. advisory group), Soc. for Values in Higher Edn., Assn. Am. Colls. (bd. dirs.), Am. Conf. Acad. Deans (bd. dirs. 1988-91), Coun. of Presidents, Assn. Governing Bds., The Annapolis Group (mem. exec. com.), Phi Beta Kappa, Phi Kappa Phi, Phi Gamma Kappa. Office Phone: 561-212-5103. Business E-Mail: srpconsulting@adelphia.net.

**PIERCE, TAMORA,** writer; b. South Connellsville, Pa., Dec. 13, 1954; d. Wayne Franklin Pierce and Jacqueline Sparks; m. Timothy Erving Liebe, Dec. 14, 1985. BA, U. Pa., 1977. Data collector Office Assessment, Kingston, NY, 1976—77; sec. Office Town Assessor, Hardenburgh and Denning, 1977—78; housemother McAuley Home for Girls, Buhl, Idaho, 1978—79; lit. agt. asst.

Harold Ober Assocs., NYC, 1979—83; sec. Chase Manhattan Bank, NYC, 1983—89, Joseph Conklin, NYC, 1990—92; freelance writer NYC, 1992—. Author: Alanna: The First Adventure, 1983, In the Hand of the Goddess, 1984, The Woman Who Rides Like A Man, 1986, Lioness Rampant, 1988, Wild Magic, 1992, Wolf- Speaker, 1994, The Emperor Mage, 1995, The Realms of the Gods, 1996, Sandry's Book, 1997, Tris's Book, 1998, Daja's Book, 1998, Briar's Book, 1999, First Test, 1999, Plain Magic in Flights of Fantasy, 1999, Magic Steps, 2000, Page, 2000, Testing in Lost and Found, 2000, Street Magic, 2001, Squire, 2001, Folquin's Folly in Disney Adventures, 2001, Elder Brother in Half Human, 2001, Cold Fire, 2002, Lady Knight, 2002, Shatterglass, 2003, Trickster's Choice, 2003, Trickster's Queen, 2004, The Will Of The Empress, 2005, The Hidden Girl in Dreams and Visions, 2006, Huntress in Firebirds Rising, 2006, Terrier in 2006, 2006; contbr. articles to profl. jours. and the Ultimate Book Guide; narrator (CD) Full Cast Audio Books; co-editor: Young Warriors, 2005, Student of Ostriches in Young Warriors, 2005. Mem. Greenpeace, 2001, World Wildlife Fedn., 1998—, Internat. Wolf Ctr., Ely, Minn., 1998—, N.Y. Ctr. Wildlife Conservation, N.Y.C., 1997—. Recipient Edward E. Smith Meml. Skylark award, Boskone 42, 2005. Mem.: ACLU, Soc. Childrens Book Writers and Illustrators, Sci. Fiction and Fantasy Writers Am., The Authors Guild, Amnesty Internat. Avocations: audio theatre and books, military history, wildlife. Personal E-mail: tampierce@aol.com.

**PIERCE, THRESIA KORTE (TISH PIERCE),** primary school educator; b. Maize, Kans. d. Herman and Marie Adeline (Lubbers) Korte; children: Judith, John, Mark. BS, Friends U., 1955; MS, U. Nev., Las Vegas, 1978. Cert./tchr., Nev., Nev. Life Ins. lic. Office worker Internat. Trust Co., Denver, Colo., 1951, Motor Equipment Co., Wichita, Kans., 1952-53; tchr. Wichita Pub. Schs., 1960-69, Clark County Sch. Dist., Las Vegas, Nev., 1970-2000. Author short stories; contbr. articles to profl. jours. Senator Clark County Edn. Assn., Clark County Classroom Tchrs. Nominee Wichita Women of Yr., 1967. Mem. NEA, Epsilon Sigma Delta (v.p. 1962). bd. dirs. Kansas Newman U., Wichita, 1966-68. Home: Bldg 6 Unit 1106 1600 S Valley View Blvd Las Vegas NV 89102-0547

**PIERCE, WILLIAM SCHULER,** cardiac surgeon; b. Wilkes-Barre, Pa., Jan. 12, 1937; s. William Harold and Doris Louis (Schuler) P.; m. Peggy Jayne Stone, June 12, 1965; children: William Stone, Jonathan Drew. BS, Lehigh U., 1958; MD, U. Pa., 1962. Intern U. Pa., 1962—63; resident in surgery Hosp. U. Pa., 1963—70; asst. prof. M.S. Hershey Med. Ctr., Pa. State U. Coll. Medicine, Hershey, 1970—73, assoc. prof., 1973—77, prof. surgery, 1977—, chief divsn. cardiothoracic surgery 1991—95; assoc. chmn. dept. surgery, dir. rsch., dept. surgery 1995—97. Contbr. over 300 articles to profl. jours. With USPHS, 1965—67. Fellow: ACS; mem.: AAAS, AMA, Soc. Clin. Surgery., Am. Surg. Assn., Soc. Univ. Surgeons. So. Pa. Assn. Thoracic Surgery, Inst. Medicine, Assn. Acad. Surgery, Am. Heart Assn., Soc. Vascular Surgery, Am. Soc. Artificial Internal Organs, Internat. Cardiovascular Soc. Achievements include invention of inventor cardiac valve, blood pump. Office: Milton S Hershey Med Ctr PO Box 850 Hershey PA 17033-0850 Office Phone: 717-531-8328. Business E-Mail: wpierce@psu.edu.

**PIERCY, GORDON CLAYTON,** bank executive; b. Takoma Park, Md., Nov. 23, 1944; s. Gordon Clayton and Dorothy Florence (Brummer) Piercy; m. Roberta Margaret Walton, 1985; children: Elizabeth Anne, Kenneth Charles, Virginia Walton, Zachary Taylor Walton. BS, Syracuse U., 1966; MBA, Pace U., 1973. Mgmt. trainee Suburban Bank, Bethesda, Md., 1962-66; mktg. planning assoc. Chemical Bank, N.Y.C., 1966-70; sr. market devel. officer Seattle-First Nat. Bank, 1970-74; product expansion adminstr., mktg. planning mgr. VISA, Inc., San Francisco, 1974-76; v.p., dir. mktg. Wash. Mutual Bank, Seattle, 1976-82; v.p., mktg. dir. First Interstate Bank Wash. N.A., Seattle, 1983-86; sr. v.p. mktg., dir. Puget Sound Nat. Bank, Tacoma, 1986-92; sr. v.p., dir. mktg. and sales Key Bank, Tacoma, 1993-94; dir. corp. sales KIRO-TV, Seattle, 1994; sr. v.p., dir. mktg. and sales Pacific N.W. Bancorp, 1994—2004; pres. Whidbey Western R.R., 1995—; prin. Whidbey Mktg., 2004—; mktg. instr. Embry-Riddle U., Oak Harbor, Wash., 2005—. Bd. dirs. Whidbey Gen Hosp. Found. Mem. found. bd. Whidbey Gen. Hosp. Mem.: Motorcar Operators West, S.W. Railcar Ltd. (mem. exec. com.), Island County Econ. Devel. Assn. (bd. dirs.), Pacific Railcar Operators, Mktg. Comm. Exec. Internat., Ctrl Whidbey Lions (treas.), Delta Mu Delta, Alpha Kappa Psi, Sigma Nu. Episcopalian. Home and Office: 750 N Snowberry Ln Coupeville WA 98239-3110

**PIERCY, MARGE,** poet, writer; b. Detroit, Mar. 31, 1936; d. Robert Douglas and Bert Bernice (Bunnin) Piercy; m. Ira Wood, 1982. AB, U. Mich., 1957; MA, Northwestern U., 1958; DHL (hon.), Hebrew Union Coll., 2004, Union Coll., 2004, Eastern Conn. State U., 2005. Instr. Gary ext. Ind. U., 1960—62; poet-in-residence U. Kans., 1971; disting. vis. lectr. Thomas Jefferson Coll., Grand Valley State Colls., 1975, 1976, 1978, 1980; vis. faculty Women's Writers Conf., Cazenovia Coll., NY; Elliston poetry fellow U. Cin., 1986. DeRoy Disting. vis. prof. U. Mich., 1992; editor Leapfrog Press, 1997—; poetry editor Lillith, 1999—; fiction editor Seattle Rev., 2003—. Author: Breaking Camp, 1968, Hard Loving, 1969, Going Down Fast, 1969, Dance the Eagle to Sleep, 1970, Small Changes, 1973, To Be of Use, 1973, Living in the Open, 1976, Woman on the Edge of Time, 1976, The High Cost of Living, 1978, Vida, 1980, The Moon is Always Female, 1980, Braided Lives, 1982, Circles on the Water, 1982, Stone, Paper, Knife, 1983, My Mother's Body, 1985, Gone to Soldiers, 1988, Available Light, 1988 (May Sarton award 1991), Summer People, 1989, He, She and It, 1991, Body of Glass, 1991 (Arthur C. Clarke award 1993), Mars and Her Children, 1992, The Longings of Women, 1994, Eight Chambers of the Heart, 1995, City of Darkness, City of Light, 1996, What Are Big Girls Made Of?, 1997 (Notable Book award ALA 1997), Storm Tide, 1998, The Art of Blessing the Day, 1999, Early Grrrl, 1999, Three Women, 1999, Sleeping With Cats, A Memoir, 2002, expanded edit., 2005, Colors Passing Through Us, 2003, Third Child, 2003, Sex Wars: A Novel of the Turbulent Post-Civil War Period, 2005; co-author: (with Ira Wood) So You Want to Write: How to Master the Craft of Writing Fiction and the Personal Narrative, 2001, 2d edit., 2005; (CD) Louder: We Can't Heed You Yet, 2004; author of poetry (16 vols.). Cons. N.Y. State Coun. on Arts, 1971, Mass. Found. for Humanities and Coun. on Arts, 1974; mem. Writer Bd., 1985-86; bd. dirs. Transition House, Mass. Found. Humanities and Pub. Policy, 1978-85, Am. ha-Yam, 1988-89, v.p., 1995-96; gov.'s appointee to Mass. Cultural Coun., 1990-91, Mass. Coun. on Arts and Humanities, 1986-89; artistic adv. bd. ALEPH Alliance for Jewish Renewal, Am. Poetry Ctr., 1988—; lit. adv. panel poetry NEA, 1989; mem. adv. bd. Carrie A. Seaman Animal Shelter. Recipient Borenstone Mountain Poetry award, 1968, 74, Lit. award Gov. Mass. Commn. on Status of Women, 1974, Nat. Endowment of Arts award, 1978, Carolyn Kizer Poetry prize, 1986, 90, Shaeffer-Eaton-PEN New Eng. award, 1989, Golden Rose Poetry prize, 1990, Brit ha-Dorot award The Shalom Ctr., 1992, Notable Book award, 1997, Paterson poetry prize, 2000. Mem.: NOW, PEN, Am. Poetry Soc., Nat. Writers Union, Authors League, Authors Guild, Citizens for the Preservation of Wellfleet, Mass. Audubon Soc., New Eng. Poetry Club. Address: PO Box 1473 Wellfleet MA 02667-1473 Personal E-mail: hagolem@c4.net.

**PIERLUISI, PEDRO R.,** lawyer; b. San Juan, PR, Apr. 26, 1959; s. Jorge A. and Doris (Urrutia) Pierluisi; m. María Elena Carrión; children: Anthony, Michael, Jacqueline, Rafael. BA, Tulane U., 1981; JD, George Washington U., 1984. Bar: D.C. 1984, U.S. Dist. Ct. D.C. 1985, U.S. Ct. Appeals (D.C. cir.) 1985, P.R. 1990, U.S. Dist. Ct. P.R. 1990, U.S. Supreme Ct. 1990, U.S. Ct. Appeals (1st cir.) 1993. Assoc. Verner, Liipfert, Bernhard, McPherson & Hand, Washington, 1984—85, Cole, Corette & Abrutyn, Washington, 1985—90; ptnr. Pierluisi Pierluisi & Mayol-Bianchi, San Juan, 1990—93; atty. gen. Govt. of P.R., 1993—96; ptnr. O'Neill & Borges, San Juan, 1997—. Chmn. bd. dirs. Jose Jaime Pierluisi Found., 2003—. Mem.: ABA (ho. of dels. 1995—96, standing com. on substance abuse 1995—98, coordinating com. on gun violence 1998—2001, state membership chmn. 2000—03), Am. Arbitration Assn. (arbitrator), Internat. Ctr. for Dispute Resolution (arbitrator), George Washington U. Internat. Law Soc. (pres. 1982—83), Nat. Assn. Attys. Gen. (chair ea. region 1996), Jose Jaime Pierluisi Found. (pres. 2003— 2003—), Puerto Rico Homebuilders Assn. (bd. dirs. 1999—2003), N.Y. Stock

Exch. (arbitrator), Phi Alpha Delta (hon.; Munoz chpt.). Avocation: jogging. Office: O'Neill & Borges 250 Ave Munoz Rivera Am Internat Plz San Juan PR 00918-1808 Office Phone: 787-282-5706. E-mail: pedro.pierluisi@oneillborges.com.

**PIERMATTI, JACK,** dentist; b. Paterson, N.J., Sept. 25, 1953; s. Matthew and Viola Piermatti; m. Carol Ann Nakashian, July 30, 1978; children: Laura Ann, Valerie Jacqueline, John Michael. BS, Fairleid Dickinson U., 1975, DMD, 1979. Cert. N.J. State Bd. Dentistry, 1979, diplomate Internat. Congress Oral Implantologists, 1997, Am. Bd. Oral Implantology, 1999, Am. Bd. Prosthodontics, 2004. Gen. practice resident St. Joseph's Hosp., Paterson, NJ, 1979—80; prosthodontics resident UMDNJ, Newark, 2001—04; pvt. practice, 1980—. Fellow. Acad. General Dentistry, 1997, Am. Acad. Implant Dentistry, 2000. Office: Dental Arts South Jersey PC 1001 Laurel Oak Rd Ste C-1 Voorhees NJ 08043 Office Phone: 856-783-5777. E-mail: jpiermatti@yahoo.com.

**PIERNO, ANTHONY ROBERT,** lawyer; s. Anthony M. and Mary Jane (Saporita) P.; m. Beverly Jean Kohn; children: Kathryn Ann, Robert Lawrence, Linda Jean Derengowski, Diane Marie Leonard. BA with highest honors, Whittier Coll., 1954; JD, Stanford U., 1959; LLD (hon.), Whittier Coll., 2000. Bar: Calif. 1960, D.C. 1979, Tex. 1994. Assoc. Adams, Duque & Hazeltine, L.A.; ptnr. Poindexter & Barger, L.A.; chief dep. commr. State of Calif., 1967-69, commr. of corps., 1969-71; ptnr. Wyman, Bautzer, Rothman & Kuchel, Beverly Hills, Calif.; sr. ptnr. Memel, Jacobs, Pierno & Gersh, L.A., 1976-86, Pillsbury, Madison & Sutro, L.A., 1986-89; sr. v.p., gen. counsel MAXXAM, Inc., L.A. and Houston, 1989-92. Author: Corporate Disaggregation, 1982; editor Stanford U. Law Rev. Trustee Whittier Coll., 1977-2000, chmn. bd. trustees, 1994-2000, chmn. presdl. selection com., 1989-90; chmn. Marymount Coll., Palos Verdes, Calif., 1989-92, trustee, 1976-93; past mem. Los Angeles County Children's Svcs. Commn. With U.S. Army, 1954-56. Recipient Emcalian award Marymount Palos Verdes Coll., 1983, Whittier Coll. Lancer Soc. Lifetime Achievement award, 1984—, Lifetime Svc. award, 2004. Mem. ABA, Los Angeles County Bar Assn., State Bar Calif. (chmn. com. on corps. 1971-75, advisor to com. on corps. 1975-76, mem. exec. com. bus. law sect. 1976-80, chmn. spl. com. on franchise law), Calif. Club (L.A.), Am. Inns of Ct. Republican. Roman Catholic. Office: 92 Avenida Lirio Blanco Rancho Mirage CA 92270 Office Phone: 760-341-7595. E-mail: arplaw@msn.com.

**PIERONI, ROBERT EDWARD,** internist, educator, military officer; b. Portland, Maine, June 20, 1937; s. Ansel Kirby and Agnes Mary (Dumais) P.; m. Dorothy Louise McDonnell, Oct. 3, 1970; children: Michelle Kirby, Robert Francis. BS, Boston Coll., 1959; MD, Pa. State U., 1971. Diplomate Am. Bd. Internal Medicine, Am. Bd. Family Practice, Am. Bd. Allergy and Immunology, Am. Bd. Quality Assurance, Am. Bd. Geriatric Medicine. Chemist Mass. Dept. Pub. Health, Boston, 1962-71, sr. bacteriologist, 1971-74; asst. prof. internal medicine U. Ala., Tuscaloosa, 1974-76, assoc. prof. dept. internal medicine and family practice, 1976-81, prof. internal medicine and family practice, 1981—; enlisted U.S. Army, 1961, advanced through grades to col., 1981. Prior cons. VA Hosp., Tuscaloosa, T. Hardin Med. Facility and Partlow State Hosp., Tuscaloosa, 1974—; cons. FDA, Dept. Def. Contbr. articles to profl. jours., chapters to books. Decorated Bronze Star, 1991, Commendation for Valor; recipient Golden Stethoscope award, 1982, Faculty Recognition award, 1986, Ala. Golden Eagle Humanitarian award Ala. Sr. Citizens Hall of Fame, 1988 and Physicians award, 1998, Wright A. Garner scientist award Ala. Acad. Sci., 1997, Designator A Proficiency award Army Surgeon Gen., 2001. Mem. AMA, ACP, Am. Coll. Allergy, Asthma and Immunology, Am. Geriatric Soc., Gerontol. Soc. Am., Am. Acad. Family Physicians, Physicians for Human Rights, VFW, Am. Legion. Democrat. Roman Catholic. Avocations: mountain trekking, scuba diving, studying medical and military history, reading. Home: 398 Riverdale Dr Tuscaloosa AL 35406-1814 Office U Ala Dept Internal Medicine PO Box 870326 Tuscaloosa AL 35487-0001 Personal E-mail: dp398@comcast.net.

**PIERRE, DWIGHT ANTHONY,** mathematician, educator; b. Queens, N.Y., Mar. 24, 1969; s. Anthony Michael and Mary Ann (Wyckoff) Pierre. BSc in Applied Math., Union Coll., 1992; MA in Math., SUNY, 1994; postgrad., Columbia U., 2003—. Adj. prof. math. Borough of Manhattan C.C., N.Y.C., 1997—2000, instr. math., 2000—. GMAT Math Instructor Dyson Coll. Arts and Scis. Pace U., N.Y.C., NY, adj. prof. math., Globe Inst. Tech., N.Y.C., Coll. New Rochelle, Bklyn., Schenectady (N.Y.) County C.C., CUNY, 1997—2000; math tchr. Mesifta Tifereth Jerusalem, N.Y.C., Fulton County Schs., Atlanta; adj. prof. academic opportunity program Union Coll., Schenectady, NY; instr. math. summer bridge program SUNY, Albany, instr. math. S.T.E.P.; cons. in field; AP calculus reader Coll. Bd., 1995—, cons. AP calculus program, 2004—. Math instr. Upward Bound Program Atlanta (Ga.) Metro. Coll. Mem.: Math. Assn. Am. Home: Ste C6 870 St Nicholas Ave New York NY 10032 Office: Borough of Manhattan CC Math Dept 199 Chambers St New York NY 10007 Office Phone: 212-220-1362. E-mail: dapierre@hotmail.com, dpierre@bmcc.cuny.edu, dap2112@columbia.edu.

**PIERRE, NATASHA UNADA,** accountant; b. San Fernando, Trinidad, June 14, 1973; d. Cleto Salazar Jamie and Leonora Shirley Pierre. BS, Jersey City State U., 1994; MBA, Seton Hall U., 1998. Acctg. specialist Prudential Ins. Co. Am., Newark, 1994—; sr. assoc. Ernst & Young LLP, Iselin, NJ, 2002. Roman Catholic. Avocations: travel, track and field.

**PIERRE, PERCY ANTHONY,** engineering educator; b. Donaldsville, La., Jan. 3, 1939; s. Percy John and Rosa (Villavaso) P.; m. Olga A. Markham, Aug. 8, 1965; children: Kristin Clare, Allison Celeste. BSEE, U. Notre Dame, 1961, MSEE, 1963, D of Engring. (hon.), 1977; PhD in Elec. Engring, Johns Hopkins U., 1967; postgrad., U. Mich., 1968; DSc (hon.), Rensselaer Poly. Inst. Asst. prof. elec. engring. So. U., 1963; instr. Johns Hopkins U., Balt., 1963-64; instr. physics Morgan State Coll., 1964-66; instr. info. and control engring. U. Mich., Ann Arbor, 1967-68; instr. systems engring. UCLA, 1968-69; research engr. in communications RAND Corp., 1968-71; White House fellow, spl. asst. Office of Pres., 1969-70; dean Sch. Engring., Howard U., Washington, 1971-77; program officer for engring. edn. Alfred P. Sloan Found., 1973-75; asst. sec. for research, devel. and acquisition U.S. Dept. Army, 1977-81; engring. mgmt. cons., 1981-83; pres. Prairie View (Tex.) Agrl. and Mech. U. System, 1983-89, Honeywell prof. elec. engring., 1989-90; v.p. rsch. and grad. studies Mich. State U., East Lansing, 1990-95, prof. elec. engring., 1995—. Dir. engring. coll. council Am. Soc. for Engring. Edn., 1973-75; mem. sci. adv. group Def. Communications Agy., 1974-75; mem. adv. panel Office Expti. Research and Devel. Incentives, NSF, 1973-74; mem. Commn. Scholars To Rev. Grad. Programs, Ill. Bd. Higher Edn., 1972-74; mem. panel on role U.S. engring. sch. in fgn. tech. assistance, 1972, co-chmn. symposium on minorities in engring., 1973; mem. rev. panel for Inst. for Applied Tech., Nat. Bur. Standards, 1973-77; chmn. com. on minorities Nat. Acad. Engring., 1976-77; cons. to dir. Energy Rsch. and Devel. Adminstrn., 1976-77; mem. Army Sci. Bd., 1984; mem. adv. bd. Sch. Engring.. Johns Hopkins U., 1981-84; cons. Office Sec. Def., 1981-84; mem. adv. bd. Lincoln Labs., MIT. Contbr. articles on communications theory to profl. publs. Trustee U. Notre Dame, 1974-77, 81—; trustee, mem. exec. com. Nat. Fund for Minority Engring. Students, 1976-77; bd. dirs. The Hitachi Found., 1987, Ctr. for Naval Analysis, 1986, Assn. Tex. Colls. and Univs.; pres. Southwest Athletic Conf., 1985-87, bd. dirs. CMS Corp., 1990—, Defense Sci., 1992-94, Old Kent Fin. Corp., 1993—, bd. trustee Aerospace Corp., 1991—. Recipient Disting. Civilian Service award Dept. Army, 1981; award of merit from Senator Proxmire, 1979. Mem. IEEE (sr. mem. Edison award com. 1978-80), Sigma Xi, Tau Beta Pi. Home: 2445 Emerald Lake Dr East Lansing MI 48823-7256 Office: Mich State U 3224 Engineering East Lansing MI 48824-1226 Business E-Mail: pierre@msu.edu.

**PIERREHUMBERT, JANET BRECKENRIDGE,** language educator; AB in Linguistics, Harvard Univ., 1975; Rotary Found. grad. fellow, Univ. of Turku, Finland, 1975—76; PhD in Linguistics, MIT, 1980. Cons., dept. linguistics and speech analysis AT&T Bell Labs, 1980—82, technical staff mem., dept. linguistics and artificial intelligence rsch., 1982—89; rsch. assoc.,

Ctr. for Cognitive Sci. MIT, 1980—82; cons. asst. prof., dept. linguistics Stanford Univ., 1984—85; faculty Linguistic Soc. of Am. Summer Inst., 1986, 1993; visitor, dept. speech transmission and music acoustics Royal Inst. of Tech., Stockholm, 1987—88; assoc prof., dept. linguistics Northwestern Univ., 1989—93, chair, 1993—96, prof., 1993—; faculty, LOT (Dutch post-grad. sch. of linguistics Univ. Nijmegen, 1997; visitor Ecole National Superieure des Telecommunications, Paris, 1996—97; poste rouge Centre Nat. de la Recherche Scientifique, 1997. Assoc. editor Jour. Phonetics, 1989—, adv. editor Oxford Surveys in Generative Phonology, 2000—; co-author (with M. Beckman): (monograph) Japanese Tone Structure, Linguistic Inquiry Monograph, 1988; co-author: (with M. Broe) (books) Papers in Laboratory Phonology V, 2000; contbr. articles to profl. journals, chapters to books. Fellow John Simon Guggenheim Mem. Found., 1996—; grantee NSF Grad. Fellowhip, 1976—79. Fellow: Am. Acad. Arts & Sci. Office: Dept Linguistics Northwestern Univ 2016 Sheridan Rd Evanston IL 60208 Office Phone: 847-467-1570. Office Fax: 847-491-3770. Business E-Mail: jbp@northwestern.edu.

**PIERSKALLA, WILLIAM PETER,** dean, finance educator, engineering educator; b. St. Cloud, Minn., Oct. 22, 1934; s. Aloys R. and Hilda A. Pierskalla; m. Carol Spargo, Children: Nicholas, William, Michael. AB in Econs., Harvard U., 1956, MBA, 1958; MS in Math., U. Pitts., 1962; PhD in Ops. Rsch., Stanford U., 1965; MA, U. Pa., 1978. Assoc. prof. Case Western Res. U., Cleve., 1965-68. So. Meth. U., Dallas, 1968-70; prof. dept. indsl. engring. and mgmt. scis. Northwestern U., Evanston, Ill., 1970-78; exec. dir. Leonard Davis Inst., U. Pa., Phila., 1978-83; prof., chmn. health care sys. dept. U. Pa., Phila., 1982-90, prof. decision sci. and systems engring., dep. dean acad. affairs Wharton Sch., 1983-89, Ronald A. Rosenfield prof., 1986-93; dir. Huntsman Ctr. Global Competition and Leadership U. Pa. Wharton Sch., 1989-91; John E. Anderson prof. UCLA, 1993—99, disting. prof., 1999—, dean John E. Anderson Grad Sch. Mgmt., 1993-97. Cons. HHS, Bethesda, Md., 1974-87, MDAX, Chgo., 1985-91, MEDICUS, Evanston, 1970-75, Sisters of Charity, Dayton, Ohio, 1982-83, Project Hope, 1990—; bd. dirs., chmn. The Bush Found.; bd. dirs. No. Wilderness Adventures, Informs. Contbr. articles to various publs. Mem. adv. bd. Lehigh U., 1986-93, U. So. Calif. Bus. Sch., 1987-93; regent St. Mary's Coll., 1998-2001, Hong Kong U. Sci. and Tech., 1992-2005. Recipient Harold Larnder Meml. prize Can. Oper. Rsch. Soc., 1993; grantee NSF, 1970-83, HHS, Washington, 1973-82, Office Naval Rsch., Arlington, Va., 1974-77. Fellow Inst. for Ops. Rsch. and Mgmt. Scis.: Mem. Ops. Rsch. Soc. Am. (pres. 1982-83, editor 1979-82, Kimball Disting. Svc. medal 1989), Inst. Mgmt. Scis. (assoc. editor 1970-77), Internat. Fedn. Operational Rsch. Soc. (pres. 1989-91), Inst. for Ops. Rsch. and Mgmt. Scis. (v.p. for publs. 2000—03), Omega Rho. Office: UCLA Anderson Grad Sch Mgmt 110 Westwood Plz Box 951481 Los Angeles CA 90095-1481 E-mail: william.pierskalla@anderson.ucla.edu.

**PIERSOL, ALLAN GERALD,** mechanical engineer; b. Pitts., June 2, 1930; s. Robert James and Irene Laticia (Dematty) Piersol; m. Gertrud Teresia Moller, June 8, 1958; children: Allan Gerald Jr., Marie Theresa, John Robert. BS in Engring. Physics, U. Ill., 1952; MS in Engring., U. Calif., 1961. Lic. profl. engr., Calif. Research engr. Douglas Aircraft Co., Santa Monica, Calif., 1952-59; mem. tech. staff Ramo Wooldridge Corp., Canoga Park, Calif., 1959-63; v.p. Measurement Analysis Corp., Santa Monica, Calif., 1963-71; prin. scientist Bolt Beranek and Newman, Inc., Conoga Park, 1971-85; sr. scientist Astron Corp., Santa Monica, 1985-88; owner Piersol Engring., Woodland Hills, Calif., 1988--. Lectr. U. So. Calif., L.A., 1965—95. Co-author: (book) Measurement and Analysis of Random Data, 1966, Random Data: Analysis and Measurement Procedures, 1971, 2000, Engineering Application of Correlation and Spectral Analysis, 1980, 1993, Shock and Vibration Handbook, 2002. Mem.: ASME, Acoustical Soc. Am., Inst. Environ. Scis. and Tech. (Irwin Vigness Meml. award 1991). Achievements include patents for method and apparatus for determining terrain surface profiles. Home: 23021 Brenford St Woodland Hills CA 91364-4830 Office: Piersol Engring Co 23021 Brenford St Woodland Hills CA 91364-4830 Office Phone: 818-591-2119. Personal E-mail: apiersol@pacbell.net.

**PIERSOL, LAWRENCE L.,** federal judge; b. Spirit Mound Township, SD, Oct. 21, 1940; s. Ralph Nelson and Mildred Alice (Millette) P.; m. Catherine Anne Vogt, June 30, 1962; children: Leah C., William M., Elizabeth J. BA, U. S.D., 1962, JD summa cum laude, 1965. Bar: S.D. 1965, U.S. Ct. Mil. Appeals, 1965, U.S. Dist. Ct. S.D. 1968, U.S. Supreme Ct. 1972, U.S. Dist. Ct. Wyo. 1980, U.S. Dist. Ct. Nebr. 1986, U.S. Dist. Ct. Mont. 1988. Ptnr. Davenport, Evans, Hurwitz & Smith, Sioux Falls, SD, 1968-93; judge U.S. Dist. Ct. SD, Sioux Falls, 1993—, chief judge, 1999—2005. Mem. budget com. Jud. Conf. U.S., 1996-2003, chair economy subcom., 2001-03; chmn. tribal ct. com., security com. 8th Cir. Jud. Coun.; editor-in-chief Law Rev.; mem. Judl. Conf. U.S.. Majority leader S.D. Ho. of Reps., Pierre, 1973-74, minority whip, 1971-72; del. Dem. Nat. Conv., 1972, 76, 80; S.D. mem. del. select commn. Dem. Nat. Com., 1971-75. Mem. ABA, State Bar S.D., Fed. Judges Assn. (bd. dirs., pres). Avocations: reading, running, painting, sailing. Office: US Dist Ct 400 S Phillips Ave Sioux Falls SD 57104-6824 Office Phone: 605-330-4505.

**PIERSON, AL** See PIZZAMIGLIO, ALBERT THEODORE

**PIERSON, ANNE BINGHAM,** physician; b. N.Y.C., June 9, 1929; d. Woodbridge and Ursula Wolcott (Griswold) Bingham; m. Richard N. Pierson Jr., July 10, 1954 (div. Aug. 1974); children: Richard N. III, Olivia Tiffany Jacobs, Alexandra deForest Griffin, Cordelia Stewart Comfort Smela; m. Richard Taliaferro Wright, Nov. 25, 1978 (div. Sept. 1997); m. Paul H. Altrocchi, May 9, 1998. Student, Katharine Branson Sch., Ross, Calif., 1943-47; BA, Vassar Coll., 1951; MD, Columbia U., 1955, MPH, 1972. Intern Lenox Hill Hosp., N.Y.C., 1955-56; substitute internship AUH, Beruit, Lebanon, 1955; mem. staff 7th Day Adventist Hosp., Taipei, Taiwan, 1957; clinic physician, med. dir. Planned Parenthood of Bergen County, Hackensack, N.J., 1960-74, also bd. dirs., 1966-69; asst. clin. prof. dept. ob-gyn. Columbia U. Coll. Physicians and Surgeons, Internat. Inst. Study of Human Reproduction, 1972-74; med. dir. Memphis Assn. for Planned Parenthood, Inc., 1974-75; staff physician N.Y. Telephone Co., 1976-87; med. dir. Planned Parenthood Assn. Hudson County, 1976-79; physician Sonalysts, Waterford, Conn., 1988—. Mem. nat. med. adv. com. Planned Parenthood-World Population, 1966-69. Pres. Vassar Class 1951, 1986-91; artist mem. Clinton Art Soc., 1989—, East Lyme Art League, 1991—; active Jr. League, 1964-69, sustainer, 1969—. Mem. AMA (Physicians Recognition award 1973—), Nat. Soc. Colonial Dames (life, assoc. sec. 1991-94, 2d v.p. 1994-97), Cosmopolitan Club, Lyme Art Assn. (treas. 1998-99, pres. 1999—), Mystic Art Assn., Essex Art Assn. Office: Sonalysts 215 Parkway N Waterford CT 06385-1209

**PIERSON, DAVID JOHN,** medical educator; b. Portland, Oreg., Aug. 22, 1943; s. John Martin Pierson and Clara Jane Chapman; m. Dona L Kienle, Apr. 13, 1968; children: Christine Marie Monteverdi-Pierson MD, Erika Louise Meek-Pierson. BA, Oreg. State U., Corvalli, 1965; MD, Johns Hopkins, Balt., 1969. Diplomate internal medicine, pulmonary medicine, critical care medicine Am. Bd. of Internal Medicine. Prof. medicine U. Wash., Seattle, 1976—; editor in chief, respiratory care Am. Assn. for Respiratory Care, Dallas, 1997—; editor, critical care alert Thomson Healthcare, Atlanta, 1993—. Chair, critical care policy and test writing com. Am. Bd. Internal Medicine, Phila. 1999—2003. Color photography, 2 Solo Exhibits; numerous permanent installations. Vol., com. mem., officer Am. Lung Assn. Wash., Seattle, 1982—2006. Maj. U.S. Army, 1974—76, Germany. Named to Pulmonary Hall of Fame, Am. Lung Assn. Wash., 2003; recipient Jimmy A Young medal (Lifetime Achievement award), Am. Assn. for Respiratory Care, 2005. Fellow: ACP, Am. Coll. Chest Physicians, Am. Assn. for Respiratory Care (life). Avocations: photography, music. Office: Harborview Med Ctr 325 Ninth Ave Box 359762 Seattle WA 98104 Office Phone: 206-731-2148. Business E-Mail: djp@u.washington.edu.

**PIERSON, EDWARD SAMUEL,** engineering educator, consultant; b. Syracuse, N.Y., June 27, 1937; s. Theodore and Marjorie O. (Bronner) P.; m. Elaine M. Grauer, June 6, 1971; 1 child, Alan. BS in Elec. Engring., Syracuse U., 1958; SM, MIT, 1960, ScD, 1964. Asst. prof., fellow MIT, 1965-66; assoc. prof., assoc. dept. head U. Ill., Chgo., 1966-75; program mgr. Argonne Nat. Labs., Ill., 1975-82; head dept. engring. Purdue U. Calumet, Hammond, Ind., 1982-95, spl. asst. to chancellor for environ. programs, 1995—. Cons. Argonne Nat. Lab., 1972-75, 82-93, Solmecs Corp., 1982-88, HMJ Corp., Washington, 1983-88, LM Mfg., 1994—. Contbr. articles to profl. jours. NSF fellow, 1958-60 Mem. IEEE, ASME, Am. Soc. Engring. Edn. Office: Purdue Univ Calumet Hammond IN 46323 Office Phone: 219-989-2467. E-mail: pierson@calumet.purdue.edu.

**PIERSON, JACK,** artist; b. Plymouth, Mass., 1960; BFA, Mass. Coll. Art, Boston. One-man shows include, Simon Watson, NY, 1990, Pat Hearn Gallery, NY, 1991, Richerd Kuhlenschmidt Gallery, LA, 1991, 1992, Tom Cugliani Gallery, NY, 1992, White Columns, NY, 1992, Jack Hanley Gallery, San Francisco, 1993, Regen Projects, LA, 1994, Edward Hopper & Jack Pierson: Am. Dreaming, Whitney Mus. Am. Art, NY, 1994, Luhring Augustine Gallery, NY, 1994, 1996, Fine Arts Work Ctr., Provincetown, Mass., 1994, Tex, Gallery, Houston, 1995, Mus. Contemporary Art, Chgo., 1995, Parco Gallery, Tokyo, 1995, White Cube, London, 1996, Galerie Philippe Rizzo, Paris, 1996, Taka Ishii Gallery, Tokyo, 1995, Pay Me In Coke, 1998, An Artifical Night, Ginza Art Space, Tokyo, 1998, exhibited in group shows at The Moderns, Feature, NY, 1995, Whitney Biennial, Whitney Mus. Am. Art, 1995, 2004, Defining the Nineties, Mus. Contemporary Art, Miami, 1996. Mailing: c/o Cheim & Read Gallery 547 West 25th St New York NY 10001

**PIERSON, JAY ARTHUR,** music educator; s. Arthur Lewis and Maxine Eleanor Pierson. B in Music Edn., Olivet Coll., 1981; MusM, Eastman Sch. Music, 1983; D in Musical Arts, Eastman Sch. Arts, 1989. Instr. Hochstein Music Sch., Rochester, NY, 1982—84; asst. prof. Bucknell U., Lewisburg, Pa., 1984—89; assoc. prof. E.Carolina U., Greenville, NC, 1989—97; instr. Santa Clara U., Calif., 2003—06. Composer: (musical) This Christmas Night, 1995, Concerto Arpaggione for Harp and Orchestra, 2005; musician (baritone soloist); N.C. Symphony, Rochester PhilHarmonic, Grand Rapids Symphony, Buffalo Philharmonic. Dir. music Disciples of Christ, San Jose, Calif., 1998—2000; asst. dir. music Old First Ch., San Francisco, 2000—05, elder, 2003. Recipient Glady's Cook award, Bucknell U., 1986. Mem.: Am. Guild Musical Artists, Am. Harp Soc., Nat. Assn. Tchrs. Singing. Presbyterian. Avocations: antiques, reading, travel. Home: 3550 Market #102 San Francisco CA 94131

**PIERSON, JEFFREY LYNN,** protective services officer; m. Sara A. Scorr, 1969; children: Christine, Jennifer, Jeffrey Jr. BS in Pub. Adminstrn., Roger Williams U., 1997; M in Adminstrv. Scis., Fairleigh Dickinson U., 2001; grad., Army War Coll., Command and Gen. Staff Coll., Field Artillery Basic and Advanced Officers Course. Staff, commd. U.S. Army Nat. Guard, 1961—2001; asst. dep. chief of staff tng. Hdqs. Fourth U.S. Army, 1985—88; exec. officer Hdqs. 50th Armored Divsn. Art., 1988—89, G3, 1989—91; mobilization readiness officer, 1991—93; dir. Mil. Personnel Office, 1993; chief of staff, asst. adj. gen. N.J. Dept. Mil. Vet. Affairs, 1993—99; undersheriff correctional divsn. Cape May County (N.J.) Sheriff's Office, 1999—. Spkr. in field on leadership, mgmt. and weapons of mass destruction; adj. prof. Fairleigh Dickinson U. Dep. chief safety and tng. Marmora Vol. Fire Co.; past. pres. Marmora Vol. Fire Dept., v.p. Ret. brigadier gen. U.S. Army, NG, N.J. Mem. Am. Correctional Assn., Am. Jail Assn. (cert. jail mgr.), N.J. Jail Wardens Assn., Fairleigh Dickinson U. Alumni Assn., Army War Coll. Alumni, Roger Williams U. Alumni, Masons (Cannon Lodge # 104 F&AM, past master). Avocations: golf, basketball, softball. Office: Cape May County Correctional Ctr 4 Moore Rd Cape May Court House NJ 08210

**PIERSON, KATRICIA GUYN,** language educator; b. Tulsa, Oct. 21, 1961; m. Michael Joe Pierson, Apr. 13, 2000; 1 child, Mera Guyn;children from previous marriage: Zacharye Welch Grider, Gabriel Harris Grider. BA, U. Wyo., Laramie, 1982; MA, U. Ark., Fayetteville, 1998, PhD, 2004. Asst. prof. English Pikeville (Ky.) Coll., 2001—04, William Woods U., Fulton, Mo., 2003—. Master: Sigma Tau Delta (life; advisor 2001—, scholarship com. mem. 2006—); mem.: Nat. Coun. Tchrs. of English, Modern Language Assn. Episcopalian. Office: William Woods U One University Ave ADM 207B Fulton MO 65251 Office Phone: 573-592-1107. Business E-mail: katricia.pierson@williamwoods.edu.

**PIERSON, MARILYN EHLE,** financial planner; b. Cleve., Feb. 27, 1931; d. Ernest John and Helen Irene (Steudel) Ehle; m. Edward G. Pierson, July 17, 1954; children: Melanie K., Edward G. III. BSBA, Miami U., 1953; grad., Coll. Fin. Planning, 1990, Inst. Cert. Divorce Planners, 1997. CFP. Sr. fin. advisor, advanced planner group Am. Express Fin. Advisors, Cleve., 1987—. Corp. presenter, fin. educator East Ohio Gas, AT&T, Cleve., Master Builders, Cleve., Preformed Line Products, Cleve., Parker Hannifin, Cleve.; guest lectr. Chagrin Valley C. of C, Chagrin Falls, Ohio; lectr. adult edn. Shaker Heights (Ohio). Fin. columnist Bainbridge Banter newspaper. Chair stewardship and resources Valley Presbyn. Ch., Bainbridge, Ohio; elder, 1991-93, planned giving chmn., 1991-95, 2000—. Mem. Fin. Planning Assn. (treas. exec. com. NE Ohio chpt. 1994-98), Exec. Women Internat. (advisor, bd. dirs. 1997, pres. 1996), Estate Planning Coun. Cleve. Avocation: travel. Home: 8178 Chagrin Mills Rd Chagrin Falls OH 44022-3807 E-mail: marilyn.e.pierson@aefa.com.

**PIERSON, RICHARD NORRIS, JR.,** medical educator; b. NYC, Sept. 22, 1929; s. Richard Norris and Dorothy (Stewart) Pierson; m. Alice Roberts, Aug. 26, 1974; children from previous marriage: Richard N., Olivia Tiffany, Alexandra de Forest, Cordelia S.C. stepchildren: Alice W. Dunn, Eric C.W. Dunn. BA, Princeton U., 1951; MD, Columbia U., 1955. Diplomate Am. Bd. Internal Medicine, Am. Bd. Nuclear Medicine. Resident St. Luke's Roosevelt Hosp., N.Y.C., 1955—61, assoc. dir., 1961—65, dir. div. nuclear medicine, 1965—89, dir. body composition unit, 1965—2003, attending physician, 1975—; clin. medicine Columbia U., 1980—; dir. medicine Hackensack Hosp., 1973—74; staff assoc. Brookhaven Nat. Lab., 1970—2002; rsch. scholar Lawrence Radiation Lab., Berkeley, Calif., 1970—71. Bioengring. inst. Columbia U., 1976—, chmn., 1989—94. Editor: Quantitative Radiocardiography, 1975; contbr. articles to profl. jours. Warden St. Paul's Ch., 1980—82; bd. dirs. Englewood Health Dept., NJ, 1966—74, Empire Blue Cross/Blue Shield, NY, 1978—91, v.p. NY, 1990—91. NIH grantee, 1973—76, 1986—99, John A. Hartford grantee, 1967—70. Fellow: ACP, N.Y. Acad. Medicine; mem.: AAAS, N.Y. County Med. Soc. (pres. 1978—79), Soc. Nuclear Medicine (greater N.Y. area pres. 1982—83, del. to AMA 1991—2001, trustee 1991—, Berson-Yalow award 1995), Alliance for Continuing Med. Edn. (pres. 1987—89), Am. Med. Rev. Rsch. Ctr. (N.Y. State del. to AMA 1978—90, pres. 1985—89), Am. Bur. Med. Advancement in China (pres. 1979—87), N.Y. County Health Serv. Rev. Orgn. (chmn. 1980—82), Am. Inst. Nutrition, Am. Physiol. Soc., P&S Alumni Assn. (pres. 1989—91), Englewood Field Club, Century Club. Home: 60 Lincoln St Englewood NJ 07631-3117 Office: St Lukes Roosevelt Hosp Ctr 1111 Amsterdam Ave New York NY 10025-1716 Office Phone: 212-523-3385. Business E-mail: RNP1@columbia.edu.

**PIERSON, ROBERT DAVID,** investor; b. Orange, NJ, Mar. 5, 1935; s. Carleton Wellington and Muriel Browning (Potter) Pierson; m. Virginia Duncan Knight, Apr. 30, 1960; children: Lisa Boles, Alexandra Mead, Robert Wellington. BA, Lehigh U., 1957. Exec. asst. 1st Nat. City Bank N.Y., N.Y.; 1958-61; asst. to pres. Cooper Labs. Inc., N.Y.C., 1961-65; dir. mktg. svcs. Arbrook divsn. Johnson & Johnson, Somerville, NJ, 1965-69; v.p. Klemtner Advt. Inc., N.Y.C., 1969-71; sr. v.p. Bowery Savs. Bank, N.Y.C., 1972-80; vice chmn., dir. Carteret Bancorp, Inc., Wilmington, Del., 1980-90; pres. No Divsn. Collective Bank, 1990-96, Collective Fin. Svcs., Inc., Harbor Mortgage Co. divsn. Collective Bank, Montclair, NJ, 1997-98; pvt. investor,

1998—. Mem. town coun. Twp. of Mendham, NJ, 1992—, mayor, 1995—96, 2003—04. With USCG, 1958—59. Mem.: Morristown Club; Morris County Golf Club. Republican. Presbyterian. Home: Green Hills Rd Mendham NJ 07945-3305

**PIERSON, STUART F.,** lawyer; b. Washington, June 25, 1943; s. W. Theodore and Barbara F. Pierson; m. Jennifer M. Pierson, June 20, 1987; children: Stuart, Jr., Sean, Jody Skye, Emily J.; m. Carole S. (div. 1985). BA cum laude, Hobart Coll., 1965; diploma, L.S. ID, 1968. Bar: D.C. 1969, N.Y. 1984, U.S. Supreme Ct. 1974. Atty. U.S. Dept. Justice Civil Rights Divsn., Washington, 1968—71, AUSA WD Washington, Washington, 1971—73 Spec. AUSA WD, Washington, 1974, Verner Liipfert, Washington, 1975—88, Davis Wright, Washington, 1988—96, Levine Pierson, Washington, 1996—98; atty. white collar crime practice Troutman Sanders LLP, Washington, 1998—. Office: Troutman Sanders LLP Ste 1000 401 9th St NW Washington DC 20004-2134 Office Phone: 202-274-2897. Office Fax: 202-654-5622. E-mail: stuart.pierson@troutmansanders.com.

**PIERSON, WAYNE GEORGE,** trust company executive; b. L.A., Nov. 5, 1950; s. Norman Einar and Annabelle Florence (McLay) P.; m. Margaret Aileen Boyle, Mar. 18, 1972; children: Heather, Dawn, Mark, Michael. BS in Bus. Adminstrn. with honors, Calif. State U., Northridge, 1973. CPA, Oreg., Calif. Audit supr. Ernst & Whinney (now Ernst & Young), L.A. and Portland, Oreg., 1973-80; treas. Gregory Affiliates, Beaverton, Oreg., 1980-82; CFO, treas. Meyer Meml. Trust, Portland, 1982—. Mem. adv. com. Vega Ptnrs., Onset Ptnrs. Chair investment com. Columbia Cascade Scout Coun. Mem. AICPA, Chartered Fin. Analysts Inst., Oreg. Soc. CPAs, Portland Soc. Fin. Analysts, Found. Fin. Officers Group (chair), Avocations: tennis, scouting, travel. Office: Meyer Memorial Trust STE 400 425 NW 10th Ave Portland OR 97209-3128

**PIESTER, DAVID L(EE),** magistrate judge; b. Lincoln City, Nebr., Nov. 18, 1947; s. George Piester; married; children. BS, U. Nebr., 1969, JD, 1972. Bar: Nebr. 1972, U.S. Dist. Ct. Nebr. 1972, U.S. Ct. Appeals (8th cir.) 1976, U.S. Supreme Ct. 1979. Staff atty. Legal Svcs. S.E. Nebr., Lincoln, 1972-73, exec. dir., 1973-79; asst. U.S. atty. Dept. Justice, Lincoln, 1979-81; magistrate judge U.S. Dist. Ct. Nebr., Lincoln, 1981—. Cons. Legal Services Corp., Nat. Legal Aid and Defender Assn., 1974-77. Mem. Lincoln Human rights commn., 1978-79. Mem. Nebr. State Bar Assn., Fed. Magistrate Judges Assn., Lincoln Bar Assn., Eighth Cir. Jud. Coun. (ex officio 1993-96). Office: US Dist Ct 100 Centennial Mall North 566 Fed Bldg Lincoln NE 68508

**PIETRI, TODD T.,** venture capitalist; Grad. cum laude, Duke U., 1989; MBA, Ga. State U. Robinson Sch. Bus. Dir. IT consulting, direct sales divsns. CompuSys., 1992—97; with Callier Interests, Houston; v.p. Legacy Securities Corp., Atlanta; co-founder Legacy's Tech. and Comm. Investment Banking Group; co-founder, gen. ptnr. Milestone Venture Ptnrs., NY, 1999—. Dir. Bizbash.com, Inc., NavTrak, Inc.; bd. observer Derivatives Portfolio Mgmt., LLC, ExpertPlan, Inc., Octagon Rsch. Solutions, Inc. Office: Milestone Venture Ptnrs 551 Madison Ave 7th Fl New York NY 10022 Office Fax: 212-223-0315.

**PIETRINI, ANDREW GABRIEL,** automotive aftermarket executive; b. Bryn Mawr, Pa., Feb. 27, 1937; s. Bernard and Irene (Norcini) P.; m. Pam Mari, Sept. 29, 1962; children: Darrin, Wayne BS, Villanova U., 1958. C.P.A., Pa. Jr. acct. Fernald & Co., Phila., 1958-60; sr. acct. O & W Audit Co., Narberth, Pa., 1960-62; asst. sec. James Talcott, Inc., N.Y.C., 1962-68; pres. UIS, Inc., N.Y.C., 1968—, dir., 1972—, chmn., CEO, pres., 1986—. Bd. dirs. Lebensfeld Found., N.Y.C., 1979— Mem. Am. Inst. C.P.A.s, Fin. Execs. Inst. Republican. Roman Catholic. Avocations: sailing, golf. Office: UIS Inc 15 Exchange Pl Ste 1120 Jersey City NJ 07302-3912

**PIETROCARLO, NICK,** artist, consultant, information technology manager; b. Buffalo, May 11, 1971; s. Shirley and Nick Pietrocarlo. BS in Mgmt., Calif. Coast U., 2003. Project Mmgt. Profl. Project Mgmt. Inst., 2002; cert. Citizen's Police Acad. Miami Police Dept., 2003, notary public Dept. State of Fla., 2004, neighborhood leadership acad. City of Miami Beach, 2004. Graphic artist Arvin Calspan Corp., Buffalo, 1988—89; film intern Hallwalls Contemporary Arts Ctr., Buffalo, 1989—90, tech. asst., 1990—92; photo lab mgr. U. of Buffalo, 1991—91; treas. Topsy Turvy, Inc, Buffalo, 1992—94; video programmer Royal Caribbean Cruises, Ltd., Miami, 1994—97, interactive tv specialist, 1997—99, project mgr., 1999—2002, program mgr., 2002—; global info. tech. ops. mgr. Island Cruises, Brighton, England, 2005—. Freelance artist, Miami, 1990—; cons. Cruise Industry and Info. Tech., Miami, 2000—; mem. cmty. emergency response team, Miami Beach, Fla. Prodr.: (multimedia show) Etc, 1990, (music video) Game of Fools, 2005; assoc. prodr. (video prodn.) Casino Royale, 1996; editor: (video documentary) Riding on the hair of a buffalo, 1992, (video wallpaer exhibits) Topsy Turvy, 1992—94, (pub. svc. announcement) AIDS Trilogy, 1993, (local TV talk show) The Pink Flamingo Show, 1993—94; dir.: (segment for Jerry Lewis Telethon) Charo, 1995; exec. prodr.: (video documentary) Laffoley's Odyssey, 2005. Grantee Video Prodn. grant, Owego Experimental T.V. Ctr, 1991, Rochester Visual Arts Ctr., 1992; NY State Coun. of Arts, 2005. Mem.: Project Mgmt. Inst. Roman Catholic. Achievements include production of conceptual device. Avocations: target shooting, walking, bicycling. Office: Royal Caribbean Cruises Ltd 1050 Caribbean Way Miami FL 33132 Office Phone: 954-517-6041. Personal E-mail: nick@pietrocarlo.com. Business E-Mail: npietrocarlo@rccl.com.

**PIETROFESA, JOHN JOSEPH,** psychologist, educator; b. N.Y.C., Sept. 12, 1940; s. Louis John and Margaret P; m (Carly Marks, June 20, 1905, children: John, Paul, Maria, Dolores. EdB cum laude, U. Miami, 1961; MEd, 1963, Ed.D., 1967. Diplomate Am. Bd. Sexology; cert. cognitive behavior therapist, forensic counselor, sex therapist; lic. psychologist, social worker. Counselor Dade County (Fla.) pub. schs., 1965-67; prof. edn. Wayne State U., Detroit, 1967—; div. head theoret. and behavioral founds., 1977-83; dept. chair counselor edn., 1999—. Cons. Nat. Football League, 2003—; cons. to various schs., hosps. and univs. Author: The Authentic Counselor, 1971, 2nd edit., 1980, School Counselor as Professional, 1971, Counseling and Guidance in the Twentieth Century, 1971, Elementary School Guidance and Counseling, 1973, Career Development, 1975, Career Education, 1976, College Student Development, 1977, Counseling: Theory Research and Practice, 1978, Guidance: An Introduction, 1980, Counseling: An Introduction, 1984; mem. editl. bd. Counseling and Values, 1972-75. 1st lt. Mil. Police Corps, AUS, 1963-65. Mem. APA, ACA, Mich. Counseling ASsn., Assn. Counselor Edn. and Supervision, Phi Delta Kappa. Home: PO Box 99 Bloomfield Hills MI 48303-0099 Office: Wayne State U 321 Education Detroit MI 48202 Office Phone: 248-642-6066.

**PIETRUSKI, JOHN MICHAEL, JR.,** pharmaceutical executive; b. Sayreville, NJ, Mar. 12, 1933; m. Roberta Jeanne Talbot, July 3, 1954; children: Glenn David, Clifford John, Susan Jane. BS with honors, Rutgers U., 1954; LLD (hon.), Concordia Coll., 1993. With Proctor and Gamble Co., 1954-63; pres. med. products div. C.R. Bard, Inc., 1963-77; with Sterling Drug, Inc., N.Y.C., 1977-88; pres. Pharm. Group, 1977-81, corp. exec. v.p., 1981-83, pres., COO, 1983-85, chmn., CEO, 1985-88; pres. Dansara Cons., 1988—; chmn. Encysive Pharms., Inc., 1990—. Bd. dirs. PDI, Inc., Xylos Corp., Trial Card, Inc. 1st lt. U.S. Army, 1955—57. Mem.: Union League Club (N.Y.C.), Phi Beta Kappa. Home: 27 Paddock Ln Colts Neck NJ 07722-1266 Office: One Penn Plaza Ste 3408 New York NY 10119 Office Phone: 212-268-5510. Personal E-mail: jmpco4@aol.com.

**PIETSCH, DOUGLAS K.,** music educator; b. Reading, Pa., Oct. 21, 1968; s. Ralph F. and Ellen M. Pietsch; m. Mia K. Pietsch, May 23, 1998; 1 child, Olivia L. BA, Susquehanna U., Selinsgrove, Pa., 1990; MA, U. Ars, Phila., 1999. Asst. band dir. Hamburg (Pa.) Area Sch. Dist., 1991—2001, instrumental music tchr., 1996—, Northampton (Pa.) Area Sch. Dist., 1993—94, Easton (Pa.) Area Sch. Dist., 1995—96; asst. band dir. Daniel Boone Sch. Dist., Birdsboro, Pa., 1994—99, Reading (Pa.) Sch. Dist., 2004—. Orch. condr.

musician various cmty. concert bands. Mem.: Pa. Music Educators, Am. Fedn. Musicians, Phi Mu Alpha Sinfonia (life). Office: Hamburg Area Sch Dist Windsor St Hamburg PA 19526 Personal E-mail: dpietsch@comcast.net.

**PIETZ, CLINT A.,** pediatrician, educator; b. Tacoma, July 5, 1964; MD, U. Tex. Health Sci. Ctr., 1992. Diplomate Am. Bd. Pediat. Asst. prof. clin. pediat. U. Iowa Hosps. and Clinics, Iowa City, 1996—99; assoc. clin. instr. U. Tex. Health Sci. Ctr., San Antonio, 1999—2003, asst. prof. 2003—; med. dir. pediatric transport team Christus Santa Rosa Children's Hosp., San Antonio. Physician Muzquiz (Mex.) Project, 2001. Mem.: Soc. Critical Care Medicine. Avocation: skeet shooting. Office: U Tex Health Sci Ctr 7703 Floyd Curl Dr San Antonio TX 78229 Office Phone: 210-567-5314. Office Fax: 210-567-5311. Business E-Mail: pietz@uthscsa.edu.

**PIETZSCH, JAN BENJAMIN,** engineering company executive; B, U. Karlsruhe, Germany, 2000; MS, Stanford U., Calif., 1998, PhD, 2004. Pres., CEO Wing Tech Inc., Potomac, Md., 2004—. Lectr. Stanford U. Dept. Mgmt. Sci. and Engring., Calif., 2004—. Dep. chmn. German Stanford Assn., Berlin, 2001. ERP scholar, German Nat. Merit Found., German Fed. Ministry of Econs. and Tech., 2000—02. Mem.: Health Tech. Assessment Internat. Internat. Soc. for Pharmacoeconomics and Outcomes Rsch., Inst. for Ops. Rsch. and the Mgmt. Scis. Achievements include patents pending for Methods and devices for modulating atrial configuration (cardiology catheter). Office: Wing Tech Inc 9916 Newhall Rd Potomac MD 20854 Office Phone: 301-983-2559. Personal E-mail: pietzsch@stanfordalumni.org. E-mail: jpietzsch@wing-tech.com.

**PIETZSCH, MICHAEL EDWARD,** lawyer; b. Burlington, Iowa, Aug. 1, 1949; s. Walter E. and Leanna (Moore) P.; m. Ellen G. Hart; children: Christine E., Catherine M. AB, Stanford U., 1971; JD, U. Chgo., 1974. Bar: Ill. 1974, Ariz. 1976. Ptnr. McCabe & Pietzsch, Phoenix, 1975-90, Pietzsch & Williams, Phoenix, 1990-95, Polese, Pietzsch, Williams & Nolan, Phoenix, 1995—. Contbr. articles to profl. jours.; speaker at profl. confs. Del. White House Conf. Small Bus., Washington, 1986, White House Savs. Summit, 1998; chmn. bd. trustees Ariz. Sci. Ctr., 1994-98; pres. The Group, Inc., 1995-98. Fellow Am. Coll. Tax Counsel, Am. Coun. on Tax Policy, Am. Coll. Employee Benefits Counsel; mem. ABA (chmn. personal svc. orgns. com. tax sect. 1986-90), Stanford Phoenix Club (pres. 1982-84). Office: 2702 N Third St Ste 3000 Phoenix AZ 85004 Office Phone: 602-604-6250. E-mail: pietzsch@ppwn.com.

**PIGA, STEPHEN MULRY,** retired lawyer; b. Bklyn., Apr. 9, 1929; s. Stephen Paul and Ella (Mulry) P.; married, Feb. 23, 1952 (div.); children: Maureen, Stephen, Susan, Elizabeth; m. Emilie Halliday, Aug. 1, 1975 (dec. Aug. 2003); 1 dau., Margaret. AB, Princeton U., 1950; LLB, Columbia U., 1955. Bar: N.J. 1955, N.Y. 1956. Assoc. White & Case, N.Y.C., 1955-63, ptnr., 1964-92; ret., 1992. Lectr. Practicing Law Inst. N.Y. and various insts., bar assns. Served to capt. USMCR, 1951-53. Mem. ABA, N.Y. State Bar Assn. (exec. com. tax sect. 1981-89, chmn. employee benefits com.), Assn. of Bar of City N.Y., N.J. Bar Assn., Am. Contract Bridge League (life master), Profl. Bowlers' Assn. Am., High Mt. Golf Club. Republican. Avocations: fishing, golf, bowling, bridge.

**PIGFORD, THOMAS HARRINGTON,** nuclear engineering educator; b. Meridian, Miss., Apr. 21, 1922; s. Lamar and Zula Vivian (Harrington) P.; m. Catherine Kennedy Cathey, Dec. 31, 1948 (dec. 1992); children: Cynthia Pigford Naylor, Julie Earnest; m. Elizabeth Hood Weekes, Nov. 12, 1994. BS in Chem. Engring., Ga. Inst. Tech.; 1943; S.M. in Chem. Engring., M.I.T., 1948, Sc.D. in Chem. Engring., 1952. Asst. prof. chem. engring., dir. Sch. Engring. Practice, M.I.T., 1950-52, asst. prof. nuclear and chem. engring., 1952-55, assoc. prof., 1955-57; head engring., dir. nuclear reactor projects and asst. dir. research lab. Gen. Atomic Co., La Jolla, Calif., 1957-59; prof. nuclear engring., chmn. dept. nuclear engring. U. Calif., Berkeley, 1959—; sr. rsch. scientist Lawrence Berkeley Lab., 1959—. Mem. panel Nat. Atomic Safety Licensing Bd. AEC-Nuclear Regulatory Commn., 1963-77; mem. Pres.'s Commn. on accident at 3-Mile Island, 1979; mem. bd. radioactive waste mgmt. and energy engring. bd., NAS-NAE, chmn. waste isolation systems panel, waste isolation pilot plant panel, fusion hybrid panel, separations and transmutations panel, transmutation of military plutonium panel, panel on health standard for radioactive waste disposal, chmn. adv. coun. Inst. Nuclear Power Op.; mem. Sec. of Energy's expert cons. group on Chernobyl accident; chmn. nuclear oversight com. Sacramento Mcpl. Utility Dist.; chmn. nuclear safety com. Gulf States Utilities Co.; mem. expert cons. group Swedish Nuclear Power Inspectorate; mem. peer rev. group for waste isolation pilot plant; mem. corp. rev. com. Oak Ridge Nat. Lab; lectr. Taiwan Nat. Sci. Found., 1990; vis. prof. Kyoto U., 1975, Kuwait U., 1976; cons. in field. Author: (with Manson Benedict) Nuclear Chemical Engineering, 1958, 2d edit., 1981; contbr. numerous articles to profl. jours.; patentee in field. Served with USNR, 1944-46. Recipient John Wesley Powell award U.S. Geol. Survey, 1981; named Outstanding Young Man of Greater Boston, Boston Jaycees, 1955; E. I. DuPont DeNemours rsch. fellow, 1948-50; Berkeley citation U. Calif., 1987; Japan Soc. for Promotion Sci. fellow, 1974-75; grantee NSF, 1960-75, EPA, 1973-78, Dept. Energy, 1979-92, Ford Found., 1974-75, Electric Power Rsch. Inst., 1974-75, Mitsubishi Metals Corp., 1990; named to Ga. Tech. Hall of Fame, 1995. Fellow Am. Nuclear Soc. (bd. dirs., Arthur H. Compton award 1971); mem. AIME, NAE, Am. Chem. Soc., Am. Inst. Chem. Engrs. (Robert E. Wilson award 1980; Service to Society award 1985), Atomic Indsl. Forum (dir.) Sigma Xi, Phi Kappa Phi, Tau Beta Pi. Home: 160 Alpine Ter Oakland CA 94618-1823 Office: U Calif Dept Nuclear Engring Berkeley CA 94720-0001 Office Phone: 510-652-0393. Business E-Mail: pigford@nuc.berkeley.edu.

**PIGGREM, GARY WAYNE,** science educator, writer; b. Proctor, Vt., Sept. 11, 1953; s. Lloyd A. Piggrem and Betty J. DuMouchel; m. Linda S. Hart, Oct. 17, 1981 (div. Apr. 2004); children: Brian, Jeff. BA in psychology, St. John Fisher Coll., Rochester, NY, 1977; MA in psychology, Ohio State, 1980. PhD in psychology, 1983. Tchg. asst. Ohio State, 1978—81; prof. Columbus (Ohio) State Cmty. Coll., 1983—; DeVry U., Columbus, Ohio, 1983—. Author (with N. Holt, W. Walker and S. Woodworth): (textbook) The Best Test Preparation Grad. Record Exam., 1993; author: (with J. McDuffie and S. Woodworth) (textbooks) The Best Test Preparation Advanced Placement Exam, 1993; author: (with K. Huffman) (textbook) Psychology in Action: Active Learning edit., 2003, textbook supplements; contbr. chapters to books, articles to profl. jours. Coach boy's recreational baseball, 1999—2000. Mem.: Nat. Inst. on the Tchg. of Psychology, Coun. of Tchrs. of Undergraduate Psychology, Nat. Bus. Edn. Assn., Am. Assn. Advancement of Sci., Columbus N-Track Model R.R. Club, Railroad R.R. Hist. Soc., Bridge Line Hist. Soc., Columbus Garden R.R. Soc., Delta Epsilon Sigma, Pi Gamma Mu. Office: DeVry University 1350 Alum Creek Dr Columbus OH 43209 Home: 6552 Emco Pl Worthington OH 43085 Business E-Mail: gpiggrem@devrycols.edu.

**PIGMAN, JACK RICHARD,** lawyer; b. Fostoria, Ohio, June 5, 1944; s. Jack R. and A. Ada (McDevitt) P.; m. Judy Lynn Price, June 19, 1968 (div. 1983); m. Carolyn Ruth Parker, May 31, 1986; children: Shaeney E. Pigman Craig, J. Ryan Pigman, Adam Parker. BA, U. Notre Dame, 1966; JD cum laude, Ohio State U., 1969. Bar: Ohio 1969, U.S. Ct. Mil. Appeals 1970. Law clk. Ohio Supreme Ct., Columbus, 1969-70; assoc. Wright, Harlor, Morris & Arnold, Columbus, 1970, 74-76; ptnr. Porter, Wright, Morris & Arthur and predecessor firms, Columbus, 1977—. Spkr. in field. Trustee Dublin Arts Coun., 2001—, pres. 2005, 06; trustee Ctr. for New Directions, 1990-96, treas., 1996; trustee United Cerebral Palsy of Columbus and Franklin County, 1976-82, pres. 1980. Capt. JAG US Army, 1970-74. Mem. Ohio State Bar Assn., Columbus Bar Assn. (chmn. bankruptcy com. 1982-84), Columbus Met. Club (trustee 1980-87, pres. 1985-86). Republican. Avocations: tennis, reading, cooking, photography. Office: Porter Wright Morris & Arthur 41 S High St Ste 2800 Columbus OH 43215-6194 Office Phone: 614-227-2119. Business E-Mail: jpigman@porterwright.com.

**PIGNATELLI, DEBORA BECKER,** state official; b. Hoboken, N.J., Oct. 25, 1947; d. Edward and Frances (Fishman) Becker; m. Michael Albert Pignatelli, Aug. 22, 1971; children: Adam Becker, Benjamin Becker. AA, Vt. Coll., 1967; BA, U. Denver, 1969. Exec. dir. Girl's Club Greater Nashua, NH, 1975-77; dir. tenant svcs. Nashua Housing Authority, 1979-80; vocat. counselor Comprehensive Rehab. Assocs., Bedford, NH, 1982-85; specialist job placement Crawford & Co., Bedford, 1985-87; mem. N.H. Ho. of Reps., Concord, 1986—91, mem. appropriations com., 1986-91, asst. minority leader, 1989—91; mem. N.H. Senate, Concord, 1992—2003, v.p. policy, Dem. whip, chair judiciary com., mem. capital budget com., chair enrolled bills com., long range capital budget overview com.; elected mem. N.H. Govs. Exec. Coun., 2005—. Del. Am. Coun. Young Polit. Leaders, Germany, 1987. Asst. coach Little League Baseball, Nashua, 1987—90; del. Dem. Nat. Conv., 1988, Gore del., 2000; mem. steering com. Gephardt for Pres. campaign, NH, 1987—88; bd. dirs. Sky Meadow Condominium Assn. Named one of 10 Most Powerful Women in N.H., N.H. Editions mag., 1999; recipient Meritorious Svc. award, N.H. Women's Lobby, 1997, John F. Kennedy award, Hillsborough County Dems., 2001, Anita and Norman Freedman award, N.H. Dems., 2004, William Paine Domestic Violence award, 2005. Mem.: Women's Lobby, N.H. Children's Lobby. Jewish. Avocations: skiing, swimming, boating. Home: 22 Appletree Grn Nashua NH 03062-2252 Office Phone: 603-271-3632.

**PIGNATO, JOSEPH MICHAEL,** composer, music educator, musician; s. Michael Joseph Pignato and Elisa Cuoco Pignato; m. Grace Margaret Begany. BA in Comm., U. Mass., 1989; MA in Music, NYU, 1996; student, Boston U., 2006—. Cert. social studies tchr. NJ. Lectr. SUNY, Oneonta, 2004—. Guest spkr., resident artist various colls. and univs., 1995—. Composer: works for chamber and improvising musicians. Mem.: Music Educators Nat. Conf., Internat. Assn. Jazz Educators, Coll. Music Soc. Office: Music Department - FA 122 State University of New York Oneonta Oneonta NY 13820 Office Phone: 607-436-3463.

**PI-GONZÁLEZ, AMAURY FRANCISCO,** announcer, journalist; b. Havana, Cuba, Oct. 4, 1944; arrived in U.S., 1961; s. Joaquin Pi and Olga Isabel González; m. Gail Ann Clardy; children: Jonathan Amaury, Geoffrey Walter Armando. Diploma, U.S. Army Audio Visual, Ft. Lewis, Wash., 1967. Spanish play-by-play broadcaster CBS Hispanic Network, San Francisco, 1986—89, Oakland (Calif.) Athletics, 1977—94, Golden State Warriors (NBA), Oakland, 1991—97; sports anchor, prodr. Telemundo Network, San Jose, Calif., 1991—95; Spanish play-by-play broadcaster San Francisco Giants baseball, 1995—; Spanish play-by-play broadcaster World Series Caracol Radio Network, 2000; Spanish play-by-play broadcaster Nat. League playoffs Latino Broadcasting Co., 2001; English play-by-play broadcaster Fox Sports Internat., L.A., 2001; Spanis play-by-play announcer Seattle Mariners Spanish Radio Network, Wash. and Oreg., 2003—. Cons. APG Sports, Fremont, Calif., 1988—; Sports Byline USA, San Francisco, 1997—98; mem. adv. com. Oakland A's All Star Game, 1997. Author: (pamphlet) Candlestick Park Years, 1999; columnist: La Oferta News, columnist, feature writer: www.latinobaseball.com, writer: www.loveofthegame.com, writer, prodr., narrator: (audio cassette) Latin Baseball Legends, 1988. Bd. dirs., v.p. Hispanic Heritage Baseball Mus., San Francisco, 1999—. With U.S. Army, 1966—68. Named Announcer of Yr., Latin Am. Awards, 1987; recipient award of merit, San Francisco Mayor Diane Feinstein, 1982. Mem.: CNP Profl. Assn. Cuban Journalists, Am. Sportscasters Assn. Republican. Roman Catholic. Achievements include being first Spanish play-by-play announcer in the USA to broadcast major league baseball and NBA games in concurrent seasons. Avocations: music, movies, collecting sports memorabilia. Office Phone: 510-579-0682. Personal E-mail: scrmeagles@aol.com.

**PIGOTT, CHARLES MCGEE,** transportation equipment manufacturing executive; b. Seattle, Apr. 21, 1929; s. Paul and Theiline (McGee) P.; m. Yvonne Flood, Apr. 18, 1953. BS, Stanford U., 1951. With PACCAR Inc, Seattle, 1959—, exec. v.p., 1962-65, pres., 1965-86, chmn., pres., 1986-87, chmn., chief exec. officer, 1987-97, also bd. dirs., chmn. emeritus, 1997—. Pres. Nat. Boy Scouts Am., 1986-88, mem. exec. bd. Mem. Bus. Council. Office: Paccar Inc 777 106th Ave NE Bellevue WA 98004-5017

**PIGOTT, MARK C.,** automotive executive; BS in Industrial Engring., Stanford U., MBA. V.p. Paccar Inc., Bellevue, Wash., 1988—89, sr. v.p., 1990—93, exec. v.p., 1993—95, dir., 1994—, vice chmn., 1995—96, chmn., CEO, 1997—; also dir. Paccar Financial Corp. Mem. exec. com. Washington Roundtable. Named a Top CEO, Institutional Investor mag., 2005; named Mgr. of the Year, Truck & Off-Hwy. Ledger, 2004. Office: Paccar Inc 777 106th Ave NE Bellevue WA 98004*

**PIKA, JOSEPH A.,** political scientist, educator, educational association administrator; m. Mary Pika. BA in Internat. Rels., MA in Internat. Rels., Johns Hopkins U., 1970; PhD in Polit. Sci., U. Wis., 1979. Tchr. Gilman Sch., Balt., 1970—73; instr. Western Md. Coll., 1976—77; vis. lectr. U. Wis., 1977—78; asst. prof. SUNY, Buffalo, 1978—81; asst. prof. dept. polit. sci. and internat. rels. U. Del., 1981—87, assoc. prof. dept. polit. and internat. rels., 1987—93, prof. dept. polit. sci., 1993—, assoc. chair, 1989—94, dept. chair, 1994—99, acting chair, 2000—02, faculty dir. Del. Social Studies Edn. Project, 1999—2001. Exec. dir. Govs. Commn. on Govt. Reorganization and Effectiveness, 1993; mem. State Bd. Edn., 1997—2001, pres., 2001—; presenter in field. Co-author (with N.C. Thomas and J. Maltese): The Politics of the Presidency, 2001; co-author: (with R. Watson) The Presidential Contest, 1996; contbr. chapters to books, articles to profl. jours. Trustee U. Del.; active Jobs for Del. Grads., Del. Law-Related Edn.; mem. H. Fletcher Brown scholarship com. Mem.: Omicron Delta Kappa, Phi Kappa Phi, Phi Beta Kappa, Golden Key. Address: State Bd Edn Townsend Bldg PO Box 1402 Dover DE 19901 Office: U Del Dept Polit Sci 180 Graham Hall Newark DE 19716-7380*

**PIKAS, CHRISTINA KIRK,** librarian, researcher; b. Wilmington, Del., Sept. 26, 1972; d. Howard Eliason and Gail Foster Kirk; m. Mark Michael Pikas, Oct. 24, 1998. B in Physics, U. Md., 1995, MLS, 2002. Libr. ASRC Aerospace, Ft. Meade, Md., 2003—03, The Johns Hopkins U. Applied Physics Lab., Laurel, Md., 2003—. Asst. editor: SciTech News, 2004—06. Lt. USN, 1995—99. Mem.: Am. Soc. for Info. Sci. and Tech., Spl. Librs. Assn., Phi Kappa Phi. Office: JHU Applied Physics Lab 11100 Johns Hopkins Rd Laurel MD 20723-6099 Office Phone: 240-228-4812. Business E-Mail: christina.pikas@jhuapl.edu.

**PIKE, BURLYN,** retired bank director, lawyer; b. Brodhead, Ky., May 28, 1921; s. John Daniel Pike and Jewel Francisco; m. Edith Nell Sanders, 1942 (div. 1971); children: Burnell True, David Alfred; m. Joan Thomason, 1983. Student, U. Louisville, 1939-43. Bar: Ky. 1944. Free lance writer The Courier Jour., Louisville, 1941-43; pub. various, 1946-51; ptnr. Taylor & Pike-Pike & Schmidt, Shepherdsville, Ky., 1952—2003; ret., 2002. Author: Railroad Town, 2d edit., 1997. Sgt. U.S. Army, 1943-46. Mem.: Omicron Delta Kappa. Republican. Roman Cath. Avocation: historical research. Office: Pike & Schmidt Law Offices 148 E 2d St Shepherdsville KY 40165 E-mail: bpike01@aol.com.

**PIKE, CHARLENE HELEN,** retired secondary school educator; b. Detroit, Feb. 26, 1947; d. Burt A. and Lorraine J. (Dobro) Engstrom; m. David Pierce Pike, July 5, 1969. BA in Social Sci., Mich. State U., 1969; MEd, Wayne State U., 1974. Tchr. L'Anse Creuse Pub. Schs., Mt. Clemens, Mich., 1969—99, ret., 1999. Mem. Birmingham (Mich.) Power Squadron, 1975—. Mem. NEA, Nat. Mid. Sch. Assn. (trustee 1985-92, pres.-elect 1993, pres. 1994), Mich. Assn. Mid. Sch. Educators (treas. 1995—, Outstanding Svc. award 1979), Mich. Coun. for Social Studies (Outstanding Tchr. of Yr. award 1985), Mich. Edn. Assn. (Mich. Tchr. of Yr. runner-up 1987), Mich. Assn. Learning Disabled Educators, L'Anse Creuse Edn. Assn. (local exec. bd 1980-99). Home: 325 S Maple Ave Royal Oak MI 48067-2426

**PIKE, GEORGE HAROLD, JR.,** religious organization administrator, clergyman; b. Summit, NJ, Jan. 14, 1933; s. George Harold and Ann Aurelia (Brewer) P.; m. Pauline Elizabeth Blair, Aug. 27, 1955; children: Elizabeth, George 3d, James. BA, Trinity Coll., Hartford, Conn., 1954; MDiv, Dubuque (Iowa) Theolog. Sch., 1957; DDiv (hon.), U. Dubuque, 1998. Ordained to ministry Presbyn. Ch. USA., 1957. Pastor 1st PResbyn. Ch., Kasson, Minn., 1956-59, 3d Presbyn. Ch., Dubuque, 1959-64; sr. pastor Presbyn. Ch., Bettendorf, Iowa, 1964-68, 1st Presbyn. Ch., Vancouver, Wash., 1968-78, Cranford, NJ, 1978-88; exec. chair Presbyn. Ch. USA, Louisville, 1988-93; interim pastor 2d Presbyn. Ch., Kansas City, Mo., 1993-95; dir. sem. devel. U. Dubuque, Iowa, 1995-98; retired, 1998; interim pastor Valley Presbyn. Ch., Green Valley, Ariz., 2000. Mem. exec. com. Consultation on Ch. Union, Princeton, 1980-89, pres., 1984-88. Dir. Bettendorf Bd. Edn., 1964-68, pres. 1967-68; bd. dirs. Southwest Wash. Hosps., Vancouver, 1969-78. Named Citizen of Yr., Jaycees, Bettendorf, 1967, Citizen of Yr., B'nai B'rith, Cranford, 1988; named to Honorable Order of Ky. Cols., 1989 Presbyterian. Avocations: golf, photography. Home: 928 W Union Bell Dr Green Valley AZ 85614-5928 Personal E-mail: Ghpike@aol.com.

**PIKE, JOHN NAZARIAN,** optical engineering consultant; b. Boston, Feb. 13, 1929; s Arthur Thorndike and Sarah Lucy (Nazarian) Pike; m. Margaretta May Horner, Dec. 28, 1957; 1 child, Susan Horner; 1 child, Sally Katharine. AB, Princeton U., 1951; PhD in Physics and Optics, U. Rochester, 1958. Staff scientist Parma (Ohio) Rsch. Ctr., Union Carbide Corp., 1956-63; mem. physics faculty Baldwin-Wallace Coll., Berea, Ohio, 1961-63; sr. scientist Tarrytown (N.Y.) Tech. Ctr., Union Carbide Corp., 1963-85; pres. J.J. Pike & Co., Pleasantville, NY, 1986—2006. Cons. indsl. optical instrumentation design. Mem. nat. com. for planned giving United Way of Am., 1997—2001; bd. dir. United Way of Westchester and Putnam, NY, 1979—85, 1995—, chmn., 1996—98, 1999—2000, 2003; bd. dirs. United Way of N.Y. State, 1999—2004, 2006—. Recipient Harold J. Marshall citation Cmty. Svc. United Way No. Westchester, 1976, Cmty. Svc. award, Union Carbide Corp., 1982, Spirit of Westchester and Putnam Vol. Leadership award, United Way Westchester and Putnam, 2001. Mem.: Sigma Xi, Phi Beta Kappa. Achievements include patents in field. Home and Office: 71 Cedar Ave Pleasantville NY 10570-1932

**PIKE, JUDITH ROBYN,** lawyer; b. Newton, July 23, 1959; d. Burton M. and Doris (Weingard) P.; m. Richard A. Miller, July 7, 1990. BA summa cum laude, Tufts U., 1981; JD, U. Pa., 1984. Bar: Mass. 1985, U.S. Dist. Ct. Mass. 1985. Assoc. Rackemann, Sawyer & Brewster, Boston, 1984-86, McDermott & Rizzo, Boston, 1986-90, Kirkpatrick & Lockhart, Boston, 1990—93; founder Law Office Judith R. Pike, Wellesley, Mass., 1993—. Named one of top Boston lawyers, Boston Mag., 2004. Mem.: Wellesley C. of C. (women's bus. network), Mass. Conveyancers Assn., ABA, Mass. Bar Assn., Boston Uncommon (women's accappella quintet) (dir.). Avocations: music, piano. Office: 462 Washington St Wellesley MA 02482 Office Phone: 781-237-2727. Office Fax: 781-237-2737. Business E-Mail: judy@judithpikelaw.com.

**PIKE, KERMIT JEROME,** cultural organization administrator; b. East Cleveland, June 19, 1941; s. Frank James and Pauline Frances (Prijatel) P.; m. Joyce Rita Massillo, June 27, 1964; children: Christopher James, Laura Elizabeth. BA, Case Western Res. U., 1963, MA, 1965. Rsch. asst. Western Res. Hist. Soc., Cleve., 1965-66, curator manuscripts, 1966-72, chief libr., 1969-75, dir. libr., 1976—2002, COO, 1997—. Adj. prof. history, libr. sci. Case Western Res. U., 1975-84. Author: Guide to the Manuscripts and Archives, 1972, Guide to Shaker Manuscripts, 1974; editor: Guide to Jewish History Sources, 1983; Compiler: Guide to Major Manuscript Collections, 1987. Mem. Super Sesquicentennial Com., Cleve., 1971, Cleve. Bicentennial History Com., 1992—96, Ohio Preservation Coun., 1997—, Ohio Hist. Records Adv. Bd., 2002—; chmn. Family Heritage Bd., Numa Corp., 1995—99; chmn. vis. com. on humanities and arts Cleve State U., 1980—82; trustee Nationalities Svc. Ctr., Cleve., 1978—86. Recipient Achievement award No. Ohio Live, Cleve., 1987; Spl. Recognition award Gov. Richard F. Celeste of Ohio, 1990. Mem. Soc. Ohio Archivists (co-founder 1968, pres. 1971-72), Black History Archives (founder 1970), Orgn. Am. Historians, Soc. Am. Archivists, Manuscripts Soc., Midwest Archives Conf., Ohio Geneal. Soc., Early Settlers Assn. of the Western Res., Rowfant Club, Lake County Farmers' Conservation Club, Lambda Chi Alpha. Roman Catholic. Home: 7066 Enfield Dr Mentor OH 44060-5160 Office: Western Res Hist Soc 10825 East Blvd Cleveland OH 44106-1777 Office Phone: 216-721-5722. Business E-Mail: kermit@wrhs.org.

**PIKE, LARRY SAMUEL,** lawyer; b. Savannah, Ga., Feb. 23, 1939; s. Abram and Ida (Feinberg) P.; m. Bonnie Jo Haykin, June 21, 1959; children: Douglas, Stacey, Scott. BA, Emory U., 1960, LLB, 1963; postgrad., Leeds U., Eng., 1960-61. Assoc. L. Jack Swertfeger Jr. Atty., Decatur Ga., 1963-65; ptnr. Swertfeger, Scott, Pike & Simmons, Decatur, 1966-75, Simmons, Pike & Warren, Decatur, 1975-76, Lefkoff, Pike & Sims, Atlanta, 1976-85, Branch, Pike & Ganz, Atlanta, 1985-95, Holland & Knight LLP, Atlanta, 1995—. Pres. Ansley Park Civic Assn., Atlanta, 1977-79, Northshore Homeowners Assn., Tybee Island, Ga., 1992-95, The Temple, Atlanta, 1979-81, trustee, 1977—, Am. Cancer Soc., DeKalb County, Ga. unit, 1970-71, crusade chmn., 1969-70; trustee Ansley Park Beautification Found., Inc., Atlanta, 1984—; treas., 2000—; trustee The Temple Endowment Fund, Atlanta, 1979-87, Atlanta Jewish Cmty. Ctr., 1973-76; bd. overseers Hebrew Union Coll., Cin., 1987-93; alumni coun. Emory U., Atlanta, 1966-72; bd. trustees Union of Am. Hebrew Congregations, 1991-99; mem. Rabbinical Placement Commn., 1994-2000; mem. St. Joseph's Hosp. Leadership Coun., 2003—; mem. planned giving adv. bd. Cmty. Found. Greater Atlanta, 2005—; mem. gift planning adv. coun. Emory U., 2006—. Editor-in-chief law jour. and newspaper; contbr. articles to profl. jours. Named Outstanding Young Man of Yr., North DeKalb Jaycees, 1968, Super Lawyer, Atlanta Mag.; named one of Legal Elite, Ga. Trend mag.; Fulbright fellow, 1960—61. Mem. ABA, State Bar Ga. (exec. coun. Young Lawyers sect. 1968-72), Atlanta Bar Assn., Decatur-DeKalb Bar Assn. (sec. 1965-66), Atlanta Legal Aid Soc. (pres. 1974-75, past bd. dirs.), Atlanta Tax Forum, Lawyers Club Atlanta, B'nai B'rith (pres. Atlanta lodge 1970-71, Ga. pres. 1974-75, dist. 5 bd. govs. 1973-76, chair Youth Orgn. Bd. 1971-73), Bryan Soc., Phi Beta Kappa, Omicron Delta Kappa. Office: Holland & Knight LLP 2000 One Atlantic Ctr Atlanta GA 30309 Business E-Mail: larry.pike@hklaw.com.

**PIKE, RALPH WEBSTER,** chemical engineer, educator, academic administrator; b. Tampa, Fla., Nov. 10, 1935; s. Ralph Webster and Macey (Adams) P.; m. Patricia Jennings, Aug. 23, 1958. B in Chem. Engring., Ga. Inst. Tech., 1957, PhD, 1962. Rsch. chem. engr. Exxon R & D Co., Baytown, Tex., 1962—64; Paul M. Horton prof. chem. engring. and sys. sci. La. State U., Baton Rouge, 1964—, assoc. vice chancellor rsch., 1967—96, dir. La. Mineral Inst., 1979—, dean engring., 1999—2001. Cons. to chem. and petroleum refining industry, fed. govt. and State of La., 1964—. Author: Formulation and Optimization of Mathematical Models, 1970, Optimization for Engineering Systems, 1986, Optimizacion en Ingenieria, 1989. Active various civic, ch. and cmty. orgns., Baton Rouge, 1964—. 2d lt. U.S. Army, 1958-60. Recipient more than 100 rsch. grants, including NASA, NSF, Dept. Interior, Dept. Def., EPA, NOAA, state agys. and pvt. industry, 1964—. Fellow AIChE (chmn. nat. program com. 1984, local sect. 1985); mem. Am. Chem. Soc. (Charles E. Coates Mem. Award, 1994), Sigma Xi. Democrat. Methodist. Avocation: skiing. Home: 6063 Hibiscus Dr Baton Rouge LA 70808-8844 Office: La State U 1139 Energy Coast and Environment Bldg Baton Rouge LA 70803-0001 Office Phone: 225-578-3428. Business E-Mail: pike@lsu.edu.

**PIKE, ROBERT WILLIAM,** insurance company executive, lawyer; b. Lorain, Ohio, July 25, 1941; s. Edward and Catherine (Stack) P.; m. Linda L. Feitz, Dec. 26, 1964; children: Catherine, Robert, Richard. BA, Bowling Green State U., 1963; JD, U. Toledo, 1966. Bar: Ohio 1966, Ill. 1973. Ptnr. Cubbon & Rice Law Firm, Toledo, 1968-72; asst. counsel Allstate Ins. Co., Northbrook, Ill., 1972-74, assoc. counsel, 1974-76, asst. sec., asst. gen. counsel, 1976-77, assoc. v.p., asst. gen. counsel, 1977-78, v.p., assoc. gen. counsel, 1978-86, sr. v.p., sec., gen. counsel, bd. dirs., 1987-99, exec. v.p.,

1999—. Bd. dirs. Allstate subs. Mem. bd. overseers Inst. for Civil Justice. Served to capt. inf. U.S. Army, 1966-68. Mem. ABA, Ill. Bar Assn., Ohio Bar Assn., Property Casualty Insurers Assn. Am. (bd. dirs., exec. com.), Ivanhoe (Ill.) Club. Roman Catholic. Home: 1795 W North Pond Ln Lake Forest IL 60045- Office: Allstate Ins Co 2775 Sanders Rd Ste F8 Northbrook IL 60062-6127

**PIKE, THOMAS HARRISON,** plant chemist; b. West Palm Beach, Florida, Oct. 9, 1950; s. Rufus Draper and Dora Marie (Thomason) P.; m. Julie Lynn (Simpson), Aug. 19, 1972; one child, Thomas Simpson. BS, Baylor Univ., 1972; MS, Calif. State U., 2001. Sci. instr. Valliant Pub. Sch., Okla., 1975—76; sch. adminstr. Swink Pub. Sch., Okla., 1976—81; plant chemist Western Farmers Electric Coop., Ft. Towson, Okla., 1981—2004; tech. editor Penn Well Pub., 2004—. Instr. dept. sci. and engring., Eastern Okla. State Coll., 1997—; mem. adv. bd. Kiamichi Vo-Tech. Sch., Idabel, Okla., 1985-87; tech. editor Penn Well Pub. Mem. adv. bd. Kiamichi Vo-Tech. Sch., Idabel, Okla., 1997—. Mem. ASME (co-chmn. task force, 1988-90); ASTM; Nat. Assn. Corrosion Engr. Achievements include rsch. in corrosion control of condensers, case history of turbine problems, improving boiler efficiency, preservation of turbines during extended outages, metal oxide transport, and water clarification; two patents in chemical process control technology. Home: R R 1 Box 299 Garvin OK 74736-9755 Office: Western Farmers Electric Coop PO Box 219 Fort Towson OK 74735-0219 Business E-Mail: t_pike@wfec.com.

**PIKE, WILLIAM EDWARD,** retired investment company executive; b. Ft. Collins, Colo., Jan. 25, 1929; s. Harry H. and Alice Francis (Swinscoe) P.; m. Catherine Broward Crawford, June 26, 1965; children: Elizabeth Catherine, Robert Crawford, Daniel William. Student, U. Colo., 1947-48; BS, U.S. Naval Acad., 1952; MBA, Harvard, 1960. Commd. ensign USN, 1952, advanced through grades to lt., 1958; ret. 1958; asst. treas. Morgan Guaranty Trust Co., N.Y.C., 1962-64, asst. v.p., 1964-66 v.p., 1966-71, sr. v.p., 1971-74, chmn. credit policy com., 1974-86; exec. v.p. J.P. Morgan & Co. Inc., 1986-89; corp. dir., trustee, pvt. investor. Bd. dirs. Global Lift Techs., Inc. Mem. Harvard Club N.Y.C. Clubs: Country (New Canaan, Conn.). Episcopalian. Home: Indian Waters Dr New Canaan CT 06840 Office: 36 Grove St New Canaan CT 06840-5329

**PIKITCH, ELLEN KAREN,** science educator; d. Benjamin and Ruth Pikitch; m. Allen Saul Zwickler, May 24, 1997; children: Adam Craig Zwickler, Randi Beth Zwickler; 1 child from previous marriage, Scott Merritt Emlen. BS, MA, CUNY, NYC, 1977; MS, Ind. U., Bloomington, 1982, PhD, 1983. Asst. prof. Oreg. State U., Newport, 1983—87, Sch. Fisheries, U. Wash., Seattle, 1987—90, assoc. prof., 1990—96, assoc. dir. rsch., dir. fisheries rsch. inst., 1992—96; dir. fisheries programs Wildlife Conservation Soc., NYC, 1996—98, dir. marine conservation programs, 1998—2002, dir. ocean strategy, 2002—03; exec. dir. Pew Inst. for Ocean Sci., NYC, 2003—; prof. U. Miami Rosenstiel Sch., Fla., 2003—. Mem. Pres. Clinton's Panel on Ocean Exploration, 2000—01; mem. sturgeon specialist group Internat. Union for the Conservation of Nature, 2002—; task force mem. Millennium Project Task Force on Environ. Sustainability, 2003—05; conservation com. mem. Sea Change Investment Fund, San Francisco, 2005—; co-founder Caviar Emptor Campaign, lead scientist. Contbr. articles to profl. jours. Named one of Outstanding Young Women Am., 1986; recipient Nehemiah Gittleson award, City Coll., CUNY, 1977, Kenyon prize for Excellence in Pure and Applied Math., 1977, Emerging Scholar award, Phi Kappa Phi, Oreg. State U. Chpt., 1987, Disting. Svc. award, Coll. Ocean and Fisheries Sci., U. Wash., 1992, Silver Anvil award, Pub. Rels. Soc. Am., 2004; Breckenridge fellow, Ind. U., 1982, Eigenmann fellow, 1982—83, Pew fellow in marine conservation, 2000—04. Mem.: AAAS, Soc. for Conservation Biology, Am. Fisheries Soc. Achievements include research in fisheries management and ocean conservation. Office: Pew Institute for Ocean Science 126 East 56th St Mezzanine New York NY 10022 Office Phone: 212-756-0042. Business E-Mail: epikitch@miami.edu.

**PILAFIAN, AUDREY KALENIAN,** music educator; b. Chgo., Sept. 19, 1929; d. Hagop and Adrine Kalenian; m. Harry Pilafian, Sept. 10, 1949; children: Martin, Jack David, Robert John, Mary Katherine. Student, Northwestern U., 1947—49; MusB, U. Miami, 1951, MEd in Supervision and Adminstrn., 1972. Cert. supr./adminstr., gifted edn., music edn., elem. edn. tchr. Fla. Elem. sch. tchr. Miami/Dade Pub. Schs., 1952—76, gifted students tchr., 1976—92; adj. supr. Fla. Internat. U., Miami, 1994—. Musician U. Miami Symphony Orch., Coral Gables, Fla., 1953—56; pvt. cello tchr., Miami, 1970—; cellist Chamber Music Prof. Agy., Miami, 1995—2005. Vol. co-dir. strings ensemble Leewood Elem. Sch., Miami, 1992—2005; state bd. mem. Odyssey of the Mind, Inc., Fla., 1983—98; supt. Sunday Sch. St. Mary Armenian Ch., Hollywood, Fla., 1953—2006. Named Dade County Tchr. of Yr., Fla. Fedn. Woman's Clubs, 1968; recipient Pontifical Blessing Encyclical, His Holiness Karenkin I, Catholicos of all Armenians, 1998. Mem.: Phi Delta Kappa (tchr.), Sigma Alpha Iota (musician/performer, editor, historian), Alpha Delta Kappa (internat. chmn. Fine Arts Grants Bd. 1991—97, internat. music chmn. 2005). Avocations: cello, chamber music, amateur radio, travel, camping. Home and Studio: 9940 SW 60 St Miami FL 33173 Office Phone: 305-271-2512.

**PILAND, NEILL FINNES,** health services economist, researcher, educator; b. Pomona, Calif., Nov. 6, 1943; s. Finnes Elmer and Sylvia Beatrice (Renick) PiL.; m. Diane Lynn Fiedor, Aug. 12, 1977; children: Evan Neill, Spencer Lowell, Arden Geneva. BA, UCLA, 1965, MPH, 1970, PhD, 1979; MA, U. Calif., Davis, 1966. Rsch. assoc. Sch. Pub. Health UCLA, 1971-73, sr. rsch. assoc., 1973; health economist Stanford Rsch. Inst., Menlo Park, Calif., 1973-77, asst. mgr. health svcs. rsch., 1974-77; dir. health ctr. study Jicarilla Apache Tribe, Dulce, N.Mex., 1978-82; dir. health systems evaluation program Lovelace Med. Found., Albuquerque, 1982-83, dir. health svcs. rsch. and edn., 1983-91; dir. Ctr. Health & Population Rsch., Albuquerque, 1991-94, Lovelace Inst. for Health and Population Rsch., Albuquerque, 1994-96; rsch. dir. Ctr. Rsch. Med. Group Mgmt. Assn., Englewood, Colo., 1996—2002; prof. and dir. Inst. Rural Health, Idaho State U., Pocatello, 2002—, rsch. prof., 2005—; clin. assoc. prof. U. Colo. Sch. Medicine; rsch. prof. U. Denver; dir. policy and rsch. Colo. Health Inst., Denver, 2004—05; rsch. prof. Inst. Rural Health Idaho State U., 2005—. Clin. asst. prof. medicine U. N.Mex., Albuquerque, 1981, clin. assoc. prof., 1994—; vis. prof. U. N.H., Durham, 1989-90; mem. commn. tobacco control, Idaho, 2003-04 Co-author: Strategic Nursing Management: Power and Responsibility in a New Era; mem. editorial bd. Jour. Managerial Issues, 1991—; co-editor: Physician Profiling: A Sourcebook for Adminstrators, Chart Accounts for Healthcare Organizations, Reinventing Medical Practice; contbr. over 100 articles to profl. jours. Mem. rsch. com. N.Mex. HealthNet, 1986-88; chair econ. issues N.Mex. Com. on Pub. Health Impact of Smoking, 1988; bd. dirs. Am. Geriat. and Gerontology, 1984-87, Healthcare for Homeless, 1988-92; mem. exec. coun. N.Mex. ASSIST Com., 1992—, sci. adv. com. N.Mex. ASSIST Project, 1992—; mem. steering com. Group Practice Improvement Network, 1996—; mem. workgroup smoking control Colo. Dept. Health and Environment, 1999-2002; scholarship interviewer NHSC, 2003-04; mem. Idaho State Commn. Tobacco Control, 2004—; bd. dirs. Vets. Med. Rsch. Found., 2002—. Recipient traineeship, USPHS, 1968-70. Mem. APHA, Am. Econ. Assn., Soc. Rsch. Adminstrs., Assn. Health Svcs. Rsch. Avocations: tennis, hockey, hiking, biking. Home: 2 Rice Ave Pocatello ID 83201 Office: Inst Rural Health Idaho State U Graveley Hall 205 Campus Box 8174 Pocatello ID 83209-8174 Office Phone: 208-282-5021 x211. Business E-Mail: pilaneil@isu.edu.

**PILARCZYK, DANIEL EDWARD,** archbishop; b. Dayton, Ohio, Aug. 12, 1934; s. Daniel Joseph and Frieda S. (Hilgefort) Pilarczyk. Student, St. Gregory Sem., Cin., 1948—53; PhB, Pontifical Urban U., Rome, 1955, PhL, 1956, STB, 1958, STL, 1960, STD, 1961; MA, Xavier U., 1965; PhD, U. Cin., 1969; LLD (hon.), Xavier U., 1975, Calumet Coll., 1982, U. Dayton, 1990, Marquette U., 1990, Thomas More Coll., 1991, Coll. Mt. St. Joseph, 1994, Hebrew Union Coll., 1997. Ordained priest Roman Catholic Ch., 1959. Asst. chancellor Archdiocese of Cin., 1961—63; synodal judge Archdiocesan

Tribunal, 1971—82; faculty Athenaeum of Ohio, St. Gregory Sem., 1963—74; v.p. Athenaeum of Ohio, 1968—74, trustee, 1974—; rector St. Gregory Sem., 1968—74; archdiocesan dir. ednl. services, 1974—82; aux. bishop of Cin., 1974—82; vicar gen., 1974—82; archbishop of Cin., 1982—. V.p. Nat. Conf. Cath. Bishops, 1986—89, pres., 1989—92, chmn. com. on doctrine, 1996—2000; U.S. rep. Episc. bd. Internat. Commn. on English in Liturgy, 1987—77, chmn., 1991—97; jt. com. Orthodox and Cath. Bishops, 2002. Author: Praepositini Cancellarii de Sacramentis et de Novissimis, 1964—65, Twelve Tough Issues, 1988, We Believe, 1989, Living in the Lord, 1990, The Parish: Where God's People Live, 1991, Forgiveness, 1992, What Must I Do?, 1993, Our Priests: Who They Are and What They Do, 1994, Sacraments, 1994, Bringing Forth Justice, 1996, 1999, Thinking Catholic, 1998, Practicing Catholic, 1999, Believing Catholic, 2000, Live Letters, 2001, Twelve Tough Issues and More, 2002, Being Catholic, 2006, When God Speaks, 2006. Trustee Cath. Health Assn., 1982—85, Cath. U. Am., 1983—91, 1997—2000, Pontifical Coll. Josephinum, 1983—92. Ohio Classical Conf. scholar, Athens, 1966. Mem.: Am. Philol. Assn. Roman Catholic. Home and Office: 100 E Eighth St Cincinnati OH 45202-2129 Office Phone: 513-421-3131.

**PILATI, STEFANO,** apparel designer; b. Milan; Intern Nino Cerruti; menswear asst. Giorgio Armani, 1993—95; with fabric and rsch. devel. Prada, 1995—98, asst. designer Miu Miu womenswear and menswear, 1998—2000; design dir. Yves St. Laurent, 2000—04; creative dir. Yves St. Laurent Rive Gauche, 2004—. Office: Yves Saint Laurent 3 E 57th St New York NY 10022-2557

**PILC, JEAN-MICHEL,** composer, musician; b. Paris, Oct. 19, 1960; s. Maurice Pilc and Elisabeth Bachrach; m. Muriel Vergnaud, Mar. 16, 1996. Diploma, Ecole Polytechnique, 1981. Composer: (songs) Trio Sonata (New Works award Chamber Music America, 2001). Recipient Django Reinhardt prize, French Jazz Acad., 2000. Office: Jean-Michel Pilc PO Box 247 Grahamsville NY 12740 Office Phone: 845-647-6694. Home Fax: 801-407-0266; Office Fax: 801-407-0266. Business E-Mail: jmpinfo@jmpilc.com.

**PILCHER, CARL B.,** astrobiologist; BS in Chemistry, Poly. Inst. Bklyn., 1968; PhD in Chemistry, MIT, Cambridge, 1973; M of Pub. Affairs in Internat. Rels., Princeton U., NJ, 1987. Mem. faculty dept. physics and astronomy U. Hawaii Inst. Astronomy, 1973—85; chief Mission from Planet Earth Study Office NASA, dir. sci. Office of Exploration, spl. asst. exploration Office of Space Sci. and Applications, chief Advanced Studies Br. in Solar Sys. Exploration Divsn., asst. assoc. administr. strategic and internat. planning Office of Space Sci., bd. dirs. Office of Space Sci., spl. asst. astrobiology, 2001, sci. prog. dir. Solar Sys. Exploration Washington, 2001—05, sr. scientist astrobiology Office of Space Sci., 2005—; dir. NASA Astrobiology Inst., 2006—. Mem. Galileo Solid State Imaging Team NASA, 1977—; guest prof. U. Vienna, Austria, 1983—84; mid-career fellow Princeton U. Woodrow Wilson Sch. Pub. and Internat. Affairs, 1985. Contbr. articles to profl. jours. Grantee MacArthur Found. fellowship, Internat. Peace and Security. Office: Office of Space Sci Code SZ NASA Hdqs 300 E St NW Washington DC 20546 E-mail: Carl.B.Pilcher@nasa.gov.*

**PILCHER, CHRISTIE W.,** special education educator; b. Jackson, Tenn, Dec. 17, 1944; d. Charles Arthur Sr. and Ruby Mazie (Pope) Walker; m. David Wayne Pilcher, Mar. 20, 1966 (div. 1974); children: David Andrew, Clayton Everett. Student, Mercer U., 1962-63; BA, North Ga. Coll., 1966; MEd, Ga. State U., 1976. Tchr. reading US Army Edn. Ctr., Munich, 1967; tchr. K.G. US Dependent Sch., Munich, 1967-68; tchr. Ga. Acad. for the Blind, Macon, 1974-79; tchr. for visually impaired Bibb County Bd. Edn., Macon, 1979-91, spl. edn. K.G., 1991-94; tchr. visually impaired Troup County Bd. Edn., LaGrange, Ga., 1994—2000, Bartow County Sch. Sys., Cartersville, Ga., 2000—01; tchr. spl. needs kindergarten Bibb County Bd. Edn., Macon, 2001—02, 2005—, tchr. mildly intellectually disabled, 2004. Parent advisor Ga. Parent Infant Network for Ednl. Svc., Clarkston, 1985—2004; tchr. summer program Ga. Bapt. Children's Home, Baxley, 1991. Vol. Ga. Radio Reading Svc., 2003—. Christian Ch. (Disciples of Christ), Deacon, Christian Edn. Com., chair 1991. Avocations: painting, reading, baking, travel, gardening. Home: 939 Clairmont Pl Macon GA 31204-1099 E-mail: christiep@bellsouth.net.

**PILCHER, GREGORY F.,** manufacturing executive, lawyer; b. Roswell, N.Mex., Mar. 10, 1960; m. Karen Pilcher. BS in bus. adminstrn., Okla. State U., 1982, MS in acctg., 1984; JD with highest honors, U. Okla., 1988. CPA Kans., 1983; bar: Okla. 1988, US Ct. Appeals 10th Cir., US Dist. Ct. We. Dist. Okla. With Edwards, Roberts & Propester PC, 1986—89; assoc. atty. Roberts, Gray, Goresen, Moriarty & Wright PC, 1989—92; with Kerr-McGee Corp., Okla. City, 1992—, from asst. to assoc. gen. counsel litig. and civil procs., 1996—98, dep. gen. counsel bus. transactions, 1998—99, v.p., gen. counsel, corp. sec., 1999—2000, sr. v.p., gen. counsel, corp. sec., 2000—. Mem.: Am. Soc. Corp. Secretaries, Okla. Assn. of Def. Counsel, Okla. County Bar Assn., Okla. Bar Assn., ABA, Order of the Coif. Office: Kerr-McGee Corp Kerr-Magee Ctr 123 Robert S Kerr Ave Oklahoma City OK 73102

**PILCHER, JAMES ERIC,** physicist; b. Toronto, Ontario, Canada, Apr. 23, 1942; came to U.S. 1965; s. Francis Eric and Isabel (Brand) P.; m. Carla Grosso, Aug. 31, 1970; children: Marc R., Daniel E., Erica M. BASc, U. Toronto, 1964, MSc, 1966; PhD, Princeton U., 1968. Rsch. assc. Princeton U., Princeton, N.J., 1968-69; visiting scientist CERN, Geneva, 1969-70; asst. prof. Harvard U., Cambridge, Mass., 1970-72; asst./assoc. prof. U. Chgo., 1972-79; scientific assc. CERN, Geneva, 1979-80; prof. U. Chgo., 1979—; dir. Enrico Fermi Inst. Member Physics Adv. Com. SSC, Dallas, 1990. Author numerous articles to profl. jours. Fellow Am. Phys. Soc. Achievements include discovery that there are exactly 3 families of light neutrinos. Office: University of Chicago Physics Dept 5640 S Ellis Ave Chicago IL 60637

**PILDES, RICHARD H.,** law educator; AB, Princeton U., 1980; JD, Harvard Law Sch., 1983. Bar: Mass. 1987. Law clk. to Judge Abner Mikva US Ct. Appeals DC Cir., 1983—84; law clk. to Justice Thurgood Marshall US Supreme Ct., 1984—85; assoc. Foley, Hoag & Eliot, Boston, 1986—87; asst. prof. U. Mich. Law Sch., 1988—93, prof., 1993—2000, NYU Sch. Law, 2000—, Sudler Family prof. constl. law. Vis. prof. U. Chgo. Law Sch., 1997, NYU Sch. Law, 1999—2000, Harvard Law Sch., 2004; sr. fellow Program in Ethics & the Professors Harvard U., 1998—99. Author (with others): The Law of Democracy: Legal Structure of the Political Process, 2001. Carnegie scholar, 2004. Office: NYU Sch Law Vanderbilt Hall Rm 507 40 Washington Sq S New York NY 10012-1099 Office Phone: 212-998-6377. E-mail: rick.pildes@nyu.edu.

**PILEGGI, DOMINIC J.,** electronics executive; BA, Rutgers U. Sales & mgmt. positions Thomas & Betts, Memphis, 1979—88, pres. electronics, 1988—94, pres. elec. products group, 1994—95; sr. exec. positions with Casco Plastic, Inc., Jordan Telecommunications, 1995—98; pres. EMS div. Viasystems Inc., 1998—2000; sr. v.p. Thomas & Betts, Memphis, 2000—02, group pres. electrical, 2000—03, pres., COO, 2003—04, pres., CEO, 2004—05, chmn., CEO, 2006—. Office: Thomas & Betts 8155 T&B Blvd Memphis TN 38125 Office Phone: 901-252-8000.*

**PILEGGI, JENNIFER WENDY,** transportation services executive; b. NYC, July 27, 1964; d. Jerome E. Rosenfeld. BA in Art History, cum laude, Yale U., 1986; JD, NYU, 1990. Bar: Calif. 1990. Assoc. Heller, Ehrman, White & McAuliffe, San Francisco, Marron, Reid & Sheehy, San Francisco; joined CNF Inc., Palo Alto, Calif., 1996; corp. counsel Menlo Worldwide Logistics subs., Redwood City, Calif., 1996—99, v.p. corp. counsel, 1999—2003, Menlo Worldwide subs., Redwood City, Calif., 2003—04; sr. v.p., gen. counsel, corp. sec. CNF Inc., 2004—. Mem.: ABA, Calif. State Bar Assn. Office: CNF Inc 2855 Campus Dr Ste 300 San Mateo CA 94403 Office Phone: 650-378-5200. Office Fax: 650-357-9160.

**PILGERAM, LAURENCE OSCAR,** biochemist; b. Great Falls, Mont., June 23, 1924; s. John Rudolph and Bertha Roslyn (Phillips) P.; m. Cynthia Ann Moore, Apr. 16, 1971; children: Karl Erich, Kurt John. AA, U. Calif., Berkeley, 1948, BA, 1949, PhD, 1953. Instr. dept. physiology U. Ill. Profl. Coll., Chgo., 1954-55; asst. prof. dept. biochemistry Stanford (Calif.) U. Sch. Medicine, 1955-57; dir. arteriosclerosis rsch. lab. U. Minn. Sch. Medicine, Mpls., 1957-65, Santa Barbara, Calif., 1965-71; dir. coagulation lab., assoc. dir. Cerebrovascular Rsch. Ctr., Baylor Coll. Medicine, Tex. Med. Ctr., Houston, 1971-75; dir. Thrombosis Control Labs., Palo Alto, Calif., 1975-79, Santa Barbara, 1979—; prof. dept. molecular biology U. Calif., Santa Barbara, 2004—. Cons. NIH, Bio-Sci. Labs., FDA; del. Coun. on Thrombosis and Coun. on Strokes, Am. Heart Assn. Assembly. Co-editor: Nutrition and Thrombosis for the Nat. Dairy Coun., 1973; contbr. sci. articles to profl. jours. Recipient CIBA award, London, 1958, Karl Thomae award, Germany, 1973; NIH grantee, 1954-75; Life Ins. Med. Rsch. Fund fellow, 1952-54. Mem. Am. Soc. for Biochemistry and Molecular Biology. Office: PO Box 1583 Goleta PO Santa Barbara CA 93116 Office Phone: 805-967-5994. Business E-Mail: pilgeram@lifesci.ucsb.edu.

**PILGRAM, SUZANNE,** artist, art educator; b. Montclair, NJ, Feb. 25, 1945; d. Hans J. and Florence Ketchum Pilgram; m. Hassan Ghavam, Sept. 3, 1973. BA in Art, Am. U., 1967, MFA in Painting, 1970. Artist, clk. US Com. for UNICEF Children's Culture Ctr., 1970—73; prof. Coll. Translation, Tehran, Iran, 1973—80, Farah Pahlavi U., Tehran, 1977—78, Trenton State Coll., NJ, 1983; assoc. prof. Georgian Court U., Lakewood, NJ, 1981—. Lectr., presenter Ocean County CC, NJ, 1980, NJ, 81, NJ, 82, Pine Shores Art Assn., N.J. State Coun. on Arts, 1998—2006, Columbia U., N.Y.C., 2001. Artwork, Columbia U. Invitational, 2001, painting collage, Trenton Artists Workshop, 2004, paintings, Phoenix Gallery, N.Y.C., 2004—06; printmaking coun. NJ Exhibit "Intolerance", 2006—. Grantee Fulbright-Hayes Group Projects Abroad, U.S. State Dept., Jamaica, 1983, Faculty Rsch. grant, Georgian Ct. U., 2004. Mem.: Trenton Artists Workshop, Women's Studio Workshop, NJ Project (Grant 1987—). Avocation: gardening. Home: 9 Robin Rd Howell NJ 07731 Office: Georgian Ct Univ 900 Lakewood Ave Lakewood NJ 08701 Office Phone: 732-987-2330. Business E-Mail: pilgrams@georgian.edu.

**PILGRIM, JILL,** lawyer, consultant; b. London, Nov. 26, 1958; came to U.S., 1969; d. Winslow and Florence L. (Hardy) P. BA, Princeton U., 1980; JD, Columbia U., 1984. Bar: N.Y. 1985. Assoc. Willkie Far & Gallagher, N.Y.C., 1984-86, Cowan Liebowitz & Latman, N.Y.C., 1986-88; of counsel Kurzman Karelsen & Frank, N.Y.C., 1988-89; pvt. practice Pilgrim & Assocs., N.Y.C., 1990—98; gen. counsel, dir. bus. affairs USA Track & Field, Inc., Indpls., 1998—. Examiner in guardianship matters, 1991—; bd. arbitrators Nat. Assn. Securities Delers, Inc.; guest speaker to law students, numerous N.Y. area law schs. Bd. editors The Partnership Handbook, 1986. Mem. Temp. N.Y. State Commn. on Bklyn. Recreation Facilities, 1994—; founder, pres. Ctr. for Protection Athletes' Rights Inc.; bd. dirs., mem. exec. com. Bklyn. Sports Found.; v.p. Friends of Princeton Track; mem. alumni coun. exec. com. Princeton U., 1993-95; bd. dirs. Griffith-Sandiford Family Assistance Fund, Inc.; mem. adv. bd. Bond Street Theater Coalition, Ltd., New Federal Theater. Recipient Essence award Essence Comm., Inc. and Colgate-Palmolive Co., 1990; named Woman of Yr., West Side Residents, 1993. Mem. ABA, Practicing Law Inst., Met. Black Bar Assn., Assn. Bar City N.Y., Assn. Black Women Attys., Sports Lawyers Assn. (bd. mem.), Indpls. Nat. Jr. Tennis Team (bd. mem.), Indpls. Bar Assn. (chairperson sports law sec.), U.S. Olympic Com. (mem. disabled sports com.) Avocations: tennis, field hockey, badminton, volleyball, basketball, track & field. Office: USA Track & Field 1 RCA Dome, Ste 140 Indianapolis IN 46225

**PILGRIM, LONNIE (BO PILGRIM),** food products executive; b. May 8, 1928; married. Ptnr. Pilgrim's Pride Corp., Pittsburg, Tex., 1953-68, CEO, 1968—98, chmn., CEO, 1998—2004, chmn., 2004—. Chmn. First State Bank Pitts. Served with U.S. Armed Forces, 1951-53. Office: Pilgrim's Pride Corp 4845 US Hwy 271 N Pittsburg TX 75686 Mailing: Pilgrim's Pride Corp PO Box 93 Pittsburg TX 75686-0093

**PILIGIAN, GEORGETTE A.,** insurance company executive; BS in bus. computer info. systems, Hofstra U. Positions with E.F. Hutton; joined MetLife Inc., 1987, v.p. e-business applications devel., now chief info. officer corp. systems, 2003—, also sr. v.p. Named one of Premier 100 IT Leaders, Computerworld, 2005. Office: MetLife Inc 200 Park Ave New York NY 10166*

**PILIGUIAN, TRO,** advertising executive; b. Egypt; naturalized, Canada; married; 2 children. Pres. Academie-Ogilvy, Montreal; chmn., CEO Ogilvy & Mather Canada, Toronto, 1990—; pres. Ogilvy & Mather NY, 1994—97; pres. CEO. Ogilvy & Mather N. Am. NYC, 1997—, fluent, 5 lang. Office: Ogilvy & Mather Worldwide Plz 309 W 49th St New York NY 10019-7316

**PILISUK, MARC,** psychology educator; b. NYC, Jan. 19, 1934; s. Louis and Charlotte (Feferholtz) P.; m. Phyllis E. Kamen, June 16, 1956; children: Tammy, Jeff. BA, Queens Coll., 1955; MA, U. Mich., 1956, PhD, 1961. Asst. prof., assoc. rsch. psychologist U. Mich., Ann Arbor, 1961-65, founder teach-in, 1965; assoc. prof. Purdue U., West Lafayette, Ind., 1965-67; prof.-in-residence U. Calif., Berkeley, 1967-77, prof. cmty. psychology Davis, 1977—. Vis. prof. U. Calif., Wright Inst., 1991—93; cons. Ctr. for Self Help Rsch., Berkeley, Calif., 1991—93; prof. psychology Saybrook Grad. Sch. & Rsch. Ctr., San Francisco, 1993—. Author: (textbooks) International Conflict and Social Policy, 1972, The Healing Web: Social Networks and Human Survival, 1986; editor: The Triple Revolution, 1969, Poor Americans, 1970, Triple Revolution Emerging, 1972, How We Lost the War on Poverty 1973 Onward, 1981, 1982—66; NIMH fellow, 1959—60; tng. grantee, Nat. Inst. Alcoholism and Drug Abuse, 1973—77. Fellow: APA (pres. divsn. peace psychology 1996—97, cadre experts on violence, Lifetime Contbn. award 2005), Am. Orthopsychiat. Assn., Soc. for Psychol. Study Social Issues (coun., Sage award 2004—05); mem.: ACLU (Presdl. award 2005), APHA, Faculty for Human Rights in C.Am., Psychologists for Social Responsibility (steering com., Disting. Svc. award 2001), Am. Soc. on Aging, Soc. for Cmty. Rsch. and Action. Business E-Mail: mpilisuk@saybrook.edu.

**PILKERTON, ARTHUR RAYMOND, JR.,** surgeon, educator; b. Washington, Mar. 27, 1935; s. Arthur Raymond and Mary Rose (Ginechesi) P.; m. Sally Ann Madden, Aug. 6, 1966; children: A. Raymond III, Joseph A., Mary, Christopher, Jeanne Marie. BS in Biology, Georgetown U., 1952-56, MD, 1960. Diplomate Am. Bd. Opthalmology. Intern. U. Pitts., 1961; fellow retina surgery Wills Eye Hosp., Phila., 1964-65; resident ophthalmology Georgetown U. Med. Ctr., Washington, 1961-64, asst. prof., 1965-70, assoc. prof., 1971-78, clin. prof., 1978—; asst. clin. prof. George Washington U., Washington, 1985—; co-founder Retina Group Washington. Chief ophthalmology Veteran's Adminstrn. Hosp., Washington, 1965-82; chief ophthalmology cons., Veterans Adminstrn., Washington, 1978-82. Served with U.S. Army, 1961-70. Named Knight of Malta, Knight Comdr. Holy Sepulchre; named one of America's Best Doctors, 2004, America's Top Ophthalmologists, 2004—05; recipient Profl. Svc. award, Prevention Blindness Soc., 2005, Hagerty awrd, No. Va. Acad. Ophthalmology. Fellow Am. Acad. Ophthalmology (councilor), ACS (councilor); mem. Retina Soc. U.S., Retina Group of Washington (co-founder), Am. Soc. Retina Specialist, Prevention Blindness Soc. (Profl. Svc. award 2005). Republican. Roman Catholic. Office: Retina Group Washington 5454 Wisconsin Ave Suite 1540 Chevy Chase MD 20815 Business E-Mail: rpilkerton@retinagroup.org.

**PILLA, ANTHONY MICHAEL,** bishop; b. Cleve., Nov. 12, 1932; s. George and Libera (Nista) P. Student, St. Gregory Coll. Sem., 1952—53, Borromeo Coll. Sem., 1955, St. Mary Sem., 1943, student, 1956—59; BA in Philosophy, John Carroll U., Cleve., 1961, MA in History, 1967. Ordained priest Roman Cath. Ch., 1959. Assoc. St. Bartholomew Parish, Middleburg Heights, Ohio, 1959—60; prof. Borromeo Sem., Wickliffe, Ohio, 1960—72, rector-pres., 1972—75; mem. Diocese Cleve. Liturgical Commn., 1964—69, asst. dir., 1969—72; sec. for svcs. to clergy and religious pers. Diocese

Cleve., 1975—79; titular bishop Scardona; and aux. bishop of Cleve. and vicar Eastern region Diocese of Cleve., 1979—80, apostolic adminstr., 1980—; bishop Cleve., 1981—; pres. Nat. Conf. Cath. Bishops, 1995—98. Trustee Borromeo Sem., 1975—79, Cath. U., 1981—84; trustee, mem. bd. overseers St. Mary Sem., 1975—79; mem. adv. bd. permanent diaconate program Diocese of Cleve., 1975—79, hospitalization and ins. bd., 1979. Bd. dirs. NCCJ, 1986—. Mem.: Greater Cleve. Roundtable (trustee 1981—), Cath. Conf. Ohio, Nat. Conf. Cath. Bishops, U.S. Cath. Conf., Nat. Cath. Edn. Assn. (dir. 1972—75). Home and Office: Chancery Office Diocese of Cleveland 1027 Superior Ave E Ste 300 Cleveland OH 44114-2503

**PILLALAMARRI, SESHASAYI,** computer scientist and engineer, researcher; b. Masulipatam, India, Mar. 4, 1946; s. Ramadas and Umabala Pillalamarri; m. Indira Dantu, Feb. 5, 1977; children: Sandhya, Sirisha, Vamsee. BS, Osmania U., 1964; B in engring., Indian Inst. Sci., 1967; M in tech., Indian Inst. Tech., 1969; MS, SUNY Stonybrook, 1972; PhD, U. Linz, 2000. Sci. officer Indian Inst. Tech., Madras, 1974—76, asst. mgr., 1976—87, mgr., computer ctr., 1987—96; rsch. scientist Siemens AG, Munich, Bavaria, 1992—93, ICSI, U. Calif., Berkeley, 1993—94, Ariz. State U., Phoenix, 1996—2002; software engr. Computer Info. Tech. Corp., 1996—2002, City of Phoenix, 2002—02. Cons. Indian Inst. of Tech., Madras, India, 1976—96. Contbr. chapters to books, 2000. Mem.: Assn. for Computing Machinery (assoc.), IEEE (assoc.). Independent. Achievements include invention of the impact of source traffic distribution on quality of service (QOS) in ATM networks; stability of RYNSORD, a decentralized algorithm for railway networks; fundamental attributes of high speed networks. Avocations: music, poetry. Home: 3524 W Buckhorn Tr Phoenix AZ 85085 Office: City of Phoenix 300 W Washington St Phoenix AZ 85003 Business E-Mail: sesh.pilla@phoenix.gov.

**PILLAY, ANAND,** education educator, researcher; b. London, Eng., May 7, 1951; s. Vallaithan and Patricia O'Leary; m. Margit Messmer, July 9, 1993; children: Kalyan, Bhanu; m. Bronislava Jedrusik, July 26, 1978 (div. Mar. 1992); 1 child, Anusha. BA, U. Oxford, 1973; MSc, U. London, 1974, PhD, 1977. Rschr. CNRS, Paris, 1978—81; temp. lectr. U. Manchester, 1981—82; vis. lectr. U. McGill, 1982—83; assoc. prof. U. Notre Dame, 1983—86, 1986—88, prof., 1988—96, U. Ill., 1996—2005; prof., Marie Curie chair Leeds U., England, 2005—. Org. Math. Sci. Rsch. Inst., 1998. Contbr. scientific papers; author: (book) An Introduction to Stability Theory, 1983; author: (edited with Ali Nesin) The Model Theory of Groups, 1989; author: (with D. Marker and M. Messmer) Model Theory of Fields; author: Geometric Stability Theory, 1996; author: (edited with D. Haskell and C. Steinhorn) Model theory, Algebra and Geometry, 2000. Sitar player WEFT radio, 1997—2003. Recipient Humboldt prize, Humboldt Found., 2001; grant, NSF, 1983—2003, Rsch. grant, 2001—. Mem.: Assn. Symbolic Logic, Am. Math. Soc., Socialist Forum. Office: Sch Math Leeds Univ Leeds LS2 9JT England Office Phone: 44 113 363 5171.

**PILLAY, GAUTAM,** chemical engineer, chemist, academic administrator; b. Buffalo, Jan. 28, 1967; s. Sivasankara K. K. and Revathi (Krishnamurthy) Pillay; m. Amy Matthews, 2004. BS, N.Mex. State U., Las Cruces, 1988; PhD, Tex. A&M U., 1993. Grad. rschr., staff mem. Los Alamos Nat. Lab., 1984-87, mem. tech. staff, 1997—2001; grad. rschr. Tex. A&M U., College Station, 1988-92; rsch. engr. Pacific N.W. Lab., Richland, Wash., 1992-95, sr. rsch. engr., 1995-97; adj. faculty Wash. State U., Richland, 1993-97; exec. dir. Inland N.W. Rsch. Alliance, Idaho Falls, Idaho, 2001—04; v.p. rsch. S.D. Sch. Mines and Tech., Rapid City, 2004—. Contbr. articles to profl. jours. Recipient Fed. Lab. Consortium award for excellence in tech. transfer, 1997; NSF Grad. Rsch. fellow, 1988—91. Mem.: AIChE (symposium chair), N.Y. Acad. Scis., Am. Nuc. Soc., Am. Chem. Soc., Electrochemical Soc. (symposium chair 1993—), mem. exec. com. 1994—, pres. Pacific N.W. sect. 1996—97, v.p. IE & EE divsn. 2002—04, pres. 2004—). Phi Kappa Phi, Alpha Chi, Omega Chi Epsilon, Tau Beta Pi. Avocations: general aviation, musician. Office: SD Sch Mines and Tech 501 E Saint Joseph St Rapid City SD 57701 Office Phone: 605-394-2493. E-mail: gautam.pillay@sdsmt.edu.

**PILLER, CHARLES LEON,** journalist; b. Chgo., Jan. 9, 1955; s. Jack H. and Alice (Shakow) P.; m. Susan Pilfer Bunnell, Aug. 21, 1984; 1 child, Nathan Bunnell Piller. BA, Lone Mountain Coll., 1977. Editor, writer U. Calif., San Francisco, 1982-89; sr. editor Macworld mag., San Francisco, 1990-96; exec. editor PC World Mag., San Francisco, 1996—97; tech. writer L.A. Times, 1996—2002, science writer computer tech. and biology, 2002—. Chair Ctr. Pub. Integrity, Washington, 1988—, also bd. dirs.; cons. US Senate, Washington, 1989-92. Author: Gene Wars, 1988, The Fail-Safe Society, 1991; contbr. numerous articles to newspapers and mags. Recipient of the John Swett Journalism award, 1993, Benjamin Fine Journalism award, 1995, Runner-Up Lincoln Steffens Journalism award, 1994. Am. Soc. of Business Press Editors (various awards). Office: LA Times 202 W First St Los Angeles CA 90012 Office Fax: 213-237-4712. Business E-Mail: charles.piller@latimes.com.

**PILLIOD, JAMES P.,** state legislator, physician; b. NYC, Aug. 9, 1930; s. James J. and Mary Alice (Phillips) P.; m. Judith Bean. BA, Yale U., 1952; MD, Duke U., 1960. Diplomate Am. Bd. Pediatrics. Staff physician Lake Regional Gen. Hosp., 1964—; mem. N.H. Ho. of Reps., Concord, 1996—. Lt. (j.g.) USN. Diplomate Acad. of Pediatrics; mem. AMA (past del.), N.H. Med. Soc. (past pres.), N.H. Hosp. Assn. (Physician Staff Mem. of Yr. 1988), N.H. Pediat. Soc. (Pub. Servant of Yr. 1997). Office: NH State Legis State House Concord NH 03301

**PILLOT, GENE MERRILL,** retired school system administrator; b. Canton, Ohio, Apr. 13, 1930; s. John D. Pillot and Vera R. Granstaff; m. Beverly Ann Shaw, June 4, 1982; children: Vera Kathleen Martin, Michael Gene, Patrick Merrill. BS in Math., Ohio State U., 1952; MEd in Adminstrn. and Supervision, Kent State U., 1957; EdD in Adminstrn. and Supervision, U. Fla., 1970. Asst. prin. North Royalton (Ohio) High Sch., 1959-61, prin., 1961-63; asst. prin. Sarasota (Fla.) Sr. High Sch., 1963-64, prin., 1964-68; dir. staff development Sarasota Dist. Schs., 1968-70, asst. supt., 1970-71, supt., 1971-80; dir. human resources Sarasota Meml Hosp., 1980-83; owner, broker Pillot Realty, Sarasota, 1986-90; commr. Sarasota City, 1989-2001, vice mayor, 1992-93, 96-97, 99-2000, mayor, 1993-94, 97-98, 2000-2001. Prof. Am. Assn. Sch. Adminstrn., Nat. Acad. Sch. Execs., 1969-73; adj. prof. U. South Fla., Tampa, 1978-81; pvt. cons. edn. orgns., 1969-76. Author (chpt.) Differentiated Staffing, Strategies for D.S., 1971; contbr. articles to profl. jours. Trustee Fla. Sch. Deaf/Blind, St. Augustine, 1980—89, chmn. bd. trustees, 1986—89; active Civil Svc. Bd., Sarasota, 1984—89; mem. adv. bd. Cath. Social Svcs., 1987—89; bd. dirs. Riverview Found., 1985—94, Girls Club, Sarasota, 1985—89, Hospice Found., Sarasota Opera Assn., Sarasota Mil. Acad., 2001—. Mem.: Phi Delta Kappa (Educator of Yr. 1980). Republican. Roman Catholic. Avocations: genealogy, ballroom dancing. Home: 10060 Cherry Hills Avenue Cir Bradenton FL 34202 E-mail: gpillot@aol.com.

**PILLSBURY, GEORGE STURGIS,** retired investment advisor; b. Crystal Bay, Minn., July 17, 1921; s. John S. and Eleanor (Lawler) P.; m. Sally Whitney, Jan. 4, 1947; children: Charles Alfred, George Sturgis, Sarah Kimball, Katharine Whitney. BA, Yale U., 1943. Mem. Lafayette Club, Woodhill Club, Minnetonka Yacht Club, Mpls. Club, River Club (NYC). Home: 1300 Bracketts Point Rd Wayzata MN 55391-9393 Office: 601 Carlson Pkwy Ste 800 Minnetonka MN 55305 Office Phone: 612-596-3276. E-mail: gspbury@aol.com.

**PILLSBURY, HAROLD CROCKETT, III,** otolaryngologist; b. Balt., Dec. 5, 1947; m. Carol Higgins Pillsbury; children: Matthew, Benjamin, Thomas. BA, George Washington U., Washington, 1970, MD, 1972. Diplomate Nat. Bd. Med. Examiners, Am. Bd. Otolaryngology; lic. Conn., N.C. Resident gen. surgery U. N.C., Chapel Hill, 1972-73, resident otolaryngology, 1973-76; fellow Kantonsspital, Zurich, Switzerland, 1977; asst. prof. otolaryngology Yale U., New Haven, Conn., 1977-81, assoc. prof. otolaryngology, 1981-82;

assoc. prof. surgery, otolayngology, head and neck surgery U. N.C. Sch. Medicine, Chapel Hill, 1982-86, prof. surgery, otolaryngology, head and neck surgery, 1986—, Thomas J. Dark Disting. Prof., 1991—. Civilian cons. USAF Surgeon Gen. for Otolaryngology-Head and Neck Surgery, 1993; hon. guest lectr. Alpha Omega Alpha Induction Ceremonies, U. N.C., Chapel Hill, 1990, 91, Sch. of Medicine Commencement Ceremony, U. N.C., 1990. Alpha Omega Alpha Induction Ceremonies, U. W. Va., 1991; Boies lectr. and prof. U. Minn. Dept. Otolaryngology, 1992, Whitehead lectr. Whitehead Med. Soc., U. N.C., 1994. Countbr. numerous articles to profl. jours. Recipient John A Kirchner Tchg. award, 1980, Harris Mosher award Am. Laryngological, Rhinological and Otological Soc., 1986. Mem. Am. Acad. Otolaryngology-Head and Neck Surgery (pres. elect 1997, Honor award 1985, Disting. Svc. award 1994), Am. Bd. Otolaryngology (bd. dirs., past pres., current pres. bd. dirs.), Alpha Omega Alpha. Office: U NC Dept Otolaryngology Head & Neck Surgery 1115 Bioinformatics Bldg 130 Mason Farm Rd CB # 7070 Chapel Hill NC 27599-7070 Office Phone: 919-966-8926.*

**PILNICK, GARY H.,** food products executive, lawyer; b. Forest Hills, N.Y., Sept. 17, 1964; m. Helen Pilnick. Grad., Lafayette Coll., 1986; law degree with honors, Duke U., 1989. Atty. Jenner and Block, Chgo., 1989—95; v.p., chief corp. counsel Specialty Foods Corp., 1995—97; chief counsel corp. devel. and fin. Sara Lee Corp., 1997—99; v.p., chief counsel Sara Lee Branded Apparel, 1999—2000; v.p., dep. gen. counsel, asst. sec. Kellogg Co., 2000—03, sr. v.p., gen. counsel corp. devel., sec., 2003—. Office: Kellogg Co Box 3599 1 Kellogg Sq Battle Creek MI 49016-3599 E-mail: gary.pilnick@kellogg.com.

**PILOUS, BETTY SCHEIBEL,** medical/surgical nurse; b. Cleve., July 30, 1948; d. Raymond W. and Dorothy E. (Groth) S.; m. Lee Alan Pilous, Sept. 11, 1970; 1 child. Diploma in nursing, Huron Rd. Hosp., Cleve., 1970; BSBA, St. Joseph's Coll., 1989, MHSA, 1996. RN, Ohio; CPHQ. Nurse Huron Rd. Hosp., Cleve., 1970-71, Hillcrest Hosp., Cleve., 1974-77; head nurse, relief supr. Oak Park Hosp., Oakwood, Ohio, 1977-81; head nurse med.-surg. Bedford Hosp., Ohio, 1981-87; dir. inpatient svcs. Meridia Euclid Hosp., Euclid, Ohio, 1987-93. Coord. hosp. info. system for nursing, chair nurse practice com., los com. nursing liaison; DON, Meridia Res.; dir. clin. svcs. Total Health, 1998, dir. HCQIP, Ohio, 1999, dir. Post Acute Svcs., 2001-; dir. cmty.based svcs. Ohio KePRO, 2005—. Former instr. ARC; chair nurse practice com. Am. Heart Assn.; mem. nursing standards com. Cmty. Hosp. of Bedford; mem. health and safety com. Twinsburg Schs., Ohio, 1984, mem. curriculum com., 1981-83; chairperson standards com. Cmty. Hosp. of Bedford; former counselor jr. high youth 1st Congl. Ch., Twinsburg; past chair adv. bd. chairperson Brecksville Rainbow Assembly for Girls, 1992; mem. Twinsburg Libr. Levy Com., 1991; mem. Gov.'s Task Force on Compassionate Care, 2003-04. Recipient Paradiam award, 1991. Mem. Ohio Citizen League Nursing Nurse Execs. Network (former sec.), Ohio Hosp. Assn., Ohio Orgn. Nurse Execs., Ohio Directors of Nursing Assocs. Long Term Care, Nat. League Nursing, Southeast Cleve. Mid Mgrs. Ohio Orgn. Nurse Exec., Acad. Med.-Surg. Nursing (charter mem.), Networking Group Nurse Mgrs. (initiated), Order Eastern Star, Sigma Theta Tau, Iota Psi. Avocations: hiking, helping children. Office Phone: 216-447-9604. Personal E-mail: bpilous@aol.com.

**PILSON, MICHAEL EDWARD QUINTON,** oceanography educator; b. Ottawa, Ont., Can., Oct. 25, 1933; came to U.S. 1958; s. Edward Charles and Frances Amelia (Ferguson) P.; m. Joan Elaine Johnstone, July 6, 1957; children: Diana Jane, John Edward Quinton. BSc, Bishops U., Lennoxville, Que., Can.; MSc, McGill U., Montreal, Que., Can., 1958; PhD, U. Calif., San Diego, 1964. Chemist Windsor Mills (Can.) Paper Co., 1954-55; asst. chemist Macdonald Coll. of McGill U., 1955-58; biologist Zool. Soc. San Diego, 1963-66; asst. prof. U. R.I., Narragansett, 1966-71, assoc. prof., 1971-78, prof., 1978-2000, prof. emeritus, 2000—. Dir. Marine Ecosystems Rsch. Lab., Narragansett, 1976-97. Contbr. articles to profl. and popular jours.; author chpts. for 6 books, 1 textbook. Grantee NSF, NOAA, EPA, NIH. Mem. AAAS, AGU, ASLO, Oceanography Soc., Am. Soc. Mammalogists, Saunderstown Yacht Club (bd. govs. 1974-87, commodore 1985-87), Brome Cougar Spotters (pres. emeritus). Home: PO Box 27 Saunderstown RI 02874-0027 Office: U RI Grad Sch Oceanography Narragansett RI 02882 Office Phone: 401-874-6104. E-mail: pilson@gso.uri.edu.

**PILZ, ALFRED NORMAN,** manufacturing executive; b. Evergreen Park, Ill., Oct. 12, 1931; s. Alfred and Erma Louise (Deane) P.; m. Constance Ney, Nov. 1957; children: Kerry, Kurt, Stephen, Matthew. BS, Ill. Inst. Tech., 1953; MBA, Harvard U., 1960. Registered profl. engr., Mass. Indsl. engr. Harnischfeger Corp., Milw., 1956-58; cons. Arthur D. Little Co., Cambridge, Mass., 1959-60; asst. to exec. v.p., mgr. prodn. engrng. Nat. Forge Co., Irvine, Pa., 1960-62; mgmt. cons. McKinsey & Co., N.Y.C. and Cleve., 1962-67; pres., gen. mgr. Ajax Iron Works div. Cooper Industries, Corry, Pa., 1967-72; pres., chief exec. officer WDP, Inc., 1972-79, Swank Refractories Co., Johnstown, Pa., 1972-77, Hyde Park (Pa.) Foundry & Machine Co., 1974-79, Shepard-Niles Corp., Montour Falls, NY, 1979-82, Acco Babcock Materials Handling, Frederick, Md., 1982-85; pmr. Fagan and Co., Ligonier, Pa. Bd. dirs. Acco Babcock, Inc., Babcock Internat., Chemung Foundry, Parnell Precision Products Co., Carre-Orban and Partners, Liberty Mut. Ins. Co., Ind. Steel and Engring. Corp., Bedford Crane Co., Shepard Niles Corp., Marine Bank, WDP, Inc., Ligonier Valley (Pa.) R.R. Soc.; chmn. Parnell Precision Products, 1980-82, Ind. Steeland Engring., Bedford Crane Co., 1981-82, pres., chmn., CEO, Greenway Products. With USN, 1948—56, Korea. Mem.: Ligonier Railroad Hist. Soc., Petroleum Equipment Supplies Assn., Modern R.R. Industry Assn., Conveyor Equipment Mfg. Assn., Hoist Mfrs. Assn., Crane Mfrs. Assn., Ligonier A.R. Hist. Soc., Nat. Trust Soc., Ft. Ligonier Assn., Navy League, Tin Can Sailors Assn., Auburn-Cord-Duesenberg Club, HYP (Pitts.). Home: 139 Ramsey Rd Ligonier PA 15658-2204 Office: 223 E Main St Ligonier PA 15658-1347 Personal E-mail: greenwayproducts@verizon.net.

**PIMENTEL, BENJAMIN IMPELIDO,** journalist; b. Manila, Philippines, June 20, 1964; s. Benjamin C. and Isabel (Impelido) P.; m. Maria Teresita Torres, Dec. 23, 1992. BA in Polit. Sci., U. The Philippines, 1985; M.Journalism, U. Calif., Berkeley, 1993. Staff writer Nat. Midweek mag., Manila, 1986-89; gen. assignment, Asian Am. affairs and transp. reporter San Francisco Chronicle, 1993—. Author: Rebolusyon: A Generation of Struggle in the Philippines, 1991; writer, prodr. Toxic Sunset: On The Trail of Hazardous Waste from Subic and Clark, Philippine Ctr. for Investigative Journalism, Manila, 1993. Mem. Asian Am. Journalists Assn. Office: San Francisco Chronicle 901 Mission St San Francisco CA 94103-2905

**PIMENTEL, DAVID,** entomologist, educator; b. Fresno, Calif., May 24, 1925; s. Frank and Marion V. (Sylva) P.; m. Marcia R. Hutchins, July, 16, 1949; children: Christina, Susan, Mark David. Student, St. John's U., Collegeville, Minn., 1943, Clark U., summer 1946; BS, U. Mass., 1948; PhD, Cornell U., 1951. Chief tropical rsch. lab. USPHS, San Juan, chief tropical research lab. P.R., 1951-54, project leader tech. devel. lab Savannah, Ga., 1954-55; postdoctoral investigator U. Chgo., winters 1954-55; postdoctoral investigator, OEEC rsch. fellow Oxford (Eng.) U., 1961; postdoctoral investigator, NSF computer scholar MIT, Cambridge, summer 1961; mem. faculty Cornell U., 1955—, prof. insect ecology, 1963-76, head dept. entomology and limnology, 1963-69, prof. entomology, ecology and systematics, 1969-76, prof. insect ecology and agrl. scis., 1976—; prof., core faculty Center Environ. Quality Mgmt., 1973-74. Cons. Office Sci. and Tech., Exec. Office Pres., 1964-67, 1969-70, EPA, 1971; co-chmn. Commn. on Mosquito Control for Developing Countries, Nat. Acad. Scis., 1972-73; mem. commn. on pesticides and pest mgmt. in Inter-Am., 1973-77; mem. Nat. Adv. Coun. on Environ. Edn., 1973-74; chmn. panel on environ. impact of herbicides EPA, 1972-74, pesticide adv. coun., 1975-78; nat. adv. coun. environ. edn. Office Edn., HEW, 1975-78, chmn., 1975; chmn. study team on interdependence of food, population, health, energy, and environment World Food and Nutrition Study, Nat. Acad. Scis., 1976-77, chmn. environ. studies bd., 1980-83, mem. Opportunities in Agrl. Rsch. com., 2001—; mem. energy rsch. adv. bd. Dept. Energy, 1979-85; mem. rsch. adv. com. USAID, 1979-82,

chmn. panel on land productivity; mem. Office of Tech. Assessment, U.S. Congress, 1979-80; hon. prof. Inst. Applied Ecology, Shengang, China, 1995—. Assoc. editor Am. Midland Naturalist; contbr. articles to profl. jours. Trustee Village of Cayuga Heights, 1974—2002; pres. Rachel Carson Coun., 2001—. Served to 2d lt., pilot USAAF, 1943-45. Recipient Disting. Svc. award Rural Sociol. Coun., 1992, Rachel Carson award Soc. Environ. Toxicology and Chemistry, 2002. Mem. AAAS (climate com. 1979-82, population, resource and environ. com. 1985-91, chmn. subcom. on food, population, and resources 1986-87), NAS (chmn. panel on biology and renewable resources, exec. bd. com. on life scis. 1966-68, com. on world food, health and population 1974-75, chmn. panel on econ. and environ. aspects of pest mgmt. in Ctrl. Am. 1974-76, chmn. bd. on sci. and tech. for internat. devel. 1975-79, com. on food and food prodn 1974-76, alt. agr. com. 1985-89, com. on role of alt. farming methods in modern productive agr. 1985-89), Entomol. Soc. Am. (gov. bd., chmn. editl. bd., pres. Eastern br. 1974-75), Ecol. Soc. Am., Am. Soc. Naturalists, Soc. Study of Evolution, Entomol. Soc. Can., Am. Soc. Zoologists, Nat. Geog. Soc. (com. on rsch. and explorations 1993-2000), Internat. Union for Conservation of Nature and Natural Resources (commn. on ecology 1981-90), Royal Swedish Acad. Scis. (bd. dirs. Beijer Inst. 1994-2000), Chinese Acad. Scis. (hon. prof., acad. com. Inst. Applied Ecology 1994—), Am. Inst. Biol. Scis. (bd. dirs. 1999—), Nat. Audubon Soc. (bd. dirs. 2000-02), Rachel Carson Coun. (pres. 2001—), Sigma Xi, Phi Kappa Phi, Gamma Alpha (nat. recorder 1960-62, AIBS bd. 1999—). Office: Cornell U Dept Ecology Comstock Hall Ithaca NY 14853

**PIMLEY, KIM JENSEN,** financial training consultant; b. Abington, Pa., Apr. 29, 1960; d. Alvin Christian Jensen and Helen Marie (Kairis) Meinken; m. Michael St. John Pimley, Nov. 10, 1988; 1 child, Oliver Jensen Pimley. BA, Emory U., 1982, MA magna cum laude, 1982; postgrad., U. Chgo., 1985—. Mgr. tng. ops. Continental Bank, Chgo., 1986-88, mgr. coll. rels., 1988-90; mgr. client svcs. The Globecon Group, NYC, 1990-92; prin. Pimley & Pimley, Inc., Princeton, NJ, 1992-93; pres. P&P Tng. Resources, Inc., Princeton, 1993—. Owner Jr. League Designer Showhouse, 1997. Contbr. poetry to various jours. Trustee Dem. Com., 1997—; chmn. silent auction Princeton Friends Sch., 2002-04; trustee Opera Festival NJ, 2000-03; bd. dirs./v.p. fin. Jewish Ctr. Princeton, 1999—, pres. 2004-05; bd. dirs. Princeton Healthcare Sys. Found., 2005—, United Jewish Fedn., Princeton, Mercer, Bucks, 2006; co-chmn. Nov. night, 2006. Scholarship U. Chgo., 1984. Mem. ACLU (NJ bd. dirs.), Oxford Club, Cambridge Club, Nassau Club. Office: P&P Tng Resources Inc 117 Library Pl Princeton NJ 08540-3019

**PIMM, STUART L.,** ecology educator; b. Derbyshire, England, Feb. 27, 1949; naturalized, U.S. m. Julia Killeffer, June 2, 1990; 2 children. BA second class honors, Oxford, England, 1971; PhD, New Mex. State Univ., 1974. Asst. prof. Clemson Univ., SC, 1974—75, Tex. Tech Univ., Lubbock, 1975—79, assoc. prof., 1979—82; assoc. prof. ecology and evolutionary biology Univ. Tenn., Knoxville, 1982—86, prof., 1986—99, Columbia Univ., NYC, 1999—2002; Doris Duke chair of conservation ecology Duke Univ., NC, 2002—. Vis. prof. Griffith Univ., Queensland, Australia, 1983—84, Inst. for Nonlinear Sci., Univ. Calif., San Diego, 1987, Sch. of Ecosystem Mgmt., Univ. New Eng., Australia, 1987, Ctr. for Population Biology, Imperial Coll., Silwood Park, England, 1990, Mammal Rsch. Inst., Pretoria, South Africa, 1996, Pretoria, 2000; sr. vis. scholar Nat. Rsch. Coun., 1995; disting. assoc. in rsch. Bernice P. Bishop Mus., Honolulu, 1997—. Contbr. articles to profl. journals. Named one of world's most highly cited scientists, Inst. Sci. Info. 2002; recipient Pew Fellowship, 1993—96, Kemp prize for disting. ecologists, 1994, Aldo Leopold Leadership Fellow, 1999. Fellow: Am. Acad. Arts & Sci. Office: Nicholas Sch Environ and Earth Sci Duke Univ Box 90328 Durham NC 27708 Office Phone: 919-613-8000. Office Fax: 919-684-8741.

**PINAC, ANDRÉ LOUIS, III,** obstetrician, gynecologist; b. New Orleans, Dec. 8, 1955; s. André Louis Jr. and Patricia Elaine (Ledet) P.; 1 child, Amy Elizabeth. BS, U. Southwestern La., 1977; MD, La. State U., New Orleans, 1981. Diplomate Am. Bd. Ob-Gyn. Resident ob-gyn La. State U. Affiliated Hosps., New Orleans, Lafayette, Lake Charles and Baton Rouge, 1981-85; practice medicine specializing in ob-gyn Opelousas, La., 1985—; chief of staff Doctor's Hosp. Opelousas, 1993-94. Participant Cmty. Health Fair, Opelousas, 1987—; bd. dirs. Drs. Hosp. of Opelousas. Safety officer St. Landry Parish; bd. dirs. Little League, 1992-94. Named Duke at Mardi Gras Festival, Opelousas Garden Club. 1994, King Mardi Gras Ball Masque King Orme, 1999. Fellow Am. Coll. Ob-Gyn; mem. AMA, So. Med. Assn., La. State Med. Soc., St. Landry Parish Med. Soc., Opelousas Cath. Soccer Assn. (pres. 1991-93), Alpha Phi Alpha (life), Sigma Alpha Epsilon. Roman Catholic. Avocations: golf, jogging, swimming, basketball, trivia. Office: 816 Cresswell Ln Ste 1 Opelousas LA 70570-5881

**PINCETIC, JOSE E.,** information technology executive; BS in Civil Engring., Univ. Chile; MBA, Univ. Dayton, 1983. Joined NCR, 1969, various positions from sales to mfg. and engring. dir., Latin Am. to mktg. dir., fin. sys. dir., Latin Am., gen. mgr. Brazil and area v.p., Caribbean; now area v.p., Caribbean, Latin Am. fin. solutions divsn. NCR Payment Solutions, Dayton, Ohio. Named one of 50 Most Important Hispanic in Tech., Bus., Hispanic Engineer and Info. Tech. mag., 2005. Office: NCR Payment Solutions 1700 S Patterson Blvd Dayton OH 45479 Office Phone: 937-445-1936.

**PINCHIN, JANE,** literature educator; BA, SUNY, Binghamton, 1964; MA, Columbia U., 1965, PhD, 1973. Instr. Bklyn. Coll., 1966—67; Thomas A. Bartlett Chair and prof. English Colgate U., Hamilton, NY, 1969—, interim pres., 2001—02, v.p. academic advancement, 2002—04. Author: Alexandria Still: Forster, Durrell and Cavafy, 1977; contbr. articles to profl. jours., chpts. to books. Office: Colgate U 306 B Lawrence Hall Hamilton NY 13346*

**PINCHING, DEBORAH ANNE ODELL,** special education educator; b. Travis AFB, California, June 28, 1954; d. John R. and Ruth A. (Patchell) Dawson; married, Jan. 6, 1996. BS in edn., N.Mex. State U., Las Cruces, N. Mex., 1976; post grad., U. N.Mex., 1991. Cert. in elem. and spl. edn. teaching, N.Mex. Tchg. asst. Las Cruces Pub. Sch., Las Cruces, N.Mex., 1976-77; tchr. spl. edn. Ft. Stanton Sch. and Hosp., N.Mex., 1977-79; Carlsbad Mcpl. Sch., N.Mex., 1979—2004. Ednl. assistive technologist Carlsbad Mcpl. Sch., 1991-2004; owner Deb's Techs., 1994—; instr. assistive tech. tchg. courses U. N.Mex., Albuquerque, 1992; presenter at profl. conf.; ret., 2004. Foster parent trainer, N.Mex. Human Svc. Dept., Carlsbad, N Mex., 1988-91, foster parent, 1984-91. Mem.: NEA (bd. mem.), Choices (bd. mem.), Coun. Exceptional Children, Pilot Club Internat. Mem.Nazarene. Avocations: crocheting, computer programming, cooking. Home: PO Box 3190 Carlsbad NM 88221-3190 E-mail: dpinching@hotmail.com.

**PINCHOT, DANIEL J.,** director; s. John P. and Joanne S. Pinchot; m. Jacqueline M. Kayla; children: Evan M., Allyson M. BA in Journalism, Speech Comm., Pa. State U., 1991, MEd in Tchg. and Curriculum, 2004. Cert. secondary edn., comms. and English tchr. Pa., 1998. Staff reporter Beaver County Times, Pa., 1992—97; freelance corr. Pitts. Post-Gazette, 1997—98; asst. dir. of univ. rels. Pa. State Beaver, Monaca, 1997—2001, dir. of enrollment, 2001— Mem. Beaver County Tourism Adv. Bd., Pa., 2000—06. Mem.: Nat. Assn. of Coll. Admissions Counseling, Pa. Assn. of Coll. Admissions Counseling. Office: Pa State Beaver 100 University Dr Monaca PA 15061 Office Phone: 724-773-3800.

**PINCHUK, ANATOLIY OLEKSIJOVYCH,** physicist; b. Chernigiv, Ukraine, July 26, 1969; s. Oleksij and Oleksandra Pinchuk; m. Lesya Viktorivna Fedorenko, Jan. 22, 1995; children: Pavlo, Mariya. Diploma, Taras Shevchenko Nat. U., 1995; degree, Inst. Surface Chemistry, 1999. Registered profl. engr. Rsch. fellow Inst. Surface Chemistry, Kyiv, Ukraine, 1997—99, Kyiv (Ukraine) Nat. Taras Shevchenko U., 1999—2002, docent, 2000—02; fellow I. Physikalisches Inst. Rwth, Aachen, Germany, 2002—. Master sgt. anti-aircraft defence Russian Army, 1988—90. Recipient award, NAS of Ukraine, 2000; Alexander von Humboldt fellow, 2002—. Home: Melatener Str 33 Aachen 52074 Germany Office: IA Physikalisches Institut der RWTH

Sommerffeldstr 18 Aachen 52056 Germany Office Phone: +49(0241)8027208. Personal E-mail: anatoly_pinchuk@hotmail.com. Business E-Mail: pinchuk@physik.rwth-aachen.de.

**PINCKNEY, CHARLES COTESWORTH,** lawyer; b. Richmond, Va., Oct. 23, 1939; s. Thomas and Charlotte (Kent) P.; m. Helen Raney, Aug. 13, 1966; children: Sarah Whitley, Thomas. BA, Yale U., 1961; LLB, U. Va., 1967. Bar: Va. 1967. Assoc. Mays, Valentine, Davenport & Moore, Richmond, 1967-72; ptnr. Mays & Valentine, LLP, Richmond, 1972-2000, Troutman Sanders LLP, Richmond, 2001—. Bd. dirs. Sweet Briar Coll., 1996-2000; pres. Sheltering Arms Hosp., Richmond, 1986-87, bd. dirs., 1970-99, 2004-; trustee William H.-John G.-Emma Scott Found., 1974-, sec., 1994-99, v.p., 1999-2004, pres. 2005-; campaign chmn. United Way Svcs., 1998. Bd. dirs., 1997-. Ensign (j.g.) USNR, 1961-63. Mem. ABA, Va. Bar Assn., Country Club of Va., Commonwealth Club (bd. dirs. 1986-92, pres. 1991-92), Richmond German (pres. 1996-98), Soc. of Cin. Republican. Episcopalian. Home: 2 Roslyn Rd Richmond VA 23226-1610 Office: Troutman Sanders LLP 1001 Haxall Pt PO Box 1122 Richmond VA 23218-1122 Office Phone: 804-697-1383. E-mail: cotes.pinckney@troutmansanders.com.

**PINCKNEY, NEAL T.,** psychologist, retired educator; b. NYC, July 26, 1935; s. Leo Allen and Jean P.; children: Andrew Allen, Jennifer Elizabeth, Matthew Ian. Cert. polit. social and hist. issues, King's Coll., U. Durham, 1957; AB, U. So. Calif., 1958, postgrad., 1958—61; PhD, Oxford U., 1966; postgrad., U. Vienna, U. Hiroshima, Stanford U. Mem. Pub. Welfare Commn., LA County, 1958—60; tchr. pub. schs., LA, 1960—61; tchr., counselor Las Vegas, 1961—62; admininstr. therapist psychiat. clinic, 1962—63; educator, dir. guidance svc. Dept. Def. Overseas Dep. Schs., Eng. and Japan, 1963—67; pvt. practice clin. psychology, 1967—87; lectr. Calif. State U., Sacramento, 1967—68, asst. prof., 1968—71, assoc. prof., 1971—77, prof. psychology and edn., 1977—87, prof. emeritus, 1987—, chmn. dept. behavioral scis., 1980—82, prof. counseling psychology, coord. grad. studies, dept. adminstrn., counseling and policy studies, 1992—; founder, clin. dir. Healing Heart Found., 1993—. Vis. prof. U. Calif.-Davis, 1979—; psychologist, instr. enforcement psychology and human rels. Calif. Hwy. Patrol, 1967-80; dir. Univ. Software Evaluation Project, 1987; tech. cons., adv. Ministry Edn. and Culture, Govt. Brazil, Brasilia, 1974-76; cons. psychologist Calif. Med. Facility, Vacaville, various law enforcement agys.; prof. U. Hawaii, lectr. U. Hawaii, Leeward CC, 1992-93; mem. profl. treatment team Preventive Medicine Rsch. Inst.-Ornish Residential Retreat for Reversing Heart Disease, 1996; sponsor, builder Makaha Chartres Labyrinth; webmaster Healing Heart Website, moderator, sponsor internet discussion group; dir. Judge Rotenberg Ednl. Ctr., 2004-06. Author: Healthy Heart Handbook, 1994, Law and Ethics in Counseling and Psychotherapy, A Casebook, 1961, 86; pub. USER, a Software Report Card, 1987; editor: Ency. of Psychology, 2d edit. Served with 3d Armored Divsn. U.S. Army, 1954-55. Queen's scholar Eng., 1956-57; scholar Dept. State Fgn. Svc. Inst., 1974; fellow Ford Found., 1960-61. Mem. APA, Brit. Psychol. Assn., Japanese Psychol. Assn., Brazilian Psychol. Assn., Am. Ednl. Rsch. Assn., Am. Assn. Counseling and Devel., Am. Radio Relay League (life), Hawaii Personal Computer Users Group (pres. 1989-91, sys. operator Electronic Bulletin Bd. Svc.), Quarter Century Wireless Assn. (life), Vegetarian Soc. of Hawaii (bd. dirs.), No. Calif. DX Club, Hawaii DX Assn., Phi Delta Kappa, Delta Phi Epsilon, Commonwealth Club San Francisco, Oxonian Club Tokyo, Toastmasters (area gov. 1962-63), Mason Home: 1650 Ala Moana Blvd 1601 Honolulu HI 96815-1411 Business E-Mail: heart@kumu.org. *Those who rush through life are merely hurrying toward their death. When one pauses to savor its many subtle varieties one begins to gain some insight and to be in awe of the wonder of it all. Then we begin to place ourselves in perspective and everything has meaning.*

**PINCKNEY, SANDRA,** TV host; b. Calif. m. Benne Herbert (div.); 1 child, Aina. Degree in Sociology and Anthropology, Ithaca Coll., NY, 1970; studied French Cult., Sorbonne; studied, Howard U., U. Pa. News anchor WJZ-TV, Baltimore. Host (TV series) SOS in Am., NBC, 1996, The Hidden Truth, FOX Network, 1996, Blue Ribbon, Turner Broadcasting System, Inc., Food Finds, Food Network, 2000—. Fellow: Code and Rating Bd., Motion Picture Assn. of Am. Avocations: travel, cooking.*

**PINCUS, HOWARD J.,** geologist, engineer, educator; b. NYC, June 24, 1922; s. Otto Max and Gertrude (Jankowsky) Pincus; m. Maud Lydia Roback, Sept. 6, 1953; children: Glenn David, Philip E. BS, CCNY, 1942; PhD, Columbia U., 1949. Rsch. assoc. Lamont Geol. Obs., Columbia U., 1949-51; geologist Ohio Dept. Natural Resources, summers 1950-61; faculty Ohio State U., 1949-67, from instr. to assoc. prof., 1954-59, prof., 1959-67, chmn. dept. geology, 1960-65; rsch. geologist U.S. Bur. Mines, 1963—67, geologist, rsch. supr., 1967-68; prof. geol. sci. and civil engring. U. Wis., Milw., 1968-87, prof. emeritus, 1987—, dean Coll. Letters and Sci., 1969-72; cons. geology and rock mechanics, 1954-67, 68—. Sr. postdoctoral fellow NSF, 1962; mem. U.S. nat. com. tunneling tech. NAE, 1972—74; mem. U.S. nat. com. rock mechanics NAS/NAE, 1975—78, 1980—89, chmn., 1985—87; mem. U.S. com. Internat. Assn. Engring. Geology/NAS, chmn., 1987—90. Tech. editor Geotechnology Testing Jour., 1992—95; mem. editl. bd. Geotechnology Testing Jour., 1996—. Served to 1st lt. CE U.S. Army, 1942—46. Recipient award for tchg. excellence, U. Wis.-Milw. Alumni Assn., 1978. Fellow: AAAS, ASTM (Reinhart award 1987, award of Merit 1989), Geol. Soc. Am. (chmn. engring. geology divsn. 1973—74); mem.: Am. Inst. Profl. Geologists (pres. Ohio sect. 1965—66), Assn. Engring. Geologists, Am. Rock Mechanics Assn., Internat. Soc. Rock Mechanics, Internat. Assn. Engring. Geology, Soc. Mining Engrs., Geol. Soc. Am., Am. Geophysical Union, Sigma Xi, Phi Beta Kappa (pres. Ohio State U. chpt. 1959—60, pres. U. Wis.-Milw. chpt. 1975—77). Home and Office: 17523 Plaza Marlena San Diego CA 92128-1807 Personal E-mail: hpincus@san.rr.com.

**PINCUS, LIONEL I.,** financial executive, entrepreneur; b. Phila., Mar. 2, 1931; s. Henry and Theresa Celia (Levit) P.; m. Suzanne Storrs Poulton (dec.). BA, U. Pa., 1953; MBA, Columbia U., 1956. Assoc. gen. ptnr. Ladenburg, Thalmann & Co., NYC, 1955-63; pres. Lionel I. Pincus & Co., Inc., NYC, 1964-66; pres., CEO E.M. Warburg & Co., Inc., NYC, 1966-70; chmn., CEO E.M. Warburg, Pincus & Co., LLC, 1970—. Trustee NY Presbyn. Hosp.; trustee, chmn. emeritus Columbia U.; trustee Sch. Am. Ballet, German Marshall Fund USA, 1982-88; mem. bd. overseers Columbia Grad. Sch. Bus.; bd. dirs. Am. Mus. Natural History, Nat. Park Found., 1995-01; mem. Partnership for NYC. Mem. Coun. Fgn. Rels., Nat. Venture Capital Assn. (Lifetime award), World Wildlife Fund (nat. coun.), Nat. Golf Links Am. Club, Meadow Club. Office: EM Warburg Pincus & Co LLC 466 Lexington Ave Fl 10 New York NY 10017-3147

**PINCUS, NANCY,** architect, web site designer; d. Samuel and Shirley Pincus; 1 child, Ava Leigh Ichikawa. BArch, The Cooper Union for the Advancement of Sci. and Art, 1986. Project arch. Gensler, N.Y.C., 1994—97; archtl. project cons. HLW Internat., N.Y.C., 1997—2001. Designer, developer, webmaster iHaus.com. Vol. Clinton-Gore Campaign, N.Y., 1991—92. Mem.: DNC. Achievements include development of iHaus.com and Babybytes.net. Avocations: painting, internet, design, writing, politics. Personal E-mail: npincus@optonline.net.

**PINCUS, ROBERT LAWRENCE,** art critic, historian; b. Bridgeport, Conn., June 5, 1953; s. Jules Robert and Carol Sylvia (Rosen) P.; m. Georgianna Manly, June 20, 1981; 1 child, Matthew Manly. BA, U. Calif., Irvine, 1976; MA, U. So. Calif., 1980, PhD, 1987. Instr. writing and Am. studies U. So. Calif., 1978-83; art critic L.A. Times, 1981-85, San Diego Union, 1985-92, San Diego Union-Tribune, 1992—. Vis. prof. art history San Diego State U., 1985-86, 92, lectr. U. San Diego, 1998-. Author: On A Scale That Competes with the World: The Art of Edward and Nancy Reddin Kienholz, 1990; co-author West Coast Duchamp, 1991, But Is It Art: The Spirit of Art as Activism, 1994, Paradise, 1994, Anne Mudge: Traces, 1996, Introduction to W.D.'s Midnight Carnival, 1988, Kitchen: Liza Lou, 1996, Manuel Neri: Early Work, 1953-78, 97, Gordas: Paintings and

Installations by Tania Candiani, 2002; contbr. reviewer, Artweek, 79; corr. editor, Art in America, 1988-. Recipient Ring Truth Prizes, Best Art Story, 1986, 1987, 1988, Chem. Bank award for Disting. Newspaper Art Criticism, 1994, Mo. Lifestyles Journalism award, 2001, Best Critical Writing award, San Diego Press Club, 1994, 2004. Mem. Internat. Assn. Art Critics, Coll. Art Assn. Democrat. Office: San Diego Union Tribune PO Box 120191 350 Camino De La Reina San Diego CA 92108-3003 Office Phone: 619-293-1831. Business E-Mail: robert.pincus@uniontrib.com.

**PINCUS, STEPHANIE HOYER,** dermatologist; b. Lakehurst, NJ, Feb. 28, 1944; d. Ernest Carl and Aviva (Silbert) Hoyer; m. David Frank Pincus, Aug. 22, 1965 (div. Dec. 1984); children: Matthew Jonah, Tamara Hope; m. Allan Roy Oseroff, Mar. 24, 1985; 1 child, Benjamin Henry Oseroff. BA, Reed Coll., 1964; MD cum laude, Harvard U., 1968; MBA, Northwestern U., 1998. Diplomate Am. Bd. Dermatology, Am. Bd. Internal Medicine. Intern Boston City Hosp., 1968-69; rsch. fellow U. Wash., Seattle, 1969-71, resident internal medicine, 1971-72; resident-fellow dermatology U. Washington, Seattle, 1972-74; fellow instr. dept. dermatology Harvard Med. Sch., Boston, 1974-75; asst. prof. medicine U. Wash., Seattle, 1975-77; lectr. Sch. Medicine Boston U., 1977-89; asst. prof. medicine Sch. Medicine Tufts U., Boston, 1977-82, mem. dept. immunology, 1977-89, asst. prof. dermatology, 1979-82, assoc. prof. dermatology and medicine, 1982-89; prof. medicine and dermatology, chairperson dermatology SUNY, Buffalo, 1989-2000; chief acad. affiliations officer Dept. Vets. Affairs, Washington, 2000—. Dermatology Found. fellow, Evanston, Ill., 1974-75, 77-78; Vets. Adminstrn. rsch. assoc., 1975-77; recipient Clin. Investigator award NIH, Bethesda, Md., 1979-81. Mem. Am. Contact Dermatitis Soc. (mem. liaison com., 1993—), Women's Dermatologic Soc. (bd. drs. 1992—), Soc. Investigative Dermatology (chmn. com. on govt. and pub. rels. 1992-96), Profs. of Dermatology (mem. program com. 1993—), Harvard Med. Alumni (pres. 1995-96), Phi Beta Kappa, Alpha Omega Alpha. Office: Dept Vets Affairs Office Acad Affiliations 810 Vermont Ave Washington DC 20420

**PINCUS, THEODORE HENRY,** public relations executive; b. Chgo., Sept. 15, 1933; s. Jacob T. and J. (Engel) Pincus; m. Sharon Barr, Jan. 16, 1988; children: Laura, Mark, Susan, Anne, Jennifer. BS in Journalism, Ind. U., 1955. Free-lance bus. writer, 1955-58; sr. exec. Harshe Rotman & Druck, Chgo., 1958-62; owner Theodore Pincus & Assocs., Chgo., 1962—, prin., owner, 2003—; chmn., CEO Fin. Rels. Bd., Inc., Chgo., 1965-98; vice chmn. BSMG Worldwide divsn. Interpub. Group, N.Y.C., 1998-2001; fin. columnist Chgo. Sun Times, 2002—. Pub. affairs advisor to Nelson Rockefeller, N.Y.C., 1960, N.Y.C., 68; advisor U.S. Info. Agy., 1993—; adj. prof. fin. MBA Sch., DePaul U., 2002—; former mem. adv. bd. NASDAQ; ind. comm. cons., 2003—. Author: Giveaway Day, 1977, On the Offensive, 2001; contbr. articles to profl. jours. including Wall St. Jour., Fortune and N.Y. Times. Active presdl. nomination campaigns; vice-chmn. Midwest Region Am. Jewish Com.; mem. adv. bd. Ind. U. Bus. Sch., The Ill. Coalition. With USAF, 1955—57. Named Entrepreneur of Yr., Ernst and Young Merrill Lynch, 1998; recipient numerous nat. awards for profl. excellence in investor rels. and corp. pub. rels., including Silver Anvil award, Pub. Rels. Soc. Am., 1966, Civic Achievement award, Am. Jewish Com., 1993, Pub. Rels. Profl. of Yr., Pub. Rels. Soc. Am., 2002. Mem.: Nat. Investor Rels. Inst. (founding), Young Press.'s Orgn., Union League, Standard Club. Office: 400 E Ohio St Chicago IL 60611-3322 Office Phone: 312-321-1202.

**PINCUS, WALTER HASKELL,** news editor; b. Bklyn., Dec. 24, 1932; s. Jonas and Clare (Glassman) Pincus; m. Betty Meskin, Sept. 12, 1954; 1 child, Andrew John; m. Ann Witsell Terry, May 1, 1965; children: Ward Haskell, Adam Witsell, Cornelia Battle Terry. BA, Yale U., 1954; JD, Georgetown U., 2001. With Wall St. Jour., 1957—58; cons. Senate Fgn. Rels. Com., 1962-63; spl. writer Washington Evening Star, 1963-66; editor, reporter Washington Post, 1966-69; chief cons. Symington subcom. Senate Fgn. Relations Com., 1969-70; assoc. editor New Republic, 1972-74; exec. editor, 1974-75; spl. writer Washington Post, 1975—; cons. NBC News, 1971-79, CBS News, 1979-86, NBC News, 1987-88, Washington Post Co., 1989—. Vis. lectr. Yale U., 1988, 2002, Stanford U., 2003—. Trustee Shakespeare Theater, 1988—, co-chmn. ed. com., 1989—91, chmn. nominating com., 1992—96, mem. exec. com., 1992—. With U.S. Army, 1955—57. Co-recipient Pulitzer prize, 2001; recipient Page One award, 1960, George Orwell award, 1977, George Polk award, 1978, Emmy award, 1981, Stewart Alsop award, 1999. Mem.: Coun. Fgn. Rels., Yale Club Washington. Home: 3202 Klingle Rd NW Washington DC 20008-3403 Office: Washington Post 1150 15th St NW Washington DC 20071-0001 Office Phone: 202-334-7429. E-mail: pincusw@washpost.com.

**PINCZUK, ARON,** physicist; b. San Martin, Argentina, Feb. 15, 1939; s. Faiwel and Ester (Wejeman) P.; m. Gladys Norma Teitelman, June 14, 1962; children: Ana Gabriela, Guillermo Fabian. Licenciado, U. Buenos Aires, Argentina, 1962; PhD, U. Pa., 1969; D (hon.), U Autonoma, Madrid, 1997. Staff mem. Nat. Rsch. Coun., Argentina, 1971-76; head physics dept. Faculty of Scis., U. Buenos Aires, Argentina, 1974; vis. scientist Max Planck Inst., Stuttgart, Germany, 1976, IBM Rsch., Yorktown Heights, NY, 1976-77; staff mem. Bell Labs., Murray Hill, NJ, 1978—; prof. Columbia U., N.Y.C., 1998—. Sec. Argentina Phys. Soc., Buenos Aires, 1972-75; editor Solid State Communications, 1989-92, assoc. editor in chief, 1992-2004, editor in chief, 2005—. Contbr. over 200 articles to profl. jours. and numerous chpts. to books. Recipient Oliver E. Buckley Condensed-Matter Physics prize Am. Physical Soc., 1994. Fellow: AAAS, Am. Phys. Soc. Achievements include use and devel. novel optical methods in studies of structural phase transitions, semiconductor interfaces and interactions of free electrons in semiconductors; discovered novel phenomena in studies of quantum electron fluids. Office: Columbia U Dept Physics and Applied Physics New York NY 10027 Office Phone: 212-854-6033. Business E-Mail: aron@phys.columbia.edu.

**PINDELL, HOWARDENA DOREEN,** artist; b. Phila., Apr. 14, 1943; d. Howard Douglas and Mildred Edith (Lewis) P. BFA, Boston U., 1965; MFA, Yale U., 1967; DFA (hon.), Mass. Coll. Art, 1997, New Sch./Parsons Sch. Design, 1999. Curatorial asst. Mus. Modern Art, N.Y.C., 1969-71, asst. curator, 1971-77, asso. curator dept. prints and illus. books, 1977-79; asso. prof. art SUNY, Stony Brook, 1979-84, prof. art, 1984—. Contbr. articles to profl. jours.; exhbns. include. Mus. Modern Art, Stockholm and 5 European mus., 1973, Fogg Art Mus., Cambridge, Mass., 1973, Indpls. Mus., Taft Mus., Cin., 1974, Gerald Piltzer Gallery, Paris, 1975, Mus. Modern Art, Paris, 1975, Vassar Coll. Art Gallery, 1977; represented in permanent collections, Mus. Modern Art, N.Y.C., Fogg Art Mus., Met. Mus., N.Y.C., Whitney Mus. Am. Art; represented in travelling exhbns. Brandeis U., U. Calif. at Riverside, Cleve. Inst. Arts, SUNY, Potsdam, New Paltz, Wesleyan U., Davison Art Ctr., others. Recipient Artist award Studio Mus. of Harlem, 1994, Joan Mitchell Painting award Joan Mitchell Found., 1994/95, Women's Caucus for Art award for Disting. Contbns. and Achievement in Arts, 1996, Cmty. Svc. award N.Y. State United Tchrs., 1998, Juneteenth award Heckscher Mus., 1999, IAM Pioneer award, 2000; Japan/U.S. Friendship fellow, 1981-82, Guggenheim fellow, 1987-88; Ariana Found. grantee, 1984-85. Mem. Arts Coun. African Studies Assn., Coll. Art Assn. (Best Exhbn./Performance award 1990), Internat. Art Critics Assn. Home: House of Japan (acad.). Office: SUNY/Stonybrook Art Dept Stony Brook NY 11794-0001 Office Phone: 631-632-7266. Office Fax: 631-632-7261. Business E-Mail: hpindell@notes.cc.sunysb.edu.

**PINDER, GEORGE FRANCIS,** engineering educator, research scientist; b. Windsor, Ont., Can., Feb. 6, 1942; s. Percy Samuel and Stella Marie P.; m. Phyllis Marie Charlton, Sept. 14, 1963; children— Wendy Marie, Justin George. B.Sc., U. Western Ont., 1965; PhD, U. Ill., 1968. Research hydrologist U.S. Geol. Survey, 1968-72; mem. faculty dept. civil engring. Princeton U., 1972-89, prof., 1972-89, chmn. dept., from 1980, dir. water resources program, 1987-89; dean Coll. Engring. and Math. U. Vt., Burlington, 1989-96, dir. Rsch. Ctr. for Groundwater Remediation Design, 1993—; disting. prof. Coll. Engring. and Math., 2005—. Recipient O.E. Meinzer award Geol. Soc. Am., 1975, WUC medal, 1992; U. Vt. Univ. scholar, 1993.

Fellow Am. Geophys. Union (Robert E. Horton award 1969,), Wessex Inst.; mem. ASCE (Julian Hinds medal 2002), Am. Geophys. Union. Home: 188 Bishop Rd Shelburne VT 05482-6933 Office: U Vt Coll Engring And Math Burlington VT 05405-0001

**PINDER, RENEE MONIQUE,** diplomat; b. Nassau, Bahamas, Nov. 21, 1967; arrived in U.S., 1999; d. Harcourt Maxwell and Hazel Mae Pinder. BSc, Ga. Coll., 1994; MBA, U. Miami, 1996; cert. in Spanish, Coll. of the Bahamas, 1997; diplomatic tng. cert., Santiago, Chile, 1999. Clk. Min. Fgn. Affairs, Nassau, The Bahamas; exec. officer Passport Office, Nassau, The Bahamas, 1986—96, supr.; adminstrv. cadet Min. Fgn. Affairs, Nassau, The Bahamas, 1996—99, asst. sec., 1999—, vice consul Miami, 1999—, N.Y., 2002—. Mem. Fgn. Affairs Investigative, Nassau, 1996—99, Diplomatic Corps. Com., Miami, 1999—. Active Bahamas Red Cross Soc., 1994— Mem.: Delta Sigma Theta (pres. 1993—94). Office: Bahamas Consulate Gen 25 SE 2nd Ave Ste 818 Miami FL 33131-1540 E-mail: bcg@bellsouth.net.

**PINDLE, ARTHUR JACKSON, JR.,** philosopher, researcher; b. Macon, Ga., May 26, 1942; s. Arthur Jackson Sr. and Beatrice Rosetta (Williams) P.; 1 child, Zhinga D. BS in Physics, Morehouse Coll., 1964; MA in Philosophy, Yale U., 1973, MPhil, 1974, PhD in Philosophy, 1978. Physicist IBM, Inc., Poughkeepsie, NY, 1964, Naval Ordinance Station, Indian Head, Md., 1966-69, Satellite Experiment Lab, Suitland, Md., 1970-71; philosophy prof. Fayetteville (N.C.) State U., 1974-83; pres. HRG, Inc., New Orleans, 1983—; dir. rsch. NITRT, Inc., New Orleans, 1993—; pres. Grael Electronics, Inc., 1998; prof. philosophy Spelman Coll., 2006. Mem. bd. advs. Inst. Philosoph. Rsch., Boulder, Colo., 1980-83. Contbr. articles to profl. jours.; patentee personal computer console. Mem. Dem. Nat. Com., 1993-98. Avocations: yoga, chess. Home: 250 10th St NE Apt 3402 Atlanta GA 30309 Personal E-mail: apindle@netscape.net.

**PINDYCK, BRUCE EBEN,** lawyer, corporate financial executive; b. N.Y.C., Sept. 21, 1945; s. Sylvester and Lillian (Breslow) P.; m. Mary Ellen Schwartz, Aug. 18, 1968; children: Ashley Beth, Eben Spencer, Blake Michael Lawrence. AB, Columbia U., 1967, JD, 1970, MBA, 1971. Bar: N.Y. 1971, Wis. 1987. Assoc. Olwine, Connelly, Chase, O'Donnell & Weyher, N.Y.C., 1971-80; asst. gen. counsel Peat, Marwick, Mitchell & Co., N.Y.C., 1980-82; ptnr. Hollyer, Jones, Pindyck, Brady & Chira, N.Y.C., 1983-87; pres., CEO Meridian Industries, Inc., Milw., 1985—, also chmn. bd. dirs.; CEO Majilite Corp., Dracut, Mass., 1987—, also chmn. bd. dirs. Mem. capital campaign com. Columbia U., 1984-87. Mem. bd. visitors Columbia Coll., 2001—; bd. dirs. Harambee Cmty. Sch., 1991—96, Milw. Ballet Co., 1993—97, Milw. Pub. Mus. 1994—98, The Private Bank, Milw., 2005—, Jr. Achievement, 2005—. Mem. Columbia Coll. Alumni Assn. (regional dir. 1988-94, v.p. 1994-98, exec. com., 1994-98), World Press.'s Orgn. Office: 100 E Wisconsin Ave Milwaukee WI 53202-4107 Office Phone: 414-224-0610. E-mail: bpindyck@meridiancompanies.com.

**PINDYCK, FRANK,** surgeon; b. N.Y., June 8, 1940; s. Sylvester and Lillian Pindyck; m. Suzanne Hock, Mar. 18, 1972; children: Lindsay Jane, Jennifer Sarah, Stephanie Lyn Pundyck-Constantino. AB, Princeton (N.J.) U., 1962; MD, SUNY, 1966. Diplomate Am. Bd. Surgery, 1977. Intern SUNY King County Med. Ctr., N.Y.C.; resident Mt. Sinai Hosp., N.Y.C.; attending surgeon Huntington Hosp., NY, 1974—2000, chief of surgery NY, 1993—2000; chief surgery VA Hosp., White River Junction, Vt., 2001—; assoc. prof. surgery Dartmouth Med. Sch., Hanover, NH, 2001—. Capt. USAF, 1968—70, Vietnam. Decorated Air Medal with oak leaf cluster USAF. Fellow: ACS; mem.: New Eng. Surg. Soc. Office Phone: 802-295-9363 x 5290. Personal E-mail: frank.pindyck@med.va.gov.

**PINE, BESSIE MIRIAM,** social worker, columnist; b. Toronto, Jan. 6, 1919; d. Moses and Annie (Rosenberg) Hadler; m. Kurt Pine, Mar 24, 1943 (dec. May 1962); children: Alfred Marc, Annie Laurie Reuveni. BA in Psychology, U. Toronto, 1939; M in Social Work, U. Pitts., 1944. Lic. social worker, N.Y. Br. dir. YM-YWHA, Toronto, 1940-42; case worker Family Svc. of Greater New Haven, Conn., 1944-47, Jewish Family Svc., Phila., 1947-49; divsn. unit supr. Ednl. Alliance, N.Y.C., 1949-51; older adult supr. Kings Bay YM-YWHA, Bklyn., 1955-59; editor pers. reporter Jewish Comty Ctr. Program Aids, dir. part time pers. bur., N.Y.C., 1962-67; assoc. dir. pers. svcs. Jewish Comty. Ctrs. Assn., N.Y.C., 1967-93. Editor: (booklet) Viewpoints on Social and Social Work Issues, 1965; author: (rsch. study) Making Retirement Count: Options and Opportunities, 1989; author: (publ.) Looking Back and Looking Forward: A 75 Year Retrospective on the Assn. of Jewish Center Workers, 1993. Recipient Florence G. Heller award Jewish Comty. Ctrs. Assn., N.Y.C., 1994. Mem. Com. to Strengthen Group Work in Jewish Comty. Ctrs. (co-chair 1992-99), Assn. of Jewish Ctr. Profls. (columnist Ask Bessie 1994-2004, Profl. of Yr., Phila. 1990, Tikkun Olam award Balt. 1993), Nat. Assn. Social Workers (cert. social worker). Home: 150 Beaumont St Brooklyn NY 11235-4119

**PINE, CHARLES JOSEPH,** clinical psychologist; b. July 13, 1951; s. Charles E. LaVern (Upton) P.; m. Mary Day, Dec. 30, 1979 (div. 1996); children: Charles Andrew, Joseph Scott, Carolyn Marie; m. Inga Marie Talbert, Feb. 11, 1998. BA in Psychology, U. Redlands, 1973; MA in Psychology, Calif. State U., L.A., 1975; PhD in Clin. Psychology, U. Wash., 1979; postdoc. in Psychology Am. and Indian studies, UCLA, 1981. Diplomate in clin. psych. Am. Bd. Profl. Psychology; lic. psychologist, Calif., Fla. Psychology technician Seattle Indian Health Bd., USPHS Hosp., 1977-78; psychology intern VA Outpatient Clinic, L.A., 1978-79; instr. psychology Okla. State U., 1979-80, asst. prof., 1980; asst. prof. psychology and Native Am. studies program Wash. State U., 1981-82; dir. behavioral health svcs. Riverside-San Bernardino County Indian Health Inc., Banning Calif. 1982-84; clin. psychologist VA Med. Ctr., Long Beach, Calif., 1984-85, clin. psychologist, psychology coord. psychiatry divsn. Sepulveda, Calif., 1985-93; clin. dir. Traumatic Stress Treatment Ctr., Thousand Oaks, Calif., 1985-93; assoc. clin. prof. UCLA Sch. Medicine, 1985-93, Fuller Grad. Sch. Psychology, Pasadena, Calif. 1985-93; pvt. practice Orlando, Fla., 1993-94; rsch. assoc. Nat. Ctr. Am. Indian and Alaska Native Mental Health Rsch., Denver, 1989—; psychologist Vets. Counseling Ctr., San Bernardino, Calif., 1997—2003, clin. coord., 1997—2003; psychologist Calif. Dept. Youth Authority, Norwalk, Calif., 2003—04, psychologist Heman G. Stark Youth Correctional Facility Chino, Calif., 2004—. Adj. assoc. prof. Calif. Sch. Profl. Psychology, L.A., 1989-95; adj. faculty mem. U. Ctrl. Fla., 1993-94; psychologist, adminstrv. coord. alcohol and drug abuse treatment program Orlando VA Outpatient divsn. Tampa VA Med. Ctr., 1993-94; cons. NIH, 1993-96; psychologist stress treatment programs Bay Pines (Fla.) VA Med. Ctr., 1994-96; mem. L.A. County Am. Indian Mental Health Task Force, 1987-92; editl. cons. White Cloud Jour., 1982-85; cons. Dept. HHS, USPHS, NIMH, 1980. Contbr. articles to profl. publs. Vol. worker Variety Boys Clubs Am., 1973-75; coach Rialto Jr. All-Am. Football League, 1974, Conejo Valley Little League, Dr. Phillips Little League, 1993—; coach Conejo Youth Flag Football Assn., pres., 1990; coach, bd. dirs. Westlake Youth Football, 1991-92; co-commn. Dr. Phillips Pop Warner football, 1993—; ret. U.S. Dept. Vet. Affairs, 2003-. Grantee U. Wash. Indian Studies, 1975-76, UCLA Inst. Am. Cultures, 1981-82. Fellow APA (chair task force on svc. delivery to ethnic minority populations bd. ethnic minority affairs 1988, bd. ethnic minority affairs 1985-87); mem. Soc. Indian Psychologists (pres. 1981-83), Nat. Register Health Svc. Providers in Psychology, Calif. Psychol. Assn. Found. (bd. dirs. 1990-92), Soc. for Psychol. Study Ethnic Minority Issues (exec. com. 1987-88, pres. 1995-96), Sigma Alpha Epsilon, Chi Sigma Chi. Roman Catholic.

**PINE, JEFFREY BARRY,** lawyer, former state attorney general; b. N.Y.C., Jan. 10, 1955; s. Henry F. Pine and Irma (Goldberg) Nass; m. Faith Marcia Scavitti, May 20, 1984; children: Bethany Arielle, Jonathan Ian Lee, Jamie Ilysse. BA in Polit. Sci., Haverford Coll., 1976; JD, George Washington U., 1979. Bar: R.I. 1979, Mass. 1979, U.S. Dist. Ct. R.I. 1979, U.S. Supreme Ct. 1994. Asst. atty. gen. R.I. Dept. Atty. Gen., Providence, 1979—89; assoc. atty. Decof & Grimm, Providence, 1990—92; atty. gen. State of R.I., 1993—99; mng. ptnr. Jeffrey B. Pine Esq., Providence, 1999—. Trustee MADD,

1987—2000; mem. Bd. Bar Overseers Mass. Named Top Prosecutor, R.I. Monthly; recipient Beta Rho Sigma award. Mem.: R.I. Trial Lawyers Assn., Assn. Am. Trial Lawyers, R.I. Bar Assn. Home: 349 Wayland Ave Providence RI 02906-4531

**PINE, WILLIAM CHARLES,** foundation executive; b. Canton, Ill., Nov. 4, 1912; s. William Charles and Katherine Pauline (Prichard) P.; m. Virginia Rae Keeley, June 14, 1945; children: William Charles, Barry Scott, Nancy Katherine Pine McMahon. BS, Monmouth Coll., Ill., 1939; DHL (hon.), Southwestern at Memphis, 1961; Dr.Laws (hon.), Mercy Coll. Detroit, 1966. Asst. dir. admissions Monmouth Coll., 1939-42; spl. agt. FBI, 1942-45; assoc. dir. Am. City Bur., N.Y.C. and Chgo., 1945-47; dir. pub. relations Lake Forest (Ill.) Coll., 1947-48, v.p., 1948-51; dir. scholarship prog. Ford Motor Co. Fund., Dearborn, Mich., 1951-72, asst. dir., 1972-75; prog. dir. The Collins Found., Portland, Oreg., 1976-79, exec. v.p., 1979-97; sr. cons. Providence St. Vincent Med. Found., 1997—. Contbr. articles to profl. jours. Mem. Historic Records Adv. Bd., Salem, Oreg., 1984-87. Mem. Soc. Former Spl. Agts. of FBI. Avocations: reading, mail order bus. Office: Providence St Vincent Med Found 9205 SW Barnes Rd Portland OR 97225-6603 Office Phone: 503-216-2198.

**PINEDA, ANSELMO,** neurosurgery educator; b. Lima, Peru, Apr. 3, 1923; s. Anselmo Vicente and Juana (Munayco)P.; m. Monique Yvonne Martin, Mar. 15, 1955; children: Patricia M., Richard A., Gilbert V., Katherine A. MD, San Marcos U., Lima, 1951; MS, Northwestern U., 1962. Diplomate Am. Bd. Neurol. Surgery. Rotating intern Loayza Hosp., Lima, 1950—51; head histology sect. Leprosy dept. Ministry Pub. Health, Lima, 1951; asst. pathologist Nat. Inst. Neoplastic Diseases, 1952; vol. asst. lab. normal and path. histology nervous sys. San Marcos U. Sch. Medicine, 1953; rotating intern gen. surgery Chgo., 1955; jr. asst. resident neurosurgery U. Chgo., 1955—56, sr. asst. resident neurosurgery, 1956—57, chief resident neurosurgery, 1957—58; assoc. instr. neurosurgery U. Tex., 1958—61; assoc. neurosurgeon John Sealy Hosp., Galveston, Tex., 1960—61, attending neurosurgeon, 1961; acting chief neurosurgery VA Hosp., Long Beach, Calif., 1962—63; asst. clin. prof. dept. neurobiology UCLA, 1963—82, assoc. clin. prof. divsn. neuro-biology/neurosurgery, 1982—. Cons. VA Hosp., Long Beach, 1966-67; chmn. Neurosurg. Peruvian American Found. NIH spl. fellow in Neuroanatomy Northwestern U., 1961-62. Fellow ACS, Am. Coll. Angiology, Royal Soc. Medicine; mem. AAUP, AAAS, AMA, Congress of Neurol. Surgeons, World Med. Assn., Am. Assn. Neurol. Surgeons, Calif. Med. Assn., Orange County Med. Assn., Am. Acad. Neurology, Am. Assn. Neuropathologists, Internat. Coll. Surgeons, Am. Assn. Anatomists, Am. Assn. Trauma, Am. Soc. Stereotaxic and Functional Neurosurgery, N.Y. Acad. Scis., Internat. Assn. Study Pain, U. Chgo. Surg. Soc., L.A. Surg. Soc., Sigma Xi. Office: 5267 Warner Ave Ste 301 Huntington Beach CA 92649 Office Phone: 562-787-2641. Personal E-mail: ap92649@aol.com.

**PINEDA, PATRICIA SALAS,** lawyer; BA, Mills Coll., 1974; JD, U. Calif., Berkeley, 1977. Bar: Calif. 1977. Dep. pub. defender Calif. State Pub. Defender, 1977-78; assoc. Crosley Heafy Roach & May, 1978-79; sr. counsel Itel Corp., 1980-84; assoc. gen. counsel New United Motor Mfr., Inc., 1984-88, gen. counsel, asst. corp. sec. Fremont, Calif., 1989—2004; group v.p., corp. comm. gen. counsel Toyota Motor North Am. Inc., 2004—. Dir. Levi Strauss & Co.; trustee Rand Corp. Bd. mem. James Irvine Found., 1994—, bd. vice chair, 2006—. Office: Toyota Motor North America Inc Ste 4900 9 W 57th St New York NY 10019-2701 Office Phone: 212-223-0303.*

**PINELESS, HAL STEVEN,** neurologist; b. Chgo., Oct. 19, 1954; s. William and Sophie (Lubnicka) P.; m. Eddy Dianne Rudnick, Mar. 10, 1985; children: Adam, Emily. BS in Zoology, U. Ill., 1976; DO, Chgo. Coll. Osteo. Medicine, 1981. Diplomate Am. Osteo. Bd. Neurology and Psychiatry. Intern Chgo. Osteo. Hosp., 1981-82; resident Loyola U. Med. Ctr./Hines (Ill.) VA Ctr., 1982-85; asst. prof. neurology Chgo. Coll. Osteo. Medicine, 1985-86; pvt. practice Winter Park, Fla., 1986—. Pres. med staff Fla. Hosp. East Orlando, 1990-93, bd. trustees, 1990-94. Contbr. articles to profl. jours and newspapers. Mem. Am. Osteo. Assn., Am. Acad. Neurology, Am. Coll. Neuropsychiatrists, Nat. Headache Found., Chgo. Coll. of Osteopathic Alumni Assn. (pres. 2000-03). Avocations: golf, swimming, computers, photography. Office: 1890 State Rd 436 Ste 255 Winter Park FL 32792-2285 Office Phone: 407-657-7900.

**PINES, ALEXANDER,** chemistry educator, researcher, consultant; b. Tel Aviv, June 22, 1945; came to US, 1968. US citizen in 1981. s. Michael and Neima (Ratner) P.; m. Ayala Malach, Aug. 31, 1967 (div. 1983); children: Itai, Shani; m. Ditsa Kafry, May 5, 1983; children: Noami, Jonathan, Talia. BSc, Hebrew U., Jerusalem, 1967; PhD in Chemical Physics, MIT, 1972; D (hon.), U. Paris "Pierre et Marie Curie", 1999, U. Rome "La Sapienza", 2001. Asst. prof. chemistry U. Calif., Berkeley, 1972-75, assoc. prof., 1975-80, prof., 1980—, Press.'s chair, 1993-97, Chandellor's rsch. prof., 1997-99, Miller rsch. prof., 1998-99, Glenn T. Seaborg prof. chemistry, 1999—. Faculty sr. scientist materials scis. div. Lawrence Berkeley Nat. Lab., 1975—; cons. Mobil Oil Co., Princeton, N.J., 1980-84, Shell Oil Co., Houston, 1981—; chmn. Bytel Corp., Berkeley, Calif., 1981-85; vis. prof. Weizmann Inst. Sci., 1982; adv. prof. East China Normal U., Shanghai, People's Rep. of China, 1985; sci. adv. Nalorac, Martinez, Calif., 1986-92; Joliot-Curie prof. Ecole Superieure de Physique et Chemie, Paris, 1987; Walter J. Chute Disting. lectr. Dalhousie U., 1989, Charles A. McDowell lectr. U. B.C., 1989, E. Leon Watkins lectr. Wichita State U., 1990; Hinshelwood lectr., U. Oxford, 1990, A.R. Gordon Disting. lectr. U. Toronto, 1990, Venable lectr. U. N.C., 1990, Max Born lectr. Hebrew U. of Jerusalem, 1990; William Draper Harkins lectr. U. Chgo., 1991, Kolthoff lectr. U. Minn., 1991; Md.-Grace lectr. U, Md. 1992; mem. adv bd Nat High Magnetic Field Lab., Inst. Theoretical Physics, U. Calif. Santa Barbara, Ctr. Pure and Applied Math. U. Calif., Berkeley; mem. adv. panel chem. Nat. Sci. Found.; Randolph T. Major Disting. Lectr. U. Conn., 1992; mem. bd. sci. advs. Weizmann Inst. Sci., 1997—; Peter Smith lectr. Duke U., 1993, Arthur William Davidson lect. U. Kansas, 1992, Arthur Birch lect. Australian Nat. U., 1993, Richard C. Lord Meml. lectr. MIT, 1993, Steacie lectr. Nat. Rsch. Coun. Can., 1993, Morris Loeb lectr. Harvard U., 1994, Clarke Boot Found. lectr., U. Nottingham, 1994, Frontiers in Chemistry lectr. Tex. A&M U., 1995, Bergman lectr. Weizmann Inst. Sci., 1995, faculty rsch. lectr. U. Calif., Berkeley, 1996, Raymond & Beverly Sackler lectr. Tel Aviv U., 1996; Priestley lectr. Pa. State U., 1997; Amy Mellon lectr. Purdue U., 1997; Rsch. frontiers chemistry lectr. U. Iowa, 1998, Moses Gomberg lectr. U. Mich., 1998, J and N Max T. Rogers, Mich. State U., 1998, Frontiers in Chemistry lectr., Wayne State U., 1998, Lord Todd Prof., Cambridge U., 1999, Abbot lectr., U. N.D., 2000, John D. Roberts lectr., Calif. Tech. U., 2000, Willard lectr., U. Wis., 2000, Cliford lectr., U. Pitts., 2000, William Lloyd Evan lectr. Ohio State U., 2000, Jacob Bigeleisen lectr. Stony Brook U., 2001, Laird lectr. U. B.C., 2001; Alan S. Tetelman fellow Yale U., 2001, Regitze Vold Meml. lectr. U. Calif., San Diego, 2001, Sammet guest prof. Goëethe U., Frankfurt, 2001. Editor Molecular Physics, 1987-91; mem. bd. editors Chem. Physics, Chem. Physics Letters, Nmr: Basic Principles and Progress, Advances in Magnetic Resonance, Accounts Chemistry Research, Concepts in Magnetic Reson; adv. editor Oxford U. Press; contbr. articles to profl. jours.; patentee in field. Recipient Strait award North Calif. Spectroscopy Soc., Outstanding Achievement award U.S. Dept. of Energy, 1983, 87, 89, 97, 98, R & D 100 awards, 1987, 89, Disting. Teaching award U. Calif., Ernest O. Lawrence award, 1988, Pitts. Spectroscopy award, 1989, Wolf prize in chemistry, Wolf Found., Israel, 1991, Donald Noyce Undergrad. Teaching award U. Calif., 1992, Robert Foster Cherry award for Great Tchrs. Baylor U., 1995, F.A. Cotton Medal for Excellence in Chemical Rsch., 1998, Dickson prize Carnegie Mellon U., 2001; Guggenheim fellow, 1988, Christensen fellow St. Catherine's Coll., Oxford, 1990; named in honor of his 50th birthday, Ampere Advanced Inst., Varenna, Italy; named to Scientific American 50 List, 2002. Fellow Am. Phys. Soc. (chmn. divsn. chem. physics), Inst. Physics; foreign fellow Royal Soc.; mem. NAS, Am. Chem. Soc. (mem. exec. com. divsn. chemistry, Nobel Signature award in Graduate Edu. 1982, Baekeland Medal for Pure Chemistry, 1985, Harrison Howe award 1991, Centennial Spkr., Jour. Physical Chemistry, 1997, Langmuir award in Chemical Physics, 1998, Remsen award (Md. sect.) 2000, Dickson prize

2001), Royal Soc. Chemistry (Bourke lectr., Bourke Medal, 1988, Centenary lectr. and medal 1994), Internat. Soc. Magnetic Resonance (v.p., pres. 1993-96), Lawrence Hall Sci. Outreach Com. Achievements include pioneering contributions to the development of nuclear magnetic resonance (NMR) spectroscopy; his techniques are widely used in chemistry and materials science. Office: U Calif Chemistry Dept D64A Hildebrand Hill Berkeley CA 94720-0001 Office Phone: 510-642-1220. Office Fax: 510-486-5744. Business E-Mail: pines@berkeley.edu.*

**PINES, BURTON YALE,** media executive; b. Chgo., Apr. 6, 1940; s. Hyman and Mary Pines. BA, U. Wis., 1961, MA, 1963, PhD, 1967. Instr. U. Wis., Madison, 1962-65; corr., bur. chief Time mag., Bonn, Saigon and Vienna, 1966-73, editor N.Y.C., 1973-81; sr. v.p. Heritage Found., Washington, 1981-92; chmn. Nat. Ctr. for Pub. Policy Rsch., Washington, 1982-94; co-founder, exec. v.p. COO NET Polit. Newstalk Network (later known as America's Voice Cable TV Network), Washington, 1992-95; pres., CEO Booknet Cable TV Network, N.Y.C., 1995—; exec. editor Internet ops. GOP Nat. Conv., 2000; sr. v.p. Nat. Exec. Svc. Corps, 2005—. Author: Back to Basics, 1982, Out of Focus, 1994; editor: Mandate for Leadership II, 1984, Mandate for Leadership III, 1988. Recipient Page One award N.Y. Newspaper Guild, 1976, 77, 78, Freedom's Found. award, 1983. Jewish. Office: BookNet 150 W 51st St Ste 1804 New York NY 10019-6848

**PINES, JESSE M.,** emergency physician, researcher; b. Washington, Nov. 30, 1972; s. Wayne L. and Nancy F. Pines; m. Lori Uscher-Pines, Sept. 10, 2005. BA, U. Pa., Phila., Pa., 1995; MD, MBA, Georgetown U., Washington, D.C., 2001; MS in Clin. Epidemiology, U. Pa., Phila., Pa., 2006. Diplomate Am. Bd. Emergency Medicine, 2006. Mem. faculty Dept. Emergency Medicine U. Pa., Phila., 2004—. Riggs Family EMF Health Policy grantee, Emergency Medicine Found., 2006—. Mem.: Soc. Academic Emergency Medicine, Am. Acad. Emergency Medicine. Office: University of Pennsylvania 3400 Spruce Street Ground Ravdin Philadelphia PA 19104 Office Phone: 215-662-4050. Personal E-mail: pinesj@hotmail.com.

**PINES, WAYNE LLOYD,** public relations executive; b. Washington, Dec. 31, 1943; s. Jerome Martin and Ethel (Schnall) Pines; m. Nancy Freitag, Apr. 16, 1966 (div. 2003); children: Noah Morris, Jesse Mireth. BA, Rutgers U., 1965; postgrad., George Washington U., 1969—71. Reporter, city editor Middletown Times Herald-Record, NY, 1965—68; copy editor Reuters News, 1968—69; assoc. editor FDC Reports, Washington, 1969—72; chief consumer edn. and info. FDA, also editor, 1972—74, dep. asst. commr. for pub. affairs, chief press rels. Rockville, Md., 1975—79, assoc. commr. pub. affairs, 1978—82; exec. editor Product Safety Letter and Devices and Diagnostics Letter, Washington, 1974—75; spl. asst. to dir. NIMH, 1982—83; sr. v.p., sr. counselor Burson-Marsteller, 1983—97, exec. v.p., dir. med. issues, 1987—93; pres. regulatory svc. APCO Worldwide, Washington, 1993—; sr. counselor Grey Healthcare Group, 1993—2004; mng. dir. Communs. Ptnr. and Assoc., 1999—2005; exec. v.p. Garden City Group, 1996—2006; pres. Bio-pharm. Forum George Washington U., 2002—04. Adj. prof. Washington Pub. Affairs Ctr., U. So. Calif., 1980—81; instr. NYU Sch. Continuing Edn., 1982—84, Profl. Devel. Inst., 1983—85; columnist Med. Advt. News, 1985—90, WebMD, 1999—2001; chmn. Therametrix, Inc., 1999—2001; ethics bd. Patient Channel, 2002—; bd. dirs. Scolr Inc., Medstar Rsch. Inst., FDA Alumni Assn. Author: The Sermons of Jerome Martin Pines, 1978, FDA Advertising and Promotion Manual, 1992, When Lightning Strikes: A How-to Crisis Manual, 1994, A Practical Guide to Food and Drug Law and Regulation, 1998, How to Work with the FDA, 2001, Crisis Communication in Healthcare: A Delicate Balance, 2002, A Framework for Pharmaceutical Risk Management, 2003, Making Your Case to the FDA, 2005, FDA Advisory Committees Perils and Profits, 2005, DTC Advertising and Promotion: The Changing Environment, 2005, FDA: A Century of Consumer Protection, 2006; contbr. articles to profl. jours. Home: 5610 Wisconsin Ave Apt 908 Chevy Chase MD 20815 Office: APCO Worldwide 700 12th St NW Washington DC 20005

**PINGPANK, ROBERT CHARLES,** retired mathematics educator; b. Waterbury, Conn., May 27, 1937; s. Henry Frederick and Mabel Jenny Pingpank; life ptnr. Richard Thomas Nolan, Sept. 14, 1955. BS, Trinity Coll., Hartford, Conn., 1959; MEd, U. of Hartford, 1964; CAS, Hartford Sem., 1970. Cert. secondary sch. adminstr. Conn., 1964. Tchr. Thomaston H.S., Thomaston, Conn., 1959—65, math. tchr., 1990—94, math. dept. head, 1967—90; tchr. Hamden Pub. Schs., Hamden, Conn., 1965—66, Cheshire Acad., Cheshire, Conn., 1966—67; adj. lectr. in math. Mattatuck C.C., Waterbury, Conn., 1970—92. V.p. The Litchfield Inst., Inc., Litchfield, Conn., 1984—96; guest spkr. Sr. Lifestyles radio program, 2005; guest lectr. Fla. Atlantic U., 2006. Author (with Richard T. Nolan): (book) Soul Mates: More Than Partners. Mem. Compass of West Palm Beach, Fla., 2004—; soc. of regents Cathedral of St. John the Divine, N.Y.C., 2002—; mem. Integrity-Palm Beach, Lake Worth, Fla., 1998—; treas. St. Paul's Episcopal Ch., Bantam, Conn., 1975—87, asst. treas., 1987—94; mem. Lambda Legal, N.Y.C., 2002—; notary pub. State of Fla., 1988—. Fellow: McCook Fellows Soc., Trinity Coll.; mem.: NEA, Compass of West Palm Beach, Harwood Soc. of Cheshire Acad., Yale Legacy Ptnrs., Integrity, Assn. Tchrs. of Math., Conn. Edn. Assn., Thomaston Edn. Assn. (treas.), Cathedral Founders Soc., Wash. Nat. Cathedral. Independent. Episcopal Church. Avocations: automobiles (history, design, mechanical, costs), Cavalier King Charles Spaniels. Home: 2527 Egret Lake Dr West Palm Beach FL 33413-2161 Personal E-mail: litchinst@aol.com.

**PINGREE, BRUCE DOUGLAS,** lawyer; b. Salt Lake City, June 6, 1947; s. Howard W. and Lois (Ivie) P.; m. Lorraine Bertelli, Oct. 11, 1981; children: Christian James, Matthew David, Alexandra Elizabeth, Meredith Gillian, Lauren Ashley, Geoffrey Nicholas. BA in Philosophy, U. Utah, 1970, JD, 1973. Bar: Ariz. 1973, Tex. 1990. Ptnr. Snell & Wilmer, Phoenix, 1973—89; shareholder Johnson & Gibbs, Dallas, 1989—93; ptnr. Gardere & Wynne, Dallas, 1993—95, Baker Botts, LLP, Dallas, 1995—. Lectr. in field. Contbr. articles to profl. jours. Served to capt. USAR Fellow Am. Coll. Employee Benefit Counsel, Inc. (charter); mem. ABA (tax sect., past chair employee benefits com., past vice chair, past chmn. various sub-coms., 1993-94, chair joint com. on employee benefits 1994-95), Tex. State Bar Assn. (chair, tax sect. benefits and compensation com. 2000), Dallas Bar Assn. (chair employee benefits sect. 2001-2002), S.W. Benefits Conf., Nat. Assn. Stock Plan Profls., Order of Coif. Episcopalian. Office: Baker & Botts LLP 2001 Ross Ave Ste 600 Dallas TX 75201-2900 Home: 4218 Rosa Ct Dallas TX 75220 Office Phone: 214-953-6878. Business E-Mail: bruce.pingree@bakerbotts.com.

**PING-ROBBINS, NANCY REGAN,** musicologist, educator; b. Nashville, Dec. 19, 1939; d. Charles Augustus and Ruby Phyllis (Perdue) Regan; m. Robert Leroy Ping, June 19, 1959 (div. 1980); children: Robert Alan, Michael Regan, Bryan Edward; m. William Edward Robbins, Jr., Mar. 14, 1981. BMusic, Ind. U., 1964; MA, U. No. Colo., 1972; PhD, U. Colo., 1979. Pvt. instr. piano and flute, 1960—; organist Armed Forces Chapels, Frankfurt, Kaiserslautern, Germany, 1962-64; staff pianist US Armed Forces Spl. Svcs. Theater, Frankfurt, 1963-65; music tchr. Fayetteville Pub. Schs., Ind., 1966-67, Stratton Pub. Schs., Colo., 1967-70; instr. piano, staff piano accompanist U. No. Colo., Greeley, 1970-72; instr. music history U. Colo., Boulder, 1974; instr., asst. prof. music U. NC, Wilmington, 1974-79; assoc. prof. music, coord. music Shaw U., Raleigh, NC, 1979-87; dir. Atlantic CC Com. Arts Sch., 1987-88. Profl. harpsichord accompanist Internat. Inst. in Early Music, 1983; adj. prof. Atlantic Christian Coll. (now Barton Coll.), 1987—88, assoc. prof., 1987—95; mem., pianist Chekker Duo, 1996—2003, 2006—. Recs. include Early Popular Music on Piano/Harpsichord, 1984, En Blanc et Noir, 2001; author: The Piano Trio in the Twentieth Century, 1984, Scott Joplin: A Guide to Research, 1998; editor, compiler: The Music of Gustave Blessner, 1985; music reviewer News and Observer, Raleigh, 1981-96, head music critic, 1999-95; contbr. articles to profl. jours. Sec. Bach Festival Com., Raleigh, 1984; dir. music Bailey United Meth. Ch., N.C., 2000—. John H. Edwards fellow Ind. U., 1961; U. Colo. grad fellow, 1972-74; Mellon Found. grantee, 1982; N.C. Arts Coun. grantee, 1985; NEH

summer seminar fellow, 1984. Mem. Am. Musicol. Soc. (sec.-treas. chpt. 1981-83), Soc. for Ethnomusicology (chmn. regional chpt. 1983-84), Wilson Piano Tchrs. Assn. (pres. 1988-90, 95-98), Soc. Am. Music (formerly Sonneck Soc., program com. 1999), Alpha Lambda Delta, Pi Kappa Lambda, Sigma Alpha Iota.

**PINGS, ANTHONY CLAUDE,** architect; b. Fresno, Calif., Dec. 16, 1951; s. Clarence Hubert and Mary (Murray) P.; m. Carole Clements, June 25, 1983; children, Adam Reed, Rebecca Mary. AA, Fresno City Coll., 1972; BArch, Calif. Poly. State U., San Luis Obispo, 1976. Lic. architect, Calif.; cert. Nat. Council Archtl. Registration Bds. Architect Aubrey Moore Jr., Fresno, 1976-81; architect, prin. Pings & Assocs., Fresno, 1981-83, 86—, Pings-Taylor Assocs., Fresno, 1983-85. Prin. works include Gollaher Profl. Office (Masonry Merit award 1985, Best Office Bldg. award 1986), Fresno Imaging Ctr. (Best Instnl. Project award 1986, Nat. Healthcare award Modern Health Care mag. 1986), Orthopedic Facility (award of honor Masonry Inst. 1987, award of merit San Joaquin chpt. AIA 1987), Modesto Imaging Ctr. (award of merit San Joaquin chpt. AIA 1991), Peachwood Med. Ctr. (award of merit San Joaquin chpt. AIA). Mem. Calif. Indsl. Tech. Edn. Consortium Calif. State Dept. Edn., 1983, 84. Recipient Excellence in Bus. award Fresno, 1999. Mem. AIA (bd. dirs. Calif. chpt. 1983-84, v.p. San Joaquin chpt. 1982, pres. 1983, Calif. Coun. evaluation team 1983, team leader Coalinga Emergency Design Assistance team), Fresno Arts (bd. dirs., counsel 1989—, pres. 1990-93), Fig Gardens Home Owners Assn. (bd. dir. 1991—, pres. 1994—). Republican. Home: 4350 N Safford Ave Fresno CA 93704-3509

**PINHEIRO, GERMANIA ARAUJO,** physician, researcher; d. Francisco Arruda and Maria da Conceicao Pinheiro; m. Vinicius Cavalcanti Antao, June 23, 2003; 1 child, Sophie Pinheiro Cavalcanti. MD, Petropolis Sch. of Medicine, Brazil, 1992; MSc, Fluminense Fed. U., Brazil, 1998; PhD, Sao Paulo U., Brazil, 2003. Cert. Pulmonologist Rio de Janeiro State U., 1996, Occupl. Medicine Specialist Gama Filho U., 1998. Assoc. prof. of pulmonology Rio de Janeiro State U., Rio de Janeiro, Rio de Janeiro, 1996—2003; prof. occupl. medicine Gama Filho U., Rio de Janeiro, 1996—2003; pulmonologist Rio de Janeiro State Office for Justice and the Interior, Rio de Janeiro, 1998—2002; mem. State Tech. Commn. of Occupl. Lung Diseases - Rio de Janeiro State Office for Health, Rio de Janeiro, 1998—2003; physician Brazilian Army Ctrl. Hosp., Rio de Janeiro, 1997—99; adj. asst. prof. W.Va. U., Morgantown, W.va., 2003—; epidemic intelligence svc. officer Nat. Inst. Occupl. Health/Ctrs. for Disease Control & Prevention, Morgantown, 2003—05, sr. svc. fellow, 2005—. Grantee Bronze Sponsorship, European Respiratory Soc., 2002. Mem.: European Respiratory Soc., Am. Thoracic Soc. Home: 132 Bakers Dr Morgantown WV 26505 Office: Nat Inst Occupl Health Ctrs for Disease Control & Prevention 1095 Willodale Rd Morgantown WV 26505 Office Phone: 304-285-6095. Office Fax: 304-285-6111. Personal E-mail: ghp6@cdc.gov.

**PINICK, SARIAH KAY,** music educator; d. Thomas Keith and Patricia Irene Pinick. MA in Music, U.Mo., Kansas City, 2003; MusB in Voice Performance magna cum laude, U.Mo., Columbia, 2000. Voice instr. Music Arts Inst., Independence, Mo., 2000—; adj. prof. in voice Blue River C.C., Independence, 2000—; adj. voice instr. Kans. City Kans. C.C., 2005—. Singer: (voice recital) Compositions of African American Women Composers, (opera singers competition) Ctr. for Contemporary Opera Internat. Opera Singers Competition (Semi-Finalist, 2004). Music ministry Anchor Point Bapt. Ch., Independence, 2004—06. Recipient Excellence in Music award, Pi Kappa Lambda, 1997, 1998. Mem.: Music Teachers Nat. Assn. (assoc.), Nat. Assn. of Teachers of Singing (assoc.), Pi Kappa Lambda (assoc.), Sigma Alpha Iota (life; v.p. 2005—06, Highest Scholastic Average award 2000). Avocations: travel, reading, cross stitch, piano. Office: Music Arts Inst 1010 S Pearl St Independence MO 64050 Office Phone: 816-836-1998.

**PINIELLA, LOUIS VICTOR,** professional baseball team manager; b. Tampa, Fla., Aug. 28, 1943; m. Anita Garcia, Apr. 12, 1967; children: Lou, Kristi, Derrick. Student, U. Tampa. Baseball player various minor-league teams, 1962-68, Cleve. Indians, 1968, Kansas City Royals, 1969-73, N.Y. Yankees, 1974-84, coach, 1984-85, mgr., 1985-87, 1988, gen. mgr., 1987-88, spl. advisor, TV announcer, 1989; mgr. Cin. Reds, 1990-92, Seattle Mariners, 1992—2002, Tampa Bay Devil Rays, 2002—05; baseball analyst ESPN, 2005—. Named to Am. League All-Star Team, 1972; recipient Ellis Island Medal of Honor, 1990; Named A.L. Rookie of the Yr Baseball Writers Assoc of Amer, 1969, Named A.L. Manager of the Yr, 1995. Office: ESPN Inc ESPN Plz 935 Middle St Bristol CT 06010*

**PINK, MICHAEL,** performing company executive; b. York, England; Trained as classical dancer, Royal Ballet Sch. Dancer English Nat. Ballet, 1975—85; founding dir. Ballet Ctrl., London, 1987—91; assoc. dir. Northern Ballet, 1988; artistic dir. Milw. Ballet. Internat. tchr. Norwegian Nat. Ballet, Aterballetto, Balleto di Toscanna Italy, The Hartford Ballet, Rozas Dance Co., London Contemporary Dance Co., White Oaks Dance Project, Ballet Rambert, English Nat. Ballet, Phoenix Dance Co., London Ballet. Recipient First Pl. in inaugural, Ursula Moreton Choreographic Competition, First Pl., Royal Soc. of Arts Competition. Office: Milwaukee Ballet 504 W National Ave Milwaukee WI 53204 E-mail: michael@milwaukeeballet.org.*

**PINK, (ALECIA B. MOORE),** singer; b. Doylestown, Pa., Sept. 8, 1979; m. Carey Hart, Jan. 7, 2006. With Arista Records, 2001—. Singer: (albums) Can't Take Me Home, 2000, M!ssundaztood, 2001, Try This, 2003, I'm Not Dead, 2006, (songs) There U Go, 2000, Most Girls, 2000, (with Mya, Lil', Kim, Christina Aguilera) Lady Marmalade, 2001 (Grammy award Song Yr., 2002, 2 MTV Video Music awards, 2001), You Make Me Sick, 2001, Get the Party Started, 2001 (2 MTV Video Music Awards, 2002), Don't Let Me Get Me, 2002, Just Like a Pill, 2002, Family Portrait, 2002, Feel Good Time, 2003, Trouble, 2003 (Grammy award, Best Female Rock Performance, 2004), God is a DJ, 2003, Stupid Girls, 2006 (MTV Video Music award for Best Pop Video, 2006); actor: (films) Rollerball, 2002, Charlie's Angels: Full Throttle, 2003. Named one of 100 Sexiest Artists, VH1, 2002; recipient World Music award for Best Am. Pop Female Artist, 2003. Office: Box #390 5701 E Circle Dr Cicero NY 13039*

**PINKARD, ANNE MERRICK,** foundation administrator; b. Baltimore, Feb. 8, 1924; d. Robert Graff M.; m. Walter Devier Pinkard, Sept. 24, 1949 (dec. June, 1994); children: Walter D. Jr., Robert Merrick, Gregory Clyde, Peter McEvoy. BA, Goucher Coll., Balt., 1946; student, Cornell U., Ithaca, N.Y., 1942—43; LLD (hon.), Johns Hopkins U., Balt., 1994. Bd. dirs. Citizens Planning and Housing, Balt., 1950-60; bd. dirs., sect. Soc. Md. Antiquities, Balt., 1955-63; pres. women's bd. Johns Hopkins Hosp., Balt., 1968-72, bd. dirs., 1976-92; pres. France Merrick Found., Balt., 2000—2004, bd. dirs. Bd. dirs. Johns Hopkins U., Balt., 1972-94, trustee, 1972-94; trustee St. Mary's Sem. and U., 1974-80. Home: 613 Brightwood Club Dr Lutherville MD 21093-3632 Office: France Merrick Found 1122 Kenilworth Dr Baltimore MD 21204-2139

**PINKEL, DONALD PAUL,** pediatrician; b. Buffalo, Sept. 7, 1926; s. Lawrence William and Ann (Richardson) P.; m. Marita Donovan, Dec. 26, 1949 (div. 1981); children: Rebecca, Nancy, Christopher, Mary, Thomas, Anne, Sara, John, Ruth; m. Cathryn Barbara Howarth, May 16, 1981; 1 child, Michael. BS, Canisius Coll., 1947; MD, U. Buffalo, 1951. Diplomate Am. Bd. Pediatrics, Pediatric Hematology and Oncology, Nat. Bd. Med. Examiners. From intern to resident to chief resident Children's Hosp., Buffalo, 1951-54; research fellow Children's Hosp. Med. Ctr., Boston, 1955-56; chief of pediatrics Roswell Park Meml. Inst., Buffalo, 1956-61; founding dir. St. Jude Children's Rsch. Hosp., Memphis, 1961-73; chmn. pediatrics Med. Coll. Wis., Milw., 1974-78; pediatrician-in-chief Milw. Children's Hosp., 1974-78; founding dir. Midwest Children's Cancer Ctr., Milw., 1974; chief. of pediatrics City of Hope Med. Ctr., Duarte, Calif., 1978-82; chmn. pediatrics Temple U. Sch. Medicine, Phila., 1982-85; prof., Kana Rsch. chair, dir. pediatric leukemia program M.D. Anderson Cancer Ctr. U. Tex., Houston, 1985-93; prof. pediat. U. Tex. Med. Sch., Houston, 1985-99; prof. emeritus U.

Tex.-M.D. Anderson Cancer Ctr., Houston, 1994—. Clin. prof. pediats. U. So. Calif., LA, 2002—; adj. prof. biol. scis. Calif. Polytechnic State U., San Luis Obispo, Calif., 2001—. Contbr. articles to profl. jours. Bd. dirs. Lee County Coop. Clinic, Mariana, Ark., 1972-74. Served with USN, 1944-45, served to 1st lt. U.S. Army, 1954-55. Recipient Albert Lasker award for Med. Rsch., Lasker Found., 1972, Windermere Lectureship Brit. Pediatric Assn., 1974, David Karnofsky award Am. Soc. Clin. Oncology, 1978, Zimmerman prize for Cancer Rsch. Zimmerman Found., 1979, Charles Kettering prize Gen. Motors Cancer Rsch., 1986, Clin. Rsch. award Am. Cancer Soc., 1988, Return of the Child award Leukemia Soc. Am., 1992, Pollin prize in pediat. rsch. N.Y. Presbyn. Hosp., 2003. Mem. Am. Soc. Clin. Oncology, Am. Pediat. Soc., Am. Assn. Cancer Rsch., Soc. Exptl. Biology and Medicine, Am. Hematology. Democrat. Roman Catholic. Avocations: swimming, sailing. Home: 275 Marlene Dr San Luis Obispo CA 93405 E-mail: donpinkel@yahoo.com.

**PINKER, STEVEN A.,** psychologist, educator; b. Montreal, Que., Can., Sept. 18, 1954; arrived in US, 1976; s. Harry and Roslyn (Wiesenfeld) P. BA in Exptl. Psychology, McGill U., Montreal, 1976; PhD, Harvard U., 1979; DSc (hon.), McGill U., 1999; DPhil (hon.), Tel Aviv U., 2003, U. Newcastle, 2005; DUniv (hon.), U. Surrey, 2003. Postdoctoral fellow Center for Cognitive Sci., MIT; asst. prof., dept. of psychology Harvard U., Cambridge, Mass., 1980-81, Stanford U., Palo Alto, Calif., 1981-82, MIT, Cambridge, 1982—85, assoc. prof., dept. of brain and cognitive sci., 1985—89; co-dir. Center for Cognitive Sci., MIT, 1985—94; prof., dept. of brain and cogniive sci. MIT; dir. McDonnell-Pew Center for Cognitive Neuroscience, MIT, 1994—99; Peter de Florez prof. MIT, Cambridge, 2000—03; Johnstone Family prof. of psychol. Harvard U., 2003—. Cons. Cognitive and Instructional Scis. Group, Xerox Corp. Palo Alto Rsch. Centers, 1981—82; vis. scholar, dept. of psychology Harvard Univ., 1987—88; vis. scholar, cognitive devel. unit Med. Rsch Coun., London, 1988; vis. scholar, dept. of psychology and linguistics Univ. Calif., Santa Barbara, 1995—96; hon. vis. prof., dept. of psychology Univ. of Auckland, New Zealand, 2001—04; spkr. in field. Author: Language Learnability and Language Development, 1984, Learnability and Cognition, 1989, The Language Instinct, 1994, How the Mind Works, 1997 (LA Times Science Book Prize, 1998, finalist for Pullitzer prize, 1998), Words and Rules, 1999, The Blank Slate, 2002 (finalist for Pulitzer prize, 2003); assoc. editor Cognition, 1984—; advisor, Am. Heritage Dictionary; serves on several advisory and editorial bds., contbr. articles to sci. jours. and chapters in books. Recipient Troland Rsch. award NAS, 1993, Golden Plate award, Am. Acad. of Achievement, 1999, Henry Dale prize Royal Instn. Gt. Britain, 2004, Henry Dale prize Royal Instn. of Gt. Britain, 2004; named Humanist Laureate Internat. Acad. Humanism, 2001, Humanist of Yr., 2006. Fellow AAAS, APA (Disting. Early Career award 1984, Boyd McCandless award 1986, William James Book prize 1995, 99, 2003, Eleanor Maccoby Book prize 2003), Am. Acad. Arts and Scis., Linguistics Soc. Am. (Linguistics, Lang. and Pub. Svcs. award 1997), Am. Psychol. Soc. Office: Dept Psychology Harvard Univ William James Hall 970 33 Kirkland St Cambridge MA 02138 Office Phone: 617-495-0831. Office Fax: 617-495-3278. Business E-Mail: pinker@wjh.harvard.edu.

**PINKERTON, A. LOUISE,** vocalist, music educator; d. John W. and Jane R. Pinkerton; m. Royce F. Blackburn, Aug. 12, 2000. MusB, Ind. U., 2001; MusM, U. N.D., 2003. Music instr. Mayville State U., ND, 2002—04, Minn. State U., Moorhead, 2004—; lectr. music U. N.D., Grand Forks, 2005—. Intern Nat. Symphony Orch. John F. Kennedy Ctr. Performing Arts, Washington, 2001; publicity coord. Met. Opera Nat. Coun. Auditions, Grand Forks, 2005—; presenter in field. Singer: (opera) Fargo-Moorhead Opera, (musical) Crimson Creek Players, (performances) Opera in the Ozarks, (performance) Contemporary Opera Lab; presenter (report) SAI Philanthropies, Inc: Kennedy Center Internship. Recipient Dist. Winner and Regional Finalist, Met. Opera Nat. Coun. Auditions, 2004, Vivian Menees Nelson award, Nat. Fedn. Music Clubs, 2004, semi-finalist, William C. Byrd Young Artist awards, 2006. Mem.: Nat. Assn. Tchrs. Singing, Pi Kappa Lambda, Sigma Alpha Iota (province officer 2000—03, Province Leadership award). Avocation: ballroom dance. Personal E-mail: louise_pinkerton@hotmail.com.

**PINKERTON, JAMES PEARSON,** columnist, political analyst; b. Cambridge, Mass., Mar. 11, 1958; s. James N. and Janet Ann (Pearson) P. BA in Polit. Sci., Stanford U., 1980. Policy analyst Reagan for Pres. of U.S. Campaign, L.A., 1979-80, Reagan-Bush Campaign, Arlington, Va., 1980; policy analyst Policy Office, The White House, Washington, 1981-82, dir. rsch. Polit. Office, 1982-83; dir. polit. staff Reagan-Bush Campaign, Washington, 1983-84; dir. rsch. Fund for Am.'s Future, Washington, 1985-87, George Bush for Pres. of U.S., 1987-88, Bush-Quayle Campaign, 1988; dir. Policy Devel. Office of Pres.-elect of U.S., Washington, 1988-89; dep. asst. for policy planning to Pres. of U.S. Washington, 1989—93; columnist Newsday, NYC, 1993—; polit. analyst FOX News Channel, Washington, 1996—, regular appearances, FOX News Watch. Columnist TechCentralStation.com. Author: What Comes Next: The End of Big Government and the New Paradigm Ahead, 1995; contbr. articles to NY TImes, Washington Post, Wall Street Journal, LA Times, USA Today, New Republic, National Review, Foreign Affairs, State.com, Space.com and others. Fellow: New Am. Found. Republican. Avocation: chess. Office: Fox News 400 N Capitol St NW Ste 550 Washington DC 20001 also: Newsday 235 Pinelawn Rd Melville NY 11747

**PINKERTON, MARJORIE JEAN,** librarian, library science educator; b. Chgo., June 15, 1934; d. Michael Seretto and Evelyn Isabel (Scott) Glass; m. James Ronald Pinkerton, June 29, 1957; children— Steven James, Kathryn Lynn. B.A. in Spanish and History, Carroll Coll., 1956; MA in Spanish, U. Wis., Madison, 1964; MA in Library Sci., U. Mo., 1973. Tchr. high sch., Pardeeville, Wis., 1956-57, Preble, Wis., 1958-59; libr. asst. Meml. Libr., U. Wis., Madison, 1959-64; substitute tchr., librarian Columbia Pub. Schs., Mo., 1965-73; ednl. materials librarian, prof. William Woods Coll., Fulton, Mo., 1973-81, assoc. prof., 1985-93, ret., 1993, dir. Dulany Libr. 1981—93. Co-author: Outdoor Recreation and Leisure, 1969. Contbr. articles to profl. jours. Mem. Bd. Adjustment, City of Columbia, 1971-75, chmn., 1973-74; dir. Nat. Ghost Ranch Found., United Presbyterian, Santa Fe, N.Mex., 1981-84; mem. Columbia Safety Coun., 1967—, pres., 1969-70. Recipient award for cmty. svc. New Democratic Coalition, Columbia, 1976, Outstanding Young Woman award, 1969. Mem. ALA, Mo. Assn. Coll. and Rsch. Libraries (chmn. 1984-85), Mo. Libr. Assn. (com. chmn. 1978-79), Mid-Mo. Associated Colls. and Univs. (chmn. libr. com. 1984-85), Nat. Coun. Tchrs. English, LWV (v.p. 1967-68, 2002—), Nat. Geneal. Soc., Beta Phi Mu (pres. 1974-76, 85-86), Peace Studies Inst., Phi Alpha Theta, Kappa Delta Pi. Presbyterian. Clubs: UN (pres. 1970—), Friends of the Libr. (Columbia, sec.-treas. 1977-78), Gertrude Matthews Soc., Jefferson Club, U. Mo. Libr. Soc. Avocations: genealogy, reading, travel, walking. Home: 1014 Westport Dr Columbia MO 65203-0744 Personal E-mail: mpmidge@aol.com.

**PINKERTON, RICHARD LADOYT,** retired management educator; b. Huron, SD, Mar. 5, 1933; s. Abner Pyle and Orral Claudine (Arneson) P.; m. Sandra Louise Lee, Aug. 28, 1965 (div. 1992); children: Elizabeth, Patricia. BA, U. Mich., 1955; MBA, Case Western Res. U., 1962; PhD, U. Wis., 1969. Sr. market rsch. analyst Harris-Intertype Corp., Cleve., 1957-61; mgr. sales devel. Triax Corp., Cleve., 1962-64; coord. mktg. program Mgmt. Inst., U. Wis., 1964-67; dir. exec. programs Mgmt. Inst., U. Wis. (Grad. Sch. Bus.), also asst. prof. mktg., 1969-74; prof. mgmt., dean Grad. Sch. Adminstrn., Capital U., Columbus, Ohio, 1974-86; prof. mgmt., dir. Univ. Bus. Ctr., Craig Sch. Bus. Calif. State U., Fresno, 1986-89, prof. mktg., 1989-2000, chmn. mktg. and logistics dept., 1996-2000, dir. London semester, prof. emeritus, 2000—. Adj. prof. Case Western Res. U., 2004-; trustee Ohio Coun. Econ. Edn., 1976-87; cons. to govt. and industry, 1960—. Co-author: The Purchasing Manager's Guide to Strategic Proactive Procurement, 1996; contbr. articles to profl. jours. Bd. govs. Hannah Neil Home for Children, Columbus, 1975—78; mem. indsl. and cmty. devel. commn. City of Strongsville, Ohio; bd. dirs. The Fresno Townhouse Assn., 1992—2001. Officer USAF, 1955—57, lt. col. USAF, 1957—78. La Verne Noyes scholar, 1952—55, Nat. Assn. Purchasing Mgmt. fellow, 1967—68. Mem.: Am. Mktg.

Assn. (chpt. pres. 1972—73), Nat. Assn. Purchasing Mgmt. (chmn. acad. planning 1979—84, rsch. symposium 1992), Nat. Assn. Contract Mgmt. (chmn. validation cert. com. 1990), Air Force Assn., Res. Officers Assn., Marines Meml. Club, Columbia Hills Country Club, Phi Gamma Delta, Alpha Kappa Psi, Beta Gamma Sigma. Home: 18487 Woodside Crossing South Strongsville OH 44149-6891 Office Phone: 440-846-1430.

**PINKERTON, ROBERT BRUCE,** mechanical engineer; b. Detroit, Feb. 10, 1941; s. George Fulwell and Janet Lois (Hedke) P.; m. Barbara Ann Bandfield, Aug. 13, 1966; 1 child, Robert Brent. BSME, Detroit Inst. Tech., 1965; MA in Engring., Chrysler Inst. Engring., 1967; JD, Wayne State U., 1976. From mech. engr. to emissions and fuel economy planning specialist Chrysler Engring. Office Chrysler Corp., Highland Park, Mich., 1967-80; dir. engring. Replacement div. TRW, Inc., Cleve., 1980-83; v.p. engring. TRW Automotive Aftermarket Group, 1983-86; v.p. engring. and rsch. Blackstone Corp., Jamestown, NY, 1986-89, pres., CEO, 1989-90, Athena Corp., Beaufort, SC, 1990—, Cedar Crest Corp., Beaufort, SC, 1990—; chmn., CEO Beaufort Land Co., 1998—. Bd. dirs. VRI, LLC, Coastal Banking Co., Inc., Low Country Nat. Bank, Village Renaissance, Inc., Carpenters Hall, Coastal Banking Co., Inc.; chmn. redevelopment commn. City Beaufort, 2004—. Mem. exec. com. Beaufort Schs. Oversight Com., 1995-99, Pvt. Industry Coun., 1996-99. Mem.: Greater Beaufort C. of C. (bd. dirs. 1997—98), Beaufort Roundtable (pres. 2000—02), Rotary (asst. dist. gov. 1997—98). Presbyterian. Home: PO Box 2417 Beaufort SC 29901-2417 Office: PO Box 2115 1203 Boundary St Beaufort SC 29902 Business E-Mail: rbp@athenacorp.com.

**PINKETT-SMITH, JADA,** actress; b. Balt., Sept. 18, 1971; m. Will Smith, Dec. 31, 1997; 2 children. Actor: (films) Menace II Society, 1993, The Inkwell, 1994, Jason's Lyric, 1994, A Low Down Dirty Shame, 1994, Demon Knight, 1995, The Nutty Professor, 1996, Set It Off, 1996, Blossoms and Veils, 1997 (also exec. prodr.), Scream 2, 1997, Woo, 1998, Return to Paradise, 1998, Bamboozled, 2000, Kingdom Come, 2001, Ali, 2001, The Matrix Reloaded, 2003, The Matrix Revolutions, 2003, Collateral, 2004, (voice) Madagascar, 2005, (TV films) If These Walls Could Talk, 1996, Maniac Magee, 2003, (TV series) A Different World, 1992-93, exec. prodr. All of Us, 2003-; exec. prodr. (films) The Seat Filler, 2004; author (children's book): Girls Hold Up This World, 2004 (NY Times Bestseller list, NAACP Image award for outstanding lit. work-children's 2006).*

**PINKHAM, DANIEL,** composer; b. Lynn, Mass., June 5, 1923; s. Daniel R. and Olive C. (White) Pinkham. AB, MA, Harvard, 1944; Litt.D. (hon.), Nebr. Wesleyan U., 1976; Mus D (hon.), Adrian Coll., 1977, Westminster Choir Coll., 1979, New Eng. Conservatory, 1993, Ithaca Coll., 1994, Boston Conservatory, 1998. Mem. faculty New Eng. Conservatory Music, 1959—; music dir. King's Chapel, Boston, 1958-2000; co-founder Cambridge Festival Orch., 1948. Composer: (songs) Triple Concerto, 2001, A Cask of Amontillado, 2001, Covenant Motets, 2001, Concerto for Organ and Wind Quintet, 2001, Collects, 2001, Concertino for Piano and Brass Quintet, 2003, The Seven Days, 2003, Conversing with Some One Invisible, 2003, Quartet for Oboe and String Trio, 2003, Magnificat, 2003, The Good Things of Life, 2003, Let the Word Go Forth, 2003, Conversing with Someone Invisible, 2003, Preludes for Piano: Book II, 2003, Irenicon, 2003, Dark Angels, 2004, Bright Angels, 2004, A Song for St. Cecilia's Day, 2004, Blue Blazes, 2004, Advent Canticles, 2004, Five Times Two, 2004, Streams, 2004, Woodwing Quartet, 2004, Oboe Quartet, 2004, Weather Reports for Orch., 2004, Partita on an Old Norwegian Folk Tune, 2004, Sonata Brevis, 2004, Romances, 2004, The Garden of Muses, 2005, Sonata for Trumpet, 2005, Lections, 2005, Sonata for Violin and Violoncello, 2005, Aerial Music, 2005, April Music, 2005, The Saint Luke Organ Book, 2005, A Symphony of Halleluias, 2006, Scenes for Trumpet and Organ, 2006, Missa Brevis, 2006, Many Waters, 2006, others. Fellow: Am. Acad. Arts and Scis.; mem.: Am. Guild Organists (past dean Boston chpt.). Home: 150 Chilton St Cambridge MA 02138-1227 Office Phone: 617-876-8375. Personal E-mail: pinkham150@comcast.net.

**PINKINS, TONYA,** actress; b. Chicago, May 30, 1962; m. Ron Brawer, Feb. 12, 1987 (div. 1987); 2 children; 4 children. Attended, Northwestern U., Summer Theater Inst., Chicago, 1978; student, Carnegie Mellon U., 1980—81; BA, Columbia Coll., Chicago, 1996; student, Calif. Western Law Sch., San Diego. Private acting instr. Montclair School of Dance, 1993; visual arts instr., 6th to 8th grades LAUSD, 2000—01; private coach voice, music performance, acting, 2002. Playwriting com. Playwrights' Preview Prodn., 1986—88; instr. cold reading Univ. Calif., San Diego, 2000. Actor: (Broadway plays) Merrily We Roll Along, 1981, Jelly's Last Jam, 1992 (Tony award best featured actress in a musical, 1992, Drama Desk award best featured actress in a musical, 1992, Clarence Derwent award, 1992, Outer Critics Circle award best featured actress in a musical, 1993), Chronicle of a Death Foretold, 1995, Play On!, 1997 (Tony nom. best actress in a musical, 1997), The Wild Party, 2000, Caroline, or Change, 2004— (Tony nom. best actress in a musical, 2004, Obie award best perf., 2004), (Off Broadway plays) Little Shop of Horrors, 1983, A...My Name Alice, 1985, Just Say No, 1988, Believin'/Psychoneurotic Fantasies, 1990, The Caucasian Chalk Circle, 1990, The Merry Wives of Windsor, 1994, The Vagina Monologues, 2000, The House of Flowers, 2003 (plays) Stealin', Joe Turner's Come and Gone, 1989, The Piano Lesson, 1989, Approximating Mother, 1991, No Niggers, No Jews, No Dogs, 2000, Thoroughly Modern Millie, 2000; (TV series) As the World Turns, 1983—86, University Hospital, 1994, All My Children, 1991—95, 2003—; (TV films) American Dream, 1981, Rage of Angels: The Story Continues, 1986, Strapped, 1993, Against Their Will: Women in Prison, 1994, (TV Guest appearances) Crime Story, 1986, The Cosby Show, 1990, Law & Order, 1990, The Guardian, 2002; (films) Beat Street, 1984, See No Evil, Hear No Evil, 1989, Above the Rim, 1994, Love Hurts, 2002, Romance & Cigarettes, 2005 Premium, 2006; voice (audio books) The Winner of Brewster Place, 1992, The Book of Virtues I and II, 1993, The Moral Compass, 1995, Chocolate for a Woman's Soul, 1997, The Silent Cradle, 1998; author: (book) Get Over Yourself: How to Drop the Drama and Claim the Life You Deserve, 2006; singer: (albums) Live @ Joe's Pub. Achievements include co-founder of OPERATION Z: zero tolerance of violence against women and children.*

**PINKLEY, THOMAS HAROLD,** lawyer; b. Shelbyville, Ind., Dec. 20, 1953; s. Thomas Harold and Elma Jean (Wilson) P.; m. Joan Morton, Mar. 18, 1978. BA, U. Tenn., 1979, JD, 1981. Bar: Tenn. 1982, Calif. 2004, U.S. Dist. Ct. (ea. dist.) Tenn. 1984, U.S. Ct. Appeals (6th cir.) 1986, U.S. Ct. Appeals (4th and 11th cirs.) 1988, U.S. Ct. Appeals (10th cir.) 1989, U.S. Ct. Appeals (7th cir.) 2001, U.S. Ct. Appeals (9th cir.) 1996, U.S. Supreme Ct. 1988, U.S. Dist Ct. (west dist.), Tenn. 2000, U.S. Dist Ct. (no. dist.), Ill. 2001, U.S. Dist Ct. (no. dist.), Calif. 2004. Law clk. Hon. H. Ted Milburn, Chattanooga, 1983-84, Hon. Frank W. Wilson, Chattanooga, 1982; assoc. Egerton, McAfee, Armisted & Davis, Knoxville, Tenn., 1984-87; ptnr. Paine, Swiney & Tarwater, Knoxville, 1987-95, Chambliss & Bahner, Chattanooga, 1995-97, Miller & Martin, Chattanooga, 1997—. Mem. ABA, Tenn. Bar Assn., Pro Bono Com., Nashville Bar Assn. Office: Miller & Martin 1200 One Nashville PL 150 4th Ave N Nashville TN 37219-2433 Office Phone: 615-244-9270. E-mail: hpinkley@millermartin.com.

**PINKNEY, ALFRED ELI,** environmental scientist; s. Irving and Gertrude Pinkney; m. Pamela Hope Sommers, Oct. 9, 1982; children: Gabriel Ray, Gregory Isaac. BS in Zoology, U. Mich., Ann Arbor, 1976; MS in Environ. Health Scis., N.Y. U., N.Y.C., 1982; PhD in Marine Estuarine Environ. Sci., U. Md., College Park, 1988. Biologist Johns Hopkins Applied Physics Lab, Shady Side, Md., 1983—85; grad. rsch. asst. Chesapeake Biol. Lab. U. Md., Solomons, 1986—88; scientist ICF, Inc., Fairfax, Va., 1988—89, Versar, Inc., Columbia, 1989—93; sr. scientist U.S. Fish and Wildlife Svc., Annapolis, 1993—. Mem. toxics sub com. Chesapeake Bay Program E.P.A., 1994—96, 2003—; mem. MS thesis com. U. Md. Ea. Shore, U. Del., U. N.H., mem. PhD thesis com. Contbr. abstracts, scientific papers, articles to profl. jours. Mgr. Takoma Pk.-Silver Spring Babe Ruth Coed Softball, Takoma Park, Md., 2001—. Recipient Eagle award, U.S. Fish and Wildlife Svc. (N.E. region), 2003. Mem.: Soc. Environ. Toxicology and Chemistry (bd. mem. Chesapeake

and Potomac regional chpt. 1997—2003, pres. Chesapeake and Potomac regional chpt. 2001—02), Anacostia Watershed Toxics Alliance. Avocations: softball, basketball, gardening, reading, home renovation. Office: US Fish and Wildlife Svc 177 Adm Cochrane Dr Annapolis MD 21401-7307

**PINKNEY, D. TIMOTHY,** investment company executive; b. Long Beach, Calif., June 6, 1948; s. Robert Patten and Mary (Chernus) P.; m. Nancy Dianne Fisher, Aug. 21, 1971; 1 child, Heather Anne. BA, Calif. Luth. U., 1970; MA, Pepperdine U., 1976. CFP. Membership mgr. Seattle C. of C., 1977—79; v.p. mktg. John L. Scott Investment, Bellevue, Wash., 1980—81, SRH Fin., Bellevue, 1981—82, Foster Investment Co., Bellevue, 1982—83; pres., CEO Footprint Fin. Planning, Bellevue, 1983—88, Sheppard & Assocs. Personal Fin. Advs., Bellevue, 1988—91; mgr. and v.p. asset mgmt. div. U.S. Bank, Tacoma, 1991—92; v.p., Calif. and Nev. mgr. trust and investment mgmt. U.S. Bank of Calif., Sacramento, 1992—96; prin. The Savant Group, Citrus Heights, Calif., 1996—; founder, CEO Wealth Link Enterprises. Invited spkr. Russian Parliament, 1992. Author: book, video and cassete series Pathways to Wealth, Yes IRA's Still Make Cent$?, 1988. Co-chmn. Fin. Independence Week, Western Wash., 1987; bd. dirs. Traveler's Aid Soc., A United Way Agy., Seattle, 1988, pacesetter United Way, 1988-91; alumni class steward Calif. Luth. U., 1992-2003; chmn. Friends Scouting, 1994, chmn. bd. 1999, v.p. finance, 1997-98, Golden Empire Coun. Boy Scouts Am., 1999-2005; chmn. investment com. Calif. State U. Sacramento Found., 1998-99; bd. dirs. McClellan Aviation Mus., 2000-05, YMCA Found, 2002—, Aerospace Mus. Calif., 2006—; pres. Sacramento Rotary Found., 2000-2002. Lt. USN, 1970-77, comdr. USNR, ret., 1992. Selected as Jr. Officer of Yr., USNR, 1984, 85; Career Achievement award Calif. Luth. U., 2002; Recipient Silver Beaver award, Boy Scouts of Am., 2003, Rotary Fellow, Sacramento, 2004. Mem. Nat. Spkrs. Assn. (bd. dirs. N.W. chpt. 1992), Internat. Assn. Fin. Planning (chmn. West Region 1987-90, pres. Western Wash. chpt. 1986-87), Seattle Soc. Fin. Planners (bd. dirs. 1985-86), Inst. CFPs, Real Estate Securities and Syndication Inst. (v.p. 1980-83), East King County and Pierce County Estate Planning Coun., Seattle Res. Officer Assn. (pres., v.p. 1983-85), Puget Sound Naval Res. Assn. (v.p. 1985-90), Sacramento Rotary (chmn. edn. com. 1994, bd. dirs. 2005—), Sacramento Rotary Found. (pres. 2000-2002, bd. dirs. 1996-2005), Seattle Rotary (bd. dirs., chmn. membership devel. com.). Avocations: flying gliders, giant pumpkin growing and sculpting, photography. Office Phone: 916-721-1400. Business E-Mail: tpinkney@thesavantgroup.com. E-mail: tpinkney@starstream.net.

**PINKNEY, JERRY,** artist, educator, illustrator; b. Phila., Dec. 22, 1939; s. James H. and Wille Mae (Landers) P.; m. Gloria Jean Maultsby, Mar. 19, 1959; children: Troy Bernardette, Jerry Brian, Scott Cannon, Myles Carter. Student, U. of the Arts, 1957-59. Designer, illustrator Rustcraft Pub. Co., Dedham, Mass., 1959-63, Barker/Black Studio, Boston, 1963-65, Kaleidoscope Studio, Boston, 1965-67, Jerry Pinkney Studio, Boston, 1967-70; illustrator, pres. Jerry Pinkney, Inc., Croton, NY, 1970—. Vis. critic RI Sch. Design, Providence, 1967—70; assoc. prof. Pratt Inst., Bklyn., 1986—87; disting. vis. prof. U. Del., Newark, 1986—88, assoc. prof. art, 1988—92; vis. prof. art U. Buffalo, 1991. One-man retrospective shows include Northeastern U., Boston, 1983, Mass. Coll. Art, Boston, 1987, Mus. Nat. Ctr. African Am. Artists, Boston, 1987, U. Del., Newark, 1987, Phila. Afro-Am. Hist. and Cultural Mus., 1988, Johnson Mus. Art, Cornell U., Ithaca, N.Y., 1988, Schomburg Ctr. for Rsch. in Black Culture, N.Y., 1990, Bethume Hall, U. Buffalo, 1991, Indpls. Mus. Art, 1991, Every Picture Tells a Story, L.A., 1991, Md. Inst. Art, Balt., 1992, Art Inst. Chgo., 1993; internat. group shows Biennale Bratislace, Czechoslovakia, 1989, 91; illustrator Patchwork Quilt, 1985 (Christopher award, 1986, Coretta Scott King award, 1986, Ezra Jack Keats New Writer award, 1986), Turtle in Julu, 1989 (award N.Y. Times 1989, Time mag. 1989), Rabbit Makes a Monkey of Lion, 1989, Mirandy and Brother Wind, 1989 (Coretta Scott King award, 1989, Caldecott honor), The Talking Eggs, 1989 (Irma S. and James H. Black award for Excellence in Children's Literature, 1989, Randolph Caldecott Medal Honor Book, 1990, Colo. Children's Book award, 1991, Golden Sower award, 1992, Georgia Children's Book award, 1993, Georgia Child Picture Story Book award, 1993, Virginia Young Readers program, 1993), The Man Who Kept His Heart in a Bucket (Gold medal Soc. of Ill., N.Y. 1991), In for Winter, Out for Spring, 1991, Homeplace, 1991 (Golden Kite award 1991), Wild Wild Sunflower Child Anna, 1991, Back Home, 1992, Drylongso, 1992 (Reading Magic award, 1992), The Adventures of Spider: West African Folktales, 1992, A Starlit Somersault Downhill, 1993, Sunday Outing, 1994 (NY Times Best Illustrated Children's Book of Yr., 1994), Mary McLeod Bethune, 1994, Tanya's Reunion, 1995, John Henry, 1994 (Aesop prize, 1994, ABC Children's Booksellers Choices award, 1995, Boston Globe-Horn Book award, 1995, Randolph Caldecott Medal Honor Book, 1995), Minty: A Story of Harriet Tubman, 1996 (Golden Kite award, 1996, Christopher award, 1997, Coretta Scott King award, 1997, Kentucky Bluegrass award, 1998), Sam and the Tigers, 1996 (ABC Children's Booksellers Choices award, 1997), The Hired Hand, 1997 (Aesop Prize 1997, Commonwealth Club of Calif. Book award, 1997, Best Illustrated Children's Book of Yr., NY Times, 1997), (illustrated and adapted by) Rikki Tikki Tavi, 1997 (ABC Children's Bestsellers Choice award, 1998), Black Cowboy, Wild Horses, 1998, Uncle Remus, 1999, Journey's with Elijah: Eight Tales of the Prophet, 1999, The Ugly Duckling, 1999 (Randolph Caldecott Medal Honor Book, 2000), (adapted and illustrated by) The Little Match Girl, 1999, Albidaro and the Mischievous Dream, 2000, Goin' Someplace Special, 2001 (ABC Children's Booksellers Choices award, 2002, Coretta Scott King award, 2002), Noah's Ark, 2002 (Caldecott honor), Song of Trees, 2003, God Bless the Child, 2004, Half a Moon and One Whole Star, Pretend You're a Cat, The Man Who Kept His Heart in a Bucket, Tonweya and the Eagles and the other Lakota Tales, I Want To Be, Aesop's Fables. Mem. US Citizens' Stamp Adv. Com., Washington, 1982—92, US Postal Svc. Quality Assurance Com., Washington, 1986—97, Nat. Coun. on Arts Natl. Endowment for Arts, Washington. Recipient Alumni award, Phila. Sch. Art & Design-U. Arts, 1992. Mem.: NY Soc. Illustrators (Hamilton King award 1993, gold medal 1993, 1994). Avocation: music. Office Phone: 914-271-5238.*

**PINKUS, ALAN R.,** engineering research psychologist; b. Dayton, Ohio, Apr. 11, 1951; s. Irwin A. and Harriet Austrian Pinkus; m. Rebecca S. Moser, June 2, 1951; children: Eric S. Kimble, Christopher L. Kimble, Barrie L. BS, Wright State U., Dayton, Oh90, 1973; MS, U. of Dayton, Ohio, 1980; PhD, Miami U., Oxford, Ohio, 1991. Sr. engring. rsch. psychologist AFRL/HECV, Wright-Patterson AFB, Ohio, 1982—. Contbr. scientific papers to profl. publs. Recipient USAF Sci. and Engring. award, 1999, Fitts Human Engring. award, USAF. Fellow: ASTM Internat. (vice-chair f7 com. 2006—, Award of Merit 2004). Achievements include patents for Vision Goggle Ambient Illumination Testing; Programmable Airdrop Infrared Decoy; Vision Device Automated Spectral Response Determination; Night Vision Device Wavelength Test Pattern; Spectral Distribution Emulation; Night Vision Device Localized Irradiance Attenuation; Night Vision Goggle Haze and Transmissivity Measurement Device; Airborne Target Designating Laser Canopy Returns; Level, Night Vision Imaging System-Weighted Irradiance Tester. Avocations: machine design and fabrication, travel. Office: Air Force Rsch Lab 2255 H St Wright Patterson Afb OH 45433-7022 Office Phone: 937-255-8767.

**PINKWATER, JULIE,** publishing executive; B, Boston U. With Sotheby's Internat. Realty, Network TV Assn; with advertising agency McCaffrey & McCall, Penchina Selkowitz, McCann Erickson; mgr. position Ladies Home Jour.; beauty dir. Allure; advertising dir. More, 1998—2000, pub., 2000—01, Fitness Mag., G&J USA, NY, 2001—04; v.p., pub. Ladies Home Jour., NY, 2004—. Office: Ladies Home Jour 125 Park Ave 20th Floor New York NY 10017-5529 Office Phone: 212-551-7153. Office Fax: 212-455-1313. E-mail: julie.pinkwater@meredith.com.*

**PINN, VIVIAN W.,** federal agency administrator, pathologist; b. Halifax, Va., 1941; BA, Wellesley Coll. 1963; MD, U. Va. 1967. Intern in pathology Mass. Gen. Hosp., Boston, 1967-68, rschr. in pathology, 1968-70; asst. pathologist Tufts U. New England Med. Ctr. Hosp., 1970-77, pathologist, 1977-82; from asst. to assoc. prof. pathology Tufts U., 1971-82, asst. dean student affairs, 1974-82; prof., dept. chair pathology Howard U., 1982-91;

first dir. Office Rsch. on Women's Health, NIH, Bethesda, Md., 1991—, assoc. dir. rsch. women's health, 1994—, dir. Office Women's Health Rsch. Pres. Nat. Med. Assn., 1989—90. Office: NIH Office Rsch on Women's Health 9000 Rockville Pike Bldg 1 Rm 201 Bethesda MD 20892 Office Phone: 301-402-1770.

**PINNADUWAGE, LAL ARIYARATNA,** physicist, researcher; b. Gonapinuwala, Sri Lanka; came to U.S., 1979; s. Noris and Eminona (Kariyawasam) P.; m. Purnima Damayanthi Senanayake, July 20, 1983; children: Sesha Nilmini, Neesha Priyangi. BS, U. Sri Lanka, Colombo, 1978; MS, U. Pitts., 1980, PhD, 1986. Asst. lectr. U. Sri Lanka, 1978-79; teaching asst. U. Pitts., 1979-80, rsch. asst., 1980-86; postdoctoral fellow U. Tenn., Knoxville, 1986-90, adj. asst. prof., 1991-95, rsch. assoc. prof., 1995-99, rsch. prof., 1999—; mem. rsch. staff Oak Ridge (Tenn.) Nat. Lab., 1999—, sr. scientist, 1999—. Contbr. articles to profl. jours. Fellow: Am. Phys. Soc. Achievements include first experiments on quasi one-dimensional highly-excited hydrogen atoms, first observation of optically-enhanced electron attachment to electronically-excited molecules, electron attachment to Rydberg molecules, stability of core-excited Rydberg molecules. Office: Oak Ridge Nat Lab Bldg 4500 S MS 6122 PO Box 2008 Oak Ridge TN 37831-2008

**PINNELL, SHELDON RICHARD,** dermatologist, researcher, retired educator; b. Dayton, Ohio, Feb. 3, 1937; s. Jacob and Nevella P.; m. Doren Madey, 1983; children: Kevin, Alden, Tyson. AB, Duke U., 1959; MD, Yale U., 1963. Intern in medicine U. Minn. Hosp., Mpls., 1963-65; resident in dermatology Harvard U., Boston, 1968-71; prof. medicine Duke U. Med. Ctr., Durham, N.C., 1978—, chief div. dermatology, 1982-97, asst. prof. biochemistry, 1988—, J. Lamar Callaway prof. dermatology, 1989—2002, prof. emeritus, 2002—. Founding scientist Fibrogen, 1994—, SkinCeuticals, 1997—, SkinResearch, 2002—04, Skin Sci. Inst., 2004—. Contbr. over 100 articles to profl. jours.; six patents in field. Office: Duke U Med Ctr PO Box 3135 Durham NC 27710-0001 E-mail: pinne002@mc.duke.edu.

**PINNEY, THOMAS CLIVE,** retired English language educator; b. Ottawa, Kans., Apr. 23, 1932; s. John James and Lorene Maude (Owen) P.; m. Sherrill Marie Ohman, Sept. 1, 1956; children—Anne, Jane, Sarah. BA, Beloit Coll., Wis., 1954; PhD, Yale U., 1960. Instr. Hamilton Coll., Clinton, NY, 1957-61; instr. English Yale U., New Haven, 1961-62; asst. prof. to prof., chmn. dept. English Pomona Coll., Claremont, Calif., 1962-97; ret., 1997. Editor: Essays of George Eliot, 1963, Selected Writings of Thomas Babington Macaulay, 1972, Letters of Macaulay, 1974-81, Kipling's India, 1986, A History of Wine in America, 1989, Kipling's Something of Myself, 1990, Letters of Rudyard Kipling, 1990,-2004 The Vineyards and Wine Cellars of California, 1994, The Wine of Santa Cruz Island, 1994, A History of Wine in America: From Prohibition to the Present, 2005. Guggenheim fellow, 1966, 84,Recipient Disting. Svc. citation Beloit Coll., 1984; fellow NEH, 1980; grantee Am. Coun. Learned Socs., 1974, 84, Am. Philos. Soc., 1968, 82, 94. Mem. MLA, Elizabethan Club (New Haven), Zamorano Club (L.A.), Phi Beta Kappa. Office: Pomona Coll Dept English Claremont CA 91711 Home: 890 E Harrison Ave 32 Pomona CA 91767

**PINNO, JOHN WALTER,** musician, educator; b. Marlin, Tex., Feb. 5, 1946; s. Walter Henry and Thelma (Mitchell) Pinno; m. Mary Evelyn Reed, Aug. 12, 1978; children: Suzanne, Elisa. BS Indsl. Arts, North Tex. State U., Denton, 1968; BA Music Classical Guitar Performance, U. Tex. El Paso, 1977; MA Music History, East Tex. State U., Commerce, 1980. Classical guitar instr. East Tex. State U., Commerce, 1977—79, McLennan C.C., Waco, Tex., 1979—82, U. Mary Hardin Baylor, Belton, Tex., 1982—, Temple Coll., Tex., 1981—. Arranger For 2 Guitars, Flute, STR, Voice, 1973—; performer (solo classical guitarist). Capt. USAF, 1969—73. Recipient 2d pl Music Competition, Barclay Arts Coun., Temple, Tex., 2004, 2005. Avocations: billiards, gardening, woodworking, photography. Office: Temple Coll 2600 S First St Temple TX 76504 also: U Mary Hardin Baylor Music Dept 900 Coll St Belton TX 76513 Office Phone: 254-295-4678, 254-298-8282. E-mail: jpinno093@hotmail.com.

**PINO, RICHARD EDMUND,** corporate financial executive; b. Bklyn., Feb. 1, 1966; s. Edward James Pino and Sherry Sue Harris. BA in Econs., St. Francis Coll., 1989; MBA in Corp. Fin., Adelphi U., 1993; attended, Walden U., 1997. Paper specialist Merrill Lynch Capital Markets, 1988—89; fin. analyst TimeWarner, 1990—91; contr. Veronis, Suhler & Assocs., 1993—96; asst. contr. MediaLink Worldwide, 1996—97; dir. Global Media Advisors, 1997—99; v.p. fin. and adminstrn. Eagle Comm., 1999—2000; CFO Ocean Records, 2000—01, Frontline Communication Internat., 2001—05, Relegance Inc., 2005—. Bd. dirs., chmn. audit com. St. Christopher's, Dobbs Ferry, NY, 1994—; bd. dirs., treas. Co-Operation Ireland, NYC, 1994—. Mem.: Nat. Assn. Credit Mgrs., Bus. Coun. NY State Inc., Fin. Exec. Network Group. Office Phone: 212-594-4404. E-mail: rpino@att.net.

**PINOVER, EUGENE ALFRED,** lawyer; b. NYC, Jan. 8, 1948; s. Maurice Alfred and Harriet (Ortner) P.; m. Diana Elzey, Feb. 14, 1974; children: Julia, Benjamin, Hannah. BA cum laude, Dartmouth Coll., 1969; JD cum laude, NYU, 1973. Bar: N.Y. 1974, U.S. Dist. Ct. (so. and ea. dists.) N.Y. 1974. Ptnr., chair Real Estate Dept. Willkie Farr & Gallagher LLP, N.Y.C. Office: Willkie Farr & Gallagher 787 7th Ave Lbby 2 New York NY 10019-6099 Business E-Mail: epinover@willkie.com.

**PINSKY, LAWRENCE STEVEN,** physics professor; b. N.Y.C., Aug. 9, 1946; s. Bernard and Katherine June (Collins) Pinsky; m. Brenda Joyce Wilson, Aug. 29, 1971; children: Jeffrey David, Joshua Abram, Jacqueline Elizabeth. BS in physics, Carnegie Mellon U., 1968; MA in physics, U. Rochester, 1969, PhD in physics, 1973; JD, U. Houston, 1997, LLM, 2001. Lic.: USPTO (patent atty.), Tex. (law). Postdoctorate fellow U. Houston, 1973—75, asst. prof. to assoc. prof. to prof. physics, 1975—, chair, dept. physics, 1994—. Adj. prof. law U. Houston Law Ctr., Houston, 2001—; computing coord. Alice-USA Collaboration, Switzerland, 2002—. Contbr. articles various profl. jours. Youth football coach Clear Lake Space Riders, Clear Lake City, Tex., 1970—2006. Cpt. U.S. Army, 1969—73. Recipient Tchr Excellence award, U. Houston, 1994, Law Review award, 1994, Order of the COIF, 1997. Mem.: AILPA, Tex. Bar Assn., AM. Physics Soc. Office: U Houston Dept Physics 4800 Calstown Blvd Houston TX 77204 Office Phone: 713-743-3552. Office Fax: 713-743-3589. E-mail: pinsky@uh.edu.

**PINSKY, MARK A.,** plastic surgeon; s. Richard and Janet Pinsky; m. Jennifer L. Sklaver, Sept. 11, 2004; 1 child, Daelan Matthew. MD, Ohio State U., Columbus, 1985. Cert. Am. Bd. Plastic Surgery, 1993. Physician pvt. practice, West Palm Beach, Fla., 1991—. Clin. investigator for silicone gel matrix breast implants Allergan, Calif., 1992—, internat. presenter on facial esthetics & breast esthetics, Calif., 2004—, clin. investigator for juvederm dermal filler, Calif., 2004—, clin. investigator for 410 cohesive gel breast implants, Calif., 2006—. Named Palm Beach Best Plastic Surgeon, Palm Beach Illus., 2004. Mem.: Inamed Breast Acad., Lipoplasty Soc. N.Am., Fla. Med. Assn., Palm Beach Med. Assn., Palm Beach County Soc. Plastic and Reconstructive Surgeons, AMA, Fla. Soc. Plastic and Reconstructive Surgeons, Am. Soc. Plastic and Reconstructive Surgeons, Inamed Facial Esthetic Acad., Am. Soc. Aesthetic Plastic Surgery. Office: Mark A Pinsky MD PA 927 45th St Ste 201 West Palm Beach FL 33407 Office Phone: 561-881-8800. Office Fax: 561-848-5878. E-mail: www.pinskymd.com.

**PINSKY, MICHAEL S.,** lawyer; b. Chgo., July 25, 1945; s. Joseph and Irene (Sodakoff) P.; m. Judy R. Rabin, Sept. 29, 1974; children: David, Susie, Jodie. BS, U. Ill., 1967; JD, DePaul U., 1971. Bar: Ill. 1971. Conferee, revenue agt. IRS, Chgo., 1967-72; ptnr. Levenfeld & Kanter, Chgo., 1972-80, Levenfeld, Eisenberg Janger, Chgo., 1980-84, Vedder Price, Kaufman & Kammholz, Chgo., 1984-88, Gottlieb & Schwartz, Chgo., 1989-92, Levin & Schreder, Chgo., 1993-97, Altheimer & Gray, Chgo., 1997-2000, Schain, Burney, Ross & Citron, Ltd., 2000—. Bd. dirs. Better Boys Found., Chgo., 1989-94; mem. planned giving com. Am. Soc. for Technion, 1997—. Mem. Am. Bar Assn.,

Assn. of Bar of State of Ill., Assn. of Bar of City of Chgo. (com. chmn. 1984-86). Office: 222 N La Salle St Ste 1910 Chicago IL 60601-1102 Home: 1212 Carol Ln Glencoe IL 60022-1105 Office Phone: 312-332-0200. Business E-Mail: mpinsky@Schainlaw.com.

**PINSON, CHARLES WRIGHT,** surgeon, educator, academic administrator; b. Albuquerque, May 29, 1952; s. Ernest Alexander and Jean Elizabeth Pinson. Student, Miami U., Oxford, Ohio, 1970-72; BA, U. Colo. Boulder, 1974, MBA, 1976; MD, Vanderbilt U., 1980. Diplomate Am. Bd. Surgery, Am. Bd. Surg. Critical Care, Nat. Bd. Med. Examiners. Resident in gen. surgery Oreg. Health Sci. U., Portland, 1980-86; fellow gastrointestinal surgery Lahey Clinic, Burlington, Mass., 1986-87; dir. liver transplant program VA Western region, Portland, 1989-90, Oreg. Health Sci. U., Portland, 1988-90; interim chmn. dept. surgery Vanderbilt U., Nashville, 1993-95, chief divsn. hepatobiliary surgery and liver transplantation, 1990—2004, vice-chmn. dept. surgery, 1995-2001; dir. Vanderbilt Transplant Ctr., Nashville, 1993—; chmn. med. bd. Vanderbilt U. Med. Ctr., Nashville, 1997-99; chief of staff Vanderbilt U. Hosp., Nashville, 1997—2004; H. William Scott prof., chmn. dept. surgery Vanderbilt U., Nashville, 2001—04; chief med. officer, assoc. vice chancellor for clin. affairs Vanderbilt U. Med. Ctr., Nashville, 2004—. Adv. bd. Pacific N.W. Transplant Bank, Portland, 1989—90, Tenn. Donor Svcs., Nashville, 1991—, sec., 2003—. Mem. editl. bd. Annals Surgery, Jour. Gastrointestinal Surgery, Liver Transplantation, HPB; contbr. articles to profl. jours., chapters to books. Chair liver and intestine allocation com. United Network Organ Sharing, 2003—05; bd. dirs. ARC, Nashville, 1992—94, Am. Liver Found., 1992—96, Ronald McDonald House, 2002—, United Network Organ Sharing, 2000—02, Hosp. Hospitality House, Nashville, 2005—. Fellow, Am. Heart Assn., 1983—84. Mem.: Internat. Hepatopancreato-biliary Assn. (exec. com. 2002—, treas. 2004—), Internat. Liver Transplantation Soc., Soc. Surgery Alimentary Tract, Assn. Acad. Surgery, N. Pacific Surg. Assn. (mem. sci. program 1990—92), Western Surg. Assn., So. Surg. Assn., Am. Surg. Assn., So. Med. Assn. (editl. bd. ann. sect.), Am. Physiologic Soc., Am. Hepatopancreatobiliary Assn. (mem. exec. com. 1997—, treas. 1999—2003, pres. elect 2001—03, pres. 2003—05), Am. Gastroent. Assn., Am. Soc. Study Liver Diseases, Am. Soc. Transplant Surgeons, Soc. Surg. Oncology, Halsted Soc., Soc. Univ. Surgeons, Phi Beta Kappa, Sigma Xi, Alpha Omega Alpha. Office: Vanderbilt U Med Ctr Ste 3810 TVC Nashville TN 37232-5545

**PINSON, LARRY LEE,** pharmacist, state agency administrator; b. Van Nuys, Calif., Dec. 5, 1947; s. Leland J. and Audrey M. (Frett) Pinson; m. Margaret K. Pinson, Mar. 18, 1972; children: Scott C., Kelly E. Student, U. Calif., Davis, 1967-69; AA, Am. River Coll., Sacramento, 1969; PharmD, U. Calif., San Francisco, 1973. Staff pharmacist/asst. dir. pharm. svcs St. Mary's Hosp., Reno, 1973-77; chief pharmacist May Ang Base USAF, 1973-77; mng. pharmacist Scolari's Food & Drug, Reno, 2001—05; exec. sec. Nev. State Bd. Pharmacy, 2005—, pres., 1996—2004, exec. sec., 2005—; pharm. therapeutics com. State Nev., 2004—. Cons. pharmacist Physicians Hosp., 1974—93, Reno Med. Plz., 1973—, Rural Calif. Hosp. Assn., 1973—74, Ford Ctr. Foot Surgery, 1980—; pharmacy coord. Intensive Pharm. Svcs., 1986—87; cons. Calif. Dept. Health & Corrections, Susanville, 1975—76, Nev. Med. Care Adv. Bd., Carson City, 1984—87; provider, reviewer Nev. State Bd. Pharmacy, Reno, 1975—84; instr. Nev. CC, 1974—76; adj. prof. Idaho State U., Pocatello, 1989—. Co-author: Care of Hickman Catheter, 1984. Softball coach Reno/Sparks Recreation Dept., 1973—92; bd. dirs. Am. Cancer Soc., 1986—90; mem. State of Nev. Pharmaceutics and Therapy Com., 2004—, Nev. Arthritis Found.; cubmaster Pack 153 Boy Scouts Am., Verdi, Nev., scoutmaster com. chmn. Reno troop 1, 1988—92. Named Pharmacist of the Yr., Nev. Pharm. Alliance, 1999; recipient Bowl of Hygeia award, Nev. Pharmacists Assn. and A. H. Robbins Co., 1984. Mem.: Greater Nev. Heatlh Sys. Agy., Nev. Profl. Stds. Rev. Orgn., Nev. Pharmacists Assn. (pres. 1981—82), Am. Pharm. Assn., Nat. Assn. Bds. Pharmacy, Kappa Psi. Avocations: skiing, fishing, backpacking, softball, golf. Home: PO Box 478 Verdi NV 89439-0478 Office: 555 Double Eagle Ct Ste 1100 Reno NV 89521 Office Phone: 775-850-1440. Personal E-mail: Rx2005@aol.com.

**PINSON, WILLIAM MEREDITH, JR.,** pastor, writer, administrator; b. Ft. Worth, Aug. 3, 1934; s. William Meredith and Ila Lee (Jones) P.; m. Bobbie Ruth Judd, June 4, 1955; children: Meredith Pinson Creasey, Allison Pinson Hopgood. BA, U. N. Tex., 1955; BD, Southwestern Bapt. Theol. Sem., Ft. Worth, 1959, ThD, 1963, MDiv, 1973; LittD (hon.), Calif. Bapt. Coll., Riverside, 1978; DD (hon.), U. Mary Hardin-Baylor, Belton, Tex., 1984; LHD (hon.), Howard Payne U., Brownwood, Tex., 1986; LittD (hon.), Dallas Bapt. U., 1990; LLD (hon.), Hardin Simmons U., 1999. Ordained to ministry Bapt. Ch., 1955. assoc. sec. Christian Life Commn., Dallas, 1957-63; prof. Christian ethics Southwestern Bapt. Theol. Sem., Ft. Worth, 1963-75; pastor First Bapt. Ch., Wichita Falls, Tex., 1975-77; pres. Golden Gate Bapt. Theol. Sem., Mill Valley, Calif., 1977-82; vol. dir. Tex. Bapt. Heritage Ctr., 2000—; disting. prof. Dallas Bapt. U., 2001—; disting. vis. prof. Baylor U., 2001—. Exec. dir. Bapt. Gen. Conv. Tex., 1982—2000, exec. dir. emeritus, 2000—; chmn. program com. Christian Life Commn. So. Bapt. Conv., spl. rschr. for home mission bd., nat. task force planned growth in giving, 1984—94, stewardship commn., 1986—96; bd. dirs. T.B. Maston Found., 1991—98, Assn. So. Bapt. Schs., 1997—2002; adj. prof. Southwestern Bapt. Theol. Sem., 1976—77; chmn. study commn. freedom, justice and peace Bapt. World Alliance, 1975—80, study commn. on ethics, 1990—95, commn. on racism, 1992—, com. on polity and heritage, 2000—05; v.p. Bapt. Gen. Conv. Tex., 1972—73, state missions commn., 1976—77, vice chmn. urban strategy com., chmn. order of bus. com., 1976, chmn. state missions Good News Tex., 1976—77, chmn. resolutions com.; spkr. in field; bd. dirs., chair centennial com. Baylor U. Health Care Sys., 2002—. Contbr. articles to profl. jours., chapters to books. Adv. bd. Bapt. History and Heritage Soc., 2002—; mem. adv. com. Sch. Leadership Dallas Bapt. U., 2003—. Named Lilly Found. scholar Southwestern Bapt. Theol. Sem., 1960-62; recipient Disting. Alumni award Southwestern Bapt. Theol. Sem., 1979, U. North Tex., 1980, Mosaic Missions award Home Mission Bd., 1984, Paraboloni award Tex. Bapt. Men, 1999, Spirit of Excellence award Houston Bapt. U., 2000, Tex. Bapt. Missions award State Missions Commn., 2000, Pioneer award Tex. Bapt. Missions Found., 2001, W. Winfred Moore award for lifetime achievement in ministry Baylor U., 2001, Officers' award Bapt. History and Heritage Soc., 2003, Elder Statesman award Independence. Assn., 2005. Mem. So. Bapt. Assn. Colls. and Schs., So. Bapt. Assn. of State Exec. Dirs. (pres. 1996-97). Baptist. Avocations: travel, reading. Office: Bapt Gen Conv Tex 333 N Washington Ave Dallas TX 75246-1782 Office Phone: 214-370-9471. Office Fax: 214-370-0228. Business E-Mail: william.pinson@bgct.org.

**PINSTRUP-ANDERSEN, PER,** economist, educator; b. Bislev, Denmark, Apr. 7, 1939; came to U.S., 1965; s. Marinus and Alma (Pinstrup) Andersen; m. Birgit Lund, June 19, 1965; 1 child: Trina. BS, Royal Vet. and Agrl. U., Copenhagen, 1965; MS, Okla. State U., 1967, PhD, 1969; Dr. Tech. Scis. (hon.), Swiss Fed. Inst. Tech., 1996; DSc (hon.), Tamil Nadu U., 1999, Animal Scis. U., 1999; LLD, U. Aberdeen, 1999; Dr. Agr. and Environment (hon.), Wageningen U., The Netherlands, 2000. Agrl. economist Centro Internacional de Agricultura Tropical, Cali, Colombia, 1969-72, head econ. unit, 1972-76; dir. agro.-econ. div. Internat. Fertilizer Devel. Ctr., Florence, Ala., 1976-77; sr. rsch. fellow, assoc. prof. Econ. Inst. Royal Vet. and Agrl. U., Copenhagen, 1977-80. prof. devel. econs., 2003—; rsch. fellow Internat. Food Policy Rsch. Inst., Washington, 1980, dir. food consumption and nutrition divsn., 1980-87, dir. gen., 1992—2002; dir. food and nutrition policy program, prof. food econs. Cornell U., Ithaca, NY, 1987-92, prof. applied econs. and mgmt., 2003—; H.E. Babcock prof. food, nutrition and pub. policy, 2003—; disting prof. Wageningen U., 2000—. Cons. The World Bank, Washington, 1978-92, Can. Internat. Devel. Agy., 1982-83, 86, UNICEF, N.Y.C.; cons. subcom. on nutrition UN, Rome, 1980-87; chmn. CGIAR Sci. Coun., 2004—. Author: more than 400 publs. including, The World Food and Agricultural Situation, 1978, Agricultural Research and Economic Development, 1979, The Role of Fertilizer in World Food Supply, 1980, Agricultural Research and Technology in Economic Development, 1982; editor: (with Magaret Biswas) Nutrition and Development, 1985, Food Subsidies in Developing Countries: Costs, Benefits, and Policy Options, 1988, Macroeconomic Policy Reforms, Poverty, and Nutrition: Analytical Methodologies, 1990, The Political Economy of Food and Nutrition Policies, 1993, (with David Pelletier and Harold Alderman) Child Growth and Nutrition in Developing Countries: Priorities for Action, 1995, Seed of Contention, 2001, The Unfinished Agenda, 2002; mem. editl. bd. coms., of several jours With Danish Army, 1958-59. Recipient cert. of appreciation People to People, 1967, competition prize Nordic Soc. agrl. Rschrs. & Norsk Hydro, 1979, cert. of merit Gamma Sigma Delta, 1991, Disting. Alumnus award U. Colo., 1993, Disting. Alumni award Okla. State U., 1998, World Food prize World Food Found., 2001; fellow Ford Found., 1965-66, Kellogg gravel fellow, 1979. Mem. AAAS (chair sect. on agr. 2004), AAEA (pres. 2005-), Am. Assn. Agrl. Econs. (PhD Thesis award 1970, Outstanding Jour. Article award 1977, bd. dirs. 1996-99), Internat. Assn. Agrl. Econs., Columbian Nat. Orgn. Profls. in Agr. (hon., Charles Black award 1998, Agronomprisen 2000, World Food prize 2001, Rosenhjaerprisen, 2002). Office: Cornell U Divsn of Nutrition 305 Savage Hall Ithaca NY 14853 Office Phone: 607-255-9429. Business E-Mail: pp94@cornell.edu.

**PINTCHMAN, TRACY,** religious studies educator; BA in Film Studies magna cum laude, Cornell U., NY, 1984; MA in Religious Studies, Boston U., 1987; PhD in Religious Studies, U. Calif., Santa Barbara, 1992. Prof. Loyola U., Chgo., 1992—. Author: Rise of the Goddess in the Hindu Tradition, 1994, Guests at God's Wedding, 2005; editor: Seeking Mahadevi, 2001; contbr. articles and book chpts. in field. Office: Loyola Univ Chicago Dept Theology 6525 N Sheridan Rd Chicago IL 60626 Home Fax: 772-508-2386; Office Fax: 773-508-2386. Business E-Mail: tpintch@luc.edu.

**PINTER, GABRIEL GEORGE,** retired physiology educator; b. Bekes, Hungary, June 23, 1925; came to U.S., 1958; s. Lajos and Regina (Szilagyi-Farkas) Pinter; m. Berit Helgesen, Dec. 19, 1958 (dec. May 1980); children: Renee Astrid, Eva Ingelill; m. Vera Lederer Dallos, May 24, 1984. MD, U. Sch. Medicine, Budapest, Hungary, 1951. Asst. prof. U. Sch. Medicine, Budapest, Hungary, 1951-56; rsch. assoc. U. Inst. Med. Rsch., Oslo, Norway, 1957-58; asst. prof. U. Tenn., Memphis, 1958-61; from asst. prof. to prof. U. Md., Balt., 1961-92; retired. Vis. prof. King's Coll., London, 1990-94. Contbr. articles to profl. jours.; translator (with wife) philos. and lit. works into Hungarian. Recipient A.V. Humboldt prize, Germany, 1980; Swedish Royal Med. Soc. fellow, Uppsala, 1972. Mem. Am. Physiol. Soc., Physiol. Soc. Gt. Brit., Scandinavian Physiol. Soc., European Soc. Microcirculation. Personal E-mail: ggvp@comcast.net.

**PINTER, NICHOLAS,** geologist; b. Palma, Mallorca, Spain, July 27, 1964; BA, Cornell U., 1986; MS, Penn State U., 1988; PhD, U. Calif., Santa Barbara, Calif., 1992. Exploration geologist Mobil Oil, Bakersfield, Calif., 1989, Mobil New Exploration Ventures, Dallas, 1990; rsch. asst. Penn State U., University Park, Pa., 1986-88; rsch., teaching asst. U. Calif., Santa Barbara, 1988-92, rschr., lectr., 1992-93; postdoctoral rschr. Yale U., 1995-96; full prof. Southern Ill. U., 1996—. Author: Exercises in Active Tectonics, 1996, Active Tectonics, 2d edit., 2002; editor: The Adria Microplate, 2006; editor The Adria Microplate, 2006; contbr. numerous articles to profl. jours. Recipient Rsch. and Writing award, John D. and Catherine T. MacArthur Found., 2002, Bessel prize, Alexander von Humboldt Found., 2003—04; fellow, Charles A. Lindbergh Found., 1999—; Fulbright fellow, 2000. Mem. AAAS, Geol. Soc. Am., Sigma Xi. Office: Southern Ill U Dept Geology Carbondale IL 62901-4324 Office Phone: 618-453-7375. Business E-Mail: npinter@geo.siu.edu.

**PINTO, JANET SUE,** music educator; b. Linden, Ind., Apr. 9, 1946; d. Carl Lester and LaVonne Olivet Norman; m. Thomas King Pinto, July 5, 1981; 1 child, Gabriella Elaine. BS, Ball State U., 1968; MME, Peabody Coll., Nashville, 1970; DA, U. No. Colo., 1979. Elem. music tchr., Ind., 1970—71; elem. and jr. h.s. music tchr. Royal Center, Ind., 1971—73; organist, choir dir. Christ Luth. Ch., Wantagh, NY, 1983—87, Cmty. United Meth. Ch., Massapequa, NY, 1987—99, St. Luke Luth. Ch., Dix Hills, NY, 1999—; presch. music tchr. Reach for the Stars Preschool, Wading River, NY, 1988—; North Shore Nursery Sch., Manhasset, Friends Together Nursery Sch., Port Washington, Our Redeemer Luth. Ch. Preschool, Seaford. Piano tchr., 1980—. Mem.: Early Childhood Music and Movement Assn., Am. Guild Organists (treas. 2003—). Home: 7 Daremy Ct Melville NY 11747

**PINTO, MAXWELL SALUSTIANO,** management consultant; b. Goa, India, Mar. 10, 1954; came to U.S., 1984; s. Maurice and Martha (Lopez) P.; m. Eusebia C. Fernandez, Jan. 25, 1987; children: Aaron Massimo, Esther Maxine BA honors, U. Leeds, Eng., 1978; PhD Bus. Adminstrn., Pacific So. U., 1987. Chartered acct., Eng. Auditor, acct. KPMG Peat Marwick Chartered Accts., London, 1978—82; dep. mgr. fin. and adminstrn. Elec. Bds. Mfg. Co., Kuwait, 1983—86; fin. cons. Tollafield & Assocs., Cyprus, 1986—87; dir. Brandon Planning & Corp. Analysis, Cyprus, 1987—88; mgmt. analyst Citgo Group Inc., N.Y.C., 1989—93; bus. assoc. in ins. and investments N.Y. Life Ins. Co., N.Y.C., 1993—96; trust acct. CI Mut. Funds, Inc., Toronto, Canada, 1998—2001; bus. cons. Toronto, 2001—. Lectr. acctg. Plato Coll., 1987, Limassol, Cyprus, econs. Americanos Coll., Limassol, 1987, mgmt. and law, Intercollege, Limassol, 1988 Author: The Management Syndrome, 1998, Management...Flirting with Disaster!, 2005. Pacific So. U. scholar, 1984 Mem. Inst. Profl. Mgrs. (life), Inst. Chartered Accts. (assoc.), Outdoor World, Coast to Coast Avocations: tennis, swimming, pool, movies. Home and Office: 169 Morrison Ave Toronto ON Canada M6E 1M6 E-mail: crespin79@hotmail.com.

**PINTO, ROSALIND,** retired secondary school educator, volunteer; b. NYC; d. Barney and Jenny Abrams; m. Jesse E. Pinto (dec.); children: Francine, Jerry, Evelyn. BA in Polit. Sci. cum laude, Hunter Coll.; MA in Polit. Sci., History, Columbia U.; postgrad., Queens Coll., LaGuardia C.C. Lic. social studies tchr. in field, NY, NY, per diem substitute; cert. secondary sch. social studies grades 7-12, NY. Substitute tchr., 1966-69, 90, 91—; tchr. social studies I.S. 126Q, LI, NY, 1969-88, Jr. HS 217 Briarwood, NYC, 1988-89; rct., 1989; part-time cluster tchr. social studies and communication arts Pub. Sch. 140, Bronx, NY, 1990-92; substitute tchr. I.S. 227Q, 1992-93. Participant seminars and workshops. Author curriculum materials; contbr. study guide for regent's competency test, 1990; author numerous poems; contbr. articles to profl. jours. Enrollment asst. Insight Heart Team, 1989; vol. receptionist Whitney Mus., N.Y.C.; mem. com. on pub. transp. Cmty. Bd. 6, Queens, 1990—96, mem. com. on history, 1990—, chmn. beautification com., 1992—, mem. com. on planning and zoning, 1996—, mem. com. on environ. sanitation, 1999—; mem. Forest Hills Action League, 1990; advocate Census 2000 participation; active Gt. Smokies Song Chase Warren-Wilson Coll., NC, 1992; mem. Queens Hist. Soc., Forest Hills Van Ct. Homeowners Assn.; bd. dirs. Ctrl. Queens Hist. Soc.; past mem. Rego Park Coalition Against Crime; mem. Forest Hills Civic Assn., 1996—97; vol. local polit. campaigns. Named to Internat. Who's Who in Poetry, 2005; recipient Cert. Appreciation for participation, Dept. Probate Cmty. Svc. Project, 1993, award for participation in Make a Difference Day, 1994—95, award for projects, Beautification Com., 1995, Rosemary Gunning award, Queens Borough Pres. for Women's History month, 2000, Cert. Appreciation Cmty. Svc., NY State Senate, 2004—05, Editor's Choice award, Best Poems and Poets, 2001, 2002, 2004, 2005, Poet of Merit award, Poetry Conv., 2002—03, 2005, Cert. Appreciation for joining graffiti cleanup, 112th Precinct Cmty. Coun., 2002, Cert. of Appreciation for help in Night Out Against Crime, 2004, 2005, poetry dibsvs. award, Noble House, 2006. Fellow: Mcpl. Art Soc. (hon. mention design 2000 award); mem.: NAFE, Internat. Soc. Poets (life; adv. panel, Internat. Poet of Merit award 1993, 2000, Editor's Choice award 2001), Ctr. for Sci. in the Pub. Interest, Robert F. Kennedy Dem. Assn. (bd. dirs., RFK Assn. cert. of appreciation for dedication 2005), Hunter Coll. HS Alumni Assn., Hunter Coll. Alumni Assn., Columbia U. Grad. Sch. Arts and Scis. Alumni Assn., NY Insight Alumni Assn. Avocations: poetry, reading, walking, art shows, plays. *Loving people and having faith in them and the possibility of happy outcomes is the greatest motivation toward achievement of goals.*

**PINTO-MARTIN, JENNIFER ANNE,** epidemiologist, educator; b. Colma, Calif., Mar. 17, 1957; d. Douglas Wellman Pinto and Elizabeth Kathleen (O'Hara) Hazard; m. Muscoe Burnett Martin, Aug. 17, 1986; children: Emily Grace Martin, Nora Mills Martin, Charlotte Elizabeth Martin, Muscoe (Jack) Burnett Martin. BS, Stanford U., 1974—78; MPH, U. Calif., Berkeley, 1980—82, PhD, 1982—84. Asst. prof. Columbia U., N.Y.C., 1984—90, U. Pa., Phila., 1990—97, assoc. prof., 1998—2005, prof., 2005—. Grantee Ctr. for Autism Rsch., CDC, 2001. Office: Univ Pennsylvania 420 Guardian Dr Philadelphia PA 19118 Office Phone: 215-898-4726. Business E-Mail: pinto@nursing.upenn.edu.

**PINTOZZI, CHESTALENE,** librarian; b. Macomb, Okla., Apr. 4, 1947; d. Otis William and Edith Marie (Jordan) Bowerman; m. Nicola Francis Xavier Pintozzi, Aug. 2, 1967 (div.). Student, U. Okla., 1965-67; BA in English, No. Ill. U., 1969; MLS, U. Tex., 1981. Geology libr. U. Tex., Austin, 1982-84; environ. libr., Am Marbut Environ. Libr. Sarasota (Fla.) County Pub. Libr. Sys., 1985-87; temporary reference libr. Sci.-Engring. Libr. U. Ariz., Tucson, 1989-90, reference libr. Sci.-Engring. Libr., 1990—. Mem. Geosci. Info. Soc., Soc. for Scholarly Pub., Beta Phi Mu, Phi Kappa Phi. Democrat. Office: U Ariz Bldg 54 Rm 216 Tucson AZ 85720 Office Phone: 602-621-6392. E-mail: pintozzic@u.library.arizona.edu.

**PIOMBINO, NICHOLAS,** psychotherapist; b. NYC, Oct. 5, 1942; s. Nicholas Bruce and Ruth Mary (Rothbart) P. BA with honors, CCNY, 1964; MSW, Fordham U., 1971; cert. in adult psychoanalysis and psychotherapy, Postgrad. Ctr. Mental Health, N.Y.C., 1982. Diplomate in clin. social work; cert. psychotherapist, social worker, N.Y. Social worker Manhattan State Hosp., N.Y.C., 1971-73; pvt. practice psychotherapy N.Y.C., 1976—; sch. social worker N.Y.C. Bd. Edn., 1974—2001; staff psychotherapist Postgrad. Ctr. Mental Health, 1978-86; supr., mem. faculty Psychoanalytic Inst. N.Y. Counseling and Guidance Svc., N.Y.C., 1987—. Author: Poems, 1988, Light Street, 1996, Theoretical Objects, 1999, (essays) The Boundary of Blur, 1993, The Boundary of Theory, 2000, Hegelion Honeymoon, 2004, numerous poems; contbr. articles to profl. jours.; Exhibited in group shows at Maryann Boesky Gallery, 2001, Harvard Dudley House, 2005. Mem. Postgrad. Psychoanalytic Soc., Soc. Clin. Social Work Psychotherapists. Office: 680 W End Ave New York NY 10025-6815 Home: 44 Prospect Park W Apt F2 Brooklyn NY 11215-2344 Office Phone: 212-316-1871. E-mail: nickpoetique@earthlink.net.

**PIONK, JEROME LEE,** federal official, trade association administrator; b. Watertown, S.D., Aug. 31, 1950; s. Jerome Ambrose and Helen Emeline Pionk; m. Song Yo Kim; childen: Jerome, Angela Pionk Curtis. BS, SUNY, Albany, 1984; MA, Liberty U., 1991; grad., Command and Gen. Staff Coll., 1997. Cert. counselor. Enlisted man U.S. Army, 1970, advanced through grades to sgt. maj., 1989, recruiter Minn., Republic of Korea, 1970—84; retention and recruiting staff specialist Army Enlistment Eligibility Activity, St. Louis, 1984—87; dir. theater army retention 8th Army, Seoul, 1987—92; sr. retention policy advisor Hdqs. Dept. Army, Washington, 1992—2000; ret., 2000; sr. def. analyst, rschr. Dept. Def. (Resource Cons. Inc.)_, Washington, 2000—03; rsch. analyst SAIC, 2003—04; chief recruiting incentives br. U.S. Army G-1, Pentagon, 2004—. Prof. Am. Mil. U., 2000—; exec. dir. Nat. Assn. Recruiters and Career Counselors, Washington, 1983—; bd. dirs. Ctr. Mil. Sociol. Studies. Author: Prairie Vignettes, 1999 (Midwest Lit. award 2000), History of Military Retention, 2001. Decorated Legion of Merit; recipient Olympic honor award Seoul Olympic Organizing Com., 1988, Order of Horatio Gates, Army Adj. Gen.'s Assn., 1992. Mem. VFW (life), DAV (life), Not Good Old Boys-Vets. Assn. (exec. dir. 1983—, Order of Merit 1994), Am. Vets. (life), Am. Legion. Republican. Avocations: skydiving, travel, writing, fencing, automobile racing. Office: Army Office Human Resource Mgmt 300 Army Pentagon Washington DC 20310 Home: 12241 Tilney Ct Woodbridge VA 22192-6611 Personal E-mail: ngob1@aol.com.

**PIONK, RICHARD CLETUS,** artist, educator; b. Minn., Apr. 26, 1936; s. Franz E. Spielmann and Esther (Dufrane) Pionk. Cert. in fine arts painting, Art Students League, 1983. Tchr. Art Students League, N.Y.C., 1991—. Mem. bd. control Art Students League, 1983-90. Exhibited in one-man shows Moran Gallery, Tulsa, 1985, Connoisseur Gallery, Rhinebeck, N.Y., 1987, 88, 89, 90, Bklyn. Pub. Libr.; exhibited in group shows Queens Mus., N.Y.C., 1982, Hermitage Found., Norfolk, Va., 1985, Monmouth Mus., Lincroft, N.J., 1985, La Societe des Pastellistes de France, Lille, 1987, Canton (Ohio) Art Inst., 1987, Friends Art Mus., Naples, Fla., 1987, Mel Vin Gallery Southern Coll., Lakeland, Fla., 1987, Wind Borne Gallery, Southport, Conn., 1987, 89, Gregory Gallery, Darien, Conn., 1990, 91, 92, 93, 94, 95, 96, Geary Gallery, Darien, 1997, 98, 99, 2000, 01, 02, The Food Show at Grand Cen. Art Gallery, N.Y.C., 1989, Quincy (Ill.) Art Club, 1989, 90, Jordane Art Gallery, Ft. Myers, Fla., 1990, Pastel Soc., N.Y.C., 1991, Allied Artists, N.Y.C., 1991, Harman-Meek Gallery, Naples, 1992, Butler Inst. Art, 2000, 2003, Nat. Acad. Design, N.Y.C., 2004, others; represented in permanent collections Butler Inst. Art, Ohio, 1st Pastel Mus., China, SalmaGundi Club, N.Y.C., Kidder-Peabody, N.Y., others. Recipient Salzman award, 1999, 2001, Bernhardt Gold medal for pastel, 2002, numerous awards, including medal, Artist's Fellowship, 2002, medal, The Pastel Soc., 2002, 2003. Mem. Pastel Soc. Am. (1st v.p. 1978-91, exhbn. chmn. 1978—, master pastellist, Hall of Fame 1997), Allied Artists Am. (bd. dirs. 1986-91, asst. corr. sec. 1986—), Audubon Artists (juror 1989—), Artists Fellowship Inc. (bd. dirs. 1988—), Nat. Arts Club (Art Spirit Silver medal 2005), Salmagundi Club (mem. curators com., chmn. art com. 1981—, pres. 1994—), Dutch Treat Club. Roman Catholic. Avocation: art. Home: 1349 Lexington Ave Apt 8B New York NY 10128-1511 Office: Studio 611 41 Union Sq W New York NY 10003-3208

**PIORKOWSKI, JOSEPH D., JR.,** lawyer, physician, educator, military officer; b. Chester, Pa., Nov. 21, 1956; s. Joseph D. Piorkowski and Elizabeth C. Bell; m. Marjorie Eldridge, Aug. 4, 1984; 1 child, Joseph D. III BA cum laude, Hofstra U., 1976; DO, Phila. Coll. Osteo. Medicine, 1980; JD magna cum laude, Georgetown U., 1988; MPH, Johns Hopkins U., 1992. Diplomate Am. Bd. Preventive Medicine, Am. Bd. Legal Medicine, Am. Osteo. Bd. Family Practice, Nat. Bd. Examiners for Osteo. Physicians and Surgeons; lic. physician, Md., D.C.; bar: Md., D.C., Tex., U.S. Dist. Ct. D.C., U.S. Dist. Ct. Md., U.S. Ct. Appeals (4th and D.C. cirs.); cert. instr. advanced trauma life support; cert. advanced cardiac life support. Commd. ensign USN, 1977, advanced through grades to capt., 1996, flight surgeon fighter squadron 31/carrier air wing THREE, staff physician U.S.S. Kennedy, substance abuse coord., 1982-84, flight surgeon Naval Air Facility, peer review coord. Navy Med. Clinics Washington, 1984-88, head Naval Air Facility Med. Clin., 1986-88; intern in psychiatry Nat. Naval Med. Ctr., Bethesda, Md., 1980-81; law clk. to Hon. Oliver Gasch US Dist. Ct. DC, 1988-89; ptnr. Williams & Connolly, Washington, 1997—2000, Shook, Hardy & Bacon, Washington, 2001—04; prin. Piorkowski Law Firm, PC, Washington, 2004—. Instr. Mil. Tng. Network, Dept. Def., 1986—; adj. prof. law Georgetown U. Law Ctr., Washington, 1992—, clin. asst. prof. dept. surgery Georgetown U. Med. Ctr., 1995-2004 Contbr. articles to profl. jours. Named one of 75 Best Lawyers in Washington, Washingtonian mag., 2002; acad. honors scholar, Hofstra U., 1976. Fellow Am. Coll. Preventive Medicine, Am. Coll. Legal Medicine, Aerospace Med. Assn. (assoc.); mem. ABA (litigation sect.), Soc. of U.S. Naval Flight Surgeons, Internat. Soc. Pharmacoepidemiology, Regulatory Affairs Profl. Soc., Assn. of Mil. Surgeons of U.S. Am. Osteo. Assn., Am. Coll. Family Practitioners, Order of Coif, Delta Omega, Psi Chi. Office: Piorkowski Law Firm 910 17th St NW Ste 800 Washington DC 20006 Office Phone: 202-223-5535. Business E-Mail: JPiorkowski@lawdoc1.com.

**PIOT, PETER,** international organization administrator; b. Leuven, Feb. 17, 1949; m. Greet Kimzeke, 1975; 2 children. MD, U. Ghent, 1974; PhD in Microbiology, U. Antwerp, 1981, PhD (hon.), 1997, Free U., 1995; DSc (hon.), U. West Indies, 2005. Sr. fellow microbiology and infectious diseases Washington, U., 1978—79; prof. microbiology Inst. Tropical Medicine, 1980—92, asst. in microbiology Antwerp, 1981—92; prof. pub. health Free U., Brussels, 1989—94; assoc. dir. Global Program AIDS/WHO, Geneva, 1995; exec. dir. Joint UN Program on HIV/AIDS, Geneva, 1995—; under sec.-gen. UN, 2002—. Dir. WHO Collaborating Ctr. AIDS, Antwerp, Project

SIDA, Kinshasa; assoc. prof. Nairobi U., STD/AIDS Project, Kenya; co-discoverer Ebola virus; Socrates chair, European Acad., Yuste, Spain, 2004; AIDS bd. Internat. Vaccine Initiative, King Boudouin Found. Editor: (with others) Chlamydial Infection, 1982, (with J.M. Mann) AIDS and HIV Infection in the Tropics, 1988, (with P. Lamptey) Handbook on AIDS Prevention in Africa, 1990, 2d edit. 1991, (with others) Basic Laboratory Procedures in Clinical Bacteriology, 1991; co-author: AIDS in Africa: A Handbook for Physicians, 1992, Reproductive Tract Infections in Women, 1992, (with K.K. Holmes)Sexually Transmitted Diseases, 1999, (with M. Carael) L'Epidemie de Sida et la Mondialisation des Risques, 2005. Knighted baron King Albert II, 1995; decorated officier l'Ordre Nat. du Léopard (Zaïre), comdr. l'Ordre du Lion (Sénégal), Nat. Order Burkina Faso and Madagascar; NATO fellow, 1978-79; recipient Kerkheer prize Medicine, 1989, Health Rsch. award, Belgium, 1989, Pub. Health award Flemish Cmty., 1990, AMICOM award Medicine, 1991, H. Breurs prize, 1992, A. Jaunioux prize, 1992, van Thiel award, 1993, Glaxo award infectious diseases, 1995, Nelson Mandela award, 2001, Gold medal Royal Acad. Arts and Scis., Belgium, 2002, E. Calderone medal Columbia U., 2003, Vlerick award, Belgium, 2004, Congl. Achievement award, Philippines, 2005, Grand Ofcl. Order Infante Don Enrique, Portugal, 2005, Acad. Alliance Found. Global Health Leadership award, NY, 2005; named Outstanding Physician, AMA, Chgo., 2004. Fellow Royal Coll. Physicians (London); mem. Royal Acad. Medicine, Royal Acad. Overseas Scis., Internat. AIDS Soc. (pres. 1992), Inst. Medicine, other European, US, and African socs. Achievements include co-discovering the Ebola virus. Office: UNAIDS 20 Ave Appla CH-1211 Geneva 27 Switzerland Office Fax: 22 7914179. Business E-Mail: executivedirector@unaids.org.

**PIOU-BREWER, MAGALIE,** psychotherapist, educator, small business owner; b. Arthabaska, Que., Can., Apr. 26, 1971; d. Edouard Louis and Jacqueline Dorcal Piou; m. Michael Alexander Brewer, July 21, 2003; 1 child, Anya Lilly Brewer. Student, Cath. U., Leuven, Belgium, 1991—92; BA in Comm., Loyola Coll., Balt., 1993, MS in Pastoral Counseling, 2000; PhD in Clinical Psychology, George Washington U., 2004. Lic. counselor. Assoc. dir. admissions Loyola Coll., Balt., 1994—2001; child psychotherapist Stevenson Psychol. Svcs., Columbia, Md., 2001—03; clin. dir. Bridgeway Counseling Svcs., Columbia, 2004—; exec. dir. MPB Group, Inc., Columbia, 2004—. Adj. asst. prof. Loyola Coll. Grad. Ctr., Columbia, 2005—; spkr. in field. Acad. fellow, George Washington U., 2000—03, Maternal/Child Health grant, Kennedy Kreiger Inst., Balt., 2003. Mem.: APA, Am. Counselors Assn., Am. Mental Health Counselors Assn. Avocations: reading, travel. Office: MPB Group Inc 9650 Santiago Rd Ste 11 Columbia MD 21045

**PIPCHICK, MARGARET HOPKINS,** advance practice psychiatric nurse, marriage and family therapist; m. Robert Pipchick; children: Christine, Kevin. BSN, Seton Hall U., 1968; MA, NYU, 1974; grad., Blanton Peale Grad. Inst., N.Y.C., 1981; PhD, The Union Inst., 2001. Cert. traumatologist Green Cross. Various staff positions hosps., NY, NJ; teaching asst. Seton Hall U., South Orange, NJ, 1971-72; staff therapist, faculty Blanton-Peale Counseling Ctr., Cranford, NJ, 1974-90; pvt. practice individual, couple and family therapy Cranford, 1981—. Adj. faculty Fairleigh Dickenson U., Teaneck, NJ, 1989-93, Kean Coll., 1994, 95. Drew U., 2003. Contbr. chpt. to Founds. Psychiat. Mental Health Nursing. Mem. ANA, NJ State Nurses Assn., Am. Assn. Marriage and Family Therapists, Soc. Advanced Practice Psychiatric Nurses (pres.), Sigma Theta Tau. Office Phone: 908-272-9088.

**PIPE, STEVEN W.,** pediatrician, educator; MD, U. Toronto, 1989. Diplomate Am. Bd. Pediat., 2001. Intern, resident in pediat. McMaster U., Hamilton, Ont., Canada, 1989—93; fellow pediat. hematology and oncology U. Mich., Ann Arbor, 1993—96, lectr. pediat., 1996—98, asst. prof. dept. pediat., 1998—2004, assoc. prof. dept. pediat., 2004—. Pediatric med. dir. Hemophilia and Coagulation Disorders Program U. Mich.; med. dir. Spl. Coagulation Lab. Achievements include patents for inactivation-resistant factor VIII. Office: University of Michigan 1500 E Medical Center Drive Ann Arbor MI 48109-0238 Office Phone: 734 647-2893. Office Fax: 734 936-7083. Business E-Mail: ummdswp@med.umich.edu.

**PIPER, ADDISON LEWIS,** securities executive; b. Mpls., Oct. 10, 1946; s. Harry Cushing and Virginia (Lewis) P.; m. Louise Wakefield (div.); children: Gretchen, Tad, William; m. Cynthia Schuneman, Nov. 14, 1979; children: Elisabeth LaBelle, Richard LaBelle. BA in Econs., Williams Coll., 1968; MBA, Stanford U., 1972. Mktg. cons. Earl Savage and Co., Mpls., 1968-69; mem. capital market dept. Piper and Jaffray, Mpls., 1969-70; asst. syndicate mgr. Piper, Jaffray and Hopwood, Mpls., 1972-73, v.p., 1973-79, dir. trading, 1973-77, dir. sales, 1977-79, exec. v.p., dir. mktg., 1979-83, chief exec. officer, chmn. mgmt. com., 1983—, chmn. bd. dirs., 1988—2003; vice chmn., dir. Piper Jaffray Cos. (spun off from U.S. Bancorp), Mpls., 2003—. Adv. com. N.Y. Stock Exch., 1966-90; bd. dirs Allina Health Systems, Greenspring Corp., Mpls., Minn. Bus. Partnership, Mpls., Abbott Northwestern Hosp., Mpls.; trustee CARE Found., Mpls. Fin. chmn. Senator Durenberger Fin. Com., Mpls., 1980-88; chmn. Minn. Pub. Radio, 1985-95. Mem. Securities Industry Assn. (bd. govs. 1986-90, tax policy com.), Country Club of the Rockies (Colo.), Mpls. Club, Ventana Canyon (Tucson), Woodhill Country Club (Wayzata). Republican. Episcopalian. Avocations: skiing, golf, hunting, tennis, horseback riding. Office: Piper Jaffray Cos J1012058 800 Nicollet Mall Ste 800 Minneapolis MN 55402-7020*

**PIPER, ADRIAN MARGARET SMITH,** philosopher, artist, educator; b. N.Y.C., Sept. 20, 1948; d. Daniel Robert and Olive Xavier (Smith) P.; m. Jeffrey Ernest Evans, June 27, 1982 (div. 1987). AA, Sch. Visual Arts, 1969; BA in Philosophy, CCNY, 1974; MA, Harvard U., 1977, PhD, 1981; student, U. Heidelberg, Germany, 1977-78; LHD (hon.), Calif. Inst. Arts, 1992, Mass. Coll. Art, 1994. Asst. prof, U. Mich. Ann Arbor 1979-86; Mellon rsch. fellow Stanford (Calif.) U., 1982-84; assoc. prof. Georgetown U., Washington, 1986-88, U. Calif., San Diego, 1988; prof. philosophy Wellesley (Mass.) Coll., 1990—. Disting. scholar Getty Rsch. Inst., 1998—; speaker, lectr. on both philosophy and art. Artist: one-woman exhbns. include N.Y. Cultural Ctr., N.Y.C., 1971, Montclair (N.J.) State Coll., 1976, Wadsworth Atheneum, Hartford, Conn., 1980, Nexus COntemporary Art Ctr., Atlanta, 1987, The Alternative Mus., N.Y.C. 1987, Goldie Paley Gallery, Phila., 1989, Power Plant Gallery, Toronto, 1990, Lowe Art Mus., Coral Gables, Fla., 1990-91, Santa Monica (Calif.) Mus. Contemporary Art, 1991, John Weber Gallery, N.Y.C., 1989, 90, 91, 92, Whitney Mus. Am. Art, N.Y.C., 1990, Hirschorn Mus., Washington, 1991, Ikon Gallery, Birmingham, Eng., 1991, Cornerhouse, Manchester, Eng., 1992, Cartwright Hall, Bradford, Eng., 1992, Kunstverein, Munich, Germany, 1992, Indpls. Ctr. Contemporary Art, 1992, Manasterio de Santa Clara, Moguer, Spain, 1992, Grey Art Gallery, N.Y.C., 1992, Paula Cooper Art Gallery, 1992, 94; group exhbns. include Paula Cooper Gallery, 1969, Dwan Gallery, N.Y.C., 1969, 70, Seattle Art Mus., 1969, Stadtisches Mus., Leverkusen, Germany, 1969, Kunsthalle Berne, Berne, Switzerland, 1969, N.Y. Cultural Ctr., 1970, Allen Mus., Oberlin, Ohio, 1970, Mus. Modern Art, N.Y.C., 1970, 88, 91, Musee d'Art Moderne, Paris, 1971, 77, 89, Inhibodress Gallery, New South Wales, Australia, 1972, Calif. Inst. Arts, Valencia, 1973, Samuel S. Fleischer Art Meml., Phila., 1974, Nova Contemporary Art, Chgo., 1975, Newberger Mus., Purchase, N.Y., 1978, Mass. Coll. Art, Boston, 1979, Artemesia Gallery, Chgo., 1979, A.I.R. Gallery, N.Y.C., 1980, Inst. Contemporary Arts, London, 1980, The New Mus., N.Y.C., 1981, 83, 85, Kenkeleba Gallery, N.Y.C., 1983, The Studio Mus. Harlem, N.Y.C., 1985, 89, Mus. Moderner Kunst, Vienna, Austria, 1985, Intar Gallery, N.Y.C., 1988, Whitney Mus. Downtown, N.Y.C., 1988, Art Gallery Ont., Toronto, 1988, Long Beach (Calif.) Art Mus., 1989, Simon Watson Gallery, N.Y.C., 1990, Feigen Gallery, Chgo., 1990, Barbara Krakow Gallery, Boston, 1990, Milw. Art Mus., 1990, Contemporary Arts Ctr., Houston, 1991, John Weber Gallery, 1991, Anne Plumb Gallery, N.Y.C., 1991, Hirschorn Mus., 1991, The Albuquerque Mus., Art Mus., 1991, The Toledo Mus. Art, 1991, Denver Art Mus., Fukui Fine Arts Mus., Fukyui-ken, Japan, 1992-93, N.J. State Mus., Trenton, 1992-93, Philippe Staib Gallery, N.Y.C., 1992, New Loom House, London, 1992, Espace-Lyonnais D'Art Contemporain, Lyon, France, 1993, Am. Acad. Inst. Arts and Letters, N.Y.C., 1993; permanent collections include Met. Mus. Art, Whitney Mus., L.A. Mus.

Contemporary Art, San Francisco Mus. Modern Art, The Bklyn. Mus., Denver Art Mus., Kunstmuseum Berne, Musee d'Art Moderne, The Mus. Contemporary Art, Chgo., The Wadsworth Atheneum, Met. Mus. Art; art performances include RISD, 1973, The Whitney Mus. Am. Art, 1975, Kurfurstendamm, Berlin, 1977, Hauptstrasse, Heidelburg, Germany, 1978, Allen Meml. Mus., Oberlin, Ohio, 1980, Contemporary Art Inst. Detroit, 1980, San Francisco Art Inst., 1985, Calif. Inst. Art, 1984, The Studio Mus. Harlem, 1988; performances on video, 1987—; contbr. articles to profl. jours. Recipient N.Y. State Coun. on Arts award, 1989, Visual Arts award, 1990, Skowhegan medal for sculptural installation, 1995, Dance Theatre Workshop award for New Genres, 2000; NEH Travel fellow, 1979, NEA Visual Artists' fellow, 1979, 82, Andrew Mellon Postdoctoral fellow, 1982-84, Woodrow Wilson Internat. Scholars fellow, 1988-89, Guggenheim Meml. fellow, 1989, non-resident fellow N.Y. Inst. for Humanities, NYU, 1996—, Wissan-schftskolleg zu Berlin Inst. Adv. Study fellow, 2005-; NEA Artists Forums grantee, 1987; rsch. fellowship NEH, 1998, Getty Rsch. Inst. Disting. scholarship, 1998-99, Internat. Forschungszentrum Kulturwissenschaften fellow Vienna, fellow Wissenschetskolleg zu Berlin Inst. Advanced Study, 2005-. Mem. AAUP, Am. Philos. Assn. (mem. ea. divsn.), Am. Soc. Polit. and Legal Philosophy, N.Am. Kant. Soc. Avocations: Medieval and Renaissance music, fiction, poetry, yoga, German. Office: Adrian Piper Rsch Archives Postfach 54 02 04 D-10042 Berlin Germany Office Phone: 49-30-308-253-18. E-mail: contact@adrianpiper.com, contak@adrianpiper.com.

**PIPER, DON COURTNEY,** political scientist, educator; b. Washington, July 29, 1932; s. Don Carlos and Alice (Courtney) Piper; m. Rowena Inez Wise, July 6, 1956; children: Sharon, Valarie. BA, U. Md., 1954, MA, 1958; PhD (James B. Duke fellow), Duke U., 1961. Research assoc. Duke U., 1961-62; exec. sec. Commonwealth-Studies Center, 1962-64; asst. prof. dept. govt. and politics U. Md., College Park, 1964-67, assoc. prof., 1967-69, prof., 1969-97, prof. emeritus, 1997—, head dept. govt. and politics, 1968-74, dir. grad. studies dept., 1982-95, mem. coun. of system faculty, 1989-90; chmn. faculty council College Park Faculty Assembly, 1974-75, chmn. campus senate, 1975-77, 89-90, univ. marshal, 1981-97, mem. Athletic Council, 1986-93, mem. senate ad hoc com. on undergrad. edn., 1986-88, chmn. chancellor's ad hoc com. on campus ceremonies, 1986-87, chmn. acad. com. of Athletic Council, 1986-89; chmn. campaign for College Park, 1988-89; chmn. retention review com. U. Md., 1990-91, chmn. budget and facilities com. athletic coun., 1991-93, chmn. senate com. on programs courses and curriculi, 1991-93, co-chair Mid. States self-study exec. com., 1995-97; teaching fellow Lilly Ctr. for Teaching Excellence, 1994-95. Rsch. asst. Am. Coun. Edn., 1966—68; mem. faculty adv. com., mem. adv. com. Md. State Bd. Higher Edn., 1977—82. Author: International Law of Great Lakes, 1967; co-author: International Law Standard and Commonwealth Developments, 1966, De Lege Pactorum, 1970, Foreign Policy Analysis, 1975; editor (with R. Taylor Cole): Post-Primary Education and Political and Economic Development, 1964; editor, author (with Ronald Terchek): Interaction: Foreign Policy and Public Policy, 1983; bd. editors World Affairs, 1971—94, mem. editl. adv. com. Internat. Legal Materials, 1977—78. Served to 1st lt. USAF, 1955—58. Mem.: Phi Beta Kappa (pres. Gamma chpt. 1978—79), Pi Sigma Alpha, Omicron Delta Kappa (faculty advisor 1997—97), Phi Kappa Phi (chpt. pres. 1982—83). Methodist. Home: 6312 Oakview Ct Hillsborough NC 27278

**PIPER, GEORGE CHILTON,** lawyer; b. Lexington, Ky., Feb. 23, 1939; s. Lewis Allie and Anna (Zink) Piper; children: Jennifer A., Geoffrey C. AB, Harvard U., 1960; JD, U. Ky., 1967; MPH, Harvard Sch. Pub. Health, 1984. Ptnr. Martin, Ockerman & Brabart, Lexington, 1966—91; founding ptnr. Piper, Wellman & Bowers, Lexington, 1991—. Gen. counsel Planned Parenthood of Bluegrass, Inc., Lexington, 1971—2004. Sgt. E-4 U.S. Army, 1961—64. Recipient Samdperil Essay award, Harvard Sch. Pub. Health, 1984. Office: Piper Wellman & Bowers 200 N Upper St Lexington KY 40507 Office Phone: 859-231-1012. Office Fax: 859-231-1015. Business E-Mail: pwb@pwblaw.com.

**PIPER, JAMI KATHLEEN,** music educator, composer, musician; b. Oakland, California, Dec. 31, 1955; d. Barry Eugene Piper and Margaret Letitia (Weis) Smythe; children: Stephanie June Hauck, Matthew Lewis Hook. MusB, U. Pacific, Stockton, Calif., 1976; MFA, Mills Coll., Oakland, Calif., 1989; postgrad., U. Colo., Boulder. Cert. K-12 tchg. credential in music U. Colo., Boulder, 1997, nat. certified tchr. of music in piano Nat. Music Tchrs. Assn. Piano accompanist, soloist contracted, Calif., 1962—; piano tchr. self employed, Calif., 1976—94, 2004—, Colo., 1996—2002; adj. educator Music Tchr. Assn. Calif., Calif., 1989—, Music Tchr. Nat. Assn., Colo., 1994—2002; vocal, instrumental music tchr. Boulder Valley Sch., Colo., 1995—2002; gen. music, theory, and history tchr. Boulder Arts Acad., Colo., 1995—98; piano accompanist, soloist contracted, Colo., 1995—2002. V.p., treas. Music Tchr. Assn. Calif., Alameda County, 1990—92, pres., 1992—94; v.p. Boulder Area Music Tchr. Assn., Colo., 1994—95; chair of auditions Colo. Music Tchr. Assn., Colo., 1996—98; Am. advisor Kitumusote, Tanzania, 2005. Composer: (hymn) Benediction, 1986, Give Him the Praise, 1986, God Almighty, God of Love, 1987; musician: (solo concert debut U.S.) Oakland, Calif., 1973, (solo concert debut Europe) Mendemblik, Noord-Holland, 1988; arranger: Doulos, 1986. Recipient U. Pacific Music Grant, U. Pacific, Stockton, Calif., 1973—76, Calif. State Scholarship, State of Calif., 1973—76, Mary M. Henry Prize, Mills Coll., Oakland, Calif., 1985—87. Mem.: Orgn. Am. Kodaly Educators, Nat. Music Tchr. Assn., Music Tchr. Assn. Calif., Pi Lambda Theta, Kappa Delta Pi. Democrat. Episcopalian. Achievements include arranger, performer, and asst. eng. for the album "Look into the Word" by Dean Ellenwood; world premier performance of "Awaken" by Ken McCaw; artist of the session, Festival Noord Holland. Avocations: sewing, gardening, ballet, figure skating. Home and Office: Music Chris Ann Ct Sacramento CA 95811 2000 Personal E-mail: jkpmuses@gmail.com.

**PIPER, JOHN RICHARD,** political science professor; b. Sewickley, Pa., Oct. 2, 1946; s. John Hubert and Carol Elizabeth (Coleman) P.; m. Hoa Thuy Pham, June 6, 1970; 1 child, Carolyn Hoa. BA, Pa. State U., 1968; MA, Cornell U., 1971, PhD, 1972. Prof. polit. sci. Blackburn Coll., Carlinville, Ill., 1972-76; asst. prof. polit. sci. U Tampa (Fla.), 1976-80, assoc. prof. polit. sci., 1980-83; prof. polit. sci. U. Tampa, Fla., 1983—, chmn. dept. history, polit. sci. and sociology Fla., 1990-96; dir. honors program, 1996—. Author: Ideologies and Institutions: American Conservative and Liberal Governance Prescriptions Since 1933, 1997, The Major Nation-States in the European Union, 2005; contbr. articles to profl. jours. V.p. Fla. Collegiate Honors Coun., 1998—99, pres., 1999—2000; mem. Tampa Bay Com. Fgn. Rels., 1990—. Recipient Outstanding Educator award Blackburn Coll., 1974, Louise Loy Hunter award U. Tampa, 1981, award for teaching excellence Sears Roebuck Found., 1990; Fulbright-Hays grantee, 1988. Mem.: Am. Polit. Sci. Assn., Pi Kappa Phi, Phi Beta Kappa, Omicron Delta Kappa. Democrat. Avocations: travel, swimming, reading. Office: Univ of Tampa 401 W Kennedy Blvd Tampa FL 33606-1490 Business E-Mail: rpiper@ut.edu.

**PIPER, KATHLEEN,** former political organization administrator; b. Ida County, Iowa; d. Pat and Rita Donahey McGuire; m. James Carl Piper, 1971; 2 children. Student, U. Iowa, Morningside Coll., Mt. Marty Coll. Co-owner Pied Piper Flower Shop, Yankton, S.D., 1986; vice chair Yankton County Dem. Com., 1980-95, state ctrl. committeewoman, 1995—; commr. Yankton County, 1996—, state ctrl. com. S.D. Dem. Party, 1989-99, exec. bd., 1992-99, chairwoman, 1996-99. Mem. health care adv. com. Senator Tom Daschle, 1991—. Nat. Dem. Com., N.Y.C., 1992; mem. Gold adv. coun. appointed by Gov., 1993-95; participant Pres. Clinton and Hillary Rodham-Clinton's Health Care Initiative Rev., White House, 1993, Gt. Plains Rural Health Summit, 1994, Pres., Clinton and SBA Chief Roundtable Discussion Small Bus. and Health Care Reform, Washington, 1994; appointed del. White House Conf. Small Bus., 1994. Recipient Woman of Yr. award Ed Yankton Daily Press and Dakota, 1986, Emerging Leader for S.D. award Sioux Falls Argus Leader, 1990. Mem. S.D. County Commr. Assn. (exec. bd. 1992-94). Roman Catholic. Home: PO Box 737 Sioux Falls SD 57101-0737 also: 4412 Woolworth Ave Omaha NE 68105-1757

**PIPER, LLOYD LLEWELLYN, II,** engineer, government and service industry executive; b. Wareham, Mass., Apr. 28, 1944; s. Lloyd Llewellyn and Mary Elizabeth (Brown) P.; m. Jane Melonie Scruggs, Apr. 30, 1965; 1 child, Michael Wayne. BSEE, 1ex. A&M U., 1966; MS in Indsl. Engring. U. Houston, 1973. Registered profl. engr., Tex.; diplomate hazardous waste mgmt. Am. Acad. Environ. Engrs. With Houston Lighting & Power Co., 1965—74; project mgr. Dow Chem. Engring. & Constrn Svcs., Houston, 1974—78, Ortloff Corp., Houston, 1978, mgr. engring., 1979—80, v.p., 1980—83; pres., CEO Plantech Engrs. & Constructors, Inc. subs. Dillingham Constrn. Corp., Houston, 1983—86; pres. Delta Plantech Co., Houston, 1985—86; dir. on-site tech. devel. Chem. Waste Mgmt., Inc., Oak Brook, Ill., 1986—88, mgr. projects Houston, 1988—94, dir. facility devel., 1994—95; asst. mgr. Richland Ops. U.S. Dept. Energy, Wash., 1995—96, dep. mgr., 1996—99, adminstr., 1999—2002, asst. mgr., 2002—03; dep. mgr. Carlsbad Field Office, U.S. Dept. Energy, 2003—. Bd. dirs., pres. Harris County Water Control and Improvement Dist., 1973—83; bd. dirs. Environ. Sci. and Tech. Found., 1997—99, United Way, 1998—2003, exec. com., 1998—2001, treas., 2000—01; bd. dirs. United Way of Carlsbad, 2004—, Ponderosa Joint Powers Agy. Harris County, 1977—83, pres., 1977—83; pres. bus. and industry adv. coun. North Harris Montgomery C. C. Dist., 1991—92. Contbr. articles to profl. jours. Recipient Disting. Svc. award Engrs. Coun. Houston, 1970; named Tex. Young Engr. of Yr., 1976, Nat. Young Engr. of Yr., 1976. Mem. IEEE (Outstanding Svc. award Houston sect. 1974), NSPE (chpt. pres. 1978, nat. chmn. engrs. in industry divsn. 1977, nat. v.p. 1977, chmn. nat. polit. action com. 1979-82, vice chmn. nat. engrs. week 1988-92, nat. treasurer life found. 1988-90), Phi Kappa Phi, Tau Beta Pi. Office: Dept Energy PO Box 3090 Carlsbad NM 88221-0550 Home: PO Box 5342 Carlsbad NM 88221

**PIPER, MARK HARRY,** retired banker; b. Flint, Mich., Apr. 17, 1931; s. James U. and Dorothy (Weed) P.; m. Wanda L. Hubbard, June 20, 1953; children: Mark T., Kathryn L. BS, St. John's Mil. Acad., 1949; AB with distinction and honors in Econs, U. Mich., 1953, JD cum laude, 1956. Bar: Mich. 1956. With Clark, Klein, Winter, Parsons & Prewitt, Detroit, 1956-57, Genesee Mchts. Bank & Trust Co., Flint, 1957-88, v.p., sr. trust officer, 1966-72, sr. v.p., 1972-88, NBD Genesee Bank (formerly United Mich. Corp.), 1985-88, cashier, sec. bd. dirs., 1985-88. Adj. instr. bus. adminstrn. U. Mich., Flint, 1976-80; interim co-pension officer Detroit Conf. United Meth. Ch, 1993-99; pres. Flint Estate Planning Coun., 1969-70; mem. Flint citizens adv. coun. U. Mich., 1974-82; vice chmn., 1975-82. Bd. dir. Retirement Homes of Detroit Ann. Conf. Meth. Ch., 1964-76, vice chmn. profl. ministry and support, 1975, mem. bd. support systems, 1975, coun. fin. and adminstrn., 1976-84, chmn. coun. fin. and adminstrn., 1980-84; bd. dirs. United Meth. Devel. Fund, 1986-90; gen. bd. pensions United Meth. Ch., 1988-96, mem. investment com., gen. bd. pensions, 1988-00; mem. investment com. United Meth. Found. of Detroit. Conf. of United Meth. Ch., 1993, 04, interim exec. dir., 2004; trustee Flint YMCA Boysfarm Found., 1964-78, chmn., 1976-78; bd. mgmt. Flint YMCA Boysfarm, 1968-74; mem. Detroit Conf. Bd. P. United Meth. Ch., 1968-76, chmn., 1972-75, 88-02, mem., 1986-02; bd. dirs. U. Mich. Devel. Coun., 1980-82; bd. dirs., asst. treas., sec.-treas. Flint Area Young Life Found., 1979-2006, Mich. Area Young Life Com., 1980-88; bd. dirs., vice chmn. The Crim Road Race Inc., 1985-87; bd. mem. Stewardship Found. Mich., 2002-. Mem. Mich. Bar Assn., Genesee County Bar Assn., Inst. Continuing Legal Edn., U. Mich.-Flint Club (bd. dirs., pres. 1973-74), Rotary Club. also: PO Box 3121 Estes Park CO 80517-3121 Personal E-mail: MHPiper3@aol.com.

**PIPER, ODESSA,** chef; m. Terry Theise. Chef L'Etoile Restaurant, Madison, Wis., 1976—. Contbr. Wis. Pub. Radio, NPR; cons. Ctr. for Integrated Agrl. Sys., U. Wis., Madison. Contbr. Fine Cooking, Food & Wine, Bon Appetit, Eating Well, Wine Spectator, Sierra. Recipient award, James Beard Found., 2001. Mem.: Women Chefs and Restaurateurs (mem. scholarship com.), Chefs Collaborative 2000 (bd. dirs.). Office: L'Etoile Restaurant 25 N Pinckney Madison WI 53711

**PIPER, ROBERT JOHNSTON,** retired architect, urban planner; b. Byron, Ill., Feb. 2, 1926; s. Leo Edward and Helen Anna (Johnston) P.; m. Carol Jane White, June 23, 1951; children— Christopher White, Brian Douglas, Eric Johnston. BS in Archit. Engring. U. Ill., 1951; M. City and Regional Planning, Cornell U., 1953. Architect, planner Orput & Assos., Rockford, Ill., 1953-61; dir. profl. services AIA, Washington, 1961-67; partner, v.p. Perkins & Will, Chgo., 1967-74; dep. dir. Northeastern Ill. Planning Commn., Chgo., 1974-76; asso. Metz, Train, Olson & Youngren, Inc., Chgo., 1976-79; dir. community devel. City of Highland Park, Ill., 1980-91; ret., 1991; coord. Chgo. '93 and Chgo. Design Consortium Chgo. Cultural Ctr., 1992—. Pres. Landmarks Preservation Council Ill., Chgo., 1976-80 Author: Careers in Architecture, vocat. guidance manuals, 1967, 71, 75, 80, 85, 93; author, editor: Architect's Handbook of Professional Practice, 7th edit., 1963; prin. works include Regional Open Space Plan, Northeastern Ill., Spring Valley Operations Breakthrough Housing Complex, Kalamazoo, CBD Streetscape and Skokie Corridor Master Plan, Highland Park. Trustee Village of Winnetka, Ill., 1978-83; mem. Potomac Planning Task Force Dept. Interior, 1967-68, Commn. on Fed. Procurement, Washington, 1970-71; mem. nat. advisory bd. cmty. characteristics HEW, 1970-78; mem. Burnham Plan 1909 Centennial Com., 1999—. Served with USNR, 1944-46, PTO. Fellow AIA (mem. Task Force Future of Inst. 1974-75, various coms., pres. AIA Ill. coun. 1986, Disting. Achievement awards AIA Ill., AIA Chgo. 1993), Am. Inst. Cert. Planners; mem. Lambda Alpha (Chgo. Chpt. Mem. of Yr. award 1999, Daniel H. Burnham Disting. Svc. award, 2004). Episcopalian. Home: 1132 Oak St Winnetka IL 60093-2132 E-mail: bobcarolpiper@aol.com.

**PIPER, THOMAS LAURENCE, III,** banker; b. Washington, June 20, 1941; s. Thomas Laurence and Edna (Milewski) P.; m. Ann Runnette, Apr. 8, 1967; children: Thomas Laurence IV, Andrew Kerr. Student, U. Va., 1959—61. Assoc. Hodgdon & Co., Inc., Washington, 1962-65; sr. v.p., dir. Hayden Stone Inc., N.Y.C., 1966-73; mng. dir. New Court Securities Corp., N.Y.C., 1974-81, Dillon, Read & Co., Inc., N.Y.C., 1981—97, UBS Warburg LLC, 1997—2000, Citigroup Pvt. Bank, 2000—03; sr. advisor The Nassau Group, 2003—04; sr. v.p. W.P. Stewart Asset Mgmt. (NA), Inc., 2005—. Chmn. fund dir. New Canaan chpt. ARC, 1978; bd. dirs. Manhattan coun. Boy Scouts Am., Waveny Care Ctr., New Canaan, Our Lady Queen of Angels, Manhattan; vice-chmn. adv. bd. U. Va. Art Mus., Charlottesville. Mem.: Bond Club NY, Investment Assn. NY (pres. 1974), Quail Valley Club, Red Stick Golf Club, Blind Brook Club, Country Club of New Canaan, Brook Club (N.Y.C.), Racquet and Tennis Club (N.Y.C.). Home: 14 Westmere Ave Norwalk CT 06853 Office Phone: 212-702-3248. Business E-Mail: tom@wpstewart.com. E-mail: tpiper3@optonline.net.

**PIPER, W. STEPHEN,** healthcare educator; b. Uniontown, Pa., June 4, 1945; s. Warren S. and Rhoda (Nixon) P.; m. Patricia Lewis, Aug. 16, 1948. BS, Lock Haven (Pa.) U., 1970; MS, SUNY, Brockport, 1978. Lakefront summer supr. Chautauqua (N.Y.) Inst., 1965-84; health tchr. Hornell (N.Y.) High Sch., 1970—. Recipient Leon Millot Red Bronze medal Am. Wine Soc., 1988, Seyual Blanc Gold medal, 1988, Chardonnay Silver medal, 1991; in top 5 health tchrs. N.Y. State Fedn. Profl. Health Educators, 1977. Methodist. Avocations: boating, wine making. Office: Hornell High Sch Maple City Dr Hornell NY 14843-2276

**PIPER, WILLIAM HOWARD,** bank executive; b. Flint, Mich., Oct. 15, 1933; s. James Underhill P. and Dorothy K. (Weed) Cooper; m. Joyce Rae Foster, June 6, 1959; children: Karen Elizabeth, William Howard, James Raymond. BA, Yale U., 1955. With NBD Genesee Bank, Flint, 1955—, pres., chief exec. officer, dir., 1985-90; sr. v.p. NBD Bancorp, 1990—; head of Fed. Mich. Banks, 1990—. Bd. dirs. U.S. Sugar Corp. Vice chmn., trustee emeritus McLaren Gen. Hosp., Flint, 1974—; trustee, vice chmn. Mott Found., 1985—; mem. adv. bd. Profl., Corp. Flint campus U. Mich., 1982—; dir. YWCA Found.; mem. Greater Flint Community Found.; mem. exec. com. Gen. Motors Inst. Bus. and Industry Ctr.; bd. dirs Flint Inst. Music, 1983—; Flint Exec. Svc. Corp., 1985-87, Flint Coll. and Cultural Devel. Ctr.; sec., treas. Genesee Area Focus Coun. Mem. Flint C. of C. (dir. 1983-87) Clubs: Flint Golf, Univ. Republican. Methodist. Office: NBD Bank PO Box 331041 Detroit MI 48232-7041 also: Mott Found 503 S Saginaw St Ste 1200 Flint MI 48502*

**PIPES, DORIS PERRY,** secondary school educator, consultant; b. Tyrone, N.Y., Dec. 21, 1923; d. Raymond James and Mildred (Wood) Perry; m. Vernon Thomas Pipes, 1951 (div. 1965); 1 child, Vernon Thomas, Jr. AA, Cerritos Coll., 1962; BA, U. Calif., Fullerton, 1964; MA, U. Calif., L.A., 1972. Cert. secondary sch. tchr. Coord. spl. programs, dept. chair program Pioneer High Sch., Whittier, Calif., 1964-65, dir. reading program, coord. tchr. tng., dept. head, 1966-67; instr. grad. sch. Whittier Coll., 1967-71; tchg. cons., classroom materials cons. Scholastic Mag., N.Y.C., 1969-73; resource splst. Calif. High Sch., Whittier, 1973-90, cons. math dept., 1988-90; ret., 1990. Vis. guest lectr., dir. elem. reading clinic Loyola U., L.A., 1967-70; cons. Inglewood High Sch., 1971-72; adminstr. field testing parallel tests in Spanish and English, 1971, 77; reading tchr. Whittier Adult Sch., 1962-66. Contbr. article to jour. Mem. PTA Calif. High Sch., 1964-90 Recipient PTA award, 1989; named Outstanding Secondary Sch. Reading Program Nat. Assn. Secondary Sch. Prins., 1972, Outstanding Secondary Educator of Yr. Outstanding Secondary Educators, 1973. Mem. Internat. Reading Assn. (pres. Rio Hondo coun. 1967), Calif. Tchrs. Assn. (chair), Calif. High Sch. Tchrs. Assn., Alpah Gamma Sigma. Avocations: travel, reading, gardening. Home: 1661 Northwood Rd Apt 274H Seal Beach CA 90740

**PIPES, PAUL RAY,** county commissioner; b. Truscott, Tex., Oct. 1, 1928; s. David and Maggie (Brown) Pipes; m. Linda Mullins, Dec. 17, 1961; children: Dana, Tricia. BBA, Sam Houston U., 1956, MEd, 1971. Acct. Pan Am. Petroleum Corp., Thibodaux, La., 1956-61; bus. tchr. Brenham H.S., Tex., 1962-90; county commr. Washington County, Brenham, 1991-98. With U.S. Army, 1951-53, Korea. Decorated Def. Disting. Svc. medal. Republican. Methodist. Avocations: gardening, nature study. Home: 2106 Jane Ln Brenham TX 77833-5331

**PIPES, ROBERT BYRON,** mechanical engineer, educator; b. Shreveport, La., Aug. 14, 1941; s. Walter H. and Mattye Mae (Wilson) P.; m. Ruth Ellen Franz, June 27, 1964; children: Christopher Franz, Mark Robert. BS, La. Poly. Inst., 1964, MS, 1965; MSE, MA, Princeton U., 1969; PhD, U. Tex., 1972. Registered profl. engr., Del. Sr. structures engr. Gen. Dynamics Corp., 1969-72; asst. prof. mech. engring. Drexel U., 1972-74; assoc. prof. mech. and aerospace engring. U. Del., 1974-80, prof., 1980-91, also dir. Center Composite Materials, 1978-85, dean Coll. Engring., 1985-91, provost, v.p. acad. affairs, 1991-93; pres. Rensselaer Polytech. Inst., NY, 1993-98; disting. vis. scientist Coll. William and Mary, 1998—2001; Goodyear prof. polymer engring. U. Akron, Ohio, 2001—04; John C. Bray disting. prof. engring. Purdue U., 2004—. Cons. in field; com. mem. NRC. Author: Experimental Mechanics of Fiber Reinforced Composite Materials, 1982, Characterization of Advanced Composite Materials, 1987, 3d edit., 2002; series editor 12 vols. Composite Materials; contbr. articles to profl. jours. Bd. dirs. Omnova Solutions, Inc., Fairlawn, Ohio, 1993—2005. Recipient Gustus Larson award, ASME, 1987. Mem. ASME (Gustus Larson award 1983), Soc. Mfg. Engrs., Soc. Advancement of Material and Processing Engring., Nat. Acad. Engring. (elected 1987), Swedish Acad. Engring., Am. Soc. Composites, ASTM, Sigma Xi, Tau Beta Pi, Pi Tau Sigma, Omicron Delta Kappa. Methodist. Achievements include pioneering work in the field of composite materials. Home and Office: 4509 Sugar Maple Dr Lafayette IN 47905 Office Phone: 765-494-5767. E-mail: bpipes@purdue.edu.

**PIPES, SALLY C.,** think-tank executive; Asst. dir. Fraser Inst., Vancouver, B.C., Canada, 1974—91; pres., CEO Pacific Rsch. Inst. for Pub. Policy, San Francisco, 1991—. Co-author (with Spencer Star): Income and Taxation in Canada, (with Michael Walker) 7 editions of Tax Facts; has appeared nationally on TV programs such as 20/20 and Politically Incorrect, Dateline, Inside Politics and PBS's Think Tank; regularly asked to comment on timely issues by radio and print journalists; opinion editls. have been published in various newspapers including San Francisco Chronicle, L.A. Times, Investor's Business Daily, L.A. Daily News, The Orange County Register; writes a bi-monthly column in Chief Executive mag. Bd. dirs. Fin. Instns. Commn. (B.C.), 1980-84 (vice chmn. 1982-84, chmn. 1989-); mem. Vancouver City Planning Commn., 1982-84; trustee St. Luke's Hosp. Found. in San Francisco; bd. dirs. Ind. Women's Forum; mem. bd. advisors Western Jour. Ctr. and Citizens for Term Limits, San Francisco Lawyers chpt. of the Federalist Soc.; commr. Calif. Commn. on Transp. Investment, 1996; bd. govs. Donner-Can. Found. Mem. Mont Pelerin Soc., Nat. Assn. Bus. Economists, Can. Assn. for Bus. Econs. (pres. or treas.), Assn. Profl. Economists of B.C. Office: Pacific Rsch Inst Pub Policy 755 Sansome St Ste 450 San Francisco CA 94111-1709 Office Phone: 415-955-6100.

**PIPKIN, JAMES HAROLD, JR.,** lawyer; b. Houston, Jan. 3, 1939; s. James Harold and Zenda Marie (Lewis) P. BA, Princeton U., 1960; JD, Harvard U., 1963; Diploma in Law, Oxford U., Eng., 1965. Bar: D.C. 1964, U.S. Supreme Ct. 1969, D.C. Ct. Appeals, 1972. Law ck. to assoc. justice U.S. Supreme Ct., Washington, 1963-64; assoc. Steptoe and Johnson, Washington, 1965-70, ptnr., 1971-93; counselor to The Sec. of the Interior U.S. Dept. of the Interior, 1993-98; U.S. spl. negotiator for Pacific Salmon, Dept. of State, 1994-2001; rank of amb. Dept. of State, 1995-96; dir. office policy analysis U.S. Dept. Interior, 1998-2001; fgn. affairs officer U.S. State Dept., 2001—02. Counsel Friends of Music, Smithsonian Inst., Washington, 1984-88; mem. Nat. Arbitration Panel, 1983-94. Author or co-author: The English Country House: A Grand Tour, 1985, The Country House Garden: A Grand Tour, 1987, Places of Tranquility, 1990; contbr. photographs and articles to mags. including House & Garden, Smithsonian mag., The Mag. Antiques, Archtl. Digest. Grand officier Confrérie des Chevaliers du Tastevin, 1989—. Mem. ABA, D.C. Bar Assn., Met. Club. Home: 6109 Davenport Ter Bethesda MD 20817-5827

**PIPKIN, MARY MARGARET,** artist; b. San Angelo, Tex., Mar. 17, 1951; d. Raymond G. and Lillie Marie (Billie) Pipkin; m. Robert A. Boisture; children: Will, John, Jamie. BFA, MFA, U. Tex.; Max Beckmann Scholar, Bklyn. Mus. Art Sch., 1973—74. One-woman shows include Addison/Ripley Gallery, Washington, Zigler Mus., Jennings, La., 2002, Louisburg Coll., NC, 2003, Art Sta., Stone Mountain, Ga., 2003, Anderson Art Ctr., Ind., 2003, Mus. S.W., Midland, Tex., 2003, US Botanic Garden, Washington, 2003, San Angelo Mus. Fine Art, Tex., 2004, Sci. Mus. We. Va., Roanoke, 2004, Olbrich Botanical Gardens, Madison, Wis., 2004, Mus. Arts & Sci., Daytona Beach, Fla., 2004, Dunedin Fine Arts Ctr., Fla., 2005, Elliot Mus., Stuart, Fla., 2005, Bob Rauschenberg Gallery, Edison Coll., Ft. Meyers, Fla., 2005. Personal E-mail: mmpipkin@aol.com.

**PIPKIN, ROBERT DONALD,** quality assurance professional, cardiologist; b. Rock Springs, Wyo., Mar. 29, 1939; s. Donald Willis and Angela Pipkin; m. Patricia Anne Fink, Aug. 21, 1969; children: Kristin, Rebecca, Sean, Donald 1 stepchild, Michael Fink. BA, BS, Regis U., 1962; MD, Harvard U., 1966. Cardiac surgeon Thomas Fogarty Inc., Palo Alto, Calif., 1974—78; cardiac surgeon, pres. Bay Area Cardiovascular Med. Group, Palo Alto and Fremont, Calif., 1978—2004; quality advisor Washington Hosp., Fremont, 2004—. With U.S. Army, 1968—70, Vietnam. Fellow: ACS, Am. Coll. Cardiology; mem.: Western Thoracic Surg. Soc., Soc. Thoracic Surgeons. Office: Washington Hosp 2000 Mowry Ave Fremont CA 94538

**PIPPEN, JENNIFER LYNN,** therapist, consultant; b. Hinsdale, Ill., Nov. 10, 1975; d. Randy Lynn and Mary Hoekstra Pippen. BA summa cum laude, North Ctrl. Coll., Ill., 1998; M in Counseling Psychology cum laude, Trinity Grad. Sch., Ill., 2002. Lic. profl. counselor Ill., 2002, clin. profl. counselor 2005. Intern therapist Cath. Charities, Waukegan, Ill., 2001—02; therapist Maine Ctr., Park Ridge, Ill., 2002—. Missionary The Navigators, 1998—99; vol. West Suburban Humane Soc., Downers Grove, Ill., 2004. Mem.: ACA, Psi Chi. Avocations: piano, cross stitch. Office: Maine Ctr 819 Busse Hwy Park Ridge IL 60068 Office Phone: 847-696-1570 326.

**PIPPENGER, NICHOLAS JOHN,** mathematician, researcher, computer scientist, educator; b. Abington, Pa., Mar. 14, 1947; s. Robert and Mary Emma Pippenger; m. Maria Margaret Klawe, May 12, 1980; children: Janek Evan Klawe, Sasha Kathleen. BS, Shimer Coll., 1965, MIT, 1967, MS, 1969, PhD, 1974. Mem. tech. staff Charles Stark Draper Lab., Cambridge, Mass., 1969—73; mem. rsch. staff IBM Corp., Yorktown Heights, NY, 1973—80, San Jose, Calif., 1980—87, fellow, 1987—89; prof. U. BC, Vancouver, Canada, 1988—2000, Princeton U., NJ, 2003—06; Harvey Mudd Coll, Claremont, Calif., 2006—; rsch. chair U. BC, Vancouver, 2000—03. Fellow: IEEE, Assn. Computing Machinery, Acad. Sci., Royal Soc. Can.; mem.: Math. Assn. of Am., Am. Math. Soc., Soc. Indsl. and Applied Math. Office: Harvey Mudd Coll Dept Math 1250 N Dartmouth Ave Claremont CA 91711 Business E-Mail: njp@math.hmc.edu.

**PIPPI, MIKEL EUGENE,** food service executive; b. Portland, Oreg., Apr. 20, 1947; BA, Lewis and Clark Coll., 1969. Founder, exec. dir. Frohman Acad. for Musical Theatre Edn., Carmel, Calif., 1982—91; producing dir. Am. Musical Theatre Festival, Monterey, Calif., 1985—91; co-founder, dir. internat. rels. Acad. Russian TV, Moscow, 1992—95; dir. spl. projects Turner Internat. Broadcasting, Moscow, 1993—95; global dir., artist recruitment and tng. Walt Disney Feature Animation, Burbank, Calif., 1996—98; exec. dir. Regional Arts and Culture Coun., Portland, Oreg., 1999—2000; dir. creative industries studies Portland (Oreg.) State U., 2000—04; exec. dir. Healthy Eating Lifestyle Principles, Inc., Monterey, Calif., 2005—. Mem. nat. policy bd. Ams. for The Arts, Washington, 1999-2001; Am. agent Russian Ministry of Culture, Moscow, 1987-92; vice chair cultural affairs St. Petersburg and LA Sister City Coms., 1991-95; founding trustee Nat. Alliance Musical Theatre Prodrs., N.Y.C., 1986-91. Avocations: travel, writing, humanitarian programs. Home: PO Box 22962 Carmel CA 93922-0962 Office Phone: 831-372-3616. Personal E-mail: pippihome@aol.com.

**PIPPIN, M. LENNY,** food products executive; m. Judy Pippin. BA, Fla. Atlantic U. CEO Albert Fischer, N.A., Dallas; pres., CEO Lykes Bros. Inc., Tampa, Fla., 1997-99, The Schwan Food Co., Marshall, Minn., 1999—. Office: The Schwan Food Co 115 W College Dr Marshall MN 56258 Office Fax: 507-537-8226.*

**PIRAINO, THOMAS ANTHONY, JR.,** lawyer; b. Cleve., July 12, 1949; s. Thomas Anthony and Margaret (Stephens) P.; m. Barbara McWilliams, Sept. 4, 1976; children: Margaret, Ann, Mary. BA in History, magna cum laude, Allegheny Coll., 1971; JD, Cornell U., 1974. Bar: Ohio 1974. Assoc. counsel Parker-Hannifin Corp., Cleve., 1981-84, assoc. gen. counsel, 1984-98, v.p., gen. counsel, sec., 1998—. Contbr. articles to legal jours. Mem. ABA, Ohio Bar Assn., Am. Corp. Counsel (sec. 1985—), Am. Soc. Corp. Secs. (pres. 1988—). Avocations: tennis, jogging. Office: Parker Hannifin Corp 6035 Parkland Blvd Cleveland OH 44124-4141

**PIRCHER, LEO JOSEPH,** lawyer, director; b. Berkeley, Calif., Jan. 4, 1933; s. Leo Charles and Christine (Moore) P.; m. Phyllis McConnell, Aug. 4, 1956 (div. Apr. 1981); children: Christopher, David, Eric; m. Nina Silverman, June 14, 1987. BS, U. Calif., Berkeley, 1954, JD, 1957. Bar: Calif. 1958, (N.Y.) 1985, cert.: Calif. Bd. Legal Specialization (cert. specialist taxation law). Assoc. Lawler, Felix & Hall, L.A., 1957-62, ptnr., 1962-65, sr. ptnr., 1965-83, Pircher, Nichols & Meeks, L.A., 1983—. Adj. prof. Loyola U. Law Sch., L.A., 1959—61; corp. sec. Am. Metal Bearing Co., Gardena, Calif., 1975—; dir. Varco Internat., Inc., Orange, Calif.; spkr. various law schs. and bar assns. edn. programs. Author (with others): (novels) Definition and Utility of Leases, 1968. Chmn. pub. fin. and taxation sect. Calif. Town Hall, L.A., 1970—71. Mem.: ABA, Nat. Assn. Real Estate Investment Trusts Inc. (cert. specialist taxation law), L.A. County Bar Assn. (exec. com. comml law sect.), N.Y. State Bar, Calif. State Bar, Regency (L.A.). Republican. Office: Pircher Nichols & Meeks Ste 1700 1925 Century Park E Los Angeles CA 90067-6022 Office Phone: 310-201-8901. Personal E-mail: lpircher@pircher.com.

**PIRES, LUIS A.,** cardiologist, researcher; s. Jose and Joana P. Pires; 1 child, Paulo A. Gomez. MD, U. Mass., Worcester, 1986. Dir. heart rhythm ctr. and vice-chief cardiology Stjohn Hosp. and Med. Ctr., Detroit, 1999—; assoc. prof. medicine Wayne State U., Detroit, 2002—. Sr. assoc. Eastside Cardiovasc. Medicine PC, Roseville, Mich., 1997—. Contbr. articles to profl. jours., chapters to books. Fellow: Am. Coll. Cardiology. Office: Eastside Cardiovascular Medicine PC 18325 Ten Mile Rd Roseville MI 48066 Office Phone: 586-775-4594. Personal E-mail: luis.pires@stjohn.org.

**PIRIE, ROBERT BURNS, JR.,** defense analyst; b. San Diego, Sept. 10, 1933; s. Robert Burns and Gertrude May (Freeman) P.; m. Joan Adams, Dec. 23, 1960; children: John Winthrop, Carl Joseph Emil, Susan Gilman. Student, Princeton U., 1950-51; BS, U.S. Naval Acad., 1955; BA, Magdalen Coll., Oxford U., 1959, MA, 1963. Commd. ensign U.S. Navy, 1955, advanced through grades to comdr., 1969; comdg. officer (U.S.S. Skipjack), 1969-72; dep. asst. dir. Congl. Budget Office, 1975-77; prin. dep. asst. sec. for manpower, res. affairs and logistics Dept. Def., Washington, 1977-79, asst. sec., 1979-81; mgmt. cons., 1981—; def. analyst Ctr. for Naval Analyses, Alexandria, Va., 1981-83; asst. v.p. Inst. for Def. Analyses, Alexandria, 1983-86, v.p., 1986-87; exec. v.p. Essex Corp., Alexandria, 1987, pres., 1987-88; sr. economist Rand Corp., Washington, 1989; dir. strategic studies group U.S. Naval War Coll., 1989-92; v.p. Ctr. Naval Analyses, Alexandria, 1992-94; asst. sec. of Navy for Installations and Environ. USN, Washington, 1994-2000, undersec. of Navy, 2000—01; sr. fellow Ctr. for Naval Analysis, 2001—. Chmn. bd. advisors Nat. Infrastructure Inst., 2004—. Vestryman St. John's Episcopal Ch., Chevy Chase, Md., 1973-76, 81, jr. warden, 1982-84, sr. warden, 1984-87; trustee U.S. Naval Acad. Found., 1980-94. Rhodes scholar, 1956 Mem. U.S. Naval Inst., U.S. Naval Acad. Alumni Assn. (trustee 1967-70), Vincent's Club, Cosmos Club. E-mail: rpirie@aol.com.

**PIRKEY, LOUIS THOMAS,** lawyer; b. Ft. Worth, Dec. 6, 1937; s. Louis F. and Juanita (Copeland) P.; m. Jewell Katherine Buchanan, Oct. 19, 1940; children— Julia Hope, Jeffry Thomas. B.S.Ch.E., U. Tex., 1960; J.D. with honors, George Washington U., 1964. Bar: Tex. 1964, U.S. Supreme Ct. 1981, U.S. Ct. Appeals (5th and 11th cirs.), U.S. Dist. Ct. (we., so. and ea. dists.) Tex. Mem. Arnold, White & Durkee, Houston, 1964—, 1969—; chmn. intellectual property law sect. State Bar of Tex., 1982-83; mem. U.S. delegation Diplomatic Conf. on Rev. of Paris Conv., 1982. Fellow Tex. Bar Found.; mem. U.S. Trademark Assn. (dir.), ABA (chmn. Fed. trademark legislation com. 1972-74), Am. Patent Law Assn., Houston Bar Assn., Houston Patent Law Assn., Travis County Bar Assn., Licensing Execs. Soc., Interam. Assn. for Protection of Intellectual Property, Internat. Assn. Protection of Intellectual Property, Order of Coif, Phi Alpha Delta. Clubs: Headliners, Capital, Westwood Country (Austin); Univ. (Houston). Office: 600 Congress Ave Ste 2300 Austin TX 78701-2977

**PIRKL, JAMES JOSEPH,** industrial designer, educator, writer; b. Nyack, N.Y., Dec. 27, 1930; s. James and Ida Bertha (Gigrich) Pirkl; m. Sarah B. W. Woolsey, June 8, 1974; children: Theo, James, Philip. Cert. in advt. design, Pratt Inst., 1951, B in Indsl. Design cum laude, 1958. Design staff GM, Warren, Mich., 1958-65, sr. designer, 1961-64, asst. chief designer, 1964-65; instr. indsl. design Center Creative Studies, Detroit, 1963-65; faculty dept. design Syracuse (N.Y.) U., 1965-92, assoc. prof., 1969-73; prof. indsl. design, 1974-92, prof. emeritus, 1992—, coord. indsl. design program, 1979-84, chmn. dept. design, 1985-91; exec. council chmn. Syr. Arch. 1976-78, 80-81; sr. rsch. fellow All-U. Gerontology Ctr., 1990-92. Prin. James J. Pirkl/Design, 1965—; cons. GE, 1967—70, N.Y. State Coun. Arts, 1968—69, Loretto Geriatric Ctr., Pulos Design Assocs., 1972—80, Fed. Prison Industries, 1974, Xerox Corp., 1975, Am. Soc. Aging, 1995, Ford Motor Design Ctr., 1992, Arthritis Found., 1993—96, Age Wave, Inc., 1993—96, GE Appliances, 1994, ProMatura Group, 1994—, universal kitchen product R.I. Sch. Design, 1996—98, Boeing Co., 2004; chmn. accreditation coun. Design Found., 1982—84; designer, project dir. Transgenerational House, 2000—03; exec. dir. Transgenerational Design Matters, 2004—; lectr. in field. Author:

Trangenerational Design: Products for an Aging Population, 1994; co-author: Guidelines and Strategies for Designing Transgenerational Products, 1988; co-designer GM Futurama Exhbn., N.Y. World's Fair, 1964—65; contbr. articles to profl. jours. Design mem. Everson Mus. Art, 1977—85; chmn. planning commn. Town of Cazenovia, 1988—93; mem. exhbns. com. Syracuse Cultural Resources Coun., 1992—93; coord. Tylenol/Arthritis Found. Student Design Awards Program, 1993—95; mem. senate Syracuse U., 1973—80, mem. adv. bd. SEARS Project, 1989—91, chmn. chancellor's citation, 1988—92. With SeaBees USN, 1951—55. Recipient Gold Indsl. Design Excellence award, Indsl. Designers Soc. Am. and Bus. Week Mag., 1994. Fellow: Indsl. Designers Soc. Am. (nat. bd. dirs. 1977—81, chmn. Ctrl. N.Y. chpt. 1977—81, v.p. Mid-East region 1978—81, chmn. NASAD liaison com. 1984—88, archives com. 1988—92, U.S. rep., del. Internat. Congress Socs. Indsl. Design 1989, chmn. universal design com. 1991—94, Edn. award 2001); mem.: Author's Guild, Am. Soc. Aging (contbr. articles to jour.), Nat. Ctr. Barrier Free Environment (adv. task force 1981), Human Factors Soc. (life), Nat. Assn. Schs. Art and Design (accreditation evaluator 1985—95), The Design Found. (chmn. accreditation coun. 1982). Achievements include patents for 4-way refrigerator handle. Home: 2007 Quail Run Dr NE Albuquerque NM 87122 Business E-Mail: jjp@transgenerational.org.

**PIRKLE, EARL CHARNELL,** retired geologist; b. nr. Buckhead, Ga., Jan. 8, 1922; s. Early Charnell and Eva Lee (Collins) P.; m. Valda Nell Armistead, July 9, 1942; children: Betty Jean, William A., Fredric L. AB, Emory U., 1943; MS, 1947; postgrad., U. Tenn., 1947-50; PhD, U. Cin., 1956. Certified profl. geologist. Prodn. coordinator, research crystallographer Pan-Electronics Labs., Inc., Atlanta, 1942-45; instr. geology U. Tenn., 1947-50; mem. faculty dept. phys. scis. and geology U. Fla., Gainesville, 1950-93, prof. emeritus, 1993—, prof., 1963—, chmn. dept. phys. scis., 1972-79; dir. Phys. Scis., 1979-82. Cons. in field; vis. prof. geology Emory U., summers 1959-65; rsch. cons. Fla. Dept. Nat. Resources Bur. Geology, 1950-70. Author: Natural Regions of the United States, 1977, 4th edit., 1985; Editor: Physical Science-Our Environment, 1968, Our Physical Environment, 1980; Contbr. articles to profl. jours. Served with AUS, 1945-46. Fellow Geol. Soc. Am., Soc. Econ. Geologists; mem. Am. Assn. Petroleum Geologists, Am. Soc. Mining, Metall. and Petroleum Engrs., Fla. Acad. Scis., Southeastern Geol. Soc., Phi Beta Kappa, Sigma Gamma Epsilon, Gamma Theta Epsilon, Sigma Chi. Democrat. Methodist.

**PIRKLE, GEORGE EMORY,** photographer, instructional media producer; b. Sept. 3, 1947; s. George Washington and Glanna Adeline (Palmer) P.; m. Karen Leigh Horn, Oct. 20, 1973; 1 child, Charity Caroline. Student, North Ga. Coll., 1965-66; BA in Journalism, U. Ga., 1969, MA, 1971. Radio announcer, sportscaster various radio stations, North Ga. area, 1968-70; TV prodr., dir. Instructional Resources Ctr., Athens, Ga., 1969-70; info. officer Southeastern Signal Sch., U.S. Army, 1971; prodr., dir. DA MoPic Svc. Continental Army Command Network and Signal Corps TV Divsn., 1972-73; pub. info. officer Ga. Dept. Revenue, Atlanta, 1973-78; coord. TV prodn. svcs. So. Co. Svcs., Inc., Birmingham, Ala., 1978-88; exec. v.p. Mgmt. and Human Devel. Assocs., Inc., Birmingham, Ala., 1984-86; prodr. Prodn. Works, Birmingham, Ala., 1984-88. Actor for various radio and TV commercials, corp. TV programs, radio dramas, stage plays, 1968—; owner Talking Rock Prodns., Cumming, Ga., 1989—; instr. Cliff Osmond Acting Program, 1989-92. Editor monthly newsletter Ga. Revenews, 1973-78; editor, dir. Bankers TV Network, 1990-92; writer, prodr., dir., exec. prodr. more than 500 corp. and pub. svc. TV and film programs; exec. prodr. videotape for Birmingham Film Coun., 1985; prodr., dir. Highway in Crisis, 1986; writer, prodr., dir. campaign film Birmingham Area United Way, 1981, 86, 87; writer, prodr., narrator, 1987 campaign film; anchor This Week in Banking, 1990-92. Master of ceremonies, gov.'s vet. awards presentation World Peace Luncheon, 1981, 82, 84, Birmingham; bd. directors Birmingham Internat. Ednl. Film Festival, 1987—91; dir., campaign film United Way, Pensacola, 1989; chmn. Sadie award com.; dir. student video competition; comml. acting instr. elan/Casablancas Modeling/Career Ctr., 1988—92; mem. tech. steering com. Forsyth Bd. Edn., 1995; bd. dirs. United Way of Forsyth County, 1995—2004; vol. Am. Cancer Soc. Relay for Life, 1996—2002; permanent mem. allocations com. United Way Forsyth County, 2000—04, v.p. allocations, 2003; chair Forsyth County Bd. Ethics, 2002—; mem. Comms. com. Birmingham Area couns. Boy Scouts Am., 1983—85, City Parks Recreation Bd., 1996—; mem. adv. bd. Sawnee Mtn. Preserve. 1st lt. U.S. Army, 1971—73. Recipient So. Superlative Outstanding employee award, So. Co. Svcs., 1986, Battles award 1988, various others. Mem.: So. Electric Sys. Visual Comms. Subcom. (founding), Internat. TV Assn. (charter pres. Birmingham chapter 1984—85, pres. pro tem 1984, editor newsletter Freeze Frame), Hist. Soc. Forsyth County (pres. 1996), Ga. Hist. Soc., Rotary Club (Paul Harris fellow 2001), Cumming/Forsyth C. of C. (Bus. Mem. of the Yr. 2002). Avocations: photography, astronomy, genealogy, history, archaeology. E-mail: trvideo@bellsouth.net.

**PIRKO, ISTVAN,** medical educator, neurologist, researcher, immunologist; b. Miskolc, Hungary, June 11, 1971; s. Jozsef Pirko and Maria Szabo; m. Dora Eva Kelemen, Jan. 16, 1997; children: Melissa T., Rebecca N., Adam B. MD, U. Med. Sch. Debrecen, Hungary, 1995. Diplomate Am. Bd. Psychiatry and Neurology. Fellow in ms and neuroimmunology Mayo Clinic, Rochester, Mich., 2001—03; fellow in neuroimaging U. Cin., 2003—04, asst. prof. neurology, 2004—. Advisor med. issues Nat. MS Soc., Cin., 2005. Achievements include research in micro-MRI of ms animal models.

**PIRL, JOERG NORBERT,** toxicologist, consultant; b. Glogau, Germany, Oct. 1, 1942; came to U.S., 1964; s. Kurt Erich and Ursula Pirl; m. Sunguriya Chengcharoen, Aug. 9, 1997; children: Savit Anthony, Sarunya Pamela. BS in Chemistry with honors, Roosevelt U., 1969, MS in Chemistry with honors, 1975; PhD in Med. Chemistry, U. Ill., 1982. Diplomate Am. Bd. Forencis Toxicology. Chemist U.S. Steel Co., Chgo., 1965-66, Cook County Coroner's Office, Chgo., 1967-69; from chemist III to chemist IV Ill. Dept. Pub. Health, Chgo., 1969-77, asst. chief toxicologist, 1977-85; chief of toxicology Ala. Dept. Forensic Scis., Birmingham, 1985-90; chief of toxicology & metabolic diseases Ill. Dept. Pub. Health, Chgo., 1990—2002. Mem. legis. writing com. Atty. Gen.'s Victim's Driving Under the Influence Task Force, Ala., 1989; lectr. U. Ill., 1978-85, U. Ala., Birmingham and Tuscaloosa, 1986-89; mem. Nat. Com. for Clin. Lab. Standards. Contbr. articles to profl. jours. Staff sgt. German Air Force, 1960-64. Mem. Internat. Assn. Forensic Toxicologists, Am. Chem. Soc., Soc. Forensic Toxicologists, Mass. Spectrometry Discussion Group, Ala. State Police Assn., Law Enforcement Assn. (pres. Tuscaloosa chpt. 1988), Rho Chi. Avocations: outdoors, boating, camping, fishing. Office Phone: 229-482-8272. E-mail: joergandsue@alltel.net.

**PIRNOT, THOMAS LEONARD,** mathematics professor; b. Scranton, Pa., Sept. 3, 1943; s. Victor Dennis and Julia (Getchonis) P.; m. Anna M. Wawrzak, Dec. 28, 1968; children: Matthew, Anthony, Joanna, Michael. Ba in Music, Wilkes Coll., 1965; PhD in Math., Pa. State U., 1970. Prof. Math. Kutztown (Pa.) U., 1970—. Cons. pvt. practice, Kutztown, 1970—. Author: Mathematics All Around, 2001, 2d edit., 2003, 3d edit, 2006; co-author with D. Hunkins: Mathematics: Tools and Models, 1977. Named to Disting. Teaching Chair Pa. State System of Higher Edn., 1979. Mem.: Nat. Coun. of Tchrs. of Math., Am. Math. Assn. Two-Yr. Colls., Math. Assn. Am. Avocations: tennis, music. Home: 201 Fairview Dr Kutztown PA 19530-1017 Office: Kutztown Univ 169 Lytle Hall Kutztown PA 19530 Office Phone: 610-683-4424. Business E-Mail: pirnot@kutztown.edu.

**PIRODSKY, DONALD MAX,** psychiatrist, educator; b. Freeport, N.Y., Feb. 2, 1945; s. Max and Doris Geilhard (Biedermann) P.; m. Gail Giufre Pallotta, Jan. 4, 1997; children: Laura Anne, Jason Donald. BA, Hofstra U., 1966; MD, SUNY, Syracuse, 1970. Diplomate Am. Bd. Psychiatry and Neurology, Nat. Bd. Med. Examiners. Intern Northwestern U. Med. Ctr., Chgo., 1970-71; resident in psychiatry Strong Meml. Hosp., Rochester, NY, 1973-74, U. Ariz. Med. Ctr., Tucson, 1974-76; instr. psychiatry SUNY Health Sci. Ctr., Syracuse, 1976-78, attending psychiatrist, 1976-91, asst. prof. psychiatry, 1978-85, mem. exec. com. of med. coll. assembly, 1979-82, clin. assoc. prof., 1985—, adj. attending psychiatrist, 1991—; pvt. practice Syracuse and

Fayetteville, NY, 1976—; staff psychiatrist, dir. consultation/liaison svc. Syracuse VA Med. Ctr., 1976-87, chmn. pharmacy rev. and therapeutic agts. com., 1980-86. Psychiat. cons. Ariz. Sch. for Deaf and Blind, Tucson, 1975-76, Syracuse Devel. Ctr., 1977—, Rochester Sch. for Deaf, 1978-81; ex-officio mem. Family Counseling Agy., Tucson, 1975-76; adj. attending psychiatrist SUNY Health Sci. Ctr., Syracuse, 1991—. Author: Primer of Clinical Psychopharmacology: A Practical Guide, 1981, (with Jerry S. Cohn) Clinical Primer of Psychopharmacology: A Practical Guide, 2d edit., 1992; contbr. articles to profl. jours., chpts. to med. books. Lt. comdr. USPHS, 1971-73. Fellow Am. Psychiat. Assn. (Disting., mem. cen. N.Y. dist. br.); mem. Am. Psychosomatic Soc., Am. Assn. Mental Retardation, Med. Soc. State of N.Y., N.Y. State Psychiat. Assn., Onondaga County Med. Soc. Episcopalian. Avocations: sports, collecting baseball cards and other sports memorabilia. Office: 7000 E Genesee St Fayetteville NY 13066-1131 Office Phone: 315-446-3001.

**PIROK, EDWARD WARREN,** lawyer, consultant; b. Chgo., June 2, 1947; s. Edward Warren and Elinor Jean Pirok; m. Christine Merk, Jan. 23, 1972; children: Edward, Christopher, Jennifer, Elizabeth. BS, Ill. Inst. Tech., 1970; JD, Loyola U., 1973. Bar: N.Y. 1988, Ill. 1973, U.S. Supreme Ct., U.S. Ct. Appeals (2d and 7th cirs.) U.S. Dist. Ct. (so. and ea. dists.) N.Y., U.S. Dist. Ct. (no. dist.) Ill. Trial atty. Burlington No., Inc., Chgo., 1975-77; asst. gen. counsel Regional Transp. Authority, Chgo., 1977-82; gen. counsel Metra, The N.E. Ill. R.R. Corp., Chgo., 1982-87; trial atty. Metro-North Commuter R.R., N.Y.C., 1987-89; of counsel Peltz & Walker, N.Y.C., 1990-93; ptnr. Frank & Pirok, Ltd., Chgo., 1999—. 1st lt. Ill. Army N.G. Mem. ATLA, Ill. Trial Lawyers Assn. Roman Catholic. Avocations: golf, tennis. Office: Frank & Pirok Ltd 734 N Wells St Chicago IL 60610 Home: 299 Mallard Point Lake Barrington IL 60010-1783 Office Phone: 312-634-9020. E-mail: epirok@frank-pirok.com.

**PIROMYA, KASIT,** ambassador; b. Bangkok, Dec. 15, 1944; m. Chintana Wajanabukka Piromya; children: Om(dec.), Prae. Student Bangkok Christian Coll.; St. Joseph's Coll., Darjeeling, India; Chulalongkorn U.; BS in Internat. Affairs, Sch. of Fgn. Svc., Georgetown U., 1968; MS in Social sci., Inst. of Social Studies, The Hague, Netherlands, 1971; student Nat. Def. Coll. of Thailand, 1990. Third sec., Dept. of Internat. Orgns. Ministry of Fgn. Affairs, Thailand, 1968—69, third sec. news analysis divsn., 1969—72, third sec., SEATO divsn., Dept. of Internat. Orgns., 1972—75; third sec. and second sec., Royal Thai Embassy, Brussels and Thai Mission to EU, 1975—79; second sec., Internat. Econ. Affairs Divsn. Dept. of Econ. Affairs Ministry of Fgn. Affairs, Thailand, 1979—80, first sec., office of dir.-gen, Dept. of Econ. Affairs, 1980—81, dir., Commerce and Industry Divsn., ASEAN Dept. Thailand, 1981—83, dir., Econ. Info. divsn., Dept. of Econ. Affairs, 1983—84, dir., Policy and Planning Divsn., Office of Permanent Sec., 1984—85, dep. dir.-gen., Dept. Econ. Affairs, 1985—88, dir. gen., Dept. of Internat Orgns., 1988—91; Thai amb. Extraordinary and Plenipotentiary to Soviet Union and Peoples Republic of Mongolia, 1991, to the Russian Federation and Mongolia, 1992—93, to Indonesia and Papua New Guinea, 1994—96, to Germany, 1997—2001, to Japan, 2001, to the U.S., 2004—. Recipient Chakrabarti Mala Medal, 1993, Grand Cross of the Order of merit, Fed. Republic of Germany, 2001, Grand Cordon of the Order of the Rising Sun, Japan, 2004. Office: Embassy of Thailand Ste 401 1024 Wisconsin Ave NW Washington DC 20007*

**PIROZZI, MILDRED JEAN,** retired nursing administrator; b. Syracuse, N.Y., Jan. 22, 1943; d. Alfred George and Mildred Erma (Tripp) Farmer; m. Robert T. Pirozzi, Jan. 25, 1969; children: Matthew Robert, Michael Thomas. Diploma, Gen. Hosp. Syracuse, 1963; BS, SUNY, Utica, 1983. RN, N.Y. Med., surg. staff nurse Gen. Hosp. Syracuse, 1963-64; staff nurse ICU U. Rochester Strong Meml. Hosp., N.Y., 1964-65; nurse ICU Upstate Med. Ctr. U. Hosp., Syracuse, 1965-69, rschr. anesthesia Upstate Med. Ctr., 1969-70; nurse recovery room Highland Hosp., Rochester, 1970-71; nurse orthopedic unit Auburn (N.Y.) Meml. Hosp., 1978-80; home dialysis tng. unit nurse SUNY Health Sci. Ctr., Syracuse, 1980-88; with home dialysis tng. unit N. Dialysis Ctr., Syracuse, 1988-91; home program coord. St. Joseph's Hops. Health Ctr., 1991—96, hemodialysis, 1996—2000, charge nurse hemodialysis, 2000—01, coord. self care/home hemo, 2001—04, charge nurse hemo, 2004—05; ret., 2005. Chmn. com. profl. edn. N.Y. chpt. Nat. Kidney Found., Syracuse, 1986-91. Co-author: Hemodialysis Training Manual for Patients and Families, 1981, CAPD Training Manual for Patients, 1982. Mem. folk ensemble St. Joseph's Ch., 1984—. Recipient Above and Beyond award Nat. Kidney Found., 1991. Mem. Am. Nephrology Nurses Assn. (pub. rels. com. 1988-91, sec., treas., pres. ctrl. N.Y. chpt. 1984-93, 96-98, N.E. regional sec. 1987-89, N.E. regional officer 2003-05, legis. rep. 1991-95). Roman Catholic. Avocations: sewing, crafts, gardening, sports, music. Home: 4699 Howlett Hill Rd Marcellus NY 13108-9762 E-mail: rpirozzi@twcny.rr.com.

**PIRRO, ALFRED ANTHONY, JR.,** emergency physician; b. Stamford, Conn., May 17, 1961; s. Alfred Anthony, Sr. and Frances (Battaglia) Pirro. BA in Natural Scis., The Johns Hopkins U., 1983; MD, U. Conn., 1987. Diplomate Am. Bd. Anesthesiology, Am. Bd. Critical Care Medicine. Resident in surgery Hosp. of St. Raphael, New Haven, 1987-90; fellow in neurosurgery Hartford Hosp., Conn., 1991-92, resident in anesthesiology, 1992-95, critical care fellow, 1995-97, staff anesthesiologist, 1997-99; emergency medicine physician Windham Hosp., Willamantic, Conn., 1991—; instr. anesthesiology John Dempsey Hosp.-U. Conn. Sch. Medicine, Hartford, 1997-99; owner Hosp. Physician Specialists, Elkton, Md., med. dir. hospitalist program 2004—. Chmn. critical care, chmn. med. records com., med. dir. hospitalist program Union Hosp.; physician monitor Md. Physician Rehab. Program, 2002—. Advisor Lally for Congress campaign, Mineola, NY, 1994. Scholar, Pitney Bowes, 1979; Beneficial-Hodson scholar, Johns Hopkins U., 1979. Mem.: AMA, Soc. Critical Care Medicine, Md. State Med. Soc. Republican. Office Phone: 443-350-4544, Personal E-mail: aapjrmd@aol.com.

**PIRRO, JEANINE FERRIS,** prosecutor; b. Elmira, N.Y., June 2, 1951; d. Leo and Esther Ferris; m. Albert J. Pirro, Aug. 23, 1975; children: Christi, Alexander. BA, U. Buffalo, 1972; JD, Albany Law Sch., 1975. Bar: N.Y. 1975. Legis. aide N.Y. State Senate, Albany, 1973-75; asst. dist. atty. Westchester County Dist. Atty. Office, White Plains, N.Y., 1975-78, chief Victim Witness Unit, 1978-79, chief domestic violence/child abuse bur., 1978-90, dist. atty., 1994—; county judge Westchester County, White Plains, 1990-93. Author, To Punish and Protect, 2003, 2d edit. 2004; contbr. articles to profl. jours. Chair Gov. Pataki's N.Y. State Commn. on Domestic Violence Fatalities Rev. Bd., 1996; bd. dirs. My Sister's Place, 1990—; bd. vis. Pace U. Sch. Law, 1994— Mem. N.Y. State Dist. Attys. Assn. (pres. 1999-2000), Nat. Mus. Women's History (bd. adv.). Republican. Roman Catholic. Office: Westchester County Dist Atty County Courthouse 111 Dr ML King Jr Blvd White Plains NY 10601-2507

**PIRRUNG, MICHAEL CRAIG,** chemistry professor, consultant; b. Cin., July 31, 1955; s. Joey Matthew and Grace (Fielman) P. BA, U. Tex., 1975; PhD, U. Calif., Berkeley, 1980. NSF postdoctoral fellow Columbia U., N.Y.C., 1980-81; asst. prof. Stanford (Calif.) U., 1981-89; sr. scientist Affymax Rsch. Inst., Palo Alto, Calif., 1989; assoc. prof. Duke U., Durham, N.C., 1989-94, prof., 1994—. Dir. Duke U. program in biol. chemistry, 1994—, dir. biotechnology for bus., 1993—; cons. Am. Cyanamid, 1992—, Wyeth-Ayerst, 1995—, Chroma Xome 1995—; sci. advisor Affymax Rsch. Inst., 1991—. Recipient Newcomb Cleveland prize AAAS, 1991, Intellectual Property Owners Disting. Inventor award, 1993, Outstanding Young Tex. Ex., U. Tex. Ex-Students Assn., 1995. Fellow AAAS, John Simon Guggenheim Mem. Found.; mem. Am. Chem. Soc., Am. Soc. Plant Phys. Achievements include invention of DNA chips; research on mechanism of ethylene biosynthesis. Office: Duke U Dept Chemistry PM Gross Lab PO Box 90346 Durham NC 27708-0346

**PIRSCH, CAROL MCBRIDE,** retired county official, state senator, community relations manager; b. Omaha, Dec. 27, 1936; d. Lyle Erwin and Hilfrie Louise (Lebeck) McBride; m. Allen I. Pirsch, Mar. 28, 1954 (dec.); children:

Pennie Elizabeth, Pamela Elaine, Patrice Eileen, Phyllis Erika, Peter Allen, Perry Andrew. Student, U. Miami, Oxford, Ohio, U. Nebr., Omaha. Former mem. data processing staff Omaha (Nebr.) Pub. Schs.; former mem. wage practices dept. Western Electric Co., Omaha; former legal sec. Omaha; former office mgr. Pirsch Food Brokerage Co., Inc., Omaha; former employment supr., mgr. pub. policy U.S. West Comm., Omaha; mem. Nebr. Senate, 1979-97; commr. Douglas County, 1997—2005, chair, 1999, 2004, vice chair, 2001, 2003. Founder, 1st pres., bd. dirs. Nebr. Coalition for Victims of Crime (Lifetime award 2002); bd. dirs. Centris Fed. Credit Union, 1st v.p., 2003—. Mem. Omaha Douglas County Bldg. Commn., 1997—2003, sec., 2000—03; cmty. cons. Omaha Jr. League, 2002—. Recipient Golden Elephant award, Kuhle award, 1986, Nebr. Coalition for Victims of Crime, Outstanding Legis. Efforts award YWCA, 1989, Breaking the Rule of Thumb award Nebr. Domestic Violence Sexual Assault Coalition, 1989, Cert. of Appreciation award U.S. Dept. Justice, 1988, Partnership award N.E. Credit Union League, 1995, Wings award LWV Greater Omaha, 1995, N.E. VFW Spl. Recognition award for Exceptional Svc., 1995, Victim Rights Week Recognition award, 1995, Victim Adv. Lifetime Achievement award, 2002; Crime Victims Adv. award Nebr. Atty. Gen., 1995. Mem. VASA, Nat. Orgn. Victim Assistance (Outstanding Legis. Leadership award 1981), Omaha Bus. and Profl. Rep. Women, Freedom Found., Douglas County Hist. Soc., Nebr. Taxpayers Assn.; Keystone Citizen Patrol (Comm. Network of Citizen Patrols award, 1995), Audubon Soc., N.W. Cmty. Club, Keystone Task Force (Keystoner of the month, 1987, Queen Keystone, 2002), Benson Rep. Women's Club, Omaha Bus. and Profl. Rep. Women.

**PISACRETA, RICHARD,** psychology professor; b. NYC, June 19, 1946; s. Joseph Ralph and Rose Ann Pisacreta; m. Lauraine Joan Sica, June 20, 1981; children: Rachel, Donna. BA, CUNY; MA, PhD, Adelphi U. Adj. instr. Adelphi U., NYC, 1976—80, York Coll., CUNY, NYC, 1976—80; asst. prof. Ferris State U., Big Rapids, Mich., 1985—present, prof., 1985—90, prof., 1990—. Vis. scholar Harvard U., Boston, 1987; presenter in field. Author 6 books in field; contbr., editor: articles to profl. jours. With USN. Recipient award, Pres.' Club, 1989, Disting. Tchr. award, 1999. Mem.: NEA, APA, Psychol. Soc. Home: 4100 Cott NE Grand Rapids MI 49525 Office Phone: 231-592-2735. Business E-Mail: pisacreta@ferris.edu.

**PISANI, ANTHONY MICHAEL,** architect; b. Cambridge, Mass., May 18, 1943; s. Anthony Joseph and Josephine Ann (Tortorella) P.; m. Emilia D'Agostino, Aug. 27, 1967; children: Emiliabianca, Giancarlo Diploma, Mus. Sch., 1966; BFA, Tufts U., 1966; MArch., Harvard U., 1971. Registered architect, Mass., Calif., Maine, Mich., N.Y., N.H., Tex., Vt. Project architect Kallmann & McKinell, Architects, Boston, 1971-73, Charles G. Hilgenhurst & Assocs., Boston, 1973-74, Desmond & Lord, Architects, Boston, 1974-77; pres. Anthony M. Pisani & Assocs., Architects, Boston, 1978—. Instr. design Boston Archtl. Center, 1971-74; vice- chmn. Boston Landmarks Commn., 1987-95. Major works in Eastern U.S., Ireland, Can., Mex., P.R., Japan; contbr. articles to profl. jours. Mem. Boston Zoning Bd. Appeal, 1998—. Mem. AIA, Boston Soc. Architects, Constrn. Specifications Inst., Urban Land Inst., Nat. Council Archtl. Registration Bds., Soc. Archtl. Historians Home: 95 Robinwood Ave Boston MA 02130-3130 Office: 374 Congress St Boston MA 02210-1807 Office Phone: 617-423-1022. E-mail: apisani@pisani.com.

**PISANI, JOSEPH,** artist, conservator; b. New Rochelle, NY, Oct. 1, 1938; s. Clemente Salvatore and Angelina Pisani; m. Nancy F. Pisani, May 22, 1965; 1 child, Lisa Marie Pasini. Student, San Francisco Art Inst., 1957; BFA, Calif. Coll. Arts/Crafts, 1961. Mil. illustrator HQ Dept. of Army Pentagon, Arlington, Va., 1962—73; owner, dir. Art Gallery 101 Ltd., Fairfax City, 1988—. Represented in permanent collections Pentagon. With U.S. Army, 1962—64. Decorated Meritorious Civilian Svc. medal U.S. Army, Dept. Def. Mem.: Portrait Soc. Am. Democrat. Roman Catholic. Avocations: painting, photography. Home: 2658 Quincy Adams Dr Herndon VA 20171 Office: Art Gallery 101 Ltd 10640 Main St Fairfax VA 22030 Office Phone: 703-273-6229. Business E-Mail: jp@artgallery101.com.

**PISANO, A. ROBERT,** former actors guild executive, former film company executive; b. San Jose, Calif., Mar. 3, 1943; s. Anthony Edward and Carmen Jeanne (Morisoli) P.; m. Carolyn Joan Pollock, May 5, 1979; children: Catherine J., Anthony Daniel, Elizabeth A., Alexandra N. BA in Pub. Administrn., San Jose State U., 1965; JD, U. Calif.-Berkeley, 1968. Bar: Calif. Assoc. O'Melveny & Myers, Los Angeles, 1968-75, ptnr., 1976-85, 92-93; exec. v.p. office of chmn., gen. counsel Paramount Pictures, Los Angeles, 1985-91; exec. v.p. Metro-Goldwyn-Mayer Inc., Santa Monica, Calif., 1993-96; vice chmn. Metro-Goldwyn-Mayer, Inc., Santa Monica, Calif., 1997-99; bus. cons., 1999—; nat. exec. dir., CEO Screen Actors Guild, LA, 2001—05; pres., COO Motion Picture Assn. Am., 2005—. Bd. dirs. Coppola Group, NetFlix.com, 2000- Bd. dirs. Info. for Pub. Affairs, Sacramento, 1983—; trustee Performing Arts Ctr., Los Angeles County, 1997—. Mem. Motion Picture Assn. Am. (bd. dirs. 1989-91, 93-99), Acad. Motion Picture Arts and Scis., Ctr. for Russian and Eurasian Studies (bd. overseers 1996-2001). Office: Motion Picture Assn Am 15503 Ventura Blvd Encino CA 91436

**PISCATELLI, NANCY KELLEY,** elementary school educator; b. Boston, Feb. 11, 1953; d. Joseph Murphy and Eleanor Elizabeth (Jeffers) Kelley; m. Thomas George Piscatelli, Apr. 17, 1976; 1 child, Thomas Joseph. BS, Bridgewater State Coll., 1975, MEd, 1979, Boston Coll., 1977; EdD, Northeastern U., 1989. Lead tchr. Boston Pub. Schs., 1975—, dir. exam sch. initiative, 2002—; cons. Boston Plan for Excellence in the Pub. Schs., 1997; dir. summer test preparation program Boston Latin Sch., 2003—. Cons. Tchrs. Corp. Network, 1979-80. Author/editor: (handbook) The Paraprofessional Handbook, 1979; contbr. articles to profl. jours. Campaign worker Dem. Com., Quincy, Mass., 1975—; active sch. vol. pet project of Mrs. Change Bush. Mem. Am. Fedn. Tchrs., Boston Tchrs. Union, MassCue. Roman Catholic. Avocations: literature, travel. Home: Pheasant Hill 10 Chickadee Dr Norfolk MA 02056-1741 Office: Boston Pub Schs 26 Court St Boston MA 02108-2505 Office Phone: 617-635-8157. Business E-Mail: npiscatelli@boston.k12.ma.us.

**PISCHINGER, FRANZ FELIX,** engineer, researcher, engineering educator; b. Waidhofen, Austria, July 18, 1930; s. Franz and Karoline (Bentz) P.; m. Elfriede Pischinger-Goessler, 1957 (2001); children: Gerhard, Martin, Stefan, Thomas, Alice; m. Elisabeth Pischinger-Froehlich, 2003. Diploma in Engring., Tech. U., Graz, Austria, 1952, DR in Internal Combustion Engines, 1954, Habilitation degree, 1958, Dr (hon.), 1994. Asst. Tech. U., Graz, 1953-58; head rsch. dept. Inst. Internal Combustion Engines (AVL), Graz, 1958-62; leading positions in rsch., devel. Kloeckner-Humboldt-Deutz AG, Cologne, Germany, 1962-70; dir. Inst. Applied Thermodynamics RWTH, Aachen, Germany, 1970-97; pres., CEO FEV Motorentechnik, Aachen, 1978—2003; chmn. bd., v.p. Deutsche Forschungsgemeinschaft, Bonn-Bad Godesberg, Germany, 2003—; Hon. prof. Dalian U., China, 2005. Contbr. articles to profl. jours. Decorated Ehrenring Sub asupiciis praesidentis republicae (Austria), 1954, Bundesverdienstkreuz 1st class (Germany), 1978; recipient Herbert Akroyd Stuard award Inst. Mech. Engrs., 1962, Carl-Engler-Medaille DGMK, Deutsche Wissenschaftliche Gesellschaft Erdöl, Erdgas Kohle, Hamburg, 1990, Austrian cross of Honor for Sci. and Art First Class, 1998, Hon. Prof., Dalian U. Tech., China, 2005. Fellow Soc. Automotive Engrs. U.S.A.; mem. ASME Internat. (Soichiro Honda medal 2000), NAE (USA) (fgn. assoc.), Verein Deutscher Ingenieure (medal of honor 1993, decoration of honor 1997), Deutsche Gesellschaft Mineralölwissenschaft U. Kohlechemie, Rheinisch-Westfälische Akademie Wissenschaften, Aachen-Frankenburg Club, Rotary. Office: FEV Motorentechnik Neuenhofstrasse 181 52078 Aachen Germany Office Phone: 49 241 5689 100.

**PISCHKE, VAIL W.,** lawyer, judge; AB, LLB, JD, U. Notre Dame. Pres., chmn. bd., gen. counsel Met. Bank, Washington; developer, owner Nationally franchised hotels and motels, Shopping Ctr.; judge State of Va.; pvt. practice Falls Church, Va. Commr. chancery Cir. County Fairfax County, vol. judge pro tem; mem. Alcohol Safety Action Project Adv. Com. Va.; presenter, moderator state-wide Va. Jud. Seminars; legal advisor various ch. denomina-

tions in No. Va. and Washington; counsel, legal advisor Prison Fellowship; gen. counsel Christian Fellowship Ch. Past pres., v.p., chmn. bd. elders, gen. counsel, chmn. bd. trustees Our Savior Luth. Ch., Arlington, Va.; past pres., v.p., chmn. bd. elders, gen. counsel, trustee St. Paul's Luth. Ch., Falls Church; pres. Luth. Ch., Arlington, Va.; past pres. Fairfax chpt. Am. Cancer Soc., Va. Soc. Crippled Children and Adults; past dir. Salvation Army; past pres. Longfellow H.S. PTA, Fairfax County, Va.; past pres., v.p. McLean Sr. H.S. PTA, Fairfax County; past bd. dirs. Juvenile Detention Commn. No. Va., No. Va. Family Bd., No. Va. YMCA; bd. dirs. Washington United Givers Fund. Recipient Cert. Outstanding Svc., Va. Supreme Ct. Appeals, Mem. Assn. Dist. Ct. Judges in Va. (hon. life), Falls Church Bar Assn. (past pres., v.p., sec.), No. Va. Trial Lawyers Assn. (past parliamentarian, bd. dirs.), Va. Judges Assn. (life), Falls Church Rotary (past pres., v.p.), Nat. PTA (life). Home: 2043 Reynolds St Falls Church VA 22043-1634

**PISCHL, ADOLPH JOHN,** school administrator; b. East Orange, NJ, Mar. 28, 1920; s. Adolph and Anna (Ellerman) P.; m. Catherine Wild, Sept. 9, 1947; 1 child, Sallyann. Certificate, Drake Coll., 1940. With Juilliard Sch. Music, NYC, 1962-86, asst. concert mgr., 1962-66; dir. pub. relations Juilliard Sch. Music, NYC, 1966-68; concert mgr. Juilliard Sch. Music, NYC, 1966-86; adminstr. Sch. Strings, NYC, 1987-88. With The Dance Mart, NYC, 1950-2005, pub. dir. Am. Dance Festival, Conn. Coll., 1964-68; mgr. Betty Jones Dances I Dance, 1966-68, Ruth Currier Dance Co., 1966-68, Anna Sokolow Dance Co., 1966-68, Julliard Sch. Bookstore, 1971-86. Founder, editor: Dance Perspectives, 1958-64, Dance Data, 1977; editor: Juilliard News Bull. and Rev. Ann, 1964-85; pub.: Dance Horizons, 1965-86 (Dance mag. award 1999); Contbr. articles to dance mags. Bd. dirs. Dance Notation Bur.; sec. bd. dirs. Walter W. Naumburg Found., Inc. With AUS, 1940-46. Home: 603 Valley View Pompton Plains NJ 07444 Personal E-mail: ajpischl@aeitv.net.

**PISCITELLI, FELICIA ANN,** librarian, musician, musicologist; b. Tinker Air Force Base, Oklahoma City, Okla., Sept. 21, 1956; d. Domenic Ralph and Frankie Lee Piscitelli. BA in Fine Arts, U. N.Mex, 1979, MusM, 1983; MLS, U. Ariz., 1990. Piano tchr., Albuquerque, 1982—84; libr. tech. asst. U. N.Mex, Albuquerque, 1984—89; original cataloger, assoc. prof. Tex. A&M U., College Station, 1991—, asst. dir. cataloging, 2004—. Contbr. articles to profl. jours., chapters to books (Walter Gerboth award music bibliography, 1994); author program notes musical concerts. Part-time organist St. Thomas Aquinas Cath. Ch., College Station, 1991-2003. Grantee Hymnody Am. Protestantism Project, Inst. Study Am. Evangelicalism, 1998. Mem.: Am. Guild Organists, Music Libr. Assn., Brazos Valley Chorale, Sigma Alpha Iota (life). Roman Catholic. Avocations: music, travel, languages. Office: Tex A&M U Sterling C Evans Libr Cataloging College Station TX 77843-5000 Office Phone: 979-845-5453. Office Fax: 979-862-1166. Business E-Mail: f-piscitelli@tamu.edu.

**PISCOPO, JOSEPH CHARLES,** actor; b. Passaic, N.J., June 17, 1951; s. Joseph P. and Edith I. (LaMagna) P.; m. Nancy, 1973 (div.); m. Kimberly Driscoll, 1997; children: Joseph, Alexandra. BS, Jones Coll., 1973. Repertory player Saturday Night Live, NBC-TV, 1980-84; founder Piscopo Prodns. Inc.; appeared numerous regional theater prodns., dinner theater circuit, South and N.E.; stand-up comedian improvisation and comic strip clubs, N.Y.C., 1976-80, NBC-TV, 1981-83, Joe Piscopo HBO Spl. 1985, Joe Piscopo N.J. Spl., 1986; radio personality Joe Piscopo at Large, 1983—; appeared in films Johnny Dangerously, 1984, Wise Guys, 1986, Dead Heat, 1988, Sidekicks, 1992, Huck and the King of Hearts, 1993, Two Bits & Pepper, 1995, Multimedia Celebrity Poker, 1995, Captain Nuke and the Bomber Boys, 1995, Open Season, 1996, Weird Al' Yankovic: The Videos, 1996, Baby Bedlam, 2000, Bartleby, 2001; (tv series) (voice) 100 Deeds for Eddie McDowd, 1999; author: The Piscopo Tapes, 1984; TV guest appearances Law & Order, 1999, 2001, Arli$$, 2000. Recipient 2 Ace awards, Miller Lite Beer commls., 1986; named Father of Yr., Nat. Father's Day Com., 1983 Office: William Morris Agy 151 El Camino Dr Beverly Hills CA 90212

**PISHCHALNIKOV, YURI A.,** researcher; b. Kemerovo, Russia, Apr. 26, 1967; m. Irina V. Pishchalnikova. PhD, Moscow State U., Russia, 1997. Jr. rschr. Dept. of Acoustics, Physics Faculty, Moscow State U., 1997—98; sr. rschr. Dept. of Acoustics, Physics Faculty, Moscow State U., 1999—2003; rsch. fellow Dept. of Anatomy and Cell Biology, Ind. U., 2003—04, rsch. assoc., 2004—. Reviewer of articles Jour. of the Acoustical Soc. of Am., Jour. of Sound and Vibration, Experiments in Fluids; mem. of the com. for m.s. theses def. Dept. of Acoustics, Physics Faculty, Moscow State U., 1997—2003. Contbr. articles to profl. jours. Recipient Best Abstract prize, Assn. AStellas, 2006; Visitor Support Program award, U.S. Office of Naval Rsch. Internat. Field Office, London, UK, 2004, Rsch. grant, NIH, 2004—, Fellowship award, Dept. of Anatomy and Cell Biolology, Ind. U., Sch. of Medicine, Indpls., 2003—04, Dept. of Anatomy and Cell Biology, Ind. U., Sch. of Medicine, Indpls., 2000—01, George Soros Doctoral Fellowship award, Internat. Soros Sci. Edn. Program, 1996, 1995, Joint stipend, Acoustical Soc. of Am. and the Russian Acoustical Soc., 1995. Mem.: Internat. Soc. for Therapeutic Ultrasound, Acoustical Soc. of Am. (mem. biomedical ultrasound tech. com. 2006—). Office: Dept of Anatomy Ind U 635 Barnhill Dr MS-5055 Indianapolis IN 46202 Office Phone: 317-274-0548. Office Fax: 317-278-2040. E-mail: yura@anatomy.iupui.edu.

**PISKOTI, CAROL LEE,** art educator; b. Stockton, Calif., Jan. 13, 1949; d. Kyman and Clara Lee; m. James Piskoti, June 16, 1984. BA in Fine Art, Calif. State U. Stanislaus, Turlock, 1971. Tchg. credential Calif. Tchr. Sacramento City Sch. Dist., 1973—. Facilitator, Calif. Tchr. Consortium for Arts Edn., Sacramento, 2002—05. Recipient Hon. Svc. award, PTA-John F. Kennedy H.S., 1989. Mem.: Crocker Art Mus, (tchr. adv. bd. 2002—), Nat. Edn. Assn., Calif. Art Edn. Assn. (chair vols. 2001, chair no. area youth art month 2004—06, Award of Merit 2001, Ruth Jansen Outstanding Visual Arts Educator of Yr. award 2004). Avocations: painting, drawing. Office: John F Kennedy HS 6715 Gloria Dr Sacramento CA 95831

**PISTER, KARL STARK,** engineering educator; b. Stockton, Calif., June 27, 1925; s. Edwin LeRoy and Mary Kimball (Smith) P.; m. Rita Olsen, Nov. 18, 1950; children: Francis, Therese, Anita, Jacinta, Claire, Kristofer. BS with honors, U. Calif., Berkeley, 1945, MS, 1948; PhD, U. Ill., 1952; D of Pub. Policy (hon.), U. Fla., 2004; LHD (hon.), U. Colo., 2005. Instr. theoretical and applied mechanics U. Ill., 1949-52; faculty U. Calif., Berkeley, 1952-62, prof. engring. scis., 1962-96, Roy W. Carlson prof. engring., 1985-90, dean Coll. Engring., 1980-90, Roy W. Carlson prof. emeritus, chancellor Santa Cruz, 1991-96, pres., chancellor emeritus, 1996—; sr. assoc. to pres. Oakland, 1996-99, v.p. ednl. outreach, 1999-2000. Richard Merton guest prof. U. Stuttgart, Germany, 1978; cons. to govt. and industry; bd. dirs. Monterey Bay Aquarium Rsch. Inst.; trustee Nat. U. Armenia, Grad. Theol. Union, Berkeley; chmn. bd. Calif. Coun. Sci. and Tech.; bd. dirs. Ctr. Future Tchg. and Learning. Contbr. articles to profl. jours.; mem. editl. bd. Jour. Optimization Theory and Applications, 1982, Ency. Phys. Sci. and Tech. With USNR, WWII. Fulbright scholar, Ireland, 1965, West Germany, 1973; recipient Wason Rsch. medal Am. Concrete Inst., 1960, Vincent Bendix Minorities in Engring. award Am. Soc. for Engring. Edn., 1988, Lamme medal, 1993, Alumni Honor award U. Ill. Coll. Engring., 1982, Disting. Engring. Alumnus award U. Calif. Berkeley Coll. Engring., 1992, Berkeley medal, 1996, U. Calif. Presdl. medal, 2003, World Tech. Network award for policy, World Tech. Coun., London, 2002 Alumnus of Yr. award Calif. Alumni Assn., Berkeley, 2006. Fellow: AAAS, ASME (Applied Mechanics award 1999, Internat. Pres.'s award 2000), Am. Acad. Arts and Scis., Am. Acad. Mechanics, Calif. Acad. Sci. (hon.); mem.: ASCE, NAE. Office: U Calif Dept Civil & Environ Engr Berkeley CA 94720 Office Phone: 510-642-3066. Business E-Mail: pister@ce.berkeley.edu.

**PISTERS, KATHERINE M.W.,** internist, medical educator; b. London, Ont., Canada, July 26, 1962; arrived in US, 1985; d. John Bethune and Rita Margaret Walker; m. Peter W.T. Pisters, June 28, 1984. MD, U. Western Ont., London, 1985. Diplomate Am. Bd. Internal Medicine/Med. Oncology. Intern Cornell Hosps., North Shore U. Hosp. and Meml. Hosp., Manhasset and

NYC, 1985—86, resident, 1986—88; med. oncology fellow Meml. Sloan-Kettering Cancer Ctr., NYC, 1988—91, chief resident, 1989—90; instr. Meml.-Sloan Kettering Hosp., NYC, 1991—94; asst. prof. U. Tex. M.D. Anderson Cancer Ctr., Houston, 1994—98, assoc. prof., 1998—2005, prof. medicine dept. thoracic/head and neck med. oncology, 2005—. Instr. thoracic oncology svc. Cornell U. Med. Coll., NYC, 1991—94; spkr., presenter, cons. in field. Contbr. numerous articles to profl. jours., chpts. to books, revs., abstracts in field; sect. editor: Lung Cancer, Current Oncology Reports, 2002—. Named one of Best Cancer Drs., Good Housekeeping, 1999; recipient Career Devel. award, Am. Cancer Soc., 1993—94; grantee, Protocols, 1997—2001; scholar, U. Western Ont., 1980—82; Borden fellow in clin. oncology, 1990—91. Fellow: ACP.

**PISTOLE, JOHN S.,** federal agency administrator; married; 2 children. Grad., Ind. U. Law Sch., 1981. Pvt. practice, Anderson, Ind., 1981—83; spl. agent Mpls. divsn. FBI, 1983—85, spl. agent NY divsn., 1985—90, supr. organized crime sect. Wash., 1990—94, field supr. white collar crime and civil rights squad, undercover coord. Indpls., 1994—99, asst. spl. agent in charge Boston, 1999—2001, inspector Wash., 2001—02, dep. asst. dir. counterterrorism divsn., 2002—03, asst. dir. counterterrorism divsn., 2003, exec. asst. dir., counterterrorism and counterintelligence, 2003—04, dep. dir., 2004—. Instr. Internat. Law Enforcement Acad., Budapest, Hungary, 1995—96; FBI rep. state dept. delegation, Sofia, Bulgaria; dir. Blue Team info. soc. working group, 2001. Office: FBI J Edgar Hoover Bldg 935 Pennsylvania Ave NW Washington DC 20535-0001

**PISTOLE, THOMAS GORDON,** microbiology professor, researcher, department chairman; b. Detroit, Sept. 17, 1942; s. Leotis Merton Pistole and Lillian Nell (Bosley) Besser; m. Donna Dulcie Straw, Sept. 11, 1965; children: James Alexander, Jennifer Katharine. PhB, Wayne State U., 1964, MS, 1966; PhD, U. Utah, 1969. Postdoctoral fellow U.S. Army, Frederick, Md., 1969-70; research assoc. U. Minn., Mpls., 1970-71; asst. prof. U. N.H., Durham, 1971-77, assoc. prof., 1977-83; prof., 1983—, chmn., 1983-92, dist. prof., 2006. Vis. scientist Weizmann Inst., Rehovot, Israel, 1979; vis. prof. U. Edinburgh, Scotland, 1998; faculty fellow Office of V.P. for Acad. Affairs U. N.H., 1996-99; mem. ad hoc study sect. U.S. Dept. Agr., 2002. Co-editor: Biomedical Application of the Horseshoe Crab, 1979; mem. editl bd.: Jour. Invertebrate Pathology, 1988—90. NRC fellow, 1969-70, NIH sr. internat. fellow, 1986; grantee NIH, 1975-77, 89-93, 96—, NSF, 1981-84. Mem.: Soc. for Leukocyte Biology, Am. Assn. Immunologists, Am. Soc. for Microbiology. Avocations: singing, collecting old sheet music, walking, cooking. Office: U NH Rudman Hall Dept Microbiology Durham NH 03824-2617 Office Phone: 603-862-0111. Business E-mail: thomas.pistole@unh.edu.

**PISTOR, KATHARINA,** law educator; b. Freiburg, Germany, May 23, 1963; m. Carsten G. Bonnemann. JD with honors, U. Freiburgw, 1988; LLM with distinction, U. London, 1989; MPA, Harvard U., 1994; Dr. Jur., U. Munich, 1998. Sr. rsch. fellow Ctrl. European U. Privatization Project, 1993—95; lectr. law Harvard Law Sch., 1994—95; rsch. assoc. Harvard Inst. for Internat. Devel., 1995—98, Max Planck Inst. for Comparative and Internat. Private Law, Hamburg, 1998—99; asst. prof. Kennedy Sch. Govt., Harvard U., 2000—01; assoc. prof. law Columbia U. Law Sch., NYC, 2001—04, prof., 2004—. Vis. prof. Study Ctr. at Gerzensee, Switzerland, 2003, U. Pa. Law Sch., 2004, Inst. for Law and Fin., Frankfurt U., Germany, 2004, Germany, 05. Contbr. articles to law jours. Office: Columbia Law Sch 435 W 116th St, Rm 643 New York NY 10027 Office Phone: 212-854-0068. Office Fax: 212-854-7946. E-mail: kpisto@law.columbia.edu.

**PISTORIUS, GEORGE,** language educator, educator; b. Prague, Czechoslovakia, Mar. 19, 1922; came to U.S., 1958, naturalized, 1964; s. Theodor and Blazena (Jiranek) P.; m. Marie Skokan, June 30, 1945; 1 dau., Erika. Student, Charles U., Prague, 1945-48; postgrad., Université de Paris, 1948-50; certificats d'etudes superieures, Université de Strasbourg, France, 1950, 1951; PhD, U. Pa., 1963. Asst. dept. comparative lit. Charles U., 1946-48; instr. Lafayette Coll., Easton, Pa., 1958-61, asst. prof. French, 1961-63; asso. prof. Williams Coll., 1963-68, prof. Romanic langs., 1968-92, chmn. dept., 1971-82, prof. emeritus, 1992—. Instr. French, Colby Coll. Summer Sch. Lang., 1959-65 Author: Bibliography of the works of F.X. Salda, 1948, Destin de la culture francaise dans une democratie populaire, 1957, L'Image de l'Allemagne dans le roman francais entre les deux guerres (1919-1939), 1964, Marcel Proust und Deutschland, Eine Bibliographie, 1981, 2d edit. 2002, André Gide und Deutschland: Eine internationale Bibliographie, 1990. Home: 54 Cluett Dr Williamstown MA 01267-2805

**PISZEL, ANTHONY S.,** corporate financial executive; BA, Rutgers U.; MBA, Golden Gate Univ. Practice fellow Fin. Acctg. Standards Bd., 1988—90; ptnr. Deloitte & Touche, 1990—93; CFO individual life ins. Prudential Fin. Inc., 1993—95, CFO instl. life ins., 1995—97, corp. v.p., 1997—98, sr. v.p., controller, 1998—2004; exec. v.p., CFO Health Net Inc., Woodland Hills, Calif., 2004—. bd. dir. RehabCare Group Inc. Mem.: AICPA, NJ State Soc. CPAs. Office: Health Net Life Insurance Co 21281 Burbank Blvd Woodland Hills CA 91367-6607*

**PITCHER, GRIFFITH FONTAINE,** lawyer; b. Balt., Nov. 1, 1937; s. William Henry and Virginia Griffith (Stein) P.; children; Virginia T. Pitcher Ballinger, L. Brooke Pitcher Fick, William T.B., Margaret W. Pitcher Saylors. BA, Johns Hopkins U., 1960; JD, U. Va., 1963. Bar: Ala. 1963, Fla. 1971, Ga. 1996. Assoc. Bradley, Arant, Rose & White, Birmingham, Ala., 1963-71; mem. Van den Berg, Gay & Burke, Orlando, Fla., 1971-76, Mahoney, Hadlow & Adams, Jacksonville, Fla., 1976-82; ptnr. Squire, Sanders & Dempsey, Miami, Fla., 1982-93; of counsel Mershon, Sawyer, Johnston, Dunwoody & Cole, Miami, Fla., 1994-95, Chamberlain, Hrdlicka, White, Williams & Martin, Atlanta, 1996—2002; Seyfarth Shaw LLP, Atlanta, 2002—. Contbr. articles to profl. jours. Vice chmn. Winter Park (Fla.) Planning & Zoning Bd., 1974-75. With Army N.G., 1961-64. Fellow: Am. Coll. Bond Counsel (founding fellow, past treas., past dir.); mem.: Ala. State Bar Assn., Ga. State Bar, Fla. Bar, Nat. Assn. Bond Lawyers, Order of Coif, Delta Phi. Republican. Office Phone: 404-888-1884.

**PITCHER, THOMAS B.,** lawyer; b. Nov. 28, 1938; BS, U. Fla., 1960; JD, Duke U., 1966. Bar: Calif. 1967. Ptnr. Gibson, Dunn & Crutcher, Irvine, Calif. Note editor: Duke Law Jour., 1965-66. Mem. ABA, L.A. County Bar Assn., Orange County Bar Assn. Office: Gibson Dunn & Crutcher 4 Park Plz Ste 1400 Irvine CA 92614-8557

**PITCHFORD, MARK B.,** lawyer; b. Washington, DC, Apr. 13, 1959; AB with distinction, Stanford U., 1981; JD cum laude, Santa Clara U., 1984. Bar: Calif., US Dist. Ct. (ea. dist.), Calif., US Dist. Ct. (no. dist.), Calif., US Ct. Appeals (9th cir.). Atty. litig. dept. Cooley Godward LLP, Palo Alto, Calif., 1984—, COO, ptnr., 2001—; dep. dist. atty. County of Santa Clara, 1989. Named one of Calif. top 20 up and coming lawyers under 40, Calif. Law & Bus., 1999. Mem.: ABA, Santa Clara County Bar Assn. Office: Cooley Godward LLP Five Palo Alto Sq 3000 El Camino Real Palo Alto CA 94306-2155 Office Phone: 650-843-5018. Office Fax: 650-857-0663. E-mail: mpitchford@cooley.com.*

**PITCHUMONI, CAPECOMORIN SANKAR,** gastroenterologist, educator; b. Madura, India, Jan. 20, 1938; came to U.S., 1967; s. Sankara and Jaya (Lekshmi) Iyer; m. Prema Iyer, Nov. 11, 1964; children: Sheila, Shoba, Suresh. Student, St. Xavier Coll., India, 1953-55; MB BS, Trivandrum Med. Coll., India, 1959, MD, 1965. Intern Med. Coll.: Trivandrum, India, 1961-63; resident in gastroenterology Yale U., 1967-69; N.Y. Med. Coll., 1969-72; practice medicine specializing in gastroenterology N.Y.C., 1972—; asst. prof. medicine Kottayam Med. Coll., India, 1967, N.Y. Med. Coll., 1972-75, assoc. prof., 1975-80, prof. clin. medicine, 1980-85, profl. medicine, 1985—, assoc. prof. preventive and social medicine, 1975-86, prof. community and preventive medicine, 1986—; chief sect. gastroenterology Our Lady of Mercy Med. Ctr., N.Y.C., 1980—, assoc. dir. medicine, 1985—, program dir. internal medicine, 1987—, dir. medicine, 1992, chmn. emeritus dept. medicine,

2002—; chief divsn. gastroenterology St. Peters U. Hosp., New Brunswick, NJ, 2002—. Contbg. author med. textbooks; contbr. articles to profl. jours. Recipient Om Prakash award Indian Soc. Gastroenterology, 1976, Outstanding Scientist of Yr. award MV Spltys., Madras, 1994, Oration award Thangavelu Endowment, 1994. Master Am. Coll. Gastroenterology (gov. 1996-2000); fellow Royal Coll. Physicians and Surgeons Can., Am. Coll. Nutrition, Am. Gastroent. Assn.; mem. Assn. Physicians India, India Soc. Gastroenterology (life), Am. Inst. Nutrition, Gastrointestinal Endoscopy, Am. Soc. for Clin. Nutrition. Hindu. Home: 1 Nevius Pl Somerset NJ 08873 Office: St Peters U Hosp New Brunswick NJ E-mail: pitchumoni@hotmail.com.

**PITERNICK, ANNE BREARLEY,** librarian, educator; b. Blackburn, Eng., Oct. 13, 1926; arrived in Can., 1956, naturalized, 1965; d. Walter and Ellen (Harris) Clayton; m. Neil Brearley, 1956 (div. 1971); m. George Piternick, May 6, 1971. BA, U. Manchester, Eng., 1948, F.L.A., 1983. Mem. library staff U. B.C., Vancouver, Can., 1956-66, head sci. div., 1960-61, head social scis. div., 1965-66, prof. Sch. Library, Archival and Info. Studies, 1966-91, prof. emerita, 1991—, assoc. dean Faculty of Arts, 1985-90. Mem. Nat. Com. Bibliog. Svcs. Can., 1975-80, chmn. com. on bibliography and info. services for social scis. and humanities, 1981-84; mem. adv. acad. panel Social Scis. and Humanities Research Council, 1981-84; mem. Nat. Adv. Com. Culture Stats., 1985-90; organizer Confs. on Can. Bibliography, 1974, 81; pres. Can. Assn. Spl. Librs. Info. Svcs., 1969-70, Can. Libr. Assn., 1976-77. Contbr. articles to profl. jours. Bd. dirs. Vancouver Friends of Chamber Music, 2001—. Recipient Queen's Silver Jubilee medal, 1977, award for Spl. Librarianship Can. Assn. Spl. Librs. and Info. Svcs., 1987, 75th Anniversary medal U.B.C., 1990, Can. 125 medal, 1993; fellow Coun. on Libr. Resources, 1980. Fellow Libr. Assn.; mem. Assn. Profs. Emeriti U. B.C. (pres. 2003-04), Coll. and Univs. Retiree Assns. Can. (bd. dirs. 2005—) Achievements include research in electronic info. svcs. and scholarly comm. Home: 1849 W 63rd Ave Vancouver BC Canada V6P 2H9 Personal E-mail: annebp@interchange.ubc.ca.

**PITINO, RICHARD,** collegiate basketball coach, former professional basketball coach; b. NYC, Sept. 18, 1952; Student, U. Mass. Asst. coach U. Hawaii, 1975-76, Syracuse U., 1976-78; coach Boston U., 1978-83; asst. coach N.Y. Knicks, 1983-85, coach, 1987-89, Providence U., 1986-87; basketball coach U. Ky., Lexington, 1989-97; head coach Boston Celtics, 1997—2001; head men's basketball coach Univ. of Louisville, 2001—. Author: (with Dick Weiss) Full Court Pressure: A Year in Kentucky Basketball, 1992. Named Coll. Coach of Yr., Sporting News, 1987. Office: Univ of Louisville Louisville KY 40292

**PITKIN, EDWARD THADDEUS,** aerospace engineer, consultant; b. Putnam, Conn., Dec. 14, 1930; s. Thaddeus Eugene and Florence Mabel (Brown) P.; m. Clara Lucy Modliszewski, June 13, 1953; children— Gayle Linda, Dale Edward. BS, U. Conn., 1952; MS (Guggenheim fellow), Princeton, 1953; PhD (NASA fellow), UCLA, 1964. Project engr. Astro Div. Marquardt Co., Los Angeles, 1954-59, mgr. space propulsion, 1959-61; engring. cons. Los Angeles, 1961-64; asso. prof. aerospace engring. U. Conn., Storrs, 1964-70, prof. mech. and aerospace engring., 1970-90, prof. emeritus, 1990—; cons. engr., 1990—; asst. dean U. Conn., Storrs, 1977-87. Contbr. articles to tech. publs. Served as lt. USAF, 1953-55. Asso. fellow AIAA Home: 115 Brookside Ln Mansfield Center CT 06250-1001 Office: U Conn Dept Mech Engring U-139 191 Auditorium Rd Storrs Mansfield CT 06269-3139

**PITKIN, ROY MACBETH,** retired obstetrician, educator; b. Anthon, Iowa, May 24, 1934; s. Roy and Pauline Allie (McBeath) Pitkin; m. Marcia Alice Jenkins, Aug. 17, 1957; children: Barbara, Robert Macbeth, Kathryn, William Charles. BA with highest distinction, U. Iowa, 1956, MD, 1959. Diplomate Am. Bd. Ob-Gyn. Intern King County Hosp., Seattle, 1959—60; resident in ob-gyn U. Iowa Hosps. and Clinics, Iowa City, 1960—63; asst. prof. ob-gyn U. Ill., 1965—68; assoc. prof. ob-gyn U. Iowa, Iowa City, 1968—72, prof., 1972—87, head dept. ob-gyn, 1977—87; prof. UCLA, 1987—97, head dept. ob-gyn., 1987—95, prof. emeritus, 1997—. Mem. residency rev. com. ob-gyn., 1981—87; chmn., 1985—87. Author: The Green Journal 50 Years On, 2003; co-editor: The Best of After Office Hours, 2003; editor-in-chief Year Book of Obstetrics and Gynecology, 1975—86, Clinical Obstetrics and Gynecology, 1979—2000; editor: Obstetrics and Gynecology, 1985—2001; editor emeritus Obstetrics and Gynecology, 2001; contbr. articles to med. jours. Served to lt. comdr. M.C. USNR, 1963—65. Recipient NIH career awardee, 1972—77, Disting. Alumni Achievement award, U. Iowa, 2002. Fellow: Royal Ob-Gyn. (ad eundem); mem.: Coun. Sci. Editors (Dist. Svc. award 2002), Inst. Medicine, NAS, Soc. Perinatal Obstetricians (pres. 1978—79), Soc. Gynecol. Investigation (pres. 1985—86), German Soc. Gyn-Ob. (hon.), Ctrl. Assn. Ob-Gyn., Am. Gyn-Ob. Soc. (pres. 1994—95), Am. Coll. Ob-Gyns., AMA (Goldberger award in clin. nutrition 1982) Presbyterian. Home: 78900 Rancho La Quinta Dr La Quinta CA 92253-6252 E-mail: r.pitkin@earthlink.net.

**PITMAN, GERALD H.,** plastic surgeon; AB, Williams Coll.; MD, U. Pa. Lic. NY, Mass., Pa, diplomate Am. Bd. of Plastic Surgery. Resident in surgery Columbia-Presbyterian Hosp., NYC; resident in plastic surgery NYC Med. Ctr.; fellow in microsurgery NYU Med. Ctr., attending plastic surgeon, Manhattan Eye, Ear and Throat Hosp. Clin. assoc. prof. surgery NYU Sch. Medicine; lectr. in field. Author: Liposuction and Aesthetic Surgery, 1993; contbr. numerous articles to profl. jours. Fellow: Am. Coll. Surgeons, NY Acad. Medicine; mem.: NY State and County Med. Socs., NY Regional Soc. Plastic and Reconstructive Surgeons, NE Soc. Plastic Surgeons, Am. Soc. Aesthetic Plastic Surgery, Am. Soc. Plastic and Reconstructive Surgeons. Avocations: boating, fishing, skiing, triathlons. Office: 170 E 73rd St New York NY 10021 Office Phone: 212-517-2600. Office Fax: 212-628-0774. Business E-mail: info@drpitman.com.

**PITMAN, LAVERN FRANK,** librarian; b. Poynette, Wis., June 8, 1943; s. George and Carolyn (Hutchinson) P.; m. Rosa Papist, Sept. 8, 1973 (dec. Oct. 1996); 1 child, Christina. BA, Wis. State U., 1965; MSLS, Catholic U. Am., 1973; MA, Frostburg State U., 1985. Cataloger copyright office Libr. Congress, Washington, 1966-71, Spanish/Italian cataloger shared divsn., 1971-79; libr. Frostburg (Md.) State U., 1980-98. Author: The Family of John and Deborah Flick Meyers, 1989, The Robertsons: A Norwegian Family in America, 1993; co-author: A Century of Commitment: Frostburg State University, 1997; editor: Civil War Diary of Jesse Meyers, Co. I, 23d Regiment, Wisconsin Volunteer Infantry, 2002. Historic Interpreter, Mt. Vernon, 1999-2004; curator Wayside Found., 1999-2000; libr. Md. Bur. Mines, 2000-02; trustee Shenandoah County Pub. Libr., Va., 2004—. Mem. Geneal. Soc. Allegany County, Geneal. Soc. Wis., State Hist. Soc. Wis., Frostburg Mus. Assn., Sons of Norway, Vesterheim Norwegian-Am. Mus., Clan Rose Soc. Am.

**PITMAN, PAMELA RAE,** psychologist; b. Aurora, Ill., Sept. 30, 1948; d. L. William and Caryl Margaret (Bloomdahl) Gonnerman; m. Reed Allen Pitman, Sept. 27, 1974; 1 child, Nathan James. BS in Edn., U. Mo., 1970; MA in Edn., Washington U., St. Louis, 1972. Counselor/English tchr. Dupo Community Unit 196, Dupo, Ill., 1970-74; rehab. counselor Jewish Employment & Vocat. Svc., St. Louis, 1975-76; counselor Wellsville-Middletown R.I., Wellsville, Mo., 1985-88; psychol. examiner Franklin County Spl. Edn. Coop., St. Clair Mo., 1988—. Cons. Project Access, Springfield, Mo., 1989—. Author: Early Childhood Evaluation Project, 1990—. Mem. Coun. for Exceptional Children. Avocations: reading, cooking, fishing, board/card games. Office: Franklin County Spl Edn 1773 W Springfield Rd Saint Clair MO 63077-4420

**PITOFSKY, ROBERT,** federal agency administrator, law educator; b. Paterson, N.J., Dec. 27, 1929; s. Morris and Sadye (Katz) P.; m. Sally Levy, June 4, 1961; children: Alexander, David, Elizabeth. BA, NYU, 1951; LLB, Columbia U., 1954; LLD (hon.), Georgetown U., 1989, Nyenrode U., Netherlands, 2002. Bar: N.Y. 1956, D.C. 1973, U.S. Supreme Ct. 1972. Atty. Dept. Justice, Washington, 1956-57; assoc. Dewey, Ballantine, Bushby,

Palmer & Wood, N.Y.C., 1957-64; prof. law NYU, 1964-70; dir. Bur. Consumer Protection, FTC, 1970-73; prof. law Georgetown U. Law Ctr., Washington, 1973—83, 1989—, dean, exec. v.p. law ctr. affairs, 1983-89; commr. FTC, Washington, 1978-81, chmn., 1995-2001; of counsel Arnold & Porter, Washington, 1973-78, 81-95, 01—. Guest scholar Brookings Instn., Washington, 1989-90; vis. prof. law Harvard Law Sch., 1975-76, Columbia Law Sch., 2005; faculty mem. Salzburg (Austria) Seminar in Am. Studies, 1975; chmn. Def. Sci. Bd. task force on antitrust aspects of def. industry downsizing, 1994. Co-author: Cases on Antitrust Law, 1967, Cases on Trade Regulation, 5th edit. 2003; co-editor: Revitalizing Antitrust in Its Second Century, 1991; contbr. articles on consumer protection and antitrust to profl. publs. Served with U.S. Army, 1954-56. Recipient Disting. Service award FTC, 1972, Hart Pub. Svc. award Cons. Fedn. Am., 2001, Kirkpatrick Lifetime Achievement award FTC, 2002; named One of Ten Outstanding Mid-Career Law Profs. Time Mag., 1977, Disting. Columbia Law Grad. in Tchg., 2005. Mem. ABA (coun. antitrust sect. 1986-89), Am. Acad. Arts and Scis., Am. Law Inst., Assn. Am. Law Schs., Columbia U. Ctr. for Law Econ. Studies (adv. bd. 1975-95). Democrat. Jewish. Home: 3809 Blackthorn St Chevy Chase MD 20815-4905 Office Phone: 202-662-9049. Business E-Mail: Robert_Pitofsky@aporter.com.

**PITONIAK, SCOTT MICHAEL,** sportswriter; b. Rome, NY, Apr. 10, 1955; s. Andrew Edward and Edna (Holloway) Pitoniak; children: Amy Leigh, Christopher Drew. BS in Pub. Comm. magna cum laude, Syracuse U., 1977. Baseball writer Evening Times, Little Falls, N.Y., 1977; sportswriter Daily Sentinel, Rome, N.Y., 1977; sportswriter, columnist Observer-Dispatch, Utica, N.Y., 1978-84; pro football writer Dem. & Chronicle, Rochester, N.Y., 1985-90, sports projects writer, 1990—. Voter Heisman Trophy Award, 1981—; corr. Gannett News Svc., 1982—, Sporting News, 1982—; journalism prof. St. John Fisher Coll., 1995—. Author: (book) The Buffalo Bills Official Trivia Book, 1989, 1991; co-author: Silver Seasons: The Story of the Rochester Red Wings, 1996, Playing Write Field, 1997, Baseball in Rochester, 2003, Syracuse University Football, 2003, Slices of Orang, 2005; contbr. articles to mags., newspapers, news svcs. including Sporting News, USA Today, Washington Post, Phila. Inquirer, AP, UPI, others; co-host (TV series) Time Warner Comm., 1994—96. Vol. Alzheimer's Assn., Rochester, 1991—. Named one of Am.'s Top 10 Sports Columnist, APSE, 2000, torchbearer, Winter Olympics, 2002; named to Rochester Sports Walk of Fame, 1999, Syracuse U. Journalism Hall of Fame, 2000; recipient Disting. Health Journalism award Gold medal 1st Pl. newspaper divsn., 1991, 1st Pl. sports, N.Y. State AP Writing Contest, 1995, 2d Pl. features, 1993, 2d Pl. sports, 1991, 1997, 2d Pl. columns, 2001, Best of Gannett award, 1996—98; others; scholar Regents. Mem.: Basketball Writers Am., Coll. Football Writers Assn. Am. (bd. dirs.), Profl. Football Writers Am. (1st Pl. enterprise reporting 1999, 1st Pl. columns 2000, 2d Pl. columns, hon. mention columns 2004), Phi Kappa Phi, Kappa Tau Alpha. Roman Catholic. Avocations: reading, sports memorabilia collecting, volunteering, coaching youth sports, baseball. Office: Gannett Rochester Newspapers 55 Exchange Blvd Rochester NY 14614-2001 Office Phone: 585-258-2455. Business E-Mail: spitoniak@aol.com.

**PITOT, HENRY CLEMENT, III,** pathologist, educator; b. N.Y.C., May 12, 1930; s. Henry Clement and Bertha (Lowe) Pitot; m. Julie S. Schutten, July 29, 1954; children: Bertha, Anita, Jeanne, Catherine, Henry, Michelle, Lisa, Patrice. BS in Chemistry, Va. Mil. Inst., 1951; MD, Tulane U., 1955, PhD in Biochemistry, 1959, DSc (hon.), 1995. Instr. pathology Med. Sch. Tulane U., New Orleans, 1955-59; postdoctoral fellow McArdle Lab. U. Wis., Madison, 1959-60, mem. faculty Med. Sch., 1960—, prof. pathology and oncology, 1966-99, prof. emeritus, 1999—, dir. McArdle Lab., 1973-91, acting dean Med. Sch., 1971-73, dir. McArdle Lab., 1973-91. Recipient Borden Undergrad. Rsch. award, 1955, Leaderle Faculty award, 1962, Career Devel. award, Nat. Cancer Inst., NIH, 1965, Parke-Davis award, 1968, Noble Found. Rsch. award, 1984, Esther Langer award, U. Chgo., 1984, Hilldale award, U. Wis., 1991, Founders award, Chem. Industry Inst. Toxicology, 1993, Midwest Regional chpt. Soc. Toxicology award, 1996, Emeritus Faculty award, U. Wis. Med. Sch., 2001, Disting. Lifetime Toxicology award, Soc. Toxicology, 2003, Gold-headed Cane award, Am. Soc. Investigative Pathology, 2005, Lifetime Disting. Alumnus award, Tulane Med. Sch., 2005, Disting. Svc. award, Assn. Pathology Chairs, 2005. Fellow: AAAS, N.Y. Acad. Scis.; mem.: Soc. Toxicologic Pathologists, Soc. Toxicology, Soc. Surg. Oncology (Lucy J. Wortham award 1981), Soc. Exptl. Biology and Medicine (pres. 1991—93), Am. Soc. Investigative Pathology (pres. 1976—77), Am. Cancer Soc. (life), Japanese Cancer Soc. (hon.), Am. Chem. Soc., Am. Soc. Biochemistry and Molecular Biology, Am. Assn. Cancer Rsch., Am. Soc. Cell Biology. Roman Catholic. Home: 314 Robin Pkwy Madison WI 53705-4931 Office: U Wis McArdle Lab Cancer Rsch 1400 University Ave Madison WI 53706-1599 Office Phone: 608-262-3247. Business E-Mail: pitot@oncology.wisc.edu. *Where and who we are today is the result of those whom we have met and known and loved until now*

**PITSTICK, SI A.,** real estate agent; m. Laura A. Pitstick; children: Roe, Drew. BS, Ohio State U., 1988. Real estate agt. West Shell, Cin., 1988—93, Cin. Comml. Realtors, Cin., 1993—. Mem.: CCIM, SIOR (treas. 2004—05, pres. 2005—06). Office: Cin Coml Realtors 4901 Hunt Rd Ste 102 Cincinnati OH 45242 Office Phone: 513-241-2300. Home Fax: 513-241-2654; Office Fax: 513-241-2654. Business E-Mail: sipitstick@c-c-r.com

**PITT, BERTRAM,** cardiologist, educator, consultant; b. Kew Gardens, N.Y., Apr. 27, 1932; s. David and Shirley (Blum) P., m. Elaine Liberstein, Aug. 10, 1962; children: Geoffrey, Jessica, Jillian Ba, Cornell U., 1953; MD, U. Basel, Switzerland, 1959. Diplomate Am. Bd. Internal Medicine, Am. Bd. Cardiology. Intern Beth Israel Hosp., N.Y.C., 1959-60, resident Boston, 1960-63; fellow in cardiology Johns Hopkins U., Balt., 1966-67, from instr. to assoc. prof., 1967-77; prof. medicine Sch. Medicine, 1991—2005, prof. medicine emeritus Sch. Medicine, 2005—; dir. heart failure rsch. William Beaumont Hosp., Royal Oak, Mich., 1977—. Author: Atlas of Cardiovascular Nuclear Medicine, 1977; editor: Cardiovascular Nuclear Medicine, 1974; co-editor: Clinical Trials in Cardiology, 1997, Current Controlled Trials in Cardiovascular Medicine, 1999—. Served to capt. U.S. Army, 1963-65. Mem. ACP, Am. Coll. Cardiology, Am. Soc. Clin. Investigation, Assn. Am. Physicians, Am. Physiol. Soc., Am. Heart Assn. (James. B. Herrick award 2005), Assn. Univ. Cardiologists, Am. Coll. Chest Physicians, Johns Hopkins U. Soc. Scholars. Home: 24 Ridgeway St Ann Arbor MI 48104-1739 Office: U Mich Divsn Cardiology 1500 E Medical Center Dr Ann Arbor MI 48109-0005 Office Phone: 734-936-5260. Business E-Mail: bpitt@umich.edu.

**PITT, BRAD,** actor; b. Shawnee, Okla., Dec. 18, 1963; s. Bill and Jane Pitt; m. Jennifer Aniston, July 29, 2000 (div. Oct. 2, 2005); Maddox Chivan Jolie-Pitt, Zahara Marley Jolie-Pitt (Adoptive children with Angelina Jolie); (one child with Angelina Jolie) Shiloh Nouvel Jolie-Pitt Actor (films) No Man's Land, 1987, Less Than Zero, 1987, Cutting Glass, 1989, Happy Together, 1990, Across the Tracks, 1991, Thelma and Louise, 1991, Johnny Suede, 1991, Contact, 1992, Cool World, 1992, A River Runs Through It, 1992, Kalifornia, 1993, True Romance, 1993, The Favor, 1994, Interview with the Vampire, 1994, Legends of the Fall, 1994, 12 Monkeys, 1995 (Golden Globe award for best supporting actor, 1996, Acad. award nominee for Best Supporting Actor 1996), Sleepers, 1996, Seven Years in Tibet, 1997, The Devil's Own, 1997, Dark Side of the Sun, 1997, Meet Joe Black, 1998, Fight Club, 1999, Snatch, 2000, The Mexican, 2001, Spy Game, 2001, Ocean's Eleven, 2001, Full Frontal, 2002, Confessions of a Dangerous Mind, 2002, (voice only) Sinbad: Legend of the Seven Seas, 2003, Troy, 2004, Ocean's Twelve, 2004, Mr. & Mrs. Smith, 2005, Babel, 2006; (TV movies) A Stoning in Fulham County, 1988, Too Young to Die, 1990; (TV series) Another World, 1987, Glory Days, 1990; (TV appearances) Growing Pains, 1987, 1989, Dallas, 1987, 1988, 21 Jump Street, 1988, Head of the Class, 1989, Freddy's Nightmares, 1989, thirtysomething, 1989, Tales from the Crypt, 1992, Friends, 2001, King of the Hill (voice only), 2003, Getaway,

2005. Named one of 50 Most Powerful People in Hollywood, Premiere mag., 2004—06; recipient Favorite Leading Man, People's Choice Awards, 2006. Office: Creative Artists Agy care Kevin Huvane 9830 Wilshire Blvd Beverly Hills CA 90212-1825*

**PITT, GEORGE,** lawyer, investment banker; b. Chgo., July 21, 1938; s. Cornelius George and Anastasia (Geocaris) P.; m. Barbara Lynn Goodrich, Dec. 21, 1963 (div. Apr. 1990); children: Elizabeth Nanette, Margaret Leigh; m. Pamela Ann Pittsford, May 19, 1990. BA, Northwestern U., 1960, JD, 1963; grad. (hon.), US Army Intelligence Sch., Ft. Holabird, Md., 1964; Leading Strategic Change course, U. Va., 1999. Bar: Ill. 1963. Assoc. Chapman and Cutler, Chgo., 1963-67; ptnr. Borge and Pitt, and predecessor, 1968-87, Katten Muchin & Zavis, Chgo., 1987-97; sr. mng. dir. Banc One Capital Markets, Inc. (formerly First Chgo. Capital Markets, Inc.), 1998-2000; mng. dir. UBS Fin. Svcs. Inc. (formerly UBS PaineWebber Inc.), Chgo., 2000—. Conf. chmn. Bond Buyer's 3d Ann. Midwest Pub. Fin. Conf., 1994; conf. co-chmn. Bond Buyer's 8th Ann. Midwest Pub. Fin. Conf., 1999. Notes and comments editor Northwestern U. Law Rev., 1962-63. 1st lt. AUS, 1964. Fellow: Am. Coll. Bond Counsel; mem.: Ill. State Bar Assn., Univ. Club. Chgo., Phi Gamma Delta, Phi Delta Phi, Eta Sigma Phi. Home: 600 N McClurg Ct Chicago IL 60611-3044 Office: UBS Fin Svcs Inc One N Wacker Dr 38th Fl Chicago IL 60606-2807 Business E-Mail: george.pitt@ubs.com.

**PITT, HARVEY LLOYD,** risk management consultant, former federal agency administrator; b. Bklyn., Feb. 28, 1945; s. Morris Jacob and Sara (Sapir) P.; m. Saree Ruffin, Jan. 7, 1984; children: Robert Garrett, Sara Dillard; children from previous marriage: Emily Laura, Jonathan Bradley. BA, CUNY, 1965; JD with honors (Univ. scholar), St. John's U., N.Y.C., 1968; LLD (hon.), St. John's U., 2002. Bar: N.Y. 1969, U.S. Supreme Ct. 1972, D.C. 1979. With SEC, Washington, 1968-78, legal asst. to commr., 1969; editor Instl. Investor Study, 1971-72; spl. counsel Office Gen. Counsel, Washington, 1971-72, chief counsel div. market regulation, 1972-73, exec. asst. to chmn., 1973-75, gen. counsel, 1975-78; ptnr. Fried, Frank, Harris, Shriver & Jacobson, Washington, 1978—2001; chmn. SEC, Washington, 2001—03; CEO Kalorama Ptnrs., LLC, 2003—. Adj. prof. law George Washington U. Nat. Law Ctr., 1974-82, U. Pa. Law Sch., 1983-84, vis. practitioner, 1984, Georgetown U. Law Ctr., 1976-84; comml. arbitrator Am. Arbitration Assn. Contbr. articles to profl. jours. V.p. Glen Haven Civic Assn., Silver Spring, Md., 1972-73, pres., 1974. Recipient Learned Hand award Inst. for Human Rels., 1988, Presdl. medal, Bklyn. Coll., 2003. Mem. ABA (past chmn. subcom. SEC practice and enforcement, past co-chmn. subcom. state takeover laws), Fed. Bar Assn. (Outstanding Young Lawyer award 1975), Adminstrv. Conf. U.S., Am. Law Inst. (project advisor on restatement law on corp. governance), Delta Sigma Rho, Tau Kappa Alpha, Phi Delta Phi. Office: Kalorama Ptnrs LLC Ste 800 1130 Connecticut Ave NW Washington DC 20036-3915 Office Phone: 202-721-0000. Business E-Mail: harvey@kaloramapartners.com.

**PITT, HENRY ANTHONY,** surgeon, researcher, medical educator; b. Elizabeth, NJ, Mar. 23, 1945; m. Elizabeth Jane Chambliss, June 21, 1969; children: Laura Elizabeth Teufel, David Andrew, Susan Clare. AB, Cornell U., 1967, MD, 1971. Diplomate Am. Bd. Surgery. Resident Johns Hopkins Hosp., Balt., 1971—73, 1975—78; asst. prof. surgery U. Calif., L.A., 1979—85; prof. surgery Johns Hopkins U., Balt., 1985—97, Med. Coll. Wis., Milw., 1997—2004, Ind. U., Indpls., 2004—. Coach Little League Baseball, Pacific Palisades, Calif., 1980—84. Lt. comdr. USN, 1973—75. Named Aprahamian Tchr. of Yr., Med. Coll. Wis., Surgery, 2002; recipient Letter in Baseball, Cornell U., 1967, Shipley award, So. Surg. Assn., 1989. Mem.: Internat. Hepato-Pancreato-Biliary Assn. (life; pres. 2004—), Soc. Surgery Alimentary Tract (life; v.p. 2004—05), Am. Surg. Assn. (life; fellowship com. 2001—), Am. Hepato-Pancreato-Biliary Assn. (life; pres. 1999—2001), Soc. Clin. Surgery (life; pres. 1998—2000), Soc. U. Surgeons (life; sec. 1985—86), Alpha Omega Alpha (life; pres. 1970—71). Achievements include research in gallstone pathogenesis. Office: Indiana University 535 Barnhill Drive RT 130D Indianapolis IN 46202 Office Phone: 317-274-2304. Office Fax: 317-274-4554. Business E-Mail: hapitt@iupui.edu.

**PITT, JANE,** medical educator; b. Frankfurt, Fed. Republic Germany, Aug. 25, 1938; came to U.S., 1939. d. Ludwig Friederich and Vera (Aberle) Ries; m. Martin Irwin Pitt, Aug. 12, 1962 (dec. 1980); children: Jennifer, Eric Jonathan; m. Robert Harry Socolow, May 25, 1986; stepchildren: David, Seth. BA, Radcliffe Coll., 1960; MD, Harvard U., 1964. Diplomate Am. Bd. Pediatrics, Am. Bd. Pediat. Infectious Diseases. Resident Children's Hosp. Med. Ctr., Boston, 1964-66; fellow Tufts U. Med. Sch., Boston, 1966-67, Harvard U. Med. Sch., Boston, 1967-69; asst. prof. SUNY Downstate Sch. Medicine, N.Y.C., 1970-71; asst. prof. Coll. Physicians and Surgeons Columbia U., N.Y.C., 1971-75, assoc. prof. Coll. Physicians and Surgeons, 1975-2000; prof. Coll. Physicians and Surgeons, 2000—. Mem. instl. rev. bd. Columbia Health Scis. Campus, N.Y.C., 1982—; mem. NIH study sect. Reviewer Jour. of Infectious Diseases, New Eng. Jour. Medicine, 1976—; contbr. articles to profl. jours. NIH grantee, 1974—. Fellow Infectious Disease Soc., Pediat. Infectious Disease Soc., Soc. Pediat. Rsch., Am. Pediatric Soc. Democrat. Steven Iddo, pres: Columbia U Coll Physicians Surgeons 630 W 168th St New York NY 10032-3702 Home: 2620 7TH St Boulder CO 80304-3206 E-mail: jp25@columbia.edu.

**PITT, WILLIAM ALEXANDER,** cardiologist; b. July 17, 1942; came to U.S., 1970; s. Reginald William and Una Sylvia (Alexander) P.; m. Judith Mae Wilson, May 21, 1965; children: William Matthew, Joanne Katharine. MD, U.B.C., Vancouver, 1967. Diplomate Royal Coll. Physicians Can. Intern Mercy Hosp., San Diego, 1967-68, resident, 1970-71, assoc. dir. cardiology, 1972-92; resident Vancouver Gen. Hosp., 1968-70, U. Calif., San Diego, 1971-72; with So. Calif. Cardiology Med. Group, San Diego, 1984—; pvt. practice Clin Care Cardiology, dir. trustees San Diego Found. for Med. Care, 1983-89, 91—, pres., chmn. bd. trustees, 1986-88, med. dir., 1991-96; trustee Pacific Found. for Med. Care, 1996—, med. dir., 1996—; bd. dirs. Mut. Assn. for Profl. Services, Phila., 1984-92; pres. Alternet Med. Svcs., Inc., 1992-95; pres. and med. dir. San Diego IPA, 1995-2005. Fellow Royal Coll. Physicians Can., Am. Coll. Cardiology (assoc.); mem. AMA, Am. Heart Assn., Calif. Med. Assn., San Diego County Med. Soc., San Diego County Heart Assn. (bd. dirs. 1982-88). Episcopalian. Office: So Calif Cardiology Med Group 6386 Alvarado Ct Ste 101 San Diego CA 92120-4906 Office Phone: 619-265-1237. Personal E-mail: wmapitt@aol.com.

**PITTA, JANINE ROSE,** elementary school educator; b. Bklyn., July 2, 1971; d. Philip Thomas and Julia Ann Pitta. A in Early Childhood, Kingsborough C.C., 1994; BA in Child Study, St. Joseph's Coll., 1996; MA, Bklyn. Coll., 2001. Tchr. 2d grade PS 216, Bklyn., 1996—2002, tchr. 3d grade, 2002—03, tchr. 5th grade, 2003—, tchr. 3rd grade. Participant, organizer PS 218, 2001—, leadership team participant, recorder of minutes, 2004—05.

**PITTELKO, ROGER DEAN,** clergyman, theology studies educator; b. Elk Reno, Okla., Aug. 18, 1932; s. Elmer Henry and Lydia Caroline (Nieman) Pittelko. AA, Concordia Coll., 1952; BA, Concordia Sem., St. Louis, 1954, MDiv, 1957, STM, 1958; postgrad, Chgo. Luth. Theol. Sem., 1959-61; ThD, Am. Div. Sch., Pineland, Fla., 1968; DMin, Faith Evang. Luth. Sem., Tacoma, 1983. Ordained to ministry Luth. Ch., 1958. Vicar St. John Luth. Ch., S.I., NY, 1955—56, asst. pastor New Orleans, 1958-59; pastor Concordia Luth. Ch., Berwyn, Ill., 1959-63, Luth. Ch. Holy Spirit, Elk Grove Village, Ill., 1962—87; chmn. Common. on Worship, Luth. Ch.-Mo. Synod, 1982—92, chmn. common. worship, 1994—98, asst. bishop Midwest region English dist., 1983, pres., bishop English dist., 1987-97, 3d v.p., 1997—2001; prof. pastoral theology Concordia Theol. Sem., Ft. Wayne, Ind., 1997—2003; pastor Trinity Luth. Ch., Villa Park, Ill., 2003—05, Grace English Luth. Ch., Chgo., 2005—. Author: Guide to Introducing Lutheran Worship; contbr. articles to jours. Mem.: Luth. Acad. for Scholarship, Concordia Hist. Inst., Itasca Country Club (Ill.), Maywood Sportsmans Club (Ill.). Republican. Lutheran. Office: Grace English Evang Luth Ch 2725 N Laramie Ave Chicago IL 60639-1698 Office Phone: 773-637-1177. Personal E-mail: emep@juno.com.

**PITTELKOW, MARK ROBERT,** physician, dermatologist, educator, medical researcher; b. Milw., Dec. 16, 1952; s. Robert Bernard and Barbara Jean (Thomas) P.; m. Gail L. Gamble, Nov. 26, 1977; children: Thomas, Cameron, Robert. BA, Northwestern U., 1975; MD, Mayo Med. Sch., 1979. Intern then resident Mayo Grad. Sch., 1979-84, post-doctoral exptl. pathology, 1981-83; from asst. to assoc. prof. dermatology Mayo Med. Sch., Rochester, Minn., 1984-95, prof. dermatology, 1995—, assoc. prof. biochemistry and molecular biology, 1992—. Cons. Mayo Clinic/Found., Rochester, 1984— Fellow Am. Acad. Dermatology; mem. AAAS, Am. Dermatol. Assn. Soc. Investigative Dermatology, Am. Burn Assn., Am. Soc. Cell Biology, N.Y. Acad. Scis., Chi Psi. Home: 721 12th Ave SW Rochester MN 55902-2027 Office: Mayo Clinic 200 1st St SW Rochester MN 55905-0002 Office Phone: 507-284-2555. Business E-Mail: pittelkow.mark@mayo.edu.

**PITTI, DONALD ROBERT,** financial consultant; b. N.Y.C., Sept. 15, 1929; s. August and Mary (Vitaglione) P.; m. Grace Allen Curtis, Aug. 14, 1954; children: Gail, Robert. BA, NYU, 1959; postgrad, Adelphi U., 1963-65. Asst. v.p. Standard & Poor's Corp., N.Y.C., 1959—65; v.p. Quotron, Inc., N.Y.C., 1965—67; pres. Wiesenberger & Co., N.Y.C., 1967—76; v.p. John Nuveen & Co., Inc., N.Y.C., 1976—87; pres. Monarch Resources, Inc., N.Y.C., 1987—88; chmn., CEO Monarch Fin. Svcs., Inc., N.Y.C., 1988—89; pres., CEO Seligman Fin. Svcs. Inc., N.Y.C., 1989—95; pres. Graydon Consulting Corp., Manhasset, NY, 1996—; dir. Fin. Svcs. Inst. St. John's U., N.Y., 1995—, adj. prof. fin. NY, 1995—. Chmn. Found. Fin. Planning, Atlanta, 1994-2000 Editor: Handbook of Financial Planning, 1988; contbr. articles to profl. publs. With USN, 1948-49, 50-52. Mem. Internat. Assn. Fin. Planning (pres.), Union League, Manhasset Bay Yacht Club, Met. Opera Club. Avocations: gardening, reading, swimming. Home: 169 Kensett Rd Manhasset NY 11030-2140

**PITTMAN, CATHERINE SYLVIA,** secondary school educator; b. Brunswick, Ga., Apr. 24, 1962; m. David Pittman; children: Drew, Meghan. BS, Ga. So. Coll., 1984, MEd, 1989, EdS, 1993. Tchr. grade 7,8 Risley Middle Sch., Glynn County, 1985-89; tchr. grades 9-12 Brunswick High Sch., Glynn County, 1989—. Named Ga. Tchr. of Yr., 1995, 1996, Milken Family Found. Nat. Educator, 1995; recipient YMCA Tribute to Women's Leaders, 1999. Mem. Glynn County Assn. of Educators, Ga. Assn. of Educators, Nat. Edn. Assn., Ga. Council of Social Studies, So. Assn. of Student Councils, Nat. Assn. of Student Activity Advisors. Home: 103 Marsh Landing Dr Brunswick GA 31523-9387 Office: Brunswick High Sch 3920 Habersham St Brunswick GA 31520-2799

**PITTMAN, CONSTANCE SHEN,** endocrinologist, educator; b. Nanking, China, Jan. 2, 1929; arrived in US, 1946. d. Leo F.-Z. and Pao Kong (Yang) Shen; m. James Allen Pittman, Jr., Feb. 19, 1955; children: James Clinton, John Merrill. AB in Chemistry, Wellesley Coll., 1951; MD, Harvard U., 1955. Diplomate Am. Bd. Internal Medicine, sub-bd. Endocrinology. Intern Baltimore City Hosp., 1955-56; resident U. Ala., Birmingham, 1956-57; instr. in medicine U. Ala. Med. Ctr., Birmingham, 1957—59, fellow dept. pharmacology, 1957-59, from asst. prof. to assoc. prof., 1959-70, prof., 1970—. Prof. medicine Georgetown U., Washington, 1972—73; mem. diabetes and metabolism tng. com. NIH, Bethesda, Md., 1972—76, mem. nat. arthritis, metabolism and digestive disease coun., 1975—78, mem. gen. clin. rsch. ctrs. com., 1979—83, 1987—90; bd. dirs. Internat. Coun. for Control of Iodine Deficiency Diseases, 1994—; mem. Iodine Deficiency Disorders Elimination Steering Com. Kiwanis Internat., 2002—; internat editor: ICCIDD Newsletter, 2004—06. Master ACP; mem. Assn. Am. Physicians, Am. Soc. for Clin. Investigation, Endocrine Soc. (coun., 1978-79, pres. women's caucus 1978-79), Am. Thyroid Assn. (pres. 1990-91), Kiwanis (mem. iodine deficiency disorders steering com.). Achievements include research in activation and metabolism of thyroid hormone; kinetics of thyroxine conversion to triiodothyrine in health and disease states; control of iodine deficiency disorders. Emails: Office: UAB Div Endocrinology/Metab Lab Med Ctr Birmingham AL 35294-0001 Office Phone: 205-934-0800. Business E-Mail: cpittman@uab.edu.

**PITTMAN, GREGORY DAVID,** pastor, musician; b. Greenville, SC, Mar. 23, 1973; s. David and Ruby Pittman; m. Christina Esther Pryor; children: Graham, Elena, Wyatt. BM, U. SC, Columbia, 1996; MM, Southwestern Bapt. Theol. Sem., Ft. Worth, Tex., 2001. Web Technologies Certificate Internat. Webmasters Assn., 2006. Asst. dir. Southwestern Sem. Oratorio Chorus/Ft. Worth Symphony Chorus, 1998—2001; interim dir. choral activities Fossil Ridge H.S., Keller, Tex., 2001; head fine arts Porter-Gaud Sch. Charleston, SC, 2001—03; assoc. pastor of worship Citadel Sq. Bapt. Ch., Charleston, SC, 2002—; adj. instr. in music Charleston So. U., SC, 2004—05. Tech. cons. SC Music Educators Assn., 2001—03. Coord. I6 Worship Renewal, Charleston, 2005—06. Mem.: Music Educators Nat. Conf., Am. Choral Directors Assn., Internat. Webmasters Assn./HTML Writers Guild. Avocations: reading, website design, racquetball. Office Phone: 843-577-3707.

**PITTMAN, IDDO, JR.,** retired lawyer; b. Cleveland, Miss., June 1, 1925; s. Iddo Pittman and Myrtle Fortenberry; m. Kathleen Killen Pittman; children: Kathleen Susann Iddo, John Carroll, Charles Ian. JD, La. State U., 1948; BA, Southeastern La. U., 1953. Bar: La. Pvt. practice, Hammond, La., 1948—2000; ret., 2000. Trustee Christian Health Ministries, New Orleans, 1992—2005. Lt. (j.g.) USN, 1943—46. Republican. Baptist. Avocations: furniture building, flying, ping pong/table tennis. Home: 122 College Dr Hammond LA 70401

**PITTMAN, JAMES ALLEN, JR.,** endocrinologist, educator; b. Orlando, Fla., Apr. 12, 1927; s. James Allen and Jean C. (Garretson) Pittman; m. Constance Ming-Chung Shen, Feb. 19, 1955; children: James Clinton, John Morrill. BE, Davidson Coll., 1948, DSc (hon.), 1981; MD, Harvard, 1952; DSc (hon.), U. Ala., Birmingham, 1984, Chung Shan Med U., Taichung, Taiwan, 2005. Intern, asst. resident medicine Mass. Gen. Hosp., Boston, 1952—54; tchg. fellow medicine Harvard U., 1953—54; clin. assoc. NIH, Bethesda, Md., 1954—56; instr. medicine George Washington U., 1955—56; chief resident U. Ala. Med. Ctr., Birmingham, 1956—58, instr. medicine, 1956—59, asst. prof., 1959—62, assoc. prof., 1962—64, prof. medicine, 1964—92, dir. endocrinology and metabolism divsn., 1962—71, co-chmn. dept. medicine, 1969—71, also prof., physiology and biophysics, 1967—92, dean, 1973—92, U. Ala. Birmingham Disting. prof., 1992—. Mem. endocrinology study sect. NIH, 1963—67; mem. nat. adv. rsch. resources coun. NIH, 1991—95; asst. chief med. dir. rsch. and edn. in medicine U.S. VA, 1971—73; prof. medicine Georgetown U. Med. Sch., Washington, 1971—73; mem. grad. med. edn. nat. adv. com. HEW, 1976—78; mem. HHS Coun. on Grad. Med. Edn., 1986—90; hon. prof. Chung Shan Med. and Dental Coll., Taiwan, 1994; sr. advisor Internat. Coun. on Ctrl. of Iodine Deficiency Diseases, 1994—96. Author: Diagnosis and Treatment of Thyroid Diseases, 1963; contbr. articles in field to profl. jours. Master: Am. Coll. Endocrinology; fellow: AAAS; mem.: ACP, Stearman Restorers Assn., Hist. Sci. Soc., Am. Soc. for the History of Medicine, So. Soc. Clin. Investigation (Founder's medal 1993), Am. Fedn. Clin. Rsch. (pres. So. sect., nat. coun. 1962—66), Am. Chem. Soc., Am. Diabetes Assn., Am. Ornithologists Union (life), N.Y. Acad. Scis. (life), Endocrine Soc. Ecuador (hon.), Soc. Nuc. Medicine, Am. Thyroid Assn., Am. Assn. Clin. Endocrinologists, Endocrine Soc., Assn. Am. Physicians, Inst. Medicine of NAS, Harvard U. Med. Alumni Assn. (pres. 1986—88), Wilson Ornithol. Club (life), Alpha Omega Alpha, Phi Beta Kappa, Omicron Delta Kappa. Office: U Ala Sch Med Pittman CAMS 1924 7th Ave S Birmingham AL 35294-0007 Office Phone: 205-934-3414. Personal E-mail: japdoc@msn.com. Business E-Mail: japdoc@uab.edu. *I hope that each time I meet a person, both of us leave the encounter the better for it.*

**PITTMAN, JAMES MORRIS (JACK PITTMAN),** cartoonist, illustrator, character designer, consultant; b. Sanford, N.C., Oct. 22, 1952; s. James Berdine and Merry Louise (Thomas) P.; m. Patricia Lynne Smith, Nov. 27, 1977; children: Jay Scott, Jonathan Patrick, Joy Elizabeth. B of Environ. Design in Arch. with honors, N.C. State U., 1974. Sports and editl. cartoonist, illustrator, courtroom artist The News and Observer, Raleigh, NC, 1974-83;

freelance cartoonist, illustrator Raleigh, 1983—. Adj. prof. Meredith Coll., Raleigh, 1993-94; advtsg. illustrator for Am. Express, Coca-Cola, Procter & Gamble, GMC, Palace Entertainment, Kellogg's, Wendy's, Carolina Hurricanes, NHL, Ericsson, Inc., Gatorade, GlaxoSmithKline, Nortel Networks. Illustrator: (book) A Dust of Snow, 1980, Are You Smart, Or What?, 2001, Darren Dwayne DeBakey and His Amazing Inventions, mags. include Nat. Geographic World, Wildlife in NC, Reader's Digest, (CD-ROM) Heavenword Children's Bible, 1997, The Birth of Kidd Millennium, 2001, (comic strip) Kidd Millennium, 2001-05; permanent collections include The Internat. Mus. of Cartoon Art, N.C. Mus. History, 2002-03. Deacon So. Bapt. Ch. Recipient various ADDY awards Triangle Advtsg. Fedn., 1983-97, 69th Exhbn. Merit; Best in Mag. Illustration award. Mem. Nat. Cartoonists Soc. (Best in Advt. and Illustration award Reuben divsn. 1995, 98, 2004), Raleigh Civitan Club. Mem. So. Bapt. Ch. Avocations: percussion, computers. Home: PO Box 10711 Raleigh NC 27605-0711 Office: J Pittman Illustrator 1740 Brooks Ave Raleigh NC 27607-6618 Office Phone: 919-785-1966. E-mail: jptoonist@aol.com, jack@jackpittman.net.

**PITTMAN, LISA,** lawyer; b. Limestone, Maine, Jan. 4, 1959; d. William Franklin and Rowena Paradis (Umphrey) P.; 1 child, Graham Edward Paradis. BA with highest honors, U. Fla., 1980, MA, 1981, JD, 1984; LLM with highest honors, George Washington U., 1988. Bar: Fla. 1984, D.C. 1993, U.S Supreme Ct. 1993. Spl. asst. to gen. counsel Nat. Oceanic and Atmospheric Adminstrn., Washington, 1984-85, atty., advisor, 1985-87; minority counsel Com. on Mcht. Marine & Fisheries, Ho. of Reps., Washington, 1987-95; dep. chief counsel Com. on Resources, U.S. Ho. of Reps., Washington, 1995-2001, chief counsel, 2001—02, chief counsel, dep. staff dir., 2002—. Contbr. articles to profl. jour. Home: 7325 Eldorado St Mc Lean VA 22102-2904 Office: US House of Reps 1320 Longworth HOB Washington DC 20515-6201

**PITTMAN, R. ALLEN,** federal agency administrator; Grad., U. Ark., 1974. Co-founder U.S. Oncology, Inc., chief adminstrv. officer, exec. v.p. human resources, 1993—2001, exec. v.p. exec. svcs., exec. dir., 2002—04; asst. sec. human resources & adminstrn. US Dept. Vets. Affairs, Washington, 2004—. Decorated Navy Commendation Medal with Combat V. Office: US Dept Veterans Affairs 810 Vermont Ave NW Washington DC 20420*

**PITTMAN, ROBERT TURNER,** retired newspaper editor; b. Gates, N.C., Sept. 24, 1929; s. Thomas Everett and Lillian (Turner) P.; m. Ruth Fike, Aug. 25, 1956; children: Laura Emily, Mary Ann, Lillian Elizabeth. BA, Washington and Lee U., 1951; MA, U. N.C. 1957. Reporter Times Dispatch, Richmond, Va., 1951; editor, pub. Daily Ranger, Glendive, Mont., 1957-58; writer editorials Times Union, Jacksonville, Fla., 1958-63; editorial editor Times, St. Petersburg, Fla., 1963-92; dir. Times Pub. Co., 1968-92. Trustee Poynter Inst. Media Studies, St. Petersburg, 1978-92. Editor: (jour.) Masthead, 1980—81. Active St. Petersburg Charter Revision Com., 1992-93; dir. Fla. Bar Found., 1994-96. Lt. (j.g.) USNR, 1951-55. Recipient Pinellas Civil Liberties award, 1993; U.N.C.-Chapel Hill scholarship established in honor, 1994, Liberty Bell award St. Petersburg Bar Assn., 1995. Mem. Nat. Conf. Editl. Writers (pres. 1978, life), Nat. Conf. Editl. Writers Found. Inc. (pres. 1984) Methodist. Home: 736 18th Ave NE Saint Petersburg FL 33704-4608

**PITTMAN, ROBERT WARREN,** investor; b. Jackson, Miss., Dec. 28, 1953; s. Warren E. and Lanita (Hurdle) P.; m. Sandra Hill, July 27, 1979; 1 child, Robert Thomas; m. Veronique Choa, Nov. 28, 1997; children: Andrew Forest, Lucy Li. Student, Millsaps Coll., 1971-72, Oakland U., 1972-73, U. Pitts., 1973-74; AMP, Harvard U., 1984-85. Disc. jockey Sta. WJDX-FM, Jackson, Miss., 1970-72, Sta. WRIT, Milw., 1972; research dir. Sta. WDRQ, Detroit, 1972-73; program dir. Sta. WPEZ, Pitts., 1973-74, Stas. WMAQ-WKQX NBC, Chgo., 1974-77, Sta. WNBC, N.Y.C., 1977-79; exec. producer Album Tracks, NBC TV, N.Y.C., 1977-78; dir., v.p., then sr. v.p. MTV Networks, N.Y.C., 1979-82, exec. v.p., COO, 1983-85, pres., CEO, 1985-86, Quantum Media, N.Y.C., 1987-89; exec. advisor Warner Communications, Inc., N.Y.C., 1989-90; pres., chief exec. officer Time Warner Enterprises, N.Y.C., 1990-95; CEO Six Flags Entertainment, 1991-95; mng. ptnr., CEO, Century 21 Real Estate, 1995-96; pres., CEO Am. On-Line Networks, 1996-97; pres., COO Am. On-Line, Inc., 1997-2001; CO-COO AOL Time Warner, 2001, COO, 2002—; ptnr. Pilot Group, 2003—. Bd. dirs. Cendant Corp., Elec. Arts, N.Y.C. Ballet, N.Y. Shakespeare Festival, chmn., 1987—94; bd. dir., vice-chmn. Robin Hood Found.; bd. dir. Alliance Lupus Rsch. Recipient Program Mgr. of Yr. Billboard, 1977, Program Dir. of Yr. Hall Radio Report, 1978, Entrepreneur award White House SB Conf., 1986, Golden Plate award Am. Acad. Achievement, 1990, medal of Excellence Miss. U. Women, 1992, Vision award Retinitis Pigmentosa International, 1992, Lifetime Achievement Internat. Monitor award Internat. Teleproduction Soc., 1993, Gold Medal award Internat. Radio of TV Soc., 2002, Cablevision Mags. 20/20 Vision award, Pres. award Bank St. Coll. Edn.; named Innovator of Yr. Performance Mag., 1981, Humanitarian of Yr., AMC, 1984, Time Mag. Man of Yr. runner-up, 1984, Esquire Mag. Under 40 Leadership, 1985; named one of Pioneers of New Am. Start-Up, Success mag., One of Five Original Thinkers of 80s, Life Mag. 1990, 8 of 50 Most Influential Baby Boomers, Life Mag., 1996, Bus. Week's Top 25 Exec. of 1998, one of 50 Pioneers and Visionaries of TV, 2002; inducted Broadcast & Cable Hall of Fame, 1999. Methodist. Office: Pilot Group LLC 745 Fifth Ave 24th Fl New York NY 10151

**PITTMAN, ROY CLINTON, JR.,** neurosurgeon, theologian, lawyer, philosopher; b. Florence, S.C., Oct. 12, 1931; s. Roy Clinton and Edna Hester (Altman) P.; m. Therese Huguette Lamarche Pittman, Apr. 1958 (div. May 1976); 1 stepdaughter, Mitch I Lois Young; children: Charlotte Elisabeth, Clinton Christopher, Russell Roy; m. Jeanne Elmore Waters Pittman, Oct. 10, 1976. *Paternal ancestor Captain Thomas Pittman left Monmouthshire England in 1649 to settle in Surry County, Virginia; one century later his great-grandson, John Pittman, migrated south during the First Great Awakening to found the first Baptist Church in the Colony of Georgia at Kiokee, and his descendants organized the Southern Baptist Convention in Augusta in 1845. Maternal ancestor Reverend Pierpont Edwards Bishop, one of the first graduates of Union Theological Seminary of Virginia after its initiation at Hampden-Sydney College, was active during the Second Great Awakening and one of the founding trustees of Davidson College in North Carolina.* BS magna cum laude, Wofford Coll., Spartanburg, S.C., 1952; MD, Med. U. S.C., Charleston, 1956; JD, Washburn U. Coll. Law, Topeka, Kans., 1991; MDiv with honors, Emory U. Candler Sch. Theology, Atlanta, 1995; DSc (hon.), The London Inst., 1973. Diplomate Am. Bd. Neurol. and Orthopedic Surgery; ordained to ministry Ea. Orthodox Ch., 2000; bar: Fla. 1992, U.S. Dist. Ct. (mid. dist.) Fla. 1992. Intern U.S. Naval Hosp., Newport, RI, 1956-57; resident in neurology U.S. Naval Hosp.-Nat. Naval Med. Ctr., Bethesda, Md., 1957-58; neurologist East Coast Neuropsychiat. Ctr.-U.S. Naval Hosp., Phila., 1958-59, head neurology Br., 1959; resident in neurosurgery Jefferson Med. Coll. Hosp., Phila., 1959-61, chief resident, 1961-62; resident in gen. surgery Hahnemann Med. Coll. Hosp., Phila., 1962-63; pvt. practice neurol. surgery Morton Plant and Mease Hosps., Clearwater-Dunedin, Fla., 1963-82, Cmty. Hosp. of New Port Richey, New Port Richey, Fla., 1978-88; pvt. practice legal medicine, med. jurisprudence & bioethics Pittman Profl. Assn., Clearwater, Fla., 1995-98, Tarpon Springs, Fla., 1995-98; pres., gen. counsel The Quintessential Corp., Tarpon Springs, 1998-2000; founder, prior Trinity House Retreat, Greek Orthodox Monastery of the Holy Trinity, 2001—. Protestant chaplain Morton Plant/Mease Countryside Hosp., Clearwater, Fla., 1997-98. Contbr. articles to profl. jours. Pres. St. Petersburg (Fla.) Coll. Alumni Assn., 1973-75. Lt. MC, USN, 1956-59, lt. comdr., 1962. Recipient Top Paper Bioethics and The Law award Washburn U. Coll. Law, Topeka, Kans., 1990, Top paper Comparative Civil Law award Cumberland Sch. Law and U. Heidelberg Germany Faculty of Law, 1990; endowed Jeanne Pittman ann. Bioethics and the Law Top Paper award Washburn U. Coll. Law, Topeka, 1995. Fellow Internat. Coll. Angiology, Royal Soc. Health, Internat. Coll. Surgeons, Am. Coll. Legal Medicine; mem. AMA, Congress Neurol. Surgeons, Fla. Med. Assn., Fla. Bar, Phi Beta Kappa, Phi Delta Phi. Jeffersonian Democrat. Avocations: stamp collecting/philately, anthropology, travel.

**PITTMAN, VIRGIL,** federal judge; b. Enterprise, Ala., Mar. 28, 1916; s. Walter Oscar and Annie Lee (Logan) P.; m. Floy Lasseter, 1944 (dec.) 2000; children— Karen Pittman Gordy, Walter Lee; m. Lily Davis Verneuille, Mar. 15, 2002. BS, U. Ala., 1939, LL.B., 1940. Bar: Ala. bar 1940. Spl. agt. FBI, 1940-44; practice law Gadsden, Ala., 1946-51; judge Ala. Circuit Ct., Circuit 16, 1951-66; U.S. dist. judge Middle and So. Dist. Ala., 1966-71; chief judge U.S. Dist. Ct. for Ala. So. Dist., 1971-81, sr. judge, 1981—. Lectr. bus. law, econs. and polit. sci. U. Ala. Center, Gadsden, 1948-66 Author: Circuit Court Proceedings in Acquisition of a Tract of Right of Way, 1959, A Judge Looks at Right of Way Condemnation Proceedings, 1960, Technical Pitfalls in Right of Way Proceedings, 1961. Mem. Ala. Bd. Edn., 1951; bd. trustees, life trustee Samford U., 1975-; past bd. dirs., chmn. bd. Bapt. Oaks. Lt. (j.g.) USN, 1944-46, USS Wharton, Pacific Supply Corp. Mem. Ala. State Bar, Etowah County Bar Assn. (pres. 1949), Omicron Delta Kappa. Democrat. Baptist. Office: US Dist Ct 113 Saint Joseph St Mobile AL 36602

**PITTMAN, VON VERON,** education educator; b. Sandersville, Ga., Feb. 1, 1945; s. Von V. and Reba (Hawkins) P.; m. Joyce Zeller, July 18, 1970; 1 child, Daniel Scott. AB in History, U. Ga., 1967, MA in U.S. History, 1972, MEd, 1978, PhD in U.S. History, 1979. Instr. Am. history Ga. Ctr. Continuing Edn., Athens, 1976-78; grad. intern office adult counseling, 1977-78; program coord. Wash. State U., Pullman, 1978-81, acting dir. office continuing univ. studies, 1981-83; dir. Ctr. Credit Programs U. Iowa, Iowa City, 1983—; adj. asst. prof. Coll. Edn., 1988—; assoc. dean credit programs div. continuing edn., 1989—. Assoc. Am. Ctr. for Study of Distance Edn., 1989—; dir. Ctr. Distance and Independent Study, U. Mo.-Columbia; chair ind. study div. Nat. Univ. Continuing Edn. Assn., 1989-90; cons. Annenberg Pub. Broadcasting project, 1989, others. Cons. editor Jour. Continuing Higher Edn1996—; mem. editl. bd. Vitae Scholasticae, 2006—; contbr. articles, papers to profl. publs., chpts. to profl. anthologies. Office: U Mo 136 Clark Hall Columbia MO 65211-4200

**PITTMAN, WILLIAM CLAUDE,** electrical engineer; b. Pontotoc, Miss., Apr. 22, 1921; s. William Claude and Maude Ella (Bennett) P.; m. Eloise Savage, Apr. 20, 1952; children: Patricia A. Pittman Ready, William Claude III, Thomas Allen. BSEE, Miss. State Coll., 1951, MSEE, 1957. From electronic engr. to supr. elec. engring. dept. U.S. Army Labs., Redstone Arsenal, Ala., 1951-59; supr. electronic engr. to aero. engring. supr. NASA/Marshall Space Flight Ctr., 1960; electronic engr. Army Missile Labs., 1962-82; program mgr. Army Labs. and R&D Ctr., Redstone Arsenal, 1982-99; vol. cons. Army Aviation and Missile Rsch., Devel. and Engring. Ctr., 1999—. Organizer numerous sci. and tech. confs. Author patents, reports, papers Sgt. USMC, 1940-46, PTO. Recipient Medal of Honor, DAR, Meritorious Civilian Svc. award Dept. Army, 1993. Fellow AIAA (assoc.; chmn. Miss.-Ala. chpt. 1981-82, Martin Schilling award 1980); mem. IEEE (sr. life), First Marine Div. Assn., DAV, IRE (chmn. Huntsville sect. 1957-58), Madison Hist. Soc., SAR (pres. Tenn. Valley chpt. 1984-85, Ala. Soc. 1990-91, Cert. 1991, Patriot medal), Tau Beta Pi, Phi Kappa Phi, Kappa Mu Epsilon. Avocations: history, genealogy. Home: 704 Desoto Rd SE Huntsville AL 35801-2032 Office: US Army Aviation Missile Command Huntsville AL 35898-5000 Office Phone: 256-876-1778. Personal E-mail: bill.pittman@amrdec.army.mi, wcpittman@comcast.net.

**PITTONI, LUKE M.,** lawyer; b. Rockville, N.Y., May 14, 1945; s. Mario and Grace (Henjes) P.; m. Mary Jo Rocque, July 8, 1972; children: Elizabeth, Katherine, Ellen. BA in Econs., Holy Cross Coll., 1967; JD, Fordham U., 1971. Bar: N.Y. 1972, U.S. Ct. Appeals (2d. cir.) 1975, U.S. Dist. Ct. (so. and ea. dists.) N.Y. 1975, U.S. Supreme Ct. 1976, U.S. Dist. Ct. Conn. 1977, Conn. 1986. Assoc. Martin, Clearwater & Bell, N.Y.C., 1972-75; trial atty. Anthony L. Schiavetti, N.Y.C., 1975-78; assoc. Alexander & Green, N.Y.C., 1978-79; ptnr. Heidell, Pittoni, Murphy & Bach, P.C., N.Y.C., 1979—. Mem. ABA, Conn. Bar Assn., N.Y. State Bar Assn., Am. Bd. Profl. Liability Attys., Am. Bd. Trial Advocates (past pres. NYC chpt.), N.Y. State Med. Def. Lawyers Assn., DRI, IADC. Home: 283 Quarry Rd Stamford CT 06903-5011 Office: Heidell Pittoni Murphy & Bach 99 Park Ave Fl 7 New York NY 10016-1506 Office Phone: 212-286-8585. Personal E-mail: lpittoni@hpmb.com.

**PITTS, ANDREW J.,** lawyer; b. Rochester, NY, Nov. 11, 1966; BA, Trinity Coll., 1988; JD summa cum laude, Boston Univ., 1994, MBA, 1995. Bar: NY 1995. Assoc. Cravath Swaine & Moore LLP, NYC, 1995—2003, ptnr., corp., 2003—. Notes editor Boston Law Rev. Recipient Alumni Achievement award, Boston Univ. Office: Cravath Swaine & Moore LLP Worldwide Plz 825 Eighth Ave New York NY 10019-7475 Office Phone: 212-474-1620. Office Fax: 212-474-3700. Business E-mail: apitts@cravath.com.

**PITTS, BEVERLEY J.,** academic administrator; m. William Pitts; 2 children. BA in English, Anderson U., 1968; MA in Journalism, Ball State U., 1971, EdD in Higher Edn., 1981. Chair, dept. comm. Anderson U., 1980—85; coord., News Editl. Sequence Ball State U., 1985—88, dir. grad. studies in journalism, 1985—88, dir. gen. studies, 1988—90, dir. academic assessment and general studies, 1990, assoc. provost, exec. dir. rsch. and undergraduate curriculum, 1990—92, acting provost, 1994, 2001, acting supr. for information technology, 2000—01, assoc. provost, 1993—2002, provost, v.p. for academic affairs, 2002, acting pres., 2004; pres. U. Indpls., 2005—. Instr. english Anderson U., 1977—80, advisor student publs., 1977—85, asst. prof. comm., 1980—85; prof. journalism Ball State U., 1985—90, prof. journalism, 1991—. Staff writer, researcher, comm. cons. Nat. Football League Players Assn., Washington, DC (Nat. Football League Players Assn. award of Excellence, 2000); contbr. articles to profl. jours. and newspapers; book review editor College Media Review, 1982—85; design editor College Media Review, 1985—86; reviewer Journalism Educator, 1990—99, grant reviewer Nat. Endowment for the Humanities, 1990, co-publisher (textbook) The Process of Media Writing, 1997, editl. bd. mem. Perspectives, Journal of the Association of General and Liberal Studies, 1997—2001, co-founder Ind. Teachers of Writing, 1981, pres., 1982—83, program chair, fall conf., 1982. Bd. dir. Family Svcs. of Delaware County, 1999—2002, Lyn St. James Found., 2000—02, Cmty. Alliance to Promote Edn., 2001—03, Delaware County CofC, 2003—, Sagamore Inst., 2004—, Ind. Youth Inst., 2000—, chair, 2005; bd. dir. Muncie Rotary Club, 2000—04, sec., 2000—01, pres.-elect, 2001—02, pres., 2002—03; mem. Cmty. Found. Muncie, Ind. Humanities Coun.; bd. dir. pres. Prof. Garfield Found., 2004—; bd. dir. Delaware County Cmty. Found., 2000—, vice-chair, 2003—04, chair-elect, 2005; and several others. Recipient Anderson U. Outstanding Alumni award, 1999, Ball State U. Alumni award, 2000, Woman of Achievement in Edn. award, Women in Communication; Ottoway Fellowship for Advanced Study, Am. Press Inst., Reston, Va., Ottoway Newspaper Found., 1986, Am. Press Inst. Fellowship for Advanced Study for Journalism Educators, 1987, Fellowship, Think Tank, Coll. of Scis. and Humanities, Ball State U., 1988, Fulbright Scholarship to study in Germany, 1994. Mem.: Assn. for General and Liberal Studies (nat. bd. dir. 1989—94, pres. 1993—94), Assn. for Edn. in Journalism and Mass Comm., Am. Conf. Academic Deans, Am. Assn. U. Adminstrators, Am. Assn. Higher Edn., Nat. Football League Players Assn. (cons. 1984—), Profl. Atheletes Found. (bd. dir. 1990—2004), Sigma Delta Chi. Office: U Indpls 1400 East Hanna Ave Indianapolis IN 46227-3697 Office Phone: 317-788-3211.

**PITTS, EDGAR THURLOW,** writer, retired educator; b. Rockport, Maine, Sept. 5, 1919; s. George Edgar and Mildred Nettie (Thurlow) Pitts; m. Elizabeth Knowlton, Dec. 21, 1942 (dec. May 1993); 1 child, Nathan Thurlow. BA with hons. in Math., U. Maine, 1942; diploma, U.S. Naval Acad., 1943; MEd in Adminstrn., U. Maine, 1953. Cert. tchr., prin., supt. schs. Maine. Math. tchr./prin. Stonington (Maine) H.S., 1946—53; prin. Ellsworth (Maine) H.S., 1953—70; supervising prin. Five Towns Sch. Dist., Western Hancock County, Maine, 1970—73; pvt. math. tchr. Eastern Maine, 1974—82. Co-author: Deer Isle Remembered, 1989, Stonington Past and Present, 1997; author: Long Ago and Far Away, 1936-45, 2d edit., 2001. Founder, chmn. Acad. Recognition Commn., State of Maine, 1959—63; various ad hoc com. chairs state, regional and local edn., Maine, 1960—98; past pres., exec. com. Main Tchrs. Assn. Lt. USNR, 1942—46. Mem.: NEA,

**PITTS, JAMES ATWATER,** finance company executive; b. Greenwich, Conn., Apr. 8, 1940; s. Jeremiah Patrick and Mary Louise (McGregor) P.; m. Noreen Mary Kiggins, July 20, 1963; children: Paul, Andrew, Sarah. BBA with honors, Niagara U., 1962; MBA, U. Conn., 1971. CPA, N.Y. Staff acct. Price Waterhouse, Stamford, Conn., 1962; tax specialist Deloitte Haskins & Sells, Rochester, NY, 1965-68; div. contr. Xerox Corp., Stamford, 1968-76; asst. corp. contr. Digital Equipment Corp., Maynard, Mass., 1976-81; v.p., corp. contr. Data Gen. Corp., Westboro, Mass., 1981-86; exec. v.p. fin. adminstrn. and strategic planning Cullinet Software, Inc., Westwood, 1986-88; v.p., chief fin. officer Bain & Co. Inc., Boston, 1988-92; v.p. fin. and adminstrn., treas., CFO Clean Harbors Inc., 1992-96; pres. The Pitts Group, Boston, 1996—; v.p. for fin. and adminstrn. The Boston Found., 1996—2004, chief investment officer, 2004, treas., 2004; ret., 2004. Bd. dirs., mem. audit com. Wainright Bank & Trust Co., 2005—. Chmn. Sudbury (Mass.) Town Fin. Com., 1984; v.p., mem. exec. com. Children's Mus. Boston, 1984-96; bd. dirs. Mus. Wharf Inc., 1988-96, Lake Winniepesaukee Assn., Wolfeboro, N.H.; chmn. Sudbury Long Range Capital Expenditures Com., 1981; trustee Lake Regional Conservation Trust, Meridith, N.H. With U.S. Army, 1963-64, USAR, 1965-90, Desert Storm, 1991. Decorated Meritorious Svc. medal, 1991; recipient Internat. Exec. Mgmt. award Internat. Mgmt. Inst. U. Geneva, 1980. Mem. AICPAs, Conn. CPA Soc., N.Y. Soc. CPAs, Fin. Execs. Inst., Harvard Bus. Sch. Assn. Boston (bd. govs. 1992-96, alumni treas. 2005—, audit com.), Nat. Assn. Corp. Dirs. (bd. dirs. New Eng. chpt. 2005—), Res. Officers Assn. (life), Soc. Mil. Compts., Bald Peak Colony Club, Officers Club Home: 8 West Hill Pl # 1 Boston MA 02114-3265 Personal E-mail: jamesapitts@aol.com.

**PITTS, JAMES T.,** lawyer; b. Mar. 21, 1949; BA, Hendrix Coll., 1970; JD, Univ. Ark., 1973; LLM, Georgetown Univ. 1984. Bar: Ark. 1973, DC 1986. Acting Securities Commr. State of Ark.; staff mem. House Commerce, Consumer and Monetary Affairs Subcom.; various positions to asst. dir. Securities/Corporate Practices Divsn., Office of Comptroller US Treasury Dept.; ptnr. Winston & Strawn, Washington, 1987—2002; ptnr., transp. law Venable LLP, Washington, 2002—. Office: Venable LLP 575 Seventh St NW Washington DC 20004 Office Phone: 202-344-4687. Office Fax: 202-344-8300. Business E-Mail: jtpitts@venable.com.

**PITTS, JOSEPH R. (JOE PITTS),** congressman; b. Lexington, Ky., Oct. 10, 1939; s. Joseph S. and Pearl Jackson Pitts; m. Virginia Pratt, 1961; children: Karen R., Carol J., Daniel J. AB in Philos. and Religion, Asbury Coll., Wilmore, Ky., 1961; MEd in Comprehensive Sci., West Chester U., Pa., 1972. Tchr. math., sci., english and phys. ed. Mortonsville Elem. Sch., Versailles, Ky., 1962—63; tchr. math. and sci. Great Valley HS, Malvern, Pa., 1969—72; mem. Pa. State Ho. Reps. from Dist. 158, 1973—97; owner, operator landscape nursery, Unionville, Pa., 1974—90; mem. US Congress from 16th Pa. dist., 1997—; mem. joint econ. com., 1998—; mem. energy and commerce com., 2001—. Transp. com. State of Pa., 1977-80, appropriations com., 1979-82, rep. policy com., chmn. labor rels. com., transp. and joint legis. budget and fin. coms., chmn. rep. appropriations com., 1989. 2nd lt. to capt. USAF, 1963—69. Decorated Air medal with five oak leaf clusters; recipient Pub. Servant award Chester-Del. Pomona Grange, 1980, Cmty. Leadership award Pa. for Biblical Morality, 1984, Disting. Govt. Svc. award Am. Mushroom Inst., 1985, Defender of Life award Pro Life Coalition S.E. Pa., 1985, William Penn award Pa. FACTS, 1985, Small Bus. Champion award Small Bus. Survival Com., 1999-2003, Best and Brightest award Am. Conservative Union, 2000, Friend of the Shareholder award Am. Shareholders Assn., 2000-2003, Taxpayer's Friend award Nat. Taxpayer's Union, 2000-2003, Silver Eagle award Pakistani Assn. N.Am., 2001. Mem.: NRA, Brandywine Valley Assn., VFW Post 5467, Rotary. Republican. Office: US Ho Reps 221 Cannon Ho Office Bldg Washington DC 20515 Office Phone: 202-225-2411.*

**PITTS, KEITH EARL,** set designer, educator; b. Kingsville, Tex., Oct. 1, 1974; s. Robert Andrew and Kathleen Florence Pitts; m. Brianne Marie Fose, July 23, 2005. BFA, Sam Houston State Coll., Huntsville, Tex., 1998; MFA, Northwestern U., Evanston, Ill., 2001. Designer Am. Theatre Co., Chgo., 2000—, Peninsula Players, Fish Creek, Wis., 2002—; mktg. staff Designlab, Chgo., 2004—; prof. Columbia Coll., Chgo., 2005—. Scenic designer: Heritage, 2006; Cradle of Man, 2006; costume designer: Chosen, 2006. Democrat.

**PITTS, LEONARD GARVEY, JR.,** columnist, writer; b. Orange, Calif., Oct. 11, 1957; s. Leonard Garvey and Agnes (Rowan) P.; m. Marilyn Vernice Pickens, June 27, 1981; children: Markise Pickens, Monique Pickens; (stepchildren) Marlon, Leonard, Onjél. BA English, U. So. Calif., 1977. Editor, writer Soul Mag., L.A., 1976-80; writer KFWB Radio, L.A., 1980-83; editor Radioscope, L.A., 1983-86; writer Westwood One Inc., Culver City, Calif., 1989-91; columnist, writer Miami (Fla.) Herald, 1991—. Writer, co-producer (broadcast) King: From Atlanta to the Mountaintop, 1986 (CEBA award 1987), (documentary) Young Black Men: A Lost Generation?, 1990 (Armstrong award 1991); writer, producer (documentary) Who We Are, 1988 (CEBA award 1989). Recipient Internat. Radio Festival award, 1991, Nat. Headliner award Arts critcism, 1991, Pulitzer Prize for commentary, 2004. Mem. Fla. Soc. Newspaper Editors (award arts criticism), Nat. Headliners, Am. Assn. Sunday and Feature Editors (award arts criticism 1991), Nat. Assn. of Black Journalists (Award of Execllence in commentary 1994, 95). Democrat. Baptist. Avocations: computer strategie games, reading. Office: Miami Herald One Herald Plaza Miami FL 33132

**PITTS, NEAL CHASE,** rheumatologist; b. Jackson, Miss., Dec. 6, 1933; s. Guy Moselely and Nancy Salina (Chase) P.; m. Nelia Annette Gnuse; children: Erin Chase Scott, Heather Anne Pitts. BA, Culver-Stockton Coll., 1956; MD, U. Miss., 1960. Intern U. Miss., 1960-61, resident medicine, 1961-63, fellow, 1963-65; fellow rheumatology Mayo Clin., 1965-66; bd. dirs. Caylor Nickel Clinic, Bluffton, Ind., 1990—, pres., 1991-93, 95-97, treas., 1994-95. Pres. Ind. Arthritis Assn. Indpls., 1978; bd. dirs. Lupus Found., Ft. Wayne, Ind., 1990—; elder Presbyn. Ch. Maj. M.C., U.S. Army, 1966-69. Fellow Am. Coll. Rheumatology; mem. Ind. SAR (trustee 1997, Ind. Patriot medal 1997), Nat. Soc. Mil. Order Stars and Bars (surgeon gen. 1995-99, genealogist Ind. soc.), Huguenot Soc. Ind. (registrar 1994-98, 2002—, pres. 1999), Ind. Soc. Colonial Wars (gov. 1993-95), Sons of Confederate Vets. (comdr. Ind. divsn. 1991-93, surgeon-in-chief 1998—, adjutant Ind. divsn. 2004—), Masons (sr. steward 1996-97, sr. warden 1999—), Order Crown Charlemagne, Assn. Ruddle's Fort Descendants, Colonial and Antebellum Bar and Bench, Soc. Descendents Washington's Army Valley Forge. Republican. Presbyterian. Avocation: genealogy. Home: 1020 Highland Park Cir Bluffton IN 46714-2807

**PITTS, ROBERT EUGENE, JR.,** finance educator, academic administrator; b. Griffin, Ga., Feb. 12, 1948; s. Robert Eugene and Oree Francis (Brown) P.; m. Cheryl Ann Belew, May 31, 1968. BBA, Ga. State U., 1970, M in Bus. Info. Systems, 1972; PhD, U. S.C., 1977. Account sect. leader Gen. Electric Corp., Atlanta, 1970-72; instr. mktg. Jacksonville (Ala.) State U., 1972-74; assoc. dir. consumer panel U. S.C., Columbia, 1974-77; asst. prof. mktg. U. Notre Dame, South Bend, Ind., 1977-82; assoc. prof. mktg. U. Miss., Oxford, 1982-83, dir. bur. bus. and econ. research, 1983-85; prof., chmn. dept. mktg. DePaul U., Chgo., 1985-97, dir. Kellstadt Ctr. Mktg. Analysis and Planning; dean Coll. Bus. Adminstrn. Creighton U., Omaha, 1997—2004, Coll. Charleston, 2004—. Cons. in mktg. strategy; expert legal witness in mktg. Author books on bank mktg.; contbr. articles on personal values in mktg. and pub. policy issues to profl. jours. Fellow Am. Mktg. Assn. (pres. acad. counsel), Assn. Mktg. Sci.; mem. Decision Sci. Inst., So. Mktg. Assn. Avocation: akido.

**PITYNSKI, ANDRZEJ PIOTR,** sculptor; b. Ulanow, Poland, Mar. 15, 1947; naturalized citizen, 1987; s. Aleksander and Stefania (Krupa) P.; m. Christina Teresa Gacek, Aug. 6, 1976; 1 child, Alexander Mark. MFA in Sculpture, Acad. Fine Arts, Cracow, Poland, 1974; postgrad., Art Students League, N.Y., 1975. Cert. tchr., N.J.; supr. modeling, mold, enlarging, resin crafts. Supr. and instr. sculpture Tech. Inst. of Sculpture - Johnson Atelier, Mercerville, NJ, 1979—; instr. sculpture Rider U., Lawrenceville, NJ, 1992—97, Rutgers U., NJ, 1998—2002. Asst. to sculptor Alexander Ettl, Sculpture House, N.Y., 1975-79 Bronze/granite monumental sculptures include Shield of Honor, Ulanow, Poland, 2004, Count J. Tarnowski, Tarnobrzeg, Poland, 2003, General Kosciuszko, St. Petersburg, Fla., 2002, Sarmatian - Spirit of Freedom, Hamilton, N.J., 2001, Flame of Freedom, Balt., 2000, Blue Army-1998, Warsaw, Poland, Katyn-1940, Jersey City, N.J., 1991-92, Pope John Paul II, Manhattan, N.Y., 1991, Ulanow, Poland, 1989, General Anders, Doylestown, Pa., 1995, Father J. Popieluszko, Trenton, N.J., 1987, Avenger, Doylestown, Pa., 1987, Portrait Bust M Curie, 1986, Bayonne, N.J.; aluminum sculpture Partisans II, Hamilton, N.J., 1999, Partisans, Boston, 1983, Ignacy Paderewski, Cracow, Poland, 1973; one-man show at Hamilton, N.J., 2000, N.Y., 2001; exhbn. Mus. of Polish Army, Warsaw, 1995, Contemporary Artists Guild, Lever House, N.Y., 1991—, Zacheta Nat. Art Gallery, Warsaw, 1991, Fedn. Internat. De La Medaille/Brit. Mus., London, 1992, Cast Iron Gallery, Soho, N.Y., 1992, Alt. Ext. Gallery, Phila., 1992, Audubon Exhibits-54th Ann. Exhbn., Fed. Hall, N.Y.C., others. Recipient Polonia Restituta Cross, R.P. London, 1989, Gold Order of Merit, Rep. of Poland, 1990, Cultural award Am. Inst. Polish Culture, Washington, 1992; named Comdr. Order Merit of Republic of Poland, 1996, The Monuments Conservancy's Perennial Wisdom award-medal, N.Y.C., 1999, Honorary Citizen of Balt., 2001. Fellow Nat. Sculpture Soc.; mem. Allied Artists of Am. (Silver medal of honor 1985, Elliot Liskin Meml. award 1989, Mems. and Assocs. award 1994), Audubon Artists (Gold Medal of Honor 1996, Silver Medal of Honor 1997, 98), Contemporary Artists Guild, Am. Medallic Sculpture Assn. Republican. Roman Catholic. Avocations: horse jumping, hunting, Judo. Office: PO Box 220380 Brooklyn NY 11222 Office Phone: 609-510-8926.

**PITZ, ROBERT WENDELL,** professor mechanical engineering; b. Aurora, Ill., Nov. 24, 1950; s. Wendell Edward and Anne (Benson) P.; m. Carol Elizabeth Armes; children: Matthew Robert, Anna Elizabeth BSME, Purdue U., 1973; MSME, U. Calif., Berkeley, 1976, PhDME, 1981. Staff scientist GE R&D, Schenectady, N.Y., 1981-86; asst. prof. Mech. Engring. Vanderbilt U., Nashville, 1986-89, assoc. prof. Mech. Engring., 1989—94, prof., 1994—. Contbr. articles to profl. jours. Recipient Presdl. Young Investigator NSF, 1987. Fellow Am. Assn. Mech. Engrs. (faculty advisor 1986); mem. AIAA, Optical Soc. Am., Am. Phys. Soc Office: Vanderbilt U Mech Engring PO Box 1592 Nashville TN 37202-0054 Office Phone: 615-322-0209.

**PITZER, BETTY BRAUN,** retired social services administrator; b. Springfield, Ohio, Aug. 7, 1912; d. Frank J. and Alnora (Hagerman) Braun; m. Elwood Gilbert Pitzer, Oct. 2, 1936; children: Philip Elwood, Richard Alan. BA in Bus. Adminstrn. cum laude, Wittenberg U., 1933, LHD (hon.), 2001. Asst. mgr. Baker's Cafeteria, Springfield, 1933—41; fin. sec. Credit Life Ins. Co., Springfield, 1933—41; pres. Ohio Assn. Alpha Delta Pi, Springfield, 1956—58; nat. treas. Alpha Delta Pi Sorority, Atlanta, 1963—79; assoc. dir. United Way Clark County, Springfield, 1965—69; exec. dir. Elderly United Springfield and Clark County, Springfield, 1969—91; ret., 1991. Com. mem. Area Agy. on Aging, Dayton, Ohio, 1979-83, Ohio Gov.'s Conf. on Aging, Columbus, 1979-81, Home Care Adv. com., Springfield, 1981-84, Ohio Commn. on Aging State Fair, Columbus, 1979-82; Clark County coord. White House Conf. on Aging, 1971. Pres. Adelphean Found., Atlanta, 1964-71; mem. fiscal rev. com. City of Springfield, 1982; mem. alumni coun. Wittenberg U., Springfield. Recipient Disting. Alumna award Wittenberg U., 1975, gov.'s award State of Ohio, 1982, Svc. to Mankind award Sertoma Club, Springfield, 1984, Meritorious Svc. award Community Hosp. Bd. Trustees, Springfield, 1977-86, Clark County Cmty. Action award, 1986, Hall of Fame award United Way Clark County, 1987, Kiwanis Cmty. Svc. award, 1991, Area Agy. Aging Svc. award, 1991, Springfield Urban League Svc. award, 1991, Clark County ADMH Bd. Svc. award, 1993, Ohio Sr. Citizen Hall of Fame, 1995, Alumni of Distinction award Springfield City Schs., 2006. Mem. Ohio Assn. Sr. Ctrs., Ohio Citizens Coun. (policy bd.), Miami Valley Coun. on Gerontology, Zonta (pres. Springfield 1970-72), Alpha Delta Pi (Alumna of Yr. award 1987). Republican. Lutheran. Home: 111 Englewood Dr Springfield OH 45504

**PITZER, JACK TODD,** purchasing agent, consultant, educator; s. Walter William and Kathryn Arvilla Pitzer; m. Tanya Lou Driver, June 22, 1963; children: LaTisha Beth Dew, Leyton Todd. BA cum laude, Lincoln U., 1969; MA, U. Mo., 1971, PhD, 1982. Cert. pub. purchasing officer. Asst. dir. purchasing Office Adminstrn. State of Mo., Jefferson City, 1973—75; chief purchasing officer dept. gen. svcs. State of Iowa, Des Moines, 1978—85; dean svcs. Lincoln U., Jefferson City, 1985—87; pub./mng. editor The Albany (Mo.) Ledger, 1987—96; dir. purchasing City of Alexandria (Va.) Purchasing Divsn., 1994—. Adj. assoc. prof. Drake U., Des Moines, 1981—85, Lincoln U., Jefferson City, 1985—87; adj. instr. Nat. Capital Region Grad. Ctr. - Fla. Inst. Tech., Alexandria, 2003; chmn. of the bd. Va. Assn. of Govtl. Purchasing Profl. Devel. Found., Richmond, 1997—2000; chmn. chief purchasing officers com. Met. Washington Coun. Govts., 1998—2000; mem. bd. examiners Universal Pub. Purchasing Certification Coun., Herndon, Va., 1999—2003. Co-author: (textbook) Leadership and Management in Public Procurement, 2005; mem. editl. bd.: Jour. Pub. Procurement, 1998—2003. Col. USAR, 1958—2001. Decorated Legion of Merit U.S. Army, Brevet Brig. Gen. (Ret) Iowa Army N.G.; named Honor Grad., U.S. Army Command and Gen. Staff Coll., 1975; fellow, Woodrow Wilson Found., 1972—73. Mem.: Nat. Assn. State Procurement Officers (life; pres. 1984—85), Alexandria Va. Rotary Club (pres. 2005—). Avocations: reading, walking, golf, travel. Home: 200 N Pickett St Alexandria VA 22304 Personal E-mail: jtpitzer@aol.com.

**PIUCCI, VIRGINIO LOUIS,** academic administrator; b. Peekskill, NY, Nov. 1, 1925; s. Virginio and Margiereta (DiGregorio) P.; m. Elizabeth-Logan, Mar. 25, 1951; children: Stephen, Mark, Matthew, Anthony, Andrew. BE, SUNY, New Paltz, 1949; MA, Columbus U., 1951; EdD, U. Fla., Gainesville, 1955; PhD (hon.), Internat. U., Vienna, Austria, 1999. Tchr. Suffern, N.Y., 1949-51; instr. SUNY, Oneonta, 1951-52, assoc. prof., 1955-56, prof. edn. Oswego, dir. edn., 1962-65; dean profl. studies, prof. R.I. Coll., Providence, 1966-70; v.p. rsch. and innovation Govs. State U., University Park, Ill., 1971-77, v.p. Inst. Rsch. and Planning, 1977-82, v.p. adminstrv. planning, prof. pub. adminstrn., 1982-92, v.p. emeritus, 1992—. Hon. prof. pedadogy Moscow External U. for Humanities; founder, pres. emeritus European-Am. U. Forum, West Ga. tech. Coll., Waco, Ga. Decorated knight Order of Merit (Italy); recipient Univ. medallion U. Sassari, Italy; U. Fla. fellow. Mem. Am. Assn. Univ. Adminstrs. (Eileen M. Tosney award for excellence in practice of higher edn. adminstrn. 1992). Democrat. Roman Catholic. Avocations: reading, politics, baseball. Home and Office: 22460 Lakeshore Dr Richton Park IL 60471-1607 Fax: 708-748-9760; E-mail: vpivcci@aol.com.

**PIUZE, MICHAEL JOSEPH,** lawyer; b. Worcester, Mass., July 31, 1944; s. Albert Charles Piuze and Pauline (Sadick); m. Marnie Smart, Apr. 24, 1971; children: Nicole, Stephanie, Kate. BA, Lake Forest Coll., 1967; JD, U. Tex., Austin, 1971. Bar: Calif. 1972. Atty. Gilbert, Kelly, Crowley & Jennett, LA, 1972—73; sr. mem. Law Offices Michael J. Piuze, LA, 1973—. Named LA Trial Lawyer of Yr., 1996, Southern Calif. Trial Lawyer of Yr., 1998, Calif. Lawyer of Yr., 2001, Winningest Lawyer in US, Nat. Law Jour., 2001, 2002; named one of Top 10 Super Lawyers, LA Mag., 2004, Top 100 LA County Super Lawyers, 2004, 2005, 2006, Top 10 Litigators, Nat. Law Jour., 2003, Top 100 Calif. Atty., Daily Jour., 2000—05, Best Lawyers in Am., 1993—2005. Mem.: LA Trial Lawyers Assn., Calif. Trial Lawyers Assn., Assn. Trial Lawyers Am. Office: The Law Offices Michael J Piuze 11755 Wilshire Blvd Ste 1170 Los Angeles CA 90025 Office Phone: 310-312-1102. Office Fax: 310-473-0708. Business E-Mail: mpiuze@mjplaw.net.

**PIVEN, FRANCES FOX,** political scientist, educator; b. Calgary, Alta., Can., Oct. 10, 1932; arrived in U.S., 1933, naturalized, 1953; d. Albert and Rachel (Paperny) F.; 1 dau., Sarah. BA, U. Chgo., 1953, MA, 1956, PhD, 1962; L.H.D. (hon.), Adelphi U., 1985. Mem. faculty Columbia, 1966-72; prof. polit. sci. Boston U., 1972-82, Grad. Ctr., CUNY, 1982—. Co-author: Regulating the Poor: The Functions of Public Welfare, 1971, 2d edit., 1993, The Politics of Turmoil: Essays on Poverty, Race and the Urban Crisis, 1974, Poor People's Movements, 1977, New Class War, 1982, The Mean Season, 1987, Why Americans Don't Vote, 1988; editor: Labor Societies in Post Industrial Societies, 1992, The Breaking of the American Social Compact, 1997, Why Americans Still Don't Vote, 2000, Work, Welfare and Politics, 2002, The War at Home, 2004, Challenging Authority, 2006. Recipient C. Wright Mills award Soc. Study Social Problems, 1971, Fulbright Disting. Lectureship award U. Bologna, 1990, President's award APHA, 1993, Annual award Nat. Assn. Sec. of State, 1994, Lifetime Achievement award Pol. Sociology Am. Sociological Assn., 1995, Disting. Career award, 2000, Pub. Understanding of Sociology award, 2003; Guggenheim fellow, 1973-74; Am. Coun. Learned Socs. awardee, 1982. Mem. ACLU, Am. Polit. Sci. Assn. (v.p. 1981-82), Soc. Study Social Problems (pres. 1980-81, Lee founders award 1992), Am. Sociol. Assn. (pres. 2006-). Home: PO Box N Millerton NY 12546-0651 Office: CUNY Grad Sch 365 5th Ave New York NY 10016-4309 Office Phone: 212-817-8674. E-mail: ffox-piven@gc.cuny.edu.

**PIVEN, JEREMY,** actor; b. New York, New York, July 26, 1965; s. Byrne and Joyce Piven. Student, Drake U. Actor: (films) Lucas, 1986, One Crazy Summer, 1986, Say Anything, 1989, Elvis Stories, 1989, The Grifters, 1990, White Palace, 1990, The Player, 1992, Body Chemistry II: The Voice of a Stranger, 1992, Bob Roberts, 1992, Singles, 1992, There Goes the Neighborhood, 1992, Judgement Night, 1993, Twenty Bucks, 1993, Car 54, Where Are You?, 1994, Floundering, 1994, PCU, 1994, Twogether, 1994, The Ticket, 1994, Miami Rhapsody, 1995, Dr. Jekyll and Ms. Hyde, 1995, Heat, 1995, Larger Than Life, 1996, Layin' Low, 1996, E=mc—2, 1996, Just Write, 1997, Grosse Pointe Blank, 1997, Livers Ain't Cheap, 1997, Kiss the Girls, 1997, Phoenix, 1998, Very Bad Things, 1998, Music From Another Room, 1998, Red Letters, 2000, The Crew, 2000, The Family Man, 2000, Rush Hour 2, 2001, Serendipity, 2001, Black Hawk Down, 2001, Highway, 2002, Me and Daphne, 2002, Old School, 2003, Runaway Jury, 2003, Scary Movie 3, Chasing Liberty, 2004, Two for the Money, 2005, Keeping Up with the Steins, 2006, (voice) Cars, 2006,: (TV films) 12:01, 1993, Don King: Only in America, 1997, Partners, 1999; (TV series) Carol & Company, 1990, Rugrats (voice), 1991, The Larry Sanders Show, 1992—93, Pride and Joy, 1995, Ellen, 1995—98, Cupid, 1998, Entourage, 2004— (Emmy award for Outstanding Supporting Actor in a comedy series, 2006); (Broadway plays) Fat Pig, 2004. Office: c/o ICM 8942 Wilshire Blvd Beverly Hills CA 90211*

**PIVEN, PETER ANTHONY,** architect, management consultant; b. Bklyn., Jan. 3, 1939; s. William Meyer and Sylvia Lee (Greenberg) P.; m. Caroline Cooper, July 9, 1961; children: Leslie Ann, Joshua Lawrence. AB, Colgate U., 1960; MArch, U. Pa., 1963; MS, Columbia U., 1964. Diplomate: cert. Nat. Coun. Archtl. Registration Bds.; registered arch., NY, Pa., NJ. Arch. Westermann-Miller Assocs., NYC, 1964-66, Bernard Rothzeid, A.I.A., NYC, 1967-68; v.p. Caudill Rowlett Scott, NYC, 1968-72; prin. Geddes Brecher Qualls Cunningham, Phila., 1972-87; pres. The Coxe Group, Inc., Phila., 1980-90, dir., prin. cons., 1980—. Adj. prof. U. Pa. Grad. Sch. Fine Arts, 1989—, Rensselaer Poly. Inst. Sch. Architecture, 1994—; vis. instr. Harvard U. Grad. Sch. Design; lectr. U. Pa. Sch. Design, 2005; mem. 14th edit. com. Architects Handbook Profl. Practice. Author: Compensation Management: A Guideline for Small Firms, 1982, Architect's Essentials of Ownership Transition, 2002; co-author: Success Strategies for Design Professionals, 1987, Architect's Essentials of Starting a Design Firm, 2003; contbg. editor: Archtl. Record and Design Intelligence; author (contbg.): Architects Handbook of Professional Practice, 1994, 2001, Architects Handbook of Professional Practice Update, 2004, 2005, 2006. Mem. NYC Cmty. Planning Bd., 1969-72. Fellow AIA (chmn. fin. mgmt. com. 1976-80, chmn. Fellows Jury 1998, mem. conv. task force 1998, mem. Nat. Ethics Coun. 1998-2004, chmn. 2004, pres. Phila. chpt. 1980); mem. Phila. C. of C. (dir. 1980-81), The Carpenters Co. of City and County of Phila. (mng. com. 1989-91). Home: Apt 10 201 Queen St Philadelphia PA 19147 Office: The Coxe Group Inc 1218 3rd Ave Seattle WA 98101-3097 Business E-Mail: ppiven@coxegroup.com.

**PIVER, M. STEVEN,** gynecologic oncologist; b. Washington, Sept. 29, 1934; s. Harry Samuel and Sonia (Bard) P.; m. Susan Myers, June 25, 1958; children: Debra Ellen, Carolyn Jan, Kenneth Stuart. BS, Gettysburg Coll., 1957; MD, Temple U., 1961. Diplomate Am. Bd. Ob-Gyn, Am. Coll. Surgeons. Intern Nazareth Hosp., Phila., 1961—62; resident Johns Hopkins U. Hosp., Balt., 1962; resident ob-gyn. Pa. Hosp. U. Pa., Phila., 1965—68; fellow gynecologic oncology Hosp. Tumor Inst. U. Tex., Houston, 1968—70; asst. prof. gynecologic oncology UNC Sch. Medicine, 1970—71; assoc. chief gynecologic oncology Roswell Park Cancer Inst., Buffalo, 1972—83, founder, dir. Gilda Radner Familial Ovarian Cancer Registry, 1981—, chief gynecologic oncology, 1984—97; clin. prof., dir. divsn. gynecologic oncology SUNY, Buffalo, 1986—87, prof. gynecology, 1998—, chair emeritus gynecologic oncology, 1998—. Cons., editor Yearbook of Cancer, 1972-88; assoc. editor Nat. Cancer Inst., PDQ, 1984—; mem. editl. bd. The Female Patient, 1989—, Oncology Reports, 1993—; author: Ovarian Malignancies: Clinical Care of Adults and Adolescents, 1983, Gilda's Disease: Sharing Personal Experiences and a Medical Perspective on Ovarian Cancer, 1996, Myths and Facts About Ovarian Cancer, 1997; editor: Ovarian Malignancies: Diagnostic and Therapeutic Advances, 1987, Manual of Gynecologic Oncology/Gynecology, 1989, Conversations About Cancer, 1990, Handbook of Gynecologic Oncology, 1995; contbr. more than 300 articles to profl. jours. Bd. dirs. United Way Buffalo Erie County, 1986-91; chmn. bd. trustees D'Youville Coll., Buffalo, 1989—; pres. Friends Night People, Buffalo, 1988-97. Capt. USAF, 1962-64. Hon. fellow Phi Beta Kappa, Gettysburg Coll., 1956, Tex. Assn. Obstetricians Gynecologists, 1990, Alpha Omega Alpha, Temple U. Sch. Medicine, 1995; named Citizen Yr., Buffalo News, 1989; recipient YMCA Leadership award Buffalo YMCA, 1990, Brotherhood/Sisterhood Award Medicine (Western NY Region), NCCJ, 1991, St. Marguerite D'Youville Coll. Cmty. Svc. award, 1992. Fellow ACS, Am. Coll. Obstetricians and Gynecologists; mem. Am. Soc. Clin. Oncology, Soc. Gynecologic Oncologists, Soc. Surg. Oncology, Am. Radium Soc., Phi Beta Kappa, Alpha Omega Alpha. Achievements include documentation of hydroxyurea as a radiation sensitizer in cervix cancer that significantly improves cure rate and that ovarian cancer can be inherited; patent for method of enhancing the efficacy of anti-tumor agents. Home: 315 Lincoln Pky Buffalo NY 14216-3127 Office: Sisters Hosp 2157 Main St Buffalo NY 14214-2692 Business E-Mail: mpiver@chsbuffalo.org.

**PIVI, MAURO,** physicist; b. Milan, Nov. 14, 1965; s. Alberto Pivi and Isabella Montuoro; life ptnr. Eva Maria Hannak. PhD, U. of Math. and Physics, Turin, 2000. Particle accelerator physicist staff Stanford Linear Accelerator Ctr. SLAC, Menlo Park, Calif., 2003—; postdoctoral in physics Lawrence Berkeley Nat. Lab., Berkeley, Calif. Contbr. articles to profl. jours. Achievements include research in Innovative studies on remedies for electron cloud effect in modern particle accelerators; development of beam physics; design of optics line design to achieve nanometer charged particle beam sizes. Office: Stanford Linear Accelerator Center SLAC 2575 Sand Hill Rd Menlo Park CA 94025 Office Phone: 650-926-3546. E-mail: mpivi@slac.stanford.edu.

**PIXLEY, SYLVIA KAY,** artist; b. Allegan, Mich., July 25, 1942; d. John Myron and Thelma Helen (Elsie) Katherler; m. Allen Cortner Pixley; children: Joy Elizabeth, April Catherine. BS in Fine Art, U. Mich., 1964. Rep. by Ann Arbor Art Ctr., Toledo (Ohio) Mus. of Art Collector's Corner, River Gallery, Chelsea, Mich. One-woman shows include Saginaw Valley State Coll., Mich., Monroe County C.C., Mich., Wesley United Ch., Fostoria, Ohio, U. Findlay, Ohio, exhibitions include The Print Show, Ann Arbor Art Ctr., 1999, 2002, Boston Mills Artfest, 2000 (Audrey Ratterman award, 2000), Columbus Chautauqua of Arts, 2000, Madison Chautauqua Festival of Arts, 2000 (3d in Fine Arts, 2000), Ferndale Art Fair, Mich., 2000 (Best of Show,

2000), Black Swamp Arts Festival, Bowling Green, Ohio, 2000—05 (awards), Boston Mills, 2001, Sonnenberg Arts at the Gardens, Canadaigua, NY, 2003, Four Bridges, Chattanooga, 2004, Art on the Square, Madison, Wis., 2004—05, St. James Ct., Louisville, 2004—06, others, Represented in permanent collections Krasl Art Fair, Art on the Bluff, St. Joseph, Mich., Monroe County Libr. Sys. Art in Loan Collection, Monroe County Bedford Libr. Collection, Monroe County C.C. Collection, Saginaw Valley State Coll. Art Collection, Minn. Ctr. for Books Arts, Mpls., Princeton U. Libr., N.J., Glenboco Mus., Calgary, Alta., Can. Recipient numerous other awards for art. Mem.: Wood Engravers Network (treas. 1994—), Ann Arbor Art Ctr., Mich. Guild of Artists and Artisans. Home: 601 Borgess Ave Monroe MI 48162

**PIZARRO, PEDRO,** electric power industry executive; married; 2 children. BS in Chemistry, magna cum laude, Harvard Univ.; PhD in Chem. Physics, Calif. Inst. Tech. Sr. engagement mgr. McKinsey & Co., LA; joined So. Calif. Edison, Rosemead, Calif., 1999—, v.p. power procurement, 2000—05, sr. v.p., 2005—, and gen. mgr., Edison Carrier Solutions. Trustee House Ear Inst.; dir. Colburn Sch. Performing Arts. Named one of 50 Most Important Hispanics in Tech., Bus., Hispanic Engineer and Info. Tech. mag., 2005. Office: So Calif Edison PO Box 999 Rosemead CA 91770

**PIZER, HOWARD CHARLES,** sports and entertainment executive; b. Chgo., Oct. 23, 1941; s. Edwin and Estyr (Seeder) P.; m. Sheila Graff, June 14, 1964; children: Jacqueline, Rachel. BBA, U. Wis., 1963; JD magna cum laude, Northwestern U., 1966. Assoc. McDermott, Will & Emery, Chgo., 1966-72; ptnr. Katten, Muchin, Zavis, Chgo., 1972-74; exec. v.p., gen. counsel Balcor Co., Skokie, Ill., 1975-80; exec. v.p. Chgo. White Sox, Chgo., 1981—. Exec. v.p. United Ctr Joint Venture. Past pres. Chgo. Spl. Olympics; bd. dirs. Chgo. Conv. and Tourism Bur., Inc., 1983—, Spl. Children's Charities, 1984—, Chgo. Baseball Cancer Charities, 1983—, Near West Side Cmty. Devel. Corp. Mem. Chgo. Bar Assn., Standard Club Chgo., Briarwood County. Home: 300 Euclid Ave Winnetka IL 60093-3606 Office: Chgo White Sox 333 W 35th St Chicago IL 60616-3651

**PIZITZ, RICHARD ALAN,** retail executive, real estate company officer; b. Birmingham, Ala., Feb. 24, 1930; s. Isadore and Hortense (Hirsch) P.; m. Joan Black; children: Richard Alan Jr., Jill Carole, Susan Lyn. BA, Washington & Lee U., 1951; MBA, Harvard U., 1953. Mdse. mgr. Pizitz Dept. Stores, Birmingham, 1953-59, v.p., 1959-66, pres., 1966-86, chmn. bd., 1986-87; chmn. Pizitz Mgmt. Group, Birmingham, 1987—. Pres. United Way, Birmingham, 1988, Ala. Commn. on Higher Edn., 1987-95; pres. Better Bus. Bur., Birmingham, 1962; mem. Ala adv. commn. U.S. Commn. on Civil Rights, 1985. Recipient Erskine Ramsay award, 1974; named Mktg. Man of Yr., Am. Mktg. Assn., 1966, Man of Yr., Young Men's Bus. Club, 1970. Mem. Ala. Commn. on Higher Edn., Birmingham C. of C. (pres. 1970), Ala. Retail Assn. (pres. 1965). Avocations: flying, skiing, tennis, scuba diving. Office: Pizitz Mgmt Group 2140 11th Ave S Ste 318 Birmingham AL 35205-2850 Address: 2936 Redmont Park Ln Birmingham AL 35205-2136

**PIZZAGALLI, JAMES,** construction executive; b. Burlington, Vt., Nov. 23, 1944; s. Angelo and Theresa (Moalli) P.; m. Judy Rock, June 21, 1969; 1 child, Michael. BS, U. Vt., 1966; JD, Boston U., 1969. Treas. Pizzagalli Constrn. Co., Burlington, Vt., 1969-76, v.p., 1976-91, chmn., CEO, 1991-98, co-chmn., 1998—. Dir. Chittenden Corp., Burlington, 1982—, AGC Edn. Found., Washington, 1992-2004, Shelburne (Vt.) Mus., 1983-92, 2000—; life dir. Assn. Gen. Contractors, Washington, 1976—, atty.-at law. Trustee U. Vt., 2000—05. Mem.: The Moles, Ethan Allen Club. Republican. Roman Catholic. Home: 3393 Harbor Rd Shelburne VT 05482-7611 Office: Pizzagalli Constrn Co PO Box 2009 South Burlington VT 05407 E-mail: jpizzagalli@pizzagalli.com.

**PIZZAMIGLIO, ALBERT THEODORE (AL PIERSON),** conductor; b. Ill. m. Nancy Alice Gilman, Mar. 27, 1978; five children. Studied music theory and composition; BA, MA, Ill. State U.; advanced music studies, U. Ill. Condr. Al Pierson Big Band U.S.A., 1975-89, Guy Lombardo's Royal Canadians, Aubrey, Tex., 1989—. Nat. youth music dir. Am. Inst. of Cooperation; co-host, owner TV show, Bloomington, Ill.; tchr. high sch. and coll. Musician, composer, arranger, vocalist, band leader; founder Al Pierson & Big Band U.S.A. (Best New Dance Band in the Country 1975, America's Number One Dance Band 1977), performed for fourteen yrs. at numerous famous ballrooms in the midwest and many prestigious pvt. parties, on twenty internat. dance tours including Europe, the Orient, the Middle East, the Caribbean, Mexico, Hawaii, Alaska and Tahiti; released 15 albums; recorded Guy Lombardo music album, 2000, now with Guy Lombardo's Royal Canadians performing throughout the continental U.S and Can. and 44 other fgn. countries; condr. PBS TV series (past three yrs. and continuing), 1977, PBS TV spls., 1994, 95, 96, 97, 2000, Presdl. Inauguration Festivities, 1994. Mem. Pres. George Bush Inauguration, 2004, Pres. Bill Clinton's Inauguration, 1992. Recipient Superman award for helping save 32 lives in snowstorm, 1997, 98, 99, Ill. State U. Disting. Alumni award, 2004; inducted into Ballroom Dancers' Hall of Fame, 1976; named amb. Music for World pres. Ill. State U., 1998. Office: Gilman Inc Artists Mgmt RR 1 Aubrey TX 76227-9801

**PIZZELLA, PATRICK,** federal agency administrator; b. New Rochelle, N.Y., May 19, 1954; BSBA, U.S.C., 1976. Dep. undersecretary mgmt. Dept. Edn., Washington, 1988—89; chief adminstrv. officer Fed. Housing Fin. Bd., 1990—95; govt. affairs counselor Preston Gates Ellis & Rouvelas Meeds LLP, 1996—2001; asst. sec. adminstrn. and mgmt. U.S. Dept. Labor, Washington, 2001—. Office: US Dept Labor 200 Constitution Ave NW Washington DC 20210

**PIZZINGRILLI, KIM,** state official, BBA Econ., U. Pitts., Johnstown, 1981; M Govtl. adminstrn., U. Pa., 1988. Auditor, acct., and asst. dir. bur. of audits Pa. Treasury Dept., 1981-87; sr. regulatory analyst Pa. Ind. Regulatory Rev. Commn., 1987-95; spl. asst. to sec. Dept. of State, Harrisburg, Pa., 1995-96, dep. sec. regulatory programs, 1996-98, acting sec., 1998-99, sec. of the commonwealth, 1999—2002; commr. Pa. Pub. Utility Comm., 2002—. Mem. Bd. of Property, Bd. of Fin. and Revenue, State of Pa.; mem. Pa. State Athletic Commn., Pa. State Nav. Commn. for the Delaware River and its Navigable Tributaries, mem. Pa. Mcpl. Retirement Bd.; keeper Great Seal of the Commonwealth. Mem. Nat. Assn. Sec. of State, Women Exec. in State Govt. Republican. Office: Pennsylvania Pub Utility Commn PO Box 3265 Harrisburg PA 17105-3265

**PIZZO, ANDREW JOSEPH,** music educator; b. Metairie, La., Jan. 15, 1977; s. Vincent Anthony and Mary Diane Pizzo. MusB, La. State U., 1995. Band dir. McKinley Middle Magnet Sch., Baton Rouge, 1999—2002, Southeast Mid. Sch., Baton Rouge, 2002—05, Sherwood Mid. Magnet Sch., Baton Rouge, 2005—. Recipient Grand prize, VH1/Toyota Music Tchr. Contest, 2001. Mem.: La. Music Educators Assn. (jazz chair 2006), Music Educators Nat. Conf., Nat. Band Directors Assn., Internat. Assn. Jazz Edn. (pres.-elect 2005). Home: 4425 Lakewood Dr Metairie LA 70002 E-mail: apizzo@ebrschools.org.

**PIZZO, PHILIP A.,** pediatrician, educator, dean; b. NYC, Dec. 6, 1944; BA, Fordham U., 1966; MD, U. Rochester, 1970. Diplomate Am. Bd. Pediat., Am. Bd. Hematology/Oncology. Intern Children's Hosp. Med. Ctr., Boston, 1970-71, jr. asst. resident, 1971-72, sr. resident, 1972-73; tchg. fellow Harvard U. Sch. Medicine, Boston, 1972-73; clin. assoc. Pediatric Oncology Br. of Nat. Cancer Inst., 1973-75, investigator, 1975-76, sr. investigator, 1976-80; head infectious disease sect. Pediatric Br. of Nat. Cancer Inst., 1980-96, chief pediat., 1982-96; sci. dir. divsn. clin. scis. Nat. Cancer Inst., 1994-96; prof. pediat. Sch. Medicine, Uniformed Svcs. U. Health Sci., 1987-96; Thomas Morgan Rotch prof., chmn. dept. pediat. Harvard U. Sch. Medicine, Boston, 1996—2001; dean Stanford U. Sch. Medicine, 2001—. Mem. clin. rsch. subpanel of Nat. Cancer Inst., 1978-81, infectious disease clin. ctr., NIH, 1978-96, transfusion com., 1984-87, pediatric core com., pediatric AIDS clin. trials group, 1988-94, sec. HIV task force, 1988; mem.

sci. adv. bd. Children's Hospice Internat., 1988-94, AIDS program Nat. Inst. Allergy and Infectious Diseases, 1988-89; mem. clin. rsch. subcom. AIDS Rsch. Adv. Com., 1990-94; physician-in-chief, chmn. dept. medicine Children's Hosp., Boston, 1996—, Myron Karon Meml. lectr., 1986, Melissa Anne Krinsky Meml. lectr., 1989. Mem. AAAS, Inst. Medicine of NAS, Am. Soc. Hematology, Am. Fedn. for Clin. Rsch., Am. Soc. for Clin. Investigation, Am. Soc. Clin. Oncology (bd. dirs. 1996-1999), Elizabeth Glaser Pediatric AIDS Found. (bd. dirs. 1996-1999), Infectious Disease Soc. Am., Infectious Disease Soc. Am., Internat. Immunocompromised Host Soc., IDSA (bd. dirs. 1996—). Office: Stanford U Sch Med 300 Pasteur Dr, Ste M121 Palo Alto CA 94305 Office Phone: 650-724-5688. E-mail: philip.pizzo@stanford.edu.*

**PIZZO, SALVATORE VINCENT,** pathologist; b. Phila., June 22, 1944; s. George J. Pizzo and Aida (Alcaro) Lepore; m. Carol Ann Kurkowski, Dec. 28, 1968 (div. 1987); children: Steven, David, Susan. Duke U., 1972; BS, St. Joseph's Coll., 1966; MD, Duke U., 1973. Asst. prof. Duke U. Med. Ctr, Durham, NC, 1976-80, assoc. prof., 1980-85, prof., 1985—, dir. med. scientist tng. program, 1987—, chmn.—, mem., chmn. program rev. com. NIH, Bethesda, Md., 1986-90; vice chmn. Gordon Conf. Proteases, Holderness, N.H., 1990, chmn., 1992-96; cons. in field, 1980—; mem. Cellular and Molecular Basis of Disease Rev. Com., 1990-96. Contbr. articles to profl. jours. Grantee NIH, 1976—, Am. Cancer Soc., 1976—; Disting. Faculty award, Duke U., 2004, Dean's award for excellence in mentoring, 2004; named one of the top 150 cited authors for jours. in the life sciences, Fellow AAAS; mem. Am. Heart Assn. (exec. com. Thrombosis coun. 1990, 92), Am. Chem. Soc., Am. Assn. Pathologists (program com. 1985-88, long range planning com. 1990-97), Am. Soc. Biological Chemists, Alpha Sigma Nu, Phi Beta Kappa, Alpha Omega Alpha, Sigma Xi. Achievements include patents in field; research in lipoproteins in coagulation and fibronolysis, a link to atherosclerosis, anticoagulation drug development; identification of ATP synthase as the target for Angiostatin action. Office: Duke U Med Ctr PO Box 3712 Durham NC 27710-0001 Office Phone: 919-684-3528. Business E-Mail: pizzo001@mc.duke.edu.

**PIZZORNO, JOSEPH, JR.,** health products executive; b. San Gabriel, Calif., Dec. 7, 1947; s. Joseph Sr. and Mary (Carmela) P.; 1 child, Raven Muir; m. Lara Elise Udell, Sept. 28, 1985; 1 child, Galen Udell. BS with Distinction, Harvey Mudd Coll., Claremont, Calif., 1969; Naturopathic Doctor with honors, Nat. Coll. Naturopathic Medicine, Portland, Oreg., 1975. Rsch. asst. Lockheed Aircraft, Ontario, Calif., 1968; rsch. technologist U. Wash., Seattle, 1970-75; practice naturopathic medicine Seattle, 1975-82; practice midwifery, 1978-82; pres. Bastyr U., Seattle, 1978-2000, pres. emeritus, 2000—; pres. Salugenecists, Inc., Seattle, 2001—. Pres. Coun. on Naturopathic Med. Edn., Portland, Oreg. 1985-87; apptd. adv. panel safety and efficacy of dietary supplements U.S. Office of Tech. Assessment, 1993-95; sr. med. advisor Alternative and Complementary Therapies, 1995-97; mem. White House Commn. Complementary and Alternative Medicine Policy, 2000-02; mem. Medicare Coverage Adv. Com., 2003-05. Author: Total Wellness, 1996; co-author: Handbook of Natural Medicine, 1985, 3d edit., 2001, Encyclopedia of Natural Medicine, 1990, 2d edit., 1998, Textbook of Natural Medicine, 2005, How to Prevent and Treat Cancer with Natural Medicine, 2002; editor: Integrative Medicine: A Clinician's Jour.; contbg. editor: Let's Live mag., 1987—; contbr. articles to profl. jours.; editor: Ency. Health Foods, 2005. Mem. Seattle/King County Bd. Health, 1996-2002; vice chair bd. dirs. Inst. for Functional Medicine. Mem.: Seattle Midwifery Sch. (edn. com. 1978—91), Wash. Assn. Naturopathic Physicians (adv. dir. 1976), Am. Assn. Naturopathic Physicians (bd. dirs. 1984—91). Libertarian. Avocations: microcomputers, basketball, ultimate frisbie. Home: 4220 NE 135th St Seattle WA 98125-3836 Office Phone: 206-368-5403. Personal E-mail: drpizzorno@salugenecists.com. Business E-Mail: president_emeritus@bastyr.edu.

**PIZZURO, SALVATORE NICHOLAS,** special education educator; b. Passaic, NJ, Jan. 25, 1945; s. John G. and Mary F. (Interdonato) P. BA, Jersey City State Coll., 1970, MA, 1973; profl. diploma, Fordham U., 1980; EdD, Columbia U., 1991. Tchr. spl. edn. Garfield (N.J.) Pub. Schs., 1970-71, Lodi (N.J.) Pub. Schs., 1971-75, 76-78; learning cons. Mt. Carmel Guild, Newark, 1976-76; instr. Columbia U., N.Y.C., 1988-91; asst. prof. spl. edn. Jersey City State Coll., 1990—; learning cons. Elmwood Park (N.J.) Dept. Special Svcs., 2000—02, Passaic County Ednl. Svcs. Commn., 2002—; cons. com. on edn. and workforce U.S. House of Reps., 2003; cons. Jersey City Pub. Schs., 2003—; founder, dir. Transition Advocacy Svcs., 2004. Rsch. chmn. Transition Coords. Network NJ; cons. Congressmen Rush Holt and Pete Stark, 2002-03; post-doctoral fellow U. Ky., 1993-94; dir. Learning Consultation Svcs., N.Y.C., 1990—; coord. pre-svcs. program in mental retardation Tchrs. Coll., Columbia U., 1990-91; rsch. assoc. U. Ill., 1991-92; chmn. Early Childhood Inclusion Conf., Phila., 1993; dir. United Learning Consultants, 1994—; chmn. conf. Assessment: Impact on Svc. Deliver, N.J., 1995; cons. Ind. Child Study Teams, Inc., 1995—; task force com. on econ. and ednl. opportunities U.S. Ho. of Reps., 1994-96, chair, cons. Com. Edn. & Workforce, 1997—; chmn. Future of Edn. in N.J. Conf., 1996; adj. faculty Kean Coll. N.J., 1997—; cons. Ednl. Resource Ctr. N.J., 1998; learning cons. Elmwood Park Dept. Spl. Svcs., 2000-02, Rutherford Dept. Spl. Svcs., 2002—; chmn. symposium on edn. funding Eagleton Inst. Politics Rutgers U., 1997; chmn. N.J. Com. on Pers. Stds. in Edn.; cons. U.S. Ho. of Reps. com. on edn. and workforce, 2002—; learning cons. Rutherford Pub. Schs., 2002-03, Jersey City Pub. Schs., 2003-05; chmn. symposium on sch. constrn. Kean U., 1998, chmn. symposium on urban edn., 1998, chmn. symposium on legis. initiatives in edn., 1998; chmn. congl. symposium on disability issues Capitol Hill, 2003. Author: The Individuals with Disabilities Education Act and the Nature of American Politics, 1999, (textbook) The Individuals with Disabilities Education Act and the Nature of American Politics, 2001, 2d edn., 2003 (state-wide technical report) Engagment in Education, Training, Living Arrangements and Community Activities among Recent Graduates of New Jersey's High Schools Special Education Program, 2004; editor: Learning Consultant Journal, 1995, 96, Policy Statement on Education in New Jersey, N.J. Coalition for the Study for School Reform, 1998; cons. editor Diagnostique, 1997—. Chmn. Walk for Hunger, 1979, NE Regional Legis. Coalition, 1984-86, Nat. AD HOC Comm. on the Reauthorization of the Individuals with Disabilities Edn. Act, chmn. Nat. Forum on Reauthorization, 1996, Conf. on Future of Edn. in N.J., 1996—, N.J. Coalition on Study of Sch. Reform, 1996—; staff mem. for U.S. Congressman Major Owens, 1997—; chmn. press conf. with U.S. Congressman Robert Menendez on sch. constrn., 1998, with U.S. Congressman Donald Payne on urban edn., 1998; polit. cons. Dem. election orgn., 1999-2000; cons. Legis. Initiatives in Edn., 2000, U.S. Congressmen Pete Start of Calif. and Rush Holt of N.J., 2002-04. Recipient award for dedication to mentally retarded Mt. Carmel Guild, 1972. Mem. Coun. for Exceptional Children, N.J. Coun. for Exceptional Children (pres. 1984-85), N.J. Divsn. on Mental Retardation (pres. 1986-87), Jersey City State Coll. Alumni Assn. (pres. 1974-75), Tchrs. Coll. Christian Fellowship (pres. 1988-90), Rehab. Engring. Soc. N.Am., Correctional Edn. Assn., Internat. Ctr. for Study of Psychiatry and Psychology. Roman Catholic. Avocations: writing nonfiction, jogging. Office Phone: 201-896-1755. Personal E-mail: sal.pizzuro@verizon.net.

**PIZZUTI, RONALD A.,** real estate developer; m. Ann Pizzuti; 3 children. BS, Kent State U., 1962. Chmn., CEO Pizzuti Cos., Columbus, Ohio, 1976—. Mem. Ohio Arts & Sports Facilities Commn.; bd. trustees Kenyon Coll.; chair bd. trustees Kent State U.; bd. dir. Kent State Found. Named one of Top 200 Collectors, ARTnews Mag., 2003—06; recipient Shining Stars of Seminole County. Lifetime Achievement award, 2002. Mem.: Columbus C. of C. (exec. com.). Avocation: Collecting modern and contemporary art. Office: Pizzuti Cos Ste 800 Two Miranova Pl Columbus OH 43215 Business E-Mail: rpizzuti@pizzuti.com.

**PLACE, JANEY,** banking consultant, former bank executive; b. Denver, Jan. 25, 1946; m. Michael Hiles. BA, MA, UCLA, PhD in semiology, 1975; attended Grad. Sch. Mgmt. Info tech. mgr. Hughes Aircraft Co.; corp. mgr. Strategic Tech. Planning Tosco Corp.; sr. v.p. internet strategy, R&D Wells Fargo Bank, 1990—94; exec. v.p. Strategic Tech. Group Bank of Am.,

1994—99; pres. Mellon Lab and Online Svcs., N.Y.C., 1999—2003; exec. v.p. Mellon Fin. Corp., N.Y.C., 1999—2003; founder, pres., CEO digitalthinking.com, 1999—. Past lectr. in sys. and comm. theory U. Calif., Santa Cruz, Calif.; bd. dirs. PortBlue; spkr. in field. Contbr. articles to profl. jours.; author: The Western Films of John Ford, 1974, The Non-Western Films of John Ford, 1979. Named One of 25 Women to Watch in Banking, U.S. Banker Mag., 2003.

**PLACE, MICHAEL D.,** priest, former health association administrator; b. 1944; MA in Ecclesiastical History, D in Sacred Theology, Cath. U. Am.; MDiv, lic. in sacred theology, St. Mary of the Lake Sem. Ordained priest Roman Cath. Ch., 1970. Assoc. pastor Most Holy Redeemer Parish, Evergreen, Ill., 1970—74; mem. faculty, adminstr. St. Mary of the Lake Sem., Mundelein, Ill., 1977—81; dean Athenaeum of Ohio, 1981—84; acad. dean Mt. St. Mary's Sem. of the West, 1981—84; consul for policy devel. Archdiocese of Chgo., 1984—98; pres., CEO Cath. Health Assn., St. Louis, 1998—2005. Named one of 100 Most Powerful People in Healthcare, Modern Healthcare mag., 2002, 2003.

**PLAČEK, ROMAN,** cellist, composer, music educator; b. Jesenik, Czech Republic, June 26, 1972; came to U.S., 1995; s. Bohumir and Marcela Plaček; m. Edita Blaskova, Apr, 15, 1976. Grad., Ostrava Conservatory, Czech Republic, 1993; grad. performing cert., Boston Conservatory, 1998; MusM, U. Mass., 2001. Ind. artist and educator, 1990—; founder, artist dir., composer Golden Mountain Chamber Ensemble, Czech Republic, 1993—, Golden Mountain Chamber Ensemble Music Acad. Inc., Amherst, Mass., 2001—06; pres. Golden Mountain Chamber Ensemble Music Acad.; co-owner, artistic dir., pres. bd. dirs. Golden Mountain Summer Internat. Inc., Chamber Music Summer Sch. and Festival, Zlaté Hory, Czech Republic, 2002; co-owner, co-dir. Hudba Bez Hranic, Music Without Borders, Inc., Czech Republic, 2002—. Mem. string trio-in-residence U. Mass., Amherst, 1998-2001. Author project Art Instn. for Czech-Am. Cultural Exch., 1999—. Mem. Amateur Chamber Music Players (bd. advisors 1998-2000). Avocations: drawing, photography, home improvement. Home: Sokolska' 290 793 76 Zlaté Hory Czech Republic Office: Sokolska' 290 793 76 Zlaté Hory Czech Republic Office Phone: +420584452530. E-mail: hbh@gmcema.com, rcmplacek@msn.com.

**PLACENTI, FRANK MICHAEL,** lawyer; b. Columbus, Ohio, Sept. 2, 1953; s. Anthony Joseph and Evelyn (Piteo) P.; m. Tobi M. Placenti, Apr. 29, 1971. BA cum laude, Ohio State U., 1975, JD summa cum laude, 1979. Bar: Ariz. 1979, U.S. Dist. Ct. Ariz. 1979, U.S. Ct. Appeals (9th cir.) 1979. Group co-dir. transactions and corp. governance Bryan Cave LLP, Phoenix. Judge pro tem Maricopa County Superior Ct., 1985—. Chmn. Super Bowl Kick-Off Luncheon, 1996, NBA All Star Kick-Off Luncheonj, 1995, Phoenix C. of C., 1991—92, Boys & Girls Clubs Met. Phoenix, 1992—93; chmn. bd. dirs. Phoenix Children's Hosp. Found., 2005—. James K. Barton Meml. scholar Ohio State U., 1977-79; named one of Outstanding Young Men in Am., 1981. Mem. ABA (litigation, communication law and young lawyers sects.), Maricopa County Bar (chmn. com., lectr. on litigation 1985-86), Greater Phoenix Leadership, Phoenix C. of C., Order of Coif, Phi Kappa Theta, Phi Kappa Tau, Phi Eta Sigma. Avocations: golf, travel, wine. Office: Bryan Cave LLP 1 Renaissance Sq Two N Ctrl Ave, Ste 2200 Phoenix AZ 85004 Office Phone: 602-364-7451. E-mail: fmplacenti@bryancave.com.

**PLACHNO, RONALD JOHN,** electrical engineer; b. Chgo., June 1, 1945; s. Joseph John Plachno; m. Valerie Lynn Zahorak; children: Kenneth, Gregory. BSEE, Ill. Inst. of Tech., 1968. Electronics design engr. Magnavox Govt. Divsn., Urbana, Ill., 1968—71; ops. dir. Motorola Cellular Ops., Schaumburg, Ill., 1971—94; v.p. Motorola, Swindon, Wiltshire, England, 1994—97, v.p. of mfg. Arlington Heights, Ill., 1997—2000; sr. v.p. of ops. Novatel Wireless Inc., San Diego, 2001—02. Treas., team mgr. Itasca Athletic Assn., Itasca, 1988—93. Scholar, State of Ill., 1963—67. Mem.: IEEE. Roman Catholic. Achievements include invention of 13 software copyrights. Avocations: software, music, travel. Home: 41451 Grand View Dr Murrieta CA 92562 Personal E-mail: plachnor@aol.com.

**PLACHTA, DAVID W.,** aerospace engineer; b. Detroit, Jan. 22, 1960; s. Alfons Walter and Anne Marie Plachta; m. Marilyn V. Van Camp, Nov. 29, 1986; children: Alexander James, Jonathan David, Gregory Thomas. BS, U. Mich., Ann Arbor, 1982. Aerospace engr. Glenn Rsch. Ctr., Cleve., 1985—. Outreach ministry, edn. Rockport, Rocky River, Ohio, 1997—2006. Recipient Exceptional Engring. Achievement award, NASA, 2002. Mem.: Cryogenic Soc. Am. (assoc.; bd. dirs. 2003—). Methodist. Achievements include development of analysis tools, configuration design, and research hardware for the efficient long-term, reduced boil-off and zero boil-off, storage of cryogenic propellants in space; enabled research of cryogenic propellants, with inherently high propulsive capability, for use in Lunar and Mar architecture studies and vehicle development. Avocations: bicycling, golf. Office: Aerospace Engr 21000 Brookpark Rd Cleveland OH 44135 Office Phone: 216-977-7126. Business E-Mail: david.w.plachta@nasa.gov.

**PLACKE, JAMES ANTHONY,** retired diplomat; b. Grand Island, Nebr., June 14, 1935; s. Gerhard F. and Florence E. (McCormick) P.; m. Mary Sabina Shea, July 25, 1959; children: Elizabeth, Stephen, Carolyn B.Sc., U. Nebr., 1957, MA, 1959. Commd. fgn. service officer Dept. State, 1958; econ. counselor Am. Embassy, Tripoli, Libya, 1970-71, Ottawa, 1977-79; fgn. service insp. Dept. State, Washington, 1971-73, dir. office food policy, 1974-76; minister Am. Embassy, Jiddah, Saudi Arabia, 1979-82; dep. asst. sec. Nr. Eastern and South Asian Affairs Bur., Dept. State, Washington, 1982-85; pvt. practice, 1986—90; dir. Cambridge Energy Rsch. Assoc., 1991-2000, sr. assoc., 2001—. Del. UN World Food Conf., 1974. Recipient Meritorious Honor award Dept. State, 1969, 71; Presdl. Meritorious Service award, 1985 Office: Ste 201 1150 Connecticut Ave NW Washington DC 20036-4104 Office Phone: 202-463-8222.

**PLAEGER, FREDERICK JOSEPH, II,** lawyer; b. New Orleans, Sept. 10, 1953; s. Edgar Leonard and Bernice Virginia (Schiwetz) P.; m. Kathleen Helen Dickson, Nov. 19, 1977; children: Douglas A., Catherine E. BS, La. State U., 1976, JD, 1977. Bar: La. 1978, Tex. 1999, U.S. Dist. Ct. (ea. dist.) La. 1978, U.S. Ct. Appeals (5th cir.) 1981, U.S. Supreme Ct. 1989. Law clk. U.S. Dist. Ct. (ea. dist.) La., New Orleans, 1977-79; assoc. Milling, Benson, Woodward, Hillyer, Pierson & Miller, New Orleans, 1979-85, ptnr., 1985-89; v.p., gen. counsel, corp. sec. La. Land and Exploration Co., New Orleans, 1989-97; v.p. gen. counsel Burlington Resources Inc., Houston, 1997—2006. Selected mem. Met. Area Com. Leadership Forum, 1986; bd. dirs. Soc. Environ. Edn., La. Natural and Sci. Ctr., 1992—94; trustee Houston Ballet, 2001—; bd. dirs. New Orleans Speech and Hearing Ctr., 1985—91, pres., 1988—90; bd. dirs. Children's Oncology Svcs. La. (Ronald McDonald Ho. of New Orleans), 1987—90. Recipient Service to Mankind award Sertoma, 1989; named Tex. Super Lawyer, Tex. Monthly Mag., 2004, 05, 06. Mem.: ABA, Tex. Gen. Counsel Forum (pres. Houston chpt. 2005—06, statewide chmn. 2006—), Am. Corp. Counsel Assn. (bd. dir. New Orleans chpt. 1995—98), La. Bar Assn., Inst. Energy Law (adv. bd. 2001—, exec. com. 2002—, chmn. 2005—), Am. Petroleum Inst. (chmn. gen. commn. law 2003—05), Lakeside Country Club, Univ. Club. Republican. Roman Catholic. Avocations: computers, fishing. Home: 5105 Longmont Dr Houston TX 77056-2417 Office: Burlington Resources Inc Ste 2100 717 Texas St Houston TX 77002-2712 Business E-Mail: rplaeger@pdq.net.

**PLAGER, S. JAY,** federal judge; b. Long Branch, N.J., May 16, 1931; s. A. L. and Clara L. Plager; children: Anna Katherine, David Alan, Daniel Tyler. AB, U. N.C., 1952; JD, U. Fla., 1958; LLM, Columbia U., 1961. Bar: Fla. 1958, Ill. 1964. Asst. prof. law U. Fla., 1958—62, assoc. prof., 1962—64; assoc. prof. law U. Ill., Champaign-Urbana, 1964—65, prof., 1965—77; dir. Office Environ. and Planning Studies, 1972—74, 1975—77; dean, prof. law Ind. U. Sch. Law, Bloomington, 1977—84, prof. law, 1984—90; counselor to undersec. U.S. Dept. Health and Human Svcs., 1986—87; assoc. dir. Office of Mgmt. and Budget Office of Mgmt. and Budget, 1987—88; adminstr. info.

and regulatory affairs Exec. Office of the Pres., 1988—89; cir. judge U.S. Ct. Appeals (fed. cir.), 1989—2000, sr. judge, 2000—. Vis. rsch. prof. law U. Wis., 1967—68; vis. scholar Stanford U., 1984—85. Author (with others): Water Law and Administration, 1968; author: Social Justice Through Law-New Approaches in the Law of Property, 1970; author: (with others) Florida Water Law, 1980. Chmn. Gainesville (Fla.) Planning Commn., 1962—63; mem. Urbana Plan Commn., 1966—70; mem. nat. air pollution manpower devel. adv. com., 1971—75; cons. Ill. Inst. for Environ. Quality, U.S. EPA; chmn. Ill. Task Force on Noise, 1972—76; vice chmn. Nat. Commn. on Jud. Discipline and Removal, 1991—93; mem. Jud. Conf. U.S. Ctrs. Budget Com., 1996—2003. With USN, 1948—70. Office: US Ct Appeals for Fed Cir The National Courts Bldg 717 Madison Pl NW Washington DC 20439-0002*

**PLAINE, DANIEL J.,** lawyer; b. Washington, Aug. 23, 1943; s. Herzel H.E. and Norma (Stein) P.; m. Susan Ambrose, Oct. 5, 1985; children: Caroline, Meredith. BA magna cum laude, Williams Coll., 1965; LLB in Internat. Law, Cambridge U., Eng., 1967; JD, Yale U., 1970. Bar: DC 1970, US Dist. Ct. DC 1970, US Ct. Appeals (DC cir.) 1970, US Ct. Appeals (fed. cir.), 1985, US Supreme Ct., 1974. Ptnr. Steptoe & Johnson, Washington, 1990—95, Gibson, Dunn & Crutcher, Washington, 1995—. Marshall scholar, 1967. Mem. ABA, Am. Soc. Internat. Law, Washington Inst. Internat. Law, Phi Beta Kappa. Office: Gibson Dunn & Crutcher LLP 1050 Connecticut Ave NW Ste 200 Washington DC 20036-5306 Office Phone: 202-955-8286. E-mail: dplaine@gibsondunn.com.

**PLAINE, LLOYD LEVA,** lawyer; b. Washington, Nov. 3, 1947; d. Marx and Shirley P. Leva; m. James W. Hill. BA, U. Pa., 1969; postgrad., Harvard U.; JD, Georgetown U., 1975. Bar: DC 1975. Legis. asst. to US Rep. Sidney Yates, 1971-72; with Sutherland, Asbill & Brennan, Washington, 1975-82, ptnr., 1982—. Fellow Am. Bar Found.; Am. Coll. Trust and Estate Counsel (past regent), Am. Coll. Tax Counsel; mem. ABA (past chmn. real property, probate and trust law sect., past coun. sect. of taxation). Office: Sutherland Asbill & Brennan Ste 6 1275 Pennsylvania Ave NW Washington DC 20004-2415 Office Phone: 202-383-0155.

**PLAISANCE, MELISSA C.,** consumer products company executive; b. Feb. 12, 1960; BSBA cum laude, Bucknell U., 1982; MBA, UCLA, 1990. With Bankers Trust Co. Corp. Fin., L.A., 1982—90; dir., investor rels. Safeway Inc., 1990—93, v.p., investor rels., 1993—94, v.p., investor rels. & pub. affairs, 1994—95, sr. v.p. fin., investor rels. & pub. affairs Pleasanton, Calif., 1995—2000, sr. v.p., fin. & investor rels., 2000—04; sr. v.p., fin. & corp. comm. Del Monte Foods Co., San Francisco, 2004—. Office: Del Monte Foods One Market at The Landmark San Francisco CA 94119-3575

**PLAISTED, JOAN M.,** diplomat; b. St. Peter, Minn., Aug. 29, 1945; d. Gerald A. and Lola May (Peters) Plaisted. Student, U. Grenoble, France, 1965—66, U. Calif., Berkeley, 1966; BA in Internat. Rels., Am. U., 1967, MA in Asian Studies, 1969; grad., Nat. War Coll., 1988. Korea desk officer Commerce Dept., Washington, 1969-72, Japan desk officer, 1972-73; comml. officer Am. Embassy, Paris, 1973-78; internat. economist Orgn. Econ. Cooperation & Devel., Paris, 1978-80; econ. officer Am. Consulate Gen., Hong Kong, 1980-83; trade negotiator White House Office of Spl. Trade Rep., Geneva, 1983-85; deputy dir. China desk State Dept., Washington, 1985-87; acting dep. dir., chief econ./comml. sect. Am. Inst. in Taiwan, Taipei, 1988-91; chargé d'affaires, dep. chief of mission Am. Embassy, Rabat, Morocco, 1991-94; dir. Thai and Burma affairs State Dept., Washington, 1994-95; sr. advisor U.S. Mission to UN N.Y.C., 1995; amb. to Republic of Marshall Islands and Republic of Kiribati, 1996—2000; amb., sr. advisor U.S. Mission to the UN, N.Y.C., 2000—04. Recipient Loadestar award, Am. U., 1993, Disting. Civilian Svc. decoration, Sec. of the Army, 2000, Alumna of Yr. award, Am. U. Sch. Internat. Svc., 2001, Supr. award, State Dept., 2002. Mem.: Am. Fgn. Svc. Assn., Asia Soc., Washington Inst. Fgn. Affairs, Hong Kong Wine Soc. (founding), Phillips Collection. Avocations: wine tasting, gastronomy, history, skiing, scuba diving.

**PLAKS, LIVIA BASCH,** foundation executive; b. Baia Mare, Romania, Apr. 29, 1947; arrived in US, 1964, naturalized, 1969; d. Kalman and Cecilia (Freund) Basch; m. Andrew H. Plaks, June 9, 1968; children: Jason, Eric. AB, Rutgers U., 1969; AM, NYU, 1971. Exec. assoc. Internat. Rsch. and Exch. Bd., Princeton, N.J., 1986-92; assoc. dir. Project on Ethnic Rels., Princeton, 1992-94, exec. dir., 1994—2005, pres., 2005—. Rapporteur Orgn. Security Cooperation in Europe on Roma issues, Warsaw, Poland, 1994; mem. U.S. Task Force on Romania, 1992—; mediation team between Romanian Govt. and Dem. Union of Hungarians in Romania, 1992—; mem. Coun. for Ethnic Accord, 1992-2000; mediation team between Slovak and ethnic Hungarian Parliamentary parties of Slovakia, 1995-2002; mediation team Serbs and Albanians of Kosovo, 1995—; testified to and for Commn. on Security and Cooperation in Europe on issues of Roma/Gypsies, 1994, 98, ethnic minorities, 2003. Recipient Certificate of Merit Pres. Romania, 1996, 2000, Govt. Hungary, 1996, Govt. Slovakia, 1998. Mem.: AAAS, Women in Internat. Security, Coun. Fgn. Rels. Avocations: music, reading, hiking. Office: Project on Ethnic Rels 15 Chambers St Princeton NJ 08542-3707 Office Phone: 609-683-5666. Business E-Mail: livia.plaks@per-usa.org.

**PLAMANN, ALFRED A.,** wholesale distribution executive; Pres., CEO Cert. Grocers Calif., Unified We. Grocers Inc., Commerce, Calif., 2000—. Office: Unified Western Grocers Inc 5200 Sheila St City Of Commerce CA 90040*

**PLAME, VALERIE ELISE,** former intelligence agent; b. Anchorage, Aug. 13, 1963; d. Samuel D. and Diane E. Plame; m. Joseph Charles Wilson IV, Apr. 3, 1998; children: Trevor Rolph, Samantha Finnell Diana. BA in Internat. Rels., Penn. State U., 1985; MA, London Sch. Economics, Coll. Europe, Belgium, 1995. Classified officer CIA, 1985—2003. Became the subject of a widespread government controversy when members of the Bush administration were accused of leaking her identity as an undercover CIA agent to members of the media; filed lawsuit against members of the Bush administration in 2006.

**PLANAS, CARLOS,** automotive executive; b. Havana, Cuba, Nov. 10, 1946; arrived in US, 1960; m. Ivette Planas; children: Juan-Carlos, Alex, Ivette, Lose Luis, Cristina. BBA, U. Miami, 1971. Pres. Tamiami Automotive Group. Office: Tamiami Automotive Group 8250 SW 8th St Miami FL 33144 Office Phone: 305-266-5500. Office Fax: 305-266-5604.*

**PLANCHON, HARRY PETER, JR.,** research development manager; b. Aurora, Mo., Aug. 28, 1941; s. Harry P. and Ruth Arminta (Eden) P.; m. Virginia Grace Sapp, June 13, 1964; children: Benjamin John, Matthew Brian. BSME, U. Mo., 1964; MS in Nuclear Engring., U. Ill., 1971, PhD in Nuclear Engring., 1974; MBA, U. Chgo., 1990. Cert. profl. engr. Rsch. assoc., asst. prof. U. Ill. Nuclear Engring. Dept., Urbana, 1970-74; sr. engr., mgr. Clinch River Breeder Reactor Plant Systems Westinghouse Advanced Reaction Div., Madison, Pa., 1974-84; mgr. reactor analysis Exptl. Breeder Reactor Div., Argonne (Ill.) Nat. Lab., 1984-90; reactor analysis div. Argonne Nat. Lab., 1984-90; assoc. dir. ENG divsn. Argonne Nat. Lab., Idaho Falls, Idaho, 1991-2000, dir. nuclear tech. divsn., 2000—. Contbr. articles to profl. jours. Lt. USN, 1964-70. Fellow Am. Nuc. Soc. (Seaborg medal 1996); mem. Am. Soc. Mech. Engrs., Beta Gamma Sigma, Tau Beta Pi, Pi Mu Epsilon, Pi Tau Sigma. Presbyterian. Avocations: hiking, skiing, photography, golf, reading. Office: Argonne National Laboratory PO Box 1625 Idaho Falls ID 83403-1625

**PLANE, DONALD RAY,** retired management science educator; b. Evansville, Ind., July 17, 1936; s. Edward L. and Margaret I. (Downen) P.; m. Rosemary Bieber, Sept. 4, 1961; children: Brian Russell, Dennis Lowell, Margaret Diane. ME, U. Cin., 1961; MBA (NDEA fellow), Ind. U., 1963, DBA (NDEA fellow), 1965. Instr. econs. U.S. Air Force Acad., 1965-67, asst. prof. econs., 1967-68; assoc. prof. mgmt. sci. U. Colo., Boulder, 1968-72, prof. mgmt. sci. and info. systems, 1972-84, head div. mgmt. sci., 1976-84;

prof. mgmt. sci. Crummer Grad. Sch. Bus., Rollins Coll., Winter Park, Fla., 1984-2000, faculty pres. Crummer Grad. Sch. Bus., 1992-93, prof. emeritus, 2000—. Vis. Fulbright prof. mgmt. sci. U. Nairobi, 1978-79; cons. in field. Co-author: (with E.B. Oppermann) Business and Economic Statistics, 3d edit., 1986; (with J. Dinkel, G. Kochenberger) Management Science: Text and Applications, 1978, Quantitative Tools for Decision Support Using IFPS, 1986, Management Science: A Spreadsheet Approach for Windows, 1996. Served with USAF, 1965-68. Ford Found. fellow, 1965 Achievements include research, publs. in field. Home: 322 Bellingrath Ter Deland FL 32724

**PLANETA, KATHLEEN M.,** music educator; d. Thomas Joseph and Joan marie Maney; m. Stephen J. Planeta, July 11, 1981; children: Nicholas, Katherine. BSN magna cum laude, U. Mass., 1985. RN Mass., 1985. RN Mass. Gen. Hosp., Boston, 1985—86, Dedham (Mass.) Express Care, 1988—96; piano tchr. Westwood, Mass., 1997—. Guest pianist Christ Episcopal Ch., Hyde Park, Mass., 1998—2003; guest organist Beechwood Congl. Ch., Cohasset, Mass., 2004; cantor, pianist, organist St. Margaret Mary's Ch., Westwood, 2001—. Mem.: Am. Guild Organists, New Eng. Piano Tchrs. Assn., Nat. Guild Piano Tchrs., Am. Coll. Musicians. E-mail: Kathyplaneta@comcast.net.

**PLANITZER, RUSSELL E.,** computer company executive; b. 1944; Student, U.S. Naval Acad, 1966, Harvard U., 1974; MBA, Harvard Bus. Sch. Chmn. bd. dirs. Computervision Corp., Bedford, Mass., 1974—; gen. ptnr. J.H. Whitney & Co., N.Y.C., 1981—93; chmn. bd. dirs., CFO DR Holdings Inc. of Del., 1990—; CEO Computervision (formerly Prime Computer); mng. prin. Lazard Tech. Ptnrs. Bd. dirs. Kubi Software, GGN, Tazz Software, Interwise, NetByTel, New River, Pass Key.com and Quantum Bridge Named CEO of Year, D.H. Brown Assocs., 1995. Office: Lazard Tech Partners 48th Floor 30 Rockefeller Plz New York NY 10020 Office Phone: 212-632-6000. Office Fax: 212-332-8677.

**PLANK, BETSY (MRS. SHERMAN V. ROSENFIELD),** public relations counsel; b. Tuscaloosa, Ala., Apr. 3, 1924; d. Richard Jeremiah and Bettye (Hood) P.; m. Sherman V. Rosenfield, Apr. 10, 1954. Continuity dir. radio sta. KQV, Pitts., 1944-47; account exec. Mitchell McKeown Orgn., Chgo., 1947-54; pub. rels. counsel Chgo. chpt. A.R.C., 1954-57; dir. pub. rels. Chgo. Coun. on Fgn. Rels., 1957-58; v.p. Ronald Goodman Pub. Rels. Counsel, Chgo., 1958-61; exec. v.p., treas., dir. Daniel J. Edelman, Inc., Chgo., 1961-73; dir. pub. rels. planning AT&T, N.Y.C., 1973-74; dir. external rels. Ill. Bell, Chgo., 1974-90; prin. Betsy Plank Pub. Rels., Chgo., 1990—. Dep. chmn. VII World Congress on Pub. Rels., 1976; co-chmn. nat. commn. on Pub. Rels. Edn., 1984-87; mem. adv. bd. Ill. Issues, 1975—. Bd. dirs. United Way Chgo., 1986-90; chmn. Citizenship Coun. Met. Chgo., 1990-96, Betsy Plank chpt. Pub. Rels. Student Soc. Am., No. Ill. U.; trustee Found. for Pub. Rels. Rsch. and Edn., 1975-80; nat. bd. dirs. Girl Scouts U.S., 1975-85. Recipient Millennium award Coll. Journalism, U. Fla., 2000, Alexander Hamilton award, Inst. Pub. Rels., 2000, Plank Ctr. Pub. Rels. Studies, U. Ala., 2005; named one of World's 40 Leading Pub. Rels. Profls., Pub. Rels. News, 1984, Pub. Rels. Hall of Fame Rowan U., 2005. Fellow Pub. Rels. Soc. Am. (accredited, nat. pres. 1973, Outstanding Profl. award 1977, Outstanding Cmty. Svc. award 1989, Disting. Svc. award 2001, Plank Nat. Scholarships); mem. Ill. Coun. on Econ. Edn. (past chmn., trustee 1974—Extraordinary Leadership award 2001), Internat. Pub. Rels. Assn., Chgo. Network (chmn. 1980-81), Arthur W. Page Soc. (lifetime achievement award 2000), Union League Club of Chgo., Econ. Club Chgo., Zeta Tau Alpha. Presbyterian. Home and Office: 421 W Melrose St Chicago IL 60657-3848

**PLANK, KEVIN A.,** apparel executive; s. William and Jayne Plank; m. Desiree Jacqueline Guerzon, Mar. 2003; 1 child, James. Grad., U. of Md.: Coll. Park, 1997. Spl. teams capt. Md. Football Team; founder, CEO, chmn. Under Armour Inc., 1996—. Bd. trustees U. of Md. Named Entrepreneur of Year award Md. mfg. category, Ernst & Young, 2003. Office: Under Armour Inc Investor Relations 1020 Hull St Baltimore MD 21230-2080 Office Phone: 617-587-8911.*

**PLANK, RAYMOND,** energy executive; b. Mpls., May 29, 1922; s. Raby and Maude (Howe) P.; children:Katherine, Michael, Pamela, Roger, Dana. BA, Yale U., 1944. Founder, partner Plank & Somekawa (accounting), 1946-53; founder, pres. Apache Corp., Houston, 1954—79, CEO 1966—2002, chmn., 1979—. Former dir. St. Paul Securities, Inc. Former chmn. U. Minn. Found.; chmn. Ucross Found.; trustee Com. for Econ. Develop., Washington. Served to 1st lt., bomber pilot USAAF, World War II So. Pacific. Mem. Beta Theta Pi. Clubs: Minneapolis, Woodhill Country. Republican. Office: Apache Corp 1 Post Oak Central Houston TX 77056*

**PLANT, ALBIN MACDONOUGH,** lawyer; b. Balt., July 30, 1937; s. Albin Joseph and Ruth E. (French) P.; m. Anne Warwick Brown, June 17, 1961; children: Katherine, Albin MacDonough Jr., Elizabeth Ashby. BA, Princeton U., N.Y., 1959; LLB, U. Va., Charlottesville, 1963; MLA, Johns Hopkins U., Balt., 1978; DHL, U. Colo., 2006. Bar: Md. 1963, U.S. Dist. Ct. Md. 1963, U.S. Ct. Appeals 1970. Assoc. Semmes, Bowen & Semmes, Balt., 1963-71, ptnr., 1971-91; Stewart, Plant & Blumenthal, Balt., 1991—. Bd. dir. T. Rowe Price Savs. Bank; adj. prof. law U. Balt., 1979, U. Md., 1979—83, 1984—85. Bd. dir. Am. Horticulture Soc., Balt. Choral Arts Soc. Mem.: Am. Coll. Trust and Estate Counsel, Am. Bar Found. (life), Wednesday Law Club, Md. Club (bd. dir.), Lawyers Roundtable. Democrat. Office: 7 St Paul St Baltimore MD 21202-1626 Office Phone: 410-347-0511. Business E-Mail: amplant@spblaw.com.

**PLANT, JOHN CHARLES,** automotive equipment company executive; b. West Bromwich, West Midlands, Eng., Aug. 1, 1953; s. John and Florence (Harrison) P.; m. Christine Ann; children: Alexa Jayne, John Alexander. B in Commerce, Econs., Acctg. and Law, Birmingham U., Eng., 1974. Auditor Touche Ross, Birmingham, 1974-77; financier Lucas Auto Ltd., Birmingham, 1977—, Burnley, Eng., 1983—; mng. dir. Lucas Varity Elec. and Electronics, 1991—97; pres. Lucas Varity Automotive, 1999; pres., CEO TRW Chassis; gen. mgr. TRW Automotive; exec. v.p. TRW, 1999—2001; co-CEO TRW Inc.; pres., CEO TRW Automotive, Livonia, Mich., 2001—. Bd. dirs. Martin Currie Portfolio Investment Trust PLC. Fellow Inst. Chartered Accts. in Eng. and Wales (mng. dir., FCA award 1981). Avocation: tennis. Office: TRW Automotive 12025 Tech Center Dr Livonia MI 48150*

**PLANT, LINDA R.,** music educator; b. Eugene, Oreg., Mar. 25, 1949; d. Robert Ward and Ruth Adeline Johnston; m. Allan F. Plant, June 15, 1968; children: Glenn A., Jason R. Piano tchr. Linda Plant Piano Studio, Springfield, Oreg., 1973—; organist Emerald Baptist Ch., Eugene, Oreg., 1989—. Vol. ARC, Oreg., 1983—, adminstr., 2001—; mem. bd., sec. Oreg. Camp Cherith, 1977—, pres., 1984-87, 89-94. Mem. Nat. Guild Piano Tchrs. (pres. 1981-84, chmn. 1985-97), Oreg. Music Tchrs. Assn. (state cert., event chmn. 1990-2000, libr. 2001—, dist. pres. 1995-97, state sec. 1996-98). Republican. Baptist. Avocation: lifeguard/canoe instructor for youth camps.

**PLANT, ROBERT ANTHONY,** singer, composer; b. Bromwich, Staffordshire, Eng., Aug. 20, 1948; Previously sang with rock groups Band of Joy and Alexis Korner, singer, composer Led Zeppelin, 1968—80, world-wide concert tours, performed (films) The Song Remains the Same, 1976; composer: (songs) Black Dog, Stairway to Heaven, D'Yer Mak'Er; albums include (with Led Zeppelin) Led Zeppelin, Led Zeppelin II, 1969, Led Zeppelin III, 1970, Led Zeppelin IV, Houses of the Holy, 1973, Physical Graffiti, 1975, The Song Remains the Same, Presence, 1976, In Through the Out Door, 1979, albums include (with Led Zepplin) Coda, 1982, solo albums include Pictures at Eleven, 1982, The Principle of Moments, Shaken N' Stirred, 1985, Now and Zen, 1988, Manic Nirvana, 1990, Fate of Nations, 29 Palms/Whole Lotta Love, 1994, No Quarter: Jimmy Page & Robert Plant Unledded, 1994, Walking into Calrksdale, 1998, Dreamland, 2002, albums (with the Honeydrippers) The Honeydrippers, Vol. I, 1985, performed at LIVE AID in Phila., with Jimmy Page and John Paul Jones, 1985; contbr.

soundtrack to movie Wayne's World 2. Named to Rock and Roll Hall of Fame, 1995; recipient Grammy nomination (Best Hard Rock Performance) for "Calling to You", 1994, Grammy, 1999. Office: care Atlantic Rec Corp 1290 Avenue Of The Americas New York NY 10104-0101

**PLANTS, WALTER DALE,** retired elementary school educator, minister; b. Middlefield, Ohio, June 8, 1942; s. William E. and Hazel A. Plants; m. Sarah A. Gaddis, July 5, 1962; children: Dale Anthony, Jeanette Marie. BD, Azusa Pacific U., 1967; MEd, U. Nev., 1970. Cert. elem. tchr., ednl. adminstr. Elem. tchr. Churchill County Sch. Dist., Fallon, Nev., 1967—69, 1970—72, elem tchr., 1988—2001; grad. asst. U. Nev., Reno, 1969-70; tchr. Kingman (Ariz.) Elem. Sch. Dist. #4, 1972-77; head sci. program E. C. Best Elem. Sch., Fallon, 1988—2001; ret., 2001. Adj. instr. Ariz. State U., Tempe, 1973-77; cons. sci. Ariz. State Dept. Edn., 1975-77. Bd. dirs. Solar Energy Commn. Mohave County, Ariz., 1974; coord. County Sci. Fair, 1988-93; active Western Regional Sci. Fair Com.; sci. fair coord. Churchill County, 1989-94; mem. com. Regional Sci. Fair, 1992-94; min. non-demoninational ch., 1969-2005. HEW fellow, 1969; NSF grantee, 1973; AIMS Found. scholar, 1988; recipient Ariz. State PTA award, 1977, Ruth Neldon award Ariz. State Dept., 1977, Conservation award Big Sandy Natural Resources Conservation Dist. Ariz., 1976, Community Builder Svc. award Masons, Fallon, 1991, Disting. Leadership award, 1991-93; named State Tchr. of Yr. Nev. PTA, 1991, Conservation Tchr. of Yr., 1991; named to Congl. Select Edn. panel U.S. Congress, 1993. Mem. NEA, AAAS, Nat. Sci. Tchrs. Assn., Nat. Coun. Tchrs. Math., Internat. Reading Assn., Churchill County Edn. Assn. (Tchr. of Yr. 1989), Internat. Platform Assn., Nat. Arbor Day Found., World Wildlife Fund, Nat. Parks and Conservation Assn., Nat. Audubon Soc., Nev. State Tchrs. of Yr. Assn. (pres, 1994-96, pres. 1996-97), Phi Delta Kappa. Personal E-mail: wpla@charter.net.

**PLAPINGER, WILLIAM A.,** lawyer; b. Washington, July 23, 1952; s. Jerome S. and Alice E. Plapinger; m. Kathleen J. Murray, Oct. 11, 1982; children: Alexander S., Elizabeth L., Thomas A. Student, Westfield Coll., U. London, 1972—73; AB, Vassar Coll., 1974; JD, NYU, 1978. Bar: NY 1979, US Dist. Ct. (ea. dist.) NY 1979, US Dist. Ct. (so. dist.) 1979, US Supreme Ct. 1983. Assoc. Sullivan & Cromwell, NY, 1976—86, ptnr. NY, 1986—87, London, 1987—95, mng. ptnr. Londin office, coord. European offices, 2000—. Trustee Vassar Coll., Poughkeepsie, 1996—, chair bd. trustees, 2006—; trustee Am. Sch., London, 1996—. Mem.: India Ho., Queenwood Golf Club, Vineyard Golf Club, Links Club. Office: Sullivan & Cromwell LLP 1 New Fetter Lane London EC4A 1AN England Address: 125 Broad St 32nd Fl New York NY 10004-2498 Office Phone: 44(0)20 7959-8900. Business E-Mail: plapingerw@sullcrom.com.

**PLAPP, BRYCE VERNON,** biochemistry educator; b. DeKalb, Ill., Sept. 11, 1939; s. Vernon Edgar and Eleanor Barbara (Kautz) P.; m. Rosemary Kuhn, June 13, 1962; children— Brendan Bryce, Laurel Andrea BS, Mich. State U., East Lansing, 1961; PhD, U. Calif.-Berkeley, 1966. Research assoc. J.W. Goethe U., Frankfurt/Main, Germany, 1966-68; research assoc. Rockefeller U., N.Y.C., 1968-70; faculty U. Iowa, Iowa City, 1970—, prof. biochemistry, 1979—. Contbr. articles to profl. jours.; mem. editorial bd. Archives Biochemistry and Biophysics. Am. Cancer Soc. fellow, 1966-68 Mem. Am. Soc. for Biochemistry and Molecular Biology, Am. Chem. Soc., Sigma Xi Avocations: travel, sports. Office: Univ Iowa Dept Biochemistry 4-712 Iowa City IA 52242 Office Phone: 319-335-7909. E-mail: bv-plapp@uiowa.edu.

**PLASIL, FRANZ,** physicist; b. Prague, Czechoslovakia, May 17, 1939; came to U.S., 1960; s. Frank and Eva (Wenger) P.; m. Catherine Logan, Feb. 15, 1964 (div. Sept. 1979); two children: Maia, David; m. Carol Baratz, Apr. 12, 1980. BS, Queen Mary Coll., U. London, 1960; PhD, U. Calif., Berkeley, 1964. Chemist Lawrence Berkeley (Calif.) Lab., 1964-65; rsch. assoc. Brookhaven Nat. Lab., Upton, NY, 1965-67; rsch. staff physics div. Oak Ridge (Tenn.) Nat. Lab., 1967-78, group leader physics div., 1978-86, sect. head physics div., 1986-99; fellow U. Tenn.-Battelle, 1999—2002; hon. rsch. prof. emeritus, 1999—. Co-author: The Western Humanities, 1991 (named articles to Annals of Physics, Phys. Rev., Phys. Rev. Letters, Nuc. Phys., Phys. Letters. Recipient Alexander von Humboldt award 1985, E. Mach medal of honor Acad. of Sci. of the Czech Republic, 1998. Fellow Am. Phys. Soc. Achievements include rsch. in fission-imposed limits on the stability of rotating nuclei and rsch. in nucleus-nucleus collisions at ultrarelativistic energies. Home: 964 W Outer Dr Oak Ridge TN 37830-8607 Personal E-mail: plasil@comcast.net.

**PLASKETT, THOMAS GEORGE,** transportation executive, director; b. Raytown, Mo., Dec. 24, 1943; s. Warren E. and Frances S. P.; m. Linda Lee Maxey, June 8, 1968; children: Kimberly, Keith. B in Indsl. Engring., Kettering U., 1965; MBA, Harvard U. Supr. indsl. engring. GM, Flint, Mich., 1968, supt. indsl. engring., 1969-73, sr. staff asst., treas. N.Y.C., 1973; asst. contr. Am. Airlines, N.Y.C., 1974, v.p. mktg. adminstrn., 1975-76, sr. v.p. fin., 1976-80, sr. v.p. mktg. Dallas, 1980—86; pres., CEO Continental Airlines Inc., Houston, until 1988; chmn., CEO, pres. Pan Am Corp., NYC, 1988—91; chmn. Fox Run Capital Assocs., 1991—; dir., interim pres., CEO, acting CFO Greyhound Lines, Inc., Dallas, 1994-95, chmn., 1995—99; vice-chmn. Legend Airlines, Dallas, 1997—2001, exec. v.p., 1999—2001; pres., CEO Probex Corp., Dallas, 1999—2000, chmn., 1999—2000. Bd. dir. Radioshack Corp., Ft. Worth, Novell, Inc. 2002-2006, non-exec. chmn., 2006-, Waltham, Mass., Provo, Utah, Alcon Inc., Ft. Worth, Smart & Final, Inc., Calif. Trustee Kettering U., Flint. Avocations: golf, skiing, squash. Office: 5215 N O Connor Blvd Ste 1070 Irving TX 75039-3738 Office Phone: 972-869-6595. Business E-Mail: tom@foxruncapital.com.

**PLASKON, JUANITA EVE,** biotechnologist; educ adm; b. Stroudsburg, Pa., Oct. 6, 1971; d. Marion Irene Thorne; m. Michael George Plaskon, May 30, 1998; children: Savannah Marie, Cole Dakota. BA, Johns Hopkins U., Balt., 1993; PhD, U. of Pitts., 2000. Faculty C.C. of Allegheny County, Pitts., 2000—. Fellow Predoctoral Minority fellow, NIH, 1997—99; scholar Undergrad. scholar, AAUW, 1989—90, J.F. Goodwin Undergrad. scholar, J.F. Goodwin Com., 1989—93. D-Liberal. Achievements include development of of the Biotechnology program for projected growth sector in Western PA. Partership established in a 2+2+2 program linking public high schools, community college, and 4-year colleges. Avocations: playing piano, birdwatching. Home: 738 Greenleaf Dr Monroeville PA 15146 Office: Community College of Allegheny County 808 Ridge Ave Pittsburgh PA 15212 Personal E-mail: jeplaskon@hotmail.com. Business E-Mail: jplaskon@ccac.edu.

**PLASTOW, EDWARD GEORGE,** business administration educator; b. Mitchell, S.D., July 8, 1952; s. Dr. and Mrs. Robert L. Plastow; m. Aug. 23, 1972; children: Virginia, Al, Jeannie, Lori, William, Carl, Etta, Sam, Robert, Sharla. BA, Dakota Wesleyan U., 1973; MBA, Nat. U., 1988; PhD in Adminstrn./Mgmt., Walden U., 1998. CPA, S.D. Sr. acct. Ernst & Ernst, CPA's, L.A., 1973-75; sr. mgr., dir. client svc. and dept. Touche Ross, CPA's, Denver and Sacramento, 1975-86; v.p. fin. Blue Anchor, Inc., Sacramento, 1986-88; prof., coach Dakota Wesleyan U., Mitchell, S.D., 1988-99; chair bus. dept., head basketball coach Southeastern Coll., Lakeland, Fla., 1999—. Faculty rep., bus. affairs com. Dakota Wesleyan U., 1988-91, 95—; ednl. tng. and CPA cons. various orgns., 1990—. Contbr. articles to local newspapers. Fin. advisor, vol. Mitchell Christian Sch., 1988-96. Named Young Alumnus of the Yr., Dakota Wesleyan U., Mitchell, 1988. Mem. AICPA, S.D. Soc. CPA's (state com. 1994-97), Rotary Internat. (bd. mem., com. chmn.). Republican. Avocations: contemporary christian music, reading, youth coaching. Home: 1102 Country Oaks Ln Lakeland FL 33810 Office: Southeastern Coll 1000 Longfellow Blvd Lakeland FL 33801

**PLATE, THOMAS GORDON,** columnist, educator; b. NYC, May 17, 1944; s. John William and Irene (Henry) P.; m. Andrea I. Margolis, Sept 22, 1979; 1 child, Ashley Alexandra. AB, Amherst Coll., 1966; MPA, Princeton U., 1968. Writer Newsweek, N.Y.C., 1968-70; editor Newsday, L.I., N.Y.,

1970-72; sr. editor N.Y. Mag., N.Y.C., 1972-75; editor edit. page L.A. Herald Examiner, 1978-82; sr. editor Time Mag., N.Y.C., 1982-83; editor in chief Family Weekly, N.Y.C., 1984-85; editor edit. pages N.Y. Newsday, N.Y.C., 1986-89, L.A. Times, 1989-95, Times Op-Ed Page columnist, contbg. editor, 1995—. Adj. prof. UCLA Pub. Policy Sch. and Letters and Scis.; mem. founders bd. UCLA Sch. Pub. Policy; founder Asia Pacific Media Network; participant World Econ. Forum, Davos. Author: Understanding Doomsday, 1971, Crime Pays!, 1975, Secret Police, 1981; co-author: Commissioner, 1978. Recipient Best Deadline Writing award Am. Soc. Newspaper Editors, 1981, Best Edit. awards L.A. Press Club, 1979, 80, 81, Best Edit. award Calif. Newspaper Pubs. Assn., 1991, 92, 94; media fellow Stanford U. Mem. Pacific Coun. on Internat. Rels., Century Assn. (N.Y.C.), Phi Beta Kappa. Avocations: tennis, photography, travel. Office: LA Times 405 Hilgard Ave Los Angeles CA 90095-9000

**PLATER, WILLIAM MARMADUKE,** literature and language professor, educator, academic administrator; b. East St. Louis, Ill., July 26, 1945; s. Everett Marmaduke and Marguerite (McBride) P.; m. Gail Maxwell, Oct. 16, 1971; children: Elizabeth Rachel, David Matthew. BA, U. Ill., 1967, MA in English, 1969, PhD in English, 1973. Asst. dir. Unit One, asst. to dean Coll. Liberal Arts and Scis. U. Ill., Urbana, 1971-72, acting dir. Unit One, 1972-73, asst. dean Coll. Arts and Scis., 1973-74, asst. dir. Sch. Humanities, 1974-77, assoc. dir., 1977-83, assoc. coordinator interdisciplinary programs, 1977-83; prof. English, dean Sch. Liberal Arts Ind U., Indpls., 1983-87; dean of faculties Ind. U.-Purdue U., Indpls., 1987—, exec. vice chancellor, 1988—, acting chancellor, 2003. Bd. dirs. Met. Indpls. Pub. Broadcasting, Inc.; cons. in field. Author: The Grim Phoenix: Reconstructing Thomas Pynchon, 1978, also articles, revs., poetry. Trustee Coun. for Adult and Experiential Learning, 1995—; bd. dirs. Ind. Com. for Humanities, 1986—92, Ind. Repertory Theatre, 1987—93, Children's Mus., 1992—2001, U. Ill. YMCA, Urbana, 1982—83, Herron Gallery Contemporary Art, 1987—93; bd. govs. Ind. U. Ctr. on Philanthropy, 1997—; bd. dirs. Midwest Univs. Consortium for Internat. Activities, Inc., 1996—98. Recipient Program Innovation prize Am. Acad. Ednl. Devel., 1982. Home: 6477 Oxbow Way Indianapolis IN 46220-Office Phone: 317-274-4500. E-mail: wplater@iupui.edu.

**PLATFOOT, CHRISTOPHER W.,** systems administrator, information technology executive; b. Greenville, Ohio, June 18, 1966; s. Willard Ralph Platfoot and Shiela Ann Coffield. A of Applied Bus., Edison State Coll., 2001. Shift supr. Clopay Corp., Russia, Ohio, 1990—99; pc coord. Upper Valley Med. Ctr., Troy, 1999—2006, sys. administr., 2005—. Condr. Fraternal Order Eagles, Minster, Ohio, 2004—06. With USN, 1998—2006. Decorated Mil. Outstanding Vol. Svc. medal USN, Coast Guard Spl. Ops. Ribbon USCG, Coast Guard Meritorious Unit Commendation, Sea Svc. Deployment Ribbon USN, Navy & Marine Corps Commendation medal Dept. of Navy, Navy & Marine Corps Achievement medal, Navy Achievement medal, Navy Conduct medal, Navy Res. Meritorious Svc., Nat. Def. medal, War on Terrorism Svc. medal USN, Armed Forces Res. medal; scholar, Local Sponsor, 2001. Mem.: Phi Theta Kappa (life Internat. Scholastic Order 2001). Roman Catholic. Avocations: travel, softball, skiing. Office: Upper Valley Med Ctr 3130 N Dixie Hwy Troy OH 45373 Office Phone: 937-440-7560. Business E-Mail: cplatfoot@uvmc.com.

**PLATIS, JAMES GEORGE,** secondary school educator; b. Detroit, Mar. 23, 1927; s. Sam and Myra (Theodore) P.; m. Mary Lou Campbell, Aug. 16, 1974. BS in Physical Edn., Ind. U., 1955, MS in Edn., 1965; postgrad., Ind. State U., 1967. Cert. physical edn. tchr., Ind. Foreman Cast Armor, Inc., East Chicago, Ind., 1951-53, Youngstown Sheet & Tube, East Chicago, 1953-54; dir., tchr. East Chicago Pub. Schs., 1955—. Sports editor East Chicago Globe/Calumet News, 1973-78, Herald Newspapers, Merrillville, Ind., 1973-78; asst. dir. No. Ind. State Sports Mus., 1984-99. Contbr. articles to newspapers, jours. Founder East Chicago Hall of Fame, 1975, Little Olympics, East Chicago, 1956; pres. Ind. Am. Amateur Baseball Congress, 1954-57, commr., 1984-98; dir. No. Ind. State Sports Mus., 1988-00. With AUS, 1945-47, ETO. Named to Ind. Amateur Baseball Hall of Fame, 1962, East Chicago Hall of Fame, 1976, All-Am. Amateur Baseball Congress, 1955, 56, The Athletic Congress Masters All-Am., 1986-98, 99, 2000, 2001-02; selected to 90 Yr. Greatest Athletes in East Chicago History, Nat. Athletic Congress, 1990; named Amateur Coach of Yr., U.S. Baseball Fedn. Inc., 1990, Amateur Runner-up Coach of Yr., 1988; recipient 53 World and 61 Nat. No. 1 track rankings, Athletic Congress Masters, 1989-98, 2000, 2001-02, 16 League Batting Titles, 12 MV League Players awards; Ind. Jr. Legion State Champions, All-State Batting Champions, MVP in tournament, Conf. Baseball Champions, 1943, 44, 45, All-Conf. Team, 1944-45, Conf. Batting Champion, 1944, Team Cptn., 1945, All-Midwest team, Best Outfielder, 1944; 23 times Ind. all-state team; Ind. Nat. Baseball State Champions; mem. team won 53 League Championships, 54 Playoff championships, 41 Ind. State Baseball Championships, 5 Ind. State Champions Runner Up, 7 World Regional Titles, 5 World Finalists, 2 runner-up World Champions, Big Ten baseball champions Ind. U., 1949, Best Outfielder Congress All-State team, Ill., Ind. Bi-State Champions, 1950; Nat. C.I.O. Baseball Championship, 1951, 12 Times League Mgr. Of The Year, 1982-96; Big Ten Baseball Champions, Ind. U., 1949; named Athlete of Yr. Ind. Masters Track and Field, 1992, World Sr. Olympic Masters Track & Field Champion, Spain, 6 gold medals, named Best Performer, 3 Masters Track & Field World Records, 1992, Fla. Masters Track and Field Athlete of Yr., 1994-98; recipient 74 State Ind. Track and Field Individual Gold medals, 1983-99, 2000-02, 84 Ind. state regional individual gold medals, 1983-98, 2000-02, 322 All Am. Masters Track and Field Certs., 1986-99, 2000-02, 39 Ill. Grand Prix individual titles, 1989-92, 45 Mid-West Track and Field individual titles, 1989-92, 5 gold medals, silver medal World Sr. Olympic Masters Track & Field, 1996, Ga., 5 Masters Track & Field World Records, 1997, 2 Masters Track & Field World Records, 1998 Nat. Senior Olympic Qualifie, 1991, 93, 95, 97, 99, 2001, 03, 4 Gold medals, 2 World Records Nat. Sr. Olympics, 1999-2001, 7 gold medals World Sr. Olympic Masters Track and Field, Sydney, Australia, 2000, 5 World Records, selected Best Performer; named Internat. Man of the Yr. in Edn., 1991-92, 93, Professional of the Yr. in Edn., 1991, Master Track and Field All-Am., 1986-2003, Northwest Ind. Intriguing Family of the Yr., 2002, 8 Decades of Baseball, Individual & Team Records in Baseball Hall of Fame, Cooperstown, N.Y., 2003, Youth award Chgo. Profl. Pitch & Hit Club, 2005. Fellow Nat. Assn. Basketball Coaches, Am. Assn. Health, Phys. Edn. and Recreation; mem. Athletic Dirs. Assn. Sportswriters Guild, VFW, Am. Legion, WWII Meml. (82nd Airborne Divsn., 1st Inf. Divsn. 1998), Mens Club Ind. U. Republican. Avocations: reading, running, baseball, writing.

**PLATNICK, NORMAN I.,** curator, entomologist; b. Bluefield, W.Va., Dec. 30, 1951; s. Philip and Fannie (Kascenewsky) P.; m. Nancy Stewart Price, June 14, 1970; 1 child, William Durin. BS in Biology, Concord Coll., 1968; MS in Zoology, Mich. State U., 1970; PhD in Biology, Harvard U., 1973. Asst. curator Am. Mus. Natural History, N.Y.C., 1973-77, assoc. curator, 1977-82, curator, 1982-98, chmn. dept. entomology, 1987-94, Peter J. Solomon Family curator, 1998—; program dir. biotic surveys and inventories NSF, 2002—03. Sci. attaché Consulate of Gondwana, N.Y.C., 1976—. Author: The World Spider Catalog; co-author: Systematics and Biogeography, 1981; co-editor: Advances in Cladistics, 1983. V.p. Ctr. Internat. de Documentation Arachnologie, 1986-89 (pres. 1995-98). Fellow Willi Hennig Soc. (founder, pres. 1990-92); mem. Am. Arachnological Soc. (charter, membership sec. 1976—2002). Office: Am Mus Natural History Central Pk W At 79th St W New York NY 10024 Office Phone: 212-769-5612. Business E-Mail: platnick@amnh.org.

**PLATSOUCAS, CHRIS DIMITRIOS,** immunologist; b. Athens, Greece, Apr. 17, 1951; came to U.S., 1973; s. Dimitrios Evagelos and Maria (Tsonidis) P.; m. Emilia L. Oleszak, Oct. 18, 1985. BS, U. Patras (Greece), 1973; postgrad., Purdue U., 1974; PhD, MIT, 1978. Rsch. fellow/assoc. Meml. Sloan-Kettering Cancer Ctr., N.Y.C., 1978—81, asst. mem., 1982—85, asst. prof., 1981-85, head lab. biol. response modifiers, 1981-85; assoc. prof. Baylor U., immunology M.D. Anderson Cancer Ctr., Houston, 1985-89, prof., dep. chmn., 1989-93, Ashbel Smith professorship, 1991-92, H.L. and O. Stringer professorship in cancer rsch., 1992-93; L.H. Carnell prof. and

chmn. dept. microbiology, immunology Temple U. Sch. Medicine, Phila., 1993—; acting dean Coll. Sci. and Tech. Temple U., Phila., 1998-2000, dean Coll. Sci. and Tech., 2000—04. Biotech. cons., sci. reviewer study sects. NIH, Bethesda, Md., 1982—. Contbr. numerous articles to profl. jours. Nat. Rsch. Svc. award NIH, 1978-79; grantee NIH, Am. Cancer Soc., State of Tex., many others. Mem. Am. Assn. Immunologists, Am. Soc. Hematology, Am. Assn. Biochem & Molecular Biology, Soc. Investigative Pathology, Am. Assn. Cancer Rsch. Greek Orthodox. Achievements include patents in field; research on human T cell immunology, on T-cell antigen receptors, on tumor-infiltrating lymphocytes in malignant melanoma and ovarian carcinoma, on organ transplantation, on chronic rejection, on AIDS, and on autoimmune diseases. Office: Temple U Sch Medicine Dept Microbiology and Immunology 3400 N Broad St Philadelphia PA 19140-5104 Office Phone: 215-707-7929. Business E-Mail: chris.platsoucas@temple.edu.

**PLATT, FRANKLIN DEWITT,** retired history professor; b. Marion, La., Nov. 15, 1932; s. Robert Baxter and Ethel Estelle (White) P.; m. Dixie Ferguson, Aug. 4, 1956; 1 dau. Dixie. BA, La. State U., 1955; Rockefeller Bros. Theol. fellow, Union Theol. Sem., 1955-56; A.M., Washington U., St. Louis, 1963, PhD, 1969. Instr. dept. humanities Mich. State U., East Lansing, 1964-69, asst. prof., 1969-72, assoc. prof., 1972-77, prof., 1977-89, asst. chmn. dept. humanities, 1971-78, chmn., 1978-80, prof. history, 1989-96, prof. emeritus, 1997—. Co-author: The Western Humanities, 1991 (named Best Coll. Textbook Bookbuilders West 1998), Readings in the Western Humanities, 1994. Served with USNR, 1956-60. also: 5190 Far Oak Cir Sarasota FL 34238-3303 Address: 1134 Southlawn Ave East Lansing MI 48823 Business E-Mail: plattf@msu.edu.

**PLATT, GEORGE MILO,** university administrator; b. Rapid City, S.D., Jan. 1, 1931; s. George Lee and Josephine M. (Paulson) P.; B.S., S.D. State U., 1953; M.A., Syracuse U., 1955, Ph.D., 1962. Asst. prof. U. S.D., 1962-65, U. Iowa, 1965-69; dir. planning and instl. research Wichita (Kans.) State U., 1969-79, assoc. v.p., 2nd assoc. prof. pub. adminstrn., 1869—97; Ford Found. adv. to secs. of local govt., East and West Pakistan, 1963, 65-66, 68. Served with AUS, 1955-57. Mem. Am. Soc. for Public Adminstrn., Western History Assn., Am. Planning Assn., Soc. for Coll. and Univ. Planning. Author: (with Richard O. Niehoff) Local Government in East Pakistan, 1964; (with Alan L. Clem) A Bibliography of South Dakota Government and Politics, 1965, (with others) Administrative Problems in Pakistan, 1966, (with others) Presdl. Ptnrs.: First Ladies of the University, 2001; contbg. author: The Coopertown Symposium on Baseball and American Culture, 2002. Office: Wichita State Univ Campus Box 155 Wichita KS 67260-0155 Office Phone: 316-978-6587. Business E-Mail: george.platt@wichita.edu.

**PLATT, JAN KAMINIS,** former county official; b. St. Petersburg, Fla., Sept. 27, 1936; d. Peter Clifton and Adele (Diamond) Kaminis; m. William R. Platt, Feb. 8, 1963; 1 child, Kevin Peter. BA, Fla. State U., 1958; postgrad., U. Fla. Law Sch., 1958-59, U. Va., 1962, Vanderbilt U., 1964. Pub. sch. tchr. Hillsborough County, Tampa, Fla., 1959-60; field dir. Girl Scouts Suncoast Coun., Tampa, 1960-62; city councilman Tampa City Coun., 1974-78; county commr. Hillsborough County, 1978—94, country commr., 1996—2004; chmn. Hillsborough County Bd. County Commrs., 1980-81, 83-84, 98-99, ret., 1994, re-elected, 1996, chmn., 1998-99, County Charter Rev. Bd., 2005—06; cp-chair Countrywide Cultural Plan, 2006—. Chmn. Tampa Bay Regional Planning Coun., 1982, West Coast Regional Water Supply Authority, Tampa, 1985, Hillsborough County Coun. Govts., 1976, 79, Agy. Bay Mgmt., Hills Environ. Protection Commn., Sunshine Amendment Drive 7th Congrl. Dist., Tampa, 1976, Cmty. Action Agy., Tampa, 1981, 83-84, chmn. pro tem Tampa Charter Revision Commn., 1975, chmn. Prison Sitting Task Force, Tampa, 1983, Tampa Housing Study Com., 1983, Met. Planning Orgn., Tampa, 1984, Bd. Tax Adjustment, Tampa, 1984, chmn. Hartline, 2002-03, Friendship Trailbridge Oversight Com., 2002-03, Tampa Bay Water, 2003-04; appointee Constn. Revision Commn., Fla., 1977, HRS Dist. IV Adv. Coun., Fla.; mem. Hillsborough County Expy. Authority, Taxicab Commn., Ch. Hills Cmty. Youth Coun.; vice chmn. steering com. Nat. Counties Environ. Task Force; pres. Suncoast Girl Scout Coun., 1973-74, Ch. Head Start Cmty. Found., 2005; chmn. County Charter Rev. Bd., 2005. Bd. dirs. March of Dimes, Tampa, The Fla. Orch., Tampa, Tampa Bay Sierra, Tampa Audubon; trustee Hillsborough County Hosp. Authority, Tampa, 1984-94; pres. Citizens Alert, Tampa, Bay View Garden Club; v.p. Hillsborough County Bar Aux.; mem. advt. bd. Northside Cmty. Mental Health Ctr.: Access House, Tampa; active Arts Coun. Tampa-Hillsborough County, 1983-85, 96-2001, Drug Abuse Coordinating Coun. Orgn., Tampa, Bd. Criminal Justice, Tampa, Fla. Coun. on Aging, Inebriate Task Force, Tampa, Tampa Downtown Devel. Authority Task Force, Tampa Sports Authority, Tampa Area Mental Health Bd., Children's Study Commn., Manahill Area Agy. on Aging, Tampa, Athena Soc., Tampa Area Com. Fgn. Affairs, LWV; pres. Hills Children's Coun., Headstart Found.; bd. dirs. Arts Coun.; exec. com. Tampa Performing Arts Ctr., chmn. charter rev. bd.; mem. Com. of 100. Recipient Athena award, Women in Comm., 1976, Spessard Holland Meml. award, Tampa Bay Com. for Good Govt., 1979, First Lady of Yr. award, Beta Sigma Phi, 1980, First Ann. Humanitarian award, Nat. Orgn. of Prevention of Animal Suffering, 1981, Women Helping Women award, Soroptimist Internat. Tampa, 1983, Good Govt. award, Tampa Jaycees, 1983, LWV, 1983, John Books Meml. award, Fla. Audubon Soc., 1989, Girl Scout Woman of Distinction award, 1996, Girl Scout Thanks award, 1996, Libney Bell award, Hillsborough County Bar Assn., 2000, Black Bear award, Suncoast and Tampa Bay Groups of the Sierra Club, 2001, Eliza Wolff award, Tampa United Meth. Ctrs., Outstanding Leadership in Local Environ. Protection, Fla. Local Environ. Resource Agys., 2002, Lifetime Achievement award for outstanding leadership in local environ. protection, 2004, Communicator of Yr., Tampa Ednl. Cable Consortium, 2005, Disting. Alumna award, Fla. State U., 2005, Tampa Bay Ethics award, Tampa U. Ctr. Ethics, 2005, Dan Hanson Conservationist Yr., Frank Sargenat Fishing Expo, 2006. Mem. Am. Judicature Soc., State Assn. County Commrs. Fla. (at-large dir.), AAUW (bd. dirs.), Mortar Board (Disting. Lifetime Mem. award 2006), Garnet Key, Phi Beta Kappa (pres. local alumni), Phi Kappa Phi. Democrat. Episcopalian. Home: 3531 Village Way Tampa FL 33629-8914 Home Fax: 813-805-9622.

**PLATT, JEFFREY LOUIS,** surgeon, director, immunologist, educator, pediatric nephrologist; b. New Rochelle, NY, Mar. 21, 1949; s. Charles Alfred and Paula Platt; m. Agnes M. Schipper. BA in Politics with honors, NYU, 1971; postgrad., Columbia U., 1971-73; MD, U. So. Calif., 1977. Diplomate Am. Bd. Pediatrics, Nat. Bd. Med. Examiners. Intern in pediatrics Children's Hosp. L.A., 1977-78, resident, 1978-79, Della M. Mudd resident, 1979-80; med. fellow in pediatric nephrology U. Minn., Mpls., 1980-85, instr. dept. pediatrics, 1985-86, asst. prof., 1986-88, assoc. prof. pediatrics and cell biology and neuroanatomy, 1988-92; prof. surgery, pediatrics and immunology depts. Duke U., Durham, NC, 1992—98, Dorothy W. and Joseph W. Beard prof. exptl. surgery, 1994—98; prof. surgery immunology and pediatrics Mayo Clinic, Rochester, Minn., 1998—, dir. transplantation biology, vice chair surgery rsch., 2006—. Mem. editl. bd.: Transplantation, Transplant Immunology, Xenotransplantation, Jour. Immunology, Cellular Immunology; contbr. over 450 articles to med. jours.; author: 4 books. Recipient Clinician-Scientist award Am. Heart Assn., 1983-88, Established Investigator award Am. Heart Assn., 1988-93, Inst. Medicine of NAS. Mem. AAAS, NIH (Merit award), Assn. Am. Physicians, Am. Heart Assn (coun. kidney in cardiovasc. disease, coun. basic sci.), Internat. Soc. Nephrology, Am. Assn. Immunologists, Am. Fedn. Clin. Rsch., Am. Soc. Nephrology, Am. Assn. Pathologists, Soc. for Devel. Biology, Clin. Immunology Soc., Soc. Pediatric Rsch., Soc. Glycobiology, Soc. Exptl. Biology and Medicine, Alpha Omega Alpha. Office: Mayo Found Medical Scis Bldg Rm 2 Rochester MN 55905-0001 Business E-Mail: platt.jeffrey@mayo.edu.

**PLATT, JONATHAN JAMES,** lawyer; b. Southampton, N.Y., Aug. 3, 1950; s. William Bangs Jr. and Edith Elizabeth (Guldi) P.; m. Linda Lee Tiska, Sept. 23, 1978. BS in Fgn. Svc., Georgetown U., 1972; JD, Fordham U., 1976. Bar: N.Y. 1977, U.S. Dist. Ct. (ea. dist.) N.Y. 1988, U.S. Ct. Appeals (2d cir.) 1988. Assoc. William B. Platt, Jr., Southampton, 1977-78; ptnr. Platt & Platt, Southampton, 1978-80, Platt, Platt & Platt, Southampton, 1980-2000; pvt.

practice Southampton, 2001—. Counsel Elks, Southampton, 1983—. Mem. ABA (gen. practice sect., probate and trust sect., real property sect., 1985—, sect. of law practice mgmt, 1993—), N.Y. State Bar Assn. (real property sect., trusts and estates law, gen. practice sect. 1977—, invited participant statewide conf. solo and small firm practitioners 1991), Suffolk County Bar Assn. (real property com., solo and small firm task force 1992-97, Pres.' award of merit 1994), Elks (hon., exalted ruler 1982-83, hon. life, dist. govt. rels. chmn. 1991-94, esquire to dist. dep. 1993-94). Republican. Roman Catholic. Avocations: photography, videography, golf, scuba diving. Office: 99 Sanford Pl Southampton NY 11968-3338 Office Phone: 631-283-0099. E-mail: jplattesq@aol.com.

**PLATT, JOSEPH BEAVEN,** former college president; b. Portland, Oreg., Aug. 12, 1915; s. William Bradbury and Mary (Beaven) P.; m. Jean Ferguson Rusk, Feb. 9, 1946; children: Ann Ferguson Walker, Elizabeth Beaven Garrow. BA, U. Rochester, 1937; PhD, Cornell U., 1942; LLD, U. So. Calif., 1969, Claremont McKenna Coll., 1982; DSc, Harvey Mudd Coll., 1981. Instr. physics U. Rochester, NY, 1941-43, from asst. prof. to prof. NY, 1946-56, assoc. chmn. dept. physics NY, 1954-56; staff mem. Radiation Lab. MIT, Cambridge, 1943-46; founding pres. Harvey Mudd Coll., Claremont, Calif., 1956-76, now part-time sr. prof. physics; pres. Claremont Grad. U., 1976-81. Trustee Aerospace Corp., 1972-85, Consortium for Advancement of Pvt. Higher Edn., 1985-92; chief physics br. AEC, 1949-51; cons. US Office Ordnance Rsch., NSF, 1953-56; mem. com. on sci. in UNESCO, NAS-NRC, 1960-62, mem. com. on internat. orgns. and programs, 1962-64, sci. advisor US Del., UNESCO Gen. Conf., Paris, 1960, alt. del., 1962, chmn. Subcom. on Sino-Am. Sci. Cooperation, 1965-79; mem. panel on internat. sci. Pres.'s Sci. Adv. Com., 1961; trustee Analytic Svcs., Inc., 1958-89, chmn., 1961-89; mem. adv. com. on sci. NSF, 1965-70, 72-76, chmn., 1969-70, 73-74, 74-75; bd. dirs. Lincoln Found., 1979-85, Bell & Howell Corp., 1978-88, Am. Mut. Fund, 1981-88, DeVry, Inc., 1984-87, Sigma Rsch., 1983-87, Jacobs Engring. Co., 1978-86. Author: Harvey Mudd College: The First Twenty Years, 1994. Trustee China Found. for Promotion of Edn. and Culture, 1966—, Carnegie Found. for Advancement Tchg., 1970-78, Ancient Bibl. Manuscript Ctr., 1980-2005; chmn. select com. Master Plan for Higher Edn. Calif., 1971-73; mem. Carnegie Coun. for Policy Studies in Higher Edn., 1975-80. Fellow Am. Phys. Soc.; mem. IEEE, Automobile Club So. Calif. (bd. dirs. 1973-90, chmn. bd. dirs. 1986-87), Calif. Club, Sunset Club, Twilight Club, Cosmos Club, Bohemian Club, Phi Beta Kappa, Sigma Xi, Phi Kappa Phi. Home: 452 W 11th St Claremont CA 91711-3833 Business E-mail: joseph_platt@hmc.edu.

**PLATT, LESLIE A.,** lawyer; b. Bronx, N.Y., Aug. 7, 1944; s. Harold and Ann (Bienstock) P.; m. Marcia Ellin Berman, Aug., 1969; 1 son, Bill Lawrence. BA, George Washington U., 1966; JD, NYU, 1969. Bar: N.Y. 1970, U.S. Dist. Ct. D.C. 1972. Atty. advisor Office Gen. Counsel HUD, Washington, 1971-72, legis. atty., 1972-75, asst. gen. counsel for legis. svcs., 1975-78, assoc. gen. counsel for legis., 1978-80; dep. gen. counsel-legal counsel and staff dir. White House Agent Orange group, 1980-81; pvt. practice Washington, 1982-91; exec. asst. to dir. NIH, 1991-92; exec. v.p., COO, gen. counsel The Inst. for Genomic Rsch., Gaithersburg, Md., 1992-95; sr. v.p.k strategic devel., gen. counsel Am. Type Culture Collection, Manassas, Va., 1996-98; prin. assurance and adv. bus. practice Ernst & Young LLP, McLean, Va., 1999—2004; prin. Itaris LLC, McLean, 2004—05. Pres. dir. Found. for Genetic Medicine, Inc., 1997—2004; adj. prof. George Mason U., 2005—. Patentee in field. Chmn. cmty. adv. bd. Fairfax Hosp. Assn. Cameron Glen Facility; chair steering com. Reston/Herndon Bus.-H.S. Partnership; mem. Loudoun County Sci. and Tech. Cabinet, 2002—04, chair, 2006—; bd. dirs. No. Va. Tech. Coun., 2002—05. Recipient Disting. Svc. award HUD, 1978. Mem. ABA, Fed. Bar Assn., Am. Jud. Soc., Fed. Sr. Exec. Svc. (charter), Internat. Bar Assn. Home: 11901 Triple Crown Rd Reston VA 20191-3015

**PLATT, NICHOLAS,** retired ambassador; b. N.Y.C., Mar. 10, 1936; s. Geoffrey and Helen (Choate) P.; m. Sheila Maynard, June 28, 1957; children: Adam, Oliver, Nicholas. BA cum laude, Harvard U., 1957; MA, Johns Hopkins U., 1959. Commd. fgn. svc. officer Dept. State, 1959; vice consul Windsor, Ont., Canada, 1959-61; Chinese lang. trainee, 1962-63; polit. officer consulate gen. Hong Kong, 1964-68; chief Asian Communist areas divsn. Bur. Intelligence and Rsch., Dept. State, Washington, 1969, chief North Asia div., 1970, dept. dir. Exec. Secretariat staff, 1971, dir. staff, 1972-73; chief polit. sect. U.S. Liaison Office, Peking, China, 1973-74; 1st sec. Am. embassy, Tokyo, 1974-77; dir. Office of Japanese Affairs, Dept. State, 1977-78; mem. staff Nat. Security Council, White House, 1978-79; dep. asst. sec. for internat. security affairs Dept. Def., 1980-81; dep. asst. sec. for internat. orgn. affairs Dept. State, 1981-82; amb. Lusaka, Zambia, 1982-84; exec. asst., spl. asst. to sec. state Dept. State, 1985-87; amb. to The Philippines Am. Embassy, Manila, 1987-91, amb. to Pakistan, 1991-92; pres. Asia Soc., N.Y.C., 1992—2004, pres. emeritus 2004—. Bd. dirs. Fiduciary Trust Internat. Recipient Meritorious award exemplary achievement pub. admin-strn. William A. Jump Found., 1973, Disting. Civilian Svc. medal Dept. Def., 1981, Presdl. Merit award, 1985, 87, Disting. Honor award U.S. Dept. State, 1987, 91, Wilbur Carr award, 1992. Mem. N.Y. Coun. Fgn. Rels., Met. Club (Washington), Century Club, Union Club. Home: 131 E 69th St New York NY 10021-5158

**PLATT, NINA,** law librarian; d. Harlan and Ethel (Byron) Thorlacius; m. Vernon Platt, Dec. 21, 1984. BS, U. ND, Grand Forks, 1980; Ms of Libr. and Info. Sci., Dominican U., River Forest, Ill., 1997. Libr. dir. Carnegie Libr., Devils Lake, ND, 1982—85; tech. svcs. mgr. Dorsey & Whitney, Mpls., 1986—95; systems libr. Minn. Office of Atty. Gen., St. Paul, 1995—97; dir. of libr. services Faegre & Benson LLP, Mpls., 1998—. Cons. Nina Platt & Associates, Prior Lake, Minn., 1993—98. Contbr. textbook Knowledge Management for the Information Professional, articles to profl. jours. and web sites. Mem.: Minn. Law Libr. Assn. (Law Librarianship award 2003), Spl. Libraries Assn. (Innovations in Tech. award 2003), Minn. Assn. Law Libraries, Am. Assn. Law Libraries (exec. bd. mem. 2002—), Minn. Libr. Assn. (assoc.), Hekla Club (pres. 1996—97). Achievements include develop-ment of Minn. appellate ct. opinions archive. Avocations: motorcycling, gardening. Office: Faegre & Benson LLP 2200 Wells Fargo Ctr 90 S 7th St Minneapolis MN 55402 Business E-mail: nplatt@faegre.com.

**PLATT, OLIVER,** actor; b. Windsor, Ont., Can., Jan. 12, 1960; s. Nicholas Platt and Sheila Maynard; m. Camilla Campbell, 1993; children: Lily, George, Claire. Attended, Tufts U. Actor: (films) Crusoe, 1988, Married to the Mob, 1988, Working Girl, 1988, Flatliners, 1990, Postcards from the Edge, 1990, Beethoven, 1992, Diggstown, 1992, Benny & Joon, 1993, Indecent Proposal, 1993, The Temp, 1993, The Three Musketeers, 1993, Tall Tale, 1995, Funny Bones, 1995, Executive Decision, 1996, A Time to Kill, 1996, Venice, 1997, Bulworth, 1997, Dangerous Beauty, 1998, Doctor Dolittle, 1998, A Small Miracle, 1998, The Impostors, 1998, Simon Birch, 1998, Three to Tango, 1999, Gun Shy, 1999, Lake Placid, 1999, Bicentennial Man, 1999, Gun Shy, 2000, Ready to Rumble, 2000, Don't Say a Word, 2001, Liberty Stands Still, 2002, ZigZag, 2002, Ash Wednesday, 2002, Pieces of April, 2003, Hope Springs, 2003, Kinsey, 2004, Loverboy, 2005, The Ice Harvest, 2005, Casanova, 2005, (TV films) The Infiltrator, 1995, Cinderella, 1999, (TV series) Deadline, 2000-01, Queens Supreme, 2003, Huff, 2004-, (Broad-way plays) Shining City, 2006. Office: c/o William Morris Agy 151 S El Camino Dr Beverly Hills CA 90212-2704*

**PLATT, RUTHERFORD HAYES,** law educator, geographer, consultant; b. N.Y.C., Nov. 1, 1940; s. Rutherford and Jean (Noyes) P.; children: Anne, Stephen. BA, Yale U., 1962; JD, U. Chgo., 1967, PhD, 1971. Bar: Ill. 1968. Staff atty. Open Lands Project, Chgo., 1968-72; prof. U. Mass., Amherst, 1972—. Cons. FEMA, World Bank, Lincoln Inst., EPA, and others; mem. 8 NRC coms., 1979—. Author: Land Use and Society, 1996, 2d edit., 2004, Disasters and Democracy, 1999; contbr. articles to profl. jours. Mem. Assn. Am. Geographers, Faculty Club (Mass.), Cosmos Club (Washington). Home: 78 Hillcrest Dr Florence MA 01062-1362

**PLATT, THOMAS COLLIER, JR.,** federal judge; b. NYC, May 29, 1925; s. Thomas Collier and Louise Platt; m. Ann Byrd Symington, June 25, 1948; children: Ann Byrd, Charles Collier, Thomas Collier, III, Elizabeth Louise. BA, Yale U., 1947, LL.B., 1950. Bar: N.Y. 1950. Assoc. Root, Ballantine, Harlan, Bushby & Palmer, N.Y.C., 1950-53; asst. U.S. atty. Bklyn., 1953-56; assoc. Bleakley, Platt, Schmidt, Hart & Fritz, N.Y.C., 1956-60, ptnr., 1960-74; judge U.S. Dist. Ct. (ea. dist.) N.Y., 1974—, chief judge Bklyn., 1988-95. Former dir. Phoenix Mut. Life Ins. Co., RAC Corp., McIntyre Aviation, Inc.; atty. Village of Laurel Hollow, N.Y., 1958-74; acting police justice Village of Lloyd Harbor, N.Y., 1958-63 Alt. del. Republican Nat. Conv., 1964, 68, 72; del. N.Y. State Rep. Conv., 1966; trustee Brooks Sch., North Andover, Mass., 1968-82, pres., 1970-74. Served with USN, 1943-46 Mem. Fed. Judges Assn. (sec., bd. dirs. 1982-91). Clubs: Phelps Assn. (New Haven) (bd. govs. 1960-98); Cold Spring Harbor Beach (N.Y.) (bd. mgrs. 1964-70); Yale of N.Y.C. Episcopalian. Office: US Dist Ct PO Box 9014 Central Islip NY 11722-9014 Office Phone: 631-712-5600.

**PLATT, WARREN E.,** lawyer; b. McNary, Ariz., Aug. 5, 1943; BA, Mich. State U., 1965; JD, U. Ariz., 1969. Bar: Ariz. 1969, Calif. 1991, Texas 1993. Atty. Snell & Wilmer, Phoenix. Mng. editor Ariz. Law Rev., 1968—69. Fellow Am. Coll. Trial Lawyers; mem. Blue Key, Order of Coif, Phi Alpha Delta Office: Snell & Wilmer One Arizona Ctr Phoenix AZ 85004-0001 also: 6000 Anton Blvd Ste 1400 Costa Mesa CA 92626 Office Phone: 602-382-6292, 714-427-7475. Business E-mail: wplatt@swlaw.com.

**PLATT, WILLIAM HENRY,** judge; b. Allentown, Pa., Jan. 25, 1940; s. Henry and Genevieve (McElroy) P.; m. Maureen Hart, Nov. 29, 1969; children: Meredith H., William H., James H. AB, Dickinson Coll., 1961; JD, U. Pa., 1964. Bar: Pa. 1967, U.S. Supreme Ct. 1971. Ptnr. Yarus and Platt, Allentown, 1967-77; asst. pub. defender Lehigh County (Pa.), 1972-75, chief pub. defender, 1975-76, dist. atty., 1976-91; ptnr. Eckert, Seamans, Cherin & Mellott, 1991-95; city solicitor City of Allentown, 1994-95; judge Ct. Common Pleas of Lehigh County, Allentown, 1996—, pres. judge, 2002—. Mem. criminal procedural rules com. Supreme Ct. Pa., 1982-92, chmn., 1986-92; mem. Gov.'s Trial Ct. Nominating Commn. Lehigh County, 1984-87; mem. Pa. Commn. on Crime and Delinquency Victim Services Adv. Com., 1983-91. Served with M.P., U.S. Army, 1964-66. Mem.: ABA, Pa. Conf. of State Trial Judges (edn. com. 1997—2002), Pa. Assn. Dist. Attys. (exec. com. 1980—86, pres. 1983—84, chmn. 1986—87, tng. inst. mem. 1986—91), Nat. Assn. Dist. Attys. (state dir. 1982—84), Lehigh County Bar Assn., Pa. Bar Assn., Pa. Bar Inst. (hon.) (life; bd. dirs. 1989—2000, exec. com. 1994—2000, pres. 1997—98). Office: Lehigh County Courthouse 455 W Hamilton St Allentown PA 18101-1614 Office Phone: 610-782-3393.

**PLATTE, MARK,** editor; BA in Journalism, U. S.C. Staff writer City and Features Desk Atlanta (Ga.) Jour. Constn., 1982—84; staff writer Broward County Edit. Miami (Fla.) Herald, 1984—88; staff writer Orange County Register, 1988—90; from mem. staff to dep. city editor LA (Calif.) Times, 1990—98, dep. city editor, 1998—2000; asst. mng. editor news Honolulu (Hawaii) Advertiser, 2000—04, exec. editor, 2004—. Office: Honolulu Advertiser PO Box 3110 Honolulu HI 96802

**PLATTNER, MARC FLOREA,** foundation administrator, editor; b. NYC, May 8, 1945; s. Irving Herman and Claire Yvette (Bakst) P.; m. Jacqueline Suzanne Stark, Sept. 19, 1976; children: David Marshall, Laura Wolcott. AB summa cum laude, Yale U., 1966; PhD in Govt., Cornell U., 1974. Mng. editor The Pub. Interest, NYC, 1971-75; program officer The Twentieth Century Fund, NYC, 1975-81; adviser econ. and social affairs US Mission to UN, NYC, 1981-83; fellow Nat. Humanities Ctr., Rsch. Triangle Pk., NC, 1983-84; dir. program Nat. Endowment Democracy, Washington, 1984-89, counselor, 1989—2002, v.p. rsch. studies, 2002—; editor Jour. Democracy, 1989—; dir. Internat. Forum Dem. Studies, 1994—. Adj. prof., Touro Coll., N.Y.C., 1973-75; cons. Exec. Coun. on Fgn. Diplomats, Armonk, N.Y., 1984-90; vis prof. Robert Schuman Ctr. Adv. Studies European U. Inst., Florence, Italy, 2002-03. Author: Rousseau's State of Nature, 1979; editor: Human Rights in Our Time, 1984; co-editor: The Global Resurgence of Democracy, 1993, Capitalism, Socialism and Democracy Revisited, 1993, Nationalism, Ethnic Conflict, and Democracy, 1994, Democratization in Africa, 1999, The Democratic Invention, 2000, The Global Divergence of Democracies, 2001, Islam and Democracy in the Middle East, 2003, World Religions and Democracy, 2005; contbr. numerous articles to various publs. Dir. issues rsch., Moynihan for Senate campaign, N.Y.C., 1976. Herbert H. Lehman fellow, 1966-70; Earhart Found. fellow, 1970-71. Mem., Polit. Sci. Assn., Coun. on Foreign Relations, Phi Beta Kappa. Office: Nat Endowment Democracy 1025 F St NW 8th Fl Washington DC 20004 Business E-mail: marc@ned.org.

**PLATTO, JAMIE SCOTT,** lawyer; s. Charles and Leslie Platto. BA, U. Chgo., 1994; MBA, Boston (Mass.) U., 2000, JD, 1999. Bar: N.Y. 2000, Mass. 2000, Calif. 2000. Intern FTC, Washington, 1998; atty. Kaye Scholer, LLP, N.Y., 2000—03, Epstein Becker & Green, P.C., San Francisco, 2003—. Mem.: ABA, Am. Health Lawyers Assn. Office: Epstein Becker & Green PC One California Street San Francisco CA 94111 Office Phone: 415-398-3500. Office Fax: 415-398-0955.

**PLATTS, HOWARD GREGORY,** cultural organization administrator, not-for-profit fundraiser; b. Aug. 14, 1947; s. Thayer Horton and Anne Elizabeth (Gregory) P.; m. Elizabeth Hertzler Murray, June 7, 1969; children: James Thayer, Christopher Wilke. AB, Harvard U., 1969; M. Pub. and Pvt. Mgmt., Yale U., 1980. Tchr. Potomac Sch., McLean, Va., 1969-72; investment officer First Am. Bank, Washington, 1972-78; fin. analyst Yale U., New Haven, 1979; fin. asst. to pres. Nat. Geog. Soc., Washington, 1980-82, asst. treas., 1982-91, sr. v.p., treas., 1992—. Trustee Nat. Presbyn. Sch., Washington, 1988-91, Decatur House, Washington, 1994-2004, Ctr. for the Study of the Presidency, Washington, 2004—; chmn., trustee regional blood svcs. ARC, Balt., 1992-2000; treas., bd. dirs. Friends of Fort Dupont, Washington, 1995-2002; governing bd. St. Albans Sch., Washington, 1997-2003 Trustee Westmoreland Congl. Ch., 1988-91. Mem. Westmoreland Soc. Investment Analysts (pres., bd. dirs. 1985-91). Home: 5302 Portsmouth Rd Bethesda MD 20816-2929 Office: Nat Geog Soc 1145 17th St NW Washington DC 20036-4701 Office Phone: 202-857-7417. Business E-mail: platts@aya.yale.edu.

**PLATTS, TODD RUSSELL,** congressman, state legislator; b. York, Pa., Mar. 5, 1962; m. Leslie Platts; 2 children. BS summa cum laude in Pub. Adminstrn., Shippensburg U. Pa., 1984; JD cum laude, Pepperdine U. Sch. Law, Malibu, Calif., 1991. Atty. Barley, Snyder, Senft & Cohen; mem. Pa. State Ho. Reps. from Dist. 196, 1993-2001, US Congress from 19th Pa. dist., 2001—, mem. transp. and infrastructure com., mem. edn. and the workforce com., mem. govt. reform com., chmn. govt. mgmt., fin. and accountability subcommittee. Mem. aging and youth edn. com. State of Pa., 1993. Republican. Episcopalian. Office: US Ho Reps 1032 Longworth Ho Office Bldg Washington DC 20515 Office Phone: 202-225-5836.*

**PLATTS-MILLS, THOMAS ALEXANDER E.,** immunologist, educator, researcher; b. Colchester, Essex, Eng., Nov. 22, 1941; came to U.S., 1982; s. John Faithful F. and Janet Katherine (Cree) P-M.; m. Roberta Rosenstock, Apr. 9, 1970; children: Eliza, Timothy, James, Oliver. BA, Balliol Coll. Oxford (Eng.) U., 1963; MB, BChir, Oxford U., 1967; PhD, London U., 1982. Registrar in medicine Bury St. Edmunds, and New Market, Suffolk, England, 1968-71; fellow in medicine Johns Hopkins U., Balt., 1971-74; staff mem. Med. Rsch. Coun., England, 1976-82; hon. cons. physician Northwick Park Hosp., London, 1978-82; prof. medicine, head divsn. allergy and clin. immunology U. Va., Charlottesville, 1982—; dir. Asthma and Allergic Diseases Ctr., 1994. Mem. immunological scis. study sect. NIH, 1988. Editl. bd. Am. Jour. Respiratory Critical Care Medicine, Clin. and Exptl. Immunol-ogy, Clin. Allergy, Jour. Immunological Methods; contbr. articles to profl. jours. Grantee NIH. Fellow Royal Coll. Physicians, Am. Acad. Allergy; mem. Assn. Am. Physicians, Am. Acad. Allergy, Asthma and Immunology (v.p.

2004—2005, pres.-elect, 2005-2006, pres. 2006-), Southeastern Allergy Assn. (Hal Davidson award 1986, pres. 1987-88), Brit. Soc. Allergy and Clin. Immunology. Office: U Va Dept Medicine PO Box 800225 Charlottesville VA 22908-0225 E-mail: tap2z@virginia.edu.*

**PLAUCHE, NANCY CAROLINE,** retired counselor; b. Lima, Ohio, Oct. 31, 1938; d. Willis Sylvanis and Mabel Louise (Neiswander) Siferd; m. Jack Plauche (div. 1979); children: Michel, Jacqueline, Jon. BFA, Ohio U., 1960; MS, Nova U., Ft. Lauderdale, Fla., 1984; PhD, The Union Inst., Cin., 1989. Counselor Pinellas county Schs., St. Petersburg, Fla., 1980—2002; smoke stopper's instr. Nat. Ctr. for Health Promotion/Morton Plant Hosp., Clearwa-ter, Fla., 1986-92; ret., 2002. Co-dir. Counseling & Profl. Cons. Svcs., St. Petersburg, 1984-88. Co-author: All About Me, 1985, Safer Parenting, 1985; contbr. articles to profl. jours. Mem. Dem. Exec. Com., Wood City W.Va., 1977-79; sustainor Jr. League St. Petersburg. Mem. APA, So. Assn. Coll. Counselors, Am. Psychol. Soc., Am. Arbitration Assn., People to People Internat., Fla. Counseling Assn., Fla. Sch. Counselors Assn., Clearwater Area Panhellenic Assn. Democrat. Avocations: painting, drawing, travel, cultural exchange.

**PLAUD, JOSEPH JULIAN,** psychology educator; b. Worcester, Mass., Mar. 25, 1965; s. Henry Emile and Barbara Ann (Perry) P.; m. Christine Marie Therlault, Mar. 14, 1987 (div. Mar. 1990); 1 child, Brianna Marie; m. Deborah Muench, Jan. 30, 1999. BA summa cum laude, Clark U., 1987; PhD in Psychology, U. Maine, 1993. Lic. clin. psychologist, Mass.; bd. cert. behavior analyst Behavior Analyst Cert. Bd. Psychology resident U. Miss. Med. Ctr., Jackson, 1992-93; asst. prof. psychology U. ND, Grand Forks, 1993-97; dir. rsch., webmaster Cambridge Ctr. for Behavioral Studies, Mass., 1999—2003; pres. Franklin D. Roosevelt Am. Heritage Ctr., Inc. Cons. ND Devel. Ctr., Grafton, 1994—, State of NH, 1999—; forensic cons., 1993—; vis. scholar Brown U., 1998—; COO New Sch. for Learning Scis.; forensic psychology cons. Applied Behavioral Cons., Inc. Author: From Behavior Theory to Behavior Therapy, 1997; editor-in-chief Jour. Behavioral Analysis and Therapy, Jour. Sexual Offender Civil Commitment: Science and the Law; contbr. articles to profl. jours. Pres. Franklin D. Roosevelt Am. Heritage Ctr., Inc. Lt. comdr. Med. Svc. Corps, USNR, 2002. Fellow APA, Behavior Therapy and Rsch. Soc. (clin.); mem. AAAS, Assn. for Advancement of Behavior Therapy, Am. Psychol. Soc., Phi Beta Kappa, Psi Chi. Democrat. Roman Catholic. Home: 44 Hickory Ln Whitinsville MA 01588-1356 E-mail: plaud@fdrheritage.org.

**PLAUT, JONATHAN VICTOR,** rabbi; b. Chgo., Oct. 7, 1942; s. W. Gunther and Elizabeth (Strauss) P.; m. Carol Ann Frankin, July 5, 1965; children: Daniel Abraham, Deborah Maxine. BA, Macalester Coll., 1964; postgrad., Hebrew Union Coll., Jerusalem, 1967-68; BHL, Hebrew Union Coll., Cin., 1968, MA, 1970, DHL, 1977; DD (hon.), 1995. Ordained rabbi, 1970. Rabbi Congregation Beth-El, Windsor, Ont., Canada, 1970-84; sr. rabbi Temple Emanu-El, San Jose, Calif., 1985-93; dir. comty. outreach and involvement Jewish Fed. of Met. Detroit, 1993-95; pres. JVP Fund Raising Cons., Inc., Farmington Hills, Mich., 1994—. Lectr. Assumption Coll. Mich., 1972-84, St. Clair Coll., 1982-84, U. Windsor, Ont., Can., 1984; adj. asst. prof. Santa Clara U., 1985-93; adj. prof. U. Detroit Mercy, 2002—; vis. Rabbinic scholar Temple Beth El, 1993—95; pres. JVP Fund Raising Cons., 1994—; rabbi emeritus Congregation Beth El, Traverse City, Mich., 1999—2004; rabbi Temple Beth Israel, Jackson, Mich., 2000—. Contbg. author: Reform Judaism in America: A Biographical Dictionary and Source-book, 1993; editor: Through the Sound of Many Voices, 1982, Jour. Can. Jewish Hist. Soc., 1976-83; also articles; host weekly program Religious Scope, Sta. CBET-TV, Religion in News, Sta. CKWW, 1971-84. Pres. Jewish Nat. Fund Windsor, 1978-81, chmn. bd. dirs., 1978-87; chmn. United Jewish Appeal Windsor, 1981-83, State of Israel Bonds, Windsor, 1980; nat. bd. dirs. Jewish Nat. Fund Can., 1972-84; pres. Reform Rabbis of Can., 1982-84; bd. dirs. Can. Jewish Congress, 1978-84, Jewish Family Svc. Santa Clara County, 1987-90, Jewish Fedn. Greater San Jose, 1986-93; chaplain San Jose Fire Dept., 1987-93; mem. exec. cabinet United Jewish Appeal, Windsor, 1971-84, mem. nat. rabbinic cabinet, 1993-95; mem. exec. com. Windsor Jewish Community Coun., 1970-84, chmn. 1975-84; mem. adv. coun. Riverview unit Windsor Hosp. Ctr., 1972-81; pres. Credit Counselling Svc. Met. Windsor, 1977-79. Honoree Jewish Nat. Fund, 1985. Mem. NCCJ, Can. Jewish Congress (nat. exec. bd. 1978-84), Can. Jewish Hist. Soc. (nat. v.p. 1974-84), Calif. Bd. Rabbis, Rabbinic Assn. Greater San Jose (chmn. 1986-87), Ctrl. Conf. Am. Rabbis, Nat. Assn. Temple Educators. Home and Office: 30208 Kingsway Dr Farmington Hills MI 48331-1648 Office Phone: 248-505-8888. Fax: (248) 788-4144. E-mail: jvplaut@earthlink.net.

**PLAVE, LEE JONATHAN,** lawyer; b. Bklyn., June 22, 1958; s. Seymour and Matty P.; m. Ilene Susan Pearlman. BA, Clark U., 1980; JD cum laude, NY Law Sch., 1983. Bar: NY 1983, DC 1987. Atty., Used Car Rule program advisor FTC, Washington, 1983—87; assoc. to ptnr. Brownstein & Zeidman, P.C., Washington, 1987—96; ptnr. DLA Piper (formerly Piper Rudnick), Washington, 1996—; ptnr., chmn. Domain Name practice group DLA Piper Rudnick Gray Cary, Washington, 2005—. Assoc. editor NY Law Sch. Jour. Internat. and Comparative Law, 1982-83; contbr. articles to profl. jours. Mem. ABA, Internat. Bar Assn., Va State Bar Assn., DC Bar Assn., NY State Bar Assn., Internat. Franchise Assn. Jewish. Avocations: ice hockey, stamp collecting/philately, politics. Office: DLA Piper 1200 19th St NW Washington DC 20036-2412 also: DLA Piper Suite 400 1775 Wiehle Ave Reston VA 20190 Office Phone: 703-773-4243. Office Fax: 703-773-5054. Business E-Mail: lee.plave@dlapiper.com.

**PLAVINSKAYA, ANNA DMITRIEVNA,** artist; b. Moscow, Nov. 26, 1960; came to U.S., 1989, naturalized, 1995; d. Dmitri Petrovich and Nina Nicolaevna; m. Gennady Ioffe, Jan 9, 1988 (div. July 1993). Diploma in Costume Design, Theatrical Art Coll., Moscow, 1976-80. Costume designer Evgeny Vahtangov Theater, Moscow, 1980-82; artist freelance Moscow, 1983-89; art restorer pvt. studio, N.Y.C., 1990-93; artist freelance N.Y.C., 1993—. Exhibited in group shows at Moscow, Gallery Moscow Artists, 1983, Ctrl. Exhbn. Hall, Moscow, 1984, 88, Kuznetzky Most Gallery, Moscow, 1985, Tbilisi Acad. Art, Georgia, 1986, Tallinna Moepaevad '87, Tallinn, Estonia, 1987, Remizovo St. Gallery, Moscow, 1988, Pushkin Sq. Gallery, Moscow, 1988, Textile Art Ctr., Chgo., 1991, Russian Nobility Assn., NYC, 1991, 11th Cleve. Internat. Drawing Biennale, Middlesbrough, Eng., 1993 (2d prize), BWA Gallery, Wroclaw, Poland, 1994, BWA Gallery, Lublin, Poland, 1994, Elblag (Poland) Gallery, 1994, Tatranska Gallery, Poprad, Tatry, Slovakia, 1994, State Gallery, Ostrova, Czech Republic, 1994, Port Royal Mus. Gallery, Naples, Fla., 1994, Art Addiction Gallery, Stockholm, 1996-98 (cert. merit 1997), Art Addiction Gallery, Venice, Italy, 1998, Internat. Platform Assn., 1998, (1st place, Best of Show), 1999 (1st place award), Le Salon, Paris, 2000, 2002, 03, 04 (Bronze medal 2000), Salon Internat. Beziers, 2001-04, 06 (Bronze medal 2001, Prix de La Societe Des Beaux Arts 2002), Salon D'Automne Internat., Luneville, France, 2001, 04, 14e annee Europ'Art Geneve Palexpo, Switzerland, 2005; represented in permanent collections Cleve. Contemporary Art Collection, Middlesbrough, Eng., Zim-merli Art Mus., Norton and Nancy Dodge Collection, NJ. Mem.: Nat. Fedn. French Culture. Russian Orthodox. Avocations: fashion design, antique textile restoration, tennis. Home: 815 W 181st St Apt 3E New York NY 10033-4530 Office Phone: 212-795-4258. Personal E-mail: annaplavinskaya@hotmail.com.

**PLAX, KAREN ANN,** lawyer; b. St. Louis, June 29, 1946; d. George J. and Evelyn G. Zell; m. Stephen E. Plax, Dec. 19, 1968; 1 child, Jonathan. BA magna cum laude, U. St. Louis, 1969; JD with distinction, U. Mo., Kansas City, 1976. Bar: Mo. 1976, U.S. Supreme Ct. 1980. Atty. Thayer, Gum & Wickert, Grandview, Mo., 1976-84, Plax & Cochet, Kansas City, Mo., 1984-87; pvt. practice Kansas City, 1987—. Past chair divsn. 3, region IV Mo. Supreme Ct. Com. to review ethical conduct of attys., 1997—98; pres. Collaborative Law Inst. Mo., 2003—06. Author: Missouri Bar Practical Skills, 1998; asst. editor: Racial Integration in the Inner Suburb, 1970; contbr. articles to profl. jours. Recipient Pub. Svc. award U. Mo. Kansas City Law Found., 1998, Woman of Yr. award Assn. Women Lawyers of Greater Kansas

City, 1999; named Family Law Practioner of Yr., Mo. Bar, 2005 Fellow: Am. Acad. Matrimonial Lawyers (pres. Mo. chpt. 1999—2001); mem.: ABA (family law sect. 1976—), Mo. Bar Family Law (legis. chair 1997—98, v.p. 1999—2000, Spl. Commendation for Legis. Role in Family Law 1998), Kansas City Met. Bar Assn. Office: Ste 300 1310 Carondelet Dr Kansas City MO 64114-4803 Office Phone: 816-942-1900. Personal E-mail: kaplax@swbell.net.

**PLAYER, THELMA B.,** librarian; b. Owosso, Mich. d. Walter B. and Grace (Willoughby) Player. BA, Western Mich. U., 1954. Reference asst. USAF Aero Chart and Info. Ctr., Washington, 1954-57; reference libr. USN Hydrographic Office, Suitland, Md., 1957-58, asst. libr., 1958-59; tech. libr.br. head USN Spl. Project Office, Washington, 1959-68, Strategic Sys. Project Office, Washington, 1969-76. Mem. ALA, AAUW, English Speaking Union, Spl. Librs. Assn., Nat. Geneal. Socl, Internat. Soc. Brit. Genealogy and Family History, Ohio Geneal. Soc. Royal Oak Found., Daus of Union Vets. of Civil War, David Ackerman Descs. Episcopalian. Home: 730 24th St NW Washington DC 20037-2519

**PLAYFAIR, DAVID MALCOLM,** vocalist, voice educator, researcher; b. Toronto, Ont., Can., Mar. 2, 1957; arrived in US, 2001; s. Harold Gilbert and Avril Elisabeth (Faulknor) Playfair; m. Gordon John Portman, Oct. 21, 2000. MusB, U. Toronto, 1991, MusM, 1997; PhD, U. Iowa, 2006. Course dir., asst. tchr. U. Toronto, 1996—97; elem. music tchr. Toronto Dist. Sch. Bd., 1998—2001; asst. prof. voice U. Wis., Superior, 2004—. Adj. prof. voice Sheridan Coll., 1993—94, Wartburg Coll., Waverly, Iowa, 2002—03; course creator, dir. Brampton Theatre Alliance, 1995—96; tchg. asst. U. Iowa Sch. Music, Iowa City, 2001—04; conductor Lake Superior Youth Chorus Concert Choir, 2004—05; pvt. practice, 1988   2003. Singer. (Operas) Shaw Festival, 1985, Opera Atelier, 1986, 1988, Kennedy Ctr., 1987, Stratford Festival, 1989, Opera Ora Now, 1990, Banff Ctr. for the Arts, 1991, Livent Corp. Cda, 1991—93, 1997, 1999, Opera Mississauga, 1995, Summer Opera Lyric Theatre, 1996, Royal Conservatory, 1996, Montrose Prodns., 1998, Cedar Rapids Opera, 2001, Martha-Ellen Tye Opera, 2002—03, Duluth Superior Symphony Orch, 2005, others. Vocal dir., tchr. Duluth Playhouse, 2005; children's choir dir. St. Anne's Anglican Ch., Toronto, 1997—99. Recipient Profl. Devel. award, U. Wis., 2005; Walker Quartet scholar, U. Iowa, 2002—04. Mem.: Nat. Assn. Tchrs. Singing. Home: 3004 N 21st St Superior WI 54880

**PLAYFAIR, JIM,** professional hockey coach; b. Vanderhoof, BC, Can., May 22, 1964; m. Roxanne Playfair; children: Dylan, Jackson, Austyn. Defenseman Portland Winter Hawks, 1981—83, Calgary Wranglers, 1983—84, Edmonton Oilers, 1984, Nova-Scotia Oilers, 1984—87, Saginaw Hawks, 1987—89, Chgo. Blackhawks, 1987—89, Indpls. Ice, 1989—92; head coach Dayton Bombers (ECHL), 1993—96, Michigan K-Wings (IHL), 1996—98, Saint John Flames (AHL), 2000—02; asst. coach Calgary Flames, 2003—06, head coach, 2006—. Recipient Minor Profl. Coach of Yr., The Hockey News, 2001. Achievements include being the head coach of Calder Cup Champion Saint John Flames, 2001. Office: Calgary Flames PO Box 1540 Stn M Calgary Canada*

**PLAYFORD, NANCY JEAN,** medical association administrator; b. Lansing, Mich., May 23, 1960; d. Jack Frederick and Doris Jean Lillrose; children: Kimberley, Kristen. Med. staff coord. Valley Luth. Hosp., Mesa, Ariz., 1984-93, Scottsdale (Ariz.) Health Sys., 1993-95, credentials supr., 1995-97; dir. med. staff svcs. Tempe (Ariz.) St. Luke's Hosp., 1997—. Mem. adv. bd. Greater Ariz. Cen. Credentialing, Phoenix, 1995—; expert witness in ct. for credentialing issues. Mem. Nat. Assn. Med. Staff Svcs. (cert. med. staff coord. 1993, cert. provider credentialing specialist 1996), Ariz. Assn. Med. Staff Svc. (pres.-elect Superstition Mountain chpt. 1995-96, pres. Superstition Mountain chpt. 1996-97). Avocations: photography, hiking, playing piano, horses. Office: Tempe St Luke's Hosp 1500 S Mill Ave Tempe AZ 85281-6699 E-mail: nplayford@isaishealthcare.com.

**PLEASANT, JAMES SCOTT,** lawyer; b. Anniston, Ala., July 14, 1943; s. James C. and Barbara (Scott) P.; m. Susan M. Pleasant, May 17, 1966; children: Deborah Kaye, Carol Ann, Julie Ruth. BS, Oreg. State U., 1965; JD summa cum laude, Williamette U., 1972. Bar: Tex. 1972, U.S. Dist. Ct. (no. dist.) Tex. 1973, U.S. Ct. Appeals (5th cir.) 1975, U.S. Supreme Ct. 1977. Ptnr. Gardere Wynne Sewell, LLP, Dallas, 1972—. Mem. Smithsonian Assn., Washington, 1985—, Dallas Mus. of Art, 1987—. Capt. U.S. Army, 1966-69, Vietnam. Mem. ABA (partnership law sect. 1969—), Tex. Bar Assn. (partnership law sect. 1989—), Vietnam Pilots Assn., Dustoff Assn. Office: Gardere Wynne Sewell LLP 1601 Elm St Ste 3000 Dallas TX 75201-4761 Office Phone: 214-999-4690. E-mail: pleja@gardere.com.

**PLEASANTS, JOHN,** Internet company executive; BA, Yale U.; MBA, Harvard U. With Frito-Lay divsn. PepsiCo; with Hughes Industries; gen. mgr., new mkts. divsn. City Search IAC / InterActive Corp, 1996; exec. v.p. new markets Ticketmaster Online-CitySearch (divsn. IAC/InterActiveCorp), Pasadena, Calif., pres. ticketing and transactions; pres. info. sys., CEO Ticketmaster, Pasadena, Calif., 2000—03; now pres., CEO Ticketmaster, Reserve Am., Ticketweb, Pasadena. Bd. dir. Ticketmaster7, Australia, The Active Network, La Jolla, Calif.

**PLEASANTS, JULIAN MCIVER,** history educator, summer school director; b. Pinehurst, NC, Nov. 12, 1938; s. James McIver and Jean (McIver) P.; m. Donna Marie Bishop, Feb. 28, 1987. BA, Davidson Coll., 1960; MA, U. NC, 1962, PhD, 1971. Asst. prof. Western Carolina U., Cullowhee, NC, 1966-67; from asst. prof. to prof. U. Fla., Gainesville, 1969—. Instr. Converse Coll., Spartanburg, SC, 1962; dir. summer sch. U. New Orleans, U. Fla., 1976-97, dir., proctor oral history program, 1996-; cons. Documentary on Frank P Graham, 1991, Author Frank P. Graham and The Senate Election of 1950 in North Carolina, 1990 (Best Book in NC History 1991), Buncombe Bob: The Life and Times of Robert Rice Reynolds, 2001, Orange Journalism: Voices From Florida Newspapers, 2003, Hanging Chads: The Inside Story of the 2000 Presidential Recount in Florida, 2004. Dir. Upward Bound program, Gainesville, 1971. 1st lt. US Army, 1962-64. Rotary Internat. fellow, 1965-66, fellow Archie K. Davis Found., 1990-91; recipient award of merit City of Innsbruck, Austria, 1985, 91; named one of 10 Outstanding Profs., Interfraternity Coun.-Omicron Delta Kappa, 1972; named Most Inspiring Prof. U. Fla., 1989. Mem. Fla. Hist. Assn., So. Hist. Assn., Golden Key (hon.), Phi Alpha Theta. Avocations: reading, walking, travel. Home: 9424 SW 21st Ave Gainesville FL 32607-3243 Office: U Fla History Dept 4103 Turlington Hall Gainesville FL 32611 Office Phone: 352-392-7168.

**PLEAU, LAWRENCE WINSLOW,** professional sports team executive; b. Boston, June 29, 1947; s. Ernest and Norma (Knowles) Pl.; m. Wendy Sargent MacDougall, May 3, 1969; children, Steven Lawrence, Shannon Lynn. Grad. high sch. Player Montreal Canadiens, 1969-72, N.Eng. Whalers, Hartford, Conn., 1972-79; asst. coach Hartford Whalers, 1979-80, coach, gen. mgr., 1980-83, asst. gen. mgr., 1983-84, coach, 1988-89; coach, gen. mgr. Binghamton Whalers, NY, 1984-88; asst. gen. mgr. player devel. NY Rangers, 1989, asst. gen. mgr., v.p. player personnel; gen. mgr. St. Louis Blues, 1997—. Player U.S. Olympic Hockey Team, Grenoble, France, 1968, U.S. Nat. Hockey Team, Stockholm, 1969, U.S.A. Hockey Team, Providence, 1976; radio, TV commentator, ESPN, Hartford, 1979-80; owner Bridge Marina Inc. With U.S. Army, 1967-69. Mem. All-Star Teams, 1973, 74, 75; named Coach of Yr. Am. Hockey League, 1986-87, Exec. of Yr., The Sporting News, 1999-2000. Democrat. Achievements include being a member of Stanley Cup Champion Montreal Canadiens, 1971. Avocations: deep sea fishing, golf, tennis. Office: St Louis Blues Hockey Club Savvis Ctr 1401 Clark Ave Saint Louis MO 63103*

**PLEHATY, PHYLLIS JULIETTE,** retired curator; b. N.Y.C., Nov. 28, 1920; d. Aaron Neumann and Lillian Caroline Nagel; m. Carl William Plehaty Jr., Oct. 28, 1942 (dec. Jan. 1995); children: Carl. W. III, Phyllis Gretchen (dec.). Student, Parsons Sch. Design. With design dept. Schumacher-Waverly,

N.Y.C., 1940—43; mgr. boutique, antiques The Place, Darien, Conn., 1957—69; archivist, vol. Darien Hist. Soc., 1960—65; photographer, tour guide Swan Ho. Atlanta Hist. Soc., 1969—71; photographer Jamaica Tourism, 1972—74; mgr., buyer Landlords Daughter Vintage '87, Yountville, Calif., 1974—76; curator collections Boulder History Mus., Colo., 1980—99; ret., 1999; antiques art dealer Niwot Antiques, Colo., 2005—. Cons. costume, collection named in hon. Boulder History Mus., 1990—; cons. exhibit Talbots Stores, 2000—; mem. adv. bd. Wise Homestead Mus., Erie, 2000—. Vol. libr. Loraine Davis Children's Libr., Erie, 2003; established Phyllis J. Plehaty Scholarship Univ. Colo.; bd. trustees Boulder Mus. Recipient CU Scholarship, Boulder History Mus. Republican. Lutheran. Avocations: jewelry design, silversmithing, blacksmithing, antiques, painting, crafts. Home: 12675 Kenosha Rd Erie CO 80516

**PLEICONES, COSTA M.,** state supreme court justice; b. Greenville, SC, Feb. 29, 1944; s. Mike and Lecha Pleicones; m. Donna Singletary; 2 children. BA in English, Wofford Coll., 1965; JD, U. SC, 1968. Bar: S.C. 1968. Pub. defender Richland County, SC; atty. Lewis, Babcock, Pleicones and Hawkins; municipal judge City of Columbia, SC; county atty. Richland County, SC; resident cir. ct. judge 5th Judicial Cir., 1991—2000; assoc. justice SC Supreme Ct., 2000—. With JAG U.S. Army, 1968—73, with USAR, 1973—99. Office: 1231 Gervais St Columbia SC 29201-3206 also: PO Box 11330 Columbia SC 29211*

**PLESE, JOSEPH MARSHALL,** education educator, actor; b. Big Spring, Tex., Oct. 21, 1980; s. Ed and Marsha Plese. BS in Edn., U. Kans., Lawrence, 2003; MFA, Ea. Mich. U., Ypsilanti. Cert. tchr. English and social studies 7-12 Kans. Tchr. Shawnee Mission South H.S., Overland Park, Kans.; program rev. analyst Ea. Mich. U., Ypsilanti, 2004—. Actor: (title role) Lady in the Dark, (Hamm) Endgame, (title role) Where To, Turelu (Kennedy Ctr.-Am. Coll. Theatre Festival Irene Ryan Acting award Nomination); singer: (countertenor soloist) Chichester Pslalms; actor: (Gato) Pinocchio. Sec. Standing Together Against Negative Displays, Lawrence, Kans., 1999—2002; cantor St. Lawrence Cath. Campus Ctr., Lawrence, 1999—2004, Holy Trinity Student Parish, Ypsilanti, 2004—06; vol. drama specialist U. of Kans, Ea. Mich. U. Theatre for Young People. Recipient Nat. Merit scholarship, U. Kans. Merit Scholarship Found., 1999—2003, Rock Chalk scholarship, U. Kans., Kans. Honors award, Kans. Bd. of Regents, Cert. of Excellence, Ednl. Testing Svc.-Praxis Series. Mem.: NEA, Am. Alliance for Theatre in Edn. Democrat. Achievements include research in Devising for TIE, Academic Service Learning in the Creative Drama Classroom, Process Drama and Literary Criticism. Home: 7872 W 153rd Terr Overland Park KS 66223 Personal E-mail: jplese@emich.edu.

**PLETCHER, CAROL H.,** chemicals executive; m. Wayne Pletcher. B in Chemistry, Juniata Coll., Huntingdon, Pa.; M in Phys. Chemistry, U. Mich.; PhD, Coll. Biol. Sciences, U. Minn. Sr. scientist Cargill, Inc., 1983—89, mgr., 1989—92, dir., 1992—93, asst. v.p., 1993—99, v.p., 1999—2001, chief innovation officer, 2001—. Mem. Coll. Biol. Sciences Alumni Soc. Bd. U. Minn., mem.steering com. for Cargill, Inc.; established with husband Pletcher Fellowship, Coll. Biol. Sciences, U. Minn. Named one of 25 Masters of Innovation, BusinessWeek; recipient Outstanding Achievement award, Coll. Biol. Sciences, U. Minn., 2003; Fellowship, Am. Assn. of U. Women. Mem.: Minn. High Tech Assn. (bd. dir. 2006—). Office: Cargill Inc PO Box 9300 Minneapolis MN 55440-9300*

**PLETCHER, ELDON,** retired cartoonist; b. Goshen, Ind., Sept. 10, 1922; s. Arthur and Dora (Cripe) P.; m. Barbara Jeanne Jones, Jan. 29, 1948; children— Thomas Lee, Ellen Irene. Student, Chgo. Acad. Fine Arts, 1941-42, U. Aberdeen, Scotland, 1945, John Herron Art Sch., Indpls., 1946-47. Editorial cartoonist Sioux City (Iowa) Jour., 1949-66; editorial cartoonist The Times-Picayune, 1966-85; free-lance gag cartoonist Sat. Eve. Post, Rotarian, Nat. Enquirer, other publs. Rep. permanent exhbns., Syracuse U., U. South Miss., U. Cin., Boston Mus. Art, Harry S. Truman Library, Lyndon B. Johnson Library, Wichita State U., John F. Kennedy Libr., Richard M. Nixon Libr., U. Mo.; cartoons appeared in The Continental Edit. of TIME (Army Weekly). Served with AUS, 1943-46. Recipient Christopher award, 1955, Freedoms Found. award, 12 years Mem. VFW, Assn. Am. Editorial Cartoonists. Democrat. Presbyterian. Personal E-mail: epletch@aol.com.

**PLETSCH, MARIE ELEANOR,** plastic surgeon; b. Walkerton, Ont., Can., May 3, 1938; came to U.S. 1962; d. Ernest John and Olive Wilhemina (Hossfeld) P.; m. Ludwig Philip Breiling, Aug. 25, 1967; children: John, Michael, Anne. MD, U. Toronto, 1962. Diplomate Am. Bd. Plastic Surgery. Intern Cook County Hosp., Chgo., 1962-63, resident, gen. surgery, 1963-64, St. Mary's Hosp., San Francisco, 1964-66; resident in plastic surgery St. Francis Hosp., San Francisco, 1966-69; practice med. specializing in plastic surgery Santa Cruz, Calif., 1969—; Monterey, Calif., 1990—; adminstr. Plasticenter, Inc., Santa Cruz, 1976-88, med. dir., 1987-88. Mem. AMA, Am. Soc. Plastic and Reconstructive Surgeons, Calif. Soc. Plastic Surgeons (mem. coun. 1986-89, sec. 1989-93, v.p. 1994-95, pres. elect 1995-96, pres. 1996-97), Am. Soc. Aesthetic Plastic Surgeons, Calif. Med. Assn., Assn. Calif. Surgery Ctrs. (pres. 1988-92), Santa Cruz County Med. Soc. (bd. govs. 1983-88, 1992-94), Santa Cruz Surgery Ctr. (bd. dir. 1988-93, 2004—). Roman Catholic. Office: Santa Cruz Can Am Med Group 1669 Dominican Way Santa Cruz CA 95065-1523: 24571 Silver Cloud Ct Monterey CA 93940 Office Phone: 831-462-1000. Personal E-mail: pletsch@pacbell.net.

**PLETZ, THOMAS GREGORY,** lawyer; b. Toledo, Oct. 3, 1943; s. Francis G. and Virginia (Connell) P.; m. Carol Elizabeth Connolly, June 27, 1969; children: Anne M., John F. BA, U. Notre Dame, 1965; JD, U. Toledo, 1971. Bar: Ohio 1971, U.S. Ct. Appeals (6th cir.) 1978, U.S. Supreme Ct. 1985. Ct. bailiff Lucas County Common Pleas Ct., Toledo, 1967-71; jud. clk. U.S. Dist. Ct. (no. dist.) Ohio, Toledo, 1971-72; assoc. Shumaker, Loop & Kendrick, Toledo, 1972-76, litigation ptnr., 1976—. Acting judge Sylvania (Ohio) Mcpl. Ct., 1990—; mem. Ohio Bar Bd. Examiners, 1993-2003, chmn., 1996-99. Active Toledo Parish Coun., 1987-2003; mem. Nat. Conf. Bar Examiners Com., 1996-2001. With USNR, 1965-92; ret. CDR. Recipient Toledo Jr. Bar award, 1995. Mem. ABA, Ohio State Bar Assn., Toledo Bar Assn. (trustee 1981-93), Diocesan Attys. Bar Assn., 6th Cir. Jud. Conf. (life). Roman Catholic. Office: Shumaker Loop & Kendrick 1000 Jackson St Toledo OH 43604-1573 Office Phone: 419-321-1231. Business E-Mail: tpletz@slk-law.com.

**PLEUGER, GUENTER,** diplomat; b. Wismar, Germany, Mar. 25, 1941; m. Gabriella Mebus-Pleuger; 2 children. Student in Law and Polit. sci., U. of Colgne and U. of Bonn, 1960—64; PhD in Law, 1966; student, Ecol Nationale d'Administration, Paris, 1966—67. Fgn. svc. trainee consulate gen., Bonn and Liverpool, U.K., 1969—70; first sec. Permanent Mission of Fed. Republic of German to UN, NYC, 1970—74; with European Communities Divsn., Federal Fgn. Office, 1974—77; embassy spokesman and head of press divsn. German Embassy, New Delhi, 1977—79; policy planning staff Federal Fgn. Office, Bonn, 1980—85; dir. in charge of Public Info and Liaison with polit. parties Federal Fgn. Min. Office, Bonn, 1985—88; min.-counsellor for polit. affairs German Embassy, Washington, 1988—93; head of directorate for UN Affairs and coord. for human rights issues Federal Fgn. Office, Bonn, 1993—95, head of directorate gen. for UN Affairs, Human Rights and Humanitarian Aid, 1995—98, dir. gen., UN Affairs, Human Rights, Humanitarian Aid and Global Issues, 1998, polit. dir. Bonn, 1998—99, state sec. Berlin, 1999—2002; perm. rep. of Germany UN, NYC, 2002—04. Office: Permanent German Mission to UN 871 UN Plaza New York NY 10017

**PLEVAN, BETTINA B.,** lawyer; b. Oceanside, N.Y., Nov. 21, 1945; BA, Wellesley Coll., 1967; JD magna cum laude, Boston U., 1970. Bar: N.Y. 1971, US Dist. Ct., (Ea. dist.)NY, US Ct. Appeals, (2nd cir.), 1975, U.S. Supreme Ct. 1977, US Ct. Appeals, (DC cir.), 1977, US Ct. Appeals, (3rd cir.), 1978, US Ct. Appeals, (So. dist.) NY, 1979, US Tax Ct., 1979, US Ct. Appeals, (5th. cir.), 1982, US Ct. Appeals (9th cir.), US Dist. Ct. (No. dist.)

NY, 1983, US Ct. Appeals, (4th cir.), 1986, US Dist. Ct. (We. dist.) NY, 1993, US Ct. Appeals, (6th cir.) Editor Boston U. law Review, 1968—70; mem. Proskauer Rose LLP (formerly Proskauer Rose Goetz & Mendelsohn), N.Y.C., 1974—. Pres. Fed. Bar Coun., 1996—98, pres. emeritus, 1998—. Named one of The Best Lawyers in NY, NY mag. Fellow: Am. Acad. Appellate Lawyers, Am. Coll. Trial Lawyers; mem.: ABA (mem. Ho. Delegates 1986—91), NY County Lawyers Assn., NY State Bar Assn., Assn. Bar of the City NY (mem., com. on state courts of superior jurisdiction 1975—78, chair 1978—81, mem. exec. com. 1981—85, chair coun. on jud. adminstrn. 1985—88, mem., long range planning com. 1988—90, chair 1992—95). Office: Proskauer Rose LLP 1585 Broadway Fl 27 New York NY 10036-8299 E-mail: bplevan@proskauer.com.*

**PLEW, PAUL TIMOTHY,** music educator, dean; s. Harlow Nelson and Dorothy Amelia Plew; m. Pamela Jean Smith, July 24, 1970; children: Paul Timothy, Janelle Jean Sonnenburg, Jason David. BS in Music, Bapt. Bible Coll., 1970; MusM, Pacific Luth. U., 1979; EdD, Nova Southeastern U., 1996. Prof. NW Bapt. Sem., Master's Sem.; dean of music dept. Master's Coll., Santa Clarita, Calif., 1979—; min. music Santa Clarita Bapt. Ch., 1990—. Regional pres. Choral Conductor's Guild, LA; co-founder So. Calif. Christian Coll. Music Faculty Conferences; choral adjudicator and clinician. Dir.: (numerous professional choral recordings);, singer various oratorio performances. Named Amb. of Goodwill for Israel, Min. Tourism, Jerusalem, 2001, 2005. Mem.: Nat. Assn. Ch. Musicians (past pres.), Nat. Assn. Schs. Music, Santa Clarita Choral Music Educators Assn. (founder), Am. Choral Dirs. Assn. Achievements include research in musicology and hymnology. Office: Master's Coll 21726 Placerita Canyon Rd Santa Clarita CA 91321

**PLIMPTON, CALVIN HASTINGS,** retired internist, university president; b. Boston, Oct. 7, 1918; s. George Arthur and Fanny (Hastings) P.; m. Ruth Talbot, Sept. 6, 1941; children: David, Thomas, George (dec.), Anne, Edward. BA cum laude, Amherst Coll., 1939; MD cum laude, Harvard, 1943, MA, 1947; Med. Sci.D., Columbia, 1951; LL.D., Williams Coll., 1960, Wesleyan U., 1961, Doshisha U., Kyoto, Japan, 1962, St. Lawrence U., 1963, Amherst U., 1971; L.H.D., U. Mass., 1962; D.Sc., Rockford Coll., 1962, St. Mary's, 1963, Trinity Coll., 1966, Grinnell Coll., Iowa, 1967; Litt.D., Am. Internat. Coll., 1965, Mich. State Coll., 1969; DSc, N.Y. Med. Coll., 1986. Diplomate: Nat. Bd. Med. Examiners, Am. Bd. Internal Medicine. Intern, asst. resident, resident medicine Presbyn. Hosp., N.Y.C., 1947-50; asst. attending physician Columbia-Presbyn. Med. Center, 1950-60; asso. medicine (Coll. Phys. and Surg.), 1950-59, asst. prof. clin. medicine, 1959-60; prof. medicine, chmn. dept. Am. U. Beirut, Am. U. Hosp., Beirut, Lebanon, 1957-59; pres. Amherst Coll., 1960-71, Downstate Med. Center, SUNY, 1971-79, dean med. sch., 1971-74, 76-79, prof. medicine, 1971-82, prof. emeritus, 1982—; pres. Am. U., Beirut, 1984-87. Vis. prof. Columbia Presbyn. Med. Center, 1976-77. Trustee Am. U. Beirut, 1960-90, trustee emeritus, 1990—, chmn. bd., 1965-82; trustee World Peace Found., 1962-77, Phillips Exeter Acad., 1963-76, Commonwealth Fund, 1962-83, Hampshire Coll., 1963-71, U. Mass., 1962-70, L.I. U., 1972-82, N.Y. Law Sch., 1976-84; mem Harvard Bd. Overseers, 1969-75. Capt. U.S. Army, 1944-46, ETO. Decorated comdr. Order of Cedars Lebanon; recipient award Nat. Geog. Soc., award New Eng. Soc., John Phillips award Phillip Exeter Acad., Battle Star Ctrl. Europe. Fellow ACP; mem. Am. Acad. Arts and Scis., Russian Fedn. Acad. Med. Tech. Scis., Coun. Fgn. Rels., Soc. Mayflower Descs., Harvey Soc., Alpha Omega Alpha, Sigma Xi. Clubs: Century, Univ. (N.Y.C.), Charaka (N.Y.C.), Riverdale Yacht (N.Y.C.), Pilgrims (N.Y.C.); Tavern Boston. also: 10 Longwood Dr Apt 411 Westwood MA 02090 Office Phone: 781-329-3961.

**PLIMPTON, MARTHA,** actress; Represented by Internat. Creative Mgmt., Beverly Hills, Calif. Actress (films) The River Rat, 1984, The Goonies, 1985, The Mosquito Coast, 1986, Shy People, 1987, Stars and Bars, 1988, Running on Empty, 1988, Another Woman, 1988, Parenthood, 1989, Silence Like Glass, 1989, Stanley & Iris, 1990, Daybreak, 1993, Josh and S.A.M., 1993, The Beans of Egypt, 1994, Mrs. Parker and the Vicious Circle, 1994, Beautiful Girls, 1996, Eye of God, 1997, (plays) Hobson's Choice, 2002 (Obie Award, 2002), The False Servant, 2005, Hurlyburly, 2005, Shining City, 2006.*

**PLIMPTON, PEGGY LUCAS,** trustee; b. Nov. 3, 1931; d. David Nicholson and Margaret (MacMillan) Lucas; m. Hollis Winslow Plimpton, June 11, 1955; children: Victoria P. Babcock, Priscilla P. Morphy, Hollis Winslow Plimpton III. AB, Duke U., 1954. Trustee Cape Cod Conservatory of Music, 1989—. Bd. trustees Carleton Williard Retirement Home, Bedford, Mass., 1968—, Cape Cod Conservatory Music, 1990—; bd. dirs. Episcopal Ch. Women, 1968-78, Brigham & Women's Hosp., Boston, 1975—; pres. Boston Lying-In Hosp., 1970-72; chmn. Mass. Nat. Cathedral Assn., Boston, 1978-80, 1985-88; pres. bd. trustees Women's Ednl. and Indsl., Boston, 1980-83. Mem. New Eng. Farm and Garden Club (bd. dirs. 1965—, pres. 1995—), Chestnut Hill Garden Club (bd. dirs. 1970-74), Jr. League Garden Club (pres. 1981-83), Colonial Dames (bd. mgrs. 1983-89, v.p. 1993-98, pres. 1998—), Vincent Club, Chilton Club. Republican. Episcopalian. Avocations: gardening, golf, bridge.

**PLIMPTON, THOMAS E.,** automotive executive; Exec. v.p. Paccar Inc., Bellevue, Wash., 1998—2002, pres., 2002—. Office: Paccar Inc 777 106th Ave Bellevue WA 98004 Mailing: Paccar Inc PO Box 1518 Bellevue WA 98009*

**PLINE, JENNIFER ALICE,** trust company executive; BA, Boston (Mass.) Coll., 1982, MBA, 1987. Chartered fin. analyst CFA Inst., 1990, chartered investment counselor Investment Counsel Assn. Am., 1990. Dir. client svc Standish Mellon Asset Mgmt., Boston, 1987—2003, v.p. trusts Harvard Mgmt. Co., Boston, 2005—. Mem. adv. bd. Fin. Dept. Boston (Mass.) Coll., 2002—06. Mem. com. fgn. rels. City Boston; trustee Beth Israel Hosp., Needham, Mass., 2005—06; chmn.'s account exec. United Way Mass. Bay, Boston, 2004—06; mem. adv. bd. Horizons for Homeless Children, Boston, 2003—06. Office: Harvard Management Company 600 Atlantic Avenue Boston MA 02210 Office Phone: 617-720-6766.

**PLISCHKE, LE MOYNE WILFRED,** chemist, researcher; b. Greensburg, Pa., Dec. 11, 1922; s. Fred and Ruth Naomi (Rumbaugh) P.; m. Joan Harper, Mar. 11, 1966. BS, Waynesburg Coll., 1948; MS, W.Va. U., 1952. Rsch. chemist U.S. Naval Ordinance Test Sta., China Lake, Calif., 1952-53; asst. prof. chemistry Commonwealth U., Richmond, Va., 1953-54; rsch. chemist E.I. du Pont, Gibbstown, N.J., 1955-57, Monsanto Chem. Co., Pensacola, Fla., 1957—. Mem.: Am. Chem. Soc. Achievements include 18 U.S. patents and 51 foreign patents in field. Home: 2100 Club House Dr Lillian AL 36549-5402 Office: Monsanto Co The Chem Group PO Box 97 Gonzalez FL 32560-0097 E-mail: plis123@gulftel.com.

**PLISHNER, MICHAEL JON,** lawyer; b. Rockville Center, NY, Jan. 22, 1948; s. Meyer J. and Lillian (Gold) P.; m. Rosalind F. Schein, Jan. 26, 1969; children: Aaron, Alexander, Elias. BA summa cum laude, Yale U., 1969, JD, 1972. Bar: Calif. 1972, U.S. Dist. Ct. (no. dist.) Calif. 1972, U.S. Ct. Appeals (9th cir.) 1972. Assoc. McCutchen, Doyle, Brown & Enersen, San Francisco, 1972-79, ptnr., 1979—2001, Bingham McCutchen, San Francisco, 2001—, dep. chmn. litig. practice group. Mem. Phi Beta Kappa. Office: Bingham McCutchen LLP 3 Embarcadero Ctr San Francisco CA 94111-4003 Office Phone: 415-393-2240. Business E-Mail: michael.plishner@bingham.com.

**PLISKOW, VITA SARI,** anesthesiologist; b. Tel Aviv, Sept. 13, 1942; arrived in Can. 1951; came to U.S., 1967; d. Henry Norman and Renee (Mushkatel) Stahl; m. Raymond Joel Pliskow, June 30, 1968; children: Tia, Kami. MD, U. B.C., Vancouver, 1967. Diplomate Am. Bd. Anesthesiology. Ptnr. Olympic Anesthesia, Bremerton, Wash., 1971-84, pres., Anesthesiologist, 1974-84; co-founder Olympic Ambulatory Surgery Ctr., Bremerton, 1977-83; ptnr., anesthesiologist Allenmore Anesthesia Assocs., Tacoma, 1983—. Staff anesthesiologist Harrison Meml. Hosp., Bremerton, 1971-95, Allenmore Hosp., Tacoma, 1983—. Trustee Tacoma Youth Symphony Assn.,

1994—; active Nat. Coun. Jewish Women, 1972—. Fellow Am. Coll. Anesthesiologists, Am. Coll. Chest Physicians; mem. Am. Soc. Anesthesiologists (del. Wash. State 1987—), Wash. State Med. Assn. (del. Pierce County 1993-94), Wash. State Soc. Anesthesiologists (pres. 1985-87), Pierce County Med. Soc. (sec.-treas. 1992). Avocations: classical music, opera, singing (mezzo soprano). Office: PO Box 65274 University Place WA 98464-1274

**PLOMP, TEUNIS (TONY PLOMP),** minister; b. Rotterdam, Netherlands, Jan. 28, 1938; arrived in Can., 1951; s. Teunis and Cornelia (Pietersma) P.; m. Margaret Louise Bone, July 21, 1962; children: Jennifer Anne, Deborah Adele. BA, U. B.C., Vancouver, Can., 1960; BD, Knox Coll., Toronto, Ont., Can., 1963, DD (hon.), 1988. Ordained to ministry Presbyn. Ch., 1963. Min. Goforth Meml. Presbyn. Ch., Saskatoon, Sask., Canada, 1963-68, Richmond (B.C.) Presbyn. Ch., 1968—2004. Clerk Presbytery of Westminster, Vancouver, 1969-2003; moderator 113th Gen. Assembly Presbyn. Ch. Can., 1987-88, dep. clk., 1988—; chaplain New Haven Correctional Centre, Burnaby, B.C., 1973-99. Contbr. mag. column You Were Asking, 1982-2002. Presbyterian. Avocations: record collecting, bicycling, swimming. Personal E-mail: tony_plomp@telus.net.

**PLONK, WILLIAM MCGUIRE,** retired minister; b. Franklin, N.C., Aug. 19, 1925; s. Thomas Motley and Mary Louise (McGuire) P.; m. Nancy Marie Moore, June 29, 1957; children: Mary Evelyn Plonk Lucas, William McGuire Plonk, Jr. BS, Davidson Coll., 1949; BD, Union Theol. Seminary, Richmond, Va., 1954. Ordained to ministry Presbyn. Ch., 1954. Pastor Lawrenceville (Va.) Presbyn. Ch., 1954-56, Rivermont Presbyn. Ch., Chester, Va., 1956-58; youth minister First Presbyn. Ch., Greensboro, N.C., 1958-61; pastor Westminster Presbyn. Ch., Columbia, S.C., 1961-66, Covenant Presbyn. Ch., Spartanburg, S.C., 1966-69, Bow Creek Presbyn. Ch., Virginia Beach, Va., 1969-72; spl. agt. Jefferson Standard Ins. Co., Norfolk, Va., 1972-73; exchange pastor St. Stevens and West Church of Scotland, Broughty Ferry, Scotland, 1972; pastor Makemie/Naomi Makemie Presbyn. Chs., Accomac, Onancock, Va., 1974-90; interim pastor Manokin Presbyn. Ch., Princess Anne, Md., 1991, 92; stated supply Clark Presbyn. Ch., Daugherty, Va., 1993—2001; interim pastor Chatham (Va.) Presbyn. Ch., 2003—. Dist. chmn. Boy Scouts Am. 1st lt. U.S. Army, 1944-46. Mem. Ruritan (pres. Onancock Club, Paul Harris Fellow 1993), Drummondtown-Lee Ruritan Club (pres.). Avocations: singing, early Amercial church history. Home: 107 Settlers Bend Martinsville VA 24112-6616 E-mail: bplonk@aol.com.

**PLONSEY, ROBERT,** electrical and biomedical engineer; b. N.Y.C., July 17, 1924; s. Louis B. and Betty (Vinograd) P.; m. Vivian V. Vucker, Oct. 1, 1948; 1 child, Daniel. BEE, Cooper Union, 1943; MSEE, NYU, 1948; PhD, U. Calif., Berkeley, 1955; postgrad. med. sch., Case Western Res. U., 1969-71; D of Technol. Scis., Slovak Acad. Scis., 1995. Registered profl. engr., Ohio. Asst. prof. elec. engring. U. Calif., Berkeley, 1955-57, Case Inst. Tech., Cleve., 1957-60, assoc. prof., 1960-66, prof., 1966-68, dir. bioengring. group, 1962-68; prof. biomed. engring. Sch. Engring. and Med. Medicine Case Western Res. U., 1968-83, chmn. dept., 1976-80; vis. prof. biomed. engring. Duke U., Durham, NC, 1980-81, prof., 1983-96, prof. biomed. engring., Hudson prof. engring., 1990-93, Pfizer-Inc.-Edmond T. Pratt Jr. Univ. prof. biomed. engring., 1993-96, Pfizer-Inc.-Edmond T. Pratt Jr. Univ. prof. emeritus, 1996—. Mem. biomed. fellowships rev. com. NIH, 1966-70; mem. tng. com. Engrs. in Medicine and Biology, 1972-73, cons., 1974-96; cons. NSF, 1973-93; mem. internat. sci. adv. com. Ragnar Granit Inst., Tampere (Finland) U. Tech., 1992—; ad hoc mem. sci. adv. com. Whitaker Found., 1989-91. Author: (with R. Collin) Principles and Applications of Electromagnetic Fields, 1961, Bioelectric Phenomena, 1969, (with J. Liebman and P. Gillette) Pediatric Electrocardiography, 1982, (with T. Pilkington) Engineering Contributions to Biophysical Electrocardiography, 1982, (with J. Liebman and Y. Rudy) Pediatric and Fundamental Electrocardiography, 1982, (with R.C. Barr) Bioelectricity: A Quantitative Approach, 1988, 2d edit., 2000, (with J. Malmivuo) Bioelectromagnetism, 1995; mem. editl. bd. Trans. IEEE, Biomed. Engring. 1965-70; assoc. editor, 1977-79; mem. editl. bd. TIT Jour. 1971-81, Electrocardiology Jour., 1974—, Med. and Biol. Engring. and Computing, 1987—Critical Revs. in Biomed. Engring., 1994—; procs. editor Engring. in Medicine and Biology, 17th Ann., Conf., 1965. Mem. com. on electrocardiography Am. Heart Assn., 1976-82; v.p. Your Schs., Cleveland Heights, Ohio, 1968-69, 73-75; provisional trustee Am. Bd. Clin. Engrs., 1973-74, pres. 1975, trustee, 1976-85. With AUS. 1944-46. Recipient award postdoctoral award NIH., 1980-81, Merit award Internat. Union Phys. and Engring. Scis. in Medicine, 1997, Ragnar Granit prize, 2003. Fellow AAAS, IEEE (chmn. Cleve. chpt. group on biomed. electronics 1962-63, chmn. publs. com. group on engring. in medicine and biology 1968-70, v.p. adminstrv. com. 1970-72, pres. 1973-74, chmn. fellows com. Engring. in Medicine and Biology Soc. 1986-88, 2000, v.p. tech. and conf. activities 1991, William S. Morlock award 1979, Centennial medal 1984, co-program chair ann. conf., Paris 1992, chmn. awards com. 1996, Millennium medal 2000, Ragnar Granit prize 2003); mem. AAUP, NAE (bioengring. peer com. 1988-91, 2001-04, chair 1990-91, 2003-04, nominating com. 1991-92, mem. com. 1992-94, program adv. com. 1996-98, NRC postdoctoral rsch. associateships evaluation panel 1987-90, Russ prize com. 2000-03), Internat. Acad. Med. and Biol. Engring. (founding mem. 1997), Am. Inst. Med. and Biol. Engring. (founding fellow 1992—), Alliance for Engring. in Medicine and Biology (treas. 1976-78), Biomed. Engring. Soc. (bd. dirs. 1975-78, 79-83, pres. 1981-82, chmn. affiliations com. 1987-89, ALZA Disting. lectr. 1988, Disting. Svc. award, 2004), Am. Physiol. Soc., Am. Soc. Engring. Edn. (bd. dirs. biomed. engring. divsn. 1978-82, chmn. 1982-83, Pilkington Outstanding Educator award, 2002). Office: Duke U Box 90281 Dept Biomed Engring Durham NC 27708-0281 Office Phone: 919-660-5131. Business E-Mail: robert.plonsey@duke.edu. *External recognition of success is not nearly so important as the inner awareness of coming to full grips with life, to be fully involved, bending all strengths to fulfill one's goals and philosophies. And of all involvements, those with people are most meaningful (to be aware of and share the feelings of colleagues, students, friends, and family—and to enrich these relationships)—and for me most difficult.*

**PLORDE, JAMES JOSEPH,** physician, educator; b. Brewster, Minn., Feb. 16, 1934; s. James Arthur and Mary Jeanette (Lutz) P.; m. Diane Sylvia Koenigs, Aug. 28, 1964 (div. July 1974); children: Lisa Marie, Michele Louise, James Joshua; m. Jo Ann Gates, Dec. 22, 1986. BA, U. Minn., 1956, BS, 1957, MD, 1959. Diplomate Am. Bd. Internal Medicine, Am. Bd. Pathology. Vol. leader Peace Corps, Gondar, Ethiopia, 1964-66; intern King County Hosp., Seattle, 1959-60; resident U. Wash., Seattle, 1960-62, fellow infectious diseases, 1962-64; chief med. resident King County Hosp., Seattle, 1966-67; asst. prof. medicine U. Wash., Seattle, 1967-71, assoc. prof., 1971-78; fellow clin. microbiology, 1972-73; prof. medicine, lab. medicine U. Wash. Sch. Medicine, Seattle, 1978-98 (ret.), prof. emeritus medicine, lab. medicine, 1998—; head clin. investigation U.S. Naval Med. Research, Addis Ababa, Ethiopia, 1968-71; chief infectious diseases VA Hosp., Seattle, 1973-89, chief clin. microbiology, 1973-98; ret., 1998. Instr. U. Wash., 1966 67; cons WHO, 1975, Suez Canal U. Faculty of Medicine, Ismailia, Arab Republic of Egypt, 1981-85. Contbr. numerous articles to profl. jours., chpts. to books. Fellow Infectious Disease Soc., ACP; mem. AAAS, Am. Soc. Microbiology, Acad. Clin. Lab. Physicians and Scientists. Home: 3164 W Laurelhurst Dr NE Seattle WA 98105-5346 Fax: 206-523-3541. E-mail: jjplorde@u.washington.edu.

**PLOSSER, CHARLES IRVING,** bank executive, economics professor; b. Birmingham, Ala., Sept. 19, 1948; s. George Gray and Dorothy (Irving) P.; m. Janet Schwert, June 26, 1976; children: Matthew, Kevin, Allison. B.E. cum laude, Vanderbilt U., 1970; MBA, U. Chgo., 1972, PhD, 1976. Cons. Citicorp Realty Cons., N.Y.C., 1972-73; lectr. Grad. Sch. Bus., U. Chgo., 1975-76; asst. prof. Grad. Sch. Bus. Stanford U., Calif., 1976-78; asst. prof. econs. W.E. Simon Grad. Sch. Bus., U. Rochester, NY, 1978-82, assoc. prof., 1982-86, prof., 1986-89, Fred H. Gowen prof. econs., 1989-92, John M. Olin Disting. prof. econs. and pub. policy, 1992—2006, acting dean, 1990-91, 92-93, dean, 1993—2003; pres. Fed. Res. Bank, Phila., 2006—. Chmn. bd. Consortium for Grad. Study in Mgmt., 1995-97; bd. dirs. ViaHealth, Inc. 1995-2000, Rochester Gas & Electric Corp, RGS Energy Group, 1996-2002, dir. adv. bd.,

2002-05; bd. dirs. Grad. Mgmt. Admission Coun., 1997-2003, chmn. bd., 2002-03; rsch. assoc. Nat. Bur. Econ. Rsch. Editor, Jour. Monetary Econs., 1983—, Carnegie-Rochester Conference Series on Public Policy, 1989—; contbr. articles to profl. jours. 1st lt., U.S. Army, 1972-73. NSF research grantee, 1982, 84. Mem. Am. Econs. Assn., Econometrics Soc., Am. Fin. Assn., Tau Beta Pi, Beta Gamma Sigma. Office: Fed Res Bank Phila Ten Independence Mall Philadelphia PA 19106

**PLOTCH, WALTER,** management consultant, fund raising counselor; b. N.Y.C., July 19, 1932; s. Harry and Belle (Lebowsky) P.; m. Yvette Gabrielle Lambert, Mar. 20, 1957; children: Allison, Jennifer, Adrienne. AB, Queens Coll., 1957; MA, Harvard U., 1959; postgrad., 1959-62. Analyst L.F. Rothschild & Co., N.Y.C. and Boston, 1962-64; cons., 1964-65; edn. dir. New Eng. Anti-Defamation League, 1965-68; nat. edn. dir., 1968-76; v.p. Brakeley, John Price Jones Inc., N.Y.C., 1976-79; sr. v.p., dir., 1979-89; sr. v.p. The Oram Group, Inc., N.Y.C., 1989-92; exec. v.p.; pres., CEO Walter Plotch Assocs., Inc., Croton-On-Hudson, NY, 1992—2005. Mem. faculty Grad. Sch. Mgmt. and Urban Affairs, New Sch. U.; lectr. Harvard U. Grad. Sch. Edn.; cons. Harcourt, Brace, Plenum Pubs. Co-editor: Pluralism in a Democratic Society, 1977; gen. editor: The Job Corps Intergroup RElations Series, 1974; contbr. articles to profl. jours.; contbg. editor mag., Jour. Sponsored Rsch. Bd. dirs. Schizophrenia Found., 1975-90; nat. bd. dirs. NCCJ, 1980-84, Nat. Charitable Info Bur.mem. exec. com. 1986-94. Served with USCGR, 1953-55, Korea. Grantee U.S. Office Edn., Dept. Labor, N.Y. Coun. Humanities; tchg. fellow Harvard U., 1959-61. Mem. Princeton Club, Phi Alpha Theta. Democrat. Jewish. Office: 39 Furnace Dock Rd Croton On Hudson NY 10520-1406

**PLOTKIN, HORACIO,** pediatric endocrinologist, orthopedic surgeon, educator; b. Buenos Aires, Dec. 23, 1964; m. Carola Rabuffetti, Mar. 23, 1999; children: Sophie Adele, Lucas Jay, Olivia Robin. BS, J.J. Urquiza, Buenos Aires, 1981; MD, U. Buenos Aires, 1987. Resident in pediats. T. Alvarez Hosp., Buenos Aires, 1988—92; fellow in pediat. endocrinology J.P. Garrahan Hosp., Buenos Aires, 1991—92; fellow in metabolic bone diseases IDIM, Buenos Aires, 1992—96; fellow in endocrinology Yale U., New Haven, 1996—97; fellow in pediat. metabolic bone diseases McGill U., Montreal, Que., Canada, 1997—2002; asst. prof. pediats. U. of Nebr. Med. Ctr., Omaha, 2002—, asst. prof. of orthopedic surgery, 2002—; dir. Metabolic Bone Diseases Clinic Children's Hosp., Omaha, 2002—, dir. Osteogenesiss Imperfecta Clinic, 2002—. Contbr. articles and cartoons to humorous publs. Named Home Town Hero, City of Omaha, 2005. Fellow: Am. Acad. of Pediats.; mem.: Endocrine Soc., Internat. Bone and Mineral Soc., Am. Soc. for Bone and Mineral Rsch. Office: Univ Nebr Med Ctr 985456 Nebraska Medical Center Omaha NE 68198-5456 Office Phone: 402-559-4056. Office Fax: 402-559-4001.

**PLOTKIN, IRVING H. (IRVING HERMAN PLOTKIN),** economist, consultant; b. Bklyn., July 19, 1941; s. Samuel H. and Dorothy (Falick) P.; m. Janet V. Bufe, July 26, 1969; children: Aaron Jacob, Joshua Benjamin. BS in Econs., U. Pa., 1963; PhD in Math. Econs., MIT, 1968. Corp. planning analyst Mobil Oil Co., N.Y.C., 1962-63, Mobil Oil Italiana, Genoa, Italy, 1965; ind. cons. econs. and ops. rsch. to banks, mut. funds, ins. cos., govt. agys. Cambridge, Mass., 1965-68; sr. economist Arthur D. Little, Inc., Cambridge, 1968—2002. Dir. regulation and econs., 1974-2002, v.p., 1979-2002; bd. dirs. Arthur D. Little Valuation, Inc.; trustee Arthur D. Little, Inc., ESOP, 1988-2002; mgr. dir. tax svc. PricewaterhouseCoopers LLP, Boston, 2002—; instr. fin. and computer scis. MIT, 1965-68; lectr. maj. univs. U.S. and abroad; expert witness U.S. Ho. of Reps. and Senate coms., U.S. Ct. Claims, U.S. Tax Ct. I.C.C., FTC, Fed. Martime Commn., Fed. Dist. Cts., Fed. Res. Bd., other fed. and state govt. agys., 1967—. NASA fellow, 1963-66, NSF fellow, 1967, Am. Bankers Assn. fellow, 1968. Mem. Am. Econ. Assn., Econometric Soc., Am. Fin. Assn., Beta Gamma Sigma, Pi Gamma Mu, Tau Delta Phi (chpt. pres. 1962-63). Home: Apt 910 975 Memorial Dr Cambridge MA 02138-5754 Office: 125 High St Boston MA 02110 Office Phone: 617-530-5332. Business E-Mail: irving.h.plotkin@us.pwc.com.

**PLOTKIN, LOREN E.,** lawyer; b. Bklyn., Feb. 8, 1943; s. Arthur and Betty Ann (Strugatz); m. Carol Baxter, Aug. 25, 1990; children: Lily, Kate. BA, Harpur Coll., SUNY, Binghamton, 1963; JD, St. John's U., N.Y.C., 1966. Bar: N.Y. 1966, U.S. Dist. Ct. (so. and ea. dists.) N.Y. 1972, U.S. Tax Ct. 1976. Law asst. appellate divsn., first dept. N.Y. State Supreme Ct.; ptnr. Lans Feinberg & Cohen, N.Y.C., 1969-81; mem. Levine & Thall, P.C., N.Y.C., 1981-84, Levine Thall and Plotkin, N.Y.C., 1984-96, Levine Thall, Plotkin & Menin, L.L.P., N.Y.C., 1996-99, Levine, Plotkin & Menin, L.L.P., N.Y.C., 2000—. Lectr. on entertainment law. Notes and comments editor St. John's U. Law Rev., 1965-66. Home: 34 Lawrence Ln Palisades NY 10964-1604 Office: Levine Plotkin & Menin LLP 1740 Broadway Fl 22 New York NY 10019-4315

**PLOTKIN, MANUEL D.,** management consultant, educator, former corporate executive, former government official; s. Jacob and Bella (Katz) P.; m. Diane Fern Weiss, Dec. 17, 1967; 1 child, Lori Ann. BS with honors, Northwestern U., 1948; MBA, U. Chgo., 1949. Price economist, survey coordinator U.S. Bur. Labor Statistics, Washington, 1949-51, Chgo., 1951-53; sr. economist Sears Roebuck & Co., Chgo., 1953-61, mgr. market research, 1961-66, chief economist, mgr. mktg. rsch., 1966-73; dir. corp. planning and research, 1973-77, exec. corp. planner, 1979-80; dir. U.S. Bur. Census, Washington, 1977-79; v.p. dir. group practice Divsn. Mgmt. Cons. Austin Co., Evanston, Ill., 1981-85; pres. M.D. Plotkin Research & Planning Co., Chgo., 1985—. Tchr. statistics Ind. U., 1953-54; tchr. econs. Wilson Jr. Coll., Chgo., 1954-55; tchr. quantitative methods and managerial econs. Northwestern U., 1955-63; tchr. mktg. rsch. and mktg. mgmt. DePaul U., Chgo., 1992-95; mem. Conf. Bd. Mktg. Rsch. Adv. Coun., 1968-77, chmn.-elect, 1977; chmn. adv. com. U.S. Census Bur., 1974-75; trustee Mktg. Sci. Inst., 1968-77; mem. Nat. Commn. Employment and Unemployment Stats., 1978-79, Adv. Coun. Edn. Stats., 1977-79, Interagy. Com. Population Rsch., 1977-79; mem. adv. coun. Kellstadt Ctr., DePaul U., 1987-92; trustee U.S. Travel Data Ctr., 1977-79. Contbr. articles to profl. jours. Served with AUS, 1943-46, ETO. Decorated Bronze Star medal with oak leaf cluster. Mem. Am. Mktg. Assn. (pres. Chgo. 1968-69, nat. dir. 1969-70, nat. v.p. mktg. rsch. 1970-72, nat. v.p. mktg. mgmt. 1981-83, pres., CEO 1985-86), Am. Statis. Assn. (pres. Chgo. 1966-67, Forecasting award 1963), Am. Econ. Assn., Nat. Assn. Bus. Economists, Planning Execs. Inst., World Future Soc., Midwest Planning Assn., U. Ill. Businessmen Rsch. Adv. Group, Chgo. Assn. Commerce and Industry, Beta Gamma Sigma, Alpha Sigma Lambda, Delta Mu Delta. Home and Office: 2650 N Lakeview Ste 3910 Chicago IL 60614-1831

**PLOTKIN, MARK ELLIOTT,** lawyer; b. Dallas, Tex., May 30, 1961; s. Stanley Bert and Carol Lynn (Schwartz) P.; m. Teresa Marie Cavalier, June 21, 1987; children: Sarah Elizabeth, Natalie Anne. BA in History summa cum laude, Yale U., 1983; JD with honors, Harvard U., 1987. Bar: Md. 1987, D.C. 1988, U.S. Dist. Ct. D.C. 1991, U.S. Dist. Ct. Md. 1994, U.S. Supreme Ct. 1994 Assoc, Covington & Burling, Washington, 1987-95, ptnr., Internet/Info. Tech. Practice Group, 1995—; co-chmn. recruitment com. Sr. editor: Jour. Internat. Banking Law, Oxford, Eng., 1992—; contr. articles to profl. jours. 1994—. Bd. mem. lawyers com. Children's Hosp. D.C., 1995—. Mem. ABA, Phi Beta Kappa. Office: Covington & Burling 1201 Pennsylvania Ave NW Washington DC 20004-2401 Office Phone: 202-662-5656. Office Fax: 202-662-6291. Business E-Mail: mplotkin@cov.com.

**PLOTKIN, STANLEY ALAN,** virologist; b. N.Y.C., May 12, 1932; s. Joseph and Lee (Fishbein) P.; m. Susan Lannon, Nov. 24, 1979; children: Michael, Alec. BA, NYU, 1952; MD, SUNY, N.Y.C., 1956; MA (hon.), U. Rouen, 2006; D honoris causa (hon.), U. Rouen, 2006. Diplomate Am. Bd. Pediat., Am. Acad. Pediat. Intern Cleve. Met. Gen. Hosp., 1956-57; resident pediat. Phila. Children's Hosp., 1961—62, dir. divsn. infectious diseases; physician, 1969—90; registrar Hosp. for Sick Children, London, 1962-63; assoc. mem. Wistar Inst., Phila., 1963-74, prof. virology, 1974—; asst. prof. pediat. U. Pa., Phila., 1966-71, assoc. prof., 1971-74, prof., 1974-91; prof. emeritus, 1991—; assoc. chmn. dept. pediat. U. Pa., Phila., 1986-88; med. and

sci. dir. Pasteur-Mérieux-Connaught Labs. (now Sanofi-Pasteur), Marnes-la-Coquette, France, 1991-97; advisor to pres. Sanofi Pasteur, Lyon, France, 1997—. Adj. prof. internat. health Johns Hopkins U., Balt., 2000—. Assoc. editor: Am. Jour. Epidemiology, 1967-87, Proc. Soc. Exptl. Biology and Medicine, 1968-85, Pediatric Infectious Disease jour., 1982-87, Vaccine jour., 1983—, Molecular and Cellular Probes jour., 1987—, Clin. Vaccine Immunology, 1996—, Biologicals, 2000—. Served as med. officer USPHS, 1957-60. Decorated Legion of Honor (France); Joseph P. Kennedy Found. grantee, 1964-66, Hartford Found. grantee, 1971-73, NIH grantee, 1973—; recipient Bruce medal ACP, 1987, Clin. Virology award Pan Am. Group Rapid Viral Diagnosis, 1995, Gold medal Sabin Found., 2002; named Disting. Physician Pediatric Infectious Diseases Soc., 1993, Disting. Alumnus, Children's Hosp. Phila., 2001, Fleming award Infectious Diseases Soc. of Am., 2004, Marshall award European Soc. Pediat. Infectious Diseases, 2006. Fellow AAAS; mem. NAS (Inst. of Medicine), Soc. Pediatric Rsch., Am. Pediatric Soc., Am. Epidemiology Soc., Am. Soc. Microbiology, Am. Acad. Pediatrics (chmn. infectious diseases com. 1987-90), World Soc. Pediatric Infectious Diseases (pres. 2003—), European Soc. Pediat. Infectious Diseases (Marshall award 2006_. Achievements include pioneering work on vaccine strains for protection against polio, rabies, rubella, rotavirus and cytomegalovirus. Office Phone: 215-297-9321. Personal E-mail: stanley.plotkin@sanofipasteur.com.

**PLOTNICK, HARVEY BARRY,** publishing executive; b. Detroit, Aug. 5, 1941; s. Isadore and Esther (Sher) Plotnick; m. Susan Regnery, Aug. 16, 1964 (div. Apr. 1977); children: Andrew, Alice; m. Elizabeth Allen, May 2, 1982; children: Teresa, Samuel. BA, U. Chgo., 1963. Editor Contemporary Books, Inc., Chgo., 1964-66, pres., pub., 1966—94; pres., CEO Paradigm Holdings, Inc., Chgo., 1994—. CEO Molecular Electronics Corpn., 2000. Trustee U. Chgo., 1994—, bd. gov., Argonne Nat. Lab., 2001—. Named one of Top 200 Collectors, ARTnews mag., 2005—06. Avocations: collecting old master prints, collecting Islamic ceramics. Office: Paradigm Holdings Inc 2 Prudential Plz Ste 3150 Chicago IL 60601-6790 Office Phone: 312-819-4015. E-mail: harvey1844@aol.com.

**PLOTNICK, ROBERT DAVID,** economic consultant, educator; b. Washington, Aug. 3, 1949; s. Theodore and Jean (Hirshfeld) P.; m. Gay Lee (Jensen), Dec. 22, 1972. BA, Princeton U., 1971; MA, U. Calif., Berkeley, 1973, PhD, 1976. Rsch. assoc. Inst. Rsch. on Poverty, Madison, Wis., 1973—75; asst. prof. Bates Coll., Lewiston, Maine, 1975—77, Dartmouth Coll., Hanover, NH, 1977—84; assoc. prof. U. Wash., Seattle, 1984—90, prof., 1990, assoc. dean, 1990—95, acting dean, 1994—95. Vis. scholar Russell Sage Found., 1990, U. NSW, 1997, London Sch. Econs., 2004; rsch. affiliate Inst. Rsch. Poverty, 1989—, Nat. Poverty Ctr., 2004—, West Coast Poverty Ctr., 2005—; chmn. Population Leadership Program, 1999—2005; dir. Ctr. for Studies in Demography and Ecology, 1997—2002; adj. fellow Pub. Policy Inst 1981—2000; cons. Wash. Dept. Social and Health Svcs., Olympia, 1984—86, 1990—96, 2000; cons. in field. Author: Progress Against Poverty, 1975; contbr. articles to profl. journals. Recipient Teaching Excellence Award U. Wash., 1985, 89. Mem. Am. Econ. Assn., Assn. Policy Analysis and Mgmt., Population Assn. Am. Avocations: hiking, birdwatching. Office: U Wash Evans Sch Pub Affairs PO Box 353055 Seattle WA 98195-3055 Office Phone: 206-685-2055. Business E-Mail: plotnick@u.washington.edu.

**PLOTNIK, ARTHUR,** writer, columnist; b. White Plains, NY, Oct. 1, 1937; s. Michael and Annabelle P.; m. Meta Von Borstel, Sept. 6, 1960 (div. 1979); children: Julia Nicole, Katya Michelle.; m. Mary Phelan, Dec. 2, 1983. BA, State U. N.Y., Binghamton, 1960; MA, U. Iowa, 1961; MS in L.S, Columbia U., 1966. Gen. reporter, reviewer Albany (N.Y.) Times Union, 1963-64; freelance writer, 1964-66; editor Librarians Office, Library of Congress, 1966-69; assoc. editor Wilson Library Bull., Bronx, NY, 1969-74; editor-in-chief Am. Libraries, Chgo., 1975-89; assoc. pub. ALA, 1989-97; editl. dir. ALA Editions, 1993-97; writer, 1997—. Adj. instr. journalism Columbia Coll., Chgo., 1988-89; speaker in field. Author: The Elements of Editing: A Modern Guide for Editors and Journalists, 1982, Jacob Shallus, Calligrapher of the Constitution, 1987, Honk If You're a Writer, 1992, The Elements of Expression, 1996, 2d edit., 2006, The Urban Tree Book, 2000, The Elements of Authorship (reprint of Honk if You're a Writer), 2000, Spunk & Bite: A Writer's Guide to Punchier, More Engaging Language and Style, 2005; contbg. editor: The Writer, 2000—; columnist: Editorial Eye, 1995—2001; exec. prodr.: Libr. Video mag., 1986—91; contbr. articles to profl. jours.; author: gen. articles, fiction and poetry. Bd. dirs. Am. Book Awards, 1979-82; bd. advs. Univ. Press of Am., 1982—1997. Served with USAR, 1962-67. Fellow Iowa Writers Workshop Creative Writing, 1961; recipient award Ednl. Press Assn. Am., 1973 (3), 77, 82, 83; cert. of excellence Internat. Reading Assn., 1970, First Pl. award Verbatim essay competition, 1986, award Am. Soc. Bus. Press Editors, 1987, First Pl. award poetry competition Irish-Am. Heritage Ctr., Chgo., 2005. Mem. ALA, ACLU, Treekeepers (Openlands Project). Home and Office: 2120 W Pensacola Ave Chicago IL 60618-1718 also: N E Pub Assocs Literary Agents PO Box 5 Chester CT 06412-0005

**PLOTTEL, GLORIA SUSANNE STONE,** marketing professional; b. N.Y.C., Feb. 16, 1966; d. Leroy Saul and Karen Lila Stone; m. Philip Benjamin Plottel, June 9, 1996. BA cum laude Univ. Profs. Program, Boston U., 1988; MS in Forest Resources Mgmt, SUNY, Syracuse, 1992; MBA, NYU, 2002. Mgr. dept. geography Boston U., 1989-90; tchg. asst. coll. environ. sci. and forestry SUNY, Syracuse, 1990-92; asst. acct. exec. Lowe and Ptnrs./SMS, N.Y.C., 1993-95; asst. mgr. Champion Internat. Corp., Stamford, Conn., 1995-97; mktg. mgr. Bus. New Haven, 1997-98; prin., mktg. and bus. cons., 2002—. Cons. Mass. Dept. Environ. Mgmt., Boston, 1993, No. Forest Lands Coun., Concord, N.H., 1993. Screenwriter: Seasoned Trails, 1989. Mem. exec. bd. U. Profs. Program, Boston U., 1997—; coun. mem. YMCA-YWCA Camping Svcs. of Greater N.Y., 1998—. SUNY internat. conf. grantee, 1991. Avocations: hiking, camping, swimming, ballroom dancing.

**PLOTTEL, JEANINE PARISIER,** foreign language educator; b. Paris, Sept. 21, 1934; came to U.S., 1943; m. Roland Plottel, 1956; children: Claudia S., Michael E., Philip B. Baccalauréat lettres, Lycée Français de N.Y., 1952; BA with honors, Barnard Coll., 1954; MA, Columbia U., 1955, PhD with distinction, 1959. Lectr. dept. French and Romance philology Columbia U., N.Y.C., 1955-59; rsch. assoc. fgn. lang. program MLA of Am., N.Y.C., 1959-60; lectr. dept. romance langs. CUNY, N.Y.C., 1960; asst. prof. div. humanities Julliard Sch. Music, N.Y.C., 1960-65; dir. lang. labs. Hunter Coll. CUNY, N.Y.C., 1965-69; asst. prof. dept. romance langs. Hunter Coll. CUNY, N.Y.C., 1965-69, assoc. prof. dept. romance langs., 1969-81, prof. dept. romance langs., 1981—2000, assoc. prof. French doctoral program grad. sch., univ. ctr., 1980-81, prof. French doctoral program grad. sch., univ. ctr., 1981—2000, prof. emeritus, 2000—. Exec. dir. AAVP NY state conf., 2002-; president's adv. coun. Barnard Coll., 2006—; Extensive adminstrv. experience in CUNY including chair dept. Romance langs. Author: Les Dialogues de Paul Valéry, 1960; pub. editor N.Y. Literary Forum, 1978-88; contbr. articles to profl. jours.; books. Pres. Maurice I. Parisier Found., Inc. Named Officer des Palmes Acad., 1999, recipient NEH fellowship, 1979; grantee N.Y. Coun. for the Humanities, 1986, Helena Rubenstein Found., 1986, Florence J. Gould Found., 1986, 88, N.Y. Times Found., 1986. Mem. AAUP (exec. dir. N.Y. State Conf. 2002-06), Maison Française (bd. dirs. Columbia U.), Peyre Inst., CUNY, Soc. French Am. Cultural Svcs. & Ednl. Aid, Hunter Coll. Art Galleries, Inst. French Studies. Home: 50 E 77th St Apt 14A New York NY 10021-1836 Office: Hunter Coll-CUNY 695 Park Ave New York NY 10021-5024 Office Phone: 212-535-6668. Personal E-mail: plottel@att.net.

**PLOTZ, CHARLES MINDELL,** physician, educator; b. N.Y.C., Dec. 6, 1921; s. Isaac and Rose (Bluestone) P.; m. Lucille Weckstein, Aug. 5, 1945; children: Richard, Thomas, Robert. BA, Columbia U., 1941, D.Sci., 1951; MD, L.I. Coll. Medicine, 1944. Diplomate Am. Bd. Internal Medicine. Intern New Haven Hosp., 1944-45; resident internal medicine Kings County Hosp., 1945-46, Maimonides Hosp., 1948-49; postdoctoral research fellow USPHS,

Columbia Coll. Phys. and Surgs., 1949-50; practice medicine, specializing in internal medicine Bklyn., 1950—; chief Arthritis Clinic, attending physician Kings County Hosp. Center, 1950-85; chief L.I. Coll. Hosp. (Arthritis Clinic), 1950-65; asst. attending physician Mt. Sinai Hosp., 1955—; chief Mt. Sinai Hosp. (Arthritis Clinic), 1955-65, Arthritis Clinic, State U., Hosp., 1967-85; asst. physician Columbia-Presbyn.Med. Center, 1949-71; attending physician Bklyn. State Hosp.; dir. ambulatory care Bklyn. Hosp.Ctr., 1991-93; emeritus prof. medicine SUNY, 1991—; professorial lectr. Mt. Sinai Sch. Medicine, 1992—; emeritus prof. in medicine SUNY, 1991—. Cons. physician Peninsula Gen. Hosp., Jamaica Hosp.; cons. on rheumatology VA Hosp., Bklyn., L.I. Coll. Hosp.; cons. family practice Luth. Med. Ctr.; vis. cons. internal medicine Jewish Gen. Hosp., Mont., Que., Can., 1965; cons. internal medicine Avicenna Hosp. and Wazir Akbar Hosp., Kabul, Afganistan, 1965; prof. medicine, dir. continuing edn., chmn. dept. family practice SUNY Downstate Med. Ctr., 1967-91, prof. emeritus medicine and family practice, 1991—; Fulbright lectr. U. Paris, 1984, 91; professorial lectr. Mt. Sinai Sch. Medicine, 1992—. Editorial adv. bd.: Pakistan Med. Forum; editor-in-chief: Clin. Rheumatology in Practice, 1981—; editor-in-chief: Advances in Rheumatology, 1986—, Rheuma21st.com, 1998—. Mem. nat. bd. govs. Arthritis Found., 1964-82, bd. govs. N.Y. chpt., 1965—, v.p. 1971-83, trustee, 1977-82, N.Y. chpt. sr. v.p., 1977-82, vice chmn. bd. trustees, 1983-85, 87—, pres., 1985-87; trustee Leo N. Levi Meml. Nat. Arthritis Hosp., Alumni Fund-Alumni Assn. SUNY Downstate Med. Center, Bklyn. Inst. Arts and Scis., Bklyn. Bot. Garden; mem. adv. bd. MEDICO, corp. mem., 1977—; treas. Internat. League Against Rheumatism, 1981-89; trustee Internat. League Against Rheumatism Trust, 1981-89. Served to capt. AUS, 1946-48. WHO fellow U. Negev, 1974; master Am. Coll. Rheumatology, 1991—; recipient Gold medal Am. Coll. Rheumatology, 1992. Master Am. Coll. Rheumatology (Gold medal 1992), fellow ACP, Am. Acad. Family Physicians (charter), N.Y. Acad. Medicine (chmn. edn. com. 1976-78); mem. AMA, (N.Y. chpt.), AAUP, Internat. Soc. for Rheumatic Therapy (chmn. 1987-89), Am. Fedn. Clin. Rsch., Am. Rheumatism Assn. (past sec.-treas.), N.Y. Rheumatism Assn. (past pres., exec. com.), Harvey Soc., (N.Y. chpt.), Kings County med. socs., Bklyn. socs. internal medicine, Soc. Tchrs. Family Medicine, N.Y. State Acads. Family Physicians, Soc. Urban Physicians, Mystery Writers Am., Sigma Xi, Alpha Omega Alpha; hon. mem. Rheumatology Soc. France, Rheumatology Soc. Japan, Rheumatology Soc. Mex., Rheumatology Soc. Brazil, Rheumatology Soc. Yugoslavia, Rheumatology Soc. Norway, Rheumatology Soc. Egypt, Med. Soc. Czechoslovakia, Cosmos Club, Heights Casino Club. Home: 184 Columbia Hts Brooklyn NY 11201-2105 also: 450 Clarkson Ave Brooklyn NY 11203-2056 E-mail: rheuma21st@aol.com.

**PLOUGH, ALONZO L.,** city health department administrator; BA in Biology, San Diego State U., 1973; MA in Sociology, Cornell U., 1975; MPH, Yale U. Sch. Medicine, 1977; PhD in Anthropology, Cornell U., 1978. Lectr., health policy and mgmt. Harvard U. Sch. Pub. Health, Cambridge, Mass., 1985—95; dep. commr., dir., pub. health Boston Dept. Health and Hosps., 1989—95; assoc. prof., health svcs. U. Wash. Sch. Pub. Health and Cmty. Medicine, 1995—; dir., health officer Seattle-King Co. Health Dept., 1995—. Mem., scientific adv. com. Nat. Ctr. for Health Statistics. Bd. dirs. Am. Lung Assn. of Wash., United Way of King Co., Wash. Dental Found.; chair, bd. Edn. Devel. Ctr., Inc.; chair, adv. com. King Co. Health Action Plan. Mem.: Nat. Assn. of City and County Health Officials. Office: Seattle-King Co Health Dept 999 Third Ave Ste 1200 Seattle WA 98104*

**PLOURDE, WILLIAM E.,** secondary school educator; s. Robert Joseph and Angela Anne Plourde. BA in Theology, Loyola Marymount U., 1982; MA in Asian Religions, U. Hawaii, 1994; MA in Theology, U. Notre Dame, 2004. Travel agt. Decker Internat., L.A., 1978—84; driver Arrow Charter Lines, 1980—84; tchr. theology Sacred Heart Acad., Honolulu, 1984—; dir. music campus ministires U. Hawaii, 1993—; sound/light tech. IATSE Local 665, 1998—. Sailing coach Sacred Heart Acad., 1999—, student coun. advisor, 2003—. Vol. Hospice Hawaii, Honolulu, 1994—; mem. chorus Hawaii Opera Theatre, 1988, 1989, 1995. Mem.: Am. Acad. Religion, Am. Choral Dirs. Assn. (life), Hawaii Yacht Club. Roman Catholic. Avocations: sailing, horseback riding, needlepoint, travel. Office: Sacred Heart Acad 3253 WaialaeAve Honolulu HI 96816

**PLOWDEN, DAVID,** photographer; b. Boston, Oct. 9, 1932; s. Roger and Mary Russell (Butler) P.; m. Pleasance Coggeshall, June 20, 1962 (div. 1976); children: John, Daniel; m. Sandra Oakes Schoellkopf, July 8th, 1977; children: Philip, Karen. BA Econs., Yale U., 1955; pvt. studies with Minor White, Rochester, N.Y., 1959-60. Asst. O. Winston Link Studio, N.Y.C., 1958-59, George Meluso Studio, N.Y.C., 1960-62; photographer, writer, 1962—. Assoc. prof. Inst. Design, Ill. Inst. Tech., Chgo., 1978-86; lectr. U. Iowa Sch. Journalism, 1985-88; vis. prof. Grand Valley State Univ., 1988-90, 91—; artist-in-residence U. Balt., 1990-91. Author and photographer: Farewell to Steam, 1968, Lincoln and His America, 1970 (Benjamin Barondess award 1971), The Hand of Man on America, 1971, 2d edit, 1974, The Floor of the Sky: the Great Plains, 1972, Bridges: the Spans of North America, 1974, 2d edit. 1984, 3d edit., 2002, Commonplace, 1974, Tugboat, 1976 (notable Children's books ALA 1976, Children's Book Showcase 1976), Steel, 1981, An American Chronology, 1982 (Notable Books ALA 1982, Booklist's Best of the 80s 1989), Industrial Landscape, 1985, A Time of Trains, 1987, A Sense of Place, 1988, End of an Era: The Last of the Great Lakes Steamboats, 1992, Small Town America, 1994, Imprints: The Photographs of David Plowden, 1997, David Plowden: The American Barn, 2003, A Handful of Dust, 2006; co-author, photographer, Nantucket, 1970, Cape May to Montauk, 1973, Desert and Plains, the Mountains and the River, 1975, The Iron Road, 1978 (notable children's books 1978, Honor list Horn Books 1979), Wayne County: the Aesthetic Heritage of a Rural Area, 1979; introduction The Gallery of World Photography/the Country, 1983; commd. illustrator Gems, 1967, The Freeway in the City, 1968, America the Vanishing, 1969, New Jersey, 1977, North Dakota, 1977, Vermont, 1979, New York, 1981, A Place of Sense, 1988; contbr. articles to numerous jours. including Time, Newsweek, Life, Audubon, Fortune, Smithsonian, Camera Arts, Lenswork; one-man shows include Columbia U., 1965, Smithsonian Instn., 1970, 71, 75, 76, 81, 89, Internat. Ctr. Photography, N.Y., 1976, Witkin Gallery, N.Y.C., 1979, Cin. Art Acad., 1979, The Gilbert Gallery, Chgo., 1980, 81, Chgo. Ctr. Contemporary Photography, 1982, Fed. Hall Mus., N.Y.C., 1982, Calif. Mus. Photography, Riverside, 1982-83, Chgo. Hist. Soc., 1985, Martin Gallery, Washington, 1987, Kunstmuseum, Luzern, Switzerland, 1987, Burchfield Ctr., Buffalo, 1987-88, Iowa State Mus., Des Moines, 1988-89, Catherine Edelman Gallery, Chgo., 1990, Grand Valley State U., 1993, Ewing Gallery, Washington, 1994, Beinecke Rare Book and Manuscript Lib. Yale U., 1997, Albright-Knox Art Gallery, 1997, Mus. Contemporary Photography, Chgo., 1998, Albin O. Kuhn Libr. & Gallery, U. Md., Balt., 1998, Tatar/Alexander Photogallery, Toronto, 1999, Lawrence Miller Gallery, N.Y.C., 2000, The Chgo. Cultural Ctr., 2002, Peter Fetterman Gallery Photographic Works of Art, Santa Monica, Calif., 2004-05, Copia, Napa, Calif., 2004; exhibited in group shows at Met. Mus. Art, N.Y.C., 1967, Kodak Gallery, N.Y.C., 1976, Currier Gallery Art, Manchester, N.H., 1978, Whitney Mus., 1979, Art Inst. Chgo., 1983-86, 87, Witkin Gallery, N.Y.C., 1988, Davenport (Iowa) Mus. Art, 1992, Mus. Contemporary Photography, Chgo., Ill., 1996, 98, 99, City, 2000, Fay Gold Gallery, Atlanta, 2003-04; represented in permanent collections Albright-Knox Gallery, Art Inst. Chgo., Calif. Mus. Photography, Ctr. Creative Photography, Chgo. Hist. Soc., Libr. Congress, Smithsonian Instn., U. Md., J.B. Speed Mus., Iowa Humanities Bd., Iowa State Hist. Dept., Burchfield Art Ctr., Buffalo and Erie County Hist. Soc., Internat. Mus. Photography George Eastman House, Internat. Ctr. Photography, Ekstrom Libr. U. Louisville, Beinecke Rare Book and Manuscript Libr., Yale U., 1995—, Mus. Contemporary Photography, Chicy, Bayly Mus. U. Va., Charlottesville. John Simon Guggenheim fellow, 1968; grantee N.Y. State Coun. Arts, 1966, 87, Smithsonian Inst., 1970-71, Dept. Transp. and Smithsonian Inst., 1975-76, H. E. Butt Found., 1977, United Bd. Homeland Ministries, 1976, Chgo. Hist. Soc., 1980-84, Seymour H. Knox Found., 1987, Baird Found., 1987, State Hist. Soc. Iowa, 1987-88, Iowa Humanities Bd., 1987-88; recipient R.R. History award, 1989, Honored Imagemaker, Soc. for Photographic Edn., 2002; subjectof PBS documentary: David Plowden:

Light, Shadow & Form, 2000. Mem. Am. Soc. Media Photographers. Home and Office: 609 Cherry St Winnetka IL 60093-2614 Office Phone: 847-446-2793. Home Fax: 847-446-2795. Personal E-mail: david@davidplowden.com.

**PLOWMAN, BOYD R.,** automotive executive; BS in Acctg., Utah State U. With Fleetwood Enterprises, Inc., Riverside, Calif., 1990—87; pres., CEO Lee & Assocs. Comml. Real Estate Svcs., 1990—97; v.p. Retail Housing Fleetwood Enterprises, Inc., 1990—2000, CFO, 2000—, exec. v.p., 2001—. Office: Fleetwood Enterprises Inc 3125 Myers St Riverside CA 92513-7638

**PLOWMAN, JACK WESLEY,** lawyer; b. Blairsville, Pa., Sept. 12, 1929; s. Ralph Waldo, Sr., and Ethel Beatrice (Nicely) P.; m. Barbara Ellen Brown, Apr. 5, 1952; children: Linda Ellen, Judith Lynn AB, U. Pitts., 1951, LL.B. with honors, 1956. Bar: Pa. 1956, U.S. Dist. Ct. (we. dist.) Pa. 1956, U.S. Ct. Appeals 1960, U.S. Supreme Ct. 1978. Assoc. Campbell, Houck & Thomas, Pitts., 1956-57; ptnr. Rose, Houston, Cooper & Schmidt, Pitts., 1957-63, Plowman & Spiegel, Pitts., 1963-2000; of counsel Bentz Law Firm, P.C., Pitts., 2000—. Adj. prof. emeritus Duquesne U. Sch. Law, 1963—80, 1983—2002. Editor-in-chief Pitts. Legal Jour., 1971—81, U. Pitts. Law Rev., 1955—56. Bd. dirs. United Meth. Pub. House, 1984-96, Ward Home for Children, United Meth. Ch. Union, 1977-83, Wesley Inst., 1977-81, Neighborhood Legal Svcs. Assn., 1969-74; chancellor emeritus Western Pa. Ann. Conf., United Meth. Ch. Capt. JAG, USAFR, 1979-2000. Fellow Am. Bar Found. (life mem.), Am. Coll. Trial Lawyers, Allegheny County Bar Found. (trustee, sec.); mem. ABA, Pa. Bar Assn., Allegheny County Bar Assn. (pres. 1982), Pa. Bar Inst. (bd. dirs. 1988-92), Am. Law Inst., Supreme Ct. Pa. Hist. Soc, (trustee, pres.). Republican. Home: 1025 Lakemont Dr Pittsburgh PA 15243-1817 Office: The Washington Ctr Bldg 680 Washington Rd Pittsburgh PA 15228 Office Phone: 412-563-4500. E-mail: jplowman@bentzlaw.com.

**PLUM, FRED,** neurologist; b. Atlantic City, Jan. 10, 1924; s. Fred and Frances (Alexander) Plum; m. Susan Butler Apr. 23, 1990; children from previous marriage: Michael, Christopher, Carol. BA, Dartmouth Coll., 1944, postgrad., 1944—45; MD, Cornell U., 1947; MD (hon.), Karolinska Inst., Stockholm, 1982; DSc (hon.), L.I. U., 1990. Resident N.Y. Hosp., 1947—50, fellow, 1950—53. Instr. neurology Sch. Medicine Cornell U., 1950—53, Anne Parrish Titzell prof. neurology, 1963—98, univ. prof., 1998—, chmn. dept. neurology, 1963—98; head neurology sect. U.S. Naval Hosp., St-Albans, NY, 1951—53; from asst. prof. to prof. neurology Sch. Medicine U. Wash., 1953—63; vis. scientist U. Lund, Sweden, 1970—71; vis. physician Rockefeller U. Hosp., 1975—85; assoc. neurosci. rsch. program MIT and Rockefeller U., 1977—87; mem. neurology study sect. NIH, 1964—68; nat. adv. coun. Nat. Inst. Neurol., Communicative Disorders and Stroke, 1984—86; founding mem. McKnight Endowment Fund for Neurosci., 1986, pres., 1986—90. Author (with J.B. Posner): Diagnosis of Stupor and Coma, 1966; author: 3d edit., 1982, Clinical Management of Seizures, 1976, 2d edit., 1983; author: (with others) Cecil Essentials of Medicine, 1986, 3d edit., 1995; editor, contbg. author: Cecil's Textbook of Medicine, 1968, chief editor neurology sect.: Contemporary Neurology series, 1980—96, founding editor: Vols. 1-40, 1966—93, Brain Dysfunction in Metabolic Disorders, 1974, mem. editl. bd.: Archives Neurology, 1958—68, chief editor:, 1972—76; editor: Annals of Neurology, 1977—85; founding editor:, 1986—; editor: Neurology Alert, 1981—; contbr. articles to sci. and profl. jours. Mem.: NAS, Assn. Am. Physicians, Assn. Rsch. Nervous Mental Diseases (pres. 1973, 1987), Am. Soc. Clin. Investigation, Soc. Neurosci., Am. Acad. Neurology (past mem. coun.), Am. Neurol. Assn. (v.p. 1974—75, pres. 1976—77, Jacoby award 1984), Inst. of Medicine, Am. Acad. Arts and Scis., Can., Brit., French, Itatlian, Swiss neurol. socs. (hon.), Alpha Omega Alpha. Achievements include research in conciousness, coma and stroke. Office: Weill-Cornell U Med Coll 525 E 68th St # A565 New York NY 10021-4870 Business E-Mail: frp2007@mail.cornell.edu.

**PLUMB, CHARLES SUMNER, III,** lawyer; b. Columbus, Ohio, Mar. 27, 1957; s. Charles Sumner II and Elaine Marcene (Wharton) P.; m. Kathleen Kendall Barry, Aug. 16, 1980; children: Joseph Quinn, Nora Kendall. BBA, So. Meth. U., 1979; JD, Ohio State U., 1982. Bar: Okla. 1982, U.S. Dist. Ct. (no., ea., and we. dists.) Okla. 1982, U.S. Ct. Appeals (10th cir.) 1982. Ptnr. Doerner, Saunders, Daniel & Andersen, Tulsa, 1982—. Editor Okla. Employment Law Letter, Tulsa, 1992—; articles editor Ohio State U. Law Jour., 1980-82. Office: Doerner Saunders Daniel & Andersen 320 S Boston Ave Ste 500 Tulsa OK 74103-3725 Office Phone: 918-591-5279. Business E-Mail: cplumb@dsda.com.

**PLUMERI, JOSEPH JAMES, II,** financial executive; b. Trenton, NJ, July 7, 1943; s. Samuel J. and Josephine (Vaccaro) Plumeri; m. Nancy Plumeri, June 18, 1966; children: Christian, Jay Michael, Leslie. BA in History, Coll. of William and Mary, 1966; postgrad., N.Y. Law Sch., 1967-69. Trainee Carter Berlind & Weill, NYC, 1968-69; stockbroker CBWL-Hayden Stone, NYC, 1968-73; br. mgr. Shearson Hayden Stone, Fort Lauderdale, Fla., 1973-74, exec. v.p. western region San Francisco, 1974-81; sr. exec. v.p. Shearson Lehman Hutton, NYC, 1981—, dir. mktng. and nat. sales, 1981-89, dir. domestic br. div., 1990-94; vice chmn., group CEO Travelers Group, Inc., NYC, 1994-2000; chmn., CEO Willis Group, Ltd., Jacksonville, Fla., 2000—, bd. mem., 2001—. Bd. visitors Coll. William & Mary, trustee endowment assn.; bd. visitors Nat. Ctr. on Addiction and Substance Abuse. Mem.: Columbus (N.Y.C.). Avocations: golf, reading. Office: Willis Group Ltd 3000 Bayport Dr Ste 300 Tampa FL 33607 Home: 455 Long Ln Far Hills NJ 07931-2742*

**PLUMEZ, JEAN PAUL,** advertising executive, consultant; b. N.Y.C., Oct. 31, 1939; s. Jean Paul and Marie Antoinette (Compagne) P; m. Jacqueline Hornor Feb. 20, 1965; children: Jean Paul, Nicole. BS in Chem. Engring., Bucknell U., 1962, BA in Chemistry, 1962; MBA, U. Pa., 1968. Product engr. Mobil Oil Co., Paulsboro, NJ, 1965-66; account mgr. Dancer Fitzgerald, Sample, Inc., N.Y.C., 1968-86, exec. v.p., 1979-86; pres. Leadership on Paper, Larchmont, NY, 1986—; founding ptnr. The Right Direction, 1987—. Served to capt. Signal Corps U.S. Army, 1962-64. Mem. Alpha Chi Sigma, Beta Gamma Sigma, Kappa Delta Rho Clubs: Larchmont Yacht, Wharton of N.Y., Princeton of N.Y. Home and Office: 90 Beechtree Dr Larchmont NY 10538-1202 Office Phone: 914-833-0332.

**PLUMMER, AHMED,** professional football player; b. Wyoming, Ohio, Mar. 26, 1976; Studied Bus. and Human Resources, The Ohio State Univ. Cornerback San Francisco 49ers. Named to All-Madden Team, 2001, All-Rookie Team, Football News, 2000. Office: San Francisco 49ers Marie P DeBartolo Sports Ctr 4949 Centennial Blvd Santa Clara CA 95054*

**PLUMMER, AMANDA,** actress; b. N.Y.C., Mar. 23, 1957; d. Christopher and Tammy (Grimes) Plummer. Student, Middlebury Coll. Has appeared in theatre roles: debut: Artichoke, 1979, A Taste of Honey, 1981(nominee for Tony award, and Drama Desk, recipient Outer Critics Circle and Theatre World awards); A Month in the Country, 1980; The Glass Menagerie, 1983-84; other theatre roles include: Agnes of God (Tony, Drama Desk award, Outer Circle Critics award, Boston Critics award), 1982; A Lie of the Mind, 1985; motion picture debut: Cattle Annie and Little Britches, 1981, The World According to Garp, 1982, Daniel, 1983, Hotel New Hampshire, 1984, Static, 1985, Riders to the Sea, 1987, Courtship, 1987, Made in Heaven, 1987, The Story of the Dancing Frog, 1989, Prisoners of Inertia, 1989, Joe Versus the Volcano, 1990, The Fisher King, 1991, Freejack, 1992, The Lounge People, 1992, So I Married an Axe Murderer, 1993, Needful Things, 1993 (Saturn award), Pax, 1994, Nostradamus, 1994, Pulp Fiction, 1994, The Final Cut, 1995, The Prophecy, 1995, Search and Destroy, 1995, Butterfly Kiss, 1995, The Vampyre Wars, 1996, Freeway, 1996, Dead Girl, 1996, American Perfekt, 1997, Drunks, 1997, A Simple Wish, 1997, You Can Thank Me Later, 1998, Hysteria, 1998,October 22, 1998, L.A. Without a Map, 1998, Elizabeth Jane, 1998, Great Sex, 1999, Eight and a Half Women, 1999, The Million Dollar Hotel, 2000, Seven Days to Live, 2000, Triggermen, 2002, Ken Park, 2002, Pulp Fiction: The Facts, 2002, My Life Without Me, 2002,

The Gray in Between, 2002, The Last Angel, 2002, Satan's Little Helper, 2004, Darkness, 2005; (TV movies) The Unforgivable Secret, 1982, The Dollmaker, 1984, True Blue, 1989, Kojak: None So Blind, 1990, Gryphon, 1990, Miss Rose White, 1992, Sidney Sheldon's The Sands of Time, 1992, Last Light, 1993, Whose Child Is This? The War for Baby Jessica, 1993, Under the Piano, 1995, Don't Look Back, 1996, The Right to Remain Silent, 1996, (voice) Hercules, 1997, The Apartment Complex, 1999, Shadow Realm, 2002, Get a Clue, 2002, Broadway: The Golden Age, by the Legends Who Were There, 2002; (TV series) Stories from My Childhood (voice), 1998; TV appearances include Hallmark Hall of Fame: Miss Rose White (Emmy award supporting actress, 1992), (TV series) Moonlighting, 1987, The Equalizer, 1988, LA Law, 1989, 1990, Tales from the Crypt, 1989, The Outer Limits, 1996, 2000 (Emmy award best guest actress, 1996), Law & Order: Special Victims Unit, 2004 (Creative Arts Primetime Emmy award outstanding guest actress in a drama, 2005), and several other appearances. Recipient Anti-Defamation League award for Women of Achievement, 1988.

**PLUMMER, CHRISTOPHER (ORME) (ARTHUR PLUMMER),** actor; b. Toronto, Ont., Can., Dec. 13, 1929; s. John and Isabella Mary (Abbott) P.; m. Tammy Grimes, Aug. 19, 1956 (div. 1960); 1 child, Amanda; m. Particia Audrew Lewis, May 4, 1962 (div. 1967); m. Elaine Taylor, 1970. Student pub. and pvt. schs., Can.; pupil Iris Warren, C. Herbertcasari; LLD (hon.), U. We. Ont., 2004; DFA (hon.), NY Julliard Sch.; PhD (hon.), U. Toronto, Ryerson and Western Ont. Stage debut in The Rivals with Can. Repertory Theatre, 1950; Broadway debut in Starcross Story, 1954, J.B.; London debut in Becket, 1961; leading actor Cymbeline, Am. Shakespeare Theatre, Stratford, Conn., 1955, Royal Shakespeare Co., London and Stratford, Avon, Eng., 1961-62, Stratford (Ont.) Shakespeare Festival, 1956, 57, 58, 60, 62, 67, Nat. Theatre Co., London; radio roles include Shakespeare, Canada; plays include Home is the Hero, 1954, Twelfth Night, 1954, 70-71, Dark is Light Enough, The Lark, Julius Caesar, The Tempest, 1955, (rearranger with Sir Neville Mariner) Henry VI, 1956, Hamlet, 1957, Winter's Tale, 1958, Much Ado About Nothing, 1958, J.B., 1958, King John, 1960, Romeo and Juliet, 1960, Richard III, 1961, Arturo Ui, 1963, The Royal Hunt of the Sun, 1965, Antony and Cleopatra, 1967, Danton's Death, 1971, Amphitryon 38, 1971, The Constant Wife, The Dark is Light Enough (Theatre World award), Medea, The Lark; (musicals) Cyrano, 1973 (Tony award for Best Actor in a Musical, 1974), The Good Doctor, 1973, Love and Master Will, 1975; performer (with Sir Neville Mariner and rearranged by Michael Lankester) A Midsummer's Night's Dream; Othello, 1982, Macbeth, 1988, No Man's Land, 1993, Barrymore, 1996 (Tony award for best actor in a play, 1997, Drama Desk, Outer Critics Cr. award, Edwin Booth award, Boston Critics' award, Chgo.'s Jefferson award, LA Ovation award best actor 1997-98), King Lear, 2004 (Tony nom. best actor in a play, 2004); made TV debut 1953; TV prodns. include Little Moon of Alban, Johnny Belinda, 1958, Cyrano de Bergerac, 1962, Oedipus Rex, After the Fall, 1974, The Doll's House, The Prince and the Pauper, Prisoner of Zenda, Hamlet at Elsinore, BBC, 1964, Time Remembered, Capt. Brassbound's Conversion, The Shadow Box, 1981, The Thornbirds, 1983, Little Gloria-Happy at Last, A Hazard of Hearts, 1987, Crossings, 1986, Danielle Steele's Secrets, 1992, Liar's Edge, 1992, On Golden Pond, 2001, Night Flight, 2002; star TV series The Moneychangers, 1977, Harrison Bergeron, 1995, We the Jury, 1996, The Conspiracy of Fear, 1996; made film debut in 1957; films include Stage Struck, 1957, Wind Across the Everglades, 1958, The Fall of the Roman Empire, 1963, Inside Daisy Clover, 1965, Sound of Music (Acad. award), 1965, Triple Cross, 1967, Nobody Runs Forever, 1969, The Battle of Britain, 1969, The Royal Hunt of the Sun, 1969, Lock up your Daughters, 1969, The Phyx, 1970, Waterloo, 1971, The Man Who Would Be King, 1975, The Return of the Pink Panther, 1975, Conduct Unbecoming, 1975, International Velvet, 1978, Murder by Decree, 1979, Starcrash, 1979, The Silent Partner, 1979, Hanover Street, 1979, Somewhere in Time, 1980, Eyewitness, 1981, The Disappearance, 1981, The Amateur, 1982, Dreamscape, 1984, Ordeal by Innocence, 1984, Lily in Love, 1985, The Boss' Wife, 1986, The Boy In Blue, 1986, An American Tail, 1986 (voice), Souvenir, 1987, Dragnet, 1987, Light Years (voice), 1988, Where the Heart Is, 1989, Fire Head, 1991, Star Trek: VI: The Undiscovered Country, 1991, Rock a Doodle, 1992 (voice), Malcolm X, 1992, Wolf, 1994, Dolores Claiborne, 1994, Twelve Monkeys, 1995, Skeletons, 1996, The Arrow, 1997, Hidden Agenda, 1998, The Clown at Midnight, 1998, Winchell (TV), 1998, Blackheart, The Insider (Boston, LA, Chgo., Las Vegas and Nat. Critics's awards), 1999, All the Fine Lines, 1999, Celebrate the Century (TV mini-series), 1999, The Dinosaur Hunter, 2000, Dracula 2000, Nuremberg (TV mini-series), 2000, American Tragedy (TV mini-series, Golden Globe nomination), 2000, A Beautiful Mind, 2001, Nicholas Nickleby, 2002, Ararat, 2002, Blizzard, 2003, Cold Creek Manor, 2003, National Treasure, 2004, Alexander, 2004, Tma, 2005, (TV) Our Fathers (Emmy Nomination), 2005, Must Love Dogs, 2005, Four Minute Mile (TV), 2005, Syriana, 2005, The New World, 2005, Inside Man, 2006, The Lake House, 2006, Rick Burns documentary film on Eugene O'Neil, and The Man in the Chair. Decorated companion Order of Can., 1968; recipient Theatre World award, 1955, Evening Std. Theatre award, 1961, Delia Austrian medal, 1973, 2 Drama Desk awards, 1973, 82, Antoinette Perry award, 1974, Emmy award Nat. Acad. TV Arts and Scis., 1977, Genie award, Can., 1980, Golden Badge of Honor, Austria, 1982, Maple Leaf award Nat. Acad. Arts and Letters, many honors Eng., Austria, Can., Two Tony awards (seven nominations), Two Emmy awards (six nominations), Gt. Britain's Evening Std. award, Can.'s Genie award, Gov. Gen's Lifetime Achievement award, 2001, William Shakespeare award (Will award) classical theatre, Nat. Bd. Rev. Career Achievement award, NY., Jason Robard's award excellence in theater as great friend, 2002; inducted in Am.'s Theatre's Hall of Fame, 1986, Can.'s Walk of Fame, 1997. Office: c/o Lou Pitt The Pitt Group 9465 Wilshire Blvd fln 400 Beverly Hills CA 90212-2612

**PLUMMER, DIRK ARNOLD,** chemical, electrical, and electronics engineer; b. Stamford, Conn., Apr. 18, 1930; s. Charles Arnold Plummer and Edwina Woodling Johnson; m. Janis Susan Lowery Stuart, Feb. 18, 1967 (div. 1973); 1 child, Julie. SBChemE, MIT, 1952; BSEE, U. Calif., Berkeley, 1961; MSEE, Monmouth U., 1995. Registered profl. engr., Conn., N.J.; cert. nondestructive test examiner of inspectors for radiography, magnetic particle, liquid penetrant and ultrasonic testing methods; cert. comml. pilot. Chem. engr. Foster Wheeler Corp., N.Y.C., 1952; project engr. The M.W. Kellogg Co., N.Y.C., 1954; project engr. Am. Machine & Fdry. Co., Greenwich, Conn., 1955-56; devel. engr. Aerojet-Gen. Corp., Azusa, Sacramento, San Ramon, Calif., 1956-61; sr. mem. tech. staff Aerospace Comm. & Controls Divsn. RCA, Burlington, Mass., 1961-62; engr. Elec. Boat Div. Gen. Dynamics Corp., Groton, Conn., 1963; electronics engr. U.S. Civil Svc., various locations, 1963-88; comm. inspector Bd. Chosen Freeholders, Freehold, NJ, 1994; pvt. practice Sea Bright, NJ, 1988—. Contbr. articles to profl. jours. Archtl. control officer Sea Bright Village Assn., 1991. 1st lt. U.S. Army, 1952-54. Recipient Meritorious Svc. medal Pres. of U.S., 1982, Cert. for Commendable Svc. Dept. Supply Agy., 1972. Mem. AAAS, NSPE, ASCE, ASME, AIChE (profl. devel. officer 1990), IEEE (chmn. nuclear and plasma sci. chpt. 1990), Am. Phys. Soc., Am. Math. Soc., Am. Math Assn., Am. Internat. Soc. Logistics, Am. Chem. Soc. Home and Office: 45 Village Rd Sea Bright NJ 07760-2233 Business E-Mail: dap@alum.mit.edu.

**PLUMMER, E. WARD,** physics professor; b. Astoria, Oregon, Oct. 30, 1940; married; 2 children. BA summa cum laude in Physics and Math., Lewis and Clark Coll., 1962; PhD in Physics, Cornell U., 1968. NRC postdoctoral fellow Nat. Bur. Standards, 1967—70, asst. sect. chief for surface physics Far Ultraviolet Sect., 1970—73; assoc. prof. physics U. Pa., 1973—77, prof., 1977—88, William Smith prof. physics, 1988—92; disting. prof. physics U. Tenn., 1992—; disting. scientist Oak Ridge Nat. Lab., 1992—; dir. Tenn. Advanced Materials Lab., 2001—. Dir. Lab. Rsch. Structure of Matter, 1990—92; vis. disting. scientist Oak Ridge Nat. Lab., 1992; mem. basic energy sci. adv. com. Dept. Energy, 2001—04; mem. exec. adv. bd. U. Pa. Materials Rsch. Sci. and Engring. Ctr., 2003—. Contbr. articles to sci. jours.; consulting editor: Chem. Physics, mem. editl. bd.: Phys. Rev. B, 1986—89, mem. editl. adv. bd.: Langmuir, 1989—93, mem. adv. editl. bd.: Chem.

Physics Letters, 1991—94. Recipient Medard W. Welch award, Sci. and Tech. Soc., 2001. Fellow: NAS (mem. solid state sci. com. 1986—89). Office: Dept Physics and Astronomy U Tenn 201 South Coll Knoxville TN 37996-1200 E-mail: eplummer@utk.edu.*

**PLUMMER, GAYTHER L.,** retired climatologist; b. Indpls., Jan. 27, 1925; s. Conley L. and Rowena H. (Huber) P.; m. H. Eileen Barr, June 3, 1950. BS, Butler U., Indpls., 1948; MS, Kans. State U., Manhattan, 1950; PhD, Purdue U., 1954. Instr. biology Knox Coll., Galesburg, Ill., 1950-51; naturalist Ind. Dept. Conservation, various locations, 1947-52; asst. prof. biology Antioch Coll., Yellow Springs, Ohio, 1954-55; prof. botany U. Ga., Athens, 1955-95, state climatologist, 1978-95. Rsch. fellow Oak Ridge (Tenn.) Inst. Nuclear Studies, 1958-62. Author: Georgia Weather Watchers, 1991, Georgia Temperatures, 1993, Georgia's Climate During 20th Century, 2001, U.S. National Climate During 20th Century, 2001; cartographer 160 vegetation maps of Ga., 1972-74; editor Ga. Jour. Sci., 1977-84; contbr. articles to profl. jours. 2d lt. USAAF, 1943-46. Fellow AAAS; mem. Ind. Acad. Sci., Ga. Acad. Sci., Soil Sci. Soc. Am., Crop Sci. Soc., Agron. Soc. Am., Sigma Xi, Phi Kappa Phi. Achievements include research in droughts in S.E. U.S. relating to astrogeophysical processes via geomagnetics; lightning history in Piedmont for over 70 million years etched in Stone Mountain granite.

**PLUMMER, JAMES D.,** electrical engineering educator; BS in elec. engring., UCLA, 1966; MS in elec. engring., Stanford U., 1967, PhD in elec. engring., 1971. Rsch. assoc. Stanford U., 1971—74, sr. rsch. assoc., 1974—78, assoc. dir. integrated circuits lab., 1974—84, dir., 1984—93, assoc. prof. elec. engring., 1978—83, prof., 1983—, John M. Fluke Prof. Elec. Engring., 1988—, prof. (by courtesy) materials sci. and engring., 1996—, sr. assoc. dean. Sch. Engring., 1993—96, dean, 1999—, chmn. elec. engring. dept., 1997—99, Frederick Emmons Terman Prof. Engring., 1999—, dir. Stanford Nanofabrication Facility, 1994—2000; nat. dir. NSF Nat. Nanofabrication Users Network, 1995—2000. Cons. to numerous semiconductor and other companies, 1970—; mem. bd. dirs. Internat. Rectifier, 1995—; mem. Cypress Semiconductor Tech. Adv. Bd., 1995—; Herbert H. Johnson lectr. in materials sci. and engring. Cornell U., 1998. Author, co-author of over 300 publs.; patentee in field. Recipient Outstanding Paper Award, Internat. Solid-State Circuits Conf., 1970, 1976, 1978, Outstanding Svc. Award, Elec. Engring. Dept., Stanford U., 1988, 2 Inventor Recognition Awards, Semiconductor Rsch. Corp., Tau Beta Pi Undergrad. Tchg. Award, Sch. Engring., Stanford U., 1992, Best Tchr. Award, Soc. Women Engineers, 1995, J.J. Ebbers award, IEEE, 2003, Aldert Van der Ziel award, 2003, Jacob Millman award, McGraw-Hill, 2004. Fellow: IEEE (Third Millenium Medal 2000); mem.: NAE, Materials Rsch. Soc., Am. Phys. Soc., Electrochem. Soc. (Solid State Sci. and Tech. Award 1991), Sigma Xi, Tau Beta Pi. Office: Stanford U Sch Engring 380 Panama Mall, 214 Terman Stanford CA 94305-4027

**PLUMMER, JASON STEVEN (JAKE PLUMMER),** professional football player; b. Boise, Idaho, Dec. 19, 1974; Student, Ariz. State U. Quarterback Ariz. Cardinals, Phoenix, 1997—2003, Denver Broncos, 2003—. Named to NFL Pro-Bowl, 1997—2003, 2005. Office: Denver Broncos 13655 Broncos Pkwy Englewood CO 80112*

**PLUMMER, KAREN ANNE,** librarian, educator; b. Sheffield, Ala., May 18, 1956; d. Gilbert S. Plummer and Margaret Jean Morris. BA, Kent State U., 1978, MLS, 1984; MA, So. Ill. U., 1979. Cert. web tech. Internat. Webmasters Assn./HTML Writers Guild. Circulation asst. Stark County Dist. Libr., Canton, Ohio, 1980—84, reference asst., 1984—90, sr. cataloger, 1990—91; tech. svcs. libr. Supreme Ct. of Ohio Law Libr., Columbus, 1991—93; catalog coord., libr. Eisenhower Nat. Clearinghouse, Columbus, 1993—2001; audiovisual/spl. materials cataloger U. Akron, Ohio, 2001—. Contract cataloger, metadata cons. Nat. Sci. Digital Libr. Project: The Learning Matrix, Columbus, 2002; cons., contract cataloger Eisenhower Nat. Clearinghouse, Columbus, 2001; presenter in field. Co-editor (column) Technical Services Quarterly; contbr. articles, revs. to profl. publs. Recipient Extra Mile Award, Eisenhower Nat. Clearinghouse, 2001; grantee, NSF, 1999. Mem.: ALA, Online Audiovisual Catalogers, Inc., Academic Libr. Assn. Ohio, Libr. and Info. Tech. Assn., Assn. Libr. Collections and Tech. Svcs., Assn. Coll. and Rsch. Librs., Richard III Soc. North Am. Conf. on Brit. Studies, Am. Hist. Assn. (assocs.), Internat. Webmasters Assn./HTML Writer's Guild, Beta Phi Mu, Phi Beta Kappa, Phi Kappa Phi. Avocations: web design, reading. Office: U Akron Bierce Library 177B Akron OH 44325-1712 Office Phone: 330-972-7244. Office Fax: 330-972-6383. Personal E-mail: karen42@sssnet.com. Business E-Mail: kplumme@uakron.edu.

**PLUMMER, LEONARD NIEL,** geochemist; b. Lexington, Ky., Aug. 13, 1945; s. Leonard Niel and Marjorie Sidney Wiest Plummer; m. Phyllis C. Mohney, Aug. 21, 1945; children: Philip Niel, Michael Ross, Rebecca Wiest Weaver, Kathryn Elizabeth Cartwright. BA, U. Ky., Lexington, 1967, MS, 1969; PhD, Northwestern U., Evanston, Ill., 1972. Asst. prof. SUNY, Buffalo, 1972—74; hydrologist U.S. Geol. Survey, Reston, Va., 1974—92, sr. rsch. scientist, 1992—. Contbr. articles to sci. publs. Recipient Meritorious Svc. award, U.S. Dept. Interior, 1987, Disting. Svc. award, 1996, Spl. Recognition award, Assn. Ground Water Scientists and Engineers, Nat. Water Well Assn., 1990. Fellow: Geol. Soc. Am. (O.E. Meinzer award 1993); mem.: Geochemical Soc., Am. Chem. Soc., Am. Geophys. Union, Sigma Xi. Achievements include development of geochemical models for simulation of water-rock reactions; ground-water dating with chlorofluorocarbons; research in hydrochemistry of major US aquifers; contaminants in ground water such as arsenic, perchlorate, volatile organic carbon compounds; co-development of concept of stoichiometric saturation in solid-solution - aqueous solution reactions; solubility of calcium carbonate in water; application of environmental tracers to interpretation of ground-water age studies with sulfur hexafluoride, tritium/helium-3, and others. Avocation: violin.

**PLUMMER, MARGUERITE REYNOLDS,** historian, educator; b. Shelby County, Tex., Nov. 6, 1929; d. Lawrence W.J. Reynolds and Edith Beatrice Martin; m. Royce Carleton Plummer, Sept. 22, 1950. BA in Comm., La. State U., Shreveport, 1981, MBA, 1984, M in Liberal Arts, 1987; PhD in Humanities, U. Tex. Dallas, Richardson, 2001. Legal sec. various firms, Marshall, Tex., 1946—55, Shreveport, 1946—55; co-owner Royce Plummer Polled Hereford Farm, Keithville, La., 1962—79; dir. Pioneer Heritage Ctr. La. State U., Shreveport, 1982—, assoc. prof. history, 1993—. Cons. to regional workshop program Smithsonian Instn., Washington, 1997; Southeastern Mus. Conf. rep. to edn. com. Am. Assn. Mus.; cons. in field; spkr. in field. Author: Historic Shreveport Bossier, 2000; contbr. chapters to books. Grantee Am. Studies Fellowship grant, La. State U. Shreveport, 1996—97. Mem.: Nat. Coun. on Pub. History, So. Assn. Women Historians, La. Assn. Mus., So. Hist. Assn., La. Hist. Assn., Southeastern Mus. Conf., Am. Assn. for State and Local History, Phi Kappa Phi, Omicron Delta Kappa. Republican. Baptist. Avocations: writing, reading. Office: La State U Shreveport 1 University Pl Shreveport LA 71115 Business E-Mail: mplummer@pilot.lsus.edu.

**PLUMMER, ORA BEATRICE,** nursing educator, consultant; b. Mexia, Tex., May 25, 1940; d. Macie Idella (Echols); children: Kimberly, Kevin, Cheryl. BSN, U. N.Mex., 1961; MS in Nursing Edn., UCLA, 1966. Nurse's aide Bataan Meml. Meth. Hosp., Albuquerque, 1958—60, staff nurse, 1961—62, 1967—68; staff nurse, charge nurse, relief supr. Hollywood Cmty. Hosp., Calif., 1962—64; instr. U. N.Mex. Coll. Nursing, Albuquerque, 1968—69; sr. instr. U. Colo. Sch. Nursing, Denver, 1971—74, asst. prof., 1974—76; staff assoc. III We. Interstate Commn. for Higher Edn., Boulder, Colo., 1976—78; DON Garden Manor Nursing Home, Lakewood, Colo., 1978—79, nurse surveyor, cons., 1979—87; ednl. coord. Colo. Dept. Health, Denver, 1987—96. Active in faculty devel. Cluster of Schs.; bd. dirs. Domestic Violence Initiative. Contbr. articles to profl. jours. Mem. adv. bd. Affiliated Children's and Family Svcs., 1977; mem. Colo. Instnl. Child Abuse and Neglect Adv. Com., 1984-92; trustee Colo. Acad., 1990-96; mem. planning com. State Wide Conf. on Black Health Concerns, 1977; mem. staff devel. com. Western Interstate Commn. for Higher Edn., 1978, mem. minority

affairs com., 1978, mem. coordinating com. for baccalaureate program, 1971-76; active in minority affairs, U. Colo. Med. Ctr., 1971-72; mem. ednl. resources com., pub. rels. com., rev. com. for reappointment, promotion and tenure U. Colo. Sch. Nursing, 1971-76, mem. regulatory tng. com., 1989-93; mem. gerontol. adv. com. Met. State Coll., 1989-94; mem. expert panel long term care tng. manual Health Care Financing Adminstrn., Balt., 1989; mem. employee diversity com. Colo. Dept. Health, 1989-96; mem. Nurse Del. to Cuba, 2000. Nominee Nightingale award, Colo., 2003. Avocation: exercise. Office: 4300 Cherry Creek South Dr Denver CO 80246-1523

**PLUMMER, WILLIAM B.,** publishing executive; BS, MIT, MS in Aeronautics and Astronautics; MBA, Stanford U. V.p. equity capital group GE Capital Corp., 1995—97; treas. Mead Corp., 1997—98, vice pres. corp. strategy and planning, 1998—2000; pres. Gilbert Paper Div., 2000; v.p., treas. Alcoa Inc., 2000—06; exec. v.p., CFO Dow Jones & Co., NYC, 2006—. Bd. dirs. John Wiley & Sons, Inc., 2003—. Office: Dow Jones & Co 1 World Financial Ctr 200 Liberty St New York NY 10281*

**PLUMMER, WILLIAM TORSCH,** optical physicist; s. William Edwin and Margaret Fairchild (Torsch) P.; m. Susan Bowman White, Sept. 9, 1961; children: Kathryn, Hilleary. BA, Johns Hopkins U., 1960, PhD, 1965. Lens designer Muffoletto Optical Co., Towson, Md., 1963-69; sr. dir. optical engring. Polaroid Corp., Cambridge, Mass., 1969—2001; pres. WTP Optics, Inc., Concord, Mass., 2002—. Asst. prof. astronomy U. Mass., Amherst, 1967-69; vis. prof. Tufts U., Medford, Mass., 1984-88; sr. lectr. MIT, 1991—. Capt. signal corps U.S. Army, 1965—67. Recipient David Richardson medal, 1980, Joseph Fraunhofer award, 1997, Robert M. Burley prize, 1997. Fellow Soc. Photo-Optical Instrumentation Engrs., Nat. Speleological Soc., Optical Soc. Am.; mem. Nat. Acad. Engring., Phi Beta Kappa. Achievements include central optical and opto-mechanical developments in Polaroid SX-70 folding SLR camera, model 600 LMS camera, spectra camera, captiva camera, and in laser-based printing devices; implemented new concepts for precision in high-volume manufacture; 96 US patents in field for optical, mechanical, electronic, and chemical inventions. Home: 129 Arena Ter Concord MA 01742-4413 Personal E-mail: plummew@yahoo.com.

**PLUMPTRE, TIM,** think-tank executive; BA with honors, U. Toronto, Can., 1965; MSc in Econs., London Sch. Econs., 1966; cert. in Mgmt. Studies, Oxford U., Eng., 1973. Founder, pres. Inst. On Governance, Ottawa, Canada, 1990—. Adj. prof. Sch. Pub. Policy and Adminstrn. Carleton U.; spkr. in field; cons. in field. Author: Beyond the Bottom Line: Management in Government, 1988. Office: Inst Governance 122 Clarence St Ottawa ON Canada K1N 5P6

**PLUNKET, DANIEL CLARK,** pediatrician, educator; b. Birmingham, Ala., May 7, 1929; s. Henry Clark and Carolyn Clark (Langford) P.; m. Lillian C. Barrington, Dec. 31, 1971; children: Dennis, Beth, Ann, Brenda, Scott. BS, Emory U., 1949, MD, 1952. Diplomate Am. Bd. Pediatrics. Intern Med. Coll. Va. Hosp., Richmond, 1952-53, resident in pediatrics, 1953-54, Tripler Army Med. Center, Honolulu, 1958-59, Walter Reed Army Inst., 1962-64; pediatrician, pediatric hematologist/oncologist acad. medicine, chief pediatric service William Beaumont Gen. Hosp., El Paso, Tex., 1959-62; commd. 1st lt. U.S. Army, 1955, advanced through grades to col., 1967; asst. chief dept. pediatrics Letterman Army Med. Center, San Francisco, 1964-65; chmn. dept. pediatrics Fitzsimons Army Med. Center, Denver, 1965-75; prof. pediat. U. Okla. Coll. Medicine, Tulsa, 1975-2000; sr. assoc. dean for clin. affairs U. Okla. Health Scis. Ctr., Tulsa, 1993-2000; chmn. dept. pediat. U. Okla. Coll. Medicine, Tulsa, 1975-96, now prof. pediat. Clin. prof. pediatrics U. Colo., Denver, 1974-75. Mem. adv. chmn. March of Dimes, Tulsa chpt., 1975-92; bd. dirs. ARC, Tulsa chpt., 1981—. Decorated Legion of Merit; Walter Reed Inst. Research fellow hematology and research, 1962-64 Mem. AMA, Acad. Pediatrics, Am. Pediatric Soc., Am. Soc. Hematology. Episcopalian. Home: 2436 E 33rd St Tulsa OK 74105-2316 Fax: 918-742-2046. Office Phone: 918-749-6729. E-mail: dan5729@aol.com.

**PLUT, STEPHEN C.,** protective equipment company executive; m. Karen Plut; 1 child, Stephanie. B in human resources, Geneva Coll. Led info. tech. services group Deloitte and Touche Consulting/ICS; joined Mine Safety Appliances Co., Pitts., 1998, now chief info. officer, also v.p., 2005—. Named one of Premier 100 IT Leaders, Computerworld, 2005. Office: Mine Safety Appliance Co RIDC Indsl Pk 121 Gamma Dr Pittsburgh PA 15238 Office Phone: 412-967-3000.*

**PLUTA, RYSZARD,** neuropathologist, educator; b. Biała Podlaska, Poland, Apr. 16, 1952; s. Marian and Antonina (Szarubko) P. Student, Humboldt U., Berlin, 1975, U. Cologne, Germany, 1976; MD, scientist, Med. Acad., Lublin, Poland, 1977; PhD, Polish Acad. Scis., Warsaw, 1983. Intern gynaecology unit State Hosp., Biała Podlaska, 1977; intern dept. pediatry Med. Acad., Warsaw, 1978; intern internal medicine and surgery units Czerniakowski Hosp., Warsaw, 1978; sci. visitor lab. of CNS Resuscitation Pathology, Inst. Gen. Reanimatology, USSR Acad. Med. Scis., Moscow, 1979; sr. rsch. asst. Polish Acad. Sci., Warsaw, 1981-87, asst. prof., 1987-94, assoc. prof., 1994—; postdoctoral fellow NIH, Bethesda, Md., 1986-88; prof. Acad. Phys. Edn., Warsaw, 1995—2002; resident neurology Med. Acad., Warsaw, 1997. Postdoctoral rsch. fellow, vis. prof. N.Y. State Inst. Basic Rsch., Staten Island, 1988—89, 1990—91, 1993—94, 1997; vice-chmn., bd. dirs State Hosp., Biała Podlaska, 1999—2000; mem. sci. coun. Acad. Phys. Edn., Warsaw, 1995—2002, mem. senate, 1996—99; mem. sci. coun. Inst. Phys. Edn. and Sport, Biala Podlaska, 1996—2002; mem. Polish com. sci. rsch. SPUB, Warsaw, 2001—. Contbr. articles to profl. jours. Mem. Polish com. sci. rsch. SPUB, Warsaw, 2001—; chief Trade Union Solidarnosc Med. Rsch. Ctr., Warsaw, 1980—90, Dem. Union, Dist. Biala Podlaska, 1990—94; candidate Polish Parliament, 1991, 1993. 2nd lt. Polish mil., 1977. Mem.: U. Sports Assn. of Acad. Phys. Edn., Polish Acad. Sci., Polish Assn. Neuropathologists, N.Y. Acad. Sci., Internat. Soc. Neuropathology, Internat. Soc. Cerebral Blood Flow and Metabolism, Internat. Soc. Brain Edema Rsch., Polish Neurosci. Soc., European Soc. Clin. Respiratory Physiology. Roman Catholic. Avocations: politics, sports, good food, cooking. Office: Med Rsch Ctr Dept Neuropath Pawińskiego Str 5 02-106 Warsaw Poland

**PLUTH, JOSEPH, JR.,** music educator; b. Hinsdale, Ill., July 8, 1979; s. Joseph Pluth, Sr. and Charlene Ruth Pluth; m. Amy Nicole Lafferty, June 9, 2006. BA in Sacred Music, Northland Bapt. Bible Coll., 2000; M in Music Edn., VanderCook Coll. Music, 2003. Music dir. Brentwood Bapt. Christian Acad., Des Plaines, Ill., 2000—02, Front Range Bapt. Ch. and Acad., Fort Collins, Colo., 2002—. Vocalist N.W. Choral Soc., Des Plaines, 2001—02, Opera Ft. Collins, 2004—05, Ft. Collins Children's Theatre, 2004; trumpet player Des Plaines Cmty. Concert Band, 2000—02, No. Colo. Concert Band, Windsor, 2004—06. Mem.: Internat. Trumpet Guild, Music Educator's Nat. Conf., Nat. Assn. Tchrs. Singing, Nat. Bapt. Mus. Bapt. Assn. Avocations: reading, sports. Home: 1024 E Swallow B-231 Fort Collins CO 80525 Office: Front Range Baptist Church and Academy 625 E Harmony Rd Fort Collins CO 80525 Office Phone: 970-223-5757. Business E-Mail: jpluth@frontrangebaptist.org

**PNIAKOWSKI, ANDREW FRANK,** structural engineer; b. Grodno, Poland, Aug. 18, 1930; s. Josef Leon and Janina (Kodzynski) Pniakowski; m. Margaret M. Czajkowski, Aug. 15, 1957; 1 child, Mary. Diploma Engr., Politechnika Warszawska, 1952. Registered prof. engr., Ont., Mass., Maine, N.H. Bridge design and field engr. Govt. of Poland, Ministry of R.R., Warsaw, 1952—57; bridge design engr. Dept. Hwys. of Ont., Toronto, Canada, 1958—66; sr. structural engr. Sverdrup & Parcel Assocs., Inc., Boston, 1967—71; chief structural engr. Louis Berger & Assocs., Inc., Needham, Mass., 1972—96; cons. engr. in transp., bridges, hwys., railroads, pub. bldgs., others. Mem.: Assn. Profl. Engrs. of Province of Ont., Prestressed Concrete Inst., Am. Concrete Inst., Am. Inst. Steel Constrn. Roman Catholic.

**PNUELI, AMIR,** computer science educator; b. Nahalal, Israel, Apr. 22, 1941; married; 3 children. BSc in Math., Technion U.; PhD in Applied Math., Weizmann Inst. Sci., 1967; doctorate (hon.), U. Uppsala, 1997, U. Joseph Fourier, 1998, Carl von Ossietzky U., 2000. Fellow Stanford U., Watson Rsch. Ctr., Yorktown; prof. computer sci. Weizmann Inst. Sci., Rehovot, Israel, sr. rschr., prof., 1981—99, head Minerva Ctr. Verification of Reactive Systems, 1998; prof. computer sci. NYU, 1999—. Co-founder Mini-Sysems, 1971; founder, chmn. dept. computer sci. Tel-Aviv U., 1973; co-founder AdCad. Author (with Z. Manna): The Temporal Logic of Reactive and Concurrent Systems: Specification, 1991, Temporal Verification of Reactive Systems: Safety, 1995. Recipient A.M. Turing award, Assn. Computing Machinery, 1996, Israel Prize in Exact Sciences, 2000. Mem.: NAE, Israeli Acad. Arts and Scis. Achievements include seminal work introducing temporal logic into computing science; outstanding contributions to program and system verification. Office: Computer Sci Dept Courant Inst Math Sci NYU 251 Mercer St New York NY 10012 Office Phone: 212-998-3225. Business E-Mail: amir@cs.nyu.edu.

**POAD, FLORA VIRGINIA,** retired librarian, retired elementary school educator; b. Roanoke, Va., Oct. 8, 1921; d. Thomas Franklin and Ethlind (Wertz) Huff; m. Stanley Theodore Benton, Dec. 24, 1942 (div. Oct. 1983); children: Peggy, Betty, Mary Jo, Lucy; m. James Joseph Poad, June 6, 1986. Student, Radford Coll., 1939—41, Ohio U., 1956—57; BS in Edn., Ohio No. U., 1960; MA in LS, U. Toledo, 1964; postgrad., Kent State U., 1964—66, postgrad., 1971. Reference asst. Roanoke Pub. Libr., 1939-42; catalog asst. Univ. Libr., Emory U., Atlanta, 1942; sec. ARC, Atlanta, 1943; catalog asst. Pickerington (Ohio) Pub. Libr., 1950-51; tchr. Celina (Ohio) Pub. Schs., 1957-62; tchr., libr. Toledo Pub. Schs., 1962-64; libr. supr. Oregon (Ohio) Pub. Schs., 1964-85; instr. U. Toledo, 1970, reference libr., 1971-86; tchr. Sylvan Learning Ctr., Toledo, 1985-92, ret., 1992. Evaluation team Ohio Dept. Edn., Columbus, 1973; rep. Ohio Gov.'s Conf. on Librs., Columbus, 1974; chmn., adv. bd. tchr. sci. dept. Cmty.-Tech. Coll., 1965-69. Editor Ohio Assn. Sch. Librs. Bull., 1968-71. Vol. Am. Cancer Soc., Toledo, 1946—48, 1986—87, Mobile Meals, Toledo, 1986—93, Helping Hands, Toledo, 1994—2001. Martha Holden Jennings scholar, 1976. Mem. Nat. Honor Soc., Delta Kappa Gamma, Pi Lambda Theta, Kappa Delta Pi, Phi Kappa Phi. Avocations: reading, walking, crafts. Home: 3544 Bayberry Pl Oregon OH 43616-2475

**POCALYKO, MICHAEL NICHOLAS,** investment banker, venture capitalist; b. Fountain Hill, Pa., Dec. 24, 1954; s. Walter and Anna Margaret (Pagats) P.; m. Barbara Wilson Snelbaker, Dec. 26, 1976; children: James Kenneth, Kathryn Laura. AB, Muhlenberg Coll., 1976; MPA, Harvard U., 1985; MBA, U. Pa., 1995. Commd. ensign USN, 1976, advanced through grades to comdr., 1992; aviation detachment officer in charge USS Pharris, 1983-84; mem. strategic concepts group Office of Chief of Naval Ops., Washington, 1985-86, spl. asst. to dep. chief of naval ops., 1986-87; aviation detachment officer in charge USS Boone, 1988-90; with Office of Sec. of Navy, Washington, 1990-92; sr. fellow Atlantic Coun. U.S., Washington, 1992-93; with Office of Sec. Def., Washington, 1993—95; founder, prin. M.N. Pocalyko Investment Bankers, 1995—97; mng. dir., CEO Monticello Capital, 1997—, corp. dir., chmn., 1997—. Audit com. chmn. Challenger Corp., 2002—; chmn. Advanced Environ. Resources Inc., 2003—, Erdevel Europa S.à r.l., 2003—, Erdevel Water Sys. S.r.l., 2004—; trustee Fairleigh Dickinson U., 2000—06. Co-editor: A John Hawkes Symposium: Design and Debris, 1977; contbr.: Reconstituting America's Defense, 1992; rapporteur: The Future of Russian-American Relations in a Pluralistic World, 1992, The Future of Ukrainian-American Relations in a Pluralistic World, 1992; co-author: The NATO Infrastructure Program, 1993; author: The New Trade Order, 1994, Trends in the International Business Competition Environment, 2001; contbr. articles, essays, op-eds to profl. publs., books, newspapers. Apptd. Fairfax County Industrial Devel. Authority, 1999—2000; apptd. mem. exec. Boy Scouts Am. Nat. Capital Area Coun., 2002—; apptd. mem. Va. Commonwealth Competition Coun., 2000—03; mem. Fairfax County Rep. Com., 1996—2004, Va. Ho. Delegates 36th dist. Rep. Com., 1996—2001, 2001—06. Recipient Eagle Scout award, 1968, Vincent Astor Found. award U.S. Naval Inst., 1983, Lamb award, Evangelical Lutheran Ch. Am., 1998, Silver Beaver award, Boy Scouts Am., 2002; decorated Navy Commendation Medal, Navy Achievement Medal, Meritorious Svc. Medal (3 awards), 16 other decorations. Mem. U.S. Naval Inst., Internat. Inst. Strategic Studies, Coun. on Fgn. Rels., Assn. Naval Aviation, Muhlenberg Coll. Alumni Assn. (exec. coun. 1986-90, chmn. 1986-90), Metropolitan Club (New York), Tower Club (Tysons Corner Va.), Am. Legion, V.F.W., Masons, Sovereign Military Order Temple Jerusalem (gran officier), Military Order Foreign Wars, Military Order Carabao, Sigma Phi Epsilon, Sigma Tau Delta. Republican. Lutheran. Avocations: fly fishing, horseback riding. Home: 12932 Oak Lawn Pl Oak Hill VA 20171-2259 Office: Monticello Capital One Fountain Sq Reston Town Ctr 11911 Freedom Dr Ste 710 Reston VA 20190-5629 Office Phone: 703-674-0500. Business E-Mail: pocalyko@monticellocapital.com.

**POCHAMPALLY, KISHORE K.,** engineering educator; b. Hyderabad, Andhra Pradesh, India, Jan. 7, 1977; s. Narasimha Rao and Sharada Pochampally. BE in Mech. Engring. with distinction, Nat. Inst. Tech., Bhopal, India, 1999; MS in Indsl. Engring., Northeastern U., Boston, 2001, PhD in Indsl. Engring., 2004. Rsch. assoc. Northeastern U., Boston, 1999—2004; post doctoral fellow MIT, Cambridge, 2004—05; asst. prof. So. N.H. U., Manchester, 2005—. Contbr. scientific papers to profl. jours. Math bee vol. North South Found., Manchester, NH, 2006—06. Recipient Best Paper award, Internat. Symposium Electronics and Environment, Outstanding Scholarly Work award, Lab. Responsible Mfg. Northeastern U. Mem.: Phi Kappa Phi, Alpha Pi Mu. Hindu. Avocation: reading. Home: Apt 36 56 Brighton Ave Allston MA 02134 Office: So NH U 2500 North River Rd Manchester NH 03106 Office Phone: 603-629-4685. Business E-Mail: k.pochampally@snhu.edu.

**POCHI, PETER ERNEST,** physician; b. Boston, Mar. 8, 1929; s. Anesti and Alice (Peterson) P.; m. Barbara Orlob, June 11, 1955; children: Alan, Rena. AB cum laude, Harvard Coll., 1950; MD, Boston U., 1955. Diplomate Am. Bd. Dermatology. Intern Boston City Hosp., 1955-56, vis. dermatologist, 1978-91, assoc. dermatol., 1967-74, 78-84, acting chief dermatology, 1984-85; resident in dermatology Boston U. Hosp., 1958-61, vis. dermatologist, 1977-91, acting chief dermatology, 1984-85; assoc. in medicine Peter Bent Brigham Hosp., Boston, 1972-78; sr. cons. in dermatology Lemuel Shattuck Hosp., Boston, 1975-91; Herbert Mescon prof. dermatology Sch. Medicine, Boston U., 1988-91, prof. emeritus, 1991—, interim chmn. dept. dermatology, 1984-85. Cons. med. service in dermatology Boston VA Hosp., 1978-82; lectr. dermatology Sch. Medicine, Tufts U., 1980-91; assoc. staff New Eng. Med. Ctr. Hosp., 1981-91. Assoc. editor Jour. Investigative Dermatology, 1968-73; contbg. editor Year Book of Dermatology, 1983-90; mem. editl. bd. Archives of Dermatology, 1979-84, Jour. Am. Acad. Dermatology, 1981-90; hon. editor Acta Dermatovenerologica Albanica, 2004—; contbr. articles to med. jours Bd. dirs. Cmty. Music Ctr., 1973-77, 97-2003, corp. mem., 1994-97, 2005—; governing bd. Boston Musical Theater, 2000-03. With USN, 1956-58. USPHS fellow, 1960-62, 62-63; USPHS grantee, 1965-84 Fellow Am. Acad. Dermatology (bd. dirs. 1981-85); mem. Am. Fedn. Clin. Research, AMA, Boston Dermatological Club (sec.-treas. 1967-69), Boston U. Sch. Medicine Alumni Assn. (pres 1979-80), Boston U. Nat. Alumni Council, Dermatology Found., Evans Med. Found. (dir., sec.), Internat. Soc. Dermatology, Mass. Acad. Dermatology, Mass. Med. Soc. (chmn. sect. dermatology 1977-78), New Eng. Dermatol. Soc., Soc. Investigative Dermatology, 1960-62, 1981-85); mem. Am. Fedn. Clin. Research, AMA, Boston Dermatological Soc. (sec.-treas. 1967-69), Boston U. Sch. Medicine Alumni Assn. Home: 333 Commonwealth Ave Boston MA 02115-1933 E-mail: pepderm@bu.edu.

**POCHI, SUBBARAYAN RAMALINGAM,** biomedical researcher; b. New Delhi, May 19, 1965; arrived in U.S., 1999; s. Ramalingam Kumaraswamy and Sundary Pochi; m. Malancha Sarkar, Sept. 2, 1994; children: ShuvamBharathy Subbarayan, Bhargavi Subbarayan. BS in Zoology, U. Madras, India, 1986, MS in Biomedical Genetics, 1988; PhD, Banaras Hindu U., Varanasi, India, 1994. Rschr. Nat. Inst. Genetics, Mishima, Shizuoka Ken, Japan, 1997—98; asst. scientist U. Miami (Fla.) Sch. Medicine, 2002—; mem. faculty in biology U. Miami and Miami Dade Coll., 2005—. Recipient Young Scientist award, Internat. Union Biochemistry and Molecular Biology, 1994,

Japanese Govt. Rsch. Awards for Fgn. Specialist, Sci. and Tech. Agy., Japan., 1995; fellow, Sci. and Tech. Agy., Govt. Japan, 1995—96. Mem.: Soc. Biol. Chemists India (life). Office: Univ Miami Sch Medicine 1550 NW 10th Ave Fox 431A (D8-4) Miami FL 33136 Office Phone: 305-243-4887. Business E-Mail: spochi@med.miami.edu.

**POCHICK, FRANCIS EDWARD,** financial consultant; b. Metuchen, NJ, May 28, 1931; s. Frank Stephen and Bertha Barbara Pochick; m. Shirley Ann Elliott, Feb. 16, 1957; children: Bonnie Lynn, Keith Francis. Student, Rutgers U., 1949-50, 54-55. Agt. New Eng. Mut. Life. Ins. Co., Newark and New Brunswick, NJ, 1958-61, Lambert M. Huppeler Co., Inc., N.Y.C., 1962-64, cons., 1964, sr. cons. employee benefits, 1967-87; fin. cons. Francis E. Pochick Assocs., N.Y.C., 1987—. Mem. adv. bd. Mercer Fund, Cmty. Found. N.J., 1986—, Rec. for the Blind, Princeton, 1989, charitable devel. officer Nat. Found., Inc., 1992, Nat. Coun. on The Aging, Planned Giving Coun. 1994; mem. com. bd. dirs. health Princeton Coun. Planned Giving, 1993; v.p. The Benefits Planning Co., Ltd., Charlottesville, Va., 1995. With USMC, 1951-54. Mem. Am. Soc. Pension Actuaries, Nat. Assn. Life Underwriters, Fin. Planning Assn., Estate Planning Coun., Nat. Assn. Philanthropic Planners, Lions, Glenmore Country Club. Home: 1451 Bremerton Ln Keswick VA 22947-9147 Office: PO Box 518 Keswick VA 22947-0518 also: No Jersey Br 30 Two Bridges Rd Fairfield NJ 07004-1550 Office Phone: 434-295-7173. E-mail: blmccann118@aol.com

**POCHINI, JUDY HAY,** interior designer, writer, editor; b. Phoenix, Mar. 16, 1932; d. Cecil Clifford and Nadine Mary (Larimer) Cook; m. Gordon Eugene Hay, June 5, 1971 (dec. 1974); m. Robert Frank Pochini, Sept. 18, 1983 (dec. 1995). BA, U. Calif., Santa Barbara, 1953; MA in Journalism, U. Calif., Berkeley, 1965. Exec. sec. Mobil Oil Corp., Mpls., 1958-60, Kaiser Aluminum & Chem. Corp., Oakland, Calif., 1960-64; asst. trade publ. editor Sunset mag., Menlo Park, Calif., 1966-68, trade publ. editor, 1968-73; owner, home furnishings editor Lifestyle West, Walnut Creek, Calif., 1974-79; interior designer Berman's Drexel-Heritage, Oakland, 1979-85, Suburban House Drexel-Heritage, Concord, Calif., 1986-87; ptnr., interior designer Judy Hay Interiors, Lafayette and Santa Barbara, Calif., 1987-95, owner, 1995—. Mem. nat. consumer action panel Carpet & Rug Industry, Dalton, Ga., 1973-75; cons. in field. Contbr. articles to profl. jours. Mem. AAUW (pres. 2002-04), Internat. Furnishings and Design Assn., Women in Comms. Inc., U. Calif. Santa Barbara Alumni Assn. (music affiliates bd.), Chi Omega. Democrat. Mem. Unity Ch. Office: 1026 Coast Village Rd 140 Santa Barbara CA 93108

**POCKALNY, ROBERT,** geophysicist, researcher; PhD, U. R.I., 1991. Marine rsch. scientist GSO/URI, Narragansett, RI, 1995—. Office: GSO/URI South Ferry Rd Narragansett RI 02882 Office Phone: 401 874-6926. Business E-Mail: robp@gso.uri.edu.

**POCKER, YESHAYAU,** chemistry and biochemistry educator; b. Kishinev, Romania, Oct. 10, 1928; came to U.S., 1961; naturalized, 1967. s. Benzion Israel and Esther Sarah (Sudit) P.; m. Anna Goldenberg, Aug. 8, 1950; children: Rona, Elon I. MSc, Hebrew U., Jerusalem, 1949; PhD, Univ. Coll., London, Eng., 1953; DSc, U. London, 1960. Rsch. assoc. Weizmann Inst. Sci., Rehovot, Israel, 1949-50; humanitarian trust fellow Univ. Coll., 1951-52, asst. lectr., 1952-54, lectr., 1954-61; vis. assoc. prof. Ind. U., Bloomington, 1960-61; prof. U. Washington, Seattle, 1961—. Bicentennial lectr. Mont. State U., Bozeman, 1976; Horizons in Chemistry lectr. U. N.C., Chapel Hill, 1977, guest lectr. U. Kyoto, Japan, 1984; Edward A. Doisy vis. prof. biochemistry St. Louis U. Med. Sch., 1990; plenary lectr. N.Y. Acad. Sci., 1983, Fast Reactions in Biol. Systems, Kyoto, Japan, 1984, NATO, 1989, Consiglio nat. delle Richerche, U. Bari, Italy, 1989, Sigma Tau, Spoleto, Italy, 1990; Internat. lectr. Purdue U., 1990; cons. NIH, 1984, 86, 88; Spl. Topic lectr. on photosynthesis, Leibniz House, Hanover, Fed. Republic Germany, 1991; enzymology, molecular biology lectr., Dublin, Ireland, 1992; 3M lectr., St. Paul, 1996; enzymology, molecular biology, retinal metabolism lectr. Deadwood, S.D., 1996, fast reactions in solutions and Bronsted symposium lectr., Copenhagen, 1997, self assembly kinetics of Alzheimer beta-amyloid peptides, ultrafast studies of insulin-insulin and insulin-receptor interactions; 1st Bannan invited lectr. Seattle U., spring, 1999; invited Bannan lectr. Seattle U., 2000, Alzheimer and Prion Proteins; internat. conf. Port Townsend, Wash. 2000, lectr. water sensing mechanisms, internat. symposium, Taos, N. Mex., 2000, internat. lectr. enzymology, molecular biology. Mem. editorial adv. bd. Inorganica Chimica Acta-Bioinorganic Chemistry, 1981-89; bd. reviewing editors Sci., 1985-2000; contbr. numerous articles to profl. jours.; pub. over 220 papers and 12 revs. Numerous awards worldwide, 1983-97. Mem. Royal Soc. Chemistry, Am. Chem. Soc. (nat. spkr. 1970, 74, 84, chmn. Pauling award com. 1978, plaque awards 1974, 84, Outstanding Svc. award 1979, chmn. selection com. Pauling award 1996), Soc. Exptl. Biology, Am. Soc. Biol. Chemists, N.Y. Acad. Scis., Sigma Xi (nat. lectr. 1971). Avocations: history, philosophy, poetry. Office: U Wash Dept Chemistry PO Box 351700 Seattle WA 98195-1700

**POCKRASS, JOSEPH CRAIG,** music educator; b. N.Y.C., May 21, 1971; s. Arlen Stuart and Evelyn Leona Pockrass; m. Jessica Ann Hegele, July 30, 1995; children: David Stuart, Benjamin Thomas, Anna Elizabeth. BS, Ball State U., 1994. Lic. tchg. K-12 gen., instrumental, and choral music Ind., 2002. Choral/computer tchr. Twin Lakes Sch. Corp., Monticello, Ind., 1994—95; spl. edn. asst. Wash. Twp. Schs., Indpls., 1995—96; choral/drama tchr. Durham Pub. Schs., N.C., 1996—97; elem. gen. music tchr. Chapel Hill-Carrboro City Schs., N.C., 1997—2001; elem. gen./instrumental music tchr. Indpls. Pub. Schs., 2001—. Piano/voice tchr. Ashley Arts Music Sch., Durham, 1998—2000; piano tchr. Meridian Music, Carmel, Ind., 2001— Finalist Tchr. of Yr., Elizabeth Blaker Sch. 55, 2004; named, Sch. 55, 2006. Mem.: Ind. State Tchrs. Assn., MENC. Achievements include conducted the first VH1 Save the Music Celebration Concert for the Indpls. Pub. Sch. Dist. Home: 271 Hampshire Ct Noblesville IN 46062 Office: Eliza Blaker School 55 1349 East 54th St Indianapolis IN 46220 Personal E-mail: jpock@aol.com. Business E-Mail: pockrasj@ips.k12.in.us.

**POCKWINSE, SHIRWIN M.,** research scientist, educator; b. Concord, N.H., Nov. 15, 1947; d. Winsor Edmund and Shirley Jane Merrill; m. Richard Carl Pockwinse, Mar. 9, 1974; 1 child, Sarah Winsor-Elizabeth. BA, U. N.H., 1969. Lab. technician U. Mass. Med. Sch., Worcester, 1969—74, profl. technician I, supr. electron microscopy facility, 1974—78, rsch. assoc., administr. electron microscopy facility, 1979—2004, faculty, 2004—. From mem. to chmn. adv. bd. U. Mass. Med. Ctr. Child Care Ctr., Worcester, 1975—93. Contbr. articles to profl. jours. Mem.: Baypath Humane Soc. (treas., sec. 1972). Republican. Avocations: skiing, gardening. Home: 2 Peg's Way Hopkinton MA 01748 Office: U Mass Med Sch Cell Biology 55 Lake Ave N Worcester MA 01655

**POCOCK, J. MICHAEL,** communications executive; B in Telecomm., U. Ky., Lexington. Various sr. mgmt. pos., consumer products divsn. GE Co., Fairfield, Conn.; mem. mgmt. team Epson Am., Torrance, Calif.; variuos sr. mgmt. pos. Murata Bus. Systems, Dallas; variuos sr. mgmt. positions including pres., CEO Quadmark Ltd. Xerox Corp., Rochester, NY, 1992—94; v.p., gen. mgr. Digital Equipment Corp., Acton, Mass., 1994—96; v.p., gen. mgr. N.Am. sales Compaq Computer Corp., Houston, 1996—99, gen. mgr. comml. products computer group, 1999, v.p. corp. strategy; pres., CEO Polaroid Corp., Waltham, Mass., 2003—06; sr. v.p., gen. mgr. Linksys Cisco Systems, Inc., Irvine, Calif., 2006—. Office: Linksys 121 Theory Dr Irvine CA 92617*

**POCOSKI, DAVID JOHN,** cardiologist; b. Waterbury, Conn., July 15, 1945; s. Edward J. and Stella E. (Kolpa) P.; m. Madelyn M. Pocoski, Sept. 25, 1971; 1 child, Sarah C. BS, U. Conn., 1967; MD magna cum laude, Upstate Med. Ctr., Syracuse, NY, 1971. From intern to fellow in cardiology U. Rochester, NY; founder, pres. Osler Clinic of Medicine, Melbourne, Fla.; chief of staff, dir. cardiac rehab. Sea Pines Rehab. Hosp.; chmn. dept. cardiology Hulmes Resident Med. Ctr., Melbourne. Commr. Holy Name Jesus Cath. Ch. Maj. USAF, 1974-76. Recipient Outstanding Scientist of the 20th Century award.

---

Fellow Am. Coll. Cardiology; mem. AMA, Alpha Omega Alpha, Phi Beta Kappa. Republican. Roman Catholic. Avocations: music, art, running, community service. Office: 930 S Harbor City Blvd Melbourne FL 32901-1963 Office Phone: 321-725-5050. Personal E-mail: fdhp93@aol.com.

**POCRASS, RICHARD DALE,** management consultant; b. Meadville, Pa., Mar. 7, 1940; s. Irving F. and Roslyn (Sperber) P.; m. Rena Levy, Feb. 3, 1968; children: Michael B., S. Douglas. BS in Math., U. Pitts., 1962, MBA in Fin., 1964. EDP sales mgr. NCR Corp., Pitts., 1962-67, retail mktg. mgr. L.A., 1972-74; v.p., dir. Nanoseconds Sys., Fairfield, Conn., 1967-69, dir., 1968-72; v.p. gen. mgr. Hart Jewelry Co., Warren, Ohio, 1969-71, dir., 1981-84; mktg. mgr. Data Source Corps subs. Hercules, Inc., El Segundo, 1974-75; pres. Webster-Pocrass & O'Neil (name changed to Pocrass Assocs. 1981), L.A., 1976—, Health Tech. Inc. Pub. CEO, chmn. bd. dirs. Chocolates a la Carte, Valencia, Calif. Author: The Recruitment Letter; author (with Maronde) Drug Abuse Study for Hoffman LaRoche, 1980. Bd. dirs. West Valley Little League, U.S. Pastry Alliance, Providence Holly Cross Med. Ctr. Found., L.A. Mission Coll. Found., Western Overseas, Inc., Long Beach, Calif. Mem. Am. Mktg. Assn. L.A. Spkrs. Bur., Soc. for Human Resource Mgmt., L.A. Area C. of C., Bank Mktg. Assn., Retail Controllers Assn., Calif. Exec. Recruiters Assn., Pers. and Indsl. Rels. Assn., Internat. Platform Assn., Rotary. Republican. Jewish. Home: 18815 Paseo Nuevo Dr Tarzana CA 91356-5136 Office: 28455 Livingston Ave Valencia CA 91355-4173 Office Phone: 661-257-3700. Personal E-mail: rick@candymaker.com

**PODAIR, JERALD E.,** history professor; b. NYC, Nov. 1, 1953; s. Simon and Selma Podair; m. Caren A. Benzer, June 23, 1985; 1 child, Julie. BA, NY U., 1974; JD, Columbia u., 1977; MA, Princeton U., 1991, PhD, 1997. Bar: NY 1978. Atty. Whitman & Ransom, NYC, 1977—79, Hahn & Hessen, NYC, 1979—83, Bankers Trust Co., NYC, 1983—88; lectr. in history Princeton U., NJ, 1997—98; asst. history prof. Lawrence U., Appleton, Wis., 1998—2003, assoc. prof. history, Robert S. French prof. Am. studies, 2005—. Author: The Strike that Changed NY: Blacks, Whites and the OceanHill-Brownsville Crisis, 2002. Recipient Allan Nevins prize, Soc. of Am. Historians, 1998, Hon. mention, Urban History Assn., 2003. Mem.: Org. of Am. Historians (Findlist Liberty Legacy award 2003), Am. Hist. Assn., Phi Beta Kappa. Home: 2700 Beechwood Ct Appleton WI 54911 Office: Lawrence U Dept History P O Box 599 Appleton WI 54912

**PODBERESKY, SAMUEL,** lawyer; b. Cremona, Italy, Mar. 16, 1946; came to U.S., 1947; s. Noah and Mina (Milikowsky) P.; m. Rosita Rubinstein, March 8, 1970; children: Daniel J., Michael A. BS in Aeronautical Engring., U. Md., 1967; JD, U. Md., Balt., 1971. Bar: Md. 1972. Flight test engr. Vertol div. Boeing Co., Phila., 1967-68; regulatory atty. FAA, Washington, 1971-78; dep. asst. gen. counsel U.S. Dept. Transp., Washington, 1978-86, asst. gen. counsel aviation enforcement and proceedings, 1986—. Author: Never the Last Road, 2003. Office: US Dept Transp 400 7th St SW Washington DC 20590-0001

**PODBOY, ALVIN MICHAEL, JR.,** law librarian, director; b. Cleve., Feb. 10, 1947; s. Alvin Michael and Josephine Esther (Nagode) P.; m. Mary Ann Gloria Esposito, Aug. 21, 1971; children: Allison Marie, Melissa Ann. AB cum laude, Ohio U., 1969, JD, Case Western Res. U., 1972, MLS, 1977. Bar: Ohio 1972, US Dist. Ct. (no. dist.) Ohio 1973, US Supreme Ct. 1992. Assoc. Joseph T. Svete Co. LPA, Chardon, Ohio, 1972-76; dir. pub. svcs. Case Western Res. Sch. Law Libr., Cleve., 1974-77, assoc. law libr., 1977-78; libr. Baker & Hostetler, LLP, Cleve., 1978-88, dir. librs., 1988—. Instr. Notre Dame Coll. of Ohio, Cleve., 1991-2002, Ursuline Coll., Cleve., 2003—, Am. Inst. Paralegal Studies, Cleve., 1991-96. Mem. (editl. adv. bd.) Law Tech. News, 1999—, Practice Innovations, 2001—. Bd. overseers Case Western Res. U., 1981-87, vis. com. sch. libr. sci., 1980-86, Westlaw. adv. bd., 1987-92, bd. govs. law sch. alumni assn., 1992-95, West's Legal Directory Ohio Adv. Panel, 1990-91; adv. com. West's Info. Innovators Inst., 1995-97; chmn. Case Western Res. Libr. Sch. Alumni Fund, 1979-80; Rep. precinct committeeman Cuyahoga County, Cleve., 1981-95, exec. com., 1984-87; Rep. precinct committeeman Portage County, Aurora, 2004—; treas. Aurora Meml. Libr. Trust, 2004-; 2nd vice comdr. Aurora Am. Legion Post 803, 2006-. 1st lt. USAF, 1972. Mem.: ABA, Arnold Air Soc., Case Western Res. U. Libr. Sch. Alumni Assn. (pres. 1981), Ohio Regional Assn. Law Librs. (pres. 1985), Am. Assn. Law Librs. (chmn. pvt. law librs. spl. interest sect. 1994—95, exec. bd. 2001—04, cert.), Cleve. Bar Assn., Ohio State Bar Assn. (chmn. librs. com. 1989—91), Phi Alpha Theta, Pi Gamma Mu. Roman Catholic. Avocation: alpine skiing. Home: 417 East Parkway Blvd Aurora OH 44202 Office: Baker & Hostetler LLP 3200 National City Ctr Cleveland OH 44114-3485 Office Phone: 216-861-7101. Business E-Mail: apodboy@bakerlaw.com

**PODD, ANN,** newspaper editor; b. Buffalo, Jan. 15, 1954; d. Edward and Florence (Bojan) P.; m. Timothy Murray, 1980; children: Laura, Gregory. AB, Syracuse U., 1976; MBA, SUNY, Buffalo, 1981. Reporter AP, 1977, Buffalo Courier-Express, 1977-80, bus. editor, 1980-82, Bergen (N.J.) Record, 1982-88, N.Y. Daily News, 1988-90, assoc. editor, 1990-92, assoc. editor, dir. human resources, 1992-93; dep. spot news editor Wall St. Jour., N.Y.C., 1994, spot news editor, 1994—2000, nat. TV editor, 2000—03, day editor, 2003—05; Hong Kong mng. editor Wall St. Jour. Asia, Hong Kong, 2005—. Office: Wall Stret Journal 25/F Central Plaza 18 Harbour Rd Hong Kong Hong Kong

**PODESCHI, AMANDA LANDACRE,** director, educator; d. Michael and Cindy Landacre; m. Richard Pasquo Podeschi, July 10, 2004. BA in Social Sci. Secondary Edn., Millikin U., 2002; MA in History, U. Ill., 2005; Grad. studies tchr. Glenwood H.S., Chatham, Ill., 2002—04; assoc. dir. devel. Millikin U., Decatur, Ill., 2004—. Instr. Millikin U., Decatur, Ill., 2005—. Adminstrv. coun. sec. Sharon United Meth. Ch., Decatur, 2005—06. Recipient Albert T. Mills prize, Millikin U., 2002, Lindsey medallion for scholarathletes, 2003, scholar, 1999—2002. Mem.: Am. Hist. Assn., Alpha Lamda Delta, Phi Alpha Theta, Phi Kappa Phi.

**PODESTA, JOHN DAVID,** law educator, former White House chief of staff; b. Chgo., Jan. 8, 1949; s. John David, Sr. and Mary (Kokoris) Podesta; m. Mary Spieczny, Nov. 4, 1978; children: Megan Rouse, Mae, Gabriel. BS, Knox Coll., 1971; JD, Georgetown U., 1976. Bar: DC 1976. Trial atty. Dept. of Justice, Washington, 1976-77; spl. asst. to dir. ACTION, Washington, 1978-79; counsel Senate Judiciary Com., Washington, 1979-81; chief minority counsel Senate Judiciary Subcom., Washington, 1981-86; chief counsel Senate Agr. Com., Washington, 1987-88; pres., gen. counsel Podesta Assocs., Inc., Washington, 1988-93; asst. to pres., staff sec. The White House, Washington, 1993-95, asst. to pres., dep. chief of staff, 1997-98, chief of staff to Pres., 1998—2001; pres., CEO Ctr. Am. Progress, Washington, 2001—. Vis. prof. law Georgetown U. Law Ctr., Washington, 1983, Washington, 1995—97, Washington, 1998—2000, Washington, 2001—; chair US Senate subcom., Task Force Privacy and Tech., Washington, 1991; mem. coun. Adminstrv. Conf. US, Washington, 1993—95; mem. Com. Protecting and Reducing Govt. Secrecy, Washington, 1995. Author: Protecting Electronic Messaging, 1990. Fellow: Natural Resources Def. Coun. (sr.); mem.: ABA (coun., sec. individual rights and responsibilities 1994—, chair 2002—03), DC Bar (chair adminstrv. law sect. 1982—83), League Conservation Voters (bd. dirs. 2001—). Democrat. Office: Ctr Am Progress 1333 H St NW 10th Fl Washington DC 20005 also: Georgetown U Law Ctr 574 McDonough Hall Washington DC 20001-2075

**PODESTA, ROGER E.,** lawyer; b. Aug. 10, 1947; BA, Columbia U., 1969; JD, Harvard U., 1973. Bar: NY 1973. Law clk. to Hon. Wilfred Feinberg US Ct. Appeals (2nd cir.), 1973-74; ptnr., head Product Liability Practice Debevoise & Plimpton LLP, NYC. Case and comments editor: Harvard Law Rev., 1972-73. Mem. ABA, Phi Beta Kappa. Office: Debevoise & Plimpton LLP 919 Third Ave New York NY 10022 Office Fax: 212-909-6836. E-mail: repodesta@debevoise.com.

---

**PODGORNY, GEORGE,** emergency physician; b. Tehran, Iran, Mar. 17, 1934; s. Emanuel and Helen (Parsian) P.; came to U.S., 1954, naturalized, 1973. B.S., Maryville Coll.; 1958; postgrad. Bowman Gray Sch. Medicine, 1958; M.D., Wake Forest U., 1962; m. Ernestine Koury, Oct. 20, 1962; children: Adele, Emanuel II, George, Gregory. Intern in surgery NC Bapt. Hosp., Winston-Salem, 1962-63, chief resident in gen. surgery, 1966-67, in cardiothoracic surgery, 1967-69; sr. med. examiner Forsyth County, N.C., 1972—; dir. dept. emergency medicine Forsyth Meml. Hosp., Winston-Salem, 1974-80; sec.-treas. Forsyth Emergency Services, Winston-Salem, 1970-80; clin. prof. emergency medicine East Carolina U. Sch. Medicine, Greenville, 1984—, chmn. residency rev. com. on emergency medicine, 1980-88; mem. Accreditation Coun. for Grad. Med. Edn. Dir. Emergency Med. Svcs. Project Region II of N.C., 1975—; chmn. bd. trustees Emergency Medicine Found.; chmn. residency rev. com. emergency medicine Accreditation Coun. Grad. Med. Edn.; founder Western Piedmont Emergency Med. Svcs. Coun., 1973; mem. N.C. Emergency Med. Svcs. Adv. Coun., 1976-81; assoc. prof. clin. surgery Bowman Gray Sch. Medicine, Wake Forest U., Winston-Salem, 1979—. Bd. dirs. Piedmont Health Systems Agy., 1975-84; trustee Forsyth County Hosp., Authority, 1974-75; bd. dirs. N.C. Health Coordinating Coun., 1975-82, Medic Alert Found. Internat. Fellow Internat. Coll. Surgeons, Internat. Coll. Angiology, Royal Soc. Health (Great Britain), Royal Soc. Medicine, Southeastern Surg. Congress; mem. Am. Coll. Emergency Physicians (charter, pres. 1978-79), AMA, (chmn. coun. of sect. emergency medicine 1978-90, alt. del. for Am. Coll. Emergency Physicians, 1990—), Am. Bd. Emergency Medicine (pres. 1976-81). Contbr. articles to profl. publs. on trauma, snake bite and history of medicine; editorial bd. Annals of Emergency Medicine. Med. Meetings. Home and Office: 2115 Georgia Ave Winston Salem NC 27104-1917 Office Phone: 336-727-1161.

**PODGORSAK, ERVIN B.,** medical physicist, educator, administrator; b. Vienna, Sept. 28, 1943; arrived in Slovenia, 1946, came to U.S., 1968, Can., 1973; s. Franc and Gabriella Podgorsak; m. Mariana Ambrozic, Oct. 23, 1965; children: Matthew, Gregor. Dipl.Ing. in Physics, U. Ljubljana, Slovenia, 1968; MSc in Physics, U. Wis., 1970, PhD in Physics, 1973. Diplomate Am. Bd. Med. Physics. Rsch. asst. U. Ljubljana, 1965-68, U. Wis., Madison, 1968-73; postdoctoral fellow U. Toronto, Ont., Canada, 1973-74; asst. prof. McGill U., Montreal, Que., Canada, 1975-79, assoc. prof., 1980-84, prof. med. physics, 1985—, dir. med. physics unit, 1991—; dir. dept. med. physics Montreal Gen. Hosp., 1979—. Hon. vis. prof. U. Ljubljana, 1995—; presenter in field. Contbr. numerous articles to sci. jours., chpts. to books. Recipient (with C. Zankowski) Sylvia Fedoruk prize in Med. Physics, 1997, (with C. Zankowski) Farrington Daniels award in Med. Physics, 1997. Fellow Can. Coll. Physicists in Medicine (bd. dirs. 1981-89, v.p. 1984-87, pres. 1987-89), Am. Assn. Physicists in Medicine (bd. dirs. 1990-93, assoc. editor Med. Physics Jour. 1989-2005, radiother. com. 1994-96, Lifetime Achievement in Med. Physics award Upstate NY chpt. 2005, William D. Coolidge award 2006); mem. Am. Coll. Med. Physics (bd. chancellors 1997-99), Can. Assn. Physicists, Can. Orgn. Med. Physics, Can. Assn. Radiation Oncologists, Can. Radiation Protection Assn., Internat. Stereotactic Radiosurgery Soc. (bd. dirs. 1991-95) Home: 1540 croissant Seville Brossard PQ Canada J4X 1J4 Office: Montreal Gen Hosp Dept Med Physics 1650 Cedar Ave Montreal PQ Canada H3G 1A4 Office Phone: 514-934-8052. E-mail: epodgorsak@medphys.mcgill.ca.

**PODHORETZ, JOHN,** editor, writer; b. NYC, Apr. 18, 1961; s. Norman Podhoretz and Midge (Decter); m. Ayala Cohen, Oct. 13, 2002. AB, U. Chgo., 1982. Former researcher, reporter Time; exec. editor news Insight Mag., Washington, 1985-87; contbg. editor U.S. News and World Report, Washington, 1987-88; speechwriter to Pres. Ronald Reagan and George H. W. Bush White House, Washington, 1988-89; spl. asst. to William Bennett Office of Nat. Drug Control Policy, 1989; asst. mng. editor Washington Times, 1989-91; sr. fellow Hudson Inst., 1991-94; contbr. FOX News Channel, 1997—. TV critic N.Y. Post, 1994-95, editor editl. page, columnist 1997—; co-founder, former dep. dir. The Weekly Std., 1995-97, currently contbg. editor; weekly columnist National Review Online; cons. editor Regan Books; co-founder White House Writers Group; author Hell of a Ride: Backstage at the White House Follies 1989-1993, 1992, Bush Country: How Dubya Became a Great President While Driving Liberals Insane, 2004; cons. (TV) West Wing. Recipient J.C. Penney/Mo. award for excellence in feature sects., 1990. Jewish. Achievements include Five-time winner on Jeopardy!. Office: FOX News Channel 1211 Ave of Americas New York NY 10036

**PODICHETTY, VINOD KUMAR,** medical researcher; arrived in U.S., 2000; s. Haricharan and Vasantha Podichetty. MBBS, Maharastra Inst. Med. Sci. & Rsch., India, 1998; MS, Cleve. State U., 2002; cert. in Protection of Human Research Subjects, U. Miami, 2002. Diplomate Indian Med. Coun., 1999. Staff physician Aware Hosps., Hyderabad, Andhra Pradesh, India, 1998; chief med. officer Aware Cancer Rsch. Inst., Hyderabad, Andhra Pradesh, India, 1999—2000; rsch. asst. Cleve. (Ohio) Clinic Found., 2000—02; coord., rsch. assoc. Cleve. Clinic Fla., Weston, Fla., 2003—04, project dir., 2004—; project lead U. Hosp. West Eng., Bristol, England, 1999. Co-director, spine symposium Cleve. Clinic Fla., Weston, Fla., 2003; dir. Primary Health Care Ctr. - Pulse Polio Program, Latur, Maharastra, India, 1997. Contbr. articles to profl. jours. Grantee, Pharm. Industry, 2002—05; scholar, Dept. Health Scis. Cleve. State U., 2000—02. Mem.: Am. Med. Writers Assn., Assn. Clin. Rsch. Profls., Am. Coll. Health Assn., Indian Soc. Human Genetics, Indian Med. Coun., Nat. Assn. Spine Specialists, N.Am. Spine Soc., Indian Student Orgn. (pres. 2002), Continuing Med. Edn. Com. Achievements include research in effectiveness of calcitonin nasal spray in the treatment of lumbar canal stenosis; thoracic microendoscopic discectomy; chronic non-malignant musculoskeletal pain in older adult: clinical issues and opioid intervention; age-based comparative studies in elderly patients receiving lumbar decompression surgery; ASA class, not age, predicts complications after minimally invasive spine surgery. Office Phone: 954-659-5630.

**PODKUL, THEODORE B., JR.,** systems support specialist; s. Theodore B. and Ida C. Podkul; m. Joan Kline, June 10, 1973; children: Jennifer, Timothy. AB, Franklin and Marshall Coll., 1967; MA, George Washington U., 1974. Cert. compliance profl. Health Ethics Trust, med. adminstr. Am. Acad. Med. Administrators. Adminstrv. resident US Dept. Vets. Affairs, Martinez, Calif., 1973—74, mgmt. analyst, 1974—75, med. dist. coord. Buffalo, 1976—78, health sys. specialist, 1979—. Mem. citizens bd. Nat. Alliance for Mentally Ill in Buffalo and Erie County, Buffalo, 1990—2005. First lt. U.S. Army, 1967—70. Decorated Combat Inf. Badge US Army, Bronze Star, Army Commendation medal, Vietnam Campaign medal, Vietnam Svc. medal, Nat. Defence Svc. medal, Jungle Expert badge, Conspicuous Svc. Cross NY State, DSM State of NJ. Fellow: Am. Inst. Inst. Healthcare Quality, Assn. Behavioral Healthcare Mgmt. (cert., bd. dirs. 1988—89, Harold C. Piepenbrink award for Exemplary Leadership and Significant Accomplishments in Behavioral Healthcare Mgmt. 2004), Am. Acad. Med. Adminstrs. (life), Am. Coll. Health Care Adminstrs. (life); mem.: VFW (life), DAV (life), AMVETS (life), Am. Bd. Quality Assurance and Utilization Rev. Physicians (cert. healthcare and mgmt., bd. dirs. 1989—2006), Health Care Compliance Assn., Assn. of Mil. Surgeons of Am. (life), Leadership VA (life), Am. Coll. Healthcare Execs. (cert. healthcare exec., cert. nursing home adminstr.), Leadership Buffalo (bd. dirs. 1989—90), Vietnam Veterans Am. (life), Combat Infantryman's Assn. (life), Am. Legion (life), 101st Airbourne Divsn. Assn. (life), Buffalo Ambassadors (life). Office Phone: 716-862-8545. Business E-Mail: theodore.podkul@med.va.gov.

**PODLESAK, THOMAS F.,** electronics engineer; b. Mineola, NY, Nov. 22, 1953; s. Gerald R. and Anna Podlesak; m. Mary C. Wessel, May 6, 1989; children: Joseph G., Mary Anna, Catherine V. Pudmore, BS cum laude, St. John's U., NYC, 1975; MS, SUNY, Buffalo, 1977; PhD, SUNY, 1984. Rsch. engr. IAP Rsch., Dayton, Ohio, 1984—86; systems engr. GE, Malta, NY, 1986; sr. engr. ITT, Easton, Pa., 1987; electronics engr. US Army Rsch. Lab. Adelphi, Md., 1988—. Gen. chmn. 24th Internat. Power Modulator Symposium, Norfolk, Va., 2000. Author: High Temperature Electronics. Officer Bishop J. Louis Flaherty Assembly KC, Manassas, Va. Recipient 1st prize paper, European Power Electronics Assn., 2004; Full Competative Academic scholar, St. John's U., 1971—75. Mem.: IEEE (1st prize paper 2005). Achievements include patents for method of detecting electrical breakdown in water cooling system; tridirectional inverter. Office: US Army Rsch Lab 2800 Powder Mill Rd Adelphi MD 20783 Office Phone: 301-394-2293. E-mail: tpodlesak@arl.army.mil.

**PODOBNIK, FRANK EDWARD,** school psychologist, educational consultant; b. Mpls., June 6, 1964; s. Frank Stanley and Violet Sarah Podobnik; m. Laura Lee Mulcahy, Aug. 3, 1985; children: Francis William, Patrick Thomas, Tanner Scott. BA, U. Mont., Missoula, 1990, MA in Sch. Psychology, 1994, Edn. Specialist in Sch. Psychology, 1995. Lic. educator Mont. Office Pub. Instrn., Helena, 1994. Sch. psychologist Gt. Falls Pub. Schs., Mont., 1994—2002, Butte Pub. Sch. Dist. 1, Mont., 2005—; sch. improvement and compliance specialist Mont. Office Pub. Instrn., 2002—05. Mem. Mont. Mental Health Oversight and Adv. Com., Helena, 2004—, Mont. Comprehensive Sys. Profl. Devel. State Panel, Helena, 2005—. Mem.: NASP, Mont. Assn. Sch. Psychologists (com. chmn. Comm. and Pub. Rels. Coms. 1996—2006, pres. 1999—2000, lobbyist 2005—06). D-Liberal. Roman Catholic. Avocations: fly fishing, rafting, auto repair, woodworking. Personal E-mail: podobnikfe@butte.k12.mt.us.

**PODOLNY, JOEL M.,** dean, management educator; AB magna cum laude, Harvard U., 1986, AM, 1989, PhD in Sociology, 1991. Asst. prof. orgnl. behavior Stanford U., 1991—95, assoc. prof., 1995—96, assoc. prof. strategic mgmt. and orgnl. behavior, 1996—99, prof., 1999—2000, William R. Timken prof. orgnl. behavior and strategic mgmt., 2000—02, sr. assoc. dean for academic affairs, 2000—02; prof. sociology and bus. adminstrn. Harvard U., Cambridge, 2002—05, Novartis Profl. leadership and mgmt.; dir. rsch. Harvard Bus. Sch., Cambridge, 2003—05; dean, William S. Beinecke prof. mgmt. Yale Sch. Mgmt., New Haven, 2005—. Co-author: Strategic Management, 2001; cons. editor American Journal of Sociology, 1992—94, mem. editl. bd. Administrative Science Quarterly, 1999—2000; mem. editl. bd. American Sociological Review, 2005; assoc. editor Industrial and Corporate Change, 1999—; contbr. articles to profl. jours. Bd. mem. Nat. Arts Stabilization. Mem.: Am. Sociol. Assn. Office: Yale Sch Mgmt 135 Prospect St Box 208200 New Haven CT 06520-8200 Office Phone: 203-432-6035. Office Fax: 203-432-5092. E-mail: joel.podolny@yale.edu.

**PODRUG, DINKO,** psychiatrist, educator; b. Zagreb, Croatia, Feb. 1, 1952; came to U.S., 1977. MD, U. Zagreb, 1975; Med ScD, SUNY, Bklyn., 1988. Diplomate Am. Bd. Psychiatry and Neurology. Resident in psychiatry NYU-Bellevue Med. Sch., N.Y.C., 1977-81; rsch. fellow SUNY Health Scis. Ctr., Bklyn., 1981-85, attending psychiatrist, 1981—, dir. psychiatry clerkship, 1985-88, dir. inpatient psychiatry, 1996—2000; pvt. practice, N.Y.C., 1981—. Co-author: Transference in Brief Psychotherapy, 1985; contbr. articles pub. to profl. jour. Office: 52 E End Ave New York NY 10028-7954 Office Phone: 212-734-3307. Personal E-mail: dpodrug@hotmail.com.

**PODSIADLIK, EDWARD,** reading educator; b. Chgo., Aug. 28, 1965; BS in Edn., St. Xavier U., Chgo., 1990; MS in Adminstrn., St. Xavier U., 2003; MS in English, Purdue U., West Lafayette, Ind., 2005. Cert. tchr. reading K-8 and 9-12, ESL tchr. K-8 Ill., tchr. English K-12 Ill. Tchr. Chgo. Archdiocese, Chgo., 1990—93, Chgo. Pub. Schs., 1993—2005, area reading coach, 2005—. Mem. tchr. adv. panel Art Inst. Chgo., 1998—2003. Contbr. articles to profl. jours. Del. Chgo. Tchr. Union, 2002—05; bd. dirs. Aqua Gold, 2003—. Named Tchr. of the Yr., GWES; recipient Outstanding Svc. award, Aqua Gold, finalist, Golden Apple. Mem.: Nat. Coun. Tchrs. Social Studies, Am. Classical League, Internat. Reading Assn., Nat. Coun. Tchrs.English. Avocations: reading, writing, gardening, piano. Office: Chicago Public Schs Area 10 4655 Dearborn Chicago IL 60603

**PODWALL, KATHRYN STANLEY,** biology professor; b. Chgo., Oct. 14; d. Frank and Marie C. Stanley. BS, U. Ill.; MA, NYU. Prof. biology Nassau C.C., Garden City, NY. Developmental reviewer West Ednl. Pub., Amesbury, Mass. and Highland Park, Ill., 1989, 91-92; reviewer AAAS, Washington, 1970—; exec. bd., advisor Women's Faculty Assn., Nassau C.C., 1990—, pres, 2000-2002; lectr. in field. Author: Tested Studies for Laboratory Teaching, vol. 5, 1993; editor: (books and cassettes) Rhyming Simon Books and Cassettes, 1990, Sight Reading Syncopation, 1998, Today's Way To Play the Standards, 2000, Today's Way To Play the Classics, 2000, (book and CD) Cartoons & Car Tunes, 2001, Cartoons & Kid Tunes, 2002, Cartoons and Christmas Tunes, 2003. Recipient L.I. Alzheimer's Found. Svc. award, 2002, Excellence award, Nat. Inst. for Staff and Orgnl. Devel., 2003, Chancellor's award excellence in tchg., SUNY, 2004. Mem. AAUW, Am. Assn. for Women in Cmty. Colls., Nat. Assn. Biology Tchrs. (life), Nat. Sci. Tchrs. Assn. (life), Soc. for Coll. Sci. Tchrs., Met. Assn. Coll. and Univ. Biologists, Nat. Cathedral Assn., N.Y. Acad. of Scis., Friends of Archives (charter), Xerces Soc., Southampton Colonial Soc., LaSalle County Hist. Soc. (life), Garden City Hist. Soc. (life), Soroptimists (bd. dirs. dist. 1 1994-96, club pres. 1992-94, Nassau County Pres. award 2001), U. Ill. Alumni Assn. (life). Avocations: travel, gardening, zoological pursuits. Office: Nassau Community College One Education Dr Garden City NY 11530 Office Phone: 516-572-7575. Business E-Mail: podwalk@ncc.edu.

**POE, DAVID RUSSELL,** lawyer; b. Columbia, Mo., Sept. 4, 1948; s. Russell Warren and Chloe Ardith (Prichard) P.; m. Constance Elizabeth Vaught, Aug. 3, 1974; children: Meghan Elizabeth, Michael Lewis. BS in Mechanical and Aerospace Engring., U. Mo., 1970; JD, Duke U., 1974. Bar: NY 1975, NC 1977, US Supreme Ct. 1985, DC 1991, US Ct. Appeals (1st, 2d, 4th, 6th and DC cirs.), US Dist. Ct. (so., ea. dists.) NY, US Dist. Ct. (ea. dist.) NC. Network engr. Southwestern Bell Telephone Co., St. Louis, 1970-71; assoc. LeBoeuf, Lamb, Leiby & MacRae, NYC, 1974-82, ptnr., 1983-89, Washington, 1989-93, LeBoeuf, Lamb, Greene & MacRae, LLP, Washington, 1994—, chmn. hydroelectric practice. Adj. faculty Columbus Sch. Law, Cath. U. Am., 1992-98. Vestry St. Paul's Ch., Englewood, NJ, 1986-89; legal advisor First Presbyn. Pre-Sch. and Kindergarten, Englewood, 1984-88; vestry St John's Ch., McLean, Va., 1996-97, 1999-2001, jr. warden 2000-01. Mem. ABA (pub. utility sect., chmn. adminstrv. law com. 1988-89, chmn. cable TV com. 1989-92, mem. coun. 1990-93, chmn. publs. com. 1993-95, chmn. ann. mtg. 1997, vice-chair 2001-02, chair-elect 2002-03, sect. chair 2003-04), Fed. Comm. Bar Assn., Fed. Energy Bar Assn. (vice chmn. jud. rev. com. 1993-95, chmn. 1995-96). Office: LeBoeuf Lamb Greene MacRae LLP Ste 1200 1875 Connecticut Ave NW Washington DC 20009-5728 Office Phone: 202-986-8039. Office Fax: 202-956-3237. Business E-Mail: dpoe@llgm.com

**POE, H. SADLER,** lawyer; b. Rock Hill, SC, Oct. 17, 1944; s. Alvis Bynum and Frances Guy (Sadler) P.; m. Mary McConnell; children: Justina Lasley, Julia Rives, Abigail Sadler. AB, Princeton U., 1967; LLB, U. Va., 1971. Bar: Ga. 1971, US Dist. Ct. (no. dist.) Ga. 1976. Assoc. Alston, Miller & Gaines, Atlanta, 1971-77, ptnr., 1977-82; ptnr. leveraged capital practice area Alston & Bird LLP, Atlanta, 1982—, chmn. bus. and fin. dept., 1988-93. Bd. dirs., pres. Hillside, Inc., Atlanta, InRoads/Atlanta, Inc., 1997-2000; presenter in field. Elder Trinity Presbyn. Ch., Atlanta, 1977-80, 92-95, 98-2001; active Leadership Atlanta, 1988, exec. com. 1991-92; trustee Ga. Assn. Pastoral Care, Atlanta, 1991-96; bd. dirs., exec. com., chair-designate Sanders Buckhead YMCA, 2000—. Mem. State Bar Ga. (chmn. securities com. 1981-88, chmn. bus. and banking law sect. 1991-92), Am. Coll. Investment Counsel. Avocations: woodworking, golf. Office: Alston & Bird LLP One Atlantic Ctr 1201 W Peachtree St NW Atlanta GA 30309-3400 Office Phone: 404-881-7564. E-mail: spoe@alston.com.

**POE, JERRY B.,** financial educator; b. Springfield, Mo., Oct. 3, 1931; s. Carlyle and Eunice P.; m. Carol J. Mussler, Sept. 9, 1959; children: Cheryl Marie, Jennifer Brenna. AB, Drury Coll., 1953; MBA (Weinheimer fellow), Washington U., St. Louis, 1957; DBA (Ford Found. fellow), Harvard U., 1963. Instr. U. Ark., spring 1957; indsl. engr. McDonnell Aircraft Corp., St. Louis, 1957; lectr. on fin. Boston U., 1959-61; asst. prof. bus. adminstrn. Drury Coll., 1961-64, assoc. prof., 1964-68, prof., 1968-74; dir. Breech Sch.

Bus. Adminstrn., 1968-74; prof. emeritus Ariz. State U., 2000—, prof. fin., 1974—2000, chmn. dept. fin., 1974-82. Vis. prof. Fla. Tech. U., 1971; examiner, mem. Higher Learning Commn. of the North Cetrl. Assn. Colls. and Schs.; dir. NDEA Inst. Econs.; cons. in field Author: Essentials of Finance: An Integrated Approach, 1995, An Introduction to the American Business Enterprise, 1969, 7th rev. edit., 1989, Cases in Financial Management, 1977, 3d rev. edit., 1987. Mem. Regional Manpower Adv. Com.; mem. bus. and profl. adv. council Empire Bank. Served to lt. comdr. USNR, 1953-55. Recipient Hall Fame, Br. Sch. Bus. Adminstrn., 2006. Mem. Fin. Mgmt. Assn., Kappa Alpha, Beta Gamma Sigma, Omicron Delta Kappa. Methodist. Office: Ariz State U Coll Bus Dept Fin Tempe AZ 85287-3906

**POE, KENNETH DONOVAN,** secondary school educator; b. Washington, May 2, 1956; s. James Donovan Jr. and Barbara Wilson Poe; m. DeLena Poe, Oct. 5, 1980; children: Joshua Donovan, Arielle DeLena. BA in Music Edn., U. Richmond, Va., 1978. Tchr., band dir. Virginia Beach City Pub. Sch., Va., 1978—. Home: 1681 Will O Wisp Dr Virginia Beach VA 23454-3126

**POE, LAURA,** nursing educator, administrator; b. Salt Lake City, July 20, 1962; d. William D. and Laree Jardine (Birch) P. Grad., Utah Tech. Coll., 1980; A degree, Brigham Young U., 1984, B, 1986, MS, 1988. Asst. dir. Divsn. Occupl. and Profl. Licensing Utah Bd. Nursing, exec. dir. Author: (with others) Geri-Assistant Care Manual; contbr. articles to profl. jours. Mem. Utah Nurses Assn. (del., chair govt. rels. com.), Nightingale Soc., Phi Kappa Phi, Sigma Theta Tau.

**POE, LUKE HARVEY, JR.,** lawyer; b. Richmond, Va., Jan. 29, 1916; s. Luke Harvey and Alice Mary (Reddy) Poe; m. Josephine Jaster, Mar. 20, 1998. BS in Math, U. Va., 1938, JD, 1941; postgrad. (Rhodes scholar) Oxford U., Eng., 1939; D.Phil., Christ Ch., 1957. Bar: Va. bar 1940, D.C. bar and D.C. Ct. Appeals bar 1967, U.S. Supreme Ct. bar 1969, Md. bar 1974. Assoc. Cravath, Swaine & Moore, N.Y.C., 1941—42; tutor St. John's Coll., Annapolis, Md., 1946—50, asst. dean, 1947—49, tenure tutor, 1953—60, dir. physics and chemistry lab., 1959—60; asst. chmn. Nat. Citizens Com. for Kennedy and Johnson and others, 1960—61, Pres.'s Inaugural Com., 1960—61; asst. to chmn. bd. Aerojet-Gen. Corp., El Monte, Calif., 1961—63; divsn. pres. Internat. Tech. Assistance and Devel. Co., Washington, 1963—66; ptnr. Howard, Poe & Bastian, Washington, 1966—83; pvt. practice law, 1983—. Bd. dirs. First Am. Bank of Md.; cons. Dept. Transp., Dept. State, NEH; lectr. War Coll. of USAF, Gen. Studies program U. Va.; seminar leader Aspen Inst. Humanistic Studies; guest panelist Panel on Sci. and Tech. of Com. on Sci. and Astronautics, U.S. Ho. of Reps., 1970; pres. bd. dirs. Watergate East, Inc., 1976-79, 90-92; organizer U. Va. Unified Liberal Arts Program, 1988—. Author: The Combat History of the Battleship U.S.S. Mississippi, 1947, The Transition From Natural Law to Natural Rights, 1957; (with others) lab. manuals Einstein's Theory of Relativity, 1957, Electro-Magnetic Theory, 1959; editor: (with others) Va. Mag., 1936-38, U. Va. Law Rev., 1940-41. Dean's adv. coun. Lehigh U., 1962-65, mem. Seminar on Sci., Tech. and Pub. Policy, Brookings Instn., 1964-66; coun. on trends and perspectives U.S. C. of C., 1966-69; chmn. bd. Bristol Property Mgmt. and Svcs., Inc., 1967-88; chmn. Annapolis Bd. Zoning Appeals, 1966-75; mem. Annapolis Mayor's Task Force, 1967-74, Md. Gov.'s Commn. on Capital City, 1970-76. Lt. comdr. USNR, 1942-46. Decorated Jhalavada Order of Durbargadh, Dhrangadhara. Mem. Am. Law Inst., AAUP, Raven Soc. (pres.), Soc. of Cincinnati, Sr. Common Room and High Table (Christ Church), Met. Club (Washington), Travellers Club (London), Brook Club (N.Y.C.), New Providence Club (Annapolis), Vincent's Club (Oxford), Phi Beta Kappa, Phi Delta Phi. Episcopalian. Home: 139 Market St Annapolis MD 21401-2628 also: 2500 Virginia Ave NW Washington DC 20037-1901 Office Phone: 202-337-3080. Personal E-mail: lharveypoe@aol.com.

**POE, RANDALL ELLSWORTH,** public relations executive, author; b. Colorado Springs, Colo., Nov. 2, 1935; s. Everett E. and Emilie (Hamburger) P.; m. M. Catherine Ferguson, June 12, 1959 (div. July 1988); 1 child, Andrea Catherine. BA in Journalism, U. Calif., San Jose, 1958. Exec. dir. The Conf. Bd., N.Y.C., 1961-68, news dir., 1968-74, news dir./media mgr., 1974-88, dir. comm., exec. dir., 1988—. Contbr. articles to maj. mags., chapters to books; columnist bus. pubs. Office: The Conf Bd 845 3rd Ave 2nd Fl New York NY 10022-6601

**POE, ROBERT ALAN,** lawyer; b. Bracken County, Ky., Apr. 25, 1951; Student, U. Ky.; BA, Centre Coll., 1973; JD, U. Va., 1976. Bar: Colo. 1976. Mem. Holland & Hart, Denver, 1976—. Adj. prof. taxation U. Denver, 1986-88. Articles editor Va. Law Rev., 1974-76. Mem. ABA, Order of Coif, Phi Beta Kappa. Office: Holland & Hart 8390 E Crescent Pkwy Ste 400 Greenwood Village CO 80111-2822 Office Phone: 303-290-1616. E-mail: apoe@hollandhart.com.

**POE, TED,** congressman, former judge; b. Temple, Tex., Oct. 13, 1948; m. Carol Poe. BA in Polit. Sci., Abilene Christian U., 1970; JD, U. Houston Law Ctr., 1973. Asst. dist. atty. Harris County, Tex., 1973—81, criminal ct. judge Tex., 1981—2003; mem. US Congress from 2nd Tex. dist., 2005—, mem. transp. and infrastructure com., mem. internat. rels. com., mem. small bus. com., founder Victims' Rights Caucus. Instr. U. Houston, FBI Nat. Acad., Quantico, Va., US Mil. Acad., West Point. Bd. mem. Nat. Children's Alliance; past bd. mem. Children's Assessment Ctr. Houston, CASA Child Advocates, Child Abuse Prevention Coun., Parents of Murdered Children, MADD, Drug Abuse Resistance Edn., Roseate Women's Ctr. for Abused Women, Abilene Christian U. Served fees. C-130 Unit USAF, 1970—76. Named Outstanding Nat. Victim Adv., Nat. Victim Ctr., Outstanding Judge, Found. for Improvement of Justice, Outstanding Instr., Tex. Dist. Atty. Assn., Best Judge, Kans. Peace Officers Assn., Outstanding Dist. Judge, Houston Police Officers Assn., Harris County Dep. Sheriffs Assn., Outstanding Young Lawyer, Houston Bar Assn.; recipient Spirit of Enterprise award, US C. of C., Congl. Partnership award, S.E. Tex. Regional Planning Commn., 2006, Social Change award, Tex. Assn. Against Sexual Assault, Morton Bard award, Nat. Orgn. Victims Assistance. Republican. Christian. Office: US Ho Reps 1605 Longworth Ho Office Bldg Washington DC 20515-4302 Office Phone: 202-225-6565.*

**POE, TERRY LYNN,** music educator; b. Asheboro, NC, Mar. 30, 1952; s. George McLamb and Christine Teague Poe. B in music edn., Wake Forest U., 1970—74. Assoc. dir. Raleigh Boychoir, Raleigh, NC, 1974—94; chapel organist St. Mary's Coll., Raleigh, 1979—84; church organist Trinity U. Meth. Ch., Raleigh, NC, 1976—; choral music tchr. Wake County Pub. Schools, 1974—. Mentor coord. Carroll Mid. Sch., Raleigh, NC, 1995—, fine arts chmn., 1979—, beta club coun. chmn., 1994—. Mem. Wake County Exec. PTA Coun., 1988—89, Boy Scouts Am., 1965—70. Mem.: Am. Guild Organists, Nat. Edn. Assn. Democrat. Bapt. Avocation: flying. Home: 704 Hampstead Pl Raleigh NC 27610 Office: Carroll Mid Sch 4520 Six Forks Rd Raleigh NC 27609 Personal E-mail: terrylpoe@aol.com.

**POE, WILLIAM CLAY,** archaeologist, educator; b. Durham, N.C., Dec. 4, 1941; s. Henry Clay and Lillian Craig Poe; m. Patricia Davis, Aug. 16, 1963 (div. 1979); children: Lynda Ruth (Talgo), David Craig; m. Sue Eileen Hayes, June 16, 1984; children: Ana Raquel, Tita. BA in Greek, Duke U., Durham, NC, 1963; MDiv in Old Testament, Princeton Theol. Sem., NJ, 1966; MA in Mediterranean Studies, Brandeis U., Waltham, Mass., PhD in Mediterranean Studies, 1971. Registered profl. archaeologist Registry Profl. Archaeologists, 1996. Area supervisor Am. Expedition to Hebron, El-Khalil, Jordan, 1966; prof. archaeology Sonoma State U., Rohnert Park, Calif., 1970—; co-dir. Am. Expedition Petra, Petra, Jordan, 1973—74; chair, divsn. soc. sci. Sonoma State U., Rohnert Park, Calif., 1975—76, dean, academic planning, dean, undergrad. studies, 1978—80; dir. Mesoamerican Archaeology Field Sch., Ujuxte, Guatemala, 1994—97, GPS Mapping Project, El Pilar Archaeological Reserve for Maya Flora Fauna, San Ignacio, Belize, 1999—2000, Archaeological Map of Belize, San Ignacio, Belize, 2000—04; co-dir. Belize Valley Archaeological Reconaissance Project, San Ignacio, Belize, 2000—04; dir. GPS Mapping Project, Chavin de Huantar, Peru, 1998. Project mapping cons., archaeologist Inst. Archaeology, Belize, 2001. Author: The Writing of a

Skillful Scribe: An introduction to hieratic Middle Egyptian through the text of The Shipwrecked Sailor. Mem. Sonoma County Orchid Soc., Santa Rosa, Calif., 2000—06. Named NDEA Title VI fellow, Brandeis U., 1967—70; recipient award for Excellence in Tchg., Sarlo Family Found., 1998; fellow Benjamin Stanton fellow in Old Testament, Princeton Theol. Sem., 1964—64, sr. fellow in Old Testament, 1965—66. Mem.: Soc. Am. Archaeology. Office: Sonoma State Univ Rohnert Park CA 94928 Office Phone: 707-664-2580.

**POEHLEIN, GARY WAYNE,** retired chemical engineering professor; b. Tell City, Ind., Oct. 17, 1936; s. Oscar Raymond and Eva Lee (Dickman) P.; m. Sharon Eileen Wood., Jan. 1, 1958; children: Steven Ray, Timothy Wayne, Valorie Ann, Sandra Lee. BSChemE, Purdue U., 1958, MSChemE, 1961, PhD, 1966. Design engr. Proctor & Gamble, Cin., 1958-61; from asst. prof. to assoc. prof. Lehigh U., Bethlehem, Pa., 1965-75, prof. chem. engring., 1975-78, co-dir. emulsion polymers inst., 1973-78; dir. sch. chem. engring. Ga. Inst. Tech., Atlanta, 1978-86, assoc. v.p. rsch., dean grad. studies, 1986-91, v.p. interdisciplinary programs, prof. chem. engring., 1991-95; prof. chem. engring., 1978-96; dir. Chem. and Transport Systems Divsn. NSF, 1996-2000; ret., 2000. Bd. dirs. Flexible Products Co., Marietta, Ga.; interim chair chem. engring. dept., vis. prof. Lehigh U., 2001—02. Contbr. over 100 articles to tech. publs. Mem. sch. bd. Bethlehem Area Sch. Dist., 1969-75. Recipient Honor Scroll award Phila. br. Am. Inst. Chemists, 1977, Mac Pruitt award Coun. for Chem. Rsch., 1989. Fellow AIChE. Avocations: woodworking, sailing. Home: 407 S Henry St Alexandria VA 22314-5901 E-mail: gspoehlein@aol.com.

**POEHLER, AMY,** comedienne, actress; b. Burlington, Mass., Sept. 17, 1971; m. Will Arnett, Aug. 29, 2003. Grad., Boston Coll. Cast mem. Second City, Chicago, 1993—96, Upright Citizen's Brigade, 1996—, Saturday Night Live, 2001—. Actor: (films) Saving Manhattan, 1998, Tomorrow Night, 1998, Deuce Bigalow: Male Gigolo, 1999, The Devil and Daniel Webster, 2001, Wet Hot American Summer, 2001, Martin & Orloff, 2002, Mean Girls, 2004, Envy, 2004; actor, writer, prodr. (films) Wild Girls Gone, 2005, actor, writer (TV series) Upright Citizens Brigade, 1998—2000, appearances include Late Night with Conan O'Brien, 1998—2000, Apt. 2F, 1997, Spin City, 1998, Undeclared, 2002, Arrested Development, 2004. Office: Saturday Night Live NBC Studios 30 Rockefeller Plz New York NY 10112*

**POEHLING, KATHERINE,** pediatrician; d. Gary Poehling; m. Timothy Peters, May 4, 1996; children: Jennifer Peters children: Robert Peters. MD, Wake Forest Sch. of Medicine, Winston-Salem, N.C., 1995; MPH, Vanderbilt U. Sch. of Medicine, Nashville, Tenn., 2001. Lic. Med. Tenn. State Bd. of Med. Examiners, 1999, cert. Bd. Am. Acad. Pediat., 1998. Fellow Vanderbilt U., Nashville, 1999—2002, asst. prof. of pediat., 2002—. Fellow: Am. Acad. Pediat.; mem.: Soc. Pediatric Rsch., Ambulatory Pediat. Assn., Infectious Disease Soc. Am., Alpha Omega Alpha. Achievements include research in Clin. rsch. on pediat. respiratory infections.

**POEHLMANN, CARL JOHN,** agronomist, researcher; b. Jamestown, Mo., Jan. 29, 1950; s. Edwin William and Lucille Albina (Neu) P.; m. Linda Kay Garner, Dec. 29, 1973; children: Anthony, Kimberly. BS, U. Mo., 1972, MS, 1978. Farmer, Jamestown, Mo., 1972-73; vocat. agrl. tchr. Linn (Mo.) Pub. Schs., 1973-75, Columbia (Mo.) Pub. Schs., 1975-78; dir., mgr. agronomy rsch. ctr. U. Mo., Columbia, 1978-2000; dir. MOAES Field Ops., 2000—. Mem. Am. Soc. Agronomy (div. A-7 chair 1985-86, bd. mem. 1991-94, cert. crop advisor 1993—), Crop Sci. Soc. Am., Soil Sci. Soc. Am., Internat. Assn. Mechanization Field Experiments. Mem. Christian Ch. (Disciples Of Christ). Office: MU Field Ops 3600 New Haven Rd Columbia MO 65201 E-mail: poehlmannc@missouri.edu.

**POEHNER, RAYMOND GLENN,** retired bank executive; b. Cleve., Oct. 2, 1923; s. Raymond Frank and Winifred (Kirchbaum) P.; m. Frances E. Dunaway Gillespie, Jan. 4, 1958 (dec. 1993); children: R. David, Jacqueline Diane, Leslie Marie, Jon Anthony, Rebecca Glen; stepchildren: Bruce Gillespie, Tony Gillespie. Student, pub. schs., Chgo. and Cleve. Enlisted USN, 1941, advanced through grades to chief petty officer, 1957, ret., 1965; with Security Pacific Nat. Bank, San Diego, 1966-80, loan officer, 1971-74, credit card officer, 1975-80, asst. br. mgr., 1974-80, asst. mgr.; ret., 1980. Mem. VFW, U.S. Naval Inst. (assoc.), Fla. Sheriff's Assn., Am. Biog. Soc. (nat. bd. advisors), R.I. Rsch. (cert. assoc.), Fleet Res. Assn., Rep. Legion of Merit, Nat. Geographic Soc., Nat. Assn. Civilian Conservation Corps Alumni, Optimist Club (dir. 1978), Fraternal Order Police (booster Fla. chpt.). Republican.

**POEL, ROBERT WALTER,** military officer, physician; b. Muskegon, Mich., July 24, 1934; s. Abel John and Fannie M. (Vanderwall) P.; m. Carol Anne Noordeloos, June 24, 1960; children: Kathryn Anne Poel Engle, James Robert, Sharon Kay Poel Thompson. BS, Calvin Coll., 1957; MD, U. Mich., 1959. Diplomate Am. Bd. Surgery. Commd. capt. USAF, 1962, advanced through grades to brig. gen., 1988, ret., 1993; comdr. Hosp. Malmstrom AFB, Great Falls, Mont., 1971-73; dir. profl. svcs. Hdqrs. Tactical Air Command Command Surgeon's Office, Langley AFB, Va., 1973-74; div. chief, med. plans Office of Air Force Surgeon Gen., Wash., 1974-78; comdr. regional hosp. Sheppard AFB, Wichita Falls, Tex., 1978-83; dir. profl. svcs. Office of Air Force Logistics Command Surgeon, Wright-Patterson AFB, Ohio, 1983-85; vice-comdr. Wilford Hall USAF Med. Ctr., San Antonio, 1985-87; chief, quality assurance, dir. plans and resources Air Force Surgeon Gen.; Bolling AFB, Wash., 1987-89; hosp. comdr. Malcolm Grow Med. Ctr., Andrews AFB, 1989-93; med. dir. near south office Meth. Occupational Healthctrs. Inc., Indpls., 1995—. Dir. Andrews Fed. Credit Union, 1991-95, vice chmn. bd. dirs., 1992-95. Advisor, bd. regents Uniformed Svcs. U. the Health Scis. Bethesda, Md., 1989-93; mem. pres. coun. Calvin Coll., 1990. Named Disting. alumnus, Calvin Coll., 1990; Paul Harris fellow Rotary Club of Wichita Falls, 1982. Mem. AMA, Am. Coll. Occupl. and Environ. Medicine, Assn. Mil. Surgeons of U.S. (life), Ret. Officers Assn. (life). Republican. Home: 12085 Waterford Ln Carmel IN 46033-5501 Office: 1101 Southeastern Ave Indianapolis IN 46202-3946 Office Phone: 317-955-2020. Personal E-mail: poelrc@indy.rr.com.

**POEN, KATHRYN LOUISE,** music educator, performing arts association administrator; b. Decorah, Iowa, Mar. 4, 1927; d. Arthur Nicolai and Emma Margaret Lomen; m. Roger Dean Walker, Nov. 25, 1949 (div. June 5, 1974); children: Bonnie Jo Walker, Marcia Lee Walker, Randall Craig Walker; m. Monte Mac Poen, May 22, 1982. BA, Iowa State Tchrs. Coll.; 1949; MusM, U. Ariz., 1968. Music educator pub. schs., Iowa, 1950—55, Mont., 1960—61, Nogales, Ariz., 1962—76, Flagstaff, Ariz., 1976—90; founder, dir. Flagstaff Light Opera Co., 1998—. Mem. Flagstaff Festival of Arts, 1992—93; dir., mem. Flagstaff chpt.Sweet Adelines, 1990—2000; owner, tchr. pvt. piano practice, 1950—. Composer songs. Mem.: Am. Choral Dirs. Assn., Ariz. Tchrs. of Music Assn., Ariz. Music Educators Assn., Music Educators Nat. Conf. Avocations: travel, collecting. Home: 3703 N Grandview Dr Flagstaff AZ 86004 Office Phone: 928-779-3810. E-mail: pianomewsik@aol.com.

**POEPPING-FAULKNER, MICHELE ANN,** pharmacist, educator; b. Salt Lake City, Jan. 5, 1970; d. Ira J. and Lucille T. Poepping. PharmD, Creighton U., Omaha, 1994. Registered pharmacist Tex., 1994, Nebr., 1998, pharmacist immunizer Am. Pharmacy Assn., 2001. Pharmacy practice resident S.W. Tex. Meth. Hosp., San Antonio, 1994—95, clin. pharmacist, 1995—98; cons. clin. pharmacist Sid Peterson Meml. Hosp., Kerrville, Tex., 1997—98; asst. prof. of pharmacy practice Creighton U., Omaha, 1998—2005, vice chair dept. pharmacy practice Sch. Pharmacy and Health Professions, 2003—04, assoc. prof. pharmacy practice, 2005—. Spkrs. bur. Boehringer Ingelheim Pharm., Inc., 2004—, Pharmacy Partnership for Tobacco Cessation, 2005—. Contbr. articles to profl. jours., chpts. to books. Grantee, Wyeth-Ayerst, 2002, Nat. Assn. Bds. of Pharmacy/Am. Assn. Colls. Pharmacy, 2003—04, 2004—05, Midwest Consortium for Svc. Learning in Higher Edn., 2006. Mem.: Midwest Consortium for Svc. Learning in Higher Edn., Health Futures Found., Am. Pharmacy Assn. (grantee 2003), Nebr. Pharm. Assn., Am. Assn. Colls. Pharmacy (grantee 2003, 2004), Am. Coll. Clin. Pharmacy (com.

mem./ambulatory care prn comm. com. 2002—03, ambulatory care budget and fin. com. 2003—04), Am. Soc. Health-System Pharmacy (faculty liaison for students at Creighton U. 2001—), Kappa Psi (life). Avocations: travel, fine dining. Business E-Mail: faulkner@creighton.edu.

**POESCH, JESSIE JEAN,** art historian; b. Postville, Iowa, May 19, 1922; parents: Edward H. and Vina (Meier) P. BA, Antioch Coll., 1944; MA, U. Del., 1956; PhD, U. Pa., 1966. Relief worker Am. Friends Svc. Com., France, Germany, Phila., 1946—54; curatorial asst. H.F. DuPont Winterthur Mus., Del., 1956-58; from asst. prof. to prof. art history Tulane U., New Orleans, 1963-92, Maxine and Ford Graham chair in fine arts, 1988-92. Guest curator Painting in the South, Va. Mus. Fine Arts, Richmond, 1980-84, Jefferson's America and Napoleon's France, New Orleans Mus. Art, 2003; curator Newcomb Pottery: An Enterprise for So. Women, 1895-1940, Newcomb Coll. Tulane U. and Smithsonian Instn. traveling exhbn. svc., 1980-87. Author: Titian Ramsay Peale, 1799-1885, and His Journals of the Wilkes Expedition, 1961, The Art of the Old South: Painting, Sculpture, Architecture and the Products of Craftsmen, 1560-1860, 1983, (with John Cuthbert) David Hunter Strother: One of the Best Draughtsmen the Country Possesses, 1997; (book/exhbn. catalogue) The Early Furniture of Louisiana, 1972, Newcomb Pottery: An Enterprise for Southern Women 1895-1940, 1984, Will Henry Stevens, 1987; editor: (with Barbara Bacot) Louisiana Buildings 1720-1948, 1997, (with Nancy E. Green) Arthur Wesley Dow and American Arts and Crafts, 1999, Newcomb Pottery and Crafts, 2003, Printmaking in New Orleans, 2006; also numerous articles and book revs. Fellow U. Del., 1954-56; Fulbright scholar U. London, 1960-62; NEH grantee, London, 1969-70. Mem. Soc. Archtl. Historians (bd. dirs. 1986-89), Coll. Art Assn. Am. Antiquarian Soc., La. Endowment for the Humanities (bd. dirs. 1984-90, La. Humanist of Yr. 1992), Victorian Soc. Am. (bd. dirs. 1988-92). Office: Tulane U. Dept Newcomb Art New Orleans LA 70118 Office Phone: 504-319-2225. Business E-Mail: jpoesch@tulane.edu.

**POESSNECKER, MYRON,** music educator; s. Paul and Gynell Poessnecker; m. Stacie Krohn, Sept. 27, 2003. BS, Wayne State Coll., Wayne, Nebr., 2000. Cert. tchr. Nebr. Music dir. Sterling Pub. Schs., Nebr., 2000—01; instrumental music dir. Logan View Pub. Schs., Hooper, Nebr., 2001—. Office: Logan View Public Schools 2163 County Rd G Hooper NE 68031

**POETTCKER, HENRY,** retired academic administrator; b. Rudnerweide, Russia, Mar. 27, 1925; s. John and Margaretha (Voth) P.; m. Aganetha Baergen, July 4, 1946; children: Victoria, Ronald, Martin. AB, Bethel Coll., North Newton, Kans., 1950; BD, Mennonite Bibl. Sem., Chgo., 1953; ThD, Princeton Theol. Sem., 1961, converted PhD, 1973. Ordained to ministry Mennonite Ch., 1948; instr. Can. Mennonite Bible Coll., Winnipeg, Man., 1954-59, pres., 1959—78, Mennonite Bibl. Sem., Elkhart, Ind., 1979—90, assoc. for devel., 1991-93. Interim dean Bluffton Coll., Ohio, 1965-66; vis. lectr. Taiwan Theol. Coll. and Tainan Theol. Coll., Taiwan, 1973-74. Editor: (with Rudy A. Regehr) Call to Faithfulness, 1972, Alumni Bull. Can. Mennonite Bible Coll, 1960-73. Pres. Gen. Conf. Mennonite Ch., Newton, Kans., 1968-74. Home: 301-475 Lindenwood Dr E Winnipeg MB Canada R3P2P3 E-mail: henr2502@mts.net. *The secret of happiness lies not in doing what one likes, but in liking what one does.*

**POFF, BORIS,** medical technician; b. Duesseldoef, Germany, Sept. 15, 1969; s. Peter Karl and Karin Katharina Poff; m. Adrianna Kocinski, Dec. 16, 2000; m. Wanda Denise Carr (div.). AA, Sacramento City Coll., Calif., 1989; BA, San Jose State U., 1993; MS, No. Ariz. U., Flagstaff, 2002; PhD, No. Ariz. U., 2006. Cert. EMT. Tech. writer, safety engr. Rockland Engring. Svcs., Sunal, Calif., 1991—94; vice-dir. Class 22 London, 1994—98; rsch. asst. No. Ariz. U., Flagstaff, 2000—03; hydrologic tech. USDA/U.S. Forest Svc., Flagstaff, 2003—. Avocations: snow boarding, kayaking, scuba diving, hiking, brewing beer. Home: 1550 N Fort Valley Rd #18 Flagstaff AZ 86001 Office: USDA Forest Service 2500 S Pineknoll Dr Flagstaff AZ 86001

**POGEDE, ALEXANDER,** consulting company executive; b. Berlin, Mar. 18, 1974; arrived in U.S., 1991; s. Viktor and Inge Pogede. Pres. Aridis Corp., L.A., 1996—98, Aridis AG, Berlin, 1998—2000, Aridis KK, Tokyo, 2000—02; chmn. Aridis Corp., Miami, Fla., 2002—. Founder Alexander Pogede Found. Office: Aridis Corp 8345 NW 66th St #2708 Miami FL 33166-2626 Office Phone: 800-741-3054. Office Fax: 800-515-8216. E-mail: alexander_pogede@aridis.com.

**POGEL, ALAN FRED,** history educator; s. Fred Erwin and Hazel Winifred Pogel; m. Mary Catherine Jasper, Nov. 4, 1989. BS in Bus., Valparaiso U., Ind., 1977, JD, 1982; MS in Edn., Niagara U., Niagara Falls, NY, 1990. Bar: Ind. 1982; cert. tchr. NY, 1998. Tchr. Valparaiso U., 1976—78; counselor, psychiat. tech. Porter Starke Svcs., 1979—82; adminstrv. asst. Town of Niagara Recreation, 1982—91; tchr., coach Niagara Wheatfield H.S., Sanborn, 1982—. Liaison, intern Niagara County Legis., Lockport, NY, 1991—. Mem. Friends Nat. Parks, Gettysburg, Pa., Found. Fellowship of Christian Athletes; mem., coach Athletes in Action, NY; liaison, tchr. Salvation Army Adopt-A-Family, Niagara Falls. NY State Empire scholar, Albany, 1989. Mem.: Delta Theta Phi, Sigma Pi. Avocations: photography, poetry, writing. Home: 3277 Andrews Rd Ransomville NY 14131 Office: Niagara Wheatfield High Sch 2292 Saunders Settlement Rd Sanborn NY 14132

**POGGI, MATTHEW MICHAEL,** radiation oncologist, researcher; b. Poughkeepsie, N.Y., Dec. 30, 1969; s. Peter V. and Patricia K. Poggi; m. Sarah Barklow Hoogen, Dec. 30, 1995; children: Eliza, Julia. BA, MA, Yale U., 1992, MD, 1996. Diplomate Am. Bd. Radiology. Resident Nat. Cancer Inst., Bethesda, Md., 1999—2003; commd. ensign USN, 1996, advanced through grades to comdr., intern San Diego, 1996—97; gen. med. officer Marine Corps Air Station, Santa Ana, Calif., 1997—99; resident Nat. Cancer Inst., Bethesda, Md., 1999—2003; asst. divsn head Nat. Naval Med. Ctr., Bethesda, Md., 2003—; residency dir. Nat. Cancer Inst., Bethesda, Md., 2003—. Staff radiation oncologist Nat. Naval Med. Ctr., Bethesda, 2003—, asst. divsn. head, 2003—. With USMC, 1996—. Recipient 2 Achievement medals, USN. Mem.: Am. Soc. Clin. Oncology, Am. Coll. Radiology, Am. Coll. Radiation Oncology. Office: Nat Navl Med Ctr 8901 Wisconsin Ave Bethesda MD 20889 Office Phone: 301-295-5000. Office Fax: 301-295-5788. Business E-Mail: mmpoggi@bethesda.med.navy.mil.

**POGGIO, TOMASO ARMANDO,** physicist, educator, computer scientist, researcher; b. Genoa, Italy, Sept. 11, 1947; came to U.S., 1981; s. Angelo and Maria Adele (Moro) P.; m. Barbara Venturini-Guerrini, July 29, 1972; children: Martino, Allegra. D in Physics summa cum laude, U. Genoa, 1971. Researcher Max Planck Inst., Federal Republic of Germany, 1971-82; assoc. prof. to prof. MIT, Cambridge, 1982-88, Uncas and Helen Whitaker prof., dept. brain and cognitive scis., 1988—. Corp. fellow Thinking Machines Corp., Cambridge, 1985—; adv. bd. MIT/Bradford Press series on Computational Models of Cognition and Perception, 1984, VNY Sci. Press series of monographs in neuroinformatics and robotics, 1984; Eugene McDermott Chair, McGovern Inst. for Brain Rsch., 2002. Assoc. editor Sys. and Control Letters, 1984; mem. editl. bd. Synapse, 1986, Visual Neurosci., 1987, Neural Computation, 1988, Network, 1989, others; adv. bd. Jour. Math. Biology, 1977, Lecture Notes in Biomathematics, 1979; contbr. over 200 sci. papers to profl. publs. Recipient Cassa di Risparmio of Genoa award, 1966, Otto-Hahn-Medaille award Max-Planck Soc., 1979, Columbus prize Istituto Internazionale delle Communicazioni Genoa, 1982, Premio Luigi Carlo Rossi award (with V. Torre) Elsag Elettronica, Italy, 1984, Max-Planck-Forschungs Preis Alexander von Humboldt-Stiftung, 1992, At&T New Rsch. Fund Award, 1996, MIT 50K Entrepreneurship Competition Award, Imagen, 1997, Gabor Award, Internat. Neural Network Soc., 2003; Angelo della Riccia grad. fellow, 1969-70, fellow CNR Lab. Biophysics and Cybernetics, Italy, 1971. Fellow: Am. Assn. Artificial Intelligence, Am. Acad. Arts and Scis.; mem.: IEEE, Soc. for Neuroscience, Italian Acad. Scis. (foreign mem.), Istituto Lombardo dell' Academia di Scienze e Lettere (foreign mem.), Optical Soc. Am., Am. Math. Soc. Office: MIT 77 Massachusetts Ave Cambridge MA 02139

**POGGIOLI, FRANCES CONSOLO MOSTEL,** business educator, medical educator, rehabilitation therapist; b. Apr. 30, 1930; d. Anthony and Mary (Iannuzzi) Consolo; m. Irving Mostel, June 26, 1954 (dec. Aug. 1969); m. Lester John Poggioli, Oct. 27, 1974. BBA, St. John's U., 1952; MS, L.I. U., 1959; postgrad., Buffalo U., U. Siena, Italy, Bklyn. Coll., 1974; doctoral equivalency, CUNY, 1974. Therapist VA Hosp., Bklyn., 1953—54; dir. N.Y. Sch. Industry, N.Y.C., 1954—57; lectr. L.I. U., Bklyn., 1959—62; bus. educator Heffley & Brown, Bklyn., 1963—65; prof. bus., med., secretarial option CUNY, Bklyn., 1965—90, recruiter-advisor, 1973—90, med. coord., 1972—, mem. employment com. bd. higher edn., 1990, coord. employment in med. field Bklyn. and N.Y.C., 1971—90, prof. emeritus, rehab. therapist emeritus, 1990—. Lectr. U. Siena, Italy, 1974. Eucharistic min. Roman Cath. Ch.; Mem. Italian-Am. Adv. Com., Bklyn., 1983-90, Bklyn., 1983—90. Fellow, CUNY Bd. Higher Edn., 1983—84. Fellow: Am. Assn. Rehab. Therapy (cert. rehab. therapist); mem.: Ea. Bus. Edn. Assn. (conf. chmn. 1983). Avocations: research, travel, writing, languages, handcrafts.

**POGNONEC, YVES MAURICE,** steel products executive; b. Rennes, Bretagne, France, Jan. 21, 1948; arrived in U.S., 1983; s. Jean P. and Simone J. (Boudot) P. M in Engring., Centrale Paris, 1970; MA in Bus., CPA, Paris, 1982. Cons. Office of Graham Parker, Paris, 1972-75; sales mgr. fittings dept. Vallourec S.A., Paris, 1975-79, mgr. engring. dept., 1980-82; v.p. mktg. and sales Vallourec Inc., Houston, 1983-88, exec. v-p., 1989-97, pres., 1998—; v.p. Vallourec & Mannesmann Tubes Corp., 1997—. Advisor French Fgn. Trade Counselors, Houston, 1987—. Bd. trustees, v.p. Awty Internat. Sch., Houston, 1997—. Lt. French Air Force, 1970-71. Mem. Assn. Ecole Centrale, Nat. Assn. Steel Pipe Distbrs. (bd. dirs.), Am. Boiler Mfrs. Assn. (chmn. internat. com.). Avocations: pilot, scuba diving, tennis. Office: Vallourec Inc 1990 Post Oak Blvd Ste 1400 Houston TX 77056-3813

**POGO, GUSTAVE JAVIER,** cardiothoracic surgeon; b. Buenos Aires, Feb. 7, 1957; came to U.S., 1964; s. Angel Oscar and Beatriz (Garcia-Tuñon) P.; m. Janis Teitler, Feb. 17, 1983; children: Michael Tyler, Katherine Elizabeth. BA, NYU, 1979, MD, 1983. Gen. surgery resident North Shore Univ. Hosp., Manhasset, NY, 1983-88; cardiothoracic surgery resident Mt. Sinai Sch. Medicine, N.Y.C., 1988-91; attending, cardiothoracic surgery North Shore Univ. Hosp., Manhasset, 1991—. Contbr. articles to profl. jours. Fellow ACS, Am. Coll. Chest Physicians, Am. Coll. Cardiology; mem. Soc. Thoracic Surgery. Office: North Shore Univ Hosp 300 Community Dr Manhasset NY 11030-3801

**POGORELOV, NIKOLAI,** physicist, researcher; b. Poltava, Ukraine, Dec. 31, 1951; s. Vladimir Pogorelov and Lyudmila Pogorelova; m. Lidia Gulyaeva, Apr. 12, 1977; 1 child, Natalia Pogorelova. MS, Moscow Inst. Physics and Tech., Dolgoprudny, Russia, 1975; PhD in Physics and Math., Inst. for Problems in Mechanics, Russian Acad. Scis., 1984; DSc in Physics and Math., Highest Certification Com. Russian Fedn., 2001. Rsch. scientist Inst. for Problems in Mechanics, Russian Acad. Scis., Moscow, 1977—90; assoc. prof. Moscow Aviation Inst. (State Tech. U.), 1985—91; sr. rsch. scientist Inst. for Problems in Mechanics, Russian Acad. Scis., Moscow, 1990—96, 1997—98, 1999—2002, prin. rsch. scientist, 2002—03; assoc. prof. Kobe (Japan) U., 1996—97, 1998—99; rsch. physicist U. Calif., Riverside, 2003—. Vis. prof. Max-Planck-Inst. Astrophysics, Garching, Germany, 1999—2002; vis. rschr. Solar-Terrestrial Environment Lab., Nagoya U., Toyokawa, Japan, 2002—03; chmn. organizing com. 1st IGPP-CalSpace Internat. Conf., Palm Springs, Calif., 2006. Author: (book) Mathematical Aspects of Numerical Solution of Hyperbolic Systems, Mathematical Problems of Numerical Solution of Hyperbolic Systems; editor: Physics of the Outer Heliosphere; contbr. articles to profl. jours. Grantee, NASA, 2005—, NSF, 2004—. Mem.: AAAS, Russian Nat. Com. Theoretical and Applied Mechanics, Am. Geophys. Union. Achievements include development of one of the most sophisticated numerical models of the heliospheric interface based on high-resolution shock-capturing methods, adaptive mesh refinement techniques and Monte Carlo simulations; performed a detailed analysis of nonevolutionary MHD shocks behavior in numerical plasma flow simulations; research in high-speed, non-equilibrium airflows near complex-shaped bodies at high angle of attack; global MHD-Boltzmann model of the outer heliosphere; multi-scale combined hybrid-magnetohydrodynamic-neutral atom code. Office: IGPP University of California 900 University Ave Riverside CA 92508 Office Phone: 951-827-5640. Business E-Mail: nikolaip@ucr.edu.

**POGREBIN, LETTY COTTIN,** writer, educator; b. NYC, June 9, 1939; d. Jacob and Cyral (Halpern) Cottin; m. Bertrand B. Pogrebin, Dec. 8, 1963; children: Abigail and Robin (twins), David. AB cum laude with spl. distinction in English and Am. Lit. Brandeis U., 1959. V.p. Bernard Geis Assocs. (book pubs.), N.Y.C., 1960-70; columnist The Working Woman column Ladies Home Jour., 1971-81; contbg. editor Tikkun mag., 1988—, Family Circle, 1989—; founding editor Ms mag., N.Y.C., 1971-87, columnist, editor at large, 1987-89, contbg. editor, 1990—; columnist The N.Y. Times, Newsday, Moment Mag., Washington, 1990—, Moment Mag., Washington, 1990—. Cons. Free to Be, You and Me projects, 1972—; lectr. women's issues and family politics, changing roles of men and women, friendship in Am., non-sexist child rearing and edn., Judaism and feminism, Mid-East politics. Author: How to Make It in a Man's World, 1970, Getting Yours: How to Make the System Work for the Working Woman, 1975, Growing Up Free, 1980, Stories for Free Children, 1982, Family Politics, 1983, Among Friends, 1986, Deborah, Golda, and Me: Being Female and Jewish in America, 1991, Getting Over Getting Older: An Intimate Journey, 1996, Three Daughters: A Novel, 2002; mem. editl. bd. Tikkun Mag.; contbr. articles to N.Y. Times, Washington Post, Nation, Chubo, The Nation, TV Guide, Family Circle, Elle, Travel & Leisure, L.A. Times, N.Y. Daily News, Harpers Bazaar, also other mags., newspapers. Pres. Author's Guild, 1998-2002; pres. Aythors Registry, 2000—; bd. dirs. Ms. Found. for Edn. and Comm., New Israel Fund, Jewish Fund for Justice, PEN Am.; mem. Task Force on Women Fedn. Jewish Philanthropies. Pointer fellow Yale U., 1982, MacDowell Colony fellow, 1979, 89, 94, 2000, Cummington Colony Arts fellow 1985, Edna St. Vincent Millay Colony fellow, 1985; recipient Matrix award Women in Comm., 1981, Gloria Steinem Women of Vision award Ms. Found. for Women, 1990, Abram L. Sachar medal Brandeis U., 1994, Woman of Valor award Jewish Fund for Justice, 1997, Woman of Achievement award N. Shore Child and Family Assn., 1997, Hannah G. Solomon award Nat. Coun. Jewish Women, 1997, Woman of Distinction award Kingsborough Coll., 1998, U.S./Israel Women-to-Women award, 1999, N.Y.C. Contr.'s Jewish Heritage award, 1999, Elle Mag. Readers prize, 2002, Barr Peace award, 2003, Mayor Michael Bloomberg Libr. award, 2003, Lion of Judah Jewish Women's Archive Pioneer award, 2004, Jane Evans Pursuit of Peace award Women of Reform Judaism, 2005; named Woman of Yr. Fifty-Plus Expo, 1997, Outstanding Scholars 21st Century, 2000, Vet. Feminists of Am., Nat. Honor Roll, 2002. Address: care Rosenstone/Wender 3 E 48th St New York NY 10017-1027

**POGUE, DAVID,** journalist; m. Jennifer Pogue; 3 children. BA in Music summa cum laude, Yale Univ., 1985. Writer, Desktop Critic column Macworld mag., 1988—2000; personal-tech. columnist NY Times, NYC, 2000—. Conductor, synthesizer programmer, arranger (Broadway plays): author: (computer books) Macs for Dummies, 1992, The iMac for Dummies, 1999, The iBook for Dummies, 1999, PalmPilot: The Ultimate Guide, 1998, Switching to the Mac: The Missing Manual, 2003, Mac OS X: The Missing Manual, 2005; co-author (with Adam Engst): Crossing Platforms, 1999; co-author: (with Joe Schorr) Macworld Mac Secrets, 2001; co-author: (with Scott Speck) (music books) Opera for Dummies, 1997, Classical Music for Dummies, 1997; author: (humor books) The Microsloth Joke Book, 1997, The Great Macintosh Easter Egg Hunt, 1998; editor: Tales from the Tech Line, 1998; author: Magic for Dummies, 1998, (novels) Hard Drive, 1995; tech. corr. CBS News Sunday Morning, 2000— (Bus. Emmy award, 2004). Mem.: Internat. Brotherhood of Magicians. Avocations: magic, music. Office: Technology Columnist NY Times 229 W 43rd St New York NY 10036*

**POGUE, DONALD CARL,** federal judge; b. 1947; BA, Dartmouth Coll., 1969; MA, JD, Yale U., 1974. Bar: Conn. 1974. Pvt. practice, 1974-75; ptnr. Kestell, Pogue & Gould, 1976-89; commr. Conn. Commn. Hosps. and Health Care, 1989-94; judge Conn. Superior Ct., 1994-95, U.S. Ct. Internat. Trade, NYC, 1995—. Office: US Ct Internat Trade One Federal Plz New York NY 10278-0001

**POGUE, JOHN MARSHALL,** physician; b. Washington, Sept. 21, 1945; s. L(loyd) Welch and Mary Ellen (Edgerton) P. *His father and mother are his guiding lights. Ancestor William Bradford "was the first American citizen of the English race who bore rule by the free choice of his brethren," the first American historian, and thus the Father of American History. Ancestor Hannah (Bradford) Ripley (Governor William Bradford's granddaughter) was America's first Physician of her gender. His uncle, Massachusetts Institute of Technology Institute Professor Harold Eugene Edgerton, enhanced his interest in Science. He worked with Harold on ultra-high-speed photography in Harold's Stroboscopic Light Laboratory and on sonar probes. The difficult Harold did at once; the impossible took a little longer.* AB with honors, Princeton U.; MD, Georgetown U. Diplomate Nat. Bd. Med. Examiners. Intern, resident Georgetown U. Hosp., Washington; editor, author Bradford Jour., 1983—; historian Gov. Bradford Compact, 1996—, surgeon, 1999—, v.p., 2005—. Spkr. and lectr. in field of cardiology. *He is a Fellow of six Scientific and Learned Societies, and he is active in numerous Cardiology Societies. He received Honors in various Medical School courses, having ranked within the top 5% of the entire Medical School class in those courses. As a premedical student at Princeton University, he achieved high academic distinction climaxed by his ranking within the top 2% of his class of 789 students in the junior year-the year that is particularly important for premedical students. He also received a Letter of Individual Commendation for his scholarship from the Dean of the College at Princeton.* Author: Herbert Martin Giffin, M.D., A Role Model Physician and a Doctor's Doctor: From Princeton to Johns Hopkins, Mayo Clinic, USN, and Yater Clinic, 2000, Sir William Osler, M.D., The Preeminent Physician: From McGill to the University of Pennsylvania, Johns Hopkins, and Oxford, 2004; designer Ofcl. Gov. William Bradford Flag, 1987 (New Constellation award Nat. Flag Found., 1996), Ofcl. Order of Descs. of Colonial Physicians and Chirurgiens Flag, 2005; editor, contbr.: Pogue/Pollock/Polk Genealogy as Mirrored in History, From Scotland to Northern Ireland/Ulster, Ohio, and Westward, 1990 (recipient 5 First Pl. Genealogy awards, recipient 2 Meritorious History awards), assoc. editor: Hereditary Soc. Blue Book, 1997—, 1998, 1999, 2000; dir.(of film): Hugo Victor Rizzoli, Preeminent Neurosurgeon, A.B. and M.D., Johns Hopkins, Neurosurg. Tng. at Johns Hopkins Hosp., 2005; contbr. articles on cardiology to med. jours. Fellow Royal Soc. Medicine, Royal Microscopical Soc. Oxford, Royal Statis. Soc., Royal Geog. Soc., Royal Soc. Arts, Internat. Soc. Holter and Noninvasive Electrocardiology; mem. Am. Heart Assn. (coun. clin. cardiology, coun. basic cardiovasc. scis.), AMA, Royal Soc. Medicine (cardiology sect., cardiothoracic sect.), Laennec Cardiovasc. Sound Soc., European Soc. Cardiology, Am. Soc. Echocardiography (coun. cardiac sonography, coun. intraoperative echocardiography), Internat. Soc. Cardiovasc. Ultrasound, Internat. Cardiac Doppler Soc., Internat. Soc. Electrocardiology (Glasgow U.), Internat. Soc. Holter and Noninvasive Electrocardiology, Internat. Acad. Cardiovasc. Scis., Can., Soc. Cardiovasc. Magnetic Resonance, Capital Area Heart Failure Soc. (founding mem. 2002), Heart Failure Soc. Am., Heart Valve Soc. Am. (cardiac imaging coun.), Internat. Soc. Cardiovasc. Pharmacotherapy, Switzerland, Internat. Soc. Heart Rsch., Can., Cardiac Muscle Soc., World Heart Fedn., Switzerland, European Assn. Cardiovasc. Prevention and Rehab., European Microscopy Soc. (Netherlands), Friends Nat. Libr. Medicine (founding mem. 1988), Friends McGill U. Osler Med. Libr., Friends Oxford U. Mus. History Sci., Ashmolean Natural History Soc. Oxford, Oxford Hist. Soc., Internat. Shakespeare Assn. (Stratford-upon-Avon), Princeton U. Alumni Assn., Princeton Tigertones Alumni, Oxford U. Bodleian Libr., Soc. Mayflower Descs. (surgeon 1998-), Order Descs. Colonial Physicians and Chirurgiens (surgeon gen. 1994-2000, chmn. hon. membership com. 1994-, v.p. gen. 2000-03, pres. gen. 2003-2006, hon. pres. gen. life, 2006—), Oxford Bibliog. Soc., Nat. Gavel Soc., Hereditary Order of Descs. of Colonial Govs. (rec. sec. gen. 2005-), Provincial Families Md., Kenwood Citizens Assn., RSM Music Soc./Royal Soc. Medicine Music Club, Royal Soc. Medicine Book Club, Princeton U. Club, Washington, Oxford Bibliographical Soc. Avocations: classical music, reading. Home and Office: 5204 Kenwood Ave Chevy Chase MD 20815-6604

**POGUE, RICHARD WELCH,** lawyer; b. Cambridge, Mass., Apr. 26, 1928; s. Lloyd Welch and Mary Ellen (Edgarton) P.; m. Patricia Ruth Raney, July 10, 1954; children: Mark, Tracy, David. BA, Cornell U., 1950; JD, Mich. Law Sch., 1953. Bar: Mich. 1953, Ohio 1957, U.S. Dist. Ct. (no. dist.) Ohio 1960, U.S. Ct. Appeals (6th cir.) 1972, U.S. Ct. Appeals (D.C. and 9th cirs.) 1979. Assoc. Jones, Day, Reavis & Pogue, Cleve., 1957-60, ptnr., 1961—, mng. ptnr., 1984-92, sr. ptnr., 1993-94, cons., 2004—; sr. advisor Dix & Eaton, Cleve., 1994—2003. Vis. prof. Mich. Law Sch., 1993-95; bd. dirs.Continental Airlines, Inc., Houston, Roten Inc., Aurora, Ohio, Viztek Inc., Twinsburg, Ohio. Chmn. Cleve. Found., 1985-89, Greater Cleve. Roundtable, 1986-89, Greater Cleve. Growth Assn., 1991-93, Univ. Hosps., 1994—, trustee 1975—, Cleve. Ballet, 1983-85, United Negro Coll. Fund., Cleve., 1979, United Way Cleve., 1989, Kulas Found., 1998-, Bus. Vol. United, 1998-2001, Nat. Inventors Hall of Fame, 1996-, Newcomen Soc. U.S.A., Phila., 2000-; mem. Adminstrv. Conf. U.S., 1974-80; vice chmn. Cleve. Tomorrow, 1988-93; trustee Case Western Res. U.; active Coun. Fgn. Rels., 1989—, Am./EC Assn. Bus. Adv. Coun., 1988-93; trustee Rock and Roll Hall of Fame and Mus., 1986—; co-chmn. 1996 Cleve. Bicentennial Commn., interim chmn. Cleve. Inst. Music, 1994. Capt. U.S. Army, 1954-57. Recipient Outstanding Alumnus award U. Mich. Club, Cleve., 1983, Torch of Liberty award Anti-Defamation League, 1989, Leadership Cleve. Vol. of Yr award, 1990, Int. Exec. Devel., Workshop award Nat. Coun. on Urban Econ. Devel., 1992, Humanitarian award Nat. Conf. Christians and Jews, 1992; named Cleve. Bus. Exec. of Yr., 2000, Cleve. United Way Vol. of Yr., 2002. Mem. ABA (chmn. antitrust sect. 1983-84), Ohio State Bar Assn. (chmn. antitrust sect. 1969-73). Clubs: Bohemian (San Francisco), Soc., Union (Cleve.). Republican. Mem. United Ch. of Christ. Office: Jones Day North Point 901 Lakeside Ave Cleveland OH 44114-1190 Office Phone: 216-586-7300. Office Fax: 216-586-7960. E-mail: rwpogue@jonesday.com.

**POGUE, VELVIE ANNE,** nephrologist, educator; d. Henry Robinson and Maggie Mandigo; m. Alfred Robert Ashford; children: Alfred C. Ashford III, Adrienne Ashford. BS, So. U., Baton Rouge, 1970; MD, Harvard U., 1974. Diplomate Am. Bd. Internal Medicine, 1978, nephrology Am. Bd. Internal Medicine, 1980. Intern in internal medicine Harlem Hosp. Ctr., N.Y.C., 1974—75, resident in attending medicine, 1975—77, fellow in clin. nephrology, 1977—79, attending physician, 1979—, chief divsn. nephrology, 1990—; assoc. prof. clin. medicine Coll. Physicians and Surgeons Columbia U., N.Y.C., 2002—. Rschr. African Am. Study of Kidney Disease and Hypertension, N.Y.C. Named to America's Leading Black Doctors, Black Enterprise Mag., 2001. Mem.: Am. Heart Assn., Nat. Kidney Found., Internat. Soc. Hypertension in Blacks, Nat. Med. Assn., Am. Soc. Nephrology. Achievements include research in complications of hypertension, including hypertensive renal disease in blacks; impact of changes in blood pressure staging on recognized severity of hypertension. Office: Harlem Hospital Center 506 Lenox Ave New York NY 10037 Business E-Mail: vap1@columbia.edu.

**POGUE, WILLIAM REID,** retired astronaut, foundation administrator, aerospace scientist, consultant; b. Okemah, Okla., Jan. 23, 1930; s. Alex W. and Margaret (McDow) P.; m. Jean Ann Pogue; children: William Richard, Layna Sue, Thomas Reid. BS in Secondary Edn., Okla. Bapt. U., 1951, DSc (hon.), 1974; MS in Math., Okla. State U., 1960. Commd. 2d lt. USAF, 1952, advanced through grades to col., 1975; combat fighter pilot Korea, 1953; gunnery instr. Luke AFB, Ariz., 1954; mem. acrobatic team USAF Thunderbirds, Luke AFB and Nellis AFB, Nev., 1955-57; asst. prof. math. USAF Acad., 1960-63; exchange test pilot Brit. Royal Aircraft Establishment, Ministry Aviation, Farnborough, Eng., 1964-65; instr. USAF Aerospace Research Pilots Sch., Edwards AFB, Calif., 1965-66; astronaut NASA

Manned Spacecraft Center, Houston, 1966-75; pilot 3d manned visit to Skylab space sta.; ret. Decorated Air medal with oak leaf cluster, D.S.M.; named to Five Civilized Tribes Hall of Fame, Choctaw descent; recipient Distinguished Service medal NASA, Collier trophy Nat. Aero. Assn.; Robert H. Goddard medal Nat. Space Club; Gen. Thomas D. White USAF Space Trophy Nat. Geog. Soc.; Halley Astronautics award, 1975; de la Vaalx medal Fedn. Aeronautique Internat., 1974; V.M. Komarov diploma, 1974; inducted into Okla. Aviation and Space Hall of Fame, 1980, U.S. Astronaut Hall of Fame, 1997. Fellow Acad. Arts and Scis. of Okla. State U., Am. Astron. Soc.; mem. Soc. Exptl. Test Pilots, Explorers Club, Sigma Xi, Pi Mu Epsilon. Baptist (deacon). Home: 4 Cromer Dr Bella Vista AR 72715-5318 E-mail: wrpogue@arkansas.net.

**POHAN, ARMAND,** transportation executive, professional hockey club executive, lawyer; b. Langley Field, Va., Apr. 28, 1944; s. Armen and Helen (Turner) P.; m. Margaret A. Neigel, Dec. 18, 1976; children: Andrew Stephen, Alicia Margaret, Amanda Turner AB, Harvard U., 1964, JD, 1967. Bar: N.J. 1967. Assoc. McCarter & English, Newark, 1968-70; asst. prosecutor Hudson County, N.J., 1970-72; assoc. McCarter & English, 1973-76, ptnr., 1976-77; v.p. A-P-A Transport Corp., North Bergen, N.J., 1977-83, pres., 1983—, Colo. Rockies Hockey Club, Denver, 1978-81; chmn. bd. dirs. NY Waterway, 2001—. Mem. Fort Lee Bd. Adjustment, N.J., 1977-78; mem. Fort Lee Planning Bd., 1979, 2002—, borough atty., Fort Lee, 1973-76, councilman, 2003—; bd. govs. Nat. Hockey League, 1978-81; trustee Bede Sch., Englewood, N.J., 1984-90; trustee Dwight-Englewood Sch., 1984-92, pres., 1985-92. Mem. N.J. Bar Assn. Office: A-P-A Transport Corp 2100 88th St North Bergen NJ 07047-4721 E-mail: apohan@aol.com.

**POHL, ADOLF LEOPOLD,** clinical chemist, quality assurance consultant; b. St. Poelten, Austria, Dec. 14, 1936; s. Adolf Theodor and Cornelia Maria Anna (Moerth) P.; m. Ingrid Maria Antonia Payer, Feb. 24, 1962 (div. Dec. 11, 1975); children: Martin, Ulrike; m. Nanako Tanaka, Mar. 14, 1989; 1 child, Anna Yumi. Grad. in classical studies, Stiftsgymnasium Melk, 1954; BSc, U. Vienna, 1957, MSc, 1965, DPhil, 1968. Rsch. asst. med. dept. I U. Vienna Med. Sch., 1967-69, asst. prof., 1969-85, head erythrocyte enzyme lab. med. dept. I, 1969-85, founder tumor marker lab., 1978, head tumor marker lab., 1984-85, assoc. prof. med. dept. I, dept. chemotherapy, 1985-87, assoc. prof. dept. clin. labs., 1987-97. Quality assurance cons. Med. Pharm. Rsch. Ctr., Vienna, 1993—. Mem. editl. bd. Cancer Molecular Biology Jour., 1994—; contbr. articles to profl. jours., chpts. to books. Recipient Austrian Med. Assn. award, 1969. Mem. Am. Assn. for Clin. Chemistry, N.Y. Acad. Scis., IEEE Computer Soc., Drug Info. Assn. Achievements include discovery in human blood serum of a new ADP-ribosyltransferase, implementation of advanced data analysis in clinical chemistry, detection by new micromethods of phospholipid metabolism in red blood cell membranes and study of its abnormalities in hemolytic anemia; research on serum glycosyltransferases as possible cancer markers and critical analysis of galactosyltransferase heterogeneity; leading of 1st foldboat expedition on Tenojoki, 1st behavioral studies of Thai ferret badger. Home: Lambrechtgasse 3/10 A-1040 Vienna Austria E-mail: adolf.pohl@chello.at.

**POHL, FREDERIK,** freelance/self-employed writer; b. N.Y.C., Nov. 26, 1919; s. Fred George and Anna (Mason) P.; m. Carol Ulf, Sept. 15, 1953 (div. 1981); children— Ann, Karen, Frederik, Kathy; m. Elizabeth Anne Hull, July 27, 1984 Editor Popular Pubs., N.Y.C., 1939-43; editor Popular Sci., N.Y.C., 1946-49; freelance writer N.Y.C., 1950-60, 80—; editor Galaxy Pubs., N.Y.C., 1961-69, Bantam Books, N.Y.C., 1973-80. Author: Man Plus, 1977 (Nebula award), Gateway, 1978 (Nebula, Hugo, Campbell awards, Prix Apollo award), Jem, 1979 (Am. Book award), The Years of the City (Campbell award 1985), Chasing Science, 2000, The Boy Who Would Live Forever, 2004, Platnum Pohl, 2005 Served to sgt. USAAF, 1943-45; Italy Recipient Popular Culture Assn. award, 1982 Fellow AAAS; mem. Sci. Fiction Writers of Am. (pres. 1974-76, Grand Master award 1993), World Sci. Fiction (pres. 1980-82), Authors Guild, Astron. Soc. Pacific. Democrat. Unitarian Universalist. Home: 855 Harvard Dr Palatine IL 60067-7026

**POHL, GUNTHER ERICH,** retired library administrator; b. Berlin, July 22, 1925; came to US, 1927; s. Erich Ernst and Martha (Seidel) P.; m. Dorothy Edna Beck, Aug. 21, 1949; children: Christine, Louise, Elizabeth, Ronald BA, NYU, 1947, MA, 1950; MLS., Columbia U., 1951. Librarian local history and genealogy divsn. N.Y. Pub. Libr., N.Y.C., 1948-69, chief local history and genealogy divsn., 1969-85, ret., 1985. Compiler: N.Y. State Biography and Portrait Index. Fellow N.Y. Geneal. and Biog. Soc.; mem. ALA (chmn. genealogy com. 1971-73, 76-78, History sect. award 1996), N.Y. Geneal. and Biog. Soc. (libr., trustee 1982-92), Sigma Phi Epsilon (trustee local chpt. 1978—). Republican. Avocations: stamps, opera, collecting new yorkiana. Home: 134 Lowry Ln Wilmore KY 40390

**POHL, HANS GEORGE,** pediatrician, urologist; b. Los Angeles, Calif., Oct. 31, 1966; s. Bernhard and Alicia Pohl. MD, George Wash. U., 1992. Urology Am. Bd. of Urology, 2004. Asst. prof., urology and pediat. George Wash. U. Sch. of Medicine, Washington, 2002—; dir. urology rsch. Children's Nat. Med. Ctr., Washington, 2002—. Fellow: Am. Acad. Pediat. Avocations: swimming, yoga. Office Phone: 202-884-5042. Office Fax: 202-844-4739.

**POHL, KATHLEEN SHARON,** editor; b. Sandusky, Mich., Apr. 7, 1951; d. Gerald Arthur and Elizabeth Louise (Neukamm) P.; m. Bruce Mark Allen Reynolds, June 11, 1982. BA in Spanish, Valparaiso U., 1973; MA in English, No. Mich. U., 1975. Producer, dir. fine arts Sta. WNMU-FM, Marquette, Mich., 1981-82; instr. communications Waukesha County (Wis.) Tech. Inst., 1983; editor Ideals mag., Milw., 1983-85; editor, mng. editor Raintree Pubs. Milw., 1985-87; mng. editor, now exec. editor Country Woman mag., Greendale, Wis., 1987—; exec. editor Country Handcrafts mag., Greendale, 1990-93, Taste of Home Mag., Greendale, Wis., 1993—; editor Talk About Pets, Greendale, 1994-95. Author nature book series, 1985-87; sr. editor: Country Woman Christmas Book, 1996—; mng. editor: Irwin the Sock (Chgo. Book Clinic award 1988); exec. editor Taste of Home's Quick Cooking Mag., 1998—, Down the Aisle Countr Style, 2000, Taste of Home's Light & Tasty Mag., 2000—. Mem. Nat. Mus. of Women in Arts, Alpha Lambda Delta (hon.). Home: N54 W26326 Lisbon Rd Sussex WI 53089-4249 Office: Country Woman Mag 5400 S 60th St Greendale WI 53129-1404

**POHL, PAUL MICHAEL,** lawyer; b. Erie, Pa., July 17, 1948; s. Joseph Paul and Mary (Strenio) P.; m. Kaya Lynn Gavriloff, Aug. 13, 1970; children: Thomas Michael, Mary Elizabeth, Michael David. AB, Princeton U., 1970; JD, U. Pitts., 1975. Bar: Pa. 1975, Ohio 1976, U.S. Dist. Ct. (we. dist.) Pa. 1975, U.S. Dist. Ct. (no. dist.) Ohio 1976, U.S. Ct. Appeals (5th cir.) 1980, U.S. Ct. Appeals (11th cir.) 1983, U.S. Ct. Appeals (1st, 3d and 6th cir.) 1993, U.S. Ct. Appeals (D.C. cir.) 1995. Reporter Erie Daily Times, 1970-71; law clk. to presiding justice Pa Supreme Ct., 1975-76; assoc. Jones, Day, Reavis & Pogue (now Jones Day), Cleve., 1976-82, ptnr., 1982—. Guest mem. faculty Sch. Law, Hofstra U., Hempstead, N.Y., 1982, 84; mem. trial advocacy program Sch. Law, Emory U., Atlanta, 1983—; bd. dirs. JURA Corp., Erie, Lord Corp., Cary, N.C.; mem. CLE bd. Supreme Ct. of Pa. Co-author: Conflicts of Interest—A Trial Lawyers Guide, 1984. Bd. dirs. Franciscan U., Steubenville, Ohio, 1991—, vice chmn., 1994—; bd. dirs. Gannon U., Erie; chmn. bd. dirs. Seton Hill Coll., Greensburg, Pa., 1997—; mem. supervisory bd. Found. Maria Thron, Gaming, Austria, 1996—. With USMC, 1971-72. Named one of Cleve.'s 78 Most Interesting People, Cleve. mag., 1978. Mem. Cleve. Bar Assn. (mem. com. task force on violent crime 1983). Roman Catholic. Office: Jones Day Reavis & Pogue 500 Grant St Pittsburgh PA 15219-2502 also: Jones Day Reavis & Pogue 901 Lakeside Ave E Cleveland OH 44114-1116

**POHL, ROBERT OTTO,** physics professor; b. Gottingen, Germany, Dec. 17, 1929; came to U.S., 1958; s. Robert Wichard and Auguste Eleonore (Madelung) P.; m. Karin Ursula Koehler, May 6, 1961; children: Helen M., Robert S., Otto C. Vordiplom, U. Freiburg, Fed. Rep. Germany, 1951;

---

diploma, U. Erlangen, Fed. Rep. Germany, 1955, Dr. rer. nat., 1957. Asst. U. Erlangen, 1957-58; rsch. assoc. Cornell U., Ithaca, NY, 1958-60, asst. prof., 1960-63, assoc. prof., 1963-68, prof., 1968-2000, Goldwin Smith prof. physics emeritus, 2000—. Vis. prof. Tech. Hochschule Stuttgart, 1966-67, Tech. U. Munchen, 1973-74, Konstanz U., Regensburg U., 1987-88, all Fed. Republic Germany; vis. scientist Nuc. Research Ctr., Juelich, Fed. Rep. Germany, 1980-81, Hahn-Meitner Inst., Berlin, 1995. Contbr. articles on solid state physics to profl. jours. Recipient Sr. Scientist award Alexander von Humboldt Found., 1980; Guggenheim Found. fellow, 1973, Erskine fellow U. Canterbury, New Zealand, 1988. Fellow AAAS, Am. Inst. Physics (O.E. Buckley award 1985); mem. NAS, Internat. Thermal Conductivity Confs. Office: Cornell U Physics Dept Ithaca NY 14853-2501 Office Phone: 607-255-3303. Business E-Mail: pohl@ccmr.cornell.edu.

**POHLAD, CARL R.,** bank executive, professional sports team executive; b. West Des Moines, Iowa, Aug. 23, 1915; m. Eloise Pohlad (dec. 2003); 3 children. Student, Gonzaga U. With MEI Diversified, Inc., Mpls., 1959—, chmn. bd., 1976—94; pres. Marquette Bank Mpls., N.A., pres., dir., Bank Shares, Inc.; owner Minn. Twins, 1985—. Bd. dirs. Meth. Hosp. Adminstrv. Group, T.G.I. Friday's, Tex. Air Corp., Ea. Airlines, Continental Airlines, Inc., Carlson Cos. Inc. Named one of Forbes' Richest Americans, 2006. Address: MN Twins Hubert H Humphrey Metrodome 34 Kirby Puckett Pl Minneapolis MN 55415-1523*

**POHLAD, ROBERT C.,** consumer products company executive; Dir. Mesaba Holdings Inc.; v.p. N.W. area Pepsi-Cola Bottling Group; pres. Pohlad Cos., 1987—2000; CEO PepsiAmericas, 2000—, vice chmn., 2001—02, chmn., 2002—. Office: PepsiAmericas 4000 Dain Rauscher Plaza 60 S Sixth St Minneapolis MN 55402

**POHLHAUS, TESS,** theater educator; b. Irene and Mark Pohlhaus. BA, Washington Coll., Chestertown, Md., 2003. Cert. secondary tchr. Md. Theatre tchr. Rising Sun HS, North East, Md., 2003—. Actor: Romeo and Juliet, 2004, Twelfth Night, 2005, Measure for Measure, 2006, (world-premiere play) Father Joy, 2006. Avocations: music, acting. Office Phone: 410-658-9115.

**POHLMAN, LYNETTE,** museum director, curator; BA, Iowa State U., 1972, MA in applied art, 1976. Dir., chief curator Univ. Mus. at Iowa State U. Adj. prof. art & design Iowa State U.; organizer Art in State Bldgs. Prog. Curator Emperors, Shoguns and Kings, 1981, Fiber to Glass, 1987, Land of Fragile Giants: Landscapes, Environments and Peoples of the Loess Hills, 1994—96, The Golden Age of Glass: 1875-1939, 1999. Recipient Christian Petersen Design Award, 2004. Mem.: Assn. Coll. and Univ. Mus. and Galleries (founding mem.). Office: Univ Mus 290 Scheman Bldg Ames IA 50011-1110 Office Phone: 515-294-3342. E-mail: lpohlma@iastate.edu.

**POHLMAN, RANDOLPH A.,** business administration educator, dean; b. Topeka, Jan. 25, 1944; s. Clarence Alvin and Martha Melissa (McElheny) P.; m. Jeanne Lucille Gebhart, Aug. 22, 1965; children— Kristina, Lisa BS, Kans. State U., 1967, MS, 1969; PhD, Okla. State U., 1976. Asst. prof., assoc. prof. fin. Kans. State U., Manhattan, 1976-82, assoc. prof., head dept. fin., 1982-84, prof., dean Coll. Bus. Administrn., 1984-90; dir. employee devel. Koch Industries, 1990-91, dir. human resources, 1991-95; dean sch. bus. and entrepreneurship Nova Southeastern Univ., Ft. Laud, Fla., 1995—. Vis. rsch. scholar UCLA, 1983; holder L.L. McAninch Chair of Entrepreneurship, 1988-90; bd. dirs. Union Nat. Bank, Manhattan, mem. investment com., 1986-87, mem. trust mgmt. com., 1988. Author: International Investment, 1977, Financial Statement Analysis and Forecasting for the Non-Financial Executive, 1990, Understanding the Bottom Line: Finance for Non-financial Managers and Supervisors. Chmn. Kans. State U., United Way, 1982; trustee Meml. Hosp., Manhattan, 1984-90; treas. Kans. State U. Found., 1980-90, mem. investments com., 1988; mem. steering com. Ctr. for Workforce Mgmt.; mem. cost containment roundtable Sedgwick County med. Soc.; mem. bd. dirs. Wichita/Sedgwick County Partnership for Growth Employment and Tng.; mem. Broward Econ. Devel. Coun., 1995; mem. exec. adv. bd. Wharton Sch. Univ. Pa., 1995. With USAF, 1971-73. Recipient Outstanding Tchr. award Coll. of Bus., Kans. State U., 1977, All-Univ. Disting. Tchg. award Kans. State U., 1977, Cutting Edge award selection com. Miami C. of C., 1995-96; investments rsch. grantee Kans. State U., 1978. Mem. Fin. Execs. Inst., Am. Fin. Assn., Am. Econ. Assn., Fin. Mgmt. Assn., Midwest Fin. Assn., Kans. State U. Alumni Assn. (treas. 1980-90, trustee 1983-90, bd. dirs.), Manhattan C. of C. (bd. dirs. 1987-90), Manhattan Country Club (bd. dirs. 1983-85), Rotary (bd. dirs. Manhattan club, 1986—, pres.-elect Manhattan chpt.). Republican. Avocations: golf, guitar playing, reading. Office: Nova Southeastern U H Wayne Huizenga Sch Bus 3301 College Ave Fort Lauderdale FL 33314 Office Phone: 954-262-5005. E-mail: pohlman@nsu.nova.edu.

**POHLMANN, EVELYN GAWLEY,** music educator, consultant; b. Pasadena, Calif., May 3, 1942; m. John Ogden Pohlmann, Aug. 8, 1964; children: Alison Pohlmann Espinosa, Victoria Elizabeth. BA, Occidental Coll., 1964. Life tchg. credential Calif. Studio piano tchr., Seal Beach, Calif., 1971—. Tchr. cons. Internat. Piano Tchg. Found., 1976—. Bd. dirs. Long Beach Symphony Assn., 1998—. Recipient Ruby Sword of Honor, Delta Province, Sigma Alpha Iota, 1964. Mem.: Music Tchrs.' Assn. Calif. (pres. 1988—90), Long Beach Symphony Guild (pres. 1994—95).

**POHOST, GERALD MICHAEL,** cardiologist, medical educator; b. Washington, Oct. 27, 1941; married; 3 children. BS, George Washington U., 1963; MD, U. Md., 1967. Diplomate Am. Bd. Internal Medicine, Am. Bd. Cardiovascular Disease, Am. Bd. Nuclear Medicine. Intern Montefiore Hosp. & Med. Ctr., Bronx, N.Y., 1967-68, asst. resident, 1968-69; sr. resident Jacobi Hosp. Albert Einstein Coll. Medicine, Bronx, 1969-70; cardiology resident Montefiore Hosp. & Med. Ctr.; clin. & rsch. fellow in medicine Mass. Gen. Hosp., Boston, 1971-73; rsch. fellow in medicine Harvard Med. Sch., Boston, 1971-73, instr. medicine, 1974-77, asst. prof., assoc. prof. medicine, 1977-83; with dept. radiology Mass. Gen. Hosp., Boston, 1977-83, asst. gen. med. svcs., 1978-82; prof. medicine, radiology U. Ala., Birmingham, 1983—; Mary Gertrude Waters chair cardiovascular medicine divsn. cardiovascular disease, 1991—, prof. cardiovascular medicine, 1991—, dir. Ctr. for NMR R&D. Cons. nuclear medicine radiology dept. Mass. Gen. Hosp., 1977-83; dir. ctr. NMR R&D U. Ala. Hosp., Birmingham, 1986—. Sr. editor: Noninvasive Cardiac Imaging, 1983, New Concepts in Cardiac Imaging, 1985, 86, 87, 88, 89, The Principles and Practice of Cardiovascular Imaging, 1991; contbr. more than 400 articles, reviews, book chpts., editls. to profl. jours.; nat. and internat. spkr. in field; mem. editl. bd. Circulation, Jour. Magnetic Resonance in Medicine, Am. Jour. Cardiology, Internat. Jour. Cardiology, NMR in BioMedicine, Coronary Artery Disease, others; editor Jour. Cardiovasc. Magnetic Resonance, 1998—; editor-in-chief Jour. Cardiovascular Magnetic Resonance, 1999—; rsch. interests in radionuclide and nuclear magnetic resonance studies of the heart, myocardial metabolism, cardiac pathophysiology. SCOR grant NIH, 1990—, tng. grant, 1992—, Dept. Energy grant, 1992—, Nat. Ctr. Rsch. Resources, 1992—. Fellow Am. Coll. Cardiology (editl. bd. jour., chmn. cardiac Imaging com. 1982-88, current procedural terminology com. 1988-94, gov. rels. com. 1989-95, trustee 1994-99); mem. AMA (chmn. panel nuclear magnetic resonance imaging 1985-88), Am. Fedn. Clin. Rsch., Am. Soc. Clin. Investigations, Am. Assn. Profs., Am. Heart Assn. (fellow coun. clin. cardiology 1975—, Mass. affiliate 1975-83, established investigator 1979-84, Richard and Hinda Rosenthal award for excellence in clin. investigation 1985, chmn. advanced cardiac tech. com. of coun. on clin. cardiology 1981-86, exec. com. 1981-95, 98—, Ala. affiliate 1983—, long range planning com. 1986-89, chmn. 1989-91, vice chmn. exec. com. coun. clin. cardiology 1989-91, nominating com. 1989-91, chmn. 1993-95, budget com. 1989-91, exec. com. 1991-93, immediate past chmn. 1994—, rsch. com. fellow subgroup A 1988-91), Soc. Nuclear Medicine (coun. nuclear cardiology 1990-92), Soc. for Cardiovasc. Magnetic Resonance (pres. 1995-98, founder 1995, exec. com. 1995-99, trustees, 1995—), Soc. Magnetic Resonance in Medicine (exec. com. 1987—, sci. program com. 1988-89, pres. 1986-87), Nat. Heart, Lung and Blood Inst. (program project rev. com. A 1984-88, cardiovascular and renal study sect.

---

1991-94, radiol. study sect. 1994-99), So. Med. Assn., NIH Reviewers Res., U.S. Nuclear Regulatory Commn. (adv. com. 1984-93), Assn. Univ. Cardiologists, Assn. Profs. Cardiology (sec. treas. 1995-96), Sigma Xi. Home: 612 N Las Palmas Ave Los Angeles CA 90004-1020 Fax: 205-975-1952.

**POIAN, EDWARD LICIO,** historian; b. Trieste, Friuli-Venezia Giulia, Italy, June 10, 1946; arrived in U.S., 1954, naturalized, 1960; s. Angelo Del Picollo and Zaira (de Bourbon-Cornelli) Poian; m. Maria del Carmen Lopez Clinton, Nov. 22, 1969 (div. Mar. 1980); children: Jeanne Marie, Nicole Anna; m. Nancy Flynn, Sept. 18, 1982. AS, U.S. Govt. Inst., 1965; BS, Mercy Coll., 1988; MS, L.I. U., 1989; PhD, U. Ariz., 1992. Chief exec. Budget Fin. Inc., Pittsfield, Mass., 1968-70; acting postmaster U.S. Postal Svc., Chappaqua, 1971-80; v.p. Lehman Bros Khun Loeb, N.Y.C., 1980-83; CEO Cosmopolitan Armaments, N.Y.C., 1983-90; intern The UN Univ., 1989-90; prof. history Mercy Coll., Dobbs Ferry, N.Y., 1991—, prof. history and polit. sci., 1991—. Cons. in field; intern UN U., 1990. Author: On the Outside Looking In, 1972, Peace and Regional Security Through Education in Africa, 1992, Problems in Coordination Among Western Donor Governments in Relations to Multilateral and Social Programmes of the United Nations System, 1990; contbr. articles to profl. jours. Rector, CEO Internat. Edul. Rsch. Found., Inc., Yonkers, NY, 1991—; trustee archeology dept. U. Trieste, 1986—; dir. history and govt. assn. Mercy Coll., 1988. With USCG, 1963—67, served to capt. USCG Res., 1968—98. Decorated Knight of Malta Cross of Gregory the Great Vatican City; recipient UN award, 1988. Fellow: World Assn. Former UN Interns and Fellows; mem.: VFW, Am. Soc. Polit. Sci., Yonker Hist. Soc., Mil. Officers Assn. Am., Navy League (N.Y. chpt.) (life), U.S. Naval Inst. (life), Fleet Res. Assn. (life), Am. Legion (life), Phi Gamma Mu, Phi Alpha Theta. Republican. Roman Catholic. Avocations: archaeology, historical research, art collector, philanthropy. Home: 1930 Hone Ave Bronx NY 10461-1304 Office: Mercy Coll Dept History and Polit Sci 555 Broadway Dobbs Ferry NY 10522-1134 Office Phone: 914-693-4500. Personal E-mail: doctorpoian@email.com.

**POILE, DAVID ROBERT,** professional sports team executive; b. Toronto, Ont., Can., Feb. 14, 1949; s. Norman Robert (dec.) and Margaret (Elizabeth) P.; m. Elizabeth Ramey, July 4, 1971; children: Brian Robert, Lauren Elizabeth. BS, Northeastern U., 1971. Asst. mgr. Atlanta Flames, 1971-80, Calgary Flames, Alta., Can., 1980-82; gen. mgr., v.p. Washington Capitals, Landover, Md., 1982-95; exec. v.p., gen. mgr. Nashville Predators, Nashville, 1997—. Office: Nashville Predators Nashville Arena 501 Broadway Nashville TN 37203-3932*

**POINAR, GEORGE ORLO, JR.,** entomologist, science educator; b. Spokane, Wash., Apr. 25, 1936; s. George O. and Helen Louise (Ladd) P.; m. Eva I. Hecht; children: Hendrik, Maya; m. 2d, Roberta Theresa Heil; 1 child, Gregory. BS, Cornell U., 1958, MS, 1960, PhD, 1962. Prof. dept. entomology U. Calif., Berkeley, 1964—95; courtesy prof. dept. zoology Oreg. State U., Corvallis, 1995—. Author: Entomogenous Nematodes, 1975, Nematodes for Biological Control of insects, 1979, The Natural History of Nematodes, 1983, co-author (with Roberta Poinar) The Quest for Life in Amber, (with Roberta Poinar) The Amber Forest, (with R. Milki) Lebanese Amber, 2001, (with G.M. Thomas) Diagnostic Manual for the Identification of Insect Pathogens, 1978, (with G.M. Thomas) Laboratory Guide to Insect Pathogens and Parasites, 1984, (with Hans-Börje Jansson) Diseases of Nematodes, Vols. 1, 2, 1988. Grantee NATO, NSF, NIH, 1962-72. Avocations: photography, piano, tennis. Office: Oreg State Univ Dept Zoology Corvallis OR 97331 Office Phone: 541-737-5356. Business E-Mail: poinarg@science.oregonstate.edu.

**POINDEXTER, WILLIAM MERSEREAU,** lawyer; b. L.A., June 16, 1925; s. Robert Wade and Irene M. Poindexter; m. Jani Jennifer Wohlgemuth, Feb. 14, 2000; children: James Wade, David Graham, Honour Hêlenê, Timothy John, Cory Todd, E.W. Greg. BA, Yale U., 1946; postgrad., U. Chgo., 1946-47; LL.B., U. Calif., Berkeley, 1949. Bar: Calif. 1952. Practiced in, San Francisco, 1952-54, Los Angeles, 1954—; mem. firm Poindexter & Doutre, Inc., 1964—. Pres. Consol. Brazing & Mfg. Co., Riverside, Calif., 1949-52. Pres. South Pasadena-San Marino (Calif.) YMCA, 1963; Mem. San Marino Sch. Bd., 1965-69, pres., 1967; pres. Conf. of Ins. Counsel, 1975. Served with USMCR, 1943. Fellow Am. Coll. Trust and Estate Counsel; mem. ABA, L.A. County Bar Assn., State Bar Calif., Yale Club (pres. So. Calif. chpt. 1961), Calif. Lincoln Clubs (L.A. downtown chpt. chmn. 1997-2003). Republican. Presbyterian. Office: 1 Wilshire Bldg Ste 2420 Los Angeles CA 90017 Office Phone: 213-628-8297.

**POINSETTE, DONALD EUGENE,** engineering executive, management consultant; b. Ft. Wayne, Ind., Aug. 17, 1914; s. Eugene Joseph and Julia Anna (Wyss) P.; m. Anne Katherine Farrell, Apr. 15, 1939 (dec.); children: Donald J., Eugene J., Leo J., Sharon Poinsette Smith, Irene Poinsette Snyder, Cynthia Poinsette West, Maryanne Poinsette Stohler, Philip J. Student, Purdue U., 1934, Ind. U., 1935-37, 64. With GE Corp., RCA, Stewart Warner Corp., 1937-39; metall. rsch. and field sales cons. P.R. Mallory Corp., 1939-49; dist. sales mgr. Derringer Metall. Corp., Chgo., 1949-50; plant engr. Cornell-Dubilier Electric Corp., Indpls., 1950-53; with Jenn-Air Corp., Indpls., 1953-74, purchasing dir., 1953-71, mgr. value engring. and quality control, 1969-74; bus. mgmt. cons. Mays and Assocs., Indpls., 1974-76. Pres. Marian Coll. Parents Club, Indpls., 1969-70; com. mem. Boy Scouts Am.; nat. trustee Xavier U., 1972-73, Dad's Club, Cin.; mem. Triad choral groups. Recipient Testimonial Golden Anniversary award Purdue U., 1987; named to U.S. Finder's List, Nat. Engrs. Register, 1956, Army Navy E award for excellence in engring. and prodn., 1944. Mem. Nat. Assn. Purchasing Mgmt., Indpls. Purchasing Mgmt. Assn., Soc. Am. Value Engrs. (cert. value specialist, sec.-treas. Cnt. Ind. chpt. 1972-73), Soc. Ret. Execs. Indpls., Ind. U. Alumni Assn., Purdue U. Alumni Assn., Columbian (pres. 1972-73), Internat. Platform Assn., Tau Kappa Epsilon, K.C. (4 deg.). Home: 8480 Craig St Apt 131 Indianapolis IN 46250

**POINTER, MARSHA G.,** principal; b. St. Louis, Oct. 24, 1950; d. Robert Lee Gentry and Clarice Anita McClure; m. James Earl Pointer, Apr. 15, 1989; children: Tiffany, James Jr. BA, Albion Coll., 1973; MA, Mich. State U., 1977; prin. lic., U. Colo., Denver, 1995. Spl. edn. endorsement EBD (emotional and behavior disorder). Dean, tchr., coach Denver Pub. Schs., 1979—95, asst. prin., 1995—2001, H.S. prin., 2001—. Pres. Manual Leadership High Ach. Bd., Denver, 2001—03. Grantee, U.S. Dept. Edn., 1974, Bill and Melinda Gates Found., 2002. Mem.: Nat. Assn. Secondary Sch. Prins., Nat. Wildlife Assn. Jehovah'S Witness. Avocations: dance, gardening, reading. Home: 12410 E 29th Ave Denver CO 80239 Office: Denver Pub Schs Manual HS 1700 E 28th Ave Denver CO 80205

**POINTER, MICHELLE PHILLIPS,** counselor, educator, consultant; d. George and Ruth Phillips; m. L.P. Pointer, Jr.; 1 child, Lyle P. B Psychology, Fisk U., 1971; M Guidance and Counseling, Bowie State U., 1977; D Counseling, George Washington U., 2001. Cert. rehab. counselor, nat. cert. counselor, lic. clin. profl. counselor. H.S. psychology tchr. Anne Arundel County Pub. Schs., 1972—73; mental health and gen. counselor Divsn. Rehab. Svcs., Rockville, Md., 1974—84; dist. supr., regional dir. Prince Georges and Montgomery Counties, Md., 1984—91, spl. asst. to asst. supt. Balt., 1991—93, dir. comms. and cmty. rels., 1992—93; state dir. divsn. vocat. rehab. State of Del., Wilmington, 1993—94; regional cons. George Washington U., Washington, 1996—99; adj. prof., instr. Coppin State Coll., Balt., 1995—2001, assoc. prof., 2001—; dir. counseling ministries Round Oak Missionary Bapt. Ch., Silver Spring, Md. Mem. nat. adv. coun. U. Okla., Norman, 1994—96, Howard U., Washington, 1994—, Very Spl. Arts, Washington, 1994—95; mem. regional adv. coun. U. Md., College Park, 2002—; nat. chmn. client svcs. Coun. State Adminstrn. Vocat. Rehab., Washington, 1994—95, regional rep., 1993—96; presenter in field. Dir.: (video) Divsn. Vocat. Rehab., 1994. Mem. Del. Alcohol, Drug Abuse and Mental Health Adv. Coun., Wilmington, 1994—96; Del. Gov.'s Com. on Employment of Individuals with Disabilities, Wilmington, 1993—96, Md. Gov.'s Com. on Employment of Individuals with Disabilities, Balt., 1991—93, Del. Gov.'s Coun. on Equal Employment Opportunities,

1994—95, Del. State Coordinating Coun. for People with Disabilities. Recipient Second Genesis award, 1984, First State Projects with Industry award, 1994, 3d annual award, Nat. Head Injury Coun., Dover, Del., 1996, numerous others. Mem.: ACA, Nat. Assn. Multuval Rehab. Counseling, Nat. Rehab. Counseling Assn., Nat. Rehab. Adminstr. Assn., Internat. Assn. Marriage and Family Counselors, Md. Rehab. Assn. (pres.-elect), Nat. Rehab. Assn., Chi Sigma Iota, Phi Delta Kappa.

**POINTER, ROSANNE ELISE,** music educator; d. Jack Edward and Bonnie Jeanne (Beary) Pointer. BSc in Vocal Music Edn., N.W. Mo. State U., Maryville, Mo., 1996. Dir. choral music Odessa (Mo.) R-7 Schs., 1996—. Instr. choral music N.W. Mo. State U., Maryville, 1996—2006; staff summer camp Ctrl. Mo. State U., Warrensburg, Mo., 2000—06. Dir. choir First Christian Ch., Odessa, 2004—. Named Most Outstanding Choral Dir., West Ctrl. Dist. MCDA, 2006. Mem.: NEA, Am. Choral Dirs. Assn., Music Educators Nat. Conf. Democrat. Home: 1232 N Ashley Dr Grain Valley MO 64029 Office: Fort Osage HS 2101 N Twyman Rd Independence MO 64029 Office Phone: 816-650-7059.

**POINTER, SAM CLYDE, JR.,** retired federal judge, lawyer; b. Birmingham, Ala., Nov. 15, 1934; s. Sam Clyde and Elizabeth Inzer (Brown) P.; m. Paula Purse, Oct. 18, 1958; children: Minge, Sam Clyde III. AB, Vanderbilt U., 1955; JD, U. Ala., 1957; LL.M., NYU, 1958. Bar: Ala. 1957. Ptnr. Brown, Pointer & Pointer, 1958—79; judge U.S. Dist. Ct. (no. dist.) Ala., Birmingham, 1970-2000, chief judge, 1982-99; judge Temp. Emergency Ct. Appeals, 1980-87; mem. Jud. Panel Multi-dist. Litigation, 1980-87; ptnr. Lightfoot, Franklin & White, 2000—. Mem. Jud. Conf. U.S., 1987-90; mem. Jud. Coun. 11th Cir., 1987-90, mem. standing com. on rules, 1988-90, chmn. adv. com. on civil rules, 1990-93. Bd. editors: Manual for Complex Litigation, 1979-91. Mem. ABA, Ala. Bar Asn., Birmingham Bar Assn., Am. Law Inst., Am. Judicature Soc., Furrah Order of Jurisprudence, Phi Beta Kappa. Episcopalian. Office: Lightfoot Franklin & White The Clark Bldg 400 N 20th St Birmingham AL 35203 E-mail: spointer@lfwlaw.com.

**POINTS, ROY WILSON,** municipal official; b. Quincy, Ill., Oct. 21, 1940; s. Jess C. and Gladys (Wilson) P.; m. Karen Lee Olsen, July 23, 1966; children: Eric, Holly. BBA, Culver Stockton Coll., 1968. Tchr., coach Lewis County C-1, Ewing, Mo., 1968-69, Community Unit 3, Camp Point, Ill., 1969-78; real estate salesman Landmark, Quincy, 1978-80; supr. of assessment County of Adams, Quincy, 1980-90; assessor City Twp. of Quincy, 1990—. Chmn. Adams County Bd. Rev., 1977—80. Bd. dirs., 1st v.p., sec. Quincy Jaycees, 1970-76, Quincy Rotary East, 1980. Mem. Cert. Ill. Assessing Officers, Internat. Assn. Assessing Officers (cert. ednl. recognition 1988), Ill. Assessors Assn. (bd. dirs. 1992—), Twp. Ofcls. Ill. (bd. dirs. 1995-2001), North Ctrl. Regional Assn. Assessing Officers (bd. dirs. 1997—). Democrat. Avocations: fishing, hunting, jogging, raising cattle. Office: Quincy Twp Assessor City Hall Annex 706 Maine St Quincy IL 62301-4013 Office Phone: 217-228-4505.

**POIRIER, LOUIS JOSEPH,** neurology educator; b. Montreal, Que., Can., Dec. 30, 1918; s. Gustave Joseph and Calixta (Brault) P.; m. Liliane Archambault, June 11, 1947; children: Guy, Michel, Louise, Esther. BSc, U. Montreal, 1942, MD, 1947; PhD, U. Mich., 1950; D (hon.), U. Rennes, France, 1973. Asst. prof. U. Montreal, 1950-55, assoc. prof., 1955-58, prof. faculty of medicine, 1958-65; chmn. dept. anatomy Faculty of Medicine, Laval U., Cité Universitaire, Que., 1970-78; prof. exptl. neurology, 1978-83; dir. Centre de Research in Neurobiology, Laval U. and Hosp. de l'Enfant-Jesus, 1977-85, prof. emeritus, 1985—. Editor: Advances in Neurology, vol. 24, 1979; contbr. articles to profl. jours. Pres. Que. Health Scis. Research Council, 1978-81. Decorated officer Order of Can.; recipient Que. sci. award, 1975; Killam commemorative scholar, 1977, 78 Mem. AAAS, Royal Soc. Belgium (hon.), Neurol. Soc. France (hon.), Am. Assn. Anatomists, Am. Physiol. Soc., Soc. for Neuroscis., Internat. Brain Research Orgn., Can. Med. Assn. (emeritus). Address: 603 Chemin Caron Lac Simon Montpellier PQ Canada J0V 1M0

**POITEVENT, EDWARD BUTTS, II,** lawyer; b. New Orleans, Oct. 19, 1949; s. Eads and Elizabeth (Schramm) P.; m. Julia Dunbar Baños, Dec. 29, 1972; children: Sarah Dunbar, Elizabeth Grehan, Edward Scott, Mary McCutchen. BA, Tulane U., 1971, JD, 1974. Assoc. Jones, Walker, Waechter, Poitevent, Carrere & Denegre, New Orleans, 1974-79, ptnr., 1979-91, Phelps Dunbar, New Orleans, 1991—2001; of counsel King & Spalding, Houston, 2002—04; sr. counsel Akin, Gump, Strauss Hower & Feld, Houston, 2004—. Mem. ad hoc com. Pipeline divsn. La. Office of Conservation; mem. adv. coun. La. Mineral Law Inst. Mem. editl. bd. Oil and Gas Law and Taxation Rev.; contbr. articles to profl. jours.; presenter in field. Pres. La. chpt. Leukemia Soc. Am., Inc., New Orleans, 1991; trustee Ea. Mineral Law Found., 1988-93; co-chmn. oil and gas sect. Rocky Mountain Mineral Law Found. 36th Ann. Inst., Santa Fe; trustee-at-large Rocky Mountain Mineral Law Found., 1995-97. Mem. ABA (sect. on natural resources, energy and environ. law natural gas and oil coms., litigation sect. energy litigation com., chair program com., editor energy litigation com. newsletter, chair energy litigation com. natural gas mktg. and trans. com., mem. coun. 1994-98, mem. nominating com. 1995-96, CLE reporter 1995-96, mem. exec. com. 1996-97), La. State Bar Assn., Fed. Energy Bar Assn., Am. Assn. Petroleum Landmen (chair ad hoc com. on model form gas Balancing Agreement), Assn. Internat. Petroleum NEgotiators (model forum govt. agreement 2002-2003). Republican. Roman Catholic. Office: Akin Gump Strauss Hauer & Feld Ste 4400 1111 Louisiana Houston TX 77002 Office Phone: 713-220-8115. Business E-mail: epoitevent@akingump.com.

**POITIER, CONSTANCE RENA,** music specialist, educator; b. Quincy, Fla., June 1, 1955; d. Leroy Cornelius and Dorothy Louise Parker Harris; m. James Poitier, July 22, 1995; children: Carla Felicia DuPont, Carl Franklin DuPont, Jr. BA, Bethune-Cookman Coll., 1977. MF, Fla. Atlantic U., 1988; ednl. specialist magna cum laude, Nova U., 2004. Nat. bd. cert. tchr. 2004, cert. nat. bd. cert. minority recruiter. Choral dir., gen. music Roosevelt Jr. H.S., West Palm Beach, Fla., 1977-81; drama coach Jupiter (Fla.) H.S., 1985; music specialist Roosevelt Elem., 1981-86, Riverview (Fla.) Elem., 1986-96; min. of music Spring Hill Bapt. Ch., Tampa, Fla., 1994-96; choral dir. Atlantic H.S., Port Orange, Fla., 1996-97; choral dir. Daytona Beach Gospel Choir Daytona Beach Bapt. Ch., Fla., 1996—; music specialist Palm Terrace Elem., Daytona Beach, Fla., 1997—, Bonner Elem., 2004—; asst. to the choral dir. Bethune Cookman Coll., 2003; proprietor Poitier Fin. Svcs. Choral dir. Progress M&E Bapt. State Choral Svc., 1973-76; choral dir., pianist 1st Bapt. Ch. College Hill, Tampa, 1986-96; choir cons., guest dir., clinician for choral workshops; concert and rec. artist; pvt. instr., voice and piano; choral festival judge; gospel music workshop clinician. Author: My Book of Poems, 1996. Fellow NEA, NAACP, Am. Choral Dirs., Westside Bus. and Profls., Fla. Vocal Assn., Fla. Music Educators Assn., Fla. Music Educators Nat. Conf., Zeta Phi Beta. Home: 3801 Birch Mtn Rd Port Orange FL 32129 Office: Bonner Elem Sch George Ingram Blvd Daytona Beach FL 32114-1253 E-mail: connie8082@bellsouth.net.

**POITIER, SIDNEY,** actor, film director; b. Miami, Fla., Feb. 20, 1927; Grew up on Cat Island, The Bahamas. At age 15 moved to Miami, and at age 16 to NYC. s. Reginald and Evelyn (Outten) Poitier; m. Juanita Hardy, Apr. 29, 1960 (div. 1965); children: Beverly, Pamela, Sherri, Gina; m. Joanna Shimkus, Jan. 23, 1976; children: Anika, Sydney. Student, The Bahamas. Accepted to Am. Negro Theatre, NYC, on second audition and made debut in Days of Our Youth, 1945. Mem. to Japan from the Bahamas, 1997; bd. dirs. Walt Disney Co., 1994—2003. Performer: (Broadway plays) Lysistrata, 1946; Anna Lucasta, 1974; A Raisin in the Sun, 1959—60 (Tony Award nomination for best actor in a play, 1960); dir.: Carry Me Back to Morningside Heights, 1968; actor: (films) No Way Out, 1950, Cry, the Beloved Country, 1951, Red Ball Express, 1952, Go, Man, Go!, 1954, Blackboard Jungle, 1955, Goodbye, My Lady, 1956, Edge of the City, 1957, Something of Value, 1957, Band of Angels, 1957, The Mark of the Hawk, 1958, The Defiant Ones, 1958 (Acad. award nomination for best actor in a leading role, 1959), Virgin Island, 1958, Porgy and Bess, 1959, All the Young Men, 1960, A Raisin in the Sun,

1961, Paris Blues, 1961, Pressure Point, 1962, Lilies of the Field, 1963 (Acad. Award for best actor in a leading role, 1964, Golden Globe Award for best motion picture actor - drama, 1964), The Long Ships, 1963, The Bedford Incident, 1965, The Greatest Story Ever Told, 1965, A Patch of Blue, 1965, The Slender Thread, 1965, Duel at Diablo, 1966, To Sir, with Love, 1967, In the Heat of the Night, 1967, Guess Who's Coming to Dinner, 1967, The Lost Man, 1969, The Call Me Mister Tibbs!, 1970, Brother John, 1971, The Organization, 1971, The Wilby Conspiracy, 1975, Shoot to Kill, 1988, Little Nikita, 1988, Sneakers, 1992, The Jackal, 1997; (TV films) Separate but Equal, 1991 (Emmy Award nomination for outstanding lead actor in a miniseries or special, 1991), Children of the Dust, 1995, To Sir, with Love II, 1996, Mandela and de Klerk, 1997 (Emmy Award nomination for outstanding lead actor in a miniseries or special, 1997), David and Lisa, 1998, The Simple Life of Noah Dearborn, 1999, The Last Brickmaker in America, 2001; actor, dir. (films) Buck and the Preacher, 1972, A Warm December, 1973, Uptown Saturday Night, 1974, Let's Do It Again, 1975, A Piece of the Action, 1977, actor, prodr. (TV films) East of Eden, 1999, actor, writer (story) (films) For Love of Ivy, 1968; dir.: (films) Stir Crazy, 1980, Hanky Panky, 1982, Fast Forward, 1985, Ghost Dad, 1990; author: (autobiography) This Life, 1980, The Measure of a Man, 2000. Served 1267th Med. Deatchment U.S. Army, 1944—45, veteran's hosp., LI. Decorated Hon. Knight Comdr. Order Brit. Empire; recipient Golden Globe Award for World Film Favorite - Male, 1969, Cecil B. DeMille Award, Golden Globe Awards, 1982, Lifetime Achievement Award, Am. Film Inst., 1992, Kennedy Ctr. Honors, 1995, Lifetime Achievement Award, Screen Actors Guild, 2000, Hall of Fame Award, NAACP, 2001, Hon. Award, Acad. Awards, 2002, Star on Hollywood Walk of Fame. Achievements include First black person to win an Acad. Award for a leading role, 1964.

**POJETA, JOHN, JR.,** geologist, researcher; b. NYC, Sept. 9, 1935; s. John and Emilie (Pilat) P.; m. Mary Louise Eberz, June 23, 1957; children: Kim Louise, John Martin. BS, Capital U., Columbus, Ohio, 1957; MS, U. Cin., 1961, PhD, 1963. Teaching fellow U. Cin., 1957-63; geologist U.S. Geol. Survey, 1963—, chief lower paleozoic studies unit, 1969-74, chief br. paleontology and stratigraphy, 1989-94. Assoc. prof., lectr. George Washington U., 1965-74; research assoc. Smithsonian Instn., 1969—; U.S. Geol. Survey-Australian Bur. Mineral Resources exchange scientist, 1974-75 Author papers in field. Pres. Potomac Woods Citizens Assn.; mem. area 4 coun. Montgomery County (Md.) Bd. Edn.; mem. bd. Citizens for Good Govt.; trustee Paleontol. Rsch. Instn., 1976—85, 1999—, v.p., 1978—79, pres., 1980—82. Fellow: AAAS (coun.), Geol. Soc. Am. (sr.); mem.: Australasian Paleontologists, Paleontol. Soc. (sec. 1982—88, pres. 1989—90, bus. mgr. spl. studies 1989—). Home: 1492 Dunster Ln Rockville MD 20854-6119 Office: US Geol Survey Smithsonian Instn Rm E-308 MRC121 Mus Natural History Washington DC 20560-0137 Office Phone: 202-633-1347. Business E-Mail: pojetaj@si.edu.

**POKEMPNER, JOSEPH KRES,** lawyer; b. Monessen, Pa., June 11, 1936; s. Leonard and Ethel Lee (Kres) P.; m. Judith Montague Stephens, Aug. 23, 1970; children: Elizabeth, Jennifer, Amy. AB, Johns Hopkins U., 1957; LLB, U. Md., 1962. Bar: Md. 1962. Law clk. to judge Supreme Bench Balt., 1960-62; field atty. 5th region NLRB, 1962-64; pvt. practice labor law Balt., 1964—; ptnr. Wolf, Pokempner & Hillman, Balt., 1972-86, Whiteford, Taylor & Preston, Balt., 1986—. Contbr. articles to legal jours. Capt. AUS, 1969-74. Mem. ABA, Fed. Bar Assn. (pres. Balt. chpt. 1979-80), Md. Bar Assn., Balt. Bar Assn. (pres. 1984-85), Serjeant's Inn Law Club. Jewish. Home: 1500 Willow Ave Baltimore MD 21204-3611 E-mail: jpokempner@wtplaw.com.

**POKORNY, ALEX DANIEL,** psychiatrist; b. Taylor, Tex., Oct. 18, 1918; s. John Robert and Olga Frances (Susen) P.; m. Jeanice Brooke Allen, Mar. 13, 1948; children: Martha, Ross, Ellen, Sally. BA, U. Tex., 1939; MD, U. Tex., Galveston, 1942. Diplomate Am. Bd. Psychiatry and Neurology. Psychiatrist VA Hosp., Houston, 1949-55, chief psychiatry and neurology svc., 1955-73; from instr. to prof. psychiatry Baylor Coll. Medicine, Houston, 1949-89, acting chmn. dept. psychiatry, 1968-72, vice chmn. dept. psychiatry, 1972-89; ret. Editor (with others) 7 books, including Phenomenology and Treatment of Anxiety, 1979, Phenomenology and Treatment of Alcoholism, 1980, Phenomenology and Treatment of Psychosexual Disorders, 1983, Phenomenology and Treatment of Psychiatric Emergencies, 1984; editor numerous publs.; contbr. 100 articles to profl. jours. Capt. U.S. Army, 1943-46. Recipient Amersa award for Excellence in Med. Edu. Assn. Med. Edn. & Rsch. Substance Abuse, 1989, Dublin award Am. Assn. Suicidology, 1992. Fellow AAAS, Am. Psychiat. Assn. (life), Am. Coll. Psychiatrists (life); mem. Soc. Psychophysiological Rsch. Home and Office: 813 Atwell St Bellaire TX 77401-4718

**POKORNY, JAN HIRD,** architect, educator; b. Brno, Czechoslovakia, May 25, 1914; came to U.S., 1940, naturalized, 1945; s. Jaroslav and Theresia (Harrer) P.; m. Marise Angelucci, 1967; 1 son, Stefan Alexander. Engr-Architect, Tech. U., Prague, 1937; MS in Architecture, Columbia U., 1941. Gen. practice architecture, Prague, 1938-39; designer Winn-Roensch & Brezner, Detroit, 1942, Leo Bauer, Detroit, 1942-44; Skidmore, Owings & Merrill, N.Y.C., 1944-45; CEO Jan Hird Pokorny (architect), N.Y.C., 1945-71, 77—; partner Pokorny & Pertz, 1971-77. Assoc. prof. Columbia Sch. Architecture, 1958-74, dir. evening program in architecture, 1957-73, prof. architecture Grad. Sch. Architecture, Planning and Preservation, 1974-82, prof. emeritus, 1982—; architect mem. Art Commn. City N.Y., 1973-77, James William Kideney award N.Y. State Assn. of Architects, 1992. Contbr. articles to profl. jours.; prin. works include: Taylor Meml. Library and Reeves Student Union Bldg. at Centenary Coll. for Women, Hackettstown, N.J., Lewisohn Hall at Columbia U., (with Damaz and Weigel) Student Union Bldg., Adminstrn. Bldg., Library and Fine Arts Bldg. at N.Y. State U., Stony Brook, (with David Todd Assts.) master plan Library, Auditorium and renovated Music Bldg., Speech and Theatre Bldg., Lehman Coll. City U. N.Y., housing at Grasslands Westchester Med. Ctr. and housing for Urban Devel. Corp., in Middletown, Elmira and Wayne County, N.Y., Corp. offices for Samuel H. Kress Found., Ambassador's Offices U.S. Mission to UN, Offices John and Harry R. Markle Found.; restoration of: Schermerhorn Row Block, South St., Seaport, N.Y.C., Monsignor McGolrick Park Shelter, Bklyn., Sloppy Louie's Restaurant, South St., Seaport, N.Y.C., Shellens Gallery of Bklyn. History, Bklyn. Hist. Soc., Firemen's Meml., N.Y.C., Church of Incarnation, N.Y.C., Morris-Jumel Mansion, N.Y.C., Century Club Facade, N.Y.C. Bd. dirs. Am. Fund for Czechoslovak Refugees, 1959—, sec. 1964-71, chmn., 1971—; trustee Grand Central Terminal Trust Fund, N.Y.C.; v.p. of Fine Arts Fedn. of N.Y.C., pres. Bohemian Benevolent and Literary Assn., N.Y.C., 1987—. Recipient Ethnic New Yorker award by Mayor of N.Y., 1985, Lifetime Preservation award Columbia Alumni, 1990, Felber Gold medal Czech Tech. U., 1991, James William Kideney award, AIA, 1992, award for Morris-Jumel restoration N.Y.C. Landmarks Commn., 1993, "Quintessential Architect" AIA N.Y. State Fellows award, 2000. Fellow AIA (awards of merit 1955, 61,74, N.Y. state assn. award 1975, Bard award 1985, Arthur Ross award); mem. Nat. Acad. Design. Clubs: Century Assn. Office: Jan Hird Pokorny Associates Inc 39 W 37th St New York NY 10018-6217 Office Phone: 212-759-6462. Office Fax: 212-759-6540. E-mail: pokorny@jhpokorny.com.

**POKORNY, JOSEPH WENCESLAUS, III,** engineer; b. Park Ridge, Ill., July 11, 1979; s. Joseph Wenceslaus Pokorny, Jr. and Marlene Pokorny. BS, U. Ill., Champaign, 2001, MS, 2003. Tchg. asst. U. Ill., Champaign, 2001—03; application support engr. The MathWorks, Inc., Natick, Mass., 2003—04, tng. engr., 2004—. Presenter in field. Recipient Lincoln Arc Welding award, James F. Lincoln Arc Welding Found., 2001. Mem.: IEEE. Democrat. Roman Catholic. Avocations: sports, fishing, travel. Home: Apt 4403 195 Binney St Cambridge MA 02142 Office: The MathWorks Inc 3 Apple Hill Dr Natick MA 01760

**POKRAS, SHEILA FRANCES,** retired judge; b. Newark, Aug. 5, 1935; m. Norman M. Pokras, 1954; children: Allison, Andrea, Larry. Student, Beaver Coll., 1953-54; BS in Edn., Temple U., 1957; JD cum laude, Pepperdine U., 1969. Bar: Calif. 1970, U.S. Dist. Ct. D.C. 1970, U.S. Dist. Ct. Calif. 1970,

U.S. Supreme Ct. 1975. Tchr. elem. and secondary schs., Phila. and Newark, 1957-59; pvt. practice law Long Beach, Calif., 1970-78; city councilwoman Lakewood, Calif., 1972-76; judge Long Beach Mcpl. Ct., 1978-80, L.A. Superior Ct., 1980-98; ret., 1998. Supervising judge, 1986; del. Calif. State Dem. Cen. Com., 1975, Calif. State Conv., 1975; mem. Com. on Gender Bias in Calif. Courts, 1986-89 Advisor Jr. League, 1980-85; mem. early childhood adv. bd. Long Beach City Coll.; bd. dirs. Long Beach Alcoholism Coun., 1979-80, Boys and Girls Club Am., 1981-89, Long Beach Symphony, 1985, Jewish Community Fedn., 1982-86, past mem. community rels. com.; active Nat. Women's Polit. Caucus, LWV. Named Woman of Yr., NOW, Long Beach, 1984; recipient Torch of Liberty award, B'nai B'rith Anti-Defamation League, 1974; honoree, Nat. Conf. Christians and Jews, 1986. Mem. ABA, AAUW, Nat. Assn. Women Judges (dist. supr. 1986), Calif. Bar Assn. (judges div.), Calif. Judges Assn. (mem. ann. seminar com. 1981-89), Mcpl. Cts. Judges Assn. (mem. Marshall com. 1979-80), L.A. County Bar Assn. (judges div., mem. arbitration com.), Women Lawyers Assn., L.A. (judges sect.), Women Lawyers Assn. Long Beach, Long Beach Legal Aid Found. (v.p. 1976-78), Long Beach Bar Assn. (active various coms., bd. govs. 1977-78, Judge of Yr. 1987), Long Beach C. of C. (bd. dirs.). Avocations: swimming, golf, jogging, classical music, movies.

**POLACCO, PATRICIA,** writer, illustrator; Works include: Meteor!, 1987, Rechenka's Eggs, 1988, The Keeping Quilt, 1988, Uncle Vova's Tree, 1989, Boatride with Lillian Two-Blossom, 1989, Thunder Cake, 1990, Just Plain Fancy, 1990, Babushka's Doll, 1990, Some Birthday!, 1991, Appelemando's Dreams, 1991, Picnic at Mudsock Meadow, 1992, Mrs. Katz & Tush, 1992, Chicken Sunday, 1992, The Bee Tree, 1993, Babushka Baba Yaga, 1993, Tikvah Means Hope, 1994, Pink & Say, 1994, My Rotten Readheaded, Older Brother, 1994, Firetalking, 1994, My Ol' Man, 1995, Babushka's Mother Goose, 1995, Aunt Chip and the Great Triple Creek Dam Affair, 1995, I Can Hear the Sun: A Modern Myth, 1996, In Enzo's Splendid Gardens, 1997, Mrs. MacK, 1998, Luba and the Wren, 1999, The Butterfly, 2000, Mommies Say Shhh!, 2005; illustrator: Casey at the Bat, 1992. Office: Penguin Putnam Inc 345 Hudson St Fl 15 New York NY 10014-4502

**POLAK, ELIJAH,** engineering educator, computer scientist; b. Bialystok, Poland, Aug. 11, 1931; came to US, 1958, naturalized, 1977; s. Isaac and Fruma (Friedman) P.; m. Virginia Ann Gray, June 11, 1961; children: Oren, Sharon. BSEE, U. Melbourne, Australia, 1957; MSEE, U. Calif., Berkeley, 1959, PhD in Elec. Engring., 1961. Instrument engr. ICIANZ, Melbourne, Australia, 1956-57; summer student IBM Rsch. Labs., San Jose, Calif., 1959-60; vis. asst. prof. MIT, fall 1964; assoc. dept. elec. engring. and computer scis. U. Calif., Berkeley, 1958-61, asst. prof. elec. engring. and computer scis., 1961-66, assoc. prof., 1966-69, prof., 1969-94, prof. grad. Sch., 1994—. Author: (with L.A. Zadeh) System Theory, 1969, (with E. Wong) Notes for a First Course on Linear Systems, 1970, (with others) Theory of Optimal Control and Mathematical Programming, 1970, Computational Methods in Optimization, 1971, Optimization: Algorithms and Consistent Approximations, 1997. Guggenheim Fellow, 1968; UK Sci. Rsch. Coun. Sr. fellow, 1972, 76, 79, 82 Fellow IEEE; mem. Soc. Indsl. and Applied Math. (assoc. editor Jour. Theory and Applications Optimization 1972—), Soc. Math. Programming. Jewish. Avocation: cross country skiing. Home: 38 Fairlawn Dr Berkeley CA 94708-2106 Office: U Calif Dept Elec Engring Cp S Berkeley CA 94720-0001 Office Phone: 510-642-2644. Business E-Mail: polak@eecs.berkeley.edu.

**POLAK, EMIL JOSEPH,** history professor, researcher; b. Bay Shore, NY, Aug. 16, 1936; s. Emil Frank and Mary Rose (Comitsky) Polak; m. Patricia Faith Leuzzi, Aug. 3, 1968. AB cum laude, U. Albany, 1957; AM, Columbia U., 1958, PhD, 1970. Lectr. Bklyn. Coll., 1961—65; instr. St. John's U., Jamaica, NY, 1965—66; lectr. S.I. C.C., 1966—67; instr. CCNY, 1967—70; asst. prof. Queensborough C.C., Bayside, NY, 1970—76, assoc. prof., 1977—81, prof., 1982—. Author: A Textual Study of Jacques de Dinant's Summa dictaminis, 1975, Medieval and Renaissance Letter Treatises and Form Letters: A Census of Manuscripts Found in Eastern Europe and the Former U.S.S.R., 1993, Medieval and Renaissance Letter Treatises and Form Letters: A Census of Manuscripts Found in Part of Western Europe, Japan and the United States of America, 1994; editor: A Medievalist's Odyssey: Helene Wieruzowski Scholar, 2004. Recipient Performance Excellence award, Queensborough C.C., 2000; fellow, Am. Acad. Rome, 1963, CUNY Rsch. Found., 1977—2006, Internat. Rsch. Exchanges Bd., 1978, 1981, 1996; grantee, Am. Coun. Learned Socs./USSR Acad. Scis., 1981, Gladys Krieble Delmas Found., 1995, NEH, 1997, Renaissance Soc. Am., 2000; Excellence in Faculty scholar, Queensborough C.C., 2002. Mem.: L.I. Maritime Mus., Internat. Soc. Classical Tradition, Medieval Latin Studies Group, Medieval Club N.Y., Am. Assn. Neo-Latin Studies, Early Book Soc., Internat. Assn. Neo-Latin Studies, Soc. Fellows Am. Acad. Rome, Am. Soc. History of Rhetoric, Internat. Soc. History of Rhetoric, Am. Hist. Assn., Medieval Acad. Am., Renaissance Soc. Am., Am. Phil. Assn., Bohemia Hist. Soc., Bayport Heritage Assn., Sayville Hist. Soc., Columbia U. Grad. Sch. Arts and Scis. Alumni Assn., U. Albany Alumni Assn., Pi Gamma Mu, Kappa Phi Kappa. Avocations: travel, theater, films. Office: Queensborough CC Dept History 222-05 56 Ave Oakland Gardens NY 11364-1497 Office Phone: 718-631-6291. Office Fax: 718-631-6372.

**POLAK, JONATHAN G.,** lawyer; b. Phila., Pa., Dec. 8, 1968; s. Joseph John Jr. and Doris Evelyn Polak; m. Rebecca C. Polak, Aug. 19, 1995; children: Elizabeth, Caroline, Andrew. BS, So. Meth. U., Dallas, 1991, JD, 1994. Assoc. Arter & Hadden, LLP, Dallas, 1994—96, Calhoun & Stacy, PC, Dallas, 1996—99; ptnr. Dann Pezar Newman & Kleiner, PC, Indpls., 2000—06, Sommer Barnard, PC, Indpls., 2006—. Chmn. bd. dirs. N Power Ind., Inc., Indpls., 2003—. Mem.: 7th Cir Bar Assn. Office: Sommer Barnard PC 1 Indiana Sq Ste 3500 Indianapolis IN 46204

**POLAKIEWICZ, LEONARD ANTHONY,** foreign language and literature educator; b. Kiev, Ukraine, Mar. 30, 1938; came to the U.S., 1950; s. Wladyslaw and Aniela (Ossowska) P.; m. Marianne Helen Swanson, Sept. 7, 1963; children: Barbara, Kathryn, Janet. BS in Russian with distinction, U. Minn., 1964, BA in Internat. Rels., 1964; MA in Russian, U. Wis., 1968; cert. Russian area studies, 1969; PhD in Slavic Langs./Lit., U. Wis., 1978; diploma in Polish Curriculum and Instrn., Curie-Sklodowska U., Lublin, Poland, 1981. Instr. U. Minn., Mpls., 1970-78, 1978-90, assoc. prof., 1990—, Morse Alumni disting. teaching assoc. prof. Slavic langs. and literatures, dir. Inst. Langs., 1991-93, chair Slavic dept., 1993—97, 1999—2000, 2006—. Vis. asst. prof. U. London, 1984; dir. U. Minn. Polish Lang. Program, Curie-Sklodowska U., Lublin, Poland, summers 1984-89, dir. Russian Faculty Exch., Herzen Pedagogical U., St. Petersburg, Russia, 1993—; mem. selection com. Fulbright Tchr. Exch. Program, USIA, 1989, Title VI Dept. Edn., 1990, NEH Tchr.- Scholar Program, 1994; reviewer divn. ednl. programs NEH, 1990, translation program, 1993, 94; mem. rev. bd. Ctr. Applied Linguistics Polish Proficiency Test, 1990; mem. exec. com. Coun. on Internat. Edn., N.Y.C., 1991-94; mem. Russian Lang. Program Acad. Policy Com. CIEE, N.Y.C., 1994-2002; mem. nat. task force Polish Studies in Am., Ind. U., 1995-96; project dir. Nat. Coun. Orgns. of Less Commonly Taught Langs. Polish Lang. Learning Framework, 1995-2001; Polish examiner Yale U. Ctr. Lang. Study, 2006—; dir. U. Minn. Curie Sklodowska U. Faculty Exch., 1988—, U. Minn. Cath. U. of Lublin Faculty Exch., 1995-2001; coord. Def. Lang. Inst. Polish Proficiency Testing, 1998; apptd. adv. bd. Am. U. Poland, 2004—; mem. nat. screening com. Fulbright-Hays Program, US Dept. State, 2006. Author: Supplemental Materials for First Year Polish, 1991, Supplemental Materials for Fifteen Modern Polish Short Stories, 1994, Directory of US Institutions of Higher Education and Faculty Offering Instruction in Polish Language, Literature and Culture, 1996-97, Intermediate Polish: A Cultural Reader with Exercises, 1999, (with Joanna Radwanska Williams and Waldemar Walczynski) Polish Language Learning Framework, 2002; assoc. editor Slavic and East European Jour., 1988-94; mem. editl. bd. The Learning and Tchg. of Slavic Langs. and Cultures: Toward the 21st Century, 1996-2000; reviewer Choice Mag., Modern Lang. Jour., Canadian Slavonic Papers, Slavic and East European Jour., Soviet and Post-Soviet Rev. Bd. dirs. Immigration Hist. Rsch. Ctr., Mpls., 1984-89, Am. Univ. in Poland, 2004—; co-founder Polish-Am.

Cultural Inst., Mpls., 1986; vice-chair Polish Am. Congress' Commn. Edn., 1987; mem. gov.'s Commn. on Ea. Europe, St. Paul, 1991. With U.S. Army, 1961-63. Ford Found. fellow, 1964-65, NDEA fellow, Title IV, 1966-68; grantee Kościuszko Found., 1981, Coun. for European Studies grantee Columbia U., 1981, 84, 86, Rsch. Assoc. grantee Russian and East European Ctr., U. Ill., 1982, 83, 84, Wasie Found. grantee, 1983, IREX Collaborative Activities and New Exchs. grantee, 1984, Ireland Travel grantee Trinity Coll., Dublin, 1984, Bush Found. Rsch. grantee, 1986-87, grantee U.S. Dept. Edn., 1988-91; Fulbright-Hays Group Projects Abroad grantee for Poland, 1989, USIA U. Linkage grantee for Poland, 1989-93, IREX Short Term Travel grantee, 1995, USIA Coll. and Univ. Affiliations grantee for Poland, 1995-2000; recipient Polanie Club of the Twin Cities Merit award, 1982, Curie-Sklodowska U. medal for acad. linkage devel., 1992, Cavalier's Cross of Order of Merit of Republic of Poland, 1999, Disting Svc. award Herzen Pedagogical U., St. Petersburg, Russia, 2002, Pres.'s Outstanding Svc. award, 2003, A. Ronald Walton award Nat. Coun. Less Commonly Taught Langs., 2006. Mem. AAUP, Am. Assn. for the Advancement Slavic Studies, Am. Assn. Tchrs. Slavic and East European Langs. and Lits. (com. on testing and profl. devel. 1997—, Excellence in Tchg. in U.S. award 1994), Internat. Czeslaw Milosz Soc. (pres. 1984-85), N.Am. Chekhov Soc., Am. Coun. Tchrs. of Russian, Polish Inst. Arts & Scis. Am. (N.Y.C., Waclaw Lednicki Humanities award com. 1996), Assn. Literary Scholars & Critics, Soc. of Lovers of the Russian Book, Irish Assn. of Russian and East European Studies, Polish Tchrs. Assn. of Am., Polish Studies Assn. (mem. biannual prize jury 1998), Bristol Group Internat. Assn. Tchrs. Polish, U. Minn. Acad. Disting. Tchrs., The Australia and New Zealand Slavists' Assn. Roman Catholic. Avocations: reading, philatelics, genealogy, touring, gardening. Home: 466 Oak Creek Dr S Vadnais Heights MN 55127-7008 Office Phone: 612-625-1384. Business E-Mail: polak001@tc.umn.edu.

**POLAKOFF, ABE,** baritone; b. Bucharest, Rumania; s. Sam and Mary P. Ousherenkova; children: David Fred, Mark Evan, Robert Ira; m. Judyth Kanner, Dec. 5, 1992. Civil engring. student, CCNY; profl. tng. program, Am. Theater Wing, 1952-54; student, N.Y. Coll. Music, 1955-57. Dir. Island Opera Players; opera recital. Arts Couns. (municipalities and schs.); cantor Progressive Shaari Zedek synagogue, Bklyn., 1972-77, Temple Emanuel, Denver, 1984-94. Debuts include Marcello in La Boheme, Milan, Florence, 1960; leading baritone Zurich Opera, 1961-63, numerous appearances with N.Y. Met. Opera, City Opera N.Y., Phila. Lyric Opera, Pitts. Opera, Seattle Opera, Berlin Deutsche Opera, Frankfurt Opera, Cinn. Opera, Hamburg, Munich Staatsoper, Stuttgart Staatsoper, The Netherlands Opera, Cin. Opera, Kansas City Lyric Opera, Canadian Opera Co., others; soloist with Mex. State Symphony Orch., Kalamazoo Symphony Orch., Winston-Salem (N.C.) Symphony, numerous concert and recital appearances Sgt. U.S. Army, 1943-46. 1st prize winner Am. Theatre Wing Vocal Profl. Scholarship award, 1954, 1st prize winner Am. Opera Auditions, 1960, Silver medal Vercelli (Italy) Internat. singing contest, 1960; Rockefeller Found. grantee, 1961-62; Bayreuth Festival Masterclass scholar. Mem. Cen. Opera Service, Am. Guild Musical Artists, Actors Equity Assn. Address: 11132 76th Ave Apt 7H Forest Hills NY 11375-6409 E-mail: judyth@nvbb.net.

**POLAMALU, TROY,** professional football player; b. Garden Grove, Calif., Apr. 19, 1981; Grad., U. So. Calif., 2003. Safety Pitts. Steelers, 2003—. Named to NFL Pro-Bowl Team, 2004, 2005, NFL All-Pro Team, 2005. Office: c/o Pittsburgh Steelers 3400 S Water St Pittsburgh PA 15203*

**POLAN, MARY LAKE,** obstetrics and gynecology educator; b. Las Vegas, N.Mex., July 17, 1943; Student, Smith Coll., Paris, 1963—64; BA cum laude, Conn. Coll., 1965; PhD in Biophysics and Biochemistry, Yale U., 1970, MD, 1975. Diplomate Am. Bd. Ob-Gyn., Am. Bd. Reproductive Endocrinology, Nat. Bd. Med. Examiners. Postdoctoral fellow dept. biology, NIH postdoctoral fellow Yale U., New Haven, 1970—72, resident dept. ob-gyn. Sch. Medicine, 1975—78, fellow in oncology, then fellow in endocrinology-infertility, 1978—80, asst. instr., then lectr. molecular biophysics-biochemistry, 1970—72, instr., then asst. prof. ob-gyn., 1978—79, 1980—85, assoc. prof., 1985—90; clin. clk. in ob-gyn. and pediat. Radcliffe Infirmary, Oxford (Eng.) U. Med. Sch., 1974; instr. Pahlavi U., Shiraz, Iran, 1978; Katharine Dexter McCormick and Stanley McCormick Meml. prof. Stanford (Calif.) Sch. Medicine, 1990—, chmn. dept. gynecology and obstetrics, 1990—. Vis. prof. Hunan Med. Coll., Changsha, China, 1986; mem. med. bd. Yale-China Assn., 1987—90; liaison com. on ethics in modern world Conn. Coll., New London, 1988—90; mem. med. adv. bd. Ova-Med Corp., Palo Alto, Calif., 1992—95, Vivus, Menlo Park, Calif., 1993—; bd. dirs. Metra Biosys., Mountain View, Quidel, San Diego, Am. Home Products, Madison, NJ, 1994—; mem. reproductive endocrinology study sect. NIH, 1989—90, co-chmn. task force on opportunities for rsch. on woman's health, 1991. Author: Second Seed, 1987; guest editor: Seminars in Reproductive Endocrinology, 1984, Infertility and Reproductive Medicine Clinics of North America: GnRH Analogues, Vol. 4, 1993; editor: with DeCherney: Surgery in Reproductive Endocrinology, 1987:; editor: (with DeCherney, S. Boyers and R. Lee) Decision Making in Infertility; ad hoc reviewer: Jour. Clin. Endocrinology and Metabolism, Fertility and Sterility, Ob-Gyn., others; contbr. chapters to books, articles to med. jours. Fellow, NSRA, 1981—82; grantee, NIRA, 1982—85, HD, 1985—90, NRSA, 1987—88, Johnson & Johnson, 1993—96; scholar, Assn. Acad. Health Ctrs., 1993—96. Fellow: ACOG (PROLOG task force for reproductive endocrinology and infertility 1988—89, rep. to CREOG coun. 1994—97); mem.: Bay Area Reproductive Endocrine Soc., San Francisco Gynecologic Soc., Inst. Medicine (com. on rsch. capabilities of acad. depts. ob-gyn. 1990—91, bd. on health scis. policy 1992—96), Am. Gynecological and Obstetric Soc., Soc. for Reproductive Endocrinologists, Soc. for Gynecologic Investigation, Am. Fertility Soc., Phi Beta Kappa. Home: 4251 Manuela Ct Palo Alto CA 94306-3731 Office: Stanford U Sch Medicine Dept Gyn OB 300 Pasteur Dr Stanford CA 94305-5317

**POLANCO, KATIUSCA,** lawyer; d. Jose Polanco and Seneida Ovalles; 1 child, Nadhya Amaris Polanco Ray. BA with honors, Rutgers U., 1997, JD, 2003. Bar: (N.J.) 2003, US Dist. Ct. for the Dist. of N.J. 2003, cert.: Legal Svcs. of N.J. (legal advocate) 1999. Fellow- dept. of edn. Ctr. for Hispanic Policy R & D, Trenton, NJ, 1995; surveyor Eagleton Inst. of Politics, Rutgers U., New Brunswick, 1996; tutor Writing Ctr., Rutgers U., New Brunswick, NJ, 1996—97; family support specialist N.J. Assn. for Retarded Citizens, North Brunswick, NJ, 1996—97; bilingual paralegal Legal Svcs. of N.J., Edison, NJ, 1997; legal adv. Middlesex County Legal Svcs., New Brunswick, NJ, 1997—2003; law clk. to the hon. Mathias E. Rodriguez, J.S.C. State of New Jersey-Judiciary, New Brunswick, NJ, 2003—04; dep. atty. gen. Dept. of Law and Pub. Safety, Trenton, NJ, 2004—05; staff atty. Ctrl. Jersey Legal Svcs., New Brunswick, NJ, 2006—. Assoc. editor Rutgers Law Record, Newark, 2001—02; evening law student rep. Assn. for Latin Am. Law Students, Newark, 2000—02; rsch. asst. Rutgers Sch. of Law-Newark, 2002—03. English instr. Our Lady of Mt. Carmel Ch., New Brunswick, NJ, 1997—98; hurricane relief vol. Religious Organ., Merida, Yucatan, Mexico, 1995; mentor Project R.I.S.E.-Rutgers U., New Brunswick, NJ, 1994; pres. Latin Am. Women's Organ., New Brunswick, 1995—96; vol. Prevention Using Student Help (P.U.S.H.), Somerset, NJ, 1990—91. Fellow Pub. Policy Leadership Inst. fellow, Ctr. for Strategic Urban Cmty. Leadership-Rutgers U., 1995; grantee law sch. grantee, Middlesex County Bar Assn., 2001; scholar scholar, Nat. Assn. of Water Co., 2001, Austin Scott scholar, 2000, Jacobs Seymour Meml., 2000, Middlesex County Bar Assn., 2001. Mem.: Middlesex County Bar Assn., N.J. Hispanic Bar Assn. (moderator 2005), N.J. State Bar Assn., Delta Sigma Pi (hon.), Phi Sigma Iota (hon.). Avocations: running, creative crafts, hiking, travel. Office: Central Jersey Legal Services Inc 317 George St Ste 201 New Brunswick NJ 08901 Office Phone: 732-249-7600. Personal E-mail: katiamaris@yahoo.com. E-mail: kpolanco@lsnj.org.

**POLANSKI, ROMAN,** film director, writer, actor; b. Paris, Aug. 18, 1933; s. Ryszard and Bule (Katz-Przedborska) P.; m. Barbara Lass (div.); m. Sharon Tate (dec.); m. Emmanuelle Seigner. Student, Art Sch., Cracow, State Film Coll., Lodz. Appeared in (children's radio show) The Merry Gang, (stage

prodn.) Son of the Regiment; dir.: (films) Two Men and a Wardrobe, 1958, When Angels Fall, 1958, Le Gros et le Maigre, 1960, Knife in the Water, 1962 (Venice Film Festival award), The Mammals, 1963 (Tours Film Festival award), Repulsion, 1965 (Berlin Film Festival award), Cul-de-Sac, 1966 (Berlin Film Festival award), The Vampire Killers, 1967, Rosemary's Baby, 1968, Macbeth, 1971, What?, 1972, Chinatown, 1974 (best Dir. award Soc. Film and TV Arts, Priz Raoul-Levy, 1975), The Tenant, 1976, Tess, 1980 (Cesar award), Pirates, 1986; dir., co-writer (films) Frantic, 1988; dir.: (films) Bitter Moon, 1994, Death and the Maiden, 1994, The Ninth Gate, 1999, The Pianist, 2002 (Best Dir. Acad. award, 2003, Best Film, British Acad. Film Award (BAFTA), 2003, The David Lean Award for Achievement in Direction, 2003, 2003), Oliver Twist, 2005; actor: (on stage) The Metamorphosis, 1988; (films) A Generation, The End of the Night, See You Tomorrow, The Innocent Sorcerers, Two Men and a Wardrobe, The Vampire Killers, What?, The Magic Christian and Andy Warhol's Death, Back in the U.S.S.R., A Pure Formality, Chinatown, The Tennant; actor, dir.: (plays) Amadeus; Warsaw, 1981; Paris, 1982; Amadeus/Italy, 1999; dir.: (Operas) Lulu, 1974, Rigoletto, 1976; (Operas, musical comedy) Tales of Hoffman, Master Class, 1996—97; (Operas) Tanz der Vampire, 1997, 2000; author: (autobiography) Roman, 1984. Office: ICM 8942 Wilshire Blvd Beverly Hills CA 90211-1934

**POLANSKY, ANDY,** public relations executive; Pres. Weber Shandwick Worldwide; reporter Bucks County Courier Times, Levittown, Pa.; writer Princeton Packet, Princeton, NJ; sports writer The Trentonian, Trenton, NJ. Office: Weber Shandwick PR Worldwide 640 Fifth Ave New York NY 10019 Business E-Mail: apolansky@webershandwick.com.

**POLANSKY, LARRY PAUL,** legal association administrator; b. Bklyn., July 24, 1932; s. Harry and Ida (Gershgom) P.; m. Eunice Kathryn Neun; children: Steven, Harriet, Bruce. BS in Acctg., Temple U., 1958, JD, 1973. Bar: Pa. 1973, U.S. Dist. Ct. (ea. dist.) Pa. 1973, U.S. Ct. Appeals (3d cir.) 1973, D.C. 1978, U.S. Supreme Ct. 1980. Acct., systems analyst City of Phila., 1956-63; data processing mgr. Jefferson Med. Coll. and Hosp., Phila., 1963-65; systems engr. IBM Corp., Phila., 1965-67; dep. ct. adminstr. Common Pleas Cts. of Phila., 1967-76; dep. state ct. adminstr. Pa. Supreme Ct., Phila., 1976-78; exec. officer D.C. Cts., Washington, 1979-90. Presdl. appt. to bd. dirs. State Justice Inst., 1985-89; bd. dirs. Search Group, Inc. Author: A Primer for the Technologically Challenged Judge, 1995; contbr. articles to profl. jours. Served as cpl. U.S. Army, 1951-53, Korea. Fellow Inst. for Ct. Mgmt., Denver, 1984; recipient Reardon award Nat. Ctr. for State Cts., 1982, Disting. Svc. award Nat. Ctr. for State Cts., 1986, Justice Tom C. Clark award Nat. Conf. of Metro. Cts., 1991, award of merit Nat. Ct. Mgmt., 1996. Mem. ABA (jud. adminstrn. divsn., chmn. com. 1991-93, 95, exec. com. lawyers conf. 1985-98, chmn. 1991-92, JAD coun. 1994-97), Conf. State Ct. Adminstrn. (bd. dirs. 1980-86, pres. 1984-85). Republican. Jewish. Avocations: tennis, skiing, computers, golf. Home and Office: PO Box 752 Lake Harmony PA 18624-0752 Office Phone: 570-722-9288. E-mail: polanskyl@aol.com.

**POLANYI, JOHN CHARLES,** chemist, educator; b. Berlin, Jan. 23, 1929; s. Michael and Magda Elizabeth (Kemeny) Polanyi; m. Anne Ferrar Davidson, 1958; 2 children. BSc, Manchester U., Eng., 1949, MSc, 1950, PhD, 1952, DSc, 1964; DSc (hon.), U. Waterloo, 1970, Meml. U., 1976, McMaster U., 1977, Carleton U., 1981, Harvard U., 1982, Rensselaer U., Brock U., 1984, Lethbridge U., Sherbrooke U., Laval U., Victoria U., Ottawa U., 1987, Manchester U. and York U., Eng., 1988, U. Montreal, Acadia U., 1989, Weizmann Inst., Israel, 1989, U. Bari, Italy, 1990, U. B.C., 1990, McGill U., 1990, Queen's U., 1992, Free U. Berlin, 1993, Laurentian U., 1995, U. Toronto, 1995, U. Liverpool, 1995; LLD (hon.), Trent U., 1977, Dalhousie U., 1983, St. Francis-Xavier U., 1984, Concordia U., 1990, Calgary U., 1994. Mem. faculty dept. chemistry U. Toronto, Ont., Canada, 1956—, prof. 1962—. William D. Harkins lectr. U. Chgo., 1970; Reilly lectr. U. Notre Dame, 1970; Purve lectr. McGill U., 1971; F.J. Toole lectr. U. N.B., 1974; Philips lectr. Haverford Coll., 1974; Kistiakowsky lectr. Harvard U., 1975; Camille and Henry Dreyfus lectr. U. Kans., 1975; J.W.T. Spinks lectr. U. Sask., Canada, 1976; Laird lectr. U. We. Ont., 1976; CIL Disting. lectr. Simon Fraser U., 1977; Gucker lectr. Ind. U., 1977; Jacob Bronowski Meml. lectr. U. Toronto, 1978; Hutchinson lectr. U. Rochester (N.Y.) U., 1979; Priestley lectr. Pa. State U., 1980; Barré lectr. U. Montreal, 1982; Sherman Fairchild disting. scholar Calif. Inst. Tech., 1982; Chute lectr. Dalhousie U., 1983; Redman lectr. McMaster U., 1983; Wiegand lectr. U. Toronto, 1984; Edward U. Condon lectr. U. Colo., 1984; John A. Allan lectr. U. Alta., 1984; John E. Willard lectr. U. Wis., 1984; Owen Holmes lectr. U. Lethbridge, 1985; Walker-Ames prof. U. Wash., 1986; John W. Cowper disting. vis. lectr. SUNY, Buffalo, 1986; vis. prof. chemistry Tex. A&M U., 1986; Disting. vis. spkr. U. Calgary, 1987; Morino lectr. U. Japan, 1987; J.T. Wilson lectr. Ont. Scil. Ctr., 1987; Welsh lectr. U. toronto, 1987; Spiers Meml. lectr. Faraday divsn. Royal Soc. Chemistry, 1987; Polanyi lectr. Internat. Union Pure and Applied Chemistry, 1988; W.B. Lewis lectr. Atomic Energy of Can. Ltd., 1988; Consol. Bathurst vis. lectr. Concordia U., 1988; Priestman lectr. U. N.B., 1988; Killam lectr. U. Windsor, 1988; Herzberg lectr. Carleton U., 1988; Falconbridge lectr. Lauretian U., 1988; DuPont lectr. Ind. U., 1989; Luther lectr. U. Regina, 1989; Franklin lectr. Rice U., 1990; Laurier lectr. Wilfred Laurier U., 1990; Pratt lectr. U. Va., 1990; Goodrich lectr. Case Western Reserve U., 1990; Phillips lectr. U. Pitts., 1991; Albert Noyes lectr. U. Tex., 1992; John and Lois Dove Meml. lectr. U. Toronto, 1992; Fritz London lectr. Duke U., 1993; Castle lectr. U. South Fla., 1993; Linus Pauling lectr. Calif. Inst. Tech., 1994; Hagey lectr. U. Waterloo, 1995; Larkin Stuart lectr. U. Toronto, 1995; Hungerford lectr. York Club, 1995; disting. lectr. ser Meml. U., 1995; John C. Polanyi Nobel Laureate lectr. U. Toronto, 1995; Floyd E. Bartell Meml. lectr. U. Mich., 1996; Christian Culture award lectr. Assumption U., 1996; Liversidge lectr. U. Sydney, 1996; disting. scientist lectr. Apotex, Inc., 1996; mem. sci. adv. bd. Max Planck Inst. Quantum Optics, Germany, 1982—92; mem. nat. adv. bd. on Sci. and Tech., 1987—89; hon. cons. Inst. Molecular Sci., Okazaki, Japan, 1989—94; bd. dirs. Steacie Inst. Molecular Scis., Ottawa, Ont.; founding mem., pres. Can. Com. of Sci. and Scholars; Beam Disting. vis. prof. U. Iowa, 1992; Charles M. and Martha Hitchcock prof. U. Calif., Berkeley, 1994; Young Meml. visitor Royal Mil. Coll., 1994; mem. Bd. of Premier's Coun., 1994; co-chair Internat. Consultative Group on Improving UN Rapid Reaction Capability. Editor (with F.G. Griffiths): The Dangers of Nuclear War, 1979; contbr. articles to jours., mags., newspapers; prodr. (film) Concepts in Reaction Dynamics, 1970. Mem. Queen's Privy Coun. for Can., 1992; founding mem. Can. Pugwash Com., 1960; Can. Ctr. for Arms Control and Disarmament. Decorated Officer Order of Can., Companion, knight Grand Cross Order St. John of Jerusalem; co-recipient (with N. Bartlett) Steacie prize, 1965, Wolf prize in chemistry, Wolf Found., 1982; recipient Marlow medal, Faraday Soc., 1962, Centenary medal, Chem. Soc. Gt. Brit., 1965, Norandaaward, Chem. Inst. Can., 1967, award, Brit. Chem. Soc., 1971, Mack award and lectureship, Ohio State U., 1969, medal, Chem. Inst. Can., 1976, Remsen award and lectureship, Am. Chem. Soc., 1978, Nobel prize in Chemistry, 1986, Izaak Walton Killam Meml. prize, 1988, C. Polanyi award, Can. State Chemistry, 1992, Floyd E. Bartell Meml. lectureship, U. Mich., 1996, Liversidge lectureship, U. Sydney, 1996, Christian Culture award and lectureship, Assumption U., 1996; fellow Sloan Found., 1959—63, Guggenheim, 1979—80, Geoffrey Frew, 1996, Disting. Anniversary, Australian Nat. U., 1996. Fellow: Royal Soc. Chemisry (Michael Polanyi medal 1989), Royal Soc. Edinburgh, Royal Soc. Can. (founding mem., pres., com. on scholarly freedom, Marshall Tory medal 1977), Trinity Coll., U. Toronto (hon.), Royal Soc. London (Royal medal 1989, Bakerian lectureship and award 1994), Chem. Inst. Can. (hon.); mem.: NAS (fgn. mem.), Croation Acad. Scis. and Arts, Russian Acad. Scis. (foreign mem.), Pontifical Acad. Scis. (Rome), Am. Acad. Arts and Scis. (mem. com. on internat. security studies, hon. fgn.). Office: U Toronto Dept Chemistry Rm 262 80 St George St Toronto ON Canada M5S 3H6*

**POLASCIK, MARY ANN,** ophthalmologist; b. Elkhorn, W.Va., Dec. 28, 1940; d. Michael and Elizabeth (Halko) Polascik; m. Joseph Elie, Oct. 2, 1973; 1 dau., Laura Elizabeth Polascik Jr. BA, Rutgers U., 1967; MD, Pritzker Sch. Medicine, 1971. Jr. pharmacologist Ciba Pharm Co., Summit, NJ, 1961-67; intern Billings Hosp., Chgo., 1971-72; resident in ophthalmol-

ogy U. Chgo. Hosp., 1972-75; practice medicine specializing in ophthalmology Dixon, Ill., 1975—. Pres. McNichols Clinic, Ltd.; cons. ophthalmology, Jack Mabley Devel. Ctr., 1976-93; mem. staff Katherine Shaw Bethea Hosp. Bd. dirs. Sinnossippi Mental Health Ctr., 1977-82, Dixon Cmty. Trust Mental Health Ctr., 1989—. Mem. Am. Acad. Ophthalmology, Alpha Sigma Lambda, Galena Territory Club. Roman Catholic. Office: 1700 S Galena Ave Dixon IL 61021-9695

**POLASEK, EDWARD JOHN,** retired electrical engineer, consultant; b. Cudahy, Wis., Oct. 12, 1927; s. John Vincent and Mary Ann (Totka) P.; m. Alice S. Nee (Harnecki), Aug. 18, 1948. BSEE, Marquette U., 1948. Registered profl. engr., Wis., Fla. Cons. engr. Eau Claire, Wis., Gainesville, Fla., 1955-60, various countries, Korea, Vietnam, Nicaragua, 1960-72; v.p., dir. Finley Engring. Co., Eau Claire, 1972-78; pres. Chippewa Devel. Co., Eau Claire, 1978-82; planning engr. Harza Engring. Co. in Cairo, Egypt and Dominican Rep., 1982-86; cons. engr. Gainesville, 1986-99; ret. Cons. Lake Altoona Rehab. Dist., Eau Claire, 1974. Author: Planning Methods, 1982, Feasibility Study, 1984; editor: Field Engineer's Handbook, 1982. Chmn. Eau Claire chpt. Am. Cancer Soc.; master gardner U. Fla. Ext. Svc., Gainesville, 1990. With USN, 1944-46, PTO. Mem. Nat. Soc. Profl. Engrs. (pres. 1956), IEEE, Audobon Soc., Tau Beta Pi, Eta Kappa Nu. Avocations: mycology, fishing, art. Address: 3532 Hwy 51 N Woodruff WI 54568 E-mail: polasek@gru.net.

**POLASKI, THOMAS BRIAN,** social studies educator, department chairman; b. Beloit, Wis., Oct. 17, 1958; s. Terry R. and Margaret M. Polaski; m. Sherry L. Polaski, June 23, 1990; children: Kristin Beadle, Tracy Follis, Weston. BA in History, Western Ill. U., Macomb, 1976—80; MA in History, No. Ill. U., DeKalb, 1982—85. Social studies tchr./coach Hononegah HS, Rockton, Ill., 1980—. Author: (historical article) Black History of Beloit, Wisconsin. Treas. Rockton Sun. Christ., 1997—2003; v.p./sec. HOPE Found., Rockton, Ill., 2000. Recipient Quest for Excellence in Edn., Ecolab, 1996, 2005, NIC-9 Coach of Yr. - Boys Track, NIC-9 Conf., 1994, 1997, 2002, 2003, Tchr. of Yr., Hononegah HS, 1992, 1994, 1999, 3M Economics in Edn. Excellence award in Ill., Ill. Coun. Econ. Edn., 2002, Semi-finalist, Golden Apple Found., 2005. Mem.: Wis. State Track Coaches Assn., Ill. Coun. Econ. Edn., Nat. Coun. for Social Studies. Home: 121 E Mechanic St Rockton IL 61072 Office: Hononegah HS 307 Salem St Rockton IL 61072 Office Phone: 815-624-2070. Business E-Mail: tpolas@hononegah.org.

**POLATTY, ROSE JACKSON,** civic worker; b. Atlanta, Sept. 17, 1922; d. James Wilmot and Esther Ann (Sweeny) Jackson; m. George Junius Polatty,Nov. 27, 1942; children: George Junius, Robert Wilmot, Rose Crystal, Richard James. AB in Journalism, U. Ga., 1943; postgrad., Oglethorpe U., 1962-63, Ga. State U., 1963. Active U. Ga. Alumni Soc.; pres. Class of 1943 Alumni, 1948-58; bd. mgr., 1966-69; v.p., 1971-73; chmn. seminar, 1971; exec. sec. Atlanta Boy Choir, 1968-69; bd. dirs. Atlanta Arts Coun., 1968-69; adv. com. Kennesaw Coll. on Wheels, 1974-78; bicentennial chmn. City of Roswell (Ga.), 1975-76; sec. hist. preservation commn., 1978-82; chmn., 1983-84. Active Ga. Trust Hist. Preservation, Ga. Conservancy. Mem. adminstrv. bd., chmn. altar guild, Roswell United Meth. Ch., 1977-89. Recipient Recognition award Nat. 4-H Alumni, 1959, Svc. award City of Roswell, 1970, Cmty. Svc. award Roswell Optimist Club, 1977, Roswell Jaycees Leadership award, 1977, Cmty. Svc. award Zion Bapt. Ch., 1977, Vol. award Friends Roswell Libr., 2000. Mem. Roswell Hist. Soc. (charter 1971), Atlanta Symphony Assocs., Colonial Dames XVII Century (charter Nicholas Wallingford chpt. 1979, v.p. 1980-81, pres. 1982-83), U.D.C. (Phillips Legion chpt.), Altanta Audubon Soc., High Mus. Art (charter), PEO (chpt. AA, Ga., charter 1977), DAR (Joseph Habersham chpt.), Roswell Women's (charter 1948, pres. 1966-68), Roswell Garden (charter 1951, pres. 1975-77), N. Fulton Coun. Garden Clubs (charter 1975, pres. 1975-77), Kappa Delta,Delta Omicron, Phi Beta Kappa, Phi Kappa Phi, Kappa Delta Pi. Home: 889 Mimosa Blvd Roswell GA 30075-4436 Personal E-mail: rosejp@aol.com.

**POLAY, BRUCE,** music educator, conductor; b. Bklyn., Mar. 22, 1949; s. Benjamin and Joan Polay; m. Louise Phillips, Dec. 17, 1983; children: Elizabeth Louise, Bruce Adam, Rachel Joanne, Jacob Benjamin, Julia Christine. MusB, U. So. Calif., 1971; MA, Calif. State U., 1977; DMA, Ariz. State U., 1989. Music dir. So. Calif. Philharm., Long Beach, 1971-81; grad. asst. in theory and orch., assoc. condr. univ. symphony Ariz. State U., Tempe, 1981-83; condr. Phoenix Symphony Guild Youth Orch., 1981-83; music dir. Knox-Galesburg (Ill.) Symphony, 1983—; prof. music Knox Coll., Galesburg, 1983—, chair music dept., 2001—05. Guest condr. in Belarus, Italy, Eng., Mexico, Romania, Russia, Ukraine, Spain; bd. dirs. Ill. Coun. of Orchs., 1992—; mem. adv. bd. Found. for New Music, 1996—; bd. advisors Barlow Endowment for Music Composition; mem. music program adv. panel Ill. Arts Coun., 2004—. Orchestral compositions include Enconium, 1986, Perspectives, 1989, Concerto for Tenor Trombone, 1990, Tranquil Cycle for Tenor and Orch., 1992, Cathedral Images, 1993, Bondi's Journey: An Orchestral Rhapsody on Jewish Themes, 1994, Pictures For an Exhibition Piano, 1995, Anniversary Mourning for a cappella choir, 1996, Sandburg Cycle for Soprano, Tenor and Piano, 2000, Semi-Suite for Vin, Cello and Piano, 2001, Golden Oldie for Orchestra, 2001, Elegy for Violin and Small Orchestra, 2002, Suite of Preludes for Organ, 2002, Illumination for Orchestra, 2003, Suite on Catalonian Folksongs for String Orchestra, 2004, 3 Violin Duets on Catalonian Folksongs, 2005, Sparkel for Orchestra, 2006. Recipient Ill. Condr. of Yr. award Ill. Coun. Orchs., 1997, 2004. Mem. ASCAP, Am. Music Ctrs., Phi Kappa Phi. Avocations: body surfing, reading, American history. Home: 1577 N Cherry St Galesburg IL 61401-1820 Office: Knox Coll Campus Box 5 Galesburg IL 61401-4999 Office Phone: 309-341-7208. Business E-Mail: bpolay@knox.edu.

**POLCHINSKI, ALYSA R.,** music educator, artist; b. Bklyn., Apr. 11, 1958; d. Robert and Marilyn P. Gritz; m. Robert E. Polchinski, Oct. 11, 1958; children: Jason E., David A., Rebecca E. BA, Bklyn. Coll., 1980; MPA, NYU, 1983. Cert. piano ajudicator Nat. Guild Of Piano Tchrs., Am. Coll. Of Musicians, 1998. Piano tchr. Polchinski Piano, S.I., NY, 1976—. Officer Bklyn. Music Tchrs. Guild, 2000—. One-woman shows include Bird And Butterfly Scenes, S.I., N.Y., 2000 (nystate coun. of arts grant, 2004), Fish Scenes, 2001—04 (SI coun. of arts premier grant, 2003), exhibited in group shows at Polish and Polish-Am. Artists, Saug Harbor, N.Y., 2001—06. Officer S.I. Artists' Fedn., NY, 2000—06. Democrat. Jewish. Avocations: reading, jogging, tennis, swimming, yoga. Office Phone: 917-846-5461.

**POLCHINSKI, JOSEPH G.,** physicist, science educator; Prof. physics U. Calif., Santa Barbara. Author: String Theory: An Introduction to the Bosonic String, 1998, String Theory: Superstring Theory and Beyond, 1998. Mem.: NAS, Kavli Inst. for Theoretical Physics. Achievements include research in D-branes in theoretical physics and their importance in String Theory. Office: Univ Calif Kavli Inst for Theoretical Physics Santa Barbara CA 93106-4030 Office Phone: 805-893-3126. Office Fax: 805-893-2431. E-mail: joep@itp.ucsb.edu.*

**POLDEN, DONALD,** dean, law educator; BBA, George Washington U.; JD cum laude, Ind. U. Sch. Law. Law clerk for Hon. William C. Hanson, Chief Justice U.S. Dist. Ct. for So. Dist. Iowa, 1975—76; of counsel Hawkins and Norris, 1978—90; prof. law Drake U. Sch. Law, 1976—93; assoc. dean U. Memphis Sch. Law, 1991—93, dean, prof law, 1993—2003, Santa Clara U. Sch. Law, 2003—. Vis. prof. U. Louisville Sch. Law, 1984. Co-author: Employment relationships: law and practice, 1998; contbr. articles to law jours. Fellow: Coll. Labor and Employment Lawyers; mem.: Am. Law Inst. (elected mem. 1993), ABA (life). Office: Santa Clara U Sch Law El Camino Real Santa Clara CA 95053 Office Phone: 408-554-4362. E-mail: dpolden@scu.edu.

**POLEBAUM, MARK NEAL,** lawyer; b. Lowell, Mass., May 1, 1952; s. Eugene Harvey and Phyllis Diane (Sherman) P.; m. Diane M. Buhl, June 6, 1982; children: Katherine Elizabeth, Jessica Leigh, Michael William. BA, Middlebury Coll., 1974; JD, NYU, 1978. Bar: Mass. 1979, U.S. Dist. Ct.

Mass. 1979. Law clk. Chief Judge John C. Godbold, U.S. Ct. Appeals (5th cir.), Montgomery, Ala., 1978-79; assoc. Hale and Dorr, Boston, 1979-83, jr. ptnr., 1983-86, sr. ptnr., 1986—2004; ptnr., co-chmn. Bankruptcy & Comml. dept. Wilmer Cutler Pickering Hale & Dorr, Boston, 2004—. Counsel bondholders com. in out of ct. restructuring of Swan Brewery, Inc.; counsel bondholders com. in chpt. 11 reorgn. of EUA Power Corp. Editor (rsch.): NYU Law Rev.; contbr. articles to profl. jours. Mem. appropriations com., City of Lexington, Mass., 1984-88. Watson Found. fellow, 1974-75; named Mass. Super Lawyer, Boston Mag., 2004; Pro Bono Turnaround award, Turnaround Mgmt. Assn. Fellow Am. Coll. Bankruptcy; mem. ABA (corp., banking and bus. law sects., ad hoc subcom. on scope of uniform comml. code), Am. Bankruptcy Inst., Mass. Bar Assn., Phi Beta Kappa, Order of the Coif. Office: Wilmer Cutler Pickering Hale & Dorr 60 State St Boston MA 02109-1816 Office Phone: 617-526-6792. Office Fax: 617-526-5000. Business E-Mail: mark.polebaum@wilmerhale.com

**POLEDNA, MATHIAS,** video artist; b. Vienna, 1965; arrived in LA, 2000; Student, U. Applied Arts, U. Vienna, Austria. Prin. works include Produktion Pop (with Martin Beck and Jon Savage), 1996, Fondazione, Generali Found., Vienna, Austria, 1998, Actualite, 2001, Sufferers' Version, 2004, exhibitions include Zones of Disturbance, Graz, Austria, 1997, Grazer Kunstverein, 2001, Richard Telles Fine Art, LA, 2002, 2005, Mus. Modern Art Found., Austria, 2003, MUMOK, Vienna, Austria, 2003, Galerie Meyer Kainer, 2004, Witte de With Ctr. Contemporary Art, Netherlands, 2006, exhibited in group shows at 3. berlin biennale, Martin-Gropius-Bau, Berlin, 2004, 20/20 Vision, Stedelijk Mus. Post CS, Amsterdam, Netherlands, 2004, Liverpool Biennial, Tate Liverpool, Eng., 2004, Occupying Space/Wasting Time, Haus der Kunst, Munich, 2005, Das Neue II., Atelier Augarten, Wien, Austria, 2005, I Really Should..., Lisson Gallery, London, 2005, Whitney Biennial: Day for Night, Whitney Mus. Am. Art, 2006. Mailing: c/o Richard Telles Fine Art 7380 Beverly Blvd Los Angeles CA 90036*

**POLEDOURIS, BASIL K.,** composer; b. Kansas City, Mo., Aug. 21, 1945; s. Konstantine John and Helen Poledouris; m. Barbara Renée Godfrey, Aug. 15, 1969; children: Zoë Renée, Alexis Elene. BA in Music and Cinema, U. So. Calif., 1967, postgrad., 1967-69. Intern Am. Film Inst., L.A., 1969; freelance composer Hollywood, Calif., 1970—; pres. Basil Poledouris, Inc., Encino, Calif., 1987—. Bd. dirs. Blowtorch Flats, Venice, Calif.; mem. adv. bd. Soc. for Preservation Film Music, L.A., 1985—. Composer (film music) 90028, 1971, Extreme Close-Up, 1973, Tintorerra, 1977, Big Wednesday, 1979, Defiance, 1979, The Blue Lagoon, 1988, The House of God, 1988, Conan the Barbarian, 1981, Summer Lovers, 1982, Making the Grade, 1984, Conan the Destroyer, 1984, Red Dawn, 1984, Protocol, 1984, Flesh and Blood, 1985, Cherry 2000, 1986, Iron Eagle, 1986, Robocop, 1987 (BMI award 1988), No Man's Land, 1987, Split Decisions, 1988, Spellbinder, 1988, Farewell to the King, 1989, Wired, 1989, Hunt for Red October, 1990 (BMI award 1991), Quigley Down Under, 1990, Flight of the Intruder, 1991, White Fang, 1992, Return to the Blue Lagoon, 1991, Harley Davidson and the Marlboro Man, 1991, Robocop III, 1992, Free Willy, 1992 (BMI award 1994, gold record 1994), Hot Shots! Part Deux, 1993, Serial Mom, 1993, On Deadly Ground, 1994, Lassie, 1994, Jungle Book, 1994, Free Willy II, 1995, Under Seige II, 1995, It's My Party, 1995, Celtic Pride, 1996, Amanda, 1996, The War at Home, 1996, Switchback, 1996, Breakdown, 1997, Starship Troopers, 1997, Les Miserables, 1998, Mickey Blue Eyes, 1999, Amanda, 1999, For Love of the Game, 1999, Cecil B DeMented, 2000, Crocodile Dundee in L.A., 2001, The Touch, 2002, (TV film music) Congratulations It's A Boy, 1973, A Whale for the Killing, 1981, Fire on the Mountain, 1981, Amazons, 1984, Single Women, Single Bars, 1984, Amerika, 1987, Intrigue, 1988, Lonesome Dove, 1989 (Emmy award 1988, BMI award 1989), Nasty Boys, 1989, Lone Justice, 1990, Return to Lonesome Dove, 1993, TV pilots Alfred Hitchcock Presents, 1985, Misfits of Science, 1986, Island Sons, 1987, Murphy's Law, L.A. Takedown, 1989, Life and Times of Ned Blessing, 1991, Zoya, 1995, Tradition of Games Opening Ceremonies, 1996 Olympics, If These Walls Could Talk II, 2000, Dark Targets, 2001, The Legend of Butch and Sundance, 2003. Recipient resolution Calif. Legislature, 1990, Orange County Bd. Suprs., 1990, Key to City, Garden Grove City Coun., 1990, Disting. Artist award Calif. State U., Long Beach, 1992. Mem. NARAS, BMI, Am. Fedn. Musicians, Acad. Motion Picture Arts and Scis., Acad. Television Arts and Scis., Soc. Lyricists and Composers. Avocations: sailing, surfing, tai chi, Qi Gong.

**POLEFKA, THOMAS GREGORY,** biochemist; b. Passaic, N.J., Mar. 12, 1952; s. Emil Stanley and Stephanie (Kroczynski) P.; m. Maryann Brigida, Aug. 29, 1981; 1 child, Sara Jane. BS, Upsala Coll., 1974; PhD, U. Medicine/Dentistry N.J., 1979. Postdoctoral rsch. fellow Boston Biomed. Rsch. Inst./Harvard U. Med. Sch., 1979-80; rsch. assoc. Colgate-Palmolive Tech. Ctr., Piscataway, 1980—, dir. skin rsch., 2000—. Asst. editor Internat. Jour. Cosmetic Sci., Jour. Cosmetic Dermatology; contbr. chpts. to books, articles to profl. jours. Mem. AAAS, Soc. Investigative Dermatology, Am. Chem. Soc., Soc. Cosmetic Chemistry, Am. Acad. Dermatology, U. Medicine/Dentistry N.J. Sch. Biomed. Scis. Alumni Assn. (exec. coun. 1990-95). Achievements include patents in field. Avocations: bicycling, fishing, gardening, outdoor activities. Home: 79 Ellison Rd Somerset NJ 08873-2257 Office: Colgate-Palmolive Tech Ctr 909 River Rd Piscataway NJ 08854-5596 Office Phone: 732-878-7548. E-mail: tpolefka@yahoo.com.

**POLEJAEVA, IRINA,** genetic cloning company executive, researcher; MS in Animal sci., Kubanski Agrl. U., Russia; PhD in Biotechnology/Stem Cell Biology, Nat. Inst. Animal Sci., Russia; postdoctoral tng., Utah State U., US. Dir., Cell Biology group and project mgr. Porcine Nuclear Transfer Program, PPL Therapeutics; chief scientific officer Genetic Savings & Clone, Inc., Sausalito, Calif., 2002—. Contbr. articles to Nature, Nature Biotechnology and Science. Mem.: Soc. of Reproduction, Internat. Embryo Transfer Soc. Manages Genetic Savings and Clone, Inc. and oversees the gene banking and the canine and feline cloning R & D. Pioneer in the field of animal cloning. In March, 2000, she led efforts to the birth of the world's first cloned pigs by somatic cell nuclear transfer. In 2002, she produced the world's first 1,3-galactosyltransferase deficient pigs. Office: Genetic Savings & Clone 80 Liberty Ship Way Ste 22 Sausalito CA 94965-3300 Office Phone: 415-298-2525. Office Fax: 415-289-2526.

**POLEMITOU, OLGA ANDREA,** accountant; b. Nicosia, Cyprus, June 28, 1950; d. Takis and Georgia (Nicolaou) Chrysanthou. BA with honors, U. London, 1971; PhD, Ind. U., Bloomington, 1981. CPA Ind. Asst. productivity officer Internat. Labor Office/Cyprus Productivity Ctr., Nicosia, 1971-74; cons. Arthur Young & Co., N.Y.C., 1981; mgr. Coopers & Lybrand, Newark, 1981-83; dir. Bell Atlantic, Reston, Va., 1983-97; v.p. corp. auditing Columbia Energy Group, Herndon, 1997—2000; pres., CEO Aristion Inc., Reston, Va., 2000—. Chairperson adv. coun. Extended Day Care Cmty. Edn., West Windsor Plainsboro, NJ, 1987-88. Contbr. articles to profl. jours. Bus. cons. project bus. Jr. Achievement, Indpls., 1984—85. Mem.: AICPAs, NAFE, Princeton Network Profl. Women, Va. Soc. CPAs, N.J. Soc. CPAs (sec. mem. in industry com.), Ind. CPA Soc., Nat. Trust Hist. Preservation. Avocations: water-skiing, tennis. Home: PO Box 2744 Reston VA 20195-0744 Office: 11921 Freedom Dr Ste 550 Reston VA 20190 Business E-Mail: opolemitou@aristion.com.

**POLEN-DORN, LINDA FRANCES,** communications executive; b. Cleve., Mar. 23, 1945; d. Stanley and Mildred (Kain) Neuger; m. Samuel O. Dorn; children: Lanelle, Brian, Adam, Dawn. BA cum laude, U. Miami, 1967; MBA, Nova Southeastern U., 1993. Reporter Miami (Fla.) News, 1966-67; writer Miamian Mag., 1967-68; dir. pub. rels. Muscular Dystrophy Assn., Miami, 1968-72; cons., adv. and pub. rels. Ft. Lauderdale, 1974-77; pub. rels. writer J. Cory and Assocs., Ft. Lauderdale, Fla., 1978-79; account supr. Maizner & Franklin, Fla., 1979-86; v.p. mktg., communications mgr. Glendale Fed. Bank, Fla., 1986-95; prod. mktg. mgr. Ryder Sys., Inc., Miami, 1995-2003; cons. Southeastern Consulting Group, LLC, Ft. Lauderdale,

---

2004—. Active Symphony of Ams. Soc., Ft. Lauderdale, 2004—, Symphony Soc. Ft. Lauderdale, 1987-2003—. Mem. Internat. Assn. Bus. Communications, Am. Mktg. Assn., Broward C. of C. (vice chmn. govt. affairs 1984-85). Avocation: travel.

**POLENOVA, TATYANA,** chemistry professor, researcher; b. Kazanlak, Bulgaria, Sept. 10, 1970; arrived in U.S., 1992; d. Evgenii Alexandrovich Polenov and Inanka Andreeva Vladimirova; m. Andrew Vladimirovich Teplyakov, July 5, 1989. BSc, Moscow State U., Russia, 1992; PhD, Columbia U., N.Y.C., 1997. Asst. prof. Hunter Coll. CUNY, N.Y.C., 1999—2003, U. Del., Newark, 2003—. Contbr. chapters to books. Grantee, NSF, 2003—. Am. Chem. Soc. Petroleum Rsch. Fund, 2003—05. Mem.: Am. Chem. Soc. Office: U Del Dept Chem and Biochem Newark DE 19716 Business E-Mail: tpolenov@udel.edu.

**POLENZ, JOANNA MAGDA,** psychiatrist; b. Cracow, Poland, Oct. 20, 1936; came to U.S., 1961; d. Mieczyslaw and Nusia (Goldberger) Uberall; m. Daryl Louis Polenz, July 8, 1962 (div. 1991); children: Teresa Ann, Daryl Philip, Elizabeth Sophia. MD, U. Sydney, Australia, 1960; MPH, Columbia U., 1992. Diplomate Am. Bd. Psychiatry and Neurology. Intern Bklyn. Hosp., 1961-62; resident in psychiatry Mt. Sinai Med. Ctr., N.Y.C., 1962-65, edni. fellow, 1965-66, rsch. assoc., 1966-67; med. dir. Tappan Zee clin. Phelps Meml. Hosp., Tarrytown, NY, 1968-71, dir. dept. psychiatry, 1972-77; sr. attending psychiatrist Meml. Hosp. Ctr., 1972-93; pvt. practice Briarcliff Manor, NY, 1971-91; physician Joint Commn. Accreditation of Healthcare Orgns., Oakbrook Terrace, Ill., 1993—2004; pres. Sch. of Health.com, N.Y.C., 1998—; assoc. dir. administn. N.Y.C. Health and Hosp. Corp., 2004—. Lectr. in field. Author: In Defense of Marriage, 1981; (with other) Test Your Marriage IQ, 1984, Test Your Success IQ, 1985, The Last Sick Generation, 2000; contbr. articles to profl. jours.; numerous TV appearances including Phil Donahue, 1988, Oprah Winfrey 1984. Grant Found. grantee, 1970. Fellow Am. Psychiat. Assn. (disting. life); mem. AMA, Westchester Psychiat. Assn. (sec. 1982-85, chmn. fellowship com. 1989-98). Avocations: travel, international affairs. Home and Office: SchoolofHealth.com 123 E 75th St Ste 10B New York NY 10021 Office Phone: 212-426-5605. Office Fax: 212-828-2507. Business E-Mail: jpolenz@nyc.rr.com.

**POLESE, KIM,** software company executive; BS, U. Calif., Berkeley, 1984; student, U. Wash. Product mgr. Sun Microsys., 1988—95; co-founder, pres., CEO Marimba, Inc., 1996—2000, chmn., 1996—2003, bd. dirs., 1996—. Bd. dirs. TechNet. Bd. dirs. Do Something, Global Security Inst., U. Calif. President's Bd. Sci. and Innovation, Carnegie Mellon Computer Sci. Advisory Coun. Named one of Time Mags. Most Influential Ams. Mem.: Silicon Valley Mfg. Group. Achievements include a pivotal role in launching Java.

**POLESKIE, STEPHEN FRANCIS,** retired art educator, artist, writer, publisher; b. Pringle, Pa., June 3, 1938; s. Stephen Francis and Antoinette Elizabeth (Chludzinski) P.; m. Jeanne Mackin, 1959. BS, Wilkes Coll., 1959; postgrad., New Sch. for Social Research, 1961. Owner Chiron Press, N.Y.C., 1961-68; instr. Sch. Visual Arts, N.Y.C., 1968; prof. art Cornell U., Ithaca, NY, 1969-2001, prof. emeritus 2001—. Vis. critic Pratt Graphic Arts Center, N.Y.C., 1965-68; vis. artist Colgate U., Hamilton, N.Y., 1973, USSR, 1979, Escuela de Bellas Artes, Honduras, 1980, Loughborough Coll. Art and Design, Eng., 1989; vis. prof. U. Calif., Berkeley, 1976; reviewer in field. Contbr. short stories to mags. and book; one-man shows include Louis K. Meisel Gallery, N.Y.C., 1978-80, Galerie Kupinski, Stuttgart, Germany, 1979, Palace of Culture and Sci., Warsaw, Poland, 1979, Sky Art Presentation, MIT, 1981, Am. Ctr., Belgrade, 1981, William and Mary Coll., 1983, McPherson Art Gallery, Victoria, B.C., Can., 1984, Studio D'Ars, Milan, 1985, Gallery Flaviana, Locarno, Switzerland, 1985, Il Salatto Gallery, Como, Italy, 1985, Galleria Schneider, Rome, 1987, Mus. Sztuki Lodz, Poland, 1987, Alternative Mus., Lido di Spina, Italy, 1987, Galerie Klaus Lea, Munich, 1987, Patricia Carega Gallery, Washington, 1988, Nine Columns Gallery, Palermo, Italy, 1988, John Hansard Gallery, Southampton, Eng., 1989, Quai Art Gallery, Isle of Wight, Eng., 1989, Lee Art Gallery, Clemson (S.C.) U., 1990, Apogeeairway, N.Y.C., 1991, Nine Columns Gallery, Brescia, Italy, 1991, Glenn Curtiss Mus., Hammondsport, N.Y., 1993, Caproni Mus., Trento, Italy, 1995, Temple U., Rome, 1995, Gallery Modern Art, Maribor, Slovenia, 1995, Palazzo Communale, Todi, Italy, 1995, Upstairs Gallery, Ithaca, NY, 2006, Palazzo Della Pretura, Piacenza, Italy, Internat. Art Ctr., Kyoto, Japan, 2006; represented in collections at Met. Mus., N.Y.C., Mus. Modern Art, N.Y.C., Victoria and Albert Mus., London, Whitney Mus., N.Y.C., Walker Art Center, Mpls., Tate Gallery, London, Fort Worth Art Center, Nat. Collection, Washington, others; pub. Onager Edits., 2004, publ. The Balloonist The Story of T.S. C. Lowe, 2005 Am. Fedn. of Arts grantee, 1965; Carnegie Found. grantee, 1967; Nat. Endowment for Arts grantee, 1973; N.Y. State Council on Arts grantee, 1973; Creative Artists Public Service Program grantee, 1978; Best Found. grantee, 1985 Home: PO Box 849 Ithaca NY 14851-0849 Office Phone: 877-275-6388. Personal E-Mail: onagereditions@aol.com.

**POLEVODA, BOGDAN V.,** research scientist; b. Skalat, Ternopil, Ukraine, Aug. 17, 1959; s. Wasyl I. and Khrystyna M. Polevoda; m. Inna M. Rublevska; 1 child, Andrew. MS, Shevchenko Kiev State U., Ukraine; PhD, Inst. of Biochemistry and Physiology of Microorganism, Puschino, Moscow reg., former USSR, 1986. Scientist Inst. for Microbiology and Virology Nat. Acad. Sci. of Ukraine, Kyiv, Ukraine, 1987—93; postdoctoral fellow U. Rochester, NY, 1993—96, rsch. asst. prof. NY, 1997—. Contbr. numerous articles and reviews to profl. jours. Grantee Rsch. grantee, Ukrainian Nat. Com. for Sci. and Tech., 1991—94. Mem.: AAAS, Am. Soc. for Biochemistry and Molecular Biology Genetics Soc. Am. Achievements include complete identification and characterization of n-terminal acetyltransferases and some metyltransferases in eukaryotes. Office: Univ Rochester Med Sch Dept Biochemistry & Biophysics PO Box 712 601 Elmwood Ave Rochester NY 14642 Office Phone: 585-275-3329. Business E-Mail: Bogdan_Polevoda@urmc.rochester.edu.

**POLEVOY, NANCY TALLY,** lawyer, social worker, genealogist; b. N.Y.C., May 27, 1944; d. Charles H. and Bernice M. (Gang) Tally; m. Martin D. Polevoy, Mar. 19, 1967; children: Jason Tally, John Gerald. Student, Mt. Holyoke Coll., 1962—64; BA, Barnard Coll., 1966; MSW, Columbia U., 1968, JD, 1986. Bar: N.Y. 1987. Caseworker unmarried mothers' svc. Louise Wise Svcs., N.Y.C., 1967, caseworker adoption dept., 1969-71; caseworker Youth Consultation Svc., N.Y.C., 1968-69; asst. rsch. scientist, psychiat. social worker NYU Med. ctr., N.Y.C., 1973-81; adv. ct. apptd. spl. advs. Manhattan Family Ct., N.Y.C., 1981-82; cons. social work, 1981-86; matrimonial assoc. Ballon, Stoll & Itzler, 1987, Herzfeld & Rubin, P.C., 1987-88; practice NYC. Contbr. articles to profl. jours. Mem. parents' adv. bd. Riverdale Country Sch., 1988—93; mem. outreach bd. Manhattan divsn. United Jewish Appeal Fedn., 1990—94, exec. bd. Manhattan divsn., 1992—94, mem. met. campaign cabinet, 1994—95, mem. task force aging, 2004—; trustee Jewish Assn. Svcs. to Aged, 1996—, v.p., 1999—2003; bd. dirs. Ctr. Jewish History, 1996—; archives com. Ctrl. Synagogue, 1994—2005; trustee Am. Jewish Hist. Soc., 1992—, asst. treas., 1995—98, v.p., 1998—2003, 2005—. Recipient French Govt. prize, 1963, honor for lifetime cmty. svc., United Jewish Appeal Fedn. N.Y., 2003. Mem.: NASW, Acad. Cert. Social Workers, N.Y. State Bar Assn., Assn. Bar City of N.Y., Barnard Coll. Alumni Assn. (v.p. 1966, class pres. 1966 1996—). Home and Office: 1155 Park Ave New York NY 10128-1209

**POLEWAY, CHRISTOPHER J.,** publishing executive; b. Bklyn., 1958; m. Poleway; 2 children. BA, St. Bonaventure Univ., Olean, NY; MBA, Fordham Univ. Mgr. fin. sys. HBO, 1982—88; gen. mgr. Corp. Fin. Reporting, 1988—91; Circulation Planning Mgr. Fortune, 1991—92, asst. bus. mgr., 1992—94, advertising bus. mgr., 1994—97, dir. of fin. and ops. 1997—99, v.p. and gen. mgr., 1999—2000, chief op. officer, 2000—01; pres. Fortune/Money Group, 2001—. Office: Time and Life Bldg Rockefeller Ctr New York NY 10020-1393*

---

**POLHAMUS, BARBARA,** nutritionist, educator; d. Helen and Leslie Polhamus. PhD, MPH, U. N.C., Chapel Hill, 1991—97. Registered dietitian Am. Dietetic Assn., 1982. Nutrition dir. Dorchester Ho. Multi-Svc. Ctr., Mass., 1982—84; nutrition dir., maternal and child health Mass. Dept. Pub. Health, Boston, 1984—91; rsch. assoc. U.N.C., Chapel Hill, 1998—2000; nutritionist CDC, Nat. Ctr. for Chronic Disease Prevention and Health Promotion, Divsn. Nutrition and Phys. Activity, Atlanta, 2000—. Tech. cons., Ukraine micronutrient survey CDC, Atlanta, 2002. Contbr. chapters to books, articles to profl. jours., sci. material for web sites. Recipient award of Excellence Pub. Health Tng. and Nutrition Team award, 2005; fellow, Dannon Inst., 1998; grantee, Inst. Nutrition, 1994. Mem.: APHA (elected sect. mem. 2002—04). Liberal. Avocations: yoga, hiking, travel. Office: CDC 4770 Buford Hwy NE MS K-25 Atlanta GA 30341 Personal E-Mail: bfp9@cdc.gov.

**POLI, KENNETH JOSEPH,** editor, writer, photographer; b. Bklyn., June 8, 1921; s. Joseph H. and Irene (Seeman) P.; m. Virginia Osk, Dec. 14, 1946; 1 child, Bruce. Student, Goddard Coll., 1938-40. Writer, photographer North Atlantic Area Office ARC, N.Y.C., 1946-49. Editorial cons., 1965— Author Critical Focus Column, 1972-83; editor: External House Mags., Internat. Nickel Co., N.Y.C., 1949-53, Leica Photography mag., E. Leitz, Inc., N.Y.C., 1953-65; assoc. editor Popular Photography mag., Ziff-Davis Pub. Co., N.Y.C., 1965-68, sr. editor, 1968-1970, editor, 1970-83, cons. 1983-87; cons. editor Photography Ann., 35-mm Photography, Photography Directory and Buying Guide, 1970-83; contbr. articles to photog. jours. and encys. With inf. U.S. Army, 1942-45, PTO. Decorated Purple Heart medal. Mem. Am. Photog. Hist. Soc., Photographic Adminstrs., Circle of Confusion, Mensa. Home and Office: Apt 6167 1 Jefferson Ferry Dr South Setauket NY 11720-4727 Personal E-Mail: heremi_2000@yahoo.com.

**POLIAHU, GEORGE,** retired music educator; b. Kapaau, Hawaii, Aug. 16, 1939; s. George Keohuhu and Mary Poliahu; m. Betty Jane Hoffman, Apr. 1, 1969; children: TamiLani Malia Mack, Gail Leilani Kamalani, Todd George, Johnathan William K. BS, Ch. Coll. of Hawaii, Laie, 1962—66; MA in Music Edn., Brigham Young U., Provo, Utah, 1977. Profl. musician, Honolulu, 1963—75; band dir. and gen. music tchr. Waimanalo Intermediate Sch., Waimanalo, Hawaii, 1967—86; instrumental music tchr. State Youth Correctional Facility, Kailua, Hawaii, 1970—71; folk and band instrument tchr. Dept. of Parks and Recreation, Kaneohe, Hawaii, 1976; band dir. Kailua Intermediate Sch., Kailua, Hawaii, 1986—2004; chair fine arts dept., 1991—2004; ret., 2004. Music arranger Ednl. TV, Honolulu, 1970; Western Assn. Schs. and Colls. accreditation team Hawaii Dept. of Edn., Lanai, Hawaii, 1970. Leader and merit badge counselor Boy Scouts of Am., Kaneohe, Hawaii, 1989—2003, asst. dist. commr., 2003—04; bishop The Ch. of Jesus Christ of Latter-day Saints, Kaneohe, Hawaii, 1992—94. Named Music Educator of the Yr., Music Found. of Hawaii, 2004; recipient On My Honor Adult Recognition, Boy Scouts of Am., 2001, Ko'olauloa Cmty. Svc. award, 2005. Mem.: Oahu Band Dirs. Assn., Music Educators Nat. Assn., NEA, Hawaii State Tchrs.Assn. (faculty rep. and grievance rep. 1970—2004). The Church of Jesus Christ Of Latter-Day Saints. Avocations: jogging, playing variety of instruments, singing, camping, hiking. Home: 45-922 Anoi Rd Kaneohe HI 96744-3301

**POLIAKOFF, GARY A.,** lawyer, educator; b. Greenville, SC, Nov. 25, 1944; s. Herman and Dorothy (Ravitz) P.; m. Barbara Shubin, June 24, 1967; children: Ryan, Keith. BS, U. S.C., 1966; JD, U. Miami, 1969. Bar: Fla. 1969, DC 1971, Colo. 1999. Founding prin. pres. Becker & Poliakoff, P.A., Hollywood, Coral Gables, Naples, Sarasota, West Palm Beach, Largo, Orlando, Ft. Walton Beach, Fla., Prague and Beijing, 1973—. Adj. prof. condominium law and practice Nova Southeastern U.; panelist Nat. Confs. Cmty. Assn.; testified before coms. of the US Senate on Condominiums; lectr. ann. condominium seminars Fla. Bar; participant Fla. Law Revision Council; cons. to State Legis. and the White House in drafting Condominium and Coop. Abuse Relief Act, 1980; mem. condominium study commn. State of Fla., 1990; chmn. State of Fla. Advisory Coun. on Condominiums, 1992, 93.; atty. Town of Southwest Ranches. Author: The Law of Condominium Operations, 1988; co-author: Florida Condominium Law and Practice, 1982, The Florida Bar Continuing Legal Education, 1982; contbr. articles to legal jour. Mem. pres. adv. group U. SC, U.S.C. Ednl. Found., 1999-2001. Recipient Judge Learned Hand award Am. Jewish Com. for devel. of co-ownership housing law, 1999; Legal Elite award Fla. Trend Mag., 2004, 05, 06, Diamond award Honoree for Excellence in Bus. Leadership So. Fla. Bus. Jour., 2002. Mem. ABA (adv. nat. conf.), Fla. Bar, Coll. Cmty. Assn. Lawyers (bd. gov.), Scribes. Office Phone: 954-985-4150. Personal E-Mail: gpoliakoff@becker-poliakoff.com.

**POLICANO, ANDREW J.,** dean, finance educator; b. July 4, 1949; m. Pamela Z. Policano; children: Emily, Keith. BS in math., SUNY, Stony Brook, 1971; MA in economics, Brown U., 1973, PhD in economics, 1976. Asst. prof. U. Iowa, Iowa City, 1975-79; assoc. prof. dept. economics, 1979-81, prof., chair dept. economics, 1984-87, sr. assoc. dean academic affairs, 1987-88; prof. dept. economics Fordham U., NYC, 1981-84, asst. chair, dir. grad. studies, 1982-83; rsch. assoc. Ctr. for Study of Futures Markets Columbia U., NYC, 1982-86; dean divsn. social & behavioral sci. SUNY, Stony Brook, 1988-91; dean Sch. Bus., U. Wis., Madison, 1991—2001, Kuechenmeister Prof. Bus. 2001—04; dean Pual Merage Sch. Bus., U. Calif., Irvine, 2004—, prof. economics/pub. policy, 2004—. Guest prof. Inst. Advanced Studies, Vienna, Austria, 1985; dir. Nat. Guardian Life, Madison, 1991- PIC Wis. 1995, Badger Mut., 1997, mmbl. Wis. Glass Ceiling Commn., 1995-2000. Recipient Disting. Alumnus award SUNY, Stony Brook, 1994. Mem. Assn. to Advance Collegiate Schools of Bus. (bd. dirs., 1997-98). Office: U Calif Irvine Grad Sch Mgmt 350 GSM Irvine CA 92697-3125 Office Phone: 949-824-8470. E-mail: dean@gsm.uci.edu.*

**POLICINSKI, CHRIS,** food products executive; BA, Univ. Notre Dame, 1980; MBA, NYU. Mgmt. positions with Pillsbury Co., Kraft Gen. Foods; v.p. strategy, bus. & internat. develop. Land O'Lakes Inc., Arden Hills, Minn., 1997—99, exec. v.p. COO dairy foods value added group, 1999—2002, exec. v.p., COO dairy foods, 2002—05, pres., CEO, 2005—. Mem. pres. council Grocery Manufacturers Am.; bd. dir. Nat. Milk Prod. Fedn., Nat. Coun. Farmer Cooperatives. Mem.: United Way, St. Paul, Mpls. Office: Land O'Lakes Inc 4001 Lexington Ave N Saint Paul MN 55126-2998 Mailing: Land O'Lakes Inc PO Box 64101 Saint Paul MN 55164-0101

**POLICINSKI, EUGENE FRANCIS,** foundation administrator, editor, radio personality, television personality, television producer; b. South Bend, Ind., Aug. 31, 1950; s. E.T. and Margaret C. (O'Neill) P.; m. Kathleen Beta O'Donnell Powell, Aug. 19, 1972; children: Ryan, David. Degree in journalism and polit. sci., Ball State U., 1972; student, Nashville Sch. Law, 2005—. Corr. Gannett News Svc., Washington, 1979-82; Washington editor USA Today, Arlington, Va., 1982-83, page one editor, 1983-85, mng. editor sports, 1989—96; spl. asst. to chmn/CEO The Freedom Forum, Arlington, Va., 1996-98; wash. editor Freedom Forum Website, 1998-99; dep. dir. First Amendment Ctr., Nashville, 1999—2004, exec. dir., 2004—. Host, commentator USA Today Sky Radio, Arlington, 1992—95; host Newseum Radio, 1998—2001; adj. faculty Winthrop U., 1999—; exec. prodr. Speaking Freely (PBS), 2001—05. Founding editor USA Today Baseball Weekly, 1991. Bd. advisors Ctr. Study Sport in Soc., 1995—; trustee U.S. Sports Acad., 1997—, Watkins Coll. Art and Design, 2001—04; dir. J-IDEAS program Ball State U., 2003—04. Named one of 100 Most Important People in Sports Sporting News, 1992-93, 95, Sports Person of the Yr., U.S. Sports Acad., 1996; named to Journalism Hall of Fame, Ball State U., 1989, Alumni of Yr., 1996. Mem. NATAS (gov. 2004), Am. Soc. Newspaper Editors, Soc. Profl. Journalists, Assn. Educators in Journalism and Mass Comms. Avocations: sailing, bicycling, golf. Office: First Amendment Center Office of Exec Dir 1207 18th Ave S Nashville TN 37212-2807 Office Phone: 615-727-1600. Business E-Mail: gpolicinski@fac.org.

**POLICY, CARMEN A.,** vintager, professional sports team executive; b. Youngstown, Ohio, Jan. 26, 1943; s. Albert and Ruby (Tisone) P.; m. Aug. 8, 1964 (div. Mar. 1989); children: James, Daniel, Edward, Kerry, Kathy; m. Gail Marie Moretti, June 27, 1991. Grad., Youngstown State U., 1963; JD, Georgetown U., 1966. Bar: Ohio 1966, Va. 1966, D.C. 1966. Assoc. Nadler & Nadler, Youngstown, 1966-68; asst. prosecutor City of Youngstown, 1968-69; ptnr. Flask & Policy, Weimer & White, Youngstown, 1969-90; spl. counsel to atty. gen. State of Ohio, 1970-91; v.p., gen. counsel San Francisco 49ers, NFL, 1983-90, pres., 1990-99; pres., CEO & co-owner Cleve. Browns, 1998—2004, consultant, 2004—. Mem. various coms. NFL, 1990—; bd. dirs. World League Am. Football, N.Y.C., 1991—. Com. mem. various charities, Youngstown, 1969-90, San Francisco, 1990—. Mem. Va. Bar Assn., Ohio Bar Assn., D.C. Bar Assn. Roman Catholic. Avocations: scuba diving, hiking.

**POLILLO, RONALD R.,** federal official; b. Honolulu, Mar. 25, 1949; s. John F. and Dolores T. Polillo; m. Marion E. Lapworth, June 16, 1983; m. Karen E. Rickards, Sept. 18, 1971 (div. Feb. 21, 1981); children: William Thomas Schweitzer, Albert M., Mazie L. Alimenti, Kimberly A., Jennifer L. BS in Math. Scis., Fla. Inst. Tech., 1972; M in Aviation Mgmt., Embry Riddle Aero. U., 1984. Mathematician US Army Ft. Belvoir, Ft. Belvoir, Va., 1974—75; mathematician, divsn. mgr. FAA, WJH Technical Center, NJ, 1975—96, aviation security lab facility mgr., 2000—01, security integrated product team lead Washington, 1996—2000; transp. security lab facility mgr. Transp. Security Adminstrn., WJH Technical Center, 2001—04; v.p. home-land security and defense Hi-Tec Systems, Inc., Egg Harbor Township, NJ, 2004—. Contbr. articles to profl. jours. Hon. comdr. USAF 105th Aeroport Squadron, McGuire AFB, NJ, 2001—03; pres. Jersey Cape Region, Antique Automobile Club Am., Ocean City, NJ, 1983—86. Recipient Outstanding Performance awards, U.S. Govt., 1975—2004; scholar, Rotary Club, 1967. Mem.: NRA (life), Air Traffic Control Assn. (assoc.), Game Preserve Estell Manor (chmn. membership com., co-chair of arrangements committe 2002—06), North Am. Hunting Club (life), Pi Kappa Alpha (chief justice and steward 1968—72). Republican. Roman Catholic. Avocations: hunting, fishing, shooting sports, antique car restoration, travel. Home: 6140 Robin Dr Mays Landing NJ 08330 Office: Hi-Tec Systems Inc Ste 108 500 Scarborough Dr Egg Harbor Township NJ 08234 Office Phone: 609-272-1515. Home Fax: 609-272-1888; Office Fax: 609-272-1888. Business E-Mail: ron.polillo@hitecsystems.com.

**POLIMENI, JOHN MATTHEW,** economics professor; b. Schenectady, N.Y., Nov. 21, 1972; s. John Joseph and Catherine Marie Polimeni; m. Raluca Ioana Iorgulescu, Aug. 14, 1968. BS in Math., Rensselaer Poly. Inst., 1994; MA in Econs., SUNY, Albany, 1996; PhD in Ecol. Econs., Rensselaer Poly. Inst., 2002. Asst. prof. econs. Albany (N.Y.) Coll. Pharmacy, 2004—. Office: Albany Coll Pharmacy 106 New Scotland Ave Albany NY 12208

**POLIMENI, REBECCA H.,** special education educator; b. Albertson, NY, Dec. 13, 1973; d. Vincent and Joan M Polimeni. BA in psychology, Hofstra U., 1995—97; MA in spl. edn., Columbia U., 1999—2001. Tchr. asst. Devel. Disabilities Inst., Young Autism Program, Smithtown, NY, 1997—98; home tutor and parent trainer Pvt. Practice, NY, 1997—; tchr. cons. Autism Help Ctr., Medford, NY, 2000—01; program coord. Devel. Disabilities Inst., Young Autism Program, Ronkonkoma, NY, 2001—03; behavior cons. LI Devel. Cons., Lake Grove, NY, 2003—; behavior consultation Pvt. Practice, NY, 2004—. Staff devel. spkr. LI Devel. Consulting and Pvt. Practice, 2003—. Recipient Adele Leonard Endowed Prize for excellence in Linguistics, Hofstra U., 1997, Provost's Scholar, Hosftra U., 1997, Dean's List, Hofstra U., 1995—97; Academic scholarship, 1995. Mem.: Counsel for Exceptional Children, Psi Chi Nat. Honor Soc., Golden Key Nat. Honor Soc. Independent. Avocations: travel, writing, music, outdoor activities, exercise. Personal E-mail: autad@cs.com.

**POLIN, JANE L.,** foundation official; b. NYC, Sept. 30, 1958; BA, Wesleyan U., Middletown, Conn., 1980; MBA, Columbia U. 1988. Asst. dir. ann. giving Wesleyan U., 1980—82; centennial fund assoc. Met. Opera Assn., N.Y.C., 1982—84; devel. officer Columbia U., N.Y.C., 1984—88; program mgr., comptr. GE Fund, Fairfield, Conn., 1988—99; v.p. cmty. devel. and corp. affairs Sperry & Hutchinson, Inc., 1999—2000, philanthropic advisor, 2001—; bd. dirs. Fred Friendly Seminars, 2005—. *Jane L. Polin brings twenty-five years of innovative leadership experience within the nonprofit and private sectors in developing and investing philanthropic resources. Now serving as a philanthropic advisor, principally in the areas of the arts, education, and public policy, her current and recent clients include: The American Music Center / Andrew W. Mellon Foundation; JF Kennedy Center for the Performing Arts; Metropolitan Opera Guild; Center for Arts Education; The Dana Foundation; Jobs For The Future; The Thomas S. Kenan Institute for the Arts; WNYC; and Young Audiences.* Panelist arts-in-edn. Nat. Endowment for Arts, Washington, 1989—90, 1994—95, NEH, 1997; adv. bd. mem. ARC, 1991—99, United Way Am., 1991—99, Inst. for Internat. Econs., 1995—99, Young Audiences, N.Y.C., 1991—2000, mem. Advt. Coun., 1998—2003; judge Frances Hesselbein Cmty. Innovation Fellows Program, 2001—02, Peter F. Drucker Award for Nonprofit Innovation, 1996—2000. Mem.: Alpha Delta Phi. Home and Office: 67 Riverside Dr Apt 7D New York NY 10024-6136 Fax: 212-873-1568. Personal E-mail: janepolin@aol.com.

**POLINER, GARY A.,** corporate financial executive; Sr. v.p., CFO Northwestern Mutual Life Ins. Co., Milw. Office: Northwestern Mutual 720 E Wisconsin Ave Milwaukee WI 53202-4797*

**POLINER, JASON M.,** lawyer; b. NYC, Oct. 1, 1954; BA, SUNY, Binghamton, 1976; JD, SUNY, Buffalo, 1979. Bar: NY 1980, US Dist. Ct. So. & Ea. Districts NY 1992. Ptnr. Wilson, Elser, Moskowitz, Edelman & Dicker LLP, NY, Albany. Office: Wilson Elser Moskowitz Edelman & Dicker LLP 23rd Fl 150 E 42nd St New York NY 10017-5639 Office Phone: 212-490-3000 ext. 2204. Office Fax: 212-490-3038. Business E-Mail: polinerj@wemed.com.

**POLING, KERMIT WILLIAM,** minister; b. Elkins, W.Va., Oct. 1, 1941; s. Durward Willis and Della Mae (Boyles) P.; m. Patricia Ann Groves, June 12, 1965; children: David Edward Elson, Mikael Erik. Diploma in Bible, Am. Bible Sch., 1966; BA in Bible, Reed Coll. Religion, 1968; AA, W.Va. U., 1970; ThD, Zion Theol. Sem., 1971; postgrad., Wesley Theol. Sem., 1974; LLD, Geneva Theol. Coll., 1980; DSL (hon.), Berean Christian Coll., 1981; postgrad., Mansfield Coll., U. Oxford, Eng., 1986, Mansfield Coll., U. Oxford, 1990, postgrad., 1991; D Ecumenical Rsch., St. Ephrem's Inst. for Oriental Studies, 1989; BRE, Am. Bible Coll., 1991; M of Herbology, Emerison Coll., 1994. Ordained to ministry United Meth. Ch., 1967. Pastor Parkersburg-Crossroads (W.Va.) Cir., 1967-70; asst. sec. W.Va. Ann. Conf. 1967-69; pastor Hope-Halleck Morgantown Cir., 1970-76, Trinity-Warren Grafton (W.Va.) Charge, 1976-83, 1st Trinity Pennsboro (W.Va.) Charge, 1983-97, South Parkersburg United Meth. Ch., 1997—2004. Editor local ch. news; instr. Bible Bodkin Bible Inst., 1975-75, United Meth. Lay Acad., 1992—2004; mem. staff Taylor County Coop. Parish, 1976-83; coord. Hughes River Coop. Parish, 1983-86; mem. chaplains com. Grafton City Hosp., 1976-82; mem. coun. Ctr. d'Etudes et d'Action Oecumeniques, 1972-74; bishop in Partibus of Tayma. Author: A Crown of Thorns, 1963, A Silver Message, 1964, History of the Halleck Church, 1970, Eastern Rite Catholicism, 1971, From Brahmin to Bishop, 1976, Cult and Occult: Data and Doctrine, 1978, The Value of Religious Education in Ancient Traditional Churches, 1993, Anniversary History of Trinity Church, Pennsboro, 1997; editor: Jane's Heirs; contbr. articles and poems to religious jours. Decorated Royal Afghanistan Order of Crown of Amanullah, Byzantine Order of Leo the Armenian, Order of Polonia Resitutia, Mystical Order of St. Peter, knight Grand Cross of the Order of St. Dennis of Zante, companion Naval Order of U.S.; recipient Good Citizenship award Doddridge County, 1954, Silver medal Ordre Universel du Merit Humain, Geneva, 1973, Commendation for Outstanding Achievement in Ministry, Ohio Ho. of Reps., 1988; recipient U.S. Heritage award, 2002; named Chief of Dynastic Ho. of Polanie-Patrikios, 1988, Prince of the Holy Roman Empire, 2005. Mem. SAR, Assn. Bible Tchrs. (founder), Internat. Platform Assn., Naval Order U.S., Sovereign

Order St. John Jerusalem, Ritchie County Ministerial Assn. (pres. 1984-97), Order Sacred Cup, Knights of Malta, Order of the Crown of Lauriers. Home: 101 E Myles Ave Pennsboro WV 26415

**POLING, SHEILA R.,** management consultant; BSBA, U. Tenn., Knoxville, 1979. V.p. Statis. Process Controls, Inc., Knoxville, Tenn., 1989—2001; mng. ptnr. and COO Pinnacle Partners, Inc., Oak Ridge, 2001—. Editor Brain Teasers monthly feature Quality mag. Author: Customer Focused Quality, 1996, Building Continual Improvement: SPC for the Service Sector, 1998, The Manufacturing Engineering Handbook, 2004, Using Lean for Faster Six Sigma Results: A Synchronized Approach, 2006. Recipient Most Read Monthly Column award, Quality mag. Mem.: Am. Mktg. Assn., Am. Mgmt. Assn., Am. Soc. Quality (quality mgmt. conf. chair 1991). Office: Pinnacle Partners Inc 36 Rivers Run Way Oak Ridge TN 37830 Personal E-mail: srpoling@att.net.

**POLINSKY, A. MITCHELL,** law and economics educator; b. Feb. 6, 1948. m. Joan Roberts, June 29, 1945; 2 children. AB in Economics, magna cum laude, Harvard U., 1970; PhD in Economics, MIT, 1973; MSL, Yale Law Sch., 1976. Asst. prof. economics and law Harvard Law Sch., 1977-79; Russell Sage Found. resident in law and social sci., Yale Law Sch., 1975-76, Harvard Law Sch., 1976-77; assoc. prof. economics Stanford U., 1979-84, prof. (by courtesy), 1984-, nat. fellow domestic studies program The Hoover Instn., 1985-86; prof. law Stanford Law Sch., 1979-84, Josephine Scott Crocker prof. law and economics, 1984—, dir. John M. Olin program in law and economics, 1979-, co-dir. Stanford Ctr. for Law, Economics, and Bus., 2002-; fellow Ctr. for Advanced Study in Behavioral Sciences, Stanford, Calif., 1997-98. Vis. prof. law and economics Harvard Law Sch., 1992-93, 2000, 03; rsch. assoc. law and economics program Nat. Bur. Econ. Rsch., 1978—, mem. editl. bd. Jour. Law, Economics, and Orgn., 1983-, Internat. Rev. Law and Economics, 1987-, Jour. Pub. Economics, 1999-, B.E. Journals of Econ. Analysis & Policy, 2001-; adv. editor Jour. Risk and Uncertainty, 1987-, Fellow, John Simon Guggenheim Meml. Found., 1993-94. Mem. Am. Law and Economics Assn. (bd. dirs. 1991-93, sec.-treas. 1991-92, v.p. 1992-93, pres. 1993-94). Office: Stanford Law Sch Crown Quadrangle 559 Nathan Abbott Way Stanford CA 94305-8610 Office Phone: 650-723-0886. Office Fax: 650-723-3557. Business E-Mail: polinsky@stanford.edu.

**POLINSKY, JANET NABOICHECK,** retired state official, retired state legislator; b. Hartford, Conn., Dec. 6, 1930; d. Louis H. and Lillian S. Naboicheck; m. Hubert N. Polinsky, Sept. 21, 1958 (div.); children: Gerald, David, Beth. BA, U. Conn., 1953; postgrad., Harvard Bus. Sch., 1954. Mem. Waterford 2d Charter Commn. (Conn.), 1967-68, Waterford Conservation Commn., 1968-69; Waterford rep. Town Meeting, 1969-71, S.E. Conn. Regional Planning Agy., 1971-73; mem. Waterford Planning and Zoning Commn., 1970-76, chmn., 1973-76; mem. Waterford Dem. Town Com., 1976-92. Del. State Dem. Conv., 1976, 78, 80, 82, 84, 86, 90, 92; mem. Conn. Ho. of Reps. from 38th Dist., 1977-82, asst. majority leader, 1981-83, chmn. appropriations com., 1983-85, 87-89, ranking mem., 1985-87, minority whip, 1985-86, dep. whip., 1989-92; dep. commr. dept. adminstrv. svcs. State of Conn., 1993-94, chmn., 1994-95, asst. sec. of state, 1995, commr. utilities ctrl. auth., 1995-97. Trustee Eugene O'Neill Meml. Theatre Ctr., 1973-76, 81-92; corporator Lawrence and Meml. Hosps., 1987-88; mem. New Eng. Bd. Higher Edn., 1981-83; mem. fiscal affairs com. Eastern Conf. Coun. State Govts., 1983-88; mem. Limoge Village Bd., 2000-02; sec. Cascades Master bd., 2000—, sec., 2002—. Named Woman of Yr., Waterford Jr. Women's Club, 1977, Nehantic Women's Bus. and Profl. Club, 1979, Legislator of Yr., Conn. Libr. Assn., 1980. Mem. Order of Women Legislators, Delta Kappa Gamma (hon.). Home: 7141 Haviland Cir Boynton Beach FL 33437-6463 Personal E-mail: naboi1@aol.com.

**POLIS, MICHAEL PHILIP,** engineering educator; b. N.Y.C., Oct. 24, 1943; s. Max and Sylvia (Goldner) P.; m. Claudette Martin, May 28, 1966; children: Melanie Bobby, Martin Pascal, Karine Melissa. BSEE, U. Fla., 1966; MSEE, Purdue U., West Lafayette, 1968, PhD, 1972. Grad. instr. elec. engring. Purdue U., West Lafayette, 1966-71; postdoctoral fellow Ecole Polytechnique, Montreal, 1972-73, asst. prof. elec. engring., 1973-74, assoc. prof., 1974-82, prof., 1982-83; program dir. sys. theory NSF, Washington, 1983-87; chmn. dept. elec. and computer engring. Wayne State U., Detroit, 1987-93; dean Sch. Engring. and Computer Sci. Oakland U., Rochester, Mich., 1993-2001, prof. elec. and systems engring., 2001—. Expert witness various law firms, 1989—; cons. Mich. Bell-Ameritech, Detroit, 1989-95, ICAM Technologies, Inc., Montreal, 1981-83; vis. rsch. assoc. LAAS, Toulouse, France, 1978. Contbr. articles to profl. jours. Mem. IEEE (sr.), IEEE Control Sys. Soc. (bd. govs. 1993-95, 98-2000, Best Paper Trans. on Automatic Control 1974-75, Disting. Mem. 1993, v.p. mem. activities 1990-91, assoc. editor 1981-82). Office: Oakland Univ Sch Engring & Computer Sci Rochester MI 48309-4778 Office Phone: 248-370-2743.

**POLISAR, LEONARD MYERS,** lawyer; b. Bklyn., Oct. 25, 1929; s. Aaron and Anna (Myers) P.; m. Judith Sarah Weisstein, Aug. 16, 1959; children: Mark Joseph, Daniel Aaron. BA, Bklyn. Coll., 1950; LLB, Yale U., 1953; LLM in Taxation, NYU, 1959. Bar: N.Y. 1954. Assoc. Hays, Podell, Algase, Crum & Feuer, N.Y.C., 1955-63; asst. to gen. counsel CIT Fin. Corp., N.Y.C., 1963-65; v.p. law and pub. affairs Mgmt. Assistance Inc., N.Y.C., 1966-72; v.p., gen. counsel Internat. Controls Corp., Fairfield, NJ, 1972-73; v.p., gen. counsel Baker Industries Inc., Parsippany, NJ, 1973-80; ptnr. Herzfeld & Rubin, P.C., N.Y.C., 1980—, co-chmn. corp. and securities law dept., 1988—, also bd. dirs. Arbitrator N.Y. Stock Exch., 1987—; speaker at computer, securities and corp. seminars. Editor Yale Law Jour., 1953. Bd. dirs. Mental Health Assn. of N.Y.C., 1960—, chmn., 1985—; trustee Union Temple Bklyn., 1988—, v.p. 1990-99; bd. dirs. Routes to Roots Found. Mem. ABA, Assn. of Bar of City of N.Y., Am. Soc. Corp. Secs. (chmn. audit com. 1989-92), Bus. Coun. for UNA (bus. adv. com.), Bus. Execs. for Nat. Security, Computer Law Assn., Citizens Union, Yale Club of N.Y., Yale Club of Montclair, Phi Beta Kappa. Jewish. Avocations: skiing, sailing, spectator sports, music, drama. Office: Gibbons DelDeo Dolan Griffinger & Vecchione 1 Pennsylvania Plaza Fl 37 New York NY 10119-3701 Office Phone: 212-554-9625. E-mail: lpolisar@gibbonslaw.com.

**POLISI, JOSEPH WILLIAM,** academic administrator; b. NYC, Dec. 30, 1947; married Elizabeth; 3 children. BA in Polit. Sci., U. Conn., 1969; MA in Internat. Relations, Tufts U., 1970, MusM, 1973, M of Mus. Arts, 1975; DMA, Yale U., 1980; DHL (hon.), Ursinus Coll., Collegetown, Pa., 1986; MusD (hon.), Curtis Inst. Music, 1990; DMA, New England Conservatory Music, 2001; DHL (hon.), Juilliard Sch., 2005. Exec. officer Yale Sch. of Music, New Haven, 1976-80; dean of faculty Manhattan Sch. of Music, NYC, 1980-83; dean Coll. Conservatory of Music U. Cin., 1983-84; pres. The Juilliard Sch., NYC, 1984—. Spkr. in field. Performances as bassoonist throughout the U.S.; contbr. articles to various publs. in U.S. and France; author: The Artist as Citizen, 2005. Dir. Edward John Noble Foundation, Irene Diamond Fund. Named Educator of Yr., Musical Am. Internat. Dir. Performing Arts, 2005. Mem.: Royal Acad. Music London (hon.). Office: Juilliard Sch Office of Pres 60 Lincoln Center Plz New York NY 10023-6588

**POLITAN, NICHOLAS H.,** lawyer; b. 1961; BA, Duke U., 1983; JD, Stanford U., 1986. Bar: Calif. 1986, D.C. 1999, N.Y. 2000. Ptnr. Bingham McCutchen LLP, N.Y.C., co-chmn. project fin. practice group. Mem.: ABA-comml. fin. svc. com. Office: Bingham McCutchen LLP 399 Park Avenue New York NY 10022-4689 Office Phone: 212-705-7726. Office Fax: 212-752-5378. Business E-mail: nick.politan@bingham.com.

**POLITANO, MARCELA SUSANA,** chemical engineer, researcher; b. Rio Cuarto, Argentina, May 21, 1968; arrived in U.S., 2001; d. Simon Telmo Politano and Miriam Susana Parsi; m. Daniel Seabra De Andrade (div.); 1 child, Daniel Seabra de Andrade; m. Pablo Marcelo Carrica, Apr. 28, 2002; 1 child, Victoria Carrica. Degree in Chem. Engring., U. Nat. de Rio Cuarto, 1993, MS in Chem. Engring., 1999; DSc in Engring., Inst. Balseiro, 2001.

Process engr. En Gevix-Engenharia, São Paulo, Brazil, 1993—94; jr. rschr. U. Nat. de Rio Cuarto, Argentina, 1994—98; asst. prof. U. Argentina de la Empresa, Buenos Aires, 2001—02; postdoctoral assoc. U. Iowa, Iowa City, 2002—04, asst. rsch. engr., 2004—. Contbr. articles to profl. jours. Fellow, Fund Improvement of Univ. Quality, 1997—99, Nat. Coun. Sci. and Tech., 1999—2002. Avocations: reading, hiking, running, cooking.

**POLITE, CARLENE HATCHER,** writer, educator; b. Detroit; d. John and Lillian Hatcher; m. James S. Patrick, July 21, 2003; children from previous marriage: Glynda Morton, Lila Ashaki. Student, Martha Graham Sch. Dance, N.Y.C., 1952-56; diploma, Acad. Leonardo da Vinci, Rome, 1980. Dancer, student Martha Graham Sch., N.Y.C., 1952-56; dancer Alvin Ailey Dance Co., N.Y.C., 1957-58, Edith Stephen Co., N.Y.C., 1958; dancer, actress Vanguard Playhouse, Detroit, 1960-62; prof. English SUNY, Buffalo, 1971—2000, chair dept. Am. Studies, 1981, prof. emerita, 2000. Tchr. Golden Dragon Kung Fu Acad., 1974-75, Himalayan Inst. Yoga, 1980-82; panelist NEA, Washington, 1981, N.Y. State Coun. Arts, N.Y.C., 1982, N.Y. Found. Arts, 1983, Seattle Arts in Pub. Places, 1989. Author: The Flagellants, 1966, Paris edit., 1967, N.Y. edit., 1968, also other European edits. (Pulitzer prize nominee, 1967, NEA grant, 1967, Rockefeller grant, 1968), Sister X and The Victims of Foul Play, 1975. Coord. Walk to Freedom with Martin Luther King, Detroit, 1963; del., participant UN-Non-Govtl.Orgns. 4th World Conf. on Women, Beijing, 1995. Recipient numerous nat. and internat. awards as artist and educator; invited 1st Ann. Conf. African Presence, Paris, 1991, Internat. Educators and Writers Oxford U., 1997. Avocation: yoga.

**POLITE, EVELYN C.,** retired elementary school educator, evangelist; b. Pineland, SC, Dec. 25, 1937; d. Martin and Mary Brantley Coger; m. Horace Polite, Jan. 1, 1958 (dec. Jan. 1987); children: Horace Lenton, Tracy Polite Floyd. BS, Allen U., 1960; M in Elem. Edn., Armstrong-Savannah (Ga.) State U., 1976; cert. specialist of arts in theology, Zoe U., Jacksonville, Fla., 2000; PhD in Christian Counseling, Zoe U., 2001. Tchr. math. Beaufort County Bd. Edn., Bluffton, SC, 1960—61, Florence County Bd. Edn., Florence, SC, 1961—63, Jasper County Bd. Edn., Ridgeland, SC, 1963—64, 1991—92, Savannah Pub. Schs., 1964—90; math. tutor Dept. Family and Children, Savannah, 1992—94; ret., 1994. Mem. curriculum devel. com. Savannah Pub. Schs., 1983—84, mem. staff devel. coun., 1983—84; test-item writer Ednl. Testing Svc., Princeton, NJ, 1990; dir. Widows Harvest Ministries, Savannah, Ga. Pres. 42d St Civic Club, Savannah, 2000—03; exec. v.p. Cuyler-Brownsville Neighborhood Orgn., Savannah, 2001—02. Recipient Outstanding Tchr. award, Math.-Sci. Roundtable, Atlanta, 1990. Mem. Ch. Of God. Avocations: world missions, travel, physical fitness, reading Christian literature. Office: Coastal Cathedral Ch of God 2208 E DeRenne Ave Savannah GA 31406 Home: 33 Wild Heron Villas Rd Savannah GA 31419-8981 Office Phone: 912-354-5225. Personal E-mail: evelyn33@bellsouth.net.

**POLITI, BETH KUKKONEN,** publishing services company executive; b. Englewood, N.J., Sept. 18, 1949; d. Andrew and Beatrice G. (Druskin) Kukkonen; m. Joseph Politi, Oct. 21, 1982; children: Andrew, Joseph. BS in Mktg., Miami U., Oxford, Ohio, 1971. Media buyer Schwab, Beatty & Porter, Inc., 1971-72; media planner Adler, Schwartz & Connes, 1972-73; media buyer/planner Schwab Beatty divsn. Marstellar, 1973-74; dir. insert advt. Benjamin Co., Inc., Elmsford, N.Y., 1975-78, prodn. mgr., 1978-80, v.p. client svcs., 1980-83, editor supr., 1979-83; v.p. Bergen County Profl. Svcs., Ft. Lee, N.J., 1983—. Assoc. pub. various books Benjamin Co., Inc., 1981-83; freelance proofreader Montage Media, Mawah, N.J., 1999-2003. Trustee bd. edn. Pascack Valley Regional H.S. Dist., 1999—2006, v.p., 2002—06, pres., 2006—; mem. dist. fee com. Office of Atty. Ethics of Supreme Ct. of NJ, 2001—05; del. exec. com. Bergen County Sch. Bd. Assn., 2003—; v.p. exec. com. Borough Bogota, 2005—, tax assessor, 2004—. Home: 4 Smoke Rise Ct Montvale NJ 07645-1139

**POLITO, ROBERT J.,** federal agency administrator; m. Michele Polito; 3 children. B in Health Edn., Pa. State U. Creator, leader Bowery Mission Transitional Ctr., N.Y.C., 1994—99; founder FaithWorks, Milw., 1999; founder, past pres. FaithWorks Internat., N.Y.C.; dir. Ctrs. for Faith-Based and Cmty. Initiatives U.S. Dept. Health and Human Svcs., Washington, 2002—. Office: US Dept HHS Ctr for Faith-Based and Cmty Initiatives 200 Independence Ave SW Rm 118F Washington DC 20201

**POLITZER, HUGH DAVID,** physicist, educator; b. NYC, Aug. 31, 1949; s. Alan A. and Valerie T. (Diamant) P. BS, U. Mich., 1969; PhD, Harvard U., 1974. Jr. fellow Harvard U. Soc. Fellows, 1974-77; mem. faculty Calif. Inst. Tech., 1977—, prof. theoretical physics, 1979—, exec. officer for physics, 1986-88. Recipient J.J. Sakurai prize, 1986; fellow NSF, 1969-74, Sloan Found., 1977-81, Woodrow Wilson grad. fellow, 1969-74, Guggenheim fellow, 1997-98; co-recipient High Energy and Particle Physics prize European Phys. Soc., 2003, Nobel Prize in Physics, 2004. Mem. Phi Beta Kappa. Achievements include discovery of asymptotic freedom in the theory of the strong interaction. Office: Calif Inst Tech High Energy Physics 1201 E California Blvd Mail Code 452-48 Pasadena CA 91106-3368 Business E-Mail: politzer@theory.caltech.edu.*

**POLK, DAVID BRENT,** pediatrician, educator; MD, U. of Ark., Little Rock, 1984. Diplomate Am. Bd. of Pediat., 1999. Dean's prof. of pediat. and cell and devel. biology Vanderbilt U., Nashville, 1990—. Office: Vanderbilt University 2215 Garland Ave MRBIV 1025 Nashville TN 37232 Office Phone: 615-322-7449. Office Fax: 615-343-5323. E-mail: d-brent.polk@vanderbilt.edu.

**POLK, GEORGE WASHINGTON,** telecommunications executive, entrepreneur; b. Washington, Apr. 21, 1963; s. William Roe and Ann (Cross) P. BA, Harvard U., 1985. Fin. analyst Merrill Lynch Capital Mkts., N.Y.C., 1986-87, asst. to chmn., 1987-88; v.p., corp. devel. Wave Systems Corp., N.Y.C., 1988-90; pres. EP Systems Corp., Rolling Meadows, Ill., 1990-93; sr. v.p., internat. networks Geotek Comm., Montvale, N.J., 1994-98; pres. Global Wireless Holdings (Latin Am.), London, 1998-2000; CEO & founder The Cloud Inc., 2003—. Dir. Colourpath Ltd., London, 1993—. Bd. govs. Middle East Inst., Washington, 1997—; mem. nominating com. George Polk Awards, N.Y.C., 1992—; mem. Coun. on Fgn. Rels. Mem. Internat. Mobile Telecomm. Assn. (vice chmn. 1998—). Office: The Cloud Networks Ltd 54 bartholomew close London ec1a 7ry England Office Phone: +44 (0)20 7710 6500.*

**POLK, HIRAM CAREY, JR.,** surgeon, educator; b. Jackson, Miss., Mar. 23, 1936; s. Hiram Carey and Dorris (Hemby) P.; m. Susan Galandiuk; children: Susan Elizabeth, Hiram Cary. BS, Millsaps Coll., 1956; MD, Harvard U., 1960. Intern Barnes Hosp., St. Louis, 1960-61, resident, 1961-65; instr. in surgery Washington U., St. Louis, 1964-65; asst. prof. surgery U. Miami, Fla., 1965-69, assoc. prof., 1969-71; prof. chmn. dept. surgery U. Louisville, 1971—; pres., chmn. bd. U. Surg. Assocs., PSC, 1971—2005; chmn. bd. Clin. Services Assn., Inc. Mem. merit rev. bd. for surgery VA, 1983—85. Author: (with H.H. Stone) Contemporary Burn Management, 1971, Hospital-Acquired Infections in Surgery, 1977; (with B. Gardner, H.H. Stone and W.L. Sugg) Basic Surgery, 1978; (with H.H. Stone and B. Gardner) 2d edit., 1983, 3d edit., 1987, 4th edit., 1992, 5th edit., 1995; (with D.C. Carter) Trauma, 1982; (with J.E. Conte Jr. and L.S. Jacob) Antibiotic Prophylaxis in Surgery: A Comprehensive Review, 1984; (with J.D. Richardson and L.M. Flint Jr.) Trauma: Clinical Care and Pathophysiology, 1987; contbr. articles to profl. jours.; mem. editl. bd. So. Med. Jour., 1970-72, Jour. Surg. Rsch., 1970-72, 75-77, 78-80, Current Problems in Surgery, 1973—, Surgery, 1975-85, Current Surgery, 1977—, Current Surg. Techniques, 1977—, Emergency Surgery: A Weekly Update, 1977—, Collected Letters in Surgery, 1978—, Brit. Jour. Surgery, 1981-94; chief editor Am. Jour. Surgery, 1986-2004. Fellow Royal Coll. Surgeons Edinburgh (hon.); mem. ACS (gov. 1972-80), AMA, Allen O. Whipple Soc. (exec. coun. 1977-80), Am. Assn. Cancer Edn. (exec. coun. 1968-72), Am. Assn. Surgery of Trauma, Am. Burn Assn., Am. Cancer Soc. (pres. Ky. div. 1989-90, nat. del. dir. 1989-92, 93-95), Am. Surg. Assn. (sec. 1984-89, pres. 2005), Acad. Surgery (pres. 1975-76), Cen. Surg. Assn., Assn. Am. Med. Colls. (chmn. ad hoc com. on Medicare and

Medicaid 1978-79), Collegium Internat. Chirurgiae Digestivae (sec.-treas. 1981-86, pres. 1986-87), Coun. on Public Higher Edn. (task group on health scis.), Halsted Soc., Jefferson County Med. Soc., Ky. Med. Assn., Ky. Surg. Soc. (pres. 1982-83), Louisville Surg. Soc. (pres. 1989-90), Residency Rev. Com. for Surgery (vice chmn. 1981-83, chmn. 1983-85), Soc. Internat. de Chirurgie, Soc. Surgery Alimentary Tract (treas. 1975-78, pres. 1985-86), Soc. Clin. Surgery, Soc. Surg. Chairmen, Soc. Surg. Oncology (pres. 1984-85), Soc. Univ. Surgeons (treas. 1971-74, pres. 1979-80), James IV Assn. Surgeons (v.p. 2002—), Southeastern Surg. Congress (exec. coun. for Ky. 1985-86, pres. 1994-95), So. Med. Assn. (vice chmn. sect. on surgery 1969-70, chmn. sect. 1972-73, sec. 1970-72, exec. coun. for Ky. 1971-77, 89-90), So. Surg. Assn. (pres. 1988-89), Alpha Omega Alpha. Home: 5609 River Knoll Dr Louisville KY 40222-5846 Office: U Louisville Dept Surgery Louisville KY 40292-0001 Office Phone: 502-852-5442. Business E-Mail: hcpolk01@gwise.louisville.edu.

**POLK, JAMES RAY,** journalist; b. Oaktown, Ind., Sept. 12, 1937; s. Raymond S. and Oeta (Fleener) P.; m. Bonnie Becker, Nov. 4, 1962; children: Geoffrey, Amy; m. Cara Bryn Saylor, June 21, 1980; 1 child, Abigail. BA, Ind. U., 1962. With A.P., Indpls., 1962-65, Milw., 1965, Madison, Wis., 1966-67, Washington, 1967-71; investigative reporter Washington Star, 1971-75; correspondent NBC News, Washington, 1975-92; sr. producer CNN Spl. Assignment, 1992—. Pres. Investigative Reporters and Editors, Inc., 1978-80, chmn. bd., 1980-82, nat. coll. chmn., 1983-90. With U.S. Navy, 1955-58. Named to Ind. Journalism Hall of Fame, 1994; recipient Pub. Affairs Reporting award, Am. Polit. Sci. Assn., 1961, Raymond Clapper Meml. award, 1972, 1974, Pulitzer prize for nat. reporting on Watergate, 1974, Sigma Delta Chi award, 1974, Nat. Headliner awards, 2d pl. award TV documentary, 1996, 2003, investigative reporting, 1993, Emmy award for coverage of Oklahoma City bombing, 1996, Ind. U. Disting. Alumni award. Mem. Phi Kappa Psi. Office: CNN Center Atlanta GA 30348

**POLK, MALCOLM,** chemistry professor; b. Chgo., Feb. 2, 1938; s. Andrew and Irene Mosley; 1 child, Irene. BS in Chemistry, U. Ill., 1960; PhD in Chemistry, U. Pa., 1964. Chemist E.I. DuPont, Wilmington, Del., 1965—67, 1968—72; assoc. prof. Prairie View (Tex.) Coll., 1967—68; polymer chemist U.S. Dept. Interior, Washington, 1982—83; assoc. prof., then prof. Atlanta U., 1973—85, Ga. Inst. Tech., Atlanta, 1984—2003, prof. emeritus, 2003—. Dir. Polymer Rsch. Ctr., Atlanta, 1980—84; mem. com. on liquid crystalline polymers NRC, 1987—89; leader conf. in field. Contbr. chapters to books. Grantee, Polymer Rsch. Ctr., Office Naval Rsch., 1980—84, Nat. Textile Ctr., 1992—95, NIH/MBS, 1978—81. Mem.: Nat. Orgn. Profl. Advancement of Black Chemists and Chem. Engrs. (Outstanding Tchr. award 1990), Fiber Soc., Am. Chem. Soc., Phi Lambda Upsilon. Achievements include invention of multidimentional crosslinear rigid-rod benzobistzole polymer fibers. Avocations: ancient history, travel, cycling, reading, playing cards. Office: Ga Inst Tech Atlanta GA 30332 Office Phone: 404-894-2490. Office Fax: 404-894-8780. E-mail: malcolmp@bellsouth.net.

**POLK, SAMUEL S.,** lawyer; Former ptnr. Milbank, Tweed, Hadley & McCloy. Former trustee Cooper Union for Advancement of Sci. & Art, Frederick R. Koch Found.; trustee Hosp. for Special Surgery, Med. Indemnity Assurance Co., Ltd., Collier Found., Westchester Land Trust; chmn., bd. dirs. NY Community Trust. Office: NY Community Trust 909 Third Ave New York NY 10022*

**POLK, WILLIAM ROE,** historian; b. Ft. Worth, Tex., Mar. 7, 1929; m. Joan Alison Cooledge, Dec. 1950; children: Milbry Catherine Polk, Alison Elizabeth Polk; m. Ann Borders Cross, June 9, 1962 (div. Oct. 1979); children: George Washington Polk, Eliza Polk; m. Baroness Elisabeth von Oppenheimer, Dec. 29, 1981. BA with honors, Harvard U., 1951, PhD, 1958; BA with honors, Oxford, Eng., 1955, MA, 1959; LLD (hon.), Lake Forest Coll., 1967. Asst. prof. Harvard Univ., 1956-61; fgn. svc. res. officer class 1, mem. policy planning coun. U.S. State Dept., 1961-65; prof. U. Chgo., 1965-73; pres. Adlai Stevenson Inst., Chgo., 1967-72; sr. dir. W.P. Carey Found.; chmn. EP Systems, N.Y.C., 1990-93, Chaika Oil Co., London and Moscow, 1993-95. Bd. dirs. Hyde Park Bank, Chgo., Microform Data Systems, Arlington Books, Cambridge, Naftex Ltd., Harris & Harris, Morrison Internat. Ltd., The Salzburg Seminar; cons. Aetna Life and Casualty, Time Inc., TWA, Crocker Nat. Bank, Wheelabrator Frye Inc., Fuller Petroleum, GTE, Teledyne, J. Henry Schroder, U.K., Power Corp., Can., Allianz Versicherungs A.G., Germany, Volkswagen A.G., Germany, Flughafen Frankfurt Main A.G., Germany, Louis Féraud & Cie, France, UN Stockholm and Vancouver Confs. on the Environment; lectr. in field. Author: What the Arabs Think, 1952, Backdrop to Tragedy, 1957, The Opening of South Lebanon, 1963, The United States and the Arab World, 1965, The United States and the Arab World, 3rd edit., 1975, Passing Brave, 1973, 1974, The Golden Ode, 1974, 1977, 1993, The Elusive Peace, 1979, The Arab World, 1980, The Arab World Today, 1991, The Vence Partitas, 1992, Neighbors and Strangers: The Fundamentals of Foreign Affairs, 1997, Polk's Folly: An American Family History, 2000, 2001, Understanding Iraq, 2005, 2006, The Birth of America, 2006, Out of Iraq: A Practical Plan for Withdrawal Now, 2006; editor: The Civilization of Islam, 1962, 1975, The Developmental Revolution, 1963, The Beginnings of Modernization in the Middle East, 1968; contbr. articles to books and profl. jours. including Fgn. Affairs, N.Y. Rev. Books, The Atlantic, etc. Bd. dirs. The Salzburg Seminar, YMCA C.C., The Middle East Inst., The Adlai Stevenson Inst., W.P. Carey Found., 2001—. Recipient Medal of Honor, Kingdom of Afghanistan, 1967; fellow Rockefeller Found., 1951-55, Ford Found., 1954, Guggenheim Found., 1961. Mem. The Century Assn., Coun. on Fgn. Rels., Middle East Studies Assn. (bd. dirs.), Soc. of the Cin. Democrat. Avocations: exploration, tennis, sailing, gardening. Home: 669 Chemin de la Sine F-06140 Vence France E-mail: williamrpolk@post.harvard.edu.

**POLL, MARTIN HARVEY,** film producer; b. NYC; s. David and Fay (Tamber) P.; m. Lee Lindenberg, May 21, 1954 (div. Oct. 10, 1967); children: Mark, Jonathan; m. Gladys Peltz Jaffe, Oct. 31, 1976; 1 son, Anthony. BS, Wharton Sch. Bus. U. Pa., 1943. Pres. Inter-Continental TV Films Inc., N.Y.C., 1952; exec. producer Theatre Network TV Inc., N.Y.C., 1953; pres. Gold Medal Studios, Bronx, N.Y., 1954-62; ind. producer, 1962—. (Named Hon. Commr. Motion Picture Arts N.Y.C. 1958, recipient David Di Donatello Best Film Producer award Pres. Italy 1968, N.Y. Film Critics award 1968, Hollywood Fgn. Press Assn. Golden Globe award 1968, Brit. Acad. award 1968); films include Love is a Ball, 1962, Sylvia, 1964, The Appointment, 1968, The Lion in Winter, 1968 (Best Picture award), The Magic Garden of Stanley Sweetheart, 1970, Night Watch, 1972, The Man Who Loved Cat Dancing, 1973, Love and Death, 1975, The Sailor Who Fell From Grace with The Sea, 1976, The Dain Curse, Somebody Killed Her Husband, 1978, Nighthawks, 1981, Arthur the King, 1984, Gimme An F, 1984, Haunted Summer, 1987, My Heroes Have Always Been Cowboys, 1991, (TV miniseries) Diana—Her True Story, 1993. Served with AUS, 1944-47. Mem. Producers Guild of Am., Acad. Motion Picture Arts and Scis., Cinema Circulus, Friends of Library U. So. Calif.

**POLL, ROBERT EUGENE, JR.,** bank executive; b. Urbana, Ill., Apr. 16, 1948; s. Robert E. Sr. and Dorothy (Baker) P.; children: Alexandra, Bianca; m. Caroline Vaughan, Sept. 20, 2003. BA, Kenyon Coll., 1970; MBA, Ind. U., 1972. V.p. Chase Manhattan Bank, N.Y.C., 1972-78; assoc. Lazard Freres & Co., N.Y.C., 1978-82; mng. dir., mgr. mcpl. divsn., 1985-98; gen. ptnr. William Blair & Co., Chgo., 1982-84; sr. mng. dir. Poll Financial, LLC, 1998—; co-chmn. Chief Consol. Mining Co., 2002; pres., CEO Bernard Techs., Inc., 2002; mng. dir., chief investment officer Castleton Ptnrs., 2005—. Adv. bd. Pub. Fin. Inst., N.Y.C., 1976, Worldvest. Trustee Citizens Budget Commn. Mem. N.Y. Acad. Sci., Tavern Club (Chgo.), N.Y. Athletic Club, Ind. U. Kelley Sch. Bus. Alumni Assn. (dir.). Home: Apt 13A 350 Central Park W New York NY 10025-6503 Office Phone: 212-832-9700. Personal E-mail: rpollfin@att.net. Business E-Mail: rpoll@pollfinancial.com.

**POLLACE, PAMELA L.,** public relations executive; b. San Jose, Calif., May 1953; BA; U. Santa Clara, 1975. Acct. mgr. mktg. comm. Oxbridge, Inc.; acct. supr. Burson Marsteller; spokesperson, mgr., dir. Intel Corp, Santa Clara, Calif., 1987-96, v.p., dir. worldwide press rels., 1996—2000; v.p. dir. corp. comms. Intel Corp., Santa Clara, Calif., 2000—. Office: Intel Corp Worldwide Press Rels PO Box 58119 Santa Clara CA 95052-8119

**POLLACK, BARBARA GRACE,** writer; b. N.Y.C., May 17, 1927; m. Merrill S. Pollack, Nov. 27, 1947; children: Elise, Diana, Steven, Anne. Student, Am. Acad. Dramatic Art, 1946, Fordham U., 1978-79, Georgetown U., 1980-81. Rsch. asst. art and archaeology dept. Princeton (N.J.) U., 1964-67; with Social Security Adminstrn. Office Hearings and Appeals U.S. Govt., N.Y.C., 1987—. Vol. coord. employee art hobby shows Social Security, NYC, 2003—04. Co-author: (with Doris Humphrey) The Art of Making Dances, 1959, The Collectors, 1962, (with Charles H. Woodford) Dance is a Moment, 1993; contbr. articles to mags. Vol. Smithsonian Instn., The White House, Cooper-Hewitt Mus., N.Y.C., ARC; vol. mentor in English lang.; Am. history and music and art. Home: 484 W 43rd St Apt 39m New York NY 10036-6342

**POLLACK, GERALD ALEXANDER,** economist, educator, federal agency administrator; b. Vienna, Jan. 14, 1929; came to U.S. 1938; s. Stephen J. and Tini (Herschel) P.; m. Patricia E. Sisterson; children: Nora P. Silverman, Carol A. BA, Swarthmore (Pa.) Coll., 1951; MA, MPA, Princeton U., 1953, PhD, 1958. Corp. economist Leeds & Northrup Co., Phila., 1958-62; officer in charge internat. payments U.S. Dept. State, Washington, 1962-63; internat. economist Joint Econ. Com. of Congress, Washington, 1963-65; chief economist Office Spl. Rep. for Trade Negotiations, 1964; dep. asst. sec. U.S. Dept. Commerce, Washington, 1965-68; v.p. Loeb, Rhoades & Co., N.Y.C., 1968-69, Bendix Corp., Southfield, Mich., 1969-70, Citibank, N.Y.C., 1970-71; internat. economist Exxon Corp., N.Y.C., 1971-86; v.p., chief economist Overseas Shipholding Group, N.Y.C., 1986-89; assoc. prof. fin. Pace U., N.Y.C., 1990-94; assoc. dir. for internat. econs. Bur. Econ. Analysis, U.S. Dept. Commerce, 1994-99. Contbr. articles to profl. jours. Bd. dirs. Jamaica Estates Assn., 1976-80, Oakwood Friends Sch., Poughkeepsie, N.Y., 1979-89; trustee Lindley Murray Fund, 1990-94; mem. Greenwich Dem. Town Com., 1992-94, 2001—; clk. Flushing Monthly Meeting Soc. of Friends, 1990-94; mem. Greenwich Rep. Town Meeting, 1999-2003. With U.S. Army, 1953-55. Mem.: Violoncello Soc., Coun. on Fgn. Rels., Phi Beta Kappa. Mem. Soc. Of Friends. Avocations: cello, classical music, photography, hiking, bicycling. Personal E-mail: gapollack@hotmail.com.

**POLLACK, GERALD LESLIE,** physicist, researcher; b. Bklyn., July 8, 1933; s. Herman and Jennie (Tenenbaum) P.; m. Antoinette Amparo Velasquez, Dec. 22, 1958; children: Harvey Anton, Samuela Juliet, Margolita Mia, Violet Amata. BS, Bklyn. Coll., 1954; Fulbright scholar, U. Gottingen, 1954-55; MS, Calif. Inst. Tech., 1957, PhD, 1962. Physics student trainee Nat. Bur. Standards, Washington, 1954-58, solid state physicist, 1961-65, cons. Boulder, Colo., 1965-70; assoc. prof. dept. physics Mich. State U., East Lansing, 1965-69, prof., 1969—2005, prof. emeritus, 2005—; cons. NRC, Ill. Dept. Nuclear Safety; physicist Naval Med. Rsch. Inst., Bethesda, Md., summer 1979. Physicist USAF Sch. Aerospace Medicine, San Antonio, Tex., summer 1987; adj. prof. Dept. Physics, Colo. Sch. Mines, Golden, 2005—. Co-author (with D.R. Stump): Electromagnetism, 2002; contbr. articles to profl. jours. Fellow Am. Phys. Soc.; mem. AAAS, Am. Assn. Physics Tchrs. Office: Colo Sch of Mines Dept Physics Golden CO 80401 Office Phone: 303-273-3920. Business E-Mail: gpollack@mines.edu, pollack@msu.edu.

**POLLACK, IAN FREDRIC,** physician, researcher; b. Holliswood, N.Y., Aug. 26, 1960; s. Jonah and Roberta Minnie (Wainick) P.; m. Constance Shenk, Aug. 15, 1982; children: Benjamin Nathan, Andrew Maxwell. BS magna cum laude, Emory U., 1980; MD, Johns Hopkins U., 1984. Intern in surgery U. Pitts., 1984-85, resident in neurosurgery, 1985-91, postgrad. fellow dept. neurobiology, 1988-90, asst. prof. dept. neurosurgery, 1990-96, assoc. prof., 1996—99, prof., 1999—, Walter Dandy prof., 2001—, co-dir. Brain Tumor Ctr., 1996—. Chmn. brain tumor strategy group. Contbr. articles to New Eng. Jour. Medicine, Cancer Rsch., Exptl. Neurology, Jour. Neurosurgery, Cancer, Jour. Neurosurgery Rsch., Neurosurgery, Brain Rsch., others. Van Wagenen fellow Am. Assn. Neurol. Surgeons, 1991; recipient Resident Rsch. award ACS, 1990, Pitts. Neurosci. Soc., 1989, Preuss award Am. Assn. Neurol. Surgeons and Congress Neurological Surgeons Joint Sect. on Tumors, 1989, Young Clinician Investigator award Am. Assn. Neurol. Surgeons, 1992. Mem. AAAS, Congress of Neurol. Surgeons, Phi Beta Kappa, Alpha Omega Alpha. Achievements include research in the growth factor response properties of human brain tumor cells in culture, the role of selective inhibitors on tumor growth in culture, molecular markers of brain tumor prognosis and immunotherapeutic strategies for brain tumors. Office: U Pitts Dept Neurosurgery 9402 Presbyn Univ Hosp 230 Lothrop St Pittsburgh PA 15213-2536 also: Childrens Hosp Pitts Dept Neurosurgery 3705 5th Ave Pittsburgh PA 15213-2583 E-mail: ian.pollack@chp.edu.

**POLLACK, IRWIN WILLIAM,** psychiatrist, educator; b. Phila., Aug. 14, 1927; s. Nathan and Rose (Bergman) P.; m. Barbara Jean Callaway, Oct. 9, 1988; children from previous marriage: Nathaniel Edward, Joshua Frank, Jonathan Daniel AB, Temple U., 1950; MA, Columbia U., 1951; student, U. Pa., 1951—52; MD, U. Vt., 1956. Diplomate: Am. Bd. Psychiatry and Neurology. Intern Grad. Hosp. U. Pa., 1956—57; asst. resident psychiatry Henry Phipps Psychiat. Clinic (John Hopkins Hosp.), 1957—60; chief resident psychiatry Johns Hopkins Hosp., 1960—61, adminstr. psychosomatic clinic, psychiat. liaison svc., 1961—64; psychiatrist-in-chief Sinai Hosp. Balt., 1964—69; mem. faculty psychiatry Coll. Medicine and Dentistry N.J. (Rutgers Med. Sch.), 1968—87, 1971—, clin. prof. psychiatry, 1998. Assoc. prof. psychiatry, 1968-70, prof. psychiatry, 1979-99, emeritus prof. psychiatry 1999—, chmn. dept. Univ. Medicine and Dentistry N.J., prof. neurology, dir. Ctr. for Cognitive Rehab.; exec. dir. Coll. Medicine and Dentistry (Cmty. Mental Health Ctr.), 1970-77 Served with USNR, 1945-46 Fellow Am. Psychiat. Assn. (life); mem. N.J. Psychiat. Assn., Am. Psychosomatic Soc., Am. Congress Rehab. Medicine, Alpha Omega Alpha Achievements include spl. research or problems of time and space perception, psychology of phys. disability, doctor-patient relationships, cognitive retraining of brain-injured persons. Home: 1499 W Shore Rd West Danville VT 05873 E-mail: iwpollack@aol.com.

**POLLACK, JEFFREY LEE,** restaurateur; b. San Francisco, May 1, 1945; s. Albert and Loretta (Popper) P.; m. Patricia Bowdle Connell, Feb. 20, 1983; children: Lizabeth Ann, Hilary Margaret, Nicholas Albert. BA, San Jose State U. Owner, surety underwriter North Beach Bonding Co., San Francisco, 1968-75; proprietor Old Waldorf, San Francisco, 1974-80, Punchline, 1978-80, Julius' Castle, San Francisco, 1980—, New Joe's, San Francisco, 1984-99, Shadows, San Francisco, 1985-95, Iron Horse, 1986-92, Pollack Group, San Francisco, 1985—, Nick's Lighthouse Restaurant, San Francisco, 1991—, Original Joe's # 2, 1992-95, O'Connell's, San Francisco, 1994, Dalla Torre, 1996—. Mem. Downtown Assn. (bd. dirs. 1987—, v.p. 1992), Union Sq. Assn., North Beach C. of C. (bd. dirs. 1989, v.p. 1992), Port Tenants Assn., Fisherman Wharf Assn., Commonwealth Club. Democrat. Avocations: classic car collecting, movies. Home: 302 Greenwich St San Francisco CA 94133-3210 Office: Pollack Group Ltd 1541 Montgomery St San Francisco CA 94133-3232

**POLLACK, JOE,** retired columnist, critic, writer; b. Bklyn., Feb. 3, 1931; s. Samuel H. and Anna (Weisman) P.; m. Joan S., Mar. 6, 1952 (div. 1964); children: Wendy, Dara, Sharon; m. Carol Atchison, Dec. 1, 1964 (dec. 1993); m. Ann Lemons, Nov. 20, 1994. BJ, U. Mo., 1952. Sports writer St. Louis Globe-Democrat, 1955-61; dir. pub. rels. St. Louis Football Cardinals, 1961-72; critic, columnist St. Louis Post-Dispatch, 1972-95. Critic Sta. KSDK-TV, St. Louis, 1973-88, Sta. KMOV-TV, St. Louis, 1988-92; commentator Sta. KMOX, St. Louis, 1960-85, Sta. KWMU, St. Louis, 1994—. Author: Joe Pollack's Guide to St. Louis Restaurants, 1988, updated, 1992, (with Ann Lemons Pollack) Beyond Toasted Ravioli, 1998, Beyond Gooey Butter Cake, 2001, The Great St. Louis Eats Book, 2005; contbr. numerous

articles to mags. Mem. Am. Theatre Critics Assn., Profl. Football Writers Assn., Am. Soc. Profl. Journalists. Home: 7417 Oxford Dr Saint Louis MO 63105-2915 Office Phone: 314-862-3321. Personal E-mail: jpalfood@aol.com.

**POLLACK, JUDY BARBARA,** special education educator; b. Chicago, Ill., Mar. 4, 1953; d. Richard B and Betty L Pollack; m. James E Weir, Oct. 6, 1979; 1 child, Jerome R Weir. BA, Elmhurst Coll., 1972—75, EdB, 1985—88; MEd, Nat. Louis U., 1996—2000. Educational Administration Ill., 2000, Special Education Ill., 1995, Secondary Education Ill., 1988. Sales rep. Prentice Hall Pub., Chgo., 1980—85; tchr. York H.S., Elmhurst, Ill., 1988—. V.p. Sch. Dist. 45, Villa Park, Ill., 1991—93; bd. mem. North Shore Club Condominiums, South Haven, Mich., 2003—. Recipient Salesmanship, Prentice Hall, Info. Divsn., 1982; scholar Ill. State Scholarship, State of Ill. 1971—75. Mem.: ASCD, Coun. of Administrators of Spl. Edn. (corr.) D-Liberal. Avocations: travel, piano, violin. Home: 206 N Cornell Ave Villa Park IL 60181 Office: York High School 355 W St Charles Rd Elmhurst IL 60126 Office Phone: 630-617-2400 7306. Personal E-mail: pollackjudy@comcast.net. E-mail: jpollack@elmhurst205.org.

**POLLACK, LARRY,** plastic surgeon; b. N.Y.C., June 6, 1956; s. Curt and Giselle Pollack; m. Lisa Arian, Sept. 4, 1983; children: Jennifer, Melanie. BA, UCLA, 1978; MD, St. George's U., Grenada, 1982. Diplomate Am. Bd. of Plastic Surgery, 1992. Sr. staff, surgery Sharp Meml. Hosp., San Diego, 1990—; dir. plastic surgery Del Mar Plastic Surgery, San Diego, 1995—; chief plastic surgery Sharp Meml. Hosp., San Diego, 2001—05. Contbr. textbook. Fellow: ACS; mem.: Calif. Soc. Plastic Surgeons, Am. Soc. Plastic Surgeons. Office: Larry Pollack MD 7930 Frost St Ste 101 San Diego CA 92123

**POLLACK, MARSHA,** secondary school educator; d. Harry and Rose Grunberg; m. Bertram Pollack, July 14, 1944; 1 child, Meredith Pollack-Richman. BA, Bklyn Coll., 1968, MS, 1973; Specialist Diploma in Adminstrn. and Supervision, Queens Coll., 2003. Cert. tchr. Nat. Bd. Profl. Tchg. Standards, 2001. Tchr. N.Y.C. Dept. of Edn., Bklyn. and Queens, 1968—2002, asst. prin. Queens, 2002—03, tchr./coach/staff devel., 2003—. L.E.A.D. tchr. N.Y.C. Dept. of Edn., 1998—2002, nat. staff devel., 2000; profl. devel. Jericho Mid. Sch., 2003; lesson plan-abstract evaluator Internat. Reading Assn., 2003—05. CAL grantee, Chase Manhattan, 2001. Mem.: Am. Fedn. Tchrs., Nat. Coun. Tchrs. English, Phi Delta Kappa, Internat. Reading Assn., ASCD. Avocations: law, educational research, writing. Office Phone: 718-831-4000. Office Fax: 718-831-4008. Personal E-mail: bjpmhp@aol.com. Business E-mail: mpollac2@nycboe.net.

**POLLACK, MARTIN D.,** lawyer; b. Newark, July 24, 1951; BA, MA, Johns Hopkins U., 1973; JD, U. Pa., 1976; LLM, NYU Sch. Law, 1979. Bar: NJ 1976, US Dist. Ct. NJ 1976, NY 1977, US Tax Ct. 1978. Ptnr., co-head tax dept. Weil, Gotshal & Manges LLP, NYC, 1995—. Assoc. adj. prof. NYU Sch. Continuing Edn., 1983—, assoc. adj. prof. tax law NYU Sch. Law, 1989—; lectr. Real Estate Inst., 1979-83; lectr. in field; mem. adv. bd. Tax Mgmt. US Income. Mem. U. Pa. Law Review 1975-1976; mem. adv. bd. Equipment Leasing newsletter.; Contbr. articles to profl. jours. Mem. ABA, NY State Bar Assn. (mem. tax sect.), NJ State Bar Assn. (mem. tax sect.), Phi Beta Kappa. Office: Weil Gotshal & Manges LLP 767 5th Ave New York NY 10153 Office Phone: 212-310-8461. Office Fax: 212-310-8007. Business E-Mail: martin.pollack@weil.com.

**POLLACK, MICHAEL,** lawyer; b. NYC, July 14, 1946; s. Irving and Bertha (Horowitz) P.; m. Barbara Linda Shore, Aug. 23, 1970; children: Matthew, Ilana. BEng, Cooper Union, 1967; MS, U. Pa., 1970; JD, Temple U., 1974. Bar: Pa. 1974, U.S. Dist. Ct. (ea. dist.) Pa. 1974, N.Y. 2000. Rsch. scientist Pa. Rsch. Assocs., Phila., 1969-70; engr. GE Co., Valley Forge, Pa., 1969-70, Burroughs Corp., Great Valley, Pa., 1970-71; assoc. Blank, Rome, Comisky & McCauley, Phila., 1974-82, ptnr., mgr. dept. real estate, 1982—. Lectr., course planner Pa. Bar Inst., Phila. Mem. ABA, Pa. Bar Assn., Phila. Bar Assn., Internat. Assn. Attys. and Execs. in Corp. Real Estate (chmn., bd. dirs.), Eta Kappa Nu, Tau Beta Pi. Republican. Avocations: music, tennis. Office: Blank Rome LLP 1 Logan Sq Philadelphia PA 19103-6998 Office Phone: 215-569-5670. E-mail: pollack@blankrome.com.

**POLLACK, MICHAEL BRUCE,** lawyer; b. Phila., Mar. 27, 1958; s. Solomon Robert and Ethel (Sutow) Pollack; m. Deborah Ann Moses, Aug. 15, 1982; children: Jennifer Cara, Benjamin Philip. BS in economics, U. Pa., 1980; postgrad., U. Pa. Law Sch., 1982-83; JD, Boston U., 1983. Bar: Pa., 1983, US Dist. Ct. Ea. Dist. Pa., 1984. Ptnr., Phila. office Reed Smith Shaw & McClay (now Reed Smith LLP), 1983—, dir. strategic planning, mem. exec. com. & mgmt. com. 1st v.p., sec. W.P. Carey & Co., Inc., 1987. Bd. dirs. Temple Sinai. Mem. ABA, Pa. Bar Assn., Beta Alpha Psi. Republican. Jewish. Avocation: golf. Office: Reed Smith LLP 2500 One Liberty Pl 1650 Market St Philadelphia PA 19103-7301 Office Phone: 215-851-8182. Office Fax: 215-851-1420. Business E-Mail: mpollack@reedsmith.com.

**POLLACK, ROBERT ELLIOT,** biologist, educator, writer; b. Bklyn., Sept. 2, 1940; s. Hyman Ephraim and Molly (Pollack) P.; m. Amy Louise Steinberg, Dec. 23, 1961; 1 child, Marya BA in Physics, Columbia U., 1961; PhD in Biology, Brandeis U., 1966. Asst. prof. pathology Med. Sch. NYU, 1967-69; sr. scientist Cold Spring Harbor Lab., NY, 1971-75; prof. microbiology Med. Sch., SUNY-Stony Brook, 1975-78; prof. biol. sci. Columbia U., N.Y.C., 1978—; dean Columbia Coll. N.Y.C., 1982-89 Dbl dir., chmn. sci. adv. bd. Tapestry Pharms., 1994—; instr. Pratt Archtl. Sch., Bklyn., 1970; lectr. psychiatry Ctr. for Psychoanalytic Trng., Columbia U., 1999—; dir. Ctr. for the Study of Sci. and Religion, 1999—; vis. prof. pharmacology Albert Einstein Coll. Medicine, Bronx, N.Y., 1977-92; dean's disting. lectr. in Humanities, Columbia Med. Sch., 2000; lectr. Rosenthal Colloquium, March of Dimes, 1989; McGregory lectr. Colgate U., 1979; du Vigneaud lectr. Med. Sch., Cornell U., 1983. Co-editor: Readings in Mammalian Cell Culture, 1973, 3d rev. edit., 1981, Signs of Life, 1984 (translations in 7 langs., Lionel Trilling award 1995), The Missing Moment, 1999, The Faith of Biology and the Biology of Faith, 2000; mng. editor BBA Revs. on Cancer, 1980-86; contbr. numerous rsch. articles on molecular cell biology to profl. jours. Trustee N.Y. Found., 1988-96, Brandeis U., 1989-94, Solomon Schechter Sch. of N.Y.C., 1996-98; fellow World Econ. Forum, 1995—; bd. overseers List Coll. of the Jewish theol. Sem. of Am., 1996-99; pres. Jewish Campus Life Fund, Columbia U., 1997-2001. Recipient Rsch. Career Devel. award NIH, 1974, Alexander Hamilton medal, 1989, Lionel Trilling award Columbia U., 1995; NIH spl. fellow Weizmann Inst., Rehovot, Israel, 1970-71; grantee Nat. Cancer Inst., NIH, 1968-92, Am. Cancer Soc., 1985-94; John Simon Guggenheim fellow, 1993. Fellow AAAS; mem. N.Y. Acad. Scis., Am. Soc. Microbiology. Office: Columbia U Fairchild Hall 1212 Amsterdam Ave # Mc2419 New York NY 10027-7003 Office Phone: 212-854-2409. Business E-Mail: pollack@columbia.edu.

**POLLACK, ROBERT HARVEY,** psychology professor; b. N.Y.C., June 26, 1927; s. Solomon and Bertha (Levy) P.; m. Martha Dee Katz, Aug. 20, 1948; children: Jonathan Keith, Lance Michael, Scott Evan. BS, CCNY, 1948; MS, Clark U., Worcester, Mass., 1950, PhD, 1953. Lectr. U. Sydney, Australia, 1953-61; spl. rsch. fellow Columbia U., N.Y.C., 1960-61; chief div. congitive devel. Inst. Juvenile Rsch., Chgo., 1961-63, dep. dir. rsch., 1963-69; from clin. asst. prof. to clin. assoc. prof. rsch. U. Ill. Coll. Medicine, Chgo., 1962-67; prof. psychology U. Ga., Athens, 1969-96, chair grad. program, exptl. psychology, 1970-78, chair grad. study com., 1978-86; prof. emeritus, 1996—; chair grad. program in life-span psychology U. Ga., Athens, 1988-96. Editor: The Experimental Psychology of Alfred Binet, 1969; contbr. over 100 articles and chpts. to profl. publs. Cpl. U.S. Army, 1945-46. Grantee Nat. Inst. Child Health and Human Devel., 1965, 67, 72, 78. Fellow AAAS, Am. Psychol. Assn.; mem. Am. Assn. Sex Edn., Counsellors and Therapists, Gerontol. Soc. Am., Australian Psychol. Soc., Soc. for Researching Child

Devel., Soc. for Sci. Study Sex, Sigma Xi. Democrat. Avocations: travel, stamp collecting/philately, opera, military history. Office: U Ga Dept Psychology Athens GA 30602 Office Phone: 706-542-3084. Business E-Mail: bpollack@uga.edu.

**POLLACK, ROBERT WILLIAM,** psychiatrist, corporate financial executive; b. N.Y.C., May 22, 1947; s. George and Esther P.; m. Pam Gregory, Sept. 15, 1984; 1 child, Jessie. BS in Biology, Yale U., 1969; MD, SUNY Downstate Med. Ctr., Bklyn.; 1973. Diplomate Am. Bd. Psychiatry and Neurology. Tng. resident U. Fla., 1973-76, chief resident dept. psychiatry, 1975-76, asst. prof. dept. psychiatry Gainesville, 1976-77; clin. asst. prof. dept. psychiatry Shands Hosp., Gainesville, 1977—; chief dept. psychiatry Fla. Hosp., Orlando, 1983, 84; clin. dir. assessment and evaluation team West Lake Hosp., Longwood, Fla., 1984-87, clin. dir. intensive evaluation unit, 1987-89; med. dir. Fla. Psychiat. Assocs., Winter Park, 1989-92, Fla. Psychiat. Mgmt., Winter Park, 1990-97; corp. med. dir. FPM Behavioral Health, 1993-97; co-founder Profl. Quality Analysts, Inc., Casselberry, Fla., 1997—2001; CEO VShift, Orlando, Fla., 2002—03; CMIO Ctrl. Fla. Healthcare Coalition, 2003—; pres. Matrix Network Tech. Group, Orlando, Fla., 2003—, Quantum Delta Enterprises, Orlando, 2004—, Nexia Strategy Corp., Orlando, 2005—; exec. v.p. Mirabilis Ventures Inc., 2005—. Med. dir. consultation, liaison svc. and spl. med. unit Winter Park Meml. Hosp., 1992; integrated surveyor Jt. Commn. for Accreditation of Healthcare Orgns., 1998—2000, sentinel event, 1999—2000; pres., CEO The Rondo Group, Longwood, Fla., 2000—; CEO, Cory Marvin Erving Found, 2001—; chief med. info. officer Ctrl. Fla. Healthcare Coalition, 2003—; bd. dirs. Analytic Data Systems, Inc.; chmn. Bd. Living Hope Ministries, 2004—; bd. dirs. Teknovation; gen. ptnr. EP JVG (Erving Pollack Joint Venture Group), BOD Teknovation, Erving Pullack Joint Venture Group Review Bd. Contbr. 4 articles to profl. jours.; author sci. reports. Chmn. Retinitis Pigmentosa Casino Night, Orlando, 1988-92; vice-chmn. nat. championship com. U.S. Blind Golfers Assn., 1991-92, chair 48th ann. championship com., 1992-93; bd. dirs. Tennis with a Different Swing, Orlando, 1989-92; mem. Seminole County Assn. on Domestic Violence, 1998-; chmn. Living Hope Internat. Ministries, 2005-. Recipient Quality Achievement award, Ctrl. Fla. Healthcare Coalition, 2003. Mem. U.S. Blind Golfers Assn. (chairperson, nat. championships 1998, 99, 2000), Alqua Country Club (bd. dirs.). Methodist. Achievements include introduction of use of computerized topographical brain mapping as a diagnostic tool in central Florida; development of Data Portals, wireless/web-based data acquisition system. Avocations: golf, winemaking. Address: Nexia Strategy Group 20 N Orange Ave Orlando FL 32801 Office: Mirabilis Ventures Inc 111 N Orange Ave Orlando FL 32801 Office Phone: 407-517-7779. Office Fax: 407-426-9191. Business E-Mail: bpollack@nexiastrategy.com.

**POLLACK, RONALD FRANK,** healthcare organization executive, lawyer; b. NYC, Feb. 21, 1944; s. Max Louis and Hanna Esther (Borchardt) Pollack Baruch; m. Rebecca Lucy Bolling, Jan. 8, 1972; children: Sarah Shoshana, Abraham Max, Martin Landrum. BA, Queens Coll., 1965; JD, NYU, 1968. Bar: N.Y. 1968, D.C. 1978, U.S. Ct. Appeals (D.C. cir) 1970, U.S. Ct. Appeals (5th cir.) 1971, U.S. Ct. Appeals (6th cir.) 1974, U.S. Supreme Ct. 1973. Atty. Ctr. on Social Welfare Policy and Law, N.Y.C., 1968-73; founder, exec. dir. Food Research and Action Ctr., N.Y.C., 1970-80; dean Antioch Sch. Law, Washington, 1980-83; exec. dir. Families U.S.A., Washington, 1983—. Sec. treas., bd. dirs. Food Research and Action Ctr., Washington, 1980—; mem. civil legal services D.C. Jud. Conf. Com., 1980-83; appointee Pres.'s Adv. Commn. on Consumer Protection and Quality in the Health Care Industry, 1997-98. Author: If We Had Ham, We Could Have Ham and Eggs...If We Had Eggs: A Study of the National School Breakfast Program, 1972, Out to Lunch: A Study of USDA's Child Care Feeding and Summer Feeding Programs, 1974; co-author: On the Other Side of Easy Street: Myths and Facts About the Economics of Old Age, 1987. Treas. Jewish Fund for Justice, 1985-88, bd. dirs., 1985-93; bd. dirs. Am. Jewish World Service, Self-Help Community Services, 1974-77; mem. domestic adv. bd., project rev. bd. U.S.A. for Africa/Hands Across Am., 1986-88; v.p. of bd. dirs. Burgundy Farm Country Day Sch., 1988-90, pres. 1990-91; bd. dirs. Americans for Health, 1986-81. Arthur Garfield Hays Civil Liberties fellow, 1967; research fellow Legal Services Corp., Washington, 1978-80 Office: Families USA 1334 G St NW Washington DC 20005-3117

**POLLACK, SEYMOUR VICTOR,** computer science educator; b. Bklyn., Aug. 3, 1933; s. Max and Sylvia (Harrison) P.; m. Sydell Altman, Jan. 23, 1955; children: Mark, Sherie. BChemE, Pratt Inst., 1954; MChemE, Bklyn. Poly. Inst., 1960. Lic. chem. engr., Ohio. Engr. Schwarz Labs., Mt. Vernon, NY, 1954-55; design engr. Curtiss-Wright, Wood-Ridge, NJ, 1955-57, Fairchild Engines, Deer Park, NY, 1957-59, GE, Evendale, Ohio, 1959-62; rsch. assoc. U. Cin., 1962-66; prof. computer sci. Washington U., St. Louis, 1966-95, prof. emeritus, 1995—. Cons. Mo. Auto Club, St. Louis, 1969-82, United Van Lines, Fenton, Mo., 1984-86, Computer Sci. Accreditation Bd., N.Y.C., 1985-93. Author: Structured Fortran, 1982, UCSD Pascal, 1984, Studies in Computer Science, 1983, The DOS Book, 1985, Turbo Pascal Programming, 1991; cons. editor Holt Rinehart & Winston, N.Y.C., 1979-86. Bd. dirs. Hillel orgn., Washington U., 1983-84. Recipient Alumni Achievement award Pratt Inst., 1966, Outstanding Teaching award Burlington Northern Found., 1987. Mem. Assn. for Computing Machinery, Am. Assn. for Engring. Edn. Jewish. Avocations: trombone, walking, classical and jazz piano, jogging. Office: Washington U PO Box 1045 Saint Louis MO 63188-1045 Business E-Mail: svp@cse.wustl.edu.

**POLLACK, STANLEY P.,** lawyer; b. N.Y.C., Apr. 23, 1928; s. Isidor and Anna (Shulman) P.; m. Susan Aronowitz, June 16, 1974; 1 child, Jane. BA, NYU, 1948; JD, Harvard U., 1951; LLM in Taxation, NYU, 1959. Bar: N.Y. 1951, U.S. Dist. Ct. (so. dist.) N.Y. 1955. Sole practice, N.Y.C., 1955-61; v.p., gen. counsel James Talcott, Inc., N.Y.C., 1961-73; sr. exec. v.p. Rosenthal & Rosenthal Inc., N.Y.C., 1973—. Served to j.g. lt. USNR, 1951-54. Mem. Bklyn. Bar Assn. (banking com.), bankruptcy com.), Fed. Bar Council, Assn. Comml. Fin. Atty.'s (pres. 1968), Factors Chain Internat. Clubs: Harvard (N.Y.C.). Home: 6 Peter Cooper Rd New York NY 10010-6701 Office: Rosenthal & Rosenthal Inc 1370 Broadway # 2 New York NY 10018-7302

**POLLACK, STEPHEN J.,** stockbroker; b. NYC, Aug. 25, 1937; s. Harold S. and Gladys H. P. BS in Econs., U. Pa., 1960. V.p. retail sales Drexel Burnham Lambert, N.Y.C., 1960-77; 1st v.p. investments Dean Witter Reynolds Inc., N.Y.C., 1978-98; 1st v.p., fin. advisor Morgan Stanley, N.Y.C., 1998—, v.p., fin. advisor, 2001—03; with Pollack Asset Management, 2004—. Pres. B'nai B'rith Cohen, N.Y.C.; exec. v.p. Cosmopolitan League of City of HOpe, v.p. circle mem. Whitney Mus., N.Y.C.; treas. Sutton Pl. Synagogue, pres. Havurah Group. With USAR, 1966. Recipient Double Chai Citation, State of Israel Bonds, 1984, Appreciation award City of Hope, 1984, Kiter Key Club award Franklin Funds, Million Dollar Club Svc. award, B'nai B'rith Internat. award. Mem. Internat. Assn. Fin. Planners, Assn. Investment Brokers (bd. dirs.), Youngmen's Philanthropic League (bd. dirs.), Internat. Study Rsch. Inst., Exec. Forum, Fin. Analysts Money Mgrs. soc., Town Club, Atrium Club, Schuylkill Country Club, Wharton Sch. Club, U. Pa. Club, Yale Club, East River Tennis Club, Fresh Meadow Country Club, Matterhorn Sports Club, East Side Rep. Club, Knickerbokker Rep. Club, Berks County Tennis Club, Penn. Club (charter). Friars Club Home: 245 E 40th St Apt 14E New York NY 10016-1714 Office: Pollack Asset Mgmnt 40th Fl 245 E 40th St New York NY 10016 Office Phone: 212-949-1476. Personal E-mail: stephenpollack12@yahoo.com.

**POLLACK, SYDNEY,** film director; b. Lafayette, Ind., July 1, 1934; s. David and Rebecca (Miller) P.; m. Claire Griswold, Sept. 22, 1958; children: Steven, Rebecca, Rachel. Grad., Neighborhood Playhouse Theatre Sch., N.Y.C., 1954. Asst. to Sanford Meisner, Neighborhood Playhouse Theatre, 1954, instr. acting, 1954-60. Exec. dir. West Coast br. The Actors Studio. Appeared in Broadway prodns.: The Dark Is Light Enough, 1954, A Stone For Danny Fisher, 1955; appeared on live TV programs: Alcoa Presents, others; toured in Stalag 17; dir. TV programs: The Chrysler Theatre, Ben Casey, 1962-63, Something About Lee Wiley, 1963-64; dir: (films) The Slender

Thread, 1965, This Property is Condemned, 1966, The Scalphunters, 1968, Castle Keep, 1969, Jeremiah Johnson, 1972, Three Days of the Condor, 1975, The Electric Horseman, 1979, The Firm, 1993; dir. prodr. They Shoot Horses, Don't They?, 1969, The Way We Were, 1973, The Yakuza, 1975, Bobby Deerfield, 1977, Absence of Malice, 1981, Out of Africa, 1985 (Academy Award for Best Picture and Dir.), Havana, 1990, The Firm, 1993, Sabrina, 1995; prodr. Songwriter, 1984, Bright Lights, Big City, 1988, The Fabulous Baker Boys, 1989, Presumed Innocent, 1990, Sliding Doors, 1998, Cold Mountain, 2003; exec. prodr.: Honeysuckle Rose, 1980, White Palace, 1990, King Ralph, 1991, Dead Again, 1991, Leaving Normal, 1992, Searching for Bobby Fischer, 1993, Flesh and Bone, 1992, Sense and Sensibility, 1995, Sliding Doors, 1997, Up at the Villa, 1998, The Talented Mr. Ripley, 1998, For Love of the Game, 1998, The Talented Mr. Ripley, 1999, Blow Dry, 2001, Birthday Girl, 2001, Iris, 2001, Heaven, 2002, The Quiet American, 2002, In the Name of Love, 2003, Forty Shades of Blue, 2005; (actor) The Player, 1992, Death Becomes Her, 1992, Husbands and Wives, 1992, The Firm, 1993, Eyes Wide Shut, 1997, Civil Action, 1998, (voice) The Majestic, 2001, Changing Lanes, 2002, (TV) Mad About You, 1998, Eyes Wide Shut, 1999; dir., prodr., actor: Tootsie, 1982, Random Hearts, 1999, The Interpreter, 2005; TV appearances include Playhouse 90, 1959, Alfred Hitchcock Presents, 1960, The Deputy, 1961, Ben Casey, 1962, (voice) Frasier, 1994, Mad About You, 1998, Will & Grace, 2000, 01, 02, Just Shoot Me!, 2000, (voice) King of the Hill, 2000, Served with U.S. Army, 1957-59. Recipient Acad. award for best dir. and best picture, 1986; John Huston award Directors Guild Am., 2000. also: Deloitte & Touche 350 S Grand Ave Los Angeles CA 90071-3406 Office: Artists Mgmt Group 9465 Wilshire Blvd Ste 519 Beverly Hills CA 90212-2604

**POLLAK, CHERYL L.,** federal judge; b. 1953; AB, Princeton U., 1975; JD, U. Chgo., 1978. Bar: N.Y. Law clk. to Hon. William H. Timbers, U.S. Ct. Appeals for 2d Circuit, 1978-79; assoc. David Polk & Wrdell, N.Y.C., 1979-86; with Office U.S. Atty. for Ea. Dist. N.Y., U.S. Dept. Justice, Bklyn. 1986-91, chief OCDETF unit, 1991-94, dept. chief criminal divsn., 1994-95, internat. and nat. security advisor, 1991-95; magistrate judge for ea. dist. N.Y., U.S. Magistrate Ct., Bklyn., 1995—. Mem.: Assn. Bar City of NY (mem. com. Women in the Legal Profession, litigation com., fed. courts com.), ABA. Office: 225 Cadman Plz E Room 538 Brooklyn NY 11201-1818 Business E-Mail: cheryl_pollak@nyed.uscourts.gov.

**POLLAK, JOANNE ELIZABETH,** lawyer; b. Cleve., July 16, 1944; m. Mark Pollak, Dec. 26, 1976; children: Elizabeth, Joshua, Rebecca, Benjamin, Jonathan. BA magna cum laude, Dickinson Coll., 1965; JD with honors, U. Md., 1976. Bar: Md. 1976. V.p., gen. counsel The Johns Hopkins Health System Corp./Johns Hopkins Medicine, Balt.; assoc., ptnr. and head of health care practice group Piper & Marbury Law Offices, 1976-93. Instr. bus. of medicine Sch. Medicine, Johns Hopkins U., Internat. Bus. Sch. Bd. dirs. Charlestown Cmty., Inc., 1992—, Mid-Atlantic affiliate Am. Heart Assn., 1991—2004, chair bd. dirs., 2002—03, chair rsch. for life campaign, 1999; mem. bd. advisors U. Md. Law Sch., 2002—. Named One of Md.'s Top Women, Daily Record, 1996, 98, 2000. Office: Johns Hopkins Health Sys Corp Broadway Rsch Bldg 733 North Broadway Ste 102 Baltimore MD 21205 Office Phone: 410-614-3322.

**POLLAK, KEVIN,** actor; b. San Francisco, Oct. 30, 1957; m. Lucy Webb, 1995. Appeared in Avalon, 1990, L.A. Story, 1992, Another You, 1991, Ricochet, 1991, A Few Good Men, 1992, Indian Summer, 1993, The Opposite Sex (And How to Live With Them), 1993, Grumpy Old Men, 1993, Clean Slate, 1994, Miami Rhapsody, 1995, The Usual Suspects, 1995, Canadian Bacon, 1995, Casino, 1995, Grumpier Old Men, 1995, House Arrest, 1996, Apt Pupil, 1997, Cannes Man, 1996, Truth or Consequences N.M., 1997, The Sex Monster, 1998, She's All That, 1999, End of Days, 1999, Deterrence, 1999, Deal of a Lifetime, 1999, The Whole Nine Yards, 2000, Steal This Movie!, 2000, The Wedding Planner, 2001, 3000 Miles to Graceland, 2001, Dr. Dolittle 2, 2001, Stolen Summer, 2002, Juwanna Mann, 2002, Mother Ghost, 2002, The Santa Clause 2, 2002, Rolling Kansas, 2003, Blizzard, 2003, Seven Times Lucky, 2004, The Whole Ten Yards, 2004, Our Time is Up, 2004, Hostage, 2005; appeared on TV in The Don's Analyst, 1997, Salute to Martin Scorsese, 1997, Ruby Bridges, 1998, From the Earth to the Moon, 1998, others, (tv series) Work with Me, 1999, Movie Lover's Road Trip, 2003, Celebrity Poker Showdown, 2003.

**POLLAK, LISA,** radio producer; Grad., U. Mich., 1990. Reporter News & Observer, Raleigh, NC, Charlotte (NC) Observer; columnist Balt. Sun, 1997—2004. Prodr.: This American Life, 2004—. Recipient Pulitzer prize for feature writing, 1997. Office: This American Life WBEZ Radio 848 E Grand Ave Chicago IL 60611

**POLLAK, LOUIS HEILPRIN,** judge, educator; b. NYC, Dec. 7, 1922; s. Walter and Marion (Heilprin) P.; m. Katherine Weiss, July 25, 1952; children: Nancy, Elizabeth, Susan, Sarah, Deborah. AB, Harvard U., 1943; LLB, Yale U., 1948; LLD (hon.), Wilkes U., 2002, Columbia U., 2004, Roger Williams U., 2005. Bar: N.Y. 1949, Conn. 1956, Pa. 1976. Law clk. to Justice Rutledge U.S. Supreme Ct., 1948-49; with Paul, Weiss, Rifkind, Wharton & Garrison, N.Y.C., 1949-51; spl. asst. to Amb. Philip C. Jessup State Dept., 1951-53; asst. counsel Amalgmated Clothing Workers Am., 1954-55; mem. faculty Yale Law Sch., 1955-74, dean, 1965-70; Greenfield prof. U. Pa., 1974-78, dean Law Sch., 1975-78, lectr., 1980—; judge U.S. Dist Ct. (ea. dist.) Pa., Phila., 1978—, now sr. judge. Vis. lectr. Howard U. Sch. Law, 1953; vis. prof. U. Mich. Law Sch., 1961; Columbia Law Sch., 1962. Author: The Constitution and the Supreme Court: A Documentary History, 1966. Mem. New Haven Bd. Edn., 1962-68; chmn. Conn. adv. com. U.S. Civil Rights Commn., 1962-63; mem. bd. NAACP Legal Def. Fund, 1960-78, v.p., 1971-78. Served with AUS, 1943-46. Mem.: ABA (mem. sect. individual rights 1970—71, Spirit of Excellence award 2003), Am. Law Inst. (coun. 1978—), Am. Acad. Polit. and Social Sci. (bd. dirs. 2001—), Am. Philos. Soc., Am. Acad. Arts and Scis., Assn. Bar City N.Y., Phila. Bar Assn., Fed. Bar Assn. Office: US Dist Ct 16613 US Courthouse 601 Market St Philadelphia PA 19106-1713 Office Phone: 215-597-9590.

**POLLAK, MARK,** lawyer; b. Paris, July 16, 1947; came to U.S., 1955; s. Joseph and Zofia (Berkowitz) P.; m. Joanne Elizabeth Harris, Dec. 26, 1976; children: Joshua David, Jonathan Stephen, Benjamin Eric, Rebecca Lynn. BA, Bklyn. Coll., 1968; MA in City Planning, U. Pa., 1972, JD, 1972. Bar: Md. 1972. Assoc. Piper & Marbury, Balt., 1972-81, ptnr., 1981-99, Wilmer, Cutler & Pickering, Washington, 1999—2004, Wilmer Cutler Pickering Hale and Dorr LLP, Washington, 2004—. Bd. dirs. Jack Kent Cook Found. Author: Sports Leagues and Teams--An Encyclopedia 1871 to 1996, 1997. Bd. dirs. Balt Children's Mus., Downtown Partnership of Balt., Inc. Mem. ABA, Md. Bar Assn., Am. Coll. Real Estate Lawyers, Am. Planning Assn. Nat. Assn. Bond Lawyers. Office: Wilmer Cutler Pickering Hale and Dorr LLP 100 Light St Baltimore MD 21202-1036 Office Phone: 410-986-2860. Business E-Mail: mark.pollak@wilmerhale.com.

**POLLAK, RAYMOND,** general and transplant surgeon; b. Johannesburg, Nov. 12, 1950; came to U.S., 1977; MB BCh, U. Witwatersrand, Johannesburg, 1973. Diplomate Am. Bd. Surgery. Rotating intern Gen. Hosp., Johannesburg, 1974; intern in surgery U. Ill. Hosps. and Clinics, Chgo., 1977-78, resident in surgery; immunology and transplant fellow U. Ill., Chgo., 1982-84, assoc. prof. surgery, chief divsn. transplant dept. surgery, 1988-98, prof. surgery dept., surgeon, 1995—, chief divsn. transplant Peoria, 2000—05; dir. Clinical Trials Dept. Edward Hosp., Naperville, Ill., 2005—. Fellow ACS, Royal Coll. Surgeons Edinburgh. Office: Edward Hosp Clinical Trials Dept 801 S Washington St Naperville IL 60540 Office Phone: 630-527-5672. Business E-Mail: rpollak@edward.org.

**POLLAK, WILLIAM L.,** newspaper publishing executive; AB cum laude, Harvard Univ., 1978, MBA, 1982. Exec. v.p. sales The New York Times, exec. v.p. circulation, 1994—98; pres. & CEO Am. Lawyer Media, 1998—. Dir. ProBono.Net; chmn. graduate bd. The Harvard Crimson. Office: Am Lawyer Media 345 Park Ave So New York NY 10010

**POLLAN, STEPHEN MICHAEL,** lawyer, writer, finance expert; b. NYC, May 19, 1929; m. Corinne Staller; children: Michael, Lori, Tracy, Dana. LLB, Bklyn. Law Sch., 1951; BBS, LI U., 1985. Bar: NY 1951. Asst. prof. Marymount Coll., 1960-70; pres. Royal Bus. Funds AMEX, 1970-76; sr. real estate cons. Nat. Westminster Bank, 1976-78; asst. prof. fin. C.W. Post Coll., LI U. Sch. Bus., 1994-96; prin. Stephen M. Pollan, P.C., NYC, 1980—; pvt. practice NYC, 2006—. Mem. President's Commn. on Small Bus. Co-author: Die Broke, Live Rich, The Total Negotiator, 1994, Lifescripts, 1996, Second Acts, 2003, It's All in Your Head, 2006, also other personal bus. books; contbr. numerous articles to nat. bus. publs. Pres. Gay Head Cmty. Coun., 1975; vice chmn. UN Com. for UN Day, 1971-72. Mem. Nat. Assn. Small Bus. Investment Cos. (regional pres. 1975, bd. govrs.). Home: 1095 Park Ave New York NY 10128-1154 Office: 400 Park Ave Ste 1420 New York NY 10022 Office Phone: 212-688-8333. Business E-Mail: stephen@stephenpollan.com.

**POLLARA, BERNARD,** pediatrician, educator, immunologist; b. Chgo., Ill. s. Joseph and Mamie Domenica PhB, Northwestern U., 1951, MS, 1954; MD, U. Minn., 1960, PhD, 1963. Intern USPHS Hosp., Seattle, 1960; resident in pediatrics U. Minn. Hosps., 1968-69; rsch. assoc. pediatrics U. Minn., 1960-63, assoc. prof. biochemistry and pediatrics, 1969; prof. pediatrics Albany (N.Y.) Med. Coll., 1969-94, chmn. dept., 1979-93; pediatrician in chief Albany Med. Ctr. Hosp., 1979-93; sabbatical leave, pediatrician Yukon Kuskokwim Regional Hosp., 1992-93; John and Aliese Price prof. pediatrics & adolescent medicine U. South Fla., Tampa, 1994—, head divsn. gen. pediatrics, dept. pediatrics, 1994—2005, interim chmn. pediats., 1999-2001, chief divsn. clin. rsch., 2005—. V.p. rsch. affairs Albany Med. Ctr., 1986-89. Dir. N.Y. State Kidney Disease Inst., 1969-79. With USN, 1945-46. Recipient Acad. Laureate award SUNY, Albany, 1991; Arthritis and Rheumatism Found. fellow, 1961-64. Fellow Am. Acad. Pediats.; mem. AAAS, Am. Assn. Immunologists, Am. Pediat. Soc., Am. Soc. Cell Biology, Clin. Immunology Soc., Ambulatory Pediat. Assn., Sigma Xi, Phi Lambda Upsilon, Alpha Omega Alpha. Office: U South Fla Sch Medicine Dept Pediatrics 17 Davis Blvd Ste 200 Tampa FL 33606-3475 Office Phone: 813-259-8752. E-mail: bpollara@health.usf.edu.

**POLLARA, JOANNE,** learning disabilities educator consultant; b. Hoboken, N.J., Apr. 18, 1954; d. Ralph Frank and Katharine Stark (Cunningham) Pollara; children: Angela, Joshua. BA, St. Joseph Coll., 1976; MA, Montclair State U., 1994. Cert. tchr. elem., spl. edn., L.D.T.C., N.J.; professionally recognized spl. educator in ednl. diagnosis; cert. supr. 4th grade tchr. Holy Trinity Sch., Hackensack, N.J., 1976-77; tchr. of handicapped Kessler Inst., West Orange, N.J., 1978-86; bedside instructor West Orange Bd. of Edn., 1976-86, spl. edn. inst. aide, 1986-88; tchr. of handicapped Redwood Sch., West Orange, N.J., 1988-97; learning disabled tchr. cons. West Orange Pub. Schs., 1997—. Mem. spl. edn. curriculum com., W. Orange, N.J., 1989, bldg. mgmt. com., 1991-92; spl. edn. rep. reading curriculum com., W. Orange, 1990; PTA faculty rep. Redwood Sch., W. Orange, 1994-95. Religious educator Our Lady of Lourdes Ch., West Orange, N.J., 1984-85, Notre Dame Ch., North Caldwell, N.J., 1992-91; girl scout leader Girl Scouts of U.S., W. Orange, N.J., 1983-84, 86-87. Mem. Coun. for Exceptional Children (learning disabilities divsn.), Coun. for Ednl. Diagnostic Svcs., Assn. Learning Consultants, Phi Kappa Phi. Avocations: reading, music (piano, guitar), swimming. Home: 23 Espy Rd Apt B5 Caldwell NJ 07006-4855 Office: Dept Student Support Svcs 179 Eagle Rock Ave West Orange NJ 07052 Office Phone: 973-669-5400 226.

**POLLARD, C. WILLIAM,** environmental services executive; m. Judy Pollard; four children. Grad., Wheaton Coll.; JD, Northwestern U. of Law. Lawyer, 1963-72; v.p., faculty Wheaton (Ill.) Coll., 1972-77; CEO The ServiceMaster Co., Downers Grove, Ill., 1983-93, chmn., 1993-99, chmn., CEO, 1999—2002, chmn. emeritus 2002—; bd. chmn. UnumProvident Corp., Chattanooga. Bd. dirs. Herman Miller, Inc., Coro, Inc., UnumProvident Corp., Inst. for Diversity in Health Mgmt.; chmn. bd. trustees Wheaton Coll.; chmn. bd. dirs. Hosp. Rsch. and Ednl. Trust; mem. adv. bd. Drucker Found. for Nonprofit Mgmt.; bd. visitors Drucker Grad. Mgmt. Ctr. at Claremont. Author: The Soul of the Firm; contbr. author books and mags. Office: UnumProvident 1 Fountain Sq Chattanooga TN 37402 Office Phone: 800-333-6678, 630-271-1300. Office Fax: 630-271-5750. Business E-Mail: billpollard@svm.com.*

**POLLARD, FRED DON,** finance company executive, director; b. Proctorsville, Vt., Sept. 15, 1931; s. Bryant Frank and Millie Viola (Brobst) P.; m. Sandra Jean Norton, Oct. 19, 1957; children: Fred Don, Bruce Gardiner, Mark Bryant. BA, Dartmouth Coll., 1953, MBA, 1954. CPA, N.Y. Staff auditor Touche, Niven, Bailey & Smart, Chgo., 1954-55, 57-58; with Hertz Corp., Chgo., 1958-60, London, 1960-62, Paris, 1962-64, N.Y.C., 1964-65; European controller Avis Rent A Car, London, 1965-69, internat. treas., 1969-71, asst. v.p., dir. fin. Garden City, NY, 1971-72, asst. treas., 1972-75; treas. Garcia Corp., Teaneck, NJ, 1975-78; v.p. fin., treas. Augsbury Orgn., Inc., Ogdensburg, NY, 1978-79, sr. v.p. fin., treas., 1979-83; pres. Corp. Fin. Assocs. No. N.Y., Canton, 1983—, Agrl. Processing Corp., Canton, 1983—; pres. and treas. AG Pro Ltd., Massena, NY, 1998—. Vis. lectr. sch. of mgmt. Clarkson U., Potsdam, 1986-87, dept. econs. St. Lawrence U., Canton, N.Y., 1987-88; cons. Whalen, Davey & Looney LLP, 1990-2000. Served with U.S. Army, 1955-57. Mem. N.Y. State Soc. CPAs, Am. Inst. CPAs, St. Lawrence county C. of C. (bd. dirs. 1997—). Lodges: Masons; Shriners. Presbyterian. Home: Old Stone House 1129 County Route 25 Canton NY 13617-6539 Office: 1129 County Rte 25 Canton NY 13617 E-mail: stonhous@northnet.org.

**POLLARD, HARVEY B.,** medical educator, neuroscientist; b. San Antonio, May 26, 1943; BA in Biology, Rice U., 1964; MS in Biochemistry, U. Chgo., 1969, MD, 1969, PhD, 1973. Rsch. assoc. NIH-Nat. Inst. Arthritis and Metabolic Diseases, Bethesda, Md., 1969-71, sr. investigator, 1972-74, 1977-79, sect. chief, 1979-81; lab. chief Nat. Inst. Diabetes, Digestive and Kidney Diseases, Bethesda, 1981-96; prof., chair dept. anatomy, physiology and genetics Uniformed Svcs. U. Sch. Medicine, Bethesda, 1997—. Contbr. over 275 articles to profl. jours. With USPHS, 1969-96. Recipient Commendation medal USPHS, 1982, Alumni award for Disting. Svc., U. Chigo. Alumni Assn., 1989, NIH Inventor's award, 1991. Mem. Biophys. Soc., Soc. for Neurosci., Am. Soc. for Pharmacology and Exptl. Therapeutics, Soc. for Cell Biology, Endocrine Soc., Am. Coll. Psychoneuropharmacology, Am. Soc. for Biochemistry and Molecular Biology, Am. Assn. Anatomists., Am. Physiol. Soc., Institute of Medicine of Washington, D.C. Office: USU Sch Med Dept Anatomy Physiology and Genetics Bethesda MD 20814-4712 E-mail: hpollard@usuhs.mil.

**POLLARD, HENRY,** arbitrator, mediator; b. NYC, Jan. 10, 1931; s. Charles and Sarah (Lanster) P.; m. Adele Ruth Brodie, June 16, 1954; children: Paul A., Lydia S. AB, CCNY, 1953; JD, Columbia U., 1954. Bar: N.Y. 1954, Calif. 1962. Assoc. Sullivan & Cromwell, N.Y.C., 1954, 56-61; ptnr. Kaplan, LIvingston, Goodwin, Berkowitz & Selvin, Beverly Hills Calif., 1962-81, Pollard, Bauman, Slome & McIntosh, Beverly Hills, 1981-87, Seyfarth, Shaw, L.A., 1987-95; of counsel Oberstein, Kibre & Horwitz, L.A., 1995-99. Arbitrator/mediator, mem. large complex case program Am. Arbitration Assn.; arbitrator/mediator, N.Y. Stock Exch., Am. Stock Exch., Pacific Stock Exch., L.A. County Dispute Resolution Svcs.; settlement officer Beverly Hills Mcpl. Ct., L.A. County Superior Ct. Editor Columbia U. Law Rev., 1953-54. Served with U.S. Army, 1954-56. Harlan Fiske Stone scholar, 1953-54. Mem. ABA, Calif. Bar Assn., Beverly Hills Bar Assn. Office Phone: 310-457-1713. Office Fax: 310-457-1713. Personal E-mail: adrpollard@aol.com.

**POLLARD, HERSCHEL NEWTON,** artist, psychologist; s. Herschel Newton and Lora Frances Pollard; m. Luz Mariela Gomez Bolanos, Oct. 10, 1997; m. Margaret Lila Kathleen Innes, 1962 (div. 1972); children: Steven Morton, Christopher Charles, Charles William, Heather Dianne, Herschel Newton. BA, Vanderbilt U., 1960; postgrad., Ga. State U., 1963—63, U. of Tenn., 1963—64, Vanderbilt Divinity Sch., 1963—64; PhD, Vanderbilt U., 1972; postgrad., Chattanooga State Tech. Coll., 1992—94. Lic. clin. psychology Tenn., forensic psychology Tenn., clin./cons. psychology Miss., Ark., Alaska, Fla. Counselor InterUniversity Psychol. and Counseling Ctr., Nashville, 1964—72; prof. Grad. Sch. Murray (Ky.) State U., 1967—69; adj. prof. St. Thomas Aquinas Coll., Nashville, 1970—71; intern Nashville Comty. Mental Health Ctr., 1971—72; pvt. practice psychologist Memphis, 1972—74; clin. dir. N.W. Miss. Regional Mental Health Sys., Clarksdale, Miss., 1975—76; dir. Kuskokwim Mental Health Svcs., Aniak, Alaska, 1976—77; clin. dir. Anchorage (Alaska) Comty. Mental Health Svcs., Anchorage, 1977—78; pvt. practice psychologist Naples, Fla., 1979—86, Chattanooga, 1986—90; owner, dir. Montlake Studios, Chattanooga, 1990—; instr. Von Liebig Ctr. for the Arts, Naples, 1990—2003, Art League of Bonita Springs, Fla., 1995—98, Cape Coral (Fla.) Arts Studio, 2002—04, Visual Arts Ctr., Punta Gorda, Fla., 2003—. Contbg rschr. Pres.'s Commn. to Investigate Civil Disturbances, Nashville, 1970; mem. Pres.'s Commn. on Mental Health, Washington, 1976—78; instr. Visual Arts Ctr., Punta Gorda, Fla., 2002—; founder Nat. Aviation Art Exhbn., Nat. Air Show, Punta Gorda, 2006. Author, dir., prodr.: (films) Dealing with Conflict (1st award Religion and Ethics Divsn., EFLA Am. Film Festival, 1964); author: (biographical commentary and docudrama) Vincent van Gogh: Love, God and Art, (rsch. monograph) The Re-emergence of a Noteworthy Baroque Painting, (drama) The Madman of Arles, (book) Pollard's Brief Handbook for Painters, (novels) Wait for the Thunder, (biography) The Art of Frances Morton Pollard, (edul. audiovisual) The Nineteen Friends of Robbie McNee (Excellence award Edni. Film Libr. Assn., 1964), (film) Turning Point, 1971; designer, pub. Pollard's Infinite Palette; exhibitions include Von Liebig Ctr. for the Arts, Naples, Fla., Cape Coral Arts Studio, Naples Nat. Art Festival, Mus. of the Everglades, Robb and Stucky Atrium, Ft. Myers, Fla., No. Trust, Naples, Impac U., Punta Gorda, Goff Gallery, Visual Arts Ctr., Ave Maria U., Naples, 1st Cmty. Nat. Bank, Port Charlotte, Preseller Gallery, Punta Gorda, Alla Prima Pastel Invitational, Naples, The 2005 H. Pollard Retrospective Exhibit, Art and Humanities Gallery, Port Charlotte, Represented in permanent collections Portrait of Sir Denis Mahon, Nat. Gallery, Gt. Britain. Rep. S.W. Fla. Arts Coun., Ft. Myers, Fla., 2003—04; originator children's art exhbn. Early Edn. Project, 2003; bd. dirs. Early Edn. Project Policy Coun., Punta Gorda, 2002—03; pres. Von Liebig Ctr. for the Arts, Naples, 2003—04, Ctr. for the Visual Arts, Punta Gorda, 2005; bd. dirs. Charlotte Artists Guild, 2004—05, pres., 2005—. Lt. (j.g.) USN, 1960—62. Named Artist of Month, Charlotte County Bd. Commrs., 2005; recipient Mitchell scholarship, Vanderbilt U., 1956—60, Tchg. fellowship, NIMH, 1964—72, 1st Prize, 2003 Plein Aire Festival, 2003, 1st Award, Visual Art Ctr., 2004, 1st Judge's award, Charlotte Nat. Art Competition, 2004, 1st Prize, Tenn. State Fair Art Competition, 1965, 1st Award, Collier County Fair Art Competition, 1970, Bowles award for portraiture, 2005, 1st award comml. aviation divsn., Nat. Aviation Art Exhbn. Mem.: APA (licentiate), Charlotte Artists Guild (pres. 2005—), Naples Art Assn. (pres. 2003—04), Am. Numis. Assn. Achievements include development of The Pollard Pain Scale; design of Pollard's Infinite Palette. Avocations: archaeology, coin collecting/numismatics, ceramics, psychology of art, art. Office: CESA Pub 179 Maria Ct Punta Gorda FL 33950 Personal E-mail: hnpollard@aol.com.

**POLLARD, JOHN OLIVER,** lawyer; b. American Falls, Idaho, Dec. 25, 1937; s. Donald Lusher Pollard and Gertrude Marie Schelecter Chaney; m. Patricia Gheen Dyer, June 10, 1961 (div. 1966); 1 child, Ariane Raquel; m. Carol Virginia Foard, Apr. 27, 1968; children: Ashley Carol, Jennifer Leigh. BA, Am. U., 1965; JD, U.N.C., 1973. Bar: N.C. 1973. Indsl. relations mgr. Carolinas Branch, Associated Gen. Contractors, Charlotte, NC, 1965-68; dir. labor relations and personnel Nello L. Teer Co., Durham, 1968-71; atty., ptnr. Blakeney & Alexander, Charlotte, 1973—98; ptnr. McGuireWoods, LLP, Charlotte, 1998—. Bd. dirs. Ingles Markets, Inc., Ashville, N.C., 1987—. Staff mem. N.C. Law Rev., Chapel Hill, N.C., 1973. Bd. mem., past chmn., legal counsel The Relatives, Inc., Charlotte, N.C., 1985—95; bd. mem., past pres. Advs. for Children in Ct., Inc., Charlotte, 1985-93; mem. Mecklenburg County Per. Commn., Charlotte, 1984-91. Mem. NC Bar Assn., Quail Hollow Country Club. Republican. Avocations: golf, hunting, fishing, backpacking. Office: McGuireWoods, LLP Bank Am Corp Ctr 100 N Tryon St, Ste 2900 Charlotte NC 28202-4011 also: Ingles Markets, Inc 2913 Hwy 70 W Black Mountain NC 28711 Office Phone: 704-373-8960. E-mail: jpollard@mcguirewoods.com.

**POLLARD, MARCUS,** professional football player; b. Valley, Ala., Feb. 8, 1972; m. Amani Pollard; children: Myles, Micah. Attended, Bradley Univ. Tight end Indianapolis Colts, 1996—2004, Detroit Lions, 2005—. Founder TRUST 81 charity. Office: Detroit Lions Inc 222 Republic Dr Allen Park MI 48101*

**POLLARD, MICHAEL ROSS,** lawyer, health science association administrator; b. Flint, Mich., Apr. 14, 1947; s. Gail Winton Pollard and Evelyn Georgeanna (LeMire) Goplen; m. Penelope Brigham, Aug. 22, 1970. AB in Polit. Sci., U. Mich., 1969; JD, Harvard U., 1972, MPH, 1974. Bar: Mass. 1972, D.C. 1975. Profl. assoc. for program devel. Nat. Acad. Scis. Inst. Medicine, Washington, 1974-77, dir. law and ethics div., 1977-78; atty. advisor Office of Policy Planning, FTC, Washington, 1978-81, asst. dir. Bur. Consumer Protection, 1981-83; dir. Office of Policy Analysis, Pharm. Mfrs. Assn., Washington, 1983-88; exec. dir. Am. Pharm. Inst., Washington, 1988-89; counsel Michaels, Wishner & Bonner, P.C., Washington, 1988-89, ptnr., 1989—2000; cons. fed. policy and regulation Medco Health Solutions, Inc., 2000—. Cons. Nat. Ctr. for Health Svcs. Rsch. Rockville, Md., 1975-80, Office Tech. Assessment U.S. Congress, 1984-95; dir. Inst. for Health Policy Solutions, 1992—. Contbr. articles to profl. jours. Treas. Nat. Leadership Coalition on AIDS, 1988-93; treas. and dir.-at-large Nat. Commn. on Cert. of Physician Assts., 1991-97, James B. Angell scholar U. Mich., 1967, 68, 69; docent Hendricks Hill Mus., 2001—; vis. com. Harvard U. Sch. Pub. Health, 2002—; mem. nat. adv. com. Calif. Health Benefits Rev. Program, 2004—; v.p. Southport Island Assn., 2004—. Mem. Rotary Internat., Phi Beta Kappa, Pi Sigma Alpha. Democrat. Avocations: running, bicycling, gardening, drawing, architecture. Home: 7300 Maple Ave Chevy Chase MD 20815-5108 also: 29 Paradise Lane Southport ME 04576 Office Phone: 202-639-1884.

**POLLARD, MORRIS,** microbiologist, educator; b. Hartford, Conn., May 24, 1916; s. Harry and Sarah (Hoffman) P.; m. Mildred Klein, Dec. 29, 1938 (dec. 2001); children: Harvey, Carol, Jonathan. D.V.M., Ohio State U., 1938; MS, Va. Poly. Inst., 1939; PhD (Nat. Found. Infantile Paralysis fellow), U. Calif.-Berkeley, 1950; DSc (hon.), Miami U., Ohio, 1981. Mem. staff Animal Disease Sta., Nat. Agrl. Research Center, Beltsville, Md., 1939-42; asst. prof. preventive medicine Med. br. U. Tex., Galveston, 1946-48, assoc. prof., 1948-50, prof., 1950-61; prof. biology U. Notre Dame, Ind., 1961-66, prof., chmn. microbiology, 1966-81, prof. emeritus, 1981—, 2001—, dir. Lobund Lab., 1961-85, Coleman dir. Lobund Lab., 1985—, Coleman Found. prof. 1985—2001. Vis. prof. Fed. U. Rio de Janeiro, Brazil, 1977; vis. prof. Katholieke U., Leuven, Belgium, 1981; mem. tng. grant com. NIH, 1965-70; mem. adv. bd. Inst. Lab. Animal Resources NRC, 1965-68; mem. adv. com. microbiology Office Naval Research, 1966-68, chmn., 1968-70; mem. sci. adv. com. United Health Found., 1966-70; cons. U. Tex., M.D. Anderson Hosp. and Tumor Inst., 1958-66; mem. colon cancer com. Nat. Cancer Inst., 1972-76, chmn. tumor immunology com., 1976-79; mem. com. cancer cause and prevention NIH, 1979-81; program rev. com. Argonne Nat. Lab, 1979-85, chmn., 1983-85; lectr. Found. Microbiology, 1978 Editor: Perspectives in Virology Vol. I to XI, 1959-80; contbr. articles to profl. jours. Served from 1st lt. to lt. col. Vet. Corps, AUS, 1942-46. Recipient Disting. Alumnus award Ohio State U., 1979, Army Commendation medal, Presdl. citation, Hope award Am. Cancer Soc., 2000; named Hon. Alumnus U. Notre Dame, 1989; McLaughlin Faculty fellow Cambridge U., 1956; Raine Found. fund U. Western Australia, 1975; vis. scientist Chinese Acad. Med. Scis., 1979, 81;

hon. prof. Chinese Acad. Med. Scis., 1982. Mem. Am. Acad. Microbiology (charter), Brazilian Acad. Scis., Soc. Exptl. Biology and Medicine, Am. Soc. Microbiology (Acad. Sci. Achievement award 1990), Am. Soc. Investigative Pathology, Am. Assn. Cancer Rsch., Am. Soc. Lab. Animal Sci., Assn. Gnotobiotics (pres.), Internat. Commn. Lab. Animal Sci., AAAS, Internat. Assn. Gnotobiology (pres.), Internat. Assn. Gnotobiotics (hon. pres. 1987), Sigma Xi, Phi Delta Epsilon (hon.), Phi Zeta (hon.). Office: Lobund Lab U Notre Dame Notre Dame IN 46556 Home: 1025 Park Pl Apt 137 Mishawaka IN 46545-3537 Office Phone: 574-631-7564.

**POLLARD, OVERTON PRICE,** retired lawyer; b. Ashland, Va., Mar. 26, 1933; s. James Madison and Annie Elizabeth (Hutchinson) Pollard; m. Anne Aloysia Meyer, Oct. 1, 1960; children: Mary O., Price, John, Anne, Charles, Andrew, David. AB in Econs., Washington and Lee U., 1954, JD, 1957. Bar: Va. Claims supr. Travelers Ins. Co., Richmond, Va., 1964-67; asst. atty. gen. State of Va., Richmond, 1967, 70-72; spl. asst. Va. Supreme Ct., Richmond, 1968-70; exec. dir. Pub. Defender Commn., Richmond, 1972—2003; ptnr. Pollard & Boice and predecessor firms, Richmond, 1972-87. Bd. govs. Va. Criminal Law Sect., Richmond, 1970—72; pres. Met. Legal Aid, Richmond, 1978; chair sr. lawyers sect. Va. State Bar, 1999—2000. Del. State Dem. Conv., Richmond, 1985; mem. Va. Commn. Family Violence Prevention, 1995; bd. dirs. Henrico County Housing Corp., 1999. With USN, 1957—59. Recipient Svc. award, Criminal Law Bd. of Govs. Pub. Defender Study, 1971, Outstanding Svc. award, Pub. Defender Commn., 1998, Carrico Professionalism award, Va. State Bar Criminal Law Sect., 2005. Fellow: Va. Law Found.; mem.: ABA, Va. Bar Assn. (Pro Bono Publico award 1995, Walker award 2005), Nat. Legal Aid and Defender Assn. (Reginald Heber Smith award 1991), Richmond Bar Assn., Va. Bar Assn. (chmn. criminal law sect. 1991—93). Democrat. Baptist. Avocation: fishing. Home: 7726 Sweetbriar Rd Richmond VA 23229-6622

**POLLARD, THOMAS DEAN,** cell biologist, educator; b. Pasadena, Calif., July 7, 1942; s. Dean Randall and Florence Alma (Dierker) Pollard; m. Patricia Elizabeth Snowden, Feb. 7, 1964; children: Katherine, Daniel. BA cum laude, Pomona Coll., Claremont, Calif., 1964; MD cum laude, Harvard Med. Sch., 1968. Intern Mass. Gen. Hosp., Boston, 1968—69; staff assoc. lab. biochemistry Nat. Heart and Lung Inst., Bethesda, Md., 1969—72; asst. prof. anatomy Harvard Med. Sch., Boston, 1972—75, assoc. prof., 1975—78; Bayard Halsted prof., dir. dept. cell biology and anatomy Johns Hopkins U. Sch. Medicine, Balt., 1977—96; pres. Salk Inst. Biol. Studies, La Jolla, Calif., 1996—2000, prof., 1996—2001, U. Calif., San Diego, 1996—2001; Eugene Higgins prof. molecular, cellular and devel. biology and cell biology Yale U., New Haven, 2001—; prof. molecular biophysics and biochemistry, 2003—. Vis. scientist Med. Rsch. Coun. Lab. Molecular Biology, Cambridge, England, 1984; mem. NRC Commn. Life Sci., 1990—97, chair, 1993—97; mem. coun. NIH Nat. Inst. Gen. Med. Sci.; adj. prof. biology, bioengineering and chemistry and biochemistry U. Calif., San Diego, 1997—2001; chair dept. molecular, cellular and devel. biology Yale U., 2004—. Contbr. articles to profl. jours.; mem. editl. bd.: Cell Biology - Internat. Reports, 1976—81, Jour. Cell Biology, 1977—82, Jour. Submicroscopic Cytology, 1978—82, Cell Motility and the Cytoskeleton, 1980—94, Jour. Muscle Rsch. and Cell Motility, 1980—88, Microscopy Rsch. and Technique, 1981—93, Current Opinion in Cell Biology, 1988—, Current Biology, 1991—, Protein Profile, 1994—97, Trends in Biochemical Scis., 1995—, Procs. NAS, 1996—98, assoc. editor: Molecular Biology of the Cell, 1991—. Co-recipient Lewis S. Rosentiel Disting. Work in Basic Med. Rsch. award, Brandeis U., 1966; recipient Rsch. Career Devel. award, US Pub. Health Svc., 1974—78, MERIT award, Nat. Inst. Gen. Med. Sci., 1988—98, Gairdner award for achievement in med. rsch., Gairdner Found., 2006; grantee Guggenheim fellowship, 1984, Winston Churchill Overseas fellowship, Churchill Coll., UK, 1984. Fellow: Am. Acad. Microbiol., AAAS (bd. dirs.). Inst. Medicine, Biophys. Soc. (mem. coun. 1977—80, pres. 1992—93, Pub. Svc. award 1997), NAS, Am. Acad. Arts & Scis.; mem.: Am. Soc. Biochemistry and Molecular Biology, Marine Biol. Lab. (trustee 1991—97), Am. Soc. Cell Biology (mem. exec. com. 1976—77, mem. coun. 1976—79, pres. 1987—88, K.R. Porter lectr. 1989, E.B. Wilson medal 2004). Achievements include patents in field. Office: Dept Molecular Cellular and Devel Biology Yale U PO Box 208103 New Haven CT 06520-8103 E-mail: thomas.pollard@yale.edu.*

**POLLARD, VERONICA,** automotive executive; m. Joel Dreyfuss; 1 child, Justin. Student, U. Wis.; Bachelor's Degree, Boston U.; Master's Degree, Columbia U. First grade tchr., NY; mgr. internat. affairs Cosmo Pub. Rels. Corp., Tokyo; staff writer San Francisco Chronicle; asst. dir. pub. affairs Newsweek Mag.; publicist ABC TV Network, mgr. bus. info.; dir. corp. comm. Capital Cities/ABC, Inc.; v.p. corp. pub. rels. ABC; v.p., external affairs Toyota Motor Corp. Services N.Am., 1998—2002; group v.p. corp. comm. Toyota Motor N.Am., Inc., 2002—. Bd. dirs. Granite Broadcasting Corp.; mem. individual investor adv. com. N.Y. Stock Exch. Former dir. Nat. YMCA of the U.S.A., YMCA Greater N.Y.; trustee Mus. for African Art, NY; active YMCA; hon. bd. mem. West Side YMCA, NY, 1990—98, bd. chair; dir. The Doe Fund, NY. Mem.: Women's Forum. Office: Toyota Motor NAm Ste 4900 Nine West 57th St New York NY 10019

**POLLARD, WANDA MEADOWS,** primary school educator; d. Fred Malcolm and Lieen Edna Meadows; m. William Frederick Pollard, May 1, 1965; children: Nathan Owen, Meadows Terri. BS, U. of Montevallo, Ala., 1961; MA, U. of Ala., Tuscaloosa, 1966; Edni. Specialist, U. of Ala., 2000. Cert. Nat. Bd. Profl. Tchg. Stds. 2000. 4th grade tchr. Hanceville Elem. Sch., Hanceville, Ala., 1961—64; 4th grade/1st grade tchr. Noble St. Sch., Anniston, Ala., 1964—66; 1st grade tchr. Guntersville Elem. Sch., Guntersville, Ala., 1966—72, Cherokee Bend Elem., Mountain Brook, Ala., 1972—73; 3rd grade tchr. Alliance Christian Sch., Birmingham, Ala., 1990—93, 7th grade tchr. Minor Elem. Sch., Birmingham, 1985—86; 1st/2nd grade tchr. Albertville Elem., Albertville, Ala., 1986—2002; kindergarten tchr. Big Spring Lake Kindergarten Sch., Albertville, Ala., 2002—05, reading specialist, 2005—. Named Tchr. of the Yr., Albertville City Elem. Sch., 2003—04, Big Spring Lake Sch., Local Walmart Tchr. of the Yr., 2004—05; named to, Ala. Tchr. Hall of Fame, 2003; Wildflower Garden grantee, Albertville Elem. Sch., Conflict Resolution grantee, 2001. Mem.: AEA, NEA. Office: Big Spring Lake Kindergarten School 257 Country Club Rf Albertville AL 35951 Office Phone: 256-878-7922. Home Fax: 256-891-6368; Office Fax: 256-891-6368. Personal E-mail: wpollard@albertk12.org.

**POLLARO, PAUL PHILIP,** artist; b. NYC, Aug. 2, 1921; s. Charles and Maria (Aprile) P.; m. Jo Ann Stover, July 16, 1962 (div. Nov. 1979); children: Lauren, Paul Jr.; m. Laura Clayton, Apr. 2, 1985. Student, Art Students League, 1945-48, Pratt Graphic Ctr., 1972. Instr. painting The New Sch. of Social Rsch., N.Y.C., 1964-69; vis. artist Notre Dame U., South Bend, Ind., 1965-67; asst. prof. art, chmn. art dept. Wagner Coll., Staten Island, NY, 1970-73; asst. dir. The MacDowell Colony, Peterborough, NH, 1973-76; pvt. practice Hancock, NH, 1976—. One-man shows include Jersey City Mus., NJ, 1966 (2d prize), S.I. Mus. Art, NY, 1973, Manchester Inst. Arts and Scis., Manchester, NH, 1970-85, Chryser Mus., Norfolk, Va., 1991, others. Sgt. U.S. Army, 1942-45, PTO. Tiffany Found. grantee, NYC, 1967, N. State Coun. Arts grantee, 1985; MacDowell Colony fellow, 1965-69. Roman Catholic. Home: Norway Hill Hancock NH 03449

**POLLEY, HARVEY LEE,** retired missionary, math and science educator; b. Wapato, Wash., Aug. 14, 1924; s. Edward Prestley and Alda June Polley; m. Corinne Weber; children: Catherine, David, Corinne, Robert. BA, Whitworth Coll., 1951; postgrad., East Wash. Coll., 1953, Berkeley Bapt. Div. Sch., 1958—59; MEd, Ctrl. Wash. Coll., 1958; postgrad., Ecole d'Adminstrn. des Affaires Africaines, Brussels, 1959—60. Tchr. Quincy Pub. Schs., Wash., 1953—57, N.W. Christian Schs., Spokane, 1958; missionary Am. Bapt. Fgn. Missionary Soc., Democratic Republic of Congo, 1958—89; tchr. Evang. Pedagogical Inst., Kimpese, Democratic Republic of Congo, 1961—69, asst. legal rep., dir., prin., supt., 1969—72; dir. BIM Hostel, Kinshasa, Democratic Republic of Congo, 1972—73; mem. staff Ctr. Agrl. Devel. Lusekele, Democratic Republic of Congo, 1975—85, dir., 1976—79, 1983—85, Plateau

Bateke Devel. Program, Kinshasa, 1985—89; ret., 1989. Author: Mpila Kele, a rural development guide written in the Kituba lang., 1989. Mem. Coun. Elders, Kimpese, 1969-72; pres. bd. adminstrn. Vanga (Zaire) Hosp., 1981-83; mem. exec. com. Nat. Human Nutrition Planning Coun. Govt. Zaire-USAID, Kikwit, 1983-85. With U.S. Army, 1946-47, USAF, 51-53. Home: 2405 W Johannsen Rd Spokane WA 99208-9616

**POLLEY, RICHARD DONALD,** microbiologist, chemist; b. Bklyn., Feb. 23, 1937; s. George Weston and Evelyn (Tuttle) P.; m. Linda R. Radford, Sept. 21, 1991; children from previous marriage: Gordon MacHeath, Jennifer Elizabeth, Tabitha Isabelle, Sean Sullivan. Student, Trinity Coll., 1954-57; BS, Hofstra U., 1960. Lic. nuclear radiation tech. U.S. Govt., 2003. Asst. advt. mgr. tech. Permatex Chem. Corp., Huntington, NY, 1960-61, Sun Chem. Corp., 1961-63; advt. mgr. Celanese Plastics Co., Newark, 1963-67; account dir. McCann Indsl. Tech. Mktg., N.Y.C., 1967-68, v.p., gen. mgr. Miami, 1968-70; pres. Intercapital Belgium S.A., Brussels, Nassau, Bahamas, Panama City, Panama, 1970-72; cons. Nuclear Regulatory Commn., Atomic City, Idaho, 1975—76; founder, pres., tech. dir. Iodinamics Corp., Lancaster, Pa., El Paso, Tex., El Paso, Tex., 1973-76; founder, CEO, COO, tech. dir., bd. dirs., chmn. Hydrodine Corp., Miami, 1976—2002, chmn., CEO, tech. dir., 1986—2002, also bd. dirs. Founder, chmn. CEO, COO, tech. dir. Polymorphic Polymers Corp., Miami, 1978—90; founder, COO, tech. dir., CEO, bd. dirs. Omnidine Corp., Miami, 1980—98, bd. dirs.; pres. and tech. dir. Skin Care Labs. Inc., Miami, 1979—90; tech. dir. Hydrodine Biotech (Far East) Ltd., Bangkok, Thailand, Hong Kong, Singapore and Kuala Lumpur, 1989—98; CEO, tech dir. Polllabs., Sao Paulo, Brazil, 1990—2000; tech. dir. Ecology Tech. do Brasil, Sao Paulo, 1993—2000; tech. dir., environ. and agrl. mgr. Environ. Tech. do Brasil, Sao Paulo, 1995—; chief internat. tech. dir. environ. microbiology San. Service. Corp., Solon, Ohio, 1993—2000; chmn., co-founder Peer Group Influencers Ltd., London, Miami, 1988—98; v.p., bd. dirs. Internat. Airlines, Long Beach, Calif., 1984—2000; tech. dir. Swiver Corp., Miami, 1994—2002; tech. dir. chief scientist Infinity Techs., Ltd., Panama City, 1996—98; founder, bd. dirs., CEO, pres., tech. dir. PolleyTech Corp., Pembroke Pines, Fla., 1998—; overseas dir. field iodine deficiency disease med. demonstration projects Beth Israel Hosp., Harvard U. Med. Sch., 1977—88; lectr. Harvard Bus. Sch., 1980; cons. water microbiology and disinfection control, water environments Pan Am. Health Orgn., others; med. and tech. dir. Enzymes Brasil, Ltd., Sao Paulo, 2001—, med. mgr., tech. dir. Guayaquil, Ecuador, 2001—; chmn. med./sci. adv. bd., found. tech. dir. RAH Found., Napa Valley, Calif., 2001—; cons. IGFA Wetlands Project, 2001—; founder, CEO, chmn. bd. dirs. Xurex Nano-Coatings Corp., Hollywood, Fla., 2005—. Mem. editl. adv. bd. Chem. Week, 1988; contbr. articles to profl. jours.; patentee. Mem. cmty. bd. Am. Heart Assn., Am. Stroke Assn., Broward County, PR. Recipient R. Buckminster Fuller Home of the Future award for paints and water system, 1976. Mem. AAAS, NRA, Am. Concrete Inst., N.Y. Acad. Scis., Internat. Iodine Inst. (chmn. bd. and tech. dir. 1976—), Associaçao de Ciencia e Tecnologia Ambiental (bd. dirs. Sao Paulo 1993—), The Nature Conservancy, World Wildlife Fund, Sierra Club, Audubon Soc., Wilderness Soc., Defenders of Wildlife, Environ. Defense Org., Fla. Wildlife Fedn., Internat. Game Fish Assn., others. Achievements include patents for farm, industrial, commercial, medical, environmental and household protective coatings and water treatment devices, nuclear industries; fields of medicine, environmental protection, agriculture and enzymes soil road building, asphalt and soil enzymes roads, lagoons, aquaculture, ponds; drinking water reservoirs, hazardous waste containment area soil reservoirs; soil aircraft landing strips. Office Phone: 954-434-5062. E-mail: rpolley@xurex.com.

**POLLICK, G. DAVID,** academic administrator, philosopher; b. Kansas City, Mo., Oct. 13, 1947; children: Dayna, Landon; m. Karen Bentley Pollick, 2002. BA in Philosophy, U. San Diego, 1971; PhL in Philosophy, St. Paul U., Ont., Can., 1973; MA in Philosophy, U. Ottawa, Can., 1973, PhD in Philosophy, 1981. Lecturer, philosophy U. San Diego, San Diego, 1972-73; tchr.-counselor, neurologically and physically handicapped Aseltine Sch. Neurol. Handicapped, 1972-73; dir. heroin rehab. ctr. Imperial County Diversion Program, El Centro, Calif., 1973-74; tchr.-counselor, emotionally handicapped Finley Elem Sch. Holtville, Calif., 1974-75; lecturer, philosophy U. Ottawa, Ottawa, Ont, Canada, 1975-77; asst. prof. philosopy, dept. chrm., acad. coordinator St. John's U., Collegeville, Minn., 1977-84; assoc. prof., dean coll. arts and scis. Seattle U., 1984—89; acting pres., provost, v.p. for acad. affairs SUNY, Cortland, 1989—93; co-CEO, pres. Art Inst. Chgo., Sch. Art Inst. Chgo., 1993—95; pres. Lebanon Valley Coll., Annville, Pa., 1996—2004, Birmingham (Ala.) So. Coll., 2004—. Pres. Big South Conf., 2004—. Author: The Work of Roman Ingarden, 1977, (with others) The Aesthetics of Roman Ingarden, 1982; co-editor Supplementary Volume on Aesthetics, 1977. With USN, 1966—68. Fellow philosophy and fine arts, Inst. Ecumenical and Culture Rsch., 1976-77; Koscjusko Found. award, 1978. Avocations: sculpture, art history, archaeology. Office: Birmingham-Southern Coll 900 Arkadelphia Rd Birmingham AL 35254

**POLLIHAN, THOMAS HENRY,** lawyer; b. St. Louis, Nov. 15, 1949; s. C.H. and Patricia Ann (O'Brien) P.; m. Donna M. Bickhaus, Aug. 25, 1973; 1 child, Emily Christine. BA in Sociology, Quincy U., 1972; JD, U. Notre Dame, 1975; Exec. Masters in Internat. Bus., St. Louis U., 1992. Bar: Mo. 1975, Ill. 1976. Jud. law clk. to judge Mo. Ct. of Appeals, St. Louis, 1975-76; from assoc. to ptnr. Greenfield, Davidson, Mandelstamm & Voorhees, St. Louis, 1976-82; asst. gen. counsel Kellwood Co., St. Louis, 1982-89, gen. counsel, sec., 1989—, v.p., 1993—2002, sr. v.p., 2002—05, exec. v.p., 2005—. Adj. prof. St. Louis U. Cook Sch. Bus., 2001—04, Trustee Quincy (Ill.) U., 1987-92, 97-2004, pres. alumni bd., 1986-87, Quincy (Ill.) U. Found., 1993-94, 97-; dir., sec. New Piasa Chautauqua, Ill., 1996-97. Named Quincy U. Alumnus of Yr., 1997. Mem. Bar Assn. Met. St. Louis. Roman Catholic. Avocations: soccer, bicycling. Office: Kellwood Co 600 Kellwood Pkwy Ste 300 Chesterfield MO 63017-5897 Home: 2080 Key Harbour Dr Lake Saint Louis MO 63367 Business E-mail: tom.pollihan@kellwood.com.

**POLLIN, BURTON RALPH,** language educator; b. Worcester, Mass. s. Louis and Rae (Cohen) P.; m. Alice Pollin, Jan. 30, 1944; children: Diana Claire, Myles Clement. BA, CCNY, 1936; PhD, Columbia U., 1962. Tchr. English NYC Bd. Edn., 1936-62, chmn. dept. English, 1956-62; lectr. English CUNY, 1957-62, assoc. prof. to full prof., 1962-73, prof. emeritus, 1973—. Lectr. on Poe NY State Coun. Humanities, 1996—99, 2003—05. Author: Education and Enlightenment in the Works of William Godwin, 1962, Godwin Criticism: A Synoptic Bibliography, 1967, Dictionary of Names and Titles in Poe's Collected Works, 1968, Discoveries in Poe, 1970, Benjamin Constant's Translation of Godwin's Political Justice, 1972, The Music for Shelley's Poems: An Annotated Bibliography of 1309 Compositions, 1974, Poe, Creator of Words, 1974, The Imaginary Voyages, vol. 1 of Collected Writings of...Poe, 1994, Word Index to Poe's Fiction, 1982, The Brevities of Poe, vol. 2 of Collected Writings of Poe, 1985, Poe's Writings in the Broadway Jour., 1986, Insights and Outlooks: Essays on Great Writers, 1986, Images of Poe's Works: A Comprehensive Descriptive Catalogue of Illustrations, 1989, The German Face of Poe (with Thomas Hansen), 1995, (with J.V. Ridgely) Poe's Writings in the Southern Literary Messenger, vol. 5 of Collected Writings of Poe, 1986, Poe's Seductive Influence on Great Writers, 2004; adv. bd. editors Poe Studies, 1980—, Poe Rev., 2000-04, (with Joseph Ridgely) Poe's Writings in the Southern Literary Messenger, vol. 2; contbr. over 200 articles to profl. jours. Founder, continuing bd. dirs. Bronxville Beautification Coun., 1980—; active Friends of NY Pub. Libr., Carnegie Hall, Libr. of Bronxville, Eastchester Arts Coun., Columbia U. Libr. Friends, Supporters of Guggenheim Found.; bd. trustees Poe Mus., Richmond, Va. Recipient Poe award, Bronx County Hist. Soc., 2001, Rotary Club award, 2002, Alice and Burton Pollin for effective beautification of Bronxville; fellow John Hay Whitney, 1947; grantee Am. Philos. Soc., US, 1964-65, London, 1965, 1968, NY State U. Rsch. Found., 1966, Carl and Lily Pforzheimer, 1966, 1969, SUNY, 1967—73, Am. Coun. Learned Socs., 1968, 1975, 1984, Guggenheim Found., 1973—74, CUNY Rsch. Found., 1973, 1980, 1986, NEH, 1983—84, Lectureship on Poe, NY State Humanities

Coun., 1996—99, 2003—05. Mem. MLA (life), Poe Studies Assn. (hon., life), Am. Lit. Assn. Avocations: literary research, piano playing, travel, environmentalism. Home: 3 Stoneleigh Plz Apt 4D Bronxville NY 10708

**POLLINGER, WILLIAM JOSHUA,** lawyer; b. Passaic, N.J., Dec. 14, 1944; s. Irving R. and Ethel (Groudan) P.; m. Helen Rizzo, May 30, 1977; children: Samantha, Zachary. BA, Rutgers U., 1966; JD, Am. U., 1969. Bar: N.J. 1969, U.S. Dist. Ct. N.J. 1969, N.Y. 1981, U.S. Supreme Ct. 1982, U.S. Ct. Appeals (3d cir.) 1986; cert. Civil Trial Atty. N.J. Supreme Ct., 1983; masters level cert. U.S.A. Track and Field Ofcl. Assoc. Krieger & Klein, Passaic, 1969-75; ptnr. Delorenzo & Pollinger, Hackensack, NJ, 1975-84; pres. William J. Pollinger, P.A., Hackensack, 1984-88, Pollinger, Fearns & Kemezis, P.A., 1988-90, Pollinger & Fearns, P.A., 1990-92, William J. Pollinger P.A., Hackensack, NJ, 1992—. Mem. Bergen County Ethics Com., NJ, 1984—88; lectr. ins. N.J.-ICLE, 1998—. Arbitrator Better Bus. Bur. of Bergen and Rockland Counties, Paramus, N.J., 1983-89, Am. Arbitration Assn., 1983—. Assoc. of Yr. award Builders Assn. No. N.J., Paramus, 1981. Master: Justice Robert L. Clifford Am. Inn of Ct.; mem.: ATLA, Def. Rsch. Inst., Am. Arbitration Assn., Trial Attys. N.J., Bergen County Bar Assn., N.J. State Bar Assn. (ins. law com.), Masons (past master), Phi Delta Phi. Avocation: track and field officiating. Office: 302 Union St Hackensack NJ 07601-4303 Office Phone: 201-487-5666.

**POLLIO, RALPH THOMAS,** managing editor, writer, magazine publishing consultant; b. Bronx, N.Y., Nov. 1, 1948; s. Thomas and Dolores (Miccioli) P.; m. Rita Lucia Napolitano, Sept. 29, 1974 (div. 1991); 1 child, Christopher. BCE, Manhattan Coll., 1978; postgrad., Columbia U., 1988—. Founding pub., editor, owner Ea. Basketball Publs., Franklin Square, N.Y., 1975-88; cons., ptnr., founder Ea. Basketball Mag., Rochester, Mich., 1988—; founding pub., owner, editor High School News, 1984, EB News, 1981; mng. editor Harman Consumer Group, Woodbury, N.Y. Contbr. articles to mags. and profl. jours., 1985—. Sgt. U.S. Army N.G., 1969-74. Mem. U.S. Basketball Writers Assn. (1st Place award for best mag. feature 1984), ASCE, Soc. Profl. Journalists, Sigma Delta Chi, Internat. Soc. Philos. Enquiry, World Lit. Acad., Mag. Pubs. Assn., Am. Soc. Mag. Editors, Mensa, and numerous other high IQ socs. Roman Catholic. Clubs: N.Y. Road Runners (N.Y.C.), Dix Hills Runners. Avocations: working out, listening to jazz, gourmet cooking, reading, film. Home: 1201 Hempstead Ave Malverne NY 11565-1213 Office Phone: 516-682-3715. Business E-Mail: rpollio@harman.com.

**POLLITT, BYRON H., JR.,** retail executive; BS in Bus. Econs., U. Calif.; MBA, Harvard U. Mgmt. cons. McKinsey & Co.; v.p. corp. ops. planning Walt Disney Co., 1990—92, v.p. bus. planning, 1992—94, CFO, 1994—95, sr. v.p., CFO Disneyland Resorts, 1995—99, exec. v.p., CFO Walt Disney Parks and Resorts, 1999—2003; exec. v.p., CFO Gap, Inc., San Francisco, 2003—. Office: Gap Inc 2 Folsom St San Francisco CA 94105*

**POLLITT, JEROME JORDAN,** art historian, educator; b. Fair Lawn, N.J., Nov. 26, 1934; s. John Kendall and Doris B. (Jordan) P.; m. Susan Baker Matheson, Feb. 10, 1977. BA, Yale U., 1957; PhD, Columbia U., 1963. Instr. history of art Yale U., New Haven, 1962-64, asst. prof., 1964-68, assoc. prof., 1969-73, prof., 1973-98, prof. emeritus, 1998—, chmn. dept. classics, 1975-77, chmn. dept. history of art, 1981-84, dean, 1986-91. Author: Art and Experience in Classical Greece, 1972, The Ancient View of Greek Art, 1975, Art in the Hellenistic Age, 1986, The Art of Greece: Sources and Documents, 1990, Personal Styles in Greek Sculpture, 1996; editor-in-chief: Am. Jour. Archaeology, 1973-77; contbr. articles to profl. jours. Mem. Archaeol. Inst. Am., Coll. Art Assn. Home: 48 Dillon Rd Woodbridge CT 06525-1219 Office: Dept Art History Yale U PO Box 208272 New Haven CT 06520-8272 Business E-Mail: Jerome.Pollitt@yale.edu.

**POLLITT, KATHA,** writer, educator, poet; b. N.Y.C., Oct. 14, 1949; d. Basil Riddiford and Leanora (Levine) P.; div.; 1 child, Sophie Pollitt-Cohen. BA, Harvard U., 1972; MFA, Columbia U., 1975. Lit. editor The Nation, N.Y.C., 1982-84, contbg. editor, 1986-92, assoc. editor, then columnist, 1992—; jr. fellow council of humanities Princeton (N.J.) U., 1984. Lectr. The New Sch., N.Y.C., 1986-90, Poetry Ctr. 92d St. YMHA and YWHA, N.Y.C., 1986-95. Author: Antarctic Traveller, 1982 (Nat. Book Critics Circle award 1983), Reasonable Creatures: Essays on Women and Feminism, 1994, Subject to Debate: Sense and Dissents on Womes, Politics and Culture, 2001; poetry appeared in The New Yorker, The New Republic, Poetry, and others; contbr. articles to jours. Maggie award, Planned Parenthood Fed Am, 1993; Whiting fellow, 1993, Guggenheim fellow 1987; recipient I.B. Lavan Younger Poet's award Acad. Am. Poets, 1984, Nat. Mag. award 1992; Fulbright grantee, 1985; grantee N.Y. Found. of the Arts, 1987, Nat. Endowment for Arts, 1984. Fellow N.Y. Inst. Humanities. Democrat.

**POLLOCK, ALEXANDER JOHN,** banker; b. Indpls., Jan. 28, 1943; s. Alex S. and Doris L. (VanHorn) P.; m. Anne M. Fryfogle, Jan. 27, 1968; children: Elizabeth, Alexander, Evelyn, James. BA, Williams Coll., 1965; MA, U. Chgo., 1966; M.P.A., Princeton U., 1969. Instr. philosophy Lake Forest Coll., Ill., 1967; with internat. banking dept. Continental Ill. Nat. Bank, Chgo., 1969-77 v.p., 1977-82, sr. v.p., 1982-85; prin. Nolan Norton & Co., Chgo., 1985-86; chief fin. officer Marine Corp., Milw., 1986; pres. Marine Bank N.A., Milw., 1987; pres., CEO Cmty. Fed. Savs., St. Louis, 1988-90; vis. scholar Fed. Res. Bank of St. Louis, 1991; pres., CEO Fed. Home Loan Bank Chgo., 1991—2004; fellow Am. Enterprise Inst. Pub. Policy Rsch., Washington, 2004—. Bd. dirs. Gt. Lakes Higher Edn. Corp., Allied Capital Corp., Chgo. Merc. Exch.; past pres. Internat. Union for Housing Fin. Trustee Ill. Coun. on Econ. Edn.; Bd. dirs. Great Books Found. Mem.: Union League Club, Univ. Club, Phi Beta Kappa. Office: Am Enterprise Inst 1150 Seventeenth St NW Washington DC 20036 Office Phone: 202-862-7190. Business E-Mail: APollock@aei.org. Omnia superans vi rationis et arte loquendi.

**POLLOCK, BRUCE GODFREY,** psychiatrist, educator; b. Toronto, Ont., Can., Aug. 18, 1952; s. Ira Justus and Sheila Joy (Godfrey) P.; m. Judith Arluk, May 18, 1982; children: Debra, Ariel. BS, U. Toronto, 1975, MD, 1979; PhD, U. Pitts., 1987. Chief resident Clarke Inst. Psychiatry, Toronto, 1982-83; fellow U. Pitts., 1983-84, asst. prof. psychiatry, 1984-90, assoc. dir. clin. pharmacology dept. psychiatry, 1987-95, assoc. prof. dept. psychiatry and pharmacology, 1990-96, dir. geriat. psychopharm. dept. psychiatry and pharmacology, 1995—, prof. depts. psychiatry, pharmacology and pharm. scis., 1997—, chief acad. divsn. geriatrics and neuropsychiatry, 2001, Sandra A. Rotman chair neuropsychiatry, 2005—; head divsn. geriatric psychiatry U. Toronto, 2005—. Contbr. chapters to books, articles to profl. jours. Centennial fellow Med. Rsch. Coun. of Can., Ottawa, 1983, Merck fellow geriatric clin. pharmacology, Am. Fedn. for Aging Rsch., N.Y.C., 1988; recipient Geriat. Mental Health award NIMH, Bethesda, Md., 1992, Ind. Scientist award, 1997, Sr. Investigation Award, Am. Assoc. for Geniatric Psychiatry, Bethesda, Md., 2003. Fellow Royal Coll. Physicians Can., Am. Psychiat. Assn. (disting.). Home: 7032 Meade St Pittsburgh PA 15208-2429 Office: Rotman Rsch Inst Baycrest 3560 Bathurst St Toronto Canada M6A 2E1 Office Phone: 412-246-6274. Business E-Mail: pollockbg@upmc.edu.

**POLLOCK, EARL EDWARD,** lawyer; b. Decatur, Nebr., Feb. 24, 1928; s. Herman and Della (Rosenthal) P.; m. Betty Sokol, Sept. 8, 1951; children: Stephen, Della, Naomi. BA, U. Minn., 1948; JD, Northwestern U., 1953; LLD (hon.), Morningside Coll., 1995. Bar: D.C. 1955, Va. 1955, Ill. 1959, U.S. Supreme Ct. 1960. Law clk., chief justices Vinson and Warren, U.S. Supreme Ct. Washington, 1953-55; atty. antitrust div. Dept. Justice, Washington, 1955-56, asst. to solicitor gen., 1956-59; ptnr. Sonnenschein Nath & Rosenthal, Chgo., 1959—. Life trustee Loyola U., Chgo., Northwestern Meml. Hosp.; pres. Fla. West Coast Symphony, Sarasota, 2004-05. Mem. Chgo. Bar Assn. (chmn. antitrust law com. 1967-68), ABA (chmn. antitrust law sect. 1979-80), Alumni Assn. Northwestern U. Sch. Law (pres. 1974-75, svc. award 1976). Office: Sonnenschein Nath 233 S Wacker Dr Ste 8000 Chicago IL 60606-6491

**POLLOCK, JOHN PHLEGER,** lawyer; b. Sacramento, Apr. 28, 1920; s. George Gordon and Irma (Phleger) P.; m. Juanita Irene Gossman, Oct. 26, 1945; children: Linda Pollock Harrison, Madeline Pollock Chiotti, John, Gordon. AB, Stanford U., 1942; JD, Harvard U., 1948. Bar: Calif. 1949, U.S. Supreme Ct. 1954. Ptnr. Musick, Peeler & Garrett, L.A., 1953-60, Pollock, Williams & Berwanger, L.A., 1960-80, Rodi, Pollock, Pettker, Galbraith & Cahill, L.A., 1980-89, of counsel, 1989—. Contbr. articles to profl. publs. Active Boy Scouts Am.; trustee Pitzer Coll., Claremont, Calif., 1968-76, Pacific Legal Found., 1981-91, Fletcher Jones Found., 1969—, Good Hope Med. Found., 1980-2006. Fellow Am. Coll. Trial Lawyers; mem. ABA, LA County Bar Assn. (trustee 1964-66). Home: 30602 Paseo Del Valle Laguna Niguel CA 92677-2317 Office: 444 S Flower St Ste 1700 Los Angeles CA 90071-2918 Personal E-mail: Phleger1@msn.com.

**POLLOCK, KAREN ANNE,** computer analyst; b. Elmhurst, Ill., Sept. 6, 1961; d. Michael Paul and Dorothy Rosella (Foskett) Pollock. BS, Elmhurst Coll., 1984; MS, North Ctrl. Coll., 1993. Formatter Nat. Data Corp., Lombard, Ill., 1985; computer specialist Dept. VA, Hines, Ill., 1985—. Lutheran. Avocations: cross-stitch, mystery books, bowling, bicycling, softball.

**POLLOCK, KEVIN ALEXANDER,** academic administrator; b. Bay City, Mich., Feb. 8, 1959; s. Alexander Welsh and Irene Elizabeth Pollock; m. D'Lynn Kay McBride, June 25, 1994; children: Sean Robert, Brendan Alexander, Mackenzie Elizabeth-Gene. BS in Edn., Ctrl. Mich. U., 1981, MA in Edn., 1988; PhD, Mich. State U., 2001. Dir. of admissions GMI Engring. and Mgmt. Inst. Flint, Mich., 1985—93, Lawrence Technol. U., Southfield, Mich., 1993—98; dir. of enrollment and recruitment Lake Superior State U., Sault Ste. Marie, Mich., 1988—2000; v.p. of student svcs. West Shore C.C., Scottville, Mich., 2000—. Lectr. in field. Contbr. articles to profl. jours. Mem.: Assn. of Coll. Adminstrn. Profls., Mich. Assn. of Coll. Registrars and Admissions Officers, Nat. Inst. for Staff and Orgnl. Devel., Coun. for the Study of Cmty. Colls., Nat. Coun. on Student Devel., Nat. Assn. of Student Pers. Adminstrs., Nat. Assn. of Coll. Admissions Counselors (assoc.), Am. Assn. of Coll. Registrars and Admissions Officers (assoc.). Home: 1425 N Wooded Lake Dr Ludington MI 49431 Office: West Shore Community College 3000 North Stiles Rd Scottville MI 49454 Office Phone: 231-845-6211. Office Fax: 231-845-3944. E-mail: kapollock@westshore.edu.

**POLLOCK, LAWRENCE I.,** retail executive, investment company executive; BS, Ohio State Univ. Pres., COO Zale Corp., 1994—96; exec. v.p., COO Home Place Inc., 1997—98, pres., CEO, 1998—99; pres. Cole Nat. Corp., 2000—03, pres., CEO, 2003—04; pres., mng. ptnr. Lucky Stars Partners LLC, 2004—. Bd. dir. Borders Group Inc., 1995—, non-exec. chmn., 2006—. Pres. Bellefaire JCB; trustee Musical Arts Assn. (Cleveland Orch.), Nat. Conf. for Cmty. & Justice No. Ohio region, WVIZ/PBS & 90.3 WCPN ideastream. Office: Borders Group Inc Bd Directors 100 Phoenix Dr Ann Arbor MI 48108*

**POLLOCK, MARGARET LANDAU PEGGY,** elementary school educator; b. Jefferson City, Mo., Oct. 18, 1936; d. William Wold and Grace Elizabeth (Creamer) Anderson; children by previous marriage: Elizabeth, Charles, Christopher, Jeffrey; m. William Whalen Pollock, Jan. 30, 1993. AA, Stephens Coll., 1956; BS in Elem. Edn., U. Mo., Columbia, 1958; MA in Reading Edn., U. Mo., Kansas City, 1987. Cert. elem. tchr., Mo. Kindergarten tchr. Columbia Schs., 1958-59, Moberly (Mo.) Schs., 1960-62; 1st grade tchr. Kansas City Schs., 1962-63; kindergarten tchr. Independence (Mo.) Schs., 1966-75; chpt. I reading specialist Thomas Hart Benton Elem. Sch., Independence, 1975-93; book reviewer Corpus Christi (Tex.) Caller Times, 1994—; children's libr. Corpus Christi Pub. Libr., 1995-97; dir. Johnson City (Tex.) Libr., 1997—. Cons., presenter in field. Bd. dirs. Boys and Girls Club, Independence, 1990-93; coord. Independence Reading Fair, 1989-93; coord. books and tutoring Salvation Army, Kansas City, 1990-92. Mem. AAUW, Internat. Reading Assn. (People to People del. to USSR 1991, local v.p 1990-91, pres. 1991-92), Internat. Platform Assn., Austin Writer's League, Archeol. Inst. Am., Tex. Libr. Assn., Earthwatch, Nature Conservancy, Sierra Club, Phi Kappa Phi, Pi Lambda Theta (pres. Beta Upsilon chpt. 1992-93). Avocations: native american history, rights and education, archeology, reading, travel, conservation. Home: PO Box 482 Johnson City TX 78636-0482

**POLLOCK, PAUL JAMES,** lawyer; b. NYC, July 11, 1960; s. Edmund and Gertrude (Weissman) P.; m. Linda Susan Chinman, Sept. 17, 1988. AB, Colgate U., 1982; JD, Fordham U., 1985. Bar: N.Y. 1986. Assoc. Willkie Farr & Gallagher, NYC, 1986-88, Brown, Raysman & Millstein, NYC, 1988; ptnr. Piper Rudnick LLP, 1996, Katten Muchin Zavis Rosenman, NYC. Mem. ABA, Assn. Bar City of N.Y., Team Redline Club (pres.). Democrat. Office: Katten Muchin Zavis Rosenman 575 Madison Ave New York NY 10022 Office Phone: 212-940-8555. Office Fax: 212-940-8776. E-mail: paul.pollock@kmzr.com.

**POLLOCK, R. JEFFREY,** lawyer; b. San Francisco, Jan. 5, 1946; BA, DePauw U., 1968; MT, Harvard U., 1971; JD, Northeastern U., 1976. Bar: Ohio 1976, Mich. 2002. Asst. sec. dept. community devel. Commonwealth of Mass., 1972—73; assoc. Burke, Haber & Berick, Cleve., 1976—84, ptnr., 1984—90; atty. McDonald, Hopkins Co. LPA, Cleve., prin., 1990—; gen. counsel Metaldyne Corp., 2001—05. Mem. ABA, Ohio State Bar Assn., Cleve. Bar Assn. Office: McDonald Hopkins 600 Superior Ave E Ste 2100 Cleveland OH 44114-2653 Office Phone: 216-348-5400. E-mail: jpollock@mcdonaldhopkins.com.

**POLLOCK, ROBERT B.,** insurance company executive; BBA, Univ. Wis., Madison, 1976. Actuary CUNA Mutual Ins. Co., 1974—81; staff actuary through sr. v.p. Assurant Employee Benefits, 1981—93; pres., CEO Assurant Employee benefits, 1993—99; exec. v.p., CFO Assurant Inc., 1999—2005, pres., COO, 2005—. Past chmn., disability ins. com. Health Ins. Assn. Am. Fellow: Soc. of Actuaries; mem.: Am. Acad. of Actuaries. Office: Assurant Inc 1 Chase Manhattan Plz New York NY 10005*

**POLLOCK, ROBERT ELWOOD,** nuclear scientist; b. Regina, Sask., Can., Mar. 2, 1936; s. Elwood Thomas and Harriet Lillian (Rooney) Pollock; m. Jean Elizabeth Virtue, Sept. 12, 1959; children: Bryan Thomas, Heather Lynn, Jeffrey Parker, Jennifer Lee. BSc (hon.), U. Man., Can., 1957; MA, Princeton U., 1959, PhD, 1963. Instr. Princeton (N.J.) U., 1961—63, asst. prof., 1964—69, rsch. physicist, 1969—70; Nat. Rsch. Coun. postdoctoral fellow Harwell, England, 1963—64; assoc. prof. Ind. U., Bloomington, 1970—73, prof., 1973—84, disting. prof., 1984—2001, prof. emeritus, 2001—, dir. Cyclotron Facility, 1973—79, mem. nuc. sci. adv. com., 1977—80. Recipient Alexander von Humboldt Sr. U.S. Scientist award, 1985—88. Fellow Am. Phys. Soc. (Bonner prize 1992). Home: 2811 Dale Ct Bloomington IN 47401-2414 Office: Ind U Swain Hall Dept Physics Bloomington IN 47405

**POLLOCK, STEPHEN MICHAEL,** operations research engineer, educator, consultant; b. N.Y.C., Feb. 15, 1936; s. Meyer and Frances R. Pollock; m. Bettina Dorn, Nov. 22, 1962; children: Joshua, Aaron, Ethan. B in Engring. Physics, Cornell U., 1958; SM, MIT, 1960, PhD in Physics and Ops. Research, 1964. Mem. tech. staff Arthur D. Little Inc., Cambridge, Mass., 1964-65; asst. prof. Naval Postgrad. Sch., Monterey, Calif., 1965-68, assoc. prof., 1968-69, U. Mich., Ann Arbor, 1969-73, prof., dept. indsl. and ops. engring., 1974—, chmn. dept., 1980-90. Cons. to over 40 orgns. Area editor Ops. Rsch. Jour., 1977-82; sr. editor Inst. Indsl. Engrs. Trans., 1985-89, Army Sci. Bd., 1994-99; contbr. more than 60 tech. papers to profl. jours. Fellow, Space Tech. Labs., 1960. Inst. Ops. Rsch. Mgmt. Sci.; sr. fellow NSF, 1975. Fellow: AAAS; mem.: Nat. Acad. Engring., Ops. Rsch. Soc. Am. (pres. 1986—87), Inst. Mgmt. Sci. Office: U of Mich Dept Indsl Ops Engring Ann Arbor MI 48109-2117

**POLLOCK, STEWART GLASSON,** lawyer, state supreme court justice; b. East Orange, NJ, Dec. 21, 1932; BA, Hamilton Coll., 1954; LLD (hon.), 1995; LLB, NYU, 1957; LLM, U. Va., 1988. Bar: NJ 1958. Asst. U.S. atty., Newark, 1958-60; ptnr. Schenck, Price, Smith & King, Morristown, NJ, 1960-74, 76-78; commr. N.J. Dept. Pub. Utilities; counsel to gov. State of N.J., Trenton, 1978-79; assoc. justice N.J. Supreme Ct., Morristown, 1979-99; of counsel Riker Danzig Hyland & Perretti, Morristown, 1999—. Mem. N.J. Commn. on Investigation, 1976-78; chmn. commn. on the rules of profl. conduct N.J. Supreme Ct., 2000—. Assoc. editor N.J. Law Jour.; contbr. articles to legal jours. Fellow Am. Coll. Comml. Arbitrators; mem. ABA (chmn. appellate judges conf. 1991-92), N.J. Bar Assn. (trustee 1973-78), Am. Judicature Soc. (dir. 1984-88), Morris County Bar Assn. (pres. 1973). Office: Riker Danzig Scherer Hyland & Perretti LLP Hdqs Plz 1 Speedwell Ave Morristown NJ 07962-1981 Office Phone: 973-538-0800. E-mail: spollock@riker.com.

**POLLOCK-O'BRIEN, LOUISE MARY,** public relations executive; b. Tarentum, Pa., Mar. 14, 1948; d. Louis P. and Marian M. (Ballay) Pollock; m. Vincent Miles O'Brien. BS, Ind. U. of Pa., 1970. Tchr. Archbishop Wood H.S., Warminster, Pa., 1970-75; spokesperson, publicist Calif. Olive Industry, Fresno, 1976-78; account exec. Ketchum Pub. Rels., N.Y.C., 1979-81, account supr., 1982-83, v.p., 1984, v.p., group mgr., 1985-88, sr. v.p., group mgr., 1988-89, assoc. dir., dir. food mktg., sr. v.p., 1990-91; chmn. Aronow & Pollock Comm., Inc., N.Y.C., 1991—2004; pres. Pollock Comm. Inc., N.Y.C., 2004—. Mem. pub. rels. adv. com. Mayor's Vol. Action Com., N.Y.C., 1986; mem. food svc. adv. bd. L.I. City Coll., Bklyn., 1987-88. V.p.; fundraiser West 76th St. Block Assn., N.Y.C., 1982. Mem. Internat. Foodservice Editl. Coun. (v.p., bd. dirs. 1984-85). Avocations: watercolor painting, skiing. Office: Pollock Comm Inc 665 Broadway New York NY 10012-4408 Office Phone: 212-941-1414. E-mail: lpollock@pollock-pr.com.

**POLON, IRA H.,** lawyer; b. NYC, Mar. 9, 1943; BA, Lehigh U., 1965; LLB, Columbia U., 1968. Bar: N.Y. 1968, D.C. 1971, U.S. Ct. Appeals (D.C. cir.) 1972. Ptnr. Dickstein Shapiro Morin & Oshinsky LLP, Washington. Mem. ABA (mem. corporation, banking and bus. law sect.), D.C. Bar, N.Y. State Bar Assn., Bar Assn. D.C. Office: Dickstein Shapiro Morin & Oshinsky LLP 2101 L St NW Washington DC 20037-1526 Office Phone: 202-828-2238. Business E-Mail: poloni@dsmo.com.

**POLONSKY, ARTHUR,** artist, educator; b. Lynn, Mass., June 6, 1925; s. Benjamin and Celia (Hurwitz) P.; children: Eli, D.L., Gabriel. Diploma with highest honors, Sch. Mus. Fine Arts, Boston, 1948. Instr. painting dept. Sch. Mus. Fine Arts, Boston, 1950-60; asst. prof. fine arts Brandeis U., 1954-65; assoc. prof. Boston U., 1965-90, prof. emeritus, 1990—. One-man shows include Boris Mirski Gallery, Boston, 1950, 1954, 1956, 1964, Durlacher Gallery, NYC, 1965, Mickelson Gallery, Washington, 1966, 1974, Boston Pub. Libr., 1969, 1990, 1993, 1996, 1999, Boston Ctr. for Arts, 1983, Starr Gallery, Boston, 1987, Fitchburg Art Mus., 1990, Kantar Fine Arts, Newton, Mass., 2002, St. Botolph Club Gallery, Boston, 2004—05, exhibited in group shows at Met. Mus., NYC, 1950, The Salon Des Jeunes Peintres, Paris, 1950, Stedelijk Mus., Amsterdam, The Netherlands, 1950, Carnegie Internat. Expn., 1951, Boston Arts Festival, 1954, 1955, 1985, Inst. Contemporary Art, Boston, 1960, Mus. Fine Arts, 1976, Expressionism in Boston, Decordova Mus., Lincoln, Mass., 1986, Palais Univ. de Strasbourg, France, 1992, Boston's Honored Artists, Danforth Mus., Framingham, Mass., 1995, Decordova Mus., Lincoln, Mass., 2002, Sagendorph Gallery, Keene State Coll., Keene, NH, 2003, Francesca Anderson Gallery, Lexington, Mass., 2004, Represented in permanent collections Mus. Fine Arts, Boston, Fogg Mus., Harvard U., Addison Gallery of Am. Art, Andover, Mass., Stedelijk Mus., Amsterdam, Walker Art Ctr., Mpls., Zimmerli Art Mus., Rutgers U., New Brunswick, NJ, Honolulu Acad. Arts, Decordova Mus., Lincoln, Mass., High Mus. Art, Atlanta, The Danforth Mus., Framingham, Mass. Recipient Louis Comfort Tiffany award for painting, 1951, 1st prize Boston Arts Festival, 1954; European travelling fellow Sch. Mus. Fine Art, Boston, 1948-50 Mem. Artists Equity Assn., Inc. (founding, former dir. New Eng. chpt.). Address: 364 Cabot St Newtonville MA 02460-2252 Office Phone: 617-969-6789.

**POLOS, IRIS STEPHANIE,** artist; b. Oakland, Calif., Feb. 14, 1947; d. Theodore C. and Catherine (Pappas) P.; 1 child Apollo Papafrangou. BFA, Calif. Coll. Arts and Crafts, Oakland, 1968, MFA, 1971. Instr. figure drawing Am. Sch. of Art, Athens, Greece, 1969-71 summers; instr. advanced drawing U. Calif. Extension Open Exchange, San Francisco, 1978-79; artist in residence Chabot Elem. Sch., Oakland, Calif., 1986-92, Mus. of Children's Art, Oakland, 1988—96; art tchr. Arrowsmith Acad., Berkeley, 1991—; instr. Oakland children's hosp. MOCHA, 1995—96. Artist: selected exhibitions include: San Francisco Mus. of Modern Art, 1971, Richmond (Calif.) Art Ctr., 1973, Calif. Coll. of Arts and Crafts, Oakland, 1973, Art for Art Sake Gallery, San Francisco, 1977, Jehu Wong Gallery, San Francisco, 1979, Triangle Gallery, San Francisco, 1981, Bond Gallery, N.Y.C., 1985, 86, Berkeley (Calif.) Art Ctr., 1987, 88, Emanuel Radnitzky, San Francisco, 1990 (2 shows), San Francisco Art Commn. Gallery, 1991, Fine Arts Ctr., Irvine, Calif., 1991, Trojanowska Gallery, San Francisco, 1991, Nelson Morales Gallery, San Francisco, 1992, Morphos Gallery, L.A., 1993, 94, Morphos Gallery, San Francisco, 1994, 95, Hotel Triton Art Fair with Morphos Gallery, San Francisco, 1995, Moreau Galeries, Notre Dame, Ind., 1995, Fort Mason Found., San Francisco, 1995, Magic Theater Lobby, San Francisco, 1995, Chgo.-Artspace, Lima, Ohio, 1997, Catherine Clark Gallery, San Francisco, 1997, 98, 99, Circle Elephant Art Gallery, L.A., 2001, 04, others; permanent collections include the Oakland Mus., Catharine Clark, Gary Noguera, Helen Salz, Daniel Soto, Caroline Zecca, di Rosa Found., Sonoma County, and others; her works also include book illustration and theatre set design; featured artist in Juxtapoz mag., Fall 1998, Chicago Art Fair with C. Clark Gallery, 2001-02, mural projects with Arrowsmith Acad. at Oakland Zoo and at St. Marks Ch., Berkeley. Grantee: Arts in Edn. grant Cultural Arts Divsn., Oakland, 1991-96, Berkeley Repertory Theater, 1995. Democrat. Home: 5801 Broadway Oakland CA 94618-1524 Office: Arrowsmith Acad Art Dept Berkeley CA 94704

**POLOZOLA, FRANK JOSEPH,** federal judge; b. Baton Rouge, La., Jan. 15, 1942; s. Steve A. Sr. and Caroline C. (Lucito) P.; m. Linda Kay White, June 9, 1962; children: Gregory Dean, Sheri Elizabeth, Gordon Damian. Student bus. adminstrn., La. State U., 1959-62, JD, 1965. Bar: La. 1965. Law clk. to US Dist. Ct. Judge E. Gordon West, 1965-66; assoc. Seale, Smith & Phelps, Baton Rouge, 1966-68, ptnr., 1968-73; part-time magistrate US Dist. Ct. (Mid. Dist.) La., Baton Rouge, 1972-73, magistrate, 1973-80, judge, 1980—, chief judge, 1998—2005. Adj. prof. Law Ctr., La. State U., 1977-95. Bd. dirs. Cath. HS. Mem. La. Bar Assn., Baton Rouge Bar Assn., Fed. Judges Assn., 5th Cir. Dist. Judges Assn., La. State U. L Club, KC, Wex Malone Inns of Ct., Omicron Delta Kappa. Roman Catholic. Office: US Dist Ct Russell B Long Fed Bldg & US Courthouse 777 Florida St Ste 313 Baton Rouge LA 70801-1717

**POLSBY, ALLEN ISAAC,** retired lawyer; b. New Haven, Nov. 4, 1937; s. Daniel II and Edythe (Woolf) P.; m. Gail Kissling, Aug. 30, 1963; children: Daniel Laurence, Abigail Starr. A.B., Brown U., 1959; J.D., George Washington U., 1962. Bar: D.C. 1962, U.S. Ct. Appeals (D.C. cir.) 1963, U.S. Supreme Ct. 1979. Assoc., Denning & Wohlstetter, Washington, 1962-63; trial atty. CAB, 1963-66; asst. counsel research, tech. programs subcom. Com. on Govt. Ops., U.S. Ho. of Reps., 1966; atty. Office Gen. Counsel, HUD, Washington, 1966-2003, acting gen. counsel, 1996, assoc. gen. counsel legis. and regulations, 1996-2000, assoc. gen. counsel appeals, 2000-03, ret., 2003; comml. arbitrator, 2003—.

**POLSBY, DANIEL D.,** dean, law educator; b. 1945; BA, Oakland U., 1964; JD, U. Minn., 1971. Bar: Minn. 1971, D.C. 1972, Ill. 1977, N.Y. 1982. Law clk. to Judge Harold Leventhal U.S. Ct. Appeals (D.C. cir.), 1971-72; assoc. Wilmer, Cutler & Pickering, Washington, 1972-74; legal adviser to atty. FCC, Washington, 1974-76; asst. prof. law Northwestern U., Chgo., 1976-78, assoc. prof., 1978-79, prof., 1979—99, Kirkland & Ellis prof., 1990—99;

prof. law George Mason U., Sch. Law, 1999—, acting dean, 2004—05, dean, 2005—. Vis. prof. Cornell U., 1981-82, U. Mich., 1982, U. So. Calif., 1990. Author: The False Promise of Gun Control, 1994. Mem. ABA, ALI, Order of Coif. Office: George Mason U Sch Law 3301 Fairfax Dr Arlington VA 22201-4426 Office Phone: 703-993-8087. E-mail: polsby@gmu.edu.

**POLSBY, GAIL K.,** psychotherapist; b. Washington, Jan. 13, 1939; d. Thomas Edward and Elise Wildman (Hammer) Kissling; m. Allen I. Polsby, Aug. 30, 1963; children: Daniel, Abigail. BA, U. Md., Balt., 1960; MSW, Cath. U., Washington, D.C., 1963. Mem. faculty Washington Sch. Psychiatry, 1967—2001, chmn. bd. dirs., 2001—; pvt. practice psychotherapy, Chevy Chase, Md., 1969—; cons. doctoral program Clin. Social Work Inst., Washington, 1999—2003. Sec., bd. dirs. Washington Sch. Psychiatry, 1995—2001, chair faculty coun. Editor quar. newspaper Washington Sch. Psychiatry News, 1997-2005. Mem. Am. Group Psychotherapy Assn., Nat. Fedn. Clin. Social Workers. Avocations: hiking, biking. Home: 5651 Bent Branch Rd Bethesda MD 20816-1049

**POLSBY, NELSON WOOLF,** political science professor; b. Norwich, Conn., Oct. 25, 1934; s. Daniel II and Edythe (Woolf) P.; m. Linda Dale Offenbach, Aug. 3, 1958; children: Lisa, Emily, Daniel R. AB, Johns Hopkins, 1956; MA, Yale U., 1958, PhD, 1961; LittD, U. Liverpool, 1992; MA, Oxford U., Eng., 1997; Dr. h.c. (hon.), Ecole Normale Superieure de Cachan, 2002. Instr. U. Wis., 1960-61; from asst. prof. to prof. Wesleyan U., Middletown, Conn., 1961-68; prof. polit. sci. U. Calif., Berkeley, 1967. Dir. Inst. Govtl. Studies U. Calif., 1989-99; vis. faculty Columbia, 1963, Yale, 1963, 67, 75, Hebrew U., Jerusalem, 1970, Stanford, 1977, Harvard U., 1986-87, Oxford U., 1994, 97-98; com. on pub. engring. policy Nat. Acad. Engring., 1973-76; commn. on behavioral and social scis. and edn. NRC, 1983-89. Author: Community Power and Political Theory, 2d edit, 1980, Congress and the Presidency, 4th edit, 1986, (with Aaron Wildavsky) Presidential Elections, 11th edit, 2004, Congress: An Introduction, 1968, Political Promises, 1974, (with Geoffrey Smith) British Government and its Discontents, 1981, Consequences of Party Reform, 1983, Political Innovation in America, 1984, (with Alan Brinkley and Kathleen Sullivan) New Federalist Papers, 1997, How Congress Evolves, 2004; editor: (with R.A. Dentler and P. Smith) Politics and Social Life, 1963, (with R.L. Peabody) New Perspectives on the House of Representatives, 4th edit, 1993, Congressional Behavior, 1971, Reapportionment in the 1970's, 1971, The Modern Presidency, 1973, (with F.I. Greenstein) Handbook of Political Science, 8 vols., 1975, What If?, 1982, (with G. Orren) Media and Momentum, 1987; book rev. editor: Transaction, 1968-71; mng. editor: Am. Polit. Sci. Rev, 1971-77; editor Ann. Rev. Polit. Sci., 1988-2005, The Forum Online; editorial adv. bd. Polit. Sci. Quar., other jours. Mem. commn. on vice presdl. selection Dem. Nat. Com., 1973-74; mem. Yale U. Coun., 1978-2000, pres., 1986-93. Fellow Social Sci. Research Council, 1959, Brookings Instn., 1959-60, Center Advanced Study Behavioral Scis., 1965-66, 85-86, Ford Found., 1970-71, John Simon Guggenheim Found., 1977-78, 85-86, Roosevelt Ctr., 1982-83; recipient Yale U. Wilbur Cross medal, 1985, Yale medal, 1997. Fellow AAAS; mem. Am. Polit. Sci. Assn. (coun. 1971-77, 88-89), Am. Acad. Arts and Scis. (coun. 1993-96), Am. Sociol. Assn., Nat. Acad. Pub. Administrn. Avocation: on Fgn. Rels., Phi Beta Kappa. Home: 1500 Le Roy Ave Berkeley CA 94708-1914 Office: U Calif Berkeley Inst Govtl Studies Berkeley CA 94720-0001 Business E-Mail: nwpolsby@berkeley.edu.

**POLSHEK, JAMES STEWART,** architect; b. Akron, Ohio, Feb. 11, 1930; s. Alex and Pearl (Beyer) P.; m. Ellyn May Margolis, June 29, 1952; children: Peter, Jennifer. BS, Case Western Res. U., 1951; MArch, Yale U., 1955. With I.M. Pei & Assocs., NYC, 1955-56, Ulrich Frazen & Assocs., NYC, 1957-60; with Westermann & Miller & Assocs., NYC, 1960-61; pvt. practice architecture NYC, 1962-80; dean Sch. Architecture and Planning, spl. advisor to pres. for design and planning Columbia U., NYC, 1972-87; prin. James Stewart Polshek & Ptnrs., NYC, 1980—. Trustee Mcpl. Art Soc., NYC Fulbright fellow, 1956-57 FAIA (1st. v.p. 1971, pres.-elect 1972) Clubs: Yale of NY, Century Assn., AAAL, 2005. Achievements include design of William J. Clinton Presdl. Ctr., Little Rock, Ark., 2004. Office: Polshek Ptnrshp Arch LLP 320 W 13th St New York NY 10014 Office Phone: 212-807-7171. Office Fax: 212-807-5917.

**POLSKY, CYNTHIA HAZEN,** artist, art collector, philanthropist; b. NYC, Feb. 16, 1939; m. Leon B. Polsky; 2 children. BA, Marymount Coll., 1978; MBA, Fordham U., 1981. Art collector arts of S.E. Asia and India, 20th century Am. and European paintings, sculpture and 19th and 20th century decorative arts; one-woman shows include U.S. galleries and mus., Represented in permanent collections Corcoran Mus., Washington, DC, Fogg Mus., Cambridge, Mass., Johnson Mus., Cornell U., Ithaca, NY, NY Acad. Scis. and Rockefeller U., NYC. Trustee Met. Mus. Art, NYC, mem. acquisitions com., mem. exec. com., chmn. membership com.; hon. life trustee Asia Soc., Storm King Art Ctr., Mountainville, NY; trustee Pierpont Morgan Libr., NYC; mem. Bryant Park Art Commn.; mem. exec. com. Rockefeller U. Coun.; mem. collector's com. Nat. Gallery Art. Office: 667 Madison Ave New York NY 10021 Office Phone: 212-751-4917.

**POLSKY, DONALD PERRY,** architect; b. Milw., Sept. 30, 1928; s. Lew and Dorothy (Geisenfeld) P.; m. Corinne Shirley Neer, Aug. 25, 1957; children: Jeffrey David, Debra Lynn. BArch, U. Nebr., Lincoln, 1951; postgrad., U. So. Calif., 1956, U. Calif., Los Angeles, 1957, U. Nebr., Omaha, 1964, U. Ill., 1965. Project architect Richard Neutra, Architect, Los Angeles, 1953-56, Daniel Dworsky, Architect, Los Angeles, 1956; dir. dept. architecture MCA, Inc., Universal City, Calif., 1962-64. Adj. prof. Coll. Arch., U. Nebr., 1998—99. Prin. works include Mills residence, 1958, apt. bldgs., 1960, Polsky residence, 1961, Milder residence, 1965 Chmn Design Control 1400 Study Mayor's Riverfront Devel., Omaha, 1969, 71; pres. Swanson Sch. Community Club, Omaha, 1972; mem. Mayor's Adv. Panel Design Services, Omaha, 1974; vice chmn. Omaha Zoning Bd. Appeals, 1976. Fellow dir. Siena/Francis House. Recipient archtl. awards Canyon Crier Newspaper, Los Angeles, 1960, House and Home Mag., Life Mag., AIA, Santa Barbara, Calif., 1962. Fellow AIA (nat., pres. Omaha chpt. 1968); mem. Nebr. Soc. Archs. (pres. 1975, awards 1964, 68, 87, 91, 93, 94, 95, 97, 01, Firm of Yr. 1997, Harry F. Cunningham Gold medal 2002). Home: 10010 Frederick St Omaha NE 68124-2651 Office Phone: 402-391-7176 ext. 15.

**POLSTON, EVA KORNBERG,** neuroscientist, educator; b. Washington, Mar. 19, 1963; d. Warren Stanley and Felice Sher Kornberg. BA, Oberlin Coll., Ohio, 1986; PhD, Boston U., 1997. Rsch. asst. Boston U., 1986—92; postdoctoral fellow Dartmouth Coll., Hanover, NH, 1997—99; postdoctoral assoc. Oreg. Nat. Primate Rsch. Ctr., Beaverton, 1999—2003; asst. investigator CIIT Ctrs. Health Rsch., Research Triangle Park, NC, 2004—06; rsch. asst. prof. Howard U., Washington, 2006—. Contbr. articles to profl. jours. Recipient Belamarich award, Boston U., 1997, Macchi award, 1995. Mem.: Women in Endocrinology, Soc. for Behavioral Neuroendocrinology, Endocrine Soc., Soc. for Neurosci. Office Phone: 919-558-1264.

**POLSTON, MARK FRANKLIN,** minister; b. Indpls., Feb. 9, 1960; s. Albert Franklin and Mildred (Wiggington) P.; m. Lisa Kaye Polston, July 21, 1984; children: Jordan Franklin, Jonathan Mark. AS, Somerset (Ky.) C. C., 1981; BS, Campbellsville Coll., 1984; JD, Ind. Sch. Law, 1995. Real estate agt. Homestead Real Estate, Somerset, 1978-89; pastor Trace Fork Separate Bapt. Ch., Liberty, Ky., 1979-81, Calvary Separate Bapt. Ch., Nancy, Ky., 1980-84, Harmony Separate Bapt. Ch., Jacksonville, Fla., 1984-85, Fairview Separate Bapt. Ch., Russell Springs, Ky., 1985-89, Calvary Separate Bapt. Ch., Nancy, Ky., 1989-91, Edinburgh (Ind.) Separate Bapt. Ch., 1991; sales rep. Sentry Ins., Somerset, 1989-91; dep. atty. gen. Ind. Atty. Gen., Indpls., 1992—. Clk. Gen. Assn. Separate Bapt. 1986-98; bd. dirs. Separate Bapt. Missions., Inc., 1988-92; adj. prof. Ind. Vocat. Tech. Coll., Indpls., 1993-95. Office: Ind Atty Gen 402 W Washington St Indianapolis IN 46204-2739 Address: Edinburgh Separate Bapt Ch 905 S Main St Edinburgh IN 46124-1311

**POLT, MICHAEL C.,** ambassador; b. Austria; married; 2 children. M in Pub. Adminstrn., U. Tenn. Various sr. level positions including dep. dir. for European security and arms control issues US Dept. State, Washington; dep. chief of mission U.S. Embassy, Bern, Switzerland, U.S. Embassy Bonn and U.S. Embassy Berlin, Germany, 1998—2001; prin. dep. asst. to sec. of state, bur. legis. affairs US Dept. State, Washington, 2002—04, U.S. ambassador to Serbia and Montenegro Belgrade, 2004—. Minister-counselor Sr. Fgn. Svc. U.S. Recipient Presdl. Meritorious Svc. award, Thomas Jefferson award for Svc. to U.S. Citizens Overseas, Am. Citizens Abroad. Office: Am Embassy Belgrade 5070 Belgrade Pl Washington DC 20521-5070

**POLTRACK, DAVID F.,** broadcast executive, marketing educator; b. June 3, 1945; BA in History magna cum laude, U. Notre Dame; MBA in Mktg., NYU. With media dept. Ted Bates Advt., until 1969; mgr. mktg. svcs., then dir. rsch. & sales promotion, dir. mktg. rsch., dir. mktg. svcs., dir. advt. CBS TV, NYC, 1969-79, v.p. mktg. svcs. network sales, 1979-82, v.p. rsch., 1982-87, v.p. mktg. CBS Mktg. Div., 1987-88, sr. v.p. planning & rsch., 1988—94, exec. v.p. rsch. and planning, 1994—2006; pres. CBS Vision, 2006—; exec. v.p., chief rsch. officer CBS Corp., 2006—. Adj. prof. mktg. Columbia U.; adj. prof. TV mgmt. Leonard Stern Sch. Bus., NYU. Author: Television Marketing: Network, Local and Cable, 1983; contbr. articles to profl. jours. Recipient Hugh Malcolm Beville Jr. award, Nat. Assn. Broadcasters & Broadcast Edn. Assn., 1994. Mem.: Mktg. Rsch. Coun. (past pres.), Internat. Radio and TV Found. (former bd. mem.), Advt. Rsch. Found. (past chmn.), Nat. Assn. TV Arts and Scis., Advt. Rsch. Coun. (v.p.), Mktg. Sci. Inst. (trustee, mem. exec. com.), Media Rating Coun. (past chair). Office: CBS Corp 530 W 57th St New York NY 10019 also: Coulmbia Bus Sch 3022 Broadway New York NY 10027 also: Leonard Stern Sch Bus Kaufman Mgmt Ctr 44 W 4th St, Ste 9-181A New York NY 10012 Office Phone: 212-854-7903, 212-854-7647, 212-998-0500, 212-995-4006. E-mail: dfp6@columbia.edu, dpoltrac@stern.nyu.edu.*

**POLUS GERSTNER, LILLIAN,** educational association administrator, director; b. Nashville, Tenn., Oct. 10, 1951; d. Moses and Rosalie Polus; m. Alan Ira Gerstner, Dec. 12, 1976; children: Michael Jacob Gerstner, Lisa Faye Gerstner. BS, Northwestern U., Evanston, Ill., 1973. Cert. tchr. secondary sch. State Bd. Edn., Ill., 1973. Adminstrv. asst. Blau Bishop & Assocs., Chgo., 1973—80; bookseller Waldenbooks, Skokie, Ill., 1986—91; site dir. Holocaust Meml. Found. Ill., Skokie, 1991—. Dir. holocaust expression theatre B'nai B'rith Youth Orgn., Great Midwest Region, Ill., 1998—2004; spkr. in field; presenter in field. Author: (plays) Pages of Testimony, 2003; editor (compiler) Books on the Holocaust for Young Readers, Bibliography & Videography for the Study of the Holocaust, (films) Films on the Holocaust for Young Viewers. Lerner fellow, Jewish Found. Righteous, 2001. Mem.: Northwestern Alumni Club Chgo. (v.p. 1989—91, pres. 1991—93, sec. 1987—89, treas. 1985—87), Assn. Holocaust Orgns. (dir. 1998—2000). Jewish. Avocations: travel, reading. Home: 10018 La Crosse Avenue Skokie IL 60077-1008 Office: Holocaust Memorial Foundation of IL 4255 Main Street Skokie IL 60076-2063 Office Phone: 847-677-4640. Personal E-mail: lilliangerstner@mac.com. Business E-Mail: lgerstner@hmfi.org.

**POLVANI, LORENZO M.,** physics professor; b. Mar. 1, 1961; PhD, MIT, Cambridge, Mass., 1988. Lectr. MIT, 1988—90; prof. Columbia U., NYC, 1990—. Office: Columbia Univ Dept Applied Physics & Applied Math New York NY 10027

**POLVERINI, PETER J.,** dean, dental educator; m. Carol Polverini. B in biology, Marquette U., 1969, DDS Dental-Oral Pathology, 1973; DMS, Harvard U. Cert. in oral and maxillofacial pathology Harvard U. Asst. prof. dept. diagnostic and surgical sciences U. Pittsburgh Sch. Dental Medicine, 1977—81; various positions Northwestern U. Med. and Dental Sch., 1981—92; prof. dentistry and chief oral and maxillofacial pathology U. Mich. Sch. Dentistry, 1992—95, chair dept. oral medicine, pathology, and surgery, 1995—96, chair dept. oral medicine, pathology, and oncology, 1996—2000, Donald A. Kerr Endowed Collegiate Prof., 1996—2000; dean U. Minn. Sch. Dentistry, 2000—03, U. Mich. Sch. Dentistry, 2003—. Mem. editl. bd. Lab. Investigation, Jour. Oral Pathology and Medicine; assoc. editor Angiogenesis. Address: U Mich Sch Dentistry 1011 N Univ Ave Ann Arbor MI 48109-1078*

**POLYAKOV, YURIY SERGEYEVICH,** engineer, researcher; b. Moscow, Sept. 3, 1980; s. Sergey Vladimirovich Polyakov and Lyubov Ivanovna Polyakova. BS in Computer Info. Systems summa cum laude, Excelsior Coll., Albany, NY, 2002; MS in Computer Sci., NJ Inst. Tech., Newark, 2003; PhD in Chem. Engring., Moscow State U. Environ. Engring., 2004. Rsch. asst. Moscow State U. Environ. Engring., 1997—98; field engr. Cross Country Land Svcs., Leavenworth, Wash., 1998—99, network adminstr., software engr., 1999—2001; network engr., software engr. Envision Technologies Inc., Wenatchee, 2001—02; rschr., engring. cons. US Poly Rsch., Ashland, Pa., 2002—. Contbr. articles to profl. jours., chapters to books. Recipient Young Scientist award, Moscow Mayor's Office, 2005. Mem.: AIChE, North Am. Membrane Soc., Am. Filtration Soc. Achievements include patents pending for Hollow Fiber Membrane Adsorber and Process for the Use Thereof; research in Novel filtration process and its theoretical study; Approximate method for nonlinear differential and integrodifferential equations. Office: USPolyResearch 906 Spruce St Ashland PA 17921 Office Phone: 570-875-3353. E-mail: ypolyakov@uspolyresearch.com

**POLYDORIDES, ALEXANDROS DEMETRIOS,** pathologist; s. Nicos Demetrios and Georgia Kontogiannopoulou Polydorides. AB, Princeton U., NJ, 1995; PhD, Rockefeller U., NYC, 2002; MD, Cornell U., NYC, 2003. Lic. MD Dept. of Pub. Health, State of Conn., 2006. Resident, anatomic pathology and chief resident NY Presbyn Hosp., Weill Cornell Med. Ctr., NYC, 2003—06, fellow oncologic pathology Meml. Sloan Kettering Cancer Ctr., N.Y.C., 2006—. Recipient Disting. Housestaff award, NY Weill Cornell Med. Ctr. Alumni Coun., 2006, Outstanding Lab. Work award, Princeton U., Dept. of Physics, 1993, Paul E. Strandjord Young Investigator award, Acad. of Clin. Lab. Physicians and Scientists, 2005, Herman L. Jacobius Prize in Pathology, Weill Med. Coll. of Cornell U., 2003, McGraw Hill award, 1996, George Khoury '65 Sr. Prize for Academic Excellence, Princeton U., Dept. of Molecular Biology, 1995; Dwight P. Green scholarship, Princeton U., 1991—93, Samuel Bayard Dod scholarship, 1993—95, grant, Hellenic Med. Soc. of NY, 2001. Mem.: Acad. of Clin. Lab. Physician and Scientists (assoc.), NY Path. Soc. (assoc.), Coll. of Am. Pathologists (assoc.), US and Can. Acad. of Pathology (assoc.), Phi Beta Kappa, Sigma Xi. Home: Apt 200 1233 York Ave New York NY 10021-6306 Office: Meml Sloan-Kettering Cancer Ctr Dept Pathology 1275 York Ave New York NY 10021 Office Phone: 212-746-2700.

**POLZONETTI, PIERPAOLO,** musicologist, music educator; b. Italy, June 27, 1969; s. Claudio and Fernanda Polzonetti; m. Lena Rose Magee, June 2, 2001. PhD, Cornell U., Ithaca, NY, 2003. Asst. prof. U. NC, Greensboro, 2003—06, U. Notre Dame, 2006—. Author: Tartini e la Musica Secondo Natura, 1999 (Internat. prize in musicology Petrassi Inst. Latina); contbr. articles to profl. jours. Recipient Alfred Einstein award, 2004, Am. Musicological Soc., 1999. Achievements include development of gastromusicology, semiotics of food in opera.

**POMBO, RICHARD WILLIAM,** congressman, rancher, farmer; b. Tracy, Calif., Jan. 8, 1961; m. Annette Cole, 1983; children: Richard Jr., Rena, Rachael. Student, Calif. State U., Pomona, 1981-83. Councilman City of Tracy, 1991-92; mayor pro-tem Tracy City Coun., 1992; mem. U.S. Congress from 11th Calif. dist., 1993—; mem. agri. com., subcom. on livestock and horticulture; mem. resources com., transp. and infrastructure com. Chmn. Pvt. Property Rights Task Force, 1993-94, Endangered Species Act Task Force, 1995-96; co-chmn. Spkr.'s Environ. Task Force, 1996. Author (with Joseph Farah) This Land Is Our Land: How to End the War on Private Property, 1996 Co-founder San Joaquin County Citizen's Land Alliance, Calif., 1986—; active San Joaquin County Econ. Devel. Assn., Tracy Bus. Improvement Dist., City Coun. (vice chmn. Cmty. Devel. Agy., Cmty. Parks

Com., and Waste Mgmt. Com.), San Joaquin County Rep. Ctrl. Com. Mem. Rotary Club. Republican. Roman Catholic. Office: US Ho Reps 2411 Rayburn Ho Office Bldg Washington DC 20515-0511 E-mail: rpombo@mail.house.gov.

**POMERANTZ, CHARLOTTE,** writer; b. Bklyn., July 24, 1930; d. Abraham L. and Phyllis (Cohen) P.; m. Carl Marzani, Nov. 12, 1966; children: Gabrielle Rose, Daniel Avram. BA, Sarah Lawrence Coll., 1953. Children's books include The Bear Who Couldn't Sleep, 1965, The Moon Pony, 1967, Ask the Windy Sea, 1968, Why You Look Like You Whereas I Look Like Me, 1968, The Day They Parachuted Cats on Borneo, 1971 (chosen for Internat. Year of the Child 1977-78), The Princess and the Admiral, 1974 (Jane Addams Children's Book award), The Piggy in the Puddle, 1974 (Featured on Reading Rainbow in Claymation, 1992, NYT Outstanding Picture Book of the Year award 1974), The Ballad of the Long Tailed Rat, 1975, Detective Poufy's First Case, 1976, The Mango Tooth, 1977 (Jr. Literary Guild Selection), The Downtown Fairy Godmother, 1978, The Tamarindo Puppy and Other Poems, 1980 (an ALA Notable Book), Noah's and Namah's Ark, 1980, If I Had a Paka, 1982 (Jane Addams Honor award 1983), Buffy and Albert, 1982, Posy, 1983 (1984 Christopher award), Whiff, Sniff, Nibble and Chew, 1984, Where's the Bear?, 1984, The Half-Birthday Party (Jr. Literary Guild Selection), 1984, All Asleep, 1984, One Duck, Another Duck, 1984, How Many Trucks Can a Tow Truck Tow? (Children's Book of the Year Libr. of Congress 1991) 1987, Timothy Tall Feather, 1987, The Chalk Doll (Top 10 Picture Books of 1989 Boston Globe, Parents Choice award, 1990) 1989, Flap Your Wings and Try, 1989, Serena Katz, 1992, The Outside Dog (One of 100 Books Recommended by the N.Y. Pub. Libr., 1993, ALA Notable) 1993, Halfway to Your House, 1993, Here Comes Henny (based on the wordplay of James Joyce), 1994, Mangaboom, 1997, You're Not My Best Friend Anymore, 1998 (Jr. Libr. Guild Selection 1998), The Birthday Letters, 2000, The Mousery, 2000 (Christopher award), Thunderboom!, 2005; co-author, lyricist play Eureka!, 1997; author radio play Whiff Sniff Nibble and Chew, 1997; contbr. stories to mags.; spl. editorial asst.: Einstein on Peace, 1960; editor: A Quarter Century of Un-Americana, 1963. Address: 260 W 21st St New York NY 10011-3447

**POMERANTZ, FREDERICK J.,** lawyer; b. Apr. 3, 1952; BA magna cum laude, CUNY, 1973; MA, Cornell U., 1975; JD, Bklyn. Law Sch., 1979. Bar: NY 1980, US Dist. Ct. Ea. Dist. NY, US Dist. Ct. So. Dist. NY, US Supreme Ct. Ptnr. fin. institutions practice group Wilson, Elser, Moskowitz, Edelman & Dicker LLP, NYC. Mem.: Fedn. Regulatory Counsel Inc., NY State Bar Assn. (torts, ins. & compensation law sect.; chmn. com. govtl. rels.), Assn. of the Bar of the City of NY, Phi Beta Kappa. Office: Wilson Elser Moskowitz Edelman & Dicker LLP 23rd Fl 150 E 42nd St New York NY 10017-5639 Office Phone: 212-490-3000 ext. 2109. Office Fax: 212-490-3038. Business E-Mail: pomerantzf@wemed.com.

**POMERANTZ, JAMES ROBERT,** psychology professor, academic administrator; b. N.Y.C., Aug. 21, 1946; s. Mihiel Charles and Elizabeth (Solheim) P.; divorced; children: Andrew Emil, William James; m. Mary B. McIntire, May 23, 1998. BA, U. Mich., 1968; PhD, Yale U., 1974. Prize teaching fellow Yale U., New Haven, 1973-74; asst. prof. psychology Johns Hopkins U., Balt., 1974-77; assoc. prof. SUNY, Buffalo, 1977-83, prof., 1983-88, chmn. dept. psychology, 1986-88, assoc. dean, 1983-86; dean social scis., Elma W. Schneider prof. psychology Rice U., Houston, 1988-95; provost, prof. cognitive and linguistic scis. Brown U., Providence, 1995-98, acting pres., 1997; adj. prof. psychology, dir. neuroscis. Rice U., Houston, 1998-99, prof. psychology, 2000—. Adj. prof. Baylor Coll. Medicine, 1992—. Editor: Perceptual Organization, 1981, The Perception of Structure, 1991. Fellow APA, Am. Psychol. Soc.; mem. Psychonomic Soc., Soc. Exptl. Psychologists. Office Phone: 713-348-3419. E-mail: pomeran@rice.edu.

**POMERANTZ, MARTIN,** chemistry educator, researcher; b. N.Y.C., May 3, 1939; s. Harry and Pauline (Sietz) P.; m. Maxine Miller, June 4, 1961; children: Lee Allan, Wendy Jane, Heidi Lauren. BS, CCNY, 1959; MS, Yale U., 1961, PhD, 1964. NSF postdoctoral fellow U. Wis.-Madison, 1963-64; asst. prof. Case Western Res. U., Cleve., 1964-69; assoc. prof. chemistry Yeshiva U., N.Y.C., 1969-74, prof., 1974-76, chmn. dept., 1971-72, 73-76; prof. chemistry U. Tex.-Arlington, 1976—; co-dir. Ctr. for Advanced Polymer Rsch., 1988-91; dir. Ctr. for Advanced Polymer Rsch., 1991—; vis. assoc. prof. U. Wis.-Madison, 1972; vis. prof. Columbia U., N.Y.C., 1970-75, Ben Gurion U. of the Negev, Beer Sheva, Israel, summers 1981, 85; program officer NSF, 2005—. Contbr. articles to sci. jours. Fellow Alfred P. Sloan Found., 1971-76, NSF and Sterling, 1962-63, Leeds and Northrup Found., 1960-62, Woodrow Wilson fellow, 1959-60; grantee NSF, Robert A. Welch Found., Def. Adv. Rsch. Projects Agy., Air Force Office Sci. Rsch., Dept. Energy, Petroleum Rsch. Fund, Tex. Advanced Tech. program, Tex. Advanced Rsch. program, Disting. Record of Rsch. award U. Tex., Arlington, 1997, also others. Mem. Am. Chem. Soc. (Wilfred T. Doherty award Dallas-Fort Worth sect. 1997), Phi Beta Kappa, Sigma Xi. Achievements include research in synthesis, reactions and properties of organo lambda-5-phosphazenes, reactions of carbenes with other molecules, with themselves and with diazo precursors; design, synthesis and study of electronically conducting polymers with enhanced properties, synthesis and study of electroluminescent (light emitting) polymers, preparation and study of polymeric ionic self-assembled monolayers (ISAMs), non-linear optical materials. Home: 5521 Williamstown Rd Dallas TX 75230-2127 Office: U Tex Dept Chemistry-Biochemistry PO Box 19065 Arlington TX 76019-0065 Office Phone: 817-272-3811. Business E-Mail: pomerantz@uta.edu.

**POMERANTZ, MARTIN ARTHUR,** astronomer, educator, physicist; b. Bklyn. Dec. 17, 1916; AB, Syracuse U., 1937; MS, U. Pa., 1939; PhD, Temple U., 1951; Fil. Dr. (hon.), U. Uppsala, Sweden, 1967; ScD (hon.), Swarthmore Coll., 1973; DSc (hon.), U. Del., 2001. Rsch. assoc. Bartol Rsch. Found., 1938—41, rsch. fellow, 1941—43, physicist, 1943—59, dir., 1959—85, pres., 1985—87; v.p. The Franklin Inst., 1967—85, exec. v.p., 1985—87, Bartol prof., 1968—89; prof. emeritus U. Del., 1990—, pres. emeritus, 1987—. Fulbright scholar, vis. prof. Muslim U., Aligarh, India, 1952—53; leader Nat. Geog. Soc. expeditions, 1948—59; chmn. U.S. Com. for Internat. Yrs. of the Quiet Sun Nat. Acad. Scis., 1962—66, mem. Com. on Polar Rsch., 1959—71, mem. Space Sci. Bd., 1963—70, mem. Geophysics Rsch. Bd., 1959—73; v.p. Com for Internat. Yrs. of the Quiet Sun Internat. Coun. Sci. Unions, v.p. Com. Internat. Geophysique, 1962—66; mem. Com. on Solar-Terrestrial Rsch. Nat. Acad. Scis., 1981—86; vis. prof. astronomy Swarthmore Coll., 1961, 64, 67; vis. prof. U. Tokyo, 1983, Potchefstroom U., South Africa, 1987; Sigma Xi nat. lectr., 68; OAS vis. prof., 73. Editor: Jour. of the Franklin Inst.; mem. editl. bd.: Space Sci. Revs.; Antarctic Rsch. Series. Recipient Centennial Gold medal, Syracuse U., 1970, Prix de la Belgica, Acad. Royal des Scis., des Lettres et des Beaux Arts de Belgique, 1985, Disting. Pub. Svc. award, NSF, 1987, medal for disting. sci. achievement, NASA, 1990. Fellow: AAAS, Am. Geophys. Union, Am. Phys. Soc.; mem.: Am. Polar Soc. (hon.), Rotary Internat., Cosmos Club, Explorers Club, Sigma Pi Sigma (hon.). Home: 100 Deer Valley Rd Apt GE San Rafael CA 94903 Personal E-mail: mapomeratz@sbcglobal.net.

**POMERANTZ, MARVIN,** thoracic surgeon; b. Suffern, NY, June 16, 1934; s. Julius and Sophie (Luksin) Pomerantz; m. Margaret Twigg, Feb. 26, 1966; children: Ben, Julie. AB, Colgate U., 1955; MD, U. Rochester, 1959. Diplomate Nat. Bd. Med. Examiners, Am. Bd. Surgery, Am. Bd. Thoracic Surgery (bd. dirs. 1989-95). Intern Duke U. Med. Ctr., Durham, NC, 1959—60, resident, 1960—61, instr. surgery, 1966—67; asst. prof. surgery U. Colo. Med. Sch., Denver, 1967—71, assoc. prof. surgery, 1971—74, assoc. clin. prof. surgery, 1974—93, prof. surgery, chief gen. thoracic surgery, 1992—; chief thoracic and cardiovascular surgery Denver Gen. Hosp., 1967—73, asst. dir. surgery, 1967—70, assoc.dir. surgery, 1970—73; pvt. practice Arapahoe CV Assocs., Denver, 1974—92; prof., chief gen. thoracic surgery sect. U. Colo. Health Sci. Ctr., 1992—; resident Duke U. Med. Ctr., Durham, NC, 1963—67. Clin. assoc. surgery br. NCI, 1961—63; mem. staff Univ. Hosp., Denver, Denver Gen. Hosp., Rose Med. Ctr., Denver, Denver VA Med. Ctr., Children's Hosp., Denver, U. Coll. Health Sci. Ctr., 1992—, bd.

dirs., 1990—96; vice chmn. Am. Bd. Thoracic Surgery, 1995—97, chmn., 1997—99. Guest editor Chest Surgery Clinics N.Am., 1993; contbr. numerous articles to profl. publs., chapters to books. Master: AMA; fellow: ACS, Am. Coll. Chest Surgeons; mem.: Soc. Vascular Surgeons, Soc. Thoracic Surgeons (nomenclature/coding com. 1991—95, standards and ethics com., govt. rels. com., chmn. program com. 1994—95), Rocky Mtgn. Traumatologic Soc., rgery Soc., Internat. Cardiovascular Soc., Denver Acad. Surgery (pres. 1980), Colo. Med. Soc., Am. Heart Assn. (bd. dirs. Colo. chpt. 1993), Am. Assn. Thoracic Surgeons (program com. 1991), Western Thoracic Surg. Assn. (v.p. 1992, pres. 1993—94, counselor-at-large 1988—90). Office: UCHSC Divsn CTS 4200 E 9th Ave # C310 Denver CO 80262-0001

**POMERANTZ, MARVIN ALVIN,** manufacturing executive; b. Des Moines, Aug. 6, 1930; s. Alex and Minnie (Landy) P.; m. Rose Lee Lipsey, Nov. 12, 1950; children: Sandy Pomerantz, Marcie Morrison, Vickie Ginsberg, Lori Long. BS in Commerce, U. Iowa, 1952. Exec. v.p. Midwest Bag Co., Des Moines, 1951-75; v.p. Continental Can Co. Inc., Greenwich, Conn., 1971-75; v.p., gen. mgr. Forest Products Brown Systems Operation (div. Continental Can Co. Inc.), Greenwich, Conn., 1975-77; pres. Diversified Group Internat. Harvester, Chgo., 1980-81, ex. v.p., 1981-82; pres., chmn., chief exec. officer The Mid-Am. Group, Des Moines, 1981—; chmn., chief exec. officer Gaylord Container Corp., Deerfield, Ill., 1986—2002. Mem. Greater Des Moines Commn.; trustee Drake U., 1978—; pres. Iowa State Bd. Regents, 1987-93, 95-96; mem. U.S. Olympic Budget and Audit Commn., Colorado Springs., Colo., 1989-92. Republican. Office: The Mid-Am Group 4700 Westown Pkwy Ste 303 West Des Moines IA 50266-6718 Office Phone: 515-224-3610.

**POMERANTZ, WENDY JANE,** pediatrician, educator; d. Martin and Maxine Pomerantz. BA in Biochemistry summa cum laude, U. Tex., Austin, 1988; MD, U. Tex. SW Med. Sch., Dallas, 1992; MS in Epidemiology, U. Cin., 1998. Bd. cert. pediat. Am. Bd. Pediat., 1995, bd. cert. pediat. emergency medicine Am. Bd. Pediat., 1998. Internship pediats. Children's Hosp. Dallas, 1992—95, residency pediats., 1992—95, fellowship 1995—98; assoc. prof. clin. pediat. Cin. Children's Hosp., U. Cin., 1998—; affiliated faculty Ctr. Epidemiology and Biostatistics Cin. Children's Hosp., 2002—. Development EMS Telemetry Protocols Children's Med. Ctr., Dallas; co-coordinator Injury Prevention & Advocacy Course Curriculum, 2002—; designer Children for Injury Free Coalition for Kids Website, 2003, content provider, 03; with Rebound Basketball Ednl. Program, 2004—. Co-dir. Injury Free Coalition for Kids in Cin., 2000—06; mem. Cin. Youth Collaborative Mentoring Program, 1997—98, Am. Red Cross Med. Assistance Team, 2000—; chariperson Ohio Emergency Med. Svcs. for Children Com., 2006; mem. Cin. Safe Kids Coalition, 1999—, chair, pub. policy com., 1999—2002; mem. Mt. Lookout Civic Club, 1999—2003; coach St. Mary's Girls Basketball, 2000—03; playground devel. Cin. Recreation Commn., 2001—06; advisor Avondale Cincy After Sch. Program, 2004—; co-dir. Safety Resources Ctr., 2004—. Recipient Nat. Merit Scholarship, 1984, Presdl. Endowed Scholarship, 1984, Panhellenic Merit Scholarship, 1986, SW Med. Found. Scholarship, 1988, Pediat. House Officers Rsch. award, 1995, Divisional Tchg. award, Cin. Children's Hosp., 1998—99, Physician's Recognition award, AMA, 1999—2000, Divisional Tchg. award, Cin. Children's Hosp., 2000—01, 2003—04, Presdl. Partnership award, Cin. Recreation Commn., 2006; Grad. scholar, U. Cin., 1996—98. Fellow: Am. Acad. Pediat. (sect. injury and poision prevention, newsletter editor 2002—06); mem.: AMA, APHA, Soc. Academic Emergency Medicine, Emergency Med. Com., Ohio Chapter, Am. Acad. Pediat. (chair, pediat. emergency medicine com. 2006—), Tex. Med. Assn., Ambulatory Pediatric Assn., Cin. Safe Kids Coalition (pub. policy chair 1999—2002), Am. Red Cross Med. Assistance Team. Avocations: travel, golf, needlepoint. Office: Cincinnati Childrens Hospital Divsn Emergency Medicine 3333 Burnet Avenue MLC 2008 Cincinnati OH 45229 Office Phone: 513-636-7966.

**POMERANZ, FELIX,** accounting educator; b. Vienna, Mar. 28, 1926; s. Joseph and Irene (Meninger) P.; m. Rita Lewin, June 14, 1953; children: Jeffrey Arthur, Andrew Joseph. BBA, CCNY, 1948; MS, Columbia U., 1949; PhD, U. Birmingham, Eng., 1992. Diplomate Am. Bd. Forensic Acctg.; CPA, NY, Va., La., NC; cert. computer profl., fraud examiner, govt. fin. mgr. Audit staff Coopers & Lybrand, CPAs, NYC, 1949-56; mgr. Marks, Grey & Shron (now Ernst & Young, CPA's), NYC, 1956-58; asst. chief auditor Am.-Standard, NYC, 1958-62; mgr. systems Westvaco Corp., NYC, 1962-66; dir. operational auditing Coopers & Lybrand, CPAs, NYC, 1966-68, ptnr., 1968-85; disting. lectr./dir. Ctr. for Acctg., Auditing, Tax Studies Fla. Internat. U., Miami, 1985-93, prof. acctg., 1993—2002, assoc. dir. sch. acctg., 1993—99, affil. faculty dept. religious studies, 1996—2002, prof. emeritus, 2003—. Author: Managing Capital Budget Projects, 1984; The Successful Audit: New Ways to Reduce Risk Exposure and Increase Efficiency, 1992; co-author: Pensions-An Accounting and Management Guide, 1976; Auditing in the Public Sector: Efficiency, Economy, and Program Results, 1976; Comparative International Auditing Standards, 1985; contbr. articles to profl. jours. Emeritus trustee Nat. Ctr. for Automated Info. Rsch.; founding mem. Ctr. for Study of Islam and Democracy; founder Afghan Inst. Accts.; mem. rev. panel Inst. Chartered Fin. Analysts of India Jour. Audit Practice. 1st lt. AUS, 1944-46, 51-52. Recipient Spear Safer Harmon faculty fellow Coll. Bus. Administrn., 1987, Outstanding Svc. award, 1998, Matriculation Merit award, 2000. Mem. AICPA, NY State Soc. CPA, Assn. Sys. Mgmt., Acad. Acctg. Historians, Assn. Govt. Accts., NY Acad. Scis., Am. Acctg. Assn., Inter-Am. Acctg. Assn., Assn. Cert. Fraud Examiners, Beta Gamma Sigma, Beta Alpha Psi (Most Disting. and Most Outstanding Profl. awards 1993, Most Supportive Profl. award 2002), Alpha Kappa Psi (life, Dr. Felix Pomeranz Faculty of Yr. award, Jenkins Esteem & Endless Work award, Loyal Mem. award 2006). Home: 250 Jacaranda Dr Apt 406 Fort Lauderdale FL 33324-2532 Office: Fla Internat U Sch Acctg University Park Miami FL 33199-0001 Office Phone: 305-348-3483. Personal E-mail: pomeranzf@bellsouth.net. Business E-mail: pomeranf@fiu.edu.

**POMERANZ, KENNETH L.,** history professor; PhD, Yale U., 1988. UCI Chancellor's prof. history U. Calif., Irvine. Author: The Making of a Hinterland: State, Society and Economy in Inland North China, 1853-1937, 1993; author: (with Steven Topik) The World that Trade Created: Society, Culture and the World Economy, 1400 to the Present, 1999; author: The Great Divergence: China, Europe and the Making of teh World Economy, 2000. Fellow: Am. Acad. Arts and Sciences. Office: Dept History Univ California Irvine 200H Murray Krieger Hall Irvine CA 92697-3275 Office Phone: 949-824-5169. Office Fax: 949-824-2865. E-mail: klpomera@uci.edu.*

**POMERANZ, MICHAEL,** newscaster; BS in Broadcast Journalism, Ariz. State U. Minor league baseball pitcher Minn. Twins, Chgo. Cubs, Balt. Orioles, Pitts. Pirates, Pitts.; reporter, fill-in anchor Sta. KRDO-TV, Colorado Springs, Colo.; anchor, reporter Sta. WATE-TV, Knoxville; anchor Sta. WFLD-TV, Chgo., Sta. WCBS-TV, N.Y.C., 2000—. Recipient Emmy nomination.

**POMERENE, JAMES HERBERT,** retired computer engineer; b. Yonkers, NY, June 22, 1920; s. Joel Pomerene and Elsie Bower; m. Edythe R. Schwenn, Dec. 1, 1944; children: James Bennett, Katherine Ellen, Andrew Thomas Stewart. BSEE, Northwestern U., 1942; postgrad., Princeton U., 1950. Elec. engr. Hazeltine Corp., Little Neck, NY, 1942-46; mem. staff electronic computer project Inst. for Advanced Study, Princeton, NJ, 1946-51, chief engr., 1951-56; sr. engr. IBM Corp., Poughkeepsie, NY, 1956-67, sr. staff mem. Armonk, NY, 1967-76. Cons. in field. Patentee in field. IBM fellow T.J. Watson Rsch. Ctr., 1976—. Fellow IEEE (Computer Pioneer award Computer Soc. 1986, Edison medal 1993, Eckert-Mauchly award 2005); mem. NAE, Sigma Xi, Tau Beta Pi. Episcopalian. Home: 403 Bedford Rd N Chappaqua NY 10514-2207 Personal E-mail: jhpomerene@aol.com.

**POMEROY, EARL RALPH,** congressman, retired commissioner; b. Valley City, ND, Sept. 2, 1952; s. Ralph and Myrtle Pomeroy; m. Laurie Kirby, Dec. 26, 1986; 2 children. Student, Valley City State U.; BA in Polit. Sci., U. ND,

1974, JD, 1979. Bar: ND 1979. Atty. Sproul, Lenaburg, Fitzner and Walker, Valley City, 1979-84; mem. ND State Ho. Reps., 1980—84; ins. commr. State of ND, Valley City, 1984-92; mem. US Congress from ND (at large), 1993—, mem. ways and means com., mem. agr. com., co-chair Ho. Dem. Social Security Task Force, co-chair Rural Health Care Coalition. Recipient Found. award Rotary, 1975, Rural Health Champions Legis. award Nat. Rural Health Assn. 2004; named Outstanding Young North Dakotan ND Jaycees, 1982. Mem. Nat. Assn. of Ins. Commrs. (chmn. midwest zone 1987-88, exec. com. 1987-88), Phi Beta Kappa. Democrat. Presbyterian. Office: US Ho Reps 1501 Longworth Ho Office Bldg Washington DC 20515 Office Phone: 202-225-2611.*

**POMEROY, LEE HARRIS,** architect; b. NYC, Nov. 19, 1932; s. Alfred and Florence Pomeroy; children: Jordana, Jeremy, Alexandra. BArch, Rensselaer Poly. Inst., 1955; MArch, Yale U., 1961. Registered arch., NY, Conn., Mass., Vt., NJ, Fla., Pa., Maine, Nat. Coun. of Registrators Bd. Arch. William Tabler, NYC, 1958-59, The Archs. Collaborative, Cambridge, Mass., 1959-60; pres. Lee Harris Pomeroy Archs., NYC, 1965-87. Prof. Sch. Architecture, CUNY, 1962-87; prin. solar rsch. group ECOSOL, Conn., Eng., Spain, 1965-84; dir. Project for Pub. Spaces, Inc., NYC, 1982-88; dean's adv. coun. Sch. Architecture, Resselaer Poly. Inst., 1991—, adv. to pres., 1994-98. Prin. works include Swiss Bank Tower and Saks Fifth Ave. ext., NYC (Arthur Ross award 1991), Teda Conv. Ctr., Tanjuin, China, Biuhoi Convention Ctr. Hotel, Teda, China; restoration of Plaza Hotel, NY, Sch. Art and Dance City Coll., NYC, 1989, New Rochelle Pub. Libr., 1980 (AIA-ALA design award 1980, NY State AIA and Urban Design awards 1980), Dutchess County Jail, Poughkeepsie, NY (AIA-ACA design award 1981), HBO Satellite Comm. Ctr., 1983 (NY State AIA design award 1984), Manitou Sta. planned cmty., 1973 (AIA and Progressive Architecture awards 1973), Henry St. studios artists housing (Progressive Architecture mag. design award 1963, AIA design award 1975), Bedford Mews housing (AIA, Owens Corning energy conservation and Record Homes design awards 1980), Fulton Mall, Bklyn., 1985 (City Club NYC Bard award for design 1985), Trinity Ch. Bridge (AIA design award 1991), Hotel Usixtu, Prague, Czech Republic, Lally Sch. of Mgmt. and Tech., Rensselaer Poly. Inst., Troy, NY, Reconstrn. of Union Square Subway, 2001, MOMA, Bleeker St.and Dekalb Ave. Stas., Fulton St. Transit Ctr., Lower Manhattan, NYC, Cosco Housing and Comml. Ctr., Shanghai, Jin Ling Hotel on Hynan Island, Parish House and St. James Ch., NYC, NY Mem. Cmty. Bd. 5, Midtown Manhattan, NYC, 1980-91; bd. dirs. Bellview Assn. with Bellview Med. Ctr., NYC, 1992—; trustee, v.p. Putnam County Hist. Soc. and Foundry Mus. 1st lt. USA Signal Corp., 1955-57. Recipient Mcpl. Arts Soc. award, NYC, 1982; Nat. Endowment for Arts grantee, NYC, 1983. Fellow AIA (bd. dirs. 1979-81), Inst. of Urban Design; mem. Royal Inst. of British Archs., Mcpl. Arts Soc., Regional Plan Assn., Yale Club, Century Club, City Club NY (co-chmn. Bard award program for excellence in urban design 1988-90, 94). Avocations: tennis, photography, travel. Home: 285 Central Park W New York NY 10024-3006 Office: 462 Broadway Fl 3 New York NY 10013-2696 Office Phone: 212-334-2600. Business E-Mail: leepom@lhparch.com.

**POMEROY, ROBERT CORTTIS,** lawyer; b. Syracuse, N.Y., Sept. 17, 1943; s. Stuart E. and Elizabeth (Corttis) Pomeroy; m. Sandra Campbell; children: Lisa, Robert Jr., Heather. AB, Hamilton Coll., 1965; LLB, Harvard U., 1968. Bar: Mass. 1968, Fla. 1981. Assoc. Goodwin Procter LLP (formerly Goodwin, Procter & Hoar LLP), Boston, 1968-76, ptnr., 1977—2005, of counsel, 2005—. Mem.: Am. Coll. Trust and Estate Counsel. Avocations: skiing, golf, sailing. Home: 3 Pier 7 Charlestown MA 02129-4225 Office: Goodwin Procter LLP Exchange Pl Boston MA 02109-2881 Office Phone: 617-570-1150. Business E-Mail: rpomeroy@goodwinprocter.com.

**POMFRET, DAVID B.,** medical educator, internist; b. Somerset, Mass., Nov. 22, 1937; s. David B. Pomfret and Rhea Chouinard; m. Anna Rafferty, Mar. 31, 1964; children: Mark, Bruce, Scott, Heidi. BS, Stonehill Coll., 1959; MD, Univ. Coll., Dublin, Ireland, 1964. Diplomate Am. Bd. Internal Medicine. Chief medicine Leonard Morse Hosp., Natick, Mass., 1968—71, chief staff, 1976—80; clin. prof. Tufts U., Boston, 1976—; prof. medicine Tumaini U., Moshi, Tanzania, 1996—2000. Author: Computer Science, 1998, Dispatches From Kilimanjaro, 2001. Fellow: ACP. Avocations: skiing, sailing, offshore racing. Home: 20 Grey Gull Rd Jamestown RI 02835-2808 Office: Kilimanjaro Christian Med Ctr Box 3010 Moshi Tanzania Office Phone: 603-374-2705. Personal E-mail: pomfret1@juno.com. Business E-Mail: pomfret1@cox.net.

**POMMIER, YVES GEORGES,** medical researcher; b. Caen, Calvados, France, Apr. 1, 1951; came to U.S., 1988; s. Roger Pommier and Marie-Therese Blais; m. Françoise Champey, Jan. 4, 1988; children: Gabriel, Elie. MS in Pharmacology, U. Paris, 1978, MD cum laude, 1981, PhD, 1986. Cert. radiation safety authorized user NIH. Resident Paris Hosps., 1978-81; pharmacology asst. U. Paris., 1979-81; vis. fellow NIH, Nat. Cancer Inst., Bethesda, Md., 1981-84, vis. scientist, 1984-95, prin. investigator, 1995—, chief lab. molecular pharmacology, 1997—. Organizer internat. conf. HIV-1 Integrase Inhibitors, 1996; lectr. in field. Mem. editl. bd. Cancer Rsch., Molecular Pharmacology, Anticancer Drug Design, others; contbr. articles to med. jours.; patentee in field. Recipient Impact Medicine Med. Dr. for Yr. 2000, 1992, Fed. Tech. Transfer award, 1994; competitive tng. grantee French Found. for Biol. Rsch., 1981, NIH intramural grantee AIDS Targeted Antiviral Program of Office of Dir., 1993-94, 95-96, 97-98. Mem. French Soc. Pharmacology, Am. Fedn. for Clin. Rsch., Am. Assn. for Cancer Rsch. (program com. 1996-99, chmn. CaiN award 1998), N.Y. Acad. Scis., NIH Apoptosis Interest Group. Democrat. Avocations: painting, tennis, coaching soccer team. Office: Ctr Cancer Rsch Lab Molecular Pharmacology Bldg 37 Rm 5068 37 Convent Dr Bethesda MD 20892-4255 Office Phone: 301-496-5944. Office Fax: 301-402-0752. E-mail: pommier@nih.gov.*

**POMORSKI, STANISLAW,** lawyer, educator; b. Lwow, Poland, Nov. 23, 1934; arrived in U.S., 1972, naturalized, 1983; s. Juliusz and Maria (Ziemba) Pomorski; m. Patricia Smith; children: Lukasz, Christopher, Maria. M.Law, U. Warsaw, 1956, D.Law, 1968. Law clk., 1958-61; pvt. practice law Warsaw, 1961-64; vis. scholar Harvard U. Law Sch., Cambridge, Mass., 1964-66; rsch. assoc. Polish Acad. Scis., 1966-72; mem. faculty Rutgers U. Law Sch., Camden, NJ, 1973—, prof. law, 1977-81, disting. prof. law, 1981—2006, disting. prof. law emeritus, 2006—. Fellow Soviet law U. Leyden, Netherlands, 1980—81; trustee Nat. Coun. Soviet and East European Rsch., Washington, 1988—94. Author: (book) American Common Law and the Principle Nullum Crimen Sine Lege, 2d edit., 1975, Restructuring the System of Ownership in the USSR, 1991, On Multiculturalism, Concepts of Crime and the De Minimis Defense, 1997, Justice in Siberia, 2001. Fellow, Ford Found., 1972—73. Office: Rutgers U Law Sch 5th And Penn St Camden NJ 08102 Office Phone: 856-225-6395. Business E-Mail: pomorski@camden.rutgers.edu.

**POMP, ALFONS,** surgeon; b. Can., Nov. 2, 1954; m. Rachel Chartrand; children: Audrey Chartrand, Genevieve Chartrand. BSc, McGill U., Montreal, 1971—76; MD, Sherbrooke U., 1980. Cert. Am. Bd. Surgery, 1987. Fellow surg. nutrition and metabolism R.I. Hosp./Brown U., 1986—88; assoc. prof. surgery U. Montreal/Hotel Dieu Hosp. Montreal, 1988—99; assoc. prof., surgery Mount Sinai Med. Sch., N.Y.C., 1999—2003; assoc. prof. Cornell Med. Coll., N.Y.C., 2003—. Contbr. articles to profl. jours. Fellow: ACS. Office: Weill Med Coll Cornell 525 E 68th St Box 294 New York NY 10021 Office Phone: 212-746-5294. E-mail: alp2104@med.cornell.edu.

**POMPADUR, I. MARTIN,** communications executive; b. Bklyn, June 25, 1935; s. Jack and Florence (Raitbord) P.; m. Joan Lynn Krassner, Dec. 18, 1960 (div. 1986); children: F. Douglas (dec.), Jana Sue; m. Marian Hackett, Dec. 23, 1987 (div. 2003); children: Chelsea Rae. BA, Williams Coll., 1955; LLB, U. Mich., 1958. Bar: Conn. 1958, NY 1961. Atty. ABC-TV Network, NYC, 1960-61, 61-66, chief adminstrv. officer, 1966-68, gen. mgr., 1968-70, v.p. broadcast div., 1970-72, corp. v.p., 1972; pres. ABC Leisure Group I, 1973-75, asst. to pres. parent co., 1975-76; also dir. parent co.; v.p., chmn., chief exec. officer GP Sta. Ptnr., Corp., 1977-78, pres., 1978-82; chmn., chief exec. officer GP Sta. Ptnr.,

1982-96; mng. gen. ptnr. TV Sta. Ptnr., 1982-96; chmn., CEO PBTV, Inc., 1984-96; mng. gen. ptnr. Northeastern TV Investors Ltd. Partnership, 1984-96; prin. owner, sec. Caribbean Internat. News Corp., 1985—; also bd. dir.; CEO, COO RP Media Mgmt., Inc., 1986; CEO ML Media Ptnr., L.P., 1986—; CEO, COO RP Opportunity Mgmt., 1988—2002; CEO ML Media Opportunity Ptnr., L.P., 1988—2002; exec. v.p. News Corp.; pres. News Corp. Ea. Ctrl. Europe; chmn. News Corp. Europe, 2000—. Prin. shareholder Hispanic Media Inc., 1986-90; prin. shareholder, vice-chmn. Hunter Pub. L.P., 1986-94; co-trustee Lidan Trust, 1983—; atty. Young & Rubicam, Inc., advt. agy., NYC, summer 1961. Mem. Stamford bd. reps., chmn. legis. and rules com., 1959-60. Office: News Corp 4th Fl 1211 Ave of the Americas New York NY 10036 also: News Corp Europe 1 Virginia St 6th Fl London England

**POMPAN, JACK MAURICE,** management consultant; b. NYC, Jan. 23, 1926; s. Maurice A. and Helen (Schmidt) P. m. Esther Terri Scharaga, July 4, 1958; children: Neil Charles, Lori Beth. BS in Indsl. Mgmt., Ga. Inst. Tech., 1948; MBA with distinction, NYU, 1973, advanced profl. cert., 1978. Trainee to budget mgr. Redmond Co., Owosso, Mich., 1948—55; mgmt. cons. Coopers and Lybrand, N.Y.C., 1955—60; contr. Hazel Bishop Inc., N.Y.C., 1960—61; treas. Floyds Stores Inc., Valley Stream, NY, 1961—66; pres. Farmers Pantry Inc., Mamaroneck, NY, 1966—68; v.p. pub. divsn. Heinst, Inc., N.Y.C., 1968—74; prin. Baxter, Pompan & Storr, Mgmt. Cons., and predecessors, Greenwich and N.Y.C., 1974—83, Jack M. Pompan, Mgmt. Cons., Rockville Centre, NY, 1983—92, Pompan & Co., Rockville Centre, 1992—; v.p. Eisner Computer Solutions, LLC, N.Y.C., 1997—98. Adj. prof. Hofstra U., 1977, Roth Grad. Sch. Bus. Adminstrn., C.W. Post Ctr., L.I. U., 1974-79, NYU, 1982-89. Bus. and econs. editor Info. Please Almanac, 1978-82. Trustee edn. chmn., v.p. Ctrl. Synagogue, Rockville Centre, NY, 1983-86, pres. 1986-88; mem. Greater NY Coun., Union for Reform Judaism, 2004—. Lt. USNR, 1943-46, 51-53. Mem. Exec. Forum at NYU (bd. dirs.), Inst. Mgmt. Accts. (cert. merit 1953), Am. Jewish Com., Princeton Club N.Y. Office: 70-01 Maine Ave Rockville Centre NY 11570-3641 Office Phone: 516-678-5206. E-mail: jpompan@optonline.net.

**POMPEO, ELLEN,** actress; b. Everett, Mass., Nov. 10, 1969; Actor: (films) 8 1/2 x 11, 1999, Coming Soon, 1999, Eventual Wife, 2000, In the Weeds, 2000, Moonlight Mile, 2002, Catch Me If You Can, 2002, Daredevil, 2003, Old School, 2003, Undermind, 2003, Nobody's Perfect, 2004, Art Heist, 2004; (TV series) Grey's Anatomy, 2005—, (TV appearances) Strangers with Candy, 1999, Law and Order, 1996, 2000, Get Real, 2000, Strong Medicine, 2001, The Job, 2001. Office: Creative Artists Agy 9830 Wilshire Blvd Beverly Hills CA 90212-1825*

**POMPER, PHILIP,** historian, educator; b. Chgo., Apr. 18, 1936; s. Solomon and Rebecca (Fenigstein) P.; m. Alice N. Epstein, Aug. 27, 1961 (div.); children: Erica, Stephen, Karen; m. Emily Meyer, June 26, 1994 (dec. July 2003). BA, U. Chgo., 1959, MA, 1961, PhD, 1965. Instr. history Wesleyan U., Middletown, Conn., 1964-65, asst. prof., 1965-71, assoc. prof., 1971-76, prof., 1976—, chmn. dept. history, 1981-84; William F. Armstrong prof. history, 1992—. Author: The Russian Revolutionary Intelligentsia, 1970, 2nd edit., 1993, Peter Lavrov and the Russian Revolutionary Movement, 1972, Sergei Nechaev, 1979 (Choice award 1979), The Structure of Mind in History: Five Major Figures in Psychohistory, 1985, Trotsky's Notebooks, 1933-35: Writings on Lenin, Dialectics and Evolutionism, 1986, Lenin, Trotsky, and Stalin: The Intelligentsia and Power, 1990; assoc. editor History and Theory, 1991—; editor: World History: Ideologies, Structures, and Identities, 1998; co-editor: History and Theory, Contemporary Readings, 1998; co-editor: The Return of Science: Evolution, History and Theory, 2002; contbr. articles on Russian history and theory of history to profl. jours. Fellow, Ford Found., 1963—64, Social Scis. Rsch. Coun., 1968, Hoover Instn., 1987, Wilson Ctr., 1988; Russian Rsch. Ctr. scholar, 1987—. Mem.: Am. Assn. for Advancement of Slavic Studies, Conn. Acad. Arts and Scis. Home: 13 Red Orange Rd Middletown CT 06457-4916 Office: History Dept Wesleyan U Middletown CT 06459-0001 Business E-Mail: ppomper@wesleyan.edu.

**POMPEY-PLUMMER, DANIELLE NICOLE,** counselor; b. Queens, N.Y., Jan. 20, 1975; d. Willie J. and Virginia E. Pompey; m. Joel I. Plummer, Oct. 11, 2003. MA in Counseling, Kean U., 2001. Lic. marriage and family therapist N.J., 2004. Ops. mgr. New Cmty. Corp., Newark, 1997—2001; clinician Trintias Hosp., Elizabeth, NJ, 2001—. Mem.: APA, Am. Counseling Assn., N.J. Psychol. Assn. Office: Trinitas Hopital 655 East Jersey Street Elizabeth NJ 07201 Office Phone: 908-994-7901.

**POND, BYRON O., JR.,** manufacturing executive; b. 1936; BSBA, Wayne State U., 1961. With Fed. Mogul Corp., Detroit, 1958-68, Maremont Corp., Chgo., 1968—86, dir. sales exhaust systems div., 1970-74, corp. v.p., 1974-76, sr. v.p. nat. accounts, 1976-78, exec. v.p., 1978-79, pres., CEO, 1979—86; exec. v.p. Arvin Industries, Columbus, Ind., 1991—93, pres., CEO, 1993—96, chmn., 1996—99; pres. Amcast Industrial Corp., 2001—02, chmn., 2002—05, pres., CEO, 2004—05; interim CEO Cooper Tire & Rubber Co., Findlay, Ohio, 2006—. Bd. dirs. Cooper Tire & Rubber Co., 1998—. Recipient Disting. Alumni award, Wayne St. U. Office: Cooper Tire & Rubber Co 701 Lima Ave Findlay OH 45840*

**POND, PATRICIA BROWN,** library and information scientist, educator; b. Mankato, Minn., Jan. 17, 1930; d. Patrick H. and Florence M. (Ruehle) Brown; m. Judson S. Pond, Aug. 24, 1959. BA, Coll. St. Catherine, St. Paul, 1952; MA, U. Minn., 1955; PhD, U. Chgo., 1982. Sch. libr., Minn., N.Y., 1952-62; asst. prof. libr. sci. U. Minn., 1962-63; reference libr. U. Mont., 1963-65; asst. prof. U. Oreg., 1967-72, assoc. prof., 1972-77; prof., dept. chair, assoc. dean Sch. Libr. and Info. Sci. U. Pitts., 1977-85. Mem. ALA (life), Phi Beta Kappa, Beta Phi Mu, Delta Phi Lambda, Kappa Gamma Pi. Home: 15829 SW Village Cir Beaverton OR 97007-3532 Personal E-mail: ppond1@mindspring.com.

**POND, THOMAS ALEXANDER,** physics professor, academic administrator; b. LA, Dec. 4, 1924; s. Arthur Francis and Florence (Alexander) P.; m. Barbara Eileen Newman, Sept. 6, 1958; children: Arthur Phillip Ward, Florence Alexandra. AB, Princeton U., 1947, AM, 1949, PhD, 1953; DSc, SUNY, Stony Brook, 1998. Instr. physics Princeton U., 1951-53; asst. prof., then assoc. prof. physics Washington U., St. Louis, 1953-62; prof. physics SUNY, Stony Brook, 1962-81, prof. emeritus, 1982—, chmn. dept., 1962-68, exec. v.p., 1967-79, acting pres., 1970, 75, 78; prof. physics Rutgers U., New Brunswick, NJ, exec. v.p., chief acad. officer, 1982-91, exec. v.p., chief acad. officer emeritus, 1991—, acting pres., 1990, prof., 1991-97, prof. emeritus, 1997—; acting sr. v.p. for acad. affairs U. Medicine and Dentistry N.J., New Brunswick, 1998. Bd. dirs. Action Com. for L.I., 1978-80, Tri-State Regional Planning Commn., 1979-82; trustee Univs. Research Assn. 1985-87; bd. dirs. Fermilab, 1987-89. Served to ensign USNR, 1943-46. Fellow AAAS; mem. Am. Phys. Soc., Phi Beta Kappa, Sigma Xi. Home: 144 Fox Run Arlington VT 05250 Personal E-mail: aandbpond@aol.com.

**PONDEL, ROGER S.,** public relations executive; BA in Pub. Rels., Calif. State U., San Jose. Pub. rels. dir. Cordon Internat. Corp., Cordura Corp., Bekins Co.; pres. Pondel/Wilkinson, Inc., LA, 1997—. Adj. faculty Pepperdine U., Malibu, Calif.; spkr. Reporter San Jose Mercury News. Mem. Nat. Investor Rels. Inst., Pub. Rels. Soc. Am., L.A. Soc. Fin. Analysts. Office: Pondel Wilkinson Inc Ste 700 1880 Century Park E Los Angeles CA 90067 Office Phone: 310-279-5980. Business E-Mail: rpondel@pondel.com.

**PONDER, ANNE,** academic administrator; b. Asheville, N.C., Apr. 26, 1950; d. Herschel Doyle and Mary Eleanor (Israel) Ponder; m. John Christopher Brookhouse, Mar. 3, 1973; stepchildren: Stephen Christopher, Nathaniel. AB, U. N.C., 1971, MA, 1973, PhD, 1979. Dir. honors Clemson U., N.C., 1977-83; assoc. acad. dean Guilford Coll., Greensboro, N.C., 1985-89; acad. dean, prof. Kenyon Coll., Gambier, Ohio, 1989—96, v.p. info. tech.; pres. Colby-

Sawyer Coll., New London, NH, 1996—2005. Mem. Nat. Collegiate Honors Coun. (pres. 1988-89), N.C. Honors Assn. (pres. 1983), Order of Valkyries. Episcopalian. Office: Colby-Sawyer Coll 541 Main St New London NH 03257

**PONDER, CATHERINE,** clergywoman; b. Hartsville, S.C., Feb. 14, 1927; d. Roy Charles and Kathleen (Parrish) Cook; 1 child, Richard. Student, Worth Bus. Coll., 1948; BS in Edn., Unity Ministerial Sch., 1956; doctorate (hon.), Unity Sch., 1976. Ordained to ministry Unity Sch. Christianity, 1958. Min. Unity Ch., Birmingham, Ala., 1958-61, founder, min. Austin, Tex., 1961-69, San Antonio, 1969-73, Palm Desert, Calif., 1973—. Author: (books) The Dynamic Laws of Prosperity, 1962, The Prosperity Secret of the Ages, 1964, The Dynamic Laws of Healing, 1966, The Healing Secret of the Ages, 1967, Pray and Grow Rich, 1968, The Millionaires of Genesis, 1976, The Millionaire Moses, 1977, The Millionaire Joshua, 1978, The Millionaire from Nazareth, 1979, The Secret of Unlimited Prosperity, 1981, Open Your Mind To Receive, 1983, Dare To Prosper!: The Prospering Power of Prayer, 1983, The Prospering Power of Love, 1984, Open Your Mind to Prosperity, 1984, The Dynamic Laws of Prayer, 1987, (memoir) Prosperity Love Story, From Rags to Enrichment, 2003. Office: 73-669 US Hwy 111 Palm Desert CA 92260-4033

**PONDER, HERMAN,** geologist; b. Light, Ark., Jan. 31, 1928; s. Herman Cook and Sylvia Adell (Cameron) P.; m. Barbara Elaine Sando, May 10, 1947; children: Teresa Elaine, David Mark. BA, U. Mo., 1955, PhD, 1959. Rsch. engr. A.P. Green Refractories Co., Mexico, Mo., 1959-61, lab mgr., 1961-63; project engr., then mgr. mining div. Colo. Sch. Mines Rsch. Inst., Golden, 1963-67, dir. rsch., 1967-70, pres., 1970-85, ATI Exploration, Golden, Colo., 1985—90; chmn. bd. dirs Analytica, Inc. V.p. Copper Range Co., White Pine, Mich., 1985-89. Served with USN, 1946-47. Recipient Disting. Alumnus award U. Mo., 1993. Home: 2725 E Papago Trl Sierra Vista AZ 85650-8112

**PONDROM, LEE GIRARD,** physicist, researcher; b. Dallas, Dec. 26, 1933; s. Levi Girard and Guinevere (Miller) P.; m. Cyrena Jo Norman, Aug. 25, 1961. BS, So. Meth. U., 1953; MS, U. Chgo., 1956, PhD, 1958. Instr., dept. physics Columbia U., N.Y.C., 1960-63; assoc. prof. dept. physics U. Wis., Madison, 1963-69, prof. physics, 1969—, Robert Williams Wood prof., 1992—. Dept. chmn. U. Wis., 1997-2000; mem. high energy adv. com. Brookhaven Nat. Lab., 1973-75, chmn. Associated Universities, Inc., vis. com., 1987; mem. physics adv. com. Fermi Nat. Accelerator Lab., 1979-82, chmn., 1981-82; adv. com. for physics NSF, 1981-84; mem. high energy adv. panel (physics) U.S. Dept. Energy, 1981-84, 87-88, chmn. subcom. on detectors, 1987-88, mem. subpanel on future facilities, high energy physics, 1983, mem. subpanel on future modes of exptl. research in high energy physics, 1987; trustee Univs. Research Assn., 1973-76, 82-85; mem. sci. policy com. Stanford Linear Accelerator Ctr., 1984-88; mem. Internat. Com. Future Accelerators, 1984-90; chmn. Snowmass 1986 Summer Study on the SSC.; chmn. User's Orgn. for the SSC, 1987-89, mem. sci. policy com. SSC Lab., 1992; mem. CDRF awards com. to scientists in former Soviet Union, 1996. Contbr. articles to profl. jours. Served to 1st Lt. USAF, 1958-60. J.S. Guggenheim Meml. fellow, 1971-72, Japan Soc. for Promotion of Sci. fellow; recipient Disting. Alumni award So. Meth. U., 1983, W.K.H. Panofsky award Am. Phys. Soc., 1994. Fellow Am. Phys. Soc. (chmn. div. particles and fields 1987, com. on status of women in physics 1989—, chmn. com. to award the Panofsky prize 1991); mem. AAAS, Phi Beta Kappa (pres. U.S. Alpha chpt. 1996-97). Episcopalian. Home: 210 Princeton Ave Madison WI 53726-4077 Office: U Wis Dept Physics Madison WI 53706 E-mail: pondrom@hep.wisc.edu. *I have been fortunate to pursue a career in research and teaching at a university and at various U.S. national laboratories, where the individual has much freedom to do whatever he or she wants. Close association with many colleagues and my work with younger people in physics have been sources of stimulation.*

**PONEMAN, DANIEL BRUCE,** lawyer; b. Toledo, Mar. 12, 1956; s. Meyer and Delores Suzanne (Shapiro) P.; m. Susan Anne Danoff, Aug. 12, 1984; children: Claire Gillian, Michael Bruder, William Meyer. AB in Govt. and Econs. magna cum laude, Harvard Coll., 1978; MLitt in Politics, Lincoln Coll., Oxford, Eng., 1981; JD cum laude, Harvard U., 1984. Bar: D.C. 1985, N.Y., 1985. Vis. fellow Internat. Inst. Strategic Studies, London, 1980-81; rsch. fellow ctr. sci. and internat. affairs Kennedy sch. govt. Harvard U., 1981-84; assoc. Covington & Burling, 1985-89; White House fellow U.S. Dept. of Energy, 1989-90; dir. def. policy and arms control NSC, Washington, 1990-93, spl. asst. to the Pres., sr. dir. nonproliferation and export controls, 1993-96; counsel Hogan & Hartson L.L.P., 1996-97, ptnr., 1999—2002; prin. The Scowcroft Group, 2001—. Author: Nuclear Power in the Developing World, 1982, Argentina: Democracy on Trial, 1987, Going Critical, 2003; contbr. articles to profl. jours. and newspapers including N.Y. Times, Washington Post, Wall Street Jour., L.A. Times, Boston Globe, Fin. Times. Mem. Commn. to Asses the Orgn. of Govt. to Combat the Proliferation of Weapons of Mass Distruction, 1997-99; mem. Pres.' Export Coun. Subcom. on Export Adminstrn. Grantee Corp. Pub. Broadcasting; Lord Crewe scholar. Mem. D.C. Bar, N.Y. Bar, Assoc. Coun. Fgn. Rels., Phi Beta Kappa. Home: 1541 Forest Ln Mc Lean VA 22101 Office: The Scowcroft Group 900 17th St NW Ste 500 Washington DC 20006 Business E-Mail: poneman@scowcroft.com.

**PONITZ, DAVID H.,** former academic administrator; b. Royal Oak, Mich., Jan. 21, 1931; s. Henry John and Jeanette (Bouwman) P.; m. Doris Jean Humes, Aug. 5, 1956; children: Catherine Anne, David Robinson. BA, U. Mich., 1952, MA, 1954; EdD, Harvard U., 1964; degree (hon.), U. Dayton, 1996. Prin. Waldron (Mich.) Area Schs., 1956-58, supt., 1958-60; cons. Harvard U., Boston Sch. Survey, 1961-63; supt. Freeport (Ill.) Pub. Schs., 1962-65; pres. Freeport C.C., 1962-65, Washtenaw C.C., 1965-75, Sinclair C.C., 1975-97, pres. emeritus, 1997—, Cons. to cmty. colls.; chmn. pres. Ohio Assn. of Tech. Ctr.; cdnl. cons., 1997—. Mem. editorial adv. bd. Nations Schs, 1963-70; chmn. adv. bd. Community Coll. Rev, 1978-89. Past chmn. Dayton Mayor's Coun. on Econ. Devel., 1977-85; mem. Nat. Adv. Coun. on Nursing; former co-chair Performing Arts Edn. Task Force; bd. dirs Alliance for Edn.; former campaign chmn. Ann Arbor and Dayton United Way; past vice chmn. Dayton Citizens Adv. Coun. for Desegregation Implementation; v.p. Miami Valley Rsch. Park; mem., past chmn. Area Progress Coun., Dayton; bd. dirs. Dayton Devel. Coun.; mem. F.S.B. bd. Citizens Fed. Banks, Universal Energy Systems Bd.; past chmn. Miami Valley Joint Labor/Mgmt. Profls., Area Progress Coun.; chmn. bd. dirs Ctr. Occupational R & D; bd. chair Wright Tech. Network; bd. dirs. Dean Family Funds; trustee Thomas B. Fordham Found.; mem. Midwestern Higher Edn. Commn.; vice chair Miami Valley Rsch. Found.; past chmn. bd. dirs. League Innovation C.C.; bd. dirs. Miami Valley Regional Planning Commn. Served with U.S. Army, 1954-56. Named Outstanding Alumnus, U. Mich., One of Top 100 Pres. in U.S. Coun. for Advancement and Support of Edn., Exec. of Yr., Bd. Realtors; named to Hall of Fame, Nat. Mgmt. Assn., 2001; recipient Presdl. medallion, Patron emeritus Hofer-Georgetown Tech. Coll., Bogie Buster Red Jacket award, 1987, Thomas J. Peters award for Excellence, Assn. Cmty. and Jr. Colls., 1988, Marie N. Martin Chief Exec. Officer award, ACCT, 1989, The Living Legend award, Martin Luther King Jr. Holiday Celebration Com., 1991, Hon. Alumnus award, Sinclair, 1991, honor, India Found., 1992, Disting. Eagle Scout award, Nat. Eagle Scout Assn., 1993, Smitty award, Anti-Defamation award, Anti-Defamation League, 1996, Citizen Legion of Honor award, 1997, hon. award, Citizen Legion, 1997, Edn. award, Gov., 1999. Mem. Am. Assn. Community and Jr. Colls. (nat. future commn., bd. dirs., chmn. 1988-89, Nat. Leadership award 2002), Ohio Tech. and Community Coll. Assn. (pres. 1979-80), Nat. Mgmt. Assn. (Hall of Fame award 2001), Rotary. Methodist. Office Phone: 937-434-6640. Business E-Mail: dponitzsinclair@woh.rr.com.

**PONITZ, JOHN ALLAN,** lawyer; b. Battle Creek, Mich., Sept. 9, 1949; m. Nancy J. Roberts, Aug. 14, 1971; children: Amy, Matthew, Julie. BA, Albion Coll., 1971; JD, Wayne State U., 1974. Bar: Mich. 1974, U.S. Dist. Ct. (ea. dist.) Mich. 1975, (we. dist.) Mich. 1986, U.S. Ct. Appeals (6th cir.) Mich. 1981, U.S. Supreme Ct. 1992. Assoc. McMachan & Kaichen, Birmingham, Mich., 1974—75; atty. Grand Trunk Western R.R., Detroit, 1975-80, sr. trial

atty., 1980-89, gen. counsel, 1990-95; ptnr. Hopkins & Sutter, Detroit, 1995-2000, Maxwell, Ponitz & Sclawy, Troy, Mich., 2000—01; of counsel Fabrizio & Brook, P.C., Troy, 2002—03; gen. counsel A&M Hospitality, Southfield, Mich., 2002—. Served to capt. USAR, 1974-82. Mem.: Mich. Bar Assn., Nat. Assn. R.R. Trial Counsel, Oakland County Bar Assn. Lutheran. Avocation: golf. Office: A&M Hospitality 24725 Greenfield Rd Southfield MI 48075 Business E-Mail: jponitz@ponitzlaw.com

**PONKO, WILLIAM REUBEN,** architect; b. Wausau, Wis., Apr. 4, 1948; s. Reuben Harrison and Ora Marie (Ranke) P.; m. Kathleen Ann Hilt, May 5, 1973; children: William Benjamin, Sarah Elizabeth. BArch magna cum laude, U. Notre Dame, 1971. Cert. Nat. Coun. Archtl. Registration Bds. V.p., arch., dir. ednl., instl. specialty Le Roy Troyer & Assocs. (now the Troyer Group), Mishawaka, Ind., 1971—; design instr. dept. arch. U. Notre Dame, 1976. Mem. Ind. State Bd. Registration for Architects, 1990—; mem. registration exam com. Nat. Coun. Archtl. Registration Bds., 1992—, vice chair 1996, chair 1997. Prin. archtl. works include: St. Peter Luth. Ch., Mishawaka, Ind., 1979, 4 brs. for South Bend Pub. Libr., 1983, Edward J. Funk & Sons office bldg. Taylor U., Upland, Ind., 1982, Taylor U. Lbir., carillon tower, 1985, Early Childhood Devel. Ctr. U. Notre Dame, 1994, Convents for Sisters of Holy Cross St. Mary's, Notre Dame, Ind., 1995. Mem. AIA (gold medal for exellence in archtl. edn. 1971), Ind. Soc. Archs. (Design Excellence award 1978, chpt. pres. 1985, Juliet Peddle award 2000). Office: The Troyer Group Inc 550 Union St Mishawaka IN 46544-2346

**PONNAMBALAM, ANANTHASEKAR,** pediatrician, gastroenterologist; arrived in U.S., 1997; s. Arumugam Ponnambalam and Lalitha Krishnaswamy; m. Kalpana Ananthasekar, July 1, 1993; children: Shivani Ananthasekar, Skandan Ananthasekar. MB, BChir, Stanley Med. Coll., Madras, 1985; Diploma in Child Health, Madras Med. Coll., 1987, MD, 1990, DM, 1993. Diplomate Am. Bd. Pediat., 2000, cert. pediat. gastroenterology Am. Bd. Pediat., 2005. Attending physician Primary Health Care, Tamilnadu, India, 1990—91; attending physician in pediat. and gastroenterology India, 1993—94; attending physician in pediat. Ministry of Health, Oman, 1994—97; resident in pediat. SUNY Downstate Med. Ctr., Bklyn., 1997—2000, fellow pediat. gastroenterology, 2000—03, rschr. Question writer Am. Bd. Pediats. Contbr. chapters to books. Fellow: Am. Acad. Pediat.; mem.: Am. Coll. Gastroenterology, Am. Gastroenterology Assn., N.Am. Soc. for Pediat. Gastroenterology Hepatology and Nutrition. Achievements include research in mast cells. Home: 1410 N Shevlin Ct Sewickley PA 15143 Office: SUNY Downstate Med Ctr 450 Clarkson Ave Box 49 Brooklyn NY 11203 Personal E-mail: ananthasekarp@hotmail.com.

**PONOROFF, LAWRENCE,** dean, law educator, consultant; b. Chgo., Sept. 10, 1953; s. Charles Melvin and Jean Eileen (Kramer) P.; m. Monica J. Moses, July 25, 1981; children: Christopher J., Devon E., Laura J., Scott C. BA, Loyola U., Chgo., 1975; JD, Stanford U., 1978. Bar: Colo. 1978, Ohio 1988, U.S. Dist. Ct. Colo., U.S. Dist. Ct. (no. dist.) Ohio, U.S. Ct. Appeals (10th cir.). Assoc. Holme Roberts & Owen, Denver, 1978-84, ptnr., 1984-86; asst. prof. law U. Toledo, 1986-88, assoc. prof. coll. of law, 1988-90, prof. law, assoc. dean academic affairs, 1990-92, prof., 1990-95, Tulane U. Sch. Law, New Orleans, 1995-00, J. Mitchell Franklin prof. pvt. and comml. law, 2000—, vice dean, 1998-2001, dean, 2001—. Vis. prof. Wayne State U. Law Sch., 1993, U. Mich. Law Sch., 1997; lectr. fed. juc. ctr.; cons. long range planning subcom. of com. on adminstrn. of bankruptcy sys. Jud. Conf. US, mem. adv. com. on bankruptcy rules, 2004—; dir. Am. Bd. Cert., 2000-06; bd. advisors editors Am. Bankruptcy Inst. Law Rev., 2000—03. Co-author: (with S.E. Snyder) Commerical Bankruptcy Litigation, 1989, (with J. Dolan) Basic Concepts in Commercial Law, 1998, (with Epstein and Markell) Making and Doing Deals: Contracts in Context, 2002, 2d edit., 2006, (with J. Colan and B. Markell) Core Concepts of Commercial Law: Past, Present and Future, 2004. Fellow Am. Coll. Bankruptcy; mem. ABA, Am. Bar Ist., Am. Law Inst., La. State Bar Assn. (bd. govs. 2001-03). Home: 6025 Pitt St New Orleans LA 70118-6010 Office: Tulane Law Sch 6329 Freret St New Orleans LA 70118 Office Phone: 504-865-5937. Business E-Mail: lponoroff@law.tulane.edu.

**PONSETI, IGNACIO VIVES,** orthopaedic surgery educator; b. Cuidadela, Balearic Islands, Spain, June 3, 1914; s. Miguel and Margarita (Vives) P.; 1 child, William Edward; m. Helena Percas, 1961. BS, U. Barcelona, 1930, MD, 1936, D honoris causa, 1984. Intern: dept. orthopaedic surgery State U. Iowa, 1944-57, prof., 1957—. Author papers and a book on cogenital and developmental skeletal deformities. Capt. M.C. Spanish Army, 1936-39. Recipient Kappa Delta award for orthopaedic rsch., 1955. Mem. Assn. Bone and Joint Surgeons, Am. Acad. Cerebral Palsy, Soc. Exptl. Biology and Medicine, Internat. Coll. Surgeons, N.Y. Acad. Sci., AMA (Ketoen gold medal 1960), Am. Acad. Orthopedic Surgeons, ACS, Am. Orthopedic Assn., Pediatric Orthopaedic Soc. (hon.), Iowa Med. Soc., Orthopedic Rsch. Soc. (Shands award 1975), Sigma Xi, Asociacion Argentina de Cirugia (hon.), Asociacion Balear de Cirugia (hon.), Sociedad de Cirujanos de Chile (hon.), Sociedad Espanola de Cirugia Ortopedica (hon.), Sociedad Brasilera de Ortopedia e Traumatologia (hon.). Home: 110 Oakridge Ave Iowa City IA 52246-2935 Office: Carver Pavilion U Iowa Hosps Iowa City IA 52242 Business E-Mail: ignacio-Ponseti@uiowa.edu.

**PONT, JOHN,** football coach, educator; b. Canton, Ohio, Nov. 13, 1927; s. Bautista and Susie (Sikurinec) P.; m. H. Sandra Stoutt, June 23, 1956; children: John W., Jennifer Ann, Jeffrey David. BS, Miami U., Oxford, Ohio, 1952, MS, 1956. Profl. football player, Canada, 1952—53; instr., coach freshman football and basketball Miami U. Oxford, 1953—55, asst. prof. head football coach, 1955—62; head football coach Yale U., 1963—65; prof., head football coach Ind. U. Bloomington, 1965—73; head coach Northwestern U., Evanston, Ill., 1973—77, athletic dir., 1974—79; head football coach, athletic dir. Hamilton, Ohio; head football coach, tennis coach, asst. athletic dir. Coll. Mt. St. Joseph, Cin.; head football coach Gakusei-Engo-Kai Inc., Tokyo; dir. football ops. Ohio Dominican U., Columbus, 2003—. Agt. Equitable Assurance Soc., U.S., 1981-82; v.p. Fin. Leasing Corp., 1983-85, Splty. Brush, Inc.; athletic dir. Jewish Community Center, Canton, 1953; v.p. NCAA Coun., 1979-80; mem. bd. dirs. Cin. chpt. Nat. Football Found. Hall Of Fame; pres. NFL Alumni-S.W. Ohio. Mem. Pres.'s Coun. on Phys. Fitness; chmn. Ind. Easter Seal, 1968-69, Ind. div. Cancer Crusade, 1969; bd. dirs. Multiple Sclerosis, N.E. Ill. counc. Boy Scouts Am., Boys Hope. Served with USN, 1945-47. Named Coach of Year Coaches Assn., 1967, Coach of Year Football Writers, 1967, Coach of Yr. Washington Touchdown Club, 1968, Coach of Yr. Walter Camp Found.; recipient Significant Sig award, 1968, elected Ind. Football Hall of Fame, 1984, Butler County Hall of Fame, 1986, Mid-Am. Conf. Hall of Fame, 1992, Ind. U. Sports Hall of Fame, 1992. Mem. Am. Football Coaches Assn. (chmn. ethics com.), Kusatsu City Football Assn. Japan (hon. chmn.), Am. Legion, Blue Key, Sigma Chi, Phi Epsilon Kappa, Omicron Delta Kappa. Republican. Home: 482 White Oak Dr Oxford OH 45056-9272 Personal E-mail: pont52@aol.com.

**PONTIFF, PAUL E.,** lawyer; b. Bklyn., June 6, 1930; s. Louis J. and Catherine A. (Menig) P.; m. Judy A. Dufour, June 13, 1998; children: Paul L., Thomas M., Matthew J., Kathy Braley, Shawna Braley, Lynn Lafond. BBA in Acctg., St. Johns U., N.Y.C., 1954; JD, 1959. Bar: N.Y. 1959, U.S. Tax Ct. 1962, U.S. Dist. Ct. (no. dist.) N.Y. 1974. Acctg. tax mgr. Ball George & Co. CPAs, Glens Falls, N.Y., 1960-62; lawyer Bartlett, Pontiff Stewart & Rhodes PC, Glens Falls, 1962—. bd. dirs. World Awareness Children's Mus., 1986—, past pres.; bd. dirs., treas. Adirondack Vets House, Inc. With U.S. Army, 1954—56. Mem. Warren County Bar Assn. (pres. 1977-78), Estate Planning Coun. Eastern N.Y. (pres. 2000-01), Glens Falls Elks, Glens Falls Rotary Club (past pres.). Avocations: mountain climbing, tennis, golf. Office: Bartlett Pontiff et al PO Box 2168 One Washington St Glens Falls NY 12801 E-mail: pep@bpsrlaw.com.

**PONTIUS, STANLEY N.,** bank holding company executive; b. Auburn, Ind., Aug. 26, 1946; s. Clayton and Frances (Beuret) P.; m. Cheryl Ann Dawson, Aug. 3, 1968; children: Jarrod B., Dorian K. BS, Ind. U., 1968; grad., Stonier Grad. Sch. of Banking, 1979. Bank One, 1968-91; dir., pres., COO 1st Fin. Bancorp, Hamilton, Ohio, 1991, dir., pres., CEO, 1992—2003, 1st Nat. Bank of Southwestern Ohio, Hamilton, 1991-97, chmn., CEO, 1997-98, chmn., 1998—2003. Bd. dirs. Health Alliance Greater Cin., Ohio Casualty Corp. (chmn., 1994-); Fort Hamilton Health Network (chmn.), Hamilton Cmty. Found. With U.S. Army, 1968-70. Mem. Am. Bankers Coun., Hamilton-Fairfield Arts Assn. Leadership Hamilton, Metropolitan Growth Alliance, "The Community Banker" magazine (adv. bd.).

**PONT MARCHESE, MARISARA,** former Puerto Rican government official; b. Río Piedras, P.R., Oct. 29, 1941; d. Rafael Pont and Sara Marchese. BA in Humanities cum laude, U. P.R., 1962-63; MS in Libr. Sci., Columbia U., 1971. Asst. to dir. med. scis. campus U. P.R., Río Piedras, 1964-72; spl. aide to Pres. Senate Commonwealth of P.R., San Juan, 1972; dep. aide in mgmt. Office of Gov. of P.R., San Juan, 1973, exec. aide to dir. of communications, 1973-74, dir. communications, 1974-76; pres. Plus Image Devel. and Pub. Rels., San Juan, 1977-86, Comstat/Rowland Pub. Rels., San Juan, 1986—; lectr. U. PR, pres. Commn. of Transition, 2004—05; sec. state Commonwealth of P.R., San Juan, 2005. Mem. Assn. Profl. Pub. Rels. Practitioners of P.R. (pres. 1984-86), Pub. Rels. Soc. Am., Overseas Press Club P.R. (co-chmn. ann. award program 1981-89), P.R. Mfrs. Assn., P.R. C. of C. (pub. rels. award 1985), Bankers Club. Roman Catholic. Business E-Mail: marisarap@comstat-pr.com.

**PONTON, MICHAEL KAMANO,** engineer, educator; s. William Fordyce and Kikue Kamano Ponton; m. Janet Renee Ponton, Jan. 2, 1981; children: Michael Lee, Kathryn Marie. EdD, George Wash. U., Washington, DC, 1996—99, MS, 1986—91; BS, Old Dominion U., Norfolk, Va., 1979—83. Mech. engr./mech. engr. trainee Applied Tech. Lab., Ft. Eustis, Va., 1981—82; acoustics engr., sr. acoustics engr. PRC-Kentron, Inc., Hampton, Va., 1983—87; adj. lectr. Thomas Nelson C.C., Hampton, Va., 1994—95; adj. prof. George Wash. U., Washington, 1998—99; aerospace engr. NASA Langley Rsch. Ctr., Hampton, Va., 1987—99; sr. rsch. & devel. engr., asst. prof. of higher edn. U. Miss., University, Miss., 1999—2001; assoc. prof. higher edn., sr. r & d engr. U. of Miss., University, Miss., 2001—. Sr. assoc. Human Resource Devel. Enterprises, Arlington, Va., 1999—. Fellow NASA Administrator's Fellowship, NASA, 1997-1998; scholar Randolph-Macon Coll. Award Scholarship, 1978—79. Mem.: AIAA, Am. Assn. for Adult and Continuing Edn., Assn. for the Study of Higher Edn., Am. Soc. of Engring. Edn. Achievements include research in NASA Langley Research Center Superior Accomplishment Award for the identification of nonlinear interactions in supersonic free jet flows; NASA Langley Research Center Group Achievement Award for performance as a member of the supersonic twin-jet resonance research team; NASA Group Achievement Award for performance as a member of the B-1B engine nozzle sonic fatigue team; NASA Group Achievement Award for performance as a member of the supersonic jet noise reduction team; development of NASA Langley Research Center Performance Award for contributions resulting in the enhancement of the research capability of the Jet Noise Laboratory; NASA Langley Research Center Superior Accomplishment Award for contributions resulting in the successful modification of the Low Speed Aeroacoustic Wind Tunnel; research in NASA Langley Research Center Turning Goals into Reality Award for performance as a member of the advanced subsonic technology engine systems noise reduction team; NASA Langley Research Center Certificate of Appreciation for efforts leading to the successful demonstration of advanced noise reduction technologies for aircraft applications.

**PONTRELLI, LAURA ALISON,** psychologist; b. Madison, Wis., July 11, 1961; d. Gene Joseph Pontrelli and Tania Lipko; m. Adam Fisher F., Oct. 1, 1994; children: Isabel, Camille. AB, Bard Coll., 1983; MA, New Sch. for Social Rsch., 1987, PhD, 1994. Psychology fellow SUNY Downstate Med. Ctr., Bklyn., 1992—94; clin. psychology instr. Columbia Coll. of Physicians and Surgeons, NYC, 1995—2002; sr. psychologist of adult svcs. Harlem Hosp. Psychiatric Emergency Rm., 1995—2002; pvt. practice Sleepy Hollow, NY, 1999—. Mem. Collaborative Analystic Multisite, NYC, 1993—2000, Project of the Am. Psychoanalytic Assn. Mem.: APA, NY State Psychol. Assn. Avocations: running, reading, jewelry making. Office: 239 N Broadway Ste 5 Tarrytown NY 10591

**PONZI KAY, MARYLOU,** human resources specialist; b. N.Y.C., Oct. 14, 1950; d. Bruno and Constance Louise (DeLuca) P.; m. William J. Kay, Jr., Oct. 24, 1993. BA, SUNY, Geneseo, 1972; MA, U. Iowa, 1974, SUNY, Buffalo, 1979; cert. in advanced study in labor rels., N.Y. Inst. Tech., 1995. Cert. sr. profl. in human resources Soc. for Human Resources Mgmt. Cert. Inst., 2002. Pers. adminstr. Michelin Tire Corp., Lake Success, N.Y., 1978-83; tech. recruiter 1st Data Resources, Lake Success, N.Y., 1983-84; mgr. human resources Chem. Bank, Jericho, N.Y., 1984-87; pers. officer J.P. Morgan Inc., N.Y.C., 1987-89; mgr. employment Am. Express Inc., N.Y.C., 1989-92; dir. human resources RockBottom Stores, Inc., 1992-95; asst. dir. human resources Canon U.S.A., Lake Success, N.Y., 1995-97, dir. human resources, 1997-2000, dir. corp. human resources and devel., 2000; dir. human resources Esselte Ams., Melville, NY, 2000—02; v.p. global compensation benefits and svcs. Esselte Corp., 2002—05; v.p. human resources Smartmatic Corp., Boca Raton, Fla., 2005—. Instr. French and Spanish, Amityville H.S. Adult Edn., 1986-96; adj. prof. human resources N.Y. Inst. Tech., 2000-05. Editor: New England Guide, 1982, Canada Guide, 1982. Pres. LeBourget Alliance, Amityville, N.Y., 1995-97; pres. bus. adv. coun. Adults and Children with Learning Disabilities, 1994-97, trustee, 1997-, bd. dir., 2005-06; sr. exec. orientation Miami C of C, 2006. Mem. ASTD, Soc. Human Resources Mgmt., Human Resources Strategic Issues Coun., World at Work. Roman Catholic. Avocations: languages, travel, cooking, sports. Office: 1001 Broken Sound Pky Boca Raton FL 33487 Office Phone: 561-862-0747 ext. 4720. Personal E-mail: mwk93@aol.com. Business E-Mail: marylou.ponzi@smartmatic.com.

**POODIACK, ROBERT D.,** mathematics professor; b. Danbury, Conn., Jan. 27, 1966; s. Robert P. and Jean A. Poodiack; m. June Nolan; children: Daniel, Thomas. PhD, U. Vt., Burlington, Vt., 1999. Grad. tchg. fellow U. Vt., Burlington, Vt., 1994—99; assoc. prof. math. Norwich U., Northfield, Vt., 1999—. Recipient Homer L. Dodge Excellence in Tchg. award, Norwich U., 2005. Mem.: Math. Assn. Am. Office: Norwich University 158 Harmon Drive Northfield VT 05663 Office Phone: 802-485-2339.

**POOL, DAVID,** software executive; BA, Wash. State U. Product mgr. Clouston LTD; prin. SPRY Inc. (acquired by CompuServe 1995), 1989-95; v.p. strategic devel. Compuserve, 1995-96; prin. DataChannel, 1996-99; founder XML Fund, Bellevue, Wash., 1999—. Bd. dirs. Aventail, Seattle. Office: XML Fund 777 108th Ave NE Ste 1870B Bellevue WA 98004-5142 Office Phone: 425-467-0111. Office Fax: 425-467-0104.

**POOL, MARY JANE,** writer, editor; d. Earl Lee and Dorothy (Matthews) P. Grad., St. de Chantal Acad., 1942; BA in Art with honors, Drury Coll., 1946; LHD (hon.), Drury U., 2002. Mem. staff Vogue mag., N.Y.C., 1946-68, assoc. merchandising editor, 1948-57, promotion dir., 1958-66, exec. editor, 1966-68; editor House and Garden mag., 1969, editor-in-chief, 1970-80. Cons. Baker Furniture Co., 1981-94, Aves Advt., Inc., 1981-94, bd. dirs.; mem. bd. govs. Decorative Arts Trust; past mem. bd. govs. Fashion Group, Inc., N.Y.C. Author: The Gardens of Venice, 1989, The Gardens of Florence, 1992, Gardens in the City-New York in Bloom, 1999; co-author: The Angel Tree, 1984, The Angel Tree—A Christmas Celebration, 1993, The Christmas Story, 2001, editor: 20th Century Decorating, Architecture, Gardens, Billy Baldwin Decorates, 26 Easy Little Gardens. Mem. bus. com. N.Y. Zool. Soc., 1979-86; trustee Drury Univ., 1971—; bd. dirs. Isabel O'Neil Found., 1978—. Recipient award Nat. Soc. Interior Designers, Disting. Alumni award Drury Coll., 1961, Edith Wharton Women of Achievement award, 1999; Pool Art Ctr. at Drury U opened 2004. Address: 1 E 66th St New York NY 10021-5854

**POOLE, D. BRUCE,** lawyer; b. Hagerstown, Md., June 17, 1959; s. David Kreigh Jr. and Janice Marie (Zaiser) P.; m. Kathleen Kay Graham, July 20, 1991; 1 child, David Graham. BA, Washington & Lee U., 1981, JD, 1985. Bar: Md. 1985. Ptnr. Poole & Poole, P.A., Hagerstown, Md., 1985—89, 1992—, Snyder & Poole, P.A., Hagerstown and Frederick, 1989-95. Mem. Md. Ho. of Dels., Annapolis, 1988-2000, house majority leader, 1991-93, mem. commerce and govt. matters com., chmn. procurement subcom., 1994-97, joint fed. rels. com., way and means com., house chmn. jt. audit com.; mem. Md. State Ethics Commn., 1999—. Assoc. mem., bd. dirs. March of Dimes of Washington County, Hagerstown, 1986-91; pres. United Dems. Washington County, Hagerstown, 1985-86; mem. Gov.'s Commn. on Drug & Alcohol Abuse and Truck Safety, Annapolis, 1989-93. Mem. Sons of American Legion, Jaycees (named one of Ten Outstanding Marylanders 1991), Elks, Rotary (fellow U. Melbourne, Australia 1981). Lutheran. Avocations: swimming, travel, history, sporting clays. Office: Poole & Poole PA 29 Franklin St Hagerstown MD 21740*

**POOLE, DAVID EVANS,** music educator, composer; b. Albuquerque, July 7, 1959; s. Robert Carlisle and Mary Helen Poole; m. Winona Carol Lockard, June 15, 1985; children: Kendra, Aaron. BA, Ind. U., 1982; MusM, U. N. Mex., 1989. Dir. de Profundis and a cappella men's ensemble La Mesa Presbyn. Ch., 1994—, dir. music, 1989—; pvt. voice instr., 1989—; composer, 1990—. Author: (book) The Rivers Bend, 1995. Mem.: Presbyn. Assn. Musicians, Pi Kappa Lamda. Avocations: fishing, fly fishing, bicycling. Home: 2815 Indian Farm Lane NW Albuquerque NM 87107 Office: La Mesa Presbyn Ch 7401 Copper Ave Albuquerque NM 87107

**POOLE, DAVID P.,** lawyer; b. Houston, Tex., Mar. 13, 1962; s. Preston L. and Shari J. Poole; 1 child, Aubrey. BSc in Petroleum Engring., Tex. Tech. U., Lubbock, 1984, JD, 1988. Bar: Tex. 1988, DC 1989, US Dist. Ct. (no. dist. Tex.) 1988. Assoc. Worsham, Forsythe Woodridge, Dallas, 1988—97, ptnr., 1997—2002, mng. ptnr., 2001—02; ptnr., mng. ptnr. Hunton & Williams LLP, Dallas, 2002—04; assoc. gen. counsel, sr. v.p. TXU Corp., Dallas, 2004—06, gen. counsel, exec. v.p., 2006—. Mem. exec. bd. Cir. 10 Coun. Boy Scouts of Am., Dallas, 2003—. Mem.: Dallas Bar Assn. (co- chair CLE Com. 2003—04). Office: TXU Corp 1601 Bryan 600 Dallas TX 75201 Office Phone: 214-812-6001.*

**POOLE, EVA DURAINE,** librarian; b. Farrell, Pa., Dec. 20, 1952; d. Leonard Milton and Polly Mae (Flint) Harris; m. Tommy Lynn Cole, May 15, 1970 (div. Sept. 1984); 1 child, Tommy Lynn Cole; m. Earnest Theodore Poole, Sept. 22, 1990; 1 child, Aleece Remelle Poole. BA in LS, Tex. Woman's U., 1974, MLS, 1976; postgrad., U. Houston, 1989. Libr. asst. Emily Fowler Pub. Libr., Denton, Tex., 1970-74; children's libr. Houston Pub. Libr., 1974-75, 1st asst. libr., 1976-77; children's libr. Ector County Libr., Odessa, Tex., 1977-80; head pub. svcs. Lee Davis Libr. San Jacinto Coll., Pasadena, Tex., 1980-84; libr. dir. San Jacinto Coll. South, Houston, 1984-90; libr. svcs. mgr. Emily Fowler Pub. Libr., Denton, 1990-93, interim dir., 1993; dir. librs. Denton Pub. Librs., 1993—. Mem. Libr. Svcs. Constrn. Act Adv. Coun., 1994-97, Libr. Svcs. Tech. Act Adv. Coun., 1997-2000; mem. TEXSHARE adv. bd. Tex. State Libr. and Archives Commn., 1999-2005, chmn., 2003-2004; bd. dirs. Denton Area Tchrs. Credit Union, 2003-06; mem. adv. bd. U. North Tex. Sch. Libr. and Info. Sci., 2000—, chair, 2006—; mem. members coun. Online Computer Libr. Ctr., 2004—; mem. presdl. search adv. com. U. North Tex., 2005-06; mem. external constituent bd. Tex. Woman's U. Sch. Libr. and Info. Studies, 2005—. Bd. dirs. Amigos Libr. Svcs., 2000-03, Girl Scouts Cross Timbers Coun., 2002-04, United Way of Denton County, 2002—, exec. com., bd. pres., 2006-, Friends of Librs. U.S.A., 2003—. Named to Outstanding Young Women of Am., 1991. Mem. ALA (chair Loleta Fyan jury com. 1999-2000) Allied Profl. Assn.(chmn. cert. pub. libr. adminstr. program 2005—), mem. com. orgn., 2005—), Pub. Libr. Assn. (mem. budget and fin. com. 1999-2002, chair budget and fin. com. 2001-2002, 2004-05, nat. conf. com. 2002-04, chair bylaws and orgn. 2002-03, mem. instnl. scholarships task force 2006), Libr. Adminstrn. and Mgmt. Assn. (program com. 1994-97, mem.-at-large bd. dirs. 2000-02, chair cultural diversity com. 2000-01, com. on orgn. 2002-05, rep. to Freedom to Read Found. 2002-03, strategic planning com. 2005-06), Tex. Libr. Assn. (pub. libr. divsn. sec. 1995-96, chair 1997-98, leadership devel. com. 1995-97, leadership devel. com. chair 1996-97, alumnae 1st class Libr. Leaders 1994, legis. com. 1997-99, Dist. 7 coun. 1996-99, exec. bd. 1998-2000, 2002-05, ad hoc comm. on pub. libr. stds. com. chair 1998-2000, 2002 conf. local arrangements com. 2001-02, chair 2000 conf. program com. 1998-2000, chair awards com. 2001-02, pres.-elect 2002-03, pres. 2003-04, chair Tocker Found. com. 2006—), Pub. Libr. Adminstrs. North Tex. (vice chair 1994-95, chair 1995-96), Tex. Mcpl. Libr. Dirs. Assn. (pres. 1995-96, grantee 1993, Libr. of Yr. 1998), Denton Rotary Club, Tex. Mcpl. League (bd. dirs. 1997-2000). Office: Denton Pub Libr 502 Oakland St Denton TX 76201 Office Phone: 940-349-8750. Business E-mail: eva.poole@cityofdenton.com

**POOLE, KEITH T.,** political science professor; b. Newport, Oreg., 1947; m. Janice K. Poole, 1972. BS in Polit. Sci., Portland State U., 1972; MA in Polit. Sci., U. Rochester, 1975, PhD in Polit. Sci., 1978. Asst. prof. polit. sci. U. Oreg., 1978—82; postdoctoral fellow in polit. economy Carnegie-Mellon U., 1981—82; vis. prof. polit. sci. divsn. humanities and social sci. Calif. Inst. Tech., 1992, 1995; prof. Grad. Sch. Indsl. Adminstrn. Carnegie-Mellon U., 1982—2000; Kenneth L. Lay prof. polit. sci. U. Houston, 2000—04; fellow Ctr. Advanced Study in Behavioral Sciences, 2003—04; prof. polit. sci. U. Calif. San Diego, 2005—. Editl. bd. Social Sci. Quarterly, 1998—, American Jour. Polit. Sci., 1998—2002, Jour. Politics, 2001—04, Legislative Studies Quarterly, 2002—05. Author (with L Harmon Zeigler): (books) Women, Public Opinion, and Politics: The Changing Political Attitudes of American Women, 1985; author: (with Howard Rosenthal) Congress: A Political-Economic History of Roll Call Voting, 1997; author: Spatial Models of Parliamentary Voting, 2005; author: (Nolan M. McCarty and Howard Rosenthal) Polarized America: The Dance of Ideology and Unequal Riches, 2006; author: (with Howard Rosental) Ideology and Congress, 2006; author: (with Nolan M. McCarty) (monograph) Income Redistribution and the Realignment of American Politics, 1997; contbr. articles to profl. journals. Recipient Warren E. Miller prize best article, 2001. Fellow: Am. Acad. Arts and Sciences. Office: Dept Political Science Univ Calif San Diego Social Sciences Bldg Rm 301 9500 Gilman Dr MC 0521 La Jolla CA 92093-0521 Office Phone: 858-534-1452. E-mail: kpoole@ucsd.edu.*

**POOLE, NANCY GEDDES,** art gallery curator, writer; b. London, Ont., Can., May 10, 1930; d. John Hardy and Kathleen Edwards (Robinson) G.; m. William Robert Poole, Aug. 15, 1952; 1 child, Andrea Mary. BA, U. Western Ont., 1956, LLD, 1990. Owner, dir. Nancy Poole's Studio, Toronto, Ont., Canada, 1969-78; acting dir. London Regional Art Gallery, Ont., Canada, 1981—, exec. dir. Ont., 1985-89; dir. London Regional Art and Hist. Museums, Ont., Canada, 1989-95. Chair governing coun. Ont. Coll. Art, 1972-73; bd. dirs. Robarts Rsch. Inst., 1995. Author: The Art of London 1939-1980, 1984; editor Jack Chambers, 1978, The Collection, 1990. Bd. govs. U. Western Ont., 1974-85; bd. dirs. Western Area Youth Svcs., 1996; chair Western Area Youth Svcs. Found., 2004, Hazel Cryderman-Wees Found., 2004. Fellow Ont. Coll. Art. Mem.: Order of Can. Office: 420 Fanshawe Park Rd London ON Canada N5X 2S9

**POOLE, RICHARD WILLIAM,** economist; b. Oklahoma City, Dec. 4, 1927; s. William Robert and Lois (Spicer) Poole; m. Bertha Lynn Mehr, July 28, 1950; children: Richard William, Laura Lynne, Mark Stephen. BS, U. Okla., 1951, MBA, 1952; postgrad., George Washington U. 1957—58; PhD, Okla. State U., 1960. Rsch. analyst Okla. Gas & Electric Co., Oklahoma City, 1952- 54; mgr. sci. and mfg. devel. dept Oklahoma City C. of C., 1954—57; mgr. Office of J.E. Webb, Washington, 1957-58; from instr. to prof. econs. Okla. State U., Stillwater, 1960-65, prof. econs., dean Coll. Bus. Adminstrn., 1965-72, v.p., prof. econs., 1972-88, Regents Disting. Svc. prof., prof. econs., 1988-93, emeritus v.p., dean, Regents Disting. Svc. prof./prof., 1993—. Cons. to adminstr. NASA, Washington, 1961—69; advisor subcom. govt. rsch. U.S. Senate, 1966—69; lectr. Intermediate Sch. Banking, Ops. Mgmt. Sch., Okla. Bankers Assn., 1969—88; lectr. internat. off-campus programs

Oklahoma City U., 1994—96. Author (with others): The Oklahoma Economy, 1963, County Building Block Data for Regional Analysis, 1965. Mem. Gov.'s Com. Devel. Ark.-Verdigris Waterway, 1970—71, Gov.'s Five-Yr. Econ. Devel. Plan, 1993; past v.p. bd. dirs., past chmn. Mid-Continent R & D Coun. 2d lt. arty. U.S. Army, 1946—48. Named to Coll. Bus. Adminstrn. Hall of Fame, Okla. State U., 1993, Stillwater Hall of Fame, Payne county Hist. Soc. and Stillwater C. of C., 1996, Okla. Higher Edn. Hall of Fame, 1998; recipient Delta Sigma Pi Gold Key award, Coll. Bus. Adminstrn. U. Okla., 1951, Tchg. award on Am. free enterprise sys., Merrick Found., 1992, Disting. Alumni award, Okla. State U., 1995, Henry G. Bennett Disting. Svc. award, 1999. Mem.: Southwestern Bus. Adminstrn. Assn. (past pres.), Nat. Assn. State Univs. and Land Grant Colls. (past chmn. commn. edn. for bus. professions), Am. Assembly Collegiate Schs. Bus. (past bd. dirs.), Southwestern Econ. Assn. (past pres.), Stillwater C. of C. (past bd. dirs., pres.), Santa Fe Trail Assn. (bd. dirs. 2001—02), Okla. C. of C. (past bd. dirs.), Okla. Heritage Assn. (bd. dirs. 2000—05), Omicron Delta Kappa, Phi Eta Sigma, Phi Kappa Phi, Beta Gamma Sigma (past bd. dirs.). Home: 14901 N Pennsylvania Apt 336 Oklahoma City OK 73134

**POOLE, ROGER CLIFF,** academic administrator, finance educator, retired military officer; b. Fayetteville, NC, Dec. 31, 1936; married. BA, The Citadel, 1959, PhD (hon.) in Bus., 2005; MBA in Mgmt., U. SC, 1962, PhD in Fin., 1974; diploma, US Army War Coll., 1981. V.p. Investors Nat. Life Insurance Co., Inc, Columbia, SC, 1963—66; instr. fin. U. SC, 1969—70; asst. prof. fin. Va. Commonwealth U., Richmond, 1970—73, coord. of fin.; v.p. fin. and adminstrn., mem. bd. dirs. Century Construction Co. Inc., Richmond; sec., treas., mem. bd. dirs. Century Constructors of Virginia, Inc., 1973—76; asst. prof. fin. U. Richmond, 1976—79, assoc. dean, dir. of grad. studies Richard S. Reynolds Grad. Sch., 1979—83, assoc. prof. fin., 1985—88, dean E. Claiborne Robins Sch. Bus., 1988—93; v.p. academic affairs, dean The Citadel, Charleston, 1993—96, 1997—99, interim pres., 1996—97, 2005, BOV disting. fellow of fin., 2005—. Dir. Transp., Troop Support & Energy Dept. Army Ops. Ctr., Desert Shield/Desert Storm. Ret. brigadier gen. USAR. Decorated Legion of Merit Award, Meritorious Svc. Medal with Oak Leaf Cluster, Army Commendation Medal with Oak Leaf Cluster, Army Reserve Components Achievement Medal with Two Oak Leaf Clusters, Nat. Defense Svc. Medal, Armed Forces Reserve Medal with 30-year Device, Army Svc. Ribbon, Army Reserve Components Overseas Training Ribbon with Numeral 3. Fellow: Southwestern Fin. Assn., Life Mgmt. Inst.; mem.: So. Risk and Insurance Assn., So. Econs. Assn., So. Fin. Assn., Soc. for Advancement of Mgmt., Fin. Execs. Inst., Acad. Internat. Bus., Am. Coll. Charter Life Underwriter, Order of St. Stanislaus. Office: The Citadel 171 Moultrie St Charleston SC 29409

**POOLE, SCOTT,** architect, educator; MArch, U. Tex., 1983. Registered arch., Va. Instr. Va. Tech., Blacksburg, 1986—, prof. arch., dir. Sch. Arch. and Design, 2004—. Lectr. Yale U., U. Va., Sch. arch., Aarhus, Denmark; Gilmore vis. lectr. U. Calgary, 2000; vis. prof. Royal Danish Acad. Art, Copenhagen; workshop presenter Royal Inst. Tech., Stockholm. Recipient Tchg. Excellence award, Vt. Coll. Arch. and Urban Studies, 2002; Fulbright scholar, Finland. Mem.: AIA. Office: Va Tech Sch Arch & Design 201 Cowgill Hall Blacksburg VA 24061 Business E-Mail: spoole@vt.edu.

**POOLE, THOMAS RICHARD,** endowment capital campaign director, fund raising counsel; b. Newark, July 15, 1947; s. Frank Baldwin and Edna Laura (Harper) Poole. BA, Ohio Wesleyan U., 1969; MEd, Wright State U., 1975. Cert. fund-raising exec., 1985. Assoc. program dir. Brakeley, John Price Jones Inc., Stamford, Conn., Newport Beach, Calif., 1976-79, program dir., 1979-81, v.p., 1981-91, sr. v.p., 1991—. Assoc. campaign dir. Columbia-Presbyn. Med. Ctr., N.Y.C., 1976-79; campaign dir. Manhattan Eye, Ear and Throat Hosp., N.Y.C., 1979-82; endowment/capital campaign dir., cons. Albany (N.Y.) Med. Ctr., 1984-89; endowment/capital campaign dir. Long Beach (Calif.) Meml. Med. Ctr., 1989-95; campaign dir. Samaritan Health Sys., Phoenix, 1995-2000; cons., 2001—. Author various corporate reports and feasibility studies. Mem. Nat. Soc. Fund-Raising Execs., Assocs. Ohio Wesleyan U. Avocations: reading, sailing, hiking, swimming. Fax: 949-721-1502. E-mail: brakeleynb@aol.com.

**POOLE, WILLIAM,** bank executive; b. Wilmington, Del., June 19, 1937; s. William and Louise (Hiller) P.; m. Mary Lynne Ahroon, June 26, 1960 (div. May 1997); children: William, Lester Allen, Jonathan Carl; m. Geraldine S. Stroud, July 12, 1997. AB, Swarthmore Coll., 1959, LLD (hon.), 1989; MBA, U. Chgo., 1963, PhD, 1966. Asst. prof. polit. economy Johns Hopkins U., Balt., 1963-69; professorial lectr. Am. U., Washington, 1970-71; assoc. professorial lectr. George Washington U., Washington, 1971-73; professorial lectr. Georgetown U., Washington, 1972; vis. lectr. Harvard U., Cambridge, Mass., 1973, MIT, Cambridge, 1974, 77; Bank Mees and Hope vis. prof. econs. Erasmus U. Rotterdam, 1991; prof. econs. Brown U., Providence, 1974-98, dir. ctr. for study fin. markets and insts., 1987-92, chmn. econs. dept., 1981-82, 85-86; economist Fed. Res. Sys., Washington, 1964, 69-70, sr. economist, 1970-74; pres., CEO Fed. Res. Bank St. Louis, 1998—. Adviser Fed. Res. Bank, Boston, 1973-74, cons., 1974-81; vis. economist Res. Bank of Australia, 1980-81; mem. Coun. Econ. Advisers, 1982-85; adj. scholar Cato Inst., 1985-98. Author: (book) Principles of Economics, 1991; contbr. articles to profl. jours. Dir. United Way Gr. St. Louis; bd. trustees Webster U. Mem. Am. Econ. Assn., Am. Fin. assn. (mem. nominating com. 1979), Western Econ. Assn. (mem. internat. exec. com. 1986-89, mem. nominating com. 1995). Office Phone: 314-444-8301.*

**POOLE, WILLIAM DANIEL,** writer, editor; b. Statesville, N.C., Nov. 3, 1932; s. William Oscar and Edna (Brewer) P.; m. Sandra Ball, June 14, 1980. BA, Wake Forest U., 1955. Reporter Norfolk (Va.) Virginian-Pilot, 1955-57, Washington Star, 1957-61, real estate editor, 1961-71, features editor, asst. mng. editor, 1971-81; v.p. Ins. Info. Inst., N.Y.C., 1981-91; pub. Insurance Rev. mag., N.Y.C., 1986-91. Contbr. articles to profl. jours. Mem. White House Corr. Assn., Nat. Assn. Real Estate Editors (pres. 1970-71), Newspaper Comics Coun. (chmn. 1975-77), Soc. Am. Travel Writers, Mystery Writers of Am., Ins. Mktg. Comms. Assn., Am. Assn. Sunday and Feature Editors, Amateur Comedy Club, Dutch Treat Club, The Players Club, Nat. Press Club (D.C.), Omicron Delta Kappa, Sigma Phi Epsilon. Republican. Baptist. Home: 139 E 63rd St New York NY 10021-7408

**POOLER, ROSEMARY S.,** federal judge; b. 1938; BA, Brooklyn Coll., 1959; MA, Univ. of Conn., 1961; JD, Univ. of Mich. Law Sch., 1965; cert. in Program for Sr. Mgrs. in Govt., Harvard Univ., 1978; degree (hon.), SUNY, Albany, 1986. With Crystal, Manes & Rifken, Syracuse, 1966—69, Michaels and Michaels, Syracuse, 1969—72; asst. corp. counsel Dir. of Consumer Affairs Unit, Syracuse, 1972—73; common counsel City of Syracuse Pub. Interest Rsch. Group, 1974—75; chmn., exec. dir. Consumer Protection Bd., 1975—80; commr. N.Y. State Pub. Services Commn., 1981—86; staff dir. N.Y. State Assembly, Com. on Corps., Authorities and Commns., 1987—94; judge Supreme Ct, 5th Jud. Dist., 1991—94; dist. judge U.S. Dist. Ct. (no. dist.) N.Y., Syracuse, 1994—98; cir. judge U.S. Ct. Appeals, 2nd cir., 1998—. Vis. prof. Syracuse Univ. Coll. of Law, 1987—88; v.p. legal affairs Atlantic States Legal Found., 1989—90. Mem.: Assn. of Supreme Ct. Justices of the State of N.Y. (sec. 1993—94), Women's Bar Assn. of the State of N.Y., N.Y. State Bar Assn., Onondaga County Bar Assn. Office: Federal Bldg 100 S Clinton St Syracuse NY 13261-7395 also: 40 Foley Square New York NY 10007*

**POOLEY, ERIC,** editor-in-chief; m. Pamela Newman Pooley; 2 children. Freelance reporter East Germany; with New York Mag., NYC, 1983—95, editorial asst., 1983—85, writer, 1985—87, sr. editor, polit. columnist, 1987—95; joined Time, Inc., NYC, 1995—; White House corr. to chief polit. corr. Time Mag., 1995—2001, Nation editor NYC, 2001—02, editor, European, Middle East, & African editions London, 2002—05; mng. editor Fortune Mag. (Time Inc.), NYC, 2005—. Finalist Nat. Mag. award, public interest reporting, 1996; recipient Soc. Prof. Journalists award, 1991, Gerald R. Ford Prize for excellence in reporting, 1998. Office: Fortune Mng Editor Time & Life Bldg Rockefeller Center New York NY 10020-1393*

**POON, CHRISTINE A.,** pharmaceutical company executive; b. Cin., June 23, 1952; d. James and Virginaia Poon; m. Mike Tweedle. BS in Biology, Northwestern U., 1973; MS in Biology and Biochemistry, St. Louis U., 1973; MBA in Fin., Boston U., 1982. Various mgmt. positions Bristol-Myers Squibb, 1985—2000, v.p., sr. v.p. for Can. and L.Am. pharm. ops., pres., gen. mgr. Squibb Diagnostics' Can. operation, 1994, pres. Med. Devices, 1997—98, pres. internat. medicines, 1998—2000; co. group chmn. pharm. group Johnson & Johnson, New Brunswick, NJ, 2000—01, worldwide chmn. pharms. group, 2001—03, worldwide chmn. medicines and nutritionals, 2003—, vice chmn., mem. exec. com., 2005—. Bd. dirs. Prudential Fin., Inc., 2006—; bd. adv. Healthcare Businesswomen's Assn. Bd. dirs. Fox Chase Cancer Ctr., Phila. Named Woman of Yr., Healthcare Businesswomen's Assn., 2004; named one of 50 Women to Watch, Wall St. Jour., 2005, Most Powerful Women, Forbes mag., 2005, 10 Most Powerful Women in NJ Bus., Star-Ledger, 2006. Office: Johnson & Johnson 1 Johnson and Johnson Plaza New Brunswick NJ 08901*

**POON, PETER TIN-YAU,** engineer, physicist; b. Hengyang, Hunan, China, May 31, 1944; came to U.S., 1967; s. Sam. Chak-Kwong and Lai (Yiu) P.; m. Mable Tsang, Apr. 13, 1974; children: Amy Wei-Ling, Brian Wing-Yan. *Parents, Sam Chak-Kwong and Lai (Yiu) Poon grew up in China. Father fought along side the Flying Tigers during World War II, and later became a US citizen. Wife, Mable, grew up in Hong Kong and completed her studies in Hawaii. She is an Office Manager, Human Resources Administration, California Institute of Technology. Daughter, Amy, completed her MD at University of California, San Francisco, and is a chief resident at Stanford University Medical Center. Son, Brian, graduated from University of California, Berkeley, in Electrical Engineering-Computer Science, and has acquired experience as a professional in software engineering.* BS, U. Hong Kong, 1965; MA, Calif. State U., Long Beach, 1969; PhD, U. So. Calif., 1974. Tech. mgr. and sr. engr. advanced tech. and missions Jet Propulsion Lab./Calif. Inst. Tech., Pasadena, 1974—83; advisor Space Sta. Ada Task NASA, 1984—85, task leader software mgmt. and assurance program, software mgmt. stds., 1986—88, element mgr. software info. sys.; from multimission sys. mgr. to telecom. and mission sys. mgr. Cassini and Mars missions Jet Propulsion Lab., 1988—2001, telecom. and mission sys. mgr. global surveyor Mars Odyssey mission, 2001—, telecomm. and mission sys. mgr. Voyager Interstellar mission, telecom. and mission sys. mgr. Ulysses mission, telecom. and mission sys. mgr. European Very Long Baseline Interferometry Network Project, Space Geodesy Project, 2001—. Del. various confs.; U.S. chmn., program mgmt. com., panel chair Internat. Software Engring. Stds. Symposium, U.K., Canada, Brazil and U.S., 1992—99, Canada, 1992—99, Brazil, 1992—99, England, 1992—99; mem. Internat. Orgn. for Standardization in Info. Tech. Subcom. and U.S. Tech. Adv. Group, 1995—; U.S. chmn., program mgmt. com., panel chair Internat. Software Quality Profl., Am. Soc. for Quality, 1998—; contbr. articles to profl. jours. Active JPL steering com. United Way, Pasadena, Calif., 1998—2005. Recipient Group awards NASA, 1977-2006, Recognition cert. Inventions and Contbns. Bd., award from Mars Global Surveyor and Mars Odyssey, 2002. Mem. IEEE (exec. com. software engring. stds. 1993-2000), Arcadia Music Club (pres. 1994-95), Sigma Xi, Eta Kappa Nu, Phi Kappa Phi, Athenaeum. Avocations: music, hiking, theater. Office: Jet Propulsion Lab Calif Inst Tech 4800 Oak Grove Dr Pasadena CA 91109-8099 Business E-Mail: peter.t.poon@jpl.nasa.gov

**POONS, LARRY,** artist; b. Tokyo, Oct. 1, 1937; came to U.S., 1938; Student, New Eng. Conservatory Music, 1955-57, Boston Mus. Fine Arts Sch., 1958. Mem. vis. faculty N.Y. Studio Sch., 1967. Lectr. in field. Author: The Structure of Color, 1971; exhibitions include Green Gallery, NYC, 1963—65, Art Inst. Chgo., 1966, Corcoran Gallery Art, Carnegie Inst., 1967, Leo Castelli Gallery, 1967—68, Documenta IV, Kassel, W. Germany, 1968, Whitney Mus. Am. Art, 1968, 1972, Lawrence Rubin Gallery, 1970—73, Whitney Biennial, 1973, Knoedler & Co., 1973—78, Knoedler Contemporary Art, N.Y.C., 1974—78, Andre Emmerlich Gallery, 1979—87, Albright-Knox Art Gallery, Buffalo, 1968, 1970, Pasadena Art Mus., 1969, Gallery 99, Bar Harbor Islands, Fla., 1981, Mus. Fine Arts, Boston, 1981—82, Galerie Montaigne, Paris, 1990, Helander Gallery, Palm Beach, Fla., 1990, Gallery Afinsa, Madrid, 1991, Salander-O'Reilly Galleries, N.Y.C., 1991—96, 1998, Frederick Spratt Gallery, San Jose, 1996—97, Ruth Bachofner Gallery, Santa Monica, 1996, Art Pub., Geneva, Switzerland, 1997, Claudia Carr Gallery, 1997, Larry Evan/James Willis and Frederick Spratt Gallery, San Francisco, 1997, exhibited in group shows at Matthew Mark, Pat Hearn, 1998, Sideshow 195, Bklyn., 1998, Art and the Am. Experience, Kalamazoo Inst. of the Arts, 1998, Staatliche Kunsthalle, Baden-Baden, Germany, 1999, Ameringe Howard Fine Art, N.Y.C., 2000, Bernard Jacobson, 2002, Jacobson Howard, NYC, 2003—04, Side Show Gallery, Bklyn., 2003, 2006, Studio 18 Gallery, NYC, 2004, Albright Knox, Buffalo, 2005, Represented in permanent collections Mus. Modern Art, N.Y.C., Allen Meml. Art Mus., Oberlin Coll. Cleve. Mus. Art, Hirschhorn Mus. and Sculpture Garden, Washington, Milw. Art Ctr., Solomon R. Guggenheim Mus., N.Y.C., Tate Gallery, London, Whitney Mus. Am. Art, Met. Mus. Art, Chgo. Art Inst., Denver Mus., Boston Mus. Fine Arts, Albright-Knox Art Gallery, Stedelijk Mus., Amsterdam, Woodward Found., Washington, David Mirvish Gallery, Toronto, Bernard Jacobson Gallery, London, one-man shows include Salander-O'Reilly Gallery, N.Y.C., 2001, Theo Waddington, Boca Raton, Fla., 2000, Galleria Metta, Madrid, 2000, Perrella Gallery, Johnstown, N.Y., 2000, Bernard Jacobson, 2002, 2004, Jacobson Howard Gallery, 2004—05, Side Show Gallery, Bklyn., 2005—06. Address: 831 Broadway New York NY 10003-4706

**POOR, ANDREW FORD,** music educator; b. Tucson, Ariz., Oct. 20, 1965; s. William Brown and Shirley Yvonne Poor; m. Marilyn Claire King; children: Kathryne, Addison. BA Music Edn., U. Fla., 1988; MMus Trumpet Performance, U. Cin., 1993, D Music Edn., 1999. Lic. tchr. Ga., 1999, cert. Clin. Educator Fla., 1996. Dir. bands Beaumont Mid. Sch., Kissimmee, Fla., 1988—91; instr. trumpet Cin. Conservatory Prep. Dept., 1992—95; dir. bands Haines City H.S., Fla., 1995—99; brass caption head Drum Corps Internat., Addison, Ill., 2000—02; dir. bands Osborne H.S., Marietta, Ga., 1999—2002. Music adjudicator Bands of Am., Schaumburg, Ill., 1996—2002; music cons. Bibb County Sch. Bd., Macon, Ga., 2002—02; music adjudicator Drum Corps Internat., 1994—2002. Composer: (musical work for band) United We Stand, 2002, (musical work for brass choir) Declarations, 2001, (musical work for band) To Challenge the Spartans, 2001, Faith!, 1999; author: (book) Middle School Music Education, 1999. Festival chmn. Fla. Bandmasters Assn., Tallahassee, 1995—98. Recipient Jim Ott Meml. Scholarship, Sponsors of Musical Enrichment, 1988; fellow, U. Cin., 1993-95. Mem.: Internat. Assn. of Jazz Educators, ASCD, Ga. Music Edn. Assn., Phi Mu Alpha Sinfonia (life; edn. leader for local chpt. 1984—87). Conservative-R. Methodist. Avocation: composing, golf, reading, drawing. Home: 4557 Darrowby Drive Powder Springs GA 30127 Office: Robert L Osborne HS 2451 Favor Rd Marietta GA 30060 Business E-Mail: andrewfpoor@cobbk12.org.

**POOR, HAROLD VINCENT,** electrical engineering educator; b. Columbus, Ga., Oct. 2, 1951; s. Harold Edgar and Virginia (Hardin) P.; m. Connie Irene Hazelwood, Sept. 1, 1973; children: Kristin Elizabeth, Lauren Alissa. BEE with highest honors, Auburn U., 1972; PhD, Princeton U., 1977. From asst. prof. to prof. U. Ill., Urbana, 1977—90; prof. dept. elec. engring. Princeton U., NJ, 1990—2003, George Van Ness Lothrop prof. engring., 2003—05, Michael Henry Strater univ. prof. elec. engring., 2005—, dir. Ctr. for Innovation in Engring. Edn., 2005—, dean engring. and applied scis., 2006. Acad. visitor Imperial Coll. London U., 1985, 2003; vis. prof. Newcastle (Australia) U., 1987, Stanford U., 2004; vis. scholar Harvard U., 2004; sr. vis. fellow Imperial Coll., London U., 1993; cons. in field. Author: An Introduction to Signal Detection and Estimation, 1988, 2d edit., 1994, Wireless Communication Systems: Advanced Techniques for Signal Reception, 2004, Wireless Networks: Multiuser Detection in Cross-Layer Design, 2005; co-editor: Wireless Communications: Signal Processing Perspectives, 1998; contbr. articles to profl. jours. Grantee NSF, Office Naval Rsch., Army Rsch. Office, 1978—; recipient Dir.'s Disting. Tchg. scholars award NSF, Disting. Alumnus award Tay Beta Pi 2005; John Simon Guggenheim Meml.

Found. fellow, 2002—05. Fellow IEEE (bd. dirs. 1991-92, pres. Info. Theory Soc. IEEE 1990, editor-in-chief IEEE Transaction Info. Theory, 2004—, Disting. Mem. award Control Sys. Soc. 1994, Third Millennium medal 2000, Joint Paper award with IEEE com. soc., 2001, Grad. Tchg. award 2001, EAB Major Ednl. Innovation award, 2004, James H. Mulligan Jr. Edn. medal 2005), AAAS, Acoustical Soc. Am., Am. Soc. Engring. Edn. (Terman award 1992, Centennial cert. 1993), Inst. Math. Stats., Optical Soc. Am.; mem. NAE, Am. Acad. Arts and Scis., Cosmos Club (Washington). Office: Princeton Univ Sch Engring and Applied Sci Princeton NJ 08544-0001 Office Phone: 609-258-2260.

**POOR, JANET MEAKIN, III**, landscape designer; b. Cin., Nov. 27, 1929; d. Cyrus Lee and Helen Keats (Meakin) Lee-Hofer; m. Edward King Poor III, June 23, 1951; children: Edward King IV, Thomas Meakin. Student, Stephens Coll., 1947-48, U. Cinn., 1949-51, Triton Coll., 1973-76. Pres. Janet Meakin Poor Landscape Design, Winnetka, Ill., 1975—, chmn. bd. dirs. Chgo. Botanic Garden. Author, editor: Plants That Merit Attention Vol. I: Trees, 1984, Vol. II: Shrubs; contbr. articles to profl. jours. Participant in long range planning City of Winnetka, 1978-82, archtl. and environ. bd., 1980-84, beautification commn., 1978-84, garden coun., 1978-82; adv. coun., Sec. of Agr. Nat. Arboretum, Washington; nat. adv. bd. Filoli, San Francisco; trustee Ctr. Plant Conservation at Mo. Bot. Garden, St. Louis, also mem. exec. com.; mem. adv. coun. The Garden Conservancy, 1989—, chmn. Open Days Program Garden Conservancy; trustee Winnetka Congl. Ch., 1978-80; bd. dirs. Lady Bird Johnson Wildflower Ctr., Austin, Tex., McKee Bot. Garden, Vero Beach, Fla. Recipient merit award Hadley Sch. Blind, 1972; named Vol. of Yr. Hadley Sch. Blind. Mem. Chgo. Hort. Soc. (chmn. bd. dirs. 1987-93, medal 1984, gold medal garden design, exec. com., chmn. rsch. com., women's bd., designer herb garden Farwell Gardens at Chgo. Botanic Garden, Hutchinson medal 1994), Am. Hort. Soc. (bd. dirs., Catherine H. Sweeney award 1985), Garden Club Am. (chmn. nat. plant exchange 1980-81, chmn. hort. com. 1981-83, bd. dirs., 1983-85, corresponding sec. 1985-87, Horticulture award Zone X1 1981, Creative Leadership award 1986), Fortnightly Club, Garden Club Am. (bd. dirs.), Garden Club Am. (v.p. 1987-89, medal awards chmn. 1991-93, Medal of Honor 1994). Republican. Avocations: gardening, writing, music, lecturing, horticulture research.

**POOR, PETER VARNUM**, television producer, television director; b. NYC, May 17, 1926; s. Henry Varnum and Bessie Breuer (Freedman) P.; m. Eloise Marcovicci Miller, Sept. 27, 1950; children: Candida Eustacia, Anna Maria, Graham Varnum. BA, Harvard U., 1947; postgrad., Centro Sperimentale di Cinematografia, Rome, 1951-52. Prodn. asst. New World Films, N.Y.C. 1948; editor, dir. Willard Pictures, N.Y.C., 1948-51; film editor, dir. and producer CBS News-Airpower, 1954-57, 7 Lively Arts, 1957-58, Twentieth Century, 1958-66, 21st Century, 1966-69, 60 Minutes, 1970-71, CBS Reports, 1971-75; sr. producer NBC News, Monitor, First Camera, White Paper, 1977-87; freelance producer and dir. Crow House Prodns., N.Y.C., 1988—. Instr. in TV journalism Fordham U., 1976-78; screening com. Fulbright Grants in Film, TV and Radio, 1965-67, chmn., 1967, 70; adj. assoc. history of documentary Columbia U. Grad. Sch. Journalism, 1987; adj. asst. prof. visual arts NYU, 1991-92. Producer-dir.: (TV documentary films) What's New at School, 1972, The IQ Myth, 1975, The Biggest Lump of Money in the World, 1985, The Japan They Don't Talk About, 1986, Nuclear Power in France, 1987, The Cronkite Report, 1993. Served with USAF, 1944-45. Recipient Emmy award Acad. TV Arts and Sci., 1961-62, 67, Lasker TV award Lasker Found., 1968-69, U.S. CEA Forum award, 1967, 87; hon. mention Robert Kennedy Journalism Award in TV, 1976; Fulbright scholar, 1951-52. Mem. Dirs. Guild Am. (coun. 1980-90), Film Editors Union, Writers Guild Am. East. Clubs: Phoenix S-K (Cambridge, Mass.). Avocations: bicycling, reading, photography, gardening. Home and Office: 1150 5th Ave New York NY 10128-0724 Office Phone: 212-722-3836.

**POOR, ROBERT**, wireless semiconductor company executive; PhD, MIT, 2001. Tech. and mgmt-level positions with Stanford Artificial Intelligence, Lucid, NeXT, and Opcode; co-founder, CTO Ember Corp., Boston, 2001—. Tech. editor IEEE 802.15.4 standards specification. Achievements include patents for self-organizing networks in 2000. Office: Ember Corp 343 Congress St 5th Fl Boston MA 02210 Office Phone: 617-951-0200. Office Fax: 617-951-0999.

**POOR, SUZANNE DONALDSON**, advertising and public relations executive; b. Somers Point, NJ, Oct. 6, 1933; d. James Watt and Roberta (Radford) Donaldson; m. Richard Sumner Poor, Mar. 19, 1955 (div. Sept. 1983); children: Jonathan Scott, Jeffrey Sumner, Sara Suzanne; m. Jasper Raul Gonzalez, Apr. 20, 1996. AB, Mt. Holyoke Coll., 1955; MA, Montclair State Coll., 1975; postgrad., NYU, 1977—83; MPhil, Drew U., 1994, PhD, 1998; photography student, New Sch. Social Rsch., 1979—82. Reporter, copy writer WFLB, WFLB-TV, Fayetteville, N.C., 1955-56; dir. public relations Montclair YMCA, N.J., 1965-69, Girl Scouts Greater Essex County, Montclair, 1969-74; assoc. pub. relations dept. Nat. League Nursing, N.Y.C., 1974; freelance public relations, photography Montclair, 1974-76; dir. communications Insts. Religion and Health, N.Y.C., 1976-78; ptnr., pres. Miller/Poor Assocs., Verona, N.J., 1978—. Freelance writer N.Y. Times, 1988—94; adj. prof. Seton Hall U., 1999—2000, NYU, 2005—. Pres. bd. trustee Doubletree Gallery, Montclair, 1977-79; trustee Friends NJ Network, 1986-93. Mem.: NAFE, Am. Soc. Media Photographers (editor Exposure newsletter 1993—), Exec. Women N.J. (bd. dirs. 1980—83), Am. Woman's Econ. Devel. Corp., Author's Guild, N.J. Ad Club (editor Ad Talk 1982—, bd. dirs. 1983, pres. 2001—03, named to Advt. Hall of Fame NJ 2002). Democrat. Episcopalian. Avocations: bicycling, swimming, tennis, furniture restoration. Home: 30 Plymouth St Montclair NJ 07042-2625 Office: Miller Poor Assocs 261 Bloomfield Ave Verona NJ 07044-2426 Office Phone: 973-857-5161. Personal E-mail: poorsue@aol.com.

**POORMAN, ROBERT LEWIS**, retired academic administrator; b. Germantown, Ohio, Dec. 9, 1926; s. Dale Lowell and Bernice Velma (Krick) P.; m. Lois May Romer, Dec. 26, 1949; children: Paula Beth, Janice Marie, Mark Leon, John Alex, Lisa Ann, Daniel Romer. Student, Ohio Wesleyan U., 1944-45, U. Va., 1945-46; BSEd., Ohio State U., 1948, MA, 1950; postgrad., U. So. Calif., 1951-53; Ed.D. (Kellogg fellow 1960-62, Disting. Scholar Tuition grantee 1960-62), UCLA, 1964. Tchr., counselor, adminstr., secondary schs., Colo., Mo., Ariz., 1948-57; registrar Phoenix Coll., 1957-60; intern Bakersfield Coll., 1960-63, asst. to pres., 1963-64, asso. dean instrn., 1964-65, dean students, 1965-67; founding pres. Lincoln Land C.C., 1967-88, pres. emeritus; edn. cons. MARA of Malaysia, 1983; higher edn. cons. Springfield, Ill., 1988—; interim pres. Parkland Coll., Champaign, Ill., 1989-90. Vis. assoc. prof. Fla. Internat. U., 1994-95; lectr. in field; cons. in field. Contbr. articles to profl. jours. Bd. dirs. (past) United Way of Springfield, bd. dirs. Urban League of Springfield, Good Will Industries of Springfield, Springfield (Ill.) Symphony, Catholic Youth Orgn., Springfield, Gov.'s Prayer Breakfast, Springfield Mental Health, Griffin H.S. Bd., Diocesan Sem.; mem. adv. bd. Sacred Heart Acad., Springfield Commn. on Internat. Visitors, Sister Cities Assn. With USNR, 1944—46. Recipient Midwest region CEO of Yr. Assn. C.C. Trustees, 1988, recognition Ill. C.C. Trustees Assn., 1988; named an Outstanding CEO for Ill. Cmty. Colls. U. Tex. Leadership Program, 1987; named a leader in shaping the century State Jour. Register, 1999; Phi Theta Kappa fellow, 1981; Fulbright Sr. scholar, Lithuania, 1993, Ukraine, 1996, China, 2000; Fulbright sr. specialist, Tanzania, 2003-04. Mem. Am. Assn. Cmty. and Jr. Colls., Ill. Coun. Pub. C.C. Pres. (sec. 1973-74, vice chmn. 1974-75, chmn. 1975-76), Coun. North Ctrl. Cmty. and Jr. Colls. (exec. bd. 1979-81), North Ctrl. Assn. (cons., evaluator 1984-88) Republican. Roman Catholic. Home and Office: 2324 Willemoore Ave Springfield IL 62704-4362 Office Phone: 217-546-1936. Home Fax: 217-793-6939. Personal E-mail: rpoorma9@netzero.net.

**POOS, LAWRENCE RAYMOND**, history educator; b. Eaton, Ohio, Feb. 8, 1954; s. Raymond Henry and Edna (Brower) P. AB, Harvard U., 1976; PhD, Cambridge (Eng.) U., 1984. Fellow Fitzwilliam Coll., Cambridge, 1980-83; prof. The Cath. U. of Am., Washington, 1983—; dean sch. of arts and scis. The Catholic U. of Am., Washington, 2002—. Author: A Rural Society After

the Black Death, 1991, Lower Ecclesiastical Jurisdiction in Late Medieval England, 2001, (with L. Bonfield) Select Cases in Manorial Courts 1250-1550: Property and Family Law, 1998; editor: Continuity and Change, 1985-00; contbr. articles to scholarly jours. Fellow Royal Hist. Soc. (London). Avocations: exercise, travel, computers. Home: 328 12th St SE Washington DC 20003-2206 Office: The Cath U of Am 620 Michigan Ave NE Washington DC 20064-0001 Office Phone: 202-319-5115. E-mail: poos@cua.edu.

**POOVEY, MARK NIXON**, lawyer; b. Durham, NC, Aug. 11, 1956; s. Jerry Postel and Ruth Eugenia (Royal) P.; m. Deborah Lou Best, Dec. 29, 1984. BA cum laude, Wake Forest U., 1978, JD cum laude, 1980. Bar: NC 1980, US Dist. Ct. We., Mid. and Ea. Districts NC 1980, US Ct Appeals 4th Cir. 1980. Ptnr. Martin & Poovey, Morganton, NC, 1980-83; with Womble, Carlyle, Sandridge & Rice PLLC, Winston-Salem, NC, 1983—, leader tech. and commerce practice group. Editor Wake Forest Law Rev., 1979. Mem. ABA, NC Bar Assn., Forsyth County Bar Assn. Republican. Baptist. Avocations: backpacking, photography, golf, snow skiing. Office: Womble Carlyle Sandridge & Rice PLLC PO Box 84 Winston Salem NC 27102 Office Phone: 336-721-3641. Office Fax: 336-733-8398. Business E-mail: mpoovey@wcsr.com.

**POP, IGGY (JAMES NEWELL OSTERBERG)**, composer, singer, musician; b. Muskegon, Mich., Apr. 21, 1947; s. James Newell and Louella Kristine (Christensen) Osterberg. Student, U. Mich., 1963-64. Drummer, lead singer, composer The Iguanas, 1966-67; lead singer, composer The Stooges, 1967-74; solo artist, 1975—; toured extensively with David Bowie and others. Composer music and lyrics for over 90 songs including China Girl (recorded by David Bowie); rec. artist, albums include The Stooges, 1970, Funhouse, 1972, Raw Power, 1973, Kill City, 1976, The Idiot, 1977, Lust for Life, 1977, TV Eye, 1977, New Values, 1979, Soldier, 1980, Party, 1982, Zombie Birdhouse, 1983, Blah, Blah, Blah, 1986, Instinct (Grammy nomination 1988), 1988, Brick by Brick, 1990, ArizonaDream, 1992, American Caesar, 1993, We Are Not Talking About Commercial Shit, 1995, Wake Up Suckers, 1995, Naughty Little Doggie, 1996, Nued & Rude: The Best of Iggy Pop, 1997, Avenue B, 1999; has recorded for Elektra, Columbia; RCA, solo albums for Arista, Chrysallis, A&M; guest appearances on television and prodns.; known as Godfather of Punk; appeared in films including Sid & Nancy, 1986, The Color of Money, 1986, Cry-Baby, 1990, Coffee and Cigarettes (Palme d'Or 1993), Tank Girl, 1995, Howard Stern's Private Parts, 1997, The Rugrats Movie (voice), 1998, Snow Day, 1999. Named Punk of the Yr. Creem Mag.

**POPA, MIHAELA ALINA**, research scientist; b. Iasi, Romania, Jan. 18, 1973; d. Maria and Ion Popa. MD, Med. Sch., Romania, 1997; M in Gerontological Studies, Miami U. Ohio, 2001. Intern physician, resident physician in geriat. St. Spiridon U. Hosp., Iasi, Romania, 1998—2001; rsch. asst. Miami U. of Ohio, Oxford, 2001—03, U. of South Fla., Tampa, 2003—06, rsch. assoc., 2006—. Author: (jour. article) Jour. of Aging and Health, (brochure) Insights on Wellness from CCRC Residents: A Focus Group Study. Grantee Grant, The Ohio Long-Term Care Rsch. Project, Scripps Gerontology Ctr., 2001—02, 2002—03, Sarasota Meml. Hosp.-Memory Disorder Clinic, 2004—05, Scholarship, The Honor Soc. of Phi Kappa Phi, the U. of South Fla. Chpt., 2006. Mem.: APHA, Gerontol. Soc. of Am.

**POPE, ALEXANDER H.**, retired lawyer; b. NYC, June 4, 1929; s. Clifford H. and Sarah H. (Davis) P.; m. Katherine Mackinlay, Sept. 14, 1985; children by previous marriage: Stephen C., Virginia L., Daniel M. AB with honors, U. Chgo., 1948, JD, 1952. Bar: Ill. 1952, Republic of Korea 1953, Calif. 1955, U.S. Supreme Ct. 1970. Pvt. practice, L.A., 1955-77, 87-96; assoc. David Ziskind, L.A., 1955; ptnr. Shadle, Kennedy & Pope, L.A., 1956, Fine & Pope, L.A., 1957-59, 61-77; legis. sec. to gov. State of Calif., 1959-61; county assessor Los Angeles County, L.A. 1978-86; ptnr. Mayer, Brown & Platt, L.A., 1987-88, Barash & Hill, L.A., 1989-92; of counsel Seyforth, Shaw, Fairweather & Geraldson, L.A., 1993-96; exec. dir. Calif. citizens budget commn. Ctr. Govtl. Studies, Los Angeles, 1997-2000. Nat. bd. mem. Vols. for Stevenson, 1952; vice-chmn. L.A. County Dem. Cen. Com., 1958-59; pres. Westchester Mental Health Clinic, 1963; mem. Calif. Hwy. Commn., 1966-70; mem. L.A. Bd. Airport Commrs., 1973-77, v.p., 1973-75, pres., 1975-76; trustee, sec. L.A. Theatre Ctr., 1984-89; trustee Spring St. Found., 1990-2004. With U.S. Army, 1952—54, Mo., Korea. Mem. ACLU, U. Chgo. Alumni Clubs Greater L.A. and San Francisco Bay area (pres. 1970-71), Population Connection, Ams. United, Sierra Club, Common Cause, Order of Coif, Phi Beta Kappa. Democrat. Unitarian. Home: 1155 Euclid Ave Berkeley CA 94708-1602 Personal E-mail: kandap@juno.com.

**POPE, ANDREW**, health science association administrator; Acting dir., sr. program officer Bd. on Neuroscience and Behavioral Health, Inst. of Med., 1998-99; dir. Bd. on Health Sciences Policy, Inst. of Medicine, 1999—; acting dir. Bd. on Neuroscience and Behavioral Health, Inst. of Med., 2003—. Office: Inst Medicine 500 5th St, NW Washington DC 20418-0007

**POPE, ANDREW JACKSON, JR., (JACK POPE)**, retired judge; b. Abilene, Tex., Apr. 18, 1913; s. Andrew Jackson and Ruth Adella (Taylor) Pope; m. Allene Esther Nichols, June 11, 1938; children: Andrew Jackson III, Walter Allen. BA, Abilene Christian U., 1934, LLD (hon.), 1980; LLB, U. Tex., 1937; LLD (hon.), Pepperdine U., 1981, St. Mary's U., San Antonio, 1982, Okla. Christian U., 1983. Bar: Tex. 1937. Practice law, Corpus Christi, 1937-46; judge 94th Dist. Ct., Corpus Christi, 1946-50; justice Ct. Civil Appeals, San Antonio, 1950-65, Supreme Ct. Tex., Austin, 1965-82, chief justice, 1982-85 (ret.), 1985. Author: John Berry & His Children, 1988; chmn. bd. editors Appellate Procedures in Texas, 1974; contbr. articles to profl. jours. Pres. Met. YMCA, San Antonio, 1956—57; chmn. Tex. State Law Libr. Bd., 1973—80; trustee Abilene Christian U., 1944—. With USNR, 1944—46. Recipient Silver Beaver award, Alamo Coun. Boy Scouts Am., 1961, Disting. Eagle award, 1983, Rosewood Gavel award, 1962, Outstanding Alumnus award, Abilene Christian U., 1965, St. Thomas More award, St. Mary's U., San Antonio, 1982, Greenhill Jud. award, Mcpl. Judges Assn., 1980, citation, Houston Bar Found., 1985, award, San Antonio Bar Found., 1985, Disting. Jurist award, Jefferson County Bar, 1985, Oustanding Alumnus award, U. Tex. Law Alumni Assn., 1988, George Washington Honor medal, Freedom Found., 1988, Disting. Lawyer award, Travis County, 1992. Fellow: Tex. Bar Found. (Law Rev. award 1979—81); mem.: ABA, State Bar Tex., Tex. Supreme Ct. Hist. Soc. (v.p.), Tex. State Hist. Assn., Am. Judicature Soc., Tex. Philos. Soc., Bexar County Bar Assn., Travis County Bar Assn., Nueces County Bar Assn. (pres. 1946), State Bar Tex. (pres. jud. sect. 1962, Oustanding Fifty Yrs. Lawyer award 1991), Christian Chronicle Coun. (chmn.), KP (grand chancellor 1946), Sons Rep. of Tex., Masons, Austin Knife and Fork (pres. 1980), Order of Coif, Pi Sigma Alpha, Phi Delta Phi, Alpha Chi. Mem. Ch. Of Christ. Home: 2803 Stratford Dr Austin TX 78746-4626

**POPE, C. LARRY**, food products executive; BBA, Coll. William & Mary, 1975, EMBA, 1994. Controller Smithfield Foods Inc., Smithfield, Va., 1980—99, v.p. fin., 1999—2000, CFO, 2000—01, pres., COO, 2001—. Bd. mem. Coll. William & Mary Bus. Sch. Found. Office: Smithfield Foods Inc 200 Commerce St Smithfield VA 23430-1204*

**POPE, CARL**, environmental organization administrator; BA summa cum laude, Harvard U., 1967. Vol. Peace Corps, Barhi Barhi, India, 1967-69; assoc. conservation dir. Sierra Club, San Francisco, polit. dir., conservation dir., exec. dir., 1992—. Author: Sahib: An American Misadventure in India, 1971, Hazardous Waste in America, 1981; co-author with Paul Rauber) Strategic Ignorance: Why the Bush Administration Is Recklessly Destroying a Century of Environmental Progress, 2004. Bd. dirs. Calif. League of Conservation Voters, 1986-87, exec. dir., 1973-83; bd. dirs. Pub. Voice, 1989-92, Nat. Clean Air Coalition, Calif. Common Cause, 1976-78, Pub.

Interest Econs., Inc., 1973-76; bd. dirs. Zero Population Growth, 1972-90, also polit. dir., 1970-73. Mem.: America Coming Together (treas.). Address: Sierra Club 85 2nd St Fl 2 San Francisco CA 94105-3456

**POPE, CHARLES C.**, computer hardware company executive; BS in Acctg., U. Utah; MBA, Brigham Young U. With Hewlett Packard Co., Diasonics Corp.; dir. budgets and analysis Seagate Technology, Scotts Valley, Calif., 1985, dir. fin. for Thailand ops., v.p. fin. Far East ops., v.p. fin., treas. Scotts Valley; v.p., gen. mgr. Seagate Magnetics; sr. v.p. storage products Seagate Technologies; sr. v.p. fin., CFO, 1998—. Office: Seagate Tech PO Box 66360 Scotts Valley CA 95067-0360

**POPE, DOROTHY MAE**, librarian; b. Waynesboro, Tenn., Nov. 16, 1952; d. Thomas Lee and Beulah Mae (Holt) Adams; m. Aaron N. Pope, June 22, 1974; children: Stephanie Rose, Amy Elizabeth. BS, U. N. Ala., 1974, MA, 1980; postgrad., Tenn. State U., 1986. Cert. elem. and sec. tchr., libr. sci. Tenn. Elem. tchr. Ethridge (Tenn.) Elem. Sch., 1974-75; jr. high sch. tchr. English and phys. edn. E.O. Coffman Sch., Lawrenceburg, Tenn., 1975-80; libr. Lawrence County High Sch., Lawrenceburg, 1980—. Mem. Tenn. Libr. Assn., Lawrenceburg Study Club (treas. 1985-88). Methodist. Avocations: antiques, reading, travel. Office: Lawrence County H S 1800 Springer Rd Lawrenceburg TN 38464-2344

**POPE, EDDIE**, professional soccer player; b. Greensboro, NC, Dec. 24, 1973; m. Corina Pope, 2000; 2 children. Attended, Univ. NC. Defender DC United, 1997—2002, NY NJ MetroStars, 2003—04, Real Salt Lake, 2005—. 80 caps, 8 goals U.S. Nat. Soccer team, 1996—; mem. U.S. World Cup team, 1998, 2002, 06. Named Major League Soccer Defender of the Yr., 1997; named to Major League Soccer All-Star team, 1997—2005, Major League Soccer All-Time Best XI, 2005. Mailing: US Soccer Fedn 1801 S Prairie Ave Chicago IL 60616*

**POPE, FRED WALLACE, JR.**, lawyer; b. Sanford, Fla., Feb. 9, 1941; s. Fred Wallace and Dorothy (Marshall) P.; m. Jane Laird Miller, Dec. 27, 1962 (div. Oct. 1986); children: Catherine W., Gregory W.; m. Christine R. Fredrick, Jan. 4, 1991. BA in Polit. Sci., U. Fla., 1962, JD with honors, 1969; AM in Internat. Rels., Boston U., 1965. Bar: Fla. 1970, U.S. Dist. Ct. (so., mid. and no. dists.) Fla., U.S. Supreme Ct. 1975, U.S. Ct. Appeals (11th cir.) 1983. Rsch. aide 2d Dist. Ct. Appeal, Lakeland, Fla., 1970; assoc. Trenam, Simmons, Kemker, Scharf & Barkin, Tampa, Fla., 1970-74; ptnr. Johnson, Pope, Bokor, Ruppel & Burns, P.A., Clearwater, Fla., 1974—. Dir. Citizens Bank Clearwater, 1986-98, First Nat. Bank of Fla., 1998-01. Trustee The Fla. Orch., Tampa, 1984—, chmn. bd. trustees, 1991-93; bd. dirs. Pinellas County Arts Coun., Clearwater, 1988-93. Capt. U.S. Army, 1962-67. Mem. ABA (coun. mem. sect. litigation 1983-86, editor, chief Litigation 1979-80), The Fla. Bar (gov. 1982-86), Clearwater Bar Assn. (pres. 1980-81). Office: Johnson Pope Bokor Ruppel & Burns LLP 911 Chestnut St Clearwater FL 33756-5643 E-mail: wallyp@jpfirm.com.

**POPE, HARRISON GRAHAM, JR.**, psychiatrist, educator; b. Lynn, Mass., Dec. 26, 1947; s. H. Graham and Alice (Rider) P.; m. Mary M. Quinn, June 7, 1974; children: Kimberly, Hilary, Courtney. AB summa cum laude, Harvard U., 1969, MPH, 1972, MD, 1974. Diplomate Am. Bd. Psychiatry and Neurology. Resident in psychiatry McLean Hosp., Belmont, Mass., 1974-77, clin. rsch. fellow Mailman Rsch. Ctr., 1977-79, asst. psychiatrist, 1979-84, assoc. psychiatrist, 1984-92, psychiatrist, 1992—, chief biol. psychiatry lab., 1984—; Dupont-Warren rsch. fellow Harvard Med. Sch., Boston, 1976-77. Instr. psychiatry Harvard Med. Sch., Boston, 1977-82, asst. prof., 1982-85, assoc. prof., 1985-99, prof. 1999—; staff psychiatrist Hampstead (N.H.) Hosp., 1976-80; vis. fellow The Maudsley Hosp., London, 1977, Hôpital. Ste. Anne, Paris, 1977; mem. Am. Psychiat. Assn., 1976-80, adv. com. on schizophrenic, paranoid and affective disorders, 1979, adv. com. on preparation of DSM-III-R, 1984, task force on nomenclature and stats., 1979, 84. Author: Voices from the Drug Culture, 1971, The Road East, 1974, (with J.I. Hudson) New Hope for Binge Eaters: Advances in the Understanding and Treatment of Bulimia, 1984; co-editor: The Psychobiology of Bulimia, 1987, Use of Anticonvulsants in Psychiatry: Recent Advances, 1988, Psychology Astray: Fallacies in Studies of "Repressed Memory" and Childhood Trauma, 1997; The Adonis Complex: The Secret Crisis of Male Body Obsession, 2000; mem. editl. bd. European Psychiatry, Paris, 1984—, Internat. Jour. of Eating Disorders, 1984—, Jour. Clin. Psychiatry, 1993-; contbr. numerous articles to profl. jours. Named one of Outstanding Americans under 40 Esquire mag., 1984; fellow Scottish Rite Schizophrenia Program, No. Masonic Jurisdiction, 1977-81, Charles A. King Trust, Boston, 1977-79. Avocation: weightlifting. Office: McLean Hosp 115 Mill St Belmont MA 02478-1048

**POPE, INGRID BLOOMQUIST**, sculptor, poet, painter; b. Arvika, Sweden; became U.S. citizen. d. Oscar Emanuel and Gerda (Henningson) Brostrom; m. Howard Richard Bloomquist, Feb. 14, 1941 (dec. Nov. 1982); children: Dennis Howard, Diane Cecile Connelly, Laurel Ann Shields; m. Marvin Hoyle Pope, May 9, 1985 (dec. June 1997). BA cum laude, Manhattanville Coll., 1979, MA in Humanities, 1981; MA in Religion Yale U., 1984. Exhbns. include Manhattanville Coll., Purchase, N.Y., Yale Div. Sch., Ch. of Sweden in N.Y.C., First Ch. of Round Hill; author: (books) Musings, 1994, Hosannah, Help Please, 1999, Blessings, 2003. Past bd. dirs. N.Y.C. Mission Soc., Greenwich YWCA, Greenwich Chaplaincy, Greenwich Acad. Parents' Assn., past pres; past trustee First Ch. Round Hill, Greenwich; pres. Ch. Women United, Greenwich, 1990-91. Mem. AAUW, Nat. Assn. Pen Women, English Speaking Union, Nat. Wildflower Assn., Yale Club N.Y.C., Lakeview Club (Austin, Tex.), Acad. Am. Poets, Nat. Mus. of Women in Arts, Yale Alumnae Club (Austin and Greenwich, Conn.). *I need to share my feelings deep inside be it in verse or prose or form or line. I need to say it, do it, show, or write and so creatively I try to do my best. I lift up brush and paint a scene, I struggle with a stone or mold in clay or write my verse just as I do today.*

**POPE, JACQUELINE PRIVETTE**, music educator; b. Darlington, S.C., Aug. 13, 1936; d. Leo Thomas Privette and Ophelia Mae Norris; m. George Wallace Kilpatrick (div.); children: George Ashley, Laurie Dawn, Andrew Wallace; m. James L. Pope, June 21, 1997. BA, Furman U., 1958; student, Bapt. Internat. Sem., 1960—61; studied with Powell Everhart, Atlanta, Ga., 1964—67, studied with Irene Harrower, 1972—74, studied with Claude Shirley, 1980—81; MusM in Voice Performance, Ga. State U., 1987; studied with Joseph Meeks, Kennesaw State U., 1995. Minister music and edn. Westminster (S.C.) Bapt. Ch., 1958—59; tchr. music Louisville (Ky.) City Schs., 1959—60, Jefferson County Schs., Louisville, 1961—62; substitute tchr. Houston (Tex.) City Schs., 1962—63; pvt. voice and piano tchr. Austell, Ga., 1964—; dir. music Southminster Presbyn. Ch., Marietta, Ga., 1983—91; music specialist Cobb County Pub. Schs., Marietta, 1987—98; chancel choir dir. Luth. Ch. Nativity, 1992—2005. Chmn. caring ministry Luth. Ch. Nativity, 1992—2004; dir. of music Cobb Children's Theater, 1972—82. Performer: (CD) Jacqueline P. Pope Sings for You. Mem.: Nat. Assn. Tchrs. Singing, Nat. Music Tchrs. Assn., Ga. Music Tchrs. Assn. (chmn. voice auditions 1980—81), South Cobb Arts Alliance, Alpha Delta Kappa (pres. 1999—2001, state pianist 2002—). Democrat. Lutheran. Avocations: gardening, painting. Home: 2565 Sloan St Austell GA 30106 Office Phone: 770-732-8666.

**POPE, JOHN CHARLES**, former airline company executive; b. Newark, Mar. 30, 1949; s. John Aris Coutant and Eleanor Laura (Porro) P. BA, Yale U., 1971; MBA, Harvard U., 1973. Dir. profit analysis and capital planning GM, N.Y.C., 1973-77; sr. v.p. fin., treas., CFO Am. Airlines, Inc., AMR Corp., Dallas-Fort Worth, 1977-88; exec. v.p., CFO UAL Corp., United Airlines (subs.), Chgo., 1988-91, pres., COO, 1991-94. Bd. dirs. Fed. Mogul Corp., Detroit, R.R. Donnelley & Sons, Chgo., Dollar Thrifty Automotive Group, Inc., Tulsa, CNF Inc., San Mateo, Calif., Dollar Thrifty Automotive Group,

Inc., Tulsa, Fed. Mogul Corp., Detroit, Kraft Foods, Northfield, Ill., R.R. Donnelley, Chgo.; chmn. bd. Waste Mgmt., Houston; bd. trustees, treas. Shedd Aquarium, Chgo. Office Phone: 847-735-0112.

**POPE, JOHN EDWIN,** editor, columnist; b. Athens, Ga., Apr. 11, 1928; s. Henry Louis and Rose (McAfee) P.; m. Eileen Pope; children: Shirley, Susan, Eddie, David. BA in Journalism, U. Ga., 1948. Sports editor Banner-Herald, Athens, Ga., 1943-48; So. sports editor UPI, Atlanta, 1948-50; sports writer Atlanta Constn., 1950-54; exec. sports editor Atlanta Jour., 1954-56; asst. sports editor Miami (Fla.) Herald, 1956-67, sports editor, 1967—2001. Author: Football's Greatest Coaches, 1956, Baseball's Greatest Managers, 1960, Encyclopedia of American Greyhound Racing, 1963, Ted Williams: The Golden Year, 1970, (with Norm Evans) On the Line, 1976, The Edwin Pope Collection, 1988; contbr. articles to popular mags. and Ency. Brittanica, World Book. Recipient Bill Corum Meml. award Thoroughbred Racing Assn., 1962, top sports column award Nat. Headliners Club, 1962, 79, 82, 86, Eclipse award Thoroughbred Racing Assn., 1976, 82, 86, Red Smith award AP Sports Editors, 1989; named to Internat. Churchmen's Sports Hall of Fame, 1976; recipient Knight-Ridder editl. excellence award, 1996, Nat. Sportswriters and Sportscasters Assn. Hall of Fame, 1995, Fla. Sports Hall of Fame, 1996, Bert McGrane award Coll. Football Hall of Fame, 2000, Dick McCann award NFL Pro Football Hall of Fame, 2002, A.J. Liebling award Boxing Writers Assn. Am., 2005; named Orange Bowl Hall of Hon., 2003. Mem. Profl. Football Writers Am. (pres. 1968-69), Football Writers Assn. Am., Golf Writers Am., Nat. Turf Writers, U.S. Tennis Writers. Presbyterian. Office: Miami Herald 235 Harbor Dr Key Biscayne FL 33149 Office Phone: 305-376-3403. E-mail: epope@herald.com, edwinpope@aol.com.

**POPE, JOHN MARVIN,** journalist; b. Hattiesburg, Miss., Nov. 5, 1948; s. Paul M. Jr. and Mary Lee (Scott) P.; m. Diana Pinckley, May 19, 1984. BA cum laude, U. Tex., 1970, MA, 1972. Copy editor The States-Item, New Orleans, 1972-73, reporter, 1973-80, The Times-Picayune, New Orleans, 1980-86, med.-health reporter, 1986—. Hearst Found. vis. fellow U. Tex., 2005. Co-author: American First Ladies: Their Lives and Their Legacy, 1996. Recipient Med. Writing award, La. State Med. Soc., 1990, 1998, 2005, Frank Allen award, La.-Miss. AP, 1989, Louise McFarland award for excellence in pub. health comm., La. Pub. Health Assn., 2003; fellow Knight Found., Ctrs. for Disease Control and Prevention, 2001; Knight Ctr. for Specialized Journalism fellow, 1999. Fellow Phi Beta Kappa; mem. Soc. Profl. Journalists, Nat. Assn. Sci. Writers, Investigative Reporters and Editors, Press Club New Orleans (4 1st pl. awards 1978-87, Alex Waller award 1987). Avocations: running, travel, aerobics. Office: The Times-Picayune 3800 Howard Ave New Orleans LA 70125-1429 Business E-mail: jpope@timespicayune.com.

**POPE, KENT SMITH,** lawyer; b. Harrisburg, Pa., Mar. 19, 1946; s. H. Ray and Mary Louise (Smith) P.; children: Kent S. Jr., Kirk M. BA, Denison U., 1968; JD, George Washington U., 1971. Bar: Pa. 1971, U.S. Dist. Ct. (we. dist.) Pa. 1971. Ptnr. Pope, Pope and Drayer, Clarion, Pa., 1971-97; sole practitioner Clarion, 1997—. Mem. Clarion Cmty. Choir, 1993—, Clarion Young Republicans, 1971-75; elder 1st Presbyn. Ch., Clarion, 1980s, 1996-2000 (deacon, 1970s). Mem. Pa. Bar Assn. (zone gov. 1996-99, ho. del. 1974-88, 99—), Clarion County Bar Assn. (pres. 1976-77), Rotary Internat. (bd. dirs., pres. 2000-01). Republican. Presbyterian. Avocations: travel, skiing, bridge. Office: 10 Grant St Ste A Clarion PA 16214-1023 Office Phone: 814-227-2100.

**POPE, KERIG RODGERS,** retired magazine executive; b. Waukesha, Wis., Sept. 30, 1935; s. Kerig James Pope and Mildred (Offerman) Troemel; m. Claudia T. Koralewski, Nov. 1961 (div. 1975); children— Kerig William, Giles Thomas; m. Beth Leslie Kasik, May 24, 1980; children: Kolin Jared, Zoe Alissa. Grad., Art Inst. Chgo., 1958. Designer Jack Denst Wallpaper Designs, Chgo., 1958-60; designer Continental Casualty Ins. Co., Chgo., 1960-62, Leo Burnett Advt. Agy., Chgo., 1962-63; art dir. Mercury Records Corp., Chgo., 1963-66; mng. art dir. Playboy mag., Chgo., 1966— Exhibited in group shows Whitney Mus. Am. Art, N.Y.C., 1969, Mus. Contemporary Art, Chgo., 1972, Bienal de Sao Paulo, Brazil, 1973, Museo de Arte Moderno, Mexico City, 1974, Nat. Collection Fine Arts, Washington, 1979, Moderno, Mexico City, 1974, Mus. Contemporary Art, Chgo., 1996; represented in permanent collections Nat. Collection Fine Arts, Washington, Mus. Contemporary Art, Chgo., Smart Mus., U. Chgo. Recipient silver medal Communigraphics, N.Y.C., 1971, gold medal, 1971, 72; award of excellence Soc. Publ. Designers, 1979, 4 awards of excellence Design Ann., 1984, Silver medal Illustrators 29, 1986, Silver medal Soc. of Illustrators, 1988. Mem.: Soc. Publ. Arts (3 Silver awards 1987), Soc. Typog. Arts (Silver medal 1998, Gold medal 1999, 2001), Art Dirs. Club N.Y., Soc. Illustrators (Gold medal 1981, 1984, Silver medal 1988, Gold medal 1991, Silver medal 1998, Gold medal 1999), Arts (Chgo.), Arts Club (Chgo.). Office: Playboy Enterprises Inc 680 N Lake Shore Dr Fl 15 Chicago IL 60611-4455

**POPE, LEAVITT JOSEPH,** broadcast company executive; b. Boston, Apr. 2, 1924; s. Joseph and Charlotte (Leavitt) P.; m. Martha Pascale, Nov. 20, 1948; children— Joseph, Daniel, Patricia, Elizabeth, Nancy, Maria, Joan, Christopher, Virginia, Matthew, Charles. BS, Mass. Inst. Tech., 1947. Adminstrv. asst. N.Y. Daily News, N.Y.C., 1947-51; asst. to gen. mgr. Sta. WPIX-TV, N.Y.C., 1951-56, v.p. ops., 1956-72, Sta. WPIX-FM, N.Y.C., 1956-72; sec. WPIX, Inc., N.Y.C., 1958-75, exec. v.p., 1972-75, pres., chief exec. officer, 1975-92, also dir. Sec., exec. v.p. Conn. Broadcasting Co., Bridgeport, 1967-75, pres., chief exec. officer, dir., 1975-87; dir. N.Y. Daily News, 1975-78, Tribune Co., 1978-81; founder Ind. Network News, 1978-89; chair N.Y.C. TV all industry com., advanced TV sys. com. HDTV; chair copyright com. NAB, 1985—. Mem. N.Y. State Regents Ednl. TV Adv. Council, 1958; bd. govs. Daytop Village, 1972—; trustee Catholic Communications Found.; St. Thomas Aquinas Coll., 1968-75; Cardinal Cooke Hosp., 1979—, vice chair, 1998—, Catholic Healthcare Network, 2001-; dir. Archdiocese N.Y. Instructional TV com. 1976—; trustee St. Patrick's Cathedral, N.Y.C., 1992—. Served with Signal Corps U.S. Army, 1942-46. Mem. Assn. Ind. TV Stats. (pres. 1976-78, bd. dirs.), ASME, Internat. Radio and TV Soc., Nat. Assn. Broadcasters (dir. 1982-86), N.Y. State Broadcasters (pres. 1976-78), Sigma Nu, Knight of Malta. Clubs: Univ. (N.Y.C.); Riverbend (Tequesta, Fla.). Home: 173 Dorchester Rd Scarsdale NY 10583-6052

**POPE, LISTON, JR.,** writer, journalist; b. New Haven, Dec. 26, 1943; s. Liston and Bennie (Purvis) P. BA in English, Duke U., 1965; postgrad., Sorbonne, Paris, 1965-70, U. Vienna, 1966-67. Probation officer Bronx (N.Y.) Supreme Ct., 1972-73; freelance journalist N.Y.C., 1972—; war correspondent World Coun. of Chs., Beirut, 1978-79, Nat. Cath. News Svc., Managua, Nicaragua, 1983-84; radio prodr. Pacifica Radio, N.Y.C., 1983-90; critic art/lit. Pacifica News, N.Y.C., 1984-89; sr. editor N.A. Gilbert & Sons Publs., N.Y.C., 1993—; pub. Mantis Press, N.Y.C., 1995—. Press agent Liston Pope & Assocs., N.Y.C., 1984-90; media dir. Casa Nicaragua, NYC, 1983—90. Author: Redemption: A Novel of War in Lebanon, 1994, Living Like the Saints: A Novel of Nicaragua, 1996, Floriane: Stages of Love, 1998, (plays) Somoza's Niece, 1987, Oratorio, 1987, Canto Epico, 1989, The Van Gogh Testament, 2005, (trilogy) Newell Gilbert's Boyhood: American Wine, Journey on the Needing, Infernal Innocence, 2006. Vis., supporting vol. Meml. Sloan-Kettering, 1972-78; recreation dir., tutor Cath. Guardian Group Home, 1975-90; life skills tchr. Harlem I Men's Shelter, N.Y.C., 1991-93; AIDS support worker St. Vincent's Supportive Care, Bellevue Visitation Program, Bellevue Pediatrics. Recipient Narrative Poetry award, NY Poetry Soc., 1972, Grand prize, Am. Poetry Assn., 1986. Home and Office: 126 W 73rd St Apt 11A New York NY 10023-3031 Office Phone: 212-874-6017. E-mail: liston4949@yahoo.com.

**POPE, MARCIA L.,** lawyer; b. St. Petersburg, Fla., May 12, 1961; AB, Harvard Univ., 1983; JD, Univ. Va., 1986. Bar: Calif. 1986. Assoc. to ptnr., Employment & Labor practice Pillsbury Winthrop Shaw Pittman, San Francisco, 1986—, employment counsel. Office: Pillsbury Winthrop Shaw Pittman 50 Fremont St San Francisco CA 94105 Office Phone: 415-983-1200. Business E-mail: marcia.pope@pillsburylaw.com.

**POPE, MARK ANDREW,** lawyer, academic administrator; b. Munster, Ind., May 22, 1952; s. Thomas A. and Eleanor E. (Miklos) P.; m. Julia Risk Pope, June 15, 1974; children: Brent Andrew, Bradley James. BA, Purdue U., 1974; JD cum laude, Ind. U., 1977. Bar: Ind. 1977, U.S. Dist. Ct. (so. dist.) Ind. 1977, U.S. Ct. Appeals (7th cir.) 1984. Assoc. Johnson & Weaver, Indpls., 1977-79, Rocap, Rocap, Reese & Young, Indpls., 1980-82, Dutton & Overman, Indpls., 1982-88, ptnr., 1988-89; asst. gen. counsel Lincoln Nat. Corp., Fort Wayne, Ind., 1989-91, sr. counsel, 1991-95, v.p. govt. rels., 1995-2001; dir. athletics Ind. U.-Purdue U., Ft. Wayne, 2001—. Bd. dirs. Ft. Wayne Bicentennial Coun.; pres., bd. dirs. ARCH, Inc., 1994-97. Bd. editors, devel. editor Ind. U. Law Rev., 1976-77 Mem. pres.'s coun. Purdue U., 1977—; applied econs. coun. Jr. Achievement, 1989—95; bd. dirs. Jr. Achievement of No. Ind., 1992—94; grad. Leadership Ft. Wayne, 1992; adv. coun. Ind. U. Bus. Sch., Purdue U., Ft. Wayne, 2000—02; trustee Allen County War Meml. Coliseum, 2002—; mem. parish coun. St. Elizabeth Ann Seton Ch., 1993—96, pres., 1993—95; bd. mem. Bishop Luers H.S., 2000—03, pres., 2002—03. Named Disting. Hoosier, Gov. of Ind., 1974. Fellow Ind. Bar Found., Indpls. Bar Found. (disting.); mem. ABA (dist. rep. young lawyers divsn. 1981-83, dir. 1983-84, liaison council. 1985-86, 87-88, exec. coun. 1981-88, cabinet 1982-88, gen. practice sect. coun. mem. 1986—; membership chmn. 1987-89, chmn. career and family com. 1990-92, dir. 1991-93), Indpls. Bar Assn. (v.p. 1983, chmn. young lawyers divsn. 1981), 500 Festival Assocs. (vice-chmn. of 500 festival parade 1985-89), Orchard Ridge Country Club (bd. dirs. 1995-2001, sec. 1996-97, pres. 1999-2001). Avocations: tennis, golf, running. Office: Ind U-Purdue U at Fort Wayne Gates Sports Ctr 2101 E Coliseum Blvd Fort Wayne IN 46805-1499 Office Phone: 260-481-5443. Business E-mail: popem@ipfw.edu.

**POPE, MARTIN,** chemist, educator; b. NYC, Aug. 22, 1918; s. Philip and Anna (Frimet) P.; m. Lillie Bellin, June 27, 1946; children: Miriam, Deborah Judith. BS in Chemistry, CCNY, 1939; PhD in Phys. Chemistry, Poly. Inst. Bklyn., 1950. Scientist Radiation Lab. Bklyn. Navy Yard, 1941—42; rsch. scientist Balco Rsch. Lab., Newark, 1946—47, tech. dir., 1951-56; sr. rsch. scientist NYU Radiation and Solid State Physics Lab., NYC, 1956-60, rsch. assoc. prof., 1960-65; assoc. prof. chemistry NYU, 1965—68, prof., 1968—88, prof. emeritus phys. chemistry, 1988—. Co-dir. NYU Radiation and Solid State Physics Lab., 1968—83, dir., 1983—88; vis. prof. U. Alexandria, Egypt, 1981. Contbr. articles to sci. jours., chapters to books; mem. editl. bd.: Molecular Crystals, 1965—97; co-author: Electronic Processes In Organic Crystals, 1982, Electronic Processes in Organic Crystals and Polymers, 1999. Pres. Ezra Jack Keats Found., NYC, 1983—. Pvt. to 1st lt. USAAF, 1942—45, WWII. Recipient Townsend Harris medalist, CUNY, 1996, Davy medal, Royal Soc., UK, 2006; grantee, Nat. Chem. Energy, 1958—88, NSF, 1960—75; honored at internat. conf., U. Rochester, 1998. Fellow: AAAS, NY Acad. Scis., Am. Phys. Soc.; mem: Am. Chem. Soc., Sigma Xi. Achievements include patents in field. Avocation: mineralogy. Office: Dept Chemistry NYU New York NY 10003 E-mail: martin.pope@nyu.edu.*

**POPE, ROBERT DEAN,** lawyer; b. Memphis, Mar. 10, 1945; s. Ben Duncan and Phyllis (Drenner) P.; m. Elizabeth Dante Cohen, June 26, 1971; 1 child, Justin Nicholas Nathanson. AB, Princeton U., 1967; Diploma in Hist. Studies, Cambridge U., 1971; JD, Yale U., 1972, PhD, 1976. Bar: Va. 1974, D.C. 1980. Assoc. Hunton & Williams, Richmond, Va., 1974-80, ptnr., 1980—. Mem. steering com. Bond Attys. Workshop, 1994—98; lectr. in law U. Va. Law Sch., 2000—02; advisor, com. on govtl. debt and fiscal policy Govt. Fin. Officers Assn., 1993—99; adj. prof. law William & Mary Law Sch., 2004—. Author: Making Good Disclosure: The Role and Responsibilities of State and Local Officials Under the Federal Securities Laws, 2001; co-author: Disclosure Roles of Counsel in State and Local Government Securities Offerings, 2d edit., 1994. Mem. adv. com. Va. Sec. of Health and Human Svcs. on Continuing Care Legislation, 1992-94; mem. Anthony Commn. on Pub. Fin.; adv. coun. dept. history Princeton U., 1987-91; mem. Mcpl. Securities Rulemaking Bd., 1996-99, vice chmn. 1998-99. Mem.: Nat. Council Cmty. Justice, Nat. Conf. Cmty. Justice (bd. dirs. Richmond), Yale Law Sch. Assn. (exec. com. 1985—88), Va. Bar Assn. (chmn. legal problems of elderly 1982—88), Am. Coll. Bond Counsel (bd. dir. 2003—), Am. Acad. Hosp. Attys., Nat. Assn. Bond Lawyers (bd. dirs. 1982—89, treas. 1984—85, sec. 1985—86, pres. 1987—88, coordinating coun. 2005—, Bernard P. Friel medal for contbns. to pub.fin. 1994), Bond Club Va. (bd. dirs. 1990—98, v.p. 1993—94, pres. 1994—95), Phi Beta Kappa. Republican. Episcopalian. Avocations: history, golf, music, book reviews. Office: Hunton & Williams 951 E Byrd Richmond VA 23219-4074 Home: 9704 Old Country Trace Richmond VA 23238 Office Phone: 804-788-8438. Business E-mail: dpope@hunton.com.

**POPE, ROBERT E(UGENE),** fraternal organization administrator; b. Wellington, Kans., Sept. 10, 1931; s. Samuel E. and Opal Irene (Davis) P. BSChemE with honors, U. Kans., 1952, MS, 1958. Registered profl. engr., Kans. Asst. instr. U. Kans., Lawrence, 1952-56; lab. technician Monsanto Co., St. Louis, 1952; project engr. Mallinckrodt, Inc., St. Louis, 1953-59; traveling sec. Theta Tau, St. Louis, 1959-62, exec. sec., 1963-84, exec. dir., 1984-96, exec. dir. emeritus, 1996—. Carillonneur, Grace United Meth. Ch., St. Louis, 1985—, chmn. adminstrv. coun., 1991-95, trustee, 1997-99; lay mem. trustee Mo. Conf., United Meth. Ch., 2000—; trustee Theta Tau Ednl. Found., 1997-2002; bd. dirs. St. Louis Cmty. Tower Bells, 2000—. Mem. Am. Soc. Assn. Execs. (life), Am. Soc. Engring. Edn., Profl. Fraternity Execs. Assn. (charter), Profl. Fraternity Assn. (exec. sec. 1977-86, Fraternity Svc. award 1995), Theta Tau (Alumni Hall of Fame 1988, mem. bd. editors The Gear of Theta Tau 1993—2001, editor-in-chief 1996—2001), Tau Beta Pi, Phi Lambda Upsilon, Omicron Delta Kappa. Democrat. United Methodist. Avocations: physical fitness, sports, photography, stamp collecting/philately, writing. Home: 13 Sona Ln Saint Louis MO 63141-7742

**POPE, THADDEUS MASON,** law educator; b. Pitts., Aug. 2, 1969; s. Lawrence Sheldon and Reina Gloria Pope; m. Linda Louise Bosse, May 2, 1998; 1 child, Phineas Lawrence. JD, MA, Georgetown U., 1997, PhD 2003. Bar: Calif. 1999. Jud. law clk. U.S. Ct. Appeals, (7th cir.), Milw., 1999—2000; atty. Arnold & Porter LLP, L.A., 2000—05; prof. law U. Memphis, 2005—. Contbr. articles to profl. jours. Pro bono atty. medicaid benefits City of L.A., 2003—05. Recipient Wiley W. Manuel award, State Bar Calif., 2004, Hon. Benjamin Aranda III Outstanding Pub. Svc. award, L.A. County Bar Assn., 2005. Mem.: Kennedy Inst. Ethics, APHA, Am. Soc. Law, Medicine & Ethics. Office: University of Memphis School of Law 3715 Central Avenue Memphis TN 38152 Office Phone: 901-678-1623. Office Fax: 901-202-7549. Business E-mail: tmpope@memphis.edu.

**POPE, W. ALAN,** psychology professor, psychotherapist; b. Abilene, Tex., Aug. 7, 1958; s. Walter Steele and Ida Vickery Pope. PhD, Duquesne U., 2000. Computer programmer Household Fin. Corp., Prospect Heights, Ill., 1980—83; systems analyst Time-Life Inc., Chgo., 1983—84, Wash. Nat. Ins. Corp., Evanston, Ill., 1984—86; asst. prof. U. West Ga., Carrollton, 2001—; psychotherapist Ielase Inst., Pitts., 1993—96. Cognitive sci. rsch. asst. U. Del., 1988—91; cons. editor Janus Head: Jour. of Interdisciplinary Studies in Lit., Continental Philosophy, and the Arts, Pitts., 1999—; tchg. fellow Duquesne U., 1996—97. Author: From Child to Elder: Personal Transformation in Becoming an Orphan at Midlife, 2006; contbr. articles to profl. publs. Organizer Padmasambhava Buddhist Ctr., Carrollton, Ga., 2004—. Grant to study Japanese culture, Asian Studies Devel. Program, NEH, 2002. Mem.: APA, Soc. for Values in Higher Edn., Inst. Noetic Scis., Assn. Asian Studies, Internat. Network on Personal Meaning, Assn. Humanistic Psychology. Achievements include research in psychospiritual transformation. Home: 527 Roy North Rd Carrollton GA 30117 Office: U West Ga Dept Psychology Carrollton GA 30118 Office Phone: 678-839-0601. Personal E-mail: wapope@hotmail.edu. Business E-mail: apope@westga.edu.

**POPENOE, HUGH LLYWELYN,** soils educator; b. Tela, Honduras, Aug. 28, 1929; s. Frederick Wilson and Dorothy (Hughes) P. BS, U. Calif. Davis, 1951; PhD, U. Fla., 1960. Mem. faculty U. Fla., Gainesville, 1960—, dir. ctr. tropical agr., 1965—2002, dir. internat. programs, 1966—92, dir. Fla. Sea Grant Coll., 1971—81. Bd. dirs. Escuela Agricola Panamericana, Zamorano, Honduras, Orgn. Tropical Studies. Contbr. numerous articles to profl. jours. Chari Assn. U.S. Univ. Dirs. Internat. Agrl. Programs, 1969-70, Joint Rsch. Com. Bd. Internat. Food and Agrl. Devel., 1977-82, Joint Com. Agrl. Rsch. and Devel., 1982-86; chair numerous reports Bd. Sci. and Tech. in Devel., 1979-84; trustee Internat. Found. for Sci., Stockholm, 1984-87; mem. sci. liaison officer Internat. Inst. for Tropical Agr., Nigeria, 1983-88; mem. adv. com. internat. programs NSF, 1985-87; bd. dirs. League for Internat. Food Edn., 1976-87. With U.S. Army, 1952-54. Recipient Sci. Pioneer prize Egyptian Vet. Assn. for Buffalo Devel., 1985. Fellow AAAS, Am. Soc. Agronomy, Am. Geog. Soc., Internat. Soil Sci. Soc., Am. Water Buffalo Assn. (pres. 1988—), Cosmos Club. Office: U Fla PO Box 110286 Gainesville FL 32611-0286 Office Phone: 352-392-2643. Business E-mail: hlp@ufl.edu.

**POPEO, R. ROBERT,** lawyer; b. Boston, Apr. 9, 1938; AB, Providence U., 1958; JD, Boston Coll., 1961. Bar: Mass. 1961, DC 1972. Law clerk US Dist. Ct. Mass., 1961-63; instr. Sch. Law Boston U., 1964-67; U.S Commr., 1967-71; asst. atty. gen. Commonwealth of Mass., 1970-74; chmn., pres. Mintz, Levin, Cohn, Ferris, Glovsky and Popeo, PC, Boston, 1989—, mem. policy com. Editor: Boston Coll. Indsl. and Comml. Law Rev., 1960—61; student editor Ann. Survey Mass. Law, 1960—61. Trustee Boston Coll.; mem. bd. overseers Boston Coll. Law Sch., Northeastern U.; mem. bd. advisors Boston Coll. Carroll Sch. Mgmt., Birmingham Bus. Sch.; mem. exec. comm. Mass. Bus. Round Table. Named one of top 100 Lawyers in Am., Nat. Law Jour. Fellow: Am. Coll. Trial Lawyers; mem.: ABA, Mass. Bar Assn., DC Bar Assn., Boston Bar Assn., Practising Law Inst. Office: Mintz Levin Cohn Ferris Glovsky & Popeo PC One Financial Center Boston MA 02111 Office Phone: 617-348-1716. Office Fax: 617-542-2241.

**POPESCU, DANIEL,** interior designer; b. Bucharest, Romania, July 22, 1943; arrived in U.S., 98; s. Eugen and Lucia Popescu; m. Luminita Serbanescu, May 7, 1975 (div. Aug. 1995); 1 child, Dinu; m. Nina Bouzanis, July 22, 2000; 1 child, Jason Bouzanis. Diploma, Archtl. Coll., Bucharest, 1972. Rsch. and design team leader R.D.I.A.D., Bucharest, 1970—82; pres. Jetset Design Interior Inc., Toronto, Ont., Canada, 1984—; chief designer, cons. Madison Design Group, Troy, Mich., 1998—; sr. design cons. Richard M. Tumis Inc., Chevy Chase, Md., 1998—. Cons., chief designer Poggempohl, Toronto, 1996—98; cons. Artcraft Kitchen, Niagara Falls, Ont., 1994—, Mazar Keer Arch., Detroit, 1998—. Over 200 comml. and residential projects in Romania, Can. and U.S. Cpl. Romanian armed forces, 1966—68. Orthodox. Avocations: art, classical music, travel, skiing, dancing. Home: 1501 Crystal Dr Apt 1029 Arlington VA 22202 Office: Richard M Tunis Inc 7032 Wisconsin Ave Bethesda MD 20815 E-mail: ninapopescu@aol.com.

**POPESCU, MIHAELA,** elementary school educator, researcher; d. Constantin and Aurica Popescu; 1 child, Ileana Alexandra Klein. BS in Math., U. Bucharest, Romania, 1991, BS in Biology, 1997; MS, U. Fla., 2004, PhD, 2005. Mathematician Nuclear Energy Reactor Inst., Bucharest, 1991—93; hs math. tchr. Bucharest, 1994; mid. sch. math. tchr. Buzau, 1997—99; rsch. asst. U. Fla., Gainesville, 1999—2005; post doc. Sintef, Tondheim, Norway, 2005—06. Cons. U. Bucharest, 1994—97. Sci. fair judge Sci. Bd. Alachua County, Gainesville, Fla., 1999, 2001. Mem.: AIAA. Avocations: music, mountain climbing. Office: Univ Fla PO Box 116250 Gainesville FL 32611

**POPHAM, TODD GORDON,** insurance company executive; b. Mpls., Jan. 18, 1957; s. Wayne Gordon and Joan (Nelson) P.; m. Alicia Ellen Sordyl, Nov. 23, 1985; children: Chelsea Nicole, Austin Gordon. BS in Econs., Gustavus Adolphus Coll., 1979. CPCU, CLU. Legis. intern Senator David Durenburger, Washington, 1979; underwriter, supr. State Farm Ins., St. Paul, 1979-83, edn. tng. analyst Bloomington, Ill., 1983-87, asst. pers. mgr. Monroe, La., 1987-88, regional pers. mgr. Columbia, Mo., 1988-90, Malta, N.Y., 1990—. Loaned exec. United Way, Monroe, 1987; chmn. Ptnrs. in Edn., Columbia, 1988. Mem. CLU Soc. (bd. dirs. 1989-90), CPCU Soc. (sec. 1987), Capital Dist. Pers. Assn., Columbia C. of C., Saratoga C. of C., Rotary, Toastmasters (pres. Bloomington area gov. 1986, Toastmaster of Yr. 1986). Republican. Roman Catholic. Avocations: politics, tennis, golf, travel, reading. Office: State Farm Ins 100 Saratoga Village Blvd PO Box 62 Ballston Spa NY 12020-0062

**POPIK, WILLIAM C,** insurance company executive; BA in psychology, Yale U.; MD, Columbia U. Coll. of Physicians and Surgeons. Bd. cert. family physician. Physician, family and emergency medicine Calif.; various positions CIGNA Healthcare, 1996; sr. v.p., chief med. officer Health Net HMO Calif.; v.p., med. affairs QualMed Plan for Health, 1990—94; sr. v.p., chief med. officer Aetna Inc. Mem.: Am. Coll. Physician Executives. Office: Aetna Inc 151 Farmington Ave Hartford CT 06156

**POPKIN, ALICE BRANDEIS,** lawyer; b. NYC; d. Jacob H. and Susan Brandeis Gilbert; m. Jordan J. Popkin; children: Susan Cahn, Anne, Louisa. AB magna cum laude, Radcliffe Coll., 1949; JD, Yale U., 1953. Bar: NY 1953, US Dist. Ct. (so. dist.) NY 1956, US Ct. Appeals (2nd cir.) 1959, US Supreme Ct. 1962, DC 1972, Mass. 1987. Assoc. Cahill Gordon & Reindel, 1953—61; dir. internat. programs Peace Corps, 1961—63; project co-dir. Georgetown Inst. Criminal Law and Procedure, 1967—72; spl. counsel Senate Sub-Com. to Investigate Juvenile Delinquency, 1972—74; atty., prof. Antioch Sch. Law, 1974—77; assoc. administr. EPA, 1977—79; pvt. practice cons. on internat. environ. issues, 1979—81; practicing atty., 1981—87; of counsel Toabe and Riley, Chatham, Mass., 1987—. Fellow Brandeis U.; trustee Radcliffe Coll.; active Chatham Harbor Mgmt. Com.; trustee Eldredge Pub. Libr., 1994—, pres. bd. trustees, 2005. Mem. ABA, Mass. Bar Assn., Barnstable County Bar Assn., Estate Planning Coun. Cape Cod, Planned Giving Coun. Cape Cod. Office: Toabe & Riley Box 707 154 Crowell Rd Chatham MA 02633-2800 Personal E-mail: adee.abp@verizon.net.

**POPKIN, JOEL,** economist, consultant; b. Trenton, NJ, July 6, 1932; s. Nathaniel Robert and Betty (Finkle) Popkin; m. Elizabeth Rose Alk, Oct. 17, 1968; children: Neil Robert, Sara Rachel. BS in Econs., U. Pa., 1954, PhD, 1965. Asst. economist Allied Chem. Co., NYC, 1957—59; lectr., rschr. U. Pa., Phila., Northwestern U., Evanston, Ill., George Washington U., Washington, 1960—64; econometrician Dept. Commerce, Washington, 1964—66; divsn. chief, asst. commr. US Bur. Labor Stats., Washington, 1966—73; sr. staff economist Pres.'s Coun. Econ. Advisors, Washington, 1973—74; dir., mem. rsch. staff Nat. Bur. Econ. Rsch., Washington, 1974—78; pres. Joel Popkin and Co., Washington, 1978—. Mem. visitors econs. dept. U. Pa., 1987—2001. Lt. USAR, 1955—57. Recipient Julius Shiskin award for contbns. to econ. stats., 1994. Fellow: Am. Statis. Assn.; mem.: Internat. Assn. Rsch. on Income and Wealth, Nat. Assn. Bus. Economists, Conf. Bus. Economists (chmn. 1989), Am. Econ. Assn., Cosmos Club, Nat. Economists Club (chmn. bd., pres. 1978—80). Home: 6706 Loring Ct Bethesda MD 20817-3148 Office: 2001 L St NW Washington DC 20036-4970 Office Phone: 202-466-9063.

**POPLAWSKA, ANNA,** artist, educator, art critic; Tchr. in field. Contbr. to monthly art columns in a the following publs.: Footlights Playbill, YogaChicago, Wednesday Jour. of Oak Park. l. freelancer Chicago Artist's News. Mem.: Chgo. Art Critics Assn. Address: 1017 S Harlem Forest Park IL 60130 E-mail: poplawska@comcast.net.

**POPLER, KENNETH,** behavioral health services administrator, psychologist; BA in Psychology, CUNY, 1967; MA in Psychology, New Sch. Social Rsch., N.Y.C., 1969, PhD in Psychology, 1974; MBA, Wagner Coll., 1994. Diplomate Am. Bd. Profl. Psychology. Case worker N.Y.C. Dept. Social Svcs., 1967-70; intern Bklyn. Psychiat. Ctrs., 1970-72; sch. psychologist N.Y.C. Bd. Edn., 1972-73; psychologist Mid Nassau Cmty. Guidance Ctr., Hicksville, NY, 1973-77; dir. St. Mary Cmty. Mental Health Ctr., Hoboken, NJ, 1978-81; pres., CEO S.I. Mental Health Soc., Inc., 1981—. Asst. rsch. scientist N.Y. State Psychiat. Inst., N.Y.C., 1971; psychometrician L.I. Hillside Jewish Med. Ctr., Queens, NY, 1972—73; vol. rsch. Manhattan Sch. Seriously Disturbed Children, N.Y.C., 1972—73; instr. CUNY, Bklyn., 1972—73; sr. psychologist dir. psychol. svcs. HHC Gouverneur Hosp.,

N.Y.C., 1973—78; pvt. practice, N.Y.C., 1976—85; asst. clin. prof. psychiatry Mt. Sinai Med. Sch., N.Y.C., 1978—95; apptg. by mayor N.Y.C. Bd. Health, 2003—. Apptd. by mayor N.Y.C. Cmty. Svcs. Bd., 1984—, chmn., 2003—; pres. Coalition Voluntary Mental Health Agys., Inc., 1991—94; sec. Head Start Sponsoring Bd. Coun., N.Y.C., 1985—92; chmn. S.I. United Way Execs. Com., 1985, Mental Health Coun., S.I., 1987—89. Mem.: Rotary. Office: SI Mental Health Soc Inc 669 Castleton Ave Staten Island NY 10301-2099

**POPNIK, MARLENE ALITA,** retired school librarian; b. Paterson, N.J., Aug. 31, 1942; d. Clarence L. and Katherine M. Borst; m. Joseph R. Popnik, Aug. 5, 1972. BS, SUNY, Geneseo, 1964. With Fonda-Fultonville Ctrl. Sch., 1964-65; libr. Spencerport (N.Y.) Ctrl. Sch., 1965-68, 69-72, U.S. Dependant Sch., Wethersfield, Eng., 1968-69, Susquehanna Twp. Schs., Harrisburg, Pa., 1973-2000; retired, 2000. Mem. ALA, Pa. Sch. Librs. Assn., Delta Kappa Gamma (Beta Theta chpt. pres.). Home: 6349 Mifflin Ave Harrisburg PA 17111-4266 E-mail: jomarlene@aol.com.

**POPOFF, EDNA SPIELER,** psychologist, consultant; d. Isidor and Rose Spieler; m. William Popoff, June 1, 1946; children: Joshua, Ross, Leslie. BA, Hunter Coll., 1941—45; MA, Columbia U., 1945—47; post grad., Queens Coll., 1958—60; degree, St. John's U., 1960—63. Spl. edn. tchr. NYC Bd. Edn., 1960—65; sch. psychologist Bur. Child Guidance, NYC 1965—87; guidance cons. Guidance Org. Dist. Office, NYC, 1987—97. Cons. AABB, Queens, NY, 1965—80. Mem.: Am. Psychol. Assn.

**POPOFSKY, MARK S.,** lawyer; s. M. Laurence and Linda Seltzer Popofsky; m. Suzanne Yelen. BA, Brown U., Providence, 1990; JD, Harvard U., Cambridge, Mass., 1993. Bar: Calif. 1994, DC 1999. Law clk., to Judge D.W. Nelson US Ct. Appeals (9th cir.), Pasadena, Calif., 1993—94; atty. antitrust divsn. US Dept. Justice, 1994—97, sr. counsel, antitrust divsn., 1998—99; ptnr. Kaye Scholer LLP, 1999—. Office: Kaye Scholer LLP 901 15th St NW Washington DC 20005 Office Phone: 202-682-3500.

**POPOFSKY, MELVIN LAURENCE,** lawyer; b. Oskaloosa, Iowa, Feb. 16, 1936; s. Samuel and Fannye Charlotte (Rosenthal) P.; m. Linda Jane Seltzer, Nov. 25, 1962; children: Mark Samuel, Kaye Sylvia. BA in History summa cum laude, U. Iowa, 1958; BA in Jurisprudence (first class honors), Oxford U., Eng., 1960; LLB cum laude, Harvard U., 1962. Bar: Calif. 1962. Assoc. Heller, Ehrman, White & McAuliffe, San Francisco, 1962-69, ptnr., 1969—, mem. exec. com., 1980-93, co-chair, 1988-93. Contbr. articles to law jours. Bd. dirs. Mt. Zion Hosp., San Francisco, 1982-88, U.S. Dist. Ct. (no. dist.) Calif. Hist. Soc., 1988-2004, Jewish Home for Aged, San Francisco, 1989-96, Golden Gate U., 1997-2000, Jewish Cmty. Fedn., 1997-2001. Recipient Anti-Defamation League's Disting. Jurisprudence award, 2000; named State Bar of Calif. Antitrust Lawyer of the Yr., 2000, Best in Calif. Antitrust, 2005, Sr. Statesman Antitrust, Chambers, 2006; Rhodes scholar, 1958. Fellow Am. Bar Found., Am. Coll. Trial Lawyers; mem. ABA, Calif. Bar Assn., San Francisco Bar Assn., Bur. Nat. Affairs (adv. bd. antitrust sect.), Calif. Acad. Appellate Lawyers. Democrat. Jewish. Home: 1940 Broadway Apt 10 San Francisco CA 94109-2216 Office: Heller Ehrman 333 Bush St Ste 3000 San Francisco CA 94104-2834 Office Phone: 415-772-6310. Business E-Mail: lpopofsky@hewm.com.

**POPOLIZIO, RICK,** music educator; b. Bronx, Sept. 8, 1949; d. Lawrence Popolizio and Irma Alvarez; 1 child, Sara. BA in Liberal Arts and Music, Fairleigh Dickinson U., Teaneck, N.J., 1973; MA in Adminstrn. and Supervision, Kean U., Morris, N.J., 1996. Tchr. pub. schs., NJ; instrumental music tchr. Park Ridge HS, NJ. Adjucator bands, NJ, 1990—96. Mem.: Music Educators of Bergen County, Music Educators Nat. Conf. Avocations: drumming, music memorabilia. Office: Park Ridge High School 2 Park Ave Park Ridge NJ 07656-1278

**POPOV, OLEG,** physicist; b. Ussurijsk, Russia, Jan. 4, 1943; arrived in U.S., 1982; s. Alexej Popov and Varvara Shedogub; m. Natalia Alyokhina Popov, Dec. 12, 1970; children: Peter, Ilya, Stanislav. BA in Elecs., Moscow Inst. Power, 1965; PhD in Plasma Physics, Moscow State U., 1977. Engr. Plasma Rsch. Inst., Ryazan, Russia, 1966—70, Moscow State U., 1971—78, Eaton Corp, Beverly, Mass., 1984—85; sr. scientist Gen. Ionics, Inc., Newburyport, 1985—86, Microsci., Inc., Norwalk, 1986—93, Matsushita Elec. Works, Woburn, 1993—. Vis. scientist Stevens Inst. Tech., Hoboken, NJ, 1983—84. Editor: High Density Plasma Sources, 1995; mem. editl. bd.: Plasma Sources Sci. & Tech. Jour., 1998—; contbr. articles to profl. jours. Fellow: Inst. Physics. Achievements include patents for lightings-plasma sources. Office: Panasonic Electric Works Lab Am Inc 216 W Cummings Pk Woburn MA 01801

**POPOVA, NINA,** dancer, choreographer, director; b. Novorossisk, USSR, 1922; Student in Paris, studied ballet with Olga Preobrajenska, Lubov Egorova, Anatole Vilzak, Anatole Oboukhov, Igor Schwezoff. Ballet debut with Ballet de la Jeunesse, Paris, London, 1937-39; soloist Original Ballet Russe, 1939-41, Ballet Theatre (now Am. Ballet), 1941-42, Ballet Russe de Monte Carlo, 1943, 47, Ballet Alicia Alonso, Cuba; mem. faculty Sch. Performing Arts, N.Y.C., from 1954; later artistic dir. Houston Ballet, 1975; tchr. Nat. Acad. Arts, Champaign, Ill., also N.Y.C., 1975—, now Eglevsky Ballet Sch., L.I.; tchr. ballet Mexico City, Mex.; asst. choreographer mus. comedy Birmingham So. Coll., Ala., 1960; numerous appearances on Broadway stage, TV; former mem. regular cast Your Show of Shows; currently tchg. N.Y.C. Address: 33 Adams St Sea Cliff NY 11579-1614

**POPOVICH, GEORGE LEE,** theater educator; s. George and Hazel Popovich; children: Wiley Thomas, Jennifer Lee. BA, Calif. State U., Fullerton, 1971, MA, 1975, U. Tex., El Paso 1980; PhD, Ohio State U., Columbus, 1987. Curr. tech. Calif. Dir. theater virtual theater lab Henry Ford CC, Dearborn, Mich., 1985—. Dir.: The Tempest, 2004 (Kennedy Center's Am. Coll. Theater Festival), The Skriker. Regional dir. Dads of Mich., Howell. Grantee, Tech. Investment Fund, 1996, 1998, 2000, 2005. Mem.: Assn. Theater Higher Edn. Libertarian. Achievements include development of a system for incorporating 3D scenery and characters into live stage performances. Avocations: gardening, travel, videography, camping. Office: Henry Ford Cmty Coll 5101 Evergreen Rd Dearborn MI 48128 Office Phone: 313-845-6478. Business E-Mail: popovich@hfcc.net.

**POPOVICH, GREGG,** professional basketball coach; b. Jan. 28, 1949; m. Erin; 2 children. Grad. in Soviet studies, Air Force Acad., 1970; MA, Univ. of Denver. Asst. coach Air Force Acad., 1975-81; head coach Pomona-Pitzer Coll., Claremont, Calif., assoc. prof.; asst. coach San Antonio Spurs, 1988-92, Golden State Warriors, 1992—94; gen. mgr. San Antonio Spurs, 1994—2002, head coach, exec. v.p. basketball ops., 1996—. Head coach USA Senior National Team, 2003; asst. coach U.S. Olympic Team, Athens, 2004. 2nd lt. USAF, 1970-73. Recipient Daily Point of Light award President George Bush, 1992. Achievements include coaching NBA Champion San Antonio Spurs, 1999, 2003, 2005. Office: San Antonio Spurs One SBC Ctr San Antonio TX 78203*

**POPOVICH, KAREN,** health facility administrator; d. Gerald C. and Patricia J. Barnard; m. Mark N Popovich, May 12, 1995; children: Steven, Joseph, Andrew. BS, Ball State U., 1976, MA, 1993. Underwriter Am. United Life, Indpls., 1976—81; employee benefits mgr. Cmty. Hosp., Indpls., 1981—86; v.p. VHA Tri-State, Indpls., 1986—90, Riverview Hosp., Noblesville, Ind., 1990—95; pres. Cardinal Health Alliance, Muncie, 1995—. Mem. faculty Ball State U., Muncie; cons. Nat. Coun. Healthcare Advisors. Author: (refereed publs.) Hospital Strategic Planning, (refereed pub.) Use of Q-Methodology for Hospital Strategic Planning. Mem. Rotary Internat., Muncie, 1999; editor Network of Women in Bus., Indpls., 1979—83; bd. mem. Tri County Mental Health Ctr., Indpls., 1991—95, HealthPoint, Indpls., 1996—2004. Recipient Touchstone, Am. Hosp. Assn., 1994. Mem.: Am. Coll. Healthcare Execs. (diplomate 1983—2006), Women in Managed Care,

Women's Health Adv. Bd. (bd. mem. 1985—87), Am. Assn. Integrated Delivery Systems, Ind. Hosp. Assn. (mem. pub. rels. coun. 1991—95). Office: Cardinal Health Alliance LLC 3711 S Madison St Muncie IN 47302 Office Phone: 765-286-2150.

**POPOVICI, ADRIAN,** law educator; b. Bucharest, Rumania, Sept. 6, 1942; came to Can., 1951; s. Adrian and Alice (Moruzi) P.; children— Adrian, Alexandra. BA, Stanislas Coll., Montreal, 1959; B.C.L., McGill U., 1962; D.E.S., U. Paris, 1965. Bar: Que. 1963. Prof. law U. Montreal, Que., Canada, 1968—. Author: L'Outrage au Tribunal, 1977, La Couleur du Mandat, 1995; editor: Problèmes de Droit Contemporain, 1974 Roman Catholic. Home: 5589 Canterbury Montreal PQ Canada H3T 1S8 Office: U Montreal Faculte de Droit CP 6128 Succursale A Montreal PQ Canada H3C 3J7 E-mail: adrian.popovici@umontreal.ca.

**POPOVICS, SANDOR,** civil engineer, educator, researcher; b. Budapest, Hungary, Dec. 24, 1921; came to U.S., 1957; s. Milan and Erzsebet (Droppa) P.; m. Lea M. Virtanen, Aug. 29, 1960; children: John, Lisa. 1st Degree in Civil Engring., Poly. U., Budapest, Hungary, 1944; Advanced Degree in Civil Engring., Poly. U., 1956; PhD, Purdue U., 1961. Registered profl. engr. Ariz., Pa. Rsch. engr. Met. Lab., Budapest, 1944-48; adj. prof. Tech. Coll., Budapest, 1949-52; rsch. engr., mgr. Inst. for Bldg. Scis., Budapest, 1949-56; grad. asst. Purdue U., Lafayette, Ind., 1957-59; prof. engring. Auburn (Ala.) U., 1959-69; prof. civil engring. No. Ariz. U., Flagstaff, 1968-76; prof. engring. King Abdulazziz U., Jeddah, Saudi Arabia, 1977-78; Samuel S. Baxter prof. civil engring. Drexel U., Phila., 1979-92, rsch. prof., 1992—Pres. Optimum Engring. Rsch. Author: Fundamentals of Portland Cement Concrete, 1982, Concrete Materials, 2d edit., 1992, Strength and Related Properties of Concrete, 1998, over 300 tech. papers. Recipient numerous grants and awards. Fellow ASCE (life), Am. Concrete Inst.; mem. ASTM, Ala. Acad. Scis., Ariz. Acad. Scis., Sigma Xi, Chi Epsilon. Avocations: jogging, music, fine art. Home and Office: 283 Congress Ave Lansdowne PA 19050-1206 Office: Drexel U Dept Civil Archtl & Environ Engring 32nd and Chestnut Philadelphia PA 19104 Office Phone: 215-895-2345. Business E-Mail: popovics@coe.drexel.edu.

**POPP, JOSEPH BRUCE,** manufacturing executive; b. Chgo., July 9, 1919; s. Peter Leon and Anna (Chomyz) P.; m. Mabel Lydia Szymanski, Oct. 23, 1941 (dec. Mar. 1993); m. Elinor A. Maves, Jan. 27, 1996; children: Dianne, Lydia, Bruce, Anita, Gregory. Founder, owner Poultry Farm, Westville, Ind., 1941-48, Gary (Ind.) Undercoating Co., 1948-51; survey analyst George S. May Co., Chgo., 1952-54; gen. sales mgr. Maurey Instrument Corp., Chgo., 1958-64; founder, owner Joe Popp Sales Co., North Riverside, Ill., 1964-89, Chart Pool USA Inc., Portage, Ind., 1966—. Bd. dirs. YMCA Camp Tecumseh, Brookston, Ind., 1973—. Sgt. U.S. Army, 1942—46. Mem. Nat. Fedn. of Ind. Bus., Greater Portage C. of C., The Gideons Internat., Nat. Inst. Animal Agr. Republican. Achievements include patents for Bloodhound Property Security System. Home: 1133 Lincoln St Hobart IN 46342-6039 Office: Chart Pool USA Inc 5695 Old Porter Rd Portage IN 46368-1194 Personal E-mail: bloodhoundidentification@yahoo.com.

**POPP, NATHANIEL,** archbishop; b. Aurora, Ill., June 12, 1940; s. Joseph and Vera (Boytor) P. BA, St. Propcopius Coll., 1962; MDiv, Pontifical Gregorian U., Rome, 1966; PhD, U. Oradea, Romania, 2003. Ordained priest Romanian Greek Cath. Ch., 1966; consecrated bishop Romanian Orthodox Episcopate of Am., 1980; elevated to archbishop, 1999. Asst. pastor St. Michael Byz Ch., Aurora, 1967; parish priest Holy Cross Romanian Orthodox Ch., Hermitage, Pa., 1975-80; aux. bishop Romanian Orthodox Episcopate of Am., Orthodox Ch. in Am., Jackson, Mich., 1980-84, ruling bishop Detroit, 1984—; mem. Holy Synod Orthodox Ch. in Am., Syosset, NY, 1980—; Episcopal moderator Pastoral Life Ministries, O.C.A., 1991—2000. Bd. dirs. Moldovita Romanian Orthodox Ch., Hayward, Calif, 1982; tchr. summer youth programs Romanian Diocese; confessor to sisterhood Holy Transfiguration Monastery; rep. Conf. on Monasticism, Cairo, 1978; participant Monastic Consultation, Cairo, 1979, Seventh Assembly, Vancouver, Can., 1983; active mem. diocesan liturgical commn.; spkr., lectr. in field. Author: Holy Icons, 1969; editor newspaper Solia; contbr. numerous articles to profl. jours. Chmn. Romanian-Am. Heritage Ctr., Grass Lake, Mich.; organizer, chmn. Help for Romania Nat. Relief Fund and Help the Children of Romania Relief Fund; chmn. Congress of Romanian Ams., 1991—; mem. adv. bd. Orthodox Christian Laity, 1999—; pres. Ctr. for Orthodox Christian Studies, St. Andrew, Detroit, 2000; Dr. Honoris Causa, U. Oradea, Romania, 2003; chmn. bd Orthodox Witness, 2003-. Romanian Orthodox. Home and Office: Romanian Orthodox Episcopate Am 2535 Grey Tower Rd Jackson MI 49201-9120 also: PO Box 305 Grass Lake MI 49240-0309 Office Phone: 517-522-4800. E-mail: hgbnpopp@aol.com, nathaniel@roea.org.

**POPPE, EUGENE DALE,** banker; b. Omaha, Nebr., June 28, 1956; s. Orville Eugene Poppe and Ophelia Goethals Torres. BA, Creighton U., Omaha, 1979, poastgrad., 1980; M of Internat. Mgmt., Am. Grad Sch., Glendale, Ariz., 1983. Emerging market trader Mfrs. Hanover Trust, NYC, 1983—87; internat. banker NCNB Tex., Dallas, 1988—91; emerging market trader European Inter Am. Corp., NYC, 1991—93; emerging market chief trader Ecoban Fin. Ltd., 1993—97; sr. acct Fremont Group, San Francisco, 2000—01. Vol. Desert Aids Project, Palm Springs, Calif., 2006. Recipient Biology Rsch. award, NSF, Creighton U., 1980. Mem.: Mensa. Avocations: rock collecting, hiking, travel, dance. Home: 69320 Nilda Dr Cathedral City CA 92234

**POPPE, PAMELA J.,** accountant; b. Breckenridge, Minn., Oct. 25, 1948; d. John T. and Anita Ruth (Knudsen) Sanker; m. James Wayne Kelly, May 10, 1969 (div. May 1993); children: Jamison Marc, Brian Lee m. James E. Poppe. Jan. 19, 2000, BA in Music Edn., Concordia Coll., Moorhead, Minn., 1969; m Indsl. Adminstrn., Iowa State U., 1980. CPA, Iowa. Band and choir tchr. Danube (Minn.) Ind. Schs., 1969-70; orch. tchr. Raleigh (N.C.) City Schs., 1972-73; French and English tchr. Bethel Acad., Kinston, N.C., 1974; jr. high sch. music tchr. Lenoir County Schs., Kinston, 1974-76; in-charge staff auditor McGladrey Pullen, Des Moines, 1980-82; internal auditing dept. Am. Fed. Savs. & Loan, Des Moines, 1982-84; v.p. fin. Gentry, Ltd., Des Moines, 1984-89; dir. property mgmt. adminstrn. R&R Investors, Ltd., West Des Moines, Iowa, 1989—96; controller Venter Spooner Inc., Johnston, Iowa, 1997—. Mem. acct. adv. bd. Am. Inst. Bus., Des Moines, 1988-94. Chairperson Holy Trinity Luth. Ch., Ankeny, Iowa, 1991. Recipient Elijah Watts Sells award AICPA, 1980. Mem. Cert. Financial Mgrs. Assn., Iowa Timberline Users Group, Iowa Soc. CPAs, Mensa, Phi Beta Kappa. Avocations: reading, needlecrafts, quilting, dance, bicycling. Home: 909 SE Kensington Rd Ankeny IA 50021-3960 Office: 6500 NW Beaver Dr Johnston IA 50131 Office Phone: 515-331-2800. E-mail: ppoppe@venterspooner.com.

**POPPEL, HARVEY LEE,** management consultant, investment banker; b. Bklyn., Dec. 18, 1937; s. Frank M. and Fannie (Axenzow) P.; m. Emily A. Daigneault, Jan. 2, 1959; children: Marc F, Clinton S. BS, Rensselaer Poly. Inst., 1958, MS, 1959. Sr. info. systems analyst Westinghouse Electric Corp., Pitts., 1959-65; mgr. industry systems Western Union, Paramus, NJ, 1965-67; from assoc. to mem. operating coun. Booz, Allen & Hamilton, N.Y.C., 1967-84; gen. ptnr. Poptech, LLC, Sarasota, Fla., 2003—. Bd. dirs. Larscom, Santa Clara, Calif., 1996-02; mng. dir. Broadview Assocs., Ft. Lee, 1984-96; mem. panel, lectr. on computers, comm. and info. industry; judge Entrepreneur of Yr., 1991, 93, 94, 95, 96; investor in start-ups. Co-author: Information Technology: The Trillion-Dollar Opportunity, 1987; contbr. articles to profl. jours. Mem. Aspen Inst. Fellows, Inst. Mgmt. Cons., Israel Cancer Assn. (exec. com.), Rep. Jewish Coalition, Palm Beach Civic Assn. (bd. dirs. 2006—)Road Runners Club, Banyan Golf Club, Marin Country Club, Breakers Ocean Club, Zeta Psi Office: 1391 6th St Sarasota FL 34236-4906 E-mail: hpoppel@msn.com.

**POPPEL, SETH RAPHAEL,** entrepreneur; b. Bklyn., Mar. 17, 1944; s. Frank M. and Fritzi R. (Axenzow) P.; m. Danine Vokt, June 30, 1974; children: Clarysa, Jared, Stacy. BS magna cum laude, L.I. U., 1965; MBA,

Columbia U., 1967. Asst. prof. L.I. U., Greenvale, N.Y., 1967-68; v.p. Synergistic Sys. Corp., N.Y.C., 1968-77; v.p., dir. corp. planning Chase Manhattan Corp., N.Y.C., 1977-90; owner, pres. Yearbook Libr., N.Y.C., 1980—; chmn., pres. Am. Vision Ctrs., N.Y.C., 1990-96. Owner harness horses Seth Poppel Stables, 1983—; founder, owner, operator Seth Poppel Yearbook Archives, 1986-2000. Recipient Claire F. Adler award in math., 1964-65, Mepham H.S. Hall of Fame award, 1993; E.I. DuPont fellow, 1965-67, Downie Muir fellow, 1965-66. Mem. U.S. Trotting Assn., Beta Gamma Sigma, Psi Chi, Omega Epsilon. Home and Office: 38 Range Dr Merrick NY 11566-3233 Office Phone: 877-HIGHSCHOOL. Personal E-mail: sethpoppel@aol.com.

**POPPENSIEK, GEORGE CHARLES,** retired veterinary scientist, retired educator; b. NYC, June 18, 1918; s. George Frederick and Emily Amelia (Miller) P.; m. Edith M. Wallace, July 3, 1943; children: Neil Allen, Leslie Marion. Student, Cornell U., 1936-37, MS, 1951; student, U. Pa., 1937-42, V.MD, 1942. Diplomate Am. Bd. Microbiology, Am. Coll. Vet. Microbiology (charter), Am. Coll. Vet. Preventive Medicine (hon.). Asst. instr. medicine U. Pa. Sch. Vet. Medicine, 1943; asst. prof. vet. sci. U. Md., 1943-44; head dept. vet. virus vaccine prodn. Lederle Labs. div. Am. Cyanamid Co., 1944-49; dir. diagnostic lab. N.Y. State Coll. Vet. Medicine Cornell U., 1949-51, research assoc. Vet. Virus Research Inst., 1951-55; veterinarian Plum Island Animal Disease Ctr., animal disease and parasite research div. Agrl. Research Service, U.S. Dept. Agr., 1955-56, acting-in-charge diagnostic investigations, 1956-58, charge immunological investigations, 1958-59; dean and prof. microbiology N.Y. State Coll. Vet. Medicine, Cornell U., 1959-74, James Law prof. comparative medicine, 1974-88, dean emeritus, James Law prof. comparative medicine emeritus, 1988—; guest prof. U. Bern, Switzerland, 1975; ret., 1988. Mem. exam. com. Nat. Bd. Vet. Med. Examiners, 1976-79; bd. dirs. Cornell Research Found., 1963-74; chmn. bd. dirs. Cornell Veterinarian, Inc., 1976-86 Recipient Certificate of Merit award U.S. Dept. Agr., 1959; citation Sch. Vet. Med., U. Pa., 1978, Centennial medals U. Pa., 1984, Ohio State U., 1985; others. Fellow AAAS, Am. Acad. Microbiology (charter); mem. AVMA, Am. Soc. Virology (charter), NY State Vet. Med. Soc. (disting. life), Am. Bd. Microbiology, US Animal Health Assn., Assn. Am. Vet. Med. Colls. (pres. 1970-71), So. Tier Vet. Med. Assn., Am. Vet. Radiology Soc., Am. Soc. for Microbiology, NY Agrl. Soc. (life), Argentine Nat. Acad. Agronomy and Vet. Medicine (hon.), Soc. Polona Medicinae Veterinariae (hon.), Sigma Xi, Phi Kappa Phi, Alpha Psi, Omega Tau Sigma, Phi Zeta. Congregationalist. Home: 32 Horizon Dr Ithaca NY 14850-9769 Personal E-mail: poppensiek@clarityconnect.com.

**POPPER, ROBERT,** lawyer, retired dean; b. N.Y.C., May 22, 1932; s. Walter G. and Dorothy B. (Kluger) P.; m. Mary Ann Schaefer, July 12, 1963; children: Julianne, Robert Gregory. BS, U. Wis., 1953; LLB, Harvard U., 1956; LLM, NYU, 1963. Bar: N.Y. 1957, U.S. Dist. Ct. (so. dist.) N.Y. 1962, U.S. Ct. Appeals (2d cir.) 1962, U.S. Supreme Ct. 1962, U.S. Dist. Ct. (ea. dist.) N.Y. 1969, U.S. Ct. Appeals (7th cir.) 1970, U.S. Ct. Appeals (8th cir.) 1971, Mo. 1971, U.S. Dist. Ct. (we. dist.) Mo. 1973. Trial atty. criminal br. N.Y.C. Legal Aid Soc., 1960-61; asst. dist. atty. N.Y. County, 1961-64; assoc. Seligson & Morris, N.Y.C., 1964-69; mem. faculty School of Law U. Mo, Kansas City, 1969-96, prof., 1973-96, acting dean, 1983-84, dean, 1984-93, dean and prof. emeritus, 1996—. Cons. and lectr. in field. Author: Post Conviction Remedies in a Nutshell, 1978, De-Nationalizing the Bill of Rights, 1979; contbr. articles to profl. jours. Bd. trustees Rsch. Psychiat. Ctr. (HCA Midwest). Fellow ABA; mem. Mo. Bar, Kansas City Met. Bar Assn., Mo. Inst. of Justice. Home: 6229 Summit St Kansas City MO 64113-1556 Office: U Mo Kansas City Sch Law 1500 Rockhill Rd Kansas City MO 64110-2467 Fax: (816) 235-5276. Office Phone: 816-235-1006. E-mail: popperr@umkc.edu.

**POPPERS, PAUL JULES,** anesthesiologist, educator; b. Enschede, Netherlands, June 30, 1929; came to U.S., 1958; naturalized, 1963; s. Meyer and Minca (Ginsburg) P.; m. Ann Feinberg, June 3, 1969; children: David Matthew, Jeremy Samuel. MD, U. Amsterdam, 1955. Diplomate Am. Bd. Anesthesiology. Instr. anesthesiology Columbia U., N.Y.C., 1962-63, assoc., 1963-65, asst. prof. anesthesiology, 1965-71, assoc. prof. anesthesiology, 1971-74; prof., vice chmn. dept. anesthesiology NYU, 1974-79; prof., chmn. dept. anesthesiology Stony Brook U., NY, 1979—97, disting. prof., chmn. dept anesthesiology, 1997—2000, disting. prof. emeritus, 2000—. Cons. Brookdale Med. Ctr., Bklyn., 1975-2000, VA Med. Ctr., Northport, N.Y., 1979-2000, The N.Y. Hosp. Med. Ctr. of Queens (formerly Booth Meml. Hosp.), Flushing, N.Y., 1979-98, L.I. Jewish Med. Ctr., New Hyde Park, N.Y., 1980-98, Ea. L.I. Hosp., Greenport, N.Y., 1995-99, Am. Hosp. Paris, 1989-93; cons., lectr. USN, 1968-85 Author: Regional Anesthesia, 1977; editor: Beta Blockade and Anaesthesia, 1979; sect. editor Jour. Clin. Anesthesia, 1990-2000; mem. editl. bd. Internat. Jour. Clin. Monitoring and Computing, 1990-2000, Anaesthesiology Digest, 1991-94, Gynecologic and Obstetric Investigation, 1996-2001; contbr. over 200 articles to profl. jours. Rsch. fellow NIH, 1961; recipient medal Polish Acad. Scis., Poland, 1987, Univ. medal Jagiellonian U., Krakow, Poland, 1987, 1st Sci. award Post-grad. Assembly in Anesthesiology; named Hon. Prof. Anesthesiology, U. Leiden, The Netherlands, 1977. Fellow Am. Coll. Anesthesiology, Am. Coll. Obgyns., Royal Soc. Medicine, Post-grad. Assembly in Anesthesiology (hon. chmn. 1989—); mem. Am. Soc. Anesthesiologists, Assn. Univ. Anesthesiologists, Internat. Anesthesia Rsch. Soc., Soc. Obstetric Anesthesia and Perinatology, Am. Soc. Regional Anesthesia, Jerusalem Acad. Medicine, Am. Soc. Pharmacology and Exptl. Therapeutics, Fedn. Am. Soc. Exptl. Biology, Sigma Xi. Personal E-mail: paulpoppers@hotmail.com.

**POPPLER, DORIS SWORDS,** lawyer; b. Billings, Mont., Nov. 10, 1924; d. Lloyd William and Edna (Mowre) Swords; m. Louis F. Poppler, June 11, 1949; children: Louis William, Kristine, Mark J., Blaine, Claire, Arminda. Student, U. Minn., 1942-44; JD, Mont. State U., 1948. Bar: Mont. 1948, U.S. Dist. Ct. Mont. 1948, U.S. Ct. Appeals (9th cir.) 1990. Pvt. practice law, Billings, 1948-49; sec., treas. Wonderpark Corp., Billings, 1959-62; atty. Yellowstone County Attys. Office, Billings, 1972-75; ptnr. Poppler and Barz, Billings, 1972-79, Davidson, Veeder, Baugh, Broeder and Poppler, Billings, 1979-84, Davidson and Poppler, P.C., Billings, 1984-90; U.S. atty. Dist. of Mont., Billings, 1990-93; field rep. Nat. Indian Gaming Commn., Washington, 1993-2000. Pres. Jr. League, 1964-65; bd. dirs., pres. Yellowstone County Metre Bd., 1982; trustee Rocky Mt. Coll., 1984-90, mem. nat. adv. bd., 1993—; mem. Mont. Human Rights Commn., 1988-90; bd. dirs. Miss Mont. Pageant, 1995—; elected to Billings City Coun. Billings, Mont., 2002; elected dep. mayor coun. woman Ward4, 2002—. Recipient Mont. Salute to Women award, Mont. Woman of Achievent award, 1975, Disting. Svc. award Rocky Mt. Coll., 1990, Disting. Female Alumna award U. Montana Law Sch., 1996, 2004, Status Women award Zonta Club, 2004. Mem. AAUW, Mont. Bar Assn., Nat. Assn. Former U.S. Attys., Nat. Rep. Lawyers Assn., Internat. Women's Forum, Yellowstone County Bar Assn. (pres. 1990, Lifetime Achievement award 2004), Alpha Chi Omega. Republican.

**POPRÁDY, GÉZA,** librarian; b. Tök, Hungary, Mar. 19, 1940; s. Géza and Ilona (Lugmayer) P.; m. Maria Wéber, July 13, 1963; children: Géza, Judit, Peter. Student, Eötvös Lorand U., Budapest, Hungary, 1958-63. Cert. librarian, tchr. Librarian Architectural Info. Ctr., Budapest, 1963-64, Ctrl. Rsch. and Design Inst. for Silicate Industry, Budapest, 1964—83; head dept. Nat. Széchényi Library, Budapest, 1984-90, dep. dir.-gen., 1990-93, acting dir.-gen., 1993-94, dir.-gen., 1994-99, counsellor, 1999—. Author: (book) The Application of Technical Information, 1977, The Systematic Catalogue, 1981, Preservation of Library Materials, 2000, Trends of Librarianship (Handbook of Librarians), 2003; contbr. articles to profl. jours. Recipient Szabó Ervin medal Min. of Culture, 1989. Mem. Assn. Hungarian Librarians (sec.-gen. 1987-90, v.p. 1990-98, award 1988). Avocations: reading, gardening. Home: Árpád vezér u 27 H-2081 Piliscsaba Hungary Office: Nat Széchényi Library Budavári Palota F-épulet 1827 Budapest Hungary E-mail: pprady@oszk.hu.

**POPRAWA, ANDREW,** diversified financial services company executive, accountant; b. Toronto, Ont., Can., Nov. 13, 1952; s. Mieczyslaw and Wanda P.; m. Rita Poprawa, Oct. 10, 1981; children: Alexandra, Jason. B in

Commerce, U. Toronto, 1975. Chartered acct., Can. CEO St. Stanislaus Credit Union, Toronto, 1980-82; dir. Office of Supt. of Fin. Instns. (Can.), Toronto, 1982-92, Ministry of Fin., Province of Ont., Toronto, 1992-93; pres., CEO Deposit Ins. Corp. of Ont., Toronto, 1993—. Mem. Inst. Chartered Accts. Ont. (cert. govt. fin. mgr.), Lakeshore Yacht Club, Toronto Bd. of Trade. Roman Catholic. Avocations: sailing, tennis, skiing, hockey. Office: Deposit Insurance Corp of Ontario 4711 Yonge St #700 Toronto ON Canada M2N 6K8 Office Phone: 416-325-9580. E-mail: apoprawa@dico.com.

**POPREN, VALERIE,** artist; b. Bronx, N.Y., Dec. 25, 1939; d. Gustave Popren and Sadie Orkin; m. Herbert Bernard Frankel, Dec. 10, 1960; children: Gayle, Marc, Gregg. Student, Suffolk C.C., Brentwood, N.Y. Exhibitions include Vanderbilt Mus., 1994, Fine Art Mus. L.I., 1995, Heckscher Mus., 2001, Represented in permanent collections Jan Voorhees Zimmerli Art Mus., New Brunswick, N.J., Nat. Assn. Women Artists, N.Y.C. Mem.: N.Y. Artists Equity Assn., N.Y. Soc. Women Artists, Nat. Assn. Women Artists. Home: 32 Frazer Dr Greenlawn NY 11740

**PORAD, FRANCINE JOY,** poet, painter; b. Seattle, Sept. 3, 1929; d. Morris H. and Gertrude (Volchok) Harvitz; m. Bernard L. Porad, June 12, 1949 (dec.); children: Laurie, Bruce, Ken, Constance, Marci, Jeffrey. BFA, U. Wash., 1976. Founder, coord. Haiku NW Poets/Readers, Mercer Isle, Wash., 1988—2000; editor Brussels Sprout, Mercer Isle, 1988-95; co-editor Haiku Northwest Anthology, Seattle, 1996, Red Moon Press, Berryville, Va., 1996. Workshop presenter Haiku Can., Toronto and Alymer, Que., Can., 1992, 95, Haiku N.Am., Calif., Toronto, 1993, 95, Haiku N.Am., Oreg., 1997, Haiku Internat., Tokyo, 1997; judge Internat. Haiku Contest New Zealand Poetry Soc., 1995, People's Haiku & Senryu Contest, Canada, 1999, San Francisco Contest for Haiku Poets of North Calif., 1992, Hawaii Edn. Assn., Honolulu, 1995, 99, PEN Women (Seattle) Internat. Poetry Contest, 2000, Fla. State Poetry Assn. Contest, 2003. Author: Connections, 1986, Pen and Inklings, 1986, After Autumn Rain, 1987, Blues on the Run, 1988, Free of Clouds, 1989, Without Haste, 1989 (Cicada Chapbook award 1990), Hundreds of Wishes, 1990, A Mural of Leaves, 1991, Joy is My Middle Name, 1993, The Patchwork Quilt, 1994 (Haiku Soc. Am. Merit Book 1994), Waterways, 1995 (Haiku Can. Sheet Book series 1995), All Eyes, 1995, Ladies and Jellyspoons, 1996, Extended Wings, 1996, Moon, Moon, 1997, Fog Lifting, 1997, All the Games, 1997, Let's Count The Trees, 1998 (Haiku Can. Sheet Selection 1998), (with M. Mountain) Cur*rent, 1998, The Perfect Worry-Stone, 2000, (with K. Kondo and M. Mountain) Other Rens, 2000, Other Rens Book Two and Book Three, 2000, Trio of Wrens, 2000, Second Blooming, 2001, Other Rens Book Five and Book Six, 2001, Other Rens Book Seven, 2001, Other Rens Book Eight, 2002, Other Rens Book Nine, 2002, Other Rens Book Ten, 2003, Probably: 'Real' Renga Sorta, 2002, Probably: 'Real' Renga Sorta 2, 2003, Sunlight Comes and Goes, 2004, (with M. Mountain) Pieces, 2005, Buzzwords, 2005. Recipient 1st prize Internat. Tanka competition Poetry Soc. Japan, Tokyo, 1993, Itoen Tea award Haiku Internat., Tokyo, 1996, 98, Cicada award for Haiku sequences by Amelia, 1999, award Mainichi Internat. Haiku Contest, Tokyo, 1999, Francine Porad's Yearly Haiku award Wash. Poets Assn., 2004, haiku contest award NC Poetry Soc., 2006; named an Hon. Curator Calif. State Libr. Am. Haiku Archive, 2005-06. Mem. Nat. League Am. Penwomen (treas. 1992-94, Owl award 1982, 92, 1st prize state art exhbn. Frye Mus. 1993, 1st pl. Haiku, 1995), Haiku Soc. Am. (pres. 1993-94, Merit book 1994, judge 1997, Brady Senryu Contest H.M. award 1997, Merit book award 2001, San Francisco Internat. Haiku award 2002, Sora award 2004), Heron's Nest award, 2003), N.W. Watercolor Soc. (treas. 1980-85), Women Painters Wash. (v.p. 1987, bd. 1985-93). Avocations: computer fun, travel. Home: 10392 NE 12th I-307 Bellevue WA 98004-4263 E-mail: poradF@aol.com.

**PORAYKO, MICHAEL,** physician, educator; s. Peter Porayko and Anne Haley; m. Karen Manoukian, June 13, 1987; children: Chris, Caitlyn. MD, U. Ill., Rockford, 1981. Diplomate Am. Bd. Internal Medicine. Assoc. prof. medicine, med. dir. liver transplantation Vanderbilt U., Nashville, 2002—. Designer exam. for hepatologists Am. Bd. Internal Medicine, Phila., 2004—06. Mem.: ACP (bd. dirs. 2004—06, Rsch.award 1985). Achievements include research in nutrition in Cirrhotic patients. Office Phone: 615-936-3730.

**PORCARO, MICHAEL FRANCIS,** advertising executive; b. NYC, Apr. 3, 1948; s. Girolamo M. and Marianna (DePasquale) P.; m. Bonnie Kerr, Apr. 7, 1972; children: Sabrina, Jon. BA in English, Rockford (Ill.) Coll., 1969. Broadcaster Sta. KFQD-AM; KENI-AM/TV, Anchorage, 1970-71, Sta. KENI-AM/TV, Anchorage, 1972-73; v.p. ops. Cook Inlet Broadcasters, Anchorage, 1973-74; owner Audio Enterprises, Anchorage, 1974-75; asst. Alaska Pub. Broadcasting Commn., Anchorage, 1975-76, exec. dir., 1976-81; CEO, ptnr. Porcaro Blankenship Advt. Corp., Anchorage, 1981-97; CEO Porcaro Comms., Anchorage, 1997—; chmn. bd. Bernholz & Graham, Pub. Rels., 2001—; ptnr. Porcaro Vancouver Ad and Pub. Rels., 2003, Porcaro L.A. (Calif.) Ad and Pub. Rels., 2004—. Cons. Arco Alaska TV sta., Anchorage, 1981; expert witness U.S. Senate Subcom. on Telecom., Washington, 1978; chmn. citizens adv. com. dept. journalism U. Alaska, 1995-96. Afternoon talk show host KENI, 2000—; contbr. articles to profl. jours.; co-author (with John Dragseth): (casebook patent law) Patents-Ilist. Perspective Served to capt. U.S. Army Res., 1968-73. Named one of top Boston lawyers, Boston Mag., 2002. Mem.: Boston Patent Law Assn. (pres. 1990—91), Fed. Ct. Bar Assn., Am. Intellectual Property Law Assn. (chmn. chem. practice subcom. legis. 1987—89, chmn. chem. practice subcom. judicial & adminstrv. decisions 1989—91, chmn. spl. practice com. 1991—92), ABA. Avocations: golf, running, downhill skiing, history, watching college football and basketball. Office: Fish & Richardson PC 225 Franklin St Fl 32 Boston MA 02110-2809 Office Phone: 617-521-7808. Office Fax: 617-542-8906. Business E-Mail: porcelli@fr.com.

**PORCELLO, LEONARD JOSEPH,** engineering research and development executive; b. NYC, Mar. 1, 1934; s. Savior James and Mary Josephine (Bacchi) P.; m. Patricia Lucille Berger, July 7, 1962 (dec. Sept. 1991); children: John Joseph, Thomas Gregory; m. Victoria Roberta Smith, June 21, 1996. BA in Physics, Cornell U., 1955; MS in Physics, U. Mich., 1957, MSEE, 1959, PhD in Elec. Engring. 1963. Research asst. U. Mich., Ann Arbor, 1955-58, instr. elec. engring., 1958-61; research engr. Radar & Optics

Lab., 1968-72; asso. dir. Willow Run Labs., 1970-72, asso. prof., 1969-72, prof., 1972-73, adj. prof., 1973-75. Dir. radar and optics divsn. Environ. Rsch. Inst. of Mich., Ann Arbor, 1973-76, v.p., 1973-76, trustee, 1975; asst. v.p., mgr. sensor sys. operation Sci. Applications Internat. Corp., Tucson, 1976-79, v.p., 1979-85, corp. v.p., 1985-87, mgr. def. sys. group, 1986-95, sr. v.p., 1987—, dep. mgr. tech. and advanced sys. sector, 1993-97, mgr. applied sys. group, 1995-2000, dep. mgr. space and tech. solutions sector, 1997-99; CFO, bd. dirs. TIAS ARMS, 2004—. Bd. dirs. Tucson Jr. Strings, 1977-79, chmn., 1978-79 Fellow IEEE; mem. Optical Soc. Am., AAAS, Sigma Xi, Eta Kappa Nu. Roman Catholic. Achievements include research on imaging radar, synthetic aperture radar systems and radar remote sensing. Home: 5072 Grandview Ave Yorba Linda CA 92886-4216 Office: Sci Applications Internat Corp Attn LJ Porcello PO Box 820 Yorba Linda CA 92885-0820 Office Phone: 714-695-1465. Business E-Mail: leonard.j.porcello@saic.com.

**PORDON, GRACE,** writer, poet, artist; life ptnr. Ezequiel Rodriguez Gallegos. Dir. Casa Poema Writer's Retreat, Jalisco, Mexico, 2000—. Dir. Casa Poema Writers' Retreat, Jalisco, Mexico, 2000—. Editor: website. Socialist. Mystic. Office: CasaPoema Writers' Retreat Jalisco Mexico Personal E-mail: casapoema@hotmail.com.

**PORDUM, FRANCIS J.,** former state legislator, educator, marketing professional; b. Lackawanna, NY; 1 child, Carolyn. BA, Colgate U., 1968; MEd, State U. Coll., Buffalo. Formerly tchr. and coach; mem. N.Y. State Assembly, 1983-96, mem. majority steering com., chmn. local govts. com., chmn. com. on state and local rels., chmn. ethics com.; v.p. mktg. and profl. svcs. Capitol Hill Mgmt. Svcs., Inc., Albany, NY, 1997—. Former mem. banking com., corrections com., ins. com., racing and wagering com., transp. com., commn. on critical transp. choices and hazardous wastes and toxic substances N.Y. County. Legislator, Erie County. Recipient Pub. Servant of Yr. award Erie County Fedn. Sportsmen, 1983, Citizen of Yr. award Am.-Polish Eagle, 1984, Legislator Citation of Merit award Nat. Columbus Day Com., 1985, Friend of Edn. award Hamburg Tchrs. Assn., 1986, others. Mem. Hamburg C. of C. (N.Y. retirement bd. del.), Profl. and Businessmen's Assn. Western N.Y., Chopin Singing Soc., Polish Am. Congress, Lackawanna Tchrs. Fedn. Address: 7476 Derby Rd Derby NY 14047-9687

**POREMBKA, MICHAEL RICHARD,** assistant principal, supervisor; b. Latrobe, Pa., Dec. 30, 1974; s. Richard D. and Carmella J. Porembka. BA in History Edn., St. Vincent Coll., Pa., 1997; MEd, Gannon U., Erie, Pa., 2002, Prin. Certification, 2004. Cert. Tchr. Pa., 1997, Adminstrv. Prin., 2002, Adminstrv. Prin. Pa., 2004, prin. cert. Gannon U., Pa., 2004. Tchr. Greater Latrobe (Pa.) Jr. HS, 1998—2006; social studies dept. coord. Greater Latrobe (Pa.) Sch. Dist., 2002—; asst. prin. Greater Latrobe (Pa.) Jr. HS, 2006—; sports/radio broadcaster WCNS Radio, Latrobe, Pa., 2001—. Track coach Greater Latrobe (Pa.) Jr. HS, 1997—2003, football coach, 1998—99, student assistance team mem., 2000—; strategic planning com. Greater Latrobe (Pa.) Sch. Dist., 2001—; asst. softball coach Greater Latrobe (Pa.) Sr. HS, 2005—06. Prodr.(co-host): (radio show) The Sunday Evening Polka Cafe; sports commentator (radio broadcast) Greater Latrobe High School Football on 1480 WCNS Radio. Platelet donor ARC, Greensburg, Pa., 1998—2006; com. mem. Westmoreland County Courthouse Com., Greensburg, Pa., 2005—06; lector St. Rose Roman Cath. Ch., Latrobe, Pa., 2002—06. Mem.: Nat. Assn. Secondary Sch. Principals (assoc.), Internat. Polka Assn. (assoc.), NEA (assoc.), Am. Greek Beneficial Soc. (assoc.), B.P.O. Elks (assoc.). Roman Catholic. Avocations: golf, cars, music. Home: 304 Skoloda Ln Loyalhanna PA 15661 Office: Greater Latrobe Sch Dist 410 Main St Latrobe PA 15650 Office Phone: 724-539-4200.

**PORFILIO, JOHN CARBONE,** federal judge; b. Denver, Oct. 14, 1934; s. Edward Alphonso Porfilio and Caroline (Carbone) Moore; m. Joan West, Aug. 1, 1959 (div. 1983); children: Edward Miles, Joseph Arthur, Jeanne Kathrine; m. Theresa Louise Berger, Dec. 28, 1983; 1 stepchild, Katrina Ann Smith. Student, Stanford U., 1952—54; BA, U. Denver, 1956, LLB, 1959, LLD (hon.), 2000. Bar: Colo. 1959, U.S. Supreme Ct. 1965. Asst. atty. gen. State of Colo., Denver, 1962—68, dep. atty. gen., 1968—72, atty. gen., 1972—74; U.S. bankruptcy judge Dist. of Colo., Denver, 1975—82; judge U.S. Dist. Ct. Colo., Denver, 1982—85, U.S. Ct. Appeals (10th cir.), Denver, 1985—99, sr. judge, 1999—. Instr. Colo. Law Enforcement Acad., Denver, 1965—70, State Patrol Acad., Denver, 1968—70; guest lectr. U. Denver Coll. Law, 1978. Committeeman Arapahoe County Rep. Com., Aurora, Colo., 1968; mgr. Dunbar for Atty. Gen., Denver, 1970. Mem.: ABA. Roman Catholic. Office: US Ct Appeals US Courthouse 2725 Rocky Mountain Ave Ste 480 Loveland CO 80538*

**PORGES, LAWRENCE MICHAEL,** editor; b. N.Y., Sept. 5, 1961; s. Walter Rudolf Porges and Jean Belle Mlotok. BA in History, Tufts U., 1983. From corp. scholarship adminstr. to dir. Youth For Understanding Internat. Exch., Washington, 1986—96, dir., program mgmt., 1993—96; pers. and adminstrn. supr. Atlanta Com. for the Olympic Games, Washington, 1996—96; from mktg. specialist, trade books to editor Nat. Geog. Soc., Washington, 1999—96, editor travel books, 2005—. Managing editor National Geographic Directions; author: (films) Larry Day; prodr.: (films) Larry Day. Jewish. Office: National Geographic Society 1145 17th St NW Washington DC 20036

**PORIES, WALTER JULIUS,** surgeon, educator; b. Munich, Jan. 18, 1930; s. Theodore Francis and Frances (Lowin) P.; m. Muriel Helen Aronson, Aug. 18, 1951; children: Susan E., Mary Jane, Carolyn A., Kathy G.; m. Mary Ann Rose McCarthy, June 4, 1977; children: Mary Lisa, Michael McCarthy. BA, Wesleyan U., Middletown, Conn., 1952; MD with honors, U. Rochester, 1955. Diplomate Am. Bd. Surgery, Am. Bd. Thoracic Surgery. Intern Strong Meml. Hosp., Rochester, NY, 1955—56, resident, 1958—62; chmn. dept. surgery Wright-Patterson AFB, Ohio, 1952—67; asst. prof. surgery and oncology U. Rochester, 1967—69; prof. surgery and assoc. chmn. dept. surgery Case Western Res. U., 1969—77; prof. surgery, biochemistry, exercise and sport medicine East Carolina U., Greenville, NC, 1977—, chmn. dept. surgery, 1977—96, chief Metabolic Inst., 2005—; chief surgery Pitt County Meml. Hosp., 1977—96, prof. surgery U. Health Scis. of Uniformed Svcs., 1982—; founder, assoc. dir. Rochester Cancer Ctr., 1967—69; founder, dir. Cleve. Cancer Ctr., 1972—77, Hospice of Cleve., 1975; founder, chmn. bd. Hospice of Greenville, 1981; med. dir. Home Health Care of Greenville, 1978—83; pres. Surg. Rev. Corp., Raleigh, 2003—. Founder, chmn. bd. Ctr. for Creative Living, 1984; chmn. Echo Mgmt. Orgn., 1994—; vis. scholar NIH, 1996; sec. treas., pres. N.C. Med. Bd. 1997-2003. Author: Clinical Applications of Zinc Metabolism, 1974; editor: Operative Surgery series, vols. 1-4, 1979-83, Office Surgery for Family Physicians, 1985; editor in chief Current Surgery, 1990-2005; editor Nat. Curriculum for Residency in Surgery, 4th edit., 1988—. Bd. dirs. Boy Scouts Am., Cleve., 1974-77, Greenville Arts Mus., 1980-82; pres. Sequoiah, Inc., 1999—; bd. dirs. East Carolina U. Found., United Meth. Homes, 2003-. Maj. USAF, 1955-67; col. USAR, 1979-91, comdr. USAF Hosp., Durham, N.C.; activated Desert Shield, 1990. Decorated Legion of Merit; Thorndyke scholar, 1948-51; recipient McLester award USAF, 1966, Miss. Magnolia Cross, 1989, Presdl. citation for Desert Shield, 1994; named to Hon. Order of Ky. Cols., 1965. Fellow ACS, Am. Coll. Cardiology, Am. Coll. Chest Physicians; mem. Soc. for Vascular Surgery, Soc. Surg. Oncology, Soc. Univ. Surgeons, Am. Surg. Assn., Soc. Environ. Geochemistry (past pres.), Residency Rev. Com. for Surgery (vice-chair 1992-98), So. Surg. Assn., Soc. for Thoracic Surgery, Ea. Carolina Health Orgn. (pres., chmn. bd. 1994-99), Assn. Programs Dirs. in Surgery (pres. 1995-96), N.C. Surg. Assn. (pres. 1995-96), Am. Soc. Bariatric Surgery (pres. 2002), Sigma Xi (O. Max Gardner prize), Phi Kappa Phi. Home: Deep Sun Farm 7464 NC 43 N Macclesfield NC 27852 Office: East Carolina U Dept Surgery Greenville NC 27858 Personal E-mail: pories@aol.com.

**PORILE, NORBERT THOMAS,** chemistry professor; BA, U. Chgo., 1952, MS, 1954, PhD, 1957. Rsch. assoc. Brookhaven Nat. Lab., Upton, NY, 1957-59, assoc. chemist, 1959-63, chemist, 1963-64; vis. prof. chemistry McGill U., 1963-65; assoc. prof. chemistry Purdue U., West Lafayette, Ind.,

1965-69, prof. chemistry, 1969—. Rsch. collaborator Brookhaven Nat. Lab., Argonne Nat. Lab., Los Alamos Sci. Lab., Lawrence Berkeley Lab.; vis. prof. Facultes des Scis., Orsay, France; fellow Soc. Promotion of Sci. in Japan, Inst. Nuclear Study, U. Kyoto, 1961. Editor: Radiochemistry of the Elements and Radiochemical Techniques, 1986-90. John Simon Guggenheim meml. fellow Institut de Physique Nucleaire Orsay, 1971-72; recipient F.D. Martin Undergrad. Teaching award, 1977; Von Humboldt Sr. U.S. Scientist award Philipps U., Marburg, W. Ger., 1982 Mem. Am. Chem. Soc., Am. Phys. Soc. Office: Purdue U Dept Chemistry Brown Lab Lafayette IN 47907

**PORITZ, DEBORAH T.,** state supreme court justice, retired state attorney general; b. Bklyn., Oct. 26, 1936; married; 2 children. BA, Brooklyn Coll., City U. NY, 1958; JD, U. Penn., 1977. Dep. atty. gen. NJ Dept. Law and Pub. Safety, 1977—81, asst. chief environ. protection section, 1981—84, dep. atty. gen. in charge of appeals, chief banking, ins. and pub. securities section, 1984—86, asst. atty. gen., dir. divsn. law, 1986—89; chief counsel to Gov. Thomas Kean, 1989—90; ptnr. Jamieson, Moore, Peskin and Spicer law firm, Princeton, 1990—94; atty. gen. State of NJ, 1994—96; chief justice NJ Supreme Ct., Trenton, 1996—. Office: Supreme Ct NJ Hughes Justice Complex PO Box 23 Trenton NJ 08625-0023 Office Phone: 609-292-2448.*

**POROMANSKA, MARGARITA KIRILOVA,** science educator, environmental scientist; b. Gabrovo, Bulgaria, Nov. 3, 1960; arrived in U.S., 2000; d. Kiril Georgiev Poromanski and Liliana Dimitrova Ralcheva; 1 child, Viktor Dimitrov Arobadjiev. MSc in Biology/Zoology, U. Sofia, Bulgaria, 1983; MSc in Environ. Sci., Ctrl. European U., Budapest, Hungary, 2000. Cert. substitute tchr. Ill. Environ. sci. expert Union Nature Conservation, Sofia, Bulgaria, 1998—99, Pearson Custom Pub., Indpls., 2004—; instr. biology Coll. DuPage, Glen Ellyn, Ill., 2001—, Waubonsee CC, Sugar Grove, 2001—, Columbia Coll., Chgo., 2002—, Nat. Louis U., 2004—; instr. environ. sci. Oakton CC, Des Plaines, 2002—. Sci. and fgn. langs. tutor W. Suburban Ednl. Assocs., Naperville, Ill., 2002—; rsch. fellow Inst. Ecology Bulgarian Acad. Scis., Sofia, 1988—96. Author: editor: New Portals to Appreciating Our Global Environment, 2005. Judge competition Malcolm X Coll., Chgo., 2004. Grantee, Open Soc. Found., 1992; scholar, 1999, Carl-Duisberg Found., 1994. Mem.: NEA, Ill. Edn. Assn., Ctrl. European U. Alumni Assn. Avocations: hiking, bicycling, birdwatching. Home: 1662 Monticello Ct # C Wheaton IL 60187 Office: Coll DuPage Natural And Appied Sci Dept 425 Fawell Blvd Glen Ellyn IL 60137-6599

**POROSOFF, HAROLD,** chemist, science administrator, research and development company executive; b. Bklyn., Apr. 3, 1946; s. Solomon and Ruth (Goldberg) P.; m. Leslie Pamela Freiman, May 19, 1948; children: Lauren, Stephen, Marc. BS, MIT, 1966; PhD, Brown U., 1970. Various rsch. and mgmt. positions fibers div. Am. Cyanamid Co., Stamford, Conn. and Milton, Fla., 1970-78, various mgmt. positions Shulton Rsch. div. Clifton, NJ, 1978-83, dir., 1983-88, v.p. R & D chem. rsch. divsn. Stamford, 1989-93; v.p. R & D Cytec Industries Inc., Stamford, 1993-95; v.p., chief tech. officer Cytec Industries, Inc., Stamford, 1995-98, cons., 1998—. Patentee in field. Mem. AAAS. Office: 22 Olmsted Rd Scarsdale NY 10583-2324 E-mail: hpphd@optonline.net.

**PORPOTAGE-SIGLER, MARYLOU M.,** academic administrator; d. Michael J. and Kathryn Porpotage; 1 child, Zac Sigler. MS, Bucknell U., 1992; BS, BS, Mansfield U., Mansfield, PA, 1969—72. Cert. supt. letter of eligibility Dept. of Edn., Pa., supr. curriculum and instrn. Dept. of Edn., Pa., secondary prin. Dept. of Edn., Pa., comprehensive English in secondary edn. Dept. of Edn., Pa. Tchr. English Mifflin County Sch. Dist., Lewistown, 1973—91, curriculum coord., 1982—90, mid. sch. asst. prin., 1991—93, mid. sch. prin., 1993—97, dir. of fed. programs and staff devel., 1997—. Task group mem. Heroin Task Group, Lewistown, 1998—2004; dir. of devel. Sacred Heart Ch., Lewistown, 2005—06; com. chair Communities That Care, Lewistown, 2000—04; fed. programs monitor Dept. of Edn., Pa., Harrisburg, 2006; mem. e-grants adv. bd. Divsn. Fed. Programs, Dept. Edn., Harrisburg; grants reviewer Divsn. Student Svcs.-Safe and Drug-Free Schs., Dept. of Edn., Harrisburg, 1998—2001. Mem.: ASCD, Pa. Assn. of Elem. and Secondary Sch. Prins., Nat. Assn. of Secondary Sch. Prins., Pa. Assn. of Fed. Programs Coords. Office: Mifflin County Sch Dist 201 Eighth St - Highland Park Lewistown PA 17044 Office Phone: 717-248-0148 8. E-mail: mms12@mcsdk12.org.

**PORRAZ, MAURICIO JIMENEZ LABORA,** civil engineer, researcher; b. Mexico City, Mar. 24, 1938; s. Manuel Guillen Porraz and Dolores Jimenez Labora; m. Margarita Lando Coindreau, Oct. 1, 1966; children: Margarita, Mauricio, Miguel. BA, La Salle U., Mexico City, 1954; degree in civil engring. with honors, Autonomous Nat. U. Mex., Mexico City, 1961; degree in ocean engring., Assn. Orgn. des Stages France, Paris, 1964; degree in petroleum offshore engring., Assn. Coop. Technique Internat. Maritime, Marseille, France, 1968; postgrad., Nat. Engring. Acad., Mex., 1977, Corpus Christi, Toledo, Spain, 1988. Pres. Orgn. Submarina Mexicana, Mexico City, 1965-2001, Equipos y Tecnicas, Mexico City, 1967-2001, Control de Erosion, Mexico City, 1971-2001, Conersa, Mexico City, 1973-91, Estructuras Marinas Concreto, Mexico City, 1979-91, Constrn., Cons. y Comercializadora, Mexico City, 1991-2001, Soluciones Ecoambientales, 2000—. Engr. in geosyntetics, introduced interconnected concrete blocks for breakwaters; patentee in field. Bd. dirs. Panam. Fedn. on Oceanic Coastal Engring., Stevens Inst. Tech., 1989; corr. mem. Royal Acad. Nice Arts and Hist. Scis., Toledo, 1989; mem. Royal Inst. Geography, Madrid, 1970-91. Lt. Mexican Infantry, 1956-57. Recipient Best Thesis in Yr. award Engring. Found. (Mex.), 1963, rsch. and invention medal Soc. for Rsch. and Invention (Paris), 1977, Internat. Coastal Engring. award ASCE, 1977, 91; named Man of Yr. Group Expansion Economy and Fins. Bus. (Mex.), 1983-84, Hon. Armed Knight Toledo, Spain, Knight Marshal D. Mexico Mil. and Hospitaller Order of St. Lazarus of Jerusalem, 1998. Fellow Mexican Assn. Architects and Engrs. (centenary 1968); mem. Venezuela's Engrs. Soc. (dir. A, goco award 1972), Panam. Fedn. Engring. Assn. (oceanic engring. com. 1981), Ctr. Profl. Actualization (prof. 1981), Mex. Acad. Engrs. Roman Catholic. Office: Acad Scis Gen Sec Pla Villa de Madrid # 3 06700 Mexico City Roma Mexico E-mail: mauricio@porraz.com, mporrazjl@hotmail.com.

**PORRECA, ANNE AGNES,** secondary school educator, counseling administrator; b. Buffalo; d. Dominick Peter and Marion (Piccone) P. BA, Canisius Coll., 1966, MA in Edn., 1969. Stenographer Canisius Coll., Buffalo, N.Y., 1949-55, sec. dean of faculty, 1956—59; sec. pres., 1959—66; tchr. Heim Middle Sch., Williamsville, N.Y., 1966-68; counselor State of N.J. Employment Svc., Camden, Vineland, 1968-71; guidance counselor Vineland (NJ) HS, 1971—77, 1978—96; counselor Royal Pers., Encino, Calif., 1977—78; South Jersey-Phila. area rep. Canisius Coll., 1997—2004. Tchr. Vineland (N.J.) Adult High Sch. Program, 1969-71. Mem. NEA, N.J. Edn. Assn., Vineland Edn. Assn., N.J. S.G.A., Alpha Delta Kappa. Democrat. Roman Catholic. Avocations: reading, travel, music, bridge, theater. Personal E-mail: anneporre7@aol.com.

**PORRECO, RICHARD PATRICK,** physician; b. Borinquen Field, PR, Aug. 27, 1946; s. Andrew Roger and Nancy Tendera Porreco; m. Terese Irene Kaske, Oct. 24, 1992; m. Jacqueline Anne Davis, June 8, 1968 (div. Apr. 29, 1989); children: Richard Christopher, Allison Christine. MD, U. Colo. Med. Ctr., Denver, Colo., 1971. Lic. Am. Bd.of Ob-gyn, 1977, Am. Bd. of Ob-gyn, Maternal-Fetal Med, 1981, Am. Bd. of Med. Genetics, 1984. Staff physician Naval Regional Med. Ctr., San Diego, 1975—77; fellow, maternal-fetal medicine U. Calif., San Diego, 1977—79; staff perinatalogist Kaiser-Permanente Med. Group, San Diego, 1979—81. Dir. maternal-fetal medicine Presbyn./St. Luke's Med. Ctr., Denver, 1981—. Joint venture com. HealthOne/HCA Joint Venture, Denver, Colo., 1999—2002. Lt. comdr. USNR, 1975—77. Named Recipient Most Outstanding Faculty Tchg. Award, U. Colo. OBGYN Dept., 1990; grantee Rsch. in Genetics, Bank of Am., Giannini, 1977-79; scholar Med. Scholarship, Clara C. Wolleson Trust, Colo. Springs, 1967-71. Fellow: ACOG (pres., colo. gyn-ob soc. 1996—97, Outstanding Program Chmn. 1989); mem.: Denver Clin. and Path. Soc., Soc. Maternal Fetal Medicine, Alpha Omega Alpha (life), Alpha Tau

Omega (life; v.p. 1966—67). Achievements include research in Over 80 various contbn. to clin. obstetrics lit; 25 years high risk obstet. care in Rocky Mtn region. Office: Obstetrix Med Group of Colo 1601 East 19th Ave Ste 5050 Denver CO 80218 Office Phone: 303-860-9990.

**PORT, SIDNEY CHARLES,** mathematician, educator; b. Chgo., Nov. 27, 1935; s. Isadore and Sarah (Landy) P.; m. Idelle Jackson, Mar. 24, 1957; children— Ethan, Jonathan, Daniel. AB, Northwestern U., 1957, MS, 1958, PhD, 1962. Staff mathematician Rand Corp., 1962-66; assoc. prof. math. U. Calif. at Los Angeles, 1966-69, prof., 1969—. Author: (with P. Hoel and C. Stone) Probability, Statistics and Stochastic Processes, 1971, (with C. Stone) Brownian Motion and Classical Potential Theory, 1978, Theoretical Probability for Applications, 1993; contbr. articles to profl. jours. Fellow Inst. Math. Statistics; mem. Am. Math. Soc. Home: 680 Kingman Ave Santa Monica CA 90402-1334 Office: UCLA Dept Math Los Angeles CA 90024 Office Phone: 310-825-4701. E-mail: sport@ucla.edu.

**PORTA, SIENA GILLANN,** sculptor, educator; b. N.Y.C., Nov. 5, 1951; d. Vincent Anthony Porta and Barbara Ann Gill Porta Hutchinson; m. Robert Christopher Dell, May 30, 1986; 1 child, Malcolm Vincent Dell. BS in Studio Arts, Bklyn. Coll., CUNY, 1977; MFA in Sculpture, Pa. State U., 1979. Sci. illustrator Columbia U./Lamont-Doherty Geol. Obs., Palisades, NY, 1980—87; scenic artist Saturday Night Live, N.Y.C., 1986—89, Met. Opera, N.Y.C., 1987—92; master scenic artist numerous Broadway prod., including Frankie and Johnny, Boiler Rm., Sorrows and Rejoicings, 1992—; adj. prof. contemporary arts Ramapo Coll., 2000—; adj. prof. art St. Thomas Aquinas, Sparkill, NY, 2000—; represented by Noho Gallery, N.Y.C., 14 Sculptors Inc., N.Y.C. Adj. prof. Bergen CC, Paramus, NJ, 1984—85; artist-in-residence Brisons Veor, Cornwall, England, 2003. One-woman shows include 14 Sculptors Gallery, NYC, 1984-85, 88, 90, Mid-Hudson Arts and Sci. Ctr., Poughkeepsie, NY, 1992-93, Dominican Coll., Blauvelt, NY, 1980, 2005, Noho Gallery, NYC, 2003, 2005; group shows at A.B. Condon Gallery, NYC, 1982-83, Terrain Gallery, NYC, 1984, Am. Cultural Ctr., Reykiavik, Iceland, 1988, Notre Dame U., South Bend, Ind., 1990, Lehigh U., Phila., Blue Hill Cult. Ctr., Pearl River, NY, 1995, Eighth Floor Gallery, NYC, 1996, NJ City U., Jersey City, Nassau C.C., Garden City, NY, The Interchurch Ctr., Riverside Dr., NY, 1998, Adelphi U., NY, 2000, St. Thomas Aquinas Coll., Sparkill, NY, 2000, Galleri Ofeigur, 2001, Noho Gallery, 2001-02, 04-05, Snaefelsness Regl. Museum, 2002, Hafnarborg Ctr. for Culture, Mus, 2002-03, Regional Mus. of Hornafjorduv, 2003, Rutgers U., 2003, 14 sculptors at McLevy Park Outdoor Installation, Bridgeport, Conn., 2004, 14 sculptures including The Lockwood Mathews Mansion Mus. Pk., Norwalk, Conn., 2005-, others; represented in collections at Fulbright Commn., Reykjavik, Bergen C.C., Paramus, NJ, 1988, St. Philip R.C. Ch., Norwalk, Conn., Jacob Riis Nat. Park US Embassy, Brisons Veor Trust Cornwall, Eng., Iceland, Hafnarborg Mus.; subject of video Me and The Mirror, 1990; contbr. articles to popular mag., Internat. Sculpture Ctr. Pa. State Arts Coun./Hershey Med. Coll. grantee, 1978-79; NY State Coun. on the Arts grantee, 1986; USIA-Ptnrs. of Ams. travel grant to St. Lucia, W.I., 1992, NY Fdn. for the Arts grantee, 2002.; artist resident Brisons Veor, Cornwall, Eng., 2003. Mem. Zen Ctr. of San Diego. Home: PO Box 46 Palisades NY 10964-0046 Personal E-mail: sportaedu@aol.com.

**PORTAL, GILBERT MARCEL ADRIEN,** oil industry executive; b. Paris, Aug. 2, 1930; came to U.S., 1982; s. Emmanuel Jules and Henriette Josephine (Bonnard) P.; m. Monique Janine Adam, July 12, 1951; children: Dominique, Veronique, Marc-Emmanuel. Baccalaureate, Lycee Charlemagne U., Paris, 1949; Ingenieur Civil des Mines, Sch. of Mines, St. Etienne, 1955; diplome du C.P.A., Ctr. Advanced Bus., Paris, 1969; auditeur 30 eme session IHEDN, Higher Studies Nat. Defense, Paris, 1978. Geophysicist Societe Nationale Elf Aquitaine, Sahara, Algeria, 1957-63, exploration mgr. north sea, 1963-65, dep. exec. v.p. Europe, 1965-68, dep. exec. v.p. North and South Am., 1968-70, chief exec. officer Iraq, 1970-72, dir., chief exec. officer Gabon, Africa, 1972-76, dep. exec. v.p. hydrocarbons, 1976-78, exec. v.p. North Africa, Mid. East, Far East, 1978-82; pres. Elf Aquitaine Petroleum, Houston, 1982-89; chmn., chief exec. officer Elf Exploration, Inc., Houston, 1989-90; sec.-gen. European Petroleum Industry Assn., 1990-95; ptnr. G.M.H. Internat. Oil and Gas Consulting, Paris, 1995—; pres. internat. devel. Howard Energy Internat. LLC, 1999—2002. Served to lt. French Army, 1955-57. Decorated Legion of Honor (France), Nat. Merit Order (France); Equatorial Star (Gabon). Mem. Cercle Royal Gaulois Artistique et Littéraire. Roman Catholic. Office Phone: (33) 1 45 58 01 02. Business E-mail: gmh@portal-consult.com.

**PORTALE, ALFRED,** chef, restaurant owner; Grad., Culinary Inst. Am., 1981. Chef, co-owner Gotham Bar and Grill, N.Y.C. Mem. Singapore Airlines Internat. Chef Panel. Author: Gotham Bar and Grill Cookbook, 1998 (Julia Child Cookbook award, 1998), 12 Seasons Cookbook, 2001. Named Best Chef in N.Y., 1993; recipient Outstanding Pastry Chef award, James Beard Found., 2006. Office: Gotham Bar & Grill 12 E 12th St New York NY 10003-4498*

**PORTE, JOEL MILES,** language educator; b. Bklyn., Nov. 13, 1933; s. Jacob I. and Frances (Derison) P.; m. Ilana D'Ancona, June 18, 1962 (div. 1977); 1 child, Susanna Maria; m. Helene Sophrin, Oct. 18, 1985. AB magna cum laude, CCNY, 1957; A.M., Harvard U., 1958, PhD, 1962. Instr. English Harvard U., Cambridge, Mass., 1962-64, prof., 1964-68, assoc. prof., 1968-69, prof., 1969-82, Bernbaum prof. lit., 1982-87, chmn. dept. English and Am. Lit., 1985-87; Frederic J. Whiton prof. English Cornell U., Ithaca, NY, 1987-89, Ernest I. White prof. Am. Studies and Humane Letters, 1989—. Vis. lectr. Am. Studies Rsch. Ctr., Hyderabad, India, spring 1976. Author: Emerson and Thoreau: Transcendentalists in Conflict, 1966, The Romance in America: Studies in Cooper, Poe, Hawthorne, Melville and James, 1969, Representative Man: Ralph Waldo Emerson in His Time, 1979, In Respect to Egotism: Studies in American Romantic Writing, 1991; editor: Emerson in His Journals, 1982, Emerson: Prospect and Retrospect, 1982, Emerson: Essays and Lectures, 1983, New Essays on Portrait of a Lady, 1990, A Cambridge Companion to Ralph Waldo Emerson (with Saundra Morris), 1999, Emerson's Prose and Poetry: A Norton Critical Edit. (with Saundra Morris), 2001, Consciousness and Culture: Emerson and Thoreau Reviewed, 2004. Scholar in Residence, Rockefeller Found., Bellagio, Italy, 1979; fellow John Simon Guggenheim Found., 1981-82. Mem. Am. Lit. Assn., Phi Beta Kappa. Home: 14 Yardley Green Ithaca NY 14850-1237 Office Phone: 607-255-6806. E-mail: jp26@cornell.edu.

**PORTELA, ANTONIO GOUVEA,** retired mechanical engineer, researcher; b. Lisbon, Portugal, Jan. 26, 1918; s. Raul Lello Portella and Esther Gouvea Portela; married, Sept. 29, 1965; 2 children. Engr. degree, Inst. Superior Tecnico, Lisbon, 1960; prof. degree, Inst. Sup. Tecn., Lisbon, 1958. Cert. mech. engring. Contbr. articles to profl. jours. Mem. AAAS, ASME, Am. Nuclear Soc., N.Y. Acad. Scis., Academia de Engenharia of Portugal. Office: Inst Superior Tecnico Av Rovisco Paes Lisbon Portugal

**PORTELL, KEITH S,** application developer, consultant; s. Sherman Melvin and Caroline Margaret Portell; m. Claudia K. Epting, July 14, 1996; children: Andrew Justin, Aaron Michael. BS in info sys. mgmt., U. Of Md. U. Coll., 1995—97; Database Systems Technologies Grad. Cert., U. of Md. U. Coll., 2001—03, MS in computer sys. mgmt., 2001—04. MCSE Microsoft, 1997, cert. Novell Master Network Engineer Novell, 1994. Supr. Six Flags Corp., Houston, 1982—88; sys. analyst Giant Food, Inc., Landover, Md., 1988—94; lan/wan engr. Bus. Network Assoc., Annapolis, Md., 1994—95; network adminstr. Micros Systems, Inc., Beltsville, Md., 1995; lead network engr. Zurich Personal Ins., Balt., 1996—97; sr. systems programmer/analyst Mayo Clinic, Jacksonville, Fla., 1997—. Contbr. articles. Mem. Air Jaycees, Annapolis, Md., 1996—98. Mem.: Health Data Warehousing Assn. (assoc.), Am. Med. Informatics Assn (assoc.). Independent. Christian. Achievements include invention of Medical Data Trust - Mayo Clinic. Avocations: travel,

reading. Home: 6935 La Loma Dr Jacksonville FL 32217 Office: Mayo Clinic 4500 San Pablo Rd #VAS153A Jacksonville FL 32224 Office Phone: 904-953-0416. Personal E-mail: keith@keithportell.net. E-mail: portell.keith@mayo.edu.

**PORTEOUS, G. THOMAS, JR.,** judge; b. 1946; BA, La. State U., 1968, JD, 1971. Spl. counsel, atty. gen., 1971-73; asst. dist. atty. Dist. Atty. Office Parish of Jefferson, 1973—84; ptnr. Edward, Porteous & Amato, Grenta, La., 1973-74, Edwards, Porteous & Lee, Grenta, 1974-76, Porteous, Lee & Mustakas, 1976-80, Porteous & Mustakas, Metairie, La., 1980-84; city atty. City of Harahan, La., 1982-84; dist. ct. judge divsn. A State of La., 1984-94; dist. judge U.S. Dist. Ct. (ea. dist.), La., 1994—. Mem. ABA, Fed. Bar Assn., La. State Bar Assn., 4th and 5th Cir. Judges Assn., Jefferson Bar Assn., Am. Judges Assn., La. Dist. Atty. Assn. Office: US Dist Ct E Dist 500 Poydras St Rm C-206 New Orleans LA 70130-3313 Office Phone: 504-589-7585.

**PORTEOUS, SKIPP,** private investigator, writer; b. Hartford, Conn., Feb. 7, 1944; s. Charles Robert and Marian Berle (Guy) P.; m. Linda Marie Silvernail, Mar. 25, 1965 (div. Feb. 1977) children: Angela Monique, Charles Mark, Marylisa; m. Barbara Ann Simon, May 1, 1983 (div. June 2002). Student, Life Bible Coll., LA, 1966-67, East LA C.C., 1969, Columbia Green C.C., Greenport, NY, 1978. Ordained ministry Elim Fellowship, 1968; cert. radio mktg. cons. Licensed private investigator, Mass., NY. Evangelist Chapel on the Strip, Hollywood, Calif., 1967-68; pastor Pasadena (Calif.) Christian Fellowship, 1968-74, West Copake (NY) Reformed Ch., 1974-76, Agape House Christian Ctr., Hillsdale, NY, 1976-77; sales exec., promoter various radio stas. newspapers, NY, Mass., 1977-84; pres. Inst. First Amendment Studies, Inc., Gt. Barrington, Mass., 1984—; pvt. investigator, owner Sherlock Investigations, NY, Mass., 1998—. Radio TV talk show guest, nationwide, 1986—; rschr. TV news networks, mags. Author: Jesus Doesn't Live Here Anymore-From Fundamentalist to Freedom Writer, 1991; co-author: Challenging, The Christian Right - The Activist's Handbook; author mag. articles, columns. Elim fellow. Democrat. Jewish. Avocations: photography, painting. Office Phone: 212-579-4302. Personal E-mail: skippporteous@gmail.com.

**PORTER, ANDREW CALVIN,** academic administrator, psychologist, educator; b. Huntington, Pa., July 10, 1942; s. Rutherford and Grace (Johnson) P.; children: Matthew, Anna, John, Joe, Kate. BS, Ind. State U., 1963; MS, U. Wis., 1965, PhD, 1967. Vis. asst. prof. Ind. State U., 1967; asst. prof. ednl. psychology Mich. State U., East Lansing, 1967—70, dir. office rsch. consultation, 1967—73, assoc. prof. ednl. psychology, 1970—74; vis. scholar Nat. Inst. Edn., Washington, 1973—74, chief measurement and methodology divsn., 1974—75; prof. ednl. psychology Mich. State U., East Lansing, 1974—88; assoc. dir. basic skills group Nat. Inst. Edn., Washington, 1975—76; dir. Sch. Advanced Studies Coll. Edn. Mich. State U., East Lansing, 1979—81, assoc. dean rsch. and grad. study Coll. Edn., 1981—85; Anderson-Bascom prof. edn., prof. ednl. psychology U. Wis., Madison, 1988—2003, dir. Wis. Ctr. Edn. Rsch., 1988—2003; Patricia and Rodes Hart prof. ednl. leadership and policy Vanderbilt U., Nashville, 2003—, dir. Learning Scis. Inst., 2003—. Mem adv. com. What Works Clearinghouse Inst. Edn. Scis., 2002-, steering com. math/sci. partnerships, Nat. Acad. Sci., 2003-2005, nat. assessment governing bd., 2004-; chmn. adv. coun. on edn. stats., U.S. Dept. Edn., 1994-2001; chair bd. Internat. Studies, Nat. Acad. Sci., Nat. Rsch. Coun., 1998-2001 Editor: (with A. Gamoran) Methodological Advances in Cross-National Surveys of Educational Achievement, 2002; mem. editl. bd. Tchrs. Coll. Record, 1995—, Am. Ednl. Rsch. Jour., 2004—. Bd. dirs. Madison Urban League, 1992-96. Recipient Disting. Alumni award, Ind. State U., 1994, Sch. Edn. Dean's Club Faculty Disting. Achievement Award, U. Wis.-Madison, 1996, Crystal Apple Award, Mich. State U., 2000, Alumni Achievement award, U. Wis., Madison, 2005. Mem. Am. Ednl. Rsch. Assn. (pres. 2001, Outstanding Reviewer award 2003), Nat. Coun. Edn. Measurement, Nat. Coun. Tchrs. Math., Nat. Acads. (lifetime nat. mem.), Nat. Acad. Edn. (v.p. 2005), Phi Delta Kappa (life). Office: Vanderbilt U Learning Scis Inst Box 59 Peabody Sta Nashville TN 37203 E-mail: andy.porter@vanderbilt.edu.

**PORTER, BIGGS C.,** corporate financial executive; B in Acctg., Duke U.; M in Profl. Acctg., U. Tex., Austin. CPA. Audit prin. Arthur Young & Co.; corp. controller, asst. treas. Vought Aircraft; CFO integrated systems sector Northrop Grumman, CFO comml. aircraft divsn.; sr. v.p., corp. controller TXU Corp., Dallas; v.p., corp. controller Raytheon Co., Waltham, Mass., 2003—, acting CFO, 2005—06. Mem.: AICPA. Office: Raytheon Co 870 Winter St Waltham MA 02451-1449 Office Phone: 781-522-3000.*

**PORTER, BLAINE ROBERT MILTON,** sociology professor, psychology professor; b. Morgan, Utah, Feb. 24, 1922; s. Brigham Ernest and Edna (Brough) P.; m. Elizabeth Taylor, Sept 27, 1943 (dec.); children: Claudia Black, Roger B., David T., Patricia A. Hintze, Corinna; m. Myrna Katherine Kennedy, Feb. 26, 1988. Student, Utah State U., 1940-41; BS, Brigham Young U., 1947, MA, 1949; PhD (Grant Found. fellow family life edn. 1951-52), Cornell U., 1952. Instr. sociology Iowa State Coll., 1949-51; asst. prof. sociology and child devel. Iowa State U., 1952-55; prof., chmn. dept. human devel. and family relationships Brigham Young U., 1955-65, dean Coll. Family Living, 1966-80, prof., 1980-87. Vis. prof. Fulbright rsch. scholar U. London, 1965-66; vis. prof. U. Wurzberg, 1980, 81, 83; facilitator human rels. workshops for the Human Devel. Inst., Denver, 1988-90, pres./CEO Families for Children Internat., Inc., 2001—. Editor: The Latterday Saint Family, 1963, rev. edit., 1966; editor quar. jour.: Family Perspective, 1966-82; contbr. articles to profl. jours. Pres. elect Iowa Coun. Family Rels., 1954-55; pres. Utah Coun. Family Rels. Coun., 1957-58; chmn. sect. marriage counseling Nat. Coun. Family Rels., 1958-59, bd. dirs., 1959-60, exec. com., 1958-72, pres., 1963-64; bd. dirs. Am, Family Soc 1975 85, Pilot USA AF, 1942 45 Recipient Prof. of Yr. award Brigham Young U., 1964. Mem. Am. Home Econs. Assn. (vice chmn. sect. family relations and child devel. 1955-56), Am. Sociol. Assn. (sec. sect. on family 1964-67), Am. Assn. Marriage and Family Therapy, Am. Psychol. Assn., Soc. Research in Child Devel., Sigma Xi, Phi Kappa Phi (chpt. pres. 1969-71) Home: 1675 Pine Ln Provo UT 84604-2163 Office: 4505 HBLL Brigham Young U Provo UT 84602 Personal E-mail: porter22@comcast.net.

**PORTER, BRUCE JACKMAN,** computer engineer, application developer, portfolio manager, civil engineer; b. El Paso, Tex., Aug. 7, 1954; s. Covington Baskin and Carolyn Fee (Bruce) P.; m. Janette Anne Brown, Oct. 19, 1985; children: Laura, Holly, Travis. BS, US Mil. Acad., 1976; MS in Computer Sci., Stanford U., 1985, MS in Civil Engring., 1985; grad., U.S. Army War Coll., 1997. Engr. in tng., Pa. Commd. 1st lt. U.S. Army, 1979-80, advanced through grades to lt. col., 1993, co-commdr. 17th armored engr. bn. Ft. Hood, Tex., 1977-80, constrn. engr. Misawa, Japan, 1981-83, orgnl. evaluator Ft. Leavenworth, Kans., 1989-90, ops. officer 5th engr. combat bn. Saudi Arabia and Iraq, 1990-91; assoc. prof. mathematics U.S. Mil. Acad., West Point, NY, 1985-88; chief concepts officer USA Engr. Sch., Ft. Leonard Wood, Mo., 1991-93; logistics assistance officer 1st Cavalry Divsn., Ft. Hood, Tex., 1993-94; comdg. officer 20th Engr. Bn., 1st Cavalry Divsn., Ft. Hood, Tex., 1994-96; sr. engr. trainer Nat. Tng. Ctr., Ft. Irwin, Calif., 1997-98; cmdr., engr. brigade 4th Infantry Divn., Ft. Hood, Tex., 1998—99; exec. officer Army chief of staff for ops. Pentagon, Washington, 1999—2001; investment rep. Edward Jones & Co., Buellton, Calif., 2001—. Pioneer new courses in computer theory and discrete math. U.S. Mil. Acad., 1987-88; proponent Army Engr. Restructive Initiative, 1991-92; panel mem. Army Study Team for Battle Dynamics, 1992; mem. Summer Study for Chief of Staff of Army, 1992. Co-author: Army Keystone Operations Field Manual, 1993; pub. papers on combat engr. reorgn., 1991-92, 98. Decorated DSM, Bronze Star, Legion of Merit. Home: 345 Meadowlark Rd Santa Ynez CA 93460 Office: 175 H McMurray Rd Buellton CA 93427 Office Phone: 805-688-9079.

**PORTER, CHARLES MICHAEL (MIKE PORTER),** business consultant, executive; b. Danville, Ill., Jan. 11, 1957; s. Charles K. Jr. and Constance K. (Kinnaman) P.; m. Kathryn S. Klein, July 15, 1990; children: Eric J., Jerry D. AA, Danville Area C.C., 1986; BS in Accountancy, U. Ill., 1988, MS in

Taxation, 1989. Owner C.M. Porter Realty, Danville, Ill., 1980-85; staff acct. Clifton Gunderson & Co., Danville, Ill., 1989; staff tax acct. McGladrey & Pullen, Peoria, Ill., 1989-91, Galesburg, Ill., 1991-95; dir. tax Dollar Gen. Corp., Goodlettsville, Tenn., 1995—2002; v.p., CFO Clear Check, Inc., Greenville, SC, 2002—06; pres., chmn. Rodeo Stockyard, Inc.; v.p., CFO BPG Group, Greenville, SC, 2006—. Owner Thunder Run Ranch. Former bd. dirs., treas. Dollar Gen. Literacy Found. Mem. Tax Execs. Inst., Internat. Mass Retailers Assn. (former chmn. tax adv. com.), Profl. Rodeo Cowboys Assn. (assoc.), Southern Extreme Bull Riding Assn., U. Ill. Alumni Assn., Am. Bucking Bull Assn. Avocations: rodeo, stock and ranch horses, rodeo bull breeding. Office: Clear Check Inc 135 Interstate Blvd Ste 6 Greenville SC 29615 Business E-Mail: mike@rodeostockyard.com.

**PORTER, DANIEL REED, III,** museum director; b. Northampton, Mass., July 2, 1930; s. Daniel Reed and Eleanor (Parsons) P.; m. Joan Joyce Dornfeld, Nov. 22, 1958; children: Leslie Marie, Andrew Gregory. BA, U. Mass., 1952; MA, U. Mich., 1956. Asst. to dir. State Hist. Soc. Wis., Madison, 1956-58; dir. Hist. Soc. York County, Pa., 1958-61; asst. dir., dir. Ohio Hist. Soc., Columbus, 1961-74; exec. dir. Preservation Soc. Newport County, R.I., 1974-78; dir., prof. Cooperstown (N.Y.) Grad. Programs, 1978-82; dir. N.Y. State Hist. Assn. Farmer's Mus. Cooperstown, 1982-92. Hist. preservation officer State of Ohio, Columbus, 1967-74. Editor: N.Y. Heritage, 1984-92; contbr. articles to publs. in field. With U.S. Army, 1952-54, Korea. Recipient Spl. award of Merit Ohio Assn. Hist. Socs., 1970. Mem. Am. Assn. Mus. (accreditation commn. 1982-88, councillor-at-large 1981-84), Am. Assn. State and Local History (coun., Nashville 1971-73, councillor 1985-87) Congregationalist.

**PORTER, DARWIN FRED,** writer; b. Greensboro, NC, Sept. 13, 1937; s. Numie Rowan and Hazel Lee (Phillips) P. BA, U. Miami, 1959. Bur. chief Miami Herald, 1959-60; v.p. Haggart Assoc., NYC, 1961-64; editor, author Arthur Frommer Inc., NYC, 1964-67, Frommer/Pasmantier Pub. Corp., NYC, 1967-86, Prentice Hall Press, NYC, 1987-90, Simon & Schuster, NYC, 1991—. Author: Frommer Travel Guides to: England, 1964, Spain, 1966, Scandinavia, 1967, Los Angeles, 1969, London, 1970, Lisbon/Madrid, 1972, Paris, 1972, Morocco, 1974, Rome, 1974, Portugal, 1968, England, 1969, Italy, 1969, Germany, 1970, France, 1970, Caribbean, Bermuda, the Bahamas, 1980, Switzerland, 1984, Austria and Hungary, 1984, Bermuda and the Bahamas, 1985, Scotland and Wales, 1985, the Virgin Islands, 1991, Scotland, 1992, Jamaica/Barbados, 1992, Puerto Rico, 1992, the Caribbean, 1993, Bermuda, 1993, the Bahamas, 1993, Austria, 1993, Madrid & the Costa del Sol, 1993, San Francisco, 1996, California, 1996, Caribbean Cruises, 1996, Caribbean Ports of Call, 1996, Georgia and the Carolinas, 1996, Charleston and Savannah, 1996, Munich and The Bavarian Alps, 1996, Vienna & the Danube, 1996, Guide to Caribbean Cruises, 1997, Frommer's Europe, 1997, Frommer's Venice, 1997, Barcelona, Madrid & Seville, 1997, Frommer's Portable London, 1998, Frommer's Portable Bahamas, 1998, Frommer's Portable Paris, 1998, Frommer's Portable Berlin, 1999; author: Butterflies in Heat, 1976, Marika, 1977, Venus, 1982, Razzle-Dazzle, 1998, Blood Moon, 1998, Frommer's Sweden, 1999, Frommer's Denmark, 1999, Midnight in Savannah, 2000, Hollywood's Silent Closet, 2000, Frommer's Frankfurt, 2001, Frommer's Great Britain, 2001, Bahamas for Dummies, 2002, Caribbean for Dummies, 2002, Rhinestone Country, 2002, Frommer's Charleston, 2003, Frommer's Savannah, 2003, Frommer's Sicily, 2003, Frommer's Norway, 2003, France for Dummies, 2003, Frommer's Cayman Islands, 2003, Frommer's Dominican Republic, 2003, The Secret Life of Humphrey Bogart, 2003, Katharine the Great, 2004, Fommer's Europe By Rail, 2004, Howard Hughes: Hell's Angel, 2004, Frommer's Seville and Southern Spain, 2005, Frommer's Andalusia, 2005, Irreverent Paris, 2005, Brando Unzipped, 2006, Frommer's Tuscany Day by Day, 2006. Recipient Silver award Internat. Film and TV Festival NY, 1977. Mem. Soc. Am. Travel Writers, Smithsonian Assoc., Nat. Trust for Hist. Preservation, Sigma Delta Chi. Home: 75 Saint Marks Pl Staten Island NY 10301-1606 Office Phone: 718-556-9410. Personal E-mail: porterandprince@hotmail.com.

**PORTER, DAVID HUGH,** musician, classicist, academic administrator, music educator; b. NYC, Oct. 29, 1935; s. Hugh B. and Ethel K. (Flentye) P.; m. Laudie Ernestine Dimmette, June 21, 1958 (dec. Nov., 1986); children: Hugh, Everett, Helen, David; m. Helen Louise Nelson, Aug. 24, 1987. BA with highest honors, Swarthmore Coll., 1958; PhD (Danforth Grad. fellow, Woodrow Wilson Grad. fellow), Princeton U., 1962; student, Phila. Conservatory Music, 1955-61. Instr. in classics and music Carleton Coll., Northfield, Minn., 1962-63, asst. prof., 1963-68, assoc. prof., 1968-73, prof., 1973-87, William H. Laird prof. liberal arts, 1974-87, pres. faculty, 1980-82, coll. pres., 1986-87; pres. Skidmore Coll., Saratoga Springs, NY, 1987—99, prof. classics, 1987—99; vis. prof. classics Williams Coll., Williamstown, Mass., 1999—, Harry C. Payne vis. prof. liberal arts, 2000—. Phi Beta Kappa vis. lectr., 1979-92, vis. scholar, 1994-95; vis. prof. classics Princeton U., 1986; recitalist, lectr., especially on contemporary music, at colls., univs. throughout U.S., U.K., on radio and TV; chmn. Hudson-Mohawk Assn., 1990-92, Inst. for Internat. Edn. of Students, 2004—. Author: Only Connect: Three Studies in Greek Tragedy, 1987, Horace's Poetic Journey: A Reading of Odes I-III, 1987, Virginia Woolf and Logan Pearsall Smith, 2002, Virginia Woolf and the Hogarth Press, 2004; editor: Carleton Remembered, 1909-86, 1987, The Not Quite Innocent Bystander: Writings of Edward Steuermann, 1989; contbr. articles to profl. jours. Rsch. fellow NEH, 1969-70, 83-84, Am. Coun. Learned Socs., 1976-77 Mem. Am. Philological Assn., Classical Assn. Atlantic States. Democrat. Mem. United Ch. Of Christ. Avocations: hiking, reading, collecting rugs and books. Home: 5 Birch Run Dr Saratoga Springs NY 12866-1023 E-mail: ddodger@skidmore.edu.

**PORTER, DAVID LINDSEY,** history and political science professor, writer; b. Holyoke, Mass., Feb. 18, 1941; s. Willis Hubert and Lora Frances (Bowen) P.; m. Marilyn Esther Platt, Nov. 28, 1970; children: Kevin, Andrea. BA magna cum laude, Franklin Coll., 1963; MA, Ohio U., 1965; PhD, Pa. State U., 1970. Asst. prof. history Rensselaer Poly. Inst., Troy, NY, 1970-75, co-dir. Am. studies program, 1972-74; ednl. adminstrv. asst. Civil Svc. Office State of N.Y., Troy, 1975-76; asst. prof. history William Penn U., Oskaloosa, Iowa, 1976-77, assoc. prof. history, 1977-82, prof. history and polit. sci., 1982-86, Louis Tuttle Shangle prof. history and polit. sci., 1986—, chmn. Sperry & Hutchinson Found. lectureship series, 1980-82, acting chair social and behavioral scis. divsn., 2000—01. Supr. legis. internship program Iowa Gen. Assembly, 1978—, records inventory project Mahaska County, 1978-79, internship program Washington Ctr., 1985—; active Franklin D. Roosevelt Meml. Commn.; chpt. adviser Phi Alpha Theta, 1977—. Author: The Seventy-sixth Congress and World War II, 1939-40, 1979, Congress and the Waning of the New Deal, 1980; co-author: The San Diego Padres Encyclopedia, 2002; contbr. Dictionary of American Biography, 1981, 1988, 1994, 1995, Directory of Teaching Innovations in History, 1981, The Book of Lists #3, 1983, Biographical Dictionary of Internationalists, 1983, The Hero in Transition, 1983, Herbert Hoover and the Republican Era: A Reconsideration, 1984, The History of Mahaska County, Iowa, 1984, Franklin D. Roosevelt, His Life and Times: An Encyclopedic View, 1985, The Rating Game in American Politics: An Interdisciplinary Approach, 1987, Sport History, 1987, Book of Days, 1988, Sports Encyclopedia North America, 1988, The Harry S. Truman Encyclopedia, 1989, Encyclopedia of Major League Baseball Team Histories: The National League, 1991, Twentieth Century Sports Champions, 1992, Statesmen Who Changed the World, 1993, Ency. Modern Social Issues, 1996, Advanced Placement U.S. History 2, 1996, Encyclopedia of United States Popular Culture, 1997, Encyclopedia of Civil Rights, 1997, Encyclopedia of Propaganda, 1997, Total Padres, 1997, The Scribner Encyclopedia of American Lives, 1998, 1999, 2001, 2002, American National Biography, 1999, The Sixties in America, 1999, Racial and Ethnic Relations in America, 1999, History of Mahaska County, Iowa, 2000, Great Athletes, rev. edit., 2001, The Scribner Encyclopedia of American Lives, Sports Figures, 2002, Great Events: 1900-2001, rev. edit., 2002, The Scribner Encyclopedia of American Lives, The 1960's, 2003, Encyclopedia of U.S. History, 2003, Dictionary of American History, 3rd. edit., 2003, Encyclopedia of the Great Depression, 2003, Native Americans in Sports, 2004, The Fifties in America, 2005, editor, contbr. Biographical Dictionary of American Sports: vols.

Baseball, 1987, Football, 1987, Outdoor Sports, 1988, Basketball and Other Indoor Sports, 1989, 1989-92 Supplement for Baseball, Football, Basketball and Other Sports, 1992, 1992-95 Supplement for Baseball, Football, Basketball and Other Sports, 1995, African-American Sports Greats, 1995, Baseball, revised and expanded edit., 3 vols., 2000, Latino and African American Athletes Today, 2004, Basketball: A Biographical Dictionary, 2005, compiler A Cumulative Index to the Biographical Dictionary of American Sports, 1993, assoc. editor (with others) American National Biography, 24 vols., 1999; contbr. articles to profl. jours., local newspapers. Mem. Franklin D. Roosevelt Meml. Commn.; participant Green Bay Packers Project, 1992; historian United Meth. Ch.; official scorer Babe Ruth State Tournament, 2000, 03. Grantee NSF, 1967, NEH, 1974, Rensselaer Poly. Inst., 1974, Eleanor Roosevelt Inst., 1981, William Penn Univ., 1986, 89, 92; recipient Choice Outstanding Acad. Book awards, 1989. Mem. AAUP, Am. Hist. Assn., Orgn. Am. Historians, N.Am. Soc. for Sport History, Soc. History Am. Fgn. Rels., Ctr. for Study of the Presidency, Soc. Am. Baseball Rsch., Friends of the Nat. Baseball Hall of Fame, Popular Culture Assn., Profl. Football Rschrs. Assn., Coll. Football Rschrs. Assn., Coll. Football Hist. Soc., State Hist. Soc. Iowa, Mahaska County Hist. Soc. (y.p.), Iowa State UN Assn. (chmn. ann. assembly 1982, nat. soc. Disting. Svc. award 1981), Mahaska County UN Assn. (v.p.), Oskaloosa Babe Ruth League (bd. dirs.), Oskaloosa Cmty. Choir, Friends of Oskaloosa Pub. Libr. (mem. nominating com.), Friends of the Nat. Baseball Hall of Fame, Phi Alpha Theta, Kappa Delta Pi. Home: 2314 Ridgeway Ave Oskaloosa IA 52577-9109 Office: William Penn Univ Dept Social and Behavioral Scis Divsn Oskaloosa IA 52577-1757

**PORTER, DIXIE LEE,** insurance company executive, consultant; b. Bountiful, Utah, June 7, 1931; d. John Lloyd and Ida May (Robinson) Mathis. BS, U. Calif., Berkeley, 1956, MBA, 1957. CLU. Personnel aide City of Berkeley, 1957-59; employment supr. Kaiser Health Found., L.A., 1959-60; personnel analyst UCLA, 1961-63; personnel mgr. Reuben H. Donnelley, Santa Monica, Calif., 1963-64; personnel officer Good Samaritan Hosp., San Jose, Calif., 1965-67; fgn. svc. officer AID, Saigon, Vietnam, 1967-71; gen. agt. Charter Life Ins. Co., L.A., 1972-77, Kennesaw Life Ins. Co., Atlanta, 1978—, Phila. Life Ins. Co., San Francisco, 1978—; pres. Womens Ins. Enterprises, Ltd., 1976—. Cons. in field. Co-chair Comprehensive Health Planning Commn. Santa Clara County, Calif., 1973-76; bd. dirs. Family Care, 1978-80, Aegis Health Corp., 1977-92, U. Calif. Sch. Bus. Adminstrn., Berkeley, 1974-76; task force on equal access to econ. power U.S. Nat. Womens Agenda, 1977—, Lake County Transp. Coun., 2000—. With USMC, 1950-52. Mem. AAUW, CLU Soc., U. Calif. Alumni Assn., U. Calif. Sch. Bus. Adminstrn. Alumni Assn., Bus. and Profl. Women, Prytanean Alumni, The Animal Soc. Los Gatos/Saratoga (pres. 1987-90), The Am. Legion, Beta Gamma Sigma, Phi Chi Theta. Republican. Episcopalian.

**PORTER, DUNCAN MACNAIR,** research scientist; b. Kelseyville, Calif., Apr. 20, 1937; s. James Duncan and Dorothy May; m. Sarah Holyoke, Sept. 10, 1966; children: Charles Holyoke, Dorothy Carr, Christina Margaret, Susannah Reaves. AB, Stanford U., 1959, AM, 1961; PhD, Harvard U., 1967. Asst. Calif. Acad. Scis., San Francisco, 1966-67; asst. prof. biology U. San Francisco, 1967-68; curator flora Panama Mo. Bot. Garden, St. Louis, 1968-72; editor-in-chief flora N.Am. project Smithsonian Inst., Washington, 1972-73; assoc. program dir. systematic biology NSF, Washington, 1973-75; assoc. prof. bot. Va. Polytech. Inst. & State U., Blacksburg, 1975-84, prof. bot., 1984—; sr. editor Darwin Corr. Project, Cambridge, England, 1991—2006, dir., 1997—2006. Rsch. assoc. biology Stanford U., 1966-68; asst. prof. bot. Washington U., 1968-70, adj. asst. prof. biology, 1970-73; sec., program chmn. Am. Soc. Plant Taxonomists, 1972-73. Author: Rare and Endangered Vascular Plant Species of Virginia, 1980; co-author: Flora of the Calapagos Islands, 1971, The Portable Darwin, 1993, Categorical Glossery for the Flora of North America Program, 2001; editor: The Correspondence of Charles Darwin, vol. 8, 1993, vol. 9, 1994, vol. 10, 1997, vol. 11, 1999, vol. 12, 2001, vol. 13, 2002, vol. 14, 2004, vol. 15, 2005. Vis. fellow U. Cambridge, 1980-81, U. Canterbury, New Zealand, 1986, Thomas Jefferson medal, Va. Mus. Natural History Found., 2004, Albert L. Sturm award Phi Beta Kappa, 1998, Lifetime Achievement in Sci. award Sci. Mus. Va., 2006. Fellow AAAS, Linnean Soc. London; mem. Calif. Bot. Soc. (bd. editors 1970-76, 78-83), History Sci. Soc., Soc. History Natural Hist., Sigma Xi. Democrat. Episcopalian. Avocations: reading, travel, walking, gardening. Home: 1002 E Roanoke St Blacksburg VA 24060 Office: Va Tech Dept Biol Scis Blacksburg VA 24061 Office Phone: 540-231-6768. Office Fax: 540-231-9307. Business E-Mail: duporter@vt.edu.

**PORTER, ELSA ALLGOOD,** writer, educator; b. Amoy, China, Dec. 19, 1928; d. Roy and Petra (Johnsen) Allgood; m. Raeford B. Liles, Mar. 19, 1949 (div. 1959); children: Barbara, Janet; m. G. Hinckley Porter, Nov. 22, 1962; children: David, Brian, Wendy. BA, Birmingham-So. Coll., 1949; MA, U. Ala., 1959; M in Pub. Adminstrn., Harvard U., 1971; LHD (hon.), U. Ala., 1986. With HEW, Washington, 1960-73; with U.S. CSC, Washington, 1973-77; asst. sec. Dept. Commerce, Washington, 1977-81; disting. practitioner in residence Washington Pub. Affairs Ctr., U. So. Calif., Washington, 1982-84; v.p. R & D The Maccoby Group, Washington, 1990-96; sr. fellow Meridian Internat. Inst., 1990—. Chair commtl. adv. subcom. NASA, 1997—2003. Fellow World Acad. Art & Scis., Nat. Acad. Pub. Adminstrs.; mem. Women's Nat. Dem. Club. Home: 2309 SW 1st Ave Apt 742 Portland OR 97201-5008

**PORTER, ETHEL MAE,** publishing executive; b. Phila., July 16, 1947; d. Everette Marmon and Ethel Mae Porter. BA in Econs., Mount Holyoke Coll., 1969; MA in Internat. Rels., Yale U., 1971, MPhil in Am. Studies, 1975, PhD in Am. Studies, 1978. Sr. account exec. CTB McGraw-Hill, Monterey, Calif., 2003—04; v.p. Riverside Pub., Itasca, Ill., 2004—. V.p. Harcourt Edul. Measurement, San Antonio, 1984—2002. Former mem. San Antonio Libr. Found., San Antonio, Tex. Recipient Educator's Hall of Fame, Phi Delta Kappa, Inc.k Gamma Tau Chpt., 1998. Mem.: Nat. Assn. of Black Sch. Educators (life Policy Fellow, Inst. for Ednl. Leadership 1979-1980). Office: Riverside Pub 425 Spring Lake Dr Itasca IL 60143 Office Phone: 630-467-6516. Office Fax: 630-467-7150. Business E-Mail: ethel_porter@hmco.com.

**PORTER, GERALD JOSEPH,** mathematician, educator; b. Elizabeth, N.J., Feb. 27, 1937; s. Fred and Tillie Florence (Friedman) P.; m. Judith Deborah Revitch, June 26, 1960; children: Daniel, Rebecca, Michael. AB, Princeton U., 1958; PhD, Cornell U., 1963; MA (hon.), U. Pa., 1971. Instr. MIT, Cambridge, 1963-65; asst. prof. math. U. Pa., Phila., 1965-69; assoc. prof., 1969-75, prof., 1975—, chmn. undergrad. affairs dept. math., 1971-73, assoc. dean computing Sch. Arts and Scis., 1981-91, dir. Interactive Math. Text Project, 1991-96. Chair-elect faculty senate U. Pa., 1992-93, chair, 1993-94, past chair, 1994-95, 2001-02; prin. investigator NSF MACMATC Grant, 1997-2001. Author: (with D.R. Hill) Interactive Linear Algebra, 1996. Mem. Dem. Com., Haverford Twp., Pa., 1976-82, ward leader, 1980-84; times., 1984-87. Postdoctoral fellow Office Naval Rsch., 1965 66. Mem. Am Math. Soc., Math. Assn. Am. (com. computers in math. edn. 1983-86, chmn. investment com. 1986-2003, bd. govs. 1980-83, 86-2002, mem. fin. com. 1986-2000, exec. com. 1992-2002, chmn. audit and budget com. 1988-90, 92, treas. 1992-2002, chair com. on profl. devel. 1995-2001, chair membership com. 2004—), Nat. Assn. Mathematicians. Democrat. Jewish. Home: 161 Whitemarsh Rd Ardmore PA 19003-1698 Office: U Pa 4N69 DRL 209 S 33rd St Philadelphia PA 19104-6395 E-mail: gjporter@math.upenn.edu.

**PORTER, HENRY HOMES, JR.,** investor; b. Chgo., Nov. 13, 1934; s. Henry H. and Mary (Kinney) P.; m. Louisa Catherine Perkins, June 10, 1961; children: Mary Porter Johnson, Catherine. AB, Yale U., 1956; MBA, Harvard U., 1962. With Gen. Mills, Inc., Mpls., 1962-76, asst. treas., 1964-67, treas., 1967-76, v.p. fin., treas., 1969-76; sr. v.p., chief fin. officer, dir. Brown & Williamson Industries, Inc., 1977-79, Batus, Inc., 1980; now ret. Chmn. bd. Active Ankle Systems, Inc.; bd. dirs. SEI Investment Co., Caldwell & Orkin Funds, Inc. Lt. (j.g.) USNR, 1957-60. Home: 8 Eaglehead Rd Manchester MA 01944-1549

**PORTER, HORACE ANTHONY,** literature educator, writer; s. Joseph and Lillie Mae Porter; m. Carla Carr, Apr. 20, 1981; 1 child, Zachary. BA magna cum laude, Amherst Coll., Mass., 1972; MPhil, Yale U., New Haven, 1977, PhD, 1981. Lectr. English and black studies Wayne State U., Detroit, 1977—79; asst./assoc. prof. English and African Am. studies Dartmouth Coll., Hanover, NH, 1979—90; assoc. prof. English Stanford U., Calif., 1990—99; prof. English, African-Am. Studies U. Iowa, Iowa City, 1999—, F. Wendell Miller prof. English and Am. studies, 2006—. Author: (literary criticism) Stealing the Fire: The Art and Protest of James Baldwin, 1989, Jazz Country: Ralph Ellison in America, 2001, (memoir) The Making of a Black Scholar: From Georgia to the Ivy League, 2003. Mem.: Alpha Phi Alpha (Faculty Mem. of Yr. award 1983). Office: University of Iowa 308 English Philosophy Building Iowa City IA 52242-1492 Office Phone: 319-353-2227. Office Fax: 319-335-2535. Business E-Mail: horace-porter@uiowa.edu.

**PORTER, J. REID,** engineering executive; BA, Colgate U., 1971; MBA in Fin., U. Chgo., 1975. With fin. analysis staff Rockwell Internat., Chgo., 1975—78; with McGraw-Edison Co., Rolling Meadows, Ill., 1978—82; various sr. exec. positions Onan Corp., Mpls., 1982—95; v.p., gen. mgr. Renewal by Anderson, Minn., 1996—98; v.p., ptnr. Hidden Creek Industries, Mpls., 1998—2001; CFO Heavy Duty Holdings, Mpls., 1998—2001; exec. v.p. IMC Global Inc., Lake Forest, Ill., 2001—, CFO, 2001—. Office: IMC Global Inc 3600 S Yosemite St Ste 900 Denver CO 80237

**PORTER, J. RIDGELY, III,** lawyer; b. Va., Apr. 28, 1948; s. John R and Mary Manning (Barclay) P.; m. DeLane Williams, 1978; 1 child, Eleanor M. BA, U. Va., 1970; JD, Washington & Lee U., 1973. Law clerk to U.S. judge, 1973-74; ptnr. Carr & Porter, 1974—; pres. Va. Internat. Terminals, 1985-92; chmn. bd. Chesapeake Gen. Hosp., 1986-96; owner Cattle Farms. Mem.: ABA, Va. Bar Assn., Met. Club (DC). Episcopalian. Office: 355 Crawford Pkwy Portsmouth VA 23704 Office Phone: 757-393-6018. Personal E-mail: ridgeporter@aol.com.

**PORTER, JACK NUSAN,** writer, sociologist, educator, political organization worker; b. Rovno, Ukraine, USSR, Dec. 2, 1944; came to U.S., 1946; s. Irving Puchtik and Faye (Merin) P.; m. Miriam Almuly, Sept. 18, 1977 (div. 2000); children: Gabriel, Danielle. Cert., Machon Inst., Jerusalem, 1963; BAS cum laude, U. Wis., Milw., 1967; MA, Northwestern U., 1969; PhD in Sociology, Northeastern U., 1971; Rabbinical tng., Acad. for Jewish Religion, 1998-99. Ordained rabbi Vaad HaRabbainim, N.Y., 2000. Rsch. assoc. Harvard U. Ukrainian Rsch. Inst., Cambridge, Mass., 1982-84; pres. The Spencer Group, Newton, Mass., 1984—; exec. dir. The Spencer Sch. Real Estate, Newton, 1986—; dir. The Spencer Inst. for Bus. and Soc., Newton, 1984—; asst. prof. Coll. of Basic Studies Boston U., 1989-90. Vis. lectr. Boston U. Met. Coll., 1987, 88, Bryant Coll., Smithfield, R.I., 1991, Bay State Coll., 2005; adj. prof. sociology U. Mass., Lowell, 1976-79, 1994-2004, Stonehill Coll., Easton, Mass., 1996-97; presenter White House Conf. on Family, 1980; mem. Gov. Dukakis' Adv. Coun., 1982-84; panelist on Comparative Genocide, The Oxford (Eng.) Conf., 1988; panelist Machon Reunion, Jerusalem, Israel, 2003; Boston area coord. Seminars on Zionist Thought, World Zionist Orgn., 1996—; cons. in non-fiction Nat. Book Critics Circle Awards, 1997-98. Author or editor 30 books and anthologies including Student Protest and the Technocratic Society: The Case of ROTC, 1972, The Study of Society, 1974, REadings in Sociology, 1975, Confronting History and Holocaust, 1983, Sexual Politics in Nazi Germany, 1991, Kids in Cults, 1977, 85, 94, Jews and the Cults, 1981, Genocide and Human Rights, 1982, (with Ruth Taplin) Conflict and Conflict Resolution: A Sociological Introduction, 1987, (with Peter Dreier) Jewish Radicalism, 1973, 2002, Jewish Partisans (2 vols.), 1982, Conflict and Conflict Resolution: A Historical Bibliography, 1982, The Jew as Outsider, 1981, 2002, The Sociology of Jewry: A Curriculum Guide, 1992, 99, The Sociology of American Jews: A Critical Anthology, 1980, 98, The Sociology of Jewry: Collected Essays, 1998, Forclosed Property (with Gerry Glazer), 1990, (with Steve Hoffman) The Sociology of Genocide and the Holocaust: A Curriculum Guide, 1992, 99, The Sociology of Business: A Curriculum Guide, 1992, Women in Chains: Sourcebook on the Agunah, 1996, A Life of Mitzvah: Rabbi Joseph Mayer Jacobson of Boston, 2001; The Genodical Mind: Toward a Sociology of the Holocaust, 2004, (collected essays) Anti-Semitism: From Deicide to Genocide, The Speeches and Writings of Jack Nusan Porter, 2004, The Soc. Imagination of American Jewry: Collected Essays, 2004, The Radical Writings of J.N. Porter, 2004; co-author: Sexual Politics in the Third Reich, 1997; contbr. chpts. in books, more than 600 articles and revs. to jours. in field; founder, pub. Jour. of the History of Sociology, 1977-85, The Sociology of Bus. Newsletter, 1977-79; mem. editl. bd. Contemporary Jewry, 1995-97; dep. editor, dep. pub. Jewish Family and Life, 1997-98; author (films) Key West Rabbi, Partisans, Dressed to Kill, Founder Holocaust Survival Video Project, Newton, Mass., 1992—; judge Nat. Jewish Book Awards, 1993-95; mem. Jewish Radical Edn. Project, 1994-99; spiritual leader Temple Emmanuel, Chelsea, Mass., 1999-2001; rabbi Cong. B'nai Zion, Key West, Fla., 2001; candidate alderman at large, Newton, 2003. John Atherton fellow Breadloaf Writers Conf., Middlebury, Vt., 1976; recipient Spl. award Boston Police Dept., 1986. Mem. PEN (newsletter com. 1992-95), Am. Sociol. Assn. (mem. coun. 2004, recipient Disting. Contbn. award 2004, Disting. Career award History of Soc. Sect.), Ea. Sociol. Soc., New Eng. Soc., Internat. Assn. of Genocide Scholars (v.p. 1996-98), Tikkun, Workman's Circle, PEN New Eng., Cong. Kehillat Israel, Brookline, Mass. Avocations: baseball card collecting, reading, spiritual thinking. Home and Office: 79 Walnut St # 4 Newtonville MA 02460 Office Phone: 617-965-8388. Personal E-mail: jacknusan@earthlink.net. *The older I get, the important things in life are my children, good health, a few good friends, my brother and sister and Mom, a good meal, and lastly - some money and a little fame. That's all I need. Oh, yes - love. One needs lots of love.*

**PORTER, JAMES KENNETH,** retired judge; b. Newport, Tenn., Apr. 6, 1934; s. John Calhoun and Bessie Betis (Crouch) P.; m. Evelyn Janet Rhodes, Sept. 17, 1955; children: Jane Caroline, James Kenneth Jr. BS, U. Tenn., Knoxville, 1955, JD, 1957. Bar: Tenn. 1957, U.S. Dist. Ct. (ea. dist.) Tenn. 1958, U.S. Ct. Appeals (6th cir.) 1971. Ptnr. Porter, Porter & Dunn, Porter & Porter, Newport, 1957-74; state rep. Tenn. Gen. Assembly, Nashville, 1961-65, minority fl. leader, 1963-65; county atty. Cocke County, Tenn., 1961-63, commr. County Election Commn. Tenn., 1966-72, chmn. Tenn., 1968-70; mem. Tenn. Senate, Nashville, 1972-74; state cir. judge 4th Jud. Cir., Newport, 1974-93; ret., 1993; state presiding judge 4th Jud. Cir., Newport, 1984-86, 88-90, 1992-93; judgeship nominee U.S. Dist. Ct. (ea. dist.), Tenn., 1986; Tenn. Ct. Appeals nominee, 1990. Del. S.E. Law Rev. Conf., Durham, N.C., 1957, Nat. Conf. State Legislator Leaders, Boston, 1963; discussion leader Nat. Jud. Coll., Reno, 1981, faculty adviser, 1982; mem. Gov.'s Correction Overcrowding Commn., Nashville, 1985-86. Contbr. articles to U. Tenn. Law Rev., 1956-57, editor in chief, 1957. Active Farm Bur., 1962-82; mem. adv. coun., trustee Walters State Community Coll., Morristown, Tenn., 1975-86. Mem. ABA (Tenn. jud. del. 1984), Tenn. Jud. Conf. (v.p. 1980-81), Tenn. Trial Judges Assn. (bd. dirs. 1976-86, pres. 1982-85), Tenn. Bar Assn. (spl. trial counsel 1973-76), Cocke County Bar Assn., Smoky Mountain Country Club (bd. dirs. 1964-67, v.p. 1966-67), Order of Coif, Sigma Alpha Epsilon (Highest Effort Law award 1986), Phi Delta Phi. Republican. Baptist. Avocations: golf, gardening, guitar. Home: 306 North St Newport TN 37821-2413 Office: 106 S Mims Ave Newport TN 37821-3125 E-mail: porterk@planetc.com.

**PORTER, JEAN MCRAE,** counselor; b. Augusta, Ga., Aug. 1, 1949; d. Hugh Burrell and Ruby Collins McRae; m. Ralph S. Porter, Jr., Aug. 17, 1975; children: Bradford Sloan, Jonathan James. BS, Augusta Coll., Ga., 1970; MEd, Clemson U., S.C., 1973. Cert. secondary adminstrn., guidance, biology, elem.; sci. tchg. Tchr. Davenport Jr. H.S., Greer, SC, 1970—71, Greer Middle Sch. 1971—73; counselor Hillcrest Middle Sch., Simpsonville, SC, 1973—75; counselor, tchr. Hughes Middle Sch., Greenville, SC, 1975—84; counselor Wade Hampton H.S., Greenville, 1984—90, Bryson Middle Sch., Simpsonville, 1990—94, Woodmont H.S., Piedmont, SC, 1994—95, Northwood Middle Sch., Taylors, SC, 1995—, 504 accommodations coord., 2002—. Facilitator Christmas Knights, 1995—. Mem.: NEA,

Nat. Assn. Mental Illness, Greenville County Edn. Assn., SC Counselors Assn., SC Edn. Assn. Democrat. Avocations: reading, hiking, raising dogs. Home: 111 Brigham Creek Dr Greer SC 29650 Office: Northwood Middle School 710 Ikes Rd Taylors SC 29687 Business E-Mail: jporter@northwd.greenville.k12.sc.us.com.

**PORTER, JEFFREY R.,** lawyer; b. 1963; m. Jill Porter; 2 children. BA with high honors in Polit. Sci., cum laude, Bates Coll., 1985; JD, Cornell U., 1988. Bar: Mass. 1988, US Dist. Ct. (Dist. Mass.). Ptnr., chair environ. law sect. Mintz, Levin, Cohn, Ferris, Glovsky & Popeo PC, Boston. Treas., bd. dirs. Boston Harbor Island Alliance; vice chmn., bd. trustees Nature Conservancy Mass. Chpt. Mem.: ABA (environ., energy and resources sect., litig. sect.), Boston Bar Assn., Phi Beta Kappa. Office: Mintz Levin Cohn Ferris Glovsky & Popeo PC One Financial Center Boston MA 02111 Office Phone: 617-348-1711. Office Fax: 617-542-2241. Business E-Mail: jporter@mintz.com.

**PORTER, JENNY LIND,** writer; b. Fort Worth, Tex., Sept. 3, 1927; d. Drue J. and Josephine Trammell Porter; m. Lawrence E. Scott. BA summa cum laude, Tex. Christian U., 1948; MA, Tex. Christian U., Ft. Worth, 1949; PhD, U. of Tex., Austin, 1955; Hon. Doctorate (hon.), Pepperdine U., 1980. Asst. prof. The U. Tenn., Knoxville, Tenn., 1958—59, West Tex. A&M U., Canyon, Tex., 1959—61; assoc. prof. Southwest Tex. State U., San Marcos, Tex., 1961—64, Tex. Luth. U., Sequin, Tex., 1964—68; prof. Huston-Tillotson Coll., Austin, Tex., 1968—96; guest prof. Pepperdine U., Malibu, Calif. 1981. Vis. prof. Pepperdine U., Malibu, Calif., 1981. Author: (numerous works including) Three Dramatic Monologues, 1980, Verses on Death, Les Vers de la Mort, 1999 (Tex. Inst. Letters Translation award, 2000), El Sol Colorado, 2001, O. Henry, Witter Bynner, and A Fog in Santone, 2002. Named Jenny Lind Porter Day in Austin, Tex. named in her honor for contbns. to lit. and the O. Henry Mus., City Coun., Austin, 1996; named to Tex. Women's Hall of Fame, Austin, 1985; recipient Piper Prof. award, Piper Found., San Antonio, Tex., 1976. Home: 51 Summit View Place Austin TX 78703

**PORTER, JILL,** journalist; b. Phila., Aug. 5, 1946; d. Sidney and Mae (Merion) Chalfin; m. Eric Porter, Mar. 7, 1970 (div. 1975); m. Fred Hamilton, Oct. 28, 1983; 1 child, Zachary. BA, Temple U., 1968. Pub. rels. Manning Smith P.R., Phila., 1968-69; reporter Norristown Times Herald, Norristown, Pa., 1969-72, The Trentonian, Trenton, NJ, 1972-75, The Phila. Daily News, Phila., 1975-79, columnist, 1979—. Instr. Temple U., 1976—80. Contbr. articles to numerous mags. Vol. Phila. Futures, 1994, 95, 96, Phila. Cares, 1997, Career Wardrobe, 2006. Recipient numerous journalism awards. Avocations: dance, biking, reading. Home: 134 Rolling Rd Bala Cynwyd PA 19004-2615 Office: Phila Newspapers Inc Phila Daily News 400 N Broad St Philadelphia PA 19130-4015 Office Phone: 215-854-5850. E-mail: porterj@phillynews.com.

**PORTER, JIM,** human resources specialist; m. Deb Porter; 4 children. Grad., Northwest Mo. State U. Various human resources positions Trane Co., La Crosse, Wis., Hoechst-Roussell Pharmaceuticals, Inc., Somerville, NJ, ELBA Corp., Denver; recruiter to sr. v.p. and chief adminstrn. officer Honneywell Internat., 1982—2003; sr. v.p. human resources Carlson Cos., Inc., Minnetonka, Minn., 2003—05, exec. v.p. human resources, 2005—. Office: Carlson Cos Inc 701 Carlson Pkwy Minnetonka MN 55305 Office Phone: 763-212-1000. Office Fax: 763-212-2219.

**PORTER, JOHN E.,** lawyer; b. Cin., Oct. 23, 1958; s. Robert Carl Jr. and Joanne (Patterson) P.; children: Rebecca Sheyne, Robin Leigh. BSEE with distinction, Stanford U., 1980, JD, 1983. Bar: Calif. 1983, U.S. Ct. Appeals (9th cir.) 1983, U.S. Dist. Ct. (cen. dist.) Calif. 1984. Law clk. to Hon. Procter Hug U.S. Ct. Appeals, ninth cir., 1983—84; ptnr. Paul, Hastings, Janofsky & Walker LLP, L.A., mem. policy com. Bd. visitors Stanford (Calif.) Law Sch., 1990-94. Mem. Stanford Law Soc. of So. Calif. (treas. 1990-95). Office: Paul Hastings Janofsky & Walker LLP 515 S Flower St Los Angeles CA 90071-2228 Office Phone: 213-683-6305. Office Fax: 213-996-3305. E-mail: johnporter@paulhastings.com.

**PORTER, JOHN EDWARD,** former congressman; b. Evanston, Ill., June 1, 1935; s. Harry H. and Beatrice V. P.; 5 children. Attended, MIT; BSBA, Northwestern U., 1958; JD with distinction, U. Mich., 1961; degree (hon.), Northwestern U., Tufts U., Mt. Sinai Sch. Medicine, Oreg. Health Scis. U., Howard U., Rush U. Bar: Ill. 1961, D.C. 2005, U.S. Supreme Ct. 1968. Former honor law grad. atty., appellate div. Dept. Justice, Washington; mem. Ill. Ho. of Reps., 1973—79, 96-106th Congresses from 10th Ill. Dist., Ill., 1980-2001; ptnr. Hogan & Hartson, Washington, 2001—. Founder, co-chmn. Congl. Human Rights Caucus; legis. sponsor Radio Free Asia; founder Congl. Coalition on Population and Devel.; chmn. Global Legislators Organized for a Balanced Environment; chmn. Commn. on Security and Cooperation in Europe; chmn. com. future roles acad. health ctrs. Inst. Medicine, NAS, chmn. com. on presdl. and fed. adv. com. sci. and tech.; co-chmn. Ctr. for Global Devel. Commn. on Weak States and Nat. Security Past editor: Mich. Law Rev. Bd. dirs., vice chair PBS, Rand Corp.; vice chair Rsch.! Am.; chair Found. for NIH; bd. dirs. Am. Heart Assn., Brookings Instn., Chgo. Botanic Gardens, Population Resource Ctr., Princeton, NJ; trustee emeritus John F. Kennedy Ctr. for Performing Arts. Recipient Best Legislator award League of Conservation Voters, 1973, Ind. Voters Ill., 1974, Chgo. Crime Commn., 1976, Lorax award Global Tomorrow Coalition, 1989, Spirit of Enterprise award U.S. C. of C., 1988, 89, 90, Golden Bulldog award Watchdogs of the Treasury, 12 times, Taxpayer's Friend award Nat. Taxpayers Union, Taxpayer Superhero award Grace Commn.'s Citizens Against Government Waste, Mary Wood Lasker award for pub. svc., Edwin C. Whitehead award Rsch! Am., Carter award Nat. Found. Infectious Diseases, Pub. Svc. award Fedn. Am. Socs. for Exptl. Biology, Svc award Am. Soc. Cell Biology, Disting. Pub. Svc. award Am. Soc. Microbiology, Pub. Svc. Excellence award Assn. Am. Med. Colls., Lifetime Achievement award Juvenile Diabetes Found., Decade of Brain award Nat. Found. Brain Rsch., Lifetime Achievement award Am. Psychiat. Assn. and Acad. Consortium, Dr. Nathan Davis award AMA, Morris K. Udall Pub. Svc. award Michael J. Fox Found., Pub. Health Continuation award Coalition for Health Funding, Beacon award Am. Soc. Assn. Execs., Henry M. Jackson Leadership award Union Couns. for Soviet Jewry, Anatoly Scharansky Freedom award Chgo. Action for Soviet Jewry, others. Mem.: Inter-Am. Dialogue, Coun. Fgn. Rels. Republican. Office: Hogan & Hartson 555 13th St NW Washington DC 20004 Office Phone: 202-637-5695. E-mail: jeporter@hhlaw.com.

**PORTER, JOHN PAUL,** artist, educator; b. Alturas, Calif., Nov. 26, 1935; s. Carlton Lewis and Bernice (Smith-Schulz) P.; m. Carol Lynn Jones, Apr. 20, 1957 (div. Apr. 1978); children: Sean Michal, Sheryl Lynn. BA in Art, Calif. State U., Chico, 1958; MA in Art, UCLA, 1962; postgrad., Calif. State U., Chico, 1958. Calif. State U., Sacramento, 1959-61, Calif. State U., Northridge, 1958-63, Calif. State U., San Jose, 1978, Stanford U., 1986. Cert. secondary tchr., Calif. Prof. art, chair dept., coord. dist. Antelope County Unified Sch. Dist. & Art, Coll., Lancaster, Calif., 1958-67; prof. art Gavilan Coll., 1967-2000, chair fine arts and humanities, 1969-75. Vis. prof. U. London, 1988; consortium prof. Calif. CC; judge various local, regional and national shows; rschr. in field. Exhbns. and one-man shows include Chico State Libr., 1958, Benny Barrio Gallery, Carmichael, Calif., 1959, Allied Arts Gallery, Lancaster, 1961, Aldous Huxley Show, Porter Show Allied Arts, 1962, Charles Parker Estates, Quartz Hill, Calif., 1963, Chic Sale Art Competition, Lancaster, 1964, Tumbleweed Gallery, Pearblossom, Calif., 1964-66, Edwards AFB, 1965, Oldfield Studio, Lancaster, 1967, Hollister Art League, 1967, 70, Gilroy Mus., 1972, 78, 80, UC Davis Student Union Gallery, 1978, Faye Dixon's Mariposa House, 1973, El Cerrito Open Studio Show, Gilroy, 2003, 75, De Saisset Gallery, 1978, Oaktree Allied Arts Gallery, 1978-80, Spring Art-Music Fesitval, 1970-78, San Jose Art League, 1980, Children's Home Soc. Benefit, 1981, Friendly Inn Art and Flower Show, Morgan Hill, 1979-80, 82, Vacaville State Art Competition, 1982, Am. Greeting Card Print Nat. Convention, San Francisco, 1983, Union Street Gallery, 1984, Russian River State Festival, Forestville, Calif., 1984-85, Bay

Area Fine Arts Exhbn., San Francisco, 1985, Steinbeck Gallery, 1986, Glen Loma Estates, 1987, Thackery House, London, 1988, Santa Clara County Fair, 1989, Avina Gallery, Sao Paolo, Brazil, 1991, Carlton House, London, 1992, Skyline Coll, 1993, San Jose Art League, 1994, Beaux Artes Show, Reno, Nev., 1995, Willows Mansion, 1996. So. Valley Symphony Benefit, 1997, Growth and Opportunity Exec. Offices, Morgan Hill, Calif., 1997, 98; mem. editl. bd. Collegiate Press, 1990-94; contbr. articles to profl. jours., chpts. to books; represented in over 1200 pvt. collections. Co-founder Mushroom Festival, Morgan Hill, 1990—; owner. City of Gilroy, 1976—76; com. mem. Santa Clara County Fair, Tapestry in Talent, 1987; active Gilroy Garlic Festival Art, 1980—99; neighborhood com. San Jose Solari Ctr.; geneology and staff cons. LDS Family History Ctr. Danforth fellow Stanford U., 1975-76; recipient Jay Stott award, 1957, Crown Zellerbach award, 1958, Nat. AVIP Tchr. of Yr. award, 1964, award Nat. Neighborhood Youth Corp., 1967, Mayoral Citation Svc. City of Gilroy, 1978, 96; named Man of Yr. Lancaster C. of C., 1967. Mem. Commonwealth Club, South Bay Scottish Soc. (acting chief, bd. govs.), San Francisco World Coun., Hearaldry Soc. Great Britain, Clan Cian Soc., Clan Boyd, Clan McNaughten, Clan McAlpin, Clan O'Neal, Nat. Thespians (award 1965). Democrat. Congregationalist. Avocations: dance, swimming, tennis, crafts. Home: Indian Palms Country-club Resort 82529 Delano Dr Indio CA 92201 E-mail: art-e-facts@webtv.net.

**PORTER, JOHN WESTON,** counselor, consultant, administrator; b. Fostoria, Ohio, Dec. 26, 1939; s. William Thomas and Ida Elizabeth (Carter) Porter. Student, U. Cin., 1958; BA, Heidelberg Coll., 1961; MA in Cmty. Psychology, U. D.C., 1973, MA in Counseling, 1975; postgrad., Antioch Coll., 1974, Frostburg U., Md., 1970, George Washington U., 1968. Cert. Nat. Bd. Cert. Counselors, DC. Claims rep. Social Security Adminstrn., Cleve. and Akron, Ohio, 1961-62; office mgr. Phoenix Cos., Washington and L.A., 1966-70; rschr. Frostburg U., U.D.C., 1970-73; edn. and career devel. specialist D.C. Pub. Schs., 1973-79, career edn. unit, 1979-83, Career Assessment Ctr., 1983-85, asst. dir. guidance and counseling, 1985-95; mem. cmty. adv. coun. Washington Hosp. Ctr., 1987—. Counseling mentor DC Pub. Schs., 1998—2003; dir. Westport Consulting, 2001—; cons. DC Pub. Sch. HiScip program, New Couns. Mentor, 2001—02. Contbr. articles to profl. jours. Vice chmn. adv. coun. Group Health Assn., Washington, 1977—79, 1981—83; sec. Md.-DC Am. Coll. Testing Coun., 1987—88, vice chair, 1988—90, chair, 1990—91, mem. exec. com., 1991—; mem. adv. com. Children's Edn. Found., 1989—93, mem. fund raising com., 1989—, exec. bd., 1992—, asst. treas., 1992—93, treas., 1993—95; pres. N.E. Hill Found., 1990—92; mem. com. DC Career and Tech. Edn. Task Force, 2000; team chmn. Wilson HS, 2002, mem. student mgmt. task force, 2002—03, grant rev. panelist, 1998, 2002—03; mem. planning com. Friends of Turkey Thicket Rec. Ctr., 2005. Lt. (j.g.) USN, 1962—66, Lt. USNR. Recipient award, Ohio Acad. Sci., 1954—57, Cleve. Plain Dealer Operation Demonstrate, 1956, Svc. award, Heidelberg Coll. Publs., 1961, Recognition cert., DC Assn. Career Devel., 1975, 1976, DC City Coun., 1982, Children's Edn. Found., 1990, Recognition award Outstanding Contbn. to Guidance and Counseling, 1987, Commn. Svc. award, Advisory Neighborhood Commn., 2004, 2005. Mem.: ACA (counselor adv.-legis.), Coun. Accreditation Counseling and Related Ednl. Programs (site visit team 2000—), Assn. Counselor Edn. and Supervision, DC Career Devel. Assn. (exec. bd. 0983—1990, treas. 1983—86), DC Sch. Counselors Assn. (Outstanding Leadership award 1994), Nat. Career Devel. Assn. (assembly del. 1984, master career coun. 2003), Am. Sch. Counselors Assn. (chair rsch. com. 1990—91, career guidance com., leadership recognition cert. 1987), Am. Counseling Assn. (chmn. govt. rels. N. Atlantic region 1980—81, cert. Outstanding Contbn. in Govt. Rels. 1982, Recognition award 1987), DC Counseling Assn. (treas. 1975—77, exec. bd. 1975—80, sec. 1977—78, pres. 1979—80, trustee 1989—92, treas. 1991—92, trustee 2003—04, counselor adv.-legis., Mem. of the Yr. 1980, Outstanding Leadership award 1980), Phi Delta Kappa (vp. recognition rep. 1993—95, v.p. membership 1995—96, pres. 1996—97, MACI project adv. coun. Hosp. Sick Children 1997—98, rev. panel DC vocat. edn. grants 1998, lic. profl. counselor, DC). Home: 821 Taylor St NE Washington DC 20017-2009 Personal E-mail: jw.wb.porter@erols.com.

**PORTER, JOHN WILSON,** educational association administrator, director; b. Ft. Wayne, Ind., Aug. 13, 1931; BA, Albion Coll., 1953; MA, Mich. State U., 1957, PhD, 1962; D in Pub. Adminstrn. (hon.) Albion Coll., 1973; LLD (hon.), Mich. State U., 1977, Cleary Coll., 1987; LHD, Adrian Coll., 1970, U. Detroit, 1979; LLD, Western Mich. U., 1971, Eastern Mich. U., 1975; HHD. Kalamazoo Coll., 1973, Detroit Coll. Bus., 1975, Madonna Coll., Livonia, Mich., 1977, DEd, Detroit Inst. Tech., 1978; AA, Schoolcraft Coll., Livonia, Mich., 1979; DBA, Lawrence Inst. Tech., 1988; LLD, Cleary Coll., 1989. Counselor Lansing (Mich.) Pub. Schs., 1953-58; cons. Mich. Dept. Pub. Instrn., 1958-61; dir. Mich. Higher Edn. Assistance Authority, 1961-65; assoc. supt. for higher edn. Mich. Dept. Edn., 1966-69, state supt. schs., 1969-79; pres. Ea. Mich. U., Ypsilanti, 1979-89; v.p. Nat. Bd. for Profl. Teaching Standards, 1989; gen. supt. Detroit Pub. Schs., 1989-91; CEO Urban Edn. Alliance, Inc., Ypsilanti, Mich., 1991—. Mem. numerous profl. commns. and bds., 1959—, including Commn. on Financing Postsecondary Edn., 1972-74, Commn. for Reform Secondary Edn., Kettering Found., 1972-75, Edn. Commn. of States, 1973-79, Nat. Commn. on Performance-Based Edn., 1974-76, Nat. Commn. on Manpower Policy, 1974-79, Mich. Employment and Tng. Svcs. Coun., 1976-79, Nat. Adv. Coun. on Social Security, 1977-79, Commn. on Ednl. Credit, Am. Coun. on Edn., 1977-80; task panel on mental health of family Commn. on Mental Health, 1977-80; mem. Nat. Coun. for Career Edn. (HEW), 1974-76; pres. bd. dirs. Chief State Sch. Officers, 1974-79; pres. Coun. Chief State Sch. Officers, 1977-78; bd. dirs. Comerica Bank; former chmn. bd. Coll. Entrance Exam. Bd., 1984-86; apptd. by Gov. John Engler, Mich. Sch. Dist. Accountability Bd., 1999, Gov. Jennifer M. Granholm, Lt. Gov.'s Commn. on Higher Edn. and Econ. Growth, 2004. Author: Mich. Internat. Student Problem Inventory. Trustee Nat. Urban League, 1973-79, Charles Stewart Mott Found, 1981, Albion Coll., 1990—, bd. dirs. Mich. Internat. Council, 1977—. Mich. Congress Parents and Tchrs.; mem. bd. overseers com. for Grad. Sch., Harvard U., 1980-88; mem. edn. com. NAACP; convener goal 6 Nat. Edn. Goals Panel, 1990—; mem. East Lansing Human Relations Commn.; chmn. Am. Assn. State Colls. and U.'s Task Force on Excellence in Edn.; mem. Mich. Martin Luther King, Jr. Holiday Commn., Gov.'s Blue Ribbon Commn. on Welfare Reform; trustee East Lansing Edgewood United Ch.; mem. Catherine McAuley Health Systems Bd., 1990—. Recipient numerous awards including Disting. Svc. award Mich. Congress Parents and Tchrs., 1963, Disting. Svc. award NAACP, Lansing, 1968; cert. of outstanding achievement Delta Kappa chpt. Phi Beta Sigma, 1970; award for disting. svc. Assn. Ind. Colls. and Univs. Mich., 1974, Disting. Alumni award Coll. Edn., Mich. State U., 1974; award for disting. svc. to edn Mich. State U., 1974; Disting. Alumni award, 1979; award for disting. svc. to edn. in Mich. Mich. Assn. Secondary Sch. Prins., 1974; Pres.'s award as disting. educator Nat. Alliance Black Sch. Educators, 1977; Marcus Foster Disting. Educator award, 1979; recognition award Mich. Ednl. Rsch. Assn., 1978; recognition award Mich. Assn. Secondary Sch. Prins., 1978; recognition award Mich. Assn. Intermediate Sch. Adminstrs., 1979; recognition award Mich. Assn. Sch. Adminstrs., 1979; Mich. Sch. Bus. Ofcls., 1979; resolution Mich. State Legislature, 1978; Anthony Wayne award Coll. Edn., Wayne State U., 1979; Educator of Decade award Mich. Assn. State and Fed. Program Specialists, 1979; Spirit of Detroit award Detroit City Coun., 1981; Disting. Svc. award Ypsilanti Area C. of C., 1988; Philip A. Hart award Mich. Women's Hall of Fame, 1988; Summit award Greater Detroit C. of C., 1991; Mich. State C. of C. award 1991; Olivet Coll. award for Leadership and Social Responsibility, 2001; Lifetime Achievement award Albion Coll., 2003; inducted Mich. Edn. Hall of Fame, 1992; John W. Porter Disting. Chair endowed at Eastern Mich. U., 1999; Coll. of Edn. bldg. at Eastern Mich. U. named for him, 1999. Mem.: NAACP (life), Lt. Gov.'s Commn. Higher Edn. and Econ. Growth, Mich. Sch. Dist. Accountability Bd., Am. Assn. Sch. Adminstrs., Am. Assn. State Colls. and Univs. (pres.'s coun., chmn. task force on excellence in edn.), Nat. Measurement Coun., Tuskegee Airmen (Disting. Svc. award 1991), Ea. Mich. U. Alumni Assn. (disting. svc. award 1997), Mich. PTA (hon. life), Mich. State C. of C. (Disting. Svc. and Leadership award 1991), Greater Detroit C. of C. (Summit award 1991), Econ. Club (dir. 1979), Sigma Pi Phi, Phi Delta Kappa.

**PORTER, JON CHRISTOPHER, SR.,** congressman; b. Fort Dodge, Iowa, May 16, 1955; m. Laurie Porter; children: J. Christopher, Nicole. Student, Briar Cliff Coll. Electronic appliance repair-distbn. store mgr., 1978—81; agt. Farmers' Ins. Grp. Corpn., 1982—88, dist. mgr., 1988—2000; mem. City Coun., Boulder City, Nev., 1983—93, mayor, 1987—91; mem. Nev. State Senate from dist. 1, 1995—2002, US Congress from 3rd Nev. dist., 2003—. Mem. U. Nev. Inst. for Ins. and Risk Mgmt., Las Vegas; Rep. majority whip US Congress, 1997, mem. edn. and the workforce com., mem. govt. reform, mem. transp. and infrastructure. Chair bd. dirs. Las Vegas Events, pres., 1993-95; charter bd. dirs. So. Nev. Water Authority; bd. dirs. Las Vegas Conv. and Visitors Authority; bd. dirs. Nev. League of Cities; mem. civilian mil. coun. Nellis AFB. Named Elected Official of Yr., Nev. League of Cities, 1988; recipient Crystal Apple award, Clark County, Nev. Sch. Dist., 1998, Friend of the Shareholder award, Am. Shareholders Assn., 2004, Hero of the Taxpayer award, Americans for Tax Reform, 2004, Small Bus. Adv. award, Small Bus. Survival Com., 2004. Republican. Roman Cath. Office: US Ho Reps 218 Cannon Ho Office Bldg Washington DC 20515-2803 Office Phone: 202-225-3252.*

**PORTER, JUDITH DEBORAH REVITCH,** sociologist; b. Phila., Mar. 26, 1940; d. Eugene and Esther (Tulchinsky) Revitch; m. Gerald Joseph Porter, June 26, 1960; children: Daniel, Rebecca, Michael. Student, Vassar Coll., 1958-60; BA, Cornell U., 1962, MA, 1963; PhD, Harvard U., 1967. Lectr. Bryn Mawr (Pa.) Coll., 1966-67, asst. prof., 1967-73, assoc. prof., 1973-79, prof. sociology, 1979—, chair dept. sociology, 1987-93. Author: Black Child, White Child: The Development of Racial Attitudes, 1971; contbr. articles to profl. jours. Committeeperson Haverford Twp. Dem. Party, 1976-96; bd. dirs. Phila. AIDS Fund, 1992-98, Phlla. Com. End Homelessness, 1984-, Women Against Abuse, 1995-; vice-chmn. exec. com. drugs and alcohol, Mayor, Phila.; vol. Congreso de Latinos Unidos, Inc., Greater Phila. Coalition Against Hunger. Recipient Shannon award NIMH, 1992-94; Ford Found. fellow, 1973-74; NSF fellow, 1967; NIDA grant Co-PI, 1998-2001. Mem. APHA, Am. Sociol. Assn., Phi Beta Kappa, Phi Kappa Phi. Jewish. Address: 161 Whitemarsh Rd Ardmore PA 19003-1634 Office: Bryn Mawr Coll Dept Sociology Bryn Mawr PA 19010 Business E-Mail: jporter@brynmawr.edu.

**PORTER, KAREN ANN,** anthropologist, educator; b. Seattle, Wash., July 14, 1960; d. George Arnold Porter and Carole Diane Mattson. BA cum laude with distinction, U. of Wash., 1986; MA, U. of Rochester, 1988, PhD, 1997. Program dir. & folklorist Arts and Cultural Coun. of Greater Rochester, Rochester, NY, 1997—98; asst. prof. U. Puget Sound, Tacoma, 1998—2005; assoc. prof. Hanover (Ind.) Coll., 2005—. Cons. in field. Editor: Demele: Making It - Migration and Adapation Among Haitian Boat People in the U.S.A., 1988; author: (manual) Folk Music, Dance, and Choreographed Dance, 1998; contbr. articles to profl. jours. Vol. Food Connections, Tacoma, 2000—02, Habitat for Humanity, Rochester, 1996—97, St. Joseph's Ho. of Hospitality, Rochester, 1994—98; vol. St. Paul's Episcopal Ch., Rochester, 1994—98, chmn. refugee resettlement task force, 1997—98. Recipient Faith In Action award, Greater Rochester Cmty. of Ch., 1997; fellow Lewis Henry Morgan fellowship in Anthropology, U. of Rochester, 1986—89, Lang. Fellowship, Cornell U. Africana Studies and Rsch Ctr., 1988—89, Fulbright Hays fellow, 1989, Rsch. in Africa fellow, Joint Com. on African Studies of the Social Sci. Rsch. Coun. & Am. Coun. of Learned Societies, 1990, Coun. of Ind. Coll. Tchg. fellowship, U.S. Dept. of Edn., 1994—95, U. of Rochester, 1996—97; grantee Geneseo Found. Rsch. Travel grant, SUNY-Geneseo, 1997, Oct. Event grant, N.Y. Coun. for the Humanities, 1998, W.M. Keck Found. & Project Kaleidoscope, 2002. Mem.: Soc. for the Anthropology of Work (gen. editor 1997—2001), Fedn. of Small Anthropology Programs, Am. Ethnol. Soc., Am. Anthrop. Assn., African Studies Assn., Inst. for Devel. Anthropology (rsch. assoc. 2001), Soc. for Applied Anthropology, YMCA, City Club, Phi Beta Kappa Soc. Avocations: gardening, travel, calligraphy. Office: Hanover College PO Box 108 Hanover IN 47243 E-mail: porterk@hanover.edu.

**PORTER, LAURIN R.,** literature and language professor; b. St. Louis, June 29, 1945; d. Helmuth and Sylvia Reininga; m. Thomas Emmett Porter, Aug. 4, 1978; children: Katherine Kilbane, Margaret Laurin. MA summa cum laude in Tchg., Harvard U., Cambridge, Mass., 1968; BA in English, U. Mo., Columbia, Mo., 1967; PhD, U. Detroit, 1976. Asst. prof. English St. Mary's U., San Antonio, 1976—78; vis. asst. prof. U. Tex., Dallas, 1984—86; prof. English Arlington, 1986—. Mem. adv. bd. Cir. Theatre, Ft. Worth, 1995—; lectr. in field. Author: The Banished Prince: Time, Memory, and Ritual in the Late Plays of Eugene O'Neill, 1988, Orphans' Home: The Voice and Vision of Horton Foote, 2003; contbr. chapters to books, articles to profl. jours. Mentor Big Bros./Big Sisters, Arlington, Tex., 2002—05. Recipient Outstanding Rsch. award, U. Tex., Arlington, 2006, Star-Telegram Outstanding Tchg. award, 2006, Provost's Profl. Devel. award, 2005, 2006; fellow, Harvard U., 1967—68, U. Detroit, 1973—76; grantee, U. Tex., Arlington, 1994, 1996, 1997, 1998; scholar, Fulbright Assn. and Charles U., Prague, Czech Republic, 2003. Mem.: MLA (assoc.), Soc. Study Am. Women Writers, Fulbright Assn., Eugene O'Neill Soc. (assoc.), Horton Foote Soc. (assoc.), Cir. Theatre, Phi Beta Delta, Phi Beta Kappa. Home: 3008 Pitkin Drive Arlington TX 76006 Office: University of Texas Arlington Box 19035 Arlington TX 76019 Office Phone: 817-272-2693. Office Fax: 817-272-2718. Personal E-mail: lporter@uta.edu.

**PORTER, LILIANA ALICIA,** artist, photographer, painter, printmaker, filmmaker; b. Buenos Aires, Oct. 6, 1941; came to U.S., 1964, naturalized, 1982; d. Julio and Margarita (Galetar) P.; m. Luis Camnitzer, 1965 (div. 1978); m. Alan B. Wiener, May 28, 1980 (div. 1991). Grad., Nat. Sch. Fine Arts, Argentina, 1963. Co-dir., instr. Studio Camnitzer-Porter summer workshops, Lucca, Italy, 1974, 75, 76, 77; prof. art Queens Coll., CUNY, N.Y.C., 1991— Adj. lectr. SUNY Coll. Old Wstbury, N.Y., 1974-76, Purchase br., 1987; co-dir. Studio Porter-Wiener, N.Y.C., 1979-87. One-woman shows of prints/paintings/photographs include Galeria Artemultiple, Buenos Aires, Argentina, 1977, 78, Galleria Arte Comunale, Adro, Brescia, Italy, 1977, Hundred Acres Gallery, N.Y.C., 1977, Mus. Modern Art, Cali, Colombia, 1978, Center for Interamerican Relations, N.Y.C., 1980, Galeria Arte Nuevo, Buenos Aires, 1980, Barbara Toll Fine Arts, N.Y.C., 1979, 81, 82, 84, Galerie Jolliet, Montreal, 1983, Museo de Arte Contemporaneo, Panama City, Panama, 1984, Dolan/Maxwell Gallery, Phila., 1985, U. Alta., Edmonton, 1985, Dolan/Maxwell Gallery, Phila., 1985, Galería Luigi Marrozzini, San Juan, P.R., 1986, Galería-Taller, Museo of Arte Moderno, Cali, Colombia, 1987, The Space, Boston, 1988, Syracuse U., N.Y., 1990, Steinbaum-Krauss Gallery, N.Y.C., 1993, Galeria Ruth Benzacar, Buenos Aires, 1994, U. Art Gallery, N.Mex. State U., Las Cruces, 1995, Monique Knowlton Gallery, 1996, Ruth Benzacar Gallery, N.Y., 1997, Mus. de Bellas Artes Juan Manuel Blanes, Montevideo, Uruguay, 1997, Espacio Minimo, Murcia, Espana, 1998, 2000, Annina Nosei Gallery, N.Y., 1999, 2000, 02, 04, Artcore Gallery, Toronto, Can., 1999, Ruth Benzacar Gallery, Buenos Aires, 2000, Sicardi Gallery, Houston, 2000, 02, 04, Ctr. Photography, Woodstock, N.Y., 2000, Phoenix Mus., 2000, Galeria Espacio/Mimimo, Madrid, 2000, 03, 04, Brito-Cimino, Sao Paulo, Brazil, 2001, Casas Riegner Gallery, Miami, Fla., 2003, Hosfelt Gallery, San Francisco, 2003, Centro Cultural Recoleta, Buenos Aires, 2003, Palacio Aguirre, Cartagena, Spain, 2004, Eli Marsh Gallery, Amherst Coll., Mass., 2004, Carrie Secrist Gallery, Chgo., 2005, Annina Nosei Gallery, N.Y.C., 2004, Galeria Ruth Benzacar, Buenos Aires, 2005, Carrie Secrist Gallery, Chgo., 2005, Sala de Veronicas, Murcia, Spain, 2005, Galeria Petrus, San Juan, P.R., 2005, Galeria Casas Riegner, Bogota, Colombia, 2005; retrospective exhibits 1968-90 Fundacion San Telmo, Buenos Aires, 1990, Museo Nacional de Artes Plasticas, Montevideo, Uruguay, 1991, Centro de Recepciones del Gobierno, San Juan, P.R., 1991, Bronx Mus. Art, N.Y.C., 1992, retrospective exhibit Archer Huntington Art Gallery U. Tex. Austin, 1993, Statler Ctr. for the Art SUNY at Stony Brook, N.Y., 1998, Centro Cultural Recoleta, Sla Cronopios, Buenos Aires, Argentina, 2003; exhibited in numerous group shows including most recently El Mus. del Barrio, N.Y.C., 2000, Casa de America, Madrid, 2000, Contemporary Mus., Balt., 2000, +'s, others, Mass. Coll. Art, Huntington Gallery, Boston, 2001, ARCO, Madrid, 2001, Centro Cultural Borges, Buenos Aires, 2001, Peter Lewis Theater, Guggenheim Mus., N.Y., 2001, Hosfelt Gallery,

San Francisco, 2001, Fundacion Telefonica, Madrid, 2001, Fundacion Joan Miro, Barcelona, 2001, Carrie Secrist Gallery, Chgo., 2001, Contemporary Art Ctr., N.Y., 2001, The Mahady Contemporary Gallery at Marywood U. Scranton, Pa., 2002, Kunst Werke, Berlin, 2003; represented in permanent collections Mus. Phila., Mus. Modern Art, N.Y.C., RCA Corp., N.Y.C., N.Y. Public Libr., N.Y.C., La Biblioteque Nationale, Paris, France, Museo del Grabado, Buenos Aires, Museo Universitario, Mexico City, Mexico, Museo de Art Moderno, Cali, Colombia, Museo de Bellas Artes, Caracas, Venezuela, Met. Mus. Art, N.Y.C. Recipient 1st prize Argentinian Art 78 Mus. Fine Arts, Buenos Aires, 1978, Grand Prix XI, Internat. Print Biennial, Cracow, Poland, 1986, 1st prize VII Latin Am. Print Biennial, San Juan, Puerto Rico, 1986; fellow Guggenheim Found., 1980-81, N.Y. Found. for the Arts, 1985, grantee, 1999. Address: 720 Greenwich St 10G New York NY 10014 Office Phone: 718-997-4800, 845-876-3472. Personal E-mail: lilianaporter@earthlink.net.

**PORTER, LOUISA S.,** federal judge; Apptd. presiding magistrate judge so. dist. U.S. Dist. Ct. Calif., 1997—2002. Mem.: Fed. Magistrate Judges Assn. (pres. 2003—04). Office: 1140 US Courthouse 940 Front St San Diego CA 92101 Office Phone: 619-557-5383. Office Fax: 619-702-9925.

**PORTER, MARC BENNETT,** auction house executive; b. July 30, 1960; BA, U. Pa., BS in Econs., 1982; JD, Yale U., New Haven, 1987. Various positions including assoc. in bus. devel. and mgr. estates and appraisals Christie's Fine Art Auctioneers, N.Y.C., 1990—96, internat. bus. dir. 19th and 20th century art, 2000—03, internat. mng. dir., 2003—; pres. Christie's Am., 2004—. Office: Christies Fine Art Auctioneers 20 Rockefeller Plz New York NY 10020 Office Phone: 212-636-2372. Personal E-mail: MarcPorter@aol.com.

**PORTER, MARGARET EVANS,** novelist, lecturer, historian; b. Macon, Ga., Mar. 4, 1959; d. Fred William Jr. and Mariann (Chappell) Evans; m. Christopher John Porter, Oct. 6, 1984 BA Theatre and English, Agnes Scott Coll., 1980; MA Radio, TV and Film, U. Ga., 1983. Instr. writing Colo. Free U., Denver, 1989—93; writer-in-residence Wesleyan Coll., Macon, 1993. Author: (novels) Heiress of Ardara, 1988, Irish Autumn, 1990, Road to Ruin, 1990, Jubilee Year, 1991, Sweet Lavender, 1992, Toast of the Town, 1993, Dangerous Diversions, 1994, The Proposal, 1998, Kissing a Stranger, 1998, The Seducer, 1999, Improper Advances, 2000; also poetry Precinct del. Jefferson City Dem., Colo., 1992; active Episcopal Diocese N.H., columnist Concord Monitor; del. N.H. Dem. Conv., 2002, 06; moderator Diocesan Coun., 2006—; parishioner St. Stephen's Episcopal Ch., Pittfield, N.H. Recipient Excellence cert. Romantic Times mag., 1991, 94; named Best New Author, Romantic Times mag., 1990 Mem. Authors Guild, Novelists, Inc., N.H. Writers Project, Romance Writers Am., Rocky Mountain Fiction Writers (v.p. 1991-93, Jasmine award 1993), Jane Austen Soc. N.Am Avocations: nature study, theater, music, travel, gardening.

**PORTER, MICHAEL E.,** competitive strategy educator; b. Ann Arbor, Mich., May 23, 1947; s. Howard Eugene and Stana (Vernerova) P. BS, Princeton U., 1969; MBA, Harvard U., 1971, PhD, 1973. Asst. prof. Grad. Sch. Bus., Harvard U., 1973-77, assoc. prof., 1977-82, prof., 1982—, C. Roland Christensen Prof. Bus. Admin., Bishop William Lawrence U. Prof., 2000—. Bd. dirs. Alpha-Beta Techs., Hyatt Mgmt. Co., Inforte, Corp.; bd. advisers, WebEx Communications Inc.; adviser to several fgn. govts., including Canada, India, Ireland, New Zealand, Portugal, the U.K. Author: Interbrand, Choice, Strategy and Bilateral Market Power, 1976, Competitive Strategy: Techniques for Analyzing Industries and Competitors, 1980 (Outstanding Acad. Book selection Choice mag. 1980-81), (with R.E. Caves and A.M. Spence) Competition in the Open Economy, 1980, Competitive Advantage: Techniques for Achieving and Sustaining Superior Performance, 1985, Competition in Global Industries, 1986, The Competitive Advantage of Nations, 1990; mem. editorial adv. bd. Long Range Planning, Antitrust Law and Econs. Rev. Mem. Presdl. Commn. on Indsl. Competitiveness, 1983, Gov's Council on Econ. Growth and Technology, Mass., 1991. Served to capt. AUS, 1969-76. Recipient David A. Wells Prize in Econs. Harvard U., 1973-74, McKinsey award for best article Harvard Bus. Rev., 1979, 87, Charles Coolidge Parlin award Am. Mktg. Assn., 1991, Adam Smith award, Nat. Assoc. Bus. Economists, 1997. Fellow Acad. Mgmt. (George R. Terry award 1985), Fin. analysts Fedn. (Graham and Dodd award 1980), Internat. Acad. Mgmt.; mem. Am. Mktg. Assn., Strategic Mgmt. Soc. Clubs: Cap and Gown. Republican. Office: Harvard Bus Sch Soldiers Field Rd Boston MA 02163-1317 *My work has sought to make a positive impact on the ability of companies to compete effectively and on the ability of government to play a constructive role in that process. I have tried to bring a new level of sophistication to the understanding of competition by combining the tools of an economist with a strong awareness of and interest in the problems of the practicing manager. I have also sought to influence public policy by bringing to its formulation a closer awareness of the realities of competition than is embodied in contemporary economic theory.*

**PORTER, MICHAEL PELL,** lawyer; b. Indpls., Mar. 31, 1940; s. Harold Troxel and Mildred Maxine (Pell) P.; m. Alliene Laura Jenkins, Sept. 23, 1967 (div.); 1 child, Genevieve Natalie Porter Eason; m. Janet Kay Smith Hayes, Feb. 13, 1983 (div.). Student, DePauw U., Greencastle, Ind., 1957-58; BA, Tulane U., New Orleans, 1961, LLB, 1963. Bar: La. 1963, U.S. Ct. Mil. Appeals 1964, N.Y. 1969. Hawaii 1971. Clk. U.S. Ct. Appeals (5th cir.), New Orleans, 1963; assoc. Sullivan & Cromwell, N.Y.C., 1968-71, Cades Schutte Fleming & Wright, Honolulu, 1971-74, ptnr., 1975-94; mem. faculty Addis Ababa (Ethiopia) U. Sch. Law, 1995-99; sr. regulatory advisor Egyptian Capital Market Authority, Cairo, 1999—2002; advisor capital market Palestinian Nat. Authority, 2002—; lectr. Arab Acad. Banking and Fin. Scis., 2003; legal adv. Securities and Exch. Commn, Bangladesh, 2001 05. Legal advisor St. Matthews Anglican Ch., Addis Ababa, Ethiopia, 1995—99; cons, Rep. of Yemen, 1997; mem. deans coun. Law Sch. Tulane U., 1981—88; dep. vice chancellor Episcopal Diocese Hawaii, 1980—88, chancellor, 1988—94, Episcopal Ch., Micronesia, 1988—95; legal cons. Bangladesh SEC, 2004—05. Author: Hawaii Corporation Law & Practice, 1989; Hawaii reporter State Limited Partnership Laws, 1992-94. Bd. dirs. U. Achievement Hawaii, Inc., 1974-84, Inst. Human Svcs., Inc., 1980-88; donor Michael P. Porter Dean's Scholastic Award, U. Hawaii Law Sch., 1977—. With JAGC, U.S. Army, 1963-66, Vietnam. Fulbright scholar, 1997-99; Tulane U. fellow, 1981; lectorship named in his honor, Addis Ababa, 1994-97; established Michael P. Porter Prizes on Ethnic Harmony and Religious Tolerance in a Dem. Soc. at Addis Ababa, 1995. Mem.: ABA, Hawaii Bar Assn. E-mail: porterconsultant@yahoo.com.

**PORTER, PHILIP DREW,** lawyer; b. Buffalo, Jan. 31, 1947; s. Verne William and Eleanor Marie Porter. BA, Canisius Coll., Buffalo, 1969; MEd, U. S.C., 1974, JD, 1982. Bar: DC 1982, Va. 1996. Tchr., guidance counselor, curriculum coord. Barnwell (S.C.) County Schs., 1969-76; coord. sec. curriculum Horry County Schs., Conway, SC, 1976-79; assoc. Shaw Pittman, Washington, 1982-86, Fenwick & West, LLP, Washington, 1986-; ptnr. Hogan & Hartson, LLP, McLean, Va., 1996—; dir. intellectual property practice group. Mem. and chair steering com. D.C. Bar, Washington, 1994-97. Contbr. articles to profl. jours. Bd. advisors George Mason U. Internet Multimedia Ctr., Fairfax, Va., 1998-2000; mem. D.C. Computer Law Forum, 1992-96. Recipient Golden Achievement awards D.C. Bar, 1995, 96, Cert. of Appreciation, 1999, Appreciation award Century Club of George Mason U., 1998. Mem. Computer Law Assn. Office: Hogan and Hartson LLP 8300 Greensboro Dr Ste 1100 Mc Lean VA 22102 Business E-Mail: pdporter@hhlaw.com.

**PORTER, PHILIP THOMAS,** retired electrical engineer; b. Clinton, Ky., Mar. 18, 1930; s. Philip Henry and Ruth Frances (Pennebaker) P.; m. Louise Monroe Jett, July 3, 1957; children: Philip C., Sara Shelby Porter Taylor. BA in Physics, Vanderbilt U., 1952, MA in Physics, 1953. Mem. tech. staff Bell Telephone Labs., Murray Hill, NJ, 1953-62, Holmdel, NJ, 1962-70, supr., 1971-78, West Long Branch, NJ, 1979-83; dir. wireless and wireline network compatiblity studies Telcordia Tech., Red Bank, NJ, 1984-94; ret., 1994. U.S. del. Consultative Com. for Internat. Radio, Geneva, 1984-93. Contbg. author:

Electronics Engineers' Handbook, 1982, History of Science and Technology in the Bell System, 1985, Digital Communications, 1986; patentee in field. Fellow IEEE. Unitarian Universalist. Avocations: group singing, bridge. Personal E-mail: pporter@triad.rr.com.

**PORTER, PHILIP WAYLAND,** geography educator; b. Hanover, N.H., July 9, 1928; s. Wayland Robinson and Bertha Maria (LaPlante) P.; m. Patricia Elizabeth Garrigus, Sept. 5, 1950; children: Janet Elizabeth, Sara Louise, Alice Catherine. AB, Middlebury Coll., 1950; MA, Syracuse U., 1955; PhD, U. London, 1957. Instr. geography U. Minn., Mpls., 1957-58, asst. prof., 1958-64, assoc. prof., 1964-66, prof., 1966-2000, prof. emeritus, 2000—; assoc. to v.p. acad. affairs, also dir. Office Internat. Programs, 1979-83. Geography panel Com. on Space Programs for Earth Observations Nat. Acad. Scis., 1967-71; liaison officer Midwest Univs. Consortium for Internat. Activities, 1979-83 Author: (with Eric S. Sheppard) A World of Difference: Society, Nature, Development, 1998, Challenging Nature: Local Knowledge, Agroscience and Food Security in Tanga Region, Tanzania, 2006; contbr. articles to profl. jours. With AUS, 1952-54. Grantee Ctrl. Rsch. Fund, 1955-56, NSF, 1961-62, 78-80, 92-93, Social Sci. Rsch. Coun., 1966-67, Rockfeller Found., 1969, 71-73, Gen. Svc. Found., 1981-83, Exxon Edn. Found., 1983-84, Fulbright, 1992-93; Bush Sabbatical fellow, 1985-86. Mem. Assn. Am. Geographers (Lifetime Achievement award 2004), Phi Beta Kappa (alumni mem.). Home: 10 Burkehaven Terr Sunapee NH 03782-2402 Office: U Minn Dept Geography Minneapolis MN 55455 Personal E-mail: pwporter@verizon.net.

**PORTER, ROGER BLAINE,** federal official, educator; b. Provo, Utah, June 19, 1946; s. Blaine Robert and Elizabeth M. (Taylor) P.; m. Ann Robinson, Jan. 6, 1972; children: Robert Roger, Stacy Ann, David R., Rachel Elizabeth. BA in History and Polit. Sci., Brigham Young U., 1969; PhB, Oxford U., 1971; MA, PhD, Harvard U., 1978; PhD (hon.), Weber State U., 2003. Asst. dean, tutor in politics Queen's Coll., Oxford U., 1971-72; spl. asst. to pres. The White House, 1974-77; rsch. assoc. Kennedy Sch. Govt. and Grad. Sch. Bus., Harvard U., Cambridge, Mass., 1977-79, asst. prof. pub. policy, 1979-81, assoc. prof., 1981, prof. govt. and bus., 1985—; spl. asst. to Pres. of U.S., 1981-82; dep. asst. to Pres. of U.S., 1982-85; dir. White Ho. Office of Policy Devel., Washington, 1982-85; counselor to sec. U.S. Treasury, 1981-85; exec. sec. Nat. Productivity Adv. Com., 1981-85, Cabinet Coun. on Econ. Affairs, 1981-85, Econ. Policy Coun., 1985; asst. to U.S. Pres. for econ. and domestic policy, 1989-93. Exec. sec. Pres.'s Econ. Policy Bd., 1974—77; sr. scholar Woodrow Wilson Internat. Ctr. for Scholars, 1993—; dir. Ctr. for Bus. and Govt. Harvard U., 1995—2000, master Dunster House, 2001—; mem. Pres.'s Commn. on White House Fellowships, 1976—2001; bd. dirs. Zions Bancorp., Pactiv Corp., Nat. Life Ins. Co., Tenneco, Inc., Mutual of Am., Extra Space Storage, Packaging Corp. Am. Author: Presidential Decision Making, 1980, U.S.-USSR Grain Agreement, 1984, Efficiency, Equity, Legitimacy: The Multilateral Trading System at the Millenium, 2001; asst. editor: Public Policy, 1979—81. Mem. Utahns for Effective Govt., Salt Lake City, 1971-72; mem. Rep. Nat. Com. Econ. Adv. Com., 1977-81; trustee Gerald R. Ford Found.; mem. adv. bd. George Bush Sch. Govt. and Pub. Svc., Tex. A&M U. Rhodes scholar, 1969; Woodrow Wilson fellow, 1969; White House fellow, 1974; recipient spl. citation U.S. Sec. Treasury, 1977, Rolex Intercollegiate Tennis Achievement award, 1996; named One of 10 Outstanding Young Men in Am., 1981 Fellow Nat. Acad. Pub. Adminstrn.; mem. White House Hist. Assn. (bd. dirs. 1995—), Phi Kappa Phi, Pi Sigma Alpha, Phi Eta Sigma, Phi Alpha Theta. Republican. Mem. Lds Ch. Avocations: classical music, basketball, tennis, travel. Home: 12 Clifton St Belmont MA 02478-3363 Office: Harvard U Kennedy Sch Govt 79 JFK St Cambridge MA 02138-5801

**PORTER, ROGER JOHN,** research and development company executive, neurologist, pharmacologist; b. Pitts., Apr. 4, 1942; s. John Keaggy and Margaret (Parker) P.; m. Candace Marie Leland, Feb. 17, 1968; children: David, Stacey. BS, Eckerd Coll., 1964; MD, Duke U., 1968. Diplomate Nat. Bd. Med. Examiners, Am. Bd. Neurology, Am. Bd. Electroencephalography. Intern U. Calif., San Diego, 1968-69; resident in neurology U. Calif., San Francisco, 1971-74; fellow rsch. tng. program Duke U., Durham, NC, 1966-67; staff assoc. sect. epilepsy Nat. Inst. Neurol. Diseases and Stroke, NIH, Bethesda, Md., 1969-71; investigator U. Calif., San Francisco, 1972-73; sr. rsch. assoc. epilepsy br. neurol. disorders program Nat. Inst. Neurol. and Communicative Disorders and Stroke, NIH, Bethesda, 1974-78, asst. chief epilepsy br., 1977-79, acting chief, 1979-80, acting chief clin. epilepsy sect., IRP, 1979-84, chief epilepsy br. neurol. disorders program, 1980-84, chief med. neurology br. and clin. epilepsy sect. IRP, 1984-87; dep. dir. Nat. Inst. Neurol. Disorders and Stroke, NIH, Bethesda, 1987-92; v.p. clin. rsch., 1997—99, v.p., dep. head clin. rsch., 1999—2002; cons., 2002—. Adj. prof. neurology U. Pa., 1993—; prof. neurology Uniformed Svcs. U. Health Scis., Bethesda, 1980-93, adj. prof. pharmacology, 1982—; cons.-lectr. neurology Nat. Naval Med. Ctr., Bethesda, 1978-93; chmn. White House Subcom. on Brain and Behavioral Scis., 1990-92; scholar-in-residence Am. Med. Colls., Washington, 1989-90; mem. NIMH/Nat. Inst. Neurol. Disorders and Stroke Coun. of Assembly of Scientists, 1983-86, pres., 1985-86; mem. pharmacy and therapeutics com. NIH, 1977-86, chmn., 1978; mem. instnl. rev. bd. human subjects Nat. Inst. Neurol. Disorders and Stroke, 1984-87, chmn., 1986-87. Mem. editl. bd. Acta Neurologica Scandanavica, 1977, Annals of Neurology, 1987-92, Epilepsia, 1982-86, Clin. Neuropharmacology, 1999-2001; contbr. articles to profl. jours., chpts. to books; writer, contbr. 5 motion pictures, 1 exhibit. Bd. trustees Eckerd Coll., 1994—97; commd. officer USPHS, 1969—92. Recipient MacArthur Outstanding Alumnus award Eckerd Coll., 1977, Fulbright Disting. Prof. award, 1985, Disting. Alumnus award Duke Duke U. Med. Ctr., 1989, USPHS Dist. Svc. Medal, 1991, USUHS Commendable Svc. Award, 2001. Fellow Coll. Physicians Phila. (mem. bd. trustees 2006—). Am. Acad. Neurology, Am. Neurol. Assn.; mem. Am. Electroencephalographic Soc., Am. Epilepsy Soc. (pres. 1989-90), Soc. Neurosci., Am. Soc. Clin. Pharmacology and Therapeutics, Am. Soc. Exptl. Neurol. Therapeutics (pres.-elect 2006), Internat. League Against Epilepsy (sec.-gen. 1989-93), Am. Soc. Pharmacology and Exptl. Therapeutics. Home and Office: 461 Timber Ln Devon PA 19333-1232 Office Phone: 610-989-3767. Business E-Mail: rjporter@aol.com.

**PORTER, STEPHEN CUMMINGS,** geologist, educator; b. Santa Barbara, Calif., Apr. 18, 1934; s. Lawrence Johnson Porter Jr. and Frances (Cummings) Seger; m. Anne Mary Higgins, Apr. 2, 1959; children: John, Maria, Susannah. BS, Yale U., 1955, MS, 1958, PhD, 1962. Asst. prof. geology U. Wash., Seattle, 1962-66, assoc. prof., 1966-71, prof., 1971—2002, dir. Quaternary Research Ctr., 1982-98, prof. emeritus, 2002—. Mem. bd. earth scis. Nat. Acad. Sci., Washington, 1983-84; vis. mem. adv. com. divsn. polar programs NSF, Washington, 1983-84; vis. fellow Clare Hall Cambridge (Eng.) U., 1980-81; guest prof. Chinese Acad. Scis., People's Republic of China, 1987—; v.p. Internat. Union Quaternary Rsch., 1992-95, pres., 1995-99. Co-author: Physical Geology, 1987, The Dynamic Earth, 1989, 1992, 1995, 1999, 2004, The Blue Planet, 1995, 1999, Environmental Geology, 1996, Dangerous Earth, 1997; editor: Late Quaternary Environments of the United States, 1983, Quaternary Rsch., 1976—2000; co-editor: The Quaternary Period in the U.S.; assoc. editor Radiocarbon, 1982—89, Am. Jour. Sci., 1997—, mem. editl. bd. Quaternary Sci. Revs., 1984, S.F. Emmons lectr. Colo. Sci. Soc., 1996; Fulbright Hays sr. rsch. fellow, New Zealand, 1973-74. Fellow Geol. Soc. Am. (Kirk Bryan award 2004, Disting. Career award 2005), Arctic Inst. N.Am. (bd. govs.), AAAS; mem. Am. Quaternary Assn. (coun., pres. 1992-94, Disting. Career award 2004). Avocations: photography, mountain climbing. Home: 18034 15th Ave NW Shoreline WA 98177-3305 Office: U Wash Dept Earth and Space Scis Seattle WA 98195-1310

**PORTER, TERRY,** professional basketball coach; b. Milw., Apr. 8, 1963; Student, U. Wis., Stevens Point, 1981-85. Guard Portland Trail Blazers, 1985-97, Minn. Timberwolves, Mpls., 1997-98, Miami Heat, 1998-99, San

Antonio Spurs, 1999—2002; head coach Milw. Bucks, 2003—05. Recipient Citizenship award, 1993; named to NBA All-Star team, 1991, 93. Achievements include holding single game record for most three point field goals without a miss-7, 1992.

**PORTER, THOMAS W.B.,** lawyer; b. Ann Arbor, Mich., July 15, 1957; s. James Morris and Helen Marie (Adams) P.; m. Anne R.P. Ballew, Aug. 2, 1980; children: Devin B., Clare B., Keith B. BA, John Carroll U., 1977; JD, U. Mich., 1980. Bar: D.C. 1980, Mich. 1985, U.S. Ct. Claims 1980, U.S. Dist. Ct. (ea. dist.) Mich. 1985, U.S. Ct. Appeals (4th cir.) 1981, U.S. Ct. Appeals (fed. cir.) 1982, U.S. Ct. Appeals (6th cir.) 1986, U.S. Ct. Appeals (9th cir.) 1991, U.S. Ct. Appeals (7th cir.) 1992, U.S. Ct. Appeals (1st cir.) 1994. Trial atty. U.S. Dept. Justice Civil Div., Washington, 1980-85; assoc. Dykema Gossett PLLC, Detroit, 1985-87, ptnr., 1988-93; gen. counsel Barton Malow Co., Southfield, Mich., 1997—98; mem. Dykema Gossett PLLC, Detroit, 1994-98; v.p., gen. counsel Barton Malow Co., Southfield, Mich., 1998—2001, sr. v.p., gen. counsel, 2001—04, exec. v.p., sec., chief legal officer, 2004—; chmn. United Integrity Assurance, Ltd., 2004—. Bd. dirs. Met. Affairs Coalition, 2004—, Design Build Inst. Am., 2005—. Recipient Spl. Achievement award U.S. Dept. Justice Civil Div., Washington, 1984. Mem. Fed. Bar Assn. (mem. chpt. exec. bd. 1992-95, program chair 1995-96, treas. 1996-97, sec. 1997-98, v.p. 1998-99, pres.-elect 1999-2000, pres. 2000-01). Office: Barton Malow Co 26500 American Dr Southfield MI 48034 Office Phone: 248-436-5040.

**PORTER, THOMAS WILLIAM, III,** lawyer; b. Dallas, Aug. 23, 1941; s. Thomas William and Ruth Mae (Campbell) P.; m. Sally Ann Shell, May 10, 1963 (div. July 1983); children: Elizabeth Elisse, Laura Christina; m. Patty Ann Sanders, Nov. 2, 1985. BBA in Fin., So. Meth. U., Dallas, 1963; LLB, Duke U., Durham, N.C., 1966. Bar: Tex. 1966, U.S. Dist. Ct. (no. dist.) Tex. 1967, U.S. Dist. Ct. (so. dist.) Tex. 1975, U.S. Dist. Ct. (we. dist.) Tex. 1977, U.S. Ct. Appeals (5th cir.) 1977. Assoc. Jackson & Walker, Dallas, 1966-72; ptnr. Bracewell & Patterson, Houston, 1972-74, Foreman & Dyess, Houston, 1974-81; sr. ptnr. Porter & Hedges LLP, Houston, 1981—, chmn., 2000—. Bd. dirs. US Concrete, Helix Energy Solutions, Copano Energy. Life mem. bd. visitors Duke U. Law Sch.; trustee Tex. Heart Inst.; dir. Alley Theatre, Hobby Ctr. Performing Arts. Fellow: Tex. Bar Found.; mem.: ABA (fed. regulation of securities com. 1979—, com. on law firms 1981—), State Bar Tex. Assn. (coun. mem. sect. bus. law 1984—86, securities and investment banking com. 1976—), Coronado Club, River Oaks Country Club. Republican. Methodist. Office: Porter & Hedges LLP Reliant Energy Plz 36th Fl 1000 Main St Houston TX 77002-6336 Office Phone: 713-226-6635. Business E-Mail: bporter@porterhedges.com.

**PORTER, WALTER ARTHUR,** retired judge; b. Dayton, Ohio, June 6, 1924; s. Claude and Estella (Raymond) P.; m. Patricia Reeves Higdon, Dec. 3, 1947; children— Scott Paul, David Bryant. BS in Engring, U. Cin., 1948, LL.B., 1949. Bar: Ohio 1949. Legal dept. Montgomery County Probate Ct., 1949-51; asst. pros. atty. Montgomery County, 1951-56; with Albert H. Scharrer (atty.), Dayton, 1956-61; mem. firm Smith & Schnacke, Dayton, 1962-85, pres., 1980-85; judge Montgomery County Common Pleas Ct., 1985-95; of counsel Thompson Hine & Flory, Dayton, 1996-2001. Served with inf. U.S. Army, 1943-45, ETO. Mem. ABA, Ohio Bar Assn. (pres. 1973-74), Dayton Bar Assn., Am. Coll. Trial Lawyers, Am. Coll. Probate Counsel, Phi Alpha Delta, Omicron Delta Kappa. Clubs: Mason. Democrat. Presbyterian. Home: 872 Timberlake Ct Kettering OH 45429-3494 Personal E-mail: wapphp@aol.com.

**PORTER, WALTER THOMAS, JR.,** retired bank executive; b. Jan. 8, 1934; s. Walter Thomas and Mary Rebecca (Brookes) P.; m. Dixie Jo Thompson, Apr. 3, 1959; children: Kimberlee Paige, Douglas Thompson, Jane-Amy Elizabeth. BS, Rutgers U., 1954; MBA, U. Wash., 1959; PhD, Columbia U., 1964. CPA, Wash., N.Y. Staff cons. Touche Ross & Co., N.Y.C., 1959-61, dir. edn., 1964-66; NDEA fellow Columbia U., 1961-64; assoc. prof. U. Wash., 1966-70, prof., 1970-74; vis. prof. N. European Mgmt. Inst., Oslo, 1974-75; nat. dir. planning Touche Ross & Co., Seattle, 1975-78, dir. exec. fin. counseling, 1978-84; exec. v.p., mgr. pvt. banking Rainier Nat. Bank, 1984-87, exec. v.p., mgr. capital mgmt. and pvt. banking, 1987-88, vice-chmn., 1988—92, Security Pacific Bank Washington, 1989-92; exec. v.p., mgr. capital mgmt. group Bank of Am., Seattle, 1992-99; chmn. Porter Investments LLC, 1999—. Vis. lectr. taxation U. Wash., 1978—85; vis. lectr. strategic planning Nat. U. Ireland, 2003; bd. dirs. Shugard Self-Storage, Coldstream Capital Mgmt., Bite, Inc. Author: 11 books, the most recent being The Bank of America Guide to Personal Financial Solutions, 2d edit., 1998, The Glory of Washington: The People and Events That Shaped the Husky Athletic Tradition, 2001; Husky Stadium: Great Games and Golden Moments, 2004. Mem. Seattle adv. bd. Salvation Army, 1975-83, 89-97, pres., 1993-95; trustee Ryther Child Ctr., 1975-85, pres., 1979-81; trustee Lakeside Sch., 1977-87, pres., 1984-86; trustee Va. Mason Med. Ctr., 1986-97, chair bd. govs., 1994-96; chair Nat. Campaign for Student Athlete U. of Wash., 1995-2000, Mus. History and Industry, 1982-83, Olympic Park Inst., 1996-2001. With U.S. Army, 1955-57. Mem. Sand Point Country Club. Congregationalist.

**PORTER, WAYNE RANDOLPH,** dermatologist; b. Washington, Jan. 10, 1948; s. James Randolph and Betty Rose (Burgess) P. BS, MIT, 1970; MD, Duke U., 1973. Diplomate Am. Bd. Internal Medicine, Am. Bd. Dermatology. Intern U. Miami (Fla.) Affiliated Hosps., 1973-74; resident in internal medicine U. Miami Sch. Medicine, 1973-76, resident in dermatology, 1976-78, clin. instr., then asst. prof. dermatology (vol.), 1978-85, assoc. prof. (vol.), 1985—2005, prof., 2005—. Adj. prof. Barry U. Sch. Grad. Medicine, 2000—; practice medicine specializing in dermatology, North Miami Beach, 1978—; mem. staff U. Miami-Jackson Meml. Hosp. Mem. med. adv. bd. Dade-Broward chpt. Lupus Found. Am. Fellow Internat. Soc. for Dermatologic Surgery, Am. Acad. Dermatology, Am. Assn. Dermatologic Surgeons; mem. AMA, ACP, Internat. Soc. Pediat. Dermatology, Fla. Med. Assn., Fla. Dermatology Soc., Miami Dermatol. Soc. (pres.), Dade County Med. Assn., So. Med. Assn., Bath Club (Miami Beach), Coral Reef Yacht Club. Office: 909 N Miami Beach Blvd Miami FL 33162-3712 Office Phone: 305-949-4223. E-mail: wrpmd@bellsouth.net.

**PORTER, WILLIAM LYMAN,** architect, educator; b. Poughkeepsie, N.Y., Feb. 19, 1934; s. William Quincy and Lois (Brown) P.; m. Lynn Rogers Porter; children: Quayny Lyman, Zoe Lynn, Eve Lyman. BA, Yale U., 1955, M.Arch., 1957; PhD, MIT, 1969. Designer, job capt. Louis I. Kahn (architect), Phila., 1960-62; urban designer, asst. chief of design Ciudad Guayana project Joint Center for Urban Studies of Harvard and MIT, Caracas, Venezuela, 1962-64; Mellon fellow dept. urban studies and planning MIT, 1964-65; Samuel Stouffer fellow Joint Center for Urban Studies, Harvard and MIT, 1966-67; asst. prof. urban design, depts. architecture and urban studies and planning MIT, 1968-70, assoc. prof. urban design, 1970-71, prof. architecture and planning, 1971—2004, Norman B. and Muriel Leventhal prof. architecture and planning, 1988—2004, prof. emeritus, 2004—, head. dept. architecture, 1987-91, dean Sch. Architecture and Planning, 1971-81; co-dir. Aga Khan Program for Islamic Architecture Harvard U.-MIT, 1979-85. Cons. in field; mem. Nat. Archtl. Accrediting Bd., 1978-80, pres., 1979; mem. Mass. Designer Selection Bd., 1978-79, chmn., 1979; mem. steering com. Aga Khan Award for Architecture, 1977-86, mem. master jury, 1989; prin. Four Architecture Inc., Boston, 1994—. Co-author: Transforming Workplace and Work Practice, 1999; co-founder, co-editor Places: A Quarterly Jour. Environ. Design, 1982-88, Facilities Engineering and Management Handbook: Commercial, Industrial and Institutional Buildings, 2000, Design Representation, 2003. Trustee Milton (Mass.) Acad., 1989-2001; mem. bd. overseers Coll. Fine Arts, U. Pa., 1984-90, Mus. Fine Arts, Boston, 1992-94. Fellow AIA; mem. Boston Soc. Architects (pres. 1973-77, 81). Clubs: Harvard Musical Assn. (Boston). Home: 17 Concord Ave Cambridge MA 02138-2321 Office: MIT Sch Architecture & Planning 77 Massachusetts Ave Cambridge MA 02139-4307 Business E-Mail: wlporter@mit.edu.

**PORTER, WILMA JEAN,** retired educational consultant; b. Sylacauga, Ala., May 30, 1931; d. Harrison Samuel and Blanche Leonard Butcher; m. Douglas Taylor Porter, Apr. 18, 1953; children: Daria Cecile, Blanche Evette, Douglas Vincent. BS, Tuskegee U., 1951; MS, Mich. State U., 1966; PhD, Iowa State U., 1980. Asst. dietitian Miss. State Tb Sanatorium, 1951-52; therapeutic dietitian dept. of hosp. City of N.Y., S.I., 1952-53; libr. asst. Mississippi Valley State Coll., Itta Bena, Miss., 1963-65; asst. prof. Grambling (La.) State U., 1966-75, Howard U., Washington, 1976-80; country dir. U.S. Peace Corps, Tonga, 1980-82; asst. dir. internat. programs Ft. Valley (Ga.) Coll., 1983-84, dir. Inst. Advancement, 1984-88; dir. Sch. Home Econs. Tenn. Technol. U., Cookeville, 1989-96; ret., 1996. Project dir. Capitol Hill Health and Homemaker, Washington, 1982-83; interim dir. Inst. Advancement Alcorn State U., Lorman, Miss., 1988-89. Author lab. manual for quantity foods, 1977; editor: (cookbook) Some Christmas Foods and Their Origins from Around the world, 1983. Convenor Nat. Issues Forums, Ga. and Tenn., 1985-90; citizen participant Nat. Issues Forums Soviet Dialogue, Newport Beach, Calif., 1988; bd. dirs. Leadership Putnam, Cookeville, 1990-94; chmn. Tenn. Technol. U. campaign United Way, 1989; mem. devel. and planning com. Peach County Ft. Valley, 1985-87; mem. Peach County Heart Fund Dr., 1986-88; participant People to People Internat. to China; ct. apptd. spl. adv. for children vol. CASA N.E. La. Title III grantee U.S. Dept. Edn., 1986, 87; Tenn. Dept. Human Svcs. grantee, 1993, 94. Mem. AAUW (program chair 1991-92, pres. Cookeville br. 1993-94), Am. Family and Consumer Scis. Assn., Am. Dietetic Assn., La. Assn. Family and Consumer Scis., La. Dietetic Assn., CASA N.E. La. Democrat. Roman Catholic. Avocations: writing, vegetable and flower gardening. Home: 1415 ML King Jr Ave Grambling LA 71245

**PORTERFIELD, CHRISTOPHER,** magazine editor, writer; b. Weston, W.Va., Apr. 3, 1937; s. James Herman and Irene (Smith) P.; m. Stephanie Brown, Jan. 20, 1962; children: Christopher Brown, Tessa Louise, Kevin Stephenson. BA, Yale U., 1958; MA, Columbia U., 1965. Music critic Time mag., N.Y.C., 1967-69, cultural correspondent London, 1969-72; exec. producer Daphne Prodns., N.Y.C., 1974-79; sr. editor Time mag., N.Y.C., 1980-93, asst. mng. editor, 1993-96; exec. editor, 1996—2003; contbr., 2003—. Co-Author: (with Dick Cavett) (books) Cavett, 1973, Eye on Cavett, 1983; contbr. articles to popular mags. and periodicals, 1975—. Mem. Writers Guild of Am. Avocations: reading, music, tennis. Home and Office: 315 Central Park W New York NY 10025-7664

**PORTERFIELD, WILLIAM WENDELL,** chemist, educator; b. Winchester, Va., Aug. 24, 1936; s. Donald Kennedy and Adelyn (Miller) P.; m. Dorothy Elizabeth Dail, Aug. 24, 1957; children: Allan Kennedy, Douglas Hunter. BS, U. N.C., 1957, PhD, 1962; MS, Calif. Inst. Tech., 1960. Sr. research chemist Hercules, Inc., Cumberland, Md., 1962-64; asst. prof. chemistry Hampden-Sydney (Va.) Coll., 1964-65, assoc. prof., 1965-68, prof. chemistry, 1968—, Charles Scott Venable prof. chemistry, 1989—, chmn. natural sci. div., 1973-77, chmn. dept. chemistry, 1982-83, 93-96, 2002—. Vis. fellow U. Durham (U.K.), 1984 Author: Concepts of Chemistry, 1972, Inorganic Chemistry, 1984, 2d edit., 1993; contbr. articles to profl. jours. Mem. Am. Chem. Soc., Royal Chem. Soc. (London, Eng.), Phi Beta Kappa Home: PO Box 697 Hampden Sydney VA 23943 Office Phone: 434-223-6179. Business E-Mail: wporterfield@hsc.edu.

**PORTERFIELD-PYATT, CHAUMONDE R.,** music educator, advocate; b. Visalia, Calif., Oct. 18, 1943; d. Roy E. and Zoisla Saladin; m. Melvin E. Pyatt, June 16, 1984; children: Michelle R. Pyatt children: Brian K. Porterfield, Erik D. Porterfield, Kevin G. Porterfield. AA, Coll. Sequoias, Visalia, Calif., 1963; post grad. with Stanley Glasser, U. London, 1981; BS, U. San Francisco, 1988; degree (hon.), Wessex Theology Coll. Cert. C.C. supr. Calif., 1988, C.C. instr. Calif., 1987, Wellstone Actions Adv. Campaign Mgmt. Sch., 2006. Prof. music Coll. Sequoias, Visalia, Calif., 1981—. Exec. dir. 49th Mozart Festival, 1982; guest soloist Grieg Piano Concerto, No. 1, Opus 16 Kings County Symphony, 1988; state legislative advocate Faculty Assn. Calif. Cmty. Colleges, 1994; conf. presenter Copyright Laws II, Lobbying 101: How to Stalk the Wild Legislator, 2002. Accompanist and singer: Desert Song, 1963, Music Man, 1963; performer (with Maestro Igor Stravinsky): Von Himmel Hoch and Symphony of Psalms, 1965; performer: (with Maestro Aaron Copland) Musica Viva with the San Francisco Symphony, 1966; performer: New J. S. Bach Chorales Premiere, 1988, recitals featuring Composers of Chopin, Rachminoff, Liszt, Debussy, J. S. Bach, and Beethoven, Piano Dedication Concert-Visalia United Methodist Church, 1984; singer: San Francisco Chorale, 1967; contbr. articles to profl. jours. Recipient cert. Appreciation, Fine Arts Divsn. Coll. Sequoias, 2000; Music fellow, Wessex Theol. Coll., Eng., 1989. Mem.: NEA, C.C. Assn. (advocacy chair 1994—, polit. action com. 1994—, lobbying com 1994—, legislation com. 1994—, exec. bd 1998—, advocate 1998—, bd. dir. dist D, W. H. O. award 2004), Music Assn. Calif. Cmty. Colleges (legis. advocacy rep. 1984, exec. bd. 1984—), Am. Theatre Organ Soc., Am. Guild Organists (conf. presenter 1984), Calif. State Tchrs. State Coun. (higher edn. rep. 2001), Calif. Teachers Assn. (life; exec. bd. 1989, advocate 1998—, higher edn. dir. at large 2004, com. higher edn. 2004, state dir. 2004—), Calif. Scholastic Fedn. (life), Mu Phi Epsilon (pres. 1967). Achievements include Invited guest to sail on the QE2 from New York to Southampton, England; featuring piano artists Eugene Istomin, Peter Orth, Michael LaGrand, Leonard Pennario and Charles Strauss; Invited guest performer on Steinway pianos once belonging to Vladimir Horowitz, Van Cliburn and Ignace Paderewski. Office: Coll Sequoias 915 S Mooney Blvd Visalia CA 93277 Office Phone: 559-730-3810.

**PORTER-KELLEY, JOHANNA MARIE,** microbiology educator, researcher; d. John Willie Porter and Helen Porter King; 1 child, Jordan Nicole Kelley. PhD, Meharry Med. Coll., Nashville, 2000. Postdoctoral fellow NIH, Bethesda, Md., 2000—02, U. Md., Balt., 2002—05; asst. prof. microbiology Winston-Salem State U., NC, 2005—. Office: Winston-Salem State U 601 Martin Luther King Blvd Winston Salem NC 27110 Office Phone: 336-750-3239. E-mail: porterkelleyj@wssu.edu.

**PORTES, FERNANDO A.,** project manager; b. Sabana de la Mar, Dominican Republic; came to U.S., 1995; s. Manuel Ulises Portes and Onfalia Antonia Pimentel Rodriguez. BS magna cum laude, U. Santo Domingo, Dominican Republic, 1986, BEng magna cum laude, 1988; MPS, MEng, Cornell U., 1991; MBA, Cath. U., Santo Domingo, 1995. Cert. quality engr., project mgmt. profl. Sr. quality engr., quality engr. supt. Baxter, Santo Domingo, 1989, 1992—95; project engr., sr. process engr., sr. procurement analyst Merck, 1990, 1995—2001; sourcing sys. mgr. J&J, Raritan, NJ, 2001—03; prin. project mgr. Wyeth, 2003—05; pres., founder Best Project Mgmt., 2005—; affiliate prof. Stevens Inst. Tech., 2005—. Mem. Merck Mgmt. Devel. Program, 1997-00. Pres. Merck Hispanic Orgn., West Point, 1998-99, treas., 2000-01. Mem. Project Mgmt. Inst. Democrat. Roman Catholic. Avocations: politics, current affairs, dance, history, sociology. Address: 380 Mountain Rd 1514 Union City NJ 07087 Office Phone: 201-617-9240. E-mail: portes@verizon.net.

**PORTES, PEDRO RENÉ,** psychology professor, department chairman; h Havana, Cuba, June 19, 1950; arrived in U.S., 1961; s. Helio B. Portes and Eulalia D. Cortada; m. Patricia Ranagan, May 28, 1977; 1 child, André Sebastian. BS in Psychology, U. Iowa, Iowa City, 1972; MS in Psychology, Nova Southeastern U., Ft. Lauderdale, Fla, 1977; PhD in Ednl. Psychology, Fla. State U., Tallahassee, 1982. Lic. prof. counselor, psychologist. Asst. to full prof. Dept. Ednl. and Counseling Psychology Coll. Edn. U. Louisville, 1982—. Mental health counselor United Behavioral, Louisville, 1995; program evaluator Ohio Valley Ednl. Coop., Shelbyville, 1999—2003; pres. Ky. Specialists in Group Work, 1986. Editor: Journal of the Society for Accelerated Learning 1992—98; author: Making Kids Smarter, 1998, Dismantling the Achievement Gap, 2005. Named Disting. Rschr., U. Louisville, 1998; Fulbright scholar, Peru, 1988, Colombia, 1996. Mem.: Ky. Counseling Assn., Am. Ednl. Rsch. Assn. (sec. 1999—2000, Rsch. award in Human Devel. 2005), Fulbright. Avocations: tennis, chess, basketball, pool, ping pong/table tennis. Office: U Louisville 320 Edn Louisville KY 40292

**PORTES, RICHARD DAVID,** economics professor; b. Chgo., Dec. 10, 1941; s. Herbert and Abra (Halperin) P.; m. Barbara Diana Frank, 1963 (div. 2005); children: Jonathan, Alison; m. Helene Mireille Rey, 2006. BA summa cum laude, Yale U., 1962; MA, Balliol and Nuffield Colls., Oxford, 1965, DPhil, 1969; DSc honoris causa, U. Libre de Bruxelles, 2000, London Guildhall U., 2000. Asst. prof. econs. and internat. affairs Princeton U., 1969-72; prof. econs. U. London, 1972-94; head dept. econs. Birkbeck Coll., 1975-77, 80-83; pres. Ctr. for Econ. Policy Rsch., 1983—; dir. Ecole des Hautes Etudes, Paris, 1978—; prof. econs. London Bus. Sch., 1995—. Disting. Global vis. prof. U. Calif., Berkeley, 1999—2000; assoc. Nat. Bur. Econ. Rsch., Cambridge, Mass., 1980—; vis. prof. Harvard U., Cambridge, 1977—78; dir. European Corp. Governance Inst., 1999—2005; Joel Stern disting. vis. prof. internat. fin. Columbia Bus. Sch., 2003—04; mem. Group of Econ. Policy Advisors to Pres. of European Commn., 2001—. Editor, author: Planning and Market Relations, 1971, The Polish Crisis, 1981, Deficits and Detente, 1983, Threats to International Financial Stability, 1987, Global Macroeconomics, 1987, Blueprints for Exchange Rate Stability, 1989, Macroeconomic Policies in an Interdependent World, 1989, External Constraints on Macroeconomic Policy, 1991, The Path of Reform in Central and Eastern Europe, 1991, Economic Transformation in Central Europe, 1993, European Union Trade with Eastern Europe, 1995, Crisis? What Crisis? Orderly Workouts for Sovereign Debtors, 1995, Crises de la dette, 2003, European Government Markets, 2006; contbr. articles to profl. jours. Decorated Comdr. Brit. Empire; Rhodes scholar; fellow Balliol Coll., 1965-69; Guggenheim fellow, 1977-78. Fellow Econometric Soc., Brit. Acad., European Econ. Assn.; mem. Coun. Royal Econ. Soc. (exec. com. 1987-92, sec.-gen. 1992—), Econ. Policy (bd. govs., sr. editor 1985—), Coun. on Fgn. Rels., Commn. Econ. de la Nation (France). Avocation: living beyond my means. Office: London Bus Sch Regents Pk London NW1 4SA England E-mail: rportes@london.edu.

**PORTIS, ALAN MARK,** physicist, researcher; b. Chgo., July 17, 1926; s. Lyon and Ruth P.; m. Beverly Portis, Sept. 5, 1948; children: Jonathan, Stephen, Sara, Eliyahu. PhB., U. Chgo., 1948; AB, U. Calif., Berkeley, 1949, PhD, 1953. Mem. faculty U. Pitts., 1953-56, U. Calif.-Berkeley, 1956—, prof. physics, 1964-95, prof. emeritus, 1995—, asst. to chancellor for research, 1966-67, assoc. dean grad. div., 1967-68, dir. Lawrence Hall Sci., 1969-72, univ. ombudsman, 1981-83, 92-94, assoc. dean Coll. Engring., 1983-87, 94-95. Author: Electromagnetic Fields/Sources and Media, 1978, Electrodynamics of High-Temperature Superconductors, 1993; contbg. author: Berkeley Physics Laboratory, 1964, 65, 66, 71. Fulbright fellow, 1961, 67, Guggenheim fellow, 1965, SERC sr. fellow, U.K., 1991-92. Fellow Am. Phys. Soc.; mem. Am. Assn. Physics Tchrs. (Robert Andrews Millikan award 1966). Business E-Mail: portis@socrates.berkeley.edu.

**PORTIS, CHARLES MCCOLL,** reporter, writer; b. El Dorado, Ark., Dec. 28, 1933; s. Samuel Palmer and Alice (Waddell) P. BA, U. Ark., 1958. Reporter The Comml. Appeal, Memphis, 1958, Ark. Gazette, Little Rock, 1959-60, N.Y. Herald Tribune, N.Y.C., 1960-64. Author: Norwood, 1966, True Grit, 1968, The Dog of the South, 1979, Masters of Atlantis, 1985, Gringos, 1991. Sgt. USMC, 1952-55, Korea. Presbyterian. Home: 7417 Kingwood Rd Little Rock AR 72207-1734

**PORTIS, CLINTON,** professional football player; b. Laurel, MS, Sept. 1, 1981; Degree, U. Miami. Running back Denver (Colo.) Broncos, 2002—03, Washington Redskins, 2004—. Named NFL Offensive Rookie of the Yr., AP, 2002; named to NFL Pro-Bowl, 2003. Achievements include being a member of NCAA Champion Miami Hurricanes, 2001. Office: 21300 Redskins Park Dr Ashburn VA 20147*

**PORTMAN, GLENN ARTHUR,** lawyer; b. Cleve., Dec. 26, 1949; s. Alvin B. and Lenore (Marsh) P.; m. Katherine Seaborn, Aug. 3, 1974 (div. 1984); m. Susan Newell, Jan. 3, 1987. BA in History, Case Western Res. U., 1968; JD, So. Meth. U., 1975. Bar: Tex. 1975, U.S. Dist. Ct. (no. dist.) Tex. 1975, U.S. Dist. Ct. (so. dist.) Tex. 1983, U.S. Dist. Ct. (we. and ea. dists.) Tex. 1988, Ct. of Appeals, Ffith Cir., 1998. Assoc. Johnson, Bromberg & Leeds, Dallas, 1975-80, ptnr., 1980-92, Arter, Hadden, Johnson & Bromberg, Dallas, 1992-95, Arter & Hadden LLP, Dallas, 1996—2003, Bennett, Weston & LaJone, PC, Dallas, 2003—. Chmn. bd. dirs Physicians Regional Hosp., 1994-96; mem. exec. bd. So. Meth. U. Sch. Law, 1994—; lectr. bankruptcy topics South Tex. Coll. Law, State Bar Tex.; mem. vis. com. Coll. Arts and Scis., Case Western Res. U., 1999-2004. Asst. editor-in-chief Southwestern Law Jour., 1974-75; contbr. articles to profl. jours. Firm rep. United Way Met. Dallas, 1982-92; treas. Lake Highlands Square Homeowners Assn., 1990-93. Mem. ABA, Am. Bankruptcy Inst., State Bar Tex., Dallas Bar Assn. Turnaround Mgmt. Assn., So. Meth. U. Law Alumni Assn. (coun. bd. dirs., v.p. 1980-86, chmn. admissions com., chmn. class agt. program 1986-89, chmn. fund raising 1989-91), 500 Club Inc., Assemblage Club. Republican. Methodist. Office: 1750 Valley View Ln Ste 120 Dallas TX 75234 Home: 1306 Bradford Dr Coppell TX 75019 Office Phone: 214-691-1776 ext. 207. Office Fax: 214-393-4007. Personal E-mail: glennportman@comcast.net. Business E-Mail: @bwlpc.com.

**PORTMAN, JOHN C., JR.,** architect, developer; b. Walhalla, S.C., Dec. 4, 1924; s. John Calvin and Edna (Rochester) P.; m. Joan Newton, Dec. 23, 1944; children: Michael Wayne, John Calvin III, Jae Phillip, Jeffrey Lin, Jana Lee, Jarel Penn. Midshipman, U.S. Naval Acad., 1944; BS in Architecture, Ga. Inst. Tech., 1950, DFA, 1993, Emory U., 1993, Atlanta Coll. Art, 1993. Diplomate: Registered architect, Ga. With Ketchum, Gina and Sharp, H.M. Heatly, Asso. (Architects), N.Y.C. and Atlanta, 1945-49, Stevens & Wilkinson, Atlanta, 1950-53; individual practice Atlanta, 1953-56; partner Edwards and Portman (Architects), Atlanta, 1956-68; prin. John Portman and Assocs., 1968—; CEO The Portman Holdings, Atlanta, chmn. bd. dirs., 1971—; chmn. bd. dirs., CEO, dir. AMERICASMART, Atlanta, 1957—; bd. dirs. National Bank, Baton Rouge, La., 2006—; pres. Central Atlanta Progress, 1970-72. Prin. works include: The Regent Hotel, Marina Sq., both Singapore, Embarcadero Center, The Pan Pacific-San Francisco, San Francisco Fashion Ctr., Hyatt Regency O'Hare Hotel, Chgo., Peachtree Center, Atlanta; George W. Woodruff Phys. Edn. Ctr., R. Howard Dobbs Student Ctr., both Emory U., Atlanta, Atlanta Merchandise Mart, Atlanta Apparel Mart, Atlanta Decorative Arts Center, Atlanta Gift Mart, Inforum, One Peachtree Ctr., Kennedy Community Center and Middle Sch, Hyatt Regency Hotel, Westin Peachtree Plaza Hotel, Atlanta Marriott Marquis, Northpark Town Ctr., Riverwood, Greenbriar Shopping Ctr., Olympic Village Housing, all Atlanta, Blue Cross-Blue Shield Bldg, Chattanooga, Ft. Worth Nat. Bank Bldg. and Garage, Brussels Internat. Trade Mart, Dana Fine Arts Bldg. at Agnes Scott Coll, Decatur, Ga., Renaissance Center, Detroit, Bonaventure Hotel, Los Angeles, N.Y. Marriott Marquis, Rockefeller Ctr. renovation, N.Y.C., Shanghai Centre, Dream Lake Villas, Hangzhou Qiantang River City, Shandong Bldg., Guomai Bldg., BAODA Bldg., Senfuli Bldg., S Renzhill Complex, Peoples Republic of China, Capital Sq., Kuala Lumpur, Malaysia. Co-author: The Architect as Developer, 1990. Hon. counsul, Denmark; sponsor Atlanta Symphony; mem. nat. adv. bd. Ga. Inst. Tech. Found. Bd. Inc.; trustee Atlanta Arts Alliance, Nat. Jewish Hosp. and Research Center; Dean's adv. coun. Emory U. Sch. Bus.; dir. Atlanta C. of C. (named famous Georgian 1991). Served with USNR, 1942-44. Decorated knight Royal Order Knights of Dannebrog, Denmark; officer Royal Order of the Crown, Belgium; recipient Ivan Allen award N. Ga. chpt. AIA, 1964; award excellence Am. Inst. Steel Constrn., 1973; Design in Steel award Am. Iron and Steel Inst., 1975; medal for hotel design AIA, 1978; Silver medal for innovative design Ga. chpt. AIA, 1981, Community Devel. award Atlanta Bus. League, 1986, others; named Outstanding Young Man of Year, Ga. Jr. C. of C., 1959; Salesman of Year, Sales and Mktg. Execs., Atlanta, 1968; recipient Exceptional Achievement award Ga. Inst. Tech. Alumni Assn., 1985, Disting. Service award Empire Real Estate Bd., Atlanta, 1984, Martin Luther King Salute to Greatness, 1993, Disting. Community Svc. award Atlanta Bus. League, 1991, Atlanta Downtown Partnership's Resurgens award and Design of Peachtree Plz. Park, 1991, Atlanta Downtown Partnership's Resurgens award Design of One Peachtree Ctr., 1993, Horatio Alger award Horatio Alger Assn., 1990, Nat. Home Furnishings Assn.

Disting. Svc. award, 1990, Shaping the City award Atlanta Convention and Visitors Bureau, 1988, Trendsetter award Foodsvc. Cons. Soc. Internat., 1987, Torch of Liberty award Anti-Defamation League, 1994; named Man of Yr. Danish Am. Soc., 1986, Father of Yr. Southeast Father's Day Council, 1986; named to Bus. Hall of Fame Coll. Bus. Adminstrn. Ga. State U., 1987, Atlanta Bus. Chronicle, 1991, Atlanta Entrepreneurs Hall of Fame Atlanta Entrepreneurs Network, 1990; named Famous Georgian, Atlanta C. of C.; Paul Harris fellow Rotary Found. Rotary Internat., 1991. Fellow AIA (Atlanta Svc. to Profession award 1992); mem. Nat. Council Archtl. Registration Bds., Am. Inst. Interior Designers (hon.), Soc. Internat. Bus. Fellows (hon.), World Trade Club (founding), Ga. Archtl. and Engring. Soc., Atlanta Rotary Club, Atlanta Action Forum, Omicron Delta Kappa, Tau Sigma Delta Clubs: Commerce (bd. dirs.). Office: Portman Holdings LLC 303 Peachtree St NE Ste 4600 Atlanta GA 30308 Office Phone: 404-614-5252. Office Fax: 404-614-5400.*

**PORTMAN, NATALIE,** actress; b. Jerusalem, June 9, 1981; d. Avner and Shelley Hershlag. BS in Psychology, Harvard U., 2003. Appeared in motion pictures including The Professional, 1994, Developing, 1995, Heat, 1995, Beautiful Girls, 1996, Everyone Says I Love You, 1996, Beautiful Girls, 1996, Mars Attacks!, 1996, Star Wars: Episode I-The Phantom Menace, 1999, Anywhere But Here, 1999, Where the Heart Is, 2000, Zoolander, 2001, Star Wars Episode II-Attack of the Clones, 2002, Cold Mountain, 2003, Garden State, 2004, True, 2004, Closer, 2004 (Golden Globe award for best supporting actress, 2005), Domino One, 2005, Star Wars: Episode III-Revenge of the Sith, 2005, Free Zone, 2005, V for Vendetta, 2006; appeared in stage prodns. including Diary of Anne Frank, 1997 (Nominee Tony award), The Seagull, 2001. Office: Creative Artists Agy 9830 Wilshire Blvd Beverly Hills CA 90212*

**PORTMAN, ROBERT JONES,** federal official, former ambassador, former congressman; b. Cin., Dec. 19, 1955; m. Jane Portman; children: Jed, Will, Sally BA, Dartmouth Coll., 1979; JD, U. Mich., 1984. Assoc. Patton Boggs LLP, Washington, 1984—86; ptnr. Graydon Head & Ritchey LLP, Cin., 1986-89, 1991—93; assoc. counsel to Pres. The White House, Washington, 1989—91, dep. asst. to Pres., dir. Office Legis. Affairs, 1989—91; mem. U.S. Del. to UN Subcom. on Human Rights, 1992, U.S. Congress from 2nd Ohio dist., 1993—2005; mem. ways & means com., budget com.,ethics com., select com. on homeland security; chmn. Rep. leadership; US Trade Rep. Exec. Office of the Pres., Washington, 2005—06, dir. Office Mgmt. & Budget, 2006—. Bd. trustees Springer Sch., The United Way, Hyde Park Community United Meth. Ch.; founding trustee Cin.-China Sister City Com.; former bd. dirs. United Home Care; vice chmn. Hamilton County George Bush for Pres. Campaign, 1988, 92; chmn. Rep. Early Bird Campaign com., 1992; del. Rep. Nat. Conv., 1988, 92; active Hamilton County Rep. Party Exec. com., Hamilton County Rep. Party Fin. Com. mem. Fed. World Trade Assn. Republican. Office: Office Mgmt & Budget 725 17th St NW Washington DC 20503*

**PORTNEY, PAUL ROGERS,** dean; BA in economics and math., Alma Coll., Mich., 1967; PhD in economics, Northwestern U., 1973. Chief economist White House Coun. on Environ. Quality, Washington, 1979-80; joined Resources for the Future, Washington, 1972—, head rsch. divisions, 1986—89, v.p., 1989-95, pres., CEO, 1995—2005; dean Eller Coll. Mgmt., U. Ariz., Tucson, 2005—, Halle chair in leadership, 2005—. Vis. prof. U. Calif., Berkeley, 1977—79, Princeton U., 1992—94. Office: U Ariz Eller Coll Mgmt McClelland Hall 1130 E Helen St Tucson AZ 85721-0108 Office Phone: 520-621-2125. Office Fax: 520-621-8105. E-mail: pportney@eller.arizona.edu.*

**PORTNOW, MARJORIE,** painter; b. NYC, Sept. 30, 1942; d. Julius J. and Bessie M. (Aptaker) P. BA in Art History, Cae-Western Res. U., 1964; MFA in Painting summa cum laude, Bklyn. Coll., 1972; postgrad., Pratt Inst., 1964-65, Skowhegan Sch. Painting, 1965. Mem. faculty Vt. Studio Sch. 1987—2005, Vt. Studio Sch., Johnson, 1987—95, U. Pa., Phila., 1988—91, Pa. Acad. Fine Arts, Phila., 1988—2003, Snowaggan Sch. Painting and Sculpture, 1989, U. Calif., Santa Cruz, 1991—93, Bklyn. Coll., 1994—96, Phila. Acad. Fine Arts, NY Studio Sch., NYC, 1994—95, Nat. Acad. Design, NYC, 2000—06. One-woman shows include Hollins U., Roanoke, Va., 2000, Peter Rose Gallery, NY, 2003, Oxbow Gallery, North Hampton, Mass., 2005, exhibited in group shows at curated by Graham Nichson, Olana, NY, 2000, fLizan Tops Gallery, East Hampton, NY, 2000, Julie Heller Gallery, Provincetown, Mass., 0201, Lower Manhattan Cultural Coun., NY, 2004, 2005, Sharon Arts Ctr., Peterborough, NH, 2005, exhibitions include Nat. Acad. Design, NY, 2005. Fellow, MacDowell Colony, 1971, 72, 75, Yaddo, 1972, 74, 77; Artists for Environment grantee 1972, Tiffany grantee, 1972-73, 78, Radcliffe Inst. grantee 1973-74, 74-75, 93, Ingram Merrill grantee 1975-76, Nat. Endowment for the Arts grantee, 1980, 94, N.Y. State Creative Artists Pub. Svc. grantee, 1981-82, N.Y. Found. for the Arts grantee, 1986, Radcliffe grantee, 1990, Fullbright grantee, 1993; named juror painting N.Y. Found. for the Arts, 1988. Mem.: Nat. Acad. Design. Office: National Acad Design 5 E 89th St New York NY 10128 Office Phone: 212-925-6321. Office Fax: 212-426-1711.

**PORTNOY, DARIN ARTHUR,** medical association administrator; b. 1962; MD, PhD, Tulane U., 1989. Diplomate Am. Bd. Family Practice. Chief of staff Indian Health Svc., N.Mex., 1992—97; med. coord. tuberculosis project Doctors Without Borders, Uzbekistan, 1997—98; physician Conejos County Med. Clinic, LaJara, Colo., 1998—. Bd. dirs., v.p. Doctors Without Borders US. Office: Conejos County Med Clinic PO Box 639 19021 State Hwy 285 S La Jara CO 81140

**PORTNOY, ELLIOTT IVAN,** lawyer; b. Morgantown, W.Va., Nov. 1, 1965; s. Donald Charles and Enid Joan (Pallant) Portnoy; m. Estee Renee Mermelstein, Sept. 6, 1992; children: Joshua Brandon, Noah Abraham, Daniela Faye. BA, Syracuse U., 1986; PhD in Politics, Oxford U., Eng., 1989; JD, Harvard U., 1992. Bar: Md. 1992, DC 1993. Staff asst., cons. dem. policy com. US Senate, Washington, 1985-88; ptnr. Arent Fox Kintner Plotkin & Kahn, Washington, 1992—2002, past head lobbying practice; ptnr. Sonnenschein Nath & Rosenthal LLP, Washington, 2002—, chair firm pub. law & policy strategies group, 2002—, chmn. elect, 2006—, mem. firm policy & planning com. Atty. Clinton-Gore presdl. transition, Washington, 1992-93. Author: Guide to Congress, 1991. Founder, pres. bd. dirs. Kids Enjoy Exercise Now Found., Washington, Oxford, 1987—; bd. dirs. Jewish Social Services Agy., Washington, 1996—; exec. com. Demo Young Lawyers Com., Washington, 1996—. Rhodes scholar, Oxford U., 1986-89; named Washingtonian of the Yr., Washingtonian Mag., 1999. Mem.: ABA (vice chair legis. process & lobbying com.). Office: Sonnenschein Nath & Rosenthal LLP Ste 600, E Tower 1301 K St NW Washington DC 20015 Office Phone: 202-408-6433. Office Fax: 202-408-6399. Business E-Mail: eportnoy@sonnenschein.com.

**PORTNOY, JEFFREY STEVEN,** lawyer; b. Bklyn., July 5, 1947; s. Bernard and Edna (Fure) Portnoy; m. Sandi Edelstein, Mar. 29, 1970; 1 child, Carrie Paige. AB in Polit sci., Syracuse U., 1969; JD, Duke U., 1972. Bar: Hawaii 72, U.S. Dist. Ct. Hawaii 72, U.S. Ct. Appeals (9th cir.) 73, U.S. Supreme Ct. 78, U.S. Dist. Ct. No. Mariana Islands 84. With Cades, Schutte, Fleming and Wright, Honolulu, 1972—78; ptnr. Cades Schutte, Honolulu, 1979—. Adj. prof. media law dept. journalism U. Hawaii, Honolulu, 1986—92; chmn. biden com. U.S. Dist. Ct., 1991—94. Former editor-in-chief Hawaii Employment Law Letter. Pres., bd. dirs Manoa Valley Theatre, Honolulu, 1980—97; mem. Honolulu Cmty. Media Coun., 1983—; chmn. Honolulu Neighborhood Commn., 1984—88, We The People; mem. Hawaii Bicentennial Commn.; pres., bd. dirs Hawaii Internat. Film Festival. Recipient Freedom of Press award, Sigma Delta Chi, 1984. Mem.: C. of C. Bd. Rsch. Inst. (DRI Amb. award 1988, Exceptional Performance award 1991—92), Hawaii Def. Lawyers assn. (lawyer del. 9th cir. jud. conf. 1989—91, assoc. dele. 1991—95, lawyer del. 9th cir. jud. conf. 2002—05), Hawaii State Bar Assn. (bd. dirs. 1990—93, del. to ABA House of Dels. 1994—96, pres.-elect

2006—, rep. adv. bd. ninth cir.). Jewish. Home: 5111 Palaole Pl Honolulu HI 96821-1530 Office: Cades Schutte 1000 Bishop St Honolulu HI 96813 Office Phone: 808-521-9221. E-mail: jportnoy@cades.com.

**PORTNOY, SARA S.,** lawyer; b. N.Y.C., Jan. 11, 1926; d. Marcus and Gussie (Raphael) Spiro; m. Alexander Portnoy, Dec. 13, 1959 (dec. 1976); children: William, Lawrence. BA, Radcliffe Coll., 1946; LLB, Columbia U., 1949. Bar: N.Y. 1949, U.S. Dist. Ct. (so. dist.) N.Y. 1952, U.S. Dist. Ct. (ea. dist.) N.Y. 1975, U.S. Ct. Appeals (2d cir.) 1975, U.S. Supreme Ct. 1975. Assoc. Seligsberg, Friedman & Berliner, N.Y.C., 1949-51; atty. AT&T, N.Y.C., 1951-61; vol. atty. Legal Aid Soc. of Westchester, NY, 1966-74; assoc. Proskauer Rose Goetz & Mendelsohn, N.Y.C., 1974-78, ptnr., 1978-94; ret., 1994. Mem. Commn. on Human Rights, White Plains, N.Y., 1973-78; mem. bd. visitors Columbia Law Sch., 1996-02; bd. dirs. Legal Aid Soc. of Westchester County, N.Y., 1975-83, Columbia Law Sch. Assn., 1990-94, Mosholu Montifiore Cmty. Ctr., 1998—; mem. Pres.'s Coun. Yaddo; dir. Muscular Dystrophy Assn., 2000-03. Mem. Assn. Bar City of N.Y. (chair com. legal support staff 1994, mem. Com. on Homeless, Sr. Lawyer's Com. and chair Pub. Svc. Network 2003-06), South Fork Country Club (dir. 1997-2006), The Children's Storefront (dir. 1998—), Legal Momentum (bd. legal advisors 2004—).

**PORTOGHESE, PHILIP SALVATORE,** medicinal chemist, educator; b. N.Y.C., June 4, 1931; s. Philip A. and Constance (Antonelli) P.; m. Christine L. Phillips, June 11, 1960; children— Stephen, Stuart, Philip. BS, Columbia U., 1953, MS, 1958; PhD, U. Wis., 1961; Dr. honoris causa, U. Catania, Italy, 1986, Royal Danish Sch. Pharmacy, Copenhagen, 1992. Asst. prof. Coll. Pharmacy, U. Minn., Mpls., 1961-64, assoc. prof., 1964-69, prof. medicinal chemistry, 1969—, prof. pharmacology, 1987—, dir. grad. study in medicinal chemistry, 1974-86, head dept., 1974-83; disting. prof. medicinal chemistry, 2000. Cons. NIMH., 1971-72; mem. med. chemistry B sect. NIH, 1972-76; mem. pharmacology, substance abuse and environ. toxicology interdisciplinary cluster President's Biomed. Research Panel, 1975; mem. expert panel of Flavor and Extract Mfrs. Assn. of U.S., 1984—. Mem. editorial adv. bd. Jour. Med. Chemistry, 1969-71; editor-in-chief, 1972—; mem. editorial adv. bd. Med. Chem. series, 1972-77. U.S. Army, 1954—56. Named Highly Cited Rschr., Inst. for Sci. Info., 2001; recipient Ernest H. Volwiler award (oustanding contbns. to pharm. scis., Am. Assn. Colls. Pharmacy, 1984, N.B. Eddy Meml. award, Coll. on Problems of Drug Dependency-NAS NRC, 1991, Recognition award, U. Wis., 1996, Merit award, NIH, 1997, Oak and the Tulip award, European Fedn. Medicinal Chemistry, 1999, Nauta award, Internat. Fedn. Medicinal Chemistry, 2006. Fellow AAAS, Acad. Pharm. Scis., Am. Assn. Pharm. Scientists (Rsch. Achievement award 1990); mem. Am. Chem. Soc. (Medicinal Chemistry award 1990, E.E. Smissman-Bristol-Meyers-Squibb award 1991, Alfred Burger award in medicinal chemistry 2000), Am. Soc. Pharm. Exptl. Therapeutics, Internat. Union Pure and Applied Chemistry (commn. on medicinal chemistry 1978-82, internat. com. med. chemistry 1982-85), Soc. Neurosci., Sigma Xi, Rho Chi (lecture award 1999), Phi Lambda Upsilon. Home: 17 Oriole Ln Saint Paul MN 55127-6334 Office: U Minn Coll of Pharmacy 308 Harvard St SE Minneapolis MN 55455-0353 Office Phone: 612-624-9174. Business E-Mail: porto001@umn.edu.

**PORTWAY, PATRICK STEPHEN,** telecommunications consulting company executive, educator; b. June 18, 1939; s. Christopher Leo and Ceciala (King) P.; m. Malle M. Portway: children by previous marriage: Shawn, Pam, Vicki. BA, U. Cin., 1963; MA, U. Md., 1973; postgrad., Columbia U. Regional ADP coord. GSA, Washington, 1963-68; mgr. strategic mkt. planning Xerox Corp., 1969-74; mgr. plans and programs System Devel. Corp., 1974-78; fin. instial. mktg. exec. Satellite Bus. Sys., 1978-80; western regional mgr. Am. Satellite Co., 1980-81; CEO Applied Bus. Telecomm., Livermore, Calif., 1981-98; prof., lectr. Golden Gate U. Grad. Sch., San Francisco, 1983—. Pub. mag. Teleconference, 1981-98; pub. (newspapers) Discovery Bay, Delta Clippers; prodr. Telecon & Ioccon Confs., 1981-98, CEO ET3 Internet Edn. Co. 1998—. Author: (with others) Teleconfencing and Distance Learning, 1992, 3rd edit., 1997. Presdl. elector Electoral Coll., Va., 1976; candidate Va. State Legislature from 19th Dist., 1971; mem. Discovery Bay Mcpl. Adv. Coun., 1992-96, chmn., 1992; mem. adv. com. Congl. Internet Caucus. 1st lt. U.S. Army, 1963-65. Recipient Internat. Rotary award for Higher Edn., Bombay, India, 1999. Mem. Internat. Teleconferencing Assn. (founder, bd. dirs. 1983-88), Nat. Univ. Teleconferencing Network (mem. adv. bd., bd. dirs. 1986-89), U.S. Distance Learning Assn. (founder, exec. dir. 1987-99), Electronic Funds Transfer Assn. (founder, bd. dirs. 1980), Satellite Profls., Internat. Internet Assn. (pres. 2001—), Internat. Higher Edn. Acad. of Sci., Global Distance Learning Assn. (founder, exec. dir., COO 1998-99), Jaycees (charter pres. Chantilly, Va., Disting. Svc. award Dale City, Va.), Commonwealth. E-mail: portwayinva@aol.com.

**PORZAK, GLENN E.,** lawyer; b. Ill., Aug. 22, 1948; m. Judy Lea McGinnis, Dec. 19, 1970; children: Lindsay and Austin. BA with distinction, U. Colo., 1970, JD, 1973. Bar: Colo. 1973. Assoc. Holme Roberts & Owen, Denver, 1973-80, ptnr., 1980-85, mng. ptnr. Boulder office, 1985-95; mng. ptnr. Porzak Browning & Bushong LLP, Boulder, 1996—. Bd. Wells Fargo Bank Boulder, Ctr. of Am. West, U. Colo. Mus., U. Colo.; presdl. search com., 2005—. Contbr. articles to profl. jours. Bd. dirs. Manor Vail Resorts Condominium Assn., 2001, pres., 2003—; bd. dirs. U Colo. Found., 2002—, vice chmn., 2004—. Named Disting. Alumnus U. Colo., 1991, U. Colo. Sch. Law, 2006. Fellow Explorers Club (bd. dirs. 1995-96, Citation of Merit 1998); mem. Am. Alpine Club (pres. 1988-91), Colo. Mtn. Club (pres. 1983, hon. mem. 1983—), Colo. Outward Bound (trustee 1992-2002, vice chmn. 1997-99, chmn. 1999-2001), Phi Beta Kappa. Achievements include reaching summit of Mt. Everest, climbing highest peak on all seven continents. Home: 405 Baseline Rd Boulder CO 80302 Office: Porzak Browning & Bushong 929 Pearl St Ste 300 Boulder CO 80302-5108 Office Phone: 303-443-6800. Business E-Mail: gporzak@pbblaw.com.

**PORZIG, ULLRICH E.,** retail executive; m. Linda K. Porzig. With May Co., 1982—93, sr. v.p. fin., CFO Foley's, 1988—93; sr. v.p., CFO, treas. Payless ShoeSource, Inc., Topeka, 1996, 1996—, Petro Stopping Ctrs. L.P., 1993—96. Office: Payless ShoeSource Inc 3231 SE 6th Ave Topeka KS 66607-2207

**PORZIO, DONALD TIMMIS,** mathematics educator; b. Long Beach, Calif., May 28, 1958; s. Arthur and Carol Ann Porzio; m. Lois Lorretta Coffe, May 29, 1983; children: Michael Timmis, Bryan Daniel. BS in Math., U. Calif., Santa Barbara, 1981; MA in Math., Ohio State U., 1985, PhD in Math. Edn., 1994, MS in Math., 1985. Tchr. math. St. Anthony's Seminar H.S., Santa Barbara, Calif., 1980—82; grad. tchg. asst. in math. Ohio State U., Columbus, 1982—85, 1991—94; asst. prof. dept. math. No. Ill. U., DeKalb, 1994—98; tchr. H.S. math. Ill. Math. and Sci. Acad., Aurora, 1998—. Textbook editor - H.S. math. Merrill Pub. Co., Westerville, Ohio, 1984—91. Mem.: Math. Assn. of Am. (dir. on sect. bd. 1998—2005, Edith May Sliffe award for outstanding H.S. tchg. 2004), Ill. Coun. of Tchrs. of Math. (dir. on state bd. 2005—), Nat. Coun. of Tchrs. of Math., Ill. Math. Coun. of Chgo. (dir. bd. 2001—02). Republican. Avocations: chess, golf, basketball, volleyball. Home: 861 Brown Ct Batavia IL 60510 Office: Ill Math and Sci Acad 1500 W Sullivan Rd Aurora IL 60506 Office Phone: 630-907-5968. Office Fax: 630-907-5976. Personal E-mail: dtpprof@comcast.net. Business E-Mail: dporzio@imsa.edu.

**POSADA, JORGE RAFAEL,** professional baseball player; b. Santurce, PR, Aug. 17, 1971; s. Jorge Posada Sr.; m. Laura Posada, Jan. 21, 2000; children: Jorge Jr., Paulina. Aa, Calhoon C.C., 1991. Profl. baseball player NY Yankees, 1995—. Co-founder Jorge Posada Found., 2000—. Named to Am. League All-Star Team, 2000—03; recipient Louisville Silver Slugger award, 2000, 2001, 2002, 2003, Thurman Munson Award, Assn. for Help of Retarded Children, 2001. Achievements include being a mem. of World Series Champions, 1998, 99, 2000. Office: NY Yankees Yankee Stadium 161st St and River Ave Bronx NY 10451

**POSAMENTIER, ALFRED STEVEN,** mathematics professor, dean; b. NYC, Oct. 18, 1942; s. Ernest and Alice (Pisk) P.; children: Lisa Joan, David Richard. AB, Hunter Coll., 1964; MA, CCNY, 1966; postgrad., Yeshiva U., N.Y.C., 1967-69; PhD, Fordham U., 1973; Nostrifizierung of Doctorate, U. Vienna, Austria, 1992. Tchr. math Theodore Roosevelt H.S., Bronx, NY, 1964-70; asst. prof. math. edn. CCNY, NYC, 1970-76, assoc. prof., 1977-80, prof., 1981—, dept. chmn. dept. secondary and continuing edn., 1974-80, chmn., 1980-86, dir. select program in sci. and engring., 1978—2002, dir. Germany/CCNY Exch. Program, 1985—, dir. Austria/CCNY Exch. Program, 1987—, dir. Czech Republic/CCNY Exch. Program, 1989—, dir. sci. lectr. program, 1981-94; assoc. dean Sch. Edn., CCNY, NYC, 1986-95, dep. dean, 1995-99, dean, 1999—; dir. initiatives program City Coll. UK, 1983—. Chmn. bd. dirs. Salvadori Ednl. Ctr. on Built Environ., 1988-99, 2005—; supr. math. and sci. Mamaroneck HS, NY, 1976-79; NSF math. devel. program for secondary sch. tchrs. math., NYC, 1978-82; project dir. numerous NSF sponsored math./sci. tchr. devel. insts., 1976-99; cons. NYC Bd. Edn., 1973-75, NYC Bd. Edn. Office of Evaluation, 1974-80, NYC Bd. Edn. Examiners, 1979-92, NYS Math Standards Comm., 2003-05, numerous others; coord. NSF NE Resource Ctr. Sci. and Engring., 1980-90; lectr. various confs.; vis. prof. U. Vienna, Austria, 1985, 87, 88, 90, Tech. U., Berlin, 1989, 95, Tech. U., Vienna, 1993-98, Pedgogical Inst., Vienna, 1993-99, Humboldt U., Berlin, 1996; dir. NYC Maths. Project, 1994—, Math for the New Millennium Project, 1995-2000. Author: A Study Guide for the Scholastic Aptitude Test in Math., 1969, Challenging Problems in Geometry, 1970, Challenging Problems in Algebra, 1970, Geometry, Its Elements and Structure, 1972, rev. edit., 1977, Geometric Constructions, 1973, Excursions in Advanced Euclidean Geometry, 1980, 2d edit., 1984, Teaching Secondary School Mathematics: Techniques and Enrichment Units, 1981, 7th edit., 2006, Uncommon Problems for Common Topics in Algebra, 1981, Unusual Problems for Usual Topics in Algebra, 1981, Math Motivators: Investigations in Pre-Algebra, 1982, Math Motivators: Investigations in Geometry, 1982, Using Computers in Mathematics, 1983, 2d edit., 1986, Math Motivators: Investigations in Algebra, 1983, Using Computers: Programming and Problem Solving, 1984, 2d edit., 1989, Advanced Geometric Constructions, 1988, Challenging Problems in Algebra, 1988, 2d edit., 1996, Arbeitsmaterialien: Mathematik, 1994, The Art of Problem Solving: A Resource for the Mathematics Teacher, 1996, Students! Get Ready for Mathematics for SAT-I: Problem Solving Strategies and Practice Tests, 1996, Teachers! Prepare Your Students for Mathematics for SAT-I: Methods and Problem-Solving Strategies, 1996, Deutsch-Englisch Mathematik Worterbuch, 1996, 2d edit., 2000, Tips for the Mathematics Teacher: Research-Based Strategies to help Students Learn, 1998, Problem-Solving Strategies for More Effective and Elegant Solutions: A Resource for the Mathematics Teacher, 1998, Making Pre-Algebra Come Alive, 2000, Making Algebra Come Alive, 2000, Making Geometry Come Alive, 2000, Advanced Euclidean Geometry: Excursions for Secondary Teachers and Students, 2002, Math Wonders: To Inspire Teachers and Students, 2003, Math Charmers: Tantalizing Tidbits for the Mind, 2003, Pi: A Biography of the World's Most Mysterious Number, 2004, What Successful Math Teachers Do, 7-12, 2005; author: (with Dr. H.A. Hauptman Nobel Laureate) Great Ideas for Introducing Key Concepts in Mathematics, 2006; author: (6 textbook series) Progress in Mathematics, 2005—; contbr. articles to profl. jours. and newspapers. Trustee Demarest Bd. Edn., 1977-80. Decorated Austrian Cross of Honor for Sci. and Art-First Class, 2004, Grand Medal of Honor, Austria, 1994; named Tchr. of Yr. CCNY Alumni Assn., 1993; hon. fellow U. South Bank, London, 1988, Ehrenbürger Vienna U. Tech., 2003; Fulbright scholar U. Vienna, 1990; recipient Medal of Distinction City of Vienna, 1996, Medal of Honor Technische Fachhochschule Berlin, 1996, 1000 Years Austria commemorative medal Govt. of Austria, 1997, Townsend Harris medal CCNY Alumni, 2006; Hon. Univ. Prof. of Austria, 1999; named to Hall of Fame, Hunter Coll., 2005. Mem. Math. Assn. Am., Nat. Coun. Tchrs. Math., (reviewer new publs., referee articles Math. Tchr. Jour.), Assn. Tchrs. Math. NY (exec. bd. 1966-67), Assn. Tchrs. Math. NY State, Assn. Tchrs. Math. NJ, Nat. Coun. Suprs. of Math. Home: 634 Caruso Ln Rivervale NJ 07675-6210 Office Phone: 212-650-5471. Personal E-mail: asp2@juno.com.

**POSEN, RICHARD L.,** lawyer; b. NYC, May 26, 1950; AB, Johns Hopkins U., 1972; JD, NYU, 1975. Bar: NY 1976. Ptnr. litig. dept. Willkie Farr & Gallagher LLP, NYC, mem. Exec. Com., 1995—. Articles editor Annual Survey Am. Law, 1974-75. Mem. Assn. Bar City NY, Fed. Bar Coun. Office: Willkie Farr & Gallagher LLP 787 7th Ave New York NY 10019-6018

**POSEN, SUSAN ORZACK,** lawyer; b. NYC, Nov. 5, 1945; BA, Sarah Lawrence Coll., 1967; JD, Bklyn. Law Sch., 1978. Bar: N.Y. 1979. Assoc. Stroock & Stroock & Lavan, N.Y.C., 1978-83, 84-86; ptnr. Stroock, Stroock & Lavan, LLP, N.Y.C., 1987-2000; asst. gen. counsel Cablevision Systems Corp., Woodbury, NY, 1983-84; co-founder, ptnr. DIVA Capital LLC, N.Y.C., 2000—01; vice chair, CEO House of Z LLC, 2001—. Office: House of Z LLC 13-17 Laight St New York NY 10013

**POSER, CHARLES MARCEL,** neurology educator; b. Antwerp, Belgium, Dec. 30, 1923; s. Maurice and Sadye (Gleitsman) P.; m. Joan Doris Crawford, Sept. 3, 1950; children: William John, Nicholas Charles. BS, CCNY, 1947; MD, Columbia U., 1951; DMS (hon.), U. Sassari, Italy, 2000. Diplomate Am. Bd. Psychiatry and Neurology. Resident in neurology Neurol. Inst. Columbia-Presbyn. Med. Center, N.Y., 1952-55; Fulbright scholar Neuropathology Inst. Bunge, Antwerp, Belgium, 1955-56; instr. through assoc. prof. neurology U. Kans. Sch. Medicine, 1956-64; prof., head div. neurology U. Mo. Sch. Medicine, Kansas City, 1964-68; prof., chmn. dept. neurology U. Vt. Coll. Medicine, 1968-81; prof. neurology Boston U. Sch. Medicine, 1981-84; lectr., 1984—; sr. neurologist Beth Israel Hosp. Cons. prof. Tex. Tech. U. Sch. Medicine, Lubbock, 1981-90; neurology lectr. Harvard Med. Sch., 1981-96, vis. prof. neurology, 1996—; neurology lectr. Tufts U. Sch. Medicine, 1982-90; cons. in neurology U.S. Army and U.S. Navy, 1963—; Cross lectr. U. Witwatersrand, Johannesburg, Republic of South Africa, 1990; Oscar Trelles meml. lectr., Lima, Peru, 1997. Editor-in-chief Jour. Tropical and Geog. Neurology, 1989-92, Neurol. Infections and Epidemiology, 1995-97; contbr. numerous articles to med. jours. Served with U.S. Army, 1943-46. Decorated officer Order of Leopold II Belgium; recipient Silver Bicentennial medal Coll. of Physicians and Surgeons, 1967; named Luis Guerrero Meml. lectr. U. Santo Tomás, Manila, 1979, Wilder Penfield lectr. Am. U., Beirut, 1983, Salmon James lectr. London Med. Soc., 1987, Kroc lectr. Rush Med. Coll., Chgo., 1987; Wu Ho-Su Meml. Lectr., Taipei, Taiwan, 1994. Fellow ACP, Am. Acad. Neurology, Am. Acad. Pediat., Royal Soc. Medicine (London), Royal Soc. Tropical Medicine and Hygiene (London), Royal Coll. Physicians (Glasgow), Royal Coll. Physicians (Eng.), Royal Coll. of Physicians (Edinburgh); hon. fellow Japanese, Belgian, Cuban, French, Icelandic, Filipino, Dutch, Uruguyan and Colombian socs. neurology, All-Russian Soc. Neurol. Sci., Uruguyan Neurological Soc., Neurol. Soc. India, Assn. Brit. Neurol.; mem. Am. Neurol. Assn. (sr.), Am. Assn. Neuropathologists, Assn. for Rsch. in Nervous and Mental Diseases, Nat. Acad. Medicine Colombia (hon.), Home: 11 Rutland Sq Boston MA 02118-3105 Office: Beth Israel Deaconess Med Ctr East Campus Dept Neurology Harvard Med Sch 330 Brookline Ave Boston MA 02215-5400 E-mail: cposer@caregroup.harvard.edu.*

**POSER, JOAN RAPPS,** artist, writer; b. Plainfield, N.J., Apr. 10, 1940; d. Mandel Max and Marion Davidson Rapps; m. Jay Sanford Poser, Nov. 15, 1964; children: Lester Philip, Toby Anne BA, U. Conn., 1962. Self-employed travel cons., Lancaster, Pa., 1976—79; tchr. McDonogh Sch., Balt., 1982—90; artist's agt. Joan E. Poser Assocs. Agts. in the Arts, Balt., 1978—; co-owner, v.p. Poser's Apparel, Inc., Pa., 1990—95; co-owner Poser's Accessories Sales Reps., 1995—; polit. speech writer, 2005—. Cons. Charmelle, Inc., San Francisco 2002—. Pres. Lancaster Town Fair, 1974, Temple Beth El Sisterhood, Lancaster, 1973—77, donor chmn., 2000—03; pres. and devel. chmn. Md. Assocs. for Dyslexic Adults and Youth, Inc., 1989—91; campaign chair Bus. and Profl. Women, Assoc. Jewish Charities, Balt., 1985; spl. events chair Cultural Arts Inst. Chizuk Amuno Congregation, 1986—90, trustee, 1986—90; chmn. Lancaster Jewish Cmty. Ctr. 50th Anniversary Gala, 1994, Temple Beth El 50th Anniversary Gala, 1995; bd. dirs. Temple Beth El, 1991—92, Janus Sch., Lancaster, 1991—94, Lancaster Jewish Cmty. Ctr., 1991—93. Mem. Hadassah Democrat. Avocations: opera, sports, architecture, travel, writing. Home: 119 Greenview Dr Lancaster PA 17601-4988 Office Phone: 717-560-7976. Personal E-mail: jerapps@localnet.com.

**POSER, NORMAN STANLEY,** law educator; b. London, May 28, 1928; came to U.S., 1939, naturalized, 1946; s. Jack and Margaret (Salomon) P.; m. Miriam Kugelman, Sept. 1, 1957 (div. 1979); children: Samuel Marc, Susan; m. Judith Eiseman Cohn, Aug. 11, 1985. AB cum laude, Harvard U., 1948, LLB cum laude, 1958. Bar: N.Y. 1958. Asso. Greenbaum, Wolff & Ernst, N.Y.C., 1958-61; atty. SEC, Washington, 1961-64, asst. dir. div. trading and markets, 1964-67; asso. Rosenman, Colin, Kaye, Petschek, Freund & Emil, N.Y.C., 1967-68; v.p. Am. Stock Exchange, N.Y.C., 1968-72, sr. v.p., 1972-75, exec. v.p., 1975-80; adj. prof. law NYU, 1975-80; prof. law Bklyn. Law Sch., 1980—. Cons. World Bank, SEC, OAS, various stock exchs.; spl. counsel N.Y. Stock Exch., 1987—. Mem. adv. bd.: Regulation & Law Report, 1979-2003, Rev. Securities and Commodities Regulation, 1975—; author: International Securities Regulation: London's "Big Bang" and the European Securities Markets, 1991, Broker-Dealer Law and Regulation, 1995, 2d edit., 1997, 3d edit. 2000, supplements, 2001-06 Served with U.S. Army, 1951-53. Mem. Am. Law Inst., ABA, N.Y.C. Bar Assn., Nat. Futures Assn. (arbitrator 1987—). Clubs: Harvard (N.Y.C.). Office: 250 Joralemon St Brooklyn NY 11201-3700 Business E-Mail: norman.poser@brooklaw.edu.

**POSES, FREDERIC M.,** engineering company executive; b. 1942; BBA in Fin., NYU, 1965. Vol. Peace Corps, 1967-69; various positions Allied Corp., 1969-85; pres. plastics and engineered materials divsn. AlliedSignal Inc., Morristown, NJ, 1985-86, pres. fibers divsn., 1986-88, exec. v.p., pres. engineered materials, 1988-98, pres. and COO, 1998-99; chmn. and CEO Am. Standard Cos., Piscataway, NJ, 1999—. Office: 1 Centennial Ave Piscataway NJ 08854-3921*

**POSEY, ADA LOUISE,** human resources specialist; BA, Carleton Coll. Expense mgmt. and pension operation staff Prudential Ins. Co., 1978—85, internal auditing staff, 1985—89; corp. budgeting staff Minn. Mut., 1989—93; assoc. dir. for gen. svcs. Office Adminstrn., The White House, Washington, 1993-96, dep. dir., 1996-97, dir., 1997-99; spl. advisor Office of Nat. Drug Control Policy, Washington, 1999—; sr. policy advisor Dept. of Energy, Washington, 1999-2001; pres. Posey Cons. Group, 2001—03; dir. diversity and compliance Raytheon Tech. Svcs., Reston, Va., 2003—. Trustee Carleton Coll.; mem. Capital City Links Chpt., Washington. Office: Raytheon Tech Svcs 12160 Sunrise Valley Dr Reston VA 21910 Office Phone: 703-295-2259. Personal E-mail: noah0496@aol.com. Business E-Mail: ada_l_posey@raytheon.com.

**POSEY, ELDON EUGENE,** mathematician, educator; b. Oneida, Tenn., Jan. 25, 1921; s. Daniel M. and Eva (Owens) P.; m. Christine K. Johnson, Dec. 25, 1943; children: Margaret Posey McQuain, Daniel Marion. BS, East Tenn. State U., 1947; MA, U. Tenn., 1949, PhD, 1954. Instr. U. Tenn., 1954—55; asst. prof. W.Va. U., Morgantown, 1955—59; assoc. prof. Va. Poly. Inst., Blacksburg, 1959—61, prof., 1961—64; prof. math. U. NC, Greensboro, 1964—88, prof. emeritus, 1988—, head dept. math., 1964—80. Served to capt. USAAF, 1941-46. Decorated Air medal with 18 oak leaf clusters, DFC, Silver Star, Purple Heart, Bronze Star with 6 oak leaf clusters. Mem.: Math. Assn. Am., Am. Math. Soc., Pi Mu Epsilonf, Sigma Xi. Home: 7 Dogwood Cir Blacksburg VA 24060-6298 Personal E-mail: eeposey@bellsouth.net.

**POSEY, PARKER,** actress; b. Balt., Nov. 8, 1968; d. Chris Posey. Student, SUNY, Purchase. Actor (films) Joey Breaker, 1993, Description of a Struggle, 1993, The Wake, 1993, Sleepless in Seattle, 1993, Dazed & Confused, 1993, Coneheads, 1993, Flirt, 1993, Dead Connection, 1994, Opera No. 1, 1994, Iris, 1994, Mixed Nuts, 1994, Amateur, 1994, Sleep With Me, 1994, Drunks, 1995, Frisk, 1995, An Eviction Notice, 1995, Party Girl, 1995, Kicking and Screaming, 1995, The doom Generation, 1995, The Daytrippers, 1996, Basquiat, 1996, Waiting for Guffman, 1996, SubUrbia, 1997, The House of Yes, 1997, Clockwatchers, 1997, Henry Fool, 1997, What Rats Won't Do, 1998, You've Got Mail, 1998, The Misadventures of Margaret, 1998, The Venice Project, 1999, Dinner at Fred's, 1999, Scream 3, 2000, Best in Show, 2000, Josie and the Pussycats, 2001, The Anniversary Party, 2001, Personal Velocity: Three Portraits, 2002, The Sweetest Thing, 2002, The Event, 2003, A Mighty Wind, 2003, Laws of Attraction, 2004, The Sisters of Mercy, 2004, Blade: Trinity, The OH in Ohio, 2006, Superman Returns, 2006; (TV series) As The World Turns, 1991-92; (TV films) First Love, Fatal Love, 1991, Tracey Takes on New York, 1993, Hell on Heels: The Battle of Mary Kay, 2002, Frankenstein, 2004; (TV miniseries) Armistead Maupin's Tales of the City, 1993, More Tales of the City, 1998, Further Tales of the City, 2001; (TV appearances) (voice only) Futurama, 2000, (voice only) The Simpsons, 2000, Will & Grace, 2001, Boston Legal, 2006; (stage) Hurlyburly, 2005, (Lucille Lortel awards, outstanding featured acress, 2005); screenwriter (with Rory Kelly) Dumb in Love, 1995; contributing editor, Open City literary mag. Recipient Spl. Jury prize Sundance Film Festival, 1997; named Queen of Indies by TIME Mag. Office: William Morris Agy 151 S El Camino Dr Beverly Hills CA 90212-2775*

**POSHARD, GLENN (GLENDAL W. POSHARD),** academic administrator, former congressman; b. Herald, Ill., Oct. 31, 1945; BA, So. Ill. U., 1970, MS, 1974, PhD, 1984. Tchr. high sch., 1970—74; asst. dir. then dir. Ill. State Regional Edn. Svc. Ctr., 1974—84; mem. Ill. State Senate, 1984-88, 101st-105th Congresses from 22nd (now 19th) Ill. Dist., 1989-98; tchr., adminstr. John A. Logan Coll., Carterville, Ill.; vice chancellor for adminstrn. So. Ill. U., Carbondale, Ill., 1999—2003, chmn. bd. trustees, 2004—05, pres., 2006—. Founder The Poshard Found. for Abused Children. Served in U.S. Army, 1962—65. Democrat. Office: So Ill U 1400 Douglas Dr Carbondale IL 62901 E-mail: poshard@notes.siu.edu.*

**POSIN, KATHRYN OLIVE,** choreographer; b. Butte, Mont, Mar. 23, 1943; d. Daniel Q. and Frances (Schweitzer) P. BA in Dance, Bennington Coll., 1965; MFA in Interdisciplinary and World Dance, NYU, 1994; studies in composition, 1965-78, studies in ballet, 1965-80, studies in modern dance, 1967-80. Mem. dance co. Am. Dance Theater at Lincoln Ctr., 1965; dancer Anna Sokolow Dance Co., 1965-73; artistic dir. Kathryn Posin Dance Co., NYC, 1972-91; choreographer Eliot Feld Ballet, NYC, 1978, Netherlands Dance Theater, Den Hague, Switzerland, 1980, Alvin Ailey Am. Dance Theater, NYC, 1980; mem. dance faculty U. Wis., Milw., 1984-86, choreographer, 1984-88; tchr., choreographer UCLA, 1988-90, Trinity Coll., Hartford, Conn., 1990-91. Mem. dance faculty, choreographer U. Calif., Santa Barbara, 1986; tchr. dance technique and performance Tchr.'s Coll. Columbia U., spring 1990; tchr. composition and technique Nat. Inst. of Arts, Taiwan, 1991; tchr. world dance Gallatin Sch. NYU; founding chair Joffrey Ballet Sch., New Sch. U. BFA in Dance, 1998. Choreographer (performing cos./orgns.) Cherry Orchard, Lincoln Ctr., NYC, 1978, Alvin Ailey Am. Dance Theater, 1981, Netherlands Dans Theater 84182, Extemporary Dance Co. London, Balletmet, Columbus, Ohio, Milw. Ballet, 1991, 1993, 1995, 1996, Cin. Ballet, 1997, Kansas City Ballet, 2004, Louisville Ballet, 2004, (prin. works) Salvation, Off-Broadway, NYC, 1969, Waves, 1975 (Am. Dance Festival commn.), The Cherry Orchard, NY Shakespeare Festival, 1979, Mary Stuart, Acting Co., 1980, Shady Grove (grantee jt. program of Ohio Arts and Humanities Couns., 1991), The Tempest, Am. Shakespeare Festival, Stratford, Conn., 1982, Midsummer Night's Dream, Arena Stage, Washington, 1982, Boys From Syracuse, Am. Repertory Theater, Harvard U., 1983, The Paper Gramophone, Hartford Stage, 1989, Of Rage and Remembrance, 1990 (Premiere of Yr. in Music and Dance, Milw. Jour.), Stepping Stones, 1993 (co-recipient Meet the Composer/Choreographer award Milw. Ballet, 1993), many others; subject of documentary Kathy's Dance. Grantee Guggenheim Found., 1978, NY State Coun. on Arts, 1977, 79, 80, Jerome Robbins Found., 1972; grantee Nat. Endowment for Arts 1981, 82, 85-87, choreography fellow, 1995-96; Doris Humphrey fellow Am. Dance Festival, New London, Conn., 1968. Office: Kathryn Posin Dance Co 20 Bond St New York NY 10012-2406 Personal E-mail: Pozndance@aol.com.

**POSITAN, WAYNE JOHN,** lawyer; b. Newark, Sept. 11, 1948; BA in Govt. magna cum laude, Boston U., 1970; JD, NYU, 1974. Bar: N.J. 1974, U.S. Dist. Ct. N.J. 1974, U.S. Dist. Ct. (ea. dist.) N.Y. 1987, U.S. Dist. Ct. (so. dist.) N.Y. 1989, U.S. Ct. Appeals (3d cir.) 1981, U.S. Supreme Ct. 1989. Assoc. Lum, Biunno & Tompkins, Newark, 1974-82; ptnr. Lum, Danzis, Drasco & Positan, Roseland, NJ, 1982—; mng. ptnr. Lum Danzis, Roseland, NJ, 1990—. Author: (with others) Business Torts Litigation, 2005, Employment Litigation Handbook, 1998, Jury Instructions in Employment Litigation, 1994, 2d edit., 2005; assoc. editor Annual Survey of American Law, 1972-73; editor-in-chief N.J. Labor and Employment Law, 1998, 2d edit., 2005. Trustee Montclair State U., 1999-2006. Staff sgt. USAR, 1970-76. Mem. ABA (ho. of dels. 2003—, chmn. employment and labor law com. sect. litig. 1990-93, chmn. sect. litig. ann. meeting 1995-96, co-chair task force on merit selection of judges 1996-97, coun. mem. sect. litig. 1997-2000, chmn. commn. multijurisdictional practice 2000-02, dir. divisn. 2001-2005, bd. govs. 2006-2009), N.J. Bar Assn. (labor and employment sect. chmn. 1995-97, gen. coun. 1989-2007, pres. 2006—), Am. Inns of Ct. (master Sidney Reitman Laborand Employment 1993-2005), Confrerie de la Chaine des Rotisseurs (vice conseiller gastronomique Saddle River Valley chpt. 1987—), Essex Fells Country Club, Phi Sigma Delta. Republican. Presbyterian. Avocations: golf, photography, fishing. Office: Lum Danzis Drasco Positan LLC 103 Eisenhower Pky Roseland NJ 07068-1049 Office Phone: 973-228-6730. E-mail: wpositan@lumlaw.com.

**POSKANZER, STEVEN GARY,** academic administrator, lawyer; b. Cortland, N.Y., Sept. 1, 1958; s. Charles Newton and Joan Rae (Mamolen) P.; m. Jane Anne Nofer; children: Jill Madeline, Craig Robert. BA, Princeton U., 1980; JD, Harvard U., 1983. Assoc. Arent, Fox, Kintner, Plotkin & Kahn, Washington, 1983-85; asst. gen. counsel U. Penn., Philadelphia, Pa., 1985—88, assoc. gen. counsel U. Penn, Philadelphia, Pa., 1988—93; spl. asst. to provost Princeton U., 1991—92; exec. asst. to pres. U. Chgo., 1993-97; assoc. provost SUNY, Albany, 1997—98, sr. assoc. provost, 1998—2000, vice provost, 2000—01, interim pres. New Paltz, 2001—03, pres., 2003—. Author: Higher Education Law: The Faculty, 2001. Mem. Phi Beta Kappa, 1980. Office: SUNY New Paltz 75 S Manheim Blvd New Paltz NY 12561 Home: 29 Cedar Ridge Rd New Paltz NY 12561-2728 Office Phone: 845-257-3288.

**POSLER, GERRY LYNN,** agronomist, educator; b. Cainsville, Mo., July 24, 1942; s. Glen L. and Helen R. Posler; m. O. Shirley Weeda, June 23, 1963; children: Mark L., Steven C., Brian D. BS. U. Mo., 1964, MS, 1966; PhD, Iowa State U., 1969. Asst. prof. Western (Macomb) Ill. U., 1969-74; assoc. prof. Kans. State U., Manhattan, 1974-80, prof., 1980—, asst. dept. head, 1982-90, dept. head, 1990-98. Contbr. articles to profl. jours. and popular publs., abstracts, book reviews. Fellow Am. Soc. Agronomy, Crop Sci. Soc. Am.; mem. Am. Forage Grassland Coun., Crop Science Soc. Am. (C-3 div. chmn. 1991), Coun. Agrl. Science Tech. (Cornerstone club), Nat. Assn. Colls. Tchrs. Agr. (tchr. fellow award 1978, ensminger interstate dist. teaching award, 1987, north cen. region dir. 1989, v.p. 1990, pres. 1991; life mem.), Kans. Assn. Colls. Tchrs. Agr. (pres. 1983-85), Kans. Forage Grassland Coun. (bd. dirs. 1989-92), Gamma Sigma Delta (Outstanding Faculty award 1991, pres. 1987). Home: 3001 Montana Ct Manhattan KS 66502-2300 Office: Kans State U Dept Agronomy Throckmorton Plant Sci Ctr Manhattan KS 66506 E-mail: gposler@oznet.ksu.edu.

**POSNER, DAVID S.,** lawyer; b. Pitts., Dec. 27, 1945; s. Mortimer B. and Lillian P.; m. Marilyn Hope Ackerman, Aug. 14, 1966; children: Morton J., Jennifer L. BS, Carnegie Mellon U., 1969; JD, U. Pitts., 1972. Bar: Pa. 1972, U.S. Supreme Ct. 1981. Ct. adminstr. Washington County, Pa., 1972-76, asst. dist. atty., 1976-79; ptnr. Goldfarb & Posner, Washington, Pa., 1979-97, Goldfarb, Posner, Beck, DeHaven & Drewitz, Washington, 1997—. Pres. Pa. Council of Trial Ct. Adminstrs., 1972-76; solicitor Clk. of Cts., Washington, 1983—. Mem. sect. 85 YMCA, Washington, 1980—85; chmn. East Washington Zoning Hearing Bd., 1992—; bd. dirs. Washington County Redevel. Authority, 2002—03, chmn., 2003; bd. dirs. United Way, 1979—85, 2004—; pres. Beth Israel Congregation, 1992—94. With USAR, 1966—72. Mem. ABA, Pa. Bar Assn. (ho. of dels. 1993—95, 1995-97), Washington County Bar Assn. (treas. 1982-83, pres. 1995), B'nai B'rith (past pres.). Home: 149 S Wade Ave Washington PA 15301-4926 Office: Goldfarb Posner Beck DeHaven & Drewitz 26 S Main St Ste 200 Washington PA 15301-6812 Office Phone: 724-222-4200. Personal E-mail: dsp@gpbdd.com.

**POSNER, ERIC A.,** law educator; b. 1965; BA, MA in Philosophy, summa cum laude, Yale U., 1988; JD magna cum laude, Harvard U., 1991. Bar: Md. 1991. Law clk. to Hon. Stephen F. Williams US Ct. Appeals DC Cir., 1991—92; atty. advisor Office Legal Counsel US Dept. Justice, 1992—93; asst. prof. law U. Pa. Law Sch., 1993—98; prof. law U. Chgo. Law Sch., 1998—, Kirkland & Ellis prof. law, 2003—, editor The Journal of Legal Studies, 1998—; mem. Com. Internat. Rels. U. Chgo., 2003—. Vis. asst. prof. law U. Chgo. Law Sch., 1997. Author: Law and Social Norms, 2000; co-author (with J. Goldsmith): The Limits of International Law, 2005; editor: Chicago Lectures in Law and Economics, 2000; co-editor (with M. Adler): Cost-Benefit Analysis: Legal, Philosophical, and Economic Perspectives, 2001. Mem.: Am. Law & Economics Assn. (bd. dirs. 2000—03). Office: U Chgo Law Sch 1111 E 60th St Chicago IL 60637 Office Phone: 773-702-0425. E-mail: eric_posner@law.uchicago.edu.

**POSNER, GARY HERBERT,** chemist, educator; b. NYC, June 2, 1943; s. Joseph M. and Rose (Klein) P.; children: Joseph, Michael. BA, Brandeis U., 1965; MA, Harvard U., 1965, PhD, 1968. Asst. prof. Johns Hopkins U., Balt., 1969-74, assoc. prof., 1974-79, prof. dept. chemistry, 1979—, Scowe prof. chemistry, 1989—, prof. dept. environ. chemistry, 1982—, chmn. dept. of chemistry, 1987-90. Mem. medicinal chemistry study sect. NIH, 1986-89; cons. Batelle Meml. Inst., Columbus, Ohio, 1983, S.W. Rsch. Inst., San Antonio, Nova Pharm. Co., Balt.; mem. Fulbright-Hays Adv. Screening Com. in Chemistry, 1978-81; Michael vis. prof. Weizmann Inst. Sci., Rehovot, Israel, 1983; leader Round Table discussion Welch Found. Conf. Chem. Rsch., Houston, 1973, 83; Novartis Chemistry lectr., 2004-2005; lectr. in field. Author: Introduction to Organic Synthesis Using Organocopper Reagents, 1980; mem. editl. bd. Organic Reactions, 1976-89; exec. editor Tetrahedron Reports, 1996-2006. Named Chemist of Yr., State of Md., 1987; fellow Japan Soc. for Promotion Sci., 1991; recipient Johns Hopkins U. Disting. Tchng. award, 1994, merit award NIH, 2006. Mem. AAAS, AAUP, AAUP, Am. Chem. Soc. (A.C. Cope Sr. Scholar award 2004), Phi Beta Kappa Office: Johns Hopkins U Dept Chemistry 3300 N Charles St Baltimore MD 21218 E-mail: ghp@jhu.edu.

**POSNER, JEROME BEEBE,** neurologist, educator; b. Cin., Mar. 20, 1932; s. Philip and Rose (Goldberg) Posner; m. Gerta Grunen, Aug. 29, 1954; children: Roslyn, Joel, P.J. BS, U. Wash., 1951, MD, 1955. Intern King County Hosp., Seattle, 1955—56; asst. resident in neurology U. Wash. Affiliated Hosps., Seattle, 1956—59, fellow in neurology, 1958—59; spl. fellow NIH, U. Wash., 1961—63; instr. medicine U. Louisville Sch. Medicine, 1959—61; attending neurologist King County Hosp., 1962—63; asst. prof. neurology Cornell U. Med. Coll., N.Y.C., 1963—67, assoc. prof., 1967—70, prof., 1970—, vice chmn. dept. neurology 1978—87; asst. attending neurologist N.Y. Hosp., 1963—67, assoc. attending neurologist, 1967—70, attending neurologist, 1970—; assoc. Cotzias Lab. of Neuro-Oncology, Sloan Kettering Inst. Cancer Research, N.Y.C., 1967—76, mem., 1976—; chief neuropsychiat. service, attending physician dept. medicine Meml. Hosp. for Cancer and Allied Diseases, 1967—75, attending physician, 1975—, chmn. dept. neurology, 1975—87, 1989—97, Cotzias chair neurooncology, 1986—; Evelyn Frew clin. rsch. prof. Am. Cancer Soc., 1996—2006. Mem. med. adv. bd. Burke Rehab. Ctr., White Plains, NY, 1973—2005; adj. prof., vis. physician Rockefeller U. and Hosp., N.Y.C., 1973—75; mem. neurology B study sect. NIH, 1972—76; coun. mem.

NINDS, 1998—2001. Author (with F. Plum): Diagnosis of Stupor and Coma, 3d edit., 1980; author: (with H. Gilbert and L. Weiss) Brain Metastasis, 1980, Neurologic Complications of Cancer, 1995; author: (with DeAngeles) Intracranial Tumor, 2002; mem. editl. bd.: Archives of Neurology, 1971—76, Annals of Neurology, 1976—80, Am. Jour. Medicine, 1978—93, Neurology, 1992—96; contbr. articles to profl. jours. Served with M.C. U.S. Army, 1959—61. Fellow: AAAS; mem.: AMA, Am. Acad. Arts and Scis., Soc. Neurocsis., Inst. Medicine N.Y. Acad. Scis., Harvey Soc., Assn. Am. Physicians, Am. Physiol. Soc., Am. Neurol. Assn. (pres. 1997—99), Am. Fedn. Clin. Rsch., Am. Assn. Cancer Rsch., Am. Acad. Neurology (Farber Brain Tumor award 1988), Can. Neurol. Soc. (hon.), Alpha Omega Alpha. Office: Meml Sloan-Kettering Cancer 1275 York Ave New York NY 10021-6094 Office Phone: 212-693-7047. Business E-mail: posnerj@mskcc.org.

**POSNER, KATHY ROBIN,** retired communications executive; b. Oceanside, N.Y., Nov. 3, 1952; d. Melvyn and Davonne Hope (Hansen) P. BA in Journalism, Econs., Manhattanville Coll., 1974. Corp. liaison Gulf States Mortgage, Atlanta, 1980-82; dir. promotion Gammon's of Chgo., 1982-83; coordinator trade show mktg. Destron, Chgo., 1983-84; pres. Postronics, Chgo., 1984-87; v.p. Martin E. Janis & Co., Inc., Chgo., 1987-90; chmn. Comm 2 Inc., Chgo., 1990—2005, ret., 2005. Editor: How to Maximize Your Profits, 1983; contbg. editor Internat. Backgammon Guide, 1974-84, Backgammon Times, 1981-84, Chgo. Advt. and Media; columnist Food Industry News. Bd. dirs. Chgo. Beautification Com., 1987, Concerned Citizens for Action, Chgo., 1987, Midwest Bd. Shaare Zedek, Med. Ctr. Jerusalem; mem. steering com. Better Boys Found.; campaign mgr. Brown for Alderman, Chgo., 1987; mem. bd. cons. Little City Found.; mem. benefit bd. C.A.U.S.E.S. Mem. NATAS, NOW, Women in Comm., Am. Soc. Profl. and Exec. Women, Women in Film-Chgo. (bd. dirs.), Mensa, Acad. Arts (v.p.), Ill. Restaurant Assn. (mem. adv. bd.), Chgo. Area Pub. Affairs Group, City Club Chgo. (bd. dirs.), Chgo. Legal Clinic (bd. dirs.). Republican. Jewish. Avocations: politics, reading. Home: 100 E Huron #3505 Chicago IL 60611 Personal E-mail: kathyposner@aol.com.

**POSNER, LOUIS JOSEPH,** lawyer, accountant; b. NYC, May 29, 1956; s. Alex Posner and Hilda G. (Gottlieb) Weinberg; m. Betty F. Osin, June 21, 1986; 1 child, Daniel. BS in Acctg., Drexel U., 1979; MS in Taxation, Pace U., 1985; JD, N.Y. Law Sch., 1989. Bar: N.Y. 1990, U.S. Ct. Appeals (2d cir.) 1993, U.S. Supreme Ct. 1994. Auditor Arthur Andersen & Co., CPAs, Phila., 1979-81; tax sr. Kenneth Leventhal & Co., CPAs, N.Y.C., 1981-82; tax mgr. Mann Judd Landau, CPAs, N.Y.C., 1983-86; tax dir. Integrated Resources, Inc., N.Y.C., 1986-89; pvt. practice N.Y.C., 1989—. Instr. Nat. Bus. Inst., 2003—; spkr. in field. Prodr., dir. Your Legal Rights. Founder, exec. dir. Voter March, 2000—. Mem.: AICPA, ABA, Nat. Lawyers Guild, N.Y. State Bar Assn. (trusts estates sect.), Assn. Atty CPA's, N.Y. County Lawyers Assn. (trusts estates sect.), N.Y. State Soc. CPA's (tax. com. 1985—90, mem. faculty NYC chpt. Found. Acctg. Edn. 1989—90), Assn. Bar. City of N.Y., Mensa (coord. spl. interest group NYC chpt. 1978—99). Home: 160 E 48th St Apt 12T New York NY 10017-1225 Office: 305 Madison Ave Ste 1740 New York NY 10165 Office Phone: 212-490-4500. Business E-mail: lawfind@verizon.net.

**POSNER, MICHAEL HOFFMAN,** lawyer; b. Chgo., Nov. 19, 1950; s. Harry Randolph and Elizabeth (Hoffman) Posner; m. Deborah Korzenik, Dec. 12, 1986. Children: Alexander Posner, Hannah Posner, Daniel Posner. BA with honors, U. Mich., 1972; JD, U. Calif., Berkeley, 1975. Bar: Calif. 1975, Ill. 1976, US Dist Ct. No. Dist. Ill. 1976. Rsch. asst. Internat. Commn. Jurists, Geneva, 1974; assoc. Sonnenschein, Nath & Rosenthal, Chgo., 1975-78; exec. dir. Human Rights First, N.Y.C., 1978—2005, pres., 2005—. Vis. lectr. Yale Law Sch., New Haven, 1981-84, Columbia Law Sch., NYC, 1984—; bd. dirs. Fair Labor Assn. Contbr. articles to profl. journals Mem.: Coun. Fgn. Rels., ABA. Democratic. Jewish. Avocations: tennis, skiing, hiking. Office: Human Rights First 333 7th Ave New York NY 10001-5004

**POSNER, RICHARD ALLEN,** federal judge; b. NYC, Jan. 11, 1939; s. Max and Blanche Posner; m. Charlene Ruth Horn, Aug. 13, 1962; children: Kenneth A., Eric A. AB, Yale U., 1959, LLD (hon.), 1996; LLB, Harvard U., 1962; LLD (hon.), Syracuse U., 1986; LLD (hon.), Georgetown U., 1992, U. Pa., 1997; LLD (hon.), Northwestern, 2001, Aristotle Univ. Thessaloniki, 2002; PhD (hon.), U. Ghent, 1995, Univ. Athens, 2002. Bar: N.Y. 1963, U.S. Supreme Ct. 1966. Law clk. to Hon. William J. Brennan Jr. U.S. Supreme Ct., Washington, 1962—63; asst. to counsel FTC, Washington, 1963—65; asst. to solicitor gen. U.S. Dept. Justice, Washington, 1965—67; gen. counsel Pres.'s Task Force on Comm. Policy, Washington, 1967—68; assoc. prof. Stanford U. Law Sch., Calif., 1968—69; prof. U. Chgo. Law Sch., 1969—78, Lee and Brena Freeman prof., 1978—81, sr. lectr., 1981—; judge US Ct. Appeals (7th Cir.), Chgo., 1981—, chief judge, 1993—2000. Rsch. assoc. Nat. Bur. Econ. Rsch., Cambridge, Mass., 1971—81; pres. Lexecon Inc., Chgo., 1977—81. Author: Antitrust Law: An Economic Perspective, 1976, The Economics of Justice, 1981, The Problems of Jurisprudence, 1990, Cardozo: A Study in Reputation, 1990, Sex and Reason, 1990, Sex and Reason, 1992, The Essential Holmes, 1992, Overcoming Law, 1995, Aging and Old Age, 1995, The Federal Courts: Challenge and Reform, 1996, Law and Legal Theory in England and America, 1996, Law and Literature, revised and enlarged edit., 1998, The Problematics of Moral and Legal Theory, 1999, An Affair of State: The Investigation, Impeachment, and Trial of President Clinton, 1999, Frontiers of Legal Theory, 2001, Breaking the Deadlock: The 2000 Election, The Constitution, and the Courts, 2001, Antitrust Law, 2d edit., 2001, Public Intellectuals, 2001, Law, Pragmatism and Democracy, 2003, Catastrophe: Risk and Response, 2004, Preventing Surprise Attacks: Intelligence Reform in the Wake of 9/11; author: (with William M. Landes) The Economic Structure of Tort Law, 1987, Economic Analysis of Law, 6th edit., 2003, The Economic Structure of Intellectual Property Law, 2003; author: (with Tomas J. Philipson) Private Choices and Public Health: The AIDS Epidemic in an Economic Perspective, 1993; pres. Harvard Law Rev., 1961—62, editor Jour. Legal Studies, 1972—81, Am. Law and Econs. Rev., 1999—. Fellow: AAAS, Brit. Acad., Am. Law Inst.; mem.: Am. Law and Econ. Assn. (pres. 1995—96), Am. Econ. Assn., Century Assn. Office: US Ct Appeals 7th Cir 219 S Dearborn St Chicago IL 60604-1702*

**POSNIACK, LEE JOSEPH,** secondary school educator; b. Bklyn., Mar. 31, 1970; s. Gregory Joseph and Diane Posniack; children: Aaron Simon, Shira Bracha. BA in Biology, Bklyn Coll., 1991; MSEd in Secondary Edn., CUNY, 1999. Cert. tchr., supr., adminstr. NY. Tchr. James Madison HS, Bklyn., 1994—2001, Haldane Jr./Sr. HS, Cold Spring, NY, 2001. Democrat. Jewish. Home: 228 Carol Ln Fishkill NY 12524-2913 Office: Haldane Jr/Sr HS 15 Craigside Dr Cold Spring NY 10516 Office Phone: 845-265-9254 220. Office Fax: 845-265-3510. Personal E-mail: ljp353@verizon.net.

**POSPICHAL, MARCIE W.,** neuroscientist, psychologist, educator; b. Great Lakes, Ill., Feb. 2, 1959; BS in Psychology, Fla. So. Coll., 1985; MA in Psychology, Neurosci., Vanderbilt U., Nashville, 1990, PhD in Psychology, 1991. Tchg. asst. Vanderbilt U., Nashville, 1988—91, faculty lectr. dept. psychology, 1991—95, rsch. assoc. dept. psychology, 1991—97, editl. asst. Jour. Comparative Neurology, 1992—97, asst. dir. programs Ctr. for Molecular Neurosci., 1996—2001, coord. grad. studies Vanderbilt Brain Inst., 1997—2001, asst. dir. programs in neurosci. edn. Vanderbilt Brain Inst., 1999—2001; adj. instr. dept. psychology Fla. So. Coll., Lakeland, 2001—. Neurosci. cons. Bd. of Nat. Health Mus., 1999; lectr. in field; condr. seminars in field; mem. neurosci. coun. com. Vanderbilt U., Nashville, 1999—2001; Assoc. Vice-Chancellor's planning com. for the 2001 Consortium on Neurogenetics Vanderbilt Med. Ctr., 1999—2001, Vice-Chancellor's Com. on Cmty. Outreach, 1998—2001; mem. neurosci. PhD curriculum com. Vanderbilt U., 1997—2001; adj. mem. Ctr. for Molecular Neurosci. Faculty Recruitment Com., 1997—2001. Contbr. articles and abstracts to profl. jours. Vol. WDCN, Nashville, 1999; mem. Safe and Drug-Free Nashville Metro Schs. Com., 1997; vol. reader for the blind WPLN Listening Libr., Nashville, 1992—93. Co-recipient NSF grantee, 1999; recipient Rsch. Svc. Award, Nat., 1995; fellow postdoctoral fellow, Vanderbilt U., 1996, 1993—94, 1991—92, grad. rsch. fellow, 1986—88, 1991; grantee Fight for Sight Postdoctoral Tng.

grantee, 1992—93. Mem.: Internat. Brain Rsch. Orgn., Soc. for Neurosci. (com. on neurosci. liberacy 2001—), Assn. of Neurosci. Depts. and Programs. Achievements include research in neurotoxic and electrolytic stereotaxic brain lesioning in rodents; pressure injectin and iontophoretic application of tract tracing substances such as HRP and its conjugates in non-human primates; tract tracing using live slice tissue preparation in non-human primates. Office: thern Coll Dept Psychology Lakeland FL

**POSPISIL, GEORGE CURTIS,** health science administrator; b. Thomas, Okla., Aug. 8, 1945; s. George Frank and Zelpha Earline (Hensley) P.; children: Heather Elizabeth, Derek Curtis; m. Hoda Nasr, Aug. 24, 2002. Student, Wheaton Coll., 1963-64; BA, U. Okla., 1968; MA, 1971. Tchr. Peace Corps, Maseru, Lesotho, 1973-74; dir. health svcs. fin. project State of Wis., Madison, 1975-76; pub. health advisor USPHS, Rockville, Md., 1977-73, program/policy analyst, 1977—81, 1984—86, congl. liaison 1989—99, clin. trials policy adv., 1998-2001, contract mgr., 1982-84, 2005—; dir. Svcs. Crime Victims/Witnesses Project, Tioga County, NY, 1986—; pub. health educator Office of the Sec., OHRP, HHS, 2001—04; health scientist Office of Rsch. Oversight, VA, Bedford, Mass., 2004—05; health sci. adminstr. NIH, Bethesda, Md., 2005—06. Guest lectr. U. Wis., Summer Inst., Carthage Coll.; analyst biomed. rsch. program NIH, 1989—; sci. editor The Johns Hopkins U. Krieger Mind/Brain Inst., 1993—95; pub. health analyst U.S. Dept. Health and Human Svcs., Office of Sec. Editor: Decde of the Brain, 1990, Maximizing Human Potential: Decade of the Brain, 1991. Mem. Rockville Humanities Commn., 1981-83; spokesperson Neighborhood Planning Com., 1980-82; coordinator mental health svcs. Cuban Refugee Project, Ft. McCoy, Wis., 1980; sec. cmty. adv. com. mental health program Montgomery House, 1982-86; rsch. and tng. adminstr. Cornell U., Ithaca, N.Y., 1986-89; bd. dirs. Family Svc. Mongomery County, 1984-86; legis fellow U.S. Senate Labor and Human Resources Com./Health Office, 1991; mem. county Spl. Olympics Com., 1982-86; mem. Citizens' Planning Subcom. Carroll County Md.; insp. gen. Civil Air Patrol; mem. adv. com. troop 321 Boy Scouts Am.; bd. dirs. Shepherd's Staff Cmty. Svc. program. Mem. Soc. Rsch. Adminstrs. Office: NIH Nat Inst on Drug Abuse 6101 Executive Blvd Bethesda MD 20892 Personal E-mail: pospisilg@nida.nih.gov.

**POSPISIL, JOANN,** historian, archivist; b. Schulenburg, Tex., Dec. 10, 1947; d. Edwin James and Jossie Annie (Mica) Krametbauer; m. Gerald Joseph Pospisil, Nov. 19, 1966; 1 child, Ryan Joseph. BA summa cum laude, U. Houston, 1992, MA, 1994. Cert. archivist Acad. Cert. Archivists, 2001. Sec. to v.p. Bohler Bros. of Am., Inc., Houston, 1972-75, asst. corp. sec., 1975-77; archival intern Sul Ross State U. Archives of the Big Bend, Alpine, Tex., 1993; rsch. asst. U. Houston Recovering U.S.-Hispanic Literary Heritage, 1993-94; archival technician Houston Acad. Medicine-Tex. Med. Ctr. Jesse H. Jones Libr., 1995-98; asst. archivist Baylor Coll. Medicine Archive, Houston, 1997—2004, archivist, 2004—. Task force mem. rsch. cons. Houston Urban Coun., 1993; contbg. historian Candelilla Wax Industry, Tex. Archeol. Rsch. Lab., 2004. Contbr. articles to profl. jours. Sec. handbook com. Clay Road Bapt. Parent-Tchr. Orgn., Houston, 1980-81; coord. Houston Police Dept., Houstonians on Watch, 1982-91; sec., membership chair, libr. aide Spring Branch Ind. Sch. Dist. Parent-Tchr. Assn., Houston, 1983-89; presenter geographical and cultural topics to classrooms in Spring Br. Elem. Sch., Northbrook H.S., 1995-98; interviewer oral history program Alliance Am. Quilts, 1999-; pres., pub. chair, sec. Spring Branch Addition Civic Assn. Inc., pres., 2005—. Recipient Spanish award Houston C.C., 1985, Josephine Del Barto scholar U. Houston, 1989-90, Helen M. Douthitt scholarship in history, 1990-91; named Sadie Iola Daniels scholar Assn. for Study of African Am. Life and History, Washington, 1990. Mem. Ctr. for Big Bend Studies, Soc. Am. Archivists, Tex. Czech Geneal. Soc. (charter), Archivists Houston Area (charter), Soc. Southwest Archivists, Tex. Hist. Assn., West Tex. Hist. Assn. (life, bd. dirs. 2006—), Tex. Oral History Assn. (v.p. 2005-06, pres. 2006—), Phi Kappa Phi, Phi Alpha Theta. Avocations: hiking, genealogy, whitewater rafting, reading non-fiction. Home: 9418 Railton St Houston TX 77080-1431 Office: Baylor Coll Medicine Archives One Baylor Plaza BCMC 177A Houston TX 77030

**POSPISIL, LEOPOLD JAROSLAV,** anthropologist, educator, law educator; b. Olomouc, Czechoslovakia, Apr. 26, 1923; came to U.S., 1949, naturalized, 1954; s. Leopold and Ludmila (Petrlak) P.; m. Zdenka Smyd, Jan. 31, 1945; children: Zdenka, Mira. Juris Universae Candidatus, Charles U., Prague, Czechoslovakia, 1947, JD, 1991; BA in Sociology, Willamette U., Salem, Oreg., 1950; MA in Anthropology, U. Oreg., 1952; PhD, Yale U., 1956; ScD (hon.), Willamette U., 1969; PhD (hon.), Charles U., Prague, Czech Rep., 1994. Instr. Yale U., New Haven, 1956-57, asst. prof., 1957-60; asst. curator Peabody Mus., 1956-65, assoc. prof., 1960-65, prof., curator, 1965-93, dir. divsn. anthropology, 1966-93; prof. anthropology, 1965-93; prof. and curator emeritus, 1993—. Dir. Peabody Mus. Anthropology Yale U., New Haven, 1966—93; Robert Merton Prof. Law U. Munich, Germany, 1978—79; vis. prof. Anthropology Charles U., Prague, Czech Republic, 1991—; vis. prof. Law Capetown U., South Africa, 1989; DFC prof. Law U. Munich, 1982. Author: Kapauku Papuans and Their Law, 1958, Kapauku Papuan Economy, 1963, Kapauku Papuans of West New Guinea, 1963, Anthropology of Law, 1971, Ethnology of Law, 1972, Anthropologie des Rechts, 1981, Sprache, Symbole und Symbolverwendungen in Ethnologie, Kulturanthropologie, Politik, Religion und Recht, 1993, Obernberg: Quantitative Analysis of a Tyrolean Economy, 1996, Etnologie Prava, 1997, Sociocultural Anthropology, 2004; contbr. articles to profl. jours. Guggenheim fellow, 1962, NSF fellow, 1962, 64-65, 67-71, NIMH fellow, 1973-79; Social Sci. Rsch. Coun. grantee, 1966. Fellow AAAS, N.Y. Acad. Scis., Am. Anthrop. Assn.; mem. NAS, Conn. Acad. Arts and Scis., Explorers Club, Czechoslovakian Acad. Arts and Scis. (past pres.), Coun. Free Czechoslovakia, Assn. for Polit. and Legal Anthropology (pres.-at-large), Assn. for Social Anthropology in Oceania, Soc. for Econ. Anthropology, Sigma Xi. Independent, Avocations: gardening, mountain climbing. Home: 554 Orange St New Haven CT 06511-3819 Office: 51 Hillhouse Ave New Haven CT 06520-3703 Office Phone: 203-432-3771. Business E-mail: anthropology@yale.edu.

**POSS, JEFFERY SCOTT,** architect, educator; b. Harvey, Ill., May 20, 1956; m. Barbara Young Cook. May 1, 1999. BAS, U. Ill., 1978, MArch, 1990. Intern architect Charles Kober Assocs., Chgo., 1980-81, Skidmore, Owings and Merrill, Chgo., 1981; designer Newman/Lustig and Assocs., Chgo., 1983-84; design assoc. Kevin Roche John Dinkeloo and Assocs., Hamden, Conn., 1985-87; project architect and designer Tai Soo Kim Assocs., Hartford, Conn., 1987-89; pvt. practice Urbana, Ill., 1989—; assoc. prof. U. Ill. Sch. Arch., Champaign-Urbana, Ill., 1989—. Vis. prof. Glasgow Sch. Art, 1999, 2001; design cons. Isaksen Glerum Wachter Archs., P.C., Urbana, 2001—; invited juror, lectr. in field. Contbr. articles to profl. jours. Recipient 1st Alt. Paris prize, Nat. Inst. for Archtl. Edn., 1981, 1st pl., Champaign Pk. Dist./AIA, 1989. Nat. Design award, Concrete Steel Reinforcing Inst./AIA, 1992, 2d pl. WWII Meml., State of Md., 1996, Merit award, Saluda Shoals Amphitheater, State of N.C., 2001; 1st Pl. Francis J. Plym Traveling fellow, U. Ill., 2004. Mem. AIA (Excellence in Edn. Honors award 1993, Ctrl. Ill. award for design excellence, 1993, 97, 2000), Am. Soc. Archtl. Perspectives (Excellence in Graphic Representation Architecture award 1990, 93). Business E-Mail: poss@uiuc.edu.

**POSS, STEPHEN DANIEL,** lawyer; b. Buffalo, Jan. 13, 1955; s. Gilbert H. and Bernice L. (Lippman) Poss; m. Jane Fitz Simon, 1990. BA magna cum laude, Amherst Coll., 1978; JD, U. Chgo., 1981. Bar: N.Y. 1982, Mass. 1988; U.S. Dist. Ct. (so. dist.) N.Y. 1984, U.S. Dist. Ct. Mass. 1988; U.S. Tax Ct. 1983; U.S. Supreme Ct. 1986; U.S. Ct. Appeals (1st cir.) 1989, U.S. Ct. Appeals (fed. cir.) 1992. Assoc. Cravath, Swaine & Moore, N.Y.C., 1981-87, Goodwin Procter LLP, Boston, 1988-89, ptnr., 1989—. Teaching asst. to prof. Henry Steele Commager, 1977; lectr. Mass. Continuing Legal Edn., 1987—; Mass. Bar Assn. Ednl. Seminars, 1992-94; seminar chmn. SEC Inst. II, 1998; lectr. Nasdaq Exec. Forum, 1998, 2001; mem. civil litigation curriculum com. Mass. Continuing Legal Edn., 1997—; lectr. SEC Inst., 1999-2001, mem. nat. adv. bd., 2001—; mem. Nasdaq Investor Rels. Forum, 2000. Advisor campaign Bill Guy for U.S. Senate from N.D., 1974, Quentick Burdick for U.S. Senate, N.D., 1976, Bill Bradley for U.S. Senate, N.J., 1978, Gary Hart for

U.S. Senate, Colo., 1980, Jeff Bingaman for U.S. Senate, N.Mex., 1982; pro bono counsel to Dem. Nat. Com., 1986-87; bd. dirs. Internat. Forum, N.Y.C., 1984; counsel of N.Y. Law Assocs., N.Y.C., 1985; assoc. dir., bd. dirs. Mass. Audubon Soc., 1997-2000, adv. counsel, 2001—. John Woodruff Simpson fellow, 1978. Mem.: ABA (vice chair securities litigation subcom. bus. law sect. 2000—), SEC Inst., Inc. (nat. adv. bd. 2001—), Boston Bar Assn., Mass. Bar Assn. (vice chair bus. litigation com. 1992—94), Internat. Churchill Soc. Office: Goodwin Procter LLP Exchange Pl Boston MA 02109-2803 E-mail: sposs@goodwinprocter.com.

**POST, AUGUST ALAN,** retired economist, artist; b. Alhambra, Calif., Sept. 17, 1914; s. Edwin R. and Edna (Stickney) P.; m. Helen E. Wills, Nov. 21, 1940; 1 child, David Wills. AB, Occidental Coll., 1938; student, Chouinard Inst. Art, 1938; MA, Princeton U., 1940; LLD, Golden Gate U., 1972, Occidental Coll., 1974, Claremont Grad. Sch., 1978. In banking bus., 1933-36; instr. econs. Occidental Coll., 1940-42; asst. prof. Am. U., 1943; economist Dept. State, 1944-45; rsch. dir. Utah Found., 1945-46; chief economist, adminstrv. analyst State of Calif., 1946-50, state legis. analyst, 1950-77. Cons. Com. Higher Edn. and State, 1964; mem. Nat. Com. Support of Pub. Schs., 1967; mem. nat. adv. panel Nat. Ctr. Higher Edn. Mgmt. Systems, 1971-72; chmn. Calif. Gov.'s Commn. on Govt. Reform, 1978; mem. faculty U. So. Calif. Grad. Sch. Pub. Adminstrn., 1978-80; Regents' prof. U. Calif., Davis, 1983, vis. prof., 1984-85; spl. cons. Touche Ross and Co., 1977-87; cons., interim exec. dir. Calif. Commn. for Rev. of Master Plan for Higher Edn., 1985; mem. adv. bd. Calif. Tomorrow nat. shows and one-man shows; dir. Crocker Art Gallery Assn., pres., 1966-67. Trustee U. Calif., Berkeley Art Mus., 1986-91; mem. adv. com. on future ops. Coun. State Govts., 1965; bd. mgrs., pres. YMCA; bd. dirs. Sacramento Civic Ballet Assn.; trustee Calif. Coll. Arts and Crafts, 1982-86; chmn. Calif. State Task Force on Water Future, 1981-82, Sacramento Regional Found., bd. dirs., 1983-91; bd. dirs. Calif. Mus. Assn., pres., 1976-77, Policy Analysis for Calif. Edn., 1985—, Senate Adv. Commn. on Control of Cost of State Govt., 1986—, Pub. Policy Inst. Calif., 1994-2004; co-chmn. Calif. Citizen's Budget Commn., 1992-99, chmn., 1999—; chmn. Citizen's Commn. on Ballot Initiatives, 1992—, Catalonia Sister State Task Force, 1988—, Commn. on Innovation, Calif. Cmty. Colls., 1992; chair Judicial Coun. Select Com. on Judicial Retirement, 1993—; mem. Supreme Ct. Select Com. Judicial Ethics, 1995-96; bd. dirs. Ctrl. Valley Found., 1994-99. With USNR, 1943-44. Mem. Nat. Acad. Pub. Adminstrn., Phi Beta Kappa, Kappa Sigma. Home: 1900 Rockwood Dr Sacramento CA 95864-1527 Personal E-mail: aphp@wnet.com.

**POST, AVERY DENISON,** retired church official; b. Norwich, Conn., July 29, 1924; s. John Palmer and Dorothy (Church) P.; m. Margaret Jane Rowland, June 8, 1946; children: Susan Post Ross, Jennifer C., Elizabeth Post Elliott, Anne Post Roy. BA, Ohio Wesleyan U., 1946; B.D., Yale U., 1949, S.T.M., 1952; L.H.D. (hon.), Lakeland Coll., Sheboygan, Wis., 1977; D.D. (hon.), Chgo. Theol. Sem., 1978, Middlebury Coll., Vt., 1978, Defiance Coll., Ohio, 1979; LL.D. (hon.), Heidelberg Coll., Ohio, 1982, Chapman Coll.; Litt.D. (hon.), Elmhurst Coll. Ordained to ministry, 1949; pastor chs. in Vt., Ohio, Conn. and N.Y., 1946-63; sr. minister Scarsdale (N.Y.) Congl. Ch., 1963-70; minister, pres. Mass. conf. United Ch. Christ, 1970-77; pres. United Ch. Christ, N.Y.C., 1977-89; mem. central com. World Council Chs., 1978-91; exec. com., bd. govs. Nat. Council Chs., 1977-89. Moderator, planning com. 7th Gen. Assembly World Coun. Chs.; lectr. Bible Adelphi Coll., Garden City, N.Y., 1958-59; Luccock lectr. Yale U. Div. Sch., 1961; lectr. homiletics Union Sem., N.Y.C., 1967-69, bd. dirs., 1967-77; trustee Andover Newton Theol. Sem., 1970-80; del. numerous internat. ch. meetings; sr. fellow Hartford Sem., 1989-93. Bd. dirs. Bridges for Peace, 1990-94; exec. dir. Bangor Theol. Sem., Hanover, N.H., 1991-93. With USNR, 1943-45. Decorated Comdr.'s Cross (Federal Republic Germany), 1990; recipient 1st Ecumenical award Mass. Coun. Chs., 1976; Disting. Achievement award Ohio Wesleyan U., 1983 Mem. PTA (life), Randolph Mountain Club (N.H.), Phi Beta Kappa, Omicron Delta Kappa. Democrat.

**POST, DAVID ALAN,** broadcast executive; b. NYC, Oct. 20, 1941; s. Emil R. and Ruth (Rosen) P.; m. Arline Goldbrum, June 10, 1962 (div. 1981); children: Randee, Lori, Jill; m. Kathleen de Monchy, Dec. 13, 1984; 1 dau., Emily Hart. Student, CCNY, 1959-61; grad., Fleigenheimer Ins. Inst., 1961, N.Y. Inst. Fin., 1968. Sales rep. Aetna Life Ins. Casualty, Hartford, Conn., 1961-63; sales mgr. Globe Rubber Products, Phila., 1963-67; ptnr. Zuckerman Smith and Co., N.Y.C., 1968-71; dir. corp. fin. Andersen and Co., N.Y.C., 1971-72; exec. v.p., dir. R.K. Pace Post Investment Bankers, N.Y.C., 1973-76; chmn., chief exec. officer, founder Page Am. Group, Inc., Hackensack, N.J., 1976-86; co-founder, bd. dirs. Cellular Sys. Inc., 1991-92; chmn., founder Channel Am. TV Network, N.Y.C., 1987-96; chmn., co-founder Can Do Woman TV & Other Media, N.Y.C., 1996-2000; chmn., CEO UMagic Systems, Inc., an Internet Tech. Co., N.Y.C., 2000—; chmn., exec. prodr. Can do Woman div. of Nextpert News, N.Y.C., 2000—; exec. prodr. Nextpert News Network, 2002—; founder, exec. prodr. Two Minute TV Network, 2004—. Contbr. articles to INC. mag.; creator several TV series. Mem. Nat. Assn. TV Programming Execs. Republican. Jewish. Avocation: writing. Office: Nextpert News Network 350 Fifth Ave Ste 5600 New York NY 10118 Home: 35 Sutton Pl 15C New York NY 10022-2464 E-mail: david@nextpert.com.

**POST, DIANA CONSTANCE,** retired librarian; b. Anoka, Minn., Oct. 17, 1929; d. Kenneth Fred and Emma Constance (Fredrickson) Davis; husband dec., June 1996; children: Leslie Post, Paul Post, Tom Post. BS, U. Minn 1970, MLS, 1976. Cert. libr., media specialist, Minn. Libr., media specialist Lake City (Minn.) H.S., 1970-94. Bd. dirs. Zumbrota (Minn.) Pub. Libr.; mem. SELCO governing bd. regional libr. sys., Rochester, Minn., 1980-86; pres. SELCO exec. com., 1984-86; SELS adv. com., 1990-94. Editor Lake City Sch. Dist. News, 1988-89. Scholar LaVerne Noyes Found., 1947-48, Delta Delta Delta, 1949. Mem. Beta Phi Mu. Avocations: golf, swimming, volunteering. Home: 695 Jefferson Dr Zumbrota MN 55992-1103 E-mail: DPost3@aol.com.

**POST, GAINES, JR.,** retired history professor, dean, academic administrator; b. Madison, Wis., Sept. 22, 1937; s. Gaines and Katherine (Rike) P.; m. Jean Wetherbee Bowers, July 19, 1969; children: Katherine Doris, Daniel Lawrence. BA, Cornell U., 1959, Oxford U., 1963; MA, Stanford U., 1964, PhD, 1969. Instr. Stanford U., 1966-69; asst. prof. history U. Tex., Austin, 1969-74, assoc. prof., 1974-83; dean faculty, sr. v.p. Claremont McKenna Coll., Calif., 1983-88, prof., 1988—99, emeritus prof., 1999—. Exec dir. Rockefeller Found. Commn. on Humanities, 1978-81. Author: The Civil Military Fabric of Weimar Foreign Policy, 1973, Dilemmas of Appeasement: British Deterrence and Defense, 1934-37, 1993, Memoirs of a Cold War Son, 2000; co-author The Humanities in American Life, 1980; editor: German Unification: Problems and Prospects, 1992. Mem. exec. com. Forming the Future Project, Austin Ind. Sch. Dist., 1982; mem. Tex. Com. for Humanities, 1981-83; mem. coun. Calif. Congl. Recognition Program, 1984-88, Calif. Coun. Humanities, 1995-2003. Rhodes scholar, 1961-63; Am. Coun. Learned Socs. fellow, 1982-83; Am. Philos. Soc. grantee, 1974.

**POST, GINA,** mathematics professor, researcher; d. Arnold Smith and Helen Carter Post; children: Kari Lynne Smith, Chad Thomas Smith. BS, U. Utah, 1970; MEd, U. Utah, Salt Lake City, 1996, PhD, 2000. Tchr. k-8 Cin. Pub. Schs., 1970—71, Phoenix Pub. Schs., 1976—77; tchr. k-6 Jordan Sch. Dist., Sandy, Utah, 1984—91, tchr. mid. sch. math., 1991—99; univ. instr. U. Utah, Salt Lake City, 1999—2004, asst. prof., 2005—. Ednl. cons. Arvada Family Psychol. Clinic, Colo., 1980—84. Fellow, U. Utah, 2004—05. Mem.: Am. Assn. Tchr. Educators, Am. Assn. Math. Educators, Utah Assn. Math. Educators (sec. 2006—), Nat. Coun. Tchrs. Math., Am. Ednl. Rsch. Assn. Home: 1235 E Laird Ave Salt Lake City UT 84105 Office: University of Utah 1705 E Campus Center Dr Rm 142 Salt Lake City UT 84112-9256 Office Phone: 801-587-7987. Home Fax: 801-581-3609; Office Fax: 801-581-2609. Personal E-mail: gina.post@ed.utah.edu. E-mail: gina.post@ed.utah.ed.

**POST, GLEN FLEMING, III,** telecommunications industry executive; b. El Dorado, Ark., Oct. 4, 1952; s. Glen F. Jr. and Mary L. (Tubberville) P.; children: Brad, Luke, Matt. BS in Acctg., La. Tech. U., 1974, MBA, 1976. Pvt. practice tax acctg., 1974-76; with CenturyTel Inc., Monroe, La., 1976—, v.p., 1982—84, sr. v.p., treas., 1984-86, sr. v.p., CFO, 1986—88, exec. v.p. & COO, 1988—90, pres. & COO, 1990—92, vice chmn., exec., CEO, 1992—2003, chmn., CEO, 2003—. Bd. dir. Yelcot Telephone Co., No. La. Regions Bank. Mem. exec. cabinet Coll. Adminstrn. & Bus., La. Tech. Univ.; bd. dir. La. Tech. Univ. Found., La. Tech. Univ. Rsch. Found. Recipient Tower Medallion award, La. Tech. Univ., 1997, Lifetime Achievement award in bus., DeGree Enterprises, 2003. Mem. Am. Mgmt. Assn., STICC (subcom. acctg.), Beta Alpha Psi. Office: CenturyTel Inc 100 Century Tel Dr Monroe LA 71203*

**POST, JEFFREY H.,** insurance company executive; BBA, Univ. Wis., Madison. Chief actuary Fireman's Fund Ins. Co., 1994—96, CFO, 1996—2001, pres., CEO, 2001—04; pres., CEO, dir. CUNA Mutual Group, Madison, Wis., 2005—. Dir. Am. Ins. Assn. Fellow: Casualty Actuarial Soc.; mem.: Am. Acad. Actuaries. Office: CUNA Mutual Group 5910 Mineral Point Rd Madison WI 53705

**POST, JERRY T,** retail executive; B in econ., Hartwick Coll. Gen. mdse. mgr., NY region Sears Roebuck and Co., 1976—80, territorial mdse. mgr., 1980—82, nat. mdse. mgr., sporting goods, 1984—87, nat. mgr. hardware stores, 1987—91, nat. mdse. mgr., automotive, 1991—92, nat. bus. mgr., home improvement, 1993—96, v.p. and gen. mgr., the gt. indoors, 1996—98, pres. hardware stores, 1998—99; sr. v.p. gen. mgr. home improvement category, 1999—2002; sr. v.p., gen. mgr. Sears off mall strategy, Sears retail for Sears Sears Roebuck and Co., 2002—

**POST, KELLY MARIE,** elementary school educator; b. Lakeside, Ariz., Feb. 16, 1979; d. Gregory Lane and Donna Jo Post. B in Elem. Edn., Ottawa U., Phoenix, 2001. 3rd grade tchr. Copper Canyon, Pendergast Sch. Dist., Avondale, Ariz., 2001—02, Rio Vista Elem. Sch., Pendergast Sch. Dist., Avondale, 2002—03, jr. high math. tchr., 2003—. Jr. high girls volleyball coach Rio Vista Elem. Sch., Avondale, 2002—04; girls soccer coach Copper Canyon H.S., Glendale, 2004—. Named Rio Vista Elem. Tchr. of Yr., Rio Vista Elem. Tchr. and Staff, 2005—06, Pendergast Sch. Dist. Tchr. of Yr., Pendergast Sch. Prins., 2005—06. Avocations: soccer, softball, bowling, golf.

**POST, MARTIQUA LEIGH,** engineering educator; b. Shakopee, Minn., Aug. 29, 1977; d. Charlotte June Post. PhD, U. Notre Dame, 2004. Vis. asst. prof. U. Notre Dame, Ind., 2004—05; asst. prof. U.S. Air Force Acad., Colo., 2005—. Mem.: AIAA. Office: HQ USAFA/DFAN 2410 Faculty Dr Ste 120 U S A F Academy CO 80840 Business E-Mail: martiqua.post@usafa.af.mil.

**POST, MIKE,** lighting designer; b. Suffern, NY, June 2, 1962; s. Dirck Hooper and Barbara Spence Post. AB, Ripon Coll., Wis., 1984; MFA in Theatre Design and Tech., U. Mont., Missoula, 1995. Asst. prodn. mgr./master electrician Ala. Shakespeare Festival, Montgomery, 1995—2004; asst. prof. lighting and sound U. So. Miss., Hattiesburg, 2004—. Assistant lighting design, Love Jerry, video design, Macbeth Military Base Tour with The Alabama Shakespeare Festival, lighting design, A Streetcar Named Desire with The Montana Rep, A Midsummer Night's Dream with Georgia Shakespeare. Office Phone: 601-266-5918. Business E-Mail: michael.post@usm.edu.

**POST, PETER L.,** marketing executive, writer; m. Patricia C. Post; 2 children. BA, U. Penn., 1972; MFA, Pratt Inst. Reporter Valley Voice, Middlebury, Vt.; dir. comm. & publications Champlain Coll., 1979—84; pres., founder PostScript, Inc., Burlington, Vt., 1984—; dir. Emily Post Inst.; columnist, Etiquette At Work, Boston Sunday Globe, 2004—, NY Times Syndication Sales Corp., 2005—; columnist, Professional Courtesy, Men's Health, 2005—. Founder Emily Post Bus. Seminar Series. Co-author: (books) The Etiquette Advantage in Business, 1999; author: Essential Manners for Men, 2003, Essential Manners for Couples, 2005. Bd. mem. Wake Robin Retirement Comty., Vt. Office: PostScript Inc 444 S Union St Burlington VT 05401 Office Phone: 802-863-2568. Office Fax: 802-863-4179. E-mail: peter@postscriptinc.com.*

**POST, RICHARD BENNETT,** retired human resources executive; b. Clyde, Ohio, July 5, 1936; s. Robert Irving and Elinor May (Bennett) P.; m. Nancy Jane Wardlow, Aug. 31, 1956; children: David Bennett, Todd McKinley, Amy Ellen, Brett Richard, Brina Marie. BS in Edn., Bowling Green State U., 1958; student, Ohio U., Athens, 1954-56; postgrad., George Washington U., 1959-60, So. Ill. U., Edwardsville, 1972-74. With U.S. Civil Svc. Commn., 1958-79, chief evaluation div. St. Louis, 1967-71, chief staffing div., 1971-74, dep. reg. dir., 1974-79; dep. assoc. dir. staffing U.S. Office Pers. Mgmt., Washington, 1979-81, assoc. dir. staffing, 1982-86, dir. Washington area svc. ctr., 1986-94; retired, 1994. Cert. lay spkr. United Meth. Ch., 1973—; treas. Meadows Homeowners Assn., 2000—. Recipient Dirs.' Disting. Svc. award U.S. Office Pers. Mgmt., 1986, Dirs.' citation for Exemplary Pub. Svc., 1994. Mem. AARP (pres. King George Area chpt. 2003-04), Sr. Execs. Assn. (life), Fed. Exec. Inst. Alumni Assn., Vienna Choral Soc. (pres. 1987-89), Masterworks Chorus, King George, Va. Avocations: woodworking, singing, gardening. E-mail: Postrn@Worldskyline.com.

**POST, ROBERT CHARLES,** law educator; b. Bklyn., Oct. 17, 1947; s. Ted and Thelma (Feifel) P.; m. Paula Franklin, Jan. 22, 1981; children: Alexander, Amelia. AB, Harvard U., 1969, PhD, 1980; JD, Yale U., 1977; LLD (hon.), Chgo.-Kent U., 1998. Bar: D.C. 1979, Calif. 1983. Law clk. to chief judge U.S. Ct. Appeals (D.C. cir.), 1977-78; law clk. to justice William Brennen Jr. U.S. Supreme Ct. D.C., 1978-79; assoc. Williams & Connelly, Washington, 1980-82; acting prof. law U. Calif., Berkeley, 1983-87, prof. law, 1987-94, Alexander F. and May T. Morrison prof. law, 1994—2003; David Boies prof. law Yale U., New Haven, 2003—. Author: Constitutional Domains, 1995; editor: Law and the Order of Culture, 1991, Censorship and Silencing: Practices of Cultural Regulation, 1998; co-editor: Race and Representation: Affirmative Action, 1998, Human Rights in Political Transistions: Gettysburg to Bosnia, 1999, Civil Society and Government, 2001; co-author: Prejudicial Appearances: the Logic of America Antidisaimation Law, 2001. Gen. counsel AAUP, 1992-94. Fellow Guggenheim Found., 1990-91, Am. Coun. Gen. Socs., 1990-91. Mem. AAUP, Am. Acad. Arts and Scis. Office: Yale Law Sch PO Box 208215 New Haven CT 06520 Office Phone: 203-432-4946. E-mail: robert.post@yale.edu.

**POST, STEPHEN GARRARD,** theologian, philosopher, educator; b. Bayshore, N.Y., May 6, 1951; s. Henry Albertson Van Zo and Marguerite Magee Post. MA in religious studies, U. Chgo., 1979; PhD in Ethics and Soc., U. Chgo., 1983. Prof. dept. humanities Marymount Coll., Tarrytown, NY, 1985—88, prof. dept. bioethics Sch. Medicine, Case Western Res. U., Cleve., 1988—. Mem. nat. ethics adv. bd. Alzheimer's Assn., Chgo., 1997—; bd. advisors John Templeton Found., Radnor, Pa., 1998—2002; pres. Inst. for Rsch. on Unltd. Love, Altruism, Compassion, Svc., Cleve., 2001—. Author: (book) The Moral Challenge of Alzheimer Disease, 2000; editor-in-chief (ency.) Ency. of Bioethics, 2003. Episcopalian. Avocations: sailing, gardening, writing. Office Phone: 216-368-6205.

**POST, STEPHEN LIGHTNER,** retired psychoanalyst, educator; b. St. Louis, May 4, 1927; s. Lawrence Tyler Post and Bernice Dorothy Clute Lightner; m. Ann Whelan, Aug. 31, 1953 (dec. Dec. 1958); m. Jane Conant, June 1960 (div. Oct. 1975); children: Nancy Whelan Post Hunter, Kenneth Conant, Louise Lightner, Eric Stephen; m. Ellen Eisendrath, Nov. 8, 1975; stepchildren: William C. Steinert, Sylvia C. Steinert, Eric C. Steinert. AB cum laude, Princeton U., 1950; MD, Columbia U., 1957; grad., Chgo. Inst. for Psychoanalysis, 1974. Diplomate Nat. Bd. Med. Examiners, Am. Psychoanalytic Assn. Intern Montefiore Hosp., N.Y.C., 1957—58; resident in psychiatry Strong Meml. Hosp., Rochester, NY, 1958, Washington U., St. Louis, 1959—61, fellow in child psychiatry, 1960—62; faculty dept. psychiatry St.

Louis U. Med. Sch., 1965—2006; ret., 2006. Mem. adv. bd. Pastoral Counseling Inst., St. Louis, 1964-74; med. dir. St. Louis Clin. Assn. for Religious and Ednl. Counseling, 1979-81, bd. dirs.; mem. faculty St. Louis Psychoanalytic Inst., 1973—, chmn. cmty. edn. com., 1980-83, chmn. inst. edn. com., 1987-91, tng. and supervising analyst, 1982—, inst. assoc. dir., 2001-05; clin. prof. psychiatry St. Louis U. Med. Sch., 1996—. Contbg. editor Psychoanalytic Inquiry, 1984-2001, issue co-editor, 1985; contbr. chpts. to books, articles to profl. jours. Fellow Am. Coll. Psychoanalysts; mem. AMA, Am. Psychoanalytic Assn. (del. to exec. coun. 1982-85, fellow bd. profl. stds. 1987-91, com. on founds. 1993—), Mo. State Med. Assn., Ea. Mo. Psychiat. Soc. (sec.-treas. 1967-69), Greater St. Louis Med. Soc., St. Louis Psychoanalytic Soc. (membership com. chmn. 1977-78, 87-88, program chmn. 1977-79, pres. 1980-82), Sigma Xi. Avocations: music, hiking, swimming. Home: 9 Southmoor Dr Clayton MO 63105-3016

**POST, WENDY,** elementary school educator; d. Larry and Susan Marlin; m. Randy Post, July 11, 1992; 1 child, Mindy. B of Elem. Edn., Ind. State U., Terre Haute, 1986. Tchr. kindergarten John D. Floyd Elem., Spring Hill, Fla., 1987—2004; tchr. kindergarten and 1st grade Mary Giella Elem., 2004—. Team leader Mary Giella Elem., Spring Hill, 2005—; treas. Hernando County Reading Coun., 1992—93; team leader John D. Floyd Elem., 1997—2003; mentor Mary Giella Elem., 2006—, John D. Floyd Elem., 2002—03, tchr. kinder camp, 2001—03. Tchr. Sunday sch. Grace Luth. Ch., Spring Hill, Fla. Mem.: United Sch. Employees Pasco, Fla. Reading Assn., Pasco County Reading Coun., Hernando County Reading Coun. (treas. 1992—93), Parent Tchr. Assn. Pasco County (life), Parent Tchr. Assn. (life; tchr. rep. 1987—88). Avocations: yoga, exercise, camping. Office: Mary Giella Elementary 14710 Shady Hills Road Spring Hill FL 34610 Office Phone: 727-774-5800.

**POST, WILLIAM JOSEPH,** utility executive; b. Salem, Ohio, Oct. 13, 1950; s. John Joseph and Barbara Louise (Walton) P.; m. Mary Kay Lane, May 2, 1987; children: Kathryn Leigh, Carly Nancy. BS, Ariz. State U., 1972. Budget mgr. Ariz. Pub. Svc., Phoenix, 1978-82, contr., 1982-85, v.p., contr., 1985-87, v.p. fin. and rates, 1987—; chmn., CEO Pinnacle West Capital Corp., 2001—. Mem. exec. com. Nuclear Energy Inst. Bd. dir. Tumbleweed, Phoenix, Tempe Leadership, 1987, YMCA, Phoenix, 1989. Staff sgt. U.S. Army, 1969-75. Republican. Presbyterian. Office: Pinnacle West Capital 400 N Fifth St Phoenix AZ 85004 Home: 4235 E Claremont St Paradise Valley AZ 85253-3948

**POSTAER, LARRY,** advertising executive; b. Chgo. Grad., U. Mo. Sch. Journalism, 1959. Catalog copywriter Sears; with Stern, Walters & Simmons, Chgo., 1962-64, creative dir., 1964-76; sr. v.p., group creative dir. Needham Harper & Steers, Chgo., 1976-81, exec. v.p., dir. creative svcs. LA, 1981-86; co-founder, exec. v.p., dir. creative svcs. Rubin Postaer and Assoc., Santa Monica, 1986—. Named Co-leader of Yr. for 1990, Western States Advt. Agys. Assn., 1991. Office: 2525 Colorado Ave Santa Monica CA 90404

**POSTE, GEORGE HENRY,** biology professor, former pharmaceutical company executive; b. Polegate, Sussex, Eng., Apr. 30, 1944; came to U.S., 1972; s. John H. and Kathleen B. (Brooke) P.; 1 child, Eleanor Kathy; m. Linda C. Suhler Lopez, Nov. 21, 1992; stepchildren: John Robert, Lisa Carolyn. DVM, U. Bristol, 1966, PhD, 1969, DSc, 1987, LLD (hon.), 1995. Lectr. U. London, 1969-72; assoc. prof. SUNY, Buffalo, 1972-76; prof. pathology Roswell Park Meml. Inst., Buffalo, 1976-80; v.p. rsch. SmithKline Beckman, Phila., 1980-82, v.p. R & D, 1982-86, v.p. worldwide rsch. and pre-clin. devel., 1987-88, pres. R & D, 1988-89; pres. R & D techs. SmithKline Beecham, King of Prussia, Pa., 1989-90, vice-chmn., exec. v.p. R & D, 1990-91, pres. and chmn. R & D, 1992-97; chief sci. and tech. officer SmithKline Beecham Corp. PLC, King of Prussia, Pa., 1997-99; CEO Health Tech. Networks, Scottsdale, Ariz., 2000—; non-exec. chmn. OrchidBioSciences Inc., Princeton, NJ, 2002—; Del E. Webb Disting. prof biology Ariz. State U., Tempe, 2003—, dir. Biodesign Inst., 2003—. Mem. pathology B study sect. NIH, Bethesda, Md., 1978-82; chmn. Gordon Conf., N.H., 1985-86, diaDeXus, 1997-2003, Cerebrus, 1997; pres. coun. U. Tex. M.D. Anderson Cancer Ctr.; bd. dirs. Monsanto, Exelixis, SmithKline Beecham Corp. PLC, Orchid BioSciences Inc., 2000-; mem. adv. coun. Beckman Ctr. for Molecular and Genetic Medicine, Stanford U.; mem. coun. Oxford Internat. Biomedical Centre; chmn. task force on bioterrorism, U.S. Dept. of Defense, 2001-04. Editor: Cell Surface Revs., New Horizons in Therapeutics, Cancer Metastasis Revs., Advanced Drug Delivery Revs., 15 books; contbr. articles to profl. jours. Mem. governing bd. UCLA Symposia, Life Sci. Rsch. Found.; mem. bd. Overseers Sch. Vet. Medicine, U. Penn., Gov.'s adv. com. Sci. and Tech., Pa.; mem. adv. bd. Natural Sci. Assn., U. Pa. Fleming fellow U. Oxford, Eng., 1995, Pitt fellow U. Cambridge, Eng., 1995; named Comdr. of British for svcs. in devel. of bioscis., 1999, Scientist of the Year, R&D mag., 2004. Fellow Royal Soc., Royal Coll. Vet. Surgeons, Royal Coll. Pathologists, Ins. Biology (London), Acad. Med. Scis. (London); mem. AAAS, Am. Soc. Cell Biology, Pathol. Soc., Nat. Assn. Biomed. Rsch. (bd. govs. 1984), Univ. Assn. Space Rsch. (mem. coun. 1984), Pharm. Mfrs. Assn. (former chmn. rsch. and devel. section 1988). Avocations: military history, foreign affairs, photography, auto racing. Office: Biodesign Inst Ariz State Univ PO Box 875001 Tempe AZ 85287-5001 Office Phone: 480-727-8662. Business E-Mail: george.poste@asu.edu.

**POSTELNEK, STEPHEN A.,** lawyer; b. NYC, Apr. 24, 1940; BSME, Columbia U., 1961; MSME, Poly. Inst. Bklyn., 1968; JD, St. John's U., 1974. Bar: NY 1975, US Supreme Ct., NY State & Fed. Courts. Design engr. Pratt and Whitney Aircraft Engring. Corp., East Hartford, Conn., Grumman Aerospace Corp., Bethpage, NY; ptnr. Wilson, Elser, Moskowitz, Edelman & Dicker LLP, NYC. Mem.: ABA, NY State Trial Lawyers Assn., Assn. of the Bar of the City of NY, St. Thomas More Inst. Legal Rsch., NY State Bar Assn. Office: Wilson Elser Moskowitz Edelman & Dicker LLP 23rd Fl 150 E 42nd St New York NY 10017-5639 Office Phone: 212-490-3000 ext. 2208. Office Fax: 212-490-3038. Business E-Mail: postelneks@wemed.com.

**POSTER, MERYL,** film company executive; With William Morris Agy.; exec. asst. to co-chmn Harvey Weinstein Miramax Film Corp., 1989—91, dir. devel., 1991—93, v.p. east coast prodn., 1993—94, sr. v.p. prodn., 1994—97, exec. v.p. prodn, 1997—98, co-pres. prodn., 1998—2005. Exec. prodr.: (films) Smoke, 1995, Marvin's Room, 1996, The Pallbearer, 1996, Cop Land, 1997, Wide Awake, 1998, Shakespeare in Love, 1998 (Acad. Award for Best Picture), Cider House Rules, 1999, Chocolat, 2000, Bounce, 2000, The Shipping News, 2001, Kate and Leopold, 2001, Blow Dry, 2001, Chicago, 2002 (Acad. Award for Best Picture), Duplex, 2003; co-prodr.: Music of the Heart, 1999.

**POSTHUMUS, RICHARD EARL,** state offical, farmer; b. Hastings, Mich., July 19, 1950; s. Earl Martin and Lola Marie (Wieland) P.; m. Pamela Ann Bartz, June 23, 1972; children: Krista, Lisa, Heather, Bryan. BS in Agrl. Econs. and Pub. Affairs Mgmt., Mich. State U., 1972. Exec. v.p. Farmers and Mfrs. Beet Sugar Assn., Saginaw, Mich., 1972-74, Mich. Beef Commn., Lansing, 1974-78; dir. constituent rels. Rep. Caucus, Mich Ho, of Reps., 1979-82, senator, Mich., 1983-98, senate majority leader, 1991-98, lt. gov., 1999-2002; self-employed farmer, 1974—. Third vice-chmn. Mich. Republican Com., 1971-73; mem. Hope Ch. of the Brethren. Mem. Alpha Gamma Rho. Republican. Office: Varnum Riddering Schmidt and Howlett Bridgewater Pl 333 Bridge St NW PO Box 352 Grand Rapids MI 49501-0352

**POSTIGLIONE, COREY M.,** artist, critic, art educator; b. Chgo., July 25, 1942; BA, U. Ill. Circle Campus; also with Martin Hurtig & Roland Ginzel; MA in 20th Century Art History, Sch. Art Inst. Chgo. Instr. painting Evanston Art Ctr., Ill., 1971—79, Ill. Inst. Tech., 1975—83, Columbia Coll., Chgo., 1979—89, Art Inst. Chgo., 1981—83, U. Ill., Chgo., 1983; instr. art history and criticism Columbia Coll., Chgo., 1990—, tenured prof., 1996—; instr. 2D design studio, 1999—. Asst. dir. Jan Cicero Gallery, Chgo., 1975—76; juror 38th Ann. Old Orchard Art Festival, 1995, 19th Elkhardt Regional, Midwest Mus. Am. Art, Elkhardt, Ind., 1997; judge Riverside Artfair '97, Riverside Art Ctr., Riverside, Ill., 1997; bd. dir. White Walls, 1992. Contbr.

editor of reviews and articles The New Art Examiner, 1976—83, Dialogue mag., 1989—, Contbr. reviews and articles New Art Assn., 1975—76, C mag., contbr. editor ArtForum, 2003; contbr. catalogue essay for Liz Langer Retrospective, Artemisia Gallery, Chgo., catalogue essay for Alexandra Domowska for the Pougialis Exhbn., Columbia Coll. Chgo. Hokin Annex Gallery, catalogue essay for Karen Lebergott one-person exhbn., Columbia Gallery, catalogue essay for John Phillips, 2005; collections arranged, Art in Chgo., 1996, 1998, 2000, 2002, one-man shows include Evanston Art Ctr., Ill., 1972, Mayer Kaplan JCC, Skokie, Ill., 1973, Jan Cicero Gallery, Chgo., Ill., 1976, 1978, 1983, 1985, 1995, 1997, Columbia Coll. Gallery, Chgo., 1981, 1997—98, Passages, Oakton Cmty. Coll., 1998, A&D Gallery, Columbia Coll., Rivereast Art Ctr., Chgo., 2005, exhibitions include New Works on Paper, Jan Cicero Gallery, 1993, Labyrinth Series, Jan Cicero Gallery, 1993, Exquisite Corpse, Transmission Gallery, Glasgow, Scotland, 1994, Lakeside Views, Evanston Art Ctr., 1994, Brad Cooper Gallery, Tampa, Fla., 2003, and others, installation work, Blink, No. Ill. U. Gallery, Chgo., 2000. Recipient Third Prize (all show), Italian Am. Exhibit, 1981, Merit award, Evanston & Vicinity Exhbn., 1998. Mem.: Am. Abstracts Artists, NY, Chgo. Art Critics Assn. Home: 4508 N Monticello Chicago IL 60625 Office: Columbia Coll Dept Art & Design 623 S Wabash Rm 1004 Chicago IL 60625 Office Phone: 312-344-7190. Business E-Mail: cpostiglione@colum.edu, cpostiglione@popmail.colum.edu.

**POSTLEWAITE, ANDREW WILLIAM,** economics professor, department chairman; b. Harvey, Ill., Aug. 23, 1943; s. Edward Homer and Margaret (Hostetler) P.; children: Justin, Kevin. BA in Economics, Ill. Wesleyan U., 1965; MS in Math., DePaul U., 1969; PhD in Applied Math., Northwestern U., 1974; LHD (hon.), Wesleyan U., 2001. Lectr. DePaul U., Chgo., 1970—73; rsch. fellow CORE, Louvain, Belgium, 1973—74; asst. prof. econs. U. Ill., Urbana, 1974—76, assoc. prof. econs, 1976—80; prof. econs. U. Pa., Phila., 1980—82, prof. econs. fin., pub. mgmt., 1982—, chmn. dept. econs., 1982—87, 1990, Harry P. Kamen prof. economics. Bd. dirs. Nat. Bur. Econ. Rsch., Cambridge, Mass.; vis. asst. prof. U. Calif. San Diego, 1976, vis. prof. Princeton U., 1979—80, Stanford Bus. Sch., 1988—89, Calif. Inst. Tech., 2002, Harvard U., 2003, Yale U., 2004; cons. in field; assoc. editor Jour. Economic Theory, 1981—87, 2005—, Jour. Games and Economic Behavior, 1990—97, 2006—; co-editor Econometrica, 1997—2005; editor Internat. Economic Rev., 1996—98; editor Organization Theory and Allocation Processes sect. Fundamentals of Pure and Applied Economics, 1985—94. Contbr. articles to profl. jours. Coun. mem. Game Theory Soc., 2005—; bd. dirs. Nat. Bur. Economic Rsch., 1986—. Grantee NSF, 1975—. Fellow: Am. Acad. Arts and Sciences, Econometric Soc. (coun. mem. 2000—05); mem.: Am. Econ. Assn. (prize com. 2002—). Office: U Pa Dept Econs 3718 Locust Walk Philadelphia PA 19104-6209 Office Phone: 215-898-7350. Office Fax: 215-573-2057. E-mail: apostlew@con.sas.upenn.edu.*

**POSTMAN, ROBERT DEREK,** mathematics educator; b. Kearny, N.J. July 13, 1941; s. Benjamin and Edith (Maw) P.; m. Elizabeth Ann Del Corso, Aug. 14, 1965; children: Chad, Blaire, Ryan. B.A., Kean Coll., 1966; M.A., Columbia U. Tchrs. Coll., 1967, Ed.D., 1971. Faculty Hunter Coll., N.Y.C., 1970-76, Tchrs. Coll. Columbia U., N.Y.C., 1977-81; prof. math. and edn. Mercy Coll., Westchester County, N.Y., 1976—, chair dept., 1978—; grad. coord. L.I. U., Westchester County, 1979—, dean grad. edn. programs, 1988—; founder, head Urban Teaching Acad.; math. cons. to sch. dists. and state edn. depts.; cons. to Psychol. Corp. for Devel. of the Calif. Achievement Test; bd. dirs. Westchester Com. for Tech. and Disabled; presenter numerous workshops and lectr. local and nat. meetings of orgns. Author: Mathematics on the Geoboard, 1974; Intermediate Mathematics, 1976; (series) Enrichment Mathamatics, 1978, Growth in Mathematics, 1980, 82; (series) Computer Programming, 1983; Collegiate Reading, 1985; (series) Mathematics Unlimited, 1986, High School Mathematics (2 volumes), 1988, Macmillan Mathematics, 1990, Mathematics Today (series), 1991, Consumer Mathematics, 1993, 12 books abouty math., 1994-2006, also computer programs, filmstrips; contbr. articles to profl. jours. Mem. Closter Bd. Edn., N.J., 1973-79; del. N.J. Sch. Bds. Assn., 1974-77; coach, organizer Closter Recreation Commn., 1973—; coach Closter Comets Soccer Team, 1984—. With USAF, 1959-63. NDEA fellow, 1966-70. Mem. Nat. Council Tchrs. of Math., Soc. Applied Learning Tech., N.Y. Acad. Scis., Assn. Tchr. Educators (exec. bd.), Assn. for Mentally Ill Children of Westchester (bd. dirs.), Kappa Delta Pi, Phi Delta Kappa. Roman Catholic. Home: 33 Julia St Closter NJ 07624-2417 Office: Mercy Coll 555 Broadway Dobbs Ferry NY 10522-1134

**POSTOL, LAWRENCE PHILIP,** lawyer; b. Bridgeport, Conn., Oct. 18, 1951; s. Sidney Samuel and Eunice Ruth (Schine) P.; m. Ellen Margaret Russell, Mar. 22, 1975; children: Raymond Russell, Stephan Russell, Carolyn Russell. BS, Cornell U., 1973, JD, 1976. Bar: Conn. 1976, D.C. 1977, U.S. Dist. Ct. D.C. 1977, U.S. Ct. Appeals (D.C. cir.) 1977, U.S. Supreme Ct. 1980, Va. 1982, U.S. Ct. Appeals (4th cir.) 1982, U.S. Dist. Ct. (ea. dist.) Va. 1985, U.S. Dist. Ct. Md. 1989, U.S. Dist. Ct. Conn. 1990. Assoc. Arent, Fox, Kintner & Plotkin, Washington, 1976-80, Seyfarth, Shaw LLP, Washington, 1980-83, ptnr., 1985—; assoc. Jones, Day, Reavis and Pogue, Washington, 1983-85. Lectr. Loyola U., New Orleans, 1983—, U. Cin., 1987-93; bd. advisers The Environ. Counselor Jour.; spl. counsel Greater Washington Bd. Trade, 1991-93. Author: Legal Guide to Handling Toxic Substances in the Workplace, 1990, Americans with Disabilities Act - A Compliance Manual for Employers, 1993. Jewish. Avocation: sports. Home: 6340 Chowning Pl Mc Lean VA 22101-4129 Office: Seyfarth Shaw LLP 815 Connecticut Ave NW Washington DC 20006-4004 Office Phone: 202-828-5385. Office Fax: 202-828-5393. Business E-Mail: lpostol@seyfarth.com.

**POSTON, ANITA OWINGS,** lawyer; b. Sylacauga, Ala., Sept. 24, 1949; d. John T. and Margaret Owings; m. Charles E. Poston, June 9, 1973; children: Charles E. Jr., John W., Margaret Elizabeth. BA, U. Md., 1971; JD, Coll. William & Mary, 1974. Bar: Va. 1974. Atty. Vandeventer Black LLP, Norfolk, Va., 1974—. Substitute judge Norfolk (Va.) Gen. Dist. Cts., 1982-90; mem. Bar Examiners Bd.; mem. bd. vistors Coll. William and Mary Mem. State Bd. C.C.s, Richmond, 1985-90, chmn. 1988-89; mem. Norfolk Sch. Bd., 1990-2002, chmn. 1998-2002; bd. dirs. WHRO Pub. Broadcasting, chair, 2002-04; bd. dirs. Access Coll. Found., Towne Bank, Norfolk. Mem. ABA (law fellows), Va. Bar Assn. (pres. 2000), Norfolk-Portsmouth Bar Assn. (pres. 1998-99), Va. Law Fellows, Am. Inst. of Ct. Office: Vandeventer Black LLP 500 World Trade Ctr Norfolk VA 23510-1679 Office Phone: 757-446-8600. Office Fax: 757-446-8670. Business E-Mail: aposton@vanblk.com.

**POSTON, WALKER SEWARD, II,** medical educator, researcher; BA in Biol. Scis., U. Calif., Davis, 1983; PhD in Psychology, U. Calif., Santa Barbara, 1990; MPH, U. Tex., Houston, Health Sci. Ctr. Clin. psychology resident USAF Med. Ctr., Wright-PAtterson AFB, Ohio, 1989-90; dir. psychology svcs., asst. chief mental health svcs. 9th Med. Group, Beale AFB, 1990-92; fellow in behavioral medicine Wilford Hall Med. Ctr., 1992-93; chief health and rehab. psychology svc. Malcolm Grow Med. Ctr., 1993-95 faculty, 1993-95; clin. asst. prof. dept. med. and clin. psychology F. Edward Herbert Sch. Medicine, Bethesda, Md., 1993-95; asst. prof. medicine Baylor Coll. Medicine, Houston, 1995-99; assoc. prof. U. Mo., Kansas City, 1999—. Rsch. exch. scientist Karolinska Inst., Stockholm, Sweden, 1997, 98. Contbr. articles to profl. jours. Recipient Minority Scientist Devel. award Am. Heart Assn., 1995; U. Calif. Doctoral scholars fellow, 1984-85, 85-86, 86-87, 88-89, Clin. fellow Wilford Hall Med. Ctr., Lackland AFB, 1992-93; Nat. Merit scholar, 1979-80. Fellow, Am. Heart Assn., North Am. Assoc. for the Study of Obesity. Office: Univ Mo 5319 Holmes St Kansas City MO 64110-2437

**POSUNKO, BARBARA,** retired elementary school educator; b. Newark, July 17, 1938; d. Joseph and Mary (Prystauk) P. BA, Rutgers U., Newark, 1960; MA, Kean U., Union, N.J., 1973; teaching cert., Seton Hall U., Newark, 1966. Cert. elem. tchr., reading specialist, N.J. Social case worker Newark City Hosp., 1960-65; elem. tchr. Plainfield Bd. Edn., NJ, 1966; elem. jr. and sr. high sch. tchr. minimum basic skills and reading Sayreville Bd. Edn., NJ, 1966-82, tchr. Chpt. I and minimum basic skills, 1982-95, cooperating tchr. to student tchr., 1983, coord. testing, 1984-95; ret., 1995. Sch. coord. for congressionally mandated study of ednl. growth and opportunity, 1991-95; mem. numerous reading coms. Recipient Outstanding Tchr. award N.J. Gov.'s Tchr. Recognition Program, 1988. Mem. NEA, Internat. Reading Assn., N.J. Reading Assn., N.J. Edn. Assn. Home: 17 Drake Rd Mendham NJ 07945-1805

**POSVAR, MILDRED MILLER,** opera singer; b. Cleve. d. William and Elsa (Friedhofer) Mueller; m. Wesley W. Posvar, Apr. 30, 1950; children: Wesley, Margot Marina, Lisa Christina. Degree in Music (hon.), Cleve. Inst. Music, 1946; doctorate (hon.), Cleve. Ins. Music, 1983; diploma, New England Conservatory Music, 1948, doctorate (hon.), 1966; MusD (hon.), Bowling Green State U., 1960; doctorate (hon.), Washington Jefferson U., 1988. Founder Opera Theater of Pitts., 1978—; mem. music faculty Carnegie-Mellon U., 1996—. Operatic debut in Peter Grimes, Tanglewood, 1946; appeared N.E. Opera Theater, Stuttgart State Theater, Germany, 1949-50, Glyndebourne Opera, Edinburgh Festival; debut as Cherubino in Figaro, Met. Opera, 1951; 23 consecutive seasons Met. Opera; radio debut Bell Telephone Hour; TV debut Voice of Firestone, 1952; appeared in films including Merry Wives of Windsor (filmed in Vienna), 1964; Vienna State Opera debut, 1963, appearances with San Francisco, Chgo. Lyric, Cin. Zoo, San Antonio, Berlin, Munich, Frankfurt, Pasadena, Ft. Worth, Kansas City, Pitts., Tulsa and St. Paul operas. Bd. dirs. Gateway to Music. Recipient Frank Huntington Beebe award for study abroad, 1949, 50, Grand Prix du Disque, 1965, Outstanding Achievements in Music award Boston C. of C., 1959, Ohioana Career medal, 1985, Outstanding Achievement in Opera award, Slippery Rock U., 1985, YWCA Ann. Tribute to Women award, 1989, Keystone Salute award Pa. Fedn. Music Clubs, 1994; named one of outstanding women of Pitts., Pitts. Press-Pitts, Post-Gazette, 1968, Person of Yr. in Music, Pitts. Jaycees, 1980. Mem. Nat. Soc. Arts and Letters (pres. 1989-90, Gold medal 1984), Disting. Daus. Pa. (pres. 1991-93), Tuesday Mus. Club, Phi Beta Kappa, Phi Delta Gamma, Sigma Alpha Iota. Office: Opera Theater of Pittsburgh PO Box 110108 Pittsburgh PA 15232-0608

**POTAMKIN, ROBERT,** automotive executive; b. Mar. 12, 1946; m. Lexi Brockway. Grad., U. Pa., 1970, JD, 1972. CEO Potamkin Cos., Phila., 1972—; co-chmn. Potamkin Auto Group, Phila.; co-chmn., co-CEO Planet Automotive Group Inc., Miami, Fla.; bd. of overseers U. Pa. Law Sch. Million Dollar Roundtable United Way; co-founder Potamkin Prize for Alzheimer's Rsch. Mem.: World Presidents Orgn. Office: Potamkin Cos 130 Spruce St Apt 30B Philadelphia PA 19106-4325 also: Planet Automotive 2333 Ponce De Leon Blvd # 50 Coral Gables FL 33134-5418

**POTASH, JEREMY WARNER,** public relations executive; b. Monrovia, Calif., June 30, 1946; d. Fenwick Bryson and Joan Antony (Blair) Warner; m. Stephen Jon Potash; 1 son, Aaron Warner. AA, Citrus Coll., 1965; BA, Pomona Coll., 1967. With Forbes Mag., NYC, 1967-69, JETRO, San Francisco, 1970-75; v.p., co-founder, pres. Potash & Co. Pub. Rels., Oakland, Calif., 1980—. Founding exec. dir. Calif.-Asia Bus. Coun., Alameda, 1991—; editor Cal-Asia Member Alert, 1991—; exec. dir. Customs Brokers and Forwarders Assn., San Francisco, 1990—; adv. bd. Asia Pacific Econ. Rev., 1996—; mem. No. Calif. Dist. Export Coun., 2000—, Pacific Coun. Internat. Policy, 2000—; mem. adv. bd. Ctr. Pacific Rim U. San Francisco, 2005—; mem. adv. bd. China-Am. Bus. and Edn. Ctr., Calif. State U. East Bay, 2005. Editor Southeast Asia Environmental Directory, 1994, Southeast Asia Infrastructure Directory, 1995-96. Co-founder J.L. Magnes docent program, 1980; pres. NorCal WAORT, 1985—86; bd. dirs. Judah L. Magnes Mus., Berkeley, 1981—94. Named Export Citizen of Yr., U.S. Dept. Commerce, 1998. Mem. Oakland Women's Lit. Soc., Book Club Calif. Office: Potash & Co Pub Rels 1050 Marina Village Pkwy Alameda CA 94501

**POTASH, MARTIN H.,** English educator; b. Balt., Md., Mar. 15, 1951; s. Albert Joseph and Helen Zelda Potash; m. Janet F. Gorelick, June 25, 1978; children: Andrew Joseph, Meredith Lee. BS, U. Md., 1973; MA, Western Md. Coll., 1979. Cert. in Sec. Administrn. Hood Coll., 1990. English and journalism instr., dept. chair Frederick County Pub. Schools, 1981—2003; asst. prin. Wash. County Pub. Schools, Smithsburg, Md., 2003—04, coord. sec. english Hagerstown, Md., 2004—. Mem., sch. improvement teams Frederick County Pub. Schools, 1997—2003; mem., staff develop. adv. group Md. State Bd. Edn., 1997. Mem. bd. trustees Beth Shalom Congregation, Frederick, Md., 1994—, v.p., 1999—2003. Recipient Disting. H.S. Tchr., Western Md. Coll., 1998. Mem.: Assn. for Supervision and Curriculum Develop., Nat. Assn. Sec. Sch. Prin. Office: Was County Pub Sch 820 Commonwealth Ave Hagerstown MD 21741

**POTASH, STEPHEN JON,** public relations executive; b. Houston, Feb. 25, 1945; s. Melvin L. and Petrice (Edelstein) P.; m. Jeremy Warner, Oct. 19, 1969; 1 child, Aaron Warner. BA in Internat. Rels., Pomona Coll., 1967. Account exec. Charles von Loewenfeldt, Inc., San Francisco, 1969-74, v.p., 1974-80; founder, pres. Potash & Co., Pub. Rels., Oakland, Calif., 1980-87, 1990—. Exec. dir. Calif. Coun. Internat. Trade, 1970-87; v.p. corp. communications APL Ltd., Oakland, 1987-90; chmn. Potash & Co., Oakland, 1990-. Bd. dir. Calif. Coun. Internat. Trade, 1987-94, Calif.-Asia Bus. Coun., 1992—; Temple Sinai, Oakland, 1979-81; adv. com. Old Mint, San Francisco Mus., Clampers-Yerba Buena. Mem.: Pub. Rels. Soc. Am. Office: Potash & Co Pub Rels 1050 Marina Village Pkwy Ste 105 Alameda CA 94501 E-mail: steve@potashco.com.

**POTE, HAROLD WILLIAM,** banker; b. Phila., Sept. 18, 1946; s. Frank Lafferty and Lucille (Bock) P.; m. Judy Elizabeth Constantine, Oct. 12, 1968. AB, Princeton U., 1968; MBA, Harvard U., 1972. Dir. investor relations Fidelcor/Fidelity Bank, Phila., 1974-76, v.p., head corp. devel. dept., 1976-78, sr. v.p., head corp devel. dept., 1970-80, exec. v.p., treas. fin. and planning dept., 1980-83, vice chmn., treas. fin. and planning dept., 1983-84; chmn. bd., chief exec. officer Fidelity Bank, Phila., 1984-88; pres., chief exec. officer Fidelcor, Inc., 1986-88; pres. and chief exec. officer First Fidelity Bancorp, Phila., 1988; chief exec. officer Spl. Situation Fund, N.Y.C., 1988-93; ptnr. The Beacon Group (acquired by J.P. Morgan), N.Y.C., 1993—2000; head, regional banking J.P. Morgan Chase & Co., 2000—04, vice chmn. retail fin. services, 2004—. Asst. prof. La Salle Coll., Phila., 1972-79; bd. dirs. Norfolk So. Corp. Trustee Pa. Ballet Assn., Phila., 1976-92; mem. exec. coun. Harvard Bus. Sch. Assn., 1986—. Mem. AICPA, Merion Golf Club, Locust Club. Office: JP Morgan 270 Park Ave New York NY 10017

**POTEMPA, KATHLEEN M.,** dean, nursing educator; b. Oct. 3, 1948; Diploma in nursing, Providence Hosp. Sch. Nursing, Southfield, Mich., 1970; BA in Psychology summa cum laude, U. Detroit, 1974; MS in Nursing, Rush U., 1978, D of Nursing Sci., 1986. Charge nurse coronary ICU Holy Cross Hosp., Ft. Lauderdale, Fla., 1970-71; staff nurse, charge nurse cardiovasc. ICU Henry Ford Hosp., Detroit, 1971-74; nurse practitioner Rush-Presbyn.-St. Luke's Med. Ctr., Chgo., 1974-75; nursing edn. coord. dept. nursing Michael Reese Hosp. and Med. Ctr., Chgo., 1975-77, nursing supr., 1977-78; asst. unit leader dept. gerontol. nursing Rush U. Coll. Nursing, Chgo., 1978-79, asst. chmn., 1979-80, assoc. chmn., asst. prof. gerontol. nursing, 1980-85, asst. prof. gerontol. nursing, 1985-86; asst. prof. nursing, dept. internal medicine, practitioner Rush Med. Coll., Rush U., 1987-88; asst. then assoc. prof. dept. med.-surg. nursing Coll. Nursing, Rush U., Ill., Chgo., 1989-90, dir. tng., pre and postdoctoral fellowship instnl. rsch., 1992—94, exec. assoc. dean Coll. Nursing, 1994-95, interim dean Coll. Nursing, 1995-96; prof., dean Sch. Nursing Oreg. Health Scis. U., Portland, 1996—2006, v.p., 2002—06; dean, prof. nursing, Sch. Nursing U. Mich., Ann Arbor, 2006—. Mem.: Robert Wood Johnson Tchg. Nursing Home Project, VA Edward Hines Jr. Hosp., Hines, Ill., 1985-86, co-dir. Exercise Rsch. Lab., 1985-86; dir. nursing Johnston R. Bowman Health Ctr. for Elderly, Rush Presbyn. St. Luke's Med. Ctr., Chgo., 1980-85. Contbr. articles to profl. jours. Recipient Oreg. Med. Rsch. Found. Mentor award, 2002, Disting. Alumni award, Rush U., 2003. Fellow Am. Acad. Nursing; mem. ANA (coun. nurse rschrs.), Am. Soc. Hypertension, Gerontol. Soc. Am., Midwest Nursing Rsch. Soc., Heart Assn. Met. Chgo., Am. Heart Assn. Oreg., Ill. Coun. Nurse Rschrs., Am. Heart

Assn. (coun. cardiovasc. nursing, coun. hypertension, coun. on strokes), Am. Assn. Coll. Nursing Bd. (sec. 2004), Sigma Theta Tau. Office: U Mich Sch Nursing 400 N Ingalls Rm 1320 Ann Arbor MI 48109*

**POTEMPA, PHILIP MATTHEW,** journalist, columnist, communications educator; b. San Pierre, Ind., Aug. 13, 1970; s. Chester John and Peggy Louise Potempa. BA, Valparaiso U., 1992. Arts and entertainment reporter Vidette-Messenger Newspaper, Valparaiso, Ind., 1991-95, Times Newspaper N.W. Ind., Munster, 1995—; adj. prof. comms. Valparaiso U., 1997—. Arts and entertainment corr. South Bend (Ind.) Tribune, 1993—; prof. comm. Purdue U., Westville, Ind., 1998—; radio commentator WLJE-FM, Ind., 2002—; corr. Indpls. Star Newspaper, 2003—. Co-author: It's a Wonderful Life: A Memory Book, 2003; author: From the Farm, 2004. Bd. dirs. Ind. Journalism Hall of Fame. Recipient Reporting award, Hoosier State Press Assn., 1995, AP Mng. Editors, 1997. Mem.: Ind. Hist. Soc., Soc. Profl. Journalists (award 1996), Chgo. Headline Club (bd. dirs.). Republican. Roman Catholic. Avocation: collecting historical autographs. Office: Times Newspaper 601 W 45th St Munster IN 46321 Home: 104 W Eliza San Pierre IN 46374 Office Phone: 800-837-3232 3247. E-mail: ppotempa@NWITimes.com.

**POTENTE, EUGENE, JR.,** interior designer; b. Kenosha, Wis., July 24, 1921; s. Eugene and Suzanne Marie (Schmit) P.; m. Joan Cioffe, Jan. 29, 1946; children: Eugene J., Peter Michael, John Francis, Suzanne Marie. PhB, Marquette U., 1943; postgrad., Stanford U., 1943, NY Sch. Interior Design, 1948; DFA, Carthage Coll., 1997; DLitt (hon.), Concordia U., 1997. Cert. lighting Nat. Coun. on Lighting Qualification. Founder, chmn. Studios of Potente, Inc., Kenosha, Wis., 1949—; pres., founder Archtl, Svcs. Assocs., Kenosha, 1978 ; Bus. Leasing Svcs. of Wis. Inc., 1978—. Past nat. pres. Inter-Faith Forum on Religion, Art and Architecture; vice chm. Wis. State Capitol and Exec. Residence Bd., 1981—. Sec. Kenosha Symphony Assn., 1968-74; bd. dirs. Ctr. for Religion and the Arts, Wesley Theol. Sem., Washington, 1983-84. With U.S. Army, 1943—46, WWII, ETO. Recipient Disting. Alumni award Marquette U., 1999; named to St. Catherine's HS Hall of Fame, 2002. Fellow Am. Soc. Interior Designers; Mem. Am. Soc. Interior Designers (treas., pres. Wis. chpt. 1985-86, 94-95, chmn. nat. pub. svc. 1986, Gold medal Wis. chpt. 2003), Interior Design Coalition Wis (pres 2003-04), Illuminating Engring. Soc. N.Am., Internat. Interior Design Assn., Elks, Am. Legion (life), Sigma Delta Chi. Roman Catholic. Home: 8609 2nd Ave Pleasant Prairie WI 53158-4720 Office: 914 60th St Kenosha WI 53140-4041 Personal E-mail: gpotente@wi.rr.com. Business E-Mail: eugene@potenteinc.com.

**POTENZA, JOSEPH MICHAEL,** lawyer; b. Stamford, Conn., June 27, 1947; s. Michael Joseph Sr. and Rose Elizabeth (Coppola) P.; m. Karen Louise Yankee, Jan. 28, 1978; children: Wendy Lynn, Chiara Micol. BSEE cum laude, Rochester Inst. Tech., 1970; JD, Georgetown U., 1975. Bar: Va. 1975, D.C. 1976, U.S. Dist. Ct. D.C., U.S. Ct. Appeals (fed. cir.), U.S. Ct. Appeals (6th cir.), U.S. Supreme Ct. Patent examiner U.S. Patent and Trademark Office, Arlington, Va., 1970-74, law clk. bd. appeals, 1974-75, law clk. to presiding judge 6th cir. U.S. Ct. Appeals, 1975-76; assoc. Banner, Birch, McKie & Beckett, Washington, 1976-80, ptnr., 1980—, Banner & Witcoff, Washington, 1995. Adj. prof. Georgetown U. Law Ctr., Washington, 1985—; faculty Nat. Inst. Trial Advocacy-Patent Inst., 1996—; task force on intangibles. Brookings Inst. Editor (monographs) Sorting Out Ownership Rights in Intellectual Property, 1980, Recent Developments in Licensing, 1981; co-author: Patent Trial Advocacy Casebook, 2006; contbg. author Patent Litigaton Strategies Handbook, Patent Misuse-The Critical Balance, A Patent Lawyer's View, Fed. Cir. Bar Jour., Vol. 15, 2005. Bd. dirs. Found. for a Creative Am., 1991—. Recipient Patent and Trademark Office Superior Performance award Dept. Commerce, 1973-75. Fellow Am. Bar Found.; mem. ABA (young lawyers divsn. exec. coun. 1979—, chmn. legis. action com. 1980—, chmn. patent trademark and copyright com. 1977—, house of dels. 1984-86, sci. and tech. sect., coun. mem. 1985—, membership chmn. 1985—, budget co-chmn. 1987—, budget officer 1988—, vice chmn. 1991—, chmn.-elect 1992-93, chmn. 1993, chmn. standing com. on pub. oversight, 1996-2005, spl. adv. on pub. oversight 2005-), IEEE, AAAS (nat. conf. lawyers and scientists), Am. Intellectual Property Law Assn. (chmn. unfair competition com. 1980-81), D.C. Bar Assn. (sec. patent, trademark, copyright sect.), Va. Bar Assn., Wash. Patent Lawyers Club (pres. 1988-89), Am. Inns of Ct. (founding mem. and exec. com. Giles S. Rich 1991—, v.p. 1997, pres. 1998-99), Phi Sigma Kappa, Alpha Sigma (pres. 1979-80), Tau Beta Pi. Home: 1238 Kirkwood Ct Herndon VA 20170-2418 Office: Banner & Witcoff 1001 G St NW Ste 1100 Washington DC 20001-4545 Office Phone: 202-824-3000. Business E-Mail: jpotenza@bannerwitcoff.com.

**POTERBA, JAMES MICHAEL,** economist, educator; b. Flushing, NY, July 13, 1958; s. William Samuel and Margaret Mary (Toale) P.; m. Nancy Lin Rose, June 23, 1984; children: Matthew Robert, Timothy James, Margaret Rose. AB, Harvard U., 1980; MPhil, Oxford U., Eng., 1982, DPhil, 1983. From asst. to assoc. prof. MIT, Cambridge, Mass., 1983-88, prof., 1988—, Mitsui prof., 1996—, dept. head, 2006—. Dir. pub. econs. rsch. program Nat. Bur. Econ. Rsch., Cambridge, 1990—; fellow Ctr. Advanced Study in Behavioral Scis., 1993-94, Hoover Instn. Stanford U., 2000-01. mem. Pres. Adv. Panel on Fed. Tax Reform, 2005; trustee Coll. Retirement Equity Fund, 2006—. Editor: Economic Policy Responses to Global Warning, 1991, International Comparisons of Household Saving, 1994, Housing Markets in the United States and Japan, 1994, Empirical Foundations of Household Taxation, 1996, Fiscal Institutions and Fiscal Performance, 1999, Jour. Pub. Econs.; contbr. articles to profl. jours. Recipient award for Excellence in Sci. Reviewing NAS, 1999; Marshall scholar, 1980-83, Batterymarch fellow, 1986. Fellow: Ctr. Advanced Study in Behavioral Scis., Econometric Soc., Am. Acad. Arts and Scis.; mem.: Am. Econ. Assn. (exec. com. 2001—03), Phi Beta Kappa. Office: MIT 50 Memorial Dr Rm E52-350 Cambridge MA 02142-1347 Office Phone: 617-253-6673. E-mail: poterba@mit.edu.

**POTH, STEFAN MICHAEL,** retired diversified financial services company executive; b. Detroit, Dec. 9, 1933; s. Stefan and Anna (Mayer) P.; m. Eileen T. McClimon, May 28, 1966; 1 child, Stefan Michael Jr. Cert. in acctg., Walsh Inst., Detroit, 1954. CPA Mich., cert. consumer credit exec. Sr. acct. Lybrand, Ross Bros. & Montgomery, Detroit, 1953-56, 58-61; with Ford Motor Credit Co., Dearborn, Mich., 1961-91, v.p. leasing truck and recreational products and tractor financing, 1973-77; v.p. cen. and western U.S. ops. Ford Motor Credit CO., Dearborn, 1977-79; v.p. mktg. and ops. svcs. Ford Motor Credit Co., Dearborn, 1979-85, v.p. bus. planning, 1985-90, v.p. credit policy 1990-91. Bd. dirs. GE Credit Auto Resale Svcs., Inc.; adv. coun. Credit Rsch. Ctr., Krannert Grad. Sch. Mgmt., Purdue U., 1984—91. Chmn. adv. coun. Credit Rsch. Ctr. Krannert Grad. Sch. Mgmt., Purdue U., 1989-90; mem. bd. dirs. Internat. Credit Assoc., 1989-91. With AUS, 1956-58. Roman Catholic. Home: 7230 Mohansic Dr Bloomfield Hills MI 48301-3550

**POTIRNICHE, GABRIEL PETRU,** mechanical engineer, researcher; PhD, Miss. State U., Mississippi State, 2003. Asst. rsch. prof. Ctr. for Advanced Vehicular Systems, Mississippi State, 2003—. Contbr. articles to profl. jours. Recipient Henry O. Fuchs award, SAE, 2002. Mem.: ASME. Office: Mississippi State University Box 5405 Mississippi State MS 39762 Personal E-mail: gpp30@yahoo.com.

**POTLURI, VENKATESWARA RAO,** medical facility administrator; b. Krishna Dist., India, Jan. 1, 1955; came to U.S., 1983; s. Venkata Krishnaiah and Bulli Ademma (Koduru) P.; m. Padma Sree Peddu, Dec. 4, 1986; children: Vani, Vamsee Krishna, Varun. BSc, ANR Coll., Gudivada, India, 1975; MSc, AU Coll. Sci. and Tech., Waltair, India, 1977; MPhil, SKU (India) U., 1979, PhD, 1982. Diplomate Am. Bd. Med. Genetics, 1984. Postdoctoral fellow Mt. Sinai Med. Ctr., N.Y.C., 1983-85, vis. asst. prof., 1985-87; lab. dir., adj. mem. med. staff Norwalk (Conn.) Hosp., 1987-98; lab. dir. Lab. Diagnostics (divsn. Cytogenetics), Norwalk, 1998—2001; lab dir.

Ctr. for Genetic Svcs. Inc. (divsn. Lab. Corp. of Am.), Corpus Christi, Tex., 2001—03, Dynagene divsn. Lab. Corp. Am., Houston, 2003—. Fellow: Am. Coll. Med. Genetics (founding); mem.: Am. Soc. Human Genetics. Avocations: classical music, Telugu literature, home improvement. Home: 4018 Blue Bonnet Blvd Apt D Houston TX 77025 Office: Dynagene 7400 Fannin Ste 1200 Houston TX 77054

**POTOCKA, KATARZYNA,** mathematics professor; d. Libert Potocki and Janina Potocka. BA in Math., Coll. N.J., 1999; MS in Math., Lehigh U., 2001, PhD in Math., 2004. Tchg. asst. Lehigh U., Bethlehem, Pa., 1999—2004; asst. prof. Ramapo Coll. N.J., Mahwah, NJ, 2004—. Spkr. in field. Contbr. articles to profl. jours.; editor: Introductory Statistics: A Problem-Solving Approach, 2005. Grantee, Ramapo Coll. N.J., 2006. Mem.: Math. Assn. Am., Am. Math. Soc., Pi Mu Epsilon. Roman Catholic. Avocations: piano, singing, classical music. Office: Ramapo Coll NJ Dept Math 505 Ramapo Valley Rd Mahwah NJ 07430

**POTSIC, AMIE SHARON,** photographer, educator, artist; b. Chgo., Dec. 11, 1971; d. William P. and Roberta K. Potsic. BA, Ind. U., 1993; MFA, San Francisco Art Inst., 1999. Cert. Teaching English as a Foreign Language to Adults U. Cambridge, 1996. Adj. faculty, photography instr. San Francisco Art Inst., 1999—; adj. faculty photography instr. U. Calif. Berkeley, 2001—; adj. faculty, photography instr. Ohlone Coll., Fremont, Calif., 2003—. Art/photography cons. Amie Potsic Photography, San Francisco, 2004—. One-woman shows include Seduce Me, Quotidian Gallery, 2000, Thin Skinned Thick, 2002, Doppelganger, The Painted Bride Art Ctr., 2003, 626 Gallery, LA, 2005, publication, exhbn., Ritual and Resilience (Second Pl. Photoessay award, San Francisco Bay Guardian, 1998), publication, Prayer - Jerusalem, Israel (Jerusalem 3000 First pl. award Jewish Exponent, 1996), Casa do Vaticano, Graficos Burti Brazil, exhibited in group shows at Documenta USA, The Mus. of New Art, 2001, Fotosemana, Meseo de Arte Moderno de Bogota, 2002, Piece Process, Athens Inst. Contemporary Art, 2004. Program coord., instr. Shooting Back, Washington, 1993—94. Recipient Award of Excellence, Manhattan Arts Internat. Mag., 1996, Award of Excellence, Coll. Photography Ann., Photographer's Forum, 1999, winner Photo Alliance Slide Competition, San Francisco Art Inst., 2004. Mem.: Coll. Art Assn. Personal E-mail: apotsic@yahoo.com.

**POTSIC, WILLIAM PAUL,** otolaryngologist, educator; b. Berwyn, Ill., May 22, 1943; s. Andrew M. and Estella (Buschak) P.; m. Roberta I. Kite; children: Amie, Jordan. BS, U. Ill., 1965; MD cum laude, Emory U., 1969; postgrad., U. Pa.; M in Med. Mgmt., Tulane U., 1998. Intern, resident U. Chgo., 1969-74; practice medicine specializing in pediatric otolaryngology Phila., 1974—; staff Presbyn. Hosp., U. Pa. Hosp., Phila., Children's Seashore House, Phila.; prof. otorhinolaryngology and human comm. U. Pa., Phila., 1974-93, E. Mortimer Newlin prof., 1993—; dir. div. otorhinolaryngology and human comm. Children's Hosp., Phila., 1975—, pres. med. staff, 1982-84, med. dir. Cochlear Implant Program, 1991—, vice-chmn. clin. affairs dept. surgery, 1995—, dir. ambulatory surg. svcs., 1997—, dir. ctr. for childhood comm., 1999. Author: Surgical Pediatric Otolaryngology, 1997; contbr. articles to profl. jours. Recipient 1st prize for clin. rsch. Am. Acad. Ophthalmology and Otolaryngology, 1977, Sylvan E. Stool award for outstanding lifetime contbns. in ear nose and throat advances in children, Presdl. award Soc. Otorhinolaryngology and Head and Neck Nurses, 2002; NIH grantee. Mem. AMA, Am. Acad. Otolaryngology Head and Neck Surgery, Am. Laryngology, Otolgy and Rhinology Soc., Am. Coll. Physician Execs., Internat. Acad. Cosmetic Surgery, Pa. Med. Soc., Phila. Coll. Physicians, Phila. County Med. Soc., Phila. Laryngol. Soc. (treas. 1983), Phila. Pediatric Soc., Am. Laryngol. Assn. (Gabriel Tucker award 2005), Phila Laryngol. Soc. (pres. 1984), Phila. Soc. Facial Plastic Surgeons, Politzer Soc., Soc. Ear, Nose and Throat Advances in Children (pres. 1983), Am. Soc. Pediatric Otolaryngology (pres. 1991, Potsic Ann. award for basic sci. rsch.), Soc. Univ. Otolaryngologists, Am. Acad. Pediat., Alpha Omega Alpha, Phi Chi. Home: 1057 Beaumont Rd Berwyn PA 19312-2007 Office: Children's Hosp Phila 34th And Civic Center Blvd Philadelphia PA 19104 Office Phone: 215-590-3450. E-mail: potsic@email.chop.edu.

**POTT, JAMES THOMAS,** retired civil engineer, consultant; b. Shanghai, China, Feb. 28, 1927; (father Am. citizen); permanent resident. s. James Hawks and Nancy (Yang) P.; m. Lois Jane Donaldson, July 16, 1955; children: Nancy, Catherine, Margaret. BSCE, Stanford U., 1949, MSCE, 1950, student, 1957—58. Registered profl. engr., Calif., Colo. Civil engr. Kennedy/Jenks/Chilton, San Francisco, 1950-60; county engr. County of Santa Clara, San Jose, Calif., 1960-77, dir. pub. works, 1963-73, dir. transp., 1973-77, asst. county exec., 1977-78; city engr., dir. pub. works City of Long Beach, Calif., 1978-84; v.p. O'Brien-Kreitzberg & Assocs., Encino, Calif., 1984-87; propr., engring. cons. James Pott & Co., Long Beach, 1987—94; ret., 1994. Patentee transit wheelchair lift. Bd. dirs. Rail Constrn. Corp. of L.A. County Transp. Commn. 1990-92. Tech. sgt. U.S. Army, 1944—46, lt. special aviation U.S. Army, 1952—53. Recipient S.I.R. award Assoc. Gen. Contractors Calif., 1976; Disting. Service award Calif. Council Civil Engrs. and Land Surveyors, 1967. Fellow: ASCE (life); mem.: AIA (hon.), hon. assoc. mem. Santa Clara Valley chpt.), Pub. Works Officers League Calif. Cities (v.p. 1983—84), Nat. Assn. County Engrs. (life; 1st v.p. 1976—77, Urban County Engr. of Yr. 1973), County Engrs. Assn. Calif. (life; pres. 1971—72), Am. Pub. Works Assn. (life; rsch. found. 1982—84, Top Ten Pub. Works award 1976), Long Beach Area C. of C. (vice chmn. 1986—90, chmn. strategic plan task force 1988), Tau Beta Pi. Republican. Anglican. Personal E-mail: dunmovin@cox.net.

**POTTASH, A. CARTER,** psychiatrist, hospital executive; b. Phila., Nov. 20, 1948; s. B. Rubin and Elizabeth (Braunschweig) P. BS with high honors, Trinity Coll., Hartford, Conn., 1970; MD, Yale U., 1974. Intern Tufts U. Sch. Medicine, Springfield, Mass., 1974-75; clin. fellow Yale-New Haven Hosp., 1977-78; fellow Yale U., New Haven, 1975-78; med. dir. Psychiatric Diagnostic Labs. Am., Summit, NJ, 1979-83. Lectr., cons. in field; vis. prof. St. Elizabeth Med. Ctr., Northeastern Ohio U. Coll Medicine, 1979; clin. prof. NYU, 1989—; pres. Fla. Consultation Svcs., P.A., West Palm Beach, 1992—, Psychiatric Assocs. N.J., P.A., Summit, N.J., 1978-93, Met. Med. Group P.C., N.Y.C., 1981-92, So. Fla. Med. Group P.A., Delray Beach, 1984-93, Stony Lodge Hosp., Inc. and Stony Lodge Med. Group P.C., Briarcliff Manor, N.Y., 1985—, Hampton Med. Group, P.A., Rancocas and Summit, N.J., 1986—; exec. med. dir. Fair Oaks Hosp., Summit, 1978-92, The Regent Hosp., N.Y.C., 1981-92, Lake Hosp of the Palm Beaches, Lake Worth, Fla., 1984-92, Fair Oaks Hosp. at Boca/Delray, Fla., 1984-92, Hampton Hosp., Rancocas, N.J., 1986-95—; chmn. Stony Lodge Hosp., Briarcliff Manor, N.Y., 1985—. Editor Psychiatry Letter, 1980-91; mem. editl. bd. Internat. Jour. Psychiatry in Medicine, 1978-87, The Psychiatric Hosp., 1982—, Jour. Nat. Assn. Pvt. Psychiatric Hosps., 1980-81, Fla. Psychiatry Newsletter, 1992—; reviewer Jour. Nervous and Mental Disorders, Alcoholism, Clin. and Exptl. Rsch., JAMA, Hosp. and Cmty. Psychiatry; contbr. articles to profl. jours. mem. adv. bd. Mothers for More Halfway Houses, N.Y.C., 1986—; cons. com. on women and alcoholism Jr. League of N.Y.C., 1987; bd. dirs. Met. Soc. Arts, N.Y.C., 1984-87. Fellow Am. Coll. Clin. Pharmacology, Assn. Clin. Scientists, Nat. Acad. Clin. Biochemistry, Am. Psychiat. Assn. (disting. fellow), The Acad. Medicine N.J.; mem. AMA, Soc. Neurosci., Nat. Acad. Clin. Biochemistry, Palm Beach County Med. Soc., Am. Acad. Clin. Psychiatrists, Brit. Brain Rsch. Assn. (hon.), European Brain and Behavioral Soc. (hon.), Am. Soc. Addiction Medicine, Am. Academy of Addiction Psychiatry (founding mem. 1987), Fla. Med. Soc., Palm Beach County Psychiat. Soc., Med. Soc. State N.Y., Med. Soc. N.J., Union County Med. Soc., N.Y. Athletic Club, Canoe Brook Country Club, Beacon Hill Club, Phi Beta Kappa, Beta Phi Alpha. Office: PO Box 511 West Palm Beach FL 33402-0511 Office Phone: 561-837-2215.

**POTTER, ALICE CATHERINE,** medical technician; b. Oil City, Pa., June 24, 1928; d. Howard Taylor and Hilda Marian (Lewis) P. BA, U. Findlay, 1949; postgrad., Springfield (Ohio) City Hosp. 1949-50. Registerd med. technologist Am. Soc. Clin. Pathologists; cert. clin. lab. scientist. Med. technologist Mercy Hosp., Springfield, 1950-54, Oil City Hosp., 1954-67;

staff med. technologist Thomas Jefferson U. Hosp., Phila., 1968-83, sr. med. technologist, 1983—97, retired, 1997—2002. Vol. Acad. Natural Scis., Phila., 1995-2000 Mem. Am. Soc. Clin. Lab. Scientists, Pa. Soc. Clin. Lab. Scientists (membership chmn. Delaware Valley chpt. 1977-78, chmn. pub. rels. 1982-94, 96-97, bd. dirs. 1989-91, 97-98, 98-99, 99-2004, pres.-elect 1991-92, pres. 1992-93, Scrimshaw award 1992) Republican. Avocations: travel, needle-crafts. Home: 1701 Wallace St Philadelphia PA 19130-3312

POTTER, ALLAN L., lawyer; b. Corpus Christi, Tex., Apr. 27, 1947; s. C. Burtt and Marion J. Potter. Student, U. Tex., 1965-67; BA, Baylor U., 1969, JD, 1971. Bar: Tex. 1971, U.S. Ct. Appeals (5th cir.) 1972, U.S. Ct. Appeals (6th and 11th cirs.), U.S. Supreme Ct. 1975; cert. in bus. and consumer bankruptcy Tex. Bd. Legal Specialization. Law clk. 13th Ct. Appeals Tex., Corpus Christi, 1972-73; ptnr. Potter & Potter, Corpus Christi, 1973-91. Pvt. trustee U.S. Bankruptcy Ct., Corpus Christi, 1975-91. Chmn. Nueces County Dem. Com., Corpus Christi, 1982-86. Mem. Corpus Christi Bankruptcy Bar Assn. (pres. 1992-93). Baptist. Office: PO Box 3159 606 N Carancahua Ste 820 Corpus Christi TX 78463-3159

POTTER, CALVIN J., retired library director; b. Sheboygan, Wis., Nov. 3, 1945; married. Student, U. Wis., Sheboygan; BA, Lakeland Coll., 1968; postgrad., U. Wis. Past Wis. state assemblyman dist. 26; with dist. 9 Wis. State Senate, 1990-98, chmn. edn. com.; asst. supt. Dept. Pub. Instrn., Madison, Wis., 1998—2003. Former tchr. Mem. Sheboygan County Hist. Soc. Mem. NEA, Wis. Edn. Assn., Izaak Walton League. Address: N6266 Rio Rd Sheboygan Falls WI 53085-2203

POTTER, CARYL A., III, lawyer; b. Norfolk, Va., Apr. 4, 1947; BA in sociology, Stanford U., 1972; JD, U. Mo., Columbia, 1973. Bar: DC 1978. Govt. contract practice, Washington, 1978—91; joined Sonnenschein Nath & Rosenthal LLP, Washington, 1991, now vice chmn. of firm, mem. policy & planning com., mem. & former head govt. contracts practice group. Capt. Judge Adv.'s Office USAF, 1973—78. Office: Sonnenschein Nath & Rosenthal LLP Ste 600, E Tower 1301 K St NW Washington DC 20015 Office Phone: 202-408-6340. Office Fax: 202-408-6399. Business E-Mail: cpotter@sonnenschein.com.

POTTER, DAN R., history educator; b. Portsmouth, Ohio, May 8, 1960; BS in Edn., Wright State U., Dayton, Ohio, 1983; MA in Edn., U. Dayton, Ohio, 1990. History tchr. Beaver Creek City Schs., Ohio, 1983—. Tennis coach Beaver Creek HS, 1984—85, volleyball coach, 1990—91, conditioning coach, 1989—91. Mem. David's United Ch. of Christ. Mem.: NEA. Office: Beavercreek HS 2660 Dayton-Xenia Rd Dayton OH 45434

POTTER, DAVID L., academic administrator; m. Pam Mathews (dec.); children: Elizabeth, Holly. Degree, Amherst Coll.; MS, PhD, Syracuse U. Instr., asst. to dir. pub. affairs program Syracuse U., NY, 1968-70; mem. staff Denison U., Ohio, 1970-81, Silliman U., The Philippines, 1970-81, State Coun. Higher Edn. Va., 1981-86; exec. asst. to pres. George Mason U., Fairfax, Va., 1986, v.p. exec. affairs, 1987-91, dean Coll. Arts and Scis., 1991-96, provost, 1996—99, prof. anthropol. theory and cultural anthropology; pres. Delta State U., Cleveland, Miss., 1999—2003; commr. higher edn. Miss. Instns. of Higher Learning, 2003—04; pres. North Ga. Coll. & State U., Dahlonega, Ga., 2005—. Mem.: So. Assn. Colls. and Schs. (exec. com. mem.), Am. Assn. State Colls. and Univs., Am. Coun. of Edn. (mem. Commn. on Leadership and Instl. Effectiveness). Office: North Ga Coll & State U 82 College Circle Dahlonega GA 30597

POTTER, DAVID SAMUEL, former automotive company executive; b. Seattle, Jan. 16, 1925; children: Diana (Mrs. Paul Bankston), Janice (Mrs. Robert Meadows), Tom, Bill; m. Nancy Shaar, Dec. 1979. BS, Yale U., 1945; PhD, U. Wash., 1951. Mem. staff Applied Physics Lab., U. Wash., 1946-60, asst. dir., 1955-60; with Gen. Motors Corp., 1960-73; chief engr. Milw. ops. GM Delco Electronics div., 1970-73; dir. research and devel. Detroit Diesel Allison div., 1973; asst. sec. for research and devel. Dept. Navy, 1973-74, under sec., 1974-76; v.p. environ. activities staff Gen. Motors Corp., Detroit, 1976-78, v.p. and group exec. public affairs group, 1978-83, v.p. in charge power products and def. ops. group, 1983-85; ret., 1985. Mem. Gov. Calif. Adv. Commn. Ocean Resources, 1964-68; mem. adv. panel Nat. Sea Grant Program, 1966; adv. bd. Naval Postgrad. Sch., Dept. Energy; bd. dirs. Sanders Assocs. Inc., Sci. Applications Internat. Co., John Fluke Mfg. Co., Lockheed Martin Corp. Served to ensign USNR, 1943-46. Mem. Nat. Acad. Engring., NSF, Marine Tech. Soc., Am. Phys. Soc., AIAA, Am. Acoustical Soc., Nat. Oceanographic Assn. (v.p. 1966), Soc. Automotive Engrs. (chmn. tech. bd. 1978-79, dir. 1981-83), Cosmos Club (Washington), Detroit Club, Birmingham Athletic Club (Mich.), Birnam Wood Country Club (Montecito, Calif.), Santa Barbara Club. Achievements include research on cosmic rays, magnetics, underwater acoustics. Home: 877 Lilac Dr Santa Barbara CA 93108-1449 Office Phone: 805-969-9371. E-mail: dpotter@impulse.net.

POTTER, EMMA JOSEPHINE HILL, language educator; b. Hackensack, N.J., July 18, 1921; d. James Silas and Martha Loretta (Fygle) Hill; m. James H. Potter, Mar. 26, 1949. AB cum laude with honors in classics, Alfred U., 1943; AM, Johns Hopkins U., 1946. Tchr. Latin, Balt. County Pub. Schs., 1943-44; instr. French and Spanish, Balt. Poly. Inst., 1950-83, instr. Spanish adult edn. classes, 1946-48; treas. Bruno-Potter, Inc. Trustee James Harry Potter Gold Medal award of ASME. Donor commemorative plaque in honor of Martha Pyle Hill to Chenango County Coun. Arts, 1996. Mem. Internat. Platform Assn., Clan Hay Soc. Scotland (Am. br.), John Hopkins U. Faculty Club. Democrat. Home: 419 3d Ave Avon By The Sea NJ 07717-1244

POTTER, FRED LEON, lawyer, retired insurance company executive; b. Kansas City, Kans., Dec. 15, 1948; s. Donald Warren and Olive Lucile (Ater) P.; m. Mertie Lorraine Scribner, June 13, 1970; children: Mark, Amy, Joy. BA, Harvard U., 1970, MBA, 1972; JD, U. Mich., 1975. Bar: N.H. 1975, U.S. Dist. Ct. N.H. 1975. Atty. Sulloway, Hollis & Soden, Concord, N.H, 1975-80, 96—; pres., gen. counsel Christian Mut. Life Ins. Co., Concord, N.H, 1980-96. Ptnr., mgmt. cons. Potter-Brock Assn., Tucson, 1969-82; trustee Gordon-Conwell Theol. Seminar, South Hamilton, Mass., 1983—; bd. dirs. N.H. Savs. Bank Corp., Concord, 1987-90; exec. dir. N.H. Health Plan, 2002—, N.H. Vaccine Assn., 2002—. Clk. Concord Union St. Dist., 1978-84; deacon 1st Bapt. Ch., Concord, 1978-85; elder Grace Bible Fellowship, 1993—; coach Concord Little League, 1985-87, 90-93. Mem. ABA, N.H. Bar Assn. (treas. 1980-84, v.p. 1984-85, pres. 1986-87, Pres. Disting. Service award 1983), Merrimack County Bar Assn. (sec. 1976-80), Christian Legal Soc., Computer Law Assn., Order of Coif. Evangelical. Achievements include completing the first-ever church mortgage loan securitization in 1990. Home: 4 Pond Place Ln Concord NH 03301-3033 Office: 9 Capitol St Concord NH 03301-6310 Office Phone: 603-223-2816. Business E-Mail: FPotter@sulloway.com

POTTER, GEORGE KENNETH, artist; b. Bakersfield, Calif., Feb. 26, 1926; s. Howard Eugene and Edythe (Keast) P.; m. Heliodora Carneiro de Mendonca, July 30, 1954 (div. July 1956); 1 child, Helen Marcia Pessoa; m. Ruth Mary Griffen, Aug. 4, 1962 (div. July 1989); children: Katherine Anne Klein, Claire Lorraine, Cynthia Ann Decker. Student, Acad. Art U., San Francisco, 1947—48, Jean Metzinger Acad. Frochot, Paris, 1950—52, Inst. Statale dei Belli Arti, Florence, Italy, 1951; BA magna cum laude, San Francisco State U., 1974. Tchr. pvt.watercolor workshops, San Francisco, Santa Fe, Hawaii, Italy, Adriatic, Sacramento Fine Arts Ctr., others; lectr. San Francisco State U.; instr. Acad. Art U., San Francisco; judge Vacaville 28th Ann., 2005, Calif. State Fair Art Exhbn., 1968. One-man shows include U. Calif.-Berkeley, 1959, U. Santa Clara, Calif., 1958, Coll. Marin, Calif.,1958, Rosacrucian Mus., San Jose, Calif., 1959, Brazilian-Am. Inst., Rio de Janeiro, 1955, Gallerie 8, Paris, 1952, Maxwell Galleries, San Francisco, 1958, 62, Gallery 5, Santa Fe, 1960, Rotunda Gallery, San Francisco, 1949, 52, Kaiser Art Ctr. Gallery, Oakland, Calif., 1980, Marin County Civic Ctr., San Rafael, Calif., 1985, Foundry Gallery, Sacramento, 2003, 20th St. Gallery, Sacramento, 2005, NutTree Gallery, Vacaville, Calif., 1987, numerous others; competitive exhibitions include Am. Watercolor Soc., N.Y.C., 1961, 74, 76,

79, 03, Phelan Awards Competition San Francisco Mus. Art, 1949, Calif. Palace Legion Honor, 1958, 60, San Francisco, 1958, 60, 63, 75, Springville (Utah) Invitational, 1963, Jack London Invitational (award 1958), Oakland, Calif., 1957-65, Calif. State Fair (awards 1958, 72, award of excellence 2006) Sacramento, 1957-58, 61-68, 70-74, 76, 79, 86, Oakland Watercolor Ann., 1948, 52, Mother Lode Ann., Sonora, Calif., 1957-58, 63, 65, Kingsley Ann., E.B. Crocker Art Mus., Sacramento, 1948, 58, 61, 62, 64, 65, Marin County Artists Ann., 1948-49, 58, 61, 65-73, 75, 77, 95-98, 04, 05, Marin County Ann. (awards 1966, 67), 1962, 65-67, 70, 71, 76, Western Assn. Mus. Shows, 1964, 67, 74, 05, 06, No. Calif. Arts Ann., 1961, 68, 88, 97, 98, 03-06, Fukuoka (Japan) Invitational Exchange Show with Oakland, 1964, Soc. Western Artists Ann. at M.H. De Young Mus., San Francisco, 1956-64, Statewide Watercolor Show (award), Santa Cruz, 1958, Watercolor U.S.A., Springfield, Mo., 1973, 74, Royal Watercolor Soc. Invitational Exhbn., London, 1975, From London to Leeds Mus. Art, Eng., 1975, Palace of the Legion of Honor, San Francisco, A City Buys Art Invitational, 1967, San Francisco Art Festival, 1975, Palo Alto Cultural Ctr. (award 1977), 1977, Calif. Modernist Watercolors of 1950's, Pasadena Mus. Calif. Art, 2006; executed murals Moore Bus. Forms, Inc., Oakland, 1963, Town Hall, Corte Madera, Calif., Macy's of Calif., Sacramento, 1963, San Mateo, 1944, Stockton, 1965, stained glass dome for Hale Meml., Soc. Calif. Pioneers, San Francisco, 1974, Calif. Dept. Motor Vehicles, Oakland, 1975, Orange County Mus. Art, Newport Beach, Calif., 2004, Calif. Heritage Mus., Santa Monica, 2004, Calif. Watercolor Assn., 2004, 06; stained glass and resin triptych U. Calif. at San Francisco Moffitt Hosp., 1976, Embassy Stes. Hotel, Sacramento (watercolor commn.), 2001, W. Robert Griswold, Jr., Tiburon, Calif. (sculpture commn.), 2002; represented in permanent collections including HUD San Francisco regional office, San Francisco Art Commn., San Diego Mus. Art; art dir. McCann-Erickson Advt. Inc., Rio de Janeiro, 1954-55, Johnson and Lewis Advt., San Francisco, 1957, Michelson Advt., Palo Alto, Calif., 1959-60; contbr. The Calif. Style-Watercolor Artists 1925-55 (McClelland and Last), 1985, The N.Y. Art Rev., 1988, Watercolors Editions Limited, 1990, California Watercolors 1850-1970, McClelland and Last, 2002. Served with USMCR, 1944-46, PTO. Recipient Macy's Art award, San Francisco, 1958, 1st award Watercolor Delta Ann., Antioch, Calif., 1969, 1st award Alameda County Fair, 1974, 79, 85, Santa Rosa 12th Ann., 1975, Best of Show Calif. Arts League Open Exhibition, 1988, 98, First Popular award Calif. Arts League Open, 1989, 2d award Calif. Art League, 1997, 1st place award, 1997, 1st place award Marin Soc. Artists Ann. Open, 1997, Watercolor Artists Sacramento Horizons, 19th ann. Grumbacher award, 1997, Valley Sculpture Artists 1st Ann. Exhbn. Merit award, 1998-99, award of excellence Opus Magnum XI, 1998, Wash. 20th Ann. Exhbn., 1998, First award sculpture, 1997, First award 1999, Award of Merit No. Calif. Arts Annual Open, 1999, Florence Ferrario Meml. award, 1998, Award of Excellence League of Carmichael Artists Annual Open, 1999, Merit award 1998, 2d Sculpture award, 1st Mixed award Calif. Art League, 2000, First award Valley Sculpture Artists Members Show, 2000, 1st Watercolor award Watercolor Artists Sacramento Open, 2000, 1st Watercolor award, 1st Mixed award Calif. Arts. League Ann. Open, 2001, Merit award Sacramento Watercolor Artists Open, 2002, 1st Ann. Meml. award Valley Sculpture, 2003, award of merit No. Calif. Arts Open, 2003, 1st award and 1st Popular award, 2004, 1st Watercolor award, 2d Print award, 3d Mixed award Calif. Art League Open, 2004, Richeson Golden Watercolor award Calif. Art League, 2005, First Watercolor award, 2005, Best of Color Open Show, 2006, First Watercolor award No. Calif. Arts Member Show, 2005, Second Watercolor award, 2005, Judge's award Magnum Opus, Best of Color Sacramento Fine Arts Ctr., 2006, Haley Meml. award, 2005, Best of Show, Watercolor Artists Sacramento Open, 2005, Best of Show Vacaville Art Fest, 2005, First award Marin Soc. Artists, 2006, Calif. State Fair award of excellence, 2006, 2d prize Vacaville Ann., 2006, others. Mem. Am. Watercolor Soc., Marin Soc. Artists (life), No. Calif. Arts, Watercolor Artists Sacramento, Valley Sculpture Artists. Address: 4824 Skyway Dr Fair Oaks CA 95628-6520 Office Phone: 916-966-8248. E-mail: kpotterart@yahoo.com.

POTTER, GEORGE WILLIAM, JR., mining executive; b. St. Louis, Aug. 5, 1930; s. George William and Fay Marguerite (Finch) P.; m. Emily Louise Withers, Feb. 11, 1956; 1 child, Anne Finch Russ. BA, U. Mo., Kansas City, 1952. Pres. Oritz Mines, Inc., Joplin, Mo., 1962—64, chmn. bd. dirs., 1964—87, Nancy Oil & Royalty Co., Joplin, 1981—86; pres., chmn. bd. dirs. Potter Industries, Inc., Joplin, 1981—90; chmn. bd. dirs. Cresset Corp., Joplin, 1986. Art exhibited in one-man shows at Barn Gallery, Kansas City, Mo., 1974, Fountain Valley Sch., Colorado Springs, Colo., 1974, U. Leyden, The Netherlands, 1977, others; author books (under pseudonym E.L. Withers): The House on the Beach, 1957, The Salazar Grant, 1959, Diminishing Returns, 1960, Heir Apparent, 1961, The Birthday, 1962, Royal Blood, 1964; fgn. edits. include Brit., French, Italian, German, Scandinavian, Japanese. Founding bd. dirs. Winfred L. and Elizabeth C. Post Meml. Art Reference Libr., 1977-82, Kansas City Ballet, 1976-79; trustee Conservatory of Music, Kansas City, 1988-2001. Recipient Mo. Writers award, U. Mo., Columbia, 1967. Mem. Authors Guild, Nat. Trust for Hist. Preservation, Soc. Fellows Nelson Gallery Found. (coun. 1988-91), Kansas City Country Club. Home: 1239 W 61st Terr Kansas City MO 64113-1327

POTTER, HAROLD CLAUDE, philosopher; b. Waukegan, Ill., Sept. 11, 1941; s. Claude Allen and Stella Eve (Zaborski) P.; m. Barbara Rae Marr, Aug. 18, 1962 (div. Sept. 1991); children: Deborah Renee, Chris Michele. BS, Ill. Inst. Tech., Chgo., 1963; MS, U. Ill., Champaign-Urbana, 1964; PhD, Cornell U., Ithaca, N.Y., 1970. Mem. tech. staff Bell Labs., Reading, Pa., 1963-77; Pvt. practice Lake County, Ill., 1977-78; pvt. practice Ky., 1978—. Author: One Realtist's Guide to Insurance-A Philosophic Commentary, 1991, A Mathematical Depiction of Simple Emotional Character, 1993, Sveta Prostronstvo: Prichinnoj Reshetkoj Otnositel'nostic, 2005. Home: 425 W Ormsby Ave #408 Louisville KY 40203-3014

POTTER, HOLLIS GROMISCH, radiologist; b. NYC, 1958; MD, NY Med. Coll., 1985. Nat. Bd. of Med. Examiners 1985, diplomate Am. Bd. Radiology, Diagnostic Radiology 1990. Intern Danbury Hosp., 1985—86; resident No. Shore U. Hosp., Manhasset, NY, 1986—90; fellow skeletal radiology NY Hosp., Cornell U. Med. Coll., NY, NY, 1990—91; fellow musculoskeletal radiology Hosp. Spl. Surgery, NYC, 1990—91, attending radiologist, chief, divsn. of magnetic resonance imaging, co-dir. rsch., 1992—, assoc. scientist-rsch. divsn.; attending radiologist NY Presbyn. Hosp. Prof. radiology Weill Med. Coll., Cornell U.; spkr. in field. Contbr. scientific papers, chapters to books; reviewer: Jour. of Am. Acad. of Orthopaedic Surgeons, Jour. of Biomechanics, Radiology, Jour. of Orthopaedic Rsch., Jour. of Bone and Joint Surgery. Recipient Editor's Recognition award with Distinction, 1996, 1997. Mem.: Am. Orthopaedic Soc. for Sports Medicine, Soc. of Skeletal Radiology, Radiological Soc. of N.Am., Internat. Soc. for Magnetic Resonance in Medicine, AMA, Am. Coll. of Radiology, Am. Acad. of Orthopaedic Surgeons, ACL Study Group, NY Roentgen Soc., Am. Roentgen Ray Soc., Phi Beta Kappa, Alpha Omega Alpha. Office: Hosp for Spl Surgery 535 E 70th St New York NY 10021-4872 Office Phone: 212-606-1023. Business E-Mail: potterh@hss.edu.

POTTER, J. STEWART, property manager; b. Ft. Worth, July 8, 1943; s. Gerald Robert Potter and Marion June (Mustain) Tombler; m. Dianne Eileen Roberb, Dec. 31, 1970 (div. Aug. 1983); 1 child, Christopher Stewart; m. Deborah Ann Blevins, Oct. 20, 1991. AA, San Diego Mesa Coll., 1967. Cert. apt. mgr., apt. property supr., housing administr. Sales mgr. Sta. KJLM, La Jolla, Calif., 1964-67; mgr. inflight catering Host Internat., San Diego, 1967-69; lead aircraft refueler Lockheed Co., San Diego, 1969-70; property mgr. Internat. Devel. and Fin Corp., La Jolla, 1970-72; mgr. bus. property BWY Constn. Co., San Diego, 1972-73; mgr. residents Coldwell Banker, San Diego, 1973-74; mgr. Grove Investments, Carlsbad, Calif., 1974-76, Villa Granada, Villa Seville Properties Ltd., Don Cohn, Chula Vista, Calif., 1976-83; gen. mgr. AFL-CIO Bldg. Trades Corp., National City, Calif., 1983—2003; instr. Cert. Apt. Mgmt. San Diego Apt. Assn., 1995-98. Bd. dirs. San Diego County Apt. Assn., 1995-97, San Diego County Policy Panel Youth Access to Alcohol, 1994-2002, San Diego Crime Victims Fund,

1998-2003, Founding Families San Diego Hist. Soc. Mem. Am. Assn. Retired Persons, San Diego County Apt. Assn. (bd. dirs.), La Jolla Monday Night Club (treas. 1984-89), La Jolla Hist. Soc. Roman Catholic. Avocation: golf. Personal E-mail: jspotter@san.rr.com.

POTTER, JACK (JOHN E. POTTER), federal agency administrator; b. NYC, 1955; m. Maureen Potter; 2 children. B in Econs., Fordham U.; M in Mgmt., MIT. With US Postal Svc., 1977—, mgr. of Capital Metro ops., 1998—2000, sr. v.p. labor rels., 1998—99, sr. v.p. ops., 1999—2000, COO, 2000—01, postmaster gen., CEO, 2001—. Recipient Bd. Governors award, US Postal Svc., 1999, Elmo R. Zumwalt Legacy award, Marrow Found., 2003, J. Edward Day award, Assn. Postal Commerce, 2003. Office: US Postal Svc 475 L'Enfant Plz Rm 5021 Washington DC 20260-0004*

POTTER, JAMES EARL, retired international hotel management company executive; b. Utica, N.Y., July 25, 1933; s. Earl Moses and Helen May Potter. BS in Hotel Mgmt. with distinction, Cornell U., 1954, postgrad., 1955-56. Owner, propr. Old Drovers Inn, Dover Plains, NY, 1956-89; various acctg. positions Inter-Continental Hotels Corp., N.Y.C., 1960-62, fin. dir. for Asia and Pacific, 1963-69; v.p. Overseas Nat. Airways Hotels, N.Y.C., 1969-71; sr. v.p. Inter-Continental Hotels Corp., N.Y.C., 1972-89, London, 1990-92. Instr. acctg. Cornell U., Ithaca, N.Y., 1957-59. Author: A Room with a World View, 1996. Trustee Opera Co. Boston, 1978-85; mem. Cornell U. Coun., 1988-91; mem. patron com. Met. Opera, N.Y.C.; bd. dirs., mem. investment com., treas. Santa Fe Opera. Mem.: Culinary Inst. Am. (trustees com. on acad. policy 1980—90), Santa Fe Opera Found. (mem. fin. com. 2002—03, trustee), Cornell Hotel Soc., Santa Fe Opera Club (bd. dirs.), Cornell Club (N.Y.C.), Met. Opera Club (bd. dirs., pres.). Presbyterian. Avocation: opera.

POTTER, JAMES MICHAEL, archaeologist, consultant; b. San Mateo, Calif., Jan. 14, 1965; s. Michael Arthur and Margaret Ann Potter. PhD, Ariz. State U., Tempe, Ariz., 1997. Project dir. SWCA Environ. Consultants, Durango, Colo., 2002—05, prin. investigator Broomfield, Colo., 2005—. Author: (novels) Mothcrazy; contbr. articles to profl. jour. Grantee Dissertation Improvement Grant, NSF, 1996. Democrat-Npl. Avocations: writing, music, travel. Home: 2130 Marion St Denver CO 80205 Office: Swca 295 Interlocken Blvd Broomfield CO 80021 Office Phone: 303-487-1183. Personal E-mail: mothcrazy@yahoo.com. E-mail: jpotter@swca.com.

POTTER, JAMES VINCENT, association executive; b. Walla Walla, Wash., July 17, 1936; s. James Floyd and Dorothy May (Turner) P.; m. Margaret Mae Fogerson, July 4, 1954 (div. Apr. 1970); children: Deborah Ann, David Allan, Rebecca Lynn, Mary Michelle, Randy J., Jonathan James; m. Paula Maureen Brutsman, Feb. 28, 1986; stepchildren: Carolyn June, Catherine Doreen, Paul Clayton, Connie Lynn. BA in Bibl. Studies, Logos Bible Coll., 1989; MA in Theology, Logos Grad. Sch., 1989; PhD, Vision Christian U., 1990, postgrad., 1991-95; PhD (hon.), Inst. Theology and Christian Therapy, 2006. Diplomate Nat. Bd. Addiction Examiners, Am. Coll. Profl. Mental Health Practitioners, Am. Coll. Forensic Counselors; lic. clin. pastoral counselor; cert. temperament therapist, doctoral addictions specialist, doctoral domestic violence specialist, diplomat clin. hypnotherapist; cert. clin. psychopathologist; cert. Christian marraige and family therapist. Lectr., nat. presenter on addiction prevention and treatment, domestic violence, family enrichment, comm. skills, lit. evang. Seventh-day Adventist Ch., Idaho, 1956-60; staff mem. U. of the Nations Family Ministries, Kailua-Kona, Hawaii, 1989; pastor Gospel of Salvation Ministries, 1989-93; dean Coll. Christian Counseling, Vision Christian U., Hilo, Hawaii, 1990-93; pres. Family Care Svcs. Internat., 1990-93; v.p., mem. faculty Vision Christian U., Ramona, Calif., 1991-92, 1998—; adminstr., clinician Hawaii Family Care Ctrs., Hilo, 1989—95; exec. dir. Agape Family Svcs., Inc., Alliance Recovery Svcs., 1995—2003, Agape Family Svcs. Family Skills Inst.; dir. Jubilee Enterprises, 2003—. Vice chmn. Teen Challenge of Hawaii, 1991-93, govtl. apptd. mem. Hawaii Area Commn. on Mental Health and Substance Abuse, 1991-94; pres. Profl. Assn. Christian Therapists, 1989-94, Internat. Christian Counselors Assn., 1988—, Am. Assn. Christian Therapists, 2003—, Calif. Bd. Addiction Examiners, 2000-03; nat. presenter comm. skills, conflict resolution, anger management, marriage enrichment, domestic violence and addictions prevention and treatment. Author: Soul Care, 1989, Untwisting Twisted Temperaments, 1991, (book and curriculum), Save Our Families, Pulling Down Strongholds, 1998, Breaking Free, 1998, Discovering Our True Selves, 1999, Mastery Over Anger, 2000, Assertiveness, Individuation and Autonomy, formerly Assertiveness & Self-Ownership, 2000, Conquering Codependencies, formerly Codependency and Self-Identity, 2000, Arrested Development & Dual Personalities, 2000, Healing Inner-Child Wounds, 2000, Toxic Shame and the Journey Out, 2002, Growing Beyond Our Genetics, Adolescence and Beyond, Relapse Prevention and Rage, 2002, Adolescence and Beyond: Growing Beyond Our Genetics, 2003, Counseling Addicts & Offenders, 2003, Bonding vs. Bondage: Marriage, Intimacy & Oneness, 2005; co-author: Family Care Center Manual, 1991, Christian Character Alignment, 1991, A Reasonable Response: Guide for Legal/Judicial Response to Domestic Violence Incidents, 2005; editor newsletter Gem-State Surveyor, 1976. Dem. nominee Idaho State Legis., House Rep., Boise, 1976, 78; vice chmn. Idaho Tech. Adv. Coun., Boise, 1976-83; pres. Idaho Assn. Land Surveyors, Boise, 1976-77; chmn. Western Fedn. Profl. Land Surveyors, 12 western states, 1979-80; nat. dir. Am. Congress Surveying Mapping, Washington, 1981-83; gov. Nat. Soc. Profl. Land Surveyors; state del. Mont./Hawaii State Rep. Conv., Turtle Bay, 1988. With USN, 1953. Am. Congress Surveying Mapping fellow, Washington, 1980. Fellow: Nat. Assn. Forensic Counselors (diplomate, cert. ednl. provider Vision Internat. U.); mem.: Family Skills Inst., World Assn. Online Educators, Am. Assn. Family Counselors, Am. Coll. Cert. Forensic Counselors (bd. govs.), Am. Assn. Christian Therapists, Christian Assn. Psychol. Studies, Am. Assn. Christian Counselors, Nat. Christian Counselors Assn. (bd. dirs. 1988), Nat. Assn. Family Counselors, Nat. Bd. Cert. Hypnotherapists, Nat. Bd. Addiction Examiners. Office: PO Box 994114 Redding CA 96099 Office Phone: 530-365-1951. Business E-Mail: dr.potter@jubileeenterprises.com. Sin, which separated man from God, is the "distortion" from all that which God intended man to be. Sin is "missing the mark" of being a fully realized child of God (Romans 8:18 27). Jesus Christ "became sin" (2 Corinthians 5:21), assuming in His flesh the distortion of humanity, that we might in Him have "the right to become restored children of God." (John 1:12). Christian ministries are called to minister this healing of personhood to a sin sick world. (Isaiah 61: 1,2). The "new-birth" experience enables an individual to reclaim his/her heritage as a child of God, and to begin to "grow-up" in the wisdom and stature thereof. A process that the entire universe-animate and inanimate is waiting for with eager anticipation (Romans 8:18-27).

POTTER, JANE FRANCES, physician; m. Dan Schafer; children: Ned Schafer, Nick Schafer. BS in Chemistry, Creighton U., 1973; MD, Creighton U. Sch. Medicine, Omaha, 1973—77. Chief, geriat. sect. U. Nebr. Med. Ctr. Omaha, 1982—, dir. geriatric fellowship program, 1982—, prof., 1997—, chair, Neumann M. & Mildred E. Harris geriatric prof., 2000—. Ad hoc reviewer NIH, Washington, 1995; mem. test com. Am. Bd. Internal Medicine, Phlla., 1998—2004; reviewer, geriatric academic career awards Dept. of Health and Human Svcs., Washington, 2003—04. Editor: (book) Geriatrics at Your Fingertips; contbr. chapters to books, articles to profl. jours. Pub. edn. spkr. U. Nebr. Med. Ctr., Omaha, 1982—2004. Lcdr U.S. Pub. Health Svc. 1980—82, Washington, D.C. Fellow, NIH, 1980—82. Fellow: Gerontol. Soc. Am.; mem.: Am. Geriat. Soc. (chair, pub. policy com. 1988, bd. dirs. 2000—, exec. com. 2004—, pres. elect 2005, pres. 2006—). Office: Univ Nebr Med Ctr 981320 Nebr Med Ctr Omaha NE 68198-1320 Office Phone: 402-559-7595.

POTTER, JOHN FRANCIS, oncologist, surgeon; b. NYC, July 26, 1925; s. John Albert and Isabelle Cecelia (Sullivan) P.; m. Tanya Agnes Kristof, Nov. 19, 1955; children: Tanya Jean, Miriam Isabelle, John Mark. MD, Georgetown Med. Sch., 1949. Intern Grasslands Hosp., Valhalla, NY, 1949-50, resident in surgery, 1949-50, Georgetown U. Hosp., Washington, 1953-56; sr. investigator Nat. Cancer Inst., Bethesda, Md., 1957-60; chief divsn. surg. oncology Georgetown Med. Ctr., Washington, 1960-85; instr, asst.prof., then assoc. prof. surgery Georgetown U. Sch. Medicine, 1957-64, prof., 1969—2000; dir. Vincent T. Lombardi Cancer Rsch. Ctr., Washington, 1967-87, U.S. Mil. Cancer Inst., Bethesda, Md., 2000—. Mem. U.S. Mil. Health Adv. Com.; presdl. apptd. mem. bd. regents Uniformed Svcs. U. of the Health Scis., 1999. Hon. prof. Universidad Cayetano Heredia, Lima, Peru, 1980. Lt. (j.g.) USNR, 1951-53. Recipient Pres.'s medal Georgetown U., 1991. Mem. Soc. Surg. Oncology (rep. adv. bd.), ACS, Assn. Am. Cancer Insts. (v.p. 1985-86, pres. 1986-87, bd. dirs. 1982, chmn. bd. dirs. 1987-88), So. Surg. Assn., Peruvian Cancer Soc. (hon.). Office: US Mil Cancer Inst Walter Reed Army Med Ctr Bldg # A109 6900 Georgia Ave NW Washington DC 20307 E-mail: john.potter.1@na.amedd.army.mil.

**POTTER, JOHN LEITH,** retired mechanical and aerospace engineer, retired educator, consultant; b. Metz, Mo., Feb. 5, 1923; s. Jay Francis Lee and Pearl Delores (Leeth) P.; m. Dorothy Jean Williams, Dec. 15, 1957; children: Stephen, Anne, Carol. BS in Aerospace Engring., U. Ala., Tuscaloosa, 1944, MS in Engring., 1949; MS in Engring. Mgmt., Vanderbilt U., 1976, PhD in Mech. Engring., 1974. Engr., educator various indsl., ednl. and govt. orgns., 1944-52; chief, flight and aerodyns. lab. Redstone Arsenal, Ala., 1952-56; mgr., div. chief, dep. tech. dir., sr. staff scientist Sverdrup Tech., Inc., Tullahoma, Tenn., 1956-83; research prof. Vanderbilt U., Nashville, 1983-92, prof. emeritus, 1992—; cons. engr. Nashville, 1983—. Convener NATO-AGARD, U.S. and Eng., 1980-82, mem. working group, 1984-88; mem. adv. com. Internat. Symposium on Rarefied Gasdynamics, 1970—; invited lectr. USSR Acad. Scis., 1967; mem. NRC com. on assessment nat. aeronautical wind tunnel facilities, 1987-88; mem. NASA working groups, 1987—; mem. Engring. Accreditation Commn., 1985-90. Editor: Rarefied Gas Dynamics, 1977. Contbr. articles to profl. publs., chpts. to books Chmn. bd. dirs. Coffee County Hist. Soc., Tenn., 1971-72; bd. dirs. Southeastern Amateur Athletic Union, 1972-73; pres. Tullahoma Swim Club, 1972-73. Recipient Outstanding Fellow award U. Ala. Aerospace Engring. Dept., 1987; elected 150th Anniversary Disting. Engring. Fellow U. Ala. Coll. Engring., 1988; USAF Arnold Engring. Devel. Ctr. fellow, 1993. Fellow AIAA (assoc. editor jour. 1970-73, publs. mem. 1973-78, assoc. editor Progress in Astronautics and Aeronautics 1981-85, Gen. H.H. Arnold award Tenn. chpt. 1964); mem. U. Ala. Capstone Engring. Soc. (regional bd. dirs. 1972-77), Sigma Xi, Tau Beta Pi, Theta Tau, Pi Tau Sigma, Sigma Gamma Tau. Home: 400 University Park Dr Apt 394 Birmingham AL 35209

**POTTER, LORRAINE K.,** career military officer; m. Robert Saunders. BS, Keuka Coll.; MDiv, Colgate Rochester Div. Sch. Former pastor, N.Y.; clin. pastoral educator Yale-New Haven Med. Ctr.; commd. 2d lt. USAF, 1971, advanced through ranks to maj., 2001; various assignments to command chaplain Hdqtrs. Air Edn./Tng. Command, Randolph AFB, Tex., 1998-99; dep. chief of Chaplain Svc. Hdqtrs. USAF, Bolling AFB, D.C., 1999—. At-large mem. Am. Bapt. Chs. Gen. Bd.; active Ministers Coun. for Chaplains and Pastoral Counselors. Office: Chief Chaplain HQ USAF/Bolling AFB 112 Luke Ave SW Washington DC 20332-5113

**POTTER, MICHAEL J.,** retail stores executive; b. Oreg., 1960; BS, U. Oreg., 1983; MBA, Capital U., Ohio. CFO, sr. v.p. Consolidated Stores Corp. (now Big Lots), Columbus, Ohio, 1991—2000; pres., CEO Big Lots, Columbus, Ohio, 2000—. Office: Big Lots 300 Phillipi Rd Columbus OH 43228-5311

**POTTER, MYRTLE S.,** research and development company executive; BA, U. Chgo. Various sales, marketing, and bus. positions Merck and Co., v.p. N.E. Region Bus. Group, 1993—96; v.p. strategy and econ. US Pharmaceuticals Group Bristol-Myers Squibb, 1996—97, group v.p. Worldwide Medicine Group, 1997—98, sr. v.p. sales, US Cardiovascular/Metabolics, 1998, pres. US Cardiovascular/Metabolics, 1998—2000; exec. v.p. Genetech, Inc., South San Francisco, 2000—01, exec. v.p. comml. ops., COO, 2001, president, commercial ops., co-chmn., product portfolio com., cons., 2004—. Bd. dirs. Calif. Healthcare Inst., 2001—, Amazon.com, 2004—. Named Top 50 Most Powerful Women In Business, Fortune, 2003, Most Powerful Black Executives in America, 15 Young Global Business Influentials, Time, Woman of Yr., Healthcare Bus. Women's Assn., 2000; named one of 50 Women to Watch, Wall St. Jour., 2005; recipient National Woman of Distinction Award, Girl Scouts of the USA, 2004. One of the architects of the Astra/Merck joint venture and led the work that set Prilosec on pace to be one of the biggest pharmaceutical products in the world; Won the Merck Chairman's Award for work on the Astra/Merck joint venture. Office: Genetech Inc 1 DNA Way South San Francisco CA 94080*

**POTTER, NICHOLAS F.,** lawyer; b. 1963; AB magna cum laude, Harvard U., 1985, JD, 1988. Bar: NY 1989. Counsel Skadden, Arps, Slate, Meagher & Flom LLP, NYC, London; mem. Debevoise & Plimpton LLP, NYC, 1998—, ptnr., co-head Insurance Industry Group, co-chair Pro Bono Com., mem. Mergers & Acquisitions Practice Group and Securities Practice Group. Mem.: ABA, Assn. Bar City NY. Office: Debevoise & Plimpton LLP 919 Third Ave New York NY 10022 Office Phone: 212-909-6459. E-mail: nfpotter@debevoise.com.

**POTTER, POLYXENI,** writer, editor; naturalized, US; d. Aristodemos and Alexandra; m. Morris E. Potter, Sept. 25, 1971; children: Alexia Jordan, Elliott Eugene. MA in Am. Studies, Purdue U., Lafayette, Ind., 1971. ESL instr. Ga. State U., Atlanta, 1977—87; bd. mem. Hellenic studies program; writer, editor Nat. Ctr. Infectious Diseases, Atlanta, 1987—89, chief pubs. activities, 1989—95; sr. mng. editor Ctrs. Disease Control and Prevention, Atlanta, 1995—. Author (founding mng. editor): Emerging Infectious Diseases Jour. (Lifetime Achievement Excellence in Health Comm. award, 2004). Tchr. modern greek lang. classes Annunciation Sch. Greek Orthodox Cathedral, Atlanta, 2001—03. Recipient Outstanding Leadership award, Am. Med. Writers Assn., 1995, Excellence in Health Comms. Lifetime Achievement award, 2004. Mem.: Am. Med. Writers Assn., Coun. Sci. Editors (mem. editl. bd. jour. 2004—06, sci. editor jour. 2004—06). Avocations: drawing, reading, gardening, cooking, travel. Office: Centers for Disease Control and Preventi 1600 Clifton Rd Atlanta GA 30333 Office Phone: 404-639-0290. Office Fax: 404-639-1954. Business E-Mail: ppotter@cdc.gov.

**POTTER, ROBERT DANIEL,** federal judge; b. Wilmington, NC, Apr. 4, 1923; s. Elisha Lindsey and Emma Louise (McLean) P.; m. Mary Catherine Neilson, Feb. 13, 1954; children: Robert Daniel Jr., Mary Louise, Catherine Ann. AB in Chemistry, Duke U., 1947, LLB, 1950; LLD (hon.), Sacred Heart Coll., Belmont, N.C., 1982. Bar: NC 1951. Pvt. practice law, Charlotte, NC, 1951-81; dist. judge US Dist. Ct. (we. dist.) NC, 1981—2001, chief judge, 1984-91, now sr. judge, 1991—. Commr. Mecklenburg County, Charlotte, 1966-68. Served as 2d lt. U.S. Army, 1944-47, ETO. Mem. N.C. Bar Assn., Charlotte City Club. Republican. Roman Catholic. Office Phone: 704-552-7742.

**POTTER, ROBERT JOSEPH,** technical and business executive; b. NYC, Oct. 29, 1932; s Mack and Ida (Bernstein) P.; married; children: Diane Gail, Suzanne Lee, David Craig. BS cum laude, Lafayette Coll., 1954; MA in Physics, U. Rochester, 1957, PhD in Optics, 1960. Cons. ANPA Research Inst., AEC Brookhaven Nat. Lab., RCA Labs., U.S. Naval Research Labs., 1952-60; mgr. optical physics and optical pattern recognition IBM Thomas J. Watson Research Center, Yorktown Heights, NY, 1960-65; assoc. dir. Applied Research Lab., Xerox Corp., Rochester, NY, 1965-67; v.p. advanced engring. Xerox Corp., 1967-68, v.p. devel. and engring., 1968-69, v.p. gen. mgr. Spl. Products and Systems divsn. Stamford, Conn., Pasadena, Calif., 1969-71, v.p. info. tech. group Rochester, 1971-73, Dallas, 1973-75, pres. Office Sys. divsn., 1975-78; sr. v.p. chief tech. officer Internat. Harvester Co., Chgo., 1978-82; group v.p. integrated office sys. Nortel Networks, Richardson, Tex., 1984—87; pres., CEO Datapoint Corp., San Antonio, 1987—90; R.J. Potter Co., Dallas, 1990—; bd. govs. various indsl. chmn. IIT Rsch. Inst., 1999—2002; chmn. Tatum CIO Ptnrs., LLP, 2000—02; adv. dir. Am. Nat. Bank, 2002—05; mem. rsch. adv. bd. U. Tex., Dallas; bd. dirs. Zebra Techs., Cree, Inc., Molex Inc., Bradshaw Group, Speed FC. Office. Contbr. articles to profl. jours. Life trustee

Ill. Inst. Tech.; trustee Alliance Higher Edn. Recipient IBM Outstanding Tech. Contbn. award, 1964, Disting. Achievement award Soc. Mfg. Engrs., 1981; Kroner scholar Lafayette Coll., 1954; Disting. Rochester scholar U. Rochester, 1995. Fellow Optical Soc. Am., Am. Phys. Soc.; mem. Phi Beta Kappa, Sigma Xi. Office: R J Potter Co 5215 N O Connor Blvd Ste 1110 Irving TX 75039-3739   Office   Phone:   972-869-8270.   Business   E-Mail: RJPotter@RJPotter.com.

**POTTER, SUSAN KUNIHOLM,** bank executive; BA, Cornell U., 1988; MBA, U. Pa. Sr. mgr. Sotheby's, 1992—94; bus. analyst McKinsey & Co., Cleve., 1994—98, engagement mgr. 1998—2002; exec. v.p. product mgmt. consumer banking group KeyCorp, Cleve., 2002—04, exec. v.p. retail bus. devel., 2004—. Named One of 25 Women to Watch, U.S. Banker Mag., 2003. Office: KeyCorp 127 Public Square Cleveland OH 44114-1306

**POTTER, TOM,** mayor; b. 1940; m. Karin Hansen; 4 children. BA, Univ. Portland. Lt. Portland Police Dept., Portland, Oreg.; mayor City of Portland. With Portland Police Sunshine Div.; chmn. Shepherd Legal Scholarship Fund Com. Driver Meals on Wheels-Portland. Mem.: Shepherd Legal Scholarship Fund Com., Parents of Friends, Lesbians & Gays. Office: Office of the Mayor Ste 340 1221 SW 4th Ave Portland OR 97204 Office Phone: 503-823-4120. Office Fax: 503-823-3588.*

**POTTER, WILLIAM BARTLETT,** diversified financial services company executive; b. Washington, Jan. 4, 1938; s. George Holland and Virginia (Bartlett) P.; m. Simone Robert, June 6, 1964; children: Eva Simone, William Bartlett. AB, Princeton U., 1960; MBA, Emory U., 1962. With Merc.-Safe Deposit & Trust Co., Balt., 1962—, asst. sec., asst. treas., 1964-66, asst. v.p., 1966-68, v.p. 1968-69, v.p., 1969-76, exec. v.p., 1976, Preston Trucking Co., 1976-77, pres., 1977-86; chmn., pres. Preston Trucking, 1986-92; Preston Corp., 1986-93, chmn., 1994—. Home: 41880 RCR 44 Steamboat Springs CO 80487 Personal E-mail: will@wbpotter.family.com.

**POTTER, WILLIAM GRAY, JR.,** library director; b. Duluth, Minn., Feb. 18, 1950; s. William Gray and Kathryn Martha (Scheuer) P.; m. Marsha Ann Munie, Sept. 23, 1982. BA, So. Ill. U., Edwardsville, 1973; MLS, MA, U. Ill., 1975, PhD, 1984; PhD (hon.), So. Ill. U., Edwardsville, 2001. Libr. U. Wis.-Whitewater, 1975-78; asst. dir. gen. svcs. U. Ill.-Urbana, 1978-85; assoc. dean librs. for tech. svcs., automation and systems Ariz. State U., Tempe, 1985-89; libr. coll. & rsch. librs. U. Ga., Athens, 2002, now univ. libr., assoc. provost. Editor: Serials Automation, 1980, Libr. Trends, 1981, Info. Tech. and Librs., 1984-89; mem. editl. bd. Multi-Media Rev., 1989-92, OCLC Micro., 1990-93, Libr. Hi-Tech., 1992—, Coll. and Rsch. Libr., 1996-2002. Contbr. articles to profl. jours. Bd. dirs. Richard B. Russell Found., 1989—, sec., 1990—, Southeastern Libr. Network, 2001—; trustee OCLC, 1994-2000; mem. adv. bd. Wiley Libr., 2000-. Recipient Disting. Alumnus of Yr. award So. Ill. U., Edwardsville, 2001. Mem. ALA (Hugh Atkinson Meml. award 1997, Blackwell scholarship award 1998, LITA/Gaylord award 2000), Libr. and Info. Tech. Assn. (pres. 1987-88), OCLC Users Coun. (del. 1990-94, pres. 1991-92), IBM (info. steering com. 1994-95, higher edn. adv. coun. 1995-96), Assn. Rsch. Librs. (bd. dirs. 1996-99), Ga. Libr. Assn. (mem. exec. com. 1994-2000, Nix-Jones award 1998), Beta Phi Mu. Home: 285 Blue Heron Dr Athens GA 30605-4961 Office: U Ga Librs U Ga Athens GA 30602-1641 Office Phone: 706-542-0621. Office Fax: 706-542-4144. E-mail: wpotter@uga.edu.

**POTTLE, STEVEN L.,** lawyer; b. Anchorage, Alaska, Nov. 3, 1960; Student, Univ. of London, Japanese Bus. and Soc. Program, Tokyo; BBA, Univ. Wash., 1983; JD, Vanderbilt Univ., 1987. CPA; bar: Ga. 1987. Acct. Ernst & Whinney; ptnr., co-chmn., tech. group, chmn., corp. health care group Alston & Bird LLP, Atlanta. Office: Alston & Bird LLP One Atlantic Ctr 1201 W Peachtree St NW Atlanta GA 30309-3424 Office Phone: 404-881-7278. Office Fax: 404-881-7777. Business E-Mail: spottle@alston.com.

**POTTORFF, JO ANN,** state legislator; b. Wichita, Kans., Mar. 7, 1936; d. John Edward McCluggage and Helen Elizabeth (Alexander) Ryan; m. Gary Nial Pottorff; children: Michael Lee, Gregory Nial. BA, Kansas State U., 1957; MA, St. Louis U., 1969. Elem. tchr. Pub. Sch., Keats and St. George, 1957-59; cons., elem. specialist Mid Continent Regional Edn. Lab., Kansas City, Mo., 1971-73; cons. Poindexter Assocs., Wichita, 1975; campaign mgr. Garner Shriver Congl. Camp, Wichita, 1976; interim dir. Wichita Area Rape Ctr., 1977; conf. coord. Biomedical Synergistics Inst., Wichita, 1977-79; real estate sales asst. Chester Kappelman Group, Wichita, 1979-98, J.P. Weigard & Sons, Wichita, 1998—; state rep. State of Kans., Topeka, 1985—. Mem. exec. com. Nat. Conf. State Legis. Com. mem. sch. bd. Wichita Pub. Schs., 1977-85; bd. dirs. Edn. Consol. and Improvement Act Adv. com., Kans. Found. for the Handicapped; mem. Children and Youth Adv. com. (bd. dirs.); active Leadership Kans.; chairperson women's network Nat. Conf., State Legislators; mem. Wichita Children's Home Bd.; vice chmn. Nat. Assessment Governing Bd.; chair edn. com. assembly on state issues Nat. Conf. State legislators. Recipient Disting. Svc. award Kans. Assn. Sch. Bds., 1983, Outstanding Svc. to Sch. Children of Nation award Coun. Urban Bds., 1984, awards Gov.'s Conf. for Prevention of Child Abuse and Neglect, Kans. Assn. Reading. Mem. Leadership Am. Alumnae (bd. dirs., sec) Found. for Agr. in Classroom (bd. dirs.), Jr. League, Vet. Aux. (pres.), Bd. Nat. State Art Agys., Rotary, Ky. Assn. Rehab. Facilities (Ann. award), Nat. Order Women in Legislature (past bd. dirs.), Nat. Conf. State Legislatures (chmn. edn. assembly state issues, exec. com.), Rotary, Chi Omega (pres.). Avocations: politics, travel. Office: Weigard 6530 E 13th St N Wichita KS 67206 1217

**POTTRUCK, DAVID STEVEN,** brokerage house executive; b. 1948; m. Emily Pottruck; 2 children. BA, U. Pa., 1970, MBA with honors, 1972. Now pres., CEO U.S. Govt., 1972-74; with Arthur Young & Co., 1974-76, sr. cons.; with Citibank N.Am., 1976-81, v.p.; with Shearson/Am. Express, 1981-84, sr. v.p. consumer mktg. and advt.; with Charles Schwab & Co., San Francisco, 1984—; exec. v.p. mktg., br. adminstr. Charles Schwab and Co., Inc.; pres. Charles Schwab & Co., 1992—94; pres., COO The Charles Schwab Corp., 1994—98, pres., co-CEO, 1998—2003, pres., CEO, 2003—04. Apptd. commr. by Congress The Advisory Commn. on Internet Commerce; bd. dirs. Intel Corp., US Trust Co., N.A., DoveBid, Inc. Co-author: Clicks and Mortar: Passion Driven Growth in an Internet Driven World. Bd. dirs. US Ski and Snowboard Team Found.; trustee U. Penn. Named Exec. of the Year, San Francisco Bus. Times, CEO of the Year, Morningstar; named one of Top 15 CEOs, Worth mag.; recipient Torch of Liberty award, Anti-Defamation League, 2000.

**POTTS, ANNIE,** actress; b. Nashville, Oct. 28, 1952; m. Steven Hartley, 1973 (div. 1978); m. B. Scott Senechal, 1980 (div. 1989); 1 child, Clay Senechal; m. James Hayman, Sept. 2, 1990; children: Doc, Harry. Student, Calif. Inst. of Arts; BFA, Stephens Coll. Appeared in films including Corvette Summer, 1978, King of the Gypsies, 1978, Heartaches, 1982, Bayou Romance, 1982, Crime of Passion, 1984, Ghostbusters, 1984, Stick, 1985, Pretty in Pink, 1986, Jumpin' Jack Flash, 1986, Pass the Ammo, 1988, Who's Harry Crumb?, 1989, Ghostbusters II, 1989, Texasville, 1990, Breaking the Rules, 1992, Elvis Has Left the Building, 2004; (voice) Toy Story 1995, Toy Story II, 1999, Hercules, 1998; plays include Richard III, Charley's Aunt, Cymbeline; TV films Black Market Baby, 1977, Ladies in Waiting, 1979, Flatbed Annie & Sweetiepei: Lady Truckers, 1979, Something So Right, 1982, Cowboy, 1983, Why Me?, 1984, It Came Upon the Midnight Clear, 1984, My Dissident Mom, 1987, Her Deadly Rival, 1995, Defending Our Kids: The Julie Posey Story, 2003, Stuck in the Middle with You, 2003; TV series include Designing Women, 1986-1993, Love and War, 1993-95 (Emmy nomination, Lead Actress - Comedy Series, 1994), Dangerous Minds, 1996, Over the Top, 1997(also prodr.), Any Day Now, 1998-2002; guest appearances Family, 1978, Goodtime Girls, 1980, Remington Steele, 1983, The Twilight Zone, 1985, Magnum P.I., 1986, Huff, 2004, Joan of Arcadia, 2004,

2005, Close to Home, 2005, Julie Reno, Bounty Hunter, 2006, Law & Order: Special Victims Unit, 2005, 2006; appeared in production Diva, Pasadena Playhouse, 2006. Spokesperson Women for the Arthritis Found.; mem. aux. bd. MADD.*

**POTTS, ANTHONY VINCENT,** optometrist, orthokeratologist; b. Detroit, Aug. 10, 1945; m. Susan Claire, July 1, 1967; 1 child, Anthony Christian. Student, Henry Ford Community Coll., 1964—65, Eastern Mich. U., 1965—66; OD, So. Coll. Optometry, 1970; MS in Health Svcs. Mgmt., LaSalle U., 1995. Practice orthokeratology and contact lenses, Troy, Mich., 1975—; head of optometry Nat. Naval Med. Ctr., Bethesda, Md. Adj. prof. optometry So.Calif. Coll. Optometry, Pa. Coll. Optometry; lectr., author orthokeratology, contact lenses and astigmatism; head optometry Nat. Naval Med. Ctr. Bethesda Md. Comdr. MSC, USN, 1992—. Fellow Internat. Orthokeratology Soc. (membership chmn. 1976-83, bd. dirs. local chpt. 1976-83, chmn. Internat. Eye Rsch. Found. sect 1981-83, bd. dirs. nat. chpt. 1985—, adminstrv. dir. nat. chpt. 1985—, chmn. nat. chpt. 1987-1992), Fellow Am. Acad. Optometry, Am. Optometric Assn.; mem. Am. Assn. Healthcare Execs., Armed Forces Optometric Soc., Nat. Eye Rsch. Found., Naval Order Am., Assn. of Mil. Surgeons of U.S., Naval Hosp. Am. Care Ctr., Am. Coll. Healthcare Execs. Roman Catholic. Office: Med Sq Troy 1575 W Big Beaver Rd Ste 11C Troy MI 48084-3525

**POTTS, BARBARA JOYCE,** retired historic site director; b. L.A., Feb. 18, 1932; d. Theodore Thomas and Helen Mae (Kelley) Elledge; m. Donald A. Potts, Dec. 27, 1953; children: Tedd, Douglas, Dwight, Laura. AA, Graceland Coll., 1951; grad., Radiol. Tech. Sch., 1953; grad. program for sr. execs. in state and local govt., Harvard U., 1989. Radiol. technician Independence (Mo.) Sanitarium and Hosp., 1953, 58-59, Mercy Hosp., Balt., 1954-55; city coun. mem.-at-large City of Independence, 1978-82, mayor, 1982-90; exec. dir. Jackson County Hist. Soc., 1991-97; ret., 1997. Chmn. Mid-Am. Regional Coun., Kansas City, Mo., 1984-85; bd. dirs. Mo. Mcpl. League, Jefferson City, 1982-90, v.p., 1986-87, pres., 1987, 88; chmn. Mo. Commn. on Local Govt. Cooperation, 1985-90; bd. dirs., Mercantile Bank, 1989-98, chair ind. adv. bd., 1997-99; bd. dirs. Women's Found. of Greater Kansas City, 1997-2003; mem. chancellor's adv. bd. UMKC Women's Ctr., 1996-; mem. adv. bd. Comprehensive Mental Health Svcs., 1997-. Author: Independence, 1985. Mem. Mo. Gov.'s Conf. Edn., 1976, Independence Charter Rev. Bd., 1977; bd. dirs. Hope House Shelter Abused Women, Independence, 1982—, Vis. Nurses Assn., 1990-93, Truman Heartland Cmty. Found., 1990-2003, bd. chmn., 1997-99, Mid-Continent coun. U.S. Girl Scouts, 1991-95, Harry S. Truman Libr. Inst., 1995—, Truman Med. Ctr., 2001—, Coun. on Philanthropy, 2001-03, Leadership 20/20 Vision; adv. bd. Ewing M. Kauffman Fund, 2002-06, Greater Kansas City Cmty. Found., 1999-02, Salvation Army, 1999—; pres. Child Placement Svcs., Independence, 1972-89, Greater Kansas City region NCCJ, 1990-2004; bd. vis. UMKC Sch. Medicine, 2002—; trustee Independence Regional Health Ctr., 1982-90, 94-2001, Park Coll., 1989-99, 2004—, chmn. bd. trustees, 1995-99. Eye Found. Kansas City, 1997-99; mem. Nat. Women's Polit. Caucus, 1978—; mem. adv. bd. Greater Mo. Focus on Leadership, mem. steering com., 1989—. Recipient George Lehr Meml. award for cmty. svc., 1989, Woman of Achievement award Mid-Continent coun. Girl Scouts U.S.A., 1983, 75th Anniversary Women of Achievement award Mid-Continent coun. Girl Scouts, 1987, Jane Addams award Hope House, 1984, Cmty. Leadership award Comprehensive Mental Health Svcs., Inc., 1984, 90, Graceland Coll. Alumni Disting. Svc. award 1991, Disting. Citizen award Independence C. of C., 1993, Outstanding Cmty. Svc. award Jackson County Inter-Agy. Coun., 1994, Outstanding Cmty. Svc. award Cmty. Svcs. League, 1996, Jackson County Humanitarian of Yr. award, 1997, Disting. Citizen award, 1997, Paul Harris award Ind. Rotary Club, 1997, Outstanding Svc. award City of Independence Human Rels. Commn., 1999, Greater Kans. City Coun. Philanthropy Vol. of Yr. award, 2000; named Friend of Edn. Indpendence NEA, 1990. Mem.: LWV (Cmty. Svc. award 1990), Jackson County Hist. Soc., Nat. Trust for Hist. Preservation. Mem. Lds Ch. Home: 18508 E 30th Ter S Independence MO 64057-1904

**POTTS, CHARLES AARON,** management executive, writer, publishing executive; b. Idaho Falls, Aug. 28, 1943; s. Verl S. and Sarah (Gray) Potts; m. Judith Samimi, 1977 (div. 1986); children: Emily Karen, Natalie Larise; m. Ann Weatherill, June 19, 1988. BA in English, Idaho State U., 1965. Lic. real estate broker Wash. Pres. Walla Walla Rental Properties, 1984—86; dir. Washington Apt. Assocs., 1984—88; owner Palouse Mgmt., Inc., Walla Walla, Wash., 1979—. Founder, dir. Litmus Inc., 1967—77; founding editor COSMEP, Berkeley, Calif., 1968; host poetry radio program Oasis NPR-KUER, Salt Lake City, 1976—77; N.W. rep. Chinese Computer Comm., Inc., Lansing, Mich., 1988—94; pres. Tsunami Inc.; founder Temple Bookstore, 2002, Temple Sch. Poetry, 2002. Author: Blues from Thurston County, 1966, Burning Snake, 1967, The Litmus Papers, 1969, Little Lord Shiva, 1969, Blue Up the Nile, 1972, Waiting in Blood, 1973, The Trancernigracion of Menzu, 1973, The Golden Calf, 1975, Charlie Kiot, 1976, The Opium Must Go Thru, 1976, Valga Krusa, 1977, Rocky Mountain Man, 1978, A Rite to the Body, 1989, The Dictatorship of the Environment, 1991, Loading Las Vegas, 1991, How the South Finally Won the Civil War, 1995, 100 Years in Idaho, 1996, Lost River Mountain, 1999, Facist Haikus, 1999, Little Lord Shiva: The Berkeley Poems, 1968, 1999, Angio Gram, 2000, Nature Lovers, 2000, prophet/profit, 2001, Slash and Burn, 2001, Across the Pacific, 2002, Lucintite, 2002, Compostrella/Star Field, 2004, Kiot: The selected early poems of Charles Potts, 1963-1977, 2005, The Portable Potts, 2005, Greatest Hits, 2005; editor: Pacific Northwestern Spiritual Poetry, 1998, The Temple, 1997—2002, Wallawalla Poetry Party, 1990—2003; columnist (with Kyushu Gleaner): Japan's Political Choices, 1995—. Rep. to exec. com. 5th Congl. Dist., Wash. State Dems., 1993—95. Recipient Profl. Achievement award, Idaho State U., 1994. Mem.: Soc. Neurolinguistic Programming (master practitioner), Chinese Lang. Computer Soc., Pacific N.W. Booksellers Assn., Toastmasters, Fukuoka Internat. Forum, Italian Heritage Assn. (ice cream chair 1990, award 1993). Avocations: tennis, raspberries. Office: Palouse Mgmt Inc 129 E Alder St PO Box 1773 Walla Walla WA 99362-1962 Office Phone: 509-524-0813. Office Fax: 509-522-0766. Business E-Mail: tsunami@innw.net. E-mail: chas@thetemplebookstore.com.

**POTTS, GERALD NEAL,** manufacturing executive; b. Franklin, N.C., Apr. 10, 1933; s. Joseph Thomas and Virgie (Bryant) Potts; m. Ann Eliza Underwood, Dec. 21, 1956 (div. 1991); children: Catherine, Thomas, Alice. BS, U. N.C., 1954; grad., Advanced Mgmt. Program, Harvard, 1973. With Vulcan Mold & Iron Co., Chgo., 1957-59, sales engr., 1959-62, gen. sales mgr. Latrobe, Pa., 1963-65, v.p. sales, 1965-68; v.p. Vulcan, Inc., Latrobe, 1968-72, exec. v.p., 1972-73, pres., 1973-85, CEO, 1977-85, chmn., 1985-93; group exec. Teledyne Inc., 1985-92; pres. Woodings Verona Tool Works Inc., 1993-97; ret. Trustee Greater Latrobe Cmty. Chest, 1970—87, pres., 1978—79; bd. dirs. Latrobe Area Hosp., chmn., 1985—88; mem. adv. bd. U. Pitts., Greensburg, Pa., 1974—80; trustee Seton Hill Coll., Greensburg, 1974—80. With U.S. Army, 1954—56. Mem.: Duquesne Club (Pa.), Chi Phi. Personal E-mail: jpotts1120@comcast.net.

**POTTS, JEFFREY THOMAS,** biomedical researcher; b. St. John, New Brunswick, Can., Dec. 26, 1958; s. Thomas Edmund and Enid Helen Potts. PhD, U. N.Tex., Ft. Worth, 1993. Fellow Johns Hopkins U. Sch. Medicine, Balt., 1993—95, U. Tex. Health Sci. Dallas, 1995—97, instr., 1997—99, asst. prof., 1999—2000, Wayne State U. Sch. Medicine, Detroit, 2000—01; assoc. prof. U. Mo. Coll. Vet. Medicine, Columbia, 2004—06. Grantee, NIH, 1998—. Mem.: Soc. Neurosci., Am. Physiol. Soc. Home: 7102 Stanwood Dr Columbia MO 65203 Office: Univ Mo 134 Research Park Dr Columbia MO 65211 Office Phone: 573-884-1798. Office Fax: 573-884-4232. Business E-Mail: pottsjt@missouri.edu.

**POTTS, JOHN THOMAS, JR.,** physician, educator; b. Phila., Jan. 19, 1932; married; 3 children. BA, LaSalle Coll, Phila., 1953; MD, U. Pa., Phila., 1957; DSc, LaSalle U. From intern to asst. resident in medicine Mass. Gen. Hosp., Boston, 1957—59; resident Nat. Heart Inst., 1959—60; rsch. fellow in medicine Mass. Gen. Hosp., Boston, 1960—63; sr. research staff Nat. Heart Inst., 1963—66, head sect. polypeptide hormones, 1968—81; from asst. to assoc. prof. medicine Harvard U. Med. Sch., Boston, 1968—75, prof., 1975—; prof. medicine Harvard-MIT Divsn. Health Sci. and Tech., 1978—, Jackson prof. Clin. Medicine, 1981—96, disting. Jackson prof. clin. medicine, 1996—; chief endocrine unit Mass. Gen. Hosp., Boston, 1968—81, physician-in-chief, 1981—96, dir. rsch., 1995—2003. Recipient Andre Lichwitz prize, Endocrine Soc., 1968. Mem.: AAAS, Am. Soc. Bone and Mineral Rsch. (William F. Neumann award 1987), Am. Soc. Clin. Investigation, Assn. Physicians, Endocrine Soc. (pres. 1987, Ernest Oppenheimer award 1968, Fred Konrad Koch award 1991), Inst. Medicine NAS. Office: Mass Gen Hosp Dir Rsch 149 13th St # 1494005 Charlestown MA 02129-2020

**POTTS, KEVIN T.**, retired chemistry professor; b. Sydney, Australia, Oct. 26, 1928; married; children: Mary Ellen, Jeannette, Karen, Susan. BSc, U. Sydney, 1950, MSc, 1951; PhD in Organic Chemistry, Oxford U., Eng., 1954, DSc, 1973. Demonstrator chemistry U. Sydney, 1950, tchg. fellow, 1951; rsch. asst. organic chemistry Oxford U., 1951-54; scientist Med. Rsch. Coun. of Eng., 1954-56; rsch. asst. organic chemistry Harvard U., 1956-58; lectr. Adelaide, 1958-61; assoc. prof. chemistry U. Louisville, 1961-65; assoc. prof. Rensselaer Poly. Inst., 1965-66, prof. chemistry, 1966-94; prof. emeritus Rensselaer Poly Inst., 1994—; chmn. dept. Rensselaer Poly. Inst., 1973-80. Contbr. articles in field organic chemistry to sci. jours. Grantee Nat. Cancer Inst., Nat. Heart Inst., Dept. Energy, NSF, Am. Chem. Soc.-Petroleum Rsch. Fund. Mem. AAAS, Am. Chem. Soc., Brit. Chem. Soc., Royal Soc. Chemistry. Home: 102 Pelican Cv Sneads Ferry NC 28460-9520 Office: Rensselaer Poly Inst Dept Chemistry 110 Eighth Troy NY 12180 E-mail: pottskt@charter.net.

**POTTS, ROBERT LESLIE**, academic administrator; b. Jan. 30, 1944; s. Frank Vines and Helen Ruth (Butler) Potts; m. Irene Elisabeth Johansson, Aug. 22, 1965; children: Julia Anna, Robert Leslie. BA, So. Coll., 1966; JD, U. Ala., 1969; LLM, Harvard U., 1971. Law clk. to chief judge U.S. Dist. Ct. (no. dist.) Ala., 1969—70; rschr. Herrick, Smith, Donald, Farley & Ketchum, Boston, 1970—71; lectr. Boston U., 1971, U. Ala., 1973—75, 1988; ptnr. Potts & Young, Florence, Ala., 1971—84; gen. counsel U. Ala. Sys., 1984—89; pres. U. North Ala., 1990—2004; chancellor ND Univ. Sys., 2004—. Mem. Nat. Adv. Com. on Instnl. Quality and Integrity, 1994—2001; com. on colls. So. Assn. Colls. and Schs., 2001—04; chmn. Nat. ROTC subcom. for Sec. of Army, 1999—2001; adv. com. rules of civil procedure Ala. Supreme Ct., 1973—88; chmn. Ala. Bd. Bar Examiners, 1983—86, Ala. Coun. Coll. and Univ. Pres., 2001—03, Nat. Conf. Bar Examiners, 1994—95. Contbr. numerous articles to profl. jours., edn. and schs. Trustee Ala. State U., 1976—79, Oakwood Coll., 1978—81; pres. Ala. Higher Edn. Loan Corp., 1988—93. Mem.: ABA (ho. of dels. 2001—03), ND State Bd. Career Technical Edn., Western Interstate commn. Higher Edn., Midwestern Higher Edn. Compact (commr.), Am. Assn. State Colls. and Univs. (bd. dirs. 2002—04), Ala. Bar Assn. (pres. young lawyers sect. 1979—80). Office: ND Univ Sys 600 E Blvd Ave Dept 215 Bismarck ND 58505-0230 Office Phone: 701-328-2963. Business E-mail: robert.potts@ndus.nodak.edu.

**POTTS, SANDRA**, library director; m. David Potts, June 26, 1983. Bachelor's degree, Coe Coll., 1969; MEd, Ctrl. Mich. U., 1975; MLS, Wayne State U., 1993. Elem. sch. tchr., Mich., 1970—74; libr. White Pine Libr. Coop., Saginaw, Mich., 1975—95; libr. dir. Northwood U., Midland, Mich., 1995—. Mem.: ALA, Midwest Archives, Mich. Libr. Assn., Alpha Xi Delta. Sentinal Party. Office: Northwood Univ Strosacker Library 4000 Whiting Dr Midland MI 48640

**POTTS, STEPHEN DEADERICK**, lawyer; b. Memphis, Nov. 20, 1930; s. Ramsay Douglas and Anne (Van Dyke) P.; m. Irene Potter, Mar. 14, 1953; children: Lori Potts-Dupre, Stephen Deaderick Jr., Stacy Potts Krogh. AB, Vanderbilt U., 1952, LLB, 1954. Bar: Tenn. 1954, D.C. 1961. Assoc. Farris, Evans & Evans, Nashville, 1957-61; ptnr. Shaw, Pittman, Potts & Trowbridge, Washington, 1961-90; dir. U.S. Office Gov. Ethics, Washington, 1990-2000; chmn. bd. dirs. Ethics Resource Ctr., Washington, 2004—. Mem. Pres.'s Commn. on the Fed. Appt. Process, 1969-70, 1991-92, Pres.'s Coun. on Integrity and Effectivity, 1990-2000. Past pres. Washington Tennis Patrons Found., 1970—72; past. chmn. USTA Olympic com. 1st lt. U.S. Army, 1954—57. Mem. ABA, U.S. Supreme Court. Bar Assn., D.C. Bar Assn., Chevy Chase Club (bd. govs. 1982-86), Met. Club (bd. govs. 2000-04), Alibi Club, U.S. Tennis Assn. (bd. govs. 5 not nat., 1 internat. father/son championships, twice ranked 1st in U.S.). Methodist. Office: Ethics Resource Ctr Ste 400 1747 Pennsylvania Ave Washington DC 20006 Office Phone: 202-872-4762. E-mail: steve@ethics.org.

**POTTS, TIMOTHY F.**, museum director; b. Australia; Dir. media and telecommunications, corp. fin. dept. Lehman Brothers, NYC, London; prof. U. Melbourne; dir. Nat. Gallery of Victoria, Australia, Kimbell Art Mus., Fort Worth, Tex., 1998—. Adj. prof. La Trobe U., Melbourne. Author: (monograph) Mesopotamia and the East: An Archaeological & Historical Study of Foreign Relations 3400-2000 BC, 1995; editor: Kimbell Art Museum: Handbook of the Collection, 2003; co-editor: Culture Through Objects: Ancient Near Eastern Studies in Honour of P. R. S. Moorey, 2003. Office: Kimbell Art Mus 3333 Camp Bowie Blvd Fort Worth TX 76107-2792

**POTVIN, ALFRED RAOUL**, engineering executive; b. 1942; m. Janet Holm, Mar. 20, 1965 BEE, Worcester Poly. Inst., 1964; MSEE, Stanford U., 1965, Engr. in EE, 1967; MS in Bioengring., U. Mich., 1970, MS in Psychology, 1970, PhD in Bioengring., 1971. Registered profl. engr., Tex. Asst. prof. elec. engring. U. Tex., Arlington, 1966—68, assoc. prof. biomed. engring. and elec. engring., 1971—76, prof., 1976—84, chmn. biomed. engring., 1972—84; dir. med. instrumentation sys. rsch. divsn. Eli Lilly & Co., Indpls., 1984—90, dir. tech. assessment and project mgmt., 1990—92, dir. engring., med. devices and diagnostics divsn., 1992—93; prof. elec. engring. Purdue Sch. Engring. and Tech., Ind. U.-Purdue U., Indpls., 1993—96; dean engring. and tech. Ind. U.-Purdue U., Indpls., 1993—95; pres. MEECO, Melbourne, Fla., 1996—. Faculty fellow life scientist, cons. NASA, Houston, 1972-76, NASA and Moffett Field, 1974-76; clin. prof. biophysics U. Tex. Health Sci. Ctr., Dallas, 1967-84; mem. phys. med. device panel FDA, Washington, 1978-84; mem. adv. bd., reviewer Biomed. Engring. NSF, Washington, 1983-89, 92-97; founding dir. Ctr. Advanced Rehab. Engring., 1983-84, mem. adv. bd., 1984-88; mem. adv. bd. Engring. Rsch. Ctrs. NSF, Washington, 1988-92. Biomed. Engr. Worcester Polytech. Inst., Mass., 1987—, Coll. Engrs. Duke U., Durham, N.C., 1987-94, U. Calif., Berkeley, 1989-92, Coll. Engrs. U. Denver, 1990-93, Sch. Engr. and Tech. Ind. U.-Purdue U., Indpls, 1992-93, med. engring. Jet Propulsion Lab., Pasadena, Calif., 1989; chmn. NIH Resource Ctr. Case Western Res. U., Cleve., 1988-96; bd. advisors Sch. of Health and Rehab. Sci., U. Pitts., 1993-97; mem. adv. com. NIH, 1987-92, 93-95; bd. dirs. Biomed. Engring. Alliance for Engring. in Medicine and Biology. Author: (with W.W. Tourtellotte) Quantitative Examination of Neurologic Functions, 1985; editl. bd. IEEE Spectrum, 1987-90, 92-95, Biomed. Sci. and Tech., 1990-93; co-editor spl. issue on biosensors IEEE Trans. on Biomed. Engring., 1986, spl. issue on status and future directions in biomed. engring. Medicine and Biol. Mag., 1989; mem. editl. bd. Biomed. Sci. and Tech., 1990-92; mem. adv. bd. The Biomed. Engring. Handbook, 1995, 2000. Mem. Masthead Property Owners Assn., Indpls., 1984-96, Manasota Key Property Owners Assn., Englewood, Fla., 1985-98. Recipient Life Scientist award NASA, 1974, Hall of Achievement award U. Tex. at Arlington, 2006; spl. fellow NIH, 1968. Fellow: IEEE (gen. chmn. annual conf. 1872, pres. Engring. in Medicine and Biology Soc. 1983, re-elected 1984, chmn. health care engring. com. 1986, editl. bd. spectrum 1987—89, founding mem. steering com. symposium on computer based med. systems 1993—94, co-editor spl. issue Medicine and Biology 1989, editl. bd. spectrum 1992—94, internat. conf. com. 1993—95, Centennial award 1984), Biomed. Engring. Soc. (chmn. edn. and pub. affairs com. 1979—83), Assn. Advancement Med. Instrumentation, Am. Inst. Med. and Biol. Engring. (bd. dirs. 1992—, vice pres. 1993—94). Fellow in Medicine and Biology (Career Achievement award 1993); mem.: Ind. Elec. Mfg. Assn.

(bd. dirs. 1993—96, Svc. to Industry award 1996), Assn. Advancement of Med. Instrumentation, Alliance Engrs. in Medicine and Biology (v.p. nat. affairs 1987—89, pres. 1989—92), Am. Soc. Engring. Edn. (chmn. biomed. engring. divsn. 1979—80), Presdl. Founders Worcester Poly. Inst., Appalachian Long Distance Hikers Assn., Appalachian Trail Club. Avocations: boating, hiking, travel, gourmet dining, skiing. Personal E-mail: arpotvin@msn.com.

**POTVIN, PIERRE**, physiologist, educator; b. Quebec City, Que., Can., Jan. 5, 1932; s. Rosario and Eva (Montreuil) P.; m. Louise Dube, Aug. 31, 1963; children: Aline, Bernard. BA, Laval U., 1950, MD, 1955; PhD, U. Toronto, 1962. Asst. prof. Faculty of Medicine Laval U., Quebec City, 1956-63, assoc. prof., 1963-68, prof., 1968-98, prof. emeritus, 1998—, vice dean exec., 1977-86, dean, 1986-94. V.p. Internat. Conf. of Deans of French-Speaking Faculties of Medicine, 1990-96, pres. evaluation coun., 1994—; hon. prof. Norman Bethune U. Med. Sci., Changchun, China, 1992. Assoc. editor Modern Medicine Can., 1958-61, Laval Med., 1962-70. Fellow Royal Coll. Physicians and Surgeons Can. (hon.), Ordre Nat. du Lion (officer), Senegal, Sahamatrei Order, Cambodia, Order Can., Ordre Nat. des Palmes académiques, Légion d'Honneur, France. Roman Catholic. Avocation: painting. Office: Laval U Faculty of Medicine Dept Anat & Physiology Quebec City PQ Canada G1K 7P4 Business E-Mail: pierre.potvin@phs.ulaval.ca.

**POUCHARD, LINE CATHERINE**, research scientist, educator; b. Caudebec-les-Elbeuf, Normandy, France, Aug. 5, 1958; arrived in U.S., 1983; d. Jean-Claude Louis Arsene and Alice Maria Pouchard; m. Erich Strohmaier, June 27, 1997 (div. July 22, 2001); m. William A. Thomas, Sept. 16, 2005. Lic., U. Haute-Normandie, Rouen, France, 1982; PhD, CUNY, 1993; MS, U. Tenn., Knoxville, 1998. Adj. lectr. Hunter Coll., N.Y.C., 1987—90, Queens Coll., N.Y.C., 1989—91; instr. U. Reading, England, 1993—95; rsch. assoc. U. Tenn., Knoxville, 1998; postdoctoral rschr. Oak Ridge (Tenn.) Nat. Lab., 1999—2001, rsch. assoc., 2001—03, staff scientist, 2003—. Mem. program com. Autonomous Agts. and Multi-Agt. Sys., 2004, Internat. Semantic Web Conf., 2005—06. Contbr. articles to profl. jours. Mem.: IEEE, Divers Alert Network, Sierra Club. Avocations: boating, scuba diving, athletics. Office: Oak Ridge Nat Lab 1 Bethel Valley Rd Oak Ridge TN 37831

**POUILLON, NORA EMANUELA**, food service executive, chef; b. Vienna, Oct. 26, 1943; came to U.S., 1965; d. Leopold and Gertraude (Mayr) Aschenbrenner; m. Pierre Pouillon, Dec. 3, 1965 (separated 1978); children: Alexis, Olivier; life ptnr. Steven Damato; children: Nina, Nadia. Baccalaureat, Neuland Schule, Vienna, 1961; Moderne Rechtechnic, Technische Hochschule, Vienna, 1962-63; Bus. Degree, Handelsakademie, Vienna, 1964; drawing cert., Corcoran Sch. Art, 1967; diploma, Internat. Sch. Interior Design, 1968. Tchr. and owner Guerilla Gourmet, Washington, 1973-76; owner Food for Friends, Washington, 1973—75; chef Tabard Inn Hotel, Washington, 1976—78; co-owner, chef Restaurant Nora, Washington, 1979—, City Cafe, Washington, 1986—94, Asia Nora, 1994—. Activist with food safety advocacy groups Green Circle Organics, Walnut Acres, Seaweb's Give North Atlantic Swordfish A Break; founding mem. Chefs Collaborative 2000; charter mem. Seafood Choices Alliance; participant Harvard Sch. Nutrition Roundtable; mem. Internat. Com. Alternative and Complementary Medicine; bd. mem. Foodfit.com, Ctr. Mind-Body Medicine, Women Chefs and Restaurateurs. Bd. mem. Amazon Conservation Team. Restaurant named Top Healthiest Restaurant, Health Mag.; named one of Zagat's Top Ten Restaurants, one of three Power Chefs, Washington Post; Chef of Yr. award of Excellence, IACP; First Book finalist for Cooking with Nora, Julia Child Cookbook award; recipient New Hope Natural Media award for Contbns. Organic Industry; Citizens for Better Health-Nora Pouillon award Sustainable Living, 2003; First Ladies of Cuisine award for Excellence, YMCA, 2004. Mem.: Internat. Assn. Culinary Profls., Les Dames d'Escoffier, Organic Trade Assn. (Spl. Pioneer Leadership award 2004). Achievements include having the first certified organic restaurant in the country. Avocations: synergy exercise, yoga, hiking, downhill and cross-country skiing. Office: Restaurant Nora 2132 Florida Ave NW Washington DC 20008-1925 Office Phone: 202-462-5143. Business E-Mail: norap@noras.com.

**POULET, ANNE LITLE**, museum director, art historian; b. Wash., Pa., Mar. 20, 1942; d. John Francis and Ruth Virginia (Kurtz) Litle; m. Francois Poulet, May 20, 1967. BA cum laude, Sweet Briar Coll., 1964; MA, Inst. Fine Arts, NYU, 1970. Curator Dept. European Decorative Arts and Sculpture Mus. Fine Arts, Boston, 1980—99; curator European Decorative Arts and Sculpture emerita Russell B. & Andrée Beauchamp Stearns, 1999—; dir. Frick Collection, NYC, 2003—. Catalogue, vol. 5, Wrightsman Collection, Met. Mus. Art, NYC, 1967—72, exhibitions include Corot to Braque, Mus. Fine Arts, Boston, 1978—80; author: (exhibit catalogue) Corot to Braque, 1978—80; editor-in-chief Jour. Mus. Fine Arts, Boston, 1989—93; co-author: (catalogue) Clodion (1738-1814), 1992; author, guest curator Jean-Antoine Houdon (1741-1828): Sculptor of the Enlightenment, Nat. Gallery Art, Washington, DC, 2003; contbr. articles to profl. jours. Recipient Iris Fedn. award for decorative arts, 2000; grantee, Ford Found., 1965, Lamb Mellon, 1990, 1998, 2000—01; Kress fellowship, 1976. Fellow: Am. Acad. Arts & Sciences; mem.: Assn. Art Mus. Dir., Am. Fedn. Arts, Assn. Art Mus., French Heritage Soc. (co-founder, former vice chmn. bd.). Office: The Frick Collection 1 E 70th St New York NY 10021-4967

**POULETTY, PHILIPPE**, health products executive; MD, U. Paris VI; degrees in immunology and virology, Inst. Pasteur. Postdoctoral fellow dept. med. microbiology and immunology Stanford U.; intern Hopitaux de Paris, 1981—84; founder, dir. rsch. Clonatec, France, 1984—88; founder SangStat, 1988—, pres., CEO, bd. dirs., 1988—95, chmn. bd. dirs., CEO, 1995—98, chmn., 1998—; founder DrugAbuse Scis., Inc., Los Altos, Calif., 1994—; chmn. bd. dirs., pres. DrugAbuse Scis. SAS. Bd. dirs. Conjuchem.

**POULEUR, HUBERT GUSTAVE**, cardiologist, consultant; b. Bouffioulx, Belgium, June 6, 1948; m. Michelle Leonet, July 7, 1973; children: Anne-Catherine, Jean-Hubert. MD, U. Louvain, Belgium, 1973, PhD, 1980. Intern, resident, then fellow in internal medicine U. Louvain, Belgium, 1973-77; Pub. Health Service internat. research fellow U. Calif, San Diego, 1977-79; asst. prof. U. Louvain, Brussels, 1979-83, assoc. prof., 1983-91, prof., 1991-94; assoc. dir. clin. rsch. Pfizer U. Louvain, 1993-95; v.p. cardiovascular clin. R&D Bristol-Myers Squibb, Princeton, NJ, 1996-2000; exec. dir. cardiovasc. and metabolic group Pfizer Inc., N.Y.C., 2001—. Disting. clin. scientist Syntex Clin. Rsch., Palo Alto, Calif., Maidenhead, U.K., 1988-93. Contbr. numerous sci. articles to profl. jours. Recipient Damman prize Damman Found., 1977, Bekales prize Bekales Found., 1986; Squibb Cardiovascular fellow Belgian Soc. Cardiology, 1982. Fellow Am. Coll. Cardiology; mem. Am. Heart Assn. (fellow Coun. of Circulation, fellow Coun. Clin. Cardiology), Atlantic Salmon Fedn., Trout Unltd. Avocation: fly fishing. Home: 43 Woodlane Rd Lawrenceville NJ 08648-5544 E-mail: hubert.pouleur@pfizer.com.

**POULIOT, ASSUNTA GALLUCCI**, retired business school owner, director, consultant; b. West Warwick, R.I., Aug. 14, 1937; d. Michael and Angelina (DeCesare) Gallucci; m. Joseph F. Pouliot Jr., July 4, 1961; children: Brenda, Mark, Jill, Michele. BS, U. R.I., 1959, MS, 1971. Bus. tchr. Cranston High Sch., R.I., 1959-61; bus. dept. chmn. Chariho Regional High Sch., Wood River Junction, R.I., 1961-73; instr. U. R.I., Kingston, 1973-78; founder, dir. Ocean State Bus. Inst., Wakefield, RI, 1977-95, fin. aid cons., 1995—2005, ednl. cons., 1996—2005. Dir. Fleet Nat. Bank, 1985-91; bd. mgrs. Bank of New Eng., 1984-85; commr. Accrediting Coun. Ind. Colls. and Schs., 1995-98, chair accreditation com. team visits, 1998-2001, intermediate rev. com., 2000-01, rev. bd., 2000—; spkr. in field including Glencoe/McGraw-Hill Pub. Co., 1995—. Ednl. author, Glencoe McGraw Hill Pub. Co., 1999-2002. Pres. St. Francis Women's Club, Wakefield, 1975; sec. St. Francis Parish Coun., Wakefield, 1980; mem. Econ. Devel. Commn., Wakefield, 1981-85; mem. South County Hosp. Corp. Wakefield, 1978-97; fin. dir. Bus. and Profl. Women's Club, Wakefield, 1982-84; chmn. Ladies Golf Charity, 1985-91; mem. Computer Info. Systems Com., Chariho Regional Career and Tech. Ctr. Mem. R.I. Bus. Edn. Assn. (newsletter editor

1979-81), New Eng. Bus. Coll. Assn. (sec. 1984-86, pres. 1985-87), R.I. Assn. Career and Tech. Schs. (treas., bd. dirs. 1979-95), Eastern Bus. Edn. Assn. (conf. leader), Nat. Bus. Edn. Assn. (conf. leader), Career Coll. Assn. (conv. speaker, pub. rels. com., govt. rels. com., membership com., key mem., nominating com., evaluator), Assn. Colls. and Schs. (commr. commn. on postsecondary schs. accreditation 1994-98), R.I. Women's Golf Assn., Am. Cancer Soc., U. R.I. Alumni Assn. (Excellence Bus. award 1992), Phi Kappa Phi, Delta Pi Epsilon (pres., newsletter editor). Clubs: Point Judith Country (past ladies golf chmn., R.I. Women's golf rep.). Roman Catholic. Avocations: golf, gardening. Office: 15835 Sandy Point Dr Fort Myers FL 33917-5464 Office Phone: 239-567-0399. Personal E-mail: sjpouliot@aol.com.

**POULOS, CLARA JEAN**, nutritionist; b. L.A., Jan. 1, 1941; d. James P. and Clara Georgie (Creighton) Hill; m. Themis Poulos, Jan. 31, 1960. PhD in Biol., Fla. State Christian U., 1974; PhD in Nutrition, Lafayette U., 1984; D in Nutritional Medicine, Hearts of Jesus and Mary Coll., 1986. Registered nutritionist, cert. hypnotherapist, clin. densitometry technician, in diabetes edn. Dir. rsch. Leapou Lab., Aptos, Calif., 1973—76, Monterey Bay Rsch. Inst., Santa Cruz, Calif., 1976—2001; nutrition specialist Santa Cruz, 1975—2001; dir. nutritional svcs., health enhancement, lifestyle planning, 1983—97; chief tech. and rsch. Osteoporosis Diagnostic Ctr., Santa Cruz, 2000—04; chief tech. rsch. Osteoporosis Care Ctr., San Jose, 2001—. Instr. Stoddard Assocs. Seminars; cons. Biol-Med. Lab., Chgo., Nutra-Med Rsch. Corp., NY, Akorn-Miller Pharmacal, Chgo.; cons. Threshold Lab. Monterey Bay Aquaculture Farms, Calif.; cons. Resurrection Lab., Calif. Author: Alcoholism-Stress-Hypoglycemia, 1976, The Relationship of Stress to Alcoholism and Hypoglycemia, 1979; assoc. editor: Internat. Jour. Bio-Social Research, Health Promotion Features; editor: Nutrition and Dietary Consultant Jour.; columnist: The Connection Newspaper; contbr. articles to profl. jours. Recipient Najulander Internat. Rsch. award, 1971, Wainwright Found. award, 1979, various state and local awards. Fellow: Internat. Acad. Nutritional Consultants, Am. Nutritionist Assn., Internat. Coll. Applied Nutrition; mem.: AAAS, Internat. Fishery Assn. (health assoc.), Calif. Acad. Sci., Am. Public Health Assn., Am. Heart Assn. (pres. Santa Cruz br. 1990—91), Internat. Platform Soc., Am. Diabetes Assn. (profl., pres. Santa Cruz chpt., editor newsletter The Daily Balance Santa Cruz chpt., sec. No. Calif. chpt.), MUSE-Computer Users Group, Am. Women's Bowling Assn., Quota, Toastmistress. E-mail: cjp1918@netscape.net.

**POULOS, JAMES THOMAS**, endocrinologist, educator; b. Lynn, Mass., Apr. 11, 1938; s. Thomas Dimitrios and Christine Julia (Zorzy) Poulos; m. Mary Margaret White, June 22, 1963; 1 child, Christopher Kreag. BS, Tufts U., 1959, MD, 1963. Diplomate Am. Bd. Internal Medicine, Am. Bd. Endocrinology and Metabolism. Intern New Eng. Med. Ctr., Boston, 1963—64, resident, 1964—65; resident and fellow in endocrinology U. Chgo., 1967—70; practice medicine specializing in endocrinology Lafayette, Ind., 1970—2004. Adj. prof. clin. pharmacology Purdue U., West Lafayette, Ind., 1976—95; chmn. therapeutics com. Ind. Dept. Medicaid, 2002—; clin. faculty Ind. U. Sch. Medicine, mem. dean's search com., 1998, mem. therapeutics com. 2004—; dir., pres. med. staff Lafayette Home Hosp., 1978—79; pres. Arnett HMO, 1986—97; bd. dirs. North Ctrl. Health Svc.; chmn. therapeutics com. State of Ind. Family and Social Svc. Adminstrn., 2002—; dir. regional diabetes ctr. Sisters of St. Francis Health Systems Inc., 1985—, Greater Lafayette Health Svc., 1985—, mem. mission com., 2005—; bd. dirs. GLHS Inc., 2005; mem. mission com. Sisters St. Francis Health Sys. Co-author: The Metabolic Influence of Progestins Advances in Metabolis Disorders, 1971; contbr. articles to profl. publ. Mem. Nat. Rep. Senatorial Com., Nat. Rep. Congrl. Com. With M.C., US Army, 1965-67. Fellow ACP (councilor-at-large Ind. chpt.), Am. Coll. Endocrinology, Am. Assn. Clin. Endocrinologists; mem. AMA, Am. Diabetes Assn. (dir. Ind. chpt. 1980—, pres. 1986-88, 96-98, bd. dirs., com. profl. practice 1987-88, pres. 1994—), Endocrine Soc., Internat. Diabetes Fedn., Am. Lung Assn. (pres. West Ctrl. Ind. 1982-83), Lafayette C. of C, Nat. Lipid Assn., Ind. Endocrine Soc., Ind. Lipid Working Group Home and Office: 1000 Windwood Ln West Lafayette IN 47906-4737 Office Phone: 765-743-1741. Personal E-mail: jpoulos@insightbb.com.

**POULOS, JOAN GRAHAM**, lawyer; b. Almena, Kans., June 7, 1936; d. Gilbert W. and Opal Z. Graham; m. John W. Poulos (div. 1978); children: John S., Alexandra J. Poulos Fullerton; m. David C. Lewis. BS, U. Kans., 1958; JD, U. Calif. Hastings Coll. of Law, 1962; MA, U. Calif., Riverside, 1978. Bar: Calif. 1963, U.S. Supreme Ct., U.S. Ct. Appeals (9th cir.), U.S. Dist. Ct. (so., ea. and no. dists.) Calif. Pvt. practice, Davis, Calif., 1978—. Dir. People Resources Inc., Yolo County, Calif., 1994-96. City coun. mem. City Davis, 1972-74, mayor, 1974-76; chmn. juvenile justice com. Mendo County, Ukiah, Calif.; commr. Nat. Commn. Uniform State Law, 1978-86; mem. Davis Chorale; musician Fisherman's Chapel Bodega Bay; past pres. Mental Health Assn. Yolo County. Mem. ABA, LWV, Am. Women for Internat. Understanding (bd. dirs.), Yolo County Bar Assn. Office: Poulos & Fullerton 1723 Oak Ave Davis CA 95616-1004 also: PO Box 1241 Bodega Bay CA 94923-1241 Fax: (530) 753-9457. Office Phone: 530-753-4450.

**POULSEN, JAMES VIGGO, III**, music educator, composer; b. Burlington, Iowa, Dec. 12, 1958; s. James Viggo and Marilyn Elizabeth (Brubaker) Poulsen; m. Lori Lynn Zender, Aug. 3, 1985; children: Christopher, Elise. BA, Buena Vista Coll., 1984; MusM, U. SD, 1985. Comml. music composer, Des Moines, 1990—. Lectr. music Simpson Coll., Indianola, Iowa, 1991—. Composer numerous works. Recipient Telly award, 1992—2003, Addy award, 1992—2003, First prize, Presbyn. Metro Ministries of Omaha Composition Contest, 1985, award for best score, Iowa Film Awards, 1994—96, 2005. Mem.: Music Tchrs. Nat. Assn. United Methodist. Avocations: history, reading, travel. Office: Simpson Coll 701 N C St Indianola IA 50125 Office Phone: 515-961-1846. Office Fax: 515-961-1637. Personal E-mail: jlpoulsen@aol.com.

**POULSON, JOHN FRANKLIN**, agricultural studies educator, consultant; b. Bryan, Ohio, Sept. 23, 1959; s. David Franklin and Florence Mae Poulson; m. Lexie Marie Zenz, July 31, 1981; children: Jessie Luella, Shane. BS in Agr., The Ohio State U., 1981, MS in Agr., 1988. Tchr. agr. Crestview H.S., Ashland, Ohio, 1981—88; orgnl. dir. Ohio Farm Bur. Fedn., Columbus, Ohio, 1988—90; instr. agr. Pettisville (Ohio) H.S., 1990—. Mem.: Nat. Assn. Agrl. Educators, Ohio Assn. Agrl. Edn. (del. com. 1994—), Agr. Soc. (dir. 2000—), Future Farmers Am. Alumni (mem. coun. 1986—, Honorary State degree Ohio chpt. 1996, Honorary Am. degree mem. 1999), Lions (officer 1982—). Home: V685 Rd 21 Archbold OH 43502 Office: Pettisville HS 232 Summit St Pettisville OH 43553

**POULSON, RICHARD JASPER METCALFE**, lawyer; b. Elizabeth City, N.C., Sept. 4, 1938; s. Richard Jasper and Dorothy (Morse) P.; m. Anne Keenan, Dec. 21, 1963 (div. 1976); m. Anne Dare Wrenn, Sept. 25, 1993; children: Richard Hugh Hundley, Anna Blair Masters. BA, U. Va., 1960; JD, Am. U., 1968; ML in Taxation, Georgetown U., 1970. Bar: Va. 1968, D.C. 1969, U.S. Supreme Ct. 1976. V.p. Am. Security & Trust Co., Washington, 1968-70; assoc. Hogan & Hartson, Washington, 1970-73, ptnr., 1973-94, sr. ptnr. London, 1990-93; chmn. Rapidan Capital Ptnrs., 1994—; sr. mng. dir. The Appian Group, Washington, 1995-98; chmn. The Animex Group, Warsaw, 1998—; exec. v.p., sr. advisor to chmn. Smithfield Foods, Inc., NYC, 1998—. Adj. prof. Georgetown U. Law Ctr., 1971-76; lectr. Law and Fgn. Svc. Schs. Georgetown U.; internat. advisor in field; active Euro-Arab Conciliation and Arbitration Sys. Trustee bd. mgrs. U. Va., Charlottesville, 1992—98, v.p., 1994—95, pres., 1995—97; dir., chmn. exec. com. Mary & Daniel Loughran Found., Washington, 1976—, pres., 2002—; chmn., dir. Montpelier Steeplechase Found., Orange, Va., 1991—98; chmn., trustee U.S. Rugby Football Found., Boston, 1988—2001. Mem. Law Soc. of Eng. and Wales, Metro. Club, Keswick Country Club, Columbia Country Club, Saratoga Golf and Polo Club, Commonwealth Club. Republican. Episcopalian. Avocations: horseback riding, hunting, steeplechase racing, thoroughbred breeding. Home: Hare Forest Farm PO Box 287 Orange VA 22960 Office: Smithfield Foods Inc 499 Park Ave 6th Fl New York NY 10022 Office Phone: 212-758-2100. Business E-Mail: dickpoulson@smithfieldfoods.com.

**POULTER, CHARLES DALE,** chemist, educator, consultant; b. Monroe, La., Aug. 29, 1942; s. Erwin and Mary Helen Poulter; m. Susan Raetzsch, Aug. 24, 1964; children: Mary Christa, Gregory Thomas. BS, La. State U., Baton Rouge, 1964; PhD, U. Calif., Berkeley, 1967. NIH postdoctoral fellow UCLA, 1967-68; asst. prof. chemistry U. Utah, Salt Lake City, 1969-75, assoc. prof., 1975-78, prof., 1978-94, John A. Widtsoe prof. chemistry, 1994—, chair dept. chemistry, 1995-2000; editor-in-chief Jour. Organic Chemistry, 2001—. Fellow AAAS, Am. Acad. Arts and Scis.; mem. Am. Chem. Soc. (organic exec. com. 1983-86, biol. divsn. councillor 1993-98, chair organic divsn. 1998, Ernest Guenther award 1991, Utah award 1992, Arthur C. Cope scholar 1998, Repligen award 2002, James Flack Norris award 2004). Office: U Utah Dept Chemistry 340 S 1500 E Rm 2020 Salt Lake City UT 84112

**POULTERER, WILLIAM TAYLOR, III,** river pilot; b. Phila., Sept. 4, 1938; s. William Taylor Jr. and Betty (Bennett) P.; m. Jane D. Fisher, Aug. 23, 1991; children: Jane D., Matthew T.; children: by previous marriage: Stacy P. Thompson, Andrew T. Student, U. Del., 1980-81, U. Richmond, 1983. Lic. first class pilot for Del. Bay and River Commonwealth of Pa., USCG. River pilot Pilots Assn. Bay and River Del., Phila., 1961—, pres., 1999—2001, Kalmar Nyokel Fon, 2004—. State legislator, mem. Del. Ho. of Reps., Dover, 1970-74; pres. bd. dirs. Edn., Inc., Salina, Kans., 1970-78; bd. dirs. Planned Parenthood, Wilmington, Del., 1972-74; mgr. Del. Franklin P. Hall re-election campaign, Richmond, Va., 1987-89; pres. Chapelcroft Civic Assn., Wilmington, 1968-70, Gates Head Civic Assn., Richmond, 1988-89, Challenge Discovery Projects, Richmond, 1989-91; pres. Kalm or Nychel Found., 2004-05, Challenge Discovery Project, Richmond, 1989 94. Named Young Rep. of Yr. New Castle County Young Reps., 1970. Mem. Am. Pilots Assn. (trustee 1994—), Pilots Soc. For Relief of Distressed and Decayed Pilots Their Widows and Children (pres. 1980-94), Phila. Pilots Assn. (bd. dirs.), Masters Mates and Pilots. Avocations: outdoor activities, skiing, tennis, travel. Home: 40 Harborview Rd Lewes DE 19958

**POUND, FRANK R., JR.,** lawyer; b. Mayo, Fla., Nov. 3, 1933; s. Frank Reese and Elizabeth (Hart) P.; m. Betty Armstrong, Aug. 31, 1957; children: Tamara, Susan, Tracy, Brittain. BS, U. Fla., 1959, JD, 1961. Bar: Fla. 1962, U.S. Dist. Ct. (mid. dist.) Fla. 1962, U.S. Supreme Ct. 1969; cert. civil trial advocate; cert. civil trial lawyer; cert. mediator. Asst. county solicitor, Orlando, Fla., 1962-64; trial assoc. Crofton, et.al., Titusville, Fla., 1964-66; assoc. Howell, et.al., Rockledge, Fla., 1966-71; ptnr., pres. Lovering, Pound & Clifton, Cocoa, Fla., 1971—90; cir. judge 18th Jud. Cir. of Fla., 1991—98. Bd. dirs. Wuesthoff Health Sys., Inc., 2000—06. Comm. Titusville Airport Authority, 1972, Sheriff's Civil Service Bd., Titusville, 1983-86, Coll. Leadership, Brevard 2000-02. Served to col. USMC res., 1952-84. Mem. Acad. Fla. Trial Lawyers, Fla. Bar Assn. (bd. govs. 1979-82), Brevard County Bar Assn. (pres. 1972-73). Lodges: Rotary (Cocoa) (pres. 1982-83), Carlton Am. Inn of Ct. (pres. 2005-06). Office: Frank Pound Mediation 1970 Michigan Ave Cocoa FL 32922-5758 Office Phone: 305-639-0505.

**POUND, JOHN BENNETT,** lawyer; b. Champaign, Ill., Nov. 17, 1946; s. William R. and Louise Catherine (Kelly) P.; m. Mary Ann Hanson, June 19, 1971; children: Meghan Elizabeth, Matthew Fitzgerald. BA, U. N. Mex., 1968; JD, Boston Coll., 1971. Bar: N. Mex. 1971, U.S. Dist. Ct. N. Mex. 1971, U.S. Ct. Appeals (10th cir.) 1972, U.S. Supreme Ct., 1993. Law clk. to Hon. Oliver Seth, US Ct. Appeals, 10th Cir., Santa Fe, 1971-72. Asst. counsel Supreme Ct. Disciplinary Bd., 1977-83, dist. rev. officer, 1984—; mem. Supreme Ct. Com. on Jud. Performance Evaluation, 1983-85; bd. dirs. Archdiocese Santa Fe Cath. Social Svcs., 1995—. Contbr. articles to profl. jours. Pres. bd. dirs. N.Mex. Ind. Coll. Fund, Santa Fe; chmn. N.Mex. Dem. Leadership Coun., 1991—; bd. dirs. Santa Fe Boys Club, 1989-92; rules com. N.Mex. Dem. Party, 1982—; v.p. Los Alamos Nat. Lab. Comm. Coun., 1985-90; fin. chmn. N.Mex. Clinton for Pres. campaign, 1992; co-chmn. Clinton-Gore Re-election Campaign, N.Mex., 1996, 2000; co-chmn. Gore for Pres., N.Mex., 2000; co-chmn. Kerry for Pres., N.Mex., 2004. Fellow Am. Bar Found., Am. Coll. Trial Lawyers, N.Mex. Bar Found.; mem. ABA, Am. Bd. Trial Advocates, N.Mex. Bar Assn. (health law sect. 1987—), Santa Fe County Bar Assn. Democrat. Roman Catholic. Avocations: history, languages, literature, swimming, baseball. Office: Long Pound Komer PA PO Box 5098 2200 Brothers Rd Santa Fe NM 87505-6903 Office Phone: 505-982-8405. Personal E-Mail: jmpound@comcast.net.

**POUND, RICHARD WILLIAM DUNCAN,** lawyer, accountant; b. St. Catharines, Ont., Can., Mar. 22, 1942; s. William Thomas and Jessie Edith Duncan (Thom) P.; m. Julie Houghton Keith, Nov. 4, 1977. B in Commerce, McGill U., Montreal, 1962, B in Civil Law, 1967; BA, U. Sir George Williams U. (now Concordia U.), Montreal, 1963; PhD (hon.), U.S. Sports Acad., 1989; LLD (hon.), U. Windsor, Can., 1997, U. We. Ont., 2004; DSA (hon.), Laurentian U., 2005. Bar: called to Que. bar 1968, Ont. bar, 1980; chartered acct., 1964, F.C.A, 2001. Auditor Riddell, Stead, Graham & Hutchinson, Montreal, 1963-65; law clk., then atty. firm Laing, Weldon, Courtois, Clarkson, Parsons, Gonthier & Tétrault, Montreal, 1965-71; mem. firm Stikeman Elliott, Montreal, Toronto, Ottawa, Calgary, Vancouver, London, N.Y.C., Sydney, 1972—. Lectr. taxation McGill U. Faculty Law; lectr. Que. Real Estate Assn.; mem. Ct. of Arbitration of Sport, Lausanne, 1991—; officer Order of Can., officer Ordre nat. du Quebec, Order of St. John of Jerusalem; Queen's Counsel, 1992. Author: Five Rings Over Korea, 1994; Chief Justice W.R. Jackett: By the Law of the Land, 1999, Stikeman Elliott The First Fifty Years, 2002, High Impact Quotations, 2004, Canadian Facts and Dates, 2004, Inside the Olympics, 2004, Inside Dope, 2006; editor-in-chief: Doing Business in Canada, 1987—, Canada Tax Cases, 2003 ; Bilin Inom Income Tax Act (annotated), author: Pound's Tax Case Notes, 1988—; Legal Notes, CGA mag., 1986-03; mem. editl. bd. Can. Tax Svc., 1972-82. Pres. Can. Olympic Assn., 1977-82, sec., 1968-76, dir., 1968—; mem. Internat. Olympic Com., 1978—, exec. bd., 1983-87, 92-2000, v.p., 1987-91, 1996-2000; bd. govs. McGill U., 1986—, chmn., 1994-99, chancellor, 1999—; gov. Martlet Found.; former trustee Stanstead Wesleyan Coll.; chmn. McGill U. Athletic Bd.; chmn. McGill U. Fund Coun.; founding chmn., pres. World Anti-Doping Agy., 1999—. Decorated knight Mil. and Hospitaler Order of St. Lazarus of Jerusalem; named to Can. Swimming Hall of Fame, 1969, Sports Fedn. Can. Hall of Fame, 1976, Can. Olympic Order, 1995, Quebec Sports Hall of Fame, 2001, Gold Medallion award Internat. Swimming Hall of Fame, 2002, B.C. Swiming Hall of Fame, 2005; named one of 100 Most Influential People of 2005, Time mag. Fellow Order of Chartered Accts.; mem. Can. Bar Assn., Can. Tax Found., Internat. Fiscal Assn.; Internat. Assn. Practicing Lawyers, Can. Squash Racquets Assn., Royal Life Savs. Soc., Alumni Assn. McGill U. (former pres.). Clubs: Montreal Amateur Athletic Assn. (pres. 1987-88), Club Atwater (Montreal); Jesters, Mt. Bruno Country. Home: 87 Arlington Ave Westmount PQ Canada H3Y 2W5 Office: Ste 4000 1155 Rene Levesque Blvd W Montreal PQ Canada H3B 3V2 Office Phone: 514-397-3037. Business E-Mail: rpound@stikeman.com.

**POUND, ROBERT VIVIAN,** physics professor; b. Ridgeway, Ont., Can., May 16, 1919; arrived in U.S., 1923, naturalized, 1932; s. Vivian Ellsworth and Gertrude C. (Prout) Pound; m. Betty Yde Andersen, June 20, 1941; 1 child, John Andrew. BA, U. Buffalo, 1941; AM (hon.), Harvard Coll., 1950; DSc (hon.), SUNY, Buffalo, 1994. Staff mem. Radiation Lab. MIT, Cambridge, 1942—46; Soc. Fellows jr. fellow Harvard U., Cambridge, 1945—48; asst. prof. physics Harvard Coll., Cambridge, 1948—50, assoc. prof., 1950—56, prof., 1956—68; chmn. dept. physics, 1968—72; Mallinckrodt prof. physics, 1968—89; emeritus, 1989—; dir. Physics Lab. Harvard U., Cambridge, 1975—83. Fulbright rsch. scholar Oxford (Eng.) U., 1951; vis. rsch. fellow Merton Coll., 1980; Fulbright lectr., Paris, 58; vis. prof. Coll. de France, 1973; vis. fellow Joint Inst. Lab. Astrophysics U. Colo., 1979—80; Zernike vis. prof. U. Groningen, The Netherlands, 1982; vis. sr. scientist Brookhaven Nat. Lab., 1986—87; vis. prof. U. Fla., 1987; W.G. Brickwedde lectr. Johns

Hopkins U., Balt., 1992; Julian Mack lectr. U. Wis., 1992. Author, editor Mmicrowave Mixers, 1948; contbr. articles to profl. jours. Associated Univs., Inc., 1976—. Recipient B.J. Thompson Meml. award, Inst. Radio Engrs., 1948, Eddington medal, Royal Astron. Soc., 1965, Nat. medal Sci., Pres. U.S., 1990; fellow John Simon Guggenheim, 1957—58, 1972—73. Fellow: AAAS, Am. Acad. Arts and Scis., Am. Phys. Soc.; mem.: NAS, French Phys. Soc. (mem. coun. 1958—61), French Acad. Scis. (assoc.; fgn.), Sigma Xi, Phi Beta Kappa. E-mail: pound@fas.harvard.edu.

**POUNDS, REGINA DOROTHEA,** writer; arrived in U.S., 1980; d. Friedrich and Herta Klein; m. Wayne C. Pounds, June 21, 1968; 1 child, Louis C. Author: Theo's Ghost, 2000, Lord Eaglebeak, 2000, Leonora, 2002, Wild Violets, 2005; contbr. articles to pubs. Mem.: Defenders of Wildlife, World Wildlife Fund. Avocations: history, languages, poetry, art. Home: 614 E Grant St Belleville IL 62220 Personal E-mail: oldberliner@yahoo.com.

**POUNDS, WILLIAM FRANK,** management educator; b. Fayette County, Pa., Apr. 9, 1928; s. Joseph Frank and Helen (Fry) P.; m. Helen Anne Means, Mar. 6, 1954; children: Thomas Mcclure, Julia Elizabeth. BSChemE, Carnegie Inst. Tech., 1950, MS in Math. Econs., 1959, PhD in Indsl. Adminstrn., 1964. Indsl. engr. Eastman Kodak Co., 1950-51, 55-57; cons. Pitts. Plate Glass Co., 1958-59, asst. to gen. mgr. Forbes finishes divsn., 1960—61; faculty Sloan Sch. Mgmt., MIT, 1966-98, prof. mgmt., 1966-98, dean, 1966-80; sr. adv. Rockefeller Family and Assocs., 1981-91. Bd. dirs. Idexx Labs., Inc., Mgmt. Scis. for Health, Inc.; bd. dir. Sunoco, Inc., 1973—2000, General Mills, Inc., 1979—91; trustee/vice chmn. Putnam Funds, 1974—2000. Chmn. bd. trustees Boston Mus. Fine Arts, 2000-03; trustee WGBH Ednl. Found., 2002—. Served as aviator lt. (j.g.) USNR, 1951-55. Fellow Am. Acad. Arts and Scis. Home: 83 Cambridge Pkwy # W1205 Cambridge MA 02142-1241

**POUNDSTONE, SALLY HILL,** library director; m. Robert Bruce Poundstone; children: Nancy Katrina, Holly Megan, Angus Bruce, Alice Heather. BA, U. Ky., 1954, MA in Libr. Sci., 1955. Asst. head ref. dept. Louisville Free Pub. Libr., 1955-59; libr. Folger Shakespeare Libr., Washington, 1959-60; chief acquisition dept. White Plains (N.Y.) Pub. Libr., 1960-62; libr. Bedford Hills (N.Y.) Pub. Elem. Sch., 1965-66; dir. Mamaroneck (N.Y.) Free Libr. and Emelin Theatre, 1966-87, Westport (Conn.) Pub. Libr., 1987-98; prin. SHP Libr. Consultants, 1998—. Instr. libr. sci. N.Y. U., 1968-69, Coll. of New Rochelle (N.Y.), 1970-71; adv. coun. mem. Pratt Inst. Grad Sch. of Libr. and Info. Sci., 1978-87; adminstrv. svcs. comm. N.Y. Met. Ref. and Res. Libr. Agy., 1977-79; bd. trustees, 1979-88, 2d v.p. and chair, 1984-85, pres., 1985-88; planning and devel. com. mem. Bibliomation, Inc., 1988-90; chair Conn. State Adv. Coun. for Libr. Planning and Devel., 1988-90. Pres. Garden Club of Mamaroneck, 1969-70, Larchmont-Mamaroneck Film Coun., 1971-72, Mamaroneck Hist. soc., 1976-77, bd. mem., 1976-87; vice chmn. Village of Upper Nyack Planning Bd., 1988-89; leadership com. and task force mem. Westchester 2000, 1988-87; com. mem. Rotary Club of Westport, 1987—; active Downtown Westport Adv. Com., 1989-90, Rep. Town. Com., Weston, Conn., 1990-93, Westport Bridge & Traffic Com., 1990-97, Honorable Order of Ky. Cols., 1995—, United Way Profl. Adv. Com., 1994-97, Westport Telecomm. Com., 1994-96, and others; v.p.; dir. Woodcock Nature Ctr., 1998—, pres., 2001—; mem. Wilton Rep. Town Com., 2000—; mem. Planning and Zoning Bd. Commns., 2000—, sec., 2004-05, vice chair 2005-. Mem. ALA, Conn. Libr. Assn., Fairfield Libr. Adminstrs. Group, Archons of Colophon, Pub. Libr. Dirs. Assn. Westchester County (various offices and chairs), N.Y. Libr. Assn. (sec. treas. adult libr. assn. 1970-72, pres. pub. librs. sect. 1981-82, chair planning com. 1984-85). Home and Office: 48 Sharp Hill Rd Wilton CT 06897-3531 Office Phone: 203-761-0291.

**POUNDSTONE, WILLIAM NICHOLAS, JR.,** writer; b. Morgantown, W.va., Sept. 29, 1955; s. William Nicholas and Doris Mae (Jamison) P. Critic N.Y. Times, N.Y.C., 1992—; The Economist, London, 1996—. Author: Big Secrets, 1983, The Recursive Universe, 1984, Labyrinths of Reason, 1988, Prisoner's Dilemma, 1992, Carl Sagan: A Life in the Cosmos, 1999, How Would You Move Mount Fuji?, 2003, Fortune's Formula: The Untold Story of the Scientific Betting System that Beat the Casinos and Wall Street, 2005; co-producer Dave Bell Assocs., LA, 1993-94, producer, 1994-95. Mem. PEN, Writer's Guild.

**POURBAIX, ALEXANDER,** energy executive; BA with distinction, U. Alta., LLB. Pres. energy TransCanada Corp., 1997—; chmn., dir. TransCanada Turbines Ltd. Mem. bd. mgmt. Alta. Econ. Devel. Authority; active Calgary Homeless Found.; bd. dirs. Jr. Achievement of So. Alta. Recipient Top 40 Under 40 award for leadership excellence, 2002—03. Office: TransCanada Corp 450 1st St SW Calgary AB Canada T2P 5H1 Office Phone: 403-920-2122. Business E-Mail: alex_pourbaix@transcanada.com.

**POURCIAU, LESTER JOHN, JR.,** retired librarian; b. Baton Rouge, Sept. 6, 1936; s. Lester John and Pearlie M. (Hogan) Pourciau; 1 child, Lester John Thomas III. BA, La. State U., 1962, MS, 1964; PhD, Ind. U., 1975. Asst. ref. libr. U. S.C., Columbia, 1963—64; ref. libr. Florence County Pub. Libr., SC, 1964—65; coord. ref. svcs. U. Fla., Gainesville, 1966—67; dir. librs. U. Memphis, 1970—99, assoc. v.p. for acad. affairs, dir. librs., 1987—91. Chmn. coun. of head librarians State Univ. and C.C. System Tenn., 1980, 87, 97; acad. assoc. Atlantic Coun. of U.S., U. Memphis; fgn. expert; vis. lectr. Beijing U. of Posts & Telecomms., Beijing Normal U., Peking U., Renmen U., Qinghua U., Chingqing Inst. Posts & Telecomms., Guizhou Normal U., Republic of China, 1993, Beijing U. Posts and Telecom, 1993, Nanjing U. Posts and Telecom, Anhui Normal U., Beijing U Posts and Telecom, 1994, People's Republic of China, 1994; cons. prof. Beijing U. of Posts and Telecom, 1996—; participant 2d Internat. Conf. Crimea 95, Librs. and Assn. in the Transient World, Republic of Crimea; participant dep. chair organizing com., 1996—; Peking U. Internat. Conf., Beijing, 1998. Contbr. articles to profl. jours. With USAF, 1955-59. Recipient Adminstrv. Staff award Memphis State U., 1981, Commendation Boy Scouts Am., 1985, Commendation Tenn. Sec. State, 1989, Honor award Tenn. Libr. Assn., 1990, Allen J. Hammond award for Disting. Svc. U. Memphis, 1999, SLIS Disting. Alumni award Ind. U., 1999, TRACES award U. Memphis Assn. Retirees, 2003; named Outstanding Alumnus, La. State U., 1988; named Libr. of Yr., Memphis Libr. Coun., 1989; fellow Higher Edn. Act Ind. U.; named to 30th Ann. Honor Roll. ALA Office Intellectual Freedom and Freedom to Read Found. U. Memphis, 1999. Mem.: ALA, Memphis Old Time Car Club (sec. 1981, pres. 1982, 1989), Mid-Am. Old Time Automobile Assn., Antique Automobile Club Am., Nat. Assn. Watch and Clock Collectors (chpt. pres. 1983, sec.-treas. 1988—89). Office: Memphis State U U Libr Memphis TN 38152-0001 Business E-Mail: pourciau@memphis.edu.

**POUSADA, LIDIA,** physician; b. Mt. Kisco, N.Y., July 21, 1957; d. Manuel and Maria Nieves (Mejuto) P.; m. Andrew Kemper Goodman, June 26, 1983 (div. Sept. 1986); 1 child, Sara Pousada Goodman; m. Wayne William Maibaum, Apr. 11, 1987 (div. July 1993); 1 child, Anna Pousada Maibaum; m. James Paul Kreindler, Mar. 2, 1996; 1 child, Victoria Pousada Kreindler. BS, CUNY, N.Y.C., 1978; MD, N.Y. Med. Coll., 1980. Diplomate Am. Bd. Internal Medicine, Am. Bd. Geriatric Medicine. Student geriatric fellowship NYU Med. Sch., N.Y.C., 1978-80; resident in internal medicine Montefiore Med. Ctr., Bronx, NY, 1980-83; dir. geriatric unit, 1986-89; with nat. health svc. North Cent. Bronx Hosp., 1983-84; Morris Heights Health Ctr., Bronx, 1985; instr. City Coll. Med. Sch., N.Y.C., 1982-85, Albert Einstein Coll. Medicine, Bronx, 1983-84, 86-89; asst. prof. medicine, 1988-89; assoc. prof. clin. medicine N.Y. Med. Coll., 1993—; pvt. practice geriatric medicine, 2002—. Dir. geriatric cons. svc. Montefiore Med. Ctr., 1987—89; assoc. chief divsn. geriatrics, 1988—92; chief divsn. geriatrics and gerontology Sound Shore Med. Ctr., 1992—2002. Author: Geriatric Diagnostics, 1983, Geriatric Medicine for the House Officer, 1986, 2d edit., 1995, Emergency Medicine for Nurses, 1989, Perioperative Medical Care of the Geriatric Patient, 1989, Case Studies in Emergency Medicine for the House Officer,

1993. Physician scholar Nat. Health Svc., 1978-80. Fellow ACP. Gerontol. Soc. Am., Am. Geriatric Soc.; mem. Physicians for Social Responsibility. Office: 141 North State Rd Briarcliff Manor NY 10510 Office Phone: 914-762-2900.

**POUSCHINE, JOHN LAURENCE,** private equity investment executive; b. Glen Cove, N.Y., Jan. 28, 1957; s. Ivan and Helen (Carlson) P.; m. Catherine Dana, Nov. 16, 1991; children: Alexander, Anna. BA, Princeton U., 1979; MBA, Harvard U., 1983. Officer's asst. JP Morgan, N.Y.C., 1979-81; assoc. Prudential Securities, Inc., N.Y.C., 1983-85; v.p. Bradford Ventures Ltd., N.Y.C., 1985-88; sr. v.p. Electra Inc., N.Y.C., 1989-96; mng. dir. Pouschine Cook Capital Mgmt., LLC, 1997—. Bd. dirs. A World of Tile, Denver, Doe & Ingalls Mgmt., Durham, NC, Latex Internat., Shelton, Conn., St. Clair Entertainment, L.A. Bd. dirs. Russian Children's Welfare Soc., N.Y.C. Mem. Bridgehampton Club, Nassau Club, Princeton Club of N.Y., Union Club. Avocation: sports. Office: Pouschine Cook Capital Mgmt 375 Park Ave Ste 3408 New York NY 10152 E-mail: jpouschine@pouschinecook.com.

**POUSSAINT, ALVIN FRANCIS,** psychiatrist, educator; b. N.Y.C., May 15, 1934; s. Christopher Thomas and Harriet (Johnston) P. BA, Columbia U., 1956; MD, Cornell U., 1960; MS, UCLA, 1964. Intern UCLA Ctr. for Health Sci., 1960-61, resident in psychiatry Neuropsychiat. Inst., 1961-64, chief resident, 1964-65; So. field dir. Med. Com. Human Rights, Jackson, Miss., 1965-66; asst. prof. psychiatry Tufts U. Med. Sch., 1966-69; assoc. prof. psychiatry, assoc. dean students Harvard Med. Sch., 1969-75, 78—, prof. psychiatry, 1993—, dean students, 1975-78. Cons. HEW, 1969-73. Author numerous articles in field. Nat. treas. Black Acad. Arts and Letters, 1969-70, Med. Com. Human Rights, 1966—. Recipient Michael Schwerner award, 1968, Am. Black Achievement award in Bus. and the Professions Johnson Pub. Co., Inc., 1986, John Jay award for Disting. Profl. Achievement Columbia Coll., 1978-87, Medgar Evers Medal of Honor Beverly Hills/Hollywood chpt. NAACP, Hollywood, Calif., 1988, and numerous hon. degrees. Fellow AAAS, Am. Orthopsychiatric Assn., Am. Psychiat. Assn. (mem. com. on Black Psychiatrists 1970-75); mem. Nat. Med. Assn., Am. Acad. of Child Psychiatry, Children's Longwood. Office: Judge Baker Ctr 53 Parker Hill Ave Boston MA 02120-3225

**POUSSOT, BERNARD JEAN,** pharmaceutical executive; m. Delphine Cecile Poussot, May 15, 1976; children: Rodolphe, Eve, Juliette. Grad., Ecole Superieure de Commerce de Paris, 1975. Deputy gen. mgr. Wyeth France, 1986, pres. gen. mgr., 1987—91; group v.p. Europe Wyeth-Ayerst Internat., Collegeville, Pa., 1991, exec. v.p., 1993, pres., 1996, pres. worldwide pharm. bus., 1997—2002; exec. v.p. Wyeth R & D Wyeth, Madison, NJ, 2002—06, pres., vice chmn., 2006—. Mem.: PhRMA (chmn. internat. section 1999). Office: Wyeth Five Giralda Farms Madison NJ 07940-0874*

**POUTRINA, EKATERINA,** optics scientist, researcher; d. Vladislav Putrin and Lesya Putrina; m. Andrei Alexandrov, Dec. 16, 2001. MS in Physics, Moscow State U., 1991; MS in Optics, U. Rochester, N.Y., 2003, PhD in Optics, 2005. Rschr. Moscow State U., 1991—95; instr. Moscow State Tech. U., 1995—97, sr. instr., 1997—98. Contbr. articles to profl. jours. Fellow, U. Rochester, 1998—2005. Mem.: IEEE, Optical Soc. Am. Home: 605 A Prospect Street New Haven CT 06511 Personal E-mail: poutrina.optics@ugrad.rochester.edu.

**POUTSMA, JOHN C.,** science educator; PhD, Purdue U., West Lafayette, Ind., 1997. Asst. prof. Coll. of William and Mary, Williamsburg, Va., 1999—2005, assoc. prof., 2005—. Recipient Award for Excellence in Undergrad. Rsch., Ind. U., 2004, Early CAREER Devel. award, NSF, 2004. Mem.: Coun. on Undergrad. Rsch., Am. Soc. for Mass Spectrometry, Am. Chem. Soc., Phi Mu Alpha (faculty advisor for William and Mary chpt. 2003—06, Bachelor Sinfonian 1991).

**POUTSMA, MARVIN L.,** retired chemical research administrator; b. Grand Rapids, Mich., Aug. 7, 1937; m. Yolanda Arco, July 20, 1968; children: John C., Julie A. BS, Calvin Coll., 1958; PhD, U. Ill., 1962. Staff scientist corp. rsch. Union Carbide, Tarrytown, N.Y., 1961-65, group leader corp. rsch., 1965-68, sr. scientist corp. rsch., 1968-73, sr. group leader corp. rsch., 1972-78; group leader chemistry divsn. Oak Ridge (Tenn.) Nat. Lab., 1978-80, sect. head chemistry divsn., 1980-83, dir. chemistry divsn., 1984-93, dir. chem. & analytical scis. divsn., 1994-2000, ret., 2000. Contbr. chpts. to books and articles to profl. jours. Fellow AAAS; mem. Am. Chem. Soc. Office: Oak Ridge Nat Lab PO Box 2008 Oak Ridge TN 37831-6197 Office Phone: 865-576-8339. Business E-Mail: poutsmaml@ornl.gov.

**POVICH, DAVID,** lawyer; b. Washington, June 8, 1935; s. Shirley Lewis and Ethyl (Friedman) Povich; m. Constance Enid Tobriner, June 14, 1959; children: Douglas, Johanna, Judith, Andrew. BA, Yale U., 1958; LLB, Columbia U., 1962. Bar: D.C. 1962, U.S. Ct. Appeals (4th cir.) 1980, U.S. Tax Ct. 1981, U.S. Ct. Appeals (5th and 11th cirs.) 1984, U.S. Dist. Ct. Md., U.S. Ct. Appeals (3d cir.) 1997. Law clk. to assoc. judge D.C. Ct. Appeals, Washington, 1962-63; exec. com. Williams & Connolly, 1986-87, ptnr., 1963—2005, of counsel, 2006—. Bd. dirs., officer Lisner Home for Aged. Mem.: ABA, Barristers (exec. com. 1992—93), Bar Assn. D.C., D.C. Bar Assn. Office: Williams & Connolly 725 12th St NW Washington DC 20005-5901 Office Phone: 202-434-5071. E-mail: dpovich@wc.com.

**POVICH, LYNN,** journalist, internet executive; b. Washington, June 4, 1943; d. Shirley and Ethyl P.; m. Stephen B. Shepard, Sept. 16, 1979; children: Sarah, Ned. AB, Vassar Coll., 1965. Rschr., reporter, writer, editor, sr. editor Newsweek mag., NYC, 1965—91; editor-in-chief Working Woman mag., NYC, 1991—96, mng. editor, sr. exec. prodr. East coast programming MSNBC Interactive, Secaucus, NJ, 1996—2001. Editor: All Those Mornings at the Post, 2006. Bd. mem. Internat. Women's Media Found., 1998—, co-chair, 2002—05; adv. com. women's rights divsn. Human Rights Watch, 2003—. Recipient Matrix award N.Y. Women in Comms., 1976; named to Acad. of Women Achievers YWCA, 1993.

**POWDERLY, WILLIAM H., III,** lawyer; b. Pitts., Feb. 23, 1930; BS, Georgetown U., 1953; LLB, U. Pitts., 1956. Bar: Pa. 1956. Ptnr. Reed Smith, LLP, Jones Day; of counsel Tucker Arensberg PC, Pitts. Office: Tucker Arensberg PC 1500 One PPG Pl Pittsburgh PA 15222 Office Phone: 412-594-3925. Business E-Mail: wpowderly@tuckerlaw.com.

**POWE, NEIL RICHARD,** physician, educator, epidemiologist, public health service officer; b. Phila., May 11, 1955; BA, Princeton U., 1976; MD, MPH, Harvard U., 1981; MBA, Wharton Grad. Sch., Phila., 1986. Intern, resident hosp. U. Pa., 1981-84, Robert Wood Johnson Clin. scholar; instr. Johns Hopkins U., Balt., 1986-88, asst. prof., 1988-94, assoc. prof., 1994-98, prof., 1998—. Dir. Welch Ctr. for Prevention, Epidemiology and Clin. Rsch., 1998—, Johns Hopkins Evidence Based Practice Ctr.; co-dir. Robert Wood Johnson Clin. Scholars Program. Contbr. articles to profl. jours. Assn. Health Svcs. Rsch. Adminstrn., 1997. Fellow: ACP (tchg. and rsch. scholar); mem.: Inst. Medicine, Am. Soc. Clin. Investigation. Office: Johns Hopkins U 2-600 2024 E Monument St Baltimore MD 21287-0007 E-mail: npower@jhsph.edu.*

**POWELL, ADAM CLAYTON,** engineering educator, consultant; b. NYC, 1970; PhD in Materials Engring., MIT, Cambridge, Mass., 1997. Metallurgist NIST, Gaithersburg, Md., 1997—99; asst. prof. MIT, Cambridge, Mass., 1999—. Musician: (gospel choir director) Boston Temple Youth Gospel Choir. Achievements include development of Method for understanding pore structure formation in polymer membranes. Office: Massachusetts Institute of Technology 77 Massachusetts Ave Rm 4-117 Cambridge MA 02139-4307 Office Phone: 617-452-2086. E-mail: hazelsct@mit.edu.

**POWELL, ALAN,** engineering educator, research scientist; b. Buxton, Derbyshire, Eng., Feb. 17, 1928; arrived in U.S. 1956; s. Frank and Gwendolen Marie (Walker) P.; m. June Sinclair, Mar. 28, 1956. Student, Buxton Coll. 1939-45; diploma in aeros., Loughborough Coll., 1948; BSc in

Engring. (hon.), London U., 1949; honours diploma 1st class, Loughborough Coll., 1949; DTech (hon.), Loughborough U. Tech., 1980; PhD, U. Southampton, 1953. Chartered engr. Engr. Percival Aircraft Co., Luton, Eng., 1949-51; from rsch. asst. to lectr. U. Southampton, Eng., 1951-56; rsch. fellow Calif. Inst. Tech., Pasadena, 1956-57; engr. Douglas Aircraft Co., 1956; assoc. prof. UCLA, 1957-62, prof. engring., 1962-65, head Aerosonics lab., 1957-65; assoc. tech. dir., head acoustics and vibration lab. David Taylor Model Basin, Dept. Navy, Washington, 1965-66, tech. dir., 1966-67, David Taylor Naval Ship Research & Devel. Center, Bethesda, Md., 1967-85; mem. Undersea Warfare Research & Devel. Council, 1966-76, chmn., 1971-72; mem. council on Fed. Labs., 1972-85; prof. mech. engring. U. Houston, 1985-2000, chmn., 1985-87, prof. emeritus, 2000—. Com. on hearing bioacoustics and biomechs. NAS-NRC, 1961-85, exec. coun., 1963-65, chmn., 1965-66, advisor, 1985-95, mem. naval studies bd. 1990-95; mem. various coms. Naval Studies Bd. and Marine Bd., 1990-96; advisor Chinese U. Devel. Project, 1989-91; cons. Douglas Aircraft Co., 1956-65, others; adv. coun. Internat. Towing Tank Conf., 1981-85; mem. advisor U.S.-Japan Program Natural Resources, 1987-90, mem. Marine Facilities Panel; gen. chmn. 3d advanced vehicles conf. AIAA and Soc. Naval Archs. and Marine Engrs., 1976; chmn. internat. conf. Computer Aided Design, Manufacture and Ops. in Marine and Offshore Industries, 1987-88; cons. Sci. Applications Internat., Inc., 1987-90; governing bd. Am. Inst. Physics, 1995-97. Contbr. articles to profl. jours. Recipient Navy Meritorious Civilian Service award, 1970; Brit. Empire scholar, 1945; named Meritorious Exec. Pres. of U.S., 1982; Capt. Robert Dexter Conrad gold medal for sci. achievement Sec. Navy, 1984; dedication spl. issue Internat. J. Aeronautics vol. 2 nos. 3/4, 2003. Fellow Royal Aero. Soc. London (Baden-Powell prize 1948, Wilbur Wright prize 1953), Acoustical Soc. Am. (biennial award 1962, assoc. editor Jour. 1962-67, chmn. edn. com. 1964-66, exec. coun. 1966-69, chmn. medals and awards com. 1978-81, v.p. elect 1981-82, v.p. 1982-83, pres. elect 1989-90, pres. 1990-91, past pres. 1991-92, Silver medal in engring. acoustics 1992, designated Nat. Spkr. in Engring. Acoustics 1994-98), Inst. Mech. Engrs., Inst. Acoustics (U.K.); mem. AIAA (assoc. fellow, Aeroacoustics award 1980), ASME (Rayleigh lectr. 1988, Per Brüel Gold medal 1991), Inst. Noise Control Engrs. (initial mem., dir. 1974-77, Disting. lectr. 1975, 83, v.p. 1981-84, bd. cert. 1993), Acoustics, Speech and Signal Processing Soc. (exec. com. 1969-72, awards com. 1971-73, bylaws com. chmn. 1973-75), Am. Soc. Naval Engrs. (life), Am. Acad. Mechanics, Tau Beta Pi (hon. life). Office: U Houston Dept Mech Engring Houston TX 77204-4006

POWELL, ALMA JOHNSON, writer, advocate, foundation administrator; b. Birmingham, Al., Oct. 27, 1937; d. Robert and Mildred Johnson; m. Colin L. Powell, Aug. 1962; children: Michael, Linda, Annemarie. BA, Fisk U., 1957; LHD (hon.), Emerson Coll., 1996. Audiologist Boston Guild Hard of Hearing, 1959—62. Author: (children's books) America's Promise, 2003, My Little Wagon, 2003. Chair nat. coun. Best Friends Found., 1989—2001; chair Alliance for Youth, 2004—. Named one of 100 Most Powerful Women in Wash., Washingtonian mag., 2001.

POWELL, ANNE ELIZABETH, editor-in-chief; b. Cheverly, Md., Nov. 11, 1951; d. Arthur Gorman and Barbara Anne (MacAran) P.; m. John Alan Ebeling Jr., 1972 (div. 1983). BS, U. Md., 1972. Reporter Fayetteville (N.C.) Times, 1973-75; home editor Columbus (Ga.) Ledger-Enquirer, 1976; assoc. editor Builder mag., Washington, 1977-78; architecture editor House Beautiful's Spl. Publs., N.Y.C., 1979-81; editor Traditional Home mag., Des Moines, 1982-87, Mid-Atlantic Country mag., Alexandria, Va., 1987-89; editor in chief publs. Nat. Trust for Hist. Preservation, Washington, 1989-95; editor-in-chief Landscape Architecture Mag., Washington, 1995-98, Civil Engring. Mag., Washington, 1998—. Author: The New England Colonial, 1988. Mem. Nat. Press Club, Am. Soc. Mag. Editors. Home: 1105 Park St NE Washington DC 20002-6317 Office: American Society of Civil Engrs Civil Engring Mag 1801 Alexander Bell Dr Reston VA 20191-4344 Office Phone: 703-295-6213.

POWELL, ARDAL, music company executive, editor; b. Bournemouth, Dorset, England, Apr. 22, 1958; BA with honors, U. Cambridge, 1980, MA, 1989, PhD, 2004. Cert. Kononklijk Conservatorium, Den Haag, 1983. Pres. Folkers & Powell, Makers Hist. Flutes, Hudson, NY, 1983—. Editor: Traverso, Hist. Flute Newsletter, 1989—; translator: The Virtuoso Flute-Player by Johann George Tromlitz; author: (monograph) The Flute, The Keyed Flute by Johann George Tromlitz; editor: The Baroque Flute Fingering Book by Margaret N. Neuhaus, (periodical collected reprint) Traverso: Historical Flute Newsletter, Volumes 1—10, 1989—98. Fellow, NEH, 1993—94. Mem.: Am. Musical Instrument Soc. (bd. govs. 2001—, Bessaraboff prize 2005), Nat. Flute Assn. (com. 1987), Juggler Meadow Morris Men. Avocation: sailing.

POWELL, BARBARA ANN, music educator, voice educator; d. Henry Joseph and Helen Marie Bochenko; m. Dennis Alan Powell, June 28, 1980; children: Daniel Alan, Matthew Evan. BA, SUNY Oneonta, 1975. Cert. Music K-12, Speech Ed K-12, Elementary Ed N-6 N.Y. State Edn. Dept., 1979. Music educator Binghamton (N.Y.) City Sch. Dist., 1976— Chairperson jr. high/mid. sch. classroom music N.Y. State Sch. Music Assn., 1996—2001; chairperson, so. tier music educators mem. HS concerto competition So. Tier Music Teachers Assn., Binghamton, NY, 2004—; mem. capital project facilities com. Maine-Endwell (N.Y.) Sch. Dist., 2005—; singer Madrigal Choir of Binghamton (N.Y.), 2005—. Musician (choral conductor, guest conductor) county/state festivals; singer (soprano soloist for american premiere): (choral work) Donal Nobis Pacem; co-author: (handbook) Assessment in Classroom Music; actor: (theater, musical) My Fair Lady and The Music Man; contbr. video for pbs. Mem.: So. Tier Music Educators Assn. (assoc.; chairperson HS concerto competition 2004—06), Music Educators Nat. Conf. (assoc.), Broome County Music Educators Assn. (assoc.), Am. Choral Dirs. Assn. (assoc.), N.Y. State Sch. Music Assn. (assoc.), state chairperson 1996—2001). Roman Catholic. Avocations: travel, gardening, reiki/healing arts, meditation. Office: West Mid Sch West Middle Ave Binghamton NY 13905-4151 Office Phone: 607-763-8423. Home Fax: none. Business E-Mail: powellb@binghamtonschools.org.

POWELL, BARRY BRUCE, classicist, educator; b. Sacramento, Apr. 30, 1942; s. Barrett Robert and Anita Louise (Burns) Powell; m. Patricia Ann Cox; children: Elena Melissa, Adam Vincent. BA in Classics, U. Calif., Berkeley, 1963, PhD, 1971; MA, Harvard U., 1965. Asst. prof. Northern Ariz. U., Flagstaff, 1970-73; from asst. prof. to prof. U. Wis., Madison, 1973—, chmn. dept. classics, 1985-92, chmn. program integrated liberal studies. Author: Composition by Theme in the Odyssey, 1973, Homer and the Origin of the Greek Alphabet, 1991, Classical Myth, 1995, 1997, 2000, 2003, New Companion to Homer, 1997, A Short Introduction to Classical Myth, 2001, Writing and the Origins of Greek Literature, 2002, Homer, 2003; author: (with Ian Morris) The Greeks: Society, Culture, History, 2004; writer screenplays; contbr. articles to profl. jours. Woodrow Wilson fellow, 1965. Mem.: Am. Acad. in Rome, Classical Assn. Midwest and South, Archeol. Inst. Am., Am. Sch. Classical Studies at Athens (mng. com.), Am. Philol. Assn., Phi Beta Kappa (former pres. Madison chpt.). Home: 1210 Sweetbriar Rd Madison WI 53705-2228 Office: Univ Wis Dept Classics Madison WI 53707 Office Phone: 608-262-2041. E-mail: bbpowell@wisc.edu.

POWELL, BENJAMIN ALBOND, federal agency administrator, lawyer; b. Apr. 1967; BSE, U. Pa.; JD, Columbia U. Bar: 1999. Law clk. to Justice Byron R. White US Supreme Ct., law clk. to Justice John Paul Stevens; assoc. Kellogg, Huber, Hansen, Todd and Evans LLP; corp. counsel Vitria Tech., Inc.; program examiner State and USIA Branch Office of Mgmt. and Budget, Exec. Office of Pres., Washington, 2002—06; gen. counsel Office Nat. Intelligence, Washington, 2006—. Captain USAF. Office: Office Nat Intelligence NEOB 725 17th St Washington DC 20500*

POWELL, BILLY, musician; b. Corpus Christi, Tex., June 3, 1952; s. Donald and Marie Powell. Roadie with Lynyrd Skynyrd, 1970—72, keyboardist, 1972—77, 1987—; band mem. Alias, 1979, The Rossington-Collins Band, 1980—82, Allen Collins Band, 1983—85, Vision, 1985—87. Musician: (albums) Second Time Around, (with Lynyrd Skynyrd) Pronounced Leh-Nerd Skin-Nerd, 1973, Smokes, 1973, Second Helping, 1974, Nuthin' Fancy, 1975, Gimme Back My Bullets, 1976, One More from the Road, 1976, Street Survivors, 1977, Southern by the Grace of God, 1988, Lynyrd Skynyrd 1991, The Last Rebel, 1993, Endangered Species, 1994, Freebird: The Movie, 1996, Southern Nights, 1996, Twenty, 1997, Lyve, 1998, Edge of Forever, 1999, Universal Masters Collection, 1999, Christmas Time Again, 2000, Vicious Cycle, 2003, (with Alias) Contraband, 1979, (with the Rossington-Collins Band) Anytime, Anyplace, Anywhere, 1980, This is the Way, 1982, (with the Allen Collins Band) Here, There & Back, 1983. Named to Rock and Roll Hall of Fame, 2006. Office: Vector Mgmt PO Box Nashville TN 37212 also: Sanctuary Records 5226 Greens Dairy Rd Raleigh NC 27616-4612*

POWELL, BRADFORD SCOTT, research scientist, educator; s. Robert Lee Powell and Joan Margaret Cline; m. Maria A. Powell; 1 child, Thais Cavalcante Guimaraes. BA magna cum laude, U. Colo., Boulder, 1983; PhD, U. Calif., Davis, 1989. Cert. regulatory affairs Hood Coll. Asst. scientist Abbott Labs., Abbott Park, Ill., 1983—85; vis. scientist U. Calif., Davis, 1989—90; postdoctoral rschr. Frederick Cancer Rsch. and Devel. Ctr. Nat. Cancer Inst., Md., 1990—97; chemist/molecular biologist European Bioinformatics Inst. and NIH, Rockville, 1997—99; lab head and prin. investigator US Army Med. Rsch. Inst. Infectious Diseases, Frederick, 1999—. Postdoctoral adviser rsch. associateship programs NRC, Washington, 2000; adj. prof. Johns Hopkins U., Balt., 2006—. Contbr. scientific papers to profl. jours., chapters to books. Recipient Excellence in Fed. Career, Outstanding Profl. Tech., Sci. and Program Support., Balt. Fed. Exec. Bd., 2002; vis. scholar, Ministry of Edn. and Sci., Japan, Tokyo U. Med. Inst., 1991—93; Internat. Rsch. fellow, NSF, 1991. Mem.: Am. Peptide Soc., Am. Soc. Microbiology, Nature Conservancy (life). Achievements include patents for methods of screening for agents that delay a cell cycle; patents pending for prophylactic and therapeutic monoclonal antibodies against plague; research in methods for protein production and analysis; methods for analysis of essential bacterial genes; specific molecular mechanisms of pathogenesis; spectroscopic analysis of protein structure and stability; pharmaceutical product development. Avocations: hiking, travel, bicycling, kayaking, mountain climbing. Office Phone: 301-619-4933. Business E-Mail: bradford.powell@amedd.army.mil.

POWELL, CARL R., academic administrator; m. Caroline Eaken; 1 child, Tiffany. BA, U. Calif., Santa Barbara, 1981; MS, Kent State U., Ohio, 1984; PhD, Cleve. State U., 2004. V.p., CIO Cuyahoga CC, Cleve., 2000—. Mem.: No. Ohio IT Roundtable (co-founder), Educause, NE Ohio Soc. Info. Mgmt. (chpt. pres. 2001—03). Office: Cuyahoga CC 2900 Community College Ave Cleveland OH 44115 Office Phone: 216-987-4596.

POWELL, CAROLYN WILKERSON, retired music educator; b. Hamburg, Ark., Oct. 9, 1920; d. Claude Kelly and Mildred (Hall) Wilkerson; m. Charles Luke Powell, Dec. 12, 1923; children: Charles Luke Jr., James David, Mark Wilkerson, Robert Hall. AB, Ctrl. Meth. U., Fayette, Mo., 1942; MA in Tchg., U. N.C., 1970. Life tchg. cert. Mo., cert. tchr. N.C. Choral dir. Maplewood-Richmond Heights Sch., St. Louis, 1943-45; pvt. piano tchr. Greensboro, NC, 1951-63; organist Presbyn. and Meth. chs., Greensboro, 1950-61; dir. ch. youth choirs, Greensboro, 1958-61; choral and humanities tchr. Page HS, Greensboro, 1963-67; choral dir. Githens Jr. HS, Durham, NC, 1967-80; mem. Durham Choral Festival N.C. Dist., 1968—78; accompanist, music dir. Altavista (Va.) Little Theatre, 1981—83; Den mother Boy Scouts Am., Greensboro, 1951—57; mem. Chapel Hill (N.C.) Preservation Soc., 1985—; vol., chapel organist, pediat. tutor U. N.C. Hosps., Chapel Hill, 1984—89; mem. Chapel Hill Hist. Soc.; Sunday and vacation schs. tchr., organist Grace Meth. Ch., Greensboro; organist St. Peter's Episcopal Ch., Altavista, 1981—83; organist Episcopal ch. svc. Carol Woods Retirement Cmty., Chapel Hill, 1999—. Mem.: AAUW, NEA, Classroom Tchrs. Assn., Am. Organists Guild, Music Educators Nat. Conf., Ackland Art Mus. Assn., Carolina Club, Nat. Federated Music Club Euterpe, Chapel Hill Country Club, Univ. Woman's Club, Delta Kappa Gamma. Avocations: reading, golf, needlecrafts, gardening, travel. Home: Apt 1113 750 Weaver Dairy Rd Chapel Hill NC 27514-1441

POWELL, CHARLES ARTHUR, III, lawyer; b. Atlanta, Apr. 8, 1940; s. Charles Arthur Jr. and Leslie (Sibley) P.; m. Nancy Watson, June 7, 1962 (div. Jan. 1982); children: Charles Arthur IV, Christopher Alan; m. Glenda Ryan, Oct. 19, 1989; stepchildren: Clarence Glen Culp Jr., Belinda Culp Williams. AB, Birmingham So. Coll., 1961; LLB, Duke U., 1964. Bar: Ala. 1964, U.S. Dist. Ct. (no., mid. and so. dists.) Ala., U.S. Ct. Appeals (4th, 5th, 6th, 8th and 11th cirs.), U.S. Supreme Ct. Assoc. Rives, Peterson, Pettus & Conway, Birmingham, 1964-65; from assoc. to ptnr. Lange, Simpson, Robinson & Somerville, Birmingham, 1965-84; proprietory Powell & Assocs., Birmingham, 1984-88; ptnr. Powell, Tally & Frederick, Birmingham, 1988-94, Powell & Frederick, Birmingham, 1994-95, Johnston, Barton, Proctor & Powell, Birmingham, 1995—. Contbg. editor: The Developing Labor Law (cumulative supplement 1971-75), 1976; editor: The Developing Labor Law, 2d edit., 1983; assoc. editor: The Developing Labor Law (fifth supplement 1982-88), 1989, The Developing Labor Law, 3d edit., 1992. Chmn. bd. mgrs. World Business Advisors. Fellow Am. Bar Found., Coll. Labor and Employment Lawyers (charter, pres. 1998, bd. gov. 1996-); mem. ABA (mgmt. co-chair com. on the devel. of the law under the nat. labor rels. act 1978-81, mgmt. co-chair insts. and meetings com. 1983-86, coun. mem. sect. of labor and employment law 1985-95, chair-elect sect. of labor and employment law 1993-94, chair sect. of labor and employment law 1994-95, bd. gov. 2003-), Ala. State Bar (state labor law sect. 1969—, mem. standing com. on Ala. rules of jud. adminstrn. 1977-94, com. on lawyer advt. and solicitation 1991-94, character and fitness com. 1992—, Ho. of Dels., bd. govs. 2003-), Birmingham Bar Assn., Ea. Mineral Law Found. (trustee 1984—), Coun. R.R. and Airline Labor Lawyers, Indsl. Rels. Rsch. Assn., Bus. Coun. Ala., Fed. Bar Assn., Am. Employment Law Coun. (founding mem.). Office: Johnston Barton Proctor Powell Suite 2900 AmSouth/Harbart Plz 1601 6th Ave N Birmingham AL 35203-2618 Office Phone: 205-458-9449.

POWELL, COLIN LUTHER, former secretary of state, former Chairman of the Joint Chiefs of Staff; b. NYC, Apr. 5, 1937; s. Luther and Maud Ariel (McKoy) P.; m. Alma Vivian Johnson, Aug. 25, 1962; children: Michael, Linda, Annemarie. BS in Geology, CUNY, 1958; MBA, George Washington U., 1971; Grad. Nat. War Coll., 1976. Commd. 2d lt. U.S. Army, 1958; advanced through grades to gen., 1989; ret., 1993; asst. to dep. dir. Office Mgmt. & Budget, Washington, 1972—73; battalion comdr. Republic of Korea, 1973—74; comdr. 2d Brigade, 101st Airborne Div., Ft. Campbell, Ky., 1976—77; exec. asst. to sec. US Dept. Energy, Washington, 1979; sr. mil. asst. to dep. sec. US Dept. Def., Washington, 1979—81, asst. div. comdr. 4th Inf. Div. Ft. Carson, Colo., 1981—83, mil. asst. to sec. def. Washington, 1983—86; assigned to U.S. V Corps, Europe, 1986—87; dep. asst. to the Pres. for nat. security affairs NSC, Washington, 1987, asst. to Pres. for nat. security affairs, 1987—89; comdr.-in-chief US Forces Command, Ft. McPherson, Ga., 1989; chmn. Joint Chiefs of Staff The Pentagon, Washington, 1989—93; sec. US Dept. State, Washington, 2001—05; strategic limited ptnr. Kleiner Perkins Caufield & Byers, Menlo Park, Calif., 2005—. Founding chair America's Promise.; pub. spkr. addressing audiences across the country and abroad; mem. Wash. Baseball Club, 2005—. Author: (with Joseph E. Persico) My American Journey (autobiography), 1995. Decorated Legion of Merit (2), Bronze Star, Air medal, Purple Heart; named hon. knight comdr. Most Honorable Order of the Bath Queen Elizabeth II, 1993; recipient Presdl. Medal of Freedom (2), Ronald Reagan Freedom award, 1993, President's Citizens Medal, Congressional Gold Medal, Sec. of State Disting. Svc. Medal, Sec. of Energy Disting. Svc. Medal, Ellis Island Family Heritage award in Govt. Svc., Statue of Liberty-Ellis Island Found., Inc, 2005, Legion of Honor, France, 2006, several sch. and other inst. have been named in his honor; The White House fellow, 1972—73. Mem. Assn. U.S. Army. Republican. Episcopalian. Office: Kleiner Perkins Caufield & Byers 909 N Washington St Ste 700 Alexandria VA 22314

POWELL, DANA LINDSLEY, art association administrator, consultant; b. West Islip, NY, May 20, 1968; d. David Lawrence Powell and Judith Ann Larsh; m. Scott Matthew Russell, July 24, 2004; 1 child, Oliver Powell Russell. BA in Visual Arts, U. Calif., San Diego, 1989; MA in Mus. Studies, John F. Kennedy U., 1991; EdD in Learning and Instrn., U. San Francisco, 2001. Asst. educator San Diego Mus. Art, 1988—89, educator sch., youth, and family programs, 1992—94; archives technician San Francisco Nat. Maritime Mus., 1989—90; exhbn. developer Ind. Exhibitions, Berkeley, Calif., 1991—92; dir. of edn. for pub. programs Kidspace Mus., Pasadena, Calif., 1991—92; curatorial asst. Security Pacific Gallery, San Francisco, 1990—91; dir. of edn. Triton Mus. Art, Santa Clara, Calif., 1996—99; dir. creative edn. program Cultural Initiatives Silicon Valley, San Jose, Calif., 1999—2006; asst. print appraiser Butterfield and Butterfield Auctioneers and Appraisers, San Francisco, 2006—. Rsch. rev. editor Tchg. Artist Jour., Chicago, 2004—06; chmn. profl. devel. com. Americans for the Arts, Washington, 2004; curriculum advisor arts edn. Calif. Coll. Arts, Oakland, 2002. Contbr. articles to profl. jours. Mem.: Calif. Alliance for Arts Edn. (chmn. pub. policy com. 2003—). Avocations: gourmet vegetarian cooking, yoga, swimming, creative arts, travel. Personal E-mail: dana@powellrussell.com.

POWELL, DAVA ANNETTE, computer educator, grant writer; d. David Troy and Annie Elizabeth Powell. BE, NE La. U., 1994; M in Ednl. Tech., Northwestern State U., 1998, Specialist in Ednl. Tech., 2003. Lab asst. NE La. U., Monroe, 1991—94; tchr. Madison Parish Schs., Tallulah, La., 1994—98; computer lab grad. asst. Northwestern State U., Natchitoches, La., 1996—98; adj. instr. Remington Coll., Baton Rouge, 1998—2000; ednl. asst. La. State Dept Edn., Baton Rouge, 1999—2002; tchr. East Baton Rouge Schs., 2002—03, City of Baker Schs., La., 2003—; tchr. upward bound math and sci. So. U., Baton Rouge, 2005—; online educator PBS Tchr. Line, Baton Rouge, 2005—. Asst. sponsor Pepsters, Baker, La., 2003—; tchr. NASA Explorer Sch. Program, Alexandria, Va., 2004—; coach Robotics Team, Baker, La., 2005—. Author: (essay) Who Am I? (Cooper Fellowship Semi-Finalist, 1993). Mem. Parents, Tchr. Orgn., Baker, 2003—06; sponsor 4-H Club, 2005—. Named Top Ten Srs., Mortar Bd., 1994, Top Ten Sophomores, Cardinal and Amber Soc., 1992; recipient Presdl. award, NE La. U., 1992; grantee McNair award, U. Houston, 2005, Northwestern State U., 1996—98; scholar John Scott Meml. Fund, Scott Found., 1990; Presdl. scholar, NE La. U., 1990, La. Edn. Majors, LA State Dept Edn., 1990. Mem.: La. Assn. Educators (acting pres. 2004—05), La. Sci. Tchr. Assn. (assoc.), La. Computer Using Educators (life), Sigma Tau Delta (life). Avocations: swimming, reading, writing, surfing the internet, dance. Office Phone: 225-775-9750.

POWELL, DAVID CHARLES, music educator, meteorologist; b. Keokuk, Iowa, May 14, 1926; s. Othello Dotson and Miriam Estella (Trittschuh) Powell; m. Judith Ann Ahrens, Feb. 2, 1950; children: Walter David, Katharine Elise. MusB, Ind. U., 1949, MusM, postgrad., Ind. U., 1951; BS, U. Utah, 1964, MA, 1968, PhD, 1974. Cert. music tchr. Instr. piano Ea. Ky. State Coll., Richmond, 1951—52; tchr. math. and music Darby (Mont.) Pub. Schs., 1953—56; pvt. piano instr. Whitefish, Mont., 1956—62; rsch. scientist, sr. scientist meteorology Battelle, Pacific NW Nat. Lab., Richland, Wash., 1968—88; pvt. piano instr. Richland, 1989—. Contbr. articles and papers to profl. publs. Cmty. educator classical music history, 1981—. With U.S. Army, 1944—46, ETO. Grad. fellow, NASA, 1965—67. Mem.: Nat. Guild Piano Tchrs., Wash. State Music Tchrs. (treas., publicity com. 1989—91), Nat. Music Tchrs. Assn., Audubon Soc. (pres. lower Columbia Basin chpt. 1975—76). Episcopalian. Achievements include development of computer programs to model atmospheric conditions. Avocations: hiking, birdwatching, camping, travel, music. Home and Office: 2110 Hudson Ave Richland WA 99354 Office Phone: 509-946-4429. E-mail: res0szlg@verizon.net.

POWELL, DEBORAH ELIZABETH, pathologist, dean; b. Lynn, Mass., Nov. 28, 1939; MD, Tufts U., 1965. Diplomate Am. Bd. Pathology. Intern Georgetown Med. Ctr., Washington, 1965-66; resident in pathology NIH, Bethesda, Md., 1966-69; exec. dean, vice-chancellor clin. affairs U. Kans. Sch. Medicine, Kansas City, 1997—2002; dean, assst. v.p. for clin. scis. U. Minn. Med. Sch., Mpls., 2002—. Past pres. U.S. & Can. Acad. Pathology, Inc.; trustee Am. Bd. Pathology. Mem.: Am. Soc. Investigative Pathologists, Inst. Medicine, Coll. Am. Pathologists. Office: U Minn Med Sch Dean's Office MMC 293 Mayo 8293 420 Delaware St SE Minneapolis MN 55455 Business E-Mail: dpowell@umn.edu.*

POWELL, DENNIS D., computer systems network executive; BBA in Acctg., Oreg. State U. Former sr. ptnr. Coopers & Lybrand LLP; v.p., corp. contr. Cisco Systems, Inc., San Jose, Calif., 1997—2002, sr. v.p. corp. fin., 2002—03, sr. v.p., CFO, 2003—. Mem. FDIC Adv. Com. on Banking Policy; expert witness on fin. reporting Senate Banking Com. and Ho. Fin. Subcom. Mem.: AICPA (task force on fin-process R&D 2000), Fin. Execs. Internat. Office: Cisco Systems Inc 170 W Tasman Dr San Jose CA 95134*

POWELL, DINA HABIB, federal agency administrator; b. Cairo, 1973; d. Onsi Habib and Hoda Soliman. BA, U. Tex. Mem. rels. coord. to rep. Dick Army U.S. Ho. of Reps., Washington; dir. congl. affairs, sr. adv. to chmn. of Rep. Nat. Com. Washington, 1999—2001; spl. asst. to pres. for presdl. personnel, Exec. Office of Pres. The White House, Washington, 2001—05; asst. sec. ednl. & cultural affairs US Dept. State, Washington, 2005—. Office: US Dept State 301 Fourth St SW Rm 800 Washington DC 20547 Office Phone: 202-203-5118. Office Fax: 202-203-7469.

POWELL, DONALD ASHMORE, clinical research psychologist; b. Spartanburg, S.C., Oct. 29, 1938; s. Russell Kermit Powell and Mignon Kathlene Cox; m. Palmyra Langston, 1961 (div. 1972); children: Donald Langston, Donetta Plamyra, Ashley Preston, Stephanie Anne; m. Shirley L. Buchanan, Aug. 17, 1992 (dec. June 1998); m. Trisha Pope, May 18, 2002. BS, U. S.C., 1960, MA, 1962, PhD, Fla. State U., 1967. Rsch. psychologist Dorn VA Med. Ctr., Columbia, S.C., 1969—, acting dir. R&D, 1996-2000; prof. U. S.C. Sch. Medicine, Columbia, 1979—. Adj. prof. U. S.C., Columbia, 1969—; cons. U.S. Heart, Lung and Blood Inst., Bethesda, 1986—; program specialist VA Mental Health and Behavioral Scis., Washington, 1984-88. Author: (with others) Eyeblink Conditioning, 1999. Rsch. fellowship NIH, 1967-69; vis. scholar NIH, 1974; recipient Merit Rsch. award Dept. of Vet. Affairs, 1996—. Mem. Soc. for Neurosci., Am. Psychol. Soc., Pavlovian Soc. (Pavlovian Rsch. award 1991), Soc. for Neurosci. (pres. S.C. chpt. 1980-81, councilor 1982-85). Democrat. Avocations: running, reading. Home: 405 Hunt Cliff Dr Columbia SC 29229 Office: Dorn VA Med Ctr 6439 Garners Ferry Rd Columbia SC 29209-1638 Office Phone: 803-695-6821. Business E-Mail: donnie.powell@med.va.gov.

POWELL, DONALD E., federal agency administrator; b. Perryton, Tex., May 2, 1941; m. Twanna C. Powell; 2 children. BS in Econs., West Tex. State U.; grad., Southwestern Sch. Banking, So. Meth. U. Loan officer, sec. First Fed. Savings & Loan, Amarillo, Tex., 1963—71; with Boatmen's First Nat. Bank, Amarillo, Tex., 1971—97, chmn., pres., CEO First Nat. Bank Amarillo, Tex., 1997—2001; chmn. bd. FDIC, Washington, 2001—05; coord. Recovery & Rebuilding in the Gulf Coast Region US Dept. Homeland Security, 2005—. Active City of Amarillo Housing Bd., Franklin Lindsay Student Aid Fund, Cal Farley's Boys Ranch; adv. bd. mem. George Bush Sch. Govt. & Public Svc.; chmn. Amarillo C. of C.; chmn. bd. regents Tex. A&M U. Sys.; past bd. dirs. High Plains Bapt. Hosp., Harrington Regional Med. Ctr.

POWELL, DURWOOD ROYCE, lawyer; b. Raleigh, N.C., Nov. 21, 1951; s. Albert Royce and Powell; m. Leej Ida Copperfield, Mar. 1, 1980. BS, U. N.C., 1974, JD, 1979; LLM in Taxation, Emory U., 1985. Bar: N.C. 1979, U.S. Dist. Ct. (ea., mid. and we. dists.) N.C. 1981, U.S. Tax Ct. 1981, U.S. Ct. Appeals (4th cir.) 1984, U.S. Ct. Claims 1984, U.S. Supreme Ct. 1984, D.C. 1988, N.Y., 1989, U.S. Ct. Appeals (D.C. cir.) 1988, N.Y. 1989. Mgmt. analyst GAO, Norfolk, Va., 1974-76; tax staff Arthur Andersen & Co., Washington, 1979-80; assoc. Biggs, Meadows, Etheridge & Johnson, Rocky

Mount, NC, 1980-82, Biggs Law Firm, Rocky Mount, 1982-83; ptnr. Maupin, Taylor, Ellis & Adams, Raleigh, NC, 1985—, also bd. dirs., 1985—. Adj. prof. corp. taxation Grad. Sch. Bus., U. N.C., Chapel Hill, 1989-92; faculty Duke U. Tax and Estate Planning Conf., 1991; mem. negotiation project Harvard U., Cambridge, Mass., 1992. Contbr. articles to profl. jours. Tax reform com. Duke U., Washington, 1988. Mem. ABA (tax, corp., banking and securities sects.), N.C. Bar Assn. (tax and corp. sects.), Phi Beta Kappa, Phi Eta Sigma. Home: 7616 Wingfoot Dr Raleigh NC 27615-5485 Office: Maupin Taylor Ellis & Adams 3200 Beech Leaf Ct Ste 500 Raleigh NC 27604-1064

**POWELL, EARL ALEXANDER, III,** art museum director; b. Spartanburg, SC, Oct. 24, 1943; s. Earl Alexander and Elizabeth (Duckworth) P.; m. Nancy Landry Powell, July 17, 1971; children: Cortney, Channing, Sumner. AB with honors, Williams Coll., 1966; AM, Harvard U., 1970, PhD, 1974; DFA (hon.), Williams Coll., 1993, Otis Parson Art Inst. Tchg. fellow in fine arts Harvard U., 1970-74; curator Michener Collection U. Tex., Austin, 1974-76, asst. prof. art history, 1974-76; mus. curator, sr. staff asst. to asst. dir. and chief curator Nat. Gallery Art, Washington, 1976-78, exec. curator, 1979-80; dir. L.A. County Mus. Art, 1980-92, Nat. Gallery Art, Washington, 1992—. Chmn. US Commn. Fine Arts; trustee Am. Fedn. Arts, Morris and Gwendolyn Cafritz Found., White House Hist. Assn., Nat. Trust Hist. Preservation; Georgia O'Keeffe Found., John F. Kennedy Ctr. for Performing Arts; nat. adv. bd. O'Keeffe Mus.; mem. com. for preservation The White House; fed. coun. Arts and Humanities; fine arts adv. panel Fed. Res. Bd.; mem. overseer's com. Visit the Art Mus., Harvard; mem. Nat. Portrait Gallery Com.; mem. Pres.'s Com. on Arts and Humanities; mem. vis. com. Williams Coll. Mus. Art. Author: American Art at Harvard, 1973, Selections from the James Michener Collection, 1975, Abstract Expressionists and Imagists: A Retrospective View, 1976, Milton Avery, 1976, The James A. Michener Collection: Twentieth Century American Painting, catalogue raisonne, 1978, Thomas Cole monograph, 1990. Mem. Nat. Coun. on the Arts; mem. Pres.'s Com on the Arts and Humanities. With U.S. Navy, 1966-69, comdr. Res., 1976-80. Decorated officier Arts and Letters,chevalier Legion of Honor; grand ofcl. Order of the Infante D. Henrique medal, 1995; recipient King Olav medal, 1978, Bicentennial medal Williams Coll., 1995; Harvard U. travelling fellow, 1973-74, Mexican Cultural award, 1996, commendatore dell'Ordine al Merito della Republica Italiana, 1998. Mem. Am. Acad. Arts and Scis., Walpole Soc., Assn. Art Mus. Dirs., Am. Philos. Soc., Friends of Art and Preservation in Embassies. Office: Nat Gallery Art 2000B S Club Dr Landover MD 20785 Office Phone: 202-842-6001.

**POWELL, EDWARD A., JR., (NED POWELL),** nonprofit organization executive; b. Richmond, Va. m. Diane Powell. BA, Washington and Lee U.; MBA, U. NC, 1978. Lic. real estate broker Va. Yeoman USN, Def. Intelligence Agy.; owner, mgr. Mechanism Design, Inc., 1989—9?; asst. sec. fin. mgmt. US Dept. Veterans Affairs, 1998—2000, acting dep. sec., 2000—01; pres., CEO USO, Arlington, Va., 2002—. Former adj. prof. U. Richmond. Recipient Disting. Fed. Exec., Assn. Govt. Accountants, 2000. Mem.: World Pres. Orgn. Office: USO 2111 Wilson Blvd Ste 1200 Arlington VA 22201*

**POWELL, ELAINE MARIE,** writer, educator; b. St. Louis, Nov. 25, 1946; d. Edsel Arthur and Jessie Louise (Whitelaw) Hatfield; m. David Eugene Powell; children: Steven, Bryan. Grad. H.S., Florissant, 1964. Sec. U. Mo., Columbia, 1969—71, Francis Howell Sch. Dist., St. Charles County, Mo., 1985—93; scrapbook instr., cons., 1996—. Author: The Family Heritage Album. Coun. tng. staff Boy Scouts Am., 1980-85, dist. tng. chmn., 1982-85; mem. long range planning coun. Francis Howell Sch. Dist., 1989-93, others. Recipient Dist. award of merit Boy Scouts Am., 1983, Howell of Fame award, 1987, Silver Beaver award Boy Scouts Am., 1991. Mem.: First Families St. Louis, Ctrl. Fla. Geneal. Soc. (pres. 2003—). Republican. Presbyterian. Home and Office: 4620 Saddleworth Cir Orlando FL 32826-4126 Personal E-Mail: TheHeritageLady@aol.com.

**POWELL, JAMES BOBBITT,** health facility administrator, pathologist; b. Burlington, NC, Aug. 28, 1938; s. Thomas Edward and Sophia (Sharpe) P.; m. Pamela Oughton, Sept. 12, 1969 (div. Sept. 1979); 1 child, Daphne P. Markcrow; m. Anne Ellington, Oct. 20, 1984; children: James Bobbitt (dec.), John Banks, James Rosser, Helen Bobbitt. BA, Va. Mil. Inst., 1960; MD, Duke U., 1964. Diplomate Am. Bd. Pathology. Intern Duke U. Med. Ctr., Durham, NC, 1964-65; resident Cornell Med. Ctr., N.Y.C., 1965-67, Englewood (N.J.) Hosp., 1967-69; founder Biomed Labs, Burlington, NC, 1969—; pres. Roche Biomed. Labs., 1982-95; pres., CEO Lab. Corp. Am. Holdings, 1995-97; CEO Tripath Imaging, Burlington, NC, 1997—2000. Bd. dirs. Mid-Carolina Bank, Living Microsystems, Warren Land Co. Contbr. articles to sci. publs. Trustee Elon U. NC, 1979—, chmn. bd. trustees; chmn. bd. dirs. Alamance Found. Maj. M.C. U.S. Army, 1969—72. Mem. Alamance Country Club. Republican. Methodist. Avocations: tennis, US military history. Office: 1573 York Pl Burlington NC 27215

**POWELL, JAMES LAWRENCE,** educational association administrator, museum director, geologist; b. Berea, Ky., July 17, 1936; s. Robert Lain and Lizena (Davis) P.; m. Joan Hartmann; children: Marla, Dirk, Joanna. AB, Berea Coll., 1958; PhD, MIT, 1962; DSc (hon.), Oberlin Coll., 1983; LHD (hon.), Tohoku Gakuin U., 1986; DSc (hon.), Beaver Coll., 1992. Asst. prof., assoc. prof., prof. Oberlin Coll., Ohio, 1962-83, chmn. geol. dept., 1965—73, v.p., provost, 1975—81, assoc. dean, 1973—75, acting pres., 1981—83; pres. Franklin and Marshall Coll., Lancaster, Pa., 1983-88, Reed Coll., Portland, Oreg., 1988-91; pres., chief exec. officer The Franklin Inst., Phila., 1991-94; pres., dir. Los Angeles County Mus. Natural History, LA, 1994—2001; exec. dir. Nat. Physical Sci. Consortium, LA, 2001—. Mem. Nat. Sci. Bd., 1986-98; adj. prof. Univ. So. Calif., 1995-2001 Author: Strontium Isotope Geology, 1972, Pathways to Leadership: Achieving and Sustaining Success: A Guide for Nonprofit Executives, 1995, Night Comes to the Cretaceous: Dinosaur Extinction and the Transformation of Modern Geology, 1998, Mysteries of Terra Firma: Age and Evolution of the Earth, 2001, Grand Canyon: Solving Earth's Greatest Puzzle, 2005. Fellow: Geol. Soc. Am.; mem.: Phi Beta Kappa, Phi Kappa Phi, Sigma Xi. Office: Nat Physical Science Consortium Ste 348 3716 S Hope Los Angeles CA 90007-4344 Business E-Mail: jpowell@usc.edu.

**POWELL, JAMES MATTHEW,** history professor; b. Cin., June 9, 1930; s. Matthew James and Mary Loretta (Weaver) P.; m. Judith Catherine Davidorf, May 29, 1954 (dec. 1992); children: James, Michael, Mark, Mary Helen, Miriam, John Ba, Xavier U., Cin., 1953, MA, 1955; postgrad., U. Cin. 1955-57; PhD, Ind. U., 1960. Instr. Kent State U., Ohio, 1959-61; asst. prof. U. Ill., Urbana, 1961-65, Syracuse U., NY, 1965-67, assoc. prof. NY, 1967-72, prof. history NY, 1972—, dir. Ranke Cataloging Project NY, 1977—. Disting. vis. prof. medieval history Rutgers U., New Brunswick, 1996—97. Author: Medieval Monarchy and Trade, 1962, Civilization of the West, 1967, Anatomy of a Crusade, 1213-1221, 1986, 2d edit., 1990, Albertanus of Brescia: The Pursuit of Happiness in the Early Thirteenth Century, 1992; translator: Liber Augustalis, 1971, The Deeds of Pope Innocent III, 2004; editor: Innocent III: Vicar of Christ or Lord of the World, 1963, revised and enlarged 2d edit., 1994, Medieval Studies, 1976, 2d edit., 1992; (with George G. Iggers) Leopold von Ranke and the Shaping of the Historical Discipline, 1989, Muslims Under Latin Rule, 1100-1300, 1990, (with Michael Gervers) Tolerance and Intolerance: Social Conflict in the Age of the Crusades, 2001; contbg. editor: New Catholic Encyclopedia, 2000—; cons. in field. Grantee NEH, 1977-84, 84, Inst. for Advanced Study, Princeton, N.J., 1989-90, Progetto Radici, Brescia, Italy, 1994-95; Fritz Thyssen Stiftung, 1986, 89; recipient John Gilmary Shea prize Am. Cath. Hist. Assn., 1987, Fellow Royal Hist. Soc. (corr.); mem. Am. Hist. Assn. (1st v.p. 2005, pres. 2006), Am. Cath. Hist. Assn., Medieval Acad. Am., Soc. for Italian Hist. Studies (coun. 1976-79, v.p. 1991-92, pres. 1993-95), Midwest Medieval Conf. (pres. 1965-66), Soc. for Study of the Crusades and the Latin East (sec. 1989-95), Haskins Soc. Democrat. Roman Catholic. Office: Syracuse U Maxwell School Syracuse NY 13244-0001

**POWELL, JEFFREY SCOTT,** endocrinologist; s. Norman Emory and Barbara Ellen Powell; m. Ellen Lynn Rothbaum, June 11, 1995; children: Abigail, Ryan. BA cum laude in Biology, Harvard U., Cambridge, Mass., 1991; MD, Albert Einstein Coll., Bronx, N.Y., 1995. Diplomate Am. Bd. Internal Medicine. Intern to resident in internal medicine Columbia Med. Ctr., N.Y.C., 1995—98; fellow in endocrinology Colubmia U., Coll. Physicians and Surgeons N.Y.C., 1998—2001; endocrinologist Mt. Kisco (N.Y.) Med. Group, 2001—. Chief divsn. endocrinology No. Westchester Hosp., Mt. Kisco, 2006—. Contbr. articles to profl. jours. Fellow: Am. Coll. Endocrinology; mem.: Am. Assn. Clin. Endocrinology, Alpha Omega Alpha. Office: Mt Kisco Med Group 90 S Bedford Rd Mount Kisco NY 10549 Office Phone: 914-241-1050. Office Fax: 914-242-2915. Personal E-Mail: jpowell@mkmg.com.

**POWELL, JERRY W.,** lawyer; b. Montgomery, Ala., Jan. 6, 1950; BA cum laude, Birmingham-So. Coll., 1972; JD, U. Ala., 1975. Bar: Ala. 1975, U.S. Dist. Ct. Ala. (No. and Mid. dist), U.S. Ct. Appeals (11th cir.). Law clk. No. Dist. Ala., 1975—76; gen. counsel, sec. Compass Bancshares, Inc., Birmingham, Ala. Mem. editl. bd.: Alabama Law Review, 1973—75. Mem.: ABA, Am. Soc. Corp. Secretaries, Am. Corp. Counsel Assn. (pres. Ala. chpt. 1984—85), Ala. State Bar Assn., Birmingham Bar Assn., Order of Coif (bench and bar). Office: Compass Bancshares Inc 15 S 20th St Birmingham AL 35233 Office Fax: 205-297-3043. Business E-Mail: jerry.powell@compassbank.com.

**POWELL, KENDALL J.,** consumer products company executive; BA, Harvard Univ., 1976; MBA, Stanford Univ., 1979. Mktg. & mgmt. positions General Mills Inc., Mpls., 1979—90; v.p. mktg. dir. Cereal Partners Worldwde, 1990—96; pres. Yoplait USA divsn. General Mills Inc., Mpls., 1996—97, pres. Big G div., 1997—99, sr. v.p., 1998 2004; CEO Cereal Partners Worldwide, Morges, Switzerland, 1999—2004; exec. v.p. Meals, Pillsbury USA, Bakeries & Foodservice General Mills Inc., Mpls., 2004—05, exec. v.p. U.S. retail, 2005—06, pres., COO, 2006—. Bd. mem. Cereal Partners Worldwide. Bd. mem. Twin Cities United Way. Office: General Mills Inc 1 General Mills Blvd Minneapolis MN 55426*

**POWELL, KENNETH GRANT,** aerospace engineering educator; b. Euclid, Ohio, July 3, 1960; s. Thomas Edward and Mary Catherine (Byrum) P.; m. Susanne Maria Krummel, Aug. 31, 1991; children: Jasmine Tara, Ryan Grant, Nicole Maia. SB in Math., MIT, 1982, SB in Aeronautics, 1982, SM in Aeronautics, 1984, ScD in Aeronautics, 1987. Asst. prof. dept. aerospace engring. U. Mich., Ann Arbor, 1987-93, assoc. prof. dept. aerospace engring., 1993-2000, prof. dept. aerospace engring., 2000—02, Arthur F. Thurnau prof., 2002—. Lectr. Von Karman Inst. for Fluid Dynamics, Brussels, 1990, 96; cons. Ford Motors, Dearborn, Mich., 1992-95; cons. Detroit Edison, 1996-98; exec. dir. Francois-Xavier Bagnoud Prize Bd., 1998-2000. Named Presdl. Young investigator NSF, 1988; recipient Tchg. Excellence award U. Mich. Coll. Engring., 1992, Outstanding Tchg. award Tau Beta Pi, 1988, 99, 2005, Tchg. Excellence award Sigma Gamma Tau, 1989, 95. Fellow AIAA (assoc.); mem. Tau Beta Pi, Sigma Xi, Sigma Gamma Tau. Home: 5531 Spring Hill Dr Ann Arbor MI 48105-9552 Office: U Mich Dept of Aerospace Engring Ann Arbor MI 48109

**POWELL, LARRY,** communications educator; b. Greenville, Ala., May 14, 1948; s. A. Harold Powell and Virginia Brown; m. Clarine Thrower, Dec. 19, 1970. BA, Auburn U., Ala., 1970; MA, Auburn U., 1971; PhD, U. Fla., 1975. From asst. prof. to prof. Miss. State U., Starkville, 1975—86; vcons. Kitchens, Powell & Kitchens, Orlando, Fla., 1987—96; owner Powell Cons., Orlando, 1996—98; prof., former chair U Ala., Birmingham, 1998—. Vis. prof. Meisei U., Hino, Japan, 1984—85; prof. Ctrl. Fla. U., Orlando, 1996—98; media pollster Birmingham News, Birmingham, 2001—; cons. in field. Co-author: Political Campaign Communication, 2003, Interviewing: Situations and Content, 2005; contbr. articles to profl. jours.; co-author: Holy Murder: Abraham, Isaac, and the Rhetoric of Sacrifice, 2006. Polit. advisor Bus. Coun. of Ala., Montgomery, 1994—96, WVTM-TV/WBRC-TV, Birmingham, 2001—02. Named one of Top 100 Comm. Rschrs., Assn. of Comm. Adminstrs., 1998; recipient Miss. Jaycee Gov. award, 1986; Ala. Dept. Pub. Health grantee, 1999—2000. Master: So. States Comm. Assn. (life; chair polit. com. 1999—2000); mem.: Nat. Comm. Assn., Religious Comm. Assn. (life). Home: 328 Shadeswood Dr Hoover AL 35226 Office: Univ of Alabama Comm Studies Dept 901 S 15th St Birmingham AL 35294 Office Phone: 205-934-8784. Business E-Mail: lpowell@uab.edu.

**POWELL, LEWIS FRANKLIN, III,** lawyer; b. Richmond, Va., Sept. 14, 1952; s. Lewis F. Jr. and Josephine (Rucker) P.; m. Lisa T. LaFata; children: Emily, Hannah, Luke. BA, Washington & Lee U., 1974; JD, U. Va., 1978. Bar: Va. 1978, U.S. Dist. Ct. (ea. and we. dists.) Va. 1979, U.S. Ct. Appeals (4th cir.) 1979, U.S. Ct. Appeals (2d cir.) 1983, U.S. Ct. Appeals (11th cir.) 1992, U.S. Supreme Ct. 1985. Law clk. to judge U.S. Dist. Ct. (ea. dist.), Richmond, 1978-79; assoc. Hunton & Williams, Richmond, 1979—86, ptnr., 1986—. Pres. young lawyers conf. Va. State Bar, 1986-87. Bd. dirs. William Byrd Cmty. Ho., Richmond, 1982-87, Boys Club of Richmond, 1984-90, Maymont Found., Richmond, 1987-92, St. Christopher's Sch., Richmond, 1989-96. Mem. Richmond Bar Assn. (chmn. improvement justice com. 1982-83), 4th Cir. Jud. Conf., Am. Law Inst. Avocations: fly fishing, mountaineering, hiking. Office: Hunton & Williams Riverfront Plz East Tower 951 E Bird St Richmond VA 23219

**POWELL, LOUIE J.,** editor-in-chief, engineer, consultant; b. Jacksonville, Fla., Sept. 26, 1945; s. Louie J., Sr. and Annie L. Powell; m. Linda L. Carnright, Aug. 26, 1972; children: David E., Jeffrey M. BEE, Ga. Inst. Tech., 1968. Cert. profl. engr., N.Y., N.J., La. Consulting engr. GE Energy Consulting, Schenectady, NY 1969 98, mgr. hi-h consulting, 1990—2004. Various one-man and group exhbns. Fellow: IEEE (Richard Harold Kaufmann Technical Field award 2001). Methodist. Home: 14 Stone Clover Dr Saratoga Springs NY 12866

**POWELL, MARSHA,** director, educator, pathologist; BS in Math., SUNY, Cortland, 1978, MS in Math., 1992. Applications programmer Cornell U., Ithaca, NY, 1978—80; sr. systems analyst Cbord Group, Inc., Ithaca, 1980—82; prof., program chmn. Tompkins Cortland Coll., Dryden, NY, 1982—; computer forensic examiner Broome County Govt. Security, Binghamton, NY, 2003—. Pres., chmn. Cayuga Chamber Chorus, Ithaca, 1993—2003; patroller Nat. Ski Patrol, Cortland, 1993—2006. Recipient Incentive award for classroom rsch., Tompkins Cortland C.C., Coll. Tchg. Ctr., 1996, NY State Chancellor's award for excellence in tchg., NY State Dept. Edn., 2004. Mem.: High Tech. Crime Investigation Assn., Internat. Assn. Computer Investigative Specialists (cert.). Office: Tompkins Cortland CC 170 North St Dryden NY 13053 Office Phone: 607-844-8211.

**POWELL, MELCHIOR DANIEL,** educational administrator, lawyer; b. NYC, July 7, 1935; children: Anthony, Vanessa. BS, NJ State U., 1957; MA, George Washington U., 1963; JD, U. Balt., 1966; PhD, U. Md., 1968. Bar: Md. 1966. Atty. City of Greenbelt, Md., 1966-67; dir. contract rsch. Nat. Assn. Counties, 1967-71; assoc. prof. urban affairs U. No. Colo., Greeley, 1971-72; dir. Appalachian region com. Office of Rsch. Mgmt., Washington, 1972-73; dean Grad. Ctr. Pub. Policy and Adminstrn. Calif. State U., Long Beach, 1973-92, prof. emeritus, 1992—. Exec. sect. We. Govtl. Rsch. Assn., 1992-95; vis. prof. Fla. Atlantic U., 1995-96; exec. dir., pres. So. Md. Higher Edn. Ctr., 1997—; cons. in field. Author: Education for the Future Pub. Svc., 1981, Achieving Closer Ties, 1984; contbr. articles to profl. jours. Mem. Mayor's Task Force City of Long Beach, 1978, mem. charter comm., 1979, bd. dirs. poverty program, 1980; mem. Calif. workers compensation rate setting comm., 1991, So. Md. Workforce Infrastructure Bd. Served to lt. (j.g.), U.S. Navy, 1959-63. Mem. Western Govt. Rsch. Assn. (pres. 1980-82, exec. sec. 1989-93), Am. Soc. Pub. Adminstrn. (pres. Md. chpt. 1972-73, program chmn. Nat. Conf. 1980, conf.chmn. 1986, 93, pres. L.A. Metro chpt. 1976-77, Dykstra award 1977, Will Baughman award 1982), Urban Affairs Assn. (pres. 1986-87), Internat. Assn. Schs. and Insts. of Adminstrn. (v.p.

N.Am. 1989—, mem. bd. mgmt., 2001—). Democrat. Roman Catholic. Home: 422 Overlook Dr Lusby MD 20657-3202 Office: SMHEC 44219 Airport Rd California MD 20619 Office Phone: 301-737-2500. Business E-Mail: mpowell@smhec.org.

**POWELL, MICHAEL KEVIN,** investment company executive, former federal official; b. Birmingham, AL, Mar. 23, 1963; s. Colin and Alma Powell; m. Jane Knott; children: Bryan, Jeffrey. BA, Coll. William and Mary, 1985; JD, Georgetown U., 1993. Policy advisor to asst. sec. def. for internat. security affairs, Washington, 1988—90; law clk. to Hon. Harry T. Edwards U.S. Ct. Appeals (D.C. cir.), Washington, 1993—94; assoc. O'Melveny & Myers LLP, 1994—96; chief of staff divsn. antitrust U.S. Dept. Justice, Washington, 1996—97; commr. FCC, Washington, 1997—2001, chmn., 2001—05; sr. advisor Providence Equity Partners, Washington, 2005—. Formed cons. firm MK Powell Group, 2005—; bd. dirs. ObjectVideo Inc., 2005—. Bd. visitors Georgetown U. Law Ctr.; bd. dirs. U.S. Telecomm. Tng. Inst. Cavalry platoon leader, troop exec. U.S. Army, 1985—88, Amberg, Germany. Recipient Freedom of Speech medal, Media Inst., 1999; Henry Crown fellow, Aspen Inst., 1999. Office: Providence Equity Partners Inc 1050 Connecticut Ave NW Ste 1250 Washington DC 20036

**POWELL, NANCY JO,** federal official, former ambassador; b. Cedar Falls, Iowa; BA, No. Iowa U., 1970. Dep. chief of mission US Embassy, Lome, Togo, 1990—92, consul gen. New Delhi, 1993—95, dep. chief of mission Khaka, Bangladesh, 1995—97; US amb. to Uganda US Dept. State, Kampala, 1997—99, prin. dep. asst. sec. for African affairs, 1999—2001, acting asst sec. African affairs, 2001, US amb. to Ghana US Dept. State, Accra, 2001—02, US amb. to Pakistan Islamabad, Pakistan, 2002—04, prin. dep. asst. sec. & acting asst. sec. for legis. affairs Washington, 2004 05, acting asst. sec. Bur. Internat. Narcotics and Law Enforcement Affairs, 2005, sr. coord. for Avian & Pandemic Influenza, 2005—06; nat. intelligence officer for South Asia, Nat. Intelligence Council Office Nat. Intelligence, Washington, 2006—. Office: Office of Dir Nat Intelligence NEOB 725 17th St Washington DC 20500*

**POWELL, NICHOLE LARAI,** chemistry professor, researcher; d. Ripton Roy Powell and Grace Monica Clarke-Powell; 1 child, Maria-Cristina Pascoe. BS, U. West Indies, Mona, Jamaica, 1995; PhD, Ga. State U., Atlanta, Ga., 2003. Instr. Ga. State U., Atlanta, 2001—03; adj. instr. Ga. Perimeter Coll., Lawrenceville, Ga., 2003—05; asst. prof. Tuskegee U., Ala., 2004—. Chmn. academic affairs com. faculty senate Tuskegee U., 2005—. Mem.: Am. Chem. Soc. (chmn. elect Auburn Local sect. 2006, sec. Auburn Local sect. 2005), Am. Soc. Microbiology, Phi Beta Delta. Office: Tuskegee University 102 Armstrong Hall Tuskegee AL 36088 Office Phone: 334-724-4489. Business E-Mail: nlpowell@tuskegee.edu.

**POWELL, RAYMOND WILLIAM,** financial planner, school administrator; b. Waterbury, Conn., June 17, 1944; s. Don C. and Kathryn (Linhard) P.; m. Janet Yasinski, June 24, 1967; 1 child, Raymond Joseph. BS, So. Conn. State Coll., New Haven, 1966, MS, 1969; postgrad., U. Bridgeport, Conn. CFP; enrolled agt. CEO R.W. Powell Enterprises, Inc., fin. and tax cons., Prospect, Conn., 1972—; dir.-owner Educators Tax Svc., Watertown, 1972—; Powell's Acctg. Svc., 1975—; Powell's Fin. Planning Svc., 1977—; supt. of schs. Winchester, Conn., 1995—. Contbr. articles to profl. jours. Vice chmn. Watertown Town Coun., 1975-76. Mem. Nat. Assn. Enrolled Agts., Internat. Assn. Fin. Planners, Am. Soc. Tax Cons., Conn. Assn. Enrolled Agts. Democrat. Office: PO Box 7077 42 Waterbury Rd Prospect CT 06712-1238 Office Phone: 203-758-5700. Business E-Mail: powells.financial@snet.net.

**POWELL, RICHARD A.,** music educator; b. Augusta, Ga., Oct. 13, 1955; m. Kay P. Patterson, June 11, 1983; children: Kathryn I., Kathleen A. BA, Lander U., Greenwood, S.C., 1977—79. Band Dire. S.C. Dept. Edn. Band dir. North HS, North, SC, 1980—83, Ware Shoals HS, 1985—87, Woodruff HS, 1987—90, Ware Shoals HS, 1990—2001, Tamassee Salem HS, 2002—04; gen. music tchr. Anderson Sch. Dist. #5, 2004—05; band dir. Lakeside Mid. Sch., Anderson, 2005—. Recipient, S.C. Gov.'s Sch. Arts. Mem.: Music Educator's Nat. Conf. (assoc.), S.C. Band Dir.'s Assn. (assoc.; region band chmn. 1998—2000). Office: 115 Pearman Dairy Rd Anderson SC 29625 Office Phone: 864-260-5135. E-mail: richardpowell@anderson5.net.

**POWELL, RICHARD GORDON,** retired lawyer; b. Rochester, N.Y., Jan. 7, 1918; BS, Harvard U. 1938; LL.B., Columbia U. 1941. Bar: N.Y. 1941, 1952-85. Former mem. bd. mgrs. Englewood (N.J.) Community Chest; trustee, elder 1st Presbyterian Ch. Mem. ABA, Assn. Bar City of N.Y., Am. Law Inst. Home: 200 E 65th St # 33N New York NY 10021-4451

**POWELL, ROBERT ELLIS,** mathematics professor, dean; b. Lansing, Mich., Mar. 16, 1936; s. James Ellis and Mary Frances (Deming) P.; children: Carl Robert, Glenn Arthur, Charles Addison; m. Lisbeth Nilsen, Nov. 21, 1992. BA, Mich. State U., 1958, MA, 1959; PhD, Lehigh U., 1966. Instr. math. Lehigh U., 1964-66; asst. prof. math. U. Kans., Lawrence, 1966-69; vis. asst. research prof. U. Ky., Lexington, 1967-68; vis. asst. prof. math. Ind. U., Bloomington, summer 1969; assoc. prof. math. Kent State U., Ohio, 1969-74, prof. math., 1974-95, dean grad. coll., 1980-92, prof. math. emeritus, dean emeritus grad. coll., 1995—; prof. math., dean grad. sch., dir. rsch. U. Scranton, Pa., 1995-2000. Mem. Ohio Bd. Regents' Adv. Com. on Grad. Study, 1980-92, chmn., 1983-84. Co-author: Summability Theory, 1973, rev. edit., 1988, Intuitive Calculus, 1973; contbr. numerous articles to profl. jours. Bd. dirs. Kent State U. Found., 1981-91. NSF summer grantee, 1964, 65; recipient Fulbright award, 1988. Mem. Midwestern Assn. Grad. Schs. (bd. dirs. 1988-92, chmn. 1990-91), Coun. Grad. Schs. (bd. dirs. 1990 91) Northea Assn. Grad. Sch. (bd. dirs. 1990-2000). Home: 3490 Wild Indigo Ln Bonita Springs FL 34134

**POWELL, RONALD ROWE,** library science educator; b. Columbia, Mo., May 24, 1944; s. Hampstead Rowe and Elizabeth Floris (Sapp) P.; m. Jeanne Ann Branstetter, Jan. 28, 1967; children: Rebecca Lynn, Angela Leigh. AB, U. Mo., 1967; MS, Western Mich. U., 1968; PhD, U. Ill., 1976. Bibliographer U. Ill., Urbana, 1968-69, asst. circulation libr., 1969-71, rsch. asst., 1971-74, rsch. assoc., 1974-75; libr. dir. U. Charleston, W.Va., 1976-79; asst. prof. U. Mich., Ann Arbor, 1979-86; assoc. prof. U. Mo., Columbia, 1986-92, dir. grad. studies 1987-90, chmn. Dept. Libr. Sci., 1990-92; prof. Wayne State U., Detroit, 1993—, interim dir., 1999. Editl. bd. Assn. Libr. & Info. Sci. Edn., Raleigh, 1984-88, dir., 1989-91; vis. prof. Universidade de Brasilia, Brazil, 1985; sec. Coll. Libr. Sect., Assn. for Coll. and Rsch. Libr., Chgo., 1982; sr. fellow Coun. Libr. Resources, Wash., 1982; guest lectr. Moscow State U. of Culture, 1996. Author: Basic Research Methods for Librarians, 1997, 4th edit., 2004; co-author: Success in Answering Reference Questions, 1987, Basic Reference Sources, 1990, The Next Library Leadership, 2003, Basic Research Methods for Librarians, 2004; co-editor: Topics in Library and Information Studies, 1989-2000, Qualitive Research in Information Management, 1992; co-editor Jour. Edn. for Libr. and Info. Sci., 1995-2001; Research Methods in Library and Information Studies, 2000—; mem. editl. bd. Jour. Academic Librarianship, 2000-02, Libr. and Info. Sci. Rsch., 2002—. Recipient Curator's scholarship U. Mo., Columbia, 1962. Mem. ALA (chmn. standing com. libr. edn. 1992-93, chair libr. rsch. round table 1996-1998), Assn. Coll. and Rsch. Libr., Assn. for Libr. and Info. Sci. Edn., Mich. Libr. Assn., Internat. Info. Acad., Beta Phi Mu. Avocations: music, reading, tennis. Office: Wayne State Univ Libr and Info Sci Program 106 Kresge Detroit MI 48202 Home: 21529 Garrison St Dearborn MI 48124-2301 Office Phone: 313-577-6199. Business E-Mail: ad5328@wayne.edu.

**POWELL, SANDY,** costume designer; b. London, Apr. 7, 1960; Studied theater design, Ctrl. Sch. Art, London. Costumer designer for films including London Story, 1980, Caravaggio, 1986, Aria, 1987, The Last of England, 1988, Stormy Monday, 1988, For Queen and Country, 1988, Venus Peter, 1989, Killing Dad, 1989, Shadow of China, 1990, The Miracle, 1991, The Pope Must Die, 1991, Edward II 1991(also actress); The Miracle, 1991, Orlando, 1992 (Nominated BAFTA Award, Academy Award; Best Costume

Design, 1994), The Crying Game, 1992, Wittgenstein, 1993, Being Human, 1993, Interview with a Vampire, 1994 (Nominated BAFTA Award, Best Costume Design, 1995), Rob Roy, 1995, Michael Collins, 1996, The Wings of a Dove, 1997 (Nominated Golden Satellite Award, BAFTA Award; Best Costume Design, 1998), The Butcher Boy, 1997, Velvet Goldmine, 1998 (Nominated Academy Award, Best Costume Design; Won Best Costume Design, British Academy Awards, 1998), Hilary and Jackie, 1998, Shakespeare in Love, 1998 (Won Academy Award, Best Costume Design; Nominated BAFTA Award, Best Costume Design, 1998), Felicia's Journey, 1999, Miss Julie, 1999, The End of the Affair, 1999, Far From Heaven, 2002, Gangs of New York, 2002, Sylvia, 2003, The Aviator, 2004 (Academy award for best costume design, 2005); guest appearances Anatomy of a Scene. Address: c/o Lynda Mamy Drury House 34-43 Russell St London WC2B 5HA England

**POWELL, SCOTT,** diversified financial services company executive; With Comml. Credit Co., 1988; dir. credit risk mgmt. Global Consumer Grp. Citigroup, Inc.; head retail lending Bank One Corpn., 2003; co-CEO home fin. J.P. Morgan Chase & Co., head Chase auto and student fin., 2005—. Bd. trustees Phipps Houses. Office: JP Morgan Chase & Co 270 Park Ave New York NY 10017-2070*

**POWELL, SHIRLEY THERESSA,** elementary school educator; b. Kingfisher, Okla., Sept. 28, 1949; d. Walter Charles and Alzadie Bessie Baker; m. Floyd Dean Powell, Feb. 22, 1969; children: Marc Len, Corey Lyndale, Ginger LaDean, Carmen LaShay. BA in Edn., Wichita State U., 1988; MA in Tchg., Friends U., Wichita, Kans., 1990. Cert. elem. tchr. Kans. State Dept. of Edn., 2004. 3d gr. tchr. Chisholm Trail Elem., Wichita, Kans., 1988—92, 4-5 gr. tchr., 1992—2002, 5th gr. tchr., 2002—. Team leader Chisholm Trail Elem., Wichita, Kans., 1995—2003, quality performance accreditation team, 1995—2003, yr. book advisor to students, 1996—, sch. store advisor to students, 1996—2003, career day amb. trainer, 1996—. Recipient Salute To Delta Gt. Tchrs. award, Delta Sigma Theta Sorority, Inc., 1992, Outstanding Svcs. to Children of Chisholm Trail Elem. award, Chisholm Trail Elem. Prin., 1993-94, Outstanding Tchr. of Yr. award, Wichita Assn. of Black Sch. Educators, 1995. Mem.: Links, Inc. (assoc.; fin. sec. 2004—, Wichita chpt.), Phi Delta Kappa (assoc.), Delta Sigma Theta (assoc.). Office: Chisholm Trail Elem Sch 6015 Independence Wichita KS 67219 Office Phone: 316-973-9452. Business E-Mail: spowell2@usd259.net.

**POWELL, SUE ROSE,** art educator; b. Erie, Pa., Mar. 22, 1928; d. Arthur John and Mayme (Marshall) Hoffman; m. Robert Gramberg (div.); 1 child, Cathy Rhea Gramberg (dec.); m. Russell Rea Powell (dec.); 1 stepchild, Lenora Powell Crundwell. Degree, Am. Acad. Art, 1950; student, Palos Hills C.C., 1978—80. Tchr. oil and porcelin paintings Palos Hills CC 1981—. Vol. Cystic Fibrosis Found., Chgo., 1957—80. Independent. Baptist. Avocation: art.

**POWELL, THOMAS ARTHUR,** publisher; b. N.Y.C., Jan. 30, 1929; s. Ernest Powell and Sophie Huber. Freelance writer, 1946—60; mgr. L&H Orchid Nursery, Summit, NJ, 1960—64; exec. dir. Horticultural Soc. N.Y., N.Y.C., 1964—68; editor, pub. The Avant Gardener, N.Y.C., 1968—. Author: Avant Gardener Handbook, 1973, Your Garden Homestead, 1975. Fellow: Garden Writers Assn. (Quill & Trowel award 1985); mem.: Mass. Horticultural Soc. (Gold Medal 1982), Garden Club Am. (Sarah Chapman Francis Medal 1978). Avocation: sailing. Home: 238 E 82nd St New York NY 10028 Office: The Avant Gardener PO Box 489 New York NY 10028

**POWELL, THOMAS EDWARD, III,** biological supply company executive, physician; b. Elon College, N.C., Aug. 1, 1936; s. Thomas Edward, Jr., and Sophia Maude (Sharpe) P.; m. Betty Durham Yeager, June 19, 1965; children: Frances Powell Barnes, Thomas Edward IV, Caroline Powell Rogers. AB in Biology, Va. Mil. Inst., 1957; MD, Duke U., 1961; MA, Harvard U., 1966. Surgeon USPHS, 1966-68; co-founder Biomed. Reference Labs., Inc., Burlington, N.C., 1969, exec. v.p., 1969-75, chmn. exec. com., 1979-82, also dir.; exec. v.p. Carolina Biol. Supply Co., Burlington, N.C., 1968-80, chmn., 1977-80, 94—, pres., 1980-94; pres. Wolfe Sales Corp., Burlington, 1980-84, Waubun Labs. Inc., Schriever, La., 1980—, Bobbitt Labs., Inc., Burlington, 1983-94; bd. mgrs. Wachovia Bank and Trust Co. N.A., Burlington. Contbr. articles to profl. jours. Bd. dirs. United Way Alamance County, Burlington, 1968—; bd. dirs. Elon Coll., N.C., 1968—, sec., 1975—; bd. dirs. Am. Cancer Soc., Burlington, 1971-81; bd. dirs. Burlington Day Sch., 1973—, pres., 1974-78, 80-84; bd. dirs. N.C. Citizens for Bus. and Industry, Raleigh, 1983-87, Nat. Found. for Study of Religion and Econs., Greensboro, 1984-88, Blue Ridge Sch., Dyke, Va., 1985-90. Served to capt. USAR, 1957-66. Recipient Citizens Service award Elon Coll. Alumni Assn., 1980. Mem. Assn. Biology Lab. Edn., N.C. Acad. Sci., Alamance-Caswell Med. Soc., N.C. Med. Soc., Assn. Venture Founders, Newcomen Soc. Democrat. Mem. United Ch. of Christ. Clubs: Alamance Country (Burlington); Capital City (Raleigh, N.C.); Congl. Country (Washington); N.C. Country (Pinehurst); Hope Valley Country (Durham, N.C.); Greensboro City.

**POWELL, WILLIAM ARNOLD, JR.,** retired bank executive; b. Verbena, Ala., July 7, 1929; s. William Arnold and Sarah Frances (Baxter) Powell; m. Barbara Ann O'Donnell, June 16, 1956; children: William Arnold III, Barbara Calhoun, Susan Thomas, Patricia Crain. BSBA, U. Ala., 1953; grad., La. State U. Sch. Banking of South, 1966. With Am. South Bank, N.A., Birmingham, Ala., 1953—93, asst. v.p., 1967, v.p., br. supr., 1968—72, sr. v.p., br. supr., 1972—73, exec. v.p., 1973—79, pres., 1979—83, vice chmn. bd., 1983—93, also bd. dirs.; pres. AmSouth Bancorp., 1979—93; ret., 1993. Bd. dirs. AmSouth Bank, Fla. Bd. dirs. United Way Found.; past pres. United Way, campaign chmn., 1987; life mem. Birmingham Met. Devel. Bd.; bd. dirs. Warrior-Tombigbee Devel. Assn.; life trustee Ala. Ind. Colls.; mem. pres.'s coun. U. Ala., Birmingham, life mem. bd. visitors. Lt. U.S. Army, 1954—56. Named William A. Powell, Jr. Endowed Professorship in his honor, U. Ala. Mem.: Met. Devel. Assn. (life; bd. dirs.), Birmingham Area C. of C. (life; bd. dirs.), Birmingham Country Club, The Club, Mountain Brook. Home: 2114 Hickory Ridge Cir Birmingham AL 35243-2925

**POWELL, WILLIAM COUNCIL, SR.,** service company executive; b. Burlington, NC, Nov. 5, 1948; s. Thomas Edward Jr. and Annabelle (Council) P.; m. Jacqueline Garrison, July 3, 1976; children: William C. Jr., Ashley C. Student, U. S.C., 1968-69; BS, Va. Mil. Inst., 1971; MBA, Wake Forest U. 1974; postgrad., Elon Coll. 1972. Lic. pilot, real estate broker. NC adminstrv. assoc. Carolina Biol. Supply Co., Inc., Burlington, 1971—91; v.p. Bobbitt Labs., Burlington, 1974-77, pres., 1977—82; owner HEADS, Inc., Elon, NC, 1978—, pres., 1984—; owner Ashwil Acres Farm, Mebane, NC, 1981—2005. Pres. Granite Diagnostics, Inc., Burlington, 1981-84, UST Specialists Inc., 1991-2000, Burlington, Warren Land Co., 1994-2005, Merrymount Property Owners Assn., Inc., 1996-2000, Merrymount Boat Slip Assn., Inc., 1996-2005, Stratonet Inc., 1996-2001, Forest Realm, Inc., 2001—, Goat Island Maritime Inc., 2001—, Powell Realm Inc., 2001—, Poignard Compact Inc., 2001-; owner Powell Real Estate, Burlington, 1979-2001, bd. dirs. Excalibur Lock Co., Inc., Waubun Labs. Inc., Schriever, La.; v.p. fin. Environ. Responsible Bus. Inc., 1992-97; bd. mgrs. Babcock Sch. Alumni Coun. Wake Forest U., 1981-85; mgr. Macon Farm, 1994-92; chmn. bd. Ensci Corp. Inc., 1991-95, ptnr. Port Assocs., 1987-2002, Port Assocs. II, 1992-2002; chmn. bd. Netpath Inc., 1995-96, bd. dirs.; filed for election N.C. Senate, 2000, 02. Bd. advisors Elon Coll. (N.C.), 1984-86, bd. visitors, 1987-92; bd. advisors Duke U. Marine Lab., Beaufort, N.C., 1985-92; nat. adv. coun. Baruch Marine Inst., 1998—; mem. adv. panel Air Quality Compliance Panel State of N.C. Dept. Environ. Health and Natural Resources, 1994—; guardian mem. Boy Scouts Am., Burlington, 1985; trustee Dr. T.E. Powell Jr. Trust, 1989-95; v.p. fin. Cherokee Coun. Boy Scouts of Am., 1990-92, exec. bd., 1990-94, exec. bd. Old N. State Coun., 1994-95; mem. Forest Bt. United Meth. Ch., Burlington, N.C. Capt. USAR, 1971-79. Recipient Bill Fish Cert. State of S.C., 1983, 2 Bill Fish Certs. State of N.C., 1990, Sower's award Duke U., 1985, N.C. Gov.'s Cup for Billfishing, 1991, 3rd Pl., Big Rock Blue Marlin Tourn., 1998. Mem. NRA (life), Newcomen Soc. N.Am. (life), Billiard Congress Am., Am. Angus Assn., Billiard and Bowling Inst. Assn., NC

Forestry Assn. (legis. affairs com. 1994—), N.C. Wildlife Habitat Found. (life), Ducks Unltd. (life sponsor, area chmn. 1985-87, 1997-2005), Safari Club Internat. (state pres. 1985-88, life), Aircraft Owners and Pilots Assn., Cessna Pilots Orgn., Atlantic Coast Conservation Assn. (life), Alamance Wildlife Club (bd. dirs. 1992-95, 2000-03, pres. 1999-2000), Rolls Royce Owners Club (life), N.Am. Hunting Club (life), Found. N.Am. Wild Sheep (life), Chaine des Rotisseurs (chevalier 1991), Brotherhood of the Knights of the Vine (master knight 1991), 10 Point Hunt Club, Am. Angus Assn., Nat. Wild Turkey Fedn., Quail Unltd. (life), NC Cattlemans Assn. (life), Nat. Cattlemans Assn., Inc., Internet Users Group Alamance, Ocean Green Assn., Debordieu Club, Nat. Soc. SAR, Sons Confederate Vets., Alamance County Cattleman's Assn., Citation Fishing Team (capt 1979—), Alamance Country Club, Debordieu Beach Club, Litchfield Carriage House Club. Home: 1109 W Front St Burlington NC 27215-3610 Office: Home Entertainment and Decor Sys Inc 945 E Haggard Ave Elon NC 27244 also: Netpath Inc 2260 S Church St Ste 601 Burlington NC 27215-5380 Personal E-Mail: wcp@netpath.net.

**POWELL GEBHARD, JOY LEE (BOK SIN LEE),** small business owner; b. Jan. 29, 1936; arrived in U.S.A., 1956, naturalized, 1962; d. Yong Joon and Chun Jal Lee; m. Jimmy Wayne Powell, Sept. 24, 1960; children: Chun Jal Lee, Miran Victoria, D. Gebhard; m. Karl Ten Eyck Gebhard, Oct. 15, 1995. Grad., Internat. Speech Acad., Pusan, Korea, 1952, Nat. U. Pusan, 1953—55, McMurry Coll., Abilene, Tex., 1956—58; BA, Wayland Bapt. U., Plainview, Tex., 1966; postgrad., Cen. State U., Okla., 1967—68. Cert. antique appraiser and cons. Nurse Rok Med. Sch., Pusan, 1950—53; news anchor Pusan Radio Sta., 1953; sec., ret. choir organizer chaplain's office U.N. Army divsn. 8069, Pusan, 1954—56, Meth. Mission, Pusan, 1955—56, U.S. A.S.C. Office, Ploydada, Tex., 1958, Am. U., Washington, 1958—60; with Washington Post, U.S. Acad. Sci., 1960; with spl. study of prejudice among children grades 1 to 12 Pub. Opinion and Propaganda, 1965—66; tchr. Oklahoma City Sch. Sys., 1968—70; head social studies dept. Dunjee H.S., 1968; tchr. Spanish Carl Albert H.S., 1969; owner Internat. Antiques, Upperville, Va., 1973—; founder, dir. Healing Inc., 1997—. Co-founder, charter mem. lit. mag. Mang Hiang. Contbr. articles to profl. jours., poetry New Voices in American Poetry, 1978, poems and essays to Korean periodicals. Mem.: World Affairs Coun. Washington, Nat. History Preservation, Smithsonian Assocs. Avocations: music, writing, swimming, collecting, travel. Home and Office: PO Box 221 Upperville VA 20185-0221

**POWELSON, GALE DAWN,** elementary school educator; b. Defiance, Ohio, Jan. 19, 1953; d. Arlo Lee and Majorie May Wagner; m. Robert Louis Powelson, Aug. 16, 1974; children: Michelle Dawn Patrick, Matthew Robert. M in ednl. adminstr., Ind. U./Purdue U., 1995—96, BSc in elem. edn., 1990—94. Classroom tchr. Meadowbrook Elem., New Haven, Ind., 1994—; elem. prin. Village Elem., Ft. Wayne, Ind., 2004. Adj. prof. Ind. U./Purdue U., Ft. Wayne, Ind., 1998—. Mem.: Nat. Reading Recovery Coun. (assoc.), Assn. of Supervision and Curriculum Devel. (assoc.), Nat. Assn. of Elem. Principals (assoc.), Internat. Reading Assn. (assoc.; local ira officer 2004—05), Delta Kappa Gamma (assoc.), Ind. U./Purdue U. Ft. Wayne Alumni Assn. (life), Kappa Delta Phi (life; pres. 1999—2005). Catholic. Avocations: travel, horticulture. Home: 10711 State Rd 101 Monroeville IN 46713 Office: East Allen County Schools US 930 East New Haven IN 46774 Personal E-mail: GPOW1234@aol.com. Business E-Mail: gppowelson@eacs.k12.in.us.

**POWELSON, JOHN JAY,** music educator; b. Fla. m. Elizabeth Powelson, Jan. 15, 2000; children: Andrew, Zachary. MusB, U. Wash., Seattle, 1996; MEd, U. Phoenix, Seattle, 2002. Cert. profl. Tchr. Wash., 1996, Ariz., 2003. Orch. dir. Liberty HS, Renton, Wash., 2003, Westwood HS, Mesa, Ariz., 2003—. Office: Westwood HS 945 W 8th St Mesa AZ 85201

**POWER, A. KATHRYN,** federal agency administrator; m. Brian Power; children: Matthew, Brendan. BA in edn., St. Joseph's Coll., Md.; MEd, Western Md. Coll.; postgrad. Harvard U. Tchr. various pub. schs.; computer systems analyst US Dept. Def.; exec. dir. RI Coun. Cmty. Mental Health Centers, 1985—90; dir. RI Anti Drug Coalition, Gov.'s Drug Program, RI Office Substance Abuse, RI Dept. Mental Health, Retardation and Hospitals, 1993—2003, Ctr. for Mental Health Services, Substance Abuse and Mental Health Adminstrn., HHS, Rockville, Md., 2003—. Pres. Nat. Assn. State Mental Health Program Directors, 1997. Capt. USNR. Recipient Award for Disting. Svc., Sec. US HHS, 2005; fellow Toll fellow, Coun. State Legislators, 1991. Office: Ctr for Mental Health Services 5600 Fishers Ln Rockville MD 20857*

**POWER, CAROLYN PORTER,** elementary school educator, principal; b. Clinton, Mo., Mar. 16, 1944; d. Hubert Dan and Rue Kathern Porter; m. Robert Allen Power, Aug. 21, 1970; children: Ronald Allen, Brian Robert. BS in Elem. Edn., Ctrl. Mo. State U., Warrensburg, 1966; M in Religious Edn., Southwestern Bapt. Theol. Sem., Ft. Worth, Tex., 1968. Cert. elem. edn., early childhood, kindergarten, mid-mgmt. Tchr. grade 1 Reed's Ferry Elem. Sch., Merrimack, NH, 1968—72; tchr. asst. APT, Title III Program, Merrimack, 1972—73; tchr. asst. grades 5-6 spl. edn. Hamilton Park Ind. Sch. Dist., Richardson, Tex., 1989—90; tchr. kindergarten Highland Park Ind. Sch. Dist., Tex., 1990—, MLA summer sch. prin., 2002—. Mem. dist. strategic planning com. Highland Park Ind. Sch. Dist., 1999—2000, 2003, curriculum writer, 06; mem. dist. leadership coun. Bradfield Elem. Sch., Highland Park, 1998—2001. Author: Dist. Math. Curriculum, Model Instrnl. Program, 1999; project mgr. curriculum manuals, 2001. Pres. YWA Mo. State Bapt. Conv., Jefferson City, 1964—65; local pres. PTA, Northrich Elem. Sch., Richardson, 1984—86; dist. PTA officer Richardson Ind. Sch. Dist. Coun., 1988—89; mem. exec. bldg. com. 1st Bapt. Ch., Richardson, 1980—85. Recipient Tchr. of Yr., Bradfield Elem. Sch., 1998—99. Mem.: Assn. Tex. Profl. Educators, Kindergarten Tchrs. Tex., Tex. PTA (hon.), Pi Lambda Theta. Baptist. Business E-Mail: powerc@hpisd.org.

**POWER, CHANDRA LYNN,** elementary school educator; b. Athens, Ga., Oct. 15, 1959; d. James Lucas and Evelyn Darthula (Patton) Power; children from previous marriage: Alexandra Adkins, Jessica Adkins, Samantha Adkins. BS in Edn., U. Ga., 1980, MEd, 1982, PhD, 1998. Tchr. Hart County HS, Hartwell, Ga., 1981—83, Washington (Ga.)-Wilkes HS, 1986, 1988—95, 1999—2001, Madison County HS, Danielsville, Ga., 2002, Clarke Ctrl. HS, Athens, Ga., 2003—, head dept. English, 2004—. Adj. prof. U. Ga., Athens, 1999—. Author: editor: Mentor Teacher, 1997. Troop leader Oglethorpe County coun. Girl Scouts US, 1999. Named Star Tchr., Wilkes County Bd. Edn., 2000, Tchr. of Yr., 2002. Mem.: Ga. Coun. Tchrs. English, Nat. Coun. Tchrs. English. Democrat. Baptist. Avocations: reading, writing, hiking, movies, music. Home: PO Box 794 Crawford GA 30630 Office: Clarke Ctrl HS 350 S Milledge Ave Athens GA 30605

**POWER, DAVID M.,** advertising executive; BA, Univ. Louisville, 1993. Pres., COO Power Creative, Louisville. Office: 11701 Commonwealth Dr Louisville KY 40299-2358

**POWER, FRANCIS WILLIAM,** newspaper publisher; b. Webster, SD, Aug. 12, 1925; s. Frank B. and Esther C. (Fowler) P.; m. Margaret Jean Atkinson, Mar. 24, 1951; children: Patricia Ann, John Michael, Kerry Jean. BBA, U. N.Mex., 1948. Display advt. sales rep. The Register, Santa Ana, Calif., 1948-51; advt. mgr. Valley Morning Star, Harlingen, Tex., 1951-62; gen. mgr. Pampa (Tex.) Daily News, 1962-69; bus. mgr. Brownsville (Tex.) Herald, 1969-75; pub. The Lima (Ohio) News, 1975-91; v.p. Freedom Comm., Inc., until 1991; ret., 1991. Served with USNR, 1943-46. Mem.: Shawnee Country Club, Elks, Rotary. Roman Catholic. Office: Freedom Comm Inc 17666 Fitch Irvine CA 92614-6022

**POWER, J.D., III, (JAMES DAVID POWER III),** marketing executive; b. Worcester, Mass., May 30, 1931; m. Julie Power (dec. 2002); 4 children; m. Joan Power, 2003. BA in English, Coll. of the Holy Cross, Worcester, Mass., 1953; MBA, U. Penn., 1959; PhD (hon.), Coll. of the Holy Cross, Calif. Lutheran U., Calif. State U. Northridge, Coll. Misericordia. Financial analyst

Ford; mktg. rsch. cons. Marplan GM; mktg. rsch. exec. J.I. Case; dir. corp. planning McCulloch Motors Inc., Los Angeles, Calif.; founder, pres. J.D. Power & Assocs., Calif., 1968—, chmn., 1996—. Adj. prof. mktg. Calif. State U. Northridge. Line officer duty U.S. Coast Guard, Arctic and Antarctica. Recipient Disting. Service Citation, Automotive Hall of Fame, 1992. Office: J D Power & Assocs 2625 Townsgate Rd Westlake Village CA 91361

**POWER, JOHN BRUCE,** lawyer; b. Glendale, Calif., Nov. 11, 1936; m. Sandra Garfield, Apr. 27, 1998; children by previous marriage: Grant, Mark, Boyd. AB magna cum laude, Occidental Coll., 1958; JD, NYU, 1961; postdoctoral, Columbia U., 1972. Bar: Calif. 1962. Assoc. O'Melveny & Myers, L.A., 1961—70, ptnr., 1970—97, resident ptnr. Paris, 1973—75; Sheffelman disting. lectr. Sch. Law, U. Wash., Seattle, 1997. Mem. Social Svcs. Commn. City of L.A., 1993, pres., 1993; pres. circle, exec. com. Occidental Coll., 1979-82, 91-94, chair, 1993-94; adj. prof. UCLA Sch. Law, 1999; mem. Tri-Bar Opinion Com., 2005-. Contbr. articles to jours. Bd. dirs. Met. L.A. YMCA, 1988—, treas., 1998-2001; bd. mgrs. Stuart Ketchum Downtown YMCA, 1985-92, pres., 1989-90; mem. L.A. County Rep. Ctrl. Com., 1962-63; trustee Occidental Coll., 1992—, vice-chmn., 1998-2001, chmn., 2001-03, acting gen. counsel, 1998-2000. Recipient YMCA Golden Book of Disting. Svc. award, 2002, Alumni Seal award Occidental Coll., 2003; Root Tilden scholar. Fellow Am. Coll. Comml. Fin. Lawyers (bd. regents 1999-03); mem. ABA (comml. fin. svcs. com., com. 3d party legal opinions, vice chair 2005-, UCC com., bus. law sect.), Am. Bar Found., Calif. Bar Assn. (chmn. partnerships and unincorporated assns. com. 1982-83, chmn. uniform commn. code com. 1983-86, chmn. opinions com. 2000-04, exec. com. 1987-91, chmn. bus. law sect. 1990-91, chmn. coun. sect. chairs 1992-93, liaison to state bar commn. on future of legal profession and state bar 1993-95, Bus. Law Sect. Lifetime Achievement award 2004), L.A. County Bar Assn. (exec. com. comml. law and bankruptcy sect. 1970-73, 86-89), Internat. Bar Assn., Fin. Lawyers Conf. (bd. govs. 1982—, pres. 1984-85), Exec. Svc. Corps (sec. 1985-00, dir. 1994-, vice-chmn. 2000—), Occidental Coll. Alumni Assn. (bd. govs. 1965-68, pres. 1967-68), Phi Beta Kappa (councilor 1982—, pres. 1990-92). Office: O Melveny & Myers 400 S Hope St Los Angeles CA 90071-2899 Personal E-mail: johnpower@earthlink.net.

**POWER, JOSEPH ALOYSIUS, JR.,** lawyer; b. Oct. 15, 1952; s. Joseph Aloysius and Mary Ellen (Cavenaugh) Power; m. Susan Vohs, Apr. 26, 1980; children: Joseph Aloysius III, Michael Anthony, Ryan Patrick, James Ian. BA, U. Notre Dame, 1974; JD, Loyola U., Chgo., Ill., 1977. Bar: Ill. 1977, U.S. Dist. Ct. (no. dist.) Ill. 1977, U.S. Ct. Appeals (7th cir.) 1994, U.S. Supreme Ct. 1992. Assoc. John D. Hayes & Assocs., Chgo., 1977—84; ptnr. Hayes & Power, Chgo., 1984—91, Power, Rogers & Lavin, Chgo., 1991—93, Power, Rogers & Smith, Chgo., 1993—. Chmn. bd. dirs. Assn. of Trial Lawyers Assurance a mutual risk retention group, 1988—2000; author, lectr. Ill. Inst. Contg. Legal Edn., Springfield, Ill., 1983—89; bd. mgrs. Trial Lawyers for Pub. Justice, 1994—, v.p., 1996—97, pres.-elect, 1997—98, pres., 1998—99. Trustee Loyola U., Chgo., 2004—; bd. dir. Ill. Pub. Action, Chgo., 1987—93. Fellow: Inner Cir. of Advocates, Internat. Acad. Trial Lawyers, Am. Coll. Trial Lawyers; mem.: U.S. Sen. Judiciary Com. (chmn.'s adv. coun. 1994, Ill. Supreme Ct. rules com. 1995—2004, chmn. 1996—2001), ATLA, Ill. Bar Assn., Ill. Trial Lawyers Assn. (author, lectr. 1984—, bd. mgrs. 1984—, chmn. membership com. 1985—87, chmn. legis. com. 1987—89, 3d v.p. 1989—90, 2d v.p. 1990—91, pres. elect 1991—92, pres. 1992—93), Chgo. Bar Assn. (chmn. young lawyers sect. fed. trial bar advocacy program No. dist. Il 1984), ABA, Chgo. Athletic Assn. Democrat. Roman Catholic. Home: 344 W Wellington Ave Chicago IL 60657-5637 Office: Power Rogers & Smith Three First National Plaza 70 West Madison St Suite 5500 Chicago IL 60602 Office Phone: 312-236-9381. Business E-Mail: joepower@prslaw.com.

**POWER, JOSEPH EDWARD,** lawyer; b. Peoria, Ill., Dec. 2, 1938; s. Joseph Edward and Margaret Elizabeth (Birkett) P.; m. Camille June Repass, Aug. 1, 1964; children— Joseph Edward, David William, James Repass Student, Knox Coll., Galesburg, Ill., 1956-58; BA, U. Iowa, 1960, JD, 1964; CAP, The Am. Coll., Bryn Mawr, Pa., 2004. Bar: Iowa 1964. Law clk. to judge U.S. Dist. Ct., 1964-65; mem. Bradshaw, Fowler, Proctor & Fairgrave, P.C., Des Moines, 1965—2005, of counsel, 2005—. Trustee Am. Inst. Bus., 1987-2002, chmn., 1992-2002; bd. dir. Iowa Law Sch. Found., 1992-2004, Plymouth Ch. Found., 1991-99; bd. dir. Des Moines Cmty. Found., 1996—, sec.-treas., 2001—; bd. dir. Iowa Natural Heritage Found., 1995—, chmn., 2003-05; mem. Des Moines Civil War Roundtable. Fellow Am. Coll. Trust and Estate Counsel (state chair 1994-2000); mem. ABA, Iowa Bar Assn. (chmn. probate, property and trust law com. 1983-87), Polk County Bar Assn., Des Moines Estate Planners Forum (pres. 1982-83), Wakonda Club, Rotary. Mem.United Ch. Of Christ. Home: 1928 Elm Cr West Des Moines IA 50265 Office: Bradshaw Fowler Proctor & Fairgrave 801 Grand Ave Ste 3700 Des Moines IA 50309 Office Phone: 515-246-5844. Business E-Mail: power.edward@bradshawlaw.com.

**POWER, MARY SUSAN,** political scientist, educator; b. Hazleton, Pa., July 5, 1935; d. Younger L. and Cleo (Brook) Power; 1 child, Catherine Laverne. BA, Wells Coll., 1957; postgrad., Exeter U., Eng., 1955-56, Yale U., 1958-59; MA, Stanford U., 1960; PhD, U. Ill., 1961. Asst. prof. Susquehanna (Pa.) U., 1961-64; assoc. prof. U. Ark., Fayetteville, 1965-68; assoc. prof. polit. sci. Ark. State U., State University, 1968-79, prof., 1979—2000, prof. emeritus, 2000—. Author: (book) Before the Convention, Religion and the Founding Fathers, 1984, Jacques Maritalm and the Quest for a New Commonwealth, 1992, Political Philosophy & Cultural Renewal: Collected Essays of Francis Wilson, 2001; columnist (newspaper) The Son, 2005—; contbr. articles to profl. jours. Mem. Fed. Edn. Commn. States, 1982—84; N.E. chair Arkansans for Progress, 1990—96; alt. del. Rep. Nat. Conv., 1972, 1976, 1988, del., 1992; mem. State com. Ark. Rep. Com., 1968—96, sec. 1978—80; mem. Craighead County Election Commn., 1986—88; chmn. Craighead County GOP, 1986—88, vice chmn., 1990—96, N.E. regional chmn., 1988—96; chmn. Craighead County Sheffield for Gov., 1990; mem. exec. com. Ark. Rep. Party, 1990—96, N.E. regional chair, 1988—96; treas. women's soc. Blessed Sacrament Ch., Jonesboro, 1996—2000, chmn. jubilee 2000; chair Silver Caths., 2002—; bd. dirs. Beacons and Bridges, 2005. Relm Found. fellow, 1960, NSF-Am. Polit. Sci. Assn. fellow, 1963, Nat. Def. Seminar fellow, Nat. War Coll., 1973, NEH fellow, 1978, Pres.'s fellow, Ark. State U., 1988—89. Mem.: AAUP (state sec. 1978—80, pres. 1983—90), So. Polit. Sci. Assn., Am. Polit. Sci. Assn., Ark. Polit. Sci. Assn. (bd. dirs., v.p. 1992—93, pres. 1993—94), Phi Kappa Phi (pres. 1991), Phi Gamma Mu (sec.-treas. 1990—2000), Phi Sigma Alpha. Republican. Roman Catholic. Personal E-mail: spower@fastdata.net.

**POWER, MICHAEL L.,** advertising executive; BA, Univ. Louisville, 1965. CEO, founder Power Creative (formerly Power Graphics), Louisville, 1976—. Office: 11701 Commonwealth Dr Louisville KY 40299-2358

**POWER, PEGGY ANN,** elementary school educator; b. Chgo., Sept. 17, 1973; d. Edward and Lois Power. BA, U. Ill., Chgo., 1994, MEd, 1996, postgrad., 2004—. Cert. elem. sch. tchr., Ill. Rsch. asst. U. Ill., Chgo., 1991-96; sales asst. Chgo. Bd. Trade, 1991-96; spl. edn. tchr. Gladstone Elem. Sch. Chgo. Bd. Edn., 1995—. Poet: Outstanding Poets of 1994, Best Poems of the 90's, 1992, Distinguished Poets of America, 1993. Active Wis. Dairy Coun., 1996—, Lawry's Menu for Success, Chgo., 1996—, Artist-Sch. Acad. Ctr., Chgo., 1996—; rep. Chgo. Tchr.'s Union, 1997—; bd. dirs., elem. v.p., 2004—, IFT/AFT del., 2004—. Recipient Gwendolyn Brookes Poet Laureat award, 1990; Baer-Darfler scholar Morgan Park Women's Assn., 1994-96; Marilyn Mucha fellow U. Ill., Chgo., 1995. Mem. ASCD, Coun. Exceptional Children, Nat. Coun. Tchrs. English, U. Ill. Chgo. Alumni Club, Pi Lambda Theta. Democrat. Roman Catholic. Avocations: Karate, poetry, pottery, kayaking. Home: Apt 407 710 Oakton St Evanston IL 60202-2927 Personal E-mail: peggypower@juno.com.

**POWER, SAMANTHA J.,** public policy educator, writer; b. Dungarvan, Ireland, 1970; Grad., Yale U., Harvard U. Law Sch. Reporter covering wars in former Yugoslavia US News & World Report and Economist, 1993—96; polit. analyst Internat. Crisis Group; prof. practice in pub. policy, JFK Sch. Govt Harvard U., founding exec. dir., Carr Ctr. for Human Rights, 1998—2002. Author: A Problem from Hell, America and the Age of Genocide, 2003 (Pulitzer prize, 2003, Nat. Book Critics Cir. award gen. nonfiction, 2003, Artur Ross prize for best book in US fgn. policy, 2003); co-editor (with Graham Allison): Realizing Human Rights, 2000; contbr. articles to pubs. such as The New Yorker, NY Rev. Books, Washington Post, NY Times. Recipient Nat. Mag. award for best reporting, 2005. Office: Carr Ctr Human Rights Policy Harvard Univ - Rubenstein-217 79 John F Kennedy St Cambridge MA 02138 E-mail: samantha_power@harvard.edu.*

**POWER, ANTHONY RICHARD, JR.,** educational sales professional; b. Chgo., June 14, 1942; s. Anthony Richard and Bernadine Rene (Schwenke) P.; m. Marianne Fugiel, Mar. 15, 1980; children: Kathleen Mary, Anthony Richard III. BA, Quincy Coll., 1964; MS, U. Notre Dame, 1974. Cert. tchr., Ill. Sci. tchr. St. Rene Sch., Chgo., 1964-70; sci. coord. Queen of All Saints Sch., Chgo., 1970-76; sci. and math. product mgr. Ideal Sch. Supply Co., Oak Lawn, Ill., 1976-79, customer svc. mgr., 1980-83, Midwest sales mgr., 1983-85; nat. sales mgr. Ednl. Teaching Aids, Vernon Hills, Ill., 1985-89, v.p., 1989-97; accounts mgr. Numerical Algorithms Group, Downers Grove, Ill., 1997-2001; midwest acct. mgr. Freedom Sci., Vernon Hills, Ill., 2001—, midwest regional mgr., 2001—04, Texthelp Sys., 2004—. Lectr., De Lourdes Coll., Des Plaines, Ill., 1970-78; sci. adviser, Archdiocese of Chgo., 1969-76. Author sci. edn. materials. Pres. Orchard Estates Condominium Assn., 1986-87; chmn. Vernon Hills Fire and Police Commn., 1995—. Mem. Northeastern Ill. Sci. Assn. (pres. 1970-75), U.S. Golf Assn., Internat. Brotherhood Magicians, K.C. Roman Catholic. Avocations: magic, music, golf. Home: 241 Tally Ho Dr Vernon Hills IL 60061-2900 Office: Texthelp Sys 241 Tally Ho Dr Vernon Hills IL 60061 Office Phone: 847-549-0344. Personal E-mail: arpnd74@aol.com. Business E-mail: dpowers@texthelp.com.

**POWERS, BRUCE RAYMOND,** writer, language educator, consultant; b. Bklyn., Dec. 10, 1927; s. George Osborne and Gertrude Joan (Bangs) P.; m. Dolores Anne Dawson, July 25, 1969; children: Christopher, Patricia Student, U. Conn., 1947—49; AB, Brown U., 1951, MA, 1965; postgrad., U. Pa., 1961. Announcer, engr. Sta. WNLC, New London, Conn., 1946—47; tng. officer CIA, Dept. Def., 1951—55; TV sales/svc. rep. NBC, 1955; TV news writer and reporter Movietone News UP Assns., Inc., 1955—56; asst. to pres. Gotham-Vladimir Advt., Inc., 1956—57; asst. account exec. D'Arcy Advt. Co., 1957—58; asst. campaign dir. Cmty. Counseling Svcs., Inc., 1958—59; dir. fund-raising campaign Tamblyn & Brown, Inc., 1959—60; instr. Brown U., Providence, 1963—65, Ryerson Poly. Inst., Toronto, 1966, Nazareth Coll., Rochester, NY, 1966—67; asst. prof. English and comm. studies Niagara U., Lewiston, NY, 1967—86, chmn. permanent curriculum com. English dept., 1970—71, assoc. prof., 1986—92, prof., 1986—92, prof. emerito, 1992—; dir. Film Repertory Ctr., 1971—92, dir. comm. studies program, 1973—87. Prodr., mng. dir. Exptl. Film Retrospective, N.Y. State Coun. Arts, Buffalo, 1972; narrator (documentary) Niagara: Fading in the Mist, 1996; panelist, judge Artists Com. 2d World Festival Animated Films, Zagreb, Yugoslavia, 1974; lectr., vis. artist ARTPARK, Lewiston, 1975; project dir. Bicentennial Symposium, N.Y. State Am. Revolution Bicentennial Commn., Buffalo, 1975-76; rsch. assoc. Ctr. Culture and Tech., U. Toronto, 1977-81; keynote spkr. Dupont de Nemours & Co. Health and Safety Conf., Buffalo, 1990; prinr. Moon Island Documentary Group, 1997— Co-author: (with Marshall McLuhan) The Global Village, Oxford, 1989; editor The Film and Study Guide, 1973-74 Served with Underwater Demolition Teams, USNR, PTO, 1945-46 Scholar, Brown U., 1961—62. Mem. MLA, Underwater Demolitions Teams/Seal Assn. Va. Beach, Broadcast Edn. Assn., Soc. Cinema Studies, Am. Soc. Journalism Sch. Adminstrs., Assn. Edn. Journalism and Mass Comm., Internat. Exptl. Film Soc. (founding pres. 1971-73), Ariz. Sr. Acad. U. Ariz., We. N.Y. Audio-Visual Assn., N.Y. Coll. English Assn., Phi Beta Kappa Roman Catholic. Home: 915 Sun Valley St North Tonawanda NY 14120-1952 Office Phone: 716-694-4815.

**POWERS, CLAUDIA MCKENNA,** state legislator; b. Key West, Fla., May 28, 1950; d. James Edward and Claudia (Antrim) McKenna; children: Gregory, Theodore, Matthew, Thurston. BA in Edn., U. Hawaii, 1972; MA, Columbia U., 1975. Cert. tchr., N.Y. Mem. Greenwich Rep. Town Meeting, Conn., 1979-93, sec. bldg. com., 1982-84, sec. legis. com., 1986—88, 1990—93; mem. Conn. Ho. of Reps., Hartford, 1993—, ranking mem. govt. adminstrn. and elections com., 1995-96, asst. minority leader, 1997-98, vice chmn. Rep. bill rev. com., 1997—2004, house minority whip, 1999—2003, dep. minority leader, 2003—, mem. spl. com. of inquiry into impeachment of the gov., 2004. Mem. editl. bd. Greenwich Mag., 1995-98. Conn. commr. Edn. Commn. of the States, 2000—, also mem. steering com.; campaign chmn. Greenwich Rep. Town Com., 1984, 85, chmn., 1986-90; sec. Rep. Round Table, Greenwich, 1988-90; bd. govs. Riverside Assn., Greenwich, 1987-91, sec., 1991-92; class mother Riverside Sch., Greenwich, 1984-90; mem. altar guild Christ Ch., Greenwich, 1990—, lay eucharistic min., 2004—; adminstrv. coord. Greenwich Teen Ctr., 1990-91; alt. del. Rep. Nat. Conv., New Orleans, 1984—, San Diego, 1996; v.p. LWV of Greenwich, 1990-91; bd. trustees Norwalk Maritime Ctr., 2001—; bd. dirs. Gov.'s Prevention Partnership, 2004—. Episcopalian. Home and Office: 15 Hendrie Ave Riverside CT 06878-1808

**POWERS, DAVID RICHARD,** educational administrator; b. Cambridge Springs, Pa., Apr. 5, 1939; s. William Herman and Elouise Fancheon (Fink) Powers; m. Mary Julia Ferguson, June 11, 1960. Student, Pa. State U., 1957-60; BA, U. Pitts., 1963, MA, 1965, PhD, 1971. Dir. CAS advising ctr. U. Pitts., 1966-68, asst. dean faculty, 1968-70, asst. to chancellor, 1970-76, assoc. provost, 1976-78 vice provost, 1970-79, v.p. for acad. affairs George Mason U., Fairfax, Va., 1979-82; vice chancellor for acad. affairs W.Va. Bd. Regents, Charleston, 1982-88; exec. dir. Minn. Higher Edn. Coord. Bd., St. Paul, 1989-94, Nebr. Coord. Commn. Post-secondary Edn., Lincoln, 1994—2005, exec. dir. emeritus, 2005. Prin. author: Making Participatory Management Work, 1983, Higher Education in Partnership with Industry, 1988; contbr. articles to Ednl. Record, Adult Learning, Forum for Applied Rsch. on Pub. Policy. Founder mem. Ed. Commn. Western Govs. U. Grantee USOE Faculty Seminar, Taiwan, 1967, ARC Ctr. for Edn. & Rsch. with Industry Appalachian Regional Commn., 1983, Republic of China Sino-Am. Seminar, 1985; recipient Award for Acad. Quality W.Va. Coun. Faculty, 1986. Mem. State Higher Edn. Exec. Officers, Western Coop. Ednl. Telecomm., Civil Air Patrol, Pi Sigma Alpha. Avocation: boating. Home: 6513 Spencer Ln Clinton WA 98236 Office Phone: 360-341-1533. Personal E-mail: davidpowers@whidbey.com.

**POWERS, EDWARD ALTON,** minister, educator; b. Jamestown, N.Y., Oct. 26, 1927; s. Leslie Edgar and Mabelle Florence (Alton) P.; children: Randall Edward, Christopher Alan, Ann Lynn. BA, Coll. of Wooster, 1948; MDiv, Yale U., 1952; EdD, Columbia U., 1973. Ordained to ministry Congl. Ch. 1951. Pastor, Hamden, Conn., 1949-53, Pleasant Hill, Ohio, 1953-56; sec. dept. youth work Congl. Christian Ch. Bd. Home Missions, 1956-60; gen. sec. divsn. Christian edn., bd. home missions Congl. and Christian Chs. 1960-61; divsn. Christian edn.; bd. homeland ministries United Ch. of Christ, 1962-73; gen. sec., divsn. evangelism, edn., ch. ext. United Ch. Bd. Homeland Ministries, 1973-79; mem. faculty Inst. Mgmt. Competency, Am. Mgmt. Assn., N.Y.C., 1980-87; affiliate faculty Milano Grad Sch., New Sch. U., 1981—. Mem. program bd. divsn. edn. and ministry Nat. Coun. Chs., 1963-80; mem. edn. working group World Coun. Chs.; chmn. Peace Priority Team, United Ch. of Christ, 1970-75, adminstr., editor sexuality study, 1977; ptnr. Cane Powers Cons., and Powers, Wayno & Assocs., 1987-2003. Author: Journey Into Faith, 1964, Signs of Shalom, 1973, (with Rey O'Day) Theatre of the Spirit, 1980, In Essentials Unity, 1982, Youth in the Global Village, 1982; also articles. Home: 13 Gramercy Park W Apt 5B New York NY 10003-1759 Office Phone: 212-229-5400 ext. 1520. Personal E-mail: powersea@aol.com.

**POWERS, ELIZABETH WHITMEL,** lawyer; b. Charleston, SC, Dec. 16, 1949; d. Francis Persse and Jane Coleman Cotten (Wham) P.; m. John Campbell Henry, June 11, 1994 (dec. Jan. 1997); m. Henry C. B. Lindh, June 16, 2000. AB, Mt. Holyoke Coll., 1971; JD, U. S.C., 1978. Bar: SC 1978, NY 1979. Law clk. to justice S.C. Cir. Ct., Columbia; assoc. Reid & Priest, N.Y.C., 1978—86, ptnr., 1986—97; of counsel LeBoeuf, Lamb, Greene & MacRae, N.Y.C., 1997—2004, ptnr., 2004—. Exec. editor S.C. Law Rev., Columbia, 1977-78. Vol. N.Y. Jr. League, N.Y.C., 1983—; bd. dirs. The Seamen's Ch. Inst., 1996—2006, sec., 1999—2006; trustee Ch. Club, 1991—94, 1997—2001, v.p., 1992—94. Mem.: Nat. Soc. Colonial Dames in State of N.Y. (pres. 1992—95), Nat. Soc. Colonial Dames of Am. (parliamentarian 1994—2000, regent Gunston Hall 2001—02), S.C. Bar Assn., ABA.

**POWERS, HELEN,** columnist, writer; b. Alton, Ill., Jan. 13, 1925; d. Charles Lawrence Rayborn and Ethel Lowder Howard; m. Henry Powers (dec.); children: Lawrence Anthony, Timothy Joseph. Columnist Florissant Valley Reporter, Mo., 1959—61; theater critic Beloit Daily News, Wis., 1961—63, Johnson County Squire, Leawood, Kans., 1963—64, Johnson County Scout, 1964—65, News Times, Danbury, Conn., 1965—72; feature writer and columnist Sunday Post, Bridgeport, 1970—73; freelance pub. rels. Candlewood Theatre, New Fairfield, Conn., 1974—81, Conn. and N.Y., 1974—81; lectr. women's clubs, 1974—93; columnist Citizen News, New Fairfield, Conn., 1990—. Author: Signs of Silence, 1972 (First prize, Conn. Press Women, 1973, Second prize, Nat. Press Women, 1973); performer: How to Live Like a Super Star, 1974 (Spkr. of Yr., Conn. Fedn. of Women's Clubs, 1980); author: Biggest Little Cat Book, 1978 (First prize, Conn. Press Women, 1979, Second prize, Nat. Press Women, 1979), Parents' Guide to the Five U.S. Svc. Acads., 1985 (cert. of appreciation, U.S. Military Acad., 1987), Winding Roads - A New Eng. Notebook of Wisdom and Wit, 1999, Winding Roads - The Perfect Prince or Just Another Frog, 2000, Winding Roads - Star Struck, 2001, Winding Roads - Treasures from an Attic in New England, 2002, (plays) A Nice Jewish Affair, 1974, Save the Seeds, Darling, 1977, Of Hearts and Hoofers, 1978, (newspaper column) Winding Roads, 1991—. Vol. Meals -on-Wheels, Wethersfield Hist. Soc., Rocky Hill Hist. Soc., Fairfield Hills Hosp.; exec. bd. Old Forge Condominiums, Rocky Hill, Conn., 1989—, sec. and newsletter. Scholar, Godfrey General. Libr. Mem.: Pyquag Writers, Wethersfield Hist. Soc., Rocky Hill Hist. Soc., DAR. Independent. Roman Catholic. Avocations: doll collecting, dollhouses, miniatures, genealogy. Home: 602 Briarwood Ct Rocky Hill CT 06067

**POWERS, HENRY MARTIN, JR.,** oil industry executive; b. Bath, Maine, July 18, 1932; s. Henry Martin and Eva (Saunders) Powers; m. Hepzibah Hinchey Reed, June 20, 1959; children: Henry Martin III, Carlton Reed. BS, Maine Maritime Acad., 1954. Marine engr. Am. Export Lines, N.Y.C., 1954-58; staff engr. Bull & Roberts Inc., N.Y.C., 1958-59; gen. sales mgr. Williams Bros., Inc., Portland, Maine, 1959-61; v.p. C. H. Sprague & Son Co., Boston, 1961-72, pres., 1972—, also chmn. bd. dirs.; chmn. bd. dirs. Sprague, Inc., Portsmouth, NH, 1999—. Chmn. Pease Devel. Authority, 1990—93; bd. dirs. Shanley Corp., Strawbery Banke Inc., 1st N.H. Banks, Seaward Constrn. Co., Santa Holding Co., Intelligent Controls, Environ. Resource Return. V.p. Seacoast United Fund, 1967—69; chmn. fuels, energy com. New Eng. Coun., 1974—75; pres. Portsmouth Coun., 1966—67; bd. visitors Maine Maritime Acad. Served to lt. USNR, 1956—58. Mem.: Mechanic Fire Soc., Navy League, Cumberland Club (Portland), Algonquin Club (Boston), Masons. Office: Sprague Inc 2 Intl Dr Ste 1 Portsmouth NH 03801-6810 Home: 100 Shepard's Cove Rd I-2 Kittery ME 03904 Office Phone: 603-431-1000. Personal E-mail: hpowers5@comcast.net.

**POWERS, JAMES G.,** corporate financial executive; With Arthur Andersen & Co., 1983—91; controller Moog Automotive, Inc., 1991—93; v.p., controller Berg Elec. Corp., 1993—95; v.p. fin. Crain Industries, Inc.; exec. v.p. Viasystems, 1997—2001, sr. v.p., chief fin. officer, 2001; chief fin. officer UniGroup, 2002—. Office: UniGroup 1 Premier Dr Fenton MO 63026

**POWERS, JAMES MATTHEW,** neuropathologist; b. Cleve., Sept. 15, 1943; s. Alfred Patrick and Margaret Anne (Gunther) P.; m. Karen P. Smith, 1983; children: Kristin, Scott, Conor. BS in Biology, Manhattan Coll., 1965; MD, Med. U. S.C., Charleston, 1969. Diplomate in anatomic pathology and neuropathology Am. Bd. Pathology. Asst. prof. pathology Med. U. S.C., Charleston, 1973-76; dir. electron micros. lab. VA Hosp., Charleston, 1973-76; assoc. prof. pathology Med. U. S.C., Charleston, 1976-80, prof. pathology, 1980-88; vice chmn. dept. pathology Columbia Coll. Physicians and Surgeons, N.Y.C., 1989-92; assoc. chair of edn. U. Rochester (N.Y.), 1994-97, dir. residency tng. program, 1994—2003, prof., dir. neuropathology, 1992—2005. Soc. Biol. Stain Commn., 1994—2001. Author: (practice guidelines) Archives Pathology and Laboratory Medicine, 1995, Greenfield's Neuropathology, 2002; mem. editl. bd.: Human Pathology, 1991—2005, Brain Pathology, 1995—2000, Acta Neuropathologica, 1995—2005, Biotech. and Histochemistry, 1994—2001, Modern Pathology, 1996—2004, Neurology, 1999—2004, Am. Jour. Surg. Pathology, 1999—2005, Jour. Neuropath. Exptl. Neurology, 2000—06; contbr. chpt. to book. Mem. Internat. Soc. Neuropathology (v.p. 1994-97), Am. Assn. Neuropathologists (pres. 1993, Moore award 1975, 76, 77, 81), U.S.-Can. Acad. Pathology. Office: U Rochester Box 626 601 Elmwood Ave Rochester NY 14642-0001 Office Phone: 585-275-3202. Business E-mail: james_powers@urmc.rochester.edu.

**POWERS, JOHN KIERAN,** lawyer; b. Schenectady, Aug. 2, 1947; s. Paul Joseph and Anne Marie (Leahy) P.; children: Erin Kelly, Megan Kerry. BS, U. Notre Dame, 1969; JD, Union U., 1972. Bar: N.Y. 1973, U.S. Dist. Ct. (no. dist.) N.Y. 1973, U.S. Dist. Ct. (so., ea. and we. dists.) N.Y. 1982, U.S. Ct. Appeals (2d cir.) 1984, U.S. Supreme Ct. 1985, U.S. Dist. Ct. (no. dist.) N.Y. 1982. Assoc. Medwin and McMahon, Albany, 1973-77; pvt. practice law Albany, 1973-80; pres. John K. Powers P.C., Albany, 1980-87; ptnr. Powers and Santola, Albany, 1987—. Contbr. articles to profl. publs. Trustee N.Y. State Lawyers Polit. Action Com., 1983-88, treas., 1989-93, chmn., 1993—; trustee ATLA Polit. Action Com., 1995-98. Fellow Roscoe Pound Found. Mem. ABA (sustaining vice-chair, legis. subcom., automobile law com., trial and ins. practice sect., state leader com. on state legis. sect.), Nat. Coll. Adv. (co-founder), ATLA (life, state del. 1990, bd. govs. 1990—, exec. com. 1995—), Am. Bd. Trial Advocates (advocate), N.Y. State Bar Assn. (sustaining, lectr., exec. com. and chmn. legis. com. trial lawyers sect.), N.Y. State Trial Lawyers Assn. (sustaining, bd. dirs. 1983-88, chmn. key person legis. com., chmn. com. atty. referral com., exec. com. 1986—, treas. 1988-89, v.p. 1989-91, 1st v.p. 1990-91, pres.-elect 1991-92, pres. 1992-93, award of merit 1990, 94, award of excellence 1991, Pres. award 1995, 96, 98, 99, 2000, dist. svc. award 1997), N.Y. Trial Lawyers Inst. (lectr. and program chmn. 1981—, treas. 1988-89, pres. 1992-93), (life) N.Y. State Head Injury Assn. (co-counsel 1983-85, bd. dirs. 1992-93, 1st v.p. 1993—), Capitol Dist. Trial Lawyers Assn. (bd. dirs. 1979-81, v.p. 1983-85, pres. 1985-86), Pa. Trial Lawyers Assn., Alban County Bar Assn. (lectr.), Chief Judge's Com. to Improve Availability of Legal Svcs., Chief Judge's Pro-Bono Monitoring Com., Civil Justice Found. (guest lectr. Law Sch. NYU, Albany Law Sch., U. Syracuse Law Sch., Albany Med. Coll.), Trial Lawyers for Pub. Justice, Lions (pres. Scotia, N.Y. chpt. 1979-80). Democrat. Roman Catholic. Home and Office: 39 N Pearl St Albany NY 12207-2785

**POWERS, JOHN T., JR.,** former mayor; Mayor City of Spokane, Wash., 2001—03. Bd. dirs. Assn. Wash. Cities, Inland Northwest Tech. Edn. Ctr., Spokane Regional Econ. Devel. Coun.; co-chair Spokane Task Force on Race Rels., U.S. Conf. Mayors; mem. Gas & Elec. Utility Restruction Task Force, Wash. State Competitiveness Coun., Assn. Northeast Wash. Mayors.

**POWERS, KENNETH,** urogynecologist; BS, Columbia U., N.Y.C., 1984, MD, 1988. Diplomate Am. Bd. Ob-Gyn. Resident in ob-gyn N.Y. U., N.Y.C., 1989—93; attending physician ob-gyn N.Y. U., Bellevue Hosp., N.Y.C., 1993—94, Jacobi, North Ctrl. Bronx Hosp., Bronx, NY, 1999—, Montefiore Med. Ctr., Jack D Weiler Hosp., Bronx, 1994—, Lincoln Med. and Mental Health Ctr., Bronx, 2001—. Chief comte. ob gyn, dept family medicane Montefiore Med. Ctr., 1994—98, dir. female pelvic medicine and reconstructive surgery,

2001—, Lincoln Med. and Mental Health Ctr., 2003—; assoc. prof. Albert Einstein Coll. Medicine, Bronx, 2006—. Reviewer: Am. Jour. Obstetrics and Gynecology, 2005—, Brit. Jour. Obstetrics and Gynecology, 2005—, Internat. Urogynecology Jour., 2005—, Jour. Pelvic Medicne and Surgery, 2005—, Jour. Reproductive Medicine, 2005—, Internat. Jour. Obstetrics and Gynecology, 2005—. Fellow: ACS, Am. Coll. Ob-Gyn.; mem.: Westchester Ob-Gyn Soc. Avocations: running, sailing, skiing, scuba diving, hiking. Office: Montefiore Med Ctr 3332 Rochambeau Ave Bronx NY 10467 Office Phone: 718-920-6311. Office Fax: 718-920-6313. Business E-Mail: kpowers@montefiore.org.

**POWERS, LINDA S.,** art association administrator; Undergraduate in Sales and Mktg., Davenport U. With Amway Corp., Digital Equipment Corp., IBM Corp.; mktg. dir. private country club; founder, pres. Arts and Crafts Assn. Am., 1999—. Office: Arts and Crafts Assn Am 4888 Cannon Woods Ct Belmont MI 49306 Office Phone: 616-874-1721. Office Fax: 616-874-1771. Business E-Mail: powers@triton.net.

**POWERS, LINDA SUE,** biophysicist, educator, biomedical engineer; b. Pitts., Feb. 8, 1948; d. Luther Thurston and Helen Grace (Currence) Powers. BS in Physics and Chemistry, Va. Poly. Inst. and State U., 1970; MA in Physics, Harvard U., 1972, PhD in Biophysics, 1976. Mem. tech. staff AT&T Bell Labs., Murray Hill, N.J., 1976-88; dir. bio-catalysis sci. ctr., prof. chemistry & biochemistry Utah State U., Logan, 1988-91, prof. elec. engring., biol. & irrigation engring., 1991—; dir. Nat. Ctr. for the Design of Molecular Function, Logan, 1991—. Adj. prof. U, Pa. Med. Sch., Phila., 1978-2000, vis. fellow Princeton U., 1981-82. Mem. editl. corr. Comments Molecular Cellular Biophysics, 1980-89; editl. bd. Biophysics Jour., 1989-96, Am. Inst. of Physics Internat. Basic and Applied Biol. Physics, 1993—, Internat. Series Basic and Applied Biol. Physics, 1994-2003, Wiley Encyclopedia of Biomedical Engineering. 2002-05; contbr. numerous articles to profl. jours. and books. Recipient 1st U.S. Bioenergetics award, 1982, State of Utah Gov.'s medal for sci. and tech., 1994. Fellow Am. Phys. Soc. (coun. divsn. biol. physics 1988-92, exec. bd. 1977-83, chmn. 1984-85), Am. Inst. Chemists; mem. IEEE (steering com. 2002-03), AAAS, NAS (com. chme. and biol. terrorism. 1997-98, com. countering agr. bioterrorism 2001-02), Biophys. Soc., Soc. Applied Spectroscopy, Sigma Pi Sigma, Phi Lambda Upsilon. Avocations: breeding and showing horses, writing music, windsurfing, snowboarding. Office: Utah State U Nat Ctr Design Molecular Function 1695 N Research Pkwy North Logan UT 84341 Office Phone: 435-797-2033.

**POWERS, MARY ELLEN,** lawyer; b. Cleve., 1955; JD, Univ. Va., 1980. Bar: DC 1980, admitted to practice: US Dist. Ct. for DC 1981, US Ct. of Appeals, DC Cir. 1982, US Ct. of Appeals, Fifth Cir. 1987, US Supreme Ct. 1996. Ptnr.-in-charge DC office Jones Day, Washington. Mem.: Women's Bar Assn. (Star of the Bar 2004), DC Bar Assn. (pro bono com.). Office: Jones Day 51 Louisiana Ave Washington DC 20001-2113 Office Phone: 202-879-3870. Office Fax: 202-626-1700. Business E-Mail: mepowers@jonesday.com.

**POWERS, MATTHEW DOUGLAS,** lawyer; b. San Francisco, July 7, 1959; BS, Northwestern U., 1979; JD cum laude, Harvard Law Sch., 1982. Bar: Calif. 1982, Dist. Ariz., US Dist. Ct., No. Dist. Calif. 1982, US Dist. Ct., Central Dist. Calif. 1983, US Ct. Appeals, 9th cir. 1983, US Dist. Ct., Ea. Dist. Calif. 1985, US Ct. Appeals for Fed. Cir. 1986, US Supreme Ct. 1988, US Ct. Internat. Trade 1990, US Dist. Ct., So. Dist. Tex. 1990, US Dist. Ct., No. Dist. Ind. 1991, US Dist. Ct., Ea. Dist. Mich. 2003. Head. mng. ptnr., global patent litigation group Weil, Gotshal & Manges, LLP, Redwood City, Calif., serves on management com. Lectr. in field; tchr. patent litigation U. Calif., Berkeley's Boalt Hall Sch. Law; lectr. patent law Stanford U., Santa Clara U.; mem. adv. bd. Inst. for Transitional Arbitration; mem. exec. com. Boalt Hall, Berkeley Ctr. for Law & Technology, Santa Clara U. Sch. Law, High Tech. Law Inst.; mem. No. Dist. Calif. Patent Rules Com., No. Dist. Calif. Patent Jury Instruction Com.; chmn. Internat. Patent Law Subcommittee, 1989; mem. ICC Commn. on Intellectual and Industrial Property, 1990. Editor-in-chief Intellectual Property & Technology Law Jour., co-editor-in-chief Jour. of Propriety Rights, editl. bd. Mealey's Litigation Reports: Intellectual Property, Internat. Litigation Quarterly, 1991, published (numerous articles). Mem. leadership coun. Am. Diabetes Assn., San Francisco; bd. dir. Greater Bay Area Make-A-Wish Found.; mem. exec. com. Orientation in In USA Law Program, U. Calif. Named a Leading Lawyer, PLC Which Lawyer?, 2006; named The "Go To" Patent Litigator in No. Calif., The Recorder, 2003, Father of the Yr., Father's Day Coun. of San Francisco, 2004, Trial Lawyer of the Yr., Santa Clara County Trial Lawyers Assn., 2005, Calif. Lawyer Atty. of the Yr. in Intellectual Property, Calif. lawyer mag., 2005; named one of 8 Star Attorneys in all fields in the US, Chambers Global Guide, 2001, Top 10 Attorneys in Silicon Valley, The Lawyer (London), 2001, Top 100 Attorneys in the country, IP Worldwide, 2002, 7 Top IP Trial Lawyers in the country, IP Worldwide, 2002, Top 25 IP Lawyers in Calif., San Francisco Daily Jour., 2003, Top 25 Attorneys in All Fields in the San Francisco Bay Area, San Francisco Chronicle, 2003, The Top 45 Attorneys Under 45, Am. Lawyer mag., 2003, Top 10 Trial Lawyers in Am., Nat. Law Jour., 2006. Mem.: ABA. Office: Weil Gotshal & Manges LLP 201 Redwood Shores Pky Redwood City CA 94065 Office Phone: 650-802-3200. Office Fax: 650-802-3100. Business E-Mail: matthew.powers@weil.com.*

**POWERS, PAULINE SMITH,** psychiatrist, educator, researcher; b. Sept. 23, 1941; m. Henry P. Powers; children: Jessica, Samantha. AB in Math., Washington U., 1963; MD, U. Iowa, 1971. Med. intern Emanuel Hosp., Portland, Oreg., 1971-72; psychiatry resident U. Iowa Iowa City, 1972-74, II Calif., Santa Barbara, 1974 (?); from asst. prof. to assoc. prof. psychiatry Coll. Medicine U. So. Fla., Tampa, 1975-85, prof., 1985—, dir. eating disorder program, 1979—, dir. psychosomatic medicine divsn., 1979—. Author: Obesity: The Regulation of Weight, 1980; editor: The Current Treatment of Anorexia Nervosa and Bulimia, 1984. Fellow: Am. Psychiat. Assn. (Rush Gold Outstanding Exhibit medal 1976, Dorfman Jour. Paper award 1987); mem.: Nat. Eating Disorders Assn. (pres.-elect 2003—05, pres. 2005—), Acad. Eating Disorders (founding pres., Women Helping Women award 1995, Profl. Excellence award 1997, Outstanding Clinician award 2000). Office: U So Fla Coll Medicine Dept Psychiatry 3515 E Fletcher Ave Tampa FL 33613-4706 Office Phone: 813-974-2926. Business E-Mail: ppowers@hsc.usf.edu.

**POWERS, RICHARD EDWARD, JR.,** lawyer; b. Evanston, Ill., July 20, 1952; s. Richard Edward and Helen Lufen Powers; m. Diane Wojda, Aug. 12, 1978. BS, Gonzaga U., 1974; JD, U. Notre Dame, 1977. Bar: DC 1977, Tex. 1979. Ptnr. Butler & Binion LLP, Washington, 1977-99, Dorsey & Whitney LLP, Washington, 1999—2005; ptnr., corp. law Venable LLP, Washington, 2005—. Bd. regents Gonzaga Univ.; mem. Bretton Woods Com.; bd. dir. Capital Partners for Educ. Mem. ABA, Tex. Bar Assn., D.C. Bar, Energy Bar Assn. Home: 5233 Elliott Rd Bethesda MD 20816-2910 Office: Venable LLP 575 7th St NW Washington DC 20004 Office Phone: 202-344-4360. Office Fax: 202-344-8300. Business E-Mail: repowers@venable.com.

**POWERS, RICHARD GERARD,** history educator; b. Rochester, NY, Jan. 26, 1949; s. Albert Dominic and Evelyn Rogers Powers; m. Patricia Marie Maslyn, May 29, 1971. BA in History, SUNY, Brockport, NY, 1971, postgrad., 1971—75. Tchr. US history, govt. and European history H.W. Schroeder H.S., Webster, NY, 1971—. Recipient Excellence Secondary Sch. Tchg. award, U. Rochester, 2000, Spl. Recognition award Excellence Tchg., Tufts U., 2000. Office: Webster Central School District 875 Ridge Road Webster NY 14580 Office Phone: 585-670-5000. Personal E-Mail: gems158@aol.com. E-Mail: dick_powers@webstersschools.org.

**POWERS, ROBERT DAVID,** physician; b. Plainfield, N.J., Nov. 6, 1953; s. John B. and Marian E. (Kuhn) P.; m. Sally Ann Harmet, 1977; children: Alison; Elizabeth, Carolyn. BA, Amherst Coll., 1975; MD, U. Va., 1979; MPH, Yale U., 1999. Intern U. Minn., Mpls., 1979-81; resident U. Va.,

Charlottesville, 1981-83, from asst. to assoc. prof., 1983-94; assoc. prof. U. Conn. Sch. Medicine, Farmington, 1994—, chief emergency medicine, 1997—2005, vice chmn. dept. trauma and emergency medicine, 1997—2005, assoc. prof., 1994-99, prof., 1999—. Fellow ACP. Office: U Va Sch Medicine Dept Emergency Medicine Charlottesville VA 22908 Business E-Mail: rdpsp@virginia.edu.

**POWERS, ROBERT LAWRENCE,** retired civilian military employee; b. Bklyn., Apr. 3, 1942; s. Lawrence Robert and Audrey Buchanan Powers; m. Susan McCormick, June 13, 1964; children: Jennifer Powers Kane, Megan Powers Dosher. BS in Chemistry, Math., U.S. Naval Acad., 1964; MS in Ops. Rsch., Naval Postgrad. Sch., Monterey, Calif., 1972. Commd. officer USN, 1964, officer, 1964-81; commdg. officer USS Fairfax County, Norfolk, Va., 1981-83; chief staff officer Amphibious Squadron 10, Norfolk, 1983-85; sr. analyst Sonalysts, Inc., Norfolk, 1985-92; tng. coord. Fleet Tactical Readings Group, Norfolk, 1992-98; sr. doctrine writer Fleet Info. Warfare Ctr., Norfolk, 1998—2000, with experimentation divsn., 2001—04. Adj. prof. U.S. Naval War Coll., Norfolk, 1985—. Co-founder Children's Coun. S. Hampton Rds., Norfolk, 1998; mem. Naval War Coll. Found. Mem. U.S. Naval Inst., Ret. Officers Assn., Kiwanis (Hixson fellow 1993, webmaster capital dist. 1998—, editor Great Bridge Kiwanis Newsletter 1998—, gov. 1998-99, Circle K internat. circle of svc.), Assn. for Ednl. Comm. and Tech. (Crystal award for distance edn. 2002), Sigma Xi. Episcopalian. Avocations: computers, naval history, war games. Home: 1100 West Rd Chesapeake VA 23323 E-mail: bpowers100@aol.com.

**POWERS, RONALD GEORGE,** management consultant; s. Lee Whitney and R. Anne Powers; m. Elizabeth Braislin McClellan, July 24, 1980. Chmn. Boardroom Advisors, Inc., Winter Park and Tampa, Fla., The Strategic Mgmt. Adv. Group, Inc., Winter Park and Tampa, Fla. Adviser to chief execs. of banks, corps. and govts. on strategic mgmt. issues, 1971—. Trustee Trinity Sch., Fla. Symphony Orch. Mem. Interlachen C. of C. Republican. Episcopalian. Home: PO Box 2174 Winter Park FL 32790-2174 Office: PO Box 1922 Winter Park FL 32790-1922 E-mail: boardroomadvisor@mindspring.com.

**POWERS, ROSS,** Olympic athlete; b. Bennington, Vt., Feb. 10, 1979; Mem. U.S. Snowboard Team; olympic gold medalist in halfpipe, 2002; founder Ross Powers Found., 2001. Named Nat. Champion, 1993, 1994, 1997, Grand Prix Champion, FIS World and Overall Champion, 1998, US Open title, 1998; recipient 2nd pl., 1992, 3rd pl., 1993, 1st pl., World Cup, 1995, 1996, 2nd pl. 1995, 3rd pl. 1995, 2nd pl., 1996, 3rd pl., 1996, 1st pl., World Championship, 1996, 2nd pl., World Cup, 1997, Bronze medal in Snowboarding (Halfpipe), Nagano Olympics, Japan, 1998, 1st pl., World Championship, 1998, Gold medal, NBC Gravity Games, 2000, TNT Winter Goodwill Games, 2000, Silver medal, ESPN X Games, 2000, Bronze medal, 2001, Gold medal in Snowboarding (Halfpipe), Olympic games, 2002. Office: The Ross Powers Found c/o Pete Carlisle P O Box 17574 Portland ME 04112

**POWERS, SCOTT,** television producer, actor; b. Chgo., Aug. 23, 1948; s. Raymond Alford and Ruby Marilyn (Ivacko) P. BS, Ithaca Coll., 1970; MBA, Fairleigh Dickinson U., 1971. Producer Young & Rubicam, Inc., NYC; account exec. Kelly, Nason, Inc., NYC; sr. account exec. Bozell & Jacobs, Inc., NYC; account supr. Foote, Cone & Belding, Inc., NYC; actor NYC, LA, 1982—; pres. Scott Powers Prodns., Inc., NYC, 1988—. Pres. CaribCom, Inc., NYC, 1996—. Author: Here's Looking At You!, 1997; contbr. articles to publs.; cartoonist Thankyounext, 1990—. Mem. Better Bus. Bur. NYC, 1991—, Knickerbocker Rep. Club, NYC, 1971—; bd. dirs. Profl. Comedians Assn., NYC, 1988-91, v.p., 1989-91; bd. dirs. One World Arts Found., 1992—; judge Internat. Film and TV Festivals, NYC, 1991—. Mem. AFTRA (bd. dirs. 1989-91), SAG, Actor's Equity Assn., NATAS (judge Emmys 1985—), NYC C.of C., Met. Club, NY Athletic Club, Players Club, Mensa, Intertel. Republican. Congregationalist. Avocations: skiing, sailing, tennis, squash, international river running. Home: 180 Central Park S New York NY 10019-1562 Office: Scott Powers Studios Inc 135 W 29th St Ste 404 New York NY 10001

**POWERS, SONIA NODLE,** psychologist, consultant; b. Canton, Ohio, May 11, 1943; d. George Bernard and Evelyn Lee (Hoyman) Nodle; m. Brad C. Thurman, June 25, 1965 (div. 1978); children: Mark Thurman, Ginger Thurman, Scott Thurman; m. Richard Mars. BS, Calif. State U., 1965; MS, Nat. U., San Diego, 1981; PhD, PSPS, San Diego, 1983. Lic. clin. psychologist Calif. Foster home supr. Children's Home Soc., Orange County, Calif., 1966-70; salesperson Red Carpet Realtors, Huntington Beach, Calif., 1972-75, mgr. Escondido, Calif., 1975-79, owner, pres. Lake Forest, Calif., 1979; psychologist in pvt. practice San Clemente, Calif., 1983—; pub. spkr., pres. Power Presentations, San Clemente, 1989—; dir. Profl. Success Seminars, San Clemente, 1981—. Cons. psychologist numerous bus. orgns. and state, county and city govt. agys., 1983—; trainer Police Officers Stds. and Tng. State of Calif., 1985—; spkr. in field. Author: (book) Charismatic Leader-...Self Esteem, 1983; contbr. articles to profl. jours.; host (TV series) Dr. Sonia Powers TV Show, 1997—98. Hon. fire fighter, 1991. Named Honored Citizen, South Orange County, 1986; scholar Johnston Found., 1982. Mem.: APA, Transformational Leadership Coun., Robbins Rsch. Internat. Avocations: travel, working with people and organizations, public speaking, writing. Office: Power Presentations 1031 South Pacific # F Oceanside CA 92054 Office Phone: 760-722-3326.

**POWERS, THOMAS MOORE,** writer; b. N.Y.C., Dec. 12, 1940; s. Joshua Bryant and Susan (Moore) P.; m. Candace Molloy, Aug. 21, 1965; children: Amanda, Susan, Cassandra. BA, Yale U., 1964. Reporter Rome (Italy) Daily American, 1965-67, U.P.I., N.Y.C., 1967-70; freelance writer, 1970—; contbg. editor The Atlantic mag.; editor, founding ptnr. Steerforth Press, So. Royalton, Vt., 1993—. Author: Diana: The Making of a Terrorist, 1971, The War at Home, 1973, The Man Who Kept the Secrets: Richard Helms and the CIA, 1979, Thinking About the Next War, 1982, Total War: What It Is, How It Got That Way, 1988, Heisenberg's War: The Secret History of the German Bomb, 1993, The Confirmation, 2000, Intelligence Wars: American Secret History from Hitler to Al Qaeda, 2002. Recipient Pulitzer prize for nat. reporting, 1971 Mem. PEN Am. Center, Council on Fgn. Relations. Address: 106 Chelsea St South Royalton VT 05068-9800 also: Lit Rep Lynn Nesbit 445 Park Ave New York NY 10022-2606 Office Phone: 802-763-8585. E-mail: tom@steerforth.com.

**POWERS, TIMOTHY EUGENE,** lawyer; b. Waukegan, Aug. 3, 1955; s. Herman Eugene and Beryl Grace (Weiskittel) P.; m. Joni Grace Helm, Mar. 21, 1987. BA, UCLA, 1977; JD, So. Meth. U., 1980. Bar: Tex. 1980. Assoc. Passman & Jones, Dallas, 1980-82; ptnr. Haynes and Boone, Dallas, 1982—, chmn., Internat. Practice Group, bd. dir. Mem. adv. bd. Southwestern Legal Found. Internat. and Comparative Law Ctr., Richardson, Tex., 1982—. Soc. Internat. Bus. fellow, 1987—. Mem.: State Bar Tex., Internat. Bar Assn. (chmn. internat. bankruptcy cooperation sub-com. 1987—95, constitution com. 2002—, vice chmn. project fin. sub-com. 2003—05), Internat. Bar Found. (trustee 2003—), Inter-Pacific Bar Assn., Am. Law Inst. (adv. internat. insolvency project 1994—2000), Japan Am. Soc. of Dallas/Ft. Worth (pres. 1992—93, bd. dir. 1990—), Coun. on Fgn. Relations, Leadership Dallas, No. Tex. Commn., Dallas C. of C. (internat. forum), Tex. Assn. Bank Counsel, Dallas Bar Assn., Tex. Bar Assn. (chmn. Internat. Law Sect. 1987—88), ABA (internat. comml. transactions com. 1988—90, governing coun., Internat. Law Sect. 1990—93, chmn. internat. comml. transactions com. 1992—96, transnational legal practice com. 1999—2001, governing coun. 1999—2005, Internat. Law and Practice Sect., chmn. fgn. investment in US real estate com.), Phi Delta Phi. Republican. Roman Catholic. Office: Hayne and Boones LLLP 901 Main St Ste 3100 Dallas TX 75202-3789 Office Phone: 214-651-5610. Office Fax: 214-200-0610. Business E-Mail: timothy.powers@haynesboone.com.

**POWERS, TIMOTHY H.,** electric power industry executive; Sr. positions ABB, Inc., BBC Brown Boveri, Inc.; sr. v.p., CFO Hubbell Inc., 1998—2001, pres., CEO, 2001—, bd. dir., 2001—, chmn., 2004—. Office: c/o Hubbell 584 Derby Milford Rd Orange CT 06477*

**POWERS, WILLIAM BRYAN,** academic administrator; b. Indpls., Ind., July 2, 1960; s. Rosalie and Anthony William Powers; m. Sarah Jayne Young, Sept. 19, 1987; 1 child, Rosemary Clair. BA, Purdue U., 1978—82; JD, Ind. U. Sch. of Law, 1982—85; LLM, The John Marshall Law Sch., 1999—2002. Bar: Ind. 1988. Asst. cons. on legal edn. ABA, Indpls., 1986—96; assoc. dean for admission and student affairs The John Marshall Law Sch., Chgo. 1996—. Author: (book review) Jour. of Computer & Info. Law; co-editor: (book) Reflections of the Chairpersons; author: Rsch. Institutes of ABA Approved Law Schools; editor: Law Sch. Facilities Reference Book; author: A Study of Contemporary Law Sch. Curricula; contbr. articles Ind. Law Rev. Mem. Ill. Lawyers Assistance Program Oper. Com., Chgo., 2001—03. Mem.: Nat. Network of Law Sch. Officers, Midwest Assn. of Law Sch. Admissions (treas. 2002—), Nat. Assn. for Law Placement, Chgo. Bar Assn., ABA (chair, student services com. 2000—02), Union League Club of Chgo. Avocations: travel, bridge. Office: The John Marshall Law Sch 315 S Plymouth Ct Chicago IL 60604 E-mail: 6powers@jmls.edu.

**POWERS, WILLIAM CHARLES, JR.,** academic administrator, law educator; b. 1946; BA, U. Calif., Berkeley, 1967; JD, Harvard U., 1973. Bar: Wash. 1974, Tex. 1980. Law clk. to Hon. E. A. Wright U.S. Ct. Appeals (9th cir.), Seattle, 1973-74; asst. prof. Wash. U., Seattle, 1974-77, assoc. prof., 1977-78; prof. law U. Tex., Austin, 1978—, assoc. dean acad. affairs, 1984—87, 1994—95, univ. disting. prof. and Hines H. Baker and Thelma Kelly Baker chair in law, 1997—, John Jeffers Rsch. Chair in law, 2000—, dean Sch. Law, 2000—06, pres., 2006—. Chair Spl. Investigation Com. Enron Corp. Author: Texas Products Liability Law, 1992; co-author: Cases and Materials in Torts, 1998, Cases and Materials in Products Liability, 2002. Mem.: Am. Law Inst. Office: U Tex at Austin Office of Pres PO Box T Austin TX 78713-8920 Home: 3600 Murillo Cir Austin TX 78703 Office Phone: 512-232-1120. Office Fax: 512-471-6987. E-mail: wpowers@law.utexas.edu.

**POWERS, WILLIAM EDWARD,** emergency physician, medical educator, surgeon; b. Atlanta, Sept. 16, 1957; s. Richard Candler and Olive Carol Osburn Powers; m. Nancy Carolyn Freeman, May 17, 1986; children: Nicole, Will. MS in Biomed. Engring., U. Ill., Chgo., 1981; MS in Aerospace Medicine, Wright State U., 1991; MD, Rush U., 1985; postgrad., U. Houston, 2001—03. Diplomate Am. Bd. Emergency Medicine, Am. Bd. Preventive Medicine. Intern in gen. surgery Orlando (Fla.) Regional Med. Ctr., 1985-86, resident in emergency medicine, 1986-88; resident in aerospace medicine Wright State U., Dayton, Ohio, 1989-91; biomed. engr., rsch. asst. U. Ill., Chgo., 1980-81; chief resident emergency medicine Orlando (Fla.) Regional Med. Ctr., 1987; assoc. dir. emergency medicine Kissimmee (Fla.) Meml. Hosp., 1988-89; asst. med. dir. Martin-Marietta Aerospace, Orlando, Fla., 1988-89; emergency med. physician, clin. instr. Wright State U. Med. Sch., Dayton, Ohio, 1989-91; med. officer, flight surgeon NASA Johnson Space Ctr., Houston, 1991-92; asst. med. dir. Cape Canaveral Hosp., Cocoa Beach, Fla., 1991-93, Twin Cities Hosp., Niceville, Fla., 1991-93; asst. prof. emergency medicine, rsch. dir. U. Tex. Med. Sch., Houston, 1993-95; asst. prof. family medicine, dir. urgent care U. Tex. Med. Br., Galveston, 1995-96; asst. prof. medicine Baylor Coll. Medicine, Houston, 1996—2001; med. dir. emergency dept. Meml. Hermann Hosp. S.E., 2002—03; flight surgeon U. Tex. Med. Branch, 2003—04, NASA, 2004—. Contbr. articles to profl. publs. Med. missionary Missionary Ventures, Honduras, 1995, 98. Fulbright Found. grantee U. Vienna, Austria, 1996. Fellow Am. Coll. Emergency Physicians, Aerospace Med. Assn. (assoc. fellow); mem. AIAA, Am. Phys. Soc., Exptl. Aircraft Assn. Avocations: flying, soccer, basketball, photography, piano. Office: Mail Code SD 2, 2101 NASA Pkwy Houston TX 77058 Office Phone: 281-483-4481. E-mail: WEPowers@aol.com.

**POWLEN, DAVID MICHAEL,** investment banker, consultant; b. Logansport, Ind., May 28, 1953; s. Daniel Thomas and Bertha Frances (Cappa) P.; m. Miriam Lango, Apr. 23, 2005; 1 child, Brooks Ryan. JD, Harvard U., 1978, AB, 2005. Bar: Ind. 1978, NY 2004, Pa. 2005, U.S. Dist. Ct. (so. dist.) Ind. 1978, U.S. Ct. Appeals (7th cir.) 1985, Bus. Bankruptcy Law Am. Bd. Cert., 2001. Assoc. Barnes & Thornburg, Indpls., 1978-84, ptnr., 1985-01, chmn., adminstr. creditors rights dept.; mng. dir., mgr. restructuring group McDonald Investments Inc., Cleve., 2001—04; sr. v.p. Mesirow Fin. Cons., NYC, 2004—06; mng. dir. Western Res. Ptnrs., Phila., 2006—. Contbr. articles to profl. jours. Mem. ABA (bus. bankruptcy com., secured creditors and chpt. 11 subcom., comml. fin. svcs. com., creditors rights subcom.), Am. Bankruptcy Inst. (chmn. fin. advisors com.), Assn. Insolvency and Restructuring Advisors (cert. insolvency and restructuring advisor 2005-), Ind. Bar Assn. (chmn. bankruptcy and creditors rights sect. 1990-91), Indpls. Bar Assn. (chmn. edn. com. 1984, chmn. ct. liaison com. 1985, bankruptcy and comml. law sect.), Turnaround Mgmt. Assn. (bd. dirs. NE Ohio chpt. 2001-04), Harvard Club, Phi Beta Kappa. Office: Western Res Ptnrs Ste P108 2001 Hamilton St Philadelphia PA 19130 Office Phone: 317-727-2211, 215-563-6870. Business E-Mail: dpowlen@wesrespartners.com.

**POWNELL, PATRICK H.,** plastic surgeon; b. Tyler, Tex., Sept. 28, 1959; s. Galyn and Helen Pownell; m. Dawn Gilliland, Dec. 29, 1984; children: Caroline, Preston, Trevor. BS, Baylor U., 1982; MD, U. Tex. Southwestern, Dallas, 1986. Pvt. practice plastic surgeon, Dallas, 1996—. Office: 7150 Greenville Ave Ste 310 Dallas TX 75231 Office Phone: 214-368-3223.

**POWSNER, EDWARD RAPHAEL,** physician; b. N.Y.C., Mar. 17, 1926; m. Rhoda Lee Moscovitz, June 8, 1950; children: Seth, Rachel, Ethan, David. SB in Elec. Engring., MIT, 1948, SM in Biology, 1949; MD, Yale U., 1953; MS in Internal Medicine, Wayne State U., 1957; MHSA, U. Mich. Diplomate Am. Bd. Nuclear Medicine, Am. Bd. Pathology in clin. pathology and anatomic pathology, Am. Bd. Internal Medicine; lic. physician, Mich. Intern Wayne County Gen. Hosp., Eloise, Mich., 1953-54, resident internal medicine, 1954-55, Detroit Receiving Hosp., 1955-56; fellow in hematology Wayne State U. and Detroit Receiving Hosp., 1957-58; clin. investigator VA Hosp., Allen Park, Mich., 1958-61, chief nuclear medicine svc., 1961-78; dir. clin. labs. Mich. State U., East Lansing, 1978-81; staff pathologist Ingham Med. Ctr., Lansing, Mich., 1978-81; dir. nuclear medicine St. John Hosp., Detroit, 1982-95. Rsch. asst. biology MIT, 1948-49, 50; asst. instr. medicine Wayne State U. Coll. Medicine, 1954-56, instr., 1959-61; assoc. prof. pathology Wayne State U. Sch. Medicine, 1961-68, assoc. medicine, 1961, prof. pathology, 1968-78; prof. pathology Mich. State U., 1978-81, assoc. chairperson, 1980-81, clin. prof., 1981-82; chief clin. labs. Detroit Gen. Hosp., 1969-73; chief lab. svcs. Health Care Inst., Wayne State U., 1976-78; mem. adv. coun. Nuclear Medicine Tech. Cert. Bd., 1990-91. Bd. editors Am. Jour. Clin. Pathology, 1963-76, 83-88; author 2 textbooks, 11 chpts., 50 peer reviewed papers, 17 abstracts and other publs. With U.S. Army, 1944-47. Mem. AMA (sect. coun. on pathology), Am. Soc. Clin. Pathologists (rep. 1987-89, 93-2000, govt. rels. com. 1993 95, mem. coun. nuclear medicine 1978-82, chmn. 1982-84), Am. Coll. Nuclear Physicians, Am. Soc. Nuclear Cardiology, Coll. Am. Pathologists, Detroit Acad. Medicine, Mich. Soc. Pathologists, Mich. State Med. Soc., Soc. Nuclear Medicine, Washtenaw County Med. Soc., Sigma Xi, Tau Beta Pi. Office: Eastside Nuclear Medicine 2370 E Stadium Blvd #315 Ann Arbor MI 48104-4810

**POWSNER, SETH,** psychiatrist, educator, medical researcher; BSEE, MIT, 1974; MD, Yale U., 1978. Cert. bd. cert. psychiatrist Amer Bd. of Psychiatry and Neurology, added qualifications in geriatric psychiatry Amer Bd. of Psychiatry and Neurology. Psychiatry resident Michael Reese Hosp., Chgo., 1978—82; pvt. practice as gen. psychiatrist Chgo., 1982—84; clin. computing Ill. State Psychiat. Inst., Chgo., 1984—85; engring. cons. sect. cardiology U. of Chgo., 1985—86; asst. prof. of psychiatry Yale U. Sch. of Medicine, New Haven, 1986—92, assoc. prof. of psychiatry, 1992—2005, prof. of psychiatry, surgery, and emergency medicine, 2005—. Recipient Biomed. Pilot Projects Initiative grant, Culpepper Found., 1998—99. Fellow: Acad. of

Psychosomatic Medicine (chair membership com. 2001—02). Achievements include patents for graphical summary of patient status. Office: Yale Psychiatry Rm 2039cb 20 York St New Haven CT 06510-3202

**POWSNER, SETH M.,** psychiatrist, educator; b. New Haven, May 29, 1953; s. Edward Raphael and Rhoda Lee (Moscovitz) P.; m. Elizabeth C. Yen, Aug. 18, 1985. BSEE, MIT, 1974; MD, Yale U., 1978. Resident in psychiatry Michael Reese Hosp., Chgo., 1978—82, 1979-82, asst. dir. psychiat. tng., 1983-84; practice medicine specializing in psychiatry, Chgo., 1982-86; unit chief Charter Barclay Hosp., Chgo., 1983-84; psychiatrist Ill. State Psychiat. Inst., Chgo., 1984-85; rsch. cons. U. Chgo. Med. Sch., Chgo., 1985-86; asst. prof. Yale Med. Sch., New Haven, 1986-92, assoc. prof. psychiatry, 1992—2005; chief psychiat. consultation svc. Yale-New Haven Hosp., 1994—2000, chief crisis intervention unit, 2000—; prof. psychiatry and surgery Yale Med. Sch., New Haven, 2006—. Contbr. articles to profl. jours. Mem. AMA, IEEE, Am. Psychiat. Assn., Assn. for Computing Machinery. Avocations: skiing, skating. Office: Yale U Dept Psychiatry 20 York St Rm 2039 New Haven CT 06510-3202

**POYDASHEFF, ROBERT STEPHEN,** lawyer; b. NYC, Feb. 13, 1930; s. Stephen Alexander Poydasheff and Pauline M. Miller; m. Anastasia Catherine Latto, Aug. 29, 1954; children: Catherine Alexandra, Robert Stephen Jr. BA in Polit. Sci., The Citadel, 1954; JD, Tulane U., 1957; MA, Boston U., 1966; diploma, Command and Gen. Staff Coll., 1969, Army War Coll., 1976. Bar: S.C. 1958, Ga. 1979, US Supreme Ct. 1964, US Ct. Mil. Appeals, US Ct. Mil. Rev. 1964, US Dist. Ct. (fed. dist.) S.C. 1988, US Dist. Ct. (fed. and mid. dists.) Ga. 1987. Commd. 2d lt. U.S. Army, 1955, advanced through grades to col., 1975, ret., 1979; sr. v.p. SunTrust Bank of West Ga., Columbus, 1979-95; pvt. practice Columbus, 1995—. Instr. bus. law Am. U. Ext. Divsn., Ft. Benning, 1961-63; adj. prof. internat. law. Am. govt., and bus. law U. Md. Ext. Divsn., Berlin, 1964-67, Vietnam, 1967-68; adj. instr. Troy State U., Ft. Benning, Ga., 1976—; cons., exec. v.p. ATI-Allied Tech. Internat. Inc., Columbus, 1995—; past legal advisor to Sec. of Army and Sec. of Def. on mil. dependent sch. and labor rels. Contbr. commentaries, papers, and analyses to profl. jours. City councilor City of Columbus, 1996-2002; mayor of Columbus, Ga., 2003; bd. dir. Springer Opera House Assn., 1998—; trustee Ga. Coun. of Humanities, exec. com. 1998—; bd. edn. Ft. Benning Sch., 1976-79, chmn. pers. actions com., 1976-79; trustee Dr. Hosp., Columbia; bd. dirs. Columbus United Way, River Ctr. Performing Arts; past pres. Chattahoochee coun. Boy Scouts Am., Columbus; past pres. Chattahoochee Valley, Assn. of US Army, Anne Elizabeth Shepherd Home, Columbus Symphony, ARC; chmn. bd. dir. Leadership Morality Inst.; chmn. Civilian Mil. Coun., Ga. Govs. Commn. on Transp. Decorated Legion of Merit with 2 oak leaf clusters, Bronze Star, commendation medal with oak leaf cluster, Vietnam Svc. medal with four bronze stars, Order of St. George, Episcopal Ch., Infantry Order of St. Maurice; parachutist badge; badge of The Army secretariet; recipient Ga. Govs. medal for the humanities, Outstanding Civilian Svc. medal U.S. Army, 2004. Fellow Leadership Morality Inst.(chair of bd.); mem. Ga. Mcpl. Assn. (bd. dirs.), Columbus Bar Assn., C. of C. (mil. affairs com., bd. dirs.), Kiwanis, Masons (32 deg.), Phi Delta Phi, Pi Sigma Alpha. Republican. Episcopalian. Avocations: jogging, reading, gymnastics. Home: 6349 Mountainview Dr Columbus GA 31904-2213 Office: 944 2d Ave Columbus GA 31902 Office Phone: 706-653-4712. E-mail: b.poydasheff@columbus.ga.org.

**POZA, ERNESTO,** management consultant, educator; b. Havana, Cuba, Mar. 27, 1950; arrived in U.S., 1961; s. Hugo Ernesto and Carmen (Valle) Poza; m. Karen Elizabeth Saum, Oct. 14, 1978; 1 child, Kali Jennette. BS in Adminstrv. Sci., Yale U., 1972; MS in Mgmt., MIT, 1974. Personnel mgr. rsch. Sherwin Williams Co., Chgo., 1974-75, orgn. specialist Cleve., 1975-77, dir. orgn. planning, 1977-79; pres., sr. mgmt. cons. E.J. Poza Assoc., Cleve., 1979—; prof. Weatherhead Sch. Mgmt. Case Western Res. U., Cleve., 1996—2006; prof. Thunderbird U., Garvin Sch. Internat. Mgmt., 2006—. Advisor Family Firm Inst., 1986; vis. lectr. Yale U., U. Chile, MIT, Sloan Sch. Mgmt.; mem. editl. bd. Family Bus. Rev., 1997—, Jour. Small Bus. Mgmt. 1997—; bd. dirs. Sky Fin. NE Ohio; mem. adv. bd. Mack Industries. Author: A la Sombra del Roble: La Empresa Privada Familiar y Su Continuidad, 1995, Smart Growth: Critical Choices for Business Continuity and Prosperity, 1997, La Empresa Familiar Por Dentro, 1998, Family Business, 2004, 2d edit., 2006, Empresas Familiares, 2006; contbg. editor: Family Bus. Mag.; mem. editl. rev. bd. Family Bur. Rev.; mem. editl. bd.: Entrepreneurship Theory & Practice; contbr. articles to profl. jours. Bd. dirs. Neighborhood Health Care, 1980, Family Firm Inst., 1990; mem. program com. United Way, Cleve., 1985, Hispanic Leadership, 1986. Fellow: Family Firm Inst. (sr.; founding mem. 1985, Richard Beckhard Practice award 1996); mem.: Acad. Mgmt. (entrepreneurship divsn. 1980—, orgn. devel. network 1975—). Office Phone: 440-247-6300, 480-538-2120. Business E-Mail: poza@family-business.com.

**POZA, HUGO BERNARDO,** aerospace company executive; b. Havana, Mar. 12, 1945; s. Hugo Ernesto and Carmen (Valle) P.; m. Mary Karen Connors, Jan. 21, 1967; children: Hugh Thomas, Sean Christopher, Vanessa Kristi. BS in Elec. Engring., U. Dayton, 1966; MS in Elec. Engring., Purdue U., 1967, PhD, 1971. Mem. tech. staff TRW Systems Group, Redondo Beach, Calif., 1971-73, dept. staff engr., 1973-75, sr. staff engr., 1975-77, asst. program mgr., 1977-80; mgr. mil. systems ops. Mil. Electronics Div. TRW, San Diego, 1981-84, v.p., gen. mgr. Mil. Electronics and Avonics Div., 1985—86; sr. v.p. M/A-COM Government Systems, 1986—88; v.p., gen. mgr., Avionics div. Lockheed Martin-Sanders, 1988—95, exec. v.p., 1995; v.p., aerospace electronic Lockheed Martin; v.p., gen. mgr., Strategic Systems div. Raytheon Co., Falls Church, Va., v.p., Homeland Security, 2002—. Mem. tech. adv. bd. Quest Tech. mag. Contbr. articles to profl. jours; patentee in field. Bd. dirs. Am. Martyrs Youth Group, 1975-78; bd. dirs. Manhattan Beach Single Young Adults, 1979-81; mem. Christian Family Movement, 1979-81, St. Gabriel's Youth Ministry, 1981—. Named one of 50 Most Important Hispanics in Tech. & Bus., Hispanic Engr. & Info. Tech. mag., 2005. Mem. IEEE, AIAA, World Affairs Council Los Angeles, Old Crows, Tau Beta Pi Clubs: Escondido, Tennis. Roman Catholic. Office: Raytheon Co 7700 Arlington Blvd Falls Church VA 22042 *I have always believed in giving all I have to anything I dedicate myself. I have strived to be the very best in all my endeavors, but never by stepping on someone else's pride. I am a positive thinker with a winning attitude. My success in life has been greatly due to the support of my family and my strong belief in the Lord.*

**POZDEEV-FREEMAN, YURI,** research scientist; s. Leon Freeman and Prima Mikson; m. Galina Denisov, June 26, 1986; children: Anya Freeman, Daniel Freeman. PhD, Kharkov Tech. U., Ukraine, 1971. Rsch. mgr. Elitan Electronics, Kharkov, Ukraine, 1981—94; prin. scientist Vishay Sprague, Sanford, Maine, 1995—. Author (papers at Passive Components meetings) Physics of tantalum and niobium capacitors (Outstanding Paper awards, 2002). Achievements include holder of 23 USSR patents and 7 U.S. patents in the field of materials for electronics. Home: 11 Garrison Oaks Dr Kennebunk ME 04043 Office Phone: 207-324-4140 308. Office Fax: 207-490-7248. Personal E-mail: freeman@gwi.net. E-mail: yuri.pozdeevfreeman@vishay.com.

**POZDRO, JOHN WALTER,** retired music educator, composer; b. Chgo., Aug. 14, 1923; s. John and Rose Anna P.; m. Shirley Allison Winans, June 12, 1954; children: John Winans, Nancy Allison Thellman. Student, Am. Conservatory Music, Chgo., 1941-42; B.M. in Music, Northwestern U.-Evanston, Ill., 1948, M.M. in Music, 1949; PhD in Music, Eastman Sch. Music, 1958. Instr. Iowa State Tchrs. Coll., Cedar Falls, 1949-50; instr. to assoc. prof. U. Kans., Lawrence, 1950-64, prof. music, 1964-93, dir. theory and composition, 1961-88; ret., 1993; teaching fellow Eastman Sch. Music, Rochester, NY, 1956-57. Chmn. symposium com. U. Kans., Lawrence, 1958-69. Representative works include Third Symphony, 1960, Piano Sonata No. 4, 1976, Malooley & Fear Monster, 1977, Impressions, Winds, Piano, 1984, Tryptich for Carillon, 1996, the Spirit of Mt. Oread, 1989. Winds of Autumn, 1996. Served with U.S. Army, 1943-46. Recipient U. Calif. Berkeley medal for Disting. Svc., 1993; grantee Ford Found., 1960, Nat. Endowment

Arts, 1976; nominated for Pulitzer prize in Music, 1960. Mem. ASCAP, Pi Kappa Lambda. Presbyterian. Avocations: golf, photography, writing. Home: 4700 Muirfield Dr Lawrence KS 66047-1820

POZEN, ROBERT CHARLES, investment company executive; b. NYC, Aug. 8, 1946; s. Morris and Miriam Pozen; m. Elizabeth Kelner, Apr. 11, 1976; children: Joanna, David. BA, Harvard U., 1968; JD, Yale U., 1972, JSD, 1973. Bar: N.Y. 1977, D.C. 1978, U.S. Supreme Ct., U.S. Ct. Appeals (4th, 5th, 7th and D.C. cirs.). Assoc. prof. law NYU, 1974-77; assoc. gen. counsel SEC, Washington, 1978-80; ptnr. Caplin & Drysdale, Washington, 1981-86; sr. v.p., gen. counsel, mng. dir. FMR Corp./Fidelity Investments, Boston, 1987—96; pres. Fidelity Mgmt. and Rsch. Co., Boston, 1997—2001; vice chmn. Fidelity Investments, Boston, 2001—02; secy. econ. affairs Commonwealth Mass., 2003; non-exec. chmn. Mass. Fin. Svcs. Investment Mgmt., Boston, 2004—. Mem. adv. bd. Securities Regulation Law Reporter Bur. Nat. Affairs, Washington, 1981; vis. lectr. Harvard Law Sch., Cambridge, Mass., 1986; mem. legal adv. com. N.Y. Stock Exchange, 1987; appt. mem., Commn. to Strengthen Social Security John Olin Visiting Prof., Harvard Law Sch. 2002-2003. Author: Financial Institutions: Investment Mgmt. Cases, Materials and Problems, 1977; contbr. articles to profl. jours. Mem. ABA (securities com. 1981—, employee retirement income secuity act 1985-86). Office: MFS 500 Boylston St Boston MA 02116-3470

POZEN, SHARIS ARNOLD, lawyer; b. Jefferson City, Mo., Jan. 31, 1964; d. John Burleigh and Mary Carolyn Arnold; m. Thorn Lord Pozen, Sept. 1, 1991; children: Hannah Carolyn, Grace Leigh. BA, Conn. Coll., 1986; JD, Washington U., 1989. Staff atty. U.S. FTC, Washington, 1989—93, asst. to dir. bur. of competition, 1993—94, atty. advisor, 1994; assoc. Hogan and Hartson LLP, Washington, 1995—99, counsel, 1999—2000, ptnr. 2000—, Editor Market Power Handbook, 2005. Chair. bd dirs. The Ballet Studio, Washington, 2004—; vice chair membership Horace Mann PTA, Washington, 2005—. Mem.: ABA Office: Hogan and Hartson LLP 555 13th St NW Washington DC 20004 Office Phone: 202-637-6948. Office Fax: 202-637-5910. Business E-Mail: sapozen@hhlaw.com.

POZNANSKI, ANDREW KAROL, pediatric radiologist; b. Czestochowa, Poland, Oct. 11, 1931; came to U.S., 1957, naturalized, 1964; s. Edmund Maurycy and Hanna Maria (Ceranka) P.; children: Diana Jean, Suzanne Christine. BSc, McGill U., 1952, MD CM, 1956. Diplomate: Am. Bd. Radiology, Royal Coll. Physicians and Surgeons Can. Intern Montreal (Que., Can.) Hosp., 1956-57; resident Henry Ford Hosp., Detroit, 1957-60, staff radiologist, 1960-68, U. Mich. Med. Center, Ann Arbor, 1968-79; co.-dir. pediatric radiology C.S. Mott Children's Hosp., Ann Arbor, 1971-79; radiologist-in-chief Children's Meml. Hosp., Chgo., 1979-99; prof. radiology U. Mich., 1971-79, Northwestern U. Med. Sch., 1979—. Bd. dirs. Nat. Coun. on Radiation Protection, 1983-90; mem. Internat. Commn. on Radiologic Protection, 1981-89; mem. adv. panel on radiologic devices FDA, 1975-77, chmn., 1976-77; trustee Am. Bd. Radiology, 1993-2003. Author: The Hand in Radiologic Diagnosis, 1974, 2d edit., 1983, Practical Approaches to Pediatric Radiology, 1976; co-author: Bone Displasias, An Atlas of Genetic Disorders of Skeletal Development, 2002 bd. editors: Skeletal Radiology, 1975-95, Radiographics, 1980-84, Pediatric Radiology, 1986-91. Mem.: AMA, Internat. Skeletal Soc. (founder, pres. 1992—94), John Caffey Soc., Radiol. Soc. N.Am., Soc. Pediatric Radiology (pres. 1980—81), Am. Roentgen Ray Soc. (pres. 1993—94), Polish Radiol. Soc. (hon.), Can. Assn. Radiologists (hon.), European Soc. Radiology (hon.), Alpha Omega Alpha. Home: 2400 N Lakeview Ave Chicago IL 60614-2747 Office: Childrens Meml Hosp 2300 N Childrens Plz Chicago IL 60614-3394 Office Phone: 773-880-3521. Business E-Mail: apoznanski@ameritech.net.

POZZATTI, RUDY OTTO, artist; b. Telluride, Colo., Jan. 14, 1925; s. Innocente and Mary L. (Mimiolla) P.; m. Dorothy I. Pozzatti, May 20, 1946; children: Valri Marie, Rudy Otto, Gina Maria, Mia Ines, Illica Lara. BFA, U. Colo., 1948, MFA, 1950, DHL, 1973. Mem. faculty dept. art U. Nebr., Lincoln, 1950-52, 53-56, Ind. U., Bloomington, 1956-91, prof. fine arts, 1964-91, disting. prof., 1975-91; ret., 1991; artist-in-residence Roswell Mus. and Art Ctr. One-man exhbns. include Cleve. Mus. Art, 1955, Whitney Mus. Am. Arts, NYC, 1961, Tyler Sch. Art, Rome, 1969, Sheldon Meml. Art Gallery U. Nebr., 1969, Mitchell Mus. Art, Mt. Vernon, Ill., 4 other sites, 1992-93, Ind. U. Art Mus., Bloomington, 2002, Evansville Mus. ARt, 2002; represented in permanent collections, Mus. Modern Art, NYC, Libr. Congress, Washington, Art Inst. Chgo., Cleve. Mus. Art. Served with AUS, 1943-46. Recipient George Norlin silver medal U. Colo., 1974; Fulbright grantee, 1952-53, 63-64, grantee US Dept. State, USSR, 1961, Yugoslavia, 1965, Brazil, 1974, Hungary, 1986; grantee Rockefeller Found., Bellagio, Italy, 1995; Guggenheim fellow, 1963-64; Fellow Ford Found., 1963, grantee, Japan, 1981. Mem. Soc. Am. Graphic Artists, Am. Color Print Soc., Coll. Art Assn. (bd. dirs.), Artists Equity Assn., Ind. Acad. (elected). Roman Catholic. Business E-Mail: rpozzatt@indiana.edu.

POZZI, LUCIO, artist, educator; b. Milan, Nov. 29, 1935; came to U.S., 1962; s. Lucio Pozzi and Ida Borletti; m. Susanna Tanger (div. 1985); children: Giordano, Eveanna; m. Elisabeth Tanger (div. 2002); 1 child, Katerina. Student, Rome U., 1955-57. Ptnr. Gramma Design Studio, Rome, 1959; tchr. Marlboro (Vt.) Coll., 1967, Cooper Union Coll., N.Y.C., 1968-74, Princeton U., N.J., 1974, Sch. Visual Arts, N.Y.C., 1974—, Tyler Sch., Phila., 1989, Md. Inst., Balt., 1989—. Sr. critic Yale MFA Sculpture, 1990. Pub. New Observations mag., 1982—; contbr. articles to books, profl. jours.; works exhibited internationally. Lt. Italian Army Calvary, 1954-55. NEA fellow, 1984. Mem. Am. Abstract Artist. Democrat. Home and Office: PO Box 689 New York NY 10012-0013

POZZO, RICCARDO, philosophy educator; b. Milan, June 7, 1959; s. Giancarlo and Carla (Rizzani) P.; m. Annette Popel, Sept. 4, 1997; 1 child, Carlo Lauren in Philosophy, U. Milan, 1983, Promotion in Philosophy, U. Saarland, Saarbrücken, 1988; Habilitation in Philosophy, U. Trier, 1995. Rsch. assoc. U. Saarland, 1984-85; fellow Deutscher Akademischer Austauschdienst, 1985-97, Herzog August Bibliothek Wolfenbüttel, 1988-90, Alexander von Humboldt-Stiftung, 1990—98; h.s. tchr. Sch. Superintendency Lombardy, Milan, 1994-96; tchr. Cath. U. Am., Washington, 1996—2003, U. Verona, 2003—. Lectr. U. Trier, 1991-96. Author: Hegel: Introductio in Philosophiam, 1989, Kant und das Problem einer Einleitung, 1989, El giro kantiano, 1998, Georg Friedrich Meiers Vernunftlehre, 2000; co-editor: The Impact of Aristotelianism on Modern Philosophy, 2004, L'autore e i uoi diritti, 2005, Aristotele Nella Società Contemporanea, 2006; co-editor: (with Karl-Otto Apel) Zur Rekonstruktion der praktischen Philosophie, 1990; (with Michael Oberhausen) Vorlesungsverzeichnisse der Universität Königsberg 1720-1804, 1999; (with Michael Oberhausen and Heinrich P. Delfosse) Vernunftkritik und Aufklärung, 2001, (with Heinrich P. Delfosse and Clemens Schwaiger) Meier-Index: Vernunftlehre, 2005; cons. editor: Longanesi Editore, 1988-89, Feltrinelli Editore, 1989—. Recipient 6th Study Tour of Japan, Japanese Ministry of Fgn. Affairs, 1984. Mem.: Soc. Filosofica Italiana (bd. dirs. 2005), Soc. Medieval and Renaissance Philosophy, Hegel Soc. N.Am., Italian Soc. Kant Studies, N.Am. Kant Soc., Alexander von Humboldt Assn. Italy (sec., bd. dirs. 2003—), Alexander von Humboldt Assn. Am. (bd. dirs. 2002—03), Am. Philos. Assn., Rotary Internat. (internat. dist. 2040 Milano Ovest 2005—06). Roman Catholic. Avocation: contemporary literature. Office: via San Francesco 22 I-37129 Verona Italy Office Phone: +39/045/8028143. Business E-Mail: riccardo.pozzo@univr.it.

PRABHAKAR, KUMKUM, biology professor; arrived in US, 1991, naturalized, 1999; d. Dalip Singh and Meena Rani Cheema; m. Sunil Prabhakar, Mar. 1, 1979; children: Pankaj, Rahul. BSc with honors in Botany, U. Delhi, India, 1973, MSc in Botany, 1975, PhD in Botany, 1980. Rsch. assoc., dept. botany U. Delhi, 1981, sr. lectr. botany Maitreyi Coll., 1982—93; instr. biology Nassau C.C., Garden City, NY, 1995—2000, asst. prof. biology, 2000—05, assoc. prof. biology, 2005—. Overseas councillor, dept. botany The Botanica, Delhi, 1998—; advisor Kingsborough C.C. Bklyn., 2005—; chmn. gen. edn. natural sci. assessment com. Nassau C.C., 2001—; cons. in field. Author: The Botany Notebook, Investigative Introductory Botany, 1st

edit.; contbr. chapters to books, articles to profl. jours. Chmn. cmty. svc. com. Nassau C.C., 2005—06, presenter sr. ctrs. Spkrs. Bur., 1999. Recipient Excellence in Tchg. award, SUNY, Albany, 2002; grantee, NSF, 2005—. Mem.: NSTA (assoc.; presenter conf., San Diego 2002), ASCD (assoc.), Met. Assn. Coll. and U. Biologists (archivist 2000—), Bot. Soc. Am., Nat. Assn. Biology Tchrs. (assoc.; Otto Burgdorf apprenticeship N.Y. chpt. 2001—03, nominee Biology Tchr. award 2006), Internat. Soc. Plant Morphologists (life; councillor 2005—), Women's Faculty Assn. at Nassau C.C. (pres. 2006—), Friends Hempstead Plains (sec. 1995—2005), Delta Kappa Gamma (assoc.; v.p. elect 2006—, Ruth and Williams scholarship 2006). Hindu. Avocations: yoga, cooking, gardening, travel. Office: Nassau Community College One Education Drive Garden City NY 11530 Office Phone: 516-572-8086. Business E-Mail: prabhak@ncc.edu.

PRABHALA, RAO H., pharmaceutical executive; b. Guntur, AP, India, July 15, 1955; s. Sastry Pk and Sesha A. Prabhala; m. Nalini R. Reddy, May 15, 1982; children: Harsha K., Nithya S., Neelima D. MSc, Nagarjuna U., India, 1977; MS, Calif. State U., Los Angeles, 1985; PhD, U. Az., 1989; Postdoctorate, Darmouth Coll., 1991. Cert. coll. tchg. Calif., 1982. Rsch. assoc. King Drew med. Ctr., Los Angeles, 1982—85; asst. prof. Midwestern U., Downers Grove, Ill., 1991—93; sr. immunologist Zonagen, Woodlands, Tex., 1993; asst. prof. Darmouth Hitchcock Med. Ctr., Lebanon, NH, 1994—97; dir. NIMI Bio Tech, Guntur, India, 1997—2000; sr. staff scientist DFCI Harvard Med. Sch., Boston, 2000—02; mgr. of microbiology Nucryst Pharmaceuticals, Wakefield, Mass., 2002—. Reader Nagarjuna U., Guntur, India, 1997—2000; mentor DFCI Harvard med. Sch., Boston, 2002. Author: Handbook of Mucosal Immunology, 1994; contbr. articles various profl. jours. Recipient Meritorious Rsch. award, AMA, 1988, Coll. Tchr. award, AP Parents Club, 1999; Immunology Training grant, NIH, 1990. Mem.: Infectious Diseases Soc. of Am., Am. Assn. of Immunology, Am. Soc. of Microbiology. Democrat. Hindu. Achievements include research in how to turn off immune system to facilitate transplantation without rejection. Avocations: running, basketball, singing, cooking, drawing. Home: 96 Manning St Needham MA 02494 Office: Nucryst Pharmaceuticals 50 Audubon Rd Ste B Wakefield MA 01880 E-mail: rprabhala@nueryst.com.

PRABHU, KRISH ANANT, telecommunications industry executive, educator; b. Ankola, India, Aug. 2, 1954; came to U.S., 1975; s. Anant K. and Indira (Mahale) P.; m. Shuba George, June 14, 1980; children: Sarita, Vinay, Sanjay. BSc with honors, Bangalore (India) U., 1973; MSc, Indian Inst. Tech., Bombay, 1975; MS, U. Pitts., 1977, PhD, 1980. Mem. tech. staff Bell Labs., Holmdel, NJ, 1980-84; mem. tech. staff, mgmt. positions Rockwell Internat., Richardson, Tex., 1984-92; v.p R & D Alcatel Network Systems, Richardson, 1992—95; pres. Alcatel Broadband Products, 1995—97; CEO Alcatel USA, Inc., 1997—99; COO Alcatel S.A., 1999—2001; venture ptnr. Morgenthaler Ventures, 2001—04; pres., CEO Tellabs, Inc., Naperville, Ill., 2004—. Adj. prof. U. Tex. at Dallas, Richardson, 1988—; mem. adv. coun. U. Tex., Arlington, 1992—. Contbr. articles to tech. jours. Mem. IEEE (sr.), NMA. Avocations: tennis, chess, reading. Office: Tellabs Inc One Tellabs Ctr 1415 W Diehl Rd Naperville IL 60563

PRABHU, VASANT, corporate financial executive; Grad., Indian Inst. Tech., Bombay, India; MBA, U. Chgo. V.p., ptnr. N.Y. office Booz, Allen & Hamilton; with Pepsico Inc., U.S., Europe, Latin Am.; sr. v.p., CFO Pepsico Internat.; pres. info. and media group McGraw-Hill Cos., Inc., 1998—2000; exec. v.p., CFO Safeway Inc., 2000—03; CFO Starwood Hotels & Resorts Worldwide Inc., 2003—. Office: Starwood Hotels & Resorts Worldwide Inc 1111 Westchester Ave White Plains NY 10604

PRABHUDESAI, MUKUND M., pathology educator, health facility administrator, researcher, academic administrator; b. Lolyem, Goa, India, Mar. 17, 1942; came to U.S., 1967; s. Madhav R. and Kusum M. Prabhudesai; m. Sarita Mukund Usha, Feb. 1, 1972; 1 child, Nitin M. MB, BS (MD), G.S. Med., Bombay, 1967, postgrad., 1973-75. Diplomate: Am. Bd. Pathology. Asst. pathologist Fordham Hosp., Bronx, NY, 1973-74, assoc. pathologist, 1974-76; assoc. dir. clin. pathology Lincoln Med., Bronx, 1976, dep. dir. pathology, 1977-79; chief pathology and lab. medicine svc., coord. R&D VA Med. Ctr., Danville, Ill., 1979—, dir. electron microscopy lab., 1987—. Senator U. Ill. Chgo.; co-investigator U. Ill. Coll. Medicine, Urbana-Champaign, clin. prof. pathology and internal medicine, 1982—. Contbr. articles to Am. Jour. Clin. Nutrition, Jour. AMA, Am. Jour. Clin. Pathology. Member Gifted Student Adv. Bd., Danville, 1984-86; v.p. Am. Cancer Soc. Vermilion County chpt., 1982, pres., 1986-88. VA rsch. grantee, 1980-82, 82-85, 83. Fellow Coll. Am. Pathology (inspector 1981-, Ill. state del. to C.A.P. Ho. Dels. 1992-; mem. reference com. 1993, chair, standard and integration com., 2000-); mem. AAAS, Am. Coll. Physician Execs., Ill. State Soc. Pathologists (bd. dirs. 1990-, chmn. membership com. 1990-). Achievements include development of cancer of bladder following portocarval shunting; research in adverse effects of alcohol on lung structure and metabolism; on effects of soy and bran on cholesterol, fish and coronary artery disease, endocrine response to soy protein, in induction and reversibility of atherosclerosis in trout, effects of ethanol on Vitamin A, lymphatics in atherosclerosis, iron in atherosclerosis, development of dermofluorometer for detection of P.V.D. Office: PO Box 3583 Placida FL 33946 Office Phone: 217-748-6272. E-mail: sarita@soltec.net, mdesaih@aol.com.

PRADA, MIUCCIA BIANCA, fashion designer; b. 1949; m. Patrizio Bertelli. PhD in Polit. sci.; student, mime performer, Teatro Piccolo, Milan, 1973—78. With family business Prada, Milan, 1978—. Introduced the following product lines to Prada handbags, 1983, women's ready-to-wear, 1989, Miu Miu line, 1992, men's wear 1995; showed product line in NYC for the first time in 1994; opened boutique in London, 1994. Named one of Time Mag. 100 Most Influential People, 2005, the 30 Most Powerful Women in Europe, Wall St. Jour., 50 Women to Watch, 2002, Top 200 Collectors, ARTnews mag., 2005—06. Office: Prada SpA 2 Via Andrea Maffei 20154 Milan Italy Address: Prada ApA 30 Via Melzi D'Eril 20100 Milan Italy Office Phone: 02 54 67 01.*

PRADELL, STEVEN, lawyer; b. Fairbanks, Alaska, June 29, 1960; s. David Edward and Lila (Charney) P. BA cum laude, Brandeis U., 1982; JD, U. Oreg., 1986. Bar: Alaska 1986, U.S. Dist. Ct. Alaska 1986, U.S. Ct. Appeals (9th cir.) 1990. Assoc. Kelly & Assocs., Anchorage, 1986-88, Birch, Horton, Bittner & Cherot, Anchorage, 1988-93; owner Pradell and Assocs., Anchorage, 1993—. Author: Winning The War Against Life Threatening Diseases, 1994, Alaska Family Law Handbook, 1998. Avocations: magic, music. Home: PO Box 102062 Anchorage AK 99510-2062 Office: Pradell & Assocs 1009 W 7th Ave Anchorage AK 99501-3323 Office Phone: 907-279-4529. E-mail: pradell@alaska.net.

PRADO, EDGAR, horse racing jockey; b. Lima, Peru, June 10, 1967; Horse racing jockey Breeder's Cup Series. Achievements include over 5,000 races won in career; winning Belmont Stakes, 2002, 2004; winning Kentucky Derby (riding Barbaro), 2006. Office: Breeders Cup PO Box 4230 Lexington KY 40544-4230*

PRADO, EDWARD CHARLES, federal judge; b. San Antonio, June 7, 1947; s. Edward L. and Bertha (Cadena) P.; m. Maria Anita Jung, Nov. 10, 1973; 1 child, Edward C. AA, San Antonio Coll., 1967; BA, U. Tex., 1969, JD, 1972. Bar: Tex. 1972. Asst. dist. atty. Bexar County Dist. Atty.'s Office, San Antonio, 1972-76; asst. pub. defender U.S. Pub. Defender's Office, San Antonio, 1976-80; judge U.S. Dist. Ct. Tex., San Antonio, 1980; U.S. atty. U.S. Dept. Justice, San Antonio, 1981—84; judge U.S. Dist. Ct. (we. dist.) Tex., San Antonio, 1984—2003, U.S. Ct. Appeals (5th cir.), San Antonio, 2003—. Served to capt. U.S. Army. Named Outstanding Young Lawyer of Bexar County, 1980. Mem. ABA, Tex. Bar Assn., San Antonio Bar Assn., San Antonio Young Lawyers Assn., Fed. Bar Assn. Republican. Roman Catholic.*

PRADO, GERALD M., investment banker; b. Langeloth, Pa., Jan. 19, 1946; s. Caesar S. and Anita A. P.; m. Judith A. Pompe, May 20, 1967; children: Dennis, Eric, Lynn, Christopher. BA, Washington and Jefferson Coll., 1963-67; MBA, U. Pitts., 1983. Sr. acct. Haskins and Sells, Pitts., 1967-72; auditor G.C. Murphy Co., McKeesport, Pa., 1972-76, asst. controller, 1976-78, treas., 1979-80, asst. v.p., treas., 1980-82, v.p., treas., 1982-85, Russell, Rea & Zappala, Pitts., 1986-87, sr. v.p., 1987-90; pres. Westinghouse Mcht. Banking, Inc., Pitts., 1990-94; prin., co-mgr. Main St. Capital Holdings L.L.C., Pitts., 1994—; Roman Catholic. Home: 205 Overlook Dr Mc Murray PA 15317-2657 Office: Main St Capital Holdings 1001Corporate Dr Ste 200 Canonsburg PA 15317 Office Phone: 724-743-5650. E-mail: prado@mainstcap.com.

PRADOS, JOHN WILLIAM, engineering educator; b. Spring Hill, Tenn., Oct. 12, 1929; s. Gustave Olivier and Elizabeth Branham Prados; m. Ruth Lynn Baird, Sept. 2, 1951; children: Elizabeth Pauline Bowman, Laura Lynn, Anne Caroline Lynch. BS in Chem. engring., U. Miss., Oxford, Miss., 1947—51; PhD, U. Tenn., Knoxville, 1954—57, MS, 1953—54. Registered Profl. Engr., State Bd. of Archtl. and Engring. Examiners/Tenn., 1964. Asst. prof. of chem. engring. The U. of Tenn., Knoxville, Tenn., 1956—59, assoc. prof. of chem. engring., 1959—64, prof. of chem. engring., 1964—, assoc. dean of engring., 1969—71, dean of admissions and records, 1971—73, acting chancellor, knoxville campus, 1973—73, v.p. for academic affairs, statewide sys., 1973—81, v.p. for academic affairs and rsch., statewide sys., 1981—88, v.p. emeritus, 1989—, u. prof., 1989—, head, chem. engring. dept., 1990—93, acting chancellor, martin campus Martin, Tenn., 1979—79; cons. Nuc. Divsn., Union Carbide Corp. Oak Ridge, Tenn., 1957—84, Martin Marietta Energy Systems, Oak Ridge, Tenn., 1984—86. Editor, jour. of engring. edn. Am. Soc. for Engring. Edn., Washington, 1996—2001; sec. Accreditation Bd. for Engring. and Tech., Inc., Baltimore, Md., 1989—90, pres., 1991—92; commr. Commn. on Colleges, So. Assn. of Colleges and Schools, Decatur, Ga., 1986—92, exec. councillor, 1986—89; trustee So. Assn. of Colleges and Schools, Decatur, Ga., 1995—98, F. W. Olin Coll. of Engring., Needham, Mass., 2002—; vice chmn. Engring. Accreditation Commn., Accreditation Bd. for Engring. and Tech., Inc., Baltimore, Md., 1981—84, chmn. 1984—85; dir. Accreditation Bd. for Engring. and Tech., Baltimore, Md., 1988—93; sr. edn. assoc. NSF, Arlington, Va., 1994. First lt. U. S. Air Force, 1951—53, Biloxi, MS; Albuquerque, NM; Limestone, ME. Recipient L. E. Grinter Award for Contributions to Engring. Edn., Accreditation Bd. for Engring. and Tehcnology, Inc., 1993, Alumni Outstanding Tchr. U. Tenn., 1967, Outstanding Engring. Alumnus, 1975, Faculty Macebearer, 1997—98, James T. Rogers Disting. Leadership award, So. Assn. Colls. and Schs., 2004. Fellow: Am. Inst. Chem. Engrs. (Knoxville-Oak Ridge Chem. Engr. of Yr. 1977, treas. 1996—2001, Knoxville-Oak Ridge Chmn. Engr. of Yr. 1999), Am. Inst. of Chemists (life), Am. Soc. for Engring. Edn. (life); mem.: Am. Chem. Soc., Tech. Soc. of Knoxville, Torch Club, Phi Kappa Phi (Disting. Mem. 1974), Tau Beta Pi (exec. coun. 1986—90), Sigma Xi, Sci. Rsch. Soc. (pres. 1983—84, treas. 1990—2002), Alpha Tau Omega. Roman Catholic. Home: 7021 Stagecoach Trail Knoxville TN 37909-1112 Office: 419 Dougherty Engineering Building 1512 Middle Drive Knoxville TN 37996-2200 Business E-Mail: jprados@utk.edu.

PRADZYNSKI, ANDRZEJ HENRYK, chemist; b. Plock, Poland, Jan. 1, 1924; arrived in U.S., 1969; s. Maurycy and Frania (Goldkind) Nejman; m. Halina Romana Bromberger, Apr. 1, 1946; children: Richard E. Neuman, Zgibniew Jacek. BS, U. Wroclaw, Poland, 1949, MS, 1951. Asst. prof. crystallography, chmn. dept. U. Wroclaw, 1948-51; sect. mgr. materials testing Inst. Aviation, Warsaw, Poland, 1951-57; adj. prof. Polish Acad. Scis., Warsaw, 1957-68; dept. dir. Atomic Energy Commn. Poland, Warsaw, 1959-68; rsch. assoc. IV nuclear reactor U. Tex., Austin, 1969-80; exec. v.p. Halinco Skin Care Products, Inc., Austin, 1980-2000. Cons. IAEA, Vienna, Austria, 1968-69. Author: Industrial Radiography (in Polish), 1957; also more than 30 articles in IAEA Conf. Procs., Nukleonika, ISA Trans., others. Mem. Am. Chem. Soc., N.Y. Acad. Scis. Achievements include patent for method and apparatus for collection and analysis of mercury in the atmosphere; developer method of photo-nuclear activation analysis of copper in ores and concentrates, synthetic standards for EDX-ray analysis, method of collection and analysis of mercury in air, method of nondestructive X-ray analysis of heavy metals in toys. Developed pre-concentration methods of trace elements in water for EDX-ray analysis.

PRAGER, STEPHEN, chemistry professor; b. Darmstadt, Germany, July 20, 1928; came to U.S., 1941, naturalized, 1953; s. William and Gertrude Ann (Heyer) P.; m. Julianne Heller, June 7, 1948. B.Sc., Brown, 1947; PhD, Cornell, 1951. Mem. faculty U. Minn., Mpls., 1952—, assoc. prof. chemistry, 1956-62, prof., 1962-90, prof. emeritus, 1990—. Cons. Union Carbide Corp., Oak Ridge, 1954-74 Asso. editor: Jour. Phys. Chemistry, 1970-79. Fulbright scholar and Guggenheim fellow, 1958, 59; Fulbright lectr. and Guggenheim fellow, 1966-67 Mem. Am. Chem. Soc., Am. Phys. Soc. Home: 3320 Dunlap St N Saint Paul MN 55112-3709 E-mail: psprager@cs.com.

PRAGER, SUSAN WESTERBERG, academic administrator, law educator; b. Sacramento, Dec. 14, 1942; d. Percy Foster Westerberg and Aileen M. (McKinley) P.; m. James Martin Prager, Dec. 14, 1973; children: McKinley Ann, Case Mahone. AB, Stanford U., 1964, MA, 1967; JD, UCLA, 1971. Bar: N.C. 1971, Calif. 1972. Atty. Powe, Porter & Alphin, Durham, NC, 1971-72; acting prof. law UCLA, 1972-77, prof. Sch. Law, 1977—, Arjay and Frances Fearing Miller prof. law, 1990—2001—06, assoc. dean Sch. Law, 1979-82, dean, 1982-98; provost Dartmouth Coll., Hanover, NH, 1999—2001; pres. Occidental Coll., 2006—. Bd. dirs. Pacific Mut. Life Holding Co., Newport Beach, Calif. Editor-in-chief, UCLA Law Rev., 1970-71. Trustee Stanford U., 1976-80, 87-97. Mem. ABA (council of sect. on legal edn. and admissions to the bar 1991-97), Assn. Am. Law Schs. (pres. 1986), Order of Coif. Office: Occidental Coll / Office of Pres 3rd Fl, Coons Adminstn Bldg 1600 Campus Rd Los Angeles CA 90041-3314 E-mail: prager@law.ucla.edu.*

PRAHALAD, C.K., finance educator, corporate strategist; b. India; BS, U. Madras, 1960. Harvey C. Fruehauf prof. bus. adminstrn. & prof. corp. strategy and internat. bus. Stephen M. Ross Sch. Bus., U. Mich. Co-author: Competing for the Future, 1994, The Future of Competition: Co-Creating Unique Value with Customers, 2004, The Fortune at the Bottom of the Pyramid: Eradicating Poverty Through Profits, 2004; contbr. articles to profl. jours. Office: Stephen M Ross Sch Bus U Mich 701 Tappan St Ann Arbor MI 48109-1234 Office Phone: 734-763-5573. Office Fax: 734-936-8715. E-mail: ckp@umich.edu.*

PRAKAPAS, EUGENE JOSEPH, art gallery director; b. Lowell, Mass., July 29, 1932; s. Joseph S. Prakapas and Viola Schensnol; m. Dorothy A. Seitner, Dec. 1, 1951. BA, Yale U., 1953; MA, Oxford U., Balliol, 1959. Editor-in-chief, v.p. Trident Press and Pocket Books divsn. Simon & Schuster, Inc., N.Y.C., 1960-70; co-dir. Carus Gallery, N.Y.C., 1973-75; dir. Prakapas Gallery, N.Y.C., 1976—. Vis. curator San Francisco Mus. Modern Art, 1986. Author: Bauhaus Photography, 1985. Lt. (s.g.) USNR, 1953-57. Fulbright fellow, 1957-59; Yale U. scholar, 1949-53. Mem. Art Dealers Assn. Am., Assn. Internat. Photography Art Dealers. Office Phone: 914-961-5091. Business E-Mail: eugeneprakapas@optonline.net.

PRAKASH, CHANDRA, gastroenterologist, researcher; s. Surjya Datta and Shanti Devi Gyawali; m. Laura Christine Johnston, June 15, 2001; children: Kyle Prakash Gyawali, Millie Christine Gyawali. MBBS, Calicut Med. Coll., 1980—85, MD, 1987—90. Bd. Cert. Am. Bd. of Internal Medicine, 1995, Bd. Cert. in Gastroenterology Am. Bd. of Internal Medicine, 1999. Jr. cons. Patan Hosp., Kathmandu, Nepal, 1990—92; sr. ho. officer in internal medicine various hospitals in the UK, 1992—93; resident in internal medicine Dept. of Medicine, Wash. U. in St. Louis, 1993—95, assoc. chief resident in medicine, 1995—96; fellow in gastroent. Divsn. of Gastroent., Wash. U. in St. Louis, 1996—99, instr. of medicine, 1999—2000, asst. prof. of medicine, 2000—. Peer rev. bd. mem. Gastrointestinal Endoscopy, Cleve., 2000—; asst. program dir. Divsn. of Gastroent., Wash. U. in St. Louis, 2001—. Editor: (handbook) A Therapeutic Guide to Common Problems in Gastroenterology. Recipient

Knowlton Incentive for Excellence award, Barnes Jewish Hosp. Found., 1996, Tchr. of the Yr. 2001, Fellows in Divsn. of Gastroent., 2001. Mem.: Royal Coll. Physicians, Am. Gastroent. Assn. (edn. and training com. 2005—), Am. Coll. of Gastroent. (mem. patient care com. 2003—), Am. Soc. for Gastrointestinal Endoscopy (peer rev. com. mem. 2000—03). Office: Washington Univ 660 South Euclid Ave Campus Box 8124 Saint Louis MO 63110 Office Phone: 314-454-8201.

**PRAKASH, JAI,** computer scientist, educator; b. Delhi, India, Feb. 11, 1959; s. Ram and Kirti Prasad; m. Namita Prakash, Jan. 31, 1993; children: Jaya, Neema. PhD, Case Western Res. U. 1990. Tech. mgr. Energizer, Gainesville, Fla., 1996—98; prof. IIT, Chgo., 1998—. Mem.: Electrochem. Soc. (chmn. energy tech. divsn. 2002—). Office: Illinois Institue of Technology 10 W 33rd Chicago IL 60616 Office Phone: 312-567-3639. Home Fax: 312-567-8874; Office Fax: 312-567-8874. E-mail: prakash@iit.edu.

**PRALLE, MARTIN ULRICH,** materials engineer, director; b. Pequanock Township, N.J., Aug. 6, 1971; s. Gert Egon and Karin Marie Pralle; m. Julia Jai Yuen Hwang, May 4, 2002; 1 child, Jucas Kurt. BS in Engring., Cornell U., Ithaca, N.Y., 1993; PhD in Engring., U. Ill., Urbana Champaign, Ill., 2000. Materials engr. Xerox, Webster, NY, 1993—95; sr. rsch. scientist Ion Optics Inc., Waltham, Mass., 2000—04; dir. engring., 2004—. Contbr. articles to profl. jours. Mem.: Optical Soc. Am., Materials Rsch. Soc. Avocations: kayaking, hiking, bicycling. Office: Ion Optics Inc 411 Waverley Oaks Rd Ste 144 Waltham MA 02452-8484

**PRANGE, ARTHUR JERGEN, JR.,** psychology professor, neuroscientist; b. Grand Rapids, Mich., Sept. 19, 1926; s. Arthur Jergen and Martha Frances (Elliott) P.; m. Sarah Elizabeth Bowen, Feb. 4, 1950; children— Christine Anne, Martha Louise, Laura Beth, David Elliott. BS, U. Mich., 1947, MD, 1950. Intern Wayne County Gen. Hosp., Elcina 1950-51; resident in psychiatry U. N.C., Chapel Hill, 1954-57, instr., 1957-60, asst. prof., 1960-64, asso. prof., 1964-68, prof. psychiatry, 1968-83, Boshamer prof. psychiatry, 1983—, acting chmn. dept. psychiatry, 1983-85, dir. NIMH Clin. Rsch. Ctr., 1979—. Vis. scientist Med. Rsch. Coun. Unit, Epson, Surrey, Eng., 1968-69; chmn. clin. projects rsch. rev. com. HEW, NIMH, 1975-76, chmn. bd. sci. counselors, 1986-87; mem. psychopharmacologic drugs adv. com. HEW, FDA, 1979-82. Editor: The Thyroid Axis, Drugs and Behavior, 74; Contbr. articles to med. jours. Recipient NIMH Career Devel. award 1961-69, Career Scientist award, 1969-95, Gold Medal award Soc. of Biol. Psychiatry, 1992, Exemplary Psychiatrist award Nat. Alliance for the Mentally Ill, 1997, Selo prize Nat. Alliance for Rsch. in Schizophrenia and Affective Disorders, 1997. Fellow Am. Psychiat. Assn. (life, Rsch. in Psychiatry award 1996), Am. Coll. Neuropsychopharmacology (life, pres. 1987, Hoch award 1995); mem. Internat. Soc. Psychoneuroendocrinology (founding mem.), N.C. Neuropsychiat. Assn., Collegium Internationale Neuropsychopharmacologicum, Royal Coll. Psychiatrists (London): Home: 6503 Meadowview Rd Hillsborough NC 27278-8314 Office: Univ NC Sch Medicine Dept Psychiatry Chapel Hill NC 27599-0001

**PRANGE, HILMAR WALTER,** neurology educator; b. Reichenbach, Germany, Aug. 4, 1944; s. Georg Friedrich Reinhold and Gertrud Wilhelmine (Mueller) P.; m. Carin Juliane Schroeter, Mar. 14, 1970; children: Klaus Richard, Juliane. MD, U. Rostock, Germany, 1969, lic. specialist neurology and psychiatry, 1974; Habilitation, Georg-August U., Goettingen, Germany, 1982. Medical diplomate. Med. resident Regional Hosp., Stralsund, Germany, 1969-71; med. asst. then psychiatrist Univ. Hosp., Rostock, 1971-75; asst. med. dir. Ev. Johannes Hosp., Bielefeld, Germany, 1975-76; head neurologic out-patient clinic Univ. Hosp., Goettingen, Germany, 1976-78, asst. med. dir. dept. neurology, 1979—87, dir. neurol. intensive care unit, 1987—. Mem. expert group German Ministry of Health. Author: Neurosyphilis, 1987, Infectious Diseases of the Central Nervous System, 1995; editor: CNS Barriers and Modern CSF Diagnostics, 1993, Systemic Infections Causing Bacterial CNS Diseases, 1997, Infectious Diseases of the Central Nervous System, 2001, Emergencies in Neurology, 2002, Neurological Intensive Medicine, 2004; contbr. articles to profl. jours. Grantee German Forschungsgemeinschaft, German Tech. Cooperation, German MS Soc. Mem.: EMEA, German Med. Assn. (mem. commn. drug security), European Neurol. Soc. Lutheran. Avocation: Cultural history, sports, jogging (marathons), swimming. Business E-Mail: hprange@gwdg.de.

**PRANGE, ROY LEONARD, JR.,** lawyer; b. Chgo., Sept. 12, 1945; s. Roy Leonard and Marjorie Rose P.; m. Carol Lynn Poels, June 5, 1971; children: David, Ellen, Susan. BA, U. Iowa, 1967; MA, Ohio State U., 1968; JD, U. Wis.-Madison, 1975. Bar: Wis. 1975, U.S. Dist. Ct. (we. and ea. dists.) Wis. 1975, U.S.C. Appeals (7th cir.) 1978, U.S. Supreme Ct. 1978. Assoc. Ross & Stevens, S.C., Madison, Wis., 1975—79, ptnr., 1979—90, Quarles & Brady, LLP, Madison, 1990—. Lectr. bankruptcy, debtor-creditor rights, U. Wis., Madison, 1982—. Contbr. Wis. Lawyer's Desk Reference Manual, 1987, Comml. Litigation in Wis. Practice Handbook, 1995, West's Bankruptcy Exemption Manual, 1997—. 1st lt. U.S. Army, 1969-72. Fellow Am. Coll. Bankruptcy; mem. ABA, Wis. State Bar (dir. bankruptcy, insolvency, creditors rights sect. 1985-91, chair 1990-92, mem. continuing legal edn. com. 1990-95), Am. Bankruptcy Inst., Lincoln's Fellowship (v.p. 1980-84). Avocations: swimming, bicycling, scuba diving. Office: Quarles & Brady LLP PO Box 2113 1 S Pinckney St Madison WI 53701-2113 Office Phone: 608-283-2485. Business E-Mail: rlp@quarles.com.

**PRANSES, ANTHONY LOUIS,** retired electric power industry executive; b. Claracq, France, May 3, 1920; s. Anthony Kasimer and Georgette (Pilon) F.; m. Margaret Louise Hamill, July 24, 1943; children— Anthony Randolph, Terry Jay, Renee Louise. Student, Sorbonne, Paris, France, 1937-39; BS in Metall. Engring. Carnegie Inst. Tech., 1942, grad. student, 1946-48. With Westinghouse Electric Corp., 1945-86, mgr. mfg. planning Lima, Ohio, 1954-57, plant mgr., 1958-59, mgr. mfg. services, 1959-72, mgr. mfg., 1972-80, cons., 1980-86. Joined Am. Youth Hostels, 1935, founder Pitts. council, 1947, pres. council, 1947-50, mem. nat. bd. dirs., 1954-72, Midwest regional v.p., 1957-59, nat. pres., 1959-62, pres. Lima council, 1962-75, 87-91, chmn. nat. bd. dirs., 1963-67. Served to capt., C.E. AUS, 1942- 45. Home: 6005 Poling Rd Lima OH 45807-9492 E-mail: pranses@wcoil.com

**PRASAD, ANANDA SHIVA,** medical educator; b. Buxar, Bihar, India, Jan. 1, 1928; came to U.S., 1952, naturalized, 1968; s. Radha Krishna and Mahesha (Kaur) Lal; m. Aryabala Ray, Jan. 6, 1952; children: Rita, Sheila, Ashok, Audrey. BSc, Patna Sci. Coll., India, 1946, MB, BChir, 1951; PhD, U. Minn., 1957; doctorate honoris causa, U. Claude Bernard of Lyon, 1999. Intern Patna Med. Coll. Hosp., 1951-52; resident St. Paul's Hosp., Dallas, 1952-53, U. Minn., 1953-56, VA Hosp., Mpls., 1956; instr. dept. medicine Univ. Hosp., U. Minn., Mpls., 1957-58; vis. assoc. medicine Shiraz Med. Faculty, Nemazee Hosp., Shiraz, Iran, 1960; asst. prof. medicine and nutrition Vanderbilt U., 1961-63; mem. faculty, dir. div. hematology dept. medicine Wayne State U., Detroit, 1963-84, assoc. prof., 1964-68, prof., 1968-2000, dir. research dept. medicine, 1984-97, disting. prof., 2000—. Mem. staff Harper-Grace Hosp., VA Hosp., Allen Park, Mich.; mem. trace elements subcom. Food and Nutrition Bd., NRC-Nat. Acad. Scis., 1965-68; chmn. trace elements com. Internat. Union Nutritional Scis.; mem. Am. Bd. Nutrition; pres. Am. Coll. Nutrition, 1991-93. Author: Zinc Metabolism, 1966, Trace Elements in Human Health and Disease, 1976, Trace Elements and Iron in Human Metabolism, 1978, Zinc in Human Nutrition, 1979, Biochemistry of Zinc, 1993; editor: Clinical, Biochemical and Nutritional Aspects of Trace Elements, 1982, Am. Jour. Hematology, Jour. Trace Elements in Exptl. Medicine; editor: Zinc Metabolism, Current Aspects in Health and Disease, 1977; co-editor: Clinical Applications of Recent Advances in Zinc Metabolism, 1982, Zinc Deficiency in Human Subjects, 1983, Essential and Toxic Trace Elements in Human Health and Disease, 1988, Essential and Toxic Trace Elements in Human Health and Disease: An Update, 1993; Jour. Am. Coll. Nutrition; contbr. articles to profl. jours., also reviewer. Trustee Detroit Internat. Inst., Detroit Gen. Hosp. Rsch. Corp., 1969—72. Recipient Rsch. Recognition award Wayne State U., 1964, award Am. Coll. Nutrition, 1976, Disting. Faculty Fellowship award Wayne State

U., 1986, Medal of Honor, City of Lyon, France, 1989, Pioneer in Sickle Cell Disease Rsch. award Nat. Heart Lung Blood Inst./NIH, 1997; Pfizer scholar, 1955-56, WCMS Spl. Recognition award for Profl. Ach., 1998, Klaus Schwartz medal Internat. Assn. Bioinorganic Scientists, 2001, Spl. Recognition award Am. Assn. Physicians India, 2001; inducted Heritage Hall of Fame, Mich., 2003. Master ACP (recipient Mich. Laureate award), Am. Coll. Nutrition; fellow AAAS, Am. Inst. Nutrition (trace elements panel), Internat. Soc. Hematology; mem. AMA (Goldberger award 1975), Internat. Soc. Trace Element Rsch. in Humans (pres. 1986-92, chmn. steering com. 1985-86, Raulin award 1989), Am. Soc. Clin. Nutrition (awards com. 1969-70), Am. Fedn. Clin. Rsch. (pres. Mich. 1969-70), Am. Physiol. Soc., Am. Soc. Clin. Investigation, Am. Soc. Hematology, Assn. Am. Physicians, European Acad. Scis., Arts and Humanities (corr.), Ctrl. Soc. Clin. Rsch., Soc. Exptl. Biology and Medicine (councillor Mich. 1967-71), Wayne State U. Acad. Scholars (pres.-elect 1997-98, pres. 1998-99), Wayne County Med. Soc., Internat. Soc. Internal Medicine, Am. Soc. Clin. Nutrition (Robert H. Herman award 1984), Nutrition Soc. India (Gopalan oration award 1988), Nat. Heart, Lung, Blood Inst. NIH (mem. coun. 2002-2004), Cosmos Club (Washington), Sigma Xi. Home: 4710 Cove Rd Orchard Lake MI 48323-3604 Office: Univ Health Ctr 5-C 4201 Saint Antoine St Detroit MI 48201-2153 Office Phone: 313-577-1597. Business E-Mail: prasada@karmanos.org.

**PRASAD, BIRENDRA (BRIAN),** mechanical engineer; b. Patna, Bihar, India, June 30, 1949; came to U.S., 1973; s. Baidyanath Prasad Gupta and Ramrati Devi; m. Pushpa Gupta, May 13, 1973; children: Rosalie, Gunjan, Palak. BSME, Bihar Coll. Engring., Patna, 1969; MSME, Indian Inst. Tech., Kanpur, 1971; DEng, Stanford U., 1975; PhD in Mech. and Aerospace Engring., Ill. Inst. Tech., 1977. Rsch. asst. Ill. Inst. Tech., Chgo., 1976—77, lectr., 1978—79; prin. rsch. scientist Ill. Rsch. Lab., Ford Motor Co., Dearborn, Mich., 1982—85; sr. cons. engr. Electronic Data Sys. Corp., Troy, Mich., 1985—98; dir. Unigraphics Solutions, Inc. Knowledge based Engring. (KBE) B, Cypress, Calif., 1998—, U. Calif. Continuing Edn., Irvine, Calif., 2001—; mng. dir. Spec2market Solutions, Tustin, Calif.; chief knowledge officer Parker Hannifin, Irvine, Calif. Author: 12 books; contbr. more than 100 articles to profl. jours. Recipient award NASA, 1981. Fellow AIAA (chmn. structural dynamics and materials conf. organizing com., treas. Mich. chpt. 1986—), ASME, ASCE (chmn., mem. control group aerospace div. conf. com.); mem. Soc. Automotive Engring. Home: 2966 Penman Tustin CA 92782-3313 Office: Spec2 market Solutions Mng Dir Knowledge Based Engring PO Box 3882 Tustin CA 92781-3882 Personal E-mail: prasadb1@cox.net.

**PRASAD, NAVIN,** ophthalmologist; MD, Darbhanga Med. Coll., India, 1990. Bd. Cert. Ophthalmology All India Inst. of Med. Scis., New Delhi, 1995, cert. U.S. Med. Lic. Exam Ednl. Commn. of Fgn. Med. Grads., 2004. Med. intern Darbhanga Med. Coll., Laheriasarai, India, 1990—91, sr. ho. officer, 1991—92; resident physician All India Inst. of Med. Scis., New Delhi, 1992—95, registrar, sr. resident, 1995—98; sr. ho. officer, ophthalmology James Cook U. Hosp., Middlesbrough, England, 2000—03; glaucoma fellow Mass. Eye & Ear Infirmary, Harvard Med. Sch., Boston, 2005—. Author: (internat. jour. article) Jour. of Cataract Refract Surgery, Eyenews, Eye, (poster in internat. conf.) Longterm intervisit intraocular pressure fluctuation following selective laser trabeculoplasty as primary therapy in open angle glaucoma. Perform cataract eye surgeries in eye camps Second Sight of UK, Bisalpur, India, 2002. Merit Scholarship, Govt. of India, 1991, 1983. Fellow: The Royal Coll. of Physicians and Surgeons of Glasgow (assoc.); mem.: The Assn. for Rsch. in Vision and Ophthalmology (assoc.), All India Ophthal. Soc. (life), Am. Acad. Ophthalmology (assoc.). Achievements include research in Study of corneal endothelial loss due to phacoemulsification in different types of anterior capsulotomies.

**PRASAD, NEIL A.,** telecommunications industry executive, computer company executive; arrived in US, 1988, naturalized, 2000; s. Ayilliyath and Annie Prasad; m. Caroline George, Dec. 27, 1992; children: Jake Joseph, Anya Joseph, Gino Joseph. BEE, Gujarat U., India, 1987; MSEE, U. Houston, 1991. Cert. profl. engr., Instn. Engrs., India, 1987, Nat. Soc. Profl. Engrs., Va., 1990, Tex. Soc. Profl. Engrs., 1991; in leadership excellence Toastmasters Internat., 2004. Software engr. Software Interfaces, Inc., Houston, 1991; sr. design engr. WilTel, Inc. Advanced Tech. Group, The Woodlands, Tex., 1991—95; sr. engr. MCI Telecom. Corp., Richardson, Tex., 1995—96; sr. mgr. Stratacom, Inc., San Jose, Calif., 1996, Cisco Sys., Inc., San Jose, Calif. 1996—; dir. IPDR.org, Nantucket, Mass., 2005—; pres. CEO Abaeca Solutions, 2006—. Amb. ATM Forum, Mountain View, Calif., 1994—99; chmn., internet protocol network mgmt. group TeleManagement Forum, Morristown, NJ, 2000—06, dir., 2006—; divsn. gov. Toastmasters Internat., Mission Viejo, Calif., 2004—05; spkr., presenter in field. Contbr. articles to profl. jours. Vol. Cisco Emergency Response Team; coun. mem. Ascension Parish, San Jose, 2006—. Recipient Project Mgmt. and Tng. Excellence award, Wiltel Inc., 1995. Mem.: IEEE, Planetary Soc., Am. Physical Soc., Assn. Computing Mahinery, Instn. Engrs. (assoc.), Mensa, Toastmasters Internat. (named Disting. Toastmaster 2006, Humorous Speech Contest winner 2006). Roman Catholic. Achievements include development and industry demonstration of network management system for data, voice, and video telecommunications services. Avocations: marathon running, travel, ice skating, literature. Home: 822 Daffodil Way San Jose CA 95117 Office: Cisco Systems Inc 170 W Tasman Dr San Jose CA 95134 Office Phone: 408-525-7209. Personal E-mail: ap4411@yahoo.com.

**PRASAD, NIRU,** physician, television personality; b. Feb. 10, 1940; s. Sadashiv and Saraswati Prasad; m. Bala Prasad, Mar. 9, 1962; children: Abhilasha, Ashish, Anjali, Ashoke. Emergency rm. physician Henry Ford Hosp., Detroit, Mich., 2002; pediatric urgent care St. Joseph Mercy Hosp., Pontiac, Mich. 2002; occupl. physician Med. Plant Physician, Auhum Hills, Mich., 2002. Contbr. (book) How to Keep Your Child Safe and Healthy; contbr. articles to profl. jours.; host (television program) Health Talk. Recipient AMA Physician Recognition Award, 1992, Svc. of Justice and Mercy Recognition Award, 1993, America's Registry of Outstanding Professionals, 2001, Physician Recognition award, 1995, Ams. Top Pediatricians, 2002—, Angel award, 2002, 2003. Home: 264 Pine Ridge Drive Bloomfield Hills MI 48304 Personal E-mail: niruprasad@hotmail.com.

**PRASAD, P.V. VARA,** agricultural studies educator, researcher; s. Janardhana Rao and Kasturi Bai Pagadala; m. Lakshmi Ganji; children: Abhinav Pagadala, Ananya Pagadala. BSc in Agr., Andhra Pradesh Agrl. U., Hyderabad, India, 1991, MSc in Agr., 1993; PhD, U. Reading, England, 1999. Rsch. assoc. Andhra Pradesh Agrl. U., Hyderabad, India, 1994—95; postdoctoral rsch. assoc. U. Fla., Gainesville, 2000—05; asst. prof. Kans. State U., Manhattan, 2005—. Editor and reviewer Communications in Biometry and Crop Sci.; reviewer Crop Sci., Agronomy Jour., New Phytologist, Jour. Exptl. Botany, Annals of Botany, Agr. Ecosystems and Environment, Field Crops Rsch., Australian Jour. Agrl. Rsch. Contbr. chapters to books, articles to profl. jours. Recipient Gold medal, Potash and Phosphate Inst. Can. - India Program, 1993; scholar, Internat. Crops Rsch. Inst. for Semi-Arid Tropics, 1991—93, Felix Found., 1996—99. Mem.: Internat. Soc. Agrl Meteorology, Am. Soc. Plant Biologists, Soil Sci. Soc. Am., Am. Soc. Agronomy, Crop Sci. Soc. Am. Office: Kansas State Univ Agronomy Dept 2004 Throckmorton Hall Manhattan KS 66506

**PRATER, EMMA LOU,** retired academic administrator; b. Tyler, Tex., July 22, 1929; d. Roy Andrew and Alice Gay Wyatt; m. Kenneth L. Prater; children: Sherry S., Sandra C. AA, Tyler Jr. Coll., Tex., 1967; BS, Tex. A&M U., 1971, MS, 1982. With advt. sales and promotion Gen. Electric, Tyler 1957—64; acct. Tyler (Tex.) Jr. Coll., 1964—77, dir. student activities, 1980—89; dir. acctg. Spring Ind. Sch. Dist., Houston, 1977—80; ret., 1980. Adv. Tex. State Govt. 600 Assn. Tex. Jr. Colls., 1989—2006; former pres. alumni bd. Nat. Jr. Coll. Cheerleader Assn., 1984; coach cheerleading Tyler Jr. Coll., 1969—89. Author: Cheerleading, 1984. Dir. adult 55+ Westwood Bapt. Ch. Recipient Black and Gold award, Tyler Jr. Coll., 1991. Mem.: Tyler Jr. Coll. Alumni Assn. Achievements include Emma Lou Prater Presdl. scholarship named in honor at Tyler Jr. Coll. Home: 509 Elmridge Tyler TX 75703

**PRATER, MARY ANNE,** special education educator, researcher; d. Herman Bates and Barbara M. Prater. MusB, U. Utah, Salt Lake City, 1975, MS, 1982; PhD, Utah State U., Logan, 1987. Asst. prof. So. Ill. U., Carbondale, 1987—90; prof., dept. chair, assoc. dean U. Hawaii at Manoa, Honolulu, 1990—2001; prof., dept. chair Brigham Young U., Provo, Utah, 2001—. Author: Developmental Disabilities in Children's Literature: Issues and Annotated Bibliography, 2000. Active Ch. of Jesus Christ of Latter-day Saints. Recipient Disting. Paper award, Hawaii Edn. Rsch. Assn., 1996, 2002, Spl. Recognition award, Devel. Disabilities Divsn. of the Coun. for Exceptional Children, 2000; Rsch. grantee, U.S. Dept. Edn., 1986—87, 2000—01, Pers. Preparation grantee, 1987—90, 2004—, Leadership Preparation grantee, 1996—2001, Post-Doctoral fellow, U. Ky., 1997. Mem.: ASCD, Coun. for Learning Disabilities, Am. Assn. Colls. Tchr. Edn., Coun. for Exceptional Children (various coms.). Office: Brigham Young University 340 MCKB Provo UT 84602 Office Phone: 801-422-1592.

**PRATHER, DEBORAH A.,** music educator; b. Carlisle, Pa., July 16, 1952; d. David Dewey and Mary Isabelle Ilgenfritz; m. Richard Wright Prather, Apr. 2, 1977; children: Abby Lynn, Andrew David. B Music Edn., Valparaiso U., Ind., 1974; M Music Edn., Butler U., Indpls., 1989. K-12 vocal music tchr. Porter County Schs., Kouts, Ind., 1974—78; 3-6 vocal music tchr. Eagle Union Schs., Zionsville, Ind., 1987—88; HS vocal music tchr. Brownsburg (Ind.) Cmty. Sch. Corp., 1988—. Dir. music Christ Luth. Ch., Zionsville, 2003—. Recipient Realizing the Dream award, Lilly Endowment, Indpls., 2003. Mem.: Ind. Choral Dirst. Assn., Ind. Music Educators Assn. (chmn. repertoire 1999—2003), Am. Choral Dirs. Assn. (mem. repertoire and stds. com. ctrl. divsn. 2004—). Lutheran. Office: Browsburg HS 1000 S Odell St Brownsburg IN 46112

**PRATHER, DONNA LYNN,** psychiatrist; b. Charlotte, N.C., Nov. 4, 1946; d. James Boyd and Ann (Joyner) P. BA, Queens Coll., Charlotte, 1968; MD, U. N.C., 1978. Supr. Meckenburg County Dept. Social Svcs., Charlotte, 1971-74; family practice intern Charlotte Meml. Hosp., 1978-79, resident in family practice, 1979-81; fellow in family medicine U. N.C., Chapel Hill, 1981-82; resident in psychiatry N.C. Meml. Hosp., Chapel Hill, 1982-85; pvt. practice psychiatry Chapel Hill, N.C., 1985—. Psychiatrist Person Counceling Ctr., Roxboro, N.C., 1983-92; med. dir. Orange-person-Chatam Mental Health Ctr., Chapel Hill, 1992—; clin. assoc. prof. U. N.C., Chapel Hill, 1985—. Mem. N.C. Psychiat. Assn., N.C. Med. Soc., Am. Psychiat. Assn., N.C. Psychiat. Assn. (chmn., com. for women 1990-91, ethics com. 1997-99). Avocation: music. Office: The Courtyard Ste 27 Chapel Hill NC 27516-2319 Office Phone: 919-929-6519.

**PRATHER, GERALD LUTHER,** management consultant, retired judge, retired military officer; b. LaGrange, Ga., Apr. 7, 1935; s. Luther Pate and Hazel Belle (McCullough) P.; m. Carolyn Pearson, Nov. 22, 1956; children: Dean Allen, Bryan Pate, Jeri Lynn, Angela BSE.E., Auburn U., 1966; MS in Mgmt., Air Force Inst. Tech., 1972; postgrad. advanced mgmt., U. Houston, 1978; grad., SQ Officer Sch., Maxwell AFB, 1963, ICAF, Washington, 1974, Ecumenical Ctr. Religion and Health, San Antonio, Tex., 2000. Enlisted USAF, 1954-56, commd. 2d lt., 1956, advanced through grades to maj. gen., 1981, various assignments as pilot, 1956-68, served in Vietnam, 1967-68, commdr. 1963d Comm. Squadron Chanute AFB, Ill., 1968-69, comdr. 1918th Comm. Squadron Scott AFB, Ill., 1969-70, dep. dir. comm.-electronics for 15th Air Force March AFB, Calif., 1970-72, chief comm. ops. div. hdqrs. Washington, 1972-75, comdr. strategic comm. div. Offutt AFB, Nebr., 1975-77, comdr. European Comm. Div. Ramstein AFB, W. Ger., 1977-80; dir. Command Control, Comm. & Computer Systems, Hdqrs. U.S. Readiness Command MacDill AFB, Fla., 1980-81; asst. chief of staff Info. Systems Hdqrs. USAF, Washington, 1981-84, comdr. Air Force Comm. Command Scott AFB, Ill., 1984-86, ret., 1986; pvt. practice mgmt. cons. Del Rio, Tex., 1986-1997; Justice of the Peace Val Verde County, Tex., 1987-97. Lectr. in field; also air traffic controller, parachutist; bd. dirs. Del Rio Internat. Airport. Speech writer Team America 1983 (Freedom Found. nat. award 1984). Scoutmaster Boy Scouts Am., Sacramento, 1963, chmn. com., 1964, cub master Auburn, Ala.; sponsor Explorer Troop, Boy Scouts Am., Scott AFB, Ill., 1969; chmn. Amistad Dist. Boy Scouts Am., 1988, Eagle Scout advancement, 1994—, Val Verde County United Way campaign, 1989, pres., bd. dirs., 1990; v.p. programs, exec. bd. BSA, 2005—; pastoral counselor St. James Ch., 2002, pastoral care specialist, 2002—; chaplain Val Verde Regional Hosp., 2002—; Juvenile Detention Ctr., 1998—. Decorated DSM with oak leaf cluster, Legion of Merit with one oak leaf cluster, DFC, Bronze Star with V device, Air medal with two oak leaf clusters, Republic of Vietnam Gallantry Cross with Palm; recipient Gen. Edwin W. Rawlings award Air Force Inst. Tech., 1972, Comdt.'s award, 1972, also numerous other decorations and awards; recipient Silver Beaver award Boy Scouts Am., 2003, Eagle Scout award, 2006; Wilma E. West fellow Boy Scouts Am., 2005. Mem.: VFW (life), Army Airways Comm. Svc. Alumni Assn. (dir. 2000—), Life Achievement award 2003, Honor award 2003), Del Rio C. of C. (v.p. 1989—90, bd. dirs. 1990—99, v.p. 1991—92, pres. 1995—96, bd. dirs. 1999—, life dir. 2005—), Air Force Assn. (Jimmy Doolittle award 1984), Telephone Pioneers of Am., Soc. Logistics Engrs., Justice of the Peace and Constables Assn., Soc. Am. Mil. Engrs., Air Traffic Control Assn., Armed Forces Comm.-Electronics Assn. (mem. com. 1981—82, chmn. ethics com. 1982—83, internat. v.p. 1982—84, assoc. dir. 1984—96, Meritorious Gold medal 1976, 1983), Non-Commd. Officers Assn. (hon.), Air Force Sgts. Assn. (hon.), Disabled Am. Vets. (life), Vietnam Vets. Assn. (life), Vietnam Vets. Am. (life), Del Rio Club, Lions (dir. 1989—94, v.p. 1994, Svc. award 1992—93, 2002—03, Helen Keller fellow 2004), Civitan, Am. Legion, Order of Daedalians (life). Avocations: singing, gardening, sketching, automotive mechanics, private pilot. Address: HC 1 Box 7 Del Rio TX 78840-9720 Office Phone: 830-774-4483.

**PRATHER, LAURA LEE,** lawyer, educator; BBA, U. Tex., 1988, JD, 1991. Jud. clk. to U.S. Dist. Judge Hayden Head Jr., Corpus Christi, Tex., 1991—92; assoc. O'Melveny & Myers, L.A., 1992—93; from assoc. to ptnr. George, Donaldson & Ford, Austin, Tex., 1993—98; ptnr. Jackson Walker, Austin, 1998—. Bd. dirs. KLRN, Austin; adj. prof. media and entertainment U. Tex., 2005, 06. Editor: (e-copyright law handbook) Aspen Law and Business; contbr. articles to law jours. Mem. adv. bd. Lifeworks, Austin, Ctr. for Child Protection, Austin. Named Best Lawyer under 40, Austin Young Men's and Women's Alliance, 2000, Tex. Rising Star, Tex. Lawyer, 1999; recipient Pres.'s award, Tex. Assn. Broadcasters, 2005. Mem.: ABA (mem. governing bd. forumon comms. law 2000—, mem. editl. bd. Litigation mag. 2004—), Tex. Bar Assn., Calif. Bar Assn., N.Y. Bar Assn. Office: Jackson Walker LLP Ste 1100 100 Congress Austin TX 78703

**PRATHER, LENORE LOVING,** former state supreme court chief justice; b. West Point, Miss., Sept. 17, 1931; d. Byron Herald and Hattie Hearn (Morris) Loving; m. Robert Brooks Prather, May 30, 1957; children: Pamela, Valerie Jo, Malinda Wayne. BS, Miss. Univ. Women, 1953; JD, U. Miss., 1955; D (hon.), Miss. Univ. Women, 2003. Bar: Miss. 1955. Practice with B. H. Loving, West Point, 1955-60; sole practice, 1960-62, 65-71; assoc. practice, 1962-65; mcpl. judge City of West Point, 1965-71; chancery ct. judge 14th dist. State of Miss., Columbus, 1971-82, supreme ct. justice Jackson, 1982-92, presiding justice, 1993-97, chief justice, 1998-2001; interim pres. Miss. U. for Women, Columbus, Miss., 2001—02. V.p. Conf. Local Bar Assn. 1956-58; sec. Clay County Bar Assn., 1956-71 1st woman in Miss. to become chancery judge, 1971, and supreme ct. justice, 1982, and chief justice, 1998-2000; recipient Miss. Bar Found. Professionalism award, 2005; named Outstanding Miss. Woman, Pres.'s Commn. on Status of Women, 1986-87. Mem. Miss. State Bar Assn. (Jud. Excellence award 2000-01), DAR, Rotary, Pilot Club, Jr. Aux. Columbus Club. Episcopalian. Achievements include first female chancellor in Mississippi; first female Supreme Court justice; first female chief justice in Mississippi. Personal E-mail: lenorepr@bellsouth.net.

**PRATHER, SUSAN LYNN,** public relations executive; b. Melrose Park, Ill. d. Horace Charles and Ruth Anna Paula (Backus) P.; divorced. BS, Ind. U., 1973, MS, 1975. Arts administr. Lyric Opera Chgo., 1975; jr. account exec.

Morton H. Kaplan Assocs., Chgo., 1976-78, sr. account exec., 1978-81; account supr. Ketchum Pub. Relations, Chgo., 1981-83, v.p., 1983-87, v.p., group mgr., 1985-87; v.p., dir. pub. relations Cramer-Krasselt, Chgo., 1987-95, sr. v.p., dir. pub. rels., 1996—. Cons. Velamints, Foster Wheeler, Kellogg Co., Battle Creek, Mich., 1985—. Village of Rosemont, Ill., PrincCo Personal Comm., Sr. Friendlys, Anti-Cruelty Soc. Chgo., Ill. State Toll Hwy. Authority; founder, prin. pratherpr, 2003-. Singer various recitals; founder, dir. Chgo. Sports Hall of Fame, 1978-81. Mem. archives com. Chgo. Symphony Orch., 1986—, mem. long term planning com., 1987-89; mem. press advance team Papal Visit to Chgo., 1978; mem. White House Press Advance Team, Chgo., 1976-80. Mem. Pub. Rels. Soc. Am. (bd. dirs. Chgo. chpt. 1987—), Internat. Pub. Rels. Assn., Publicity Club (bd. dirs. 1986—, Merit award 1982, Golden Trumpet awards, Silver Trumpet awards), Bus. and Profl. Assn. Lutheran. Avocation: figure skating. Home: 155 N Harbor Dr Apt 2212 Chicago IL 60601-7321

**PRATHER, WILLIAM C., III,** lawyer, writer; b. Toledo, Ill., Feb. 20, 1921; s. Hollie Cartmill and Effie Fern (Deppen) P. BA, U. Ill., 1942, JD, 1947. Bar: Ill. 1947, U.S. Supreme Ct. 1978. Co-pres. student govt. U. Ill., 1942, asst. dean, 1942-43; atty. First Nat. Bank Chgo., 1947-51; asst. gen. counsel U.S. Savs. and Loan League, Chgo., 1951-59; gen. counsel U.S. League of Savs. Instns., Chgo., 1959-82, gen. counsel emeritus, 1982—; sole practice Cumberland County, Ill., 1981—. Sem. lectr. in law, banking. Editor: The Legal Bulletin, 1951-81, The Federal Guide, 1954-81; author: Savings Accounts, 8th edit., 1981; contbr. articles to publs. Lt. U.S. Armed Forces, 1943-45. Decorated Bronze Star. Mem. ABA, FBA, Internat. Bar Assn., Ill. Bar Assn., Chgo. Bar Assn., Union Internat. des Avocats, Nat. Lawyers Club Washington, Cosmos Club, Univ. Club Chgo., Kiwanis, Mattoon Golf and Country Club, Exeter and County Club (Eng.), Am. Club Riviera (France), Tennis Club de Beaulieu (France), Soc. Colonial Wars, St. Andrew's Soc., Am. Legion, Phi Delta Phi, Phi Gamma Delta, Phi Eta Sigma, Phi Alpha Chi. Home: Applewood Farm PO Box 157 Toledo IL 62468-0157 also: L'Orangeraie 42 Av General Leclerc Villefranche-sur-Mer 06230 France Office: 142 Courthouse Sq Toledo IL 62468

**PRATHER, WILLIAM DOYLE,** electronics engineer, researcher; b. Odessa, Tex., Mar. 9, 1947; s. William Bradford and Edna Mae Prather; m. Selma Andrea Robertson, May 12, 2001; children: Kellie Dawn Robinson, Lara Fay Garcia, Elizabeth Rose, John Bradford. BSEE, U. N.Mex, Albuquerque, 1970, MSEE, 1975. Electronics engr. Air Force Weapons Lab., Kirtland Air Force Base, N.Mex., 1970—89; dep. divsn. chief Air Force Phillips Lab., 1990—94; br. chief Air Force Rsch. Lab., 1994—2005, tech. advisor, 2005—. Contbr. articles to profl. jours. Elder Immanuel Presbyn. Ch., Albuquerque, 1986—2006. Recipient R. Earl Good award, Air Force Rsch. Lab., 2003. Fellow: EMP Soc.; mem.: IEEE, Internat. Radio Sci. Union, Directed Energy Profl. Soc., Eta Kappa Nu (life). Conservative. Presbyterian. Achievements include development of Methods for testing the integrity of electromagnetically shielded aircraft; Techniques for identifying objects behind walls; Wideband microwave sources; research in Electromagnetic coupling into aircraft. Avocations: backpacking, fishing, music. Office: Air Force Research Laboratory High Power Microwave Division Kirtland Afb NM 87117 Office Phone: 505-846-0416. E-mail: william.prather@ieee.org.

**PRATKANIS, ANTHONY RICHARD,** social psychologist, educator; b. Portsmouth, Va., Apr. 2, 1957; s. Thomas R. and Rosemarie (Gray) P. BS summa cum laude, Ea. Menonite Coll., 1979; MA, Ohio State U., 1981, PhD, 1984. Rsch. assoc. Ohio State U., Columbus, 1981-83; asst. prof. indsl. adminstrn. & psychology Carnegie Mellon, 1984—87; asst. prof., then assoc. prof. psychology U. Calif., Santa Cruz, 1987-95, prof., 1995—. Expert legal witness; reviewer acad. jours. Co-author: (with E. Aronson) The Age of Propaganda, 1992, (with D. Shadel) Weapons of Fraud, 2005; co-editor: (with A. Greenwald and S. Breckler) Attitude Structure and Function; contbr. articles to profl. papers, book chpts Postdoctor fellow Carnegie-Mellon U., Pitts., 1983-84; J.B. Smith scholar Ea. Mennonite Coll., Harristonburg, Va., 1975-79. Fellow APA, Soc. Personality and Social Psychology; mem. Midwestern Psychol. Assn., Soc. Exptl. Social Psychology. Democrat. Research includes attitudes, persuasion, social influence. Home: 166 Montclair Dr Santa Cruz CA 95060-1025 Office: U Calif Bd Psychology Santa Cruz CA 95064 Business E-Mail: peitho@cats.ucsc.edu.

**PRATS, MICHAEL,** petroleum engineer, educator; b. Tampa, Fla., Dec. 18, 1925; s. Miguel and Maria (Carbó) P.; m. Mary Blanche Flaherty, Apr. 7, 1951; children: Delicia Anne, Barbara Eileen, Teresa Kaye, Steven Michael. BS in Physics, U. Tex., 1949, MA in Physics, 1951. With Shell Devel. Co., Houston, 1950—, cons. rsch. engr., then sr. rsch. assoc., 1972-89; pres. Michael Prats & Associates, Houston, 1989—. Cons. prof. petroleum engring. dept. Stanford U., 1997—99; adj. prof. dept. geosystems petroleum engring. U. Tex., Austin, 1991—2001; participant scientist exch. Royal/Dutch Shell Lab., Amsterdam, Netherlands, 1954, 55, Shell Internat. Petroleum, The Hague, Netherlands, 1981, Maraven, S.A., Caracas, Venezuela, 1981-83. Author: Thermal Recovery, 1982, Spanish transl., 1987; contbr. articles to profl. jours.; 2 patents in field. Served to staff sgt. USAAF, 1944-46, PTO. Recipient Diploma of Honor Pi Epsilon Tau, 1986, Disting. Svc. award Rep. Honduras, 1989, Thermal Recovery Disting. Achievement award SPE Thermal Ops. Symposium, 1991, KAPITSA medal Acad. Natural Scis. (Moscow), 1995; named to Internat. Hall of Fame, 1998. Mem. AIME (hon.), NAE, Soc. Petroleum Engrs. (hon., bd. dirs. 1976-79, sr. tech. editor 1987-90, Enhanced Oil Recovery Pioneer 1986, Uren award 1974, Disting. Mem. award 1983, Anthony F. Lucas Gold medal 1993), Acad. Medicine, Engring. and Sci. of Tex., Can. Inst. Mining, Asociacion de Ingenieros Petroleros de Mexico, Mex. Nat. Acad. Engring. (corr.), Acad. Engring. Armenia (fgn. mem.), Russian Acad. Nat. Scis. (fgn.), Pi Epsilon Tau (hon.). Avocation: travel. Address: 2834 Bellefontaine St Houston TX 77025-1610 E-mail: mikep@mprats.com

**PRATT, CARIN,** television executive; b. Marshfield, Mass., Aug. 22, 1956; m. John Echeverria; children: Nicholas, Edward. BA, Harvard U., 1978. Staff mem. Nieman Found. Harvard U., Boston, 1977-79; staff mem. Tex. R.R. Commn. Campaign, 1979-80; asst. to Tex. bur. chief Washington Post, Austin, 1981-83, rschr., 1981-83, editor, 1981-83; asst. to assoc. prodr. Face the Nation CBS News, N.Y.C., 1984-87, sr. prodr. Face the Nation, 1987-93, exec. prodr., Face the Nation with Bob Schieffer, 1993—. Office: CBS News 2020 M St NW Washington DC 20036-3369

**PRATT, CAROLYN KAY,** retired literature and language educator, retired mathematics educator; b. Madison, W.Va., Apr. 30, 1943; d. Leonne Clifford and Patty (Hicks) Miller; m. Michael Pratt, Dec. 23, 1967 (div. June 1989). BS in Elem. Edn., Concord Coll., Athens, W.Va., 1964; MA in Edn., Salem-Teykyo U., 1995. Cert. elem. educator. Tchr. Boone County Schs. Madison, W.Va., 1964-69; tchr. title I lang. arts/math Mercer County Schs., Princeton, W.Va., 1969-99; ret., 1999. Presenter W.Va. State Reading Conf., White Sulphur Springs, W.Va., 1991, 93, Nat. Coun. Tchrs. Math. Conf., Charleston, W.Va., 1994, W.Va. State Math. Conf., 1995; adj. prof., supr. student tchrs. Concord Univ., 1999—; academic math coach, 2005 Author, editor: (booklet) Math Can Be Fun, 1991; author: (poems) The New American Poetry Anthology, 1991 (cert. of merit 1991), Treasured Poems of America, 1993; contbr. poems to The Coming of Dawn, 1995, Best Poems of 1996, articles to profl. jours. Newsletter editor Read Aloud Mercer County, 1999—, sec., 2000—; active Project Teach; condr. parent involvement programs Grantee Greater Kanawha Valley Found., 1988, Kellog Co., 1993, 94, Cynthia Lorentz-Cook Found., 1995. Mem. W.Va. State Reading Coun. (pub. info. com. chair 1989-90, citations and awards com. chair 1991-95, registration com. chair 1996-98, internat. programs com. chair 1998-1999, mem. exec. bd. 1991-1999, Eddie C. Kennedy Tchr. of Yr. 1990), W.Va. Coun. Tchrs. Math., Mercer County Reading Coun. (corr. sec. 1987-90, Reading Tchr. of Yr. 1989, recording sec. 1995-96), Delta Kappa Gamma (com. chair Zeta chpt. 1994-96, 2d v.p. 2000-01, 1st v.p. 2002-03, pres. 2000—), Princeton Lions Club (2d v.p. 2003-04, 1st v.p. 2004-05 Avocations: writing, reading, cross stitch, walking, photography. Home: 124 Valley View St Princeton WV 24740-2314

**PRATT, DANA JOSEPH,** publishing consultant; b. Cambridge, Mass., Dec. 9, 1926; s. Carroll Cornelius and Marjory (Bates) P.; m. Therese Louis, July 14, 1957; children: Joseph Caldwell, Michael Louis, Benjamin Lyon B.Naval Sci., Tufts U., 1946. BA, 1948. Mgmt. trainee N.J. Bell Telephone Co., Newark, 1948-50; sales asst. Princeton U. Press, NJ, 1950-53; sales mgr. U. Ill. Press, Urbana, 1953-55; field cons. Franklin Book Programs, N.Y.C., 1955-59; staff assoc. Am. Book Pubs. Council, N.Y.C., 1959-62; exec. sec. Assn. Am. Univ. Presses, N.Y.C., 1962-66; asst. dir. Yale U. Press, New Haven, 1966-78; dir. pub. Library of Congress, Washington, 1978-93. Co-founder Internat. Group Pub. Librs. Contbr. articles to profl. jours. Served as ensign USNR, comdg. officer PC 566, 1946-47 Recipient Award for Superior Svc. Libr. of Congress, 1993. Mem. Washington Book Pubs. (pres. 1984-85), Soc. for Scholarly Pub. (bd. dirs. 1982-86), Washington Map Soc., Washington Rare Book Group. Home and office: The Towers 514E 4201 Cathedral Ave NW Washington DC 20016-4901 Office Phone: 202-237-1380. E-mail: danajpratt@msn.com.

**PRATT, DAVID WIXON,** chemistry professor; b. Providence, Sept. 14, 1937; s. Norman Twombly and Barbara Frances (Fisher) P.; children: Susan Rounds, Jonathan Wixon; m. Kathleen Cummings, Oct. 2, 1994. AB, Princeton U., 1959; PhD, U. Calif., Berkeley, 1967. Postdoctoral fellow U. Calif., Santa Barbara, 1967-68; asst. prof. U. Pitts., 1968-73, assoc. prof., 1973-78, prof., 1978—. Contbr. over 100 articles to profl. jours. Lt. USN, 1959-62. NIH postdoctoral fellow, 1967, Fulbright fellow, 1979, Guggenheim fellow, 1985, Japan Soc. Promotion of Sci. fellow, 1987, Am. Phys. Soc. fellow, 1990, AAAS fellow, 1993, Exeter Coll., Oxford U. fellow, 1996; recipient Merck Found. Faculty Devel. award, 1969 Mem. AAAS, AAUP, Am. Chem. Soc. (Pittsburgh award 2005), Am. Phys. Soc. (Earle K. Plyler prize 1999), Sigma Xi. Office: U Pitts Dept Chemistry Pittsburgh PA 15260 E-mail: pratt@pitt.edu.

**PRATT, DONALD DWAYNE,** protective services official; b. Clewiston, Fla., July 10, 1957; s. Donald Ellsworth and Elsie Christine Pratt; m. Nancy Rene' Curtis, Sept. 29, 1979; children: Kyndel, Nathan, Lucas. Cert. firefighter II, Fla. State Fire Coll., Ocala, 1995—; cert. Fla. state fire safety inspector, Fla. State Fire Coll., 2006. Ordained deacon Bapt. ch., 2000. SOD foreman A. Duda & Sons, Inc., LaBelle, Fla., 1979—81; fieldman Tropicana Products, Bradenton, Fla., 1981—85; warehouse mgr. Terra Internat. Inc., LaBelle, 1986—94; fire chief City of LaBelle, 1994—. Chmn. Hendry County Comty. Traffic Safety Team, LaBelle, 1998—; mem. adv. com. Red Cross Palm Beach County, West Palm Beach, Fla., 2000—; deacon Eastside Bapt. Ch., LaBelle, 2000—. Mem.: LaBelle Quarterback Club. Baptist. Avocations: fishing, hunting, water-skiing. Home: 950 Galonga Estates Dr Labelle FL 33935 Office: LaBelle Fire Dept 290 S Main St Labelle FL 33935

**PRATT, DONALD GEORGE,** physician; b. Higgins, Tex., Oct. 19, 1946; s. George Horace and Esta Vici (Barker) P. BS in Biomed. Sci., West Tex. State U., 1970; MD, U. Tex., Galveston, 1974. Diplomate Am. Bd. Family Practice, Am. Bd. Radiology (Radiation Oncology). Intern Scott & White Meml. Hosp., Temple, Tex., 1974-75, resident in gen. surgery and pathology, 1975-77, physician, 1979-83; resident in family practice McLennan County Med. Edn. and Rsch. Found., Waco, Tex., 1977-79; physician Family Practice Assocs., El Paso, Tex., 1983; owner, pvt. contractor Minor Emergency Ctrs., Amarillo, Tex., 1983-85; resident in radiation therapy U. Tex., Galveston, 1985-88; ptnr. Cons. in Radiation Oncology, P.A., Amarillo, 1988—2003, pres., 1994—2003, Cons. in Radiation Oncology, 1994—2003; dir. dept. radiation oncology Harrington Cancer Ctr., Amarillo, 1994—2003, pres. staff, bd. dirs., 1995-99; prin. investigator Radiation Oncology group, 1988-95; pres. of staff Harrington Cancer Ctr., 1995—99; ptnr. Cons. in Radiation Oncology, P.A., Amarillo, 1988—2003, pres., 1994—2003; cons. in radiation oncology, 1994—2003. Dir. Dept. Radiation Oncology Harrington Cancer Ctr., Amarillo, Tex., 1994—2003. Mem. AMA, Am. Soc. Therapeutic Radiology and Oncology, Tex. Med. Assn., Potter/Randall County Med. Soc., Tex. Radiol. Soc. Home: 261 S Timbercreek Dr Amarillo TX 79118-3751

**PRATT, GARY WAYNE,** music educator, musician; b. LA, Feb. 11, 1958; s. James Leon and Sallie Pratt (Stepmother). MFA, Calif. Inst. Arts, Valencia, 1982. Co-dir. jazz studies Calif. State U., Northridge, 1981—, chmn. Northridge wind area, dir. orchs., composer, arranger Nuveau. Dir. Pink Pop Internat. Jazz Exch., Ibbenburen, Germany, 1995—2003, tchr., bd. mem.; adjudicator LA Music Ctr., NARAS Found., Grammy Signature Schs.; guest condr. in field. Musician (bass): Louie Bellson (Grammy nomination), Louie Bellson Jam; performer (with): Lionel Hampton, Snooky Young, Conti Candoli, Pearl Bailey, Bobby Shew, Don Menza, Blue Mitchell, Pete Christlieb, Cat Anderson, Bob Florence, Kim Richmond, Billy Mintz, Mary Bond Davis, Sandra Booker, Cathy Segal-Garcia, Brian Swartz, Matt Otto, Clay Jenkins, Rob Lockart, Matt Harris. Office Phone: 818-677-2743. Business E-Mail: gary.pratt@csun.edu.

**PRATT, GEORGE CHENEY,** law educator, retired judge; b. Corning, N.Y., May 22, 1928; s. George Wollage and Muriel (Cheney) Pratt; m. Carol June Hoffman, Aug. 16, 1952; children: George W., Lisa M., Marcia Pratt Burke, William T. BA, Yale U., 1950, JD, 1953. Bar: N.Y. 1953, U.S. Supreme Ct. 1964, U.S. Ct. Appeals 1974. Law clk. to Charles W. Froessel (Judge of N.Y. Ct. Appeals), 1953—55; assoc. then ptnr. Sprague & Stern, Mineola, NY, 1956—60; ptnr. Andromidas, Pratt & Pitcher, Mineola, 1960—65, Pratt, Caemmerer & Cleary, Mineola, 1965—75; partner Farrell, Fritz, Pratt, Caemmerer & Cleary, 1975—76; judge U.S. Dist. Ct. (Ea. Dist. of N.Y.), 1976—82, US Cir Ct Appeals for N.Y. (Uniondale), NY, 1982—93; sr. circ. judge U.S. Cir. of Appeals for 2d Cir., NY, 1993—95; counsel Parnon & Pratt L.L.P., N.Y.C., 1995—2000, Farrell Fritz PC, 2001—. Prof. Touro Law Sch., Huntington, NY, 1993—2003. Fellow: Coll. Comml. Arbitrators; mem.: ABA, Reins. and Ins. Arbitration Soc., Nassau County Bar Assn., N.Y. State Bar Assn. United Ch. Of Christ. Office: Farrell Fritz PC 1320 Reckson Plz Uniondale NY 11556 Office Phone: 516-227-0604. Business E-Mail: gpratt@farrellfritz.com.

**PRATT, HARRY DAVIS,** retired entomologist; b. North Adams, Mass., Apr. 13, 1915; s. Harry Edward and Ethel Mae (Davis) P.; m. Caroline Georgine Kreiss, Apr. 13, 1944 (dec. May 1951); children: Harry Davis Jr., Katherine Maria Pratt Garrison, George Kreiss; m. Dora Belle Ford, Nov. 29, 1952 (dec. July 1998). BS, Mass. State Coll., 1936, MS, 1938; PhD, U. Minn., St. Paul, 1941. Registered prof. entomologist. Asst. entomologist USPHS Malaria Control War Areas, San Juan, PR, 1942-46; chief med. entomol. lab. USPHS Communicable Disease Ctr., Atlanta, 1946-53, chief insect rodent tng., 1953-63, chief Aedes aegypti control tng., 1964-68; chief insect rodent control tng. Environ. Control Agy., Atlanta, 1968-72; cons., tchr., writer Atlanta, 1972—. Spl. cons. Econ. Coop. Administrn., Saigon, Vietnam, 1950, WHO, Geneva, 1966, Kuala Lumpur, Malaysia, 1969. Fellow Entomol. Soc. Am. (life); mem. Am. Mosquito Control Assn. (pres. 1967), Entol. Soc. Washington, Ga. Entomol. Soc. Mem. Christian Ch. (Disciples Of Christ). Home: 104 So Almond Dr Simpsonville SC 29681 Office Phone: 864-228-4941.

**PRATT, JOHN JACKSON,** property manager, retired utilities worker; b. Benton Harbor, Mich., July 25, 1946; s. Harry Adelbert Pratt and Edith Jane Monteverde; m. Binh-An Thi Pham; children: Joseph, Harold. AA, N.Mex. Mil. Inst., 1966. Lic. real estate salesperson Calif. Assn. Realtors. Lineman, cable splicer installer, repairman Pacific Bell, Riverside, Calif., 1973-2000; property mgr. John J. Pratt Properties, Riverside, 1978—; mem. grower Sunkist Coop. Growers, 1984—. With USAF, 1967-71; res. ret., 1994. Mem. Apt. Assn. of Greater Inland Empire, Comms. Workers of Am. (local 9400), Am. Legion (post 289). Avocation: history studies especially world war ii and general world history. Home: PO Box 70122 Riverside CA 92513-0122 Office: JJP Properties 7929 Bolton Ave Riverside CA 92503-3125 Personal E-mail: johnj.pratt@yahoo.com.

**PRATT, JOHN PATRICK,** lawyer; b. Managua, Nicaragua, Nov. 19, 1967; s. Alfred Sidney Pratt and Thelma Reyes; 1 child, Patrick Alexander. BA in Philosophy, Fla. State U., 1994; JD, Tulane U., 1997. Bar: Fla. 1998, D.C. 1999, U.S. Dist. Ct. (so. dist.) Fla. 1998, U.S. Ct. Appeals (11th cir.) 1998, U.S. Supreme Ct. 2001, U.S. Ct. Appeals (9th cir.) 2002; cert. 1. Bar (immigration and nationality law). Law clk. Office of Dist. Counsel IRS, St. Paul, 1995; law clk. Office of Asst. Chief Counsel U.S. Customs Svc., New Orleans, 1996-97; assoc. Zyne, Saleeby & Saleh, P.A., Miami, 1997-98, Montiel Davis & Woodward Kimber, P.A., Miami, 1998-2000, Leaf & Assocs., P.A., Miami, 2000-01, Kurzban, Kurzban, Weinger & Tetzeli, P.A., 2001—. Cons. Beacon Coun., Miami. Mem. ABA, Am. Immigration Lawyers Assn., Hispanic Nat. Bar Assn., Beacon Coun. Roman Catholic. Avocations: reading, tennis. Office: Kurzban Kurzban Weinger & Tetzeli PA 2650 SW 27 Ave Ste 200 Miami FL 33133 Office Phone: 305-444-0060. Personal E-mail: jpatrickpratt@aol.com. Business E-Mail: jpratt@kkwtlaw.com.

**PRATT, JON,** not-for-profit executive; JD, Antioch Sch. Law; MPA, Harvard U. Atty., lobbyist Minn. Pub. Interest Rsch. Group; regional dir. Youth Project; dir. Philanthropy Project; founder, exec. dir. Minn. Coun. Nonprofits, Saint Paul, 1987—. Adv. com. mem. Nat. Ctr. for Charitable Statistics, Johns Hopkins U. State of Sector Project. Consult. editor Nonprofit Quarterly; contbr. articles to profl. jours. Mem.: Nat. Coun. Nonprofit Assns. (co-chair Pub. Policy Com.). Office: Minn Coun Nonprofits 2314 University Ave W #20 Saint Paul MN 55114 Office Phone: 651-642-1904. Office Fax: 651-642-1517.

**PRATT, LEIGHTON CALVIN,** retired state legislator; b. Hartford, Conn., Apr. 23, 1923; s. Calvin and Jessie (White) P.; m. Sally Burgess, Oct. 21, 1961; children: Randall Leighton, Bruce Charles. BS, U. Vt., 1951; MS, U. R.I., 1953. Plant pathologist Vt. Dept. Agr., Montpelier, 1952-62; tchr. sci. Cabot HS and Jr. HS, Vt., 1962-65; tchr. biology, asst. prin. Newport HS, Vt., 1965-67; tchr. biology North Country Union HS, Newport, 1967-79; Coos agrl. ext. agt. U. NH, Durham, 1969-88, prof. emeritus ext. edn., 1988—; mem. NH House of Reps., Concord, 1991—2005; ret., 2005; lobbyist agt. NH Legis. and Senate, 2004—. Named hon. state farmer Future Farmers Am., 1986. Mem. Rotary (dir. exch. to Brazil dist. 1986, pres. Lancaster, N.H.), Epsilon Sigma Phi. Republican. Congregationalist. Avocations: travel, gardening. Home: 63 Water St Lancaster NH 03584-3129

**PRATT, MARY LOUISE,** librarian, writer; b. Iowa City, Iowa, May 31, 1953; d. William Winston and Helen Virginia Pratt. BA in Eng., Pa. State U., 1977; MLS, Clarion U. Pa., 1987. Dir. writer comts. The Fine Arts Connection, State College, Pa., 1980—81; mgr. Unimarts, Inc., State College, 1981—84; reference libr. Evansville-Vanderburgh County Pub. Libr., Ind., 1987—88; ref. libr. Cabell County Pub. Libr., Huntington, W.Va., 1989—96, adult svcs. coord., 1996—. Cons. br. libr. Cabell County Pub. Libr., Huntington, 1989—; pub. computer instr. 1998—. Actor: (plays) A Christmas Carol, Deathtrap, The Boys Next Door, Ransom of Red Chief; editor: Rural Libraries; columnist: Who Said it?; author: (poem) Mr. Lonely in the City (1st pl. Ctrl. Pa. Festival of Arts Poetry Competition., 1977, 1st pl. Calamity Cafe Poetry Slam, 1999); contbr. articles to profl. jours. Active Cabell-Huntington Coalition for the Homeless, W.Va., 1998—. Mem.: W.Va. Libr. Assn., ALA, Guyandotte Poets, Acad. Am. Poets (assoc.). Democrat. Presbyterian. Avocations: acting, autograph collecting, hiking, travel. Home: 1368 13th St Huntington WV 25701 Office: Cabell County Pub Libr 455 9th St Plaza Huntington WV 25701 Office Phone: 304-528-5700. Personal E-mail: mlpratt007@aol.com. E-mail: mpratt@cabell.lib.wv.us.

**PRATT, MURRAY LESTER,** manufacturing executive; b. Mt. Holly, N.J., Mar. 11, 1956; B. John N. and Mildred E. P.; m. Sharon Louise Busby, Aug. 13, 1988; children: Kevin Harrison, Brian Gavel, Melissa Anne, Heather Marie. BS in Indsl. Engring., Northwestern U., 1976; MS in Computer Sci., Ill. Inst. Tech., 1983. Sys. analyst Gen. Foods USA, Chgo., 1981—84, sys. specialist, 1984—87, mgr. computer integrated mfg., 1987—91; mgr. KF logistics sys. Kraft Foods, Northfield, Ill., 1991—99, mgr. supply chain optimization, 1999—2001, program mgr. collaborative planning, forecasting and replenishment and vendor mng. inventory, 2001—06, assoc. dir. customer supply chain integration, assoc. dir. RFID, 2006—. Presbyterian. Avocations: current affairs, tennis, volleyball, hiking. Office: Kraft Foods Three Lakes Dr Northfield IL 60093-2753 Home: 2508 Violet Blvd Glenview IL 60026 Office Phone: 847-646-6779. Business E-Mail: mpratt@kraft.com.

**PRATT, ROBERT CRANFORD,** political scientist, educator; b. Montreal, Que., Can., Oct. 8, 1926; s. Robert Goodwin and Henrietta (Freeman) P.; m. Renate Hecht, July 15, 1956; children: Gerhard, Marcus, Anna. BA, McGill U., Montreal, 1947; postgrad., Inst. Science Politique, Paris, 1948; MPhil, Oxford U., Eng., 1952. Lectr. McGill U., 1952-54, 56-58, Makerere U., Uganda, 1954-56; rsch. officer Oxford Inst. Commonwealth Studies, 1958-60; prin. Univ. Coll., Dar-es-Salaam, Tanzania, 1961-65; chmn. internat. studies program U. Toronto, Ont., Can., 1966-71, prof. polit. sci., 1966—. Spl. asst. to pres., Tanzania, 1965, 69, rsch. fellow Internat. Devel. Rsch. Ctr., 1978; commonwealth vis. prof. U. London, 1979-80; dir. Rsch. Project on Western Mid. Powers and Global Poverty, 1985-89; vis. fellow Devel. Ctr. Orgn. for Econ. Cooperation and Devel., Paris, 1986-87. Author: (with Anthony Low) Buganda and British Overrule, 1960, The Critical Phase in Tanzania, Nyerere and the Emergence of a Socialist Strategy, 1976, Towards Socialism in Tanzania, 1979, (with Robert Matthews) Human Rights in Canadian Foreign Policy, 1988, Internationalism Under Strain: The North-South Policies of Canada, The Netherlands, Norway and Sweden, 1989; (with Roger Hutchinson) Christian Faith and Economic Justice: A Canadian Perspective, 1989); Middle Power Internationalism: The North-South Dimension 1990, Canadian International Development Assistance Policies: An Appraisal, 1994, 2d edit., 1996. Decorated officer Order of Can.; recipient Killam award Can. Coun., 1968, Ludwik and Estelle Jus Meml. Human Rights award, 1995; Rhodes scholar Oxford U., 1950. Fellow Royal Soc. Can.; mem. Can. Polit. Sci. Assn., Can. African Studies Assn. (past pres.), Can. Assn. for Study of Internat. Devel. (mem. exec. coun.), Ecumenical Forum Can. (past chmn.). Democrat. Home: 205 Cottingham St Toronto ON Canada M4V 1C4 Office: U Toronto Dept Polit Sci Toronto ON Canada M5S 1A1 E-mail: cranford.pratt@utoronto.ca.

**PRATT, ROBERT WINDSOR,** lawyer; b. Findlay, Ohio, Mar. 6, 1950; s. John Windsor and Isabelle (Vance) P.; m. Catherine Camak Baker, Sept. 3, 1977; children: Andrew Windsor, David Camak, James Robert. AB, Wittenberg U., Springfield, Ohio, 1972; JD, Yale U., 1975. Bar: Ill. 1975, U.S. Dist. Ct. (no. dist.) Ill. 1976, U.S. Dist. Ct. (we. dist.) Mich. 1995, U.S. Ct. Appeals (fed. cir.) 1984, U.S. Ct. Appeals (7th cir.) 1996, U.S. Ct. Appeals (D.C. cir.) 2004. Assoc. Keck, Mahin & Cate, Chgo., 1975—81, ptnr., 1981—97; pvt. practice Wilmette, Ill., 1998—99; sr. asst. atty. gen. Office Ill. Atty. Gen., 1999—2001, chief antitrust bur., 2001—. Bd. dirs. Chgo. region ARC, 1985-96, vice chmn., 1988-92, chmn., 1992-96, bd. dirs. Mid-Am. chpt., 1992-96. Mem. ABA, Yale Club (Chgo.). Office Phone: 312-814-3722. Business E-Mail: rpratt@atg.state.il.us.

**PRATT, WILLIAM,** lawyer; BA magna cum laude, phi beta kappa, Tulane U., 1974; JD with honors, Columbia U., 1977. Bar: Ill. 1975, NY 1990. Named one of Am. Leading Bus. Lawyers Litig./Gen. Cmml., Chambers USA, 2004—05. Fellow: Am. Coll. Trial Lawyers; mem.: Bd. Visitors Columbia Sch. Law. Office: Kirkland & Ellis LLP Citigroup Ctr 153 E 53rd St New York NY 10022-4611 Office Phone: 212-446-4862. Office Fax: 212-446-4900.

**PRATT, WILLIAM CROUCH, JR.,** literature and language professor, writer; b. Shawnee, Okla., Oct. 5, 1927; s. William Crouch and Irene (Johnston) P.; m. Anne Cullen Rich, Oct. 2, 1954; children: Catherine Cullen, William Stuart, Randall Johnston. BA, U. Okla., 1949; MA, Vanderbilt U., 1951, PhD, 1957. Rotary Internat. Fellow U. Glasgow, Scotland, 1951-52; instr. English Vanderbilt U., 1955-57, Miami U., Oxford, Ohio, 1957-59, asst. prof., 1959-64, assoc. prof., dir. freshman English 1964-68, prof., 1968—98;

prof. emeritus Mami U., 1998—. Fulbright-Hays lectr. Am. lit., prof. Am. lit. Univ. Coll., Dublin, Ireland, 1975-76; resident scholar Miami U. European Ctr., Luxembourg, fall 1976; lectr. Yeats Internat. Summer Sch., Sligo, Ireland, 1979, 81, 82, 83, James Joyce Summer Sch., Dublin, 1996; writer-in-residence Tyrone Guthrie Ctr., County Monaghan, Ireland, summer 1992, 96. Author: The Imagist Poem, 1963, rev. edit., 2001, The Fugitive Poets, 1965, rev. edit., 1991, The College Writer, 1969, College Days at Old Miami, 1984, The Influence of French Symbolism on Modern American Poetry, 1985, Miami Poets, 1988, Homage to Imagism, 1992, The Big Ballad Jamboree, 1996, Singing the Chaos: Madness and Wisdom in Modern Poetry, 1996, Miami University: A Personal History, 1998, Ezra Pound, Nature and Myth, 2002; contbr. essays, translations, poems, revs. to lit. jours., books. Served to lt. USNR, 1953-55. Mem.: Internat. Contemporary Lit. and Theatre Soc., Ezra Pound Internat. Conf. (sec. 1991—2005), Omicron Delta Kappa, Sigma Alpha Epsilon, Phi Beta Kappa. Republican. Home: 212 Oakhill Dr Oxford OH 45056-2710 Personal E-mail: wmcpratt@aol.com. *True happiness is to live in the understanding of what we love, the pursuit of what we believe in.*

**PRATTE, ROBERT JOHN,** lawyer; b. Victoria, B.C., Can., Feb. 14, 1948; s. Arthur Louis Jr. and Marie Bertha (Latremouille) P.; children: Merie Elise, Jessica Louise, Allison Adele, Chelsea Nicole. BA, Northwestern U., 1970; JD, Tulane U., 1976. Bar: Minn. 1976, Ariz. 1997. Ptnr. Best & Flanagan, Mpls., 1976-84, Briggs & Morgan, Mpls., 1985—; head mortgage banking group. Editor: Mortgage Lending in Minnesota—A Desktop Reference Guide, 1990. Ex-officio mem. Wilderness Inquiry, Minn.; pres. Twin Cities Northwestern U. Alumni Assn., 1978; active Wayzata Cmty. Ch., Mpls. Fellow Am. Coll. Mortgage Attys. (regent) Home: 19900 Manor Rd Excelsior MN 55331-9256 Office: Briggs & Morgan 80 S 8th St #2200 Minneapolis MN 55402-2157 Office Phone: 612-977-8537. Business E-Mail: rpratte@briggs.com. *Undertake with enthusiasm and pursue to completion the tasks that others are unwilling or unable to do. Never be satisfied with mediocrity. Surround yourself with those who are smarter than you; have the patience and judgement to let them succeed. Success can be measured by the hours you spend with your children--reading, fishing, and playing.*

**PRATTIS, SUSAN MARIE,** veterinarian, educator; BA, Amherst Coll.; VMD, U. Pa., 1985; PhD, NC State U., 1992; cert. in info. tech., Bay Path Coll., Longmeadow, Mass., 1994. Diplomate Am. Coll. Lab. Animal Medicine, lic. veterinarian Mass., Pa., NY. Instr. comparative medicine U. Chgo., 1992—94; clin. vet. Northwestern U., Chgo., 1994—95; adj., clin. asst. prof. Sch. Vet. Medicine Tufts U., North Medford, Mass., 1995—96; assoc. dir., lab. animal medicine Mass. Gen. Hosp., Boston, 1995—96; asst. prof. health Hampshire Coll., Amherst, Mass., 1997—2001; asst. prof. neurosci., honors prof. Yeshiva U., N.Y.C., NY, 2001—04; asst. prof. biology, honors prof. Adelphi U., Garden City, NY, 2004—. Cons. Spelman Coll.; owner Small Wonders Animal Healthcare, Easthampton, NY. Mem.: AAAS, Fed. Am. Soc. for Exptl. Biology, Am. Vet. Med. Assn. Home: 27 Hisgen Ave Easthampton MA 01027 Office: Adelphi U 1 South Ave Garden City NY 11530

**PRATT-JOHNSON, YVONNE KAREN,** education professor; b. Bklyn., Feb. 20, 1954; d. Cyril and Jennie Pratt; m. Raphael Nathaniel Johnson, Feb. 15, 1949; children: Jonathan Leslie Johnson, Michael Raphael Johnson. BA, Stony Brook U., NY, 1975; MS, Georgetown U., Washington, DC, 1977; MA, Columbia U., NYC, 1978, MEd, 1980, Ed.D, 1986. Prof. Borough of Manhattan CC of CUNY, NYC, 1978—2003; prof. edn. St. John's U., Queens, NY, 2003—. Tchr. trainer Hunter Coll. the CUNY, NYC, 1991—94. Recipient Excellence Award for Tchg. and Rsch., Nat. Inst. for Staff and Orgnl. Devel. Excellence; grantee The Rockefeller Fellow Award, Rockefeller Rsch. Found. Mem.: ASCD, Internat. Assn. Tchrs. English as a Fgn. Lang., Am. Edni. Rsch Assn. Avocation: travel. Home: 90 La Salle St 12F New York NY 10027 Office: St John's Univ 8000 Utopia Pky Jamaica NY 11439 Home Fax: 212-222-1823. Personal E-mail: yypj15@aol.com. E-mail: prattjoy@stjohns.edu.

**PRAUSNITZ, JOHN MICHAEL,** chemical engineer, educator; b. Berlin, Jan. 7, 1928; arrived in U.S. 1937, naturalized, 1944; s. Paul Georg and Susi Prausnitz; m. Susan Prausnitz, June 10, 1956; children: Stephanie, Mark Robert. B Chem. Engring., Cornell U., 1950; MS, U. Rochester, 1951; PhD, Princeton, 1955; Dr. Ing., U. L'Aquila, 1983, Tech. U. Berlin, 1989, U. Padova, 2004; DSc, Princeton U., 1995. Mem. faculty U. Calif., Berkeley, 1955—, prof. chem. engring., 1963—. Cons. to cryogenic, polymer, petroleum and petrochem. industries; Miller rsch. prof., 1966, 78; sr. investigator Lawrence Berkeley Nat. Lab., Berkeley; Wilhelm lectr. Princeton U., 1980; W.K. Lewis lectr. MIT, 1993; Edward Mason lectr. Brown U., 1999; Danckwerts lectr. Royal Acad. Engring., London, 2000; hon. prof. Tech. U. Shanghai, 2001; Dodge lectr. Yale U., 2004. Author: (with others) Computer Calculations for Multicomponent Vapor-Liquid Equilibria, 1967, (Computer Calculations for High-Pressure Vapor-Liquid Equilibria, 1968, Molecular Thermodynamics of Fluid-Phase Equilibria, 1969, 2d edit., 1986, 3d edit., 1999, Regular and Related Solutions, 1970, Properties of Gases and Liquids, 3d edit., 1977, 4th edit., 1987, 5th edit., 2000, Computer Calculations for Multicomponent Vapor-Liquid and Liquid-Liquid Equilibria, 1980; contbr. to profl. jours. Recipient Alexander von Humboldt Sr. Scientist award, 1976, Carl von Linde Gold Meml. medal, German Inst. for Cryogenics, 1987, Solvay prize, Solvay Found. for Chem. Scis., 1990, Corcoran award, Am. Soc. for Engring. Edn., 1991, 1999, D.L. Katz award, Gas Processors Assn., 1992, Waterman award, Tech. U. Delft, 1998, Rossini award, Internat. Union of Pure and Applied Chemistry, 2002, Nat. medal of Sci., 2005; Guggenheim fellow, 1962, 1973, fellow, Inst. Advanced Study, Berlin, 1985, Christensen fellow, St. Catherine's Coll. Oxford U., 1994, Erskine fellow, U. Canterbury, Christchurch, New Zealand, 1996. Mem.: NAS, NAE, AIChE (Colburn award 1962, Walker award 1967, Inst. Lectr. award 1994), Am. Acad. Arts and Scis., Am. Chem. Soc. (E.V. Murphee award 1979, Petroleum Chemistry Rsch. award 1995). Office: U Calif 308 Gilman HI Berkeley CA 94720-1462 Office Phone: 510-642-3592. Business E-Mail: prausnit@cchem.berkeley.edu.

**PRAVEL, BERNARR ROE,** lawyer; b. Feb. 10, 1924; BSChemE, Rice U., 1947; JD, George Washington U., 1951. Bar: D.C. 1951, Tex. 1951, U.S. Supreme Ct. 1951. Ptnr. Pravel, Hewitt firm, 1956—99; sr. counsel Akin, Gump, Houston, 1999—2002; inc., 2006. Patent editor George Washington U. Law Rev., 1950. Precinct chmn. Houston Rep. Com., 1972-74. Served to lt. (j.g.) USNR. Fellow Am. Bar Found., Tex. Bar Found.; mem. ABA (chair intellectual property sect. 1991-92), Tex. Bar Assn. (chmn. patent, trademark sect. 1968-69, bd. dirs. 1976-79, Outstanding Contbn. 1982), Nat. Coun. Patent Law (chmn. 1970-71), Am. Intellectual Property Law Assn. (pres. 1983-84), Houston Intellectual Property Law Assn. (pres. 1983-84, Outstanding Svc. award 1986), Order of Coif, Kiwanis, Tau Beta Pi. Home: 10806 Oak Hollow St Houston TX 77024-3017 Personal E-mail: bpravel@sbcglobal.net.

**PRAY, LLOYD CHARLES,** geologist, educator; b. Chgo., June 25, 1919; s. Allan Theron and Helen (Palmer) P.; m. Carrel Myers, Sept. 14, 1946; children: Lawrence Myers, John Allan, Kenneth Palmer, Douglas Carrel. DA magna cum laude, Carleton Coll., 1941; MS, Calif. Inst. Tech., 1943, PhD (NRC fellow 1946-49), 1952. Geologist Magnolia Petroleum Co., summer 1942, U.S. Geol. Survey, 1943-44; hydrographic officer USN, 1944-46; Geologist U.S. Geol. Survey, 1946-56 part time; instr. to assoc. prof. geology Calif. Inst. Tech., 1949-56; sr. research geologist Denver Research Ctr., Marathon Oil Co., 1956-62, research assoc., 1962-68; prof. geology U. Wis., Madison 1968-88; emeritus prof. geology, 1989—. Short course vis. prof. U. Tex., Austin, 1964, U. Miami, 1967, U. Miami, 1971, U. Alta., 1969, Colo. Sch. Mines, 1985; vis. scientist Imperial Coll. Sci. and Tech., London, 1977, U. Calif. Santa Cruz, 1987, Nat. Park Svc. Geology panel, 1993. Author articles sedimentary carbonates, the Permian Reef complex, stratigraphy and structural geology So. N.M. and W. Tex., porosity of carbonate facies, Calif. rare earth mineral deposits. Pres. Colo. Diabetes Assn., 1963-67, v.p., 1968; mem. adv. panel earth scis. NSF, 1973-76. Served as hydrographic officer USNR, 1944-46. Named Layman of Year Am. Diabetes Assn., 1968; recipient Disting. Teaching award U. Wis. Madison, 1988, Disting. Achievement citation Carleton Coll., 1991, Wallace Pratt Resources Stewardship award

---

Guadalupe Mountains Nat. Pk., 1998. Fellow Geol. Soc. Am. (rsch. grants com. 1965-67, com. on nominations 1973, com.Penrose medal 1979-81); mem. Am. Assn. Petroleum Geologists (rsch. com. 1958-61, lectr. continuing edn. program 1966-69, continuing edn. com. 1978-80, Levorsen award 1966, Matson trophy 1967, Disting. lectr. 1986-87, 87-88, Disting. Educator award 1998), Soc. Sedimentary Geologists (hon. life mem. Penman Basin sect. 1977, hon. mem. internat. soc. 1982, sec.-treas. 1961-63, v.p. 1966-67, pres. 1969-70, Twenhofel award 1999), Am. Geol. Inst. (edn. com. 1966-68, ho. bd. dels. 1970-72), West Tex. Geol. Soc. (Disting. Svc. award 2005, Pioneer award 2006), Phi Beta Kappa. Office: Univ Wis Dept Geology Madison WI 53706 Personal E-mail: praylude@webtv.net.

**PRAY, RALPH EMERSON,** metallurgical engineer; b. Troy, N.Y., May 12, 1926; s. George Emerson and Jansje Cornelius (Owejan) P.; m. Beverley Margaret Ramsey, May 10, 1959; children: Maxwell, Ross, Leslie, Marlene. Student, N.Mex. Inst. Mining & Tech., Socorro, 1953-56, U. N.Mex., Albuquerque, 1956; BS, U. Alaska, 1961; DSc, Colo. Sch. Mines, Golden, 1966. Electrician, miner, 1944—47; chief party, field courtographer planning survey dept. N.Mex State Hwy., 1949—50; engr.-in-charge Dept. Mines and Minerals, Ketchikan, Alaska, 1957-61; asst. mgr. mfg. rsch. Universal Atlas Cement div. U.S. Steel Corp., Gary, Ind., 1965-66; rsch. metallurgist Inland Steel Co., Hammond, Ind., 1966-67; owner, dir. Mineral Rsch. Lab., Monrovia, Calif., 1968—. Pres., Keystone Canyon Mining Co., Inc., Pasadena, Calif., 1972-79, U.S. Western Mines, 1973—, Silveroil Rsch. Inc., 1980-85, v.p. Mineral Drill Inc., 1981-90; pres., CEO Copper de Mex. S.A. de C.V.; prime contractor def. logistics agy. U.S. Dept. def., 1989-92; designer Vanavara Electrolytic Gold Refinery, Krasnoyarsk, Russia, 1995; owner Precision Plastics, 1973-82; bd. dirs. Bagdad-Chase Inc., 1972-75; ptnr. Mineral R&D Co., 1981-86; lectr. Purdue U., Hammond, Ind., 1966-67, Nat. Mining Seminar, Barstow (Calif.) Coll., 1969-70; guest lectr. Calif. State Poly. U., 1977-81, Western Placer Mining Conf., Reno, Nev., 1983, Dredging and Miner Conf., Reno, 1985, others; v.p. dir. Wilbur Foote Plastics, Pasadena, 1968-72; strategic minerals del. People to People, Rep. South Africa, 1983; expert witness, cons. Bur. Land Mgmt., U.S. Dept. of Interior, 2000-2002; hist. cons. gold mining History TV Channel, 1999; guest spkr. Greater L.A. County Svc. Clubs, 1980-81; workshop condr. King Abdullaziz U., Jeddah, Saudi Arabia, 2002; v.p., tech. dir. U.S. Mining and Minerals Corp., 2006. Author: Jingu, The Hidden Princess, 2002; guest editor Calif. Mining Jour., 1978—; contbr. articles to profl. jours.; contbr. author Bre-x Gold Today, Gone Tomorrow, 1997. Vol. Monrovia Police Dept.; city coord. Neighborhood Watch., 1990-99, Citizen Patrol, 1997-99. With U.S. Army, 1950-52. Recipient Disting. Svc. medal Monrovia Police Dept., 1998. Fellow Geol. Mining and Metall. Soc. India (life), Am. Inst. Chemists, South African Inst. Mining and Metallurgy; mem. Soc. Mining Engrs., Am. Chem. Soc., Am. Inst. Mining, Metall. and Petroleum Engrs., NSPE, Can. Inst. Mining and Metallurgy, Geol. Soc. South Africa, Soc. Mineral Analysts, Sigma Xi, Sigma Mu. Achievements include research on recovery of metals from refractory ores, benefication plant design, construction and operation, underground and surface mine development and operation, mine and process plant management; syndication of natural resource assets with finance sources; freelance fiction and nonfiction writer; patents for chemical processing and steel manufacture; measurement of residual mercury in ancient and modern mine wastes of Chile. Office: 805 S Shamrock Ave Monrovia CA 91016-3651 Office Phone: 626-357-6511.

**PRAY, RALPH MARBLE, III,** lawyer; b. San Diego, June 7, 1938; s. Ralph Marble, Jr. and Doris (Thomson) Pray; m. Karen L. Pray (div. May 1988); children: Matthew Thomson, Kristen Leigh; m. Sandra Anne Shaw, June 7, 1988. BS, U. Redlands, 1960; JD, U. Calif., San Francisco, 1967. Bar: Calif. 1967, U.S. Dist. Ct. (so. dist.) Calif. 1968, U.S. Supreme Ct. 1972, U.S. Dist. Ct. (ea. dist.) Calif. 1985, U.S. Dist. Ct. (ctrl. dist.) Calif. 1989, U.S. Dist. Ct. (no. dist.) Calif. 1992. Assoc. Gray, Cary, Ware & Friedenrich and predecessor, San Diego, 1967-73, ptnr., 1973—; mem. mgmt. com. Gary, Cary, Ames & Frye, San Diego, 1975-80. Arbiter Superior Ct., San Diego, 1984—. Lt. USN, 1960—64. Mem.: NRA, SAR, ABA, Am. Arbitration Soc. (arbiter), Calif. Bar Assn., Thurston Soc., San Diego Zool. Soc., Ducks Unltd., Club of Coronado, Rotary, Order of Coif. Republican. Episcopalian. Home: 535 C Ave Coronado CA 92118-1824 Office: DLA Piper Rudnick Gray Gary US LLP 4365 Exec Dr Ste 1100 San Diego CA 92121-2133 Office Phone: 858-638-6890.

**PRAYTOR, KENT DWAYNE,** career planning administrator; b. Pitts., Aug. 9, 1963; s. Hubert Henry and Juanita Pecola Praytor. BA in Psychology, California U. of Pa., 1991; EdM, Bowie State U., 1996. Cert. guidance and counseling Harrisburg, Pa., 1996. Acad. counselor Pitts. Pub. Sch., 1990—. Author: Closer Than Skin. With USN, 1981—85. Recipient medal, DAR. Home: 3519 Centralia St Pittsburgh PA 15204 Office: Columbus Middle School 1805 Buena Vista St Pittsburgh PA 15212 E-mail: kdpraytor@yahoo.com.

**PREBLE, LAURENCE GEORGE,** lawyer; b. Denver, Apr. 24, 1939; s. George Enos and Ruth (Jewett) Preble; m. Deborah Joan Horton, Aug. 24, 1963; children: Robin Lee, Randall Laurence. B in Petroleum Refining Engring., Colo. Sch. Mines, 1961; JD cum laude, Loyola U., Los Angeles, 1968. Bar: Calif. 1969, D.C. 1983, N.Y. 1987, U.S. Dist. Ct. (cen. dist.) Calif. 1969. Assoc. firm O'Melveny & Myers, Los Angeles, 1968-76, ptnr. L.A., 1976—2000; dir. devel. KUD Internat. LLC, 2001—. Adj. prof. law Southwestern U., 1970-75, Loyola U. of L.A. Sch. Law, 1984-92, 99-2000, Fordham U. Sch. Law, 1992-98, Calif. Continuing Edn. of the Bar; lectr., author Practicing Law Inst. Trustee Harvey Mudd Coll., 1991-94, Citizens Bidget Commn. N.Y.C., 1994-98, Ho. Ear Inst., 1998—, vice-chmn., 2001—. Recipient Disting. Achievement medal, Colo. Sch. Mines, 1998. Mem. Los Angeles County Bar Assn. (chmn. real property sect. 1979-80, Outstanding Leadership award 1999), Assn. Bar City of N.Y. (real property sect. exec. com. 1993-96), N.Y. State Bar Assn. (exec. com. real property sect. 1996-), Calif. Bar Assn. (mem. exec. com. real property sect.), ABA, Am. Coll. Real Estate Lawyers (bd. govs. 1986—), Anglo-Am. Real Property Inst., La Canada-Flintridge C. of C. (pres. 1974-75), Loyola Law Sch. Alumni Assn. (pres. 1978). Office: KUD Internat LLC STE 950 100 Wilshire Blvd Santa Monica CA 90401-1145

**PREBLE, ROBERT CURTIS, JR.,** insurance executive; b. Oak Park, Ill., Dec. 19, 1922; s. Robert Curtis and Dorothy (Seidel) P.; m. Lidia Blazik, May 29, 1963. BA, Amherst Coll., 1947; MBA, Harvard U., 1949, postgrad., 1971. CLU, Chartered Fin. Cons. Pvt. to 1st lt. U.S. Army, 1943—46; 33d divsn. capt. Nat. Guard, Ill., 1950—53; asst. to gen. supt., asst. buyer Carson Pirie Scott & Co., Chgo., 1949—52; with sales dept. Northwestern Mut. Life Ins. Co., Chgo., 1952—53, Nat. Life Ins. Co., Chgo., 1953—59; prin. Preble Assocs., Chgo., 1959—; pres., treas. Savs. Plans Inc., Chgo., 1980—. Cons. Iowa Savs. & Loan League, 1959-82; consul of Colombia, 1981-86, Bolivia, 1965-70; bd. dirs. chmn. fin. com. Guardsman Life Ins. Co., 1962-74; chmn. exec. com. World Book Life Ins. Co., 1974-83; gov.'s adv. bd. Ill. Dept. Ins., 1965-70; dir. Scandia Savs. & Loan Assn., 1968-83, Chgo. Coun. on Fgn. Rels., 1971-77, Chgo. Estate Planning Coun., 1977-80. Dept. regional chmn. Dem. Nat. Fin. Com., 1952; bd. dirs. Sr. Ctrs. Met. Chgo., 1974—77, McCormick Theol. Sem., 1977—83; deacon 4th Presbyn. Ch. of Chgo., 1967—70. Recipient Svc. award, Chgo. coun. Boy Scouts Am.f, 1962; record holder, Ill. Masters Swimming, 2003. Mem. Soc. Fin. Svc. Profls. (past pres. Chgo. chpt., Huebner scholar 1991, Grauer award 1998), Million Dollar Roundtable (life), Nat. Assn. of Insurance and Fin. Advisors, Assn. for Advanced Life Underwriting (founding pres. 1957), Harvard Bus. Sch. Assn. (alumni coun. 1977-82), Harvard Alumni Assn. (dir. 1980-82), Inst. Internat. Edn. (midwest adv. bd., 1979-99), Found. Study Cycles (internat. adv. bd.), Soc. Colonial Wars (coun.), Mil. Order World Wars, Univ. Club (Lifetime Achievement award 2004), Chgo. Club, Harvard Bus. Sch. Club (past pres.), Amherst Club (past chmn. ednl. trust, pres. 1992-95, Svc. award 1986). Home: 4208 Fleet Landing Blvd Atlantic Beach FL 32233

---

**PREBLE, SARAH HAMILTON,** art librarian, author, writer; b. N.Y.C., Sept. 19, 1939; d. John Leonard and Elizabeth (Collier) Hamilton; m. Duane Preble, Mar. 13, 1961; children: Jeffrey Hamilton, Kristen Malia Yang. BA in Psychology, U. Hawaii, 1962, MLS, 1980. Reference libr. U. Hawaii, Honolulu, 1981-89; libr. Manoa Pub. Libr., Honolulu, 1989-90; art libr. Hawaii State Libr., Honolulu, 1990—2000; res., 2000. Co-author: (book) Artforms, 2d edit., 1978, 6th edit., 1998. Bd. dirs. Life of the Land, Honolulu, 1972. Mem.: Maui Arts & Cultural Ctr., Librs. Assn. Hawaii, Honolulu Acad. Arts, Bishop Mus., Maui Hist. Soc., Hawaiian Mission Childrens Soc., Contemporary Mus. Home: 3347 Anoai Pl Honolulu HI 96822-1419

**PRECELLA, JANE WESTBROOK,** museum shop director; b. Brady, Tex., Jan. 6, 1955; d. Warren Ganey and Gertrude Nelson Westbrook; m. Michael J. Precella, Mar. 12, 1978; children: Jay Barrett, Alexander Joseph. BS in Edn, Curriculum and Devel. Tex. A&M U., 1973—77, grad sch., 1977—78. Grad. tchg. asst. Tex. A&M U., Coll. Sta., 1977—78; English tchr., dept. chair LaMonte Sch., LaMonte, Md., 1979—83; writing instr. Pima Cmty. Coll., Tucson, 1984—85; tchr. Knob Noster R VIII Sch., Md., 1990—93; mus. shop dir. Joslyn Art Mus., Omaha 1999—. Chmn. Boy Scouts, Colo. Springs, 1993—95. Mem.: Mus. Store Assn. Avocations: reading, soccer. Home: 904 Haverford Dr Papillion NE 68046 Office: Joslyn Art Mus 2200 Dodge St Omaha NE 68112 Office Phone: 402-342-3300. Business E-Mail: jprescella@joslyn.org.

**PRECKEL, PAUL VEITCH,** agricultural economics educator, researcher; b. Cumberland, Md., Mar. 30, 1954; s. Ralph Frederick and Margaret (McAuley) P. BS in Math. Scis., Ohio State U., 1977; MS in Ops. Rsch., Stanford U., 1979, PhD in Ops. Rsch., 1983. Asst. prof. agrl. econs. Purdue U., West Lafayette, Ind., 1983-89, assoc. prof., 1989—. Cons. Electric Power Rsch. Inst., Palo Alto, Calif., 1980-83, Control Analysis Corp., Palo Alto, 1980-81, Hudson Inst., Hudson-on-Croton, N.Y., 1982. Contbr. articles and abstracts to profl. jours. Grad. engring. fellow Stanford U., 1977. Mem. Am. Agrl. Econs. Assn. (assoc. editor Jour. 1991—), Math. Programming Soc. Avocations: scuba diving, bicycling. Office: Purdue U 639 Krannert West Lafayette IN 47907

**PRECOURT, CHARLES J.,** astronaut, retired military officer; b. Waltham, Mass., June 29, 1955; s. Charles and Helen Precourt; m. Lynne Denise Mungle; 3 children. BS in Aeronautical Engring., USAF Acad., Colo. Springs, 0977; MS in Engring. Mgmt., Golden Gate U., 1988; MA in Nat. Security Affairs, Strategic Studies, US Naval War Coll., 1990. Commd. 2d lt. USAF, 1977; advanced through grades to Col. USAF (ret.); student pilot USAF, Reese AFB, Tex., 1977—78, instr. pilot T-37, 1979—82; pilot F-15 USAF Bitburg Air Base, Germany, 1982—84; student test pilot sch. USAF, Edwards AFB, Calif., 1985; test pilot USAF, Edwards AFB, 1985—89; postgrad. studies U.S. Naval War Coll., Newport, RI, 1989—90; astronaut NASA Johnson Space Ctr., Houston, 1990—. Decorated Disting. Flying Cross USAF, 4 Space Flight medals NASA; recipient David B. Barnes award, USAF Test Pilot Sch., 1989. Mem.: Soc. Exptl. Test Pilots, Exptl. Aircraft Assn., Assn. Space Explorers (v.p.). Achievements include 4 space flights; over 7000 flight hours in 60 types of civil and military aircraft; approximately 40 days spent in space.

**PREDDY, RAYMOND RANDALL,** retired newspaper publisher, educator; b. Texarkana, Ark., Feb. 1, 1940; s. Raymond Watson and Dorothy Belle (Long) P.; m. Sarah Elizabeth Mitchell, Nov. 20, 1965; children: Lewis, Tiffany. BS, Northwestern U., 1961, MS in Journalism, 1962. Copy editor Louisville Courier-Jour., 1965-69; with Dayton (Ohio) Daily News, 1969-74, asst. city editor, 1971, met. editor, 1971-74; systems mgr. Dayton Newspapers, Inc., 1974-76; bus. mgr. Waco (Tex.) Tribune-Herald, 1976-77, asst. pub., 1977-78; pub. Waco Tribune-Herald, 1978-96. Part time journalism instr. Baylor U., Waco. Pres. Waco United Way, 1986, Waco Found., 1984-86, Waco Symphony Assn., 1985-86; moderator Grace Presbytery, 2005. Served with USN, 1962-65; capt. Res. (ret.) Named Tex. Newspaper Leader of 1994; recipient Pat Taggart award from Tex. Daily Newspaper Assn. Mem.: Rotary. Presbyterian. Personal E-mail: rrpreddy@aol.com.

**PREDMORE, MICHAEL PENNOCK,** Spanish language and literature educator; b. New Brunswick, N.J., Feb. 5, 1938; s. Richard Lionel and Catherine (Pennock) P.; m. Izvara Kleinhempel, Apr. 12, 1969; 1 child, Michael Kleinhempel Predmore. BA, Swarthmore Coll., 1959; MA, U. Wis., 1961, PhD, 1965. Asst. prof. U. Wash., Seattle, 1965-69, assoc. prof., 1969-74, prof., 1974-86, Stanford (Calif.) U., 1986—, chair Spanish and Portuguese, 1987-94. Elected corporator Internat. Inst., Madrid, 1985—; vis. prof. U. Calif., San Diego, 1986, Princeton U., 1998; nat. selection com. Am. Coun. Learned Socs., Washington, 1987—. Author: La Obra en prosa de J.R. Jimenez, 1966, La Poesia Hermetica de J.R. Jimenez, 1973, Una España Joven en la Poesia de A. Macnado, 1981; editor: Platero y yo de J.R. Jimenez, 1978, rev. edit., 1995; mem. editl. staff Discurso Literario, 1985—; editor: Diarieo de un poeta reciencasado de J.R. Jimenez (1916), 1998, (bilingual edit.) Diary of a Newlywed Poet of J.R. Jimenez, 2003; cons. numerous jours. Fellow Humanities Inst., U. Wis., 1968-69, John Simon Guggenheim Found., U. Wash., 1975-76, NEH, Stanford U., 1990-91, Stanford Humanities Ctr., 1990-91. Mem. MLA (exec. com. divsn. on 20th century Spanish lit. 1981-85, sec. 1983, chair 1984), Am. Assn. of Tchrs. of Spanish and Portuguese. Avocations: tennis, swimming, hiking. Home: 81 Peter Coutts Cir Stanford CA 94305-2512 Office: Stanford U Dept Spanish & Portuguese Bldg 260 Stanford CA 94305 E-mail: predmore@stanford.edu.

**PREECE, SCOTT,** food products executive; From mem. staff to pres., COO WinCo Foods, Woodburn, Oreg., 1969—2001, pres., 2001—, COO, 2001—. Office: WinCo Foods Woodburn Distbn Ctr PO Box 400 Woodburn OR 97071

**PREEDOM, BARRY MASON,** physicist, researcher; b. Stamford, Conn., Dec. 31, 1940; children: Bonnie Marie, Lawrence Richard. BS, Spring Hill Coll., 1962; MS, U. Tenn., 1964, PhD, 1967. Grad. fellow Oak Ridge (Tenn.) Nat. Lab., 1964-67; rsch. assoc. Mich. State U., East Lansing, 1967-70; asst. prof., then assoc. prof. U. S.C., Columbia, 1970-76, prof. physics, 1976—, Carolina rsch. prof., 1986-95, Carolina Disting. prof., 1995—, assoc. dean for rsch., 2002—. Vis. prof. Swiss Inst. Nuclear Rsch., Villigen, 1976; vis. staff Los Alamos (N.Mex.) Nat. Lab., 1972-91, tech. adv. panel, 1982-85; guest scientist Brookhaven Nat. Lab., Upton, N.Y., 1987—. Contbr. rsch. articles to sci. publs. Sr. teaching fellow Lilly Found., 1994-95; grantee Rsch. Corp. 1971, Office Naval Rsch., 1972-75, NSF, 1975—; recipient Mortar Bd. award for Excellence in Teaching, 1993. Mem. Am. Phys. Soc., Sigma Xi, Alpha Sigma Nu. Achievements include research and study of nuclear reaction mechanisms and nuclear structure, reaction probes including gamma rays, mesons, protons, deuterons and light ions. Office: Univ SC Dept Physics Columbia SC 29208-0001 Office Phone: 803-777-4121. E-mail: preedom@sc.edu.

**PREGERSON, HARRY,** federal judge; b. LA, Oct. 13, 1923; s. Abraham and Bessie (Rubin) P.; m. Bernardine Seyma Chapkis, June 28, 1947; children: Dean Douglas, Kathryn Ann. BA, UCLA, 1947; LL.B., U. Calif.-Berkeley, 1950. Bar: Calif. 1951. Pvt. practice, Los Angeles, 1951—53; Assoc. Morris D. Coppersmith, 1953; ptnr. Pregerson & Costley, Van Nuys, 1953—65; judge Los Angeles Mcpl. Ct., 1965—66, Los Angeles Superior Ct., 1966—67, U.S. Dist. Ct. Central Dist. Calif., 1967—79, U.S. Ct. Appeals for 9th Circuit, Woodland Hills, 1979—. Faculty mem., seminar for newly appointed distr. Judges Fed. Jud. Center, Washington, 1970—72; mem. faculty Am. Soc. Pub. Adminstrn., Inst. for Ct. Mgmt., Denver, 1973—; panelist L.A. chpt. FBA, 1989, Calif. Continuing Edn. of Bar, 9th Ann. Fed. Practice Inst., San Francisco, 1986, Internat. Acad. Trial Lawyers, L.A., 1983; lectr. seminars for newly-appointed Fed. judges, 1970—71. Author: over 450 published legal opinions. Mem. Community Rels. Com., Jewish Fedn. Coun., 1984—, Temple Judea, Encino, 1955—; bd. trustees Devil Pups Inc., 1988—; adv. bd. Internat. Orphans Inc., 1966—; Jewish Big Brothers Assn., 1970, Salvation Army, Los Angeles Met. area, 1988—; worked with U.S. Govt. Gen. Svcs. to establish the Bell Shelter for the homeless Child Day Care Ctr., the Food Partnership and Westwood Transitional Village; bd. dirs. Marine Corps Res. Toys for Tots Program, 1965—, Greater Los Angeles Partnership for the Homeless, 1988—. 1st lt. USMCR, 1944—46. Decorated Purple Heart, Medal of Valor Apache Tribe; recipient Promotion of Justice Civic award, City of San Fernando, 1965, award, San Fernando Valley Jewish Fedn. Coun., 1966, Profl. Achievement award, Los Angeles Athletic Club, 1980, Profl. Achievement award UCLA Alumni Assn., 1985, Louis D. Brandeis award, Am. Friends of Hebrew U., 1987, award of merit, Inner City Law Ctr., 1987, Appreciation award, Navajo Nation and USMC for Toys for Tots program, 1987, Humanitarian award, Los Angeles Fed. Exec. Bd., 1987—88, Grateful Acknowledgement award, Bet Tzedek Legal Svcs., 1988, Commendation award, Bd. Suprs. Los Angeles County, 1988, Others award, Salvation Army, 1988. Mem.: ABA, Marines Corps Res. Officers Assn., State Bar Calif., San Fernando Valley Bar Assn., L.A. County Bar Assn., Am. Legion (Van Nuys Post), DAV (Birmingham chpt.). Office: US Ct Appeals 9th Cir 21800 Oxnard St Ste 1140 Woodland Hills CA 91367-7919*

**PREISER, WOLFGANG FRIEDRICH ERNST,** architect, educator, consultant, researcher; b. Freiburg, Germany, June 26, 1941; came to U.S., 1967; s. Gerhard Friedrich and Ursula Helene (von Huelsen) P.; m. Cecilia M. Fenoglio, Feb. 16, 1985; children: Johanna, Timothy, Andreas, Nicholas. Student, Vienna Tech. U., 1963; diploma in Engring., Architecture, U. Karlsruhe, 1967; M.Arch., Va. Poly. Inst. and State U., 1969; PhD in Man-Environ. Relations, Pa. State U., 1973. Architect, Germany, Austria, Eng., 1960-66; prof. architecture Va. Poly. Inst. and State U., Pa. State U., U. Ill., U. N.Mex., U. Cin., 1970—; research architect constrn. engring. research lab. U.S. Army, 1973-76; co-dir. Inst. Environ. Edn., U. N.Mex., 1976-86; dir. Ctr. for R & D, U. N.Mex., Albuquerque, 1986-90; dir. research Archit. Research Cons. Inc., 1976—; pres. Planning Rsch. Inst., Albuquerque, 1980—90; prin. Preiser Cons., Cin., 1990—. Lectr. ednl., profl. and civic groups worldwide; v.p. faculty club U. N.Mex., 1976-78; pres. Internat. Club, Va. Poly. Inst. and State U., 1968-69; rschr. in field. Contbr. chapters to books, articles to profl. jours.; co-author: Post-Occupancy Evaluation, 1988; editor: Facility Programming, 1982, Programming the Built Environment, 1985, Building Evaluation, 1989, Pueblo Style and Regional Architecture, 1989, Design Intervention: Toward A More Humane Architecture, 1991, Professional Practice in Facility Programming, 1993, Design Review: Challenging Urban Aesthetic Control, 1994, New Direction in Urban Public Housing, 1998, Directions in Person-Environment Research and Practice, 1999; Universal Design Handbook, 2001, Improving Building Performance, 2003, Assessing Building Performance, 2005. Trustee Cin. Chamber Orch., 1992-98, v.p., 1995-98. Recipient Outstanding Svc. award Coll. Design, Arch., Art, and Planning U. Cinn., 2005, Career award Environ. Design Rsch. Assn., 1999, Ann. Rieveschl award, U. Cin., 1999, MCB Univ. Press (U.K.) award for excellence, 1998, Faculty Devel. award for rsch. U. Cin., 1992, Faculty Achievement award, 1995, Pogue/Wheeler Traveling award, 1993, Dean's Spl. award, 1994, Finland's Inst. Tech. award, 1966, awards Am. Iron and Steel Inst., 1968, Progressive Arch. Ann., 1985, 89, undergrad. teaching award U. Ill., 1976, hon. mention 1st Kyoto award Internat. Coun. of Soc. for Indsl. Design, 1979; Fulbright fellow, 1967, 87, Ford Found. fellow, 1968, Nat. Endowment for Arts fellow, 1979, 82; grad. fellow U. Cin., 1996 Mem. Soc. Human Ecology (pres. 1980-86), Environ. Design Research Assn. (vice chmn. 1974-76, sec. 1973-74), Nat. Acad. Scis. (chmn. com. on programming and post-occupancy evaluation, bldg. research bd. 1985-86), U. Cin. Grad. Fellows (elected), Phi Kappa Phi. Office: Univ Cin Coll Daap Sch Arch Cincinnati OH 45221-0016 Office Phone: 513-556-6743. Business E-Mail: wolfgang.preiser@uc.edu.

**PREISS, JACK,** biochemistry professor; b. Bklyn, June 2, 1932; s. Erool and Gilda (Friedman) P.; m. Karen Sue; children: Jennifer Ellen, Jeremy Oscar, Jessica Michelle. BS in Chemistry, CCNY, 1953; PhD in Biochemistry, Duke U., 1957. Scientist NIH, Bethesda, Md., 1960-62; asst. prof. dept. biochemistry, biophysics U. Calif., Davis, 1962-65, assoc. prof., 1965-68, prof., 1968-85, chair dept. biochemistry, 1971-74, 77-81; prof. dept. biochemistry Mich. State U., East Lansing, 1985-2000, chair dept., 1985-89, Univ. Disting. Prof., 2001—. 16th loomis lectr. Iowa State U., 1997—98. Mem. editl. bd.: Jour. Bacteriology, 1969—74, Arch. Biochem. Biophysics, 1969—, Plant Physiology, 1969—74, 1977—80, assoc. editor., 1980—92; editor, 1993—95, Jour. Biol. Chemistry 1971—76, 1978—83, 1994—99, 2000—05, Plant Physiol. Biochemistry, 1997—2003. Recipient Camille and Henry Dreyfus Disting. scholar award Calif. State U., 1983, Alexander von Humboldt Stiftung Sr. US Scientist award, 1984, Award of Merit, Japanese Soc. Starch Sci., 1992, Disting. Faculty Mem. award Mich. Assn. Governing Bds. of State Univ. 1997, Mich. Sci. of Yr. award Impressions 5 Mus., 1997, Pan-Am. Biochemistry and Molecular Biology award lectr. Spanish Biochem. Soc., 2000; Alsberg-Schoch Meml. lectr. Am. Assn. Cereal Chemists, 1990, Nat. Sci. Coun. lectr. Republic of China, 1988; Guggenheim Meml. fellow, 1969-70, Japan Soc. for Promotion of Sci. fellow, 1992-93; grantee NIH, 1963-97, NSF, 1978-89, Dept. of Energy, 1993-2005, USDA, 1988—. Mem. AAAS, Am. Chem. Soc. (Charles Pfizer award in enzyme chemistry 1971), Biochem. Soc., Am. Soc. Biol. Chemists and Molecular Biology, Am. Soc. Microbiologists, Am. Soc. Plant Physiologists, Soc. for Complex Carbohydrates, Protein Soc., Pan Am. Soc. Biochemistry and Molecular Biology (sec. gen., 1994-96, vice chmn. 1997-99, chmn. 2000-02, past chmn. 2003-05). Office: Mich State Univ Dept Of Biochemistry & Molecular Biology East Lansing MI 48824 Office Phone: 517-353-3137. Business E-Mail: preiss@msu.edu.

**PREISTER, DONALD GEORGE,** state legislator, greeting card manufacturer; b. Columbus, Nebr., Dec. 23, 1946; s. Maurice J. Preister and Leona T. (Dusel) Chereck. BS in Edn., U. Nebr., 1977. Unit idr. Boys' Clubs of Omaha, 1973-83; dep. city clk. City of Omaha, 1984-85; tchr. The Great Peace March, U.S., 1986; founder, owner Joy Creations, Co., Omaha, 1988—; mem. Nebr. Legislature from 5th dist., Lincoln, 1992—. Instr. Metro C.C., Omaha, 1979-80. Author: (sect.) Drug Abuse Prevention, 1977. Troop leader Boy Scouts Am., Omaha, 1973-83. Served with U.S. Army, 1966-68, Vietnam. Decorated Bronze Star. Mem. Vets. for Peace, Nebr. Sustainable Agr. Soc., Optimist. Democrat. Roman Catholic. Avocations: gardening, running, horses. Home: 4522 Borman St Omaha NE 68157-2318 Office: State Capitol Dist 5 Lincoln NE 68509

**PREJEAN, SISTER HELEN THERESA,** human rights advocate, writer, lecturer; b. Baton Rouge, Apr. 21, 1939; d. Louis Sebastian and Gusta Mae (Bourg) P. BA in English, St. Mary's Dominican Coll., 1962; MA in Religious Edn., St. Paul's U., 1973; more than 30, hon. degrees. Joined Congregation of St. Joseph of Medaille, Roman Cath. Ch., 1957. Tchr. St. Frances Cabrini Sch., New Orleans, 1962-66; dir. religious edn. St. Frances Cabrini Parish, New Orleans, 1968-75; dir. novices Sisters St. Joseph Medaille, New Orleans, 1975-81; tchr. Hope House Adult Learning Ctr., New Orleans, 1981-84; chmn. bd. Nat. Coalition to Abolish the Death Penalty, 1993—. Spiritual advisor to death row inmates and murder victims' families, 1982—. Author: Dead Man Walking: An Eyewitness Account of the Death Penalty in the US, 1993 (nominated for Pulitzer Prize), The Death of Innocents, 2004. Recipient Sanctity of Life award So. Christian Leadership Conf., 1990, Abolitionist award Nat. Coalition to Abolish the Death Penalty, 1992, Champion of Liberty award Nat. Assn. Criminal Def. Lawyers, 1994, Ben Smith award, ACLU New Orleans, 1998, Bishop Dingman Peace award Catholic Peace Ministry, Des Moines, Iowa, 2000, Harry F. Fagan Roundtable award, 2001, Ut Diligatis Invicem award Gannon Univ., Erie, Pa., 2002, Cardinal Suenens award John Carroll Univ., 2004, Death Penalty Focus award, 2005; named among America's 20 Most Confident Women, McCalls mag., 1993, dozens of other awards; life and work profiled by N.Y. Times Mag., 1993. Business E-Mail: sisterhelen@deathpenaltydiscourse.org.*

**PREM, F. HERBERT, JR.,** retired lawyer; b. NYC, Jan. 14, 1932; s. F. Herbert Prem Sr. and Sybil Gertrude (Nichols) Prem; m. Patricia Ryan, Nov. 18, 1978; children from previous marriage: Julia Nichols, F. Herbert III(dec.). AB, Yale U., 1953; JD, Harvard U., 1959. Bar: NY 1960. Assoc. Whitman and Ransom, NYC, 1959-66, ptnr., 1967-93, co-chmn. exec. com., 1988-92, chmn., 1993, Whitman Breed Abbott & Morgan LLP, NYC, 1993-99, of

counsel, 2000; ret., 2000. Bd. dirs. Fuji Photo Film U.S.A., Inc., Fuji Film Med. Sys. U.S.A., Inc., Scoville Meml. Libr., Salisbury Visiting Nurse Assn.; pres. Crescendo, Inc., 2005—06. Vol. atty. The Legal Aid Soc., NYC, 2000—03; vol. chaplain Sharon Hosp., Conn., 2003—05; bd. dirs. Bagaduce Music Lending Libr., Inc., 1988—95, pres., 1989—93; bd. dirs. The Health Care Chaplaincy, Inc., 1998—2004, Inter Faith Neighbors, Inc., 2001—03, Legal Aid Soc., NYC, 1969—73, Cmty. Action for Legal Svc., Inc., 1967—70, treas. Lt. j.g. USNR, 1953—56. Mem. ABA, Assn. Bar City NY (sec. 1967-69), NY State Bar Assn. Am. Law Inst. (life), Union Club, Yale Club. Episcopalian.

**PREMA, NITYA,** marriage and family therapist, artist; b. LA, June 15, 1941; d. James Nicholson and Phyllis Wickersham; children: Fritjof Swenson, Derek Swenson, Krista Mills. AS, Santa Rosa Jr. Coll., Calif., 1977; BA, Sonoma State U., Rohnert Park, Calif., 1980; MA, Profl. Sch. of Psychology, San Francisco, 1983. Lic. marrage and family therapist Bd. of Behavioral Sci., Calif., 1982; psychiat. technician, Bd. of Vocat. Nursing, 1979. Owner, designer and mfr. Nitya Visionary Designs and Gallery, Forestville and Sebastopol, Calif., 1982—92; therapist/social worker O'Connor Hosp. Vista's Program, San Jose, Calif., 1997—99; psychotherapist San Jose Jails/Mental Health, Calif., 1998—2000; pvt. practice family therapist San Andreas and Visalia, Calif., 2000—. Spkr. Internat. Transpersonal Conf., Ireland, 1994; spkr.'s bur. Calif. Assn. of Marriage and Family Therapists, Santa Rosa, 1996. Author: The Spiral Labyrinth Journey: A Pilgrimage into Sacred Space. Activist Rainbow Labyrinth Journey. Mem.: Ebbets Pass Forest Watch, Brewster Kaleidoscope Soc. Achievements include artist and designer of Magic wands and Kaleidoscopes. Office: North Main St San Andreas CA 95249 Office Phone: 209-795-0755. Personal E-mail: artglasscompany@yahoo.com.

**PREMACK, ANN J.,** writer; b. Shanghai, Jan. 5, 1929; interned in Japanese detention ctr., 1943-45; came to the U.S., 1945; d. John Joseph James and Mae Victoria Parker; m. David Premack, Oct. 26, 1951; children: Ben, Lisa, Tim. BS with distinction, U. Minn., 1951. Author: Why Chimps Can Read, 1975; co-author (with D. Premack): The Mind of An Ape, 1983; co-editor: Causal Cognition: A Multidisciplinary Debate, 1995; co-author (with D. Premack): Original Intelligence: Unlocking the Mystery of Who We Are, 2003, French translation, 2003, Japanese translation, 2005; contbr. chapters to books, articles to profl. jours. Avocation: owning and running an avocado grove. Home: 6163 Heatherton Dr Somis CA 93066-9716 Personal E-mail: dpremack@aol.com, dpremack@msn.com.

**PREMACK, DAVID,** psychologist; b. Aberdeen, S.D., Oct. 26, 1925; s. Leonard B. and Sonja (Liese) P.; m. Ann M. James, Oct. 26, 1951; children: Ben, Lisa, Timothy. BA magna cum laude, U. Minn., 1949 PhD, 1955. Rsch. assoc. Yerkes Labs. Primate Biology, Orange Park. Fla., 1955; rsch. assoc., asst. prof. psychology U. Mo., Columbia, 1956-58, assoc. prof., 1959-62, prof., 1963-64, U. Calif., Santa Barbara, 1965-75; vis. prof. Harvard U., 1970-71; prof. U. Pa., 1975—. Artist-in-residence Yaddo, Saratoga Springs, N.Y., 1955; fellow Van Leer Jerusalem Inst., 1980, Inst. for Advanced Study, Berlin, 1985-86; vis. scientist Japan Soc. for Promotion Sci., 1980; univ. rsch. lectr. U. Calif., Santa Barbara, 1973; mem. sci. adv. bd. Fyssen Found., Paris, 1989—; assoc. neurosci. rsch. program, La. Jolla, Calif., 1991—. Author: Intelligence in Ape and Man, 1976, (with Ann James Premack) The Mind of an Ape, 1983, Gavagai! Or the Future History of the Animal Language Controversy, 1986 (with Dan Sperber and Ann James Premack) Causal Cognition: A Multidisciplinary Debate, 1995, (with Ann James Premack) Original Intelligence: Unlocking the Mystery of Who We Are, 2003, French translation, 2003, Japanese translation, 2005; mem. editl. bd. Jour. Exptl. Psychology: Animal Processes, 1976—, Cognition, 1977—, Brain and Behavior Sci., 1978—, Jour. Cognitive Neurosci. Served with U.S. Army, 1943-46. Ford Found. tchg. intern, 1954; USPHS postdoctoral fellow, 1956-59; Social Sci. Rsch. Coun. fellow, summer 1963; Ctr. for Advanced Study in Behavioral Scis. fellow, 1972-73; Guggenheim fellow, 1979-80; grantee NSF, 1961—, USPHS, 1960-80; recipient Kenneth Craik Resch. award St. John's Coll.-Cambridge U., 1987, Internat. Sci. prize Fyssen Found., Paris, 1987. Fellow AAAS; mem. Am. Psychol. Soc. (William James fellow 2005), Soc. Exptl. Psychologists. Personal E-mail: dpremack@aol.com.

**PREMCHAND, ARIGAPUDI,** retired financial consultant; b. Kadavakollu, India, Aug. 22, 1933; arrived in U.S., 1970; s. Venkataramiah and Manikyamma Arigapudi; m. Rama Premchand, May 8, 1953; 2 children. Diploma in econ. adminstrn., Delhi Sch. Econs., 1954; MA, Andhra U., 1953; DLitt (hon.), Krishna Devaraya U., 2002. Lectr. Andhra (India) U., 1954—57; rsch. officer Union Min. Fin., Delhi, 1957—68; cons. Ford Found., 1968—70; economist to asst. dir. Internat. Monetary Fund, Washington, 1970—98; cons. Asian Devel. Bank, 1998—2003, World Bank, 1998—, Kennedy Sch., 1998—2004; ret., 2004. Author, editor: 12 books; contbr. chapters to books. Fellow, Indian Inst. Econs., 1960, Oxford U., 1980. Hindu. Avocations: reading, writing. Home: 5 Sonrisa Irvine CA 92620-7915 Home Fax: 714-669-9374. E-mail: apremchand@cox.net.

**PREMO, PAUL MARK,** oil industry executive; b. Syracuse, NY, Nov. 20, 1942; s. Matthias George and Kathryn (Whitbread) P.; m. Mary Catherine Hennessy, June 19, 1965; children: Deborah, Mark. BSChemE, Manhattan Coll., Riverdale, N.Y., 1964; MS in Chem. Engring., MIT, 1965. Chem. engr. Chevron Rsch., Richmond, Calif., 1965-69; fin. analyst Chevron Corp., San Francisco, 1969-72, coord., mgr. supply and distbn., 1972-79; mgr. petroleum regulations Chevron USA, San Francisco, 1979-81, sec.-treas., 1981-85, mgr. property tax adminstrn., 1985-86, mgr. natural gas regulatory affairs, 1986-92; exec. cons. Resource Mgmt. Internat., San Rafael, Calif., 1992-95; v.p, Foster Assocs. Inc., San Francisco, 1995-97; prin. Energy Econs. Consulting, Mill Valley, Calif., 1998—. Dir. Ky. Agrl. Energy Corp., Franklin. Trustee Calif. Tax Found., 1985-. Mem. State C. of C. (tax com.), Western Oil and Gas Assn., Am. Petroleum Inst. (property tax com.), Natural Gas Supply Assn., Inst. Property Taxation, Calif. Taxpayers Assn. (bd. dirs. 1985-), MIT Alumni Assn., Commonwealth (San Francisco), Sigma Xi, Tau Beta Pi. Avocations: investments, carpentry, travel. Home: 310 Hazel Ave Mill Valley CA 94941-5054 Personal E-mail: paulpremo@msn.com.

**PRENDERGAST, FRANKLYN G.,** health facility administrator, medical educator; b. Linstead, Jamaica, 1945; MD, U. West Indies, 1968; PhD in biochemistry, U. Minn., 1977; BA in physiology, Oxford U., 1971, MA in physiology, 1979; DSc (hon.), Purdue U., 1994. With Mayo Clinic, Rochester, Minn., 1975—; instr. Mayo Med. Sch., Rochester, Minn., 1975—77, asst. prof. in pharmacology, 1977—81, assoc. prof. pharmacology, 1981—86, prof. in pharmacology, biochemistry, and molecular biology, 1986—, Edmond and Marion Guggenheim Prof. of Biochemistry and Molecular Biology, 1987—; named Mayo Disting. Investigator, 1988; assoc. cons. pharmacology Mayo Found., Rochester, Minn., 1977—81, cons. pharmacology, 1981—85, named cons. and chair dept. biochemistry and molecular biology, 1985, bd. trustees; named dir. rsch. Mayo Clinic, Rochester, Minn., 1992; dir. Mayo Clinic Comprehensive Cancer Ctr, Rochester, Minn., 1995—. Bd. dirs. Eli Lilly & Co., 1995—; mem. Bd. on Radiation Effects Rsch. NAS. Contbr. articles to profl. jours. Named a Disting. Alumnus, U. West Indies, 1991; recipient E.E. Just Award, Am. Soc. Exptl. Biology, 1997, Musgrave Gold Medal, Inst. Jamaica, 2003; Rhodes Scholar, 1969, Minnesota Heart Postdoctoral Fellow, 1975—77, Searle Foundation Fellow, 1980—83. Mem.: Sigma Xi, Am. Soc. Biochemistry and Molecular Biology, Biophysical Soc., AAAS, Am. Soc. Photobiology, Am. Chem. Soc. Office: Mayo Cancer Ctr 200 1st St SW Rochester MN 55905-0001

**PRENDERGAST, GEORGE C.,** cancer biologist, researcher; b. Phila., Aug. 25, 1961; s. George A. and Mary C. P.; m. Kristine Kushmeider, Oct. 25, 1986. BA magna cum laude, U. Pa., 1983; MS, Yale U., 1984; PhD, Princeton U., 1989. Postdoctoral fellow NYU Med. Ctr. Am. Cancer Soc., 1989-91; sr. rsch. biochemist Am. Cancer Soc. Merck and Co., Inc., West Point, Pa., 1991-93; asst. prof. Wistar Inst., U. Pa., Phila., 1993-97, assoc. prof., 1997—2001; sr. dir. cancer rsch. DuPont Pharms. Co., Glenolden, Pa.,

1999—2001; prof. Lankenau Inst. Med. Rsch., 2002—, pres., CEO, 2004—; prof. Thomas Jefferson U., Phila., 2002—. Dep. editor jour. Cancer Rsch.; contbr. articles to profl. jours.; patentee in field. Recipient Jr. Faculty award Am. Cancer Soc., 1995—97, Biomed. Scholar award Pew Charitable Trusts, 1995-99, Rsch. award NIH, 1995—, CaPCURE Prostate Cancer award, 1996, 97; Pfizer traveling fellow, 1997. Mem. Am. Assn. Cancer Rsch. Office: Lankenau Inst for Med Rsch 100 Lancaster Ave Wynnewood PA 19096 Office Phone: 610-645-8475. Business E-Mail: prendergastg@limr.org.

**PRENDERGAST, KENNETH LEE MICHAEL, JR.,** career officer; b. Macdill Air Force Base, Fla., Sept. 16, 1956; s. Kenneth Lee and Pauline Ann (Hall) P.; m. Naomi Sue Kincade, Aug. 6, 1976; children: Melissa Ann, Robert Anthony. BA, Jacksonville State U., 1986; BS, U. N.Y., 1986; MA, U. Fla., 1990; MPA, Troy State U., 1997; M of Strategic Studies, U.S. Army War Coll., 2003. Enlisted U.S. Army, 1978, commd. 2d lt. mil. police corps, 1982; advanced through ranks to col., 2003; exec. officer Company D 1st Bn., Ft. McClellan, Ala., 1983; aide de camp to dep. comdg. gen., M.P. sch. commandant Ft. McClellan, Ala., 1984-85; ops. tng. officer Provost Marshal's Office U.S. Army WESTCOM, Ft. Shafter, Hawaii, 1987; co. commdr. mil. police U.S. Army Support Commd., Ft. Shafter, 1988-89; ops. officer Provost Marshal's Office U.S. Army Law Enforcement Command, Ft. Shafter, Hawaii, 1989; fgn. area officer U.S. Embassy, Kinshasa, Zaire, 1991—92, Yaounde, Cameroon, 1992-93; internat. officer instr. U.S. Army Command and Gen. Staff Coll., Ft. Leavenworth, Kans., 1993; joint task force 161 and ARFOR plans officer Guantanamo Bay, Cuba, 1994; MP long range plans officer 89th Mil Police Brigade, Ft. Hood, Tex., 1994-95, exec. officer 720th Mil. Police Battalion, Ft. Hood, 1995-96; Am. Polit. Sci. Assn. congrl. fellow Senator Bob Graham, Washington, 1996-97; chief of plans and ops. office Chief of Legis. Liaison Office of Sec., U.S. Army, Washington, 1997-98; dir. legis. strategy Washington, 1998-99; bn. comdr. 19th Mil. Police Bn., Seoul, Republic of Korea, 1999—2001; provost marshal and task force comdr., joint task force patriot Ft. George G. Meade, Md., 2001—02; provost marshal, dir. operational protection Third US Army, US Army Forces Ctrl. Command, and Coalition Forces Land Component Command, Camp Arifjan, Kuwait, 2003—05; brigade comdr. 202nd Mil. Police Group (CID), Seckenheim, Germany, 2005—. Vol. coach youth football, soccer, baseball, 1974—; leader Boy Scouts Am., Ft. Hood, 1989—, mem. com., 1994-96. Decorated Legion of Merit (with one oak leaf cluster), Bronze Star Medal. Mem. VFW, Ret. Officers Assn., Korean-Am. Assn., Assn. U.S. Army, 720th Mil. Police Battalion Reunion Assn. (life), Mil. Police Regimental Assn. (life), Mil. Officers Assn. Am., Fgn. Area Officer Assn. (founding), U. Fla. Nat. Alumni Assn. (life), Jacksonville State U. Alumni Assn. (life), Am. Polit. Sci. Assn., Am. C. of C. in Korea, Harley Owners Group (life), Alpha Kappa Delta. Roman Catholic. Avocations: sailing, scuba diving, water-skiing, skydiving, foreign travel. Home and Office: 202nd MP Group Unit 29201 Box 52 APO AE 09102 Business E-Mail: kenneth.prendergast@us.army.mil.

**PRENDERGAST, SIR KIERAN,** former international organization official; b. Campbeltown, Scotland, 1942; married; 4 children. BA, St. Patricks Coll., Strathfield, Sydney; MA, Salesian Coll. and St. Edmond Hall, Oxford. Posted NATO Dept. at the Fgn. Office, 1967—69, NATO in Nicosia, Cyprus, 1969—72; second sec. NATO, 1969—72, first sec. to desk officer, 1973—76; asst. pvt. sec. Sec. of State for Fgn.and Commonwealth Affairs, 1976—79; posted United Kingdom Mission to the UN, 1979—82; Counselor and Consul gen. Tel Aviv, 1982—86; high commr. to Zimbabwe, 1989—92, to Kenya, 1992—95; amb. to Turkey, 1995—97; Under-Sec.- Gen. for polit. affairs UN, 1997—2005. Office: UN Headquarters First Ave at 46th St New York NY 10017

**PRENDERGAST, THOMAS A.,** investments consultant, management consultant; b. Dec. 10, 1933; m. Mary Alice Peinado; children: Elizabeth Jane Mettler, Laura Ann Gordon. BS, Fordham U., 1955; postgrad., U. Tex., El Paso, 1960. CPA, Tex. Pvt. practice acctg., 1957-61; v.p. fin. Farah Mfg., Inc., 1961-71; chmn. bd. Billy the Kid, Inc., 1971-81, Jetco, 1972-74, Fashion Enterpreses, Inc., 1982-84, Air Cargo Equipment Corp., 1983-88, investments, mgmt. cons.; chmn. bd. El Paso Gibson's, Inc., 1988—92; chmn. Sunland Audio Ltd. Co., 1994—98, N.Am. Bender, Inc., 1995—2000. Chmn. bd. dirs. Baron Chem., Inc., Clinitech, Inc., 1986-91, Steel Corp. Tex., Texzona Industries, Inc., True Blue Sky, Inc.; bd. dirs. Market Guide Inc., Air Cargo Inc., Fischback and Moore Inc., Double Eagle Petroleum, Inc., Intellicheck, Inc.; chmn. Market Guide, 1997-2000. Composer; author poetry, film criticsm; contbr. articles to profl. jours. Founder, pres. bd. trustees El Paso Community Coll, 1969-82. Home: 725 Montoya Oak El Paso TX 79932 Office Phone: 915-544-7722.

**PRENDERGAST, WILLIAM JOHN,** ophthalmologist; b. Portland, Oreg., June 12, 1942; s. William John and Marjorie (Scott) P.; m. Carolyn Grace Perkins, Aug. 17, 1963 (div. 1990); children: William John, Scott; m. Sherryl Irene Guenther, Aug. 25, 1991. BS, U. Oreg., Eugene, 1964; MD, U. Oreg., Portland, 1967. Diplomate Am. Bd. Ophthalmology. Resident in ophthalmology U. Oreg., Portland, 1970-73; pvt. practice specializing in ophthalmology Portland, 1973-82; physician, founder, ptnr. Eye Health NW (formerly Oreg. Med. Eye Clinic), Portland, 1983—; also bd. dirs.; founder, pres. (Focus Group) Inc. Focus Group Inc., Ophthalmic Clinic Networking Venture, Portland, 1991—. Clin. asst. prof. ophthalmology Oreg. Health Sci. U., 1985—; dir. Eye Health Ptnrs. Med. Optometric Managed Eye Care Venture, 1998. Vol. surgeon, Hosp. de la Familia, Nuevo Progreso, Guatemala, 2001-05, vol. surgeon N.W. Med. Teams, Oaxaca, Mexico, 1989-90. With USPHS, 1968-70. Fellow Am. Acad. Ophthalmology; mem. Met. Bus. Assn., Multnomah Athletic Club, Mazamas Mountaineering Club, Portland Yacht Club, Phi Beta Kappa, Alpha Omega Alpha. Avocations: sailing, mountain climbing. Office: Eye Health NW 1955 NW Northrup St Portland OR 97209-1614 Office Phone: 503-227-2020. Business E-Mail: prenderw@ehnpc.com.

**PRENSKY, ARTHUR LAWRENCE,** pediatric neurologist, educator; b. N.Y.C., Aug. 31, 1930; s. Herman and Pearl (Newman) P.; m. Sheila Carr, Nov. 13, 1969. AB, Cornell U., 1951; MD, N.Y. U., 1955. Diplomate: Am. Bd. Psychiatry and Neurology. Intern Barnes Hosp., St. Louis, 1955-56; resident and research fellow in neurology Harvard U., Mass. Gen. Hosp., Boston, 1959-66; instr. neurology Harvard Med. Sch., 1966-67; mem. faculty Washington U. Sch. Medicine, St. Louis, 1967—, prof. pediatrics and neurology, to 1975, Allen P. and Josephine B. Green prof. pediatric neurology, 1975-2000, prof. emeritus of neurology, 2000—; pediatrician St. Louis Children's Hosp.; neurologist Barnes and Allied Hosps., Jewish Hosp., St. Louis. Author: (with others) Nutrition and the Developing Nervous System, 1975; editor: (with others) Neurological Pathophysiology, 2d edit, 1978, Advances in Neurology, 1976; mem. editorial bd. Pediatric Neurology, 1984-90, Jour. Child Neurology, 1985—. Served with USAF, 1957-59. Fellow Am. Acad. Neurology; mem. Am. Neurol. Assn., Am. Soc. Neurochemistry (mem. council 1973-77), Central Soc. Neurol. Rsch. (pres. 1977-78), Child Neurology Soc. (pres. 1979-80, Hower award 2000), Am. Pediatric Soc., Internat. Child Neurology Assn., Japanese Soc. Child Neurology, Profs. Child Neurology (pres. 1984-86) Home: 15 Monarch Hill Ct Chesterfield MO 63005-4004 Office: 1 Children's Pl Saint Louis MO 63110-1014 Office Phone: 314-454-6120. Business E-Mail: prenskya@neuro.wustl.edu.

**PRENTKE, RICHARD OTTESEN,** lawyer; b. Cleve., Sept. 8, 1945; s. Herbert E. and Melva B. P.; m. Susan Ottesen, June 9, 1974; children: Catherine, Elizabeth. BSE, Princeton U., 1967; JD, Harvard U., 1974. Assoc. Perkins Coie, Seattle, 1974-80, ptnr., 1981—, CFO, 1989-94. Author: School Construction Law Deskbook, 1989, rev. 2d edit. 1998; contbr. articles to profl. jours. Pres., trustee Seattle County Day Sch., 1990-95; trustee Pocock Rowing Found., 1996-02. Lt. USN, 1967—70. Fellow Leadership Tomorrow, Seattle, 1985-86. Mem. ABA, Wash. State Bar Assn. (mem. jud. screening com. 1985-91, chmn 1987-91), Seattle-King County Bar Assn. (chmn. jud. task force 1990-93), Am. Arbitration Assn. (arbitrator 1988—), Princeton U. Rowing Assn. (pres. 1993-02, trustee 1976—), Rainier Club, Princeton Varsity Club (trustee 2003-), Princeton Varsity Club Wash. (trustee 1986-95, pres. 1990-92), Seattle Tennis Club. Avocations: art, carpentry, travel, rowing, sports. Office: Perkins Coie 1201 3rd Ave Fl 40 Seattle WA 98101-3029 Office Phone: 206-359-8888. Business E-Mail: rprentke@perkinscoie.com.

**PREOBRAZHENSKY, ALEXANDER ANATOLIYEVICH,** biochemist; b. Chita, Russia, Sept. 29, 1946; s. Anatoliy Nikolayevich and Magdalina Sergeyevna (Knyaginicheva) P.; m. Ekaterina Sergeyevna Grigoriyan, Mar. 14, 1970 (div. Jan. 1981); 1 child, Elena; m. Olga Stefanovna Zakharova, Dec. 22, 1984; 1 child, Sergei. Student, Moscow State U., 1970, PhD in Biology, 1976, DSc, 1996. Rsch. asst. Inst. for Protein Rsch., Pouschino, Russia, 1970-72; rsch. assoc. A.N. Bach Inst. of Biochemistry, Moscow, 1975-86, sr. scientist, 1986—. Grantee Ministry of Sci. and Tech., 1989, Russian Found. for Fundamental Rsch., 1994, 97, Internat. Sci. Found. Mem.: Mem. Russian Biochem. Soc., N.Y. Acad. Scis. Avocations: hiking, internet, orienteering, reading. Office: 2540 Olentangy River Rd Columbus OH 43202-1505 E-mail: apreobraz@cas.org.

**PREONAS, GEORGE ELIAS,** lawyer; b. Dayton, Ohio, Oct. 5, 1943; s. Louis D. and Mary (Drakos) P.; m. Aileen Strike, June 1, 1944; children: Annemarie, Michael, Stephen. BA, Stanford U., 1965; JD, U. Mich., 1968. Bar: Ill. 1968, Nev. 1969, Calif. 1974. Ptnr. Seyfarth, Shaw, Fairweather & Geraldson, L.A., 1968—. Mem. ABA, L.A. County Bar Assn., Calif. Bar Assn., Ill. Bar Assn., Nev. Bar Assn. Office: Seyfarth Shaw 2029 Century Park E Ste 3300 Los Angeles CA 90067-3019

**PRESANT, SANFORD CALVIN,** lawyer, educator, writer, tax specialist; b. Buffalo, Nov. 15, 1952; s. Allen and Reeta Presant; children: Jarrett, Danny, Lauren; m. Nancy Loeb. BA, Cornell U., 1973; JD cum laude, SUNY, Buffalo, 1976; LLM in Taxation, Georgetown U., NYU, 1981. Bar: N.Y. 1977, D.C. 1977, U.S. Tax Ct. 1977, U.S. Ct. Claims 1978, Calif. 1992, U.S. Supreme Ct. 1982. Staff atty. SEC Options Task Force, Washington, 1976-78; assoc. Barrett Smith Schapiro, NYC, 1978-80, Trubin Sillcocks, NYC, 1980-81; ptnr. Carro, Spanbock, Fass, Geller, Kaster, NYC, 1981-86, Finley, Kumble, Wagner, Heine, Underberg, Manley, Myerson & Casey, NYC, 1987, Kaye, Scholer, Fierman, Hays & Handler, NYC, 1987-95, Battle Fowler LLP, LA, 1995-2000, Ernst & Young, LA, 2000; nat. dir. real estate tax strategies, opportunity funds Ernst & Young LLP, LA, 2000; ptnr. DLA Piper Rudnick Gray Cary US LLP, LA, 2005—. Adj. assoc. prof. real estate NYU, 1984-00; frequent lectr. in tax law; regular TV appearances Nightly Bus. Report, PBS, 1986-88; co-chmn. NYU Conf. Fed. Taxation Real Estate Trans., 1987, PLI Advanced Tax Planning Real Estate, 1987, PLI Ann. Real Estate Tax Forum, 1999—; program dir. Nareit Law and Acctg. Conf., 2003; conf. chmn. various confs. in field. Author: Realty Joint Ventures, 1980-86, Tax Sheltered Investments Handbook-Special Update on Tax Reform Act of 1984, Real Estate Syndication Handbook, 1986, The Tax Reform Act of 1986, 1987, Real Estate Syndication Tax Handbook, 1987, Understanding Partnership Tax Allocations, 1987, The Final Partnership Nonrecourse Debt Allocation Regulations, 1987, Taxation of Real Estate Investments, 1987, Understanding Partnership Tax Allocations, 1987, Tax Aspects of Environmental (Superfund) Settlements, 1994, The Proposed Publicly Traded Partnership Regulations, 1995, (with others) Tax Aspects of Real Investments, 2002, Structuring Real Estate Private Equity Funds, 2005, Joint Ventures With Tax-Exempt Entities, 2005, others. Kripke Securities Law fellow NYU, 1976. Mem. ABA (nat. chmn. audit subcom. of tax sect. partnership com. 1984-86, partnership tax allocation subcom. chmn. 1986-90, nat. chmn. partnership com. 1992-94, chmn. task force publicly traded partnerships 1995—, others), N.Y. State Bar Assn. (tax sect. partnership com. 1980—), Assn. Bar City of N.Y. Republican. Jewish. Office: Real Estate Capital Markets DLA Piper Rudnick Gray Cary US LLP 1999 Avenue of the Stars Fourth Fl Los Angeles CA 90067-5403 Office Phone: 213-977-3303, 310-595-3190. Office Fax: 866-222-9401, 310-595-3490. Business E-Mail: sanford.presant@ey.com, susan.teague@dlapiper.com.

**PRESBY, J. THOMAS,** financial advisor, director, arbitrator; b. Newark, Feb. 15, 1940; s. George and Shirley (Ansel) P.; m. Elaine Merle Smith, Aug. 19, 1961; children: Philip, Terry, Mona. BSEE, Rutgers U., 1961; MBA in Indsl. Adminstrn., Carnegie-Mellon U., 1963. CPA, Ohio, N.Y. Ptnr. Touche Ross, N.Y.C., 1972-76; regional ptnr. Touche Ross Internat., Paris, 1976-79, nat. dir. client svcs., 1979-81, exec. dir. internat., 1981-82, ptnr.-in-charge fin. svcs. ctr., 1982-90, mng. ptnr. Ea. Europe, Brussels, 1990-94, chief exec. officer Europe, Paris, 1991-95; COO Deloitte Touche Tohmatsu Internat., N.Y.C., 1995—, dep. chmn., chief oper. officer, 1997, chief staff, mem. exec. group, 1999—2002. Mem. bus. adv. coun. Grad. Sch. Indsl. Adminstrn., Carnegie-Mellon U., Pitts., 1984-2001; trustee Rutgers U., New Brunswick, N.J., 1985-90; bd. dirs. Tiffany & Co., Amvescap PLC, Am. Eagle Outfitters, World Fuel Services, Turbochef Technologies, German Marshall Fund. Mem. AICPA, Ohio Soc. CPAs, N.Y. Soc. CPAs, Harmonie Club. Avocations: antique autos, racquetball, squash, motorcycling, fly fishing. Home: 6 Holton Ln Essex Fells NJ 07021-1709 Office: 655 Madison Ave Ste 2300 New York NY 10021 Office Phone: 646-358-3043. E-mail: tom.presby@verizon.net.

**PRESCOTT, DANA E.,** lawyer; b. Aug. 1958; BA, Western New Eng. Coll.; JD, Vt. Law Sch. Bar: Maine 1983. Atty. Prescott Lemoine Jamieson & Nelson, PA, Saco, Maine. Mem.: Maine State Bar Assn. (pres.-elect 2003, pres. 2004). Office: Prescott Lemoine Jamieson and Nelson 37 Beach St PO Box 1190 Saco ME 04072-1190

**PRESCOTT, DARRELL,** lawyer; b. Montpelier, Vt., May 17, 1949; AB magna cum laude, Harvard Law Alumni Ass, 1971, JD, 1975. Bar: NY 1976, US Ct. Appeals (2d cir.) 1985, US Ct. Appeals (11th cir,) 1996, US Ct. Appeals (Fed. cir.) 2000, US Supreme Ct. 1996. Ptnr. Baker & McKenzie LLP, NYC. Contbr. articles to profl. jours.; co-editor: Joint Ventures in the Internat. Arena, ABA, 2003. Knox fellow. Fellow: Am. Bar Found. (sec., liaison officer 2005—06); mem.: ABA (programs officer, Sect. Internat. law, CLE award, Sect. Internat. Law 2004), Assn. Bar City of NY, Phi Beta Kappa. Office: Baker & McKenzie LLP 1114 Ave of the Americas New York NY 10036 Office Fax: 212-316-1637. E-mail: darrell.prescott@bakernet.com.

**PRESCOTT, DAVID L. C., JR.,** music educator; s. David L. C. Prescott, Sr. and Lavina Hall Prescott. BS in Bus. Adminstrn., Old Dominion U., 1981, MusB in Music Edn., 1992, MS in Secondary Edn., Choral Conducting, 2002. Acct. W. E. Moulton, Jr. & Assocs., Portsmouth, Va., 1981—90; music specialist Tanners Creek Elem. Sch., Norfolk, Va., 1992—93; dir. choral activities Ocean Lakes H.S., Virginia Beach, Va., 1993—97, Kempsville H.S. Virginia Beach, Va., 1997—. Guest clinician, condr. Various Churches And Civic Choirs, Va., 1992—; dir. music Holland Rd. Bapt. Ch., Virginia Beach, 1983—97, Faith Wesleyan Ch., Norfolk, 1995—2005, Thalia United Meth. Ch., Virginia Beach, 2005—. King herod: (musical theatre) Jesus Christ Superstar; costumer (dramas and musical theatre works) A Man for All Seasons, Christ and St. Luke's Arts Guild, 2000, Our Town, Christ and St. Luke's Art Guild, 1999, Jesus Christ Superstar, Christ and St. Luke's Art Guild, 2001, Guys and Dolls, Wizard of Oz, Annie Get Your Gun, Mame, Pippin, Carousel Cinderella, Kempsville H.S., 1999—2005. Mem. bd. dirs. Virginia Beach Ballet, 1990—93. Recipient Award of Distinction - Choral Conducting, Fest. Music Competitions, 1999. Mem.: Music Educators Nat. Conf., Va. Music Educators Assn., Am. Choral Dir.'s Assn., Phi Mu Alpha Sinfonia. Wesleyan. Avocations: antiques, flower arranging. Office: Kempsville High School 5194 Chief Trail Virginia Beach VA 23464 Office Phone: 757-474-8400 ext. 58104. E-mail: dlpresco@vbschools.com.

**PRESCOTT, EDWARD C.,** economist, educator; b. 1940; BA in Mathematics, Swarthmore Coll., 1962; MS in Operations Rsch., Case-Western Reserve U., 1963; PhD in Economics, Carnegie Mellon U., 1967. Lectr. U. Penn, 1966—67; asst. prof. Economics Dept. U. Penn., 1967—71; asst. prof. Grad. Sch. Indsl. Admin. Carnegie Mellon U., 1971—72, assoc. prof., 1972—75; vis. prof. Economics Norwegian Sch. Bus. and Economics, 1974—75; prof. Economics Grad. Sch. Indsl. Admin. Carnegie Mellon U., 1975—80; Ford

vis. rsch. prof. U. Chgo., 1978—79; vis. prof. Economics Northwestern U., 1979—80; vis. prof. Finance Kellogg Grad. Sch. Mgmt. Northwestern U., 1980—82; sr. advisor rsch. dept. Fed. Reserve Bank, Mpls., 1980—2003; prof. Economics U. Minn., 1980—98, U. Chgo., 1998—99, U. Minn., 1999—2003; prof. dept. Economics Ariz. State U., 2003—; sr. monetary advisor Fed. Reserve Bank, Mpls., 2003—. Leader NBER/NSF Workshop in Indsl. Orgn., 1977—84; rsch. assoc. Nat. Bureau of Economic Rsch.; spkr. in field. Author (with S.L. Parente): Barriers to Riches, 2000; co-editor: Economic Theory, 1991; assoc. editor: Jour. Econometrics, 1976—82, Internat. Economic Review, 1980—90, Jour. Economic Theory, 1990—92; contbr. articles to profl. jours. Named Regents' Prof., U. Minn., 1996, McKnight Presidential Chair in Economics, 2003, W.P. Carey Chair, U. Ariz., 2003; recipient Erwin Plein Nemmers prize in Econ., Northwestern U., 2002, Laurea Honoris Causa in Economica, U. Rome, 2002, Nobel Prize for Econ. Sciences, 2004; fellow, Econometric Society, 1980, Am. Acad. Arts & Scis., 1992; Brookings Economic Policy Fellow, 1969—70, Guggenheim Fellow, 1974—75. Mem.: Soc. Advancement of Econ. Theory (pres. 1992—94), Soc. Econ. Dynamics and Control (pres. 1992—95). Office: Ariz State U Dept Econs Tempe AZ 85287-3806*

**PRESCOTT, JOHN MACK,** biochemist, retired university administrator; b. San Marcos, Tex., Jan. 22, 1921; s. John Mack and Maude (Raborn) P.; m. Kathryn Ann Kelly, June 8, 1946; children: Stephen Michael, Donald Wyatt. BS in Chemistry, S.W. Tex. State Coll., 1941; MS in Biochemistry and Nutrition, Tex. A&M U., 1949; PhD in Biochemistry, U. Wis., 1952. Lab. asst. Dow Chem. Co., Freeport, Tex., 1942-43; faculty Tex. A&M U., College Station, 1946-49, 52-85, prof. biochemistry, 1959-85, dean Coll. Sci., 1970-77, v.p. for acad. affairs, 1977-81, dir. Inst. Occupational and Environ. Medicine, 1981-87, prof. med. biochemistry, 1981-85, prof. emeritus, 1985—, spl. asst. to dep. chancellor for biotech. devel., 1987; research asst. U. Wis.-Madison, 1949-51, 1 yr., Austin, 1951-52; vis. prof. Harvard Med. Sch., 1982. Contbr. articles profl. jours. Mem. Tex. Bd. Examiners in Basic Scis., 1974-79, Tex. State Bd. Edn., 1984-88. Served to lt. USAAF, 1943-46; lt. col. USAF Res., 1946-68. Mem. Am. Soc. for Biochemistry and Molecular Biology, Soc. for Exptl. Biology and Medicine, Sigma Xi, Phi Lambda Upsilon. Home: 31 Forest Dr College Station TX 77840-2337

**PRESCOTT, PERRY DON,** psychology professor, counselor; b. Jasper, Ala., Mar. 15, 1952; s. Howard J. and Mary Lou Prescott; m. Hazel Ann Prescott, June 12, 1975; children: Justin H., Nigel A., Trevor G. BS, U. Ala., 1974, MA, 1978; PhD, 1984. Asst. prof. psychology Miss. Coll., Clinton, 1988-89; asst. prof. counseling U. Ga., Athens, 1989-90, U. Guam, Mangilao, 1990-91; pvt. practice Tuscaloosa, Ala., 1991-92; asst. prof. psychology McNeese State U., Lake Charles, La., 1992-93; counselor, tchr. State of Ala. Schs., Jasper, Double Springs, 1993-97; PACE psychology prof. Navy program Ctrl. Tex. Coll., San Diego, 1997—2002; psychotherapist, consortium between Auburn U. and UJ. Ala. Montgomery State of Ala., 2002—. Cons. Profl. Counseling Svcs., Jasper, Ala., 1994, Walker Regional Hosp., Jasper, 1994. Contbr. articles to profl. jours. including Ala. Assn. Counselors Jour., Jour. Reading. With USAR, 1972-78. Named one of Outstanding Young Men in Am., Jaycees, 1982. Mem So. Assn. Coll. Student Adminstrs. (com. 1986-87), William Glasser Inst. (cert.), Phi Delta Kappa, Kappa Delta Pi. Avocations: travel, foreign languages, reading. Home and Office: 11531 Shalom Rd Duncanville AL 35456-2533

**PRESCOTT, RICHARD CHAMBERS,** writer; b. Houston, Apr. 1, 1952; s. Chambers Richard and Dorothy Mae (Bashara) P.; m. Sarah Elisabeth Grace, Oct. 13, 1981. Author: The Sage, 1975, Moonstar, 1975, Neuf Songes (Nine Dreams), 1976, 2d edit., 1991, The Carouse of Soma, 1977, Lions and Kings, 1977, Allah Wake Up, 1978, 2d edit., 1994, Night Reaper, 1979, Dragon Tales, 1983, Dragon Dreams, 1986, 2d edit., 1990, Dragon Prayers, 1988, 2d edit., 1990, Dragon Songs, 1988, 2d edit., 1990, Dragon Maker, 1989, 2d edit., 1990, Dragon Thoughts, 1990, Tales of Recognition, 1991, Kings and Sages, 1991, Dragon Sight: A Cremation Poem, 1992, Three Waves, 1992, Years of Wonder, 1992, Dream Appearances, 1992, Remembrance Recognition and Return, 1992, Spare Advice, 1992, The Imperishable, 1993, The Dark Deitess, 1993, Disturbing Delights: Waves of The Great Goddess, 1993, The Immortal: Racopa and the Rooms of Light, 1993, Hanging Baskets, 1993, Writer's Block and Other Gray Matters, 1993, The Resurrection of Quantum Joe, 1993, The Horse and the Carriage, 1993, Kalee Bhava: The Goddess and Her Moods, 1995, The Skills of Kalee, 1995, Because of Atma, 1995, Measuring Sky Without Ground, 1996, The Goddess And The God Man, 1996, Kalee: The Allayer of Sorrows, 1996, Living Sakti, 1997, The Mirage and the Mirror, 1998, Inherent Solutions to Spiritual Obscurations, 1999, The Ancient Method, 1999, Quantum Kamakala, 2000; contbr. articles to profl. jours.

**PRESCOTT, THOMAS W.,** bank executive; b. Oct. 24, 1954; BBA in Acctg., Columbus Coll., 1976. From v.p. fin. to exec. v.p., CFO Synovus Fin. Corp., Columbus, Ga., 1987—96, exec. v.p., 1996—, CFO, 1996—. Bd. dir. Family Counseling Ctr. Mem.: Ga. Soc. CPAs, Kiwanis Club N.Columbus. Office: Synovus Financial Corp 1 Arsenal Place 901 Front Ave Ste 301 Columbus GA 31901

**PRESKA, LORETTA A.,** federal judge; b. 1949; BA, Coll. of St. Rose, 1970; JD, Fordham U., 1973; LLM, NYU, 1978; LHD (hon.), Coll. of St. Rose, 1995. Assoc. Cahill, Gordon & Reindel, NYC, 1973-82; ptnr. Hertzog, Calamari & Gleason, NYC, 1982-92; fed. judge U.S. Dist. Ct. (So. Dist.), NY, 1992—. Mem. N.Y. State Bar Assn., N.Y. County Lawyers Assn., Fed. Bar Coun., Fordham Law Alumni Assn. (v.p.). Office: US Courthouse 500 Pearl St Rm 1320 New York NY 10007-1316

**PRESKA, MARGARET LOUISE ROBINSON,** historian, educational association administrator; b. Parma, N.Y., Jan. 23, 1938; d. Ralph Craven and Ellen Elvira (Niemi) Robinson; m. Daniel C. Preska, Jan. 24, 1959; children: Robert, William, Ellen Preska Steck. BS summa cum laude, SUNY, 1957, MA, Pa. State U., 1961; PhD, Claremont Grad. Sch., 1969. Instr. LaVerne (Calif.) Coll., 1968-75, asst. prof., assoc. prof., acad. dean, 1972-75; instr. Starr King Sch. for Ministry, Berkeley, Calif., summer, 1975; v.p. acad. affairs, equal opportunity officer Minn. State U., Mankato, 1975-79, pres., 1979-92; project dir. Kaliningrad (Russia) Mil. Re-Tng., 1992-96; disting. svc. prof. Minn. State U. Sys., 1993—; pres. Trust for Effective Tchg. Minn. State U., Winona, 1993—98; owner BuildaBikeInc.com, 2002—. Bd. dirs. XCEL Energy Co., Milkweed Edits.; pres. emerita Minn. State U., Mankato, 1992—; provost, CEO AbuDhabi Campus, Zayed U., United Arab Emirates, 1997-99. Pres. Pomona Valley chpt. UN Assn., 1968-69, Unitarian Soc. Pomona Valley, 1968-69, PTA Lincoln Elem. Sch., Pomona, 1973-74; pres., chmn. bd. Nat. Camp Fire Boys and Girls, 1984-88; mem. Pomona City Charter Revision Commn., 1972; chmn. The Fielding Inst., Santa Barbara, 1983-86; bd. dirs. Elderhostel Internat., 1983-87, Minn. Agrl. Interpretive Ctr. (Farmam.), 1983-92, Am. Assn. State Colls. and Univs., Moscow on the Mississippi - Minn. Meets the Soviet Union; nat. pres. Campfire, Inc. 1985-87; chmn. Gov.'s Coun. on Youth, Minn., 1983-86, Minn. Edn. Forum, 1984; mem. Gov.'s Commn. on Econ. Future of Minn., 1985—, NCAA Pres. Commn., 1986-92, NCAA Cost Cutting Commn., Minn. Brainpower Compact, 1985; commr. Great Lakes Govs.' Econ. Devel. Coun., 1986, Minn Gov.'s Commn. on Forestry. Carnegie Found. grantee Am. Coun. Edn. Deans Inst., 1974; recipient Outstanding Alumni award Pa. State, Outstanding Alumni award Claremont Grad. Sch., YWCA Leader award 1982, Exch. Club Book of Golden Deeds award, 1987; named One of top 100 alumni, SUNY, 1895-1985, 1985, Hall of Heritage award, 1988, Wohelo Camp Fire award, 1989. Fellow Fielding Inst.; mem. AAUW (pres. Mankato 1990-92), LWV, Women's Econ. Roundtable, St. Paul/Mpls. Com. on Fgn. Rels., Am. Assn. Univ. Adminstrs., Rotary, Horizon 100. Unitarian Universalist. Home: 10 Sumner Hls Mankato MN 56001-3931 E-mail: mpreska@hickorytech.net.

**PRESKILL, JOHN PHILLIP,** physics professor; b. Highland Park, Ill., Jan. 19, 1953; m. Roberta M. Gross, June 22, 1975; children: Carina Lou, Micaela Marie. AB in Physics, Princeton U., 1975; AM in Physics, Harvard U., 1976,

PhD in Physics, 1980. Jr. fellow Harvard Soc. Fellows, 1980-81; asst. prof. physics Harvard U., Cambridge, Mass., 1981-82, assoc. prof., 1982-83; assoc. prof. theoretical physics Calif. Inst. Tech., Pasadena, 1983-90, prof., 1990—; dir. Inst. Quantum Info., 2000—; John D. MacArthur prof., 2002—; dir. Ctr. for Physics of Info., 2003— Andrejewski lectr. Humbolt U., Berlin, 2001; Lorentz chair U. Leiden, 2002; Rouse Ball lectr. U. Cambridge, 2005. Recipient Presdl. Young Investigator award NSF, 1984-89; fellow NSF, 1975-78, Alfred P. Sloan Found., 1982-86. Fellow Am. Phys. Soc. Office: Calif Inst Tech 452-48 Div Physics Math & Astronomy Pasadena CA 91125-0001 Office Phone: 626-395-6691. Office Fax: 626-568-8473. E-mail: preskill@theory.caltech.edu, preskill@iqi.caltech.edu.

**PRESLAND-BYRNE, PETER,** mortgage company executive; Exec. v.p. application devel. Countrywide Fin. Corp. Named one of Premier 100 IT Leaders, Computerworld, 2005. Office: Countrywide Fin Corp 4500 Park Granada Calabasas CA 91302-1613 Office Phone: 818-225-3000. Office Fax: 818-225-4051.*

**PRESLAR, LEN BROUGHTON, JR.,** hospital administrator; b. Concord, N.C., Aug. 13, 1947; s. Len B. and Billie M. (James) P.; m. Joyce W. Whittington, July 11, 1971; children: Bradley E., Whitney A., Andrew C. BA, Wake Forest U., 1971; MBA, U. N.C., Greensboro, 1980. Admissions clk. N.C. Bapt. Hosp., Winston-Salem, 1969-71, systems analyst, 1971-72, budget mgr., 1973, contr., 1973-75, v.p. fin. mgmt., 1975-88, pres., chief exec. officer, 1988—. Bd. dirs. Univ. Healthsystem Consortium; bd. mgrs. Wachovia Bank; mem. owenrs and affiliate rels. com. Premier, Inc. Deacon local Bapt. ch. Fellow Hosp. Fin. Mgmt. Assn.; mem. N.C. Hosp. Assn. (bd. dirs.). Republican. Baptist. Avocations: gardening, golf. Office: NC Bapt Hosp Medical Center Blvd Winston Salem NC 27157-0001

**PRESLEY, BRIAN,** investment company executive; b. Evansville, Ind., Dec. 28, 1941; s. Harry and Ruth P.; m. Mary Nell Minyard, Aug. 17, 1972; children: Debra, Cynthia, David, Jeffrey, Clark, Gregory, Steven. BSBA, U. Evansville, 1963; MBA, Mich. State U., 1964; diploma, Wharton Sch., U. Pa., 1995. Market rsch. analyst Stanley Works, New Britain, Conn., 1964-68; tax shelter coord. F.I. Dupont, Memphis, 1968-73; v.p. Bullington Schas, Memphis, 1973-75; pres., mng. ptnr. Presley Assocs., Memphis, 1965-93; pres., CFO CSG, Inc., Memphis, 1975—. Gen. ptnr. various real estate and oil and gas partnerships, 1974-1986; pres. Cooper St. Group Securities, Inc., 1983-86; divsn. mgr. Advantage Capital Corp. (divsn. AIG Advisors, Inc.), 1986-89, reg. v.p., 1989, CEO 1990-94, mng. dir., mktg. strategist, 1995; pres. Presley Adv. Inc., 1995—, pub. Presley Adv. Letter; instr. fin. divsn. continuing edn. Memphis U. Bd. dirs. Apt. Coun. Tenn., 1980-86, sec.-treas., 1982-83; pres. Memphis Apt. Coun., 1983; mem., U. Evansville Nat. Alumni Bd., 1988-91; prodr. 2 daily radio stock market commentary shows, 1988; fin. commentator Sta. WEVU-TV (ABC), Ft. Myers/Naples, 1988-89; host syndicated radio show for sr. citizens, 1979-81; mem. found. bd. and fin. com. Fla. Gulf Coast U., 2001—. Mem. Leadership Charlotte; chmn. Charlotte County Econ. Devel. Coun., 1999-2002; pres. Enterprise Charlotte Found., 2002—; chmn. Angels Found. Charlotte County, 2002-2005; bd. dirs. Charlotte County Cmty. Found., 2005—. Recipient Richard L. McLaughlin award, Econ. Devel. Coun., Fla., 2002. Mem. Internat. Assn. Fin. Planners (broker dealer adv. coun. 1993-97), Admirals Club (life, bd. dirs.), Naples Jazz Soc. (chmn. bd. dirs. 1993-96), Naples Sailing and Yacht Club (bd. dirs.1991-96), Pi Sigma Epsilon, Beta Gamma Sigma, Tau Kappa Epsilon Alumni Assn. (pres. Memphis area 1979-80), Isles Yacht Club (bd. dirs. 2001-04). Presbyterian. Home and Office: Acorn Ranch 5161 Acorn Ranch Rd Punta Gorda FL 33982-9511 Office Phone: 941-505-9017. Business E-Mail: brian@presleyadvisoryinc.com.

**PRESLEY, JAMES WRIGHT,** writer, environmentalist; b. Nash, Tex., Jan. 13, 1930; s. James Alexander and Lola Opal (Wright) Presley; m. Fran Burton, Jan. 13, 1962; children: John Francis, Ann Burton. BA, East Tex. State Tchrs. Coll., 1950; MA, U. Tex., 1955, Mexico City Coll., 1955; PhD, U. Tex., Austin, 1991. Reporter Texarkana (Tex.-Ark.) Gazette, 1947—49; asst. news editor Amarillo (Tex.) Globe-Times, 1956; staff writer Shreveport (La.) Times, 1958—59; copy editor The Light, San Antonio, 1959—61, 1969; part-time news editor Texarkana Gazette, 1969—71; polit. cons. Texarkana, 1960—; freelance writer, 1961—. Contbg. editor, editl. adv. bd. Tex. Observer, Austin, 1960—80; mgmt. cons. Red River Regional Coun. Alcoholism, Texarkana, 1975; spkr. workshops, Tex. and Ark. Co-author: Center of the Storm, 1967, Please Doctor, Do Something!, 1972, Vitamin B6: The Doctor's Report, 1973, Public Defender, 1974, Human Life Styling, 1975, Food Power, 1978; author: A Saga of Wealth: Rise of the Texas Oilmen, 1978, Never in Doubt, 1981; featured interviewee PBS-TV Documentary series on Tex., 1986; featured interviewee: other documentaries. Co-founder, pres., etc. Texarkana Anti-Pollution Soc.; co-founder, bd. dirs., etc. Friends United for a Safe Environ., Tex.-Ark., 1988—; press aide Henry Gonzalez-for-Gov., San Antonio, 1958. Staff sgt. USAF, 1950—53. Recipient various news prizes, AP, various other news assns., 1969—71, Anson Jones award, Tex. Med. Assn., 1971, John H. McGinnis Meml. award, Southwest Rev., 1981. Mem.: Am. Med. Writers Assn., N.Y. Acad. Scis., Oral History Assn., Soc. Environ. Journalists, Internat. Soc. Fluoride Rsch., Am. Assn. History of Medicine. Democrat. Achievements include author history of diabetes mellitus in the U.S. (1880-1990), 1991, 2 vols; led numerous environmental campaigns. Avocations: book collecting, investigating unsolved cases, fencing, running. Home and Office: 417 W 27th St Texarkana TX 75503-4232

**PRESLEY, JOHN WOODROW,** academic administrator; b. Jonesboro, Ark., Mar. 24, 1948; s. Marvin Woodrow and Willa Louise (Taylor) P.; m. Katherine Bailey Harrison, Oct. 17, 1978. BSE, Ark. State U., 1970; MA, So. Ill. U., 1972, PhD, 1975; postgrad., Johns Hopkins U., 1976, U. Tex., 1980. From asst. prof. to prof., asst. v.p. acad. affairs Augusta State U., 1974—89; assoc. provost Lafayette Coll., 1989—92; dean Coll. of Arts, Scis. and Letters U. Mich., Dearborn, 1992-99; provost, v.p. acad. affairs SUNY at Oswego, 1999—2003; v.p. acad. affairs, provost Ill. State U., 2003—. Author and presenter in fields of modern lit. and higher edn. adminstrn. Author: The Robert Graves Letters and Manuscripts at Southern Illinois University, 1976. NDEA fellow, 1972. Office: Ill State Univ 410 Hovey Hall Normal IL 61790 Office Phone: 309-438-7018. E-mail: jwpresl@ilstu.edu.

**PRESLEY, LISA MARIE,** singer; b. Memphis, Tenn., Feb. 1, 1968; d. Elvis and Priscilla Presley; m. Danny Keough, Oct. 3, 1988 (div. 1994); children: Danielle Riley Keough, Benjamin Storm Keough; m. Michael Jackson, May 18, 1994 (div. Jan. 18, 1996); m. Nicholas Cage, Aug. 10, 2002 (div. May 16, 2004); m. Michael Lockwood, Jan. 22, 2006. Mgmt. Michael Presley Trust; owner, chmn. bd. the Elvis Presley Enterprises, Inc.; co-owner with mother Priscilla Elvis Presley's Memphis nightclub, operated by Paisley Estate, 1997—2003. Singer: (albums) To Whom It May Concern, 2003 (cert. Gold), Lights Out, 2003, Now What, 2005; actor: (music video) You Are Not Alone, Michael Jackson, (car commercial), 1989; appeared on (cover of Vogue mag.), 1996, (cover of Vogue mag. with mother and daughter), 2004, featured in (TV) Elvis by the Presleys, 2005. Internat. spokesperson Citizens Commn. on Human Rights; co-founder (with Isaac Hayes) LEAP (Literacy, Edn., and Ability Program); involved with Fight for Kids. Office: Elvis Presley Enterprises Inc PO Box 16508 3734 Elvis Presley Blvd Memphis TN 38186-0508*

**PRESLEY, PRISCILLA (PRICILLA ANN WAGNER, PRISCILLA BEAULIEU PRESLEY),** actress; b. Bklyn., May 24, 1945; m. Elvis Presley, 1967 (div. 1973); 1 child, Lisa Marie; 1 child (with Marco Garibaldi), Navarone. Studied with Milton Katselas; student, Steven Peck Theatre Art Sch., Chuck Norris Karate Sch.; HHD (hon.), Rhodes Coll., Memphis, 1998. Co-owner Bis and Beau Boutique, 1973—76; co-executor, pres. Elvis Presley Enterprise, Inc. (acquired by CKX, Inc.), Memphis, 1979—2005, founder, 1980—2005, exec. chmn. bd.; bd. dir. CKX, Inc., Las Vegas, Nev., 2005—. Launched & developed internat. fragrance line, 1988—, Moments, 1990, Experiences, 1994, Indian Summer, 1996; designer of jewelry line; launched website, 2005—; bd. dir. Metro-Goldwyn-Mayer Inc., 2000—; lectr. SMART TALK. Appearances include (films) The Naked Gun: From the Files of Police Squad!, 1988, The Adventures of Ford Fairlaine, 1990, The Naked Gun 2 1/2, 1991, The Naked Gun 33 1/3: The Final Insult, 1994, (TV series) Those Amazing Animals, 1980-81, Dallas, 1983-88, Melrose Place, 1996, (TV movies) Love Is Forever, 1983, Breakfast With Einstein, 1998 (also exec. prodr.), Hayley Wagner, Star, 1999, After Dallas, 2002; exec. prodr. (TV movie) Elvis and Me, 1988, The Road to Graceland, 1998, Finding Graceland, 1998; co-prodr.(TV mini series) Elvis, 1990; host, Elvis: The Great Performances, 1992; featured in (TV) Elvis 85, 1984, Elvis: Life and Times, 1997, After Dallas, 2002, Elvis by the Presleys, 2005, (TV mini series) Between the Lines, 2004; guest appearances include The Fall Guy, 1983, Tales from the Crypt, 1993, Touched by an Angel, 1997, Spin City, 1999, After They Were Famous, 2002, Oprah Winfrey Show, 2005; author: Elvis and Me, 1987. Amb. Dream Found., 2000—; mem. Citizen's Commn. on Human Rights. Named one of 50 Most Beautiful People in the World, People Mag., 1992. Office: Paul Bloch & Michelle Bega c/o Rogers & Cowan 8687 Melrose Ave 7th Fl West Hollywood CA 90069 Address: Norman Brokaw c/o William Morris Agency 151 El Camino Beverly Hills CA 90212 Office Phone: 310-850-4206, 310-854-8100.

**PRESNIAKOV, ALEXANDER,** artist, sculptor, inventor, writer; b. San Francisco, June 28, 1963; s. Alexander Alexandervich and Nina (Hanova) P. Student, Acad. of Art Coll., San Francisco, 1979-82. Curator Gen. Svcs. Adminstrn., Washington, 1983; artist Washington, 1984-85, San Francisco, 1986—. Songwriter Hilltop Records, L.A., 1996—, Amerecord, L.A., 1996—, Premier Melodies, N.Y.C. Commd. to paint life-size portraits of Prince Charles, Princess Diana, Miss Dame Barbara Cartland, Amb. Gerald Posner Carmen, presdl. candidates for 1985 Polit. Conservative Action Conf., Sheraton Hotel, Washington, Pres. Ronald Reagan, San Francisco mayor Willie Brown; series Women in Love Cycle, 1986—; author: Eagle's Nest, 2001, Lords of Death, 2005, 8 others; screenwriter. Recipient Literary Excellence award Iliad Press, 1995; named Prof. and Corr. Academician Dept. Arts Accademia Internazionale, Italy. Mem. Internat. Soc. Poets (disting. mem., Hall of Fame 1997-98), Legion of Honor Mus., De Young Mus., Gallery Marabella (hon.). Republican. Russian Orthodox. Achievements include invention of Manshield Deflector; artistic ideal ultrafictionilization used in all U.S. govt. agencies. Avocations: tennis, golf, equestrian. Home: 499 Thirty-third Ave Apt 206 San Francisco CA 94121 Office Phone: 415-595-8927. Personal E-mail: AlexanderPresniakov@gmail.com.

**PRESS, AIDA KABATZNICK,** retired editor, poet, writer; b. Boston, Nov. 18, 1926; m. Newton Press, June 5, 1947; children: David, Dina Press Weber, Benjamin Presskreischer. BA, Radcliffe Coll., 1948. Reporter Waltham (Mass.) News-Tribune, 1960-63; freelance writer, 1960-63; editl. cons. Mass. Dept. Mental Health, Boston, 1966-72; Waltham/Watertown reporter Boston Herald Traveler, 1963-70; dir. news and publs. Harvard Grad. Sch. Design, Cambridge, Mass., 1972-78; publs. editor Radcliffe Coll., Cambridge, 1978-81, dir., editor of publs., 1981-83, editor Radcliffe Quar., 1971-93; dir. pub. info., 1983-93; cons. editor Regis Coll. Alumnae Mag., Weston, Mass., 1994. Editor emerita Radcliffe Quar., 1993—; contbr. articles to newspapers and mags. Recipient Publs. Distinction award Am. Alumni Coun., 1974, Top 5 coll. Mag., Coun. for Advancement and Support of Edn., 1984, Top 10 Univ Mags., 1991, Gold medal Coll. Mags., 1991, Alumnae Achievement award Radcliffe Coll., 1994, Radcliffe Coll. Presdl. Commendation, 1992. Mem. Phi Beta Kappa. Avocations: hiking, playing recorder.

**PRESS, BARRY HARRIS JAY,** plastic surgeon; s. Robert Alfred and Phyllis Elaine (Rovner) P.; m. Cynthia Jane Witz, Aug. 11, 1973; children: Sarah Jane, Rachel Ann. BS in Microbiology with honors, U. Iowa, 1973, MD, 1977. Diplomate Am. Bd. Med. Examiners, Am. Bd. Surgery, Am. Bd. Plastic Surgery. Intern U. Minn. Hosps., 1977—78, resident otolaryngology, 1979—80, resident surgery, 1980—85; resident plastic surgery Med. Ctr. NYU, 1985—87; asst. prof. plastic surgery Stanford (Calif.) U. Sch. Medicine, 1987—94; assoc. chief plastic surgery, med. dir. Burn Ctr. Santa Clara Valley Med. Ctr., San Jose, Calif., 1987—95; assoc. prof. plastic surgery Stanford (Calif.) U. Sch. Medicine, 1994—95; surgeon, owner Plastic Surgeons Inst., Mountain View, Calif., 1995—99, Barry Press, M.D., San Jose, 1999—. Contbr. chapters to books, articles to profl. jours. Fellow ACS; mem. AMA, Am. Soc. Plastic and Reconstructive Surgeons, Am. Burn Assn., Calif. Med. Assn., Santa Clara County Med. Assn., Calif. Soc. of Plastic Surgeons, Am. Soc. for Surgery of the Hand, San Jose Surg. Soc. Office: Barry Press MD Ste A 2550 Samaritan Dr San Jose CA 95124-4104 Office Phone: 408-356-1148. Office Fax: 408-356-1140. Business E-mail: bpressmd@ix.netcom.com.

**PRESS, CHARLES,** retired political science professor; b. St. Louis, Sept. 12, 1922; s. Otto Ernst and Laura (Irion) P.; m. Nancy Miller, June 10, 1950; children: Edward Paul, William David, Thomas Leigh, Laura Mary. Student, Elmhurst Coll., Ill.; B of Journalism, U. Mo., 1948; MA, U. Minn., 1951, PhD, 1953. Faculty N.D. Agrl. Coll., 1954-56; dir. Grand Rapids Area Study, 1956-57; with Bur. Govt., U. Wis., 1957-58; faculty Mich. State U., East Lansing, 1958-91, prof. polit. sci., 1964-91; emeritus, 1991—; chmn. dept. Mich. State U., 1966-73. Cons. Mich. Constl. Conv., 1962-63; supr. Ingham County, 1966-72; tchr. summers, London; U. N.S.W., Sydney, Mich. State U. Author: Main Street Politics, 1962, (with Charles Adrian) The American Government Process, 1965, Governing Urban America, 1968, 5th edit., 1977, American Politics Reappraised, 1974, (with Kenneth VerBurg) States and Community Governments in a Federal System, 1979, 3d edit., 1991, American Policy Studies, 1981, The Political Cartoon, 1982, (with others) Michigan Political Atlas 1984, (with Kenneth VerBurg) American Politicians and Journalists, 1988, (with Kenneth VerBurg) Looking Over Sir Arthur's Shoulder, How Doyle Turned the Trick, 2004, (weekly newspaper column) The Pros and Cons of Politics. Sec. Ingham County Bd. Health, 1983-93; chmn., mem. East Lansing Bd. Rev., 1966-86; bd. dirs. Urban League, 1971-73; mem. East Lansing Housing and Urban Devel. Commn., 1988-93. Served with AUS, 1943-45. Recipient Disting. Prof. award Mich. State U., 1980, Alumni Merit award Elmhurst (Ill.) Coll., 1995. Mem. Am. Polit. Sci. Assn., Midwest Polit. Sci. Assn. (pres. 1974-75), So. Polit. Sci. Assn., Mich. Conf. Polit. Scientists (pres. 1972-73), Nat. Municipal League, B.S.I. Home: 987 Lantern Hill Dr East Lansing MI 48823-2831 Personal E-mail: pressc@msu.edu.

**PRESS, FRANK,** geophysicist; b. Bklyn., Dec. 4, 1924; s. Solomon and Dora (Steinholz) Press; m. Billie Kallick, June 9, 1946; children: William Henry, Paula Evelyn. BS, CCNY, 1944, LLD (hon.), 1972; MA, Columbia U., 1946, PhD, 1949; DSc (hon.), 28 univs. Rsch. assoc. Columbia U., 1946—49, instr. geology, 1949—51, asst. prof. geology, 1951—52, assoc. prof., 1952—55; prof. geophysics Calif. Inst. Tech., 1955—65, dir. seismol. lab., 1957—65; prof. geophysics, chmn. dept. earth and planetary scis. MIT, Cambridge, 1965—77, inst. prof., 1981—93; sci. advisor to pres., dir. Office Sci. and Tech. Policy, Washington, 1977—81; pres. NAS, 1981—93, pres. emeritus, 2000—; Cecil & Ida Green sr. fellow Carnegie Inst. of Washington, 1993—97; ptnr. Washington Adv. Group, 1996—. Mem. Pres.'s Sci. Adv. Com., 1961—64, Com. on Anticipated Advances in Sci. and Tech., 1974—76, Nat. Sci. Bd., 1970—76; mem. lunar and planetary missions bd. NASA; participant bilateral scis. agreement with Peoples Republic of China and USSR; mem. U.S. delegation to Nuc. Test Ban Negotiations, Geneva and Moscow; prof. emeritus MIT, 2000—. Author (with M. Ewing, W.s. Jardetsky): Propagation of Elastic Waves in Layered Media, 1957; author: (with R. Siever) Earth, 1986; author: Understanding Earth, 2003; author: (contbr.) articles to over 160 publs. Decorated cross of Merit Germany, Legion of Honor France; named Sherman Fairchild Disting. scholar, Calif. Inst. Tech., 1994, A.D. White prof., Cornell U.; recipient Columbia medal Excellence, 1960, Pub. Svc. award, U.S. Dept. Interior, 1972, Gold medal, Royal Astron. Soc., 1972, Pub. Svc. medal, NASA, 1973, Japan prize, Sci. and Tech. Found. Japan, 1993, Pupin medal, Columbia U., 1993, Nat. medal of Sci., Pres. U.S., 1994, Philip Hauge Abelson prize, AAAS, 1995, Lomonosov Gold medal, Russian Acad. Sci., 1998. Mem.: NAS, Engring. Acad. Japan (fgn. assoc.), Acad.Scis. Russia (fgn. mem.), Royal Soc. U.K., French Acad. Scis., Am. Philos. Soc., Seismol. Soc. Am. (pres. 1963), Soc. Exploration Geophysicists,

Am. Geophys. Union, Geol. Soc. Am. (councilor), Am. Acad. Arts and Scis. Office: Ste 616 South 2500 Virginia Ave Washington DC 20037-1901 Office Phone: 202-682-0164. Business E-mail: fpress@nas.edu.

**PRESS, FRED,** artist; b. Boston, Oct. 14, 1919; s. Samuel and Rose Press; m. Alice Bernadette, Nov. 4, 1942; children: David, Peter, Christopher. Student, Vesper George Sch. Art, Boston, 1938-39. Founder, chief designer sculpture collection Contemporary Arts, Inc., Boston, 1937-62; tchr. Vesper George Sch. Art, Boston, 1945—50; chief designer, exec. v.p. sales agy. N.Y.C., 1951—70; freelance in design field, 1970—85. Mem. Mass. Art Commn. One-man shows include Stuart Art Gallery, Boston, 1947, Jaffrey Civic Ctr., 1989, Granary Gallery, Martha's Vineyard, Mass., 1990, exhibited in group shows at NAD, N.Y.C., Delgado Mus. Art, New Orleans, Springfield Art League, Mass., Pan Am. Soc., Boston, Conn. Acad. Fine Arts, Allied Artists, N.Y., Vose Galleries, Boston, Boston Mus. Fine Arts, Silvermine Guild Artists, Conn., Mus. Contemporary Art, Boston, Ky. Derby Mus., Nat. Art League, Olin Art Ctr., Hoyt Inst. Fine Arts, Sharon Arts Ctr., Represented in permanent collections Worcester (Mass.) Art Mus., prin. works include 2 Bronze Reliefs, U.S. Navy Meml., Washington, individual pvt. collections; featured in Am. Artist Mag., Christian Sci. Monitor, Dance Mag.; author: (book) Sculpture at Your Fingertips, 1961; mng. editor: Ofcl. 6th Air Force Mag., 1944—45. Tech. sgt. USAF, 1942—45. Recipient ann. awards for soap sculpture, Proctor and Gamble Co., 1936—39, 1st prize for Slave sculpture, Delgado Mus. Art, 1946; scholar, HS Commerce. Home: 262 Hadley Rd Jaffrey NH 03452

**PRESS, JAMES E.,** automotive executive; b. Calif., Oct. 4, 1946; m. Linda Press; 1 children. BA in Bus. Adminstrn., Kans. State U., 1968. With Ford Motor Co., 1968—70; joined Toyota Motor Corp., Torrance, Calif., 1970; exec. v.p. Toyota Motor Sales, U.S.A., Inc., 1999—2005, COO, 1999—2005, pres., 2005—; mng. officer Toyota Motor Corp., 2003—, pres. Toyota North Am., 2006—. Avocations: boating, motorcycling, auto racing, skiing, scuba diving. Office: Toyota North America 9 W 57th St Ste 4900 New York NY 10019*

**PRESS, RON,** marketing professional; b. Framingham, Mass., June 18, 1965; s. Sylvia Press; m. Nina Opperman, Dec. 1, 2004; 1 child, Makaela. BSEE, U. Mass., Amherst, 1987. Lead engr., mgr. Raytheon Co., Marlboro, Mass., 1984—95, Harris RF Comm., Rochester, NY, 1995—97; tech. mktg. mgr. Mentor Graphics Corp, Wilsonville, Oreg., 1997—. Mem. steering com. Internat. Test Conf., 2006; tech. cons. Am. Soc. Test Engrs., 2000. Recipient Inventor's award, Raytheon Co., 1993. Achievements include patents for glitch free selection of a clock from multiple asynchronous clocks; patents pending for reduced pin count testing. Home: 10720 SW Willow St Tualatin OR 97062 Office: Mentor Graphics Corp 8005 SW Boeckman Rd Wilsonville OR 97070 Office Phone: 503-685-7954. Business E-Mail: ron_press@mentor.com.

**PRESS, TERRY,** marketing executive; children: Gracie, Ethan. Head mktg. DreamWorks SKG. Faculty mem. UCLA Film Sch. Named one of most powerful women in entertainment, Hollywood Reporter, 2005. Office: DreamWorks SKG 100 Universal City Plz # 5121 Universal City CA 91608*

**PRESS, WILLIAM HENRY,** physicist, computer scientist; b. NYC, May 23, 1948; s. Frank and Billie (Kallick) P.; m. Margaret Ann Lauritsen, 1969 (div. 1982); 1 dau., Sara Linda; m. Jeffrey Foden Howell, Apr. 19, 1991; 1 son, James Howell. AB, Harvard Coll., 1969; MS, Calif. Inst. Tech., 1971, PhD, 1972. Asst. prof. theoretical physics Calif. Inst. Tech., 1973-74; asst. prof. physics Princeton (N.J.) U., 1974-76; prof. astronomy and physics Harvard U., Cambridge, Mass., 1976-98, chmn. dept. astronomy, 1982-85; dep. lab. dir. Los Alamos Nat. Lab., 1998—2004, sr. fellow, 2004—. Mem. numerous adv. coms. and panels NSF, NASA, NAS, NRC; vis. mem. Inst. Advanced Study, 1983-94; mem. Def. Sci. Bd., 1985-89, sci. adv. com. Packard Found., 1988—; program com. Sloan Found., 1985-91; chmn. adv. bd. NSF Inst. Theoretical Physics, 1986-87; mem. Computer Sci. and Telecomm. Bd., 1991-96; U.S. del. IUPAP Gen. Assembly, 1996; cons. MITRE Corp., 1977—; trustee Inst. Def. Analysis, 1988—, exec. com., 1990—; chief naval ops. Exec. Panel, 1994-2000. Author: Numerical Recipes, 1986; contbr. articles to profl. jours. Sloan Found. research fellow, 1974-78 Fellow: Am. Phys. Soc., Am. Acad. Arts and Scis.; mem.: NAS, Coun. on Fgn. Rels., Assn. for Computing Machinery, Internat. Soc. Relativity and Gravitation, Internat. Astron. Union, Am. Astron. Soc. (Helen B. Warner prize 1981). Office: Los Alamos Nat Lab MS F 600 Los Alamos NM 87545-0001

**PRESSER, HARRIET BETTY,** social studies educator; b. Bklyn., Aug. 29, 1936; d. Phillip Rubinoff and Rose (Gudowitz) Jabish; m. Neil Nathan Presser, Dec. 16, 1956 (div.); 1 child, Sheryl Lynn. BA, George Washington U., 1959; MA, U. N.C., 1962; PhD, U. Calif., Berkeley, 1969. Statistician Bur. Census, Washington, 1959; research assoc. Inst. Life Ins., N.Y.C., 1962-64; lectr. demography U. Sussex, Brighton, England, 1967-68; staff assoc. Population Council, N.Y.C., 1968-69; asst. prof. sociomed. scis. Columbia U., N.Y.C., 1969-73, assoc. prof. sociomed. scis., 1973-76; prof. sociology U. Md., College Park, 1976—99, dir. Ctr. on Population, Gender, and Social Inequality, 1988—2001, disting. faculty rsch. fellow, 1993-94, disting. univ. prof., 1999—; fellow in residence Netherlands Inst. for Advanced Study in Humanities & Social Sci., Wassenaar, The Netherlands, 1994-95. Fellow-in-residence Ctr. for Advanced Study in the Behavioral Scis., Stanford, Calif., 1986-87, 91-92, 2003-04; scholar-in-residence Russell Sage Found., NYC, 1998, 99, 2000; resident scholar Bellagio Study and Conf. Ctr., Rockefeller Found., 2000; acad. visitor Gender Inst. London Sch. Econs and Polit. Scis., 2000. Editl. bd. Time and Soc., 1991-95, Social Forces, 1981-87, Signs, 1975-85, Applied Population and Policy, 2002-, Rose Monograph Series, 2003-05, Jour. of Marriage and the Family, 2002; assoc. editor Jour. Health and Social Behavior, 1975-78; co-editor (with Gita Sen) Women's Empowerment and Demographic Processes: Moving Beyond Cairo, 2000; author: Working in a 24/7 Economy: Challenges for Am. Families, 2003; editor: Population Studies and Demographic Change, Transaction Pubs., 2005-. Nat. Inst. for Child Health and Devel. grantee, 1972-78, 83-88, Population Coun. grantee, 1976-79, NSF grantee, 1982-83, 90-94, 2000-03, Rockefeller Found. grantee, 1983-85, 88-94, William and Flora Hewlett Found. grantee, 1989—, Andrew W. Mellon Found. grantee, 1994-95, W. T. Grant Found., 1996-99, Russell Sage Found., 1976-79, 2003-04; recipient Rosabeth Moss Kanter award for excellence in work-family rsch., 2001, Lawrence R. Klein award, 2003. Fellow AAAS, Sociol. Rsch. Assn.; mem. APHA (coun. mem. population sect. 1976-79), Population Assn. Am. (bd. dirs. 1972-75, 2nd v.p. 1983, 1st v.p. 1985, pres.-elect 1988, pres. 1989), Am. Sociol. Assn. (coun. mem. at large 1990-93, chmn., coun. mem. population sect. 1978-83). Office: U Maryland Dept Sociology College Park MD 20742-0001

**PRESSER, STANLEY,** social sciences educator, researcher; b. Bklyn., Feb. 18, 1950; s. Sidney and Sydonia (Cohen) P.; m. Yan Yu; 1 child, Solomon Zhi-Qian. AB, Brown U., 1971; PhD, U. Mich., 1977. Rsch. investigator Survey Rsch. Ctr., U. Mich., 1977-78, head field office, 1981-83; rsch. assoc. Inst. Rsch. Social Sci., U. N.C., 1978-81; dir. Detroit Area Study, U. Mich., 1983-85; assoc. dir. sociology program NSF, 1985-87, dir., 1987-88; prof. sociology U. Md., 1989—; dir. Survey Rsch. Ctr., 1989-2000. Vis. prof. sociology U. Md., 1988-89; dir. Joint U. Md. and U. Mich. program in Survey Methodology, 1992-96; bd. overseers Nat. Opinion Rsch. Ctr. Gen. Social Survey, 1984-85, 93-97; spl. cons. Nat. Econ Rsch. Assocs., 1986-89; cons. U.S. Dept. Justice, 1995, Dept. Commerce, 1991, GAO, 1988-89, EEO Commn., 1985, NOAA, 1991-94, State of Alaska Atty. Gen., 1989-92. Co-author: Questions and Answers in Attitude surveys, 1981, Survey Questions: Handcrafting the Standardized Questionaire, 1986, Valuing Oil Spill Prevention, 2004; editor Pub. Opinion Quar., 1993-97; co-editor: Sourcebook of Harris National Surveys, 1981, Survey Rsch. Methods, 1989, Methods for Testing and Evaluating Survey Questions, 2004; mem. editl. bd. Pub. Opinion Quar., 1983-87, Sociol. Methods and Rsch., 1980-83, Social Psychology Quar., 1979-82; contbr. articles to profl. jours. Fellow: Am. Statis. Assn.;

mem.: Social Rsch. Assn., Am. Sociol. Assn. (chair profl. ethics com. 1999—2001), Am. Assn. Pub. Opinion Rsch. (pres. 1993—94). Office: U of Md Sociology Dept College Park MD 20742-1315

**PRESSER, STEPHEN BRUCE,** lawyer, educator; b. Chattanooga, Aug. 10, 1946; s. Sidney and Estelle (Shapiro) P.; m. Carole Smith, June 18, 1968 (div. 1987); children: David Carter, Elisabeth Catherine; m. ArLynn Leiber, Dec. 13, 1987; children: Joseph Leiber, Eastman Leiber. AB, Harvard U., 1968, JD, 1971. Bar: Mass. 1971, DC 1972. Law clk. to Judge Malcolm Richard Wilkey U.S. Ct. Appeals (D.C. cir.), 1971-72; assoc. Wilmer, Cutler & Pickering, Washington, 1972-74; asst. prof. law Rutgers U., Camden, NJ, 1974-76; vis. assoc. prof. U. Va., 1976-77; prof. Northwestern U., Chgo., 1977—, class 1940 rsch. prof., 1992-93, Raoul Berger prof. legal history, 1992—, assoc. dean acad. affairs Sch. Law, 1982-85. Prof. bus. law Kellogg Sch. Mgmt., Northwestern U., Chgo., 1992—. Author: (with Jamil S. Zainaldin) Law and Jurisprudence in American History, 1980, 6th edit., 2006, Studies in the History of the United States Courts of the Third Circuit, 1982, The Original Misunderstanding: The English, The Americans and the Dialectic of Federalist Jurisprudence, 1991, Piercing the Corporate Veil, 1991, revised ann., (with Ralph Ferrara and Meredith Brown) Takeovers: A Strategist's Manual, 2d edit., 1993, Recapturing the Constitution, 1994, (with Douglas W. Kmiec, John Eastman and Raymond Marcin) The American Constitutional Order: History, Cases, and Philosophy, 1998, 2d edit., 2004, An Introduction to the Law of Business Organizations, 2005; assoc. articles editor Guide to American Law, 1985. Trustee Village Winnetka, Ill., 2000-04, police and fire commr., 2004-; mem. acad. adv. bd. Washington Legal Found. Recipient summer stipend NEH, 1975; Fulbright Sr. scholar Univ. Coll., London Sch. Econs. and Polit. Sci., 1983-84, Inst. Advanced Legal Studics, 1996. Adams fellow Inst. U.S. Studies, London, 1996; assoc. rsch. fellow Inst. U.S. Studies, 1999—. Mem. Am. Soc. Legal History (bd. dirs. 1979-82), Am. Law Inst., Univ. Club Chgo. (bd. dirs. 1997-99, sec. 1999), Legal Club Chgo., Reform Club (London), Mich. Shores Club (Wilmette). Office: Northwestern U Law Sch 357 E Chicago Ave Chicago IL 60611-3069 E-mail: s-presser@law.northwestern.edu.

**PRESSLER, LARRY,** former senator, lawyer; b. Humboldt, S.D., Mar. 29, 1942; s. Antoine Lewis and Loretta Geneive (Claussen) P.; m. Harriet Dent, 1982; 1 child, Laura. BA, U. S.D., 1964; diploma (Rhodes scholar), Oxford U., Eng., 1965; MA in Govt., Harvard U., 1971, JD, 1971. Bar: N.Y., D.C. Mem. 94th-95th Congresses from 1st S.D. Dist., 1974-78, U.S. Senate from S.D., 1979-97; pres. Pressler and Assocs., U.S. del. Inter-Parliamentary Union for 97th Congress; mem. bd. visitors all mil. svc. academies; chmn. commerce, sci. and transp. coms. U.S. Senate, 1995-96; founder telecomm. group Pressler & Assocs., Washington, 1997—. Prin. sponsor Telecomm. Act of 1996, Pressler Telecomm. Act; mem. fgn. rels. com., 1980-95; congl. del. to UN Gen. Assembly, 1986, 92; former bus. cons. McKinsey & Co.; former atty. U.S. State Dept. Legal Advisor's Office; sr. fellow U. Calif., L.A., 2000—; vis. prof. Fudan U., Shanghai, 2005; lectr. Am. govt. U.S. Naval Acad., 2005. Author: U.S. Senators from the Prairie, 1982, Star Wars: The SDI Debates in Congress, 1986. 1st lt. U.S. Army, 1966-68, Vietnam. Mem. Am Assn. Rhodes Scholars, D.C. Bar Assn., N.Y. State Bar Assn., VFW, ABA, Century Club (N.Y.), Met. Club (Washington), St. Albans Tennis Club, Bohemian Club Calif., Cosmos Club, 25th Infantry Divsn. Assn., Phi Beta Kappa. Avocations: golf, tennis, rowing. Office Phone: 202-333-5856.

**PRESSLER, PAUL S.,** retail executive; b. 1956; m. Mindy Pressler; 2 children. BS in Bus. Economics, SUNY, Oneonta. V.p. mktg. and design Kenner-Parker Toys; v.p. mktg. & design Walt Disney Co., 1987—90, sr. v.p. licensing, 1990—92, sr. v.p. consumer products, 1992—94, exec. v.p., gen. mgr. Disneyland Parks & Hotels, 1994—98, pres. Walt Disney Parks and Resorts, 1998—2002; pres., CEO Gap, Inc., 2002—. Dir. Avon Products Inc. Adv. bd. Children Affected by AIDS Found.; bd. dirs. Resources Children with Spl. Needs, Big Bros. Big Sisters Greater LA, Disney GOALS, Anaheim, Calif. Office: Gap Inc 2 Folsom St San Francisco CA 94105*

**PRESSLEY, DELORIS N.,** literacy educator; b. Nesmith, S.C., Aug. 14, 1950; d. Murray Vanderbilt Nesmith, Sr. and Blanche Lamar Nesmith; m. Booker Theodore Pressley, Mar. 5, 1976; children: Malcolm L., Marquis B. B in Elem. Edn., Allen U., 1972; MEd, U. S.C., 1976; postgrad., U. S.C., Francis Marion U., 1995. Cert. elem. edn. Part-time curriculum and instrn. facilitator Battery Park Elem. Sch., Nesmith, 2003—04, literacy coach, 2004—05, elem. edn. tchr., 2005. Chairperson Williamsburg County Sch. Dist. Tchr. Forum, Kingstree, SC, 2000—02; rep. Pee Dee Edn. Tchr. Forum, Florence, SC, 2000—02. Named Tchr. of Yr., Battery Pk. Elem. Sch., 1986, 2000, Williamsburg County Dist. Tchr. of Yr., 2000; recipient mini grant, Pee Dee Edn. Found., 1990, 1994; grantee, Ednl. Improvement Act, 1999. Mem.: NEA, S.C. Internat. Reading Assn., Nat. Coun. Tchrs. English, Internat. Reading Assn. Democrat. United Methodist. Avocations: reading, gardening. Home: 721 Nesmith Corner Rd Nesmith SC 29580 Office Phone: 843-558-5233.

**PRESSLEY, FRED G., JR.,** lawyer; b. N.Y.C., June 19, 1953; s. Fred G. Sr. and Frances (Sanders) P.; m. Cynthia Denise Hill, Sept. 5, 1981. BA cum laude, Union Coll., 1975; JD, Northwestern U., 1978. Bar: Ohio 1978, U.S. Dist. Ct. (so. dist.) Ohio 1979, U.S. Dist. Ct. (no. dist.) Ohio 1989, U.S. Dist. Ct. (ea. dist.) Wis. 1980, U.S. Ct. Appeals (6th cir.). Assoc. Porter, Wright, Morris & Arthur, Columbus, Ohio, 1978-85, ptnr., 1985—. Bd. dirs. Columbus Area Leadership Program, 1981-84, Franklin County Bd. Mental Retardation and Devel. Disabilities, Columbus, 1989-97, Union Coll., Schenectady, N.Y., 1992—. Recipient Civic Achievement award Ohio Ho. of Reps., 1988. Mem. ABA. Avocations: jogging, golf, basketball, history. Office: Porter Wright Morris & Arthur 41 S High St Ste 2800 Columbus OH 43215 6101

**PRESSLY, THOMAS JAMES,** history professor; b. Troy, Tenn., Jan. 18, 1919; s. James Wallace and Martha Belle (Bittick) P.; m. Lillian Cameron, Apr. 30, 1943; children: Thomas James II, Stephanie Suzuki. AB, Harvard U., 1940, AM, 1941, PhD, 1950; LLD (hon.), Whitman Coll., 1981. Instr. history Princeton (NJ) U., 1946-49; asst. prof. U. Wash., 1949-54, assoc. prof., 1954-60, prof., 1960-87, prof. emeritus, 1987—. Vis. assoc. prof. Princeton U., 1953-54, Johns Hopkins U., 1969-70. Author: Americans Interpret Their Civil War, 1954; editor: (with W.H. Scofield) Farm Real Estate Values in the United States, 1965, (with others) American Political Behavior, 1974, Diary of George Templeton Strong (abridged), 1988, (with Glenn M. Linden) Voices From the House Divided, 1995, (with Maclyn P. Burg) The Great War at Home and Abroad, 1999. With U.S. Army, 1941—45. Ford Found. Faculty fellow, 1951-52; Ctr. for Advanced Study in Behavioral Scis. fellow, 1955-56. Mem. Am. Hist. Assn., So. Hist. Assn. (editl. bd. Jour. So. History 1957), Orgn. Am. Historians. Home and Office: 4545 E Laurel Dr NE Seattle WA 98105-3838 Office Phone: 206-543-5790.

**PRESSMAN, ANDY,** architecture educator; BArch, Rensselaer Poly. Inst.; M in Design Studies, Harvard U. Registered arch., N.Y., 1983, Ill., 1987, N.J., 1989, N.Mex., 1996, Maine, 1997, Nat. Coun. Archtl. Registration Bds. 1983. With Norman Rosenfeld, FAIA, Archs., 1983—; prin. Andrew Pressman, FAIA, Archs., 1983—. Adj. asst. prof. U. Wis.-Milw. Sch. Arch. and Urban Planning, 1987—91; asst.-in-instrn. Harvard U. Grad. Sch. Design, 1993—94; with U. N.Mex. Sch. Arch. and Planning, Albuquerque, 1995—, assoc. prof., 1998—2003, prof., 2003—, dir. arch. program, 2000—. Author: Architecture 101: A Guide to the Design Studio, 1993, 2000, 2003, The Fountainheadache: The Politics of Architect-Client Relations, 1995, Professional Practice 101: A Compendium of Business and Management Strategies in Architecture, 1997, Architectural Design Portable Handbook: A Guide to Excellent Practices, 2001, 2002. Nominee Outstanding Tchr. of Yr. award, U. N.Mex. Enhancement Com. on Awards and Fellowships, 1997; recipient First Pl. award Internat. Housing Design Competition, Bldg. Ctr. Japan and Misawa Homes, Tokyo, 1982, citation Evanston 2063 Design Competition, Evanston Art Ctr., 1983, Gen. Libr. Recognition award, U. N.Mex., 1997, Disting. Svc. award, N.Mex./AIA, 1997, Alumni Assn. Faculty award, U. N.Mex., 1998, Svc. award, Assn. Collegiate Schs. Arch., 1999, Dean's award for excellence in rsch. and creative work, U. N.Mex., 1997. Fellow: AIA (bd. dirs. Albuquerque chpt. 2000—, award for outstanding support and contbns. Albuquerque chpt. 1996). Office: Univ NMex Sch Arch and Planning 2414 Central Ave SE Albuquerque NM 87131

**PRESSMAN, JACOB,** retired rabbi; b. Phila., Oct. 26, 1919; s. Solomon David and Dora (Levin) P.; m. Marjorie Steinberg, June 14, 1942; children: Daniel David, Joel David, Judith Sharon. BA, U. Pa., 1940; MHL, Jewish Theol. Sem., 1944, Dr.Hebrew Letters, 1960, Dr. Humane Letters, 1979. Ordained rabbi, 1945. Rabbi Forest Hills Jewish Ctr., N.Y.C., 1944-46, Congregation Sinai, L.A., 1946-50, Temple Beth Am, L.A., 1950—85; ret. Dir. Bonds of Israel, L.A., 1988-90, city chmn., 1990-91; vice chmn. bd. govs. L.A. Jewish Fedn. Coun., 1988—; founder U. Judaism, L.A. Hebrew High Sch., Herzl Sch., Camp Ramah at Ojai, Akiba Acad., Rabbi Jacob Pressman Acad. Author: Dear Friends, 2001, This Wild and Crazy World, 2001. Recipient Simon Greenberg award for Outstanding Achievement in Rabbinate, Ziegler Sch. Rabbinic Studies, U. Judaism, L.A., 2004. Mem. Rabbinical Assembly Western Region (pres. 1954-56), Bd. Rabbis So. Calif. (pres. 1958-61). Office Phone: 310-652-7353. E-mail: jpress6511@aol.com. *God is. God is good. His creation is good, and so, mankind, being of His creation is good. As an act of grace, God gives man the power to choose between good and evil in his ways, and with even greater grace gives man the awareness that he has this choice. Man is perfectible. His perfect stage, the Messianic era, is coming; but it will always be coming, never at a moment in time to arrive, but always inviting us to progress to newer and higher goals personally and as a society, each new mountaintop of human progress toward that nobler future merely opens our eyes to visions of even greater and more God-like human life.*

**PRESSMAN, RONALD R.,** utilities executive; b. NYC, Apr. 11, 1958; m. Mary Pressman; 3 children. Grad., Hamilton College, NY, 1980. Gen. mgr. ctr. and ea. Europe GE, London, 1990—92; CEO GE Power Sys. Europe, 1992—95, CEO Power Sys. global mktg., 1995—96; pres., CEO GE Capital Real Estate, 1997; sr. v.p. GE Co., 2000—; pres., CEO G.E. Employers Reinsurance Co., 2000—. Bd. dirs. A Better Chance, Kansas City Civic Coun.; mem. exec. bd. Nat. Realty Com., Wharton Real Estate Bus. Sch. Recipient Crown American Golden Crown award, 1998, Fin. Svcs. Exec. of Yr., Comml. Property News. Office: GE Employers Reinsurance Co PO Box 2991 Shawnee Mission KS 66201-1391

**PRESTAGE, JAMES JORDAN,** university chancellor; b. Deweyville, Tex., Apr. 29, 1926; s. James J. and Mona (Wilkins) P.; m. Jewel Limar, Aug. 12, 1953; children— Terri, James Grady, Eric, Karen, Jay BS cum laude, So. U., Baton Rouge, 1950; MS, U. Iowa, 1955, PhD, 1959. Instr. biology Prairie View Coll., Tex., 1955-56; asst. prof. So. U., Baton Rouge, 1959, assoc. prof. biology, 1959-61, prof. biology, 1961—, dir. computer sci. ctr., 1968-71, 72-73, dean acad. affairs, v.p. acad. affairs, 1973-81, exec. v.p., 1981-82, chancellor, 1982-85, univ. disting. prof. emeritus 1985—; univ. disting. prof. biology Dillard U., New Orleans, 1987—. Chair divsn. natural scis. Dillard U., 1990—97; asst. dir. La. Coordinating Council for Higher Edn., Baton Rouge, 1971—72; mem. commn. on scholars Ill. Bd. Higher Edn., 1975—82; mem. com. on off-campus instrn. La. Bd. Regents, 1975—; mem. La. Data Processing Coun., Baton Rouge, 1979—82; vis. prof. biology Dillard U., New Orleans; trustee Am. Coll. Testing Program, 1983—86; faculty assoc. Danforth Found., 1966—70; cons. in field. Mem. exec. bd. Istrouma council Boy Scouts Am.; vice chmn. bd. trustees Greater Mt. Carmel Baptist Ch., Baton Rouge; bd. dirs. Capital Area United Way, Baton Rouge. Served with USN, 1944-46, 50-52; ETO, Korea Named Most Outstanding Faculty Mem. So. U., 1966-67; Nat. Med. Fellowships fellow U. Iowa, Iowa City, 1956-59; NIH grantee, 1960-65 Mem. Conf. Acad. Deans So. States. NAACP, Sigma Xi, Alpha Chi, Alpha Phi Alpha (chpt. pres.), Sigma Pi Phi Democrat. Avocations: fishing, reading, gardening. Home: 2145 77th Ave Baton Rouge LA 70807-5508 Office: So Br PO Box 9222 Baton Rouge LA 70813

**PRESTBO, JOHN ANDREW,** editor, writer, journalist; b. Northwood, N.D., Sept. 26, 1941; s. Oscar Bernt and Jeanne (Schol) P.; m. Darlene Parrish, Aug. 14, 1965; children: Bradford Jonathan, Laura Christine. BS, Northwestern U., 1963, MS, 1964. Reporter, writer Wall Street Jour., Chgo., 1964-74, staff editor, Page 1 N.Y.C., 1974-75, commodities editor, 1975-77, bur. chief Cleve., 1977-81, markets editor N.Y.C., 1984—, editor Dow Jones Indexes, 1993—; v.p. editorial Dow Jones Radio 2, Inc., Princeton, NJ, 1981-83; exec. dir. Dow Jones Indexes, Princeton, 2006—. Author: Sleuthing, 1976; co-author: (with Frederick C. Klein) News and the Market, 1974, (with Douglas R. Sease) Barron's Guide to Making Investment Decisions, 1994, 2nd edit., 1998, The Wall Street Jour. Book of Internat. Investing, 1997; editor: This Abundant Land, 1975, Dow Jones Commodities Handbook, 1976-79, The Dow Jones Guide to the World Stock Market, 1994-98, The Market's Measure, 1999, Dow Jones Indexes, 2006—. Served with USAFR, 1966-73. Recipient Econ. Reporting award Ind. Natural Gas Assn., U. Mo., 1967; recipient Achievement-bur. writing award G.M. Loeb, 1968 Home: 14 Charleston Dr Skillman NJ 08558-1801 Office: 4300 Rte 1 Monmouth Junction NJ 08852 Office Phone: 609-520-7079. Business E-Mail: john.prestbo@dowjones.com.

**PRESTIFILIPPO, JOHN,** air transportation executive; m. Debra Prestifilippo; 3 children. Student, U. Md., U. Calif., Stockton State U. Airframe and powerplant license. V.p. tech. svcs. and ops. Continental Express Airlines, 1986—2001; sr. v.p. maintenance US Airways Inc., Arlington, Va., 2002—. With USAF. Office: US Airways 2345 Crystal Dr Arlington VA 22227

**PRESTINE, JOAN SINGLETON,** writer, educator, editor; b. Salt Lake City, Mar. 11, 1944; d. Herbert William and Frances Bowdidge Singleton; m. Douglas C. Prestine, Apr. 5, 1963; children: Scott, Deb, Jeffrey. BA, Univ. So. Calif., L.A., 1965. Freelance editor Children's Picture Book, 1989—. Pub. cons., 1987—; lectr. Santa Monica Coll., Pierce Coll., West LA Coll., Ventura Coll., Coll. of Canyons, Moorpark Coll., Oxnard Coll., Learning Tree U., U. Colo., Denver U., 1987—. Author: (picture books My Special Feelings series) I Want This and This and This, 1987, Love Me Anyway, 1987, My Parents Go On a Trip, 1987, Someone Special Died, 1987, Me First, 1987, Sometimes I'm Afraid, 1987, Match Who You Are With What You Do, 1987, How to Write Picture Books for Fun and Profit, 1987, Chipper Chipmunk Cruises, 1989, (picture books Kids Have Feelings Too series) Someone Special Died, 1993, 2003, Sometimes I Feel Awful, 1993, 2003, It's Hard to Share My Teacher, 1994, 2003, Mom and Dad Break Up, 1996, 2003, Moving Is Hard, 1997, 2003, (resource guides) Family Day Care Activities from A to Z, 1989, Earthquake Preparedness, 1990, (Helping Children Understand Their Feeling series) Helping Children Cope with Death, 1993, Helping Children Understand Their Feelings, 1993, Helping Children Share Their Teacher, 1994, Helping Children Understand Divorce, 1996, Helping Children Cope With Moving, 1997, Easy Activities for Every Kid, 2001. With Jr. League LA, 1976—, St. Joseph Ctr. chair, 1991—, sustainer pres., 2004—; founder Investments Plus, 1983, pres., 1983—86, rec. sec., 1986—; benefactor Huntington Libr.; bd. mem. Parrots Internat., 2005—; mem. Boy Scouts Am., 1972—84, Girl Scouts Am., 1975—80, Peterson Automotive Mus., Nat. Charity League, Checkered Flag 200, 2003—, Pres. Cir. Orthop. Hosp., 2004—; life mem. 11-99 Found., 2002—. Named PTA Parent of Yr., Bellagio Rd. Sch., 1977, Parent of Yr., Parent Tchr. Student Assn., U. HS, 1983; recipient Parenting Shelf, Parents Choice Mag., 1994, 1996, Vol. Cir., St. Joseph Ctr., 1996, Dir.'s award, Early Childhood News, 1997, Carolyn Helman Lichtenberg Crest award, 2002. Mem.: FOCAL, Westside Writer's Guild, Pubs. Mktg. Assn., Soc. Children's Book Writers and Illustrators, So. Calif. Children's Book Writers and Illustrators, Internat. Reading Assn., Childrens Author Network, Book Publicists of So. Calif., Authors Guild, Nat. Assn. Edn. of Young Children (life), Pi Beta Phi (alumni bd., pres. 1996—99, program chair 1993—96, Carolyn Helman Lichtenberg Disting. Alumnae Achievement award 2002). Avocations: car rallies, reading, travel, walking. Office: 2070 South 7th Street, Suite E San Jose CA 95112 Personal E-mail: joanprestine@msn.com.

**PRESTON, ANDREW JOSEPH,** pharmacist, drug company executive; b. Bklyn., Apr. 19, 1922; s. Charles A. and Josephine (Rizzutto) Pumo; m. Martha Jeanne Happ, Oct. 10, 1953; children: Andrew Joseph Jr., Charles Richard, Carolyn Louise, Frank Arthur, Joanne Marie, Barbara Jeanne. BSc, St. John's U., 1943. Cert. bus. intermediary Internat. Bus. Brokers Assn. Mgr. Press Club, Bklyn. Nat. League Baseball Club, 1941-42; purchasing agt. Drug and Pharm. divsn. Intrassind, Inc., 1947; chief pharmacist Hendershot Pharmacy, Newton, NJ, 1949; agt. Bur. of Narcotics, U.S. Treasury Dept., 1948-49; owner Preston Drug & Surg. Co., Boonton, NJ, 1949-86; CEO Preston Pharmaceutics, Inc., Butler, NJ, 1970-80, Preston Bus. Cons., Inc., Kinnelon, NJ, 1987—. Commr. NJ State Bd. Pharmacy, 1970—72; pres., 1973; organizer State of NJ Drug Abuse Spkrs. Program, 1970—76; chmn. Morris County Drug Abuse Coun., 1969—70; lectr. drug abuse and narcotic addiction various cmty. orgns., 1968—78; mem. adv. bd. Nat. Cmty. Bank, Boonton, 1973. Contbr. editls. to profl. jours. Chmn. bldg. fund com. Riverside Hosp., Boonton, 1963; mem. exec. com. Gov. Tom Kean Ann. Ball, 1985—86; chmn. Pharmacists of NJ for election of Pres. Ford, 1976, Pharmacists for Gov. Tom Kean, 1981—84, NJ Pharmacists for Reagan/Bush, 1984; mem. exec. com. Morris County Overall Econ. Devel. Com., 1976—82; chmn. Pharmacists for Fenwick, 1982, v.p. Kinnelon (NJ) Rep. Club, 1980; Rep. com. Kinnelon, 1990; mem. adv. com. to Congressman Dean Gallo on Pres. Clinton's Health Security Plan, 1994; mem. Morris County (NJ) Rep. Fin. Com., 1972; pres. Ronald Reagan NJ Re-Election Adv. Bd., 1984. Lt. (j.g.) USNR, 1943—46. Recipient Bowl Hygeia award, Robbins Co., 1969, Pres.'s award, E.R. Squibb, 1968, Square Club award, NJ Pharm., 1969, Andrew J. Preston award for Polit. Action established in his honor, 1999, Spl. NJ Pharmacists award for loyal svc., NJ Pharm. Assn., NJ Polit. Action Com., 2002. Mem.: VFW, Morris-Sussex Pharmacists Soc., Morris County Pharm. Assn., NJ Pub. Health Assn., Pharmacists Guild NJ, Pharmacists Guild Am. (pres. NY divsn. 1946—47), Inst. Bus. Appraisers, Internat. Bus. Brokers Assn., NJ Narcotic Enforcement Officers Assn., Internat. Narcotic Enforcement Officers Assn., Nat. Cmty. Pharmacists Assn., NJ Pharm. Assn. (econs. com. 1960—65, pres. 1967—68, Oscar Singer Meml. award 1987, William H. McNeil award 1994, Presdl. Citation award 2000, Spl. NJ Pharmacists award 2002), Am. Pharm. Assn., St. John's Alumni Assn., NJ Assn. Realtors, Nat. Assn. Realtors, Morris County Bd. Realtors, Am. Legion, Smoke Rise Club, KC (4th Degree 2005), Elks. Roman Catholic. Home and Office: 507 Pepperidge Tree Ln Kinnelon NJ 07405-2223 Office Phone: 973-838-5342.

**PRESTON, CHARLES MICHAEL,** lawyer; b. Balt., Oct. 11, 1945; s. Carlton Edward and Jeannette Thorn (Baker) P.; m. Carol Ann Armacost, June 21, 1969 (div. Dec. 1978). BA, Western Md. Coll., 1967; JD, U. Balt., 1970. Bar: Md. 1970, U.S. Dist. Ct. Md. 1972, U.S. Supreme Ct. 1974, U.S. Dist. Ct. (trial bar) 1984. Law clk. to Hon. E.O. Weant, Jr., Westminster, Md., 1970-71; assoc. Hoffman & Hoffman, Westminster, 1972-75; ptnr. Hoffman, Hoffman & Preston, Westminster, 1976-77, Hoffman, Stoner & Preston, Westminster, 1978-79; ptnr., v.p. Stoner, Preston & Boswell Chartered, Westminster, 1980—. Rev. bd., panel mem. Atty. Grievance Commn., Annapolis, Md., 1978-95; mem. Md. Ct. Appeals Commn. on alternate dispute resolution, 1998-2000, adv. bd., Md. Mediation and Conflict Resolution Office (co-chair, Circuit Courts Com.), 2001-, Md. Ct. of Appeals Task Force on Professionalism, 2002-. Contbr. articles to profl. jours. Mem. Carroll County Gen. Hosp., Westminster, 1983—; trustee Raymond I. Richardson Found., Middleburg, Md., 1979-93; bd. dirs. Carroll County Agrl. Ctr., Westminster, 1975—; dir. N.W. dist. ARC, Balt., 1987-95; trustee Balt. Opera Co., 1998-2001. With U.S. Army, 1970-71. Fellow Md. Bar Found. (dir. 1998-, sec., treas. 2005-), Am. Bar Found.; mem. ABA (del. ho. of dels. 1997-00), Md. State Bar Assn. (treas. 1991-96, bd. govs. 1985-86, 91-00, pres.-elect 1997, pres. 98), Carroll County Bar Assn. (pres. 1985), Pro Bono Resource Ctr. Md. (bd. dirs. 1997-00), Elks. Presbyterian. Avocations: skiing, ice skating, woodworking, music, travel. Office: Stoner Preston & Boswell PO Box 389 188 E Main St Westminster MD 21157-5017

**PRESTON, FORREST L.,** healthcare executive; Founder, chmn. Life Care Centers of Am., Cleveland, Tenn., 1970—. Office: Life Care Centers of Am PO Box 3480 3570 Keith St NW Cleveland TN 37320-3480*

**PRESTON, FRANCES WILLIAMS,** music company executive; b. Nashville, Aug. 27, 1934; children: Kirk, David, Donald. Degree (hon.), Lincoln Coll., Ill., Berklee Sch. Music. With BMI (Broadcast Music Inc.), Nashville, 1958—, v.p., 1964-85, sr. v.p. performing rights N.Y.C., 1985, exec. v.p., CEO, 1986, pres., CEO, 1986—2004, pres. emeritus, 2004—. Bd. dirs. Bionovo Inc., 2006—. Mem. Film, Entertainment and Music Commn. Adv. Council State of Tenn.; founding mem. bd. dirs. Leadership Nashville; past pres. bd. dirs. John Work Meml. Found.; chmn. bd. dirs. Country Music Found., Inc., 1983-85, trustee, past pres., chmn. bldg. com.; mem. Commn. on White House Record Library, Carter adminstrn., Pres.'s Panama Canal Study Com., Carter adminstrn.; bd. dirs. Rock & Roll Hall of Fame; mem. adminstrv. council Internat. Confedn. of Socs. of Authors and Composers; v.p. Nat. Music Council; past bd. dirs. Peabody Awards; hon. trustee Nat. Acad. Popular Music; pres. T.J. Martell Fedn. for Leukemia, Cancer and AIDS Rsch.; established Frances Williams Preston Rsch. Labs. for T.J. Martell Fedn., 1993; bd. dirs. R&B Found. Recipient achievement award Women's Equity Action League, spl. citation award NATAS, Golden Baton award Young Musicians Found., Humanitarian award Internat. Achievement in Arts award, 1995, Creative Achievement award Elaine Kaufman Cultural Ctr., 1996, Lester Sill Humanitarian award, 1996, Nat. Trustees award Grammys, 1998; named one of Am.'s 50 Most Powerful Women Ladies' Home Jour.; named to Country Music Hall of Fame. Mem. Country Music Assn. (life mem. bd. dirs., Irving Waugh Award of Excellence), Nashville Symphony Assn. (past sec., bd. dirs.), NARAS Found. (bd. dirs. pres.'s adv. bd.), Nashville Songwriters Assn. (life mem., bd. dirs.), Gospel Music Assn. (life mem. bd. past chmn. past pres.), Am. Women in Radio and TV (past nat. dir.). Clubs: (Friars Found. Applause award). Lodges: Rotary (1st woman mem. Nashville club), Friars. Presbyterian. Office: BMI 320 W 57th St Fl 3 New York NY 10019-3790

**PRESTON, JEROME, JR.,** retired lawyer; b. Staten Island, NY, Nov. 15, 1922; s. Jerome and Iva (Stone) P.; m. Dorothy Greeno McCann, Oct. 3, 1953; children: Richard M., Douglas J., David G. AB, Harvard U., 1947; LL.B. Yale U., 1950. Bar: Mass. 1951. Ptnr. Foley Hoag LLP, Boston, 1956—92, ret. sr. ptnr., 1992—. Trustee Eaton-Vance Income Fund of Boston, Inc., 1976-95. Trustee Univ. Hosp., 1956-96, overseer, 1996—; bd. dirs. Cambridge Sch. of Weston, 1973-78, pres., 1975-77; mem. Wellesley (Mass.) Planning Bd., 1962-70, chmn., 1966-68. Served to 1st lt. Signal Corps AUS, 1943-46. Mem. ABA, Mass. Bar Assn., Boston Bar Assn., Am. Law Inst., Handel and Haydn Soc. (pres. 1988-92, pres. emeritus 1992-, gov. 1988-92), Tavern Club. Democrat. Home: 1010 Memorial Dr Apt 2G Cambridge MA 02138-4853 Office: Foley Hoag LLP 155 Seaport Blvd Ste 1600 Boston MA 02210-4853 Office Phone: 617-832-1149. Personal E-mail: jprestonh@aol.com.

**PRESTON, JOHN ELWOOD,** lawyer; b. Celina, Ohio, Sept. 15, 1941; s. Homer Harlan and Nancy Alice (Boroff) P.; m. Alexandra Learned, Aug. 7, 1965. BA, Ohio U., 1962; LLB, George Washington U., Washington, 1965. Bar: D.C. 1967, Calif. 1973, U.S. Dist. Ct. D.C. 1967, U.S. Dist. Ct. (cen. dist.) Calif. 1984. Staff asst. Office of U.S. Senator Thomas H. Kuchel, Washington, 1964-66; atty. advisor Office of Gen. Counsel, GAO, Washington, 1966-71; mem. legislation study group Commn. on Govt. Procurement, Washington, 1970-71; div. counsel Litton Industries, Beverly Hills, Calif., 1971-79, group v.p., 1979-88, asst. gen. counsel, 1988-89, assoc. gen. counsel, 1989-90, v.p., assoc. gen. counsel, 1990-93, sr. v.p., gen. counsel, 1993—. Bd. dirs. Parks Jaeger Aerospace, Orlando, Fla., 1988-92; arbitrator Am. Arbitration Assn., L.A., 1986—. Contbr. articles to profl. jours. Mem. ABA (chmn. various coms.), Soc. Internat. Lawyers, Fed. Bar Assn., Nat. Contract Mgmt. Assn., Phi Alpha Delta. Avocations: golf, tennis, music, theater. Office: Litton Industries Inc 21240 Burbank Blvd Woodland Hills CA 91367-6675

**PRESTON, JULIA,** journalist; BA in Latin American Studies, Yale Univ., 1976. Latin Am. corr. Washington Post, 1986—92, U.N. corr., 1993—95; Mexico corr. The New York Times, 1995—2001, U.N. Bureau chief corr., 2002—03, dep. investigations ed., 2003—. Author: (Book) What Duarte Won, 1985, The Trial that Shook Cuba, 1989, The Battle for San Salvador, 1990, The Case of the Cesna 310: An Exchange, 1990, The Defeat of the Sandanistas, 1990. Recipient Robert F Kennedy award for Humanitarian Journalism, 1994, Maria Moors Cabot Prize for disting. coverage of Latin Am., 1997, Pulitzer Prize for Journalism, 1998. Office: The New York Times 229 W 43rd St New York NY 10036 Office Phone: 212-566-1251. Office Fax: 212-566-3690.*

**PRESTON, KELLY,** actress; b. Honolulu, Oct. 13, 1962; m. Kevin Gage, 1986 (div. 1988); 1 child; m. John Travolta, 1991; children: Jett, Ella Bleu. Student, U. So. Calif., UCLA. Represented by Internat. Creative Mgmt., Beverly Hills, Calif. Actor: (films) Mischief, 1985, Space Camp, 1986, 52 Pick-Up, 1986, A Tiger's Tale, 1987, Spellbinder, 1988, Twins, 1988, The Experts, 1989, Run, 1991, Love is a Gun, 1994, Jerry Macguire, 1996, Citizen Ruth, 1997, Addicted to Love, 1997, Nothing to Lose, 1997, The Holy Man, 1998, Jack Frost, 1998, For Love of the Game, 1999, Battlefield Earth, 2000, Daddy and Them, 2001, View from the Top, 2003, What a Girl Wants, 2003, The Cat in the Hat, 2003, Eulogy, 2004, Return to Sender, 2004, Sky High, 2005. Involved with Fight for Kids.

**PRESTON, LINDA CAROL KNIGHT,** retired English educator; b. LaGrange, Ga., Dec. 25, 1941; d. James Albert and Charlsie Myrtis (Holland) Knight; m. James A. Preston, Oct. 6, 1959 (dec. April 20, 2005); children: Sharon Grace, Terri Elizabeth. AA, Thornton C.C., 1972; BA, Purdue U., 1974, MA, 1977; AAS, Thornton C.C., 1986. Cert. secondary English tchr., tchr. of gifted, Ga. Tchg. asst. Purdue U. Calumet, Hammond, Ind., 1974-77; editl. asst. Pathotox Pub., Park Forest South, Ill., 1979-80; instr. Purdue U. Calumet, 1980-82, Prairie State Coll., Chicago Heights, Ill., 1983-84; paralegal Environ. Control divsn. Office of Ill. Atty. Gen., Chgo., 1986-87; tchr. Troup County Sch. Sys., La Grange, Ga., 1987—2004; ret., 2004. Mem. Applied Comm. Consortium, 1996—; adviser Nat. Honor Soc., Troup H.S., 1991-95. Contbr. poems, essays and short stories to jours., newsletters and mags. Mem. MLA, Profl. Assn. Ga. Educators, Nat. Coun. Tchrs. English, Edn., Ga. Coun. Tchrs. English, Phi Delta Kappa. Avocations: gardening, travel, reading.

**PRESTON, RICHARD ARTHUR,** historian; b. Middlesbrough, England, Oct. 4, 1910; s. Frank and Florence Rachel (Carter) P.; m. Marjorie Fishwick, Sept. 2, 1939; children— David Frank, Carol Jane, Peter Eric. BA, Leeds U., 1931, MA, 1932, Dip.Ed.; 1933; PhD, Yale U., New Haven, Conn., 1936; LL.D., Royal Mil. Coll. Can., 1977. Mem. faculty U. Toronto, 1936-38, U., Coll. South Wales, 1938-45, U. Toronto, 1945-48; mem. faculty Royal Mil. Coll. Can., Kingston, 1948-65; prof. history, to 1965, Duke U., Durham, N.C., 1965-80, 1st N.K. Boyd prof. history, 1980—, dir. Can. studies, 1973-79. Author: Gorges of Plymouth Fort, 1953, Men in Arms, 1956-91, Royal Fort Frontenac, 1958, Kingston Before the War of 1812, 1958, Canada in World Affairs, 1959-61, 1965, Canada and Imperial Defense, 1967, Canada's R.M.C., 1969, For Friends at Home, 1974, Defence of the Undefended Border, 1977, Perspectives in the History of Military Education and Professionalism, 1980, the Squat Pyramid: Canadian Studies in the U.S, 1980, To Serve Canada, 1991. Served with RAF, 1940-45, Commonwealth Fund fellow, 1933-36; Can. Coun. fellow, 1963-64; Social Sci. Rsch. Coun. fellow, 1963-64; Guggenheim fellow, 1972-73; recipient Achievement award City Kingston, 1959, Can. Confedn. medal, 1967, Queen's Jubilee medal, 1975, Donner medal, 1977, No. Telecom. Internat. Can. Studies award and Gold medal, 1983, Kingston Hist. Soc. Centennial award, 1994. Mem. Can. Hist. Assn. (pres. 1961-62), Assn. Can. Studies U.S. (founding pres. 1971-72), Am. Mil. Inst. Home: Olsen # 245 2701 Pickett Rd Durham NC 27705-5648

**PRESTON, RICHARD MCKIM,** lawyer; b. Balt., June 2, 1947; s. Wilbur Day Jr. and May Virginia (Honemann) P.; m. Trisa Jean Thompson, Apr. 28, 1961. BA, Washington & Lee U., 1969, JD cum laude, 1976; MA cum laude, Fairleigh Dickinson U., 1973. Assoc. vomBaur, Coburn, Simmons & Turtle, Washington, 1976-79, Seyfarth, Shaw, Washington, 1979-82, ptnr., 1982—. Mng. ptnr. Constrn. Group, 1987—; bd. govs. Washington Bldg. Congress, 1997—. Contbr. articles to profl. publs., chpt. to book. Bd. advisors Jubilee Support Found., Washington, 1989—; mem. Washington & Lee Law Coun., Lexington, Va., 1986-93. Mem. River Bend Golf and Country Club, Sankaty Head Golf Club, Metro. Club (D.C.). Office: Seyfarth Shaw 815 Connecticut Ave NW Washington DC 20006-4004 Office Phone: 202-828-5370. Business E-Mail: rpreston@seyfarth.com.

**PRESTON, SEYMOUR STOTLER, III,** chemicals executive; b. Media, Pa., Sept. 11, 1933; s. Seymour Stotler and Mary Alicia (Harper) P.; m. Jean Ellen Holman, Sept. 8, 1956; children: Courtney J., Katherine E., Alicia D., Shelley S. BA, Williams Coll., 1956; MBA, Harvard Coll., 1958. With Pennwalt Corp., Phila., 1961-89, exec. v.p. in charge of chems. and equipment ops., worldwide, 1975-77, pres., COO, 1977-89; pres., CEO Elf Atochem N.Am., Inc. (formerly Atochem N.A.), Phila., 1990-93. Chmn. AAC Engineered Sys. Inc., 1994-2003; bd. dirs. Scott Splty. Gases, Inc., Albermarle Corp., Tufco Techs., Inc., Ocean Power Tech. Inc.; non-exec. chmn. Ind. Publs., Inc., 2004—. Trustee Shipley Sch., Bryn Mawr, Pa., 1976-88, Phila. Orch. Assn., 1992-95; trustee Acad. Natural Scis., 1980—, chmn., 1995-2000, pres., CEO, 2000-02; bd. mgrs. Franklin Inst., Phila. 1980-92; bd. dirs. Lawrenceville (NJ) Sch., 1982-99, Wistar Inst., 1997—, Barra Found., 1998—, chmn., 2004—. 1st lt. USAF, 1958-61. Mem. Soc. for Chem. Industry, Greater Phila. C. of C. (bd. dirs. 1979-94), Radnor Hunt Club (Malvern, Pa.). Office Phone: 610-889-3980. Personal E-mail: spmillrace@aol.com.

**PRESTON, SHAWN,** lawyer; s. Michael Preston and Darlene Umland; m. Greta Adam, Dec. 4, 2004. JD, St. Mary's Sch. of Law, San Antonio, 1997; BA, Pepperdine U., Malibu, 1993. Bar: Fla. 1999, DC 2001, U.S. Supreme Ct. 2003. Assoc. atty. Becker & Poliakoff, PA, Ft. Lauderdale, 1998—2000; corp. counsel RaceWay Net, LLC, Boca Raton, 2000—02; worldwide licensing counsel The Coca-Cola Co., Atlanta, 2002—03; gen. counsel Benefit Ptnrs., Inc., Dallas, 2003—05; divsn. counsel Flowserve Corp., Irving, Tex., 2006—. Mem.: DC Bar Assn. (assoc.), Fla. Bar Assn. (assoc.), ABA (assoc.). Conservative. Roman Catholic. Avocations: travel, sports, wine tasting. Home: 6819 Park Ln Dallas TX 75225 Office Phone: 469-420-4027.

**PRESTON, STEPHANIE DANETTE,** science educator, researcher; d. Johnell and Althea Preston. BS, Xavier U. La., New Orleans, 1999, MA, 2003; PhD, Pa. State U., University Park, 2003. Tchr. sci. Xavier U. Prep. Sch., New Orleans, 1999—2003; grad. asst. Pa. State U., University Park, 2003—. Fellow, Pa. State U., 2003—. Mem. Nat. Rschrs. Sci. Tchg., Am. Ednl. Rschrs. Assn. (assoc.), Pi Lambda Theta (assoc.), Delta Sigma Theta (life; pres. 2005—). Office: The Pennsylvania State University 170 Chambers Building University Park PA 16802

**PRESTON, STEPHEN W.,** lawyer; b. May 30, 1957; BA summa cum laude, Yale U., 1979; diploma with first class honors, Trinity Coll., Univ. Dublin, 1980; JD magna cum laude, Harvard U., 1983. Bar: DC 1983. Law clk. to Hon. Phyllis A. Kravitch U.S. Ct. Appeals (11th cir.), 1983—84; vis. fellow Ctr. for Law in Pub. Interest, Washington, 1984—85; ptnr. Wilmer, Cutler & Pickering, Washington, 1986—93; prin. dep. gen. counsel, acting gen. counsel Dept. of Def., 1993—95; dep. asst. atty. gen. Dept. of Justice, 1995—98; gen. counsel Dept. of Navy, 1998—2000; ptnr., vice-chmn. Def. Nat. Security & Govt. Contracts dept. Wilmer Cutler Pickering Hale & Dorr, Washington, 2001—. Editor: Harvard Law Rev. Recipient Disting. Pub. Svc. medal Dept. of Def., 1995, 2000, Dept. of Navy, 2000. Fellow: Am. Bar Found.; mem.: ABA (mem. standing com. on law, adv. com. nat. security),

Council on Fgn. Rels., Phi Beta Kappa. Office: Wilmer Cutler Pickering Hale & Dorr LLP 2445 M St NW Washington DC 20037-1420 Office Phone: 202-663-6900. Office Fax: 202-663-6363. Business E-Mail: stephen.preston@wilmerhale.com.

**PRESTON, STEVEN C.,** federal agency administrator, former service company executive; b. Aug. 4, 1960; BA in Polit. Sci. with highest distinction, Northwestern U., 1982; MBA, U. Chgo., 1985; student, Ludwig Maximillian U., Munich, Germany. Investment banker Lehman Bros., 1985-93; sr. v.p., corp. treas. First Data Corp.; CFO The ServiceMaster Co., Downers Grove, Ill., 1997—2003, exec. v.p., 2003—06; adminstr. SBA (Small Bus. Adminstrn.), Washington, 2006—. Vice chmn. bd. visitors Northwestern U. Weinberg Coll. Arts & Sciences; bd. dirs. Hinsdale Hosp. Found; mem. adv. bd. Tri-Artisan Partners, Concentric Equity Partners. Office: SBA 409 3rd St SW Rm 7000 Washington DC 20416*

**PRESTON, THOMAS RONALD,** language educator, researcher; b. Oct. 31, 1936; s. Thomas and Marie Katherine (Nettlow) P.; m. Mary Ruth Atkinson, June 4, 1960; children: Lorel, Mary, Thomas BA, U. Detroit, 1958; MA, Rice U., 1960, PhD, 1962. Asst. prof. English Duquesne U., Pitts., 1962-63; Asst. prof. English U. Fla., Gainseville, 1963-67; assoc. prof., chmn. dept. Loyola U., New Orleans, 1967-69; prof., chmn. dept. U. Tenn., Chattanooga, 1969-73, U. Wyo., Laramie, 1973-82; prof., dean arts and scis. U. North Tex., Denton, 1982-92, prof. English, 1992—. Chmn. Wyo. Council for Humanities, Laramie, 1976-77 Author: Not in Timon's Manner, 1975; editor U. Ga. edit. of Smollett's Humphry Clinker, 1990; contbr. articles on 18th century lit. to profl. jours. Recipient John W. Gardner award Rice U., 1962; George Duke Humphrey award U. Wyo., 1982; NEH grantee, 1979; Am. Council of Learned Socs. grantee, 1980 Mem Am Soc for 18th Century Studies, South Ctrl. Soc. for 18th Century Studies (pres. 1986-87). Democrat. Anglican. Office: U North Tex Dept English Box 311307 Denton TX 76203 Office Phone: 940-565-2050. Personal E-mail: trpatlake@cs.com.

**PRESTOWITZ, CLYDE VINCENT, JR.,** economist, researcher; b. Wilmington, Del., Sept. 6, 1941; s. Clyde Vincent and Lillian (Lang) Prestowitz; m. Carol Ann Jay, Mar. 29, 1964; children: Anne, Clyde, Brian. BA with honors, Swarthmore Coll., 1963; MA, U. Hawaii, 1965; MBA, U. Pa., 1980. Mgr. market devel. Scott Paper Co., Phila., 1968—72, dir. planning Europe Brussels, 1972—76; v.p Japan Egon Zehnder Internat., Tokyo, 1976—78; dir. mktg. Am. Can Co., Greenwich, Conn., 1978—79; pres. Prestowitz Assocs., New Canaan, Conn., 1979—81; dep. asst. sec. internat. econ. policy U.S. Dept. Commerce, Washington, 1981—82, acting asst. sec. internat. econ. policy, 1982—83, counselor to sec., 1983—86; Wilson fellow, 1986—87; sr. assoc. Carnegie Endowment for Internat. Peace, Washington, 1987—89; founder, pres. Econ. Strategy Inst., Washington, 1989—. Vice-chmn. Pacific Basin Econ. Coun., 1989—; vice chmn., presdl. com. U.S./Pacific Trade and Investment Policy. Author: Trading Places: How We Are Giving Our Future to Japan and How to Reclaim It, 1993, Rogue Nation: American Unilateralism and the Failure of Good Intentions, 2003, Three Billion New Capitalists: The Great Shift of Wealth and Power to the East, 2005; co-author: The New North American Order, 1991, Future of the Auto Industry: It Can Compete, Can It Survive?, 1992, Powernomics: Economics and Strategy After the Cold War, 2000. Republican. Presbyterian. Office: Econ Strategy Inst 3050 K St NW Washington DC 20007 Office Phone: 202-295-4645. Office Fax: 202-339-0880. Business E-Mail: presto@econstrat.org.

**PRETE, GAYLE COMPTON,** advertising and marketing executive; b. Washington, Nov. 28, 1956; d. Walter Dale and Jeanne (Parker) C.; m. Lanny Ross Huff, May 22, 1982 (div. 2002); m. James G. Prete, May 30, 2005. B in Gen. Studies, U. Mich., 1978. Mgr. br. merchandising CBS Records, Chgo., 1978, local promotion, mktg. mgr. Indpls., Boston, N.Y.C., 1978-81; spl. projects supr. Pickwick Internat. Musicland Group, Mpls., 1981-82; account exec. Campbell-Mithun Advt., Mpls., 1982-85; mktg. mgr., communications Universal Foods Corp., Milw., 1985-86; nat. advt. mgr. Thorobred Advt. Agy. (Jockey Internat., Inc.), Wis., 1986-88, dir. consumer and trade advt., 1988-89, v.p advt., 1990-92; dir. mktg./advt. Allen-Edmonds Shoe Co., Port Washington, Wis., 1993-95; v.p., dir. Fin. Mktg. Plus Direct Mktg. Group, Libertyville, Ill., 1995-97; dir. mktg. & merchandising AR Accessories Group Inc., Milw., 1997-98; v.p. creative svcs. Tucker-Knapp Integrated Mktg. Comms., Schaumburg, Ill., 1998-2000; sr. mgr. creative svcs. Discover Fin. Svcs. (Morgan Stanley Dean Witter), Riverwoods, Ill., 2000—04, dir. mktg. prodn. svcs., 2004—. V.p., sec. Java Masters, Inc., 1992-2005. Mem. Traffic Audit Bur. for Media Measurement (bd. dirs. 1988-93), Assn. Nat. Advertisers (print adv. com., out of home advt. com. 1989-92). Avocations: dance, gymnastics, conga drumming, autocross. Office: Discover Fin Svcs 2500 Lake Cook Rd # 2W Deerfield IL 60015-3851 Personal E-mail: javanuts@aol.com. Business E-Mail: gaylehuff@discoverfinancial.com.

**PRETTYMAN, ELIJAH BARRETT, JR.,** lawyer; b. Washington, June 1, 1925; s. Elijah Barrett and Lucy Courtney (Hill) P.; m. Noreen Prettyman; children by previous marriage: Elijah Barrett III, Jill Savage Lukoschek. BA, Yale U., 1949; LLB, U. Va., 1953. Bar: Wash., D.C. 1954, U.S. Supreme Ct. 1957. Pvt. practice, Washington, 1955—; law clk. to Hon. Justices Jackson, Frankfurter and Harlan U.S. Supreme Ct., Washington, 1953-55; assoc. Hogan & Hartson, Washington, 1955—63, ptnr., 1964—2001, of counsel, 2002—; inspector gen. Dist. of Colo., Washington, 1998—99. Spl. asst. to Atty. Gen. U.S., 1963; White House, 1963-64; also Pres. rep. to Interagy. Com. on Transport Mergers; spl. cons. subcom. to investigate problems connected with refugees and escapees, U.S. Senate Judiciary Com., Vietnam, 1967-68; outside cons. to subcom. on oversight and investigations, Ho. of Reps. com. on internal and fgn. commerce, 1978; spl. cons. for ABSCAM investigation to Com. on Standards of Ofcl. Conduct, U.S. Ho. of Reps., 1980-81; trustee emeritus, past exec com. Am. U., Washington; past trustee, mem. exec. com. Washington Journalism Ctr.; past adv. com Media Law Reporter. Author: Death and the Supreme Court, 1961 (Edgar Allan Poe award); Editor: (with William E. Jackson) The Supreme Court in the American System of Government (Justice Robert H. Jackson), 1955; contbr. articles to profl. jours. Past corp. mem. Salvation Army; past mem. adv. com. Procedures of Jud. Coun., DC; past mem. adv. bd. Inst. Comm. Law Studies, Cath. U.; bd. govs. St. Albans Sch., 1957-63, 65-72, chmn., 1965-67; past mem. nat. adv. com., Nat. Inst. for Citizen Edn. in Law; bd. dirs., past pres. PEN/Faulkner Found.; v.p., past chmn. publ. com. Supreme Ct. Hist. Soc.; bd. dirs. Robert H. Jackson Ctr., Jamestown, NY, 2006-; past internat. adv. group Toshiba Corp.; past commr. Supreme Ct. Jud. Fellows Commn., chmn., 2003-05. With AUS, 1943—45. Chmn. recipient Pub. Achievement award Common Cause, 1999, Justice Potter Stewart award Coun. for Ct. Excellence, 2000, disting. pub. svc. award D.C. 1999. Fellow: ABA; mem.: D.C. Cir. Hist. Soc. (pres. 2000—02, chmn. 2003—), Am. Acad. Appellate Lawyers (past pres.), Am. Judicature Soc. (past vice chair, exec. com.), Met. Washington Bd. Trade, DC Bar Assn. (bd. govs., Lawyer of Yr. award 1998), DC Bar Found. (pres. 1983—84), Jud. Conf. DC Cir., Am. Coll. Trial Lawyers, Chevy Chase Club, Met. Club, Alfalfa Club, Barristers Club, Lawyers Club (past pres.). Methodist. Home: 2737 Devonshire Pl NW # 424 Washington DC 20008-5148 Office: Columbia Sq 555 13th St NW Washington DC 20004-1109 Office Phone: 202-637-5685. Business E-Mail: ebprettyman@hhlaw.com.

**PRETZEL, MARK WILLIAM,** musician; BM, MM, U. Cin., 1979—86; MM, Bowling Green State U., Ohio, 1986—88; DMA, U. Mo., Kansas City, 1988—95. Adj. prof. music U. Mo., Kansas City, Mo., 1990—2000, Johnson County C.C., Overland Park, Kans., 1997—. V.p. U. Mo. Conservatory Alumni Assn., Kansas City, 2002. Home: 16633 W 145th St Olathe KS 66062 Office: Johnson County Comty Coll 12345 College Blvd Overland Park KS 66062 Office Phone: 913-469-8500 6533. Personal E-mail: mwpretzel@aol.com. Business E-Mail: mpretzel@jccc.edu.

**PREUCIL, DORIS BOGEN,** music educator; b. Milw., Wis., Dec. 10, 1932; d. Walter Leopold and Adele Anne (Jarvis) Bogen; m. William Warren Preucil, Sept. 4, 1954; children: William, Jr., Walter, Anne, Jeanne. MusB

with distinction, Eastman Sch. Music, Rochester, N.Y., 1954; MusM, U. Iowa, 1968; studied with Shinichi Suzuki, Talent Edn. Inst., Japan, 1982. Violinist Rochester Philharm. Orch., 1952—54, Nat. Symphony Orch., Washington, 1954—56; freelance violinist & tchr. Iowa City, 1956—72; asst. prof. Western Ill. U., Macomb, 1972—76; founder, dir., master tchr. Preucil Sch. Music, Iowa City, 1975—97, dir. emerita, tchr., 1997—. Suzuki Professorial chair U. Wis., Stevens Point, 1986; hon. bd. mgrs. Eastman Sch. Music, Rochester, 2005—. Musician (1st violinist): Milw. Symphony, 1948—50, Rochester Philharm., 1952—54, Tri-City Symphony, 1958—72; concertmaster:, 1971—72; musician: Eastman Faculty Quartet, 1951—54, Lydian Trio, 1972—75, Preucil Family Players, 1975—84; author, editor: The Suzuki Viola Sch., 1976—; arranger: The Solo with Orchestra series 2004-. Trustee Nat. Guild Cmty. Schs. Arts, 1988—91; bd. dirs. Amateur Chamber Music Found., 1998—; elder, deacon 1st Presbyn. Ch., Iowa City, 1964—. Named Tchr. of the Yr., Iowa State Music Tchrs. Assn., 2005; recipient Lifetime Achievement award, Eastman Sch. Music, 2004. Mem.: Internat. Suzuki Assn. (founding bd. mem. 1983—95), Suzuki Assn. Am. (cert. tchr., trainer 1980—, pres. 1982—84, Disting. Svc. award 1992), Rotary (mem. music commn. 1989—). Avocations: music, reading, travel. Home: 317 Windsor Dr Iowa City IA 52245 Personal E-mail: wdpreucil@mchsi.com.

**PREUIT, THERESA,** librarian; b. Florence, Ala., Mar. 6, 1960; d. Richard Gordon and Rose Mary Preuit. BA, Judson Coll., 1981; MLS, U. of Ala., 1982. Reference libr. U. of Ala. Librs., Tuscaloosa, Ala., 1982—85; humanities reference libr. U. of West Fla., Pensacola, Fla., 1985—89, interim libr. campus libr. Fort Walton Beach, Fla., 1989, humanities reference libr. Pensacola, 1990—93, head circulation dept., 1993—99; head, access services dept. Old Dominion U., Norfolk, Va., 1999—2001; assoc. dir. for pub. svcs. and collections Mercer U. Libraries, Macon, Ga., 2001—. Sec., treas. Innovative Users Group, 2003—; editor, the southeastern libr. Southeastern Libr. Assn., Atlanta, 1993—97, chair, southeastern libr. editl. bd., 1998—99; editor, fla. chpt. newsletter Assn. of Coll. and Rsch. Libraries, Pensacola, Fla., 1988—95; editor, coll., u., and spl. libraries divsn. page Ala. Libr. Assn., Tuscaloosa, Ala., 1984—85, mem., ala. libr. exec. bd., 1984—85; asst. to libr. dir. U. West Fla., Pensacola, 1988—90; online rsch. coord. U. Ala. Librs., Tuscaloosa, 1984—85. Mem.: ALA, Ala. Libr. Assn. (chmn. pubs. com. 1985—85), Fla. Libr. Assn. (bd. mem. academic librs. caucus 1988—95, chmn. Fla. electronic access com. 1999—99), Va. Libr. Assn. (chmn. pub. svcs. forum 1999—2000), Ga. Libr. Assn., Assn.Coll. and Rsch. Librs., Gulf Coast Online and Automated Librs. (sec., treas. 1986—87, v.p 1988—89, pres. 1989—99, pres. elect 1988—89), Beta Phi Mu. Office: Mercer University Jack Tarver Library 1300 Edgewood Avenue Macon GA 31207 Office Phone: 478-301-2031. Business E-Mail: preuit_t@mercer.edu.

**PREUL, HERBERT C.,** engineering educator, consultant; b. Mo. s. Frederich Charles Preul; m. Audrey Anne Van Roekel; 1 child, Mark C. BS in Civil Engring., U. Iowa, Iowa City, 1950; MS in Civil and Hydraulic Engring., U. Minn., Mpls., 1955, PhD in Civil Engring., 1964. Profl. engr., Ohio, 1964, Ky., Ariz. Hydraulic engr. US Corps Engrs., St. Paul, 1952—55, supr. civil engring. Omaha, 1955—60; prof. civil, environ. engring. U. Cin., 1964—2000; consulting engr. H.C. Preul Civil and Environ. Engr., Cin., 1964—. Profl. baseball pitcher NY Yankee Baseball Sys., Minor League Cities. Contbr. articles to profl. and tech. publs. Sgt. inf. U.S. Army, 1944—46, USA. Mem.: Internat. Assn. Hydraulic Engring., Internat. Water Assn., Am. Waterworks Assn. (life), Water Environ. Fedn. (life), Am. Soc. Civil Engrs. (life). Achievements include patents for wastewater source control system. Office Phone: 513-221-5291. E-mail: h.preul@uc.edu.

**PREUS, DAVID WALTER,** bishop, minister; b. Madison, Wis., May 28, 1922; s. Ove Jacob Hjort and Magdalene (Forde) P.; m. Ann Madsen, June 26, 1951; children: Martha, David, Stephen, Louise, Laura. BA, Luther Coll., Decorah, Iowa, 1943, DD (hon.), 1969; postgrad., U. Minn., 1946-47; BTh, Luther Sem., St. Paul, 1950; postgrad., Union Sem., 1951, Edinburgh U., 1951-52; LLD (hon.), Wagner Coll., 1973, Gettysburg Coll., 1976; DD (hon.), Pacific Luth. Coll., 1974, St. Olaf Coll., 1974, Dana Coll., 1979, Tex. Luth. Coll., 1994; LHD (hon.), Macalester Coll., 1976; DD (hon.), Luther Coll. 1969. Ordained to ministry Luth. Ch., 1950; asst. pastor First Luth. Ch., Brookings, SD, 1950-51; pastor Trinity Luth. Ch., Vermillion, SD, 1952-57; campus pastor U. Minn., Mpls., 1957-58; pastor Univ. Luth. Ch. of Hope, Mpls.; 1958-73; v.p. Am. Luth. Ch., 1968-73, pres., presiding bishop, 1973-87; exec. dir. Global Mission Inst. Luther Northwestern Theol. Sem., St. Paul. Disting. vis. prof. Luther-Northwestern Sem., St. Paul, 1988-94; Luccock vis. pastor Yale Div. Sch., 1969; chmn. bd. youth activity Am. Luth. Ch., 1960-68; mem. exec. com. Luth. Council U.S.A.; v.p. Luth. World Fedn., 1977-90; mem. cen. com. World Council Chs., 1973-75, 80-90; Luth. del. White House Conf. on Equal Opportunity Chmn. Greater Mpls. Fair Housing Com., Mpls. Council Chs., 1960-64; mem. Mpls. Planning Commn., 1965-67; mem. Mpls. Sch. Bd., 1965-74, chmn., 1967-69; mem. Mpls. Bd. Estimate and Taxation, 1968-73, Mpls. Urban Coalition; sr. public adv. U.S. del. Madrid Conf. of Conf. on Security and Cooperation in Europe, 1980-81; bd. dirs. Mpls. Inst. Art, Walker Art Center, Hennepin County United Fund, Ams. for Childrens Relief, Luth. Student Found., Research Council of Gt. City Schs., Urban League, NAACP; bd. regents Augsburg Coll., Mpls. Served with Signal Corps AUS, 1943-46, PTO. Decorated comdr.'s cross Royal Norwegian Order St. Olav, Order of St. George 1st deg. Orthodox Ch. of Georgia (USSR); 1989; recipient Regents medal Augustana Coll., Sioux Falls, S.D., 1973, Torch of Liberty award Anti-Defamation League, 1973, St. Thomas Aquinas award St. Thomas U., Pax Christi award St. John's Univ/. Collegeville, Minn., 1997. Lutheran.

**PREUSS, CHARLES FREDERICK,** lawyer; b. Santa Barbara, Calif. Feb. 27, 1941, BA, Dartmouth Coll., 1962, JD, Stanford U., 1969. Bar: Calif. 1970. Atty. Bronson, Bronson & McKinnon, 1969—93; ptnr. Preuss Walker & Shanagher, San Francisco, 1993-98, Preuss, Shanagher, Zvoleff & Zimmer, San Francisco, 1998; mng. ptnr., head West Coast offices Drinker Biddle & Reath LLP, San Francisco, and ptnr., products liability practice group. Mem. Product Liability Adv. Coun., Inc., bd. dir., Def. Rsch. Inst., 1996-99. Mem. Am. Bd. Trial Advocates, Internat. Assn. Def. Counsel. Office: Drinker Biddle & Reath LLP 50 Fremont St San Francisco CA 94105-2235 Office Phone: 415-591-7566. Office Fax: 415-591-7510. Business E-Mail: charles.preuss@dbr.com.

**PREUSS, MARY HERGE,** Spanish educator; b. Ellwood City, Pa., Aug. 04; d. William J. and Imogene (Lewis) Herge; m. Franklin A. Preuss, Mar. 21, 1964. BA, U. Pitts., 1959, MEd, 1965, cert. Latin Am. studies, 1977, PhD, 1981. Cert. Spanish and English tchr., Pa. Tchr. Spanish Mars (Pa.) Area High Sch., 1959-62, Wilkinsburg High Sch., Pitts., 1962-64, North Hills High Sch., Pitts., 1967-77; lectr. Spanish Chatham Coll., Pitts., 1977, Carlow Coll., Pitts.; prof. Spanish Geneva Coll., Beaver Falls, Pa., 1981-89, chmn. dept. fgn. langs., coord. Latin Am. bus. studies, 1983-89; prof. Pa. State U., McKeesport, 1989—, chair fgn. langs. Author: Gods of the Popol Vuh, 1988, Dioses del Popol Vuh, 1988, Yucatan Maya Stories: From Chen Ja' to the Milpa, 2005; editor Hummingbird Lore and Other Selected Papers from the VI Internat. Symposium on Latin Am. Indian Lits., 1989, LAIL SPEAKS: Selected Papers from the VII Internat. Symposium on Latin Am. Indian Lits., 1989, Past, Present and Future, Selected Papers on Latin Am. Indian Lit., 1991, Stories Yucatec Maya: From Chen Ja' to Milpa, 2005; contbr. numerous articles to profl. jours. Mem. Ross Twp. (Pa.) Rep. Com., 1970-79, Ross Twp. Drug Abuse Team, 1972-75; bd. dirs. North Hills Youth Ministry, Pitts., 1970-75, Friends Hillman Libr., U. Pitts., 1976-80. Am. Philos. Soc. grantee, Geneva Coll. grantee, Pa. State U. grantee. Mem. DAR, Latin Am. Indian Lit. Assn. (founding pres. 1983-87, bd. dirs. 1982—, symposium chmn. 1983-95, editor newsletter 1982-85, editor Latin Am. Indian Lit. Jour. 1985—), MLA, Mid-Atlantic Coun. Latin Am. Studies, Delta Kappa Gamma (scholarship chmn. 1979-80, Laura Braun award 1978, 79). Lutheran. Avocations: travel, reading, gardening, guitar. Home: 145 Timberlane Dr Pittsburgh PA 15229-1058 Office: Pa State U Dept Spanish 6000 University Dr Mc Keesport PA 15132 E-mail: mhpl@psu.edu.

**PREUSS, ROGER EMIL,** artist; b. Waterville, Minn., Jan. 29, 1922; s. Emil W. and Edna (Rosenau) P.; m. MarDee Ann Germundson, Dec. 31, 1954 (dec. Mar. 1981). Student, Mankato Comml. Coll., Mpls. Sch. Art. Emeritus instr. Mpls. Coll. Art and Design; emeritus Mpls. Inst. Arts Speakers Bur.; former judge Goodyear Nat. Conservation Awards Program; founder U.S. Fed. Roger Preuss Waterfowl Prodn. Area, LeSueur County, Minn., 1997; former advisor Wildlife Forever Nat. Fish-Art Contest. One-man shows include St. Paul Fine Art Galleries, 1959, Albert Lea Art Ctr., 1963, Hist. Soc. Mont., Helena, 1964, Brotherhood Fine Arts Ctr., 1965, Le Sueur County Hist. Soc. Mus., Elysian, Minn., 1976, Merrill's Gallery Fine Art, Taos, N.Mex., 1980; exhbns. include Mpls. Inst. Art Msa exhibit, 1946, Midwest Wildlife Conf. Exhbn., Kerr's Beverly Hills, Calif., 1947, Laguna Art Mus., Calif., 1947, Joslyn Meml. Mus., Omaha, 1948, Hollywood Fine Arts Center, 1948, Minn. Centennial, 1949, Federated Chaparral Authors, 1951, Nat. Wildlife Art, 1951-52, N.Am. Wildlife Art, dir. exposition, 1952, Ducks Unltd. Waterfowl exhibit, 1953-54, St. Paul Winter Carnival, 1954, St. Paul Gallery Art Mart, 1954, Harris Fine Arts Ctr., Provo, Utah, 1969, Galerie Internat., N.Y.C., 1972, Holy Land Conservation Fund, N.Y.C., 1976, Faribault Art Ctr., 1981, Wildlife Artists of the World Exhbn., Bend, Oreg., 1984, U. Art Mus., U. Minn., Mpls., 1990, Rochester Art Ctr., 1991, Minn. Hist. Soc.-Hill House, 1992, Bemidji Art Ctr., 1992, Jack London Ctr., Dawson City, Yukon Territory, Can., 1992, Weyerhaeuser Meml. Mus., Little Falls, Minn., 1995, Minn. Valley Nat. Wildlife Refuge Ctr., Bloomington, 1995, Sagebrush Artists Exhbn., Klamath Falls, Oreg., 1995, Smithsonian Inst., Blauvelt Art Mus.; represented in-permanent collections: Demarest Meml. Mus., Hackensack, N.J., N.Y. Jour. Commerce, Mont. Hist. Soc., Inland Bird Banding Assn., Minn. Capitol Bldg., Mont. State U., Wildlife Am. Collection, LeSueur Hist. Soc., Voyageurs Nat Park Interpretive Ctr., Krause-Hartig VFW Post, Mpls., Nat. Wildlife Fedn. Collection, Minn. Ceremonial House, U.S. Wildlife Svc. Fed. Bldg., Fort Snelling, Minn., Crater Lake Nat. Park Visitors Ctr., VA Hosp., Mpls., Luxton Collection, Banff, Alta., Can., Internat. Inst. Arts, Geneva, Mont. Capitol Bldg., People of Century-Goldblatt Collection, Lyons, Ill., Harlem Savings Collection, N.Y.C., Weisman Art Mus., Mpls., Minn. Vets. Home, Mpls., Roger Preuss Art Collection, Augustana Ctr. for Western Studies, Sioux Falls, S.D., Minn. Mus. Am. Art, St. Paul, U. Minn. Art Mus., C.M. Russell Mus., Great Falls, Mont., Le Sueur County Courthouse, Le Center, Minn., others, numerous galleries and pvt. collections; designer: Fed. Duck Stamp, U.S. Dept. Interior, 1949, Commemorative Centennial Pheasant Stamp, 1981, Gold Waterfowl medallion Franklin Mint, 1983, Gold Stamp medallion Wildlife Mint, 1983, 40th Anniverary Commemorative Fed. Duck Stamp etching, 1989; panelist: Sportsman's Roundtable, Sta. WTCN-TV, Mpls. (emeritus), from 1953; author: Is Wildlife Art Recognized Fine Art?, 1986; contbr.: Christmas Echos, 1955, Wing Shooting, Trap & Skeet, 1955, Along the Trout Stream, 1979; contbr. Art Impressions mag., Can., Wildlife Art, U.S.; contbr. illustrations and articles in Nat. Wildlife; assoc. editor emeritus: Out-of-Doors mag.; compiler and artist: Outdoor Horizons, 1957, Twilight over the Wilderness, 1972, 75 limited edition prints Wildlife of America, from 1950; contbr. paintings and text Minnesota Today; creator paintings and text Preuss Wildlife Calendar; inventor: paintings and text Wildlife Am. Calendar; featured artist Art West, 1980-84, Wildlife Art; featured in films Your BFA-Care and Maintenance, Black Ducks Along the Border Former del. Nat. Wildlife Conf.; bd. dirs. emeritus Voyageurs Nat. Park Assn., Deep-Portage Conservation Found.; former bd. dirs. Wetlands for Wildlife Foundation; active Wildlife Am.; co-organizer, v.p., bd. dirs. Minn. Conservation Fedn., 1952-54; mem. U.S. Hospitalized Vets. Venison Program, 1957—; trustee Liberty Bell Edn. Found.; Waseca Arts Coun.; founder, dir. Roger Preuss Conservation Preserve for Study of Nature, 1990—; adv. Wildlife Forever. With USNR, WWII. Recipient Stamp Design award U.S. Fish and Wildlife Svc., 1994, Minn. Outdoor award, 1956, Patron of Conservation award, 1956, award for contbns. conservation Minn. Statehood Centennial Commn., 1958, 1st award for Wildlife award U.S. Fish and Wildlife Svc., 1994; named Wildlife Conservationist of the Yr., Sears Found.-Nat. Wildlife Fedn. program, 1966, Am. Bicentennial Wildlife Artist, Am. Heritage Assn., 1976; hon. mem. Ont. Chippewa Nation of Can., 1957; named Knight of Mark Twain for contbns. to Am. art Mark Twain Soc., 1978; named to Water, Woods and Wildlife Hall of Fame, named Dean of Wildfowl Artists, 1981, Hon. Ky. Col.; recipient hon. degree U.S. Vets. Venison program, 1980, Western Am. award significant contbns. to preservation arts and history No. Prairie Plains, Augustana Coll. Ctr. for Western Studies, Sioux Falls, S.D., 1992, Pub. Svc. award U.S. Dept. Interior, 1996, Marshall award 2004; named creator first signed, numbered photolithographic modern print pub. in N.Am., 1959; documented Colorado Springs Fine Arts Ctr., 1993, colleague of Frederick R. Weisman Mus., Mpls., 1994; grantee NEH, 1995, Prairie Lakes Arts Coun., 1995. Fellow Internat. Inst. Arts (life), Nat. Wildlife Fedn. (past nat. wildlife week chmn. Minn.), Minn. Ducks Unltd. (bd. dirs. emeritus), Minn. Artists Assn. (v.p., bd. dirs. 1953-59), Minn. Mycol. Soc. (pres. emeritus, hon. life), Le Sueur County Hist. Soc. (hon. life), Minn. Conservation Fedn. (hon. life), Wildlife Artists World (charter, emeritus internat. v.p., chmn. fine arts bd.), Prairie Chicken Soc. (patron), Mission Oceanic Arctic, Minn. Press Club (emeritus), Silver Lake Sports (hon.), Wildlife Rehab. Ctr. Minn. Office: care Wildlife Am PO Box 580004-a Minneapolis MN 55458-0004 *With a modicum of natural skills in painting and writing, my basic goal throughout all my work has been to help people appreciate and understand nature. If I as a naturalist am a small voice for our world's waters, woods, and wildlife, if I have influenced many children and adults to become more environment conscious, if my art brings to others a measure of joy, then my best aspirations for my creations have been fulfilled.*

**PREVE, ROBERTA JEAN,** librarian, researcher; b. Wilmington, Del., Feb. 27, 1954; d. Burton Hugo Sundem and Betty (Kay) Klein; m. Thomas Alan Preve, Sept. 23, 1978; children: Stephanie Jean, Melanie Marie. BA, U. NH, 1975; MLS, Simmons Coll., 1985. Rschr. U. N.H., Durham, 1974-75; rsch. asst. Eikonix Corp., Burlington, Mass., 1976-79; asst. cashier, credit dept. mgr. Dania (Fla.) Bank, 1980-83; rsch. assoc. Ctr. for Strategy Rsch., Cambridge, Mass., 1984-86; info. svcs. Braxton Assocs., Boston, 1986-87; mktg. adminstr. Summit Tech., Waltham, Mass., 1987-91; mgr. market rsch. AT&T Capital Corp., Framingham, Mass., 1991-95; mgr. Bus. Info. Ctr. Raytheon Co., Lexington, Mass., 1995—. Co-owner T&R Pest Mgmt., Attleboro, Mass., 1988—95. Mem. Spl. Librs. Assn., New England Online (dir., logistics chair 1986-90), Beta Phi Mu. Avocations: hiking, reading, needlecrafts, sports. Office: Raytheon Co Bus Info Ctr 870 Winter St Waltham MA 02451 Business E-Mail: roberta_j_preve@raytheon.com.

**PREVIDI, MICHAEL,** meteorologist, research scientist; b. Englewood, NJ, Aug. 19, 1979; BS in Meteorology, Rutgers U., New Brunswick, NJ, 2001, PhD in Enviromental Sci, 2006. Tchg. asst. Rutgers U., New Brunswick, NJ, 2001—02, grad. rsch. asst., 2002—06, postdoctoral assoc., 2006—. Grantee Tchg. assistantship Rutgers U. Dept. of Environ. Sci, 2001—02, Grad. Rsch. assistantship, Rutgers U. Dept. of Environ. Sci., 2002—05. Mem.: AAAS, Am. Meteorol. Soc., Am. Geophys. Union. Achievements include research in atmospheric science. Avocation: basketball. Office: Rutgers University 71 Dudley Rd New Brunswick NJ 08901 Office Phone: 732-932-6555 253. Business E-Mail: mprevidi@marine.rutgers.edu.

**PREVIN, ANDRÉ (ANDRE LUDWIG PREWIN),** composer, conductor, pianist; b. Berlin, Apr. 6, 1929; came to U.S. 1938, naturalized, 1943; s. Jack and Charlotte (Epstein) P.; m. Dory Previn, 1958 (div. 1965); m. Betty Bennett (div.); 2 children; m. Mia Farrow, Sept. 10, 1970 (div. 1979); children: Matthew and Sascha (twins), Fletcher, Lark, Daisy; m. Heather Hales, Jan. 1982 (div. 1999); 1 child, Lukas; m. Anne-Sophie Mutter, 2002-. Student, Berlin Conservatory, Paris Conservatory; privately with, Pierre Monteux, Mario Castelnuovo-Tedesco. Mem. faculty Guildhall Sch., London, Curtis Inst., Phila., Berkshire Music Ctr. Rec. artist classical music for RCA, EMI, Phillips, Telarc, Deutsche Gramophone, 1946—; composer (orchestra) Concerto for Cello, 1960, Concerto for Guitar Concerto, 1960, Principia, 1980, Reflections, 1981, Concerto for Piano, 1985 Honey and Rue, 1992, The Magic Number, 1995, Vocalise, 1994, Sallie Chisum Remembers Billy the

Kid, 1995, Diversions, 1999, Violin Concerto (Anne-Sophie), 2001, Double Concerto for Violin, Double Bass and Orchestra, 2004; composer (chamber/solo) Two Little Serenades, 1970, Paraphase on a Theme of William Walton, 1973, Four Outings for Brass, 1974, Peaches, 1978, Matthew's Piano Book, 1979, Triolet for Brass, 1985, A Wedding Waltz, 1986, Variations on a Theme by Haydn, 1990, Cello Sonata, 1993, Sonata for Violin, Vineyard, 1994, Trio for Piano, Oboe, and Bassoon, 1994, Bassoon Sonata, 1997, Hoch soil Er Leben, 1997, Tango Song and Dance, 1998, String Quartet with Soprano, 2003; composer (vocal) Five Songs, 1977, Four Songs, 1994, Three Arias from the Streetcar Named Desire, 1998, Two Rememberances, 1995, Three Dickinson Songs, 1999, The Giraffes Go to Hamburg, 2000, String Quartet (with Soprano), 2003; composer (musicals) Coco, 1960, The Good Companions, 1964; composer (cadenzas) W.A. Mozart: Concerto for Flute and Harp, C major, K 299, W.A. Mozart: Piano Concerto No. 20, D minor, K 466 (3rd mvt.), W.A. Mozart: Piano Concerto No. 24, C minor, K 491 (1st mvt.); composer (movie scores) The Sun Comes Up, 1949 (also musical dir.), Scene of the Crime, 1949, Challenge to Lassie, 1949, Tension, 1950, The Outriders, 1950, Shadow on the Wall, 1950, Three Little Words, 1950 (also musical dir.), Dial 1119 (also musical dir.), 1950, Kim, 1950, Cause for Alarm!, 1951, The Girl Who Had Everything, 1953, Bad Day at Black Rock, 1955, It's Always Fair Weather, 1955 (also condr., music supervisor), Invitation to the Dance, 1956, The Catered Affair, 1956, The Fastest Gun Alive, 1956, Hot Summer Night, 1957, Designing Women, 1957, House of Numbers, 1957, Who Was That Lady?, 1960, The Subterraneans, 1960, Elmer Gantry, 1960, Pepe, 1960 (also condr.), All in a Night's Work, 1961, One, Two, Three, 1961 (also condr.), Four Horseman of the Apocalypse, 1962, Long Day's Journey Into Night, 1962, Two for the Seesaw, 1962, Irma la Douce, 1963(Academy award, 193), Dead Ringer, 1964, Goodbye Charlie, 1964, Kiss Me Stupid, 1964, Inside Daisy Clover, 1965, Harper, 1966, The Fortune Cookie, 1966, The Swinger, 1966, Throughly Modern Millie, 1967, Valley of the Dolls, 1967, Paint Your Wagon, 1969, Mrs. Pollifax-Spy, 1971, Bang Bang, 1973, (TV mini series) Jennie: Lady Randolph Churchill, 1974, Léon, 1994, (opera and TV) A Streetcar Named Desire, San Francisco Opera, 1998 (also condr.), Fight Club, 1999, Return to the Arena: The Making of Rollerball, 2000; musical dir. (films) Act of Violence, 1948, Big Jack, 1949, The Secret Garden, 1949, The Great Sinner, 1949, Border Incident, 1949, Small Town Girl, 1953, Kiss Me Kate, 1953, Give a Girl a Break, 1953, Invitation to the Dance, 1956; condr. (films) Malaya, 1949, Above and Beyond, 1952, The Way West, 1967, The Music Lovers, 1970, Jesus Christ Superstar, 1973, Elephant Man, 1980; musician (film) Young at Heart, 1954; condr., music supervisor Kismet, 1955, Silk Stockings, 1957, GiGi, 1958 (Academy award, 1958), Porgy and Bess, 1959 (Academy award, 1959), My Fair Lady, 1964 (Academy award, 1964); music supervisor, musical dir., Bells Are Ringing, 1960; condr., musical dir. Rollerball, 1975; musical dir. (TV) 26th Annual Academy Awards, 1954, 28th Annual Academy Awards, 1956, 32nd Annual Academy Awards, 1960, 33rd Annual Academy Awards, 1961; condr.-in-chief Houston Symphony, 1967-70; music dir. London Symphony Orch., 1969-79, condr. laureate 1993-, Royal Philharm. Orch., Eng., 1988-91 (also music dir. 1985-88); music dir. South Bank Music Festival, London, 1972-74, Pitts. Symphony, 1976-84, L.A. Philharm., 1985-89; composer (theatre) Every Good Boy Deserves Favour, 1976, Oslo Philharmonic, 2002-03; guest condr. maj. symphony orchs. and festivals in U.S. and Europe including: festivals in Salzburg, Edinburgh, Flanders, Vienna, Osaka, Prague, Berlin, Bergen; appears annually with Boston Symphony Orchestra, N.Y. Philharmonic, Vienna Philharmonic, and others; recordings include Andre Previn/Royal Philharmonic Orchestra Holst: The Planets, Andre Previn/Royal Philharmonic Orchestra Vaughan Williams: Symphony No. 2, Andre Previn/Los Angeles Philharmonic Orchestra Prokofiev: Alexander Nevsky & Lt. Kije, Andre Previn/Royal Philharmonic Orchestra Vaughan Williams: Symphony No. 5 & Tallis Fantasia, Andre Previn/Vienna Philharmonic Orchestra Strauss: Also sprach Zarathustra & Tod und Verklarung, Andre Previn/Los Angeles Philharmonic Orchestra Bartok: Concerto for Orchestra / Janacek: Sinfonietta, Andre Previn/Vienna Philharmonic Orchestra/Arleen Auger Strauss: Ein Heldenleben & Four Last Songs, Andre Previn/Royal Philharmonic Orchestra/Horacio Guiterrez Brahms: Piano Conc. No. 2 & Haydn Variations, Andre Previn/Vienna Philharmonic Orchestra Strauss: Alpine Symphony, Andre Previn/Los Angeles Philharmonic Orchestra Dvorak: Symphony No. 9 New World & Carnival Overture, Andre Previn/Royal Philharmonic Orchestra/Horacio Guiterrez Brahms: Piano Concerto No. 1 & Tragic Overture, Andre Previn/Vienna Philharmonic Orchestra/Franz Bartolomey Strauss: Don Juan & Don Quixote, Andre Previn/Vienna Philharmonic Orchestra The Essential Richard Strauss, Andre Previn/Joe Pass/Ray Brown After Hours: Jazz Standards, Andre Previn/Ray Brown/Mundell Lowe Uptown: Songs of Harold Arlen, Duke Ellington & others, Andre Previn/Mundell Lowe/Ray Brown Old Friends, Andre Previn Triple Play, Ludwig van Beethoven String Quartet op. 131(Version for String Orchestra) Wiener Philharmoniker André Previn, Richard Strauss Der Rosenkavalier Le Chevalier à la Rose Il cavaliere della rosa (Suite) Orchestermusik Orchestral Music aus/from Intermezzo Salome Capriccio Wiener Philharmoniker André Previn, 1993, Frédéric Chopin Klavierkonzert Piano Concerto Concerto pour Piano Concerto per pianoforte: No. 2 24 Préludes op. 28 Maria João Pires Royal Philharmonic Orchestra André Previn, 1994(Grand Prix du Disque Frédéric Chopin - Warsaw, 1995), Samuel Barber Violinkonzert Violin Concerto Concerto pour Violon op. 14 Gil Shaham London Symphony Orchestra André Previn, 1994 (Cannes Classical award, 1995), Carl Orff Carmina Burana, 1994, Jean Sibelius Violinkonzert Violin Concerto Concerto pour Violon Concerto per violino 2 Serenaden Serenades op. 69 Humoresque op. 87 No. 1, Anne-Sophie Mutter Staatskapelle Dresden André Previn, 1995 (Edison award, 1997), Serge Prokofiev Violinkonzerte Violin Concertos Concertos pour Violon Concerti per violino: Nos. 1 and 2 Sonate für Violine solo Sonata for Solo Violin op. 115, Gil Shaham London Symphony Orchestra André Previn, 1996 (Gran Premio del Disco "Ritmo" (Madrid), 1996, Grand Prix de la Nouvelle Académie, 1996), Erich Korngold Symphony op. 40 Much Ado about Nothing op. 11 (Suite for Chamber Orchestra) London Symphony Orchestra André Previn, 1997, Richard Strauss, Horn Concertos No. 1 and No. 2 Oboe Concerto Duet Concertino for Clariner and Bassoon with String Orchestra, George Gershwin Songbook, 1998, Duke Ellington We Got It Good and That Ain't Bad, An Ellington Songbook, André Previn A Streetcar Named Desire, 1998 (Echo award, 1999), Maurice Ravel L'Enfant et les Sortilèges Ma Mère l'Oye, 1999, Anne-Sophie Mutter, Back to the Future, 2000, André Previn Diversions, 2001, Erich Korngold, 2002, Anne Sophie Mutter Tango Song and Dance, 2003, André Previn Violin Concerto & Bernstein Serenade, 2003 (Grammy award, 2005), Tchaikovsky-Korngold Violin Concertos; author: Music Face to Face, 1971, No Minor Chords, 1991; editor Orchestra, 1979, André Previn's Guide to Music, 1983, André Previn's Guide to the Orchestra: With Chapters on the Voice, Keyboards, Mechanical and Electronic Instruments, 1986. Served with AUS, 1950-51. Knighted (KBE), Her Majesty Queen Elizabeth II, 1996; recipient awards Nat. Grammophone Soc., Kennedy Ctr. Honoree, 1998, Glenn Gould prize, 2005; decorated Germany's Commander's Cross of the Order of Merit; named Musician of Yr., Musical America. Mem. Acad. Motion Picture Arts and Scis., Dramatists Guild, Brit. Composers Guild, Nat. Composers and Condrs. League, Degrees Curtis Inst., Royal Acad., Guild Hall Sch./Duquesne U. Office: care Columbia Artists 165 W 57th St New York NY 10019-2201

**PREVITE, ROBERT,** composer, musician; b. Niagara Falls, NY, July 16, 1959; s. Vincent James and Angela Previte; 1 child, Katherine. BA, SUNY, Buffalo. Musician, 1985—. Composer: The 23 Constellations of Joan Miró, 2002, Counterclockwise, 2003, The Coalition of the Willing, 2006, Dialed-In, 2006. Recipient composition award, NEA, Jerome Found., 2005; fellow, MacDowell Colony, 1999, 2000, 2001, 2003, 2005. Mem.: ASCAP. E-mail: etiverp@rcn.com.

**PREVITS, GARY JOHN,** finance educator, consultant; b. Cleve., Oct. 23, 1942; s. J.A. and L.M. (Guta) P.; m. F.A. Porubsky, Oct. 3, 1964; children: Robert, Susan, Joanne, Michelle. BSBA, John Carroll U., 1963; M Acctg., Ohio State U., 1964; PhD, U. Fla., 1972. CPA, Ohio, Ala. Mem. staff Deloitte, Cleve., 1963-68; asst. prof. Augusta (Ga.) Coll., 1968-70; instr. U. Fla., Gainesville, 1970-72; prof. U. Ala., 1973—79; prof. acctg. Case Western Res U., Cleve., 1979—, assoc. dean undergrad. program, 1994—. Vis. assoc.

prof., Northwestern U., 1977. Author: (with others) A History of Accounting in America, 1979, 98; editor Acctg. Historians Jour., 1977-80, 87-89, Ohio CPA Jour., 1982-85, Rsch. in Acctg. Reg., 1987-2004. Coach Rocky River (Ohio) Baseball Recreation, 1980-81; mem. nat. com. career exploring Boy Scouts Am., 1985-91; mem. Rocky River City Charter Rev. Com., 1990, 2002; chmn. Rocky River Mayor's Vision Com., 1995, 99. 1st U. S. Army, 1965-67. Mem. AICPA (governing coun. 1986-87, 89—, bd. dirs. 1995-98, Outstanding Educator 1996), Internat. Assn. Fin Execs. Inst. (fin. ethics com. 1997-2000, comm. com. 2000-02, edn. policy commn. 2002-04), Acad. Acctg. Historians (pres. 1974-78, Hourglass award 1980), Am. Acctg. Assn. (v.p. Ohio region 1983-84, dir. edn., exec. com. 1987-89), Ohio Soc. CPAs (v.p. 1987-88, pers. 1993-94, Gold medal 2002), Playhouse Club, VFW, KC. Roman Catholic. Avocations: reading, handball, jogging. Home: 3420 Bradfords Gate Cleveland OH 44116-3804 Office: Case Western Res U Weatherhead Sch Mgmt Dept Acctg Cleveland OH 44106-7235 Office Phone: 216-368-2074. Personal E-mail: gary_previts@email.com.

**PREVITTI, JAMES P.,** real estate executive; Founder Forecast Group, Rancho Cucamonga, Calif., 1971—, pres., CEO, 1989—. Recipient Fair Housing award L.A. Times; named Builder of Yr., Real Estate Entrepreneur of Yr. Mem. Calif. Bldg. Industry Assn. (pres., Medal of Honor). Office: Forecast 3536 Concours Ste 320 Ontario CA 91764-5593

**PREVOST, ROXANE LISE,** music theory educator; d. Roger Andre and Lise Houle Prevost. BA, U. Guelph, Ont., 1992; MusB, U. Ottawa, 1997; MusM, U. Western Ont., 1999; PhD, SUNY at Buffalo, 2003. Tchg. asst. U. Western Ont., London, 1997—99, SUNY, Buffalo, 1999—2001, instr., 2001—02; asst. prof. dept. music U. Ottawa, 2003—. Chair music grad. symposium SUNY, Buffalo, 2002—03; presenter in field; publ. in field. Ont. Grad. scholar, Govt. Ont., 1997—99, Pres. scholar, U. Western Ont. 1997—99, Social Scis. and Humanities Rsch. Coun. of Can. Doctoral fellow, Govt. Can., 2002—03, Coll. of Arts and Scis. Dissertation fellow, SUNY at Buffalo, 2002—03. Mem.: Music Theory Soc. N.Y. State, Can. U. Music Soc., Soc. for Music Theory. Roman Catholic. Avocations: violin, piano. Office: U Ottawa Dept Music 50 University Ottawa ON K1N 6N5 Canada Personal E-mail: rprevost@uottawa.ca.

**PREVOZNIK, MICHAEL E.,** health facility administrator, lawyer; BS, U. Notre Dame, 1983; MBA, U. Chgo., 1985, JD magna cum laude, 1988. With Dechert Price & Rhodes; chief legal compliance officer SBCL, 1994—96; v.p., chief legal compliance officer SmithKline Beecham Healthcare Svcs., 1996—98, v.p. compliance, 1998—99; v.p. legal Quest Diagnostics, Teterboro, NJ, 1999—, gen. counsel compliance, 1999—. Office: Quest Diagnostics One Malcolm Ave Teterboro NJ 07608 Business E-Mail: Michael.E.Prevoznik@questdiagnostics.com.

**PREWITT, CHARLES THOMPSON,** geochemist; b. Lexington, Ky., Mar. 3, 1933; s. John Burton and Margaret (Thompson) P.; m. Gretchen B. Hansen, Jan. 31, 1958; children: Daniel Hansen. SB, MIT, 1955, SM, 1960, PhD, 1962. Rsch. scientist E.I. DuPont De Nemours & Co. Inc., Wilmington, Del., 1962-69; assoc. prof. SUNY, Stony Brook, 1969-71, prof., 1971-86, chmn. dept. earth and space scis., 1977-80; dir. Geophys. Lab., Carnegie Inst. of Washington, 1986-98, mem. rsch. staff, 1998—2003; adj. prof. Dept. Geoscis. U. Ariz., Tucson, 2003—. Sec.-treas. U.S. Nat. Com. for Crystallography, Washington, 1983-85, 99—; gen. chmn. 14th Meeting of Internat. Mineral Assn., Stanford, Calif., 1986; chmn. NRC/NAS com. on physics and chemistry of earth materials, 1985-87; mem. bd. govs. Consortium for Advanced Radiation Svcs.; co-dir. NSF Ctr. for High Pressure Rsch., 1991—; disting. vis. prof. chemistry Ariz. State U., 1983. Editor: (jour.) Physics and Chemistry of Minerals, 1976-85; contbr. more than 180 articles to profl. jours. Bd. dirs. Internat. Ctr. for Diffraction Data, 1998-2002. Capt. USAR, 1956-65. NATO sr. postdoctoral fellow, 1975, Churchill overseas fellow, 1975, Japan Soc. for Promotion of Sci. fellow, 1983, Ernst Cloos Meml. scholar Johns Hopkins U., 2002-. Fellow AAAS, Mineral. Soc. Am. (pres. 1983-84, Roebling medal 2003), Am. Geophys. Union, Internat. Centre Diffraction Data; mem. Geol. Soc. Am., Am. Crystallographic Assn., Materials Rsch. Soc., Mineral. Soc. Gt. Britain and Ireland, Cosmos Club. Office: Dept Geoscis Univ Arizona Tucson AZ 85721-0077 Office Phone: 520-621-9993.

**PREWITT, JEAN,** not-for-profit organization executive; Degree, Harvard U.; degree in law, Georgetown U. Formerly lawyer Donovan Leisure Newton & Irvine; sr. v.p., gen. counsel United Internat. Pictures, 1982—89; with Nat. Telecomm. and Info. Adminstrn. U.S. Dept. Commerce, 1989—94; prin. Podesta Assocs., Washington, 1994—99; pres. Indep. Film & TV Alliance, L.A. 2000—01, CEO, 2001—; chair Film LA, LA, 2006—. Pres. Casa De Los Amigos, LA, 2003—. Adv. bd. Friends of Cancer Rsch., Washington, 2003—. Office: 10850 Wilshire Blvd 9th Fl Los Angeles CA 90024-4321 Business E-Mail: jprewitt@ifta-online.org.

**PREWITT, KENNETH,** political science professor, foundation administrator; b. Alton, Ill., Mar. 16, 1936; s. Carl Kenneth and Louise (Carpenter) P.; children: Jennifer Ann, Geoffrey Douglas. BA, So. Meth. U., 1958; MA, Washington U., St. Louis, 1959; PhD, Stanford U., 1963. Prof. polit. sci. U. Chgo., 1964-80, chmn. dept. polit. sci., 1975-76; dir. Nat. Opinion Rsch. Ctr. 1976-79; pres. Social Sci. Rsch. Coun., N.Y.C., 1979-85, 95-98; sr. v.p. Rockefeller Found., N.Y.C., 1985-95; dir. U.S. Census Bur., Washington, 1998-2001; dean grad. faculty New Sch. U., N.Y.C., 2001—02; Carnegie Prof. of Public Affairs School of International and Public Affairs, Columbia Univ., N.Y.C., 2002—. Vis. scholar U. Nairobi, Kenya, 1968-71; bd. dirs Washington U., So. Meth. U., Energy Found., Ctr. Advanced Study Behavioral Scis. Author: Political Socialization, 1969, Ruling Elites, 1973, Labryrinths of Democracy, 1973, Politics and Science in Census-Taking, 2003. Guggenheim fellow, 1983; fellow Center Advanced Study in Behavioral Scis., 1983; recipient Officer's Cross of Order of Merit, Rep. of Germany. Fellow AAAS, Am. Acad. Arts and Scis.; mem. Am. Polit. Sci. Assn., Coun. on Fgn. Rels. E-mail: kp2058@columbia.edu.

**PREWITT, WILLIAM CHANDLER,** finance company executive; b. Phila., Aug. 23, 1946; s. Richard Hickman and Jean Mary (Simpkins) Prewitt; m. Karen Ruth Padgett, May 15, 1971. BA in History, Transylvania Coll., 1968; cert., Coll. Fin. Planning, 1985; MS in Fin. Planning, Coll. for Fin. Planning, 1991. Dist. exec. Cen. N.C. Coun., Albemarle, 1971-74, Transatlantic Coun., Heidelburg, Fed. Republic Germany, 1974-78; field dir. Dutchess City Coun., Hyde Park, NY, 1978-80; prin. Prewitt Properties, Charleston, SC, 1980—, William C. Prewitt Cert. Fin. Planner, Charleston, SC, 1986—2004; owner Charleston Fin. Adv., LLC, 2005—; registered rep. First Investors Corp., Charleston, SC, 1982-83. Lectr. Coll. of Charleston, 1987—, Trident Tech. Coll., Charleston, 1987—, Charleston So. U. Sec. Hist. Ansonborough Neighborhood Assn., Charleston, 1987—90, v.p., 1999, pres., 1999—2000; bd. dirs. Christian Family Y, 1991—99, pres., 1995—97; treas. South Carolinians to Limit Congl. Terms, 1991—2000; deacon 1st Presbyn. Ch., Rockingham, NC, 1972—74; elder 1st Scots Ch., Charleston, 1990—93, meml. fund trustee, 1990—2000; exec. bd. Coastal Carolina Coun. Boy Scouts Am., 2001—04. 1st lt. Res. USMC, 1968—71. Named One of 300 Best Fin. Advisors, Worth Mag., 1996, 1997, 1998, One of 120 Best Fin. Advisors for Drs., Med. Econs. Mag., 1998. Mem.: SCV, SAR (chpt. pres. 1996—2003, chpt. pres. 2004—06), Nat. Assn. Personal Fin. Advisors (pres. region 1994—96, chmn. ethics and stds. com. 1996—99, nat. bd. dirs. 1996—99, chmn. compensation com. 1999—, Robert J. Underwood award 2005), Internat. Assn. Fin. Planners (registry 1986—92), Inst. Cert. Fin. Planners, S.C. Soc. Cert. Fin. Planners (pres. 1985—87, chmn. bd. dirs. 1988—90), St. David's Soc., Internat. Churchill Soc., Société Francaise (sec. 1999—2001, pres. 2001—02), Navy League (pres. 1992, chmn. bd. dirs. 1993, mem. Charleston Coun.), Carolina Yacht Club, Cruising Club Charleston (navigator 2003—04, vice comdr. 2004—05, comdr. 2005—06), Rotary (bd. dirs. 2000—02). Republican. Avocation: Mysteries, historic restorations. Home: 33 Hasell St Charleston SC 29401-1604 Office: 15 Broad St Charleston SC 29401-3030 Office Phone: 843-722-3331. E-mail: bill@charlestonfinancial.net.

**PREWOZNIK, JEROME FRANK,** retired lawyer; b. Detroit, July 15, 1934; s. Frank Joseph and Loretta Ann (Parzych) Prewoznik; m. Marilyn Ruth Johnson, 1970; 1 child, Frank Joseph II. AB cum laude, U. Detroit, 1955; JD with distinction, U. Mich., 1958. Bar: Calif. 1959. Pvt. practice, Calif., 1960-91. Served in U.S. Army, 1958—60. Mem.: State Bar Calif. Republican.

**PREY, BARBARA ERNST,** artist; b. N.Y.C., Apr. 17, 1957; d. Herbert Henry and Margaret (Joubert) Ernst; m. Jeffrey Drew Prey, Jan. 11, 1986; children: Austin William Ernst Prey, Emily Elizabeth Prey. BA with honors, Williams Coll., 1979; MDiv, Harvard U., 1986. Sales staff Tiffany and Co., N.Y.C., summer 1977; intern Met. Mus. Art, N.Y.C., summer 1979; pers. asst. Prince Albrecht Castell, Castell, Germany, 1980-81; with modern painting dept. Sotheby's Auction House, N.Y.C., 1981-82; sales asst. Marlborough Gallery, N.Y.C., 1982; tchg. asst. Boston Coll., 1984, Harvard U., Cambridge, Mass., 1984-85; vis. lectr. Tainan (Taiwan) Coll. and Sem., 1986-87; artist Oyster Bay, NY, 1987—. Artist-in-residence Westminster Sch., Simsbury, Conn., 1998; art juror Washington and Jefferson Coll., Washington, 1990; chmn.'s coun. Heckscher Mus.; presenter in field. Illustrator Boys Harbor Cookbook, 1988, A Dream Became You, A City Grows Up, 1991, (cover) Am. Artist Mag., 1994, Barbara Ernst Prey: Watercolors, 1998, Internat. Art Newspaper, 2001, N.Y. Post, 2001, N.Y. Daily News, (PBS) True North, 2001, (PBS) Metro Section, 2001, Arts and Antiques Mag., 2001, 2003, Barbara Ernst Prey: A Trace in the Mind, 2002, NY Times, 2002; illustrator: cover NY Times, 2003; illustrator (cover) NY Times, 2004, 2005, Newsday, 2002, Artwork in the American Embassy Prague, 2002, Artwork in the American Embassy Oslo, 2003, The Robb Report, 2003, LA Times, 2004, White House Christmas Card, 2003, The New Yorker, 2004, Larry King Live CNN, 2004, (PBS) WLIW-NY, 2005, Style Soc1., Washington Post, 2005, The New York Times, 2005, NPR, 2005; one-woman shows include Harvard-Yale-Princeton Club, Pitts., 1991, Jensen Fine Arts, NYC, 1999, 2001, exhibited in group shows at Kennedy Space Ctr., Nassau County, N.Y., 1988, Nat. Arts Club, N.Y.C., 1988, Gallery One, Rockland, Maine, 1992, Williams Coll., Williamstown, Mass., 1993, Johnstown (Pa.) Art Mus., 1993, Blair Art Mus., Holidaysburg, Pa., 1993, Phila. Mus. Art Gallery, 1995, Mus. Fine Arts, Westmoreland Mus. Am. Art, Greensburg, Pa., 1996 (Best in Show award), Mus. the Southwest, Midland, Tex., Farnsworth Mus. Art, Rockland, Maine, 1997, Guild Hall Mus., East Hampton, NY, 1998, Portland (Maine) Mus. Art, 1998, U.S. Embassy, Prague, 2002, Heckscher Mus. Art, Huntington, N.Y., 2002, Guild Hall Mus., East Hampton, NY, 2002, 2004, Gilcrease Mus., Tulsa, 2002, NASA Commn.: The Internat. Space Station, 2003, The White House, Collection of Pres. and Mrs. George Bush, 2003, 2004, Kennedy Space Ctr., 2003—06, U.S. Embassy, Oslo, Prague, Liberia, Belarus, 2003, 2004, 2005, U. S. Embassy, Paris, Madrid, 2006, NASA Commn X-43.: Columbia Tribute, 2004, US Embassy, Minsk, 2004, Madrid, 2006, Paris, 2006, NASA Commn: Shuttle Discovery Relaunch, U.S. Embassy, 2005, Kennedy Space Ctr., 2006, Represented in permanent collections Pres. and Mrs. George Bush Farnsworth Mus. Art, NASA, Kennedy Space Ctr., displayed 1997 Holiday Card on 80,000 screens worldwide Bloomberg Bus. Newss; featured on Fox TV News, 1999; contbr. to popular mags., local newspapers. Class agt. Williams Coll., Williamstown, Mass., 1981—91; mem. chmn.'s coun. Heckscher Mus.; lectr. Nat. Gallery Art, Washington, 2005; mem. chmn.'s coun. Heckscher Mus.; active 1st Presby. Ch., Oyster Bay, NY. Fulbright scholar, Germany, 1979-80; grantee Roothbert Fund, Chataugua, N.Y., 1982-84; recipient Ch. History award Gordan-Conwell Sem., S. Hamilton, Mass., 1984, Henry Luce Found., Taiwan, 1986-87, Jean Thoburn award, 1994, Women of Distinction award, N.Y. State Senate, 2004, Women of Distinction award, Distinction Mag., 2005. Mem. Pitts. Watercolor Soc. (Jean Thoburn award 1994), Nat. Mus. Women in the Arts. Avocations: tennis, skiing, birdwatching, reading, squash. Home and Office: 22 Pearl St Oyster Bay NY 11771-2305 E-mail: bprey@optonline.net.

**PREYSZ, LOUIS ROBERT FONSS, III,** management consultant, educator; b. Quantico, Va., Aug. 1, 1944; s. Louis Robert Fonss, Jr. and Lucille (Parks) P.; m. Patricia Dianne Yelland; children: Louis Robert Fonss IV, Christine Elizabeth, Michael Anthony, Daniel Timothy. BA, U. Wis., 1968; MBA, U. Utah, 1973; postgrad., Rutgers U., 1983; grad., Command and Gen. Staff Coll., 1986. Tchg. and rsch. asst. U. Utah, Salt Lake City, 1972—73; mktg. and pers. officer Security 1st Nat. Bank of Sheboygan, Wis., 1973—76; mktg. dir. 1st Nat. Bank Rock Island, Ill., 1976—77; asst. v.p. mktg. sales mgr. 1st Nat. Bank Birmingham, Ala., 1977—78; v.p. mktg. mgr. Sun 1st Nat. Bank Orlando, Fla., 1978—80; adj. prof. Disney U., Orlando, 1978—79; pres. Preysz Assocs., Saint Augustine, Fla., 1980—. Assoc. prof. mgmt. and banking Flagler Coll., Saint Augustine, Fla., 1982—; faculty U. Wis., Sheboygan, 1973-76, Fla. Inst. Tech., 1976-77, St. Ambrose Coll., Davenport, Iowa, 1976-77, U. Ctrl. Fla., 1979-81, Columbia (Mo.) Coll., 1981-82; mem. tng. and profl. devel. coun. Bank Mktg. Assn., 1976-78, chmn., 1978; mem. mktg. and pub. rels. com. Wis. Bankers Assn., 1975; v.p. Ala. Automated Clearing House Assn., 1977-78; spkr. in field; host to daily FM radio program Money Issues. Author: How to Introduce a New Service, 1976, Energy Efficiency Programs and Lending Practices for Florida's Financial Institutions, 1980, Credit Union Marketing, 1981, An Effective Management Structure for Multi-Holding Companies, 1983, Credit Union Strategic Marketing, 1993; contbg. editor: Target Market, an Instructional Approach to Bank Cross Selling of Services, New Accounts Training Manual, 1977, Tested Techniques in Bank Marketing, 1977; contbg. author: Rapid Debt Reduction Strategies, 1990, The Debt Free Army, 1993; mem. editl rev. bd. SAM Advanced Mgmt. Jour.; contbg. reviewer Professional Selling in the Buyer's Era, Human Resource Management, 8th edit.; contbr. articles to mags. Bd. dirs. Cath. Charities Bur. Inc., 1988—89, v.p., 1989; bd. dirs. United Way St. Johns County, 1989—95, chmn., 1991—95; charter mem. U.S. Com. for Battle Normandy Mus., 1989, Nat. WWII Meml.; mem. Reagan Presdl. Libr., 1989, Rep. Presdl. Task Force, 1982—86, Rep. Nat. Com., 1980—89, 2000—, Rep. Nat. Com. Victory, 2000; charter mem. George W. Bush for Pres.; bd. dirs., treas., deacon Grace Cmty. Ch., 1996—99; fin. chair Billy Graham Crusade, Jacksonville Crusade. Capt. U.S. Army, 1966—72, officer Florida Army N.G. Recipient Congrl. Order Merit, Rep. Congrl. Com., 2003. Fellow: Soc. Advancement Mgmt. Honor Soc. (internat. v.p., bd. dir., cons., Mgmt. Excellence award 1990); mem.: Ronald Reagan Presdl. Libr., Nat. World War II Mus., Nat. D-Day Mus. (charter), Friends of Collections Soc. Pres. Harrison Home, Nat. Mus. U.S. Army, Civil War Preservation Trust, Civil War Soc., U.S. Holocaust Meml. Mus. (charter), U. Wis. Alumni Assn., U. Utah Alumni Assn., Nat. Guard Officers Assn. Fla., Nat. Guard Assn. U.S., Nat. Trust Hist. Preservation, St. Augustine Officers Club, U.S. Army Hist. Found. (charter), Rotary (Paul Harris fellow), Sigma Beta Delta, Omicron Delta Kappa, Phi Gamma Delta. Republican. Mem. Christian Ch. Avocations: military history, exercise, civil war history, sports. Office: PO Box 1027 Saint Augustine FL 32085-1027 Office Phone: 904-819-6243. Personal E-mail: mosserrs@aol.com. Business E-Mail: preyszlr@flagler.edu.

**PREZIOSO, GIOVANNI P.,** lawyer; b. 1957; B, Harvard Coll., 1979; JD magna cum laude, Harvard Law Sch. Assoc. Cleary, Gottlieb, Steen & Hamilton LLP, Washington, 1982—91, ptnr., 1991—2002, 2006—; gen. counsel, chief legal officer SEC, Washington, 2002—06. Office: Cleary Gottlieb Steen & Hamilton LLP 2000 Pennsylvania Ave NW Washington DC 20006 Office Phone: 202-974-1650.

**PRIBOR, HUGO CASIMER,** physician; b. Detroit, June 12, 1928; s. Benjamin Harrison and Wanda Frances (Mioskowski) P.; m. Judith Elinor Smith, Dec. 22, 1955; children: Jeffrey D., Elizabeth F., Katheryn A. BS, St. Mary's Coll., 1949; MS, St. Louis U., 1951, PhD, 1954, MD, 1955. Diplomate Am. Bd. Pathology; cert. age mgmt. medicine. Intern Providence Hosp., Detroit, 1955-56; resident pathologic anatomy and clin. pathology NIH, Bethesda, Md., 1956-59; field investigator gastric cytology rsch. project Nat. Cancer Inst., Bowman-Gray Sch. Medicine, Winston-Salem, NC, 1959-60; assoc. pathologist dir. clin. lab. Bon Secours Hosp., Grosse Pointe, Mich., 1960-63; pathologist, dir. labs. Samaritan Hosp. Assn., East Side Gen. Hosp., Detroit, 1963-64, Anderson Meml. Hosp., Mt. Clemens, Mich., 1963-64; cons. pathologist Middlesex County Med. Examiners Office, New Brunswick, NJ, 1964-73; dir. dept. labs., chief pathologist, sr. attending physician Perth Amboy (N.J.) Gen. Hosp., 1964-73; chmn., CEO Ctr. Lab. Medicine, Inc.,

Metuchen, NJ, 1968-77; v.p. med. affairs Damon Corp., Med. Svcs. Group, 1977-78; exec. med. dir. MDS Health Group, Inc., Red Bank, NJ, 1978-80; med. dir. Internat. Clin. Labs., Inc., Nashville, 1981-88, SmithKline Beechman Clin. Labs., Nashville, 1988—96, Quest Diagnostics, Inc., Nashville, 1996—; med. dir., physician Pribor & Assocs., Tampa, 2003—. Physician, pathologist Assoc. Pathologists (P.C.), Nashville, 1981-2003; rsch. assoc. dept. pathology St. Louis U. Sch. Medicine, 1954-55; instr. pathology Bowman-Gray Sch. Medicine, Winston-Salem, N.C., 1959-60; asst. prof. chemistry U. Detroit, 1961-64; instr. pathology Wayne State U. Sch. Medicine, Detroit, 1961-64; clin. assoc. prof. dept. pathology Med. Sch. Rutgers U., The State U., New Brunswick, N.J., 1966-68; cons. Health Facilities Planning and Constrn. Svc., USPHS, HEW, Rockville, Md., 1970-71; prof. biomed. engring. Coll. Engring., Rutgers, The State U., New Brunswick, N.J., 1971-75, 80-82; chmn. bd. trustees St. Mary's Coll., Winona, Minn., 1972-74, chmn. fin. com., 1971-72; clin. prof. pathology Vanderbilt U. Sch. Medicine, Nashville, 1981-2003. Author: (with G. Morrell and G. H. Scherr) Drug Monitoring and Pharmacokinetic Data, 1980, The Laboratory Consultant, 1992; contbr. articles to profl. jours. Fellow Am. Soc. Clin. Pathologists (Silver award 1968); mem. AMA, Am. Assn. Exptl. Pathology, Coll. Am. Pathologists (chmn. subcom. 1974-78), Internat. Acad. Pathology, Pan Am. Med. Assn. (life), N.J. State Med. Soc., Acad. Medicine N.J. (chmn. clin. pathology sect. 1965-67), N.J. Soc. Pathologists (exec. com. 1965-67), Sigma Xi. Republican. Roman Catholic. Home: 5700 Mariner St Unit 704 Tampa FL 33609-3458 Office Phone: 813-282-7173. E-mail: hpribor@mindspring.com, DrPribor@hpribor.com.

PRIBRAM, KARL HARRY, neuroscience and psychology educator, brain researcher; b. Feb. 25, 1919; BS, U. Chgo., 1938, MD, 1941; PhD in Psychology (hon.), U. Montreal, Can., 1992; PhD in Philosophy (hon.), U. Bremen, 1996. Diplomate Am. Bd. Neurol. Surgery, Am. Bd. Med. Psychotherapists. Lectr. Yale U., New Haven, 1951-58; dir. psychology Inst. of Living, Hartford, Conn., 1951-58; fellow Ctr. for Advanced Studies in Behavioral Sci., Stanford (Calif.) U., 1958-59, assoc. prof., 1959-62, NIH lifetime rsch. career prof., 1962-89, prof. emeritus, 1989—; eminent scholar Radford (Va.) U., 1989—2006, prof. emeritus, 2006—. Vis. scholar, hon. lectr. MIT, 1954, Clark U., 1956, Harvard, 1956, Haverford Coll., 1961, U. So. Calif., 1961, U. Leningrad, 1962, U. Moscow, 1962, U. Alta., Can., 1968, Ctr. for Study Dem. Insts., 1967-75, U. Coll., London, 1972, U. Chgo., 1973, Menninger Sch. Psychiatry, 1973-76, Ohio State U., 1975; vis. lectr. Grass Found., 1977; Phillips lectr., Haverford Coll., 1979; Lashley lectr., Queens Coll., 1979; Hubert Humphrey lectr. Macalester Coll., 1981; lectr. Internat. Mgmt. Inst., Geneva, Switzerland, 1987, Inst. Med. Psychology, Naples, 1988; disting. lectr. Second Annual Symposium of the Mind, Arlington, Tex., 1988; disting. prof. Georgetown U., George Mason U., 2006—; hon. lectr. Sirius Seminaries, Paris, 1988, Bielefeld, Germany, 1990, numerous others. Author: Brain and Behavior, vol. 1-4, 1969, What Makes Man Human, 1971, Languages of the Brain: Experimental Paradoxes and Principles in Neuropsychology, 1971; The Neurosciences: Third Study Program, 1971, Brain and Perception: Holonomy and Structure in Figural Processing, 1991, Rethinking Neural Networks: Quantum Fields and Biological Data, 1993, Origins: Brain and Self Organization, 1994, Scale in Conscious Experience: Is the Brain Too Important to be Left to Specialists to Study?, 1995, Freud's Project Reassessed, 1976; editor, mem. consulting bd. Neuropsychologia Jour. Math. Biology, Internat. Jour. Neurosci., Behavioral and Brain Scis., Jour. Mental Imagery, Jour. Human Movement Studies, Jour. Social and Biol. Structures, ReVision, STSM Quar., Indian Jour. Psychophysiology, Internat. Jour. Psychophysiology, Cognition and Brain Theory; contbr. over 400 articles to profl. jours. Recipient Lifetime Rsch. Career award in neurosci. NIH, 1962-89, Humanitarian award INTA, 1980, Realia honor Inst. Advanced Philosophic Rsch., 1986, 93, Outstanding Contbrs. award Am. Bd. Med. Psychotherapists, Neural Network Leadership award Internat. Neural Network, 1996, Dagmar and Vaclev Havel prize, 1989. Fellow Am. Acad. Arts and Scis., N.Y. Acad. Scis. (hon. life); mem. AAUP, AMA, AAAS, APA (pres. div. physiol. and comparative psychology 1967-68, pres. div. theoretical and philos. psychology 1979-80), Internat. Neuropsychol. Soc. (founding pres. 1967-69), Internat. Assn. Study of Pain, Soc. Exptl. Psychologists (Anderson Lifetime Achievement award 2005), Am. Psychol. Soc., Am. Psychopathological Assn. (Paul Hoch award 1975), Am. Acad. Psychoanalysis, Soc. Biol. psychiatry (Manfred Sakel award 1976), Soc. Clin. and Exptl. Hypnosis (Henry Guze award 1991), Soc. Neurosci., Sigma Xi. Home: PO Box 679 Warrenton VA 20188-0679 E-mail: pribramk@georgetown.edu.

PRICE, ALFRED LEE, lawyer, mining executive; b. Little Rock, May 19, 1935; s. Dewey Ernest and Dorothy Ava (Cooper) P.; m. Magdalena Torres, June 20, 1958; children: Gregory L., Ana Maria. BA, Hendrix Coll., 1956; JD, Tulane U., 1967. Bar: La. 1967, Miss. 1974, D.C., U.S. Supreme Ct., 1980, U.S. Tax Ct., 1977, cert. arbitrator, mediator, Am. Arbitration Assn. and Better Bus. Bur., Nat. Arbitration Forum. Office mgr., dir. personnel Petroleum Helicopters Co., Lafayette, La. and New Orleans, 1956-67; atty. Offshore Navigation and Petroleum Helicopters Co., New Orleans, 1967-74; gen. counsel First Miss. Corp., Jackson, 1974-93, corp. sec., 1988-93; commr. Miss. Employment Commn., Jackson, 1994—2002. Arbitrator Am. Arbitration Assn., 1998—. Mem. Jackson Co of C., chmn. legislative com., 1991-94. Recipient Arbitrator of Yr., Better Bus. Bureau, 1998. Mem. ABA, La. Bar Assn., Miss. Bar Assn., Hinds County Bar Assn., Miss. Mfrs. Assn. (bd. dirs.), Miss. Econ. Coun. (chmn. tort reform com.), River Hills Club. Methodist.

PRICE, ALICIA HEMMALIN, retired psychotherapist, alcohol/drug abuse services professional; b. New Bedford, Mass., Nov. 24, 1937; d. William Alton Disbury and Hazel Rogers; m. John Paul Hemmalin, Aug. 11, 1957 (div. 1970); m. John Barrett Price, Nov. 3, 1983 (dec. 1998); children: Karen, Roxanne, Eric. Student, Mass. Coll. Art, 1957—58; BA in Psychology/Art, U. R.I., 1972; MA in Counseling R I Coll., 1978; cert. Jungian/Depth Psychology Counseling, Interfaith Counseling Ctr., Providence, 1990. Cert. chem. dependency profl. Internat. Cert. Reciprocity Consortium for Alcoholism and Other Drug Dependencies. Therapist creative arts Health Care Industry, RI, 1976—87, Mass.; family counselor Family Focus Program, Edgehill Newport, RI, 1987—93; social worker Thundermist Health Assoc., Woonsocket, RI, 1990—91; clinician rsch. team Miriam Hosp., Providence, 1991—2004, ret. Spkr. in field. Mem.: Jean Baker Miller Tng. Inst. Stone Ctr. Wellesly Coll., East Providence Substance Abuse Prevention Task Force, Nat. Assoc. for Alcoholism and Drug Abuse Counselors, Nat. Mus. Women Artists, Providence Art Club. Independent. Avocations: photography, writing, dance, bicycling. Personal E-mail: adisburyprice@hotmail.com.

PRICE, AMELIA RUTH, not-for-profit foundation president, artist, small business owner; b. Bklyn., Sept. 4, 1942; d. Dr. Alphonse Frederick Pagano and Adele Marie Savarese; 1 child, Ean James. BA, Georgian Ct. Coll., Lakewood, NJ, 1964; MA in Art Hist., Cath. U. of Am., Washington, DC, 1968. Cert. Permanent Certificate, Art State of N.Y. Edn. Dept., 1971. Art tchr. Bd. Coop. Ednl. Svcs., Patchogue, NY, 1967—68; art director Roland Advt. Co., N.Y.C., 1968—69; art dept. chair Bd. Coop. Ednl. Svcs. II, Deer Park, NY, 1969—78; v.p. Delicious Selections Ltd, White Plains, NY, 1991—95; pres., owner Parker Commodities Ltd, Kings Park, NY, 1995—; owner Bubbling Oaks Samoyeds, Commack, NY, 1974—. Co-founder bubbling oaks samoyeds kennels Bubbling Oaks Samoyeds, Commack, NY, 1974—2002. Samoyed Newsletter and other publs.featuring Samoyeds, 1999—; contbr. articles on Samoyeds and their care to various publs., 1999—. Pres. Samoyed Club of Am. Edn. and Rsch. Found., Inc., Madison, Wis., 2001—, v.p., 1997—2001. Recipient # 1 Samoyed Bitch, Kennel Rev., 1974, 1975, 1976, 1977, 1978, 1983, 1984, # 3 Samoyed, Dogs in Canada, 1976, Top Winning Team, Orgn. for the Working Samoyed Inc., 1986, 1988. Mem. Habour Lights Painter, Decorative Artists LI, Soc. Decorative Painters, Nat. Assn. Woman Bus. Owners (pub. affairs com. 2003—), Suffolk County Kennel Club Inc. (chmn. hospitality 1989—99, bd. dirs. 1996—99), Westbury Kennel Association (chmn. of trophies 1985, chmn. judges' transport. 2000), Samoyed Club of America Inc. (pres. 1997—99, Top Winning Bitch 1975, 1976, 1985, Top Winning Team 1985, Top Winning Bitch 1986, Top Winning Team 1987). Home: 128 Cowie Rd Commack NY 11725

PRICE, ARDYTHE BERNADEANE, nurse; b. Two Hills, Alta., Can., Sept. 27, 1948; d. Peter Cecil and Doris Eunice Tym; children: Shelley, Steven. AS, Pacific Union Coll., 1972; BA in English, Loma Linda U., 1973. RN Calif. RN Agnews State Hosp., Santa Clara, Calif., 1975—80, Kaiser, San Jose, Calif., 1980—90, Fremont Riedout, 1991—92, Sierra Nursing Registry, various cities, Calif., 1992—2002, Res-Care/Sierra Nurses, Yuba City, Calif., 1995—2002; RN, long term care Maxims Registry, Sacramento, 2006—. Rep. Calif. Nursing Assn., San Jose, Calif., 1974; various coms. and bds. Agnews State Hosp., San Jose, Calif., 1979—80; pvt. nurse, Yuba City, Calif. Vol. Salvation Army, Marysville, Calif., 1996; mem. Sutter County Dem. Ctrl. Com., Yuba City, Calif., 1996—; sec. Yuba Sutter Dem. Club, Marysville, Calif., 2001—04; bd. dirs. comms. Samaritan Village, Yuba City, Calif., 1996—. Mem.: Sutter County Dem. Women's Club, Women of the Moose (chmn. ednl. advancement 2004—05). Democrat. Seventh Day Adventist. Avocations: ballroom dancing, reading, swimming, exercise, party planning. Home: 1445 Stabler Ln # 4 Yuba City CA 95993 Office Phone: 530-218-3478, 916-974-2599. Personal a092748@yahoo.com, ardytheprice@aol.com. E-mail: ardyteprice04@hotmail.com.

PRICE, ARNOLD HEREWARD, historian; b. Bonn, Germany, July 1, 1912; arrived in U.S., 1933; s. Hereward Thimbleby and Liese Price; children: Jeffrey Thomas, John Brigham(dec.), William Frederick Stephen. BA, U. Mich., MA in History, PhD in History, U. Mich. Asst. supt. U. Mich. Arch. Lab. W.P.A., Ann Arbor; analyst Libr. of Congress, Washington; intelligence analyst OSS, Washington; rsch. tchr. U.S. Army, Ft. Eustis, Va.; intelligence State Dept., Washington; spl. historian supr. Libr. of Congress, Washington; chief bibliographer Am. Hist. Assn., Washington. Author: The Evolution of the Zollverein, 1949, Missionary to the Malagasy, 1980, The Germanic Warrior Cults, 1996, My Twentieth Century, 2003; contbr. articles to profl. jours. Sgt. U.S. Army. Recipient Bronson-Thomas award, U. Mich., 1935, honoree, ABC-Clio Hist. Soc., 1985. Mem.: Assn. for the Bibliography of History, Am. Hist. Assn., OSS Soc. Home: 7470 Spring Village Dr Unit RG1409 Springfield VA 22150-4487

PRICE, B. BYRON, historian; BS, U.S. Mil. Acad., 1970; MA in Mus. Sci., Tex. Tech. U., 1977; postgrad., Am. U., Washington, 1975. Tchg. asst. Tex. Tech. U., Lubbock, 1975, rsch. coord. Ranching Heritage Ctr./Mus., 1976-77; curator of history Panhandle-Plains Hist. Mus., Canyon, Tex., 1977-82, exec. dir., 1982-86, Nat. Cowboy Hall of Fame and Western Heritage Ctr., Oklahoma City, 1987-96, Buffalo Bill Hist. Ctr., Cody, Wyo., 1996—. Lectr. in field; condr. seminars in field; cons. in field. Advisory editor: The Handbook of Texas, 1986-96; editl. bd. N.Mex. Hist. Rev., 1990-93, Jour. Ariz. History, 1993-95; assoc. editor The Ency. of the West, 1996; author: Cowboys of the American West, 1996, Crafting a Southwestern Masterpiece, 1986, Imagining the Open Range: Erwin E. Smith, Cowboy Photographer, 1997, Longheed: A Painter's Painter, 1991, The National Cowboy Hall of Fame Chuck Wagon Cook Book, 1995, She Doesn't Write Like a Woman: Mari Sandoz and the Cattlemen, 1996, Fine Art of the West, 2004; co-author: The Golden Spread: An Illustrated History of Amarillo and the Texas Panhandle, 1986; co-editor: Cowboy Justice, 1997, Adventuring with the Old-Timers: Trails Traveled and Tales Told, 1979; contbr. articles to profl. jours. Mem. tourism task force Okla. Dept. Commerce, 1987; mem. Okla. Film Adv. Commn., 1988-90; bd. dirs. Okla. Ctr. for the Book, 1990—; judge Arts for the Parks Ann. Exhbn., 1992-93; mem. cultural opportunities work group Okla. Futures, 1993; mem. Oklahoma City Conv. and Visitors Commn., 1996—. Recipient Gov.'s Arts award State of Okla., 1994. Mem. Tex. Assn. Mus. (exec. coun. 1985-86), Okla. Mus. Assn. (v.p. 1993-95), Mus. West Consortium (pres. 1996—), Western History Assn. (mem. program com. 1997), Am. Assn. Mus., Tex. State Hist. Assn., Western Writers of Am., Panhandle Plains Hist. Soc. Office: Buffalo Bill Hist Ctr 720 Sheridan Ave Cody WY 82414-3428

PRICE, BERNICE IRENE, retired elementary school educator; b. Creston, Iowa, Apr. 17, 1922; d. Theodore Morton Hayden and Mabel Pearl Reed; m. Robert Henry Johnson, July 15, 1945 (dec.); children: Jeanine Kae Johnson, Roger Hayden Johnson, Julie Anne Johnson; m. Clarence Howard Price, Oct. 12, 1990; stepchildren: Stanley, Janet, Lou Ann, Daniel. Cert. in elem. edn., Simpson Coll., 1941; BS, Drake U., 1965; libr. cert., U. Utah, 1970. 3d and 4th grade tchr. Ellston (Iowa) Consolidated Sch., 1941—42; 4th and 5th grade tchr. Laurel (Iowa) Consolidated Sch., 1942—44; 4th grade tchr. Knoxville (Iowa) Sch., 1944—45; tchr. kindergarten and 4th grade Kellogg (Iowa) Sch., 1961—69; Thomas Jefferson libr. Newton (Iowa) Cmty. Sch., 1969—86; hosp. vol. Marshalltown (Iowa) Med. and Surg. Ctr., 1989—90. Author: Grandpa's Threshing Run, 1999. Vol. Heifer Project, Ark., 1991, Navajo Indian Reservation, 1985; del. Iowa State Rep. Conv.; dist. chairwoman Evang. United Brethren Ch. Mem.: Ret. Sch. Pers. Assn., Mayflower Soc. Methodist. Avocations: travel, reading, singing, lay speaking at church. Home: 2001 Skyline Dr Marshalltown IA 50158

PRICE, BETTY JEANNE, chimes musician; b. Long Beach, Calif., June 12, 1942; d. Grant E. and Miriam A. (Francis) Sickles; m. Harvey H. Price, Aug. 6, 1975; children: Thomas Neil Gering, Timothy Ray(dec.), Pamela Kay(dec.). Degree in Acctg.. Northland Pioneer Coll., Show Low, Ariz., 1977. Youth missionary Open Bible Standard Missions, Trinidad, 1958-59; typographer Joel H. Weldon & Assocs., Scottsdale, Ariz., 1980-89; exec. chief acct. Pubs. Devel. Corp., San Diego, 1991-93; coord. music and worship College Ave. Bapt. Ch., San Diego, 1994-95; ChoirChime soloist, 1986—; exec. acct. Advance Reprographics, San Diego, 1996—2003. Chime musician and writer. Author: 101 Ways to Fix Broccoli, 1994, ABC's of Abundant Living, 1995; contbg. author God's Vitamin C for the Spirit, 1995, BounceBook, 1997, You Can Bounce Back Too, 1998, Breaking Free from Financial Bondage: A Guide to Living Debt Free, 2004; musical arranger: handbell/chime Classical Sounds, 2005, A Musical Tour Around the World, 2005, Music for Special Occasions, 2005, Sounds of Christmas, 2005, A Musical Christmas Story, 2005, Hymns of Faith, 2005; musician: (CD) Classical Chimes, 2005, Chimes of Faith, 2005, Christmas Chimes, 2005. Mem.: ASCAP, Am. Guild English Handbell Ringers. Business E-Mail: chimesoloist@aol.com

PRICE, CHARLES H., II, former ambassador; b. Kansas City, Mo., Apr. 1, 1931; s. Charles Harry and Virginia (Ogden) P.; m. Carol Ann Swanson, Jan. 10, 1969; children: Caroline Lee, Melissa Marie, Charles H., II B., Pickette. Student, U. Mo., 1951-53; LLD (hon.), Westminster Coll., 1984, U. Mo., 1988; LHD (hon.), Baker U., 1991; DSc (hon.), U. Buckingham, Eng., 1993. Chmn. bd. dir. Price Candy Co., Kansas City, 1969-81, Am. Bancorp., Kansas City, 1973-81; chmn., chief exec. officer Am. Bank & Trust Co., Kansas City, 1973-81; ambassador to Belgium Brussels, 1981-83; Am. ambassador to U.K. London, 1983-89. Chmn. bd. Americanc, Inc., St. Joseph, Mo., 1989—92, pres., CEO, 1990—92; chmn. bd. Merc. Bank Kansas City, Mo., 1992—96; bd. dirs. Palmer Capital Assocs., Ltd., London. Trustee Midwest Rsch. Inst., Kansas City, chmn., 1990-93. Hon. fellow Regent's Coll., London, 1986; recipient William Booth award Salvation Army, 1985, World Citizen of Yr. award Mayor of Kansas City, 1985, Trustee Citation award Midwest Rsch. Inst., 1987, Disting. Svc. award Internat. Rels. Coun., 1989, Mankind award Cystic Fibrosis Found., 1990, Gold Good Citizenship award SAR, 1991, Chancellor's medal U. Mo. Kansas City, 1992, William F. Yates medallion William Jewell Coll., 1996. Mem.: The Vintage Country Club, White's Club, Swinley Forest Club, Kansas City Country Club, Eldorado Country Club, Brook Club, Cypress Point Club, Los Angeles County Club, River Club, Sigma Alpha Epsilon. Republican. Episcopalian. Office: 1 W Armour Blvd Ste 300 Kansas City MO 64111-2087 Office Phone: 816-360-6175.

PRICE, CLIFFORD WARREN, retired metallurgist, researcher; b. Denver, Apr. 22, 1935; s. Warren Wilson and Vivian Fredricka (Cady) P.; m. Carole Joyce Watermon, June 14, 1969; children: Carla Beth, Krista Lynn Price. MetE, Colo. Sch. Mines, 1957; MS, Ohio State U., 1970, PhD, 1973. Design engr. Sundstrand Aviation-Denver, 1957-60; materials specialist Denver Rsch. Inst., 1960-63; sr. metallurgist Rocky Flats div. Dow Chem. Co., Golden, Colo., 1963-66; staff metallurgist Battelle Columbus (Ohio) Labs.,

1966-75; sr. scientist Owens-Corning Fiberglas, Granville, Ohio, 1975-80; metallurgist Lawrence Livermore (Calif.) Nat. Lab., 1980-93; retired, 1993. Contbr. articles to profl. jours. Battelle Columbus Labs. fellow, 1974-75. Mem. Metall. Soc. AIME, Microscopy Soc. Am. (treas. Denver 1961-62), Am. Soc. Metals Internat. Achievements include research on electron, scanning probe and optical microscopy, secondary ion mass spectroscopy, deformation, fracture and recrystallization mechanisms in metals, recrystallization kinetics. E-mail: clifford.price@comcast.net.

PRICE, DANA KENNETH, foreman, automotive executive; b. Santa Clara, Calif., Dec. 18, 1964; s. Orval L. (Stepfather) and Margaret E. Petersen; m. Stacy Jo Lisher, Feb. 21, 1999; children: Brandon Lee, Ryan Mitchel. Comm. sgt., combat ops. US Army, Clarksville, Ky., 1984—92; shipping and sales foreman Safeway, Clackamas, Oreg., 1992—. Owner, operator NW Barracudas Parts and Trim Restorations, Boring, Oreg., 2000—. Contbr. articles to profl. jours. Decorated Army Commendation medal with 2 oak leaf clusters. Mem.: 1967 to 1969 Plymouth Barracuda Owners Group (life; adminstr. 2002—06). Christian. Achievements include invention of new and creative ways to restore very old automotive trim parts that were not intended to be restored when they were produced; paints to match the old paints using new materials. Avocations: automotive restoration, building bikes. Home: 10625 SE 362nd Ave SP C-23 Boring OR 97009 Office Phone: 971-645-9063. E-mail: nwcudaman@earthlink.net.

PRICE, DANIEL MARTIN, lawyer; b. St. Louis, Aug. 23, 1955; s. Albert and Edith S. (Werner) P.; m. Kim Ellen Heebner, July 15, 1984; children: Emma Rachel, Joseph Armin, Joshua Simon. BA, Haverford Coll., 1977; diploma in law, Cambridge U., 1979, JD, Harvard U., 1981. Bar: D.C. 1981, Pa. 1986, US Supreme Ct. 1999. Assoc. Drinker, Biddle & Reath, Phila., 1981-82, 86-89; dep. gen. counsel Office of U.S. Trade Rep., Washington, 1989-92; ptnr. Powell, Goldstein, Frazer & Murphy, Washington, 1992—2002; ptnr. and mem. exec. com. Sidley Austin Brown & Wood LLP, Washington, 2002—, and chair, Internat. Trade and Dispute Resolution practice. Atty., adviser Dept. State, Washington, 1982-84; dep. agt. U.S. Iran-U.S. Claims Tribunal, Hague, The Netherlands, 1984-86; lectr. Haverford Coll., 1982; mem. adv. bd. Can.-U.S. Law Inst., British Inst. of Internat and Comparative Law, European Inst., Georgetown Univ. Law Ctr. Inst. of Internat. Econ. Law. Articles editor Harvard Law Rev., 1980-81; contbr. articles to profl. jours. including Am. Jour. Internat. Law, Internat. Lawyer, Internat. Fin. Law Rev., Harvard Internat. Law Jour., others. Mem. Bush-Cheney Transition Team, 1999—2000. Am. Keasbey scholar Cambridge U., 1977-78. Mem. ABA, Internat. Bus. Forum (legal adv. bd. 1987-89), Am. Arbitration Assn. (panel arbitrators), Internat. C. of C. (arbitrator), Orgn. for Internat. Investment (counsel), Coun. on Fgn. Rels., Phi Beta Kappa, Internat. Ctr. for Settlement of Investment Disputes (mem. panel of arbitrators), Dept. of State Adv. Com. on Intl. Econ. Policy. Office: Sidley Austin Brown & Wood LLP 1501 K St NW Washington DC 20005 Office Phone: 202-736-8226. Office Fax: 202-736-8711. Business E-Mail: dmprice@sidley.com.

PRICE, DAVID B., JR., management consultant; b. St. Louis, Nov. 9, 1945; s. David B. and Ethyl (Armstrong) P.; m. Joyce Jacobs, Dec. 3, 1966; children: Danyale, Jason. BSCE, U. Mo., Rolla, 1968; MBA, Harvard U., 1976. Structural design engr. Monsanto Co., St. Louis, 1972-74, v.p., gen. mgr. specialty chem. divsn., 1987-90, v.p., gen. mgr. performance products divsn., 1991-93, v.p., gen. mgr. indsl. products group comml. ops., 1993-95, pres. performance materials, 1995-97; pres. Noveon Inc., 2001; exec. v.p. BF Goodrich Co., Richfield, Ohio, 1997, pres., COO performance materials Brecksville, Ohio, 1997—2001; pres., CEO Birdet Price, LLC, St. Louis, 2001—. Bd. dirs. Tenneco Automotive, Inc., 1999-, Am. Plastics Coun.; mem. adv. bd. Chem. & Engring. News. Mem. No. Ohio Minority Bus. Coun., Exec. Leadership Coun.; bd. dirs. Cleve. Tomorrow, United Way Svcs. of Cleve., First Tee of Cleve.; trustee Cleve. Playhouse Square Found., Sta. WVIZ-TV, pub. TV. Mem. Chem. Mfrs. Assn. (bd. dirs.). Avocations: golf, music, reading.*

PRICE, DAVID CECIL LONG, physicist, researcher; b. London, Jan. 17, 1940; came to U.S., 1966; s. Cecil Long and Freda (Salusbury) P.; m. Marie-Louise Saboungi, Nov. 24, 1989; children: Morgan, Alkes. BA, Cambridge U., 1961, MA, 1962, PhD, 1966. Rsch. assoc. Brookhaven Nat. Lab., Upton, NY, 1966-68; mem. staff Argonne (Ill.) Nat. Lab., 1968—2001, dir. solid state sci. divsn., 1974-79, dir. intense pulsed neutron source program, 1979-81, sr. physicist, 1981—2001; exec. dir. high-flux isotope reactor Oak Ridge (Tenn.) Nat. Lab., 2004—05; dir. rsch. CRMHT, Orleans, France, 2001—04, 2005—. Vis. prof. Japanese Soc. Promotion Sci., 1977; disting. vis. prof.Grad. U. for Adv. Studies, Hayama, Japan, 2000; mem. panel research opportunities with low energy neutrons Nat. Acad. Scis., 1976-77; sr. sci. advisor physics panel Energy Research Adv. Bd., Dept. Energy, 1986-87. Editor: Neutron Scattering (Methods of Experimental Physics, vols. 23 A, B, C), 1986-87. Recipient U. Chgo. award for disting. performance at Argonne Nat. Lab., 1988, Warren prize Am. Cryst. Assn., 1997, Alexander von Humboldt Rsch. award, 1998. Fellow Am. Phys. Soc., Inst. Physics (U.K.). Home: 5492 S Everett Ave Chicago IL 60615-5918 Office: CRMHT 45071 Orleans France Office Phone: 33-238-255531. E-mail: price@cnrs-orleans.fr.

PRICE, DAVID EUGENE, congressman, education educator; b. Johnson City, Tenn., Aug. 17, 1940; s. Albert Lee and Elna (Harrell) Price; m. Lisa Beth Kanwit, July 27, 1968; children: Karen Elizabeth, Michael Edmond. Student, Mars Hill Coll., NC, 1957—59; BA in Am. Hist. and Math., U. NC, 1961; BD in Theology, Yale U., 1964, PhD in Polit. Sci., 1969. Legis. aide Staff of US Senator Edward Lewis Bartlett of Alaska, 1963-67; prof. polit. sci. and pub. policy Duke U., Durham, NC, 1973-86; mem. US Congress from 4th NC dist. 1987—95, 1997—; mem. appropriations com., ranking Dem. democracy assistance commn., co-chair Dem. budget grp. Exec. dir. NC Dem. Party, Raleigh, 1979-80, chmn., 1983-84; mem. 1983—; staff dir. nat. com. on presdl. nomination Dem. Party, 1981-82 Author: Who Makes the Laws, 1972, Bringing Back the Parties, 1984, Policymaking in Congl. Coms., 1979, The Congressional Experience: A View From the Hill, 2000. Named a Champion of Sci., Sci. Coalition, 2002, 2004; recipient Engring. Deans Coun. award, Am. Soc. Engring. Edn., 2003, Charles Dick Medal of Merit, NC Nat Guard, Hubert H. Humphrey Pub. Svc. award, Am. Polit. Sci. Assn. Mem. Am. Polit. Sci. Assn.; recipient Values in Higher Edn., Phi Beta Kappa, Kiwanis. Democrat. Baptist. Avocations: jogging, music. Office: US Ho Reps 2162 Rayburn Ho Office Bldg Washington DC 20515-3304 Office Phone: 202-225-1784.*

PRICE, DAVID W, physician, educator, reseachrer; MD, Rutgers U., 1985. Diplomate Am. Bd. Family Medicine. Dir. edn., clinician rschr. Colo. Permanente Med. Group, Denver, 1998—; assoc. prof., family medicine U Colo. Health Sciences Ctr., Denver, 1999; clin. lead, profl. edn. and depression Kaiser Permanente Care Mgmt. Inst., Oakland, 2001—; chairelect Am. Bd. Family Medicine, Lexington, 2006—. Named Tchr. of Yr., Colo. Acad. Family Physicians, 1991, Superhero Colo. Family Medicine, 1998. Fellow: Am. Acad. Family Physicians. Achievements include design of multiple physician and ealth professional training curricula. Avocation: running. Office: Colorado Permanente Medical Group 10065 East Harvard Ave Denver CO 80231 Office Phone: 303-614-1308.

PRICE, DENNIS LEE, industrial engineer, educator; b. Taber, Alberta, Can., Oct. 24, 1930; s. Walter and Wilma Harlan (Nance) P.; m. Barbara Ann Shelton; children: Denice Lynn Price Tsugawa, Philip Walter. BA, Bob Jones U., 1952; BD, MA, Am. Bapt. Sem. of the West, Berkeley, Calif., 1955; MA, Calif. State U., Long Beach, 1967; PhD in Indsl. Engring., Tex. A&M U. 1974. Cert. product safety mgr., hazard control mgr., human factors profl. Clergyman Am. Bapt. Conv., Calif., 1953-56; tech. staff autonetics divsn. Rockwell Internat. Anaheim, Calif., 1966-69; sr. engr. Martin Marietta Aerospace, Orlando, Fla., 1969-72; rsch. assoc. Tex. A&M U., College Station, 1972-74; tchg. asst. Calif. State U., Long Beach, 1963-66; asst. prof. dept. indsl. engring. and systems engring., 1979—83, prof., 1984-95, prof. emeritus, 1996—, dir. safety projects office, 1975-95, coord.

Human Factors Engring. Ctr., 1986-95. Expert witness in safety engring. and human factors, 1978—; mem. U.S. Nuclear Waste Tech. Rev. Bd., 1989-95; U.S. tech. adv. group Internat. Stds. Tech. Com. 159 Ergonomics, 1987-94; chmn. com. on transp. of hazardous materials NRC, 1981-87; chmn. group 3 coun. emerging issues subcom. Transp. Rsch. Bd., 1987-89; chmn. task force on pipeline safety NAS, 1986 Mem. editorial bd. Human Factors, Santa Monica, Calif.. 1989-95; author: (with K.B. Johns, J.W. Bain) Transportation of Hazardous Materials, 1983, (with W. Hammer) Occupational Safety Management and Engineering, 2000; author: Why Christ is the Only Way, 2003, Death, That's Life, 2005; contbr. chpts. to books, articles to profl. jours.; reviewer in field. Recipient Disting. Svc. award Nat. Rsch. Coun. NAS, 1987, 89, Outstanding Svc. commendation Transp. Rsch. Bd. NAS, 1981, Jack A. Kraft Innovator award Human Factors and Ergonomics Soc., 1996, Best Book award San Diego Christian Writers Guild, 2004; grantee NIOSH, Va. Dept. Transp. and Safety, 1977-82, 86-87, IBM, 1981-84, USN Office of Naval Rsch., 1978-80, USN Naval Systems Weapons Command, 1978-79. Mem. Inst. Indsl. Engrs. (sr.), Am. Soc. Safety Engrs. (profl.), Human Factors Soc. (rep. to rev. panel Guideline for the Preparation of Material Safety Data Sheets), System Safety Soc. (Educator of Yr. 1993), Alpha Pi Mu. Avocation: flying. Home: 15204 Moonglow Dr Ramona CA 92065-4529 Office: Va Poly Inst and State Univ Dept Indsl and Sys Engring Blacksburg VA 24061

**PRICE, DONALD DENNIS**, neuroscientist, psychologist; b. Pasadena, Calif., Aug. 3, 1942; s. Donald Raymon and Geraldine Marie Price; m. Elizabeth Coleman, Aug. 2, 1997; 1 child, Amy Rose. BA, U. Calif., Davis, 1965, PhD, 1969. Post doctoral student UCLA, 1969—70; asst. prof. Med. Coll. of Va., 1971—74, prof., 1980—97; rsch. psychologist, physiologist NIH, 1975—79; prof. oral surgery and neuroscience U. Fla., Gainesville, 1997—. Contbr. articles to profl. jours. Recipient Founders award, Am. Acad. Pain Medicine, 2004, John Bonica award, Ea. Pain Soc., 2004; Rsch. grantee, NIH, 1971—74, 1981—84, 1987—. Mem.: Soc. for Neurosci., Internat. Assn. for the Study of Pain, Am. Pain Soc. (com. mem., Kerr award 2004). Achievements include development of pain measurement methods; discovery of neurons, pathways, and brain regions that process pain, mechanisms of pain relief by placebo/hypnosis; patents in field. Avocations: cartooning, philosophy. Office: Univ Fla PO Box 100416 1600 SW Archer Rd Gainesville FL 32610-0416 Office Phone: 352-846-2718. Office Fax: 352-846-0588. Business E-Mail: dprice@dental.ufl.edu.

**PRICE, DONALD RAY**, academic administrator, researcher, agricultural engineer; b. Rockville, Ind., July 20, 1939; s. Ernest M. and Violet Noreen (Measel) P.; m. Joyce Ann Gerald, Sept. 14, 1963; children: John Allen, Karen Sue, Kimberly Ann, Daniel Lee BS in Agrl. Engring., Purdue U., 1961, PhD in Agrl. Engring., 1971; MS in Agrl. Engring., Cornell U., 1963. Registered profl. engr., Fla. From asst. prof. to prof. Cornell U., Ithaca, N.Y., 1962-80, dir. energy programs, 1975-77, 78-80; program mgr. Dept. Energy, Washington, 1977-78, cons.; assoc. dean research U. Fla., Gainesville, 1980-83, dean Grad. Sch., 1983-84, v.p. rsch., 1984—; pres. U. Fla. Rsch. Found., Inc.; program dir. NSF, 2003—. Chmn. bd. dirs. Progress Research, Inc.; cons. to Pres. Carter, Washington, 1978; bd. dirs. Nat. Food and Engring. Council, Columbia, Mo., 1978-85, S.E. Healthcare Found., Gainesville, Fla., 1985 Contbr. numerous articles on engring. to profl. jours.; patentee mech. device Mem. Ithaca Sch. Bd., N.Y., 1979-80; elder Ch. of Christ, Gainesville, Fla., 1983—. Recipient citation Pres. Carter, 1979, Disting. Alumnus award Purdue U., 1990. Fellow Am. Soc. Agrl. Engrs. (dir. 1990, paper awards 1963, 77, 78, Young Engr. of Yr. award 1980); mem. Soc. Research Adminstrs., Nat. Assn. Univ. Research Adminstrs., S.E. Univ. Research Assn., Research Univs. Network Lodges: Rotary. Democrat. Avocations: tennis, jogging, woodworking. Office: NSF 4201 Wilson Blvd Arlington VA 22203 Home: 1505 Fort Clarke Blvd Apt 7105 Gainesville FL 32606-9104 E-mail: dprice@nsf.gov.

**PRICE, DONNA B.**, special education services professional; b. San Antonio, Sept. 24, 1943; d. Herman David Zweiban; m. Harry Roger Price, Aug. 16, 1964; children: Martin, Brian, Eric. BS in Edn., Ind. U., 1964; EdM, U. Houston, 1977. Lic. profl. counselor Tex., marriage and family therapist Tex., cert. counselor Nat. Bd. Cert. Counselors, career counselor Nat. Bd. Cert. Counselors. Secondary English and Latin tchr. Speedway HS, Indpls., 1964—67; ednl. therapist St. Joseph Hosp., Houston, 1977—78; job placement program dir. Jewish Family Svc., Houston, 1978—83; therapist Greenway Psychotherapy Assn., Houston, 1983—92; ADA counselor Houston CC Sys., 1992—99, ADA coord., 1999—. Mem. Gov.'s Adv. Coun. Tech. and Vocat. Edn., Austin, 1999—2000. V.p. Women's Am. Ort. Houston, 2003, Hadassah, Houston, 2003, Nat. Coun. Jewish Women, Houston, 2003; bd. mem. Mental Health and Mental Retardation Assn., Houston, 1994—99. Mem.: Tex. Assn. for Higher Edn. and Disabilities (dir. 1990—93), Assn. for Higher Edn. and Adults with Disabilities (bd. mem. 1995—97). Avocations: walking, travel, swimming, raising standard poodles. Office Phone: 713-718-5165. E-mail: donnaprice@houston.rr.com.

**PRICE, EDGAR HILLEARY, JR.**, manufacturing executive, consultant; b. Jacksonville, Fla., Jan. 1, 1918; s. Edgar Hilleary and Mary Williams (Phillips) P.; m. Elise Ingram, June 24, 1947; 1 son, Jerald Steven. Student, U. Fla., 1937-38. Mgr. comml. flower farm, 1945-49, Fla. Gladiolus Growers Assn., 1949-55; exec. v.p. Tropicana Products, Inc., Bradenton, Fla., 1955-73, dir. div. govt. and industry regulations, to 1979; dir.; exec. v.p. Indsl. Glass Co., Inc., Bradenton, 1963-73; pres., chmn. bd. Price Co., Inc., Bradenton, cons., 1973—. Dir. emeritus F.P.L. Group, Inc.; past chmn. Fla. Citrus Commn., Fla. Gov.'s Freeze Damage Survey Team, Spl. Commn. for Study Abolition Death Penalty; bd. dirs. Fla. Power and Light Co., Fla. Fair Assn., Fla. Citrus Expn., Fla. Fruit and Vegetable Assn., G.T.E. Fla., Fla. Cyprus Gardens, Ellis Bank Co.; past chmn. Joint Citrus Legis. Com.; past mem. Fla. Plant Bd., Fla. Bd. Control, Fla. Legis. Coun.; exec. com. Growers and Shippers League Fla., Fla. Agrl. Council, Spl. Health Agrl. Research and Edn.; past pres., chmn. bd. Fla. Hort. Soc. Past chmn., commr. census 12th Jud. Circuit; mem. Gov. Fla. Com. Rehab. Handicapped, Fla. Commn. on Ethics, 1976-77, Pres. Carter inaugural Fin. com., 1977, Ea. 5th Circuit U.S. Jud. Nominating Commn., 1977—; Fla. Senate from 36th Dist., 1958-66; past chmn. Manatee County Bd. Sch. Dist. Trustees, Local Housing Authority Bradenton, Bradenton Sub. Std. Housing Bd., Bradenton Charter Adv. Com.; del. Dem. Nat. Conv., 1960, dist. del., 1964; past trustee, mem. exec. com. Stetson U.; former trustee New Coll., Aurora Found. Served to 1st lt. USAAF, 1941-45. Named Boss of Yr., Nat. Secs. Assn., 1959, Man of Yr. for Fla. agr. Progressive Farmer mag., 1959; recipient merit award Am. Flag Assn., 1962, Gamma Sigma Delta, 1965, leadership award Fla. Agrl. Ext. Svc., 1963, Outstanding Senator award Fla. Radio Broadcasters, 1965, Allen Morris award s most valuable mem. Fla. Legislature, 1965, Most Valuable Mem. award Fla. Senate, St. Petersburg Times, 1965, Brotherhood award Sarasota chpt. NCCJ, 1966, Disting. Citizen award Manatee County, 1970, Disting. Alumnus award U. Fla., 1972, Svc. to Mankind award Sertoma Internat., 1976, Goodwill Disting. Citizen award, 1979, Crystal Shield award Salvation Army, 1996; inducted into Fla. Agrl. Hall of Fame, 1992, Tampa Bay Bus. Hall of Fame, 1992. Mem. Fla. C. of C. (bd. dirs. emeritus and past chmn.), Manatee C. of C. (past pres.), Fla. Hort. Soc. (past pres., chmn. bd.), Fla. Flower Assn., ARC Clara Barton Soc., Blue Key (hon.), Omicron Delta Kappa (hon.), Kiwanis (pres. 1955), Sigma Alpha Epsilon. Home: 3009 Riverview Blvd W Bradenton FL 34205-3420 Office: PO Box 9270 Bradenton FL 34206-9270 *The turning point in my life came at the age of 32 when I accepted Jesus Christ as my personal Lord and Saviour. I believe every person should live his life up to the fullest extent of his God-given talents and ability. I think we have a responsibility to "pay our dues" for the privilege of living in a free land by being actively involved in our government.*

**PRICE, EDWARD WARREN**, aerospace engineer, educator; b. Detroit, Dec. 6, 1920; s. Frank E. and Elizabeth Alleyne (Rattray) P.; m. Mary Kate Howard, June 21, 1952; children: Douglas Brian, Alison Tamara, Carolyn Louise. BA in Physics, Math, UCLA, 1948. Ballistician Calif. Inst. Tech., 1944-49; physicist U.S. Naval Weapons Ctr., China Lake, Calif., 1946-74; prof. aerospace engring. Ga. Inst. Tech., Atlanta, 1967—68, 1974—. V.p. tech. AIAA, mem. Am. Acad. Scis.-Nat. Rsch. Coun. Space Shuttle

Booster Redesign Rev. Panel, 1986-89; cons. in field. Contbr. articles to profl. jours. With USN, 1944—46. Recipient Pub. Svc. award, Astronauts award NASA, 1987. Fellow AIAA (Rsch., Pendrary, Goddard awards 1966, 71, 76); mem. AAAS, NAE, Combustion Inst., Sigma Xi. Achievements include numerous contributions to science in areas of rocket propulsion and combustion. Home: 5058 Highpoint Rd NE Atlanta GA 30342-2313 Office: Ga Inst Tech 225 North Ave Mail Code 0150 Atlanta GA 30332

**PRICE, ELIZABETH ANNE**, lawyer; b. Macon, Ga. Aug. 23, 1960; BA, George Washington U., 1983, JD with honors, 1986. Bar: Ga. 1986, U.S. Dist. Ct. (no. dist.) Ga. 1986, U.S. Ct. Appeals (11th cir.) 1986, U.S. Supreme Ct. 1995. Ptnr., litig., trial practice Alston & Bird LLP, Atlanta, 1986—. With U.S. Army, interrogator/Arabic linguist, 1978-81. Mem. State Bar Ga. (access to justice com., ct. futures com.), Atlanta Bar Assn. (bd. dirs. 1996—, pres.). Office: Alston & Bird 1 Atlantic Ctr 1201 W Peachtree St NW Atlanta GA 30309-3400 Office Phone: 404-881-7264. Business E-Mail: lprice@alston.com.

**PRICE, ELY**, dermatologist; b. NYC, Aug. 9, 1932; s. Jacob and Mary (Flattau) P.; m. Ilona Brodie, Apr. 30, 1989; children from previous marriage: Jeremy, Andrew. BS cum laude, CCNY, 1953; AM, Ind. U., 1956; MD, U. Lausanne, Switzerland, 1964. Diplomate Am. Bd. Dermatology. Intern Brookdale Hosp. Med. Ctr., Bklyn., 1964-65, resident internal medicine, 1965-66; fellow Mt. Sinai Hosp., N.Y.C., 1965-66; resident in dermatology Kings County Hosp., Bklyn., 1966-69; practice dermatology Bay Ridge Skin and Cancer Dermatology, P.C., Bklyn., 1969—; attending-in-charge, head dermatology Maimonides Med. Ctr., Bklyn., 1985—; clin. assoc. prof. dermatology SUNY Sci. Ctr., Bklyn., 1985—. Cons. in medicine Luth. Med. Ctr., Bklyn., 1988—; cons. in dermatology Victory Med. Hosp., Bklyn., 1989—. Fellow ACP, Am. Acad. Dermatology, Am. Soc. Dermatol. Surgery, N.Y. Acad. Medicine. Avocation: golf. Office: Bay Ridge Skin & Cancer Dermatology PC 9921 4th Ave Brooklyn NY 11209-8347 Home: 5598 Vista Del Mando S Unit B Laguna Woods CA 92637-6923 E-mail: elyilona@aol.com.

**PRICE, EMMETT GEORGE, III**, musicologist, educator, music minister; b. LA, Jan. 13, 1975; s. Emmett George and Carolyn Jean Price; m. Nicole Gayle Price, Sept. 1, 2001; children: Emmett George IV, Nicholas Robert. BA in Music, U. Calif., Berkeley, 1996; MA in Music (ethnomusicology), U. Pitts., 1999, PhD in Music (ethnomusicology), 2000. Vis. asst. prof. Northeastern U., Boston, 2001—02, asst. prof., 2002. Min. of music Western Ave. Bapt. Ch., Cambridge, Mass., 2003—04; asst. to the pastor (music, worship & the arts) Ebenezer Bapt. Ch., Boston, 2004—; assoc. scholar Primary Source, Watertown, Mass., 2003—; consulting scholar The Rhythm & Blues Project, 2003—; bd. dirs. Freedom Ho., Mass., 2001—03, Project: Think Different, Mass. 2002—04; rsch. assoc. African Am. Cultural Ctr. of Greater Pitts., Pittsburgh, Mass., 2001; ind. cons. Am. Jazz Mus., Kansas City, Mo. 2001. Contbr. articles to profl. jours. and encys. Min. of music Western Ave. Bapt. Ch., Cambridge, Mass., 2003—04; asst. to the pastor (music, worship & the arts) Ebenezer Bapt. Ch., Boston, 2004—05; mem. Project: Think Different, Mass., 2002—04 Freedom Ho., Mass., 2001—03. Fellow, Wash. U., St. Louis, 2000—01, Ind. U, Bloomington, 2000; W.E.B. Du Bois Inst. for African and African Ameircan Rsch. fellow, Harvard U., 2004—05. Mem.: Soc. for Ethnomusicology (assoc.), Soc. for Am. Music (assoc.), Internat. Assn. for the Study of Popular Music (assoc.; editor-in-chief Jour. Popular Music Studies 2003—), Ctr. for Black Music Rsch. (assoc.), Alpha Phi Alpha (assoc.). Avocations: music, reading, travel. Office: Northeastern Univ 351 Ryder Hall Boston MA 02115 Office Phone: 617-373-7700.

**PRICE, FRANK**, motion picture and television company executive; b. Decatur, Ill., May 17, 1930; s. William F. and Winifred A. (Moran) P.; m. Katherine Huggins, May 15, 1965; children: Stephen, David, Roy, William. Student, Mich. State U., 1949-51, HHD (hon.), 2003. Writer, story editor CBS-TV, NYC, 1951-53, Columbia Pictures, Hollywood, Calif., 1953-57, NBC-TV, Hollywood, Calif., 1957-58; producer, writer ZIV-TV, Hollywood, Calif., 1958, Universal Television, Universal City, Calif., 1959-64, v.p., 1964-71, sr. v.p., 1971-73, exec. v.p. in charge of production, 1973-74, pres., 1974-78; v.p., dir. MCA, Inc., 1976-78; pres. Columbia Pictures Prodn., 1978-79; chmn., chief exec. officer Columbia Pictures, 1979-84, also bd. dirs.; chmn. MCA Motion Picture Group, 1984-86; chmn., chief exec. officer Price Entertainment Inc., 1987-90; chmn. Columbia Pictures, 1990-91; chmn., chief exec. officer Price Entertainment, 1991—; prodr. The Tuskegee Airmen, 1996. Trustee U. So. Calif., 1996—, chmn. bd. counselors Sch. of Cinema-TV, 1990—. With USN, 1948-49. Recipient Peabody award, 1996, NAACP Image award, 1996. Mem. Writers Guild Am. West, N.Y. State Soc. Cin. Office: Price Entertainment Inc 527 Spoleto Dr Pacific Palisades CA 90272-4517

**PRICE, GEORGIANNA THROWER**, elementary school educator; b. Hardin, Mont., May 2, 1951; d. Rex Burton and Georgia Knight Thrower; m. Bruce Eugene Price, Aug. 27, 1971. Student, Mont. State U., 1969—71; BS in Edn., Black Hills State U., 1973, MS in Curriculum Instruction, 1992. Elem. tchr., Sturgis, SD, 1973—75, Lead-Deadwood, SD, 1975—2006. Mem.: Pahasapa Reading Coun. (treas.), Internat. Reading Coun. (local treas. 1993—), Delta Kappa Gamma. Home: 12356 Nemo Rd Nemo SD 57759

**PRICE, GLENDA DELORES**, dean, college president; b. York, Pa., Oct. 10, 1939; d. William B. Price and Zelma E. Holmes McGeary. BS, Temple U., 1961, MEd, 1969, PhD, 1979. Clin. lab. specialist. Cytotechnologist Temple U. Hosp., Phila., 1961-67, prof. clin. lab. sci.; faculty Coll. Allied Health Professions, Temple U., Phila., 1967-79, asst. dean allied health, 1979-86; dean allied health Sch. Allied Health Professions, U. Conn., Storrs, 1986—; pres. Marygrove Coll., Detroit, 1998. Pres. Am. Soc. Clin. Lab. Contbr. over 20 articles to profl. jours., chpts. to books. Bd. trustees U. New Eng., Biddeford, Maine, 1989—; bd. dirs. Windham Hosp., Willimantic, Conn., 1989—, E. Hartford VNA, 1989—; allied health adv. Pew Health Prof. Commn., Durham, N.C., 1991—. Recipient Leadership award SUNY-Buffalo, 1982; named Mem. of the Yr., Pa. Soc. Med. Tech., 1979; decorated Legion of Honor, Chapel of Four Chaplains, 1977. Mem. Am. Soc. Allied Health Professions (sec. 1985-87), Am. Soc. Med. Tech. (pres. 1979-80), Alpha Kappa Alpha, Alpha Mu Tau, Alpha Eta, Phi Kappa Phi. Democrat. Baptist. Home and Office: U Conn 358 Mansfield Rd Storrs Mansfield CT 06269-9000

**PRICE, GRIFFITH BALEY, JR.**, lawyer; b. Lawrence, Kans. Aug. 15, 1942; s. Griffith Baley and Cora Lee (Beers) P.; m. Maria Helena Martin, June 29, 1968 (div.); children: Andrew Griffith, Alexandra Helena; m. Nancy Culver Rhodes, Aug. 17, 1997; children: Carolyn Rhodes, Sarah Culver. AB (cum laude), Harvard U., 1964; LLB, NYU, 1967. Bar: N.Y. 1967, D.C. 1991, U.S. Ct. Appeals (6th cir.) 1975, U.S. Ct. Appeals (2nd cir.) 1978, U.S. Ct. Appeals (3d, 5th and 11th cirs.) 1981, U.S. Ct. Appeals (1st cir.) 2002, U.S. Ct. Appeals (fed. cir.) 1984, U.S. Supreme Ct. 2001. Assoc. Dewey, Ballantine, Bushby, Palmer & Wood, N.Y.C., 1967-75; ptnr. Milgrim Thomajan & Lee, N.Y.C., 1976-86; of counsel, ptnr. Finnegan, Henderson, Farabow, Garrett & Dunner, LLP, Washington, 1987—. Adj. prof., lectr. George Washington U. Law Ctr., Washington, 1989—93; mem., chair pub. adv. com. U.S. Patent and Trademark Office, 1999—2004; lectr., spkr. in field. Author: (with others, treatise) Milgrim on Trade Secrets, 1986; contbr. articles to profl. jours. Root-Tilden scholar NYU Law Sch., 1964-67. Fellow: Am. Intellectual Property Law Assn. (bd. dirs., com. chmn.); mem.: ABA (intellectual property sec., com. chmn.), Assn. Interamerican Indsl. Property, Fed. Cir. Bar Assn., Licensing Execs. Soc., Internat. Trademark Assn. (bd. dirs., com. chmn.). Cosmos Club, Nat. Press Club, Harvard Club (Washington), N.Y. Athletic Club, Unitarian Universalist. Office: Finnegan Henderson Farabow Garrett & Dunner LLP 901 New York Ave NW Washington DC 20001-4413 Office Phone: 202-408-4071. Business E-Mail: gbprice@finnegan.com.

**PRICE, HELEN BURDON (LOIS BURDAN PRICE)**, artist, retired nursing educator; b. St. Louis, Sept. 23, 1926; d. Kenneth Livingston and Estelle Lois (Pemberton) Burdon; m. John Bryan Price, Jr.; children: Diane Price Baker, Jeannette B., John Bryan III. BS, La. State U., 1946; BS, RN, Johns Hopkins U., 1949; postgrad., Boston U., 1951-52. Head nurse in pediatrics Johns Hopkins Hosp., Balt., 1949-51; instr. nursing sch. Boston Children's Hosp., 1951-52; physician's aide, sec. U.S. Army-Osaka (Japan) Hosp., 1952-54; instr. pediat. nursing Holy Name Hosp., Teaneck, N.J., 1965-67; primary nurse Englewood (N.J.) Hosp., 1974-79; dir.- curator Vineyard Theatre Gallery, N.Y.C., 1980-90; bd. mem., coord. pub. lecture series Ward Nasse Gallery, N.Y.C., 1987-92. Program planner, judge, panel participant, curator Salute to Women in the Arts, Bergen County, N.J., 1977-95. Fund raiser Women's Aux., Presbyn. Med. Ctr., N.Y. Hosp. Fund, N.Y.C., 1982-90. Mem. Nat. Assn. Women Artists (past sec., v.p., pres., permanent advisor, Akston Found. award 1987, Blake award 1991, Bronze medal 1995, Kreindler Meml. award 1998, Blum Meml. award 1999). Avocations: birdwatching, mycology. Personal E-Mail: hbp31@aol.com.

**PRICE, HENRY ESCOE**, broadcast executive; b. Jackson, Miss., Oct. 13, 1947; s. Henry E. Price Sr. and Alma Kate (Merrill) Noto; m. Maria Diane Harper, Apr. 8, 1972; children: Henry E. III, Norman Harper. BS in Radio, TV, Film, Journalism, U. So. Miss., 1972. Announcer, news dir. Sta. WROA Radio, Gulfport, Miss., 1967-69; comml. producer Sta. WJTV-TV, Jackson, Miss., 1969-73; prodn. mgr. Sta. WAAY-TV, Huntsville, Ala., 1973-77, Sta. WPEC-TV, West Palm Beach, Fla., 1977-79; dir. promotion Sta. WPTV-TV, Palm Beach, Fla., 1979-81; TV cons. Frank Magid Assoc., Marion, Iowa, 1981-83; dir. advt. and promotion Sta. WJLA-TV, Washington, 1983-84; v.p., dir. programming Sta. WUSA-TV, Gannett TV, Washington, 1984-88; pres., gen. mgr. Sta. WFMY-TV, Gannett TV, Greensboro, N.C., 1988-91, Sta. KARE-TV, Mpls., 1991-96; v.p., gen. mgr. Sta. WBBM-TV, CBS TV Stas., Chgo., 1996—. Pres. Carolina News Network, 1988-91; adj. faculty media mgmt. Ctr. Northwestern U., 2000—. Vice chair, bd. dirs. The Courage Ctr., Mpls.; regional dir. Nat. Conf.; mem. exec. com., bd. dirs. The Minn. Orch.; Pacesetter program chair Mpls. United Way Campaign; active Twin Cities Dunkers, Twin Cities Comm. Coun., 11 Who Care. Mem. Chgo. C. of C. (bd. dirs.), Ill. Broadcasters Assn. (bd. dirs.). Avocations: furniture design and construction, reading, walking, bicycling. Home: PO Box 11847 Winston Salem NC 27116-1847

**PRICE, ILENE ROSENBERG**, lawyer; b. Jersey City, July 2, 1951; d. Irwin Daniel and Mildred (Riesberg) Rosenberg; m. Jeffrey Paul Price, Feb. 18, 1973. AB, U. Mich., 1972; JD, U. Pa., 1977. Bar: Pa. 1977, DC 1978, U.S. Dist. Ct. DC 1979, U.S. Ct. Appeals (D.C. cir.) 1979. Assoc. Haley, Bader & Potts, Washington, 1977-80; staff atty. Mut. Broadcasting System Inc., Arlington, Va., 1980-82, asst. gen. counsel, 1982-85; gen. counsel Multi-Comm Telecommunications Corp., Arlington, 1985-88; east coast counsel Westwood One, Inc., Arlington, 1988-91; gen. counsel Resource Dynamics Corp., Vienna, Va., 1991—2001; legal search cons. The McCormick Group, Arlington, 2001—03; gen. counsel Bluewave Resources, LLC, McLean, Va., 2003—. Mem. Fed. Communications Bar Assn., Wash. Met. Area Corp. Counsel Assn., Women's Bar Assn. D.C. (bd. dirs. 1984-87). Office: Bluewave Resources LLC Ste 310 6830 Elm St Mc Lean VA 22101 Office Phone: 703-448-3400. Business E-Mail: ileneprice@bwres.com.

**PRICE, JAMES GORDON**, physician, educator; b. Brush, Colo., June 20, 1926; s. John Hoover and Rachel Laurette Price; m. Janet Alice McSween, June 19, 1949; children: James Gordon II, Richard Christian, Mary Laurette, Janet Lynn. BA, U. Colo., 1948, MD, 1951. Diplomate charter Am. Bd. Family Practice. Intern Denver Gen. Hosp., 1951—52; practice medicine specializing in family medicine Brush Co., 1952—78; prof. family practice U. Kans. Med. Ctr., 1978—93; chmn. dept. U. Kans. Med. Center, 1982—90, exec. dean, 1990—93, prof. emeritus in family practice, 1993—. Dir., pres. Am. Bd. Family Practice, 1979; mem. Inst. Medicine of NAS, 1973—. Med. editor: Gen. Learning Corp., 1973—92, mem. editl. bd.: Med. World News, 1969—79; editor: Am. Acad. Family Physician Home Study Self Assessment Program, 1978—83; columnist: Your Family Physician, 1973—90. Trustee Family Health Found. Am., 1970—82; vol. physician St. Jude's Hosp., St. Lucia, West Indies, 1998—99. With USNR, 1943—46. Fellow: Am. Acad. Family Physicians (charter, pres. 1973); mem.: Phi Beta Kappa, Alpha Omega Alpha. Home: 12205 Mohawk Rd Shawnee Mission KS 66209-2137 Business E-Mail: jimtad@sbcglobal.net.

**PRICE, JAMES TUCKER**, lawyer; b. Springfield, Mo., June 22, 1955; s. Billy L. and Jeanne Adele Price; m. Francine Beth Warkow, June 8, 1980; children: Rachel Leah, Ashley Elizabeth. BJ, U. Mo., 1977; JD, Harvard U., 1980. Bar: Mo. 1980. Assoc. firm Spencer Fane Britt & Browne, Kansas City, 1980-86; ptnr. Spencer Fane Britt & Browne LLP, Kansas City, 1987—, chair environ. practice group, 1994—, mem. exec. com., 1997—. Mem. Brownfields Commn., Kansas City, 1999—; mem. steering com. Kansas City Bi-State Brownfields Initiative, 1997—. Contbr. to monographs, other legal publs. Mem. ABA (coun. sect. environ. energy and resources 1992-95, vice chmn. solid and hazardous waste com. 1985-90, chmn. 1990-92, chmn. brownfields task force 1995-97, vice chmn. environ. transactions and brownfield com. 1998-2000), Mo. Bar Assn., Kansas City Met. Bar Assn. (chmn. environ. law com. 1985-86), Greater Kansas City C. of C. (co-chair Brownfields Working Group, 1996-98, chmn. energy and environ. com. 1987-89). Office: Spencer Fane Britt & Browne LLP 1000 Walnut St Ste 1400 Kansas City MO 64106-2140 Office Phone: 816-292-8228. Business E-Mail: jprice@spencerfane.com

**PRICE, JOE D.**, pipeline developer; m. Etsuko Price. Founder Shin'enKan Found. for Japanese art, Corona del Mar, Calif. Bd. dir. Friends of Kebyar, 1983—. Named one of Top 200 Collectors, ARTnews Mag., 2004. Avocation: Collecting Edo-period Japanese art. Mailing: PO Box 1111 Bartlesville OK 74005 Office Phone: 949-759-8550.

**PRICE, JOHN ALEY**, lawyer; b. Maryville, Mo., Oct. 7, 1947; s. Donald Leroy and Julia Catherine (Aley) P.; m. Deborah Diadra Gunter, Aug. 12, 1995; children: Theodore John, Joseph Andrew. BS, N.W. Mo. State U., 1969; JD, U. Kans., 1972. Bar: Kans. 1972, N.C. 2006, U.S. Dist. Ct. Kans. 1972, U.S. Ct. Appeals (10th cir.) 1972, Tex. 1984, U.S. Ct. Appeals (5th cir.) 1984, U.S. Supreme Ct. 1987; cert. civil trial law Tex. Bd. Legal Specialization, pro bono atty. Tex., 1992. Law clk. U.S. Dist. Ct. Kans., Wichita, 1972-74; from assoc. to ptnr. Weeks, Thomas and Lysaught, Kansas City, Kans., 1974-82; ptnr. Winstead, Sechrest & Minick, Dallas, 1982-96, litigation sect. coord., 1990-92, intellectual property sect. litigation coord., 1993-95; gen. counsel Travelhost Inc., Dallas, 1996—, Club Co., Inc., 1999-2001. Pres. Umansys, Inc., Dallas, 2000—04; spl. prosecutor Leavenworth County Office Dist. Atty., 1970-71, Sedgwick County Offce Dist. Atty., Wichita, Kans., 1971-72. Author: Our Boundless Self (A Call to Awake), 1992, A Gathering of Light: Eternal Wisdom for a Time of Transformation, 1993; co-author: Soular Reunion: Journey to the Beloved, 1998; editor (mag.) Academic Analyst, 1968-69; assoc. editor U. Kans. Law Rev., 1971-72, Dallas Bus. Jour.; contbr. articles to profl. jours. Co-dir. Douglas County Legal Aid Soc., Lawrence, Kans., 1971-72; co-pres. Northwood Hills PTA, Dallas, 1984, Westwood Jr. H.S. PTA, 1989-90; founder New Frontiers Found., 1993; co-founder Wings of Spirit Found., 1994, dir., v.p. 1994—. Recipient Tex. Super Lawyer, Law and Politics and Tex. Monthly Mag., 2003, 2006, Mem. ABA, Kans. Bar Assn. (mem. task force for penal reform; Pres.'s Outstanding Svc. award 1981), Tex. Bar Assn., Pro Bono Coll., State Bar Tex., World Bus. Acad., Inst. Noetic Scis., UN Assn. (human rights com. Dallas chpt. 1991-93, bd. dirs 1991-93), Campaign for the Earth (chpt. coord. Global Report 1991-92, coord. govt. and polit. area 1991-92), Blue Key, Order of Coif, Phi Delta Phi, Sigma Tau Gamma (v.p. 1968-69), Mem. Unity Ch. Office: Travelhost Inc 10701 N Stemmons Fwy Dallas TX 75220-2419 Office Phone: 972-556-0541. Personal E-Mail: japrice@travelhost.com. *We create our reality every moment of existence. Our only limitations are those we choose to accept.*

**PRICE, JOHN R.**, lawyer, educator; b. Indpls., Nov. 28, 1934; s. Carl Lee and Agnes I. P.; m. Suzanne A. Leslie, June 22, 1963; children: John D., Steven V. BA with high honors, U. Fla., 1958; LL.B. with honors, NYU, 1961. Bar: Wash. 1977, U.S. Ct. Appeals (9th cir.), U.S. Dist. Ct. (we. dist.) Wash. Assoc. McCutchen, Doyle, Brown & Enersen, San Francisco, 1961-69; prof. law U. Wash., Seattle, 1969-97, dean, 1982-88; of counsel Perkins Coie, Seattle, 1976–2004. Author: Contemporary Estate Planning, 1983, Price on Contemporary Estate Planning, 1992, 2d edit., 2000, Conflicts, Confidentiality and Other Ethical Issues, 2000. Served with U.S. Army, 1953-55 Root-Tilden fellow NYU Sch. Law, 1958-61 Fellow Am. Coll. Trust and Estate Counsel (former regent); mem. ABA, Am. Law Inst., Order of Coif, Phi Beta Kappa. Congregationalist. Home: 3794 NE 97th St Seattle WA 98115-2564 Office: 1201 3rd Ave Ste 4800 Seattle WA 98101-3099 E-mail: jprice@perkinscoie.com.

**PRICE, JOHN RANDOLPH**, writer; b. Alice, Tex., Feb. 12, 1932; s. John Randolph and Eva Mae (Boney) P.; m. Janis Bryant Price, June 20, 1953; children: Susan Lynn, Leslie Anne. BS, U. Houston, 1957; PhD (hon.), Emerson Inst., 2001; DHL (hon.), Holmes Inst., 2003. Dir. advt. Gates Radio Corp., Quincy, Ill., 1957-62; v.p. Sander Rodkin, Ltd., Chgo., 1962-64; exec. v.p. Stewart, Price, Tomlin, Inc., Chgo., 1964-67; v.p. Goodwin, Dannenbaum, Littman & Wingfield, Inc., Houston, 1967-70; pres. O'Neill, Price, Anderson, Fouchard, Inc., Houston, 1970-74, John Price & Co., Houston, 1974-79, Arnan, Inc., Austin, 1979-81; chmn. bd. The Quartus Found. Inc., Boerne, Tex., 1981—. Author: The Superbeings, 1981, The Manifestation Process, 1983, The Planetary Commission, 1984, Practical Spirituality, 1985, With Wings as Eagles, 1987, The Abundance Book, 1987, Prayer, Principles & Power, 1987, A Spiritual Philosophy for the New World, 1990, Empowerment, 1992, The Angels Within Us, 1993, Angel Energy, 1995, Living a Life of Joy, 1997, The Success Book, 1998, The Wellness Book, 1998, The Meditation Book, 1998, The Love Book, 1998, The Jesus Code, 2000, The Alchemist's Handbook, 2000, Removing the Masks That Bind Us, 2001, Nothing Is Too Good to Be True, 2003. Staff sgt. USAF, 1952-56. Recipient Joseph S. Cullinan award U. Houston, 1956, Grand Prix Best Consumer Mag. Advt. award, 1970. Mem. Internat. New Thought Alliance (Humanitarian award 1992, Joseph Murphy award 1994). Achievements include organizer of first annual World Peace day on December 31, 1986. Office: The Quartus Found Inc PO Box 1768 Boerne TX 78006-6768 Office Phone: 830-249-3985. Business E-Mail: quartus@quartus.org.

**PRICE, JONATHAN G.**, geologist; b. Danville, Pa., Feb. 1, 1950; s. A. Barney and Flora (Best) P.; m. Elisabeth McKinley, June 3, 1972; children: Alexander D., Argenta M. BA in Geology and German, Lehigh U., 1972; MA, U. Calif., Berkeley, 1975, PhD, 1977. Cert. profl. geologist. Geologist Anaconda Copper Co., Yerington, Nev., 1974-75, U.S. Steel Corp., Salt Lake City, 1977, Corpus Christi, 1978-81; rsch. assoc. Bur. Econ. Geology, U. Tex., Austin, 1981-85, rsch. sci., 1984-88, program dir., 1987-88; dir. Tex. Mining & Mineral Resources Rsch. Inst., Austin, 1984-88; dir., state geologist Nev. Bur. Mines & Geology, U. Nev., Reno, 1988-92, 95—. Staff dir. Bd. on Earth Scis. & Resources Nat. Rsch. Coun., Washington, 1993-95; asst. prof. Bucknell U., Lewisburg, 1977-78; chair We. States Seismic Policy coun., 1998-2002. Author: editor: Igneous Geology of Trans-Pecos Texas, 1986. Vol. instr. CPR and first aid ARC, 1983-95, bd. dirs. Sierra Nev. chpt., 1991-92. German Acad. Exch. Svc. fellow U. Heidelberg, 1972-73; recipient Explorer award Am. Geol. Inst., 1995. Fellow Geol. Soc. Am., Soc. Econ. Geologists (nat. pres. 2003); mem. Am. Inst. Profl. Geologists (Nev. sect. pres. 1992, nat. pres. 1997, John T. Galey Sr. Meml. pub. Svc. award 1999), Assn. Am. State Geologists (pres. 2000-01), Mineral. Soc. Am., Phi Beta Kappa. Office: Nev Bur Mines & Geology UNR Ms 178 Reno NV 89557-0088 Office Phone: 775-784-6691 x126. Business E-Mail: jprice@unr.edu.

**PRICE, JOSEPH HUBBARD**, lawyer; b. Montgomery, Ala., Jan. 31, 1939; s. Aaron Joseph and Minnie Jule (Reynolds) P.; m. Cynthia Winant Ramsey, Sept. 14, 1963 (div. 1980); children: Victoria Reynolds, Ramsey Winant; m. Courtney McFadden, Apr. 25, 1980. AB, U. Ala., 1961; LLB, Harvard U., 1964; postgrad., London Sch. Econs., 1964-65. Bar: Ala. 1964, D.C. 1968. Law clk. to justice Hugo L. Black U.S. Supreme Ct., Washington, 1967-68; assoc. Leva, Hawes, Symington, Martin & Oppenheimer, Washington, 1968-71; v.p. Overseas Pvt. Investment Corp., Washington, 1971-73; ptnr. Leva, Hawes, et. al., Washington, 1973-83; ptnr., internat. law Gibson, Dunn & Crutcher, Washington, 1983—2005. Capt. U.S. Army, 1966—67, Vietnam. Decorated Bronze Star; Frank Knox Meml. fellow London Sch. Econs., 1964-65. Mem. ABA, Am. Soc. Internat. Law, Supreme Ct. Hist. Soc., Phi Beta Kappa, Met. Club. Office: Gibson Dunn & Crutcher 1050 Connecticut Ave NW Ste 900 Washington DC 20036-5306

**PRICE, JOSEPH MICHAEL**, lawyer; b. St. Paul, Dec. 2, 1947; s. Leon and Rose (Kaufman) P.; m. Louise Rebecca Braunstein, Dec. 19, 1971; children: Lisa, Laurie, Julie. BA, U. Minn., 1969, JD, 1972. Bar: Minn. 1972, U.S. Dist. Ct. Minn. 1974. Ptnr. Faegre & Benson, Mpls., 1972—. Mem. Minn. Bar Assn., Hennepin County Bar Assn. Home: 4407 Country Club Rd Minneapolis MN 55424-1148 Office: Faegre & Benson 2200 Wells Fargo Ctr 90 S 7th St Ste 2200 Minneapolis MN 55402-3901 Office Phone: 612-766-8617. Business E-Mail: Jprice@faegre.com.

**PRICE, JUDITH HOLM**, educational psychologist; b. Milw., Nov. 6, 1937; d. Paul James and Dorothy Ruth (Munton) Holm; m. Thomas Munro Price, Aug. 8, 1959; children: Scott Michael, Andrea Lynn. BA, Carroll Coll., 1959; MA, U. Iowa, 1973; PhD, U. Wyo., 1980. Nat. cert. sch. psychologist. Tchr. Waukesha Pub. Sch., Wis., 1959, Madison Pub. Sch., 1959-63; preschool assessment specialist Grant Wood Area Edn. Agy. 10, Cedar Rapids, Iowa, 1976-78; Ednl. Resource Ctr. facilitator Albany County Sch. Dist. 1, Laramie, Wyo., 1980-89, dir. spl. svc., 1989—93; acad. dean Brush Ranch Sch., Tererro, N.Mex., 1993—96; hist. home renovator Yerington, Nev., 1997—. Substitute tchr. Melbourne (Australia) Sch. 1979; temporary prof. U. Wyo., Laramie, 1981, 84; mem. computer com. Wyo. Dept. Edn., Casper, 1984-85, com. for devel. spl. edn. database, 1987, task force cert. standards for early childhood spl. edn. tchr., 1988; speaker Wyo. Fedn. CEC, Riverton, 1986, task force on specific learning disability criteria, 1988; conf. mem. Council for Exceptional Children Software Conf., Washington, 1986; provider state-wide inservice Specific Learning Disability Criteria, 1988. Spl. edn. rules and regulations task force Wyo. Dept. Edn., 1990—92; mem. Wyo. gov. Early Intervention Coun., 1990—93; governing bd. mem. South Lyon Health Ctr., Inc., 2003—. Mem. Nat. Assn. Sch. Psychologists (alt. del. 1983), Wyo. Sch. Psychoednl. Assn., Council for Exceptional Children (com. specific learning disability 1987-88, speaker 1988, pres. Frontier chpt. 1989), Assn. Curriculum Devel., N.Mex. Assn. Non-Pub. Sch., Phi Kappa Phi, Phi Delta Kappa, 2003. Avocations: computers, skiing, camping, travel. Office: The Nordyke House 727 State Route 339 Yerington NV 89447-9553

**PRICE, KENNETH L.**, mathematics professor; b. Mt. Vernon, Ill., July 26, 1968; s. Larry K. and Cathy M. Price; m. Paula M. Lovell, May 27, 2006. BS, Western Ill. U., Macomb, Ill., 1990; MS, U. Wis., Milw., 1991, D, 1997. Vis. asst. prof. Truman State U., Kirksville, Mo., 1997—99; assoc. prof. of math. U. Wis., Oshkosh, 1999—. Dir. of student activities Math. Assn. of Am. (Wis. Sect.), Wis., 2005—. Contbr. articles to profl. jour., presentations to profl. confs. Grantee Undergraduate Student and Faculty Collaborative Rsch. Program, UW Oshkosh Faculty Devel. Program, 2004, Rsch. Component Award, 2002, Off-Campus Program Award. Office: Uf Wisc Oshkosh 800 Algoma Blvd Oshkosh WI 54091 Office Phone: 920-424-1057. Home Fax: 920-424-7317; Office Fax: 920-424-7317.

**PRICE, KENNETH MARSDEN**, humanities educator; b. Pomona, Calif., Apr. 22, 1954; s. Marsden and Barbara (Cunningham) P.; m. Renee Arlene Hall, Aug. 1, 1981; children: Ashley, Gillian. BA, Whitman Coll., 1976; MA, U. Chgo., 1977, PhD, 1981. From asst. to full prof. Tex. A&M U., College Station, 1981-93; prof. Coll. William and Mary, Williamsburg, Va., 1994-2000; Hillegass chair Am. lit. U. Nebr., Lincoln, 2000—. Guest prof. Ruhr U., Bochum, Germany, 1990; pres. Rsch. Soc. for Am. Periodicals, 1995-97. Author: Whitman and Tradition, 1990, To Walt Whitman, 2004; editor: Walt

Whitman: The Contemporary Reviews, 1996; co-editor (CD-ROM) Major Authors on CD-ROM: Walt Whitman, 1997, (online database) Walt Whitman Hypertext Archive, 1995—. Fund for the Improvement of Postsecondary Edn. grantee U.S. Dept. Edn., 1997-2000.. Nat. Endowment Humanities, 2000, 2003-2005. Mem. MLA, South Ctrl. MLA (editor South Ctrl. Rev. 1988-92, dir. 1993), Edith Wharton Soc. (exec. bd. 1998—), Instit. for Mus. and Lib. Svcs., 2002-2004. Avocation: tennis. Home: 1036 Fall Creek Rd Lincoln NE 68510-4944 Office: Dept English 202 Andrews Hall Lincoln NE 68588 Fax: 402-472-9771. E-mail: kprce@unlotes.unl.edu.

**PRICE, LAWRENCE WAYNE, II**, artist, educator; s. Lawrence Wayne Price and Margaret June Hurd. BS in edn., No. Ill. U., 1967, MA in painting, 1969, MFA in painting, 1971. Adj. instr. art Coll. DuPage, Glen Ellyn, Ill., 1982—99, William Rainey Harper Coll., Palatine, Ill., 1987—. Computer art, Spectrum: The Best in Contemporary Fantastic Art, 9th nat. computer art invitational, (accepted into the Traveling Exhbn., Ea. Wash. U.); sound composer The Lost Pleiad (Played on New Sounds (WNYC-FM), John Schaefer, Host, NYC), Enigmatic Birds (Sounds From Chgo., a series produced by Exptl. Sound Studio, Chgo.); sound & slides performance, Dragon Vortex (Chances in Time: Random Ops. in Film, San Francisco Cinematheque). Mem.: Assn. of Sci. Fiction & Fantasy Artists, Coll. Art Assn. Office Phone: 847-925-6000 ext 7242. Personal E-mail: larry@larrypriceart.com.

**PRICE, LEONTYNE (MARY VIOLET LEONTYNE PRICE)**, retired concert and opera singer, soprano; b. Laurel, Miss., Feb. 10, 1927; d. James A. and Kate (Baker) Price; m. William Warfield, Aug. 31, 1952 (div. 1973). BA, Central State Coll., Wilberforce, Ohio, 1949, DMus, 1968; student, Juilliard Sch. Music, 1949-52; pupil, Florence Page Kimball; LHD, Dartmouth Coll., 1962, Fordham U., 1969, Yale U., 1979; MusD, Howard U., 1962; Dr. Humanities, Rust Coll., 1968. Singer: (Operas) (debut) in 4 Saints in 3 Acts, 1952, (appeared) Bess in Porgy and Bess, Vienna, Berlin, Paris, London, under auspices U.S. State Dept., N.Y.C. and U.S. tour, 1952—54; recitalist, soloist (symphonies) U.S., Can., Australia, Europe, 1954—, appeared concerts in India, 1956, 1964, soloist Hollywood Bowl, 1955—59, 1966, Berlin Festival, 1960, role as Mme. Lidoine in Dialogues des Carmelites, San Francisco Opera, 1957; singer: (Operas) NBC-TV, 1955—58, 1960, 1962, 1964, San Francisco Opera Co., 1957—59, 1960—61, 1963, 1965, 1967, 1968, 1971, as Aida at La Scala, 1957;: (Operas) Vienna Staatsoper, 1958—59, 1960, 1961, Berlin Opera, 1964, Rome Opera, 1966, 1968, (recital) Brussels Internat. Fair, auspices State Dept., 1958, Verona Opera Arena, 1958—59, Yugoslavia for, State Dept., 1958; rec. artist RCA-Victor, 1958—, appeared Covent Garden, London, 1958-59, 70, Chgo. Lyric Theatre, 1959, 60, 65, Oakland (Calif.) Symphony, 1980, soloist Salzburg Festival, 1959—63, appeared Tetro alla Scala, Milano, 1960-61, 63, 67, Met. Opera, N.Y.C., 1961-62, 64, 66, 75, 76, since resident mem., until 1985, soloist Salzburg Festival, 1950, 60, debut Teatre Dell'Opera, Rome, 1967, Teatro Colon, Buenos Aires, Argentina, 1969, Hamburg Opera, 1970, recordings A Christmas Offering with Karajani, God Bless America with Charles Gerhardt, Arias from Don Giovanni, Turandot, Aida, Emani, Messa di Requiem, Trovatore, Live at Ordway, The Prima Donna Collection, A Program of Song with D. Garvey, Right as the Rain with André Previn. Co-chmn. Rust Coll. Upward Thrust Campaign; trustee Internat. House.; hon. vice-chmn. U.S. com. UNESCO; Hon. bd. dirs. Campfire Girls. Decorated Order at Ment Italy; named Musician of Year, Mus. Am. mag., 1961; recipient Merit award for role of Tosca in NBC-TV Opera, Mademoiselle mag., 1955, 20 Grammy awards for classical vocal recs. Nat. Acad. Rec. Arts and Scis., citation YWCA, 1961, Spirit of Achievement award Albert Einstein Coll. Medicine, 1962, Presdl. medal of freedom, 1964, Springarn medal NAACP, 1965, Schwann Catalog award, 1968, Nat. Medal of Arts, 1985, Essence award, 1991, others. Fellow: Am. Acad. Arts and Sci.; mem.: AFTRA, Actors Equity Assn., Am. Guild Mus. Artists, Delta Sigma Theta, Sigma Alpha Iota. Inducted into Am. Classical Music Hall of Fame, 1998. Office: Price Enterprises 1133 Broadway Ste 920 New York NY 10010-7901

**PRICE, LEW PAXTON**, writer, engineer; b. Takoma Park, Md., Dec. 19, 1938; s. Raymond Miller and Clarene Pearl (Morris) P.; m. Sherrie Darlene Sellers, June 25, 1960 (div. Apr. 1979); children: Terilyn Ann, Heather Rae, Crystal Alene. BS, U.S. Air Force Acad., Colorado Springs, Colo., 1960. Hon. Ho-O Ryu Bushido 6th Dan Master. Electronics engr. Pacific Telephone, Sacramento, Calif., 1965-66, engring. coord., bldgs., 1966-85; pres., design engr. Condor Aeroplane Works, Ltd., Sacramento, 1983-85; engring. coord. Tuttle Engring. and Constrn. Consultants, El Dorado Hills, Calif., 1989-92; scientist, flute design cons., writer, flutemaker Fair Oaks, Garden Valley, Calif., 1977—. Cons. flute design and physics. Author: The Cosmic Stradivarius, 1974, Aquarian Anastasis, 1975, The Music of Life, 1984, Dimensions in Astrology, 1986, Native North American Flutes, 1990, Secrets of the Flute (Math, Physics & Design), 1991, Creating & Using the Native American Love Flute, 1994, Creating & Using Grandfather's Flute, 1995, The Oldest Magic (Prehistory & Influence of Music), 1995, Creating & Using Older Native American Flutes, 1995, Creating & Using Smaller Native American Flutes, 1995, Creating & Using the Native American Concert Flute, 1996, More Secrets of the Flute, 1997, Creating and Using Larger Native American Flutes, 1998, Creating and Using the Largest Native American Flutes, 1998, Creating and Using Very Small Native American Flutes, 1998, Behind Light's Illusion (7-book series), 1999, 2000, 2001, Climbing on Course, 2003, (biography) When a Man is a Man, 2003; author, programmer: (computer program) Flute Design (Native American), 1996. Co-advisor Aviation Explorers, archery/space/sci. merit badge instr./examiner, Boy Scouts Am., North Highlands, Calif., 1968-70; panelist United Crusade, Sacramento, Calif., 1971; rifle/pistol/shotgun safety instr. NRA, Fair Oaks, Calif., 1970-72. Capt. USAF, 1960-65. Mem. No. Calif. Flute Circle (co-organizer 1996), Oreg. Native Am. Flute Circle (hon.). Avocations: flying, singing, flute, hiking, archery. Home and Office: PO Box 88 Garden Valley CA 95633-0088 Personal E-mail: lewprice@softcom.net.

**PRICE, (WILLIAM) MARK**, professional basketball player; b. Bartlesville, Okla., Feb. 15, 1964; Student, Ga. Inst. Tech. With Dallas Mavericks, 1986; guard Cleve. Cavaliers, 1986-95, Washington Bullets, 1995-96, Golden State Warriors, 1996-97, Orlando Magic, 1997—. Winner NBA Long Distance Shootout, 1993, 94; named to NBA All-Star team, 1989, 92, 93, 94, NBA First Team, 1993, Dream Team II, 1994. Holder career record for highest free-throw percentages during regular and playoff seasons. Office: Orlando Magic Orlando Arena 8701 Maitland Summit Blvd Orlando FL 32810-5915

**PRICE, MARLA**, museum director, curator; PhD in art hist. Assoc. curator of 20th-century art Nat. Gallery Art, Washington, DC; chief curator Modern Art Mus. Fort Worth, Tex., 1986—91, dir. Tex., 1991—. Office: Modern Art Mus Fort Worth 3200 Darnell St Fort Worth TX 76107-2872 E-mail: mprice@themodern.org.

**PRICE, MARY SUE SWEENEY**, museum director; d. William Robert Sweeney; m. Clement A. Price, 1988. BA in English, Allegheny Coll., 1973; D.H.C. (hon.), Caldwell Coll. With textbook pub. co., NYC; supr. pub. rels. Newark Mus., 1975, dep. dir., 1990—93, dir., 1993—. Past pres. ArtTable Inc.; v.p. ArtPrice NJ Inc.; bd. dirs. St. Vincent Acad., Newark Arts Coun. Mem.: Assn. Art Mus. Dirs., Am. Assn. Mus., NJ Assn. Mus. (bd. dirs.). Office: Newark Mus 49 Washington St Newark NJ 07102 Office Phone: 973-596-6550.

**PRICE, MICHAEL F.**, money management executive; b. 1952; div., 3 sons. Graduate, U. Okla., 1975. Rsch. asst., mgr. to CEO Heine Securities, Short Hills, NJ, 1975-97; CEO Franklin Mutual Advs. Inc. (formerly Heine Securities), Short Hills, NJ, 1997; pvt. investor, 1998—. Pres., chmn. bd. dirs. Franklin Mutual Series Fund Inc. Named one of Forbes' Richest Americans, 2006. Office: Franklin Mutual Advisers Inc 51 John F Kennedy Pkwy Short Hills NJ 07078-2702*

**PRICE, MICHAEL HOWARD**, journalist, critic, composer; b. Amarillo, Tex., Sept. 14, 1947; s. John Andrew and Thelma Adeline (Wilson) P.; m. Christina Renteria, Aug. 31, 1980. BA in Journalism, West Tex. State U., 1970. Edn. writer Amarillo Globe-News, 1968-74, fin. editor, 1974-76, city editor, 1976-77; adminstr. Amarillo Coll., 1977-80; bur. chief Ft. Worth Star-Telegram, 1980-83, features editor, 1983-85, film critic, 1985-98; dir. motion picture programming Sundance Sq. Entertainment Dist., Ft. Worth, 1998—2002; critic-at-large Ft. Worth Bus. Press, 2002—. Cons. journalism West Tex. State U., Canyon, 1977-90, Tex. Tech U., Lubbock, 1982-85; dirs. The Harvey Awards comic-book profls. awards, 1990—; syndicated columnist N.Y. Times News Svc., 1990-98; critic-in-residence Sta. KRLD Newsradio, Dallas-Ft. Worth, 1998—; columnist Fangoria mag., 2002—. Author: (CD-ROMs) A Century of Fantastic Cinema, 1995, Silver Screen Sensations, 1996; (albums) Cognitive Dissonance, 1994, The Last Temptation of Price, 1995, R. Crumb—The Musical, 1995, Swingmasters Revue, 1995, Claus & Effect, 1996, Diddy Wah Diddy, 1997, Big Hoedown Tonight!, 1999, From Hell to Texas, 1999, Arghlebargle, 2001; (books) Forgotten Horrors: The Definitive Edition, 1999, Forgotten Horrors II, 2001, Hollywood and the Piano, 2001, Spawn of Skull Island, 2002, Human Monsters in the Movies, 1994, Krime Duzzin't Pay, 1995, The Guitar in Jazz, 1996, Stitches, 1996, Frights Genuine & Fancied, 1996; (novels) The Prowler, 1989, Carnival of Souls, 1991, Holiday for Screams, 1992, Lon Chaney, Jr.: A Critical Biography, 1997; co-author: The Big Book of Biker Flicks, 2002; screen actor: Ramming Speed, 1997, Southern Fried Homicide, 1998, Beauty & the Beasts, 1998, Vincent Price: A Critical Biography, 1998, It's Christmastime at the Movies, 1998. Creative dir. Tex. Gridiron Show, Fort Worth, 1984-85, 92-93; pres. Ft. Worth Film Festival, Inc. 1997—; Grad. fellow in journalism U. Mo., 1975; inducted into Tex. Tornados Blues Hall of Fame, 1995. Mem. ASCAP, Soc. Profl. Journalists (bd. dirs. 1992-94), Soc. Film Critics. Office: Sundance Square Management 201 Main St Ste 700 Fort Worth TX 76102-3134 *People who believe that writing is a glamour gig often ask, "How do you become a writer?" as if in search of some magical formula. The only answer is: "WRITE." For whatever purpose and however large or small a readership: WRITE.*

**PRICE, MICHAEL WITWER**, art gallery owner, lawyer; b. Bronxville, NY, Dec. 30, 1941; s. Will James and Jeanette Witwer Price; children: Freyzewd Negussie, Seth, Rachel, Lucero. BA, Yale U., 1964; MS in City Planning, MIT, 1970; JD, Boston U., 1983. Bar: Mass. 1983. Dir. legal and social svc. Am. Friends Svc. Com., East Jerusalem, 1972—75; asst. dir. admissions Yale U., New Haven, 1976—78; pvt. practice law Boston, 1983—90; counsel Mass. Dept. Pub. Health Hosps., Boston, 1990—94; arts coord. Internat. Inst., Boston, 1996—98; owner MPG Contemporary, Boston, 1998—. Co-author: Boston's Immigrants 1840-1925, 2000. Bd. dirs. West End Boys and Girls Club, Boston, 2004—. Mem.: St. Botulph Club. Avocations: sailing, reading. Home: 7 Westford St Boston MA 02134 Office: MPG Contemporary 450 Harrison Ave Boston MA 02118

**PRICE, MITCH**, biology professor; arrived in U.S., 1996; s. Dow and Marjorie Price. BS (hons.), U. New Brunswick (Can.); PhD, Queens U., Can., 1996. Postdoctoral fellow Pa. State U., 1996—99, asst. prof. Biology, 1999—. Office: Pa State Univ Biology Dept 208 Mueller Lab University Park PA 16802

**PRICE, MITCHELL R.**, pediatric surgeon; MD, U. Chgo., 1986. Intern in surgery NYU Sch. of Medicine, N.Y.C., 1986—87, resident in surgery, 1987—88, 1991—94; Extracorporeal Membrane Oxygenation fellow Columbia Babies Hosp., N.Y.C., 1988—91; fellow pediatric surgery U. Colo. Denver Children's Hosp., 1994—96; asst. prof. divsn. pediat. surgery UMDNJ-Robert Wood Johnson Med. Sch., New Brunswick, NJ, 1996—. Office: Robert Wood Johnson Med Sch 1 Robert Wood Johnson Pl New Brunswick NJ 08903-0019 Office Phone: 732-235-7821.

**PRICE, NELSON (JOHN NELSON PRICE)**, author, journalist; b. Augusta, Ga., May 7, 1957; s. John Paul and Joy Gertrude (Scheck) P. BA in Journalism and Psychology, Ind. U., 1978. City hall reporter Lawrence (Kans.) Journal-World, 1978-79; fed. cts. reporter, social issues writer Fort Wayne (Ind.) Journal-Gazette, 1979-80; edn. writer Indpls. News, 1981-85; columnist, feature writer Indpls. Star-News, 1985—2002. Bd. dirs. The Sagamore, Indpls.; adj. prof. journalism Ind. U.-Purdue U., Indpls., 2003-05. Author: Indiana Legends: Famous Hoosiers from Johnny Appleseed to David Letterman, hardcover 1997, softcover 2005, Indianapolis: Leading the Way, 2000, Legendary Hoosiers: Famous Folks from the State of Indiana, 2001, Indianapolis Then and Now, 2004; contbr. articles to profl. jours., chapters to books. Recipient Sagamore of the Wabash award Gov. Ind., 1995, 2002, Martin Luther King Jr. award Indpls. Edn. Assn., 1986, Best Sports Writing award Hoosier State Press Assn., 1994, Best Column award, 1994, Best Feature Story award, 1994, Best Personality Profile award, 1994. Mem. Soc. Profl. Journalists (awards), Mental Health Assn. Marion County (awards).

**PRICE, NICK**, professional golfer; b. Durban, South Africa, Jan. 28, 1957; m. Sue Price; children: Gregory, Robyn Frances, Kimberly. Profl. golfer PGA, 1977—. Winner Asseng Invitational, 1979, Canon European Masters, 1980, Italian Open, 1981, South African Masters, Vaals Reef Open, 1982, World Series of Golf, 1983, Trophee Lancome, 1985, ICL Internat. Open, West End South Australian Open, 1989, GTE Byron Nelson Golf Classic, 1991, Canadian Open, Air New Zealand/Shell Open, 1992, PGA Championship, 1992, 1994, H.E.B. Tex. Open, The Players Championship, 1993, Canon Greater Hartford Open, Sprint Western Open, Fed. Express St. Jude Classic, HondaClassic, 1994, Southwestern Bell Colonial, Motorola Western Open, Bell Canadian Open, Alfred Dunhill Challenge Hassan II Golf Trophy, Zimbabwe Open, British Open, 1994, MCI Classic, 1997, Dimension Data Pro-Am, 1997, 97, Suntory Open, 1999; 3rd PGA Tour Money Leader, 1992, PGA Tour Money Leader, 1993, 10 USPGA Tour Victories, 26 World Wide Victories; recipient Vardon Trophy, 1993; named Player of Yr., 1993; recipient, Payne Stewart award, 2002; ASAP/Jim Murray award, 2002; named to World Golf Hall of Fame, 2003. Achievements include holding PGA Tournament record for lowest score (269), 1994.

**PRICE, PAUL BUFORD**, physicist, researcher; b. Memphis, Nov. 8, 1932; s. Paul Buford and Eva (Dupuy) P.; m. JoAnn Margaret Baum, June 28, 1958; children— Paul Buford III, Heather Alynn, Pamela Margaret, Alison Gaynor. BS summa cum laude, Davidson Coll., 1954, DSc (hon.), 1973; MS in Physics, U. Va., 1956, PhD in Physics, 1958. Fulbright scholar U. (Eng.) Bristol, 1958-59; NSF postdoctoral fellow Cambridge (Eng.) U., 1959-60; physicist R&D Ctr., GE, Schenectady, 1960—69; prof. physics U. Calif., Berkeley, 1969—, Miller rsch. prof., 1972—73, chmn. dept. physics, 1987—91, McAdams prof. physics, 1990—92, dean phys. scis., 1992—2001, dir. Space Scis. Lab., 1979—85, prof. grad. sch. Dept. Physics, 2002—. Vis. com. Bartol Rsch. Inst., 1991-94; adj. bd. Indian Inst. Astrophysics, Bangalore, 1993-95; cons. to lunar sample analysis planning team NASA; space sci. bd. Nat. Acad. Scis.; adj. prof. physics Rensselaer Poly. Inst., 1967-68; vis. prof. Tata Inst. Fundamental Rsch., Bombay, 1965-66, U. Rome, 1983, 92; sci. assoc. Ctr. d'Etude Rsch. Nuclear, 1984; mem. polar rsch. bd. NAS; rschr. in high-energy neutrino astrophysics, climatology, microbial life in extreme environments; mem. U.S. Ice Core Working Group, 2002-05; mem. libr. adv. bd. U. Calif. Berkeley. Author: (with others) Nuclear Tracks in Solids; Contbr. (with others) articles to profl. jours. Regional dir. Calif. Alliance for Minority Participation, 1993-2004. Recipient Disting. Svc. award Am. Nuclear Soc., 1964, Indsl. Rsch. awards, 1964, 65, 71, E.O. Lawrence Meml. award AEC, 1971, medal for exceptional sci. achievement NASA, 1973; Sci. Symposium in honor of 65th birthday, Aug 23-24, 1997, Berkeley Leadership and Rsch. Distinction citation, 2002; John Simon Guggenheim fellow, 1976-77. Fellow: Am. Geophys. Union, Am. Phys. Soc., Indian Inst. Astrophysics (hon.); mem.: NAS (chmn. geophysics sect. 1981—84, sec. class phys.-math. scis. 1985—88, chmn. 1988—91), Bohemian Club. Achievements include discovery of nuclear tracks in solids; invention of nucleopore filters for microbiology; fission track geochronology; optical dust logger; biospectral logger; nine patents; invention of instrument for radon detection. Avocation: travel. Office: U Calif Dept Physics 285 Evans Hall Berkeley CA 94720 Business E-Mail: bprice@berkeley.edu.

**PRICE, RAY HAMPTON,** mathematics professor; b. Charlotte, Oct. 29, 1952; s. Robert Hampton and Frances Humphries; m. Ann Rankin Price, Aug. 29, 1981; children: Caroline, Mary. BS in Math, Wofford Coll., 1974; MS in Math, Wake Forest U., 1978; PhD in Math, Virginia Tech., 1987. Math tchr. Juaben Secondary Sch., Ghana, 1975—77; asst. prof. math Judsor Coll., Marion, Ala., 1979—81, prof. math, dept head, 1987—. Office: Dept Math Judson Coll Marion AL 36756 Business E-Mail: rprice@judson.edu.

**PRICE, REYNOLDS,** writer, educator; b. Macon, N.C., Feb. 1, 1933; s. William Solomon and Elizabeth (Rodwell) P. AB summa cum laude (Angier Duke scholar), Duke, 1955; BLitt (Rhodes scholar), Merton Coll., Oxford U., Eng., 1958; LittD, St. Andrews Presbyn. Coll., 1978, Wake Forest U., 1979, Washington and Lee U., 1991, Davidson Coll., 1992; LittD, Elon Coll., U. N.C., 2003. Mem. faculty English Duke U., 1958—; asst. prof., 1961-68; assoc. prof., 1968-72; prof., 1972-77; James B. Duke prof., 1977—; acting chmn., 1983; writer in residence U. N.C., Chapel Hill, 1965, U. Kans., 1967, 69, 80, U.N.C., Greensboro, 1971; Glasgow prof. Washington and Lee U., 1971; faculty Salzburg Seminar, 1977. Author: A Long and Happy Life, 1962, The Names and Faces of Heroes, 1963, A Generous Man, 1966, Love and Work, 1968, Permanent Errors, 1970, Things Themselves, 1972, The Surface of Earth, 1975, Early Dark, 1977, A Palpable God, 1978, The Source of Light, 1981, Vital Provisions, 1982, Private Contentment, 1984, Kate Vaiden, 1986, The Laws of Ice, 1986, A Common Room, 1987, Good Hearts, 1988, Clear Pictures, 1989, The Tongues of Angels, 1990, The Use of Fire, 1990, New Music, 1990, The Foreseeable Future, 1991, Conversations with Reynolds Price, 1991, Blue Calhoun, 1992, Full Moon, 1993, The Collected Stories, 1993, A Whole New Life, 1994, The Promise of Rest, 1995, Three Gospels, 1996, The Collected Poems, 1997, Roxanna Slade, 1998, Learning a Trade, 1998, Letter to a Man in the Fire, 1999, A Perfect Friend, 2000, Feasting the Heart, 2000, Noble Norfleet, 2002, The God Priest's Son, 2005. A Serious Way of Wondering, 2003, Recipient William Faulkner Found. award notable 1st novel, 1962, Sir Walter Raleigh award, 1962, 76, 81, 84, 86, award Nat. Assn. Ind. Schs., 1964, Roanoke-Chowan Poetry award, 1982; Guggenheim fellow, 1964-65; fellow Nat. Endowment for Arts, 1967-68, lit. advt. panel, 1973-76, chmn., 1976; recipient Nat. Inst. Arts and Letters award, 1971, Bellamann Found. award, 1972, Lillian Smith award, 1976, N.C. award, 1977, Nat. Book Critics Circle award, 1986, Elmer H. Bobst award, 1988, R. Hunt Parker award N.C. Lit. and Hist. Soc., 1991, Northcarolinana award, 1999, Caldwell award NC Humanities Coun., 2002. Mem. Am. Acad. Arts and Scis., Am. Acad. Arts and Letters, Phi Beta Kappa, Phi Delta Theta. Home: PO Box 99014 Durham NC 27708-9014 Office: care Harriet Wasserman Lit Agy Inc 137 E 36th St New York NY 10016-3528

**PRICE, RICHARD EDWARD,** lawyer; b. Stanford, Calif., Apr. 30, 1969; s. Richard Maxwell and Mary Frances Price; m. Brook Renee Gauntz, Sept. 14, 2002. BA, U. Mass., 1991; JD, George Washington U., 1994; LLM, Cambridge U., England, 1995. Bar: N.Y. 1995, Mass. 1995, D.C. 1996, U.S. Ct. Appeals (D.C. cir.) 1997. Atty. Koteen & Naftalin, L.L.P., Washington, 1996—99, Vinson & Elkins L.L.P., 1999—2005; assoc. gen. counsel One Communications Corp., 2005—. Mem.: Federalist Soc., Conn. Bar Assn., Genesee Valley Club, U. Club of Wash., DC, Golden Key, Pi Sigma Alpha. Office: One Communications Corp 100 Chestnut St Rochester NY 14604

**PRICE, RICHARD GALEN,** sound recording engineer, music producer, conductor; b. Ann Arbor, Mich., Jan. 31, 1956; s. Galen B. and Nina Ruth (Hudson) Price; m. Margaret Addison Bowles, July 6, 1985; 1 child, Hannah Leigh. MusB in Horn Performance, U. Mich., Ann Arbor, 1977; postgrad., The Juilliard Sch., N.Y.C., 1977—79, Pierre Monteux Domaine Sch., Hancock, Maine, 1987. Hornist, founding mem. Borealis Wind Quintet, N.Y.C., 1976—91; freelance musician various orgns., N.Y.C., 1977—91; interim chair dir.a nd baritone soloist 2d Congl. Ch., Greenwich, Conn., 1988—95; sr. rec. engr., prodr. Squires Prodns., Elmsford, NY, 1991—; music dir., conductor Danbury Concert Chorus, Conn., 2002—. Arranger: Brass quintet music Carols for Brass, 1976—80. Bd. mem. Pro Arte Singers, New Canaan, Conn., 1995—97, Conn. Folklife Project, Danbury, 2005—. Nominee many Grammy nominations as prodr., engr., editor. Avocations: woodworking, boating, fishing. Home: 29 Lake Dr S New Fairfield CT 06812 Office: Squires Prodns Inc 2 Westchester Plaza Elmsford NY 10523 Personal E-mail: rchdprice@aol.com.

**PRICE, ROBERT,** media and communications executive, investment banker, lawyer; b. NYC, Aug. 27, 1932; s. Solomon and Frances (Berger) P.; m. Margery Beth Weiner, Dec. 18, 1955 (div.); children: Eileen Marcia, Steven. AB, NYU, 1953; LLD, Columbia U., 1958. Bar: NY 1958, U.S. Dist. Ct. 1958, U.S. Ct. Appeals 1958, U.S. Supreme Ct. 1958, ICC: 1958, FCC: 1958, IRS: 1958. With R.H. Macy & Co., Inc., 1955-58; practiced in N.Y.C., 1958—; law clk. to judge U.S. Dist. Ct. (so. dist.) N.Y., 1958-59; asst. U.S. atty. So. Dist. N.Y., 1959-60; ptnr. Kupferman & Price, 1960-65; dep. mayor N.Y.C., 1965-66; exec. v.p. dir. Dreyfus Corp., N.Y.C., 1966-69; v.p., investment officer Dreyfus Fund, until 1969; gen. ptnr. Lazard, Freres & Co., 1972-82; pres. N.Y. Law Jour., Nat. Law Jour.; pres., treas., dir. Price Comm. Corp., 1979—; chmn., pres., dir. PriCellular Corp., 1988-95; pres., dir. TLM Corp., 1989—2000. Mem. adv. com. Bankers Trust Co. N.Y.; dir. Holly Sugar Corp., Lane Bryant, Inc., Graphic Scanning Corp.; chmn. N.Y. Port Authority Negotiating Com. for World Trade Ctr., 1965-66; spl. counsel N.Y. State Joint Legis. Com. on Ct. Reorgn.; asst. counsel N.Y. State Joint Legis. Com. on N.Y. Banking Laws; mem. The N.Y. State Mcpl. Assistance Corp., 1996-2000; commr. N.Y. State Commn. of Investigations, N.Y.C., 2000—. Contbr. articles to profl. publs. Trustee CUNY, 1996-98; chmn. govt. and civil svc. divsn. United Jewish Appeal Greater N.Y., 1966; co-chmn. met. N.Y. blood drive ARC, 1966; campaign mgr. John V. Lindsay, Campaigns for Congressman, N.Y.C., 1958, 60, 62, 64, 69, for Nelson A. Rockefeller Oreg. Rep. presdl. primary campaign, 1964, Lindsay campaign for mayor, N.Y.C., 1965; del. N.Y. Rep. State Conv., 1962, 66; del. Rep. Nat. Conv., 1988, 92, 96; lectr. Rep. Nat. Com., 1966; bd. dirs. Am. Friends Hebrew U.; past trustee Columbia U. Sch. Pharm. Scis. With U.S. Army, 1953-55. Recipient Yeshiva U. Heritage award, Pub. Svc. award, Queens Catholic War Vets. Mem. ABA, FCC Bar Assn., Assn. Bar City NY, NY State Dist. Attys. Assn., Coun. Fgn. Rels., Columbia Law Sch. Alumni Assn. (dir.); Scribes, Tau Kappa Alpha. Home: 25 E 86th St New York NY 10028-0553 Office: Price Communications Corp 45 Rockefeller Plz Ste 3200 New York NY 10111-0100 Office Phone: 212-757-5600.

**PRICE, ROBERT EBEN,** judge; b. Waco, Tex., Jan. 13, 1931; s. Robert Eben and Mary Hamilton (Barnett) P.; m. Ann Hodges, June 4, 1954; children— Eben, Mary, Ann, Emily. BA, So. Methodist U., 1952, JD, 1954, LL.M., 1972; postgrad., Air War Coll., 1976. Bar: Tex. 1954, U.S. Supreme Ct., U.S. Ct. Mil. Appeals, U.S. Ct. Claims, U.S. Dist. Ct. (no. dist.) Tex. 1954. Mem. firm Taylor, Mizell, Price, Corrigan & Smith, Dallas, 1956-86; judge Dallas County Probate Ct. No. 2, 1986—. Lectr. continuing legal edn. program U. Houston Law Found., 1993—; lectr. law So Meth. U. Law Sch., 1973-74, faculty paralegal cert. program Sch. Continuing Edn., 1987-89; lectr. practice skills program State Bar Tex., 1974-78. Editor-in-chief: Southwestern Law Jour., 1953-54. Trustee and sec. St. Michael and All Angels Found., 1984-88; bd. dirs. Downtown Ministry, Diocese of Dallas Episcopal, 1986-88; chmn. legis. and legal awareness subcom., vice chmn. Tex. Gov's Com. on Employment of Handicapped, 1978-82. Served as legal officer USAF, 1954-56; col. JAGC Res. ret. Fellow: Tex. Bar Found., Am. Coll. Trust and Estate Counsel; mem.: ABA (nat. conf. spl. ct. judges com. on probate and surrogates cts. 1992—), Tex. Coll. Probate Judges (mem. faculty), State Bar Tex. (lectr. profl. devel. program 1988—), Dallas Bar Assn., Coll. State Bar Tex., Nat. Coll. Probate Judges, Phi Delta Theta, Phi

Eta Sigma, Phi Alpha Delta. Episcopalian. Home: 4300 Arcady Ave Dallas TX 75205-3704 Office: Probate Ct 2 ste 211 509 Main St Dallas TX 75202-3508 Office Phone: 214-653-7138.

**PRICE, ROBERT F.,** lawyer; BS in Acctg., Loyola Coll., 1969; JD, U. NC, 1974. Bar: Md. 1974. Asst. gen. counsel USF&G; mng. dir., gen. counsel Alex Brown & Sons, Inc.; sr. v.p., gen. counsel Legg Mason, Inc., Balt., 1998—. Mem. exec. com. compliance and legal divisn. Securities Industry Assn., mem. fed. regulation com.; mem. legal adv. bd. NASD; bd. dirs. St. Ignatious Loyola Acad. Office: Legg Mason Cds Inv Serv PO Box 55214 Boston MA 02205-5214 Office Phone: 410-539-0000. E-mail: rfprice@leggmason.com.

**PRICE, ROBERT IRA,** coast guard officer; b. N.Y.C., Sept. 22, 1921; s. Alfred and Mary Edna (Schweitzer) P.; m. Virginia Louise Miller, June 20, 1946; children: Andrea Jean, Keven Virginia. BBA, CCNY, 1942; BS, U.S. Coast Guard Acad., 1945; postgrad., M.I.T., 1950-53. Registered profl. engr., D.C. Commd. ensign U.S. Coast Guard, 1945, advanced through grades to vice adm., 1978; asst. chief Mcht. Marine Tech. Div., Washington, 1965-67; chief planning staff Office Mcht. Marine Safety, 1967-71; capt. Port of Phila., 1971-73; chief Office Marine Environ. Washington, 1974-76; comdr. 11th Coast Guard Dist. Long Beach, Calif., 1976-78; comdr. Atlantic Area and 3d Coast Guard Dist. N.Y.C., 1978-81; ret., 1981; sr. v.p. J.J. Henry Co. (marine engrs.), N.Y.C., 1981-86; maritime cons., 1986—. Prin. U.S. negotiator to tech. programs Intergovtl. Maritime Consultative Orgn., UN, 1962-71 Contbg. author: Ship Design and Construction, 1980; Contbr. articles to profl. jours. Decorated D.S.M. with gold star, Legion of Merit with gold star, Meritorious Service medal with gold star, Coast Guard Commendation medal. Fellow Royal Instn. Naval Architects, Soc. Naval Architects (Land medalist 1982); mem. Sigma Xi. Clubs: Propeller, Army Navy, N.Y. Yacht. Office Phone: 321-751-4666.

**PRICE, ROBERT J,** corporate financial executive; BS, Pa. State U. CPA. Former audit ptnr. Price Waterhouse; various positions Aetna Inc., 1989—2000, sr. v.p., CFO, 1998—2000; pres., CEO CitiInsurance, 2000—01; sr. v.p., controller The Hartford Fin. Svcs. Group, Inc., 2002—. Bd. mem. Greater Hartford Arts Coun.; Bushnell Park Carousel Soc. Mem.: Conn. Soc. of Cert. Pub. Accountants, Am. Inst. Office: Hartford Fin Svcs Group Hartford Plaza 690 Asylum Ave Hartford CT 06115

**PRICE, ROBERT STANLEY,** lawyer; b. Phila., Jan. 21, 1937; s. Benjamin and Estelle B. (Muchnick) P.; m. Emilie W. Kirschbaum, June 27, 1965 (dec. Mar. 1998); children: Louise P. Kelly, Marianna R. BA, Kenyon Coll., 1958; LLB, Yale U., 1961. Bar: Pa. 1963, U.S. Dist. Ct. (ea. dist.) Pa. 1963, U.S. Ct. Appeals (3d cir.) 1963, N.Y. 1993. Assoc. Dechert, Price & Rhoads, Phila., 1961-63; asst tax atty. Smith, Kline & French, Phila., 1963-67; tax atty. Pa. Ctrl. Transp. Co., Phila., 1967-70; tax counsel IU Internat., Phila., 1970-72; ptnr. Townsend, Elliott & Munson, Phila., 1972-76, Pepper, Hamilton & Scheetz, Phila., 1977-86, Saul, Ewing, Remick & Saul, Phila., 1986-93; spl. cons. Saul, Ewing, Remick & Saul (now Saul Ewing LLP), Phila., 1994—2001. Inst. tax cons. Fischbein-Badillo-Wagner-Harding, N.Y.C., 1998—2001, Mintz, Levin, Cohn, Ferris, Glovsky and Popeo, P.C., N.Y.C., 2001—. Author: ABCs of Industrial Development Bonds, 1981, 5th edit., 1990; contbr. articles to profl. jours. Pres. Samuel Eells Lit. and Ednl. Found., 1980—. With U.S. Army, 1961—62. Mem. ABA (tax exempt fin. com.), Pa. Bar, Phila. Bar Assn., N.Y. Bar, Racquet Club Phila. (v.p. 1987-88), Alpha Delta Phi (pres. 1975-78). Office: 3800 Centre Sq W Philadelphia PA 19102-2186 E-mail: rpricedj@verizon.net.

**PRICE, ROBERT WILLIAM,** school superintendent, consultant; b. Ogden, Utah, May 13, 1950; s. William Robert and Eileen Louise (Rabe) P.; m. Sally Sandman, Sept. 20, 1975; children: Geoffrey Thomas, Caitlin Elizabeth. BS in Child Devel., Calif. State U., Hayward, 1973, MS in Sch. Adminstrn., 1986; EdD, U. Pacific, 1998. Cert. elem. tchr., Calif. Tchr. Turlock (Calif.) Sch. Dist., 1974-81; asst. prin. Monte Vista Mid. Sch., Tracy, Calif. 1981-82, prin., 1982-87; asst. supt. instrn. Tracy Pub. Schs., 1987-90, 91-93, interim supt., 1990-91; supt. Empire Union Sch. Dist., Modesto, Calif., 1993—. Cons. Campfire, Tracy, 1983; founding mem. Tracy Exch. Club, 1985; co-founder Project Bus. & Edn. Together, Tracy, 1985; bd. dirs. Boys and Girls Club of Tracy, 1987-93. Recipient Adminstrv. Leadership award Calif. Media & Libr. Educators Assn., 1994. Mem. Assn. Calif. Sch. Adminstrs. (planning com. supts. symposium 1995—, v.p. programs Region 7 1994—), Calif. League Mid. Schs. (adv. panel Region 6 1993—, chair legis. action 1994-95, Region 6 Educator of Yr. 1991). Democrat. Office: Empire Union Sch Dist 116 N Mcclure Rd Modesto CA 95357-1329 E-mail: bprice@empire.k12.ca.us.

**PRICE, STEVEN,** venture capitalist, communications executive, lawyer; b. NYC, Feb. 14, 1962; s. Robert and Margery Price; m. Tina Gitlin, Mar. 16, 1991. BS magna cum laude, Brown U., 1984; JD, Columbia U. Sch. Law, 1989. Spl. asst. to US Amb. to the START Talks in Geneva US Dept. State, 1989—90; assoc. Davis Polk & Wardell, 1991; with mergers and acquisitions group Goldman, Sachs & Co.; COO PriCellular Corp., 1994—97, bd. dirs., 1996, pres., CEO, 1997—2001; deputy asst. sec. def. spectrum and command, control and communications policy US Dept. Def., 2001—03; pres., CEO LiveWire Capital, 2003—04; gen. partner Spectrum Equity Investors, 2004—. Dir. Met. Coun. Poverty, 1999—, UJA Fedn. NY, 2000—, US Nat. Archives Bd., 2003—; advisory bd. for computing and IT Brown U., 2003—; cons. Office Sec. Def. and Def. Sci. Bd., 2003—. Co-founder Brown U. Ctr. for Combat Casualty Recovery. Mem.: ABA, Bar Assn. Wash., DC, Assn. Bar NY, Phi Beta Kappa. Office: Spectrum Equity Investors One International Place Boston MA 02110 Office Phone: 617-464-4600. Office Fax: 617-464-4601. Business E-Mail: steven@spectrumequity.com.

**PRICE, TERESA ANNETTE,** elementary school educator; b. Riverdale, Md., Jan. 13, 1961; d. Carl William and Mary Helen Gohr; m. Darryl Scott Price, Nov. 20, 1982 (div. Oct. 2003); children: John, Mark. BS in Elem. Edn., U. Md., College Park, 1979—85; MS in Curriculum and Instrn., We. Md. Coll., 1992—98. Cert. natl. bd. early childhood generalist 2000. Elem. tchr. Prince George's County Pub. Sch. Upper Marlboro, Md., 1986—88, Charles County Pub. Sch. - Indian Head Elem., Indian Head, Md., 1988—; So. regional network 1 faciliator/ coord. Md. State Dept. Edn. - Nat. Bd. Profl. Tchg. Standards, Brandywine, 2002—; second grade team leader Indian Head Elem., Md., 2002—; curriculum design grad. course, instr. curriculum and instruction McDaniel Coll., Westminster, Md., 2003—. Curriculum developer/writer Charles County Pub. Sch., LaPlata, 1998—99; del. Nat. Edn. Assn./Edn. Assn. Charles County, LaPlata, 2000—01, Md. State Tchr. Assn., LaPlata, 2003—, "I Can Do It" classroom mgmt. trainer, Annapolis, 2000—; adv. bd. com. grad. curriculum and instrn. McDaniel Coll., 2001—; summer enrichment reading tchr. Charles County Pub. Sch., Waldorf, Md., 2002—. Avocations: camping, golf, reading, crafts, fishing. Home: 2805 Lohengrin Ct Waldorf MD 20601 Office: Charles County Pub Sch IHES 4200 Indian Head Hwy Indian Head MD 20640 Personal E-mail: turbotepee13@aol.com. Business E-Mail: tprice@ccboe.com.

**PRICE, THEODORA HADZISTELIOU,** individual, child and family therapist; b. Athens, Greece, Oct. 1, 1938; arrived in U.S., 1967; d. Ioannis and Evangelia (Emmanuel) Hadzisteliou; m. David C. Long Price, Dec. 26, 1966 (div. 1989); children: Morgan N., Alkes D. L. Diploma in piano tchg., Nat. Conservatory, Athens, 1958; BA in History/Archaeology, U. Athens, 1961; DPhil, U. Oxford, Eng., 1966; MA in Clin. Social Work, U. Chgo., 1988. LCSW, bd. cert. diplomate in clin. social work. Mus. asst., resident tutor U. Sydney, Australia, 1966-67; instr. anthropology Adelphi U., N.Y.C., 1967-68; archaeologist Hebrew Union Coll., Gezer, Israel, 1968; asst. prof. classical archaeology/art U. Chgo., 1968-70; jr. rsch. fellow Harvard Ctr. Hellenic Studies, Washington, 1970-71; clin. social worker Harbor Light Ctr., Salvation Army, Chgo., 1988-89; therapist Inst. Motivational Devel., Lombard, Ill., 1989-90; caseworker Jewish Family & Cmty. Svc., Chgo., 1989-90; staff therapist Family Svc. Ctrs. of South Cook County, Chicago Heights,

1990-91; pvt. practice child, adolescent, family therapy Bolingbrook, Ill., 1991—; dir. counseling svcs., clin. supr., psychotherapist Family Link, Inc., Chgo., 1993; staff therapist Cen. Bapt. Family Svcs., Gracell Rehab., Chgo., 1991, 92-93; casework supr., counselor Epilepsy Found. Greater Chgo., Chgo., 1992-93; therapist children, adolescents and families dept. foster care Cath. Charities, Chgo., 1993-94; individual and family therapist South Ctrl. Cmty. Svcs. Individual-Family Counseling Svcs., Chgo., 1994-97. Bd. dirs. counselor Naperville Sch. Gifted and Talented, 1982—84; lectr. in field. Author: (monograph) Kourotrophos, Cults and Representations of the Greek Nursing Deities, 1978; contbr. articles to profl. jours. Eleutherios Venizelos scholar, 1962—65, Meyerstein Traveling grantee, Oxford, Eng., 1963, 1964. Mem.: NASW, Am. Bd. Clin. Soc. Workers, Ill. Clin. Social Workers, Nat. Acad. Clin. Social Workers. Avocations: piano, Byzantine chanting, writing. Home and Office: 10 Pebble Ct Bolingbrook IL 60440-1557 Office Phone: 630-378-1187. *Nobody stands alone, for each of us partakes and contributes to universal energy and creation. Every thought or action has progressively timeless impact. Therefore, working in helping people is influencing the flow of creation.*

**PRICE, THOMAS E.,** congressman; b. Lansing, Mich., Oct. 8, 1954; m. Elizabeth; 1 child, Robert. Bachelor's, MD, U. Mich. Intern in surgery Emory U. Affiliated Hosps., resident in orthop. surgery; founder Compass Orthop. (formerly North Fulton Orthop. Clinic); mem. Ga. Senate, Atlanta, 1996—2004, majority leader, 2002—03; mem. US Congress from 6th Ga. dist., 2005—; mem. Edn. and Workforce com., Fin. Svcs. com. Rep. health care task force Am. Legis. Enterprise Coun.; bd. dirs. Northside Bank. Mem. bd. dirs. North Metro YMCA; active Roswell Presbyn. Ch., Ga. Ensemble Theatre, Chattahoochee Nature Ctr. Mem. Rotary (bd. dirs.). Republican. Presbyterian. Office: US Ho Reps 506 Cannon Ho Office Bldg Washington DC 20515-1006 also: Dist Office Ste 50 3750 Roswell Rd Marietta GA 30062 Office Phone: 202-225-4501. Office Fax: 202-225-4656.*

**PRICE, THOMAS FREDERICK,** theater educator; b. Salt Lake City, June 19, 1937; s. Thomas William P. and Caryl Susan Brown; children: Devin, Jennifer. BA in Drama, Pomona Coll., 1960; MA in Theatre, San Francisco State U., 1962; PhD in Drama, Stanford U., 1968; student, Columbia U. Rare Book Sch., 1983. Asst. prof. English U. of the Pacific, Stockton, Calif., 1968-70; asst. prof. drama U.S. Internat. U., Sch. Performing Arts, San Diego, 1970-74; archivist, curator The Philibrick Theatre Libr., Los Altos Hills, Calif., 1975-85; vis. prof. English Tianjin Normal U., China, 1985-87; adj. prof. English Sussex County CC, Newton, NJ, 1991; adj. prof. theatre So. Oreg. State U., Ashland, 1991-92; assoc. prof. English Tamkang U., Taipei, Taiwan, 1993—2004; adj. prof. U. Laverne, Calif., 2004—06. Ednl. broadcaster KPFA-FM, LA, 1959—62, KSRO-FM, Ashland, Oreg., 1990—92; dramaturge Caligula, Old Globe Theatre, San Diego, 1973; organizer Gordon Craig retrospective Stanford U. Dept Spl. Collections, 1985; dramaturge Mother Courage & Her Children, Allen Theatre, Claremont Coll., 2004. Author: Edward Gordon Craig Revisited, 1984, Edward Gordon Craig and the Theatre of the Imagination, 1985, Dramatic Structure and Meaning, 1992, rev. edit., 1999; editor: Critical Edition of the Jealous Wife and Polly Honeycombe by George Colman the Elder, 1997; contbr. articles to profl. jours. Recipient Taiwan Nat. Sci. Found., 1998, Disting. Tchr. award Tamkang U., 1998, Emma May Shiel Fellow, Stanford U. Mem.: Calif. Scholarship Fedn. Personal E-mail: ecripto@yahoo.com.

**PRICE, TIMOTHY R.,** accountant; b. Reigate, Eng., Jan. 26, 1943; m. Frances Baird; 4 children. BA, U. Victoria, Can., 1964. Chartered acct. Touche Ross & Co., Montreal, 1965-69; pres., COO Mico Enterprises Ltd., 1970-80; pres., CEO Hees Internat. Bancorp Inc., Toronto, 1980-88, mng. ptnr., chmn., 1988—96; chmn. The Edper Group Ltd., Toronto, 1997, Trilon Fin. Corp., Toronto, 1997—2002, Brascan Fin. Corp., Toronto, 2002—04, Funds Mgmt. Brookfield Asset Mgmt. Inc., Toronto, 2005—. Bd. dirs. Astral Media Inc., Morguard REIT, Brookfield Homes Corp., Q9 Networks Inc.; chmn. Brascan Found., 1997—. Bd. dirs. St. Michael's Hosp. Found.; bd. govs. York U., Can.; chmn. Ctr. for Addiction and Mental Health Found. Office: Brookfield Asset Mgmt Inc PO Box 771 BCE Pl 181 Bay St Ste 300 Toronto ON Canada M5J 2T3 Office Phone: 416-363-9491.

**PRICE, TOM,** journalist; b. Pitts., May 26, 1946; s. H. Samuel and Anna Mae (Nicholson) P.; m. Susan Crites; 1 child, Julianna Margaret. BS in Journalism, Ohio U., 1968. Writer, editor Athens (Ohio) Messenger, 1968-73; freelance writer, 1973-75; politics writer Dayton (Ohio) Jour. Herald, 1975-82; corr. Washington bur. Cox Newspapers, Washington, 1982-96; freelance writer politics, govt., tech., bus. and edn., 1996—; Washington columnist Optics and Photonics News, 2002—; contbg. writer Congl. Quar. Rschr., 2004—. Author: Frommer's Washington, D.C. for Dummies, 2003, 3d edit., 2005, The Irreverent Guide to Washington, DC, 5th edit., 2005; co-author: (with Susan Crites Price) The Working Parents Help Book, 1994 (Parent's Choice award, Scholastic Book Club selection), rev. edit., 1996, (with Tony Hall) Changing the Face of Hunger, 2006; co-author Working Solutions Internet Column; nat. newspaper columnist Working Parents Lifeline, 1996-98. Mem.: Washington Ind. Writers, Am. Soc. Journalists and Authors. Presbyterian. Avocations: photography, hiking, travel, reading.

**PRICE, TREVOR ROBERT PRYCE,** psychiatrist, educator; b. Concord, N.H., Nov. 29, 1943; BA, Yale U., 1965; MD, Columbia U., 1969. Diplomate Am. Bd. Psychiatry and Neurology (sr. examiner 1985—), with Geriatric Psychiatry, Am. Bd. Internal Medicine, Nat. Bd. Med. Examiners. Intern in medicine Med. Ctr. of U. Calif., San Francisco, 1969-70; resident in internal medicine Med. Ctr. of U. Calif., San Francisco, 1972-74; resident in psychiatry Dartmouth Med. Sch., Hanover, N.H., 1974-77, asst. prof., assoc. prof. psychiatry and medicine, 1977-85; assoc. prof., prof. psychiatry U. Pa. Sch. Medicine, Phila., 1985—88; dir. psychiat. in-patient svcs. Hosp. of U. Pa., 1985-88; prof. psychiatry Med. Coll. Pa., Pitts., 1989-90, prof. psychiatry and medicine, 1991-95, 1993—2002; chmn. dept. psychiatry Med. Coll. Pa. and Hahnemann U., Pitts., 1989-95, sr. assoc. dean, 1993-95; pres., CEO Allegheny Neuropsychiat. Inst., Pitts., 1994—98, exec. dir., 1994—; chmn. dept. psychiatry Med. Coll. Pa. Hahnemann Sch. Medicine, Phila., 1995—2002; prof. psychiatry and med. Drexel U. Coll. Med., Phila., 2002—03, chmn. dept. psychiatry, 2002; pvt. practice Bryn Mawr, Pa., 2002—04; pres., treas. Price & Price Practices Psychiatry, PC, Bryn Mawr, 2003—. Bd. dirs. Coll. Health Consortium, Inc., Phila., Highland Dr. Rsch. and Edn. Found., Yale Club Pitts., Pitts. Psychoanalytic Found., Med. Coll. Pa. Hosp.; mem. blue ribbon bd. Alzheimer's Disease Alliance, Western Pa., 1989-97; mem. governing bd. Med. Coll. of Pa. Hosp., 1999-2002. Mem. editl. bd. Convulsive Therapy, 1984-94, Jour. Neuropsychiatry and Clin. Neurosci., 1992—, Allegheny Gen. Hosp. Jour. Neurosci., 1992-98, Seminars in Neuropsychiatry, 1995—; editl. reviewer 15 psychiat. and med. jours., 1978; contbr. chpts. to books and articles in profl. jours. Mem. N.H. Commn. on Laws Effecting Mental Health, 1974-75; bd. dirs. Advanced Studies Program, Friends of St. Paul's Sch., Concord, N.H., 1983-87. Recipient William C. Menninger award Ctrl. Neuropsychiat. Assn., 1977, Faculty Teaching award dept. psychiatry Dartmouth Med. Sch., 1984, Pres. award for Exceptional Achievement AHERF, 1994, numerous grants. Fellow: Am. Coll. Psychiatrists, Am. Neuropsychiat. Assn. (bd. dirs. 1993—95, exec. dir. 1995), Am. Psychiat. Assn. (disting. fellow); mem.: Am. Medicine and Psychiatry, Assn. Convulsive Therapy, Assn. Acad. Psychiatry, Am. Assn. Dirs. Psychiat. Residency Tng., Assn. for Acad. Psychiatry, Soc. Biol. Psychiatry, Am. Assn. Chairmen of Depts. Psychiatry, Pa. Psychiat. Assn., Columbia Club of Phila., Yale Club Phila., H-Y-P Club Pitts., Yale Club Pitts. Avocations: fly fishing, tennis, reading, piano, kayaking. Office: 950 Haverford Rd Ste 302 Bryn Mawr PA 19010 Office Phone: 610-527-5926. Personal E-mail: myTwins2@verizon.net. *Life at its best is being continually challenged and fully engaged, yet not self-absorbed.*

**PRICE, VINCENT,** communications educator, department chairman; s. Edward and Joan Price; m. Annette Newmeyer, July 23, 1983; children: Sarah, Alexander. BA, Santa Clara U., Calif., 1979; AM, Stanford U., Calif., 1985, PhD, 1987. Steven H. Chaffee prof. U. Pa., Annenberg Sch. Comm., Phila. 1999—; chair faculty senate U. Pa., 2006—. Chair dept. comm. studies

U. Mich., Ann Arbor, 1995—98. Author: (book) Public Opinion; contbr. articles to profl. jours. Recipient Robert M. Worchester award, World Assn. Pub. Opinion Rsch., 1997; fellow, Stanford U., 1983—87; grantee, Pew Charitable Trusts, NSF, 1999—2006. Mem.: Am. Assn. Pub. Opinion Rsch., Internat. Comm. Assn., Alpha Sigma Nu. Office: Annenberg School for Communication University of Pennsylvania 3260 Walnut Philadelphia PA 19104-6220 Office Phone: 215-573-1963.

**PRICE, WILLIAM CHARLIE,** lawyer; b. Bristol, Va., Oct. 28, 1956; BA, Duke U., 1978; JD, Yale U., 1981. Law clerk to Hon. Stanley A. Weigel US Dist. Ct. (no. dist.) Calif., 1981—82; asst. US atty. major crimes unit and pub. fraud and corruption unit, Dist. Oreg. US Dept. Justice, 1985—88; ptnr. Quinn Emanuel Urquhart Oliver & Hedges, LLP, L.A., 1988—. Instr. Nat. Inst. Trial Advocacy. Named one of Top 10 Trial Lawyers in Am., Nat. Law Jour., 2004, 2006; recipient John Fletcher Caskey prize, 1981. Mem.: State Bar Calif., Phi Beta Kappa. Achievements include won verdict in excess of $250 million against Bertelsmann & former CEO on breach of contract and other claims arising out of formation of AOL Europe joint venture; largest verdict awarded to individual plaintiffs, 2003. Office: Quinn Emanuel Urquhart Oliver & Hedges LLP 865 S Figueroa St Los Angeles CA 90017 Office Phone: 213-624-7707. E-mail: williamprice@quinnemanuel.com.*

**PRICE, WILLIAM JAMES, IV,** investment banker; b. Balt., Oct. 6, 1924; s. William James 3d and Frances (Robbins) P.; m. Marjorie Beard, Dec. 6, 1952; children: Marjorie, Jonathan Robbins, William James V, Juliet Robbins. BS, Yale U., 1949. Propr. Price & Co., 1949-52; with Alex. Brown & Sons, Balt., 1952-98, gen. partner, 1959-84, mng. dir., 1984-89. Chmn. Sonitrol Security Svcs., Inc., NC. Trustee Washington Coll., St. Paul's Sch. and St. Paul's Sch. for Girls, Eugene B. Casey Found. With inf. AUS, 1943—46, ETO. Decorated Bronze Star, Purple Heart with oak leaf cluster, Combat Infantry badge. Mem.: Nat. Assn. Securities Dealers (bd. govs. 1964—66, vice chmn. 1966).

**PRICE, WILLIAM RAY, JR.,** state supreme court justice; b. Fairfield, Iowa, Jan. 30, 1952; s. William Ray and Evelyn Jean (Darnell) P.; m. Susan Marie Trainor, Jan. 4, 1975; children: Emily Margret, William Joseph Dodds. BA with distinction, U. Iowa, 1974; postgrad., Yale U., 1974-75; JD cum laude, Washington and Lee U., 1978. Bar: Mo. 1978, U.S. Dist. Ct. (we. dist.) Mo. 1978, U.S. Ct. Claims 1978, U.S. Ct. Appeals (8th cir.) 1985. Assoc. Lathrop & Norquist, Kansas City, Mo., 1978-84, ptnr., 1984-92, chmn. bus. litigation sect., 1987-88, 90-92, exec. com., 1989-92; judge Mo. Supreme Ct., Jefferson City, 1992—, chief justice, 1999—2001. G.L.V. Zumwalt monitoring com. U.S. Dist. Ct. (we. dist.) Mo., Kansas City. Pres. Kansas City Bd. Police Commrs.; mem. Together Ctr. & Family Devel. Ctr., Kansas City; chmn. merit selection com. U.S. marshal Western Dist. of Mo., Kansas City; bd. dirs. Truman Med. Ctr., Kansas City. Rockefeller fellow, 1974-75; Burks scholar Washington & Lee U., 1976. Mem. Christian Ch. Office: Supreme Ct Mo PO Box 150 207 W High St Jefferson City MO 65102-0150*

**PRICE BODAY, MARY KATHRYN,** choreographer, small business owner, educator; b. Ft. Bragg, N.C., May 20, 1945; d. Max Edward and Katharine (Jordan) Price; m. Les Boday (div. 1982); children: Shawn Leon Boday, Irmali Ferecho Boday; m. Richard A. Weil, May 1, 1986. BFA, U. Okla., 1968, MFA, 1970; studies with David Howard, 1972-74. Soloist dancer Mary Anthony Dance Co., N.Y.C., 1971-74, Larry Richardson Dance Co., N.Y.C., 1971-73; dancer Pearl Lang Dance Co., N.Y.C., 1971-73, Gaku Dance Theater, N.Y.C., 1972-74; ballet mistress and soloist dancer St. Gallen Ballet, Switzerland, 1974-75; dancer, tchr. Zurich Ballet, Switzerland, 1975-76; asst. prof. U. Ill., Champaign-Urbana, 1976-79; artist-in-residence Cornish Inst., Seattle, 1979-80; pres. The Dance Works, Inc., Seattle, 1981-90; dir. Seahurst Ballet, 1982-84; pres. The Dance Works, Inc., Erie, Pa., 1990-94; dir. dance dept., asst. prof. Mercyhurst Coll., Erie, Pa., 1990-94; dir. Peoria Ballet, 1994-99; asst. prof. Bradley U., Peoria, 1994—; dir. Ill. Ballet (formerly Ctrl. Ill. Ballet), 1999—; assoc. prof. Ann Lacy Sch. Am. Dance and Arts Mgmt., Oklahoma City U. Tchr. Harkness Ballet NY, Mary Anthony Dance Sch., Zurich Ballet, Nat. Acad. Arts Ill., Summer Dance lab., Kneeland Workshops, Port Townsend, Wash., 1968, Pa. Gov.'s Sch. of Arts, 1991, 92, 94; tchr., choreographer Jefferson HS Performing Arts, Portland; choreographer Mary K. Price Dance Co., U. Ill., Nat. Acad. Arts, Cornish Inst., Seahurst Ballet; tchr., co-dir. Kneeland Seminars, Las Vegas, Nev., Port Townsend, 1989, Port Townsend, 90, Oklahoma City U., 1990, Am. Coll. Dance Festival, 1991—93; tchr. David Howard summer seminar, Mercyhurst Coll., 1992; tchr. David Howard summer workshop Tulsa Ballet Theatre, 1993, 94; tchr. David Howard workshop Seattle tchrs., 1996, U. Ill., 1997, Western Mich. U., 1999; guest artist, asst. prof. Slippery Rock U., 1994; owner Dance Works, Peoria, Ill., 1994—; guest artist So. Ballet Theatre, 2000, 01, David Howard and Mary Price Boday Summer Intensives, Worcester, 2000—02, Mt. Hood Ballet Acad., 2002—03; lectr. Knox Coll., 2000—; assoc. prof. Oklahoma City U., 2005—. Choreographer (ballets) Ballet Co. St. Gallen, 1988, The Nutcracker, Warner Theater Erie, Gloria, Ill. Ballet with Bradley U. Chorale, 2002, Liebeslieder Waltzes, 2003, Carmina Burana, 2005, Peoria Ballet, Nutcracker, 1995, 30 Yr. Gala, 1995, Alice in Wonderland, 1996, Little Mermaid of Lake Peoria, 1997, Rudolph the Red Nose Reindeer, Ill. Ballet, Shrine Mosque, 2000, Evanston Dance Ctr., 2004, Rock Ballet, Peoria Civic Ctr. Theatre, The Lion, Witch, and Wardrobe, 2001, Sleeping Beauty, 2003, Hansel and Gretel, 2002, Power of Dance, 2002, Coppella, 2002, Nut. Ballet Panama, 2003, Mary & Friends, Seattle, 1990, co-choreographer (ballets) The Nutcracker Ballet, 1991—93, Coppella, 1993, The Little Mermaid of Lake Erie, Warner Theater, 1994, staged Swan Lake, 1999, 2004. Named one of Outstanding Young Women of Am., 1977, 25 Women in Leadership, Week TV, 2003; recipient Outstanding Dancer award, U. Okla., 1968. Office: Ann Lacy Sch Am Dance and Arts Mgmt Okla City Univ 2501 N Blackwelder Oklahoma City OK 73106 Office Phone: 405-208-5523. Business E-Mail: mboday@okcu.edu.

**PRICER, WAYNE FRANCIS,** counseling consultant; b. Bogue, Kans., Feb. 11, 1935; s. William C. and Lena I. (Hecke) P.; m. Alice M. Fitzpatrick, July 25, 1964; children: Wayne F. Jr., Elizabeth Anne. AB, Ft. Hays State U., 1957; MEd, U. N.D., 1963; postgrad., Wayne State U. Nat. cert. counselor; nat. cert. career counselor; nat. cert. sch. counselor; lic. prof. counselor Mich.; master career counselor. Tchr. Bogue (Kans.) Grade Sch., 1958-62; counselor Lamphere High Sch., 1963-64, 69-75; asst. prin. Page Jr. High, Madison Heights, Mich., 1964-68, prin., 1968-69; adj. counselor Oakland Community Coll., Bloomfield Hills, Mich., 1969—; dir. guidance Lamphere Schs., Madison Heights, Mich., 1975-99; adj. prof. Oakland C.C., 1969—; counseling cons. Royal Oak, Mich., 1999—. Bd. dirs., 2d v.p., v.p. Haviland Collectors Internat. Ednl. Found. Contbr. articles to prof. jours. Bd. dirs., 2d v.p. Haviland Collectors Internat., 1997—99, Mich. Assn. Retired Sch. Personnel. Named Counselor of Yr. Oakland Counseling Assn., 1999, Lifetime Achievement award MCDA, 1999. Mem. ACA, Am. Mental Health Counselors Assn., Alliance for Ret. Americans, Assn. for Career and Tech. Edn., Assn. for Counselor Edn. and Supervision, Am. Coll. Counselors Assn., Am. Fedn. Tchrs., Am. Sch. Coun. Assn., Assn. for Adult Devel. and Aging, Assn. for Assessment in Counseling, Lamphere Fedn. Teachers, Assn. Mich. Sch. Counselors, Mich. Assn. for Adult Devel. and Aging, Mich. Assn. Coll. Admission Counselors, Mich. Counseling Assn., Mich. Assn. for Counselor Edn. and Supervision, Mich. Assn. for Measurement and Evaluation in Guidance (pres.), Mich. Assn. Specialists in Group Work, Mich. Career Devel. Assn. (treas. 1994-2000), Mich. Assn. Ret. Sch. Pers., Mich. Assn. Career and Tech. Edn., Mich. Mental Health Counselors Assn., Mich. Sch. Counselors Assn., Mich. Assn. for Humanistic Edn. and Develop., Mich. Assn. for Multi-Cultural Develop., Nat. Assn. Coll. Admission Counselors, Nat. Career Devel. Assn., Oakland Assn. for Counseling and Devel. (former pres.), Mich. Fedn. Tchrs., Suburban Assn. of Retired Sch. Personnel, Mich. Coll. Counseling Assn., Assn. Mich. Sch. Counselors, Mich. Fedn. Tchrs., Phi Delta Kappa. Office: 719 S Washington Ave Royal Oak MI 48067-3829 Office Phone: 248-246-2464. E-mail: wfpricer@aol.com.

**PRICHARD, PETER S.,** newspaper editor; b. Auburn, Calif., Dec. 18, 1944; s. Jarvis B. and Floris C. (Smith) P.; m. Ann O'Donnell, Nov. 13, 1971; children: Oliver W., Lindsay M. AB, Dartmouth Coll., 1966. Wire editor Greenwich (Conn.) Time, 1970-72; reporter Democrat and Chronicle, Rochester, N.Y., 1972-75; assoc. news dir. WOKR TV, Rochester, N.Y., 1975-76; reporter Times Union, Rochester, 1976-78; asst. to chmn. communications Gannett Co. Inc., Rochester, 1980-82, dir. communications, Office of Chief Exec., 1980-82; columns editor USA Today, Washington, 1982-83, dep. assoc. editorial dir., 1983-84, assoc. editorial dir., 1984-86, mng. editor spl. projects, 1986-87, sr. editor, 1988, editor, sr. v.p., news, 1988—; sr. v.p. News Gannett Co. Inc., Washington, 1988—, chief news exec., 1990—. Author: The Making of McPaper: The Inside Story of USA Today, 1987 (Frank Luther Moh Rsch. award Kappa Tau Alpha 1987). Vice chmn., bd. trustees Washington Journalism Ctr., 1989—. With U.S. Army, 1967-69, Vietnam. Decorated Bronze Star. Mem. Nat. Press Club, Am. Soc. Newspaper Editors (Reston, Va.) (various coms. 1985—). Office: USA Today 7950 Jones Branch Dr Mc Lean VA 22108-0001

**PRICKETT, DAVID CLINTON,** physician; b. Fairmont, W.Va., Nov. 26, 1918; s. Clinton Everett and Mary Anna (Gottschalk) Prickett; m. Mary Ellen Holt, June 29, 1940 (dec. Feb. 1987); children: David C., Rebecca Ellen, William Radcliffe, Mary Anne, James Thomas, Sara Elizabeth; m. Pamela S. Blackstone, Nov. 17, 1991 (dec. Mar. 2002). Student, Fairmont State Coll., 1940—42; AB, W.Va. U., 1944; MD, U. Louisville, 1946; MPH, U. Pitts., 1955. Pres. Prickett Chem. Co., 1938-43; acct. W.Va. Conservation Commn. and Fed. Works Agy., 1941, 42; lab. asst., instr. chemistry W.Va. U., 1943; intern Louisville Gen. Hosp., 1947; surg. resident St. Joseph's Hosp., Parkersburg, W.Va., 1948-49; gen. practice W.Va., 1948 50, 55-61; mem. staff Fairmont (W.Va.) Gen. Hosp., 1955-60, Fairmont Emergency Hosp., 1955-60; physician USAF, N.Mex. and Calif., 1961-62, U.S. Army, Fort Ord, Calif., 1963-64; resident physician San Luis Obispo County Hosp., 1965-66; pvt. practice LA, 1967—; mem. staff St. Francis Hosp., LA, 1970-71; physician So. Calif. Edison Co., 1981-84. Physician Bethlehem Mines Corp., Idamay, W.Va., 1956; resident physician Sedgwick County Hosp., Wichita, Kans., 1964-65; med. dir. South Gate auto assembly plant GM, 1969-71; staff physician City of LA, 1971-76; relief med. practice Appalachia summer seasons, W.Va. and Ky., 1977, 86, 88-97. Author: The Newer Epidemiology, 1962, rev., 1990, Public Health, A Science Resolvable by Mathematics, 1965; contbr. articles to profl. jours. Med. officer USPHS, Navajo Indian Reservation, Tohatchi (N.Mex.) Health Ctr., 1953-55, surgeon, res. officer, 1957-59; pres. W.Va. Pub. Health Assn., 1951-52; sec. indsl. and pub. health sect. W.Va. Med. Assn., 1956; W.Va. dist. 4 health officer; health officer Marion County, W.Va., 1951-53; dist. health officer Allegheny County, Pa., 1957; officer Aux. Civil Def. Police, W.Va., 1942; med. advisor Boy Scouts Am., W.Va., 1956-57, N.Mex., 1954; mem. Med. Rsv. Corps of L.A., 2005—. 2d lt. AUS, 1943-46. Dr. Thomas Parran fellow U. Pitts. Sch. Pub. Health, 1955; named to Hon. Order Ky. Cols. Fellow APHA; mem. AMA, Am. Occupl. Med. Assn., Am. Acad. Family Physicians, Western Occupl. Med. Assn., Calif. Med. Assn., Los Angeles County Med. Assn., SAR, W.Va., Am. Legion, Elks, Phi Chi, Rio Hondo Symphony Guild, Phi Chi. Avocations: photography, auto repairs, amateur radio, square dancing. Address: PO Box 4032 Whittier CA 90607-4032 Office Phone: 626-330-4106.

**PRIDDY, EVELYN J.,** education educator; b. Bluffton, Ind., Jan. 4, 1950; d. Robert Ray and Helen Rosalie Priddy. BS in Elem. Edn., Huntington U., 1972; MS in Edn., Ind. U., Ft. Wayne, 1976; EdD, Ball State U., 1989. Tchr. Bluffton (Ind.)- Harrison Met. Sch. Dist., 1972—84, reading coord., 1984—90; prof. edn. Huntington (Ind.) U., 1990—. Pres. Huntington County Literacy Assn., 2001. Mem.: Kiwanis, Phi Delta Kappa, Kappa Delta Pi, Delta Kappa Gamma (chpt. pres. 1999—2001). Office: Huntington U 2303 College Ave Huntington IN 46750

**PRIDE, BENJAMIN DAVID,** sales executive; b. Staten Island, NY, Sept. 20, 1952; s. Benjamin David and Evelyn Marie (Dann) Pride; m. Jane Jeanette Adams, Oct. 12, 2002; stepchildren: Emily Adams, Phillip Adams. BA, St. Francis Coll., Bklyn., 1974. Office mgr., prodn. estimator Leber Katz Ptnrs., N.Y.C., 1975-76; prodn. estimator, media planner, out-of-home media buyer, sports buyer Dancer, Fitzgerald & Sample, N.Y.C., 1976-81; v.p. sports and promotion Backer, Spielvogel, Bates Worldwide, N.Y.C., 1981-95, Zenith Media, N.Y.C., 1995-96; ptnr. Schineller & Pride, N.Y.C., 1996-97; account exec. Newport Media, N.Y.C., 1997-99; asst. mgr., sr. membership dir. UCC Total Home, Eatontown, NJ, 2001—03; advt. cons. Rosnik Pub., Inc., NYC, 2003—04; bus. devel. mgr. Securitas Security Svcs. USA, Inc., 2004—. Divsn. capt. USCG Aux., 2000. Republican. Roman Catholic. Avocations: boating, fishing. Office Phone: 718-855-8880. Personal E-mail: bdpjjp@aol.com

**PRIDE, DENA BETH,** small business owner; b. Pomona, Calif., Aug. 21, 1965; d. James Garfield and Patsy Lorriane Pride; children: Cullena Brittany Clement, Valorie Rose Clement. Diploma, Sch. Tax Preparation, Atlanta, 1997; AAS in Constrn. Mgmt., C.C. So. Nev., 2004; AA in Divinity, Universal Ministries, 2004. Asst. to gen. mgr. Lassen Internat., Las Vegas, 1994—97; vacation coord. Vegas Golfer, Las Vegas, 1998—99; office mgr. Evergreen Corp., 1999—2000; project asst. R & O Constrn., 2000—04; owner Dena Woodworks, 2004—; with MP Constrn., 2004—05, Plise Devel. and Constrn., Las Vegas, 2005—. Editor (pub.): (booklet of poems) Just a Few Poems. Notary pub. State of Nev., 1999—; deacon Seventh-Day Adventist Ch. Republican. Avocations: woodworking, sewing, music, crafts, race cars. Personal E-mail: cowgirl_865@hotmail.com.

**PRIDHAM, THOMAS GRENVILLE,** retired microbiologist; b. Chgo., Oct. 10, 1920; s. Grenville and Gladys Ethoral (Giles) P.; m. Phyllis Sue Hokamp, July 1, 1943 (dec. Feb. 1994); children: Pamela Sue, Thomas Foster, Grenville Thomas, Rolf Thomas, Montgomery Thomas; m. Edna Lee Boudreaux, Mar. 6, 1995 (dec. Apr. 2006). BS Chemistry, U. Ill., 1943, PhD Bacteriology, 1949. Instr. bacteriology U. Ill., Champaign-Urbana, 1947; rsch. microbiologist No. Regional Rsch. Lab., USDA, Peoria, Ill., 1948—51, No. Regional Rsch. Lab. USDA, Peoria, 1953—65, U.S. Indsl. Chem., Balt., 1951—52; supr. tech. ops. Acme Vitamins, Inc., Joliet, Ill., 1952—53; sr. rsch. biologist U.S. Borax Rsch. Corp., Anaheim, Calif., 1965—67; supervisory rsch. microbiologist No. Regional Rsch. Ctr. USDA, Peoria, 1967—81, head agrl. rsch. culture collection No. Regional Rsch. Lab., 1967—81; ret., 1991. Cons. Mycogen Corp., San Diego, 1985-87; U.S. sr. scientist Germany, Darmstadt, 1977 Contbg. author: Actinomycetales: The Boundary Microorganisms, 1974, Bergey's Manual of Determinative Bacteriology, 1974, Synopsis and Classification of Living Organisms, 1982; mem. editl. bd. Jour. Antibiotics, 1969-81; contbr. articles to Jour. Bacteriology, Applied Microbiology, Phytopathology, Actinomycetes, Mycologia, Devel. Indsl. Microbiology, Jour. Antibiotics, Internat. Bull. Bacteriological Nomenclature Taxonomy, Antibiotics Ann., Antimicrobial Agts., Chemotherapy, also others With USNR, 1943-45, with Rsch. Res., 1945-54, lt. ret. Fulbright scholar, Italy, 1952; grantee Soc. Am. Bacteriologists, 1957 Fellow: Am. Acad. Microbiology; mem.: Alexander von Humboldt Assn. Episcopalian. Achievements include patents in fermentative production of riboflavin and of antibiotics; research in microbial culture collection technology and management, systematics of streptomycetes, industrial microbiology. Home: 16645 S Pacific PO Box 1098 Sunset Beach CA 90742

**PRIDMORE, ROY DAVIS,** retired federal official; b. Gaffney, S.C., May 18, 1925; s. Davis Bailey and Ethel (Hughes) P.; m. Doris Hedy Glatzl, July 16, 1960 (dec. Aug. 5, 2000); children: Lisa Ann, David Michael. Cert. Columbus U., Washington, 1949, Am. Inst., 1953, U.S. Dept. Agr. Grad. Sch., 1957. Pers. asst. Dept. Army, Fort Myer, Va., 1955-58; staff asst. D.C. Hwy. Dept., Washington, 1962-67; adminstrv. asst. Dept. Transp., Washington, 1958-62, adminstrv. officer, 1967-94, ret., 1994. Vice pres. Springboard Swim Club, Springfield, Va., 1984-85. Served with U.S. Army, 1946-47; mem. Res. (ret.) Decorated Legion of Merit. Democrat. Roman Catholic. Avocations: swimming, gardening.

**PRIEBE, CEDRIC JOSEPH, JR.,** pediatric surgeon; b. N.Y.C., Feb. 7, 1930; s. Cedric Joseph and Mary Martha (O'Beirne) P.; m. Cynthia Amelia Cali, June 11, 1955; children: Diane Marie, Janice Marie, Cedric Joseph III, Catherine Marie, Michael Stephen, Gregory Paul, Marta Marcella. BS cum laude, Fordham U., 1951; MD, Cornell U., 1955. Bd. cert. Am. Bd. Surgery, 1961, Pediat. Surgery, 1976, Pediat. Surgery, 1984, Pediat. Surgery, 1993, Pediat. Surgery, 2003. Resident surgery Roosevelt Hosp., N.Y.C., 1955—60; resident pediat. surgery Ohio State U., Children's Hosp., Columbus, 1965—67; pediat. surgeon, asst. and assoc. prof. Roosevelt Hosp., Colombia U., N.Y.C., 1967—79; chief pediat. surgery La. State U., Charity Hosp., New Orleans, 1979—82; dir. surg. edn. Children's Hosp. New Orleans, 1979—82; chief pediat. surgery, prof. surgery SUNY, U. Hosp., Stony Brook, 1982—; adminstrv. vice chmn. dept. surgery Stony Brook Sch. Medicine, 2002—, faculty senate, 1991—, apptd. mem. promotion and tenure com., 2001—, exec.com., 1999—, pres., 2003—. Sr. clin. trainee in cancer control NIH, Washington, 1963—65. Editl. cons. Jour. Pediat. Surgery, Phila., 1994—; author: (with others) Neoplasia in Childhood, 1966; contbr. articles to profl. jours Maj. USAF, 1956—65. Mem.: ACS, Med. Soc. State N.Y., N.Y. Soc. Pediat. Surgery (v.p. 1976—78, pres. 1978—79), Children's Oncology Group, Pediat. Oncology Group (cancer control com. 1992—2000), Am. Pediat. Surg. Assn. (membership com. 1990—93, by-laws com. 1993—95, cancer com. 1996—99), Am. Acad. Pediat. (surg. sect. publs. com. 1989—92, chair publs. com. 1992), Soc. for Surgery Alimentary Tract, Am. Burn Assn. Republican. Roman Catholic. Avocations: tennis, squash racquets, travel. Home: 9 Woodhull Cove Ln Setauket NY 11733-1643 Office: SUNY at Stony Brook HSC T 19 Stony Brook NY 11794-8191 Office Phone: 631-444-7950. Personal E-mail: priebe@optonline.net. Business E-Mail: cedric.priebe@stonybrook.edu, cjpriebe@notes.cc.sunysb.edu.

**PRIEM, RICHARD GREGORY,** writer, information technology executive; b. Munich, Sept. 18, 1949; arrived in U.S., 1953; s. Richard Stanley and Elizabeth Teresa (Thompson) Priem; m. Janice Lynne Holland, July 27, 1976; children: Michael John, Matthew Warren(dec.), Kathryn Elizabeth Guthrie. BS in Radio-TV-Film, U. Tex., 1970; MEd in Ednl. Tech., U. Ga., 1979; postgrad., Coll. William and Mary, 1981-82. Cert. fraud examiner. Radio personality, sales exec. KOKE, Inc., Austin, Tex., 1968-73; numerous positions including asst. prof. dept. behavioral scis. and leadership U.S. Mil. Acad., anti-terrorism staff officer and insp. gen. U.S. Army, 1973-94; dep. divsn. mgr. Sci. Applications Internat. Corp., Vienna, Va., 1994-97; asst. v.p. SAIC, 2003—. Cons. Dallas Cowboys Football Club, 1981; scouting coord. Army Football, 1983-85; cons. in field of anti-terrorism. Contbr. articles to profl. jours. Mem. Assn. Cert. Fraud Examiners, Internat. Soc. for Performance Improvement, Phi Kappa Phi, Kappa Delta Pi, Internat. Assn. Bomb Technicians and Investigators. Home: 13505 Trail Vista Ct Ne Albuquerque NM 87111-9248 Personal E-mail: rpriem@earthlink.net.

**PRIESAND, SALLY JANE,** rabbi; b. Cleve., June 27, 1946; d. Irving Theodore and Rosetta Elizabeth (Welch) P. BA in English, U. Cin., 1968; B.Hebrew Letters, Hebrew Union Coll.-Jewish Inst. Religion, 1971, MA in Hebrew Letters, 1972; D.H.L. (hon.), Fla. Internat. U., 1973; DD (hon.), Hebrew Union Coll., 1997. Ordained rabbi 1972. Student rabbi Sinai Temple, Champaign, Ill., 1968, Congregation B'nai Israel, Hattiesburg, Miss., 1969-70, Congregation Shalom, Milw., 1970, Temple Beth Israel, Jackson, Mich., 1970-71; rabbinic intern Isaac M. Wise Temple, Cin., 1971-72; asst. rabbi Stephen Wise Free Synagogue, N.Y.C., 1972-77, assoc. rabbi, 1977-79; rabbi Temple Beth El, Elizabeth, NJ, 1979-81, Monmouth Reform Temple, Tinton Falls, 1981—2006, rabbi emeritus, 2006—; chaplain Lenox Hill Hosp., N.Y.C., 1979-81. Author: Judaism and the New Woman, 1975. Mem. commn. on synagogue rels. Fedn. Jewish Philanthropies N.Y., 1972-79; mem. com. on aged commn. synagogue rels., 1972-75; mem. task force on equality of women in Judaism pub. affairs com. N.Y. Fedn. Reform Synagogues, 1972-75; mem. com. on resolutions Ctrl. Conf. Am. Rabbis, 1975-77, com. on cults, 1976-78, admissions com., 1983-89; chmn. Task Force on Women in Rabbinate, 1977-83, chmn. 1977-79, mem. exec. bd., 1977-79, com. on resolutions, 1989-92, chmn. com. on conv. program, 1993-96; mem. joint commn. on Jewish edn. Ctrl. Conf. Am. Rabbis-Union Am. Hebrew Congregations, 1974-77; mem. task force on Jewish singles Commn. Synagogue Rels., 1975-77; mem. N.Y. Bd. Rabbis, 1975—, Shore Area Bd. Rabbis, 1981—; mem. interim steering com. Clergy and Laity Concerned, 1979-81; bd. dirs. NCCJ, N.Y.C., 1980-82, Jewish Fedn. Greater Monmouth County, trustee, 1988-2000, strategic planning commn., 1996—, hon. v.p., 2000—; trustee Planned Parenthood of Monmouth County, 1982-90; v.p. Interfaith Neighbors, 1988-96, pres., 1997—; mem. UAHC-CCAR Joint Commn. on Synagogue Affiliation, 1992-2002; bd. govs. Hebrew Union Coll.-Jewish Inst. Religion, 1993-2005; trustee Union Am. Hebrew Congregations, 1994-98. Cited by B'nai Brith Women, 1971; named Woman of Yr. Temple Israel, Columbus, Ohio, 1972, Woman of Yr. Ladies Aux. N.Y. chpt. Jewish War Vets., 1973, Woman for All Seasons N. L.I. region Women's Am. ORT, 1973, Extraordinary Women of Achievement NCCJ, 1978, Woman of Achievement Monmouth County Adv. Commn. on Status Women, 1988; recipient Quality of Life award Dist. One chpt. B'nai B'rith Women, 1973, Medallion Judaic Heritage Soc., 1978, Eleanor Roosevelt Humanities award Women's div. State of Israel Bonds, 1980, Rabbinical award Coun. Jewish Fedn., 1988, Woman of Leadership award Monmouth Coun. Girl Scouts U.S., 1991, The Woman Who Dares award Nat. Coun. Jewish Women, 1993, Women's Studies Disting. Alumnae award Friends of Women's Studies U. Cin., 1997; named to Alumni Hall of Fame, Fairview Park H.S., 2002. Mem. Hadassah (life), Ctrl. Conf. Am. Rabbis, NOW, Am. Jewish Congress, Am. Jewish Com., Assn. Reform Zionists Am., Jewish Women Internat. (life), Jewish Peace Fellowship, Women's Rabbinic Network, Nat. Breast Cancer Coalition, HUC-JIR Rabbinic Alumni Assn. (sec., treas. 1997-99, v.p. 1999-2001, pres. 2001-03, past pres., 2003-05). Achievements include being the first US women rabbi. Home: 10 Wedgewood Cir Eatontown NJ 07724-1205 Office: 332 Hance Ave Eatontown NJ 07724-2730 Office Phone: 732-747-9365. E-mail: spriesand@monmouth.com.

**PRIEST, DANA,** journalist; married; 2 children. BA, U. Calif., Santa Cruz. Intelligence reporter, Nat. News Desk Washington Post, 1987—. Author: The Mission: Waging War & Keeping Peace with America's Military, 2003 (Pulitzer prize finalist for gen. non-fiction, 2004). Recipient MacArthur Found. Rsch. & Writing grant, 2001, Gerald R. Ford prize for Disting. Reporting on Nat. Def., 2001, Excellence in Journalism award, State Dept., 2001, George Polk award for nat. reporting, 2006, Pulitzer Prize for beat reporting, 2006, Bob Considine award, Overseas Press Club, 2006. Office: Washington Post Nat News Desk 1150 15th St Washington DC 20071-0070 Office Phone: 202-334-4490. Office Fax: 202-496-3883. E-mail: priestd@washpost.com.*

**PRIEST, GEORGE L.,** law educator; b. 1947; BA, Yale U., 1969; JD, U. Chgo., 1973. Assoc. prof. U. Puget Sound, Tacoma, 1973-75; law and econ. fellow U. Chgo., 1975-77; prof. U. Buffalo, 1977-80, UCLA, 1980-81, Yale U., New Haven, 1981—; John M. Olin Prof. Law and Econs., 1986—, dir. John M. Olin Ctr. for Law, Econs. and Pub. Policy, 1986—. Dir. program in civil liability; John M. Olin prof. law and econs., 1986—. Mem. Pres.' Com. on Privatization, 1987-88. Office: PO Box 208215 New Haven CT 06520-8215 E-mail: george.priest@yale.edu.

**PRIEST, JEFFREY ARNOLD,** music educator; b. Sangerville, Maine, Apr. 6, 1962; s. Irving Arnold and Roselyn Morril Priest; children: Megan C., Jason M. BS in Music Edn., Berklee Coll. Music, U. Maine, Orono. Dir. bands Mattanawcook Acad., Lincoln, Maine, 1985—89, Old Town (Maine) H.S., 1989—, head K-12 dept. Old Town Schs. Music, U. Maine, Orono. Guest condr. festivals. Office: Old Town H S 203 Stillwater Ave Old Town ME 04468

**PRIEST, JESSIE SHAW,** media specialist; d. Shaw Wesley and Shaw McFadden (Teddie) James; m. David Priest, Dec. 27, 1972; children: David, LaDawndrea Catoria. Cert. edn. tchr. SC State Dept. of Edn., 1967. Reading tchr. Chavis Elem. Sch., Hemmingway, SC 1967—70; elem. tchr., 1967—73; media specialist Planterville Elem. Sch., Georgetown, SC, 1970—2005.

**PRIEST, SHARON DEVLIN,** retired state official, not-for-profit developer; b. Montreal, Can. m. Bill Priest; one son Adam. Tax preparer, instr. H & R Block, Little Rock, 1976-78; owner, founder Devlin Co., Ark., 1983-86; account exec. Greater Little Rock C. of C., 1990-94; vice mayor Little Rock, 1989-90, mayor, 1991-92; Sec. of State State of Ark., 1994—2002; exec. dir. The Downtown Partnership, 2002—. Bd. dir. Invesco Inc., New Futures. Bd. dirs., past pres. Metroplan (Environ. Svc. Award 1982), YMCA, Southwest Hosp.; bd. dirs. Fed. Reserve Bank St. Louis; mem. Carter-Baker Comm. Fed. Election Reform Commn., Advt. and Promotion commn., Ark. Internat. Visitors Coun., Pulaski Are Transp. Svc. Policy Com., St. Theresa's Parish Coun., Exec. com. for Ark. Mcpl. League, Nat. League of Cities Trans. and Comm. Steering Com. and Policy Com., adv. bd. M.M. Cohn., Little Rock City Beautiful Commn., 1980-86, Carter Barker Election Reform Commn., 2005, BP Ind. Safety Panel, 2005-06; former bd. dir. Downtown Partnership, S.W. YMCA, 1984, 86, sec.; former mem. Cmty. Housing Resource Bd., 1984-86, Pub. Facilities Bd. S.W. Hosp., 1985-86, S.W. Merchants' Assn., 1985—, 2d v.p., 1985; chmn. Little Rock Arts and Humanities Promotion Commn.; led petition dr. for appropriation for Fourche Creek Plan 7A. Recipient of the Fighting Back Freedom Fighter Award, 1995; Environ. Svc. Award from the Little Rock Metroplan Comm.. 1982. Mem. Leadership Inst. Alumni Assn. (4 Bernard de la Harpe Awards), Rotary. Achievements include being selected by Ark. Bus. as one of the Top 100 Women in Ark. Office: Downtown Partnership PO Box 1937 Little Rock AR 72203 Office Phone: 501-375-0121. Business E-Mail: spriest@downtownlr.com.

**PRIESTLEY, JASON (JASON BRADFORD PRIESTLEY),** actor; b. Vancouver, B.C., Can., Aug. 28, 1969; m. Ashlee Petersen, Feb. 2, 1999 (div. Jan. 2, 2000); m. Naomi Lowde, May 14, 2005. Driver Kelley Racing, 2002. Actor: (TV series) Sister Kate, 1989-90, Beverly Hills 90210, 1990-1998 (Golden Globe award nominee for best actor in a drama series 1993)(also dir. 15 episodes, 1993-97, prodr.. dir. episodes in 1995-96; prodr. 58 episodes 1996-97, exec. prodr. 1997-98), Eek! The Cat(voice), 1992, Tru Calling, 2003; (TV movies) Teen Angel, 1989, Choice of the Heart: The Margaret Sanger Story, 1995, Vanishing Point, 1997, Kiss Tomorrow Goodbye, 2000 (also exec. prodr.. dir.), Teen Angel Returns, 1990, Common Ground, 2000, Homicide: The Movie, 2000, Warning: Parental Advisory, 2002, The True Meaning of Christmas Specials, 2002, I Want to Marry Ryan Banks, 2004, Sleep Murder, 2004, Murder at the Presidio, 2005, Colditz, 2005; (films) The Boy Who Could Fly, 1986, Watchers, 1988, Nowhere To Run, 1989, Calendar Girl, 1993, Tombstone, 1993, Cold-Blooded, 1995, Love and Death on Long Island, 1997, Hacks, 1997, The Thin Pink Line, 1998, Conversations in Limbo, 1998, Choose Life, 1999, Dill Scallion, 1999, Standing On Fishes, 1999, Eye of the Beholder, 1999, Barenacked in America, 1999 (also prodr.. dir.), The Highwayman, 2000 (also prodr.), Lion of Oz (voice), 2000, Herschel Hopper: New York Rabbit (voice), 2000, Zigs, 2001, The Fourth Angel, 2001, Cherish, 2002, Cover Story, 2002, Darkness Falling, 2002, Time of the Wolf, 2002, Fancy Dancing, 2002, Die, Mommie Die, 2003, Chicks with Sticks, 2004, Going the Distance, 2004; guest appearances include Airwolf, 1987, 21 Jump Street, 1987, The Outer Limits, 1997 (also dir.), MacGyver, 1988, Quantum Leap, 1989, Superman, 1998, Grace Point, 2001 (also dir.), Spin City, 2001 & 2003, 8 Simple Rules...for Dating My Teenage Daughter, 2002, Celebrities Uncensored, 2003, 04, American Idol, 2004, Overhaulin, 2004 Named one of the 50 Most Beautiful People in the World, People Mag., 1991, 1992, TV's 25 Greatest Teen Idols, TV Guide, 2005; won 1998 Grand-Am race, Mid-Ohio Sports Car Course. Avocations: hockey, race car driving.

**PRIETO, CLAUDIO R.,** academic administrator, lawyer; b. Caguas, P.R., Aug. 17, 1933; s. Claudio Prieto and Carmen (Gutierrez) del Arroyo; m. Myrna Irizarry; children: Claudio, Carmen, Isabel, Rosa, Anna, Alfonso. BS, U. P.R., 1954, JD, 1971. Bar: P.R. Asst. prof. U. P.R., Rio Piedras, 1956-70, coord. student affairs, 1957-59, dir. extension div., 1959-61, assoc. prof. Sch. Law, 1970-71; dir. edn. press Commonwealth of Puerto Rico, Rio Piedras, 1961-65, asst. sec. edn., 1965-67, asst. to gov. San Juan, 1967-68; asst. to dep. commr. Dept. Edn. State of N.Y., Albany, 1977-78, asst. commr., 1978-88; chancellor Turabo U., Gurabo, P.R., 1989-93; exec. dir. office of equity and acccess policy studies N.Y. State Dept. Edn., Albany, 1993-94; dep. asst. sec. for higher edn. programs Dept. Edn., Washington, 1994—2001; chancellor InterAmerican U. of PR - Met. Campus, 2001—. Cons. to chancellor U. P.R., 1969, legal plannning and adminstrn. Tech. Svcs. P.R., 1973-76. Columnist San Juan Star, 1973-76, 1992— Trustee Ewald B. Nyquist Meml. Fund, Albany, 1990—; bd. overseers Regents Coll., 1989-93. Named Edn. Exec. of Yr. Sales and Mktg. Assn., P.R., 1989. Mem. Intercollegiate Athletic League (bd. govs.). Democrat. Roman Catholic.

**PRIETO, MONIQUE N.,** artist; b. LA, 1962; BFA, UCLA, 1987, Calif. Inst. Arts, 1992, MFA, 1994. One-woman shows include ACME, Santa Monica, Calif., 1994, 1995, 1996, 1997, 1999, 2000, 2001, Bravin Post Lee, N.Y.C., 1996, Anderson Gallery, Va. Commonwealth U., Richmond, 1997, Pat Hearn Gallery, N.Y.C., 1998, Robert Prime, London, 1998, Corvi-Mora, London, Eng., 2000, 2002, Cheim & Read, NY, 2002, 2005, Il Capricorno, Venice, Italy, 2003, Out of the Blue, ACME Gallery, LA, 2004, Scottsdale Mus. Contemporary Art, 2005, exhibited in group shows at Wight Gallery, UCLA, 1987, Bacilla Hernandez Gallery, Long Beach, Calif., 1989, Lockheed Gallery, Valencia, Calif., 1994, Pat Hearn Gallery, N.Y.C., 1996, 1997, Factory Place Gallery, L.A., 1996, Armand Hammer Sales and Rental Gallery, 1997, ACME, Santa Monica, 1997, Orange County Mus. Art, Newport Beach, Calif., 1997, Abstract Painting, Once Removed, Contemporary Arts Mus., Houston, Tex., 1998, Etcetera, Spacex Gallery, Exeter, Eng., 1999, Facts & Fiction II: LA, Arco, Torino, Italy, 1999, Ambient Fiction, Pat Hearn Gallery, NY, 2001, The Figure in the Landscape, Lehmann Maupin Gallery, 2001, The Sensational Line, Mus. Contemporary Art, Denver, 2001, Flatline, Cirrus Gallery, LA, 2002, The Galleries Show, Royal Acad., London, 2002, Before and After Science, Marella Art Contemporanea, Milan, 2003, Drunk vx. Stoned, Gavin Brown's Enterprise, NY, 2005, Extreme Abstraction, Albright-Knox Art Gallery, Buffalo, NY, 2005, Tet a Tete, Greenberg Van Doren, NY, 2005. Herb Alpert scholar, 1992—93, Philip Morris fellow, 1992—94, Skowbegan Sch. Painting and Sculpture fellow, 1994, Louis Comfort Tiffany Found grant, 1998. Mailing: c/o Chem & Read Gallery 547 West 25th St New York NY 10001*

**PRIEUR, C. JAMES,** insurance company executive; BA, Coll. Militaire Royal de S. Jean, Quebec; MBA, Univ. We. Ontario, 1975. Equity analyst & portfolio mgr. Sun Life Fin. Inc., 1979—85, head Canadian private placements, 1985—88, v.p. securities investments Canada, 1988—91, v.p. investments Canada, 1991—92, v.p. investments U.S., 1992—97, sr. v.p. gen. mgr. U.S. ops., 1997—99, pres., COO, 1999—2006; CEO Conseco Inc., Carmel, Ind., 2006—. Bd. LIRMA Internat. Inc. Office: Conseco Inc 11825 N Pennsylvania St Carmel IN 46032*

**PRILLELTENSKY, ISAAC,** dean; b. Cordoba, Argentina, Sept. 18, 1959; s. Jacobo Prilleltensky and Betty Priyoltensky; m. Ora Rappoport, Dec. 14, 1982; 1 child, Matan. PhD, U. Man., Winnipeg, 1989. Prof. Peabody Coll., Vanderbilt U., Nashville, 2003—06; dean U. Miam, Sch. Edn., Coral Gables, 2006—. Fellow, APA, 1996. Office: U Miami Sch Edn PO Box 248065 Coral Gables FL 33124-2040 Office Phone: 305-284-3505. E-mail: isaacp@miami.edu.

**PRIMEAU, KEITH,** retired professional hockey player; b. Toronto, Nov. 24, 1971; m. Lisa Primeau; 4 children. Center Detroit Red Wings, 1990—96, Hartford Whalers, 1996—97, Carolina Hurricanes, 1997—99, Phila. Flyers, 2000—06. Mem. Team Can.: Olympic Games, Nagano, Japan, 1998; player NHL All-Star Game, 1999, 2004. Office: c/o Phila Flyers 3601 S Broad St Philadelphia PA 19148*

**PRIMEAU, RONALD,** literature educator, writer; b. Chgo., Feb. 6, 1946; s. Armand L. and Lucille Fortier Primeau; m. Katherine D. Dreyer, Apr. 11, 1970; children: Elizabeth Hopson, Sarah. BA in English (hon.), U. Ill., 1968, MA in English, U. Ill., Urbana-Champaign, 1969, PhD in English, 1971. Tchg. asst. U. Ill., Urbana-Champaign, 1968—71; prof. English Ctrl. Mich.

U., Mt. Pleasant, 1971—, interim assoc. dean, coll. grad. studies and office rsch., 1992—94; instr. Elderhostel Internat., 1987—95; exch. lectr. Middlesex U., London, 1989. Dir. MA of Arts in Humanities program Ctrl. Mich. U., 1996—; cons. in field. Author: Writing in the Margin, 1976, The Rhetoric of Television, 1979, Beyond Spoon River: The Legacy of Edgar Lee Masters, 1981, Romance of the Road, 1996, Herbert Woodward Martin and the African American Tradition in Poetry, 2004; co-editor: The Great Lakes Review, 1978—84, In His Own Words: The Dramatic and Other Uncollected Works of Paul Laurence Dunbar, 2002; editor: Influx: Essays on Literary Influence, 1979. Recipient Excellence in Tchg. award, Ctrl. Mich. U., 2001; grantee, Nat. Endowment for the Humanities, 1973, 1980, Mich. Coun. for Humanities, 1974. Mem.: Coll. English Assn., Midwest Modern Languages Assn., Soc. Study Midwestern Lit. (Mid Am. award 2002). Office: Ctrl Mich Univ Mount Pleasant MI 48859

**PRIMEAUX, HENRY, III,** automotive executive, author, speaker; b. New Orleans, Nov. 16, 1941; s. Henry Jr. and Ethel (Ritter) P.; m. Jane Cathrine Velcich, July 23, 1960; children: Joann Primeaux Longa, Lisa Primeaux Lotz, Henry Joseph. Student, La. State U., New Orleans, 1959-63. Compt. Jimco, New Orleans, 1965-66; owner, mgr. Picone Seafood, New Orleans, 1966-67; v.p. NADW Inc., Metairie, La., 1967-78, Am. Warranty Corp., L.A., 1978-80; pres. F&I Warranty Corp., Arlington, Tex., 1980-87; exec. v.p. F&I Mgmt. Corp., Arlington, 1980-87; pres., CEO Primco Corp., Arlington, 1987-91; owner Flavors Restaurant, Tulsa, Okla., Primeaux Mktg. Mng. ptnr. Crown Auto World, Bristow; founder, Pimeaux Family Found., 1998; mgr., Primeaux Family Dealerships; mng. ptnr., Primeaux Family Realty; cons., corr. Wards Auto Dealer, Detroit, 1987-95, weekly TV program Automotive Satellite TV Network; cons. Nissan Motor Co., L.A., 1988-89, Convergent div. Unisys, Hunt Valley, Md., 1988-90; cons. Mercedes-Benz N.Am.; exec. com. Okla. Workforce Investment Bd.; chmn. Tulsa Workforce Investment Bd.; owner Tusla Talons AF2 Football, 2004. Writer Auto Age mag., Dealer mag., 2003-; author: F&I Handbook. Mem. Rep. Task Force Okla. Workforce Devel. Com.; bd. dirs. John Starks Found., Boy Scouts U.S.; mem. nat. adv. bd. Automotive Yes Sch. to Work Initiative; mem. Okla. Sch. to Work Commn.; bd. regents Okla. State U., Tulsa. With USN, 1959-61. Recipient Automotive Yes Dealer Yr., 2004. Mem. Am. Internat. Automobile Dealers Assn., Assn. of F&I Profls. (bd. dirs. 1990—, pres. 1994), Nat. Auto Dealers Assn. (pres. Tulsa chpt. 1994, Time Quality Dealer of Yr. 1994), Okla. State C. of C. (bd. dirs.), Met. Tulsa C. of C. (bd. dirs. 1998-2000). Roman Catholic. Office: Crown Bristow 901 S Roland Bristow OK 74010 Home: 6201 E 108th St Tulsa OK 74137-8903 Office Phone: 918-367-3423. E-mail: primeaux1@aol.com, crownhen@aol.com, henry@crownbristow.com.

**PRIMERANO, LAVINA S.,** volunteer; b. Snow Camp, N.C., June 20, 1918; d. Passmore Harrison Stephens and Manie Mae Culberson-Stephens; widowed; children: Joseph Stephens, Jane Roberta. BS Guilford Coll., 1938, MA U. Ky., 1941. Cert. tchr. NC. Tchr. Pine Hall (N.C.) H.S., 1939—40; dean Blackstone (Va.) Jr. Coll., 1940—42; substitute Morris County (N.J.) Schs., 1960—62; 3d grade tchr. Jefferson Twp., NJ, 1962—64, math tchr. NJ, 1964—76, dept. chmn. NJ, 1969—70; ret., 1976. Vol. tchr. St. Lucie County Schs., Ft. Pierce, Fla., 1985—; svc. officer Nat. Assn. Ret. Fed. Employees, 1993—; pres. River Park Homeowners Assn., Port St. Lucie, Fla., 1994—99, 2002—04. Recipient Good Neighbor award, McDonald's, 1999—; Prime Time award, RSVP, St. Lucie County, 1995—96. Mem.: Pi Mu Epsilon.

**PRIMI, DON ALEXIS,** advertising executive, public relations executive, rail transportation executive; b. N.Y.C., Jan. 14, 1947; s. John Prosper, Sr. and Eileen Mary Primi. A in Advt., State U. N.Y., 1967; BS in Mktg. and Advt., Hofstra U., 1971; advanced astron. studies degree, Vanderbilt Mus. and Planetarium, 1967. Ordained deacon Holy Roman Cath. Ch., Soc. of the Virgin Mary, 2005. Gen. mgr. Recreational Pub. Corp.; pres., owner Fantasia Trains/REE R.R. Equipment Exchange, 1980, Don Primi Designs, 1984, Rail Industries, Rail Fin. Corp., 1987, Gold Coast Ltd/Royal Rail, 1987, Rail Enterprises, 1990, LPA North Am., 1992, Alexis Daniels, 1992, Salon Promotions, 1992, Trans Fla. Express, Inc., 2001. Cons. in field, ry. industry, brick and clay products industry; designer corp. identity programs. Recipient awards, Printing Industries Met. N.Y., Gold Boli advt. awards, Kimberly-Clark Graphic excellence awards, Astrophoto awards. Mem.: Astron Soc. L.I. (pres., pub. rels. dir.), Sales and Mktg. Execs., Nat. R.R. Assn. Passengers, R.R. Pub. Rels. Assn., Assn. Ry. Progress Inst., Rail Mktg. Club N.Y. Achievements include designs published in periodicals. Home: 4065 Old Settlement Rd Merritt Island FL 32952-6211 Office: 160 5th Ave New York NY 10010-7003 E-mail: dprail21@brevard.net.

**PRIMM, EARL RUSSELL, III,** publishing executive; b. Rhinelander, Wis., Oct. 24, 1958; s. Earl Russell and Betty Joan (Dennis) P. AB in Classics (hon.), Loyola U. Chgo., 1980; MA in Libr. Sci., U. Chgo., 1990. Asst. to edn. dir. J.G. Ferguson Pub. Co., Chgo., 1981-84; prodn. mgr. Joint Commn. on Accreditation of Hosps., Chgo., 1984-85; sr. editor J.G. Ferguson Pub. Co., Chgo., 1985-87; asst. editor U. Chgo. Press., 1987-88; editorial dir. J.G. Ferguson Pub. Co., Chgo., 1988-89; project mgr. Children's Press, Chgo., 1989-92; exec. editor Franklin Watts, Inc., N.Y.C., 1992-95; editl. dir. Grolier Children's Pub., Danbury, Conn., 1995-97; pres. Editl. Directions, Inc., Chgo., 1997—. Mem. adv. bd. U. Chgo. Pub. Program, 1990-2000; judge Lambda Lit. awards, Washington, 1994-2000; guest lectr. Sch. Edn. Harvard U., 2004. Editl. chief: Career Discovery Encyclopedia, 1990, Favorite Children's Authors and Illustrators, 1992; editor: Civil Rights Movement in America, 2nd edit., 1991, Extraordinary Hispanic Americans, 1991; editl. dir. The Child's World, 2002, Tradition Books, 2002. Mem. crisis counselor Nat. Runaway Switchboard, Chgo., 1985-88; Horizon's hotline counselor, Chgo., 1987-88; bd. dirs. Gerber/Hart Libr. and Archives, Chgo., 1992-94. Named Honors Sr. of Yr., Loyola U. Chgo., 1980; recipient Mertz Latin Scholarship key Loyola U. Chgo., 1980. Mem. Am. Libr. Assn. Democrat. Home: 1000 W Washington Blvd #147 Chicago IL 60607-2148 Office: 1000 W Washington Blvd # 203 Chicago IL 60607 Office Phone: 312-829-5456. E-mail: russell@editorialdirections.com.

**PRIMM, RICHARD KIRBY,** physician; b. Thomasville, NC, May 23, 1944; s. Richard Wesley and Gertrude (Berrier) P.; m. Sharon Kay Lucas, Dec. 28, 1968; children: Heather, Lucas. BA, Duke U., 1966; postgrad., Baylor U., 1966-67; MD, U. N.C., 1970. Intern internal medicine Vanderbilt U. Hosp., Nashville, 1970-71, resident in internal medicine, 1973-75, chief resident, 1975-76; fellow cardiovascular diseases U. Ala., Birmingham, 1976-78, chief fellow, instr. medicine, 1978-79; asst. prof. medicine Vanderbilt U. Sch. Medicine, Nashville, 1979-84; staff cardiologist Wenatchee (Wash.) Valley Clinic, 1984—. Clin. asst. prof. medicine U. Wash., Seattle, 1985-91, clin. assoc. medicine, 1991-2003, clin. prof. medicine, 2003—; adminstrv. lead dept. cardiology Wenatchee Valley Clinic, 1987-91, 1997-2006. Contbr. articles to profl. jours. Capt. U.S. Army, 1971-73. Recipient Heusner Pupil award U. N.C., 1969, Hillman Teaching Excellence award Vanderbilt U., 1976. Fellow: Am. Coll. Cardiology (gov. Wash. chpt. 2002—05); mem.: AHA, Wash. Heart Assn. (trustee 1990—94), North Pacific Soc. Internal Medicine, Physicians for Social Responsibility, Alpha Omega Alpha. Avocations: downhill skiing, backpacking. Office: Wenatchee Valley Med Ctr 820 N Chelan Ave Wenatchee WA 98801-2028 Office Phone: 509-663-8711. Business E-Mail: rprimm@wvclinic.com.

**PRIMMER, LILLIAN JUANDA,** science educator; d. Melvin Palmer and Amanda Severina (Olstad) Bekkum; m. Donald Gale Primmer, June 17, 1967; children: Donald Guy, Jacqueline Juanda Gruber. BS, U. Wis., 1990, MEd, 1993. Tchr. Clintonville Pub. Schs., Wis., 1990—96; part-time tchr. Christa McAuliffe Acad., Appleton, Wis., 2002, 2004. Part-time tchr. Enstein Acad., Green Bay, Wis., 1991; participant/tchr.-facilitator Sci. World, Drummond, Wis., 1994—99; pres. Wis. Elem. & Middle Level Sci. Tchrs., Wis., 1998—99. Merit badge counselor Boy Scouts/Girl Scouts, Clintonville, Wis., 1990—; hunter safety instr. Dept. Nat. Resources, Clintonville, 1994—; fundraiser, participating survivor Relay for Life, Clintonville, Viroqua. Recipient Disting. Tchr. Sci., Wis. Elem. Sci. Tchrs., 1995; grantee Earth-

watch grant, Wis. Acad. Scis., Arts & Letters, 1994. Mem.: NSTA, Wis. Soc. Sci. Tchrs. (co-chair forum com., Outstanding Tchr. Sci. 1996). Avocations: hunting, fishing, camping, volleyball, knitting. Home: 69 Ninth St Clintonville WI 54929

**PRIMO, DAVID MARTIN,** political science professor; s. Mauro and Elda Primo; m. Neeta Primo. BA in Polit. Sci. and Econs., Brown U., Providence, 1998, MA in Polit. Sci., 1998; MA in Econs., Stanford U., Calif., 2001, PhD in Polit. Sci., 2002. Asst. prof. polit. sci. U. Rochester, NY, 2002—. Author: The Plane Truth: Airline Crashes, the Media, and Transportation Policy, 2003; contbr. articles to profl. jours. Named Undergraduate Prof. of Yr., U. Rochester Students' Assn., 2005; recipient Goergen award for Disting. Artistry in Undergraduate Edn., U. Rochester, 2005. Mem.: Phi Beta Kappa, Omicron Delta Epsilon. Office: Univ Rochester Political Science Dept Harkness Hall 333 Rochester NY 14627-0146 Office Phone: 585-273-4779.

**PRIMO, JOAN ERWINA,** retail and real estate consulting business owner; b. Detroit, Aug. 28, 1959; d. Joseph Carmen and Marie Ann (Nash) P.; m. David James Yared, 1982; 1 son, Benjamin Primo Yared. BA, Wellesley Coll., 1981; MBA, Harvard U., 1985. Acct. exec. Michigan Bell, Detroit, 1981—82, AT&T Info. Sys., Southfield, Mich., 1983; planning analyst Gen. Motors, Detroit, 1984; v.p. Howard L. Green & Assocs., Troy, Mich., 1985—89; prin., founder Strategic Edge, Inc., Southfield, 1989—. Contbr. articles to profl. jours. Mem. founders soc. Detroit Inst. Arts, 1989—; rsch. advisory task force com. officer Mich. State U; v.p. Detroit County Day Sch., 2005—. Mem.: Internat. Coun. Shopping Ctrs. (faculty, seminar leader 1987—, Mich. state com. officer, rsch. adv. task force), Detroit Country Day Sch.-Lower Sch. Parents Assn. (bd. dirs. 2004—05, v.p. 2005—06, pres. 2006—), Ivy Club Detroit (bd. dirs. 1994—, sec. 1995—99), Harvard Bus. Sch. Club Detroit (bd. dirs. 1994—98, v.p. 1995—96, exec. v.p. 1996—97), Wellesley Club Southeastern Mich. (pres. 1994—98). Republican. Avocations: antiques, travel, theater, gourmet cooking. Home: 224 Woodwind Dr Bloomfield Hills MI 48304-2172 Office: The Strategic Edge 24333 Southfield Rd Ste 211 Southfield MI 48075-2849 Office Phone: 248-557-1664. Business E-Mail: jprimo@thestrategicedge.com.

**PRIMO, QUINTIN E., III,** real estate company executive; BS in Fin. with honors, Ind. U.; MBA, Harvard U. Former mng. dir. Q. Primo & Co., Inc., CEO, co-founder, co-chmn. Capri Capital L.P., Chgo., 1992—. Chmn. Urban Family and Cmty. Ctrs.; chmn. Com. of 100 Ill. Pub. Policy Caucus. Mem.: Urban Land Inst., Pension Real Estate Assn., Real Estate Roundtable (dir.). Office: Capri Capital LP Ste 3430 875 N Michigan Ave Chicago IL 60611*

**PRIMOSCH, JAMES THOMAS,** music educator, composer, musician; b. Cleve., Oct. 29, 1956; s. Edward Joseph and Rose Marie (Potochar) P.; m. Mary Marguerite Murphy, April 5, 1986. BA in Composition magna cum laude, Cleve. State U., 1978; MA in Composition, U. Pa., 1980; DMA in Composition awarded with distinction, Columbia U., 1988; studied piano privately with Lambert Orkis, Phila., 1978-80; studied composition with John Harbison, Tanglewood, 1984. Asst. prof. music U. Pa., 1988—94, assoc. prof. music, 1994—2001, prof. music, 2001—. Grad. assistantships Columbia-Princeton Electronic Music Ctr., 1982-84, 86-87, preceptorship Columbia U., 1984-85; residency Va. Ctr. Creative Arts, 1985, MacDowell Colony, 1988, Bellagio Conf. Ctr., 1992; regional vis. artist Am. Acad. in Rome, 1994; composer in residence Marlboro Music Festival, 1994. Composer more than 50 compositions and 26 published works; compositions performed by Chgo. Symphony Orch., LA Philharm., St. Paul Chamber Orch., Cleve. Chamber Symphony, NY New Music Ensemble; compositions performed at Carnegie Hall, Dorothy Chandler Pavilion, Town Hall, Weill (Carnegie) Recital Hall, others; reviewer High Performance Rev. Mag., 1987-95. Recipient 3rd prize, People's prize Internat. Gaudeamus Competition, The Netherlands, 1977, Helen L. Weiss prize U. Pa., 1979, David Halstead prize U. Penn., 1980, 3rd prize Shreveport Symphony Composer's Competition, 1980-81, John H. Bearns prize, 1981, 1st. prize Holtkamp Organ Composition Contest, 1982, Eda and Boris Rappoport prize Columbia U., 1984, Tanglewood prize in Composition Berkshire Music Ctr., 1984, Cleve. Arts prize, 1992, Elise Stoeger prize Chamber Music Soc. Lincoln Ctr., 1999; recipient Recognition award Mader Meml. Fund, 1980, BMI Student Composers award, 1982; New Music Consort Composition Contest winner, 1987, League of Composers ISCM winner, 1988; Fine Arts scholar Cleve. State U., 1974-78, scholar Cleve. Fortnightly Music Club, 1976-78, Arthur Loesser Meml. scholar, 1977-78, Yale Composer's Workshop at Norfolk, 1981, Columbia U. scholar, 1981-82, Charles Ives scholar Am. Acad. Inst. Arts & Letters, 1985; U. fellow U. Penn., 1978-79, Composers Conf. Johnson Vt., 1979-80, CBS Found. fellow U. Penn., 1979-80, Margaret Lee Crofts fellow Berkshire Music Ctr. Tanglewood, 1984, Guggenheim fellow, 1985, NEA, 1991-92, Goddard Lieberson fellow Am. Acad. Arts and Letters, 1993, Pew fellow in arts, 1996, Independence Found. Arts fellow, 2005; ASCAP Found. Young Composers grant, 1984, 82, Meet The Composer grant 1980, 82, 85, 87, 89-90, 94, 96-97, Am. Music Ctr. Copying Assistance grant, 1985, 90, Pa. Coun. on the Arts, 1990, 98, 02, Presser Found. grantee U. Pa. Mem. BMI, Pi Kappa Lambda. Roman Catholic. Avocation: reading.

**PRIMOZIC, DANIEL THOMAS,** dean; PhD in Philosophy, U. N.Mex, Albuquerque, 1986. Chair and assoc. prof. philosophy Elmhurst Coll., Ill., 1996—2003; dean liberal and fine arts Santa Fe C.C., 2003—. Mem. Bd. Examiners Quality N.Mex., Albuquerque, 2006—. Office: Santa Fe CC 6401 Richards Ave Santa Fe NM 87508

**PRIMPS, WILLIAM GUTHRIE,** lawyer; b. Ossining, NY, Sept. 8, 1949; s. Richard Byrd and Mary Elizabeth (Guthrie) P.; m. Sophia Elizabeth Beutel, Aug. 25, 1973; children: Emily Ann, Elizabeth Armstrong, William Andrew. BA, Yale U., 1971; JD, Harvard U., 1974. Bar: N.Y., 1975. Assoc. LeBoeuf, Lamb, Leiby & MacRae LLP, NYC, 1974-82, ptnr., chmn. recruiting com., 1983—. Counsel to Bd. Zoning Appeals, Bronxville, 1988-89, chmn., 1989-91. Class coun. New Haven, 1991; trustee Village of Bronxville, 1991-97, dep. mayor, 1995-97; deacon Reformed Ch. Bronxville, 1989-94, elder, 1998-2002; bd. dirs. Bronxville Sch. Fdn. 1998—, v.p., 2003—, Ivy Football Assn., 2003—, mem. adv. coun. Atlantic Legal Found. Inc., 2002-; counsel to ethics bd., Bronxville, 2004—. Mem. ABA, N.Y. State Bar Assn., Assn. Yale Alumni (class 1971), Yale Club, Bronxville Field Club. Republican. Office: LeBoeuf Lamb Greene & MacRae 125 W 55th St New York NY 10019-5369 Office Phone: 212-424-8827. Office Fax: 212-424-8500. Business E-Mail: wprimps@llgm.com.

**PRINA, L(OUIS) EDGAR,** journalist; b. West New York, N.J., Oct. 7, 1917; s. Louis Edgar and Marion (Duggan) P.; m. Frances Lee Lorick, Feb. 14, 1947; 1 dau., Lee Lorick II. AB, Syracuse U., 1938, MA, 1940. Copy editor, asst. night city editor N.Y. Sun, N.Y.C., 1946-48, Washington corr., 1948-50; nat. affairs writer Washington Star, 1950-66; mil. affairs writer/editor Copley News Svc., Washington, 1966-77, bur. chief, 1977-84, sr. corr., 1984-87; editor Navy mag., Washington, 1961-68; columnist Sea Power mag., 1968—. Author: The Political Virgin, 1958, Flew to South Pole for Overnight Visit, 1966. Served with USN, 1941-46, 51-53; capt. Res. (ret.). Recipient honorable mentionHeywood Broun award, 1956, Disting. Public Svc. award USN, 1965, Alfred Thayer Mahan award Navy League U.S., 1987, Copley Ring of Truth award, 1971, 74-76, 79, 80-81, Chancellor's Sr. Alumni award Syracuse U., 1998; nominated for Pulitzer Prize (twice). Mem. U.S. Naval Inst., Nat. Press Club (chmn. bd. govs.), White House Corrs. Assn., Explorers Club, Soc. Profl. Journalists (pres. Washington chpt., named to Hall of Fame 1999), Kappa Sigma, Phi Kappa Phi. Clubs: Gridiron, Chevy Chase, Met. of Washington. Roman Catholic. Home: 4813 Quebec St NW Washington DC 20016-3228 Office: The Metro Club Box 47 1700 H St NW Washington DC 20006-4689

**PRINCE, ALICE SARA,** pediatrician, educator; b. NYC, Dec. 6, 1949; d. Leon and Adelaide Wald Prince; widowed; children: Daniel Jacob Hopkins, Benjamin David Hopkins. MD, Columbia U., NYC, 1975. Prof. Columbia U., NYC, 1997—. Office: Columbia University 650 W 168th Street New York NY 10032 Office Phone: 212-305-4193.

**PRINCE, ANDREW STEVEN,** lawyer, retired government agency administrator; b. Bklyn., Oct. 9, 1943; s. Milton S. and Beatrice M. (Ratkin) P.; m. Rochelle Moskowitz, July 4, 1973; children: Brett, Kenneth. BS, U.S. Naval Acad., 1965; MBA, JD, Harvard U., 1974. Bar: N.Y. 1975, U.S. Supreme Ct. 1980. Assoc. firm Shearman & Sterling, N.Y.C., 1974-81; dep. asst. sec. Navy Dept., Washington, 1981-86; exec. v.p., gen. counsel Urquhart and Co., Inc., McLean, Va., 1986-94; mng. dir. Nat. Capital Cos. LLC, Bethesda, Md., 1997-2000; mng. dir., COO HFS Capital LLC, McLean, Va., 2000—02; CEO, pres. Bretken Enterprises, 2002—03, Prince Strategic Group LC, McLean, Va., 2003—. Sec. Potash Import & Chem. Corp., N.Y.C., 1979-81; mem. panel of arbitrators Am. Arbitration Assn., N.Y.C., 1979- Bd. dirs. Harvard Coop. Soc., Cambridge, Mass., 1972-74; bd. dirs. USO, Washington, 1982-86, N.Y.C., 1979-81. Served with USN, 1965-70. Capt. Res., ret Mem. Harvard Bus. Sch. Club, Washington, DC (bd. dir., pres.), Mil Order World Wars (judge adv.), Naval Acad. Alumni Assn., Naval Acad. Found. (dir.). E-mail: aprince65@hotmail.com, aprince@princestrategic.com.

**PRINCE, ANNA LOU,** composer, music publisher, construction executive; b. Isabella, Tenn., May 28, 1935; d. Ulysses Gordon and Della Carrie (Hawkins) P.; children: Sandra, Teresa, Vandi. Diploma, Carolina Sch. Broadcasting, 1966; Zion diploma, Israel Bible Sch., Jerusalem, 1970; diploma, S.W. Tech. Coll., 1970; student, United Christian Assn., 1976; MusD, London Inst. Applied Rsch., 1991; diplomatic diploma, Acad. Argentina de Diplomacia, 1993; PhD (hon.), Australian Inst. Coord. Rsch., Victoria, 1993; diploma of honors on internat. affairs, Inst. Des Affaires Internat., Paris, 1994. Lic. Bible tchr. United Christian Acad. Songwriter Hank Locklin Music Co., Nashville, 1963-70; entertainer 1982 World's Fair, Knoxville, Tenn., 1982; ptnr., owner Prince Wholesale Bait Co., Canton, N.C., 1976-82, Grad Builders, Canton, 1982-86, Prince TV Co., Canton, 1986—. Music pub. Broadcast Music, Inc., Nashville, 1982—; mem. prodn. staff, talent coord. (TV series) Down Home, Down Under, 1989-90; host TV show Real Hereos of Country Music in Nashville, 1997-2003. Songs recorded on RCA: I Feel a Cry Coming On, 1965 (#1 in Eng.), Best Part of Loving You, (#1 in Eng.), Anna, 1969 (Billboard 1970, recorded in Ireland 1974, hit in Europe and New Zealand); singer, composer I'm In Love With You, 1995; over 20 songs recorded to date; appeared Grand Ole Opry, 1970; exec. prodr., host TV talk show, Real Hereos of Country Music, 1989— (Emmy nomination 1997). Cand. for county commr. Dem. Party Macon County, N.C., 1984; bd. dirs. Macon County Taxpayers Assn., Inc., 1984, v.p., 1984-86; bd. dirs. Head Start, Topton, N.C., 1969-73. Nominated Disting. Women N.C., N.C. Coun. Coun. on Status of Women, 1984, Jefferson award WYFF TV and Am. Inst. for Pub. Svc., Outstanding Bus. Woman Small Bus. Adminstrn., 1984. Mem. BMI, Internat. Parliament Safety and Peace (life, dept. fgn. affairs, dep. mem. assembly), Nashville Songwriters Assn. Internat. (moderator, tchr. 1984-86), Country Music Assn., Reunion Profl. Entertainers, Fraternal Order Police, C. of C., Order of Knight of Templars (dame) Lofsensic Order (dame), Maison Internat. des Intellectuals. Democrat.

**PRINCE, CHARLES O., III, (CHUCK PRINCE),** diversified financial services company executive; b. Lynwood, Calif., Jan. 13, 1950; s. Charles Prince Jr.; m. Margaret L. Wolff, Sept. 20, 2003. BA, U. So. Calif., 1971, MA, JD, 1975; LLM, Georgetown U., 1983. Bar: Pa. 1975, Md. 1979, Minn. 1982. Atty. U.S. Steel Coll., 1975—79; gen. counsel Commercial Credit Co., 1979—86; exec. v.p., gen. counsel, sec. Traveler's Group, NYC, 1986-98; co-gen. counsel, sec. Citigroup (merger of Traveler's Group and Citibank), NYC, 1998—2000; chief admin. officer Citigroup, Inc., NYC, 2000, COO, 2001—02, CEO, 2003—, chmn., 2006—, chmn. & CEO, Global Corp. & Investment Bank Group, 2002—03. Mem. Coun. Fgn. Rels.; bd. dirs. Johnson & Johnson, New Brunswick, NJ, 2006—. Bd. dirs. United Negro Coll. Fund; trustee Columbia U., Juilliard Sch.; bd. mem. Joan & Sanford I. Weill Med. Coll., Cornell U. Office: Citigroup Inc 399 Park Ave New York NY 10022 also: Citigroup 153 E 53rd St New York NY 10043-0001*

**PRINCE, DANFORTH,** publishing executive, journalist; b. Toledo, June 14, 1953; s. Edward Mitchell Prince and Elizabeth Jane Danforth. BA, Hamilton Coll., Clinton, N.Y., 1975. V.p., treas. Porter & Prince Corp., 1983—; pres., CEO Blood Moon Prodn., N.Y.C., 1997—, Ga. Lit. Assn., N.Y.C., 1997—. Co-author (dir. rsch.): Europe & Caribbean Series of The Frommer Guides, 1983—. Mem.: North Am. Travel Journalists Assn. Office: Blood Moon Productions Ltd 75 Saint Marks Pl Staten Island NY 10301 Office Phone: 718-556-9410. Office Fax: 718-816-4092. E-mail: DanforthPrince@hotmail.com.

**PRINCE, DAVID CANNON,** lawyer; b. Hawkinsville, Ga., July 4, 1950; s. Carl Willis and Carobel (Cannon) P.; m. Mary MacIntyre, June 30, 1973. BA in Econs., Clemson U., 1972; JD, St. John's U., Jamaica, N.Y., 1980. Bar: N.Y. 1981, Ga. 1982, U.S. Dist. Ct. (no. dist.) Ga. 1982. Atty. enforcement SEC, Atlanta, 1981-86; regional counsel Shearson Lehman Bros. Inc., Atlanta, 1986-92; gen. counsel Robinson-Humphrey Co., Inc., Atlanta, 1992—2001; chief legal officer SunTrust Capital Markets, Inc., 2001—. Capt. USAF, 1972-78. Mem. ABA (co-chairperson young lawyers div. 1986-88). Democrat. Avocations: sailing, running. Home: 1824 Lenox Rd NE Atlanta GA 30306-3031 Office: Suntrust Capital Markets Inc 303 Peachtree St 36t Flr Atlanta GA 30306-1070 Office Phone: 404-926-5570.

**PRINCE, GEORGE EDWARD,** retired pediatrician; b. Erwin, N.C., Nov. 25, 1921; s. Hugh Williamson and Helen Herman (Hood) P.; m. Millie Elizabeth Mann, Nov. 26, 1944; children: Helen Elizabeth, Millie Mann, Susan Hood, Mary Lois, MD, Duke U., 1944. Diplomate Am. Bd. Pediatrics, Am. Bd. Med. Examiners. Intern Boston Children's Hosp. Harvard Svc., Boston, 1944-45; resident pediatrics Children's Hosp., Louisville, 1945-47; instr. pediatrics U. Louisville, 1947; founder Gastonia (N.C.) Children's Clinic, 1947, pediatrician, 1947-86; pub. health physician Gaston County Health Dept., Gastonia, N.C., 1986-98, med. dir., 1995-98, ret., 1998. Chmn. bd. dirs. Carolina State Bank; bd. dirs. So. Nat. Bank, Gastonia, 1979-95, Hospice, Gastonia, 1987-92; organizer, dir. AIDS Adv. Coun., Gaston County, N.C., 1988-94; coord. N.C. state Pediatric Rsch. in Office Setting, 1986-92. Contbr. articles to profl. jours. Mem. Gaston County Human Rels. Com., Gastonia, 1966; mem. Sch. Health Adv. Coun., Gaston County, 1980-97. Maj. USAF, 1955-57. Recipient Balthis Heart Assn. award, Gaston County, 1981, 1998, Good Amb. award, Health Dept., 1986, Family Adv. award, Commn. on the Family, Gastonia, 1995, commendation, City of Gastonia, 2001, Gaston County Bd. Commrs., 2001. Fellow Am. Acad. Pediatrics (pres. N.C. chpt. 1984-86); mem. AMA, N.C. Pediatric Soc. (hon., pres. 1970), N.C. Med. Soc. (pres. 1966), Gaston County Med. Soc. (pres. 1984), County Club (bd. dirs. 1975-76). Democrat. Methodist. Avocations: golf, skiing, sailing, bridge. E-mail: gep2@aol.com.

**PRINCE, GREGORY SMITH, JR.,** retired college president; b. Washington, May 7, 1939; s. Gregory Smith and Margaret (Minor) P.; m. Toni Layton Brewer; children: Tara Wyndom, Gregory S. III. BA, Yale U., 1961, M in Philosophy, 1969, PhD, 1973; cert. in teaching English as a Second Language, Georgetown U., 1961; DHL (hon.), LLD (hon.), Amherst Coll., 1991. Instr. New Asia Coll., Kowloon, Hong Kong, 1961-62, Chinese U., Kowloon, 1962-63, Yale China Assn., Kowloon, 1961-63, Woodberry Forest (Va.) Sch., 1963-65; dean summer programs Dartmouth Coll., Hanover, NH, 1970-72, asst. dean faculty, 1972-78, assoc. dean faculty, 1978-89; pres. Hampshire Coll., Amherst, Mass., 1989—2005; ice. coun. Pathways to Coll., 2005—. Vice chair coun. on racial and ethnic justice ABA; bd. dirs. Mass Ventures. Producer: (film) A Way of Learning, 1988. Trustee Montshire Mus. Sci., Hanover, 1973-89, Washington Campus, 1978—; trustee, chmn. Univ. Press New England, Hanover, 1983-84; trustee, pres. Yale-China Assn., New Haven, 1969-84; bd. dirs. Five Colls., Inc., Amherst, 1989-2005; bd. dirs. Mass. Internat. Festival for Arts, 1994-98; chmn. bd. dirs. Assn. Ind. Colls.

and Univs. Mass., 1994-95; chair commn. on accreditation Am. Coun. Edn.; bd. dirs. Mass. Nature Conservancy, 1996—; bd. dirs. Nat. Assn. Ind. Colls. and Univs., 1999-2001, Friendship House, 2002—. Coe fellow Stanford U., 1965, Woodrow Wilson fellow Yale U., 1966, NDEA fellow, 1967-70. Mem. Internat. Assn. of Chiefs Police Found. (bd. dirs. 1991-95), Nat. Assn. of Ind. Colls. and Univs. Democrat. Episcopalian. Office: Hampshire Coll 893 West St Amherst MA 01002-3372 Home: 24 Academy Rd Norwich VT 05055-9480

**PRINCE, HAROLD,** theatrical director, producer; b. NYC, Jan. 30, 1928; s. Milton A. and Blanche (Stern) P.; m. Judith Chaplin, Oct. 26, 1962; children: Charles, Daisy. AB, U. Pa., 1948, DFA (hon.), 1971; LittD, Emerson Coll., 1971. Chmn. Performing Arts Libr., NYC; participant, Voices of the Arts Kennedy Ctr. for Performing Arts, Washington, 2005. Co-prodr.: Pajama Game, 1954-56 (Antoinette Perry award), Damn Yankees, 1955-57 (Antoinette Perry award), New Girl in Town, 1957-58, West Side Story, 1957-59, A Swim in the Sea, 1958, Fiorello, 1959-61 (Antoinette Perry award, Pulitzer prize), Tenderloin, 1960-61, A Call on Kuprin, 1961, They Might Be Giants, London, 1961, Side by Side by Sondheim, 1977; prodr.: Take Her, She's Mine, 1961-62, A Funny Thing Happened on the Way to the Forum, 1962-64 (Antoinette Perry award), Fiddler on the Roof, 1964-72 (Antoinette Perry award), Poor Bitos, 1964, Flora the Red Menace, 1965; dir., prodr.: She Loves Me, 1963-64, London, 1964, Superman, 1966, Cabaret, 1966-69 (Antoinette Perry award 1968), Zorba, 1968-69, Company, 1970-72 (Antoinette Perry award 1972), A Little Night Music, 1973-74 (Antoinette Perry award 1975), Pacific Overtures, 1976, A Doll's Life, 1982; co-dir., prodr.: Follies, 1971-72 (Tony award for directing), Faust, 1990; co-prodr., dir.: Candide, 1974-75 (Tony award for directing), Merrily We Roll Along, 1981; dir.: A Family Affair, 1962, Baker Street, 1965, Great God Brown, 1972-73, The Visit, 1973-74, Love for Love, 1974-75, Ashmedai, 1976, Some of My Best Friends, 1977, On The Twentieth Century, 1978, La Fanciulla Del West, 1978, Evita, London, 1979, N.Y.C., 1980, L.A., 1982, Australia, 1980, Chgo., 1980, Detroit, 1982, Sweeney Todd, The Demon Barber of Fleet Street, Broadway, 1979, London, 1980, Silverlake, 1980, Willie Stark, 1981, Candide, 1982, 94, 97, Madama Butterfly, 1983, Turandot, 1983, Play Memory, 1984, End of the World, 1984, Grind, 1985, Cabaret Revival, 1987, Roza, 1987, Phantom of the Opera, London, 1986, N.Y.C., (Antoinette Perry award) 1988, Kiss of the Spider Woman, Toronto, 1992, London, 1992, N.Y.C., 1993, Show Boat, Toronto, 1993, N.Y.C., 1994 (Tony award for directing), La Fanciula del West, Don Giovanni, N.Y. City Opera, 1989, Faust, Met. Opera, 1990, The Petrified Prince, 1994, (off broadway) Diamonds, 1984; adapter, dir. (off broadway) Grandchild of Kings, 1992, Candide, Broadway, 1997, Parade, Broadway, 1998, Hollywood Arms, Broadway, 2002, Bounce, Chgo., Wash. 2003, The Phantom of the Opera, 2004, Fiddler on the Roof, 2004; co-prodr: (films) The Pajama Game, 1957, Damn Yankees, 1958; dir.: (films) Something for Everyone, 1970, A Little Night Music, 1978, 3Hree, Phila. & L.A. Mem. coun. Nat. Endowment Arts; pres. League N.Y. Theatres, 1964-66; chmn. Performing Arts Libr., N.Y.C. Recipient 20 Antoinette Perry (Tony) Meml. awards, Critics Circle awards, Pulitzer prize, 1961, Best Mus. awards London Evening Std., Kennedy Ctr. Honors, 1994, Spl. Tony award lifetime achievement in theatre, 2006. Office: Harold Prince 10 Rockefeller Plz Ste 1104 New York NY 10020-1903*

**PRINCE, JONATHAN D.,** social worker, educator; b. Orange, N.J., Dec. 3, 1965; s. Carl E. and Sue G. Prince; m. Jackie R. Dowd, Nov. 19, 2005. PhD, U. Calif., Berkeley, 2002. Prof. Sch. Social Work Rutgers U., New Brunswick, NJ, 2002—. Assoc. mem. Inst. Health, Health Care Policy, and Aging Rsch. Rutgers U., New Brunswick, 2005—06. Contbr. articles to profl. jours. Grantee, NIH. Office: Rutgers University 536 George St New Brunswick NJ 08901 Business E-Mail: jdprince@rci.rutgers.edu.

**PRINCE, KENNETH STEPHEN,** lawyer; b. Newton, Mass., Jan. 28, 1950; s. Samuel and Edna L. Prince; m. Patricia Denning, Jan. 15, 1977 (div. Nov. 1985); 1 child, Kenneth Stephen Jr.; m. Jane M. McCabe, Sept. 5, 1987; 1 child, Allison Pamela. BA, U. Pa., 1972; JD, Boston Coll., 1975. Bar: N.Y. 1976, Mass. 1975, U.S. Dist. Ct. (so. and ea. dists.) N.Y. 1978. Assoc. Shearman & Sterling, NYC, 1975-83, ptnr., 1984—; antitrust group practice leader, 1992—2003, 2005—. Mem. N.Y. Law Inst. (exec. com. 1984-96), Order of Coif. Home: 15 Dellwood Rd Darien CT 06820-2915 Office Phone: 212-848-4139. Business E-Mail: kprince@shearman.com.

**PRINCE, LARRY L.,** automotive parts and supplies company executive; b. 1937; With Genuine Parts Co., Atlanta, 1958—, v.p., then group v.p., 1977-83, exec. v.p., 1983-86, pres., chief oper. officer, 1986-90, chief exec. officer, 1989—2004, bd. chmn., 2000—2005, chmn. exec. com., 2005—. Office: Genuine Parts Co 2999 Circle 75 Pky NW Atlanta GA 30339

**PRINCE, LEAH FANCHON,** lab administrator, executive secretary; b. Hartford, Conn., Aug. 12, 1939; d. Meyer and Annie (Forman) Berman; m. Herbert N. Prince, Jan. 30, 1955; children: Daniel L., Richard N., Robert G. Student, U. Conn., 1957—59, Rutgers U., 1962; BFA, Fairleigh Dickinson U., 1970; postgrad., Caldwell Coll. for Women, 1973—75, Parsons Sch. of Design, N.Y.C., 1978. Cert. tchr. art, N.J. Tchr. art Caldwell-West Caldwell Pub. Schs., NJ, 1970—75; pres. Britannia Imports Ltd., Fairfield, NJ, 1979—89; tchr. religious studies Bohrer-Kaufman Hebrew Acad., Randolph, NJ, 1981—82; co-founder, corp. sec. Gibraltar Biol. Labs., Inc., Fairfield, 1970—; dir., co-founder Gibraltar Inst. for Rsch. and Tng., Fairfield, 1984—. Cons. Internat. Antiques and Fine Arts Industries, U.K., 1979-89; cons. in art exhibitry Passaic County Coll., Paterson, N.J., 1989-93; art curator Fairleigh Dickinson U., Rutherford, N.J., 1972-74; curator history of nursing 20th century Bloomfield (N.J.) Coll., 1990-91; lectr. Am. Soc. Microbiology, New Orleans 1989; sptkr in field, Exhibited in group shows at Bloomfield (N.J.) Coll., 1990, Caldwell Women's Club, N.J., 1991, State Fedn. Women's Clubs Ann. Show, 1992 (1st pl. award 1992), Newark Art Mus., 1992, West (N.J.) Essex Art Assn., 1990, Somerset (N.J.) Art Assn., 1994, Mortimer Gallery, Gladstone, N.J., 1994 (1st pl. award 1998), Tewksbury Hist. Soc. (1st pl. award 1994, 2004), Tewksbury Hist. Soc., 2001,02, 04, 05, Nat. Meeting Am. Pen Women, Calif., 2002, Washington, 2004 (1st pl. award); one-woman shows include Passaic County Coll., N.J., 1990, Caldwell Coll., 1990; author children's stories. Chair ann. juried art awards Arts Coun. of Essex Bd. Trustees, Montclair, N.J., 1984-90; chair fundraising Arts Coun. Essex County, N.J., 1989. Recipient 1st place award, N.J. Tewksbury Hist. Soc., 1994, 1998, 2004—05, Juried Art award, 2001—02, 2004, 2005. Mem. AAUW, Soc. Childrens Book Writers and Illustrators, Somerset Art Assn., Nat. League Am. Pen Women (pres. N.J. br., Juried Art award 2001, 2004), Barnegat Light Yacht Club. Republican. Avocations: boating, tennis, opera, painting, travel. Home: 5 Standish Dr Mendham Twp Morristown NJ 07960-3224

**PRINCE, M(ORRIS) DAVID,** retired electronics research and technical manager, computer graphics pioneer; b. Greensboro, N.C., Mar. 27, 1926; m. Fay Wright, June 8, 1947; children: Stephen, Nicholas, Timothy, Rebecca. BEE, Ga. Inst. Tech., 1946, MSEE, 1949. Project mgr. Ga. Tech. Engring. Expt. Sta., Atlanta, 1952-57; sr. tech. staff ITT Labs., Atlanta, 1957-59; rsch. lab. dir., sr. staff specialist Lockheed-Ga. Co., Marietta, 1959-95; ret. 1995. Prof. Ga. Inst. Tech., 1980-90, adj. prof., 1990—; cons. Sys. Cons. Assocs., Atlanta, 1970-; chmn. Electronics Automation Program, Computer-Aided Mfg. Internat., 1982-83; adj. prof. Ga. Tech. Coll. Computing, 1995—. Author: Interactive Graphics for Computer-Aided Design, 1971 (pioneer text CAD, translated to Japanese, Russian and Chinese langs.); contbr. articles to profl. jours.; patentee computers and electronics; invited worldwide speaker; co-inventor velocity modulation TV for enhancing picture detail utilized by manufacturers in an estimated 100 million TV sets. With USNR, 1944-48. Recipient NASA Group Achievement Award, 1984. Named Engr.-Scientist of Yr., Lockheed-Ga. Co., 1983; named to Ga. Inst. Tech. Engring. Hall of Fame, 2004. Fellow IEEE (life). Avocations: astronomy, book collecting. Home: 3132 Frontenac Ct NE Atlanta GA 30319-2414 Personal E-mail: mdprince@mindspring.com.

**PRINCE, RICHARD,** artist; b. Panama Canal Zone, Republic of Panama, Aug. 6, 1949; came to U.S., 1956; s. Louis and Virginia (McLeod) P. Odd jobs Time Life, N.Y.C., 1973—85; edited cover photog. Mademoiselle Mag., N.Y.C., 1985; full-time artist N.Y.C., 1985—. Mem. "Picture" Generation of artists 1970s, N.Y.C. Exhibitions include Last Picture Show: Artists Using Photography 1960-1982, Walker Art Ctr., Mpls., 2003; author: Why I Go To The Movies Alone, 1995; editor: Wild History, 1985; exhibitions include Whitney Biennial, Whitney Mus. Am. Art, NY, 2004, Barbara Gladstone Gallery, N.Y.C., 2003, Patrick Painter Inc., Santa Monica, Calif., 2002, Galerie Micheline Szwajcer, Antwerp, Belgium, 2001, Skarstedt Fine Art, N.Y.C., 2001, Regen Projects, L.A., 2001, Sadie Coles, HQ, London, 2001. Recipient Nat. Endowment award, 1985. Mem. The Offices, N.Y. (pres. 1979-80). Avocation: Avid book collector: purchased 1820 bldg. to house collection of books & his art; will be open to public.

**PRINCE, THOMAS E.,** bank executive; b. 1947; With Security Pacific Corp., LA, 1968-92, sr. v.p., controller, 1984—92; exec. v.p., treas. Downey Savs Loan Assn., Newport Beach, Calif., 1992—2004, CFO, 1992—, COO, 2004—. Office: Downey Savs Loan Assn 3501 Jamboree Rd Ste 5000 Newport Beach CA 92660-2980 Mailing: Downey Savings Loan Assn PO Box 6000 Newport Beach CA 92658-6000 Office Phone: 949-509-4440. Office Fax: 949-854-8162.*

**PRINCE, THOMAS RICHARD,** accountant, educator; b. New Albany, Miss., Dec. 7, 1934; s. James Thompson and Callie Florence (Howell) P.; m. Eleanor Carol Polkoff, July 14, 1962; children: Thomas Andrew, John Michael, Adrienne Carol. BS, Miss. State U., 1956, MS, 1957; PhD in Accountancy, U. Ill., 1962. CPA, Ill. Instr. U. Ill., 1960—62; mem. faculty Northwestern U. Kellogg Grad. Sch. Mgmt., 1962—, prof. acctg. info. and mgmt., 1969—, chmn. dept. acctg. info. and mgmt., 1968—75; prof. health industry mgmt. Northwestern U., 1990—; cons. in field. Dir. Applied Rsch. Sys., Inc. Author: Extension of the Boundaries of Accounting Theory, 1962, Information Systems for Management Planning and Control, 3d edit, 1975, Financial Reporting and Cost Control for Health Care Entities, 1992, Product Life-Cycle Costing and Management of Large-Scale Medical Systems Investments, 1997, Strategic Management for Health Care Entities: Creative Frameworks for Financial and Operational Analysis, 1998. Served to 1st lt. AUS, 1957-60. Mem. AICPA, INFORMS, AHA, HFMA, HIMMS, AUPHA, Am. Accounting Assn., Am. Econ. Assn., Fin. Execs. Inst., AAAS, Ill. Soc. CPA, Inst. Mgmt. Acct., Alpha Tau Omega, Phi Kappa Phi, Omicron Delta Kappa, Delta Sigma Pi, Beta Alpha Psi. Congregationalist. Home: 303 Richmond Rd Kenilworth IL 60043-1138 Office: Northwestern U Leverone Hl Evanston IL 60208-2002 Office Phone: 847-251-4339. Business E-Mail: t-prince@kellogg.northwestern.edu.

**PRINCE, WILLIAM B.,** lawyer; b. Albuquerque, Feb. 7, 1949; BS cum laude, Brigham Young U., 1973; JD, U. Utah, 1978. Bar: Utah 1978. Ptnr. Holme Roberts & Owen, Salt Lake City; ptnr.-in-charge, co-chmn., environ., natural resources, energy practice Dorsey & Whitney LLP, Salt Lake City, 1996—. Mem. Office of Exception and Appeals Fed. Energy Adminstrn., 1974-75. Co-author: Utah Environmental and Land Use Permits Manual, 1981; assoc. editor Jour. Contemporary Law U. Utah, 1977-78. Mem. ABA (natural resources, energy and environ. law sect., chmn. hard minerals com. 1991—), Utah State Bar (past chmn. energy, natural resources and environ. law 1986-87), Northwest Mining assn., Air and Waste Mgmt. Assn. (Rocky Mountain sect., treas. Great Basin chpt. 1991—). Office: Dorsey & Whitney LLP Ste 925 Wells Fargo Plz 170 S Main St Salt Lake City UT 84101-1655 Office Phone: 801-933-7370. Office Fax: 801-933-7373. Business E-Mail: prince.william@dorsey.com.

**PRINCE, (PRINCE ROGERS NELSON),** musician, actor; b. Mpls., June 7, 1958; s. John L. and Mattie D. (Shaw) Nelson; m. Mayte Garcia, 1996 (div., 2000); 1 son (dec.); m. Manuela Testolini, Dec. 31, 2001 (separated, 2006) Singer, songwriter, actor. Albums include For You, 1978, Dirty Mind, 1979, Controversy, 1981, 1999, 1983, film star and soundtrack Purple Rain, 1984 (Academy Award for best original score, 1984), Around the World in a Day, 1985 (Best Soul/Rhythm and Blues Album of the Yr., Downbeat readers poll, 1985), Parade, 1986, Chaos and Disorder, 1996, Sign O' the Times, 1987, Lovesexy, 1988, Batman: Motion Picture Soundtrack, 1989 (Soundtrack of Yr. award Playboy mag. readers' poll, Best Pop/Rock album Downbeat mag. readers' poll), (with the New Power Generation) Diamonds and Pearls, 1991, (symbol as title), 1992, Come, 1995, The Greatest Romance Ever Sold, 1999, 94 East, 2000, The Very Best of Prince, 2001, Beautiful Experience, 2001, The Rainbow Children, 2001, One Night Alone...Live!, 2002, N.E.W.S., 2003, Musicology, 2004, 3121, 2006; films include Purple Rain, 1984, film star and soundtrack Under the Cherry Moon, 1986, film star and soundtrack Sign O' the Times, 1987; film appearance and soundtrack Graffiti Bridge, 1990 (ASCAP award for most performed songs from a motion picture, 1991); formerly mem. group Prince and the Revolution (Best Soul/Rhythm and Blues Group of Yr. Downbeat mag. readers poll 1985); composer Showgirls, 1995, Girl 6, 1996, The Gold Experience, 1995, Crystal Ball, 1998, Rave Un2 the Joy Fantastic, 1999, Bamboozled, 2000. Recipient 3 Grammy awards, 1985, Am. Music Achievement award for infuence on look and sound of the 80's, NAACP Spl. Achievement award, 1997, Webby Lifetime Achievement award, Internat. Acad. Digital Arts and Sciences, 2006, Best Male R&B award, Black Entertainment TV (BET), 2006; named Rhythm and Blues Musician of Yr. Down Beat mag. readers' poll, 1984, 1992; inducted Rock and Roll Hall of Fame, 2004. Office: Paisley Park Studios 7801 Audubon Rd Chanhassen MN 55317-8201

**PRINCE-RAMUS, JOSHUA,** architect; BA in Philosophy, Yale U., 1991; MArch, Harvard U., 1996. With Office Met. Architecture, 1996—2006; ptnr., founder Office Met. Architecture NYC, 2001—06; founder Ramus Ella Architects, 2006—. Partner-in-charge Mus. Plaza, Louisville, Dee and Charles Wyly Theater, Dallas, Annenberg Ctr. Info. Sci. and Tech., Pasadena, Calif. Office: Ramus Ella Architects PC 160 Varick St 10th Fl New York NY 10013 Office Phone: 646-230-6557, 646-230-6558. E-mail: jramus@rex-ny.com.*

**PRINCETON, JOY CAROL,** retired nursing educator; b. St. Paul, Minn., Dec. 8, 1935; d. Eugene Russell Princeton and Margaret Edna Ehlers Princeton; children: Todd A. Myers, Michael D. Myers, Sarah C. Mooney. BSN, U. Colo., 1969, MSN, 1970, MA in Anthropology, 1975, PhD in Anthropology, 1977. RN Minn., Colo., N.C., Utah. Head nurse, obstetrics Abbott Hosp., Mpls., 1958—65; supr. obstetrics Boulder Meml. Hosp., Colo., 1965—68; asst. prof. U. Co. Sch. Nursing, Denver, 1970—73; assoc. prof. Duke U. Sch. Nursing, Durham, NC, 1978—81; prof. U. Utah Coll. Nursing, Salt Lake City, 1982—95; assoc. dir. U. Hosp., Salt Lake City, 1987—91. Mem. White House Com. on Children & Youth, Colo. Chpt., Denver, 1970—73; expert panel mem. Am. Acad. Nursing, Culturally Competent and Sensitive Health Care, Washington, 1991—93; cons. U. N.C. Med. Sch., Chapel Hill, NC, 1984—85, U. Rochester Sch. of Nursing, NY, 1988, NIH, Nat. Ctr. Nursing Rsch., 1988, U. Capetown Sch. Medicine, South Africa, 1990—91, HHS, PHS Divsn. Nursing, Rockville, Md., 1987—88, 1990—91, St. Louis U. Med. Ctr., 1990—91, Regis Coll. Sch. of Nursing, Denver, 1990—91; adv. Utah State Dept. Health, Salt Lake City, 1991—92; cons. in field, grad. student mentor, 1995—. Author: Maternity Nursing Today, 1973—77 (Parent/Child Nursing, 1973); mem. editl. bd.: Health Care for Women, 1984—94, Medical Anthro Quar., 1984—88, 1993—94, Scholarly Inquiry for Nursing Practice, 1985—90, Jour. Profl. Nursing, 1985—91, 1994—97, Jour. Nursing Edn., 1991—94, Nursing Outlook Jour., 1993—94; contbr. articles to profl. jours.; review panel mem. profl. jours., 1995—2006. Named Nurse of Yr., NC Nurses Assn., 1980; grantee, Dept. Health and Human Svcs., 1982—95; Ednl. grants, Dept. Health, Edn. and Welfare, U. Colo. Programs, 1970—73, grants for master's and doctoral edn., U.S. Pub. Health Svc., 1982—95. Fellow: Soc. Applied Anthropology, Am. Acad. Nursing. Democrat. Avocations: library work, hiking, camping, travel. Home: 2720 14th St Boulder CO 80304 Office Phone: 303-444-8163.

**PRINCIPAL, VICTORIA (VICTORIA REE PRINCIPALE),** actress, film producer, writer; b. Fukuoka, Japan, Jan. 3, 1946; d. Victor and Ree (Veal) P.; m. Christopher Skinner (div.) m. Harry Glassman, 1985 (separated 2006) Attended, Miami-Dade Community Coll.; studied, Royal Acad. Ballet; studied acting with Max Croft, Al Sacks and Estelle Harman, Jean Scott, Royal Acad. Dramatic Arts. Created product line Principal Secret Skin Care, Color Principal Makeup. Worked as model, including TV commls.; appearences include (film) The Life and Times of Judge Roy Bean, 1972 (Golden Globe Nominee for Most Promising Newcomer), The Naked Ape, 1973, Earthquake, 1974, I Will I Will For Now, 1976, Vigilante Force, 1976, Michael Kael In Katango, 1998; (TV movies) Last Hours Before Morning, 1975, Fantasy Island, 1977, The Night They Took Miss Beautiful, 1977, Pleasure Palace, 1980, Not Just Another Affair, 1982, Mistress, 1987, Naked Lie, 1989 (also exec. prodr.), Blind Witness, 1989 (also co-exec. prodr.), The Burden of Proof, 1990, Sparks: The Price of Passion, 1990, Don't Touch My Daughter, 1991(also exec. prodr.), Just Life, 1992, Seduction: Three Tales from the Inner Sanctum, 1993 (also exec. prodr.), River of Rage: The Taking of Maggie Keene, 1993 (also exec. prodr.), Beyond Obsession, 1994, Dancing in the Dark, 1995, The Abduction, 1996, Love in Another Town, 1997, Time Flies, An Evening of Comic One-Acts; guest host An Evening at the Improv, 1982; exec. prodr. Midnight's Child, 1991; (TV series) Dallas, 1978-87; (theatre) Time Flies, LA Theatre Works, Love Letters, Canon Theatre, LA and Coral Gables Theatre, Fla., Mere Mortals, Second City, Chgo.; (TV miniseries) Greatest Heros of the Bible, 1978; guest appearances Hawaii Five-O, 1979, Fridays, 1982, Home Improvement, 1994, Chicago Hope, 1998, Tracey Takes On, 1999, Just Shoot Me!, 1999, Jack & Jill, 1999, 2001, Titans, 2000, The Practice, 2000, Family Guy (voice), 2000, Providence, 2000, Dallas Reunion: Return to Southfork, 2004: guest lead The Tracy Ullman Show, The Garry Shandling Show; author: The Body Principal, 1983, The Beauty Principal, 1984, The Diet Principal, 1987, Living Principal, 2001 Hon. chairperson, amb. Arthritis Found.; co-chair Victory Over Violence; mem. cmty. adv. coun. LA County Domestic Violence Coun.*

**PRINCIPI, ANTHONY JOSEPH,** pharmaceutical company executive, former secretary of veterans affairs; b. NYC, Apr. 16, 1944; s. Antonio Joseph and Theresa (Princiotta) P.; m. Elizabeth Ann Ahlering, June 26, 1971; children: Anthony, Ryan, John BS. U.S. Naval Acad., 1967; JD, Seton Hall U., 1975. Commd. 2d lt. U.S. Navy, 1967, advanced through grades to comdr., 1984, line officer Washington, 1967-72; atty. JAGC, San Diego, 1975-80: counsel Com. on Armed Service U.S. Senate, Washington, 1980-83, staff dir. Com. on Vet.'s Affairs, 1984—88: dep. adminstr. congl. & pub. affairs VA. Washington, 1983-84; dep. sec. US Dept. Veterans Affairs, Washington, 1989-90. acting sec., 1992—93, sec. 2001—05; ptnr. Luce, Forward. Hamilton & Scripps, San Diego, 1990-95; sr. v.p. CEO Lockheed Martin IMS Integrated Solutions Co., Santa Clara, Calif., 1995-2001; pres. QTC Medical Services, 2001; v.p. govt. rels. Pfizer Inc., Washington, 2005— Chmn. Base Realignment & Closure (BRAC) Commn., 2005. Decorated Bronze Star with combat "V", Vietnamese Cross of Gallantry, Navy Commendation medal with combat "V" (3); recipient Meritorious Service medal VA. 1983 Mem. ABA (chmn. subcom. gen. practice sect. 1985—) Republican. Roman Catholic. Avocations: gardening, skiing. Office: Pfizer Inc 325 Seveth St NW Ste 120 Washington DC 20004

**PRINDLE, WILLIAM ROSCOE,** retired glass company executive; b. San Francisco, Dec. 19, 1926; s. Vivian Arthur and Harriette Alnora (Nickerson) P.; m. June Laverne Anderson, June 20, 1947; children— Carol Susan, William Alastair. BS. U. Calif., Berkeley, 1948, MS. 1950; Sc.D., M.I.T., 1955. asst. tech. dir. Hazel-Atlas Glass Co., 1954-56; mgr. research Hazel-Atlas Glass div. Continental Can Co., Wheeling, W.va., 1956-58, gen. mgr. research and devel., 1959-62; mgr. materials research Am. Optical Co., Southbridge, Mass., 1962-65; v.p. research Southbridge and Framingham, Mass., 1971-76; dir. research Ferro Corp., Cleve., 1966-67, v.p. research, 1967-71; exec. dir. Nat. Materials Adv. Bd., NRC-NAS, Washington, 1976-80: dir. adminstrv. and tech. svcs. R & D div. Corning Glass Works, NY, 1980-85, dir. materials rsch. NY, 1985-87; assoc. dir. R & D, Engring. div. Corning Glass Works (now Corning, Inc.), NY, 1987-90; div. v.p., assoc. dir. tech. group Corning Inc., NY, 1990-92; ret. Pres. XII Internat. Glass Congress, 1980, Internat. Commn. on Glass, 1985-88. Served with U.S. Navy, 1944-46. Named Disting. Ceramist of New Eng., New Eng. sect. Am. Ceramic Soc., 1974, Toledo Glass and Ceramic award NW Ohio sect., 1986, Albert Victor Bleininger Meml. award Pitts. sect., 1989, Phoenix award as Glass Industry Man of Yr., 1983; Friedberg Meml. lecture Nat. Inst. Ceramic Engrs., 1990, Graeves Walker award, 2004. Fellow Am. Ceramic Soc. (disting. life, pres. 1980-81), Soc. Glass Tech., Am. Soc. for Metals Internat.; mem. NAE, AAAS, World Acad. of Ceramics, Cosmos Club (Washington), Sigma Xi. Phi Gamma Delta. Home: 1556 Crestline Dr Santa Barbara CA 93105-4611 Personal E-mail: wprindle@aol.com.

**PRING, ROBERT BRADFORD,** banker, financial consultant; b. St. Louis, July 22, 1951; s. Charles Branscombe Pring and A Helen Crosson Reim; m. Bernice Rosalyn Crisp, Oct. 25, 1975 (div. Dec. 2001); children: Robert Bradford III, Jennifer Christiane; m. Linda Colleen Mueller, Aug. 10, 2002. BS in Agr., U. Mo.. Columbia, 1973: postgrad., U. Mo., 1973. Lic. life, accident and health ins agt; cert. fin planner, stockbroker, registered investment advisor rep. Ptnr. Prings Nursery, St. Louis, 1973-74; dist. sales mgr Curtis Circulation Co., Nashville, 1974-75, reg. mktg. mgr. Orlando, Fla., 1975-77, West Coast account exec. West Caldwell, NJ, 1977-79, div. mktg. supr. St. Louis, 1979-81; trust mktg. officer Commerce Bank, St. Louis, 1982-84; v.p. bus. devel./comml. lending Commerce Bank St. Charles County, N.A., St. Peters. Mo.. 1984—97; v.p., comml. devel. officer Commerce Bank St. Louis, St. Peters. Mo.. 1991-97; bus. mgr. program First State Bank St. Charles, St. Charles. Mo.. 1997-2001; fin. advisor, investment mgr., personal fin. planning INVEST Fin. Corp., 2001—02; ins. cons. fin. advice, mortgage banking Robert B. Pring & Assocs., 2002—04; v.p. comml. lending, br. mgr. CBC Bank, St. Peters, 2004—05; asst. v.p. Bank of Old Monroe, 2005—. Prodr., dir. St. Charles County, A World of Opportunity, 1987. Pres., chmn. United Serv Handicapped, St. Charles, 1988—89; treas. bd. dirs YMCA St. Charles County, 1989—99, chmn. bd. dirs., 1991—92; treas. Citizens St. Charles County C.C., 1990, co-chmn., 1991, scholarship com., pres. search coun., chair bd. devel. com., 2005—; bd. dirs. YMCA Greater Met. S.t Louis, 1991—92, Mid-Am Theatre Co., St. Charles, St. Charles YMCA, 1985—2000, St. Charles C.C. Found., 1994—, past chmn., treas. sec. chmn. bd., major gifts com., exec. dir. search com., chmn. nominating, devel. com., 2005—. Recipient Meritorious Serv Award, United Servs Handicapped, 1989, Bell Vol Award, St Charles County Community Coun and Southwestern Bell, 1990. Mem.: Fin. Planning Assn., inst. Cert. Fin. Planners, Greater St. Louis Soc. Cert. Fin. Planners (bd dirs 1990—91), St. Peters C. of C. (past dir, pres, chmn 1988, Disting Leadership Award 1990), Rotary (bd dirs St Charles chpt 1992). Presbyterian. Avocations: flying, soaring, water sports. Home and Office: 2163 Roselake Cir Saint Peters MO 63376-7772 Office Phone: 636-665-5601. E-mail: rbpring@charter.net.

**PRINGLE. CURT,** mayor; m. Alexis Pringle; children: Katie, Kyle. BBA, MPA, Calif. State U., Long Beach. Pres. Curt Pringle and Assocs., LLC, Irvine, Calif.; mayor Anaheim, Calif., 2003—. Vis. faculty mem. U. Calif., Irvine. Bd. mem. Leadership Traq; mem. Calif. Film Commn., 1996—99, Calif. State Assembly, 1988—90, 1992—98, Rep. leader, Rep. Caucus chair, chmn. appropriations com., chmn. ruies com., vice chmn. budget com.; nominee Calif. State Treas., 1998; Calif. del. Nat. Rep. Conv., 1996; active Calif. Rep. Ctrl. Com. Office: Anaheim City Hall 200 S Anaheim Blvd Anaheim CA 92805 Office Phone: 714-765-5247.

**PRINGLE, LAURENCE PATRICK,** writer; b. Rochester, NY, Nov. 26, 1935; s. Laurence Erin and Marleah Elizabeth (Rosehill) P.; m. Judith Malanowicz, June 23, 1962 (div. 1970); children: Heidi Elizabeth, Jeffrey Laurence, Sean Edmund; m. Alison Newhouse, July 14, 1971 (div. 1975); m. Susan Deborah Klein, Mar. 13, 1983; children: Jesse Erin, Rebecca Anne. BS in Wildlife Biology, Cornell U., 1958; MS in Wildlife Biology, U. Mass., 1961. Tchr. sci. Lima (N.Y.) Cen. Sch., 1961-62; editor Nature and Sci. mag.

Am. Mus. Natural History, N.Y.C., 1963-70; free-lance writer, 1970—. Writer-in-residence Kean College, Union, N.J., 1985-86. Author: (children's books) Dinosaurs and Their World, 1968, The Only Earth We Have, 1969, From Field to Forest, 1970, In a Beaver Valley, 1970, One Earth, Many People, 1971, Ecology: Science of Survival, 1971, Cockroaches: Here, There, Everywhere, 1971, From Pond to Prairie, 1972, This Is a River, 1972, Pests and People: The Search for Sensible Pest Control, 1972, Estuaries: Where Rivers Meet the Sea, 1973, Into the Woods: Exploring the Forest Ecosystem, 1973, Follow a Fisher, 1973, Twist, Wiggle and Squirm: A Book about Earthworms, 1973, Recycling Resources, 1974, Energy: Power for People, 1975, City and Suburb: Exploring an Ecosystem, 1975, Chains, Webs and Pyramids: The Flow of Energy in Nature, 1975, Water Plants, 1975, The Minnow Family: Chubs, Dace, Minnows and Shiners, 1976, Listen to the Crows, 1976, Our Hungry Earth: The World Food Crisis, 1976, Death is Natural, 1977, The Hidden World: Life Under a Rock, 1977, The Controversial Coyote: Predation, Politics and Ecology, 1977, The Gentle Desert: Exploring an Ecosystem, 1977, Animals and Their Niches: How Species Share Resources, 1977, The Economic Growth Debate: Are There Limits to Growth?, 1978, Dinosaurs and People: Fossils, Facts and Fantasies, 1978, Wild Foods, 1978, Nuclear Power: From Physics to Politics, 1979, Natural Fire: Its Ecology in Forests, 1979, Lives at Stake: The Science and Politics of Environmental Health, 1980, What Shall We Do with the Land?: Choices for America, 1981, Frost Hollows and Other Microclimates, 1981, Vampire Bats, 1982, Water: The Next Great Resource Battle, 1982, Radiation: Waves and Particles/Benefits and Risks, 1983, Wolfman: Exploring the World of Wolves, 1983, Feral: Tame Animals Gone Wild, 1983, The Earth Is Flat—and Other Great Mistakes, 1983, Being a Plant, 1983, Nuclear War: From Hiroshima to Nuclear Winter, 1985, Animals at Play, 1985, Here Come the Killer Bees, 1986, Throwing Things Away: From Middens to Resource Recovery, 1986, Restoring Our Earth, 1987, Home: How Animals Find Comfort and Safety, 1987, Rain of Troubles: The Science and Politics of Acid Rain, 1988, Living in a Risky World, 1989, Nuclear Energy: Troubled Past, Uncertain Future, 1989, Bearman: Exploring the World of Black Bears, 1989, The Animal Rights Controversy, 1989, Saving Our Wildlife, 1990, Global Warming: Assessing the Greenhouse Threat, 1990, The Golden Book of Insects and Spiders, 1990, Killer Bees (rev. edit.), 1991, Batman: Exploring the World of Bats, 1991, Living Treasure: Saving Earth's Threatened Biodiversity, 1991, Antarctica: The Last Unspoiled Continent, 1992, The Golden Book of Volcanoes, Earthquakes, and Powerful Storms, 1992, Chemical and Biological Warfare: The Cruelest Weapons, 1993, revised edit.. 2000, Oil Spills: Damage, Recovery, and Prevention, 1993, Jackal Woman: Exploring the World of Jackals, 1993, Scorpion Man: Exploring the World of Scorpions, 1994, Dinosaurs! Strange and Wonderful, 1995, Vanishing Ozone: Protecting Earth from Ultraviolet Radiation, 1995, Coral Reefs: Earth's Undersea Treasures, 1995, Dolphin Man: Exploring the World of Dolphins, 1995, rev. edit., 2002, Fire in the Forest: A Cycle of Growth and Renewai, 1995, Taking Care of the Earth: Kids in Action, 1996, Smoking: A Risky Business, 1996. An Extraordinary Life: The Story of a Monarch Butterfly, 1997, Nature! Wild and Wonderful, 1997, Everybody Has a Bellybutton: Your Life Before You Were Born, 1997, Elephant Woman: Cynthia Moss Explores The World of Elephants, 1997, Drinking: A Risky Business, 1997, One Room School, 1998, Explore Your Senses: SIGHT, 1999, Explore Your Senses: HEARING, 1999, Explore Your Senses: TASTE, 1999, Explore Your Senses: TOUCH, 1999, Explore Your Senses: SMELL, 1999, BATS! Strange and Wonderful, 2000, The Environmental Movement: From Its Roots to the Challenges of a New Century, 2000, Sharks! Strange and Wonderful, 2001, Global Warming: The Threat of Earth's Changing Climate, 2001, A Dragon in the Sky: The Story of a Green Darner Dragonfly, 2001, Scholastic Encyclopedia of Animals, 2001, Strange Animals, New to Science, 2002, Crows! Strange and Wonderful, 2002, Dog of Discovery: A Newfoundland's Adventures with Lewis and Clark, 2002, Whales! Strange and Wonderful, 2003, Snakes! Strange and Wonderful, 2004, American Slave, American Hero: York of the Lewis and Clark Expedition, 2006, (fiction) Jesse Builds a Road, 1989, Octopus Hug, 1993, Naming the Cat, 1997, Bear Hug, 2003, (adult books) Wild River, 1972, Rivers and Lakes, 1985. Recipient Spl. Conservation award, Nat. Wildlife Fedn., 1978, Eva L. Gordon award, Am. Nature Study Soc., 1983, Orbis Pictus award, Nat. Coun. Tchrs. English, 1998, Nonfiction award, Washington Post/Children's Book Guild, 1999, Lifetime Achievement prize for excellence in sci. books, AAAS, 2005; fellow, John Simon Guggenheim Meml. Found., 2006. Mem.: The Authors Guild. Home and Office: PO Box 252 West Nyack NY 10994-0252 Office Phone: 845-623-7275.

**PRINGLE, LEWIS GORDON,** marketing professional, educator; b. Lansing, Mich., Feb. 13, 1941; s. Gordon Henry and Lucile Roxana (Drake) P.; children: Lewis Gordon Jr., William Davis, Thomas Benjamin. BA, Harvard U., 1963; MS, MIT, 1965, PhD, 1969. V.p., dir. mktg. sci. BBDO, Inc., N.Y.C., 1968—73; asst. prof. mktg. Carnegie-Mellon U., Pitts., 1973—74; exec. v.p., dir. rsch. svcs., corp. dir. BBDO, Inc., N.Y.C., 1974—91; exec. v.p. BBDO Worldwide, 1986—91; chmn., CEO BBDO Europe, 1986—91, LG Pringle and Assocs., 1992—95; Joseph C. Seibert prof. mktg. Farmer Sch. Bus. Adminstrn., Miami U., Oxford, Ohio, 1995—2000. Bd. dirs. Yorktown U., prof.; mem. vis com. Sloan Sch. Mgmt., MIT. Assoc. editor Jour. Advt. Rsch.; mem. editl. bd. Jour. Mktg. Sci.; mem. editl. bd. Jour. Market Rsch.; contbr. numerous articles to Harvard Bus. Rev., Mktg. Scis., others. Active local Boy Scouts am. Ford Found. fellow, 1967 Fellow Royal Statis. Soc.; mem. INFORMS (chmn. mktg. strategy com.), Market Rsch. Coun., Am. Psychol. Assn., European Soc. Mktg. and Opinion Rsch., Am. Mktg. Assn., Inst. Ops. Rsch. and Mgmt. Sci. Office: Silver Creek Farm 2858 N Stout Rd Liberty IN 47353 Business E-Mail: lewpring@direcway.com.

**PRINGLE, ORAN ALLAN,** mechanical and aerospace engineering educator; b. Lawrence, Kan., Sept. 14, 1923; s. Oran Allan and Mae (McClell) P.; m. Billie Hansen, June 25, 1947; children— Allan, Billie, James, Rebecca. BS in Mech. Engring, U. Kan., 1947; MS, U. Wis., 1948, PhD, 1967. Registered profl. engr., Mo. Mech. engr. Black and Veatch (cons. engrs.), Kansas City, Mo., 1947-48; engr. Boeing Airplane Co., Wichita, 1952—; prof. U. Mo., Columbia, 1948—90, prof. emeritus, 1991—. Co-author: Engineering Metallurgy, 1957; contbr. articles to profl. lit. Bd. dirs. United Cerebral Palsy Boone County, Mo. Served with AUS, 1943-45. Ford Found. grantee. Mem. ASME (chmn. fastening and joining com., disting engring. div.), Sigma Xi. Home: 1820 University Ave Columbia MO 65201-6004 Office: Dept Mech and Aerospace Engring U Mo Columbia MO 65201

**PRINGLE, PAUL C.,** lawyer; b. 1943; AB, Dartmouth Coll., 1965; JD, Univ. Mich., 1968. Bar: NY 1969, Calif. 1972. Ptnr. corp. securities Sidley Austin Brown & Wood LLP, San Francisco and LA. Office: Sidley Austin Brown & Wood Ste 2000 555 California St San Francisco CA 94104-1715 Office Phone: 415-772-1249. Office Fax: 415-772-7400. Business E-Mail: ppringle@sidley.com.

**PRINGLE, ROBERT MAXWELL,** diplomat; b. N.Y.C., Nov. 12, 1936; s. Henry Fowles and Helena Huntington (Smith) Pringle; m. Barbara Ann Cade, Sept. 26, 1964; children: James Maxwell, Anne Elizabeth, BA, Harvard U., 1958; PhD, Cornell U., 1967. Dir. econ. policy staff Bur. African Affairs Dept. State, 1981-83; dep. chief mission Ouagadougou, Burkina Faso, 1983-85, Port Moresby, Papua New Guinea, 1985-87; ambassador to Mali, 1987-90; dir. cen. African affairs U.S. Dept. State, 1990-93; dir. ecology and terrestrial conservation U.S. Dept. of State, 1993-95; dir. sr. seminar U.S. Dept. State, 1995-96; dep. chief of mission Dept. State, Pretoria, 1996-99; prof. nat. security policy Nat. War Coll., 1999—2001. Author: Rajahs and Rebels: The Ibans of Sarawak Under Brooke Rule, 1970, Indonesia and the Philippines: American Interests in Island Southwest Asia, 1980, A Short History of Bali, 2004. Mem.: African Studies Assn., Assn. Asian Studies. Avocations: photography, gardening, scuba diving. Home: 216 Wolfe St Alexandria VA 22314-3858 Office Phone: 703-519-8252. E-mail: pringler@post.harvard.edu.

**PRINN, RONALD G.,** atmospheric science educator; b. Hamilton, New Zealand, June 11, 1945; BSc, U. Auckland, New Zealand, 1967, MSc with 1st honors, 1968; ScD, MIT, 1971. Asst. prof. MIT, Cambridge, Mass., 1971-76,

assoc. prof., 1976-82, prof., 1982-93, Tepco prof., 1993—, head dept. earth, atmospheric and planetary scis., 1998—2003. Chair com. on earth sci. NAS, Washington, 1982-84; chair Internat. Global Atmospheric Chemistry Project, Stockholm, 1988-95. Recipient Vernadsky Meml. lectr. Russian Acad. Sci., Moscow, 1984. Fellow Am. Geophys. Union (Macelwane medal 1981), AAAS (chmn. atmospheric and hydrospheric scis. 1999). Office: MIT Bldg 54-1312 Cambridge MA 02139 Business E-Mail: rprinn@mit.edu.

**PRINS, RICHARD T.,** lawyer; b. Grand Rapids, Mich., 1950; BA summa cum laude, Calvin Coll., 1972; JD cum laude, U. Mich., 1977. Bar: NY 1979. Pntr., co-heads investment mgmt. matters, mergers and acquisitions, securities and general corporate matters Skadden, Arps, Slate, Meagher & Flom LLP, NYC. Office: Skadden Arps Slate Meagher & Flom LLP 4 Times Sq New York NY 10036 Office Phone: 212-735-2790. Office Fax: 917-777-2790. Business E-Mail: rprins@skadden.com.

**PRINS, ROBERT JACK,** retired academic administrator; b. Grand Rapids, Mich., Oct. 12, 1932; s. Jacob and Marie (Vanden Brink) P.; m. Ruth Ellen John, Oct. 10, 1950; children: Linda, Douglas, Debra, Nancy, Eric, Sarah. BA, Hope Coll., 1954; DBA, Coll. Emporia, 1974; DHL, Iowa Wesleyan U., 1999. With Mich. Bell Tel. Co., Detroit area, 1954—64, Chesapeake and Potomac Tel. Co., 1964—66; dir. devel. Bethesda Hosp., Denver, 1966-68; v.p. planning and devel. Park Coll., Parkville, Mo., 1969-70; chief adminstrv. officer Coll. of Emporia, Kans., 1970-75; dir. fin. and devel. The Abbey Sch., Canon City, Colo., 1975-79; dir. devel. Kirksville Coll. Osteo. Medicine, Mo., 1979-84; v.p. devel. McKendree Coll., Lebanon, Ill., 1984-86; pres. Iowa Weslyan Coll., Mt. Pleasant, 1986-99, pres. emeritus, 1999—; exec. dir. Internat. Student Svcs., Canon City, Colo., 1999—. Bd. dirs. Iowa Coll. Found., Iowa Commn. on Vol. Svc.; mem. Iowa Assn. Ind. Colls. and Univs.; former chmn., mem. bd. Potomac Worldwide, Taipei, Taiwan. Mem. Nat. Assn. Ind. Colls. and Univs., Coun. for Advancement and Support Edn.

**PRINSTER, GORDON D.,** psychologist; b. St. Charles, Mo., July 4, 1968; s. Gordon David and Elinor Alger Prinster; m. Bernadette Brown, Apr. 13, 1996; 1 child, Callum James. BA in Psychology, U. Mo., 1992; EdD in Sch. Psychology, Seattle U., 1999. Cert. ednl. staff assoc. sch. psychology Wash. State. Counselor WA St Juvenile Rehab. Adminstrn., Snoqualmie, Wash.; sch. psychologist Seattle Pub. Sch, Seattle. Mem.: NASP (assoc.), D-Liberal. Avocations: mountaineering, aviation, travel. Home: 233 Williams Ave N Renton WA 98055 Office: Seattle Pub Sch Seattle WA 98055 Office Phone: 206-250-4673. Personal E-mail: gprinster@yahoo.com.

**PRINZ, RICHARD ALLEN,** surgeon; MD, Loyola U., Chgo., 1972. Diplomate Am. Bd. Surgery, bd. dirs., 1994—. Intern Barnes Hosp., St. Louis, 1972-73, resident in surgery, 1973-74, Loyola U., Chgo., 1974-77, attending surgeon, 1980-93: staff Rush Presbyn.-St. Luke's Med. Ctr., Chgo., 1993—; Helen Shedd Keith prof., chmn. dept. gen. surgery Rush U., Chgo., 1993—. Mem. Am. Surg. Assn., Am. Assn. Endocrine Surgeons (pres. 1996), Midwest Surg. Assn. (pres. 1997), Western Surg. Assn. (treas. 1993-97, pres. 2002-), Chgo. Surg. Soc. (pres.-elect 2002-, pres. 2003). Office: Rush U 818 Proffl Bldg 1725 W Harrison St Chicago IL 60612-3828 Office Phone: 312-942-6511. Business E-Mail: rprinz@rush.edu.

**PRIOR, CORNELIUS BERNARD, JR.,** utilities executive, financial consultant; b. Hartford, Conn., Feb. 26, 1934; s. Cornelius B. Sr. and Katherine (Daly) P.; m. Trudie Yolleck, 1993; children: Elizabeth, Michael, Sarah. AB, Holy Cross Coll., 1956; LLB, Harvard U., 1962. Bar: NY 1963. Assoc. atty. Sullivan and Cromwell, NYC, 1963-68; gen. counsel Private Investment Co. for Asia, Tokyo, 1969-71; v.p. Drexel Firestone, NYC, 1971-75; sr. v.p. Blythe Eastman Dillon, NYC, 1975—78; mng. dir. Paine Webber, NYC, 1978—80, Kidder, Peabody and Co., NYC, 1980-87; chmn. & CEO Atlantic Tele-Network, Inc., St. Thomas, V.I. Bd. dirs. Atlantic Telenetwork Co., St. Thomas. Bd. dirs., trustee Holy Cross Coll.; mem. vis. com. Harvard Law Sch., dean's adv. coun.; trustee, chair capital campaigns Antilles Sch.; chmn. Caribbean Assn. of Nat. Telephone Orgns.; mem. adv. bd. Peter Gruber Found.; trustee, treas., mem. exec. com. Caribbean and C.Am. Action. Served to lt (j.g.) USN, 1956-59. Fulbright scholar, 1962—63. Mem.: Bar Assn. of NY, Univ. Club (NYC). Roman Catholic. Office: Atlantic TeleNetwork Inc PO Box 12030 St Thomas VI 00801 Office Phone: 340-774-2260. E-mail: cbpriorjr@viaccess.net.

**PRIOR, DAVID B.,** academic administrator; m. Anny Prior; children: Kylie, Jonathan. BA, Queen's U. Belfast, No. Ireland, 1964, PhD in Geomorphology, 1968. Dir. Atlantic Geosci. Ctr. Bedford Inst. Oceanography, Halifax; prof. geology and geophysics Tex. A&M U., College Station, 1996—97, dean, 1997—2002, provost 2002—. Fellow: Geol. Soc. London. Office: Office Exec VP and Provost Tex A&M Univ 1248 TAMU College Station TX 77843-1248

**PRIOR, GARY L.,** lawyer; b. Niagara Falls, N.Y., June 26, 1943; s. Harold D. and Adeline Thelma (Lee) Prior; m. Nancy O'Shaughnessy, Aug. 23, 1975; children: Joseph Lee, Julia Elizabeth. BS, Tulane U., 1965; JD, U. Chgo., 1968. Bar: Ill. 1968, U.S. Dist. Ct. (no. dist.), Ill. 1968, U.S. Ct. Appeals (7th cir.) 1973, U.S. Ct. Appeals (3d cir.) 1974, U.S. Trial Bar 1983, U.S. Supreme Ct. 1989, U.S. Dist. Ct. (we. dist.) Wis. 1992, U.S. Dist. Ct. (ea. dist.) Wis. 1993, U.S. Dist. Ct. Minn. 1994, U.S. Ct. Appeals (fed. cir.) 2002. Assoc. Rooks, Pitts, and Poust, Chgo., 1968-71, McDermott, Will, and Emery, Chgo., 1971-74, ptnr, 1974—2002, dir. trial dept. tng., 1980-85, mem. securities approval com., 1986—94, mem. nominating com., chmn., 1988-89, partnership com., 1989-92, mem mgmt. com., 1991-93; of counsel Tabet, DiVito, and Rothstein, LLC, Chgo., 2002—03, ptnr., 2004—. Trustee Prior Family Charitable Found., Furry Friends Found. Mem.: Fed. Cir. Bar Assn., Ill. State Bar Assn., Ill. Appellate Lawyers Assn. Avocations: history, farming, scuba diving. Home: 2512 N Burling St Chicago IL 60614-2510 Office: Tabet DiVito & Rothstein The Rookery 209 S LaSalle Ste 700 Chicago IL 60604 Office Phone: 312-762-9472. Business E-Mail: gprior@tdrlawfirm.com

**PRIOR, JOHN THOMPSON,** pathology educator; b. St. Albans, Vt., Oct. 8, 1917; s. Thomas William and Pauline Thompson Prior; m. Elizabeth Titus Troy, July 24, 1948; children: Anne, Polly, John Jr., Thomas, Jeffrey, Timothy. BS, U. Vt., 1939, MD, 1943. Diplomate Am. Bd. Pathology. Resident in pathology Binghamton (N.Y.) City Hosp., 1946-47; fellow in pathology Syracuse (N.Y.) U. Med. Coll., 1947-49; asst. prof. pathology SUNY, Syracuse, 1949-54, assoc. prof., 1954-63, prof., 1963-72, clin. prof. pathology, 1972—. Active ARC Blood Bank, Syracuse, 1966-70; pres. N.Y. State Assoc. Lab., Syracuse, 1959-60; med. dir. PSRO Ctrl. N.Y., Syracuse, 1983-84; mem. N.Y. State Hosp. Rev. & Planning Assn., Albany, 1980-82; bd. dirs. Am. Med. Peer Rev. Assn., 1985-90. Contbr. articles to profl. jours. Bd. dirs. Lung Assn. Ctrl. N.Y., Syracuse, 1994—. Col. M.C., U.S. Army, 1944-77. Decorated Bronze Star, Silver Star, Legion of Merit, Belgian Croix de Guerre; recipient William Hammond Citation, N.Y. State Jour. Medicine, N.Y.C., 1984, Disting. Alumnus award U. Vt., Burlington, 1994. Mem. Onondaga County Med. Soc. (pres. 1958), dir. disting. svc. award 1987). Avocations: golf, tennis. Home: 4615 Pewter Ln Manlius NY 13104-9329

**PRIOR, MARK,** professional baseball player; b. San Diego, Calif., Sept. 7, 1980; Attended, Vanderbilt, 1998—99; MBA, U. So. Calif., 2001. Pitcher Chgo. Cubs, 2002—. Named to NL All-Star Team, 2003; recipient Golden Spikes award for Best Coll. Baseball Player, 2001. Office: Chgo Cubs Wrigley Field 1060 W Addisson Chicago IL 60613*

**PRIOR, WILLIAM ALLEN,** electronics company executive; b. Benton Harbor, Mich., Jan. 14, 1927; s. Allen Ames and Madeline Isabel (Taylor) P.; m. Nancy Norton Sayles, July 5, 1951 (div. Oct. 1971); children: Stephanie Sayles, Alexandra Taylor, Robert Eames, Eleanor Norton; m. Carol Luise Becker-Ehmck, Oct. 30, 1971; children: Michael Becker-Ehmck, Jeffrey Renner. AB in Physics, Harvard Coll., 1950, MBA, 1954. Salesman IBM, Mineola, L.I., NY, 1950-52; sales engr. Lincoln Electric Co., Cleve., 1954-57; ptnr. Hammond Kennedy & Co., N.Y.C., 1957-66; v.p. The Singer Co.,

N.Y.C., 1967-68; pres. Tansitor Electronics, Bennington, Vt., 1969-71, Aerotron Inc., Raleigh, NC, 1971-82; v.p. J. Lee Peeler & Co., Durham, NC, 1986-89; pres. Accudyne, Inc., Raleigh, 1990-99. Chmn. Royal Blue Capital, Inc., Raleigh; bd. dirs. NeoDyne, Inc., Raleigh. Cpl. USAAF, 1945-46, Germany. Mem. IEEE, North Ridge Country Club (Raleigh), Raleigh Racquet Club, Harvard Club of N.Y.C., 50 Group. Republican. Avocations: tennis, skiing, computer programming. Home: 329 Meeting House Cir Raleigh NC 27615-3133 Personal E-mail: wprior@mbal954.hbs.edu.

**PRIORE, CHRISTOPHER ANSELMO,** artist; b. Buffalo, Apr. 28, 1959; s. Robert Michael and Annetta Anselmo Priore. Studied, Tyler Sch. Art/Temple U., Rome, 1979—80; BFA, Carnegie Mellon U., Pitts., 1981. One-man shows include Pitts. Ctr. for the Arts, 1990, Searfone Gallery, U. Tampa, Fla., 1994, E.M. Donahue, NYC, 1997, Cardozo Gallery, Benjamin N. Cardozo Sch. Law, Yeshiva U., NYC, 2000, Museo ItaloAmericano, San Francisco, 2004, Italian Am. Mus., NYC, 2004, The McKinney Ave. Contemporary, Dallas, 2005, exhibited in group shows at Carnegie Mus. Art, Pitts., 1986, So. Alleghenies Mus. Art, Loretto, Pa., 1988, Albright-Knox Art Gallery, Buffalo, NY, 1990, Fukuya Art Gallery, Hiroshima, Japan, 1995, Kunstun Technik, Berlin, 1998, L Gallery, Moscow, 1998, Del. Ctr. for Contemp. Arts, Wilmington, 2003, Kim Foster Gallery, NYC, 2005, prin. works include "SKY", The Pitts. Children's Mus., 1988—98, "Rise!", MTA NYC Transit, 1997—98, Represented in permanent collections Singer's Forum, NYC, Westinghouse Energy Ctr., Monroeville, Pa., Italian Am. Mus., N.Y.C. Grantee, Richard King Mellon Found., 1988, Eben Demarest Trust, 1988, 1991, N.Y. Found. Arts. Artist Sponsorship Program, 1997—98, 1999. Democrat. Roman Catholic. Avocations: weightlifting, swimming. Studio: 579 Fort Washington Ave Ste 3E New York NY 10033 Office Phone: 212-568-2836. E-mail: christopherpriore@earthlink.net.

**PRIORY, RICHARD BALDWIN,** former electric power industry executive; b. Lakehurst, N.J., May 15, 1946; s. Joseph Albert Jr. and Betty (Baldwin) P.; m. Joan Ellen Rourke, May 30, 1968; children: Jennifer Joan, Richard Baldwin Jr. BSCE magna cum laude, W.Va. Inst. Tech., 1969; MS in Engring., Princeton U., 1973; grad. utility exec. program, U. Mich., 1982; grad. advanced mgmt. program, Harvard U., 1991. Registered profl. engr., N.C., S.C. Design engr., project engr. Union Carbide Corp., 1969-72; asst. prof. structural engring. U. N.C., Charlotte, 1973-76; design engr. Duke Power Co., Charlotte, N.C., 1976-78, prin. engr., 1978-81, mgr. project mgmt. divsn., 1981-84, v.p. design engring., 1984-88, sr. v.p. generation and info. svcs., 1988-91, exec. v.p. power generation group, 1991-94, pres., COO 1994-97; chmn., CEO Duke Energy Corp. (formerly Duke Power Co.), Charlotte, 1997—2003. Bd. dirs. Duke Energy Corp., Dana Corp., EEI AEIC; mem. Duke Fluor Daniel Mgmt. Com. Bd. visitors U. N.C., Charlotte; past chmn. bd. dirs. Charlotte-Mecklenburg Edn. Found.; pres., bd. trustees Discovery Place, Inc., 1992-93; past mem. Charlotte-Mecklenburg Pub. Broadcasting Found.; vice chmn. campaign drive United Way Ctrl. Carolinas, Inc., 1990; adv. coun. N.C. Alliance for Competitive Technologies. Mem. ASCE, Nat. Acad. Engring, Charlotte Engrs. Club. Avocation: golf.

**PRISCHMANN GRYNIEWICZ, DEBORAH ANNE,** voice educator, vocalist; d. Richard D. Prischmann and Carole Anne Frascone; m. Ronald Joseph Gryniewicz, Mar. 13, 1962. B in Music Edn., U. Ariz., 1979; MusM in Opera/Vocal Pedagogy, Temple U., 1985. Cert. N.J. Dept. Edn., 1984. Vocal solo artist Jubilant Voice Ministry, Doylestown, Pa., 1990—; dir., instr. Meadow Lark Vocal Studio, Doylestown, 1990—; vocalist in Voices of Pops Peter Nero and the Philly Pops, Phila., 2001—; prof. voice U. of the Arts, Phila., 2005—. Gen. music tchr. Lebanon (N.J.) Boro Sch., 1987—91; dir. music Washington's Crossing (Pa.) United Meth. Ch., 1987—88; youth chorus dir. Musica Arts Acad., Doylestown, 1997—99; musical vocal dir. Ctrl. Bucks West H.S., Doylestown, 1998—99; worship leader Doylestown United Meth. Ch., 1999—2001; vocal worship cons. Calvary Chapel, Chalfont, Pa., 2001—03; vocal clinician William Penn H.S., Newark, 2004—04. Composer: (solo debut vocal album) Light My Way, (vocal solo album) Deborah - Christmas at America's Keswick - live!, (solo vocal contemporary christian album) The Me God Sees, (solo contemporary christian album) The Way, The Truth, The Life. Dir. music Ctrl. Schwenkfelder Ch., Worcestor, Pa., 1979—82. Finalist Outstanding Sr. award, U. Ariz., 1979; recipient Ruby Sword of Honor for outstanding leadership, Sigma Alpha Iota, 1979, Grad. Tchg. Assistantship, Temple U., 1980; Full Gen. Music scholar, U. Ariz., 1976. Mem.: ASCAP, Nat. Assn. Tchrs. Singing (vocal adjudicator 1992—93). Republican. Avocations: travel, equestrian, gardening, birdwatching. Office: University of the Arts 320 South Broad St Philadelphia PA 19102 Office Phone: 215-717-6000.

**PRISCO, DOROTHY DESTENO,** academic administrator; b. Hoboken, N.J., Jan. 27, 1942; d. Dominick and Martha (Balacco) DeSteno; m. Salvatore Prisco, July 15, 1967; 1 child, Lisa Natalie. BA, Bard Coll., 1964; MA, Jersey City Stat Coll., 1968; MS, U. Ala., Tuscaloosa, 1975; EdD, Rutgers U., 1983. Cert. English tchr., N.J. Tchr. English, Sacred Heart Acad., Hoboken, N.J., 1964-65, North Bergen (N.J.) High Sch., 1965-69, Tuscaloosa Acad., 1969-70; editor, copywriter McCall's Needlework and Crafts mag., N.Y.C., 1974-77; mem. faculty and divsn. chmn. Centenary Coll., Hackettstown, NJ, 1977—84, exec. asst. to pres., 1985—86, v.p. acad. affairs and dean coll., 1986—92, Wesley Coll., Dover, Del., 1992—97, Gwynedd-Mercy Coll., Gwynedd Valley, Pa., 1997—2000; dean sch. grad. and continuing studies, Coll. St. Elizabeth, Morristown, NJ, 2000—. Manuscript cons. Prentice Hall and John Wiley Pub., N.Y.C., 1983-86; mem. evaluation team Mid. States Assn., Phila., 1991—; lectr. series in the humanities funded by N.J. Dept. Higher Edn., 1985-86. Co-author: Fashion Merchandise Information, 1986; contbg. author: (Elizabeth Carteret biography) in Past and Promise: Lives of N.J. Women, 1990; mem. editorial bd. Nat. Assn. Women in Edn., 1991—93. Coord. community svc. Centenary Coll. and United Meth. Ch., Hackettstown, 1989-91. Recipient Disting. Svc. award Rutgers U., 1989; grantee United Meth. Ch., 1989 90, N.J. Dept. Higher Edn., 1989 90, Roncleo Corp., 1990. Mem. Coun. Ind. Colls. (program participant 1991—), Am. Coun. on Edn. (rep. to nat. identification program for advancement women in higher edn. adminstrn. 1985—), Rutgers U. Grad. Sch. Edn. Alumni Assn. (pres. 1991-92). Office: Coll St Elizabeth 2 Convent Rd Morristown NJ 07960

**PRISELAC, THOMAS M.,** health facility executive, educator; BA in Biology, Washington & Jefferson Coll.; MPH Health Svcs. Adminstrn. and Planning, U. Pitts. Asst. adminstr. Cedars-Sinai Med. Ctr., L.A., 1979—81, assoc. adminstr., 1981—82, sr. assoc. adminstr., 1982—83, v.p adminstrn., 1983—85, sr. v.p. ops., 1985—91, exec. v.p., COO, 1988—94, pres., CEO, 1994—. Adj. lectr. UCLA Sch. Pub. Health; tchr., principles of orgn. leadership Master of Pub. Health for Health Professionals; past chmn. Coun. of Teaching Hosp. of Assn. of Am. Med. Coll.; chmn. Calif. Healthcare Assn., Healthcare Assn. of Southern Calif.; bd. dirs. Am. Hosp. Assn., VHA, Inc., Nat. Com. for Quality Healthcare, Calif. Healthcare Found.; lectr. in field. Bd. dirs. Blue Cross Calif. Office: Cedars Sinai Med Ctr 8700 Beverly Blvd Rm 2628 Los Angeles CA 90048 Address: UCLA Sch Pub Health Dept Health Services Box 951772 Los Angeles CA 90095-1772 Office Phone: 310-423-5711, 310-206-3435. Office Fax: 310-423-0120, 310-206-4722. Business E-Mail: tmp@cshs.org.*

**PRISINZANO, THOMAS EDWARD,** chemistry professor, researcher; b. NYC, July 19, 1973; s. Paul Robert and Eileen Gilleece Prisinzano; m. Deanna Olech Olech, Sept. 30, 1973; children: Sara Marie, Joseph Paul. BS, U. Del., Newark, 1995; PhD, Va. Commonwealth U., Richmond, 2000. Grad. asst. Va. Commonwealth U., 1995—2000; asst. prof. U. Iowa, Iowa City, 2003—. Faculty mem. U. Biocatalysis and Bioprocessing, Iowa City, 2003—, U. Iowa Pain Rsch. Program, 2003—. Co-author: (textbook) Comprehensive Medicinal Chemistry Second Edition, Recipient J. Doyle Smith award, Va. Commonwealth U. Sch. Pharmacy, 1998, Early Career Investigator award, Coll. Problems Drug Dependence, 2003, D. John Faulkner award, Am. Soc. Pharmacognosy, 2005, Travel award, Internat. Narcotics Rsch. Conf., 2005; fellow, Nat. Inst. Diabetes and Digestive and Kidney Diseases, 2000—03; grantee, Nat. Inst. Drug Abuse, 2005. Mem.: Internat. Narcotics Rsch. Conf., Soc. Neurosci., Am. Assn. Pharm. Scientists, Coll.

Problems Drug Dependence, Am. Soc. Pharmacognosy, Am. Chem. Soc., Theta Xi (life). Roman Catholic. Achievements include patents pending for Novel Opioid Receptor Ligands; discovery of Novel Scaffold for Mu Opioid Receptor Ligands; Mu Opioid with Altered Receptor Regulation; research in Method for the Detection of Salvinorin A in Biological Fluids; patents pending for Novel Opiate Agonists That Do Not Promote Receptor Regulation as Analgesics with Limited Tolerance Liability. Office: U Iowa 115 S Grand Ave Iowa City IA 52242 Office Phone: 319-335-6920. Office Fax: 319-335-8766. E-mail: thomas-prisinzano@uiowa.edu.

**PRISSEL, BARBARA ANN,** paralegal, law educator; b. Plum City, Wis., July 7, 1946; d. John Henry and Mary Ann Louise (Dankers) Seipel; m. Stephen Joseph Prissel, Dec. 16, 1967; children: Angela, Benjamin. Grad. with honors, Mpls. Bus. Coll., 1966; at, Moraine Park Tech. Coll., 1983— Cert. interactive TV, adult edn. instr. Legal sec. Mott, Grose, Von Holtum & Hefferan, Mpls., 1966-67, Whelan, Morey & Morey Attys. at Law, Durand, Wis., 1967-70, Murry Law Office, River Falls, Wis., 1968-70, Potter, Wefel & Nettesheim, Wisconsin Rapids, Wis., 1970-71; paralegal Kilgore Law Office, Ripon, Wis., 1985—2004; sec. to adminstr. Moraine Park Tech. Coll., Fond du Lac, Wis., 1971—72; legal sec. instr., 1995—. Chmn. legal adv. com. Moraine Park Tech. Coll., Fond du Lac, 1996-98, mem. adminstrv. assts. adv. com., 1984-86, mem. legal adv. commn. 1984-. Contbr. poems to newspapers. Ch. rep. Ch. Women United, Ripon, 1984-87; pianist Christian Women's Orgn., Ripon, 1985-95; pianist, organist Our Lady of Lake Ch., Green Lake, Wis., 1987—. Mem.: NAFE, Legal Profls. Assn. (East Ctrl. Wis. pres. 1994—95, sec. 1995—96, chmn. Day-In-Ct. 1999, NALS Fedn. liaison 2000—02, sec. 2001—02, state legal edn. task force 2003—04, v.p. 2003—04, pres. 2003—, v.p East Ctrl. Wis. chpt. 2004—, chmn. edn. liaison com., Legal award of Excellence 1995—96), Wis. Assn. Legal Profession (state legal edn. liaison com. 1997—98, state legal edn. task force 2003—04, ann. meeting com. mem. 2005, mem. nominations and elections com. 2005—06), Nat. Assn. Legal Profession, Nat. Women's History Mus. Roman Catholic. Avocations: teaching and playing piano, creative writing, cooking, swimming, exercising. Home: 129 Wolverton Ave Ripon WI 54971-1144

**PRITCHARD, BENJAMIN CHADWICK,** music educator; s. Claude Chadwick and Christal Carol Pritchard; m. Christina Marie Caiazzo, Oct. 5, 2002. MusB in Music Edn., Shenandoah U., 1999, M Music Edn., 2001. Cert. tchr. Pa., Va. Prof. music Shenandoah U. Music Conservatory, Winchester, Va., 2001; band dir. grades 3-8 Future Musicians Inc., Cranford, NJ, 2001—02; band dir. grades 7-8 Stroudsburg (Pa.) Area Sch. Dist., 2002—; asst. HS marching band dir. Stroudsburg Area Sch. Dist., 2002—, jr. HS jazz band dir., 2002—. Pvt. saxophone instr., 2002—; pvt. jazz piano instr., 2002—. Mem.: Pa. State Educators Assn., Pa. Music Educators Assn., Kappa Kappa Psi (life; v.p. 2001—02).

**PRITCHARD, CLAUDIUS HORNBY, JR.,** retired university president; b. Charleston, W.Va., June 28, 1927; s. Claudius Hornby and Katherine (Ellison) P.; m. Marjorie Walker Pullen, Aug. 9, 1952; children: Virginia Aiken, Katherine Winston, Olivia Reynolds, Claudius V. BA, Hampden-Sydney Coll., 1950; MA, Longwood U., 1965; PhD, Fla. State U., 1971. Comml. loan teller Am. Nat. Bank and Trust Co., Danville, Va., 1950-53; asst. cashier Planters Bank & Trust Co., Farmville, Va., 1953-55; asst. to pres. Hampden-Sydney (Va.) Coll., 1955-57, bus. mgr. and treas., 1957-67, v.p. devel., 1967-71; sr. budget analyst-edn. State of Fla., Tallahassee, 1971-72; pres. Sullins Coll., Bristol, Va., 1972-76; v.p adminstrn. Maryville U., St. Louis, 1976-77, pres., 1977-92, pres. emeritus, 1992—. Adv. dir. Commerce Bank of St. Louis, 1982—92. Author: Col. D. Wyatt Aiken (1828-1887) South Carolina's Militant Agrarian, 1970; contbr. articles to profl. jours. Mem. bd. visitors Charleston So. U., 1993—2005; chmn. Summerville Comml. Design Rev. Bd., 1999—; bd. dirs. West St. Louis County YMCA, Chesterfield, Mo., 1985—92. With USNR, 1945—46. Fla. State U. fellow, 1969-70, Arthur Vining Davis fellow Am. Council on Edn., 1974; recipient Disting. Svc. award Charleston Southern U., 2000; named Citizen of Year Chesterfield, Md., 1986. Mem. AAUP, SCV, Am. Assn. Higher Edn., So. Hist. Assn., S.C. Hist. Soc., Mo. Colls. Fund (bd. dirs., chmn. 1987-88), Mil. Order of the Stars and Bars, Ind. Colls. and Univs. Mo., Chesterfield C. of C. (pres. 1987, Chesterfield Citizen of Yr. award 1986), Rotary. Republican. Presbyterian.

**PRITCHARD, DALTON HAROLD,** retired electronics executive; b. Crystal Springs, Miss., Sept. 1, 1921; s. Cecil Harold and Marvie Prudence (Lofton) P.; m. Caroline Ann Hnatuk, Apr. 27, 1947; 1 child, Mary Ann Pritchard Poole. BSE.E., Miss. State U., 1943; postgrad., Harvard, MIT Radar Sch., 1943-44. Mem. tech. staff RCA Labs., Riverhead, NY, 1946-50, mem. tech. staff Princeton, NJ, 1950-75, fellow tech. staff, 1975-87. Session chmn., mem. program com. Internat. Conf. on Consumer Electronics, Chgo., 1980-85 Contbr. articles to profl. jours.; patentee in field. Mem. N.J. Gov.'s Sci. Adv. Council, Princeton, 1981-85. Served to capt. U.S. Army Signal Corps Decorated Bronze Star; recipient Eduard Rhein prize Edward Rhein Found., Berlin, Fed. Republic of Germany, 1980; Disting. Engring. fellow Miss. State U., 1991. Fellow IEEE (Vladimir Zworykin award 1977, David Sarnoff award 1981), Soc. Info. Display, Nat. Assn. Engrs., Nat. Acad. Engring., Sigma Xi, Tau Beta Pi, Kappa Mu Epsilon Republican. Baptist. Avocations: amateur radio, tennis. Home: 3 Bent Tree Ln Hilton Head Island SC 29926-1906 Office Phone: 843-681-3904.

**PRITCHARD, DAVID EDWARD,** physics professor; b. NYC, Oct. 15, 1941; m. Andrea Hasler; children: Orion, Alexander. BS, Calif. Inst. Tech., 1962; PhD, Harvard U., 1968. Postdoctoral fellow MIT, Cambridge, Mass., 1968, instr., 1968-70, asst. prof., 1970-75, assoc. prof., 1975-80, prof., 1980—, Cecil and Ida Chair, 2001—. Vis. scientist Stanford Rsch. Inst., 1975; vis. prof. U. Paris Sud Orsay, 1983; disting. visitor Joint Inst. for Lab. Astrophysics, 1989, 98, mem subpanel, 1990 91, chmn., 1994, co chair First Quantum Electronic and Laser Sci. Conf., 1989; chair Internat. Conf. on Atomic Physics, 2002; Selby Travelling lectr. of Australia, 04. Div. assoc. editor Phys. Rev. Letters, 1983-88; contbr. articles to profl. jours. Polaroid fellow Harvard U., 1962-63, NSF predoctoral fellow, 1963-68. Fellow: AAAS, Optical Soc. Am. (bd. dirs. 1998—2001, Max Born award 2004), Am. Acad. Arts and Scis., Am. Phys. Soc. (disting. traveling lectr. laser sci. topical group 1992—94, rep. steering com. laser sci. topical group, rep. joint coun. on quantum electronics, Broida prize 1991, Centennial spkr. 1999, Schawlow prize 2003); mem.: NAS, Am. Assn. Physics Tchrs. (rsch. in physics edn. com.), Effective Educational Tech., Inc. (co-founder), Tiverton Yacht Club (R.I.). Avocations: sailing, carpentry. Home: 88 Washington Ave Cambridge MA 02140-2708 Office: MIT Rm 26-241 Dept Physics Cambridge MA 02139 Office Phone: 617-253-6812. Business E-Mail: dpritch@mit.edu.

**PRITCHARD, ELSIE TOMLINSON,** librarian; b. Dothan, Ala., Nov. 14, 1947; d. Eugene and Merle (Coleman) Tomlinson; m. Robert Donald Pritchard II, Dec. 23, 1966; children: Claire, Alison. BS, Old Dominion U., 1969; MLS, U. Miss., 1972; MusM, Morehead State U., 1990. Tech. svcs. libr. Boston Conservatory, 1978-79; music cataloger Morehead (Ky.) State U., 1972-78, 82-86, acquisitions libr., 1986-92; head libr. Camden Sch. Svcs., 1993—2005, dean libr. svc., 2005—. Elder Morehead Presbyn. Ch., 1982—. Mem. ALA, Ky. Libr. Assn., Assn. Coll. and Rsch. Librs. Office: Camden Carroll Libr Morehead St # U Morehead KY 40351

**PRITCHARD, HUW OWEN,** chemist, educator; b. Bangor, Wales, July 23, 1928; s. Owen and Lilian Venetia P.; m. Margaret Ramsden, Nov. 3, 1956; children— Karen, David. B.Sc., U. Manchester, 1948, M.Sc., 1949, PhD, 1951, D.Sc., 1964. Asst. lectr. chemistry Manchester (Eng.) U., 1951-54, lectr., 1954-65; prof. chemistry York U., Ont., Can., 1965-97, prof. emeritus Can., 1997—. Contbr. articles to profl. jours. Fellow: Royal Soc. Can. Office: Chemistry Dept York Univ Toronto ON Canada M3J 1P3 Business E-Mail: huw@yorku.ca.

**PRITCHARD, JOHN F.,** lawyer; b. Libertyville, Ill., Jan. 20, 1943; BA, Yale U., 1965; JD, U. Calif., Berkeley, 1968. Bar: N.Y. 1970. Ptnr., leader Litigation practice Pillsbury Winthrop Shaw Pittman, NYC. Articles editor

Calif. Law Review, 1966-68. Office: Pillsbury Winthrop Shaw Pittman 1540 Broadway New York NY 10036 Office Phone: 212-858-1620. Office Fax: 212-858-1500. Business E-mail: john.pritchard@pillsburylaw.com.

**PRITCHARD, KATHLEEN JO,** not-for-profit association administrator; b. Milw., Feb. 6, 1951; d. Owen J. and Madelon (Coogan) P.; m. William A. Durkin Jr., Oct. 22, 1982; children: Elizabeth Durkin, Christine Durkin, W. Ryan Durkin. BA in Anthropology, U. Wis., Oshkosh, 1973; MA in Pub. Adminstrn., U. Wis., 1980; PhD in Polit. Sci., U. Wis., Milw., 1986. Rsch. analyst Wis. Coun. on Criminal Justice, Madison, 1974-77; planning analyst Wis. Dept. Health and Social Svcs., Madison, 1977-80; assoc. lectr. U. Wis., Milw., 1980-89; vis. asst. prof. Marquette U., Milw., 1986, 90-91; policy cons. dept. adminstrn. City of Milw., 1992; Outcomes Project dir. United Way of Greater Milw., 1992-96, dir. impact and evaluation, 1997—; chmn. United Way of Am. Forum on Outcomes II, 1997. Faculty advisor Model OAS, UN advisor, Milw., 1986-91; campus rep. adv. Wis. Inst. for Study of War, Peace and Global Cooperation, Milw., 1989-90; mem. United Way Am. Task Force on Impact, 1995—; instr. Nat. Acad. Volunteerism, 1996; bd. dirs. North Shore Fire Dept. Contbr. articles to profl. jours., chpts. to books Dir. cmty impact United Way of Greater Milw., 1998; trustee Pub. Policy Forum, 2000—, NonProfit Mgmt. Fund, 2000—03, NonProfit Mgmt. Edn. Ctr., 2000—03; pres. Whitefish Bay Village, 2002—; dir. cmty. impact, product devel. United Way Am.; mem. exec. coun. Met. Milw. Sewerage Dist.; mem. Lakefront Devel. Com., 2004—; bd. dirs. North Shore Fire Dept., 2005—; mem. exec. steering com. Partnership for Healthy Milw., 2001—04; bd. dirs. Counseling Ctr. of Greater Milw., 2004—, Planning Coun. for Health & Human Svcs. Recipient Alice Paul Dissertation award Women's Caucus for Polit. Sci., 1984; Grad. Sch. fellow U. Wis., Milw., 1983, fellow Kenyon Coll. Summer Inst., 1983. Mem. Phi Kappa Phi (chpt. officer 1989). Personal E-mail: pritchardkj@aol.com.

**PRITCHARD, LLEWELYN GEORGE,** lawyer; b. NYC, Aug. 13, 1937; s. Llewelyn and Anne Mary (Streib) P.; m. Joan Ashby, June 20, 1959; children: David Ashby, Jennifer Pritchard Vick, Andrew Harrison, William Llewellyn. AB with honors, Drew U., 1958; LLB, Duke U., 1961. Ptnr. Helsell & Fetterman, Seattle. Trustee Allied Arts Found., pres. 2005—; pres., trustee, corp. counsel Allied Arts Seattle, 1973-76; dir. Fifth Ave. Theatre, 2005-; trustee Meth. Ednl. Found., 1970-85, pres.; 1991-92; life trustee PONCHO Patrons of Pacific N.W. Civil, Cultural and Charitable Orgns., pres., 1972-73; bd. dirs. Planned Parenthood of Seattle/King County, 1972-78; trustee Seattle Symphony Orch., 1979-83, chmn. bd., 1980-82, life trustee; trustee U. Puget Sound., 1972-99, exec. com., 1973-96, chmn. bd. visitors to Law Sch., 1984-88; trustee Mus. of Glass, 2000—; chancellor Pacific N.W. Ann. conf. United Meth. Ch. 1969—. Fellow Am. Bar Found. (life, state chmn. 1988-98); mem. ABA (state del. 1982-86, bd. govs. 1986-89, chmn. program com. 1988-89, exec. com. 1988-89, Ho. of Dels. 1979—, nat. dir. young lawyers divsn. 1971, chmn. sect. of individual rights and responsibilities 1975-76, exec. coun. family law sect. 2002-05, chair standing com. on legal aid and indigent defendants 1973-75, chair legal needs study 1995-98, chair adv. com. to pro bono immigration project 1991-01, dir. Ctr. for Human Rights 2001-), Commn. Rule of Law Initiatives, Wash. State Bar Assn. (bd. govs. King County 1972-75), King County Bar Assn. (chair young lawyers sect. 1970). Avocations: reading, art collector. Home: 5229 140th Ave NE Bellevue WA 98005-1024 Office: Helsell & Fetterman 1001 Fourth Ave Ste 4200 Seattle WA 98154 Office Phone: 206-292-1144. Business E-Mail: lpritchard@helsell.com.

**PRITCHARD, SARAH MARGARET,** library director; b. Boston, Feb. 8, 1955; d. Wilbur Louis and Kathleen Hunton (Moss) P.; m. Timothy John Brennan, Aug. 20, 1977 (div. 1993); m. Neal Edward Blair, July 15, 2005. BA, U. Md., 1975; MA in French, U. Wis., 1976, MLS, 1977. Intern Libr. Congress, Washington, 1977-78, reference specialist in women's studies, 1978-88, head microform reading rm., 1988-90; sr. program officer Assn. Rsch. Librs., Washington, 1990-91; assoc. exec. dir., 1991-92; acad. libr. mgmt. intern Coun on Libr. Resources Princeton U., NJ, 1988-89; dir. librs. Smith Coll., Northampton, Mass., 1992-99; univ. libr. U. Calif., Santa Barbara, 1999—2006; libr. Northwestern U., Evanston, Ill., 2006—. Editl. advisor Women's Rsch. and Edn. Inst., Washington, 1987-92; bd. dirs. Western Mass. Regional Libr. Sys., 1997-98; bd. dirs. U. Calif. So. Regional Libr. Facility, Gold Coast Libr. Network, Libr. Calif.; mem. steering com. Scholarly Pub. and Academic Resources Coalition, 2006—. *Sarah Pritchard is widely active in regional and national library consortia and associations. She is the author of over sixty articles, reviews, and compilations and serves on many editorial boards and grant review panels. She has lectured and consulted in North America, Europe, and Asia on library management, electronic services, collection development, women's studies, and other professional issues.* Editor: The Women's Annual, 1984; compiler ARL Stats., 1990-92; contbr. articles to profl. jours.; mem. editl. bd. Jour. Acad. Librarianship, 1993-99, Portal: Libr. and the Acad., 2000—; contbg. editor Libr. Issues, 1994-99. Trustee Leroy C. Merritt Humanitarian Fund, 1991-94. Named Wis. Alumni Rsch. Found. fellow, 1975-77, Outstanding Alumna U. Wis. Sch. of Libr. and Info. Studies, 1997. Mem. ALA (chair machine assisted reference sect. 1986-87, chair women's studies sect. 1989-90, coun. 1990-98, 2000-2004, chair stds. com. 1998-2002, chair ethics com. 2002-06, Equality award 1997), Scholarly Pub. and Academic Resources Coalition (mem. steering com. 2006—), Nat. Women's Studies Assn., Cosmos Club. Democrat. Office: Northwestern Univ Libr Evanston IL 60208

**PRITCHARD, THERESE D.,** lawyer; AB, Bryn Mawr Coll., 1975; JD, Boston Coll., 1978. Bar: Mass. 1978. Asst. dir. Enforcement SEC, 1990—91; dep. chief counsel for enforcement Office of Thrift Supervision, 1991—94; ptnr., group leader Securities Enforcement, Compliance and Litig. Bryan Cave LLP, Washington, DC. Office: Bryan Cave LLP 700 Thirteenth Street NW Washington DC 20005 Office Phone: 202-508-6252. E-mail: tdpritchard@bryancave.com.

**PRITCHARD, WILLIAM H.,** literature educator, writer; AB, Amherst Coll., 1953; MA, Harvard Univ., 1956, PhD, 1960. Henry Clay Folger prof. of English Amherst Coll. Author: (books) Wyndham Lewis, 1968, W.B. Years, 1972, Seeing Through Everything: English Writers 1918-1940, 1977, Frost: A Literary Life Reconsidered, 1984, Randall Jarrell: A Literary Life, 1990, Playing It By Ear: Literary Essays & Reviews, 1994, English Papers: A Teaching Life, 1995, Under Criticism: Essays for William H. Pritchard, 1998, Talking Back to Emily Dickinson & Other Essays, 1998, Lives of the Modern Poets, 1980, 1997, Updike: America's Man of Letters, 2000, 2005, Shelf Life: Literary Essays and Reviews, 2003. Fellow: Am. Acad. Arts & Sci. Office: Dept English Amherst College Amherst MA 01002-5000 Office Phone: 413-542-2000. Business E-Mail: whpritchard@amherst.edu.

**PRITCHARD, WILLIAM ROY,** former university systems administrator; b. Portage, Wis., Nov. 15, 1924; s. William Roy and Lillian Edith (Roberts) P.; m. Deanna Elaine Pritchard; children: Rosan June, William Roy, Caryl Jean, Alyn Evan, Cynthia Bedeau. Student, U. Wis., 1942-43; DVM, Kans. State U., 1946; PhD, U. Minn., 1953; JD, Ind. U., 1957; DSc (hon.), Kans. State U., 1970, Tufts U., 1988, Purdue U., 1977, U. Guelph, 1998. Asst. prof. U. Wis., 1946-49; assoc. prof. U. Minn., 1949-53; prof. U. Minn., 1949-53; prof., head vet. sci. U. Fla., 1957-61; assoc. dir. Vet. Med. Rsch. Inst., Ia. State U., 1961-62; assoc. dir. Agrl. Expt. Sta., 1962-72; coord. internat. agrl. programs U. Calif. system, 1977-81. Vis. fellow Woodrow Wilson Sch. Pub. and Internat. Affairs, Princeton, 1968-69; John Thomson lectr. U. Queensland, 1966; co-dir. nat. vet. edn. program Duke U., 1987-92; spl. research hemmorrhagic disease animals. Cons. Dept. Agr., Def. Dept., USPHS, Va, Calif. Dept. Health, FDA, 1962-97; bd. cons. agr. Rockefeller Found., 1962-66; nat. med. cons. surgeon gen. 1962-64; mem. FAO/WHO Expert Panel Vet. Edn., Pres.'s Sci. Adv. Com. Panel World Food Supply, 1966-67, President's Sci. Adv. Com. Panel Biology and Med. Sci., 1969-70, Joint Rsch. Com. Bd. Internat. Food and Agr. AID, 1977-81; Recognition lectr. Assn. Am. Vet. Med. Colls., 2005. With U.S. Army, 1942-44. Recipient Gov. Fla. award, 1961, Disting. Svc. award Kans. State U., 1963, Outstanding

Achievement award U. Minn., 1976, Disting. Pub. Svc. award U. Calif., Davis, 1991, Gold Headed Cane award Am. Soc. Vet. Epidemiology, 1992. Mem. AAAS, APHA, Am. Vet. Med. Assn. (Internat. Vet. Congress award 1988), Nat. Acad. of Practice in Vet. Medicine (elected 1986), Am. Soc. Vet. Epidemiologists, Conf. of Pub. Health Vets. (hon. life), U.S. Animal Health Assn., Nat. Assn. State Univs. and Land-Grant Colls. (internat. affairs com. 1965-70), Order of Coif, Sigma Xi, Phi Zeta, Gamma Alpha. Home: 2409 Madrid Ct Davis CA 95616-0141

**PRITCHARD WOOD, GRACE RUTH,** elementary school educator; b. Oakland, Calif., May 11, 1956; d. James Henry and Gloria Ethel Pritchard. BS in Elem. Edn., U. Colo., 1978; MEd, U. Ariz. West, 2002. Cert. tchr. K-8 State of Ariz., 1988, Nat. Bd. Profl. Tchg. Stds., 2000. Tchr. k-8 Schoolhouse for Homeless Children, Phoenix, 1988—92; tchr. 4th grade Wash. Elem. Dist., 1992—, tchr. English lang. learners tng., cadre leader mentoring program for 2d yr. tchrs., mem. reading curriculum com. Asst. prof. Ariz. State U. West, Glendale, 2003—; mem. Alta Vista Site Coun., 2003—04, mem. leadership team, 2004—. Recipient Plight of the Little Ones award, B'nai Brith, 1989. Mem.: ASCD, Nat. Coun. Tchrs. Math., Internat. Reading Assn. Democrat. Avocation: reading. Office: Alta Vista Elem Sch 8710 N 31st Ave Phoenix AZ 85051 Office Phone: 602-347-2070. Office Fax: 602-347-2020. Personal E-mail: gwoodfleming@aol.com. E-mail: gwood@av.wesd.k12.az.us.

**PRITCHETT, DANIEL R.,** music educator; b. Indpls., Feb. 22, 1954; s. Jewell and Ruth Pritchett; children: Katie, Josh. BS, Ball State U., 1975; MA in Liberal Studies, Valparaiso U., 1978. Lic. tchr. Ind. Math tchr. Valparaiso (Ind.) H.S., 1975—86, assoc. dir. bands, 1975—95, dir. bands, chmn. music dept., 1995—; pvt. saxophone instr. Valparaiso, 1975—; profl. musician Ind. Named Oustanding H.S. Music Tchr., Ind. Music Educators Assn., 2004; named one of Fifty Directors Who Make A Difference, Sch. Band and Orch. Mag., 2001, 2005; recipient Music Alumni award, Ball State U., 1992, Greater Chicagoland H.S. Band Dir. ward, Quinalan & Fabish Music Co., 2005. Mem.: Internat. Assn. Jazz Educators, Coll. Band Dirs. Assn., Ind. State Sch. Music Assn. (pres. 1995), Ind. Bandmasters Assn. (pres. 1991—92, 1997—98), Pi Kappa Lambda, Phi Beta Mu, Phi Mu Alpha Sinfonia. Avocations: travel, music, fitness. Office: Valparaiso HS 2727 Campbell St Valparaiso IN 46385 Office Phone: 219-531-3070.

**PRITCHETT, SAMUEL TRAVIS,** finance and insurance educator, researcher, consultant; b. Emporia, Va., Dec. 18, 1938; s. Harvey Eugene and Mary (Brown) P.; m. Bertha Yates, Feb. 20, 1960; children: John Travis, Meri Katherine. BSBA, Va. Poly. Inst. and State U., 1960, MSBA, 1967; DBA, Ind. U., 1969. CLU, ChFC, CPCU. Claim rep. Equitable Life Assurance Soc., Richmond, Va., 1960-64, asst. div. claim mgr., 1964-65; asst. prof. bus. adminstrn. U. Richmond, 1969-70; asst. prof. ins. Va. Commonwealth U., Richmond, 1970-72, assoc. prof. ins., 1972-73; assoc. prof. fin. and ins. U. S.C., Columbia, 1973-76, prof. fin. and ins., 1976-99, J.H. Fellers prof., 1981-83, W.F. Hipp prof. ins., 1983-2000, program dir., chair banking, fin., ins. and real estate, 1977-83, 99-00, acad. dir. MBA program, 1993-95, disting. prof. finance and ins., 1999-2000, disting. prof. emeritus, 2000—. Vis. prof. ins. Ind. U., Bloomington, 1995-96; chmn. Risk Theory Soc., Columbus, Ohio, 1987-88; acad. dir. internat. exec. devel. program Bamerindus Seguros, Curtiba, Brazil, 1995; mem., investment commr. S.C. Retirement Sys., 2005—. Author: Risk Management and Insurance, 7th edit., 1996, Stock Life Insurance Company Profitability, 1986, Individual Annuities as a Source of Retirement Income, 2d edit., 1982, An Economic Analysis of Workers' Compensation in South Carolina, 1994; assoc. editor Jour. Risk and Ins., 1982-86, editor, 1987-91; assoc. editor Fin. Svcs. Rev., 1989-95, 97-99; asst. editor Jour. Am. Soc. CLU and ChFC, 1993-98; mem. acad. rev. bd. Jour. Fin. Planning, 1990-91; mem. editl. bd. Jour. Bus. Rsch., 1976-83, Am. Jour. Small Bus., 1975-79; contbr. articles to profl. jours. Active U.S. Joint Ins. Study Com., 1981-86, 89-95; commr. S.C. Retirement Systems Investment Commn., 2005—; bd. dirs. Rialto Re, 2006. Mem. Am. Risk and Ins. Assn. (pres. 1980-81), Acad. Fin. Svcs. (pres. 1987-88), So. Risk and Ins. Assn. (pres. 1977-78), Fin. Mgmt. Assn., Profl. Ins. Agts. Found. (named Ins. Educator of Yr. 1989), Beta Gamma Sigma (pres. chpt. 1980-81), Gamma Iota Sigma (nat. trustee 1976-92), State Retirees Assn., (bd. mem., 2004—). Office: U SC Moore Sch Bus Columbia SC 29208-0001 Office Phone: 843-762-2645. Personal E-mail: tpritch@comcast.net. *Apply to others religious values such as honesty, humility, respect, and service. Cultivate a strong work ethic and select admirable mentors.*

**PRITCHETT, THOMAS RONALD,** retired metal and chemical company executive; b. Colorado City, Tex., Sept. 2, 1925; s. John Thomas and Meddie Omeira (Terry) P.; m. Mary Margaret Hallenbeck, Dec. 23, 1948; children: Rhonda Jean, Thomas Rand, Rebecca Ann. BS in Chemistry and ChemE., U. Tex., 1948, MS, 1949, PhD, 1951. Registered profl. engr. Calif. Rsch. chemist Def. Rsch. Lab., Austin, Tex., 1948-51, Monsanto Chem. Co., Dayton, Ohio, 1951-52; sect. head, rsch. investigator, asst. dir., tech. mgr. Kaiser Aluminum & Chem. Corp., Pleasanton, Calif., 1952-68, v.p., dir. rsch., 1968-89; metall. and corrosion cons. Alamo, Tex., 1989—. Contbr. articles to profl. jours. Mem. adv. bd. Sch. Engring. U. Calif.-Berkeley. Served with U.S. Army, 1944-46. Fellow Am. Soc. Metals; mem. AIME, Aluminum Assn. (chmn. tech. com. and acad. com.), Nat. Assn. Corrosion Engrs., Am. Chem. Soc., Electrochem. Soc., Materials Properties Council (bd. dirs.), Sigma Xi, Phi Lambda Upsilon. Home and Office: 325 Diana Dr ACC 403 Alamo TX 78516 Office Phone: 956-787-0919.

**PRITIKIN, DAVID T.,** lawyer; b. Freeport, Ill., May 2, 1949; BA summa cum laude, Cornell U., 1971; JD magna cum laude, Harvard U., 1974. Bar: Ill. 1974, US Ct. Appeals (9th cir.) 1975, US Ct. Appeals (7th cir.) 1976, U.S. Supreme Ct. 1977, US Ct. Appeals (fed. cir.) 1993. Ptnr. Sidley Austin LLP, Chgo., chair, nat. intellectual property practice. Fellow: Am. Coll. of Trial Lawyers. Office: Sidley Austin LLP 1 S Dearborn St Chicago IL 60603 Office Phone: 312-853-7359. Office Fax: 312-853-7036. Business E-Mail: dpritikin@sidley.com.

**PRITT, JEFFREY DOUGLAS,** contractor, protective services official; b. Elkins, W.Va., Mar. 13, 1976; s. Howard Kenneth and Brenda Jean Pritt. BA, W.Va. U., Morgantown, W.Va., 1996. Mgr. product group Valley Supply Co., Elkins, W.Va., 1996—97; firefighter Beverly (W.Va.) Vol. Fire Dept., 1996—, fire chief, 2001—; contractor Residential Creations, Elkins, W.Va., 1997—. Mem. Haz-Mat Team Randolph County, Elkins, 2005—. Named Fireman of Yr., Randolph County, 2001. Mem.: Nat. Fire Protection Assn., Internat. Assn. Fire Chiefs, Randolph County Fire Assn. (v.p. 2002—), Randolph County 4-H Leaders (pres. 1998—99). Republican. Bapt. Office: Beverly UFD Beverly WV 26253

**PRITTS, GLORIA PICCIA,** historian; d. Oreste Poccia and Alisa DeLitta; m. Harry U. Pritts, Apr. 28, 1946; children: Harry "Dutch", John J., Amy M. BS in History, SUNY, Ardsley, 2004. System's audio visual mgr. Mamaronek Pub. Schs., NY, 1961—91; historian Mamaroneck Village, NY, 1989—. Prodr.: (video programs) Historical Local, 1984— (Ann Sullivan award, 1993). Educator 1816 Schoolhouse, Mamaronck Hist. Soc. NY, 1994—; sec., bookkeeper Most Holy Trinity Religious Edn. NY, 2004—. Office: Village of Mamaroneck 123 Mamaroneck Ave Mamaroneck NY 10543 E-mail: gppritts@aol.com.

**PRITZKER, JEAN,** film producer; Formerly with BBC; co-owner Dee Gee Entertainment. Prodr.: (films) The Phantom of the Opera, 1989, Simple Justice, 1990, Hostile Intent, 1997, Ricochet River, 1998, Wedding Planner, 2001, The Wedding Planner 2001, Mean Creek, 2004, Hooligans, 2005, The Living Hell, 2006. Office: Dee Gee Entertainment Coronet Theater 366 N La Cienega Blvd Los Angeles CA 90048*

**PRITZKER, JOHN A.,** leisure services executive; s. Robert Pritzker; m. Lisa S. Pritzker; 3 children. Grad., Menlo Coll., U. Denver Coll. Hotel and Restaurant Mgmt. Various positions to divisional v.p. Calif. Hyatt; pres. Hyatt Ventures, Inc.; founder, pres. Red Sail Sports, Inc., 1988—. Exec. v.p. bus.

devel. Key3Media Events, Inc., 2000; bd. dirs. Zoomedia Inc. Trustee San Francisco Mus. Modern Art; dir. Pritzker Found., Pritzker Cousins Found., Children Now; bd. dirs. U. Calif. San Francisco Found. Named one of Forbes Richest Americans, 2006, Top 200 Collectors, ARTnews mag., 2005—06. Office: Red Sail Sports 1 Ferry Bldg Ste 255 San Francisco CA 94111*

**PRITZKER, NICHOLAS J.,** diversified financial services company executive; BA, Lake Forest Coll.; JD, Univ. Chgo. Bar: Ill. 1975. Joined Hyatt Corp., 1978, formerly exec. v.p. devel. Hyatt Corp., Chgo., 1981—99, chmn., 1999—; and vice chmn. Hyatt Internat. and Hyatt Corp., Chgo.; also ptnr. Pritzker & Pritzker law, Chgo. Chmn. bd. Eos Biotechnology, San Francisco, 2000—. Named one of Forbes' Richest Americans, 2006. Office: Hyatt Devel Corp 200 W Madison St Chicago IL 60606-3414*

**PRITZKER, PENNY,** investor; b. Chgo., May 2, 1959; d. Donald N. and Sue Ann (Sandel) Pritzker; m. Bryan Traubert, Sept. 10, 1988; children: Donald Pritzker Traubert, Rose Pritzker Traubert. B in Econs., Harvard U. 1981; JD, MBA, Stanford U., 1985. Bar: Ill. 1985. Mgr. Hyatt Devel. Corp. Chgo., 1985-87; pres. Classic Residence by Hyatt, Chgo., 1987—; ptnr. Pritzker & Pritzker, Chgo., 1987—; pres. Pritzker Realty Grp. (formerly Penguin Group, L.P.), Chgo., 1990—; chmn. TransUnion Corp., 2005—. Chmn. exec. com. Encore Sr. Living, Portland, Oreg.; corp. adv. bd. mem. Mayor Daley's Exec. Fellows Prog., Chgo.; mem. Mayor Daley's fin. com.; bd. dirs. William Wrigley, Jr. Co., Chgo., Coast-to-Coast Fin. Corp., NYC, Nat. Investment Conf., Washington. Chair Mus. Contemporary Art, Chgo.; adv. bd. dirs. Chgo. Cares; mem. dean's coun. Harvard U.; mem. Women's Issues Network, Chgo., 1991—, The Chgo. Network, 1992—, Internat. Women's Forum, Chgo., Coun. Fgn. Rels., NY. Named one of 50 Women to Watch, Wall St. Jour., 2005, 100 Most Powerful Women in World, Forbes mag., 2005, 400 Richest Ams., 2006; recipient Brick & Mortar award, Chgo. Equity Fund, 1991, Disting. Svc. award, REIA Kellogg, 1995. Mem. Nat. Assn. Sr. Living Industry Execs. (bd. dirs. 1989-91), Urban Land Inst., Young Pres.'s Orgn. Office: Classic Residence By Hyatt 71 S Wacker Dr Ste 900 Chicago IL 60606-4637*

**PRITZKER, THOMAS JAY,** hotel business executive; b. Chgo., June 6, 1950; s. Jay Arthur and Marian (Friend) P.; m. Margot Lyn Barrow-Sicree, Sept. 4, 1977; 3 children. BA, Claremont Men's Coll., 1971; MBA, U. Chgo., 1976, JD, 1976. Assoc. Katten, Muchin, Zavis, Pearl and Galler, Chgo., 1976-77; exec. v.p. Hyatt Corp., Chgo., 1977-80, pres., 1980—2002, chmn., CEO, 1999—2006; chmn. Hyatt Hotels Corp., 1980—2002, Hyatt Internat. Corp., 1999—2004; ptnr. Pritzker & Pritzker, Chgo., 1980—; chmn., CEO Global Hyatt Corp., 2005—. Chmn. bd. dirs. The Pritzker Orgn., 1998—; bd. dirs. Royal Caribbean Cruises Ltd. Bd. trustees, vice chmn. Art Inst. Chgo., 1988—; bd. trustees U. Chgo. Named one of Forbes' Richest Americans, 2006. Mem. ABA, Ill. Bar Assn., Chgo. Bar Assn., Standard Club, Lake Shore Country Club. Office: Hyatt Ctr 71 S Wacker Dr Ste 4700 Chicago IL 60606 Office Phone: 312-873-4901.*

**PRIVAT, RUBY (RUBY THIBODEAUX),** elementary school educator; b. Rayne, La., Nov. 4, 1954; d. Cleveland Joseph and Mable (Monceaux) Thibodeaux; m. Pierre A. Privat, Dec. 2, 1972; children: Tiffany, James, George, Jennifer. BS in elem. edn., U. S.W. La., Lafayette, 1987; M in Adminstrn., U. of La. at Lafayette, 2003. Account receivable mgr. Badger Oil Corp., Lafayette, La.; 7th grade reading tchr. Rayne (La.) Cath. Elem. Sch.; 1st grade tchr. Egan (La.) Elem. Sch., 6,7,8 grade tchr., math, social studies. Home: 723 E 2nd St Crowley LA 70526-5217

**PRIVES, CAROL,** biologist, educator; PhD, McGill U. Prof. biology Columbia U., N.Y.C., NY, chmn. Dept. Biol. Scis. Mem. Damon Runyon Fellowship Com.; mem. sci. adv. bd. NIH Virology Study Section, N.J. Cancer Commn., Howard Hughes Med. Inst., GeminX. Mem. editl. bd.: Cell, Genes & Devel., Jour. Biology, Chemistry and Cancer Rsch.; editor: Jour. Virology, 1991—99. Fellow: Am. Acad. Arts and Scis.; mem.: Inst. Medicine. Office: Dept Biological Scis Columbia Univ 816 Fairchild Center MC422 1212 Amsterdam Ave New York NY 10027*

**PRIVETT, STEPHEN A.,** academic administrator, priest; b. San Francisco, Calif. BA in Philosophy and Classics, Gonzaga U., 1966; MDiv, U. Calif., Berkeley, 1972; postgrad., U. Calif., Santa Barbara, 1973—74; MA in Catechetics/Religious Edn., Cath. U. Am., 1982, PhD in Catechetics, 1985. Entered Soc. of Jesus, 1960. Instr. Latin, western civilization and religion Jesuit H.S., Sacramento, 1966—69; dir. Project 50 Santa Clara U., 1970—71; asst. dir. novices Coll. Queen of Peace, Santa Barbara, 1972—73; instr. modern European history, Latin and English Bellarmine Coll. Preparatory, San Jose, Calif., 1974—80, prin., 1975—80; asst. prof. religious studies dept. Santa Clara U., 1985—90, assoc. prof. religious studies dept., 1990—2000, co-dir. The Eastside Project, 1985—91, dir. Voice of the Voiceless: Inst. on Human Rights and Social Justice, 1989—91, v.p. acad. affairs, 1991—97, provost, v.p. acad. affairs, 1997—2000; pres. U. San Francisco, 2000—. Mem. U.S. Cath. Conf. on Certification and Accreditation, 1990—99; mem. Strategic Planning Commn. Calif. Province of the Soc. of Jesus, 1996—2002; mem. Nat. Seminar on Jesuit Higher Edn. U. Scranton, 1999—. Contbr. articles to profl. jours.; author: The U.S. Catholic Church and Its Hispanic Members: The Pastoral Vision of Robert E. Lucey, 1988. Vol. pastoral worker Jesuit Refugee Svc., El Salvador, 1988; bd. dirs. Jesuit Vol. Corps S.W. 1987—95, chair, 1988—91; bd. dirs. Christians for Peace in El Salvador, 1997—2000, Fromm Inst. for Lifelong Learning, U. San Francisco, 2000—; trustee Brophy Coll. Preparatory, Phoenix, 1996—, Seattle U., 2000—, U. Iberoamericana, Mexico City, 2001—; hon. mem. San Francisco Host Com., 2000—. Mem.: Assn. Grad. Programs in Ministry, Assn. Profs. and Rschrs. in Religious Edn. (mem. Cath. Assembly), Religious Edn. Assn., Assn. Cath. Colls. and Univs. (bd. dirs. 2002—), Assn. Jesuit Colls. and Univs. (bd. dirs. 2000—), Commonwealth Club Calif. (bd. govs.). Office: Univ San Francisco Office of the Pres 2130 Fulton St San Francisco CA 94117 Office Phone: 415-422-6762.*

**PRIVITERA, JOSEPH F.,** retired foreign service official, writer, researcher; b. N.Y.C., Feb. 22, 1914; s. Luigi and Grazia (Paparcuri) Privitera; m. Bettina La Marca, June 30, 1935; children: Joseph Henry, Stephen Louis. BS with honors, NYU, 1935, PhD, 1938; cert. phonetics course, U. Paris, 1936; cert., U. Mex., Mexico City, 1939. Instr. French, NYU, N.Y.C., 1938; asst. prof. Romance langs. St. Louis U., 1939-45; fgn. svcs. officer, dir. Bi-Nat. Cultural Ctr., U.S. Dept. State, Sao Paulo, Brazil, 1945-47; fgn. svc. officer Am. Consulate Gen., Sao Paulo, 1947-50, Am. Embassy, Quito, Ecuador, 1950-52; dir. Italian broadcasts Voice of Am., U.S. Dept. State, N.Y.C., 1955-76; ret., 1976. Author: Charles Chevillet de Chmpmeslé, 1942-1701, 1938, The Latin American Front, 1945, Portrait of America, 1947, Perfil Cultural de America, 1951, Luigi Pirandello, His Plays in Sicilian, 1998, Beginner's Sicilian, 1998; author: (in Italian and English) A Treasury of Italian Cuisine, 1998; author: Faustus in Love, and Other Poems in English and Other Tongues, 1998, Italy, An Illustrated History, 2000, Beginner's Italian, 2000, Sicily, An Illustrated History, 2001; editor (translator): Reference Grammar of Medieval Italian with a Dual Language Edition of the Thirty-One Poems of Dante's Vita Nova, 2001; author: If I Were Minister of Education and Other Poems, Mellen, 2001; author: (with Bettina Privitera) The Mystery of the Sanfratellan Dialect, the Sicilians Legos, 2001; author: Sicilian Dictionary and Phrase Book Hippocrene, 2003, Hippocreue, 2003, The Sicilian Language, 2004, Canti Siciliani, Original Poems in Sicilian and English translation, 2004, Al Qaida, The Early Years, 2004, The Subconscious, Oedipus To Abu Ghraib, 800 B.C.-2004 A.D., 2004, Canti Lidiani, Original Love Poems, 2005, (seri-comic mini opera) EPIC Song of Love and Lust, 2006; co-author: Language as Historical Determinant-The Normans in Sicily, 1060-1200, 1995, Songs of Love and of the Times, 2006. Mem.: Diplomats and Consular Officers Ret. Avocations: salon photographer, amateur flutist. Home and Office: 7110 Minstrel Way Apt 326 Columbia MD 21045

**PRIZZI, JACK ANTHONY,** investment banking executive; b. Rochester, N.Y., July 5, 1935; s. Samuel Anthony and Mary Ann (Emanuele) P.; m. Geraldine A. Bias, Feb. 16, 1957 (div. 1971); children: Lynne Marie, Michael Vincent, Karen Annette; m. Serafina M. Iacono, Sept. 30, 1995. BS in Chemistry, Va. Mil. Inst., 1956; MS in Phys. Chemistry, U. Va., 1961, MBA, 1963. Chem. engr. E.I. duPont DeNemours & Co., Inc., Niagara Falls, N.Y., 1956-57; engr. Project Mercury, NASA, 1959; mgr. planning and devel. PPG Industries, Pitts., 1963-68; gen. mgr. Process Components Inc., Norfolk, Va., 1968-70; ptrn. Alan Patricof Assocs., N.Y.C., 1970-74, Beacon Ptnrs., N.Y.C., 1974-76, 77-79, Stuart Bros., N.Y.C., 1976-77; v.p. Walter E. Heller & Co.; exec. v.p. Heller Capital Svcs. Inc., N.Y.C., 1979-84; sr. v.p. DnC Am. Banking Corp., N.Y.C., 1984-86; mng. dir. DnC Capital Corp., 1986-89; pres., CEO Jack A. Prizzi & Co., 1989-98. Founder, mng. dir. CoE Assocs., L.L.C., N.Y.C., 1998—; spl. ltd. ptnr. Harvest Ptnrs., 1993-97; instr. advanced grades N.Y. Power Squadron; bd. dirs. Meridian Resource Corp., 1993-2004. Capt. U.S. Army, 1958-59. Capt. U.S. Army, 1958—59. Grantee Office Naval Rsch., 1960, Calif. Rsch. Corp., 1960-61. Mem. Assn. for Corp. Growth, Natl. Assn. of Corp. Dir., Am. Chem. Soc., Raven Soc. Office: CoE Assocs LLC 156 W 56th St Ste 1401 New York NY 10019-3800 Office Phone: 212-265-7474 209. E-mail: info@coeassociatesllc.com.

**PRO, PHILIP MARTIN,** judge; b. Richmond, Calif., Dec. 12, 1946; s. Leo Martin and Mildred Louise (Beck) P.; m. Dori Sue Hallas, Nov. 13, 1982; 1 child, Brenda Kay. BA, San Francisco State U., 1968; JD, Golden Gate U. 1972. Bar: Calif. 1972, Nev. 1973, U.S. Ct. Appeals (9th cir.) 1973, U.S. Dist. Ct. Nev. 1973, U.S. Supreme Ct. 1976. Pub. defender, Las Vegas, 1973-75; asst. U.S. atty. Dist. Nev., Las Vegas, 1975-78; dep. atty. gen. State of Nev., Carson City, 1979-80; magistrate US Dist. Ct. Nev., Las Vegas, 1980-87, judge, 1987—, chief judge, 2002—. Instr. Atty. Gen.'s Advocacy Inst., Nat. Inst. Trial Advocacy, 1992; chmn. com. adminstrn. of magistrate judge system Jud. Conf. U.S., 1993—. Bd. dirs. NCCJ, Las Vegas, 1982—, mem. program com. and issues in justice com. Mem. ABA, Fed. Judges Assn. (bd. dirs. 1992—, v.p. 1997-2001), Nev. State Bar Assn., Calif. State Bar Assn., Nev. Judges Assn. (instr.), Assn. Trial Lawyers Am., Nev. Am. Inn Ct. (pres. 1989-91), Ninth Cir. Jury (instructions com.), Nat. Conf. U.S. Magistrates (sec.). Republican. Office: US Dist Ct 7015 Fed Bldg 300 Las Vegas Blvd S Ste 4650 Las Vegas NV 89101-5883 Office Phone: 702-464-5510. Business E-Mail: Philip_Pro@nvd.uscourts.gov.

**PROBERT, EDWARD WHITFORD,** foundation executive, volunteer; b. Orange, NJ, May 27, 1936; s. George Ernest and Ethel Loring (Whitford) P.; m. Ann Schuyler Linen, July 2, 1960; children: Edward Whitford Jr., Leslie P. Sirbaugh, David Linen. BA, Yale U., 1958; LLB, U. Va., 1961. With Morgan Guaranty Trust Co. of N.Y., N.Y.C., 1961-68, v.p., 1970-88; from v.p. to pres. Fannie E. Rippel Found., Basking Ridge, NJ, 1988—95, CEO, pres., 1996—, chmn., 2004. Sec. Intersearch Inst., Inc., Annandale, N.J., 1989-93; bd. assocs. Whitehead Inst. for Biomed. Rsch., Cambridge, Mass., 1996-2004. Co-chmn. capital campaign Jersey Battered Women's Svc., Morris Plains, N.J., 1996-99, bd. dirs., 2002-2005; chmn. capital campaign St. Peter's Episcopal Ch., Morristown, 2001-2003. Mem. Royal Dornoch Golf Club, Mountain Lake Club, Morristown Club and Morristown Field Club, Somerset Hills C.C. (bd. govs., golf chmn. 1981-90). Republican. Episcopalian. Avocations: golf, swimming, scuba diving, reading, singing. Home: 14 Miller Rd New Vernon NJ 07976 Office: Fannie E Rippel Found 180 Mount Airy Rd Ste 200 Basking Ridge NJ 07920-2021 E-mail: tprobert@patmedia.net.

**PROBST, LAWRENCE F., III,** game systems company executive; BS, U. Del., 1972. Dist. sales mgr. Johnson & Johnson, 1972-80; nat. accounts mgr. The Clorox Co., 1980-82, Mediagenic (formerly Activision Inc.), 1982-84; v.p. sales Electronic Arts, Inc., 1984—86, sr. v.p., distbn., 1987—91, pres., 1991—98, dir., 1991—, CEO Redwood City, Calif., 1991—, chmn., 1994—. Bd. dir. MP3.com, Inc., 1999—. Office: Electronic Arts Inc 209 Redwood Shores Pkwy Redwood City CA 94065*

**PROBSTEIN, RONALD FILMORE,** mechanical engineering educator; b. NYC, Mar. 11, 1928; s. Sidney and Sally (Rosenstein) P.; m. Irene Weindling, July 30, 1950; 1 child, Sidney. BME, NYU, 1948; MSE, Princeton U., NJ, 1950, AM, 1951, PhD, 1952; ScD (hon.), Brown U., 1997. Rsch. asst. physics NYU, 1946-48, instr. engring. mechanics, 1947-48; rsch. asst. dept. aero. engring. Princeton U., 1948-52, rsch. assoc., 1952-53, asst. prof., 1953-54; asst. prof. divs. engring., applied math. Brown U., 1954-55, assoc. prof., 1955-59, prof., 1959-62; prof. mech. engring. MIT, Cambridge, 1962—89, Ford prof. engring., 1989-96, prof. mech. engring., 1996—2001, Ford prof. engring. emeritus, 1996—; Disting. prof. engring. U. Utah, 1973; sr. ptnr. Water Purification Assoc., Cambridge, 1974-82; chmn. bd. Water Gen. Corp., Cambridge, 1982-83; sr. corp. tech. advisor Foster-Miller, Inc., 1983-91. Commr. commn. on engring. and tech. systems NRC, 1980-83, mem. space studies bd., 2004—; sci. advisor to bd. Corrpro Scs., 1993-2001. Author: Hypersonic Flow Theory, 1959, Hypersonic Flow, Inviscid Flows, 1966, 03, Water in Synthetic Fuel Production, 1978, Synthetic Fuels, 1982, 2006, Physicochemical Hydrodynamics, 1989, 03; editor: Introduction to Hypersonic Flow, 1961, Physics of Shock Waves, 1966, 02, Jour. PhysicoChem. Hydrodynamics, 1987-89; contbr. articles to profl. jours.; patentee in field. Guggenheim fellow, 1960-61; R.F. Probstein Lecture Series in Engring. Sci., MIT, established 1999. Fellow AAAS, AIAA, Am. Acad. Arts and Sci. (councilor 1975-79), Am. Phys. Soc., ASME (Freeman award 1971); mem. AIChE, NAS (chmn. engring. sci. sect. 2005—), NAE (com. membership 2001-05, chmn. 2005), Internat. Acad. Astronautics. Home: 5 Seaver St Brookline MA 02445-5714 Office: 77 Massachusetts Ave Cambridge MA 02139-4301 Office Phone: 617-253-2240. Business E-Mail: rfprobst@mit.edu.

**PROBUS, MICHAEL MAURICE, JR.,** lawyer; b. Louisville, Jan. 26, 1963; s. Michael Maurice and Jerilyn Ann (Burks) P.; m. Luz Marie Probus, May 22, 1985; children: Michael Julian, Lauren Michael. BA, U. Dallas, 1985; JD, U. Tex., 1988. Bar: Tex. 1988, U.S. Dist. Ct. (we. dist.) Tex. 1990, U.S. Ct. Appeals (5th cir.) 1993. Jud. law clk. to chief judge U.S. Dist. Ct. Tex., Houston, 1988-90; assoc. Law Offices of Michael A. Wash, Austin, Tex., 1990-97; pvt. practice, Austin, 1997—. Pro bono atty. Vol. Legal Svcs., Austin, 1994—. Mem.: Travis County Bar Assn. Democrat. Roman Catholic. Office: Law Office M Probus 111 Congress Ave Ste 2230 Austin TX 78701 Office Phone: 512-480-9504. E-mail: mprobusjr@msn.com.

**PROCHASKA, ALICE,** historian, librarian; m. Franklyn Kimmel Prochaska, June 25, 1971; children: Elizabeth, William. BA in Modern History, Somerville Coll., U. Oxford, 1968; DPhil in Modern History, U. Oxford, 1975. Asst. keeper Pub. Record Office, England, 1975—84; sec. & libr. Inst. Hist. Rsch. U. London, 1984—92; dir. spl. collections Brit. Libr., 1992—2001; univ. libr. Yale U., New Haven, 2001—. Author: History of the General Federation of Trade Unions, 1982, Irish History from 1700: A Guide to Sources in the Public Record Office, 1986; co-editor (with Frank Prochaska): Margaretta Acworth's Georgian Cookery Book, 1987; contbr. numerous articles in scholarly and profl. jours. Named an Hon. Fellow, Royal Holloway U. of London, 2002, Inst. Hist. Rsch. U. London, 2001. Fellow: Royal Hist. Soc. (v.p. 1995—99). Office: Libr Adminstrv Services Sterling Meml Libr Yale U 130 Wall St PO Box 208240 New Haven CT 06520-8240 Office Phone: 203-432-1818. Business E-Mail: alice.prochaska@yale.edu.*

**PROCHNOW, DOUGLAS LEE,** lawyer; b. Omaha, Jan. 9, 1952; s. Albert Delmer and Betty Jean (Wood) Prochnow. BA with high distinction, U. Nebr., 1974; JD, Northwestern U., 1977. Bar: Ill. 1977, U.S. Dist. Ct. (no. dist.) Ill. 1977, U.S. Ct. Appeals (7th cir.) 1989, U.S. Supreme Ct. 2000. Assoc. Wildman, Harrold, Allen & Dixon, Chgo., 1977-84, ptnr., 1985—. Spl. asst. corp. counsel City of Chgo., 1986—87; adj. prof. law Northwestern U. Sch. Law, 2005—. Pres. Chgo. bd. Prevent Child Abuse Am. Mem. ABA, ATLA (assoc.), Ill. Bar Assn., Chgo. Bar Assn., Soc. Trial Lawyers, Def. Rsch. Inst., Am. Health Lawyers Assn., Phi Beta Kappa, Phi Eta Sigma. Home: 1230 N

State Pky Apt 6D Chicago IL 60610-2261 Office: Wildman Harrold Allen & Dixon 225 W Wacker Dr Ste 2700 Chicago IL 60606-1224 Office Phone: 312-201-2526. Business E-Mail: prochnow@wildmanharrold.com.

**PROCHNOW, HERBERT VICTOR, JR.,** retired lawyer; b. Evanston, Ill., May 26, 1931; s. Herbert V. and Laura (Stinson) P.; m. Lucia Boyden, Aug. 6, 1966; children: Thomas Herbert, Laura. AB, Harvard U., 1953, JD, 1956; A.M., U. Chgo., 1958. Bar: Ill. 1957, U.S. Dist. Ct. (no. dist.) Ill. 1961. With 1st Nat. Bank Chgo., 1958-91, atty., 1961-70, sr. atty., 1971-73, counsel, 1973-91, adminstrv. asst. to chmn. bd., 1978-81; pvt. practice, 1991—; ret., 2003. Author: (with Herbert V. Prochnow) A Treasury of Humorous Quotations, 1969, The Changing World of Banking, 1974, The Public Speaker's Treasure Chest, 1986, The Toastmaster's Treasure Chest, 1988; also articles in legal publs. Mem.: Am. Soc. Internat. Law, Chgo. Bar Assn. (chmn. com. internat. law 1970—71), Ill. Bar Assn., ABA, Chgo. Club, Lawyers Club (Chgo.), Harvard Club (N.Y.C.), Univ. Club (Chgo.). Econ. Club, Onwentsia, Phi Beta Kappa. Home: 949 Woodbine Pl Lake Forest IL 60045-2275 Office Phone: 312-616-8110. E-mail: hvprochnow@aol.com.

**PROCKOP, DARWIN JOHNSON,** biochemist, medical educator; b. Palmerton, Pa., Aug. 31, 1929; s. John and Sophie (Gurski) Prockop; m. Elinor Sacks, Apr. 15, 1961; children: Susan Elizabeth, David John. AB, Haverford Coll., 1951; MA, Oxford U., 1953; MD, U. Pa., 1956; PhD, George Washington U., 1962; DSc (hon.) (hon.), U. Oulu, Finland, 1983, U. So. Fla., 1993. Investigator NIH, 1957—61; assoc., asst. prof., asso. prof., prof. medicine and biochemistry U. Pa., Phila., 1961—72; prof., chmn. dept. biochemistry U. Medicine and Dentistry of N.J. (Rutgers Med. Sch.), Piscataway, NJ, 1972—86; prof., chmn. dept. biochemistry and molecular biology Jefferson Med. Coll., Phila., 1986–96; dir. Jefferson Inst. Molecular Medicine, 1986—96; prof., dir. Ctr. for Gene Therapy, MCP/Hahnemann Med. Coll., Phila., 1996—2000; prof., dir. Ctr. Gene Therapy Tulane U. Med. Ctr., New Orleans, 2000—. Contbr. Served with USPHS, 1958—61. Named hon. companion, U. Manchester, 1999; recipient Disting. Alumnus award, George Washington U., 1991, U. Pa., 1994, Hopkins Meml. medal., Brit. Biochem. Soc, 1998; fellow Fulbright Found., 1951—53; grantee, NIH, 1961—. Mem.: NAS, Am. Assn. Physicians, Am. Soc. Clin. Investigation, Am. Soc. Biol. Chemists, Acad. Finland, Inst. Medicine, Alpha Omega Alpha, Phi Beta Kappa. Achievements include research in on collagen and gene therapy. Home: 291 Locust St Philadelphia PA 19106-3913 Office: Ctr Gene Therapy Tulane U Med Ctr 1430 Tulane Ave New Orleans LA 70112-2699 E-mail: dprocko@tulane.edu.

**PROCOPE, ERNESTA GERTRUDE,** insurance company executive; b. Bklyn. d. Clarence and Eudora Forster; m. Albin Bowman (dec. 1952); m. John L. Procope, July 3, 1954. Student, Bklyn. Coll., Coll. Ins., Pohs Inst. Ins.; LLD (hon.), Adelphi U., Marymount Manhattan Coll., 1987, Howard U., 1989; HHD (hon.), Morgan State U., 1978. Founder, pres., CEO E.G. Bowman Co. Inc. NYC, 1953—. Panelist corp. governance and advancement of women US Dept. Labor, 1981. Amb. 10th anniversary independence celebration Republic of Gambia, 1975; trustee NY Zool. Soc., Cornell U., Adelphi U. Named disting. Black Woman in Corp. Role, Nat. Coun. Negro Women, Inc., 1981, Bus. Person of Yr., Urban Bankers Coalition, 1990; named to African Am. Bus. Hall of Fame & Mus., 2003, Minority Bus. Hall of Fame and Mus., 2006; recipient Achievement award, Thelma T. Johnson Meml. Scholarship Fund, 1972, Interracial Coun. for Bus. Opportunity, 1973, Women of the Yr. award, presented at White House by First Lady Patricia Nixon, 1972, Cmty. Svc. award, F & M Schaefer Brewing Co., 1974, Sojourner Truth award, Negro Bus. and Profl. Women's Club, Inc., 1974, Bus. Achievement award, Nat. Bus. League, 1976, Catalyst award, Women Dirs. of Corps., 1977, Torch of Liberty award, Anti-Defammation League, 1990, Disting. Svc. award, NAACP, 1991, Entrepreneurial Excellence award, Dow Jones/Wall Street Jour., 1992, Whitney M. Young, Jr. award, 1992, Trumpet award, Turner Broadcasting Sys., 2002, Essence Power award, 2004, Women of Power Legacy award, Black Enterprise Mag., 2006. Mem.: Nat. Assn. Ins. Women, Nat. Assn. Ins. Brokers, Cosmopolitan Club, Women's Forum, Alpha Kappa Alpha (hon.). Presbyterian. Office: EG Bowman Co Inc 97 Wall St New York NY 10005-4302 Office Phone: 212-425-8150. Business E-Mail: procope@egbowman.com.

**PROCTOR, ALLEN JOSEPH,** management consultant, economist; s. David Goodridge and Bertha Margaret (Coskie) Proctor; m. Gail Anne Walter, Apr. 9, 1983; children: Catherine, Franklyn. AB, Harvard Coll., 1974; MA, U. Wis., 1978, PhD, 1981. Rsch. asst. World Bank, Washington, 1973—75; chief Fed. Res. Bank N.Y., N.Y.C., 1980—87; dep. dir. Office of Mgmt. and Budget, City of N.Y., 1987—89; exec. dir. NY State Fin. Control Bd., N.Y.C., 1990—94; v.p. for fin. Harvard U., Cambridge, Mass., 1994—96; exec. dir. Ohio Police and Fire Pension Fund, Columbus, 1997—2001; prin. Allen Proctor Consulting, LLC, Worthington, Ohio, 2001—. Adj. prof. Columbia Grad. Sch. Bus., 1992—93; lectr. Kennedy Sch. Govt., Harvard U., 1994—97; reviewer Ford Found. Innovations in Government, 1993—96; mem. Nat. Adv. Coun. on State and Local Budgeting, Washington, 1995—97; econ. adv. panel City of Columbus, Ohio, 2001—02; Sarbanes-Oxley audit com. fin. expert Kahiki Foods, Inc., Gahanna, Ohio, 2004—. Author: Linking Mission to Money, 2004, Structural Balance, 1991 (Louisville award for Fin. Innovation, 1993). Treas. Wayland Acad., Beaver Dam, 1997—; dir. CAPA, Inc., Columbus, 2000—; investment chair Columbus Rotary Found., 1999—; investment com. OhioHealth Corp., Columbus, 1999—. Recipient Spl. Recognition citation, Ohio Ho. Reps., 2001, Alumni Achievement award, Wayland Acad., 1995. Mem.: Govt. Fin. Officers Assn., Fin. Executives Internat., Kit Kat Club (pres. 2004—05). Avocation: percussionist. Office: Allen Proctor Consulting LLC 471 Highgate Ave Worthington OH 43085 Office Phone: 614-208-5403. Office Fax: 614-888-8287. Business E-Mail: allen@proctorconsulting.org.

**PROCTOR, BARBARA GARDNER,** advertising agency executive, writer; b. Ashville, NC; d. William and Bernice (Baxter) Gardner; m. Carl L. Proctor, July 20, 1961 (div. Nov. 1963); 1 son, Morgan Eugene. BA, Talladega Coll., Ala., 1954. Music critic, contbg. editor Down Beat Mag., Chgo., 1958—; internat. dir. Vee Jay Records, Chgo., 1961-64; copy supr. Post-Keyes-Gardner Advt., Inc., Chgo., 1965-68, Gene Taylor Assos., Chgo., 1968-69, North Advt. Agt., Chgo., 1969-70; contbr. to gen. periodicals, 1952—; founder Proctor & Gardner Advt. (divsn. Proctor Comm. Network), Chgo., 1970—, pres., CEO. Pres., CEO Proctor Comm. Network, Chgo.; Mem. Chgo. Urban League, Chgo. Econ. Devel. Corp.; cons. pub. rels. and promotion, record industry; bd. dir. Window to the World Comm., Inc.; bd. trustee 98.7WFMT, WTTW11. Author: (TV documentary) Blues for a Gardenia, 1963. Bd. dirs. People United to Save Humanity, Better Bus. Bur., Window to the World Comm., Inc., Ill. Bell Telephone Co., Northwestern Hosp., Mid-City Nat. Bank, Coun. Chgo. Better Bus. Bur., Louisville Courier-Jour., United Way, Econ. Club; Mem. NARAS, USIA, Chgo. Media Women, Women's Advt. Club, NY Art Dirs. Club, Woman's Day Club, Cosmopolitan C. of C. (dir.); bd. trustee 98.7WFMT, WTTW11; co-chair, State Ill. Gannon-Proctor Commn.; governing coun. mem. Ill. State Bar Assn. Inst. for Pub. Affairs. Recipient Armstrong Creative Writing award, 1954; awards Chgo. Fedn. Advt., Frederick Douglas Humanitarian award, 1975, Headliner award, Assn. for Women in Comm., 1978; named Chgo. Advt. Woman of Yr., 1974; named to Smithsonian Instn. "Black Women Achievements Against the Odds" Hall of Fame and the series' poster-calendar traveling exhbn. Mem. Female Execs. Assn., Internat. Platform Assn., Smithsonian Instn. Assn.

**PROCTOR, CONRAD ARNOLD,** physician; b. Ann Arbor, Mich., July 14, 1934; s. Bruce and Luena Marie (Crawford) P.; m. Phyllis Darlene Anderson, June 23, 1956; children: Sharon Heimbach Pins, Barbara Jan Brown, David Conrad, Todd Bruce. MD, U. Mich., 1959, MS, 1964. Cert. Am. Bd. Otolaryngology. Intern St. Joseph Mercy Hosp., Ann Arbor, 1959-60; jr. clin. instr. Univ. Hosp., Ann Arbor, 1961-63, sr. clin. instr., 1963-65; chief dept. otolaryngology Munson Army Hosp., Ft. Leavenworth, Kans., 1965-67; mem. attending staff William Beaumont Hosp., Royal Oak, Mich., 1967—. Instr. Am. Acad. Otolaryngology, Washington, 1968-82, guest examiner,

---

Chgo., 1978-79. Author: Current Therapy in Otolaryngology, 1984-85; (booklet) Dietary Treatment of Meniere's Syndrome, 1983, Hyperinsulinemia and Tinnitus, 1988; (manual) Hereditary Sensorineural Hearing Loss, 1978, Etiology, Treatment of Fluid Retention in Meniere's Syndrome, 1992; (med. jour.) Abnormal Insulin Levels and Vertigo, 1981. Dir. Christian edn. Bloomfield Hills (Mich.) Bapt. Ch., 1969-72, fin. chmn., 1975-78, Sunday sch. tchr., 1967—. Served to capt. U.S. Army, 1965-67. Recipient 1st pl. award for med. rsch. Students Am. Med. Assn., 1959, Merit award Am. Acad. Otolaryngology, 1978; holder 7 world records Internat. Game Fish Assn., 6 world records Nat. Fresh Water Fishing Hall Fame Mem. AMA, Mich. State Med. Assn., Oakland County Med. Assn., Am. Bd. Otolaryngology, ACS, Triological Soc., Otosclerosis Study Group, Internat. Game Fish Assn. (Nat. Fresh Water Fishing Hall of Fame), Am. Legion, U.S. Tennis Assn., U.S. Golf Assn., Panangling Ltd. (Jonesboro, Maine), Victors and Presidents Club (Ann Arbor), Audubon Soc., Phi Eta Sigma, Phi Kappa Phi, Phi Beta Kappa. Republican. Avocations: baseball, football, tennis, Arctic exploration, fishing. Office: 3535 W 13 Mile Rd Ste 307 Royal Oak MI 48073-6710 Office Phone: 248-288-2137.

**PROCTOR, DEBORAH DENISE,** gastroenterologist, educator; b. Cleve., July 23, 1957; d. Frank David and Barbara Elizabeth Motil; m. Robert Bruce Proctor, Feb. 9, 1991; children: Charles Robert, David William. BS in Biology, Toledo U., 1978; MD, U. Cin., 1982. Diplomate Am. Bd. Internal Medicine, 1993. Intern in pediat. Ea. Va. U., Norfolk, Va., 1982—83; intern and resident internal medicine Beth Israel Hosp., Harvard Med. Sch., Boston, 1987—90, fellow in gastroenterology, 1990—92; asst. prof. medicine East Carolina U., Greenville, NC, 1992—97, assoc. prof. medicine, 1997—98; asst. prof. medicine Yale U., New Haven, 1998—99, assoc. prof. medicine, 1999—. Gastroenterology fellowship program dir. Yale U., New Haven, 2000—. Coach Odyssey of the Mind, Durham, Conn., 2003—06. Lt. comdr. USN, 1983—87, Norfolk, VA. Named Yale-New Haven All-Star, Yale-New Haven Hosp., 2003, 2005; named one of Best Doctors in Am., 2005. Fellow: Am. Coll. of Gastroenterology; mem.: Am. Gastroent. Assn. (chair and vice chair 2002—06, chair tng. subcommittee 2003—06, chair gie subcommittee 2006—, chair gi fellowship match ad hoc com. 2004—05). Achievements include research in hereditary hemorrhagic telangiectasia and GI bleeding research; inflammatory bowel disease patient preferences survey. Office: Yale U Sch Medicine 333 Cedar St 1080 LMP New Haven CT 06520 Office Phone: 203-785-2052.

**PROCTOR, GEORGANNE C.,** investment company executive; b. 1956; m. Robert Proctor. BS in Bus. Mgmt., U. S.D.; MBA in Fin., Calif. State U., Hayward. From fin. analyst Bechtel Financing Svcs. (now part of Bechtel Enterprises), 1982-89; mgr. Bechtel Info. Tech. Group., 1989-91, mgr. project cost controls for Disney MGM Studio project Paris, 1991; dir. fin. & acctg. Buena Vista Home Video Internat., 1991-93; dir. project & divsn. fin. Walt Disney Imagineering, 1993-94; CFO Bechtel Enterprises, 1994-97; sr. v.p., CFO Bechtel Group, Inc., San Francisco, 1997—2002; exec. v.p., CFO Golden West Fin. Corp., 2002—06, Teachers Ins. & Annuity Found. Coll. Retirement Equities Fund (TIAA-CREF), NYC, 2006—. Bd. dirs. The Bechtel Group, 1994—2002. Amb. Calif. State U., Hayward. Office: TIAA-CREF 730 3rd Ave New York NY 10017*

**PROCTOR, JAMES DAVID,** environmental scientist, educator; b. Canyonville, Oreg., Dec. 27, 1957; s. Robert Edward and Virginia Belle Proctor; children: Nonjabulo Joy, Elise Simangele. PhD, U. Calif., Berkeley, 1992. Prof. of geography U. Calif., Santa Barbara, 1992—2005; prof. and dir. of environ. studies Lewis & Clark Coll., Portland, 2005—. Pres., bd. dirs. Alder Creek Children's Forest, Canyonville, Oreg., 2002—06. Office: Lewis & Clark College 0615 SW Palatine Hill Rd Portland OR 97219 Office Phone: 503.768.7707.

**PROCTOR, JOHN JAMES,** electrical engineer; b. Castro Valley, Calif., June 3, 1960; s. Della Mary and Marvin Arthur Proctor; m. Stephanie Anne Sibilia, Aug. 26, 1984. BSEE, U. Calif., Santa Barbara, 1983. Application engr. Nat. Semiconductor Corp., Santa Clara, Calif., 1983—86; design engr. Grass Valley Group, Calif., 1986—93; tech. lead design engr. 3COM, Advanced Devel. Ctr., Grass Valley, 1993—99; sr. r&d enging. mgr. Cisco Systems, Inc., Petaluma, Calif., 1999—. Spkr. in field. Contbr. articles to profl. jours. Vol. Petaluma Am. Little League, Calif., 2000—06; asst. coach Petaluma Youth Soccer League, 2004—05, Petaluma Crusaders Soccer Club, 2006. Mem.: IEEE, IEEE Signal Processing Soc., IEEE Comm. Soc., IEEE Engring. Mgmt. Soc. (sr.). Achievements include patents for method of and apparatus for processing a shaped video signal to add a simulated shadow; method for generating a compressed video signal video signal shadow; method for adjusting the quality of a video coder; video encoder/decoder system. Avocations: soccer, guitar, running. Office Phone: 707-799-0816.

**PROCTOR, JUNE,** retired religious organization administrator, writer; b. Lehigh, Okla., June 20, 1936; d. Lowell Lawrence and Martha Fay (Winn) Whitlock; m. Richard Owen Proctor, Nov. 19, 1955; children: Michael Lee, Terrell Glen, Tanya Marie, Richard Lowell, Sheilia Renè, Roger Owen. BA in Psychology, Okla. City U., 1956; MA in Religious Edn. cum laude, Wesley Sch. Theology, 1973; postgrad., U. So. Miss., 1997; MA in History, Tex. A&M U., 2003. Cert. dir. religious edn. US Army Bd. Chaplains, 1984. Dir. religious edn. US Army Post Chapel, Ft. Huachuca, Ariz., 1984—85, Westminster United Meth. Ch., Md., 1981—82, Calvary United Meth. Ch., Paris, Tex., 1995—96; ret., 1996; co-owner Whispering Oaks Ranch, Paris, Tex. Rep. 3d military family symposium US Army War Coll., DC, 1982; curriculum selection com. Bd. US Army Chaplains, Ft. Monroe, Va., 1985; leadership trainer Paris C. of C., 1996. Author: (book) The Night the Angels Cried, 2003 (1st Press Woman Tex., 2004); columnist Stay Tuned with June, 2004 (Nat. Fedn. Press Winn p, 2d Place, 2003), Prof. Baden-Wurttemberg Dist. Protestant Women of Chapel, Kelley Barracks, Germany, 1980—81; chair youth vols. Am. Red Cross, Ft. Huachuca, 1983—85. Decorated Outstanding Civilian Svc. medal US Dept. Army; recipient Helping Hand Medallion award, VII Corps. Headquarters, Kelley Barracks, 1981, 1st Pl. inspirational books, Press Woman Tex., 2004, 1st Pl. personality profile article, 2005, 1st Pl. personal essay column, 2005, 2d Pl. inspirational books, Nat. Fedn. Press Women, 2004. Mem.: Okla. Writers Fedn., Inc., Nat. Fedn. Press Women, Press Women Tex., US Army War Coll. Assn. (student wife rep. 1982—83), Tex. Archeol. Soc. Field Soc. (registrar 2005—), Valley Caddo Archeol. Soc. (registrar 2003—), Officer's Wives Club, US Army (pres. 1980—81). United Methodist. Avocations: archaeology, writing, public speaking. Home: 18921 FM 1497 Paris TX 75462

**PROCTOR, KENNETH DONALD,** lawyer; b. Balt., Apr. 28, 1944; s. Kenneth Chauncey and Sarah Elizabeth (Kent) P.; m. Judith Danner Harris, Aug. 2, 1969; children: Kenneth Scott, Kent Harris, Janet Cameron BS, Lehigh U., 1966; JD, U. Md., 1969. Bar: Md. 1969, U.S. Dist. Ct. Md. 1970, U.S. Supreme Ct. 1974, U.S. Ct. Appeals (4th cir.) 1980. Law clk. to judge Md. Ct. Appeals, 1969-70; assoc. Miles & Stockbridge, Balt., 1970-73, 74-76, ptnr., 1976-81, Towson, Md., 1981-96; asst. atty. gen. State of Md., Balt., 1973-74. Trustee Gilman Sch., Balt., 1982-85. Mem. ABA, Md. Bar Assn. Baltimore County Bar Assn. Democrat. Episcopalian. Office: Proctor & McKee PA 102 W Pennsylvania Ave Ste 505 Towson MD 21204-4542 Office Phone: 410-823-2258. E-mail: kdproctor@proctorlaw.com.

**PROCTOR, RICHARD JAMES,** geologist, consultant; b. LA, Aug. 2, 1931; s. George Arthur and Margaret Y. (Goodman) P.; m. Ena McLaren, Feb. 12, 1955; children: Mitchell, Jill, Randall. BA, Calif. State U., L.A., 1954; MA, UCLA, 1958. Engring. geologist, Calif.; cert. profl. geologist Am. Inst. Profl. Geologists. Chief geologist Met. Water Dist., L.A., 1958-80; pres., cons. geologist Richard J. Proctor, Inc., Arcadia, Calif., 1980-95. Vis. assoc. prof. Calif. Inst. Tech., Pasadena, 1975-78. Author: History of AIPG, 2003, co-author: Citizens Guide to Geologic Hazards, 1993; editor: Professional Practice Guidelines, 1985, Engineering Geology Practice in Southern California, 1992, (screenplays) My Friend Tom Finn, 2005, Stopping by Woods, 2006. Pres., dir. Arcadia Hist. Soc., 1993-96. Fellow Geol. Soc. Am. (Burwell

---

Meml. award 1972); mem. Assn. Engring. Geologists (hon., pres. 1979), Am. Inst. Profl. Geologists (hon., pres. 1989, Van Couvering Meml. award 1990, Parker Meml. medal 2003), Am. Geol. Inst. (sec.-treas. 1979-83), Conf. Calif. Hist. Socs. (pres. 2004-06).

**PROCTOR, RICHARD JEROME, JR.,** business educator, expert witness, accountant; b. NYC, Oct. 6, 1941; s. Richard Jerome and Edith (Decker) P.; m. Elfriede N. Neundorfer, Aug. 19, 1967; children: Courtney, John, David. BS, Columbia U., 1963, MBA, 1970. CPA, N.Y., Conn.; cert. valuation analyst, cert. govt. fin. mgr.; cert. forensic acct. Am. Bd. Forensic Acctg. Sr. acct. Arthur Andersen, N.Y.C., 1970-72; dir. acctg. N.Y. Stock Exchange, N.Y.C., 1972-75; chief fin. officer Executrans, Greenwich, Conn., 1975-77; dir. planning Irvin Industries, Stamford, Conn., 1977-79; asst. prof. acctg. and taxation U. Hartford (Conn.), 1979-82; prof., dir. Ctr. for Fin. Forensics Western Conn. State U., Danbury, 1983—. Pvt. practice, 1979—; cons., expert witness in field. Author (textbook): Proli Footwear-A Team Based Audit Simulation. 2002. Mem. AICPA, Conn. Soc. CPAs (Disting. Disc. cons., mem.), Nat. Assn. Cert. Valuation Analysts, Inst. Bus. Appraisers, Am. Acctg. Assn., Inst. Mgmt. Accts., Am. Bd. Forensic Acctg. (diplomate). Home: 31 Cooper Hill Rd Ridgefield CT 06877-5903 Office: Western Conn State U 181 White St Danbury CT 06810-6826 Office Phone: 203-438-7742.

**PROCTOR, RICHARD OWEN,** historian, health facility administrator, military officer; b. Austin, Tex., Nov. 18, 1935; s. William Owen and Arlene Gertrude (Holdeman) P.; m. Martha June Whitlock, Nov. 19, 1955; children: Tanya Marie, Sheilia Renee, Michael Lee, Terry Glen, Richard Lowell, Roger Owen. BA, Oklahoma City U., 1957; MS, MD, Baylor U. Coll. Medicine, Houston, 1964; MPH and 1M, Tulane U., 1970; diploma, U.S. Army War Coll., 1983; MS in History, Tex. A&M U., Commerce, 2001. Diplomate Am. Bd. Pediatrics, Am. Bd. Preventive Medicine. Commd. capt. U.S. Army, 1964, advanced through grades to brig. gen.; instr. Imperial Ethiopian Coll. A&M Arts, Alemaya, 1957-59; dep. comdr. U.S. Army Hosp., Kagnew Station, Ethiopia, 1967-69, U.S Army Med. Lab., Ft. Sam Houston, Tex., 1973-75; instr. U.S. Army Acad. Health Scis., Ft. Sam Houston, 1975-77; surgeon U.S Army VII Corps, Moeringen, Fed. Republic Germany, 1978-81; prof., chmn., comdt. of students Uniformed Svcs. U. of Health Scis., Bethesda, Md., 1981-82; comdr. Raymond Bliss Army Community Hosp., Ft. Huachuca, Ariz., 1983-85; surgeon U.S Army Tng. and Doctrine Command, Ft. Monroe, Va., 1985-88; comdg. gen. William Beaumont Army Med. Ctr., El Paso, Tex., 1988-91; dir. pub. health Region 6 Tex. Dept. Health, Houston, 1991-96; co-owner, rancher Whispering Oaks, Tex., 1985—. Cons. WHO/PAHO, Bolivia, 1971; lectr. on archeol. and history; past adj. or clin. faculty positions Baylor U., Tulane U., U. Tex., Tex. A&M U.; archaeol. steward Tex. Hist. Commn., Archaeol. Conservancy. Author: (with others) Principles of Pediatrics: Healthcare of the Young, 1978, Current Pediatrics Diagnosis and Treatment, 1978, 80, Primary Pediatric Care, 1987, 3d edit., 1997, Comprehensive Adolescent Health Care, 1992; author multiple articles on viremia with Sabin polio vaccines. Asst. scout master Boy Scouts Am., Bowie, Md., 1971-73; scout committeeman Boy Scouts Am., Moeringen, 1978-81. Decorated D.S.M., Legion of Merit (twice); recipient scholarship Broadhurst Found., Tulsa, 1953-57; rsch. fellow NIH, 1960-61; Tropical Medicine fellow La. State U., 1970. Fellow Am. Acad. Pediatrics; mem. (life) Nat. Eagle Scout Assn., Tex. State Hist. Assn., Tex. Archaeol. Soc., Okla. Hist. Soc., Okla. Anthrop. Soc., Ark. Archaeol. Soc., Tex. Map Soc. Methodist. Avocations: conservation, living history, archaeology. Home: RR 4 Box 1193 Paris TX 75462-9708

**PROCTOR, ROBERT NEEL,** history educator; b. Corpus Christi, Tex., June 25, 1954; s. Norman Neel Proctor and Eugenia K. (Milton) P.; children: Jonathan N. Proctor, Geoffrey R. Schiebinger. BS in Biology, Ind. U., 1976; MA in History of Sci., Harvard U., 1977, PhD History of Sci., 1984. Instr. and teaching fellow biology, history of sci. Harvard U., Cambridge, Mass., 1976-84; Andrew Mellon postdoctoral fellow history of sci. program Stanford (Calif.) U., 1984-86; faculty mem./organizer program in sci., tech. and power Eugene Lang Coll., New Sch. for Social Rsch., N.Y.C., 1986-90; assoc. prof. dept. history Pa. State U., University Park, 1990-93, prof. history, 1993-2000, disting. prof. history, 2000—. Vis. asst. prof. history Va. Poly. Inst. and State U., Blacksburg, summer 1984; vis. lectr. dept. history U. Calif.-Berkeley, Fall 1985. Author: Racial Hygiene: Medicine Under the Nazis, 1988, Value-Free Science? Purity and Power in Modern Knowledge, 1991, Cancer Wars: How Politics Shapes What We Know and Don't Know About Cancer, 1995, The Nazi War on Cancer, 1999. Recipient Disting. Alumni Svc. award Ind. U., 1975, Viseltear prize, 1999; Fulbright grad. scholar, Free U., Berlin, 1980-81; NSF grad. fellow, 1976-79, Charlotte W. Newcombe doctoral dissertation fellow, 1982-83, Andrew Mellon postdoctoral fellow, Stanford U., 1984-86, Ctr. for Advanced Study in the Behavioral Scis. summer fellow, 1986, George A. and Eliza Gardner Howard Found. fellow, 1989-90, Max Planck Inst. for History of Sci. fellow 1999-2000; NEH summer stipend, 1989; grantee ACLS, 1989, Nat. Ctr. Human Genome Rsch. 1992-93; sr. scholar in residence U.S. Holocaust Meml. Mus., 1994. Mem. Am. Acad. Arts and Scis., Phi Beta Kappa.

**PROCTOR, WILLIAM GILBERT, JR.,** writer, editor; b. Atlanta, Oct. 11, 1941; s. William Gilbert and Maud (Moore) P. AB. magna cum laude in History, Harvard U., 1963, J.D., 1966; m. Priscilla Adrian Moore, June 17, 1967. Admitted to Tex. bar, 1966; reporter NY Daily News, 1969-73; editor-in-chief Ch. Bus. Report, NYC, 1976-82; pres. Inkslingers, Inc.; free-lance writer, NYC and Fla., 1973-; writer, lectr.-in-residence Teen Writers Workshop, Vero Beach, Fla., 2000-; works include Survival on the Campus, 1972, Help Wanted: Faith Required, 1974, The Commune Kidnapping, 1975, Women in the Pulpit, 1976, PDA-Personal Death Awareness, 1976, On the Trail of God, 1977, The Born-Again Christian Catalog, 1979, Return of the Star of Bethlehem, 1980, The Mean to Die, 1982, The Preconception Gender Diet, 1982, Adventures in Immortality, 1982, How to Go From Rags to Riches in Real Estate, 1982, The Templeton Touch, 1983, The Ethical Executive, 1984, Beyond the Relaxation Response, 1984, Forecast 2000, 1984, Beyond Reason, 1984, The Great American Success Story, 1985, Tough Marriage, 1986, The G-Index Diet, 1993, The Terrible Speller, 1993, Work a 4-Hour Day, 1994, Patient Power, 1996, The Resurrection Report, 1998, The Last Star, 2000, The Gospel According to the New York Times, 2000, Moongate, 2002, The Breakout Principle, 2003; writer, collaborator, Kenneth H. Cooper's Controlling Cholesterol, 1989, Charles Schwab's How to Be Your Own Stockbroker, 1991, Art Linkletter's Yes You Can!, 1982, Warren Avis's Take a Chance to Be First, 1987; editor The Light Speed Study Bible, 2005; Served with USMC, 1966-69. Mem. Authors Guild, Tex. Bar, NYC Bar Assn. Address: PO Box 643511 Vero Beach FL 32964

**PROCTOR, WILLIAM LEE,** college chancellor; b. Atlanta, Jan. 27, 1933; s. Samuel Cook and Rose Elizabeth (Nottingham) P.; m. Pamela Evans Duke; children: Samuel Matthews (dec.), Priscilla Nottingham. BS, Fla. State U., 1956, MS, 1964, PhD, 1968; DHL (hon.), Nova Southeastern U., 2003; LLD (hon.), Flagler Coll., 2004. Tchr. Seminole County Pub. Schs., Longwood, Fla., 1956-57, 58-62, Orange County Fla. Pub. Schs., Orlando, 1957-58; athletic coach Fla. State U., Tallahassee, 1962-65, asst. dean men, 1965-67, grad. fellow, 1967-68; supt. of schs. Rock Hill (S.C.) Sch. Dist. #3, 1968-69; dean of men U. Ctrl. Fla., Orlando, 1969-71; pres. Flagler Coll., St. Augustine, Fla., 1971-2001, chancellor, 2001—; mem. representing Dist. 20, Fla. Ho. of Reps., 2004. Cons. on higher edn. policy Heritage Found., Washington, 1983—, Fla. Bd. Edn., 2001-03, State Bd. Edn., 2003-2004; mem. Commn. on Colls., So. Assn. Colls. and Schs., 1995-2000; dir. Tchr. Edn. Accreditation Coun. Vice-chmn. Fla. Edn. Stds. Commn., 1995-2001; bd. dirs. Penney Retirement Cmty., chmn., 2004; bd. dirs. Vicar's Landing Retirement Cmty., chmn., 1992-95, bd., 1990-96; trustee, chmn. Fla. Sch. for Deaf and Blind, St. Augustine, 1984-2001; adv. coun. Salvation Army, St. Johns County; devel. coun. First Coast Work Force, 1998-2001; mem. Bus./Higher Edn. Partnership, 2000-01; chmn. Cmtys. in Schs., St. Johns County, Fla., 2002—; elected mem. Fla. Ho. Reps. Dist. 20, 2004. Recipient Disting. Educator award Fla. State U. Coll. Edn., 1989, Phil Carrol award Soc. for Advancement Mgmt., 1990, Disting. Svc. award Fla. Sch. for Deaf and Blind, 1992, Patrick Henry Medallion patriotic achievement Mil.

Order of World Wars, 1991, Stetson S Club Achievement award, 1993, Order of the South So. Acad. Letters, Arts, and Scis., Excellence in Mgmt. award Soc. for Advancement of Mgmt., 2000, Lifetime Edn. Achievement award, 2001, Disting. Svc. award Fla. Assn. Colls. and Univs., 2002, Sec. Jim Horne's Life Edn. Leadership award; named to Fla. State U. Athletic Hall of Fame, 1988, Order of La Florida, 2001. Mem. Am. Assn. Pres. of Ind. Colls., State Hist. Assn., Ind. Colls. and Univs. of Fla. (legis. chmn. 1974-77, vice chmn. 1976-77, chmn. 1978-79, Liberty Bell award 2003), Rotary (pres. 1978-79, bd. govs. dist. 697 1988-89). Republican. Presbyterian. Avocations: history, jogging, Karate. Office: Flagler Coll Office of the Chancellor PO Box 1027 Saint Augustine FL 32085-1027 Office Phone: 904-669-2018. Business E-Mail: proctorw@flagler.edu.

**PROEBSTING, EDWARD LOUIS, JR.,** retired horticulturist; b. Woodland, Calif., Mar. 2, 1926; s. Edward Louis and Dorothy (Critzer) P.; m. Patricia Jean Connolly, June 28, 1947; children: William Martin, Patricia Louise, Thomas Alan (dec.). BS, U. Calif., Davis, 1948; PhD, Mich. State U., 1951. Asst. horticulturist Wash. State U., Prosser, 1951-57, assoc. horticulturist, 1957-63, horticulturist, 1963-93, supt. Irrigated Agrl. Rsch. and Ext. Ctr., 1990-93; ret., 1993. Vis. prof. Cornell U., Ithaca, N.Y., 1966; vis. scientist Hokkaido U., Sapporo, Japan, 1978, Victoria Dept. Agr., Tatura, Australia, 1986—. Contbr. numerous articles to profl. jours. Scoutmaster Boy Scouts Am., Prosser, 1963-76, dist. chmn., 1976-78. Served to lt. USNR, 1943-46, 52-54. Recipient Silver Beaver award Boy Scouts Am.; fellow Japan Soc. Promotion Sci., Sapporo, 1978, Res. Bank. Australia, 1986. Fellow AAAS, Am. Soc. Hort. Sci. (pres. 1983-84, sci. editor jour. 1993-98). Methodist. Avocations: backpacking, native plants. Home: 1929 Miller Ave Prosser WA 99350-1532

**PROEFROCK, CARL KENNETH,** academic medical administrator; b. Curtis, Ill., Mar. 30, 1928; s. Carl Robert and Anna Lorraine (Hagel) Proefrock; m. Margaret Muntz (dec. Apr. 1984); 4 children; m. Janelle Dillon, Sept. 8, 1988 (dec. Sept. 2001). BA, Carthage Coll., Kenosha, Wis., 1949; MDiv, Chgo. Luth. Sem., 1953. Pastor Evang. Luth. Ch. Am., 1953—66; sr. comm. orgn. specialist N.Y.C. Housing and Devel. Adminstrn., 1966-68; exec. dir. Model Cities Program, Manchester, NH, 1968-70, Health Assn. Rochester and Monroe (N.Y.), 1970-73, Mahoning Shenango Area Health Edn. Network, Youngstown, Ohio, 1973-78; spl. asst. to dean Northeastern Ohio Univs. Coll. Medicine, Rootstown, 1978-79; v.p. Med. Coll. Ohio, Toledo, 1979-88, sr. v.p. govtl. affairs, 1988-93; pres. KPA Assocs., Inc., 1993—. V.p. Found. for Applied Rsch., Washington, 1976; chmn. adv. bd. Ohio AHEC, Columbus, 1976; program adminstr. Ohio Statewide Area Health Edn. Ctr., Toledo, 1988-93. Chmn. Toledo Area Coun. Tech., 1986; spl. asst. to clergy All Saints Parish, Pawleys Island, S.C., 1998-2000. Mem. Nat. Area Health Edn. Ctrs. Assn. (bd. dir. 1988-95), Nat. Assn. Univ. Rsch. Administrs., Soc. Rsch. Administrs., Internat. Assn. Univ. Rsch. Parks, Soc. Univ. Patent Administrs., Nat. Assn. Health Manpower Edn. Systems, Northeastern Ohio Med. Educators Assn. (bd. dir.), Rotary. Anglican. Home: 46 Pawleys Pl Dr Pawleys Island SC 29585-7254 Office: KPA Assocs PO Box 194 Pawleys Island SC 29585-0194 E-mail: kenkpa@sccoast.net.

**PROEHL, RICKY,** professional football player; b. Hillsborough, NJ, Mar. 7, 1968; BA in Speech Comm., Wake Forest Univ., 1989. Wide receiver Phoenix Cardinals, 1990—93, Ariz. Cardinals, 1994, Seattle Seahawks, 1995—96, Chgo. Bears, 1997, St. Louis Rams, 1998—2002, Carolina Panthers, 2003—. Achievements include record-holding career yardage and TD catches, Wake Forest Univ. Office: Carolina Panthers 800 So Mint St Charlotte NC 28202*

**PROFETA, SALVATORE, JR.,** chemist, educator; m. Catherine Mary Cherry, Sept. 20, 1980; children: Luisa, Theresa. BA in Pharm. Chemistry, Temple U., 1973; PhD in Phys. Organic Chemistry, U. Ga., 1978. Fellow chemistry dept. Fla. State U., Tallahassee, 1979-80; fellow pharm. chemistry dept. U. Calif., San Francisco, 1980-81, teaching fellow, 1981-82; instr. chemistry dept. La. State U., Baton Rouge, 1982-84; sr. scientist Allergan Pharms., Inc., Irvine, Calif., 1984-87; project mgr. computational chemistry Glaxo Rsch. Inst., Research Triangle Park, N.C., 1987-90, head chemistry systems, 1990-93; dir. N.C. Supercomputing Ctr. Rsch. Inst. at MCNC, Research Triangle Park, N.C., 1993-95; prin. computational chemist Monsanto, St. Louis, 1996-2000; dir. computational chemistry and structural biology Millennium Pharm., Cambridge, Mass., 2000—02; assoc. prof. Dept. Pharm. Chemistry U. S.C., Columbia, SC, 2003—. Cons. CADD-CAMM Smith, Kline & French, Phila., 1980-82, Squibb Rsch. Inst., Princeton, N.J., 1982-84; allocation com. N.C. Supercomputing Ctr., 1989-94; adj. prof. chemistry and computer sci. and engring U. SC, Columbia, 2006—. Mem. editl. bd. Jour. Molecular Graphics, 1989-2000; contbg. editor Chem. Design Automation News, 1991-2000; contbr. articles to Jour. Am. Chem. Soc. NSF fellow, 1976-78; Petroleum Rsch. Found. grantee, 1984-88. Mem. Am. Chem. Soc., Am. Crystal. Assn. Achievements include patents in anticancer drug design; co-author MM1, MM2, MM3 and AMBER molecular mechanical force fields. Office Phone: 803-808-2701. Business E-Mail: sprofetajr@netscape.net.

**PROFFER, ANDREW,** psychologist; b. Portland, Oreg., Sept. 26, 1963; s. Carl Ray Proffer and Janet Meisel. Student, Western Mich. U., 1981—83; BA in Psychology, U. Mich., 1985; MA/PhD in Clin. Psychology, Adelphi U., 1992. Psychology intern Bklyn. Family Ct. Clinic, 1987—88; co-editor newsletter Derner Inst. Adelphi U., 1988—90, tchg. asst., 1989—90, staff psychotherapist Ctr. Psychol. Svcs., 1989—90; psychology extern South Oaks Hosp., 1988—89; sch. psychologist Glen Cove Pub. Schs., 1988, 1989; pvt. practice psychology Park Slope, Bklyn., 1993—95; staff psychologist Herbert G. Birch Early Childhood Ctr., Springfield Gardens, NY, 1991—93, chief psychologist, 1993—94; sr. psychologist Child Psychiat. Inst., John Umstead Hosp., Butner, NC, 1994—95; pvt. practice psychology Proffer Psychol. Svcs., Durham, NC, 1995—98; staff psychologistDevel. and Psychol. Ctr. Moses Cone Hosp., Greensboro, NC, 1995—98; clin. psychologist Green Valley Psychiat. Group PA, 1998—2000; pvt. practice psychology Greensboro, 1999—. Contbr. articles to profl. publs. Mem.: APA. Avocations: basketball, cycling, skiing, travel. Office: 701 S Lindell Rd Greensboro NC 27403 E-mail: aproffer@triad.rr.com.

**PROFFITT, WILLIAM ROBERT,** orthodontics educator; b. Harnett County, N.C., Apr. 19, 1936; s. Glenn Theodore and Edna Marie (Queener) P.; m. Sara Thomas, Sept. 20, 1953; children: Lola Ann, Edward Thomas, Glenn Theodore. BS, U. N.C., 1956, DDS, 1959; student, Campbell Coll., Buies Creek, N.C., 1952-53; PhD, Med. Coll. Va., 1962; MS, U. Wash., 1963; FDS, Royal Coll. Surgeons, 1990. Cert. Am. Bd. Orthodontics. Investigator Nat. Inst. Dental Research, Bethesda, Md., 1963-65; asst. prof. orthodontics U. Ky., Lexington, 1965-68, assoc. prof., 1968-71; prof. U.Ky., Lexington, 1971-73; prof. orthodontics U. Fla., Gainesville, 1973-75; prof., chmn. dept. orthodontics U. NC, Chapel Hill, 1975—, Kenan prof., 1992. Cons. NIH, Bethesda, 1974— Author: Contemporary Orthodontics, 1986, 4th edit., 2006: co-author: Surgical Correction of Dentofacial Deformity, 1980, Surgical-Orthodontic Treatment, 1990, Contemporary Treatment of Dentofacial Deformity, 2003; contbr. articles to sci. jours. Served to lt. comdr. USPHS, 1963-65. Fulbright research scholar U. Adelaide, Australia, 1972 Mem. ADA, Am. Assn. Orthodontists (coun. on rsch. 1970-76), Internat. Assn. Dental Rsch., Phi Beta Kappa. Democrat. Presbyterian. Home: 620 Rock Creek Rd Chapel Hill NC 27514-6716 Office: UNC Sch Dentistry Dept Orthodontics Chapel Hill NC 27599-7450 Office Phone: 919-966-4428. E-mail: william_proffit@dentistry.unc.edu.

**PROFFITT, JOHN DANIEL, JR.,** education educator; b. Lynchburg, Va., July 16, 1981; s. John Daniel and Sharon Overstreet Proffitt; m. Tracy Jo Earley, Aug. 7, 2004. BA in music edn., Va. Tech., 2004. Tchr., music dir. Appomattox U.) County Schs., 2004—. Mem.: Va. Music Educator's Assn., Music Educators Nat. Conf. Republican. Baptist. Home: 100 Irvington St Lynchburg VA 24503

**PROFFITT, JOHN RICHARD,** information technology executive, educator, public official; b. Grand Junction, Colo., Sept. 12, 1930; s. Hillus D. and Joy Elaine (Lindsay) P.; m. Claire Boyer Miller, May 8, 1965 (div. 1992); children: Cameron Lindsay, William Boyer. BA in Edn., U. Ky., 1953, MA in Polit. Sci., 1961; postgrad., U. Mich., 1959-65. Asst. dean of men, instr. polit. sci. dept. U. Ky., Lexington, 1957-59; teaching fellow U. Mich., Ann Arbor, 1961-63, 63-65; asst. dir. Nat. Commn. on Accrediting, Washington, 1966-68; dir. accreditation and eligibility staff U.S. Dept. HEW, Washington, 1968-75; dir. divsn. eligibility and agy. evaluation U.S. Dept. Edn., Washington, 1975-80, dir. divsn. instnl. and state incentive programs, 1980-82; pres. The Clairion Corp., Bethesda, Md., 1982-84, Nat. Asbestos Removal, Inc., Beltsville, Md., 1985-90, Commonwealth Environ. Svcs., Inc., Alexandria, Va., 1987-91, also chmn. bd. dirs.; chmn. Internat. Environ. Engrs., Inc., Alexandria, Va., 1991-92; pres. Canterbury Internat., Vienna, Va., 1992-95; cons., 1995-99; v.p. E-Pass Techs., Inc., McLean, Va., 1999—. Cons. Conn. State Common. Higher Edn., Hartford, 1967, Am. Coun. Edn., Washington, 1970; cons. U.S. Dept. Hew, 1967, 68; mem. study steering com. Am. Vocat. Assn., Washington, 1968; exec. sec. Nat. Adv. Com. on Accreditation and Instnl. Eligibility, Washington, 1968-80; mem. gen. com. Nat. Study Sch. evaluation, Alexandria, 1970-78; mem. task force Edn. Commn. of the States, Denver, 1972; subcom. chmn. Fed. Interagy. Com. on Edn., Washington, 1974-76; lectr., presenter profl. confs.; chmn. Commn. Accrediting. Co-author: Accreditation and Certification in Relation to Allied Health Manpower, 1971; contbg. author: Health Manpower: Adapting in the Seventies, 1971, Accreditation in Teacher Education, 1975, Transferring Experiential Credit, 1979; contbr. articles to profl. and govtl. agy. publs., 1968-79. Bd. dirs. and chmn. accrediting common. Nat. Accreditation Coun. for Agys. Serving the Blind, N.Y.C., 1983-89, v.p. and bd. dirs., 1985-89; pres., chmn. bd. dirs. Found. for Advancement of Quality Svcs. for the Blind, Alexandria, 1988. 1st lt. USAF, 1953-55, Japan and Korea. Higher edn. fellow Univ. Mich., 1959. Mem. Optimist Club (Lexington, Ky.), Club Internat. (Chgo.), Island Club (Hobe Sound, Fla.), Thoroughbred Club Am. (Lexington), Tower Club (Vienna, Va.), Sigma Nu, Omicron Delta Kappa. Democrat. Episcopalian. Avocations: travel, antiques, art, animal welfare, conservation. Home: 515 Beall Ave Rockville MD 20850-2106 Office Phone: 703-744-1468. E-mail: john.proffitt@e-pass.com.

**PROFFITT, KEVIN,** archivist; b. Hamilton, Ohio, Dec. 24, 1956; s. Henry C. and Marjorie O. (Elam) P.; m. Joan Moriarity, May 17, 1986. BA, Miami U., Oxford, Ohio, 1979; MA, Wright State U., 1980; MLS, U. Ky., 1998. Archivist Am. Jewish Archives, Cin., 1981—. Contbr. articles to profl. jours. Mem. Soc. Am. Archivists, Acad. Cert. Archivists (cert.), Midwest Archives Conf., Soc. Ohio Archivists (pres. 1987-89). Office: Am Jewish Archives 3101 Clifton Ave Cincinnati OH 45220-2404

**PROFFITT, WALDO, JR.,** newspaper editor; b. Plainview, Tex., Oct. 8, 1924; s. Waldo and Susan Ann (Smith) P.; m. Marjorie Baltzegar, Sept. 14, 1946 (div. 1963); children: Ann Herbert, Deborah, Geoffrey Harrison, Laurence Scott; m. Anne Collier Greene, Feb. 6, 1966; 1 child, Robert Waldo. BA cum laude, Harvard U., 1948. Reporter Bangor (Maine) Commercial, 1948-50; assoc. dir. Harvard News Office, Cambridge, Mass., 1952-54; city editor Charlotte (N.C.) News, 1954-58; mng. editor Journal, Lorain, Ohio, 1958-61; editorial dir. Sarasota (Fla.) Herald-Tribune, 1961-84; editor, 1984-98; columnist Sarasota-Herald Tribune, 1998—. Lt. U.S. Army, 1943-46, ETO, lt. USAF, 1950-52. Recipient Global Media Lifetime Achievement award, Population Inst., 2003. Mem. Am. Soc. Newspaper Editors, Fla. Soc. Newspaper Editors (pres. 1978). Democrat. Unitarian Universalist. Home: 1581 Hillview Dr Sarasota FL 34239-2047 Office: Sarasota Herald-Tribune PO Box 1719 Sarasota FL 34230-1719 Personal E-mail: wproffitt@comcast.net.

**PROFIT, LORETHA SPURS,** retired elementary school educator; b. Monroe, La., Aug. 15, 1947; d. James and Willie Mae (Kiper) Spurs; m. Simon Profit Jr., June 6, 1966; children: Anthony Simeon, Adriane Sirena, Simon III. BA, N.E. La. U., 1976. From sst. mgr. to co-owner Nelsons Drive In and Motel, Monroe, 1966—84; tchr. 2d grade Woodlawn Elem. Sch., West Monroe, La., 1976—90, Lincoln Elem. Sch., Monroe, 1990—2005; ret., 2005. Substitute tchr., vol. tutor Ouachita Parish Sch. Bd., Monroe, 1968—69; paraprofl. Swayze Elem. Sch., Monroe, 1973—76. Ptnr. Spl. Olympics, La. Named Hon. Citizen, Girls and Boys Town. Mem.: NEA, Internat. Platform Assn., Smithsonian Nat. Assoc., La. Assn. Educators Black Caucus (lead tchr. La. challange grant), Monroe City Assn. Educators (faculty rep.), La. Assn. Educators, ULM Alumni Assn., Nat. Coun. Negro Women, Inc., Breeze Gospel Group, Order Eastern Star, Delta Sigma Theta. Home: 4005 Gaston St Monroe LA 71203-5819 Mailing: PO Box 5059 Monroe LA 71211-5059

**PROFITT, DONALD RALPH,** secondary school educator; b. Dayton, Jan. 23, 1949; s. Everett Ralph and Mary Francis Profitt; m. Karen Sue Freeman, Feb. 16, 1998; m. Karen Sue McDermott; children: Chad McDermott, Mathew McDermott, Shelly McDermott. BS, Bowling Green State U., Ohio, 1972; MA, Mich. State U., Mich., 1976; EdD, Nova Southeastern U., Fla., 1996. Profl. Educator Fla. Dept. of Edn., 2004. Prin. Elem. Sch., Edinburg, Tex., 1982—92, Elem. Prin., Pasadena, Fla., 1992—95; tchr. Orange County Pub. Schs., Orlando, Fla., 1998—. Author: (book on edn.) Teaching: A Survival Manual for the First Year Teacher (Sam's Club Tchr. Yr. in Fla., 1999). Recipient Excellence In Tchg., Sci. Am., 2002. Mem.: Orange County Classroom Tchrs. Assn. (assoc. Tchr. of the Yr. 2005). Home: 10624 Denali Dr Clermont FL 34711-9127 Office: Colonial 9th Grade Ctr 7775 Valencia College Ln Orlando FL Office Phone: 407-249-6369. Personal E-mail: dprofitt@cfl.rr.com. Business E-Mail: profitd@ocps.net.

**PROFUSEK, ROBERT ALAN,** lawyer; b. Cleve., Jan. 14, 1950; s. George John and Geraldine (Hobl) P.; m. Linda Gail Schmidt, May 7, 1972; children: Robert Charles, Kathryn Anne. BA, Cornell U., 1972; JD, NYU, 1975. Bar: Ohio 1975, Tex. 1981, NY 1994. Assoc. Jones Day, Cleve., 1975-81, Dallas, 1981-82, ptnr., 1982—, NY, 1993. bd. dirs., CTS Corporcitum and Valero, LP; Contbr. articles to profl. jours.; spkr. in field. Mem. ABA, NY Bar Assn., Assn. Bar City of NY, Tex. Bar Assn., Greenwich Country Club. Republican. Episcopalian. Home: 541 North St Greenwich CT 06830-3424 Office: Jones Day 222 E 41st St 15th Fl New York NY 10017 Office Phone: 212-326-3800. Office Fax: 212-755-7306. E-mail: raprofusek@jonesday.com.

**PROGER, PHILLIP A.,** lawyer; b. NYC, Apr. 8, 1948; s. BA, Univ. Maryland, 1969, JD with honors, 1973. Bar: Ohio 1973, D.C. 1978, U.S. Supreme Ct. 1978. Head Antitrust Divsn. Jones Day, Washington. Adj. prof. Georgetown Univ. Law Ctr., 1983-84; adv. bds. BNA (antitrust & trade regulation report), M&A Lawyer. Mem. editl. bd. Law Rev. Moot Ct., 1973; contbr. articles to profl. jours. Fellow Am. Bar Found.; mem. ABA (chmn. Antitrust Law sect. 1998-99, bd. gov. 2003-), Am. Law Inst., Ohio State Bar Assn., D.C. Bar Assn., Am. Acad. Hosp. Attys. (pres. 1994-95). Office: Jones Day 5th Fl 51 Louisiana Ave Washington DC 20001-2113 Office Phone: 202-879-4668. Office Fax: 202-626-1700. Business E-Mail: paproger@jonesday.com.

**PROHOVNIK, ISAK,** medical educator; b. 1950; s. Julius Litner and Hanna Prohovnik; m. Lauren Fleischer; children: Maya, Dana. PhD, Lund U., Sweden, 1980. Assoc. prof. Coll. Physicians and Surgeons Columbia U., N.Y.C., 1989—95; prof. adj. diagnostic radiology Yale U., New Haven, 2000—; prof. psychiatry and radiology Mt. Sinai Sch. Medicine, N.Y.C., 2000—.

**PROKASY, WILLIAM FREDERICK,** academic administrator; b. Cleve., Nov. 27, 1930; s. William Frederick and Margaret Lovinia (Chapman) P.; m. Pamela Pearson; children: Kathi Lynn, Cheryl Anne; stepchildrenm: Lisa Wier Cauthen, Kevin Wier. BA, Baldwin-Wallace Coll., 1952; MA, Kent State U., 1954; PhD, U. Wis., 1957. Grad. asst. Kent State U., 1953-54; W.A.R.F. fellow U. Wis., 1954-55, teaching asst., 1955-57; asst. prof., then assc. prof. Pa. State U., 1957-66; prof. psychology, chmn. dept. U. Utah, 1966-69, Disting. rsch. prof., 1971-72, dean social and behavioral sci.,

1968-70; dean U. Utah (Coll. Social and Behavioral Sci.), 1970-79; acting dean U. Utah (Grad. Sch. Social Work), 1979-80; prof. psychology dean Coll. Liberal Arts and Scis., U. Ill., Champaign-Urbana, 1980-88; prof., v.p. for acad. affairs U. Ga., 1988-98. Cons. in field. Editor: Classical Conditioning, 1965, (with A.H. Black) Classical Conditioning II, 1971, (with D. Raskin) Electrodermal Responding in Psychological Research, 1973, Psychophysiology, 1974-77; editor (with I. Gormezano and R. Thompson) Classical Conditioning III, 1986; assoc. editor Learning and Motivation, 1969-76; cons. editor Jour. Exptl. Psychology, 1968-80. Trustee Utah Planned Parenthood Assn., 1977—80; Utah bd. dirs. ACLU, 1978—80; v.p. bd. dirs. Champaign-Urbana Symphony, 1986—88; mem. bd. advisors Ga. Mus. Art, 1989—95, U. Ga. Performing Arts Ctr., 1998—2003; mem. bd. visitors U. Ga. Librs., 1998—; mem. Athens-Clarke County Libr. Bd., 1999—; treas. Athens Opera Co. Guild, 2001—; pres. Friends Ga. Mus. Art, 2002—03, Athens-Clarke County Libr. Bd., 2003—04, Friends of Drama, 2003—04; v.p. Athens-Clarke County Libr. Endowment Bd., 2003—; mem. Classic Ctr. Cultural Found., 2003—, treas., 2006—; mem. adv. bd. Franklin Coll. Arts and Scis., 2003—06; del. Utah Dem. Conv., 1968—70, 1972—74; mem. Athens Regional Libr., 2002—, chmn. Recipient Alumni Merit award Baldwin Wallace Coll., 1992, Disting. Alumni award Piedmont Coll., 1998, U. Ga. Alumni award of excellence, 1998; NSF sr. postdoctoral fellow, 1963-64. Fellow AAAS, Am. Psychol. Assn. (chmn. bd. sci. affairs 1977-78, coun. of reps. 1980-86, bd. dirs. 1983-86, bd. ednl. affairs 1993-96); mem. Fedn. Behavioral, Psychol. and Cognitive Scis. (v.p. 1984-85, pres. 1985-87), coun. of Sci. Soc. Pres.'s (exec. bd. 1987-91, chmn. 1990), Psychonomic Soc., Coun. Rsch. Librs. (bd. dirs. 1990-96), NASULGC (exec. com. coun. on acad. affairs 1995-96), Am. Assn. Higher Edn., Soc. Psychophysiol. Rsch. (bd. dirs. 1978-84, pres. 1982-83), Utah Psychol. Assn. (bd. dirs. 1970-80, pres. 1971-72), Assn. Advancement Psychology (bd. dirs. 1982-83), Sigma Xi (pres. U. Utah chpt. 1972-73), Phi Kappa Phi. Personal E-mail: wfp@charter.net.

**PROKOPCHAK, PETER A.,** music educator; b. N.Y.C., Dec. 11, 1956; s. Michael and Julia Prokopchak; children: Susan, Michelle. AS, SUNY Orange, Middletown, 1977; BS, Westchester Coll., Pa., 1979; MS, SUNY New Paltz, 1985; M +30, Coll. St. Rose, Albany, N.Y., 1998. Tchr. music Eldred Ctrl. Schs., NY, 1981—88, Pine Bush Ctrl. Schs., NY, 1988—. Mem.: Eagles, Elks (exalted ruler, trustee, dist. chair, leading knight, esquire), Phi Mu Alpha. Avocations: skiing, volleyball, ping pong/table tennis, softball. Office: Crispell Mid Sch Rte 302 Pine Bush NY 12566 Home: PO Box 2352 Middletown NY 10940

**PROKOPIS, EMMANUEL CHARLES,** computer company executive; b. Peabody, Mass., July 5, 1942; s. Charles Emmanuel and Stevia (Kassotis) P.; m. Mary Catherine Dudeck, Dec. 6, 1969; children: Peter Matthew, Christina Prokopis Leonard. BBA, U. Mass., 1966. Mgr., pricing, budgeting, acctg. The Mitre Corp., Mass., Va., 1969-74; mgr. contracts liaison Pratt & Whitney Aircraft, Conn., Fla., 1974-78; mgr. fin. planning, corp. office United Techs. Corp., Hartford, Conn., 1978-81, contr. magnet wire and insulation div. Fort Wayne, Ind., 1981-83, v.p. fin., chief fin. officer The Mostek Corp. (subs.) Carrollton, Tex., 1983-85; sr. v.p. fin. and ops., chief fin. officer The Lotus Devel. Corp., Cambridge, Mass., 1985-87, fin. mgr. mfg. and engring., 1987-91; v.p. budgeting Digital Equipment Corp., 1991-92; exec. v.p. MAST Industries, 1992, Ziff Comm., 1992-93; v.p. corp. contr. Digital Equipment Corp., 1994-96; COO, CFO, treas. IONA Technologies, 1996-97, COO, 1997-99; ret., 1999. 1st lt. U.S. Army, 1966-69, Vietnam. Decorated Bronze Star. Greek Orthodox.

**PROMISLO, DANIEL,** lawyer, small business owner; b. Bryn Mawr, Pa., Nov. 15, 1932; s. Charles and Pearl (Backman) Promislo; m. Estelle Carasso, June 10, 1961 (dec. Apr. 2006); children: Mark, Jacqueline, Steven. BSBA, Drexel U., 1955; JD magna cum laude, U. Pa., 1966. Bar: Pa. 1966. Pres. owner Hist. Souvenir Co., Phila., 1957—; assoc. Wolf, Block, Schorr & Solis-Cohen, Phila., 1966-70, ptnr., 1977-94, exec. com., 1987-89, mng. dir., 1997-2001, of counsel, 1994—; founder, pres. dir. Inst. Paralegal Tng., Phila., 1970-75, cons., 1975-77; pres., owner Hist. Documents Co., 1992—. Editor: Corporate Law, 1970, Real Estate Law, 1971, Estates and Trusts, 1971, Civil Litigation, 1972, Employee Benefit Plans, 1973, Criminal Law, 1974; contbr. articles to profl. jours. Bd. dirs. Phila. Drama Guild, 1977—95, chmn., 1982—86; bd. dirs. Phila. Israel Econ. Devel. Program, 1983—88, Inst. Arts in Edn., 1990—93, WHYY, Inc., 1994—2003, vice-chmn., 1995—96, chmn., 1996—97; bd. dirs. U.S. Physicians, Inc., 1995—98; trustee Resource Asset Investment Trust (name now RAIT Investment Trust), 1997—; bd. advisors Drexel U. Coll. Arts and Scis., 2001—. Mem.: Drexel U. 100, Blue Key, Order of Coif, Phi Kappa Phi. Democrat. Jewish. Avocations: movies, basketball, tennis, golf. Office: Wolf Block Schorr & Solis-Cohen 1650 Arch St Fl 22 Philadelphia PA 19103-2097 E-mail: dpromislo@comcast.net.

**PRONGER, CHRIS,** professional hockey player; b. Dryden, Ont., Can., Oct. 10, 1974; m. Lauren Pronger, 2001. Defenseman Hartford Whalers, 1993—95, St. Louis Blues, 1995—2005, Edmonton Oilers, 2005—06, Anaheim Ducks, 2006—; mem. Can. Nat. Hockey Team, 1992—93, 1996—97, 1997—98, 2001—02. Member NHL All-Rookie Team, 1994; player NHL All-star game, 1999, 2000, 02, 04. Finalist Lester B. Pearson award, 2000; recipient Hart medal, Can. Under 18 Team, Phoenix Cup, 1991, World Jr. Hockey Championship, 1993, World Championship, 1997, Bud Ice Plus-Minus award, 1997—98, Norris Trophy, 2000, Hart Trophy, 2000. Achievements include mem. Gold medal Can. Hockey team, Salt Lake City Olympic Games, 2002. Office: Anaheim Ducks 2695 E Katella Ave Anaheim CA 92806*

**PRONIN, ANATOLY,** photographer; b. St. Petersburg, Russia, Oct. 28, 1939; s. Alexey N. and Bronislava (Turovskaya) Pronin; m. Valeria Golovchanskaya Pronin, Mar. 4, 1967; children: Marsha, Katya. Student, State U., Leningrad, 1962—65. Asst. prof. photography Mukhina Coll. Fine and Indsl. Art, Leningrad, Russia, 1965—69, staff photographer, 1973—78, Restoring Co. Ancient Russian Art and Architecture, 1969—73; free-lance photographer NYC, 1979—. Photographer (exhibitions) Art Dir. Club NJ, 1988 (Cert. of Excellence, 1988), Photographic Assn. Calcutta, India, 1989, Johannesburg Internat. Photo Salon, South Africa, 1990, Edinburg Photographic Soc., Scotland, 1990, NJ State Coun. Arts, 1990 (Fellowship grants), 1999, Nat. Jewish Mus., Washington, 1992, Michael Ingbar Gallery, NYC, 2002, Art Hall of the Pacific Design Ctr., LA, 2004, (permanent collections) Mus. of History, St. Petersburg, Russia, State Russian Mus., St. Petersburg, Bibliotheque Nationale, Paris, France, Staatliche Museen zu Berlin, Germany, NY Pub. Libr., NYC, Bklyn. Mus., Libr. of Congress, Washington, Met. Mus. Art, NYC, Portland Art Mus., Mass. Inst. Tech. and Harvard U., Cambridge, Salvador Dali Mus., St. Petersburg, Fla., George Balanchine Found., N.Y.C., (publs.) Graphis mag., Alberta Edn., Asics Co., Brunott Art Pub., Routledge, Mus. Jewish Diaspora, McGraw-Hill, W.W. Norton, Simon & Schuster, Harcourt Brace, Prentice Hall, Ency. Britannica, Microsoft Encarta, NER, Geo. Recipient Silver medal internat. photo exhbn., Berlin, 1971, First Pl. photo exhbns., Moscow, 1977, 1978. Home: 315 Eastern St Apt D-1613 New Haven CT 06513 E-mail: apronin@apronin.com.

**PRONZINI, BILL JOHN (WILLIAM PRONZINI),** writer; b. Petaluma, Calif., Apr. 13, 1943; s. Joseph and Helene (Guder) P.; m. Marcia Muller. Author: 67 novels (including under pseudonyms), 4 books of non-fiction, 19 collections of short stories, 1971—; first novel, The Stalker, 1971; editor 80 anthologies; contbr. numerous short stories to publs. Recipient 6 scroll awards Mystery Writers Am., Life Achievement award Pvt. Eye Writers Am., 1987. Office: PO Box 2536 Petaluma CA 94953-2536 E-mail: pronhack@sbcglobal.net.

**PROPERZIO, PAUL J.,** classicist, educator; b. Keene, N.H., May 20, 1947; s. Joseph M. and Virginia T. Properzio; m. Deborah E. Jewett. Jan. 31, 1970; 1 child, Lucy A. BA in Latin and Greek, U. NH, 1969; PhD in Classical Studies, Loyola U. Chgo., 1982. Lic. educator Mass. Chair, assoc. prof. classics Drew U., Madison, NJ, 1975—87; tchr. Latin Hanover HS, NH, 1987—88; tchr. Latin, history, mythology Reading Meml. HS, Mass.,

1988—93; assoc. prof. classics and humanities St. Anselm Coll., Manchester, NH, 1993—97; tchr. Latin and Greek Boston Latin Acad., 1997—. V.p. Archaeol. Inst. of Am. (Boston Soc.), Boston, 2002—. Editor: (jour.) Am. Classical League Newsletter, 2003—; contbr. presentation,; author: (book chpt.) Heroic Epithets in Early Greek and Han Chinese Literature, New Light on the Cults of Apollo and Artemis in Marseilles, Heroic Honor and Responsibility: The Iliad as a Reflection of Global Conflict, Social Values, and Human Interaction in the Modern World; contbr. presentations, presentation, articles to profl. jours. Lector St. Joseph's Ch., Andover, Mass., 1988—. Capt. M.I. U.S. Army, 1971—79. Recipient Rome and China Participant grant, NEH, 2000—02, Elaine G. Batting Meml. scholarship, Mass. Fgn. Lang. Assn., 2003, Arthur P. McKinley scholarship, Am. Classical League, 2002, FIPSE (Fund for Improvement of Post Secondary Edn.) fellowship, Woodrow Wilson Found., Princeton U., 1985; Fulbright scholar, Italy, 1969. Mem.: Classical Assn. of the Atlantic States (pres. 1984—85), Classical Assn. of New Eng. (pres. 1993—94), Am. Philol Assn. (minority students scholarship com. 2002—05), Prof. John C. Rouman Classical Lecture Series, U. of N.H. (adv. bd. 1997—). Independent. Roman Catholic. Avocations: travel, cooking, tennis, theater, walking. Home: 15 Ballardvale Rd Andover MA 01810 Office: Boston Latin Acad 205 Townsend St Boston MA 02121 Office Phone: 617-635-9957. Home Fax: 603-864-2496; Office Fax: 617-635-6696. Personal E-mail: pjpropertius@comcast.net.

**PROPP, STEVEN H.,** legal analyst; b. Berkeley, Calif., Oct. 2, 1955; s. Harry and Dorothy S. Propp; m. Nancy L. Jones Slaughter, Mar. 3, 2005. BA, Calif. State U., Sacramento, 1978. Legis. mgr. Pub. Employees' Retirement Sys., Sacramento, 1979—, Author; Work, Death and Taxes, 2000, Tattered Pilgrims, 2001, Inquiries: Philosophical, 2002, Beyond Heaven and Earth, 2003, Utopia On the 6th Floor: Work, Death and Taxes Part 2, 2004, A Multicultural Christmas, 2005, Josué, Prisoner At Shalem, 2005, Family Lessons, 2006, Saved By Philosophy, 2006. Avocations: music, reading. Personal E-mail: stevenhpropp@hotmail.com.

**PROPST, CATHERINE LAMB,** biotechnology company executive, pharmaceutical company executive; b. Charlotte, NC, Mar. 10, 1946; d. James Pinckney and Eliza M. Propst. BA magna cum laude, Vanderbilt U., 1967; M of Philosophy, Yale U., 1970, PhD, 1973. Head microbiology div. GTE Labs., Waltham, Mass., 1974-77; various sr. mgmt. positions Abbott Labs., North Chicago, Ill., 1977-80; v.p. rsch. and devel. Ayerst (Wyeth) Labs., Plainview, NY, 1980-83; v.p. rsch. and devel. worldwide Flow Gen. Inc., McLean, Va., 1983-85; pres., CEO Affiliated Sci. Inc., Ingleside, Ill., 1985-97; pres., chmn., CEO Tex. Biotech. Found., Hempstead, Tex., 1997—. Vis. prof. genetics U. Ill., Chgo., 1989—90; founder, exec. dir. Ctr for Biotech., Northwestern U., 1990—95; pres. Ill. Biotech. Ctr., 1995—97; bd. dirs. several cos.; bd. dirs., mem. sci. adv. bd. Keystone Symposia on Molecular and Cellular Biology, 1997—2002. Author, editor Computer-Aided Drug Design, 1989, Nucleic Acid Targeted Drug Design, 1992; contbr. articles to profl. jours. Named to Outstanding Working Women in the U.S., 1982; recipient many sci. and bus. awards. Fellow: Soc. Indsl. Microbiology (bd. dirs. 1990—93), Nat. Coun. Biotech Ctrs. (bd. dirs. 1995—97); mem.: AAAS, Nat. Wildlife Fedn., Consortium for Plant Biotech. Rsch. (bd. dirs. 1994—99), Phi Beta Kappa, Sigma Xi. Episcopalian. Avocations: horseback riding, skiing, raising Black Angus and Black Brangus cattle. Office: Texas Biotech Found PO Box 17 Hempstead TX 77445-0017 Office Phone: 979-826-3075. Office Fax: 979-826-9710.

**PROPST, HAROLD DEAN,** retired academic administrator; b. Newton, N.C., Feb. 7, 1934; s. Charles Clayton and Sarah Isabel (Hilderbrand) P. BA, Wake Forest Coll., 1956; MA, Peabody Coll., 1959, PhD, 1964; LLD, Mercer U., 1985; LittD, Armstrong Atlantic State U., 2003. Tchr. Vandalia Pub. Schs., Ohio, 1959-60; instr. Wake Forest Coll., Winston-Salem, N.C., 1960-61; asst. prof. English, Radford Coll., Va., 1962-64, assoc. prof. Va., 1964-65, prof. Va., 1965-69, chmn. dept. English Va., 1965-66, 68-69; dean Armstrong State Coll., Savannah, Ga., 1969-76, v.p. for acad. affairs, 1976-79; vice chancellor for acad. devel. Univ. System Ga., Atlanta, 1979-81, exec. vice chancellor, 1981-85, chancellor, 1985-94. Editor: (novel) John Brent, 1970; contbr. articles to profl. jours.; monographs, books Bd. visitors Radford Coll., 1970-74; former pres. bd. Family Counseling Ctr., Savannah; former pres. bd. Family Counseling Ctr., Savannah; former bd. dirs. Savannah Symphony, Savannah Heart Assn., Alliance Theatre, Atlanta; mem. So. Region Edn. Bd., 1985-94; mem. adv. bd. Peabody Coll. Vanderbilt U., 1994-98; mem. adv. bd. Mars Hill Coll., 1996-2002. With USN, 1956-58. Fellow Carnegie Found., 1958, Ford Found. fellow, 1960; recipient Disting. Alumnus award Wake Forest U., 1986, Disting. Svc. award Mens Hill Coll., 1997, Disting. Alumnus award Peabody Coll. Vanderbilt U., 2003. Mem. Am. Assn. State Colls and Univs. (com. on accreditation 1982-86), Acad. for Ednl. Devel. (study com. on campus govt. 1976-77) Baptist.

**PROPST, M. TERESA CARSON,** historian; b. Balt., Jan. 7, 1976; d. John Rian and Maria Patricia (Romagnoli) Carson; m. Anthony Michael Propst, Nov. 10, 2001. BA, Towson U., 1999. Patient svcs. rep. Advanced Radiology, Towson, 1999—. Adult youth ministry vol. St. William of York Cath. Ch., Balt., 2000—04. Mem.: Order of Omega, Golden Key Nat. Honor Soc., Phi Alpha Theta, Alpha Xi Delta (chpt. life advisor Towson U. 2003—04, programs adv. 2005—). Democrat. Roman Catholic. Avocations: entertaining, travel, camping. Home: 439 Old Home Rd Baltimore MD 21206 Office: Advanced Radiology 124 Sister Pierre Dr Towson MD 21204

**PROPST, MICHAEL TRUMAN,** pathologist; b. Lebanon, Oreg., July 3, 1940; s. Lynn Edward and Vera Ruth (Forbes) P.; m. Susan Jean Joesting, Dec. 26, 1974; children: Christopher M., Andrew J., Matthew A., Michael Jonathan, Edwin Cam. BS, Oreg. State U., 1962; MD, U. Oreg., 1966. Diplomate Am. Bd. Pathology. Pathologist Humana Hosp., Anchorage, 1974—84; med. examiner State of Alaska, Anchorage, 1975—94; med. dir. Physicians Med. Lab., Anchorage, 1984—94; chief med. examiner State of Alaska, Anchorage, 1994—2001; cons. forensic pathology, 2001—. Served to maj. USAF, 1971-74. Fellow Coll. Am. Pathologists, Am. Soc. Clin. Pathologists, Am. Acad. Forensic Scientists, Royal Soc. Medicine (Gr. Britain),; mem. Nat. Assn. Med. Examiners. Lutheran. Office Phone: 541-469-2317. E-mail: mpropstmd@charter.net.

**PROSPER, PIERRE-RICHARD,** federal agency administrator; b. Denver, 1963; BA, Boston Coll.; JD, Pepperdine U. Bar: Calif. Dep. dst. atty. L.A. County, 1989—94; asst. U.S. atty. State of Calif., ctrl. dist., 1994—96; war crimes prosecutor U.N. Internat. Criminal Tribunal for Rwanda, 1996—98; spl. asst. to asst. atty. gen. for criminal divsn. State Dept.; spl. counsel, policy adviser Office of War Crimes, 1999—2001; amb. at large for war crimes issues U.S. Dept. of State, Washington, 2001—. Recipient Alumni award of Excellence, Boston Coll., 1999, Dist. Alumnus award, Pepperdine U. Sch. Law Alumni, 2000; fellow Wasserstein fellow, Harvard U., 2000—01. Office: US Dept of State Ambassador at large for War Crimes Issue 2201 C St NW Washington DC 20520-7512

**PROSSER, DAVID THOMAS, JR.,** state supreme court justice, former state legislator; b. Chgo., Dec. 24, 1942; s. David Thomas, Sr. and Elizabeth Averell (Patterson) Prosser. BA, DePauw U., 1965; JD, U. Wis., 1968. Bar: Wis. 1968. Lectr. Ind. U., Indpls., 1968-69; advisor U.S. Dept. Justice, Washington, 1969-72; adminstrv. asst. to U.S. Rep. Harold V. Froehlich, Washington, 1973-74; pvt. practice Washington, 1975, Appleton, Wis., 1976; dist. atty. Outagamie County Wis., Appleton, 1977-78; state rep. State of Wis., Madison, 1979-96; commr. Tax Appeals Commn., 1997-98; justice Supreme Ct. Wis., 1998—. Jud. Coun., 2002—06. Commr. Nat. Conf. Commrs. Uniform State Laws, 1982—96, 2005; mem. Wis. Sesquicentennial Commn., Madison, 1993—99; minority leader Wis. Assembly, 1989—94, spkr., 1995—96. Mem.: Outagamie Bar Assn., Milw. Bar Assn., Dane Bar Assn., Wis. Bar Assn. Presbyterian. Avocation: art collector of American prints. Office: Supreme Ct Wis PO Box 1688 Madison WI 53701-1688

**PROSSER, FRANKLIN PIERCE,** computer scientist; b. Atlanta, July 4, 1935; s. Edward Theron and Eunice (McDaniel) P.; m. Brenda Mary Lau, June 16, 1960; children: Edward, Andrea. BS, Ga. Inst. Tech., 1956, MS, 1958; PhD, Pa. State U., 1961. Prof. computer sci. Ind. U., Bloomington, 1969-99; asso. dir. Wrubel Computing Center, 1969-81, chmn. dept. computer sci., 1971-77, 87-93, spl. asst. for acad. computing, 1979-81; v.p. Logic Design, Inc., 1982-92. Cons. Lockheed Theoretical Physics Lab., Palo Alto, Calif., 1967 Home: 1200 S Longwood Dr Bloomington IN 47401-6072 Office: Ind U Dept Computer Sci Bloomington IN 47405

**PROSSER, JOHN MARTIN,** architecture educator; b. Wichita, Kans., Dec. 28, 1932; s. Francis Ware and Harriet Corinne (Osborne) P.; m. Judith Adams, Aug. 28, 1954 (dec. 1982); children: Thomas, Anne, Edward; m. Karen Ann Cleary, Dec. 30, 1983; 1 child, Jennifer. BArch, U. Kans., 1955; MArch, Carnegie Mellon U., 1961. Registered architect, Kans., Colo. Architect Robinson and Hissem, Wichita, 1954-56, Guirey, Srnka, and Arnold, Phoenix, 1961-62, James Sudler Assocs., Denver, 1962-68; ptnr., architect Nuzum, Prosser and Vetter, Boulder, 1969-73; from asst. prof. to prof. U. Colo., Boulder and Denver, 1968—, acting dean, 1980-84, dean, 1984, dir. environ. design Boulder, 1969-72, dir. urban design, 1972-85. Cons. John M. Prosser Assocs., Boulder and Denver, 1974—; vis. prof. urban design Oxford Brooks, Eng., 1979; vis. critic Carnegie Mellon U., U. N.Mex., Colo. Coll.; pres. Denver chpt. AIA, 1983; prin. investigator Fitsimmons-U. Colo. Health Scis. City Rsch. Study, 1997-99; vis. urban design scholar Nat. Univ. Ireland, 2003-05; vis. fellow Urban Inst. Ireland, 2003-04 Author, narrator: (PBS TV documentary) Cities Are For Kids, Too, 1984; prin. works include (with others) hist. redesign Mus. Western Art, Denver, Villa Italia, Lakewood, Colo., Denver, Auraria Higher Edn. Ctr., Pueblo C.C. campus plan and new acad. facilities, comprehensive campus plan Denver U., Ft. Lewis Coll., Westminster Golf Course Cmty., Denver Botanic Gardens 20-Yr. Concept Plan, Colo. Coll. Historic Preservation Plan, Buffalo Hills Ranch Golf Course Cmty., Fountain Valley Sch., Urban Design, Ctrl. Colo. Springs 2001—; urban design cons. McDonough & Ptnrs., New China City, 2005—. Bd. dirs. Denver Parks and Recreation Bd., 1987-93, 96-2003; chmn. design rev. bd. univs. Colo., Boulder, Denver, Aurora, and Colorado Springs, 1981—; archtl. control com. Denver Tech. Ctr., 1984—, Meridian Internat. Bus. Ctr., 1984—, DTC West, 1991—, Denver Internat. Bus. Ctr., 1993—, Nat. Renewable Energy Lab., 1995—; planning cons. Denver Internat. Airport Environs., 1984—; Nucleus co-founder U. Colo. Real Estate Ctr., 1989-2000. Capt. USAF, 1956—59. Co-recipient 2d pl. award Am. Soc. Interior Designers, 1984; recipient Honor award Colo. Soc. Architects, 1984. Mem. Urban Land Inst. (panel adv. svcs. 1990, 2001, 02, 04, 06), Denver Country Club (bd. dirs. 1984-88, pres. 1986-87), Beta Theta Pi Democrat. Avocations: skiing, golf, hiking. Home: 390 Emerson St Denver CO 80218 Office: 1512 Larimer St Denver CO 80202-1610 Office Phone: 303-892-9013. Personal E-mail: jmpros@aol.com.

**PROSSER, MICHAEL HUBERT,** communications educator; b. Indpls., Mar. 29, 1936; s. Marshall Herbert and Clydia Catharine (O'Dea) P.; m. Carol Mary Hogle, Nov. 27, 1958 (div. 1983); children: Michelle Ann Prosser-Evans, Leo Michael, Louis Mark; m. Joan Ann Kirkeby, Dec. 6, 1996 (div. 2001). BA, Ball State U., 1958, MA, 1959; PhD, U. Ill., 1964. Tchr. Latin Urbana (Ill.) Jr. High Sch., 1960-63; asst. prof. speech SUNY, Buffalo, 1963-69; assoc. prof. speech U. Bloomington, 1969-72; prof. rhetoric and comm. U. Va., Charlottesville, 1972-2001, chair, 1972-77, prof. emeritus, 2001—; William A. Kern prof. in comm. Rochester Inst. Tech., 1994—98. Vis. lectr. comm. CUNY Queens Coll., 1966—67; vis. assoc. prof. speech Calif. State U., Hayward, 1971; vis. prof. curriculum Meml. U., Newfoundland, St. John's U., 1972, St. Paul U., 1975, U. Ottawa, Canada, 1975; cons. U.S. Info. Agy., Washington, 1977; disting. vis. prof. speech State U., Kent, Ohio, 1978; fullbright prof. English U. Swaziland, Kwalusene, 1990—91; disting. vis. prof. comm. Rochester Inst. Tech., 1998—2001; adj prof. SUNY, Brockport, 1998—99; prof. English Yangzhou U., 2001—02; disting. prof. English Beijing Lang. and Culture U., China, 2002—05, Shanghai Internat. Studies U., China, 2005—. Author: The Cultural Dialogue, 1978 (translated into Japanese 1982); co-author: Diplomatic Discourse: International Conflict at the United Nations: Addresses and Analysis, 1997; editor: An Ethic for Survival: Adlai Stevenson Speaks on International Affairs, 1936-65, 1969, Sow the Wind, Reap the Whirlwind: Heads of State Address the United Nations (2 vols.), 1970, Intercommunication Among Nations and Peoples, 1973; co-editor: Readings in Classical Rhetoric, 1969, Readings in Medieval Rhetoric, 1973, Civic Discourse: Multiculturalism, Cultural Diversity, and Global Communication, 1998, Civic Discourse: Intercultural, International and global Media, 1999, Sino-American Compositions of Shared Topics, 2003; series editor Civic Discourse for the Third Millennium, 1998-2003, Ablex Pub. Co. Chair AFS Global Awareness Day, U. Va., 1983-1990, RIT Global Awareness Day, 1995-98; bd. dirs., v.p. Assn. Rochester UN, 1996-97, pres., 1997-98; pres. Rochester Area Fulbright Chpt., 1995-97; mem. Nat. Comm. Assn. Recipient Disting. Alumnus award Ball State U., 1978, Prosser-Sitarim award of excellence in internat. comm. theory, 2000. Mem. Internat. Soc. for Intercultural Edn., Tng. and Rsch. (pres. 1984-86, Citizen of World 1986, Outstanding Sr. Interculturalist 1990), Internat. Comm. Assn. (v.p., Disting. Svc. award 1978), UN Assn. U.S.A., Fulbright Assn., Nat. Comm. Assn., UN Assn. of Rochester (bd. dirs., v.p., pres.), Am. Field Svc. (pres. intercultural programs 1982-86, Charlottesville). Democrat. Roman Catholic. Avocation: travel. Office: Shanghai Internat Studies Univ Dept English 121 Guanglingyilu Shanghai 200083 China Office Phone: 086-21-6542-3070 ext. 1303. Office Fax: 86-21-6544-8852. Personal E-mail: michaelprosser@yahoo.com.

**PROSSER, MICHAEL JOSEPH,** college librarian; b. Syracuse, N.Y., May 9, 1948; s. Palmer Adelbert and Viola Mary (Clairmont) P. AA, Riverside (Calif.) City Coll. 1971; BA in History Calif. State Coll. San Bernardino, 1977; MSLS, U. So. Calif., L.A., 1981. Cert. comm. coll. instr., librarian, Calif. Libr. clk. Riverside C.C., 1968-81, learning resources asst., 1981—. Author: California and the Pacific Plate: A Bibliography, 1979. Tutor, Queen of Angels Ch., Riverside, 1985—, facilitator/patrons, 1985—; photographer With U.S. Army, 1969-71. Mem. ASCD, Internat. Soc. Poets, Calif. Libr. Assn. Democrat. Roman Catholic. Home: 6800 Palos Dr Riverside CA 92503-1330 Office: Riverside Cmty Coll 4800 Magnolia Ave Riverside CA 92506-1242

**PROST, MARY JANE,** school nurse; d. George and Mary Anne (Zigon) Klobucher; m. William Andrew Prost, July 17, 1954; children: Willy, Peggy, Beth. Diploma, Canonsburg Gen. Hosp., 1953; BS, California U., Pa., 1973; MA in Psychology, Washington-Jefferson Coll., 1976. Cert. sch. nurse Pa. Mes., surg. nurse Canonsburg Gen. Hosp., Pa., 1953—71; mental health nurse Washington Hosp., 1971—73; sch. nurse Keystone Oaks Sch. Dist., Dorment, 1973—97; ret. Sch. nurse coord. Keystone Oaks Sch. Dist., 1993—97; spkr. in field. Tchr. 1st aid classes ARC, 1975—85, Am. Heart Assn., 1975—90. Named Pa. Sch. Nurse of Yr., Pa. Sch. Nurses Assn., 1995. Mem.: Pa. Western Region Sch. Nurse Assn. (past pres.), Nat. Sch. Nurses Assn., St. Patrick's Women Guild. Home: 419 W McMurray Rd Canonsburg PA 15317

**PROST, SHARON,** federal judge; b. Newburyport, Mass., May 24, 1951; m. Kenneth F. Greene, June 24, 1984; 1 child, Matthew Prost-Greene. BS, Cornell U., 1973; MBA, George Washington U., 1975, LLM in Taxation, 1984; JD, Am. U., 1979. Bar: D.C. Labor rels. specialist Office of Personnel Mgmt., 1973-76; with Gen. Acctg. Office, 1976-79; trial atty. Fed. Labor Rels. Authority, 1980-83; atty. chief counsel's office Dept. of Treasury, 1983-84; assoc. solicitor Nat. Labor Rels. Bd., 1984-89; chief minority labor counsel Senate Com. on Labor and Human Resources, 1989-93; minority chief counsel Senate Com. on the Judiciary, 1993—2001; judge U.S. Court of Appeals, Federal Cir., 2001—. Office: US Court Appeals Fed Cir 717 Madison Pl NW Washington DC 20439*

**PROTSCH, ELIOT G.,** utilities executive, corporate financial executive; BBA in Econs. and Fin., U. S.D., Vermillion, 1975, MBA, 1976. Cert. Fin. Analyst 1981. With Mut. of Omaha Ins. Co., 1976—78; asst. treas. treasury dept. Wis. Power & Light Co. (now Alliant Energy Corp.), Madison, Wis.,

1978—85, dist. mgr. Dane County, 1985—89, v.p. and gen. mgr. energy svc., 1989—92, v.p. customer sales and svc., 1992—93, sr. v.p., 1993—98; exec. v.p. energy delivery Interstate Power & Light (now Alliant Energy Corp.), Cedar Rapids, Iowa, 1998—2003, pres., 1998—; sr. exec. v.p. and CFO Alliant Energy Corp., Madison, Wis., 2004—. Bd. dir. Nuclear Mgmt. Co., Am. Family Ins., chair audit com., 2000—; bd. dir. Capstone MicroTurbine Corp., Alliant Energy Found. Mem. Iowa Bus. Coun., 2000—, chair, 2004—; bd. dir. Mercy Med. Ctr., Cedar Rapids, 1997—, Cedar Rapids C. of C., 2002—; bd. dirs. Iowa Natural Heritage Found., Des Moines, 2000—. Office: Alliant Energy Corp 4902 N Biltmore Ln Madison WI 53718

**PROUD, ROBERT DONALD (ROBERT PAYTON),** broadcast executive; b. Cleve., Nov. 1, 1949; s. Lloyd Donald and Eleanore Matilda (Cihon) Proud; m. K. Diane Siler, Feb. 17, 1979; 1 child, James S. Owen. Grad., Cleve. Inst. Broadcasting, 1969; student, U. N.Mex., 1982, Instituto Bilingue Cultural, 1989-90. Program dir. Sta. WGCL-FM, Cleve., 1972-74; mgr. Sta. WRBR-FM, South Bend, Ind., 1974-75. Sta. XEROK, Juarez, Mexico, 1975-77; program dir. Sta. WZZP-FM, Cleve., 1977-78; gen. mgr. Sta. KELP, El Paso, Tex., 1978-82; sales mgr. Sta. KAMZ-FM, El Paso 1982-86; gen. mgr. Stas. KAMA/KAMZ-FM, El Paso, 1982-86; dir. nat. sales Thrash Broadcasting, El Paso, Lubbock, Tex., 1987-88; gen. mgr. Sta. KVIV, El Paso, 1987-89; v.p., gen. mgr. Sta. KEZB, El Paso, Tex., 1989-91; gen. mgr. Sta. KFRR, Denver, 1991-92; gen. sta. mgr. Sta. KQQK, Houston, 1992-95; v.p., gen. mgr. Entravision Comm., Dallas, 1995—2003; v.p. sales OM Media Networks, Sacramento, 2003—04; v.p. ops. Border Media Ptnrs., Tex., 2004—. Office: 8828 North Stemmons Dallas TX 75247 Office Phone: 214-689-3111. Personal E-mail: krvabob@aol.com. Business E-Mail: bproud@bmpradio.com

**PROULX, (EDNA) ANNIE,** writer; b. Norwich, Conn., Aug. 22, 1935; d. George Napolean and Lois Nellie (Gill) Proulx; m. James Hamilton Lang, June 22, 1969 (div. 1990); children: Sylvia Marion Bullock Clarkson, Jonathan Edward Lang, Gillis Crowell Lang, Morgan Hamilton Lang. BA cum laude, U. Vt., 1969; MA, Sir George Williams U., Montreal, Can., 1973; DHL (hon.), U. Maine, 1994; LLD, Concordia U., Montreal, 2002; DLitt (hon.), U. Toronto, 2000. Author: Heart Songs and Other Stories, 1988, Postcards, 1991 (PEN/Faulkner award 1993), The Shipping News, 1993 (Chgo. Tribune Heartland award 1993, Irish Times Internat. Fiction award 1993, Nat. Book award for fiction 1994, Pulitzer Prize for fiction 1994), Accordion Crimes, 1996 (Dos Passos prize for lit. 1996), Brokeback Mountain, 1998 (Nat. Mag. award 1998), Brokeback Mountain, 1998 (later adapted into film), Close Range: Wyoming Stories, 1999, That Old Ace in the Hole, 2002, Bad Dirt: Wyoming Stories 2, 2004; contbr. more than 50 articles to mags. and jours.; editor: Best American Short Stories of 1997. Recipient Dos Passos prize for Lit., Longwood Coll., 1997, Ambassador Book award English Speaking Union, 2000, Best Fiction 1999 Book award The New Yorker, 2000, Willa award, 2000, Evil Companions Lit. award, 2001; Kress fellow Harvard U., 1974, fellow Vt. Coun. Arts, 1989, NEA, 1991, Guggenheim Found., 1992; rsch. grantee Inter.-U. Ctr., 1975; resident Ucross Found., 1990, 92. Mem. PEN Am. Ctr., Phi Beta Kappa, Phi Alpha Theta. Avocations: canoeing, reading, fishing.*

**PROUNIS, OTHON A.,** lawyer; b. NYC, July 23, 1961; AB, Columbia Univ., 1983, JD, 1986. Bar: N.Y. 1987. Ptnr. Reboul MacMurray Hewitt & Maynard; ptnr. corp. dept. & co-head private equity practice group Ropes & Gray, N.Y.C., 2003—. Mem.: ABA. Office: Ropes & Gray 45 Rockefeller Plz New York NY 10111-0087 Office Phone: 212-841-5785. Office Fax: 212-841-5725. Business E-Mail: othon.prounis@ropesgray.com.

**PROUST, JOYCELYN ANN,** retired librarian; d. Merry Aylor and Alice Wilhelmina (Morgan); m. George Edward Proust (dec.); children: Gabrielle Cynara, Bertrand Gerard. BA, U. Denver, 1950, MA, 1955; cert., U. Paris Sorbonne, 1953. Lifetime French tchg. credential Calif. C.C., lifetime libr. credential C.C. Libr. Colo. Sch. Mines, Golden, 1955—62; prof. libr. sci. Long Beach (Calif.) City Coll., 1962—92, prof. emerita, 1992—. Chair Calif. C.C. Libr. Cooperative, 1968—75; exec. dir., pres. Libr./Learning Resources Assn., Calif., 1985—86. Bd. mem. Long Beach Mozart Festival, 1975—95, chair; active 1976 Bicentennial Com., L.A., 1976. Mem.: Alpha Gamma Delta, Phi Sigma Iota, Alpha Lambda Delta. Unitarian. Home: 5249 Village Rd Long Beach CA 90808

**PROUT, CURTIS,** internist, educator; b. Swampscott, Mass., Oct. 13, 1915; s. Henry Byrd and Eloise (Willett) P.; m. Daphne Brooks, June 27, 1939 (div. 1985); children: Diana P. Cherot, Daphne P. Cook, Rosamond P. Warren, Phyllis P.; m. Diane Neal Emmons, Dec. 7, 1985. AB, Harvard U., 1937, MD, 1941. Diplomate Am. Bd. Internal Medicine. Intern Peter Bent Brigham Hosp., Boston, 1942; resident in internal medicine Johns Hopkins Hosp., Balt., 1943; research fellow Mass. Gen. Hosp., Boston, 1944—45; practice medicine specializing in internal medicine, 1945—; asst. dir. Univ. Health Services Harvard U., Cambridge, Mass., 1961-72; dir. prison health project Office of Econ. Opportunity, 1972-74; asst. dean Harvard Med. Sch., Boston, 1980-94, asst. clin. prof. medicine, 1975-82. Trustee Humane Soc. Mass., Boston, 1975-2005, pres., 2004; bd. dirs. Nat. Commn. on Correctional Health Care, 1980-98, chmn., 1990; dir., trustee The Med. Found., Boston, 1980-98. Chmn. Bd. Health, Dover, Mass., 1960-75. Fellow ACP, Mass. Med. Soc.; mem. AMA, Am. Clin. and Climatol. Assn., Tavern Club of Boston (pres. 1980-82). Avocations: sailing, writing. Home: 115 School St Manchester MA 01944-1232 Office: 319 Longwood Ave Boston MA 02115-5728 E-mail: cprout_02115@yahoo.com.

**PROUT, GEORGE RUSSELL, JR.,** medical educator, urologist; b. Boston, July 23, 1924; s. George Russell and Marion (Snow) P.; m. Lou Katherine Wheatley, Oct. 17, 1950; children: George Russell III, Elizabeth Louise. Student, Union Coll., 1943, DSc (hon.), 1990; MD, Albany Med. Coll., 1947, DSc (hon.), 1988; MA (hon.), Harvard U., 1969. Intern Grasslands Hosp., Valhalla, NY, 1947-48; asst. resident in surgery, 1948-50; surg. resident Grasslands Hosp., Valhalla, NY, 1948-50; resident N.Y. Hosp., N.Y.C., 1952-56; fellow in surgery Meml. Ctr. Cancer & Allied Diseases, 1954—55; asst. attending physician Meml. Ctr. for Cancer and Allied Disease, N.Y.C., 1956-57; asst. clinician in surgery James Ewing Hosp., N.Y.C., 1956-57; assoc. prof., chmn. div. urology U. Miami, 1957-60; prof., chmn. div. urology Med. Coll. Va., 1960-69; chief urol. svc. Mass. Gen. Hosp., Boston, 1969-89; prof. surgery Harvard Med. Sch., 1969-89, emeritus prof. surgery Boston, 1989—; hon. urologist Mass. Gen. Hosp., Boston, 1989—. Chmn. Adjuvants in Surg. Treatment of Bladder Cancer; mem. adv. task force Nat. Cancer Inst. 1968—, cons., 1990—; expert cons. divsn. surveillance, 1991—; Finland coop. ATBC study, 1991—; chmn. Nat. Bladder Cancer Group, 1973—86. Editor-in-chief: Urologic Oncology, 1994—2000. With USNR, 1950-52. Fellow ACS, Acad. Medicine Toronto (corr.); mem. AMA, AAUP, Am. Urol. Assn., Can. Urol. Assn., Japanese Urol. Soc. (hon.), Am. Cancer Soc., Soc. Surg. Oncology, Soc. Univ. Urologists, Dallas So. Clin. Soc. (hon.), Am. Assn. Genitourinary Surgeons, Soc. Pediat. Urology, Soc. Urol. Oncology, Soc. Internat. Urologists, Soc. Basic Urol. Rsch., Alpha Omega Alpha. Home (Winter): 224 Corsair Rd Duck Key FL 33050 Home: 1800 River Watch Dr Annapolis MD 21401 Office Phone: 305-289-0770, 410-266-1086. Personal E-mail: drurocsal@aol.com.

**PROUT, ROBERT STEPHEN,** higher education consultant, law enforcement consultant; b. June 24, 1944; Degree in law, LaSalle Ext. U., Chgo., 1967; BA, Muskingum Coll., 1969; MEd, Ohio U., 1970; PhD, Ohio State U., 1972. State trooper Ohio Hwy. Patrol, Akron, Ohio, 1965-68; coord. Zane State Coll., Zanesville, Ohio, 1972; dept. chair criminal justice St. Cloud (Minn.) State U., 1972—96, 2002—, dir. grad. program criminal justice, 1988—. Adj. faculty St. John's U., Coll. St. Thomas, U. Louisville; chmn. Govs. Com. on Crime Prevention-Region D, Minn., 1976-77. Author: Meeting Ohio's Law Enforcement Needs, 1973; contbr. articles to profl. jours. Recipient Tchr. of Yr. award, 1988. Office: St Cloud State U 241 Stewart Hall Saint Cloud MN 56301 Office Phone: 320-308-5541. Business E-Mail: prout@stcloudstate.edu.

**PROVENCHER, JEANNE STANSFIELD,** secondary school educator; b. Methuen, Mass., June 30, 1948; d. Ernest Daniel and Rita Marie (Vayo) Stansfield; m. Richard Leonard Provencher, Dec. 15, 1978; children: Matthew, Ryan. BA, Newton Coll. (now Boston Coll.), Chestnut Hill, Mass., 1970; MA, Rivier Coll., Nashua, N.H., 1990. Cert. tchr., Mass.; cert. experienced educator, N.H. Tchr. St. Francis Acad., Nevada, Mo., 1970-71, Salem (NH) H.S., 1971-72, Pelham (NH) Meml. Sch., 1983-87; tchr. English and women's studies Nashua (N.H.) HS South, 1987—. Critical reader Grammar Workshop, 1994; contbg. reader Adventures in Appreciation, 1994; reader/evaluator A.P. Lang. Exams, 2003—06; presenter in field. Lector St. Kathryn Ch., Hudson, N.H., 1988—. Mem. NOW, N.H. NOW, Nat. Coun. Tchrs. English (state judge for student lit. mags. 1994—), New Eng. Coun. Tchrs. English, N.H. Coun. Tchrs. English. Avocations: reading, gardening, bicycling. Office: Nashua HS South 36 RIverside Dr Nashua NH 03062 Office Phone: 603-589-1566. Business E-mail: provencherj@nashua.edu.

**PROVENCIO, ROBERTO ENRIQUE,** music educator, music minister; b. El Paso, Tex., July 14, 1957; s. Jesus Roberto and Velia Rivero Provencio; m. Linda Kay Johnson, Aug. 18, 1984; children: Robert Phillip, Charles Raymond, Elizabeth Anne, Victoria Lynn. MusB, U. Ariz., 1980; MusM, Tex. State U., 1986; D Musical Arts, U. Colo., 1993. Prof. music Calif. State U., Bakersfield, 1988—; min. music First Presbyn. Ch., Bakersfield, 1995—. Pvt. practice cons., Bakersfield, 1980—. Mem. editl. bd. The Choral Jour.; translator: History of the Choral Movement of Venezuela; author: Releasing the Artist Within: Mnemonics for Achieving Artistic Choral Performance. Mem. Adult Rehab. Ctr. Salvation Army, Bakersfield, 1999; bd. dirs. The Beethoven Festival, Bakersfield, 1992—95. Named Outstanding Hispanic Alumnus, Tex. State U., 1994, Outstanding Music Educator, Calif. Music Educators Assn., 1994, Outstanding Prof., 2001; Calif. State U. fellow, 1988—92, Choral Rsch. fellow, U. of Colo., Boulder, 1986—88. Mem.: Nat. Assn. Ch. Musicians (bd. govs. 1998—, chair publs. com. jour.), Internat. Fedn. Choral Music, Am. Choral Directors Assn. (life; chair multicultural perspectives western divsn. 1992—96, mem. editl. bd. 1995—), Rotary (dir., scholarship chair 1994, Bakersfield East), Pi Kappa Lambda (life). Conservative. Avocations: motorcycle touring, fly fishing, tennis, photography, tobacciana. Home: 101 Camino del Oeste Bakersfield CA 93309 Office: Calif State U 9001 Stockdale Hwy Bakersfield CA 93311 Office Phone: 661-664-3073. E-mail: rprovencio@csub.edu.

**PROVENSEN, ALICE,** artist, writer; b. Chgo. d. Jay Horace and Kathryn (Zelanis) Twitchell; m. Martin Provensen, Apr. 17, 1944 (dec.); 1 child, Karen Anna. Student, Art Inst. of Chgo., 1930-31, U. Calif., L.A., 1939, Art Student League, N.Y., 1940-41; D.H.L. (hon.), Marist Coll., 1986. With Walter Lanz Studios, Los Angeles, 1942-43; OSS, 1944-45. Author, illustrator Karen's Opposites, 1963, Karen's Curiosity, 1963, What is a Color?, 1967, author, illustrator (with Martin Provensen) Who's in the Egg?, 1970, author, illustrator The Provensen Book of Fairy Tales, 1971, Play on Words, 1972, My Little Hen, 1973, Roses are Red, 1973, Our Animal Friends, 1974, The Year at Maple Hill Farm, 1978, A Horse and a Hound, A Goat and a Gander, 1979, The Owl and Three Pussycats, 1981, Town and Country, 1984, Shaker Lane, 1987, The Buck Stops Here, 1990, Punch in New York, 1991 (Best Books N.Y. Times, 1991), My Fellow Americans, 1995, Count on Me, 1998 (Book of Yr. Parenting Mag., 1998), The Master Swordsman, 2001, The Magic Doorway, 2001, A Day in the Life of Murphy, 2003 (named One of the Three Best Childrens Books, 2003), Klondike Gold, 2005 (Spur award Western Writers Am., 2006), illustrator (with Martin Provensen) Mother Goose Book, 1976, illustrator Old Mother Hubbard, 1977, A Peaceable Kingdom, 1978, The Golden Serpent, 1980, A Visit to William Blake's Inn, 1981 (Caldecott honor book, 1981), Birds, Beasts and the Third Thing, 1982, The Glorious Flight, 1984 (Caldecott medal, 1984), The Voyage of Ludgate Hill, 1987, also textbooks; exhibitions include with Martin Provensen Balt. Mus., 1954, exhibitions include Am. Inst. Graphic Arts, NYC, 1959, Botolph Group, Boston, 1964, Eric Carle Mus., Amherst, Mass., 2005—06, one-woman shows include Henry Feiwel Gallery, NYC, 1991, Children's Mus., Washington, 1991, Moscarelle Mus. Art, Williamsburg, Va., 1991, Eric Carle Mus. Picture Book Art, Amherst, Mass., 2005—06; books represented Fifty Book of Yr. selections Am. Inst. Graphic Arts, 1947, 1948, 1952 (The Charge of the Light Brigade named Best Illustrated Children's Book of Yr. N.Y. Times, 1964, co-recipient medal Soc. Illustrators, 1960). Named to Soc. Illustrators Hall of Fame, 2000; recipient Empire State award, Youth Svcs. sect. NY Libr. Assn., 2004.

**PROVINE, JOHN CALHOUN,** retired lawyer; b. Asheville, NC, May 15, 1938; s. Robert Calhoun and Harriet Josephine (Thoms) P.; m. Martha Ann Monson, Aug. 26, 1966 (div. Jan. 1975); m. Nancy Frances Lunsford, Apr. 17, 1976 (div. Mar. 1996); children: Robert, Frances, Harriet. AB, Harvard U., 1960; JD, U. Mich., 1966; MBA, NYU, 1972, LLM in Taxation, 1975. Bar: NY, Tenn., US Dist. Ct. (so. and ea. dists.) NY, US Ct. Appeals (2nd and 6th cirs.), US Dist. Ct. (mid. dist.) Tenn., US Supreme Ct. From assoc. to ptnr. White & Case, NYC, 1966—74, ptnr., 1974—82, 1992—94, Jakarta and Ankara, 1982—91; counsel Dearborn & Ewing, Nashville, 1981—82; ret., 1994. Lt. USN, 1960-63. Mem. ABA, NY Bar Assn., Tenn. Bar Assn., Assn. of Bar of City of NY Avocations: bluegrass music, rural activities. Home and Office: 6630 Manley Ln Brentwood TN 37027-3401 Personal E-mail: jprovine@bellsouth.net.

**PROVINE, LORRAINE,** retired mathematics educator; b. Altus, Okla., Oct. 6, 1944; d. Claud Edward and Emmie Lorraine (Gasper) Allmon; m. Joe A. Provine, Aug. 14, 1966; children: Sharon Kay, John David. BS, U. Okla., 1966; MS, Okla. State U., 1984. Tchr. math U.S. Grant High Sch., Oklahoma City Schs., 1966-69; tchr. East Jr. High Sch., Ponca City (Okla.) Schs., 1969-70; tchr. Ponca City High Sch., 1978-79, 81-96; lectr. dept. math. Okla. State U., Stillwater, 1996-99. Mem.: Cleve. McClain County Ret. Educators Assn., Ponca City Assn. Classroom Tchrs. (treas. 1983—86, 1991—96), Assn. Women in Math, Okla. Coun. Tchrs. Math, Okla. Edn. Assn., Sch. Sci. and Math Assn., Nat. Coun. Tchrs. Math, Math Assn. Am., Internat. Soc. Tech. in Edn., Coun. for Exceptional Children, Okla. Ret. Educators Assn. (life), Okla. State U. Alumni Assn. (life), U. Okla. Alumni Assn. (life), Okla. Assn. Mothers Club (life; state bd. dirs. 1977—87, pres. 1984—85), Delta Kappa Gamma Soc. Internat. (Delta chpt. treas. 1996—98, chmn. Gamma state essay com. 2005, Eta chpt. treas. 2000—04, Eta chpt. pres. 2004—, chmn. Gamma state essay com. 2005—). Republican. Baptist. Avocations: reading, knitting, sewing, genealogy, quilting. Home: 1019 Greenway Cir Norman OK 73072-6125 Personal E-mail: lorraineprovine@cox.net.

**PROVINE, WILLIAM B.,** biology professor; BS, U. Chgo., 1962, MA in Hist. of Sci., 1965, PhD, 1970. Asst. prof. hist. Cornell U., Ithaca, NY, 1969, mem. faculty divsn. biol. scis., 1974, mem. faculty sect. ecology and systematics, 1986, Charles A. Alexander prof. biol. scis. dept. ecology and evolutionary biology. Contbr. articles to profl. jours., chapters to books; author: The Origins of Theoretical Population Genetics, 1971, Sewall Wright and Evolutionary Biology, 1986; co-editor: The Evolutionary Synthesis, 1980; editor: Evolution: Selected Papers by Sewall Wright, 1986. Grantee Guggenheim fellowship, 1984. Fellow: AAAS, Am. Acad. Arts & Scis. Office: Dept Ecology and Evolutionary Biology Cornell U E139 Corson Hall Ithaca NY 14853 E-mail: wbp2@cornell.edu.*

**PROVORNY, FREDERICK ALAN,** lawyer, educator; b. Bklyn., Sept. 7, 1946; s. Daniel and Anna (Wurm) P.; m. Nancy Ileene Wilkins, Nov. 21, 1971; children: Michelle C., Cheryl A., Lisa T., Robert D. BS summa cum laude, NYU, 1966; JD magna cum laude, Columbia U., 1969. Bar: NY 1970, US Supreme Ct. 1973, DC 1975, Mo. 1977, Md. 1987, Calif. 1989; CPA, Md., Mo. Law clk. to Judge Harold R. Medina U.S. Ct. Appeals (2d cir.), NYC, 1969-70; asst. prof. law Syracuse (NY) U., 1970-72; assoc. Debevoise, Plimpton, Lyons & Gates, N.Y.C., 1972-75, Cole & Groner PC, Washington, 1975-76; with Monsanto Co., St. Louis, 1976-86, asst. co. counsel, 1978-86; pvt. practice Washington, 1986-89; ptnr. Provorny & Jacoby, Washington, 1989-91; counsel Shaw, Pittman, Potts & Trowbridge, Washington, 1991-93; ptnr. Tydings & Rosenberg, Balt., 1993-94; pvt. practice Balt., 1994—98; Harold R. Tyler prof. law and tech. Sci. and Tech. Law Ctr., Albany (NY) Law Sch., 1998—2004, dir., 1998—2003; pres. Empire State Venture Group, Inc., 2001—03; dir. Md. Intellectual Property Legal Resource Ctr., Rockville, 2004—. Vis. prof. U. Md. Sch. Law, 2004-; lectr. Bklyn Law Sch., 1973-74; adj. prof. U. Balt. Sch. of Law, 1996-98, Rensselaer Poly Inst., 2004; pres. Sci. and Tech. Assocs., Inc., 1986-91. Contbr. articles to profl. jours. Trustee Christian Woman's Benevolent Assn. Youth Home, 1979-83, Jewish Family Svcs. of N.E. NY, 1999—2004. Mem. ABA, Am. Law Inst., Am. Arbitration Assn. (panel comml. abitrators), Am. Intellectual Property Lawyers Assn., Licensing Execs. Soc. (U.S., Can.), Assn. Univ. Tech. Mgrs., Philo-Mt. Sinai Lodge 968, Masons, Beta Gamma Sigma. Jewish. Home: 11803 Kemp Mill Rd Silver Spring MD 20902-1511 Office: U Md Sch Law 500 W Baltimore St Baltimore MD 21201 also: Md Intellectual Property Legal Resource Ctr 9700 Great Seneca Hwy Rockville MD 20850 Office Phone: 410-706-1190, 240-453-6246. E-mail: fprovorny@law.umaryland.edu.

**PROVOST, THOMAS TAYLOR,** dermatology educator, researcher; b. Pitts., Mar. 21, 1938; s. Charles Thomas and Marcelle K. (Taylor) P.; m. Carol Sara Christie, July 2, 1960; children: Charles T., Christie Lynn, Thomas Wright. AB, U. Pitts., 1958, MD, 1962. Intern Mary Hitchcock Meml. Hosp., Hanover, N.H., 1962-63; resident in dermatology Dartmouth Med. Ctr., Hanover, N.H., 1966-67, U. Oreg. Med. Ctr., Portland, 1967-68; fellow in immunology SUNY, Buffalo, 1969-72, asst. prof. dermatology, 1972-75, assoc. prof., 1975-78, Johns Hopkins U. Med. Sch., Balt., 1978-82, prof. dermatology, 1982—, chmn. dept. dermatology, 1997—. Lt. commdr. US-PHS, 1962-64. Mem. Soc. Investigative Dermatology, Soc. Clin. Investigation. Avocation: boating. Home: PO Box 230 Milton DE 19968-0230

**PROWN, JULES DAVID,** art historian, educator; b. Freehold, N.J., Mar. 14, 1930; s. Max and Matilda (Cassileth) P.; m. Shirley Ann Martin, June 23, 1956; children: Elizabeth Anderson, David Martin, Jonathan, Peter Cassileth, Sarah Peiter. AB, Lafayette Coll., 1951, DFA (hon.), 1979; AM, U. Del., 1956, Harvard U., 1953, PhD, 1961. Dir. Hist. Soc. Old Newbury, Newburyport, Mass., 1957-58, Old Gaol Mus., York, Maine, 1958-59; asst. to dir. Harvard U., Fogg Art Mus., Cambridge, Mass., 1959-61; instr. to Paul Mellon prof. history of art Yale U., New Haven, 1961-99, Paul Mellon prof. emeritus history of art, 1999—; curator Am. art Yale U. Art Gallery, New Haven, 1963-68; vis. lectr. Smith Coll., Northampton, Mass., 1966-67; dir. Yale Ctr. for Brit. Art, New Haven, 1968-76, sr. rsch. fellow, 1999—; assoc. dir. Nat. Humanities Inst., New Haven, 1977. Trustee Whitney Mus., N.Y.C., 1975-94; mem. editorial adv. bd. Am. Art-Smithsonian, Washington, 1986-2001, On Common Ground, 1993—; mem. vis. com. Harvard U. Art Museums, 1993-98. Author: John Singleton Copley, 2 Vols., 1966, American Painting from Its Beginnings to the Armory Show, 1969, The Architecture of the Yale Center for British Art, 1977; Art as Evidence: Writings on Art and Material Culture, 2002, (catalogue) American Art from Alumni Collections, 1968; editor (with Kenneth Haltman) American Artifacts: Essays in Material Culture, 2000. Recipient George Washington Kidd award Lafayette Coll., 1986, recipient Iris Found. award outstanding contbns. to the decorative arts, 2001, Lawrence A. Fleischman award Scholarly Excellence Am. Art History, 2001, William Clyde DeVane award Scholarship and Tchg. Phi Beta Kappa, Yale U., 2005. Fellow The Athenaeum of Phila. (hon.); mem. Am. Antiquarian Soc., Coll. Art Assn. (Disting. Tchg. of Art History award 1996), Am. Studies Assn., Conn. Acad. Arts & Scis., Walpole Soc., Royal Soc. Arts. Office: Yale Ctr for Brit Art PO Box 208280 New Haven CT 06520-8280 Business E-Mail: jules.prown@yale.edu.

**PROZES, ANDREW,** publishing executive; b. Jan. 21, 1946; BA in Math, U. Waterloo, Ont., Can.; MBA, York U., Toronto. Former group pres. Southam Inc., Don Mills, Ont., Can.; exec. v.p., COO Westlaw, The West Group (subs. Thomson Corp.), Eagan, Minn., 1997-99; CEO global legal pub. & info. divsn. Reed Elsevier, N.Y.C., 2000—. Mem. bd. dirs. Reed Elsevier Group plc and Reed Elsevier PLC, 2000—. Office: Reed Elsevier 125 Park Ave 23rd fl New York NY 10017

**PRUCHA, INGMAR R.,** economist, educator; s. Rudolf and Walpurga Prucha; m. Ingeborg Bock; 1 child, Markus W. Bock. PhD, U. Tech. Vienna, 1977. Prof. econs. U. Md., Coll. Pk., Md., 1991—. Co-author: Dynamic Nonlinear Econometric Models: Asymptotic Theory; assoc. editor: Econometric Theory, 2000—, Jour. Econometrics, 2004—; contbr. over 50 articles to profl. jours. Office Phone: 301-405-3499.

**PRUCHA, JOHN JAMES,** geologist, educator; b. River Falls, Wis., Sept. 22, 1924; s. Edward Joseph and Katharine (Schladweiler) P.; m. Mary Elizabeth Helfrich, June 12, 1948; children: David, Stephen, Katharine, Carol, Mark, Barbara, Margaret, Christopher, Anne, Andrew. Student, Wis. State U., River Falls, 1941—43; PhB, U. Wis., 1945, PhM, 1946; MA, Princeton U., 1948, PhD, 1950. Asst. prof. geology Rutgers U., 1948-51; sr. geologist NY State Geol. Survey, 1951-56; rsch. geologist Shell Devel. Co., 1956-63; prof. geology Syracuse (NY) U., 1963-90, prof. emeritus, 1990—; chmn. dept., 1963-70, 88-89, dean Coll. Arts and Scis., 1970-72, vice chancellor acad. affairs, 1972-85; pres. Syracuse U. Press, 1973-85, bd. dirs., 1985-90. Author: Basement Tectonics of Rocky Mountains, 1965, Structural Behavior of Salt, 1967, Stratigraphy and Structure of Southeastern New York, 1959, Fracture Patterns, 1979, Zones of Structural Weakness, 1992, (with Norman A. Foss) Kinnickinnic Years, 1993. Trustee Le Moyne Coll., 1971-78; bd. dirs. Cultural Resources Coun., Syracuse, 1974—, pres., 1978-80; bd. dirs. Everson Mus. Art, Syracuse, 1977-83, v.p., 1980-81; mem. regents vis. com. NY State Mus., 1993-96. Recipient John Mason Clarke medal NY State Geol. Survey, 1990. Fellow AAAS, Geol. Soc. Am.; mem. Am. Assn. Petroleum Geologists, Am. Geophys. Union, NY State Coun. Profl. Geologists. Home: 112 Ardsley Dr Syracuse NY 13214-2110 Office: Syracuse Univ 204 Heroy Geology Lab Syracuse NY 13244-0001

**PRUDEN, ANN LORETTE,** chemical engineer, researcher, management consultant; b. Norfolk, Va., Sept. 3, 1948; d. James Otis and Elora Maie Pruden; m. Alan Todd Royer, Aug. 13, 1983; children: James Sebastian Royer, Annabelle Grace Royer. BS in Chemistry, Maryville (Tenn.) Coll., 1970; MA in Chem. Engring., Princeton (N.J.) U., 1978; PhD, 1981. Rsch. and develop. chemist and chem. engr. Mobil Corp., Princeton, 1970—92; supr. Mobil Chem. Co., Edison, N.J., 1992-97, lab. mgr., 1997-2000, rsch. mgmt. team, 1997-2000; prin. Inventive Strategies, 2000—. Mem. Process Effectiveness Network, Indsl. Rsch. Inst., Washington, 1992-98. Contbg. author: Photocatalytic Purification and Treatment of Water and Air, 1993; contbr. articles to profl. jours. Fellow Mobil R&D Corp., Princeton, N.J., 1976-79. Mem.: AIChE, Nat. Spkrs. Assn., Inst. Mgmt. Cons., Am. Chem. Soc. Achievements include organizational effectiveness, platform speaking and catalysis research. Office Phone: 908-359-4787. Business E-Mail: pruden@inv-strat.com.

**PRUDEN, JAMES NORFLEET, III,** lawyer; b. Edenton, N.C., Sept. 1, 1948; s. James Norfleet Jr. and Helen (Goodwin) P.; m. Cynthia Haines Gridley, Aug. 7, 1971; children: Matthew Gridley, Haines Goodwin. AB, U. N.C., 1970; JD, U. Va., 1973. Assoc. Kennedy Covington Lobdell & Hickman, Charlotte, N.C., 1973-78, ptnr., 1979—. Author manuscripts for continuing legal edn. programs, 1979—. Mem. county selection com. John Motley Morehead Found., Chapel Hill, N.C., 1990-92, chmn. 1993-95; vestryman Christ Episcopal Ch., 1990-92, 2000-02, sr. warden, 2002. Recipient John Motley Morehead award, 1966-70. Mem. ABA, N.C. Bar Assn. (chmn. bus. law sect. 1991-92, pres. 2002-03). Democrat. Home: 1139 Queens Rd Charlotte NC 28207-1849 Office: Kennedy Covington Hearst Tower 214 N Tryon St 47th Fl Charlotte NC 28202

**PRUDICH, GREGORY S.,** lawyer; b. Bluefield, W.Va., Sept. 13, 1960; s. William and Phyllis H. (Houck) P.; m. Penny Luanne Black, Jan. 11, 1962; children: Joshua, Justin, Janie, Jenna. BA cum laude, Concord Coll., 1982; JD, South Tex. Coll. Law, 1985. Law clk. Law Offices of Sanford B. Kahn, Houston, 1983-85; ptnr. Sanders, Austin, Prudich & Flanigan, Princeton, W.Va., 1986—. Sec. Mercer County Fire Svc. Bd., Princeton, 2004—; pres. Princeton (W.Va.) Little League, 1999—2001; v.p. soccer boosters Princeton (W.Va.) Sr. H.S., 2005—; pres., past chmn., bd. dirs. C.A.S.E. of W. Va., Bluefield, 1988—98; pres. Mercer County Fire Svc. Bd., Princeton, 1989—95, 2004—; mem. Mercer County Bd. Edn., 1998—, v.p. 2004—; Princeton H.S. Baseball. Mem. ATLA, Nat. Orgn. Social Security Claimants Reps., W.Va. Trial Lawyers. Democrat. Roman Catholic. Avocations: outdoor activities, skiing, little league baseball. Office: Sanders Austin Prudich and Flanigan 320 Courthouse Rd Princeton WV 24740-2421 Office Phone: 304-487-2456. E-mail: gprudich@sapf-law.com.

**PRUEHER, JOSEPH W.,** retired military officer, former ambassador; b. Nashville, Nov. 25, 1942; Grad., U.S. Naval Acad., Annapolis, Md., 1964. Commd. ensign USN, advanced through grades to adm.; commdr. in chief U.S. Pacific Command, Camp H.M. Smith, Hawaii, 1996-99; amb. to People's Republic of China Dept. of State, Beijing, 1999—2001; cons. prof. Stanford-Harvard Preventive Def. Project, 2001—. Bd. dirs. Merrill Lynch & Co.; bd. mem. N.Y. Life Ins. Co., Emerson Electric Co., Fluor Corp.; mem. bd. govs. The Nature Conservancy. Home: Apt 30 148 142nd St New York NY 10030-3504

**PRUEHSNER, WILLIAM ROBERT,** biomedical engineer; b. June 12, 1957; s. Robert Edward and Lois Gay Pruehsner; m. Mary Ann Millsback, 1991. AS, Norwalk Tech. Coll., 1978—80; BS, U. of New Haven, 1980—85; MSc, U. of Conn., 1996—2002. Mech. engr. Flgitronics, Shelton, 1980—85; chief engr. Wallach Surg. Devices, Milford, Conn., 1985—89; mfg. engr. Anton Bauer, Shelton, 1989—91; project engr./engr. Corometrics Med. Systems, Wallingford, Conn., 1991—96; grad. student U. of Conn., 1996—2002, doctoral candidate, 2002—. Biomedical engring. cons. Euro-Tech Mfg., Kernnersville, NC, 2000—. Editor: (hiking guide) Harriman Trails, 1990, New York Walk Book, 1992. Mem. Freemasons, Meriden, Conn., 1995—. Recipient Pro Deo Et Patria, Boy Scouts of Am., 1971, Eagle Scout, 1973, Bronze Palm, 1974, NY Long Path thru Kike to End award, Conn. 400 Club, 1993. Mem.: Rocky Mountain Biomedical Symposium (bd. mem. 2001—, exec. bd. mem. 2005—, student paper com. 2003—). Achievements include 5 patents pending for Fetal Pulse Oximeter in 1995. Avocations: hiking, letterboxing, long-distance backpacking, volksmarching, state high point hiking. Business E-Mail: pruehsnr@engr.uconn.edu.

**PRUETT, JAMES WORRELL,** librarian, educator, musicologist; b. Mt. Airy, NC, Dec. 23, 1932; s. Samuel Richard and Gladys Dorne (Worrell) P.; m. Lilian Maria-Irene Pibernik, July 20, 1957; children— Mark, Ellen. BA, U. N.C., Chapel Hill 1955, MA, 1957, PhD, 1962. Mem. faculty U. N.C., Chapel Hill, 1961-87, prof. music, 1974-87, music librarian, 1961-76, chmn. dept. music, 1976-86; chief music dir. Library of Congress, Washington, 1987-95. Vis. prof. U. Toronto, 1976; cons. in music, 1995—. Editor: Studies in the History, Style and Bibliography of Music in Memory of Glen Haydon, 1969; author: Research Guide to Musicology, 1985. Contbr. profl. jours., encys. Newberry Libr. fellow, 1966. Mem. Internat. Musicol. Soc., Am. Musicol. Soc. (chpt. chmn. 1964-66, mem. coun. 1974-77), Music Libr. Assn. (pres. 1973-75, editor jour. 1974-77), Cosmos Club (Washington). Home: 343 Wesley Dr Chapel Hill NC 27516-1520

**PRUETT-LAWSON, JO ANN,** marketing professional, special events coordinator; b. Jacksonville, Fla., Feb. 27, 1961; d. Billy Earl Pruett and Mildred Ann (Reedy) Jewell. AS in Bus. Adminstrn., Fla. C.C., Jacksonville, 1991; BS in Bus. Adminstrn. and Mktg., U. North Fla., Jacksonville, 1993; nail technician lic., Roffler, Jacksonville, Fla., 1994. Cert. image cons., makeup artist, promotional mgr., driving instr. Owner, CEO Black and White Prodns., Jacksonville, 1991—, Depeche Mktg. Group, Inc., Jacksonville, 1996—. Color and makeup cons. Carol Jackson-Color Me Beautiful, Fla., 1990, Fernand Aubrey, Fla., 1990; educator Advanced Edn. for Nail Profls. Jacksonville, 1993—; territory supr. Mktg. Force, Jacksonville, 1993-95; specialty events mgr., Jacksonville, 1993—; sales rep. KMart Corp., Jacksonville, 1995-97; specialty events mgr. Greater Jacksonville Agrl. Fair, 1996. Pres., bd. dirs. Sutton Pl. Homeowners Assn., 1997—; adv. bd. Ronald McDonald Ho., Jacksonville, 2000—; vol. Amelia Island Concour d' Elegance BMW and RM Auction, 2000—. Mem.: First Coast Car Coun. (v.p., show chmn. 14th Ann. Car, Truck, and Motorcycle Show 2001, v.p., show chmn. 2005), Suncoast Jaguar Club, South Fla. Jaguar Club, Jaguar Clubs of N. Am. (mem. BMWCCA First Coast chpt. 1998—, activities dir. 2002—, sanctioned chief judge 2003—, regional v.p. 2006—), Jaguar Car Club North Fla. (pres. 2000—03, founder, chief judge 2000—).

**PRUETZ, ADRIAN MARY,** lawyer; b. Nov. 13, 1948; Student, U. Wis. 1966—69; BA, Loyola U., Chgo., 1972, postgrad., 1972—73; JD magna cum laude, Marquette U., 1982. Bar: Wis. 1982, Calif. 1985. With Quinn Emanuel et al, LA; assoc. Whyte and Hirschboeck, SC, 1982—84, Morrison and Foerster, 1984—88, ptnr., 1988—94, Quinn Emanuel Urquhart Oliver & Hedges, LLP, LA, 1994—, co-chair Intellectual Property Litigation Group. Spkr., lectr. Price Waterhouse Intellectual Property Forum, Licensing Execs. Soc., Am. Soc. Indsl. Security. Named one of One of Calif. Top 50 Litigators, LA Daily Jour., 2001—05, Most Influential Trial Lawyers in Calif., 2002—05, State's Top Intellectual Property Lawyers, 2003—05, Calif.'s Most Successful Lawyers, Calif. Law Bus. Mem.: ABA (past chair com. U.S. lit. affecting internat. patent problems, past chair com. impact 1991 amendments), Los Angeles County Bar, State Bar Calif., Fed. Bar Assn. (spkr., lectr.). Office: 865 S Figueroa St 10th Fl Los Angeles CA 90017 Office Phone: 213-443-3134. E-mail: adrianpruetz@quinnemanuel.com.

**PRUGH, WILLIAM BYRON,** lawyer; b. Kansas City, Mo., Jan. 3, 1945; s. Byron E. and Helen Prugh; m. Linda Stuart, Aug. 12, 1968; 1 child, K. Niccole. BA, U. Mo., Kansas City, 1966, JD, 1969, LLM in Taxation, 1971. Bar: Mo. 1969, U.S. Tax Ct. 1975, U.S. Supreme Ct. 1975, Kans. 1982. Mem. Shughart Thomson & Kilroy, P.C., Kansas City, 1969—. Author, editor: Missouri Corporation Law and Practice, 1985, Missouri Taxation Law and Practice, 1987, 3d edit., 1996. Mem.: ABA, Kansas City Met. Bar Assn. (chmn. tax com. 1989—90, chmn. computer law com. 1989—91, Pres. award 1988), Mo. Bar Assn. (chmn. taxation com. 1988—90, chmn. computer tech. com. 1989—90). Republican. Methodist. Office: Shughart Thomson & Kilroy 12 Wyandotte Plz 120 W 12th St Fl 18 Kansas City MO 64105-1902 Office Phone: 816-421-3355 3570. Business E-Mail: wprugh@stklaw.com.

**PRUIS, JOHN J.,** manufacturing executive; b. Borculo, Mich., Dec. 13, 1923; s. Ties J. and Trientje (Koop) P.; m. Angeline Rosemary Zull, Sept. 14, 1944; children: David Lofton, Daniel J., Dirk Thomas. BS, Western Mich. U., 1947; MA, Northwestern U., 1949, PhD, 1951; Litt.D. (hon.), Yeungnam U., Taegu, Korea, Ind. State U.; LL.D. (hon.), Ball State U., U. So. Ind.; DHL (hon.), Keuka Coll. Tchr. pub. schs., Mich., 1942-43; supervising tchr. Campus Sch., Western Mich. U., 1947-48; instr. speech U. No La., 1951-52; from asst. prof. to assoc. prof. speech So. Ill. U., 1952-55; mem. faculty Western Mich. U., 1955-68, sec. bd. trustees, 1964-68, v.p. adminstrn., 1966-68; pres. Ball State U., 1968-78; v.p. corp. rels. Ball Corp., 1978-88. Cons., examiner North Central Assn., 1959-78; also bd. dirs. N. Central Assn. V.p. Country dr. chmn. Kalamazoo Cmty. Chest, 1964; bd. dirs. Kalamazoo chpt. Am. Cancer Soc., 1963-68, Del. County United Way, Muncie Symphony Assn., Ball Meml. Hosp., Big Bros./Big Sisters, Ind. Legal Found.; trustee U. So. Ind., 1985-90; exec. v.p. George and Frances Ball Found. With USNR, 1943-46; capt. Res., ret. Mem. Am. Assn. Higher Edn., Speech Communication Assn., Muncie C. of C., Blue Key, Rotary, Phi Delta Kappa, Omicron Delta Kappa, Beta Gamma Sigma Presbyterian. Personal e-mail: jjpruis@iquest.net.

**PRUITT, ALICE FAY,** mathematician, engineer; b. Montgomery, Ala., Dec. 17, 1943; d. Virgil Edwin and Ocie Victoria (Mobley) Maye; m. Mickey Don Pruitt, Nov. 5, 1967; children: Derrell Gene, Christine Marie. BS in Math, U. Ala., Huntsville, 1977; postgrad., Calif. State U. Northridge, 1978—79. Instr. math. Antelope Valley Coll., Quartz Hill, Calif., 1977—78; space shuttle engr. Rockwell Internat., Palmdale, Calif., 1979—81; programmer-analyst Sci. Support Svcs., Inc., Paso Robles, Calif., 1982—85; sr. engring. specialist Loral Vought Sys. Corp., Dallas, 1985—92; dir. concepts and analysis, advanced sys. engring. Nichols Rsch. Corp., Huntsville, Ala., 1992-99; sr. prin. engr. Computer Sci. Corp., Huntsville, 1999—. Mem. DeSoto (Tex.) Coun. Cultural Arts, 1987-89. Mem. AAUW (sch. bd. rep. 1982, legal advocacy fund chairperson 1989-91), Toastmasters, Phi Kappa Phi. Republican. Methodist. Avocations: dance, gourmet cooking. Office: PO Box 400002 4090 S Memorial Pky Ste A Huntsville AL 35815-1502 Business E-Mail: apruitt@csc.com.

**PRUITT, ANNE LORING,** academic administrator, education educator; b. Bainbridge, Ga., Sept. 19, 1929; d. Loring Alphonzo and Anne Lee (Ward) Smith; m. Harold G. Logan; 1 child, Leslie; stepchildren: Dianne, Pamela, Sharon, Ralph Pruitt, Jr., Harold, Minda, Andrew Logan. BS, Howard U., Washington, 1949; MA, Columbia U., N.Y.C., 1950, EdD, 1964; HumD hon., Ctrl. State U., Wilberforce, Ohio, 1982. Counsel for women Howard U., 1950-52; tchr., dir. guidance Hutto H.S., Bainbridge, 1952-55; dean students Albany State Coll., Ga., 1955-59, Fisk U., Nashville, 1959-61; prof. edn. Case Western Res. U., Cleve., 1963-79; prof. ednl. policy and leadership Ohio State U., Columbus, 1979-95, prof. emeritus, 1995—; assoc. dean Ohio State U. Grad. Sch., Columbus, 1979-84; assoc. provost Ohio State U. Columbus, 1984-86, dir. Ctr. for Tchg. Excellence, 1986-94; dean in residence Coun. Grad. Schs., Washington, 1994-96, scholar in residence, 1996—2002. Cons. So. Regional Edn. Bd., Atlanta, 1967-78, So. Edn. Found., Atlanta, 1978-87; co-dir. Preparing Future Faculty program, 1994-2002. Author: New Students and Coordinated Counseling, 1973, Black Employees in Traditionally White Institutions in the Adams States 1975-77, 1981, In Pursuit of Equality in Higher Education, 1987; co-author: (with Paul Isaac) Student Services for the Changing Graduate Student Population, 1995, (with Jerry Gaff and Richard Weibl) Building the Faculty We Need: Colleges and Universities Working Together, 2000, (with Jerry Gaff and Joyce Jentoff) Preparing Future Faculty in the Sciences and Mathematics, 2002, (with Jerry Gaff, Leslie Sims and Daniel Denecke) Preparing Future Faculty in the Humanities and Social Sciences: A Guide for Change, 2003. Trustee Urban League, Cleve., 1965-71, Ctrl. State U., 1973-82, Case Western Res. U., 1987-02, Columbus Area Leadership Program, 1988-91; bd. dirs. ARC, Cleve., 1978-79, Am. West Airlines Found., 1992-95; mem. adv. com. USCG Acad., New London, Conn., 1980-83; Ohio State U. rep. to AAUW, 1989-94; univ. co-chairperson United Way, 1990-91; trustee Marburn Acad., 1991-95; mem. Columbus 1992 Edn. Com., 1988-92; mem. edn. subcom. Columbus Found., 1991-94; mem. exec. com. Renaissance League, 1992-94; mem. vis. panel on rsch., Ednl. Testing Svc., 1996-02; mem. Commn. on Future Clemson U., 1997-98; bd. dirs. Black Women's Agenda, Inc., 1997-, pres. 1998-2002; deacon Peoples Congregational United Ch. of Christ, 1998—; mem. B.E.S.T. Expert Panel, 2002-04; evaluation external expert NSF Grad. Tchg. Fellows in K-12 Edn. Program, 2002-04. Named sr. scholar, Am. Coll. Pers. Assns., 1989, Godmother of Minority Grad. Edn., Black Issues in Higher Edn., 1995, inducted, Ohio State U. Coll. Edn. Hall of Fame, 2004; named one of Am.'s Top 100 Black Bus. and Profl. Women, Dollars & Sense Mag., 1986; recipient Outstanding Alumnus award, Howard U. Alumni Assn., 1975, Disting. Affirmative Action award, Ohio State U., 1988, Disting. Svc. award, 2005, Woman of Achievement award, YMCA, 1993; fellow Am. Coun. on Edn., 1977. Mem. NSF (mem. com. on equal opportunities in sci. and engring. 1989-95), Am. Coll. Pers. Assn. (pres. 1976-77), Coun. Grad. Schs. in U.S. (chairperson com. on minority grad. edn. 1980-84), Am. Ednl. Rsch. Assn., Ohio Assn. Counselor Edn. (pres. 1966-67), Links Inc., Cosmos Club, Alpha Kappa Alpha.

**PRUITT, BASIL ARTHUR, JR.,** surgeon, retired military officer; b. Nyack, NY, Aug. 21, 1930; s. Basil Arthur and Myrtle Flo (Knowles) P.; m. Mary Sessions Gibson, Sept. 4, 1954; children: Scott Knowles, Laura Sessions, Jeffrey Hamilton. AB, Harvard U., 1952, postgrad., 1952—53; MD, Tufts U., 1957. Diplomate Am. Bd. Surgery. Intern Boston City Hosp., 1957—58, resident surgery, 1958—59, 1961—62; commd. capt., M.C. U.S. Army, 1959, advanced through grades to col., 1972; resident Brooke Gen. Hosp., Ft. Sam Houston, Tex., 1962—64; chief clin. divsn. Inst. Surg. Rsch., Ft. Sam Houston, 1965—67; chief profl. svcs. 12th Evacuation Hosp., Vietnam, 1967—68; comdr., dir. U.S. Army Inst. Surg. Rsch., Brooke Army Med. Ctr., Ft. Sam Houston, 1968—95, ret., 1995; clin. prof. gen. surgery U. Tex. Health Sci. Ctr., San Antonio, 1975—; prof. surgery Uniformed Svcs. U. Health Scis., Bethesda, Md., 1978—. Mem. surgery, anaesthesiology and trauma study sect. NIH, 1978—82; mem. Shriners Burns Adv. Bd., 1985—92, Shriners Med. Adv. Bd., 1992—95, Shriners Rsch. Adv. Bd., 1996—, Shriners Clin. Outcomes Studies Adv. Bd., 1999—; merit recv. bd. for surgery VA, 1990—93; bd. dirs. Am. Bd. Surgery, 1982—88, sr. mem., 1989—. Author med. books; contbr. chpts. to textbooks, articles to profl. jours.; mem. editl. bd. Jour. Trauma, 1975-94, editor, 1995—; mem. editl. bd.: Archives Surgery, 1981-93, Consultations in Surgery, Correspondence Society of Surgeons, Collected Letters, 1978-2000, Circulatory Shock, 1985-93, Jour. Burn Care and Rehab., 1984-87, Jour. Investigative Surgery, 1987-97, Shock, 1993—, Current Opinion in Surg. Infections, 1993-2001, Sepsis, 1996-2002, Injury, 1998-2003, Turkish Jour. Trauma, 2002—, English edit. Chinese Jour. Traumatology, 1998—, Med. Jour. Chinese People's Liberation Army, 2005—. Decorated Bronze Star, Legion of Merit, DSM; recipient ISS/SIC Danis prize, 1995, G. Whitaker Internat. Burns prize, 2000, Tanner-Vandeput-Boswick Burn prize, 2006. Fellow: ACS (pre and postoperative care com. 1969—79, vice chmn. 1973—75, gov. 1973—79, com. on trauma 1974—84, internat. rels. com. 1983—93, chmn. 1987—89), Am. Coll. Critical Care Medicine (Disting. Investigator award 2000); mem.: We. Trauma Assn., La. Assn. Surgery Trauma, N.Am. Burn Soc. (pres. 1993—94), Shock Soc. (clin. counselor 1995—98, pres.-elect 2006, chmn. 2005 program com.), Internat. Surg. Group, Surg. Infection Soc. (recorder 1980—84, pres. 1985—86), Assn. Acad. Surgery, Internat. Soc. Surgery, Surg. Biol. Club III, Am. Assn. Surgery Trauma (recorder 1976—80, pres. 1982—83), Halsted Soc. (pres. 1985—86), So. Surg. Assn. (pres. 2004—05), We. Surg. Assn. (dist. rep. 1984—88, pres. 1993—94), Tex. Surg. Assn., Am. Surg. Assn. (2d v.p. 1980—81, pres. 1999—2000. Medallion 1998), Soc. Univ. Surgeon, Am. Trauma Soc. (pres. Tex. divsn. 1974—75, dir. 1974—, sec. 1986—88, v.p. 1988—90, pres.-elect 1990—92, pres. 1992—94), Smoke Burn and Fire Assn. (adv. coun.), Internat. Soc. Burn Injuries (nat. rep. 1974—82, co-chmn. disaster planning com. 1982—86, pres.-elect 1990—94, pres. 1994—98), Am. Burn Assn. (pres. 1975—76), Mediterranean Club Burns and Fire Disasters (regional rep. Ams.), Surgeons' Travel Club (pres. 2002—03). Home: 402 Tidecrest Dr San Antonio TX 78239-2517 Office: U Tex Health Sci Ctr Dept Surgery 7703 Floyd Curl Dr San Antonio TX 78229-3900 also: Editl Office Jour Trauma 7330 San Pedro Ste 654 San Antonio TX 78216-6236 Office Phone: 210-342-7903. Business E-Mail: pruitt@uthscsa.edu.

**PRUITT, DAVID R.,** music educator, musician; b. Chgo., Oct. 1955; s. Ralph O. and Marjorie A. Pruitt; children: Cori Ann Porter, Scott David, Megan Elizabeth. BA, We. Ill. U., Macomb, Ill., 1978. Cert. music educator State Bd. Edn., Ill., 1978. Studio percussion instr. Pk. Forest Conservatory of Music & Dance, Park Forest, Ill., 1977—78; instr. music Bluffs Unit 2 Schs., Bluffs, Ill., 1978—80, PORTA Unit 202 Schs., Petersburg, Ill., 1980—90, Unit 15 Schs., Williamsville, Ill., 1990—. Pvt. music instr., Springfield, Ill., 1978—; adj. instr. LincolnLand C.C., Springfield, 2003—06. Grantee, We. Ill. U., 1975—78. Mem.: NEA, Internat. Assn. Jazz Educators (guest condr. 1997—2006), Am. Fedn. Musicians, Ill. Edn. Assn. (assoc.; pres. local chpt. 1988—90), Ill. Music Educator's Assn. (assoc.; various offices 1978—2006). Home: 2 Hollybrook Drive Springfield IL 62702 Office: Williamsville Unit 15 Schools 900 South Walnut Williamsville IL 62693 Office Phone: 217-566-2014. Business E-Mail: pruitt@wcusd15.org.

**PRUITT, DEAN GARNER,** psychologist, educator; b. Phila., Dec. 26, 1930; s. Dudley McConnell and Grace (Garner) P.; m. France Juliard, Dec. 27, 1959; children: Andre Juliard, Paul Dudley, Charles Alexandre. AB, Oberlin Coll., 1952; MS, Yale U., 1954, PhD, 1957. Postdoctoral fellow U. Mich., 1957-59; rsch. assoc. Northwestern U., 1959-61; asst. prof., then assoc. prof. U. Del., 1961-66; assoc. prof. to prof. SUNY, Buffalo, 1966—96, SUNY Disting. prof., 1996—2001, SUNY Disting. prof. emeritus, 2001—; dir. grad. program in social psychology, 1969—73, 1976—77, 1985—88, 1998—2001; disting. scholar in residence George Mason U., 2001—. Author:

Negotiation Behavior, 1981, (with J. Z. Rubin and S.H. Kim) Social Conflict, 1986, 94, 2004, (with P.J. Carnevale) Negotiation in Social Conflict, 1993; editor; (with R.C. Snyder) Theory and Research on the Causes of War, 1969, (with K. Kressel) Mediation Research, 1989. Grantee Office Naval Rsch., 1965, NIMH, 1969, NSF, 1969, 74, 76, 80, 83, 86, 88, 93, Guggenheim Found., 1978-79. Fellow APA, Am. Psychol. Soc., Soc. for Psychol. Study Social Issues; mem. Internat. Assn. for Conflict Mgmt. (pres. 1990-92, Lifetime Achievement award 1997), Internat. Soc. Polit. Psychology (v.p. 1984-85, Harold D. Lasswell award 1992), Phi Beta Kappa, Sigma Xi. Home: 9006 Friars Rd Bethesda MD 20817-3320 Office: George Mason U Inst Conflict Analysis and Resolution Fairfax VA 22030-4444 E-mail: dean@pruittfamily.com.

**PRUITT, GARY B.,** publishing company executive; m. Abby Pruitt; children: Katherine, Allison. BA summa cum laude, U. Fla., 1978; MA in Pub. Policy, U. Calif. Berkeley, 1981, JD, 1982. Counsel The McClatchy Co., 1984—87, gen. counsel, corp. sec., 1987—91, pub. The Fresno Bee, 1991-94, v.p. ops. and tech., 1994-95, pres., 1995—, COO, 1995—96, CEO, 1996—, chmn., 2001—. Mem. chancellors com. U. Calif., Berkeley, mem. bd. advisors Goldman Sch. Pub. Policy. Mem.: James Irvine Found. (vice chmn. 2003—05), Newspaper Assn. Am (treas.), Phi Betta Kappa. Office: The McClatchy Co 2100 Q St Sacramento CA 95816-6816*

**PRUITT, GEORGE ALBERT,** college president; b. Canton, Miss., July 9, 1946; s. Joseph Henry and Lillie Irene (Carmichael) P.; m. Pamela Young; 1 child, Shayla Nicole. BS, Ill. State U., 1968, MS, 1970, DHL (hon.), 1994; PhD, Union Grad. Sch., Cin., 1974; D Pub. Svc. (hon.), Bridgewater State Coll., 1990, MA (hon.) 1990; LLD (hon.), Ill. State U., 1994; DHL (hon.), SUNY Empire State Coll., 1996. Asst. to v.p. for acad. affairs Ill. State U., Normal, 1968-70, dir. high potential students program, 1968-70; dean students Towson State U., 1970-72; v.p., exec. asst. to pres., assoc. prof. urban affairs Morgan State U., 1972-75; v.p., prof. Tenn. State U., 1975-81; exec. v.p. Council for Advancement Experiential Learning, Columbia, Md., 1981-82; pres. Thomas A. Edison State Coll., Trenton, 1982—. Commn. on ednl. credit and credentials, labor/higher edn. coun. Am. Coun. on Edn.; advisor group XII, Nat. Fellowship program W.K. Kellogg Found., 1990-94, advisor group XV, 1995-99; bd. dirs. SEEDCO, Sun Nat. Bank, Vineland, N.J.; nat. adv. com. on instnl. quality and integrity U.S. Dept. Edn., 1994—; chmn. N.J. Pres. Coun., 2004-2006; chair N.J. Capital Region Conv. and Vis. Bur., 2004-2006. Past chair Mercer County Chamber of Commerce; mem. Govs. Edn. Cabinet, 2002—05, N.J. State Planning Commn., 2002—; trustee Union Inst., Cin., 1988—, Rider U., Lawrenceville, NJ, 2001—, Econ. Devel. Corp., Trenton, 2001—06; bd. dirs. N.J. Assn. Colls. and Univs. Recipient Resolution of Commendation Bd., Trustees Morgan State U., 1975, Outstanding Svc. to Edn. award Tenn. State U., 1981, Gubernatorial citation Gov. of Tenn., 1981, Good Guy award George Washington coun. Boy Scouts Am., 1991, Humanitarian award NCCJ, 1992, Educator of Yr. award Black N.J. Mag., 1993, Disting. Alumni award Ill. State U., 1996; apptd. hon. mem. Gen. Assembly Tenn., 1981, hon. mem. U.S. Congress from 5th Tenn. dist., 1981; named ofcr. of the Most Effective Coll. Pres. in U.S., Exxon Edn. Found. Study, 1986; named to Coll. of Edn. Hall of Fame, Ill. State U., 1995; named Mercer Co. N.J. Citizen of Yr., Mercer Co. C. of C., 1997. Mem. Coun. for Advancement Exptl. Learning, Am. Assn. State Colls.and Univs., Coun. for Advancement and Support of Edn., Am. Coun. Edn., Mid. States Assn. Colls. and Schs. (accreditation evaluator commn. on higher edn.). Office: Thomas Edison Coll 101 W State St Trenton NJ 08608-1176 Office Phone: 609-984-1105. E-mail: gpruitt@tesc.edu.

**PRUITT, HOLLIS EARL,** language educator; s. Elijah Danley and Augusta Walker; m. Lynn Magalhaes, Nov. 5, 1988; 1 child, Alberta Shanzia. BA, U. Ark., Little Rock, 1979; MA, U. Tenn., 1994. English instr. Job Corps, Knoxville, Tenn., 1987—88, Knoxville Coll., 1991—97; coord. of retention, English instr. Sullivan County C.C., Loche Sheldrake, NY, 1999—2001; asst. English prof. Thomas Nelson C.C., Hampton, Va., 2001—. Author: The Handbook of the Elves, (anthology, selected poems) Revisited: Pormethus, Among Men, Black Mary, (anthology, short story) The Tree of Life. With U.S. Army, 1972—75. W.E.B. DuBois fellow, 1995. Mem.: Va. Collegiate Honors Coun., Nat. Soc. for Collegiate Scholars (life). Avocations: poetry, world mythology, fishing. Office: Thomas Nelson Community College Thomas Nelson Rd PO Box 9407 Hampton VA 23670 Office Phone: 757-825-2781. E-mail: pruitt6@cox.net.

**PRUITT, ROBERT A.,** artist; b. Houston, 1975; BFA, Tex. So. U.; MFA, U. Tex., Austin. Mem. Otabenga Jones & Assocs., Houston, 2002—; arts coord. Project Row Houses, Houston. Prin. works include This Do in Remembrance of Me, 2005, exhibited in group shows at Splat Boom Pow!: The Influence of Cartoons in Contemporary Art, Contemporary Art Mus., Come Forward: Emerging Art in Tex., Dallas Mus. Art, Whitney Biennial: Day for Night, Whitney Mus. Am. Art, 2006, exhibitions include I Call My Brother Sun Because He Shines Like One, Clementine Gallery, NYC. Recipient Artadia award, 2004. Mailing: Project Row Houses 2500 Holman PO Box 1011 Houston TX 77251-1011*

**PRUITT, STEPHEN WALLACE,** finance educator; b. Indpls., Feb. 3, 1957; s. Harry Wallace and Dorothy (Thorp) P.; m. Mary Melinda Settle, Dec. 19, 1981; children: Rebecca Elizabeth, Victoria Barrick. BS in Mgmt., Purdue U., 1979; MBA in Fin., Ohio State U., 1980; PhD in Fin., Fla. State U., 1987. Internat. cash mgr. Marathon Oil Co., Findlay, Ohio, 1980-81; fin. analyst Nat. Svc. Industries, Crawfordsville, Ind., 1981-83; asst. prof. fin. U. Miss. Oxford, 1986-88, Ind. U., Bloomington, 1988-93; assoc. prof. fin. U. Memphis, 1993-96, prof. fin., 1996—2000; Arvin Gottlieb/Mo. chmn. in bus. econs. and fin. U. Mo., Kansas City, 2005—. Cons. in field. Contbr. articles to profl. jours. Bd. dirs. Art Mus. U Memphis, 1995-2000, treas.; Memphis Print Club, 1995-2000. Mem. So. Fin. Assn., Fin. Mgmt. Assn. Avocations: collecting art and antiques, recording original music. Office: U Mo Henry W Bloch Sch Bus & Pub 5100 Rockhill Rd Kansas City MO 64110-2481 Home: 5316 W 140th St Overland Park KS 66224 Office Phone: 816-235-2334. E-mail: pruittst@umkc.edu.

**PRUKESATONKUL, KAMOL,** music educator; b. Bangkok, Feb. 14, 1951; s. Richard and Chee Shim Yip. BA, Bangkok Coll., 1974. Piano tchr., L.A., 1977—. Mem.: Music Tchr. Assn. Calif., Music Tchr. Nat. Assn. Avocations: reading, swimming, golf, hiking, travel. Home and Office: 825 Hampton ST Glendora CA 91740

**PRUNES, FERNANDO,** plastic surgeon, educator; b. Chihuahua, Mex. m. Linda R. Underwood; children: Alexander, Ariadne, Anthony. MD, Chihuahua, Mex., 1968. Surg. intern Booth Meml. Med. Ctr., Flushing, NY, 1971-72; resident in gen. surgery Tucson Hosps. Med. Edn. Program, 1972-76; resident in plastic surgery Mayo Grad. Sch. Medicine, 1979-81; chief divsn. plastic surgery Kern Med. Ctr., Bakersfield, Calif., 1983—. Asst. clin. prof. surgery U. Calif., San Diego, 1983-98. Mem. Am. Soc. Plastic Surgeons, Mayo Alumni Assn. Avocations: golf, computers. Office: Kern Med Ctr 1830 Flower St Bakersfield CA 93305-4186 Office Phone: 661-326-2274.

**PRUSINER, STANLEY BEN,** neurologist, biochemist, virologist, educator; b. Des Moines, May 28, 1942; s. Lawrence Albert and Miriam (Spigel) Prusiner; children: Helen Chloe, Leah Anne. AB cum laude, U. Pa., 1964, MD, 1968, DS (hon.), 1998; PhD (hon.), Hebrew U., Jerusalem, 1994, René Descartes U., Paris, 1996; DS (hon.), Dartmouth Coll., 1999, U. Liege, 2000; MD (hon.), U. Bologna, Italy, 2000; DSc (hon.), Fla. State U., 2001; DVM (hon.), U. Cardenal Herrera, 2005. Diplomate Am. Bd. Neurology. Intern in medicine U. Calif., San Francisco, 1968—69, resident in neurology, 1972—74, asst. prof. neurology, 1974—80, assoc. prof., 1980—84, prof., 1984—, prof. biochemistry, 1988—, acad. senate faculty rsch. lectr., 1989—90, prof. virology Berkeley, 1984—, dir. Inst. for Neurodegenerative Diseases, 1999—; founder, chmn. bd. dirs. InPro Biotech., Inc., South San Francisco, Calif., 2001—. Mem. neurology rev. com. Nat. Inst. for Neurodegenerative Diseases, NIH, Bethesda, Md., 1982—86, Bethesda, 1990—92;

mem. Coun. Nat. Inst. Aging, NIH, Bethesda, Md., 2001—04; mem. sci. adv. bd. French Found., L.A., 1985—, chmn. sci. adv. bd., 1996—; mem. sci. rev. com. Alzheimer's Disease Diagnostic Ctr. & Rsch Grant Program, State of Calif., 1985—89; chmn. sci. adv. bd. Am. Health Assistance Found., Rockville, Md., 1986—2000, hon. mem. bd. dirs., 2001—; mem. spongiform encephalopathy adv. com. FDA, 1997—2001; mem. sci. adv. bd.Family Survival Project for Adults with Chronic Brain Disorders, San Francisco, 1982—90; mem. adv. bd. San Francisco chpt. Alzheimer's Disease and Related Disorders Found., 1985—91; mem. bd. dirs. Fromm Inst. for Lifelong Learning, San Francisco, 2002—; cons. Inst. of Medicine Com. on Advancing Prion Sci., Washington, 2002—03; mem. bd. govs. Found. for Biomed. Rsch., Washington, 2002—; bd. dirs. Internat. Longevity Ctr., N.Y.C., 2003—. Editor: The Enzymes of Glutamine Metabolism, 1973, Slow Transmissible Diseases of the Nervous System, 2 vols., 1979, Prions--Novel Infectious Pathogens Causing Scrapie and CJD, 1987, Prion Diseases of Humans and Animals, 1992, Molecular and Genetic Basis of Neurologic Disease, 3d edit., 2003, Prions Prions Prions, 1996, Prion Biology and Diseases, 2d edit., 2004; contbr. more than 350 articles to profl. jours. Trustee U. Pa., 2000—05, Congregation Sherith Israel, San Francisco, 1999—2002. Lt. comdr. USPHS, 1969—72. Recipient Leadership and Excellence for Alzheimer's Disease award, NIH, 1990—97, Potamkin prize for Alzheimer's Disease Rsch., 1991, Med. Rsch. award, Met. Life Found., 1992, Christopher Columbus Discovery award, NIH and Med. Soc. Genoa, Italy, 1992, Charles A. Dana award, 1992, Dickson prize, U. Pitts., 1992, Max Planck Rsch. award, Alexander von Humboldt Found. and Max Planck Soc., 1992, Gairdner Found. Internat. award, 1993, Disting. Achievement in Neurosci. Rsch. award, Bristol-Myers Squibb, 1994, Albert Lasker award for Basic Med. Rsch., 1994, Caledonian Rsch. Found. prize, Royal Soc. Edinburgh, 1995, Paul Ehrlich and Ludwig Darmstaedter award, Germany, 1995, Paul Hoch award, Am. Psychopathol. Assn., 1995, Wolf prize in medicine, 1996, ICN Virology prize, 1996, Victor and Clara Soriano award, World Fedn. Neurology, 1996, Pasarow Found. prize, 1996, Charles Leopole Mayer prize, French Acad. Scis., 1996, Keio Internat. prize, 1996, Baxter award, Am. Assn. Med. Colls., 1996, Louisa Gross Horwitz prize, Columbia U., 1997, Nobel Prize for Medicine, 1997, K.J. Zulch prize, Gertrude Reemtsma Found., 1997, Benjamin Franklin medal, Franklin Inst., 1998, Jubilee medal, Swedish Med. Soc., 1998, Prize Lecture medal, U. Coll. London, 1999, Sir Hans Krebs medal, Fedn. European Biochem. Socs., 1999, Ellen Browning Scripps medal, 2000, Disting. Alumni award, Coll. Arts and Scis., U. of Pa., 2003, Commonwealth award, 2004, William Beaumont medal, 2005, Disting. Med. Grad. award, U. Pa. Sch. Medicine, 1991; fellow Alfred P. Sloan Rsch. fellow, U. Calif., 1976—78; grantee Med. Investigator grantee, Howard Hughes Med. Inst., 1976—81, grantee for excellence in neurosci., Senator Jacob Javits Ctr., NIH, 1985—90. Fellow: AAAS, Royal Coll. Physicians, Am. Acad. Arts & Scis., Am. Soc. Microbiology; mem.: NAS (Inst. Medicine, Richard Lounsbery award for extraordinary achievements in biology and medicine 1993), World Jewish Acad. Scis., Serbian Acad. Scis., Protein Soc. (Amgen award 1997), Royal Soc. London, Am. Philos. Soc., Am. Soc. Molecular Biol. Biochemistry, Am. Soc. Cellular Biology, Am. Soc. Cell Biology, Genetics Soc. Am., Am. Soc. Human Genetics, Soc. Neurosci., Am. Chem. Soc., Am. Soc. Biochemistry and Molecular Biology, Am. Soc. Clin. Investigation, Am. Neurol. Assn., Am. Soc. Virology, Am. Soc. Neurochemistry, Am. Soc. Neurochemistry, Am. Assn. Physicians, Am. Acad. Neurology (George Cotzias award for outstanding rsch. 1987, Presdl. award 1993, Disting. Achievement award 1998), Bohemian Club, Concordia Argonaut Club (bd. dirs. 1997—2005).

**PRUSSIN, JEFFREY A.,** management consultant; b. Bklyn., Aug. 11, 1943; s. Samuel and Shirley (Solomon) P.; m. Judith H. May; children: Aaron Justin, Leya Monique. AB, UCLA, 1965; MA, Johns Hopkins U., 1967. Dir. edn. and tng. Group Health Assn. Am., Washington, 1971-72; mgr. prog. devel. Health System div. Westinghouse, Columbia, Md., 1972-73; prin. Health Care Orgn., Delivery & Fin. System, Kensington, Md., 1973-80; exec. asst. for policy Bur. Health Facilities, HHS, Washington, 1980-81; exec. v.p. Comprehensive Am. Care, Miami, Fla., 1981-84; sr. v.p. Internat. Med. Ctrs., Miami, 1984-86; pres. Health Sys. Devel. Corp., South Miami, Fla., 1986-99, J&JP Funding Corp., Jacksonville, Fla., 1999—. Cons. in field; lectr. in field; adj. prof. U. Miami, Fla., 1982-99; vis. asst. prof. Oreg. State U., Eugene, 1970; adj. asst. prof. Linfield Coll., Oreg., 1969-70, Portland State U., 1969-70. Contbr. numerous articles to profl. jours.; author: Health Maintenance Organization Legislation in 1973-74, 1974, Employee Health Benefits: HMOs and Mandatory Dual Choide, 1976, Results of a State-of-the-Art Review of Health Assurance for the Elderly, 1979, (with Judith M. Prussin), Health Services and the Elderly: A Comprehensive, Annotated Bibliography, 1982, (with Jack C. Wood), Topics in Health Care Financing: Private Third Party Reimbursement, 1975. Mem. Fla. Assn. Health, Maint. Orgns. (pres. 1985-86), Group Health Assn. Am. Office: J & JP Funding Corp PO Box 600580 Jacksonville FL 32260-0580

**PRUSSING, LAUREL LUNT,** mayor, economist; b. NYC, Feb. 21, 1941; d. Richard Valentine and Maria (Rinaldi) Lunt; m. John Edward Prussing, May 29, 1965; children: Heidi Elizabeth, Erica Stephanie, Victoria Nicole Johanna. AB, Wellesley Coll., 1962; MA, Boston U., 1964; postgrad., U. Calif., San Diego, 1968-69, U. Ill., 1970-76. Economist Arthur D. Little, Cambridge, Mass., 1963-67, U. Ill., Urbana, 1971-72; mem. county bd. Champaign County, Urbana, 1972-76, county auditor, 1976-92; legis. dir. ERA Ill., 2002—03; founder ERA Yes!, 2003. Mem. local audit adv. bd. Office Ill. Compt., Chgo., 1984-92. Contbr. to Illinois Local Government: A Handbook, 1990. Founding mem. Citizens Forum on Gambling and Campaign Fin. Reform, 1999; downstate program dir. Citizen Action/Ill., 1999; legis. dir. AAUW, Ill., 2001, lobbyist, 2004; active Champaign-Urbana Mass Transit Dist. Bd., 2004—05; state rep. 103d dist. Ill. Gen. Assembly, 1993—95; Dem. nominee Ill. 15th dist. U.S. Congress, 1996—98, mayor Urbana, 2005—. Named Best Freshman Legislator Ind. Voters Ill., 1994; recipient Friend of Agriculture award Ill. Farm Bur., 1994; named to Legis. Honor Roll Ill. Environ. Coun., 1994. Mem. AAUW, NAACP, LWV, Govt. Fin. Officers Assn., U.S. and Can. (cons. on acctg., auditing and fin. reporting 1980-88, Fin. Reporting award 1981-91, Disting. Budget award 1986), Nat. Assn. Local Govt. Auditors (charter), Ill. Assn. County Auditors (pres. 1984-85). Democrat. Home: 2106 Grange Dr Urbana IL 61801-6609 Office Phone: 217-328-2071.

**PRUTER, MARGARET FRANSON,** editor; b. Oak Park, Ill., Jan. 16; d. Frederick G. and Margaret K. (Svoboda) Franson; m. Robert D. Pruter, July 22, 1972; 1 child, Robin. AB, Dominican U., 1961; MA, Northwestern U., 1965. Asst. editor Am. People's Ency., Chgo., 1961-62; tech. assoc. AMA, Chgo., 1962-63; asst. editor New Standard Ency., Chgo., 1964-66, assoc. editor, 1966-75, sr. editor, 1975-96; editl. dir. Elmhurst (Ill.) Editl. Svcs., 1996—2005; editor McDougal Littell, Evanston, Ill., 1997—2004; sr. editor The Book Edit Group, 2005—. Exec. dir. Militaria Archives, Elmhurst, Ill., 1972—. Co-author: DuPage Roots, 1985 (Ill. State Hist. Publ. award 1986); contbr. chpts. to books. Mem. Elmhurst Hist. Commn., 1981—, v.p., 1995—2000, pres., 2000—01; mem. Friends of Elmhurst Pub. Libr., Elmhurst Art Mus. Found.; exec. bd. North Ctrl. Coll. Parents Assn., 1995—98; bd. dirs. DuPage County Hist. Soc., Wheaton, Ill., 1982—, 1st v.p., 2004—; bd. dirs. DuPage County Sesquicentennial Com., Wheaton, Ill., 1988—89. Mem.: AAUW (bd. dirs. Elmhurst br. 1995—99), Ocean Conservancy, Nature Conservancy, Arch. Conservancy, Am. Studies Assn., Nat. Women's History Mus., Nat. Trust Historic Preservation, Orgn. Am. Historians, Nat. Wildlife Fedn., Ill. Hist. Soc., Elmhurst Hist. Soc., Chgo. Hist. Soc., World Wildlife Fedn., Chgo. Women in Pub., Sisters in Crime, Chgo. Architecture Found., Byrd's Nest Chapel Questers (pres. 1992—94, 2003—), Nat. Parks and Conservation Assn., Sierra Club. Office: The Book Edit Group PO Box 245 Elmhurst IL 60126-0768 E-mail: bookedit1@yahoo.com.

**PRUTER, ROBERT DOUGLAS,** librarian; b. Phila., July 1, 1944; s. Hugo Rehling and Nancy Lee (Taylor) P.; m. Margaret Franson; 1 child, Robin Franson. BA, Roosevelt U., 1967, MA, 1976; MLS, Dominican U., 2000. Asst. editor New Std Ency., Chgo., 1969-74, assoc. editor, 1974-79, sr. editor, 1979-96; sr. rsch. assoc. Planning Commn., 1996-97; asst. editor Charles D.

Spencer & Assocs., Chgo., 1997-98, assoc. editor, 1999-2001; govt. documents lib. Lewis U., Romeoville, Ill., 2001—. Author: Chicago Soul, 1991, Doowop: The Chicago Scene, 1996; editor: Blackwell Guide to Soul Recordings, 1993; adv. editor Popular Music and Society, 1995—; rhythm and blues editor Goldmine Mag., 1984—. Mem. adv. com. Chgo. Blues Festival, 1992—. Served U.S. Army, 1967-69, Vietnam. Mem.: NARAS, Soc. Midland Authors, Chgo. Hist. Soc., Ill. Hist. Soc., N.Am. Soc. for Sport History. Democrat. Avocations: collecting records, sports history rsch. Office Phone: 815-836-5664. Personal E-mail: pruterro@lewisu.edu.

**PRUZAN, IRENE,** musician, educator, public relations executive, art association administrator; b. Watertown, N.Y., Jan. 3, 1949; d. John Edward and Esther (Coahn) P.; m. Charles G. Ullery, Jan. 30, 1972 (div. 1978); m. Charles Robert Freeman, May 20, 1988 (dec. Sept. 2005). Student U. Ariz., Tucson, 1966-68; MusB, U. So. Calif., 1971; postgrad., San Francisco State U., Calif., 1972-74, U. Minn., 1976-80. Tchr. flute, coach chamber music MacPhail Ctr. for Arts, U. Minn., Mpls., 1976-85, coordinator instrumental music, 1978-81, program dir. instrumental music, 1982-85, div. head of programs, 1985-86; regional dir. Music On The Move, Inc., Valley Cottage, NY, 1986-87; pres. Music On the Move Minn., Inc., St. Paul, 1987—2002; dir. pub. rels. Nat. Flute Assn., 2004—. Founding mem. Crocus Hill Trio, 1976-2004; pub. rels. cons. Sch. of Music, U. Minn., 1991; faculty Nat. Music Camp, Interlochen, Mich., 1983, 84; cons. edn. and festival Ordway Music Theatre, St. Paul, 1985-87; mgr. Sartory String Quartet, Mpls., 1986-93; developer numerous master classes; cons. in field. Writer teaching materials for flute. Bd. directors Twin Cities Friends of Chamber Music, 1982—89; mem. Ariz. Chamber Orch., Tucson, 1967, San Gabriel (Calif.) Symphony, 1968—71; extra player St. Paul Chamber Orch., 1977—91; organizer German jazz residency USIA, Minn. and Wis., 1986; edn. com. Orlando Philharm., 2001—04; cons., program dir. Young Audiences Minn., Mpls., 1986—88. Mem.: AAUW (Orlando br. pub. rels. and web master 2003—), Orlando Musicians Union, Twin Cities Musicians Union, Nat. Flute Assn. (dir. mktg. 1987—90).

**PRUZANSKY, JOSHUA MURDOCK,** lawyer; b. NYC, Mar. 16, 1940; s. Louis and Rose (Murdock) P.; m. Susan R. Bernstein, Aug. 31, 1980; 1 child, Dina Gabrielle. BA, Columbia Coll., 1960, JD, 1965. Bar: N.Y., 1965, U.S. Dist. Ct. (ea. and so. dists.) N.Y., 1968, U.S. Supreme Ct., 1980. Ptnr. Scheinberg, DePetris & Pruzansky, Riverhead, NY, 1965-85, Greshin, Ziegler & Pruzansky, Smithtown, NY, 1985-2000, Pruzansky & Besunder, LLP, Islandia, NY, 2000—. NY State Bar Assoc. Pres., ho. dels. 1982-, exec. com. 1992-99, spl com. women and law 1986-91, task force on small firms 1991-1992, spl. com. on MDP 1999-2000, chair spl. com., fiduciary appts., 2003—, trusts and estates sect., gen. practice, elder law sects.), 1997-98; mem. exec. coun. NY State Conf. Bar Leaders, 1984—, chmn., 1988-89; mem. grievance com. Appellate Divsn. 10th Judicial Dist., 1992-96; mem. adv. bd. Ticor Title Guarantee Co., 1992-2001; mem. LI adv. bd. HSBC Bank, 1995—; dir. NY State Com. for Modern Ct., 1998—; mem. adv. task force NY Dept. State Corps., 1998—. Mem. bd. visitors Columbia Law Sch., 1998—; chair bd. visitors Touro Law Sch., 1998-2004; dir., sec. L.I. Mus., 1998-2004. Fellow ABA Found., NY State Bar Found. (bd. dir. 1994-2003); mem. ABA (ho. of dels. 1997-2003, probate and real property sect., standing com. on solo and small firm practitioners 1998-2000, NY state del. Caucus of State Bar Assns.), Suffolk County Bar Assn. (bd. dir. 1979-89, pres. 1985-86), Nassau County Bar Assn. Office: Pruzansky & Besunder LLP One Suffolk Sq Ste 315 Islandia NY 11749 Office Phone: 631-234-9240. Business E-Mail: jmp@prubeslaw.com.

**PRYCE, DEBORAH DENINE,** congresswoman; b. Warren, Ohio, July 29, 1951; m. Randy Walker (div.); 1 child. BA cum laude, Ohio State U., 1973; JD with honors, Capital U. Law Sch., 1976. Bar: Ohio 1976. Adminstrv. law judge Ohio State Dept. Ins., 1976—78; first asst. city prosecutor, sr. asst. city atty., asst. city mgr. Columbus City Atty.'s Office, Ohio, 1978—85; judge Franklin County Mcpl. Ct., Columbus, 1989, 1990, 1992; mem. US Congress from 15th Ohio dist., 1993—, chair Ho. Rep. Conf., 2003—, mem. fin. svcs. com., chair domestic and internat. monetary policy subcommittee, dep. whip, co-chair cancer caucus. Republican. Presbyterian. Avocation: skiing. Office: US Ho Reps 204 Cannon Ho Office Bldg Washington DC 20515-0001 Office Phone: 202-225-2015.*

**PRYCE, JONATHAN,** actor; b. North Wales, June 1, 1947; Appearances include (stage) Liverpool Everyman, 1972, Nottingham Playhouse, Comedians, 1977 (Tony award, Theatre World award), 1980, Hamlet (Olivier award), 1986, Macbeth, The Caretaker, 1981, Accidental Death of an Anarchist, 1984, The Seagull, 1986, Uncle Vanya, 1989, Miss Saigon, 1991 (Tony award, Olivier award), Oliver, 1995, My Fair Lady, 2001-02, A Reckoning, 2003, The Goat or Who Is Sylvia, 2004, Dirty Rotten Scoundrels, N.Y.C., 2006; (films) Voyage of the Damned, 1976, Breaking Glass, 1980, Loophole, 1981, Praying Mantis, 1982, The Plowman's Lunch, 1983, Something Wicked This Way Comes, 1983, Brazil, 1985, The Doctor and the Devils, 1985, Haunted Honeymoon, 1986, Jumpin Jack Flash, 1986, Hotel London, 1987, Man On Fire, 1987, The Adventures of Baron Munchausen, 1988, Consuming Passions, 1988, The Rachel Papers, 1989, Glengarry Glen Ross, 1992, The Age of Innocence, 1993, Shopping, 1994, A Business Affair, 1994, Carrington, 1996 (Best Actor award Cannes Film Festival 1995), Evita, 1996, Tomorrow Never Dies, 1997, Regeneration, 1997, Ronin, 1998, Stigmata, 1999, Very Annie Mary, 2001, Unconditional Love, 2001, Bride of the Wind, 2002, The Affair of the Necklace, 2002, What a Girl Wants, 2003, Pirates of the Caribbean, 2003, De Lovely, 2004, The Brothers Grimm, 2004, The New World, 2005, Pirates of the Caribbean 2: Dead Man's Chest, 2006; (TV movie) Barbarians at the Gate, HBO, 1993 (Emmy nomination, Supporting Actor - Miniseries or Special, 1993), David, 1997, Confessions of an Ugly Stepsister, 2002. Recipient BAFTA Cymru spl. award, 2002. Address: UTA 9560 Wilshire Blvd Beverly Hills CA 90212 Mailing: Julian Belfrage Assocs ADAM House 16 New Burlington St London W1S 3BQ England

**PRYOR, DAVID BRAM,** health science association administrator; b. Charleston, SC, Oct. 18, 1951; s. Sydney and Grace Prystowsky; m. Christin Marie Kennedy; children: Rebecca Whitaker, Rachel Celia, Grace Eileen. Attended, U. Mich., Ann Arbor, 1969—72; MD, U. Mich. Med. Sch., 1972—76. Cert. Am. Bd. Internal Medicine, 1979, bd. cert. cardiovascular diseases 1983, lic. Pa., 1976, NC, 1979, Mass., 1994, Minn., 1996, Mo., 2004. Intern in medicine Pa. Hosp., Phila., 1976—77, resident in medicine, 1977—79; fellow in cardiology Duke U. Med. Ctr., Durham, NC, 1979—81, asst. prof. medicine, 1983—89, assoc. prof. medicine, 1989—94; sr. staff mem. cardiovascular divsn. Duke U., Durham, NC, 1981—94, dir. section clinical epidemiology and biostatistics, 1984—89, dir. clinical program devel., 1993—94; pres. New England Med. Ctr. Hosp., Boston, 1994—95; prof. medicine Tufts U. Sch. Medicine, 1994—97; sr. v.p./chief info. officer Allina Health Sys., Mpls., 1995—2001; sr. v.p. clinical excellence Ascension Health, St. Louis, 2001—. Program com. and biometry track chair 11th Symposium on Computer Applications in Med. Care, 1987; bd. dir. Clinical Rsch. Internat., Inc., 1990—, PatientKeeper (Virtmed) Inc., 2001—; chmn. task force reducing med. uncertainty Joint Commn. Accreditation Healthcare Orgn., 1989—91, adv. coun. performance measurement, 1995—, chmn. adv. coun. performance measurement, 1998—2003, mem. performance measurement coord. com., 1998—2000; chmn. epidemiology and prevention track Am. Coll. Cardiology Sci. Session Com., 1991—92, chmn. health svc. delivery track, 1991—92; mem. exec. com. and steering com. Health Care Financing Adminstrn., Coop. Cardiovascular Project, 1992—94; chmn. ops. com. Acad. Med. Ctr. Consortium, 1992—94; mem. sci. session program com. Am. Heart Assn., 1994—96; chmn. bd. dir. Strategicare, Inc., 1996—99; bd. gov. Bioengineering Inst., U. Minn., Mpls., 1996—2002; mem. 2000 Spring Congress Sci. Program com. Am. Med. Informatics Assn. (AMIA), 1999—2000; mem. IT expert adv. panel Nat. Quality Forum (NQF) Nat. Forum for Health Care Quality Measurement and Reporting, 2001—02; mem. adv. bd. Ctr. Info. Tech. Leadership (CITL), 2001—; cons. prof. Cardiovascular Inst., Favaloro Found., Buenos Aires, 1994—91; cons. prof. medicine Duke U. Med. Ctr., 1994—; adj. prof. epidemiology U. Minn. Sch. Pub. Health, Mpls., 1996—2002; pres. New England Med. Ctr., Boston,

1994—95; adj. prof. St. Louis U. Sch. Pub. Health; numerous positions with Allina Health Sys., Mpls., 1995—2001; reviewer numerous jour. and rsch. grants; presenter in field; mem. numerous nat. and internat. com.; cons. in field. Contbr. articles to jour., chapters to books. Named Laureate, Computerworld Smithsonian award, Allina Health Sys., 1999; named one of 100 Most Powerful People in Healthcare, Modern Healthcare, 2002; recipient Innovations in IT awards, 2nd place, HIMMS and Deloitte and Touche (Allina Health Sys.), 1998, Tng. for Future, 3rd place, Allina Health Sys., 1998, Quest for Best award, 2000, Silver award, 2001; fellow, Am. Coll. Med. Informatics, 1986, Am. Soc. Clinical Investigation, 1992. Fellow: Am. Coll. Med. Informatics, Am. Coll. Physicians, Am. Coll. Cardiology; mem.: Am. Med. Informatics Assn., Am. Heart Assn. (fellow coun. on clinical cardiology), Am. Soc. Clinical Investigation, Am. Fedn. Clinical Rsch. Office: Ascension Health 4600 Edmundson Rd Saint Louis MO 63134 Office Phone: 314-733-8192, 314-733-8196. Business E-Mail: dpryor@ascensionhealth.org.

**PRYOR, ERIC JON,** minister, writer; b. Suffern, N.Y., July 16, 1959; s. Peter Anthony Pryor and Joanne Carol Roefs, Nancy Long (Stepmother) and Walter Little Brown (Stepfather); m. Renee Serpa, July 16, 1997; children: Christopher Borg, Sarah Borg. MFA, N.Y. Ctr. Media Arts, 1986; DDiv (hon.), Earth Star Temple, 1987. Ordained to ministry Jubilee Christian Ctr., 1995. Founder, min. Nefom Temple, Woodstock, NY, 1980—2004, New Earth Temple, San Francisco, 1987—90; founder, CEO Christian Gladiators Ministry, Sparks, Nev., 1991—2004, Peculiar Nation Prodns., Sparks, 1997—. Media cons. Jubilee Christian Ctr., San Jose, Calif., 1990—2004. Author: Book of Pagan Rituals, Crash and Burn, What is a Witch Really, My Testemony From My Own Mouth; The Ruelle Tarot; prodr.: (video) Satan Unvieled, Law Enforcement Guide to Satanic Cults, From Pagan to Pentecost; contbr. video. Spokesperson Pagan Religious Cmty., San Francisco, 1987—90. Conservative. Achievements include first to develop the worlds largest networking temples for the practicing Pagan, and Occultist community. Avocations: fishing, drag racing, horseback riding, scuba diving, skydiving. Office Phone: 408-262-0900. Personal E-mail: ohwiseone1@yahoo.com.

**PRYOR, HAROLD S.,** retired college president; b. Overton County, Tenn., Oct. 3, 1920; s. Hubert S. and Ethel (Stockton) P.; m. LaRue Vaughn, June 26, 1946. BS, Austin Peay State U., 1946; MA, George Peabody Coll., 1947; Ed.D., U. Tenn., 1951. Instr. George Peabody Coll., Vanderbilt U., 1946-47, E. Tenn. State U., 1947-49, U. Tenn., Knoxville, 1949-51; head dept. edn. Austin Peay State U., 1952, dir. tchr. edn., 1954-68; pres. Columbia (Tenn.) State Community Coll., 1968-84, now pres. emeritus, 1984—. Dir. First Farmers and Merchants Nat. Bank, Columbia, 1970—, First Farmers and Mchts. Corp., 1982—; Columbia State Found., 1971—. Contbr. articles to profl. jours. With U.S. Army, 1943-46. Grantee Dept. Labor; Grantee HEW. Mem. NEA, Tenn. Coll. Assn. (past pres.), Tenn. Edn. Assn., Am. Assn. Higher Edn., Comparative Edn. Soc., Graymere Country Club, Kiwanis, Kappa Delta Pi, Phi Delta Kappa. Democrat. Presbyterian.

**PRYOR, HUBERT,** editor, writer, consultant; b. Buenos Aires, Mar. 18, 1916; (parents am. citizens); s. John W. and Hilda A. (Cowes) P.; m. Ellen M. Ach, 1940 (div. 1959); children: Alan, Gerald, David. Grad., St. George's Coll., Argentina, 1932; student, U. London, Eng., 1934-36. Corr. in S.Am. for United Press, 1937-39; pub. relations rep. Pan Am. Airways in Buenos Aires, 1939-40; reporter N.Y. Herald Tribune, 1940-41; writer, dir. short-wave newsroom CBS, 1941-46; asst. mng. editor Knickerbocker Weekly, 1946-47; sr. editor Look mag., 1947-62; creative supr. Wilson, Haight & Welch, 1962-63; editor Science Digest, 1963-67; mng. editor Med. World News, 1967; editor NRTA jour. Modern Maturity, 1967-82; editl. dir. Dynamic Years, 1977-82; publs. coord. Modern Maturity, Dynamic Years, 1982-84; editl. cons., writer, 1985—. Author: Soul Talk, 1995, Eleanor of Palm Beach, 2002. Lt. USNR, 1943-46. Mem. Am. Soc. Mag. Editors, Author's Guild, Overseas Press Club. Home: 3560 S Ocean Blvd Palm Beach FL 33480-5772

**PRYOR, KENNETH,** meteorologist; b. Silver Spring, Md., Feb. 16, 1967; MS, U. Md., 0204. Weather forecaster USAF, Fayetteville, NC, 1997—2000; rsch. meteorologist Nat. Oceanic and Atmospheric Adminstrn, Nat. Environ. Satellite Data and Info. Svc. Ctr. for Satellite Applications and Rsch., Camp Springs, Md., 2000—. Contbr. articles to profl. jours. Lt. USN, 1989—93. Mem.: Am. Meteorol. Soc., Nat. Weather Assn. Achievements include research in meteorological index to predict the magnitude of convective downbursts associated with thunderstorms; analysis of the College Park, Maryland, tornado of September 24, 2001. Office: NOAA/NESDIS/STAR 5200 Auth Rd Camp Springs MD 20746-4304 Office Phone: 301-763-8204. Office Fax: 301-763-8580. Personal E-mail: kpryor@terpalum.umd.edu. E-mail: ken.pryor@noaa.gov.

**PRYOR, MARK LUNSFORD,** senator; b. Fayetteville, Ark., Jan. 10, 1963; s. David H. Pryor; m. Jill Pryor; children: Adams, Porter. BA in History, U. Ark., 1985, JD, 1988. Pvt. practice Wright, Lindsey & Jennings, Little Rock, 1988—97; mem. Ark. Ho. of Reps., 1990—98, chmn. Freshman Caucus, mem. judiciary com., com. on aging and legis. affairs; atty. gen. State of Ark., 1999—2002; US Senator from Ark., 2003—. Mem. com. commerce, sci. and transp. US Senate, com. homeland security and govt. affairs, com. small bus. and entrepreneurship, spl. com. ethics. Chmn. Alliance to Save Energy; mem. cardiovascular cabinet Ark. Heart Assn.; mem. Friends of Carousel. Recipient Spirit of Enterprise award, US C. of C., 2005. Democrat. Presbyterian. Office: US Senate 217 Russell Senate Office Building Washington DC 20510 also: The River Market Ste 401 500 President Clinton Ave Little Rock AR 72201-1745 Office Phone: 202-224-2353, 501-324-6336. Office Fax: 202-228-0908, 501-324-5320.*

**PRYOR, RICHARD WALTER,** telecommunications executive, retired air force officer; b. Poplar Bluff, Mo., Nov. 6, 1932; s. Walter V. and Mary (Clifford) P.; m. Barbara LeCompte, Feb. 19, 1955; children: Richard, Susan Davis, Robert, William. B in Gen. Studies, U. Nebr., Omaha, 1972; MA, Webster Coll., St. Louis, 1975. Commd. 2d lt. USAF, 1953, advanced through grades to maj. gen., 1982, ret., 1982; instr. U.S. Air Force Acad.; DVMT engr. space and missile systems USAF, chief of staff Comm. Svcs.; dir. worldwide def. comm. sys. Def. Comm. Agy., 1980-81; pres. ITT World Comm., N.Y.C., 1982-84, ITT Indsl. Transmission Co., N.Y.C.; sr. v.p. engring. ops. ITT Comm. Svcs. GP; pres., gen. mgr. ITT Christian Rovsing-Copenhagen DK, 1984-86; chmn. Christian-Rovsing Inc., Tulsa; exec. v.p. Electronic Data Sys. (EDS) Comm. Corp., Dallas, 1986-89; pres., COO IMM Corp.-Interdigital AMEX, Phila., 1989-92; chmn., CEO. officer Ultranav Corp, Dallas, 1992—; chmn. Prism Video, Dallas, 1994—; pres. Trans-Tech Holdings Corp., Dallas, 1996—; pres., CEO Unison Corp., Dallas, 1998—, Video Net, Addison, Tex.; chmn., CEO Mega Link Tech., L.A., 2003—, MIUSA, L.A., 2003—. Dir. RPost, L.A., 2000—. Contbr. articles to tech. publs. assoc. dir. Boy Soucts Am., N.Y.C., 1983. Recipient Cert. of Appreciation Okla. Mental Health Assn., 1979, Kansas City Lions Club, 1974. Mem. Armed Forces Communications and Electronics Assn. (pres. N.Y.C. 1983, nat. bd.), Air Force Assn., Oklahoma City Soc. Profl. Engrs., Canoe Brook Country Club, Army-Navy Club, Phi Alpha Theta. Republican. Roman Catholic. Office: 3333 Wilshire Blvd Los Angeles CA 90010

**PRYOR, STEFAN I.,** city manager, real estate developer; b. NYC, Jan. 14, 1972; JD, Yale U., 1998. Policy adv. to mayor City of New Haven; v.p. Partnership for NYC, exec. dir. sch. reform program; sr. v.p. policy and programs Lower Manhattan Devel. Corp., NYC, 2001—05, pres., 2005—06; dep. mayor for econ. devel. City of Newark, NJ, 2006—. Founder ReStart Ctrl., NYC, Achievement First; co-founder Amistad Acad., New Haven. Grantee John V. Lindsay Pub. Svc. Fellowship, Yale U., 2000. Office: City Hall 920 Broad St Ste 200 Newark NJ 07102*

**PRYOR, TOMMI THORNBURY,** marketing professional; b. Pikeville, Ky., Oct. 21, 1950; d. Joe Warren and Francisanna (Huffman) T. BS in Speech and Journalism, U.S. Wis., 1972; MA in Comms. Studies, U. Mo, Kansas City, 1980. Registered lobbyist Calif., 2001. Various mktg. positions to CEO

Infobahn Industries, Inc., Orange County, Calif., 1995—97; CEO TLC Comms., Ltd., Orange County, Calif., 1998—2002. Dir. Family Entertainment Am., Inc., Laguna Beach, Calif., 1988—90. Author; editor: A Complete How-To Guide for Planning and Implementing a Sucessful Direct Mail Program for Student Recruitment, 1981, A Complete Training Program for Recruiting Students by Telephone, 1981. Cons. Reagan-Bush campaign, Washington, 1984; bd. dirs. Inst. for Christian Statesmanship, Washington, 1985—. Named an Outstanding Young Career Woman of Ea. Kans., Kansas City Bus. and Profl. Women's Clubs, 1976; named to Order of Ky. Cols., Gov. of Ky., 1997. Mem. Direct Mktg. Assn. Washington, Women in Leadership, League Rep. Women, Renaissance Women. Evangelical Christian. Club: Capitol Hill. Avocation: writing, gourmet cooking, travel, antiquing.

**PRYOR, WILLIAM DANIEL LEE,** humanities educator; b. Lakeland, Fla., Oct. 29, 1926; s. Dahl and Lottie Mae (Merchant) P. AB, Fla. So. Coll., 1949; MA, Fla. State U., 1950, PhD, 1959; postgrad., U. N.C., Chapel Hill, 1952—53; pvt. art studies with Florence Wilde; pvt. voice studies with Colin O'More, Anna Kaskas; pvt. piano studies with Waldemar Hille and studied piano master classes of Ernst von Dohnányi. Asst. prof. English, dir. drama Bridgewater (Va.) Coll., 1950-52; grad. tchg. fellow humanities Fla. State U., Tallahassee, 1953-55, 57-58; instr. English U. Houston, University Park, Houston, 1955-59, asst. prof. University Park, 1959-62, assoc. prof., 1962-71, prof., 1971-97, prof. emeritus, 1997. Vis. instr. English, Fla. So. Coll., Lakeland, MacDill Army Air Base, Tampa, Fla., summer 1951, Tex. So. U., 1961-63; vis. instr. humanities, govt. U. Tex. Dental Br., Houston, 1962-63; lectr. The Women's Inst., Houston, 1967-72; lectr. humanities series Jewish Cmty. Ctr., Houston, 1972-73; originator, moderator TV and radio program The Arts in Houston Stas. KUHT-TV and KUHF-FM, 1956-57, 58-63. Author: An Examination of the Southern Milieu in Representative Plays by Southern Dramatists, 1963; contbg. author: National Poetry Anthology, 1952, Panorama das Literaturas das Americas, vol. 2, 1958-60, Perspectives on Ernst von Dohnányi, 2005; assoc. editor Forum, 1967, editor, 1967-82; contbr. articles to profl. jours.; dir. Murder in the Cathedral (T.S. Elliot), U. Houston, 1965; performed in opera as Sir Edgar in Der Junge Lord (Henze), Houston Grand Opera Assn., 1967; played the title role in Aella (Chatterton), Am. premiere, U. Houston, 1970. Bd. dir., founding mem. Contemporary Music Soc., Houston, 1958-63, Houston Shakespeare Soc., 1964-67; bd. dirs., founding mem., program annotator Houston Chamber Orch. Soc., 1964-76; narrator Houston Symphony Orch., Houston Summer Symphony Orch., Houston Chamber Orch. (with Charles Rosekrans), U. Houston Symphony Orch., St. Stephen's Music Festival Symphony Orch., New Harmony, Ind.; narrator world premier of the Bells (Jerry McCathern), 1969, U. Houston Symphony Orch., 1969, Am. premier Symphony No. Seven, Antartica (Vaughn-Williams), Houston Symphony Orch. (with Andre Previn), 1967, L'Histoire du Soldat (Stravinski), U. Houston Symphony Orch., 1957, Am. premier Babar the Elephant (Poulenc-Francais), Houston Chamber Orch. (with Charles Rosekrans), 1967, Le Roi David (Honegger), 1979, Voice of God in opera Noye's Fludde (Britten), St. Stephen's Music Festival, 1981; bd. dir., program annotator Music Guild, Houston, 1960-67, v.p., 1963-67, adv. bd., 1967-70; mem.-at-large, bd. dir. Houston Grand Opera Assn., 1966-67; repertory com. Houston Grand Opera Assn., 1967-70; bd. dir. Houston Grand Opera, 1970-75, adv. bd. 1978-79; cultural adv. com. Jewish Cmty. Ctr., 1960-66; bd. dir. Houston Friends Pub. Libr., 1962-67, 73-75, 1st v.p., 1963-67; adv. mem. cultural affairs com. Houston C. of C., 1972-75; adv. bd. dir. The Wilhelm Schole, 1980-98, Buffalo Bayou Support Com., 1985-87, bd. dir. Moores Sch. Music Soc., 1998—, trustee, 2002-04, advisory bd. dir., 2004—; bd. dir. U. Houston Retiree Assn., 1999-2001, v.p., 2000-2001; founding bd. dir. Internat. Dohnányi Rsch. Ctr., Inc., 2002-. Recipient Master Tchg. award Coll. Humanities and Fine Arts U., Houston, 1980, Favorite Prof. award Bapt. Student Union, U. Houston, 1991. Mem. MLA, AAUP, Coll. English Assn., L'Alliance Francaise, English-Speaking Union, Alumni Assn. Fla. So. Coll., Fla. State U., South Ctrl. MLA, Conf. Editors Learned Jours., Coll. Conf. Tchrs. English, Nat. Coun. Tchrs. English, Am. Studies Assn., Shepard Soc. Rice U., Nature Conservancy, Nat. Trust for Hist. Preservation, Inst. Internat. Edn., Century Club, Fla. So. Coll., President's Club, James D. Westcott Legacy Soc., Fla. State U., Tex. Ret. Tchrs. Assn., Phi Beta (patron), Phi Mu Alpha Sinfonia, Alpha Psi Omega, Pi Kappa Alpha, Sigma Tau Delta (Outstanding Prof. English U. Houston chpt. 1990), 1927 Soc. U. Houston, Houston Philos. Soc., Caledonian Club (London), Tau Kappa Alpha, Phi Kappa Phi. Episcopalian. Avocations: tennis, racquetball, swimming, travel. Home: 2625 Arbuckle St West University Place TX 77005-3929 Office: U Houston Dept English Univ Park 3801 Cullen Blvd Houston TX 77004-2602 *My commitment is to the humanities. I believe that the most important thing that a teacher can do is to help a student to stand on his/her own intellectual hind legs; to help him/her to learn how to aquire facts; to help him/her to learn how to organize and utilize these facts in intelligent, responsible ways.*

**PRYOR, WILLIAM HOLCOMBE, JR.,** federal judge, former state attorney general; b. Mobile, Ala., Apr. 26, 1962; s. William Holcombe Sr. and Laura Louise (Bowles) Pryor; m. Kristan Camille Wilson, Aug. 15, 1987; children: Caroline Elizabeth, Victoria Camille. BA in Legal Studies with honors, N.E. La. U., 1984; JD with honors, Tulane U., 1987. Law clk. U.S. Ct. Appeals (5th cir.), Judge John Minor Wisdom, New Orleans, 1987—88; assoc. Cabaniss, Johnston, Gardner, Dumas & O'Neil, Birmingham, Ala., 1988—91, Walston, Stabler, Wells, Anderson & Bains, Birmingham, 1991—95; dep. atty. gen. State of Ala., Montgomery, 1995—97, atty. gen., 1997—2004; judge U.S. Ct. Appeals (11th cir.), 2004—. Adj. prof. Samford U. Cumberland Sch. Law, Birmingham, 1989—94. Bd. student editors: Tulane Law Rev., 1985—86, editor-in-chief.; 1986—87, bd. adv. editors:; 1995—. La. nat. com. Young Rep. Nat. Fedn., 1984—86; mem. Ala. Rep. Exec. Com., 1994—95. Mem.: Federalist Soc. (assoc.), Amer. Law Inst. (assoc.), Order of Coif, Omicron Delta Kappa, Phi Kappa Phi. Republican. Roman Catholic. Office: US Court of Appeals 900 Federal Courthouse 1729 5th Ave N Birmingham AL 35203*

**PRZEMIENIECKI, JANUSZ STANISLAW,** engineering executive, former government senior executive and college dean; b. Lipno, Poland, Jan. 30, 1927; came to U.S., 1961, naturalized, 1967; s. Leon and Maria (Sarnacka) P.; m. Stefania (Fiona) Rudnicka, July 17, 1954; children: Anita, Christopher. BS, U. London, 1949, PhD, 1958; diploma in Aeros., Imperial Coll. Sci. and Tech., 1953; DSc in Engring., U. London, 1988; doctorate (hon.), Warsaw U. Tech., 1999. Registered profl. engr., Ohio. Head structural R & D sect. Bristol Aircraft Ltd., Eng., 1954-61; from assoc. prof. to prof. mechanics Sch. Engring., Air Force Inst. Tech., Wright-Patterson AFB, Ohio, 1961-66, from asst. dean, assoc. dean rsch. to dean, 1966-89, sr. dean, 1970-95; pres. Astra Technologies, Inc., Fla., 1996—. Cons. in field. Author: Theory of Matrix Structural Analysis, 1968, Mathematical Methods in Defense Analyses, 3d edit., 2000, Defense Analyses Software, 1991; assoc. editor: Jour. Aircraft, 1970-71; editl. bd.: Internat. Jour. Numerical Methods in Engring., 1969-75; editor: Mechanics of Structural Systems (textbook series) 1973-89; editor: Critical Technologies for Nat. Defense, 1991, Acquisition of Defense Systems, 1993; contbr. articles to profl. jours. Chmn. bd. trustees The Air Force Inst. Tech. Found., Ohio, 1987-88, trustee, 1993-95; trustee Engring. and Sci. Found. of Dayton, 1984-95. Decorated Polish Underground Army Cross, Warsaw Uprising Cross, Armed Forces medal; recipient USAF superior performance award, 1965, exceptional civilian svc. decoration, 1978, Presdl. rank of Meritorious Exec., 1981, Disting. Exec., 1982, Outstanding Engr. award Dayton Engring. and Sci. Found., 1986, Outstanding Civilian Svc. medal, 1995, Comdrs. Cross of the Polonia Restituta Order by Pres. of Poland, 1995, Disting. Svc. award, Am. Inst. of Polish Culture, 1997. Fellow Royal Aeros. Soc. (Usborne Meml. prize 1959), AIAA (editor-in-chief edition. series 1981—, Pendray medal 1992), City and Guilds of London Inst.; mem. Am. Soc. Engring. Edn., Ohio Acad. Sci., Polish Inst. Arts and Scis., Tau Beta Pi. Home: 510 Pennyroyal Pl Venice FL 34293-7233

**PRZYBYLSKI, SANDRA MARIE,** speech pathologist; b. Berwyn, Ill. d. Raymond and Julie Marie (Vocelka) Hammers; m. James Przybylski, children: Eric, Sara. BS, U. Iowa, 1968; MA, U. Ill., 1971. Cert. clin. speech pathologist; speech/lang., educable mentally retarded education, learning disabilites and elem. tchr., life, Mo. Speech, lang. pathologist LaPlata Sch. Dist., Mo., 1974—87, Maysville Sch. Dist., Mo., 1990—92, Bucklin Sch. Dist., Mo., 1992—2005; speech therapist Ability Network, Sainte Genevieve, Mo., 2002—05, Schuyler County Sch. Dist., Mo., 2005—. Named to Disting. Svc. Registry-Speech and Hearing, 1990. Mem. Am. Speech, Lang., Hearing Assn., Autism Soc. Am., Mo. State Tchrs. Assn., Mo. Speech, Lang. and Hearing Assn. Personal E-mail: sprzy02@yahoo.com.

PRZYDZIAL, CELINE J., mathematics professor; b. Reading, Pa., June 16, 1954; d. Theodore A. and Mary G. Kroener; m. Leonard W. Przydzial, Oct. 30, 1976; children: Jennifer M., Matthew L. BA, Alvernia Coll., Reading, Pa., 1976; MEd, Kutztown U., Pa., 1988. Instr. math. Kutztown U., 1993—. Co-founder, co-advisor NCTM Kutztown U. Student Affiliate, 2003—. Grantee, Kutztown U., 2006. Mem.: Assn. Math. Tchrs., Pa. Coun. Tchrs. Math., Nat. Coun. Tchrs. Math. Office: Kutztown U PO Box 730 Kutztown PA 19530 Office Phone: 610-683-4406. Business E-Mail: przydzia@kutztown.edu.

PRZYPYSZNY, JOHN R., lawyer; b. Chgo., 1965; AB, Georgetown Univ., 1987, JD, 1990. Bar: Ill. 1990, DC 1991. Negotiator US Dept. Edn.; ptnr., head, edn. law practice group Drinker Biddle & Reath LLP, Washington, 2001—. Frequent lectr. in field. Office: Drinker Biddle & Reath LLP Ste 1100 1500 K St NW Washington DC 20005-1209 Office Phone: 202-842-8858. Office Fax: 202-842-8465. Business E-Mail: john.przypyszny@dbr.com.

PSALTIS, HELEN, medical/surgical nurse; b. Rockford, Ill., Nov. 27, 1931; d. Harry and Martha (Triantafelakis) P. Diploma, St. Margaret Hosp., Hammond, Ind., 1953; BSN, DePaul U., 1961; MS in Health Edn., Purdue U., 1971; MSN, Purdue U., Calumet, Ind., 1988. RN, Ind., cert. sch. nurse, Ind. Staff nurse U. Ill. Hosp./Chgo. Hosp., 1959—61, U. Chgo. Hosp., Billings, Ill., 1962; sch. nurse Pub. Sch. City of East Chicago, Ind.; asst. supr., staff nurse, instr. St. Catherine Hosp., East Chicago, Ind., 1962—63; instr., head nurse, staff nurse St Margaret Hosp., Hammond, 1953—58, 1989—, 1963; staff nurse U. Ill. Rsch. Hosp./Chgo. Hosp., 1959—61; asst. supr., staff nurse, inst. St. Catherine Hosp., East Chicago, 1981—91. Mem. ANA, AACCN, Soc. of Critical Care Nursing, Nat. League for Nursing, Sigma Theta Tau. Home: 4303 Ivy St East Chicago IN 46312-3026

PSIHARIS, NICHOLAS See HARRICE, CY

PSOMIADES, HARRY JOHN, political science professor; b. Boston, Sept. 8, 1928; s. John and Koula (Yalmanides) P.; m. Dorothy Smith, Aug. 18, 1962 (dec. Aug. 27, 1984); children— Kathy Alexis, Christine Anne. BA, Boston U., 1953; M.Internat. Affairs, Columbia U., 1955; cert., Middle East Inst., 1956, PhD (Ford Found. fellow), 1962; Litt.D. (hon.), Holy Cross/Hellenic Coll., 1985. Lectr. govt. Columbia U., 1959-65, asst. dean Grad. Sch. Internat. Affairs, 1959-65, dir. Carnegie Endowment Fellowships in Diplomacy, 1959-71; assoc. prof. poli. sci. Queens Coll., City U. N.Y., 1965-69, prof., 1970—2003, chmn. dept. polit. sci., 1967-71, dep. exec. officer Ph.D. program in polit. sci., 1975-76, program dir. seminar on the modern Greek state, 1976—2004; dir. Ctr. Byzantine and Modern Greek Studies, 1976—2004. Cons. faculty U.S. Army Command and Gen. Staff Coll., 1968-86; U.S. Dept. State Fgn. Service Inst., 1968-71; mem. screening com. Fgn. Area Fellowships Program for Asia and Middle East Joint Com., Social Sci. Research Council and Am. Council Learned Socs., 1967-69 Author: Greece and Turkey: Mutual Economic Interests, 1964, (with Thomas Spelios) A Pictorial History of the Greeks, 1967, The Eastern Question: The Last Phase, 1968, 2d edition, 2000, Greek edit., 2004, (with T.A. Couloumbis) Foreign Interference in Greek Polics: An Historical Perspective, 1976, (with A. Scourby) The Greek American Community in Transition, 1982, (with R.S. Orfanos) Education and Greek Americans: Proccess and Prospects, 1987, (with S. Thomadakes) Greece, The New Europe and the Changing International Order, 1993, (with Van Coufoudakis) Greece and the New Balkans: Challenges and Opportunities, 1999, (with Sam Tsemberis) Greek American Familiies: Traditions and Transformations, 1999; editor: Jour. Modern Hellenism, 1984—; contbr. articles to profl. jours. Served with U.S. Army, 1946-50; to col. AUS, 1950-83. Hon. fellow Soc. Macedonian Studies, Thessaloniki, Greece, 1970—; named Comdr. Order of Honor The Republic of Greece, 1996. Fellow Middle East Studies Assn. N.Am.; mem. Am. Polit. Sci. Assn., Middle East Inst., Modern Greek Studies Assn. (mem. exec. com. 1972-76), Phi Beta Kappa. Greek Orthodox. Home: 440 Riverside Dr New York NY 10027-6828

PSUTY, NORBERT PHILLIP, marine sciences educator; b. Hamtramck, Mich., June 13, 1937; s. Phillip and Jessie (Proszkowski) P.; m. Sylvia Helen Zurinsky, June 13, 1959; children: Eric Anthony, Scott Patrick, Ross Phillip. BS, Wayne State U., 1959; MS, Miami U., Oxford, Ohio, 1960; PhD, La. State U., 1966. Rsch. assoc. Coastal Studies Inst., La. State U., Baton Rouge, 1962-64; instr. dept. geography and dept. geology U. Miami, Coral Gables, Fla., 1964-65; asst. prof. geography U. Wis., Madison, 1965-69; assoc. prof. geography and geol. scis. Rutgers U., New Brunswick, NJ, 1969-73, prof., 1973—2002, chmn. dept. marine and coastal scis., 1991-99, prof. marine and coastal scis., geog., geol. scis., 1989—2002, dir. Marine Scis. Ctr., 1972-76, dir. Ctr. for Coastal and Environ. Studies, 1976-90; assoc. dir. Inst. Marine and Coastal Scis., New Brunswick, 1990—2002; prof. emeritus Rutgers U., 2002—; dir. Sandy Hook Coop. Programs, 2002—. Mem. sci. com. Thalassas, Vigo, Spain, 1985—. Co-author: Living with the New Jersey Shore, 1986, Coastal Dunes, 1990, Coastal Hazard Management, 2002, Coastal Dune Ecology, 2004; mem. editl. bd. Coastal Mgmt., 1981—, Jour. Coastal Rsch., 1987—, Jour. of Coastal Conservation, 1996—; contbr. numerous articles to scholarly jours., chapters to books, monographs. Mem. Water Policy Bd., East Brunswick, NJ, 1981—83, N.J. Shoreline Adv. Bd., Trenton, 1984—86; chmn. N.J. Gov.'s Sea Level Rise Com. Trenton 1987 90; mem. N.J. State Beach Erosion Commn., 1994—99; coll. volleyball ref. Recipient Disting. Pub. Svc. award Pres. of Rutgers U. 1988, Mel Marcus Disting. Career award, 2003; numerous grants including NSF, Nat. Park Svc., EPA, Office Naval Rsch., Nat. Sea Grant Program, NOAA, 1961—. Mem.: AAAS, N.J. Acad. Sci. (pres. 1982), Internat. Geog. Union (editor newsletter 1984—96, vice chair commn. on coastal environment 1988—92, chmn. commn. on coastal systems 1992—96, editor newsletter 2002—), Coastal Soc. (pres. 1980—82), Assn. Am. Geographers (Honors award 1993), Profl. Assn. Volleyball Ofcls. (chair N.J. bd. 2000—). Avocations: gardening, reading. Office: Rutgers U Inst Marine & Coastal Scis 74 Magruder Rd Highlands NJ 07732 Office Phone: 732-708-1462.

PTACEK, WILLIAM H., library director; BA in English and Psychology, U. Ill., 1972; MLS, SUNY, Geneseo, 1974; cert. of advanced study, U. Ill., Chgo., 1979. Reference libr. South Br. Chgo. Pub. Libr., 1974-75, head libr. Mt. Greenwood br., 1975-76, head system-wide circulation, 1976-77, asst. dir. personnel, 1977-78, chief Northeast Dist., 1978-79; dir. Idaho Falls Pub. Libr., 1979-83, Louisville Free Pub. Libr., 1984-89, King County Libr. Sys., Seattle, 1989—. Co-author: (with Peggy Sullivan) Public Libraries: Smart Practices in Personnel, 1982; contbr. articles to profl. jours. Mem.: Pub. Libr. Assn., Bellevue Rotary Club (pres. 2002—03). Office: King County Libr Sys 960 Newport Way NW Issaquah WA 98027-2702 Office Phone: 425-369-3232. E-mail: billp@kcls.org.*

PTAK, FRANK STANLEY, manufacturing executive; b. Chgo., Apr. 23, 1943; s. Frank J. and Stella R. (Los) P.; m. Karen M. Novoselsky, May 2, 1971; children: Jeffrey B., Jacquelyn F., Russell E. BSc, De Paul U., 1965. CPA, Ill. Sr. auditor Arthur Young & Co., Chgo., 1965-69; sr. rsch. econs. Kemper Fin. Svcs., Chgo., 1969-71; asst. sec., mgr. acquisitions Sara Lee Corp., Chgo., 1971-73, asst. treas., 1973-74, asst. to chmn., 1974, v.p. planning, 1974-75; bus. devel. mgr. ITW Conex, Des Plaines, Ill., 1975-77; mktg. mgr. ITW Shakeproof, Elgin, Ill., 1977-78, group press., 1977-78, ITW Metal Components Cos., Glenview, Ill., 1978-91; exec. v.p. Global Automotive Components ITW Corp., Glenview, 1991-95, vice-chmn., 1996—2005, pres., CEO, The Marmon Group, Inc., Chgo., 2006—. Bd. dirs. The Marmon Group; adv. coun. DePaul U. Coll. Commerce, Chgo., 1998. Patentee in field.

Mem. AICPA, Assn. Corp. Growth, ITW Patent Soc. Jewish. Home: 849 Edgewood Ct Highland Park IL 60035-3714 Office: The Marmon Group 225 W Washington St Chicago IL 60606 Business E-Mail: fptak@itw.com.

PTASHNE, MARK STEVEN, molecular biology professor; b. Chgo., June 5, 1940; s. Fred and Mildred P.; m. Lucy Gordon, 1994. BA, Reed Coll., 1961; PhD, Harvard U., 1968. Lectr. biochemistry Harvard U., Cambridge, Mass., 1968-71, prof., 1971—73, chmn. dept. biochemistry and molecular biology, 1980-83, Herchel Smith prof. of molecular biology, 1993-97; Ludwig prof. molecular biology Sloan Kettering Cancer Rsch. Ctr., N.Y.C. 1997—. Feodor Lynen lectr. U. Miami, Fla., 1988. Author: A Genetic Switch, 1986; contbr. numerous articles to sci. jours. Recipient Eli Lilly award, 1975, prix. Charles-Leopold Mayer Acad. des Scis., Inst. de France, 1977, Louisa Gross Horwitz prize Bd. Trustees Columbia U., 1985, Gairdner Found. Internat. award, 1985, Albert Lasker award for Basic Med. Rsch., Lasker Found., 1997; co-recipient Ledle award Harvard U., 1986, GM Sloan prize, 1990. Fellow N.Y. Acad. Sci., Am. Acad. Sci.; mem. NAS, Fedn. Am. Scis. (bd. sponsors 1981). Avocations: opera, classical music, violin. Office: Sloan Kettering Cancer Rsch Ctr 1275 York Ave # New York NY 10021-6094*

PTASYNSKI, HARRY, geologist, oil industry executive; b. Milw., May 26, 1926; s. Stanley S. and Frances V. (Stawicki) Ptasynski; m. Nola G. Whitestine, Sept. 15, 1951; children: Rosa F., Lisa Joy. BS, Stanford U., 1950. Cert. profl. geologist, petroleum geologist. Dist. geologist Pure Oil Co., Amarillo, Tex., 1951-55, Casper, Wyo., 1955-58; ind. geologist, oil prodr. Casper, 1958—. With USN, 1943—46, PTO. Mem.: Soc. Petroleum Engrs., Rocky Mountain Oil and Gas Assn. (bd. dirs., mem. exec. com 1980—96), Ind. Petroleum Assn. Mountain States (v.p., bd. dirs. 1976—80), Ind. Petroleum Assn. Am. (v.p., bd. dirs. 1976—85), Am. Inst. Profl. Geologists, Am. Assn. Petroleum Geologists. Republican. Episcopalian. Avocations: tennis, trout and salmon fishing, western history, golf. Home: 1515 Brookview Dr Casper WY 82604-4895 Office: 123 W 1st St Ste 560 Casper WY 82601-2483 Office Phone: 307-234-8392. Business E-Mail: hptasyn@tribcsp.com.

PU, CALTON, computer scientist; BS in Physics, U. Sao Paulo, Brazil, 1978, BS in Computer Sci., 1979; MS, U. Wash., 1983, PhD, 1986. From asst. to assoc. prof. dept. computer sci. Columbia U., 1986-92; assoc. prof. dept. computer sci. and engring. Oreg. Grad. Inst. Sci. and Tech., Portland, 1993-96, prof. dept. computer sci. and engring., 1996-99; prof., John P. Imlay Jr. chair in software Ga. Inst. Tech., Atlanta, 1999—. Vis. rsch. scientist IBM T.J. Watson Rsch. Ctr., summer 1990-91; co-gen. chair Internat. Conf. on Data Engring., 1997, co-PC chair, 1999; vice-chair Heterogeneous Sys. Interoperability, 1995, program com. 1993-95; program. com. Internat. Conf. on Partial Evaluation and Program Manipulation, 1997, Internat. Conf. on Distributed Computing Sys., 1989, 91, 93, 97; co-chair program com. Am. and Pacific Rim Internat. Symposium on Reliable Distributed Sys., 1995, 2003; presenter in field. Mem. editl. bd. Internat. Jour. Digital Libr., 1995—; Jour. Brazilian Computer Soc.; patentee apparatus and method for certifying the delivery of information. Grantee NSF, 1991—, DARPA, 1994—. Mem. ACM; sr. mem. IEEE; fellow AAAS. Office: Ga Inst Tech Coll of Computing 801 Atlantic Dr Atlanta GA 30332-0280 Office Phone: 404-385-1106. Business E-Mail: calton.pu@cc.gatech.edu.

PUCCI, ANTHONY J., English language educator; b. Lawrence, Mass. BA, Merrimack Coll., 1971; MS, Elmira Coll., 1979. Cert. tchr. English 7-12. English tchr. assoc. Duquesne U., Pitts., 1971-73; English tchr. Gill/St. Bernard's Upper Sch., Bernardsville, N.J., 1973-74; English tchr./chmn. Notre Dame High Sch., Elmira, N.Y., 1974—. Freelance copywriter, proof-reader. Writer mystery novel, poetry, book revs.; developer curriculum in field. Bd. appeals Town of Vet. Zoning. Mem. Nat. Coun. Tchrs. English, Friends of Steele Meml. Libr. Avocations: reading, travel, photography. Office: Notre Dame High Sch 1400 Maple Ave Elmira NY 14904-3008

PUCCI, GABRIELLE JENNINE, historian, educator; b. Bklyn., Dec. 19, 1978; d. William Stuart and Denise Ellen Pucci. BA in Social Studies Edn., St. Francis Coll., Bklyn., N.Y., 2002; postgrad. in Educ. St. Johns U., Queens, N.Y., 2006—. Cert. secondary social studies tchr. N.Y. Tchr. N.Y.C. Dept. Edn., Bklyn., 2002—; intern sch. libr. media specialist, 2005—06. Coord. Boston Overnight Trip, Bklyn., 2002—; advisor Econ. Bowl Team, Bklyn., 2004—. Mem.: ALA, Phi Alpha Theta. Home: 1631 E 33d St Brooklyn NY 11234 E-mail: gabp29@aol.com.

PUCCINELLI, ANDREW JAMES, lawyer; b. Elko, Nev., July 21, 1953; BA cum laude, U. of the Pacific, 1975, JD, 1978. Bar: Nev. 1978. Ptnr. Puccinelli & Puccinelli, Elko, Nev., 1978—2002; dist. judge 4th Judicial Dist. Ct., 2002—. Bus. law adj. prof. No. Nev. C.C., 1982-93; legal advisor Nev. Home Health Svcs., 1980-88. Bd. dirs. Nev. Legal Svcs., 1986-93. Mem. ATLA, Nev. Trial Lawyers Assn., Nev. State Bar Assn. (bd. govs. 1993-2000, v.p. 1996-97, pres.-elect 1997-98, pres. 1998-99, No. Nev. disciplinary bd. 1988-93, CLE com. 1981-85), Elko County Bar Assn. (pres. 1985-86), Phi Delta Phi. Office: 4th Jud Dist Ct Elko County Cthse 571 Idaho St Elko NV 89801 Office Phone: 775-753-4602.

PUCCINELLI, DANIELE, research scientist; b. Pietrasanta, Italy, Dec. 23, 1977; s. Brunello Puccinelli and Maria Grazia Chicca. Laurea, U. of Pisa, Italy, 2001; MSc, U. of Notre Dame du Lac, Ind., 2005. Application engr. Fiat-GM Powertrain, Torino, Italy, 2001—03; tchg. and rsch. asst. U. of Notre Dame, 2003—. Contbr. tech. articles to profl. jours. Named Tchg. Asst. of the Yr., Dept. Elec. Engring. at U. of Notre Dame, 2004; recipient Outstanding Grad. Tchg. Asst. award, Kaneb Ctr. at U. of Notre Dame, 2004. Office Phone: 574 631 0340

PUCEL, ROBERT ALBIN, electronics engineer, researcher; b. Ely, Minn., Dec. 27, 1926; s. Joseph and Theresa (Francel) P.; m. Catherine Ann Silva, June 30, 1952; children: Robert W., James J., Valerie A., Marc R., David J. BS, MS, MIT, 1951, DSc, 1955. With rsch. div. Research div. Raytheon Co., Lexington, Mass., 1955-93, staff mem. microwave tube group, 1951-55, solid state physics group, 1955-65, project mgr. microwave semicondr. group, 1965-70, cons. to microwave semicondr. group, 1970-74, cons. scientist semicondr. group, 1974-93; pres. RCP Cons., Jewett City, Conn., 1994—. Editor: Monolithic Microwave Integrated Circuits, 1985; contbg. author: Advances in Electronics and Electron Physics, vol. 38, 1975, Gallium Arsenide Technology, 1985. Served with USNR, 1945-46. Recipient Excellence in Technology award, Raytheon, 1988. Fellow IEEE (life; Third Millenium medal, 2000); mem. Microwave Theory and Techniques Soc. (editl. rev. bd., nat. lectr. 1980-81, Microwave prize 1976, Microwave Career award, 1990, Microwave Pioneer award, 2000), Nat. Acad. Engring., Electron Devices Soc. Inventor low-distortion FET; co-inventor Spacistor, Overlay FET. Home and Office: RCP Cons 45 Vandy Dr Jewett City CT 06351 Office Phone: 860-376-1339. Personal E-Mail: bobpucel@yahoo.com.

PUCHALSKI, CHRISTINA M., physician, medical educator; d. Anthony R. and Krystyna J. Puchalski. BS, UCLA, 1976, MA, 1977; MD, George Washington U., 1994. Rsch. chemist NIH, Bethesda, Md., 1977—84, adj. scientist, 1984—90; intern George Wash. U. Med. Ctr., 1994—95, resident in internal medicine/primary care, 1997—98; fellowship in primary care, 1997—98; dir. edn. NIHR (Nat. Inst. Healthcare Rsch.), Bethesda, Md., 1997—2001; dir., founder George Washington Inst. for Spirituality and Health, 2001—. Asst. prof. medicine George Washington U. Sch. Medicine, Washington, 1998—2003, assoc. prof. medicine and healthcare scis., clin. leadership and mgmt., 2003—. V.p. bd. dirs. Virginia Square Condo, Arlington, Va., 1999—2002, pres. bd. dirs., 2002—. Recipient Humanitarian in Medicine award, Pfizer-AAMC, 1999, John Templeton award, John Templeton Found., 2001—; Humanitarian award, N.J. Healthcare Found., 2002; grantee, NIH, 2002. Fellow: ACP. Roman Catholic. Avocations: piano, hiking. Office: George Washington Univ 2150 Pennsylvania Ave NW Washington DC 20037

PUCIE, CHARLES R., JR., public affairs executive; b. Asheville, N.C., Oct. 8, 1943; BSFS in Internat. Affairs, Georgetown U., 1965. Fin. analyst Chase Manhattan Bank, 1969-70; account exec. Doremus, 1970-73, v.p., 1973-80, sr. v.p., regional mgr. Washington, 1980-85; sr. v.p., group dir., internat. counseling Hill and Knowlton, 1986-90, exec. v.p., 1991; founder, CEO Capitoline Internat. Group, Washington, 1991-98; chmn., CEO C.I.H. Ltd., 1992-98; CEO Capitoline/MS&L, G.P., 1994-98; v.p. pub. affairs supreme coun. KC, Washington, 1998-2001; sr. counselor Fleishman-Hillard, Washington, 2001—. Capt., aviator U.S. Army, 1966-69, Vietnam. Office: Fleishman Hillard 1615 L St NW Ste 1000 Washington DC 20036-5610

PUCK, WOLFGANG, chef; b. St. Veit, Austria, July 8, 1949; m. Marie France, 1976 (div. 1979); m. Barbara Lazaroff, 1984 (div. Nov. 27, 2002); children: Cameron, Bryon; life ptnr. Gelila Assefa; 1 child, Oliver Wolfgang. Doctor of Culinary Arts (hon.), Johnson & Wales U., Providence, RI, 1998. Former chef Hotel de Paris, Monaco, Maxim's, Paris, L'Oustau de Baumanière, Provence; chef, part owner Ma Maison, L.A., 1975—; exec. chef, ptnr. Spago, 1982—, Chinois on Main, Santa Monica, 1983—; Postrio, San Francisco, 1989—, Granita, Malibu, Calif., 1991—; owner Wolfgang Puck Express; exec. chef, ptnr. Spago Las Vegas, 1992—; owner Wolfgang Puck Cafes, 1993—; exec. chef, ptnr. Chinois Las Vegas, 1998—, Postrio Las Vegas, 1998—, Trattoria del Lupo, Las Vegas, 1989—, Wolfgang Puck Bar & Grill, Las Vegas, 2004—; (numerous others); owner, chef Wolfgang Puck Catering, 1998—; ptnr. Wolfgang Puck Worldwide, Inc., 2000—. Fund raising Meals on Wheels, A. Cancer Soc. L.A. Author: Modern French Cooking for the American Kitchen, 1982, The Wolfgang Puck Cookbook: Recipes from Spago and Chinois, 1986, Adventures in the Kitchen with Wolfgang Puck, 1991, Pizza, Pasta and More!, 2000, Live, Love, Eat! The Best of Wolfgang Puck, 2002, Wolfgang Puck Makes It Easy, 2004; producer (instructional cooking video) Spago Cooking with Wolfgang Puck; appeared in TV series Wolfgang Puck, 2001 (Daytime Emmy for Outstanding Service Show), Wolfgang Puck's Cooking Class, 2003; actor: (guest appearances) (films) The Weather Man, 2005, (TV series) Who's the Boss?, 1987, Blossom, 1991, Tales from the Crypt, 1992, Ellen, 1996, Frasier, 2000, 2002, (voice) The Simpsons, 2002. Founder Puck-Lazaroff Charitable Found., 1982—. Named Outstanding Chef of the Yr., James Beard Found., 1991; recipient Humanitarian of Yr. award, 1994, Bus. Statesman of Yr. award, Harvard Bus. Sch. of So. Calif., 2001, Smithfield Foods Outstanding Service award, James Beard Found., 2005.*

PUCKETT, CHARLES LINWOOD, plastic surgeon, educator; b. Burlington, N.C., Oct. 19, 1940; s. Harry W. and Lula C. Puckett; m. Florence Elizabeth Loy, June 18, 1961 (div. 1976); children: Loy C., Lisa A., Leslie A.; m. Patricia Louise Wells, June 17, 1984 (div. 1994); 1 child, Harry James; m. Teresa G. Teel, Nov. 24, 1995. Student, Elon Coll., 1959—62; MD, Wake Forest Coll., 1966. Diplomate in plastic surgery and surgery of the hand Am. Bd. Plastic Surgery, Am. Bd. Surgery. Intern Duke U., Durham, NC, 1966—67, jr. asst. resident gen. and thoracic surgery, 1967—68, sr. asst. resident gen. surgery, 1968—70, chief resident, instr. surgery, 1970—71, fellow gen. and thoracic surgery, 1971—72, asst. resident plastic surgery, 1973—75, instr., chief resident plastic surgery, 1975—76; fellow hand surgery U. Louisville Hosps., 1974; assoc. prof. plastic surgery U. Mo. Health Scis. Ctr., 1976—80, prof. plastic surgery, 1980—, vice chmn. dept. surgery, 1986—. Instr. surgery Duke Hosp., 1970—72, assoc. surgery, 1972—73. Contbr. articles to profl. jours. Maj. U.S. Army, 1971—76. Fellow: ACS (gov. 1991—97, Mo. chpt.); mem.: AMA, So. Med. Assn., Plastic Surgery Rsch. Coun., Plastic Surgery Ednl. Found., Lipolysis Soc. N.Am. Inc., Internat. Microsurgical Soc., Assn. Acad. Chmn. Plastic Surgery (bd. dirs. 1985—87, pres.-elect 1986—87, pres. 1987—88), Am. Trauma Soc., Am. Soc. Plastic Surgeons, Inc. (bd. dirs. member-at-large 1985—88, asst. sec. 1988—89, trustee 1989—92, 2003—, chmn. bd. trustees 1991—92, parliamentarian 1992—93, historian 1994—95, sec. 1995—97, v.p. 1997—98, pres.-elect 1998—99, pres. 1999—2000, Spl. Hon. Citation 2002), Am. Soc. Surgery of the Hand, Am. Soc. for Aesthetic Plastic Surgery, Inc. (bd. dirs. 1989—2000, traveling prof. 2002), Am. Cleft Palate Assn., Am. Bd. Plastic Surgery (dir. 1988—94, chmn. 1993—94), Am. Assn. Plastic Surgeons (trustee 1995—98), Am. Assn. Hand Surgery (bd. dirs. 1982—84, 1990, 1991, v.p. 1986—87, pres.-elect 1987—88, pres. 1988—89, parliamentarian 1992), Alpha Omega Alpha, Sigma Xi. Republican. Avocation: cattle and horse farming. Office: Univ Mo Divsn Plastic Surgery One Hospital Dr Columbia MO 65212

PUCKETT, DEREK LEE, biologist, researcher; MS, U. Tenn., 1999, PhD, 2002. Lic. civil engr. Rsch. scientist Dept. Energy, New Ellenton, S.C., 2002—04; biol. scientist USDA, Asheville, N.C., 2004—. Translator: UN Disaster Relief Task Force, 2001 (Outstanding Meritorious Relief Work, 2001). Vol. ARC, 1997—, Habitat for Humanity. Mem.: AAAS, Sci. Com. on Problems of Environment, UN Ednl. Sci. Cultural Orgn. Am. Southeastern Biologists, Internat. Union Pure Applied Chemists, Internat. Union Forest Rsch. Orgn., Internat. Soc. for Molecular Plant-Microbe Interactions, Food and Agrl. Orgn., Soc. Am. Foresters, Entomol. Soc. Am., Conv. on Biol. Diversity, Defenders of Wildlife, CARE, Internat., Nature Conservancy, S.E. Exotic Pest Plant Coun., Conservation Internat., Smithsonian Inst., Nat. Geog. Soc., African Wildlife Found., Ducks Unltd., So. Lepidopterists' Soc., UN Children's Fund, Nat. Wildlife Fedn., Sigma Xi, Phi Kappa Phi (pres. 1996—). Office: USDA 200 WT Weaver Blvd Asheville NC 28804 Office Fax: 828-257-4856.

PUCKETT, ELIZABETH ANN, law librarian, educator; b. Evansville, Ind., Nov. 10, 1943; d. Buell Charles and Lula Ruth (Gray) P.; m. Joel E. Hendricks, June 1, 1964 (div. June 1973); 1 child, Andrew Charles; m. Thomas A. Wilson, July 19, 1985. BS in Edn., Eastern Ill. U., 1964; JD, U. Ill., 1977, MS in L.S. 1977. Bar: Kans. 1978, Ill. 1979. Acquisitions/reader services librarian U. Kans. Law Library, Lawrence, 1979-79, asst. reader services librarian So. Ill. U. Law Library, Carbondale, 1979-81, reader services librarian, 1981-83; assoc. dir. Northwestern U. Law Library, Chgo., 1983-86, co-acting dir., 1986-87; dir./assoc. prof. South Tex. Coll. Law Library, Houston, 1987-89; dir./prof. South Tex. Coll. Law Libr., Houston, 1990-94, U. Ga. Law Libr., Athens, 1994—. Co-author: Evaluation of System-Provided Library Services to State Correctional Centers in Illinois, 1983; co-editor Uniform Commercial Code: Confidential Drafts, 1993. Mem. ABA, Am. Assn. Law Librs. (mem. exec. bd. 1993-96). Avocations: reading, antiques. Office: U Georgia Law Libr Athens GA 30602-6018 Office Phone: 706-542-5078. E-mail: apuckett@uga.edu.

PUCKETT, MARY ALICE, primary school educator, consultant; d. Bernard Louis and Alida Josepha Stork; m. Gary Michael Puckett, Dec. 27, 1981; 1 child, Sean. BS in Edn., North Tex. State U., 1976; MA in Edn., Tex. Wesleyan U., 1989. Cert. tchr. Tex. State Bd. Edn. 1st grade tchr.-Hill Arlington (Tex.) Ind. Sch. Dist., 1977—2000, 1st grade tchr.-Amos, 2000—01, 1st grade tchr.-Goodman, 2001—03, 1st grade tchr.-Pope, 2003—. Author: (video) It Takes Two Mainstreaming, 1989 (Ptnrs. in Mainstreaming award, 1990), (booklet) The Happy Teacher Campaign, 2000. Vol. Riding Unlimited, Keller, Tex., 1991; editl. cons. Met Adventist Cmty. Svc., Grand Prairie, Tex., 2000. Mem.: Courage to Teach, Alpha Delta Kappa. Avocations: reading tutor, travel, writing, attending retreats. Home: 1901 Montana Trail Grand Prairie TX 75052

PUCKETT, RICHARD EDWARD, artist, consultant, former recreation executive; b. Klamath Falls, Oreg., Sept. 9, 1932; s. Vernon Elijah P., Leona Belle (Clevenger) P.; m. Velma Faye Hamrick, Apr. 14, 1957 (dec. 1985); children: Katherine Michelle Briggs, Deborah Alison Bolinger, Susan Lin Rowland, Gregory Richard. Student, So. Oreg. Coll. Edn., 1951—56, Lake Forest Coll., 1957—58, Hartnell Jr. Coll., 1960—70; BA, U. San Francisco, 1978. Acting arts and crafts dir., Ft. Leonard Wood, Mo., 1956-57; arts and crafts dir., asst. spl. svcs. officer, mus. dir. F. Sheridan, Ill., 1957-59; arts and crafts dir. Ft. Irwin, Calif., 1959-60, Ft. Ord, Calif., 1960-86; dir. arts and crafts br. Art Gallery, Arts and Crafts Ctr. Materials Sales Store, 1960; opening dir. Presidio Monterey Army Mus., 1963; dir. Model Army Area Arts and Crafts Program. One-man shows include Seaside City Hall, 1967—86, 2002, Ft. Ord Arts and Crafts Ctr. Gallery, 1967, 1973, 1979, 1981, 1984, 1986,

Presidio of Monterey Art Gallery, Del Messa Gallery, Carmel, Calif., 1998, So. Oreg. Art Gallery, Medford, 2000, Country Rose Gallery, Hollister, Calif., 2001—03, Walter Avery Gallery Seaside City Hall, 2002, Sasoontsi Gallery, Salinas, Calif., 2004, also pvt. collections, designed and opened first Ft. Sheridan Army Mus., Presidio of Monterey Mus., exhibited in group shows at Salinas Valley Art Gallery, Glass on Holiday, Gatlinburg, Tenn., 1981—82, Internat. Congress on Arts and Comm., 1997, Del Messa Gallery, 2001—06. Recipient 1st pl. Dept. Army and U.S. Army Forces Command awards for programming and publicity, 1979-81, 83-85 (exhibited in Smithsonian), 1st and 3d pl. sculpture awards Monterey County Fair Fine Arts Exhibit, 1979, Comdrs. medal civilian svcs., 1986, Golden Acad. award, Internat. Man of Yr. award, 1991-92, others. Mem.: Internat. Soc. Acrylic Painters, Ft. Ord Alumni Assn., Salinas Valley Art Assn. (pres. 2000—), Monterey Peninsula Art Mus. Assn. Home: 210 San Miguel Ave Salinas CA 93901-3021

**PUCKETT, SUSAN,** newspaper editor; Exec. food editor features desk Atlanta Jour. and Constn., 1990-97, food editor, 1997—. Author: (cookbooks) A Cook's Tour of Mississippi, 1980, A Cook's Tour of Iowa, 1990, Dips: Great Recipes for Spreads, Salsas, Fondues and Other Party Fare, 1995; co-author: The 5:30 Challenge, 2005. Office: Atlanta Jour and Constn 72 Marietta St NW Atlanta GA 30303-2804 Business E-Mail: spucknat@ajc.com.

**PUCKNAT, JOHN GODFREY,** chemist, researcher; b. N.Y.C., Feb. 22, 1931; s. William and Margaret Marie (Rittig) P.; m. Mary E. Murphy, Nov. 8, 1951 (div. Mar. 1959); 1 child, Eugene; m. Alice Winifred Dillon, Jan. 30, 1960. BS cum laude, CCNY, 1957; MS, NYU, 1962, PhD, 1966. Chemist Interchem. Corp., N.Y.C., 1957—63; sr. chemist Argus Chem. Corp., N.Y.C., 1969—70; rsch. assoc. Inmont div. BASF, Clifton, NJ, 1970—90; product devel. specialist Sun Chem. Corp., Carlstadt, 1991—92, scientist, 1992—96; ret., 1996. Contbr. articles to profl. jours. Mem. Union of Concerned Scientists, Cambridge, 1987. Sgt. U.S. Army, 1951-53. Rsch. fellowship Israel Inst. Tech., 1966-67, U. Zurich, Switzerland, 1967-68. Mem. Am. Chem. Soc., N.Y. Acad. Scis., Phi Beta Kappa, Sigma Xi. Achievements include patents for coating formulations; research interests include water-based coatings and printing inks. Home: 565 W End Ave New York NY 10024-2705 Personal E-Mail: johnpucknat@aol.com.

**PUDLIN, HELEN POMERANTZ,** lawyer; b. NYC, June 26, 1949; d. George and Claire Pomerantz; m. David B. Pudlin, Dec. 23, 1973; children: Alexander R., Julia H. BA cum laude, U. Pa., 1970, MS, 1971, JD, 1974. Bar: Pa. 1974. Lectr. U. Pa. Law Sch., 1983-87; asssoc. Ballard, Spahr, Andreas & Ingersoll, Phila., 1974-81, ptnr., 1981-89; gen. counsel Provident Nat. Bank, Phila., 1989-93; sr. v.p., dep. gen. counsel PNC Fin. Corp., Pitts., 1992-93; sr. v.p., mng. gen. counsel PNC Bank Corp., Pitts., 1993; sr. v.p., gen. counsel The PNC Fin. Svc. Group, Pitts., 1993—. Speaker in field. Author: (with others) Review of Antitrust Laws and Procedures, 1983, Criminal Antitrust Litigation Manual, 1983, Pennsylvania Medical Society Handbook, 1989; co-author: Joint Ventures in Healthcare. Former mem. Bd. of Ethics City of Phila.; former mem. bd. dirs. Phila. Facilities Mgmt. Corp.; bd. advisors Pub. Interest Law Ctr. Phila.; former mem. bd. overseers U. Pa.; former bd. mgrs. Wistar Inst. Mem. ABA (antitrust sect., litigation sect., bus. law sect.), Pa. Bar Assn. (former mem. ho. of dels., judiciary com.), Phila. Bar Assn. (bd. govs. 1989-91, fed. cts. com., bus. law sect.), Acad. Natural Scis. (former bd. dirs., trustee), Duquesne Club. Office: The PNC Financial Service Group 249 5th Ave Pittsburgh PA 15222-2709

**PUDLO, STEVEN EDWARD,** computer technician; s. Chester Joseph and Mary Ann Pudlo; life ptnr. Linda Sue Jacobsen; 1 child, Julia Briggs. AS in Data Processing, Thames Valley State Tech. Coll., Norwich, Conn., 1982; BS in Computer Sci., Ea. Conn. State U., Willimantic, Conn., 1985—86; AS in Indsl. Mgmt., Three Rivers CC, Norwich, 1986—87; MBA, Rensselaer Polytech, Hartford, Conn., 1992—95. Asst dir. IT Three Rivers CC, 1985—. Contbr. book. Sec. Ancient Accepted Scottich Rite, Preston, Conn., 1998—2006; mem. Norwich Rep. Town Com., 1990—94; master Somerset-St. James Lodge #34, Preston, 2000—03. Mem.: Masonic Motorcycle Assn. Australia, Patriot Guard Riders, Masonic Motorcycle Club, Internat. R-Consevative. Avocations: motorcycling, travel. Home: 59 Saint Regis Ave Norwich CT 06360 Office: Three Rivers CC 574 New London Turnpike Norwich CT 06360 Office Fax: 860-886-4960. Business E-Mail: spudlo@trcc.commnet.edu.

**PUESCHEL, SIEGFRIED M.,** pediatrician, educator; b. Waldenburg, Germany, July 28, 1931; came to U.S., 1961; naturalized, 1971; widowed. Student, Braunschweig Coll., Germany, 1953-55, Leibniz Coll., Tubingen, Germany, 1955-56, U. Tubingen, Germany, 1955-57, Free U., Berlin, 1957-58, U. Freiburg, Germany, 1958; MD summa cum laude, Med. Acad., Dusseldorf, Germany, 1960; MPH, Harvard U., 1967; PhD, U. R.I., 1985; JD, So. New Eng. Sch. Law, 1996. Diplomate Am. Bd. Pediatrics, Am. Bd. Med. Genetics. Intern Mercer Hosp., Trenton, NJ, 1961-62; jr. resident in pediatrics Children's Hosp., Honolulu, 1962-63; asst. resident in pediatrics Children's Hosp. Med. Ctr., Boston, 1963-64, asst. in mental retardation, 1967-68, assoc. in mental retardation, 1968-75, dir. Down Syndrome Program, 1970-75, dir. PKU Clinic, 1972-75; sr. resident in pediatrics Montreal Children's Hosp., 1964-65, fellow in biochemical genetics/metabolism, 1965-66; assoc. physician R.I. Hosp., Providence, 1975-79; dir. child devel. ctr., 1975-94, dir. PKU and Amino Acid Program, 1975—, dir. Down Syndrome Program, 1978—, physician, 1979—. Instr. pediatrics Harvard U., Cambridge, Mass., 1968-74, asst. prof. in pediatrics, 1974-75, lectr. in pediatrics, 1975—; asst. prof. in pediatrics Brown U., Providence, 1975-77, assoc. prof. in pediatrics, 1977-85, prof. in pediatrics, 1985—; consulting pediatrician Waltham (Mass.) Hosp., 1968-75; cons. in genetics Lying in Hosp., Boston, 1969-75, Women and Infants Hosp., Providence, 1975—; cons. Devel. Evaluation Clinic Children's Hosp. Med. Ctr., Boston, 1975—; mem. prevention of mental retardation com. Internat. League of Socs. for Persons with Mental Handicaps; mem. rsch., prevention and program svc. com. Assn. for Retarded Citizens U.S.; mem. nat. conf. on rsch. perspectives in down syndrome Nat. Inst. Child Health and Rehab. Svcs.; mem. state-of-the-art conf. on down syndrome Office Spl. Edn. and Rehab. Svcs. U.S. Dept. Edn.; mem. nat. adv. child health and human devel. coun. NIH, Washington; mem. sub-com. on tng., edn. and quality assurance-tech. assistance Devel. Disabilities Coun., R.I.; mem. med. adv. com. Spl. Olympics. Author chpts. to books; mem. editl. bd. Down Syndrome Papers and Abstracts for Profls., Exceptional Parents, Down's Syndrome: Rsch. and Practice; reviewer numerous jours.; contbr. articles to profl. jours. Grantee Mass. Dept. Health, 1968, Vigneron Meml. Fund, 1984-85, Charlotte Taylor Fund, 1985-86, Dept. Health and Human Svcs., 1982-86, March of Dimes Nat. Found., 1987-89, Sigma-Tau Pharm., Inc., 1990-93; recipient Recognition award March of Dimes, 1976, Fogarty Founders award, 1988, Edn. award Muscular Dystrophy Assn., 1985, 86, Muscular Dystrophy Tchg. award, 1988, Recognition award Devel. Ctr. for Handicapped Personsn-Utah State U., 1986, Down Syndrome Assn. of Greater Cin. award, 1986, Colegion John Langdown Down award Mexico City, 1987, Disting. Rsch. award Assn. for Retarded Citizens of U.S., 1990, Conn. Down Syndrome Assn. award, 1991, Sindrome de Down award Asociación Down de Monterrey (Mexico), 1994. Fellow Am. Acad. Pediatrics, Am. Coll. Med. Genetics (founder); mem. AAAS, Am. Assn. Mental Retardation (Profl. Contbn. award 1991), Am. Acad. Cerebral Palsy and Devel. Medicine, Am. Pediatric Soc., Am. Soc. Human Genetics, Nat. Down Syndrome Congress (past pres.), Recognition for Disting. Svc. award 1980, Mid-Hudson Valley award 1983, Achievement in Rsch. award 1988, Outstanding Physician award 1991), N.Y. Acad. Sci., R.I. Med. Soc., New Eng. Regional Genetics Group, Soc. Inherited Metabolic Disorders, Down Syndrome Soc. R.I. (award 1985), Assn. for Children with Down Syndrome (bd. dirs.). Office: RI Hosp Child Devel Ctr 593 Eddy St Providence RI 02903-4923 Office Phone: 401-444-8477.

**PUETZ, PAMELA ANN,** human resources executive; b. Lawrence, Mass., Aug. 17, 1949; d. Gregory and Eleanor Christine Bedrosian; m. Tracy Barnum Braun, Jan. 26, 1974 (div. 1985); 1 child, Susannah; m. Dan Lee Puetz, May 31, 1986. AS, Fisher Jr. Coll., Boston, 1969; BS in Mgmt. with high distinction, Babson Coll., Wellesley, Mass., 1973. Br. mgr. First Security Bank of Utah, N.A., Salt Lake City, 1974-76; bus. mgr. U.S. Ski Team, Inc., Park City, Utah, 1976-77; banking specialist Tracy Collins Bank, Salt Lake City, 1980-83; instr. Fitness Inst., LDS Hosp., Salt Lake City, 1983-85; owner/operator Grapevine Svcs., Redondo Beach, Calif., 1987-88; human resources adminstr. PacifiCare Health Systems, Inc., Cypress, Calif., 1988-89, human resources analyst, 1989-91, human resources project mgr., 1991-93, human resources mgr., 1993—94; sr. mgr. human resources systems Mattel, Inc., El Segundo, Calif., 1994-95; sr. cons., HRIS mgr. PacifiCare Health Systems, Inc., Cypress, Calif., 1995-96, dir. Employee Svc. Ctr., 1996—2004, v.p. human resources, 2004—. Bd. dirs. Human Options, 2004—. Mem. Internat. Human Resources Info. Mgmt. Assn., Soc. for Human Resources Mgmt., World At Work. Avocations: scuba, skiing.

**PUFFER, JAMES C.,** sports medicine physician, educator, medical association administrator; married. BS, UCLA, MD, 1976. Prof., chief, divsn. family medicine UCLA; prof., family medicine Univ. Ky., Lexington; exec. dir., sec. Am. Bd. Family Medicine, Lexington, Ky., 2003—05, pres., CEO, 2005—. Physician US Winter Olympic Team, Sarajevo, 1984; head team physician US Summer Olympic Team, Seoul, 1988; mem., sports medicine, sports sci. coun. US Olympic Com., 1985—92; com. mem. NCAA Com. on Competitive Safeguards and Med. Aspects of Sports, 1985—90; cons. Pres. Coun. on Physical Fitness and Sports, 1988—90. Assoc. editor Medicine and Science in Sports and Exercise, 1989—98, editor-in-chief Sports Medicine Digest, 1992—, editl. bd. mem., peer reviewer numerous profl. jours. Recipient Duke Paoa Kahanamoku award, USA Water Polo, 2004. Fellow: Am. Coll. Sports Medicine; mem.: US Olympic Sports Medicine Soc. (bd. dir. 1993—96), Am. Med. Soc. for Sports Medicine (pres. 1996—97, founding mem.), Am. Bd. Family Medicine (bd. dir. 1989—94, exec. com. mem.-at-large 1993—94, v.p. 1993—94). Avocation: water polo. Office: ABFM 2228 Young Dr Lexington KY 40505-4294 Office Phone: 859-269-5626. Business E-Mail: jpuffer@theabfm.org.*

**PUFFER, RICHARD JUDSON,** retired college chancellor; b. Chgo., Aug. 20, 1931; s. Noble Judson and Lillian Katherine (Olson) P.; m. Alison Foster Cope, June 28, 1952; children— Lynn, Mark, Andrew. Ph.B., Ill. Wesleyan U., 1953; MS in Edn, Ill. State U., 1962; PhD (Roy Clark Meml. scholar), Northwestern U., 1967. Asst. plant supt. J.A. Olson Co., Winona, Miss., 1957-59; tchr. Leroy Community Unit Dist. (Ill.), 1959-60; tchr., prin. Community Unit, Dist. 7, Lexington, Ill., 1960-62; asst. county supt. schs. Cook County, Ill., 1962-65; dean arts and scis. Kirkwood Community Coll., Cedar Rapids, Iowa, 1967-69; v.p. Black Hawk Coll., Moline, Ill., 1969-77, pres., 1977-82, chancellor, 1982-87; pres. The Ark Computer Ctr., 1989-92. Dir. W. Ctrl. Ill. Ednl. TV Corp., Springfield, Ill., 1977-87; cons. examiner North Central Assn., 1978-87. Editor: Cook County Ednl. Digest, 1962-65. Bd. dirs. Cedar Rapids Symphony, 1967-69, United Way of Rock Island and Scott Counties, Ill., 1978-80, Unitarian Universalist Dist. of Mich., 1995-98; bd. dirs., sec. West Shore Unitarian Universalist Congregation, 1996-99; sec., treas. Ill. Ednl. Retirement Cts., 1987-91; vice-chmn. Illini Hosp. Bd., 1988-93, chmn., 1993-95; bd. dirs. Illowa coun. Boy Scouts Am., 1979-83, v.p., 1981-83. With USNR, 1953-57. Mem. Rotary (pres. 1975-76, East Moline, Ill.), Green Medallion, Blue Key, Phi Delta Kappa, Pi Gamma Mu. Home and Office: 6191 Grace Ave Ludington MI 49431-8629

**PUGH, ARTHUR JAMES (JAY PUGH),** retired retail executive; b. Glen Morrison, W.Va., Sept. 24, 1937; s. Arthur James and Mary Pugh; m. Sharon Hubacher, Sept. 26, 1961; children: James Gregory, Mary Elizabeth. BSBA, W.Va. U., 1959; Master of Retailing, U. Pitts., 1960. Mgmt. trainee, buyer Woodward & Lothrop, Washington, 1960-71, v.p., 1971-77, sr. v.p., 1977-80, exec. v.p., 1980-87, Coun. of Better Bus. Bur., Arlington, Va., 1987-90, bd. dir.; cons., bd. dir. Fairfax, Va., 1990—. Trustee, chmn. audit com. Calvert Mut. Funds, Washington, 1983—; bd. dirs. Acacia Capital Corp., Washington; bd. dirs., exec. com. compensation com., chmn. investment com. Acacia Fed. Savs. Bank, Falls Church, Va. Chmn. bd. dirs. Better Bus. Bur. Met. Washington, 1987. Mem. Rotary Found. of Washington (pres. 1990-91), Nat. Retail Mchts. Assn. (bd. dirs. 1986), W.Va. U. Alumni Assn. (bd. dirs. 1993-98), Fairfax Country Club (bd. dirs. 1990-92), Rotary Club of Washington (Rotarian of Yr. 1982, pres. 1984). Republican. Presbyterian. Avocations: tennis, skiing, swimming. Home and Office: 4823 Prestwick Dr Fairfax VA 22030-4533 Office Phone: 703-385-1312. Personal E-mail: jaypugh@prodigy.net.

**PUGH, CARLA M.,** surgeon, educator; b. Oakland, Calif., Feb. 3, 1966; d. Tillman and Helen (Abram) Pugh; m. Joseph D. Towels, Aug. 16. BA, U. Calif., Berkeley, 1988; MD, Howard U., Washington, 1992; PhD, Stanford U., Calif., 2001. Surg. intern Howard U. Hosp., 1992—93, resident in surgery, 1993—98; staff surgeon Kaiser Med. Group, Redwood City, Calif., 1998—2003; rsch. assoc. Stanford U. Sch. Med., 2002—03; assoc. dir., asst. prof. edn. and surgery Northwestern U., Chgo., 2003—; staff surgeon Chgo. VA Westside, 2004—. Home: 201 E Huron St Chicago IL 60611-3197

**PUGH, DAVID L.,** manufacturing executive; b. Lynchburg, Va. m. Barbara Pugh; 2 children. BSEE, Duke U. Former chief mktg. officer, v.p. and gen. mgr. power equipment bus. unit Square D Co.; former plant mgr., v.p. constrn. sales Westinghouse Electric Corp.; sr. v.p. indsl control group Rockwell Automation, 1994-99; pres., COO Applied Indsl. Technologies, Cleve., 1999-2000, chmn., CEO, 2000—. Bd. dir. J.L.G. Industries, R.W. Beckett Corp. Office: Applied Indsl Techs 1 Applied Plz Cleveland OH 44115*

**PUGH, DOROTHY GUNTHER,** artistic director; b. Memphis, May 8, 1951; Grad. magna cum laude, Vanderbilt U., 1973; studied with Raymond Clay, studied with Donna Carver, studied with David Howard; student, Royal Acad. Dancing, London. Founder Ballet Memphis, 1985, also artistic dir., 1985—. Named one of city's influential citizens, Memphis Mag.; recipient Woman of Achievement award for Initiative, 1987, Gordon Holl Artistic Adminstr. of Yr. award, State of Tenn., 1999. Office: Ballet Memphis PO Box 3675 Cordova TN 38088-3675 E-mail: info@balletmemphis.com.*

**PUGH, EMERSON WILLIAM,** electrical engineer; b. Pasadena, Calif., May 1, 1929; s. Emerson Martindale and Ruth Hazel (Edgin) P.; m. Elizabeth Burnam Russell; children: William Russell, Sarah Elizabeth, David Emerson. BS in Physics, Carnegie Mellon U., 1951, PhD in Physics, 1956. Asst. prof. physics Carnegie Mellon U., Pitts., 1956-57; with IBM, 1957-93, rsch. staff mem. rsch. div., Poughkeepsie, N.Y., 1957-61, engring. mgr. components div., 1962-65, group dir. data processing group, Harrison, N.Y., 1965-66, dir. tech. planning rsch. div., Yorktown Heights, N.Y., 1966-68, asst. to v.p. IBM Corp., Armonk, N.Y., 1968-71, rsch. mgr. rsch. div., Yorktown Heights, 1971-85, mgr. tech. history, 1985-93. Vis. scientist IBM Lab., Zurich, Switzerland, 1961-62; mem. United Engring. Trustees Bd., N.Y.C., 1986-92; mem. Engring. Soc. Libr. Bd., N.Y.C., 1986-89; trustee Chalres Babbage Found., 1990—, Samuel Morse Hist. Site, 1998-99. Author: Principles of Electricity and Magnetism, 1960, Memories That Shaped an Industry, 1984, IBM's Early Computers, 1986, IBM's 360 and Early 370 Systems, 1991, Building IBM, 1995; also articles; 10 patents. Fellow IEEE (pres. 1989, mem. friends com. Ctr. for History Elec. Engring. 1991-94, chmn. history com. 1995-98, dir. Found. 1996-2005, pres. found. 2000-04), AAAS, Am. Phys. Soc. Home: 3 Rock St Cold Spring NY 10516-2911

**PUGH, GEORGE WILLARD,** law educator; b. Napoleonville, La., Aug. 17, 1925; s. William Whitmell and Evelyn (Foley) P.; m. Jean Earle Hemphill, Sept. 6, 1952; children: William Whitmell III, George Willard Jr., David Nicholls, James Hemphill. BA, La. State U., 1947, JD, 1950; J.S.D., Yale U., New Haven, Conn., 1952; Dr. h.c., U. Aix-Marseille III, France, 1984. Bar: La. 1950. Instr. La. State U. Law Sch., 1950, mem. faculty, 1952-94, prof. law, 1959-94, Julius B. Nachman prof. law, 1984-94; prof. law emeritus, 1994—. Faculty U. Thessaloniki Greece 1974, Aix-en-Provence, France, 1985, 91; faculty U. San Diego, Paris, 1977; rsch. cons. La. State Law Inst., 1953-54; 1st jud. adminstr. Jud. Coun. Supreme Ct. La., 1954-56; vis. prof. U.

Tex., 1961; vis. Doherty prof. law U. Va., 1966-67; faculty orientation program in Am. law Assn. Am. Law Schs., 1968, law teaching clinic, 1969; vis. prof. U. Aix-Marseille III, France, 1983, 1987, U. Catholique de Louvain, Belgium, 1987; cons. La. State U.S. Vietnam Legal Adminstrn. Project, 1969; coord.; reporter Code of Evidence for La., 1981-95. Author: Louisiana Evidence Law, 1974, supplement, 1978; co-author: Cases and Materials on the Adminstration of Criminal Justice, 2d edit., 1969, Handbook on Louisiana Evidence Law, 1989, 19th edit., 2006. Bd. dirs. Legal Aid Soc. Baton Rouge, 1965-89, chmn., 1963-64; adv. bd. St. Alban's Episcopal Student Ctr., La. State U., 1965-68, 70-72. Served with AUS, World War II. Named George W. and Jean H. Pugh Inst. for Justice in his honor, La. State U. Law Ctr., 1997; fellow, Comparative Study Adminstrn. Justice, 1962—65. Mem. Am., La., Baton Rouge bar assns., Order of Coif, Omicron Delta Kappa, Lambda Chi Alpha. Democrat. Episcopalian. Home: 167 Sunset Blvd Baton Rouge LA 70808-5073

**PUGH, JOHN ROBERT,** academic administrator, educator, retired state official; b. New Orleans, Dec. 20, 1945; s. Edward Nicholls and Yvonne Marie (Duplantier) P.; m. Margaret Louise McMullen, Aug. 26, 1975; children— Margaret Elizabeth, John Robert. BA in Philosophy, Baylor U., 1967; M. in Social Work, U. Tex.-Austin, 1970. Program dir. McLaughlin Youth Ctr., Anchorage, Alaska, 1973-78; dep. dir. Alaska Div. Social Services, Juneau, 1978-80; dir. Alaska Family and Youth Services, Juneau, 1980-83; dep. commr. Alaska Dept. Health and Social Services, Juneau, 1983, commr., 1983-86; dean, Sch. of Education Univ. Alaska Southeast, Juneau, 1986-95, chancellor, 1995—. Cons., lectr. in field Mem., Blue Ribbon Commn. for Revision of Children's Code, 1975-77; supt. Sunday Sch., No. Light United Ch., Juneau, 1979—; mem. Gov.'s Council for Handicapped and Gifted, 1980-84; mem. precinct com. Greater Juneau Democratic Com., 1983—; bd. dirs. Alaska State Fin. Corp., 1985—; coach Juneau Little League, 1984—. Served to capt. USAF, 1969-73 Mem. Nat. Assn. Social Workers (mem. 1975-76), Am. Pub. Welfare Assn., Am. Correctional Assn., Alaska Pub. Employees Assn. (pres. 1977-79), Acad. Cert. Social Workers (cert.) Methodist. Avocations: fishing, sports. Office: U Alaska Southeast 11120 Glacier Hwy Juneau AK 99801

**PUGH, RICHARD CRAWFORD,** lawyer, educator; b. Phila., Apr. 28, 1929; s. William and Myrtle P.; m. Nanette Bannen, Feb. 27, 1954; children: Richard Crawford, Andrew Lembert, Catherine Elizabeth. AB summa cum laude, Dartmouth Coll., 1951; BA in Jurisprudence, Oxford U., Eng., 1953; LLB, Columbia U., 1958. Bar: N.Y. 1958. Assoc. firm Cleary, Gottlieb, Steen & Hamilton, N.Y.C., 1958—61, ptnr., 1969—89; disting. prof. law U. San Diego, 1989—, univ. prof., 1998—99. Mem. faculty Law Sch. Columbia U., 1961-89, prof., 1964-69, adj. prof., 1969-89; lectr. Columbia-Amsterdam-Leyden (Netherlands) summer program Am. law, 1963, 79; dep. asst. atty. gen. tax div. U.S. Dept. Justice, 1966-68; Cons. fiscal and fin. br. UN Secretariat, 1962, 64. Editor: Columbia Law Rev., 1957—58; co-editor: Legal Aspects of Foreign Investment, 1959, International Income Taxation, Code and Regulations, 2006; co-author: International Law, 2001, Taxation of Business Enterprises, 2002, Taxation of International Transactions, 2005. With USNR, 1954—56. Rhodes scholar, 1951-53. Mem. ABA, Am. Law Inst., Am. Coll. Tax Counsel, Internat. Fiscal Assn. (pres. U.S. br. 1978-79). Home: 7335 Encelia Dr La Jolla CA 92037-5729 Office: U San Diego Sch Law Alcala Park San Diego CA 92110-2429 Business E-Mail: rpugh@sandiego.edu.

**PUGH, THOMAS DOERING,** architecture educator, educator; b. Jacksonville, Fla., May 27, 1948; s. William Edward Jr. and Lina Lillian (Doering) P.; children: Rachel McRae, Jordan Faith, Nathan Calder; m. Jackie M. Hargrove, Dec. 2004. B in Design, U. Fla., 1971, MA in Architecture, 1974. Asst. prof. architecture U. Ark., Fayetteville, 1976-78; pres. Thomas D. Pugh Constrn. Co., Inc., Fayetteville, Ark., 1978-87; assoc. prof. Fla. A&M U. Sch. Architecture, Tallahassee, 1987—; interim dir. Inst. Bldg. Scis. Fla. Argl. and Mech. U., Tallahassee, 1991-93, dir., 1993—. Vis. rsch. fellow Tech. U. Eindhoven, The Netherlands, 1993-94; chmn. radon adv. bd. Fla. State U. Sys., 1988-94; mem. Fla. Coordinating Coun. on Radon Protection; juror Progressive Arch.-AIA Nat. Archtl. Rsch. Awards, 1995; mem. rsch. policy bd. AIA/Assn. Collegiate Schs. of Arch., 1996—; mem. edn. com. Odyssey Sci. Ctr., Tallahassee, 1995—. Bd. dir. Tallahassee Habitat for Humanity, 1987-92; crew leader Habitat for Humanity Internat., Americus, Ga., 1988, 90. Recipient Bronze medal Fla. Assn. AIA, Gainesville, 1975; Named Vol. of Yr. Tallahassee Dem. and Vol. Tallahassee, Inc., 1991. Mem. ASCE (sec. spl. task com. radon mitigation 1990-91), Assn. Collegiate Schs. Architecture (coun. on archtl. rsch. 1994). Democrat. Avocations: sailing, woodworking. Office: Fla A&M Univ Sch Architecture 1936 S Martin Luther King Jr B Tallahassee FL 32307-4200 Office Phone: 850-599-3007. Business E-Mail: thomas.pugh@famu.edu. E-mail: tpugh@famusoa.net.

**PUGH, THOMAS WILFRED,** lawyer; b. St. Paul, Minn., Aug. 3, 1949; s. Thomas Leslie and Joann Marie (Tauer) P.; m. Susan Elizabeth Beattie, Sept. 12, 1971; children: Aimee Elizabeth, Douglas Thomas. AB cum laude, Dartmouth Coll., 1971; JD cum laude, U. Minn., 1976. Assoc. Thuet & Lynch, South St. Paul, 1976-79; ptnr. Thuet, Lynch & Pugh, South St. Paul, 1980-85; atty., pres. Thuet, Pugh, Rogosheske & Atkins, Ltd., South St. Paul, 1986—; mem. Minn. Ho. of Reps., St. Paul, 1989—2004, Dem. leader, 1999—2002; commr. Minn. Pub. Utilities Commn., 2004—. Mem. Supreme Ct. Task Force Conciliation Ct., St. Paul, 1992, Dakota County Tech. Coll. Adv. Bd., 1991-96. Bd. dirs. Wakota Arena, South St. Paul, 1984-87; pres. Luther Meml. Ch., South St. Paul, 1983-84; Daniel Webster scholar Dartmouth Coll., 1970, Rufus Choate scholar, 1971. Mem. Minn. State Bar Assn., 1st Dist. Bar Assn., Ducks Unltd., Pheasants Forever, South St. Paul C. of C. (local issues chair 1982, Dedicated Svc. award 1983), South St. Paul Jaycees (pres. 1978-79, Key award 1979), Lions. Lutheran. Avocations: tennis, golf, hunting, fishing, reading. Office: Thuet Pugh & Rogosheske 222 Grand Ave South Saint Paul MN 55075-2237

**PUGH, WILLIAM WHITMELL HILL, III,** lawyer; b. Baton Rouge, La., June 25, 1954; s. George Willard and Jean (Hemphill) P.; m. Beth Smith, Mar. 12, 1983; children: Brendan Kelly, Bryan Clayton, Katharine Elaine. BA, U. Va., 1976; JD, La. State U., 1979. Bar: La. 1979, U.S. Supreme Ct. 1986, U.S. Ct. Appeals (5th and 11th cirs.) 1983. Law clk. to presiding justice U.S. Ct. Appeals (5th cir.), New Orleans, 1979-80. Editor-in-chief La. Law Rev., 1978-79. Mem. Maritime Law Assn., La. Assn. Def. Counsel, La. State Bar Assn., Coun. of La. State Law Inst. (young lawyers rep. 1988-91), mem. 1992—). Office: Liskow & Lewis Three Allen Ctr 333 Clay St Ste 3485 Houston TX 77002 Office Phone: 713-651-2949. Business E-Mail: wwpugh@liskow.com.

**PUGIA, MICHAEL J.,** research scientist, educator; BS in Chemistry, Clarkson Univ., 1982; PhD in Chemistry, Tex. Tech. Univ., 1986. Dir. Bayer HealthCare, Elkhart, Ind., 1986—. Vis. scholar Univ. of Notre Dame, Ind., 2004—06. Office: Bayer HealthCare 1884 Miles Ave Elkhart IN 46515

**PUGLIESE, ROBERT FRANCIS,** lawyer, manufacturing executive; b. Jan. 15, 1933; BS, U. Scranton, 1954; LLB, Georgetown U., 1957, LLM, 1959; grad. advanced mgmt. program, Harvard U., 1976. Bar: D.C. 1957, U.S. Dist. Ct. 1957, U.S. Ct. Claims 1958, U.S. Tax Ct. 1957, U.S. Ct. Appeals 1957. Assoc. Hedrick & Lane, Washington, 1957-60; tax counsel Westinghouse Electric Corp., Pitts., 1961-70, gen. tax counsel, 1970-75, v.p., gen. tax counsel, 1975-76, v.p. gen. counsel, sec., 1976-86, sr. v.p., 1987—92; spl. counsel Eckert, Seamans, Cherin & Mellott, Pitts., 1993—. Mem. Assn. Gen. Counsel. Office: Eckert Seamans Cherin & Mellott 600 Grant St Ste 4500 Pittsburgh PA 15219-2703 Business E-Mail: rpugliese@eckertseamans.com.

**PUGLISE, J. MICHAEL,** management consultant; s. John Santo and Mary Christine (Fett) P.; m. Kandi Kay Lucas, Feb. 14, 1969; children: Scott Michael, Jason Matthew, Melissa Anne. BA with distinction, Ohio No. U., Ada, 1975; post grad., Xavier U., Cin. Lic. ins. Ohio, 2002; gen. securities rep. Series 7, 2003, cert. uniform combined state fed. law exam series 66

2003, AAMS profl. Coll. Fin. Planning, 2004. Pers. mgr. Airfoil Divsn. Textron, Inc., Lima, Ohio, 1980—82, indsl. rels. mgr., 1982—87, v.p. human resources, 1987—95; mgr. labor rels. Aro divsn. Ingersoll-Rand Co., Bryan, 1995—96, v.p. human resources Steelcraft divsn. Cin., 1997—2001; pres., prin. J.M. Puglise Co., Cin., 2001—. Dir. Health Systems Agency, lima, Oh. Mem. Soc. for Human Resource Mgmt., Lima Personnel Assn. (pres. 1984-85). Republican. Avocations: reading, sports. Address: 9112 Coachtrail Ln Cincinnati OH 45242 Office Phone: 513-794-0319. E-mail: jmpuglise@aol.com.

**PUGLISI, MELANY P.,** marine chemical ecologist, researcher; b. West Palm Beach, Fla., Mar. 10, 1968; d. George W. Puglisi and Marsha J. Gorman; m. Frederick J. Weening, Jan. 11, 1967. BA in Chemistry, Southampton Coll., N.Y., 1988—91; MS in Biology, U. Guam, 1993—95; PhD in Pharmacognosy, U. Miss., Oxford, 1996—2001. Postdoctoral fellow Scripps Inst. Oceanography, La Jolla, Calif., 2001—03; asst. prof. Lake Erie Coll. Osteo. Medicine, Pa., 2003—04; postdoctoral fellow Smithsonian Rsch. Sta., Fort Pierce, Fla., 2004—05. Contbr. papers to profl. jours. and pubs. Office: Shannon Point Marine Ctr WWU 1900 Shannon Point Rd Anacortes WA 98221 Office Phone: 360-293-2188. Office Fax: 390-293-1083. Business E-Mail: melany.puglisi@wwu.edu.

**PUGSLEY, RICHARD DALLAS,** mathematics professor; b. Cheyenne, Wyo., Apr. 25, 1965; s. Larry Dean and Margaret Mary Pugsley; m. Judith F. Rybarczyk, May 14, 1988; children: Andrew Richard, Caitlyn Elizabeth, Matthew Peyton. AS in Engring., Tidewater C.C., Virginia Beach, Va., 1991; MS in Secondary Edn., Old Dominion U., Norfolk, Va., 2004; AA in Counseling and Applied Psychology, Coastline C.C., Fountain Lake, Calif., 2005, AA in Mgmt., 2005. Cert. master tng. specialist USN, 1997. MMC-M(SS) USN, Norfolk, Va., 1983—2005; math educator Tidewater Tech., Virginia Beach, 2005, Tidewater C.C., Virginia Beach, 2005—, ITT Tech. Svcs., Norfolk, 2005—. Mem.: VMATYC (assoc.), AMATYC (assoc.), MAA (assoc.), Nat. Coun. Tchrs. Math. (assoc.). Office: Tidewater Community College 1700 College Crescent Virginia Beach VA 23464

**PUHL, JENNIFER JOYCE,** physiologist; d. William and Catherine Marie Veek Puhl; m. Kurt Douglas Winkler, May 5, 2006. BS, U. Miami, Coral Gables, Fla., 1994, MS in Edn., 2000. Cert. First Aid/CPR/AED instr. ARC. Facility supr., fitness trainer, intramural ofcl. Wellness & Recreation, Coral Gables, 1992—96; grad. asst. human performance lab Exercise & Sports Sci. U. Miami, Coral Gables, 1994—96; student fitness ctr. coord. Campus Recreation Fla. Internat. U., Miami, 1996—2003; asst. dir. recreation Austin Peay State U., Clarksville, Tenn., 2003—. Statis. sports info. Fla. Internat. U. Athletics, Miami, 1998—2003; statis. video rm. Miami Heat, 2000—02; presenter in field. Co-author: (textbook) APSU 1000 Providing the Foundations for University Success; contbr. articles to profl. jours. First aid/cpr/aed instr. ARC, Miami, 1995—2003, Clarksville, Tenn., 2003; occasional instr. adult Sunday sch. Sango United Meth. Ch., Clarksville; mem. wellness task force APSU, Clarksville, mem. student affairs assessment com., 2005—06. Recipient Campus Recreation Employee of the Yr., Fla. Internat. U., 1989—90. Mem.: Nat. Health and Wellness Club, Coll. Student Educators Internat., Nat. Intramural-Recreational Sports Assn. (registry task force 2001—06), IDEA Health and Fitness Resource, ACSM Health and Fitness Assn., Nat. Strength and Conditioning Assn., Am. Coll. Sports Medicine (cert. health fitness instr.). Avocations: reading, sports, drawing. Office: Austin Peay State U University Recreation Box 4398 Clarksville TN 37044 Office Phone: 931-221-1242. Office Fax: 931-221-7950.

**PUJANA, MARIA JOSE,** neurologist; MD, Universidad Complutense, Madrid. Former chief resident, neurophysiology dept. Veteran Hosp., Madrid; adj. instructor Ctr. for Global Hlth. and Diseases, Sch. of Med., Case Western Reserve U., 1994—. Pres., designer Marise Jewelry Designs. Former v.p. of council Cleve. Ballet; adv. bd. mem. Cleve. Inst. of Art; trustee Cleve. Found., 2002—; mem. cmty. adv. bd. Rock and Roll Hall of Fame and Museum; bd. mem. Cuyahoga Cmty. Coll. Found., MetroHealth Found., Beck Ctr. for Arts, Cleve. Red Cross. Office: Case Sch of Med 10900 Euclid Ave Cleveland OH 44106*

**PUJOL, ERNESTO,** artist; b. Havana, Cuba, 1957; BA in Visual Arts magna cum laude, U. Puerto Rico, 1979; postgrad., Pratt Inst., 1987, Hunter Coll. Artist The Marketplace Program, Bronx Mus. Arts, NY, 1991. One-man shows include Taller D'Jevarez, San Juan, 1984, Cavin-Morris, N.Y.C., 1993, INTAR, 1994, Galeria Ramis Barquet, Monterrey, Mex., 1995, Casa de las Americas, Havana, 1995, Frederic Snitzer Gallery, Miami, Fla., 1995, Iturralde Gallery, L.A., 1996, exhibited in group shows at Galeria Interamericana, P.R., 1984, Nat. Arts Club, N.Y.C., 1990, Hudson Guild Gallery, 1991, Cavin Morris Gallery, 1992, The Space, Boston, 1992, Paine Weber Gallery, N.Y., 1992, Reed Coll. Art Gallery, Portland, Oreg., 1994, Seton Hill Coll., Pa., 1995, Iturralde Gallery, L.A., 1995, Spectrum Gallery, Rochester, N.Y., 1996, PS 122, N.Y.C., 1996, numerous others, Represented in permanent collections Casa de las Americas, Havana, El Museo del Barrio, N.Y., Assn. Artistas Plasticas de Cuba, Havana, Mus. Art, Ft. Lauderdale, Fla., Cintas Found. Fellows Collective, Art Mus., Fla., Internat. U. Miami, Bronx Coun. Arts, Longwood, N.Y. Recipient Breakthrough award for creativity, Acad. Ednl. Devel., Washington, 1990, Cert. of Appreciation, Dept. Cultural Affairs, L.A., 1995; fellow Cintas Found. fellow, Arts Internat., Inst. Internat. Edn., 1991, Visual Arts fellow, Pollock-Krasner Found., 1993, Regional fellow in painting, Mid-Atlantic Arts Found./Nat. Endowment Arts, 1994; scholar Studio scholar, Bronx Coun. Arts, 1991. Office: Galeria Ramis Barquet 41 E 57th St New York NY 10022-1908

**PUJOLS, ALBERT,** professional baseball player; b. Santo Domingo, Dominican Republic, Jan. 16, 1980; m. Dieter Pujols, Jan. 1, 2000, 3 children. Profl. baseball player St. Louis Cardinals, 2001—. First basemen Team Dominican Republic, World Baseball Classic, 2006. Founder Pujols Family Found. Named Nat. League Rookie of the Yr., 2001; named to Nat. League All-Star Team, 2001, 2003—06; recipient Best MLB Player, ESPY awards, 2005, 2006, Best Internat. Player, 2006, NL MVP award, 2005. Achievements include won the National League in batting title (.359 average) 2003; leading the National League in runs (137), 2003; being fourth player in MLB history to start career with 4 straight 100 RBI season's, 2004; being first player in MLB history to hit 30 HR and 100 RBI's in first 5 seasons, 2004; tying consecutive record for at-bats resulting in a HR, 2006. Office: Busch Stadium 250 Stadium Plaza Saint Louis MO 63102*

**PULANCO, TONYA BETH,** special education educator; b. Portland, Oreg., Apr. 17, 1933; d. Anthony Lorenzo and Adelfa Elizabeth (Dewey) P. BA, San Jose State U., 1955; MA, Columbia U., 1966. Occupl. therapist Langley Porter Hosp., San Francisco, 1958-60; writer ednl. sub-contracts Columbia U., N.Y.C., 1961-64; from tchr. to dir. edn. Gateway Sch. N.Y., N.Y.C., 1965—. Mem. Assn. for Children with Learning Disabilities, Am. Occupl. Therapy Assn., Japanese Am. Citizens League. Avocations: tap dancing, walkathons, silversmithing, jazz, opera. Office: Gateway Sch NY 236 2d Ave New York NY 10003 E-mail: tobytap@aol.com.

**PULEO, FRANK CHARLES,** lawyer; b. Montclair, N.J., Nov. 25, 1945; s. Frank and Kathren (Despenzerie) P.; m. Alice Kathren Leek, June 1, 1968; children— Frank C., Richard James. B.S.E., cum laude, Princeton U., 1967; J.D., N.Y.U., 1970. Bar: N.Y., 1971. Assoc., Milbank, Tweed, Hadley & McCloy, N.Y.C., 1970—76, ptnr. 1976-; mem. exec. com. 1982-91 & 1996-2002, co-chmn. Global Fin. group. Mem. ABA (mem. com. on fed. regulation securities), N.Y. State Bar Assn. Office: Milbank Tweed Hadley & McCloy 1 Chase Manhattan Plz Fl 49 New York NY 10005-1413 Office Phone: 212-530-5134. Office Fax: 212-530-5219. Business E-Mail: fpuleo@milbank.com.

**PULGRAM, ERNST,** language educator; b. Vienna, Sept. 18, 1915; came to U.S. 1939, naturalized 1943; s. Sigmund and Gisela (Bauer) P.; m. Frances McSparran, Nov. 29, 1985. Dr. Phil. in Romance and Classical Philology, U.

Vienna, 1947, Dr. phil. honoris causa, 1990; PhD in Comparative Linguistics, Harvard U., 1946. Asst. prof. Union Coll., Schenectady, N.Y., 1946; asst. prof. U. Mich., Ann Arbor, 1948-51, assoc. prof., 1951-56, prof., 1956—, H. Keniston disting. prof. romance and classical linguistics, 1979-86, prof. emeritus, 1986—. Vis. prof. U. Florence, Italy, 1956-57, U. Cologne, Germany, 1970, U. Heidelberg, Germany, 1972, U. Regensburg, Germany, 1975, U. Vienna, 1977, Internat. Christian U., Tokyo, 1982, U. Innsbruck, Austria, 1983. U. Munich, Germany, 1987; lectr. numerous univs., internat. linguistic congresses; cons. Sch. Langs. and Linguistics, Georgetown U., Washington Author: Theory of Names, 1951, The Tongues of Italy, 1958, Introduction to Spectrography of Speech, 1959, Syllable, Word, Nexus, Cursus, 1970, Latin-Romance Phonology, Prosodics and Metrics, 1975, Italic, Latin, Italian: 600 B.C.-A.D. 1250, 1978, Practicing Linguist, Essays 1950-1985 (2 vols.), 1986; editor: Studies Presented to Joshua Whatmough, 1957, Romanitas: Studies in Romance Linguistics, 1984; contbr. articles to profl. jours.; author revs.; mem. editorial bd. Current Issues in Linguistic Theory (Amsterdam), Mich. Germanic Studies, Jour. Linguistics and Philology, Mediteranean Language Rev. Served to pvt. inf. U.S. Army, 1942-44; PTO Fellow Am. Council of Learned Socs., 1951-52, 59-60, Guggenheim Found., 1954-55, 62-63; recipient Henry Russell award U. Mich., 1951, Festschrift, Amsterdam, 1980 Mem. Linguistic Soc. Am. (exec. com., com. on appointment of hon. mems., program com.), Internat. Linguistic Assn., Internat. Phonetics Assn., Linguistic Assn. Can. and the U.S. (founding mem., pres. 1978-79) Avocations: art, hiking, swimming. Home: 1 Harvard Pl Ann Arbor MI 48104-1726 Business E-Mail: mcsparra@umich.edu.

**PULGRAM, WILLIAM LEOPOLD,** architect, space designer; b. Vienna, Jan. 1, 1921; came to U.S., 1940; s. Sigmund and Gisela (Bauer) P.; married, Jan. 12, 1952; children: Deirdre, Laurence, Anthony, Christopher. BS, Ga. Inst. Tech., 1949, BArch, 1950; postgrad., Ecole des Beaux Arts, Fontainebleau, France, 1951. Archtl. designer various firms, Atlanta, 1951-58; assoc. chief interior design FABR&P, Atlanta, 1958-63; exec. v.p., gen. mgr. Associated Space Design Inc., Atlanta, 1963-70, pres., CEO, 1971-85, chmn., CEO, 1985-86, chmn. emeritus, 1986-88; arch., cons. Atlanta, 1988—. Cons. UN, 1986; com. mem. NAS, 1980-84; lectr. at colls., univs., U.S. and abroad. Author: Designing the Automated Office, 1984, Japanese transl., 1985; contbr. articles to jours. in field. Mem., lectr. High Mus. Art, Atlanta, 1970—. With U.S. Army, 1943-46. Named to Hall of Fame Interior Design mag., 1986. Fellow AIA (chmn. interiors 1978-84, archtl. res. coun. AIA Found. 1983-85); mem. Archs., Designers and Planners for Social Responsibility (nat. bd. dirs. 1989-93), Am. Soc. Interior Designers, Atlanta C. of C., Atlanta City Club, Lake Lanier Sailing Club. Mem. Unitarian Universalist Ch. Home and Office: W L Pulgram FAIA Cons 4317 E Conway Dr NW Atlanta GA 30327-3528 E-mail: pulgramga@mindspring.com.

**PULHAMUS, MARLENE LOUISE,** retired elementary school educator; b. Paterson, NJ, Sept. 11, 1937; d. David Weeder and Elfrieda (Ehler) Wemmell; m. Aaron R. Pulhamus, Aug. 20, 1960; children: Steven, Thomas, Nancy. Student, Trenton State U., 1957; BS, William Paterson U., 1959; postgrad., Rutgers U., 1992. Cert. elem. tchr., NJ. Kindergarten tchr. Wayne Bd. Edn., NJ, 1959-63; Paterson Bd. Edn., 1974-75, 2d grade tchr., 1975-81; basic skills instr. Paterson Pub. Schs., 1981—; tchr. accelerated program 1st grade, 1992—; cons. lang. arts, literacy Kendall Hunt Pegasus, Wayne; ret., 1997. Trainer for insvc. groups of learning ctrs. and math. with manipulatives for local pub. schs., trainer for local pub. schs. Contbr. Lessons 4Mat in Action, 3d edit., 4Mat: A Quest for Wholeness, 1977—. Pres. Friends of Eisenhower Libr., Totowa, NJ, 1975-77; coord. ch. sch. Preakness Reformed Ch., Wayne, 1990-93, elder, chair outreach commn.; exec. bd. United Meth. Women Altar GUild, Asbury United Meth. Ch.; sec. VTTC Homeowners Assn., Salisbury, Md. Recipient Gov.'s award for tchg. excellence State of NJ Commn. Edn., 1991, 4Mation program award, 1994. Mem. ASCD, NEA, AAUW, Nat. Coun. Tchrs. Math., Nat. Assn. for Edn. Young Children, NJ Edn. Assn., Passaic County Edn. Assn., Paterson Edn. Assn. (mem. exec. bd., 1985-89, legis. chmn. 1986-89). Personal E-mail: mylilycat@verizon.net.

**PULIAFITO, CARMEN ANTHONY,** ophthalmologist, healthcare executive; b. Buffalo, Jan. 5, 1951; s. Dominic F. and Marie A. (Nigro) P.; m. Janet H. Pine, May 19, 1979 AB cum laude, Harvard Coll., 1973, MD magna cum laude, 1978; MBA, U. Pa., 1997. Diplomate Am. Bd. Ophthalmology. Intern Faulkner Hosp., Tufts U. Sch. Medicine, 1978-79; resident Mass. Eye and Ear Infirmary, Boston, 1979-82, retina fellow, 1982-83; instr. Harvard Med. Sch., Boston, 1983-85, asst. prof., 1985-89, assoc. prof., 1989-91, dir. divsn. continuing edn. dept. ophthalmology, 1989-91; dir. Bascom Palmer Eye Inst., Miami, 2001—. Vis. scientist MIT Regional Laser Ctr., Cambridge, 1982—; asst. prof. health scis. and tech. program, 1987-89, assoc. prof., 1989-91; mem. staff Mass. Eye and Ear Infirmary, Boston, 1983; dir. Morse Laser Ctr. Mass. Eye and Ear Infirmary, 1986-91, dir. New Eng. Eye Ctr., 1991-2001; prof., chmn. dept. ophthalmology Tufts U. Sch. Medicine, 1991-2001, prof. ophthalmology and health mgmt., 1997-2001; adj. prof. biomed. engring. Tufts U., 1991—; chmn. med. bd. New Eng. Med. Ctr. Hosps., 1994-95, ophthalmologist in chief, 1991-2001; assoc. examiner Am. Bd. Ophthalmology, 1990—; sr. v.p. for network devel. Lifespan, 1997-2001; prof., chmn. dept. ophthalmology U. Miami Sch. Medicine, 2001—; med. dir. Anne Bates Leach Eye Hosp., 2001—. Author: (with D. Albert) Foundations of Ophthalmic Pathology, 1979, (with R. Steinert) Principles and Practice of Ophthalmic YAG Laser Surgery, 1984, Lasers in Surgery and Medicine: Principles and Practice, 1996, (with M.R. Hee, J.S. Schuman and J.G. Fujimoto) Optical Coherence Tomography of Ocular Diseases, 1996, (with E. Reichel) Atlas of Indocyanine Green Angiography, 1996; editor in chief Lasers in Surgery and Medicine, 1987-95, Ophthalmic Surgery and Lasers, 1995—; contbr. about 120 articles to profl. jours. Pres. Am. Soc. for Laser Medicine and Surgery, 1994-95; v.p. Mass. Soc. Eye Physicians and Surgeons, 1994-96; assoc. examiner Am. Bd. Ophthalmology, 1990—; retina trustee Assn. Rsch. in Vision and Ophthalmology, 1995-99, pres., 2000-01. Recipient Richard and Hinda Rosenthal award in visual scis., 1994, Man of Vision award Boston Aid to the Blind, 1993, Leon Goldman award Biomed. Optics Soc., 1993, I Migliori award Pirandello Lyceum of Mass., 1994. Fellow Am. Acad. Ophthalmology, Am. Soc. for Laser Medicine and Surgery (pres. 1994-95); mem. Assn. Rsch. in Vision and Ophthalmology (pres.-elect 1998-99, pres. 1999-2000, immediate past pres. 2000-2001), Mass. Soc. Eye Physicians and Surgeons (v.p. 1994-96). Roman Catholic. Home: 9321 SW 63rd Ct Miami FL 33156-1814 Office: Bascom Palmer Eye Inst 900 NW 17th St Miami FL 33136 Office Phone: 305-326-6303. Business E-Mail: cpuliafito@miami.edu.

**PULIDO, JOSE S.,** physician; b. Apr. 29, 1956; BA with hons., U. Chgo., 1976, MS, 1977; MD, Tulane U., New Orleans, 1981; MBA, U. Iowa, 1993; MPH, U. Ill., 2005. Diplomate Am. Bd. Ophthalmology. Intern Tulane Affil. Hosps.-Charity Hosp., New Orleans, 1981-82; resident in ophthalmology U. Ill., Chgo., 1982-85, chief resident in ophthalmology, 1985-86; fellow vitreoretinal surgery Bascome Palmer Eye Inst./U. Miami Sch. Medicine, 1986-87, fellow retina rsch., 1987; fellow ocular oncology Wills Eye Hosp./Thomas Jefferson U. Sch. Medicine, Phila., 1988; head and prof. dept. ophthalmology and visual scis. U. Ill., Chgo., 1998—. Instr. organic chemistry U. Chgo., 1976-77; asst. prof. ophthalmology Coll. of Medicine, U. Iowa, Iowa City, 1987-92, assoc. prof., 1992-97, prof. 1997-98; prof. and chmn. U. Ill., 1998-2004; prof. Mayo Clinic, 2005. Reviewer numerous jours., including: Archives of Ophthalmology, 1985—, Ophthalmology, 1987—, Am. Jour. of Ophthalmology, 1992—, others; abstract editor: Diabetes 2000 Newsletter, 1992—, Ophthalmology World News, 1994-96, others; editor: Evidence-Based Eye Care, 1998—; contbr. articles to profl. jours. Mem. Am. Diabetes Assn. (del.), Am. Acad. Ophthalmology, Pan-Am. Acad. Ophthalmology, Retina Soc., Vitreous Soc., Fluorescein Reading and Macular Evaluation, Assn. for Rsch. in Vision and Ophthalmology, Am. Coll. Surgeons, Schepens Internat. Soc., Am. Ophthal. Soc., Macula Soc. Office: Mayo Clinic 200 First St SW Rochester MN 55905

**PULIDO-RAGUS, ELISA S.,** secondary school educator, department chairman; b. L.A., Apr. 28, 1953; d. Venustiano and Ruth C. (Downey) Pulido; m. Tim Ragus; children: Tom Ragus, Cassidy Ragus. BA in English, UCLA, 1975, MA in English, 1978. Nat. bd. cert. English lang. arts. English tchr. Corvallis H.S., Studio City, Calif., 1979—86, Granada Hills (Calif.) H.S., 1986—, dept. chair, 1997—. Office: Granada Hills HS 10535 Zelzah Ave Granada Hills CA 91344-5999

**PULITZER, EMILY RAUH (MRS. JOSEPH PULITZER JR.),** art historian, consultant; b. Cin., July 23, 1933; d. Frederick and Harriet (Frank) Rauh; m. Joseph Pulitzer Jr., 1973 (dec. 1993). AB, Bryn Mawr Coll., 1955; student, Ecole du Louvre, Paris, 1955-56; MA, Harvard U., 1963; LHD honoris causa (hon.), U. Mo., 1989; DFA honoris causa (hon.), Aquinas Inst., St. Louis, 2002, St. Louis U., 2003; HHD honoris causa (hon.), Washington U., St. Louis 2005. Mem. staff Cin. Art Mus., 1956-57; asst. curator drawings Harvard U. Fogg Art Mus., 1957-64, asst. to dir., 1962-63; curator City Art Mus., St. Louis, 1964-73; mem. painting and sculpture com. Mus. Modern Art, 1975—; chmn. visual arts com. Mo. Arts Coun., 1976-81; bd. mem. Inst. Mus. Svcs., 1979-84; commr. St. Louis Art Mus., 1981-88, vice chmn., 1988; bd. dir. Pulitzer, Inc., 1993—2005. Bd. dirs. Contemporary Art Mus., St. Louis, 1980-2003, 2004-, pres., 1990-94; bd. dirs. Mark Rothko Found., 1976-88, Grand Ctr., 1993-95, 99—, St. Louis Symphony Orch., 1994—; bd. dirs. arts in transit com. Bi-State Devel. Agy., vice-chmn., 1990-94; mem. Leadership St. Louis, 1990-91; mem. overseers com. to visit Harvard Art Mus., 1990—, chair 2004-; trustee Mus. Modern Art, 1994—. Named one of Top 200 Collectors, ARTnews Mag., 2003—06; recipient St. Louis award, Contbn. to Arts Cmty., 2003. Mem. Am. Fedn. Arts (dir. 1976-89), St Louis Mercantile Libr. Assn. (bd. dirs. 1987-93), Mo. Women's Forum.

**PULKKINEN, ANTTI ALEKSI,** research scientist; b. Oulu, Finland, Mar. 14, 1974; s. Aimo Antero and Hilkka Helmi Valpuri Pulkkinen. PhD, U. Helsinki, Finland, 2003. Scientist Finnish Meteorol. Inst., Space Rsch. Unit, Helsinki, 1999—2004; NASA postdoctoral fellow NASA/Goddard Space Flight Ctr., Greenbelt, Md., 2004—. Contbr. articles to profl. jours. Recipient award for post-doctoral rsch. at NASA/GSFC, US NRC, 2004, 2005. Office: NASA Goddard Space Flight Center Code 6122 Greebelt Rd Greenbelt MD 20771 Business E-Mail: antti.pulkkinen@gsfc.nasa.gov.

**PULLEN, DAVID JOHN,** physicist, researcher; b. Merton, Surrey, Eng., June 28, 1936; came to U.S. 1963; s. Arthur Lester and Alexandra Q. (Griffiths) P.; m. Heather Morgan, Aug. 6, 1960; children: Katrina, Adrian, Lester, Andrew. BSc with first class honors, London U., 1958; DPhil, Oxford U., Eng., 1963. "1851" rsch. fellow Oxford U., 1961-63; instr. MIT, 1963-65; asst. prof. physics U. Pa., Phila., 1965-70; assoc. prof. Lowell (Mass.) Tech. Inst., 1970-73; prof. physics U. Mass. Lowell, 1973—2002, prof. emeritus, 2002—. Ptnr. CPS Nuc., 1990—; cons. Internat. Atomic Energy Agy., Vienna, 1991—99. Author: Physics Laboratory Experiments, 1975, 6th edit., 2006; contbr. over 70 articles to profl. jours. Royal Commn. for Exhbn. of 1851 rsch. fellowship, 1961-63. Mem. Am. Phys. Soc., Am. Assn. Physics Tchrs., Sigma Xi. Home: 2 Reeves Rd Bedford MA 01730-1335 Office: U Mass Lowell 1 University Ave Lowell MA 01854-5009 Office Phone: 978-934-3765. Business E-Mail: david_pullen@uml.edu.

**PULLEN, PENNY LYNNE,** non-profit organization administrator, retired state legislator; b. Buffalo, Mar. 2, 1947; d. John William and Alice Nettie (McConkey) P. BA in Speech, U. Ill., 1969. Tv technician Office Instnl. Resources, U. Ill., 1966-68; cmty. newspaper reporter Des Plaines (Ill.) Pub. Co., 1967-72; legis. asst. to Ill. legislators, 1968-77; mem. Ill. Ho. of Reps., 1977-93, chmn. ho. exec. com., 1981-82, minority whip, 1983-87, asst. minority leader, 1987-93; pres., founder Life Advocacy Resource Project, Arlington Heights, Ill., 1992—. Exec. dir. Ill. Family Inst., 1993-94; dir. Legal Svcs. Corp., 1989-93; mem. Pres.'s Commn. on AIDS Epidemic, 1987-88; mem. Ill. Goodwill Del. to Republic of China, 1987. Summit conf. observer as mem. adhoc Women for SDI, Geneva, 1985; active Nat. Coun. Ednl. Rsch., 1983—88; dir. Eagle Forum of Ill., 1990—2003, pres., 2003—; del. Rep. Nat. Conv., 1984; mem. Rep. Nat. Com., 1984—88; bd. Atlantic Alliance Young Polit. Leaders, Brussels, 1977; pres. Maine Twp. Rep. Women's Club, 1997—99, Rep. Women of Park Ridge, Ill., 2001—03, Rep. Women of Wheeling Twp., Ill., 2004—. Recipient George Washington Honor medal Freedoms Found., 1978, Dwight Eisenhower Freedom medal Chgo. Captive Nations Com., 1977, Outstanding Legislator awards Ill. Press Assn., Ill. Podiatry Soc., Ill. Coroners Assn., Ill. County Clks. Assn., Ill. Hosp. Assn., Ill. Health Care Assn.; named Ill. Young Republican, 1968, Outstanding Young Person, Park Ridge Jaycees, 1981, One of 10 Outstanding Young Persons, Ill. Jaycees, 1981. Mem. DAR, Am. Legis. Exch. Coun. (dir. 1977-91, exec. com. 1978-83, 2d vice chmn. 1980-83), Com. on the Status of Women (sec. 1997—).

**PULLEN, TIMOTHY L.,** corporate financial executive; BS, Rochester Inst. Tech.; MBA, Seattle Univ. Positions through v.p. fin. Hillhaven Corp., 1983—95; v.p., controller Tenet Healthcare Corp., Dallas, 1995—99, sr. v.p., controller, 1999—2003, exec. v.p., chief acctg. officer, 2003—, interim CFO, 2005. Office: Tenet Healthcare Corp Ste 100 13737 Noel Rd Dallas TX 75240*

**PULLENZA, PATRICIA,** English educator, writer, designer; b. Phoenix, July 23, 1950; d. George Anthony and Miyuki (Sase) Pullenza; m. Anthony Pullnza, Mar. 31, 1975; children: Alexandra P., Max. BA, Ariz. State U., 1972, MA, 1976. Equal edn. opportunity specialist Dept. of Edn. State of Ariz., Phoenix, 1975; dir. ESL program, mining div. ARCO, Inguaran, Michoacan, Mexico, 1975-76; dir. Instituto Americano, Cananea, Sonora, Mexico, 1977-79; faculty assoc. Ariz. State U., Tempe, 1979-90, design; owner Patrice Pullenza Collection, Mesa, Ariz., 1987—; instr. Mesa (Ariz.) Community Coll., 1991—. Organizer plenary session USIA English as a Fgn. Lang. Inst., Tempe, 1984; co-dir. ESL Program, Mesaa Com. Coll., 2000-. Contbr. articles to profl. jours. Mem. Good Samaritan Med. Ctr. Aux., Phoenix, 1985—, Ariz. State U. Asian Faculty Staff Assn., Entrepreneurial Mothers Assn., Mesa, 1987-88; leadership team Nat. Sci. Found. Grant for Comm. Sci. Inquirt Project, 2005-. Mem. Ariz. Asian Am. Assn., Ariz. State U. Faculty Women's Assn., Ariz. State U. Faculty Assn. (bd. dirs. 1985-87, bd. trustees 1988), Maricopa Com. Coll., Phoenix Sister Cities; Ariz. Quilter's Guild, Nat. Quilter's Assn. Democrat. Roman Catholic. Office: dept English Mesa Community Coll 1833 W Southern Ave Mesa AZ 85202-4822

**PULLEY, J. WAVERLY, III, (WAVERLY PULLEY),** lawyer; b. Franklin, Va., May 19, 1946; BA in English, Univ. Richmond, 1968, JD, 1972. Bar: Va. 1972. Ptnr., capital fin., real estate Hunton & Williams LLP, Richmond, Va. Editor-in-chief Univ. Richmond Law Rev., 1971—72. Fellow: Am. Bar Found.; mem.: ABA, Va. State Bar Assn., McNeill Law Soc., Phi Delta Phi, Omicron Delta Kappa. Office: Hunton & Williams LLP Riverfront Plz East Tower 951 E Byrd St Richmond VA 23219-4074 Office Phone: 804-788-8783. Office Fax: 804-788-8218. Business E-Mail: wpulley@hunton.com.

**PULLIAM, FREDERICK CAMERON,** educational administrator; b. Mesa, Ariz., Jan. 5, 1936; s. Frederick Posy and Nathana Laura (Cameron) P.; m. Deborah Jean Botts, June 1, 1979; 1 child, Sarah Elizabeth; children by previous marraige: Cameron Dale, Joy Renee. AA, Hannibal LaGrange Coll., 1955; AB, Grand Canyon Coll., 1958; MEd, U. Mo., 1966, EdS, 1976, EdD, 1981. Ordained to ministry So. Bapt. Conv., 1955. Tchr. Centerview (Mo.) Pub. Scsh., 1958-59; min. Bethel Bapt. Ch., Kansas City, Mo., 1959-61; adminstr. Fiti'uta Manu'a Sch., Am. Samoa, 1966-68; cons. in fin. Mo. State Tchrs. Assn., Columbia, 1969-79; supt. schs. Midway Heights C-VII, Columbia, 1979-83; dir. elem. edn. Brentwood (Mo.) Pub. Schs., 1983-90; pres. Life Long Learning Sys. St. Louis, Mt. Vernon, Mo., 1989—; dir. clin. and field experiences in tchr. edn. Mo. So. State Coll., 1994—99. Pastor Patten Chapel and Miller (Mo.) United Meth. Chs., 1997-2001; assoc. pastor First United Meth. Ch., Mt. Vernon, Mo., 2002-03, Saint Paul's United Meth. Ch., Joplin, Mo., 2003-05, pastor emeritus, 2005—; founder, coord. Mo. Computer-Using Educators Conf., 1982-84; contbg. writer St. Louis Computing News,

1984-95; adj. asst. profl. ednl. studies U. Mo., St. Louis, 1986-90; adj. assoc. prof. grad. studies S.W. Bapt. U., 1991-98; cons. sch. fin., curriculum improvement. Contbr. articles to profl. jours. Mem. Columbia Am. Revolution Bicentennial Commn.; mem. edn. adv. com. Mo. Gov.'s Transition Team, 1992-93. Inst. Devel. Ednl. Activity fellow, 1969, 1978—84. Mem.: ACLU, ASCD (bd. dirs. 1984—90), Am. Assn. Ret. Persons, Mo. Ret. Tchrs. Assn., Nat. Middle Sch. Assn., Nat. Assn. Gifted Children, Assn. Childhood Edn. Internat., Rotary Internat., Phi Delta Kappa. Democrat. Home: 102 Rocky Cir Carl Junction MO 64834 Personal E-mail: cpulliam@mchsi.com.

**PULLIAM, LARRY G.,** food products executive; b. Grapevine, Tex. m. Cynthia Pulliam; 2 children. With a regional food svc. co., Ft. Worth, 1974—87, Sysco Corp., L.A., 1987—91, v.p. ops., 1991—95, exec. v.p., CEO Balt., 1995—97, v.p. cheif info. officer Houston, 1997—2000, pres., CEO 2000—02, sr. v.p. mdse. svcs., 2002—. Mem. dirs. coun. Sysco Corp.; bd. dirs. Capital Bank. Bd. dirs. End Hunger Network. Office: Sysco Corp 1390 Enclave Pky Houston TX 77077-2099

**PULLIAM, RENE E.,** performing arts educator; d. Louis H. and Florence Pulliam; m. Christopher J. Schager. MusB, Whittier Coll., Calif., 1974; MFA in Dance, Mills Coll., Oakland, Calif., 1992. Cert. assoc. Fitzmaurice voice tchr. 2006. Instr. Chabot Coll., Hayward, Calif., 1985—89; assoc. prof. U. Miss., University, 1993—. Mem.: Miss. Dance Assn. (pres. 1996—2001). Determination Party. Home: 20 County Rd 220 Oxford MS 38655 Office: Univ Miss Dept Theatre Arts Isom 110 University MS 38655 Business E-Mail: rpulliam@olemiss.edu.

**PULLIAM PLUMMER, JOYCE,** medical technician; Lab. tech., Brook Army Med. Army Sch., 1972—73. Lab. tech. quality control Technicon Corp., Middletown, Va., 1980—82; tech./limited x-ray Selma Med. Assoc., Winchester, Va., 1982—. Author poetry. With U.S. Army, 1972—80. Mem.: Am. Soc. for Clin. Lab. Sci., Am. Assn. Bioanalysts (assoc.). Avocations: poetry, painting, gardening, crafts. Home: PO Box 372 Stephens City VA 22655 Office: Selma Med Assoc Inc 104 Selma Dr Winchester VA 22601

**PULLIN, TANYA,** state representative; b. South Shore, Ky, Sept. 15, 1957; d. Norman Keith and Mildred Pauline (Williams) P. JD, Univ. of Ky., 1986; MA, Duke Univ., 1985; BS, Univ. of Ky., 1980. Bar: Ky., 1986, U.S. Ct. Appeals Fed. Cir. 1987. State Rep. House of Rep., Dist. 98, Ky., 2000—; employed Baker & McKenzie, Hong Kong, China, 1995—97, Deacons, Hong Kong, China, 1990—95, Morgan & Finnegan, 1986—90. Bd. dirs., State YMCA of Ky., Frankfort, 1987—. Toll fellow, 2002, Elliott fellow, 2003; recipient Law Day award, 2003. Mem. NY Soc. Ky. Women (treas. 1988—), Kentuckians NY (dinner chmn. 1989—), Rainbow Girls (majority mem.). Democrat. Office: Capitol Capitol Annex Rm 432C Frankfort KY 40601 also: Dist Rural Rt 1 PO Box 486 South Shore KY 41175

**PULLING, THOMAS LEFFINGWELL,** investment advisor; b. NYC, May 1, 1939; s. T.J. Edward and Lucy (Leffingwell) P.; m. Lisa Canby, Sept. 14, 1962 (div. 1968); children: Elizabeth, Edward L.; m. Sheila Sonne, Mar. 12, 1970 (div. 1980); children: Victoria, Diana, Christopher; m. Eileen Kingsbury-Smith, Dec. 21, 1989. BA cum laude, Princeton U., 1961. Asst. treas. J.P. Morgan & Co. Inc., N.Y.C., 1962-68; v.p. N.Y. Securities Co., N.Y.C., 1968-71, L.M. Rosenthal & Co., N.Y.C., 1971-76; mng. dir. Citigroup Asset Mgmt., N.Y.C., 1976—. Bd. dirs. Henry Luce Found., 1988—, Woodlawn Cemetery, 1980—; trustee Long Island U., 1995—. With USMC, 1962-67. Mem.: Coun. on Fgn. Rels., Pilgrims of U.S. (N.Y.C.), The Bohemian Club (San Francisco), The Brook Club (N.Y.C.), Univ. Club (N.Y.C.), La Gorce Country Club (Miami), Surf Club (Miami, Fla.), Piping Rock Club (Locust Valley, NY). Republican. Episcopalian.

**PULLMAN, ALAN,** architect; b. N.Y. BArch, Syracuse U. Registered arch., Calif. Design dir. MCG Arch., Beverly Hills Calif.; joined Perkowitz & Ruth, Long Beach, Calif., 1999, design dir. Studio One Eleven, 1999—, assoc. 2000—. Advisor Long Beach Village Arts Dist.; bd. mem. Lonb Beach Conservation Corp. Mem.: AIA, Smart Growth Network, Calif. Redevelopment Assn., Nat. Main St. Ctr., Urban Land Inst. Office: Studio One Eleven @ Perkowitz & Ruth 18th Fl 111 W Ocean Blvd Long Beach CA 90802

**PULLMAN, BILL,** actor; b. Hornell, NY, Dec. 17, 1953; m. Tamara Hurwitz, 1987; children: Maesa, Jack, Louis. BFA, SUNY, Oneonta; MFA, U. Mass., Amherst. Theatre instr. Mont. State U., Bozeman. Actor: (theatre) The Rover, 1981, Ah, Wilderness!, 1983, The Old Flag, 1983, Dramathon '84, 1984, Curse of the Starving Class, 1985, All My Sons, 1986, Barabbas, 1986, Nanawatai, 1986, Demon Wine, 1988, Control Freaks, 1993, The Subject Was Roses, 2006; (films) Ruthless People, 1986, Spaceballs, 1987, The Serpent and the Rainbow, 1988, Rocket Gibraltar, 1988, The Accidental Tourist, 1989, Cold Feet, 1989, Brain Dead, 1989, Sibling Rivalry, 1990, Going Under, 1991, Bright Angel, 1991, Newsies, 1992, A League of Their Own, 1992, Singles, 1992, Sommersby, 1993, Sleepless in Seattle, 1993, Malice, 1993, Mr. Jones, 1993, The Favor, 1994, Wyatt Earp, 1994, While You Were Sleeping, 1995, Casper, 1995, Mr. Wrong, 1996, Independence Day, 1996, Lost Highway, 1997, The End of Violence, 1997, The Thin Red Line, 1998, Brokedown Palace, 1998, Zero Effect, 1998, A Man is Mostly Water, 1999, History Is Made at Night, 1999, The Guilt, 1999, Brokedown Palace, 1999, Lake Placid, 1999, (voice) Coming to Light: Edward S. Curtis and the North American Indians, 2000, (voice) Titan A.E., 2000, Numbers, 2000, Ignition, 2001, Igby Goes Down, 2002, 29 Palms, 2002, Rick, 2003, The Grudge, 2004, The Orphan King, 2005, Dear Wendy, 2005, Scary Movie 4, 2006; (TV movies) Home Fires Burning, 1989, Crazy in Love, 1992, The Last Seduction, 1994, Mistrial, 1996, Merry Christmas George Bailey, 1997, The Virginian, 2000, Tiger Cruise, 2004; (TV series) Revelations, 2005-. Office: UTA care JJ Harris 9560 Wilshire Blvd Ste 500 Beverly Hills CA 90212-2427 also: Big Town Prodns Ste 80 6201 Sunset Blvd Los Angeles CA 90028-8704*

**PULLMAN, JENNIFER KING,** art educator, artist; d. John Lindsay King, Jr. and Leila Luening King; 1 child, Ian Thomas. BA, Stockton Coll. N.J., 1978; MA in Tchg., Marygrove Coll., 1999; postgrad., Walden U., 2002—. Cert. elem. educator N.J., art edn. N.J. Artist, interior designer, Pomona, NJ, 1978—, Egg Harbor, 1978—, McKee City, 1978—; tchr. kindergarten Our Lady of Sea Sch., Atlantic City, 1985—89; tchr. 3d grade Atlantic City Pub. Schs., 1989—93, educator art, 1993—. Leader curriculum task force Atlantic City Pub. Schs., 2001—02, new tchr. mentor, 1992—, advisor art club, 1993—. Contbg. editor: Jour. of Educational Practice and Social Change, 2006—. Recipient Govs. Recognition award, N.J. Edn. Dept., 1998, Recognition award, Atlantic City Edn. Found., 2006. Mem.: N.J. Art Educators Assn., Nat. Art Educators Assn., Galloway Cultural Arts Ctr., Noyes Mus. Art, Atlantic City Art Ctr., Phi Delta Kappa (v.p. programs 2004—). Avocations: interior decorating, singing, guitar, gardening, exercise. Home: 1306 W Amaranth St Egg Harbor City NJ 08215 Office: NY Ave Sch 411 N NY Ave Atlantic City NJ 08401 Office Phone: 609-343-7200. Personal E-mail: cyberhen@verizon.net.

**PULLMAN, MAYNARD EDWARD,** biochemist; b. Chgo., Oct. 26, 1927; s. Harry and Gertrude (Atlas) P.; m. E. Phyllis Light, Sept. 12, 1948; children: H. Cydney, B. Valerie, Jacky Leigh. BS, U. Ill., 1948, MS, 1950; PhD (NIH fellow), Johns Hopkins U., 1953. Fellow in pediatrics Johns Hopkins Hosp., 1953-54; asst. Pub. Health Rsch. Inst., City N.Y., 1954-56, assoc., 1956-61, assoc. mem., 1961-65, mem., 1965-89, chief, 1973-87, assoc. dir., 1983-89; sr. rsch. scientist Dept. Physicians and Surgeons Columbia U., 1989-92. Vis. prof. biochemistry U. São Paulo (Brazil) Sch. Medicine, 1963-64; research assoc. prof. biochemistry Sch. Medicine NYU, 1966-76, research prof., 1976-90; biochemistry study section mem. NIH, 1969-73. Editorial bd.: Jour. Biol. Chemistry, 1967-71, 78-80. NIH grantee, 1956-85; Shubert Found. grantee, 1972-74. Fellow N.Y. Acad. Scis.; mem. AAAS, Am. Soc. Biol. Chemistry and Molecular Biology, Brit. Biochem. Soc., Am. Chem. Soc. Home and Office: 338 Archer St Freeport NY 11520-4233 E-mail: mep2658@aol.com.

**PULLMAN, PHILIP NICHOLAS,** writer, educator; b. Norwich, Norfolk, Eng., Oct. 19, 1946; s. Alfred Outram and Audrey Evelyn (Merrifield) Pullman; m. Judith Speller, Aug. 15, 1970; children: James, Thomas. BA, Oxford U., l968. Tchr. Oxfordshire Edn. Authority, Oxford, Eng., 1972-88; lectr. Westminster Coll., Oxford, 1988-96. Author: Count Karlstein, 1982, The Ruby in the Smoke, 1987 (Best Book award Internat. Reading Assn., 1988), Shadow in the North, 1988, The Tiger in the Well, 1991, Spring-Heeled Jack, 1991, The Broken Bridge, 1992, The White Mercedes, 1993, The Subtle Knife, 1997, Clockwork or All Wound Up, 1998, I Was a Rat!, 1999, The Amber Spyglass, 2000 (Whitbread Book of Yr., 2001), The Golden Compass, 2001 (Guardian Children's Fiction award, 1996, Carnegie medal, 1996), Lyra's Oxford, 2003. Recipient Astrid Lindgren Meml. award lit., Govt. Sweden, 2005. Avocations: music, drawing.

**PULOS, VIRGINIA KATE,** actress, consultant; b. Dayton, Ohio, Oct. 12, 1947; d. James C. and Mary M. Pulos; m. Georgios S. Georgiou; 1 child, Kate Elizabeth Chiemingo. BFA in Music summa cum laude, U. Cin., 1970. Singer, actor Broadway, Off Broadway, Stock, Film, Regional Theatre, more, 1970-89; founder, pres. Ginny Pulos Comms., Inc., 1989—. Speech, media and tng. cons.; asst. prof comm. NYU Sch. Continuing and Prolf. Studies; speaker confs. in field. Actress: Portrait of Jenny (Eugene O'Neil award, Richard Rodgers award), regular appearances on TV shows: All My Children, As the World Turns, The Doctors, 1982-88; numerous major opera and musical theatre roles, including: (Broadway) A Little Night Music, (Regional) My Fair Lady, others, 1970—; numerous radio and TV commls., 1970-80; guest soloist: Bklyn. Kingsboro Symphony in the Parks, 1984, 85, others. Program chair The Matrix Awards, 1993, 95, 96, others. Named Corbett Found. Internat. Opera fellow, Hamburg, Germany, 1969, N.Y.C., 1970-77. Mem. SAG, Actors Equity Assn., Am. Fedn. TV and Radio Actors, Pub. Rels. Soc. Am. (pres.-elect internat. sect 2005), N.Y. Women in Comm. (bd. dirs. 1992-99). Office: Ginny Pulos Comms Inc 4th Fl 1120 Ave of the Americas New York NY 10036-6700 Office Phone: 212-626-6597. Business E-Mail: info@ginnypulos.com.

**PULS, ELAINE ALLISON,** retired librarian; b. Grand Junction, Colo., Mar. 14, 1927; d. Ross Edgar and Bertha Margaret (Johns) Allison; m. Gerald Eugene Puls, Sept. 18, 1949; children: Allen Dale, Theodore Joseph. AA, Mesa Jr. Coll., 1947; student, Western State Coll., 1947—48; BLS, U. Denver, 1949. Libr. Denver Pub. Libr., 1949—54; reading guidance libr. Fitzsimmons Army Hosp., Denver, 1954—56; libr. dir. Meeker Grade Sch., Colo., 1958, Rangely Coll. Libr., Colo., 1962—63; acquisitions libr. Colo. Gen. Hosp., Denver, 1963—65; libr. U. Wash., Seattle, 1965—66, VA Hosp. Libr., Seattle, 1965—66; libr. dir. Loveland Pub. Libr., Colo., 1968—89. Chmn. libr. sect. Colo. Mspl. League, 1971—72. Recipient scholarship to Western State Coll., Mesa Jr. Coll., 1947. Mem.: Colo. Libr. Assn. (Lifetime Achievement award 1989). Home: 1634 Weatherby Ln Pueblo CO 81008-1900

**PULSE, RONALD H.,** agricultural studies educator; s. Ronald, Sr. H. and Mary Ann P. Pulse; m. Linda F. Quist; children: Ronda L., Rachelle L. Zavatter, Grant M. BS, U. Wyo., 1972, MS, 1977. Lic. realtor Nat. Assn. Realtors, 1996. Tchr. Crook County Sch. Dist. #1, Hulett, Wyo., 1972—76; prof. Laramie Co. County C.C., Cheyenne, 1977. Advisor Wyo. FFA Assn., Cheyenne, 1985. Bd. dirs. First United Meth. Ch., Cheyenne, 2005—. Mem. NEA (assoc.). Methodist. Avocations: baseball coach, boy scout merit badge counselor, leather work. Office: Laramie County C C 1400 E College Dr Cheyenne WY 82007 Office Phone: 307-778-1192.

**PULSIFER, EDGAR DARLING,** retired leasing and sales company executive; b. Natick, Mass., Jan. 11, 1934; s. Howard George and Elvie Marion (Morris) P.; m. Alice Minarik, Feb. 16, 1957 (div. Oct. 1979); children: Mark Edgar, Audrey Carol, Lee Howard; m. Barbara Ann Chuhak, Apr. 19, 1980. BSEE, MIT, 1955. With sales and service dept. Beckman Instruments, Fullerton, Calif., 1956-59; regional sales mgr. Hewlett Packard, Palo Alto, Calif., 1959-72, Gen. Automation, Anaheim, Calif., 1973-74; exec. v.p. Systems Mktg., Elk Grove Vlg., Ill., 1975-79; pres. Consol. Funding, Mt. Prospect, Ill., 1979—. Served as 1st lt. U.S. Army, 1956. Mem. MENSA, Coast Guard Auxiliary. Clubs: North Shore Country (Glenview, Ill.). Republican. Episcopalian. Avocations: coins, stamps, curling, scuba diving, golf. Home and Office: Consol Funding Corp 3914 Dundee Rd Northbrook IL 60062 Personal E-mail: edpulsifer@comcast.net. Business E-Mail: consfunding@comcast.net.

**PULTE, DIANE MARIE,** music educator; b. Gainsville, Tex., Apr. 29, 1966; d. Robert Joseph and Coralee Fuhrman Pulte. Mus B, Univ. North Tex., Denton, 1989; Mus M, Southeastern La. Univ., Hammond, 1997; Mus D, Ohio State Univ., Columbus, 2005. Tchg. asst. Southeastern La. Univ., Hammond, 1996—98, Ohio State Univ., Columbus, 1998—2001; adj. prof. Muskingum Coll., New Concord, 2001—02, Kenyon Coll., Gambier, 2001—02, Otterbein Coll., Westerville, 2002—03; prof. music Tenn. Tech. Univ., Cookville, 2003—. Rsch. asst. Longitudinal Study Voice Range Profile, 2001. Recipient Margaret Speaks award, Ohio State univ., 2003. Mem.: Nat. Assn. Tchrs. Singing.

**PULTE, WILLIAM J.,** construction executive; Founder, pres. William J. Pulte, Inc., 1950—69; pres. Pulte Homes Corp. (formerly William J. Pulte, Inc.), 1969—, chmn. of exec. com. bd. 1972—90, chmn., 1991—99, 2001—. Named one of Forbes' Richest Americans, 2006. Office: Pulte Homes 100 Bloomfield Hills Pkwy Ste 300 Bloomfield Hills MI 48304*

**PUMARIEGA, ANDRES JULIO,** medical educator, researcher; b. Matanzas, Cuba, Jan. 25, 1953; came to U.S., 1962; s. Andrès Augustin and America Maria (Mechoso) P.; m. JoAnne Buttacavoli, Dec. 26, 1975; children: Christina Marie, Nicole Marie. BS, U. Miami, Coral Gables, Fla., 1973; MD, U. Miami, Fla., 1976. Resident in psychiatry Duke U., Durham, N.C., 1976-78, fellow in child psychiatry, 1978-80; dir. child psychiatry consultation/liaison svc. Vanderbilt U., Nashville, 1980-83; dir. pediat. psychiatry consultation/liaison svc. Tex. Children's Hosp. Baylor Coll. Medicine, Houston, 1983-86; dir. divsn. child adolescent psychiatry U. Tex. Med. Bd., Galveston, 1986-91, dir. residency program, 1987-92; prof. neuropsychiatry and behavioral scis. U. S.C., Columbia, 1992-96, dir. divsn. child and adolescent psychiatry, 1992-96, vice-chmn. dept. neuropsychiatry and behavior sci., 1994-96; assoc. dir. William S. Hall Psychiat. Inst., Columbia, 1992-96; prof. psychiatry and behavioral scis. East Tenn. State U., Johnson City, 1996—2006, chmn. dept. psychiatry and behavioral scis., 1996-2001, dir. divsn. child and adolescent psychiatry, 1996—2006, dir. Ctr. of Excellence Children in Custody, 2002—06; chmn. dept. psychiatry Reading Hosp. and Med. Ctr., 2006—; clin. prof. psychiatry Temple U., Phila., 2006—; chair dept. psychiatry Reading Hosp. and Med. Ctr., Pa., 2006—. Examiner in child psychiatry and gen. psychiatry Am. Bd. Psychiatry and Neurology, Chgo., 1983—; co-investigator, mem. exec. com. Ctr. Cross-Cultural Rsch., Galveston, 1989-91; chmn. rsch. com. and exec. bd. S.C. Pub. Acad. Mental Health Consortium, 1994-96; chair Nat. Latin Behavioral Work Group, 1995—2000; chair Hispanic panel managed care initiative Ctr. for Mental Health Svcs. Abuse and MH Adminstrn., 1996—2000; cons. Ctr. for Substance Abuse Treatment USPHS, 1995-96; mem. nat. adv. coun. Ctr. Mental Health Svcs., Substance Abuse and Mental Health Adminstrn. U.S. Dept. HHS, 1997-2001. Editor: (with H. Vance) Clinical Assessment of Child and Adolescent Behavior, 2001; (with N. Winters) Handbook of Child and Adolescent Systems of Care: The New Community Psychiatry, 2003; editor Psychline Jour. Hispanic Am. Psychiatry, 2005—; assoc. editor Child and Family Studies, 1996-2002, Am. Jour. Orthopschiatry, 2005-; contbr. over 150 articles, chpts., monographs, and over 150 abstracts to profl. jours. Bd. dirs. Tex. Network for Children, Austin, 1986-88; mem. adv. coun. Ptnrs. Advocacy Network, 1990-92. Named to Alumni Hall of Fame, U. Miami Sch. Medicine, 1999; recipient Exemplary Psychiatrist award, Nat. Alliance for Mentally Ill, 1993, 1997, cert. of merit for beneficiary svc., Health Care Fin. Adminstrn., U.S. Dept. HHS, 1996; grantee, Ctr. for Cross-Cultural Rsch., NIMH, Bethesda, Md., 1988—92, Fullerton Found., 1993—95; Minority Child Psychiatrist Tng. grant, NIMH,

1988—92, site coord., grantee, Nat. Assn. State Mental Health Dir. Rsch. Fellowship, 1993—, Forest Pharm., 2000. Fellow: Am. Psychiat. Assn. (disting.) (chair Hispanic com. 2006—, Simon Bolivar award 2004, Silver award outstanding svcs. 2004), Acad. Psychosomatic Medicine, Am. Acad. Child Psychiatry (chmn. work group on std. of care 1995—2001, chmn. cmty. psych. com. 2001—, Outstanding Mentor award 1990, Catchers in the Rye award 2001), Am. Acad. Pediat.; mem.: Am. Orthopsychiat. Assn. (bd. dir. 2004—), Tenn. Coun. Child and Adolescent Psychiatry (pres. 2000—16), S.C. Soc. Child and Adolescent Psychiatry (founding pres. 1996—97), Tex. Mental Health Assn. (mem. children's adv. com. 1991—92), Tenn. Soc. Child Psychiatry (sec. 1982—83, pres. 2001—06), Bay Area Pediat. Soc. (pres. 1990—91), Soc. Profs. of Child Psychiatry, Am. Assn. Cmty. Psychiatrists (bd. dir. 1996—2006, Ethics in Pub. Managed Care award 2000), Am. Coll. Psychiatrists, Nat. Mental Health Assn. (bd. dir. 1999). Roman Catholic. Avocations: swimming, political history, public affairs. Home: 27 Linree Ave Reading PA 19606-9075 Office: Reading Hosp & Med Ctr Dept Psychiatry Sixth Ave and Spruce St Reading PA 19611 Office Phone: 610-988-9318. E-mail: pumariega@aol.com.

**PUMARIEGA, JOANNE BUTTACAVOLI,** mathematics educator; b. Coral Gables, Fla., May 27, 1952; d. Ciro Charles and Rosaria Frances (Calabrese) Buttacavoli; m. Andres Julio Pumariega, Dec. 26, 1975; children: Christina Marie, Nicole Marie. BA in Math. and Edn. magna cum laude, U. Miami, 1973, MA in Math., 1974; postgrad., U. Houston, 1991-92. Cert. secondary math. tchr., Tex., Fla., Tenn., N.C. Grad. tchg. asst. U. Miami, Coral Gables, 1973-74; substitute tchr. Dade County Pub. Schs., Miami, 1975; math. instr. Miami Dade C.C., 1975-76; math. and G.E.D. instr. Durham (N.C.) Tech. Inst., 1976-77; math. instr. Durham H.S., 1977-78, Durham Acad., 1978-80, Univ. Sch. of Nashville, 1980-83; pvt. practice math. instr. Houston, 1984-86; tutor Clear Lake Tutoring Svc., Houston, 1987-90; pvt. practice, S.A.T, lang. instr. League City, Tex., 1990-92; pvt. practice math. and S.A.T. instr. Johnson City, Tenn., 1996—; lang. instr. Nelson Elem. Sch., Columbia, 1993-96. Instr. fgn. langs. and math. Lonnie B. Nelson Elem. Sch., Columbia, SC; faculty math. East Tenn. State U., 1999-2006, Pa. State-Berks., 2006—. Author (with F. Rodriguez and A. Pumariega): HIV/AIDS in Children and Adolescents, 1999; co-author (with A. Pumariega): Risk Factors of Mental Illness and Addiction Amongst Hispanic Immigrant Youth, 2002; contbr. articles to profl. jours. Chair bd. edn. St. Mary Parish, League City, 1988-90, lector, 1992, v.p. coun. Cath. Women, Johnson City, 1997-99; C.C.E. instr. St. John Neumann Cath. Ch., Columbia, SC & Johnson City, Tenn., 1993-95, lector, 1992-96; lector St. Mary's Ch., Johnson City, 1996—2006; treas. St. Thomas More Women's Club, Houston, 1985-86; v.p., then pres. housestaff med. wives Duke U., Durham, NC, 1978-80; mem. Wash./Unicoi/Johnson County Med. Alliance, 1999-2004, chair pub. rels. com., 1999-2002, asst. treas., 2002-03, membership chair, 2003-04, co-chair caring com., 2004-05, corr. sec., 2005-06; co-chair Am. Med. Assn., 2004-05. Recipient Above and Beyond award, East Tenn. State U., 2002. Mem. Newcomers of Greater Columbia (chmn. pub. rels. chpt. 1993,95), Newcomers of Greater Colo. (com. chair coord. 1994-95), Welcome Neighbors of Bay Area (v.p., program chmn. 1991-92), Tex. Med. Aux., Bay Area Med. Wives, East Tenn. State U. Women's Club (v.p. 1997-98, pres. 1998-99, parliamentarian 1999-2000), U. S.C. Faculty Women's Club (v.p. 1993-94, pres. 1994-95, parliamentarian advisor 1995-96), Phi Kappa Phi, Kappa Delta Pi, Delta Kappa Gamma (corr. sec. Gamma chpt. 2004-06), Alpha Lamba Delta (Woman of Yr. 1972). Roman Catholic. Avocations: reading, travel. Home: 27 Linree Ave Reading PA 19606-9075 Personal E-mail: pumarieg@verizon.net.

**PUNDMANN, ED JOHN, JR.,** automotive company executive; b. St. Charles, Mo., Feb. 24, 1939; s. Ed J. Sr. and Ruth O. (Brehme) P.; m. Dolores Anne Lienau, June 15, 1963 (dec.); children: Mary Ann, Steven A., Susan K. BA, Westminster Coll., 1961. Jr. accountant Peat, Marwick & Mitchell, St. Louis, 1961-62; salesman Pundmann Ford, St. Charles, 1962-82, gen. mgr., 1982-92, pres., 1992—. Bd. dirs., chmn. First State Bank; mem. St. Charles City Tax Incremental Financing Commn., 1990-99; mem. Ford Motor Dispute Settlement Bd., 1993-94, St. Charles County Work Force Devel. Bd., 2002-05, Ford Motor Co. Nat. Dealer Coun., 2001-03. Treas. St. Charles City Charter Commn., 1981; mem. St. Charles City Park Bd., 1981-82; chmn. St. Charles City Econ. Devel. Commn.; mem. St. Charles City Park Found. Bd., 1985—, also past pres.; St. Louis Regional Commerce and Growth Assn.; adv. bd. St. Charles County; mem. Handicapped Facilities Bd. St. Charles County, 1986-94, also past pres.; active St. Charles County Road Bd., 1996-2005; past pres. St. John United Ch. of Christ; bd. dirs. Emmaus Homes, 1981-91, Parkside Meadows Retirement Facility, 1982-2001; chmn. St. Charles City Charter Rev. Commn., 1991; bd. dirs. St. Charles Jaycee Village Retirement Home, 1980-90, Boone Ctr. Workshop, 1982-92, Parkside Found., 2001-, St. Charles City Schs. Found., 1995-2006, St. Charles Crime Stoppers, 1999—; dist. chmn. Boy Scouts Am., 1979-82. Recipient Gov. of Mo. award, 1989, Mo. Time Quality Dealer award, 1995, United Ch. of Christ award, 1993, Jefferson award TV Sta. KSDK, St. Louis, 1996, Profl. Excellence Achievement award St. Charles C.C., 2002. Mem. Mo. Auto Dealers Assn. (bd. dirs. 1983—, treas. 1997-98, 2d v.p. 1998-99, 1st v.p. 1999-2000, pres. 2000-2001), Greater St. Louis Ford Dealers Assn. (past pres.), St. Charles C. of C. (past bd. dirs., pres., Citizen of Yr. award 1986, Small Bus. Person of Yr. 2002), Rotary (past pres.). Lodges: Rotary. Home: 3304 Lennox Dr Saint Charles MO 63301-0632 Office: Pundmann Ford 2727 W Clay St Saint Charles MO 63301-2566 Business E-Mail: edp@pundmannford.com.

**PUNDT, RICHARD ARTHUR,** lawyer; b. Apr. 18, 1944; s. Arthur Herman and Johanna Celeste (Pasterik) Pundt; m. Joyce Kay Schoenfelder, Dec. 1, 1968; children: Vincent Arthur, Jennifer Johanna, Heather Ann. BA, State U. Iowa, 1966; JD, State U., 1969. Temporary claims dep. Iowa Employment Security Commn., 1968—69; admitted to Iowa bar, 1969; staff atty. Polk County Legal Aid Office Econ. Opportunity, 1969; spl. agt. FBI 1969—71; prin. Richard A. Pundt. Law Office; pres. and CEO enlighten techs., Inc. (IP video network); pres. Lawchek Ltd. Dir. Cedar Rapids Profl. Football Corp., 1972—73, pres., 1972—73. Exec. dir. Iowans for Rockefeller, 1968, Polk County Republican Com., 1968—69; mem. Linn County Rep. Ctrl. Com., 1972—78; chmn. Linn County Rep. party, 1977—78; asst. prosecuting atty. Linn County, 1972—76. Mem.: Linn County Bar Assn., Iowa Bar Assn., Am. Iowa Bar Assn., Metro Athletic Assn. (dir. 1976—), Sertoma. Roman Catholic. Home: 3851 Hickory Ridge Ln SE Cedar Rapids IA 52403-3765 Office: 330 1st St SE Cedar Rapids IA 52401-1702 Office Phone: 319-363-8800. Business E-Mail: rpundt@lawchek.net.

**PUNIELLO, FRANÇOISE SARA,** librarian; b. Boston, June 3, 1947; d. Solomon and Carmen Henriette (Bary) Lebovitz; m. Anthony John Puniello, June 27, 1970; children: Damian Alexander, Orin Timothy. BA, RI Coll., 1969; MLS, Rutgers U., 1970, MA in Art History, 1977. Audio visual cataloguer RI Dept. Libr. Svc., Providence, 1970-71; reference libr. Mabel Smith Douglass Libr. Rutgers U., New Brunswick, NJ, 1971—, assoc. dir., dir., 1987—97, assoc. dir., campus libr. 1997—2003, acting dir., campus libr., 2003—. Author: (books) Elsie Driggs in Past and Promise: Lives of New Jersey Women, 1990, Women Painters Born After 1900 in Women in the United States, 1990; co-author: Abstract Expressionist Women Painters: An Annotated Bibliography, 1996. Mem.: Lama, Bldgs. for Colls. and Univs., Am. Coun. Rsch. Librs., ALA (steering com. undergrad. libdrs. 1991—92). Home: 302 Harrison Ave Highland Park NJ 08904-1836 Office: Rutgers University Alexander Library 169 College Avenue New Brunswick NJ 08904 Office Phone: 732-932-7129 173. Business E-Mail: puniello@rci.rutgers.edu.

**PUNNOOSE, ALEX,** physics professor; b. Marika, Kerala, India, May 21, 1968; arrived in U.S., 1999; s. Punnoose Chacko and Mary Punnoose; m. Tina Kurian, Apr. 21, 1996; children: Catherine Alex, Paul Alex. BS, Mahatma Gandhi U., India, 1988; MS, Aligarh Muslim U., India, 1990, MPhil, 1992, D in physics, 1994. Lectr. in physics Mahatma Gandhi U., Kottayam, Kerala, 1994—97; postdoctoral rsch. assoc. W.Va. U., Morgantown, 1999—2002; asst. prof. of physics Boise State U., 2002—. Mem. of sci. com. and rev. bd. Internat. Cmty. for Composites Engring., New Orleans, 2002—; mem. awards and honors com. Boise State U., 2002—; presenter in field. Contbr. articles to profl. jours. Prayer leader St. Marks Cath. Ch., Boise, 2002—03. Mem.:

Asia-Pacific Electron Paramagnetic Resonance Soc. (founding mem.), Am. Phys. Soc., Internat. Electron Spin Resonance Soc. Achievements include discovery of ferromagnetism at room temperature in semiconducting Co doped Titanium Oxide; development of noval procedure to employ electron magnetic resonance to measure magnetic hysteresis of exchange coupled magnetic nanostructures employed in spintronic devices; research in catalysts, magnetic nanostructures, semiconductors, nanoparticles, and magnetic materials; new mechanism based on Four Spin Cyclic Exchange for high temperature superconductors. Office: Boise State U 1910 University Dr Boise ID 83725 E-mail: apunnoos@boisestate.edu

**PUNT, LEONARD CORNELIS,** educational services company executive; b. Bongondza, Zaire, Nov. 16, 1940; arrived in US, 1954, naturalized, 1960; s. Harry Marius and Clara VandeGevel Punt; m. Sarah Elizabeth Walton, Dec. 18, 1966; children: John, Amy, Brian. BA, Wheaton Coll., Ill., 1964; MEd, Loyola U., Chgo., 1981. Owner, dir. The Reading Tree Inc., Downers Grove, Ill., 1976—; v.p. Am. Bus. Comm., Downers Grove, 1978—. Contbr. articles to profl. jours.; author: Dyslexia: Definition and Solutions, 2005. Mem.: Naperville C. of C. Office: Reading Tree Inc 5117 Main St Ste D Downers Grove IL 60515-4654 Office Phone: 630-964-5444. E-mail: readingtree2@sbcglobal.net.

**PUNYANUNT-CARTER, NARISSRA,** communications educator; BA, Tex. Tech. U., 1995, MA, 1996; PhD, Kent State U., Ohio, 2000. Asst. prof. Tex. Tech U., Lubbock, 2002—. Recipient Tchr. of Yr. award nominee, Nat. Spkrs. Assn., 2005, Grad. Student Senate Dissertation award, Kent State U., Grad. Sch., 2003, Dissertation award, Kent State U., Sch. Comm., 2003, Rsch. award, 2002, Kent State U., Grad. Student Senate, 2002, Kent State U., Sch. of Comm. Studies, 2001, Summer Dissertation Fellow sScholarship, Kent State U., 2001, Leadership Excellence award, 2001, Outstanding Tchg. Asst. award, Internat. Comm. Assn., 2000. Mem.: Nat. Comm. Assn. Office: Texas Tech U Dept Comms PO Box 43083 Lubbock TX 79409-3083 E-mail: n.punyanunt@ttu.edu.

**PUNYASENA, MUNASINGHE ARACHCHIGE,** physicist, educator; b. Kirillawala, We. Province, Sri Lanka, Dec. 6, 1961; s. Ekmon Singho Munasinghe and Podihamine Konpiti Kankanamalage; m. Udeni Chandrika Munasinghe, May 23, 1997; children: Mayanthi Munasinghe, Nimanthi Munasinghe. BSc (hon.), U. Kelaniya, 1990; MSc, U. Alta., 1993, PhD, 1996. Cert. Phys. Scientist Inst. of Physics, Sri Lanka, 1997, Chartered Physicst Inst. of Physics, Sri Lanka, 1997. Demonstrator U. Kelaniya, We. Province, Sri Lanka, 1990—91, probationary lectr., 1991—96, sr. lectr. grade ii, 1996—2001, 2001—. Student councillor U. Kelaniya, 1998—2001, dep. chief student councillor, 2002—. Author: (book) Knowledge Dissemination; contbr. articles to profl. jours. Pres. Social Welfare Soc., Kirillawala, We. Province, Sri Lanka, 2003—05. 2d lt. Sri Lanka Navy, 1986—87. Scholar, Commonwealth Scholarship Commn., 1991. Mem.: Chief Examiner Panel (chief examiner 1999—2005), Inst. Physics Sri Lanka (life), Sri Lanka Assn. Advancement of Sci. (life). Buddhism. Achievements include development of Commissioning of a Magnetic Spectrometer at TRIUMF Laboratory in Canada to Measure Medium Energy Nuclear Reactions; discovery of Nuclear Pion Production Cross Sections have been measured for Five Different Nuclear Reactions using Medium Heavy Nuclear Targets and Polarized and Unpolarized Proton Beams at Medium Energies. Avocations: farming, camping, singing, watching tv. Home: Kirillawala Weboda 108/5 Sri Lanka Office: Univ Kelaniya Kandy Road Kelaniya WP 11600 Sri Lanka Office Phone: 94-011-2914495. Office Fax: 94-011-2911916. E-mail: sena@kln.ac.lk.

**PUOTINEN, ARTHUR EDWIN,** college president, minister; b. Crystal Falls, Mich., Sept. 7, 1941; s. Kaleva Weikko and Ines Pauline (Maki) P.; m. Judith Cathleen Kapoun, Aug. 8, 1964; children: Anne, Marjetta, Sara. AA, Suomi Coll., 1961; BA, Augustana Coll., Rock Island, Ill., 1963; MDiv, Luth. Sch. Theology, Chgo., 1967; MA, U. Chgo., 1969, PhD, 1973; MBA, Wake Forest U., 1984. Pastor Trinity Luth. Ch., Chgo., 1968-70; asst. prof. religion Cen. Mich. U., Mt. Pleasant, 1971-74; dean faculty Suomi Coll., Hancock, Mich., 1974-78; v.p. acad. affairs Lenoir-Rhyne Coll., Hickory, N.C., 1978-83; assoc. dean acad. affairs Roanoke Coll., Salem, Va., 1983-84; exec. dir. Luth. Ednl. Conf. of N.Am., Washington, 1984-88; pres. Grand View Coll., Des Moines, 1988-96; v.p. provost Finlandia U., Hancock, Mich., 1996—. Pastor ELCA No. Great Lakes Synod, Evang.-Luth. Ch. Am. Author: Finnish Radicals..., 1979; contbr. articles to books and jours. Grantee NEH, U.S. Dept. Democrat. Avocations: jogging, reading, travel. Home: 2885 Weld Rd Elgin IL 60123-8067

**PUPKIN, BARRY A.,** lawyer; b. Chgo., 1950; AB summa cum laude, Calif. State U. - San Diego, 1972; JD, Stanford U., 1975. Bar: Calif. 1976, DC 1976. Trial atty. Fed. Trade Commn., 1975—76; ptnr. Squire, Sanders & Dempsey LLP, Washington, chmn., Econ. Regulation Practice Group. Bd. adv. The Antitrust Counselor. Office: Squire Sanders & Dempsey LLP 1201 Pennsylvania Ave NW PO Box 407 Washington DC 20044-0407 Office Phone: 202-626-6662. Office Fax: 202-626-6780. Business E-mail: bpupkin@ssd.com.

**PURANDARE, YESHWANT K.,** chemistry educator, consultant; b. Poona, Purandare, India, Sept. 19, 1934; came to U.S., 1961; s. Kashinath Purandare and Indira Deshpande; m. Margarita Renella, Feb. 8, 1964; children: Sarita, Amar, Jasmine, Ravi. BS with honors, U. Bombay, 1956; MS, U. Poona, 1960, Fordham U., 1964; PhD, NYU, 1981; MD, Spartan Health Sci. U., St. Lucia, B.W.I., 1985. Cert. clin. lab. specialist; cert. lab. dir. Grad. teaching asst. Fergusson Coll., Poona, 1956-60; quality control chemist Sardesai Bros., Bilimora, India, 1960-61; part time clin. chemist Brunswick Hosp., Amityville, N.Y., 1965-81; instr. chemistry Coll. Tech., SUNY, Farmingdale, N.Y., 1964-67, asst. prof., 1967-69, assoc. prof., 1969-74, prof., 1974—2000, chmn. dept. chemistry, 1984—99 Cons Boat Life Industries Oil De__, __, 1906—. Author (manuals) Experiments in Physiol. Chemistry, 1985, Lecture Notes on Physiological Chemistry, 1986. Leader Boy Scouts of Am., 1974—. Mem. Am. Chem. Soc., Am. Assn. Clin. Chemistry (cert.), Am. Soc. Clin. Pathologists (cert. chemistry specialist), Rotary (Farmingdale pres. 1989-90, Paul Harris fellow 1992). Office: SUNY Coll Tech Chemistry Dept Lupton Hall Farmingdale NY 11735 Office Phone: 631-420-2221.

**PURCELL, AARON D.,** archivist, historian; b. Lexington, Ky., May 30, 1972; s. R.D. and Betty A. Purcell; m. Laura Stevralia Purcell, June 30, 2000; 1 child, Samuel Sullivan. BS in Edn., Cumberland Coll., 1994; MA in History, U. Louisville, 1996; MLS in Archives, U. Md., 1999; PhD in History, U. Tenn., 2006. Univ. archivist U. Tenn., Knoxville, 2000—. Grantee nat. leadership grantee, Inst. Mus. and Libr. Svcs., 2005—. Mem.: Soc. Am. Archivists. Office: Spl Collections Libr 1401 Cumberland Ave Knoxville TN 37996 Office Phone: 865-974-3674. Office Fax: 865-974-0560. E-mail: apurcel2@utk.edu.

**PURCELL, ANN RUSHING,** state legislator, human services manager; b. Reidsville, Ga., May 12, 1945; d. William Robert and Katie (Dasher) Rushing; m. Dent Wiley Purcell, May 26, 1966; children: Edwin Wiley, Mieke Ann, Mikki Marie. BS in Edn., Ga. So. Coll., 1966; degree (hon.), Ga. Future Farmers Am., 1999. Cert. secondary tchr. Tchr. math. Evans (Ga.) High Sch., 1966-68; tchr. math., earth and sci. Beaumont Jr. High Sch., Lexington, Ky., 1969-70; substitute tchr. Tallahassee, 1970's; agt. Noblin Realty, Tallahassee, 1970's; office mgr. Radiation Therapy Assocs., PC, Savannah, Ga., 1979—; state legislator Ho. of Reps. Ga. Gen. Assembly, Atlanta, 1991—2005. Author: Purcells of South Georgia and Other Related Families, 1976. Bd. dir. Med. Assn. Ga. Polit. Action Com., Atlanta, 1988-89, Girl Scout Coun. Savannah, 1991-93, Effingham YMCA, 1999-; Effingham County fin. chmn. State YMCA, 1991-05, vice chmn. steering com., 1999, bd. dir., 1999; bd. trustees Ga. So. Found., 1992—, Armstrong Atlantic U. Found., 2004-05, sec., 2005—; mem. adv. com. Effingham County Extension Svc., 1992—; chmn. steering com. Effingham YMCA Bd., 2004, 05, 06, chmn. fin. devel. 2005-; mem. adv. com. Treutlin Home, 1999-04; bd. adv. Claxton Youth Detention Ctr. Hon. comdr. 165th Ga. Air Guard Airlift,

1997-04; hon. mem. Civil Air Patrol, 2001-, Ga. State Patrol, 2001; state bd. mem. Ga. Dept. Tech. and Adult Edn., 2005-. Decorated WA-PO-HE award Ga. Nat. Air Guard, Minuteman award, Dept. Def. Commendatino medal; named Ga.'s Legislator of Yr., Ga. Sch. Counselors Assn., 1996, Ga. Legislator of Yr., Coastal Conservation Assn. Ga., 1998, Vol. of Yr., Effingham YMCA, 2006; named to Hon. Ga. State Patrol, 2001; recipient Friend of Medicine award, Med. Assn. Ga., 1991, 1993, 1994, 1996, Ga. Vet. award, 2003, Guardian of Small Bus. award, Nat. Fedn. Ind. Bus., 1992, 1994, 1996, Commendation cert., Ga. Emergency Mgmt. Agy., 1995, Vol. of Yr. award, Effingham 4-H, 1998, Nat. Am. hon. degree, Future Farmers Am., 1999, Friend of State 4-H award, 1999, Svc. award, Effingham Recreation Dept., 2000, Cmty. Svc. award, Guyton Masonic Lodge, 2000, Hon. Family Consumer Cmty. Leaders of Ga. award, 2001, Ga. Pub. Health award, 2003, Effingham Jr. Adv. Family Connection award, 2003, 2004, Environ. Leadership award, Ga. Conservation Voters, 2003, 2004, Pub. Rels. award, Ga. Ext. Assn. of Family and Consumer Scis., 2003, Leadership award, Ga. Water Coalition, 2003, 2004, Charles Dick award, U.S. Nat. Guard, 2003, Air Nat. Guardsmen award, Savannah Assn. Flying, 2003, City of Pembroke award, 2004, Bryan County Svc. award, 2004, Friend of Effingham 4-H award, 2005, Friends award, Ga. Med. Soc., 2005. Mem. Aux. to the Med. Assn. Ga. (pres. 1985), Aux. to the Ga. Med. Soc. (pres. 1981-82), Ga. Salzburger Soc. (bd. dirs. 2005, v.p. 2005-), Effingham County Pub. Ofcls. Assn., Rotary Internat. (Paul Harris fellow 2003), Ga. Peace Officers assn. (hon.), Rincon Noon Lions Club, Exch. Club. Republican. Methodist. Avocations: painting, genealogy, fishing. Home: 410 Willowpeg Way Rincon GA 31326-9157

**PURCELL, BILL,** mayor; b. Phila., Oct. 25, 1953; s. William Paxson Jr. and Mary (Hamilton) Purcell; m Deborah Lee Miller, Aug. 9, 1986; 1 child, Jesse Miller. AB, Hamilton Coll., 1976; JD, Vanderbilt U., 1979. Bar: Tenn. 1979, U.S. Ct. Appeals (6th cir.) 1985, U.S. Supreme Ct. 1988. Staff atty. W. Tenn. Legal Svcs., Jackson, 1979—81; asst. pub. defender Metro Pub. Defender, Nashville, 1981—84, sr. asst. pub. defender, 1984—85; assoc. Lionel R. Barrett, P.C., Nashville, 1985—86; ptnr. Farmer, Berry & Purcell, Nashville, 1986—90; mem. Tenn. Ho. of Reps., Nashville, 1986—96, also majority leader, 1990—96; dir. child and family policy ctr. Inst. Pub. Policy Studies, Vanderbilt U. Nashville, 1996—99; mayor Met. Govt. of Nashville and Davidson County, 1999—. Chmn. select com. on children and youth Tenn. Gen. Assembly, 1989—96; exec. dir. Vanderbilt Legal Aid Soc., 1978—79; chmn. NCSL Assembly State Issues, 1995; chmn. policy makers' program adv. bd. Danforth Found., 1993—2002; mem. adv. bd. U.S. Conf. Mayors, 2001—02, trustee, 2002—, chmn. task force hunger and homelessness, 2001—05. Vice chmn. Nat. League Cities, 2000—02, chmn. coun. youth, edn. and families, 2003—; chmn. human svcs. com. Nat. Conf. State Legislatures, Washington, 1993; mem. exec. com. Dem. Nat. Com., 1994—97; exec. com. 6th Dist. Dems., Nashville, 1986—88; mem. Tenn. State Gen. Assembly, Nashville, 1986—96, majority leader, 1990—96; chmn. Dem. Legis. Campaign Com., 1994—96. Named Legislator of Yr., Dist. Atty.'s Gen. Conf., 1989, Tenn. Conservation League, 1991; recipient Disting. Alumnus award, Vanderbilt Law Sch., 2004; Toll fellow, Coun. State Govts., 1988. Mem.: ABA, Nashville Bar Assn., Tenn. Bar Assn. Methodist. Office Phone: 615-862-6000. Office Fax: 615-862-6040. Business E-Mail: mayor@nashville.gov.

**PURCELL, BRADFORD MOORE,** publishing company executive; b. Garden City, N.Y., Oct. 1, 1929; s. William Lawrence and Margaret (Moore) P.; m. Louise Rauth, July 10, 1954; children: Margaret, Philip, Mark, Louisa, Christopher. BA, Williams Coll., 1951; MBA, Columbia U., 1957. Sr. v.p. devel. McGraw Hill, Inc., 1976-79, sr. v.p., 1979-81, group v.p. tng. systems, 1981-83, sr. v.p. mktg., 1983-85; pres. W.H. Smith Pubs Inc., N.Y.C., 1985-91; v.p. admin. and fin. Rsch. Books Inc., 1992. Served to 1st lt. USAF 1951-53. Home: 106 Tantumorantum Rd Lyme CT 06371-3137 Office: Rsch Books Inc PO Box 555 Old Saybrook CT 06475 E-mail: bradfordpurcell@yahoo.com.

**PURCELL, GEORGE RICHARD,** artist; b. Clayton, NY, May 4, 1921; s. George Thomas and Katherine Eileen (Eagan) P.; m. Mary Sutter, Apr. 3, 1961. BS, Niagara U., 1947; postgrad., Syracuse U., 1952-53, 55-56. With Eagan Real Estate, Syracuse, 1948-49; claims interviewer N.Y. State Divsn. Unemployment ins., 1949-50, 52; with U.S. Postal Svc., Syracuse, 1957—; cert. classifier of mails, 1975-77, with registry dept., 1977—. Tutor in philosophy, 1971—; mem. world peace and diplomacy forum Internat. Biog. Ctr., Cambridge, Eng., rsch. coun. Exhibited in Ctrl. NY Art Open, 1981, Drake Gallery, Fayetteville, NY, 1982, Assoc. Artists Gallery, Syracuse, 1983, 91, Fayetteville Art Festival, 1984, Recreation Generation Art Exhibit, 1982—, DeWitt (NY) Libr., 1986-94, NY State Fair, 1990, 99, Art Telauc WCNY-TV, Syracuse, 1990-01, Cazenovia Coll. Art Auction, 1994, Old Forge (NY) Art Show, 2005. Founder, pres. Syracuse chpt. Cath. Med. Mission Bd., 1973-76, rep., 1976—; del. Presdl. Trust, 1992; active Cath. Near-East Welfare Assn., Book Mission Program, New Mems. Art Show Manlius Libr., 1991, Rep. Nat. Com., Heritage Found., Washington; dep. dir. gen. Internat. Biog. Assn., Cambridge, Eng. Served with U.S. Army, 1943-46. Decorated capt. Legion of the Eagle of the Sea, Order of Holy Cross of Jerusalem, knight Order of Lofsensian Ursinius, baron Royal Order of Bohemian Crown, knight Holy Cross of Jerusalem-Grand Priory of US: named to Hall of Fame, Am. Biog. Inst., Raleigh, NC; NY State War Svc. scholar, 1955. Fellow: Australian Inst. Coordinated Rsch. (life); mem.: French Nat. Acad., Confedn. Chivalry (chevalier), Italian Acad. Arts and Scis., Order of Templar (knight), Sovereign and Mil. Order of the Holy Sepulcher (knight), Order Holy Grail (knight), Acad. of Ho. of Internat. Intellectuals, Cross of Gold, Albert Sweitzer Austrian Soc., Alliance Universal for Peace (hon. prof.), Inst. High Studies, World Jewish Congress, Am. Biog. Inst. (life assoc., rsch. bd. advisors nat. divsn., apptd. dep. dir., editl. adv. bd., nat. bd. advisors). Roman Catholic.

**PURCELL, JAMES NELSON, JR.,** cultural organization administrator; b. Nashville, July 16, 1938; s. James Nelson and Mary Helen P.; m. Walda Jean Primm, July 16, 1961; children: Deirdre Ann, Carole Elizabeth. BA in Polit. Sci., Furman U., 1961; M.P.A. (Maxwell Grad. Sch. fellow), Syracuse U., 1962. Mgmt. intern U.S. AEC, N.Y.C., Washington, Oak Ridge, 1962, budget analyst Oak Ridge, Washington, 1962-66; mgmt. analyst AID, State Dept., Washington, 1966-68; budget preparation specialist Office Mgmt. and Budget/Exec. Office of the Pres., 1968-69, dept. chief budget preparation, 1969-72, sr. budget examiner Internat. Ednl. Exch. program, 1972-74, chief Justice-Treasury br., 1974-76; chief resources programming and mgmt. div. Bur. Ednl. and Cultural Affairs, Dept. State, Washington, 1976-77; exec. dir. Bur. Adminstrn., Dept. State, Washington, 1978-79; dep. asst. sec. Bur. Refugee Programs, Dept. State, Washington 1979-82, dir., 1982-87; dir. gen. Internat. Orgn. for Migration, Geneva, 1988-98; internat. cons., 1998—; CEO Opine Pub., Columbia, Md., 2002—. Bd. dirs. Coun. for Cmty. of Democracies; sr. adv. Inst. for Study of Internat. Migration, Georgetown U. Mem. Am. Soc. Pub. Adminstrn. Home: 5113 W Running Brook Rd Columbia MD 21044 Office Phone: 443-745-2380. Personal E-mail: jpurcelatcol@comcast.net.

**PURCELL, JOHN F.,** lawyer; b. Bellingham, Wash., Apr. 25, 1954; AB with honors, Stanford U., 1976; JD, Lewis and Clark Coll., 1980. Bar: Oreg. 1980. Ptnr. Miller Nash LLP, Portland, 1987—. Mem. Oreg. State Bar. Office: Miller Nash LLP 111 SW 5th Ave Ste 3500 Portland OR 97204-3638 Office Phone: 503-224-5858.

**PURCELL, JOHN PATRICK, JR.,** writer, art educator; b. Chgo., Dec. 31, 1969; s. John Patrick and Vera Ann. B in English and Art cum laude, Colby Coll., Waterville, Maine, 1992; MS in Edn., U. So. Calif., L.A., 2003, EdD in Edn., 2006. Various artistic positions self-employed, 1992—97; tchr, visual art cons. Los Angeles Unified Sch. Dist., 1997—. Creative cons. pvt. practice, 2000—. Contbr. articles; musician: (songs) Should Have Known, High, 1994. Morris scholar, U. So. Calif., Rudolph and Hazel Hatton Endowed scholar. Mem.: Am. Edn. Rsch. Assn., Phi Delta Kappa (scholar, fellow 2004). Avocations: movies, music, art, writing, literature. E-mail: jpurcell@usc.edu.

**PURCELL, KAREN BARLAR,** naturopathic physician, nutritionist, opera singer, writer; b. Miami, Fla., Dec. 31, 1947; d. Raymond and Elita (Kitzmiller) Barlar; m. John A. Purcell, June 11, 1977 (div. Dec. 1986); 1 child, Carl; m. Roy Gene Autry Dec. 31, 1987 (dec. Mar. 2003). MusB, U. Cin., 1969; MusM, New Eng. Conservatory Music, Boston, 1971; postgrad., Bastyr U., Seattle, 1997-98; D in Naturopathy, Natural Health Acad. Healing Arts, Tenafly, NJ, 1991. Diplomate Am. Bd. Naturopathic Physicians, 1997, cert. master herbalist, Dallas; ordained to mninstry Progressive Universal Life Ch., 1998. Assoc. prof. U. Miami, 1974-77, Dade County Jr. Coll., Miami, 1974—77; pvt. practice, N.Y.C., 1990—. Assoc. prof. NYU, 1988-92, Strasberg Theater Inst., N.Y.C, NY, 1988-92, UN Internat. Sch., N.Y.C., 1992-96; star mgr. Nature's Sunshine Products; spkr. in field Author: Simplified Nutritional Handbook, 1996, How to Survive a Nuclear Disaster, 2002; opera singer, 1970—. Founder WINS Found. for Moderate to Severe Brain Disorders, 1999—. Mem. Am. Naturopathic Med. Assn., Internat. and Am. Assn. Clin. Nutritionists, Internat. and Am. Assn. Counselors and Therapists, Nat. Spkrs. Assn. Avocations: botany, cooking, travel. Office: 666 West End Ave Ste 15S New York NY 10025-7357 Office Phone: 212-580-3051.

**PURCELL, LEE (LEE JEUNE WILLIAMS),** actress, film producer; b. Cherry Point, NC, June 15, 1957; m. Alexander Sarenguevo, May 10, 1996 (div.); 1 child, Dylan D. Purcell. Studies with Margot Lister, London; studies with Milton Katselas, Jeff Corey, U.S. Pres., owner Silver Strand Entertainment, L.A., 1995—. Appeared in (films) Adam at 6 A.M., 1970, The Toy Factory, 1971, Dirty Little Billy, 1972, Kid Blue, 1973, Mr. Majestyk, 1974, Almost Summer, Big Wednesday, 1978, Stir Crazy, 1980, Valley Girl, Eddie Macon's Run, 1983, Laura's Dream, 1986, Airplane II, 1989, Trackers, 1990, Money & Murder, 1993, The Joke, 1994, Malaika, 1997, Dizzyland, 1998, The Unknown, 2003, (TV) Hijack, 1973, Stranger in Our House, 1978, Howard, The Amazing Mr. Hughes, 1979, Kenny Rogers as the Gambler, 1980, Killing At Hell's Gate, 1981, My Wicked Wicked Ways: The Legend of Errol Flynn, 1986, Betrayed by Innocence, 1989, Long Road Home (Emmy nominee Lead Actress-Special), 1991, To Heal a Nation, 1992, Dazzle, 1993, Secret Sins of the Father (Emmy nominee Supporting Actress-Special), 1994, Due South (recurring role), 1995-96, Promised Land, 1999, (stage) One Flew Over the Cuckoo's Nest, Richard III, A Streetcar Named Desire, The Taming of the Shrew, A Midsummer's Night Dream. Recipient Bronze Star Halo Career Achievement award So. Calif. Motion Picture Council, 1985, Golden Star Halo award, 1986, Silver Medal award N.Y. Film and TV Festival, 1987. Mem. Actors' Equity Assn., Screen Actors Guild, AFTRA, Acad. Motion Picture Arts and Scis., Acad. TV Arts And Scis. Avocations: writing, collecting antiques and art. Office: PO Box 12581 La Crescenta CA 91224-5581

**PURCELL, MARY HAMILTON,** speech educator; b. Ft. Worth; d. Josseph Hants and Letha (Gibson) Hamilton; m. William Paxson Purcell, Jr., Dec. 28, 1950; children: William Paxson III, David Hamilton. BA, Mary Hardin-Baylor Coll., 1947, HHD (hon.), 1986; MA, La. State U., 1948; HHD (hon.), U. New Eng., 2000. Instr. dept speech and dramatic arts Temple U., Phila., 1948-53, 60-61; part-time instr. speech Cushing Jr. Coll., Bryn Mawr, Pa., 1966-78. Pres. Pa. Program for Women and Girl Offend, 1968—73, Nether Providence Parent Tchr. Orgn., 1975—76; treas. Virginia Gildersleeve Internat. Fund U. Women, 1975—81, bd. dirs., 1987—93; mem. U.S. del. UN Commn. on Status of Women, 1996; co-chmn. NGO Com. for UNICEF, 1994—2000, mem. global forum, 2001—; mem. Wallingford-Swarthmore Dist. Sch. Bd., 1977—83; bd. dirs. Ministers and Missionaries Fund Am. Bapt. Conv., 1985—94, pres., 1995—2003, Internat. Baptist Church, 1986—; bd. dirs. Nat. Peace Inst. Found., 1983—86; Big Bros./Big Sisters of Am., 1985—90; bd. dirs. Citizens Crime Commn. of Phila., 1976—, Pa. Women's Campaign Fund, 1985—88, 1993—. Named Outstanding Alumna, Mary Hardin-Baylor Coll., 1972, Disting. Dau. Pa., 1982, v.p., 1994—95, pres., 1995—97, Woman of Yr., DECO Women's Corp., 1998; recipient Eleanor Schnurr award, UNA/USA. 2000. Mem. AAUW (Pa. state pres. 1968-70, v.p. mid. Atlantic region, 1973-77, program v.p. 1979-81, pres. 1981-85, rep. to UN 1985-89), Internat. Fedn. Univ. Women (1st v.p. 1986-89, pres. 1989-92, rep. to UN 1992-2005; pres. UN Dept. Pub. Info. Non Govt. Orgn. ann. conf. 1993), Speech Assn. Am. (Zeta Phi Eta award for excellence in comm. 1983), Pi Kappa Delta, Pi Gamma Mu, Delta Sigma Rho, Alpha Psi Omega, Alpha Chi. Democrat. Baptist. Home: 10 Willowbrook Ave Lansdowne PA 19050 E-mail: mjd1926@aol.com.

**PURCELL, MARY LOUISE GERLINGER,** retired adult education educator; b. Thief River Falls, Minn., July 17, 1923; d. Frank and Lajla (Dale) Gerlinger; m. Walter A. Kuyawski, June 9, 1950 (dec. July 1954); children: Amelia Allerton, Jon Allerton; m. Dale Purcell, Aug. 26, 1962 (dec. Nov. 2005). Student, Yankton Coll., 1941-45, Yale Div. Sch., 1949-50, NYU, 1949; MA, Columbia U., 1959, EdD, 1963. Teenage program dir. YWCA, New Haven, 1945-52; dir. program in family rels. Earlham Coll., Richmond, Ind., 1959-62, asst. prof. sociology and psychology, 1959-62, conf. coord. undergrad. edn. for women, 1962; chmn. divsn. home and cmty. Stephens Coll., Columbia, Mo., 1962-73, chmn. family and cmty. studies, 1962-78; dir. continuing edn. women Learning Unltd., 1974-78; prof. Auburn (Ala.) U., 1978-88, head dept. family and child devel., 1978-84, chmn. search com. for v.p. acad. affairs, 1984, spl. asst. to v.p. acad. affairs, 1985-86, prof. emerita, 1988—. Developer course, cons. Contemporary Am. Woman, 1962; vis. prof. Ind. U. Summer Sch, 1970; cons. student pers. svcs. Trenton (N.J.) State Coll., 1958—59, 1961. Contbr. articles to coll. bulls., jours. V.p. Falls Villate-Canaan Hist. Soc., 1998—2001, pres., 2002—. Recipient Alumni Achievement award, Yankton Coll., 1975; Alumni fellow, Tchrs. Coll. Columbia U., 1959. Mem.: AAUW, Nat. Coun. Family Rels., Groves Conf. Family (nat. program chmn. 1977, dir., chmn.-elect affiliated couns. 1981—82, chmn. 1982—84, chmn film awards chmn., chmn. spl. emphasis sect., bd. dirs.), Am. Home Econs. Assn. (bd. dirs. 1967-69, chair 1st subject matter unit 1969, family rels. and child devel. sect. 1986—89), Falls Village Can. Hist. Soc. (v.p. 1998—2001, pres. 2002—), Litchfield County Univ. Club (mem. scholarship com. 2001—, bd. dirs. 2001—), Housatonic Camera Club (co-pres. 1996—2000), Delta Kappa Gamma. Congregationalist. Home: 120 Belden St Falls Village CT 06031-1124 E-mail: mlgp@sbcglobal.net.

**PURCELL, PATRICK JOSEPH,** newspaper publisher; b. NYC, Nov. 9, 1947; s. Patrick Joseph and Sarah (Muller) P.; m. Maureen T. Shuart, Aug. 8, 1970; children: Kathleen, Erin, Patrick, Kerry. BBA, St. John's U., 1969; MBA, Hofstra U., 1977. Various supr. positions N.Y. Daily News, N.Y.C., 1969-80; assoc. pub. Village Voice, N.Y.C., 1980-82; v.p. advt. N.Y. Post, N.Y.C., 1982-83; v.p. sales and mktg. Skyband Inc., N.Y.C., 1983; pres., pub. Boston Herald, 1984—, owner, 1994—; pub. The N.Y. Post, 1986-88; exec. v.p. News Am./Newspapers, 1986-90, pres., 1990-93, CEO, 1993-94; East Coast pres. Am. Ireland Fund, 1996—. Bd. dirs. Bay Bank, MetroWest Sub. Regional Bd., The Genesis Fund. Bd. dirs. NCCJ, Boston, 1984-85, Cath. Charitable Bur., Boston, 1984-86, John F. Kennedy Found.; mem. Greater Boston Assn. Retarded Citizens, 1984-86; chmn. Boston Against Drugs, 1988—; mem. White House Conf. for a Drug Free Am., 1987. Mem. Boston Better Bus. Bur., Am. Newspaper Pub. Assn., New Eng. Newspaper Assn., Boston C. of C. (bd. dirs. 1984-86), Downtown Crossing Assn. (bd. dirs.) Clubs: Publicity, Ad (Boston). Roman Catholic. Avocations: jogging, skiing. Office: Boston Herald PO Box 55843 Boston MA 02205-5843

**PURCELL, PHILIP JAMES,** retired diversified financial services company executive; b. Salt Lake City, Sept. 5, 1943; m. Anne Marie Mc Namara, Apr. 2, 1964; 7 children. BBA, U. Notre Dame, 1964; M.Sc. in Econs., London Sch. Econs. and Polit. Sci., U. London, 1966; MBA, U. Chgo., 1967. Mng. dir., cons. McKinsey & Co., Inc., Chgo., 1967-78; sr. v.p. corp. planning and adminstrn. Sears, Roebuck and Co., Chgo., 1978-82; from pres., CEO, to chmn., CEO Dean Witter Discover & Co., N.Y.C., 1982-97; chmn., CEO Morgan Stanley (name changed from Morgan Stanley, Dean Witter & Co. 2002), N.Y.C., 1997—2005. Dir. N.Y. Stock Exch., 1995-96, AMR Corp., 2000-; mem. coun. U. Chgo. Grad. Sch. Bus. Trustee U. Notre Dame. With USNR. Mem. Econ. Club Chgo., Chgo. Club, Links. Roman Catholic.

**PURCELL, ROBERT HARRY,** virologist, researcher; b. Keokuk, Iowa, Dec. 19, 1935; s. Edward Harold and Elsie Thelma (Melzl) P.; children: David Edward, John Leslie. BA in Chemistry, Okla. State U., 1957; MS Biochemistry, Baylor U., 1960; MD, Duke U., 1962. Intern in pediatrics Duke U. Hosp., Durham, NC, 1962-63; officer USPHS, 1963; with Epidemic Intelligence Svc., Communicable Disease Ctr. Atlanta; assigned to vaccine br. Nat. Inst. Allergy and Infectious Diseases, Bethesda, Md., 1963-65; sr. surgeon Lab. Infectious Diseases, NIH, Bethesda, Md., 1965-69, med. officer, 1969-72, med. dir., 1972-74, head hepatitis viruses sect., 1974-2001, co-chief, 2001—. Organizer, invited participant, speaker numerous nat. and internat. symposia, confs., workshops, meetings; temporary advisor WHO, 1967—; expert cons. in hepatitis U.S.—China, U.S.—Taiwan, U.S.—Japan, U.S.—Russia, U.S.—India, U.S.—Pakistan Bilateral Sci. Agreements; lectr. various virology classes. Reviewer numerous sci. jours.; contbr. 700 articles to profl. jours., chpts. to books; 40 patents in field. Recipient Superior Svc. award USPHS, 1972, Meritorious Svc. medal USPHS, 1974, Gorgas medal, 1977, Disting. Svc. medal USPHS, 1978, Disting. Alumni award Duke U. Sch. Medicine, 1978, Eppinger prize 5th Internat. FALK Symposium on Virus and Liver, Switzerland, 1979, Medal of City of Turin, Italy, 1983, Gold medal Can. Liver Found., 1984, King Faisal Internat. prize for Medicine, 1998, Rsch. Sci. award Hepatitis Found. Internats., 1999; named to Alumni Hall of Fame East Okla. State Coll., 1996. Fellow AAAS, Washington Acad. Scis., Am. Acad. Microbiology, Molecular Medicine Soc.; mem. Am. Epidemiology Soc., Am. Soc. Microbiology, Am. Soc. Virology, Soc. Epidemiol. Rsch., Infectious Diseases Soc. Am. (Squibb award 1980), N.Y. Acad. Scis., Am. Soc. Clin. Investigation, Assn. Am. Physicians, Am. Coll. Epidemiology, Am. Assn. Study of Liver Diseases (Disting. Achievement award 2000), Internat. Assn. Study and Prevention Virus Associated Cancers, Internat. Assn. Biol. Standardization, Internat. Assn. Study Liver, Soc. Exptl. Biology and Medicine (Disting. Scientist award 1986), Nat. Acad. Scis. (Washington chpt.). Office: NIH Lab Infectious Diseases 50 S Dr MSC 8009 Rm 6523 Bethesda MD 20892-8009 Office Phone: 301-496-5090. Business E-Mail: rpurcell@niaid.nih.gov.

**PURCELL, STEVEN RICHARD,** international management consultant, engineer, economist; B of Mech. and Indsl. Engring., NYU Coll. Engring., 1950; MS in Indsl. Engring., Columbia U., 1951; EdM, Harvard U., 1968. Registered profl. engr., Can. Lectr. engring. NYU Coll. Engring., N.Y.C., 1948-50; gen. mgr. Dapol Plastics Co., Inc., Boston, 1956-58; gen. div. mgr. Am. Cyanamid Co., Sanford, Maine, 1958-61; sr. prin., mgmt. cons. investment banking Purcell & Assocs., N.Y.C., 1961-66; prof., chmn. Bristol Coll., Fall River, Mass., 1966-68; assoc. dean grad. faculty adminstrv. studies York U., Toronto, Ont., Can., 1969-71; chief economist Dept. Manpower and Immigration, Ottawa, Ont., Can., 1970-71; cons. Treasury Bd., Ottawa, 1971-72; dir. urban and internat. environ. policy Ministry of State for Urban Affairs Internat. Activities, Ottawa, 1973-74; mem. com. on challenges of modern soc. NATO, Ottawa, 1973-74; mem. sci., econ. policy com. OECD UN, Ottawa, 1973-74; prof. Grad. Sch. Bus. Adminstrn. and Econs. Algonquin Coll., Ottawa, 1974-76; advisor, cons. House of Commons, 1976-77; sr. prin. Purcell & Assocs., Internat. Mgmt. Cons., Washington, 1977-80; chmn., CEO, 1981—, Phoenix Internat. Capital Associates, Washington, 1981—; exec. dir. nat. coastal zone mgmt. adv. com. NOAA U.S. Dept. Commerce, Washington, 1980-81. Profl. lectr. Northeastern U. Grad. Sch. Bus. Adminstrn., Boston, 1953-56, U. Toronto, 1968-69, George Washington U. Grad. Sch. Bus. Adminstrn., Washington, 1979; vis. prof. Rensselaer Poly. Inst. Advanced Mgmt. Program, 1967, U. Ottawa Grad. Sch. Bus. Adminstrn., 1971-74; lectr. Council for Internat. Progress in Mgmt., N.Y.C., 1960, Royal Bank Can. Mgmt. Assn., Toronto, Ont., 1970; corp. appointment cons. Harvard U., Cambridge, Mass., 1967-68; cons. Govt. Venezuela, 1967-68, Can. Inst. Bankers, Toronto, 1969-70; internat. sr. adviser NASA, 1985-86, mem. nat. adv. bd. Ctr. for Nat. Policy; dir. Rental Resource Corp., 1986-89. Contbr. articles on indsl. orgn., sci. policy and fin. to profl. jours. Lt. AC, USNR, 1943-46. Mem. UN Assn. Soc. for Advancement of Mgmt. (pres. 1949-50, leadership award 1950), Tau Beta Pi, Alpha Pi Mu (v.p. 1949-50), Columbia Univ. Club (Washington, trustee 1982-84, chmn., sr. trustee 1984-85), Harvard Univ. Club. Office: PO Box 2928 Petaluma CA 94953-2928

**PURCHASE-OWENS, FRANCENA,** marketing professional, consultant, educator; b. Milw., Nov. 14, 1960; d. Johnny Purchase Sr. and Arlene (Roberts) Pleas Brown. Cert., Mich. Profl. Sch. Modeling, 1980; AA cum laude, Bryant Stratton Coll., 1982; BS in Applied Liberal Studies, Western Mich. U., 1997, M in Ednl. Leadership, cum laude, 2004; MBA, U. Phoenix, Grand Rapids, Mich., 2006. Various office/clerical positions, 1972—84; investment mgmt. sec. M&I Bank, Milw., 1984-85; cons. United Devel. Corp., Milw., 1986-88; paraprofessional Grand Rapids (Mich.) Pub. Schs., 1990-92; temp. helper Dayton Hudson, Grand Rapids, Mich., 1990; customer svc. rep. Kent County Conv. and Visitors Bur., Grand Rapids, 1995; mktg. rschr. Wirthlin Worldwide, Grand Rapids, 1996-98; pres. Creative Works, Grand Rapids, 1988—, Francena Purchase Internat. Honor Soc., Grand Rapids, 1999—, Francena Purchase Internat. Applied Studies, 1999—, Francena Purchase Internat. Applied Profl. Studies Soc., 2000—, cons.; pres. Purchase Bus. Inst., Kentwood, 1999—; cons. Urban Bus. X-Change, Grand Rapids, 2005—; adminstrv. asst. to Elizabeth Kubler-Ross Ga. State U., 1980. Sec. Mich. Nat. Bank, Grand Rapids, 1980-81, Volt. Tech. Svcs., Milw., 1980; asst. exec. sec. Manpower Internat. Inc., Milw., 1982-84; cons. NASW; sec., cons. United Devel. Corp; human resource asst., computer programmer, sec., Patricia Stevens Coll., Milw., 1985-86; asst. to pres. Alissia Cosmetics, Miss Black Pageant, 1980; legal sec. to atty. David Clowers, Milw., 1980; student asst. gerontology dept., Ga. State U., Atlanta, 1980; student asst. main office, Ottawa Hills H.S., Grand Rapids, 1976-77; mem. contract divsn. Fed. Govt., Grand Rapids, 1977-78; grad. student adv. bd. Western Mich. U., Kalamazoo, 2000; mem. Nat. Honor Soc. Iroquois Mid. Sch., 1974-75, Grand Rapids, Ottawa Hills H.S., 1976-79; cons. in field. Co-editor: Smoke Signal, 1975; contbr. articles to profl. jours. Vol. United Way, Grand Rapids, 1990, TV (GVSU-TV) fundraiser, vol. Grand Valley State U.; vol. Cmty. Media Ctr. (GRTV), Cmty. Media Ctr. Scholarships; reading condr. S.E. Neighborhood Assn., Grand Rapids, 1990, Cmty. Media Ctr., GRTV; mem. literacy coun. Kent County Literacy Coun., Grand Rapids, 1991—, task force Dwelling Pl., Grand Rapids, 1999, First Call Help United Way, Grand Rapids, 1992; model Miss J. Fashion bd. Jacobson's Dept. store, East Grand Rapids Mich., 1979; finalist Miss Black Wis. pageant, Milw., 1981; bd. dirs. Program and Quality Com., Pers. Com., Fin. Com., Consumer Adv. bd., Touchstone innovaré mental health, Grand Rapids, 2000—, Kent County Cmty. Mental Health, 1999—; mem. Task Force Herkimer Apartment Projects, Weston Apartments Dwelling place of Grand Rapids, 1999; reading program asst. S.E. End Neigborhood Assn., Grand Rapids, 1993, mem. exec. bd. dirs, 2006; rehab. asst. Kent Comty. Hosp. Complex, Grand Rapids, 1991; intake asst. Baxter Comty. Ctr., Grand Rapids, 1989; tutor Kent County Literacy Coun., Grand Rapids, 1988; facilitator trainer Employers Coalition for Healing Racism, Grand Rapids, 1997, Citizens Cirs. Resource Ctr., Grand Rapids, 1998, Ptnrs. in Pub. Edn., Grand Rapids, 1999, United Way Champions of Diversity, Grand Rapids, 1999; project help tutor Iroquois Mid. Sch., Grand Rapids, 1975; student tutor Washington Elem., Kalamazoo, 1974; fundraiser Spl. Olympics Office Edn. Assn. Ottawa Hills HS, 1978; exec. bd. dirs., asst. sec. First Missionary Bapt. Ch., 2005—; chair cmty. investment coun. United Way, 2006—; pastors asst. First Missionary Bapt. Ch., Grand Rapids, 2005—; vol. Cancer Soc. Recipient Creative Writing award, 1975, Shorthand award Ottawa Hills HS, 1979, Shorthand awards Milw. Stratton Coll., 1981-82, Century award, 1982, Machine Transcription award Milw. Area Tech. Coll., 1981; Phillip Morris scholar Alverno Coll., 1981; Nontraditional Student grantee Western Mich. U., 1994, 00, Thurgood Marshall Profl. Tuition grantee; Thurgood Marshall Assistanship scholar Western Mich. U.1989, 1998; 1st place spkr., 3rd place typist and secretarial job application Office Edn. Assn. Extemporaneous Speaking; 1st Pl. with Letter of Recognition from Senator Berger of Wis. Milw. Area Tech. Coll., 1981; Internat. finalist theatre arts, Milw., 1986; others. Mem.: Parkinson's Assn., Alzheimer's Assn., Western Mich. U. Alumni, Phi Lambda Theta. Avocations: modern dancing, reading, tennis. Address: PO Box 7421 Grand Rapids MI 49510-7421

**PURCIFULL, DAN ELWOOD,** retired plant virologist, retired educator; b. Woodland, Calif., July 1, 1935; s. Ernest Lee and Virginia (Margaroli) P.; m. Marcia Ann Weatherby, Sept. 7, 1966; children: Scott, Douglas. BS, U. Calif., Davis, 1957, MS, 1959, PhD, 1964. Asst. prof. plant pathology U. Fla., Gainesville, 1964-69, assoc. prof., 1969-75, prof., 1975-99, prof. emeritus, 2000—; ret., 2000. Plant virus subcom. Internat. Com. for Taxonomy of Viruses, 1973-75, mem. potyvirus study group, 1987-93; mem. plant virology adv. com. Am. Type Culture Collection, 1993-99; mem. Internat. Legume Virus Working Group, 1999. Assoc. editor Phytopathology, 1971-73, Plant Disease, 1987-89; contbr. articles to profl. jours. Mem. Morningside Nature Center Commn., City of Gainesville, 1978-81, treas., 1981. With U.S. Army, 1957. Fellow AAAS, Am. Phytopathol. Soc. (Lee Hutchins award 1981, Ruth Allen award 1992); mem. Fla. State Hort. Soc., N.Y. Acad. Sci., Am. Soc. Virology, Phytopathol. Soc. Japan, Brazilian Phytopathol. Soc., Australasian Plant Pathology Soc., U.S. Golf Assn., Nat. Wildlife Fedn. (assoc.), The Nature Conservancy, Nat. Geographic Soc., Smithsonian Instn. (assoc.), Sigma Xi, Gamma Sigma Delta. Home: 3106 NW 1st Ave Gainesville FL 32607-2504 Personal E-mail: depurc@aol.com.

**PURCIFULL, ROBERT OTIS,** insurance company executive; b. Grinnell, Iowa, July 1, 1932; s. Chauncey O. and Mildred E. (Clendenen) P.; m. Mary G. White, Sept. 12, 1953; children: Jane, Robert Otis, Patricia, Elizabeth. BA, Grinnell Coll., 1954. C.L.U. With Occidental Life Ins. Co., Calif., 1960-78, 1st. v.p. charge agys. Los Angeles, 1968-71, exec. v.p. sales, 1971-76; pres., chief exec. officer Transmerica Ins. Mgmt., Inc., Los Angeles, 1972-78; Countrywide Life Ins. Co., Los Angeles, 1973-76, dir., 1973-78; chmn. bd., pres. Plaza Ins. Sales Inc., San Francisco; pres., chief exec. officer Occidental Life of Can., 1977-78; pres., chief operating officer, dir. Penn Mut. Life Ins. Co., Phila., 1979-80. Sr. v.p. life divsn. Am. Gen. Corp., 1981-82; pres. Lincoln Am. Life Ins. Co., Am. Gen. Life Ins. Co. Del., Am. Gen. Life Ins. Co. Tex., Am. Amicable Life Ins. Co., Pioneer Am., 1982-84; vice chmn. Pioneer Security Life Ins. Co., 1982-84; pres., CEO Gulf Life Ins. Co., Interstate Fire Co., Jacksonville, Fla., 1984-88, also dir.; pres. Am. Gen. Group Ins. Co. Fla., 1986-89; vice chmn. Gulf Life Ins. Co., 1988-91; chmn., CEO ROP & Assocs. Past pres. Vols. of Am., LA; trustee Life Underwriters Tng. Coun., Washington, 1975—78; campaign chmn. Jacksonville United Way, 1988, 1989, chmn., 1989—90; pres. Jacksonville U. Coun., 1992, 1993, Jacksonville Symphony Orch., 1993—94; chmn. bus. adv. coun. U. North Fla.; councilman City of Upper Arlington, Ohio, 1962—66; chmn. Conservative Order for Good Govt., San Diego County, Calif., 2001. Mem. Life Ins. Mktg. and Rsch. Assn. (bd. dirs. 1982-85). Home: 12285 Fairway Pointe Row San Diego CA 92128-3230 E-mail: Purcifull@aol.com.

**PURDES, ALICE MARIE,** retired adult education educator; b. St. Louis, Jan. 8, 1931; d. Joseph Louis and Angeline Cecilia (Mozier) P. AA, Belleville Area Coll., 1951; BS, Ill. State U., Normal, 1953, MS, 1954; cert., Sorbonne U., Paris, 1964; PhD, Fla. State U., Tallahassee, 1976. Cert. in music edn., elem. edn., secondary edn., adult edn. Tchg. and grad. asst. Ill. State U., 1953-54; music supr. Princeton (Ill.) Pub. Schs., 1954-55; music dir. Venice (Ill.) Pub. Schs., 1955-72, secondary vocal music dir., 1955-72; coord. literacy program Venice-Lincoln Tech. Ctr., 1983-86, chmn. lang. arts dept., 1983-96; ret., 1996. Tchr. in space candidate, 1985. Mem. St. Louis chpt. World Affairs Coun., UN Assn., Nat. Mus. of Women in the Arts, Humane Soc. of Am.; charter mem. St. Louis Sci. Ctr., Harry S. Truman Inst.; contbr. Old Six Mile Mus., 1981, Midland Repertory Players, Alton, Ill., 1991; chair Cystic Fibrosis Spring Bike-A-Thon, Madison, Ill., 1981, Granite City, Ill., 1985. Named to Ill. Sr. Hall of Fame, 2001, Gov's Sr. Hall of Fame, 2001; recipient Gold medal, Nat. Senior Olympics, 1989, 600 others, Sr. World Games, Generations of Success Alumni award, Belleville Area Coll., 1998, several scholarships. Mem.: AAUW, Am. Fedn. Tchrs. (pres. 1957—58), Ill. Adult and Continuing Educators Assn., Am. Choral Dirs. Assn., Ill. Music Educators Assn. (exec. award 2002), Music Educators Nat. Conf., Ill. State U. Alumni Assn., Slavic and East European Friends (life), Fla. State Alumni Assn., Lovejoy Libr. Friends, Nat. Space Soc., Western Cath. Union, Croatian Fraternal Union, St. Louis Numis. Assn., Friends St. Louis Art Mus., Archaeol. Inst. Am., Travelers Abroad (pres. 1966—68, 1989—), Madison Rotary Club (internat. amb., Humanitarian award 1975). Roman Catholic. Avocations: bowling, travel. Home: 1610 4th St Madison IL 62060

**PURDOM, PAUL WALTON, JR.,** computer scientist; b. Atlanta, Apr. 5, 1940; s. Paul Walton and Bettie (Miller) P.; m. Donna Armstrong; children: Barbara, Linda, Paul BS, Calif. Inst. Tech., 1961, MS, 1962, PhD, 1966. Asst. prof. computer sci. U. Wis.-Madison, 1965-70, asst. prof., 1970-71; mem. tech. staff Bell Telephone Labs., Naperville, Ill., 1970-71; assoc. prof., chmn. computer sci. dept. Ind. U., Bloomington, 1977-82, prof. computer sci., 1982—. Grant researcher FAW, Ulm, Germany. Author: (with Cynthia Brown) The Analysis of Algorithms; assoc. editor: Computer Surveys; contbr. articles to profl. jours. NSF grantee, 1979, 81, 83, 92, 94. Mem. AAAS, Soc. for Indsl. and Applied Math., Assn. Computing Machinery, Sigma Xi. Democrat. Methodist. Home: 2212 S Belhaven Ct Bloomington IN 47401-6803 Office: Ind U Dept Computer Science 215 Lindley Hall Bloomington IN 47405-4101 Office Phone: 812-855-1501. Business E-Mail: pwp@cs.indiana.edu.

**PURDOM, THOMAS JAMES,** lawyer; b. Seymour, Tex., Apr. 7, 1937; s. Thomas Exer and Juanita Florida (Kuykendall) P.; m. Betty Marie Shoemaker, May 31, 1969; 1 son, James Robert. Student, U. Syracuse, 1956—57, U. Md., 1958—59; BA, Tex. Tech. Coll., 1962; JD, Georgetown U., 1966. Bar: Tex. 1966, U.S. Supreme Ct. 1978, U.S. Ct. Appeals (5th cir.) 1983. Ptnr. Griffith & Purdom, Lubbock, Tex., 1966-67; asst. dist. atty. 72d Jud. Dist., Lubbock, 1967-68; county atty. Lubbock County, Tex., 1968-72; pres. Purdom Law Offices, P.C., Lubbock, 1972—. Mem. com. for 5 pattern jury charges, 1988-97. Author: West's Texas Forms Vols. 16, 17, 18, 1984-96, Family Law, Texas Practice and Procedure, 1981. Served with USAF, 1956-60. Recipient Sam Emison award Tex. Acad. Family Law Specialists, 2000. Fellow Tex. Bar Found.; mem. ABA, Lubbock County Bar Assn. (bd. dirs. 1970, Disting. Sr. Lawyer award 2000), State Bar Assn. Tex. (sec. family law sect. 1974-75, chmn. family law sect. 1975-76, mem. examining commn. for family law specialization), Am. Acad. Matrimonial Lawyers (cert. family law, Tex. bd. legal specialization), Delta Theta Phi. Democrat. Baptist. Home: 3619 55th St Lubbock TX 79413-4713 Office: Purdom Law Offices PC 3619 55th St Lubbock TX 79413-5713 E-mail: purdom6@aol.com.

**PURDY, ALAN HARRIS,** biomedical engineer; b. Mt. Clemens, Mich., Dec. 13, 1923; s. Harry Martin and Elinor (Harris) P.; m. Anna Elizabeth Sohn, Aug. 16, 1968 (dec.); children: Catherine, Charles, Susan, Harry; m. Margaret Josephine Kelley, Mar. 5, 1997. BSME, U. Miami, 1954; MS in Physiology, UCLA, 1967; PhD in Engring., U. Mo., 1970. Cert. clin. engr., Washington. Project engr. in acoustics Arvin Industries, Columbus, Ind., 1954-56, AC Spark Plug Co., Flint, Mich., 1956-60; asst. prof. engring. Calif. Poly. U., Pomona, 1960-62; assoc. dir. biomed. engring. U. Mo., Columbia, 1967-71; dep. assoc. dir., assoc. dir. Nat. Inst. for Occupational Safety and Health, Rockville, Md., 1971-81, scientist, biomed. engr. Cin., 1983-86; asst. dir. Fla. Inst. Oceanography, St. Petersburg, 1981-83; pres. Alpha Beta R & D Corp., San Marcos, Calif., 1986—. Cons. Smithy Muffler Corp., L.A., 1961-62, Statham Instruments, L.A., 1966; cons. faculty, Tex. Tech. U., Lubbock, 1972-73; lectr. U. Cin., 1980. Patentee in diving, acoustical and occupational safety fields. Pilot CG Aux., 1989-98. With USAF, 1942-43. Nat. Heart Inst. spl. fellow, 1963-67; Fulbright scholar, Yugoslavia, 1984. Mem. Acoustical Soc. Am., Biomed. Engring. Soc., Am. Inst. Physics, Exptl. Aircraft Assn., Aircraft Owners and Pilots Assn., DAV. Democrat. Home and Office: 941 Cycad Dr San Marcos CA 92078-5013 E-mail: ahpurdy@nethere.com.

**PURDY, DAVID LAWRENCE,** medical products executive; b. N.Y.C., Sept. 18, 1928; s. Earl and Mabel (Roberts) Purdy; m. Margaret Anne Rye, July 7, 1951; children: Susan Lee, John F.(dec.), Ross David(dec.), Thomas Griffith. BME, Cornell U., 1951; degree in advanced & creative engring., GE, 1955, degree in profl. bus. mgmt., 1956. Devel. engr. GE, Valley Forge, Pa., 1953—64; mgr. energy conversion divsn. Nuc. Materials and Equipment Corp. (acquired by ARCO), Apollo, Pa., 1964—69, Atlantic Richfield Corp., Apollo, 1969—72; founder, pres., chmn. Biocontrol Tech., Inc., Indiana, Pa., 1972—2000; chmn., treas. Diasense, Inc. Biomedical Engring., Indiana, 1989—2000; pres., founder Purdy Tech., Inc., Marion Center, Pa., 2000—. Contbr. articles to profl. jours. 1st lt. USAF, 1961—63. Fellow: ASME (life); mem.: AAAS. Achievements include 32 patents in field; patents for generator of electrical energy by radioisotope thermoelectric conversion; radioisotope powered cardiac pacemaker; radioisotope powered artificial heart; thermoelectric apparatus for high thermoelectric efficiency by cascading materials; method of metals joining and articles produced by such method including brazing copper to tungsten; rate responsive pacemaker; artificial pancreas; noninvasive glucose sensor; multi-leaflet heart valve. Office: Purdy Tech Inc 1482 Ambrose Rd Marion Center PA 15759 E-mail: penllwyn@yourinter.net.

**PURDY, JAMES AARON,** medical physics professor; b. Tyler, Tex., July 16, 1941; s. Walter Bethel and Florence (Neal) P.; m. Marilyn Janette Coers, Jan. 29, 1965; children: Katherine, Laura. BS, Lamar U., 1967; MA, U. Tex., 1968, PhD, 1971. Asst. rsch. scientist U. Tex., Austin, 1969-71; rsch. asst. M.D. Anderson Hosp. and Tumor Inst., Houston, 1968-69, fellow in med. physics, 1972-73; from instr. physics to prof. Sch. of Medicine, Washington U., St. Louis, 1973—83, chief physics sect., 1976—2004, prof., 1983—2004, assoc. dir. Radiation Oncology U. Calif., Davis, 2004—. Mem. NIH Radiaton Study sect. Divsn. Rsch. Grantes, 1991-95; Landauer lectr., Oakland, Calif., 1991. Editor: Three Dimensional Treatment Planning, 1991, Advances in Radiation Oncology, 1992, 3D Radiation Treatment Planning and Conformal Therapy, 1995, A Practical Guide to 3D Planning and Conformal Radiation Therapy, 1999, 3-D Conformal and Intensity Modulated Radiation Therapy: Physics and Clinical Applications, 2001; sr. physics editor: Internat. Jour. Radiation Oncology, Biology, and Physics, 1996—2003. With USMC, 1961-64. Fellow Am. Assn. Physicists in Medicine (pres. 1985, William D. Coolidge award 1997), Am. Coll. Radiology (ACR Gold Medal 2002), Am. Coll. Med. Physics (chmn. bd. chancellors 1990, Marvin M.D. Williams award 1996); mem. Am. Inst. Physics, Am. Bd. Med. Physics (vice chmn. 1988-92), Am. Bd. Radiology, Am. Soc. Therapeutic Radiology and Oncology (ASTRO Gold medal 2000). Methodist. Avocation: travel. Home: 918 Eucalyptus St Davis CA 95616 Office: Univ Calif Davis Med Ctr Dept Rad Oncolog 4501 X St Ste G126 Sacramento CA 95817 Office Phone: 916-734-3932. Business E-Mail: james.purdy@ucdmc.ucdavis.edu.

**PURDY, KEVIN MOORE,** estate planner; b. Escondido, Calif., Jan. 26, 1952; s. Kenneth C. and Helen M. (Moore) P.; m. Janice M. Cook, May 12, 1982. BA in Philosophy, Psychology, U. Redlands, 1974. Pres. Timeline Pub., San Diego, Calif., 1980-90; estate planner Sagemark Cons., San Diego, Calif. 1990—. Pub. spkr.; digital artist. Author: A Brief History of the Earth and Mankind, 1986, A Brief History of Mankind, 1987. Avocations: photography, music, travel, investment analysis. E-mail: kpurdy@home.com.

**PURDY, LAURA,** philosopher, educator; m. John Coleman. At, U. Md., Frankfurt, Germany, 1966—69; BA, San Jose State U., Calif., 1970, MS, 1971; PhD, Stanford U., Calif., 1974. Postdoctoral assoc. Cornell U., Ithaca, NY, 1975—77; irwin chair Hamilton Coll., Clinton, NY, 1988—89; bioethicist U. of Toronto Joint Ctr. Bioethics, Toronto, Ontario, 1997—2000; prof. of philosophy Wells Coll., Aurora, NY, 1979—. Author: (book) In Their Best Interest? The Case Against Equal Rights for Children; editor: Feminist Perspectives in Medical Ethics (with Helen B. Holmes); author: Reproducing Persons; editor: (text) Bioethics, Justice, and Health Care (with Wanda Teays). Recipient Excellence in Tchg., Wells Coll., 1993. Home: 75 Turkey Hill Rd Ithaca NY 14850 Office: Wells Coll Main St Aurora NY 13026 Office Phone: 315-364-3244. Personal E-Mail: lpurdy@wells.edu.

**PURDY, MARY ROSILAND,** music educator; b. Ada, Okla., May 31, 1953; d. Jack and Colleen (Ladonia) Purdy. EdB in Music, East Central U., 1976; MusM, U. Okla., 1981. Dir. bands Healdton (Okla.) Pub. Schs., 1976—78, Byna Pub. Schs., Ada, 1985—91; dir. bands, HS vocal dir. Meeker (Okla.) Pub. Schs., 1991—99; dir. bands Stratford (Okla.) Pub. Schs., 1999—2001, Davis (Okla.) Pub. Schs., 2001—02, Ada Pub. Schs., 2002—03; chair dept. music, instrumental and vocal tchr. Wayne (Okla.) Pub. Schs., 2004—. Musician: Jazz Combo, 1976—; composer (brass quintet): Basic Doo-Wah; composer: (vocal) Sing to the Lord. Vol. Salvation Army, Ada, 2003, Red Cross, Ada, 2004; exec. sec. Okla. chpt. Internat. Assn. Jazz Educators; organist. dir. handbells First United Meth. Ch., Ada, 1995—. Named Tchr. of Yr., Meeker Pub. Sch., 1995, Golden Apple Tchr. of Yr., Meeker C. of C., 1996, Outstanding Jazz Educator in Okla., Internat. Assn. Jazz Educators, 1997. Mem.: Ada Arts and Humanities Coun., Music Educators Nat. Conf., Okla. Music Educators Assn. Methodist. Avocations: movies, fishing, interior decorating, music. Home: 705 E 14 Ada OK 74820 Office: Wayne Pub Sch PO Box 40 Wayne OK 73095

**PURDY, WILLIAM RICHARD,** lawyer; b. Statesville, N.C., May 3, 1946; s. Frank Kerr and Catherine Ritchie Purdy; m. Susan Clark Smith, Aug. 18, 1968; children: Kathryn Blythe Purdy Barton, Susanna Grey. BA, U. N.C., 1972, JD, 1975. Assoc. Smith, Currie & Hancock, Atlanta, 1975—77; v.p. Southeastern Svcs., Inc., Jackson, Miss., 1977—80; founding ptnr., prin. Ott & Purdy, P.A., Jackson, Miss., 1980—2003; founding ptnr., mem. Purdy & Germany, PLLC, Jackson, 2003—. Gen. counsel Miss. Rd. Bldrs. Assn., Jackson, 1993—, Assoc. Gen. Contrs. of Miss., Jackson, 1995—, Miss. Asphalt Pavers Assn., Jackson, 1998—; lectr. in field. Author (editor): Contractor's Desk Book on Mississippi Construction Law, 1996. 1st lt. USMC, 1968—72. Decorated Bronze Star; named Master of the Bench, Charles Clark Inn, Am. Inns of Ct., 1994—; recipient Commendation for Disting. Profl. Achievement, Joint Resolution of Miss. Senate and Ho. of Reps., 2000. Fellow: Miss. Bar Found., Internat. Soc. Barristers, Am. Coll. Constrn. Lawyers; mem.: ABA (mem. pub. contract law sect., state chair 1980—83, mem. forum com. on constrn. law 1980—), Best Lawyers in Am. (Best Lawyer in Am. 2003). Avocations: jogging, rock and roll, college sports. Office: Purdy & Germany PLLC PO Drawer 1079 Jackson MS 39215-1079 Office Phone: 601-969-4140.

**PURE, PAMELA J.,** information technology executive; B in Health Adminstrn., U. NC. Various mgmt., product devel. and mktg. positions Shared Med. Sys. (now Siemens); COO Channel Health Subs. IDX Systems, 1999—2001; grp. pres. product devel. and support McKesson Corp., San Francisco, 2001—02, COO McKesson Info. Solutions, 2002—04, exec. v.p., pres. McKesson Provider Technologies, 2004—. Named Woman of Yr. Tech. (enterprise bus.), (WIT) Women in Technology, 2005. Office: McKesson Corpn 1 Post St San Francisco CA 94104 Office Phone: 415-983-8300. Office Fax: 415-983-9400.*

**PUREVDORJ-GAGE, LAURA BOLOROO,** research scientist; b. Ulaanbaatar, Mongolia, Aug. 31, 1978; d. Purevdorj Tserenkhuu and Tserendulam Davgabazar; m. Justin Patrick Gage, Aug. 18, 2003; children: Brandon Purevdorj Gage, Bridger Robert Gage. PhD, Mont. State U., Bozeman, 2000—04. Internship Ctr. Biofilm Engring., Bozeman, Mont., 1999—2000; grad. rsch. asst. Mont. State U., 2000—04, postdoctoral rsch. assoc., 2005—06; postdoctoral scholar Stanford U., Calif., 2006—. Contbr. articles to profl. jours. Mem.: AAAS. Home: 1010 Noel Dr Apt #29 Menlo Park CA 94025 Office: Stanford Univ Sherman Fairchild Bldg 299 Campus Dr Stanford CA 94305-5124 Business E-Mail: laurap1@stanford.edu.

**PURI, MADAN LAL,** mathematics professor; b. Sialkot, Feb. 20, 1929; came to U.S., 1957, naturalized, 1973; s. Ganesh Das and S. W. P.; m. Uma Kapur, Aug. 24, 1962; 3 children. BA, Punjab U., India, 1948, MA, 1950, D.Sc., 1975; PhD, U. Calif. at Berkeley, 1962. Head dept. math. D.A.V. Coll., Punjab U., 1955-57; instr. U. Colo., 1957-58; tchg. asst., rsch. asst., jr. rsch. statistician U. Calif. at Berkeley, 1958-62; asst. prof., assoc. prof. math. Courant Inst., NYU, 1962-68; vis. assoc. prof. U. N.C., summers 1966-67; prof. math. Ind. U., Bloomington, 1968—, Coll. Arts and Scis. Disting. Rsch. scholar, 2004—. Guest prof. stats. U. Gottingen, West Germany, 1972,

Alexander von Humboldt guest prof., 1974-75; guest prof. U. Dortmund, West Germany, 1972, Technische Hochschule Aachen, West Germany, 1973, U. Goteborg, Chalmers U. Tech., both Sweden, 1974; vis. prof. U. Auckland, N.Z., 1977, U. Calif., Irvine, 1978, U. Wash., Seattle, 1978-79, U. Bern (Switzerland), 1982, Va. Poly. Inst., 1988; disting. visitor London Sch. Econs. and Polit. Sci., 1991; vis. prof. U. Göttingen, Germany, 1991, June-July 1992; rsch. fellow Katholieke U., Nijmegen, The Netherlands, 1992; vis. prof. U. Des Scis. et Tech. de Lille, France, 1994, U. Basel, Switzerland, 1995—, U. New South Wales, Australia, 1996; vis. univ. fellow Australian Nat. U., Canberra, Australia, 1999; guest prof. U. Konstanz, Germany, 2000, U. Gottingen, 2001. Co-author: Non Parametric Methods in Multivariate Analysis, 1971, Non Parametric Methods in General Linear Models, 1985. Editor Stochastic Process and Related Topics, 1975, Statistical Inference and Related Topics, 1975, Non Parametric Techniques in Statistical Inference, 1970; co-editor: Nonparametric Statistical Inference, Vols. I and II, 1982, New Perspectives in Theoretical and Applied Statistics, 1987, Mathematical Statistics and Probability Theory, Vol. A, 1987, Statistical Sciences and Data Analysis, 1993, Recent Advances in Statistics and Probability, 1994, Asymptotics in Statistics and Probability, 2000, Probability, Statistics and their Applications, 2003. Recipient Sr. U.S. Scientist award, Humboldt Preis, 1974-75, 83, Rsch. award Humboldt Found., U. Göttingen, 2001. Fellow Royal Statis. Soc. (adv. editor statistics book series, 2005), Inst. Math. Statistics, Am. Statis. Assn., Internat. Indian Statis. Assn. (hon.); mem. Internat. Statis. Inst., Bernoulli Soc. Math. Stats. and Probability Office: Ind U Dept Math Rawles Hall Bloomington IN 47405 Business E-Mail: puri@indiana.edu.

PURI, RAJENDRA KUMAR, business and tax specialist, consultant; b. Hoshiarpur, Punjab, India, Dec. 22, 1932; came to the U.S., 1965, naturalized, 1969; s. Harbans Lal and Satya Vati (Jerath) P.; children: Neena, Veena, Ram. BS, Agra U., 1952; diploma in Russian lang. and lit., U. Dehli, 1958; BA, U. Wash., 1968, MBA, 1969; MS in Taxation, Golden Gate U., 1982. Customs officer Govt. of India, New Delhi, 1955-60; asst. treas. Merc. Bank Ltd., New Delhi, 1960-65; mem. staff Peat, Marwick, Mitchell & Co., CPAs, Seattle, 1969-70; state examiner State of Wash., Seattle, 1970-72, asst. supervising state examiner, 1972-74, supervising state examiner, 1974-77; sr. internal auditor Lockheed Corp., Sunnyvale, Calif., 1977-79; sci. programming analyst Lockheed Missile and Space Co., Sunnyvale, 1979-80, data processing specialist, 1980-84, sci. programming specialist, 1984-88; chief acct. Tex. Dept. Health, Austin, 1989-90; dir. internal audit, internal auditor Tex. Workers' Compensation Commn., Austin, 1990-95; bus. and tax cons., 1996—2003. Del. Wash. State Rep. Conv., 1976, Snohomish County Rep. Conv., 1976; Rep. nominee for state auditor, Wash., 1976; spl. advisor U.S. Congl. Adv. Bd., 1982-83. Mem. AICPA. Home: 2608 Hunlac Cove Round Rock TX 78681-7107 E-mail: rkpi_2000@yahoo.com.

PURIS, MARTIN FORD, media company executive; b. Chgo., Feb. 22, 1939; s. Martin and Virginia Lee (Farmer) Puris; m. Mary M. Herrmann; children: Kimberly Mayo, Jason Patterson, Mary Elizabeth. Student, DePauw U., 1961. With Campbell-Ewald Co., Detroit, 1962—64, Young & Rubicam, Inc., N.Y.C., 1964-66; v.p. Carl Ally, Inc. N.Y.C., 1966-74; pres., CEO Ammirati & Puris, Inc., N.Y.C., 1974-94; chmn., CEO, chief creative officer Ammirati, Puris, Lintas, N.Y.C., 1995—99; chmn., CEO Not Traditional Media, NYC, 2004—. Media advisor Pres. George Bush; dir. IPG Group, 1995—99; vice chmn. Sheltering Arms; mng. dir. New Things Investment Group; treasurer Hampton Classic; exec. com The Quills. Author: Comeback: How Seven Straight-Shooting CEO's Turned Around Troubled Companies, 1999. Recipient awards Art Dir. Club, Copy Club, N.Y.C., Cannes Film Festival. Mem.: Devon Yacht Club, Union Club, Am. Yacht Club, Nantucket Yacht Club, N.Y. Yacht Club. Republican. Roman Catholic. Avocations: sailing, tennis, horseback riding, hunting. Office: NTM Inc 32 E 57th St 10th Fl New York NY 10022 Office Phone: 212-371-0088. Office Fax: 212-371-8884.

PURKAYASTHA, ARINDAM, surgeon; b. India, Apr. 1, 1940; arrived in US, 1967; s. Arabinda and Jyotsna Purkayastha; married, May 27, 1973; children: Tania, Amrita. B Medicine and Surgery, U. Calcutta, India, 1963; MS, U. Delhi, India, 1967. Diplomate Am. Bd. Gen. Surgery. Gen. surgeon Barnes Kasson Hosp., Susquehanna, Pa., 1970—. Contbr. articles to profl. jours. Fellow: ACS. Home: 5 Castle Dr Windsor NY 13865 Office: Barnes Kasson Hosp 400 Turnpike St Susquehanna PA 18847 Office Phone: 570-853-3135.

PURKAYASTHA, DAS D., biostatistics director; s. D. Lal and Nandita Purkayastha. Pre U. Sci., GC Coll., India, 1969—70; BS in physics, math., stats., with honors, GC Coll., Guwahati U., 1970—73; MS, Guwahati U., India, 1973—76; MA, Monmouth U., N.J.; M, PhD, U. Buffalo, 1982—87. Computer Programming IASRI, New Delhi, 1978, Statistical Analysis Systems (SAS) SAS Inst., USA, 1999; Clinical Trial Statistician Course Pharm. Edn. Rsch. Inst., 1998, Clinical Trial Project Management George Wash. U., 2000, Clinical/Drug Development Training Novartis, USA, 1999, FDA Drug Regulatory Requirements Novartis, USA, 1998; Faculty Development Program U. of Buffalo, NY, 1986, Regulatory Studies Mich. State U., East Lansing, MI., 1990. Sr. rsch. fellow IASRI, Indian Statis. Rsch. Inst., New Delhi, Delhi, 1977—81; tchg., rsch. asst. U. Buffalo, 1982—86, vis. lectr., 1987—88; scientist grade Argonne Nat. Lab., U. Chgo., Ill., 1988—89; econometrician, statistician Pub. Svc. Commn., Washington D.C., DC, 1989—94; adj. faculty George Wash. U., Washington DC, 1994; dir. biostatsitical applications Cardiology Rsch. Ctr., Washington D.C., DC, 1995—97; sr. biostatstician Novartis Pharmaceuticals, East Hanover, NJ, 1997—99, prin. biostatsitician 1999—2001, assoc. dir., biostatistics, 2001—. Contbr. scientific papers, articles to profl. jours. Cmty. svc., charity, children welfare. Recipient Above and Beyond awards, Novartis, 1997—2003, Social and Cultural Club, Drama and Debating Societies, Art and Theatre, 1960—82, Indian Rsch. Svc. Exam., Indian Agr Scientist Recruitment Bd (IARB), 1980, Indian Stats. Svc. Exam., Union Pub. Svc. Commn., IAS Exam. Excellence Award, Recognition on FDA submission and approval of Pediatric Drug Exclusivity, Clin. Devel. Med. Affair, Novartis, 2003; State Merit Academic Grant, Guwahati U., 1973—76, Nat. Merit Scholarship, Bd. of Secondary Edn., 1969—73, Sr. Rsch. fellowship, Indian Coun. of Rsch., 1977. Mem.: AAAS, Am. Statis. Assn. Avocations: writing, swimming, yoga. Office: Novartis One Health Plaza East Hanover NJ 07936

PURKERSON, MABEL LOUISE, physician, educator, physiologist; b. Goldville, SC, Apr. 3, 1931; d. James Clifton and Louise (Smith) P. AB, Erskine Coll., 1951; MD, U. SC, Charleston, 1956. Diplomate Am. Bd. Pediat. Instr. pediat. Washington U. Sch. Medicine, St. Louis, 1961-67, instr. medicine, 1966-67, asst. prof. pediat., 1967-98, asst. prof. medicine, 1967-76, assoc. prof. medicine, 1976-89, prof., 1989-98, prof. emerita, 1998—, assoc. dean curriculum, 1976-94, assoc. dean acad. projects, 1994-98. Cons. in field. Editl. bd. Am. Jour. Kidney Diseases, 1981-87; contbr. articles to profl. jours. Mem. bd. counselors Erskine Coll., 1971—87, trustee, 2000—96; historian St. Louis Symphony Orch., trustee. USPHS spl. fellow, 1971-72. Mem. Am. Heart Assn. Coun. on the Kidney (exec. com. 1973-81), Am. Physiol. Soc., Am. Soc. Nephrology, Internat. Soc. Nephrology, Ctrl. Soc. Clin. Rsch., Am. Soc. Renal Biochemistry and Metabolism, Internat. Assn. History Nephrology, Am. Osler Soc., Explorer's Club (chair St. Louis chpt., 2005-), Sigma Xi (chpt. sec. 1974, Alpha Omega Alpha. Home: 20 Haven View Dr Saint Louis MO 63141-7902 Office: Bernard Becker Med Libr Renal Div Dept PO Box 8132 Saint Louis MO 63110-1093 Office Phone: 314-362-4234. Business E-Mail: purkerm@msnotes.wustl.edu.

PURL, O. THOMAS, retired electronics company executive; b. East St. Louis, Ill., June 5, 1924; s. Ruthford Keith and Muriel Agnes (Thompson) P.; m. Martha Elaine Smalley, Feb. 21, 1948; children— Thomas Keith, Jeanne Marie Purl Elder. BS, U. Ill., 1948, BS, 1951, MS, 1952, PhD, 1955. Head high-power traveling wave tube sect., mem. tech. staff Hughes Research Lab., Culver City, Calif., 1955-58; sect. head, dept. mgr., group v.p., v.p. shareholder relations and planning coordination Watkins-Johnson Co., Palo Alto, Calif., 1958-86. Contbr. articles to profl. jours.; patentee in field. Chmn.

career guidance com. Santa Clara Valley Joint Engring. Council, 1971-73; bd. dirs. Jr. Achievement of Santa Clara County, 1975-79. Served to 1st lt. USAAF, 1943-46. Fellow IEEE (chmn. Santa Clara Valley subsect. 1972); mem. Sigma Xi, Eta Kappa Nu, Phi Kappa Phi, Sigma Tau. Clubs: Commonwealth of Calif. Home: 300 Hot Springs Rd K220 Montecito CA 93108

PURNELL, CHARLES GILES, lawyer; b. Aug. 16, 1921; s. Charles Stewart and Ginevra (Locke) P.; m. Sally Hupp (dec.); children: Mimi, Sarah Elizabeth, Charles H., John W.; m. Jane Carter. Student, Rice Inst., 1938-39; BA, U. Tex., 1941; student, Harvard Bus. Sch., 1942; LLB, Yale U., 1947. Bar: Tex. 1948. Ptnr. Locke, Purnell, Boren, Laney & Neely, Dallas, 1947-89, Locke, Purnell, Rain & Harrell, Dallas, 1989-90, of counsel, 1990-99, Locke, Liddell & Sapp, Dallas, 1999—. Exec. asst. to Gov. of Tex., Austin, 1973-75. Bd. dirs. Trinity River Authority of Tex., 1975-81; vice chmn. Tex. Energy Adv. Council, 1974. Served to lt. U.S. Navy, 1942-45; PTO. Mem. ABA, Tex. Bar Assn., Tex. Bar Found, Yale Club, Dallas Country Club, Dallas Petroleum Club, La Jolla (Calif.) Beach and Tennis Club. Episcopalian. Home: 1 Saint Laurent Pl Dallas TX 75225-8128 Office: Locke Lidell & Sapp 2200 Ross Ave Ste 2200 Dallas TX 75201-6776

PURNELL, ELISSA T., biology professor; d. Charles and Mildred Purnell. BS, Savannah State Coll., Ga., 1990; MS, West Ga. Coll., Carrollton, 1992; PhD, Med. U. SC, Charleston, 2001. Instr. biology Savannah State Coll., 1994—96; rsch. assoc. Savannah State U., 2001—04, asst. prof. biology, 2004—. Patrica Roberts Harris fellow, West Ga. Coll., 1990—92, Phineas Roberts scholar, Savannah State Coll., 1986—87. Mem.: Beta Beta Beta (life; advisor 2004). Episcopalian. Avocations: piano, reading, cake decorating, flute. Office: Savannah State University 3219 College Street Savannah GA 31404 Office Phone: 912-361-6662. E-mail: purnelle@savstate.edu.

PURNELL, MAURICE EUGENE, JR., lawyer; b. Dallas, Feb. 17, 1940; s. Maurice Eugene Sr. and Marjorie (Maillot) P.; m. Diane Blake, Aug. 19, 1966; children: Maurice Eugene III, Blake Maillot. BA, Washington and Lee U., 1961; MBA, U. Pa., 1963; LLB, So. Meth. U., 1966. Bar: Tex. 1966. Ptnr. Locke, Purnell, Boren, Laney & Neely, Dallas, 1966-87; shareholder Locke Purnell Rain Harrell PC, Dallas, 1987-99; ptnr. Locke Liddell & Sapp LLP, Dallas, 1999—2002, of counsel, 2002—. Bd. dirs. Leggett & Platt, Inc. Bd. dirs. Dallas Summer Musicals. Mem. ABA, Tex. Bar Assn., Tex. Bar Found., Dallas Bar Assn. Am. Judicature Soc., Dallas C. of C, Brook Hollow Golf Club. Home: 4409 S Versailles Ave Dallas TX 75205-3044 Office: Locke Liddell & Sapp LLP 2200 Ross Ave Ste 2200 Dallas TX 75201-6776 Office Phone: 214-740-8444.

PURNELL, OLIVER JAMES, III, judge; b. Richmond, Va., Jan. 18, 1949; s. Oliver James Jr. and Margaret Helen (Hodges) P.; m. Cheryl Naomi Williams, June 30, 1973; children: Oliver James IV, Amy Susan. AA, U. Hartford, 1969; AB, Middlebury Coll., 1972; MSLS, Case Western Res. U., 1976; JD, Western New England Sch. Law, 1982. Bar: Conn. 1982, U.S. Dist. Ct. Conn. 1982. Dir., pharmacy libr. U. Conn. Sch. Pharmacy, Storrs, Conn., 1977-81; assoc. Lavitt, Hutchinson & Kaplan, Vernon, Conn., 1981-84, DuBeau & Ryan, Vernon, Conn., 1984-87, Howard, Kohn Sprague & Fitzgerald, Hartford, Conn., 1987-89; pvt. practice Vernon, 1989-92; reference libr. U. Conn. Sch. Law, Hartford, 1992-98; regional info. mgr. Lexis-Nexis, Vernon, 1998—99; judge Ellington Dist. Probate Ct., Vernon, 1999. Adj. prof. U. Hartford. Contbr. articles to profl. jours. Scoutmaster Boy Scouts Am., Rockville, Conn., 1990—; trustee Rockville (Conn.) Pub. Libr.; corporator Ea. Conn. Health Network; mem. U. Hartford Alumni Coun.; mem. Hillyer Coll. Bd. Vis. Mem. Am. Assn. Law Libraries, So. New England Law Libr. Assn. (pres. 1998-99), Conn. Bar Assn. (coun. of bar pres. 1995-96), Tolland County Bar Assn. (pres. 1995-96), Nat. Coll. Probate Judges, Masonic Lodge, A.F. & A.M. (master Fayette Lodge 1970) Avocations: skiing, camping, hiking, church organist. Office: 1257 Hartford Tpke Vernon Rockville CT 06066 Office Phone: 860-870-1000. Personal E-mail: jpurnell3@att.net.

PURPURA, DOMINICK P., dean, neuroscientist; b. NYC, Apr. 2, 1927; m. Florence Williams, 1948; children: Craig, Kent, Keith, Allyson. AB, Columbia U., 1949; MD, Harvard U., 1953. Intern Presbyn Hosp., NYC, 1953—54; asst. resident in neurology Neurol. Inst., NYC, 1954—55; prof., chmn. dept. anatomy Albert Einstein Coll. Medicine, Yeshiva U., NYC, 1967—74, sci. dir. Kennedy Ctr., 1970—72, dir. Kennedy Ctr., 1972—82, prof., chmn. dept. neurosci., 1974—82, dean, 1984—2006, dean emeritus, 2006—; dean Stanford U., 1982—84. Editor-in-chief Brain Rsch. Revs., 1975—2000, Developmental Brain Rsch., 1981—2000, Molecular Brain Rsch., 1985—2000, Cognitive Brain Rsch., 1991—2000, Brain Rsch., 1975—2000, mem. editl. bd., 1965—2000. Served with USAAF, 1945-47. Fellow N.Y. Acad. Scis.; mem. NAS, Inst. Medicine of NAS, Am. Acad. Neurology, Am. Assn. Anatomists, Am. Assn. Neurol. Surgeons, Am. Epilepsy Soc., Am. Physiol. Soc., Assn. Rsch. in Nervous and Mental Disease, Soc. Neurosci., Sigma Xi. Office: Albert Einstein Coll Medicine Dept Neurosci 1300 Morris Park Ave Kennedy 912D Bronx NY 10461-1926 Office Phone: 718-430-2801. Office Fax: 718-430-8822. Business E-Mail: dpurpura@aecomyu.edu.

PURPURA, GRACE, artist, retired art educator; b. N.Y.C., Nov. 3, 1929; d. Michael and Carmela Maligno Purpura; children: Marina, Diana and Valerie Andriola. Student, Cooper Union Sch. Art & Arch., 1946-49, CUNY, 1952, San Jose State U., 1969. Cert. elem., secondary, art tchr., Calif. Art tchr. L.A. City Schs., 1957-62; design instr. L.A. City College, 1960; bilingual tchr. Alum Rock Sch. Dist., San Jose, 1969-91; arts commr. City of San Jose, Calif., 1994-98. Mentor tchr. State of Calif. Dept. Edn., Sacramento, 1984-87; mem. Fulbright Scholar L.Am. project Stanford U., China and Korea/Calif. Dept. Edn., 1987, Calif. Internat. Studies mem., 1985. Exhibited paintings, sculptures and drawings at numerous shows, galleries, mus. and internat. including Synopsys, Inc., Mountain View, Calif., Lifescan, Milpitas, Calif., Network Gen. Corp., Menlo Park, Calif., Ohlone Coll., Fremont, Calif., Works Gallery, San Jose; Inst. for Contemporary Art, San Jose, Triton Mus., Santa Clara, Calif., de Saisset Mus., Santa Clara, Denver Art Mus., Raychem Corp., Menlo Park, Forum Art Gallery, N.Y.C.; one-woman shows include San Jose Art League, Casa de la Cultura, Livorno, Italy, Hayward, Calif. City Hall Art Gallery, 2003, Pacific Grove, Calif Art Ctr., 2004, Inst. for Contemporary Art, Calif., 2004, Movimiento Arte y Cultura Latino Americano, Calif., 2004; bd. dirs. San Jose Art League, 1985-88; arts commr. City of San Jose, 1994-98. Mem. Calif. Art Edn. Assn., Calif. Tchrs. Assn., Paper Gem Printmakers of Silicon Valley (co-founder). Avocations: arts, photography, children's picture books. Home: 2364 Stokes St San Jose CA 95128-4262 Office Phone: 408-971-7588.

PURSCELL, KEITH WILLIAM, minister; b. Council Bluffs, Iowa, Feb. 12, 1931; s. Benjamin William and Marie Esther (Lowe) Purscell; m. Mary Louise Elliott, May 16, 1952 (dec. Jan. 22, 1993); children: Kenneth, Sally, David, Glenda; m. Helen Margaret Duncan, June 17, 1994. Student, Johnson Bible Coll., Knoxville, Tenn., 1949—51; BA, Nebr. Christian Coll., Norfolk, 1953; postgrad. studies, Lincoln Christian Coll. Sem., Ill., 1953—54; MDiv., Phillips Grad. Sem., Enid, Okla., 1970. Ordained Clergy The Christian Ch. 1951. Pastor First Christian Ch., Spencer, Iowa, 1970—79, Broadway Christian Ch., Wichita, Kans., 1979—82, 1st Christian Ch. Independence, Kans., 1982—86, La Junta, Colo., 1986—90, Mankato, Minn., 1990—96; interim pastor Congl. UCC Ch., Webster City, Iowa, 1998—99, Fairmont, Minn., 2005, St. Lukes Fairbault, Minn., 1999—2000; retired; interim pastor United Ch. Mapleton, Minn., 2005—06. Vice moderator Christian Ch. in the Upper-Midwest Region, 1976—79; chmn. com. on scholarships for ministry Disciples of Christ, Kans., 1979—86; chmn. com. on ministry Disciples of Christ Colo., and Wyoming, 1989—90; organising pres., v.p. Living at Home Block Nurse Program, Mankato, Minn., 1991—2005; chaplin NW Iowa Alcoholism & Drug Treatment Unit, Spencer, Iowa, 1991—98; pres. Mankato State U. for Srs. Orgn., 2005—06. Co-author: (devotional prayer) Secret Place, 1982; contbr. articles to Christian mags., 1955—95. Named Disting. alumus, Phillips U. Alumni, 2001. Disciples Of Christ. Achievements include Helped create senior center and county transportation for Clay County, Iowa,

1976-79; designed regional policy on sexual abuse by clergy or staff for Christian Church in the Central Rockies Region. Avocation: photography. Home and Office: PO Box 3639 Mankato MN 56002

PURSE, CHARLES ROE, investment banker; b. Redhill, Surrey, Eng., May 19, 1960; arrived in U.S., 1960; s. James Nathanial II and Rolande Marie-Louise (Redon) Purse; m. Carole Lynn Sadler, July 5, 1986; children: Hayley Elizabeth, Cameron James, Andrew Lang. BA, Dartmouth Coll., 1982; MBA, Northwestern U., 1985. Account officer No. Trust Bank, Chgo., 1982—85; asst. v.p. Citicorp Real Estate, Inc., Chgo., 1985—88; v.p. Citibank, Ltd., Sydney, Australia, 1988—91, Citibank Realty Investment Advisors, NYC, 1991—94; sr. v.p. Yarmouth Group, NYC, 1994—96; mng. dir. DRA Advisors, Inc., NYC, 1996—2000; mng. dir. real estate pvt. fund group Credit Suisse First Boston, NYC, 2000—05; mng. prin. Park Hill Real Estate Group, LLC, NYC, 2005—. Active alumni bd. We. Res. Acad., Hudson, Ohio, 2002. Mem.: Pension Real Estate Assn., Bald Peak Colony Club, Belle Haven Club, Hillsboro Club (Hillsboro Beach, Fla.), Cromer Golf Club (Sydney), Country Club (Cleve.). Republican. Avocations: golf, photography, skiing, tennis. Office: Park Hill Real Estate Group LLC 345 Park Ave 15th Fl New York NY 10154

PURSEL, DAVID G., lawyer; b. ND, 1945; BS, U. Wash., 1971; JD, Seattle U., 1979. Bar: Wash. 1979, Mass. 1986, Tex. 1996, U.S. Ct. Appeals (Fed. cir.), U.S. Ct. Appeals (9th cir.), registered: U.S. Patent and Trademark Office. Various legal positions Advanced Micro Devices, Digital Equipment Corp., Boeing Co.; with LSI Logic Corp., Milpitas, Calif., 1996—, assoc. gen. counsel, chief intellecutal property counsel, asst. sec., v.p., gen. counsel, 2000—. Mem.: SVAGC, ACCA, Am. Soc. Corp. Secretaries. Office: LSI Logic Corp 1621 Barber Ln Milpitas CA 95035 Office Phone: 408-433-3192. Office Fax: 866-574-5742. E-mail: dpursel@lsil.com.

PURSELL, CARROLL WIRTH, history educator; b. Visalia, Calif., Sept. 4, 1932; s. Carroll Wirth and Ruth Irene (Crowell) P.; m. Joan Young, Jan. 28, 1956 (dec. 1985); children: Rebecca Elizabeth, Matthew Carroll; m. Angela Woollacott, Dec. 20, 1986. BA, U. Calif., Berkeley, 1956, PhD, 1962; MA, U. Del., 1958. Asst. prof. history Case Inst. Tech., Cleve., 1963-65; asst. prof. U. Calif., Santa Barbara, 1965-69, asso. prof., 1969-76, prof., 1976-88; Adeline Barry Davee Disting. prof. history Case Western Res. U., Cleve., 1988—, chair history dept., 1998—. Mellon prof. Lehigh U., Bethlehem, Pa., 1974-76; vis. research scholar Smithsonian Instn., 1970 Author: Early Stationary Stem Engines in America, 1969, Military Industrial Complex, 1972, From Conservation to Ecology, 1973, White Heat, 1994, The Machine in America, 1995, American Technology, 2001. Fellow: AAAS; mem.: Am. Hist. Assn., Orgn. Am. Historians, Soc. History of Tech. (pres. 1990—92, pres. internat. com.for history of tech. 1998—2001, Leonardo da Vinci medal 1991), Phi Beta Kappa. Democrat.*

PURSEY, DEREK LINDSAY, retired physics professor; b. Glasgow, Scotland, Oct. 22, 1927; came to U.S., 1964; s. Henry Edwin and Margaret Martin (Lindsay) P.; m. Barbara Ann Parker, Aug. 4, 1962; 1 child, John BS, U. Glasgow, 1948, PhD, 1952. Asst. lectr. theoretical physics King's Coll., London, 1951-54; lectr. math. physics U. Edinburgh, Scotland, 1954-59; vis. lectr. UCLA, 1959-60; mem. sch. math. Inst. for Advanced Studies, Princeton, 1960-61; lectr. in theoretical physics U. Glasgow, Scotland, 1961-64; vis. prof. Iowa State U., Ames, 1964-65, prof. physics, 1965-93, emeritus prof. physics, 1993—. Vis. prof. UCLA, 1979-80. Contbr. articles to profl. jours. Fellow Royal Soc. Edinburgh, Am. Phys. Soc.; mem. AAAS, Presbyn. Assn. on Sci., Tech. and Christian Faith (sec.-treas. 1998-2002, pres. 2002—), Sigma Xi. Democrat. Presbyterian. Avocations: church-related activities, photography, music, reading, wilderness camping. E-mail: dlpursey@mchsi.com.

PURSLEY, FRANK JAMES, retired personal development specialist; b. Durham, N.C., May 5, 1927; s. James Alton and Vesta Andwers Pursley; m. Dymple Edwards (dec.); children: Cynthia, Susan, Frank Jr.; m. Barbara Jean Pursley; children: Charles, Keith, Vanessa. AA, Ctrl. Va. C.C., Lynchburg, 1978. Sales mgr. WLVA-T Inc., Lynchburg, 1953—75; pers. devel. Va. Dept. Transp., Lynchburg, 1976—98; ret., 1998. Mem. adv. bd. Va. C.C., Lynchburg, adj. instr., 1998—2002; chmn. Svc. Corps. Ret. Exec. (SCORE) 529, 2003—. Mem. adv. bd. Local Red Cross, Lynchburg; active Rep. Nat. Com.; chair adminstrv. bd. Ct. St. Meth. Ch., Lynchburg, 1978—80. 1st. lt. U.S. Army, 1956, col. U.S. Army, 1980. Mem.: Mil. Order World Wars, Oakwood Country Club (golf com. 2000—). Avocations: golf, music, fishing, hunting. Home: 517 Midvale St Lynchburg VA 24502 Office: Score 529 Fed bldg Ste A42 1101 Court St Lynchburg VA 24504 Office Phone: 434-846-3235. Personal E-mail: fpurs17868@aol.com.

PURSLEY, JACK STEPHEN, lawyer, consultant; s. Jack Keith and Sara Stephens Pursley; m. Amber Anne Nolen, Aug. 7, 2004; 1 child, Nolen Jackson. JD, U. Tulsa, Okla., 2003; Masters of Dispute Resolution, Pepperdine U., Straus Inst., Malibu, Calif., 2004. Bar: Supreme Ct. Tex. 2004, DC Ct. Appeals 2005, US Ct. Appeals (5th cir.) 2005, US Dist. Ct. (so. dist.) 2005. Pres. Online Commerce Corp., Houston, 1997—2000; law firm mgr. Pursley Law Firm, PLLC, 2004—. Author: The Waco Tragedy: Communication or An Exercise In Social Conditioning?, Strategic Negotiation Planning for the Acquisition Side of a Unique Land Speculation Opportunity, Anatomy of a Divorce Conflict, Face Negotiation and Genderlect Conversation Theory in Divorce Mediation, Deception and Manipulation: Contrasted in Litigation and Mediation. Recipient Excellence for the Future Mediation award, Ctr. Computer Assisted Legal Instrn., 2003, Excellence for the Future Social Psychology of Conflict award, 2003. Mem. ABA, Houston Trial Lawyers Assn., Assn. Am. Trial Lawyers, Houston Bar Assn., Wash. DC Bar Assn., Tex. Bar Assn., Phi Delta Phi. Methodist. Avocations: golf, tennis, skiing, travel. Office: Pursley Law Firm PLLC 4615 Southwest Freeway Ste 600 Houston TX 77027 Office Phone: 713-893-0022. Office Fax: 713-893-2508. Business E-Mail: jsp@pursleylaw.com.

PURSLEY, MICHAEL BADER, engineering educator, communications systems researcher, consultant; b. Winchester, Ind., Aug. 10, 1945; s. Bader F. and Evelyn L. (Bennett) P.; m. Lou Ann Hinchman, July 6, 1968; 1 child, Jessica Ann. BS, Purdue U., 1967, MS, 1968; PhD, U. So. Calif., 1974. Mem. tech. staff Hughes Aircraft Co., Los Angeles, 1967; engr. Northrop Co., Hawthorne, Calif., 1968; staff engr. Hughes Aircraft Co., Los Angeles, 1968-74; acting asst. prof. UCLA, 1974; asst. prof., then assoc. prof. elec. engring. U. Ill., Urbana, 1974-80, prof., 1980-93; Holcombe prof. elec. and computer engring. Clemson (S.C.) U., 1992—; assoc. Ctr. Advanced Study, 1980-81; vis. prof. UCLA, 1985; cons. U.S. Army, Huntsville, Ala., 1977, Ft. Monmouth, NJ, 1983-86, 91, ITT, Ft. Wayne, Ind., 1979—; pres. SIGCOM, Inc., 1986-90; prin. scientist Techno-Scis. Inc., 1990—96. Author: Random Processes in Linear Systems, 2002, Introduction to Digital Communications, 2005; contbr. chapters to books. Recipient Fred W. Ellersick award Comms. Soc., 1996, Tech. Achievement award Mil. Comm. Conf., 1999, Edwin Howard Armstrong Achievement award, 2002. Fellow IEEE (pres. info. theory group 1983, Centennial medal 1984, Millennium medal 2000); mem. Inst. Math. Stats. Office: Clemson U 303 Fluor Daniel Bldg Dept ECE Clemson SC 29634

PURTAN, DICK (PAUL PURTAN), radio personality; b. Buffalo; Broadcaster WWOL-FM 104.1, Buffalo, 1958—60, WSAI-AM 1530, Cinn., 1960—65, CKLW-AM 800, Detroit-Windsor, 1965—77, WXYZ-FM, Detroit, 1977—81, WKQI-FM 95.5, Detroit, 1981—96, WOMC-FM 104.3, Detroit, 1996—. Active Vincent & Sarah Fisher Home for Children, Mich.; bd. dirs. Children's Hosp. Mich.; mem. adv. coun. Inst. Prevention of Sports Injuries, Ann Arbor, Mich.; hon. chmn. Mental Illness Rsch. Assn. Named Best Air Personality, Internat. Radio Festival, 1986, Michiganian of Yr., Detroit News, 1993; named to Nat. Radio Hall of Fame, 2004, Mass. Broadcasters Hall of Fame, 2006; recipient Marconi Radio award for Major Market Personality of Yr., Nat. Assn. Broadcasters, 1993, Industry Achievement award for Oldies Personality of Yr., Radio & Records, 1999, 2000. Office: WOMC 2201 Woodward Heights Ferndale MI 48220 Office Phone: 248-546-9600. E-mail: dickpurtan@womc.com.*

**PURTELL, LAWRENCE ROBERT,** lawyer; b. Quincy, Mass., May 2, 1947; s. Lawrence Joseph and Louise Maria (Loria) P.; m. Cheryl Lynn Tynon, Aug. 3, 1968; children: Lisa Ann, Susan Elizabeth. AB, Villanova U., 1969; JD, Columbia U., 1972. Bar: N.Y. 1973, N.J. 1978, Conn. 1988. Assoc. White & Case, NYC, 1972-73; judge advocate USMC, Washington, 1973-76; assoc. White & Case, NYC, 1977-79; corp. counsel Great Atlantic & Pacific Tea Co., Montvale, N.J., 1979-81; asst. gen. counsel United Techs. Corp., Hartford, Conn., 1981-84; assoc. gen. counsel, 1984-92; sec., gen. counsel, 1989-92; v.p., gen. counsel and sec. Carrier Corp., 1992-93; sr. v.p., gen. counsel and corp. sec. Mc Dermott Internat., New Orleans, 1993-96; sr. v.p., gen. counsel Koch Industries, Wichita, Kans., 1996-97; exec. v.p., gen. counsel Alcoa, Pitts., 1997—. Capt. USMC, 1973-76. Roman Catholic. Avocation: running. Home: 637 Shoreline Dr Naples FL 34119 Office: Alcoa 390 Park Ave New York NY 10022

**PURTLE, DOROTHY L.,** religious studies educator; b. Douglas, Wyo., Oct. 5, 1953; d. Silas I and Irene M McGehee; m. Dwight A Purtle, May 23, 1975; children: James, Lynette, Karen. BA in english, Kans. City. Coll of Bible Sch., 1977, BA in music edn., 1994. Instr. Overland Christian Sch., Overland Pk., Kans., 1986—95; registrar, instr. Kans. City Coll. and Bible Sch., 1994—. Recipient Disting. Svc. award, Kans. City Coll. and Bible Sch., 1999. Mem.: Am. Assn. of Collegiate Registrar and Admissions Officers. Avocation: music. Business E-Mail: registrar@kccbs.edu.

**PURTLE, JOHN INGRAM,** lawyer, former state supreme court justice; b. Enola, Ark., Sept. 7, 1923; s. John Wesley and Edna Gertrude (Ingram) P.; m. Marian Ruth White, Dec. 31, 1951 (dec. 1995); children: Jeffrey, Lisa K.; m. Phyllis Kelly Purtle. Student, U. Ctrl. Ark., 1946—47; LLB, U. Ark., 1950. Bar: Ark. 1950, U.S. Dist. Ct. (ea dist.) Ark. 1950. Pvt. practice, Conway, Ark., 1950-53, Little Rock, 1953—78, 1990—; mem. Ark. State Legislature, 1951-52, 69-70; assoc. justice Ark. Supreme Ct., 1979-90. Tchr., deacon Baptist Ch. Served with U.S. Army, 1940-45. Mem. ABA, Ark. Bar Assn., Am. Judicature Soc., Ark. Jud. Coun. Democrat.

**PURVES, DENNIS PATRICK,** library director; b. Elizabeth, N.J., Dec. 25, 1970; s. Dennis Patrick and Mary Theresa Purves. BA, Seton Hall U., 1993; MLS, Rutgers U., 1994. Libr. page Linden (N.J.) Pub. Libr., 1987—95, libr., 1996—2004, sr. libr., 2004—; libr. Alexander Libr. Rutgers U., New Brunswick, NJ, 1995; freelance subject cataloger Bowker-Reed Reference, New Providence, NJ, 1996—97. Mem.: ALA, Librs. of Union County Consortium (v.p. 2005, pres. 2006), N.J. Libr. Assn. Roman Catholic. Home: 38 E Elm Street Apt 3A Linden NJ 07036 Office: Linden Pub Libr 31 E Henry St Linden NJ 07036 Office Phone: 908-298-3830 11. Business E-Mail: dpurves@lindenpl.org.

**PURVIN, JACK MITCHELL,** physician; b. Bklyn., May 27, 1953; s. Saul and Sylvia (Masey) P. BA in Psychology, U. Denver, 1975; postgrad., U. Autonoma de Guadalajara, Mex., 1978-81; MD, Dominica Sch. of Medicine, 1983. Pres. P.E.C. Inc., Del. Developer diabetic food products, pmlis sys. Patentee in field. Owner Jack M. Purvin Found. Mem. Am. Diabetes Assn., Montana Hist. Soc. Avocations: chess, coin collecting/numismatics, philatelic collections, rare documents, sports. Home: 1901 84th St Apt 4A Brooklyn NY 11214-3032 Office: PEC Inc PO Box 140028 Brooklyn NY 11214-0028 Office Phone: 718-333-9198. Personal E-Mail: jackpurvin@aol.com.

**PURVIS, GAIL,** elementary school educator; b. Chgo., June 26, 1945; d. Arthur J. and Elaine (Herron) Hoffman; 1 child, Leo II. BFA, BS in Edn., U. Cinn., 1967; MS in Edn. with honors, U. Miami, 1982; psychology, art edn., fine arts, U. Ill., 1967, DBAE Art Specialist, 1991. Cert. K-12 art tchr., Fla. Instr., art Broward County Schs., Coral Springs, Fla.; art instr. St. Johns Coll., Nassau, Bahamas; tchr. pottery specialist Queens Coll., Nassau; youth planning specialist Broward Employment Tng. Adminstrn., Ft. Lauderdale, Fla. Adj. prof. Nova So. U., Ft. Lauderdale, Fla., Barry U., Miami Lakes, Fla. Mem. Nat. Art Edn. Assn., Fla. Art. Edn. Assn., Assn. Supervision Curriculum Devel. E-mail: purvis@nsu.nova.edu.

**PURVIS, GEORGE FRANK, JR.,** life insurance company executive; b. Rayville, La., Nov. 22, 1914; s. George Frank and Ann Mamie (Womble) P.; m. Virginia Winston Wendt, May 16, 1942 (dec. Feb. 3, 2001); children: Virginia Reese (Mrs. William H. Freshwater), Winston Wendt, George Frank III; m. Helen Negrotte, May 15, 2004. AA, Kemper Mil. Sch., 1932; LLB, La. State U., 1935; DHL (hon.), LLD (hon.) U. Southwestern La., 1997; DHL (hon.), U. S.W. La., 1997. Bar: La. 1935. Sole practice, Rayville, 1935-37; atty. Office Sec. State State of La., Baton Rouge, 1937-41, also dep. ins. commr., 1945-49; atty. La. Ins. Dept., also spl. asst. to atty. gen., 1937-41; with Pan-Am. Life Ins. Co., New Orleans, 1949—, exec. v.p., 1962-64, pres., chief exec. officer, 1964—, chmn. bd., 1969—; bd. dirs. Pres., bd. dirs. Compania de Seguros Panamericana, S.Am.; pres. Pan-Am. de Colombia Compania de Seguros de Vida, S.A.; chmn., bd. govs. Internat. Ins. Seminars, Inc., 1984—; mem. Industry Sector Adv. Com. for Trade Policy Matters, 1986; lectr. ins. law Tulane U., New Orleans, 1949-56; bd. dirs. 1st Nat. Bank Commerce in New ORleans, Republic Airlines Inc., 1st Commerce Corp., So. Airlines-Republic Airlines, Pan Am de Mex. Cos. de Seguros Sobre la Vida, S.A., 1964-88; dir. Northwest Airlines, 1986-87. Compiler, author: Louisiana Insurance Code, 1948; contbr. articles to profl. jours. Chmn. big donors com. New Orleans Christmas Seal Campaign, 1961, gen. campaign chmn., 1962, chmn. profl. group VIII 1963; vice chmn. New Orleans United Fund campaign, 1965, gen. chmn., 1967; pres. Tb Assn. Greater New Orleans, 1967, La. State U. Found., 1967, YMCA, New Orleans, 1968—; Internat. House, 1977, Met. Area Com., 1979; geog. chmn. U.S. Savs. Bond Campaign, Greater New Orleans, 1971; mem. Bd. City Park Commrs., 1965-79, mem. bd. commrs. Port of New Orleans, 1979—, pres. bd. commrs., 1982; chmn. S.S. Huebner Found. Ins. Edn., 1977—; Bus. Task Force on Edn., Inc., 1980—; mem. adv. bd. Bapt. Hosp., 1985—; Salvation Army, 1986—; bd. dirs. Family Svc. Soc. New Orleans, Council for a Better La., New Orleans Philharm. Symphony Soc., Summer Pop Concerts, Bur. Govt. Rsch. New Orleans; mem. Govs. Cost Control Commn., 1981-89; trustee Greater New Orleans Found., 1987—, chmn. bd. trustees La. Ind. Coll. Fund Inc., 1987-88, mem. 1987—. Served with USNR, 1941-45. Decorated Order of Vasco Nunez de Balboa (Panama); named Alumnus of Yr., La. State U., 1975, role model Young Leadership Coun., 1993; recipient award Inst. for Human Understanding, 1975, Weiss Meml. award, 1976, Vol. Activist award, 1978, award of excellence Greater New Orleans Fedn. Chs., 1983, Disting. Svc. award Navy League, 1983, Humanitarian award Nat. Jewish Hosp./Nat. Asthma Ctr., 1984, internat. ins. award Internat. Ins. Adv. Coun., 1986, 1st ann. award for outstanding efforts in promoting trade with L.Am., Rotary Club, 1987, Hall of Fame award La. State U., 1987, Man of Yr. award Fedn. Ins. and Corp. Counsel, 1988, Integritas Vitae award Loyola U. of South, 1991, Bus. Hall of Fame award Jr. Achievement, 1993, cert. of appreciation La. Air N.G., 1995, Paul M. Hebert Law Ctr.'s Disting. Alumnus of 1998, La. State U., Exec. of Yr. award Bus. Assn. Latin Am. Studies, 1999, East Jefferson Gen. Hosp. Aux. Great Gentleman's award, 2000, Cert. of Life Membership award Salvation Army Bd., 2000; selected role model Young Bus. Leadership Coun., 1993; honored as a founding mem. in Soc. of St. Ignatius, Loyola U., 1996. Mem.: ABA, Internat. Trade Adminstrn. (industry sector and functional adv. coms. for trade policy matters), New Orleans Assn. Life Underwriters (award for Loyal and Unselfish Svc. to the Ins. Industry 1987), La. Assn. Legal Res. Life Ins. Cos. (pres. 1963—68), Ins. Econs. Soc. Am. (chmn. 1980—81), Health Ins. Assn. Am. (dir., chmn. 1970), Am. Life Conv. (past chmn. legal sect., exec. com., v.p. La., chmn. 1972), Assn. Life Ins. Counsel, Am. Judicature Soc., La. Law Inst., La. Bar Found. Am. (v.p. La.), Assn. of C. of Commerce New Orleans Area (dir., pres. 1970), Delta Kappa Epsilon (Disting. Alumnus award Zeta Zeta chpt. 2001), Omicron Delta Kappa, Phi Delta Phi. Episcopalian.

**PURVIS, KAREN R.,** sanitary engineer; b. Quinter, Kans., July 13, 1958; d. Harley L. and Vera E. Beaver; m. Mark E. Purvis, Nov. 22, 1980; children: Jennifer L., Michael R. BS, Ft. Hays State U., 1981. Registered sanitarian State of Kans., 2000. Sanitarian Ellis County Environ., Hays, Kans., 1992—. Coun. advisor 4-H County Coun., Hays, 1998—2005; leader 4-H Shooting Sports, Hays, 2000—06; bell choir dir. Trinity Luth. Ch., Hays, Kans., 1994—2005. Recipient Spl. Recognition award, Kansas Assoc. Sanitarians. Mem.: Kans. Environ. Health Assn. (assoc.; pres. 2002—03). R-Consevative. Lutheran. Avocation: shooting. Office: Ellis County Environ 601 Main St Suite C Hays KS 67601 Office Phone: 785-628-9449. Office Fax: 785-628-9449. E-mail: karen@ellisco.net.

**PURVIS, RONALD SCOTT,** financial planner, real estate company officer; b. Cleve., Apr. 17, 1928; s. Samuel Martin Jr. and Dorothea (Scott) P.; m. Lynne Willis, Dec. 20, 1963; children: Ward S., Blair P. Snyder, Heather Leigh Ann. BS, U.S. Naval Acad., 1953; B Individualized Study, George Mason U., 1984. CLU, Chartered Fin. Cons. Enlisted USN, 1946, advanced through grades to lt. comdr., 1966, hon. discharged, 1972; served in destroyer with task force 77 Korea, 1953; flight instr., 1955-56; vx-6 squadron pilot, parachutist in-charge U.S. Naval Support Force Team, Antarctica, 1956-58; to McMurdo and South Pole, 1957-58; in charge of all-weather fighter detachment, 1958-59; with Office of the CNO (Op-007) Navy Dept., 1960-63; aide to pres. Kennedy, 1961-63; in charge of ordnance Handling, Flight Deck of aircraft carrier in the Mediterranean, 1963-64; in charge of pub. affairs NBC warfare def. NAS, Fla., 1965—67, in charge of 5 def. combat MoPic teams, US Mil. assistance command, 1968—69, dir. internal rels. CNO (Op-007), 1969—72; gen. agt. Can. Life Assurance, Washington, 1972-88; pres. RSVP Realty, Annandale, Va., 1985-2000, Purvis Corp., Falls Church, Va., 1986—2003. Del. Rep. Convs., Va., 1975—. Purvis Peak, Antarctic mountain, named in his honor. Mem. D.C. Soc., SAR (asst. registrar 1982-84, chaplain 1989-91, treas. 1991-92, state sec. 1992-94, sr. v.p. 1994-95, state pres. 1995-96, alt. nat. soc. trustee 1996-97, nat. soc. trustee 1997-98, registrar 1998-2000, mgmt. bd. 2000—), Assn. Naval Aviation, Masons, Shriners. Avocations: skiing, flying, scuba diving, golf, dance. Home: 27310 Baylys Neck Rd Accomac VA 23301 Office: 3415 Lakeside View Dr Falls Church VA 22041-2454 Office Phone: 703-820-3832. Business E-Mail: purvispeak@juno.com.

**PURYEAR, JAMES BURTON,** college administrator; b. Jackson, Miss., Sept. 2, 1938; s. Harry Henton and Doris (Smith) P.; m. Joan Copeland, June 13, 1965; children: John James, Jeffrey Burton, Joel Harry. BS, Miss. State U., Miss. State, 1960, MEd, 1961; PhD, Fla. State U., Tallahassee, 1969. Lic. profl. counselor, Ga. Assoc. dir. YMCA Miss. State U., Starkville, 1962-64; dir. YMCA, Starkville, Miss., 1964-65; dir. fin. aid Fla. State U., Tallahassee, 1967-69; asst. dir. student affairs Med. Coll. of Ga., Augusta, 1969-70, dir. student affairs, 1970-86, v.p. student affairs, 1986-2000, v.p. emeritus, student affairs, 2000—. mem. adv. bd. Ga. Fed. Bank, Augusta, 1978-85; deacon, 1971-, chmn. bd. First Bapt. Ch., Augusta, 1978-80; pres. Learning Disabilities Assn., Augusta, 1987, PTA, 1994, Band Assn.,1996; bd. dirs. Augusta Tng. Shop for Handicapped, 1994-98; mem. exec. bd., v.p. Boy Scouts Am., 1996-02; mem. bd. Consumer Credit Counseling Svc., 2004-. Yearbook Dedication MCG Student Yearbook, 1975; scholar Med. Coll. Ga., 1988; recipient Svc. to Mankind award Sertoma, 1988. Mem. Nat. Assn. Student Pers. (S.E. regional bd. 1985), Am. Coll. Pers. Assn., So. Assn. Coll. Student Affairs, Rotary (pres. 1978, dist. lt. gov. 1997-99, dist. gov. 2001-02, Paul Harris fellow 1985, Will Watt fellow). Baptist. Avocations: golf, photography, scouting.

**PURYEAR, JOAN COPELAND,** academic administrator; b. Columbus, Miss., May 10, 1944; d. John Thomas and Mamie (Cunningham) Copeland.; m. James Burton Puryear, June 13, 1965; children: John James, Jeffrey Burton, Joel Harry. BA summa cum laude, Miss. State U., Starkville, 1965; MA, Fla. State U., 1969; EdD, U. Ga., 1987. Instr. English, Fla. State U., Tallahassee, 1965-69, Augusta State U., 1987-88; head English dept. Augusta Tech. Coll., 1989-93, chairperson gen. edn. and devel. studies, 1993-96, mem. dean's coun., mgmt. team, 1994—, dean gen. edn. and devel. studies, 1997—, dean allied health scis., 1997—2004. Chmn. State Exec. Bd. English, Ga., 1990-92, East Ctrl. Consortium English, Ga., 1990-92; facilitator Total Quality Mgmt. Tech. Tng.; mem. exec. steering com. Continous Improvement Coun., 1996-02; mem. and co-chmn. Continuous Improvement Coun., 1996-97. Mem. Cmtys. in Schs., 1996—; trustee Augusta Tech. Inst. Found. Bd., 1996—; mem. founding bd. Junior Achievement, 2001-02; co-pres. Davidson Fine Arts Sch. PTA, 1995, co-pres. bd. assn., 1996; pres. Med. Coll. Spouse's Club, Augusta, 1972; dir. Women's Mission Orgn., First Bapt. Ch., Augusta, 1982, dir. youth Sunday Sch., 1992-98, chmn. 175th Anniversary, 1992, deacon, 1996—, vice moderator, 1998-99, mem. ministerial adv. com., 1992-2001, chair, 2003, vice chmn. scholarship and edn. com., 2002, chmn. nominating com., 2004, Sunday Sch. tchr.; mem. found. bd. Walton Rehab. Ctr. Mem.: Rotary (chmn. dist. membership 2003—, asst. dist. gov. 2006—), Augusta South Rotary Club (pres. 2002—03), Phi Theta Kappa (advisor 1992—, Horizon regional award for outstanding advisor 1997). Baptist. Avocations: flower arranging, home decorating, reading, travel. Office: Augusta Tech Coll 3200 Augusta Tech Dr Augusta GA 30906-3375

**PURYEAR, MARTIN,** artist, educator; b. Washington, May 23, 1941; s. Reginald Thomas and Martina Alice (Morse) P. BA, Cath. U., 1963; postgrad., Swedish Royal Acad., Stockholm, 1966-68; M.F.A., Yale U., 1971, Doctorate (hon.), 1994. Mem. Peace Corps, Sierra Leone, 1964—66; asst. prof. Fisk U., Nashville, 1971-73, U. Md., College Park, 1974-77; assoc. prof. art U. Ill., Chgo., 1978-86, prof., 1986-88; staff Calder Atelier, Saché, France, 1992—93; resident Am. Acad., Rome, 1997; represented by Donald Young Gallery, Chgo. Exhibited in group shows at Whitney Biennial Exhbn., 1979, 81, 89, Whitney Mus. Am. Art, N.Y., Guggenheim Mus., N.Y.C., 1978, 85, 87, Mus. Modern Art, N.Y.C., 1984, St Louis Art Mus., 1988, Donald Young Gallery, Chgo., 2002, 03, McKee Gallery, N.Y.C., 2002, Irish Mus. Modern Art, Dublin, 2004, others; one-man shows include Corcoran Gallery Art, 1977, Joslyn Art Mus., 1980, Univ. Art Mus., 1985, Bklyn. Mus., 1988; commd. sculptures include Bodard Art, Nathan Manila Sculpture Pk., Govs. State U., University Park, Ill., Chevy Chase Garden Pla., Md.; traveling retrospective Art Inst. Chgo., Hirshorn Museum, Washington, D.C., Museum of Contemporary Art, Los Angeles, 1991-92; Documenta IX, Kassel, Germany, 1992. Recipient Purchase prize Balt. Mus. Art, 1962, award Francis J. Greenburger Found., 1988, Best Artist prize Sao Paulo Bienal, 1989, Creative Arts award for sculpture Brandeis U., 1989, medal for sculpture Skowhegan Sch. Painting & Sculpture, 1990, award Coll. Art Assn.; Louis Comfort Tiffany Found. grantee, 1981; Guggenheim fellow, 1982 Mem.: Am. Acad. and Inst. Arts and Letters.

**PUSATERI, DAVID P.,** lawyer; b. Pitts., 1959; BA, U. Notre Dame, 1981, JD, 1984. Bar: Pa. 1984, US Dist. Ct. We. Dist. Pa. 1986. Law clk. to Hon. Gustave Diamond US Dist. Ct. We. Dist. Pa., 1984—86; ptnr., real estate & environ. dept. McGuireWoods LLP, Pitts., 2001—, co-mng. ptnr. Pitts. office, 2001—02, mng. ptnr., 2002—. Recipient Internat. Acad. Trial Lawyers Award. Fellow: Allegheny County Bar Found.; mem.: ABA (environment, energy & resources sect., bus. law sect.), Pa. Bar Assn. (environ. mineral & natural resource law sect.), Allegheny County Bar Assn. (bus. law sect., environ. law sect.). Office: McGuireWoods LLP Dominion Tower 23rd Fl 625 Liberty Ave Pittsburgh PA 15222-3142 Office Phone: 412-667-7924. Office Fax: 412-667-7963. Business E-Mail: DPusateri@mcguirewoods.com.

**PUSCHEL, PHILIP P.,** textiles executive; m. Roberta J. Green. AB, Hamilton Coll., 1960; MBA, Stanford U., 1962. V.p. F Schumacher & Co., N.Y.C., 1971, pres., CEO, 1981, chmn. bd., 1981—, CEO officer, 1989—99. With USN, 1962-65. Office: F Schumacher & Co 79 Madison Ave Fl 15 New York NY 10016-7802

**PUSCHETT, JULES B.,** nephrology educator, researcher; b. Hazelton, Pa., Mar. 13, 1934; m. Diane Puschett; children: Mitchell, Lynne. BA magna cum laude, Lehigh U., 1955; MD, U. Pa., 1959. Intern Jackson Meml. Hosp., Miami, 1959-60; resident, fellow endrocrinology and metabolism Univ. Hosp., Balt., 1963-66; postdoctoral fellow in medicine NIH Inst. Arthritis and Metabolic Disease, Bethesda, Md., 1966-68; fellow, renal-electrolyte sect. U. Pa. Sch. Medicine, Phila., 1966-68; rsch. assoc. VA Hosp., Phila., 1968-70, staff to chief renal-electrolyte sect. dept. medicine, 1968-73, clin. investigator, 1970-73; head renal-electrolyte divsn. Allegheny Gen. Hosp., Pitts., 1973-78; dir. renal-electrolyte divsn. fellowship tng. program U. Pitts. Sch. Medicine, 1976-78; chief renal-electrolyte divsn. dept. medicine U. Ark. for Med. Scis., Little Rock, 1979-80, U. Pitts. Sch. Medicine, 1980-90; interim chief sect. nephrology dept. medicine Tulane U. Sch. Medicine, New Orleans, 1990-92, prof. chmn. dept. medicine, 1990—, asst. dean network affairs, 1996—, Harry B. Greenberg, MD chair in internal medicine, 1999—. Instr. medicine U. Pa. Sch. Medicine 1967-79, assoc. in medicine 1969-70, asst. prof. medicine 1970-73; clin. assoc. prof. medicine U. Pitts. Med. Sch. 1973-78; prof. medicine U. Ark. Med. Scis. 1979-80; prof. medicine U. Pitts. Sch. Medicine 1980-90; adj. prof. dept. pharmacology Tulane U. Sch. Medicine, New Orleans, 2002—. Editor: The Diuretic Manual, 1984, Diuretics: chemistry, Pharmacology and Clinical Applications, 1984, Disorders of Fluid and Electrolyte Balance: diagnosis and Management, 1985, Diuretics II: Chemistry, Pharmacology and Clinical Applications, 1986, Diuretics III, 1989, Diuretics IV, 1993; contbr. over 170 articles to profl. jours.; spkr. and presenter in field; editl. bd. Am. Jour. Med. Scis., Am. Jour. Nephrology (sect. editor Physiology for the Nephrologist), Cardiovasc. Risk Factors, Internat. Jour. Artificial Organs, Southern Med. Jour. Chmn. 1st Ann. Kidney Ball, Nat. Kidney Found. of Western Pa., 1988, chmn. 2d Ann. Kidney Ball, 1989. With USN 1960-63. Recipient Gloria P. Walsh award for Tchg. Excellence, Graduating Class/Tulane U. Sch. Medicine, 1998; named Outstanding Tchr. Yr., Owl Club, Tulane U., 1991, 94; Coxe Meml. scholar Lehigh U., 1951. Fellow ACP; mem. AMA, AAAS, Am. Fedn. Clin. Rsch., Am. Soc. Artificial Internal Organs, Am. Soc. Nephrology (chmn. audit com. 1992), Nat. Kidney Found. (pub. policy com. 1989, vol. svc. award 1990), Internat. Soc. Nephrology, Am. Heart Assn. Coun. on the Kidney in Cardiovasc. Disease (chmn. sucom. on scientific confs. 1991-92, exec. com. 1991-95, long-range planning com. 1992-94, vice chair 1998-2000, chair-elect 1999-2000, chair 2000—), Am. Heart Assn. Coun. for High Blood Pressure Rsch., Am. Physiol. Soc., Fedn. Am. Socs. for Exptl. Bioiogy, Am. Geriat. Soc., Cntl. Soc. for Clin. Rsch., Soc. for Exptl. Biology and Medicine, Am. Soc. Clin. Pharmacology and Therapeutics, Am. Coll. Clin. Pharmacoiogy, Endocrine Soc., Am. Soc. Renal Biochemistry and Metabolism, Am. Soc. Hypertension (Outstanding Tchr. Yr. 1986), Internat. Soc. Nutrition and Metabolism in Renal Disease, Am. Soc. Bone and Mineral Rsch., European Dialysis and Transpiant Assn., Nat. Kidney Found. of Western Pa. (med. adv. com. 1981, chmn. 1981-83, Gift of Life award 1991), Nat. Kidney Found. of La. (mem.-at-large, trustee 1991), So. Med. Assn., So. Soc. Clin. Investigation (councilor 1992-94, sec.-treas. 1994-99, pres.-elect 1998-99, pres. 1999-2000), La. State Med. Soc., Orleans Parish Med. Soc. (membership com. 1993, long-range planning com. 1993), La. Soc. Internal Medicine, S.E. Clin. Club, Midwestern Salt and Water Club, Phi Beta Kappa, Alpha Epsilon Delta, Alpha Omega Alpha. Office: Tulane Univ Sch Medicine Dept Medicine SL 12 1430 Tulane Ave New Orleans LA 70112-2699 E-mail: jpusche@tulane.edu.

**PUSEY, WILLIAM ANDERSON,** lawyer; b. Richmond, Va., Mar. 17, 1936; s. Paul H. and Vernelle (Barnes) P.; m. Patricia Powell, Sept. 3, 1960; children: Patricia Brent, William A. Jr., Margaret Glen. AB, Princeton U., 1958; JD, U. Va., 1962. Bar: Va. 1964. Assoc. McCutchen, Brown, et al, San Francisco, 1962-63; dep. dist. atty. Alameda County, Oakland, Calif., 1963-64; assoc., ptnr., sr. counsel Hunton & Williams, Washington, Fairfax and Richmond, Va., 1964—. Trustee Ea. Mineral Law Found., pres., 1987-88. Chmn. bd. dirs. Presbyn. Sch. Christian Edn., Richmond, 1984-85. Mem. Am. Hort. Soc. (bd. dirs. and sec. 1995-2002, gen. counsel 2002—), Order of Coif, Phi Beta Kappa, Omicron Delta Kappa. Office: Hunton & Williams 1900 K St NW Washington DC 20006-1110 Home: 57 E Square Ln Richmond VA 23238

**PUSKAR, MILAN,** pharmaceuticals executive; b. 1935; Grad., Youngstown State U., 1961. V.p. Mylan Pharm. Inc., 1961-72; divsn. v.p. ICN Pharms., Inc., 1972-75; pres., CEO, chmn. Mylan Lab. Inc., 1976-2000, chmn., CEO, 2000—. Vice chmn. bd. Mylan Lab. Inc., 1980-93, chmn. bd., 1993—. Office: STE 400 1500 Corporate DR Canonsburg PA 15317-8580

**PUST, RONALD E.,** physician, educator; b. Sidney, Mont., May 5, 1941; s. Erich W. Pust and Marie Leis; m. Karen J. Blomquist, June 12, 1966; children: Joel E., Sara M. Meza, Rachel K. Durazo, Brian P. BA, Wheaton Coll., Ill., 1962; MD, U. Wash., Seattle, 1962—66. Cert. Am. Bd. Preventive Medicine, 1973, Amercan Bd. Family Medicine, 1978, qualification Am. Soc. Tropical Medicine & Hygiene, 2000. TB control physician Indian Health Svc., Window Rock, Ariz., 1969—71; med. epidemiologist CDC, USPHS, Enugu, Nigeria, 1971—73; med. officer, dir. Immanuel Luth. Hosp., Wapenamanda, Papua New Guinea, 1973—79; prof. family medicine and pub. health U. Ariz., Tucson, 1979—. Pres. Global Health Edn. Consortium, N.Y.C., 1992—93; prof. and head family health Moi U., Eldoret, Kenya, 2004—05. Med. missionary to Papua New Guinea Luth. Ch., St Louis, 1973—79. Recipient Smallpox Target Zero, WHO, 1980. Democrat. Presyterian. Avocations: travel, photography. Business E-Mail: rpust@email.arizona.edu.

**PUSTER, JOHN C.,** music educator; b. Ashland, Ohio, July 4, 1969; s. Stanley W. and Frances A. Puster; m. Melissa Ann Purdy, June 29, 1991; 1 child, Anna Grace. B of Music Edn., Coll. Wooster, 1991; M of Music Edn., U. Akron, 1993. Cert. music tchr. Ohio. Part-time music tchr. Wayne County Schs., Wooster, Ohio, 1992—93; music tchr., band dir. Jackson Local Schs., Massillon, Ohio, 1993—95, Triway Local Schs., Wooster, Ohio, 1995—. Profl. mentor Triway Local Schs./Coll. of Wooster, 1998—; home-based bus. cons. Storms Enterprises, Lakeville, Ohio, 1998—. Composer, arranger: jazz band music Jammy-Jams, 2006. Mem. ch. coun. St. John Luth. Ch., McZera, Ohio, 1996—. Mem.: Ohio Music Edn. Assn. Avocations: gardening, golf, church activities, playing Euchre, spending time with family.

**PUTH, DAVID W.,** diversified financial services company executive; 3 children. With Bank New Eng., 1980; v.p. fgn. exch. Citigroup; mng. dir., global head FX Connect; global head currencies J.P. Morgan Chase & Co., global head fgn. exch. and commodities, mng. dir., head North Am. rates, mng. dir., head North Am. FX trading. Chmn. fgn. exch. com. Fed. Res. Bank, 2000—. Office: JP Morgan Chase & Co 270 Park Ave New York NY 10017-2070*

**PUTH, JOHN WELLS,** manufacturing executive, consultant; b. Orange, N.J., Mar. 14, 1929; s. Leonard G. and Elizabeth R. (Wells) P.; m. Betsey Leeds Tait, Mar.1, 1952; children: David Wells, Jonathan Craig, Alison Leeds. BS cum laude, Lehigh U., 1952. Dir. mktg. Puroiator Products, Rahway, NJ, 1955-61; pres., chief exec. officer Bridgeport (Conn.) Hardware Mfg. Co. subs. Purolator, 1962-65; group v.p. H.K. Porter Co., Pitts., 1965-72; pres., CEO Disston Inc., Pitts., 1972-75, Vapor Corp., Niles, Ill., 1975-83; chmn., pres., CEO Clevite Industries Inc., Glenview, Ill., 1983-89; pres. JW Puth Assocs., Skokie, Ill., 1989—. Bd. dirs. Adam Street Ptnrs., L.B. Foster, Pitts., A.M. Castle & Co., Franklin Park, Ill., V.J. Growers Inc., Apopka, Fla., George W. Schmidt Inc., Niles, Ill., Guy & O'Neil, Fredonia, Wis.; advisor GTCR Funds, Golfserve Inc., Chgo. Chmn. bd. trustees Hadley Sch. for Blind, Winnetka, Ill., 1982-84; former trustee Lehigh U., Kenilworth Union Ch.; bd. dirs. Iaccoca Inst. With U.S. Army, 1946—47. Mem.: Loblolly Pines Club, Old Elm Club, Indian Hill Country Club, Comml. Club, Chgo. Club. Republican. Presbyterian. Home: 180 De Windt Rd Winnetka IL 60093-3744

**PUTHENPURAKAL, JOSEPH MATHEW,** information technology executive; b. Changanacherry, India, Feb. 12, 1949; arrived in U.S., 1978; s. Mathew Joseph and Teresa Mathew P.; m. Mary Jose Shirly, Aug. 21, 1977; children: Mathew Joseph, Thomas Joseph, Sherin Jose. BS, Kerala U., India,

1976; MS, Kerala U., 1978; AA, Dupage Coll., Glen Ellyn, Ill., 1982; BA, North Cen. Coll., Naperville, Ill., 1984; MBA, Thornewood U., Amsterdam, Netherlands, 1998, PhD, 2001. Software engr. AT&T Tech., Lisle, Ill., 1983-84; mem. tech. staff AT&T Bell Labs., Naperville, Ill., 1984-87; info. systems cons. Indecon, Inc., Chicago, 1987-89; pres. Chicagoland Star Telephone Co., 1988, Global Resources Co., Chgo., 1988—; mgr. Jewel Info. Systems Group, Melrose Park, Ill., 1989—91; pres. Optimum Techs. Inc., Lisle, Ill., 1992—; owner Optimum Real Estate, 2003—. Trustee Rep. Presdl. Task Force, Washington, 1986. Mem. Data Processing Mgmt. Assn., Am. Entrepreneurs Assn., Internat. Traders. Avocations: reading, travel, swimming. Home: 1230 Golfview Dr Woodridge IL 60517 Office: Optimum Techs Inc 1230 Golfview Dr Woodridge IL 60517 E-mail: jputhen@aol.com.

**PUTKA, ANDREW CHARLES**, lawyer; b. Cleve., Nov. 14, 1926; s. Andrew George and Lillian M. (Koryta) Putka. Student, John Carroll U., 1944, U.S. Naval Acad., 1945-46; AB, Adelbert Coll., Western Res. U., 1949, JD, 1952. Bar: Ohio 1952. Practice law, Cleve.; instr. govt. Notre Dame Coll.; v.p. Koryta Bros. Coal Co., Cleve., 1952-56; supt. divsn. bldg. and loan assns. Ohio Dept. Commerce, 1959-63; pres., chmn. bd., CEO Am. Nat. Bank, Parma, Ohio, 1963-69; dir. fin. City of Cleve., 1971-74; dir. port control, 1974-78; dir. Cleve. Hopkins Internat. Airport, 1974-78. Mem. Ohio Ho. of Reps., 1953-56, Ohio Senate, 1957-58; dep. auditor, acting sec. Cuyahoga County Bd. Revision, 1970-71; mem. exec. com. Cuyahoga County Democratic Com., 1973-81, Assn. Ind. Colls. and Univs. Ohio, 1983-89; bd. govs. Sch. Law, Western Res. U., 1953-56; mem. exec. com. World Service Student Fund, 1950-52; U.S. rep. Internat. Pax Romana Congress, Amsterdam, 1950, Toronto, 1952; mem. lay adv. bd. Notre Dame Coll., 1968-90, trustee, 1990-93, hon. trustee, 1993—, life mem., 1993—; mem. adv. bd. St. Andrew's Abbey, 1976-88; trustee Case-Western Res. U., Newman Found. No. Ohio, 1980-93, hon. trustee, life mem., 1993—; 1st v.p. First Cath. Slovak Union of U.S., 1977-80; pres. USO Council of Cuyahoga County, 1980-83. Voted an outstanding legislator Ohio Press Corrs., 1953; named to 'All-Star Legislative team Ohio Newspaper Corrs.', 1955; named one of Fabulous Clevelanders Cleve. Plain Dealer, John Henry Newman honor Soc. Mem. Cuyahoga County, Cleve. Bar Assn., Nat. Assn. State Savs. and Loan Suprs. (past. nat. pres.), U.S. Savs. and Loan League (mem. legis com, 1960-63), Am. Legion, Ohio Mcpl. League (bd. trustees 1973), Parma C. of C. (bd. dirs., treas. 1965-67), Newman Fedn. (past nat. pres.), NCCJ, Catholic Lawyers Guild (treas.), Am. Ohio Bankers Assn., Am. Inst. Banking, Adelbert Alumni Assn. (exec. com.), Cathedral Latin Alumni Assn. (trustee 1952—), Internat. Order of Alhambra (internat. parliamentarian 1971—, past grand comdr., supreme advocate 1973), Amvets, KC, Pi Kappa Alpha, Delta Theta Phi (past. pres. Cleve. alumni senate, master inspector 1975). Office: 28 Pond Dr Cleveland OH 44116-1062 Office Phone: 440-331-5532.

**PUTMAN, CAROL JEAN**, photographer, artist; b. San Francisco, Jan. 1, 1943; d. Joe Alfred and Jessie Jane (Harris) P. BA, Calif. State U., Hayward, 1968. Photographer, artist, Clayton, Calif., 1975—; exec. sec. Bank of Am., San Francisco, 1980; group sec. physics dept. Lawrence Berkeley Lab. U. Calif., Berkeley, 1974-75, sec. civil engring. dept., 1981-84, faculty sec. journalism dept., 1984-85, adminstrv. asst., sec. Dept. Math., 1985-86, 87-88. Exhibitions include Walnut Creek (Calif.) Civic Arts, 1982, Bedford Gallery, Walnut Creek, Calif., 2005, Ironstone Vineyards, Murphys, Calif., 2006, Sanchez Art Ctr., Pacifica, Calif., 2006. Avocations: sailing, bicycling.

**PUTMAN, DALE CORNELIUS**, management consultant, lawyer; b. Ponca, Nebr., Apr. 29, 1927; s. Merle H. and Catherine V. (Sheahan) P.; m. Alice Anselmi, Sept. 8, 1951; children: Mark, Lee, Neil, Bruce, Kirk, Nancy, Wendy. BS, U. Nebr., 1949, LL.D., 1951. Bar: Nebr. 1951, Iowa 1951, Mo. 1977. Mgr. Interstate Assn. Credit Mgmt., Sioux City, Iowa, 1951-52; sec., legal counsel Metz Baking Co., Sioux City, 1953-66, v.p., 1966-69, exec. v.p., 1969-72, pres., 1972-76; chief operating officer Interstate Brands Corp., Kansas City, Mo., 1976-77, pres., dir., 1977-80, pres., chief exec. officer, 1980-84; chmn., chief exec. officer, pres., dir. Interstate Bakeries (formerly DPF, Inc.), 1980-84; pvt. practice mgmt. cons., 1984—. Served with U.S. Army, 1945-46. Knight, Order of the Holy Sepulchre of Jerusalem, knight Order of Malta. Mem. KC (4th degree), Serra Internat., Mensa. Republican. Roman Catholic. Home: 8405 Reinhardt Ln Shawnee Mission KS 66206-1316 Personal E-mail: putman9752@aol.com.

**PUTMAN, JEFFREY SCOTT**, academic administrator; b. Bronx, NY, Jan. 5, 1975; s. Michael R and Phyllis P. Putman. BA summa cum laude, SUNY, Purchase, 1996; MA, Columbia U., NYC, 1997, MEd, 1998. Asst. to the v.p. for student affairs Purchase Coll., SUNY, Purchase, NY, 1996—99, asst. dean for student affairs, 1999—2003, adj. lectr. in polit. sci., 2000, acting dir. of student devel. & campus activities, 2001, asst. dean for student affairs / ombudsperson, 2004—, interim dean of students, 2003—04; tchg. asst., orgn. and leadership Teachers Coll., Columbia U., New York, NY, 2002—02. Mem., region ii adv. bd. Nat. Assn. of Student Pers. Administrs. (NASPA), Washington, 1997—; profl. del. United U. Professions (UUP), Albany, NY, 1997—. Active Tchrs. Coll., Columbia U. Alumni Coun., NYC, 2004—. Recipient Chancellor's Award for Excellence in Profl. Svc., SUNY, 2001. Mem.: Am. Coll. Pers. Assn. (assoc.), Nat. Assn. of Student Pers. Administrators (assoc.; mem., regional adv. bd., region ii 1997—2005), United U. Professions (assoc.; profl. del. 1997—2005), Purchase Coll. Alumni Assn. Inc. (assoc.; pres. emeritus 2003—05), Kappa Delta Pi (assoc.). Office: Purchase College SUNY 735 Anderson Hill Rd Purchase NY 10577 Office Phone: 914-251-6030. E-mail: jeffrey.putman@purchase.edu.

**PUTMAN, JOHN A.**, biofeedback practitioner, consultant; b. Burbank, Calif., Apr. 4, 1958; s. James Albert and Heather (Murray) Putman. BA in Math., Calif. State U., Northridge, 1980; MA in Psychology, Antioch U., 1982; MS in Electro-med. Sci., Nova U., 1998. Lic. marriage and family therapist, cert. biofeedback practitioner, EEG biofeedback specialist, lic. pvt. pilot. Gymnast Nat. Collegiate Athletic Assn. Matador Inst., Calif. State U., Northridge, Calif., 1975—77; aerospace technician Marquardt Co., Van Nuys, Calif., 1977; resident counselor Pennylane Home for Adolescents, Sepulveda, Calif., 1978—81; psychology intern/MFT Ctr. for Human Problems, Tarzana, Calif., 1982—93; therapist, inst. dir. Aviva Ctr., LA, 1985—90; marriage and family therapist, biofeedback practitioner, cons. LA, 1994—. Biofeedback practitioner Bellwood Hosp., Bellflower, Calif., 1992—96; therapist, supr. Psychiat. Mgmt. Resources, L.A., 1997—2000; EEG biofeedback practitioner EEG Inst., L.A., 1999—; presenter in field. Contbr. articles to profl. jours. Tutor, rsch. counselor Penny Lane Adolescent Placement, Sepulveda, Calif., 1978—80, Pacific Lodge Boys Home, Woodland Hills, Calif., 1984—85. Fellow: Soc. for Neurol. Regulation; mem.: Aviation Psychology Assn., Calif. Assn. Marriage Family Therapists. Avocations: musician, flying, backpacking, yoga. Office: EEG Inst 22020 Clarendon St Ste 305 Woodland Hills CA 90046 Office Phone: 818-754-4223. Office Fax: 818-373-1331. E-mail: JPutman905@aol.com

**PUTMAN, MARK**, theater educator; s. William and Sarah Putman. BA, Tex. Luth. Coll., Seguin, 1976; MFA, U. Calif., Davis, 1992. Profl. staff N.Mex State U., Las Cruces, 1985—89, U. N.Mex, Albuquerque, 1992—95; assoc. prof. Mo. State U., Springfield, 1995—. Lighting and scenic designer St. Louis Black Repertory Co.; carpenter/welder Santa Fe Opera; tech. dir. Intiman Theatre Co., Seattle; asst. tech. dir. Goodspeed Operahouse, East Haddam, Conn.; Hartford Stage Co., Conn. Mem.: US Inst. for Theatre Tech. Office Phone: 417-836-6824.

**PUTNAM, ADAM HUGHES**, congressman, farmer, rancher; b. Bartow, Fla., July 31, 1974; s. William Dudley and Sara Elizabeth (Hughes) P.; m. Melissa Putnam; children: Abbie Anna, Elizabeth Langford, Emma Katherine. BS in Food and Resource Econs., U. Fla., 1995. Co-owner Dudley Putnam, Inc., Bartow, Fla., 1988—. Fla. Ho. of Reps., Tallahassee, 1996—2000, U.S. Congress from 12th Fla. dist., Washington, 2001—, mem. budget com., rules com., 2004—, chmn. Rep. policy com., 2006—. V.p. Fla.

4-H Found., 1997—. Mem. Fla. Cattlemen's Assn., Fla. Farm Bur., Bartow Kiwanis Club. Republican. Episcopalian. Avocations: hunting, fishing, reading. Office: US Ho of Reps 1213 Longworth HOB Washington DC 20515-0912

**PUTNAM, ALFRED W., JR.**, lawyer; b. Phila., 1951; married; 1 child. AB summa cum laude, Harvard Univ., 1973; BA, Univ. Oxford, Oxford, Eng., 1975; JD, Univ. Pa., 1978. Bar: Pa. 1978. Assoc. Drinker Biddle & Reath LLP, Phila., 1979—85, ptnr., civil litig., 1985—, chmn. bd., 2005—. Sec., gen. counsel People for John Heinz; southeastern fin. chmn. Rick Santorum polit. campaign. Trustee, chmn. Lankenau Hosp., Main Line Health Sys., Jefferson Health Sys., 2004—. Mem.: Univ. Pa. Law Sch. Am. Inn of Ct. (pres.). Republican. Office: Drinker Biddle & Reath LLP One Logan Sq 18th & Cherry Sts Philadelphia PA 19103-6996 Office Phone: 215-988-2907. Office Fax: 215-988-2757. E-mail: alfred.putnam@dbr.com.

**PUTNAM, FRANK WILLIAM**, biochemistry educator, immunologist, educator; b. New Britain, Conn., Aug. 3, 1917; s. Frank and Henrietta (Holzmann) P.; m. Dorothy Alice Linder, Nov. 18, 1942; children— Frank William, Beverly Susan. BA, Wesleyan U., Middletown, Conn., 1939, MA, 1940; PhD, U. Minn., 1942; MA (hon.), Cambridge U., Eng., 1973. Instr., research asso. Duke U. Med. Sch., 1942-46; biochemist CWS, Camp Detrick, Md., 1946; asst. prof. U. Chgo., then assoc. prof. biochemistry, 1947-55; Lasdon research fellow Cambridge U., 1952-53; prof. biochemistry, head dept. U. Fla., 1955-65; prof. biology, dir. div. biol. scis. Ind. U., Bloomington, 1965-69, prof. molecular biology and zoology, 1972-74, disting. prof. molecular biology and biochemistry, 1974-88, prof. emeritus, 1989—. Bd. visitors Duke U. Med. Ctr., 1970-75; chmn. com. nomenclature of human immunoglobulins Internat. Union Immunol. Socs., 1971-76; chmn. basic sci. rev. bd. VA, 1972-76; chmn. cancer cause and prevention adv. com. Nat. Cancer Inst., 1974-75; sci. adv. com. Papanicolaou Cancer Research Inst., 1976-82; rsch. rev. com. ARC, 1973-77; sci. com. Brussels Colloquium on Protides of Biol. Fluids, 1970-90; chmn. virus cancer program adv. com. Nat. Cancer Inst., 1975-77; sr. med. adv. group VA, 1976-80; coun. divsn. biol. scis. and Pritzker Med. Sch., U. Chgo., 1977-87; chmn. Assembly Life Scis. Nat. Acad. Scis., 1977-81; mem. U.S. Nat. Com. Biochemistry, 1973-79; pres. sci. adv. com. G.E.R.M.I., Lyon, France, 1981-87. Co-author, editor: The Plasma Proteins, vol. 1, Isolation, Characterization and Function, 1960, vol. 2, Biosynthesis, Metabolism, Alterations in Disease, 1960, The Plasma Proteins, 2d edit., Structure, Function, and Genetic Control, Vol. 1, 1975. Vol. 2, 1975, Vol. 3, 1977, Vol. 4, 1984, Vol. 5, 1987; mem. editorial bd. Archives of Biochemistry and Biophysics, 1954-59, Science, 1968-82, Immunochemistry, 1972-75, Biomed. News, 1969-73, Fedn. Proc, 1958-63; Author numerous research papers. Trustee Argonne Univs. Assn., 1981-82; bd. govs. U. Chgo. Argonne Nat. Lab., 1983-89, chmn. Sci. and tech. com., 1983-87; bd. dirs. Radiation Rsch. Found., 1981-87. Markle scholar med. scis., 1950-56; Guggenheim fellow, 1970; fellow Churchill Coll., Cambridge U., 1973—; recipient Distinguished award teaching and research Wesleyan U., 1964, Distinguished Service award in medicine U. Chgo., 1968; Outstanding Achievement award U. Minn., 1974 Fellow AAAS, N.Y. Acad. Scis.; mem. Nat. Acad. Scis., Am. Acad. Arts and Scis. (Midwest council 1975-84), Pan-Am. Assn. Biomed. Scis. (sec.-gen. 1975-78), Japan Electrophoresis Soc. (hon.), Am. Inst. Biol. Scis. (life), Am. Soc. Biol. Chemists (sec. 1958-63), Soc. Exptl. Biology and Medicine, Am. Assn. Immunologists, Am. Chem. Soc. (chmn. div. biol. chemistry 1966-67), Soc. Peruana de Patologia (hon.), Fedn. Socs. Exptl. Biology (chmn. secs. com. 1958-63), Protein Soc., Internat. Soc. Thrombosis Haemostasis, Phi Beta Kappa, Sigma Xi, Phi Lambda Upsilon, Delta Sigma Rho. Clubs: Cosmos. Address: 11130 Springfield Pike Apt B423 Cincinnati OH 45246-4193

**PUTNAM, FREDERICK WARREN, JR.**, bishop; b. Red Wing. Minn., June 17, 1917; s. Frederick W. and Margaret (Bunting) P.; m. Helen Kathryn Prouse, Sept. 24, 1942; children: James Douglas, John Frederick, Andrew Warren. BA, U. Minn., 1939; M.Div., Seabury-Western Theol. Sem., 1942, D.D., 1963; postgrad., State U. Iowa, 1946-47, Mpls. Coll. of Art & Design, 1984-97. Ordained to ministry Episcopal Ch. as deacon, priest, 1942. Pastor in, Windom and Worthington, Minn., 1942-43, Iowa City, 1943-47, Evanston, Ill., 1947-59, Wichita, Kans., 1960-63; Episc. chaplain State U. Iowa, 1943-47; suffragan bishop Episcopal Diocese, Okla., 1963-79; bishop Episcopal Ch. in, Navajoland, 1979-83; asst. bishop Diocese of N.C., 1983, Diocese of Minn., 1983-89, 96-99; acting rector St. George's Episcopal, Pearl Harbor, Hawaii, 1984-85, 96, St. Clement's, Honolulu, 1986, St. John's, Kula, Maui, Hawaii, 1988, 98, St. Elizabeth's, Honolulu, 1990; interim rector St. Stephen's Episcopal Ch., Edina, Minn., 1991-92, Trinity Episcopal Ch., Pocatello, Idaho, 1994; vis. bishop Diocese of N.J., 1995. Bd. dirs. Kiyosoto Ednl. Experiment Program, 1954-91, Mobile Outreach Ministry, 1998—, v.p., 1989-91; cons. Oklahoma City Community Relation Commn., 1966-70; Pres. Okla. Conf. Religion and Race, 1963-67; v.p. Greater Oklahoma City Council Chs., 1966-67; nat. chaplain Brotherhood of St. Andrew, 1967-79, mem. brotherhood legion, 1972—; priest assoc. Order Holy Cross, 1942—; exec. com. Conf. Diocesan Execs., 1969-76, pres., 1972-74; mem. Okla. Commn. United Ministries in Higher Edn., 1970-79, pres., 1973-75; mem. nat. com. on Indian work Episc. Ch., 1977-80; chaplain Okla. Assn. Alcoholism and Alcohol Abuse, 1974-78; hon. life mem. Oklahoma City and County Criminal Justice Council, 1978—; Bechtel lectr. U. Denver, 1966. Editor: (pub.) Sharers Mag.. 1957-63; contbr. articles to profl. publs. Founder, pres. Oklahoma City Met. Alliance for Safer City, 1971-78; Trustee Seabury-Western Theol. Sem., 1959-65, Episcopal Theol. Sem. Southwest, 1966-69, St. Simeon's Episcopal Home, 1963-79, St. Crispins Episcopal Conf. Ctr., 1963-79, Casady Sch., 1963-79, Holland Hall Sch., 1963-79, Episcopal Soc. Cultural and Racial Unity, 1967-70; trustee Neighborhood Services Orgn., treas., 1969; founder, 1st pres. Friends of Wichita Pub. Libr., 1962; bd. dirs. Minn. Photographic Exhn.; chmn. Mpls. St. Paul Internat. Photog. Exhhn., 1987, 89; State Bd. Minn. Common Cause, 1989—, state chmn., 1993-95—; bd. dirs. Minn. Com. for Pub. Edn. Recipient Disting. Service award Evanston Jr. C. of C., 1952; Merit award Photog. Soc. Am. Fellow Coll. Preachers; mem. ACLU, Assoc. Parishes (pres. 1960-64), Mpls. Soc. Fine Arts (mem. photo coun.), Photog. Soc. Am., Am. Com. for KEEP (vis. 1961-70, 90), Walker Art Ctr., Sierra Club, Met. Sr. Fedn., Audubon Club, Am. Assn. Ret. Persons, Minn. Hort. Soc., Hist. Soc. Episcopal Ch., Archaeol. Conservancy, Ancient Bibl. Manuscripts Ctr., Claremont, Calif., World Future Soc., Photographic Soc. Am. (assoc. 1989—, mem. v.p., 1995-97—), Twin Cities Assn. Camera Clubs (v.p. 1987), U. Minn. Alumni Assn., Minn. Hist. Soc., St. Paul Camera Club, Crosstown Camera Club, N.Am. Rights Fund., People for the Am. Way, Episcopal Peace Fellowship, Amnesty Internat., Greenpeace, Liturgical Conf., Living Th. Found., Worldwatch Inst., Clan Douglas Soc., Northwest Racquet and Swim Club, Explorers Club, Phi Kappa Psi. Clubs: Normandale Tennis and Swim. Episcopalian. Home: 5229 Meadow Rdg Edina MN 55439-1412

**PUTNAM, GENE CHUMLEY**, music educator; b. Laurens, S.C., Nov. 20, 1935; d. Richard E. and Sara W. (Word) Chumley; (div.); children: David Martin Putnam, Ashley Paige Goodwin. BS, Winthrop Coll., 1956; MA in Tchg., Rollins Coll., 1974. Tchr. Anderson Jr. High. Sch., 1956-57, Liberty Elem., S.C., 1957-59, Whispering Hills Elem., 1965-66, Ocean Breeze Elem., 1972-73, Northwood Middle Sch., 1973-85, J.L. Mann H.S., 1985-88; pvt. tchr. Ft. Lauderdale, Fla., 1988—. Author of musical revs. Actress, dir. Little Theatre Prodn., 1956-88. Recipient award Nat. Found. for the Advancement in the Arts, 1994. Mem. Music Tchrs. Nat. Assn. (sec. Broward County chpt. 1990-94), Fla. State Music Tchrs. Assn., Broward County Music Tchrs. Assn., Lauderdale Yacht Club. Republican. Episcopalian. Home: 1259 Cordora Rd Fort Lauderdale FL 33316

**PUTNAM, GEORGE W., JR.**, retired army officer; b. Ft. Fairfield, Maine, May 5, 1920; s. George W. and Rae B. (Merrithew) P.; m. Elaine Anderson (dec. 1973); m. Claudine Mahin (div. 1995); m. Helen Guerin, 1995; children: James M., J. Glenn; stepchildren: Philip Mahin, Leslie Mahin. Enlisted man U.S. Army, 1941-42, commd. 2d lt., 1942, advanced through grades to maj. gen., 1970; comdg. gen. 1st Aviation Brigade, Vietnam, 1970, 1st Cav. Divsn., Vietnam, 1970-71; dir. Mil. Personnel Mgmt., Hdqrs. Dept. Army, Washing-

ton, 1971-75; comdg. gen. U.S. Army So. European Task Force, Vicenza, Italy, 1975-77, U.S. Army Phys. Disability Agy., Washington, 1977-81; ret. U.S. Army, 1981. Dir. Army Coun. Rev. Bds., 1977-81; pres. Nat. Capital Retiree Coun., 1982-85. Internat. judge 5th and 6th World Helicopter Championships, 1986, 89, 94, chief judge 7th World Championship, 1992; U.S. mem. Internat. Helicopter com. Fedn. Aeronautique Internationale, 1988-91, 93-95; bd. dirs. Army Aviation Mus. Found., 1987—, pres., 1993-96; chmn. bd. trustees Army Aviation Hall of Fame, 1996-2001. Recipient Elder Statesman of Aviation award, 1998; inducted Army Aviation Hall of Fame, 1980. Mem. Nat. Aero. Assn. (sr. v.p. 1991-98, Fedn. Aero. Internat. (v.p. 1995-98), Army Aviation Assn. Am. (sr. v.p., pres. 1983-87, pres. scholarship found. 1991-93), Helicopter Club Am. (pres. 1988-90). Home: 4106 N Richmond St Arlington VA 22207-4816 Personal E-mail: gputj@aol.com.

**PUTNAM, J. STEPHEN**, corporate financial executive; 3 children. BA, Bowdoin Coll., 1965. Former pres., COO Raymond James Fin. Svcs. Inc., now exec. v.p. bd. dirs. F.L. Putnam Securities. Former chmn. bd. St. Joseph's Coll., North Windham, Maine; former chmn. Scholarship Am.; former pres. Palm Harbor (Fla.) Cmty. Svc. Agy.; former chmn. Boston Stock Exch., Nat. Assn. Securities Dealers, Inc. Decorated Bronze Star, Army Commendation medal, Combat Infantryman's badge, Vietnam Cross. Office: Raymond James Fin Inc Tower 4 2d Fl 880 Carillon Pkwy Saint Petersburg FL 33716-1100 Office Phone: 727-567-5345. E-mail: Steve.Putnam@RaymondJames.com.

**PUTNAM, JERRY (GERALD D. PUTNAM)**, stock exchange executive; b. May 21, 1958; BS, U. Pa., 1981. With Walsh Greenwood, 1983—87, Jefferies & Co., PaineWebber, Prudential, Geldermann Securities, Inc.; founder, pres. Terra Nova, 1994—99; founder, CEO Archipelago Holdings, Inc., Chgo., 1999—2006; pres., co-COO NYSE Group, Inc., NYC, 2006—. Named one of Outstanding Innovators, Time mag., 2000; named to Entrepreneurship Hall of Fame, U. Ill., 2000. Avocation: hunting. Office: NYSE Group Inc 11 Wall St New York NY 10005

**PUTNAM, KERI**, film company executive; married; 2 children. Grad. Harvard U. Asst. HBO; with literary dept. Arena Stage, Washington; dir. develop. Devillier Donegan Enterprises, Washington; dir. devel. HBO, 1992—95; v.p. NYC Productions HBO Films, 1995—99, sr. v.p. LA, 1999—2004, exec. v.p., 2004—06; pres. prodn. Miramax Film Unit Walt Disney Co., 2006—. Recipient Excellence in Media award, Women in Film, 2005. Office: Miramax 375 Greenwich St New York NY 10013*

**PUTNAM, MARLENE EVANS**, artist; b. Hartford, Conn., Nov. 2, 1941; d. Charles Evans and Adrienne Edmay Levasseur; m. Harold Barnes Putnam, Jr., Mar. 9, 1980. Student, U. Hartford, 1960-63, Mus. of Fine Arts, Boston, 1971-77. Profl. artist Rockport (Mass.) Art Assn., 1986—, North Shore Art Assn., Gloucester, Mass., 1980—, Internat. Soc. of Marine Painters, Bradenton, Fla., 1983—, Art of the Sea, Rockland, Maine, 1995—, Tequesta (Fla.) Galleries, 1986—; fellow Am. Artist Profl. League, N.Y.S., 1996—. One-woman shows include Elliott Mus., 1993, Vero Beach Mus. Art, 1992, Art of the Sea, S. Thomaston, Maine, 1995; permanant collections at Harvard Law Sch., Dartmouth Coll., Nat. Wildlife Refuge, Cape Canaveral, Fla., Fla. Supreme Ct., Elliott Mus., Stuart, Fla., Vero Beach Mus. Art. Recipient over 50 awards in Fla. and Mass. Fellow Am. Artist Profl. League; mem. Rotary. Democrat. Avocations: learning and playing the viola, reading, computers, gardening, hiking.

**PUTNAM, MICHAEL COURTNEY JENKINS**, classics educator; b. Springfield, Mass., Sept. 20, 1933; s. Roger Lowell and Caroline (Jenkins) P. AB, Harvard U., Cambridge, Mass., 1954, AM, 1956, PhD, 1959; LLD (hon.), Lawrence U., Appleton, Wis., 1985. Instr. classics Smith Coll., Northampton, Mass., 1959-60; faculty classics Brown U., Providence, 1960—, prof., 1967—, chmn., 2000-2001, prof. comparative lit., 1980—, MacMillan prof. of classics, 1985—; acting dir. Ctr. for Hellenic Studies, Harvard U., 1961-62, sr. fellow, 1971-86; Townsend prof. classics Cornell U., 1985; Mellon prof.-in-charge Am. Acad. in Rome, 1989-91; Martin classical lectr. Oberlin Coll., 2004. Scholar in residence Am. Acad. in Rome, 1969-70, classical jury, 1982-83, trustee, 1991—; assoc. univ. seminar on classical civilization Columbia U., N.Y.C., 1972—; mem. cath. Commn. on Intellectual and Cultural Affairs, 1969—; adv. coun. dept. classics Princeton U., 1981-87, chmn., 1983-87; cons. Am. Coun. Learned Socs., 1987-89; mem. Inst. for Advanced Study, 1987-88; vis. scholar Phi Beta Kappa, 1994-95; councillor Assn. of Lit. Scholars and Critics, 1996-99. Author: The Poetry of the Aeneid, 1965, Virgil's Pastoral Art, 1970, Tibullus: A Commentary, 1973, Virgil's Poem of the Earth, 1979, Essays on Latin Lyric, Elegy and Epic, 1982, Artifices of Eternity: Horace's Fourth Book of Odes, 1986, Virgil's Aeneid: Interpretation and Influence, 1995, Virgil's Epic Designs, 1998, Horace's Carmen Saeculare, 2000, Maffeo Vegio: Short Epics, 2004, Poetic Interplay: Catullus and Horace, 2006; contbr. articles to profl. jours. Trustee Lowell Obs., Flagstaff, Ariz., 1967-87, bd. advisors, 1987—; trustee Bay Chamber Concerts, Camden, Maine, 1972-88, incorporator, 1988-94; mem. bd. cons. Portsmouth Abbey Sch., 1985-89; hon. sec. Keats-Shelley Meml. Assn., Rome, 1989-91. Rome Prize fellow Am. Acad. in Rome, 1963-64; Guggenheim Meml. fellow, 1966-67; sr. fellow NEH, 1973-74, cons. 1974-78, 87-90; Am. Council Learned Soc. fellow, 1983-84. Fellow Am. Acad. Arts and Sci. 1996—; mem. Am. Philol. Assn. (bd. dir. 1972-75, mem. com. on award of merit 1975-78, chmn. 1977-78, 1st v.p. 1981, pres. 1982, del. Am. Coun. Learned Soc. 1984-87, Charles J. Goodwin award of merit 1971, fin. trustee 1997-2004), mem. Am. Philosophical Soc., 1998—; Archaeol. Inst. Am., Classical Assn. New Eng., Medieval Acad. Am., Vergilian Soc. Am. (trustee 1969-73, v.p. 1974-76), Accademia Nazionale Virgiliana, Art Club. Office: Brown U Dept Classics Providence RI 02912-1856 E-mail: michael_putnam@brown.edu.

**PUTNAM, PAUL ADIN**, federal agency administrator; b. Springfield, Vt., July 12, 1930; s. Horace Adin and Beatrice Nellie (Baldwin) P.; m. Elsie Mae (Ramseyer) June 12, 1956; children: Pamela Ann, Penelope Jayne, Adin Tyler II, Paula Anna. BS, U. Vt., 1952; MS, Wash. State U., 1954; PhD, Cornell U., 1957. Research animal scientist Agrl. Rsch. Svc., USDA, Beltsville, Md., 1957-66, investigation leader beef cattle nutrition, 1966-68, chief beef cattle research br., 1968-72; asst. dir. Beltsville Agrl. Rsch. Ctr., 1972-80, dir., 1980-84; dir. cen. plains area Ames, Iowa, 1984-87; assoc. dir. mid. south area Stoneville, Miss., 1987-88; dir. mid south area, 1988-94; ret., 1994; selectman Town of Springfield, Vt., 2000, 2004—. Contbr. articles to profl. jours. Recipient Kidder medal U. Vt.; Outstanding Performance awards USDA, also cert. merit; Danforth fellow; Borden fellow; Purina Research fellow. Fellow AAAS (rep. sect. O), Am. Soc. Animal Sci. (pres., North Atlantic sect., chmn. various coms., N.E. sect. Disting. Service award); mem. Am. Dairy Sci. Assn., Orgn. Profl. Employees USDA (pres. Beltsville chpt.), Council for Agrl. Sci. and Tech. Home: 36 Putnam Rd Springfield VT 05156-9115 E-mail: pputnam8@vermontel.net.

**PUTNAM, RICHARD**, dentist, educator; b. Lima, Peru, June 10, 1968; arrived in Peru, 1994; s. Jorge A. and Rosa V. Putnam; m. Cheryl Ordway Putnam, Aug. 21, 1997; children: Carina, Nathaniel. DDS, Cayetano Heredia U., Lima, Peru, 1991; cert., U. Conn., Farmington, 1997; DMD, Boston U., 2000. Dentist Ramon Castillo, MS, DDS, Lima, Peru, 1992—94, Hugo Mautino, DDS; resident U. Conn., Farmington, Conn., 1994—97; intern Robert Lindberg, DMD, Waltham, Mass., 1999—2000; dentist Robert B. Stocks, Vernon, Conn., 2000—02; dentist, faculty U. Conn., 2002—. Dir. dentist site Manchester Cmty. Dental Svcs., Conn., 2003—. Recipient Implant award, Boston U., 2000. Mem.: Conn. State Dental Assn., Acad. of Gen. Dentistry, Am. Dental Assn. Home: 28 Box Mt Dr Vernon Rockville CT 06066 Personal E-mail: rputnam100@hotmail.com.

**PUTNAM, ROBERT D.**, education educator; m. Rosemary Werner; children: Jonathan, Lara. BA, Swarthmore Coll., 1963; Fellowship, Oxford U., Eng., 1964; MA, Yale U., New Haven, 1965, PhD with distinction, 1970;

LLD (hon.), Swarthmore Coll., 1990; PhD (hon.), Stockholm U., 1993, Ohio State U., 2000, U. Antwerp, 2000, U. Edinburgh, 2003, John Cabot U., Rome, 2006. From lectr. to prof. polit. sci. U. Mich., Ann Arbor, 1968—79; prof. govt. Harvard U., Cambridge, Mass., 1979—, chmn. dept. govt., 1984—88, assoc. dean faculty arts and scis., 1986—88, 1992—94, stanfield prof. internat. peace, 1996—2000, Peter and Isabel Malkin prof. pub. policy, 2000—; dir. Ctr. for Int'l Affairs, Harvard U., Cambridge, Mass., 1993—96; dir., saguaro seminar civic engagement in Am. Harvard U., JFK Sch. Govt., Cambridge, Mass., 1995—, dean, 1989—91. Mem. Coun. on Fgn. Rels., 1981—. Internat. Inst. Strategic Studies, 1986—, Trilateral Commn., 1990—98; exec. com. Brit. Politics Group, 1974—79, Coun. on European Studies, 1983—86; pres. Conf. Group on Italian Politics, 1981—83; adv. coun. on environmentally sustainable devel. World Bank, 1992—96; adv. bd. Swedish Collegium for Advanced Study in the Social Sciences, 1987—89, Westchester Children's Mus., NY, Thomas C. Wales Found., Seattle; Leverhulme vis. prof. faculty history St. Johns Coll. Cambridge U., 2002—03; vis. prof. of polit. sci. U. Catania, Italy, 1977, Stockholm U., 1974; cons. in field. Author: Better Together: Restoring the American Community; mem. editl. bd.: Am. Polit. Sci. Rev., 1971—76, Brit. Jour. Polit. Sci., 1975—79, Comparative Polit. Studies, 1982—2005, Legislative Studies Quar., 1983—89, Internat. Orgn., 1989, Nonprofit and Voluntary Sector Qrly., 2000—04, Am. Sociol. Rev., 2004—, Critical Rev., 2004—. Staff US NSC, Washington, 1978; active President's Coun. on Svc. & Civic Participation, Washington, 2003; pres.-elect. Am. Polit. Sci. Assn., 2000—01, pres., 2001—02, v.p., 1997—98; adv. bd. Anne E. Borghesani Cmty. Found., Lexington, Mass. Recipient Louis Brownlow Book award, Nat. Acad. Pub. Adminstrn., 1993, Gregory Luebbert award, Am. Polit. Sci. Assn., 1994, Ithiel de Sola Pool award, 1995, Charles H. Levin award, Internat. Polit. Sci. Assn., 1994, Wilbur Lucius Cross medal, Yale U. Grad. Sch. Arts & Science, 2003, Commendatore in the Order of the Star of Italian Solidarity, Pres., Italian Republic, 2004, Johan Skytte prize, Statsvetenskapliga Inst., Uppsala U., 2006; fellow, SSRC-ACLS, 1966—68, Ford Found., 1970, Ctr. for Advanced Study in the Behavioral Sciences, 1974—75, 1988—89, Woodrow Wilson Internat. Ctr. for Scholars, 1977, 1979, Coun. on Fgn. Rels., 1977—78, German Marshall Fund, 1979, SSRC-Fulbright, 1982, SSRC-Foreign Policy Studies, 1988—89, Guggenheim fellow, 1988—89; Fulbright fellow, 1964—65, 1977, Marshall Lectr. fellow, U. Cambridge, 1999. Fellow: Nat. Acad. Pub. Adminstrn., Am. Acad. Arts & Sciences, Brit. Acad. (corr.); mem.: Coun. on Fgn. Rels., Am. Acad. of Polit. & Social Sci., NAS (assembly of behavioral & social sciences 1978—81), Phi Beta Kappa, Am. Philos. Soc. Office: Harvard Univ JFK Sch Govt 79 JFK St T370 Cambridge MA 02139 Office Phone: 617-495-1148.

**PUTNAM, ROBERT ERVIN,** chemist, consultant; b. Northampton, Mass., Oct. 18, 1927; s. Ervin Earl and Mary Gertrude (Connelly) P.; m. Caroline Wright, Aug. 23, 1952; children: David Earl, Mary Caroline, Robert Edward, Andrew Wright. BS in Chemistry, U. Mass., 1950; PhD in Organic Chemistry, U. Ill., 1953. Rsch. chemist E.I. du Pont de Nemours, Wilmington, Del., 1953-59, rsch. supr., 1959-65, sr. rsch. supr., 1965-67, Parkersburg, W.Va., 1967-78, rsch. lab. supr., 1978-82, rsch. mgr., 1982-85; adj. faculty Washington State C.C., Marietta, Ohio, 1985-95; pvt. practice Marietta, 1985-95. Alumni adv. coun. dept. chemistry U. Mass., Amherst, 1975-78; instr. chemistry Marietta Coll., 1982-89, adv. coun., 1989-95, dir. Inst. for Learning in Retirement, 1995-98. Editor Bull. Am. Friends of Puttenham, 1984—; contbr. 20 articles to profl. jours. With USNR, 1945-46. NSF fellow, U. Ill., 1952-53. Fellow AAAS; mem. Am. Chem. Soc. (chmn. Ohio Valley sect. 1976-78), Rsch. Soc. Am., Valley Renaissance Consort, Mid-Ohio Valley Aviation Assn., Sigma Xi, Gamma Alpha, Phi Lambda Upsilon. Democrat. Mem. Unitarian Ch. Achievements include patents on fluorine containing polymers and monomers, ion exchange resins; research on industrial processes for nylon, polyacetals, acrylics, rubber toughened plastics, fluorinated plastics. Address: 100 Alden Ave Marietta OH 45750-1138 Office Phone: 740-373-4510. E-mail: putnamr@charter.net.

**PUTNAM, SAMUEL PATRICK,** psychologist; b. Vermillion, SD, Dec. 14, 1968; s. Patrick Francis Putnam and Marlene Kay Brown; m. Jane Kathleen Wallingford, May 28, 1994; children: Sara Julianna, Amy Helene. BS in Psychology, U. Iowa, Iowa City, 1992; PhD in Human Devel. and Family Studies, Pa. State U., College Park, 1999. Rsch. assoc. U. Oreg., Eugene, 1999—2001; asst. prof. Bowdoin Coll., Brunswick, Maine, 2001—. Dissertation grantee in devel. psychopathology, NIMH, 1998, Emotion Rsch. Tng. Postdoctoral fellow, 1999—2001. Office: Bowdoin Coll 6900 College Sta Brunswick ME 04011 Office Phone: 207-725-3152. Office Fax: 207-725-3892. E-mail: sputnam@bowdoin.edu.

**PUTNAM, WILLIAM LOWELL,** science association administrator; b. Springfield, Mass., Oct. 25, 1924; s. Roger Lowell and Caroline Plant (Jenkins) P.; m. Joan Fitzgerald, Sept. 29, 1951 (dec. April 1993); children: Katherine Elizabeth Putnam Delaney, W. Lowell, Erica A. Broman; m. Katherine E. Flynn, Sept. 18, 1999. Grad., Harvard Coll., 1945. With Springfield C. of C., 1950-52; founder, chmn. Springfield TV Corp., 1952-84; with Carroll Travel Bur., 1984-98. Vice chmn. Assn. Maximum Svc. Telecasters, 1975-84; sec.-treas. NBC Affiliates, 1980-83. Sole trustee Lowell Obs., Flagstaff, Ariz.; chmn. Springfield Park Commn., 1991-95. 1st lt. U.S. Army, 1943-45. Decorated Silver Star, Bronze Star, Purple Heart. Mem. Assn. Canadian Mountain Guides (hon.), Alpine Club Can. (hon.), Appalachian Mountain Club (hon.), Am. Alpine Club (pres. 1974-76, treas. 1977-91, hon.), Internat. Union Alpine Clubs (hon., Am. del., v.p. 2002). Avocation: alpinism.

**PUTNEY, MARK WILLIAM,** lawyer, utilities executive; b. Marshalltown, Iowa, Jan. 25, 1929; s. Lawrence Francis and Geneva (Eldridge) P.; m. Ray Ann Bartnek, May 25, 1962 (dec. Feb. 2000); children: Andi Bartnek, William Bradford, Blake Reinhart; m. Linda Phelps, July 21, 2003. BA, U. Iowa, 1951, JD, 1957. Bar: Iowa 1957, U.S. Supreme Ct. 1960. Ptnr. Bradshaw, Fowler, Proctor & Fairgrave, Des Moines, 1961-72, of counsel, 1992-94; chmn., CEO Bradford & Blake Ltd., Dakota Dunes, SD, 1992—; pres., chmn., chief exec. officer Iowa Resources, Inc., 1984-90; chmn., chief exec. officer Iowa Power & Light Co., 1984-90, Iowa Gas Co., 1984-85, Midwest Resources Inc., 1990-92. Civilian aide to Sec. Army for Iowa, 1975-77; bd. dirs. Greater Des Moines YMCA, 1976-86, Boys' Home Iowa, 1982-86, Hoover Presdle. Libr. Assn., 1983—, U. Iowa Found., 1984—, Edison Electric Inst., 1986-89, Greater Des Moines Com., 1984—, pres. 1988; bd. dirs. Assoc. Edison Illuminating Cos., 1988-93, pres., 1991-92; chmn. Iowa Com. Employer Support of Guard and Res., 1979-86; bd. dirs. Des Moines Devel. Corp., 1984-92, chmn., 1989-90. With USAF, 1951-53. Recipient Disting. Alumnus award U. Iowa, 1995. Mem. Iowa Utilities Assn. (chmn. 1989, dir.), Des Moines Club (pres. 1977), Desert Forest Golf Club (Carefree, Ariz.), Masons, Shriners, Delta Chi, Phi Delta Phi. Republican. Episcopalian. Home: PO Box 1126 Carefree AZ 85377 Office Phone: 602-549-7731. Personal E-mail: markwputney@aol.com.

**PUTNEY, MARY LYNN,** bank administrator, educator; b. N.Y.C., Feb. 26, 1948; d. Joseph John Berry and Evelyn Marie (Geoghegan) Schneir; m. Paul Michael McCaffery, May 18, 1968 (div. June 1976); children: Melissa Berry McCaffery, Paul David McCaffery; m. Frederick Bates Putney, May 30, 1992. MBA in Fin., Columbia U., 1982. Various positions Citibank, N.Y.C., 1974-85, v.p. fgn. exch., 1985-88, v.p. leveraged capital, 1988-92, mng. dir. pvt. banking, 1992-95, mng. dir. global equity, 1995—; adj. prof. Columbia Bus. Sch., N.Y.C., 1986—. Dir. Sinter Metal Corp., Cleve.; mem. adv. bd. AIG Millenium Fund, Russia, CVC/Opportunity Ptnrs., Brazil. Contbr. articles to profl. jours. Dir. Project Renewal, N.Y.C., 1995—, Mary Knoll Sch. Theology, Ossining, N.Y., 1994-95. Mem. Emily's List, Women's Campaign Fund, Sleepy Hollow Country Club, Sea Pines Country Club, Beta Gamma Sigma. Avocations: golf, bridge. Office: Citibank NA 153 E 53rd St New York NY 10022-4611

**PUTTER, IRVING,** retired French language educator; b. N.Y.C., Dec. 3, 1917; s. Joseph and Anna (Schrank) P.; children— Paul Stephen, Candace Anne Putter. BA, CCNY, 1938; MA, State U. Iowa, 1941; PhD, Yale U., 1949. Mem. faculty U. Calif. at Berkeley, 1947-88, prof. French, 1961-88, chmn.

dept., 1968-71, humanities research fellow, 1971-72, 78-79, 84-85; ret., 1988. Author: Leconte de Lisle and His Contemporaries, 1951, The Pessimism of Leconte de Lisle: Sources and Evolution, 1954, The Pessimism of Leconte de Lisle: The Work and The Time, 1961, La Dernière Illusion de Leconte de Lisle: Lettres Inédites a Emilie Leforestier, 1968; also numerous articles.; editor, translator: Chateaubriand: Atala, René, 1952. Guggenheim fellow, 1955-56; Fulbright fellow, 1955-56 Home: 115 Saint James Dr Piedmont CA 94611-3603

**PUTTERMAN, CHAIM,** rheumatologist, researcher; b. Elizabeth, NJ; MD, Technion-Israel Inst. Tech., Haifa, 1985. Diplomate rheumatology Am. Bd. Internal Medicine. Int. Ramban Med. Ctr., Haifa, Israel, 1985; res. Hadassah Hosp., Ein-Kerem, Jerusalem, 1990—93; chief rheumatology divsn. Albert Einstein Coll. of Medicine, 2004—; chief Rheumatology Divsn. Montefiore Med. Ctr., 2004—. Mem. med. and sci. bd. Systemic Lupus Erythematosus Found., N.Y.C.; mem. med. and sci. com. Arthritis Found.-N.Y. Chpt., N.Y.C. Recipient Physician-Scientist Career Devel. award, Arthritis Found., 1994—97, Robert Wood Johnson Charitable Trust SLE Young Scholar award, 1997—2000, Hulda Irene Duggan Arthritis Investigator award, 2000—05, Rsch. Steps to a Cure Leadership award, 2002, Clin. Scientist award, NIH, 1997—2002, Lupus Rsch. Inst. Novel Rsch. Project in Lupus award, SLE Found., 2001—04. Fellow: Am. Coll. Rheumatology; mem.: Am. Assn. Immunologists. Achievements include research in the renal pathogenicity of anti-DNA antibodies in lupus nephritis. Office: Albert Einstein Coll Medicine Div RheumatolForscheimer 701 AE Com 1300 Morris Park Ave Bronx NY 10461

**PUTTERMAN, LOUIS G.,** economics professor; b. N.Y.C., Apr. 27, 1952; s. Milton and Eileen L. (Goldstein) P.; (div.); 1 child, Laura Lee; m. Vivian Tseng, Apr. 5, 1981; children: Serena Rose, Mark Isaac. BA summa cum laude, Columbia U., 1976; MA in Internat. Relations, Yale U., 1978, PhD in Econs., 1980; MA (hon.), Brown U., 1983. From asst. prof. to prof. econs. Brown U., R.I., 1980—; rsch. assoc., Ctr. for East Asian Rsch. Harvard U., Cambridge, Mass., 1987-93. Author: Peasants, Collectives and Choice, 1986, Division of Labor and Welfare, 1990, Continuity and Change in China's Rural Development: Collective and Reform Eras in Perspective, 1993, Dollars and Change: Economics in Context, 2001; co-author: Economics of Cooperation and the Labor-Managed Economy, 1987; editor: The Economic Nature of the Firm, 1986, (with Randall Kroszner) 2d edit., 1996, (with Dietrich Rueschemeyer) State and Market in Development: Synergy or Rivalry, (with Avner Ben-Ner) Economics, Values and Organization, 1998; mem. editl. bd. Modern China, 1990—, Comparative Economic Studies, 1991-93, Annals of Public and Cooperative Economics, 1992—, Jour. Comparative Econs., 1989-91, 97-99, China Econ. Rev., 2001—; assoc. editor Pacific Econ. Rev., 1996-2004. Recipient Sloan Rsch. fellow, Alfred P. Sloan Found., 1983, Fellow in Chinese Studies, Wang Inst., 1986, Am. Coun. Learned Socs., 1997. Mem. Am. Economic Assn., Assn. for Comparative Economic Studies, Phi Beta Kappa. Office: Brown U Dept Econs 64 Waterman St Providence RI 02912-9029 Business E-mail: Louis_Putterman@brown.edu.

**PUTTLER, BENJAMIN,** entomologist; b. Bronx, Dec. 21, 1930; s. Isodor Puttler and Ida Lehrer; m. Virginia Witten Puttler, Oct. 6, 1961; children: Donna, Shari. BS in Agrl., U. Calif., 1955. Rsch. entomologist U.S. Dept. Agrl., Albany, Calif., 1955—57, Riverside, Calif., 1957—59, Moorestown, NJ, 1959—64, Columbia, Mo., 1964—89; extension entomologist U. Mo., Columbia, Mo., 1989—95, emeritus asst. prof., 1995. Contbr. articles over 60 scientific jours. Recipient Superior Svc. award, U.S. Dept. Agrl., 1987, Cert. Appreciation, U. Mo., Dept. Entomology, 1988, Faculty Staff award, 1999, 2000, 2002. Mem.: C.V. Riley Entomological Soc., Internat. Organ. Biological Control, Entomological Soc. Am. Independent. Jewish. Achievements include patents for virus to kill insects 1990; discovery of explorations for beneficial insects resulting in discovery of new species. Avocations: golf, stamp collecting/philately, coin collecting/numismatics. Home: 505 Bourn Ave Columbia MO 65203 Office: U Mo Divsn Plant Scis 1 31 Agrl Bldg Columbia MO 65211 Office Phone: 573-882-1457. Business E-mail: puttlerb@missouri.edu.

**PUTTLITZ, DONALD HERBERT,** microbiologist; b. Kingston, NY, Apr. 21, 1938; s. Adalbert Siegfried and Elizabeth Ann (Barthel) P.; m. Barbara Ann Dingman, July 19, 1969; children: Michelle, Brian, Laura. BS with distinction, SUNY, New Paltz, 1959; MS, SUNY, Albany, 1961; PhD, Cornell U., 1965. Diplomate Am. Bd. Med. Microbiology. Assoc. microbiologist Beth Israel Med. Ctr., N.Y.C., 1967-85; supr. microbiology Jamaica (N.Y.) Hosp., 1985-92; instr. physician asst. program Touro Coll., N.Y.C., 1986-88; supr. microbiology Sound Shore Med. Ctr. of Westchester, New Rochelle, NY, 1993-97. Mem. faculty Mt. Sinai Coll. Medicine, 1972-85. Mem. N.Y.C. Bd. Edn., 1997—. Predoctoral traineeship fellow NIH, 1964-65, postdoctoral traineeship fellow USPHS, 1965-67. Mem. Am. Soc. Microbiology, N.Y.C. Soc. Microbiology. Roman Catholic. Home: 116 Horace Harding Blvd Great Neck NY 11020-1107

**PUTZEL, CONSTANCE KELLNER,** lawyer; b. Balt., Sept. 5, 1922; d. William Stummer and Corinne (Strauss) Kellner; m. William L. Putzel, Aug. 28, 1945; 1 son, Arthur William. AB, Goucher Coll., 1942; LLB, U. Md., 1945, JD, 1969. Bar: Md. 1945. Social worker Balt. Dept. Pub. Welfare, 1945-46; pvt. practice Am. New Amsterdam Casualty Co., Balt., 1947; staff atty. Legal Aid Bur., Balt., 1947-49; mem. Putzel & Putzel, P.A., Balt., 1950-89; pvt. practice Balt., 1989—; instr. U. Balt. Sch. Law, 1975-77, Goucher Coll., 1976-77. Chair character com. Ct. Appeals for 3d Cir., 1976-97. Author: A Practice Guide to Divorce, 1999, Representing the Older Client in Divorce, 1992. Commr. Md. Com. on Status of Women, 1972-76, Com. to Implement ERA, 1973-76; Pres. U. Md. Law Alumni Assn., 1978; bd. dirs. Legal Aid Bur., 1951-52, 71-73. Fellow Am. Acad. Matrimonial Lawyers (chair elder issues com. 1996); mem. ABA (co-chair elder issues com., mem. coun. sr. lawyers divsn. 1996-2000, editl. bd. 1996-99, family law sect.), Md. Bar Assn. (bd. govs. 1972-73, chmn. family law sect. 1978-79, chair sr. lawyers divsn. 2001-03). Home: 7121 Park Heights Ave Unit 401 Baltimore MD 21215-1610 Office: 3835 Naylor s Ln Pikesville MD 21208 Office Phone: 410-602-4012. Personal E-mail: lawtowson@aol.com.

**PUTZEL, MICHAEL,** journalist, editor; b. Washington, Sept. 16, 1942; s. Max and Nell (Converse) P.; m. Ann Blackman, Feb. 23, 1974; children: Leila Elizabeth, Christof Blackman. BA, UNC in Polit. Sci., 1967. Reporter Charleston (W.Va.) Gazette, 1963-66; newsman AP, Raleigh, NC, 1967-68, N.Y.C., 1968-69, war corr. Vietnam, 1969-72, reporter Washington, 1972-79; asst. metro editor Washington Post, Washington, 1979; White House corr. AP, Washington, 1979-84, chief White House corr., 1984-87, chief of bur. Moscow, 1987—90, diplomatic corr. Washington, 1990-91; Washington bureau chief Boston Globe, 1991-92, White House corr. Washington, 1993-94; columnist "Plugged In", 1994-95; founder, CEO Trysail, Inc., Washington, 1996—; founder, pres. Milestones Inc., Washington, 1999—2000; web doctor Washington, 2003—. Lectr. Georgetown U., Washington, 1999—. With USAR, 1964-65. Recipient AP Mgn. Editors citation, 1975, 81, Merriman Smith Meml. award White House Corr. Assn., 1986. Home: 4938 Quebec St NW Washington DC 20016-3231 Office Phone: 202-362-3133. Personal E-mail: mputzel@trysail.com.

**PUYAU, FRANCIS ALBERT,** retired radiology educator, physician; b. New Orleans, Dec. 1, 1928; s. Frank Albert and Rose Sue (Jones) P.; m. Geraldine Sally diBenedetto, June 6, 1951; children: Michael, Stephen, Jeanne Marie, Julie, Melissa. BS, Notre Dame U., 1948; MD, La. State U., 1952. Diplomate Am. Bd. Pediat., Am. Bd. Pediat. Cardiology, Am. Bd. Radiology. Intern Charity Hosp., New Orleans, 1952-53, resident in pediat., 1955-57; from instr. pediat. to prof. radiology and pediat. La. State U. Sch. Medicine, New Orleans, 1957-74, acting head dept. radiology, 1971-72, head dept., 1972-74; asst. prof. pediat. Vanderbilt U., 1961-68; fellow dept. diagnostic radiology Charity Hosp., New Orleans, 1968-70; prof. radiology and pediat. Tulane U. Sch. Medicine, New Orleans, 1974-97, prof. medicine, 1974-95, acting chmn.

dept. pediat., 1976-78; cons. St. Tammany Hosps., Covington, La., 1968-81; dir. cardiac catheterization lab. dept. cardiology Charity Hosp., New Orleans, 1970-85; staff radiologist Our Lady of the Lake Regional Med. Ctr., Baton Rouge, 1986-93, ret., 1997. Mem. staff Hotel Dieu, New Orleans, 1973-80; head x-ray dept. Children's Hosp. of New Orleans, 1976-82. Contbr. articles to profl. jours. With USPHS, 1953-55. Fellow Am. Coll. Cardiology, Am. Coll. Radiology; mem. East Baton Rouge Med. Soc., So. Soc. Pediatric Research, Am. Coll. Radiology, La. Radiology Soc., New Orleans Radiology Soc. (pres. 1985), New Orleans Pediatric Soc., So. Chmn. Acad. Radiology Depts., Radiol. Soc. N.Am., Am. Roentgen Ray Soc., Assn. Univ. Radiologists, Southern Yacht Club (New Orleans), Alpha Omega Alpha. Roman Catholic. Home: 458 Shady Lake Pkwy Baton Rouge LA 70810-4322

**PUZDER, ANDREW F.,** food service executive, lawyer; b. Cleve., July 11, 1950; s. Andrew F. and Winifried M. Puzder; m. Deanna L. Descher, Sept. 26, 1987. BA, Cleve. State U., 1975; JD, Washington U., 1978. Atty. Offices of Morris A. Shenker, 1978—84, Stolar Partnership, 1984—91; ptnr. Lewis, D'Amato, Brisbois, & Bisgaard, 1991—94, Yocca, Carlson & Rauth, 1994—95; exec. v.p., gen. counsel Fidelity Nat. Fin., Inc., 1995—97; CEO Santa Barbara Restaurant Group, 1997—2000; gen. counsel, exec. v.p. CKE Restaurants, Inc., Carpinteria, Calif., 1997-99, pres., CEO, 2000—; CEO Hardee's Food Systems, Inc., 2000—. Editor Washington U. Law Quarterly, 1977-78. Mem. State Bar Nev., The Mo. Bar, State Bar Calif., Phi Alpha Theta. Office: CKE Restaurants Inc Ste A 6307 Carpinteria Ave Carpinteria CA 93013*

**PUZIA, THOMAS H.,** astronomer, researcher; Dr. rer. nat., Ludwig-Maximilians U., Munich, Germany. Rsch. fellow Space Telescope Sci. Inst., Balt. Prin. investigator Space Telescope Sci. Inst., Balt. Rsch. fellow, European So. Obs., 2000, German Sci. Found., 2000, European Space Agy., 2003. Mem.: Am. Astron. Soc. (small rsch. grantee 2005). Achievements include discovery of intermediate-age globular clusters in early-type galaxies. Office: Space Telescope Sci Inst 3700 San Martin Dr Baltimore MD 21218 Office Phone: +1-410-338-4352.

**PUZZO, JOSEPH ANTHONY, JR.,** middle school educator; b. Red Bank, N.J., May 7, 1959; s. Joseph Anthony Puzzo, Sr. and Rita Ann (Scala) Puzzo. BA, Rutgers U., 1981; MA, Nova Southeastern U., 2003. Lic. English tchr. N.J. Fitness instr. Matawan Athletic Club, NJ, 1989—90; fitness instr., personal trainer The Racquetplace, Matawan, 1990—95, Powerhouse Gym, Matawan, 1995—96; full-time substitute tchr. Middletown Twp. Schs., NJ, 1996—97; tchr. lang. arts Middletown Twp. Sch. Port Monmouth, NJ, 1997—. Ednl. advisor Jr. Nat. Young Leaders Conf., Washington, 2003—. Author: (monthly fitness column) Shape Up, 1990—92. Mem.: Middletown Twp. Ednl. Assn., N.J. Ednl. Assn., Nat. Coun. Tchrs. English. Roman Catholic. Avocations: writing, films, music, sports, fitness. Personal E-mail: joepuzzo@comcast.net.

**PYATT, EVERETT ARNO,** federal official; b. Kansas City, Mo., July 22, 1939; s. Arno Doyne and Myrl Elizabeth (Osborn) P.; m. Susan Evelyn Kristal, Sept. 28, 1968; children: Jennifer, Laura, Jeffrey. B.E., BS, Yale U., 1962; MBA, U. Pa., 1977. Staff engr. office dir. def. research and devel. Office Sec. Def., Dept. Def., Washington, 1962-72; dir. acquisition planning Office Asst. Sec. Def. for Program Analysis and Evaluation, 1972-75; dir. logistics resources Office Asst. Sec. Def. for Installations and Logistics, 1975-77; prin. asst. sec. for logistics Dept. Navy, Washington, 1977-79, prin. dep. asst. sec. for shipbldg. and logistics, 1981-84, asst. sec. for shipbldg. and logistics, 1984-89; exec. advisor Coopers & Lybrand, 1989—; pres. EV Ventures; dep. chief fin. officer Dept. Energy, 1979-81; dir. Dept. Energy (Office of Alcohol Fuels), 1980. Recipient Disting. Civilian Svc. medal USN, 1980-81, 87, Superior Civilian Svc. medal, 1981, Outstanding Svc. medal Dept. Energy, 1981; Pres.'s award of meritorious excellence, 1983, Disting. Civilian Pub. Svc. award Dept. Def., 1989; Office of Sec. Def. fellow, 1975-77. Mem.: IEEE, Yale Club. Home: 4560 25th Rd N Arlington VA 22207-4147 Office: Coopers & Lybrand 12902 Federal Systems Park Dr Fairfax VA 22033-4421 Office Phone: 703-841-8318. Personal E-mail: epyatt1@comcast.net.

**PYATT, KEDAR DAVIS, JR.,** research and development company executive; b. Wadesboro, NC, May 20, 1933; s. Kedar D. and Frances (Hales) P.; m. Mary Mackenzie, June 2, 1956; children: Geoffrey, Kira, David, Rebecca. BS in Physics, Duke U., 1955; PhD in Physics, Yale U., 1960. With Gen. Atomic, San Diego, 1959-67; sr. v.p. Fed. sys. divsn. Maxwell Techs., San Diego, 1967—2001, sr. v.p. just Sys. Divsn.; chief scientist SAIC, San Diego, 2001—. Recipient Exceptional Pub. Svc. medal Dept. Def., 1985, Lifetime Achievement medal DSWA, 1997. Office Phone: 858-826-1629. Personal E-mail: bud-mary@att.net. Business E-mail: kedar.d.pyatt@saic.com. E-mail: bud@maxwell.com.

**PYATT, LEO ANTHONY,** retired real estate broker; b. Key Port, N.J., Oct. 20, 1925; s. Ralph James and Anna Regina (Kussmaul) Pyatt; m. Geraldine Genevive Gibb, May 31, 1947; children: Steven Lee, Rebecca Lynn. Student, Franklin U., 1947-49. Salesperson Standard Oil Co., Columbus, Ohio, 1947-49, Borden Dairy Co., Columbus, 1950-57, Frito-Lay, Inc., Columbus, 1958-74; sec., treas. Snack Time, Inc., Columbus, 1975-86; agt. N. NE Realty Co., Columbus, 1976-86; owner-broker Pyatt's Rose Realty Co., Columbus, 1986—2003; ret., 2003. Mem. Citizens for An Alternative Tax Sys. With U.S. Naval Air Force, 1943—46, PTO. Decorated DFC, Air medal with silver star, Philippine Liberation award; inducted into Combat Aircrew Hall of Fame. Roman Catholic. Avocations: writing, travel, reading. Home: 4400 Wanda Lane Rd Columbus OH 43224-1026

**PYE, GORDON BRUCE,** economist; b. Oak Park, Ill., Oct. 30, 1933; s. Harold Charles and Florence Martha P. BS in Chem. Engring. M.I.T., 1955, PhD in Econs, 1963. Asst. prof. bus. adminstrn. U. Calif., Berkeley, 1963-66, assoc. prof., 1966-69, prof., 1969-72; econ. cons. Standard Oil Co. Calif. (name changed to Chevron Corp.), San Francisco, 1972-74; v.p., sr. economist Irving Trust Co., N.Y.C., 1974-78, sr. v.p., mgr. econ. research and planning div., 1978-89; prin. Gordon B. Pye Assocs., N.Y.C., 1990—. Assoc. editor: Fin. Analysts Jour, 1972-89 Mem. Forecasters Club N.Y. (pres. 1980-81) Home: 230 E 50th St New York NY 10022-7702 Personal E-mail: GBPye@aol.com.

**PYE, LENWOOD DAVID,** materials science educator, researcher, consultant; b. Little Falls, NY, May 16, 1937; s. Lenwood George and Elizabeth Marie Pye; m. Constance Lee Lanphere, Sept. 6, 1958; children: DeAnn, Lorie, Lisa, Brien. BS, Alfred U., 1959, PhD, 1968. Rsch. engr. PPG Industries, Pitts., 1959-60; rsch. scientist Bausch & Lomb, Rochester, NY, 1960-61, 62-64; prof. glass sci. N.Y. State Coll. Ceramics Alfred U., 1968—2003, dir. Inst. Glass Sci. and Engring., 1984-96, dir. Industry-Univ. Ctr. Glass Rsch., 1986-96, dean N.Y. State Coll. Ceramics, 1996—2002, dean and prof. emeritus, 2003—. Pres. Internat. Commn. on Glass, 1997-00; vis. scientist Johns Hopkins U., 2005-. 1st lt. U.S. Army, 1960—62. Recipient Dominick Labino lectr. 1995, Phoenix award as Glassman of Yr., 1996, Excellence in Tchg. award lectr., NYSCC, 2005, Glass Art Soc. award. Fellow Am. Ceramics Soc. (trustee 1992-95), U.K. Soc. Glass Tech. (hon.); mem. Worldwide Acad. Ceramics, German Soc. Glass Tech. (hon.) Office: NY State Coll Ceramics Alfred Univ 2 Pine St Alfred NY 14802-1214 E-mail: pye@alfred.edu.

**PYE, LUCIAN WILMOT,** political science professor; b. Shansi, China, Oct. 21, 1921; s. Watts Orson and Gertrude (Chaney) P.; m. Mary Toombs Waddill, Dec. 24, 1944; children: Evelyn, L. Christopher, Virginia. BA, Carleton Coll., 1943, LLD, 1982; MA, Yale U., 1949, PhD, 1951. From instr. to asst. prof. polit. sci. Washington U., St. Louis, 1949-52; rsch. assoc. Yale U., 1951-52, Princeton, 1952-56; vis. lectr. Columbia U., 1956; faculty Mass. Inst. Tech., 1956-92, prof. polit. sci., 1960-92, Ford prof., 1972-92, chmn. sect., 1961-63; sr. staff mem. Mass. Inst. Tech. (Center Internat. Studies), 1956—. Vis. assoc.

prof. Yale U., 1959-61; vis. prof. George Washington U., 1993, Balliol Coll., Oxford U., 1994, Fletcher Sch., Tufts U., 1994; chmn. com. comparative politics Social Sci. Rsch. Coun., 1963-73; assoc. Fairbank Ctr., Harvard U., 1995—; mem. adv. com. adminstr. AID, 1961-68; cons. Dept. State, 1962-68, NSC, 1968-72; trustee Asia Found., 1963-2002; gov. East-West Ctr., Honolulu, 1976-80; bd. dirs., v.p. Nat. Com. U.S.-China Rels. Author: Guerrilla Communism in Malaya, 1956, Politics, Personality and Nation Building, 1961, Aspects of Political Developments, 1966, Southeast Asia's Political Systems, 1967, The Spirit of Chinese Politics, 1968, Warlord Politics, 1971, China: An Introduction, 1972, Mao Tse-tung: The Man in The Leader, 1976, Dynamics of Chinese Politics, 1982, Asian Power and Politics, 1985; co-author: The Politics of the Developing Areas, 1960, The Emerging Nations, 1961; Editor: Communications and Political Development, 1963, Political Culture and Political Development, 1965, Political Science and Area Studies, 1975. 1st Lt. USMCR, 1945-46. Fellow Center Advanced Study Behavioral Scis., 1963 Fellow Am. Acad. Arts and Scis., Am. Philos. Soc.; mem. Asian Studies (dir.), Am. Polit. Sci. Assn. (dir., pres. 1989), Council Fgn. Relations (dir.), Asia Soc. (dir.), Pilgrim Soc., Phi Beta Kappa. Clubs: Cosmos. Unitarian Universalist. Home: 72 Fletcher Rd Belmont MA 02478-2017 Office: Mass Inst Tech Dept Polit Sci Cambridge MA 02139 Office Phone: 617-253-3379. Business E-Mail: pye@mit.edu.

**PYERITZ, REED EDWIN,** geneticist, educator, medical researcher; b. Pitts., Nov. 2, 1947; s. Paul L. and Ida Mae (Meier) P.; m. Jane Ellen Tumpson, May 28, 1972; 2 children. SB in Chemistry, U. Del., 1968; AM, Harvard U., 1971, PhD in Biochemistry, 1972, MD, 1975. Diplomate Am. Bd. Internal Medicine, Am. Bd. Med. Genetics. Intern Peter Bent Brigham Hosp., Boston, 1975-76; resident Peter Bent Bingham Hosp., Boston, 1976-77, Johns Hopkins Hosp., Balt., 1977-78; from instr. to prof. medicine and pediatrics Sch. Medicine, John Hopkins Hosp., Balt., 1977-93, chair dept. human genetics, 1994-00, prof. human genetics, medicine and pediatrics, 1994-01, MCP Hahnemann Sch. Medicine, 1993-00; prof. medicine and genetics U. Pa. Sch. Medicine, Phila., 2001—, chief divsn. med. genetics, 2001—, chair com. on appointments and promotions, 2004—, mem. faculty senate, 2006—. Dir. Inst. Genetics, Allegheny U. Health Sci., 1993-99; dir. Ctr. for Med. Genetics, Allegheny Gen. Hosp., 1995-00; chief physician Md. Athletic Commn., Balt., 1978-93; med. adv. bd. Nat. Marfan Found., N.Y.C., 1982—, chmn. 1982-93, clin. care adv. bd., Nat. Neurofibromatosis Found., 1985—; med. advisor Alliance of Genetic Support Groups, 1994-01; mem. rsch. adv. bd. Nat. Orgn. Rare Disorders, 1989-00; mem. rsch. adv. com. Am. Heart Assn., 1996-98; mem. genetic adv. bd. Nat. Cancer Inst., 1996-99; mem. med. adv. bd. Can. Marfan Assn., 1999—, chmn., 2003-; mem. sci. adv. bd. Hereditary Hemorrhagic Telangiectasia Found., 2003—, chair med. adv. bd., Canadian Marfan Assn., 2003-, Can. Inst. Health Rsch., 2005-. Co-editor Principles and Practice of Medical Genetics, 1992-; mem. editl. bd. New Eng. Jour. Medicine, 1993-96, JAMA, 1997-2001, Circulation, 2004—; contbr. over 300 articles to profl. publs. Lt. col. USAR Med. Corp., 1981—91. NIH grantee. Fellow: ACP, Am. Coll. Med. Genetics (dir. 1992—94, pres.-elect 1995—96, pres. 1997—98, past pres. 1999—2000); mem.: AAAS, AMA, Coll. Physicians Phila., Am. Med. Accred. Program (spl. adv. com. 1998—2000), Assn. Profs. Human Med. Genetics (pres. elect 1998—99, pres. 2000—02), Assn. Am. Physicians, Am. Soc. Clin. Investigation, Am. Fedn. Med. Rsch., Physician Consortium for Performance Improvement, Am. Heart Assn., Am. Soc. Human Genetics (chmn. program com. 1994—95, bd. dirs. 2005—). Office: Divsn Med Genetics Maloney 538 U Pa Sch Medicine 3400 Spruce St Philadelphia PA 19104-4283 Office Phone: 215-662-4740. Business E-Mail: reed.pyeritz@uphs.upenn.edu.

**PYKE, THOMAS NICHOLAS, JR.,** science administrator; b. Washington, July 16, 1942; s. Thomas Nicholas and Pauline Marie (Pingitore) Pyke; m. Carol June Renville, June 22, 1968 (dec. Oct. 2002); children: Christopher Renville, Alexander Nicholas. BS, Carnegie Inst. Tech., 1964; MS in Engring., U. Pa., 1965. Electronic engr. Nat. Bur. Standards, Gaithersburg, Md., 1964-69, chief computer networking sect., 1969-75, chief computer systems engring. div., 1975-79, dir. ctr. for computer systems engring., 1979-81, dir. ctr. programming sci. and tech., 1981-86; asst. adminstr. for satellite and info. services NOAA, Washington, 1986-92, dir. high performance computing and com., 1992-00, dir. The Globe Program, 1994—2002, chief info. officer, dir. high performance computing and com., 2000—01; chief info. officer US Dept. Commerce, 2001—05, US Dept. Energy, 2005—. Organizer profl. computer confs., 1970-86; mem. Presdl. Adv. Com. on Networking Structure and Function, 1980, Interagy. com. on Info. Resources Mgmt., 1983-84, bd. dirs., 1984-87, vice chmn. 1986-87 (Exec. Excellence award 1991), chmn. Interagy. Working Group on Data Mgmt. for Global Change, 1987-93; speaker in field. Mem. editl. bd. Computer Networks Jour., 1976-86; contbr. articles to profl. jours. Mem. Task Force on Computers in Schs., Arlington 1982—85; co-pres. Jamestown Elem. Sch. PTA, Arlington, 1984—85; bd. dirs. Glebe Commons Assn., Arlington, Va., 1976—79, v.p., 1977—79. Recipient silver medal Dept. Commerce, 1973, gold medal, 1995; award for exemplary achievement in pub. adminstrn. William A. Jump Found., 1975, 76, Presdl. Rank award of Meritorious Exec., 1988, 99; Westinghouse scholar Carnegie Inst. Tech., 1960-64; Ford Found. fellow U. Pa., 1964-66. Fellow Washington Acad. Scis. (Engring. Sci. award 1974); mem. IEEE (sr. mem.), Computer Soc. of IEEE (bd. govs. 1971-73, 75-77, vice chmn. tech. com. on personal computing 1982-86, chmn. 1986-87), AAAS, Assn. Computing Machinery, Sigma Xi, Eta Kappa Nu, Omicron Delta Kappa, Pi Kappa Alpha (chpt. v.p. 1963-64) Episcopalian. Office: US Dept Energy 1000 Independence Ave SW Washington DC 20585 Business E-Mail: tom.pyke@hq.doe.gov.

**PYLE, ARTIMUS (THOMAS DELMAR PYLE),** musician; b. Louisville, Ky., July 15, 1948; s. Clarence and Mildred Pyle. Drummer Volunteer Jam, Marshall Tucker Band, Lynyrd Skynyrd, 1975—77, 1987—92; founder Artimus Pyle Band 1981—. Musician: (album) A.P.B. 1982, Nightmares, 1985, Live from Planet Earth, 2000, (with Lynyrd Skynyrd) Nuthin' Fancy, 1975, Gimme Back My Bullets, 1976, One More from the Road, 1976, Street Survivors, 1977, Southern by the Grace of God, 1988, Lynyrd Skynyrd 1991, Freebird: The Movie, 1996. USMC, 1968. Named to Rock and Roll Hall of Fame, 2006. Office: Lustig Talent Enterprises Inc PO Box 770850 Orlando FL 32877 Office Phone: 407-816-8960. Office Fax: 407-816-8959. E-mail: artimus@artimuspyle.com.*

**PYLE, BENJAMIN MALREY,** investor; b. Apple Springs, Tex., Sept. 27, 1927; s. Uria Malrey Pyle, Nora Etta Burran; m. Mary Ellen Hartmann, Jan. 31, 1932; children: Malrey Nathan, Dwight Dana. BBA in Banking/Fin., U. Houston, 1960; postgrad., So. Meth. U., 1965-66; non-traditional degree, Beverly Hills U., 1985; MS in Econs., U. So. Calif./ MA, Liberty U., Lynchburg, Va., 1993. Banking exec., dir. Comml. Banking, Houston and Baytown, Tex., 1960—83; adminstrv. exec. Hill & Hill Transp., Houston, 1983—85; farm credit examiner Farm Credit Adminstrn., McLean, Va., 1986—87, asst. receiver Sugarland, Tex., 1988—91; entrepreneur/investor Baytown, Tex., 1994—. Bus. cons. Pyle Bros., Baytown, Tex., 1992—; adv. bd. So. Partison Mag., Columbia, SC, 1995—96. Contbr. articles to profl. jours. Polit. activist, precinct chmn. Rep. Party, Trinity County, Tex., 1998—; exec. bd. Episcop. Dioces. of Tex., Camp Allen, 1997—98; pres., bd. dirs. Civil War Round Table, Lufkin, Tex., 1999—; bd. regents Liberty U., 1994; mem. Trinity County Hist. Commn., 1991—; with U.S. Maritime Svc., 1944—46. With U.S. Merchant Marines, 1944—46, with USMC, 1946—57. Recipient Outstanding Leadership award, Mt. Zion Cemetery Assn. Mem.: SPJST (pres. 1977—94), Coll. of Bus. Adminstrn. Alumni U. Houston (charter). Republican. Episcopalian. Avocations: farming, ranching, hunting, lecturing. Mailing: 13529 FM 357 Groveton TX 75845-3203

**PYLE, DONALD NORRIS, II,** biologist; m. Christina M. Peregoy. AS in Biology, York Coll. Pa., 2004, BS in Biology, 2005; degree Combat Med. Specialist, US Army Med. Dept., 1995. Cert. basic life support instr. Am. Heart Assn., 2005, registered med. technician Nat. Registry Emergency Med. Technicians, 1995, cert. plasma collection sys. intermediate servicing Haemonetics, 2000, plasmapheresis freezer servicing Thermogenesis, 2000. Plasmapheresis asst. ctr. dir. SeraCare, Inc., Toledo, 1997—2000; Plasma-

pheresis ctr. mgr. BioLife Plasma Svcs., Harrisburg, Pa., 2000—02; intern York (Pa.) Hosp., 2003—05; vascular access technician Meml. Hosp., York, 2003—06. Rschr., presenter in field. Contbr. abstract in profl. jour. Com. mem. Meml. Hosp., Disaster Preparedness Com., 2005—06. Cpl. U.S Army, 1995—99, cpl. US Army Nat. Guard, 1999—2003. Decorated Svc. Ribbon US Army, Army Commendation medal (2), Army Achievement medal (4), Nat. Def. Svc. medal, Expert Field Med. Badge, Overseas Svc. Ribbon, UN medal, Air Assault Badge, Good Conduct medal; recipient Departmental Recognition award, York Coll. Pa., Dept. Biol. Sci., 2005. Mem.: VFW (life), Mil. and Vets. Soc. York (liaison 2004—05), Diplomat Com. of Harrisburg Regional C. of C., Am. Soc. Microbiology, Am. Chem. Soc., Am. Legion, Fraternal Order of Police (assoc.), York Coll., Tri-Beta (historian coll. chpt. 2003—05).

**PYLE, GERALD FREDRIC,** geographer, educator; b. Akron, Ohio, Dec. 22, 1937; s. Russell Roy and Ruth (Martin) P.; m. Carole Wood, Aug. 29, 1959; children: Eric, Frances. BA, Kent State U., 1963; MA, U. Chgo., 1968, PhD, 1970. Cartographer Rand McNally, Chgo., 1962-64; rsch. geographer Ency. Brit., Chgo., 1964-65; cartographer U. Chgo., 1965-70; from asst. prof. to prof. U. Akron, 1970-80; prof. geography and earth sci. U. N.C., Charlotte, 1980-98, prof. health promotion, 1995—2002, prof. health behavior and adminstrn., 2002—04, emeritus prof., 2004—. Vis. fellow Macquarie U., Sydney, Australia, 1988; rsch. dir. Ctr. for Urban Studies, Akron, Ohio, 1973—80; tech. dir. Akron Area Census File, 1974—80; vis. scholar U. SC, 1977; interim dir. health adminstrn. program U. NC, Charlotte, 2001—02. Author: Heart Disease, Cancer and Stroke in Chicago, 1971, Spatial Dynamics of Crime, 1974, Applied Medical Geography, 1979, Diffusion of Influenza: Patterns and Paradigms, 1986, (with Shannon and Bashshur) The Geography of AIDS, 1990, (with shannon) Medical Atlas of the Twentieth Century, 1993; sr. editor Med. Geography, Social Sci. and Medicine, 1977-84; book rev. editor Social Sci. and Medicine, 1990-2005. Recipient Scholars medal First Citizens Bank, 1992; grantee Ill. Regional Med., 1969, Law Enforcement Adminstrn. Agy., 1972, 74, NSF, 1979, 82, Nat. Geog. Soc., 1988, NRC, 1995, Smart Start 1999-2001. Fellow Ohio Acad. Sci.; mem. APHA, Am. Coll. Epidemiology, Assn. Am. Geographers (Rsch. Honors S.E. divsn. 1994), Phi Kappa Phi. Democrat. Anglican. Achievements include research in spatial diffusion of infectious diseases and the location of health care delivery facilities. Home: PO Box 641 Matthews NC 28106 Office: U NC Dept Health Behavior and Adminstrn 9201 University City Blvd Charlotte NC 28223-0002 Office Phone: 704-687-4262. Personal E-mail: gfpyle@msn.com. Business E-Mail: gfpyle@email.uncc.edu.

**PYLE, GREGORY E.,** Native American tribal leader; b. Ft. Bragg, Calif., Apr. 25, 1949; s. Alvin Pyle and Juanita Wilmouth; m. Pat Baker, Sept. 1971; children: Andrea, Eric. Student, Murray State Coll.; BS in bus., Southeastern Okla. State U., 1972. Named personnel dir. Choctaw Nation of Okla., 1982, asst. chief., 1983—97, chief, 1997—. Office: Choctaw Nation of Okla PO Drawer 1210 Durant OK 74701-1210 Office Phone: 580-924-8280.*

**PYLE, HOWARD,** lawyer, consultant; b. Richmond, Va., Feb. 1, 1940; s. Wilfrid and Anne Woolston (Roller) P.; m. Victoria M. Sheffield; children: Elizabeth Roller Ross, Howard. AB, Princeton U., 1962; JD, U. Va., 1967. Bar: Va. 1967, D.C. 1969. Career trainee CIA, Washington, 1967-69; adminstrv. asst. to Congressman Odin Langen, U.S. Ho. of Reps., Washington, 1969-70, to Congressman Hastings Keith, 1971; asst. to sec. Dept. Interior, Washington, 1971-73; Washington rep. Std. Oil Co. Ind., 1973-77; mgr. fed. pub. affairs R.J. Reynolds Industries, Inc., Winston-Salem, NC, 1977-80; dir. fed. rels. Houston Industries, Washington, 1980-99; pres. HPYLE Cons., Alexandria, Va., 1999—. Mem.: SAR, NRA, Va. Bar, DC Bar, Res. Officers Assn., Naval Res. Assn., Va. Country Club, Delta Theta Phi. Republican. Episcopalian. Home: 125 N Lee St Alexandria VA 22314-3260 also: PO Box 19645 Alexandria VA 22320-0645 Office: HPYLE Cons Po Box 19645 Alexandria VA 22320-0645 Office Phone: 703-608-4742. E-mail: hpyle@alumni.princeton.edu.

**PYLE, MATTHEW JARED,** secondary school educator; b. Joplin, Mo., Aug. 25, 1972; s. Michael Glen Pyle and Connie Sue Braschler; m. Ashli Ann Pyle, June 5, 2003. BS in Phys. Edn., Mo. State U., Springfield, 1997, MS in Secondary Edn., 1999. Grad. asst. Mo. State U.; tchr. spl. needs adaptive phys. edn. Houston Pub. Sch.; tchr. phys. edn., coach Warren County Pub. Sch.; tchr. phys. edn. Kansas City Pub. Schs., coach football, athletic dir. Democrat. Office: Northeast High Sch 415 S Va Brunt Ave Kansas City MO 64124

**PYLE, ROBERT NOBLE,** public relations executive; b. Wilmington, Del., Oct. 23, 1926; s. Joseph Lybr and LaVerne Ruth (Noble) Pyle; life ptnr. Patricia Carlile Pyle, Jan. 21, 2006; children: Robert Noble Jr., Mark C., Nicholas A., Louis P. Crosier, Sarah P. Moore. BA, Dickinson Coll., 1948; postgrad., Wharton Sch., U. Pa., 1949, U. Minn. Pres. Robert N. Pyle, Inc., Wilmington, 1949-52; adminstrv. asst. to U.S. Congress, Washington, 1952-63; chmn., bus. and polit. cons. and lobbyist Robert N. Pyle & Assoc., Washington, 1970—; cons. Ind. Bakers Assn., 1981—, chmn. Sec./treas. Bulgarian Am. Bus. Ctr. Contbr. numerous articles to profl. jours.; reporter covering Nurnburg Trials, Paris Peace Conf. for, Stars & Stripes, Europe, 1946. V.p. La Quinta Sr. Ctr.; part-time field man Rep. Nat. Congl. Com., 1959—74. With U.S. Army, 1945—46, ETO. Mem.: Kenwood Country Club, City Tavern Club, La Quinta Resort and Club, Lincoln Club. Presbyterian. Home: 50255 Via Simpatico La Quinta CA 92253 Office: 1223 Potomac St NW Washington DC 20007-3212 Office Phone: 202-333-8190. Personal E-mail: carliz8@verizon.net.

**PYLE, THOMAS ALTON,** broadcast executive; b. Phoenix, Sept. 8, 1933; s. Thomas Virgil and Evelyn B. (Redden) P.; m. Victoria K. Bileck, Apr. 21, 1957 (dec.), children: Pamela V., Brett I.; m. Marilyn Ann Miller, May 12, 2001. BA, Ariz. State U., 1956. Freelance unit mgr., casting dir., pay master motion picture industry MGM, Universal, 20th Century Fox, Paramount and others, L.A. and N.Y.C., 1956—60; v.p. sales Depicto Films Corp., NYC, 1960—65; prodr. John Sutherland Prodn., LA, 1965—67; v.p. mktg. Audio Prodn. Ednl. Svc., NYC, 1967—71; exec. v.p. mktg. Data Plex Systems, NYC, 1971—74; divsn. pres., exec. prodr. Sterling Inst. Video Prodns., Washington, D.C., 1974—80; founder and pres./ Applied Video Concepts, Inc., Washington, 1980—83; pres./ CEO Nat. Sci. Ctr. Found., Burke, Va., Augusta, Ga., 1983—85, tng. and edn. cons. to industry, govt. and military Washington, 1985—87; exec. dir., CEO Network for Instrnl. TV, Inc., Reston, Va. and Phoenix, 1987—. Built 88 new TV channels for K-12 sch. in 13 states and DC, 1997 started 1st highspeed wireless delivery of Internet to urban pub. sch., 1998 launched TeachersFirst.com an advertising supported free Internet svc. to K-12 teachers; launched TeachersAndFamilies.com, 2002 for parents, teachers, and pre-school children; founder, pres. New Century Comm., an ITFS/EBS leasing adv. svcs., 2004—; bd. dir. Natl. ITFS Assn., So. Fla. Instrnl. TV, Inc., Del. Valley Ednl. Telecom. Network, Inc., Instrnl. Opportunities, Inc., St. Louis, Mo., Cons. Wireless Cable Industry. Writer, dir., producer over 200 motion pictures, commd. for film on Pres. John F. Kennedy, 1962; prodr.: (films, on) Pres. Lyndon B. Johnson, 1964; singer: over 1500 performances on Broadway, stock, concerts, opera, radio and TV appearing with Leonard Berstein, Fred Warring, Robert Shaw, Ralph Hunter, under mgmt. to Red and Enda Skelton, 1951—55, Nat. Artists Corp., 1955—60. V.p. Dexter Park Assn., Spring Valley, NY, 1968-74, Solaridge Cluster Assn., Reston, Va., 1990-99. Recipient 27 awards from nat. and internat. film and video festivals, 2 Commendation awards White House, 1970, 2 Acad. award nominations. Mem. AAAS, Internat. Platform Assn., NY Acad. of Sci. Republican. Achievements include research in increasing productivity through education teaching and information relay and their effects on technology, science, communications, and defense. Avocation: photography. Office: New Century Communications 34111 N 7th St Phoenix AZ 85085 Office Phone: 623-434-3500.

**PYLES, LEE ALLAN,** cardiologist, biomedical researcher; s. H. and P. Pyles; m. Marie Elizabeth Steiner, July 15, 1989; children: Richard, Cynthia. BS in Chemistry, W.Va. U., Morgantown, 1979, MD, 1983. Diplomate Am.

Bd. Pediat., Am. Bd. Pediat. Cardiology. Intern pediat. U. Minn. Sch. Medicine, Mpls., 1983—84, resident pediat., 1984—86; fellow pediat. cardiology U. Minn., Mpls., 1986—89, asst. prof. pediat., 1998—; asst. prof. pediat. sect. pediat. cardiology and pediat. critical care W.Va. U., 1990—90, assoc. prof. pediat. sect. pediat. cardiology and pediat. critical care, 1995—96; assoc. prof. pediat. with tenure W.Va. U. Sch. Medicine, Morgantown, 1996—98. Privacy and security officer U. Minn. Physicians, Mpls., 2002—. Dir.(grant principal investigator): Minnesota Emergency Medical Services for Children Information System. Named one of Best Doctors in Am., Best Doctors, Inc, 1998—2005, Twin Cities Top Docs, Twin Cities Mag., 2004—05; recipient Samuel L. Channel award for Excellence in EMS, W.Va. EMS Tech. Support Network, 2000. Fellow: Am. Coll. Cardiology, Am. Acad. Pediat. (disting. svc. citation 1996—2002). Avocations: swimming, camping. Office: U Minn Mayo Mail Code # 94 420 Delaware St Minneapolis MN 55455 Office Phone: 612-626-2755. Business E-Mail: pyles001@umn.edu.

**PYLES, RODNEY ALLEN,** archivist, county official; b. Morgantown, W.Va., June 21, 1945; s. Melford John and Luci L. (Scarcella) P.; m. Carol Louise Wrobleski, May 20, 1972; 1 child, Janessa Louise. BA, MA (Benedum scholar 1966-67, grad. research asst. 1967-68, grad. teaching fellow 1968-69), W.Va. U., 1967, 69. Instr. polit. sci. Alderson-Broaddus Coll., Philippi, W.Va., 1969-71; asst. curator W.Va. U. Library, 1971-77; dir. archives and history div. W.Va. Dept. Culture and History, 1977-85; dep. chief Assessor's Office Monongalia County, 1985-88; assessor Monongalia County, 1989—. Mng. editor: W.Va. History quar, 1977-85 Mem. Morgantown (W.Va.) Dem. exec. com., 1966-69, Monongalia County (W.Va.) Dem. exec. com., 1972-76; mem. Morgantown Libr. Bd., 1988 91, Morgantown Hist. Landmarks Commn., 1986—; trustee W.Va. Pub. Theatre, 1999—, treas., 2004. Mem. Soc. Am. Archivists, W.Va. Hist. Soc. (exec. sec. 1977-90, bd. dirs. 1990—), Am. Assn. State and Local History (state awards chmn. 1980-85, state membership com. 1981-87), Monongalia Hist. Soc. (pres. 1986-88, bd. dirs. 1988—), W.Va. Polit. Sci. Assn. (treas. 1991—), W.Va. Assessors' Assn. (pres. 1992-93, bd. dirs. 2005—), KC (pres. bowling league 1995-96, 4th deg., faithful capt. 1996—, chancellor 1998-2000, dep. Grand Knight 2000-02, Grand Knight, 2002-), Sons of Italy (treas. 1995—). Roman Catholic. Home: 536 Harvard Ave Morgantown WV 26505-2157 Office: County Court House Rm 215 Morgantown WV 26505 Office Phone: 304-291-7222. E-mail: rapone@sbccom.com, rpyles@assessor.org.

**PYLES, SELMA BROADWAY,** music educator; b. Columbus, Ohio, June 7, 1955; d. Norman James and Ruth (Demarest) Broadway; m. Michael Lee Pyles, Aug. 4, 1990. MusB Edn., Ohio State U., 1977. Cert. tchr. Ohio Dept. Edn., 1977. Mid. sch. orch. tchr. South-We. City Sch. Dist., Grove City, Ohio, 1977—88; asst. h.s. orch. tchr. Hilliard City Sch. Dist., Ohio, 1988—2001, mid. sch. orch. tchr., 1988—2001, elem. orch. tchr., 2001—. Orch. coordr. Columbus Symphony Cadet Youth Orch., Ohio, 1989—90; orch. tchr. Ohio String Tchrs. Assn. Mid. Sch. Orch. Summer Camp, Columbus, 1988—97. Contbr. book. Choir dir. Westgate Friends Ch., Columbus, 1980—95, Youth Musicale, Canton, Ohio, 1980—82, Sounds of Celebration, Elyria, Ohio, 1984—86; orch. dir. N.W. Bible Ch., Hilliard, Ohio, 1998—2004, interim choir dir., 2002—04. Recipient Pub. Sch. Orch. Tchr. of Yr., Ohio Orch. and String Tchrs. Assn., 2003. Mem.: NEA (assoc.), Am. String Tchr. Assn. (assoc.), Ohio Orch. and String Tchrs. Assn. (assoc. Pub. Sch. Orch. Tchr. of the Yr. 2003), Ohio Edn. Assn. (assoc.). Achievements include Middle School Large Group Contests Superior Ratings 1989-2001. Avocations: church music, bible study, violin. Home: 4266 Ongaro Dr Columbus OH 43204 Office: Hilliard City Sch Dist 4681 Leap Road Hilliard OH 43026 Office Phone: 614-334-1600. E-mail: selma_pyles@fclass.hilliard.k12.oh.us.

**PYLIPOW, STANLEY ROSS,** retired manufacturing company executive; b. Coudersport, Pa., Apr. 4, 1936; s. Stanley Edward and Helen L. (Haskins) P.; m. Phyllis Beverly Moore, Dec. 1, 1956; children— David, James, Vicky, Kenneth, Sandra BBA in Acctg. cum laude, St. Bonaventure U., 1957. Various fin. positions Chicopee Mfg., New Brunswick, NJ, 1957-65; various positions to v.p.; gen. mgr. Domestic Coatings div. Mobil Chem. Co., N.Y.C., 1965-73; asst. corp. controller Monsanto Co., St. Louis, 1974-76; controller, dir. planning Monsanto Comml. Products, St. Louis, 1976-79; sr. v.p., bd. dirs., chief fin. officer Fisher Controls Internat., Inc., St. Louis, 1979-92; ret., 1992; bd. dirs. RBA Group. Treas. Ulster Project, St. Louis, 1998—2002. Treas., City of Town and Country, Mo., 1980-84; bd. dirs. Ecumenical Housing Prodn. Corp., St. Louis, 1980-90; mem. Acctg. Edn. Change Commn., 1992-96. Served to 1st lt., U.S. Army, 1958. Named Exec. of Yr., Profl. Secs. Internat., 1982 Mem. Inst. Mgmt. Accts. (pres. 1990-91, chmn. 1991-92), Fin. Execs. Inst., Winghaven Country Club, Silverthorn Country Club. Republican. Avocations: golf, exercise, spectator sports. Office Phone: 352-796-6903. Personal E-mail: stanpylipow@centurytel.net.

**PYM, BRUCE MICHAEL,** lawyer; b. Alameda, Calif., Sept. 29, 1942; s. Leonard A. and Willamay (Strandberg) P. B.B.A., U. Wash., 1964, J.D., 1967. Bar: Wash. 1967, U.S. Dist. Ct. (we. dist.) Wash. 1968, U.S. Ct. Appeals (9th cir.) 1968, U.S. Tax Ct. 1969, U.S. Supreme Ct. 1971. Law clk. Wash. State Supreme Ct., Olympia, 1967-68; assoc. Graham & Dunn, Seattle, 1968-73, shareholder, 1973-92; ptnr. Heller Ehrman LLP, Seattle, 1992—; mng. ptnr. Northwest Offices, 1994-99. Bd. dirs. United Way of King County, 1986-92, chmn., 1990. Mem. ABA, Wash. State Bar Assn., King County Bar Assn. (pres. 1984-85). Office: Heller Ehrman LLP 701 5th Ave Ste 6100 Seattle WA 98104-7098 Business E-Mail: bruce.pym@hellerehrman.com.

**PYNE-GEITHMAN, GAIL JEAN,** medical educator, researcher; b. London, July 19, 1974; d. Raymond and Jean Iris Pyne; m. Randolph B. Geithman, May 31, 2003; 1 child, David William Geithman. BSc in Biochemistry, U. Coll. London, 1995, PhD, U. Oxford, England, 1999. Supernumary post-doctoral scientist Med. Rsch. Coun. Ctr., London, 1998—99; post-doctoral fellow Dept. Molecular and Cellular Physiology U. Cin., 1999—2002; rsch. scientist Dept. Neurology U. Cin., 2002—05, rsch. asst. prof., 2005—. Author: Cerebral Vasospasm. Vol. Am. Heart Assn., Cin., 1999—2006. Recipient Sasakawa award, Sasakawa Found., 1997; fellow, Am. Heart Assn., 1999—2000; grantee, The Neuroscience Inst., 2002, 2005, NIH and Nat. Inst. Neurological Disorders and Stroke, 2005—. Mem.: Physiol. Soc., Internat. Stroke Assn., Am. Physiol. Soc., Biophys. Soc., Am. Heart Assn. Achievements include research in elucidation of the pathway by which hemorrhagic stroke causes delayed neurological deficit. Office: U Cin Dept Neurology Vontz Ctr 3125 Eden Ave Cincinnati OH 45267-0536 Office Phone: 513-558-7358. Business E-Mail: pynegj@email.uc.edu.

**PYOTT, DAVID EDMUND IAN,** pharmaceutical executive; b. London, Eng., Oct. 13, 1953; married; 4 children. MA, U. Edinburgh, 1975; diploma in German and European Law, U. Amsterdam, 1976; MBA, London Bus. Sch., 1980. Numerous positions Sandoz Nutrition, Barcelona, 1980-90, gen. mgr., 1990-92; pres., CEO Sandoz Nutrition Corp., Mpls., 1992-95; head divsn. nutrition Sandoz Internat. AG, 1995—97; mem., exec. com. Novartis AG (merger Sandoz and Ciba), 1995—97; pres. Allergan, Inc., Irvine, Calif., 1998—2006, CEO, 1998—, chmn., 2001—. Bd. dirs. PhRMA, Avery Dennison Corp., Edwards Lifescis. Corp., Advanced Med. Optics, Inc.; chmn. Calif. Healthcare Inst.; mem. Med. Adv. Coun. U. Calif. (Irvine) Grad. Sch. Mgmt.; mem.LA Bus. Advisors; vice-chair Chief Exec. Roundtable for UCI Bd. dirs. Internat. Coun. of Ophthalmology Found., Eyecare Am.; pres. Pan-Am. Ophthalmological Found. Mem. Pharm. Rsch. and Mfrs. Am. (bd. dirs., Allergan rep.), Pan Am. Assn. Ophthalmology (bd. dirs.), L.A. Bus. Advisors. Achievements include transforming Botox, an obsure treatment for rare muscular diseases, into a cultural and medical phenomenon. Office: Allergan Inc 2525 Dupont Dr Irvine CA 92612-1531 Address: Allergan Inc PO Box 19534 Irvine CA 92623*

**PYSH, GREGORY M.,** music educator; b. Sharon, Pa., Nov. 3, 1958; s. Michael J. and Anne L. Pysh; m. Kathy Lynne Baldwin, Sept. 5, 1981; children: Danya Lynne, Matthew Konstantin. B of Music summa cum laude, Youngstown State U., 1980; MusM, Bowling Green State U., 1982. Dir. music First Presbyn. Ch., Morristown, Tenn., 1983—96, min. music Midland,

Tex., 1996—. Adj. faculty Walters State C.C., Morristown, 1990—96, Midland Coll., Tex., 1997—. Composer: (handbell) Lead Me, Lord, 1995, Patapan, 2006, Cancion Jubiloso, 2006, (choral) O Come Before the Lord, our God, 1986, A Psalm of Ascents, 2003, When I Can Read My Title Clear, 2006. Pres. Midland Opera Theater, 2000. Mem.: Nat. Assn. Tchrs. Singing, Tex. Choral Dirs. Assn., Am. Choral Dirs. Assn. Avocation: collecting sports cards. Home: 1615 Shell Midland TX 79705 Office: First Presbyn Ch 800 W Texas Midland TX 79701 Business E-Mail: gpysh@fpcmid.org.

**PYSH, JOSEPH JOHN,** neurologist; b. Olyphant, Pa., Nov. 14, 1935; s. John Andrew and Anna Mary (Marusin) P.; m. Deborah Ann Prass, Dec. 15, 1991. BA in Biology, Wayne State U., 1958; DO, Chgo. Coll. Osteo. Medicine, 1962; PhD in Neuroanatomy, Northwestern U., Chgo., 1967. From instr. to assoc. prof. anatomy Northwestern U., Chgo., 1966-86, acting chmn. cell biology and anatomy, 1978-81, resident physician in neurology 1983-86; assoc. prof. neurology Mich. State U., East Lansing, 1986-95, prof. neurology, 1995—, dir. neurology residency program, 2001—03. Grant referee NSF, Washington, 1974—; frequent CME neurology speaker in field. Contbr. numerous articles to profl. jours; manuscript reviewer various orgns., Washington and N.Y.C. Recipient Tchg. award Northwestern U.; NIH grantee, 1969-82. Fellow Am. Coll. Neuropsychiatrists; mem. AAAS (life), NIH (mem. rsch. grant neurology study sect. 1976-77), Am. Acad. Neurology, Am. Soc. Cell Biology, Am. Assn. Anatomists, Soc. Neurosci., Sigma Xi. Republican. Achievements include research in synaptic transmission and brain development. Avocations: rare book collecting, sailing. Office: Mich State U Coll Osteo Medicine Dept Neurology 138 Service Rd A217 Clin East Lansing MI 48824 Office Phone: 517-353-8122. Business E-Mail: pysh@msu.edu.

**PYSHER, ALAN GUY,** retired nurse anesthetist; b. East Stroudsburg, Pa., Sept. 10, 1946; s. Kermit Joseph and Fern Elizabeth (Blake) P.; m. Branda Ann Petraitis, June 3, 1973 (div. 1984); 1 child, Lynne Claire. AAS, Northampton C.C., 1973; BA, Stephens Coll., 1984; MEd, U. So. Miss., 1988. RN; cert. registered nurse anesthetist. Nurse anesthetist Tinker AFB Hosp., Oklahoma City, 1981-84; chief nurse anesthetist Lajes Field Hosp., Azores, Portugal, 1984-85; asst. chief nurse anesthetist Kessler Med. Ctr., Biloxi, Miss., 1985-88; chief nurse anesthetist Cannon AFB Hosp., Clovis, N.Mex., 1988-91, Wilford Hall Med. Ctr., San Antonio, 1991-95; program dir. David Grant Med. Ctr., Fairfield, Calif., 1995-98; anesthesia element chief Wright-Patterson AFB, Dayton, Ohio, 1998-2000; comdr. surg. ops. squadron, dir. nurse anesthesia edn. Wilford Hall Med. Ctr., Lackland AFB, San Antonio, 2000—02; comdr. edn. and tng. squadron Wilford Hall Med Ctr., Lackland AFB, San Antonio, 2002—04; ret., 2004. Assoc. clin. prof. Uniformed Svcs. U. Health Scis., Bethesda, Md., 1998—2001. Col. USAF, 1973—2004. Mem. ANA, Am. Assn. Nurse Anesthetists, Aerospace Med. Assn., Air War Coll. Alumni Assn., VFW, Purple Heart Assn. Republican. Lutheran. Avocations: golf, martial arts. Home: 8910 Shady Hls San Antonio TX 78254-5525 E-mail: pyshera@aol.com.

**PYSHER, ZANE KERMIT,** retired counselor; b. Pen Argyl, Pa., Mar. 19, 1943; s. Kermit Joseph and Fern Elizabeth Pysher; m. Marcia Ann Cook, July 9, 1966; children: Erica Ann, Zane-Alan. BA, Albright Coll., 1965; MA, Kean Coll., 1970. Cert. tchr. English and history, N.J., Pa., Mass.; cert. student personnel guidance svcs. N.J., Pa. Tchr. English, reading, libr. sci. Warren Hills Sch., Washington, NJ, 1965—69; counselor, dir. guidance Roxbury Twp. Schs., Succasunna, NJ, 1969—2005. Sec., pres. bd. edn. com. Good Shepherd Nursery Sch., Easton, Pa., 1996-98 Mem. ch. coun. Good Shepherd Luth. Ch., Easton, 1992—94, mem. mut. ministry com., 2000—. Recipient Morris County Tchr. Recognition award Morris County Assn. Sch. Adminstrs., 1999; named Eisenhower Sch. Tchr. of Yr., 1999 Mem.: NEA, Morris County Edn. Assn., Roxbury Edn. Assn. (sch. bldg. rep. 1972—75, mem. scholarship com. 1978—2005, sch. test coord. 1987—2005), Morris County Guidance Assn., NJ Edn. Assn. Democrat. Lutheran. Avocations: photography, golf, bowling, sports cards collecting, coin collecting/numismatics. Home: 2311 Ben Jon Rd Easton PA 18040 E-mail: ezpysh@webtv.net.

**PYTELL, ROBERT HENRY,** retired lawyer, former judge; b. Detroit, Sept. 27, 1926; s. Henry Carl and Helen (Zielinski) P.; m. Laurie Mazur, June 2, 1956; children: Mary Beth, Mark Henry, Robert Michael. JD, U. Detroit, 1951. Bar: Mich. 1952. Of counsel Pytell & Varchetti, P.C., Detroit, 1952-2001; asst. U.S. atty. Ea. Dist. Mich., 1962-65; judge Mcpl. Ct., Grosse Pointe Farms, Mich., 1967-85. With USNR, 1945-46. Mem. Am. Coll. Trust and Estate Coun., State Bar Mich. (mem. probate coun. probate sect. 1998-2000), Crescent Sail Yacht Club (Grosse Pointe), Delta Theta Phi. Roman Catholic.

**PYTKA, STEPHEN MILTON,** office equipment executive; b. Ludlow, Mass., Apr. 29, 1947; s. Milton Ignatius and Jean Marie (Kmiecik) P.; m. Linda Rachel Madsen, May 25, 1969; children: Jonathan Stephen, Justin Stephen, Brendan Stephen. BSEE, Worcester Poly. Inst., 1968; MBA, Dartmouth Coll., 1977. Design engr. AT&T, Whippany, N.J., 1968-69, Kwajalein, Marshall Islands, 1970-71, Greensboro, N.C., 1969-70, Langdon, N.D., 1971-73; sys. engr. GE, Pittsfield, Mass., 1973-75; planning mgr. Xerox Corp., Rochester, N.Y., 1977-81; mktg. mgr. Wang Labs., Inc., 1982-83; exec. v.p. Cap. Internat., Marshfield, Mass., 1983—; mng. ptnr. Consilium Ptnrs. LLC, Boston, 2004—. Co-founder P&R Microtech, 1982-83; exec. v.p. BIS Cap Internat., 1983-89; pres., chief ops. officer BISCOM, Inc., 1990-96; v.p. The Onstott Group, 1997-98; chmn., CEO Streamware, Inc., 1998-2000; pres., CEO eChinaLink, 2000-01; CEO Talksender, Inc., 2000-01, Hellotech, 2001-02, Gazelle Systems, Inc., 2002-03; mng dir., Consilium Ptnrs., 2004; mem. exec. bd. WPI Venture Forum; mem Touch Applications, HUB Angels, Common Angels; panelist MIT Enterprise Forum; trustee Andover YMCA; spkr. in field. Mem. Am. Mgmt. Assn, HubAngels, CommonAngels. Republican. Roman Catholic. Home: 9 Langley Ln Andover MA 01810-4259 Office: Consilium Ptnrs 399 Boylston St Boston MA 02116

**PYTLINSKI, JERZY TEODOR,** physicist, educator, research scientist; b. Warsaw, Apr. 1, 1938; s. Stanislaw and Natalia (Matuszewska) P.; m. Bonnie Laurie Bennett, Dec. 30, 1969; 1 child, Christine Barbara. MS, Tech. U. Warsaw, 1962; PhD Plasma Physics with distinction, U. Paris, 1967. Program mgr., acting divsn. head N.Mex. State U., Las Cruces, 1977—80; sr. scientist, divsn. head U P.R., Mayaguez, 1981—83; program dir., sr. scientist San Juan, 1983—86, sr. scientist, founding dir. Univ.-Industry Rsch. Ctr. Tampa, Fla., 1986—89; pres. Univ.-Industry Rsch. Ctr., Tampa, Fla., 1989—, prof. 1989—. Mem.adv. bd. on solar energy UNESCO, 1979-85; referee Am. Jour. Physics, 1980—, Solar Energy Jour., 1983-87, 38th Internat. Sci. and Engring. Fair, 1987; mem. U.S. tech. adv. group of ISO TC-180, 1981—. Mem. editl. bd. Internat. Jour. Energy, Environ. Econs., 1990—; co-editor Procs. Internat. Conf. Energy for Ams., 1987; contbr. more than 85 articles to profl. jours. and procs Grantee state and fed. agys., various edn. and rsch. founds.; Postdoctoral fellow U. Liverpool, Eng., 1968-69; recipient commendation State of Kans., 1977. Mem. Am. Phys. Soc., Nat. Coun. Univ. Rsch. Adminstrs., Soc. Rsch. Adminstrs., Internat. Solar Energy Soc., Internat. Energy Soc. (sci. coun. 1985—), Sigma Phi Sigma Republican. Roman Catholic. Achievements include pioneering research in plasma physics and alternative energy sources research. Avocations: reading, tennis, travel.

**PYTTE, AGNAR,** physicist, retired academic administrator; b. Kongsberg, Norway, Dec. 23, 1932; arrived in U.S., 1949, naturalized, 1965; s. Ole and Edith (Christiansen) Pytte; m. Anah Currie Loeb, June 18, 1955; children: Anders H., Anthony M., Alyson C. AB, Princeton U., 1953; AM, Harvard U., 1954, PhD, 1958. Faculty Dartmouth Coll., 1958—87, prof. physics, 1967—87, chmn. dept. physics and astronomy 1971—75, assoc. dean faculty, 1975—78, dean grad. studies, 1975—78, provost, 1982—87; pres. Case Western Res. U., Cleve., 1987—99; adj. prof. physics Dartmouth Coll., 1999—. Active in plasma physics; mem. Project Matterhorn Princeton U., 1959—60, 1978—79, U. Brussels, 1966—67. Bd. dirs. Goodyear Tire and Rubber Co., 1988—2004, Accreditation Coun. for Grad. Med. Edn.,

2000—04, Environ. Careers Orgn., 2003—06, A.O. Smith Corp., 2001—2003, Sherman Fairchild Found., Inc., 1987—2006. Mem.: Am. Phys. Soc., Sigma Xi, Phi Beta Kappa. Personal E-mail: agnar.x.pytte@dartmouth.edu.

**QASIM, IMAD ISA,** lawyer; b. Tripoli, Libya, Sept. 14, 1957; came to U.S., 1973; s. Isa and Nawal Q.; m. Nancy Meloy Qasim, May 19, 1990. AB, Hamilton Coll., 1979; JD, Georgetown U., 1982. Bar: N.Y. 1983, Ill. 1987, D.C. 1989. Assoc. Sidley & Austin, Chgo., 1983, 85-88, Muscat, Oman, 1983-85, Washington, 1988-91, ptnr., 1991—2001, Sidley Austin Brown & Wood, Chicago, 2001—. Mem. ABA (mem. securities law sect.), D.C. Bar Assn. Office: Sidley Austin Brown & Wood Bank One Plz 10 S Dearborn St Chicago IL 60603 Office Phone: 312-853-7000.

**QAZI, ASHRAF JEHANGIR,** ambassador; b. Pakistan, 1942; married; 2 children. With Fgn. Svc. of Pakistan, 1965—; ambassador of Pakistan to Syria, 1986—88, East Germany, 1990—91, Russia, 1991—94, China, 1994—97, India, 1997—2002, U.S.A, 2002—04, Iraq, 2004—. Various diplomatic assignments Copenhagen, Tokyo, Cairo, Tripoli, London. Office: c/o UN Headquarters First Avenue at 46th Street New York NY 10017 Office Phone: 212-963-1234. Office Fax: 212-963-4879.

**QAZI, MUJTABA A.,** ophthalmologist; b. Karachi, Pakistan, Jan. 5, 1971; arrived in US, 1975; s. Asghar H. and Rehana Qazi; m. Erum Qazi, Aug. 3, 1995; children: Amaan, Rida, Ameen. BA, NYU, 1993, MD, 1997. Diplomate Am. Bd. Ophthaalmology. Intern St. Vincent's Hosp., N.Y.C., 1997—98; resident dept. ophthalmology Boston U. Med. Ctr., 1998—2001; chief resident dept. ophthalmology Boston VA Med. Ctr., 2000; fellow in corneal, anterior segment and refractive surgery Pepose Vision Inst., Chesterfield, Mo., 2001—02. Dir. clin. studies Pepose Vision Inst.; clin. instr. Washington U. Sch. Medicine, St. Louis. Author: Principles of Managing Ophthalmic Injury, 2000, Scleral Expansion Band Segments for the Treatment of Presbyopia, 2002; reviewer Am. Jour. Ophthalmology, Jour. of Refractive Surgery; co-editor refractive surgery sect.: Current Opinions in Ophthalmology. Bd. mem. Midwest Cornea Rsch. Found. Finalist Leadership scholarship, Nat. Assn. Asian Am. Profls., 1989; NYU Coll. Arts & Scis. Pres. scholar, 1989—93, Empire State Acad. scholar, 1989—93. Mem.: Internat. Soc. Refractive Surgeons, Am. Soc. Cataract & Refractive Surgery, Am. Acad. Ophthalmology. Office: Pepose Vision Inst PC 16216 Baxter Rd Ste 205 Chesterfield MO 63017 Home: 300 Remington Way Dr Ballwin MO 63021 Office Phone: 636-728-0111. E-mail: mqazi@peposevision.com.

**QI, HUAQING,** special education educator; d. Zhenhua Qi and Qingduo Sun; m. Matthew Schlecht; 1 child, Isaac Schlecht; 1 child, Peter Li. MEd, Belmont U., Nashville, 1992, Vanderbilt U., 1998, PhD, 2001. Cert. early childhood spl. edn. Nashville. Asst. prof. West Chester U., Pa., 2001—04, U. of N.Mex, Albuquerque, 2004—. Grant reviewer, jour. reviewer profl. agys. Editor: Editing for a Professional Newsletter; contbr. articles to profl. jours. (Fredrick Douglass scholarship, 2000). Mem.: CEC, Autism Soc. of Am., Am. Assn. of Mental Retardation, Soc. of Rsch. and Children Devel., Am. Speech, Lang., and Hearing Assn. (travel fellowship 2002, 2003). Office: Univ NMex Dept Ednl Specialties Hokona Hall 248 Albuquerque NM 87131 Office Phone: 505-277-4452. Business E-Mail: hqi@unm.edu.

**QI, JIANWEI,** mechanical engineer, researcher; b. Wuxi, Jiangsu, China, Mar. 11, 1967; s. Guoqin Qi and Yaqin Huang; m. Xinwei Dong; children: Yun, Yuan. BS, Nanjing (China) U. Aeronautics and Astronautics, 1989; M.E., Zhejiang U., Hangzhou, China, 1991; PhD, Tsinghua U., Beijing, China, 1996. Rsch. asst. Inst. Fluid Engring., Zhejiang U., Hangzhou, Zhejiang, China, 1989—91; rsch. and tching. asst. Tsinghua U., Beijing, 1992—94, lectr., 1995—96; engr. China Packaging Corp., Beijing, 1996—97; rschr. Nat. Inst. Advanced Indsl. Sci. and Tech., Tsukuba, Ibaraki, Japan, 1998—2000; postdoctoral rschr. The Johns Hopkins U., Balt., 2000; rsch. scientist, lab mgr. U. Md., College Park, 2000—. Sci. and tech. cons. Author: The First Prize in Sci. and Tech. Progress by State Edn. Commn, China, 1996; contbr. articles to profl. jours. (The Excellent Engring Prize by Tsinghua U., 1996). Mem.: IMAPS, AAAS, ASME, Japan Sci. and Tech. Corp. Achievements include contributions to developing Advanced Thermal Technology for electronics, energy, advanced materials process and green environmental systems. Office: U Md 2181 Martin Hall College Park MD 20742

**QI, XIAONING,** electrical engineer, electronics engineer, researcher; PhD, Stanford U., Calif. Sr. engr. R&D Sun Microsystems, Inc., Sunnyvale, Calif., 2001—05; staff engr. R&D Synopsys, Inc., Mountain View, Calif., 2005—. Mem.: IEEE.

**QI, ZHIGANG,** materials scientist, chemist; s. Pengling Qi and Fengzhi Jing; children: Lydia Cong Zhang, Albert Jie Qi, Brian Lin. BSc in Chemistry, U. Sci. and Tech., Beijing, 1985; PhD, McGill U., 1996. Post-doctoral fellow Meml. U. of Newfoundland, St. John's, Newfoundland, Canada, 1996—97; sr. staff scientist H Power Corp., Belleville, NJ, 1997—2003; fellow Plug Power Inc., Latham, NY, 2003—. Contbr. articles to profl. jours.; mem. editl. bd.: Jour. Power Sources. Mem.: Am. Chem. Soc., The Electrochem. Soc. Achievements include first to ground breaking research in PEM fuel cells and conductive polymers; patents in field. Office Phone: 518-738-0229. Home Fax: 518-207-5273. E-mail: zhigang_qi@plugpower.com.

**QIAN, LIJUN,** electrical engineer, educator; b. Rutgers U., 2001. Rsch. scientist Bell Labs., Murray Hill, NJ, 2001—03; prof. Prairie View (Tex.) A&M U., 2003—. Dir. Wireless Comm. Lab., Prairie View, 2003—. Recipient Ctrl. Bell Labs. award, Bell Labs., 2003. Office: Prairie View A&M U Dept Elec Engring Prairie View TX 77446 Office Phone: 936-857-9915. Business E-Mail: lijunqian@ieee.org.

**QIAN, YONGCHANG,** molecular toxicologist; s. Desheng Qian and Qinguo Shen; m. Ying Zheng, July 4, 1988; 1 child, Shaofeng. PhD, Chinese Acad. of Scis., Shanghai, 1990. Contbr. articles to profl. jours. Recipient Postdoctoral present award, Gulf Coast Soc. of Toxicology, 1999, Signature Program award, Tex. A&M U., 2000, Concept award, Dept. of Def., 2005—06. Mem.: Soc. for Neurosci., Soc. of Toxicology (assoc). Achievements include research in Identification of Heavy Metal-Targeted Molecular Proteins. Office: Texas A&M Univ Rm107 VMA Bldg Texas A&M Univ College Station TX 77843 Office Phone: 979-862-4973. Personal E-mail: qian3906@yahoo.com. E-mail: yqian@cvm.tamu.edu.

**QIANG, XIAO,** advocate; BS, U. Sci. and Tech. China; student, U. Notre Dame, 1986—89. Human rights worker Ind. Fedn. Chinese Students and Scholars, Washington; exec. dir. Human Rights in China, N.Y.C. Spkr. Chinese human rights UN Commn. on Human Rights, 1993—; lectr. in field in various countries.

**QIAO, FENGXIANG,** transportation engineer, educator; b. Taizhou, Jiangsu Province, China, Sept. 26, 1963; s. Deheng Qiao and Sufang Shen; m. Jinghong Ma, Sept. 28, 1988; 1 child, Yijun. Bachelor of Engring. in Automatic Control, Nanjing Inst. Tech. (renamed S.E. U.), China, 1985; Master of Engring. in Mech. Engring., S.E. U., China, 1988; PhD in Civil Engring., Hong Kong U. Sci. and Tech., 2000. Asst. prof. and dir. transp. lab S.E. U., Nanjing, 1988—97; rsch. and tching. asst. Hong Kong U. Sci. and Tech., Hong Kong, 1997—2000; post doctoral rsch. assoc. and rsch. asst. prof. Tex. So. U., Houston, 2000—06, asst. prof., 2005—. Recipient 2d Pl. award for transp. planning, City of Zhenzhou, Henan Province, China, 1992, 2d Pl. award for sci. and tech. progress, Chinese Edn. Com., 1992; Tex. So. U. Seed grantee, Tex. So. U., 2006. Master: Houston Area Nat. Summer Transp. Inst. (mentor 2002—06), United Assns. Chinese Alumni in Greater Houston Area (life; pres. 2005—06); mem.: N.Am. China Overseas Transp. Assn., Transp. Rsch. Bd., Am. Assn. Civil Engring. (assoc.), Tex. Dept. Transp. (mem. tech. adv. panel), SW. Region U. Transp. Ctr. (prin. investigator 2004—06, Award for rsch. on vehicle emission testing 2004, Award for

rsch. on intelligent transp. sys. data compression 2005). Achievements include first to Developed Wavelet Transformation based approach for Intelligent Transportation System data aggregation and compression; research in Collected and evaluated on-road vehicle emission for mobile source air quality control; Computer simulation based optimization strategy for evacuation under unexpected events in large urban areas; Improved framework and systematic calibration for intersection left-turn yellow intervals including red clearance time; Intelligent intersection delay estimation methogology by using Fuzzy logic theory. Home: 5606 Bissonet St # 12 Houston TX 77081 Office: Texas Southern University Transp D 3100 Cleburne Ave Houston TX 77004 Office Phone: 713-313-1915. Office Fax: 713-313-1856. Personal E-mail: ceqfx@yahoo.com. Business E-Mail: qiao_fg@tsu.edu.

**QIAO, JIAN-HUA,** pathologist, researcher; b. Shanghai, Sept. 17, 1960; m. Mei-Qian Guan, Sept. 27, 1985; children: Mona G., George S. Qiao-Guan. MD, Shanghai Med. U., 1984. Diplomate Am. Bd. Pathology, AP/CP, 2003, cert. med. lic. Med. Bd. Calif., 2000. Resident diagnostic radiology Children's Hosp., Shanghai Med. U., 1984—90, chief resident diagnostic radiology, 1988—90; rsch. fellow cardiology Cedars-Sinai Med. Ctr., LA, 1990—91, resident pathology, 1997—2002; asst. rschr. cardiology UCLA Med. Ctr., 1991—97, clin. fellow pathology, 2002—03, clin. instr., 2003—04; staff attending pathologist Mercy Hosp., Bakersfield, Calif., 2004—06, Calif. Hosp. Med. Ctr., 2006—. Contbr. articles to profl. jours. Recipient Physician Recognition award, AMA, 2001—, Nathan B. Friedman, M.D. prize for rsch., Cedars-Sinai Med. Ctr., 2002. Fellow: Am. Soc. Clin. Pathology, Coll. Am. Pathologists; mem.: US and Can. Acad. Pathology. Achievements include research in size of atherosclerotic plaque in coronary arteries in patients who died from acute myocardial infarction; rejection in cardiac transplantation, heart diesease and HIV infection; mouse models for atherosclerosis; discovery of define genetic determination of arterial calcification; describe cartilage cells in artery wall in human calcified diabetic peripheral vascular disease; research in imaging studies of pulmonary hypertension in Chinese children with congenital heart disease; gated MRI in diagnosis of congenital heart disease in children in Shanghai. Avocations: swimming, bicycling, stamp collecting/philately, photography. Office: Calif Hosp Med Ctr Dept Pathology 1401 S Grand Ave Los Angeles CA 90015 Office Phone: 213-742-5791. Personal E-mail: jianhuaqiao@yahoo.com. Business E-Mail: jianhua.qiao@chw.edu.

**QIU, HAI,** research scientist; b. Pingjiang, Hunan, China, Oct. 30, 1974; s. Kangxia Huang and Yumei Qiu; m. Rui Dong, Dec. 19, 1972; children: Annie Rui, David Tian. PhD, Xi'an Jiaotong U., China, 1999. Postdoctoral rschr. Tongji U., Shanghai, 2000—01, NSF Ctr. for Intelligent Maintenance Sys., U. Wis., Milw., 2001; vis. rschr. United Techs. Rsch. Ctr., East Hartford, Conn., 2001—02; lead rschr. NSF Ctr. for Intelligent Maintenance Sys., U. Wis., Milw., 2002—05; rsch. asst. prof. U. of Cin., 2005—06; rsch. scientist GE Global Rsch. Ctr., Niskayuna, NY, 2006—. Contbr. articles to profl. jours. Recipient Nat. Technol. Invention award, State Dept. of China, 2004, Chinese Excellent Patent award, State Intellectual Property Office of China, 2003, Technol. and Sci. Innovation award, Ministry of Edn., 2003, Sci. and Tech. award, China Instrument and Control Soc., 2004. Mem.: IEEE (corr.), ASME (corr.). Achievements include patents for Rotor Holo-Balancing Method. Office Phone: 518-387-5271.

**QIU, LARRY DONGXIAO,** economics professor; b. Luchun, Guangxi, China, Oct. 6, 1961; s. Peilung Qiu and Meijian Chen; m. Denise Jinglian Qiu, Jan. 9, 1987; children: Alice W., Jennifer Z. BS, Zhongshan U., Guangzhou, China, 1983; MA, U. B.C., Vancouver, Can., 1989, PhD, 1993. Asst. prof. Hong Kong U. Sci. and Tech., 1993-2001, assoc. prof., 2001—. Cons. Hong Kong Govt., 1996-98, Asian Devel. Bank, Manila, 1997-98. Contbr. articles to profl. jours. Mem. Am. Econ. Assn., Royal Econ. Soc., Econometric Soc., European Econ. Assn., Internat. Econs. and Fin. Soc. Avocations: tennis, soccer, music. Office: Dept Econs Hong Kong U Sci & Tech Kowloon Hong Kong Office Phone: 852-2358-7628. Office Fax: 852-2358-2084. E-mail: larryqiu@ust.hk.

**QIU, LI-HUI,** music educator, actress; b. Shanghai; arrived in U.S., 1997; d. Jian-Fei Qiu and Ping-Hua Wan; m. Liang Yun, Jan. 1, 1962; children: Gang, Xiao. BA, Shanghai Music U., China, 1962. Nat. 2nd class actress Shanghai Orch., China, 1962—97; vocal actress Shanghai Ballet Troupe, China, 1975—76; tchr. music Edison (NJ) Chinese Sch., 1998—2001, Everbright Chinese Sch., Edison, NJ, 2001—; pvt. instr. vocal, keyboard and piano, 1990—. Benefit performances NJ Chinese Festival, 1999, Montvale High Sch., 1998, Woodbridge (NJ) Housing Authority, 2001—06; adv. The Cultural Festival on Mother's Day, NYC, 1998. Mem.: Shanghai Keyboard Assn., Nat. Musician Soc. of China (Shanghai chapt.), Music Tchrs. Nat. Assn. Home and Studio: Apt 4J 55 Brook St Woodbridge NJ 07095 Personal E-mail: liangyun@yahoo.com.

**QIU, LILI,** science educator; d. Mingxin Qiu and Yueming Feng; m. Yin Zhang, Apr. 26, 1974. BS in Physics, U. Bridgeport, 1996, BS in Computer Sci., 1996; PhD, Cornell U., 2001. Rschr. Microsoft Rsch., Redmond, Wash., 2001—04; asst. prof. U. Tex., Austin, 2005—. Contbr. more than 30 sci. papers to leading confs. and jours. Mem.: IEEE, ACM, Upsilon Pi Epsilon. Achievements include 10 patents pending in field. Office: U Tex CS Dept 1 Univ Sta C0500 Austin TX 78712

**QIU, PEIHUA,** statistician, researcher, educator; b. Shanghai, Oct. 17, 1965; arrived in U.S., 1991; s. Hongde Ren, Qibao Li; m. Yan Zhang, May 7, 1977; children: Andrew, Alan. BS in Math., Fudan U., China, 1986; PhD, U. Wis., 1996. Asst. prof. Fudan U., Shanghai, 1989—91; sr. rsch. consulting statistician Ohio State U., Columbus, 1996—98; asst. prof. U. Minn., Mpls., 1998—2002, assoc. prof., 2002—. Author: Image Processing and Jump Regression Analysis, 2005; contbr. chapters to books, articles to profl. jours. Recipient best paper winner of the 5th ISI competition for young statistician, Internat. Statis. Inst., 1991. Mem.: Bernoulli Soc., Inst. Math. Stats., Am. Statis. Assn. Home: 6768 Carlisle Curve Shakopee MN 55379 Office Phone: 612-625-5819. Business E-Mail: qiu@stat.umn.edu.

**QU, RONGDA,** biologist, educator; b. Tianjin, China, May 29, 1946; s. Chuanrui Qu and Liqing Xu; m. Hong Gu, Feb. 4, 1983; 1 child, Helen. BS in Forestry, Beijing Forestry Inst., 1970; MS in Plant Genetics, CAS, Beijing, 1982; PhD in Plant Cell and Molecular Biology, U. SC, Columbia, 1989. Asst. rschr. Genetics Inst. Chinese Acad. Scis., Beijing, 1982—84; postdoctoral rsch. assoc. Wash. U. St. Louis, 1989—91; sr. rsch. assoc. Scripps Rsch. Inst., La Jolla, Calif., 1991—94; asst. rsch. prof. Mont. State U., Bozeman, Mont., 1994—96; asst. prof. NC State U., Raleigh, NC, 1996—2002, assoc. prof., 2002—. Mem.: AAAS, Crop Sci. Soc. Am., Am. Soc. Plant Biologists. Achievements include patents pending for a strong and costitutive rice rubi3 promoter; a method to express useful proteins in plants; research in grass and cereal biotechnology; intron-mediated gene expression enhancement; biomass crop improvement. Office: North Carolina State Univ Dept Crop Science 100 Derieux Pl Raleigh NC 27695-7620 Office Fax: 919-515-7959. Business E-Mail: rongda_qu@ncsu.edu.

**QU, RONGHAI,** electrical engineer; b. Heilongjiang, China; s. Baoshen Qu and Guilan Wang; m. Dongning Sun, Jan. 29, 1996; children: Chen, Jeffrey. PhD, U. Wis., Madison, 2002. Faculty mem. Tsinghua U., Beijing, 1996—98; sr. devel. engr. Northland, a Scott Fetzer Co., Watertown, NY, 2002—03; elec. engr. in sr. profl. band GE Global Rsch. Ctr., Niskayuna, NY, 2003—. Com. mem. Tech. Com. on Energy and Power Systems, Internat. Assn. of Sci. and Tech. for Devel., 2004—. Recipient Mgmt. award, GE Global Rsch. Ctr, 2004. Mem.: IEEE (com. mem. elec. machines com. 2002—), Sigma Xi. Achievements include patents for 2 patents on electrical machines; 12 patents pending on electrical machines; 8 inventions on electrical mahcines, working with attorneys to file patent applications. Office: EP 118A GE Global Rsch Ctr 1 Research Cir Niskayuna NY 12309 Office Phone: 518-387-4471.

**QUAAL, WARD LOUIS,** broadcast executive; b. Ishpeming, Mich., Apr. 7, 1919; s. Sigfred Emil and Alma Charlotte (Larson) Q.; m. Dorothy J. Graham, Mar. 9, 1944; children: Graham Ward, Jennifer Anne. AB, U. Mich., 1941; LL.D. (hon.), Mundelein Coll., 1962, No. Mich. U., 1967; D.Pub.Svc., Elmhurst Coll., 1967; D.H.L. (hon.), Lincoln Coll., 1968, DePaul U., 1974. Announcer-writer Sta. WBEO (now sta. WDMJ), Marquette, Mich., 1936—37; announcer, writer, producer Sta. WJR, Detroit, 1937—41; spl. events announcer-producer WGN, Chgo., 1941—42, asst. to gen. mgr., 1945—49; exec. dir. Clear Channel Broadcasting Service, Washington, 1949—52, pres., chief exec. officer, 1964—74; v.p., asst. gen. mgr. Crosley Broadcasting Corp., Cin., 1952—56; v.p., gen. mgr., mem. bd. WGN Inc., Chgo., 1956; exec. v.p., then pres. WGN Continental Broadcasting Co. (now Tribune Broadcasting Co.), 1960—75; pres. Ward L. Quaal Co., 1975—; dir. Tribune Co., 1961—75; dir., mem. exec. com. U.S. Satellite Broadcasting Co., 1982—2000. Bd. dirs. Christine Valmy Inc.; chmn. exec. com., dir. WLW Radio Inc., Cin., 1975-81; co-founder, dir. Universal Resources Inc., 1961-86; mem. FCC Adv. Com. on Advanced TV Sys., 1988-96. Author: (with others) Broadcast Management, 1968, rev. edit., 1979, new edit. 1997; co-prodr. (Broadway play) Teddy and Alice, 1988. Mem., Hoover Commn. Exec. Br. Task Force, 1949-59; mem. U.S.-Japan Cultural Exchange Commn., 1960-70; mem. Pres.'s Council Phys. Fitness and Sports, 1983-93; bd. dirs. Farm Found., 1963-73; bd. trustees Hollywood (Calif.) Mus., 1964-78, MacCormac Jr. Coll., Chgo., 1974-80; chmn. exec. com. Council for TV Devel., 1969-72; mem. bus. adv. coun. Chgo. Urban League, 1964-74; bd. dirs. Broadcasters Found., Internat. Radio and TV Found., Sears Roebuck Found., 1970-73; trustee Mundelein Coll., 1962-72, Hillsdale Coll., 1966-72. Served as It. USNR, 1942-45. Named Radio Man of Yr., Am. Coll. Radio, Arts, Crafts & Scis., 1961, Laureate in Order of Lincoln, Lincoln Acad. Ill., 1965, Communicator of Yr., Jewish United Fund, 1969, Advt. Club Man of Yr., 1973; named one of Top 100 Mems., Delta Tau Delta, 1999, 1st 100 5th Estaters, Broadcasting 20th Century, 1999, First 50 Giants of Broadcasting, Libr. Am. Broadcasting, 2003; named to Delta Tau Delta Disting. Svc. Chpt., 1970, Broadcasting Mag. Hall of Fame, 1991, Mgmt. Hall of Fame, NATAS/TV Bur. Advt., 2003; recipient Disting. Bd. Gov.'s award, NATAS, 1966, 1987, Inaugural Inductee Mgmt. Hall of Fame, 2003, Freedoms Found. award, Valley Forge, 1966, 1968, 1970, Disting. Alumnus award, U. Mich., 1967, Loyola U. Key, 1970, Advt. Man of Yr. Gold medallion, Chgo. Advt. Club, 1968, Disting. Svc. award, Nat. Assn. Broadcasters, 1973, Ill. Broadcaster of Yr. award, 1973, Press Vet. of Yr. award, 1973, Comm. award of distinction, Brandeis U., 1973, Founder & Leadership award, Broadcast Pioneers Libr., 1991, 1st recipient Sterling medal, Barren Found., 1985, Lifetime Achievement award in broadcasting, Ill. Broadcasters Assn., 1989, Lifetime Achievement award, WGN TV, 1998, 1st person named to Better Bus. Bur. Hall of Fame, Coun. on Better Bus. Burs., Inc., 1975. Mem. NATAS (bd. govs. 1966-76, Silver Circle award 1993), Nat. Press Found. (bd. dirs. 1991-99), Nat. Assn. Broadcasters (bd. dirs. 1952-56), Fed. Commn. Bar Assn., Broadcast Music Inc. (bd. dirs. 1953-70), Assn. Maximum Svc. Telecasters Inc. (bd. dirs. 1952-72), Broadcast Pioneers (pres., bd. dirs. 1962-73), Broadcast Pioneers Libr. (pres. 1981-84), Broadcast Pioneers Ednl. Fund Inc., Broadcasters Found. (chmn. bd. 1996-99). Office: Ward L Quaal Co PO Box 336 Winnetka IL 60093 Office Phone: 847-446-4697.

**QUACKENBUSH, JUSTIN LOWE,** federal judge; b. Spokane, Wash., Oct. 3, 1929; s. Carl Clifford and Marian Huldah (Lowe) Q.; m. Marie McAtee; children: Karl Justin, Kathleen Marie, Robert Craig. Student, U. Ill., 1947-49; BA, U. Idaho, 1951; LLB, Gonzaga U., Spokane, 1957. Bar: Wash. 1957. Dep. pros. atty., Spokane County, 1957-59; ptnr. Quackenbush, Dean, Bailey & Henderson, Spokane, 1959-80; dist. judge U.S. Dist. Ct. (ea. dist.) Wash., Spokane, 1980—, now sr. judge. Part-time instr. Gonzaga U. Law Sch., 1960-67 Chmn. Spokane County Planning Commn., 1969-73. Served with USN, 1951-54. Mem. Wash. Bar Assn., Spokane County Bar Assn. (trustee 1976-78), Internat. Footprint Assn. (nat. pres. 1967), Shriners. Episcopalian. Office: US Dist Ct PO Box 1432 Spokane WA 99210-1432 Office Phone: 509-353-2180.

**QUACKENBUSH, MARGERY CLOUSER,** psychoanalyst, researcher; b. Reading, Pa., Apr. 30, 1938; d. Carl Brumbach and Katherine Elvina (Althouse) Clouser; m. Robert Mead Quackenbush, July 3, 1971; 1 child, Piet Robert. BFA, Pratt Inst., 1960; MA, Calif. Grad. Inst., 1982; PhD in Psychoanalysis, Internat. U. Grad. Studies, N.Y.C., 2001. Cert. in psychoanalysis Ctr. for Modern Psychoanalytic Studies, 1992. Instr. Pratt Inst., Bklyn., 1978-79, Fashion Inst. of Tech., N.Y.C., 1980-81; counselor Wiltwyck, Bronx Ctr., 1981-82; exec. dir. Nat. Assn. for Advancement of Psychoanalysis, N.Y.C., 1982—; pvt. practice in psychoanalysis N.Y.C. 1980—. Adj. prof. Union Inst. Mem. Lenox Hill Dem. Club, N.Y.C., 1993-95; spkr. various cmty. groups, 1991—. Recipient Maison Blanche award, 1959, Miriam Berkman Spotnitz award, 1992, Am. Bd. Accreditation Profl. Svc. award, 2000-04. Mem. Nat. Assn. for Advancement of Psychoanalysis, Nat. Soc. DAR, Alumni Assn. of the Ctr. for Modern Psych. Studies (sec. 1992-94, Alumni Assn. program dir., v.p. 1995-98), Soc. Modern Psychoanalysts. Democrat. Avocations: reading, writing, golf, horseback riding. Home: 460 E 79th St Apt 14E New York NY 10021-1447 Office: Nat Assn Advancement Psychoanalysis 80 8th Ave # 1501 New York NY 10011-5126 Office Phone: 212-741-0515. Business E-Mail: mq@naap.org.

**QUACKENBUSH, ROBERT MEAD,** artist, writer, psychoanalyst; b. Hollywood, Calif., July 23, 1929; s. Roy Maynard and Virginia (Arbogast) Q.; m. Margery Clouser, July 3, 1971; 1 child: Piet Robert. B of Profl. Arts, Art Ctr. Coll. of Design, Pasadena, Calif., 1956; grad., Ctr. Modern Psychoanalytic Studies, N.Y.C., 1991; MSW, Fordham U., 1994; PhD, Internat. U. Grad. Studies, 1999. Art dir. Scandinavian Airlines Sys., N.Y.C. and Stockholm, 1956-61; pvt. practice N.Y.C., 1961—; psychoanalyst/psychtherapist New Hope Guild Ctr. for Emotionally Disturbed Children, Bklyn., 1994-2000. Educator Robert Quackenbush Studios, N.Y.C.; lectr. U.S., Europe, Middle East and South Am.; TV performer Ednl. TV; mem. faculty N.J. Ctr. for Modern Psychoanalysis. Author/artist: over 180 books including; author: (novels) Robert Quackenbush's Treasury of Humor, 1990, Benjamin Franklin and His Friends, 1991, Evil Under the Sea, 1992, James Madison & Dolly Madison and Their Times, 1993, Arthur Ashe and His Match with History, 1994, Clara Barton and Her Victory Over Fear, 1995, Batbaby, 1997 (Gradiva award, 1998), (under pen name Richard Gobbletree) Treasure Hunt, 1997, Two Miss Mallard Mysteries: Surfboard to Peril and Stage Door to Terror, 1998, Daughter of Liberty, 1999, Flamenco to Mischief: A Miss Mallard Mystery, 2000, Miss Mallard's Case Book, 2000, Batbaby Finds a Home, 2001, Mishap in Kaiserslautern: A Miss Mallard Mystery, 2001, Henry's Awful Mistake, 2005, The Return of Pete Pack Rat, 2005; prodr.: (TV series) Dear Mr. Quackenbush and The Great American Storybook, 1988; Represented in permanent collections Whitney Mus., The Smithsonian Inst., numerous pvt. collections; prodr.: (TV series) The Miss Mallard Mysteries, 1999; (TV series, DVD) Miss Mallard Rides to the Rescue, 2005, Miss Mallard Meets Masters of Mischief, 2005. With U.S. Army, 1951—53. Recipient 2 Citations for outstanding Troop Info. & Edn. instrn. from commdg. gen. 31st Inf. Divsn. 1953. Am. Flag Inst. award, 1976, 77, 81, 99, Edgar Allen Poe Spl. award, 1982, Gradiva award, 1998, Holland Soc. Gold medal for distinction in art and lit., 2000, Nat. Assn. for Advancement of Psychoanalysis Vison award, 2004 Mem. Mystery Writers of Am., Authors' Guild, Authors' League of Am., Holland Soc. of N.Y., Nat. Assn. for Advancement of Psychoanalysis (trustee, v.p. pub. info., founder, chair Gradiva awards), Soc. Modern Psychoanalysts, Soc. of Illustrators. Avocations: travel, antique restoration. Home: 460 E 79th St Apt 14E New York NY 10021-1447 Office: Robert Quackenbush Studios 223 E 78th St New York NY 10021-1222 Office Phone: 212-744-3822. Personal E-mail: rqstudios@aol.com. *Humor became a way to survival in my family when I was growing up during the depression and World War II. Thus humor became the keynote of all the books I write and illustrate - I want young readers to know that as long as we keep our sense of humor, our spirits cannot be crushed. In my analytic practice I encourage children to verbalize their emotional conflicts through art and writing projects.*

**QUACKENBUSH, ROGER E.,** retired secondary school educator; b. Cooperstown, N.Y., Jan. 22, 1940; s. Eugene W. and Marion I. (Clark) Q.; m. Cathy E. Quackenbush, Mar. 31, 1973; children: Michele, Stacey, Thomas. BS, SUNY, Albany, 1961, MS, 1966; PhD, Columbia Pacific U., San Rafael, Calif., 1984; postgrad., numerous univs. Cert. permanent biology and gen. sci. tchr., N.Y. Tchr. gen. sci. and math Troy (N.Y.) Pub. Sch. System, 1961-64; tchr. earth sci. and biology Schuylerville (N.Y.) Cen. H.S., 1964-66; tchr. biology Bethlehem Cen. H.S., Delmar, N.Y, 1966-95; cons. advanced placement biology Niskayuna (N.Y.) H.S., 1995-96; instr. anatomy and physiology lab. Russell Sage Coll., Troy, NY, 1996-97. Mentor student tchrs., 1968-90; instr. Tchr. Expectation Student Achievement program, 1985-91; lectr. on marine mammals SUNY, Albany, 1986; instr. DNA Sci. and Tech. for h.s. students SUNY, Albany, 1996; lectr. on whales; workshop leader on use microcomputers in classroom; former mem. Mid States Commn. on Evaluation Local H.S.'s; past mem. adv. bd. Upstate N.Y. Jr. Sci. and Humanities Symposium; test writer Regents biology exams. N.Y. State Dept. Edn.; presenter/cons. N.Y. State Edn. Dept. alt. assessment writer's workshop, 1994; leader, naturalist for whale watch trips and Kenya safaris; presenter for DNA-molecular biology lab. techniques; presenter on use of Tex. Instruments calculator and the Calculator-Based Lab. sys. in the sci. classroom; mem Select Seminar on Evaluating Tchrs., 1985; mem. Wells Conf. Regents Biology Syllabus Revision, 1991; faculty cons. AP Biology reading Coll. Bd. Advanced Placement Program, 1997-98; cons. DNA molecular biology technology Greater Capital Region Tchr. Ctr., 1988-2001; instnl. animal care and use com. N.Y. State Health Dept., 1999-2001. Author: Once Upon a Yesterday, 2000, Adrift Upon the Air, 2001, Sketches of the Mind, 2002; editor/writer of alternative assessments for N.Y. State Edn. Dept., 1993-94; contbr. articles to profl. jours.; author: Swahili Phrasebook, 1993. Hon. admisssions liaison officer USAF Acad., 1988. Named Hon. Grad. Marshal, 1991, 1994, hon. NY State Biology Mentor, 1995, Fla. Master Naturalist, 2006; recipient Eagle award, Boy Scouts Am., 1956, Excellence in Tchg. award, 1989, letter of commendation, U. Chgo., 1978, MIT, 1985, US Army, 1989, Tufts U., 1990, 1994, 1997, Tchr. of Yr. award, 1985, Golub Tchr.-Scholar award, SUNY, 1991, 1996, hon. mention, Tandy Tech. Scholar award, 1994, Tandy Tech. Scholar prize for excellence in sci. tchg., 1995, Outstanding Tchr. award, U. Chgo., 1995; grantee NSF, 1965, 1967, 1968, 1972, 1987, 1990, Future Directions, 1990, Greenwall Found., 1993; Chpt. II grantee, NY State Dept. Edn., 1987. Mem.: SAR, BALSA, NEA, NEA of NY, Sci. Tchrs. Assn. NY State (past sec. dir., past state bd. dirs.), Cetacean Soc. Internat., Am. Cetacean Soc., Soc. Marine Mammalogy, Nat. Assn. Biology Tchrs., Sons of Union Vets. of the Civil War, Phi Delta Kappa. Home: 2930 Banyan Hill Ln Land O Lakes FL 34639-6785 E-mail: rogquacken@yahoo.com.

**QUADAY-GRAY, AILENE DIANN,** retired speech pathology/audiology services professional; b. Blue Earth, Minn., Aug. 26, 1937; d. Carl Frederick Quaday and Arlene Alice Pringle; m. Maurice Clayton Maine, Aug. 18, 1956 (div. May 1975); children: Keith Maurice, Kevin Richard; m. Francis Moulton Gray Jr., May 7, 1989 (dec. Dec. 1994) BA, St. Cloud State U., Minn., 1971; postgrad., San Diego State U., 1979—81, various colls., 1971—85, West Hills and Fresno Pacific, 1987—94. Lic. speech pathologist Calif., cert. presch. tchr. Calif. Speech pathologist Comprehensive Health Ctrs., Inc., San Diego, 1981—82; speech pathologist pilot project Kings Rehab. Ctr., Inc., Hanford, Calif., 1983; tchr., dir. First Luth Ch. Presch., Hanford, 1983—85; speech specialist Fresno County Office Edn., Calif., 1985—87, Kings County Office of Edn., Hanford, 1987—91, Reef-Sunset Unified Sch. Dist., Avenal, Kettleman City, Calif., 1991—94, Kingsburg Joint Union Charter Elem. Schs., Calif., 1994—2001; part-time presch. speech therapist Sanger Unified Sch. Dist., Calif., 2001—02. Cons. Headstart: Tech. Assistance Mgmt., 1971-72; speech therapist Selma (Calif.) Unified Sch. Dist., 2001-04 Vice chmn. bd. edn. St. James Luth., San Diego, 1979-80; del. Consortium on County Health Needs, Wright County, Minn., 1972-75; advisor Wright County Minn. Commrs. on Handicapped, 1973-75; vol. children's waiting rm. Navy Hosp., Bremerton, Wash., 1976-77 Democrat. Methodist. Avocations: playing flute, teaching language, reading, poetry. Home: 2408-25th St # 47 Spirit Lake IA 51360

**QUADE, ROBERT THOMAS,** finance educator; b. Elizabeth, N.J., Feb. 12, 1929; s. Joseph M. and Myra (Tetter) Q.; m. Rita Elizabeth Kaiser; children: James Ross, Christopher Sean, C. Corey Ian. BA, U. Ozarks, Clarksville, Ark., 1950; MBA, State U. Iowa, Ames, 1953; AS (hon.), Churchmans Coll., Easton, Pa., 2002. Instr. U. Ark., Fayetteville, 1953-54; mktg. rsch. mgr. Am Type Founders, Elizabeth, N.J., 1954-55, Sinclair & Valentine, N.Y.C., 1955-56, Ethicon, Inc., Somerville, N.J., 1956-64, new products mgr., 1966-70; sales mgr. Arbrook, Inc., Somerville, 1964-66; dir. product devel./evaluation N.Y.C. Health and Hosp. Corp., 1970-87; chair undergrad. bus. Centenary Coll., Hackettstown, NJ, 1987—2002, exec. in residence coord., 1988—; dir. life learning, 1997—; Adj. instr. Rutgers U., New Brunswick, N.J., Fairleigh Dickinson U., Madison, N.J., 1955-80; coord. Asian Mgmt. Tng. Inst., Hackettstown, 1992; cons. Exxon, C.R. Bard, Quest Internat., French Govt., Port Authority of N.Y./N.J. Patentee (2) in field of medicine. Pres., mem. Bd. of Edn., Bernardsville, N.J., 1963-70; conferee Gov.'s Conf. on Edn., Trenton, N.J., 1968; survey cons. ARC, Girl Scouts U.S., NOW, Mayor of Hackettstown and of Morristown, 1975—, Andover Regional Sch. Dist., 1999, Warren County C. of C., 2000, Karen Ann Quinlan Hospice; mem. acad. advising coun. Thomas Edison State Coll., Trenton, 1993—; apptd. nat. adv. bd. Fordham U., N.Y.C. Recipient Minority Rights Commendation, Mayor Koch of N.Y.C., 1985. Mem. N.J. Collegiate Bus. Adminstrs. Assn. (v.p., pres. 1992-94), Middle-Atlantic Assn. Colls. of Bus. Adminstrn., Alpha Sigma Lambda (advisor 1992-97, sec., v.p. mid-Atlantic region Internat. Assembly of Collegiate Bus. Edn. 2002—), Rotary (sec. Hackettstown chpt.). Avocations: stamp collecting/philately, coaching college wrestling. Home: 37 Oak Pl Bernardsville NJ 07924-1806 Office: Centenary College 400 Jefferson St Hackettstown NJ 07840-2100 E-mail: profq1@aol.com, quader@centenarycollege.edu.

**QUADE, VICKI,** editor, writer, playwright, theater producer; b. Chgo., Aug. 15, 1953; d. Victor and Virginia (Uryasz) Q.; m. Charles J. White III, Feb. 15, 1986 (div. Aug. 1996); children: Michael, David, Catherine. BS in Journalism, No. Ill. U., 1974. Staff reporter news divsn. The News-Tribune, LaSalle, Ill., 1975-77; staff writer news divsn. The News-Sun, Waukegan, Ill., 1977-81; staff writer ABA Jour., Chgo., 1981-85; mng. editor ABA Press, Chgo., 1985-90, editor, 1990-2000, sr. editor, 1994-2000. Author: (poetry) Rain and Other Poems, 1976, Laughing Eyes, 1979, Two Under the Covers, 1981, (biography) I Remember Bob Collins, 2000; playwright Late Nite Catechism, 1993, Room for Advancement, 1994, Mr. Nanny, 1997, (musical) Lost in Wonderland, 1998, (musical) Here Come the Famous Brothers, 2001, Put the Nuns in Charge!, 2005; prodr. Late Nite Catechism, Mr. Nanny, Here Come the Famous Brothers, Christopher Carter Messes With Your Mind, Forever Plaid, Cast on a Hot Tin Roof, Verbatim Verboten, Put the Nuns in Charge; U.S. premiere of Drapes, 2005; contbr. to numerous anthologies and publs.; contbd. to: 20th Century Chicago: 100 Years, 100 Voices (contbd. the year 1953), owner/operator Crossroads Theater, Naperville, Ill Recipient numerous awards from Soc. Nat. Assn. Publs., AP, UPI, Spirit of Benedict award Benedictine Sisters Chgo., 2003, Partners in Mission award Sisters of the Living Word, 2005 Mem. Am. Soc. Bus. Press Editors (award), Chgo. Newspaper Guild (award), Am. Soc. Assn. Execs. (Gold Circle award 1989, 90). Avocations: travel, photography.

**QUADROS, PAUL D.,** health products executive; BA in Fin., Calif. State U., Fullerton; MBA, UCLA. Securities analyst, instnl. portfolio mgr.; asst. treas.The Times Mirror Co.; sr. v.p. Pub. Storage, Inc., 1981—84; exec. v.p. Amreal Securities Corp., 1984—85; officer Tech. Funding, 1985—86, gen. ptnr., 1986—95, dir. rsch. and dir. equity investments, chmn. med. investment com., 1990—94; chmn. bd., CFO and sec. GenStar Therapeutics Corp., San Diego, 1995—97, pres., CEO, 1997—98, chmn. bd., CFO, 1998—. Office: Genstar 780 Montague Expy Ste 601 San Jose CA 95131-1320

**QUAID, DENNIS,** actor; b. Houston, Apr. 9, 1954; s. William Rudy and Juanita B.; m. P.J. Soles, Nov. 25, 1978 (div. Jan. 23, 1983); m. Meg Ryan, Feb. 14, 1991 (div. July 16, 2001); 1 child, Jack Henry; m. Kimberly Buffington, July 4, 2004. Student, U. Houston, 1972-75. Actor (films) Crazy Mama, 1975, I Never Promised You A Rosegarden, 1977, Sept. 30, 1955, 1977, Our Winning Season, 1978, The Seniors, 1978, Breaking Away, 1979, G.O.R.P., 1980, The Long Riders, 1980, Caveman, 1981, All Night Long, 1981, The Night the Lights Went Out in Georgia, 1981, Tough Enough, 1983, Jaws 3-D, 1983, The Right Stuff, 1983, Dreamscape, 1984, Enemy Mine, 1985, Innerspace, 1987, The Big Easy, 1987, Suspect, 1987, D.O.A., 1988, Everybody's All-American, 1988, Great Balls of Fire, 1989, Postcards from the Edge, 1990, Come See the Paradise, 1990, Undercover Blues, 1993, Wilder Napalm, 1993, Flesh and Bone, 1993, Wyatt Earp, 1994, Something to Talk About, 1995, Dragonheart, 1996, Criminal Element, 1997, Going West, 1997, Gang Related, 1997, Savior, 1997, Switchback, 1997, The Parent Trap, 1998, On Any Given Sunday, 1999, Frequency, 2000, Traffic, 2000, The Rookie, 2002, Far From Heaven, 2002, Cold Creek Manor, 2003, The Alamo, 2004, The Day After Tomorrow, 2004, Flight of the Phoenix, 2004, In Good Company, 2004, Yours, Mine and Ours, 2005, Am. Dreamz, 2006; (theatre) The Last of the Knucklemen, 1983, True West, 1984; (TV movies) Are You In the House Alone?, 1978, Amateur Night at the Dixie Bar and Grill, 1979, Bill, 1981, Johnny Belinda, 1982, Bill: On His Own, 1983, Everything That Rises (also dir. prod.), 1998, Dinner with Friends, 2001; (TV appearances) Baretta, 1977. Named Hollywood Walk of Fame, 2005. Office: The William Morris Agy One William Morris Pl Beverly Hills CA 90212 *An artist must take chances in performing his craft. If he is to succeed he must be willing to fall flat on his face.*

**QUAID, RANDY,** actor; b. Houston, Oct. 1, 1950; s. William R. and Juanita B. Quaid; m. Ella Marie Jolly, May 11, 1980 (div. 1985); 1 child; Evi Quaid, Oct. 5, 1989. Student, Houston Baptist Coll., 1969-70; U. Houston, 1970-71. Film appearances include Targets, 1968, The Last Picture Show, 1971, What's Up Doc, 1972, Lolly Madonna XXX, 1972, The Last Detail, 1973 (Acad. award, Golden Globe nominations for best supporting actor), Paper Moon, 1973, Apprenticeship of Duddy Kravitz, 1974, Breakout, 1974, Missouri Breaks, 1975, Bound for Glory, 1976, The Choirboys, 1977, Three Warriors, 1978, Midnight Express, 1979, Foxes, 1980, Long Riders, 1980, Heart Beeps, 1981, National Lampoon's Vacation, 1983, The Wild Life, 1984, The Slugger's Wife, 1985, Fool for Love, 1986, The Wraith, 1986, Caddyshack II, 1988, Moving, 1988, Parents, 1989, Out Cold, 1989, Blood Hounds of Broadway, 1989, National Lampoon's Christmas Vacation, 1989, Quick Change, 1990, Martians Go Home, 1990, Days of Thunder, 1990, Quick Change, 1990, Texasville, 1990, Freaked, 1993, The Paper, 1994, Bye Bye, Love, 1995, Woman Undone, 1995, Legends of the North, 1995, Last Dance, 1996, Kingpin, 1996, Independence Day, 1996, Vegas Vacation, 1997, P.U.N.K.S., 1998, Bug Buster, 1998, Hard Rain, 1998, The Debtors, 1999, The Adventures of Rocky & Bullwinkle, 2000, Home on the Range (voice), 2004, Brokeback Mountain, 2005, The Ice Harvest, 2005; appeared in TV films Getting Away From It All, 1972, The Great Niagara, 1974, The Last Ride of the Dalton Gang, 1979, To Race the Wind, 1980, Guayana Tragedy: The Story of Jim Jones, 1980, Of Mice and Men, 1981, Inside the Third Reich, 1982, Cowboy, 1983, A Street Car Named Desire, 1984, LBJ: The Early Years, 1986, Dead Solid Perfect, 1988, Evil in Clear River, 1988, Murder in the Heartland, 1993, Frankenstein, 1993, Next Door, 1994, Ruby Ridge: An American Tragedy, 1996, Moonshine Highway, 1996, Roommates, 1994, Ed McBain's 87th Precinct: Lightning, 1995, Streets of Laredo, 1995, Gun, 1997, Purgatory West of the Pecos, 1998, Mail to the Chief, 2000, The Thin Blue Line, 2000, The Day the World Ended, 2001, Christmas Vacation 2: Cousin Eddie's Island Adventure, 2003, Five Days to Midnight, 2004, Category 6: Day of Destruction, 2004, Elvis, 2005, Category 7: The End of the World, 2005; TV series Saturday Night Live, 1985-87, Davis Rules, 1991-92, The Magical Legend of the Leprechauns, 1999; off-Broadway play True West, 1983 Mem. Acad. Motion Picture Arts and Scis.*

**QUAINI, DUANE C.,** lawyer; b. Napa, Calif., Mar. 30, 1945; BA summa cum laude, Claremont Men's Coll., 1967; JD, Stanford U., 1970. Bar: Ill. 1970. Assoc. Sonnenschein Nath & Rosenthal LLP, Chgo., 1970—76, ptnr., 1976—, chmn., 1997—. Note editor Stanford Law Rev., 1969-70. Mem. exec. com. bd. visitors Stanford Law Sch., 1995—, chmn.; vice chmn. bd. Jane Addams Juvenile Ct. Found.; dir. emeritus Les Turner ALS Found. Office: Sonnenschein Nath & Rosenthal LLP 8000 Sears Tower 233 S Wacker Dr Chicago IL 60606 Office Phone: 312-876-8051. Office Fax: 312-876-7934. Business E-Mail: dquaini@sonnenschein.com.

**QUAINTON, ANTHONY CECIL EDEN,** diplomat; b. Seattle, Apr. 4, 1934; s. Cecil Eden and Marjorie Josephine (Oates) Q.; m. Susan Long, Aug. 7, 1958; children: Katherine, Eden, Elizabeth. BA, Princeton U., 1955; BLitt, Oxford U., Eng., 1958. Rsch. fellow St. Antony's Coll., Oxford, 1958-59; with Fgn. Svc., State Dept., 1959-97; vice consul Sydney, Australia, 1960-62; Urdu lang. trainee, 1962-63; 2d sec., econ. officer Am. embassy, Karachi, Pakistan, 1963-64, Rawalpindi, Pakistan, 1964-66, 2d sec., polit. officer New Delhi, 1966-69; sr. polit. officer for India Dept. State, Washington, 1969-72; 1st sec. Am. embassy, Paris, 1972-73, counselor, dep. chief mission Kathmandu, Nepal, 1973-76; amb. to Ctrl. African Empire, Bangui, 1976-78, Managua, Nicaragua, 1982—84, Kuwait, 1984—87; dir. Office for Combating Terrorism, Dept. State, Washington, 1978-81; dep. insp. gen. Dept. State, 1987-89; amb. Lima, Peru, 1989-92; asst. sec. of state for diplomatic security Dept. State, Washington, 1992-95, dir. gen. fgn. svc., 1995-97. Exec. dir. Una Chapman Cox Found., 1998—99; vis. lectr. Princeton U., 1998—99; pres., CEO Nat. Policy Assn., 1999—2003; diplomat in residence Am. U., 2003—; cons. internat. policy com. U.S. Conf. Cath. Bishops, 1999—2005; chmn. bd. dirs. Washington Theol. Consortium bd. dirs. Int. Faith Conf. of Washington, project dir. Am. Acad. Diplomacy, 2004—05. V.p., treas. Washington Lions Found.; v.p. Pub. Diplomacy Coun. English Speaking Union fellow, 1951-52; Marshall scholar, 1955-58; recipient Rivkin award, 1972, Herter award, 1984, Disting. Honor award Dept. State, 1997. Fellow Fgn. Policy Assn.; mem. Coun. on Fgn. Rels., Am. Fgn. Svc. Assn., Washington Inst. Fgn. Affairs, Lions Internat., Met. Club, Phi Beta Kappa. Home: 3424 Porter St NW Washington DC 20016-3126 Office Phone: 303-885-1669. Personal E-mail: aquainton@aol.com.

**QUAKE, STEPHEN R.,** physics professor, researcher; BS in physics, Stanford U., 1991, MS in math., 1991; PhD in physics, U. Oxford, 1994. Asst. prof. applied physics Calif. Inst. Tech., 1996—99, assoc. prof. applied physics, 1999—2002; assoc. prof. applied physics and physics, 2002—03; prof. applied physics and physics, 2003—04; Thomas E. and Doris Everhard prof. applied physics and physics, 2004—; prof. bioengineering Stanford U. Mem. Quake Group, Calif. Inst. Tech., Pasadena, CSULA-Calif. Inst. Tech. Partnerships for Rsch. and Edn. in Materials (PREM) Collaborative, 2004—; co-founder Fluidigm Corp. Contbr. articles to profl. jour. Named to TR100 "Young Innovators that will create the Future", MIT Tech. Review Mag., 2002; recipient R29 "First" award, NIH, 1997, Pioneer award, 2004, Career award, 1997; Packard fellow, 1994. Achievements include research in fundamental and applied topics in biophysics, specifically single molecule science. Office: Calif Inst Tech 154 Watson MC 128-95 Pasadena CA 91125 Office Phone: 626-395-3362. E-mail: quake@caltech.edu.

**QUALE, JOHN CARTER,** lawyer; b. Boston, Aug. 16, 1946; s. Andrew C. and Luella (Meland) Q.; m. Diane Zipursky, Jan. 19, 1992; children: Virginia Ann, Jane Harris, John Andrew; stepchildren: Rachel Goldman, Alisa Goldman. AB cum laude, Harvard U., 1968, JD cum laude, 1971. Bar: Mass. 1971, D.C. 1972. Assoc. Kirkland & Ellis, Washington, 1971-78, ptnr., 1978-83, Wiley, Rein & Fielding, Washington, 1983-96, Skadden, Arps, Slate, Meagher & Flom L.L.P., Washington, 1996—. Spkr. mass media trade groups. Contbr. articles to profl. jours. Trustee Fed. Comm. Bar Assn. Found., 1992-93. Mem. ABA, Fed. Comm. Bar Assn. (treas. 1982-83, 98-99, mem. exec. com. 1993-98), Barristers, Met. Club. College: Skadden Arps Slate Meagher & Flom LLP 1440 New York Ave NW Washington DC 20005-2111 Office Phone: 202-371-7200. Business E-Mail: jquale@skadden.com.

**QUALLEY, CHARLES ALBERT,** art educator; b. Creston, Iowa, Mar. 19, 1930; s. Albert Olaf and Cleora (Dietrick) Q.; m. Betty Jean Griffith, Nov. 26, 1954; children: Janet Lynn, John Stuart. BFA, Drake U., 1952; MA, U. Iowa, 1956, MFA, 1958; EdD, Ill. State U., 1967. Art tchr. Des Moines Pub. Schs., 1952, 1954—55; critic art tchr. U. Iowa, 1955-57; prof. fine arts U. Colo., Boulder, 1958-90, prof. emeritus, 1990—, chmn. dept. fine arts, 1968-71, assoc. chmn., 1981-82. Vis. prof. Inst. for Shipboard Edn., semester at sea, 1979, vis. disting. prof. Ill. State U., 1985. Author: Safety in the Art Room, 1986; contbg. editor Sch. Arts, 1978-85, mem. editl. adv. bd., 1985-87; author column Safetypoint, 1981-85. Served with AUS, 1952-54, Korea. Fellow Nat. Art Edn. Assn. (v.p. 1980-82, pres. 1987-89, dir. conv. svcs. 1990-99, Art Educator of Yr. 1993); mem. Nat. Art Edn. Found. (trustee 1987—, chair bd. trustees 1996-2004), Colo. Art Edn. Assn. (editor 1965-67, 75, pres. 1976-78), Delta Phi Delta, Omicron Delta Kappa, Pi Kappa Delta. Home: 9025 Natalie Ave NE Albuquerque NM 87111-3131

**QUALLS, ROBERT L.,** manufacturing executive, bank executive, educator, retired state official; b. Burnsville, Miss., Nov. 6, 1933; s. Wes E. and Letha (Parker) Q.; m. Carolyn Morgan, Feb. 10, 1979 (dec. July 1996); 1 child, Stephanie Elizabeth; m. Nancy Martin, Sept. 11, 1999. BS, Miss. State U., 1954, MS, 1958; PhD, La. State U., 1962; LLD, Whitworth Coll., 1974; DBA (hon.), U. of the Ozarks, 1984. Prof., chmn. div. econs. and bus. Belhaven Coll., Jackson, Miss., 1962-66, asst. to pres., 1965-66; asst. prof. finance Miss. State U., State College, 1967-69, adj. prof., 1969-73; sr. v.p., chmn. venture com. Bancorp South, Tupelo, Miss., 1969-73; v.p. Wesleyan Coll., Macon, Ga., 1974; pres. U. of the Ozarks, Clarksville, Ark., 1974-79; mem. cabinet Bill Clinton Gov. of Ark., 1979-80; exec. v.p. Bank of America, Little Rock, 1980-85, chmn., CEO, dir. Harrison, Ark., 1985-86; pres., dir. First Bank Fin. Services, Inc., 1980-85, Advt. Assocs., Inc., 1980-85; pres., chief oper. officer Baldor Electric Co., Ft. Smith, Ark., 1986-91, CEO, 1992-97, vice chmn., 1998—2000, dir., mem. exec. com., 1987—, chmn. corp. governance com., presiding non-mgmt. dir., 2004—. Mktg. coms. Ill. Central Industries, Chgo., 1964; mem. faculty, thesis examiner Stonier Grad. Sch. Banking, Rutgers U., 1973-86; mem. faculty Miss. Sch. Banking, U. Miss., 1973-78; course coord. Sch. Banking of the South, La. State U., 1978-88, Banking Sch., Duke U., 1977; lectr. Southwestern Sch. Banking, So. Meth. U., 1983; adj. prof. bus. adminstrn. U. Central Ark., 1985-86; bd. dirs., mem. audit com., chmn. corp. governance com. Bank of Ozarks, presiding ind. dir., 2003—. Author: Entrepreneurial Wit and Wisdom, 1986; co-author: Strategic Planning for Colleges and Universities: A Systems Approach to Planning and Resource Allocation, 1979; mem. editorial adv. bd.: Bank Mktg. Mag., 1984-86. Chmn. cmty. svc. and continuing edn. com. Tupelo Cmty. Devel. Found., 1972-73; mem. Miss. 4-H adv. coun., 1969; active Boys Scouts Am.; mem. Lee County Dem. Exec. Com., 1973-74; trustee Walton Family Found., 1975-79, Oklahoma City U., 1990-95; trustee, mem. exec. com. U. Ozarks, 1982-88, chmn. bd., 2000-03; mem. Pres.'s Roundtable U. Ctrl. Ark., 1982-87; mem. exec. com. Coll. Bus. Adv. Bd., U. Ark., Little Rock, 1980-85; bd. dirs. U. Ark. Med. Sch. Found., 1991-97, Ark. Inst., 1991-94; chmn. bd. Petit Jean Youth Found., 2001-03; mem. Clarksville Light and Water Commn., 2000-01; elder Clarksville Presbyn. Ch., 1997-2000; bd. dirs. Vera Lloyd Presbyn. Home and Family Svcs., 2004-05. Lt. AUS, 1954-56. Found. for Econ. Edn. fellow, 1964; Ford Found. faculty research fellow Vanderbilt U., 1963-64; recipient Pillar of Progress award Johnson County, 1977 Mem. Am. Bankers Assn. (mktg. planning and rsch. com. 1972-73, Ark. Coun. Ind. Colls. and Univs. (chmn. 1978-79), Johnson County C. of C. (pres. 1977), Fort Smith C. of C. (dir. 1995-98), Blue Key, Omicron Delta Kappa, Delta Sigma Pi, Sigma Phi Epsilon (citation 1977), Beta Gamma Sigma, Masons (32 deg.), Clarksville Rotary (pres. 1979). Presbyterian. Office Phone: 501-661-9095. Personal E-mail: nancy_qualls@msn.com.

**QUALLS, ROXANNE,** mayor; D (hon.), Cin. State Tech. and C.C., 1996. Former exec. dir. Women Helping Women; former dir. No. Ky. Rape Crisis Ctr.; former dir. Cin. office Ohio Citizen Action; councilwoman City of Cin., 1991-93, mayor, 1993-98, founder youth summer jobs program Artworks, Cin. Homeownership Partnership. Former chairperson Cin. City Council's Intergovtl. Affairs and Environment Com.; former vice chairperson Community Devel., Housing and Zoning Com.; mem. Gov.'s Commn. on Storage and Use of Toxic and Hazardous Materials, Solid Waste Adv. Com. of State of Ohio, Gov.'s Waste Minimization Task Force; former chair bd. commrs. Cin. Met. Housing Authority; bd. dirs. Shuttlesworth Housing Found. Hon. chair Friends of Women's Studies; mem. Jr. League Adv. Coun.; bd. dirs. Nat. Underground Railroad Freedom Ctr., Ctr. Voting and Democracy; past bd. didrs. No. Ky. Cult. Commn. Soc. Justice. Recipient Woman of Distinction award Girl Scouts U.S., 1992, Woman of Distinction award Soroptomists, 1993, Outstanding Achievement award Cin. Woman's Polit. Caucus, 1993, Women of Achievement award YWCA, 1994, Outstanding Svc. award Ohio Pub. Employees Lawyers Assn., 1996, Pub. Offcl. of Yr. award State of Cinn., 1996, Nat. Assn. Soc. Workers, 1996, Nat. Homebuilders Assn., 1997. Mem. Nat. Assn. Regional Couns. (former pres. 1st v.p., 2d v.p.), Ohio Ky. Ind. Regional Coun. Govts. (1st v.p., 2d v.p.). Home: 810 Matson Pl Ph 2 Cincinnati OH 45204-1482 Fax: 513-352-5201.

**QUALSET, CALVIN O.,** agronomist, educator; b. Newman Grove, Nebr., Apr. 24, 1937; s. Herman Qualset and Adeline (Hanson) Vakoc; m. Kathleen Boehler; children: Douglas, Cheryl, Gary. BS, U. Nebr., 1958; MS, U. Calif., Davis, 1960, PhD, 1964. Asst. prof. U. Tenn., Knoxville, 1964-67; asst. prof. to assoc. prof. U. Calif., Davis, 1967, prof., 1973-94, prof. emeritus, 1994—, chmn. dept. agronomy and range sci., 1975-81, 91-94, assoc. dean Coll. Agrl. and Environ. Sci., 1981-86, dir. Genetic Resources Conservation Program, 1985—2002, dir. Agrl. Sustainability Inst., 2005—. Sci. liaison officer U.S. Agy. Internat. Devel., Washington, 1985-93, rsch. adv. com., 1989-92; nat. plant genetic resources bd. USDA, Washington, 1982-88; bd. trustees Am. Type Culture Collection, 1993-99, Internat. Rice Rsch. Inst., 1999-2004, Agronomic Sci. Found., 1999-. Contbr. over 300 articles to profl. jours. and tech. publs. Bd. dirs. Auksuciai Found., 1999—; contbr. to wheat improvement in Mex. citation, 1988. Fulbright fellow, Australia, 1976, Yugoslavia, 1984; recipient Pub. Plant Breeding award U.S. Coun. Comml. Plant Breeders, 1996, Master Alumni award U. Nebr., 1997, Charles Black award Coun. Agrl. Sci. and Tech., 2002, William L. Brown award Mo. Bot. Garden, 2002, Citation for Excellence, U. Calif., Calif. Aggie Alumni Assn., 2003, Citation for contbns. to Calif. agr. State Calif. Senate, 2003, award of excellence Coll. Agrl. and Environ. Sci., U. Calif., Davis, 2003, Citation for contbns. to agr. in Lithuania, 2004. Fellow AAAS (chmn. agr. sect. 1992), Am. Soc. Agronomy (pres. 1994, agronomy honoree Calif. sect. 2001), Crop Sci. Soc. Am. (pres. 1989, editor-in-chief 1980-84); mem. Soc. Conservation Biology, Soc. Econ. Botany, Genetic Soc. Am., Internat. Union Biol. Scis. (mem. U.S. nat. com. 2000—), Am. Genetic Assn., U. Nebr. Alumni Assn. Achievements include development of more than 15 cultivars of wheat, oat, triticale. Office: U Calif Genetic Res Conserv Prog One Shields Ave Davis CA 95616

**QUAM, LOIS,** healthcare company executive; m. Matt Entenza; children: Ben, Steve. BA magna cum laude, Macalaster Coll., Minn.; MA in Philos., Politics, Econs., U. Oxford, 1985. Dir. rsch. and eval. United HealthCare, 1989-93, v.p. pub. sector svcs., 1993; sr. adv. White House Task Force Nat. Health Care Reform, 1993-96; CEO AARP/United divsn. United HealthCare, 1996-98; CEO Ovations (formerly Retiree and Sr. Svcs. Co. United Health-Care), Minnetonka, Minn., 1998—. Bd. dirs. George C. Marshall Found., Coun. Fgn. Rels.; adv. com. Am. Democracy Inst. Mem. editl. bd.: British Med. Jour.; contbr. articles to profl. jours. Bd. trustees Macalester Coll. Recipient America-Norway Heritage Fund award, Nordmann-Forbundett Norway-Am. Assn. Office: Ovations UnitedHealth Grp 500 Opus Ctr 9900 Bren Rd E Minnetonka MN 55343-9664*

**QUAM, RYAN,** application developer; s. Gary Quam and Dianne Trankel-Schwien. BS in Computer Sci., S.D. State U., Brookings, 1997. Sr. software engr. CyberSource Corp., Sioux Falls, SD, 1998—. Author: The Unabashed

Wordgame Dictionary for Cheaters. Mem.: Aircraft Owners and Pilots Assn., Mensa. Achievements include patents pending for stored value processing system. Avocations: aviation, tennis. Home: 4404 S Birchwood Ave Sioux Falls SD 57103

**QUAM, TERI,** school psychologist; d. David and Donna Sleeth; m. Steve Quam, Apr. 25, 1981; children: Stefani, Staci. BA in Elem. Edn. and Edn. Hearing Impaired, Bowling Green State U., Ohio, 1979; M in Ednl. Psychology, cert. in Sch. Psychology, U. Wis., Milw., 1991. Elem. tchr., tchr. hearing impaired Madison Pub. Schs., Wis., 1979—86; early childhood hearing impaired tchr. Waukesha (Wis.) Pub. Schs., 1986—89, sch. psycholo-gist, mentor, 2006—; sch. psychologist Milw. Pub. Schs.-Congress Elem. Schs., 1991—. Practicum psychologist supr. Milw. Pub. Schs.-Congress Elem. Schs., 1994—2002, new psychologist, mentor, 2001—; student tchr. supr. Madison Pub. Schs., 1982—85. Sec. Catch A Rising Star Found., Milw., 2004—06, treas., 2004—06; profl. devel. plan reviewer Dept. Pub. Instrn., Wis., 2006. Mem.: NASP, Wis. Sch. Psychologist Assn. Avocations: travel, reading, tai chi. Business E-mail: quamta@milwaukee.k12.wi.us.

**QUAN, STUART FUN,** internist, educator; b. San Francisco, May 16, 1949; s. Stuart Fun and Mabel (Wing) Q.; m. Diana Lee, Dec. 18, 1971; children: Jason Stuart, Jeremy Ryan-Stuart. AB, U. Calif., Berkeley, 1970; MD, U. Calif., San Francisco, 1974. Diplomate Am. Bd. Internal Medicine, Am. Bd. Pulmonary Diseases, Am. Bd. Critical Care Medicine, Am. Bd. Sleep Medicine. Intern in internal medicine U. Wis., Madison, 1974-75, resident, 1975-77; fellow in critical care and emergency medicine U. Calif., San Francisco, 1977-79; fellow in pulmonary medicine U. Ariz., Tucson, 1979-80, from instr. to asst. prof. medicine, 1980-86, assoc. prof. medicine, 1986-1992, prof. medicine & anesthesiology, 1992—, med. dir. respiratory care, 1980—; med. dir. ICU Univ. Med. Ctr., Tucson, 1980-87, med. dir. Kindred Hosp., Tucson, 1994—; dir. Sleep Disorders Ctr. U. Ariz., Tucson, 1984—, chief pulmonary and crit. care medicine sect., 1987—, assoc. head dept. medicine, 1995—2006, prof. pub. health, 2002—. Chmn. and cons. adv. panel on anesthesia and respiratory devices FDA, 1987-89; mem. Am. Bd. Sleep Medicine, 1991-96; mem. adv. bd. Nat. Ctr. Sleep Disorder Rsch., 2002—; mem. rev. com. internal medicine ACGME, 2005—; co-chmn. test writing com. sleep medicine Am. Bd. Internal Medicine. Co-author: Respiratory Diseases--A Pathophysiological Approach, 1984; contbd. chpts. to various books; contbr. numerous articles to med. jours. Pres. Gymnastics Support Orgn., Tucson, 1985-87. Fellow Am. Coll. Chest Physicians, Am. Acad. Sleep Medicine (chmn. accreditation com. 1995-96, pres. 1999-2000, bd. dirs. 1996-2005); mem. Am. Thoracic Soc., Am. Fedn. Clin. Rsch., Nat. Assn. Med. Dirs. Respiratory Care, Soc. for Critical Care Medicine, Phi Beta Kappa, Alpha Omega Alpha. Avocations: skiing, hiking, swimming. Office: U Ariz Div Respiratory Scis 1501 N Campbell Ave Tucson AZ 85724-0001 E-mail: squan@arc.arizona.edu.

**QUANDT, JOSEPH EDWARD,** lawyer, educator; b. Port Huron, Mich., May 21, 1963; s. Herbert Raymond and Mary Katherine (West) Q.; m. Christine Ann Reilly, Aug. 21, 1993. BA, Oakland U., 1990; JD, Thomas M. Cooley Law Sch., Lansing, Mich., 1993. Bar: Mich. 1994, U.S. Dist. Ct. (ea. and we. dists.) Mich. 1994. Exec. dir. Lord & Taylor, Sterling Heights, Mich., 1985-90; compliance and enforcement specialist Mich. Dept. Environ. Quality, Lansing, 1990-93, adv. bd., 1997—; assoc. Stowe, Draling & Boyd, Traverse City, Mich., 1993-94, Smith & Johnson, Traverse City, 1994-98; ptnr. Menmuir, Zimmerman, Kuhn, Taylor and Quandt, Traverse City, 1998—. Lectr., commentator Inst. CLE, Ann Arbor, Mich., 1994—; adj. prof. Thomas M. Cooley Law Sch., 1997—; co-chair environ. law sect., mem. Environ. Law Coun. State Bar Mich., chair, natural resources sect. Contbr. articles to profl. jours. Bd. dirs. Involved Citizens Enterprises, Traverse City, 1995—. Mem. Nat. Honor Soc. for Polit. Scientists, Ancient Order Hibernians, Pi Sigma Alpha. Republican. Roman Catholic. Avocations: ice hockey, golf, fly fishing. Office: Zimmerman Kuhn Darling Boyd Taylor and Quandt PLC 412 S Union St Traverse City MI 49684-2404 Office Phone: 231-947-7900. Business E-mail: jequandt@zimmerman-kuhn.com.

**QUANDT, RICHARD EMERIC,** economics professor; b. Budapest, Hungary, June 1, 1930; came to U.S., 1949, naturalized, 1954; s. Richard F. and Elisabeth Q.; m. Jean H. Briggs, Aug. 6, 1955; 1 son, Stephen. BA, Princeton U., 1952; MA, Harvard U., 1955, PhD, 1957; Dr. Econs. (hon.), Budapest U. Econs. Scis., 1991, Kossuth Lajos U., Hungary, 1994, Gödöllő Agrl. U., 1995, Comenius U., Slovakia, 1996; DrLaws (hon.), Queens U., Can., 1996. Mem. faculty Princeton U., 1956-95, prof. econs., 1964-95, prof. emeritus, sr. rsch. economist, 1995—; chmn. dept. Princeton U., 1968-71, 85-88; dir. Fin. Rsch. Ctr., 1982-95; rsch. profl. Ford Found., 1967-68; prof. emeritus, sr. rsch. economist Princeton U., 1990—. Cons. Alderson Assocs., 1959-61; sr. cons. Mathematica, Inc., 1961-67; cons. Internat. Air Transport Assn., 1974-75, N.Y. Stock Exch., 1976-77, N.Y. State Dept. Edn., 1978; adviser Am.-Hungarian Found., 1977-78; editl. advisor Holt, Rinehart & Winston, 1968-72; fin. adviser Inst. for Rsch. in History, 1986; sr. advisor Andrew W. Mellon Found., 1989—; mem. adv. coun. Budapest U. Econ. Scis., 1992-93; vis. prof. Birkbeck Coll., 1981, U. Leicester, 1989-92; mem. Census Adv. Com., 1983-86; mem. adv. com. Coll. Fin. and Acctg., Budapest, 1993-94; bd. dirs. Ctr. for Econ. Rsch. and Grad. Edn.-Econ. Inst. Found., Prague, 2002-05. Author: (with J. M. Henderson) Microeconomic Theory: A Mathematical Approach, 1958, 2d edit., 1971, 3d edit., 1980, (with W.L. Thorp) The New Inflation, 1959, (with B.G. Malkiel) Strategies and Rational Decisions in the Securities Option Market, 1969; editor: The Demand for Travel: Theory and Measurement, 1970; (with S.M. Goldfeld) Nonlinear Methods in Economet-rics, 1972, Studies in Nonlinear Estimation, 1976; (with P. Asch) Racetrack Betting: The Professor's Guide to Strategies, 1986, (with M. Peston) Prices, Competition and Equilibrium, 1986, The Econometrics of Disequilibrium, 1988, (with H.S. Rosen) The Conflict Between Equilibrium and Disequilibrium Theories, 1988, (with R. Ekman) Technology and Scholarly Communication, 1999, The Changing Landscape in Eastern Europe: A Personal Perspective on Philanthropy and Technology Transfer, 2002, (with A. Lass) Union Catalogs at the Crossroad, 2004, (transl.) If Dogs Could Talk (by V. Csányi), 2005; mem. editl. bd. Applied Econs., Econs. Planning, Rev. Econ. and Stats., 1980-91; assoc. editor Econometrica, 1976-80, Jour. Am. Statis. Assn. 1974-80, Bell Jour. Econs., Jour. of Comparative Econs., 1988-91, Empirica, 1988-93; exec. editor Oxford U. Press, 2001—; contbr. articles to profl. jours Trustee Corvina Found., 1992— Recipient merit citation Jagiel-lonian U., Poland, 1991, Gold medal Eötvös Lóránd U., Budapest, 1991, Order of Merit, Govt. of Republic of Hungary, 1997, Medal Merentibus, Jagiellonian U., Poland, 1998, Karel Englis medal, Czech Acad. Sci., 2002; Guggenheim fellow, 1958-59; McCosh fellow, 1964; NSF sr. postdoctoral fellow, 1971-72. Fellow Am. Statis. Assn., Econometric Soc. (mem. coun. 1985-88), Am. Acad. Arts and Scis.; mem. Am. Econ. Assn., Am. Philos. Soc., Hungarian Libr. Assn. (hon.). Home: 162 Springdale Rd Princeton NJ 08540-4948 Office: Princeton U Dept Econs Princeton NJ 08544-1021

**QUANDT, WILLIAM BAUER,** political scientist; b. LA, Nov. 23, 1941; s. William Carl and Dorothy Elaine (Bauer) Q.; m. Anna Spitzer, June 21, 1964 (div. 1980); m. Helena Cobban, Apr. 21, 1984; 1 child, Lorna. BA, Stanford U., 1963; PhD, MIT, 1968. Researcher Rand Corp., Santa Monica, Calif., 1968-72; staff mem. Nat. Security Council, Washington, 1972-74, sr. staff mem., 1977-79; assoc. prof. U. Pa., Phila., 1974-76; sr. fellow Brookings Instn., Washington, 1979-94; prof. govt. and fgn. affairs U. Va., Charlottes-ville, 1994—, and vice provost internat. affairs, 2000-03. Sr. assoc., Cambridge Energy Research Assocs., Mass., 1983-90. Author: Revolution and Political Leadership: Algeria, 1954-68, The Politics of Palestinian Nationalism, 1973, Decade of Decisions, 1977, Saudi Arabia in the 1980's, 1981, Camp David: Peacemaking and Politics, 1986, The United States and Egypt, 1990, Peace Process, 1993, revised edit., 2001, 3rd. edit., 2005, Between Ballots and Bullets, 1998. Social Scis. Research Council fellow, 1966; Council Fgn. Relations fellow, 1972; NDEA fellow, 1963 Fellow: Am.

Acad. Arts & Sci. Mem. Council Fgn. Relations, Middle East Inst., Middle East Studies Assn. (pres. 1987-88). Avocations: tennis, travel, photography. Office: U Va Dept Politics Cabell Hall 255 Charlottesville VA 22901 Business E-Mail: wbq8f@virginia.edu.

**QUANN, MEGAN,** Olympic athlete; b. Tacoma, Wash., Jan. 15, 1984; Recipient Gold medal 100-meter breaststroke, 4 x 100-meter medley (team) Sydney Olympics, 2000, Silver medal 100-meter breaststroke Pan Pacific Championships, 1999; set Am. record for 100-meter breaststroke U.S. Open Swimming Championships, San Antonio, 1999; winner 100-meter breast-stroke title U.S. Swim Nats., 1998, 99, 1st pl. 100m breast stroke, Nat. Championships, 2003. Office: USA Swimming 1 Olympic Plz Colorado Springs CO 80909-5746

**QUANT, HAROLD EDWARD,** retired financial services company execu-tive, rancher; b. Aug. 21, 1948; s. Harold Atwell and Dorothy Ann Quant; m. Michelle Bumpers, June 27, 1982; children: Andrew, Angela, Emily. BSBA, San Jose State U., 1976. Account exec. Dun & Bradstreet, San Jose, Calif., 1970-81; pres. Telecredit Collection Svcs., Inc., L.A., 1981-85; v.p. FCA, Arlington, Tex., 1986-90; pres., CEO Creditwatch, Inc., Arlington, 1990-2000, chmn. bd. dirs.; ret., 2000. Sgt. USMC, 1965—70, Vietnam. Mem.: City Club. Republican. Mem. United Ch. Of God. Avocation: horses.

**QUARANTA, PHILIP,** lawyer; b. 1960; BA, Fordham U., 1981; JD with honors, Pace U., 1985. Bar: NY 1985, US Dist. Ct. No. Dist. NY, US Dist. Ct. So. Dist. NY, US Dist. Ct. Ea. Dist. NY, registered; Japan (Gaikokuho Jimu Bengoshi). Ptnr. Wilson, Elser, Moskowitz, Edelman & Dicker LLP, White Plains, NYC, past mng. ptnr. Tokyo office. Mem.: ABA, Inter-Pacific Bar Assn., Def. Rsch. Inst., Soc. for Advancement Automotive Medicine, Soc. Automotive Engineers, NY State Bar Assn. Office: Wilson Elser Moskowitz Edelman & Dicker LLP 3 Gannett Dr White Plains NY 10604 Office Phone: 914-323-7000 ext. 4238. Office Fax: 914-323-7001. Business E-mail: quarantap@wemed.com.

**QUARLES, CARROLL ADAIR, JR.,** physicist, researcher; b. Abilene, Tex., Nov. 24, 1938; s. Carroll Adair and Marguerite Marie (Vollmers) Q.; m. Sonja Gale Bandy, May 14, 1971; children: Jennifer Anne, John Patrick. BA, Tex. Christian U., 1960; PhD, Princeton U., 1964. Rsch. physicist Brookhaven Nat. Lab., Upton, NY, 1964-67; mem. faculty Tex. Christian U., Ft.Worth, 1967—, asst. prof. physics Ft. Worth, 1970-76, prof. Ft.Worth, 1976—, W.A. Moncrief Jr. prof. physics, 1986—, chmn. dept. physics Ft. Worth, 1978-84, 96-99, assoc. dean Coll. Arts and Scis. Ft.Worth, 1974-78. Contbr. articles to profl. jours. Mem. AAAS, Am. Phys. Soc. (sec.-treas. Tex. sect. 1993-99, chair Tex. sect. 2003, mem. exec. com. Forum on Physics and Soc., 1999-2002), Am. Assn. Physics Tchrs. (pres. Tex. sect. 1984), Sigma Xi, Phi Beta Kappa (pres. Delta of Tex. chpt. 1982-84). Roman Catholic. Office: Tex Christian U Dept Physics Fort Worth TX 76129-0001 Business E-Mail: c.quarles@tcu.edu.

**QUARLES, JAMES LINWOOD, III,** lawyer; b. Huntington, W.Va., Oct. 12, 1946; s. James Linwood Jr. and Beatrice (Hardwick) Q.; m. Sharon Taft, Dec. 20, 1969; children: Jessica, Matthew. BS cum laude, Denison U., 1968; JD cum laude, Harvard U., 1972. Bar: Mass. 1974, U.S. Dist. Ct. Mass. 1975, U.S. Ct. Appeals (D.C. cir.) 1975, U.S. Ct. Appeals (6th cir.) 1979, U.S. Supreme Ct. 1980, D.C. 1981, U.S. Ct. Appeals (2d cir.) 1981, U.S. Ct. Appeals (1st and 4th cirs.) 1983, Md. 1985, Va. 2000. Law clk. Judge Frank A. Kaufman, U.S. Dist. Ct. Md., Balt., 1972-73; asst. spl. prosecutor Watergate Spl. Pros. Force, Washington, 1973-75; from assoc. to sr. ptnr. Wilmer Cutler Pickering Hale & Dorr, Washington, 1975—, co-chmn. Appellate & Supreme Ct. Litigation group, mem. exec. com. Mem. Am. Law Inst., ABA, DC Bar Assn., Mass. Bar Assn., Boston Bar Assn., Phi Beta Kappa. Democrat. Office Phone: 202-663-6236. Business E-Mail: james.quarles@wilmerhale.com.

**QUARLES, JEANNE C.,** psychology professor; b. Calif. d. John and Shirley Markel; m. Junior Quarles; children: Diane Whitely, Ann Meyer. BA in Psychology, Calif. State U., Long Beach, Calif., 1974; MS in Clin. and Cmty. Psychology, Calif. State U., Fullerton, Calif., 1977. Instr. psychology Oreg. Coast C.C., Newport, Oreg., 1992—. Contbr. articles to jours. Mem.: APA. Office: Oregon Coast Community College 332 SW Coast Hwy Newport OR 97365 Office Phone: 541-574-7134.

**QUARLES, RANDAL KEITH,** federal agency administrator, lawyer; b. San Francisco, Sept. 5, 1957; s. Ralph Ray and Beverly Kay (Hulse) Q.; m. C. Hope Eccles, Sept. 13, 1997; children: Randal, Spencer, Hope. AB, Columbia U., 1981; JD, Yale U., 1984. Assoc. Davis Polk & Wardwell, N.Y.C., 1984-91, ptnr., 1993—2001; spl. asst. to sec. US Dept. Treasury, Washington, 1991-92, deputy asst. sec., fin. insts. policy, 1992-93, asst. sec. internat. affairs, 2002—05, under sec. for domestic fin., 2005—. U.S. exec. dir. IMF, 2001—02, European Bank Reconstrn. and Devel., 2002; mem. bd. dirs. Overseas Pvt. Investment Corp., 2004—05. Mem. fin. adv. com. Dole Presdl. Campaign, Washington, 1996. Mem. Yale Club, Salt Lake Country Club. Mem. Lds Ch. Avocations: aviation, skiing. Office: US Dept Treasury Under Sec Domestic Fin 1500 Pennsylvania Ave NW Washington DC 20220 Office Phone: 202-622-1703. E-mail: randal.quarles@do.treas.gov.

**QUARTARARO, PHILIP, JR.,** mathematics professor; s. Philip Quartararo and Laura Nicoll, Joseph Nicoll (Stepfather), Angeline S. Quartararo (Step-mother); m. Dorothy Marie Morvant; children: Philip III, Sharon Campbell, Deborah Michael, Beth Davis. B of Math., La. State U., New Orleans, 1964, M of Math., 1966, PhD of Math., 1972. Instr. asst. prof., assoc. prof. So. U., Baton Rouge, 1967—76, prof. math., 1976—2002; ret., 2002. Asst. to vice chancellor acad. affairs So. U., 1989—91. Co-author: (textbooks) College Algebra: The UNCPAL Approach, Elementary Applied Mathematics. Bd. chair Lamar YMCA, 2006—, bd. dirs., 1971—85. Recipient grants in field. Mem.: Math. Edn. Reform, Nat. Coun. Tchrs. Math., Am. Math. Soc., Math. Assn. Am. (chmn. LA-MS sect. 1995—96), Kiwanis Internat. (life; bd. dirs., lt. gov., pres., cert. leadership trainer), Phi Delta Kappa. Presbyterian. Avocations: swimming, home repair projects, small goat farm, gardening, golf. Office: So U PO Box 9261 Baton Rouge LA 70813 Office Phone: 225-933-6057. Personal E-mail: pquartjr@yahoo.com.

**QUARTERMAN, CYNTHIA LOUISE,** lawyer; b. Savannah, Ga., Apr. 6, 1961; d. Rudolph V. and Bernice Q.; m. Pantelis Michalopoulos, Nov. 2, 1993. BS, Northwestern U., 1983; JD, Columbia U., 1987. Atty. Benson & McKay, Kansas City, 1987-88, Steptoe & Johnson, Washington, 1988—93; dep. dir. Minerals Mgmt. Svc., Dept. Interior, Washington, 1993-95; dir., 1995-99; ptnr. Steptoe & Johnson, Washington, 1999—. mem. adv. bd. Inst. for Energy Law, co-chair ann. inst. Mem. ABA (vice chair sect. on environment, energy, resources, oil and natural gas exploration and prodn. com. 2002—03), Energy Bar Assn. (chair environment and pub. lands com. 2002—03), Women's Coun. Energy and Environment. Home: 1337 21st St NW Washington DC 20036-1503 E-mail: cquarter@steptoe.com.

**QUATAERT, DONALD,** historian, educator; b. Rochester, N.Y., Sept. 10, 1941; s. William Leonard and Norine Louise (Katzenberger) Q.; m. 1963 (div.); 1 child, Laurie; m. Jean H. Grebler, Jan. 24, 1970; 1 child, Eliot. AB, Boston U., 1966; MA, Harvard U., 1968; PhD, UCLA, 1974. Asst. prof. U. Houston, 1974-79, assoc. prof., 1979-87, Binghamton (N.Y.) U., 1988-94, prof., 1994—. Vis. assoc. prof. Binghamton U., 1987-88. Author: Social Disintegration, 1983, Manufacturing and Technology, 1992, Ottoman Manu-facturing, 1993; co-editor: An Economic and Social History of the Ottoman Empire, 1300-1914, 1994, The Ottoman Empire 1700-1922, 2000, 2d edit., 2005, Coal Miners and the State in the Ottoman Empire, 2006. NEH Sr. fellow, 1985-86, 1999-2000, Social Sci. Rsch. fellow, 1985-86, 1998, Fgn. Area fellow, 1985-86, Guggenheim fellow, 2004—05. Mem. Am. Hist. Assn., Mid. East Studies Assn., Turkish Studies Assn. Avocations: tennis, golf, stamp collecting/philately, birdwatching. Home: 4600 Deerfield Pl Vestal NY 13850-3757 Business E-Mail: dquataer@binghamton.edu.

**QUATE, CALVIN FORREST,** engineering educator; b. Baker, Nev., Dec. 7, 1923; s. Graham Shepard and Margie (Lake) Quate; m. Dorothy Marshall, June 28, 1945 (div. 1985); children: Robin, Claudia, Holly, Rhodalee; m. Arnice Streit, Jan. 1987; children: Christine, Carol, Richard. BS in Elec. Engring. U. Utah, 1944; PhD, Stanford U., 1950. Mem. tech. staff Bell Telephone Labs., Murray Hill, NJ, 1949-58; dir. research Sandia Corp., Albuquerque, 1959-60, v.p. research, 1960-61; prof. dept. applied physics and elec. engring. Stanford (Calif.) U., 1961-95, chmn. applied physics 1969-72, 78-81, Leland T. Edwards prof. engring., 1986—, assoc. dean Sch. Humanities and Scis., 1972-74, 82-83, rsch. prof. dept. elec. engring., 1995—. Sr. rsch. fellow Xerox Rsch. Ctr., Palo Alto, Calif., 1984—94. Served as lt. (j.g.) USNR, 1944—46. Recipient Rank prize for Opto-electronics, 1982, Pres.'s Nat. medal of Sci., 1992. Fellow: Acoustical Soc., Am. Acad. Arts and Scis., IEEE (Morris N. Liebmann award 1981, IEEE medal of honor 1988, Third Millennium award 2000, Ultrasonics Rayleigh award 2002); mem.: Royal Soc., Royal Microscop. Soc., Am. Phys. Soc. (Keithly award), NAS, NAE, Tau Beta Pi, Sigma Xi. Office: Stanford U E L Ginzton Lab Palo Alto CA 94305-4085 Office Phone: 650-723-0213.

**QUATRANO, ANNE,** chef, restaurant owner; Grad., Calif. Culinary Acad., San Francisco. Chef, co-owner Bacchanalia, Atlanta, Floataway Cafe, Atlanta, Star Provisions, Atlanta; chef Grolier Club, NY, Bimini Twist, La Petit Ferme. Elected mem. James Beard Found. Office: 1198 Howell Mill Rd Atlanta GA 30301

**QUATTLEBAUM, ROBERT BASKIN,** urologist; b. Roanoke, Ala., Mar. 6, 1933; s. Robert Baskin and Lucy Mathews Quattlebaum; m. Nelle Fall Binford, Dec. 18, 1959; children: Robyn, Jane, Blake, George, Elizabeth. BS, Vanderbilt U., Nashville, 1955; MD, Med. Coll. Ala., Birmingham, 1961. Diplomate Am. Bd. Urology. Intern Guthrie Clinic, Robert Packer Hosp., Sayre, Pa., 1961—62; resident U. Hosp., Hillnian Clinic, Birmingham, Ala., 1962—67; staff mem. Candler Hosp., St. Joseph Hosp., Meml. Hosp., Savannah, Ga.; pvt. practice urology Savannah, Ga. Contbr. articles to profl. jours. Bd. dirs. Salvation Army, Savannah, 2000—04, Savannah Christian Prep Sch. 2d lt. USAF. Named to Am. Registry of Outstanding Profs., 2002. Fellow: ACS; mem.: Am. Urol Assn. (past pres. southeastern sect.), Ga. Med. Soc. (past pres.), Rotary (dir. 1994). Avocations: golf, gardening, fishing.

**QUATTRONE, RICHARD DOUGLAS,** physician, military officer; b. Camden, N.J., Mar. 31, 1966; s. Richard Anthony and Rose Marie Quattrone; m. Evelyn Marie Quattrone, Oct. 19, 1996. BA in Biology, LaSalle U., 1988; D in Osteopathic Medicine, U. Medicine and Dentistry N.J., 1992; postgrad., U. N.C., 2005—. Lic. osteopathic Calif., cert. family med. physician. Commd. ensign USN, 1992, advanced through grades to commdr., family med. intern Camp Pendleton, Calif., 1992—93, family med. resident Camp Pendleton, Calif., 1996—98, flight surgeon Atsugi, Japan, 1993—96, family med. physician Toboshika, Japan, 1998—2001, Seattle, 2001—03, family med. tchg. staff Camp Lejeune, NC, 2003—05, aerospace medicine resident Chapel Hill, NC, 2005—; faculty Uniformed Svcs. U. Health Med. Sch., Seattle, 2003—05, Pikeville (Tenn.) Coll. Osteopathic, 2004—05. Mem.: Am. Acad. Family Physicians, Assn. Health Care Exec., Am. Mil. Osteo. Physicians and Surgeons, Am. Osteo. Assn. Republican. Roman Catholic. Avocations: skiing, running, cooking, travel, bicycling.

**QUATTRONE-CARROLL, DIANE ROSE,** clinical social worker; b. NYC, July 18, 1949; d. Mario Anthony and Filomena (Serpico) Quattrone; m. Rene Eugene Carroll Jr., June 7, 1980; children: Jenna Cristine, Jonathan Rene. BA cum laude, Bklyn. Coll., 1971; MSW, Rutgers U., 1974. Lic. marriage and family counselor, lic. clin. social worker, N.J.; bd. cert. diplomate in clin. social work. Clin. social worker, field instr. Essex County Guidance Ctr., East Orange, N.J., 1974-82; exec. dir. Psychotherapy Info. and Referral Svc., Madison, N.J., 1982-87; pvt. practice Sparta, N.J., 1982—. Nat. Assn. Social Workers. Avocation: travel. Office Phone: 973-729-2442.

**QUAY, THOMAS EMERY,** lawyer; b. Cleve., Apr. 3, 1934; s. Harold Emery and Esther Ann (Thomas) Q.; divorced; children: Martha Wyndham, Glynis Cobb, Eliza Emery; m. Winnifred B. Cutler, May 13, 1989. AB in Humanities magna cum laude (Univ. scholar), Princeton U., 1956; LLB (Univ. scholar), U. Pa., 1963. Bar: Pa. 1964. Assoc. Pepper, Hamilton & Scheetz, Phila., 1963-65; with William H. Rorer, Inc., Ft. Washington, Pa., 1965—, sec., counsel, 1974-79, v.p., gen. counsel, sec., 1979-88; v.p. legal planning and adminstrn. Rorer Group, 1988-90; counsel Reed Smith Shaw and McClay, Phila., 1991-93; v.p., gen. counsel Athena Inst., Chester Springs, Pa., 1993—. Bd. dirs. Main Line YMCA, Ardmore, Pa., 1971-73, chmn. bd., 1972-73; editor 10th Reunion Book Princeton Class of 1956, 1966, 25th Reunion Book, 1981—, class sec., 1966-71, class v.p., 1971-81, pres., 1981-86. Lt. (j.g.) USNR, 1957-60. Recipient Commendation award, Main Line YMCA, 1984. Mem. ABA, Pa. Bar Assn., Phila. Bar Assn., Pharm. Mfrs. Assn. (chmn. law sect. 1983), Pa. Biotech. Assn. (chmn. legis. com., mem. exec. com. 1991-93), Phila. Drug Exch. (chmn. legis. com. 1975-78), Cannon Club of Princeton U., Sharswood Law Club of U. Pa., Princeton Club of Phila. Democrat. Presbyterian.

**QUAYLE, DAN (JAMES DANFORTH QUAYLE),** former vice president United States; b. Indpls., Feb. 4, 1947; s. James C. and Corinne (Pulliam) Q.; m. Marilyn Tucker, Nov. 18, 1972; children: Tucker Danforth, Benjamin Eugene, Mary Corinne. BS in Polit. Sci., DePauw U., Greencastle, Ind., 1969; JD, Ind. U., 1974. Bar: Ind. 1974. Ct. reporter, pressman Huntington (Ind.) Herald-Press, 1965-69; assoc. pub., gen. mgr., 1974-76; with consumer protection divn. Office Atty. Gen., State of Ind., 1970-71; adminstrv. asst. to gov. State of Ind., 1971-73; dir. Inheritance Tax Div., 1973-74; tchr. bus. law Huntington Coll., 1975; mem. 95th-96th Congresses from 4th Dist. Ind., Washington; U.S. Senator from Ind. U.S. Senate, Washington, 1981-89; v.p. with Pres. George Bush U.S., Washington, 1989-93; founder BTC, 1994 chmn. Global Investment; Cerebrus Capital. Chmn. Cerberus Global Investments, NYC, 2000—; author, speaker, corp. bds.; disting. vis. prof. Am. Grad. Sch. Internat. Mgmt., 1997-99; cons. in field. Author: Standing Firm, 1994, The American Family, 1996, Worth Fighting For, 1999. Chmn. Campaign Am., 1995-99; hon. trustee emeriti Hudson Inst. With Ind. Army N.G., 1970-76. Office: Cerberus Investments 7001 N Scottsdale Rd Ste 2010 Scottsdale AZ 85253-3644

**QUAYLE, DWIGHT W.,** lawyer; b. Apr. 21, 1951; BA magna cum laude, Williams Coll., 1973; JD cum laude, George Washington Univ., 1978; MTS, Harvard Divinity Sch. Bar: Mass. 1978. Assoc. Ropes & Gray, Boston, 1978—87, ptnr., 1987—, chmn. corp. dept. Lectr. Boston Coll. Law Sch. Mem. bd. deacons & minister search com. First Parish in Lincoln, Mass. Mem.: Phi Beta Kappa. Office: Ropes & Gray 1 International Pl Boston MA 02110-2624 Office Phone: 617-951-7406. Office Fax: 617-951-7050. Business E-Mail: dwight.quayle@ropesgray.com.

**QUAYLE, MARILYN TUCKER,** wife of former United States vice president, lawyer; b. 1949; d. Warren S. and Mary Alice (Craig) Tucker; m. J. Danforth Quayle, Nov. 18, 1972; children: Tucker Danforth, Benjamin Eugene, Mary Corinne. BA in Polit. Sci., Purdue U., 1971; JD, Ind. U., 1974. Pvt. practice atty., Huntington, Ind., 1974—77; ptnr. Krieg, DeVault, Alexander & Capehart, Indpls., 1993—2001; pres. BTC Inc., Phoenix, 2001—. Author (with Nancy T. Northcott): Embrace the Serpent, 1992; author: The Campaign, 1996. Office: Quayle and Associates Ste 2010 7001 N Scottsdale Rd Scottsdale AZ 85253-3644*

**QUDDUS, MOHAMMED TANVIR,** electrical engineer, researcher; b. Comilla, Bangladesh, July 1, 1966; U.S., 1995; s. Mohammed Abdul Quddus and Khodeja Begum; m. Farhana Hussain. BS, Bangladesh U. Engring. and Tech., Dhaka, 1991, MS, 1993; PhD, Ariz. State U., 1999. Lectr. Bangladesh U. Engring. and Tech., Dhaka, Bangladesh, 1991—93, asst. prof., 1993—95; sr. staff engr. ON Semiconductor, Phoenix, 2000—. Contbr. articles to profl. jours. Pres. Bangladesh Student Assn., Ariz. State U., Tempe, Ariz., 1998—99. Recipient Pres. award, Govt. Bangladesh, 1984; scholar, Ariz.

State U., 1997—98, 1999—2000. Mem.: IEEE, Am. Chem. Soc., Phi Kappa Phi. Achievements include patents in field. Office: ON Semiconductor 5005 E Mcdowell Rd Phoenix AZ 85008 Home: 474 W Seagull Dr Chandler AZ 85248-2799 Personal E-mail: tanvir@fastq.com. Business E-Mail: tanvir.quddus@onsemi.com.

**QUEALLY, PAUL B.,** venture capitalist; b. Glen Cove, N.Y., Mar. 30, 1964; s. Francis Xavier and Claire (Doyule) Q.; m. Anne-Marie Flinn, Apr. 3, 1990; 1 child, P. Brian. BA, U. Richmond, 1986; MBA, Columbia U., 1990. Analyst Donaldson, Lufkin & Jenrette, N.Y.C., 1986—88, assoc., 1988—90, v.p., 1991—96; gen. ptnr. Welsh, Carson, Anderson & Stowe, N.Y.C., 1996—. Bd. dirs. E & B Marine, Inc., Edison, N.J., Champion Healthcare, Inc., Houston, Alphagraphics, Inc., Tucson, Cardiovascular Ventures, Inc., Stuart, Fla., United Signal Ptnrs., AmComp, Inc., AmeriSafe, Inc., Concentra Managed Care, Inc., Lab One, Inc., MedCath Corp., SHPS, Inc., AmeriPath, Inc., acting chmn., 2004— Mem. Phi Beta Kappa, Omicron Delta Epsilon. Republican. Roman Catholic. Avocations: golf, reading, antique shopping. Office: Welsh Carson Anderson 320 Park Ave Bsmt New York NY 10022

**QUEEN, JAMES E.,** automotive executive; b. Zanesville, Ohio, Feb. 4, 1949; B in Aero. and Aerospace Engring., U.S. Naval Acad., 1971. Mgr. customer satisfaction and engring. Buick, 1985—86; sr. staff engr. Buick Car Group Powertrain Divsn., Detroit, 1986—88; asst. chief engr. GM, 1988—91, Buick-Oldsmobile-Cadillac Lansing Automotive Divsn., 1991—95; engring. dir. N. Am. GM Tech. Ctr., Warren, Mich., 1995—97; group dir. engring. GM Small Car Group, 1997—99; v.p./group dir. engring. GM N. Am., 1999—2001; v.p. GM. N. Am. Engring., 2001—. Served USMC, 1971—77.

**QUEEN, JOYCE,** elementary school educator; b. Cleve., Mar. 17, 1945; d. Wilbur and Mae Closterhouse; m. Robert Graham Queen, Mar. 17, 1973. BA in Biology, Macalester Coll., 1966; MS in Conservation and Natural Resource Mgmt., U. Mich., 1968. Cert. tchr. biol. and earth scis., Ohio. Exhibitor, docent, coord. Grand Rapids (Mich.) Pub. Mus., 1967-68; tchr., naturalist Rose Tree-Media (Pa.) Outdoor Edn., 1967, Willoughby-Eastlake (Ohio) Schs., 1969-70, Independence (Ohio) Schs., 1970-78; sci. tchr. Hathaway Brown Sch., Cleve., 1970—, chmn. dept. primary sci., 1998—. Designer Courtland Woods nature trail, 1986, designer sci. greenhouse, 1990-92; designer sci. classroom Stan Wyke Architects/Hathaway Brown Sch., 1990-92; designer, coord. Dampeer Primary sci. courtyard, 1993, Oliva Herb Garden, 1998, Colini Landscape Design/Hathaway Brown Sch., Shaker Hts., Ohio; edn. adv. com. William G. Mather Vessel Mus., Cleve., 1992, Holden Arboretum, Kirtland, Ohio, 1992-97, Shaker Lakes Nature Ctr., 2005-06; youth divsn. judge Cleve. Botanic Garden Show, 1999, 2000, 02, 05, NOAA Live From Antarctica, 2003; presenter in field. Contbr. articles to profl. jours. Design cons. Cleve. Bot. Garden and Floral Scape, 1998, judge, 1998, 2000, 02, 05; active Belize (Ctrl. Am.) Tchrs. Workshop, 1994; Sagamore Adirondack Great Camps Workshop, 2003; vol. PARI Radio Telescope, 2005; task force, agrl. edn. commn. HB Engring., 2005-06. Catalyst grant Hathaway Brown Sch. Gt. Lks. Curriculum, 1991; recipient Environ. Edn. award Ohio Alliance for Environment, 1986, Presdl. Excellence in Elem. Sci. Tchg. award NSF, 1992, Sheldon Exemplary Equipment and Facilities award, 1992, Garden Club Am. Hall award, 2005; Great Lakes Lighthouse Keepers Assn. scholar, Marine Ecology scholar Marine Resources, Inc., 1989, Internat. Space Sta. Conf. scholar, 2000, Maine Salt Marsh Ecology Curriculum scholar, 2001, Calif. Coastal Wetlands and Desert Study scholar, 2002, Sagamore Inst. Adirondacks scholar, 2003, NASA Mars Mission Scholar, 2006, Hong Kong-Sci./Tech. China scholar, 2006. Mem. NSTA (recipient Exemplary Environ. and Facilities award with Sheldon Mfg. Co. 1992), Cleve. Regional Coun. Sci. Tchrs., Cleve. Coun. Ind. Schs., Cleve. Natural Hist. Mus., Cleve. Zool. Park, Ind. Sch. Assn. Ctrl. Sts., Internat. Pen Pal Exchange Progam, Great Lakes Sci. Ctr. Holden Arboretum. Presbyterian. Avocations: orchardist, naturalist, horticulturist. Office: Hathaway Brown Sch 19600 N Park Blvd Cleveland OH 44122-1899

**QUEENEY, DEBORAH ANN,** special education educator; b. Allentown, Pa., Feb. 4, 1949; d. William and Jane Swartz; m. Stephen Francis Queeney, Aug. 5, 1978; children: Nicole Ellen, Jessica Elaine. BSc, Kutztown State Coll., 1972; MEd, U. Pitts., 1975. Tchr. blind, multi-handicapped Lincoln Intermediate Unit 12, York, Pa., 1973—74; tchr. Monmouth Assn. Retarded Children, Shrewsbury, NJ, 1975—78; instr. assoc. tutor Amherst Sch. Dist. Regional Svcs. and Edn. Ctr., NH, 1988—91; spl. needs tchr. Milford (N.H.) Sch. Dist., 1991—. Named NH Tchr. of Yr., Assn. Retarded Citizens NH, 1994; recipient Monmouth County Tchr. of Yr., Monmouth Assn. Retarded Citizens, 1977, Excellence in Edn. award, Nat. Ctr. Low Incidence Disabilities, Denver, 2004. Mem.: NH Connections. Avocations: seashell collecting, sketching. Home: 7 Roberts Rd Amherst NH 03031 Office: Milford Mid Sch 33 Osgood Rd Milford NH 03055

**QUEEN LATIFAH, (DANA OWENS),** recording artist, actress; b. NJ, Mar. 18, 1970; d. Lance and Rita O. Student, Borough of Manhattan C.C. CEO Flavor Unit Entertainment; spokeswoman Revlon. TV appearances include: Living Single, 1993, Fresh Prince of Bel Air, In Living Color, Ellen, Hangin' with Mr. Cooper, Mad TV, The Arsenio Hall Show, The Queen Latifah Show, 1999-2001 (exec. prodr.), Spin City, 2001, (miniseries) Living with the Dead, 2002, Kung Faux, 2003, (TV films) Mama Flora's Family, 1998, (voice) Crash Nebula, 2004, The Muppets' Wonderful Wizard of Oz, 2005; film appearances include: House Party 2, 1991, Jungle Fever, 1991, Juice, 1992, Who's the Man, 1993, My Life, 1993, Set It Off, 1996, Hoodlum, 1997, The Wizard of Oz, 1998, Living Out Loud, 1998, Sphere, 1998, The Bone Collector, 1999, (voice) Bringing Out the Dead, 1999, The Country Bears, 2002, Brown Sugar, 2002 (also composer), (voice) Pinocchio, 2002, Chicago, 2002 (Acad. award best sup. actress nom., 2003), Bringing Down the House, 2003 (also exec. prodr., composer), Scary Movie 3, Barbershop 2: Back in Business, 2004, The Cookout, 2004 (writer, prodr.), Taxi, 2004, Beauty Shop, 2005 (also prodr.), Last Holiday, 2006, (voice) Ice Age: The Meltdown, 2006; composer (films) New Jack City, 1991, White Man Can't Jump, 1992, Girls Town, 1996; albums include All Hail the Queen, 1990, The Nature of Sista, 1991, X-tra Naked, 1992, Black Reign, 1994, Order In The Court, 1998, She's a Queen: A Collection of Hits, 2002. Named Best New Artist, New Music Seminar, 1990, Best Female Rapper, Rolling Stone Readers' Poll, 1990; recipient Grammy award nomination, 1990, Soul Train Music award, 1995, Sammy Davis Jr. award, 1995, Entertainer of Yr. award, 1995, Grammy award for best rap solo performance, 1995, named one of 50 Most Influential African-Americans, Ebony Magazine 2004, named to Hollywood Walk of Fame, 2005. Achievements include becoming first hip-hop artist honored with star on the Hollywood Walk of Fame. Office: Flavor Unit Entertainment 155 Morgan St Jersey City NJ 07302-2932*

**QUELER, EVE,** conductor; b. NYC; Student, Mannes Coll. Music, CCNY. Music staff N.Y.C. Opera, 1958-70; assoc. condr. Ft. Wayne (Ind.) Philharm., 1970-71; founder, music dir. Opera Orch., N.Y., 1968; condr. Lake George Opera Festival, Glen Falls, N.Y., 1971-72, Oberlin (Ohio) Music Festival, 1972, Romantic Festival, Indpls., 1972, Mostly Mozart Festival, Lincoln Center, 1972, New Philharmonia, London, 1974, Teatro Liceu, Barcelona, 1974, 77, San Antonio Symphony, 1975; guest condr. Paris Radio Orch., 1972, P.R. Symphony Orch., 1975, 77, Mich. Chamber Orch., 1975, Phila. Orch., 1976, Montreal Symphony, 1977, Cleve. Orch., 1977 (Recipient Martha Baird Rockefeller Fund for Music award 1968, named Musician of Month Mus. Am. Mag. 1972), N.Y.C. Opera, 1978, Opera Las Palmas, 1978, Opera de Nice, 1979, Nat. Theatre of Prague, 1980, Opera Caracas, Venezuela, 1981, San Diego Opera, 1984, Australian Opera, Sydney, 1985, Kirov Opera, St. Petersburg, Russia, 1993, Hamburg Opera, Germany, 1994, Pretoria, South Africa, 1994, 1995, Hamilton, Ont., 1995, Hawaii Philharmonic, 1997, Hong Kong Sinfonietta, 1998, Hong Kong Philharmonic, 1999, Orch. dello Stato de Mexico, 1999-2002, Macau Festival, 2000, Festival Euro Mediteranneo, Italy, 2002; Opei Bonn, 1994-96; recording CBS Masterworks, 1974, 76, Hungaroton Records, 1982-85. Decorated Chevalier de l'ordre des Arts et des Lettres; named Woman in Music, N.Y.C., 2002; recipient Beatrice award, Licia Albanese-Puccini Foundation, 1995. Office: Opera Orch 239 W 72nd St Ste 2R New York NY 10023-2734

**QUELLO, JAMES HENRY,** government official; b. Laurium, Mich., Apr. 21, 1914; s. Bartholomew and Mary Katherine (Cochis) Q.; m. Mary Elizabeth Butler, Sept. 14, 1937 (dec. 1999); children: James Michael, Richard Butler. BA, Mich. State U., 1935, D of Humanities (hon.), 1977; D of Pub. Svc. (hon.), No. Mich. U., 1975. V.p., sta. mgr. Goodwill Stas., Inc., Detroit, 1947-72; v.p. Capital Cities Comm. Corp., 1968; commr. FCC, Washington, 1974—98. Comm. cons., Detroit, 1972-74; commr. Detroit Housing and Urban Renewal Commn., 1951-72 Contbr. articles to mags., newspapers. Bd. dirs. Greater Detroit Hosp. Assn.; trustee Mich. Vet. Trust Fund; mem. Gov.'s Spl. Commn. on Urban Problems, Mich., Gov.'s Spl. Study Com. on Legis. Compensation, Mayor's Com. on Human Relations; bd. dirs. Am. Negro Emancipation Centennial; mem. exec. bd. Boy Scouts Am.; TV-radio chmn. United Found. Lt. col. AUS, 1940-45. Decorated Bronze Star with oak leaf cluster, Croix de Guerre (France); recipient Internat. Pres.'s award Nat. Assn. TV Program Execs., 1985, Silver Satellite award Am. Women in Radio and TV, 1988, 93, Sol Taishoff award Washington Area Broadcasters Assn., 1989, 93, Pub. Svc. award Fed. Comm. Bar Assn., 1993, Disting. Svc. award Media Inst., 1993, Golden Eagle Amb. award Pa. Assn. Broadcasters, 1993, Disting. Alumni award Mich. State U., Club Dir. award Detroit Adcraft Club, 1993, L.I. Coalition for Fair Broadcasting award, 1993, Nat. Disting. Svc. award Nat. Assn. Pub. TV, 1993, Obie award Ohio Ednl. TV Stas., 1993, Gold Eagle Leadership award Wireless Cable Assn. Internat., 1993, Pres. award Alaska Broadcasting Assn., 1994, Chmn. award Nat. Religious Broadcasters, 1994, Ga. Broadcasters award Broadcasters of Am., 1994, 1st Amendment award Radio & TV News Dirs. Found., 1994. Mem. Nat. Assn. Broadcaster (gov. liaison com. 1964-72, Keystone award 1990, Disting. Svc. award 1994, Honor award for protecting the technical integrity of radio and TV 1994, Broadcasting Cable Hall of Fame, 1995, Nat. Radio Hall of Fame 1996), Mich. Assn. Broadcasters (pres. 1958, legis. chmn. 1959-72, dir., Outstanding Mich. Citizen 1989, Pioneer award 1994, Ellis Island honor award 1997), Greater Detroit Bd. Commerce, Sigma Alpha Epsilon. Clubs: Adcraft (Detroit); Detroit Athletic, Army and Navy Country; Nat. Press (Washington). Office: FCC Wiley Rein and Fielding 1776 K St NW Washington DC 20006-2304 Office Phone: 202-719-7052. Personal E-mail: jquello@wrf.com.

**QUENEAU, PAUL ETIENNE,** metallurgical engineering educator; b. Phila., Mar. 20, 1911; s. Augustin L. and Jean (Blaisdell) Q.; m. Joan Osgood Hodges, May 20, 1939; children: Paul Blaisdell, Josephine Downs. BA, Columbia U., 1931, BSc, 1932, M of Engring., 1933; postgrad., Cambridge U., Eng., 1934; DSc, Delft U. Tech., Netherlands, 1971. With INCO, 1934-69; rsch. supt. Internat. Nickel Co., 1940-41, 46-48, v.p., 1958-69, chief tech. officer, tech. asst. to pres., 1956-66, asst. to chmn., 1967-69; vis. scientist Delft U. Tech., 1970-71; prof. engring. Dartmouth Coll., 1971-87, prof. emeritus, 1987—. Cons. engr., 1972—; vis. prof. U. Minn., 1974-75, U. Utah, 1987-91; geographer Perry River Arctic Expdn., 1949; chmn. arctic rsch. adv. com. USN, 1957; gov. Arctic Inst. N. Am., 1969-72; mem. engring. coun. Columbia U., 1965-70; mem. vis. com. MIT, Cambridge, 1967-70; mem. extractive metallurgy and mineral processing panels NAS; pres. Q-S Oxygen Processes Inc., 1974-79, also bd. dir. author: (with Hanson) Geography, Birds and Mammals of the Perry River Region, 1956; Cobalt and the Nickeliferous Limonites, 1971; editor: Extractive Metallurgy of Copper, Nickel and Cobalt, 1961; (with Anderson) Pyrometallurgical Processes in Nonferrous Metallurgy, 1965; The Winning of Nickel, 1967; contbr. articles to profl. jours.; patentee 500 internat. patents, 36 U.S. patents including processes and apparatus employed in the pyrometallurgy, hydrometallurgy and vapometallurgy of nickel, copper, cobalt, lead, zinc, iron and steel, extractive metallurgy oxygen tech. including INCO oxygen flash smelting, oxygen top-blown rotary converter, lateritic ore matte smelting, nickel high pressure carbonyl and iron ore recovery processes; co-inventor Lurgi QSL direct lead-making, QSOP direct coppermaking and nickelmaking reactors, Lurgi direct steelmaking reactors, and Dravo oxygen sprinkle smelting copper furnaces. Bd. dir. Engring. Found., 1966-76, chmn. bd. dir., 1973-75. With C.E. U.S. Army, 1937—45, ETO, to col. USAR, 1945—71. Decorated Bronze Star, ETO medal with 5 Battlestars, Army Commendation medal; Evans fellow Cambridge U., 1933-34; recipient Egleston medal Columbia U., 1965, Fletcher award Dartmouth Coll., 1991, McGraw-Hill Chem. Engring. award Personal Achievement in Chem. Engring. McGraw Hill, 1996. Fellow Metall. Soc. of AIME (dir. 1964, 68-71, pres. 1969, Extractive Metallurgy Lecture award 1977, Paul E. Queneau TMS Internat. Symposium on Extractive Metallurgy of Copper, Nickel and Cobalt 1993); mem. AIME (Douglas Gold medal 1968, v.p. 1970, dir. 1968-71, Henry Krumb lectr. 1984, keynote lectr. ann. meeting 1990, McGraw Hill award personal achievement in chem. engring.), NAE, NSPE, Can. Inst. Mining and Metallurgy, Inst. Mining and Metallurgy U.K. (overseas mem. council 1970-80, Gold medal 1980), Sigma Xi, Tau Beta Pi. Achievements include 36 U.S. patents and 500 foreign patents. Office: Dartmouth Coll Thayer Sch Engring Hanover NH 03755

**QUENELLE, SUSANNAH SHERMAN,** music educator; b. Albion, NY, Apr. 4, 1955; d. Moses H. and Margaret (McKirdy) Sherman; m. Anthony M. Quenelle, July 23, 1983; children: Kayla N., Taylor R. Mus B in Edn., SUNY, Potsdam, 1977; Mus M in Edn., SUNY, 1983. Tchr. K-6 music Gen. Brown Sch. Dist., Brownville, NY, 1978—83; tchr. 9-12 music St. Anne Inst., Albany, 1983—87; tchr. 6-8 music, vocal theater East Greenbush Sch. Dist., 1987—2006; tchr. 9-12 vocal music, theatre Columbia H.S., 2006—. Music dir. East Greenbush Youth Theatre, 2003—04; bd. dirs. Spotlight Players. Mem. soloist First United Meth. Ch., 1992—; conducted Rensselaer County Elem. Choir, 1998. Recipient Tchr. Recognition award, Albany Civic Theater, 2004. Mem.: Music Educators Nat. Conf., Am. Choral Dir. Assn. Methodist. Avocations: reading, exercise. Office: Columbia HS 962 Luther Rd East Greenbush NY 12061

**QUENNELL, NICHOLAS,** landscape architect, educator; b. London, Sept. 30, 1935; s. Cecil William and Beatrice Irene Quennell; m. Grace Tankersley, Apr. 30, 1983. AA, Archtl. Assn., London, 1957; MLA, Harvard U., 1969. Registered architect, N.Y., Pa., N.J., Conn., U.K.; registered landscape architect, N.Y., N.J., Conn., Mass., N.C. Architect London County Coun., 1959-61, Jose Luis Sert, Cambridge, Mass., 1961-62, Lawrence Halprin & Assocs., San Francisco, 1962-65, Vollmer Assocs., N.Y.C., 1965-68; prin. Nicholas Quennell Assocs., N.Y.C., 1968-79, Quennell Rothschild Assocs., N.Y.C., 1979-97, Quennell, Rothschild & Ptnrs., N.Y.C., 1998—. V.p. The Mcpl. Art Soc. (dir. 1978-85), N.Y.C., 1985-92, dir. The Archtl. League, N.Y.C., 1984-89 Bd. dirs. Nat. Assn. for Olmsted Pks., Washington, 1988-97, chmn., 1990-93; mem. Art Commn. of City of N.Y., 1992-97, pres., 1993-97. Fellow Am. Soc. of Landscape Architects; mem. Century Assn. Office: Quennell Rothschild & Ptnrs 118 W 22nd St New York NY 10011-2416 E-mail: quennell@qrpartners.com

**QUENNEVILLE, JOEL,** professional hockey coach; b. Windsor, Ont., Can., Sept. 15, 1958; m. Elizabeth Quenneville; children: Dylan, Lily, Anna. Hockey player, player coach St. John's Maple Leafs, 79-92; head coach Springfield Indians, Am. Hockey League, 1993-94; asst. coach Colorado Avalanche, 1995-96; head coach St. Louis Blues, 1997—2004, Colo. Avalanche, 2004—. Named Most Valuable Defensemen, 1985, 86, Coach of Yr., NHL, 1999-2000. Office: c/o Colorado Avalanche Pepsi Center 1000 Chopper Circle Denver CO 80204

**QUENTEL, ALBERT DREW,** lawyer; b. Miami, Fla., Nov. 27, 1934; s. Charles Edward Jr. and Alberta Amelia (Drew) Q.; m. Paula Staelin Hagar, Feb. 9, 1957 (dec. Mar. 1998); children: Albert D. Jr., Stephen C., Marshall Lee, Paul G., Peter E., Michael J. BA, U. Fla., 1956, JD with honors, 1959. Bar: Fla. 1959. Assoc. Mershon, Sawyer, Johnston, Dunwody & Cole, Miami, 1959-64, ptnr., 1965-71; ptnr., shareholder Greenberg Traurig P.A., Miami, 1971—. Editor-in-chief U. Fla. Law Rev., 1959; contbg. author: Florida Real Property Practice, 1965, Real Estate Partnerships Selected Problems and Solutions, 1991, Commercial Real Estate Finance, 1993. Mem. Gov.'s Growth Mgmt. Adv. Com., Tallahassee, 1985-87; bd. dirs. Nat. Parkinson Found., Miami, 1980-98, v.p. 1985-97. Mem. NRA (life mem. 1989—), Am. Coll. Real Estate Lawyers, Fla. Bar Assn. (chmn. pub. rels. com. 1970-72, chmn. editorial com. jour. 1972-73), Lions (pres. Key Biscayne, Fla. club 1973),

Miami Club (pres. 1991-92), Bath Club, Blue Key, Beta Theta Pi (pres. local chpt. 1954-55), Phi Eta Sigma, Phi Kappa Phi. Republican. Congregationalist. Avocations: reading, shooting, photography. Home: 825 Algeria Ave Coral Gables FL 33134-2401 Office: Greenberg Traurig 1221 Brickell Ave Miami FL 33131-3224 Office Phone: 305-579-0505. Business E-Mail: QuentelA@gtlaw.com.

**QURESHI, MOHAMMED YOUNUS,** retired psychology professor; b. Haripur Hazara, Pakistan, Dec. 12, 1929; arrived in U.S., 1953; s. Mohammed Noor and Meryam Khatoon Qureshi; m. Nora Jane Knapp, May 27, 1958 (div. Nov. 1979); children: Ahmed, Amna, Shukria, Shawn; m. Farzana Kaukab, May 17, 1980; children: Ajmel, Sabeeha, Azem. PhD, U. Ill., 1958. Lic. psychologist Wis.; diplomate Am. Bd. Psychol. Specialties: Asst. prof. psychology U. Minn., Duluth, 1960-62, U. N.D., Grand Forks, 1962-64; assoc. prof. psychology Marquette U., Milw., 1964-70, prof., 1970—2003, prof. emeritus psychology, 2003—, chmn. dept. psychology, 1971-77. Cons. psychologist. Author: Statistics and Behavior: An Introduction, 1980, 2d edit., 1991; contbr. articles to sci. and profl. jours. Pres. 81st St. Sch. PTA, 1968—88; merit badge counselor Milwaukee County coun. Boy Scouts Am., 1973—88; pres. Islamic Assn. Greater Milw., 1978—83; chmn. bd. trustees Islamic Soc. Milw., 2004—. Grantee, NIH, 1962—69, TOPS Club, 1969—76, Office of Edn., 1970—71. Mem.: Psychometric Soc., Am. Psychol. Assn., Sigma Xi. Home: 15660 Monet Ct Brookfield WI 53005-5125 Office: Marquette U Schroeder Health Complex PO Box 1881 Milwaukee WI 53201-1881 Office Phone: 414-288-7468.

**QUERY, LANCE D.,** dean, university librarian; EdB in History, Spanish, Univ. Mo., 1969; MA in Latin Am. History, Ind. Univ., PhD; MLS, Univ. Chgo. Acting univ. libr. Northwestern Univ., Chgo.; asst. univ. libr., planning and adminstrn. We. Mich. Univ., and faculty, history dept., to dean, univ. libraries; dean libraries and academic info. resources Tulane Univ., New Orleans, 2000—. Office: Dean Libr Academic Info Resources Tulane Univ 6823 St Charles Ave New Orleans LA 70118-5698 Office Phone: 504-865-5131. Office Fax: 504-865-6773. Business E-Mail: lquery@tulane.edu.*

**QUESENBERRY, KENNETH HAYS,** agronomy educator; b. Springfield, Tenn., Feb. 28, 1947; s. James William and Cora Geneva (Moore) Quesenberry; m. Joyce Ann Kaze; children: James Kenneth, Kendra Joyce. BS, Western Ky. U., 1969; PhD, U. Ky., 1975. D.F. Jones predoctoral fellow U. Ky., Lexington, 1972—75; asst. prof. U. Fla., Gainesville, 1975—80, assoc. prof. agronomy, 1980—86, prof. agronomy, 1986—. Contbr. articles to profl. jours. With U.S. Army, 1969—71, Vietnam. Fellow: Crop Sci. Soc. Am. (chair divsn. C-8 1993—94), Am. Soc. Agronomy. Achievements include research in germplasm enhancement of forages with release of four cultivars of tropical grasses and three clovers and genetic transformation of clovers; specialist Trifolium species germplasm and forage breeding and genetics. Avocations: sports, antique furniture refinishing. Office: U Fla PO Box 110500 Gainesville FL 32611-0500 Office Phone: 351-392-1811 ext. 213. Business E-Mail: clover@ifas.ufl.edu.

**QUESENBERY, ERIKA LYNN,** media specialist, curator; b. Balt., Apr. 29, 1969; d. Lonnie Ray Quesenbery Jr. and Ruth Ann Pierce. Student, Harford C.C., 1987—89; degree in mass. comm. News dir. Delmarva Broadcasting, Sta. WXCY, Havre de Grace, Md., 1989—91; editor The Rising Sun Herald and Herald County edit. Octoraro Pub. Co., Rising Sun, Md., 1995—2000; grant writer, media rels. specialist Boys & Girls Club of Cecil County, North East, Md., 2000—05; exec. asst. Stewart Assoc., Perryville, Md., 2005—. Curator Paw Paw Mus., Port Deposit Heritage Corp., Port Deposit, Md., 1998—. Author (researcher): (non-fiction historical book) A Snowball's Chance: Captain Alonzo Snow's 1st Maryland Light Artillery, Battery B, 1861-1865; contbr. non-fiction historical book. Co-founder Tome Sch. Clean-Up Volunteers at the former NTC Bainbridge, Port Deposit, 1997—2000; vol., tour guide, first civilian mem. USNTC Bainbridge Hist. Assn., Port Deposit, 1999—2006; bd. dirs., former tour com. chair, vol. Port Deposit Heritage Corp., Port Deposit, 1996—98. Recipient Non-Metro Radio Editl. Writing award, AP, Balt., 1989, Non-Metro Radio Enterprise in Reporting award, 1990, Sch. Bell award for media coverage of edn., Md. State Tchrs.' Assn., 1997, U.S. Navy Civilian Citizen Recognition for Bainbridge/NAPS and Tome Sch. Clean-Up Volunteers, USN, 2000. Green Party. Presbyterian. Avocations: historic preservation, local and regional history, genealogy, Irish heritage, travel. Home: 704 Main St Delta PA 17314 Office: Stewart Assoc 1723 Principio Furnace Rd Perryville MD 21903 Office Phone: 410-642-3074. Personal E-mail: historacle@verizon.net. E-mail: erikaq@stewartrealestatedev.com.

**QUESNEL-VALLÉE, AMÉLIE,** social sciences educator, medical educator; d. Jacques Vallée and Lise Quesnel; m. Frédéric Bouchard, July 22, 2000. PhD, Duke U., 2004. Asst. prof. sociology and epidemiology McGill U., Montreal, Que., 2005—. Recipient doctoral fellowship, Fulbright Found., 1999—2002, Social Scis. and Humanities Rsch. Coun. Can., 1999—2003, Vorsanger Smith award, Duke U., Dept. Sociology, 2003, Student Paper award, Am. Sociol. Assn. Sect. on Aging and Life Course, 2004, Grad. Student Paper award in social demography, Am. Sociol. Assn. Sect. on Sociology of Population, 2003, doctoral fellowship, Program for Advanced Rsch. in Social Scis., Duke U., 2003—04, Young Investigator Career award, Que. Fund for Health Rsch., 2005—09.

**QUESTER, GEORGE HERMAN,** political science professor; b. Bklyn., July 14, 1936; s. Jacob George and Elizabeth (Mattern) Q.; m. Aline Marie Olson, June 20, 1964; children: Theodore, Amanda. AB, Columbia U., 1958; MA, Harvard U., 1964, PhD, 1965. Instr., then asst. prof. govt. Harvard U., 1965-70; assoc. prof. govt. Cornell U., 1970-73, prof., 1973-82; prof. polit. sci. U. Md., College Park, 1982—. Vis. prof. U.S. Naval Acad., Annapolis, Md., 1991-93. Author: Deterrence Before Hiroshima, 1966, Nuclear Diplomacy, 1970, The Politics of Nuclear Proliferation, 1973, The Continuing Problem of International Relations, 1974, Offense and Defense in the International System, 1977, American Foreign Policy: The Lost Consensus, 1982, The Future of Nuclear Deterrence, 1986, The International Politics of Television, 1990, Nuclear Monopoly, 2000, Before and After The Cold War, 2002, Nuclear First Strike, 2006. Served with USAF, 1958-61. Fellow Center Advanced Study Behavioral Scis., 1974-75 Mem. Council Fgn. Relations, Inst. Strategic Studies, Am. Polit. Sci. Assn. Home: 5124 37th St N Arlington VA 22207-1862 Office: Univ Md 3140 Tydings College Park MD 20742-0001 Office Phone: 301-405-4146. Business E-Mail: gqueste@gvpt.umd.edu.

**QUESTROM, ALLEN I.,** retail executive; b. Newton, Mass., Apr. 13, 1941; s. Irving Allen and Natalie (Chadbourne) Questrom; m. Kelli Questrom. BS, Boston U., 1964. From exec. trainee to div. mdse. mgr. Abraham & Straus, Bklyn., 1965-73; v.p., gen. mdse. mgr. home store Bullock's, L.A., 1973-74, sr. v.p., gen. mdse. mgr. all stores, 1974-77; exec. v.p. Bullock's div. Federated Dept. Stores, L.A., 1977-78, pres. Rich's div. Atlanta, 1978-80, chmn. bd., chief exec. officer, 1980-84, chmn. bd., chief exec. officer Bullock's/Bullocks Wilshire div., 1984-88, corp. exec. v.p. Cin., 1987-88, vice-chmn., 1988; also chmn., CEO Allied Stores Corp., Cin., 1990-97; pres., CEO Neiman Marcus Group Inc., Dallas, 1988-90; chmn., CEO Federated Dept. Stores Inc., Cin., 1990-97; chmn., pres., CEO Barneys New York, 1999—2000; chmn., CEO J.C. Penney Co., Inc., Plano, Tex., 2000—. Prin. AEA Investors Inc.; ptnr. Mellon Ventures. Avocations: skiing, golf, travel. Office: JC Penney Corp Inc 6501 Legacy Dr Plano TX 75024-3698

**QUIALA, MARIBEL,** psychotherapist, consultant; d. Guillermo H. Quiala and Neris Aroche; m. Jesus A. Rios, Apr. 24, 1993; children: Natalie, Jesus. BA in Psychology and Music, Seton Hall U., 1985; MSW, Barry U., 1995. LCSW, bd. cert. Fla. Pvt. pracitce psychotherapy, Miami, Fla., 2000—, S.E. regional coord. Nat. Latina Health Network, Washington, 2000—; field instr. Barry U., Miami, Fla., 2000—, Fla. Internat. U., Miami, 2000—, Nova Southeastern U., Ft. Lauderdale, Fla., 2000—, Carlos Albizu U., Miami, 2000—; internship dir. Psychiat. Solutions Inc., Ft. Lauderdale, 2000—; mem. adv. com. Minority Tobacco Control Task Force, Dept. Health, Fla.,

1999—2002; spokesperson HIV/AIDS Awareness Campaign, State Fla., Breast/Cervical Cancer Campaign, State Fla., Hispanic Heart Healthy Day Campaign, S.E. Region. Named Most Dynamic Woman, Am. Cancer Soc., 2005. Mem.: NASW (mem. MSW Gosnell Meml. Scholarship Panel 2003—06, mem. nat. com. on women's issues 2005—), Am. Coll. Musicians, Nat. Guild Piano Tchrs. Roman Catholic. Avocations: dance, piano, meditation.

**QUIAT, GERALD M.,** lawyer; b. Denver, Jan. 9, 1924; s. Ira L. and Esther (Greenblatt) Q.; m. Roberta M. Nicholson, Sept. 26, 1962; children: James M., Audrey R., Melinda A., Daniel P., Ilana L., Leonard E. AA, U. Calif., Berkeley, 1942; AB, LLB, U. Denver, 1948, changed to JD, 1970. Bar: Colo. 1948, Fed. Ct. 1948, U.S. Dist. Ct. Colo. 1948, U.S. Ct. Appeals (10th cir.) 1948, U.S. Surpeme Ct. 1970. Dep. dist. atty. City and Co. of Denver, Colo., 1949-52; partner firm Quiat, Seeman & Quiat, Denver, 1952-67, Quiat & Quiat (later changed to Quiat, Bucholtz & Bull, P.C.), 1968; pres. Quiat, Bucholtz & Bull & Laff, P.C. (and predecessors), Denver, 1968-85; pvt. practice Denver, 1985—. Bd. dirs., past chmn. audit com. Guaranty Bank & Trust Co., Denver. Past trustee Holding Co.; pres., chmn. bd. dirs. Rose Med. Ctr., Denver, 1976—79; mem. Colo. Civil Rights Com., 1963—71, chmn., 1966—67, 1969—70, hearing officer, 1963—71; bd. dirs. AMC Cancer Rsch. Ctr., Denver, 1971—2004, chmn. bd., 1991—93, sec. treas., 2000—04; chmn. bd. Am. Med. Ctr., 1993—95; hon. mem. nat. civil rights com. Anti-Defamation League, hon. mem. nat. exec. com., hon. nat. commr.; chmn. Mountain State region, 1980—82; mem. exec. com., bd. mem. Mountain States region Anti-Defamation League. With inf. U.S. Army, 1942—45. Decorated Combat Infantry Badge, Bronze Star. Mem. ABA, Colo. Bar Assn., Am. Legion (comdr. Leyden-Chiles-Wickersham post 1 1955-56, past judge adv. Colo. dept.). Home: 5361 Nassau Cir E Englewood CO 80110-5100 Office: 1873 S Bellaire St Ste 900 Denver CO 80222-4304 Office Phone: 303-759-1000 ext. 102. E-mail: gqph@aol.com.

**QUIAT, MARSHALL,** lawyer; b. Denver, Mar. 10, 1922; s. Ira Louis and Esther Quiat; m. Ruth Laura Saunders, Nov. 26, 1950 (dec. Nov. 1995); 1 child, Matthew Philip; m. Jane Cooley, May 1, 1996 (dec. Mar. 2004). BA, U. Colo., 1947, JD, 1948. Bar: Colo. 1949, U.S. Dist. Ct. Colo. 1949, U.S. Ct. Appeals (10th cir.) 1968. Pvt. practice, Denver, 1949—. Judge Gilpin County (Colo.) Ct., 1956, 1st Jud. Dist. Ct., Golden, Colo., 1959; mem. com. on jud. reform Colo. Legis. Commn., 1958. Mem. Colo. Ho. of Reps., Denver, 1949-51; bd. dirs. Luth. Med. Ctr., Denver, 1961-87. 1st lt. F.A., U.S. Army, 1941-46, MTO, ETO. Mem. Am. Radio Relay League (nat. bd. dirs. 1986-99, honorary v.p. 1999—), Pi Gamma Mu, Delta Sigma Rho, Phi Alpha Delta. Avocations: amateur radio, skiing, mathematics, history. Home: 714 Pontiac St Denver CO 80220-5540 Office: PO Box 200878 Denver CO 80220-0878 E-mail: quiat@msn.com.

**QUICK, DANNY RICHARD,** computer systems engineer; b. Millen, Ga., Aug. 7, 1948; s. John Francis and Olene (Crane) Q.; m. Donna Kay Nobles, Oct. 13, 1973; children: Dexter Brian, Debby Kim. Cert. data processing, Strayer Coll., 1989. Enlisted USAF, 1967, advanced through grades to sr. master sgt., 1984; chief Message Processing Br. Orgn. Joints Chiefs of Staff, Pentagon, Washington, 1984—88, ret., 1988; sys. analyst Potomac Sys. Engring., Annandale, Va., 1988—89; sr. sys. cons. Wang Labs., Inc., Bethesda, Md., 1989—93; prin. sys. engr. Computer Scis. Corp., Falls Church, Va., 1993—2002; computer specialist Dept. of State, Washington, 2002—. Mem. methods & procedures panel U.S. Mil. Comm.-Electronics Bd., Washington, 1984-88, mem. call signs panel, 1984-88. Recipient Def. Meritorious Svc. medal Sec. Def., Washington, 1987, Meritorious Svc. medal Sec. Air Force, Washington, 1980; named one of 50 Outstanding Airmen of Yr., Airforce Mil. Pers. Ctr., Randolph AFB, Tex., 1983-84. Mem.: Am. Legion (editor Post-O-Gram 1983—84, exec. com. 1984—86). Republican. Methodist. Achievements include merge of the principal officers e-mail system and the foreign affairs information systems networks; led the Dept. of State test and deploy team in testing and deploying a Lotus Notes locally developed database program, which is installed on a Microsoft Windows NT/2000/2003 LAN, for distributing inbound and transmitting outbound diplomatic telegrams, throughout the Department of State and at American embassies and consulates worldwide; provide Tier 4 IT support for domestic and overseas operations. Home: 4 Caledon Ct Stafford VA 22556-1608 Office: Dept of State IRM/OPS/MSO/MSP/TD 7374 Boston Blvd Springfield VA 22153-2804 Personal E-mail: catpaws777@aol.com.

**QUICK, EDWARD RAYMOND,** museum director, educator, curator; b. L.A., Mar. 22, 1943; s. Donald Russell Quick and Gertrude Ruth (Albin) Thornbrough; m. Ruth Ann Lessig; children: Jeannette Lee, Russell Raymond. BA, U. Calif., Santa Barbara, 1971, MA, 1977. Adminstr. supr. Civil Service, Santa Ana, Calif., 1971-75; sr. computer operator Santa Barbara Rsch. Ctr., 1975-77; asst. collections curator Santa Barbara Mus. Art, 1977-78; collections mgr. Montgomery (Ala.) Mus. Fine Arts, 1978-80; asst. dir. Joslyn Art Mus., Omaha, 1980-85; dir. Sheldon Swope Art Mus., Terre Haute, Ind., 1985-95, Berman Mus., Anniston, Ala., 1995-97; mus. curator National Archives, Washington, 1998-2000, William Clinton Presdl. Libr. and Mus., 2000—04; staff curator mus. mgmt. Nat. Archives Office Presdl. Librs., Washington, 2004—. Adv. Ind. Arts Commn., Indpls., 1986-91; mem. Arts in Pub. Places Commn., Terre Haute, Ind., 1986-93; pres. Friends Vigo County Pub. Libr., 1988-95, treas., 1990-93. Author: Code of Practice for Couriering Museum Objects, 1985, Gilbert Brown Wilson and Herman Melville's "Moby Dick", 1993, The American West in the Berman Collections, 1997, Cattle Drive, 1997 others; co-author: Registrars in Record, 1987; contbg. author: Dante Marioni: Blown Glass, 2000. Bd. dirs. Vol. Action Ctr., Terre Haute, 1987-90, Terre Haute Cmty. Relief Effort for Environ. and Civic Spirit, 1989. With USAF, 1961-65, Air N.G., 1979-96. Mem. Am. Assn. Mus. (adv. 1994—, mgmt. and long-range planning com. 1994—), Assn. Ind. Mus., Am. Assn. State and Local History, Internat. Coun. Mus., Washington D.C. Print Club, Rotary Internat., Kiwanis Internat., Alpha Gamma Sigma. Avocation: museum administrative research. Office: Nat Archives Presdl Librs 8601 Adelphi Rd Rm 1320 College Park MD 20740-6001 Office Phone: 301-837-0611. Business E-Mail: edward.quick@nara.gov.

**QUICK, ELIZABETH L.,** lawyer; b. Izmir, Turkey, May 22, 1948; BA, Duke U., 1970; JD with honors, U. NC, 1974. Bar: NC 1974. Mem., trusts & estates Womble Carlyle Sandridge & Rice, Winston-Salem, NC; mem. mgmt. com. Vis. lectr. U. NC Sch. Law, 1977. Mem. U. NC Law Review, 1973—74, co-author, editor NC Estate Adminstrn. Manual, 1984; contbr. articles to profl. jours. Bd. dir. Cannon Found., Concord, NC, Reynolda House, inc., Winston-Salem, NC; bd. trustee Salem Coll. & Acad., Winston-Salem, NC; mem. Winston-Salem Found. Com. Federal Tax, com. Coll. Trust and Estate Counsel (bd chmn.); mem. ABA, NC Bar Assn. (pres. 1997-98), Forsyth County Bar Assn. (treas.), Order of Coif. Mailing: Womble Carlyle Sandridge & Rice PLLC PO Box 84 Winston Salem NC 27102 Office: Womble Carlyle Sandridge & Rice PLLC One West 4th St Winston Salem NC 27101 Office Phone: 336-721-3638. Office Fax: 336-733-8359. Business E-Mail: equick@wcsr.com.

**QUICK, PETER,** stock exchange executive; married. BS in Engring., U. Va.; postgrad., Stanford U. With U.S. Clearing Corp., 1983-94, pres., 1990-94, Quick & Reilly Group, Inc., 1994-96, Quick & Reilly, Inc., NYC, 1996—2000, Am. Stock Exch., NYC, 2000—, also bd. govs. Bd. dirs. Securities Industry Automation Corp., Reckson Associates Realty Corp. Bd. dirs. St. Francis Hospital, Good Shepherd Hospice; trustee Securities Industry Inst., Wharton Sch. U. Penn.; mem. nat. selection com. Jefferson scholar program U. Va.; trustee Museum of Am. Financial History. Recipient Ellis Island Medal of Honor award, 2001. Office: The Am Stock Exch 86 Trinity Pl New York NY 10006

**QUICK, THOMAS CLARKSON,** brokerage house executive; b. Westbury, N.Y., Feb. 26, 1955; s. Leslie Charles and Regina (Clarkson) Q. BS in Bus. Fairfield U., 1977. Br. mgr. Quick & Reilly Inc., Palm Beach, Fla., 1977-81; dir. The Quick & Reilly Group, N.Y.C., 1981-85; v.p. Quick & Reilly Inc., Palm Beach, 1981-86, pres., dir. N.Y.C., 1985-96, also bd. dirs.; COO Quick & Reilly/Fleet Securities, Inc., 1996-98; also bd. dirs.; pres., COO

Quick & Reilly Group Inc., 1998-2001. Trustee Security Industry Found. for Econ. Edn., Securities Industry Inst.; bd. dirs. Senesco Techs., corcoran.com., MindArrow Systems.com. Treas. Nat. Corp. Theater Fund, Alcoholism Coun. of N.Y.C; trustee U.S. Com.; bd. trustees Fairfield U.; mem. investment adv. bd. and endowment com. St. Jude Children's Rsch. Hosp., Memphis, 2001—; chmn. com. Wall Street Friends of St. Jude Children's Rsch. Hosp., 1979—, mem. endowment com.; bd. dirs. Best Buddies, Am. Ireland Fund. Mem. The Investment Assn. N.Y., N.Y. Stock Exch., Securities and Industry Assn. (econ. edn. com.), Am. Assn. of Sovereign Mil., Order of Malta, Young Pres.'s Orgn., Univ. Club, Friendly Sons of St. Patrick, Apawamis Country Club (Rye, N.Y.), The Beach Club (Palm Beach, Fla.), Chgo. Athletic Club., New York Yacht Club, Lotus Club, Lost Tree Club. Home: 291 El Vedado Way Palm Beach FL 33480 Office: 230 S County Rd Ste C Palm Beach FL 33480 E-mail: tquick@quick-reilly.com.

**QUICK, WILLIAM THOMAS,** writer, scriptwriter; b. Muncie, Ind., May 30, 1946; s. Clifford Willett and Della May (Ellis) Quick. Student, Ind. U., 1964-66. Pres. Iceberg Prodns., San Francisco, 1986—. Author: Dreams of Flesh and Sand, 1988, Dreams of God and Men, 1989, Yesterday's Pawn, 1989, Systems, 1989, Singularities, 1990; author: (as Quentin Thomas) Chains of Light, 1992, Ascensions, 1997; author: (as Margaret Allan) The Mammoth Stone, 1993, Keeper of the Stone, 1994, The Last Mammoth, 1995, Spirits Walking Woman, 1997; author: (as W.T. Quick) Star Control: Interbellum, 1996, American Gothic: Family, 1996, Sister of the Sky, 1998; co-author (with William Shatner): Quest for Tomorrow: Delta Search, 1997, Quest for Tomorrow: In Alien Hands, 1997, Quest for Tomorrow: Step Into Chaos, 1999, Quest for Tomorrow: Beyond the Stars, 2000, Shadow Planet, 2003; co-author: (with Richard Curtis) How to Get Your E-Book Published, 2001; author (as Sean Kiernan): Roar, 1998, Roar: The Cauldron, 1998, Roar: The Talisman, 1998, Mortal Kombat: Noob Saibot, 1999, The Hollow Man, 2000, Planet of the Apes, 2001, Planet of the Apes: The Fall, 2002, Planet of the Apes: Colony, 2003, Inner Cirlces, 2005. Mem.: Authors Guild, Sci. Fiction and Fantasy Writers Am. Home: 118 Dolphin Ct San Francisco CA 94124-2945

**QUICKSILVER, WILLIAM TODD,** lawyer; b. St. Louis, July 26, 1952; AB magna cum laude, Princeton U., 1974; JD, U. Chgo., 1978. Bar: Calif. 1978. COO, dep. mng. ptnr. Manatt, Phelps & Phillips, LLP. Dir. Pub. Counsel Law Ctr.; spkr. in field. Mem.: ABA, Century City Bar Assn. Office: Manatt Phelps & Phillips LLP 1135 W Olympic Blvd Los Angeles CA 90064-1614 Office Phone: 310-312-4210. Office Fax: 310-312-4224. E-mail: wquicksilver@manatt.com.*

**QUIE, PAUL GERHARDT,** pediatrician, educator; b. Dennison, Minn., Feb. 3, 1925; s. Albert Knute and Nettie Marie (Jacobson) Quie; m. Elizabeth Holmes, Aug. 10, 1951; children: Katie, Bill, Paul, David. BA, St. Olaf Coll., 1949; MD, Yale U., 1953; PhD (hon.), U. Lund, 1993. Diplomate Am. Bd. Pediat., Nat. Bd. Med. Examiners (mem.). Intern Hennepin County Hosp., 1953—54; pediatric resident U. Minn. Hosps., 1957—59; mem. faculty U. Minn. Med. Sch., 1959—, prof. pediatrics, 1968—99, prof. microbiology, 1974—99, assoc. dean of students, 1992—. Am. Legion meml. heart research prof., 1974—91, Regents prof., 1991; Regent's prof. emeritus, 1999—; interim dir. Ctr. for Biomed. Ethics U. Minn. Med. Sch., 1985—86; attending physician Hennepin County Hosp., 1959—91. Cons. U. Minn. Nursery Sch., 1959—91; chief of staff U. Minn. Hosp., 1979—84; vis. physician Radcliffe Infirmary, Oxford, England, 1971—72; mem. Adv. Allergy and Infectious Disease Coun., 1976—80; mem. pediat. com. NRC, 1978; mem. bd. sci. counselors Gamble Inst., 1985—90; vis. prof. U. Bergen, 1991; hon. prof. U. Hong Kong Med. Sch., 1995; vis. prof. pediat. Chubu Hosp., Nagasaki, Japan, 1996; co-dir. internat. med. edn. and rsch. program U. Minn. Med. Sch., 1998—. Editl. bd. Pediat., 1970—76, Rev. Infectious Diseases, 1989—92. Pres. Fairview Found., 1998—99; bd. dirs. Ctr. for Victims of Torture. Med. officer USNR, 1954—57. Recipient E. Mead-Johnson award, Am. Acad. Pediat., 1971, Shotwell award, Hennipen Med. Soc., 2001, Gold Headed Cane award in Pediatrics, 2005; fellow Guggenheim, 1971—72, Alexander von Humboldt, 1986; scholar John and Mary R. Markle, 1960—65. Mem.: Eliz Glaser Pediat. AIDS Found., Minn. Acad. Medicine (pres. 1993—94), Assn. Am. Physicians, Am. Acad. Pediat., Minn. Acad. Pediat., Am. Soc. Clin. Investigation, Am. Pediatric Soc. (coun. 1976—83, pres. 1987—88), Soc. Pediatric Rsch., Infectious Diseases Soc. Am. (coun. 1977—82, pres. 1985, Bristol award 1994), Am. Soc. Microbiology, Am. Fedn. Clin. Rsch., Minn. Med. Found. (pres. 1986—88), N.W. Pediat. Soc., Inst. Medicine of NAS. Achievements include research in function of human leukocytes and international medical education and research. Home: 2154 Commonwealth Ave Saint Paul MN 55108-1717 Office: PO Box 293 Minneapolis MN 55440-0293 Office Phone: 612-626-2558. Business E-Mail: quiex001@umn.edu.

**QUIGGINS, LARRY DALE,** theater educator; b. St. Louis, Jan. 6, 1962; s. Walter Louis Quiggins and Mildred Hoskinson; m. Elizabeth Marie McEvoy, May 30, 1986; children: Benjamin T'omas, James Tiberious. A in Comm., Florissant Valley C.C., St. Louis, 1983; BA, Lindenwood U., St. Charles, Mo., 1998, MFA, 2000. Owner Bug's Comics & Games, Inc., St. Louis, 1991—; prof. Lindenwood U., 2001—. Tour dir. Florissant Valley C.C., St. Louis, 1984—91, Off the Cuff Prodns., 2000—01. Author: (theatrical play: adaptation) Scrooge: A Christmas Carol, (children's play) The Adventures of Cookie-Man; actor: (improvisation troupe) NIghtshift Improv Troupe; dir.: The Nick of Time Players. Avocations: theater, comic book collecting, creative writing, music. Home: 3218 Catesby Ln Saint Charles MO 63301 Office: Lindenwood U 209 S Kings Hwy Saint Charles MO 63301 Office Phone: 636-949-4850. Personal E-Mail: nevellah@msn.com. E-mail: lquiggins@lindenwood.edu.

**QUIGLEY, DEBORAH HEWITT,** adult education educator; d. Merritt Lambert and Gertrude Bush Hewitt; m. Edward James Quigley, III; children: Margaret Sarah, Edward James IV. AA, Coll. Marin, 1972; BA in History with honors, U. Calif., Davis, 1974; multiple subject credential, Dominican Coll., 1975. Clear subject credential with supplementary added math. Calif., 2005, cert. multiple subject tchg. credential with supplementary authorization to math. State of Calif. Commn. on Tchr. Credentialing, 2005. Tchr. Ladybug Presch., Kentfield, Calif., 1975—77; head tchr. Buttons & Bows Nursery Sch., San Rafael, Calif., 1977—78; parent edn. tchr. Nat. City (Calif.) Adult Sch., 1987—, child devel. tchr., 1996—2002, older adult tchr., 2002—. Mem. parent edn. Western Assn. Sch. and Colls. com. Sweetwater Union H.S. Dist., Chula Vista, Calif., 1997—98. Counselor, asst. leader, scout leader Boy Scouts and Girl Scouts, San Diego, 1986—2002; parent assn. mem., newsletter editor Marian Cath. H.S., San Diego, 1998—2002. Lt. j.g. USN, 1978—81. Named Parent Educator of Yr., San Diego Assn. Parenting Educators, 1995, Marian Cath. H.S., 2000, 2002. Mem.: NEA, Calif. Coun. for Adult Edn., Nat. Assn. for the Edn. Young Children. Avocations: reading, sewing, ice skating. Office: Nat City Adult Edn Ctr 517 Miles of Cars Way National City CA 91950 Personal E-Mail: quigleydebbie@hotmail.com.

**QUIGLEY, JAMES B.,** diversified financial services company executive; BS in Internat. Econs., George Washington U. Elliott Sch. Internat. Affairs. With NY Syndicate Grp. Merrill Lynch, 1983, exec. dir. London Syndicate Grp., head US High Grade Syndicate Grp., head Debt Transactions Grp., head global issuer client grp. for global debt markets, sr. v.p., head client strategies for global debt markets, vice chmn. exec. client coverage grp., 2002—, head L.Am. global markets and investment banking, 2006—, pres. Merrill Lynch Internat., Inc. Office: Merrill Lynch 4 World Fin Ctr 250 Vesey St New York NY 10080*

**QUIGLEY, JAMES H.,** finance company executive; b. Utah, 1953; m. Bonnie Quigley; 3 children. BS, Utah State U., 1974; PhD in comml. sci. (hon.), Bentley Coll., Waltham, Mass., 2005. With Deloitte & Touche USA LLP, 1974—; asst. to chmn., sec. to bd. dirs., chief staff to office of chmn., nat. industry leader mfg. practice, vice chmn., regional mng. ptnr. N.E. practice, 1999—2003, CEO, 2003—; also bd. dirs.; bd. dirs. Deloitte Touche Tohmatsu. Bd. dirs. US C. of C., Catalyst; bd. trustees Fin. Acctg. Found. Bd. dirs. Partnership for NYC; bd. trustees Ctrl. Park Conservancy; nat. adv. coun.

Brigham Young U. Marriott Sch. Mgmt.; mem leadership com. Lincoln Ctr. Corp. Fund. Mem.: Union League Club, Econ. Club NY. Office: Deloitte & Touche USA LLP 1633 Broadway New York NY 10019-6754 Office Phone: 212-489-1600. Office Fax: 212-489-1687.*

**QUIGLEY, JOHN BERNARD,** law educator; b. St. Louis, Oct. 1, 1940; s. John Bernard and Ruth Rosina (Schieber) Q. BA, Harvard U., 1962, MA, LLB, 1966. Bar: Ohio 1973, Mass. 1967, U.S. Dist. Ct. (so. dist.) Ohio 1976, U.S. Ct. Appeals (6th cir.) 1986, U.S. Supreme Ct. 1989. Research assoc. Harvard U. Law Sch., Cambridge, Mass., 1967-69; prof. law Ohio State U., Columbus, 1969—. Author: Basic Laws on the Structure of the Soviet State, 1969, The Soviet Foreign Trade Monopoly, 1974, Palestine and Israel: A Challenge to Justice, 1990, The Ruses for War: American Interventionism since World War II, 1992, Flight into the Maelstrom: Soviet Immigration to Israel and Middle East Peace, 1997, Genocide in Cambodia, 2000, The Case for Palestine: An International Law Perspective, 2005, The Genocide Convention: An International Law Analysis, 2006. Mem. Nat. Lawyers Guild (v.p. 1977-79), Am. Soc. Internat. Law, AAUP. Avocations: tennis, speed skating, violin. Office: Ohio State U Coll of Law Coll of Law 55 W 12th Ave Columbus OH 43210-1338

**QUIGLEY, JOHN MICHAEL,** economist, educator; b. NYC, Feb. 12, 1942; BS with distinction, U.S. Air Force Acad., 1964; MSc with honors, U. Stockholm, Sweden, 1965; AM, Harvard U., 1971, PhD, 1972. Commd. 2d lt. USAF, 1964, advanced through grades to capt., 1968; asst. prof. econs. Yale U., 1972-74, assoc. prof., 1974-81; prof. pub. policy U. Calif., Berkeley, 1979—, prof. econs., 1981—, Chancellor's prof., 1997—, I. Donald Terner disting. prof., 1999—, chmn. dept. econs., 1992-95; vis. prof. econs. and stats. U. Gothenberg, 1978. Cons. numerous govt. agys. and pvt. firms; econometrician Hdqrs. U.S. Air Force, Pentagon, 1965-68; research assoc. Nat. Bur. Econ. Research, N.Y.C., 1968-78; mem. com. on nat. urban policy NAS, 1985-93. Author, editor, contbr. articles to profl. jours.; editor in chief Reg. Sci. and Urban Econs., 1987-2003; mem. editl. bd. many sci. and scholarly jours. Fulbright scholar, 1964-65; fellow NSF, 1968-69, Woodrow Wilson, 1968-71, Harvard IBM, 1969-71, NDEA, 1969-71, Thord-Gray Am. Scandinavian Found. 1971-72, Social Sci. Research Council, 1971-72. Mem. Am. Econ. Assn., Econometric Soc., Regional Sci. Assn. (bd. dirs. 1986—), Nat. Tax Assn., Assn. for Pub. Policy and Mgmt. (bd. dirs. 1986-89, v.p. 1987-89), Am. Real Estate and Urban Econs. Assn. (bd. dirs. 1987-2001, pres. 1995-97). Home: 875 Hilldale Ave Berkeley CA 94708-1319 Office: U Calif 2607 Hearst Ave Berkeley CA 94720-7305 Business E-Mail: quigley@econ.berkeley.edu.

**QUIGLEY, LEONARD VINCENT,** lawyer; b. Kansas City, Mo., June 21, 1933; s. Joseph Vincent and Rosemary (Cannon) Q.; m. Lynn Mathis Pfohl, May 23, 1964; children: Leonard Matthew, Cannon Louise, Daniel Pfohl, Megan Mathis. AB, Coll. Holy Cross, 1953; LL.B. magna cum laude, Harvard U., 1959; LL.M. in Internat. Law, NYU, 1962. Bar: N.Y. 1960. Assoc. Cravath, Swaine & Moore, N.Y.C., 1959-67; ptnr. Paul, Weiss, Rifkind, Wharton & Garrison, N.Y.C., 1968—2004; gen. counsel Archaeol. Inst. Am., Boston. Served to lt. USN, 1953-56. Mem. ABA, Can. Bar Assn., N.Y. State Bar, Coun. Fgn. Rels., Assn. Bar City N.Y., Harvard Club (N.Y.C.), West Side Tennis Club (Forest Hills, N.Y.). Office Phone: 212-373-3320. Business E-Mail: lquigley@paulweiss.com.

**QUIGLEY, MARTIN SCHOFIELD,** writer, educator; b. Chgo., Nov. 24, 1917; s. Martin Joseph and Gertrude Margaret (Schofield) Q.; m. Katherine J. Dunphy, July 2, 1946; children: Martin, Elin, William, Kevin, Karen, Patricia, John, Mary Katherine, Peter. AB magna cum laude, Georgetown U., 1939; MA, Columbia U., 1973, EdD, 1975. Reporter Motion Picture Herald, N.Y.C. and Hollywood, Calif., 1939-41; with overseas br. OWI, 1942; secret war work U.S. Govt., 1943-45; various editl. and mgmt. posts Quigley Pub. Co., Inc., N.Y.C., 1946—2001, pres., 1964-2001, chmn., 2001—; staff. dept. higher and adult edn. Tchrs. Coll., 1974-75; prof. higher edn. grad. courses Baruch Coll. CUNY, 1977-89; prof. higher edn. grad. courses Tchrs. Coll. Columbia U., 1979-80, 90; prof. higher edn. grad. courses Seton Hall U. 1981-82. Pres. QWS, Inc., 1975-80; ednl. cons.; cons. supt. schs. N.Y. Archdiocese, 1962-70 Author: Great Gaels, 1944, 2d edit. 1997, Roman Notes, 1946, Magic Shadows--the story of the origin of motion pictures, 1948, Government Relations of Five Universities in Washington, D.C., 1975, Peace Without Hiroshima-Secret Action at the Vatican in Spring of 1945, 1991, First Century of Film, 1995, A U.S. Spy in Ireland, 1999, Community College Movement in Perspective, 2003, Glory Days of American Film-1915-65, 2006; co-author: Catholic Action in Practice, 1962, Films in America, 1969; editor: New Screen Techniques, 1953. Pres. N.Y. Christian Family Movement, 1960-62, mem. nat. exec. com., 1960-65; founder, chmn. N.Y. Ind. Schs. Opportunity Project, 1965-77; pres. Found. Internat. Coop., 1960-65; bd. dirs. Will Rogers Inst., Motion Picture Pioneers; treas. Religious Edn. Assn. U.S. and Can., 1975-81, chmn., 1981-84; trustee Village of Larchmont, N.Y., 1977-79, mayor, 1980-84; mem. Laymen's Nat. Bible Assn., 1981—; trustee Am. Bible Soc., 1984—; bd. dirs. William J. Donovan Meml. Found., 1994-2001. Mem.: Larchmont Yacht. Roman Catholic. Home: 8 Pheasant Run Larchmont NY 10538-3423 Personal E-mail: greatgaels@aol.com.

**QUIGLEY, MICHAEL,** lawyer; b. Flushing, NY; AB, Univ. Calif., Berkeley, 1980; JD cum laude, Pepperdine Univ., 1980. Bar: Calif. 1983, US Ct. of Fed. Claims 1987, US Tax Ct. 1988, DC 1989, US Supreme Ct. 1991, US Ct. of Appeals (fed. cir.) 1991. Trial atty., tax divsn. US Dept. Justice; ptnr., internat. taxation and mem. mgmt. com. Akin Gump Strauss Hauer & Feld LLP, Washington; ptnr., head tax controversy practice White & Case LLP, Washington, 2006—. Mem.: ABA, DC Bar Assn., State Bar of Calif., Fed. Bar Assn. (chmn. sect. taxation 1993—94, 1995—96). Office: White & Case LLP 701 Thirteenth St NW Washington DC 20005 E-mail: michaelquigley@whitecase.com.

**QUIGLEY, ROB WELLINGTON,** architect; b. Calif., 1945; B, Univ. Utah, 1969. Registered Architect, Calif., 1976. Architect Peace Corps, Chile; prin. Quigley Architects, San Diego, Palo Alto, 1974—. Adj. prof. arch. Univ. Calif., San Diego; vis. design prof. Harvard Univ. Grad. Sch. Design, 1991, Univ. Tex., Austin, 1994, Univ. Calif., Berkeley, 1997, 98; appt. in field; invited juror and advisor. Prin. works include San Diego New Main Libr. (Honor award, AIA San Diego, 1998), Sherman Heights Cmty. Ctr. (Citation, AIA San Diego, 1990, Orchid, San Diego Orch. AIA, 1992, Merit award, AIA San Diego, 1996), Golden Hill Community Ctr., Baltic Inn, San Diego (Honor award, AIA San Diego, 1987, Panda award, City of San Diego, 1988), 202 Island Inn (One of "Ten Best Designs of 1992," Time Mag., 1993, Nat. AIA Honor award, 1993, Merit award. AIA San Diego, 1993, Honor award with Distinction, AIA Calif. Coun., 1994), Solana Beach Transit Sta. (Orchid, San Diego Chpt., AIA, 1996, Honor award, AIA Calif. Coun., 1998), Escondido Transit Sta. (Citation, AIA San Diego, 1990, Orchid, AIA San Diego, 1991, Beautification award, City of Escondido, 1990), San Diego Children's Mus., Calif., Student Academic Services Facility, U. Calif. San Diego, San Diego Historic Harbor Front, West Valley Branch Libr. (Divine Detail, AIA San Diego, 2003, Merit award, AIA Santa Clara, 2004), Leslie Shao-ming Sun Field Station, Stanford U. (Merit award, AIA San Diego, 2003, Honor award, AIA Santa Clara, 2004, COTE Top Ten Green Buildings, Nat. AIA, 2005), Opportunity Ctr. for the Midpeninsula (Advocacy Planning award, Northern Sect. Am. Planning Assn., 2003), Shaw Lopez Park, Casa Feliz, and several others, solo exhibitions, Retrospective, So. Calif. Inst. of Architecture, Santa Monica, 1982, Exhibit of Recent Work, UCLA, 1984, Recent Work, Portland State U., 1991, exhibitions include Visual Communication Towards Architecture, Installation Gallery, San Diego, 1982, Don Clos Pegase Competition, San Francisco Mus. Contemporary Art, 1985, The Emerging Generation in the USA, Global Architecture Gallery, Tokyo, Japan, 1987, Five Choose Five, Nat. AIA Conf., St. Louis, 1989, Fabrications, San Francisco Mus. Modern Art, 1998, Books, Bytes and Mortar, Mus. Contemporary Art, San Diego, 2001, Modern Trains and Splendid Stations, Art Inst. Chgo., 2002, and several others; co-author: (monograph) Buildings & Projects, 1996. Named Headliner of Yr. in Architecture, San Diego Press Club, 1995; named one of 100

Foremost Architects of the World, AD 100, Architectural Digest, 1991, 88 San Diegans to Watch in '88', San Diego Mag., 1988, The San Diego 50 People to Watch in 1997, 1997; recipient Presdl. Commendation for Exemplary Cmty. Svc., 1988, Firm award, AIA Calif. Coun., 1995, Maybeck award, 2005, The Irving Gill award, AIA San Diego, 1997, several mag. and cmty. program awards, several awards for design excellence from the Nat. AIA, AIA Santa Clara, AIA San Diego, and AIA Calif. Coun.; fellow Inst. for Urban Design, 1996. Fellow: AIA; mem.: NAD. Office: Quigley Architects 434 W Cedar St San Diego CA 92101 also: 210 High St Palo Alto CA 94301 Office Phone: 619-232-0888, 650-328-8030. E-mail: office@robquigley.com.

**QUIGLEY, ROBERT CHARLES,** insurance industry consultant; b. Phila. 1949; s. James and Kathrine Regina (Kinckiner) Q.; m. Barbara Jeanne Browne, 1971; children: Robert J., Michael J., Brian A., Jason T. BS in Acctg., Pa. State U., 1970. CPA, Pa., NJ. Sr. acct. Touche Ross & Co., Phila., 1970—72; dir. acctg. policy and rsch. Ins. Co. of N.Am., Phila., 1972—81; asst. treas. Reliance Ins. Co., Phila., 1981—85; v.p., treas. Mut. Fire Marine and Inland Ins. Co., Phila., 1985—86; owner Quigley & Assocs., Hatboro, Pa., 1987—. Team leader accreditation Nat. Assn. of Ins. Commrs., Kansas City, 1992—. Author: (with others) Property and Liability Insurance Accounting, 5th edit., 1991. With USMCR, 1967. Mem.: AICPAs, Internat. Assn. Ins. Receivers, AIDA Reinsurance and Ins. Arbitration Soc. U.S. (cert. arbitrator), Soc. of Ins. Fin. Mgmt. Republican. Presbyterian. Avocations: reading, writing. Office: PO Box 147 Hatboro PA 19040-0147 Business E-Mail: RCQCPA@aol.com.

**QUIGLEY, STEPHEN HOWARD,** executive editor; b. Boston, May 29, 1951; s. John Joseph Sr. and Anne Margaret (O'Brien) Quigley; m. Suzanne Elizabeth Daley, July 8, 1980; children: Benjamin Parker, Theodore Hunter, Margaret Hunter. BA in French and Internat. Rels., Dartmouth Coll., 1973. Sales rep. Addison-Wesley Pub. Co., Inc., Reading, Mass., 1973—75, math. editor, 1975—81, regional sales mgr., 1981—85; sr. math editor Scott, Foresman and Co., Chgo., 1985—88, PWS-KENT Pub. Co., Boston, 1988—95; exec. editor math. and stats. sci., tech. and med. pub. divsn. John Wiley and Sons, Inc., Marblehead, Mass., 1995—. Mem. Independence Day Celebration Commn., 1987—88; mem. Eveleth Sch. liaison Sch. PTA, Marblehead, Mass., 1989—90, vice chair sch. com., 1991—92, chair sch. comm., 1992—93; water safety chmn., bd. dirs. Greater Lynn chpt. ARC, 1978—81; leader Boy Scouts Am., Explorers Group, Marblehead, 1976—79; swim ofcl. Ill. High Sch. Ofcls. Assn., 1984—88; lector Star of Sea Ch., Marblehead, 1988—; dir. Goldthwait Reservation, Marblehead; vol. Marblehead Little Theatre, 2001—; Marblehead/Swampscott YMCA Nostalgia Weekend Swim Off, 2005. Recipient Club of Yr. award. Darmouth Coll., 1988, Disting. Book award, Assn. Am. Publ., 1999, 2001, 2003. Mem.: ASCD, Nat. Coun. Tchrs. Math., Nat. Fedn. Interscholastic Ofcls. Assn., Am. Math. Assn. Two-Yr. Colls., Am. Statis. Assn., Math. Assn. Am., Am. Math. Soc., Geol. Soc. Am., Glenview C. of C. (mem. accreditation team 1988), Friends of the Performing Arts, North Shore Friends in Pub. (founding group), Chgo. Dartmouth Club (pres. 1988—89), North Shore (Mass.) Dartmouth Club, Corinthian Yacht Club (rec. chair, operating com. 1997—2000), Rotary (bd. dirs. Boston 1990—95, Svc. award 1988). Republican. Roman Catholic. Avocations: swimming, sailing, tennis, singing, computers. Home: 10 Leicester Rd Marblehead MA 01945-1817 Office: Wiley Pub 2 Hooper St Marblehead MA 01945-3431 Office Phone: 781-631-0062. Business E-Mail: squigley@wiley.com.

**QUIGLEY, THOMAS J.,** lawyer; b. Mt. Carmel, Pa., July 22, 1923; s. James S. and Helen C. (Laughlin) Q.; m. Joan R. Reifke, Aug. 11, 1956; children: Thomas J., Jr., Joan E. James S. AB, Bucknell U., 1947; LLB, Yale U., 1950. Bar: Ohio, U.S. Dist. Ct. Ohio, U.S. Ct. Appeals (6th and D.C. cirs.). With Squire, Sanders & Dempsey, 1950—, adminstr. labor dept., 1971-80, mng. ptnr., Washington, 1980-85; nat. vice chmn., 1985-86; nat. chmn., 1986-90. Past pres., dir. Nat. Symphony Orch., nat. trustee Musical Arts Assn. Cleve.; bd. dirs. Belgian Am. C. of C. 1st lt. USAAF, 1942-45. Decorated D.F.C., Air medal with oak leaf cluster, Belgium's Order of the Crown. Mem. ABA, Ohio Bar Assn., D.C. Bar Assn., Cleve. Bar Assn., Fed. City Coun., Yale Law Sch. Alumni Assn. Roman Catholic. Clubs: Yale (N.Y.C.), Edgartown Yacht (Mass.), Edgartown Reading Room, Chevy Chase, Metropolitan (Wash.). Office: Squire Sanders & Dempsey PO Box 407 1201 Pennsylvania Ave NW Washington DC 20004-2491 also: Key Tower Bldg Cleveland OH 44114

**QUIGNEY, THERESA ANN,** special education educator; b. East Cleveland, Ohio, June 19, 1952; d. James and Lenora Mary (McDonald) Q.; m. Joseph Carl Lang, July 23, 1983. BA, Notre Dame Coll., 1974; MEd, Cleve. State U., 1980; PhD, Kent State U., 1992. Cert. tchr. handicapped K-12; cert. ednl. adminstrv. specialist edn. of exceptional pupils; cert. ednl. supr.; cert. elem. prin.; cert. h.s. prin. cert. tchr. French K-12, Ohio. Spl. edn. tchr. Newbury (Ohio) Local Schs., 1974—80; county supr., specific learning disabilities and behavior handicaps Geauga County Bd. Edn., Chardon, Ohio, 1980—86, 1987—88; asst. prof. spl. edn. West Chester (Pa.) U., 1992—93; asst. prof. edn. Heidelberg Coll., Tiffin, Ohio, 1993—94; assoc. prof. spl. edn. Cleve. State U., 1994—, coord. spl. edn. program Coll. Edn., 2000—02. Ednl. rschr.; presenter in field. Contbr. articles to profl. jours., chapters to books. Vol. cons. Tchrs. for Action Rsch. South Euclid/Lyndhurst (Ohio) Sch. Dist., 1996—; past participant issues task force Ohio Coun. for Exceptional Children; presenter, participant Oxford Round Table, Oxford U., England; past bd. mem. Camp Sue Osborne, Lake County, Ohio; mem. steering com. State Improvement Grant (Edn.), 2000—02. Grantee Ohio State Supt.'s Task Force on Spl. Edn., 1997, Cleve. State U. Coll. Edn., 1997, Am. Sch. Counselor's Assn.; recipient achievement recognition Assn. for Children and Adults with Learning Disabilities, Ohio, 1980. Mem. CEC, ASCD, Am. Ednl. Rsch. Assn., Learning Disabilities Assn., Mid-We. Ednl. Rsch. Assn., Coun. for Learning Disabilities, Kappa Delta Pi, Phi Delta Kappa, Pi Lambda Theta. Avocations: travel, writing, reading, sketching. Office: Cleveland State Univ Euclid Ave at E 24th St Cleveland OH 44115 Business E-Mail: t.quigney@csuohio.edu.

**QUILLEN, CECIL DYER, JR.,** lawyer, consultant; b. Kingsport, Tenn., Jan. 21, 1937; s. Cecil D. and Mary Louise (Carter) Q.; m. Vicey Ann Childress, Apr. 1, 1961; children: Cecil D. III, Ann C. BS, Va. Poly. Inst., 1958; LLB, U. Va., 1962. Bar: Va. 1962, N.Y. 1963, Tenn. 1974. Atty. patent dept. Eastman Kodak Co., Rochester, NY, 1962—65; atty. patent sect. Tenn. Eastman Co. (divsn. Eastman Kodak), Kingsport, 1965—69, mgr. patent sect., 1969—72, mgr. licensing, 1972—74, sec. and asst. chief counsel, 1974—76, v.p., chief counsel, 1983—85; dir. patent litigation Eastman Kodak, 1976—82, dir. antitrust litigation, 1978—82, v.p., assoc. gen. counsel, 1986. sr. v.p., gen. counsel, dir., 1986—92; sr. advisor Putnam, Hayes, Bartlett and PHB Hagler Bailly, Washington, 1992—2000, Cornerstone Rsch., Washington, 2000—. Bd. dirs. Pub. Patent Found., 2006—. Mem. ABA, Va. State Bar, Am. Intellectual Property Law Assn., Va. Poly. Inst. Com. of 100. Assn. Gen. Counsel, Phi Kappa Phi, Omicron Delta Kappa, Tau Beta Pi, Phi Lambda Upsilon. Office Phone: 202-912-8930. Personal E-Mail: cecilquillen@prodigy.net. Business E-Mail: cquillen@cornerstone.com.

**QUILLEN, CECIL DYER, III,** lawyer; b. Rochester, N.Y., Aug. 15, 1963; s. Cecil Dyer, Jr. and Vicey Ann (Childress) Q.; m. Mary Stuart Humes, Oct. 20, 1990; children: Caroline, James C.D., George, Elizabeth. AB magna cum laude, Harvard U., 1985; JD, U. Va., 1988. Bar: N.Y. 1989, D.C. 1991, U.S. Ct. Appeals (4th cir.) 1989. Law clk., Sr. Cir. Judge U.S. Ct. Appeals (4th cir.), Richmond, Va., 1988-89; assoc. Sullivan & Cromwell, N.Y.C., 1989-95, Linklaters, N.Y.C., 1995-96, ptnr., 1996—, ptnr. London office, 2000—. Spkr. various profl. confs. Notes editor Va. Law Rev., 1987-88. Mem. ABA, N.Y. State Bar Assn., Assn. Bar City of N.Y., Raven Soc., Order of Coif, Phi Beta Kappa. Office: Linklaters One Silk St London EC2Y 8HQ England

**QUILLEN, LLOYD DOUGLAS,** oil and gas executive; b. Red House, Ky., Sept. 9, 1943; s. Carter Livingston and Irene (Bolson) Q.; m. Leslie J. Johnson (div. Jan. 1980); children: Tracey, David; m. Debra Gale Wagner, Aug. 7, 1982; children: Justin, Meghan, Bradley. BA, U. Ky., 1965, JD, 1969; student,

Emory U., 1966-67. Bar: Ky., 1970, Tex., 1986. Atty. Phillips Petroleum Co., Denver, 1970-76; mgr. real estate and claims Phillips Petroleum Co. Euro. Afr., London, 1976-79; dir. govt. and comml. affairs Phillips Petroleum Co. & Subs., Lagos, Nigeria, 1979-82; mgr. internat. gas devel. Phillips Petroleum Co., Bartlesville, Okla., 1982-84; dir. laws and regulations Phillips 66 Natural Gas Co., Bartlesville, Okla., 1984-88; mgr. bus. devel. and mktg. HUFFCO/VICO Indonesia Co., Jakarta, Indonesia, 1988-93; v.p. Lng Texaco Natural Gas Internat., 1997; sr. v.p. Texaco Global Gas and Power, 1997—2001; sr. LNG comml. advisor Chevron, 2002—. Cons. Govt. of Nigeria, Lagos, 1977-82; gas cons. LNG/Internat. Gas, Houston, 1993-97. Charter mem. Statue of Liberty Ellis Island Found., N.Y.C., 1983; pro bono counsel Landmark Preservation Coun., Bartlesville, 1986-87, Washington County Sr. Citizens, Inc., Bartlesville, 1987—, Pro Bono Coll., Tex. Bar Assn., 1997-2004; cubmaster Boy Scouts Am.; pres. Pine Brook Cmty. Assn., NASA Little League coach. Recipient Speak Out award Am. Petroleum Inst., 1972; named to hon. order Ky. Cols., 1969. Mem.: Houston Vols. Lawyers Assn., Tex. Bar Assn. Republican. Avocations: woodworking, gardening, sailing, scuba diving, travel. Office Phone: 281-480-7874. E-mail: guillld@houston.rr.com.

**QUILLEN, MICHAEL J.,** energy executive; Grad., Va. Tech. Univ. Pres., CEO Addington Inc.; v.p. ops. NERCO Coal Corp.; v.p. AMVEST Corp.; pres. Pittston Coal Sales Corp.; v.p. ops. Pittston Coal Co.; exec. v.p. ops. Am. Metals & Coal Internat., 1998—2002; pres. Alpha Natural Resources LLC, Abingdon, Va., 2002—, CEO, 2003—; pres. ANR Holdings Inc., Abingdon, Va., 2002—, CEO, 2003—; pres. Alpha Natural Resources Inc., Abingdon, Va., 2004—. Office: Alpha Natural Resources 1 Alpha Pl PO Box 2345 Abingdon VA 24212*

**QUILLEN, WILLIAM TATEM,** retired judge, lawyer, educator; b. Camden, NJ, Jan. 15, 1935; s. Robert James and Gladys Collings (Tatem) Quillen; m. Marcia Everhart Stirling, June 27, 1959; children: Carol Everhart, Tracey Tatem. BA, Williams Coll., 1956; LLB, Harvard U., 1959; LLM, U. Va., 1982; LLD (hon.), Widener U. Sch. Law, 2002. Bar: Del. 1959. Assoc. Richards, Layton & Finger, Wilmington, Del., 1963—64; adminstrv. asst. to Gov. of Del., 1965; assoc. judge Superior Ct. of Del., 1966—73; chancellor State of Del., 1973—76; sr. v.p. Wilmington Trust Co., 1976—78; justice Supreme Ct. of Del., 1978—83; ptnr. Potter Anderson & Corroon, Wilmington, 1983—86; gen. counsel, v.p. Howard Hughes Med. Inst., 1986—91; sec. of state State of Del., Dover, 1993—94; assoc. judge Superior Ct. Del., Wilmington, 1994—2000; of counsel Drinker Biddle & Reath, Wilmington, 2003—. Mem. adj. faculty Widener U. Sch. Law, Wilmington, 1976—83, 1985—86, 1995—2000, 2002—, disting. vis. prof. law, 1992—94, 2001—02. Trustee Widener U., 1979—91; Dem. candidate for gov. Del., 1984. With JAGC USAF, 1959—62. Mem.: ABA, Del. State Bar Assn., Wilmington Club, Phi Beta Kappa. Democrat. Presbyterian. Office Phone: 302-467-4219. Business E-Mail: william.quillen@dbr.com.

**QUILLIAN, J. KIRK,** lawyer; b. Akron, Ohio, Mar. 1, 1946; BA, Emory U., 1968; JD, U. Va., 1973. Bar: Ga. 1973. Assoc. Troutman Sanders LLP, Atlanta, 1973—77, ptnr., 1978—; practice group leader, complex litig. Named a Super Lawyer, Atlanta Mag., 2004, Legal Elite in business litig., Ga. Trend Mag., 2004. Mem. ABA, State Bar Ga. (mem. bar-media conf. 1990—), Atlanta Bar Assn. (chmn. continuing legal edn. com. 1987-88), fellow, Am. Bar Found.; Am. Inn of Ct. Master, Lamar Inn of Ct. Founding Master, Lawyers Club Atlanta. Office: Troutman Sanders LLP 600 Peachtree St NE Ste 5200 Atlanta GA 30308-2216 Office Phone: 404-885-3204. Office Fax: 404-962-6660. Business E-Mail: kirk.quillian@troutmansanders.com.

**QUILLIAN, WARREN WILSON, II,** pediatrician, educator; b. Miami, Fla., Jan. 21, 1936; s. Warren Wilson and Rosabel (Brown) Q.; m. Sallie Ruth Creel, July 26, 1958; children: Rutledge, Ruth, Warren C., Frances. MD, Emory U., 1961. Diplomate Am. Bd. Pediat. (examiner 1966—, bd. dirs. 1974-80, 1992-98, treas. 1978, v.p. 1979, pres. 1980). Intern in pediat. Vanderbilt U., Nashville, 1961-62; resident Children's Hosp. Med. Ctr., Harvard U., Boston, 1962-63; chief resident Grady Meml. Hosp., Emory U., Atlanta, 1963-64; pvt. practice Coral Gables, Fla., 1966. Instr. asst. clin. prof., assoc. clin. prof., now clin. prof. pediat. U. Miami Med. Sch., 1966—; active staff, bd. dirs. Miami Children's Hosp.; active staff Jackson Meml. Hosp.; past chief pediat. Doctors' Hosp.; mem. courtesy staff Mercy Hosp., Bapt. Hosp., South Miami Hosp.; chmn. health adv. com. Dade County Schs.; bd. dirs., v.p. Am. Bd. Pediat. Found., 1991-98; mem. adv. bd. McGlannon Sch.; cons. Fla. Divsn. Med. Svcs.; bd. dirs. Bank Coral Gables. Contbr. articles to med. jours. Hon. bd. dirs. Soc. for Abused Children of Children's Home Soc., Miami, 1980-84; mem. Coral Gables Code Enforcement Bd., 1986-88; team-sch. physician Coral Gables Sr. H.G., 1980-88; bd. dirs. Dade County March of Dimes, Miami, 1968-72; bd. advisors Dade County Assn. Retarded Children, 1968-76; trustee Emory U., 1991-97; mem. coun. ministries, youth coord., mem. fin. com., Sunday Sch. tchr. United Meth. Ch. Coral Gables, 1966—; chair staff parish rels. com.; mem. bd. advisors The Growing Place; mem. Citizens Bd. U. Miami, 1997—; v.p. bd. Good Hope Equestrian Tng. Ctr. for Retarded, 1999—. Capt. M.C., U.S. Army, 1964-66. Recipient citation of merit Emory U., 1980, alumni commendation Miami Children's Hosp., 1983, Tchg. award U. Miami Sch. Medicine, 1995, 2002, 06, Winston Churchhill medal, 1999; named to CGHS Athletic Hall of Fame, 1996, Wisdom Hall of Fame, 1998; finalist Rotary Citizen of Yr., 2005. Fellow Am. Acad. Pediat.; mem. AMA, Fla. Med. Assn. (sch. health com.), Fla. Pediat. Soc. (past chmn. sch. health com.), So. Med. Assn., Dade County Med. Assn. (sch. health com., continuing edn. com.), Empirical Soc. (past pres.), Soc. for Pediat. Rsch., So. Perinatal Soc., Greater Miami Pediat. Soc. (past pres., chmn. legis. and sch. health com., Hall of Fame), Miami Med. Forum (past pres., Haverfield Cup 1985, Mansfield Trophy 1983, 88, 98), Sr. Soc. Emory U. Biscayne Bay Yacht Club (commodore, bd. govs.), DVS St. Honor Soc., Alpha Omega Alpha, Omicron Delta Kappa, Alpha Epsilon Upsilon, Phi Delta Theta. Democrat. Avocations: fishing, golf, boating. Office: 355 Granello Ave Coral Gables FL 33146-1806

**QUILLIGAN, EDWARD JAMES,** retired obstetrician, gynecologist, educator; b. Cleve., June 18, 1925; s. James Joseph and Maude Elvira (Ryan) Q.; m. Betty Jane Cleaton. Dec. 14, 1946; children: Bruce, Jay, Carol, Christopher, Linda, Ted. BA, MD, Ohio State U., 1951; MA (hon.), Yale, 1967. Intern Ohio State U. Hosp., 1951-52, resident, 1952-54, Western Res. U. Hosps., 1954-56; asst. prof. obstetrics and gynecology Western Res. U., 1957-63, prof., 1963-65; prof. obstetrics and gynecology UCLA, 1965-66; prof., chmn. dept. Ob-Gyn Yale U., 1966-69, U. So. Calif., 1969-78, asso. v.p. med. affairs, 1978-79; prof. Ob-Gyn. U. Calif., Irvine, 1980-83, vice chancellor health affairs, dean Sch. Medicine, 1987-89; prof., chmn. ob-gyn. dept. U. Wis., 1983-85; prof., chmn. Ob-Gyn Davis Med. Ctr. U. Calif., Sacramento, 1985-87, vice chancellor Health Scis., dean Coll. Med. Irvine, 1987-89, prof. ob-gyn, 1987-94, prof. emeritus ob-gyn., 1994; exec. dir. med. edn. Long Beach (Calif.) Meml. Health Svcs., 1995—2005; ret., 2005. Contbr. articles to med. jours.; editor-in-chief emeritus: Am. Jour. Obstetrics and Gynecology. Served to 2d lt. AUS, 1944—46. Recipient Centennial award Ohio State U., 1970 Mem. Soc. Gynecologic Investigation, Am. Gynecol. Soc., Am. Coll. Obstetrics & Gynecology, Sigma Xi. Home: 1 Goldenglow Irvine CA 92612-4077 E-mail: equilligan@cox.net.

**QUIMBY, FRED WILLIAM,** pathology educator, veterinarian; b. Providence, Sept. 19, 1945; s. Edward Harold and Isabel (Farber) Q.; m. Cynthia Claire Connelly, Aug. 21, 1965; children: Kelly Ann, Cynthia Jane. VMD, U. Pa., 1970, PhD, 1974. Diplomate Am. Coll. Lab. Animal Medicine. Hematology fellow New Eng. Med. Ctr., Boston, 1974-75, instr. pathology, 1975-76, asst. prof., 1976-79; assoc. prof. pathology Cornell Med. Coll., N.Y.C., 1979-92, prof. pathology, 1993-2000. Dir. lab. animal medicine Tufts-New Eng. Med. Ctr., Boston, 1975—79; dir. Ctr. Rsch. Animal Resources Cornell U., Ithaca, 1979—2001; assoc. v.p., sr. dir. Animal Rsch. Ctr. Rockefeller U., 2001—. Editor Animal Welfare, 1992, Lab. Animal Sci., 1992-93, consulting editor, 1993-95; editor: Clinical Chemistry of Laboratory Animals, 2d edit., 1999, Laboratory Animal Medicine, 2d edit., 2002; guest editor Applied Animal Behavior Sci., 1997; chmn. editl. bd. ILAr

News, 1988-91; contbr. over 120 sci. papers and abstracts. Recipient Focused Giving award, Johnson and Johnson, 1987—90; Greenfield Trust scholar, 1966—70, N.H. Rural Rehab. Corp. scholar, 1966—70, U. Pa. scholar, 1969—70. Mem. Am. Vet. Med. Assn. (Charles River prize 1995), Am. Assn. Lab. Animal Sci. (pres. N.E. br. 1978-79, B. Trum award 1979), Am. Soc. Lab. Animal Practitioners (Rsch. award 2004), World Vet. Assn. (sec. exec. com. animal welfare 1990-96). Roman Catholic. Home: Apt 24P 504 E 63d St New York NY 10021-7919 Office Phone: 212-327-8535. Business E-Mail: quimby@rockefeller.edu.

**QUIN, LOUIS DUBOSE,** chemist, educator; b. Charleston, S.C., Mar. 5, 1928; s. Louis DuBose and Olga vonOven (Jatho) Q.; children: Gordon, Howard, Carol. BS, The Citadel, 1947; MA, U. N.C., 1949, PhD, 1952. Research chemist Am. Cyanamid Co., Stamford, Conn., 1949-50; research project leader FMC Corp., South Charleston, W.Va., 1952-54, 56; mem. faculty dept. chemistry Duke U., Durham, NC, 1956-86, prof., 1967-81, James B. Duke prof. chemistry, 1981-86, chmn. dept., 1970-76; prof. chemistry U. Mass., Amherst, 1986-96, prof. emeritus, 1996—, head dept., 1986-94; adj. prof., disting. vis. prof. chemistry U. N.C., Wilmington, 1996—. Mem. Durham Human Relations Commn., 1978-81 Author: Heterocyclic Chemistry of Phosphorus, 1981, (with J.G. Verkade) Phosphorus-31 NMR Spectroscopy in Stereochemical Analysis, 1987, Phosphorus-31 NMR Spectral Properties in Compound Characterization and Structural Analysis, 1994, A Guide to Organophosphorus Chemistry, 2000, Practical Interpretation of P-31 NMR Spectra and Computer Assisted Structure Verification, 2004. Served to 1st lt. U.S. Army, 1954-56. Recipient Arbusovs award in phosphorus chemistry, 1997. Fellow AAAS; mem. Am. Chem. Soc. Office: 124 White Oak Bluffs Stella NC 28582

**QUINBY, WILLIAM ALBERT,** lawyer, arbitrator, mediator; b. Oakland, Calif., May 28, 1941; s. George W. and Marge (Diaz) Q.; m. Marion Bach, Nov. 27, 1964; 1 child, Michelle Kathleen. BA, Harvard U., 1963; JD, U. Calif., San Francisco, 1967. Bar: Calif. 1967. V.p., dir., shareholder Crosby, Heafey, Roach & May, Oakland, 1967-96; mediator, arbitrator Am. Arbitration Assn. and AAA Ctr. for Mediation, San Francisco, 1996—; ptnr. Wulff, Quinby & Sochynsky, 2001—. Bd. dirs. Haws Drinking Faucet Co., Berkeley, Calif.; mem. faculty Hastings Coll. Advocacy, San Francisco, 1980, instr. Boalt Hall Sch. Law, 1997; co-moderator Counsel Connect's Calif. ADR Discussion Group; lectr. currents devels. in banking arbitration and mediation; mem. fellowship rev. com. HEW; mem. mediation panel Nat. Assn. Securities Dealers; trustee Nat. Pre-Suit Mediation Program; adj. prof. Hastings Coll. of the Law, U. Calif., 1998, 99. Author: Six Reasons--Besides Time and Money--to Mediate Rather Than Litigate, Why Health Care Parties Should Mediate Rather Than Litigate, Starting an ADR Practice Group in a Law Firm, Mediation Process Can Amicably Solve Business Disputes and Not a Gold Rush (But Silver, Maybe), ADR Practice in a Large Law Firm Produces No Overnight Bonanzas, Making The Most of Mediation (Effective Mediation Advocacy). Bd. dirs. Big Bros. East Bay, Oakland, 1983-87, Easter Seals Soc. East Bay, 1973; past bd. dirs. Oakland East Bay Symphony, Oakland Pub. Libr. Found.; chmn. bd. dirs. Bay Area Tumor Inst. Scholar Harvard U., 1962-63. Fellow Coll. Comml. Arbitrators; mem. ABA (sect. on dispute resolution, chair programs, mediation coms.), Calif. Bar Assn., Alameda County Bar Assn., San Francisco Bar Assn., Contra Costa County Bar Assn., Calif. Bus. Trial Lawyers Assn., Am. Arbitration Assn. (large, complex case panel, comml. mediation and arbitration panels), Oakland C. of C. (past bd. dirs., exec. com.), Alameda County Barristers Club (bd. dirs., pres. 1972), Harvard Club, San Francisco Calimari Club. Republican. Avocations: running, skiing, tennis, travel, gardening. Office: Wulff Quinby & Sochynsky Dispute Resolution 1901 Harrison St Ste 1420 Oakland CA 94612-3582 Office Phone: 510-663-5220. Personal E-mail: wquinby@aol.com.

**QUINCE, PEGGY A.,** judge; b. Norfolk, Va., Jan. 3, 1948; m. Fred L. Buckine; children: Peggy LaVerne, Laura LaVerne. BS in Zoology, Howard U., 1970; JD, Cath. U. of Am., 1975; LLD (hon.), Stetson U., 1999, St. Thomas U., 2004. Hearing officer Rental Accomodations Office, Washington; pvt. practice Norfolk, 1977-78, Bradenton, Fla., 1978-80; asst. atty. gen. criminal divsn. Atty. Gen.'s Office, 1980; apptd. 2d Dist. Ct. of Appeals, 1994-98; justice Fla. Supreme Ct., 1998—. Lectr. in field. Former asst. Sunday sch. tchr., former mem. #3 usher bd. New Hope Missionary Bapt. Ch.; active Jack and Jill of Am., Inc., Urban League, NAACP, Tampa Orgn. for Black Affairs. Recipient award Cath.'s Neighborhood Legal Svcs. Clinic. Mem. Nat. Bar Assn., Fla. Bar, Va. State Bar, George Edgecomb Bar Assn., Fla. Assn. Women Lawyers, Tallahassee Women Lawyers, William H. Stafford Inn. Ct., Alpha Kappa Alpha. Office: Fla Supreme Ct 500 S Duval St Tallahassee FL 32399-1925 Office Phone: 850-922-5624. Business E-Mail: Larryg@flcourts.org.

**QUINDLEN, ANNA,** journalist, writer; b. Phila., July 8, 1952; d. Robert V. and Prudence Quindlen; m. Gerald Krovatin; children: Quindlen Krovatin, Christopher Krovatin, Maria Krovatin. BA, Barnard Coll., 1974. Reporter New York Post, NYC, 1974-77; gen. assignment, city hall reporter New York Times, NYC, 1977-81, columnist About New York, 1981-83, dep. met. editor, 1983-85, columnist Life in the 30's syndicated, 1986-89, columnist Public and Private, 1990-94; full-time novelist, 1995—; columnist, "Last Word" Newsweek mag. Author: (novels) Object Lessons, 1991, One True Thing, 1994, Black and Blue, 1998, Blessings, 2000, Rise and Shine, 2006, (non-fiction) A Short Guide to a Happy Life, 2000, Being Perfect, 2005 (Publishers Weekly Bestseller non-fiction list, 2005), (children's books) The Tree That Came to Stay, 1992, Happily Ever After, 1997, (compilation) Living Out Loud, 1988, Thinking Out Loud, 1993, Loud and Clear, 2004; wrote text for: coffee table pictorial Naked Babies, 1996, Siblings, 1998. Bd. mem. Nightingale-Bamford Sch., NYC, NARAL Found. Named Woman of Yr., Glamour Mag., 1991; recipient Mike Berger award for disting. reporting, 1983, Pulitzer Prize for commentary, 1992. Mem.: Planned Parenthood Fedn. of Am. (bd. adv.), Author's Guild (coun. mem.), Bd Trustees, Barnard Coll. (chmn. 2003—). Achievements include being first writer to ever appear on fiction, nonfiction & self-help NewYork Times Best Seller lists. Office: c/o ICM 40 W 57th St New York NY 10019-4001*

**QUIN-HARKIN, JANET ELIZABETH (RHYS BOWEN),** writer; b. Bath, Somerset, Eng., Sept. 24, 1941; d. Frank Newcombe Lee, Margery Lee; m. John Quin-Harkin; children: Clare Broyles, Anne, Jane Hansen, Dominic. BA with honors, U. London, 1963. Author: (children's picture book) Peter Penny's Dance, 1976 (NY Times Best Book of Yr., ALA Book of Internat. Note, 1977), Heartbreak Cafe series novels, Sweet Dreams series, Wanted Date for Saturday Night, 1985 (Reader's Choice award, 1986), Madam Sarah, 1990, Fool's Gold, 1991, Amazing Grace, 1992; author: (as Rhys Bowen) (novels) Evans Above, 1997, Evans He Lives, 1998 (nominated--Barry award, best mystery novel, 1999), Evanly Choirs, 1999, Evan and Elle, 2000, Evan Can Wait, 2001, Murphy's Law, 2001 (Agatha award, 2002, Herodohis award, Reviewer's Choice award, 2002), Death of Riley, 2002 (nominated for Agatha award, nominated for Reviewer's Choice award), For the Love of Mike, 2003 (Anthony award, Bruce Alexander award), Evans Gate, 2004 (Edgar award nominee for best novel, 2005), In Like Flynn: A Molly Murphy Mystery, 2005, Evan Blessed: A Constable Evans Mystery, 2005, Oh Danny Boy, 2006, Evanly Bodies, 2006. Treas. Daughters of the Brit. Empire, San Rafael, 1998—2000. Recipient award for best screenplay, Marin Arts Coun., 1995. Mem.: Soc. Children's Bookwriters, Sisters in Crime, Mystery Writers Am. (regional pres. No. Calif. chpt. 2001). Roman Catholic. Avocations: travel, hiking, singing, tennis. Office: c/o Meg Ruley Jane Rotrosen Agy 318 E 51st St New York NY 10022 Office Phone: 212-593-4330. Personal E-mail: rhys@rhysbowen.com.*

**QUINLAN, FRANCIS E.,** lawyer; BA, U. Wis., Madison, 1970; JD, Southwestern U., 1978; LLM in Taxation, Boston U., 1980. Bar: Calif. 1982. Spl. agt. FBI, 1979-82; founding ptnr. Kester & Quinlan, LLP, Corona Del Mar, Calif., 1982—. Brig. gen. USMCR, 1969—. Office: 680 Newport Center Dr #G100 Newport Beach CA 92660-6431

**QUINLAN, GUY CHRISTIAN,** lawyer; b. Cambridge, Mass., Oct. 28, 1939; s. Guy Thomas and Yvonne (Carver) Q.; m. Mary-Ella Holst, Apr. 18, 1987. AB, Harvard Coll., 1960; JD, Harvard U., 1963. Bar: N.Y. 1964, U.S. Dist. Ct. (so. and ea. dists.) N.Y. 1965, U.S. Ct. Appeals (2d cir.) 1967, U.S. Supreme Ct. 1969, U.S. Ct. Appeals (8th cir.) 1973, (10th cir.) 1977, (4th cir.) 1993, (11th cir.) 1995, U.S. Tax Ct. 1977. Assoc. Clifford Chance, N.Y.C., 1963-70, ptnr., 1970—90, of counsel NYC, 1991—. Past pres. Unitarian Universalist Svc. Com., Yorkville Common Pantry; Unitarian Universalist Dist. of Met. N.Y.; mem. adv. council on ministerial studies Harvard U. Div. Sch.; chair nuclear disarmament task force All Souls Unitarian Ch. Mem.: ABA, Lawyers Com. on Nuclear Policy, Amnesty Internat. Legal Network, Arm Control Assn., Harvard Club. Democrat. Office: Clifford Chance US LLP 31 W 52d St New York NY 10019-6131 Office Phone: 212-878-8219. Business E-Mail: guy.quinlan@cliffordchance.com.

**QUINLAN, J(OSEPH) MICHAEL,** lawyer; b. Rockville Centre, N.Y., Nov. 2, 1941; s. Joseph Charles Quinlan and Harriet Veronica (Gorman) Greene; m. Agnes Mary Quinlan, May 5, 1973; children: Kara Quinlan Davis, Kristen Quinlan Calder. BS in Social Sci., Fairfield U., 1963; JD, Fordham U., 1966; LLM, George Washington U., 1970. Bar: N.Y. 1966, D.C. 1967, Va. 1993, U.S. Ct. Mil. Appeals 1967, U.S. Supreme Ct. 1970. Exec. asst. to warden U.S. Penitentiary, Leavenworth, Kans., 1973-74; of counsel N.E. region U.S. Bur. Prisons, Phila., 1974-75, exec. asst. to dir. Washington, 1975-78; supt. Fed. Prison Camp, Eglin AFB, Fla., 1978-80; warden Fed. Correctional Inst., Otisville, NY, 1980-85; from dep. asst. dir. to dir. U.S. Bur. Prisons, Washington, 1985-92; dir. strategic planning Corrections Corp. Am., 1993-97; dir., bd. dirs. U.K. Detention Svcs., London, 1993-97; vice-chmn., bd. trustees Prison Realty Trust, 1997-99. 1st vice-chmn. bd. dirs. Horton Meml. Hosp., Middletown, N.Y., 1982-85; CEO Prison Realty Trust, 1997-99; pres. Corrections Corp. of Am., 1999-2000, exec. v.p., COO, 2000-02, sr. v.p., 2002—. Bd. advisors BI Inc., 2001—. Lt. col. USAFR, 1966-93. Recipient SES Presdl. Disting. Rank award, 1988, SES Presdl. Meritorious Rank award, 1991, Exceptional Leadership award U.S. Atty. Gen., 1991, Nat. Pub. Svc. award Nat. Acad. Pub. Adminstrn./Am. Soc. Pub. Adminstrn., 1992, John Marshall award Dept. Justice, 1993, E.R. Cass award ACA, 2003. Fellow Nat. Acad. Pub. Adminstrn. (chair prisons com.); mem. ABA (corrections and sentencing com. 1985—), Am. Correctional Assn. (mem. awards com.), Nat. Com. Comm. Corrections, N.Y. Bar Assn., D.C. Bar Assn., Va. Bar Assn. Roman Catholic. Avocation: reading. Home: 420 Elmington Ave # 507 Nashville TN 37205 E-mail: mike.quinlan@correctionscorp.com

**QUINLAN, KATHLEEN,** actress; b. Pasadena, Calif., Nov. 19, 1954; d. Robert and Josephine Quinlan; m. Bruce Abbott, Apr. 12, 1994; 2 children. Actress: (theatre) Taken in Marriage, 1979 (Theatre World award 1979), Accent on Youth, 1983, Les Liaisons Dangereuses, 1988, (feature films) One is a Lonely Number, 1972, American Graffiti, 1973, Lifeguard, 1976, Airport '77, 1977, I Never Promised You a Rose Garden, 1977, The Promise, 1979, The Runner Stumbles, 1979, Sunday Lovers, 1981, Hanky Panky, 1982, Independence Day, 1982, Twilight Zone: The Movie, 1983, The Last Winter, 1983, Warning Sign, 1985, Wild Thing, 1987, Sunset, 1988, Clara's Heart, 1988, The Doors, 1991, Trial by Jury, 1994, Apollo 13, 1995 (Acad. award nominee for best actress 1996), Zeus and Roxanne, 1997, Event Horizon, 1997, Lawn Dogs, 1997, A Civil Action, 1998, My Giant, 1998, The Battle of Shaker Heights, 2003, The Hills Have Eyes, 2006; (TV movies) Can Ellen Be Saved?, 1974, Lucas Tanner, 1974, Where Have All the People Gone?, 1974, The Missing Are Deadly, 1975, The Turning Point of Jim Malloy, 1975, The Abduction of Saint Anne, 1975, Little Ladies of the Night, 1977, She's in the Army Now, 1981, When She Says No, 1984, Blackout, 1985, Children of the Night, 1985, Dreams Lost, Dreams Found, 1987, Trapped, 1989, The Operation, 1990, Strays, 1991, An American Story, 1992, Stolen Babies, 1993, Last Light, 1993, Perfect Alibi, 1994, Breakdown, 1996, In the Lake of the Woods, 1996, The Doris Duke Story, 1998, Blessings, 2003, The Riverman, 2004, The Dead Will Tell, 2004; (TV series) Family Law, 1999-2002. Mem. Actors' Equity Assn., Screen Actors Guild.*

**QUINLAN, KENNETH J., JR.,** military officer; BS civil engring., U.R.I.; MS military art and sci., U.S. Army Command & Gen. Staff Coll.; grad. School Advanced Mil. Studies, Army War Coll. Advanced through ranks to maj. gen. U.S. Army; platoon comdr., ops. officer Delta Troop, 1st Cav., Alaska; ops. officer D Troop, 1st Squadron, 26th Cav. Regiment; chief force integration 101st Airborne Div., Fort Campbell; 101st Aviation Brigade S-3 Op. Desert Shield/Desert Storm; chief strategic plans div., strategic planning, policy dir. U.S. Pacific Command; commandant Joint Forces Staff Coll., 2003. Decorated Defense Superior Service Medal U.S. Army, Legion of Merit, Bronze Star, Army Commendation Medal, Expert Infantryman's Badge U.S. Army, Ranger Tab, Sr. Parachutist Badge, Air Assault Badge; recipient Meritorious Svc. Medal. Office: Joint Forces Staff Coll 7800 Hampton Blvd Norfolk VA 23511-1701

**QUINLAN, MARK,** credit agency executive; BA in Bus. Adminstrn, U. Rochester, MBA. V.p. First Fidelity Bancorp; sr. v.p. Star Bancorp; v.p. info. and human svcs. Union Ctrl. Ins. and Investments; sr. v.p., chief info. officer Charter One Fin. Inc., 2003—. Office: Charter One Fin Inc 1215 Superior Ave Cleveland OH 44114

**QUINLAN, MARY LOU,** former advertising executive, consultant; b. 1953; BA, St. Joseph's U., 1975; MBA, Fordham U., 1982; doctorate (hon.), Alvernia Coll., 1996. Dir. comm. St. Joseph's U., 1975-78; dir. advtg. Avon Products, 1978-89; sr. v.p. Ally & Gargan, 1989-91; exec. v.p., mng. ptnr. DDB Needham N.Y., 1991-94; pres N.W. Ayer & Ptnrs., NYC, 1994-99, CEO, 1995—99; vice chairperson The MacManus Group, NYC, 1999; founder, CEO Just Ask a Woman, NYC, 1999—. Bd. dirs. 1800flowers.com, 2002—; trustee, lectr. St. Joseph's U., 2004—. Author: Just Ask a Woman: Cracking the Code of What Woman Want and How They Buy, 2003, Time Off for Good Behavior: Hardworking Women Can Take a Break and Change Their Lives, 2005. Bd. dirs. St. Joseph's U., Phila. Named Advt. Woman of Yr., Advt. Women of N.Y., 1995. Mem.: N.Y. Women in Comm. (Matrix Award for Advt. 1997). Office: Just Ask a Woman 670 Broadway Ste 301 New York NY 10012

**QUINLAN, ROBERT CONRAD,** real estate developer; married. Grad., Yale Univ., 1954. Ptnr. Quinlan & Field Real Estate, NYC. Bd. trustees Whitney Mus. Am. Art, NYC, Preservation League of NY State; bd. dir. NY Landmarks Conservancy, Hist. House Trust, Friends of Upper East Side Hist. Dist.; chmn. Columbus Ave. Bus. Improvement Dist. Office: Quinlan & Field 2N 101 W 70th St New York NY 10023

**QUINN, AIDAN,** actor; b. Chgo., Mar. 8, 1959; m. Elizabeth Bracco; children: Ava, Mia. Actor: (films) Reckless, 1984, Desperately Seeking Susan, 1985, The Mission, 1986, Stakeout, 1987, Crusoe, 1989, The Handmaid's Tale, 1990, The Lemon Sisters, 1990, Avalon, 1990, At Play in the Fields of the Lord, 1991, The Playboys, 1992, Benny & Joon, 1993, Blink, 1994, Legends of the Fall, 1994, Mary Shelley's Frankenstein, 1994, Out of Ireland (voice), 1994, The Stars Fell on Henrietta, 1994, Haunted, 1994, Michael Collins, 1996, Looking for Richard, 1996, Commandments, 1996, Lumière et compagnie, 1995, The Assignment, 1997, Wings Against the Wind, 1998, Practical Magic, 1998, Blue Vision, 1998, The Impostors, 1998, 50 Violins, 1999, In Dreams, 1999, The Messiah XXI, 2000, Stolen Summer, 2002, Evelyn, 2002, Song for a Raggy Boy, 2003, Proud, 2003, Bobby Jones, Stroke of Genius, 2004, Cavedweller, 2004, Shadow of Fear, 2004; (plays) The Man in 605, Fool for Love, 1983, Hamlet, 1984, A Lie of the Mind, 1985, A Streetcar Named Desire, 1988 (Theatre World award 1988), Scheherazade, The Irish Hebrew Lesson, (TV) An Early Frost, 1985 (Emmy award nominee 1985), Perfect Witness, 1989, Lies of the Twins, 1991, A Private Matter, 1992, Two of Us, 2000, See You in My Dreams, 2000, The Prince and the Pauper, 2000, Benedict Arnold: A Question of Honor, 2003, Plainsong, 2004; actor, prodr.: This Is My Father, 1998. Address: William Morris Agy 151 S El Camino Dr Beverly Hills CA 90212 also: David Seltzer Industry Entertainment 3rd Fl 955 S Carrilo Dr Los Angeles CA 90048

**QUINN, AMELIA TURNER,** writer; b. Crawfordsville, Ark., Apr. 21, 1948; d. George (dec.) and Erma Lee Turner; children: Donald Levelle, Monique Dunell Dominiguez, David Lewis Jr. V.p. Quinn's Exterminating Co., Inc., Lynwood, Calif., 1978—2001. Author: (copyrighted brochures) Volume No. 1 - (various titles). Avocations: benevolent works, travel, reading. Home: 304 N Montgomery St Apt #2 Memphis TN 38104 Office: Mt Truth Christian Fellowship PO Box 40143 Memphis TN 38174-0143

**QUINN, ANDREW PETER, JR.,** lawyer, retired insurance company executive; b. Providence, Oct. 22, 1923; s. Andrew Peter and Margaret (Canning) Q.; m. Sara G. Bullard, May 30, 1952 (dec. Feb. 2004); 1 child, Emily H. AB, Brown U., 1945; LLB, Yale U., 1950. Bar: R.I. 1949, Mass. 1960, U.S. Tax Ct. 1960, U.S. Supreme Ct. 1986. Pvt. practice, Providence, 1950-59; ptnr. Letts & Quinn, 1950-59; with Mass. Mut. Life Ins. Co., Springfield, 1959—88, exec. v.p., gen. counsel, 1971-88; of counsel Day, Berry & Howard, Hartford, Conn. and Boston, 1988-99; retired, 1999. Pres., trustee MML Series Investment Fund, 1971-88; pres. Sargasso Mut. Ins. Co., Ltd., 1986-89, chmn. bd. dirs., 1989-93. Trustee, MacDuffie Sch., 1974-87, chmn. bd., 1978-85; trustee Baystate Med., Springfield, 1977-80. Lt. (j.g.) USNR, 1944-46. Mem. ABA (co-chmn. nat. conf. lawyers and life ins. cos. 1973), Assn. Life Ins. Counsel (pres. 1983-84, Anderson Disting. Svc. award 1998), Am. Coun. Life Ins. (chmn. legal sect. 1971), Life Ins. Assn. Mass. (chmn. exec. com. 1975-77), Brown U. Alumni Assn. (bd. dirs. 1969-72), NY Yacht Club, Dunes Club, Hillsboro Club. Home: 1205 Meadow Ridge Redding CT 06896

**QUINN, ART JAY,** retired veterinarian, educator; b. Bennington, Kans., Aug. 2, 1936; s. Arthur Jess and Edith Mae (Reigle) Q. BS, Kans. State U., 1959, DVM, 1961. Diplomate Am. Coll. Vet. Ophthalmologists. Pvt. practice, Albuquerque, 1961-75; field rep. Am. Animal Hosp. Assn., Denver, 1968-69; prof. Coll. Vet. Medicine, Okla. State U., Stillwater, 1975-95, prof. emeritus, 1995—. Contbr. articles to profl. jours. Capt. U.S. Army, 1962-64. Recipient Small Animal Proficiency award, Kans. Vet. Med. Assn., 1961, Upjohn award, 1961, Western Region Practitioner award, AAHA, 1993, Meritorious Svc. award, Western Vet. Conf., 2002; grantee, Sarkey Found. grantee, 1981. Mem.: AVMA, Am. Coll. Vet. Ophthalmologists, Am. Animal Hosp. Assn. Democrat. Home: 210 Cedar Ln Diamond Head Sand Springs OK 74063-5309 Office Phone: 918-865-3419.

**QUINN, BRIAN GRANT,** art educator, sculptor; b. Wahoo, Nebr., Oct. 21, 1950; s. Grant Scott and Goldie Maxine Quinn; m. Jennifer Ann Jackels. BA, Nebr. Wesleyan U., 1973; MFA, Ariz. State U., 1975. Preparator Phoenix Art Mus., Phoenix, 1975; artist-in-residence NEA, Mesa, Ariz., 1975—76; vis. instr. sculture Glendale C.C., Glendale, Ariz., 1976—90; lectr. sculpture Ariz. State U., Tempe, Ariz., 1980—81; prof. sculture and jewelry Glendale C. C., 1990—94; curator art collection, 1990—94; vis. instr. art hist. Scottsdale C. C., Scottsdale, Ariz., 1996—; instr. visual arts Scottsdale Pub. Sch., 1996—2006. Represented in numerous permanent collections. Fulbright Meml. Fund Scholarship, Fulbright Inst., Japan, 2001, scholarship, Tchr. Inst. Contemporary Art, 2005, Chgo. Art Inst., 2005, NEA, 2005. Mem.: Japanese Sword Soc. of U.S. (bd. dir. 1994—2004, pres. 2004—). Avocations: sculpting, painting, antiques, visual arts. Home: 6132 E Lincoln Dr Paradise Valley AZ 85253 E-mail: swords@cox.net.

**QUINN, CHARLES NICHOLAS,** journalist; b. Utica, N.Y., July 28, 1930; s. Charles Dunaway and Elsa (Zarth) Q.; children—Diana David, Ben, Jane. BA, Cornell U., 1951; MS, Columbia U. Sch. Journalism, 1954. Reporter Providence Jour., 1954-56, N.Y. Herald Tribune, 1956-62; corr. NBC News, N.Y.C., 1962-66, Washington, 1966-71, Rome, 1971-74; mng. editor, chief corr. NBC Radio News, Washington, 1978-80; corr. Ind. Network News, Washington, 1980-81; electronic media rep. Am. Petroleum Inst., Washington, 1981-91. Reported on hunger in U.S. on: Huntley-Brinkley Report, (co-recipient Emmy 1969). Served with arty. U.S. Army, 1951-53. Mem. Nat. Press Club (bd. govs. 1990-91).

**QUINN, CHRISTINE CALLAGHAN,** councilwoman; b. Glen Cove, NY, July 25, 1966; d. Mary and Lawrence Quinn; life ptnr. Kim Catullo. BA in Urban Studies and Edn., Trinity Coll., Hartford, Conn., 1988. With Assn. Neighborhood and Housing Develop., 1989—91; chief staff Councilman Thomas K. Duane, 1992—96; exec. dir. NYC Gay and Lesbian Anti-Violence Project, 1996—98; city councilwoman Dist. 3 NYC, 1999—, council speaker, 2006—. Mem. NYC Police/Community Relations Task Force; del. DNC, 2000, mem. platform com., 04. Named one of Fifty Most Powerful Women in NYC, NY Post, Forty Under Forty, Gotham Mag. Avocation: reading. Office: Dist Office Christine Quinn 224 W 30th St Ste 1206 New York NY 10001*

**QUINN, COLLEEN M.,** reading specialist; b. Phila., July 9, 1961; d. Edward J. and Jane Maryann (Comly) Quinn. AA, Delaware County C.C., 1984; BA, Temple U., Phila., 1986, MEd, 1995. Cert. reading specialist 1998. Office mgr. Temple U., Phila., 1984—86; rsch. asst. Eastern Pa. Psychiatric Inst., East Falls, 1986—91; coord. Hearing Discovery Ctr., Darby, Pa., 1993—98; tchr., special edn. Archbishop Ryan Sch. for the Deaf, Norwood, Pa., 1995—2001; reading specialist Holy Family Learning, Ambler, Pa., 2001—. Mem. Self Help for Hard of Hearing, Delaware County, Pa. Nominee Dist. Alumni award, Del. County Cmty., 2004; named Woman of Yr., Quota Club Internat., 1996. Mem.: ASCD, Nat. Coun. Tchrs. English, Internat. Reading Assn. Democrat. Avocations: reading, writing, bicycling, exercise. Office: Holy Family Learning 701 S Bethlehem Pike Ambler PA 19002 Office Phone: 215-643-7676 ext. 6288. E-mail: cqiam@juno.com.

**QUINN, DENNIS MICHAEL,** history professor; b. Pasadena, Calif., Mar. 26, 1944; s. Daniel Donald Pena-Quinn and Joyce Cola Workman; m. Janice L. Darley, June 20, 1967 (div. Jan. 1986); children: Mary, Lisa, Adam, Moshe. BA in English, Philosophy, Brigham Young U., 1968; MA in Hist., U. Utah, 1973; MPhil in Hist., Yale U., 1975, PhD in Hist., 1976; cert. of completion, Inst. Quantative Hist., Newberry Libr., 1982. Tchg. fellow III Yale U., Hist. Dept., New Haven, 1974—75; asst. prof. to assoc. prof. Brigham Young U., Hist. Dept., Provo, Utah, 1976—84, prof., 1984—88, dir. grad. program, 1986—88; vis. scholar Claremont (Calif.) Grad. U., 2000; affiliated scholar U. Southern Calif., Ctr. for Feminist Rsch., Los Angeles, 2000—02; Beinecke fellow, assoc. history dept. Yale U., New Haven, 2002—03; external mem., doctoral com. Tex. A&M U., Hist. Dept., Coll. Sta., 2004—. Adv. coun. Redd Ctr. Western Studies, Provo, 1980—86; assoc. dir. Study Abroad Program, Vienna, 1983; documentary cons. various TV broadcasts, 1990. Author: Early Mormonism and the Magic World View, 1987; editor: The New Mormon History: Revisionist Essays on the Past, 1992; contbr. articles various profl. jours.; author: The Mormon Hierarchy: Origins of Power, 1994, Same-Sex Dynamics Among Nineteenth-Century Americans: A Mormon Example, 1996, The Mormon Hierarchy: Extensions of Power, 1997, Elder Statesman: A Biography of J. Reuben Clark, 2002. Speaker various cmty. activities. Salt Lake City, 1981; bd. trustees Leonard J. Arrington Found., Salt Lake City, 1982—83; vol. One INst. and Archives, Los Angeles, 2000—02. Contra intelligence agent mil. intelligence, 1968—71, Germany. Named Outstanding Tchr., Brigham Young U., 1986, Dist. Historian, Organ. Am. Historians, 2004; recipient Samuel F. Bemis prize, Yale U., 1974, George W. Egleston prize, 1976, Frederick W. Beinecke prize, 1976, Svc. award, One Inst., 2001; fellow, Mrs. Giles Whiting Found., 1975—76; grantee Glenn W. Irwin fellowship, Ind. U., Purdue U., 1990—91; Summer fellow, NEH, 1977, Giles Mead Dist. fellowship, Henry E. Huntington Libr., 1980, Dorothy Collins Brown fellowship, 1992—93, fellowship, NEH, 1993—94, Sr. fellowship, Yale U., 2002—03. Mem.: Am. Civil Liberties Union, Organ. Am. Historians, John Whitmer Hist. Assn., Mormon Hist. Assn., Utah State Hist. Soc., Affirmation: Gay and Lesbian Mormons (awards com. 2000—02), Western Hist. Assn. (program com. 1981—82), Am. Acad. Religion, Move-On Organ., Southern Poverty Ctr., Human Rights Campaign, Ctr. Lesbian and Gay Studies, Amnesty Internat., Greenpeace. Democrat. Mormon. Avocation: photography. Home: 8348A Gabriel Dr Rancho Cucamonga CA 91730 Personal E-mail: mike.quinn@finefriends.net.

**QUINN, EUGENE FREDERICK,** diplomat, minister; b. Oil City, Pa., Sept. 16, 1935; s. Eugene Frederick and Wilma (Scott) Q.; m. Charlotte Alison Smith, Aug. 25, 1965 (dec. June 2000); children: Christopher Edward Vermilye, Alison Moore; m. Carolyn Tanner Irish, June 14, 2001. AB, Allegheny Coll., 1957; MA in African studies, UCLA, 1966, MA in History, 1969, PhD in History, 1970; diploma in theol. studies, Va. Theol. Sem., 1974. Ordained to ministry Episcopal Ch., 1975. Info. officer Am. Embassy, Rabat, Morocco, 1958-59, cultural affairs officer Port-au-Prince, Haiti, 1959-61; country pub. affairs officer Ouagadougou, Upper Volta, 1961-63; field rep. Joint U.S. Affairs Office, Saigon, Vietnam, 1964-66; country pub. affairs officer Am. embassy, Yaounde, Cameroon, 1966-68, counselor embassy for press and cultural affairs Prague, Czechoslovakia, 1975-78; apptd. career mem. Sr. Fgn. service with class of counselor, 1981, minister-counselor, 1986; dir. fgn. service personnel Voice of Am., Washington, 1981-83; dep. asst. sec. pub. affairs Dept. Transp., 1983-85; dir. Office Pub. Affairs Voice of Am., 1985-86; internat. coord. for Bicentennial U.S. Constn., dir.'s office U.S. Info. Agy., 1986-91; cons. internat. affairs, 1992—. Dir. rule of law programs, conf. on security and cooperation in Europe, Office of Dem. Instns. and Human Rights, Warsaw, 1993-95. Author: Federalist Papers' Reader, 1992, To Heal the Earth, 1994, Democracy at Dawn, Notes From Poland and Points East, 1998, Human Rights and You, 1998, French Overseas Empire, 2000, To Be A Pilgrim, The Anglican Ethos in History, 2001, African Saints, Martyrs and Holy People, 2002, Courthouse at Indian Creek, 2002; co-author: Pride, Faith and Fear: Islam in Africa, 2003, Building the Goodly Fellowship of Faith, and History of the Episcopal Church in Utah 1867-1996, 2004, In Search of Salt, a History of the Beti People 1970-1960, 2006; editor: Diplomacy for the Seventies, 1969; mem. editl. bd. Fgn. Svc. Jour., 1972-75, Dept. State Open Forum Jour., 1982-83; contbr. articles to profl. jours., chpts. to books. Trustee N.J. Ednl. Consortium, 1970-72; coord. USIA Yorktown Bicentennial Activities, 1981; assisting clergyman St. Columba's Ch., Washington, 1973-75, 78-81, St. Cathedral, Washington, 1981-82, 95-2001, Grace Ch., Silver Spring, Md., 1981-82, Epiphany Ch., Washington, 1983, 86-92; chaplain Anglo-Am. Diplomatic Cmty., Prague, 1975-78, Warsaw, 1993-95; vicar St. James Ch., Bowie, Md., 1983-84; rector Christ Ch., Accokeek, Md., 1985, St. John's Ch., Pomonkey, Md., 1985; assisting clergyman All Saints Ch., Chevy Chase, Md., 1981-82, 86-90; interim pastor Ch. of Holy Communion, Washington, 1992-93, St. Andrew's Leonardtown, Md., 1998-99; chair environ. com. Episcopal Diocese of Washington Peace Commn., 1991-92; mem. Environ. Stewardship Team, Episcopal Ch., 1992-95. Recipient Meritorious Honor award USIA, 1964, 66, 85; Merit medal Republic of Vietnam, 1965, medal of honor 2d class, 1966 Home and Office: 48W 300 S # 2601 N Salt Lake City UT 84101

**QUINN, FRANCIS A.,** bishop; b. LA, Sept. 11, 1921; Student, St. Joseph's Coll., Mountain View, Calif., St. Patrick's Sem., Menlo Park, Calif., Cath. U., Washington, U. Calif., Berkeley. Ordained priest Roman Cath. Ch., 1946, ordained titular bishop of Numana and aux. bishop of San Francisco Roman Cath. Ch., 1978. Bishop Diocese of Sacramento, 1979—94, bishop emeritus, 1994—. Roman Catholic. Office: 2110 Broadway Sacramento CA 95818-2518 Office Phone: 916-733-0200.

**QUINN, FRANCIS FLAHERTY,** lawyer; b. Phila., Jan. 22, 1946; AB, St. Joseph's U., 1967; JD, U. Pa., 1971. Bar: Pa. 1972, N.J. 1993, N.Y. 1995, U.S. Supreme Ct. 1985. Law clk. to Hon. Daniel H. Huyett III U.S. Dist. Ct. (ea. dist.) Pa., 1971-73; ptnr. Lavin, O'Neill, Ricci, Cedrone & DiSipio, N.Y.C., 1973—. Lectr. in field. Mem. Phila. Bar Assn., Def. Rsch. and Trial Lawyers Assn., N.Y. Assn. Def. Counsel, Bar Assn. City of N.Y., N.Y. State Bar Assn. Office: Lavin O'Neil Ricci Cedrone & DiSipio 420 Lexington Ave Ste 2900 New York NY 10170 Office Phone: 212-415-8201. Business E-Mail: fquinn@lavin-law.com.

**QUINN, FRANCIS XAVIER,** arbitrator, consultant, mediator, writer, law educator; b. Dunmore, Pa., June 9, 1932; s. Frank T. and Alice B. (Maher) Q.; m. Marlene Stoker Quinn; children: Kimberly, Catherine, Cameron, Lindsay, Megan, Savannah, Jackson Blair. BA, Fordham U., 1956, MA, 1958; STB, Woodstock Coll., 1964; MS in Indsl. Rels., Loyola U., Chgo., 1966; PhD in Indsl. Rels., Calif. Western U., 1976. Assoc. dir. Inst. Indsl. Rels. St. Joseph's Coll., Phila., 1966-68; Manpower fellow Temple U., Phila., 1969-74, asst. to dean Sch. Bus. Adminstrn., 1972-78. Arbitrator Fed. Mediation and Conciliation Svc., Nat. Mediation Bd., Am. Arbitration Assn., Nat. Assn. Railroad Referees, Dem. Nat. Steering Com.; apptd. to Presdl. Emergency Bd., 1975 to Fgn. Svc. Grievance Bd., 1976, 78, 80. Author: The Ethical Aftermath of Automation, 1963, Ethics and Advertising, 1965, Population Ethics, 1968, The Evolving Role of Women in the World of Work, 1969, Developing Community Responsibility, 1970; editor: The Ethical Aftermath Series; contbr. articles to profl. jours. Chmn. Tulsa City-County Mayor's Task Force to Combat Homelessness, 1991-92; mem. exec. bd. Tulsa Met. Ministries, 1990-92, Labor-Religion Coun. Okla., 1990-98; pres. pastoral coun. Ft. Worth Holy Family Roman Cath. Ch., 2000-03, formation adv. bd., 2002-05. Named Tchr. of Yr. Freedom Found., 1959; recipient Human Rels. award City of Phila., 1970; inducted into Hall of Fame, Internat. Police Assn., 2000. Fellow Coll. of Labor and Employment Lawyers; mem. Nat. Acad. Arbitrators (v.p. 1999-2001), Indsl. Rels. Rsch. Assn., Assn. for Social Econs., Soc. for Dispute Resolution, Am. Arbitration Assn. (arbitrator), Nat. Assn. Railroad Refs. (pres. 2000-04), Internat. Soc. Labor and Social Security. Democrat. Home: 4213 Blackhaw Ave Fort Worth TX 76109-1618 Personal E-mail: Quinnfrank@msn.com.

**QUINN, HELEN RHODA ARNOLD,** physicist; b. Melbourne, Victoria, Australia, May 19, 1943; came to U.S. 1961; d. Ted Adamson and Helen Ruth (Down) Arnold; m. Daniel James Quinn, Oct. 8, 1966; children: Elizabeth Helen, James Arnold. BS in Physics, Stanford U., 1963, MS in Physics, 1964, PhD in Physics, 1967; DSc (hon.), Notre Dame U., 2002, U. Melbourne, 2005. Rsch. assoc. Stanford Linear Accelerator Ctr., 1967—68 1978—79, mem. permanent rsch. staff, 1979 2005, edn. coord., 1988—93, asst. to dir. edn. and pub. outreach, 1998—2003, prof. physics, 2003—; hon. rsch. fellow Harvard U., 1971, rsch. fellow, 1971—72, asst. prof. physics, 1972—76, assoc. prof. physics, 1976—77. Guest scientist (non German postdoctoral rschr.) Deutsches Elektronen Sychrotron, Hamburg, 1968—70; vis. assoc. prof. Stanford U., 1976—78; vis. scientist Stanford Linear Accelerator Ctr., 1977—78. Contbr. articles to profl. jours. Pres. Contemporary Physics Edn. Project, Portola Valley, Calif., 1989-95; vol., chair Town of Portola Valley Trails Com., 1988-98; pres. Am. Phys. Soc., 2004. Decorated Hon. officer Order of Australia, 2005; recipient DIRAC medal Internat. Ctr. Theoretical Physics, Trieste, Italy, 2000; fellow Alfred Sloan Found., 1975-79. Fellow AAAS, Am. Phys. Soc. (pres. 2004); mem. Nat. Acad. Sci. Avocations: hiking, native plants. Business E-Mail: quinn@slac.stanford.edu.

**QUINN, HOLLI JO BARDO,** social worker, educator, librarian; b. Muncy, Pa., Jan. 7, 1961; d. Emerson David and Beverly Bair Bardo; m. Joel Paul Quinn, Oct. 15, 1983; children: Tara Jo, Austin Paul. BA in Comm., Shippensburg U., 1982; MS in Bible, Phila. Bibl. U., 1997; MA in Religion, Temple U., 1999, postgrad. in Feminist Studies, 2000—01. Mktg. asst. Lower Bucks Cablevision, Levittown, Pa., 1984—87; English composition instr. Temple U., Phila., 1998, Bible instr., 1999; case worker Bucks County Head Start, Bensalem, Pa., 2001—04; prof. humanities Strayer U., Trevose, Pa., 2003—; mgr. Learning Resource Ctr., 2005—06; career svcs. advisor Sunford Brown Inst., Trevose, Pa., 2006—. Impact study rep. Bucks County Head Start, Morrisville, Pa., 2002—04. Author: Sacrifical Offerrings, 1989, Fishing, 1995. Vol. A Woman's Place, Doylestown, Pa., 2002; spkr. Women's Ink, Phila., 1989; campaign chair United Way Bucks County Head Start, Bensalem, Pa., 2002, mem. family partnership planning Morrisville, Pa., 2003; active Safety Coun., Bensalem, 2003—04; founding mem. Nat. Campaign for Tolerance, Montgomery, Ala., 2004—06; mem. leadership coun. So. Poverty Law Ctr., Montgomery, 2005—06. Named Wall of Tolerance honoree, So. Poverty Law Ctr., Montgomery, 2005—06; recipient Discovery award in fiction, Bucks County C.C., 1989, Senatorial citation, Pa. Senate, 1992. Republican. Avocations: gardening, landscaping, writing, reading, swimming. Home: 2224 Bent Rd Langhorne PA 19053 Office: Brown Inst 3600 Horison Blvd Ste GL-1 Trevose PA 19053 Office Phone: 215-436-6942.

**QUINN, JACK (JOHN FRANCIS QUINN),** former congressman, English language educator; b. South Buffalo, N.Y., Apr. 13, 1951; s. Jack Sr. and Norma Ide Q.; m. Mary Beth McAndrews, 1974; children: Jack III, Kara. BA, Siena Coll.; MA in Edn., SUNY, Buffalo. English language tchr. Orchard Park (N.Y.) Schs., 1973—83; town councilman Town of Hamburg, 1982—84, also town supv.; mem. U.S. Congress from 30th N.Y. Dist., 1993—2002, U.S. Congress from 27th N.Y. Dist., 2003—05; mem. transp. and infrastructure com., chmn. subcom. on railroads, mem. vet. affairs com.; pres. Cassidy & Associates, Washington, 2005—. Recipient Humanitarian award Erie County for the Disabled, Pub. Svc. award Niagara Frontier Parks and Recreation Soc., Disting. Grad. award Nat. Cath. Edn. Assn., Bronze Good Citizen medal SAR, New Horizons award Drug Edn. of Internat. Assn. of Lions Club, Red, White and Blue award Am. Legion of N.Y., Honor medal Hilbert Coll. Fin. Reporting award Govt. Fin. Officer's Assn., Disting. Career Svc. award Siena Coll., 1995. Mem. Hamburg C. of C., Greater Buffalo C. of C., Buffalo KC, Hamburg Kiwanis Club. Republican. Roman Catholic. Office: Cassidy & Associates 700 13th St NW Washington DC 20005

**QUINN, JAMES E.,** retail executive; m. Diane Quinn; 2 children. BA in comm., Hofstra U.; MBA in fin. mgmt., Lubin Sch. Bus., Pace U. V.p. corp. sales Tiffany & Co., 1986—90, sr. v.p. corp. divsn., 1990—92, exec. v.p., 1992—98, dir., 1995—, vice chmn., 1998—2003, pres., 2003—. Mem. bd. dirs. BNY Hamilton Funds, Inc., Mutual Am. Capital Mgmt.; chmn. Smurfit Sch. Bus., U. Coll. Dublin, 2003. Mem. adv. com. Bus. Coun. United Nations; bd. dirs. Fifth Ave. Bus. Improvement Dist.; trustee Mus. City NY. Office: Tiffany & Co 727 5th Ave New York NY 10022

**QUINN, JAMES F.,** social studies educator; b. Cheverly, Md., Aug. 31, 1955; m. Carla Mullen, May 30, 1986. PhD, La. State U., Baton Rouge, 1986. Prof. U. of North Tex., Denton, 1988—. Contbr. articles to profl. jours., chapters to books. Recipient, Thrasher award for gang rsch., 1994. Achievements include research in crime and corrections. Home: PO Box 309882 Denton TX 76203 Office: University of North Texas PO Box 311456 Denton TX 76203 Office Phone: 940-565-2743. Office Fax: 940-565-3960. Personal E-mail: jquinn@unt.edu. E-mail: quinn@pacs.unt.edu.

**QUINN, JAMES W.,** lawyer; b. Bronxville, NY, Oct. 1, 1945; s. James Joseph Quinn and Marie Joan (Blossy) Tisi; m. Kathleen Manning, Kellianne, Christopher, Tierney, Kerrin. AB cum laude, U. Notre Dame, 1967; LLB, Fordham U. Sch. Law, 1971. Bar: NY 1972, US Dist. Ct. (So. and Ea. Dists.) NY 1973, US Ct. Appeals (2nd cir.) 1974, US Supreme Ct. 1984, US Ct. Appeals (3rd cir.) 1984, US Ct. Appeals (7th cir.) 1985, US Ct. Appeals (9th cir.) 1986, US Ct. Appeals (8th cir.) 1991, US Ct. Appeals for the Fed. Cir. 2000, US Ct. Appeals (11th cir.) 2004. Assoc. Weil, Gotshal & Manges LLP, NYC, 1971-77, 78-79, ptnr. to sr. ptnr., global chair litigation/regulatory dept., 1979—, mem. mgmt. com.; ptnr. Fleisher & Quinn, NYC, 1977-78. Adj. assoc. prof. law Fordham U., NYC, 1985-87; spkr. and lectr. in field. Co-author: ABA's Corporate Litigator, 1989, Corporate Counsellor's Deskbook, 1990, Litigating Complex Careers, 1997, ABA's Business and Commercial Litigation in Fed. Courts, 1998; editor: Fordham U. Law Rev., 1969—71; contbr. articles to profl. jours. Bd. dir. Am. Diabetes Assn., Landmark Found., The Respect for Law Alliance. Named one of Ten Top Trial Lawyers in the US ("Winning: Successful Strategies From 10 of the Nation's Top Litigators), Nat. Law Jour., 1993, 2003. Fellow Internat. Acad. Trial Lawyers, Am. Coll. Trial Lawyers, NY Bar Found.; mem. ABA (forum com. on the entertainment and sports industries 1982-85, co-chmn. subcom. alternate dispute resolution, com. corp. counsel 1983-90, litigation sect., program chmn. and chmn. of sports and entertainment subcommittee of the trial practice com. 1985-92), Assn. of Bar of City of NY (com. of state jurisdiction 1979-81, com. on entertainment & sports 1984-87, com. on anti-trust regulation 1987-89, chmn. com. sports law 1993-96); mem. adv. bd. Nat. Jud. Coll., Panel of Distinguished Neutrals of the Ctr. for Pub. Resources, Fed. Bar Coun. Avocations: golf, running, reading. Home: 1 Maple Way Armonk NY 10504-2602 Office Phone: 212-310-8385. Office Fax: 212-310-8007. Business E-Mail: james.quinn@weil.com.

**QUINN, JANE BRYANT,** journalist, writer; b. Niagara Falls, NY, Feb. 5, 1939; d. Frank Leonard and Ada (Laurie) Bryant; m. David Conrad Quinn, June 10, 1967; children: Matthew Alexander, Justin Bryant. BA magna cum laude, Middlebury Coll., 1960. Assoc. editor Insiders Newsletter, NYC, 1962-65, co-editor, 1966-67; sr. editor Cowles Book Co., NYC, 1968; editor-in-chief Bus. Week Letter, NYC, 1969-73, gen. mgr., 1973-74; syndicated fin. columnist Wash. Post Writers Group, 1974—2001; contbr. fin. column to Women's Day mag., 1974-95, Good Housekeeping, 1995—; contbr. NBC News and Info. Service, 1976-77; bus. corr. WCBS-TV, NYC, 1979, CBS-TV News, 1980-87, ABC-TV Home Show, 1991-93; contbg. editor Newsweek mag., 1978. Host PBS personal fin. series Take Charge!, 1988; dir. bd. dirs. Bloomberg LP. Author: Everyone's Money Book, 1979, 2d edit., 1980, Making the Most of Your Money, 1991, 2d edit., 1997, A Hole in the Market, 1994, Smart and Simple Financial Strategies for Busy People, 2006; contbr. (software program) Quicken Financial Planner, 1995. Dean's coun. Harvard Sch. Pub. Health; mem. bd. advisors Jerome Levy Econs. Inst. Bard Coll. Named one of 25 Most Influential Women in US, World Almanac; recipient Emmy award for outstanding coverage fin. on TV, Gerald Loeb award for lifetime achievement and disting. bus. and fin. journalism, John Hancock award for excellence in bus. and fin. journalism, Janus award for excellence in TV and bus. reporting, Journalism award for excellence in personal fin. reporting, ICI-Am. U., three-time winner Nat. Press Club award for consumer journalism, two-time winner Nat. Headliner award, honored for outstanding consumer media svc., Consumer Fedn. Am. Mem. Phi Beta Kappa. Office: Newsweek Inc 251 W 57th St New York NY 10019-1802

**QUINN, JARUS WILLIAM,** physicist, former association executive; b. West Grove, Pa., Aug. 25, 1930; s. William G. and Ellen C. (DuRoss) Q.; m. Margaret M. McNerney, June 27, 1953; children: J. Kevin, Megan, Jennifer, Colin, Kristin. BS, St. Joseph's Coll., 1952; postgrad., Johns Hopkins U., 1952-55; PhD, Cath. U. Am., 1964. Rsch. assoc. physics Johns Hopkins U., 1954-55; staff scientist Rsch. Inst. Advanced Study, 1956-57; rsch. assoc. physics Cath. U. Am., 1958-60, instr., 1961-64, asst. prof., 1965-69; exec. dir. Optical Soc. Am., Washington, 1969-93; governing bd. Am. Inst. Physics, 1973-94; pres. Stellar Focus, Sunnyvale, Calif., 1994-95. Bd. govs. Am. Assn. Engring. Socs., 1990-93. Fellow Optical Soc. Am. (Distinguished Service Award, 1993), mem. Am. Phys. Soc., Coun. Engring. and Sci. Soc. Execs. Home: 15 Forsythia Ct Durham NC 27705 E-mail: optics2010@yahoo.com.

**QUINN, JEFFRY N.,** chemicals executive, lawyer; BS, Univ. Ky., 1981, JD, 1984. Sr. v.p. sec., gen. counsel Arch Coal Inc.; exec. v.p., chief adminstrv. officer, sec., gen. counsel Premcor Inc.; sr. v.p., gen. counsel, chief restructuring officer Solutia Inc., St. Louis, 2004—, pres., CEO, 2004—. Office: Solutia Inc 575 Maryville Centre Dr Saint Louis MO 63166

**QUINN, JOHN ALBERT,** chemical engineering professor; b. Springfield, Ill., Sept. 3, 1932; s. Edward Joseph and Marie (Von de Bur) Q.; m. Frances Wilkie Daly, June 22, 1957; children: Sarah D., Rebecca V., John E. BSChemE, U. Ill., 1954; PhDChemE, Princeton U., 1959. Mem. faculty chem. engring. U. Ill., Urbana, 1958-70; prof. U. Pa., Phila., 1971—, Robert D. Bent prof., 1978—, chmn. dept. chem. engring., 1980-85. Vis. prof. Imperial Coll. U. London, 1965-66; vis. scientist MIT, 1980; vis. prof. U. Rome/La Sapienza, 1992; mem. sci. adv. bds. Sepracor, Inc., Marlborough, Mass., 1984—, Whitaker Found., Mechanicsburg, Pa., 1987—; Mason lectr. Stanford U., 1981; Katz lectr. U. Mich., 1985; Reilly lectr. U. Notre Dame, 1987; Michael's lectr. MIT, 2001. Contbr. articles to profl. publs.; editl. advisor Jour. Membrane Sci., 1975—, Indsl. and Chem. Engring. Rsch., 1987-88, Revs. in Chem. Engring., 1980—; pioneer rschr. on mass transfer and interfacial phenomena. Sr. postdoctoral fellow NSF, 1965-66; Sherman Fairchild scholar Calif. Inst. Tech., 1985. Fellow AAAS, Am. Inst. Med. and Biol. Engring.; mem. NAE, AIChE (Allan P. Colburn award 1966, Alpha Chi Sigma award 1978), Am. Acad. Arts and Scis., Am. Chem. Soc., Internat. Soc.

Oxygen Transport to Tissue, Sigma X, Phi Lambda Upsilon, Tau Beta Pi. Home: 275 E Wynnewood Rd Merion Station PA 19066-1627 Office: Univ Pa Towne Bldg 220 S 33rd St Philadelphia PA 19104-6393 Office Phone: 215-898-8503.

**QUINN, JOHN B.,** lawyer; b. Ft. Belvoir, Va., June 20, 1951; BA magna cum laude, Claremont Men's Coll., 1973; JD cum laude, Harvard U., 1976. Bar: NY 1978, Calif. 1979. Assoc. Cravath, Swaine & Moore, 1976—79; founding ptnr. Quinn Emanuel Urquhart Oliver & Hedges, LLP, 1979—. Gen. counsel Acad. Motion Picture Arts and Scis., 1987—; instr. Brigham Young U. Sch. Law, 1977; lectr. fed. practice Calif. Continuing Ed. of Bar; mem. Fed. Courts and Practice Com., Com. on Fed. Courts, Million Dollar Advocates Forum; dir. Rose Bowl Operating Co. Fellow: Internat. Acad. Trial Lawyers; mem.: ABA, Calif. Bar Assn., NY Bar Assn., Union Internationale Des Avocats, LA County Bar Assn. Office: Quinn Emanuel Urquhart Oliver & Hedges LLP 865 South Figueroa St 10th Fl Los Angeles CA 90017 Office Phone: 213-443-3000. Office Fax: 213-443-3100. E-mail: johnquinn@quinnemanuel.com.*

**QUINN, JOHN COLLINS,** publishing executive, editor; b. Providence, Oct. 24, 1925; s. John A. and Kathryn H. (Collins) Q.; m. Lois R. Richardson, June 20, 1953; children: John Collins, Lo-anne, Richard B., Christopher A. AB, Providence Coll., 1945; MS, Columbia U. Sch. Journalism, 1946. Successively copy boy, reporter, asst. city editor, Washington corr., asst. mng. editor, day mng. editor Providence Jour.-Bull., 1943-66; with Gannett Co. Inc., Rochester, NY, 1966-90; exec. editor Rochester Democrat & Chronicle, Times-Union, 1966-71; gen. mgr. Gannett News Service, 1967-80, pres., 1980-88, v.p. parent co., 1971-75, sr. v.p. news and info., 1975-80, sr. v.p., chief news exec. parent co., editor USA TODAY, 1983-89; exec. v.p. Gannett Co., Arlington, Va., 1983-90; trustee Gannett Found., Arlington, 1988-91; dep. chmn. Freedom Forum, Arlington 1991-97, trustee, 1991—. Named to R.I. Hall of Fame, 1975, Editor of Yr. Nat. Press Found., 1986; recipient William Allen White citation, 1987, Women in Communications Headliner award, 1986; Paul Miller/Okla. State U. medallion, 1988. Mem. AP Mng. Editors (past dir., nat. pres. 1973-74), Am. Soc. Newspaper Editors (dir., chmn. editorial bd., chmn. conv. program, nat. pres. 1982-83) Roman Catholic. Home: 365 S Atlantic Ave Cocoa Beach FL 32931-2719 Office: Freedom Forum 1101 Wilson Blvd Ste 2300 Arlington VA 22209-2265 Office Phone: 703-284-2871.

**QUINN, JOHN J.,** lawyer; b. Sept. 19, 1932; BA, Univ. So. Calif., 1954, JD, 1959. Bar: Calif. 1959, US Supreme Ct. 1965. Ptnr., LA Office Mgmt. Arnold & Porter, LA. Past chmn. US Senator Barbara Boxer Fed. Judicial Selection Com.; chmn., Disciplinary Com. US Dist. Ct., Ctrl. Calif., 1995—2001. Recipient Learned Hand award, Am. Jewish Com., Disting. Svc. award, U.S. Ct. Appeals, Ninth Cir. Fellow: Am. Col. Trial Lawyers; mem.: ABA (mem. Ho. of Dels. 1977—82), L.A. County Bar Assn. (pres. 1976—77, Shattuck-Price award), Am. Bd. Trial Advocates, Order of the Coif. Office: Arnold & Porter 777 S Figueroa St Los Angeles CA 90017-2513 Office Phone: 213-243-4080. Office Fax: 213-243-4199. Business E-Mail: john.j.quinn@aporter.com.

**QUINN, JOHN MICHAEL,** physicist, geophysicist; b. Denver, May 8, 1946; s. Leonard Simon and Winifred Ruth (Doolan) Q.; m. Pamela Dagmar Shield, May 28, 1983. BS in Physics, U. Va., 1968; MS in Physics, U. Colo., 1982. Physicist U.S. Naval Rsch. Lab., Washington, 1967—73; prin. engr. Singer Simulation Products, Silver Spring, Md., 1973—74; rsch. physicist U.S. Naval Rsch. Lab, Washington, 1979—80; geophysicist U.S. Naval Oceanog. Office, Stennis Space Ctr., Miss., 1974—79, 1982—85, geophysicist, mathematician, 1985—95; rsch. geophysicist U.S. Geol. Survey, Denver, 1995—2002; ret., 2002. Investigator Polar Orbiting Geomagnetic Survey Experiment, 1990-94; prin. investigator Def. Meteorol. Satellite Program Polar Orbiting Geomagnetic Survey Ext., 1991-2002; chmn. com. on earth and planetary geomagnetic survey satellites Internat. Assn. Geomagnetism and Aeronomy, 1991-99, mem. internat. geomagnetic ref. field com., 1989-2002; U.S. del. UN Internat. Stds. Orgn., 2000-2002; project coord. USN Project MAGNET; vis. scientist Nat. Oceanic and Atmospheric Adminstrn., 2003—; cons. in field. Author: Epoch World Geomagnetic Model, 1985, 90, 95, 2000. With U.S. Army, 1968—71. Mem. Am. Geophys. Union, Am. Math. Soc., European Geophys. Soc., Math. Assn. Am. Achievements include devel. of official Dept. of Def. world magnetic models which are used by military and civilian agencies for navigational purposes and basic rsch. of earth's magnetic field, specialized remote geomagnetic sensing/modeling techniques to detect, in the lithosphere, magnetization due to meteorite impact shocks and hotspot basalt flows; engaged in geodynamo research, yielding high-resolution fluid-flow models at the core-mantle-boundary. Determined global lithspheric 3-D structure of the Earth to 200 kilometers depth by inverse modeling of CHAMP satellite magnetic field data. Home: 2732 S Braun Way Lakewood CO 80228-4954 Personal E-mail: p-j_quinn@comcast.net.

**QUINN, KATHERINE SARAH,** psychologist; d. George and Esther Blank; m. Ed Quinn (div. 1994); children: Adam(dec.), Molly Quinn Panepinto. BA in Psychology, U. Nev., 1982, MA in Psychology, 1987; PhD in Psychology (hon.), Calif. Sch. Profl. Psychology, 1999. Intern Children's Behavioral Svcs., Las Vegas, 1980—83, child devel. specialist, 1984—85; rsch. devel. coord. San Diego County Mental Health, 1988—97; intern Southwood Hosp., San Diego, 1991—92; therapist Child Sexual Abuse Treatment Ctr., San Diego, 1992—93; post-doctoral intern Neuropsychological Assessment and Psychotherapy, Solana Beach, Calif., 1999—2002; pvt. practice Solana Beach, 2002—04, Del Mar, Calif., 2004—. Mem.: APA, San Diego Psychol. Assn. Roman Catholic. Avocations: music, opera, theater, hiking. Home: 721 Genter St La Jolla CA 92037 Offic: 240 9th St Del Mar CA 92014 Office Phone: 858-720-0682. Business E-Mail: quinnphd@san.rr.com.

**QUINN, KENNETH PHILLIP,** lawyer; b. Chgo., Nov. 12, 1960; s. James Aloysius and Mary Elizabeth Quinn; m. Pamela Joy Smith, July 22, 2001; children: Danielle, Brigid, Caitlin, Natalie, Patrick. BS, No. Ill. U., DeKalb, 1982; JD, DePaul U., 1985. Bar: Ill. 1985, D.C. 2005. Assoc. Sidley Austin, Chgo., 1985—88; sr. advisor Office of Pres.-elect, Washington, 1988—89; counselor to sec. Dept. of Transp., Washington, 1989—91; chief counsel FAA, Washington, 1991—93; ptnr. Pillsbury Winthrop Shaw Pittman, Washington, 1993—. Bd. dirs. DePaul Internat. Aviation Law Inst.; gen. counsel, sec. Flight Safety Found. Editor-in-chief The Air and Space Lawyer, ABA, 1997—. Chair ABA Forum on Air and Space Law, 1995—98; mem. Bush-Cheney Lawyers Task Force, Washington, 2004—05, Federalist Soc. Fellow: Royal Aero. Soc.; mem.: K. of C. Republican. Roman Catholic. Avocations: golf, tennis, skiing, basketball, writing. Office: Pillsbury Winthrop Shaw Pittman 2300 N St NW Washington DC 20027 Office Phone: 202-663-8898. E-mail: kquinn@pillsburylaw.com.

**QUINN, MARY M.,** communications executive, marketing director; b. Bklyn., May 28, 1955; BA in Journalism, L.I. U., 1976; MBA in Mktg., Fordham U., 1984; postgrad., U. London, 1975. 2d v.p., mgr. pub. rels. Chase Manhattan Bank, L.I., NY, 1984—87; pres. Prase Mktg., L.I., N.Y., 1987-92; v.p. corp. comm. Fleet Bank, Melville, NY, 1992—2000; dir. mktg. Jones Lang Wootton U.S.A., NYC, 1995—2000; dir. global mktg. and pub. rels. Apax Ptnrs., 2000—02; chief pub. rels. officer NY Inst. Tech., Old Westbury, 2004—06; exec. dir. comm. and agy. planning Nassau BOCES, Garden City, NY, 2006—. Adj. prof. mktg. Concordia Coll., Westchester, NY, 1992—. Recipient award for internat. understanding Rotary Found., 1987, Gov.'s Vol. Svc. award, 1993; L.I. U. scholar, 1972-76, N.Y. State Regents scholar, 1972-76. Mem.: Internat. Pub. Rels. Dirs. (mem. coun.), Chief Mktg. Officers (mem. coun.).

**QUINN, MICHAEL,** economics professor; s. Quinn. BA, Fairfield U., Conn., 1996; PhD in Econs., U. N.C. Chapel Hill, 2002. Asst. prof. of econs. Bentley Coll., Waltham, Mass., 2002—. Contbr. articles to profl. jours. Recipient Taner award for Excellence in Tchg., U. N.C.-Chapel Hill, 2000, Econ. Dept. award for Excellence in Tchg., 1999, Hohmann award in Econs...

Fairfield U., 1996, Gregory Zec award in Econs., So. Conn. Bus. Economists, 1996; grantee Tech. Enhancement grantee, IBM and U. N.C., 2000; scholar Malcolm Baldrige scholar in Internat. Trade, Conn. Bus. and Industry Assn., 1994. Mem.: So. Econ. Assn., Am. Econ. Assn. Office: Bentley College 175 Forest St Waltham MA 02452 Office Phone: 781-891-2938. Office Fax: 781-891-2896. E-mail: mquinn@bentley.edu.

**QUINN, MICHAEL DESMOND,** diversified financial services executive; b. Balt., Sept. 4, 1936; s. Michael Joseph and Gladys (Baldwin) Quinn; m. Mary Annette McHenry, Apr. 11, 1961; children: Caitlin A., Maureen K., Patricia B., Marianne P. BA, U. Md., 1970. With Weaver Bros., Inc. of Md., Balt., 1960—; investment v.p., corp. dir. interim loan dept. Weaver Bros., Balt., 1978—86; chmn. of bd. Wye Mortgage Co.,L.P., 1977—, Christiana Capital Group, Balt.; chmn., CEO Alliance Recovery Group, Balt., 1990—, Estate Trust Co., Inc., Balt. Mem. faculty evening coll. Johns. Hopkins U., Balt., 1967—, Essex Cmty. Coll., Balt., 1967—. Mem. Gov.'s task force Md. Housing Ins. Fund; mem. Md. Health Claims Arbitration Panel; bd. visitors U. Md.; dist. adv. coun. U.S. Small Bus.Asminstrn. With USN, 1956—58. Mem.: Soc. Cert. Sr. Advisors, N. am. Soc. Corp. Planning, Md.Bankers Assn., Home Builders Assn., Real Estate Bd. Greater Balt. (bd. dirs.), Md. Mortgage Bankers Assn. (pres. bd. govs.), Balt. County C. of C. (bd. dirs.), Balt. Jr. Assn. Commerce (Richard Troja Merit award. 1967, Outstanding Young Man of Balt. 1969), Ancent Order Hibernians, Greater Balt. Com., Balt. Econ. Soc. Home: 8207 Robin Hood Ct Baltimore MD 21204-1900 Office: 7400 York Rd Ste 300 Baltimore MD 21204-7502 Office Phone: 800-456-5100. Personal E-mail: eti7400@aol.com. Business E-mail: mdquinn@estatetrustinc.com.

**QUINN, NIGEL WILLIAM TREVELYAN,** research scientist; b. Belfast, Northern Ireland, Dec. 28, 1955; arrived in U.S., 1978; s. Stanley Quinn and Elaine Elizabeth Hayes. BSc with honors, Cranfield U., 1977; MS, Iowa State U., 1981; PhD, Cornell U., 1987. Registered profl. engr., Calif. GE fellow Cornell U., 1984—86, sr. rsch. assoc., 1987—90; lead groundwater modeler San Joaquin Valley Drainage Program, 1987—90; geol. scientist, group leader Hydro Ecol. Engring. Advanced Decision Support Berkeley (Calif.) Nat. Lab., 1990—. Convener Calif. Water and Environ. Modeling Forum, Sacramento, 2002—; bd. dirs. Internat. Symposium on Environ. Software Sys., Germany; adj. prof. Calif. Water Inst.; assoc. rsch. prof. Calif. State U., Fresno; rsch. engr. U. Calif., Merced. Contbr. chapters to books, articles to profl. jours. Dir. UN Assn., Ames, 1978—81. Recipient Hunting Challenge Cup, Cranfield U., 1977. Mem.: ASCE, Calif. Water Inst., Water Environment Fedn., Am. Water Resources Assn., Am. Geophysical Union, Berkeley Yacht Club, Yolo Polo Club. Unitarian. Avocations: sailing, travel, polo. Home: 1123 Lochbrae Rd Sacramento CA 95815 Office: Berkeley Nat Lab 70A-3317H 1 Cyclotron Rd Berkeley CA 95815 Office Phone: 510-486-7056. Business E-Mail: nwquinn@lbl.gov.

**QUINN, PAT (JOHN BRIAN PATRICK QUINN),** former professional hockey coach; b. Hamilton, Ont., Can., Jan. 29, 1943; s. John Ernest and Jean (Ireland) Q.; m. Sandra Georgia Baker, May 1, 1963; children: Valerie, Kathleen. BA in Econs., York U., 1972; JD, Del. Law Sch., 1987. Player Toronto Maple Leafs, Ont., 1968-70, Vancouver Canucks, B.C., Can., 1970-72, Atlanta Flames, 1972-77; coach Phila. Flyers, 1977-82, L.A. Kings, 1984-86; pres., gen. mgr. Vancouver Canucks, 1987-97, head coach, 1990-97, Toronto Maple Leafs, 1997-2006. Player rep. NHL, Atlanta, 1973-77, bd. govs., 1987-, head coach, Team Can., Salt Lake City Olympic Games, 2002, World Cup of Hockey, 2004, Torino Olympic Games, 2006. Named Def. Man of Yr., Vancouver Canucks, 1971, Coach of Yr. NHL, 1979-80, Coach of Yr., Sporting News, 1980, 92, Coach of the Yr. Hockey News, 1980, 92, Coach of the Yr. Acad. Awards of Sports, named to the Longest Unbeaten Record in Profl. Sports of 35 Games, 1979-80: recipient Jake Milford award, 1994, Jack Diamond award, 1994. Roman Catholic. Avocations: sports, reading.*

**QUINN, PATRICIA K.,** literary agent; b. Chico, Calif. d. Donald Joseph and Kathleen (Alexander) Q. BA, Bennington Coll.; MFA in Drama, Yale U. Prodr., devel. exec. various Off-Broadway and regional theatres, 1976-84; devel. cons. Sundance Film Inst., Utah, 1983—85; theatrical agt. I.C.M., LA, 1985-90; v.p. comedy devel. Warner Bros. TV, Burbank, Calif., 1990-92; lit. and packaging agt. Met. Talent Agy., LA, 1995—2000. Instr. UCLA Ext., 1995—; spkr., lectr. Nat. Assn. of TV Programming Execs., Fla. Bar, NATAS, Media Xchange (Internat.); mem. TV com. Brit. Acad. Film and TV Arts, 2002-; prof. reps. peer group com. NATAS, 2002-04. Founding mem. TV Theatre Workshop, N.Y.C., 1980—86. Mem.: Women in Film (v.p. 1995—2001, bd. dirs. 2005—). Office: 330 S Spalding Dr #403 Beverly Hills CA 90212 Office Phone: 310-656-5141. E-mail: p_quinn@sbcglobal.net.

**QUINN, PATRICK,** lieutenant governor; b. Sept. 22, 1948; BS, Georgetown U.; JD Northwestern U. Sch. of Law. Commr. Cook County Bd. of Tax Appeal, 1982; treas. State of Ill., 1990—94, lt. gov., 2003—. Chmn. Ill. River Coordinating Counc., Ill. Rural Affairs Counc., Ill. Rural Bond Bank. Democrat. Office: Office Lt Governor James R Thompson Ctr 100 W Randolph Ste 15-200 Chicago IL 60601 also: Office Lt Governor State Capitol 214 State House Springfield IL 62706 Office Phone: 312-814-5220, 217-782-7884. Office Fax: 312-814-4862, 217-524-6262.*

**QUINN, PATRICK,** transportation executive; BA, U. Nebr., 1968, JD, 1971. From assoc. to ptnr. Nelson & Harding, Lincoln, Nebr., 1971-77; gen. counsel S.W. Motor Freight, Chattanooga, 1977-85; pres., co-chmn. U.S Xpress Enterprises, Inc., Chattanooga, Tenn., 1985—. Office: US Xpress Enterprises Inc 4080 Jenkins Rd Chattanooga TN 37421-1174 Office Phone: 423-510-3000.

**QUINN, PEGGY ARMSTRONG,** elementary school educator, writer; b. Gorman, Tex., Nov. 12, 1943; d. Lowell Rogers and Alice Humphrey Armstrong; m. Robert Michael Quinn, Aug. 12, 1979; 2 children. BS, Tex. Woman's U., 1965; MEd, San Diego State U., 1976. Cert. elem. tchr. Calif. Dept. Educator, 1975, reading specialist Calif. Dept. Educator, 1975, kindergarten tchr. Calif. Dept. Educator, 1975, elem. tchr. Tex. Dept. Educator, 1981, kindergarten tchr. Tex. Dept. Educator, 1981, ESL tchr. Tex. Dept. Educator, 2001, Learning Resource Specialist Tex. Dept. Educator, 2001. Kindergarten tchr. North Hanover Schs., Wrightstown, N.J., 1966—69; elem. tchr., reading specialist San Diego City Schs., 1970—80; elem. tchr. Garland ISD, Tex., 1986—. Mem. AFT/CIO Educators Group, Dallas, 1987—. Author: (articles) Writer's Digest, 1984 (contest winner), Amazing Weekly, 1985. Mem., supporter Weaver PTA, Garland, 1982—; vol. pianist Western Hills Nursing Home, Denton, Tex., 1980—, Comanche, Tex., 2004—05; supporter Dem. Party, Dallas, 2005. Democrat. Baptist. Avocations: music, writing. Home: 8602 Liberty Grove Rd Rowlett TX 75089 Office: Weaver Elem Sch 805 Pleasant Valley Rd Garland TX 75040 Office Phone: 972-494-8311. E-mail: pegqn@yahoo.com.

**QUINN, THOMAS H.,** lawyer; b. Pawtucket, RI, 1937; AB, Providence Coll., 1959; LLB, Georgetown Univ., 1963. Bar: RI 1964. Atty., legis. counsel, Office Comptroller Currency US Treasury Dept., 1963—66; ptnr. legis. and regulatory practice O'Connor & Hannan, Washington; ptnr., legis. affairs group Venable LLP, Washington, 2001—. Apptd. mem. US Govt. Bd Internat. Broadcasting, 1974—82; alt. US observer Internat. Fund for Ireland, 1993; trustee Dem. Senatorial Campaign Com., House Dem. Congl. Campaign Com. Mem.: ABA, RI Bar Assn., DC Bar Assn. Democrat. Office: Venable LLP 575 Seventh St NW Washington DC 20004 Office Phone: 202-344-4701. Office Fax: 202-344-8300. Business E-Mail: thquinn@venable.com.

**QUINN, WILLIAM (CHIP) GORMAN,** biology professor, researcher; b. Brynn Mawr, Pa., Feb. 15, 1944; s. William Gorman and Nan Shirley Quinn; m. Ho-Wen Hsu, Apr. 21, 1984; children: Rose Wen-Hsiang, William Wen-An, Grace Wen-Hua. PhD, Princeton U., Princeton, NJ, 1971. Postdoctoral fellow Calif. Inst. of Tech., Pasadena, Calif., 1971—74; asst. prof. Princeton U., NJ, 1974—81, assoc. prof., 1981, MIT, Cambridge, Mass.,

1981, prof., 1999—. Democrat-Npl. Avocation: music. Home: 19 Meadow View Rd Wayland MA 01778 Office: 46-5009 Mit 77 Mass Ave Cambridge MA 02139 Office Phone: 617-256-6307. Business E-Mail: cquinn@mit.edu.

**QUINN, YVONNE SUSAN,** lawyer; b. Spring Valley, Ill., May 13, 1951; d. Robert Leslie and Shirley Eilene (Morse) Quinn. BA, U. Ill., 1973; JD, U. Mich., 1976, MA in Econs., 1977. Bar: NY 1978, US Dist. Ct. (ea. and so. dists.) NY 1978,US Ct. Appeals (3d, 5th, 9th, 10th and DC cirs.) 1982, US Ct. Appeals (2d cir.) 1992, US Ct. Appeals (4th cir.) 1994, US Supreme Ct. 1982. Assoc. Cravath, Swaine & Moore, NYC, 1977-80, Sullivan & Cromwell, NYC, 1980-84, ptnr. litig., 1984—, and coord. antitrust practice area. Mem. ABA, Assn. of Bar of City of NY Office: Sullivan & Cromwell 125 Broad St New York NY 10004-2489 Office Phone: 212-558-3736. Office Fax: 212-558-3588. Business E-Mail: quinny@sullcrom.com.

**QUINNAN, GERALD VINCENT, JR.,** medical educator; b. Boston, Sept. 7, 1947; s. Gerald Vincent and Mary (Lally) Q.; children: Kevin, Kylie, Kathleen, John, Gerald; m. Leigh A. Sawyer. AB in Chemistry, Coll. Holy Cross, 1969; MD cum laude, St. Louis U., 1973. Diplomate Am. Bd. Internal Medicine. Intern, resident, fellow Boston U. Med. Ctr., 1973-77; med. officer Bur. Biologics, USPHS, Bethesda, Md., 1977; advanced through grades to asst. surgeon gen. USPHS, 1992; dir. herpes virus br., dep. dir. div. virology Bur. Biologics, Bethesda, 1980-81; dir. div. virology Ctr. for Drugs and Biologics, Bethesda, 1981-88; dep. dir. Ctr. Biologics Evaluation and Rsch., Bethesda, 1988-93, acting dir., 1990-92; prof. Uniformed Svcs. U. Health Scis., Bethesda, 1993—, chair preventive medicine, 2002—. Contbr. chpts. to books, numerous articles to profl. jours.; editl. bd./reviewer several jours. Fellow Infectious Diseases Soc. Am.; mem. AAAS, Am. Soc. for Microbiology, Am. Soc. for Clin. Investigation, Sigma Xi, Alpha Omega Alpha. Roman Catholic. Office: Uniformed Svcs U Hlth Scis Dept Preventive Medicine & Biometrics 4301 Jones Bridge Rd Bethesda MD 20814-4712 Office Phone: 301-295-3173. Business E-Mail: gquinnan@usuhs.mil.

**QUINN TRANK, CHRISTINE,** education educator; b. Waterloo, Iowa, Feb. 27, 1953; d. Richard Peter and Irene Christine Quinn; m. Douglas Monty Trank, Jan. 15, 2001. BA, U. Iowa, Iowa City, 1975, PhD, 2001. Program asst., adminstrv. asst., coord. acad. adminstrn. U. Iowa, 1981; asst. prof. Tex. Tech U., Lubbock, 2004—. Mem. editl. bd. Acadm. Mgmt. Jour., 2004—, Acad. Mgmt. Learning and Edn., 2004—. Contbr. articles to profl. jours. Mem.: Acad. Mgmt., Am. Sociol. Assn. Office: Tex Tech U Lubbock TX 79409

**QUIÑONES KEBER, ELOISE,** art historian, educator; b. LA; d. Rudy Jr. and Margaret Q. BA, Immaculate Heart Coll., 1966; MA, UCLA, 1967, Columbia U., 1979, PhD, 1984. Lectr. Columbia U., N.Y.C., 1984-86; prof. art history Baruch Coll., The Grad. Ctr., CUNY, 1986—. Author: Codex Telleriano Remensis: Ritual, Divination, and History in a Pictorial Aztec Manuscript, 1995 (Getty Grant Program Publ. Subvention award, 1992); co-author: Art of Aztec Mexico: Treasures of Tenochtitlan, 1983; editor: Chipping Away on Earth: Studies in Prehispanic and Colonial Mexico in Honor of Arthur J.O. Anderson and Charles E. Dibble, 1995, In Chalchihuitl in Quetzalli: Mesoamerican Studies in Honor of Doris Heyden, 2000, Representing Aztec Ritual: Performance, Text, and Image in the Work of Sahaquín, 2002; co-editor: The Work of Bernardino de Sahagun: Pioneed Ethnographer of 16th-Century Aztec Mexico, 1988, Mixteca-Puebla: Discoveries and Research in Mesoamerican Archaeology and Art, 1994; contrb. articles to profl. jours. Mellon postdoctoral fellow Columbia U., 1984-86, fellow Ford Found./NRC, 1986-87, Am. Coun. of Learned Socs. fellow, 1987-88, 93-94, grantee, 1985, 95, NEH fellow, 1993-94, grantee, 1986, 91; grantee Am. Philos. Soc., 1986; fellow Guggenheim Found., 1998; recipient Ralph Waldo Emerson award Phi Beta Kappa Soc., 1996. Mem. Coll. Art Assn., Assn. Latin Am. Art, Am. Soc. for Ethnohistory. Office: CUNY Grad Ctr Art History Program 365 Fifth Ave New York NY 10016 also: CUNY Baruch Coll Dept Fine and Performing Arts 1 Bernard Baruch Way New York NY 10010-1703 Business E-Mail: EQuinones-Keber@gc.cuny.edu. E-mail: equinones@mindspring.com.

**QUINSON, BRUNO ANDRE,** painter, retired publishing executive; b. Norwich, Conn., Jan. 1, 1938; s. Louis Jean and Suzanne Marie (Richard) Q.; m. Mary Ann Goodman, May 3, 1980; children by previous marriage: Timothy Bruno, Marc Albert (dec.), Christopher Louis; stepchildren: J Geoffrey Taylor, Luke J. Taylor (dec.), Adam J. Taylor, Joshua P. Taylor. BA, Williams Coll., 1958; postgrad., NYU, 1960-61. Product mgr. Simon & Schuster, NYC, 1960-65; pub., gen. mgr. Golden Press (div. Western Pub. Co., Inc.), 1965-70; pres. Larousse & Co., NYC, 1970-82, also bd. dirs.; pres. trade and reference div. Macmillan Pub. Co., NYC, 1982-88; pres., chief exec. officer Henry Holt & Co. Inc., NYC, 1988-96, ret., 1996—. Bd. dirs. Nat. Book Found., chmn., 1993-96; treas. Columbia U. Press, 1994-03, vice chmn., 1997-03; exec. bd. Macmillan Ltd., 1995-96; nat. coun. Graywolf Press, 2005—. Exhibitions include Nat. Acad. Art, Century Assn., NYC, Meeting House, Southfield, Mass., IS 183, Interlaken, Mass., Norfolk Libr.Conn., Frost Pl., Franconia, N.H. Bd. dirs. Rye (NY) Art Ctr., treas., 1973-74; bd. dirs. Northside Ctr. for Child Devel., 1981-89, chmn., 1987-89, adv. bd., 1990—; bd. dirs. 1115 Fifth Ave. Corp., 1983-94, 96-04, pres., 1998-03; bd. dirs. Mus. of the City of NY, 1999—, Lycee Francais NY, 1994-96, Vol. Cons. Group, 1997, Each Child a Reader Found., 1996; founding mem. Barrington Stage Co.; founding mem., bd. dirs. Interlaken Sch. Art, 1998-01; nat. adv. bd. Eudora Welty Found., 2002—; trustee Leopold Schepp Found., 2001—, PEN Am. Ctr., 2003-; bd. dirs. Manhattan Theater Club, 1991-97, emeritus 1997— Decorated chevalier Des Arts et Lettres (France). Mem. Am. Assn. Pubs. (bd. dirs. 1991-95), Pubs.' Lunch Club (pres. 1990-93), Century Assn., Norfolk Country Club, The River Club. Office: 2 E 93rd St New York NY 10128-0610

**QUINT, ARNOLD HARRIS,** lawyer; b. Boston, Jan. 3, 1942; s. Milton and Esther Quint; m. Susan Arenson, July 23, 1967; children: Edward, Michael. AB, Haverford Coll., Pa., 1963; LLB, Yale U., 1966. Bar: D.C. 1967. Supervisory atty. Power Commn., Washington, 1967-70; assoc. Hunton & Williams, Washington, 1970-74, ptnr., 1974—. Mem. ABA, Energy Bar Assn. (com. chmn. 1979-83, bd. dirs. 1989-92) Office: Hunton & Williams 1900 K St NW Washington DC 20006-1110 Office Phone: 202-955-1542. E-mail: aquint@hunton.com.

**QUINT, DAVID PAUL,** investment banking executive; b. Independence, Iowa, July 24, 1950; s. Paul Theodore and Mary Ann (Connoly) Q.; m. Kathleen Mary Stern, May 25, 1973; children: Jennifer, Angela, David, Geoffrey. BA in Modern Langs., U. Notre Dame, 1972, JD, 1975. Assoc. Arter & Hadden, Cleve., 1975-82; mng. dir. Belden & Blake, London, 1983-92; pres., CEO RP&C Internat., London, 1992—. Mem. Notre Dame Law Rev., 1974. Rotary Internat. fellow, 1978. Mem. Ohio State Bar Assn. Republican. Roman Catholic. Avocation: travel. Home: Avallon East Rd KT1 30LF Weybridge Surrey England Office: RP&C Internat 31A St James Square SW1Y 4JR London England Office Phone: 011 44 207 766 7000. E-mail: dquint@rpcint.co.uk.

**QUINT, IRA,** retail executive; b. NYC, May 29, 1930; s. Theodore Isaac and Rebecca (Ginandes) Q.; m. Carol Ann Goldsmith (div. Feb. 1984); children: Susan Amy, Stephanie Ann. BS, NYU, 1951; MBA, Harvard U., 1954. Group nat. mdse. mgr. Sears Roebuck & Co., Chgo., 1954-78; pres. Colonial Corp. Am., N.Y.C., 1978-79; pres., CEO Venture Stores, St. Louis, 1979-81; exec. v.p. Montgomery Ward, Chgo., 1981-85; pres. Lane Bryant Stores, N.Y.C., 1985-90; pres., chief exec. officer Conston Corp., Phila., 1990-92; pres. Quint Consultancy, NYC. Mem.: Harvard (N.Y.C.). Home and Office: 130 E 67th St New York NY 10021-6136

**QUINTANILLA, ANTONIO PAULET,** retired physician, educator; b. Feb. 8, 1927; came to U.S., 1963, naturalized, 1974; s. Leandro Marino and Edel Paulet Quintanilla; m. Mary Parker Rodriguez, May 2, 1958; children: Antonio Paulet, Angela, Francis, Cecilia, John. PhD, San Marcos U., 1948,

MD, 1957. Assoc. prof. physiology U. Arequipa, Peru, 1960-63; assoc. in physiology Cornell U., N.Y., 1963-64; prof. physiology U. Arequipa, 1964-68; assoc. prof. medicine Northwestern U., 1969-80, prof., 1980-2000; ret., 2000. Chief renal sect. VA Lakeside Hosp., 1976-90; cons. nephrologist Northwestern Meml. Hosp., Evanston Hosp., 1990-98, sr. attending emeritus; lectr. nat. Ctr. Advanced Med. Edn., Chgo.; mem. adv. bd. Am. Fedn. Clin. Rsch. Contbr. articles on renal disease to med. jours.; author books in English and Spanish, poetry, short stories. Fellow ACP; mem. Ctrl. Soc. Clin. Rsch., Internat. Soc. Nephrology, Am. Soc. Nephrology, Am. Physiol. Soc. Home: 650 S River Rd Unit 411 Des Plaines IL 60016-8428 Personal E-mail: a.p.quintanilla@worldnet.att.net.

**QUINTANILLA-VILLANUEVA, ROSALINDA,** economist; b. Monterrey, Mex., Feb. 22, 1959; came to U.S., 1978; d. Ernesto Quintanilla and Marina Villanueva. BA in Econs. with high honors, Inst. Tech. Monterrey, 1976; MA in Econs., U. Wis., Milw., 1979; PhD in Econs., U. Minn., 1988. Rsch. assoc. Econometric Unit Inst. Tech. Monterrey, 1976; cons. Grupo Indsl. ALFA, Monterrey, 1977; assoc. prof. econs. U. Autonoma Metropolitana, Mexico City, 1977-78; economist, working with countries in L.Am., Asia, Ea. Europe World Bank, Washington, 1991—. Nat. Coun. Sci. and Technology fellow, 1978-82. Avocations: painting, Mexican history, world history. Office: World Bank 1818 H St NW Washington DC 20433-0001

**QUINTERO, RONALD GARY,** management consultant; b. Detroit, Jan. 5, 1954; s. John Urdiales and Jean Lorraine (Morton) Q.; children: Jean Marie, Alexandra Lisa; m. Ellen Robin Leventhal, Sept. 2, 2004; stepchildren: Adam Leventhal, Daniel Leventhal. AB, Lafayette Coll., 1975; MS, NYU, 1976, APC, 1978. CPA, CFA, CFP, cert. mgmt. acct., cert. fraud examiner, cert. insolvency, cert. turnaround profl., cert. in distressed bus. valuation; accreditation in bus. valuation. Sr. mgr. Peat, Marwick, Mitchell & Co., N.Y.C., 1975-85; workout cons. Zolfo, Cooper & Co., N.Y.C., 1985-87; assoc. Bear, Stearns & Co., Inc., N.Y.C., 1987-88; prin. R. G. Quintero & Co., N.Y.C., 1988—. Mng. dir. Chartered Capital Advisers, Inc., N.Y.C., 1988—; adj. prof. New Sch. for Social Rsch., N.Y.C., 1983-85; internat. lectr.; adj. prof. N.Y. Inst. Fin., N.Y.C., 1988—; instr. Ctr. for Profl. Edn., Berwyn, Pa., 1991—; leading provider CFA Sems. Author: (book and cassette) Mergers and Acquisitions, 1990, CFA Review Notes, 2001, Q-Notes, 2002; contbg. author several books; contbr. articles to profl. jours.; creator: Quintero Index of Bankrupt Stocks. Mem. AICPAs, Am. Bankruptcy Inst., N.Y. Soc. CPAs (chmn. com. 1990-91, Max Block Disting. Article award 1990, Outstanding Discussion Leader 1991), Turnaround Mgmt. Assn. (bd. dirs., exec. com.). Avocations: squash, softball, running, computers, reading. Office: R G Quintero & Co 145 4th Ave New York NY 10003-4906 Office Phone: 212-505-9743. Business E-Mail: q@rgquintero.com.

**QUINT SEHAT, ARLENE,** art history educator, curator, museum administrator; b. Chgo., Sept. 4, 1944; d. Milton and Ruth Quint; m. Kourosh Sehat, July 11, 1938. BA in Art History, U. Calif., 1966, MA in Art History, 1969, PhD in Art History, 1974. Asst. prof. Calif. State U., L.A., 1969-76, assoc. prof., 1976-79; fine arts mgmt. specialist, curator of collections U.S. gen. svcs. adminstrn. Washington, 1980-88; assoc. prof. Coll. Notre Dame, Balt., 1988-90; vis. assoc. prof. Lincoln U., Pa., 1993-95; lectr. in art history Morgan State U., Balt., 1994—. Vis. assoc. prof. HUC Skirball Mus., L.A., 1975-77; cataloger, rschr. NYU, N.Y.C., 1969; rschr. Los Angeles County Mus. Art, 1964-66; chancellor's tchr. fellow U. Calif., 1966-67; adj. prof. Towson U., Balt. Contbr. articles to profl. jours. R & D grantee Coll. Notre Dame, Balt. Mem. Am. Assn. Museums, Internat. Coun. Museums (mem. documentation working group, internat. coord. conservation documentation), Coll. Art Assn., Arts Club Washington (chmn. edn. and scholarship com., admissions and membership com.).

**QUINTYN, CONRAD BEZEKIAH,** anthropologist, educator; s. Walter Hezekiah and Joycelyn Orlena Quintyn. BA in Anthropology, Baylor U., 1991; MA in Anthropology, U. Mich., 1993, PhD in Anthropology, 1999. Asst. prof. Washtenaw C.C., Ann Arbor, Mich., 2000—03, Iowa State U., Ames, 2000—01; rsch. scientist U. Mich., Ann Arbor, 2002—. Forensic anthropologist U.S. Army Ctrl. ID Lab, Honolulu, 2001—02; asst. prof. SUNY, Oswego, 2003. Author: The Father of Man: Meeting the True Adam, 2003; editor: Gardens of Youth, 2003, Theatre of the Mind, 2003. With USN, 1983—87. Decorated Good Conduct ribbon, Sea Svc. ribbon, Fleet Marine Force ribbon; fellow Rackham Merit fellow, U. Mich., 1992—97; grantee, 1996, Rackham Dissertation grantee, 1999, Irene Sala Levi Care Archaeological Found., 1997. Mem.: Am. Mus. Natural History (assoc.), Nat. Geog. Soc. (assoc.), Am. Assn. Phys. Anthropologists (assoc.), Am. Anthrop. Assn. (assoc.), VFW (assoc.) Achievements include Recovery and identification of the remains of a U.S. pilot shot down in Rabaul Is, New Guinea in 1942, during WWII. Recovery and identification of the remains of a U.S. pilot missing in Laos,1971. Office: U Mich Dept Anthropology Ann Arbor MI 48109 E-mail: darnoc@umich.edu, CBQuintyn@hotmail.com.

**QUINZII, MARTINE,** economics professor; d. Jean Julien Ricard and Marie Blanche Robert; m. Michel Quinzii (div.). Diploma, U. Paris VI, 1970, diploma, 1972; D in Econs., U. Paris II, 1986. Lectr. math. Lycée H. Daumier, Marseille, France, 1972—75; asst. dept. math. U. Marseille, Luminy, France, 1975—79; rsch. assoc. Laboratoire d'Econométrie et l'Ecole Polytechnique, 1979—86; maitre asst. dept. econs. U. Aix-Marseille III, 1979—83; maitre conf. dept. econs. U. Paris II 1983—86; vis. assoc. prof. U. So. Calif., LA 1986—87, assoc. prof., 1987—91; prof. U. Calif., Davis, 1991—, chair dept. econs., 1995—99. Vis. scholar U. Warwick, 1976, U. Bonn, 1977, vis. assoc. prof., 90, workshop instr., 92, vis. prof., 94; Cowles Found. vis. scholar Yale U., 1982, Cowles Found. vis. prof., 2002; workshop instr. Stanford U., 1984, 87, 1996—99, Cowles Found., 1992; vis. assoc. prof. U. Copenhagen, 1990; vis. prof. CORE, Louvain La Neuve, Belgium, 1994. Author: Rednements Croissants et Efficacité Economique, 1988, Increasing Returns and Efficiency, 1992, Theory of Incomplete Markets, 1996; assoc. editor: Jour. Math. Econs., 1989—95, Econometrae, 1991—2003, Math. Social Scis., 1994—, Annals Fin., 2005—; contbr. articles to profl. jours. Grantee, French Commissariat Gen. au Plan, 1981—83, 1983—84, 1984—85, NSF, 1987-89, 1989—91. Fellow: Econometric Soc. Office: U Calif Davis Dept Econs 1 Shields Ave Davis CA 95616

**QUIRCH, GUILLERMO, JR., (BILL QUIRCH),** food distribution executive; s. Guillermo Quirch; children: Guillermo III, Igancio, Mauricio. Co-founder Quirch Foods Co., 1967—, now pres. Office: Quirch Foods Co 7600 NW 82nd Pl Medley FL 33166 Office Phone: 305-691-3535. Office Fax: 305-593-0272.*

**QUIRINO, PEDRO,** counselor; s. Teodoro Quirino and Florencia Morales. BS, U. Autonoma Mex., Mexico City, 1995; MA in Psychology, U. Mary Hardin-Baylor, Belton, Tex., 2002. Cert. Art Therapy Inst., Dallas, 2006; early intervention specialist Tex., 2002. Mid. sch. tchr. Sch. Casa del Nino, Uruapan, Michoacan, Mexico, 1989—94, mid. sch. prin., 1994—96; h.s. tchr. Sem. Jesus Maestro, Santiago de Queretaro, Queretaro, Mexico, 1997—98; prof. Escuela Normal Superior, Zacatecas, Mexico, 1998—99; elem. sch. tchr. Liceo Guadalupe, Zacatecas, Mexico, 1998—99; early intervention specialist Early Childhood Intervention Program, Temple, Tex., 2001—05, profl. counselor, 2005—. Choir mem. St. Luke's Episcopal Ch., Belton, Tex., 2000—06. Mem.: Am. Art Therapy Assn. (assoc.). Office Phone: 254-773-6787.

**QUIRK, ALFRED P., JR.,** corporate financial executive; BA in econ., Holy Cross, 1980, MBA, Cornell U., 1984. Investment analyst, bond investment dept. Aetna Inc., 1984—, sr. investment officer, 1988, asst. v.p., corp. fin., 1991, v.p., 1996, v.p., fin., treas., 1999—. Office: Aetna Inc 151 Farmington Ave Hartford CT 06156

**QUIRK, FRANK JOSEPH,** management consulting company executive; b. NYC, Feb. 27, 1941; s. Frank J. and Madeline B. Quirk; m. Betty Josephine Mauldin, Jan. 7, 1967; children: Laura Josephine, Katherine Elizabeth. BA,

Cornell U., 1962, MBA, 1964. Assoc. Booz, Allen & Hamilton, Inc., Chgo. and Washington, 1967-72; exec. v.p. Macro Internat., Inc., Calverton, Md., 1972-79, pres., CEO, 1980-98, CEO, 1998—2006, chmn., 1998—; exec. v.p. Opinion Rsch. Corp., Princeton, NJ, 1999—2003, pres., 2003—05; chmn. Alexandria Buick Pontiac GMC, 2005—. Bd. dirs. Opinion Rsch. Corp. Bd. dirs. Smithsonian Inst. Libr. Capt. U.S. Army, 1964—66. Mem.: Belle Haven Country Club. Home: 2110 Foresthill Rd Alexandria VA 22307-1128 Office: Macro Internat Inc 11785 Beltsville Dr Beltsville MD 20705-3121

**QUIRK, JOHN JAMES,** investment company executive; b. NYC, July 10, 1943; s. Francis J. and Madeline A. (Meizinger) Q.; m. Kathryn Anne O'Brien, Mar. 21, 1963; children: John James, Ashlin Carter, Merritt Andrew. BA, Georgetown U., 1965; MBA, U. Va., 1967. Asst. treas., mgr. corp. fin. dept. W.R. Grace & Co., N.Y.C., 1967-74; asst. v.p., asst. treas. City Investing Co., N.Y.C., 1974-77, v.p., treas., 1978-81, sr. v.p., treas., 1982-85; chmn. bd. Quirk Carson Peppet Inc., 1985-98; prin. Churchill Capital, Inc., 1999—2001; mng. dir. Morgan, Joseph & Co. Inc., 2001—. Bd. dirs. Environ. Opportunities Fund., Ltd., City Investing Co. Liquidating Trust. Mem.: Racquet and Tennis; Wee Burn (Conn.). Home: 445 Hollow Tree Ridge Rd Darien CT 06820-3030 Office: 600 5th Ave Fl 19 New York NY 10020-2302 Office Phone: 212-218-3726. Business E-Mail: jquirk@morganjoseph.com.

**QUIRK, KATHLEEN L.,** mining executive; BS in Acctg., La. State U. With Mobil Oil Corp., Dallas; from mem. staff to treas. Freeport-McMoRan Copper & Gold Inc., New Orleans, 1989—2000, treas., 2000—, sr. v.p., 2003—, CFO, 2003—.

**QUIRK, KENNETH PAUL,** accountant; b. Lake Charles, La., Aug. 29, 1953; s. Charles Patrick and Helen (Lejeune) Q.; m. Teresa Ann Tucker, Mar. 26, 1982 (div. Mar. 1988); 1 child, Heather Marie; m. Ava Marie Angelle, July 13, 2002. BS in Acctg., McNeese State U., 1978; MBA, U. Phoenix, 1998. CPA, La.; cert. Microsoft product specialist in Windows NT 4.0., cert. info. tech. profl., AICPA, 2000. Staff acct. Quirk, Cargile, Hicks & Reddin, Lake Charles, 1979-80, Browning-Ferris Industries, Lake Charles, 1980-81, La. Savs. Assn., Lake Charles, 1981-90, Calcasieu Marine Nat. Bank, Lake Charles, 1990-96, Hibernia Nat. Bank, Lake Charles, 1996-97; pres. Acctg. Tech. Strategies, 1997—2003; ptnr. Quirk and Associates, LLC, 2005—. Instr. U. Phoenix-Online, 1999—. Author: fin. acctg. software sys. Mem. Young Men's Bus. Club, Lake Charles, 1986-90, Girl Scouts U.S., Lake Charles, 1989-90; bd. dirs. Ednl. and Treatment Coun., Inc., 2001—. Mem.: AICPA (cert. 1994), Inf. Systems Audit and Control Assn., Computer Soc. IEEE, Assn. Computing Machinery, Soc. La. CPAs (task force com. 2000—01), Assn. Cert. Fraud Examiners (assoc.). Republican. Episcopalian. Avocations: jazz drumming, genealogy, hunting.

**QUIRK, RAYMOND R,** investment company executive; married; 3 children. Former cty. mgr., regional mgr., divsn. one mgr., COO Fidelity, 1985, now pres., 2003—. Mem. bd. dirs. Fidelity Nat. Title, Alamo Title, Chgo. Title, Home Warranty subsidiaries of Fidelity Nat. Fin. Avocation: golf.

**QUIRMBACH, HERMAN CHARLES,** economics professor; b. St. Paul, Minn., Oct. 6, 1950; s. William Herman and Elizabeth Lou (Ziegler) Q. AB in Govt. cum laude, Harvard U., 1972; AM in Econs., Princeton U., 1980, PhD in Econs., 1983. Assoc. economist, cons. Rand Corp., Santa Monica, Calif., 1981—; assoc. prof. econs. Iowa State U., Ames, 1990—. Vis. asst. prof. econs. U. Wis., Madison, 1983—84; mem. numerous coms. Iowa State Senate. Contbr. articles to profl. jours. Treas. Story County Dem. Party, Ames, 1992-94; councilman 4th ward Ames City Coun., 1995-03; pres. Iowa Civil Liberties Union, 2001-02, bd. dirs., 1996-02; bd. dirs. Ames Mcpl. Utility Retirement Sys., 1996-03, Ames Conv. and Visitors Bur., 1997-99; Ames mayor pro tem, 2002; mem. Iowa Coll. Student Aid Commn., 2003—; mem. Iowa Property Tax Implementation Com., 2003-04; state senator Iowa Dist. 23, 2003—; co-chair Ames Vets. Meml. Com., 2001—; mem. Gov's Task Force on Local Governance, 2005, Iowa Tobacco Use Prevention and Control Commn., 2005—. Recipient Don Biggs award for polit. leadership, 1998-99. Mem. AAUP, ACLU, Ames LWV, Am. Econ. Assn., Econometric Soc., Ames C. of C., Appalachian Mountain Club, White Mountain Four Thousand Footer Club, Ames Kiwanis Club, Ames Patriotic Coun. Office: Iowa State Senate The Statehouse Des Moines IA 50319

**QUIROGA, ALICIA ESPINOSA,** physiatrist; b. Manila; d. Eugenio Rillo and Felisa Padiernos (Espinosa) Q. BS, U. Philippines, 1969, MD, 1973. Rotating intern Philippine Gen. Hosp., Manila, 1973-74, resident dept. pediatrics, 1975-77; resident dept. phys. medicine and rehab. U. Md., Balt., 1977-80; fellow in pediatrics & rehab. Children's Hosp. Nat. Med. Ctr., Washington, 1980-81; fellow George Washington U. Hosp., Washington, 1980-81; attending physiatrist, asst. prof. U. Md. Sch. Medicine, Balt., 1981-86; attending physiatrist Sinai Hosp. of Balt., 1986-87; chief rehab. medicine svc. VA Med. Ctr., Augusta, Ga., 1987—. Fellow Am. Acad. Phys. Medicine and Rehab.; mem. Assn. Acad. Physiatrists. also: Macon Rehab Ctr 3330 Northside Dr Macon GA 31210-2559 Home: 11899 Marla Ln Seminole FL 33772-2219

**QUIROS-TEJEIRA, RUBEN ELOY,** pediatrician, educator; b. Panama, July 5, 1962; s. Felix A. Quiros and Olimpia Tejeira de Quiros; m. Nubia Noemi Navarrete, Nov. 12, 1994; children: Ruben Eloy Quiros Jr., Jonathan Elias Quiros, Jacob Eli Quiros. MD, Nat. U. Panama, 1986. Cert. Am. Bd. Pediat., 1995, diplomate Am. Bd. Hosp. Physicians, 2005, Am. Coll. Ethical Physicians, 2005. Resident Children's Hosp. Panama, 1988—91; sci. rschr. duPont Hosp. Children, Thomas Jefferson U., Wilmington, Del., 1992; resident Thomas Jefferson U., Phila., 1993—95; asst. prof. pediat. U. Rochester, NY, 2000—01, dir. pediatric hepatology, 2000—01; asst. prof. pediat. and surgery Baylor Coll. Medicine, Houston, 2001—04, med. dir. pediatric liver transplantation, 2001—04, assoc. prof. pediat. and surgery U. Tex., 2004—, med. dir. pediatric liver, intestinal transplantation, 2004—, dir. pediatric hepatology, 2004—; assoc. prof. pediat. U.T. M.D. Anderson Cancer Ctr., Houston, 2005—. Chmn. med. adv. com. Am. Liver Found., South Tex. Chpt., Houston, 2004—, bd. dirs.; reviewer peer rev. jour. Am. Jour. Transplantation, Edmonton, Canada, 2004—, Jour. Pediatric Gastroent. and Nutrition, Denver, 2004—, Archives Med. Rsch., Mexico D.F., 2003—, Bone Marrow Transplantation Jour., London, 2002—, Jour. Pediat., Cin., 2004—; med. adv. bd. mem. Life Gift Organ Donation Ctr., Houston, 2002—, Alagille Syndrome Alliance, Tualatin, Oreg., 2004—, Hepatitis Mag., Houston, 2005—; internat. com. mem. N.Am. Soc. Pediatric Gastroent., Hepatology and Nutrition, Flourtown, Pa., 2004—. Contbr. articles to profl. jours. Mem. focus group Tex. Gulf Digestive Disease Ctr., 2004—. Recipient Herman Roseblum award, Thomas jefferson U., 1994—95; fellow, UCLA, 1995—98, 1998—2000; grantee, NIH. Fellow: AMA (assoc.), Am. Acad. Pediatric (assoc.; mem.: AAAS (assoc.), Assn. Med. Students U. Panama (assoc.), Am. Med. Assn. Panama (hon.), Panamanian Pediatric Soc. (hon.), Harris County Med. Soc. (assoc.), Internat. Liver Transplantation Soc. (assoc.), Am. Gastroent. Assn. (assoc.), Tex. Med. Assn. (assoc.), Am. Assn. Study Liver Disease (assoc.), Am. Soc. Transplantation (assoc.), N.Am. Soc. Pediatric Gastroent., Hepatology and Nutrition (assoc.), Internat. Pediatric Transplant Assn. (assoc.), Am. Liver Found. (assoc.), Jefferson Med. Coll. Alumni Assn. (hon.). Roman Catholic. Office: U Tex 6431 Fannin St MSB 3140A Houston TX 77030 Office Phone: 713-500-6142. Office Fax: 713-500-5750.

**QUISENBERRY, NANCY LOU,** academic administrator, educator; b. Washington, Ind., Jan. 29, 1938; d. Joseph Franklin and Maud Helen (Fitch) Forbes; m. James D. Quisenberry, Feb. 6, 1960; 1 child, James Paul. BS in Home Econs., Ind. State Tchrs. Coll., 1960, MS in Home Econs., 1962; EdD, Ind. U., 1971. Cert. tchr. Ind. Home economics tchr. Honey Creek High Sch., Terre Haute, Ind., 1961-62; third grade tchr. Public Sch., 1962-64; substitute tchr. Dep. of Def., Baumholder, Fed. Republic Germany, 1964-65; first grade tchr. Wayne Twp. Schs., Indpls., 1966-67; assoc. faculty lang. arts Ind. U.-Purdue U., Indpls., spring 1970; prof. curriculum and instruction So. Ill. U., Carbondale, 1971—98, assoc. dean Coll. of Edn., 1976-96, interim dean, 1996-98; exec. dir. Orpheum Children's Sci. Mus., Champaign, Ill.,

2004—. Cons. U. N.C., Durham, 1977, Ministry Edn., Bangkok, 1980, Bangkok, 84, DePaul U., 1990, Ill. State U., 2002, U. Miss., 2001, Loyola U., 2002, Gov.'s State U., 2002; dir. tech. and tng. assistance grant Head Start-OCD, Carbondale, 1972—74, Cameroon project USAID, Carbondale, 1984—86; mem. Ill. State Tchr. Cert. Bd.; 1981—84, 1984—87. Co-author: Early Childhood Education Programs: Developmental Objectives and Their Use, 1975, Play as Development, 1978, Educators Healing Racism, 1999, Racism in the Classroom: Case Studies, 2002. Bd. dirs. Jackson County YMCA, 1988; chair candidacy com. Ctrl. So. Ill. Synod Evang. Luth. Ch. Am., Springfield, 1987—90, sec. multisynodical com. Chgo., 1987—90, synod coun., 1992—95; pres. Epiphany Luth. Ch. Coun., Carbondale, 1984—85, 1992—95, 1994—96. Recipient Dare To Be Great award, Ill. Women Adminstrs. and So. Ill. Region, 1989, Woman of Distinction award, So. Ill. U., 1992; grantee, Bur. Educationally Handicapped, 1979—82, 1990—95. Mem.: World Orgn. for Pre-sch. Edn. (U.S. nat. com., treas. 1997—99, chmn. strategic planning commn. 1999—2002, webmaster 2000—), Assn. Tchr. Educators (chair com. racism from a healing perspective 1995—98), Ill. Assn. Colls. for Tchr. Edn. (pres 1984—86), Am. Assn. Colls. for Tchr. Edn. (bd. dirs. 1986—88, chair adv. coun. state reps. 1987—88, bd. dirs. 1991—94), Nat. Coun. for Accreditation Tchr. Edn. (bd. examiners 1987—98, new profl. tchr. project elem. edn. stds. drafting com. 1996—98, transition team elem. stds. 1998—2000, chair Rubics devel. com. 2001, exec. bd. 2002—, chair Coun. Profl. Preparation of Educators 2003—), Assn. Childhood Edn. Internat. (chair tchr. edn. com. 1989—93, folio rev. coord. elem. edn. 1989—2001, sec.-treas. 1996—, pres.-elect 1998—2000, pres. 2001—03, past pres. 2003—04, folio rev. coord. elem. edn. 2004—), Internat. Coun. on Edn. for Tchg. (N.Am. v.p 1992—94, pres.-elect 1997—2000, pres. 2000—02, bd. dirs.) Rotary (pres. Urbana chpt. 2005—). Avocations: gardening, flute, sewing, walking, organ. Home: 1713 E Mumford Dr Urbana IL 61802-8605 Office: So Ill U Coll Edn Carbondale IL 62901-4624 Business E-Mail: nancyq@siu.edu.

**QUISGARD, LIZ WHITNEY,** artist, sculptor; b. Phila., Oct. 23, 1929; d. Kenneth E. and Elizabeth (Warwick) Whitney; children: Kristin, Berit. Grad. night sch., Md. Inst. Coll. Art, 1947, grad. day sch., 1949; student, Johns Hopkins U., evenings 1952-58; pupil of, Morris Louis, 1958-60; BFA in Painting, Md. Inst., 1966, MFA in Sculpture, 1966. Pvt. tchr. painting, Balt., 1955-65. Tchr. Balt. Hebrew Congregation, 1962-80; mem. faculty Md. Inst. Coll. Art, 1965-76, Goucher Coll., 1966-68, Balt. Jewish Community Ctr., 1974-78, Villa Julie Coll., Stevenson, Md., 1978-80; art critic Balt. Sun, 1969-71, Craft Horizons, 1972, The Paper, 1971-72; designer prodns. Center Stage, Goucher Coll., Johns Hopkins U.; lectr. in Md., Va., W.Va., Pa., Ark., Ohio, N.Y., N.J. One-woman exhbns. include Jefferson Pl. Gallery, Washington, 1960, Emmerich Gallery, N.Y.C., 1962, Goucher Coll., Balt., 1966, U. Md., 1969, Gallery, 707, Los Angeles, 1974, Arts and Sci. Center, Nashua, N.H., 1975, Mechanic Gallery, Balt., 1978, Marymount Manhattan Coll., N.Y.C., 1983; Tiffany's windows, N.Y.C., 1984, Starkman Gallery, N.Y.C., 1984, Fordham U., N.Y.C., 1985, Henri Gallery, Washington, 1987, Artemisia Gallery, Chgo., 1987, Savannah (Ga.) Coll. Art and Design, 1987, Life of Maryland Gallery, Balt., 1988, Franz Bader Gallery, Washington, 1989, Fairleigh Dickinson U., N.J., 1990, Herr-Chambliss Gallery, Hot Springs, Ark., 1990, Huntington (Ind.) Coll., 1991, Bergdorf Goodman Windows, 1991, Coll. of New Rochelle, N.Y., 1992, Broadway windows, N.Y.C., 1992, Nexus Found., Phila., 1993, Carnegie Arts Ctr., Leavenworth, Kans., 1994, Asheville (N.C.) Mus., 1995; group exhbns. include, Balt. Mus., 1951-53, 58, Corcoran Gallery Area Show, 1956, 64, Corcoran Biennial Show, 1963, Peale Mus., Balt., 1947, 56, Butler Inst. Am. Art, Youngstown, Ohio, 1957, Provincetown (Mass.) Art Assn., 1955, Pa. Acad. Am. Art ann., 1964, Chgo. Art Inst., 1965, Gallery 707, 1973, S. Houston St. Gallery, N.Y.C., 1974, Balt. Mus. travelling show, 1978, Mus. of Hudson Highlands, Cornwall, N.Y., 1983; represented in permanent collections U. Ariz., U. Md., U. Balt., Johns Hopkins U., Lever House, N.Y.C., Center Club, Balt., Libyan Mission to UN, Englewood, N.J., Datalogix Corp., Valhalla, N.Y., Gt. Northern Nekoosa Corp., Norwalk, Conn., Quality Inns, Newark, Can. Imperial Bank of Commerce, N.Y.C., Rosenberg Diamond Co., N.Y.C., Marsh, Inc., Indpls., Kirkpatrick and Lockhart, Pitts., Fordham U., N.Y.C., Atlantic Realty, Atlanta, Miss. Mus. Art, Jackson, St. Joseph Health Ctr., Hot Springs, Ark., Dermatology Assocs., Pitts., Scudder, Stevens & Clark, Boston, also pvt. collections; executed mural William Fell Elem. Sch., Balt., 1980, Urban Wall, Atlanta, 1990, floor painting Vet.'s Stadium, Phila., 1992, mural Med. Coll. Va., Richmond, 1994. Recipient Best in Show award Loyola Coll. Invitational, Balt., 1966, Florsheim Purchase Grant, 1991; scholar Md. Inst. 1947-49; Rinehart fellow in sculpture, 1964-66. Address: 113 Elizabeth St #B New York NY 10013

**QUIST, ARJAN,** biotechnologist, director; b. Amstelveen, Netherlands, Mar. 25, 1970; PhD, Uppsala U., Sweden, 1992—97. Sr. scientist Uppsala U., 1999—2003; rschr. U. Calif., Santa Barbara, 2003—06; dir. nanotechnology Richmond Chem. Corp., Oak Brook, Ill., 2006—. Contbr. over 25 papers to profl. jours. and pubs. Achievements include patents for Surface nano biotechnology related patents. Office: Richmond Chem Corp 2210 Midwest Rd Ste 100 Oak Brook IL 60523 Office Phone: 630-572-2500.

**QUIST, GORDON JAY,** federal judge; b. Grand Rapids, Mich., Nov. 12, 1937; s. George J. and Ida F. (Hoekstra) Q.; m. Martha Jane Capito, Mar. 10, 1962; children: Scot D., George J., Susan E., Martha J., Peter K. BA, Mich. State U., 1959; JD with honors, George Washington U., 1962. Bar: DC 1962, Ill. 1964, US Dist. Ct. (no. dist.) Ill. 1964, US Supreme Ct. 1965, Mich. 1967, US Dist. Ct. (we. dist.) Mich. 1967, US Ct. Appeals (6th cir.) 1967. Assoc. Hollabaugh & Jacobs, Washington, 1962-64, Sonnenschein, Levinson, Carlin, Nath & Rosenthal, Chgo., 1964-66, Miller, Johnson, Snell & Cummiskey, Grand Rapids, 1967-72, ptnr., 1972-92, mng. ptnr., 1986-92; judge US Dist. Ct. (we. dist.) Mich., Grand Rapids, 1992—. Mem. Code of Conduct com. U.S. Cts., 2004—2007. Bd. dirs. Wedgewood Acres-Ch. Youth Home, 1968-74, Mary Free Bed Hosp., 1979-88, Christian Ref. Publs., 1968-78, 82-88, Opera Grand Rapids, 1986-92, Mary Free Bed Brace Shop, 1988-92, Better Bus. Bur., 1972-80, Calvin Theol. Sem., 1992-93; bd. dirs Indian Trails Camp, 1970-78, 82-88, pres., 1978, 88. Recipient Disting. Alumnus award George Washington U. Law Sch. 1998 Mem. Fed. Bar Assn. Am. Judicature Soc., Mich. State Bar Found., Univ. Club Grand Rapids, Order of Coif. Avocations: reading, travel. Office: 482 Ford Fed Courthouse 110 Michigan St NW Grand Rapids MI 49503-2313 Business E-Mail: Gordon_J_Quist@miwd.uscourts.gov.

**QUITTMEYER, PETER CHARLES,** lawyer; b. Charlottesville, Va., Oct. 9, 1957; s. Charles L. and Maureen (Rankin) Q.; children: Charles Lake, Laura Slater. BA with high distinction, U. Va., Charlottesville, 1979, JD, 1982. Bar: Ga. 1985. Assoc. King & Spalding, Atlanta, 1982-87; shareholder Trotter, Smith & Jacobs, Atlanta, 1987-91; ptnr. Nelson Mullins Riley & Scarborough, Atlanta, 1991—2001, Sutherland Asbill & Brennan, Atlanta, 2001—. Adj. prof. computer law Emory U. Sch. Law, Atlanta, 1996, 98, 2000. Author: Computer Software Agreements, 1985—; mem. editl. bd. Va. Law Rev., 1981-82; contbr. articles to profl. jours. Vol. gen. counsel, dir. Ga. chpt. Arthritis Found. Recipient Vol. award, Ga. chpt. Arthritis Found., 2005; Nat. Merit scholar semifinalist, Westinghouse Sci. Talent Contest. Mem. ABA, Ga. Bar Assn., Raven Soc., Order of Coif, Phi Beta Kappa. Office: Sutherland Asbill & Brennan 999 Peachtree St NE Ste 2300 Atlanta GA 30309 Office Phone: 404-853-8186. Business E-Mail: peter.quittmeyer@sablaw.com.

**QUITTNER, JOSH,** editor; m. Michelle Slatalla; 3 children. Grad., Grinnell Coll., Columbia U. With Bergen Record, NJ, Albuquerque Jour., Newsday; joined TIME, 1995, mng. editor time.com, mng. editor ON Mag., tech. editor; editor in chief Bus. 2.0, N.Y.C., 2002—. Co-author (with M. Slatalla): Flame Wars: A Cyberthriller, 1995, Masters of Deception: The Gang That Ruled Cyberspace, 1997, Speeding the Net: The Inside Story of Netscape and How It Challenged Microsoft, 1998. Office: Business 2.0 One California St, 29th Fl San Francisco CA 94111 Office Phone: 415-293-4800.

**QUIVERS, ROBIN,** radio personality; b. Balt., Aug. 8, 1952; d. Charles and Louise Quivers. Student, U. Md., 1974. Morning anchor W100, Carlisle, Pa., 1980; co-host Howard Stern Show, 1981—; with WWDC, Wash., DC, 1981, WNBC, NYC, 1982—85, WXRK-FM, NYC, 1985—2005, Sirius Satellite Radio, NYC, 2006—. Co-author: Quivers: A Life, 1995; actor: (films) Private Parts, 1997; (TV films) Deadly Web, 1996; co-host (TV series) The Howard Stern Show (WOR-TV), 1990—92, The Howard Stern Show (E!), 1994—2005, Howard Stern On Demand, 2005—; guest appearance: (TV series) The Fresh Prince of Bel-Air, 1993; The Larry Sanders Show, 1993; The Magic Hour, 1998. RN, advanced through ranks to capt. USAF. Office: Sirius Satellite Radio 1221 Ave of the Americas New York NY 10020*

**QUON, MICHAEL JAMES,** medical researcher, internist; b. Oakland, Calif, Apr. 26, 1960; s. Jimmie Earl and Helen (Tang) Quon; m. Huison Kim, June 22, 1985; children: Hana, James. BS in Biomed. Engring., Northwestern U., 1982, PhD in Biomed. Engring., 1987, MD, 1988. Diplomate Nat. Bd. Med. Examiners, Am. Bd. Internal Medicine. Resident in internal medicine U. Chgo., 1988—90; fellow in endocrinology NIH, Bethesda, Md., 1990—93, sr. clin. investigator, 1993—95, sr. investigator Nat. Heart, Lung and Blood Inst., 1995—2002, chief diabetes unit NCCAM, 2002—. Contbr. articles to profl. jours. Capt. USPHS, 1990—. Mem.: ACP, Juvenile Diabetes Found. Internat., Coun. for High Blood Pressure, Am. Heart Assn., Am. Diabetes Assn. (Rsch. award grant 1994—). Avocations: piano, violin. Office: NIH NCCAM Bldg 10 rm 6C 205 Bethesda MD 20892-0001

**QUOQUOI, GADEMA K.,** computer consultant; b. Gbata, Liberia, Oct. 02; arrived in U.S., 1974, s. Tanoon Wiliiyan and Koluboi Quoquoi; m. Juliette Quoquoi, 1985 (separated); children: Tanoon, Gadema, Kabeh. Student, LIU, N.Y. Inst. Tech. Bookkeeper Liberia Mining Co., Lamco, Nimba, Liberia, 1973—74; field engr. Mergen the Lar Lino Type, N.Y.C., 1978—79; pres. Compuline Internat., Inc., N.Y.C., 1998—2000, Compuline Com, Inc., N.Y.C., 2000. E-mail: gkquoquoi@yahoo.com.

**QURAISHI, MOHAMMED SAYEED,** retired health facility administrator, research scientist; b. Jodhpur, India, June 23, 1924; arrived in US, 1946, naturalized, 1973; s. Mohammed Latif and Akhtar Jahan Q.; m. Akhtar Imtiaz, Nov. 12, 1953; children: Rana, Naveed, Sabah (dec.). B.Sc., St. John's Coll., 1942; M.Sc., Aligarh Muslim U., 1944; PhD, U. Mass., 1948. Sr. mem. UN, WHO Team to Bangladesh, 1949-51; entomologist Malaria Inst. Pakistan, 1951-55; sr. rsch. officer Pakistan Council Sci. and Indsl. Rsch., 1955-60; sr. sci. officer Pakistan AEC, 1960-64; assoc. prof. entomology U. Man., 1964-66, N.D. State U., Fargo, 1966-70, prof., 1970-74; chief scientist biology N.Y. State Sci. Svc., Albany, 1974-75; entomologist, toxicologist, chief pest control and consultation sect. NIH, Bethesda, Md., 1976-84; health scientist adminstr., exec. sec. microbiology and infectious disease rsch. com. Nat. Inst. Allergy and Infectious Diseases, Bethesda, Md., 1984-88, sci. rev. adminstr. spl. revs., 1988-96, sci. rev. adminstr. AIDS clin. epidemiol. rsch. rev. br., 1996-2000; ret., 2000; sr. scientist Inst. Nuclear Sci., CENTO, Tehran, Iran, 1960-64; program mgr. interdepartmental contract Project THEMIS, Dept. Def., 1968-74. Cons. breast cancer rsch. program UIS Dept. Def., 2001; vis. scientist Harvard Sch. Pub. Health, 1995. Author: Biochemical Insect Control: Its Impact on Economy, Environment and Natural Selection, 1977; mem. editorial bd. Jour. Environ. Toxicology and Chemistry, 1981-84; author numerous sci. papers. Chmn. NIH Asian-Am. Cultural Assn., 1980—81; mem. Montgomery County Bd. Social Svcs., 2002. Recipient Sustained High Quality Performance award, 1980, Merit Pay Performance awards, 1984, 86, 87, Recognition and Appreciation of Spl. Achievement award NIH, 1988, Spl. Recognition award for Svcs. to NIH, Asian Am. Cultural Com., 1989, Appreciation in Recognition of Outstanding Support for Combined Fed. Campaign, 1991. Mem. Am. Chem. Soc., Soc. Environ. Toxicology and Chemistry (mem. pubs. com. in charge spl. publs. 1982-84), Sigma Xi, Phi Kappa Phi. Home: 19813 Cochrane Way Gaithersburg MD 20879-1637 Personal E-mail: sayeedquraishi@aol.com.

**QUREISHI, A. SALAM,** computer company executive; b. Aligarh, India, July 1, 1936; s. M.A. Jabbar and Saira (Sattar) Q.; m. Naheed Fatima; children: Lubna, Leila. BS in Physics and Math., Aligarth U., India, 1954; MS in Stats., Patna U., India, 1957. Mgr. applications IBM Corp., Palo Alto, Calif., 1961-67; founder, pres., chmn. bd. Optimum Sys., Inc., Palo Alto, Calif., 1967-71; CEO Sysorex Internat., Inc., Mountain View, Calif., 1972—. Republican. Home: 925 Mountain Home Rd Woodside CA 94062-2519 Office: A Salam Qureishi 506 Clyde Ave Mountain View CA 94043-2212

**QUTUB, AMINA ANN,** biomedical researcher, entrepreneur; d. Shehryar and Nancy Qutub. BS, Rice U., Houston, Tex., 1999; PhD, U. Calif., Berkeley and San Francisco, 2004. Grad. rschr. U. Calif., San Francisco, 2000—04; founder, CEO B3io, Berkeley, Calif., 2002—03; postdoctoral fellow Sch. Medicine Johns Hopkins U., Balt., 2004—. Contbr. articles to profl. jours. Vol. dir. corp. partnerships Found. Internat. Med. Relief Children, 2005, v.p. adminstrn., 2004—05. Finalist Haas Bus. Plan Competition, U. Calif., Berkeley, 2002, Innovator's Challenge Competition, Berkeley and Stanford U., 2003; recipient Poster award, Gordon Rsch. Conf., 2004; fellow, Whitaker Found., 1999—2004; scholar Chem. Engring. Thomas Moore scholarship, Rice U., 1999; Ruth L. Kirschstein Nat. Svc. Rsch. grant, NIH, 2006—. Mem.: Am. Assn. Cancer Rsch. Achievements include first to agent-based blood-brain barrier model; research in intracellular oxygen-sensing computational model. Personal E-mail: aminaq@gmail.com.

**QUTUB, EILEEN,** state legislator, real estate appraiser; b. York, Nebr., Mar. 2, 1948; m. Abe Qutub. BA in Mgmt. Human Resources, George Fox Coll. Pres., owner Hairtel Internat., Inc., Portland, 1978—83; sales assoc., Realtor Allen Tate Realtors, Charlotte, NC, 1984—87; real estate appraiser City of Charlotte, NC, 1988—91; appraiser III Clark County Assessor's Office, Vancouver, Wash., 1993—94; state rep. Oreg. Dist. 8, Beaverton, Oreg., 1995; state sen. Oregon Dist. 4, Beaverton, Tigarg, Oreg., 1997—2001; exec. dir. spl. projects Robert D. & Marcia H. Randall Charitable Trust, Randall Realty Corp., Portland, 2001—03; dir. of sch. advancement Heritage Christian Sch., Hillsboro, Oreg., 2003; non-profit cons. Robert D. & Marcia H. Randall Charitable Trust, Portland, 2003—04; real estate broker Re-Max Equity Group, Beaverton, 2005—. Spkr. and fundraiser in field Precint Com., Charlotte, NC; chair. bd. dirs. Pregnancy Resource Ctr. of Greater Portland; bd. dirs. Portland Rescue Mission, Portland, Oregon Right to Life Polit. Action Com., Metro Policy Chaplaincy; advisory bd. dirs. Capital Ministries of Oreg. Republican. Home: 11135 Sw Patridge Loop Beaverton OR 97007 Office: S 210 State Capitol Salem OR 97310 E-mail: qutub.sen@state.or.us.

**QUTUB, MUSA YACUB,** hydrogeologist, educator, consultant; b. Jerusalem, June 2, 1940; came to U.S., 1960; s. Yacub and Sarah Qutub; married; children: Hanhia, Jennan, Sarmad, Muntaser, Aya, Saif, Tasneem. BA in Geology, Simpson Coll., Indianola, Iowa, 1964; MS in Hydrogeology, Colo. State U., 1966; PhD in Water Resources, Iowa State U. Sci. and Tech., 1969. Instr. earth sci. Iowa State U., Ames, 1966-69; from asst. prof. to prof. Northeastern Ill., Chgo., 1969-80, prof. geography and environ. studies, 1980—. Cons. hydrogeology, Des Plaines, Ill., 1970—; sr. adviser Saudi Arabian Ministry Planning, Riyadh, 1977-78; leader U.S. environ. sci. del. to People's Republic of China, 1984; pres., founder Islamic Info. Ctr. Am. Author: Secondary Environmental Science Methods, 1973; contbr. numerous articles to profl. jours.; editor Environ. Resource, Directory Environ. Educators and Cons. World. NSF grantee, 1970-71, 71-72, 72-73, 75, 76, Hew grantee, 1974, grantee Ill. Dept. Edn., 1970. Mem. AAAS, NSF (cons.), Am. Waterworks Assn., Am. Men and Women Sci., Nat. Assn. Geology Tchrs. (pres. central sect. 1974), Environ. Sci. Inst. (edn. com.), Internat. Assn. Advancement of Earth and Environ Sci. (pres. 1975—, founder), Ill. Earth Sci. Edn. (pres. 1971-73, founder), Phi Delta Kappa. Moslem. Avocations: tennis, track, cross country, soccer.

**RA, HYUNGSHIM YOO,** biologist, researcher; b. Kimje, Cheonrabook-Do, Republic of Korea, Jan. 12, 1964; d. Dolyi Ra and Bokdong Seo; m. Sunhee Yoo, June 10, 1989; children: Suran Yoo, Aran Yoo, Daeyeon Yoo. B. Paichai U., Republic of Korea, 1986; M, Sungshin Women's U., Republic of Korea, 1991; PhD, U. Ill., 2002. Cert. Achieve. U. Ill., Bus. Mgmt. U. Ill., Grad. Tchrs. U. Ill. Rschr. U. Ill., Urbana-Champaign, 2002—. Contbr. articles various rsch. papers. Treas. Ch. in Champaign, Ill., 2004—05; bd. dirs. Nat. Women's Hist. Mus., Wash, DC, 2005; rsch. bd. adv. Am. Biog. Inst., Inc., Raleigh, NC, 2005. Recipient Internat. Peace prize, United Cultural Conv., 2005. Mem.: AAUW (assoc.), Am. Bryological and Lichenological Soc. (assoc.), Am. Chem. Soc. (assoc.), Nat. Assn. for Female Executives (assoc.), Microscopy of Am. (assoc. Presdl. Student award 2002), So. Poverty Law Ctr. (assoc.), Dem. Nat. Com., Nat. Com. to Preserve Social Security and Medicare (assoc.), Habitat for Humanity (assoc.), The Nature Conservancy (assoc.), Christian Appalachian Project (assoc.), Sierra Club (assoc.). Consumer. Office: U Illinois 265 Morrill Hall 505 S Goodwin Ave Urbana IL 61801 Home: 3906 Turnberry Dr Champaign IL 61821 Business E-Mail: hs-yoo@life.uiuc.edu.

**RAAB, DIANE,** special education educator; BA, Lewis and Clark Coll., 1987; MA, U. Ariz., 2005. Cert. tchr. Alaska, Ariz. Reporter Anchorage Times, 1990—92, Juneau Empire, Alaska, 1993—94; tchr. Annette Island Sch. Dist., Metlakatla, Alaska, 1994—96; city govt. reporter Sedona Red Rock News, Ariz., 1996—98; devel. dir. KRBD, Ketchikan, Alaska, 1999—2000; news reporter KAZM 780 AM, Sedona, Ariz., 2001; campaign mgr. Middag for State Senate, Ketchikan, Alaska, 2000; tchr. Ariz. Sch. for Blind, Tucson, 2001—. Counselor Am. Cancer Soc., Ariz., 2002, Ariz., 2003; deacon St. Mark's Presbyn. Ch., Tucson, 2006. Avocations: caving, hiking. Office: Ariz Sch for Deaf and Blind 1200 W Speedway Blvd Tucson AZ 85745 Personal E-mail: diane_raab@hotmail.com.*

**RAAB, GAIL BARBARA,** painter, educator; b. NYC, Jan. 15, 1934; d. Sydney Leff and Rita Zion; m. Martin David Raab, Jan. 8, 1956; children: Jonathan, Nina Fox. Attended. U. Colo., 1953, Mexico City Coll., 1954, Queens Coll.; BFA in fine arts, Tyler Sch. of Fine Arts, Temple U., 1955. Artist Chaite Studios, N.Y.C., NY; instr. Whitney Mus., Art Reach Program, N.Y.C.; instr. Seventeen Mag., N.Y.C., one-woman shows include Bachelier, Conn., 1996, Pepper Gallery, Mass., 1999, OK Harris Gallery, N.Y., 2000, O.K. Harris, N.Y.C., 2002, 2004, Ute Stebich Gallery, Lenox, Mass., 2001, Pepper Gallery, Boston, 2003, SKH Gallery, Great Barrington, Mass., 2005, others, exhibitions include Scherling-Plough Corp., 1988, UTE Steback Gallery, Mass., 2003, O.K. Harris, N.Y.C., 2004, Hidell Brooks Gallery, NC, 2004, Phila. Museum, SKH Gallery, Great Barrington, Mass., 2005—06, others, prin. works include CBS Recordings, N.Y.C., 1986. Recipient Charlotte Winston award, 1987, Sara WilsonZMeml. award, 1990, Morre Greenblatt award, 1991, Martha Reed Meml. award, 1992, Hon. medal, Nat. Assn. Women Artists, 1993, Eve Helman award, 1995, Cecil Shapiro Meml. award, 1996. Mem.: Long Island Craftsman Guild, Nat. Assn. Women Artists (exec. bd., Medal of Honor 1980, C Winston Mem. prize 1988, Martha Reed Mem. award). Home: 300 E 74th St 25G New York NY 10021 Office: OK Harris Gallery 383 W Broadway New York NY 10012 also: Pepper Gallery 38 Newbury St Boston MA 02116 Office Phone: 212-744-5768.

**RAAB, HARRY FREDERICK, JR.,** retired physicist; b. Johnstown, Pa., May 9, 1926; s. Harry Frederick and Marjorie Eleanor (Stiff) R.; m. Phebe Ann Duerr, June 16, 1951; children: Constance Diane, Harry Frederick, Cynthia Ann Raab Morgenthaler. Student, Navy Electronics Tech. Sch., 1944-45; SB and SM E.E., MIT, 1951; postgrad., Oak Ridge Sch. Reactor Tech., 1954-55. Reactor control engr. Bettis Atomic Power Lab Westinghouse Electric Corp., West Mifflin, Pa., 1951-54, mgr. surface ship physics, 1956—62, mgr. light water breeder reactor physics, 1962-72; chief physicist Navy Nuc. Propulsion Directorate, Washington, 1972-95, ret., 1995. Patentee light water breeder reactor. Active Laymen's Missionary League, Episc. Diocese of Pitts., 1957-72; lay eucharistic min., lay intercessor and lector Episc. Ch. of Good Shepherd, Burke, Va., 1972-, Sunday sch. tchr., 1957-72, dir. liturgy, 1987-97, stewardship chmn., 1979-82, 84, 92-93, chmn. presch. bd., 1994-97, healing ministry, 1989—, sr. warden, 1983, 85, 97, Stephen Ministry leader, 1998—; mem. stewardship com. Diocese of Va., 1983—, chmn. stewardship, 1995-2002; chaplain for mentally retarded No. Va. Tng. Ctr., 1983—, treas. religious adv bd., 1998—; bd. dirs. Phoenix Cmty. Svcs., 1995-99; lay pediat. chaplain Fairfax Hosp., 1995—. With USNR, 1944-46 Fellow Am. Nuc. Soc.; mem. Masons, Sigma Xi, Tau Beta Pi, Eta Kappa Nu. Republican. Home: 8202 Ector Ct Annandale VA 22003-1342 E-mail: hraabjr@aol.com. *Always treat others with respect. Strive for excellence. Always act with honesty and integrity. Remember Henry Ford's observation: "If you say that you can, or if you say you cannot, you are right."*

**RAAB, IRA JERRY,** lawyer, judge; b. N.Y.C., June 20, 1935; s. Benjamin and Fannie (Kirschner) R.; m. Regina Schneider, June 4, 1957 (div. 1978); children: Michael, Shelley; m. Katie Rachel McKeever, June 30, 1979 (div. 1991); children: Julie, Jennifer, Joseph; m. Gloria Silverman, Nov. 7, 1996; children: Jill, Todd, John. BBA, CCNY, 1955; JD, Bklyn. Law Sch., 1957; MPA, NYU, 1959, postgrad.; MS in Pub. Adminstrn., L.I. U., 1961; MBA, Adelphi U., 1990. Bar: N.Y. 1958, U.S. Dist. Ct. (so. and ea. dists.) N.Y. 1960, U.S. Supreme Ct. 1967, U.S. Tax Ct. 1976, U.S. Ct. Appeals (2d cir.) 1977. Pvt. practice, Woodmere, NY, 1958-96, 2003—; asst. Westchester County Soc. Prevention of Cruelty to Children, White Plains, 1958; counsel Dept. Correction City of N.Y., 1959, trial commr. Dept. Correction, 1976, asst. corp. counsel Tort divsn. N.Y.C. Law Dept., 1963-70; staff counsel SBA, N.Y.C., 1961-63; counsel Investigation Com. on Willowbrook State Sch., Boro Hall, S.I., N.Y., 1970; gen. counsel Richmond County Soc. Prevention of Cruelty to Children, Boro Hall, 1970-81; pro bono counsel N.Y.C. Patrolmen's Benevolent Assn., 1974-81; rep. to UN Internat. Criminal Ct., 1977-78; arbitrator Small Claims Ct. Day Cts., N.Y.C., 1970-96; arbitrator L.I. Better Bus. Bur., 1976-93, Nassau County Dist. Ct., 1978-93, arbitrator Small Claims Ct., 1978-96; spl. master N.Y. County Supreme Ct., 1977-96; judge N.Y.C. Parking Violations Bur., 1991-93; arbitrator, 2003—; hearing ofcl. Nassau County Supreme Ct., 1982—96, 2003—. Small claims arbitrator N.Y.C. Civil Ct., 1970-96; arbitrator U.S. Dist. Ct. (ea. dist.) N.Y., 1986-96, 2003—; tchr. cmty. and ednl. orgns.; instr. paralegal course Lawrence Sch. Dist., N.Y., 1982-84; law prof. Briarcliff Coll., Bethpage, N.Y., 1997; arbitrator Nat. Arbitration and Mediation, Inc., 2003-, NASD, 2003-. Chmn. Businessmen's Luncheon Club, Wall St. Synagogue, 1968-79; exec. sec. Cmty. Mediation Ctr., Suffolk County, 1978-80, exec. v.p. 1980-81; vice chmn. Woodmere Inc., Com., 1980-81; mem. adv. bd. Nassau Expressway Com., 1979-80; bd. dirs. Woodmere Mchts. Assn., 1979-80, v.p., 1979-83, chmn., 1984-93; sec. Congregation Aish Kodesh, Woodmere, 1992-2002; candidate for dist. ct. judge Nassau County, 1987, 88, 89, 91, 93, 94, 96; candidate for supreme ct. justice Nassau and Suffolk Counties, 1995, 98; elected judge Nassau County Dist. Ct., 1997-99; candidate for county ct., Nassau County, 1997; elected presiding judge dist. ct., 1999-2000; elected justice Nassau County Supreme Ct., 2000-03; arbitrator Nat. Arbitration and Mediation Inc., 2003—. Recipient Consumer Protection award FTC, 1974, 76, 79, Recognition award Pres. Ronald Reagan, 1986, Man of Yr. award L.I. Coun. of Chambers, 1987, N.Y. State Ct. Reporters Assn., 1999. Mem. ABA (chmn. cts. and comty. com. 1988-93, exec. com. jud. adminstrn. divsn. lawyers conf. 1989-95), Am. Judges Assn. (rep. to UN 2000—, bd. govs. 1973-78, 83, 89-96, 97-2003, nat. treas. 1978-82, chmn. civil ct. ops. com. 1975-76, chmn. ednl. film com. 1974-77, editl. bd. Ct. Rev. mag. 1975-79, 82-86, chmn. spkrs. bur. com. 1976-77, chmn. legis. com. 1983-95, chmn. resolutions com. 1995-98, 2000-2002, chmn. jud. concerns com. 1997-99, historian 1988—, William H. Burnett award 1983), Am. Judges Found. (pres. 1977-79, chmn. bd. trustees 1979-83, treas. 1974-75, 76-77, trustee 1983-97, 2000—), Assn. Arbitrators of Civil Ct. City of N.Y. (past pres.), N.Y. State Bar Assn. (sec. dist., city, town and village cts. sect.), Nassau County Bar Assn. (criminal cts. com., matrimonial and family ct. com., ct. com., ethics com., Supreme Ct. com.), Profl. Group Legal Svc. Assn. (past pres.), Internat. Assn. Jewish Lawyers and Jurists (com. to draft Internat. Bill of Rights to

Privacy 1982, coun. 1981-95, bd. govs. 1984-95), adv. bd. comty. dispute ctr. 1979-81), K.P. (past chancellor comdr.). Democrat. Roman Catholic. Address: 9452 Lantern Bay Cir West Palm Beach FL 33411 Office Phone: 561-514-1047. Personal E-mail: irajraab@yahoo.com.

**RAAB, JENNIFER J.,** city commissioner; AB with distinction, Cornell U., 1977; MPA, Princeton U., 1979; JD cum laude, Harvard U., 1985. Spl. projects mgr. S. Bronx Devel. Org., 1979-81; dir. pub. affairs Planning commn. City of N.Y., 1981-82, chmn. Landmarks Preservation commn., 1994—2001; litigation assoc. Cravath, Swaine & Moore, N.Y.C., 1985-90; campaign dir. Rose State Senate Campaign, 1988; issues dir. Giuliani Mayorial Campaign, 1989; litigation assoc. Paul, Weiss, Rifkind, Wharton & Garrison, N.Y.C., 1990-94; pres. Hunter Coll., 2001—. Bd. dirs Argus Cmty., Inc., Bronx, N.Y., 1987-94, City Vol. Corps, 1994; active Manhattan Cmty. Bd. 5, 1990-94; pres. E. 154-155th St. Housing Corp., Bronx, 1992-94; vol. arbitrator Small Claims divsn. Bronx Civil Ct., 1993-94; mem. citizen's adv. coun., Mid-Town Cmty. Ct., 1994. Mem. Phi Beta Kappa. Office: Hunter College Room E1700 695 Park Ave New York NY 10021

**RAAB, SHELDON,** lawyer; b. Bklyn., Nov. 30, 1937; s. Morris and Eva (Shereshevsky) Raab; m. Judith Deutsch, Dec. 15, 1963; children: Michael Kenneth, Elisabeth Louise, Andrew John. AB, Columbia U., 1958; LLB cum laude, Harvard U., 1961. Bar: N.Y. 1961, U.S. Ct. Appeals (2d cir.) 1963, U.S. Dist. Ct. (so. and ea. dists.) 1967. Dep. asst. atty. gen. State of N.Y., 1961—63, asst. atty. gen., 1963—64; assoc. Frank, Harris, Shriver & Jacobson LLP (and predecessor firm), N.Y.C., 1964—69, ptnr., 1970—81, inc. ptnr., 1981—93, of counsel, 1993—. Mem. exec. com. lawyers' divsn. United Jewish Appeal, 1982—93. Mem.: ABA, Assn. of Bar of City of N.Y. (adminstrv. law com. 1968—71, spl. com. electric power and environment 1971—73, chmn. energy com. 1974—79, fed. cts. com. 1981—84, state superior cts. juris. com. 1985—88), N.Y. State Bar Assn. (trial lawyers sect. 1968—), Am. Law Inst. Democrat. Office: Fried Frank Harris Shriver & Jacobson LLP 1 New York Plz New York NY 10004-1980 Office Phone: 212-859-8090. Business E-Mail: raabsh@ffhsj.com.

**RAABE, GERHARD KARL,** epidemiologist; b. Flushing, NY, Feb. 24, 1948; s. Oscar Albert and Eugenie (Loehr) R.; m. Barbara Irene Douglas, Nov. 27, 1969; children: Andrew John, Emily Jean. BA in Biology, Hofstra U., 1969; MS in Computer Sci., Pratt Inst., 1971; DrPH, Columbia U., 1987. Sr. rsch. scientist N.Y. State Dept. Mental Hygiene, N.Y.C., 1970-77; med. systems analyst Mobil Oil Corp., N.Y.C., 1977-79, indsl. med. advisor, 1979-81, mgr. epidemiology and med. info. svcs., 1982-89, dir. epidemiology and med. info. svcs. Princeton, N.J., 1990-97; dir. med. info. and health risk assessment Global Med. Svcs., Mobil Bus. Resources Corp., 1997-99; pres., prin. scientist occupl. and environ. health Health Risk Scis., Inc., New Hope, Pa., 1999—. Cons. spl. studies Cornell U. Med. Ctr., N.Y.C., 1973-77; cons. N.Y.C. Health Systems Agy., 1976; chmn. occupational health com. Fla. Phosphate Coun., Lakeland, 1979-85; reviewer profl. jours.; expert panelist WHO, IARC, U.S. EPA. Contbr. articles to profl. jours., chpts. to books. Fellow Am. Coll. Epidemiology (mem. policy com.); mem. AAAS, Soc. for Epidemiologic Rsch., Internat. Soc. for Environ. Epidemiology, Am. Statis. Assn., Am. Petroleum Inst. (chmn. epidemiology 1985-88, chmn. health and product stewardship 1996-2000), N.Y. Acad. Scis., Soc. for Risk Analysis, Indsl. Epidemiology Forum (chmn. 1991), Internat. Commn. on Occupl. Health. Republican. Lutheran. Avocations: science fiction, tennis. Home: 2215 Aquetong Rd New Hope PA 18938-1149 Office: Health Risk Scis Inc PO Box 189 New Hope PA 18938-0189 Office Phone: 215-862-5718. Personal E-mail: gkraabe@cs.com.

**RAABE, WILLIAM ALAN,** tax writer, business educator; b. Milw., Dec. 14, 1953; s. William Arthur and Shirley R.; m. Nancy Elizabeth Miller, Mar 1989; children: Margaret Elisabeth, Martin William. BS, Carroll Coll., 1975; MAS, U. Ill., 1976, PhD, 1979. Wis. Disting. prof. U. Wis., Milw., 1979-96; tax edn. cons. Price Waterhouse Coopers, N.Y.C., 1985—; prof., dir. acctg. programs Samford U., Birmingham, Ala., 1997-2001; founding dean Sch. Mgmt., disting. prof. Capital U., Columbus, Ohio, 2001—02; mem. tax faculty Fisher Coll. Bus. Ohio State U., Columbus, 2002—. Vis. assoc. prof. Ariz. State U., Tempe, 1985; vis. faculty Ernst & Young, N.Y.C., 1990—, Deloitte & Touche, N.Y.C., 1998—, Calif. CPA Found., 1986, AICPA, 1984-94, Wis. Bar Assn., 1992, Capital U. Law Sch., 2002—; developer Estate Tax Planner, McGraw Hill Software, N.Y.C., 1980-88; expert witness, 1985—; cons. corp. income tax State Ala., 1997-01, State of Wis., 1995, 99; dir. Fisher/Ohio State U. Tax Clinic, 2003—. Author West's Federal Taxation, 1985—, Federal Tax Research, 1986—, Income Shifting After Tax Reform, 1987, Multistate Corporate Tax Guide, 1985-96, California Income Taxation, 1999—, Schedule M-3, 2006; editor CCH, 2005—, Price Waterhouse Coopers Tax Case Studies; contbr. articles to profl. jours. Bd. dirs., pres. Luth. High Sch. Assn. Milw., 1991-96, Bethesda Luth. Home, Watertown, Wis., 1989-91, Luth. Counseling and Family Svcs., 1982-88, Concord Chamber Orch., Milw., 1983-88; mem. Econ. Devel. Com., Wauwatosa, Wis., 1986-89; faculty athletic rep. to NCAA from U. Wis. Milw., 1990-96; mem. Milw. Symphony Chorus, Master Singers of Milw., Samford Master Singers, Samford Die Kantorei; vice chair faculty senate Samford U., 2000-01. Named to Alumni Hall Fame, Milw. (Wis.) Luth. H.S., 1995, Carroll Coll., 2005; fellow, U. Ill., 1978, Nat. Ctr. Tax Edn. and Rsch., 1981: Fellow Am. Acctg. Assn., Wis. Inst. CPAs (Educator of Yr. 1987), Ala. Acctg. Educators Assn. (pres. 1999-2000). Office: Fisher Coll Bus 2100 Neil Ave Columbus OH 43210-1144 Office Phone: 614-292-4023. Business E-Mail: raabe.12@osu.edu.

**RAAD, VIRGINIA,** pianist, educator; b. Salem, W.Va., Aug. 13, 1925; d. Joseph M. and Martha (Joseph) R. BA in Art History, Wellesley Coll., 1947; spl. student, New Eng. Conservatory Music, 1947-48; diplôme, Ecole Normale de Musique, Paris, 1950; Doctorate with honors (French Govt. grantee 1950-52, 54-55), U. Paris, 1955; student, Alfred Cortot, Jeanne Blancard, Berthe Bert, Jacques Chailley. Artist in residence Salem Coll., W.Va., 1957-70; ind. concert pianist, 1960—; musician in residence at cmty. colls. NC Arts Coun., 1971—. Adjudicator Nat. Guild Piano Tchrs., Nat. Fedn. Music Clubs; panelist, grant reviewer NEH, 1978-84, 92—; mem. com. Nat. Endowment Arts, 1978; mem. rep. Debussy Centennial Colloque, Paris, 1962. Perfomances, concerts, lectrs. master classes at West Ga. Coll., Carrollton, La Grange Coll., Ga., Columbus Coll., Ga., Young Harris Coll., Ga., U. Fla., Gainesville, Norton Gallery, Palm Beach, Fla., Alliance Française de Rollins Coll., Winter Park, Fla., Dixon Gallery and Gardens, Memphis, St. Jude Children's Rsch. Hosp., Memphis, Cleveland State CC, Tenn., Sampson Tech. Inst., Clinton, NC, Wayne CC, Goldsboro, NC, Brevard Coll., NC, Ctrl. Wesleyan Coll., SC, Ky. Wesleyan Coll., Owensboro, Berea Ky., Coll., Alice Lloyd Coll., Pippa Passes, Ky., Coll. of William and Mary, Williamsburg, Va., Eastern Mennonite Coll., Harrisonburg, Va., The Phillips Gallery, Washington, Trinity Coll., Washington, Manhattanville Coll., Purchase, NY, Elmira Coll., NY, Fordham U., NYC, The Piano Tchrs. Congress of NY, Middlebury Coll., Vt., St. Anselm's Coll., Manchester, N.H., Mount St. Mary's Coll., Hooksett, NH, Wellesley Coll., Mass., Curry Coll., Milton, Mass., So. Conn. State U., New Haven, Slippery Rock U., Pa., Seton Hill Coll., Greensboro, Pa., Alliance Française de Pitts. and U. Pitts., Channel 13 WQED (PBS) Pitts., Lincoln U., Oxford, Pa., The Grier Sch., Tyrone, Pa., Mount de Chantal Acad., Wheeling W.Va., Wheeling Jesuit U., among other colls. and univs.; contbg. author: Debussy and the Evolution de la Musique au XX Siècle, 1965; author: The Piano Sonority of Claude Debussy, 1994; recording artist: EDUCO, 1995—; contbr. articles to profl. jours. Active Amnesty Internat. Urgent Action Network; alumna regional rep. Wellesley Coll.; mem bd. visitors New Eng. Conservatory of Music, 2004—. Named Outstanding W.Va. Woman Educator Delta Kappa Gamma, 1965; presented biography to Schlesinger Library on History of Women in Am. Radcliffe Coll., 1967; grantee Govt. France, Am. Coun. Learned Socs. Mem. Soc. Française de Musicologie, Am. Musicol. Soc. (regional officer 1960-65), Am. Coll. Musicians, Internat. Musicol. Soc., Music Tchrs. Nat. Assn. (adjudicator, musicology program chair 1983-87), W.Va. Music Tchrs. Assn., Audubon

Activist, Alpha Delta Kappa (hon.). Republican. Roman Catholic. Avocations: hiking, gardening, birding. Address: 60 Terrace Ave Salem WV 26426-1116 Office Phone: 304-782-2274. Personal E-mail: virginiaraad@aol.com.

**RAAF, JOHN HART,** surgeon, educator, health facility administrator; b. Portland, Oreg., Aug. 10, 1941; s. John E. and Lorene (Rardin) R.; m. Heather Neilson, June 15, 1965; children— Jennifer, John, Sabrina AB magna cum laude, Harvard U., 1963, MD cum laude, 1970; D.Phil., Oxford U., 1966. Diplomate Am. Bd. Surgery. Intern Mass. Gen. Hosp., Boston, 1970-71, resident in surgery, 1971-73, 75-77; research fellow Sloan-Kettering Inst., N.Y.C., 1973-75; fellow in immunology Meml. Hosp., N.Y.C., 1973-74; faculty assoc. in surgery M.D. Anderson Hosp. and Tumor Inst., Houston, 1977-78, asst. prof. surgery, 1978-79, Cornell U. Med. Coll., N.Y.C., 1979-81; assoc. prof. surgery Meml. Sloan-Kettering Cancer Ctr., N.Y.C., 1981-85; dir. Cleve. Clinic Cancer Ctr., 1985-90; chmn. dept. surgery Meridia Huron Hosp., Cleve., 1991-94; chief surg. svc. VA Med. Ctr. Cleve., 1994-2001; prof. surgery Case Western Res. U., 1994—, vice chmn. dept. surgery, 1994-2001. Mem. selection coms. for Rhodes scholarships, Vt., 1969-71, New Eng., 1969-71, La., 1977, Tex., 1978, Ohio, 1989-94; mem. soft tissue sarcoma discussion group Nat. Cancer Inst., 1980; mem. clin. trials com. Nat. Cancer Inst., NIH, 1984-88 Co-author Meml. Sloan-Kettering Cancer Ctr. publs., 1980; also numerous articles, chpts., abstracts, letters, short papers, movies, med. photographs; editor: Diagnosis and Treatment of Soft Tissue Sarcomas, 1993; editor-in-chief Primary Care and Cancer, 1981-92; mem. editorial bd. Meml. Sloan-Kettering Cancer Ctr. Clin. Bull., 1979-82; assoc. editor Oncology mag., 1987-92; mem. editorial bd. Cleve Clinic Jour. Medicine, 1987-90. Rhodes scholar Oxford U., Eng., 1963; nat. scholar Harvard U. Med. Sch., 1966-70; Am. Cancer Soc. postdoctoral scholar Harvard U. Med. Sch., 1969-70; ACS scholar Mass. Gen. Hosp., Boston, 1975-77; Am. Cancer Soc. jr. faculty clin. fellow, 1980-83. Fellow ACS; mem. Am. Assn. Cancer Research, Am. Assn. Endocrine Surgeons, Am. Soc. Clin. Oncology, Assn. Acad. Surgery, Assn. Am. Rhodes Scholars, Cen. Surg. Assn., Cleve. Surg. Soc., Soc. Surg. Oncology (publs. com. 1981-84, working group on edn. 1982, membership com. 2000), Meml. Hosp. Alumni Soc. (chmn. program com. 1982), Cleve. Skating Club, Charaka Club (N.Y.C.). Home: 12501 Fairhill Rd Cleveland OH 44120-1017

**RAAFLAUB, KURT ARNOLD,** classics educator; b. Buea, Cameroon, Feb. 15, 1941; s. Fritz and Heidi (Ninck) R.; m. Deborah Dickmann Boedeker, July 14, 1978. MA, U. Basel, Switzerland, 1967, PhD, 1970. Asst. prof. ancient history Free U. Berlin, 1972-78, Brown U., Providence, 1978-80, assoc. prof. classics and history, 1980-83, prof., 1983—, John Rowe Workman Disting. prof. classics and humanistic tradition, 1989-92, David Herlihy Univ. prof., 2001—, Royce Family prof. excellence in tchg., 2005—, chmn. dept. classics, 1984-89; co-dir. Ctr. for Hellenic Studies, Washington, 1992-2000, chmn. program in ancient studies, 2000—. Author: Dignitatis Contentio, 1974, Die Entdeckung der Freiheit, 1985, The Discovery of Freedom in Ancient Greece, 2004; co-author: Studien zum Attischen Seebund, 1984, Aspects of Athenian Democracy, 1990, Ancient History: Recent Work and New Directions, 1997, Origins of Democracy in Ancient, 2007; editor or co-editor: Social Struggles in Archaic Rome, 1986, Between Republic and Empire: Interpretations of Augustus and His Principate, 1990, Athens and Rome, Florence and Venice: City-States in Classical Antiquity and Medieval Italy, 1991, Anfänge politischen Denkens in der Antike: Die nahöstlichen Kulturen und die Griechen, 1993, Studies in the Ancient Greek Polis, 1995, More Studies in the Ancient Greek Polis, 1996, Democracy 2500: Questions and Challenges, 1998, Democracy, Empire and the Arts in Fifth-Century Athens, 1998, War and Society in the Ancient and Medieval Worlds, 1999; contbr. articles to profl. jours. Mem. Historisches Kolleg Munich, 1989-90. Am. Coun. Learned Socs. fellow, 1983-84, Ctr. for Hellenic Studies fellow, 1976-77, NEH fellow, 1989; faculty fellow U. New England, Armidale, Australia, 1996. Mem. Philol. Assn., Assn. Ancient Historians, Am. Inst. Archaeology, German Archaeol. Inst. (corr.). Avocation: music. Home: 495 Lloyd Ave Providence RI 02906-4547 Office: Brown U Dept Classics Providence RI 02912-1856 Office Phone: 401-863-2123. E-mail: kurt_raaflaub@brown.edu.

**RA'ANAN, URI (HEINZ FELIX FRISCHWASSER),** international politics educator; b. June 10, 1926; m. Estelle Khan, 1949; children: Gavriel, Michael. BA, MA, MLitt, Oxford U. Polit. journalist, 1950-57; positions in internat. diplomacy, 1958-64; sr. fellow Rsch. Inst. on Communist Affairs, Columbia U., N.Y.C., 1964-66, lectr. in govt., 1965-66; assoc. Ctr. for Internat. Studies MIT, Boston, 1966-76, vis. prof. polit. sci., 1966-68; prof. internat. politics, dir. Internat. Security Studies Fletcher Sch. Law and Diplomacy, Tufts U., Boston, 1967-87; univ. prof. Boston U., 1988—, dir. Inst. for Study of Conflict, Ideology and Policy, 1988—. Assoc. Davis Ctr. for Russian Studies, Harvard U.; cons. Nat. Inst. Justice and Temple U. Rsch. Program on Organized Crime, 1981-83, Battelle Columbus Labs./U.S. Army Ballistic Missile Def. Program, 1976-77, U.S. Senate Subcom. on Nat. Security, 1972; mem. Ronald Reagan's Fgn. Affairs and Def. Adv. Team, 1980. Author, editor 25 books; mem. adv. bd. Polit. Warfare; contbr. chpts. to numerous books, articles to profl. jours.; numerous appearances on TV and radio Mem. Am. Assn. Advancement of Slavic Studies, Internat. Inst. of Strategic Studies Office: Inst for Study of Conflict Ideology and Policy 141 Bay State Rd Boston MA 02215-1708 Office Phone: 617-353-5815. Business E-Mail: raanan@bu.edu.

**RAAS, DANIEL ALAN,** lawyer; b. Portland, Oreg., July 6, 1947; s. Alan Charles and Mitzi (Cooper) R.; m. Deborah Ann Becker, Aug. 5, 1973; children: Amanda Beth, Adam Louis. BA, Reed Coll., 1969; JD, NYU, 1972. Bar: Wash. 1973, Calif. 1973, U.S. Dist. Ct. (we. dist.) Wash. 1973, U.S. Ct. Appeals (9th cir.) 1975, U.S. Supreme Ct. 1977, U.S. Tax Ct. 1983, U.S. Ct. Claims 1984. Atty. Seattle Legal Svcs, VISTA, 1972-73; reservation atty. Quinault Indian Nation, Taholah, Wash., 1973-76, Lummi Indian Nation, Bellingham, Wash., 1976-97, spl. counsel, 1997—; mem. Raas, Johnsen & Stuen, P.S., Bellingham, 1982—; judge Tulalip Indian Tribe Ct. Appeals, 2004—. Cons. Falmouth Inst., Fairfax, Va., 1992-2000, Nat. Am. Ind. Ct. Judges Assn., McLean, Va., 1976-80. Rules chmn. Whatcom County Dem. Conv., Bellingham, 1988, 92, 94, 96, 2004; bd. dirs. Congregation Beth Israel, Bellingham, 1985-2000, pres., 1990-92; adv. com. legal asst. program Bellingham Vocat. Tech. Inst., 1985-91; trustee Whatcom County Law Libr., 1978-2002; pres. Vol. Lawyer Program, 1990-93, bd. dirs., 1988-94; pres. Cliffside Cmty. Assn., 1978-80, bd. dirs., 1977-89; bd. dirs. Friends Maritime Heritage Ctr., 1983-86, Samish Camp Fire Coun., 1988-94, pres. 1991-94, v.p. 1989-91, regional v.p. Union Am. Hebrew Congregations, 1986-93, nat. trustee, 1995—, exec. com., 1995-99, sec. Pacific N.W. region, 1993-95, pres., 1995-99. John Ben Snow scholar, NYU, 1969-70, Root-Tilden scholar, NYU, 1970-72. Mem. Wash. State Bar Assn. (trustee Ind. law sect. 1989-95, Pro Bono award 1991), Whatcom County Bar Assn. (v.p. 1981, pres. 1982, Pro Bono award 1991), Grays Harbor Bar Assn. (v.p. 1976). Home: 1929 Lake Crest Dr Bellingham WA 98229-4510 Office: Raas Johnsen & Stuen PS 1503 E St Bellingham WA 98225-3007 Office Phone: 360-647-0234.

**RAB, GEORGE T.,** pediatric orthopedic surgeon; b. Cleve., Nov. 11, 1946; s. Thomas P. and Patricia S. Rab; m. Wendy Andereson Rab, Aug. 31, 1968; children: Geoffrey R. Nicholas A. BS, Northwestern U., Chgo., 1968; MD, Northwestern U., 1970; MS, U. Minn., Mpls., 1975. Lic. physician Calif., diplomate Am. Bd. Orthop. Surgery, Nat. Bd. Med. Examiners. Intern in surgery Chgo. Wesley Meml. Hosp., 1970—71; resident in orthop surgery Mayo Clinic, Rochester, Minn., 1971—75; resident in pediat. orthop. surgery Gillette Children's Hosp., St. Paul, 1974; asst. prof. dept. orthop. surgery Sch. Medicine, U. Calif., Davis, 1977—82, assoc. prof. dept. orthop. Surgery, 1982—88, prof. dept. orthop., 1988—, Ben Ali chair in pediat. orthop., 1998—, chair dept. orthop. surgery, 2000—. Guest lectr. Shriners Hosp. for Crippled Children and Sch. Medicine Oreg. Health Scis. U., Portland, 1985, Duncan Seminar Children's Orthop. Hosp. and Med. Ctr., Seattle, 1987; vis. prof., guest lectr. dept. orthop. Children's Hosp. Med. Ctr., Cin. 1986; vis. prof., guest lectr. Carrie Tingley Hosp. Annual Meeting, Albuquerque, 1992; vis. prof., guest lectr. Robert Samilson lectr., San Francisco, 96; vis. prof. U. Calif., Irvine, 1998, U. Colo., 1999, New Eng. Med. Ctr., 1999, Children's Hosp. Med. Ctr. of Akron, Ohio, 2001; Arthur A. Thibodeau vis. prof. Tufts

U. Sch. Medicine, 1999; John M. Roberts vis. prof. Children's Hosp. of New Orleans, 1999; vis. prof., Leslie Meyers lectr. Shriners Hosp., Greenville, SC, 2001; Charles LeRoy Lowman vis. prof. Orthop. Hosp., LA, 2002; orthop. surgeon, med. dir. motion analysis lab. Shriners Hosp. for Children, 1995—; pediat. orthop. specialist Sutter Cmty. Hosps., Sacramento, 1987—; vis. assoc. prof. dept. orthop. Harvard Med. Sch., Boston, 1983—84; rsch. fellow gait lab. Children's Hosp., Boston, 1983—84; editl. cons. Am. Jour. Diseases of Children, 1990—93; cons., rev. com. Orthop. Rsch. and Edn. Found., 1994—99; civilian cons. med. specialist in pediat. orthop. surgery Oakland Naval Hosp., Calif., 1990—95; pediat. orthop. cons. Kaiser Permanente Hosp., Sacramento, 1977—98. Mem. internat. editl. bd. Gait & Posture, 1992—97, bd. editors Jour. Biomechanics, 1992—97. Bd. dirs Sacramento Make-A-Wish Found., Inc., 1988—92. Maj. U.S. Army, 1975—77. Named Outstanding Clin. Instr., U. Calif. Davis Sch. Medicine, 1980, Outstanding Tchr. of Yr. in Orthop. Surgery, 1991, 1996; named one of Best Drs. in Am., 2005—06; recipient Goldsmith Intern Humanitarian award, Chgo. Wesley Meml. Hosp., 1971, Frank Stitchfield award, Hip Soc., 1976, annual award for excellence in tchg. clin. scis., Kaiser Found. Hosp., 1978, Best Poster award, Gait and Clin. Analysis Soc. Meeting, 2000; Berg-Sloat Traveling fellow, 1977. Fellow: Am. Acad. Pediat., Am. Acad. Orthop. Surgeons (con. on biomed. engring. 1980—82, com. on psychomotor skills 1980—87, com. ednl. content 1981—82, sec. com. on biomed. engring. 1982—85, subcom. on pediat. of com. on exams. and evaluations 1985—91, chmn. com. on biomed. engring. 1986—87); mem.: Sierra Sacramento Valley Med. Soc., Sacramento Pediat. Soc., Paul R. Lipscomb Soc., West Coast Gait Lab. Group, Western Orthop. Assn., Calif. Med. Assn., Am. Orthop. Assn., Pediat. Orthop. Soc. N.Am. (com. on computer applications in pediat. orthop. 1985—90), Orthop. Rsch. Soc., Internat. Soc. Electrophysiol. Kinesiology, Internat. Pediat. Orthop. Think Tank (site selection com. 1998—2003), Gait and Clin. Movement Analysis Soc. (awards com. 2001—02), Am. Soc. Biomechanics (arrangements com. annual meeting 1987, pres.-elect 1989—90, exec. com. 1989—93, pres. 1990—91), Am. Bd. Orthop. Surgery (certifying examiner 1984—92), Am. Acad. Cerebral Palsy and Devel. Medicine (nominating com. 1990—94). Avocations: bicycling, sailing, hiking, cooking. Office: Dept Orthop Surgery U Calif-Davis 4860 Y St # 3800 Sacramento CA 95817 Office Phone: 916-734-2958. Office Fax: 916-734-7904. E-mail: george.rab@ucdmc.ucdavis.edu.

**RABADEAU, MARY FRANCES,** protective services official; b. Elizabeth, N.J., July 13, 1948; d. Russell John and Frances (Hanley) R. Student, Union Coll., 1967-69; MEd, Kean Coll., 1976. Officer City of Elizabeth Police Dept., NJ, 1978-82, detective NJ, 1982-83, sgt. NJ, 1983-87, lt. NJ, 1987-91, capt. NJ, 1991-92, dir., 1993-95, dep. chief, 1994; chief N.J. Transit Police Dept., Maplewood, 1995—. Instr. Union County Police Acad. Trustee Blessed Sacrament Ch., Elizabeth, N.J., 1989-99; bd. acad. advisors N.J. state police grad. studies program Seton Hall U.; bd. trustees Benedictine Acad., Elizabeth, N.J. Named one of Outstanding Young Women in Am., 1983, Woman Leader N.J. Assn. Women Bus. Owners, 1997; recipient John H. Stamler Police Acad. Svc. award, 1992, Cert. of Recognition award YWCA, 1992, Disting. Grad. award Nat. Cath. Ednl. Assn., 1995; honoree Union County Commn. on the Status of Women, 1993, Hispanic Law Enforcement Assn. of Union County, 1995, Women Helping Women Recognition award Soroptimist Internat. Ams., 2001. Mem. NAACP, Internat. Assn. Chiefs of Police, N.J. State Chiefs of Police, Essex County Chiefs Assn., N.E. Assn. Women Police (cert., Merit award), Elizabeth Police Patrolman's Benevolent Assn., Elizabeth Police Superior Officers Assn. (treas. 1983-91, v.p. 1991), Am. Soc. Law Enforcement Trainers, Emerald Soc., Union County Urban League, Italian Law Enforcement Officers Assn., Fellas Inc. (hon.), Union County Men's Svc. Orgn., Nat. Assn. of Women Law Enforcement Execs. Democrat. Roman Catholic. Office: NJ Transit Police Dept 180 Boyden Ave Maplewood NJ 07040-2494 Home: 184 Riveredge Dr Chatham NJ 07928-3112

**RABADI, GHAITH,** engineering educator, consultant; b. Ajloun, Jordan, 1969; BSc in Indsl. Engring., U. Jordan, Amman, 1992; MS in Indsl. Engring., U. Ctrl. Fla., Orlando, 1996, PhD in Indsl. Engring., 2000. Rsch. assoc., developer Lucent Technologies (currently Agere Sys), Orlando, 1996—2000; vis. prof., rschr. U. of Ctrl. Fla., Indsl. Engring. Dept, 2000—01; tech. mgr. Productivity Apex, 2001—02; asst. prof. Old Dominion U., Dept. Engring. Mgmt. and Sys., Norfolk, Va., 2002—. Contbr. articles to profl. jours. Grantee, MITRE Corp., 2006—, Va. Port Auth., Old Dominion U., 2005—, US Dept. of Homeland Security, 2004—, NASA Langley Rsch. Ctr., 2002—05, Sentara Leigh Hosp., 2003—04; Faculty fellow, NASA, 2003, Faculty Innovator grant, Ctr. Learning Technologies at Old Dominion U., 2006. Mem.: Assn. Engring. Mgmt. (assoc.), Inst. Indsl. Engrs. (assoc.), Inst. Ops. Rsch. and Mgmt. Sci. (assoc.). Achievements include invention of NASA-GEM-FLO software invention: generic simulation environment for modeling future space launch operations. Office: Old Dominion U 241 Kaufman Hall Norfolk VA 23529 Office Phone: 757-683-4918. Office Fax: 757-683-5640. E-mail: grabadi@odu.edu.

**RABASSA, GREGORY,** language educator, translator, poet; b. Yonkers, NY, Mar. 9, 1922; m. Clementine Christos, 1966; children: Kate, Clara. AB, Dartmouth Coll., 1945, Litt.D. hon., 1982; MA, Columbia U., 1947, PhD in Portuguese, 1954; Litt.D. (hon.), U. Hartford, 2005. Instr. Spanish Columbia U., 1947-52, assoc., 1952-58, asst. prof., 1958-63, assoc. prof. Spanish and Portuguese, 1963-68; prof. Romance langs. Queens Coll., CUNY Grad. Sch., Flushing, NY, 1968-86, Disting. prof., 1986—. Assoc. editor Odyssey Rev., 1961-64 Contbr. articles to profl. jours.; author If This be Treason: Translation and Its Dyscontents, 2005, A Cloudy Day in Gray Minor, Early Poems, 1945-1948, 1992. Staff sgt. OSS, 1942-45. Decorated Croce al Merito di Guerra Italy, Order of San Carlos Colombia; recipient Nat. Book award for transl., 1967, Transl. prize, Pub. Edn. Network Am. Ctr., 1977, Wheatland Found., 1988, Gold award, Am. Transl. Assn., 1980, Pub. Edn. Network Transl medal, 1982, Arts award N.Y. Gov., 1983, Lit. award, Am. Acad. and Inst. Arts and Letters, 1989, Presdl. medal, Dartmouth Coll., 1991, Ivan Sandrof award, The Nat. Book Critics Cir., 1993, Lit. Lion award, N.Y. Pub. Libr., 1993, Mellon Humanities award, Loyola U., Chgo., 1995, Gabriela Mistral prize, Chile, 1996, Gregory Kolovakos award, Pub. Edn. Network, 2001, Martha Albrand award Art of Memoir, 2006, John Steinbeck Writers award, Southampton Coll., 2002, Machado de Assis medal, Union if Brazilian Writers, N.Y., 2005, Aurora Borealis award, Internat. Fedn. Translators, 2005; fellow Fulbright-Hays fellow, 1965—66, NEH fellow, 1979—80, Guggenheim fellow, 1988—89. Mem. Renaissance Soc. Am., MLA, Am. Assn. Tchrs. Spanish and Portuguese, Latin Am. Studies Assn., Am. Lit. Translators Assn., Hispanic Soc. Am., Century Assoc., PEN Club, Phi Beta Kappa. Office: Dept Hispanic Langs & Lits CUNY Queens Coll Flushing NY 11367 Office Phone: 212-439-6636.

**RABAUT, THOMAS W.,** defense industry executive; b. Detroit, 1948; m. Sheila Rabaut; 3 children. BS, U.S. Mil. Acad., 1970; MBA, Harvard U., 1977. Trainee mfg. dept. dr. divsn., various mfg./mgmt. positions FMC, 1977-81, planning mgr. fluid control divsn., 1982, mfg. mgr., ops. mgr. fluid control divsn., mgr. steel products divsn., 1986-88, dir. ops. ground sys. divsn., 1989; gen. mgr. def. sys. group FMC Corp., 1993, v.p., 1994; pres., CEO United Defense Industries, Inc., Arlington, Va., 1994—. With U.S. Army, 1970-75. Mem. Am. Def. Preparedness Assn., Assn. of U.S. Army, Navy League, Surface Navy Assn. Office: United Defense Industries Inc 1525 Wilson Blvd Arlington VA 22209

**RABB, BRUCE,** lawyer; b. Cambridge, Mass., Oct. 4, 1941; s. Maxwell M. and Ruth (Criedenberg) R.; m. Harriet Rachel Schaffer, Jan. 4, 1970; children: Alexander Charles, Katherine Anne. AB, Harvard U., 1962; Cert. d'Etudes Politiques, Institut d'Etudes Politiques, Paris, 1963; LLB, Columbia U., 1966. Bar: N.Y. 1966. Law clk. to judge U.S. Ct. Appeals (5th cir.), 1966-67; assoc. Stroock & Stroock & Lavan, N.Y.C., 1967-68, 71-75, ptnr., 1976-91, Kramer Levin Naftalis & Frankel LLP, N.Y.C., 1991—2003, counsel, 2003—; sr. v.p., gen counsel North Am. Bioenergy Resources, LLC, 2003—. Staff asst. to Pres. U.S., 1969-70; supr. bd. dirs Agora-Gazeta, sp.zo.o., 1993-98, Agora-Druk, sp.zo.o., 1995-98, Agora, SA, 2006—; pub. mem. Adminstv. Conf.

U.S., 1982-86, 89-92, spl. counsel, 1986-88; bd. dirs. Helicor, Inc. 2005-. Sec. Lehrman Inst., 1978-88; bd. dirs. Citizens Union of N.Y., 1981-87, 88-94, 95-2001, 2002—, treas. 2002-05. Am. Friends of Alliance Israelite Universelle, 1987-2001, Welfare Law Ctr., 1997-, Sabre Found., 2003—. Nat. Com. on Am. Fgn. Policy, 2004-05, Human Rights Watch, Helsinki, 1985-97, Fund for Free Expression, 1987-97, Human Rights Watch, Middle East No. Africa, 1989—, vice chmn., 1990—, Human Rights Watch, Asia, 2003—, Human Rights Watch, LGBT, 2005—, Human Rights Watch, US, 2004—, Human Rights Watch, 1988-2003, dir. emeritus, 2003—, sec., 2003—; Human Rights First (formerly Lawyers Com. Human Rights), 1977-95, nat. coun., 1996—; mem. internat. adv. com. Internat. Parliamentary Group for Human Rights in the Soviet Union, 1984-88, Prin. of the Coun. for Excellence in Govt., 1990—; mem. adv. coun. Doctors of the World USA, 1996—; mem. adv. coun. FilmAid Internat., 2000-03, dir., sec., 2003—; adv. com. Watch, Ams., 1982—; bd. dirs Cinereach, 2006—. With USCGR, 1967—72. Mem. ABA (adv. panel Internat. Human Rights Trial Observer project), Am. Law Inst., Assn. of Bar of City of N.Y. (fed. legis., internat. law chair 1992-95, internat. human rights, civil rights, legal edn. and admission to bar, internat. trade coms., coun. fgn. affairs, energy), Coun. Fgn. Rels., Harvard Club N.Y.C., Met. Club of Washington. Office: 1177 Ave Americas New York NY 10036-2714 Office Phone: 212-715-9484. Business E-Mail: brabb@kramerlevin.com.

**RABB, GEORGE BERNARD,** zoologist, conservationist; b. Charleston, S.C., Jan. 2, 1930; s. Joseph and Teresa C. (Redmond) R.; m. Mary Sughrue, June 10, 1953. BS, Coll. Charleston, 1951, LHD (hon.), 1995; MA, U. Mich., 1952, PhD, 1957. Teaching fellow zoology U. Mich., 1954-56; curator, coord. rsch. Chgo. Zool. Park, Brookfield Ill., 1956 61, assoc. dir. rsch. and edn., 1964-75, dep. dir., 1969-75, dir., 1976—2003, dir. emeritus, 2003—. Rsch. assoc. Field Mus., 1965—; lectr. dept. biology U. Chgo., 1965-89; mem. Com. on Evolutionary Biology, 1969—; pres. Chgo. Zool. Soc., 1976-2003, pres. emeritus, 2004—; mem. steering com. Species Survival Commn., Internat. Union Conservation of Nature/World Conservation Union, 1983—, vice-chmn. for N.Am., 1986-88, dep. chmn., 1987-89, chmn., 1989-96, vice-chmn. comms., 1997—; chmn. policy adv. group Internat. Species Info. System, 1974-89, chmn. bd., 1989-92; pres. bd. dirs. Chgo. Wilderness Mag., 1999—; v.p. Fauna and Flora Internat., 1998—; chmn. bd. Ill. State Mus., 1999—. Bd. dirs. Defenders of Wildlife, 2002—. Fellow AAAS; mem. Am. Soc. Ichthyologists and Herpetologists (pres. 1978), Herpetologists League, Soc. Systematic Zoology, Soc. Mammalogists, Soc. Study Evolution, Ecol. Soc. Am., Soc. Conservation Biology (council mem. 1986), Soc. for Integrative and Comparative Zoology, Soc. Study Animal Behavior, Am. Assn. Museums, Am. Soc. Naturalists, Am. Assn. Zool. Parks and Aquariums (dir. 1979-80), World Assn. Zoos and Aquariums, World Conservation Union (hon. mem.), Chgo. Coun. Fgn. Rels. (Chgo. com.), Sigma Xi. Office: 9236 Broadway Brookfield IL 60513 Personal E-mail: georgerabb@sbcglobal.net.

**RABB, HARRIET SCHAFFER,** academic administrator, lawyer; b. Houston, Sept. 12, 1941; d. Samuel S. and Helen G. Schaffer; m. Bruce Rabb, Jan. 4, 1970; children: Alexander, Katherine. BA in Govt., Barnard Coll., 1963; JD, Columbia U., 1966. Bar: N.Y. 1966, U.S. Supreme Ct. 1969, D.C. 1970. Instr. seminar on constl. litig. Rutgers Law Sch., 1966-67; staff atty. Ctr. for Constl. Rights, 1966-69; spl. counsel to commr. consumer affairs NYC Dept. Consumer Affairs, 1969-70; sr. staff atty. Stern Cmty. Law Firm, Washington, 1970-71; asst. dean urban affairs Law Sch., Columbia U., NYC, 1971-84, prof. law, dir. clin. edn., 1994-99, George M. Jaffen prof. law and social responsibility, 1991-99, vice dean, 1992-93; gen. counsel Dept. Health and Human Svcs., Washington, 1993—2001; v.p., gen. counsel Rockefeller U., NYC, 2001—. Mem. faculty employment and tng. policy Harvard Summer Inst., Cambridge, Mass., 1975-79. Author: (with Agid, Cooper and Rubin) Fair Employment Litigation Manual, 1975, (with Cooper and Rubin) Fair Employment Litigation, 1975. Bd. dirs. Ford Found., 1977-89, NY Civil Liberties Union, 1972-83, Lawyers Com. for Civil Rights Under Law, 1978-86, Legal Def. Fund NAACP, 1978-93, Mex. Am. Legal Def. and Edn. Fund, 1986-90, Legal Aid Soc., 1990-93, The Hastings Ctr., 2004-; mem. exec. com. Human Rights Watch, 1991-93; trustee Trinity Episcopal Sch. Corp., 1991-93; mem. external adv. bd. Columbia U. Ctr. Bioethics, 2002-. Office: Rockefeller U 1230 York Ave New York NY 10021 Office Phone: 212-327-8070. Business E-Mail: hrabb@rockefeller.edu.

**RABB, THEODORE K.,** historian, educator; b. Teplice-Sanov, Czechoslovakia, Mar. 5, 1937; came to U.S., 1956, naturalized, 1978; s. Oskar Kwasnik and Rose (Oliner) Rabinowicz; m. Tamar Miriam Janowsky, June 7, 1959; children: Susannah Rabb Bailin, Jonathan Richard, Jeremy David. BA, Queen's Coll. Oxford U., Eng., 1958; MA, Queen's Coll. Oxford U., 1962, Princeton U., 1960, PhD, 1961. Instr. Stanford U., 1961-62; instr. Northwestern U., 1962-63; asst. prof. Harvard U., 1963-67; mem. faculty Princeton U., 1967—, prof. history, 1976—. Vis. assoc. prof. Johns Hopkins U., 1969, SUNY-Binghamton, 1973-74; visitor Inst. Advanced Studies, Princeton, 1973, 82; mem. nat. bd. cons. NEH, Nat. Coun. History Edn. (chair); N.J. Com. for Humanities (chair); chief historian Renaissance Television Series; bd. dirs. Humanities West, Save Venice, Inc.; juror Rome Prize; cons. in field. Author: The Thirty Years War, 2d edit. 1972, Enterprise and Empire, 1967, The Struggle for Stability in Early Modern Europe, 1975, The Origins of Modern Nations, 1981, Renaissance Lives: Portraits of an Age, 1993, rev. edit., 2000, Origins of the Modern West, 1993, Jacobean Gentleman, 1998; co-author: The Western Experience, 8th edit., 2003, Peoples and Nations, 1982; editor: Jour. Interdisciplinary History, 1970—; co-editor: Action and Conviction in Early Modern Europe, 1969, The Family in History, 1973, Marriage and Fertility, 1981, Industrialization and Urbanization, 1981, Climate and History, 1981, The New History, 1982, Hunger and History, 1985, Population and Economy, 1986, Art and History, 1988, La Fame nella storia, 1991, Origin and Prevention of Major Wars, 1988, The Making and Unmaking of Democracy, 2003, The Last Days of the Renaissance, 2006. Bd. govs. Hebrew U. Fellow and/or grantee Folger Shakespeare Library, Am. Philos. Soc., Social Sci. Research Council, Am. Council Learned Socs., Guggenheim Found., NEH. Mem. Am. Hist. Assn. (chmn. com. quantitative rsch. history, chmn. nominating com.), Social Sci. History Assn. (exec. com., treas.), Am. Assn. Advancement Humanities (dir., sec.-treas.), Nat. Coun. History Stds., C.C. Humanities Assn. (steering com.), Royal Hist. Soc., Internat. Commn. History Parliamentary and Rep. Instns., Renaissance Soc. Am., Hakluyt Soc., Nat. Coun. History Edn. (chair), Historians Early Modern Europe, Conf. Brit. Studies. Office: Princeton University History Dept Princeton NJ 08544-1017 Business E-Mail: tkr@princeton.edu.

**RABBAT, GUY,** electronics executive, consultant; b. Cairo, Jan. 30, 1943; came to U.S., 1972; s. Victor and Alice R.; m. Elfriede Freitag, Aug. 3, 1968; children: Ralph, Shirley; m. Nadia Kobinger, Feb. 8, 1992; children: Richard, Jacques, Laurent. Baccalaureate, France; BS, Queen's U., Eng., 1967, MS, 1969, PhD in Elec. Engring. with honors, 1971. Design supr. Siemens AG, Germany, 1964-68; asst. lectr. Queens U., England, 1968-72; dir. ops. IBM, 1972-84; v.p. Austin ops., CAE system div. Tektronix, 1984-86; head elec. engring. GM Corp., Mich., 1986-87; pres., chief exec. officer Modular Computer Systems, Inc. (MODCOMP), Ft. Lauderdale, Fla., 1987-92; mng. dir., exec. bd. dirs Rank Xerox, Ltd., Welwyn Garden City, Herts, England, 1992-96; corp. v.p. Gen. Elec. Co., Milw., 1996-98; chief tech. officer, chief info. officer Gen. Elec. Med. Sys., Milw., 1996-98; sr. v.p. Solectron Corp., 1998—2003; chmn., gen. ptnr. Corcica Tech. Ventures, 2001—; pres., CEO HTC Corp., Sunnyvale, Calif., 2002—. Chmn. Internat. IEEE Conf. on Cirs. and Computers, 1980, Internat. IEEE Conf. on Computer Design, 1983; bd. dirs. indsl. affiliates Mich. State U., 1986-88; pres. Am. Automation Assn., 1984-86; chmn., founder High Tech. Consortium Yr. 2000 and Beyond, 1998-02. Author: Hardware and Software Concepts in VLSI, 1983, Advanced Semiconductor Technology and Computer Systems, 1988; contbr. numerous scis. tech. papers; patentee in field. Fellow: Royal Engring. Coun. (London), IEEE (Eng. chpt., editor-in-chief, chmn. editl. bd. Circuits and Devices Mag. 1984—86, invention and outstanding contbn. awards). Avocations: history, archaeology, poetry, jogging. Home: 110 W 5th Ave San Mateo CA 94402 Office: Htc Corporation 110 W 5th Ave San Mateo CA 94402-2005 Office Phone: 408-218-4393. Business E-Mail: guy.rabbat@htc-corp.com.

**RABBE, DAVID ELLSWORTH,** oil industry executive; b. Alexandria, Va., Dec. 17, 1955; s. Raymond Leed and Judith Ann (Ayers) R.; m. Maryann Degroot, Sept. 25, 1982; children: Lisa Ann, Chelsea Nicole, Jamison David. BCE, U. Md., 1979. From terminal trainee to mgr. Amerada Hess Corp., Balt. 1980—87, mgr. gas station maintenance Woodbridge, NJ, 1987—91; from project mgr. to pres. Tierra Solutions, Inc., East Brunswick, NJ, 1991—. Mem. editl. bd., editor: Soil and Sediment Contamination, 2002—. Mem.: Md. Soc. Surveyors, World Affairs Coun. Republican. Episcopalian. Avocations: woodworking, sailing. Home: 33 Sorrel Run Mount Laurel NJ 08054-4819 Personal E-mail: Davermxs@aol.com.

**RABCHENUK, PAUL THOMAS,** lawyer; b. Salem, Mass. s. Nicholas and Apolonia Pauline (Napierski) R. BA, Suffolk U., 1962; MPA, U. Pitts., 1964; JD, New Eng. Law Sch., 1981; postgrad., Tufts U. Bar: Mass. 1981, U.S. Dist. Ct. 1982, U.S. Ct. Appeals 1982, U.S. Supreme Ct. 1986, U.S. Ct. Internat. Trade, 1999. Clk. Essex Superior Ct, Salem, Mass., 1958-61; negotiator Commonwealth of Mass., Boston, 1962-63; realty specialist D.C. Redevel. Agy., Washington, 1964-65; rsch. assoc. Boston Mcpl. Rsch. Bur., 1966-67; urban renewal dir. City of Nashua, N.H., 1967-68, City of Haverhill, Mass., 1969-73; town adminstr. North Reading, Mass., 1973-78; town mgr. Town of Saugus, Mass., 1982-87; pvt. practice law Salem, Mass., 1981—. Cons. numerous pub. entities, 1966-85; vis. prof. civil rights Salem (Mass.) State Coll., 2001—. Chmn. Topsfield (Mass.) Housing Authority, 1978-83, Mass. Bay Tranportation Authority, Boston, 1973-86. Mem. ATLA, Mass. Bar Assn. Avocation: Eastern European history. Home: 37 Glendale Rd Marblehead MA 01945-1804 Office: Rabchenuk Law Offices 81 Washington St Ste 311 Salem MA 01970-3514 Office Phone: 978-741-1163. Business E-Mail: rablaw@verizon.net.

**RABENBERG, JOHN,** farmer, political organization worker; Farmer, Fort Peck, Mont.; chmn. Mont. Rep. Party, Helena, Mont., 2003—. Chmn. Mont. Essential Air Svc. Task Force; bd. pres. Fort Peck Paleontology, Inc. Mailing: Montana Republican Party Chmn 921 Euclid Ave Helena MT 59601

**RABENSTEIN, DALLAS LEROY,** chemistry professor; b. Portland, Oreg., June 13, 1942; 8. Melvin Leroy and Rose Marie (Nelson) R.; m. Gloria Carolyn Duncan, Aug. 30, 1964; children: Mark, Lisa. BS, U. Wash., 1964; PhD, U. Wis., 1968. Lectr. U. Wis., Madison, 1967-68; research chemist Chevron Research Co., Richmond, Calif., 1968-69; from asst. prof. to prof. chemistry U. Alta., Edmonton, Can., 1969-85; prof. U. Calif., Riverside, 1985-97, chmn. dept. chemistry, 1989—92, 1998—2000, 2002—03, dean Coll. Natural and Agrl. Scis., 1993-94, disting. prof. chemistry, 1997—; dean grad. div., 2003—. Vis. prof. U. Oxford, 1976-77, U. Western Ont., 1982; McElvain lectr. U. Wis., 1981; Dow lectr. U. B.C., 1988; Eli Lilly lectr., Ind. U., 1993; faculty rsch. lectr. U. Calif., Riverside, 2000; cons. in field. Contbr. articles to profl. jours. NIH and NSF grantee. Fellow AAAS, Chem. Inst. Can. (Fisher Sci. Lecture award 1984); mem. Am. Chem. Soc., Internat. Soc. Magnetic Resource. Avocations: reading, gardening, music. Home: 5162 Palisade Cir Riverside CA 92506-1521 Office: U Calif Dept Chemistry Riverside CA 92521-0001 Office Phone: 951-827-4302. Business E-Mail: dallas.rabenstein@ucr.edu.

**RABIC, JAMES WILLIAM,** music educator, personal trainer; b. Latrobe, Pa., Mar. 7, 1949; s. Andy Rabic and Elsie Marie Carnes; m. Linda Jean Ventriglia, July 31, 1971; 1 child, James Andrew. BA in Music Edn., Combs Coll. Music, 1971. Cert. personal fitness trainer AFI, 1999. Instrumental music tchr. Cherry Hill (N.J.) Pub. Sch., 1971—; band dir. Cath. Ch. St. Mary, Cherry Hill, 1990—. Computer music cons. Midimates, Cherry Hill, NJ, 1989—; personal trainer Smart Bodies Fitness, Marlton, NJ, 1998—. Musician (conductor): All Cherry Hill Band. Vice chmn. sect. piano Nat. Pastoral Musicians, Cherry Hill, 2005—. Mem.: NEA, N.J. Edn. Assn., N.J. Music Educators Assn., Music Educators Nat. Conf., KC (4th degree knight 1998), IJFM. Avocation: fitness. Home: 93 Greensward Ln Cherry Hill NJ 08002 Office: Beck Mid Sch 950 Cropwell Rd Cherry Hill NJ 08002 Office Phone: 856-424-4505. Business E-Mail: jrabic@chclc.org.

**RABIDEAU, MARGARET CATHERINE,** retired media center director; b. Chgo., Nov. 24, 1930; d. Nicholas and Mary Agnes (Burke) Oberle; m. Gerald Thomas Rabideau, Nov. 27, 1954; children: Mary, Margaret, Michelle, Gregory, Marsha, Grant. BA cum laude, U. Toledo, 1952, MA in Ednl. Media Tech., 1978. Cert. tchr. K-12 media tech., super. ednl. media, tchr. English and journalism, specialist in ednl. Asst. dir. pub. rels. U. Toledo, 1952-55; publicity writer United Way, Toledo, 1974-75; tchr. Toledo Pub. Schs., 1975-80, libr., media specialist, 1980-90; dir. media svcs. Sylvania (Ohio) Schs., 1990—2002, ret., 2002. Task force to evaluate coll. programs Ohio Dept. Edn., 1987; on-site evaluation team, Hiram Coll., Ohio, 1991; north ctrl. evaluation team Northwestern Ohio, 1985—. Citizen task force Toledo/Lucas County Libr., Ohio, 1991; mem. friends of the libr., 1990—; task force Sta. WGTE-TV PBS Sta., Toledo, 1993; mem. tech. com. strategic plan Sylvania Schs., 1997; instr. U. Toledo, 1990—. Recipient Disting. Educator for Art Edn. award N.W. Ohio Art Edn. Assn., 1997; nmamed Educator of Yr., Sylvania Schs., 2001. Mem. ALA, U. Toledo Alumni Assn., Ohio Ednl. Libr. Media Assn. (N.W. dir. 1993—, vocat. dir. 1985-89, Libr. Media Specialist of Yr. 1993, disting. educator art edn. 1999), Am. Ednl. Comm. and Tech., Ednl. Leadership Assn. (bd. dirs.), Maumee Valley Computer Assn. (task force), Phi Delta Kappa (Outstanding Newsletter Nat. award 1990, pres. Toledo chpt., svc. key award, 1998). Avocations: running, travel, cross stitching. Home: 1038 Olson St Toledo OH 43612-2828

**RABIDEAU, MARILYN ANN,** elementary school educator; b. Green Bay, Wis., Sept. 23, 1939; d. Henry John and Irma Tornow Fink; m. Kenneth Francis Rabideau, June 9, 1961; children: Neil Kenneth Rabideau, Laurie Ann Rabideau Kleisinger. BS in Edn., U. Wis., 1961; MEd, Nat. Louis U., 1996. Life license elem. sch. tchr. grades 1-8 Wis. Dept. Pub. Instrn. Elem. educator Janesville (Wis.) Pub. Schs., 1961-2001, retired, 2001. Pres. Rock County (Wis.) Ext. Homemakers, 1968-70; pres., coun. mem. Faith Luth. Ch., Janesville, 1983-88; officer, bd. dirs Faith Lutheran Endowment Found., 1996-2002. Recipient Cert. of Excellence, Wis. Ctr. for Academically Talented Youth, Inc., Madison, 1995. Mem. Phi Beta Kappa, Delta Kappa Gamma (chpt. pres. 1998-2000, 02). Avocations: writing, music, drawing, sports, handicrafts.

**RABIDEAU, PETER WAYNE,** dean, chemistry professor, educator; b. Johnstown, Pa., Mar. 4, 1940; s. Peter Nelson and Monica (Smalley) R.; m. Therese Charlene Newquist, Sept. 1, 1962 (div.); children: Steven, Michael, Christine, Susan; m. Jennifer Lee Mooney, Nov. 15, 1986; children: Mark, Leah. BS, Loyola U., Chgo., 1964; MS, Case Inst. Tech., Cleve., 1967; PhD, Case Western Res. U., Cleve., 1968. Postdoctoral asst. U. Chgo., 1968-69, instr., 1969-70; asst. prof. Ind. U.-Purdue U., Indpls., 1970-73, assoc. prof., 1973-76, prof., 1976-90, chmn. dept. chemistry, 1985-90; dean Coll. Basic Scis. La. State U., Baton Rouge, 1990-99; dean Coll. Liberal Arts and Scis. Iowa State U., Ames, 1999—2003; provost, v.p. acad. affairs Miss. State U., 2003—. Program officer NSF, 1988-89. Contbr. numerous articles to profl. jours. Recipient rsch. award Purdue Sch. Sci. at Indpls., 1983, Outstanding Alumnus award chemistry dept. Case Western U., 2001. Fellow AAAS; mem. Am. Chem. Soc. (chmn. Ind. sect. 1974, councilor 1981-90). Home: 105 Derbyshire Rd Starkville MS 39759 Office: Miss State U PO Box BQ Mississippi State MS 39762 E-mail: prabideau@provost.msstate.edu.

**RABIL, ALBERT, JR.,** humanities educator; b. Rocky Mount, N.C., May 8, 1934; s. Albert and Sophie Mae (Safy) R.; m. Janet Spain, Aug. 29, 1956; children: Albert III, J. Alison. Ba, Duke U., 1957; MDiv, Union Theol. Sem., 1960; PhD, Columbia U., 1964. Instr. religion Trinity Coll., Hartford, Conn., 1964-65, asst. prof., 1965-68; asst. prof. hist. theology Chgo. Theol. Sem., 1969-71; assoc. prof. SUNY-Old Westbury, 1971-74, prof., 1974-77, disting. tchg. prof. humanities, 1977-98, emeritus prof., 1998. Program dir. NEH Summer Inst., 1992, 94, 95, 96, 98, 2000, 01, 03, 04, 05. Author: Merleau-Ponty, 1967 (Ansley award 1964), Erasmus and the New Testament, 1972, Laura Cereta, 1981, (with others) Her Immaculate Hand, 1983, Erasmus'

Paraphrases of Romans and Galatians, 1983, Erasmus' Annotations on Romans, 1994; editor: Renaissance Humanism (3 vols.), 1988; editor, translator: Knowledge, Goodness, and Power, 1991, Henricus Cornelius Agrippa Declamation on the Nobility and Preeminence of the Female Sex, 1996; co-editor Renaissance Quarterly, 1992-97; series co-editor The Other Voice in Early Modern Europe, 1993—; mem. editl. bd. Soundings: An Interdisciplinary Jour., 1992-94. Travelling fellow Union Theol. Sem., 1960, Soc. for Values in Higher Edn., 1961; grantee Fulbright Found., 1961, NEH, 1974, 81, 94, 2002, 03, 04. Mem. Erasmus Rotterdam Soc. (mem. editl. bd. 1980—), Soc. for Values in Higher Edn. (bd. dirs. 1981-90), Renaissance Soc. Am. (bd. dirs. 1991-97). Democrat. Home and Office: 2305 Honeysuckle Rd Chapel Hill NC 27514-1716 Office Phone: 919-967-0231. Personal E-mail: arabil@nc.rr.com.

**RABIL, MITCHELL JOSEPH,** lawyer; b. Smithfield, N.C., Sept. 19, 1931; s. Albert G. and Eva (Nassif) R.; m. Antoinette M. Olivry, Nov. 25, 1956 (div. Oct. 1986); children: Elizabeth, Nathalie, Marcus, Gregory; m. Delores E. Bleam, Jan. 21, 1989; children: Susan Starr Vermes, Scott Starr. BS, Wake Forest Coll., 1953; LLB, Georgetown U., 1961. Bar: N.C. 1961, N.J. 1967, D.C. 1980, Pa. 1981, U.S. Tax Ct. 1962, U.S. Supreme Ct. 1979; CPA, N.J., N.C. Supervisory acct. GAO, Washington, 1956—60; fin. analyst, staff acct. SEC, Washington, 1960—62; tax atty. Office of Chief Counsel, IRS, Phila. and N.Y.C., 1962—66; assoc. Archer, Greiner, Hunter & Read, Camden, NJ, 1966—71; ptnr. Myers, Matteo, Rabil, Norcross & Landgraf, Cherry Hill, NJ, 1971—89, Montgomery, McCracken, Walker and Rhoads, Cherry Hill, 1989—95; sole stockholder, pres. Mitchell J. Rabil & Assocs., P.A., Cherry Hill, 1995—2000; mem. Rabil & Harris LLC, Cherry Hill, 1998—2000, Rabil & Ropka, LLC, Cherry Hill, 2000—02, Rabil, Ropka, Kingett & Hatzell LLC, Cherry Hill, 2002—04, Rabil, Ropka, Kingett & Stewart LLC, 2005—. Mcpl. chmn. Riverton (N.J.) Rep. Com., 1976-83; chmn. area 2 Burlington County Rep. Com., 1976-82; bd. dirs. West Jersey Chamber Music Soc., 1990-91, Zurbrugg Meml. Hosp., 1991-93; mem. N.J. New Capital Sources Bd., 1996-2000. With AUS, 1953-55 Mem. AICPA, N.J. Bar Assn., N.J. Soc. CPA, Phila. Bar Assn., Am. Assoc. Atty. CPA (bd. dirs., past pres.) Cherry Hill C. of C. (bd. dirs. 1990-94), World Affairs Coun. Phila., Union League (Phila.), Riverton Country Club, Rotary (pres. Cherry Hill chpt. 1980-81, past dir.). Roman Catholic. Home: 107 Waugle Ct Delran NJ 08075-2000 Office: 215 Fries Mill Rd Turnersville NJ 08012

**RABIN, ALAN A.,** economics professor; b. N.Y.C., June 16, 1947; s. Sidney and Claire Rabin. BA, Hamilton Coll., 1969; PhD, U. Va., 1977. NSF trainee U. Va., 1970—71, 1971—72; intern Coun. Econ. Advisors, 1971; instr. Calif. State U., Northridge, 1973-74, Georgetown U., Washington, 1975; assoc. prof. econs. U. Tenn., Chattanooga, 1977-81, assoc. prof., 1981-86, prof., 1986—. Author: Monetary Theory, 2004; contbr. articles to profl. jours. NDEA fellow, 1969-70; U. Tenn.-Chatanooga faculty rsch. grantee, 1982. Mem. Am. Econs. Assn., So. Econs. Assn., Atlantic Econs. Soc. W. Econs. Assn., U. Tenn. Chattanooga Coun. Scholars, Omicron Delta Epsilon. Avocations: sports, stamp collecting/philately, theater. Home: 1175 Pineville Rd Apt 161 Chattanooga TN 37405-2653 Office: U Tenn-Chattanooga Dept Economics Chattanooga TN 37403 Office Phone: 423-425-4360. E-mail: alan-rabin@utc.edu.

**RABIN, HERBERT,** physicist, educator, dean; b. Milw., Nov. 14, 1928; 2 children. BS, U. Wis., 1950; MS, U. Ill., 1951; PhD in Physics, U. Md., 1959. Physicist elec. divsn. U.S. Naval Rsch. Lab., 1952-54, physicist solid state physics divsn., 1954-62, head radiation effects sect. optical materials br., 1962-67, head quantum optics sect., applied optics br., 1967-68, head quantum optics br., 1968-71, assoc. dir. rsch. for space sci. and tech., 1971-77, assoc. dir. rsch. for space and comm. sci. and tech., 1977-79; dep. asst. sec. for rsch., applied and space tech. Office of Navy Secretariat, Washington, 1979-83; dir. engring. rsch. ctr., prof. elec. engring., assoc. dean Coll. Engring., U. Md., College Park, 1983—, interim dean coll. engring., 1999-2000. Dir. GRC Internat., 1988—98, Washington Aluminum Co., 1992—95, Yurie Sys. Inc., 1995—98, VT Linx Multimedia Sys., Inc., 2000—02; vis. scientist Technisch Hochschule, Stuttgart, Germany, 1960—61; mem. staff physics dept. George Washington U., 1955—73; cons. Sch. Engring. Sao Carlos U., Sao Paulo, Brazil, 1964, Sao Paulo, 70; trustee Nat. Technol. U., 1984—2000, life trustee, 2000—03; vis. fellow SEEDA, England, 2003. Contbr. articles to tech. jours. Recipient Meritorious Civilian Svc. award, USN, 1969, Disting. Civilian Svc. award, 1976, 1993, Dept. Def., 1979, Cert. of Commendation, NASA, 1986, Centennial medal, U. Md. Coll. Engring., 1994. Fellow: AIAA, AAAS, Optical Soc. Am., Am. Phys. Soc.; mem.: IEEE (sr.), Brazilian Acad. Scis. (corr.). Achievements include patents in field. Home: 7109 Radnor Rd Bethesda MD 20817-6332 Office: U Md Engring Rsch Ctr College Park MD 20742-0001 Office Phone: 301-405-3906.

**RABIN, JACK,** lawyer; b. Aug. 19, 1930; s. Leo and Bertha Rabin; m. Roberta Edith Libson, Oct. 25, 1953; children: Keith Warren, Michael Jay, Adam Douglas. Student, Bklyn. Coll., 1948-50; LLB, Bklyn. Law Sch., 1953. Bar: N.Y. 1953, U.S. Tax Ct. 1960, U.S. Claims 1964, U.S. Supreme Ct. 1964, U.S. Ct. Appeals (2d cir.) 1968. Ptnr. Hoffberg, Rabin & Engler and predecessor firms, N.Y.C., 1968-82, Javits, Hinckley, Rabin & Engler, N.Y.C., 1982-84, Phillips, Nizer, Benjamin, Krim & Ballon, N.Y.C., 1984-94, counsel, 1994—. Arbitrator gen. comml. and constrn. panel Am. Arbitration Assn., 1968—; instr. Real Estate Inst., NYU, 1976-78; ct. apptd. mediator U.S. Dist. Ct. (so. dist.), N.Y., 1994—; N.Y. Supreme Ct., N.Y. County, 1999. Assoc. editor Bklyn. Law Rev., 1952, editor-in-chief, 1953, also author law rev. note. 1st lt. JAGC, U.S. Army, 1954-57, col. res., ret., 1983. Mem. N.Y. State Bar Assn., Res. Officers Assn. U.S. (pres. Rockland County chpt. 1967-68), B'nai B'rith (pres. New City, N.Y. 1965-66). Jewish. Office: 10 W 66th St Ste 8lg New York NY 10023 Office Phone: 212-724-1050. E-mail: sutleg@earthlink.net.

**RABIN, JOSEPH HARRY,** marketing research company executive; b. Chgo., Dec. 12, 1927; s. Morris and Libby (Broder) Rabinovitz; m. Barbara E. Leader, Oct. 31, 1954; children: Marc Jay, Michelle Ann, Deborah Susan. BSc, Roosevelt U., 1950; MBA, DePaul U., 1951. Account exec. Gould, Gleiss & Benn, 1951-56; asst. dir. mktg. rsch. Paper Mate Co., Chgo., 1956-63; pres. Rabin Rsch. Co., Chgo., 1963—. Pres. Mather H.S. Coun., 1972-74; mem. adv. coun. U. Toledo, 1976-77, Kellstadt Ctr. DePaul U., 1986-93; mem. adv. com. Bur. of the Census, 1978-83; bd. dirs. Market Rsch. Inst., 1973-75, Ner Tamid Synagogue, 1976—, Jewish Vocat. Svc., 1977-80. With AUS, 1946-47. Mem. Am. Mktg. Assn. (pres. Chgo. chpt. 1961-62, nat. dir. 1973-75, nat. v.p. mktg. rsch. 1978-79, nat. pres. 1981-82), Am. Assn. Consumer Rsch., Am. Statis. Assn. (pres. Chgo. chpt. 1962-63), Am. Assn. Pub. Opinion Rsch. Home: 7061 N Kedzie Ave Chicago IL 60645-2846 Office: Rabin Rsch Co 150 E Huron St Chicago IL 60611-2999 Office Phone: 312-482-8500. Business E-Mail: jrabin@rabin-research.com.

**RABIN, MONROE STEPHEN ZANE,** physicist; b. Bklyn., Dec. 19, 1939; s. Louis and Helen (Haspel) R.; m. Joan Greenblatt, Feb. 27, 1965; children: Elaine Judith, Carolyn Sandra. AB, Columbia Coll., 1961; PhD, Rutgers U., 1967. Physicist Lawrence Berkeley (Calif.) Lab., 1967-72; assoc. prof. physics U Mass., Amherst, 1972-81, prof. physics, 1981—; vis. physicist Stanford Linear Accelerator Ctr., Palo Alto, Calif., 1979-80; vis. scientist Physics Dept. Harvard U., Cambridge, Mass., 1986-87; Soriano scholar in radiol. physics, radiation therapy dept. Mass. Gen. Hosp., Boston, 1986-87. Mem. oversight panel Proton Therapy Med. Facility, Mass. Gen. Hosp., Boston, 1991-96. Contbr. articles to Physical Rev., Physical Rev. Letters, Physics Letters, Nuclear Instruments and Methods. Mem. Am. Phys. Soc., Sigma Xi. Achievements include research in experimental particle physics, medical physics, cancer therapy using accelerated protons, ductal carcinoma in situ and heavy-ion physics. Home: 21 Atwater Cir Amherst MA 01002-3205 Office: U Mass Dept Physics Amherst MA 01003 Office Phone: 413-545-0424. Business E-Mail: rabin@physics.umass.edu.

**RABIN, ROBERT L.,** law educator; b. 1939; BS, Northwestern U., 1960, JD, 1963, PhD in Polit. Sci., 1967. Bar: Ill. 1963. Asst. prof. law U. Wis., Madison, 1966-69, assoc. prof., 1969-70; vis. assoc. prof. Stanford Law Sch.,

Calif., 1970-71, assoc. prof. Calif., 1971-73, prof. Calif., 1973-84, A. Calder Mackay prof. Calif., 1984—. Sr. environ. fellow EPA, 1979—80; vis. fellow Centre Sociolegal Studies Wolfson Coll., Oxford U., 1982; vis. prof. Harvard Law Sch., 1987—88, NYU Law Sch., 1999—2000; Jack N. Pritzker disting. vis. prof. Northwestern Sch. Law., 1994. Author: Perspectives on the Administrative Process, 1979, Perspective on Tort Law, 1995; co-author: Smoking Policy: Law, Politics and Culture, 1993, Cases and Materials on Tort Law and Alternatives, 2001, Regulating Tobacco, 2001, Torts Stories, 2003. Office: Stanford Law Sch Crown Quadrangle 559 Nathan Abbott Way Stanford CA 94305-8610 Office Phone: 650-723-3073. Business E-Mail: rrabin@stanford.edu.

**RABIN, STANLEY ARTHUR,** metal products manufacturer; b. N.Y.C., 1938; BA, BS in Metall. Engring., Columbia U., 1958; MBA, U. Santa Clara, 1969. With Comml. Metals Co., Inc., Irving, 1970—, pres., 1978—2006, CEO, 1979—2006, chmn., 1999—. Mailing: Commercial Metals Co PO Box 1046 Dallas TX 75221-1046 Office: Commercial Metals Co Ste 800 6565 N MacArthur Blvd Irving TX 75039*

**RABINOVICH, EGLA CONSUELO,** pediatrician, rheumatologist; d. Sergio and Nelly Rabinovich; m. Kenneth Wayne Jordan, May 3, 1986; children: Danielle Jordan, Nicholas Jordan, Kyle Jordan. BS, U. Ill., Champaign-Urbana, 1981; MD, So. Ill. U., 1985; MPH, U. NC, Chapel Hill, 1991. Assoc. pediat. Duke U., Durham, NC, 1991—93; asst. prof. U. Chgo., 1993—2001, Duke U., 2001—. Mem.: Am. Coll. Rheumatology (pediatric exec. com. 1992—2006, Amgen/REF Vis. Professorship 2006). Office: Duke U Med Ctr Box 3212 Durham NC 27710 Office Phone: 919-684-6475. Office Fax: 919-684-6616.

**RABINOVICH, SERGIO,** physician, educator; b. Lima, Peru, Apr. 8, 1928; m. Nelly; children— Gina, Sergio, Norca, Egla. MD, San Fernando Med. Sch., U. San Marcos, Lima, Peru, 1953. Intern San Fernando Med. Sch., U. San Marcos, Lima, 1947-54; resident in medicine Grasslands Hosp., Valhalla, NY, 1954-57, Henry Ford Hosp., Detroit; prof., head dept. internal medicine U. Arequipa Med. Sch., 1960-61; assist. prof. dept. internal medicine U. Iowa, Iowa City, 1963-65, asst. prof., 1965-69; attending physician and cons. VA Hosp., Iowa City, 1965-73; assoc. prof. U. Iowa, 1969-73; prof., chief dept. medicine div. infectious disease So. Ill. U. Sch. Medicine, Springfield, 1973-96, prof., chmn. dept. medicine, 1974-88, pres. Faculty Coun., 1992-93, prof. emeritus, 1996. Author: (with I.M. Smith, S.T. Donta) Antibiotics and Infection, 1974. Fellow ACP, Infectious Disease Soc. Am.; mem. AMA, Am. Soc. Microbiology, N.Y. Acad. Sci., Am. Fedn. Clin. Research, AAAS, Am. Thoracic Soc., Ill. Thoracic Soc. (pres. 1978-79), Central Soc. Clin. Research, Sigma Xi. Office: So Ill U Sch Medicine 800 N Rutledge St Springfield IL 62794-9636 Office Phone: 217-545-0181. Personal E-mail: sergiorabinovich@aol.com.

**RABINOVITCH, BENTON SEYMOUR,** chemist, educator emeritus; b. Montreal, Que., Can., Feb. 19, 1919; came to U.S., 1946; s. Samuel and Rachel (Schachter) R.; m. Marilyn Werby, Sept. 18, 1949; children: Peter Samuel, Ruth Anne, Judith Nancy, Frank Benjamin; m. Flora Reitman, 1980. BSc, McGill U., 1939, PhD, 1942; DSc (hon.), Technion Inst., Haifa, 1991. Postdoctoral fellow Harvard, 1946-48; mem. faculty U. Wash., Seattle, 1948—, prof. chemistry, 1957—, prof. chemistry emeritus, 1985—. Cons. and/or mem. sci. adv. panels, coms. NSF, Nat. Acad. Scis–NRC; adv. com. phys. chemistry Nat. Bur. Standards. Author Antique Silver Servers, 1991, Contemporary Silver, 2000, Contemporary Silver Part II 2005; co-author: Physical Chemistry, 1964; former editor: Ann. Rev. Phys. Chemistry; mem. editorial bd.: Internat. Jour. Chem. Kinetics, Rev. of Chem. Intermediates, Jour. Phys. Chemistry Served to capt. Canadian Army, 1942-46, ETO. Nat. Research Council Can. fellow, 1940-42; Royal Soc. Can. Research fellow, 1946-47; Milton Research fellow Harvard, 1948; Guggenheim fellow, 1961; vis. fellow Trinity Coll., Oxford, 1971; recipient Sigma Xi award for original research, Debye award in phys. chemistry, 1984, Polanyi medal Royal Soc. Chemistry; named hon. liveryman Worshipful Co. of Goldsmiths, London, 2000. Fellow Am. Phys. Soc., Am. Acad. Arts and Scis., Royal Soc. London; mem. Am. Chem. Soc. (past chmn. Puget Sound sect., past chmn. phys. chemistry divsn., assoc. editor 1965-71), Faraday Soc. Achievements include rsch. in Unimolecular gas phase reaction and history and design of silver implements. Home: 12530 42nd Ave NE Seattle WA 98125-4621 Office: Univ Washington Chemistry Box 351700 Seattle WA 98195 Fax: 206-685-8665. Office Phone: 206-543-1636.

**RABINOVITZ, BRUCE H.,** lawyer; b. Spokane, Wash., Dec. 15, 1945; BA, Washington U., 1967; JD with honors, George Washington U., 1971. Bar: Va. 1971, D.C. 1977, Calif. 1982. Atty.-advisor procurement divsn. Gen. Svcs. Adminstrn., Washington, 1971-72; rates and agreements divsn. Office Gen. Counsel Civil Aeronautics Bd., Washington, 1972-76; atty. Ginsburg, Feldman and Bress, Washington; ptnr., chmn. Aviation dept. Wilmer Cutler Pickering Hale & Dorr, Washington. Mem. D.C. Bar, State Bar Calif., Fed. Bar Assn., Va. State Bar, Order of the Coif. Office: Wilmer Cutler Pickering Hale & Dorr 1899 Pennsylvania Ave NW Washington DC 20006 Mailing: Wilmer Cutler Pickering Hale & Dorr 2445 M St NW Washington DC 20037 Office Phone: 202-663-6960. Office Fax: 202-663-6363. Business E-Mail: bruce.rabinovitz@wilmerhale.com.

**RABINOVITZ, JOEL,** lawyer, educator; b. 1939; AB, Cornell U., 1960; LLB, Harvard U., 1963. Bar: N.Y. 1963, Calif. 1981. Asst. prof. U. Fla., Gainesville, Fla., 1966—68; vis. assoc. prof. UCLA, 1968—69, acting prof., 1969—72, prof., 1972—79; vis. prof. NYU, 1976; dep. Internat. Tax Counsel, Dept. Treasury, 1980—81; ptnr. with Irell & Manella LLP, L.A., 1981—. Office: Irell & Manella LLP 1800 Avenue Of The Stars Los Angeles CA 90067-4212

**RABINOWITZ, DOROTHY,** television critic; b. N.Y.C. BA, Queens Coll., N.Y.C.; postgrad., NYU, Pratt Inst. Freelance writer, syndicated columnist, commentator Sta. WWOR-TV News, N.Y.C.; editl. page writer and television critic Wall St. Jour.; mem. editl. bd. Author: Home Life, 1970, New Lives, 1976, No Crueler Tyrannies: Accusation, False Witness, and Other Terrors of Our Times, 2003; columnist Dorothy Rabinowitz's Media Log. Recipient Pulitzer prize for Disting. Commentary, 2001. Office: Wall St Jour 1155 Ave of the Americas 5th fl New York NY 10036

**RABINOWITZ, JACK GRANT,** radiologist, educator; b. Monticello, N.Y., July 9, 1927; s. Abraham and Bessie (Sussman) R.; m. Rica Gedalia Arnon, Oct. 19, 1972; children— Antoine, Anne, Pierre, Yaron, Tal. BA, UCLA, 1949; MD, U. Berne, Switzerland, 1955. Diplomate: Am. Bd. Radiology. Intern Kings County Hosp., Bklyn., 1955-56, resident, 1956-59; instr. radiology Downstate Med. Center, Bklyn., 1960-61, asst. prof. radiology, 1967-70, prof. radiology, 1970-73; asst. radiologist Mt. Sinai Sch. Medicine, N.Y.C., 1962-65, asst. prof. radiology, 1965-66, assoc. prof. radiology, 1966-67, prof., chmn. dept. radiology, 1978-95, prof., 1995—. Asso. attending radiologist Mt. Sinai Hosp., N.Y.C., 1965-67, dir. radiology, 1978—; radiologist-in-chief Bklyn.-Cumberland Med. Center, Bklyn., 1967-70; dir. diagnostic radiology Kings County Hosp. Center, Bklyn., 1970-73; prof., chmn. dept. diagnostic radiology U. Tenn., Memphis, 1973-78; cons. in radiology VA Hosp., Bronx, N.Y. Author: Pediatric Radiology, 1978, Radiology for the Primary and Emergency Care of Physicians, 1981. Fellow Am. Coll. Radiology; mem. Radiol. Soc. N. Am., Am. Roentgen Ray Soc., Assn. Univ. Radiologists, AMA, Soc. Chmn. Acad. Radiology Depts. Office: Mt Sinai Hosp 1 Gustave L Levy Pl New York NY 10029-6500 Office Phone: 212-241-7427. Business E-Mail: jack-rabinowitz@msnyu.health.org.

**RABINOWITZ, MARK I.,** lawyer; b. Phila., Feb. 7, 1955; BS, Pa. State U., 1981; JD summa cum laude, Temple U., 1988. Bar: Pa. 1988, NJ 1988, Fla. 1990. Law clerk Blank Rome LLP, Phila., 1987, ptnr., practice group leader, fin. svcs. group, 1988—. Co-author: Golden Books Case Creates New Golden Rule for Lessors, 2002, The Case of the Continuing Guaranty, 2000, How Effective Is An Acceptance Certificate Under Article 2A?, 1999, Georgia

Upholds the Integrity of Hell or High Water, 1998. Mem.: Equipment Leasing Assn. (former bd. mem. legal com., former bd. mem. ea. regional com.), Ea. Assn. of Equipment Lessors, Pa. Bar Assn. (former vice-chmn. Article 2A Task Force, mem. bus. section), Fla. Bar Assn., NJ Bar Assn., Phila. Bar Assn. Office: Blank Rome LLP One Logan Sq Philadelphia PA 19103-6998 Office Phone: 215-569-5629. Office Fax: 215-832-5629. E-mail: mrabinowitz@BlankRome.com.

**RABINOWITZ, STEPHEN L.,** lawyer; b. Bklyn., June 8, 1962; AB, Brandeis Univ., 1983; JD, Am. Univ., Washington, 1986. Bar: NY 1987. Law clk. to Chief Judge, James C. Turk US Dist. Ct. (we. dist.) Va., 1986; shareholder, real estate dept., bd. dir. Greenberg Traurig LLP, NYC. Adj. prof. NY Law Sch. Office: Greenberg Traurig MetLife Bldg 200 Park Ave New York NY 10166-1400 Office Phone: 212-801-9295. Office Fax: 212-801-6400. Business E-Mail: rabinowitzs@gtlaw.com.

**RABIU, BADRU I.O.,** federal official; b. Lagos, Nigeria, Aug. 18, 1935; came to U.S., 1972; divorced; six children. Polit., labor specialist Am. Embassy, Lagos, 1951-72; dir. Liberty Immigration and Citizenship Svc., N.Y.C., 1984—. Adminstrv. asst. Arlington (Va.) County, 1981-83; labor writer U.S. Dept. Labor, Washington, 1979-80. Contbr. articles to profl. jours. Mem. Rep. Nat. Com. (life), Rep. Senatorial Inner Circle, Nigeria Muslim Orgn., UN Assn. of U.S. Moslem. Home: 2840 Ocean Pkwy Apt 9E Brooklyn NY 11235-7956 Office: 72 Maiden Ln Ste 312 New York NY 10038

**RABKIN, MITCHELL THORNTON,** physician, educator, hospital administrator; b. Boston, Nov. 27, 1930; s. Morris Aaron and Esther (Quint) Rabkin; m. Adrienne M. Najarian, June 24, 1956; children: Julia Margaret, David Gregory. AB magna cum laude, Harvard U., 1951, MD cum laude, 1955; DSc (hon.), Brandeis U., 1983; DPharm (hon.), Mass. Coll. Pharmacy, 2003; DSc (hon.), Curry Coll., 1989, Northeastern U., 1994; DHumLet (hon.), Salem State Coll., Mass., 1995. Intern Mass. Gen. Hosp., Boston, 1955—56, resident in internal medicine, 1956—57, 1959—60, chief resident, 1962, mem. staff, 1963—72, bd. consultation, 1972—86; CEO CareGroup, Boston, 1996—98; now disting. inst. scholar Carl J. Shapiro Inst. for Edn. and Rsch. Harvard Med. Sch. and Beth Israel Deaconess Med. Ctr., Boston, 1996—; dir. Washington Adv. Group LECG, 1999—. Asst. prof. medicine Harvard U., 1969—70, assoc. prof., 1971—83, prof., 1983—, pres. med. alumni coun., 2002—03; v.p. NYU Sch. Medicine Found. Bd.; chmn. Albert Schweitzer Fellowship, 2005—, bd. dirs. With USPHS, 1957—59. Fellow: AAAS, ACP, Am. Acad. Arts and Scis.; mem.: Inst. Medicine of NAS, Assn. Am. Med. Colls. (chmn. 1996—97), Soc. Med. Adminstrs., Mass. Med. Soc., Tavern Club Boston, Harvard Club of Boston. Jewish. Office: Beth Israel Deaconess Med Ctr/Harvard U Shapiro Inst Edn and Rsch 330 Brookline Ave Boston MA 02215-5400 Office Phone: 617-667-9400. Personal E-mail: mtrabkin@mindspring.com. Business E-Mail: mrabkin@bidmc.harvard.edu.

**RABNER, STUART JEFF,** state attorney general, lawyer; b. Passaic, N.J., June 30, 1960; s. George and Stella (Litwok) R.; m. Deborah Wiener, July 2, 1989; children: Erica, Carly, Jacob. AB, Princeton U., 1982; JD, Harvard U., 1985. Bar: N.J. 1986, N.Y. 1986, U.S. Dist. Ct. N.J. 1986, U.S. Ct. Appeals (3d cir.) 1986. Law clk. to Hon. Dickinson R. Debevoise U.S. Dist. Ct. N.J., 1985-86; asst. U.S. atty. US Dept. Justice, Newark, dep. chief criminal divsn., 1991—2005, dep. chief spl. prosecutions divsn., exec. asst. U.S. atty., chief criminal divsn.; chief counsel to gov. State of NJ, Trenton, 2006, atty. gen., 2006—. Chmn. Holocaust Resource Ctr., Clifton, N.J., 1986—. Office: Office Atty Gen Richard J Hughes Justice Complex 25 Market St CN 080 Trenton NJ 08625

**RABÓ, JULE ANTHONY,** research scientist, consultant; b. Budapest, Hungary; came to U.S., 1957; m. Sheelagh Ennis; children: Benedict, Sebastian. BSChemE, U. Budapest, 1946, DSc in Chemistry, 1949, D honoris causa, 1986, U. Veszprem, Hungary, 2002. From asst. prof. to assoc. prof. Poly. U., Budapest, 1946—54; assoc. dir. Hydrocarbon Rsch. Inst., Budapest, 1951—56; rsch. assoc. Union Carbide Corp., Buffalo, 1957-60, rsch. mgr. Tarrytown, NY, 1960-72, corp. fellow, 1969-82, sr. corp. rsch. fellow, 1982—, UOP, Tarrytown, 1988—. Cons. in chemistry and catalysis, Armonk, N.Y.; former mem. adv. bd. Ctr. for Advanced Materials, Lawrence-Berkeley Lab.; mem. adv. bd. dept. chemistry Lehigh U. Author: Zeolite Chemistry and Catalysts; former mem. editorial bd. Jour. Catalysis, Applied Catalysis; contbr. articles to profl. jours.; patentee in field. Recipient Kossuth award Govt. of Hungary, 1953, Excellence in Catalysis award N.Y. Catalysis Soc., 1982, Humboldt award, Fed. Republic of Germany, 1990. Mem. Am. Chem. Soc. (E.V. Murphree award 1988), Am. Catalysis Soc. (Eugene J. Houdry award 1989), Hungarian Acad. Sci. (Varga medal 1991), Am. Inst. Chemists (Chem. Pioneer award 1993).

**RABOLD, BARBARA ANN,** artist, writer, systems analyst; b. Germantown, Ohio, Apr. 15, 1939; d. George Crone and Gertrude Faye (Marshall) Carr; divorced; children: Matthew Theodore, Teresa Marie. Student, Sinclair C.C., Dayton, Ohio, 1990-92. Former saleswoman House of Stuart Cosmetics, McNess Home Products, Sarah Coventry Jewelry, Amway Products. Choir dir. for 14 yrs.; distbr. nutraceuticals Mannatech, 1998; tchr. art W. Carrollton City Recreation. Exhibited in group shows at Miamisburg (Ohio) Art Gallery, 1970-87, Salem and Dayton Malls, Dayton, 1975-78, Beachmont Mall, Cin., 1975-78, Indpls. Mall, 1975-78. Vol. tutor West Carrollton Sch. Sys., 1970-78, Miami Valley Literacy Coun., Dayton, 1988-2000; pub. spkr.; discussion moderator Parents Without Ptnrs., Dayton, 1980-82, 89-90; asst. group leader Alzheimer Assn., Dayton, 1990; pastoral svc. vol. local hosp. Recipient 600 vol. hours. svc. award Miami Valley Literacy Coun., 1991, more than 600 svc. hours Southview Hosp. Avocations: swimming, reading, gourmet cooking, dance, boating. Home and Office: 102 1/2 Home Ave West Carrollton OH 45449-1206

**RABOLD, CHARLENE FRANKLIN,** librarian; b. Glasgow, Ky., Dec. 1, 1947; d. Carl Paul and Macie (Anderson) Franklin; m. Billy Depp Shoultz, June 29, 1968 (dec. 1971); 1 child, David Paul; m. James A. Griffin Oct. 26, 1974 (div. June 1987); m. David Earl Rabold, Aug. 8, 1987. BS, Western Ky. U., 1969, MA, 1970, Rank I, 1982. Cert. sch. adminstr., standard elem. tchr., 1-8 endorsement for elem. sch. libr., Ky. Libr. Warren County Bd. Edn., Bowling Green, Ky., 1970—. Reference libr. Bowling Green Pub. Libr., 1989-2006; instr. Western Ky. U. Bowling Green, 1989, 95, 2002, 04; sales assoc. Embry's Bowling Green, 1991-92; realtor CryeLeike Exec. Realty, Bowling Green, 2004— Editor So. Ky. Fair Catalog, 1979. Pres. Bowling Green-Warren Count Jaycees, 1981-82, Bowling Green Women's Club, 1988-89; v.p. Warren County Jr. Miss, Inc., 1985-89; chmn. sch. issues Ky. Fedn. Woman's Clubs, Louisville, 1990-92. Recipient Outstanding Young Educator award Delafield Elem. Sch., 1971, 74, Cynthia Jeanette award So. Ky. Fair Bd., 1979, Officer of Yr. award Bowling Green Jayceeites, 1979, 81, Outstanding Local Pres. award Ky. Jaycees, 1982, U.S. Jaycees Congress award U.S. Jaycees, 1984. Mem. NEA, Ky. Edn. Assn., Warren County Edn. Assn. (faculty rep. 1988—, pres. 2001-06), Ky. Libr. Assn., Ky. Sch. Media Assn., Internat. Reading Assn., So. Ky. Reading Assn. (v.p. coun. 1991-93), Three Springs Reading Assn. (pres. 1988-89, 92-93), 3d Dist. Librs. Assn (pres. 1992-93), Warren County Librs. (pres. 1983-2006), Landmark Assn. Bowling Green, Ky. Col. Assn., 3d Dist. Edn. Assn. (pres. 2006). Democrat. Avocations: sewing, crafts, reading. Home: 113 Alpine Ct Bowling Green KY 42104-5301 Office: Crye-Leike Exec Realty 1278 Campbell Ln Bowling Green KY 42104 Office Phone: 270-467-3169. Personal E-mail: crabold@bellsouth.net. Business E-Mail: charlene.rabold@crye.lake.com.

**RABON, WILLIAM JAMES, JR.,** architect; b. Marion, SC, Feb. 7, 1931; s. Williams James and Beatrice (Baker) R.; m. Martha Ann Hibbitts, Mar. 6, 1987. BS in Arch., Clemson Coll., 1951; BArch, MIT, 1956; postgrad., Inst. Urbanistico, Rome, 1957-58. Registered architect, Calif., N.C., Ohio, Pa., Ga. Designer archtl. firms, N.Y.C. & Birmingham, Mich., 1958-61; designer, assoc. John Carl Warnecke &

Assocs., San Francisco, 1961-63, 64-66; designer, assoc. Keyes, Lethbridge & Condon, Washington, 1966-68; prin. archtl. ptnr. A.M. Kinney Assocs. & William J. Rabon, Cin., 1968-85; v.p., dir. archtl. design A.M. Kinney Inc., Cin., 1977-85; v.p., dir. programming svcs. Design Art Corp., 1977-85; sr. architect John Portman & Assocs., Atlanta, 1985-88; dir. archtl. design Robert & Co., Atlanta, 1988-89; design prin. Carlson Assocs., Atlanta, 1990-93; prin., dir. rsch. & med. facilities programming & design Rosser Internat., 1993-97, William J. Rabon, Arch., 1995—. Lectr. U. Calif., Berkeley, 1963-65; asst. prof. archtl. design Cath. U. Am., 1967-68; planning cons. Nat. Bur. Stds. Lab., China, 1982. Prin. works include Kaiser Tech. Ctr., Pleasanton, Calif., 1970 (Rsch. Devel. Lab. of Yr. award), Clermont Nat. Bank, Milford, Ohio, 1971, Pavilion Bldg. Children's Hosp. Med. Ctr., Cin., 1973 (Cin. AIA design award), EG&G, Hydrospace, Inc., Rockville, Md., 1970 (Potomac Valley AIA design award), Mead Johnson Pk., Evansville, Inc., 1973 (Rsch. Devel. lab. of Yr. merit award), Hamilton County Vocat. Sch., Cin., 1972, Hdqrs. Hall. EPA, 1975, Arapahoe Chem. Co. Rsch. Ctr., Boulder, Colo., 1976 (Rsch. Devel. lab. of Yr. award, 1976, Concrete Reinforced Steel Inst. Nat. Design award, Regional AIA design award), Corp. Hdqrs. Ohio River Co., Cin., 1977, Children's Hosp. Therapy Ctr., 1981 (Cin. AIA design award), 1978, award of merit Am. Hosp. Assoc., 1981), Va. Hosp. addition (Cin. ASHRAE Design award, 1980), NALCO Chem. Co. Rsch. Ctr., Naperville, Ill., 1980 (Ohio and Cin. AIA design awards, 1980, 1981), NALCO Chem. Co. Co. Hdqs., 1987, Proctor and Gamble-Winton Hill Tunnel, Cin., 1978 (Ohio AIA design award), Toyota Regional Ctr., Blue Ash, Ohio (Ohio AIA and Ohio Masonry Coun. combined design award, 1981), U. Cin. Med. Ctr. Lab., Cin., 1981, Children's Hosp. Ambulatory Svc. Ctr., 1984, East and West fleethdqrs. and Data Ctr. Librs. of Royal Saudi Arabian Navy, 1985, corp. hdqrs. The Drackett Co., Cin., 1983, corp. hdqrs. Brown & Williamson, Louisville, 1984, Children's Hosp. Med. Ctr. Ambulatory Svcs. Ctr., Cin., 1984, Olin Corp. Rsch. Ctr., Cheshire, Conn., 1985, Inst. Paper Sci. & Tech., Atlanta, 1989, Citicorp. Data Ctr., Napa, Calif., 1992, Sci. Complex, Athens, Ga., 1996, Biocontainment Rsch. Ctr., 1998. 1st lt., co. comdr., Battalion S-2 and Platoon leader AUS, 1951—53, Korean War. Company awarded Presdl. Unit Citation; recipient Silver Star, Bronze Star for Valor, Bronze Star for Meritorious Svc., Purple Heart with bronze cluster; MIT Grad. scholar, 1956; Fulbright scholar, Italy, 1957-58. Mem. AIA, Nat. Coun. Archtl. Registration Bds.

**RABORN, MARCIA MACARTHUR,** primary school educator; b. Birmingham, Ala., Jan. 8, 1945; d. Lee Maurance MacArthur, Jr. and Velma Bosworth Dowling; m. Francis Raborn, Aug. 8, 1970; children: Stephen Francis, Emily Louise. BA, U. Calif., Berkeley, 1968; MA, Oakland U., 1976. Flight attendant World Airways, Oakland, Calif., 1968—70; auditor No. Bancorporation, Detroit, 1973—75; dir. religious edn. Christ Ch., Los Altos Hills, Calif., 1989—90, preschool tchr., 1990—93; preschool, kindergarten tchr. Village Green Day Sch., Great Falls, Va., 1998—. Author: Parents and Children Learning Together, 1976. Parenting instr. Cabrini Coll., Wayne, Pa., 1975—76; mem. Assn. Jr. Leagues, 1976—; mem. adv. bd. United Way, Phila., 1981—84; cmty. v.p. Jr. League Phila., 1982—88; cmty. leader 4H, Los Altos, 1986—92; various bd. positions U.S Pony Club, Great Falls, Va., 1994—2002; sustainer bd. Jr. League Washington, 2002—03; bd. mem. PTA, 1980—2002; Sunday sch. tchr. various locations, 1978—94. Mem.: Nat. Mus. Women in the Arts. Episcopalian. Avocations: hiking, travel, reading.

**RABOSKY, JOSEPH GEORGE,** engineering consulting company executive; b. Sewickley, Pa., May 20, 1944; m. Suzanne Lazzelle, Aug. 23, 1969. BS, Pa. State U., 1966; MS in Engring., W.Va. U., 1969; MSCE, U. Pitts., 1973, PhD, 1984. Registered profl. engr., Pa., W.Va., Ohio. Project engr. Chester Engrs., Coraopolis, Pa., 1969-70, mgr., 1989-92; project engr. Calgon Corp., Pitts., 1970-73, sect. leader, 1979-85, mktg. mgr., 1985-86; sr. environ. specialist Mobay Chem. Corp., Pitts., 1975-79; project engr. Morris Knowles, Inc., Pitts., 1973-74; project mgr. Penn Environ. Cons., 1974-75; engring. mgr. Baker/TSA, Inc., Pitts., 1986-89; pres. AquaTerra, Inc., Moon Twp., Pa., 1992-95, Rabosky & Assocs., Moon Twp., Pa., 1995—. Adj. prof. U. Pitts., 1985-88, Pa. State U.-Beaver, McKeesport and New Kensington campuses, 1985—, Youngstown State U., 2003. Mem. Am. Acad. Environ. Engrs. (diplomate, cert. water supply wastewater engr.), Western Pa. Water Pollution Control Assn. (officer 1984-94, pres. 1992-93), Internat. Water Conf. (mem. exec. bd. 1989-94, gen. chmn. 1992-93), Pa. Water Environ. Assn. (pres. 1996-97). Home: 104 Wynview Dr Moon Township PA 15108-1033 Personal E-mail: joera1co@aol.com.

**RABSON, ALAN SAUL,** federal agency administrator, pathologist, educator; b. N.Y.C., July 1, 1926; s. Abraham and Florence (Shulman) Rabson; m. Ruth L. Kirschstein, June 11, 1950; 1 child, Arnold. BA, U. Rochester, 1948; MD, SUNY, Bklyn., 1950. Intern Mass. Meml. Hosp., Boston, 1951—52; resident in pathology NYU Hosp., 1952—54, USPHS Hosp., New Orleans, 1954—55; pathologist Nat. Cancer Inst., Bethesda, Md., 1955—; prof. pathology Georgetown U. Med. Sch., 1974—, Uniformed Services U. Health Scis., 1978—, George Washington U., 1978—; dep. dir. Nat. Cancer Inst., Bethesda, 1995—, acting dir., 2001—02. Contbr. articles to med. jours. Mem.: Am. Assn. Pathologists, Alpha Omega Alpha, Sigma Xi, Phi Beta Kappa. Address: NIH-Nat Cancer Inst 9000 Rockville Pike Bldg 31 Bethesda MD 20892-0001

**RABSTEJNEK, GEORGE JOHN,** manufacturing executive; b. Queens, N.Y., June 14, 1932; s. George John and Rose Anna (Krasa) R.; m. Patsy Kidd, July 17, 1964; 1 child, Marley Ann. B in Indsl. Engring., Ga. Inst. Tech., 1954; postgrad., U. Conn. Sch. Law, 1960, NYU Sch. Bus., 1965-69; advanced mgmt. program, Harvard U., 1975. Dir. material mgmt. svcs. divsn. Harbridge House, Inc., Boston, 1965-69, v.p., group head, 1969-75, exec. v.p., 1975-76, pres., 1976-83, CEO, 1983-92, chmn., 1983-93, ret., 1993. Chmn. bd. dirs. R.P.W., Inc., Bluelight, Inc.; chmn. B.O.D. Ctr. for Tech. Commercialization 2002; founder, mem. once con [illegible] Nat'l Prevention Assn. th. Contbr. articles to profl. jours. Vice chmn. World Affairs Coun. Boston, 1988, pres., 1984-87; trustee Internat. Coord. Coun., Boston 1984-2003; trustee, chmn. bd. dirs. Mass. Eye and Ear Infirmary, Boston, 1984—, vice chmn. bd. dirs., chmn. emeritus; bd. emeritus Draper Labs. Corp., 1994, chmn. bd. dirs., 2002; mem. adv. bd. Town of Cohasset, Mass., 1975; chmn. nat. adv. bd. Ga. Inst. Tech., 1991-92; mem. exec. adv. bd. Ivan Allen Coll.; mem. bd. visitors Northeastern U.; chmn. bd. dirs. Ctr. for Tech. Commercialization. Comdr. USNR, 1954-75, ret. Recipient Disting. Alumni award Ga. Inst. Indsl. and Sys. Engring., Ga. Inst. Tech., named to Acad. Disting. Engring. Alumni. Mem. Am. Inst. Indsl. Engrs., Nat. Security Indsl. Assn. (v.p. 1987—), Nat. Def. Transp. Assn. (Def. Transp. award 1980), Assn. Naval Aviators, Navy League, Reynolds Soc. (chmn.), Nat. Security Industry Assn. (trustee 1990-93), Harvard Club, Algonquin Club (Boston), Cohasset Golf Club (Mass.), Cohasset Yacht Club, Cohasset Tennis and Squash Club, Mill Reef Club, Antigua, B.W.I., Comml. Club, F St. Club (Washington), Phi Kappa Sigma. Republican. Unitarian Universalist. Home: 181 Border St Cohasset MA 02025-2043 Personal E-mail: gjrab@comcast.net.

**RABUN, JOHN BREWTON, JR.,** criminal justice agency administrator; b. Augusta, Ga., Aug. 16, 1946; s. John Brewton and Alsie Imor (Bateman) R.; m. Anna Betsy Park, Dec. 27, 1967; children: Kerry Kristin, John Candler. BA, Mercer U., 1967; postgrad., So. Bapt. Them. Sem., 1967—70; MSW, U. Louisville, 1971. Cert. social worker, Ky., D.C. Exec. dir. Ky. Civil Liberties Union, Louisville, 1971—72; dir. Cmty. Residential Treatment Svcs., Louisville, 1973—78; program mgr. Field Svcs., Louisville, 1978—80; Exploited and Missing Child Unit, Louisville, 1980—84; v.p. Nat. Ctr. for Missing and Exploited Children, Washington, 1984—2006, COO, 1984—, exec. v.p., 2006—. Mem. Alderman's Task Force on Social Svcs., Louisville, 1982, Mayor's City Youth Commn., Louisville, 1983-84; trainer and/or cons. to numerous agys. in U.S., U.K., Can., Mex., Belgium, Germany, Austria, Netherlands. Contbr. articles to profl. jours., chapters to books. Recipient Key to City of Louisville, 1983, Disting. Alumnus award U. Louisville, 1985, 2003, Russell L. Colling Lit. award Internat. Assn. for Healthcare Security and Safety, 1991; named hon. chief of police City of Louisville, 1982; Alumni fellow U. Louisville, 1999. Mem. ACLU, NASW, Nat. Sheriff's Assn., Nat. Coun. Juvenile and Family Ct. Judges, Internat. Juvenile Officers Assn., Acad.

Cert. Social Workers, Internat. Assn. Healthcare Safety and Security, Am. Soc. Indsl. Security, Internat. Assn. Chiefs of Police. Baptist (deacon). Avocations: photography, hunting, fishing, internet. Home: 13519 Oak Ivy Ln Fairfax VA 22033-1230 Office: Nat Ctr for Missing and Exploited Children 699 Prince St Alexandria VA 22314-3117 Office Phone: 703-837-6216. Business E-Mail: jrabun@ncmec.org.

**RABUS, DOMINIK GERHARD,** electrical engineer, researcher; b. Stuttgart, Germany, July 21, 1973; arrived in U.S., 2005; s. Gerhard Eugen and Rosemarie Irmgard Rabus; m. Regina Maria Elisabeth Fischer-Fels, July 20, 2002; children: Anouk Marjorie, Tizian Dominik. Dipl.-Ing., U. Stuttgart, 1999; Dr.-Ing., Tech. U. Berlin, 2002. Rsch. assoc. Fraunhofer Inst. for Telecom., Heinrich-Hertz-Inst., Berlin, 1999—2002, postdoctoral rsch. fellow, 2002—03; sr. rsch. scientist Forschungszentrum Karlsruhe (Germany) GmbH, 2003—05; Feodor Lynen fellow U. Calif., Santa Cruz, 2006—. Reviewer European Commn., Directorate Gen. Info. Soc., Natural Sciences and Engring. Rsch. Coun. Can. With Germany Navy, 1993—94. Recipient Exceptional reward "power engring.", 28. Landeswettbewerb of "Jugend forscht", 1993, Environ. award, City of Stuttgart, 1992, Umweltwettbewerb der Terratec, 1993. Mem.: IEEE Laser and Electro-optics Soc., Conv. of Socs. of Elec. Engrs. of Europe, Assn. for Elec., Electronic and Info. Techs./Info. Tech. Soc. Achievements include patents in field; patents pending in field. Avocations: sailing, motor biking, windsurfing. Office: University of California Santa Cruz 1156 High St Santa Cruz CA 95064 Office Fax: 18314594829. Business E-Mail: rabus@soe.ucsc.edu.

**RABUZZI, DANIEL D.,** medical association administrator; b. Pitts., June 19, 1935; s. Daniel Ralph and Victoria (Bruni) R.; m. Kathryn Allen, June 11, 1958; children: Daniel, Matthew, Douglas. AB, Harvard Coll., 1957; MD, U. Pa., 1961. Diplomate Am. Bd. Otolaryngology. Instr. otolaryngology U. Md., Balt., 1967-68; asst. prof. SUNY, Syracuse, 1968-71, assoc. prof., 1971-77, prof., 1977-81, clin. prof. otolaryngology, 1984-97, emeritus prof., 1997—; prof., chmn. N.Y. Med. Coll. and N.Y. Eye & Ear Infirmary, N.Y.C., 1981-84. Pres. St. Joseph's Hops. Med. Staff, Syracuse, 1990-92; med. dir. Harrison Surgery Ctr., 1996—. Contbr. 55 articles to profl. jours., chpts. to books. Capt. U.S. Army, 1966-68. Fellow ACS; mem. Am. Soc. Head and Neck Surgery, Am. Acad. Otolaryngology, Am. Cancer Soc. (pres. County unit 1978-80), Onondaga County Med. Soc. (pres. 1987-88). Avocations: roman archeology, european travel, golf, historical readings. Office: Harrison Outpatient Surgery Ctr 550 Harrison St Ste 230 Syracuse NY 13202-3064 Office Phone: 315-472-4424. Personal E-mail: buzdoc@verizon.net.

**RABY, JOHN CORNELIUS,** secondary school educator; b. N.Y.C., May 18, 1944; s. John Cornelius and Adele Lambrose Raby; m. Betty Louise Hays, July 31, 1971; 1 child, John Hays. BA in History, Stanford U., 1966; MA in History, Columbia U Tchr. Coll., 1968. Cert. teach social studies N.Y., N.J., Calif. History tchr. Mountain HS, West Orange, NJ, 1968—71; faculty mem. The. Gov. Sch. of N.J. for Pub. Issues, West Long Branch, 1983—88, 1990, 1992—93, 1995; history tchr. James Caldwell HS, West Caldwell, NJ, 1973—89, The Pingry Sch., Martinsville, NJ, 1989—. Cross-country coach The Pingry Sch., Martinsville, NJ, 1993—. Mem. Dem. Com., Warren, NJ, 1995—, treas., 2002—03. Recipient U.S. Presdl. Tchr. award, NEA, 1986, Nat. Tchr. award Finalist, The Disney Corp., 1994; fellow, Soc. For Values In Higher Edn., 1994—. Mem.: Organization of Am. Historians, Soc. For Values In Higher Edn. (Nat. Bd. Mem. 2003), Am. Historical Assoc. (assoc.). Democrat. Avocations: running, travel, gardening, reading. Office: The Pingry School Box 366 Martinsville Rd Martinsville NJ 08836

**RABY, JULIAN,** art gallery director; b. London, Eng., 1950; m. Lorna Raby. PhD in Oriental Stdues, Univ. Oxford, 1981. Lectr. in Islamic Art & Architecture Univ. Oxford, England, 1979—2002; chmn. of curators Oriental Inst., 1991—93, 1995—2000, chmn. of bd, faculty of Oriental Studies, 1993—95; dir. Freer Gallery of Art and Arthur M. Sackler Gallery, Smithsonian Instn., Washington, 2002—. Founder, former co-owner Azimuth Editors publisher. Series founder and editor Oxford Studies in Islamic Art; author: Venice, Durer, and the Oriental Mode, 1982, IZNIK: The Pottery of Ottoman Turkey, 1989, Turkish Bookbinding in the 15th Century, The foundation of a Court Style, 1993, Qajar Portraits, 1999. Fellow: Soc. of Antiquaries; mem.: Coun. of Britis Inst. of Archaeology and History, Amman, Jordan. Office: Freer Gallery of Art Smithsonian Instn MCR707 PO Box 37012 Washington DC 20013-7012 Office Phone: 202-633-4880. Office Fax: 202-357-4911.

**RABY, WILLIAM LOUIS,** writer, consultant; b. Chgo., July 16, 1927; s. Gustave E. and Helen (Burgess) R.; m. Norma Claire Schreiner, Sept. 8, 1956; children: Burgess, Marianne, Marlene. BSBA, Northwestern U., 1949; MBA, U. Ariz., 1961, PhD, 1971. Prtn. VAR CPA Firms, 1950-76, Touche Ross & Co., N.Y.C., 1977-87; ret. ptnr. Deloitte & Touche, N.Y.C. Pres. Ariz. State Bd. Accountancy, 1993-94; mem. Ariz. State Bd. Tax Appeals, 1994-06, chmn., 1997-99, 2003-05; prof. acctg. emeritus Ariz. State U.; columnist Tax Notes mag., Arlington, Va., 1990—; cons. on video and audio tax edn. tapes Bisk Pub. Co., 1992—. Author: The Income Tax and Business Decisions, 1964, Building and Maintaining a Successful Tax Practice, 1964, The Reluctant Taxpayer, 1970, Tax Practice Management, 1974, Introduction to Federal Taxation, annually, 1980-91, Tax Practice Management: Client Servicing, 1986; editor: Raby Report on Tax Practice, 1986-96, PPC Guide To Successful Tax Practice, 1991; mem. editorial adv. bd. Practical Tax Strategies; contbr. articles to profl. jours. Mem. AICPA (chmn. fed. tax divsn. 1980-83, v.p. 1983-84, coun. 1983-90), Tax Ct. Bar. Presbyterian (elder, United Presbyn. Ch. chmn. adv. coun. on ch. and soc. 1979-81). Office: PO Box 26846 Tempe AZ 85285-6846 Office Phone: 480-967-1501. E-mail: rabyw@aol.com.

**RACCAH, DOMINIQUE MARCELLE,** publisher; b. Paris, Aug. 24, [illegible]; arrived in U.S., 1964; d. Paul Mordechai and Colette Bracha (Madar) Raccah; m. Raymond W. Bennett, Aug. 20, 1980; 3 children. BA, U. Ill., Chgo., 1978; MS, U. Ill., Champaign-Urbana, 1981. Rsch. analyst Leo Burnett Advt., Chgo., 1980-81, rsch. supr., 1981-84, assoc. rsch. dir., 1984-87; pres., pub., owner Sourcebooks, Inc., Naperville, Ill., 1987—; co-CEO Login Pubs. Consortium, Chgo., 1990-99. Author: Financial Sourcebooks' Sources, 1987; editor: Poetry Speaks, 2001, Poetry Speaks to Children, 2005, The Sourcebooks Shakespeare, 2005. Bd. dirs. Com. of 200, Book Industry Study Group. Recipient Blue Chip Enterprise award, 2000, Ernst & Young Entrepreneur of Yr. Ill. and N.W. Ind., 2000; named to Inc. 500 list; inducted into Univ. Ill. Entrepreneurship Hall of Fame, 2001. Mem. Pubs. Mktg. Assn., Am. Booksellers Assn., Am. Assn. Pubs. Office: Sourcebooks Inc 1935 Brookdale Rd # 139 Naperville IL 60563-9245 Office Phone: 630-961-3900. Business E-Mail: dominique.raccah@sourcebooks.com.

**RACE, GEORGE JUSTICE,** pathology educator; b. Everman, Tex., Mar. 2, 1926; s. Claude Ernest and Lila Eunice (Bunch) R.; m. Annette Isabelle Rinker, Dec. 21, 1946; children: George William Daryl, Jonathan Clark, Mark Christopher, Jennifer Anne (dec.). Elizabeth Margaret Rinker. MD, U. Tex., Southwestern Med. Sch., 1947; MS in Pub. Health, U. N.C., 1953; PhD in Ultrastructural Anatomy and Microbiology, Baylor U., 1969. Intern Duke Hosp., 1947-48, asst. resident pathology, 1951-53; intern Boston City Hosp., 1948-49; asst. pathologist Peter Bent Brigham Hosp., Boston, 1953-54; pathologist St. Anthony's Hosp., St. Petersburg, Fla., 1954-55; staff pathologist Children's Med. Center, Dallas, 1955-59; dir. labs. Baylor U. Med. Center, Dallas, 1959-86, chief dept. pathology, 1959-86, vice chmn. exec. com. med. bd., 1970-72; cons. pathologist VA Hosp., Dallas, 1955-71; adj. prof. anthropology and biology So. Meth. U., Dallas, 1969; instr. pathology Duke, 1951-53, Harvard Med. Sch., 1953-54; asst. prof. pathology U Tex. Southwestern Med. Sch., 1955-58, clin. assoc. prof., 1958-64, clin. prof., 1964-72, prof., 1973-94, prof. emeritus, 1994—, dir. Cancer Center, 1973-76, assoc. dean for continuing edn., 1973-94, emeritus assoc. dean, 1994—. Pathologist-in-chief Baylor U. Med. Ctr., 1959-86, prof. biomed. studies Baylor Grad. sch., 1989-94; chmn. Baylor Rsch. Found., 1986-89; prof. microbiology Baylor Coll. Dentistry, 1962-68, prof. pathology, 1964-68, prof., chmn. dept. pathology 1969-73, dean A. Webb Roberts Continuing Edn., 1973-94; spl. advisor on human and animal diseases to gov. State of

Tex., 1979-83. Editor: Laboratory Medicine (4 vols.), 1973, 10th edit., 1983; Contbr. articles to profl. jours., chpts. to textbooks. Pres., Tex. div. Am. Cancer Soc., 1970; chmn. Gov.'s Task Force on Higher Edn., 1981. Served with AUS, 1944-46; flight surgeon USAF, 1948-51, Korea. Decorated Air medal. Fellow AAAS, Coll. Am. Pathologists, Am. Soc. Clin. Pathologists; mem. AMA (chmn. multiple discipline research forum 1969), Am. Assn. Pathologists, Internat. Acad. Pathology, Am. Assn. Med. Colls., Explorers Club (dir., v.p. 1993-2000), Sigma Xi, Alpha Omega Alpha.

**RACE, TIM,** editor; BA, Miami Univ., 1978; MA, Bowling Green State Univ., 1980; MS in journalism, Am. Univ., 1983. Editor CMP Publications; exec. editor Comm. Week; editor, Bus. World sect. New York Times, 1989—91, info. tech. & media editor, 1991—97, founding editor, Circuits sect., 1997—98, editor, Monday Bus. sect., 1998—2004, tech. & health care editor, 2004—. Office: New York Times 229 W 43d St New York NY 10036 Office Phone: 212-556-1526. Office Fax: 212-556-1448. Business E-Mail: timrace@nytimes.com.*

**RACETTE, NANCY KELLY,** research and development company executive, consultant; b. Albany, N.Y., Aug. 4, 1960; d. Barbara Maaloe Kelly-Yeardon and David Peter Kelly; m. John Michael Racette, June 27, 1987; children: Kelly Ann, Casey John. BS, Boston U., 1982. Cert. Fund Raising Exec. Assn. of Fundraising Profls., 1996, JFK Sch. of Govt., Harvard U., 2000. Dir. devel. and mktg. Hudson Valley Girl Scout Coun., Albany, NY, 1990—94; sr. dir. devel. Am. Nat. Red Cross, Washington, 1996—2001; exec. vice pres., prin. Devel. Resources, Inc., Arlington, Va., 2001—. Directorship AFP Found. for Philanthropy, Alexandria, Va., 1997—. Mem.: AFP/DC (assoc.; edn. chair 2003—). Avocations: swimming, tennis, travel. Home: 3337 Holloman Rd Falls Church VA 22042 Office: Devel Resources Inc 1601 N Kent St Arlington VA 22209 Personal E-mail: racette@dri.cc.

**RACHANOW, GERALD MARVIN,** lawyer, pharmacist; b. Balt., Aug. 7, 1942; s. Louis and Lillyan (Binstock) R.; m. Sally Davis, July 26, 1964; children: Mindy, Shelly, Gary. BS in Pharmacy, U. Md., 1965; JD, U. Balt., 1972. Bar: Md. 1973, U.S. Dist. Ct. Md. 1977, U.S. Supreme Ct. 1977. Consumer safety officer FDA, Rockville, Md., 1973-96, dep. dir. divsn. OTC drug evaluation, 1978-96, regulatory counsel divsn. OTC drug products, 1996—2005, regulatory counsel office nonprescription products, 2005—; ptnr. Rachanow & Wolfson, Owings Mills, Eldersburg, Md., 1975—. Contbr. fed. drug law exam. Nat. Assn. Bds. Pharmacy, 1985. Contbr. articles to profl. jours. Fellow Am. Soc. Pharmacy Law; mem. ABA, Soc. FDA Pharmacists, Heuisler Honor Soc. Avocations: chess, stamp and coin collecting, sports. Home: 6700 Sweet Clover Ct Eldersburg MD 21784-6385 Office: US FDA 10903 New Hampshire Ave Bldg 22 Rm 5496 Silver Spring MD 20903-0002 Office Phone: 301-796-0977. Business E-Mail: gerald.rachanow@fda.hhs.gov.

**RACHELEFSKY, GARY STUART,** medical educator; b. NYC, 1942; BS, Columbia Coll., 1963. Intern Bellevue Hosp. Ctr., N.Y.C., 1967-68; resident in pediatrics Johns Hopkins Hosp., 1968-70, Ctr. Disease Control, 1970-72; fellow UCLA Med. Ctr., 1972-74; clin. prof., assoc. dir. A/I Tng. Program UCLA. Fellow Am. Acad. Allergy, Asthma and Immunology (bd. dirs., past pres.). Office: 11620 Wilshire Blvd Ste 200 Los Angeles CA 90025-1767 Personal E-mail: rachruss@ix.netcom.com. Business E-Mail: gr@allergymedicalclinic.com.

**RACHERLA, GOPAL,** computer scientist, researcher; b. India; Prin. network arch. Iospan Wireless, San Jose, Calif., 2000—02; program mgr. Gen. Atomics, San Diego, 2002—. Rsch. engr. SRI Internat., Menlo Park, Calif., 1999—2000. Contbr. articles to profl. jours. Mem.: ACM, IEEE. Personal E-mail: gopalracherla@yahoo.com.

**RACHLIN, HARVEY BRANT,** writer; b. Phila., June 23, 1951; s. Philip and Mazie (Drucker) R.; m. Marla Sivak Goldwert, June 28, 1987; 1 child, Glenn. BA in Biology, Hofstra U., Hempstead, N.Y., 1973. With music pub. cos., 1973—; owner Western Hemisphere Music Co., Ellipsis Music Mgmt. Co., Manhasset Hills, NY, 1975—, pres., 1982-92; mem. faculty Five Towns Coll., Seaford, NY, 1978-84, Manhattanville Coll., Purchase, NY, 1995—. Author: The Songwriter's Handbook, 1977 (N.Y. Pub. Libr. Book for Teen Age 1979-82); The Encyclopedia of the Music Business, 1981 (Outstanding Music Reference Source ALA 1981, ASCAP-Deems Taylor award 1982, Writer's Digest Book Club Spl. Selection, included in Selected Bibliography for Musicians Libr. of Congress); Love Grams, 1983; The Money Encyclopedia, 1984 (Outstanding Fin. Reference Book, Libr. Jour., 1984, Ency. Britannica Home Libr. selection); The Kennedys: A Chronological History 1823–, 1986; The Songwriter's and Musician's Guide to Making Great Demos, 1988 (N.Y. Pub. Libr. Book for Teen Age 1989); The Making of a Cop, 1991 (N.Y. Pub. Libr. Book for Teen Age, 1992); The Songwriter's Workshop, 1991, The TV and Movie Business: An Encyclopedia of Careers, Technologies, and Practices, 1991 (Fireside Theatre Book Club main selection), The Making of a Detective, 1995 (featured on Good Morning America, NYPD Retired Detectives Assn. award), Lucy's Bones, Sacred Stones, and Einstein's Brain, 1996 (History Book Club selection, named one of best books in print The Reader's Catalog, Pub. Libr Catalog, 1999, Sr. HS Libr. Catalog, 1997-02); co-writer, cons. adapted as three-part TV mini-series History's Lost and Found (now daily series on The History Channel, CineGold Eagle award 2000), Jumbo's Hide, Elvis's Ride, and the Tooth of Buddha, 2000 (Book-of-the-Month Club's Quality Paperback Book Club selection); free-lance music journalist; contbr. Songwriter Mag., 1978—, Law and Order Mag., 1992—, Songwriter's Market, 1979, 80, 87, 92, The Writer 2005, guest on The Old Franklin Show, 1977, 81, The Dinah Shore Show, 1978, Nine Broadcast Plaza, 1991, The Sally Jessy Raphael Show, 1993, The Late Late Show with Tom Snyder, 1996; compositions performed L.I. Mandolin and Guitar Orch., 1988; featured in N.Y. Times, 1982, 96, Pro-Music, 1982, Valley Stream Herald, 1995, 96, 98, Writer's Market, 1994, Newsday, 1996, 99, Sarasota Herald-Tribune, 1996, Coral Springs Forum, 1997, L.I. Lifestyles, 2000, City Line News, 2001, Recess for Tchrs., 2005. Recipient Outstanding Reference Book of Yr. award, ALA, 1981, award, Libr. Jour., 1984. Mem.: Am. Soc. Journalists and Authors. Home: 878 Warner Rd Valley Stream NY 11580-1526 Office Phone: 516-568-1795. Personal E-mail: hbrachlin@msn.com.

**RACHLIN, JEANNE-MARIE,** mathematics educator; b. Baton Rouge, La., Nov. 10, 1948; m. Neal Rachlin, May 18, 1969; children: Sean, Aron. BA Math, San Jose State Univ., Calif., 1971. Standard Secondary Credential Calif. Math tchr. R.J. Fisher Sch., Los Gatos, Calif., 1971—81, Los Gatos High, 1981—85; math tchr. Los Gatos/Saratoga High 1985—. Math dept. chair R.J. Fisher Sch., 1978—81, Los Gatos High, 2002—. Recipient Educator of the Yr., Home & Sch. Club, 2000, Tchr. of the Yr., Los Gatos/Saratoga High, 2005. Avocations: reading, travel, yoga, photography. Office: Los Gatos High 20 High Sch Ct Los Gatos CA 95030

**RACHLIN, LAUREN DAVID,** lawyer; b. Buffalo, Feb. 6, 1929; s. Harry A. and Thelma (Goldberg) R.; m. Jean K. Rachlin, June 27, 1954; children: Laura Gail, Ellen Joan, James N. BS, U. Buffalo, 1948; JD, Harvard U., 1951. Bar: NY 1952, U.S. Dist. Ct. (no. and we. dists.) NY 1952, U.S. Tax Ct. 1952, U.S. Supreme Ct. 1958, U.S. Ct. Appeals (2d cir.) 1967, U.S. Ct. Internat. Trade 1978. Ptnr. Rachlin & Rachlin, Buffalo, 1952—81; sr. ptnr. Kavinoky & Cook, Buffalo, 1981—2003; ptnr. Hodgson Russ, LLP, Buffalo and Toronto, 2003—. U.S. appointee to Bi-nat. Dispute Settlement Panel created under U.S.-Can. Free Trade Agreement, 1989-93; U.S. appointee N.Am. Free Trade Agreement Bi-Nat. Dispute Settlement Panel, 1994-96, 2004-; arbitrator Internat. C. of C., Am. Arbitration Assn.; founder and dir. Can./U.S. Border Alliance regionalizing the bi-national trade corridor linking Toronto, Hamilton, Buffalo, Syracuse and Rochester, 1996—; founder, past pres., dir. World Trade Ctr-Buffalo Niagara, 1986—; lectr. in field. U.S. del. to UN Human Rights Commn., 1970; cons. to temporary commn. NY State Constl. Conv.; mem. Erie County Charter Rev. Commn.; mem.-at-large U.S. Nat.

Commn. for UNESCO, 1972-76, chmn. human rights task force; mem. industry functional adv. com. Customs for Trade Policy Matters of U.S. Dept. Commerce, Office U.S. Trade Rep., 1987—. Mem. ABA (fgn. investment in U.S. real estate com., internat. bus. law com., subcom. on trade import), NY State Bar Assn. (founding chmn. internat. sect. 1987-89, chmn. internat. divsn. 1989-94, chair legal edn. and admission to bar com. 1999-2002, award for distinction in internat. law and affairs Internat. Law and Practice sect. 2005), World Arbitration Inst. (adv. bd., bd. dirs.), Am. Assn. Exporters & Importers (trade policy com.), Interpacific Bar Assn., Interam. Bar Assn., Customs and Internat. Trade Bar Assn., Erie County Bar Assn, Industry Trade Adv. Commn. on Customs and Trade Facilitation, US Dept. Commerce. Office: Hodgson Russ LLP Ste 2000 1 M & T Plz Buffalo NY 14203-2391 Address: Ste 2309 150 King St W Toronto ON M5H 1J9 Canada Office Phone: 716-848-1460.

RACHOFSKY, DAVID J., lawyer; b. Oceanside, N.Y., Nov. 17, 1936; s. Lester M. and Marjorie A.; m. Faith Allen; children: Robert, Patricia, Edward. BSEE, MIT, 1958; JD, Temple U., 1968. Bar: Pa., U.S. Dist. Ct. (ea. dist.) Pa., U.S. Tax. Ct., U.S. Ct. Fed. Claims, Pa. Supreme Ct. 1968. Of counsel Dechert LLP, Phila., 1968—. Lectr. law Temple U. Law Sch., 1976-95. Contbr. articles to profl. jours. With USAF, 1969-72. Mem. ABA, Phila. Bar Assn., Internat. Fiscal Assn. (chmn. mid-Atlantic region 1985-87, mem. coun. 1986—, mem. exec. com. 1992—, v.p., sec. 1992-96, exec. v.p. 1996-98, pres. 1998-2000). Office: Dechert LLP 2929 Arch St Philadelphia PA 19104-2808

RACHOFSKY, HOWARD, retired investor, art collector, patron; m. Cindy Rachofsky, 2000; children: Meghan, Matthew. Former bd. chmn. Regal Securities Investment, L.P. Bd. dirs. Dallas Symphony Assn., Dallas Mus. Art, NYC Dia Ctr. for the Arts, East Dallas Cmty. Sch., Tate Lecture Series, So. Methodist U.; adv. dir. Booker T. Washington Magnet HS for the Performing and Visual Arts, Dallas Theater Ctr., Dallas Archtl. Found., U. Tex. Sch. Architecture; founder, bd. dirs. Dallas Ctr. for the Performing Arts Found.; chair, site design com.; mem. adv. bd. Wharton Club, Dallas/Ft. Worth, Dallas Bus. Com. for the Arts; founder Howard Earl Rachofsky Found.; mem. investment com. St. Phillips Acad. Named one of Top 200 Collectors, ARTnews mag., 2003—06. Avocation: Collector of Contemporary Art. Address: Dallas Ctr for the Performing Arts Found 2106 Boll St Dallas TX 75204

RACHOR, JEFFREY C., automotive executive; Region v.p. mid-south Sonic Automotive Inc., Charlotte, NC, 1997—98, v.p. retail ops., 1998—99, exec. v.p. retail ops., 1999—2002, exec. v.p., COO, 2002—04, pres, COO, 2004—. Office: Sonic Automotive Inc 5401 Independence Blvd Charlotte NC 28212*

RACHOW, LOUIS A(UGUST), librarian; b. Shickley, Nebr., Jan. 21, 1927; s. John Louis and Mable (Dondlinger) R. BS, York Coll., 1948; MS in L.S., Columbia U., 1959. Librarian York Coll., Nebr., 1949-54; instr. library asst. Queens Coll., N.Y.C., 1956-57; serials acquisition asst. Columbia U. Law Library, N.Y.C., 1957-58; asst. librarian Univ. Club, N.Y.C., 1958-62; librarian Hampden-Booth Theatre Library at the Players, N.Y.C., 1962-86, curator, 1986-88; library dir. Internat. Theatre Inst. U.S., N.Y.C., 1989—2002. Cons. theatre sect. U. Calif., San Diego, new campuses program, 1964, Music Ctr. Operating Archives, Los Angeles, 1985; mem. library adv. bd. Eugene O'Neill Meml. Theatre Center, 1966— Editor, compiler: Guide to Performing Arts, 1968; assoc. editor Am. Notes and Queries, 1971-74, asst. editor, 1967-71; mem. editorial adv. bd. Nat. Dir. for Performing Arts and Civic Ctrs.; editor Performing Arts series Gale Info. Guide, 1976-83, Theatre and Performing Arts Collections, 1981; contbr. articles and revs. to profl. jours. Mem. adv. bd. Am. Theatre Co., OKC Theatre Prodns. Served with AUS, 1954-56 Mem. Theatre Libr. Assn. (rec. sec. 1966-67, pres. 1967-72, 81-83, v.p. 1976-80, editor Broadside 1973-81), ALA, Spl. Librs. Assn. (sec.-treas. mus. group N.Y.C. chpt. 1964-66), N.Y. Libr. Club (pres. 1979-80), Am. Theatre Assn., New Drama Forum Assn. (pres. 1983-86), Am. Soc. Theatre Rsch., N.Y. Tech. Svcs. Librs., Archons of Colophon (convener 1982-83), Episcopal Actors Guild Am. (bd. dirs. 1976-2002, v.p. 2002—), Drama Desk, Broadway Theatre Inst. Outer Critics Circle (treas. 1998—), Players Club, The Lambs Club. Home: 528 W 114th St New York NY 10025-7841

RACHOW, SHARON DIANNE, realtor; b. St. Joseph, Mo., Apr. 12, 1939; d. Norman DeLos Zancker and Sylvia Lavina (Hawkins) Trouel; m. Thomas Eugene Rachow, Oct. 22, 1968; children: Todd A, Tiffany K. Student, So. Ill. U., 1969-72. Sec. Westab, Inc. (now Mead), St. Joseph, 1957-60, Seitz Packing Co. (now Sara Lee), St. Joseph, 1960-66; exec. asst. to v. gen. mgr. Kansas City (Mo.) Chiefs, 1972; co-owner, mgr. Pool 'N Patio Plus, St. Joseph, 1973-84; realtor Coldwell Banker Gen. Realtors, St. Joseph, 1984-93, RE/MAX, 1993—2004, Evans Realty, 2004—. Trustee Nat. Multiple Sclerosis Soc., Mid Am. chpt., Midland M.S. Express Br., 1993-98. Mem.: Real Estate Buyers Agt. Coun. (accredited buyers rep. 1996—), St. Joseph Regional Bd. Realtors (residential specialist 1987—, Multi-List com. 1993—2002, bd. dirs. 1994, forms com. 1994—2002, Top Residential Sales award 1986—, Top 10), Multi Million Dollar Club (quality svc. cert. 2001, quality svc. cert. 2003). Republican. Lutheran. Home: 4211 Country Ln Saint Joseph MO 64506-2454 Office: Evans Realty 606 S Woodbine Rd Saint Joseph MO 64507 Office Phone: 816-390-8000. Business E-Mail: sharonr@stjoelive.com.

RACICOT, MARC F., insurance association executive, lawyer, former governor; b. Thompson Falls, Mont., July 24, 1948; s. William E. and Patricia E. (Bentley) Racicot; m. Theresa J. Barber, July 25, 1970; children: Ann, Timothy, Mary Catherine, Theresa, Joseph. BA, Carroll Coll., Helena, Mont., 1970; JD, U. Mont., 1973; postgrad., U. Va., 1973, Cornell U., 1977. Bar: Mont. 1973. Prosecutor, JAG Corp. US Army, 1973—76; dep. county atty. Missoula (Mont.) County, 1976—77; bur. chief County Prosecutor Svcs. Bur., Helena, Mont., 1977—89; asst. atty. gen. State of Mont., Helena, 1977—89, spl. prosecutor for the Atty. Gen.'s Office, atty. gen., 1989—93, gov., 1993—2001; ptnr. Bracewell & Patterson LLP, Washington, 2001—, chmn. Repub. Nat. Com., Washington, 2002—03, Bush-Cheney Re-election campaign, 2003—04; pres. The Am. Insurance Assn., Washington, 2005—. Founder Missoula Drug Treatment Program, 1977; active United Way, Helena; bd. visitors U. Mont. Sch. Law. Capt. U.S. Army, 1973—76. Named to Basketball Hall of Fame, Carroll Coll., 1982. Mem.: Mont. Bar Assn. Republican. Roman Catholic. Office: Bracewell & Patterson LLP 2000 K St NW Ste 500 Washington DC 20006-1872 also: Am Insurance Assn 1130 Connecticut Ave NW Ste 1000 Washington DC 20036

RACINE, KARL A., lawyer; b. Port au Prince, Haiti, Dec. 14, 1962; Student French, French civilization, Sorbonne, Paris; BA in Economics, U. Pa., 1985; JD, U. Va., 1989. Bar: Md. 1989, DC 1992. Litig. assoc. Venable LLP, Washington, 1989—92, ptnr., corp. and civil litig. groups, 2002—, dep. mng. ptnr., 2005—06, mng. ptnr., 2006—; staff atty. Pub. Defender Svc., Washington, 1992—94; ptnr. Cacheris & Treanor, Washington, 1994—97; assoc. counsel The White House, Washington, 1997—2000. Achievements include co-producing the first Haitian/Creole/English legal dictionary, 1994. Office: Venable LLP 575 Seventh St NW Washington DC 20004 Office Phone: 202-344-8322. Office Fax: 202-344-8300. E-mail: karacine@venable.com.

RACINE, RICHARD B., lawyer; b. Cleve., Mar. 20, 1956; BS in Chem., Georgetown U., 1978; JD, Case Western Reserve U., 1981. Bar: Ohio 1981, DC 1984, registered: US Patent & Trademark Office. Ptnr. Finnegan, Henderson, Farabow, Garrett & Dunner LLP, Washington, mng. ptnr., leader, chem. practice group, mem. mgmt. com. Mem.: ABA (subcom. chmn. atty. opinions com. 1993—94), Southwestern Legal Found. (lectr. 1993—94), Fed. Cir. Bar Assn., Am. Chem. Soc. (program chmn. 1991—93, divsn. chmn. elect 1993, divsn. chmn. 1994), Am. Intellectual Property Law Assn., Bar Assn. DC, DC Bar. Office: Finnegan Henderson Farabow Garrett Dunner LLP 901 New York Ave NW Washington DC 20001-3315 Office Phone: 202-408-4038. Office Fax: 202-408-4400. Business E-Mail: rich.racine@finnegan.com.

RACINE, SCOTT H., lawyer; b. Chgo. BA, Bradley Univ., 1972; JD cum laude, Pepperdine Univ., 1978; LLM in Tax., NYU, 1979. Bar: Calif. 1978, US Dist. Ct. (ctrl., so. districts) Calif., US Ct. of Appeals (9th cir.), US Tax Ct., US Ct. of Claims. Law clk. Judge William M. Drennen US Tax Ct., 1979—80; shareholder tax specialty firm, LA; ptnr., chair, tax practice group LA Akin Gump Strauss Hauer & Feld LLP, LA. Adj. prof. law Pepperdine Univ., 1980—, Univ. San Diego, 1983—87, Loyola Univ., 2000—. Student writings editor Pepperdine Law Rev., 1976—78; author: numerous articles for profl. publs. Bd. visitors Pepperdine Univ. Sch. Law; bd. adv. Loyola Univ. Sch. Law; planning com. Univ. So. Calif. Tax Inst. Mem.: ABA (sect. on tax.), Calif. Bar Assn. (sect. on tax.), LA County Bar Assn. (sect. on tax.). Office: Akin Gump Strauss Hauer & Feld LLP Ste 2400 2029 Century Pk E Los Angeles CA 90067-3012 Office Phone: 310-229-1059. Office Fax: 310-229-1001. Business E-Mail: sracine@akingump.com.

RACITI, CHERIE, artist; b. Chgo., June 17, 1942; d. Russell J. and Jacque (Crimmins) R. Student, Memphis Coll. Art, 1963-65; BA in Art, San Francisco State U., 1968; M.F.A., Mills Coll., 1979. Assoc. prof. art San Francisco State U., 1984-89, prof., 1989—. Lectr. Calif. State U., Hayward, 1974, San Francisco Art Inst., 1978; mem. artist com. San Francisco Art Inst., 1974-85, sec., 1980-81. One woman shows include U. Calif., Berkeley, 1972, Nicholas Wilder Gallery, L.A., 1975, San Francisco Art Inst., 1977, Marianne Deson Gallery, Chgo., 1980, Site 375, San Francisco, 1989, Reese Bullen Gallery, Humboldt State U., Arcata, Calif., 1990, Mills Coll. Art Mus., Oakland, Calif., 1998; group shows include Whitney Mus. Art, 1975, San Francisco Sci. Fiction, The Clocktower, N.Y.C., Otis-Parsons Gallery, Los Angeles, 1984-85, San Francisco Art Inst., 1985, Artists Space, N.Y.C., 1988, Angles Gallery, Santa Monica, 1987, Terrain Gallery, San Francisco, 1992, Ctr. for the Arts, San Francisco, 1993, Santa Monica Coll., 1998, 25/25 25th Anniversary Exhbn., So. Exposure Gallery, San Francisco, 1999, Santa Cruz Mus., 2003, Thacher Gallery U. San Francisco, 2004. Bd. dirs. New Langton Arts, 1988-92. Eureka fellow Fleishhacker Found., San Francisco, Va.Ctr. for Creative Arts fellow, Amherst, Va., 2005; recipient Adaline Kent award San Francisco Art Inst., 1976, Djerassi resident, 1994, Tyrone Guthrie Ctr. resident, Ireland, 1995, Millay Colony for Arts resident 1999, Juror's award Artadia San Francisco. Office: San Francisco State U Art Dept 1600 Holloway Ave San Francisco CA 94132-1722 Office Phone: 415-338-6318. Business E-Mail: craciti@sfsu.edu.

RACKE, MICHAEL KARL, academic administrator; b. Morristown, N.J., Oct. 2, 1959; m. Amy E. Lovett-Racke, Mar. 3, 1965. BS, Haverford Coll., Pa., 1981; MD, U. Medicine and Dentistry N.J., Newark, 1985. Lic. neurology Am. Bd. of Neurology and Psychiatry. Postdoctoral fellow NIH, Bethesda, Md., 1989—94; asst. prof. Washington U. Sch. of Medicine, St. Louis, 1994—99; prof. U. of Tex. Southwestern Med. Ctr., Dallas, 1999—2006; chmn. of neurology Ohio State U. Med. Ctr., Columbus, 2006—. Named Am. Acad. Neurology Edn. and Rsch. Found. Young Investigator in Multiple Sclerosis, Harry Weaver Neurosci. Scholar of Nat. Multiple Sclerosis Soc. Avocation: sailing. Office: Ohio State Univ Med Ctr 445 Means Hall 1654 Upham Dr Columbus OH 43210-1228 Office Phone: 614-293-4036. Office Fax: 614-293-9029. Business E-Mail: michael.racke@osumc.edu.

RACKLIN, BARBARA COHEN, fundraising consultant; b. N.Y.C., Dec. 3, 1950; d. Harry Cohen and Shari Lillian (Greene) Cohen; m. Arthur Michael Racklin, Aug. 19, 1979 (div.); 1 child, Nicholas Michael. BA in Math., U. Tex., 1972; postgrad., U. LaVerne, 1981-82. Cert. histocompatability technologist, Am. Bd. Histocompatability and Immunogenetics; cert. fundraising exec. Asst. dir. transplant lab. Med. br. U. Tex., Galveston, 1974-76; transplant immunology specialist Montefiore Hosp., Bronx, N.Y., 1976-77; dir. pediat. immunology lab. Cedar Sinai Hosp., L.A., 1977-79; supr. pathology lab. City of Hope Nat. Med. Ctr., Duarte, Calif., 1979-82, rsch. specialist transplant lab., 1982-85; staff coord. vol. devel. City of Hope Devel. Ctr., L.A., 1986-88; coord. fin. devel. events ARC, Pasadena, Calif., 1995-99; co-owner benefit specialists Fundraising Cons., La Cañada, Calif., 1995-99; chief devel. officer San Gabriel chpt. ARC, 1999—2002; devel. dir. PSW region Anti-Defamation League, 2002—05; assoc. v.p. advancement Music Ctr. L.A. County, 2005—. Tour chmn. City of Hope Ann. Conv., Duarte, 1987, 89, 91. Contbr. or co-contbr. articles to profl. publs. Bd. dirs. City of Hope Med. Ctr., 1986-89, mem. bd. govs., 1991-93; mem. steering com. local parcel tax election, La Cañada, 1992, local sch. bd. election, 1995; mem. sch. bd. La Cañada Unified Sch. Dist., 1997-2001, clk. governing bd., 1999-2000, pres. gov. bd. 2000-01; pres. La Cañada Coun. PTA, 1995-97, City of Hope Aux., 1988-90; bd. dirs. LCF Ednl. Found., past pres., v.p., 1991-97; sec. Children's Hosp. Aux., 1994-97; auditor 1st Dist. PTA, 1997; chairperson youth com. Pasadena Temple, 1996-97; v.p. governing bd. La Canada Unified Sch. Dist., 1998-99; bd. dirs. southwest reg. B'nai B'rith Youth Orgn.; participant Leadership Pasadena, 1999-2000. Recipient Hon. Svc. award La Cañada Coun. PTA, 1996, Svc. award LCF Ednl. Found., 1995, Golden Apple award La Canada Unified Sch. Dist., 1996, Golden Bear award for Fundraising Excellence Am. Red Cross, 2001 Mem.: L.A. World Affairs Coun., Nat. Coun. Planned Giving, Calif. Advancement Rschrs. Assn., Assn. Fundraising Profls. Avocations: skiing, bowling, reading. Office: Music Ctr LA County 135 N Grand Ave Los Angeles CA 90012 Business E-Mail: bracklin@musiccenter.org.

RACKOW, ERIC C., hospital administrator; Graduate, Franklin and Marshall Coll.; MD, SUNY, Downstate Med. Ctr., Brooklyn, 1971. Bd. cert. internal medicine, cardiovasc. diseases, critical care medicine, internal medicine, 1975, cardiology, 1977, critical care, 1987. Residency Kings County Hosp. Ctr., 1970—72, chief residency, 1972—73, clin. fellow, 1973—75; dir. clin. trials NYU Hosp. Ctr.; prof. heath care mgmt. NYU Med. Ctr., Sch. Medicine; sr. v.p., chief med. officer NYU Hosp. Ctr., NYC, 2000—04, pres., 2004—. Adj. prof. medicine NY Med. Coll.; chmn. emeritus St. Vincent's Hosp. & Med. Ctr. of NY, Dept. Medicine; hon. role, Physician-in-Chief Inst. Critical Care Medicine; past pres. Soc. Critical Care Medicine; past chair Am. Bd. Internal Medicine, Critical Care Medicine Subspecialty Bd. Contbr. articles to profl. jours. Office: NYU Hosps Ctr Sch Med HCC15 550 First Ave New York NY 10016 Office Phone: 212-263-2606. Business E-Mail: eric.rackow@nyumc.org.*

RACKOW, JULIAN PAUL, lawyer; b. Phila., Dec. 16, 1941; s. Lawrence Lionel and Blanche (Wachman) R.; m. Paulette Schorr, June 23, 1963; children: Jeffrey A., Andrea B. AB, Cornell U., 1963; JD, Harvard U., 1966. Bar: Pa. 1966, U.S. Dist. Ct. (ea. dist.) Pa. 1966. Assoc. atty. Goodis, Greenfield, Narin & Mann, Phila., 1966-69; ptnr., co-chmn. dept. real estate Blank, Rome LLP, Phila., 1970—. Exec. com., bd. dirs. Ctrl. Phila. Devel. Corp., 1990—, pres. 1996-2000, chmn., 2000—; bd. dirs. Ave of the Arts, Inc., 2000—, Parkway Coun. Found., 2004—. Mem. Phila. Bar Assn., Harvard Law Sch. Assn. Phila., Am. Coll. Real Estate Lawyers, Ave of the Arts, Inc. Avocations: tennis, travel, piano. Office: Blank Rome LLP One Logan Sq Philadelphia PA 19103-6998 Office Phone: 215-569-5671. Business E-Mail: rackow@blankrome.com.

RACTLIFFE, ROBERT EDWARD GEORGE, management executive; b. Hertfordshire, Eng., July 25, 1943; came to U.S., 1965; s. Augustus David John and Veronica Phyllis (Jones) R.; m. Nancy Jane Brumbaugh, June 29, 1968; children: Richard Alban, Tiffany Elizabeth, Courtney Veronica. BS with honors, U. London, 1965; MSEE, U. Pitts., 1969, MBA with honors, 1972; PMD, Harvard U., 1975. Engr. Westinghouse Electric Corp., Pitts., 1965-69, sales mgr. LRA Div., 1969-73, mfg. engr. mgr. LRA Div., 1974-76, dept. mgr. Hydrogenerator Dept., 1976-78, mgr. product mktg. Steam Turbine Generator Div. Phila., 1979-81, mgr. strategic planning Power Generation Bus. Unit, 1981-84, gen. mgr. Power Generation Comml. Div. Orlando, Fla., 1984-86; pres., North Am. Ops. United Tech. Carrier Corp., Syracuse, N.Y., 1986-88; pres., chief exec. officer NORDYNE Inc., St. Louis, 1989—. Patentee in field; contbr. articles to profl. jours. Mem. AAIM (bd. dirs.), Gas Appliance Mfrs. Assn. (co. rep.), Manufactured Housing Inst. (co. rep.), Air Conditioning and Refrigeration Inst. (bd. dirs., v.p. exec. com., com. chmn., co. rep.). Republican. Episcopalian. Avocations: golf, tennis, skiing. Office: NORDYNE Inc PO Box 8809 O Fallon MO 63366-8809

RACZ, IRENE, public relations executive; b. Bethlehem, Pa., June 22, 1951; d. Alexander John and Olga Krivy Racz; m. Glenn Michael Gershaneck, Aug. 27, 1978; children: Nathan Racz Gershaneck, Trina Racz Gershaneck. BA magna cum laude, Ithaca Coll., Ithaca, N.Y., 1973. Adminstrv. asst. New Eng. Resource Ctr. for Occupl. Edn., Cambridge, Mass., 1973—74; reporter, editor Times Argus, Barre, Vt., 1975—79; rsch. analyst Vt. State Employees Assn., Montpelier, 1979—80; city editor Times Argus, Barre, 1980—83; asst. sunday editor Sunday Times Argus/Rutland Herald, Barre, 1983—85; ptnr. PressKit, Montpelier, 1985—97; dir. of pub. affairs Vt. Student Assistance Corp., Winooski, 1997—. Intern U.S. Senator Harold Hughes, Washington, 1971; free-lance writer, Montpelier, Vt., 1985—; publicist Contemporary Dance & Fitness Studio, Montpelier, 1996—; tchg. asst. Ithaca Coll., 1972. Parent outreach assoc. Johns Hopkins Ctr. for Talented Youth, Balt., 1999—; vol., chaperone Montpelier to Thailand Isaarn Scholarship Fund, Montpelier, Vt., 2004—; chair Ice and Water flood relief com., Montpelier, Vt., 1992; mem. Property Tax Relief Study Com., Montpelier, Vt., 1992; co-coord. Environ. Learning for the Future, Montpelier, Vt., 1997—98; vol. Planned Parenthood of No. New Eng., Williston, Vt., 1996—; mem. Vt. Women Working for Clinton/Gore, Montpelier, Vt., 1992; mem., chair The Giving Tree, Barre, Vt., 1983—86; mem. Kids'Fest, Montpelier, Vt., 1987—90; mem., com. chair Planned Parenthood of No. New Eng., Williston, Vt., 1990—96; mem. Pyralisk Arts Ctr., Montpelier, Vt., 2001—02. Recipient Bus./Econ. Reporting award, New Eng. Press Assn., 1982, 1984. D-Liberal. Avocations: travel, writing, dance, yoga, theater. Home: 12 Mountainview St Montpelier VT 05602 Office: Vermont Student Assistance Corporation 10 East Allen St Winooski VT 05404 Office Phone: 802-655-9602. Office Fax: 802-654-3779. E-mail: racz@vsac.org.

RADA, DAVID CHARLES, dermatologist; b. Chgo., Apr. 8, 1954; s. Irwin C. and Mary A. Rada; m. Christina Lynne Fogle, Mar. 27, 1981; children: Matthew D., Megan E., Rebecca C. BS in Microbiology, U. Nebr., 1976; MD, U. Nebr., Omaha, 1980. Diplomate Am. Bd. Dermatology. Resident in dermatology U. Kans. Med. Ctr., 1982—85; pvt. practice Kansas City, Mo., 1985—; pres. CryoHist, Inc., Kansas City, 1995—. Inventor (in field). Fellow: Am. Soc. Dermatologic Surgery, Am. Acad. Dermatology; mem.: Kansas City Dermatologic Soc., Mo. Dermatologic Soc. Achievements include invention of technology to get the surface cut by the surgeon's knife onto glass slides for histologic margins, a technique applicable for cancer resection margins using frozen sections. Office: 4320 Wornall Rd Ste 728 Kansas City MO 64111 Office Phone: 816-561-3641. E-mail: camargin@cryohist.com.

RADA, RUTH BYERS, retired dean; b. LA, Oct. 3, 1923; d. George and Gerda Marie (Lihm) Byers; children: Kaaren Ruth, Georgene Melanie. AB, U. So. Calif., 1944, MA, 1945; EdD, Nova U., 1976. Asst. dean instrn. and evening East L.A. Coll., 1964-69, dean instrn., 1969-70; dean student personnel L.A. Harbor Coll., 1970-73, East L.A. Coll., 1973-77, L.A. Mission Coll., 1977-83; prof. biol. sci. East L.A. C.C., 1945-69, ret., 1983. Author: Water Biology, 1950, (with others) Human Body in Health and Disease, 1969, Structure and Function of Human Body, 1970, Laboratory Manual for Introductory Microbiology, 1963. Mem. Calif. Cmty. and Jr. Coll. Assn. (area pres. 1973-74), Calif. Woman Adminstrs. Assn., Los Angeles Coll. Adminstrs. Assn. (sec. 1973-74), Phi Beta Kappa, Phi Kappa Phi, Pi Lambda Theta, Phi Sigma. Republican. Mem. Ch. of Religious Sci.

RADAKOVICH, DANIEL I., communications executive, consultant; b. Easton, Pa., Sept. 27, 1958; s. Daniel L. and Nancy A. Radakovich. BA in History, Pa. State U., University Park, 1979. Overseas mktg. mgr. Investment and Income-Producing Properties Internat., Inc., Denver, 1983—84, exec. v.p. LA, 1984—85; substitute tchr. Philipsburg Sch. Dist., NJ, 1985—87; asst. warehouse mgr. Steelcrete, North Royalton, Ohio, 1991—93; v.p. Swing-Sling Inc., Strongsville, Ohio, 1994—96; rschr. DesertSun Films LLC, Garfield, NJ, 2003—04; sr. exec. v.p. prodn. DesertSun Films, LLC, Garfield, NJ, 2004—, chief rsch. officer, 2005—. Cons. Strategicon, Inc., Fullerton, Calif., 1981—85, Diverse Talents Inc., LA, 1985, New Universe Project SF Convs., Fullerton, 1986—88, GuardTower Games, Brunswick, Ohio, 1999—2005; spl. cons. HollyDanWorks, Belgrade, 2003—04, Ontario, 2003—04, lead specialist cons., 2005—06; staff mem. Alpha Young Writer's Workshop, Greensburg, Pa., 2003—06. Actor: (films) Darkest Days (NY Ind. Film Festival Best thriller award, 2005); contbr. articles to profl. jours. Mem. Cleve. Ams. Mid. Ea. Origin, 1997—2001, Polish-Ams., Inc., Cleve., 1997—2001; exec. com. mem. Cuyahoga County Dems., Cleve., 1994—2000; mem. Cosmopolitan Dem. League, Cleve., 1997—2001, Ward 15 Dem. Club, Cleve., 1998—2001; Dem. candidate 2000 US senate primary. Mem.: Pitts. Area Scientifiction Colloquy, KC. Democrat. Roman Catholic. Avocations: reading, writing, strategic gaming, acting, politics. Office: DesertSun Films LLC TDS Studios 31 4th Ave Westwood NJ 07675 Office Phone: 862-703-3090. Business E-Mail: info@teamdesertsun.com, hollydanworks@gmail.com.

RADANOVICH, GEORGE P., congressman; b. Mariposa, Calif., June 20, 1955; s. Joan and George F.; m. Ethie Weaver; 1 child, George King. BS in Agr. Bus. Mgmt., Calif. State Polytechnic U., 1978. County supr. County Planning Comm., 1988-92; mem. U.S. Congress from 19th Calif. dist., Washington, 1995—; mem. energy and com. resources com., chmn. natural parks subcom. Chmn. Water and Power Sub Com.; co-chair Congl. Wine Caucus. Mem. Calif. Agrl. Leadership Program Class XXI, Rotary (Paul Harris Fellowship). Republican. Roman Catholic. Office: US Ho Reps 438 Cannon Ho Office Bldg Washington DC 20515-0519

RADCLIFF, JOYCE B., librarian; d. Robert and Rosanna Bullard; m. Doc Radcliff, June 24, 1968; children: Nicole Lynn, Rasheda Asia. BA, U. South Ala., 1973, MLS, 1996. Tech. asst. U. S. Ala., Mobile, 1974—99; cataloging libr. U. So. Miss., Hattiesburg, 1999—2001; serials libr. Tenn. State U., Nashville, 2001—; cons. Libr. of Congress, Washington, 1996; mem. exec. bd. Reading Is Fundamental, Nashville, 2004—. Exec. bd. Libr. Sch. Assn. U. Ala., 1997—2002. Contbr. articles to profl. jours. Advisor ABeneefuo KUO Honor Soc., 1989—99; greeter Frist Mus., Nashville, 2002—; advisor Girl Scouts Am., Mobile, 1982—86. Named Staff of Yr., U. S. Ala., 1999; recipient Award of Appreciation, Libr. Congress, Washington, 1996, Congress award, Congressman Sonny Callahan, 2000. Mem.: ALA, Tenn. Libr. Assn., Delta Sigma Theta. Avocations: walking, reading, travel, computers. Office: Tenn State Univ 330 10th Ave N Nashville TN 37203 Office Phone: 615-963-7383.

RADCLIFFE, DANIEL, actor; b. London, July 23, 1989; Actor: (films) Tailor of Panama, 2001, Harry Potter and the Sorcerer's Stone, 2001, Harry Potter and the Chamber of Secret's, 2002, Harry Potter and the Prisoner of Azkaban, 2004, Harry Potter and the Goblet of Fire, 2005; appearances (TV) The Today Show, 2001, The Oprah Winfrey Show, 2001, Late Night with Conan O'Brien, 2004, (TV special) David Copperfield, 1999. Office: c/o ICM 4-6 Soho Sq London W1D 3PZ England*

RADCLIFFE, GLENA ELOISE, lyricist, poet, composer; b. Washington, June 7, 1941; d. Harold Glenn and Dorothy Dean (McGinnis) Snyder; m. Russell Traverse Radcliffe, Sept. 19, 1963; children: Melanie Christine McCabe, Lori Victoria Meyers. Grad. HS, Bradenton, Fla. Pvt. practice, Colo., 1980—87. Author: (albums) Come'n on Down the Line, 1983. Bd. dirs. North Fork coun. The Arts and Humanities, Read, Colo., 1981—83; bd. dirs. Thunder Mountain Theatre, Paonia, Colo., 1981—83. Democrat. Avocations: piano, guitar, writing poetry and music, birdwatching, ATV riding. Home: 1215 Coronado Rd Corrales NM 87048-3108 Mailing: PO Box 3108 Corrales NM 87048

**RADCLIFFE, MARK FLOHN,** lawyer; b. Dayton, Ohio, Mar. 11, 1952; Cert. of completion, Sorbonne, Paris, 1972; BS in Chem. magna cum laude, U. Mich., 1974; JD, Harvard U., 1981. Bar: Calif. 1982. Law clk. to chief judge U.S. Dist. Ct. (so. dist.) Calif., San Diego, 1981-82; assoc. Brobeck, Phleger & Harrison, San Francisco, 1982-86; assoc. to ptnr. Gray Cary Ware & Freidenrich, Palo Alto, Calif., 1986—2004; ptnr., co-chmn. Tech. Transactions practice group DLA Piper Rudnick Gray Cary, Ea. Palo Alto, Calif., 2005—. Gen. counsel The Open Source Initiative. Mem. editorial bd.: Computer Lawyer, 1988—, Cyberspace Lawyer; mem. adv. bd. BNA Electronic Commerce & Law Report, Global Intellectual Property Asset Mgmt. Report; country contr. European Intellectual Property Rev.; contbr. articles to profl. law jours. Lt. (j.g.) USNR, 1974-77. Named one of Am. 100 Most Influential Lawyers, Nat. Law Jour., 1997, World's Leading Trademark Lawyers, Expert Guide, 2003, No. Calif Super Lawyer & one of Top 100 No. Calif. IP Lawyers, San Francisco mag., 2004, Best Lawyers in Am., 2005—06, Am. Leading Lawyers for Bus., Chanbers USA, 2006; recipient Disting. Alumni award, Harvard Univ., 1998. Mem. ABA (chmn. subcom. 1985-88), Am. Intellectual Property Law Assn., Internat. Trademark Assn., San Francisco Bar Assn. (chmn. computer law sect. 1985-86), Computer Law Assn. (dir.), Licensing Exec. Soc., South Bay Trademark Lawyers Assn. (founder), Harvard Club. Office: DLA Piper Rudnick Gray Cary 2000 University Ave Palo Alto CA 94303 Office Phone: 650-833-2266. Office Fax: 650-833-2001. Business E-Mail: mark.radcliffe@dlapiper.com.

**RADCLIFFE, REDONIA (DONNIE RADCLIFFE),** journalist, writer; m. Robert C. Radcliffe; 1 child, M. Donnel Nunes. BA, San Jose State U., Calif., 1951. Reporter, women's editor, county editor The Salinas Californian, 1951-59; free-lance writer Europe, 1959—66; reporter Washington Star, 1967-72, White Ho. reporter, columnist Washington Post, 1972-95. Author: Simply Barbara Bush: A Portrait of America's Candid First Lady, 1989, Hillary Rodham Clinton: A First Lady for Our Time, 1993, reissued as Hillary Rodham Clinton: The Evolution of a First Lady, 1999; The Fall of a President, 1974, Guide to Washington, 1989. Trustee Calvert County (Md.) Libr.; bd. dirs. Nat. 1st Ladies' Libr. E-mail: redrad@erols.com.

**RADDING, ANDREW,** lawyer; b. N.Y.C., Nov. 30, 1944; m. Bonnie A. Levinson, Oct. 7, 1972; children: Judith Lynne, Joshua David. BBA, CCNY-Baruch Sch., 1965; JD, Boston U., 1969. Bar: N.Y. 1968, Md. 1977, D.C. 1977, U.S. Supreme Ct. Grad. fellow Northwestern U. Sch. Law, 1968-69; asst. counsel U.S. Ho. of Reps. Select Com. on Crime, 1969-72; asst. U.S. atty. for Dist. Md., 1972-77; ptnr. Francomano, Radding & Mannes, Balt., 1977-80, Burke, Gerber, Wilen, Francomano & Radding, Balt., 1980-85, Blades & Rosenfeld P.A., Balt., 1985-97, Adelberg, Rudow, Dorf and Hendler LLC, Balt., 1997—. Mem. adj. faculty clin. practice skills, criminal law, fed. criminal practice U. Balt. Sch. Law, 1980—; mem. trial experience com. U.S. Dist. ct., 1986-88; apptd. by gov. State Adminstrv. Bd. of Election Laws, 1995-96; instr. professionalism course Md. State Bar Assn., 1999—; mem. inquiry panel and peer rev. panel Atty. Grievance Commn., 1991—. Bd. dirs. Copper Hill Condominium, 1979-82, pres., 1981-82; vice chair Lawyers for Erlich for Gov. Com., 2002; mem. subcom. Md. Republican Conv., 1981; sen. C.M. Mathias Jud. Selection com., 1986; chmn. U.S. Dist. Ct. Bicentennial Program, 1989-90; mem. Mayor's Domestic Violence Coord. com., 2001—. Mem.: ABA, Nat. Arbitration Forum (arbitrator), U.S. Arbitration and Mediation, Md. Inst. Continuing Profl. Edn. for Lawyers (bd. govs. 1987—92), U.S. Atty. Alumni Assn. Md. (pres. 1978—), Fed. Bar Assn. (Balt. chpt. pres. 1986—87), Balt. City Bar Assn. (jud. selection com. 1990—92, chmn. 1996—97, co-chmn. membership com. 1999—2000, exec. coun. 2000—, 2000—, chmn. fee arbitration com. 2001—02, chmn. jud. selection com. 2004—, exec. coun.), Md. Bar Assn. (CLE com. 2002—, program com. 2003—, bd. govs. 2005—). Jewish. Office: Adelberg Rudow et al LLC 7 St Paul St Baltimore MD 21202 Office Phone: 410-986-0824. Business E-Mail: aradding@adelbergrudow.com.

**RADEBOLDT-DALY, KAREN ELAINE,** retired medical/surgical nurse; b. Bklyn., Mar. 3, 1944; d. Harry Phillip and Lillian Florence (Renton) McAnaney; m. Richard William Radeboldt, Aug. 19, 1968 (dec. Aug. 1985); children: Karyn, Kellianne, Kimberly, Kristi-Jo, Richard; m. William J. Daly, Sr., Jan. 22, 1995. Lic. practical nurse, Wyckoff Heights Sch. Nursing, Bklyn., 1968; RN, Orange County C.C., Middletown, N.Y., 1990. LPN, N.Y., RN, N.Y.; cert. med.-surg. nurse, N.Y. Nurses aide, lic. practical nurse Wyckoff Heights Hosp., Bklyn., 1967-90; staff nurse, med.-surg. nurse Westchester Med. Ctr., Valhalla, N.Y., 1990—96, staff nurse, trauma unit, 1996—98, staff nurse, critical care-trauma ICU, 1988—2004; ret., 2004. Mem. Am. Jour. Nursing. Adventist. Avocations: reading, sewing, bowling, walking, motorcycling. Home: 101 Daly Rd Middletown NY 10940-7356

**RADEL, EVA,** pediatrician, hematologist; b. Vienna, Apr. 10, 1934; came to U.S., 1939; d. Ernest O. and Marian (Feiks) Grossman; m. Stanley Robert Radel, May 31, 1954; children: Carol, Laura. AB, N.Y. U., 1954, MD, 1958. Pediatric intern, resident Bronx Mcpl. Hosp. Ctr., 1958-61; pediatric hematology rsch. fellow Albert Einstein Coll. Medicine, Bronx, 1961-63; pediatrician, head pediatric hematology Morrisania city Hosp., Bronx, 1963-76; assoc. dir. pediatrics Met. Ctr. Bronx Hosp., 1978-82; attending physician pediatric hemetology out patients Montefiore Med. Ctr., Bronx, 1965-79, svc. head pediatric hematology-oncology, 1979—2004; head pediatric hematology North Cen. Bronx Hosp., 1976-97. Responsible investigator Children's Cancer Study Group, 1980-2001; dir. pediatric hematology-oncology Albert Einstein Coll. Medicine, Bronx, 1980-2004; prin. investigator Children's Oncology Group, 2001-05 Fellow Am. Acad Pediatrics; mem. Am. Soc. Hematology, Am. Pediatric Hematology-Oncology, Soc. for the Study of Blood. Office: Childrens Hosp at Montefiore Sect Pediat Hematology-Oncology 3415 Bainbridge Ave Bronx NY 10467-2401 Office Phone: 718-741-2342. Business E-Mail: eradel@montefiore.org.

**RADEMAKER, STEPHEN GEOFFREY,** legislative staff member, former federal agency administrator; b. Balt., July 18, 1959; s. Thomas Joseph and Ruth Virginia (Wentz) R.; m. Danielle Pletka; children: Andrew, Olivia, Sophia, Nicola. BA with highest distinction, U. Va., 1981, JD, 1984, MA in Fgn. Affairs, 1985. Bar: Va. 1984, D.C. 1985. Assoc. Covington & Burling LLP, Washington, 1984-86; law clk. to Hon. James L. Buckley US Ct. Appeals (D.C. Cir.), Washington, 1986; counsel to vice chmn. US Internat. Trade Commn., Washington, 1986-87; spl. asst. to asst. sec. for Inter-Am. affairs US Dept. State, Washington, 1987-89; assoc. counsel to Pres. of U.S. and dep. legal advisor to NSC, Washington, 1989-92; gen. counsel Peace Corps, Washington, 1992-93; Rep. chief counsel Com. Fgn. Affairs US Ho. of Reps., Washington, 1993-95, chief counsel Com. Internat. Rels., 1995—2001, dep. staff dir., chief counsel Com. Internat. Rels., 2001—02, chief counsel Select Com. on Homeland Security, 2002; asst. sec. for arms control US Dept. State, Washington, 2002—05, acting asst. sec. for internat. security & nonproliferation, 2005—06; dir. nat. security for Senator Bill Frist US Senate, Washington, 2006—. Mem. UN Sec. Gen.'s Adv. Bd. on Disarmament Matters, 2003—. Recipient Raven award U. Va., 1984; S. Philip Heiner scholar U. Va., 1983. Mem. Va. Bar Assn., D.C. Bar Assn., Phi Beta Kappa, Omicron Delta Kappa. Republican. Lutheran. Avocations: skiing, bicycling, scuba diving. Office: 509 Hart Senate Office Bldg Washington DC 20510*

**RADER, DOTSON CARLYLE,** writer, journalist; b. Minn., July 25, 1941; s. Paul Carlyle and Lois (Schacht) R. Student, Columbia, 1962-68. Editor Defiance: A Radical Rev. (Warner Communications, Inc.), 1969-71; contbg. editor Evergreen Rev., 1969-73, Esquire, N.Y.C., 1973-77, N.Y. mag., 1977-80; cons. Nat. Com. for Lit. Arts at Lincoln Center, N.Y.C., 1980—. Mem. sponsoring bd. New Politics, 1972—; host Free Time Show, WNET-TV, N.Y.C., 1972-73 Author: I Ain't Marchin' Anymore!, 1969, Government Inspected Meat and Other Fun Summer Things, 1971, Blood Dues, 1973, Tennessee: Cry of the Heart; An Intimate Memoir of Tennessee Williams, 1985; screenplay The Bronze Lily, 1974, The Dream's on Me: A Love Story, 1976, Miracle, 1978; novel Beau Monde, 1981; play (with Mike Miller) Shattered Glass, 1990; contbg. editor Parade Mag., 1984— Mem. Student Peace Union, 1961-63, Students for a Democratic Soc., 1964-69, War Resisters League, 1970—; pres. Humanitas, Columbia, 1963-67; vice chmn.

Peoples Coalition for Peace and Justice, 1972. Named hon. ambassador State of W. Va., 1982; recipient award for nat. journalism Odyssey Inst., 1982, Spl. Olympics award for nat. journalism Joseph P. Kennedy Found., 1985 Mem. PEN, Overseas Press Club, The Dramatists Guild.

**RADER, NANCY LOUISE DE VILLIERS,** psychology professor, consultant; b. Danbury, Conn., May 21, 1948; d. Martin Anthony and Elsie Concetta (Lauricella) R.; m. David Strutt de Villiers, Sept. 6, 1975; 1 child, Alyssa Jane. AB magna cum laude, Smith Coll., 1970; PhD, Cornell U., 1976. Asst. prof. psychology UCLA, 1974-82, dir. Infant and Child Lab., 1979-82, scholar Found. for Child Devel., 1982-83, postdoctoral fellow, rsch. psychologist Neuropsychiat. Inst., 1983-84; vis. scholar Cornell U., Ithaca, N.Y., 1979, rsch. assoc., 1984-85; asst. prof. Ithaca Coll., 1985-90, assoc. prof., 1990—2004, prof., 2004—, chair psychology dept., 2000—03. Contbr. articles to profl. jours., chpts. to books. Bd. dirs. Coddington Community Ctr., Ithaca, 1991-94, Family and Children Svcs., 1999-2002. Fellow NDEA, 1968, 71-74, Ford Found., 1970-74; grantee NIMH, 1982, NSF, 2001—. Mem. APA, Am. Psychol. Soc., Soc. for Rsch. in Child Devel., Internat. Soc. for Study Behavioral Devel., Internat. Soc. for Ecol. Psychology, Ea. Psychol. Assn., Sigma Xi (pres. Ithaca Coll. chpt. 1988-89), Phi Kappa Phi. Avocations: gardening, mystery. Home: 201 Eastman Hill Rd Willseyville NY 13864-1229 Office: Ithaca Coll Psychology Dept Ithaca NY 14850 Office Phone: 607-274-3510. E-mail: rader@ithaca.edu.

**RADER, RALPH TERRANCE,** lawyer; b. Clarksburg, W.Va., Dec. 5, 1947; s. Ralph Coolidge and Jeanne (Cover) R.; m. Rebecca Jo Vorderman, Mar. 22, 1969; children: Melissa Michelle, Allison Suzanne. BSME, Va. Poly. Inst., 1970; JD, Am. U., 1974. Bar: Va. 1975, U.S. Ct. Customs and Patent Appeals, 1977, U.S. Dist. Ct. (ea. dist.) Mich. 1978, Mich. 1979, U.S. Ct. Appeals (6th cir.) 1979, U.S. Dist. Ct. (we. dist.) Mich. 1981, U.S. Ct. Appeals (fed. cir.) 1983. Supervisory patent examiner U.S. Patent Office, Washington, 1970-77; patent atty., ptnr. Cullen, Sloman, Cantor, Grauer, Scott & Rutherford, Detroit, 1977-88; ptnr. Dykema, Gossett, Detroit, 1989-96; founder, ptnr. Rader, Fishman & Grauer, Bloomfield Hills, Mich., 1996—. Contbr. articles to profl. jours. Mem. adminstrv. bd. 1st United Meth. Ch., Birmingham, Mich., 1980—, With U.S. Army, 1970-76. Mem. ABA, Am. Patent Law Assn., Mich. Patent Law Assn., Mich. Bar (governing coun. patent, trademark and copyright law sect. 1981-84), Engring. Soc. Detroit, Masons, Tau Beta Pi, Pi Tau Sigma, Phi Kappa Phi. Methodist. Home: 4713 Riverchase Dr Troy MI 48098-4186 Office: Rader Fishman & Grauer 39533 Woodward Ave Ste 140 Bloomfield Hills MI 48304-5098 Office Phone: 248-594-0620. Business E-Mail: rtr@raderfishman.com.

**RADER, RANDALL RAY,** federal judge; b. Hastings, Nebr., Apr. 21, 1949; BA magna cum laude, BYU, 1974; JD with honors, George Washington U., 1978. Bar: D.C., U.S. Ct. Appeals (fed. cir.) 1990, U.S. Claims Ct., U.S. Supreme Ct. Legis. asst. to Congresswoman Virginia Smith U.S. Ho. of Reps., 1975—78; mem. staff Ways and Means Com. U.S. Ho. Reps., 1978—81; chief counsel subcom. on Constn. U.S. Senate Judiciary Com., 1981—86, chief counsel, staff dir. subcom. on patents, copyrights and trademarks, 1987—88; counsel to Senator Orrin Hatch, 1981—88; judge U.S. Ct. Claims, Washington, 1988—90, U.S. Ct. Appeals (fed. cir.), Washington, 1990—. Lectr. patent law U. Va. Sch. Law, 1993—99; lectr. trial advocacy, lectr. George Washington U. Nat. Law Ctr., Washington, 1993—97; lectr. comparative patent law Georgetown U. Law Ctr., Washington, 1998—99. Co-author: Patent Law, 1997; co-editor: Criminal Justice Reform, 1983; contbr. articles to profl. jours. Mem.: FBA. Office: US Ct Appeals Fed Cir 717 Madison Pl NW Ste 913 Washington DC 20439-0002*

**RADER, STEVEN PALMER,** lawyer; b. Charlotte, N.C., Dec. 30, 1952; s. Alvin Marion Jr. and Shirley Ninabelle (Palmer) Rader; m. Victoria Rolinsky, 2001; 1 child, Tudor R. AB, Duke U., 1975; postgrad., Stetson U., 1975-76; JD, Wake Forest U., 1978. Bar: N.C. 1978, U.S. Dist. Ct. (ea. dist.) N.C. 1979. Assoc. Wilkinson and Vosburgh, Washington, N.C., 1978-81; pvt. practice Washington, 1981-88; spl. asst. to sec. N.C. Dept. Human Resources, Raleigh, 1988-89, asst. dir. office legal affairs, 1989-91, gen. counsel, 1991-93; ptnr. Wilkinson & Rader, P.A., Washington, 1993—. Commr. Nat. Conf. Commrs. on Uniform State Laws, 1985-93; gen. counsel N.C. Rep. Party, 1992-97; commr. N.C. Rules Rev. Commn., 1997-99. Mem., sec. City of Washington Human Rels. Coun., 1981-83; chmn. Beaufort County Rep. party, Washington, 1983-87, 1st Congl. Dist. Rep. party, N.C., 1985-92; v.p. East Main St. Area Neighborhood Assn., 1983-85, 1st v.p., Ocean Villas Homeowners Assn., 1999-2003, pres. 2003—; del. Rep. Nat. Conv., 1984, 88, 92; Presdl. elector from N.C., U.S. Electoral Coll., 2000. Mem. N.C. State Bar, 2d Jud. Dist. Bar, Beaufort County Hist. Soc. (v.p. 1981-85, pres. 1985-86). Lutheran. Avocations: boating, classic automobiles, travel. Home: PO Box 1901 Washington NC 27889-1901 Office: Wilkinson & Rader PA PO Box 732 Washington NC 27889-0732 Office Phone: 252-946-7167.

**RADEV, DRAGOMIR RADKOV,** computer scientist, educator; b. Sofia, Bulgaria, Aug. 7, 1968; arrived in U.S., 1991; s. Radko Dimitrov Radev and Elena Petrova Loungova; m. Axinia T. Radeva, Aug. 27, 1994; children: Laura, Victoria. BA, U. Maine, Orono, 1993; MS, Columbia U., NYC, 1996; PhD, Columbia U., 1999. Rsch. staff mem. IBM Rsch., Hawthorne, NY, 1998—99; asst. prof. U. Mich., Ann Arbor, 2000—05, assoc. prof. dept. computer sci., Sch. Info., 2005—. Mem. editl. bd. Jour. Artificial Intelligence Rsch. Recipient Tchg. award, Columbia U., 1998, Outstanding Rsch. Mentorship award, U. Mich., 2004; grantee, NSF, 2000—, NIH, 2003—. Mem.: Assn. for Computing Machinery, Assn. for Computational Linguistics (sec.). Avocations: reading, Internet, movies. Home: 2907 Philadelphia Dr Ann Arbor MI 48103 Office: Univ Michigan Dept Computer Science and Engineering Ann Arbor MI 48109

**RADFORD, R. S.,** lawyer, law educator; b. Independence, Kans., July 30, 1945; s. Lloyd Raymond and Arlene (Bacon) R.; m. Sharon L. Browne, Nov. 24, 1992; children: Jessica Siegel, Jacob Siegel. BS in Bus. Adminstrn., Rockhurst Coll., 1974; MA in Econs., U. So. Calif., 1976; JD, 1988. Bar: Calif. 1988, Supreme Ct. 1992. Prin. atty. Pacific Legal Found., Sacramento, Calif., 1988—; dir. progrm for jud. awareness, 1999—. Adj. prof. law U. Pacific McGeorge Sch. Law, Sacramento, 2001—. Contbr. numerous articles to profl. jours. Named Laywer of Yr. Calif. Lawyer, 1997 Fax: (916) 362-2932. E-mail: radford@cal.com, rsr@pacificlegal.org.

**RADFORD, VIRGINIA RODRIGUEZ,** retired secondary school educator, librarian; b. Willcox, Ariz., Nov. 17, 1917; d. Domingo Acosta and Maria Ceveriana (Lopez) Rodriguez; m. John Houston Radford, June 5, 1942; children: Mary Jane, Ann Christine, Patricia Mae. BA, BS, U. Kans., 1940, univ. tchrs. diploma, 1940; Librarianship, Benedictine Coll., Atchinson, Kans., 1972-76. Cert. life. tchr. K-12, Kans., master tchrs., 1970. Tchr. Spanish, French, English Horton (Kans.) High Schs., 1957-60; 4th and 5th grade tchr. St. Leo's Parochial Sch., Horton, 1961-62; tchr. Spanish, French/librarian Horton High Sch., 1962-82. Translator U.S. War Dept., San Antonio, 1942; past pres. Brown County Ret. Tchrs. Assn., People-to-People (Horton chpt.); silver haired legislator Brown County Northeast Area Agy. on Aging, 2005—; commd. lay min. St. Leo's Ch., 1990; mem. St. Leo's Altar Soc.; pres. bd. dirs. Horton Libr., 1975; bd. dirs. Tri-County Manor, Horton, 2001; adv. bd. mem. Alta Care Corp. Tri County Manor, Horton, Kans. Named Outstanding Secondary Educator of Am., 1975; inducted Kans. Tchrs. Hall of Fame, 1984. Mem.: AAUW, Brown County Assn. Ret. Sch. Pers., Bus. and Profl. Women, Am. Legion Auxiliary, Friends of Libr., Horton Hosp. Aux. (life), Horton Sr. Citizens Club, Inc. (trustee), VFW Aux. Post 3021 (life; v.p.), Delta Kappa Gamma (pres. Alpha Kappa chpt.). Roman Catholic. Avocations: reading, music, travel, photography, collecting letter openers. Home: 439 W 8th St Horton KS 66439-1515 Office Phone: 785-486-3514. Personal E-mail: vradford@carsoncomm.com.

**RADHAKRISHNAN, ANAND,** aerospace engineer, researcher; b. Manipal, Karnatake, India, Nov. 14, 1979; s. Radhakrishnan Mylapore Guruswami and Meera Radhakrishnan. B in Engring., U. Madras, Chennai, India, 2000, B in

Aerospace Engring., 2000; MS in Aerospace Engring., U. Md., 2004. Grad. tchg. asst. U. Md., College Park, 2000—01, grad. rsch. asst., 2001—. Presenter in field. Contbr. articles to profl. jours. Recipient First Pl. in Am. Helicopter Soc./NASA Student Design Competition, 2003. Mem.: AIAA, Am. Helicopter Soc. Achievements include design of Urban Disaster Rescue Vehicle. Office: Univ Maryland Dept Aerospace Engring College Park MD 20742 Home: 1723 Church St Nw Washington DC 20036-1301 Office Phone: 301-405-1151. Personal E-mail: anandroid@gmail.com. Business E-Mail: anand@eng.umd.edu.

**RADI, ZAHER,** pathologist; DVM, MS, PhD, Iowa State U. Lic. anatomic pathology ACVP. Clin. instr. Va. Tech, Blacksburg; asst. prof. U. of Ga., Athens, 2002—04; toxicologic pathologist Pfizer Global R&D, Ann Arbor, Mich., 2004—. Achievements include research in Inflammation. Office Phone: 734-994-1841.

**RADICE, ANNE-IMELDA MARINO,** museum director, former federal agency administrator; b. Buffalo, Feb. 29, 1948; d. Lawrence and Anne (Marino) R. AB, Wheaton Coll., 1969; MA, Villa SchiFanoia, Florence, Italy, 1971; PhD, U. N.C., 1976; MBA, AM. U., 1984. Asst. curator, staff lectr. Nat. Gallery of Art, Washington, 1972-76; archtl. historian U.S. Capitol, Washington, 1976—81, curator Office of Architect, 1981—85; dir. Nat. Mus. Women in the Arts, 1985-89; chief divsn. of creative arts USIA, 1989-91; sr. dep. chmn. Nat. Endowment for Arts, Washington, 1991-92, acting chmn., 1992-93; exec. v.p. Gray & Co. II, Miami, Fla., 1993; prodr. World Affairs TV Prodn., 1994; assoc. producer Think Tank, 1994; chief spl. projects, confidential adviser Courtney Sale Ross, 1994-96; v.p., COO ICL Internat., 1996; exec. dir. Friends of Dresden Inc., 1998—2001; exec. dir. appeal Conscience Found., NYC, 2001—03; chief staff to sec. US Dept. Edn., Washington, 2003—05; acting asst. chmn. for programs Nat. Endowment Humanities, Washington, 2005—06; dir. The Inst. Mus. & Library Services, Washington, 2006—. Cons. in pub. rels. and TV, 1994—. Contbr. articles to profl. jours. Office: The Inst Mus & Library Services 1800 M St NW 9th Fl Washington DC 20036*

**RADICE, FRANK J.,** communications executive; b. Washington, Dec. 13, 1949; m. Vida S. Radice, July 4, 1995. Student, U. Md., 1968-72. Film editor WRC/NBC-TV, Washington, 1971-72, ABC News, Washington, 1972, assignment editor, 1976, assoc. prodr. Good Morning Am., 1978, ops. prodr. World News Tonight, 1979-80; prodr. Nightline N.Y.C., 1980-83; program prodr. The Last Word ABC News, N.Y.C., 1983; field dir. Entertainment Tonight Paramount Motion Pictures, N.Y.C., 1984; prodr., developer Live At 5:00 WRC/NBC-TV, Washington, 1985; exec. prodr. Entertainment News, Cable News Network, N.Y.C., 1987-89; InterActive sr. producer/product devel., producer advt. and promotion ABC News, N.Y.C., 1989-91; advt. mgr. WCBS-TV, N.Y.C., 1991; v.p. advt. and promotion NBC Entertainment, N.Y.C., 1996; sr. v.p. The NBC Agy., 2000—. Exec. prodr. NBC on Ted, 2004—05, NBC Inflight on United Airlines, 1984—2005; v.p. Vida F.R. Co., 1999; chmn. mktg. Nat. Acad. TV Arts and Scis., 2005—. Author: (with Vida Radice) Sam Katz On The Loose, 2005, On the Loose, 2005; prodr. A Line in the Sand, War of Peace, War in the Gulf; writer, prodr., 1992; co-exec. prodr. (CD): The Best of The Today Show Summer Concerts, Vols. 1 and 2, 2006. Bd. govs. N.Y. Festivals, 2003—. Recipient award Coll. Emergency Physicians, 1983, Emmy award NATAS, 1984, 1990, 7 NY Festival awards, 2000-03; Alfred I Dupont grantee Columbia U., NYC, 1984, 91, Mobius award, 1998, 2005, Cine Golden Eagle award 2002-04; Brand Builder award, B & C, 2003; inductee Promax Hall of Fame, 2004. Mem. Broadcast Music Inc. (writer affiliate), AFTRA, Nat. Assn. Broadcast Employees and Technicians, Internat. Alliance Theatrical and Stage Employees, Writers Guild Am., Dirs. Guild Am., Congressional Country Club, Friars (N.Y.C.). Democrat. Roman Catholic. Office: NBC Ste 1891E 30 Rockefeller Plz New York NY 10112-0002 Office Phone: 212-664-3555. Business E-Mail: frank.radice@nbc.com.

**RADIGAN, FRANK XAVIER,** retired pharmaceutical executive; b. Paterson, NJ, Apr. 13, 1933; s. John Joseph and Susan Clair (Brett) R.; m. Julia Lou Smith, Aug. 27, 1960 (div. Nov. 1988); children: Francis Gregory, Patricia Louise, Brett Frasier; m. Carol E. Berkley, June 26, 1992; children: Dana, Traci. AB in Sociology, Seton Hall U., 1955; MBA Mktg., U. Hartford, 1968. Asst. mgr. Beneficial Fin. Co., Newark, 1955-57; hosp. rep. Becton-Dickinson Co., Rutherford, N.J., 1957-58; dist. mgr. Merck Human Health Divsn., West Point, Pa., 1958-98; ret., 1998. Horse breeder, 1976—86. Active Greater Balt. SCORE; mem. Passaic County Dem. Com., 1955—56; chmn. St. John the Baptist Social Justice, New Freedom, Pa., 1981—85, Balt. USAR. Mem.: Md. Mental Health Assn. (legis. com. 1969—73), Balt. Pharm. Assn. (hon. pres. 1989), W.Va. Pharm. Soc., Md. Pharmacists Assn. (past chmn. indsl. rels. com., hon. pres. 1999—2000), Am. Mgmt. Assn., Am. Pharm. Assn., Hopewell Fish and Game Assn., Bon Air Country Club, Lions (pres. Glen Rock 1975—76, 1986—88), Elks. Roman Catholic. Home: 2440 Bradenbaugh Rd White Hall MD 21161-9661 Personal E-mail: fxr333@msn.com.

**RADIN, ALEX,** former association executive, consultant; b. Chattanooga, June 14, 1921; s. Joseph and Mollie (Pernat) R.; m. Sara Leah Gordon, Sept. 6, 1943 (dec. Nov. 20, 1964); children—Jay Jacob, William Gordon m. Carol Nita Schuman, Sept. 21, 1979 BA, U. Chattanooga, 1947. Reporter Chattanooga Times, Chattanooga, 1938-42; adminstrv. asst. Office of Price Administrn., Washington, 1942-43; adminstrv. analyst Dept. of State, Washington, 1945-48; asst. to gen. mgr. Am. Pub. Power Assn., Washington, 1948-51, exec. dir., 1951-86; pres. Radin & Assocs. Inc., 1986—. Cons. U.S. Senate Com. on Interior and Insular Affairs, Washington, 1959; mem. exec. com. Am. Nuclear Energy Coun., Washington, 1973-88; v.p. Consumer Fedn. Am., Washington, 1978-80; mem. bd. States Energy Bd.'s Adv. Coun. on TVA, 1986-87; chmn. Monitored Retrievable Storage Rev. Commn., 1988-89; rep., sec. U.S. Dept. Energy, Independent Mgmt. and Fin. Rev. of Yucca Mt. (Nev.) Project, 1994-95; mem. adv. bd. Ford Found. Energy Policy Project, 1973-74; bd. dirs. Consumer Energy Coun. Am., 1999—. Columnist, Pub. Power Mag.; contbr. articles to newspapers and mags.; author Public Power, Private Life, 2003. Mem. adv. bd. Dance Theatre of Harlem, N.Y.C., 1985—. Recipient Leland Olds award Western States Water and Power Consumers Conf., 1970, Philip Hart Disting. Consumer Svc. award Consumer Fedn. Am., 1985, Alex Radin Disting. Svc. award Am. Pub. Power Assn., 1986, named Disting. Alumnus of 2001 U. Tenn. Chattanooga, 2001, Lifetime Achievement award Energy Daily, 2003. Mem. Alpha Soc. Clubs: Nat. Press. Democrat. Jewish. Avocations: photography, music, art, hiking. Home: 2510 Virginia Ave NW Apt 610N Washington DC 20037-1904 Office: Radin & Assocs Inc Ste 609 2510 Virginia Ave NW Washington DC 20037-1904 Office Phone: 202-338-0607.

**RADIN, AMY JANINE,** financial services company executive; b. Mar. 30, 1958; d. Harold I. and Selma M. Friedman; m. Mitchell E. Radin, Nov. 1984; 3 children. BA magna cum laude, Coll. Letters and Spanish, Wesleyan U., MBA, Wharton Sch., U. Pa. Mktg. develop. mgr. KMG Main Hurdman, NY; various positions in mgmt., customer loyalty, market develop, and channel mgmt. American Express; exec. v.p., chief mktg. officer Dime Savings Bank of NY; exec. v.p., citi cards e-business Citigroup, Inc., 2000, exec. v.p., customer engagement, 2005, chief innovation officer, global consumer group, 2005—, mem. mgmt. com., mem. global consumer group planning com. Spkr. in field. Trustee The Healthcare Chaplaincy, 2006—; founder, pres. The Small Acts of Kindness Found., Inc. Named one of 25 Masters of Innovation, BusinessWeek. Office: Citigroup Inc 399 Park Ave New York NY 10043*

**RADIN, MARGARET JANE,** law educator; b. 1941; AB, Stanford U., 1963; MFA in Music, Brandeis U., 1965; doctoral studies in Music History, U. Calif., Berkeley, 1965—68; JD, U. So. Calif. Law Ctr., 1976; LLD (hon.), Ill. Inst. Tech. Chgo.-Kent Sch. Law, 1993. Bar: Calif. 1976. Adj. prof. law U. Oreg. Sch. Law, 1976—78; assoc. prof. U. So. Calif. Law Ctr., 1979—82, prof., 1982—87, Carolyn Craig Franklin prof. law, 1987—89; prof. Stanford Law Sch., 1989—96, William Benjamin Scott & Luna M. Scott prof. law,

1996—, founder & co-dir. Ctr. for E-Commerce, 2002—, co-dir. program in law, science and tech., 1997—2001, dir., 2001—01, dir. LLM program in law, science and tech., 2001—04. Vis. prof. law UCLA Law Sch., 1978—79, Harvard Law Sch., 1984—85, U. So. Calif. Law Ctr., 1989—90, U. Mich. Law Sch., 2004—05. Author: Reinterpreting Property, 1993, Contested Commodities, 1996; co-author: Internet Commerce: The Emerging Legal Framework, 2002. Mem.: Law Professors for the Rule of Law (co-founder), The Copyright Soc. of USA, Computer Law Soc., Am. Intellectual Property Lawyers Assn., Am. Soc. Polit. and Legal Philosophy, Assn. Computing Machinery (law and tech. policy com.). Office: Stanford Law Sch Crown Quadrangle 559 Nathan Abbott Way Stanford CA 94305-8610 Office Phone: 650-725-3803. Business E-Mail: mjradin@stanford.edu.

**RADIN, SAM,** lawyer, land use planner; b. N.Y.C., Aug. 1, 1951; s. Clarence and Marjorie (Rembar) R.; m. Pamela Anderson, Sept. 13, 1981; children: Clarence Anderson, Elizabeth Rebecca. BA, Columbia U., 1973; JD, Boston U., 1976. Bar: N.J. 1976, U.S. Dist. Ct. N.J. 1976, N.Y. 1978, U.S. Dist. Ct. (so. dist.) N.Y. 1978, U.S. Ct. Appeals (D.C. cir.) 1978, U.S. Supreme Ct. 1980. Assoc. Burns, Van Kirk, N.Y.C., 1976-79, Lovejoy Wasson successor to Burns, Van Kirk, N.Y.C., 1979-80; pvt. practice, N.Y.C., 1980-84; v.p., gen. counsel Nat. Madison Group, Inc., N.Y.C., 1984-99, pres., 1999—. Contbg. author: Executive Compensation Answer Book, 1998; contbg. author, editor: Estate and Retirement Planning Answer Book, 1999; also articles. Bd. dirs. Student Athletes Inc., N.Y.C., 1992-98, Westchester Conservatory Music, White Plains, N.Y., 1995-97; trustee Payomet Performing Arts Charitable Trust, 1999—, Nat. Lighthouse Ctr. and Mus., 2000—, pres., 2001—. Recipient Nathan Burkan Meml. prize ASCAP, 1975. Mem. ABA (subcom. on life ins. tax sect. 1996—), N.Y. State Bar Assn., Assn. Bar City N.Y., Assn. Advanced Life Underwriting, Comm. on Estate Taxation. Avocations: salt water fly fishing, collecting books, skiing, running. Home: 71 Greenacres Ave Scarsdale NY 10583-1442 Office: Nat Madison Group Inc 200 Pk Ave 21st Flr New York NY 10166-2401 E-mail: sradin@nationalmadison.com.

**RADISAVLJEVIC-GAJIC, VERICA,** mechanical engineer, educator; d. Miroljub and Ljiljana Radisavljevic; m. Zoran Gajic, Sept. 19, 1992; children: Zoran Z. Gajic, Maria Gajic. PhD, Rutgers U., Piscataway, N.J., 2001. Vis. prof. Rutgers U., Piscataway, 2001—04; vis. asst. prof. Lafayette Coll., Easton, Pa., 2004—. Mem.: ASME. Office: Lafayette Collage AEB High Street Easton PA Office Phone: 610-330-5434. Business E-Mail: gajicv@lafayette.edu.

**RADISKY, DEREK CHARLES,** biomedical researcher, educator; b. San Francisco, Calif., Feb. 29, 1968; s. Robert Charles and Karen Rice Radisky; m. Evette Sanborn Radisky, Dec. 26, 1987; 1 child, Abigail Karen. PhD, U. Utah, Salt Lake City, 1999. Postdoctoral rschr. Lawrence Berkeley Nat. Lab., Berkeley, Calif., 1999—2005; asst. prof. Mayo Clinic Cancer Ctr., Jacksonville, Fla., 2005—. Achievements include discovery of microenvironmental influences on breast cancer development. Home: 13439 Ellsworth Lane Jacksonville FL 32225 Office: Mayo Clinic Cancer Center 4500 San Pablo Road Jacksonville FL 32224 Office Phone: 904-953-6913. Business E-Mail: radisky.derek@mayo.edu.

**RADKE, KIRK A.,** lawyer; b. Mar. 21, 1958; m. Erin M. Radke. BA, Stanford U., 1980; JD, MBA, U. Va., 1984. Bar: Ill. 1985, NY 1991. Ptnr, mem. NY ops. Kirkland & Ellis LLP. Adj. prof. VCPE, HBS, Inc. Office: Kirkland & Ellis LLP Citigroup Ctr 153 E 53rd St New York NY 10022-4675 Office Phone: 212-446-4940. Office Fax: 212-446-4900. Business E-Mail: kradke@kirkland.com.

**RADKE, STEPHEN LEWIS,** social services administrator; b. Upper Darby, Pa., June 23, 1956; s. George Edward Radke and Anita Irene Fleet; m. Cathy Jane Russo, Sept. 7, 1987; children: Melissa Ashley, Jennifer Colleen. Assoc. in Sci., Del. County C.C., Media, Pa., 1976; BS in Agr., U. Del., Newark, 1979; MS, U. of N.H., Durham, 1983. Cert. instr. N.J. Divsn. of Criminal Justice, Police Tng. Commn. Rsch. asst. U. of N.H., Durham, 1979—81, lab instr., 1981—82; marine docent N.H. Sea Grant Program, Durham, 1982—83; claims rep. trainee Social Security Adminstrn., Portsmouth, NH, 1983—85; sci. instr. GED program Portsmouth Sch. Dist., 1983; vol. entomologist US Peace Corps, La Plaine, Dominica, 1985—86; caseworker Divsn. of Youth and Family Svcs., Clifton, NJ, 1987—90; sci. instr. Upward Bound, Durham, 1983; ct. liaison Divsn. of Youth and Family Svcs., Paterson, NJ, 1990—95, litigation specialist, 1995—99, intake supr., 1999—2000, spl. response unit coord., 2000—02, adoption unit supr., 2002—04; county svcs. specialist Office of Children's Svcs., Paterson, 2004—06, asst. regional adminstr., 2006—. Biology adj. William Paterson U., Wayne, NJ, 1997—. Registered parent Girl Scouts of Am., Little Falls, NJ, 2002—06. Office: Office of Children's Svcs 9th Fl 100 Hamilton Plz Paterson NJ 07505 Office Phone: 973-977-4480.

**RADLAUER, STEVE,** freelance writer, journalist, producer; b. N.Y.C., Nov. 2, 1948; s. Marvin and Gladys (Steltzer) R.; m. Kerry K. Willis, June 7, 1985; 1 child, Kate. Student, Union Coll., Schenectady, NY; BS, U. State of NY. Dir. A-Space, Toronto, Ontario, Canada, 1971-73; co-owner The Ritz Cafe, Toronto, Ontario, Canada, 1973-77; program dir. Dry Salvages Film Group, NYC, 1978-85. Co-author: The Hist. Shops and Restaurants of NY, 2002; editor-in-chief (online news comedy site) Today's Other News on American Online, 1996; co-author: Dan Quayle: Airhead Apparent, 1992, Special Moments, 1984; freelance writer articles for various pubs. incl. N.Y. Mag., Spy, Esquire, N.Y. Times, L.A. Times. Mem. Authors Guild. E-mail: steve@radz.org.

**RADLO, EDWARD JOHN,** lawyer, mathematician; b. Pawtucket, R.I., Mar. 7, 1946; s. Edward Zygmund and Sue Mary (Borek) Radlo; m. Patricia Jackson, Feb. 22, 1989; children: Heather Sue, Graeme Michael, Connor Andrew. BS, MIT, 1967; JD, Harvard U., 1972. Bar: Calif. 1972, U.S. Dist. Ct. (no. dist.) Calif. 1972, R.I. 1973, U.S. Patent Office 1973, Can. Patent Office 1974. Staff. dir. Atty. Gen.'s Adv. Commn. on Juvenile Code Revision, Boston, 1970—72; law clk. R.I. Supreme Ct., 1972—73; patent atty. Honeywell Info. Systems, Waltham, Mass., 1973—74, Varian Assoc., Palo Alto, Calif., 1974—78, Ford Aerospace Corp., 1978—83, patent counsel, 1983—90; ptnr. Fenwick & West LLP, Mountain View, Calif., 1991—2004, Sonnenschein Nath & Rosenthal LLP, San Francisco, 2004—. Lectr. U. Calif., San Jose State U., U. Santa Clara, 1975—78. Organizer So. Peninsula Emergency Comm. Sys., 1970; mem. Los Altos Hills (Calif.) Emergency Comm. Com, Lawyers' Alliance for Nuclear Arms Control, 1982—83, Environ. Def. Fund, 1979; bd. dir. Tomahawks Lacrosse Club, Menlo Park, Calif., 2002—05; bd. dirs. No. Calif. Jr. Lacrosse Assn., Corte Madera, Calif., 2004—05. Lt. (jg.) USPHS, 1967—69. Mem.: ABA, Calif. Bar (intellectual property sect.), Silicon Valley Intellectual Property Lawyers Assn., Assn. Radio Amateurs of So. New England Inc. (sec. 1962—63), No. Calif. Contest Club (pres. 1984—85), Sigma Xi. Home: 28040 Elena Rd Los Altos Hills CA 94022-2454 Office: Sonnenschein Nath & Rosenthal LLP 525 Market St San Francisco CA 94105

**RADLOFF, ROBERT ALBERT,** real estate company executive; b. Chgo., Mar. 30, 1947; s. Henry O. and Virginia G. (Grothus) R.; m. Ann Macy Beha, June 21, 1975; children: Macy, Allison. BS in Fin., Boston U., 1969. V.p. Kuras & Co., Inc., Boston, 1971-76; sr. v.p. Boston Co. Real Estate Counsel, Inc., 1976-81, pres., 1981-89, chmn., 1989-91; real estate investments counselor Boston, 1991—. Bd. dirs. Mass. Cultural Coun., 1992, Friends of Vieilles Maison Francais, 1992, The Augustus Saint-Gaudens Meml.; trustee Isabella Stewart Gardner Mus., 1995; chmn., bd. overseers WGBH Ednl. Found. Mem. Am. Soc. Real Estate Counselors (cert.), Somerset Club. Avocations: art, tennis, travel. Office: 33 Kingston St Boston MA 02111-2208

**RADMER, MICHAEL JOHN,** lawyer, educator; b. Wisconsin Rapids, Wis., Apr. 28, 1945; s. Donald Richard and Thelma Loretta (Donahue) R.; children from previous marriage: Christina Nicole, Ryan Michael; m. Laurie J. Anshus, Dec. 22, 1983; 1 child, Michael John BS, Northwestern U., 1967; JD,

Harvard U., 1970. Bar: Minn. 1970. Assoc. Dorsey & Whitney, Mpls., 1970-75, ptnr., corp. practice group, 1976—, and co-chmn., funds practice. Lectr. law Hamline U. Law Sch., St. Paul, 1981-84; gen. counsel, rep., sec./asst. sec. 52 federally registered investment cos., Mpls. and St. Paul, 1977—. Contbr. articles to legal jours. Active legal work Hennepin County Legal Advice Clinic, Mpls., 1971—. Mem. ABA, Minn. Bar Assn., Hennepin County Bar Assn., Mpls. Athletic Club. Office: Dorsey & Whitney 50 South 6th St Ste 1500 Minneapolis MN 55402 Office Phone: 612-340-2724. Office Fax: 612-340-8738. Business E-Mail: radmer.michael@dorsey.com. *A key to a successful and happy life is achieving a balance. Intellectual, academic and vocational goals are important, but their pursuit should be balanced with ample time spent with family and friends, travel and enjoying reading, music, art and sports. Don't be afraid to try something new; realize that education should be a lifelong pursuit. Much frustration can be avoided by realizing that life is full of trade-offs. You can't experience the joy of raising children and have the complete freedom of the child-free. Finally, while you should strive for perfection, be content with less. We are only human, and live in an imperfect, yet wonderful, world.*

**RADMILOVIC, VELIMIR,** materials scientist, researcher; arrived in U.S., 1986; s. Radivoje and Jelena Radmilovic; m. Vesna Mihailovic, Nov. 18, 1978; 1 child, Vuk. BS in Metallurgy, U. Belgrade, Yugoslavia, MS in Phys. Metallurgy, PhD, 1985. Prof. U. Belgrade, Belgrade, Serbia and Montenegro, 1985—2002; staff scientist Nat. Ctr. for Electron Microscopy, Lawrence Berkeley Nat. Lab., U. Calif., Berkeley, 2002—. V.p. Yugoslav Materials Rsch. Soc., Belgrade, 1996—, Yugoslav Microscopical Soc., Belgrade. Contbr. over 200 articles to profl. jours. Fulbright scholar, 1986. Mem.: ASM Internat., TMS, Microscopical Soc. Am., Materials Rsch. Soc. Office Phone: 510-486-5663. E-mail: vrradmilovic@lbl.gov.

**RADNER, ROY,** economist, educator, researcher; b. Chgo., June 29, 1927; s. Samuel and Ella (Kulansky) R.; m. Virginia L. Honoski, July 26, 1949 (dec. Apr. 1976); children: Hilary A., Erica H. (dec.), Amy E., Ephraim L.; m. Charlotte Virginia Kuh, Jan. 22, 1978. PhB with honors, U. Chgo, 1945, BS in Math., 1950, MS in Math., 1951, PhD in Math. Stats., 1956. Rsch. asst. Cowles Commn. for Rsch. in Econs. U. Chgo., 1951, rsch. assoc., 1951-54, asst. prof., 1954-55; mem. Cowles Found. for Rsch. in Econs. Yale U., New Haven, 1955-57, asst. prof. econs., 1955-57; assoc. prof. econs. and stats. U. Calif., Berkeley, 1957-61, prof. econs. and stats., 1961-79, chmn. dept. econs., 1966-69; Taussig prof. econs. Harvard U., Cambridge, Mass., 1977-78, vis. prof. Kennedy Sch. Govt., 1978-79; mem. tech. staff AT&T Bell Labs, Murray Hill, NJ, 1979-84, disting. mem. tech. staff, 1985-95; rsch. prof. econs. NYU, NYC, 1983—95, prof. econs. and info. sys., 1995, L.N. Stern Sch. prof. bus., 1996—. Com. on fundamental rsch. relevant to edn. NRC-NAS, 1976-77, commn. on human resources, 1976-79; mem. assembly of behavioral and social scis. NRC, 1979-82, com. on risk and decision making, 1980-81, working group on basic rsch. in behavioral and social scis., 1985-86, com. on info. tech. workforce, 1999-2000, com. on geophys. and environ. data, 2001—; panel on contingent valuation methology NOAA, U.S. Dept. Commerce, 1992-93; steering com. Enjeux et Procedures de Decentralization Commisariat du Plan, Paris, 1992-95; mem. Com. on Prevention of Nuclear War; com. on Info. Tech. workforce NRC, others Author: Notes on Theory of Econ. Planning, 1963; co-author (with D. Jorgensen and J.J. McCall): Optimal Replacement Policy, 1967; co-author: (with J. Marshack) Econ. Theory of Teams, 1972; co-author: (with L.S. Miller) Demand and Supply in U.S. Higher Edn., 1975; co-author: (with C.V.Kuh) Mathematicians in Academia, 1980; co-editor: Decision and Orgn., 1972, Edn. as an Industry, 1976, Info., Incentives and Econ. Mechanisms, 1987, Perspectives on Deterrence, 1989, Bargaining with Incomplete Info., 1992; assoc. editor: Info. Sys. Frontier, assoc. editor: Theoretical Econs.; contbr. articles to profl. jours. 2d lt. U.S. Army, 1945-48, PTO. William Cook scholar U. Chgo., 1944-45; fellow Ctr. Advanced Study in Behavioral Scis., Stanford, Calif., 1955-56, Guggenheim Found. fellow, 1961-62, 65-66, overseas fellow Churchill Coll., Cambridge U., Eng., 1969-70, 89. Fellow AAAS (disting. fellow), Econometric Soc. (v.p. 1970-72, pres. 1972-73), Am. Acad. Arts and Scis., Am. Econ. Assn. (disting. fellow); mem. NAS (chair econ. sect. 1994-97, sec. class 5 2004—), Inst. Math. Stats. Avocations: music, hiking, cross country skiing. Home: 3203 Davenport St NW Washington DC 20008-2211 Business E-Mail: rradner@stern.nyu.edu.

**RADNER, SIDNEY HOLLIS,** retired retail executive; b. Holyoke, Mass., Dec. 8, 1919; s. William I. Radner; m. Helen Jane Cohen, Dec. 12, 1946; children: William Marc, Richard Scott. Student, Yale U., 1941. Ret. pres. Am. Rug Co., Holyoke. Lectr., cons., investigator on crooked gambling U.S. Armed Forces, Govt. of Can., state and mcpl. police squads; dir. Houdini Magical Hall of Fame, Niagara Falls, Ont., Canada; dir., organizer Ann. Ofcl. Houdini Seance. Author: Radner on Poker, Radner on Dice, Radner on Roulette and Casino Games, How to Detect Card Sharks; contbr. articles to profl. jours.; appeared in (TV series) Turn of a Card, 1953, Tonight Show, 1956, BBC Omnibus: Houdini, 1971, CNN, 1993—94, Today Show, Merv Griffin Show, CNBC, PBS, CBC, In Search Of..., Can. Discovery on magic, 1998, History Channel on Houdini, 2000, Ripley's Believe It or Not, History Channel, 2000, (TV series) Today Show, 2004, BBC History of Magic, 2004, cons. (TV films) Houdini, 1998, cons., participant (TV Spl.) A&E Houdini, 1996, appeared in (TV spl.) E Network Houdini documentary, 1998; cons., participant: (TV spl.) History Channel show on the world's largest Houdini collection, 2005; cons., participant (TV films) Discovery Channel documentary, 1997. Past pres. Holyoke C. of C.; co-founder Volleyball Hall of Fame; past bd. dirs. Greater Springfield (Mass.) Better Bus. Bur.; hon. curator, dir. Houdini Hist. Ctr., Appleton, Wis. With criminal investigation divsn. U.S. Army, 1942—46. Named to Volleyball Hall of Fame, 1999. Mem.: Acad. Magical Arts, Nat. Assn. Bunco Investigators, Magicians Guild (charter), Magic Cir. London (mem. Inner Magic Cir.), Internat. Brotherhood Magicians, Soc. Am. Magicians (mem. occult investigation com.), Profls. Against Confidence Crime, China-Burma-India Vets. Assn. (life), Magic Collector's Assn. (charter, Honor award 1992), Houdini Club Wis. (hon.), Shriners, Masons, Rotary, Soc. Osaris (hon.). Jewish. Mailing: 3200 S Ocean Blvd 203C Palm Beach FL 33480 Home (Winter): 1050 Northampton St Holyoke MA 01040-1321 Home: 3200 S Ocean Blvd Apt C203 Palm Beach FL 33480-6670 Office Phone: 413-533-3000.

**RADNOR, ALAN T.,** lawyer; b. Cleve., Mar. 10, 1946; s. Robert Clark and Rose (Chester) R.; m. Carol Sue Hirsch, June 22, 1969; children: Melanie, Joshua, Joanna. BA, Kenyon Coll., 1967; MS in Anatomy, Ohio State U., 1969, JD, 1972. Bar: Ohio 1972. Ptnr. Vorys, Sater, Seymour & Pease, Columbus, Ohio, 1972—. Adj. prof. law Ohio State U., Columbus, 1979-99. Author: Cross-Examining Doctors: A Practical Guide, 1999; contbr. articles to profl. jours. Bd. dirs. Congregation Tifereth Israel, Columbus, 1975—, pres., 1985-87; trustee Columbus Mus. Art, 1995-98; pres. The Thurber House., 2004. Named Boss or Yr., Columbus Assn. Legal Secs., 1983. Fellow Am. Coll. Trial Lawyers; mem. ABA, Ohio State Bar Assn., Columbus Bar Assn., Def. Rsch. Inst., Internat. Assn. Def. Counsel. Avocations: reading, sculpture. Home: 400 S Columbia Ave Columbus OH 43209-1629 Office: Vorys Sater Seymour & Pease 52 E Gay St PO Box 1008 Columbus OH 43216-1008

**RADO, PETER THOMAS,** lawyer; b. Berlin, Nov. 12, 1928; came to U.S., 1931; naturalized, 1937; s. Sandor and Emmy (Chrisler) R.; m. Jacqueline Danenberg, Sept. 11, 1977. AB, HArvard U., 1949, LLB, 1952, LLM, 1953. Bar: N.Y. 1952. Assoc. Ide, Haigney & Rado, N.Y.C., 1956-61, ptnr., 1961—. With U.S. Army, 1953-55. Mem. ABA, N.Y. State Bar Assn., Assn. of Bar of City of N.Y., Harvard Club (N.Y.C.). Home: 176 E 71st St New York NY 10021-5159 Office: Ide Haigney & Rado 176 E 71st St New York NY 10021-5159 E-mail: radopandj@aol.com.

**RADOFF, LEONARD IRVING,** librarian, consultant; b. Houston, Jan. 9, 1927; s. Morris Aaron and Jenny (Goldberg) R.; m. Lisel Ruth Ephraim, July 25, 1953; 1 child, Lesley Radoff Rappaport BA, Rice U., Houston, 1949; M.L.S., U. Tex., Austin, 1965. Cert. secondary sch. tchr., Tex. Tchr. math Aldine Ind. Sch. Dist., Houston, 1959-61, sch. librarian, 1961-63; head pub.

services Abilene Pub. Library, Tex., 1964-65; library dir. Pasadena Pub. Library, Tex., 1966-70; chief br. services Houston Pub. Library, 1971-92, ret., 1992; library bldg. cons. Houston, 1975—. Treas. Literacy Vol. Am., Houston, 1984-85; mem. Northside Interests, Houston, 1982-85. Served with USN, 1945-46 Hoenthal scholar, 1948 Mem. Tex. Library Assn., ALA, Freedom to Read Found., Houston Great Books Council (leader trainer 1953-59, pres. 1967-69) Avocations: tutoring, music, stamp collecting/philately. Home: 4013 Gano St Houston TX 77009-4119

**RADOMSKI, ROBYN L.,** marketing executive; b. Pitts., 1956; d. Robert G. and Helen L. Moses; m. A. David Radomski; children: Lauren E., Kristen L. BA in Journalism, Pa. State U., 1975; MBA in Mktg., DePaul U., 1989. Dir. Sedwick-James, Inc., Chgo., 1977-81; v.p. Edelman Worldwide, Chgo., 1981-84, Playboy Enterprises, Inc., Chgo., 1984-91; sr. v.p. Bozell World-wide, Chgo., 1991-92; v.p. mktg. Fluid Mgmt., L.P., Wheeling, Ill., 1992-96, Wace, The Imaging Network, Chgo., 1998; CMO, v.p. mktg., pub. rels. and physician svcs. Northwestern Meml. Hosp., 1998—99; chief mktg. officer Sonnenschein Nath & Rosenthal, Chgo., 1999—; comm. worldwide mktg. Lex Mundi, North Am., 2003—. Bd. dirs. Playboy Found., Chgo. Mem. Am. Mktg. Assn., Nat. Investor Rels. Assn., Pub. Rels. Soc. Am., Pub. Rels. Clinic. Internat. Assn. Bus. Communicators (bd. dirs.), Sigma Delta Chi. Avocation: yacht sailing. Office: Sonnenschein Nath & Rosenthal 8000 Sears Tower Chicago IL 60606

**RADON, JENIK RICHARD,** lawyer; b. Berlin, Jan. 14, 1946; arrived in U.S., 1951, naturalized, 1956; s. Louis and Irmgard (Hinz) R.; m. Heidi B. Duerbeck, June 10, 1971 (dec. Sept. 1999); 1 child, Kaara H.D. BA, Columbia Coll., 1967; MCP, U. Calif., Berkeley, 1971; JD, Stanford U., 1971. Bar: Calif. 1972, NY 1975, U.S. Ct. Appeals (2d cir.) 1975, U.S. Dist. Ct. (so. dist.) NY 1975. Atty. Radon & Ishizumi, NYC, 1975—. Bd. dirs. Gland Pharma Ltd., India, Excorp Med. China, 2005—; pub. Baltic Rev., 1993-2004, City Paper (Baltic), 1993-2003; trustee, executor Vetter Pharma, Germany, 1999—; adj. faculty Sch. of Law Stanford U., 2000-02, Bus. Sch., 2000-01, Sch. Internat. Pub. Affairs Columbia U., 2002-, Indira Gandhi Inst. for Devel. Rsch., Bombay, 2004—; lectr. in field Editor-in-chief Stanford Jour. Internat. Studies, 1970-71; contbr. The Internat. Acquisitions Handbook, 1987, Negotiating and Financing Joint Ventures Abroad, 1989, How to Form and Manage Successful Strategic Alliances, 1990, Risks Mgmt. in Internat. Bus. 1991, Investing in Reform, 1991, Comrade Goes Pvt., 1992, Covering Energy and Development. A Reporter's Handbook, 2005; contbr. articles to profl. jours. Active Am. Coun. on Germany, NYC, 1978—; vice-chmn. U.S.-Polish Econ. Coun., 1989-93; mem. exec. com. Afghanistan Relief Com., NYC, 1980-95; bd. dirs. Columbia Coll. Alumni Assn., 1988-92, nat. coun., 1996-98, Freedom Medicine, 1987-94, chmn., 1989-94; trustee Direct Relief Internat., Santa Barbara, Calif., 1987-89; founder and dir. Eesti and Eurasian Fellowship of Columbia U., 1990—; advisor Estonian Ministry Economy, Reform and Justice, 1991-95; advisor to Parliament Republic of Georgia, 1996-98, to Pres. of Georgia, 1999-2003; advisor Min. of Fin. of Georgia, 1998-2000, Georgian Internat. Oil Corp., 1998—2004; chmn. Estonian-Am. C. of C., 1990-93, Deutsche Stiftung fuer internationale rechtliche Zusammenarbeit, Estonia Commn., Beirat, 1992-94, Ctr. for Global Change and Governance at Rutgers U., 2004-. Recipient Order of Honor award Republic of Georgia, 2000. Mem. ABA, German-Am. Law Assn. Roman Catholic. Office: Radon & Ishizumi 269 W 71st St New York NY 10023-3701

**RADOVIC, MILADIN,** engineering educator, researcher; s. Nedeljko and Milica Radovic. BSME, U. Belgrade, Serbia, 1992, MSME, 1997; PhD in Materials Engring., Drexel U., Phila., 2001. Tchg. asst., rsch. assoc. U. Belgrade, 1992—98; rsch. asst., assoc. dept. materials engring. Drexel U., Phila., 1998—2001; postdoctoral fellow Oak Ridge Nat. Lab., Tenn., 2001—06; asst. prof. dept. mech. engring. Tex. A&M U., College Station, 2006—. Guest scientist Nat. Inst. Stds. and Tech., Gaithersburg, Md., 1991—2001. Recipient A.W. Grosvenor award Acad. Performance, Drexel U., 2001; scholar, Ministry Sci. and Tech. Republic of Serbia, 1993, Gordon Rsch. Conf., Solid State Studies Ceramics, 2001. Mem.: ASM, European Structural Integrity Soc., Am. Ceramic Soc. Achievements include research in processing and characterization of nano-laminated MAX phases; reliability and durability of materials and components for solid oxide fuel cells; processing and characterization of the high-tempera. Office: Texas A&M Univ 3123 Tamu College Station TX 77843-3123 Office Phone: 979-845-5114. Office Fax: 979-845-3081. Business E-Mail: mradovic@tamu.edu.

**RADOVICH, DONALD,** painter, illustrator, retired art educator; b. Nazareth, Pa., Jan. 3, 1932; s. Zivan and Angeline (Trumich) R.; m. Sheryl Ann Nash; children: Steven Michael, Nicholas Daniel. BFA, U. N.Mex., 1956, MA in Painting, 1960; postgrad., San Miguel Allende, Gto, Mex., 1970. Instr. of art to prof. of art Western State Coll., Gunnison, Colo., 1964-88, prof. emeritus, 1988—; owner Canyon Creek Gallery, Ouray, Colo. Illustrator N.Mex. Press, 1963, Western State Press, 1980, Reader's Digest Funds, 1990, Phil. Acad. of Sci., 1990, Denver Colo. Sci., 1990, Nat. Wildlife Fedn., 1990, Birds of West Indies, 1998, Birds of Western Colorado, 2004, many others; invitational exhibit Wave Hill Mus., 1982; one person exhibit Nat. Wildlife Fedn., 1988, two person, Tohono Chul Pk. Gallery, Tucson, 2003. With US Army, 1956-58. Avocation: gardening. Home: 17232 Woodgate Rd Montrose CO 81401-7722 Office Phone: 970-325-4888.

**RADUNZ, PAUL A.,** transportation executive; BA, St. Olaf Coll. Sr. v.p., chief info. officer GE Card Svcs., GE Capital Fleet Svcs.; v.p., chief info. officer CH Robinson, Eden Prairie, Minn., 2001—. Office: CH Robinson 8100 Mitchell Rd Eden Prairie MN 55344-2248

**RADWIN, JEROME J.,** public health service officer; BA in Polit. sci., Idaho State U., 1965. Fundraiser March of Dimes Birth Defects Found., NY, 1967, dir., gen. solicitation N.Y.C., dir., devel. Chgo., 1971—74, exec. dir., 1974, exec. dir., nat. field svcs. dir., 1974—78, exec. dir., nat. field svcs. dir., asst. v.p., chpt. programs for nat. office, 1978, dir., chpt. N.Y.C., v.p., corp. comms. and v.p., planning and mktg., 1984—88; founder J. Radwin Cons. Svc., 1989—; exec. dir. Nat. Victim Ctr., 1990—93; v.p., opers. Am. Found. for AIDS Rsch., N.Y.C., 1993, sr. v.p., 1993—95, sr. v.p., COO, 1995—97, exec. v.p., CEO, 1997—2000, CEO, 2000—. Office: Am Found for AIDS Rsch 120 Wall St 13th fl New York NY 10005-3902 E-mail: jerry.radwin@amfar.org.*

**RADY, ERNEST S.,** thrift and loan association executive; b. 1938; Chmn. bd. Western Fin. Bank, Orange, Calif., 1982—, CEO, 1994—96, exec., chmn. bd., CEO Westcorp, Irvine, Calif., 1973—, pres., 1982—96, 1998—99. Named one of Forbes' Richest Americans, 2004, 2006. Office: Westcorp 23 Pasteur Irvine CA 92618-3816*

**RADZIK, ALBIN F.,** military analyst, consultant; b. Berwyn, Ill., Oct. 21, 1947; s. Albin F. and Evelyn Clara Radzik; children: Melanie Rose, Amy Marie. BS, Northwestern U.; MBA, Georgetown U., 1994; HHD (hon.), Kalinin U. St. Petersburg, 1995. Analyst U.S. Govt., Washington, 1976—, mil. cons., 1978—2001. Author: (poetry) Love and Distance, 1967 (Hole Creative Writing award, 1967). Mem. and vol. Cambodian Land Mine Relief Org.; vol. Chechnya Refugee Org.; open space com. City of Redlands, Calif. 1985—86. Served to capt. U.S. Army, 1966—82. Decorated Bronze Star, Purple Heart, DSC, Army Commendation medal, Air medal, Combat Inf. badge, Parachutist badge; recipient Cold War Recognition cert., U.S. Sec. Def., 2003. Mem.: MENSA, VFW, Royal Order of the Purple Heart. Office Phone: 909-478-0659. Personal E-mail: aradzik@netzero.net.

**RADZINOWICZ, MARY ANN,** language educator; b. Champaign, Ill., Apr. 18, 1925; d. Arthur Seymour and Ann (Stacy) Nevins; m. Leon Radzinowicz, June 16, 1958 (dec. 1999); children: Ann Stacy Radzinowicz Prior, William Francis Henry. BA, Radcliffe Coll., 1945; MA, Columbia U., 1947, PhD, 1953; MA (hon.), U. Cambridge, Eng., 1960. Prof. Vassar Coll., Poughkeepsie, NY, 1947-50, 52-59, Girton Coll., Cambridge, England, 1960-80, U. Cambridge, 1973-80, Cornell U., Ithaca, NY, 1980-90, Jacob Gould Schurman prof. English emeritus, 1990—. Mem. adv. bd. 2d, 3d, 4th Internat. Milton Symposia, 1985—. Author: Toward Samson Agonistes, 1978 (Hanford prize 1979), Milton's Epics and Psalms, 1989, Milton and the Tragic Women of Genesis, 1995 (Hanford prize); editor American Colonial Prose, 1984, Paradise Lost, Book VIII, 1974; mem. editl. bd. Milton Quar., 1981-2005, Christianity and Lit., 1989—. Mem. MLA, Renaissance Soc. Am., Milton Soc. Am. (honored scholar 1987), John Donne Soc. Home: Ballyconry House Ballyvaughan County Clare Ireland Office: Cornell U Dept English Lit Ithaca NY 14850 Office Phone: 353-65-7077-085. E-mail: manr@eircom.net.

**RAE, BARBARA JOYCE,** employee placement company executive; b. Prince George, B.C., Can., May 17, 1930; d. Alfred and Lottie Kathleen (Davis) Holmwood; m. George Suart, Feb. 14, 1984; children: James, Glenn, John. MBA, Simon Fraser U., Burnaby, B.C., 1975, LLD (hon.), 1998. Chmn., CEO Adia Can., Ltd., Vancouver, 1953-95; CEO Dekora Staging Inc., Vancouver, B.C., 2003—. Bd. dirs. emeritus Can. Imperial Bank Commerce, Grosvenor Internat. Ltd., Noranda, Inc., Telus, Xerox Can.; dir. VLINX.Com., Can. Inst. Adv. Rsch., 1995-2001, KTCS Pub. Broadcasting; bd. govs. Multiple Sclerosis Soc., 1995—; mem. Fed. Task Force on Future of Can. Fin. Svcs. Sector, 1997-98; past chmn. B.C. Women's Hosp. Found., 1994-97. Chancellor Simon Fraser U., 1987—93; mem. Jud. Appts. Com., B.C., 1988—90; commr. Triennial Commn. Judges Salaries and Benefits; mem. Premier's Econ. Adv. Coun., B.C., 1987—91, Prime Minister's Com. on Sci. and Tech., 1989—94; gen. chmn. United Way Lower Mainland, 1987; chair Salvation Army Red Shield Vancouver Campaign, 1986; bd. dirs. Vancouver Bd. Trade, 1972—76; dir. Royal B.C. Mus.; patron Can. Coun. Christians and Jews; mem. adv. bd. Salvation Army, 1985—2004. Decorated Order of Can., Order of B.C.; recipient Outstanding Alumnae award Simon Fraser U., 1985, Disting. Alumni Svc. award, 1995, Bus. Women of Yr. award Vancouver YWCA, 1986, West Vancouver Achievers award, 1987, B.C. Entrepreneur of Yr. award, 1987, Nat. Vol. award, 1990, Can. Woman Entrepreneur B.C. award, 1992, Queen's Jubilee medal, 2003, Clan Leader award Simon Fraser U., 2004. Home: 3355 Osprey Box 508 Whistler Canada V0N 1B3 Personal E-mail: brae@dekora.com.

**RAE, JENEANNE,** new product development and innovation development consultant, educator; married; 2 children. BS in Commerce, U. Va.; MBA, Harvard Bus. Sch. Prin., sr. mgmt. team mem. IDEO, Palo Alto, Calif.; co-founder Peer Insight, LLC, Alexandria, Va. Adj. prof. mktg. Georgetown U. McDonough Sch. Bus. Contbr. articles to profl. jours. Named one of Magnificent Seven Gurus of Innovation, BusinessWeek, 2005. Office: Peer Insight LLC 901 King St Ste 400 Alexandria VA 22314 Office Phone: 703-778-5543. Office Fax: 703-535-8176. Business E-Mail: jrae@peerinsight.com.*

**RAE, JOHN GIBSON, III,** biology professor; s. John Gibson Jr. and Mona Rae; m. Susan Irene Poche, Apr. 12, 1969; children: Ian Christopher, Sean Gibson. BS in Biology, SUNY, Stony Brook, 1968; MS in Marine Biology, U. of Pacific, Stockton, Calif., 1977; PhD in Zoology, Ohio U., Athens, 1981. Asst. prof. Fla. Inst. Tech., Jensen Beach, 1981—86; tchr. Martin County HS, Stuart, Fla., 1986; state pk. mgr. Fla. Dept. Natural Resources, Fort Pierce, 1987—88; from asst. prof. to prof. biology Francis Marion U., Florence, SC, 1988—, Shirley Malloy endowed chair biology, 2001—. Mem. Lynches Scenic River Adv. Coun., Olanta, SC, 1994—, Environ. Ctr. Coun., Florence, 2004—; presenter in field. Contbr. articles to profl. publs. Staff sgt. USAF, 1968—72. Recipient Shared Governance award, AAUP, 2002; grantee, Francis Marion U., 1988—. Mem.: Am. Soc. Zoologists (Best Paper award 1981), SC Acad. Scis., Assn. Southeastern Biologists (Best Paper award 1989, 1994), N.Am. Benthological Soc., Ecol. Soc. Am., Sierra Club (vice chmn. Pee Dee group 1998—2000, chmn. 2001—02). Avocations: reading, photography, orchids, collecting Native American art, travel. Office: Francis Marion U Dept Biology Florence SC 29501 Office Phone: 843-661-1410. Office Fax: 843-661-4660. E-mail: jrae@fmarion.edu.

**RAE, MATTHEW SANDERSON, JR.,** lawyer; b. Pitts., Sept. 12, 1922; s. Matthew Sanderson and Olive (Waite) R.; m. Janet Hettman, May 2, 1953; children: Mary-Anna, Margaret Rae Mallory, Janet S. Rae Dupree. AB, Duke, 1946, LLB, 1947; postgrad. Stanford U., 1951. Bar: Md. 1948, Calif. 1951. Asst. to dean Duke Sch. Law, Durham, NC, 1947-48; assoc. Karl F. Steinmann, Balt., 1948-49, Guthrie, Darling & Shattuck, L.A., 1953-54; nat. field rep. Phi Alpha Delta Law Frat., L.A., 1949-51; research atty. Calif. Supreme Ct., San Francisco, 1951-52; ptnr. Darling, Hall & Rae (and predecessor firms), L.A., 1955—. Mem. Calif. Commn. Uniform State Laws, 1985—, chmn., 1993-94; chmn. drafting com. for revision Uniform Prin. and Income Act of Nat. Conf., 1991-97, Probate and Mental Health Task Force, Jud. Coun. Calif., 1996-2000. Vice pres. L.A. County Rep. Assembly, 1959-64; mem. L.A. County Rep. Ctrl. Com., 1960-64, 77-90, 2000—, exec. com., 1977-90; vice chmn. 17th Congl. Dist., 1960-62, 28th Congl. Dist., 1962-64; chmn. 46th Assy. Dist., 1962-64, 27th Senatorial Dist., 1977-85, 29th Senatorial Dist., 1985-90, sec. 53d Assembly Dist., 2000—; mem. Calif. Rep. State Ctrl. Com., 1966—, exec. com., 1966-67; pres. Calif. Rep. League, 1966-67; trustee Rep. Assocs., 1979-94, pres., 1983-85, chmn. bd. dirs., 1985-87. 2d lt. USAAF, WWII. Fellow Am. Coll. Trust and Estate Counsel; academician Internat. Acad. Estate and Trust Law (exec. coun. 1974-78); mem. ABA, L.A. County Bar Assn. (chmn. probate and trust law com. 1964-66, chmn. legis. com. 1980-86, chmn. program com. 1981-82, chmn. membership retention com. 1982-83, trustee 1983-85, dir. Bar Found., 1987-93, Arthur K. Marshall award probate and trust law sect. 1984, Shattuck-Price Meml. award 1990), South Bay Bar Assn., State Bar of Calif. (chmn. state bar jour. com. 1970-71, probate com. 1974-75; exec. com. estate planning trust and probate law sect. 1977-83, chmn. legis. com. 1977-89; co-chmn. 1991-92; probate law cons. group Calif. Bd. Legal Specialization 1977-88; chmn. conf. dels. resolutions com. 1987, exec. com. conf. dels. 1987-90), Lawyers Club L.A. (bd. govs. 1981-87, 1st v.p. 1982-83), Am. Legion (comdr. Allied post 1969-70), Legion Lex (bd. dirs. 1964-99, pres. 1969-71), Air Force Assn., Aircraft Owners and Pilots Assn., Town Hall (gov. 1970-78, pres. 1975), World Affairs Coun., Internat. Platform Assn., Breakfast Club (law, pres. 1989-90), Commonwealth Club, Chancery Club (pres. 1996-97), Rotary, Phi Beta Kappa (councilor Alpha Assn. 1983—, pres. 1996), Omicron Delta Kappa, Phi Alpha Delta (supreme justice 1972-74, elected to Disting. Svc. chpt. 1978), Sigma Nu. Presbyterian. Home: 600 John St Manhattan Beach CA 90266-5837 Office: Darling Hall & Rae LLP 520 S Grand Ave Fl 7 Los Angeles CA 90071-2645

**RAE, NANCY A.,** human resources specialist, automotive executive; 1 child. Diploma in Bus. Adminstrn., Ea. Mich. U., M in Indsl. Rels. Interviewer Chrysler Corp., Warren, Mich., 1978; various positions DaimlerChrysler Corp., Auburn Hills, Mich., 1978—92, group personnel exec.; procurement and supply and product strategy and regulatory affairs, 1992—94, mgr. workforce diversity and econ. equality, 1994, group personnel mgr., Chrysler Tech. Ctr., 1994—96, group human resources mgr. tech. ops., 1996—98, mgr. health ins. and disability, 1998, v.p. compensation and benefits, 1998—2000, sr. v.p. human resources, 2000—. Office: DaimlerChrysler Corp 1000 Chrysler Dr Auburn Hills MI 48326-2766 Office Phone: 248-576-5741. Office Fax: 248-576-4742.

**RAEBER, JOHN ARTHUR,** architect, construction consultant; b. St. Louis, Nov. 24, 1947; s. Arthur William and Marie (Laux) R. AA, Jefferson Coll., 1968; AB, Washington U., 1970, MArch, 1973. Registered architect, Calif., Mo.; cert. constrn. specifier; cert. Nat. Coun. Arch. Specification writer Hellmuth, Obata & Kassabaum, St. Louis, 1973-78, constrn. adminstr., 1978-79; mgr. of specifications Gensler & Assocs., San Francisco, 1979-82; ind. constrn. specifier San Francisco, 1982—. Adj. prof. architecture Calif. Coll. Arts and Crafts, San Francisco, 1986—; access code advisor Constrn. Industry & Owners, 1982—; spkr., instr. seminars orgns., univs., 1982—; mem. Calif. State Bldg. Standards Commn. Accessibility Adv. Panel, Sacramento, 1981, Calif. Subcom. Rights of Disabled Adv. Panel, Sacramento, 1993; cons. Nat. Inst. Bldg. Scis., 1996—. Author: CAL/ABL: Interpretative Manual to California's Access Barriers Laws, 1982; co-author: (with Peter S. Hopf) Access for the Handicapped, 1984; columnist Constrn. Specifier Mag.,

1988-95. Vol. Calif. Office Emergency Svcs. Safety Assessment, Sacramento, 1991—. Fellow AIA (San Francisco chpt. codes com., Calif. coun. codes and standards com., nat. masterspec rev. com. 1982-84, nat. codes com. corr.), Contrns. Specifications Inst. (cert., columnist newsletter San Francisco chpt. 1984-95, Ben John Small award for Outstanding Stature as practicing specifications writer 1994, pres. St. Louis chpt. 1978-79, pres. San Francisco chpt. 1993-94, tech. com., edn. com., publs. com., Specifications Proficiency award San Francisco chpt. 1989, Tech. Commendation award 1987); mem. Specifications Cons. in Ind. Practice (nat. pres. 1990-92, nat. sec./treas. 1988-90), Internat. Conf. Bldg. Officials, Phi Theta Kappa. Avocations: history, anthropology, science fiction. Home and Office: 3962 26th St San Francisco CA 94131-2002

**RAEBURN, ANDREW HARVEY,** performing arts consultant, recording industry executive; b. London, July 22, 1933; arrived in U.S., 1964, Can., 1993; s. Walter Augustus Leopold and Dora Adelaide Harvey (Williams) R. BA in History, King's Coll., Cambridge U., 1958, MA, 1962; diploma in music performance (hon.), Mt. Royal Coll., 1998; LLD (hon.), U. Calgary, 2005. Mus. dir. Argo Record Co., London, 1959—64; asst. to music dir., program editor Boston Symphony Orch., 1964—73; dir. artists and repertory New World Records, N.Y.C., 1975—79; artistic adminstr. Detroit Symphony Orch., 1979—82; exec. dir. Van Cliburn Found. Inc., Ft. Worth, 1982—85; performing arts cons., 1985—93; exec. v.p. The Peter Pan Children's Fund, 1990—91; exec. dir. Esther Honens Internat. Piano Competition Found., 1993—95, pres., 1995—99, vice chmn., artistic dir., 1999—2001, pres., artistic dir., 2001—04; freelance cons. Calgary, Canada, 2004—. Cons. music; radio and TV commentator; mem. faculty Boston U., 1966-67; condr. New World String Orch., 1978; v.p. World Fedn. Internat. Music Compctitions, 2003-06. Author record liner notes, Argo, RCA, Time-Life records, 1960-79, program notes, Boston Symphony Orch., 1968-73. Served with Royal Arty. Brit. Army, 1952-55; founding dean Prague Mozart Acad. 1992-93. Recipient Lifetime Achievement award, World Fedn. Internat. Music Competitions, 2006. Home and Office: 702 235 15th Ave SW Calgary AB Canada T2R 0P6 Office Phone: 403-263-9939. Personal E-mail: araeburn@telus.net, ar@andrewraeburn.com.

**RAEBURN, JOHN HAY,** language educator; b. Indpls., July 18, 1941; s. Gordon Maurice and Katherine (Calwell) R.; m. Gillian Kimble, Aug. 18, 1963 (div. July 1979); children: Daniel Kennedy, Nicholas Kimble; m. Kathleen Kamerick, July 5, 1986. AB with honors, Ind. U., 1963; A.M., U. Pa., 1964, PhD, 1969. Asst. prof. U. Mich., Ann Arbor, 1967-74; vis. lectr. U. Iowa, Iowa City, 1974-75, assoc. prof., 1976-83, prof. English, 1983—; chmn. Am. Studies dept., 1983-85, 94-2000; chmn. English dept. U. Iowa, Iowa City, 1985-91; assoc. prof. U. Louisville, 1975-76. Author: Fame Became of Him: Hemingway as Public Writer, 1984, A Staggering Revolution: A Cultural History of Thirties Photography, 2006; editor: (with others) Frank Capra: The Man and His Films, 1975. Mem.: Am. Studies Assn., Orgn. Am. Historians. Democrat. Home: 321 Hutchinson Ave Iowa City IA 52246-2407 Office: U Iowa Dept Am Studies 210 Jefferson Bldg Iowa City IA 52242-1418 Office Phone: 319-335-0320. Business E-Mail: john-raeburn@iowa.edu.

**RAEBURN, PAUL,** editor, writer; b. Nov. 26, 1950; 2 children. BA in Physics, Mass. Inst. Tech. With Boston Phoenix, Mass., Lowell Sun, Mass.; sci. editor, chief sci. correspondent AP, 1981—96; sr. editor BusinessWeek, 1996—2004. Past pres. Nat. Assn. Sci. Writers, Inc.; officer Coun. Advancement of Sci. Writing; commentator Morning Edit. Nat. Pub. Radio; sci. writer-in-residence U. Wis., U. Calif. Contbr. articles to profl. publs. including Popular Science, The New York Times, Allure, American Health, Technology Review; author: (book) The Last Harvest: The Genetic Gamble that Threatens to Destroy American Culture, 1997, Mars: Uncovering the Secrets of the Red Planet, 1998, Acquainted with the Night: A Parent's Quest to Understand Depression and Bipolar Disorder in His Children, 2004; actor:. Recipient Sci. in Soc. award, Nat. Assn. Sci. Writers, Inc., John. P. McGovern award Excellence in Med. Comm., Am. Med. Writers Assn.; fellow Journalism, U. Md. Mem.: Sigma Xi (hon.).

**RAEDER, MYRNA SHARON,** lawyer, educator; b. NYC, Feb. 4, 1947; d. Samuel and Estelle (Auslander) R.; m. Terry Oliver Kelly, July 13, 1975; children: Thomas Oliver, Michael Lawrence. BA, Hunter Coll., 1968; JD, NYU, 1971; LLM, Georgetown U., 1975. Bar: N.Y. 1972, D.C. 1972, Calif. 1972. Spl. asst. U.S. atty. U.S. Atty's Office, Washington, 1972-73; asst. prof. U. San Fransisco Sch. Law, 1973-75; assoc. O'Melveny & Myers, L.A., 1975-79; assoc. prof. Southwestern U. Sch. Law., L.A., 1979-82, prof., 1983—; Irwin R. Buchalter prof. law, 1990, Paul E. Treusch prof. law, 2002; mem. faculty Nat. Judicial Coll., 1993—. Prettyman fellow Georgetown Law Ctr., Washington, 1971—73. Author: Federal Pretrial Practice, 3d edit., 2000; co-author: Evidence, State and Federal Rules in a Nutshell, 4th edit., 2003, Evidence, Cases, Materials and Problems, 2d edit., 1998. Named to Alumni Hall of Fame, Hunter Coll., 2005. Mem.: ABA (trial evidence com. litigation sect. 1980—, criminal justice sect. 1994—97, adv. to nat. conf. commrs. uniform state laws drafting com. 1996—99, vice-chair planning 1997—98, chair elect 1997—98, chair 1998—99, mem. mag. bd. 2000—, co-chair ad hoc innocence com. 2002—, Commn. Women in the Profession, Margaret Brent Women Lawyers of Achievement award 2002), Youth at Risk Commn., Am. Law Inst., Assn. Am. Law Schs. (chair women in legal edn. sect. 1982, com. on sects. 1984—87, chair elect evidence sect. 1996, chair 1997), Nat. Assn. Women Lawyers (bd. dirs. 1991—98, pres.-elect 1993, pres. 1994—96), Women Lawyers Assn. L.A. (coord. mothers support group 1987—96, bd. dirs., Ernestine Stallhutt award 2003), Am. Bar Found. (life), Order of Coif, Phi Beta Kappa. Office: Southwestern U Sch Law 675 S Westmoreland Ave Los Angeles CA 90005-3905 Business E-Mail: mraeder@swlaw.edu.

**RAEL, HENRY SYLVESTER, SR.,** retired health administrator, financial and management consultant; b. Pueblo, Colo., Oct. 2, 1928; s. Daniel and Grace (Abeyta) R.; m. Helen Warner Loring Brace, June 30, 1956 (dec. Aug. 1980); children: Henry Sylvester Jr., Loring Victoria, Thomas Warner Bush. AB, U. So. Colo., 1955; BA in Bus. Adminstrn., U. Denver, 1957, MBA, 1958. Sr. boys counselor Denver Juvenile Hall, 1955-58; adminstrv. asst. to pres. Stanley Aviation Corp., Denver, 1958-61; Titan III budget and fin. control supr. Martin Marietta Corp., Denver, 1961-65; mgmt. adv. services officer U. Colo. Med. Center, Denver, 1965-72; v.p. fin., treas. Loretto Heights Coll., Denver, 1972-73; dir. fin. and adminstrn. Colo. Found. for Med. Care, 1973-86, Tri-County Health Dept., 1987—96; ret., 1996. Instr. fin. mgmt., mem. fin. com. Am. Assn. Profl. Standards Rev. orgn., 1980-85; speaker systems devel., design assns., univs., 1947-71. Mem. budget lay adv. com. Park Hill Elem. Sch., Denver, 1967-68, chmn., 1968-69; vol. worker Boy and Girl Scouts, 1967-73; bd. dirs. Community Arts Symphony, 1981-83, 85-87; controller St. John's Episcopal Cathedral, 1982-83; charter mem. Pueblo (Colo.) Coll. Young Democrats, 1954-55; block worker Republican Party, Denver, 1965-68, precinct committeeman, 1978-84; trustee Van Nattan Scholarship Fund, 1974-96; bd. dirs. Vis. Nurse Assn., 1977-84, treas., 1982-84; cons. to dir. Clayton Found., 1996; cons. Colo. Dept. Health Center. 1997. Served with USAF, 1947-53, res. 1954-61. Recipient Disting. Service award Denver Astron. Soc., 1968, Citation Chamberlin Obs., 1985; Stanley Aviation masters scholar, 1957; Ballard scholar, 1956. Mem.: Nat. Astronomers Assn. (exec. bd. 1965—97), Am. Assn. Founds. for Med. Care (fin. com. 1981—82), Denver Astron. Soc. (pres. 1965—66, bd. dirs. 1982—94), Colo. Pub. Employees Retirement Assn. (bd. dirs. 1993), Budget Execs. Inst. (sec. 1963—64, v.p. chpt. 1964—65), Hosp. Systems Mgmt. Soc., Assn. Systems Mgmt. (pres. 1971—72), Whispering Pines of Denver Homeowners Assn. (pres. bd. dirs. 1998, dir.-at-large 2001), Brandy Chase Homeowners Assn. (bd. dirs. 1997), Delta Psi Omega, Epsilon Xi. Home: 7755 E Quincy Ave Apt 57 Denver CO 80237-2312

**RAESSLER, KENNETH RAY,** music educator, university administrator, writer; b. Highspire, Pa., Aug. 17, 1932; s. Rufus Ray and Grace Mary; m. Joyce Elaine Bond, Aug. 20, 1960; children: Laurie Elaine Raessler Denison, Todd Ray. BS, West Chester U., Pa., 1954; MM, Temple U., Phila., 1959;

PhD, Mich. State U., East Lansing, 1967. Music dir. Belvidere Sch. Dist., NJ, 1954—57; choral music dir. East Stoudsburg Area HS, East Stoudsburg, 1957—61, Hatboro-Horsham H.S., Hatboro, Pa., 1962—63; assoc. prof. music Gettysburg Coll., Pa., 1963—73; dir. music edn. Williamsport Area Sch. Dist., Pa., 1973—89; dir. sch. music Tex. Christian U., Fort Worth, 1989—2001, prof. music, 1989—2001. Cons. Wenger Corp., Owatonna, Minn., 1991, Korg Corp., L.A., 1991, Yamaha Corp., Grand Rapids, Mich., 1986—96; keynote spkr.; conf. clinician. Author: Aspiring to Excel; contbr. articles to profl. jours. Pres. Williamsport Rotary Club, Williamsport, Pa., 1985. Recipient Cmty. Svc. award, Williamsport Rotary Club, 1989, Disting. Alumni award West Chester U., 2002, Sch. of Music Disting. Alumni award, 2003. Mem.: Tex. Christian U. Retirees Assn. (pres. 2006—), Tex. Assn. Music Schs. (pres.), Van Cliburn Found. (exec. bd. 1989—2002), Phi Mu Alpha Sinfonia (trustee 1998—, v.p. 2000—04). Democrat. Christian. Avocations: golf, swimming. Home: 2913 Park Arbor Ct Fort Worth TX 76116 Office Phone: 817-738-2944. E-mail: k.raessler@tcu.edu.

**RAFAJKO, ROBERT RICHARD,** science administrator; b. Chgo., Sept. 3, 1931; s. Edward Michael and Mildred Eleanor (Simo) R.; m. Mary Ann Filipi, June 24, 1954 (div. 1979); children: Rorie Rae, Ronald Raymond, Robin Rene, Rod Richard, Rebecca Rae.; m. Anne Thorne Sloan, Jan. 26, 1982; 1 son, Andrew Sloan. BA, Coe Coll., 1953; MS, U. Iowa, 1958, PhD, 1960. Rsch. assoc. Merck Sharp and Dohme, West Point, Pa., 1960-61; rsch. scientist Microbiol. Assos., Bethesda, Md., 1961-66; v.p., gen. mgr. Med. Rsch. Cons., Rockville, Md., 1966-69; v.p. R & D, N.Am. Biols., Rockville, 1969-74; pres. Biofluids, Inc., Rockville, 1974-99, Bonheur Inc., Keswick, Va., 1999—. Pres. Tysan Serum, Inc., Rockville, 1974-2000, Kytaron Inc, Rockville, 1987-99; breeder thoroughbred horses, 1980—. Contbr. 23 articles to profl. jours. Chmn. PVAAU Swimming Program, Washington, Md. and Va., 1973-76; bd. dirs. Montgomery County Swim League, Montgomery County, Md., 1968-76. Served with USAF, 1954-55. Mem. AAAS, N.Y. Acad. Scis., Am. Soc. Microbiology, Tissue Culture Assn., Am. Horse Council, Horsemans Benevolent and Protective Assn. Republican. Presbyterian. Avocations: scuba diving, photography, collecting stamps, travel. Home and Office: 1349 Queenscroft Keswick VA 22947-2731 Personal E-mail: bonheur421@aol.com.

**RAFEEDIE, EDWARD,** federal judge; b. Orange, NJ, Jan. 6, 1929; s. Fred and Nabeeha (Hishmeh) R.; m. Ruth Alice Horton, Oct. 8, 1961; children: Fredrick Alexander, Jennifer Ann. BS in Law, U. So. Calif., 1957, JD, 1959; LLD (hon.), Pepperdine U., 1978. Bar: Calif. 1960. Pvt. practice, Santa Monica, Calif., 1960-60; mcpl. ct. judge Santa Monica Jud. Dist., 1969-71; judge Superior Ct. State of Calif., L.A., 1971-82; dist. judge U.S. Dist. Court (cen. dist.) Calif., L.A., 1982-96, sr. judge, 1996—. With U.S. Army, 1950-52, Korea. Office: US Dist Ct 312 N Spring St Ste 244P Los Angeles CA 90012-4704 Office Phone: 213-894-6927.

**RAFEYAN, ROUEEN,** psychiatrist, educator; b. Tehran, Iran, Oct. 1, 1961; came to U.S., 1979; s. Majid Rafeyan and Nezhat Babanoury; m. Helena Linda Hernandez, Feb. 15, 1991; 1 child, Ryan Michael. BA, Knox Coll., 1981; MD, U. Istanbul, Turkey, 1989. Cert. Am. Bd. Psychiatry & Neurology, 2001; Am. Bd. Psychiatry and Neurology. Resident U. Ill. Chgo., 1996; dir. outpatient clin. svcs., dir. med. student edn. Michael Reese Hosp., Chgo., 1996-99; med. dir. Rush Presbyn., Chgo., 1997—; asst. clin. prof. psychiatry U. Ill., Chgo., 1996—; asst. prof psychiatry Rush U., 2005—. Cons. Threshold Cmty. Mental Health Ctr., Chgo., 1996—. Mem. AMA, Am. Psychiatric Assn., Ill. Psychiatric Soc., Chgo. Med. Soc. Avocations: tennis, music, world history. Office: Michael Reese Hosp 2959 S Cottage Grove Ave Chicago IL 60616 Office Phone: 312-791-3930. E-mail: roueen@msn.com.

**RAFF, DANIEL MARTIN GORODETSKY,** economist, historian, educator; b. Washington, Sept. 23, 1951; s. Morton Spencer and Miriam Susan (Gore) R.; m. Susan Claire Adelman, May 18, 1986; 1 child, Anna Amelia Gorodetsky. BA, New Coll., Sarasota, Fla.; 1973; MPA, Princeton U., 1976; BPhil, Oxford U., 1978; PhD, MIT, 1987. Vis. lectr. econs. Brasenose Coll., Oxford, 1982; lectr. econs. Magdalen Coll., Oxford, 1983-85; rsch. assoc. Harvard U. Grad. Sch. Bus. Adminstrn., Cambridge, Mass., 1986-87, asst. prof. bus. adminstrn., 1987-93; assoc. prof. mgmt. The Wharton Sch., U. Pa., Phila.. 1993—. Vis. assoc. prof. bus. adminstrn. Columbia U., N.Y.C., 1992-94, lectr. in law, 1994; faculty rsch. fellow Nat. Bur. Econ. Rsch., Cambridge, 1988—. Contbr. articles to profl. jours., chpts. to books. Mem.: Bus. History Conf., Econ. History Assn., Am. Econ. Assn., Cliometric Soc., Am. Hist. Soc. Office: U Pa Wharton Sch Dept Mgmt Philadelphia PA 19104-6370

**RAFFAY, STEPHEN JOSEPH,** manufacturing executive, director; b. McAdoo, Pa., Oct. 25, 1927; s. Stephen John and Stephanie (Severa) R.; m. Audree Eugenia Kuehne, Sept. 12, 1953; children: Andrea, Stephen, Leslie. BA, Columbia U., N.Y.C., 1950, MS, 1951. C.P.A., N.Y. Sr. accountant Arthur Andersen & Co., N.Y.C., 1951-56; asst. controller Emhart Corp., Farmington, Conn., 1956-61, asst. treas., 1961-63, treas., 1963-67, v.p. internat., 1967-72, v.p., group press., 1972-79, exec. v.p., 1979-84, vice chmn., chief adminstrv. officer, 1984-87, 1980-87; sr. v.p. Dexter Corp., Windsor Locks, Conn., 1987-90. Bd. dirs. United Plumbing Tech. Inc., Rossi Enterprises, Inc., EDAC Techs. Inc. Bd. dirs. Hartford Symphony Soc. With AUS, 1946-47. Mem. AICPA, Conn. Soc. CPAs. Home: 93 Westmont St West Hartford CT 06117-2929

**RAFFEGEAU, JEAN MICHEL,** audit and consulting company executive; b. St. Germain en Laye, Yvelines, France, Sept. 24, 1930; s. Louis and Irene (Pithon) R.; m. Nicole Laporte, Jan. 19, 1962; children: Catherine, Brigitte. Diploma in law, Sorbonne U., Paris, 1954; diploma in bus. adminstrn., HEC, Paris, 1954. Chartered acct. Commissaire aux Comptes, 1966. Asst. mgr. Banque de Paris et des Pays-Bas, Paris, 1955-57; adminstrv. and fin. mgr. Société Industrielle de Transmissions, 1958-66; chmn., mng. dir. Befec, Paris, 1966-89, Befec-Price Waterhouse, 1989-94; regional mng. pntr. French-speaking Europe and Africa Price Waterhouse, Paris, 1994-96, hon. pres., 1995—. Legal expert Court Appeal, Paris, 1979, adminstv. court, Paris, 1982. Co-author: L'Audit Opérationnel, 1993; co-author, editor: Les Comptes Consolidés, 1989, Guide du Financement des Entreprises, 1993, Le Mémento Comptable, 1997, Evaluation of Enterprise, 4th edit., 2003. Recipient Silver medal Order of Experts Comptables, Paris, 1979, Chevalier de la Légion d'Honneur, Govt. France, Paris, 1995. Mem. Chartered Accountancy Exams. Jury, Rotary (Paris) (treas. 1987-88), Cercle Union Interalliée. Avocations: reading, cinema, photography. Office Phone: 33-1-47-47-80-45. E-mail: j.raffegeau@free.fr.

**RAFFEL, BURTON NATHAN,** literature educator, poet, translator; b. NYC, 1928; married, six children. BA cum laude, Bklyn. Coll., 1948; MA, Ohio State U., 1949; JD, Yale U., 1958. Lawyer Milbank, Tweed, Hadley & McCloy, N.Y.C., 1958-60; editor Foundation News, 1960-63; instr. English SUNY, Stony Brook, 1964-65, asst. prof. of English, 1965-66, assoc. prof. English Buffalo, 1966-68; prof. English and Classics U. Tex., Austin, 1969-71; sr. tutor, dean Ont. Coll. Art, Toronto, Can., 1971-72; prof. English U. Denver, 1975-87; dir. Adirondack Mountain Found., 1987-89; Disting. prof. arts and humanities, prof. English U. La., Lafayette, 1989—2003; assoc. prof. English U. Haifa, 1968—69. Lectr. English dept. Bklyn. Coll., 1950-51; instr. Ford Found. English Lang. Tchr. Tng. program in Indonesia, resident in Makassar, 1953-55; vis. prof. Humanities York U., Toronto, 1972-75, vis. prof. English Emory U., 1974; sr. editor, cons. McDonnell Douglas Computer-Based Systems Tng. Group, Denver, 1985-87; lectr. in law U. Denver, 1986-87. Author: The Development of Modern Indonesian Poetry, 1967, Mia Poems, 1968, The Forked Tongue: A Study of the Translation Process, 1971, Why Re-Create?, 1973, Four Humours, 1979, (film) The Legend of Alfred Packer, 1979, Robert Lowell, 1981, T.S. Eliot, 1982, Changing the Angle of the Sun-Dial, 1984, Grice, 1985, Evenly Distributed Rubble, 1985, Ezra Pound: The Prime Minister of Poetry, 1985, The Art of Translating Poetry, 1988, American Victorians: Exploration in Emotional History, 1984, Possum and Ole Ez in the Public Eye, 1985, After Such Ignorance, 1986, Man as a Social Animal, 1986, Artists All, 1986, Politicians,

Poets, and Con Men, 1986, Founder's Fury, 1988, The Art of Translating Poetry, 1988, Founder's Fortune, 1989, From Stress to Stress: An Autobiography of English Prosody, 1992, The Art of Translating Prose, 1994, The Annotated Milton, 1999, Beethoven in Denver and Other Poems, 1999, The Annotated Hamlet, 2003, The Annotated Romeo and Juliet, 2004, Macbeth, 2005, Midsummer Night's Dream, 2005, Othello, 2005, Taming of the Shrew, 2005, The Tempest, 2006, Henry IV, Part One, 2006, The Merchant of Venice, 2006, Julius Ceasar, 2006; mem. editl. bd. Oral Tradition 1983—, Literature East and West, 1967-70; adv. editor The Lit. Rev., 1987-03; reviewer/writer Asian Wall St. Jour., 1978-85; contbr. articles to profl. jours. Mem. Bar of the State of N.Y., The Nat. Faculty. Home: 203 S Mannering Ave Lafayette LA 70508-4829 E-mail: bnraffel@cox.net.

**RAFFEL, COREY,** neurosurgeon, pediatrician; m. Kathleen Raffel, June 16, 1974; children: Forrest Kanye, Colin Abraham. MD, PhD, U. Calif. San Diego, La Jolla, 1980. Bd. cert. Neurologic Surgery, 1990. Asst. and assoc. prof. U. So. Calif. Sch. Medicine, LA, 1987—95; prof. neurologic surgery Mayo Sch. Medicine, Rochester, Minn., 1995—. Office: Mayo Clinic Dept Neurologic Surgery Go8S 200 First St SW Rochester MN 55905 Office Phone: 507-284-8167.

**RAFFEL, LEROY B.,** real estate developer; b. Zanesville, Ohio, Mar. 13, 1927; s. Jacob E. and Anne M. (Oliker) R.; m. Shirley Balbot, Sept. 11, 1949; children: Kenneth, Janet, James, Nancy. BS, U. Pa., 1949. Pres. Raffel Bros., Inc., Youngstown, Ohio, 1949-78; York Mahoning Co., Youngstown, 1950-64, Arby's, Inc., Youngstown, 1964-70, chmn. bd., 1971-79; pres. Brom Equity Devel., Inc., Miami, Fla., 1979—. Served with USNR, 1945-46. Home: 2141 NE 190th Ter North Miami Beach FL 33179-4352 Office: Brom Equity Devel Inc Ste 207 1380 NE Miami Gardens Dr Miami FL 33179-4709 Office Phone: 305-949-6445.

**RAFFERTY, EMILY KERNAN,** museum administrator; b. NYC, Mar. 18, 1949; m. John Rafferty; children: Nicholas, Sara. BA cum laude, Boston U., 1971. Arts and philanthropy asst. to David Rockefeller, Jr., Boston, 1971; deputy dir. edn. Inst. Contemporary Art, Boston, 1973—75; adminstr. corp., found. and individual fundraising Met. Mus. of Art, NYC, 1976—81, mgr. devel., 1981—84, v.p. devel. and membership, 1984—96, sr. v.p. devel. and membership, 1996—99, sr. v.p. external affairs, 1999—2005, pres., 2005—. Mem. blue ribbon com Am. Cancer Soc. Found., 1999—2000; lifetime honorary trustee Convent of the Sacred Heart; v.p. bd. Independent Sch. Chmn. Assoc.; pres. Blue Hill Troupe, 1998—99. Mem.: Independent Sector (Met. Mus. rep.), Am. Assn. Museums (devel. com. 1984—94), Women in Financial Devel., Assn. Fundraising Professionals, ArtTable (bd. dirs. 1991—94). Office: Met Museum of Art 1000 Fifth Ave New York NY 10028-1098*

**RAFFERTY, JAMES PAUL,** telecommunications executive; b. Hartford, Conn., Oct. 26, 1952; s. James Paul and Kathleen Marie (LeHane) R.; m. Lucinda Anne Link, Sept. 16, 1989. BS in Mgmt. Engring., Rensselaer Poly. Inst., 1974, M in Mgmt. Engring., 1975. MIS analyst Burroughs, Danbury, Conn., 1977—80, MIS project leader, 1981—83, mgr. resource planning, 1984, mgr. materials, 1985—86; mgr. product program Fujitsu, Danbury, 1987—88, mgr. R&D, 1989—92; pres. Human Comm., 1992—99; sr. mgr. product Cantata Tech., Needham, Mass., 2000—05, 2006—. Pub. industry newsletter Human Comm. Digest, 1992-99, Human Commn. Stds. Update, 1996-99; U.S. del. Internat. Telecomms. Union Study Group 8, 1993-2000, Study Group 16, 2000—; vice chair Internet Engring. Task Force, 1997-2000; dir. Internat. Bus. Communicators Assn., 1999-2000. Editor Enterprise Computer Telephony Forum, 1995-2000; co-author: IETF RFC 2301, 2302, 2306, 3250, 3302, 3949, 3950; contbr. articles to profl. jours. Active Caucus of Conn. Dems., 1986; pres. Deer Ridge Condo Assn., Danbury, 1987-90; merit badge counselor Boy Scouts Am., 2003—. Recipient Computer Facsimile Industry award, 1996. Mem. Internat. Packet Comm. Consortium, Electronic Messaging Assn. (Disting. Svc. award 1998), Telecom. Industry Assn., Danbury Golf League (team capt. 1984-85), Alliance Francaise, Epsilon Delta Sigma (fed. ch. endowment com. 2003—). Avocations: golf, cooking, hiking, music, skiing. Office: Cantata Tech 410 1st Ave Needham MA 02494-2815 Office Phone: 781-449-4100. Personal E-mail: jrafferty@humancomm.com. Business E-mail: jraff@cantata.com.

**RAFFERTY, THOMAS G.,** lawyer; b. Rockaway Beach, NY, Mar. 23, 1955; BA, SUNY, Old Westbury, 1985; JD, Harvard Univ., 1988. Bar: NY 1989. Assoc. Cravath Swaine & Moore LLP, NYC, 1988—94, ptnr., litig., 1994—. Office: Cravath Swaine & Moore LLP Worldwide Plz 825 Eighth Ave New York NY 10019-7475 Office Phone: 212-474-1837. Office Fax: 212-474-3700. Business E-mail: trafferty@cravath.com.

**RAFFIN, THOMAS A.,** physician; b. San Francisco, Jan. 25, 1947; s. Bennett L. and Carolyn M. Raffin; m. Michele Raffin, June 19, 1987; children: Elizabeth S., Ross Daniel, Jason Bennett, Nicholas Ethan. AB in Biol. Sci., Stanford Med. Sch., 1968, MD, 1973. Diplomate Am. Bd. Pulmonary Medicine, Am. Bd. Internal Medicine (also in Critical Care Medicine). Intern Peter Bent Brigham Hosp., 1973-75; fellow in respiratory medicine sch. medicine Stanford U., Stanford, Calif., 1975-78, med. fiberoptic bronchoscopy service dir. med. ctr., 1978—, acting asst. prof. sch. medicine 1978-80, assoc. dir. med. ctr. intensive care units, med. dir. dept. respiratory therapy hosp., 1978—, assoc. prof. medicine sch. medicine, 1986-95, acting chief div. respiratory medicine, 1988—2004, chief divsn. pulmonary and critical care, 1990—2004, prof. of medicine, 1995—, Colleen and Robert Haas emeritus prof. medicine/biomed. ethics, 1999—; dir. emeritus Stanford U. Ctr. for Biomed. Ethics, 1989—; co-founder Rigel Pharms., Inc. Gen. ptnr. Telegraph Hill Ptnrs., 2002; bd. dirs. New Link Genetics, Angio Score, Interface Assocs. Author: Intensive Care: Facing the Critical Choices, 1988; contbr. articles to profl. jours. V.p. lung cancer com., No. Calif. Oncology Group, 1983-85; com. mem. NIH Workshop, 1984. Recipient award, Henry J. Kaiser Found., 1981, 1984, 1988, 1997, Arthur L. Bloomfield award, 1981. Fellow ACP (rep. coun. subsplty. socs. 1986), Am. Coll. Chest Physicians (program com. mem. 1985-86); mem. AAAS, Am. Fedn. for Clin. Rsch., Am. Thoracic Soc., Santa Clara County Lung Assn. and Med. Soc., Calif. Med. Assn. (chmn. sect. chest diseases 1984-85), Soc. for Critical Care Medicine, Calif. Thoracic Soc. (bd. dirs., membership, gardening, raising miniature donkeys. Home: 13468 Three Forks Ln Los Altos CA 94022-2432 Office: Stanford Ctr For Biomedical 701 Welch Rd Ste A1105 Palo Alto CA 94304-1709 Office Phone: 415-765-6985. Business E-Mail: tar@stanford.edu.

**RAFI, MOSTAFA,** ophthalmologist; b. Oujda, Morocco, May 20, 1947; s. Miloud Rafi and Fatna (Hemri) R.; m. Amina Samir Rafi, Aug. 5, 1973; children: Fedoua, Nada. PhD in Medicine, U. Rabat, 1974; diploma in Ophthalmology, U. Paris, 1976. Cert. ophthalmologist Paris. Asst. prof., Sale, 1976; prof. Auicenne's Hosp., Rabat, 1980-86, Specialty Hosp., Rabat, 1986-97; head pvt. med., 1990—; pvt. practice Clinique d'Ophthalmologie, Rabat. Dir. Sale's Hosp., 1983-85; head of OTO-Neuro-Ophthalmology Dept., 1990—; pres. 1982-85, v.p., 1986-89, Moroccan Ophthalmological Soc., pres. Qualification's Commn. in Ophthalmology, 1987-93. Mem. Direction of the Social Assn. Anjoad, 1983—; pres. Assn. Against Blindness, 1993—. Recipient Gov.'s award, Oujda, 1989, Settat, 1975, Honor award Moroccan Soc. of Ophthalmology, 2004. Avocations: golf, hunting, tennis. Home: 252 rue Beni Garfat Rabat Morocco Office: Specialty Hosp Afdal Rabat Morocco Office Phone: 212 37660389/90.

**RAFTER, TRACY,** publishing executive; m. Michael Rafter; 1 child, Haley. With advt. sales mgr., Idaho; gen. mgr. St. Louis; pub. Pa.; group pub. Taunton Daily Gazette and The Herald News, Fall River, Mass.; co-owner Valley Times, Milton-Freewater, Oreg., 1999—2002; sr. v.p. advt. and mktg. L.A. Newspaper Group, 2001—04; pub., CEO L.A. Daily News, 2004—. Office: LA Daily News 21221 Oxnard St POBox 4200 Woodland Hills CA 91365

**RAFUSE, NANCY E.,** lawyer, director; b. Columbia, SC, Dec. 14, 1966; m. Mark Rafuse; 2 children. BBA cum laude, U. Ga., 1988, JD magna cum laude, 1991. Ptnr., chair dept. employment law Paul, Hastings, Janofsky & Walker, Atlanta, 1991—2003; co-founder, mng. ptnr. Ashe, Rafuse & Hill, Atlanta, 2003—. Spkr. in field; mem. bar coun. and disciplinary com. No. Dist. Ga., 2002—05. Contbr. articles to profl. jours. Bd. dirs. Atlanta Urban League, Zoo Atlanta; mem. Atlanta United Way Women's Leadership Coun. Named one of Georgia's Legal Elite, Georgia Trend mag., 2003—04, Top 40 Lawyers Under 40, Nat. Law Jour., 2005. Mem.: ABA (mem. labor and employment law sect.), Atlanta Bar Assn. (mem. labor and employment law sect.), State Bar Ga. (mem. labor and employment law sect.). Office: Ashe Rafuse & Hill LLP 1355 Peachtree St Ste 500 Atlanta GA 30309 Office Phone:    404-253-6002.    Office    Fax:    404-253-6060.    E-mail: nancyrafuse@asherafuse.com.

**RAGAN, AMANDA,** state senator; b. Mason City, Sept. 1954; m. James Ragan; children: Edith, Charles. AA, N. Iowa Area CC; BA in Human Svcs., cum laude, Buena Vista U. Legis. asst. to Rep. Ed Parker; co-chair Ho. Majority Leader John Groninga, 1987—89; dist. rep. Iowa Dem. State Ctrl. Com., 1992—2002; legis. page Iowa State Senate, 1973, mem. DesMoines, 2002—, asst. leader, co-chair human resources com., mem. agr. com., mem. econ. growth com., mem. rules and adminstrn. com., mem. appropriations com., mem. health & human svcs. com., mem. budget com.; co-chair Senate Human Resources Com. Active Mason City Sesquicentennial Com., Sesquicentennial Com.; mem. Birth Defects Adv. Bd., HAWK-I Bd.; exec. dir. Meals on Wheels, Mason City, Cmty. Kitchen North Iowa, Inc., Mason City; mem. N. Iowa Band Festival Planning Com., Buena Vista Alumni Found., Coun. Social Agencies, Maternal Health Adv. Coun.; active Iowa Dem. Party State Ctrl. Com.; asst. leader Dem. Caucus; mem. Cerro Gordo County Dem. Ctrl. Com.; past chair. Cerro Gordo Re-Elect Clinton-Gore Com.; bd. dirs. Charles City C. of C., Osage C. of C., Francis Lauer Youth Svc. Mem.: N Iowa Fund-Raising Profls. Assn., Mason City C. of C., Mason City Sunrise Rotary (bd. dirs.). Office: State Capitol Bldg East 12th and Grand Des Moines IA 50319 Home: 20 Granite Ct Mason City IA 50401

**RAGAN, AMY K.,** secondary school educator; b. Atlanta, Mar. 28, 1970; d. Ed and Patty C. Ragan. BS in Biology, U. Tex., Austin, Tex., 1992. Cert. tchr. secondary edn. Tex., 1992, tchr. composite sci. Tex., 1992. Tchr. sci. Lake Travis H.S., Austin, Tex., 1992—96, chmn. dept., 1992—96; tchr. sci. Cedar Pk. (Tex.) H.S., 1996—, chmn. dept., 1996—. Charity promotions Ctrl. Tex. Parrotheads, Austin, 2004—06. Woodrow Wilson fellow. Mem.: ATPE (campus rep. 1996—2006). Home: 1604 Texas Oak Way Cedar Park TX 78613 Office: Cedar Park High School 2150 Cypress Creek Road Cedar Park TX 78613 Office Phone: 512-435-8451. Home Fax: 512-435-8305. Personal E-mail: amy.ragan@leanderisd.org.

**RAGAN, ANN TALMADGE,** media and production consultant, actor; b. Raleigh, NC, July 6, 1951; d. Samuel Talmadge and Marjorie Lois (Upham) R.; m. L. Worth Keeter III, Aug. 22, 1992. Student, U. N.C. 1969-71, Finch Coll., 1972-73, New Sch. Social Rsch., 1973-74, Western Wash. U., 1978. Acct. estimator Benton & Bowles Inc., NYC, 1971-72, media buyer, 1974-77; speechwriter, press aide Senator Robert Morgan, Washington, 1978-79; asst. prodr., casting dir. John F. Murray Inc., NYC, 1979—80; prod., sales dir. Grant St. Films, NYC, 1980-84; ind. prod. for various clients NYC, 1984-86; asst. pub. The Pilot, Inc., Southern Pines, NC, 1986-96, bd. dirs. Prodn. mgr. Anglo Am. Media Workshops, London, 1988—90; dir. SAG Conservatory Am. Film Inst., L.A., 2003—, coach Film Camp, 2005—, cons.; mgr., exec. prodr. films, commercials, audio books Blue Kiss, LLC, 2000—; workshop leader in field. Contbr. articles to newspapers and jours. Life mem. Roanoke Island Hist. Assn.; mem.Moore County Arts Coun., 1986-89. Mem.: SAG (conservatory com., rec. sec. 1997—2006, cons., vice-chair 2003—), AF-TRA, Women in Film, Women in Theatre (adminstrv. dir. 1995—97, treas. 1997—99, bd. dirs. 1997—99, pres. 2004—), Actors Equity Assn., Ind. Feature Project West, Kings and Clowns Ednl. Shakespeare Alliance (treas. bd. dirs. 1999—), Pi Beta Phi. Democrat. Methodist. Home and Office: 10542 Bloomfield St Toluca Lake CA 91602-2813 Office Phone: 818-762-6339. E-mail: bluekissllc@aol.com.

**RAGAN, BETTY SAPP,** artist, educator; b. Birmingham, Ala., Mar. 15, 1937; d. Robert William and Emma Mildred (O'Neal) Sapp; m. Thaxton Drew Ragan, Apr. 1958 (div. Aug. 1986); 1 child, Robert McClearan. BA cum laude, Birmingham-So. Coll., 1958; student, Allegheny Coll., 1971-72, Auburn U., 1980-83; MFA, Pratt Inst., 1985. Teachng asst. Pratt Inst., Bklyn., 1985; vis. asst. prof. dept. art Auburn U., 1985-89; asst. prof. dept. art U. Puget Sound, 1989-91, assoc. prof. photography and printmaking, dept. art, 1992—98, prof., 1998—. Panel moderator Soc. for Photo Edn. N.W., Tacoma, 1993; co-curator But Is It Art, Tacoma, 1993. Exhibited photography in solo shows at Maude Kerns Gallery, Eugene, Oreg., 1995, Helen Smith Gallery, Green River C.C., Auburn, Wash., 1996, others; group shows include Hanson Gallery, New Orleans, 1980, Montgomery (Ala.) Mus. Fine Arts, 1981, Ga. State U., Atlanta, 1981, Park Ave Atrium, N.Y.C., 1985, Carnegie Art Ctr., Walla Walla, Wash., 1990, Definitive Image Gallery, Seattle, 1992, Seattle Ctr. Pavilion, 1993, San Diego Art Inst., 1993, Eagle Gallery, Murray, Ky., 1994, B St. Pier Gallery, San Diego, 1995, Camera Club N.Y., 2002, numerous others; artist/photographer various collage series; co-curator But Is It Art?, Tacoma, 1993. Recipient numerous awards for art including Merit award Fine Arts Mus. of the South, Mobile, 1983, Dirk Andrew Phibbs Rsch. award U. Puget Sound, Tacoma, 1994, Disting. Prof. award, 2003. Mem. Soc. for Photog. Edn., Soc. Photog. Edn./N.W. (sec. 1990-93), Artist Trust, Women's Caucus for Art, Coll. Art Assn., Seattle Women's Caucus for Art. Unitarian Universalist. Avocations: entomology, hiking, gardening, existential philosophy. Office: U Puget Sound Dept Art 1500 N Warner St Tacoma WA 98416-0001

**RAGAN, CHARLES RANSOM,** lawyer; b. NYC, Aug. 13, 1947; s. Charles Alexander Jr. and Josephine Forbes (Parker) R.; m. Barbara Thiel McMahon, Aug. 30, 1969; children: Alexandra Watson, Madeline McCue. AB, Princeton U., 1969; JD, Fordham U., 1974. Bar: N.Y. 1975, U.S. Ct. Appeals (3d cir.) 1975, Calif. 1976, U.S. Ct. Appeals (9th cir.) 1976, U.S. Dist. Ct. (no. dist.) Calif. 1976, U.S. Supreme Ct. 1981, U.S. Dist. Ct. (so. dist.) N.Y. 1982, U.S. Ct. Appeals (2d cir.) 1984. Law clk. to Hon. R.J. Aldisert U.S. Ct. Appeals (3rd cir.), 1974-76; assoc. Pillsbury, Madison & Sutro, San Francisco, 1976-81, ptnr., 1982-97, Palo Alto, 1997-2000, Pillsbury Winthrop, Palo Alto, San Francisco, 2001—05; founder, ptnr. Redgrave Daley Ragan & Wagner, 2005—. Mem. exec. com. 9th Cir. Judicial Conf., 1987-91. Avocations: bicycling, swimming, sports. Office: Redgrave Daley Ragan & Wagner LLP 1750 Montgomery St San Francisco CA 94111 Office Phone: 612-455-4403. Business E-Mail: cragan@rdrw.com.

**RAGAN, CHARLOTTE ANN,** music educator; b. Elberton, Ga., May 4, 1929; d. Harry Sanders and Pauline Melissa (Edwards) Bell; m. Gordon Billy Ragan (dec.); children: Gordon Billy Jr., Evelyn Melissa Swanson. BFA, U. Ga., 1950; MA, Columbia U., 1954. Pvt. piano tchr. Dir. hand bells First Bapt. Ch., Milledgeville, Ga., pianist for Merri Maker Choir. Mem.: DAR (state curator 1994—96, state hist. 2001—99, state chorus dir. 2002—), Music Tchrs. Nat. Assn., C. of C., U. Ga. (Sigma Lamda chpt., treas. mortar bd.), Milledgeville Music Club (pres. 1968—70), Alpha Omicron Pi, Sigma Alpha Iota. Baptist. Avocations: dance, bridge, reading. Home: 330 Doles Blvd Milledgeville GA 31061 Office Phone: 478-452-1674.

**RAGAN, DAVID,** publishing company executive; b. Jackson, Tenn., Aug. 26, 1925; s. Amos and Esther Lee (Tacker) R.; m. Violet Claire Sills, Dec. 27, 1948; children—David Nathaniel, Sarah Sills, Jennifer Leigh. BA in English, Union U., Jackson, 1947; M. Theatre Arts, Calif. Sch. Theatre, 1950. Radio writer Grand Central Sta., 1950; syndicated columnist Hollywood South Side News, 1951; mng. editor Tele-Views mag., 1952; free-lance writer, 1952-57, 74-77, 82—; editor TV and Movie Screen Sterling Group, Inc., N.Y.C., 1957-61; mng. editor Motion Picture mag. Fawcett Pub. Co., N.Y.C., 1961-64; editor TV Radio Mirror, Macfadden-Bartell Pub. Co., N.Y.C., 1964-71; pub., editorial dir. Movie Digest, Words and Music, Planet mags. Nat. Periodical

Publs. (Warner Communications), N.Y.C., 1971-74; editorial dir. Photoplay, Motion Picture, TV Mirror mags.; Macfadden Women's Group, N.Y.C., 1977-79; entertainment editor Globe Nat. Weekly, N.Y.C., 1979-82. Author: Who's Who in Hollywood 1900-1976, 1977, Movie Stars of the '30s, 1985, Movie Stars of the '40s, 1985, Mel Gibson: An Intimate Biography, 1985, Who's Who in Hollywood: The Largest Cast of Film Personalities Ever Assembled, rev., 1992; co-author: Richard Pryor: This Cat's Got Nine Lives, 1982; contbr. articles to profl. jours. Served with U.S. Army, 1952-54. Mem. Screen Actors Guild, TV Acad., Alpha Tau Omega, Tau Kappa Alpha. Republican. Presbyterian. Home: Landmark Apts Apt 2-M 232 Main St Port Washington NY 11050

**RAGAN, DENNIS M.,** mathematics educator; b. Rusville, Nebr., June 1, 1945; s. Joseph E. and Anne M. Ragan. BSc in Math., Ill. State U., 1966; MA in Math. (Tchg.), San Diego State U., 1971. Cert. Tchr. Ill. Math. tchr. Shabbona HS, Ill., 1966—70, 1972—81, Elgin Acad., Ill., 1971—72, Kishwaukee Coll., Malta, Ill., 1981—. Village trustee Village of Lee, Ill., 1991—; Diabetes state chair Lions of Ill. Found., Sycamore, 1998—. Recipient Kishwaukee Coll. Bd. Trustees award of excellence, Kishwaukee Coll., Malta, 1993; Melvin Jones fellow, Lions Internat. Mem.: Ill. Math. Assn. Cmty. Colls., Ill. Fedn. Tchrs., Am. Fedn. Tchrs., Nat. Coun. Tchrs. Math. (life). Office: Kishwaukee Coll Malta IL 60150

**RAGAN, JAMES THOMAS,** communications executive; b. San Diego, Mar. 15, 1929; m. Susan Held, Nov. 9, 1957; children: James, Maria, Carey, Andrew. BA, Oxford U., Eng., 1951, MA, 1955; elect. engring. vocat. cert., U. State of N.Y., 1954. With Gen. Electric Co., 1954-69; pres., chief operating officer Athena Communications Corp. subs. Gulf & Western Industries, Inc., N.Y.C., 1969-74; v.p. broadcast services Western Union Telegraph Co., 1974-76, v.p. satellite services, 1976-82, pres. Western Union personal communications corp., v.p. communication systems group, 1982-85; pres. Associated Info. Services Corp., 1985-86, Bunting, Inc., 1985-88; ptnr. Pierce Kennedy Hearth, 1988-91; CEO Nat. Lang. Assocs. Lanarea Pub., Guilford, Conn., 1990—. Patentee recreational sports equipment; author: The Ultimate Diet, The First Alaskans, A Guide to the Geography of the Native Languages, Cultures, Their Communities, and Populations, 1996. Pres. Wilton Pop Warner Football League, Wilton, Conn., 1972—73. Maj. USMCR, 1952—54, Korea. Home: PO Box 1112 Green Valley AZ 85622 Office: Nat Lang Assocs PO Box 1112 Green Valley AZ 85622 Office Phone: 520-399-2294. Personal E-mail: jtrnla@aol.com.

**RAGAN, ROBERT ALLISON,** private investment executive, financial consultant; b. Gastonia, N.C., Aug. 21, 1938; s. Caldwell and Jocelyn (Sikes) R. BS in Bus. Adminstrn., U. NC, 1961; postgrad., Rutgers U., 1968. V.p. N.C. Nat. Bank (now Bank of Am.), Charlotte, 1961-81; pres., treas. R.A. Ragan & Co., Inc., Charlotte, 1981—. Dir. Carolina Mills, Inc., Maiden, N.C., 1977—. Author, pub.: The Ragans of Gastonia (1790-1995), 1995, The Textile Heritage of Gaston County, N.C. (1848-2000), 2000. Founder, pres. bd. govs. The Gaston Soc. of Mecklenburg County, Charlotte, NC, 1999—; trustee, bd. visitors Darlington Sch., Rome, Ga., 1981—; mem. bd. visitors Daniel Stowe Bot. Gardens, Belmont, NC, 2001—; pres. bd. trustees Gaston County Mus. Art and History, Dallas, NC, 1978—81, 1997—99. Mem. Charlotte City Club, DeBordieu Colony Country Club (Georgetown, S.C.), Linville (N.C.) Ridge Country Club. Republican. Presbyn. Avocations: preservation and recording of local and North Carolina history, especially industrial history, travel. Home: 227 Fenton Pl Charlotte NC 28207-1913 Office: R A Ragan & Co PO Drawer 6158 Charlotte NC 28207-0001 also: 407 DeBordieu Blvd Georgetown SC 29440 Personal E-mail: robertragan@carolina.rr.com.

**RAGANS, ROSALIND DOROTHY,** writer, artist, retired educator; b. Bklyn., Feb. 28, 1933; d. Sidney Guy Gordon and Beatrice (Zuckerman) Safier; m. John Franklin Ragans, July 31, 1965; 1 child, John Lee. BFA, CUNY-Hunter Coll., 1955; MEd, Ga. So. Coll., 1967; EdD, U. Ga., 1971. Cert. tchr. art, Ga. Tchr. art Union City (N.J.) Bd. Edn., 1956-62; tchr. 1st grade Chatham Bd. Edn., Savannah, Ga., 1962-64; instr. art Ga. So. U., Statesboro, 1964-69, asst. prof., 1969-76, assoc. prof., 1976-89, prof. emeritus, 1989—. Keynote speaker art edn. confs.; presenter in field. Author: (textbooks) ArtTalk, 1988, 4th edit., 2005, Introducing Art, 1997, 2d edit., 2005, Exploring Art, 1990, 3d edit., 2005, Understanding the Arts, 1990, 3d edit., 2005; sr. author Art Connections K-5, 1997, 2d edit., 2000, K-6. 3d edit., 2005 Mem. Nat. Assn. Educators (life), Ga. Assn. Educators (life), Nat. Art Edn. Assn. (Southeastern Art Educator of Yr. 1991, Nat. Art Educator of Yr. 1992), Ga. Art Edn. Assn. (Ga. Art Educator of Yr. 1990), Pilot Club Internat. (Ga. dist., Ga. Profl. Handicapped Woman of Yr. 1988). Jewish. Avocation: painting. E-mail: RozRagans@comcast.net.

**RAGATZ, THOMAS GEORGE,** lawyer; b. Madison, Wis., Feb. 18, 1934; s. Wilmer Leroy and Rosanna (Kindschi) Ragatz; m. Karen Christensen, Dec. 19, 1965; children: Thomas Rolf, William Leslie, Erik Douglas. BBA, U. Wis., 1957, LLB, 1961. CPA Wis.; bar: Wis. 1961, U.S. Dist. Ct. (e.a. and we. dists.) Wis. 1961, U.S. Tax Ct. 1963, U.S. Ct. Appeals (7th cir.) 1965, U.S. Supreme Ct. 1968. Staff acct. Peat, Marwick, Mitchell & Co., Mpls., 1958; instr. Sch. Bus., U. Wis., Madison, 1958-60; formerly lectr. in acctg. and law Law Sch. U. Wis.; law clk. Wis. Supreme Ct., 1961-62; assoc. Boardman Suhr Curry & Field, Madison, 1962-64, ptnr., 1965-78, Foley & Lardner, Madison, 1978—2002, mng. ptnr., 1984-93, chmn. budget com., 1994-99. Bd. dirs. Wolf Appliance Co., LLC, Sub-Zero Freezer Co., Inc., Norman Bassett Found., Wis. Sports Found., United Way Found.; pres. Courtier Found.; bd. dirs., pres. Wis. Sports Devel. Corp.; lectr. seminars on tax subjects. Editor-in-chief Wis. Law Rev., 1960—61, chmn. Nat. Conf. Law Revs., 1960—61; author: The Ragatz History, 1989; contbr. articles to profl. jours. Formerly dir. United Way, Meth. Hosp. Found.; mem. U. Wis. Found.; chmn. site selection com. U. Wis. Hosp. Com.; past pres., past moderator 1st Congl. Ch.; bd. dirs. Found. for Madison Pub. Schs.; pres. Bus. and Edn. Partnership, 1983—89, bd. dirs.; past pres., vice pres. HospiceCare Found.; bd. regents U. Wis., panel provision of legal svcs.; bd. dirs. Met. YMCA, Madison, 1983—90. Fellow: Am. Bar Found.; mem.: ABA, Dane County Bar Assn. (pres. 1978—79, chmn. jud. qualification com.), Wis. Inst. CPAs, State Bar Wis. (sec. 1969—70, bd. govs. 1971—75, chmn. fin. com. 1975—80, chmn. tax sect., chmn. spl. com. on comms., chmn. svcs. for lawyers com.), Wis. Bar Found., Seventh Cir. Bar Assn., Am. Judicature Soc., Order of Constantine, Bascom Hill Soc., Order of Coif, Madison Club (pres. 1980—81), Madison Club House Corp. (pres. 1999—, bd. dirs.), Sigma Chi, Beta Gamma Sigma. Republican. Home: 3334 Lake Mendota Dr Madison WI 53705-1469 Office: Foley & Lardner LLP PO Box 1497 Madison WI 53701-1497 also: Foley & Lardner LLP 1st Wisconsin Ctr 777 E Wisconsin Ave Ste 3800 Milwaukee WI 53202-5302 E-mail: tgragatz@yahoo.com.

**RAGAUSS, PETER A.,** oil industry executive; b. mech. engring., Mich. State U., 1980; MBA, Harvard U., 1987. V.p. corp. devel. Tenneco Energy Inc.; v.p. fin. El Paso Energy Internat. Corp.; v.p. & portfolio mgmt. Amoco Energy Internat.; asst to grp. chief exec. BP plc, 1998; CEO Air BP; segment contr. refining & mktg. BP plc, London, 2003—06; sr. v.p. & CFO Baker Hughes Inc., Houston, 2006—. Office: Baker Hughes Inc 3900 Essex Ln Houston TX 77027-5177 Office Phone: 713-439-8600. Office Fax: 713-439-8699.*

**RAGAVAN, ANPALAKI JEYABALASINKHAM,** software developer, researcher; arrived in U.S., 1992; d. George Nagularajah and Thangaranee Veluppillai Jeyabalasingham; m. Ragavan Vinasithamby, July 1, 1993. BS (hon.), U. Sri Lanka, 1985, MPhil (hon.) in Hydrology, 1989; MS in Hydrogeology (hon.), U. Nev., 1996, MS in Civil Engring., 2003, MS in Math., 2004—, MS in Hydrology, 2005, postgrad, 2000—. Cert. BASIC computer programmer, 1992, Visual Basic programmer, GIS and web design, well drilling with LS 100. Asst. prof. U. Sri Lanka, Kilinochchi, Jaffna, 1989—92; rsch. asst. Ind. State U., Tere Haute, 1992—93; rsch./tchg. asst. U. of Nev., Reno, 1993—96; software developer Bur. Labor Stats., Washington, 1996—99; rsch. asst. U. of Nev., Reno, 1999—. Grad. fellow U. Nev., Reno, 1993—96; presenter in field. Contbr.

articles to profl. jours. (Excellence in Abstract Submission award Am. Jour. Pub. Health, 2001); author: (book) Introductory Statistics, Lab-Guide - SAS, 1st edition., 1993, (Nev. health divsn. quar. report) Impact Of Discharge Planning On Adherence to Treatment for Inmates with HIV/AIDS in Nevada, 2001, Surveillance Update: Discharge Planning For Inmates with HIV/AIDS in Nevada, 2002. Named to Great Women of the 21st Century; recipient Excellence in Abstract Submission, APHA, HIV/AIDS Sect., 2001, Cert. Of Appreciation, Nev. State Mental Health and Devel. Services, 2000, Overseas Devel. administr. scholarship, Govt. Of UK, 1986—89; grantee, State of Nev., 2002; scholar, Asian Inst. Of Tech. in Thailand, 1991, Ind. State U., 1992—93, U. of Nev., Reno, 1993—; Soroptimist Internat. of Reno, Sierra Nev. Region, 2000, Water Resources Assn., 2005, Grad. Student Assn., 2005; Outstanding Grad. Student Rschr. scholar, Grad. Student Assn., U. Nev., Reno, 2006. Mem.: AAAS, Nature Pub. Group, Am. Geophys. Union, Nat. Ground Water Assn., Nev. Water Resources Assn., Am. Math. Soc., Am. Statis. Assn., Geol. Soc. Am., Great Women of the 21st Century (profl. women's adv. bd.), Alumni Assn. U. Nev. (mem. profl. women's adv. bd.). Mem. Lds Ch. Avocations: dance, music, guitar, swimming, sports. Office: U Nev Dept Internal Med Reno NV 89512 Home: 3952 Clear Acre Ln #276 Reno NV 89512-1202 Office Phone: 775-784-4433. Business E-mail: ragavan@unr.edu.

**RAGENT, BORIS,** physicist; b. Cleve., Mar. 2, 1924; s. Samuel and Bertha (Lev) R.; m. Dorothy Kohn, Sept. 11, 1949; children: David Stefan, Lawrence Stanton, Jesse Ron. Student, Ohio State U., 1941—44; BSEE, Marquette U., 1944; PhD in Physics, U. Calif., Berkeley, 1953. Registered profl. engr., Calif. Engr. Victoreen Instrument Co., Cleve., 1946-48; engr., physicist Radiation Lab., U. Calif. Berkeley, 1948-53; physicist Livermore, Calif., 1953-56, Broadview Rsch. Corp., Burlingame, Calif., 1956-59, Vidya divsn. Itek Corp., Palo Alto, Calif., 1959-66, Ames Rsch. Ctr., NASA, Moffett Field, Calif., 1966-87, San Jose (Calif.) State U. Found., 1987-98. Lectr. Stanford U., U. Calif. Ext. Served in USNR, 1944-46. Mem. AAAS, Am. Phys. Soc., Optical Soc. Am., Am. Geophys. Union, Sigma Xi.

**RAGGI, REENA,** federal judge; b. Jersey City, May 11, 1951; BA, Wellesley Coll., 1973; JD cum laude, Harvard U., 1976. Bar: N.Y. 1977, U.S. Dist. Ct. (ea. dist.) N.Y. 1987, U.S. Ct. Appeals (2d cir.) 2002. Law clerk US Ct. of Appeals, 7th Circuit, 1976—77; assoc. Cahill, Gordon & Reindel, NY, 1977—79; asst. U.S. atty. Dept. Justice, Bklyn., 1979—86; ptnr. Windels, Marx, Davies & Ives, N.Y.C., 1986—87; judge U.S. Dist. Ct. (Ea. dist.) N.Y., 1987—2002, U.S. Ct. Appeals (2nd Cir.), N.Y.C., 2002—. Office: US Courthouse 225 Cadman Plz E Brooklyn NY 11201*

**RAGGIO, WILLIAM JOHN,** state legislator; b. Reno, Oct. 30, 1926; s. William John and Clara M. (Cardelli) R.; m. Dorothy Brigman, August 15, 1948 (dec. Apr. 1998); children: Leslie Ann, Tracy Lynn, Mark William. Student, La. Poly. Inst., 1944-45, U. Okla., 1945-46; BA, U. Nev., 1948; JD, U. Calif. at Hastings, 1951. Bar: Nev. 1951, U.S. Supreme Ct. 1959. Atty., Reno and Las Vegas; asst. dist. atty. Washoe County, Nev., 1952-58; dist. atty., 1958-71; ptnr. firm Wiener, Goldwater, Galatz & Raggio, Ltd., 1971-72, Raggio, Walker & Woovster, Reno and Las Vegas, 1974-78, Raggio, Wooster & Lindell, 1978-92; sr. ptnr. Vargas & Bartlett, 1992-98; then Jones-Vargas (formerly Vargas & Bartlett), 1998—; mem. Nev. Senate, Washoe Dist. 3, Carson City, 1973—. Mem. Nev. Senate, 1973—, minority floor leader, 1977-81, 82-87, 91, majority flr. leader, 1987—; mem. legis. commn., vice chmn. criminal law and administrn. com. council State Govts., 1972-75; v.p., dir. Archon Corp. Mem. Nev. Am. Revolutionary Bicentennial Commn., 1975-81; mem. Republican State Cen. Com.; past nat. chmn., current dir. Am. Legislative Exchange Council, dir. Sierra Health Svcs.; republican candidate for U.S. Senate, 1970. Served with USNR, 1944-46; to 2d lt. USMCR, 1946-47. Named Young Man of Yr., Reno-Sparks Jr. C. of C., 1959, Alumnus of Yr. U. Nev. Reno, 2000, Civic Leader of Yr Greater Reno C. of C., Disting. Eagle Scout, 1989; named to Jr. Achievement of Nev. Hall of Fame, 1999, Reg. Trans. Commn. Hall of Fame; recipient Disting. Nevadan award, 1968, Fellows award The Salvation Army, Torch of Liberty award The Anti-Defamation League, SIR award Assoc. Gen. Contractors, 1995, Outstanding Svc. award Airport Authority of Washor County, Pres.'s medal UNLV, 2000. Fellow Am. Bd. Criminal Lawyers; mem. ABA (state chmn. jr. bar conf. 1957-60, ho. dels.) Am. Judicature Soc., Am. Coll. Trail Lawyers, Am. Bd. Trial Advocates, Am. Inns of Ct., Navy League, Air Force Assn., Nat. (nat. pres. 1967-68; named Outstanding Prosecutor 1965) Nev. State (sec. 1959, pres. 1960-63) Dist. Attys. Assn., NCJ (Brotherhood award 1965), Nev. Peace Officers Assn., Internat. Assn. Chiefs Police, Am. Leg. Exch. Coun. (nat. chmn. 1991-92), Coll. of Edn. U. Nev. (life), Am. Legion, Elks, Lion Club, Prospectors Club, Alpha Tau Omega, Phi Alpha Delta. Republican. Roman Catholic. Home: PO Box 281 Reno NV 89504-0281

**RAGHAVAN, ASURI,** construction executive; BSEE, U. Madras; MS in Computer Sci., Temple U. Sr. v.p., pres. equipment divsn. Kulicke & Soffa, until 1998; pres., CEO Gasonics, San Jose, Calif., 1998—.

**RAGHAVAN, DEREK,** oncologist, medical researcher and educator; b. Aug. 11, 1949; came to U.S., 1991; divorced; 2 children. MB, BS with honors, Sydney U., 1974; PhD, London U., 1984. Cert. Royal Australian Coll. Physicians, Fgn. Lic. Exam Coun., Ednl. Coun. Fgn. Med. Grads., Gen. Med. Coun. (U.K.), NSW Med. Bd. (Australia). Resident, registrar Royal Prince Alfred Hosp., Sydney, 1974-77; lectr., sr. registrar Royal Marsden Hosp., London, 1978-80; rsch. fellow Ludwig Inst. Cancer Rsch., London, 1978-80; med. rsch. specialist U. Minn., Mpls., 1980-81; sr. specialist med. oncology Royal Prince Alfred Hosp., Sydney, 1981-91; prof., chief solid tumor oncology and investigational therapeutics Roswell Park Cancer Inst. and RPMI, Buffalo, 1991-97; prof. medicine and urology U. So. Calif., L.A., 1997—2003, chief divsn. med. oncology, 1997—2003, assoc. dir. Norris Cancer Ctr., 1997—2004; prof., dir. Cleve. Clinic Taussig Cancer Ctr., 2004—. Pres. med. staff Roswell Park Cancer Inst., Buffalo, 1995—96; mem. oncology drug adv. com. FDA, 1996—2000; mem. cancer ctrs. support rev. com. Nat. Cancer Inst., 2000—; prof. medicine SUNY, Buffalo, 1991—97, prof. urology, 1996—97; assoc. dir. U. So. Calif.-Norris Cancer Ctr. U. So. Calif., 1997—2003; mem. sci. adv. bd. Southwest Oncology Group, 1998—2005, bd. govs., 1998—2004, vice chair genitourinary com., 1998—2006; vice chair genitouring cancer com. Radiation Therapy Oncology Group, 1995—97; mem. sci. adv. com. European Orgn. for Rsch. and Treatment of Cancer, 2000—, mem. external sci. audit com., 2001—; mem. external adv. bd. Comprehensive Cancer Ctr. U. Ala., Birmingham, 2002—04; mem. external sci. bd. Ohio State U. James Comprehensive Cancer Ctr., 2002—; mem. clin. trials and awards adv. com. Cancer Rsch. UK, 2002—06. Editor: The Management of Bladder Cancer, 1988, Textbook of Uncommon Cancer, 1988, 3d edit. 2006, Principles and Practice of Genitourinary Oncology, 1997, ACS Atlas of Clinical Oncology-Germ Cell Tumors, 2002, Fast Facts: Bladder Cancer, 2006; assoc. editor Urologic Oncology, 1995—, Clin. Cancer Rsch., 1996—; mem. editl. bd. Jour. Clin. Oncology, 1990-94, 2006—, European Jour. Cancer, The Prostate, The Breast, Prostate Cancer, Advances in Oncology, Abstracts in Hematology and Oncology, 1998-2000; mem. editl. bd. Oncology; bd. cons. Jour. Urology, 1996—; contbr. numerous articles to profl. jours. Rsch. grantee Nat. Health amd Med. Rsch. Coun., Australia, 1983-90; traveling fellow NSW Cancer Coun., Sydney, 1978; named Hospice Physician of Yr., Hospice of Buffalo, 1994. Fellow: ACP (MKSAP XI com. 1997—98, sci. program com. 2000), Royal Australian Coll. Physicians (chair specialist adv. com. in med. oncology 1988—90); mem.: Sydney U. Med. Soc. (pres. 1974), Med. Oncology Group Australia (chmn. 1988—90), Soc. Urologic Oncology, Am. Assn. Cancer Rsch., Am. Soc. Clin. Oncology (liaison mem. joint com. on cancer 1995—2000, AJCC liaison 1995—2000, chair cancer comms. com. 1998—2000, program com. 1999—2000, mem. pub. issues com. 2000—02, chair Diversity Working Party 2006—, assoc. editor People Living With Cancer Website). Avocations: tennis, squash. Office: Cleve Clinic Taussig Cancer Ctr Euclid Ave Cleveland OH 44195 Office Phone: 216-445-6888.

**RAGHAVAN, PRABHAKAR,** Internet company executive; BSEE, Indian Inst. of Tech., Madras, India; PhD in Computer Sci., U. Calif. Berkeley. Several managerial and technical positions IBM, 1986—2000; with IBM, T.J. Watson Rsch. Ctr., 1986—94; former head, computer science principles dept., rschr. IBM, Almaden Rsch. Ctr., San Jose, Calif., 1995; chief scientist, v.p. emerging technologies Verity, Inc., Sunnyvale, Calif., 2000—01, v.p., chief technology officer, 2001—04, sr. v.p., chief technology officer, 2004—05; head rsch. Yahoo, Inc., Sunnyvale, Calif., 2005—. Taught at Yale; currently consulting prof., computer sci. Stanford U.; mem. Nat. Sci. Found. panels; v.p. cons. svcs. Cardiff, NCR; lectr. in field. Editor-in-chief Journal of Assn. for Computing Machinery, mem. editl. bd. Internat. Mathematics, SIAM Journal of Computing; co-author (with R. Motwani): Randomized Algorithms; author: Making Connections, 2003, Not A Small World After All, 2003; contbr. articles to profl. jours. Mem. adv. bds. of several leading universities. Fellow: IEEE, Assn. for Computing Machinery (mem. spl. interest group algorithms and computation, mem. exec. bd.). Achievements include patents in field. Office: Yahoo Inc 701 First Avenue Sunnyvale CA 94089

**RAGHAVAN, SIVAKUMAR,** food scientist; s. Raghavan; m. Mahalakshmi Vasan. BS in Food and Fermentation, U. Dept. Chem. Tech., Mumbai, India, 2000; BS in Chemistry, U. Madras, India, 1997; D, U. Mass., Amherst, 2004. Cert. hazard analysis and critical control pt. Rsch. assoc. U. Wis., Madison, 2004—05, U. Fla., Gainesville, 2005—. Contbr. articles to profl. jours. Mem.: Sigma Xi, Inst. Food Tech., Am. Oil Chemists Soc. (member-at-large 2005—). Achievements include research in lipid and protein chemistry. Office: University of Florida 359 FSHN Building Newell Drive Gainesville FL 32611 Office Phone: 352-392-1991 ext. 501. Personal E-mail: siva.kr@gmail.com. Business E-mail: siva2000@ufl.edu.

**RAGHAVAN, SUDHEER,** hotel executive; b. Singapore; MS, Cranfield Inst. Tech. Various postions including jr. exec., and sr. v.p. cargo co. Singapore Airlines, 1981—2005, corp. v.p. worldwide revenue mgmt., v.p. Singapore, v.p. ea. U.S. and S.Am. region; pres. Millennium Hotels and Resorts, 2005—. Avocation: reading. Office: Millennium Hotels and Resorts 145 W 44th St New York NY 10036

**RAGHEB, SAMIA,** immunologist, educator; d. Shafik and Carmen Ragheb. BA, U. Pa., Phila., 1980; PhD, Wayne State U., Detroit, 1988. Post-doctoral fellow Wayne State U., Detroit, 1988—92, asst. prof. neurology, 1992—, assoc. immunology and microbiology, 1993—. Contbr. articles to profl. jours. Interviewer U. Pa. alumni secondary sch. com. network U. Pa., Phila., 2004—06. Osserman Rsch. fellow, Myasthenia Gravis Found., 1992. Mem.: Am. Assn. Immunologists. Avocations: travel, cooking, gardening.

**RAGHUNATHAN, PRATIMA LALITA,** epidemiologist; b. Gainesville, Fla. d. Y. and Sita L. Raghunathan. BS summa cum laude, Yale Coll., New Haven, Conn., 1989; MPH, U. Calif., Berkeley, 1998; PhD, U. Calif., San Francisco, 1997. Epidemiologist Ctrs. Disease Control and Prevention, Atlanta, 2002—04, country dir. Mutengene, Southwest Province, Cameroon 2004—. Exec. dir., co-founder Sustainable Scis. Inst., San Francisco, 1998—2000. Comdr. US Pub. Health Svc., 2000. Recipient Paul C. Schnitker Internat. Health award, Ctrs. Disease Control and Prevention, 2003; Predoctoral fellow, Howard Hughes Med. Inst., 1990—95. Mem.: AAAS, Am. Soc. Tropical Medicine and Hygiene. Office: Ctrs Disease Control and Prevention Buea Rd Southwest Province Mutengene Cameroon Office Phone: 237 335 1691.

**RAGINSKY, NINA,** artist; d. Bernard Boris and Helen Theresa R.; 1 child, Sofya Katrina. BA, Rutgers U., 1962; studied painting with, Roy Lichtenstein; studied sculpture with, George Segal; studied Art History with Allan Kaprow, Rutgers U. Freelance photographer Nat. Film Bd., Ottawa, Ont., Canada, 1963-81; instr. metaphysics Emily Car Coll. Art, Vancouver, B.C., Canada, 1973-81; painter Salt Spring Island, B.C., 1989—. Sr. artist, jury Can. Coun.; selected Can. rep. in Sweden for Sweden Now Mag., 1979; tchr., lectr. in field, 1973—. One woman shows include Vancouver Art Gallery, Victoria Art Gallery, Edmonton Art Gallery, Art Gallery Ont., San Francisco Mus. Art, Acadia U., Nancy Hoffman Gallery, N.Y.C., Meml. U. Newfoundland Art Gallery; exhibited in group shows at Rutgers U., 1962, Montreal Mus. Fine Arts, 1963, Nat. Film Bd., Ottawa, 1964, 65, 67, 70, 71, 76, 77, Internat. Salon Photography, Bordeaux, France, 1968, Nat. Gallery Ottawa, 1968, Eastman House, Rochester, N.Y., 1969, Vancouver Art Gallery, 1973, 80, Mural for Conf. Ctr. Ottawa, 1973, Field Mus., Chgo., 1976, Edmonton Art Gallery, 1978, 79, Walter Philips Gallery, 1979, Glenbow Mus. Gallery, 1979, Harbour Front Community Gallery, 1980, Hamilton Art Gallery, 1980, Musée Maisil de St. Lambert, 1981, Mendel Art Gallery, 1981, Dunlop Art Gallery, Regina, Can., 1981, Vancouver Art Gallery, 2001; represented in permanent collections Nat. Film Bd. Stills divsn., Ottawa, Ont., Banff (Alta.) Sch. Fine Arts, Nat Gallery Ottawa, Can., George Eastman House, Rochester, NY, Wadsworth Atheneum, Conn., Edmonton Art Gallery, U. Victoria, B.C., various pvt. collections. Bd. dirs. Island Watch, Salt Spring Island, B.C., 1993; founder, coord. Salt Spring Island Ecosys. Stewardship Project, 1993; founder, coord. Salt Spring Island Waterbird Watch Collective, 1994—. Decorated officer Order of Can.; 1984; recipient Kees Vermeer award for edn. and conservation Simon Fraser U., 1997, Burns Bog award for environ. excellence, Vancouver, 2005. Mem.: Soc. for Advancement of Slow, Royal Can. Acad. Arts. Avocations: gardening, birding, subject of numerous publs. Home and Office: 272 Beddis Rd Salt Spring Island BC Canada V8K 2J1

**RAGLAND, GEORGE A.,** lawyer; b. Charleston, W.Va., May 14, 1943; BS, U. Va., 1965; LLB cum laude, Washington & Lee U., 1968. Bar: NC 1978. With Wachovia Bank & Trust Co., Winston-Salem, NC, 1968—78; mem. Womble Carlyle Sandridge & Rice PLLC Winston-Salem, trust & estate practice group leader. Fellow Am. Coll. Trust and Estate Counsel; mem. ABA, NC Bar Assn. (chair estate planning and fiduciary law sect., 1990-91), Forsyth County Bar Assn., Phi Delta Phi. Office: Womble Carlyle Sandridge & Rice PLLC PO Box 84 Winston Salem NC 27102 Office Phone: 336-721-3646. Office Fax: 336-733-8401. Business E-mail: gragland@wcsr.com.

**RAGLAND, JACK WHITNEY,** artist; b. El Monte, Calif., Feb. 25, 1938; s. Jack Rider and Dorsey (Whitney) R.; m. Marilee J. Weaver, July 31, 1969; children— Roxanne, Natasha. BA, Ariz. State U., 1960, MA, 1964; postgrad., UCLA, 1961-64. Grad. asst. tchr. Ariz. State U., 1960-61; grad. teaching asst. UCLA, 1961-64; head art dept. Simpson Coll., Indianola, Iowa, 1964-76. Demonstrator Nat. Art Materials Trade Assn., Denver, 1993, Pasadena Conv. Ctr., 1994 One-man shows include Kleine Gallery, Vienna, Austria, Simpson Coll., Internat. Art Svc., Pan Paciific Hotel, San Diego, Lakes Art Ctr., Okaboji, Iowa, Hilltop Ctr., Fallbrook, 1996-98, Desert Art Source Gallery, 1999-2006; exhibited in group shows, Lyn Kottler Gallery, N.Y.C., Phoenix Art Mus., Tucson Festival Art, Talisman Gallery, Bartlesville, Okla., Exhibiting Artists Fedn., Poultney, Vt., Des Moines Art Center, Joslyn Mus. Art, Omaha, Lagerquist Gallery, Atlanta, Desert Art Source Gallery, Palm Desert, Calif., Desert Pleine Air Show, La Quinta, Calif., San Diego, NAMTA Art Show, San Francisco 1995, Christian Art Show Jubilee 2000, 04, Fall Brook, Calif., Pleine Air Show San Diego/Calif. Art Club, La Quinta Festival, 2000, Eagle Gallery, La Jolla, Galerie Internat., Solana Beach, Calif., Encouragment Gallery, Fallbrook, Calif., Show Case Houses, Pasadena, Rancho Santa Fe, Calif., 1995, 96, Palm Springs Paradise, 2000, San Diego, 97, 98, 99, French Gallery, Fallbrook, 2005, Monarch Gallery, La Jolla, 2005; represented in permanent collections, Albertina Museum, Vienna, Kunstmus., Basel, Switzerland, Bibliothèque National, Paris, Los Angeles County Mus., Simpson Coll., Phoenix Art Mus., Ariz. State collection, Graphische Bundes Versuchsanstalt, Vienna, Austria, Equitable ns. Co., Des Moines, also pvt. collections, works include stained glass windows, Meth. Ch., Perry, Iowa.; works reproduced Applause mag. 1971, New Woman mag, 1974, Artists of Cen. and No. Calif., Vol. II, San Diego Better Homes and Gardens Lifestyles mag., 1995, San Diego Decorating mag., 1995, 98, Pasadena Showcase House Design Mag., 1995, San Diego Decor and Style, 1996, 97, 98, Sci. of Mind Mag., 1997, Desert Art Scene Mag., 1999-; poster artist Vintage Car Show,

Fallbrook, 2003-. Selected for Calif. State Fair, Sacramento, 2005, recipient grand purchase prize Ariz. Ann. Art Show, 1961, 1st prize in prints Iowa State Fair, 1974, 1st prize So. Calif. Expn., Del Mar, 1984, 1st prize Fall Brook Art Assn., 2000, Best of Show, 2003, 1st prize San Diego County Fair, 2005, 3rd prize, Best of Show, 1st, 3d, hon. mention, 2006, others; featured in Am. Artist mag. Oct. 1993, San Diego Decor and Style mag. June 2005. Mem. Calif. Art Club. Home and Office: 5555 8th St Fallbrook CA 92028-9619 Office Phone: 760-728-9503. E-mail: jwragland@aol.com, jackragland@sbcglobal.net.

**RAGLAND, ROBERT ALLEN,** lawyer; b. Bartlesville, Okla., Apr. 18, 1954; s. Thomas Martin and Joan Ethel (Murphy) R. BA, U. Md., 1976; JD, George Mason Sch. of Law, 1980. Dir. regulatory reform and govt. orgn. Nat. Assn. Mfrs., Washington, 1979-82, asst. v.p. taxation, 1983-86; mgr. congl. rels. The Clorox Co., Oakland, Calif., 1982-83; dir. tax rsch. U.S. C. of C., Washington, 1988-93; v.p., officer Wachovia Bank, 1995—2004; v.p. Sun-Trust Bank, Orlando, Fla., 2004—05, Fifth Third Bank, Cin., 2006—. Chief tax counsel, mng. dir. Nat. Chamber Found., Washington, 1989-93. Author: Transportation Reform, 1980, Employee Stock Ownership Plans, 1989, Taxation of Foreign Source Income, Distributional Impact of Excise Taxes, 1990; editor Taxation of Intercorporate Profits, 1990, Jour. Regulation and Social Costs, 1992-93, Jour. Regulation, 1992-93. Active Boy Scouts Am., Washington, 1967—, bd. dirs. nat. capital area coun.; dep. dir. duPont for Pres., 1987-88; v.p. Nat. Chamber Found. U.S. C. of C., 1989-93, dir., Liz Lerman Dance Exchange, 1993-2001, dir. Our House, Inc., 1988-2000. Republican. Roman Catholic. Home: The Waverly 803 322 E Central Blvd Orlando FL 32801

**RAGLAND, WILLIAM MCKENZIE, JR.,** lawyer, real estate developer; b. Raleigh, N.C., Feb. 12, 1960; s. William McKenzie and Elizabeth White (Johnson) R. AB, U. N.C., 1982; JD, U. Va., 1986. Bar: Ga. 1986, D.C. 1987, U.S. Dist. Ct. (no. dist.) Ga. 1987, U.S. Dist. Ct. Calif. (no. dist.) 1987, U.S. Ct. Appeals (11th cir.) 1987, U.S. Ct. Appeals (D.C. and Fed. cirs.) 1990, U.S. Supreme Ct. 1990. Staff asst. Com. on Commerce, Sci. and Transp., U.S. Senate, Washington, 1982-83; legis. asst. U.S. Rep. Jim Cooper, Washington, 1983; assoc. Powell, Goldstein, Frazer & Murphy, Atlanta, 1986—. Faculty Atlanta Coll. of Trial Advocacy, 1994—. Sr. editor Jour. of Law and Politics, 1984-86; contbr. articles to profl. publs. Mem. ABA, State Bar Ga. (cofounder products liability sect.), Fed. Cir. Bar Assn., Atlanta Bar Assn. (vice-chmn./chmn.-elect 1997-98, sec./treas. 1996, dir.—, litigation sect., bd. dirs. 1997—, trustee 1997—), D.C. Bar Assn., Am. Inns. Ct. Episcopalian. Home: 2 Albemarle Dr NW Atlanta GA 30327-1856

**RAGO, ANN D'AMICO,** academic administrator, public relations executive; b. Pitts., Aug. 24, 1957; d. Jack and Florence D'Amico; m. John Rago; children: Annie J., Emily J., John Henry. BA, Duquesne U., Pitts., 1979, MA, 1987. From comm. assoc. to dir. pub. rels. Duquesne U., 1979—89, coord. univ. rels., 1989—93, adj. prof. comm., 1990—2000, exec. dir. pub. affairs, 1993—2002; v.p. instnl. rels. Carlow Coll., Pitts., 2002—. Editor University Record, 1989 (silver medal). Bd. dirs. Support, Pitts. 1989-91; sch. dir. Carylnton Sch. Bd., Pitts., 1989-93, pres. sch. bd., 1990. Recipient Gold award for publs./external prospectus 9th Ann. Admissions Advt. Awards, 1994, Gold award for Total Pub. Rels. Campaign, 10th Ann. Admissions Advt. Awards, 1995, Gold award for Total Pub. Rels. Campaign, 11th Ann. Admissions Awards, 1996, 1st Place award in Category 35, Internal Pub. Rels. Campaign, Pitts. chpt. Women in Comm., Inc., 1996, Bronze Cert. for logo and letterhead for Duquesne U.'s Capital Campaign and cert. merit for Duquesne U.'s internal publ. 14th Ann. Admissions Advt. Awards, 1998, Clarion award Assn. for Women in Communications, 2003. Mem. Pub. Rels. Soc. Am. (1st place award 1993), Internat. Assn. Bus. Communicators (award of excellence 1991, award of honor 1993, award of merit 1994), Am. Mgmt. Assn., Assn. for Women in Comm. (Clarion award 2003), Press Club Western Pa., Sigma Delta Chi. Office: Carlow Coll Institutional Relations 3333 Fifth Ave Pittsburgh PA 15213 Office Phone: 412-578-2090. Personal E-mail: adr824@aol.com. Business E-mail: arago@carlow.edu.

**RAGON, ROBERT RONALD,** clergyman; b. Flintstone, Ga., Sept. 10, 1939; s. Robert Emmett and Frances Cora (Stoner) R.; m. Judith Ann Ward, Apr. 27, 1962; children: Ronald Russell, Regina Renee. BS, U. Chattanooga, 1962; BDiv, MDiv, Columbia Theol. Sem., Decatur, Ga., 1967. Ordained to ministry Presbyn. Ch., 1967. Pastor Trion (Ga.) Presbyn. Ch., 1967-72; dir. pastor Chattooga County Presbyn. Ministries, Trion, 1971-72; pastor Brainerd Presbyn. Ch., Chattanooga, 1972—. Moderator Knoxville Presbytery, 1979-80; founder An Order of Slaves of Christ, Chattanooga, 1970; stated clk. Presbytery of S.E., 1990-93, moderator, 1995-96. Author: Covenant Agreement: O.S.C., 1970, The Journey, 1990. Trustee King Coll., Bristol, Tenn., 1983-86. Mem. Masons (Ga. chaplain 1980), KT (sec. 1991), Shriners, Kiwanis (bd. dirs. Chattanooga 1986-90). Republican. Presbyterian. Avocation: investments. Home: 4229 Happy Valley Rd Flintstone GA 30725-2222 Office: Brainerd Presbyterian Church 1624 Jenkins Rd Chattanooga TN 37421-3249 Office Phone: 423-899-2424. E-mail: rjragon@earthlink.net.

**RAGONE, DAVID VINCENT,** former university president; b. NYC, May 16, 1930; s. Armando Frederick and Mary (Napier) R.; m. Katherine H. Spaulding, Dec. 18, 1954; children: Christine M., Peter V. BS, MIT, 1951, MS, 1952, DSc, 1953. Asst. prof. chem. and metall. engring. U. Mich., Ann Arbor, 1953-57, assoc. prof., 1957-61, prof., 1961-62; asst. dir. John J. Hopkins Lab. for Pure and Applied Sci., also chmn. metallurgy dept. Gen. Atomic divsn. Gen. Dynamics, La Jolla, 1962-67; Alcoa prof. metallurgy Carnegie-Mellon U., Pitts., 1967-69; assoc. dean Sch. Urban and Pub. Affairs, 1969-70; dean Thayer Sch. Engring. Dartmouth Coll., 1970-72; dean Coll. Engring. U. Mich., 1972-80; pres. Case Western Res. U., Cleve., 1980-87; vis. prof. dept. materials sci. and engring. MIT Cambridge, 1987 88, dir. instit. dept. materials sci. and engring., 1988-98; gen. ptnr. Ampersand Ventures, 1988-92, ptnr., 1992—2006. Mem. Nat. Sci. Bd., 1978-84; mem. tech adv. bd. US Dept. Commerce, 1967-75; chmn. adv. com. advanced auto power systems Coun. on Environ. Quality, 1971-75; trustee Henry Luce Found. Named Outstanding Young Engr., Engring. Soc. Detroit, 1957. Mem. Univ. Club (NYC), Longwood Cricket Club (Boston), Sigma Xi, Tau Beta Pi. Business E-mail: ragone@mit.edu.

**RAGONE, TARA ADAMS,** lawyer; b. Paterson, NJ, Apr. 24, 1974; d. John Joseph and Maryellen Adams; m. Alexander B. Ragone, July 6, 1996; children: Elisabeth Alexandra, Evan Philip, Claire May. BA, Coll. William and Mary, Williamsburg, Va., 1996; JD, NYU, NYC, 2001. Bar: NJ 2001, NY 2002. Rsch. assist. Brookings Instn., Washington, 1996—99; law clerk US Ct. (ea. cir. NY), Bklyn., 2001—02, US Ct. Appeals (2d cir.), NYC, 2002—03; dep. atty. gen. State N.J., 2003—. Contbr. articles in field. Office Phone: 973-648-7093.

**RAGSDALE, FRANK WAYNE,** voice educator, singer; b. Dallas, Dec. 10, 1965; s. Dorothy Joyce Goodall and Dannie Murle Ragsdale, Ronald Goodall (Stepfather) and Lynda Ragsdale (Stepmother). MusB, Atlantic Union Coll., South Lancaster, Mass. (Hons) MusM, Longy Sch. of Music, Cambridge, Mass., 1994; D in Mus. Arts, U. Miami, Fla., 2004. Asst. prof. of voice Columbia Union Coll., Takoma Park, Md. 1994—98, Oklahoma City U., 2004—; tchg. asst. U. Miami, Coral Gables, Fla., 2001—04. Young artist studio mgr. Fla. Grand Opera, Coral Gables, 1999—2001; dramatic interpretation coach U. of Miami in Salzburg, Salzburg, Austria, 2003—; performer in venues including Carnegie Hall, N.Y., Avery Fischer Hall, N.Y., Cairo Opera House, Notre Dame, Paris and Martin-in-the-Fields, London. Singer (rodolfo): (opera) La Boheme; singer: (alfredo) La Traviata; singer: (don ottavio) Don Giovanni; singer: (garrison) Walker; singer: (tony) (musical) West Side Story. Mem.: Coll. Music Soc., Nat. Assn. of Teachers of Singing, Pi Kappa Lambda (hon.). D-Liberal. Achievements include research in belting and nonclassical styles of singing. Avocations: cooking, reading, exercise. Home: 249 NW Eubanks St Oklahoma City OK 73118 Office: Oklahoma City University 2501 North Backkwelder Oklahoma City OK 73106 Office Phone: 405-208-5297. Office Fax: 405-521-5971. Personal E-mail: frankragsdale@cox.net. E-mail: fragsdale@okcu.edu.

**RAGUSA, ELYSIA,** real estate company executive; V.p. Lincoln Property Co.; pres. S.W. corp. svcs. The Staubach Co., Addison, Tex., pres., COO. Grad. Leadership Dallas; assoc. mem. Dallas Citizens Coun.; bd. dirs. Dallas County C.C. Found., Vis. Nurse Assn.; bd. mem. United Way Met. Dallas, former chmn. ctrl. budget com., former mem. exec. com. Mem.: Internat. Women's Forum, Dallas Breakfast Group. Office: The Staubach Co Ste 400 15601 Dallas Pkwy Addison TX 75001

**RAHALL, NICK JOE, II, (NICK RAHALL),** congressman; b. Beckley, W.Va., May 20, 1949; s. N. Joe and Alice Rahall; m. Melinda Ross; children: Rebecca Ashley, Nick Joe III, Suzanne Nicole. BA, Duke U., 1971. Asst. Staff of US Senator Robert C. Byrd, 1971-74; sales rep. Sta. WWNR, Beckley, 1974; pres. Mountaineer Travel Co., Beckley, 1975-77, W.Va. Broadcasting, 1980; mem. US Congress from 3rd W.Va. dist., 1977—, ranking mem. resources com., mem. transp. and infrastructure com. Bd. dirs. Rahall Comm. Corpn.; served on US Constn. Bicentennial Commn. of Mo. Del. Dem. Nat. Conv., 1972, 74, 78, 80, 84, 88, 92, 96; W.Va. chmn. March of Dimes, 1979; mem. profl. adv. bd. Alsac-St. Jude Children's Rsch. Hosp. Named Young Man of Yr. Beckley Jaycees, 1972; Outstanding Young Man in W.Va. W.Va. Jaycees, 1977; recipient Achievement award Logan Cripple Children Soc., 1978; Citizenship award KC, 1978, Disting. Svc. award Am. Fedn. Govt. Employees W.Va., 1984, Young Dem. of Yr. Dem. Nat. Conv., 1980, Outfitter of Yr. Profl. Outfitters, 1987, Seneca award Sierra Club, 1988, River Conservation award Am. River, 1988; named Coal Man of Yr. Coal Industry News, 1979, W.Va. Son of Yr., W.Va. Soc. of Washington, 1996. Mem. NAACP, NRA (life), Elks, Moose, Masons (33rd degree) Shriners. Democrat. Presbyterian. Office: US Ho Reps 2307 Rayburn Ho Office Bldg Washington DC 20515-4803 Office Phone: 202-225-3452.*

**RAHARINAIVO, ANDRÉ LÉON,** research scientist, educator; b. Tananarive, Madagascar, Sept. 1, 1940; arrived in France, 1954; s. Ignace Léon and Marthe (Rasoazanamalala) R.; m. Christiane Martine Laurent, May 7, 1966 (div. June 1994); 1 child, Jacques Yves. Engr. mining and metallurgy, Ecole des Mines, Nancy, France, 1964; degree superior scientific studies, U. Nancy, France, 1964; PhD, U. Compiegne, France, 1982. Cert. engr. Head sect. Lab. Ctrl. Ponts et Chaussées, Paris, 1971-80, dep. head dept., 1980-83, sec. sci. coun., 1983-91, rsch. mgr., 1991—. Prof. U. Paris-Sud, Orsay, France, 1981; lectr. Ecole Nat. Ponts et Chaussées, Paris, 1977. Author: Fracture Mechanics and Mechanisms, 1990; patentee in field. Capt. Equipment, 1967-69, France. Mem. Cir. Français Anticorrosion, Nat. Assn. Corrosion Engrs. Avocation: singing gospel music. Home: 378 rue de Vaugirard F-75015 Paris France E-mail: andraha@aol.com.

**RAHE, MARIBETH SEMBACH,** investment management executive; b. Evanston, Ill., Oct. 3, 1948; d. Daniel F. and Boysie (Beebe) Sembach; m. Martin E. Rahe, May 31, 1975. BA, Bowling Green State U., 1970; postgrad., Ohio State U., 1970—72; MBA, Thunderbird Garvin Grad. Sch. Internat. Mgmt., 1974. Internat. banking officer Harris Bank, Chgo., 1974-77, asst. v.p. London, 1977-80; v.p. Morgan Guaranty Trust Co., London, 1980-83, N.Y.C., 1983-84; sr. rep. Sparebanken Oslo Akershus, N.Y.C., 1984-85; v.p. Morgan Guaranty Trust Co., N.Y.C., 1985-87, J.P. Morgan Investment Mgmt., N.Y.C., 1987-88; sr. v.p. Harris Bank, Chgo., 1988-91, dept. exec., 1991-94, sr. exec. v.p., 1994-95, vice chmn. bd., 1995-97; vice chmn. U.S. Trust Co. N.Y. 1997—2001, pres., 2001—02; pres., CEO Fort Washington Investment Advisors, Cin., 2003—. Bd. dirs. N.Y. Landmark Conservancy, Rush Presbyn. Hosp., Nat. Trust, Thunderbird Garvin Grad. Sch. Internat. Mgmt.; com. 200 Found. Bd.; mem. investment oversight com. United Way; mem. Fin. Svcs. Roundtable, The Chgo. Network, Women's Forum, Inc. Recipient Outstanding Alumni award, Thunderbird Garvin Am. Grad. Sch., 1991. Mem.: Chgo. Women's Network, Econ. Club N.Y., Econ. Club Chgo., Am. Bankers Assn., Univ. Club, Queen City Club, Chgo. Club, Republican. Lutheran. Office Phone: 513-361-7619. Business E-Mail: maribeth.rahe@fortwashington.com.

**RAHER, PATRICK MICHAEL,** lawyer; b. Kalamazoo, Mich., June 15, 1947; BBA, U. Notre Dame, 1969; JD, Georgetown U., 1972. Bar: Va. 1972, D.C. 1973. Prof. legal rsch. and creditors rights Internat. Sch. Law, Washington, 1972-75; law clk. to Hon. Roger Robb U.S. Ct. Appeals, Washington, 1972-73; ptnr. Hogan & Hartson LLP, Washington, environ. practice group dir. Vice chair DC Jud. Disabilities and Tenure Commn., 1986-92; mem. EPA Clean Air Act Adv. Com., 1994—. Mem. ABA, DC Bar. Office: Hogan & Hartson LLP Columbia Sq 555 13th St NW 13E-300 Washington DC 20004-1161 Office Phone: 202-637-5682. Office Fax: 202-637-5910. Business E-Mail: pmraher@hhlaw.com.

**RAHHAL, DONALD K.,** obstetrician, gynecologist; b. Clinton, Oklahoma, 1942; MD, U. Okla., 1971. Diplomate Am. Bd. Ob., Gyn. (bd. dir. 1992-2000). Resident Ind. U. Hosp., Indpls., 1971-74; ob-gyn Mercy Health Ctr., Okla. City, 1981—, chief of staff, 2003; ob-gyn Deaconess Hosp., Okla. City, 1981—; clin. prof. U. Okla. Coll. Medicine, Okla. City, 1981—. Mem. ACOG, AMA. Office: 4140 W Memorial Rd Ste 500 Oklahoma City OK 73120-8376

**RAHIMAN, KARLA MOLINA,** school counselor; b. Escondido, Calif., June 5, 1975; d. Baltasar and Estela Molina; m. Feroz Rahiman, Dec. 18, 1999. BS in Psychology with honors, U. LaVerne, Calif., 1997; EdM with credential in Counseling, Azusa Pacific U., Calif., 2000. Prog. coord. children and youth Foothill Cmty. Mental Health, Glendora, Calif., 1996—99; therapist Rsch. and Treatment Ctr., Claremont, 1999—2000; sch. counselor East Whittier City Sch. Dist., 2000—. Poet: Across the Universe, 1996. Mentor deaf and hard of hearing divsn. Catholic Big Brothers Big Sisters, L.A., 2004—. Recipient Chula Vista's Young Woman of Yr., 1993, San Diego Young Woman of Yr., 1993; Presidential scholar, U. LaVerne, 1993. Mem.: Nat. Assn. Sch. Psychologists, Psi Chi. Avocations: crocheting, scrapbooks. Office: E Whittier City Sch Dist 14535 E Whittier Blvd Whittier CA 90605

**RAHM, SUSAN BERKMAN,** lawyer; b. Pitts., June 25, 1943; d. Allen Hugh and Selma (Wiener) Berkman; m. David Alan Rahm, Nov. 23, 1972; children: Katherine, William. BA with honors, Wellesley Coll., 1965; postgrad., Harvard U., 1966-68; JD, NYU, 1973. Bar: N.Y. 1974, D.C. 1988. Assoc. Marshall, Bratter, Greene, Allison & Tucker, N.Y.C., 1973-81, ptnr., 1981-82, Kaye Scholer LLP, NYC, 1982—2005, ptnr, chair real estate dept., 1993—98, chair internat. practice group, 1999—2005. N.Y. adv. bd., Chgo. Title Ins. Co., 1995. Editor: New York Real Property Service, 1987. Bd. dirs. Girls Inc., 1989-93; mem. aux. bd. Mt. Sinai Hosp., N.Y.C., 1976-78. Recipient cert. of outstanding svc. D.C. Redevel. Land Agy., 1969, She Knows Where She's Going award Girls' Clubs of Am., 1987, Woman of Yr. award CREW.NY, 1999 Mem. ABA, Assn. Bar City N.Y., N.Y. Bar Assn. (real property law com., co-chmn. real-estate devel. 1987-91), Am. Coll. Real Estate Lawyers, WX formerly known as Comml. Real Estate Women N.Y. (bd. dirs. 1988-94, v.p. 1988-91, pres. 1991-93), Assn. Fgn. Investors in Real Estate, Assn. Real Estate Women (Outstanding Achievement award 2003). Office: Kaye Scholer LLP 425 Park Ave New York NY 10022-3506

**RAHMAN, ABU TAYEB RAFIQUR,** former United Nations official; b. Ashrafpur, Feni, Bangladesh, July 1, 1936; came to U.S., 1958; s. Abidur Rahman and Fatima Begum; m. Saleha Choudhury, Sept. l, 1963; children: Farhana, Tamanna, Nashra. M Polit. Sci., Dacca U., 1956; MPA, Karachi U., 1958; PhD, Duke U., 1969. Expert in pub. adminstrn. Rural Devel. Acad. Comilla, Bangladesh; assoc. prof. polit. sci. Dacca U., Bangladesh, 1969-71; assoc. dir. Internat. Rsch. Ctr., Ottawa, Ont., Can., 1971-80. sr. cons., 1971-72; sr. econ. affairs officer devel. adminstrn. div. UN, NYC, 1981-88, former chief div., now consultant, div. of governance, public. admin. & fin. Now adjunct prof. Baruch Coll., John Jay Coll. of Criminal Justice; guest lecturer Harvard Inst. of Internat. Develop. Pres. Bangladesh-Can. Soc., Ottawa, 1976, Deshantari Community Group, Ottawa, 1977. Mem. Bangladesh Polit. Sci. Assn., Bangladesh Devel. Forum, East Pakistan Polit. Sci. Assn. (sec. 1970).

**RAHMAN, MUHAMMAD ABDUR,** mechanical engineer; b. Sylhet, Assam, India, Mar. 1, 1930; came to U.S., 1950; s. Haji Sajjad Ali Khan and Momotaj Khanom. BSME, U. Toledo, 1953, MSME, 1968; PhD in Engring., Calif. Coast U., 1985. Registered profl. engr., Calif. Mech. design engr. various cons. firms, L.A., 1955-61; aerospace engr. Douglas Aircraft Co., Santa Monica, Calif., 1962-63, N.Am. Aviation, inc., L.A., 1963-64, NASA Manned Spacecraft Ctr. Gemini & Apollo Program Office, Houston, 1964-70; safety engr. U.S. Dept. Labor, OSHA, Washington, 1975-86; invention researcher Arlington, Va., 1987—. Contbr. articles to profl. jours. Mem. N.Y. Acad. Scis. Democrat. Moslem. Achievements include patent for solar energy collector, supersonic MHD generator system; copyrights for hypothesis on unified field theory and creation of the universe, on the gravitoenergy in the creation of cosmic matters in the space, on the mechanism of superconductivity, a note of caution for superconductivity in reference to permeability and permitivity, concentration on suggesting methods to build superconductors and biomedical engineering instrumentation for cancer in particular, others. Home and Office: 1805 Crystal Dr Apt 1013 Arlington VA 22202-4407

**RAHMAN, RAFIQ UR,** oncologist, educator; b. Mirali, Pakistan, Mar. 3, 1957; came to U.S., 1985; s. Rakhman and Bibi (Sana) Gul; m. Shamim Ara Bangash; children: Maryam, Hassan, Haider. BS, MB, U. Peshawar, Pakistan, 1980. Bd. cert. internal medicine, med. oncology, hematology; lic. physician Pa., Ala., Ky. House officer in internal medicine Khyber Tchg. Hosp.-U. Peshawar, 1980-81, house officer in gen. surgery, 1981, jr. registrar med. ICU, 1983-84; jr. registrar internal medicine Khyber Tchg. Hosp., 1981-82; sr. registrar internal medicine Khyber Tchg. Hosp.-Lady Reading Hosp. & Postgrad. Inst., Peshawar, 1984-85; Audrey Meyer Mars fellow in med. oncology Roswell Park Cancer Inst., Buffalo, 1985-86; resident in internal medicine SUNY-Buffalo Gen. Hosp.-Erie County Med. Ctr.-VA Med. Ctr., 1986-88; chief resident in internal medicine SUNY-Buffalo-Erie County Med. Ctr., 1988; fellow in hematology and med. oncology SUNY-Buffalo-Roswell Park Cancer Inst., 1989-90; hematologist, med. oncologist Daniel Boone Clinic and Harlan A.R.H., 1991-92; clin. asst. prof. medicine U. Ky., 1991—; attending physician, hematology, med. oncologist Hardin Meml. Hosp., Elizabethtown, Ky., 1993—, chief medicine, 1996, pres.-elect med. staff, 2001—02, pres. med. staff, 2002—03. Tchr. med. students Med. Sch., SUNY; participant CALGB protocol studies Roswell Park Cancer Inst., investigator. Editor English sect. Cenna mag.; contbr. articles to profl. jours. Founder Cmty. Uplift Program, Pakistan; founding dir. Pakistan Human Devel. Fund, Pakistan Am. Leadership Ctr., Washington. Mem.: Assn. Pakistan Physicians Ky. and Ind. (pres. 2002—03), Ky. Med. Assn. Avocations: travel, aeromodeling, swimming, studying political science and history. Home: 400 Briarwood Cir Elizabethtown KY 42701-6915 Office: 1107 Woodland Dr Ste 105 Elizabethtown KY 42701-2789 Office Phone: 270-769-6665. Personal E-mail: rahmanrafiq@hotmail.com.

**RAHMAN, YUEH-ERH,** biologist; b. Kwangtung, China, June 10, 1928; came to U.S., 1960; d. Khon and Kwei-Phan (Chan) Li; m. Aneesur Rahman, Nov. 3, 1956; 1 dau., Aneesa. BS, U. Paris, 1950; MD magna cum laude, U. Louvain, Belgium, 1956. Clin. and postdoctoral research fellow Louvain U., 1956-60; mem. staff Argonne (Ill.) Nat. Lab., 1960-72, biologist, 1972-81, sr. biologist, 1981-85; prof. pharmaceutics Coll. Pharmacy, U. Minn., Mpls., 1985—2002, prof. emeritus, 2002—, dir. grad. studies, pharmaceutics, 1989-92, head dept. pharmaceutics, 1991-96, 97-98. Vis. scientist State U. Utrecht, Netherlands, 1968-69; adj. prof. No. Ill. U., DeKalb, 1971-85; cons. NIH.; Mem. com. of rev. group, div. research grants NIH, 1979-83 Author; patentee in field. Recipient IR-100 award, 1976; grantee Nat. Cancer Inst., Nat. Inst. Arthritis, Metabolic and Digestive Diseases. Fellow Am. Assn. Pharm. Scientists; mem. AAAS, Am. Soc. Cell Biology, N.Y. Acad. Scis., Radiation Rsch. Soc., Assn. for Women in Sci. (1st pres. Chgo. area chpt. 1978-79). Unitarian Universalist. Home: 939 Coast Blvd Unit 6G La Jolla CA 92037-4115

**RAHMANI, CAROL HIPP,** school system administrator, psychologist; b. Loris, SC, May 4, 1950; d. James Chester and Edith Bedenbaugh Hipp; m. Abdul Manan Rahmani, May 18, 1985. BA, NC State U., 1972, MS, 1976, PhD, 1981. Lic. psychologist NC, sch. psychologist NC, cert. health svcs. provider-psychologist NC. Sch. psychologist Wake County Pub. Sch. Sys., Raleigh, NC, 1978—80, coord. psychol. svcs., 1980—90, sr. dir. related svcs., 1990—2003, sr. dir. counseling and student svcs., 2003—. Mem.: Nat. Assn. Sch. Psychologists, NC Sch. Psychology Assn. (Practitioner of Yr. 1998). Democrat. Methodist. Avocations: beach-combing, tennis, reading, sports, walking. Home: 6802 Phillips Ct Raleigh NC 27607 Office: Wake County Public School Sysem Crossroads II 110 Corning Rd Cary NC 27511 Office Fax: 919-858-1700. Personal E-mail: acrahmani@bellsouth.net. Business E-Mail: crahmani@wcpss.net.

**RAHMANI, KIA M.,** surgeon; b. London, Nov. 24, 1964; s. Abdfazel and Fereshteh Rahmani; m. Jitka Lom, Feb. 5, 1994; children: Adam, Leila, Arya. BS, Trinity Coll., Toronto, 1987; MD, Queens U., Kingston, Can., 1991. Staff surgeon Mercy Health Sys. Kans., 1995—98, Hafa Adai Specialist Group, Tamuning, Guam, 1998—. Mem.: AMA, Soc. Laproendoscopic Surgeons, Am. Cancer Soc. (vice chair 2002—), Am. Coll. Surgeons. Avocations: golf, video games, skiing, reading, travel. Office: HASG 280 Pale San Citores Rd Tamuning GU 96913-3615

**RAHMANI, RAMIN KHOSRAVI,** mechanical engineer, researcher; s. Rasoul Khosravi Rahmani and Nayereh Lajevardi Qamsari; m. Anahita Ayasoufi, May 5, 1997; 1 child, Cyrus Khosravi. BS in Mech. Engring., Sharif U. Tech., 1994, MS in Mech. Engring., 1997; PhD in Mech. Engring., U. Toledo, 2004. Project mgr. and rschr. Niroo Rsch. Inst., Tehran, 1997—99; computational fluid dynamics engr. Ill. Tool Works, Maumee, Ohio, 2001—04. Mem.: IAIAA, ASME. Achievements include research in new grid generation algorithm; new algorithm to solve heat conduction. Office: U Ala Birmingham 1530 3rd Ave S Birmingham AL 35294 Personal E-mail: rrahmani@uab.edu.

**RAHMEIER, LYNNE JILLSON,** primary school educator, secondary school educator; b. Detroit, May 23, 1940; d. Lyman Walter and Phyllis Eloise Jillson; m. Paul Wilfred Rahmeier, June 21, 1961; children: Karen Sue, Laurie Lynne, Timothy Paul. BA, U. Mich., 1962; MA, Drew U., 1968. Tchr. English grades 9-12 Fremonts HS, Vermilion, Ohio, 1962—64; tchr. music grades 7-9 Winchester (Mass.) Pub. Schs., 1977; tchr. music grades k-6 Lexington (Mass.) Pub. Schs.; tchr. music grades k-8 Brookline (Mass.) Pub. Schs., 1979—85; dir. music grades k-12 Winchester (Mass.) Pub. Schs., 1985—2005. Adj. faculty tchr. tng. U. Mass., Lowell, 1978—86; adj. faculty movement Boston Conservatory, 1984—85; adj. faculty childrens eurhythmics Longy Sch. Music, Cambridge, Mass., 1980. Adv. Winchester Cmty. Music Sch., 1980—. Mem.: Am. Choral Dirs. Assn., Mass. Music Educators Assn. Congregationalist. Avocations: travel, gardening, sewing, walking, reading. Home: 39 Thornberry Rd Winchester MA 01890

**RAHMING, ETTA LORRAINE,** social worker, consultant, psychotherapist, counseling administrator; b. Bronx, Mar. 6, 1957; d. Henry Lewis and Irene (Linen) R. BA in Sociology, CCNY, 1979; MSW, Howard U., 1981. Lic. social worker, N.Y.; lic. counselor, N.Y., alchohol and substance abuse counselor. Investigative probation officer N.Y.C. Dept. Probation, 1981-85; social worker E.N.T.E.R. Alcoholism O.P.D., 1985-86; psychiat. social worker Bronx Lebanon Alcoholism O.P.D., 1986-88; clin. supr. residential treatment program E.N.T.E.R. Inc., 1988-89; supr. Comprehensive Employment Opportunity Support Ctr. Fedn. Employment Guidance Ctr., 1989-92; therapist Our Lady of Mercy Mental Health Clinic, Bronx, 1994—96; sch. psychologist intern Dept, of Svcs. Virgin Islands Dist., 1997—. Dist. mgr. Dept. Human Svc., 1997—. Mem. NASW, Nat. Assn. Black Social Workers, Inc., N.Y. Fedn. Alcoholism Counselors, Nat. Black Alcoholism Coun., N.Y. Women in Criminal Justice. Office Phone: 340-774-0920 4243. Personal E-mail: ettarahming@yahoo.com.

**RAHMING, JOHN CHRISTOPHER,** investment company executive, consultant; b. Mt. Vernon, Ohio, Oct. 25, 1937; s. Norris Walton and Mary Catherine (Arndt) Rahming; m. Ann Gail Smith, June 12, 1959 (div. Aug. 1974); children: Charles, Jennifer; m. Penelope Watson Bevan, Dec. 17, 1988; 1 child, Jason Bevan. BA, Harvard U. Cambridge, Mass., 1959; MBA, Harvard U., Boston, 1965. Mgr Citibank, N.Y.C. and Buenos Aires, 1966-70; v.p. Security Pacific Bank, London and L.A., 1970-76, Alexander Proudfoot, L.A., Paris, London, 1976-81; mng. dir. London Interstate Bank, 1981-88; ops. mgr. Inter-Am. Investment Corp., Washington, 1989-93, gen. mgr., 1993-99, cons., 2000—06. Chmn. bd. dirs. Environ. Enterprise Assistance Fund, Ctrl. Am. Small Enterprise Investment Fund. Lt. USN, 1959-63. Mem. Met. Club, Harvard Club (N.Y.C.), Harvard Bus. Sch. Club, Roehampton Club (London). Avocations: sailing, skiing, golf, music, theater. Home: 400 Madison St Apt 1202 Alexandria VA 22314-1721

**RAHNEMA, FARZAD,** engineering educator, department chairman; m. Mahnaz Rahnema; children: Tina, Nina, Sara. PhD, UCLA, 1981. Prin. engr. GE Nuc. Energy, San Jose, Calif., 1981—92; prof., chair nuc. engring. Ga. Inst. Tech., Atlanta, 1992—. Cons. Can. Nuc. Safety Commn., Atlanta, 1998—2006. Contbr. articles to profl. jours. Fellow: Am. Nuc. Soc.; mem.: Am. Assn. Physicist Medicine. Office: Ga Inst Tech Atlanta GA 30332-0405 Office Phone: 404-894-3731. Personal E-mail: farzad@nazconsulting.com. Business E-Mail: farzad@gatech.edu.

**RAHNFELD, VINCENT D.,** counseling administrator; b. Chgo. m. Amy L. Rahnfeld; children: Michelle, Kim. BMus, U. Cin. Coll. Conservatory of Music, 1980; MEd, Xavier U., Cin., 1991. Tchr. music Milford Village Schs., Ohio, 1980—82, New Richmond Village Schs., Ohio, 1982—89, Sycamore Cmty. Sch., Cin., 1989—97, sch. counselor, 1997—. Adj. instr. Xavier U., Cin., 2004—; musician, Cin., 1979—82; counselor adv. bd. Miami U., Oxford, Ohio, 2004—; out-of-state counselor adv. bd. U. Buffalo/SUNY, 2005—. Mem.: NACAC, ASCD, Ohio Assn. Coll. Admissions Counselors, Am. Sch. Counselor Assn., Music Educators Nat. Conf. Avocations: running, cycling. Office: Sycamore High School 7400 Cornell Rd Cincinnati OH 45242

**RAHR, STEWART,** health related products executive; b. Feb. 19, 1948; m. Carol Rahr. BA, N.Y. Univ., 1968. Owner Kinray Inc., Whitestone, NY, 1975—, pres., 1978—, also CEO, 1984—. Named one of Top 200 Collectors, ARTnews Mag., 2004, 400 Richest Americans, Forbes, 2006. Avocation: Collector of Impressionist and Modern Art. Office: Kinray Inc 152-35 10th Ave Whitestone NY 11357-1233*

**RAI, AISHWARYA,** actress; b. Mangalore, Karnataka, India, Nov. 1, 1973; Jury mem. Cannes Internat. Film Festival. Actor: (films) Mamagaru, 1991, Iruvar, 1997, ...Aur Pyaar Ho Gaya, 1997, Jeans, 1998, Let's Go Back, 1999, Straight from the Heart, 1999, Taal, 1999, I Have Found it, 2000, Josh, 2000, You Have My Heart, 2000, Dhaai Akshar Prem Ke, 2000, Love Stories, 2000, Albela, 2001, Devdas, 2002, Hum Kisi Se Kum Nahin, 2002, Shakti: The Power, 2002, Heart of Gold, 2003, Choker Bali: A Passion Play, 2003, Don't Say a Word, 2003, The Uniform, 2004, Raincoat, 2004, Kyun...! Ho Gaya Na, 2004, Bride and Prejudice, 2004, Shabd, 2004. Achievements include being crowned Miss World 1994 (also named Miss Photogenic); being first actress and performer from India to appear on cover of Time Mag.(as one of 100 most influential people in world), 2004; being fluent in English, Hindi, Kannada, Tamil and Urdu. Mailing: c/o Wm Morris Agy 1 Wm Morris Pl Beverly Hills CA 90212

**RAI, MAQBOOL AHMAD,** civil engineer, consultant; b. Shorkot, Pakistan, Apr. 15, 1937; s. M. Bahadur and Bakht Bhari R.; m. Samra Rubina Rani, Feb. 2, 1966; 4 children. Registered profl. engr. Asst. engr. Karachi Devel. Authority, 1963-68; dist. engr. Dist. Coun., Gujrat, Sargodha, 1968-69, Mianwali, Campbellpur, 1971-72; asst. mcpl. engr. Mcpl. Corp., Lahore, 1972-74, mcpl. engr. Gujranwala, Multan, Lahore, 1975-78; deputy dir. Lahore Devel. Auth.; mcpl. engr. Mcpl. Corp., Lahore, 1978-82; project engr. Hamad M. Al-Qahtany Est., Saudi Arabia, 1982-84; officer on spl. duty Punjab Local Govt. Bd.; mcpl. engr., chief engr. Mcpl. Corp., Lahore, 1984, mcpl. engr. Sialkot, Sheikhupura, 1984-87, Met. Corp., Lahore, 1987-91, superintending engr., 1991-93; chief engr. Mcpl. Corp., Rawalpindi, 1993-94, Faisalabad, 1994-95, Met. Corp., Lahore, Pakistan, 1995-97; additional dir. gen. inspections local govt. dept. Govt. of Punjab, 1995; chmn. Landmark Cons., Lahore, 1997—. Recipient prizes in English and Perusian, German first class first with distinction, U. Karachi, Higher Level Appreciations and awards for meritorious svcs. in Engring. Realsm. Mem.: ASCE, Steel Engr. Inst., Am. Water Works Assn., Inst. Engrs. Home and Office: Landmark Cons 232 Pak Block Allama Iqbal Town Lahore Pakistan Office Phone: 5417871. Personal E-mail: maq232@yahoo.com.

**RAI, RAJAT,** health facility administrator; BSME, Regional Engring. Coll.; MBA in Fin., Wayne State U. From mem. staff to pres. Option Care, Inc., Buffalo Grove, Ill., 1992—2000, pres., 2000—, CEO, 2001—, bd. dirs. Office: Option Care Inc 485 Half Day Rd Ste 300 Buffalo Grove IL 60089

**RAIBLEY, PARVIN RUDOLPH,** dentist; b. Boonville, Ind., Nov. 19, 1926; s. Otto Sr. and Hallie Marie (Hedges) R.; m. Mary Helen Holder, Aug. 31, 1946; children: Bruce D., Brian L., Brent A. Student, Purdue U., 1945, U. Evansville, 1946—50; BS in Dentistry, Ind. U., 1951, DDS, 1954. Practice gen. dentistry, Evansville, Ind., 1954—; pres. Parvin Raibley Profl. Dental Corp. Counselor Boy Scouts Am. With U.S. Army, 1944-45. Named Dentist of Yr. Ind. Acad. Gen. Dentistry, 1992. Fellow Acad. Gen. Dentistry, Am. Soc. Dentistry Children, Internat. Coll. Dentists; mem. ADA, First Dist. Dental Soc., Ind. Dental Assn., Am. Acad. Pediatric Dentistry, Ind. Acad. Gen. Dentistry, S.W. Ind. Oral Health Found. (disbursement com.), Masons. Republican. Methodist. Avocations: farming, forestry, fishing, poetry, gardening. Home: 7100 Olive St Evansville IN 47715-3625 Office: 207 S Green River Rd Evansville IN 47715-7334 Personal E-mail: praibley@aol.com.

**RAICHLE, MARCUS EDWARD,** radiology, neurology educator; b. Hoquiam, Wash., Mar. 15, 1937; m. Mary Elizabeth Rupert, 1964; children: Marcus Edward, Timothy Stephen, Sarah Elizabeth, Katherine Ann. BS, U. Wash., 1960, MD, 1964. Diplomate Am. Bd. Psychiatry and Neurology. Intern Balt. City Hosps., 1964—65, resident, 1965—66; asst. neurologist N.Y. Hosp. Cornell Med. Ctr., N.Y.C., 1966—68, neurologist, chief resident, 1968—69; clin. instr. dept. medicine divsn. neurosci. U. Tex. Med. Sch., San Antonio, 1969—70; rsch. instr. Washington U. Sch. Med., St. Louis, 1971—72, from asst. prof. neurology to assoc. prof. neurology, 1972—78, from asst. prof. radiology (radiation scis.) to assoc. prof. radiology Edward Mallinckrodt Inst. Radiology, 1972—79, from asst. prof. to assoc. prof. biomedical engring., 1974-79, prof. neurology, 1978—, prof. radiology Edward Mallinckrodt Inst. Radiology, 1979—, prof. biomedical engring., 1979—, and prof. psychology Washington Univ., St. Louis, 2000—. Instr. dept. neurology Cornell U. Med. Coll., N.Y.C., 1968—69; asst. neurologist Barnes Hosp., St. Louis, 1971—75, assoc. neurologist, 1975—78, neurologist, 1978—; cons. neurologist St. Louis Children's Hosp., 1975—; neurologist Jewish Hosp., St. Louis, 1984—, St. Louis Regional Hosp., St. Louis, 1984—; mem. neurology study sect. A NIH, 1975—79; mem. com. cerebrovascular diseases Nat. Inst. Neurol. Diseases and Stroke, long range planning effort, 1978, basic sci. task force, 78; mem ad hoc adv. panel Nat. Inst. Neurol. Diseases and Stroke, 1983, chmn. PET grants spl. rev. com., 85; mem. adv. bd. McDonnell-Pew Program cognitive neuroscience, 1989; other coms. Mem. editl. bd.: Stroke, 1982, Neurology, 1976—82, Annals of Neurology, 1979—86, Brain, 1985—90, Journal Cerebral Blood Flow and Metabolism, 1983—86, dep. chief editor;, 1981—83, mem. editl. bd.: Human Neurobiology, 1985—87, Brain Rsch., 1985—90, Synapse, 1987—90, Jour. Neurosci., 1989—95, Jour. Cognitive Neurosci., 1989—, Cerebral Cortex, 1990—, Jour. Nuclear Medicine, 1990—96. Maj. USAF, 1969—71. Recipient umerous awards, lectrs., fellows including Charles A. Dana award for pioneering achievements in health and edn., Dana Found., 1996. Fellow: Am. Assn. Advancement of Sci.; mem.: NAS, Inst. Medicine of NAS.

**RAIJMAN, ISAAC,** gastroenterologist, educator; b. Empalme, Sonora, Mex., July 6, 1959; came to U.S., 1985; s. Jose and Amalia (Langsam) R. MD, Nat. Autonomous U., Mexico City, 1985; postgrad., Nat. U. Houston, U. Wis., 1985. Diplomate Am. Bd. Internal Medicine, Am. Bd. Gastroenterology. Resident in medicine Mt. Sinai Hosp., Milw., 1986-88, chief resident, 1989; clin. fellow in therapeutic endoscopy Wellesley Hosp., Toronto, Ont., Canada, 1992-93; rsch. fellow in gastroenterology U. Tex., Houston, 1989-90, clin. fellow, 1990-92, asst. prof. medicine, 1993-97, dir. therapeutic endoscopy, 1993-97, asst. prof. M.D. Anderson Cancer Ctr., 1993—2000, dir. ann. therapeutic endoscopy course, 1995-97; assoc. prof. Med. U. Tex., 2002—; dir. therapeutic endoscopy U. Tex., 2002—. Chair Ann. Therapeutic Endoscopy Meeting; chair gastroenterology and endoscopy sub. com., GI subcom. on endoscopic credentialing and quality assurance Hermann Hosp., Houston. Author: Pancreas, 1993, Bockus Textbook of Gastroenterology, 1993; also numerous articles; reviewer jours. in field. Mem. Am. Coll. Gastroenterology, Am. Gastroenterological Assn., Internat. Assn. Pancreatology, Am. Soc. Gastrointestinal Endoscopy, Am. Soc. Internal Medicine. Avocation: painting. Office: 6620 Main Ste 1510 Houston TX 77030 Office Phone: 713-795-4444. E-mail: iraijman@dahpa.com.

**RAIKES, CHARLES FITZGERALD,** retired lawyer; b. Mpls., Oct. 6, 1930; s. Arthur FitzGerald and Margaret (Hawthorne) R.; m. Antonia Raikes, Dec. 20, 1969; children: Jennifer Catherine, Victoria Samantha. BA, Washington U., 1952; MA, Harvard U., 1955, LL.B., 1958. Bar: N.Y. State 1959. Assoc. White & Case, N.Y.C., 1958-69; assoc. gen. counsel Dun & Bradstreet, Inc., N.Y.C., 1969-72, v.p., gen. counsel, 1972-73, The Dun & Bradstreet Corp., N.Y.C., 1973-76, sr. v.p., gen. counsel, 1976-94, of counsel, 1994-95; ret., 1995. Cons. Bd. Govs. Fed. Reserve System, 1958-95. Served with U.S. Army, 1952-54. Woodrow Wilson fellow, 1952 Mem. Assn. Bar City of N.Y., Harvard Club, Phi Beta Kappa. Home: 26 Crooked Trl Norwalk CT 06853-1106

**RAILSBACK, SHERRIE LEE,** management consultant, educator; b. Phila., Mar. 12, 1942; children: Ricky, Cindy. BBA, U. Ky., 1981. Sales mgr. Marjo Cosmetics, Ft. Wayne, Ind.; asst. dir. patient fin. svcs Riverside Meth. Hosp., Columbus, Ohio; cons. Railsback and Assocs., Long Beach, Calif.; adoption search/reunion assn., educator Spirited Comm., L.A. Mem.: ASTD, NAFE, Book Publicists So. Calif., Nat. Spkrs. Assn. Office Phone: 310-967-1337.

**RAILTON, PETER ALBERT,** philosophy educator; b. Elgin, Ill., May 23, 1950; s. Arthur Roy and Marjorie Elizabeth Marks Railton; m. Rebecca Jarvis Scott, Apr. 21, 1978; children: John Scott-Railton, Thomas Scott-Railton. AB magna cum laude, Harvard U., 1971; PhD, Princeton U., 1980. From asst. prof. philosophy to assoc. prof. U. Mich., Ann Arbor, 1979—90, prof. philosophy, 1990—, Nelson prof., 1999—2001, Perrin Collegiate prof., 2001—, dept. chair, 2002—05. Vis. prof. U. Calif., Berkeley, 1984-85, Princeton (N.J.) U., 1990; mem. Coun. for Philos. Studies, N.Y.C., 1992-94; rsch. assoc. Ecole Poly., Paris, 1995—. Co-editor, author: Moral Discourse and Practice, 1997; author: Facts, Values and Norms, 2003; mem. editl. bd.: Ethics, Utilitas; contbr. articles to profl. jours. Am. Coun. Learned Socs. fellow, 1988-89, 2000, NEH fellow, 1999, Guggenheim fellow, 2001-2002, Am. Acad. Arts and Scis. fellow, 2004—. Mem. Am. Philos. Assn. (various coms. 1978—), Am. Soc. for Polit. and Legal Philosophy, Philosophy of Scis. Assn. (com. mem. 1978—), Soc. for Philosophy and Psychology, Mich. Soc. Fellows (jr. fellow 1979-82, sr. fellow 2005-). Office: U Mich Dept Philosophy 2215 Angell Hall Ann Arbor MI 48109 Office Phone: 734-764-6285.

**RAILTON, W. SCOTT (WILLIAM SCOTT RAILTON),** commissioner; b. Newark, July 30, 1935; s. William Scott and Carolyn Elizabeth (Guiberson) R.; m. Karen Elizabeth Walsh, Mar. 31, 1979; 1 son, William August; children by previous marriage: William Scott, Anne Greenwood. BSEE, U. Wash., 1962; JD with honors, George Washington U., 1965. Bar: D.C. 1966, Md. 1966, Va. 1993, U.S. Patent Office 1966. Assoc., then ptnr. Kemon, Palmer & Estabrook, Washington, 1966-70; sr. trial atty. Dept. Labor, Washington, 1970-71, asst. counsel for trial litigation, 1971-72; chief counsel U.S. Occupational Safety and Health Rev. Commn., Washington, 1972-77, acting gen. counsel, 1975-77; ptnr. Reed Smith LLP, Pitts., 1977—2002, ret., 2002; commr., chmn. U.S. Occupl. Safety and Health Rev. Commn., 2002—. Lectr. George Washington U. Law Sch., 1977-79, seminar chmn. Occupational Safety and Health Act, Govt. Inst., 1979-96; lectr. Practicing Law Inst., 1976-79. Author: (legal handbooks) The Examination System and the Backlog, 1965, The OSHA General Duty Clause, 1977, The OSHA Health Standards, 1977; OSHA Compliance Handbook, 1992; contbg. author: Occupational Safety and Health Law, 1988, 93. Regional chmn. Montgomery County (Md.) Republican party, 1968-70; pres. Montgomery Sq. Citizens Assn., 1970-71; bd. dirs., pres. Foxvale Farms Homeowners Assn., 1979-82; pres. Orchards on the Potomac Homeowners Assn., 1990-92; dir. Great Falls Hist. Soc., 1991-94; scoutmaster Troop 55 Boy Scouts Am., 1993-98. With USMC, 1953-58. Recipient Meritorious Achievement medal Dept. Labor, 1972, Outstanding Service award OSHA Rev. Commn., 1977, elected fell. Coll. Labor and Employment Lawyers, 1998. Fellow Coll. Labor and Employment Lawyers; mem. ABA (mgmt. co-chmn. occupational safety and health law com. 1995-98), Md. Bar Assn., Va. Bar Assn., Bar Assn. D.C. (vice chmn. young lawyers sect. 1971), Order of Coif, Sigma Phi Epsilon, Phi Delta Phi. Home: 10102 Walker Lake Dr Great Falls VA 22066-3502 Office: US Occupational Safety and Health Rev Commn 1120 20th Street NW Washington DC 20036 Business E-Mail: srailton@oshrc.gov. *Lawsuits are won by pre-trial preparation. A litigator should be candid with his clients and honest in his dealings with associates, opponents and the courts; an attorney should also volunteer his service to the community of which he is a part.*

**RAIM, DAVID MATTHEW,** lawyer; b. NYC, Mar. 11, 1953; s. Murray S. and Joan D. (Feldman) Raim; m. Linda K. Glushien, Jan. 12, 1982. BA cum laude, JD cum laude, U. Pa., 1978. Bar: NY 1979, US Dist. Ct. (So. & Ea. Dist.) NY 1979, US Ct. Appeals (2nd Cir.) 1981, US Supreme Ct. 1982, DC 1985, US Dist. Ct. (Dist. DC) 1985, US Ct. Appeals (3rd Cir.) 1988. Asst. dir. nat. law dept. Anti-Defamation League of B'nai B'rith, NYC, 1981-82, chmn. civil rights com.; assoc. Leboeuf, Lamb, Leiby & McRae, NYC and Washington, 1978-81, 83-86; Hughes Hubbard & Reed PC, Washington, 1986—88; ptnr. Chadbourne & Parke LLP, Washington, chmn., Reinsurance & Ins. Practice Group, 1989—. Contbr. articles to profl. jour.; lectr. in field. Mem.: DC Bar (chmn. members benefit com. 1988—94). Office: Chadbourne & Parke LLP 1200 New Hampshire Ave NW Washington DC 20036 Office Phone: 202-974-5625. Office Fax: 202-974-5602. Business E-Mail: draim@chadbourne.com.

**RAIMAN, ROSEMARY A.,** advocate; d. Claude and Emma Butch; m. John L. Davidson (div.); children: Jennifer Lynne Davidson, Jacqueline Rose Davidson; m. Irwin Raiman, Aug. 29, 1981. Cert. nat. victims acad. Am. U., 1998, victim assistance specialist Greenville, SC, 2000, trauma svcs. specialist Irmo, SC, 2001, clinically cert. domestic violence counselor Am. Coll. Cert. Forensic Counselors, South Bend, Ind., 2001, credentialed advocate Nat. Advocate Credential, Washington, DC, 2004, cert. roper victim asst. U. Balt., 2004. Program coord. Del. Opportunities Inc., Delhi, NY, 1977—81; dir. Title IIIC Nutrition/Supportive Svcs. for Elderly, Delhi, 1981—85; office mgr. Reliance Comm., Inc., Latham, Md., 1991—94; agy. receptionist Sanders Ins. Agy., LaPiata, Md., 1994—96; cert. victim advocate/admin. asst. Ctr. for Abused Persons, Waldorf, Md., 1996—. Chairperson Charles County Dept. Social Svcs., 1996—2005, bd. mem., 1996—2005; mem. Md. Divsn. Parole and Probation Victim's Adv. Bd., 1998—2001; bd. mem. Md. Assn. Social Svc., 1999—2003; founder Silent Witness Program for Charles County, 1999—, co-coord., 1999—; bd. mem. Md. Network Against Domestic Violence, Bowie, Md., 2000—; crisis respondent Charles County Sheriff's Victim Svc. Unit, LaPlata, 2001—; bd. chair Md. Assn. Social Svc., 2002—03; mem. Family Violence Coord. Coun. Charles County, 2003—; mem. pro bono legal svcs. com., 2003—; co-chairperson Legal Advocates Task Force, Bowie, Md., 2004—; chair Charles County Commn. for Women, 2004—. Nominee Spirit of Cmty. award, Med. Ctr.; recipient Silver Tray of Appointment, Del. Opportunities Inc., Outstanding Svc. award, Psychol. Svcs. Inc., Cert.

Appreciation, Ctr. for Abused Persons, Charles County Commissioners, Md. Most Beautiful Nominee and 1st Runner-Up, Silent Witness Plaque award, Charles County Co-Coord., Cmty. Svc. award, Commn. for Women, Gov. Victim Assistance award, Crime Control and Prevention Bd. Victims Svc. Bd. Mem. of Yr., Dept. Social Svc., Cmty. Svc. award, Dept. Social Svcs. Appreciation Plaque, Md. State Bd. Mem., Svc. Award Plaque, Ctr. for Abused Persons, Plaque of Appreciation, Charles County Sheriff's Dept. Achievement award, Md. Coalition Against Sexal Assault, 2006. Mem.: Assn. Traumatic Stress Specialist. Republican. Methodist. Office: Ctr for Abused Persons 2670 Crain Hwy Ste 303 Waldorf MD 20601

**RAIMI, BURTON LOUIS,** lawyer; b. Detroit, May 5, 1938; s. Irving and Rae (Abel) R.; m. Judith Morse, Mar. 31, 1963 (div. Mar. 1985); children: Diane L., and Matthew D. BA, Brandeis U., 1960; JD with honors, U. Mich., 1963; LLM, George Washington U., 1964. Bar: Mich. 1963, D.C. 1964, Fla. 1991, U.S. Ct. Appeals (4th, 7th, 8th, 9th, 10th, 11th and DC cirs.), U.S. Ct. of Fed. Claims, U.S. Supreme Ct. Atty. appelate ct. sect. NLRB, Washington, 1964-69; assoc. Morgan, Lewis & Bockius, Washington, 1969-71; dep. gen. counsel FDIC, Washington, 1971-78; ptnr. Rosenman and Colin, Washington, 1978-86, Dechert Price & Rhoads, Washington, 1986-93; shareholder McCaffrey & Raimi, P.A., Naples and Sarasota, Fla., 1994—2002, Law Offices of Burton L. Raimi PA, Sarasota, Fla., 2003—05; gen. counsel Washington Mgmt. Corp., 2005—. Spkr. various insts. Mem. ABA (past chmn. bank receiverships subcom. of banking com.), D.C. Bar Assn. (past chmn. banking law com., com. on interest on lawyers trust accounts), Fla. Bar (bus. law com.), Am. Arbitration Assn. (cert arbitrator), Nat. Arbitration Forum (arbitrator) Avocations: travel, golf, fishing. Office: 1101 Vermont Ave NW Washington DC 20005 Home: 3131 Connecticut Ave Apt 2508 Washington DC 20008 Office Phone: 202-842-5663. Office Fax: 202-842-5672. Personal E-mail: burt@moneylaw.com. Business E-Mail: braimi@washmgt.com.

**RAIMI, SAMUEL M.,** film director; b. Royal Oak, Mich., Oct. 23, 1959; s. Leonard Ronald and Celia Barbara (Abrams) R.; m. Gillian Greene, 1993; 4 children. Student in humanities study, Mich. State U., East Lansing, 1977-79. V.p. Renaissance Pictures, Ferndale, Mich., 1979—. Writer, dir. (films) Crimewave, 1985 (Best Dir. award 1986), Evil Dead II, 1986, Darkman, 1990, Army of Darkness: Evil Dead 3, 1993; co-writer: (screenplay) The Hudsucker Proxy, 1994; prodr. Hard Target, 1993, Timecop, 1994, Boogeyman, 2005; dir. (films) The Quick and the Dead, 1995, A Simple Plan, 1998, For Love of the Game, 1999, The Gift, 2000, Spider-Man, 2002, Spider-Man 2, 2004; appeared in films Spies Like Us, 1985, Thou Shall Not Kill...Except, 1987, Maniac Cop, 1988, Miller's Crossing, 1990, Innocent Blood, 1992, Intruder, 1994, Terminal Force, 1995, others: exec. prodr., writer, dir.: (films) The Evil Dead, 1981; exec. prodr., writer (films) Easy Wheels, 1989, (TV films) M.A.N.T.I.S., 1994; exec. prodr. (films) Lunatics: A love Story, 1991, Hard Target, 1993, The Grudge, 2004,(TV series) Hercules: The Legendary Journeys, 1995-99, Xena: Warrior Princess, 1995-2001, American Gothic, 1995-96, Spy Game, 1997, Young Hercules, 1998, Jack of All Trades, 2000, Cleopatra 2525, 2000-2001. Recipient Best Horror Film, Knokke'heist Film Festival Belgium, 1982, Best Horror Film and Best Spl. Effects, Sitges Film Festival, Spain, 1982, 1st Prize of the Critics, 1st Prize of the Pub., Paris Festival Sci. Fiction, Fantasy and Horror, 1983, Best Horror Film of Yr., Fangoria Mag., 1983; named one of 50 Most Powerful People in Hollywood Premiere mag., 2004-06. Mem. Mich. State U. Soc. for Creative Film Making (founder, pres. 1978, 79), Calif. Rare Fruit Growers.*

**RAIMO, BERNARD (BERNIE RAIMO),** lawyer; b. Kansas City, Mo., May 29, 1944; m. Sharon Marie Brady, Aug. 23, 1974; children: Sarah Elizabeth, Peter Bernard. BA, U. Notre Dame, 1967; JD with honors, U. Md., 1967 JD with honors, George Washington U., 1972. Bar: D.C. Staff asst. to Sen. Stuart Symington, Mo., 1968-72; asst. corp. counsel D.C., Washington, 1972-76; legis. analyst Am. Petroleum Inst., 1976-78; counsel Permanent Select Com. Intelligence U.S. Ho. Reps., Washington, 1978-91, chief counsel Ho. Com. Standards of Official Conduct, 1991-95; minority counsel Ho. Com. Standards of Official Conduct, 1995-97; counsel to Dem. leader U.S. Ho. of Reps., 1997—. Office Ofc of the Dem Leader H-204 The Capitol Washington DC 20515-0001 E-mail: bernard.raimo@mail.house.gov.

**RAIMONDI, RUGGERO,** opera singer; b. Bologna, Italy, Oct. 3, 1941; m. Isabel Maier, 1987. Studies with, Teresa Pediconi, Armando Piervenanzi. Debut in La Boheme, Spoleto, Italy, 1964; singer in major houses, Europe and US; Met. debut in Ernani, NYC, 1970; favorite roles include Don Giovanni, Philip II, Boris and Don Quichotte; recorded Verdi Requiem, Vespri Siciliani, La Boheme, Aida, Attila, Don Carlos, Macbeth, Simon Boccanegra, Don Giovanni, Boris Godunov, Tosca, Turandot, Barbiere di Siviglia, Mosè, Nozze di Figaro, Italiana in Algieri, Cenerentola, Il Viaggio a Reims, and others; appeared in films Don Giovanni (Joseph Losey), 1979, Six Characters in Search of a Singer (Maurice Bejart), 1983, Carmen (Francesco Rosi), 1986, Tosca (B. Jaquot), 2001, others: opera prodn. since, 1986—. Decorated Comdr. Arts et Lettres, Officier de la Légion d'Honneur (France), chevalier Ordre de Malte, Grand Ufficiale della Repubblica Italiana, comdr. Mérite Culturel (Monaco), others; named Citizen of Honor, City of Athens, Greece. Office: 140 bis rue Lecourbe F-75015 Paris France

**RAIN, See JEONG, JI-HOON**

**RAINAL, ATTILIO JOSEPH,** retired electronics engineer; b. Marion Heights, Pa., Feb. 14, 1930; m. Violet Dorothy Robel, June 29, 1957; children: Valery, Eric. BS in Engring. Sci., Pa. State U., 1956; MSEE, Drexel U., 1959; D of Elec. Engring., Johns Hopkins U., 1963. Engr. Applied Physics Lab. Johns Hopkins U., Silver Spring, Md., 1955; engr. Martin Co., Balt., 1956-59; mem. rsch. staff Carlyle Barton Lab. Johns Hopkins U., Balt., 1959-64; mem. tech. staff R & D AT&T Bell Labs., Whippany, Murray Hill, NJ, 1964-83, mem. disting. tech. staff R & D 1983—2003; ret., 2003. Contbr. articles to profl. jours. With USAF, 1948—52. Mem.: IEEE (life), Info. Theory, Component, Hybrids and Mfg. Tech. Achievements include research in noise theory; signal detection and estimation; radiometry; radar; FM; first passage times of random processes; crosstalk; voltage breakdown; current carrying capacity of printed wires; performance limits of electrical interconnections; patents for balanced interconnections; laser intensity modulation; patents in field. Home: 28 Woodruff Rd Morristown NJ 07960-4620

**RAINE, MELINDA L.,** school librarian; b. Boston, Feb. 4, 1951; d. James Agee and Marjorie Elizabeth (Gilstrap) Raine; m. Stephen Richard Brogden, Jan. 1, 1983; 1 child, Nathan Raine Brogden. BA, U. Iowa, 1973, MA, 1974. Info. specialist Pub. Libr. Des Moines, 1974-82, libr. mgr., 1982-90; task force coord. Visio 2020 Project, Conejo Future Found., Thousand Oaks, Calif., 1991-92; mgr. engring. libr. Metters Industries, Camarillo, Calif., 1992-94; govt. pubis. libr. Pepperdine U., Malibu, Calif., 1994-98, coord. info. resources, 1998—; assoc. libr. pub. svcs. and programs Pepperdine U. Librs., 2006—. Author: Options for Our Endangered Environment, 1992, Water: Liquid Gold, 1992, The Housing Crisis, 1992, Solid Ideas for Solid Waste, 1992; co-author (with Elizabeth parang and Trisha Stevenson): Redesigning Freshman Seminar Library Instruction Based on Information Competencies in Research Strategies, 2001. Mem. ALA, AAUW (pub. policy chair 1993-96, v.p. programming 1992-93), Calif. Libr. Assn., Calif. Acad. and Rsch. Librs. Office: Pepperdine U 24255 Pacific Coast Hwy Malibu CA 90263-4786 Business E-Mail: melinda.raine@pepperdine.edu.

**RAINER, REX KELLY,** civil engineer, educator; b. Montgomery, Ala., July 17, 1924; s. Kelly Kenyon and Pearl (Jones) R.; m. Betty Ann Page, Aug. 28, 1945; children: Rex Kelly, John Kenyon. BS, Auburn U., Ala., 1944, MS, 1946; PhD, Okla. State U., 1967. Asst. engr. L. & N. R.R. Co., Cin., 1944-45; design engr. Polglaze & Basenberg, Birmingham, Ala., 1945-51; pres., chmn. Rainer Co., Inc., Orlando, Fla., 1951-62; prof. civil engring. Auburn U., 1962-67, head civil engring. dept., 1967; exec. v.p., 1980; hwy. dir. State of Ala., 1979-80, fin. dir., 1981-82; spl. asst. to gov. of Ala., 1981-82; dir. Office for Advancement Devel. Industry U. Ala., Birmingham, 1982-86; pres., cons. engr. Rex K. Rainer, Inc., 1982-98, ret., 1998. Cons. to ins. cos., constrn.

engring. firms; mem. Ala. Bd. Registration Profl. Engrs. and Land Surveyors, 1977-89. Contbr. articles to profl. jours Mem. Municipal Planning Bd., 1963-65, Indsl. Park Devel. Bd., 1969-71, So. Regional Edn. Bd., 1982-86. Served with AUS, 1943. Fellow ASCE (sec., treas. 1970, pres. Ala. chpt. 1976-77, chmn. Constrn. Rsch. Coun., chmn. hwy. div. publs. com.; Civil Govt. award 1981); mem. Assn. Gen. Contractors Am. (bd. dirs. 1955), Am. Soc. for Engring. Edn. (chmn. constrn. engring. com.), Am. Pub. Works Assn., Phi Kappa Phi, Tau Beta Pi, Chi Epsilon. Personal E-mail: rkrainer@charter.net.

**RAINER, THOMAS SPRATLING,** pastor; b. Union Springs, Ala., July 16, 1955; s. Samuel Solomon Sr. and Amelia Nan (Keller) R.; m. Nellie Jo King, Dec. 17, 1977; children: Samuel III, Arthur, Jess. BS summa cum laude, U. Ala., Tuscaloosa, 1977; MDiv, So. Bapt. Theol. Sem., 1985, PhD, 1988. Ordained to ministry So. Bapt. Conv., 1984. Pastor Hopewell Bapt. Ch., Madison, Ind., 1984-86, Louisville, 1986-88; sr. pastor Azalea Bapt. Ch., St. Petersburg, Fla., 1988-90, Green Valley Bapt. Ch., Birmingham, Ala., 1990-94; dean Billy Graham Sch. Missions, Evangelism and Ch. Growth The So. Bapt. Theol. Sem., Louisville, 1994—. Trustee Bay Area Pregnancy Ctr., Clearwater, Fla., 1988-90; mem. bd. overseers Criswell Coll., Dallas, 1991—; adj. prof. Beeson Div. Sch., Samford U., Birmingham, 1991-94. Author/editor: Evangelism in the 21st Century, 1989, The Book of Church Growth, 1993, Eating the Elephant, 1994, Breakout Churches: Discover How to Make the Leap, 2005; contbr. revs. and articles to profl. jours. Garrett fellow So. Bapt. Theol. Sem., 1986-88. Mem. Acad. for Evangelism in Theol. Edn., Beta Gamma Sigma, Omicron Delta Epsilon. Home: 13505 Rock Bay Ct Louisville KY 40245-2097 Office: The Southern Bapt Theol Sem 2825 Lexington Rd Louisville KY 40207 *Life is a series of never-ending choices which compete for our limited resource of time. I have found that my life takes on its fullest meaning when my priorities for time are my God, my family, and my church.*

**RAINER, WILLIAM GERALD,** cardiac surgeon; b. Gordo, Ala., Nov. 13, 1927; s. Jamie Flournoy and Lula (Davis) R.; m. Lois Sayre, Oct. 7, 1950; children: Vickie, Bill, Julia, Leslie. Student, Emory U., Atlanta, Ga., 1943-44, U. Ala., 1944-45; MD, U. Tenn., Memphis, 1948; MS in Surgery, U. Colo., Denver, 1958. Diplomate Am. Bd. Surgery, Am. Bd. Thoracic Surgery. Intern Wesley Hosp., Chgo., 1949; gen. practice medicine Blue Island, Ill., 1950-52; resident Denver VA Hosp., 1954-59; practice medicine specializing in cardiac surgery Denver, 1960—. Bd. dirs. St. Joseph Hosp. Found., Denver; disting. clin. prof. surgery U. Colo. Health Sci. Ctr. Contbr. articles to profl. jours. Active Colo. Symphony Assn.; dir. emeritus St. Joseph Hosp. Found. Bd. Lt. U.S. Army, 1952-54. Decorated Bronze Star; recipient Disting. Alumnus award U. Tenn. Health Sci. Ctr., 1992, Florence Sabin award U. Colo. Health Sci. Ctr., 1998, Disting. Svc. award U. Colo., 2004, Disting. Svc. award We. Thoracic Surg. Assn., 2006. Mem. Soc. Thoracic Surgeons (sec. 1980-85, pres. 1989, historian 1992—, Disting. Svc. award 1998), Colo. Med. Soc. (pres. 1984-85), Denver Med. Soc. (pres. 1984), Denver Clin. and Pathology Soc. (pres. 1997), Am. Coll. Chest Physicians (pres. 1984), Am. Bd. Thoracic Surgeons (bd. dirs. 1982-88), Am. Surg. Assn., Am. Assn. Thoracic Surgery, Société Internationale de Chirugie, Cactus Club. Avocations: photography, travel. Office: 2552 E Alameda 48 Denver CO 80209 Office Phone: 303-601-0532. Personal E-mail: wrainer@qwest.net.

**RAINES, EDGAR FRANK, JR.,** historian; b. Murphysboro, Ill., Aug. 17, 1944; s. Edgar Frank and Mary Bernice (Mohlenbrock) R.; m. Gretchen Rose Beuscher, Aug. 9, 1975 (div. Dec. 1982); 1 child, Edgar Jacob; m. Rebecca Celia Robbins, June 20, 1987. BA, So. Ill. U., 1966, MA, 1968; PhD, U. Wis., 1976. Asst. acad. dean Silver Lake Coll., Manitowoc, Wis., 1976-79; historian Office of Air Force History, Washington, 1979-80, U.S. Army Ctr. of Mil. History, Washington, 1980—. Chmn. book selection com. Mil. Classics Seminar, Washington, 1984-86, 89-92; pres. Mil. Classics Seminar, Washington, 2001-02 Co-author: The Army and the Joint Chiefs of Staff, 1986; author: Eyes of Artillery, 2000. Sec. of the Army fellow Dept. of the Army, 1987. Mem. Am. Hist. Assn., Orgn. Am. Historians, Soc. Mil. History, Soc. History in the Fed. Govt., Wis. Hist. Soc., Soc. Historians Am. Fgn. Rels. Office: US Army Ctr of Mil History 103 3d Ave Fort Mcnair DC 20319-5058 Office Phone: 202-685-2094. E-mail: edgar.raines@hqda.army.mil.

**RAINES, FRANKLIN DELANO,** former finance company executive; b. Seattle, Jan. 14, 1949; s. Delno Thomas and Ida Mae Raines; m. Wendy Farrow. BA magna cum laude, Harvard U., 1971, JD cum laude, 1976; postgrad., Oxford U., 1971-73. Assoc. dir. Seattle Model Cities Program, 1972-73; assoc. Preston, Thorgrimson, Ellis, Holman & Fletcher, Seattle, 1976-77; asst. dir. White House Domestic Policy Staff, Washington, 1977-78; assoc. dir. Office Mgmt. & Budget Exec. Office of the Pres., Washington, 1978-79; v.p. Lazard, Freres & Co., N.Y.C., 1979-82, sr. v.p., 1983-84, ptnr., 1985—91; dir. Office Mgmt. & Budget Exec. Office of the Pres., Washington, 1996-98; vice-chmn. Fannie Mae, Washington, 1991-96, chmn., CEO, 1999—2004. Vice chmn. bd. dirs. Revolution Health Group LLC. Former pres. bd. overseers Harvard U.; former chmn. Fannie Mae Found.; former co-chmn. Bus. Roundtable; vice-chmn. bus. council Nat. Urban League; Enterprise Found.; Black Student Fund. Rhodes scholar, 1971. Mem. AAAS, Coun. Fgn. Rels., Nat. Acad. Social Ins., Washington State Bar Assn., D.C. Bar Assn. Avocations: running, golf.

**RAINES, HOWELL HIRAM,** former newspaper editor, journalist; b. Birmingham, Ala., Feb. 5, 1943; s. W.S. and Bertha Estelle (Walker) R.; m. Laure Susan Woodley, Mar. 22, 1969 (div.); children: Ben Hayes, Jeffrey Howell; m. Krystyna Anna Stachowiak, March 8, 2003 BA, Birmingham So. Coll., 1964; MA, U. Ala., 1973. Reporter Birmingham Post-Herald, 1964-65, Sta. WBRC-TV, Birmingham, 1965-67, Tuscaloosa News, Ala., 1968-69, Birmingham News, 1970-71, polit. editor Atlanta Constitution, 1971-74, St. Petersburg (Fla.) Times, 1976-78; Atlanta bur. chief NY Times, 1978-80, White Ho. corr., 1980-82, nat. polit. corr., 1982-84; dep. Washington editor, 1985-86, London bur. chief, 1987-88, Washington editor, 1988-92, editl. page editor NYC, 1993—2001, exec. editor, 2001—03; polit. commentator The Guardian. Author: Whiskey Man, 1977, My Soul is Rested: Movement Days in the Deep South Remembered, 1977, Fly Fishing Through the Midlife Crisis, 1993, The One That Got Away: A Memoir, 2006. Recipient Pulitzer Prize for feature writing, 1992.*

**RAINES, JEFF,** biomedical scientist, medical research director; b. N.Y.C., Sept. 5, 1943; s. Otis J. and Mildred C. (Wetzler) Raines; children: Gretchen Christena, Victoria Jean. BSME, Clemson U., 1965; MME, U. Fla., 1967; PhD in Biomed. Engring., MIT, 1972. Mem. staff MIT, Cambridge, 1968—70; biophysicist dept. surgery Mass. Gen. Hosp., Boston, 1972—77, dir. Vascular Lab., 1972—77; instr. surgery Harvard Med. Sch., Boston, 1973—77; preceptor Harvard/MIT Sch. Health Scis., 1976—77; rsch. dir., dir. Vascular Lab. (Miami Fla.) Heart Inst., Miami Beach, 1977—88; adj. prof. bioengring. U. Miami, Coral Gables, 1977—; prof. surgery U. Miami (Fla.) Sch. Medicine, 1977—; with Miami Vein Ctr., 2004—. Prin. investigator series NIH programs and pharm. firms, 1977—; Harvard Travelling fellow lectr. in Europe, 1975. Contbr. numerous articles on biomechanics, cardiovasc. diagnosis, dynamics and instrumentation to sci. jours. Recipient Apollo Achievement award, NASA, 1969; fellow, NIH, 1972. Fellow: Am. Assn. Physicists in Medicine, Am. Coll. Radiology, Am. Coll. Cardiology; mem.: ASME, AAAS, Cardiovasc. Sys. Dynamics Soc. (founding mem., editor 1976—, pres. 1980—82), Internat. Cardiovasc. Soc., Instrument Soc. Am., Biomed. Engring. Soc., New Eng. Cardiovasc. Soc., Am. Heart Assn., MIT Club, Harvard Club, Coral Gables Club, Kiwanis, Sigma Xi, Tau Beta Pi. Republican. Presbyterian. Achievements include patents for medical devices; development of mathematical models of arterial hemodynamics and clinical use of autotransfusion. Office Phone: 305-854-1555. E-mail: drjraines@yahoo.com.

**RAINES, ROBERT RANDLE,** music educator; b. Tulsa, Okla., June 16, 1952; s. Robert Randle and Mary Alice Owens R.; m. Debra Aaron, June 19, 1986; 1 child, Aaron Randle. B of Music Edn., U. Okla., 1975; MusM, U. Kans., 1981; postgrad., Baker U., 1998, U. NE Kearney, Nebr., 2005. Music instr. Unified Sch. Dist. 495, Larned, Kans., 1975—77; dir. bands Panhandle State U., Goodwell, Okla., 1977—82, U. NC, Chapel Hill, 1982—85, McCook (Nebr.) Schs., 1983—91, Scottsbluff (Nebr.) Schs., 1991—94, Arkansas City (Kans.) Schs., 1994—97, Gering (Nebr.) Schs., 1997—. Mem.: Nat. Band Assn., Internat. Assn. Jazz Educators (sec. Nebr. chpt. 2005—06), Music Educators Nat. Conf., Lions, Kiwanis. Democrat. Presbyterian. Avocations: bicycling, fishing, tennis, photography. Home: 1475 Quail Ridge Rd Gering NE 69341 Office: Gering Schs 1500 U St Gering NE 69341 Office Phone: 308-436-3129. E-mail: rraines@geringschools.net.

**RAINES, SHIRLEY CAROL,** academic administrator; b. Jackson, Tenn., Apr. 15, 1945; m. Robert J. Canady; 1 stepchild, Brian Scott Smith. BS, U. Tenn., Martin; MS, EdD, U. Tenn., Knoxville; grad. mgmt. program, Harvard Grad. Sch. of Edn. Dept. head Northeastern State U, 1983—87; assoc. prof. edn. George Mason U., Fairfax, Va., 1987—92; prof. and chmn. dept. of childhood/ lang. arts/ reading U. South Fla., 1992—95; prof. U. Ky. Coll. of Edn., 1995—2001, vice chancellor academic svcs. and dean of coll. 1998—2001; pres. U. Memphis, 2001—. Author books; contbr. articles to profl. jours. Recipient Dist. Svc. to Edn., Phi Delta Kappa, Dist. Paper awards, Ednl. Rsch. Assn. Office: U Memphis 341 Adminstrn Bldg Memphis TN 38152

**RAINES, TIM D.,** real estate company executive; b. Everett, Wash., May 8, 1950; s. Richard Thomas and Arvilla Mae (Chick) R.; m. Virginia N. McLaurin, July 20, 1977. BA. U. Ala., Tuscaloosa, 1968-72; MA, U. Ala., Birmingham, 1977; postgrad., U. Calif., Berkeley, 1976-77. Cmty. planner HUD, Birmingham, 1972-77, dir., program planning and eval. Atlanta, 1977-83, dir. regional housing ops. div., 1983-87; exec. v.p., COO Sanbury Corp., Atlanta, 1987-92; prin. Profit, Inc., 1992—. Pres. Stonington Home-owners Assn., Atlanta, 1980-83; patron Atlanta Ballet, 1978—; sponsor Pub. TV (WPBA), Atlanta, 1980—; mem. adv. bd. Salvation Army, 1997-2003; mem. Ga. Affordable Housing Coalition, 1993-98, Sandy Springs Coun. of Neighborhoods, 2005-. Recipient Cert. of Recognition William A. Jump Found., 1978. Mem. Am. Soc. Pub. Adminstrs., Am. Mgmt. Assn., Atlanta Zool. Soc. Avocations: travel, gardening, harmonica, custom cars, custom knives. Home: 8315 Ison Rd Atlanta GA 30350-3129

**RAINESS, ALAN EDWARD,** psychiatrist, neurologist, educator; b. NYC, Sept. 24, 1935; s. George W. and Ida Rainess; m. Alice Maree Haber, June 5, 1968; children: Alice Jeanne Rainess Jordan, James Alan (dec.). AB, Columbia Coll., 1957; MD, U. Paris, 1965. Diplomate Am. Bd. Psychiatry and Neurology. Intern Meadowbrook Hosp., East Meadow, L.I., 1965-66; resident in psychiatry NY VA Hosp., NYC, 1966-67; teaching fellow in psychiatry Harvard Med. Sch., Boston, 1967; chief resident in psychiatry Boston City Hosp., 1967; psychiatrist U.S. Army Hosp., Heidelberg, Germany, 1968—70; resident in psychiatry Walter Reed Med. Ctr., Washington, 1970-72; clin. dir. Noyes Divsn. St. Elizabeths Hosp., Washington, 1973-76; asst. chief psychiatry Andrews AFB Hosp., Camp Springs, Md., 1976-80, chief neurology, 1989-91; resident in neurology Wilford Hall USAF Med. Ctr., San Antonio, 1980-83; chief medicine and neuropsychiatry Air Univ. Hosp., Maxwell AFB, Ala., 1983-89, chief neurology, 1991-94; psychiatrist Manhattan Psychiat. Ctr., NYC, 1994—97, 1999—2002, clin. dir., 1997-99; psychiatrist Prison Health Svcs., Riker's Island, NYC, 2002—. Asst. clin. prof. psychiatry Georgetown U. Med. Sch., Washington, 1974-79, NYU Sch. Medicine, 1997-2002; assoc. prof. neurology and asst. prof. psychiatry Uniformed Svcs. U. Health Scis., Bethesda, Md., 1989-94. Maj. U.S. Army, 1968-73, col. USAF, 1976-94, ret. Fellow: Am. Psychiat. Assn. (disting. life); mem.: AMA, Harvard Club (NYC). Personal E-mail: alan.rainess@verizon.net. NY Office Phone: 718-546-6580. Office: OBCC Riker's Island New York

**RAINEY, GORDON FRYER, JR.,** lawyer; b. Oklahoma City, Apr. 26, 1940; s. Gordon F. and Esther (Bliss) R.; m. Selina Norman, Aug. 3, 1968; children: Kate, Melissa, Gordon III. BA in English, U. Va., 1962, LLB, 1967. Bar: Okla. 1967, Va. 1968. Assoc. Rainey, Flynn, Wallace, Ross & Cooper, Oklahoma City, 1967-68, Hunton & Williams LLP, Richmond, Va., 1968-75, ptnr., 1975—, chmn. exec. com., 1994—2006, chmn. emeritus, 2006—. Chmn. emeritus Hunton & Williams; rector U. Va.; bd. dirs. Bon Secours Richmond Health Sys., Inc., SunTrust MidAtlantic, Colonial Williamsburg Co.; bd. visitors, past rector U. Va. Past pres. U. Va. Alumni Assn.; trustee Colonial Williamsburg Found., Va. Found. Ind. Colls.; mem. Gov.'s Blue Ribbon Commn. on Higher Edn.; campaign chmn. United Way of Greater Richmond, 1982, trustee, 1981-84; bd. dirs., past pres. Sheltering Arms Hosp., 1984; trustee Sheltering Arms Found.; chmn. Gov.'s Econ. Devel. Adv. Coun. Dist. 12; mem. Gov.'s Adv. Com. for Va. Strategy on Econ. Devel.; mem. Bd. Housing and Cmty. Devel.; past mem. bd. govs. St. Catherine's Sch.; past chmn. bd. dirs. Leadership Met. Richmond.; past pres., bd. dirs. Met. Bus. Found. 1st lt. U.S. Army, 1962-64, Korea. Recipient Disting. Grad. award Casady Sch., Comm. and Leadership award toastmasters Internat., 1983, Humanitarian award Nat. Conf. Cmty. and Justice, 2003, Disting. Alumni award U. Va. Coll. Found., 2005, Ukrop Cmty. Vision award, 2006. Mem. ABA (sect. on bus. law, banking law com., com. on devel. in investment svcs.), Richmond Metro C. of C. (bd. dirs., past chmn.), Commonwealth Club, Country Club of Va., The Brook (NYC), Forum Club (Richmond). Republican. Episcopalian. Office: Hunton & Williams Riverfront Plz East Tower PO Box 1535 Richmond VA 23219-4074 Office Phone: 804-788-8275. Office Fax: 804-788-8218. Business E-Mail: grainey@hunton.com.

**RAINEY, JEAN OSGOOD,** public relations executive; b. Lansing, Mich., Apr. 5, 1925; d. Earle Victor and Blanche Mae (Eberly) Osgood; m. John Larimer Rainey, Nov. 29, 1957 (dec. Oct. 1991); children: Cynthia, John Larimer, Ruth. Grad., Lansing Bus. U., 1942. Pub. rels. dir. Nat. Assn. Food Chains, Washington, 1954-59; v.p. pub. rels. Manchester Orgns., Washington, 1959-61; ptnr. Rainey, McEnroe & Manning, Washington, 1962-73; v.p. Manning, Selvage & Lee, Washington, 1973-79, pres. Washington divsn., 1979-84, sr. counsellor, 1985; owner Jean Rainey Assocs., Washington, 1986-87; sr. v.p. Daniel J. Edelman Inc., 1987-96; owner Jean Rainey Assocs., Washington, 1996—. Chmn. bd. Windward Mortgage, 1997—2001. Author: How to Shop for Food, 1972. Pres. Hyde Home and Sch. Assn., Washington, 1969-71; co-chmn. Nat. Adv. Com. for Reelection of the Pres., 1972; chmn. bd. trustees St. John's Presch., 1996-99, vice chair, 2003-04; pres. Sherwood Forest Endowment Fund, 1995-97; adminstr. A Few Good Women-Advancing the Cause of Women in Govt., 1969-74, 97-; bd. dirs. Westchester Corp., 2001-04. Mem. Internat. Women's Forum, Pub. Rels. Soc. Am. (accredited, Hall of Fame 1999), Am. Women in Radio and TV (pres. Washington chpt. 1962-63, mem. nat. bd. 1963-65), Am. News Women's Club (pres. 1973-75), City Tavern Club. Republican. Episcopalian. Home: 4000 Cathedral Ave NW Apt 250B Washington DC 20016-5279 Office: PO Box 251 Main Lobby W 4000 Cathedral Ave NW Washington DC 20016-5249 E-mail: jorainey@aol.com.

**RAINEY, SUSAN J.,** school system administrator; m. Jack Rainey; 1 child, Jordan. BA, MA, U. Redlands; PhD, U. So. Calif. Tchr. Moore Jr. H.S., Redlands Unified Sch. Dist.; tchr. Palo Alto, Calif., Yucaipa H.S., 1972—76, dir. activities, 1976—78; asst. prin. Monrovia H.S.; h.s. prin. Brea, Calif.; asst. supt. for adminstrv. svcs. Helmet Unified Sch. Dist., asst. supt. for personnel svcs., assoc. supt.; supt. Charter Oak Unified Sch. Dist., Covina, Calif., 1991—98; sutp. Riverside Unified Sch. Dist., 1998—. Office: Riverside Unified Sch Dist 3380 14th St Riverside CA 92501

**RAINEY, WILLIAM JOEL,** lawyer; b. Flint, Mich., Oct. 11, 1946; s. Ralph Jefferson and Elsie Matilda (Erickson) R.; m. Cynthia Hetsko, June 15, 1968; children: Joel Michael, Allison Elizabeth. AB, Harvard U., 1968; JD, U. Mich., 1971. Bar: N.Y. 1973, Wash. 1977, Ariz. 1987, Mass. 1992, U.S. Dist. Ct. (so. and ea. dists.) N.Y. 1973, U.S. Ct. Appeals (2nd cir.) N.Y. 1973, U.S. Dist. Ct. (we. dist.) Wash. 1977, U.S. Supreme Ct. 1976, U.S. Ct. Appeals (9th cir.) Wash. 1978, U.S. Dist. Ct. Ariz. 1987, U.S. Dist. Ct. Mass. 1992; registered in-house counsel, Calif., 2005. Assoc. atty. Curtis, Mallet-Prevost, Colt & Mosle, N.Y.C., 1971-76; atty., asst. corp. sec. Weyerhaeuser Co., Tacoma, 1976-85; v.p., corp. sec., gen. counsel Southwest Forest Industries

Inc., Phoenix, 1985-87; sr. v.p., corp. sec., gen. counsel Valley Nat. Corp. and Valley Nat. Bank, Phoenix, 1987-91; v.p., gen. counsel Cabot Corp., Boston, 1991-93; exec. v.p., gen. counsel, corp. sec. Fourth Fin. Corp., Wichita, Kans., 1994-96; sr. v.p., gen. counsel, corp. sec. Payless ShoeSource, Inc., Topeka, 1996—2003, Longs Drug Stores Corp., Walnut Creek, Calif., 2003—. Editor U. Mich. Jour. Law Reform, 1970-71. Bd. dirs. Big Bros./Big Sisters, 1994—96. Maj. USAR, 1970—91. Mem. ABA (chmn. task force 1984-91, com. of corp. gen. counsel, 1993—), Wash. State Bar Assn., State Bar of Ariz., Assn. Bank Holding Cos. (steering com. 1989-91, chmn. lawyers com. 1990-91), Assn. Corporate Coun., Am. Soc. Corp. Secs., Harvard Club of Phoenix (bd. dirs. 1989-91). Avocations: hiking, running, bicycling. Home: 1208 Bridlewood Ct Clayton CA 94517 Office: Longs Drug Stores Corp 141 N Civic Dr Walnut Creek CA 94596 Office Phone: 925-210-6720. Business E-Mail: brainey@longs.com.

**RAINIER, ROBERT PAUL,** publisher, consultant; b. Adrian, Mich., Oct. 19, 1940; s. Paul Leslie and Mildred Sofia (Magdefrau) R.; m. Dorothy Krauss, May 28, 1966; children: Michele Carole, Kenneth Charles. BA, Northwestern U., 1962, MA, 1964. From mem. staff to editor-in-chief McGraw Hill Book Co., N.Y.C., 1964—74, editor-in-chief humanities, 1974—79; edit. exec. CBS Coll. Pub., N.Y.C., 1979—86, v.p., editor in chief, 1984-86; dir. publs. AICPA, N.Y.C., 1986-97, dir. prof. devel., 1997-99, sr. cons. strategic devel., 1999—2003; pres. Rainier Assocs., 2003—. Vestryman St. Johns Episcopal Ch., Larchmont, N.Y., 1987-90, fundraiser, 1988-89. Staff sgt. N.Y. N.G., 1964-70. Mem. The Dessoff Choirs (pres. 2000-04), Soc. Nat. Assn. Publs. (pres. 1992-93). Democrat. Episcopalian. Avocations: music, sports. Home: 21 Summit Ave Larchmont NY 10538-2913 Office Phone: 914-643-0994. Personal E-mail: rainier.inc@verizon.net.

**RAINIS, EUGENE CHARLES,** bank executive; b. NYC, Sept. 24, 1940; s. Charles William and Louise Theresa (Nold) Rainis; m. Jane Margaret Micucci, Nov. 28, 1964; children: Ellen, David, Mark. BS, Fordham U., 1962; MBA, U. Pa., 1964. Security analyst trainee Merrill, Lynch Pierce Fenner & Smith, N.Y.C., 1963-65; ptnr. Brown Bros. Harriman & Co., N.Y.C., 1965—. Bd. dirs. Bio-Brite, Inc. Trustee Robert Brunner Found., Gregorian U. Found., St. Vincents Cath. Med. Ctrs., Cristo Rey NY HS, NYC, Montefiore Med. Sys., Our Lady of Mercy Hosp.; trustee fellow Fordham U. Mem.: Inst. Chartered Fin. Analysts, Knights of Malta, Down Town Assn. (N.Y.C.), Harbour Ridge Golf Club (Palm City, Fla.). Republican. Roman Catholic. Avocations: fishing, golf. Office: Brown Bros Harriman & Co 140 Broadway New York NY 10005 Office Phone: 212-493-7830.

**RAINS, BAXTER SMITH,** sculptor, consultant; b. Atlanta, July 2, 1938; s. Baxter, Jr. and Elinor (Nelson) Rains; m. Barbara Osmundsen, Sept. 20, 1986; children: Anne Douglass, David Sinclair, Elinor Houston, Holly Christine Delaney. Studied, Ga. Inst. Tech., Atlanta, 1964—65, Atlanta Coll. Art, 1966—68; B of Visual Arts, Ga. State U., Atlanta, 1968; MFA, U. Guanajuato, San Miguel de Allende, Mex., 1975. Tchr. The Westminster Schs., Atlanta, 1969—71; instr. Atlanta Coll. Art, 1969—71, U. Guanajuato, San Miguel de Allende, Mexico, 1972—75, Brevard Art Ctr. and Mus., Melbourne, Fla., 1992; prof. Ctr. for the Arts, Vero Beach, Fla., 2000—02; adj. prof. Indian River CC, Fort Pierce, Fla., 2000—. Dir., evening sch. Atlanta Coll. Art, 1970; founder, exec. dir. Sculptural Arts Mus., Atlanta, 1980—82; cons. U.S. Pres.'s Coun. on Handicapped, 1981—82, Brevard Cultural Alliance, Viera, Fla., 2003, Brevard Mus. Art and Sci., Melbourne, Fla., 2003—04; bd. dirs. Arts Festival of Atlanta, 1982—85; artist-in-charge Hope Dragon Found., Merritt Island, Fla., 1996. One-man shows include Ga. State U., Atlanta, 1967—68, The Westminster Schs., 1969, 1971, Galeria Roma, San Miguel de Allende, Mex., 1973—74, Pine Valley Ranch, Pine, Colo., 1977, El Rancho, Colo., 1977, Gallery Danielli, Toronto, 1979, Washington World Galleries, 1979, Southside Studio Sculpture Show, Richmond, Va., 1990—91, Fifth Ave. Art Gallery, Melbourne, Fla., 1992, Brevard Mus. Art & Sci., 2003, Indian River Sculpture Gallery, Vero Beach, Fla., 2004, Vero Beach (Fla.) Mus. Art, 2005, exhibitions include High Mus. Art, Atlanta, 1969, Mint Mus. Art, Charlotte, N.C., 1970, Galeria Del Conde, San Miguel de Allende, 1972—73, Fiesta de Santa Fe, 1977, Mus. of Touch, Atlanta, 1980, Christian-Brydon Gallery, Richmond, Va., 1989—91, Brigantine Gallery, Cocoa Beach, Fla., 1993, Raleigh Gallery, Design Ctr. of Ams., Dania, Fla., 1992—95, Gaier Contemp. Gallery, Orlando, Fla., 1994—96, Raleigh Gallery, Boca Raton, Fla., 1995—97, Vero Beach Mus. Art, 2000—03, Represented in permanent collections Brevard Mus. Art & Sci., Melbourne, Fla., Radford U. Sculpture Garden, Va., The Westminster Schs., Atlanta, Piedmont Hosp., Ga. State U. Mus., The Trane Corp., Our Lady of Perpetual Help Hosp., Bklyn., City of Atlanta, Office of the Mayor, First Presbyn. Ch., Atlanta, St. Francis Gardens, Albuquerque, Holy Name of Jesus Cath. Ch., Melbourne, Fla., commissioned, Parkway Indsl. Pk., Balt., 1987, Freedom 7 Cmty. Ctr., Cocoa Beach, Fla., 1992, Child Care Assn. of Brevard, Cocoa, Fla., 2004. Mem. Internat. Sculpture Ctr., Washington, 1988—94; bd. govs. Vector Arts Endowment, Indian Harbour Beach, Fla., 1997—. Avocations: archery, gardening. Studio: Osmundsen-Rains Studios PO Box 372628 Satellite Beach FL 32937 Personal E-mail: baxterrains@yahoo.com.

**RAINS, CAMERON JAY,** lawyer; BA cum laude, Coll. Holy Cross, 1978; JD summa cum laude, Notre Dame Univ., 1981. Bar: Calif. 1981, US Dist. Ct. (so. dist. Calif.) 1981. Ptnr., co-chmn. Corp. & Securities practice group DLA Piper Rudnick Gray Cary US LLP, San Diego. Editor (assoc.): Notre Dame Lawyer. Mem.: State Bar Calif., San Diego County Bar Assn., U.S. Golf Assn. (mem. exec. com., chmn. 2008 U.S. Open Com.), Century Club San Diego (past pres., gen. chmn. 2008 Buick Invitational), Phi Alpha Delta. Office: DLA Piper Rudnick Gray Cary US LLP 4365 Executive Dr Ste 1100 San Diego CA 92121 Office Phone: 858-677-1476. Office Fax: 858-677-1401. Business E-Mail: jay.rains@dlapiper.com.

**RAINS, M. NEAL,** lawyer; b. Burlington, Iowa, July 26, 1943; s. Merritt and Lucille Rains; children: Robert Baldwin, Kathleen Kellogg. BA in Polit. Sci. with honors, U. Iowa, 1965; JD, Northwestern U., 1968. Bar: Ohio 1968. Assoc. Arter & Hadden, Cleve., 1968-76, ptnr., 1976—2001, mem. exec. com., 1981-90, Cleve. mng. ptnr., 1990-92; ptnr. Frantz Ward LLP, Cleve., 2001—. Lectr. on profl. topics, including alternative dispute resolution, distbn. law, litigation practice and procedure, and antitrust. Contbr. articles to profl. jours. With U.S. Army, 1968-70 Fellow: Am. Bar Found.; mem.: ABA, William K. Thomas Am. Inn Ct. (pres. 1999—2000), Cleve. Bar Found. (pres. 2005—), Bar Assn. Greater Cleve. (chmn. young lawyers sect. 1975—76, chmn. CLE com.), Ohio Bar Assn., Rowfant Club, Union Club, City Club, Print Club (trustee 2001—), Phi Delta Phi, Omicron Delta Kappa, Phi Beta Kappa. Home: 18400 Shelburne Rd Shaker Heights OH 44118 Office: Frantz Ward LLP 2500 Key Ctr 127 Public Sq Cleveland OH 44114 Office Phone: 216-515-1660. Business E-Mail: nrains@frantzward.com.

**RAINS, MARY JO,** banker; b. Konawa, Okla., Oct. 27, 1935; d. Albert Wood and Mary Leona (Winfield) Starns; m. Billy Z. Rains June 17, 1956; one child, Nicky Z. Student, Okla. Sch. Banking, 1969, Seminole Jr. Coll., 1970—72, East Ctrl. State U., 1978—79; diploma, Am. Inst. Banking, 1981—83; student, Okla. State U., 1987, Adult Vocat. Tech. Ctr., Pontotoc County, 1987. With acctg. divsn. Universal C.I.T., Okla. City, 1953—56; cashier Okla. State Bank (now Bancfirst), Konawa, 1957—89, sr. v.p., 1989—95; sr. v.p. mgr. Bancfirst, Konawa, 1995—2002; bd. sec. Seminole County Election Bd., Okla., 2003—. Sec. First Bapt. Ch., Konawa Okla. 1969-79, budgeting com., 1982-92, chmn. fin. com. 1994-2004, lectureship adminstr.; fin. bd. Kennedy Libr., 1997—; bd. dir. Sacred Heart Mission Hist. Soc.; mem. exec. bd. Okla. Family Med. Ctr., 2004-, fin. com., 2004- Mem. Okla. Bankers Assn. (dir. women's divsn. 1974-76), Konawa C. of C., Am. Legion, Wewoka C. of C. Home: RR 2 Box 28 Konawa OK 74849 Office: Courthouse Ste 101 Wewoka OK 74884 Office Phone: 405-257-2786.

**RAINWATER, ERIC,** composer, music educator; b. Long Beach, Calif., July 23, 1955; s. Paul Eugene Rainwater and Billye Reé Wallace; m. Candy Marie Layne, Mar. 29, 1980; children: Autumn, Crescent, Shiloh. BA in Music Composition, Azusa Pacific U., Calif., 1988. Dir. 5 home sch. choirs,

Sacramento, 1992—; owner Rainwater Music Co., Sacramento, 1995—; dir. 3 home sch. bands Sacramento, 1997—. Music dir. River Ridge Neighborhood Ch., Elk Grove, Calif., 2004—; children's dir., seminar spkr. various music conventions, 1993—. Author, songwriter, arranger: children's musical The Not-So-Silent Night!, 1998 (Top Best Selling Musical award); Samson, The Day God Brought Down the House, 1997 (Top Best Selling Musical award); composer 25 adult, teen and children's musicals; author, songwriter, arranger: children's musical Check Out That Star!, 1995 (Top Best Selling Musical award); arranger: I've Been Working on the Railroad, Sacramento Light Rail Assn. Recipient Hall of Fame award, Azusa Pacific U., 2000, 1st Pl. Novelty Song award, Christian Artists Sem. in Rockies, Estes Park, Colo., 1989. Mem.: Yellowstone Assn. Socialist. Avocations: hiking, swimming. Home: 932 Shellwood Way Sacramento CA 95831 Office Phone: 800-428-2056.

**RAINWATER, FREDDIE BARRETT,** volunteer worker; b. Pensacola, Fla., Aug. 25, 1947; d. Bernard Sr. and Blanche L. Barrett; m. Crawford Rainwater, Jan. 24, 1970. BS, U. Tex., 1970, postgrad.; MS, U. S.C., 1972. Founder Favor House Spouse Abuse Shelter, Pensacola, Fla., 1979-85; co-organizer Manna Food Bank, Pensacola, 1981—; co-founder Friendship Scholarships, Gulf Breeze, Fla., 1989—. Mem. reorganizing bd. Wildlife Sanctuary N.W. Fla., Pensacola; pres. Panhandle Tiger Bay Club, Pensacola, 1999-2000; chmn. Escambia and Santa Rosa Counties George Bush for Pres. Campaign, Pensacola, 1979-80; reorganizer Santa Rosa County Rep. Party, Milton, Fla., 1979-80; chmn. Santa Rosa County Party Reorgn., Milton, Fla. Recipient Svc. to Mankind award Liberty Sertoma Club, Pensacola, 1986, Liberty Bell award Escambia-Santa Rosa Counties Bar Assn., 1991, Cmty. Leader of Yr. award Pensacola C. of C., 1992, Woman of Yr. award Pensacola YWCA, 1987, Multi County Shelter for Abused Women dedicated to Freddie Rainwater, 1996. Home: 616 Baycliff Rd Gulf Breeze FL 32561

**RAINWATER, GARY L.,** electric power industry executive; BSEE, U. Mo., Columbia; M of Systems Mgmt., U. So. Calif. Engr. electric transmission and distbn. Union Electric Co. (now Ameren Corp.), v.p. corp. planning, 1993—97; exec. v.p. Ameren CIPS, 1997, pres., CEO, 1997—2001, Ameren CILCO, 2000—01; pres., COO Ameren Corp., St. Louis, 2001—04, chmn., pres., CEO, 2004—. Mem. dean's adv. coun. U. Mo. Sch. Engring.; mem. adv. coun. engring. mgmt. and engring. tech. Washington U.; bd. dirs. AmerenUE, Ameren CILCO, Ameren CIPS and other Ameren subs., Mo. Hist. Soc., St. Louis USO, Ill. Energy Assn., Urban League Met. St. Louis, US Bank. Recipient Mo. Honor award for disting. svc. in engring., U. Mo.-Columbia Coll. Engring., 2000. Mem.: Engrs.' Club (Knight of St. Patrick 2000). Office: Ameren 1901 Chouteau Saint Louis MO 63166-6149*

**RAINWATER, R. STEVEN,** systems engineer; b. Tyler. Tex., Dec. 13, 1962; s. Clois Miles and Nancy Jane Rainwater; m. Susan C. Chance, May 11, 1991. AA, Northlake Coll., Irving, Tex., 1981-83; student, U. Tex., 1983-88. Programmer Profl. Info. Libr., Dallas, Tex., 1984-89; systems engr. Kimball Computer Video Tech., Irving, Tex., 1989-91; pres. Network Cybernetics Corp., Irving, 1992—. Sys. operator The Interocitor BBS, Irving, 1990-94; editor new site, 2001-. Author computer software. Mem. Soc. Motion Picture and TV Engrs., Dallas Personal Robotics Group. Avocation: artificial intelligence rsch. Home: 2821 Vassar Dr Irving TX 75062-4575 Office: Network Cybernetics Corp 3720 Canton St Ste 202 Dallas TX 75226

**RAINWATER, RICHARD EDWARD,** financial consultant, investor; b. Ft. Worth, June 15, 1944; m. Darla D. Moore; 3 children. BA in Math., U. Tex., 1966; MBA in Fin. and Mktg., Stanford U., 1968. With Goldman, Sachs & Co., N.Y.C., Dallas; chief fin. arch. Bass Corp., Ft. Worth, 1970-86; ind. investor Ft. Worth, 1986-94; founder ENSCO Internat. Inc., 1986; co-founder Columbia Hosp. Corp. (now Columbia/HCA Healthcare Corp.), 1988, Mid Ocean Ltd.; founder, chmn. bd. Crescent Real Estate Equities, Inc., Ft. Worth, 1994—; chief investor Mesa Inc., 1994—. Spkr. Harvard Bus. Sch., Stanford U., U. Tex. Bus. Sch. Appeared on cover of Bus. Week mag., Oct. 1986; recipient Man of Yr. award, 1989, Kupfer Disting. Exec. award Tex. A&M U., 1991, Golden Plate award Am. Acad. Achievement, 1992; named one of Forbes' Richest Americans, 2006. Office: Crescent Real Estate Equities Co 777 Main St Ste 2100 Fort Worth TX 76102-5325*

**RAIRDIN, CRAIG ALLEN,** software company executive, software developer; b. Cedar Rapids, Iowa, Oct. 23, 1959; s. Ernie W. and Sherryl E. (Asklund) R.; m. Johnna L. Miller, Jan. 9, 1982. BS in Computer Sci. with distinction, U. Iowa, 1981. Software engr. Rockwell Internat., Cedar Rapids, 1982-88; divsn. dir. Parsons Tech., Cedar Rapids, 1988-90, v.p., 1990-98; ind. software developer, 1999—; pres. Laridian, Cedar Rapids, 1999—. Cons. Creative Computer Systems, Cedar Rapids, 1987-90. Author: (software) Juliet, 1987, QuickVerse, 1988, Bible Illustrator, 1990, Standard Template for Electronic Publishing (STEP), 1995, PalmBible, 1998, PocketBible, 2000. Chmn. Area Liaison Com., Campus Bible Fellowship, Iowa City, 1983-90; precinct chmn. Linn. County Rep. Party, Cedar Rapids, 1986-90; founder Bible Software Industry Standards Group, 1995; vol. pilot Angel Flight Ctrl., 2001—. Republican. Christian. Avocations: church, amateur radio, flying.

**RAISBECK, GORDON,** systems engineer, consultant; b. N.Y.C., May 4, 1925; s. Milton Joseph and Marcelle (Ellinger) R.; m. Barbara Wiener, Dec. 22, 1948; children: Michael Norbert, Lucy Margaret, Alison Jane, Timothy Gordon, James Gregory. Rhodes scholar, Oxford U., Eng., 1947-48; BA, Stanford U., 1944; PhD, MIT, 1949. Registered profl. engr., Mass., Maine. Instr. M.I.T., Cambridge, 1948-49; mem. tech. staff Bell Telephone Labs., Inc., Murray Hill, NJ, 1949-61; dir. transmission line research Bell Telephone Labs., Inc. (now Lucent), 1954-61; mem. profl. staff research and devel. Advanced Research Projects Agy., Washington, 1959-60; mem. profl. staff Arthur D. Little, Inc., Cambridge, 1961-86, dir. systems engring., 1966-70, dir. phys. systems research, 1970-75, v.p. systems engring., 1973-86, part-time 1982-86; cons. mgmt. of technol. innovation, 1982-94; ret., 2004. Instr. Drew U., Stanford U., MIT. Contbr. articles to profl. jours.; author: Information Theory: An Introduction for Engineers and Scientists, 1964; patentee in field (22). Served to lt. (j.g.) USNR, 1944-46, ATO, PTO. Rhodes scholar, 1947 Fellow IEEE, Acoustical Soc. Am.; mem. Oceanic Engring. Soc. IEEE (sec. 1988-92), New Coll. Soc., Oxford Soc., Assn. Am. Rhodes Scholars, Amateur Chamber Music Players, Chamber Music Am., Sigma Xi. Democrat. Episcopalian. Home and Office: 4 Drake Ln Scarborough ME 04074-7414 Office Phone: 207-885-5174. E-mail: raisbeck9@netscape.net.

**RAISH, CAROL BROOKS,** anthropologist, archaeologist; b. Tulsa, Okla., Oct. 20, 1946; d. Horace Brooks and Julia Ann (Duff) Gotcher; m. Gordon Kent Raish, Jan. 17, 1970 (div. May 1978); 1 child, Susan Brooks Raish Sehlmeyer. BA in Spanish and Secondary Edn., Washburn U., 1968; MA in Anthropology, U. Nebr., 1979; PhD of Anthropology, U. N.Mex., 1988. Archeologist Midwest Archeol. Ctr. U.S. Nat. Park Svc., Lincoln, Nebr., 1978—79; archeologist Cibola Nat. Forest U.S. Forest Svc., Albuquerque, 1982—86; archeologist, editor Midwest Archeol. Ctr. U.S. Nat. Park Svc., Lincoln, 1988—89; anthropologist, archeologist Heritage Resource Staff Jemez Ranger Dist. Santa Fe Nat. Forest U.S. Forest Svc., Jemez Springs, N.Mex., 1989—95, anthropologist, rsch. social scientist Rocky Mountain Rsch. Sta. Albuquerque, 1995—. Author: Domestic Animals and Stability in Pre-State Farming Societies, 1992; co-editor: Livestock Management in the American Southwest, 2000; contbr. articles to profl. jours. Asst. troop leader Girl Scouts Am., Albuquerque, 1982—87. Mem.: N.Mex. Archeol. Coun. (sec. 1990—91), Soc. Am. Archaeology, Soc. Human Ecology. Democrat. Avocations: hiking, needlecrafts. Home: 10504 Monte Rosso Pl NW Albuquerque NM 87114 Office: Rocky Mountain Rsch Sta USDA Forest Svc 333 Broadway SE Ste 115 Albuquerque NM 87102-3497

**RAISH, DAVID LANGDON,** lawyer; b. Cleve., Mar. 12, 1947; s. John E. Raish and Roslyn V. (Skeels) Pettibone; m. Roslyn Anne Dinnick, Sept. 12, 1969; children: David Jr., Anne, Julia. BA, Yale U., 1969; JD, Harvard U., 1973. Bar: Mass. 1975, D.C. 1981. Law clk. to hon. James R. Browning U.S. Ct. Appeals-9th Cir., San Francisco, 1973-74; assoc. Ropes & Gray, Boston,

1974-82, ptnr., 1982—. Mem. ABA Tax sect. 1991—, mem. Employee Benefits Com., 1993—, mem. coun., 1999-2004, vice chair, 2002-04. Author: Cafeteria Plans, 2000, Cash or Deferred Arrangements, 1997, Compensation and Benefits for Key Employees of Tax-Exempt Organizations, 1995; bd. advisors Jour. Taxation of Employee Benefits, 1990-2000. Tenor Tanglewood Festival Chorus. Office: Ropes & Gray One International Pl Boston MA 02110 Business E-Mail: draish@ropesgray.com.

**RAISH, STEPHEN E,** retail executive; m. Jane Raish; children: John, Sarah. BA in physics, Carleton Coll., 1972. Various store positions J.C. Penney Corp., 1972—91, mgr. store systems and inventory, 1991, dir. geog. markets, 1993, dir. stores coord., 1996, divisional v.p., home and leisure divsn., 1997—; pres., home and leisure divsn., 1998—; pres., ACT divsn. J.C. Penney Corp., 1999—, exec. v.p., CIO, 2001—. Office: JC Penney Corp Inc 6501 Legacy Dr Plano TX 75024-3698

**RAISIAN, JOHN,** academic administrator, economist; b. Conneaut, Ohio, July 30, 1949; s. Ernest James and Ruby Lee (Owens) Raisian; m. Joyce Ann Klak, Aug. 17, 1984; children: Alison Kathleen, Sarah Elizabeth. BA, Ohio U., 1971; PhD, UCLA, 1978; LLD (hon.), Albertson Coll. Idaho, 1995. Rsch. assoc. Human Resources Rsch. Ctr., U. So. Calif., L.A., 1972—73; cons. Rand Corp., Santa Monica, Calif., 1974—75; vis. asst. prof. econs. U. Wash., Seattle, 1975—76; asst. prof. econs. U. Houston, 1976—80; sr. economist Office Rsch. and Evaluation, U.S. Bur. Labor Stats., Washington, 1980—81; spl. asst. for econ. policy Office Asst. Sc. for Policy, U.S. Dept. Labor, Washington, 1981—83, dir. rsch. and tech. support, 1981—84; pres. Unicon Rsch. Corp., L.A., 1984-86; sr. fellow Hoover Instn., Stanford, Calif., 1986—, assoc. dir., dep. dir., 1986—90 dir., 1990—. Advisor Nat. Coun. on Handicapped, Washington, 1985—86, Nat. Commn. on Employment Policy, Washington, 1987—88; chmn. minimum wage bd. Calif. Indsl. Welfare Commn., 1987; mem. nat. adv. com. Student Fin. Assistance, Washington, 1987—89; corp. mem. Blue Shield Calif., 1994—96; bd. dirs. Sentinel Groups Fund, Inc., 1997—; mem. Pacific Coun. Internat. Policy; nat. adv. bd. City Innovation. Editor (editl. bd.): (jour.) Jour. Labor Rsch., 1983—; contbr. articles to profl. jours. Exec. dir. Presdl. Task Force on Food Assistance, Washington, 1983—84. Recipient Best Publ. of Yr. award, Econ. Inquiry, Western Econ. Assn., 1979, Disting. Tchg. award, U. Houston Coll. Social Scis., 1980, Disting. Svc. award, U.S. Dept. Labor, 1983; fellow predoctoral fellow, Rand Corp., 1976. Mem.: Nat. Assn. Scholars, Coun. on Fgn. Rels., Mont Pelerin Soc., World Affairs Coun., Commonwealth Club of Calif., We. Econs. Assn., Am. Econs. Assn., Phi Beta Kappa. Republican. Avocation: wine collecting, sports enthusiast. Office: Hoover Instn Stanford Univ Museum Way & Lomita Stanford CA 94305

**RAISIG, PAUL JONES, JR.,** lawyer; b. Jamestown, N.Y., June 21, 1932; s. Paul Jones and Marian Elizabeth (Christian) R.; m. Carolyn Virginia Sides, June 12, 1955; children: Dawn Virginia, Paul Christian, Anne Sibley. B.G.E., U. Nebr., 1961; MBA, U. Ala., 1965; JD, Campbell U., 1989. Bar: N.C. 1989, D.C. 1991, U.S. Supreme Ct. 1992. Commd. 2d lt. U.S. Army, 1953, advanced through grades to col., 1973, ret., 1977, served in Vietnam, 1963, btn. comdr., Vietnam, 1968; dep. dir. U.S. Army Reorganization, 1973; v.p. Armed Forces Relief and Benefit Assn., Washington, 1977-79; sr. cons. Dept. Def., Washington, 1979-80; exec. dir. Am. Fedn. Info. Processing Socs., Arlington, Va., 1980-84; v.p., dir. Designs, Ltd., Alexandria, Va., 1985-86; ptnr. Barrington, Herndon & Raisig, P.A., Fayetteville, NC, 1989-92. Adj. prof. bus. law and bus. mgmt. Campbell U., 1992-2004; cons. in field; mediator for Superior Ct. and arbitrator for Dist. Ct. Decorated Legion of Merit (3), Bronze Star medal (2), Air medal (5), Purple Heart (2), Meritorious Service medal, Army Commendation medal with V Device (3), Combat Inf. badge. Mem. U.S. Coun. for World Comms., Beta Gamma Sigma. Home and Office: Buffalo Lake 325 Mallard Rd Sanford NC 27332-1142 *As we go about climbing the mountains in our lives, we must always remember to take the high road - for that is the only way to truly reach the top.*

**RAISLER, KENNETH MARK,** lawyer; b. New Rochelle, NY, May 15, 1951; s. Herbert A. and Norma (Glaubach) R.; m. Sara Ann Kelsey, June 11, 1978; children: Caroline Elisabeth, Katharine Kelsey, David Mark. BSBA, Yale Coll., 1973; JD, NYU, 1976. Bar: NY 1977, D.C. 1977, U.S. Dist. Ct. (so. dist.) NY 1977, U.S. Dist. Ct. D.C. 1977, U.S. Ct. Appeals (2d cir.) 1977, U.S. Ct. Appeals (D.C. cir.) 1977, U.S. Ct. Appeals (7th cir.) 1982, U.S. Ct. Appeals (10th cir.) 1983, U.S. Supreme Ct. 1985. Law clk. U.S. Dist. Ct. (so. dist.) NY, NYC, 1976-77; asst. U.S. atty., Washington, 1977-82; dep. gen. counsel Commodity Futures Trading Commn., Washington, 1982-83, gen. counsel, 1983-87; ptnr. Rogers & Wells, NYC, 1987-92, Sullivan & Cromwell, NYC, 1992—, and coord. commodities, futures and derivatives practice area. Mem. Assn. of Bar of City of NY (chair futures regulation com. 1988-91). Office: Sullivan & Cromwell 125 Broad St 33d Fl New York NY 10004-2498 Office Phone: 212-558-4675. Office Fax: 212-558-3588. Business E-Mail: raislerk@sullcrom.com.

**RAITT, BONNIE LYNN,** singer, musician; b. Burbank, Calif., Nov. 8, 1949; Student, Radcliffe Coll. Performer: blues clubs, East Coast, concert tours in Britain, 1976, 1977; albums include Bonnie Raitt, 1971, Give It Up, 1972, Takin' My Time, 1973, Streetlights, 1974, Home Plate, 1975, Sweet Forgiveness, 1977, The Glow, 1979, Green Light, 1982, Nine Lives, 1986, Nick of Time, 1989 (Grammys 1990, Rock-Best Vocal Performance, Female, Pop-Best Vocal Performance, Female, Album of Yr., 1990), I'm in the Mood (with John Lee Hooker) (Grammy 1990), Blues-Best Traditional Record, 1990), The Bonnie Raitt Collection, 1990, Luck of the Draw, 1991 (Grammy, Rock-Best Vocal Performance, Female, Grammy for Best Duet with Delbert McClinton, 1992), Longing In Their Hearts, 1994 (Grammy award Best Pop Album, 1994), Road Tested, 1996, Fundamental, I Can't Make You Love Me, 1999, Silver Lining, 2002, songs include Something to Talk About (Grammy, Best Pop Vocal Performance, Female, 1992), Good Man, Good Woman (with Delbert McClinton) (Grammy, Rock-Best Vocal by a Duo or Group, 1992). Founding mem. Musicians United for Safe Energy, Rhythm and Blues Found.

**RAITT, MERRITT,** cardiologist; m. Susan Shattuc; children: Isabel, Jay. AB, Stanford U., Calif., 1982; MD, U. of Calif., San Diego, 1986. Cardiologist, dir. of EP lab. Portland (Oreg.) VA Med. Ctr., 1994—. Achievements include research in Atrial Fibrisallation And Implantable Defibrillators. Office: Portland VA Med Ctr P-3-CARD 3710 SW US Veterans Rd Portland OR 97239 Office Phone: 503-220-8262.

**RAIZEN, SENTA AMON,** educational association administrator, researcher; b. Vienna, Oct. 28, 1924; came to U.S., 1940; d. John and Helen (Krys) Amon; m. Abraham A. Raizen, Apr. 18, 1948; children: Helen S., Michael B., Daniel J. BS, Guilford Coll., 1944; MA, Bryn Mawr, 1945; Tchr. Cert., U. Va. 1960. Rsch. chemist Sun Oil Co., Norwood, Pa., 1945-48; rsch. asst. NAS, Washington, 1960-62; assoc. program dir. NSF, Washington, 1962-69, spl. asst., 1969-72; sr. researcher The Rand Corp., Washington, 1972-74; assoc. dir. Nat. Inst. Edn., Washington, 1974-78; ind. cons. Washington, 1978-80; study dir. NAS, Washington, 1980-88; dir. Ctr. for Improving Sci. Edn., Washington, 1988—. Cons. Nat. Ctr. for Edn. Stats., Washington, 1987—; Ednl. Testing Svc., Princeton, N.J., 1988—; Nat. Goals Panel, Washington, 1990-2000, Third Internat. Math. and Sci. Study, Internat. Assn. Evaluation Ednl. Achievement, The Netherlands, 1990—; SRI Internat., 1998—; Orgns. for Econ. Cooperation and Devel., Paris, 1998—. Contbr. articles to profl. jours., encys., books, reports in field. Pres. Cooperative Nursery Sch., Arlington, Va., 1953-57; leader Brownies, Girl Scouts U.S. and Cub Scouts, Boy Scouts, Am., Arlington, 1958-64. Recipient Disting. Lifetime award WestEd, 2000; grantee NSF, U.S. Dept. Edn., US Dept. Energy, pvt. founds., 1988-2000, fellowship for grad. study NSF, 1944-45, Meritorious Svc. award, 1968, The Network Pres.' award, 1991. Fellow AAAS; mem. Am. Chem. Soc., Am. Ednl. Rsch. Assn. Avocations: dance, swimming, reading, knitting, stitchery. Home: 5513 31st St N Arlington VA 22207-1532 Office: Nat Ctr Improving Sci Edn 1940 Wilson Blvd Ste 400 Arlington VA 22201 Office Phone: 703-875-0496.

**RAJ, SELVA J.,** religious studies educator; s. Joachim and Mary A.S. PhD, U. Chgo., 1994. Prof. of religious studies Albion Coll., Mich., 1995—. Author: (book) Popular Christianity in India; Dealing with Deities. Pres. Soc. for Hindu-Christian Studies, South Bend, Ind., 2000—02. Mem.: Am. Acad. of Religion (sect. co-chair 2002—06, Midwest chpt. pres. 2002—04). Office: Albion College 611 E Porter St Albion MI 49224 Office Phone: 517-629-0400. E-mail: sraj@albion.edu.

**RAJ, TILAK D.,** anesthesiologist, educator; arrived in US, 1999; s. Premavathy Dharmaraj; m. Catherine C. O'Donovan, June 12, 1994; children: Vijay M., Anushka M., Kieran T., Roshan A. MB, BChir, Madras U., Chennai, 1982. Diplomate Am. Bd. Anesthesiology, 1996. Resident St. Mary's Hosp., London; assoc. prof. dept. anesthesiology Okla. U. Health Scis. Ctr., Oklahoma City, 2000—, dir. rsch. dept. anesthesiology, 2003—. Contbr. articles to profl. jours. Fellow: Royal Coll. Anaesthetists; mem.: Obstetric Anaesthetists Assn., Soc. Cardiovasc. Anesthesiologist, Internat. Anesthesia Rsch. Soc., Am. Soc. Anesthesiology. Home: 2008 Morning Star Edmond OK 73034 Office: Oklahoma Univ Health Sciences Ctr Rm WP 2530 920 Stanton L Young Blvd Oklahoma City OK 73104 Office Phone: 405-271-4351.

**RAJA, RAJENDRAN,** physicist; b. Guruvayur, Kerala, India, July 14, 1948; arrived in US, 1974; s. P.K. Sreeveerarayan and Chandramathi Raja; m. Selitha Barbara Freundorfer, 1976; 1 child, Anjali. BA with honors, Cambridge U., Eng., 1970, MA with honors, 1974, PhD, 1974. Rsch. assoc. Fermilab, Batavia, Ill., 1975—78, assoc. scientist, 1978—83, scientist I, 1983—88, scientist II, 1988—. Monte Carlo convenor DO Expt., 1986—97, top quark physics convenor, 1990—94; head DO Software Support Group, 1986—93, DO Electron ID Group, 1989—94; head emittance exch./ring coolers group Muon Collider/Neutrino Factory Collaboration, 2001—03; spokesman Mipp Expt. Fermilab, Batavia, 2001—; fellow Trinity Coll. Cambridge U., 1973. Contbr. over 300 articles to profl. jours. Pres. Cambridge U. India Soc., 1969—70. Mem.: AAAS, Planetary Soc., Am. Phys. Soc. Achievements include discovery of top quark. Home: 1304 Margate Ct Naperville IL 60540 Office: Fermi Nat Accelerator Lab PO Box 500 Batavia IL 60510 Office Phone: 630-840-4092. Business E-Mail: raja@fnal.gov.

**RAJAGOPAL, CHITRA P.,** engineering educator; b. Thirupapuliyur, Tamil Nadu; d. Kannankote and Padma Seshadri; m. Parthasarathy Rajagopal, Oct. 12, 1989; 1 child, Jayasai Ram. MS in Elec. Engring., Youngstown State U., Ohio, 1992. Asst. prof. Kent State U., New Philadelphia, 2004—. Adj. prof. Kent State U., Warren-Kent, 1993—2004. Organizer, participant The Hindu Soc. Northeastern Ohio, Youngstown, 1989, Sri Sathaya Sai Ctr., Cleve./Canton, 1989. Mem.: IEEE (assoc.; treas. 2003), Soc. Women Engrs. Office Phone: 330-308-7513. Personal E-mail: chitrapartha@gmail.com.

**RAJAGOPALAN, DILIP,** pharmaceutical executive; b. Madras, India, May 7, 1964; s. Tuticorin G. and Meera Rajagopalan; m. Lini Sharda Kadaba, Jan. 18, 1989; 1 child, Rohan Kadaba. BSChemE, U. Bombay, 1985; MS, Northwestern U., 1987; PhD, MIT, 1991. Engr. Mobil R&D, Paulsboro, NJ, Dupont R&D, Wilmington, Del., 1994—2002; investigator bioinformatics GlaxoSmithKline, King of Prussia, Pa., 2002—05, mgr. bioinformatics 2005—. Contbr. articles to profl. jours. Achievements include patents in field.

**RAJAMANI, VIGNESH,** electrical engineer; b. Vellore, India, June 3, 1981; s. Rajamani and Bhama Venkataraman. Postgrad., Okla. State U., Stillwater, 2002—. Cert. elec. engr. Rsch. asst. Okla. State U., Stillwater, 2002—. Mem.: IEEE. Achievements include patents for innovation in RFID. Home: 80 S University Pl Apt # 8 Stillwater OK 74075 Office: Okla State U 202 Engineering South OSU Stillwater OK 74078 Personal E-Mail: vignesh.rajamani@okstate.edu.

**RAJAN, LATHA,** microbiologist, educator; d. P B Kurup and J Rajam; m. Ramnannair Mahasenan, Apr. 24, 1983; children: Navya Nair, Keshav Nair. MBBS, U. Kerala, India, 1982; MD, AIIMS, India, 1988; DipRCPath, Royal Coll. Pathology, England, 1997; MPH&TM, Tulane U., 2000. Medicine Indian Med. Coun., 1982. Jr. resident RM Lohia Hosp., New Delhi, 1984—85, AIIMS, New Delhi, 1985—88; specialist, asst. dir. Ministry of Health, New Delhi, New Delhi, 1989—94; rsch. scientist ICMR, New Delhi, New Delhi, 1988—89; lectr. U. Malaya, Kuala Lumpur, 1994—99; asst. prof. Tulane U., New Orleans, 2002—. Tech. expert Govt. of India, New Delhi, 1990—91; adj. faculty Seameo-Tropmed, Kuala Lumpur, Malaysia, 1995—99; speaker's bur. Pfizer Inc, Kuala Lumpur, Malaysia, 1997—99; clin. cons. PORIM, Kuala Lumpur, Malaysia, 1997—99; assoc. dir. of microbiology Tulane U. Hosp., New Orleans, 2005—. Reviewer (various profl. jours.); contbr. articles various profl. jours. Exec. com. Kerala Cultural Assn., New Orleans, 2004—05; organizer Tsunami Fund Raising, New Orleans, 2005—. Recipient Best Student in Surgery award, Med. Coll., Trivandrum, 1981; fellow Travel award, CDC/Fogarty, 1991; scholar, Dept. of Biotechnology, 1989. Mem.: HIV Med. Assn., Am. Soc. of Microbiology, Am. Soc. of Tropicla Medicine and Hygiene, Infectious Disease Soc. of Am., Delta Omega Nat. Pub. Health Honor Soc. (life; sec., v.p., pres. 2003—05). Office: Tulane U Sch Public Health 1440 Canal St Ste 2210 New Orleans LA 70112 Office Phone: 504-988-7970. Office Fax: 504-988-7313. E-mail: lrajan@tulane.edu.

**RAJANI, PREM RAJARAM,** transportation company financial executive; b. Bombay, Nov. 9, 1949; came to U.S., 1973; s. Rajaram N. and Devibai Rajani; m. Rekha Rohera, Apr. 21, 1977; children: Anand, Harshada. B Tech., Indian Inst. Tech., Bombay, 1973; MBA in Acctg. and Fin., Columbia U., 1975. Sr. ops. auditor Pfizer, Inc., N.Y.C., 1975-78; sr. projects fin. analyst Sea Land Industrial Corp., Edison, NJ, 1978-80; fin. mgr. joint ventures, 1980-81, mgr. corp. planning and analysis, 1981-84; mgr. corp. fin. Sea-Land Corp., Edison, 1984-87; asst. treas.-internat. Sea-Land Svc. Inc. subs. CSX Corp., Edison, 1987-88, asst. treas.-domestic, 1988, staff v.p., treas., 1988-94, staff v.p. fin. and planning Americas, 1994-97, staff v.p. fin. projects, 1998—2001, fin. cons., 2001—. E-mail: prajani@carolina.rr.com.

**RAJAPAKSA, TRIKANTE N.,** medical educator; b. Oct. 5, 1945; s. Vernon Henry Gunnasekera and Nalini De Alwis; m. Anura Rajapaksa, Dec. 3, 1970; 1 child, Roshini. MB BS, U. Sri Lanka, Colombo, 1970. Clin. asst. prof. medicine N.Y. Med. Coll., Valhalla, 1986—. Fellow: ACP, Am. Coll. Gastroenterology. Address: Apt 24K 1965 Broadway New York NY 10023-5980 Office: 3117 Kingsbridge Ave Bronx NY 10463 Office Phone: 718-543-5514.

**RAJARAM, SRI-SUJANTHY,** internist, medical educator; arrived in US, 1993, permanent resident, 1998; d. Vel and Sribalasaras Veluppillai; m. K. Rajaram, June 4, 1989; children: Sanjev, Sweda. MBBS, U. Jaffna, Srilanka, 1989. Diplomate Am. Bd. of Internal Medicine 1996, Critical Care 1998, Am. Acad. Sleep Medicine 2003. Asst. prof. medicine Albert Einstein Sch. Medicine, Bronx, NY, 1998—2003; med. dir. Cardio Sleep Ctr., Oldbridge, NJ, 2003—04; intensivist Robertwood Johnson U. Hosp., New Brunswick, NJ, 2003—05; asst. prof. medicine Robertwood Johnson Med. Sch. UMDNJ, NJ, 2003—05; asst. prof. medicine Cooper U. Hosp., NJ, 2005—, intensivist, 2005—. Intern, pediats. ob-gyn. U. Colombo, Sri Lanka, 1991—92, sr. house officer, anesthesiology, 1992; residency, internal medicine LI Coll. Hosp., NY, 1993—96; fellowship, critical care medicine Mt. Siani Sch. Medicine, 1996—98; sleep medicine NJ Neuro-Sleep Inst., JFK Med. Ctr., Edison, NJ, 2001—02. Contbr. chapters to books, articles to profl. jours., abstracts to profl. jours. Cmty. svc. project, primary health care svcs. to Sri Lanka, 2004, 2005; bd. dir. Internat. Med. Health Orgn. USA, 2003—; dir., continuous med. edn. Internat. Med. Health Orgn., 2004—; NJ coordinator Internat. Med. Health Orgn. USA, 2003—. Fellow: Am. Acad. Sleep Medicine, American Coll. Chest Physicians (Gov.'s Cmty. Svc. award 2004); mem.: Soc. Critical Care Medicine. Hindu. Home: 5 Rushton Ct West Windsor NJ 08550 Office: Cooper U Hosp One Cooper Plaza Camden NJ 08103 Business E-Mail: rajaram-sri-sujanthy@cooperhealth.edu.

**RAJASEKAR, ARCOT,** computer scientist; s. Kuppuswamy and Sakunthala Arcot; m. Malini Govindaraj Purasawalkam, Aug. 21, 1989; 1 child, Bhairavi. B with honors in engring., Coll. of Engring., U. of Madras, India, 1979; MS, Indian Inst. of Tech., India, 1982; PhD, U. Md., 1984. Post doctoral rsch. assoc. U. Md. Inst. for Advanced Computer Studies, Coll. Pk., Md., 1989—90; asst. prof. U. Ky., Lexington, 1990—96; scientist to principle scientist San Diego Supercomputer Ctr., La Jolla, Calif., 1996—2001, dir., data grid technologies group, 2001—. Vice thrust area liaison Nat. Partnership for Advanced Computational Infrastructure, La Jolla, Calif., 1997—2003; reviewer NSF, Washington, 2000—02. Author: (research monograph) Foundations of Disjunctive Logic Programming; guest editor Annals of Mathematics and Artificial Intelligence; contbr. articles various profl. jours., chapters to books various profl. text. Various scientific grants, NSF, 1991—2007, Storage Resource Broker Performance Optimization grant, Dept. of Def., 2000-2001, Biomedical Imaging Rsch. Network Coordinating Ctr. grant, NIH, 2001—, Portal Web Services: Support of DOE SciDAC Collaborations grant, Dept. of Energy, 2002-2005, Rsch. in String-oriented Databases grant, Dept. of Def., 1996. Mem.: Global Grid Forum. Hindu. Achievements include development of storage resource broker; patents for collection-based persistent digital archive; development of MCAT - a metadata catalog; research in data grid technology; logic programming. Avocations: reading, fish-breeding, web-surfing, camping, hiking. Office: San Diego Supercomputer Ctr UCSD 9500 Gilman Dr La Jolla CA 92014-0505 Office Phone: 858-534-8378. Business E-Mail: sekar@sdsc.edu.

**RAJENDRA, KUNWAR,** retired engineering educator, consultant; PhD, Mich. State U., 1980. Cert. prof. engr., Mich., 1976, Engr. Sarvajanik Nirman Vibhag, Lucknow, Uttar Paradesh, India, 1962—71; project engr. high energy physics Mich. State U., East Lansing, Mich., 1972—76; transp. planning dir. City of Lansing, Mich., 1976—88; engr. transp. sys. State of Mich., 1991—2002; adj. prof. Mich. State U., East Lansing, 2003—. Program dir. Intelligent Transportation Sys., Mich. Fellow, ASCE, 2002, Inst. of Transp. Engrs., 2002. Office Phone: 517-353-9562. Office Fax: 517-353-1980.

**RAJENDRAN, KADIAMPATTI NATARAJAN,** marketing educator; b. Begunia, West Bengal, India, Oct. 18, 1949; s. Kadiampatti Subramania Iyer and Meenakshi Natarajan; m. Mythili Sundaram, Nov. 10, 1976; children: Hari, Aditi. BSc in Engring., Banaras Hindu U., Varanasi, India, 1971, M in Bus. Mgmt., 1973; PhD in Bus. Mgmt., Mktg., U. No. Iowa, Iowa City, 1990. Cert. Indian Inst. Bankers, 1982. Probationary officer State Bank India, India, 1974—76, officer, consultancy cell Chennai, Tamil Nadu, India, 1976—81, dep. mgr., sib divsn. Tirupur, Tamil Nadu, India, mgr., pb divsn. Avanashi, Tamil Nadu, India, 1982—83; asst. prof., mktg. U. No. Iowa, Cedar Falls, 1988—96, assoc. prof., mktg., 1996—. Faculty trng. programs for bankers World Bank, 1979—82. Contbr. articles to profl. jours., chapters to books. Fellow: Acad. of Mktg. Sci.; mem.: Mktg. Mgmt. Assn., Inst. Ops. Rsch. Mgmt. Sci., Am. Mktg. Assn. Home: 2510 Neola Street Cedar Falls IA 50613 Office: Univ No Iowa 342 Curris Business Bldg Cedar Falls IA 50614 Office Phone: 319-273-6011. Office Fax: 319-273-2922. Personal E-mail: raj@cfu.net. Business E-Mail: raj.rajendran@uni.edu.

**RAJENDRAN, SRIVIDHYA,** computer scientist, researcher; d. Trichengodu Krishnaswami and Bhagyalakshmi Rajendran; m. Prashant Kumar Tarun, June 7, 2006. BE in Computer Sci. and Engring., Sardar Patel U., Birla Vishwakarma Mahavidyalay, Anand, Gujarat, India, 1998; MS in Computer Sci. and Engring., U. Tex., Arlington, 2003. Software engr. Larsen and Toubro- Sargent and Lundy India Ltd., Baroda, Gujarat, India, 1998—2000; grad. rsch. asst. Computer Sci. and Engring. Dept., Univ. of Tex., Arlington, 2003—03, 2004—. Contbr. articles to profl. jours. Vol. Mission Arlington, Tex., 2001—06. Scholar STEM Rsch. scholar, U. of Tex. at Arlington, 2005—. Mem.: AAAI, Tau Beta Pi (life). Hindu. Avocations: swimming, badminton.

**RAJPUT, FARZAN,** cardiologist; Cardiovasc. fellow Drexel U. Coll. Medicine, Phila., 2001—; cardiologist Pacific Coast Cardiology, Newport Beach, Calif., 2004—.

**RAJSKI, PEGGY,** film director, film producer; b. Stevens Point, Wis. Attended, U. Wis. Films include: (prodn. mgr.): Lianna, 1982, Almost You, 1984; (prodr., prodn. mgr.) The Brother From Another Planet, 1984, Matewan, 1987, (co-prodr., prodn. mgr.) Eight Men Out, 1988; (co-prodr.) The Grifters, 1990, (prodr.) Little Man Tate, 1991 (also 2nd. unit dir.), Used People, 1992, Home for the Holidays, 1995; (prodr. video) Bruce Springsteen's Glory Days; (dir.) Trevor, 1994 (Acad. award for Best Live Action Short Film).

**RAJU, MINNIE M.,** nursing administrator, critical care nurse; arrived in U.S., 1974; d. Pazhavilla I. and Mary Raju. BS in Biology, Albany State U., 1994; ADN, Rockland CC, Suffern, N.Y., 1997; BSN, U. Md., 2003, MS in Nursing Informatics, 2005. RN N.Y., Md., DC. Clin. nurse Nyack (N.Y.) Hosp., 1997—99, Washington Hosp. Ctr., 1999—2004, clin. mgr., 2004—. Mem.: Am. Assn. Critical Care Nurses, Health Info. Mgmt. Sys. Soc., Am. Med. Informatics Assn., Greater Washington Area Chamber Am. Assn. Critical Care Nurses, Sigma Theta Tau. Seventh Day Adventist. Avocations: reading, cooking. Office: Washington Hosp Ctr 110 Irving St NW Washington DC 20010

**RAJUPALEPU, RAHI K.,** technologist, consultant; s. Seshagiri Rao Venkata and Padmavathi Rajupalepu; m. Vidya Vidyakumar, Oct. 18, 2001; children: Pranav, Mayukha Anasuya. B of Engring., Osmania U., 1995; MBA, Am. Intercontinental U. Programmer Beechwood Computing/ Deloitte, Norwalk, Calif. 1996—97; sr. tech. cons. Sapient Corp., Boston, Mass., 1998—2000; sr. tech. cons. arch. Commerceone, Arlington/Columbia, Va., 2000—02; sr. tech. cons., arch. Plateau Systems Ltd, Arlington, 2002—05; pres., CEO Prometheus Technologies LLC, Ashburn, 2003—. Pres. Prometheus Technologies LLC, Ashburn, 2003—. Contbr. Rajdhani Mandir, Chantilly, Va. Achievements include various patents pending for technological ideas. Office Phone: 703-975-7244. Personal E-Mail: rrajupalepu@yahoo.com. E-mail: contact@prometheusllc.com.

**RAJYAGURU, VRAJLAL LALJIBHAI,** anesthesiologist; b. Jam Raval, India, Nov. 24, 1961; arrived in U.S., 1987; s. Laljibhai Rajyaguru and Devkiben L. (Joshi) Rajyaguru; m. Kalpana S. Thanki, Mar. 12, 1986; children: Neal, Parth. MB, BS, M.P. Shah Med. Coll., India, 1986; MD, N.Y. Med. Coll., 1994. Diplomate Am. Bd. Anesthesiology (fellow). Intern in surgery St. Vincent's Hosp., N.Y.C., 1989-90; resident in surgery L.I. Jewish Med. Ctr., New Hyde Pk., NY, 1990-91; resident in anesthesiology and pain mgmt. N.Y. Med. Coll., Valhalla, 1991-94; pvt. practice. Rschr. laser application in vascular surgery, 1989. Co-chmn. physician adv. bd. Nat. Rep. Congl. Com., 2001. Named Fla. Businessman of the Yr., Nat. Rep. Congl. Com., 2001. Fellow: Am. Bd. Disability Analysis, Am. Acad. Pain Mgmt., Am. Bd. Pain Medicine; mem.: AMA, Neuromodulation Soc. (advisor). Address: Advanced Pain Clin PO Box 3129 Kissimmee FL 34742

**RAK, LINDA MARIE,** elementary school educator, consultant; b. Dunkirk, N.Y. d. Felix Joseph and Helen (Dudek) Ruzycki; m. Joseph John Rak, Oct. 11, 1969; children: Joel, Seth. BA in Edn., SUNY, Fredonia, 1969, MS in Edn., 1974; postgrad., SUNY, Brockport, 1980-84, SUNY, Buffalo, 1988-90. Cert. reading and spl. edn. tchr., NY. Tchr. 1st grade Webster Central Sch. Dist., NY, 1969-72; tchr. kindergarten and reading Williamson Central Sch. Dist., 1973-76; instr. in GED Orleans County Job Devel. Agy., Albion, 1979-83; adult basic edn. coord. SUNY, Brockport, 1980-85; tchr. remedial reading, lang. arts coord. Kendall Central Sch. Dist., 1985—, spl. edn. tchr., 1988—. In-svc. presenter Kendall Elem. Sch., NY, 1984—2002; workshop presenter Monroe #2 Orleans BOCES, Spenceport, 1988—91, Genesee Wyoming Bd. of Coop. Ednl. Svcs. (BOCES), 1988—91, NY State Whole Lang. Conf., 1993; reading recovery tchr. Kendall Elem. Sch., 1996—2003; adj. prof. dept. edn. and human devel. SUNY, Brockport, 2001—; early intervention tchr., cons. Kendall (N.Y.) Elem. Sch., 2003—, co-chmn. 2d grade level, 2004—05, literacy summer sch. coord., 1999—2003, 2005—. Nursery sch. treas. AAUW, Orleans and Niagara Counties, NY, 1977-79; tchr. Sunday sch. St. Joseph's Ch., Lyndonville, NY, 1978-95, mem. parish coun., 1996—. Recipient Cert. of Appreciation, Congressman John J. La False, 1985, Roy L. Bubb award for excellence in tchg. and supervision SUNY Brockport, 2006; named Religious Educator of the Yr., Diocese of Buffalo, 1987. Mem. Internat. Reading Assn., Rochester Area Reading Coordinators (pres. 1992-96), Genesee Valley Devel. Learning Group (satellite rep. 1987-88), Lit. Vols. Orleans County (v.p. 1981-84, Outstanding Leadership award 1984), Somerset Hist. Soc., Reading Recovery Coun. Roman Cath. Avocation: home restoration. Home: 64 N Main St # 329 Lyndonville NY 14098-9672 Office: Kendall Cen Sch Dist 1932 Kendall Rd Kendall NY 14476-9775 Personal E-mail: lrak@localnet.com. Business E-mail: lrak@brockport.edu.

**RAKEL, ROBERT EDWIN,** physician, educator; b. Cin., July 13, 1932; s. Edwin J. and Elsie (Machino) R.; m. Peggy Klare; children: Barbara, Cindy, Linda, David. BS in Zoology, U. Cin., 1954, MD, 1958. Diplomate Am. Bd. Family Practice. Intern St. Mary's Hosp., Cin., 1958-59; resident in internal medicine USPHS Hosp., Seattle, 1959-61; resident in gen. practice Monterey County Hosp., Salinas, Calif., 1961-62; practice medicine Newport Beach, Calif., 1962-69; chmn. family practice program U. Calif., Irvine, 1969-71; prof., head dept. family practice U. Iowa, 1971-85; assoc. dean acad. and clin. affairs, Richard M. Kleberg, Sr. prof., chmn. dept. family medicine Baylor Coll. Medicine, Houston, 1985-97, prof. dept. family and cmty. medicine, 1997—. Dir. family practice residency program Hoag Meml. Hosp., Newport Beach, 1969-71; med. staff Mercy Hosp., Iowa City, 1971-85; chief family practice svc. St. Luke's Episc. Hosp., The Meth. Hosp., Houston, 1985-97; trustee The Hospice of Tex. Med. Ctr., 1986-97, Inst. of Religion Tex. Author forward: Neurology for the Everyday Practice of Medicine, R.G. Feldman, 1984; author: selected References in Family Medicine, 1973; editor (with H.F. Conn & T.W. Johnson): Family Practice, 1973; editor: (with H.F. Conn) Textbook of Family Practice, 1978; editor: Textbook of Family Practice, 3d edit., 1984, Textbook of Family Practice, 5th edit., 1995, Textbook of Family Practice, 6th edit., 2002, Principles of Family Medicine, 1977, Conn's Current Therapy, 1984—, Yearbook of Family Practice, 1977—90, (series) Procedures for Your Practice Patient Care, Vol. 18, Essentials of Family Practice, 1992, 2d edit., 1998, Saunders Manual Med. Practice, 1996, Saunders Manual Med. Practice, 2d edit., 2000, Essential Family Medicine, 3rd edit., 2006; mem. 13 editorial bds. med. jours.; contbr. articles to med. jours., Encyclopedia Britannica, 1995, Dictionary of Am. Med. Biography Vols. I and II, 1984. Served with USPHS, 1959-61. Recipient Mead-Johnson Scholar award in Gen. Practice, 1971, Max Cheplove award, NY Acad. Family Physicians, 2001, Lifetime Achievement award, Am. Med. Student Assn., 2002, McGovern award, Am. Med. Writers Assn., 2004. Fellow Am. Acad. Family Physicians (pres. Orange County chpt. Calif. 1969, commn. on edn. 1970-76, Thomas W. Johnson award 1973); mem. AMA (sect. on med. schs. 1985-97, gov. coun. of sect. 1986-88), Tex. Med. Assn., Am. Bd. Family Practice (bd. dirs. 1973-79, v.p. 1977-79, chmn. exam. com. 1974-79, recert. com. 1973-79, others), Am. Bd. Med. Spltys. (com. splty. evaluation 1978-81), Nat. Bd. Med. Examiners (bd. dirs. 1975-79), Soc. Tchrs. Family Medicine (dir. 1971-79, sec. 1971-73, F. Marian Bishop Leadership award, 1992), Coun. Acad. Socs., Assn. Am. Med. Colls., History of Medicine Soc. (founder, chmn. U. Iowa 1978-85, founder, chmn. Baylor Coll. Medicine 1986—), Am. Osler Soc. (bd. dirs. 1989-96, pres. 1994). Roman Catholic. Home: 2420 Underwood St Houston TX 77030-3506 Office: Baylor College Medicine Dept Family and Cmty Medicine 3701 Kirby Dr Ste 600 Houston TX 77098 Business E-Mail: rrakel@bcm.edu.

**RAKER, IRMA S.,** judge; b. Bklyn. m. Samuel K. Raker. BA, Syracuse U., 1959; cert. of attendance (hon.), Hague (The Netherlands) Acad. Internat. Law, 1959; JD, Am. U., 1972. Bar: Md. 1973, D.C. 1974, U.S. Dist. Ct. Md. 1977, U.S. Ct. Appeals (4th cir.) 1977. Asst. state's atty. State's Atty.'s Office Montgomery County, Md., 1973-79; ptnr. Sachs, Greenebaum & Tayler, Washington, 1979-80; judge Dist. Ct., Rockville, 1980-82, Cir. Ct. for Montgomery County, Md., 1982-94, Md. Ct. of Appeals, 1994—. Adj. prof. Washington Coll. Law, Am. U., 1980—; mem. faculty Md. Jud. Inst., Nat. Criminal Def. Inst., 1980, 81, 82; mem. legis. com. Md. Jud. Conf., mem. exec. com., 1985-89, mem. commn. to study bail bond and surety industry in Md.; mem. spl. com. to revise article 27 on crimes and punishment State of Md., 1991—; mem. inquiry com. atty. Grievance Commn. Md., 1978-81; chair jud. compensation com. Md. Jud. Conf., 1997—. Treas., v.p. West Bradley Citizens Assn., 1964-68; mem. adv. com. to county exec. on child abuse Montgomery County, 1976-77, mem. adv. com. to county exec. on battered spouses, 1977-78, mem. adv. com. on environ. protection, 1980; mem. citizens adv. bd. Montgomery County Crisis Ctr., 1980. Recipient Robert C. Heeney award Md. State Bar Assn., 1993, Dorothy Beatty Meml. award Women's Law Ctr., 1994, Rita Davidson award Women's Bar Md., 1995, Margaret Brent Trailblazers award ABA Commn. on Women in the Profession/Women's Bar Assn. Md., 1995, Elizabeth Dole Woman of Achievement award ARC, 1998, Leadership in Law award The Daily Record, 2001, Nat. Assn. Social Workers' Pub. Citizen of Yr. award, 2001, others; named of Md.'s Top 100 Women Warfield's Bus. Record, 1997, 99, 2001. Fellow Md. Bar Found.; mem. ABA (chair criminal justice stds. com. 1995-96, mem. coun. criminal law sect. 1997—, del. nat. conf. state trial judges, active various coms.), Am. Law Rev., Md. State Bar Assn. (chair coun. criminal law and practice sect., mem. bd. govs. 1981, 82, 85, 86, 90, mem. coun. litigation sect., active coms., chair com. to draft pattern jury instrns. in civil and criminal cases 1980—), Nat. Assn. Women Judges, Internat. Acad. Trial Judges, Am. Law Inst., Montgomery County Bar Assn. (chair criminal law sect. 1978-79, mem. exec. com. 1979-80, active other coms., Outstanding Jurist award 2000), Montgomery County Bar Leaders, Women's Bar Assn. Md., Women's Bar Assn. D.C., Hadassah Women's Orgn. (life), Pioneer Women Na'amat (Celebration of Women award 1985), Pi Sigma Alpha. Office: Ct of Appeals of Md 50 Maryland Ave Rockville MD 20850-2320*

**RAKES, JOHN PATRICK,** music educator; b. Portsmouth, Va., Oct. 16, 1981; s. John William and Helen Rakes. B in Music Edn., Wheaton Coll., 2003. Cert. tchr. Ill. Music tchr. Cmty. Consolidated Sch. Dist. 15, Palatine, Ill., 2004—; choir dir. Faith Christian Reformed Ch., Elmhurst, Ill., 2004—. Mem.: Music Educators Nat. Conv., Am. Choral Dir.'s Assn.

**RAKES, RANDI LEE,** elementary school educator, test developer; b. Edison, N.J., June 24, 1969; d. Edward Eli and Florence (Yatrofsky) Leviten; children: Allyson B., Randy R. Jr. 1 stepchild, Laura M. BA in Psychology, Rutgers U., 1991; MEd in Spl. Edn., Trenton State Coll., 1998. Cert. spl. edn., elem. edn., N.J. Substitute tchr. Woodbridge Bd. Edn., NJ, 1989-91, Pemberton Twp. Schs., Browns Mills, NJ, 1991-92, tchr., 1992-93; test developer N.J. Dept. Pers., Trenton, 1993—95; tchr. Pemberton Twp. Schs., Browns Mills, 1995—. Gov.'s Teaching scholar State of N.J., 1987; Recipient Citation for Outstanding Svc. to Children of Cmty. N.J. Legislature, 1999. Mem. N.J. Edn. Assn., Kappa Delta Phi. Roman Catholic. Avocations: crafts, computers, camping, collecting, hunting. Home: 412 Pardee Blvd Browns Mills NJ 08015-1137 Personal E-mail: randi_rakes@yahoo.com. E-mail: rrakes@pemb.org.

**RAKHNO, IGOR,** physicist; s. Leonid and Elena Rakhno; m. Olga Kopeliovich, Nov. 24, 1984; 1 child, Eugenia. MS in Physics, Belarusian State U., Minsk, Belarus, 1981; postgrad. in nuc. engring., Nuc. Power Engring. Inst., Minsk, 1988. PhD Diploma Supreme Exam. Bd., Moscow, 1991. Jr. scientist Nuc. Power Engring. Inst., Minsk, 1981—91; scientist Radiation Physics and Chemistry Problems Inst., Minsk, 1991—93, sr. scientist, 1993—2000; tech. assoc. Fermi Nat. Accelerator Lab., Batavia, Ill., 2000—03, guest scientist, 2004—; rsch. assoc. U. Ill., Urbana-Champaign, 2003—04. Fellow, Matsumae Internat. Found., Tokyo, 1994. Achievements include research in theoretical and experimental research on nuclear waste transmutation with low-energy neutrons and high-energy hadrons; theoretical research on radiation environment in high-luminosity regions in the Large Hadron Collider to be built at CERN (Geneva, Switzerland) to study

proton-proton collisions at 14 TeV. Office: Fermi National Accelerator Lab MS 220 PO Box 500 Batavia IL 60510-0500 Office Phone: 630-840-6763. Office Fax: 630-840-6039. Business E-Mail: rakhno@fnal.gov.

**RAKITA, LOUIS,** retired cardiologist; b. Montreal, Que., Can., July 2, 1922; came to U.S., 1951, naturalized, 1962; s. S. and Rose (Weinman) R.; m. G. Blanche Michlin, Dec. 4, 1945; 1 son. Robert M. BA, Sir George Williams Coll., Montreal, 1942; MD, C.M., McGill U., 1949. Diplomate: Am. Bd. Internal Medicine. Intern Montreal Gen. Hosp., 1949-50; resident in medicine Jewish Gen. Hosp., Montreal, 1950-51; fellow in medicine Alton Ochsner Med. Found., New Orleans, 1951-52; chief resident in medicine Cleve. City Hosp., 1952-53, Am. Heart Assn. fellow, 1954-55, Inst. for Med. Research, Cedars of Lebanon Hosp., Los Angeles, 1953-54; practice medicine specializing in internal medicine and cardiology Cleve., 1954—; instr. medicine Western Res. U., Cleve., 1954-55, sr. instr., 1955-57, asst. prof., 1957-61, asso. prof., 1961-71; asst. vis. physician Cleve. City Hosp., 1954-57, vis. physician, 1957—; advanced fellow Cleve. Met. Gen. Hosp., 1959-61, dir. cardiology, 1966-87, immediate past dir., div. cardiology, 1987—2005; asso. div. of research in med. edn. Case Western Res. U., Cleve., 1969-75, prof. medicine, 1971-93, prof. emeritus medicine, 1993. Chmn. Phase IIA Cardiovascular com. Case Western Res. U., 1965-70, Faculty Senate Subcom. for Devel. and Evaluation of Ednl. Methods, 1969, chmn. Univ. Com. on Ednl. Planning, 1971-73, Faculty Coun. Sch. Medicine, 1979-80, Faculty Coun., chmn. Steering Com. Sch. Medicine, 1979-80, mem. bd. trustees Coun. on Univ. Plans, 1971-73, Faculty Senate, Exec. Coun.; cons. in cardiology Luth. Med. Ctr., Cleve., 1970—, Crile VA Hosp., Cleve., 1969—; vis. cardiologist Sunny Acres Hosp., Cleve., 1973—; cardiologist rep. of del. to USSR, 1973. Author: (with M. Broder) Cardiac Arrhythmias, 1970, (with M. Kaplan) Immunological Diseases, 1972; Contbr. (with M. Kaplan) articles on cardiovascular diseases to profl. publs. Served with RCAF, 1942-45. Recipient Research Career Devel. award USPHS, 1962-69, Saltzman award Mt. Sinai Med. Health Found., 1997. Fellow ACP (Laureate award Ohio chpt. 1992), Am. Coll. Cardiology, Royal Coll. Physicians and Surgeons Can. (cert.), Am. Heart Assn. (mem. exec. com. N.E. Ohio chpt. 1972—, trustee 1969—, pres. N.E. Ohio chpt. 1972-74, coun. on clin. cardiology 1972—, chmn. various coms., v.p. North Ctrl. Region 1985-86, bd. dirs. 1985-86, hon. life trustee Northeast Ohio affiliate, vice chmn. task force on product licensing feasibility 1987—, Award of Merit 1987, Gold Heart award 1989); mem. AAUP, Am. Fedn. Clin. Rsch., Ctrl. Soc. Clin. Rsch., Soc. Exptl. Biology and Medicine, Cleve. Med. Libr. Assn. (trustee 1972—), Nat. Bd. Med. Examiners, The Press of Case Western Res. U. (adv. com. 1970), Nat. Heart and Lung Inst., Nat. Insts. Health (left ventricular assist device clin. trial program divsn. extramural affairs, data rev. bd. 1981—, adv. com. med. devices applications program 1971-75), Sigma Xi. Home: 24151 S Woodland Rd Cleveland OH 44122-3315 E-mail: lrakita@earthlink.net.

**RAKO, SUSAN,** psychiatrist, writer; b. Springfield, Mass., Sept. 4, 1939; d. Robert and Ann (Melnikoff) Mandell; 1 child, Jennifer Sarah. Student, Wellesley Coll., 1957-60; BS, U. Cin. 1961; MS in Film, Boston U., 1988; MD, Albert Einstein Coll. Medicine, 1966. Med. rsch. asst. neuroendocrinology Worcester Found. Exptl. Biology, Shrewsbury, Mass., 1959; med. rsch. asst. May Inst., Cin., 1961-62; intern in medicine, surgery Mt. Auburn Hosp., Cambridge, Mass., 1966-67; resident in adult psychiatry Mass. Mental Health Ctr., Boston, 1967-69; tchg. fellow in psychiatry Harvard Med. Sch., Boston, 1967-69, clin. fellow in psychiatry, 1969-70; pvt. practice Newton, Mass., 1970—; clin. instr. psychiatry Harvard Med. Sch., Boston, 1970-75; resident in child and adult psychiatry Beth Israel Hosp., Boston, 1969-70; psychiatrist Mass. Mental Health Ctr., Boston, 1970-77, Newton-Wellesley Hosp., 1982. Cons. Cutler Counseling Ctr., Norwood, Mass., 1983, VA Hosp., San Juan, PR, 1990—94; founder, pres. Women's Health on Alert, Inc., 2003—; spkr. in field. Author: No More Periods? The Risks of Menstrual Suppression, 2003, The Hormone of Desire: The Truth About Testosterone, Sexuality, and Menopause, 1996, 2d edit., 1999, That's How the Light Gets In: Memoir of a Psychiatrist, 2005, The Blessings of the Curse, 2006; co-editor: Semrad: The Heart of a Therapist, 1980, (paperback) 2004; film maker Susan and Jenni, 1987; exec. prodr. play Hysterics, 2005. Business E-Mail: susanrako@aol.com.

**RAKOFF, JED SAUL,** federal judge, author; b. Phila., Aug. 1, 1943; s. Abraham Edward and Doris Tobiah (Michell) R.; m. Ann Rosenberg, Aug. 4, 1974; children: Jena Lynn, Elana Beth, Keira Jan. BA, Swarthmore Coll. 1964, LLD (hon.), 2003; MPhil, Balliol Coll., Oxford U., Eng., 1966; JD, Harvard U., 1969; LLD (hon.), St. Francis U., 2005. Bar: N.Y. 1971, D.C. 1983, U.S. Supreme Ct. 1986. Law clk. U.S. Ct. Appeals (3rd cir.), Phila., 1969-70; assoc. Debevoise, Plimpton, Lyons & Gates, N.Y.C., 1970-73; asst. U.S. atty. So. Dist. N.Y., N.Y.C., 1973-80, chief bus. and securities fraud prosecutions U.S. Atty.'s Office, 1978-80; ptnr. Mudge Rose Guthrie Alexander & Ferdon, N.Y.C., 1980-90, Fried Frank Harris Shriver & Jacobson, N.Y.C., 1990-96; judge U.S. Dist. Ct. (So. Dist.), 1996—. Lectr. in law Columbia Law Sch., 1988-; mem. bd. mgrs. Swarthmore Coll., 2003-. Author: (with S. Arkin et al) Business Crime, 6 vols., 1982, Criminal Defense Techniques, 6 vols., 1982, (with H. Goldstein) RICO: Civil and Criminal Law and Strategy, 1989, (with L. Blumkin and R. Sauber) Corporate Sentencing Guidelines; Compliance and Mitigation, 1993; editor-in-chief Bus. Crimes Bull., 1994-95; columnist N.Y. Law Jour., 1985-95; contbr. numerous articles to law revs. Mem. exec. bd. N.Y. chpt. Am. Jewish Com., 1971-95. Fellow Am. Coll. Trial Lawyers (chmn. N.Y. State 1993-94), Am. Bd. Criminal Lawyers; mem. ABA, N.Y. State Bar Assn., Assn. of Bar of City of N.Y. (chmn. criminal law com. 1986-89), Fed. Bar Coun., N.Y. Coun. Def. Lawyers (dir. 1990-94). Democrat. Jewish. Office: US Courthouse 500 Pearl St Rm 1340 New York NY 10007-1316 Office Phone: 212-805-0401. Business E-Mail: Jed_S_Rakoff@nysd.uscourts.gov.

**RAKOS, BALÁZS,** physicist, researcher; b. Budapest, Hungary, Oct. 21, 1975; s. Miklós Rakos and Zsuzsanna Szendro. MS in Physics, U. Debrecen, Hungary, 2001; PhD, U. Notre Dame, 2006. Rsch. asst. U. Notre Dame, Ind., 2001—06; rschr. Inst. Isotopes, Hungarian Acad. Sci., Budapest, 2006—. Home: 76/A Szeher ut Budapest 1021 Hungary Personal E-mail: rakos@iki.kfki.hu.

**RAKOTOBE-JOEL, THIERRY,** engineering educator, researcher, department chairman; s. Max Hoambinintsoa Rakotobe and Lydia Nicole Rajoely; m. Andoveloniaina Rasolofo, Jan. 8, 2000. MS in Engring., U. Madagascar, Antananarivo, 1994; PhD, U. Cin., 2000. Rsch. assoc. U. of Sheffield, England, 1998—2000; rsch. fellow U. of Warwick, Coventry, England, 1999—2001; asst. prof. mgmt. Ramapo Coll. of N.J., Mahwah, NJ, 2001—03, assoc. prof. mgmt., 2003—, chmn. dept. mgmt., 2005—. Editor: (book) Complex Systems and Complexity in Industry; newsletter editor divsn. internat. mgmt. Acad. Mgmt., 1999—2003; contbr. articles to profl. jours. (Highly Commended award, MCB Univ. Press, 2001). Fellow Sam Walton fellow, WalMart Found., 2001; scholar Fulbright scholar, Inst. of Internat. Edn. Mem.: Acad. of Mgmt. (newsletter editor 2000—03), Decision Sci. Inst. (assoc.), Am. Coun. for Que. Studies (assoc.), Inst. for Ops. Rsch. and Mgmt. Sci. (assoc.), Phi Beta Delta. Office: Ramapo College of New Jersey 505 Ramapo Valley Rd Mahwah NJ 07430 Personal E-mail: trakotobe@aol.com.

**RAKOVE, JACK NORMAN,** history professor; b. Chgo., June 4, 1947; s. Milton Leon and Shirley (Bloom) R.; m. Helen Scharf, June 22, 1969; children: Robert, Daniel. AB, Haverford Coll., 1968; PhD, Harvard U., 1975. Asst. prof. history Colgate U., Hamilton, N.Y., 1975-80; from asst. to assoc. prof. history Stanford (Calif.) U., 1980-90, prof., 1990—, Coe prof. history and Am. studies, 1996—, prof. polit. sci., 1999—. Author: Beginnings of National Politics, 1979, James Madison and The Creation of the American Republic, 1990, Original Meanings, 1996 (Pulitzer prize for History, 1997), Declaring Rights, 1997; editor: Interpreting the Constitution, 1990, James Madison Writings, 1999, The Unfinished Election of 1800, 2001, The Federalist, 2003. Commr. Calif. Bicentennial Commn., 1986-87. With USAR, 1968-74. NEH fellow, 1985-86, Stanford Humanities Ctr. fellow, 1988-89,

2000-01. Mem. Am. Hist. Assn., Orgn. Am. Historians, Soc. Am. Historians, Am. Polit. Sci. Assn., Am. Acad. Arts & Scis., Am. Antiquarian Soc., Soc. History of Early Am. Rep (pres. 2002).

**RAKOW, JAY,** lawyer, film company executive; AB, NYU, 1974; JD, Cornell U., 1977. Bar: Calif. 1980, DC 1980. Assoc. Dewey, Ballantine, 1977—80, Wyman, Bautzer, Christensen, Kuchel & Silbert; ptnr. Christensen, Miller, Fink, Jacobs, Glaser, Weil & Shapiro, LLP, 1988—93, 1996—2000; sr. v.p., gen. counsel Paramount Pictures Corp., 1993—96; sr. exec. v.p., gen. counsel Metro-Goldwyn-Mayer Inc., LA, 2000—05, mediator, arbitrator, 2005—. Office: 1925 Century Park East Ste 1975 Los Angeles CA 90067 Office Phone: 310-277-3669.

**RAKSIN, ALEX,** reporter, writer; b. Nov. 9, 1960; m. Victoria Hendrick; children: Tobias, Leonid. BA in Journalism, U. So. Calif., 1984. Columnist LA Times, 1985—93, dep. book editor, 1993—96, editl. writer, 1996—2005, sci. corr., 2005—. Freelance writer, 1984—93; instr. UCLA Ext., 1986—89; dir. Lit. awards PEN USA West, 1998—2000. Recipient Outstanding Media award for Editl. Writing, Nat. Alliance for Mentally Ill, 2001, Nat. Headliner award for Editl. Writing, Calif. Alliance for Mentally Ill, 2001, 1999, Aaron Price Child Health and Welfare Scholarship and Journalism award, 1999, Sigma Delta Chi award for editl. writing, 2002, Pulitzer prize for editl. writing, 2002, L.A. Times prize for best editl. series, 2004. Mem.: Nat. Conf. Editl. Writers, Nat. Com. Concerned Journalists, Nat. Book Critics Cir. Office: LA Times 202 W 1st St Los Angeles CA 90012

**RALEIGH, CECIL BARING,** geophysicist; b. Little Rock, Ark, Aug. 11, 1934; s. Cecil Baring and Lucile Nell (Stewart) R.; m. Diane Lauster, July 17, 1982; children: Alison, Marianne, Lawrence, David. BA, Pomona Coll., Calif., 1956; MA, Claremont Grad. Sch., Calif., 1958; PhD, UCLA, 1963. Fellow Research Sch. Phys. Sci., Australian Nat. U., Canberra, 1963-66; geophysicist U.S. Geol. Survey, Menlo Park, Calif., 1966-80, program mgr. for earthquake prediction research program, 1980-81; dir. Lamont-Doherty Geol. Obs. and prof. geol. scis. Columbia U., Palisades, NY, 1981-89; dean Sch. Ocean and Earth Sci. and Tech. U. Hawaii, Honolulu, 1989—2003; rschr. Hawaii Nat. Energy Inst. U. Hawaii, 2003—. CEO Ctr. for a Sustainable Future, Inc., 1996-2005, HR Biopetroleum, 2004—; mem. Gov.'s Task Force on Sci. Tech., 1996-98; mem. NAS/NRC Ocean Studies Bd.; chmn. NAS/NRC Yucca Mountain Panel. Author papers control earthquakes, rheology of the mantle, mechanics of faulting, crystal plasticity. Trustee Bishop Mus., 1997—2003. Recipient Interdisciplinary award U.S. Nat. Com. Rock Mechanics, 1969, 74; Meritorious Service award Dept. Interior, 1974; Barrows Centennial Dist. Alumnus award Pomona Coll. Fellow Am. Geophys. Union, Geol. Soc. Am. Democrat. Inventor formation fracturing method. Office: U Hawaii Sch Ocean Earth Sci & Tech Honolulu HI 96822

**RALES, MITCHELL P.,** automotive parts company executive; b. 1956; married; 2 children. B, DePauw U.; grad., Miami U., Ohio, 1978. Ptnr. Equity Grp. Holdings, Washington, 1979—; pres. Danaher Corpn., Washington, 1984—, bd. dirs., chmn. exec. com., 1990—; founder, dir. Colfax Corpn., 1995—. Chmn. Capital Campaign for Hosp. Sick Children; treas., trustee, chmn. Capital Campaign of Norwood Sch.; mem. assoc. adv. coun. Miami U., Ohio; bd. trustees Hirshorn Mus. and Sculpture Garden; mem. trustees coun. Nat. Gallery Art. Named one of Top 200 Collectors, ARTnews mag., 2003—06, Forbes' Richest Americans, 2006. Avocation: Collector of Modern and Contemporary Art. Office: Danaher Corpn 2099 Pennsylvania Ave NW 12th Fl Washington DC 20006-6800*

**RALES, STEVEN M.,** automotive parts company executive; b. Pitts., Mar. 31, 1951; m. Christine Plank Rales (div. 2002). BA, DePauw U., 1973; JD, America U., 1978. Ptnr. Equity Grp. Holdings, Washington, 1979—; chmn., CEO Danaher Corpn., Washington, 1984—2001, chmn., 2001—. Named one of Top 200 Collectors, ARTnews mag., 2003—06, Forbes' Richest Americans, 2006. Avocation: Collector of Impressionism, Modern and Contemporary Art. Office: Danaher Corpn 2099 Pennsylvania Ave NW 12th Fl Washington DC 20006*

**RALEY, BENNETT WILLIAM,** former federal agency administrator; b. 1956; BS in Agrl. Bus., Colo. State U., 1979, JD, 1983. Assoc. Davis, Graham & Stubbs, Denver, 1983, ptnr. 1990; shareholder Trout & Raley, P.C. (formerly known as Hobbs, Trout & Raley, P.C.), 1992—2001; gen. counsel No. Colo. Water Conservancy Dist.; spl. asst. atty. gen. State of N.Mex., 1998—2001; asst. sec. water and sci. US Dept. Interior, Washington, 2001—04. Staff counsel US Senator Hank Brown (Rep.-Colo.), 1991—92; chief counsel US Senate Judiciary Subcom. on Constn., Federalism and Property Rights, 1995; co-chair Fed. Water Rights Task Force.

**RALEY, JOHN WESLEY, JR.,** lawyer; b. May 23, 1932; s. John Wesley and Helen Thames; children: John Wesley III, Robert Thames. AB, Okla. Baptist U., 1954; JD, U. Okla., 1959. Bar: Okla. 1959, U.S. Supreme Ct. 1973, U.S. Ct. Appeals (10th cir.), 1962, U.S. Dist. (we. dist.) Okla. 1961, U.S. Dist. Ct. (no. dist.) Okla. 1988, U.S. Dist. Ct. (ea. dist.) Okla. 1989. Asst. U.S. atty. We. Dist. Okla. U.S. Dept. Justice, 1961-69; ptnr. Northcutt, Raley, Clark and Gardner, Ponca City, Okla., 1969-90; U.S. atty. Ea. Dist. Okla. U.S. Dept. Justice, 1990-97; of counsel Northcutt, Clark, Gardner & Hron, Ponca City, 1997—; mcpl. ct. judge Ponca City, 2001—05. Mayor of Ponca City, Okla., 1980-83; mem. Okla. Ethics Commn., 2003—, chmn., 2005-06. Capt. USNR, 1950-84, ret. Recipient George Washington Honor medal Freedoms Found. at Valley Forge, 1971, Spl. Initiative award U.S. Dept. Justice, 1994, Outstanding Alumni Achievement award Okla. Bapt. U., 1981, Outstanding Citizen award Ponca City, 1984. Fellow Am. Coll. Trial Lawyers; mem. ABA, Am. Bd. Trial Advs. (pres. Okla. chpt. 2005), Okla. Bar Assn. (bd. govs. 1988-90), Kay County Bar Assn. (pres. 1980), Am. Legion, Masons, Res. Officers Assn., Naval Res. Assn., VFW. Republican. Southern Baptist. Office: 400 E Central Ave Ste 401 Ponca City OK 74601-5428 Address: PO Box 1412 Ponca City OK 74602-1412 Office Phone: 580-762-1655. E-mail: jraley@northcuttlawfirm.com.

**RALEY, JOHN WESLEY, III,** lawyer; b. Oklahoma City, Oct. 19, 1959; s. John Wesley Raley Jr. and Mary Lane Mallett; m. Kelly Elaine Williams, Sept. 22, 1984; children: Katherine Elise, William Thomas, James Wesley. BA summa cum laude, U. Okla., 1981, JD, 1984; LLM, U. Aberdeen, Scotland, 1988. Bar: Tex. 1985, U.S. Dist. Ct. (so. dist.) Tex. 1985, U.S. Ct. Appeals (5th cir.) 1985; bd. cert. personal injury trial law Tex. Bd. Legal Specialization. With Fulbright & Jaworski, LLP, Houston, 1985-96, ptnr., 1996-2000; shareholder, mng. ptnr. Cooper & Scully, P.C., Houston, 2001—. Lectr. civil litigation U. Houston CLE, 1995—; bd. dirs. Houston Pub. TV, on-air spokesman, 1996—. Vol. Habitat for Humanity, Houston, 1998. Fellow Tex. Bar Found. (life); mem. ABA, State Bar Tex., Houston Bar Assn. (interdisciplinary ednl. alliance, spkrs. bur.), U. Okla. Varsity O Club, Phi Beta Kappa. Avocations: basketball, golf, tennis, local amateur drama performances. Home: 1 Stayton Cir Houston TX 77024 Office: 700 Louisiana St Ste 3850 Houston TX 77002 Office Phone: 713-236-6800. E-mail: john.raley@coopersally.com.

**RALL, JOSEPH EDWARD,** physician; b. Naperville, Ill., Feb. 3, 1920; s. Edward Everett and Nell (Platt) R.; m. Caroline Domm, Sept. 28, 1944 (dec. Apr. 1976); children: Priscilla, Edward Christian. BA, North Central Coll., 1940, D.Sc. (hon.), 1966; MS, Northwestern U., 1944, MD, 1945; PhD, U. Minn., 1952; Dr. honoris causa, Faculty of Medicine, Free U. Brussels, Belgium, 1975; MD (hon.), U. Naples, 1985. Assoc. mem. Sloan Kettering Inst., N.Y.C., 1950-55; chief clin. endocrinology Nat. Inst. Arthritis, Metabolism and Digestive Diseases, NIH, 1955-62; dir. intramural research Nat. Inst. Arthritis, Diabetes and Kidney Diseases, 1962-83; dep. dir. intramural research NIH, 1983-91; sr. investigator Nat. Inst. Diabetes and Digestive and Kidney Diseases, NIH, 1991; scientist emeritus NIH, 1995. Mem. NRC, 1960-65 Author numerous articles, chpts. in books on thyroid gland nuc. hormone receptors, and radiation. Chmn. Coun. of Scientists for Internat. Human Frontier Sci. Program, 1989-93. Served to capt. M.C. AUS,

1946-48. Recipient Van Meter prize Am. Goiter Assn., 1950, Fleming award, 1959, Outstanding Achievement award Mayo Clinic and U. Minn., 1964; Disting. Service award Am. Thyroid Assn., 1967; Disting. Service award HEW, 1968, Disting. Exec. rank, sr. exec. service, 1980, R.H. Williams Disting. Leadership award in endocrinology, 1983, Disting. Achievement award N.Y. Hosp., Cornell Med. Ctr., 1987; named Outstanding Alumnus N. Central Coll., 1966 Mem. NAS, AAAS, Am. Acad. Arts and Scis., Am. Soc. Clin. Investigation, Am. Phys. Soc., Endocrine Soc., Assn. Am. Physicians, Societe de Biologie (France), Royal Acad. Medicine (Brussels). Home: 3947 Baltimore St Kensington MD 20895-3913 Office: NIH Bldg 10 Rm 7C432 Bethesda MD 20892 Office Phone: 301-402-2486. E-mail: joseph_rall@nih.gov.

**RALLI, CONSTANTINE PANDIA,** lawyer; b. Bronxville, NY, Apr. 6, 1948; s. Pandia C. and Mary (Motter) R.; m. Alison Rhoads, Aug. 11, 1973; children: Pandia C., Christopher A. BA, Middlebury Coll., 1970; JD, Fordham U., 1973; LLM in Taxation, NYU, 1986. Bar: NY 1974, US Ct. Appeals (2nd cir.) 1974, US Dist. Ct. (so. and ea. dists.) NY 1975, US Tax Ct. 1977, Fla. 1985, Conn. 1985, US Dist. Ct. Conn. 1987. Assoc. Davis Polk & Wardwell, NYC, 1973-81; ptnr. Hall, McNicol, Hamilton & Clark, NYC, 1981-88, LeBoeuf, Lamb, Greene & MacRae LLP, NYC, 1988—, chmn. trust & estates dept. Sec., bd. dirs. Fairfield-Maxwell Ltd., Campo Tankers SA, N.Y.C., 1987—95. Bd. dirs. Samaritan Counseling Ctr., Rye, NY, 1987-90, Rye Free Reading Room, 1990-93, Rye Presbyn. Ch., 1986-89. Mem. Union Club, Am. Yacht Club, Ekwanok Country Club (Manchester, Vt.). Republican. Presbyterian. Office: LeBoeuf Lamb Greene & MacRae 125 W 55th St New York NY 10019-5369 Office Phone: 212-424-8394. Office Fax: 212-424-8500. Business E-Mail: cralli@llgm.com.

**RALLO, JAMES GILBERT,** management company executive; b. Balt., Mar. 1, 1942; s. James Vincent and Thelma Mary (Hannahs) R.; m. Frances Elaine Petro, June 13, 1965; children: James Michael, Robert Francis. BS, U. Md., 1965; postgrad., George Washington U., 1967—. Mktg. trainee Chessie Sys., Balt., 1965—66; market analyst Bendix Corp., Balt., 1966—68, contract administr. N.Y.C., 1968—70; account exec. Peterson, Howell & Heather, Inc. (name changed to PHH Arval) PHH Vehicle Mgmt. Svcs., Hunt Valley, Md., 1970—75; regional mgr. Peterson, Howell & Heather, Inc., Hunt Valley, 1975—80, v.p. sales, 1980—83, v.p. sales and client rels., 1983—87, sr. v.p. sales and client rels., 1987—91, sr. v.p. client and industry rels., 1991—94, v.p. industry rels., 1994—2003, v.p. strategic partnership, 2003—. Sponsor Industry Standards Project, 2001—. Bd. dirs., mem. fin. com. Towson YMCA, Md., 1981-93, mem. fundraising com., mem. budget com.; coach Cockeysville-Springlake Recreation Coun., 1973-82; advisor Jr. Achievement, 1975-76; fund solicitor United Way, 1983-84; v.p. NAFA Found., 1995—. Mem.: Am. Automotive Leasing Assn. (sponsor Industry Standards project), Automotive Fleet and Leasing Assn. (dir. lessors 1993—95, conf. com. 1993—2001, v.p. 1999—2000, exec. v.p. 2000—01, pres. 2001—02, bd. dirs., ednl. com.), Nat. Assn. Fleet Adminstrs. (affiliate chmn. intercounty chpt. 1978—80, nat. affiliate com. 1990—2000, editl. com. 1992—96, mem. conf./program com. 1993—98, bd. govs. 1993—, chmn. affiliates com. 1995—97, co-chair ednl. com. 1999—2001, affiliate trustee 2000—03, bd. trustees 2001—03, Hon. award for disting. svc. 1997), Optimists Club (v.p. Springdale-Cockeysville 1982—84, chmn. fundraising com.). Avocations: skiing, sports, classic cars, reading, golf. Office: PHH Arval 940 Ridgebrook Rd Sparks MD 21152 Office Phone: 410-771-2371. Business E-Mail: jim.rallo@phh.com.

**RALPH, DAMANI,** professional soccer player; b. Kingston, Jamaica, Nov. 6, 1980; Attended, Merdian Cmty. Coll., Miss., 1999—2001, U. Conn. 2001—03. Forward, men's soccer Meridian Cmty. Coll., 1999—2001, U. Conn., 2001—03; forward DC United Major League Soccer, Washington, 2004—. Named MVP, Nat. Junior Coll. Athletic Assn. Tournament, 2000. Offensive Player of Yr., Big East, 2002; named to First Team, Big East, 2002; recipient Finalist, Hermann Trophy, MO Athletic Commn., 2002. Achievements include team leader in goals scored (10) and points (26) for men's soccer at the U. Conn. in 2001. Office: Soldier Stadium 425 E McFetridge Dr Chicago IL 60605

**RALPH, DAVID CLINTON,** communications educator; b. Muskogee, Okla., Jan. 12, 1922; s. Earl Clinton and Rea Jane (Potter) R.; m. Kathryn Juanita Wicklund, Nov. 29, 1947; children: David Randall, Steven Wicklund. AA, Muskogee Jr. Coll., 1941; BS in Theatre, Northwestern U., 1947, MA in Theatre, 1948, PhD in Speech, 1953. Lectr. Ind. U., Hammond, 1947-48; instr. speech U. Mo., Columbia, 1948-53; tchr. debate-forensics summer program for high sch. students Northwestern U., Evanston, Ill., 1949-51; asst. prof. speech Mich. State U., East Lansing, 1953-57, assoc. prof., 1957-64, prof. speech and theatre, 1964-68, prof. communication, 1968-94, prof. emeritus, 1994—, dir. comm. undergrad. program, 1968-88. Cons. in field. Co-author: Group Discussion, 1954, 2d edit., 1956, Principles of Speaking, 1962, 3d edit., 1975; contbr. articles to profl. jours., chpts. to books. Coach Jr. League Boys' Baseball, Lansing, Mich., 1958-74; mem. civilian aux. to Lansing Fire Dept., 1987—. Lt. USNR, 1942-46, PTO, ETO. Named Hon. State Farmer, Future Farmers Am., 1965; recipient Community Svc. award Mich. State U. Sr. Class Coun., 1979, Outstanding Faculty award, 1987, 91; Teaching Excellence award State of Mich., 1990. Mem. AAUP, Nat. Communication Assn., Cen. States Communication Assn., Golden Key (hon., faculty advisor), Omicron Delta Kappa. Democrat. Methodist. Avocation: model trains and fire engines. Office: Mich State U Dept Communication East Lansing MI 48824

**RALPH, NANCYJO,** retired music educator; d. Alfred M. and Phyllis L. Niles; m. Dwight G. Ralph, Mar. 28, 1970; children: Victoria L. Fortna, Erik C. MusB in Edn., Grove City Coll., Pa., 1969; M in Elem. Edn., Edinboro U. Pa., 1974; postgrad. in Music Edn., Kent State U., Ohio, 1989, Registered music educator, Penn. music tchr. Lakeview Sch. Dist., Sandy Lake, Pa., 1969; h.s. music tchr. Cambridge Springs H.S., Penncrest Sch. Dist., Pa., 1970—2000, elem. music tchr., 2000—05; pvt. piano tchr. Vol. music tchr. Cornerstone Day Care and Penncrest Day Care Ctrs., Penncrest Day Care; with Tool City Bell Ringers, 2005—. Choir mem., pianist, various com. Saegertown (Pa.) United Meth. Ch., 1970—; dir. Justified By Faith, Saegertown, 2002—. Mem.: Pa. Music Educators Assn. (curriculum and instrn. chair dist. 2 1993—2003), Pa. State Edn. Assn. (alt. profl. rights and responsibilities commn. 2001—), Penncrest Area Edn. Assn. (assoc.; v.p. 1982—84, negotiator 1982—86, pres. 1984—86, negotiator 2000—01, v.p. 2001—02, pres. 2001—03), Tool City Ringers. Methodist. Avocations: music, reading, painting. Home: 17768 Grange Center Rd Saegertown PA 16433-4506 Personal E-mail: schoolmarm@zoominternet.net.

**RALPH, STANLEY LEE,** performing arts educator, musician; b. Waterbury, Conn., Mar. 12, 1931; s. George Timothy and Julia Ward Ralph; m. Ivy Mayhew Ralph, June 18, 1955; children: Sheryl Lee Hughes, Stanley Lee Jr., Michael O'Neil, George Timothy. B in Music Edn., Howard U., 1953; MA, NYU, 1957; postgrad., Fairfield U., Conn., 1965; EdD, U. Sarasota, Fla., 1976. Music tchr. Waterbury Pub. Schs., 1954—65; music tchr., prin. Wyandanch (NY) UFSD # 9 HS, 1965—72; adj. prof. Nassau C.C., Garden City, NY, 1973—80; asst. to v.p. SUNY, Farmingdale, 1973—80; administr. Hempstead (NY) Pub. Schs., 1980—89; supr. Hofstra U., Hempstead, 1989—90; asst. dean SUNY Rockland, Suffern, 1991—96, prof., 1996—. Min. of music Meml. Presbyn. Ch., Roosevelt, NY, 1976—2003, 1st Presbyn. Ch. in Jamaica, NY. Composer: (cantata) The Nutmeg, 2002; actor: All My Children (ABC-TV), 1985. Founder Visions for the Children of Jamaica, Long Island, NY, 1994. Named Educator of Yr., Hempstead Adminstrs. Assn. Mem.: AFTRA, Alpha Phi Alpha. Avocation: travel. Home: 63 Jane Ct Westbury NY 11590-1410 Office: SUNY Rockland 145 College Rd Suffern NY 10901 Office Phone: 845-574-4471.

**RALSTON, ANTHONY,** computer scientist, mathematician, educator; b. N.Y.C., Dec. 24, 1930; s. Alfred Joseph and Ruth (Bien) R.; m. Jayne Madeleine Rosenthal, Feb. 14, 1958; children: Jonathan, Geoffrey, Steven, Elizabeth. BS, MIT, 1952, PhD, 1956. Mem. tech. staff Bell Tel. Labs.,

1956-59; lectr. U. Leeds, 1959-60; mgr. tech. computing Am. Cyanamid Co., 1960-61; assoc. prof. math. Stevens Inst. Tech., 1961-64, prof., 1964-65; dir. computer svcs. SUNY, Buffalo, 1965-70, prof., 1965-95, chmn. dept. computer sci., 1967-80, prof. emeritus, 1995—. Bd. examiners Grad. Record Exam in Computer Sci., 1976-82; mem. computer sci. and tech. bd. NRC, 1976-79, math. sci. edn. bd., 1985-89; acad. visitor Imperial Coll., London, 1995-2003. Author: A First Course in Numerical Analysis, 1965, 2d edit., 1978, Introduction to Programming and Computer Science, 1971, Discrete Algorithmic Mathematics, 1991, 3d edit., 2004, Algorithms, 1999; editor: Ency. of Computer Science, 1976, 2d edit., 1982, 3d edit., 1992, 4th edit., 2000, concise edit., 2004, ABACUS, 1983-88; co-editor: Mathematical Methods for Digital Computers, Vol. 1, 1960, Vol. 2, 1967, Vol. 3, 1977, The Influence of Computers and Informatics in Mathematics and Its Teaching, 1993. 2d lt. U.S. Army, 1957. Fellow AAAS, Royal Soc. of Arts, Assn. Computing Machinery (pres. 1972-74, mem. coun. 1968-76, Disting. Svc. award 1982); mem. Math. Assn. Am. (bd. govs. 1984-87), Am. Fedn. Info. Processing Soc. (pres. 1975-76), Com. Concerned Scientists (bd. dirs.). Home: Flat 4 58 Prince Consort Rd London SW7 2BA England Office Phone: 44-20-75892195. E-mail: ar9@doc.ic.ac.uk.

**RALSTON, BARBARA JO,** bank executive; b. Youngstown, Ohio, Apr. 11, 1940; d. Fred Kenneth and Juanita Ruth (Welch) Roof; m. Donald Gene Ralston, Jan. 9, 1960; children: Mark David, Lori Sue. Cert., Pacific Coast Banking Sch. U. Wash., Seattle, 1981; AA in fin., Maricopa County CC. Sec. Bank of Scottsdale, Ariz., 1962-66; administrn. asst. Talley Industries, Mesa, Ariz., 1966-73; asst. mgr. Continental Bank, Phoenix, 1973-77; exec. v.p. Continental Bank Service Corp., Phoenix, 1977-85, pres., dir., 1985—86; chmn., pres. to sr. v.p. electronic and convenience banking to exec. v.p. personal banking group Chase Bank of Ariz., exec. v.p., COO; exec. v.p. northeast Ariz. retail area First Interstate Bank, 1994—95, Phoenix area pres., 1995—96; sr. v.p. mgr. in-store banking Wells Fargo Bank, Ariz., 1996—97; founder, pres., CEO Camelback Cmty. Bank, Phoenix, 1998—. Pres. Ariz. Bus. Leadership. Bd. dirs. Valley Big Bros.-Big Sisters, Phoenix, 1986; mem. Ariz. Acad., Phoenix, 1984; treas. Phoenix Together Town Hall, 1986; chair Am. West Airlines Edn. Found.; immediate past chair, Fresh State Women's Found.; past chair Ariz. Town Hall; past internat. pres. Financial Women Internat. Recipient You Too Can Make A Difference award Valley Christian Ctrs., Phoenix, 1985. Mem. Nat. Assn. Bank Women (state pres. 1981-82), Am. Inst. Banking (state edn. chmn. Ariz. chpt. 1984), Tumbleweed (pres. 1983); Am. Bankers Assn. (state membership chair for Ariz., chair ABA Edn. Found. 2003-), Ariz Bankers Assn. (bd. dirs., 2001-03, pres., 2001-02. Lodges: Soroptimists (pres. 1982, Women Helping Women award 1984). Republican. Methodist. Avocations: reading, travel, sewing. Office: Camelback Cmty Bank 2777 E Camelback Rd Ste 100 Phoenix AZ 85016

**RALSTON, JOANNE SMOOT,** public relations executive; b. Phoenix, May 13, 1939; d. A. Glen and Viriginia (Lee) Smoot; m. W. Hamilton Weigelt, Aug. 15, 1991 (dec.). BA in Journalism, Ariz. State U., 1960. Reporter The Ariz. Rep., Phoenix, 1960-62; co-owner, pub. rels. dir. The Patton Agy., Phoenix, 1962-71; founder, pres., owner Joanne Ralston & Assocs., Inc., Phoenix, 1971-87, 92—. Pres. Nelson Ralston Robb Commn., Phoenix, 1987—91, Joanne Ralston & Assocs., Inc., Scottsdale, 1991—, Kapaau, Hawaii, 2000—. Contbr. articles to profl. jours. Bd. dirs. Ariz. Parklands Found., 1984-86, Gov.'s Coun. on Health, Phys. Fitness and Sports, 1984-86; mem. task force Water and Natural Resources Coun., Phoenix, 1984-86; mem. Hawaii Gov.'s Adv. Bd., 2003-05, Hawaii Gov.'s Coun. Advisors, 2005—, others. Recipient Lulu awards (36) L.A. Advt. Women, 1964—, Gold Quill (2) Internat. Assn. Bus. Communicators, Excellence awards Fin. World mag., 1982-93, others; named to Walter Cronkite Sch. Journalism Hall of Fame, Coll. Pub. Programs Ariz. State U., 1987; named one of 25 Most Influential Arizonians, Phoenix Mag., 1991. Mem. Pub. Rels. Soc. Am. (counselor sect.), Internat. Assn. Bus. Communicators, Phoenix Press Club (pres. &c.), Investor Rels. Inst., Phoenix Met. C. of C. (bd. dirs. 1977-84, 85-91), Rotary Internat. Republican. Avocations: horses, dog training. Address: PO Box 808 Kapaau HI 96755-0808 Office Phone: 808-889-6433. Personal E-mail: joanne-ralston@juno.com.

**RALSTON, JOHN PETER,** theoretical physicist, educator; b. Reno, Nev., Aug. 8, 1951; s. Robert Lee and Katherine A. (Casserly) R.; m. Cherie Wagner, Sept. 1, 1973; children: Amy, John Charles, Joseph. PhD, U. Oreg., 1980. Design engr. Hamilton Co., Reno, 1974; postdoctoral fellow McGill U., Montreal, Can., 1980-82; rsch. assoc. Argonne (Ill.) Nat. Lab., 1982-84; asst. prof. U. Kans., Lawrence, 1984-88, assoc. prof., 1988-93, prof., 1993—. Sci. assoc. CERN, Geneva, Switzerland, summer 1991, CEN Saclay, France, summer, 1990, Stanford (Calif.) Linear Accelerator Ctr., summer 1989. Contbr. numerous articles to profl. jours. Recipient Maitre de Recherche Ecole Polytechnique, France, 1990-91, 2001. Achievements include studies in quantum chromodynamics, high energy physics and particle-astrophysics; patents in field. Office: U Kans Dept Physics And Astro Malott Hall 1251 Wescoe Hall Dr Rm 1082 Lawrence KS 66045-7582

**RALSTON, JOSEPH FREDERICK, JR.,** internist; b. Fayetteville, Tenn., Apr. 25, 1954; s. Joseph Frederick Ralston and Clara Bernadette Ralston-Wolfhard; m. Farris Lynch, Feb. 17, 1990; children: James David, Willis Farris. BA in Polit. Sci., Yale U., New Haven, Conn., 1976; MD, U. Tenn., Memphis, 1980. Diplomate Am. Bd. Internal Medicine. Resident in internal medicine Bapt. Meml. Hosp., Memphis, 1980—83; pvt. practice Fayetteville, Tenn., 1983—; dir. CCU Lincoln Med. Ctr., Fayetteville, 1984—. Active Lincoln County unit Am. Cancer Soc., Fayetteville, 1984-97, bd. dirs., pres., 1988-89; deacon, elder First Presbyn. Ch., Fayetteville, 1988-99; trustee Lincoln Regional Hosp., Fayetteville, 1989-2001. Fellow ACP (publ. com. 2001-03, vice-chmn. 2002-03, parliamentarian select 2002-03, 04—, parliamentarian 2003-04, vice-chmn. health pub. policy com. 2003-04, chmn. bd. govs. 2007—, chmn. nom. 2004-05, exec. com. bd. regents 2004—,); mem. AMA (Tenn. del., chair young physicians sect. 1991-92), Tenn. Med. Assn. (rural caucus 1984—, chair 1991-92, 97-98, del. 1985—, comm. com. 1988-99, co-chair 1992-95, chair 1995-99, judicial coun. 1988-92, chair 1990-92, legis. com. 1992—, bd. trustees 1998-2001, chmn. bd. trustees 2000-01, chair Tenn. care reform task force). Home: 51 Timberlake Dr Fayetteville TN 37334 Office: Fayetteville Med Assocs PC 207 S Elk Ave Fayetteville TN 37334 Office Fax: (931) 438-0069. E-mail: ralston@fayelectric.com.

**RALSTON, JOSEPH W.,** retired military officer; b. Hopkinsville, Ky., Nov. 4, 1943; m. Diane Dougherty; children: Christopher, Paige, David, Sarah. BA in Chemistry, Miami (Ohio) U., 1965; MA in Pers. Mgmt., Ctrl. Mich. U., 1976; student, Army Command and Gen. Staff Coll., Ft. Leavenworth, Kans., 1975—76, Nat. War Coll., Ft. McNair, Wash. DC, 1983—84, Harvard U., 1989. Commd. 2d lt. res. officer tng. corps. program USAF, 1965, advanced through grades to gen., 1995, ret., 2003, student pilot training Laughlin AFB, Tex., 1965—66, student, F-105 combat crew training sch. Nellis AFB, Nev., 1966—67, F-105 combat crew mem. 67th Tactical Fighter Squardron later 12th Tactical Fighter Squadron Kadena AFB, Japan, 1967—69, student, F-105 combat crew training sch. Nellis AFB, Nev., 1969, F-105 Wild Weasel instr. pilot 66th Fighter Weapons Squadron, 1970—71, F-105 Wild Weasel pilot, 354th Tactical Fighter Takhli Royal Thai AFB, Thailand, 1970, fighter requirements officer & project officer for F-15 & lightweight fighter programs, Office of the Dep. Chief of Staff for requirements Langley AFB, 1971—73, asst. ops. officer, 335th Tactical Fighter Squandron, the chief Standardization & Evaluation, 4th Tactical Fighter Wing Seymour Johnson AFB, NC, 1973—75, tactical fighter requirements officer, Office of the Dep. Chief of Staff for Rsch. & Devel. Washington, 1976—79, ops. officer later comdr. 68th Tactical fighter Squandron Moody AFB, Ga., 1979—80, spl. asst. later exec. officer to the comdr. Hdqs. Tactical Air Command Langley AFB, 1980—83, spl. asst. for low observables tech., Office of Dep. Chief of Staff for Rsch., Devel. & Acquisition Washington, 1984—86, comdr., 56th tactical training wing MacDill AFB, Fla., 1986—87, asst. dep. chief of staff for ops., later dep. chief of staff for requirements, Hdqs. Tactical Air Command Langley AFB, Va., 1987—90, dir. tactical programs Office of the Asst. Sec. for acquisition Washington, 1990—91, dir. operational requirements, Office

of the Dep. Chief of Staff for plans & ops., 1991—92, comdr. Alaskan Command, Alaskan N. Am. Aerospace Def. Command Region, 11th Air Force & Joint Task Force Elmendorf AFB, Alaska, 1992—94, dep. chief of staff plans & ops., 1994—95, comdr., Hdqs. Air Combat Command Langley AFB, Va., 1995—96; vice chmn. Joint Chiefs of Staff The Pentagon, Washington, 1996—2000; comdr. US European Command, Mons, Belgium, 2000—03; Supreme Allied Comdr. NATO, 2000—03; vice chmn. The Cohen Group, Washington, 2003—. Recipient Def. Disting. Svc. medal with oak leaf cluster, Disting. Svc. medal, Legion of Merit with two oak leaf cluster, Disting. Flying Cross with three oak leaf cluster, Meritorious Svc. medal with two oak leaf cluster, Air medal with 19 oak leaf cluster, Air Force Commendation medal with four oak leaf cluster Office: The Cohen Group 1200 19th St NW Ste 400 Washington DC 20036 E-mail: jralston@cohengroup.net.

**RALSTON, RONALD LEE,** manufacturing tradesman; b. Vincennes, Ind., May 22, 1942; s. Joe Franklin and Anna Lee Ralston. Student, Purdue U., 1963—66; degree in indsl. mgmt., Ivy Tech., Indpls., 1980. Machinist Allison Aircraft & Transmission, Indpls., 1962—78; skilled tradesman Allison Transmission Plants, Indpls., 1978—. Sgt./tank comdr. U.S. Army, 1966—68. Mem.: Shriners, Scottish Rite, Masons. Republican. Methodist. Avocation: woodworking. Home: 1814 Inisheer Ct Indianapolis IN 46217 Office Phone: 317-242-7470. Personal E-mail: mrronralston@aol.com.

**RALSTON, STEVEN PHILIP,** portfolio manager, financial analyst; b. Trenton, N.J., Mar. 29, 1954; s. George and Edith Martha Ralston; m. Miriam Mercedes Font, July 14, 1979. BS, MIT, 1975. CFA. Account exec. Merrill, Lynch, Pierce, Fenner & Smith, Balt., 1979—80; security analyst Fidelity and Deposit Co. of Md., Balt., 1980—83; security analyst, v.p. First Nat. Bank of Md., Balt., 1983—95; dir. rsch. 1st Nat. Bank of Md., Balt., 1990—95; portfolio mgr., analyst, v.p. Gen. Accident, Phila., 1995—98; equity investment mgr., v.p. BlackRock, Phila., 1998—2003; pres. Ralston Fin. Mgmt., Glenside, Pa., 2003—. Instr. Johns Hopkins U., Balt., 1985—87. Mem. Howard County Hist. Soc., Ellicott City, Md., 1969-92; mem. Lake Falls Improvement Assn., 1984-95, treas., 1987, pres., 1988; mem. Northwoods Assn., 1995—, bd. dirs. 1996-2006, pres. 2006—; mem. Springfield Twp. Hist. Soc., 1997—. Mem. Inst. Chartered Fin. Analysts, Balt. Security Analysts Soc. (bd. dirs., v.p. 1984-89), Fin. Analysts Phila., Fin. Analysts Fedn., Assn. for Investment Mgmt. and Rsch., Consumer Analysts Group N.Y. Avocation: auctions. Home: 515 Edann Rd Glenside PA 19038-1404 Office Phone: 215-887-2965. E-mail: sralston@ralstonfinancial.com.

**RAM, CHITTA VENKATA,** physician; b. Machilipatnam, India, Oct. 24, 1948; s. Chitta M. Row and Chitta (Cheruvu) Sarojini; m. Ashalata Ram, Feb. 17, 1979; children: Gita, Radha. B.Sci, Marathwada U., Aurangabad, India, 1966; MD, Osmania U., Hyderabad, India, 1972. Diplomate Am. Bd. Internal Medicine. Resident in internal medicine Brown U., R.I. Hosp., Providence, 1974-76; fellow in hypertension Hosp. U. Pa., Phila., 1976-77; faculty assoc. U. Tex. Southwestern Med. Ctr., Dallas, 1977-78, asst. prof., 1978-83, assoc. prof., 1983-89, prof. internal medicine, 1989—. Dir. Tex. Blood Pressure Inst., Dallas; dir. rsch. and edn. Dallas Nephrology Assocs.; dir. hypertension clinic Parkland Meml. Hosp., Dallas, hypertension unit St. Paul Med. Ctr., Dallas, dir. continuing med. edn. dept., 1996-98, chmn. instnl. rev. com., 1996-98, pres. med. staff, 1997-98; dir. Tex. Blood Pressure Inst., Dallas. Contbr. numerous articles to profl. jours. and chpts. to textbooks; editl. cons., reviewer numerous nat. and internat. jours. and pubs. Pres. Tex. IndoAm. Physician Soc., Dallas, 1988; trustee Dallas/Ft. Worth Hindu Temple Soc., Dallas, 1988. Named Outstanding Tchr. St. Paul Med. Ctr., 1982; recipient Mother of India award, 1992. Master ACP; fellow Am. Coll. Cardiology, Am. Coll. Chest Physicians (regent), Am. Coll. Clin. Pharmacology; mem. Am. Assn. Physicians from India (pres.-elect 1994-95, pres. 1995-96), Tex. Indo-Am. Physicians Soc.

**RAMACHANDRA, GOUTHAM K.,** software architect, software developer; s. K. T. and Venkatasamy Vijayalakshmi Ramachandra. M in Engring., Indian Inst. Sci., Bangalore, 1993. V.p. Goldman Sachs Japan Ltd., Tokyo, 1998—2002, Goldman Sachs and Co., NYC, 2002—. Recipient Merit cert. Outstanding Achievements, Govt. of India. Mem.: IEEE (assoc.; assoc. mem. 1993). Achievements include development of financial software. Office: Goldman Sachs and Co 85 Broad St New York NY 10004 Office Phone: 917-699-6384.

**RAMACHANDRAN, VASAN SRINI,** medical educator; b. Madras, India, Jan. 8, 1959; arrived in U.S., 1992; m. Sudha Seshadri; 1 child, Aditi. MBBS, All India Inst. Med. Sci., New Delhi, 1983; MD, All India Inst. Med. Sci., 1986, DM, 1990. Lic. physician India. Resident in internal medicine All India Inst. Med. Sci., New Delhi, 1983—86, fellow in cardiology, 1986—88; fellow in echocardiography Washington Hosp. Ctr., Washington, 1992—93; rsch. fellow in cardiology Framingham Heart Study, 1993—96; asst. prof. cardiology All India Inst. Med. Sci., 1991—92; assoc. prof. medicine Sri Chitra Tinnal Inst. Med. Sci., Trivandrum, 1996—98; clin. assoc. prof. medicine Boston U., 1998—2006, prof. medicine, 2006—. Staff cardiologist Sitaram Bhartia Inst. Med. Sci., New Delhi, 1996, All India Inst. Med. Sci., 1990—92; co-dir. echocardiography lab. Framingham Heart Study, 1998—, co-dir. fellowship program in cardiovascular epidemiology, 2001—; dir. MPH course coord. Achutha Menon Ctr. for Health Sci. Studies, Trivandrum, 1996—98; mem. K-23-K34 rev. panel study sect. NIH, NHLBI, Washington, 2000—; ad hoc reviewer Health Rsch. Bd. Iceland, 2004—. Med. Rsch. Coun. U.K., 2004—; guest editor Current Sci., 1998, Biomarkers of Congestive Heart Failure, 2005; assoc. editor Circulation, 2004; jour. reviewer Annals of Internal Medicine, 1995—, Lancet, 1995—, Jour. Hypertension, 1995—, Nat. Med. Jour. India, 1995—, Circulation, 1998—, Am. Jour. Medicine, 1998—, Am. Jour. Hypertension, 1998—, Hypertension, 1999—, New Eng. Jour. Medicine, 2002—, European Jour. Medicine, 2004—; lectr. in field. Contbr. over 150 articles to profl. jours., chapters to books; author: Textbook of Internal Medicine, 1998, Medicine at a Glance - a companion to Textbook of Internal Medicine, 1999; contbr. abstracts. Recipient Dorabjee Tata award for excellence in biochemistry, All India Inst. Med. Sci., 1979, Inst. prize for excellence in gen. surgery, 1982, Jagdish Lal Kapila Gold Medal for excellence in cardiology, 1989, Searle award, Cardiology Soc. India, 1989. Fellow: Am. Heart Assn./Coun. on Epidemiology and Prevention, Am. Coll. Cardiology. Home: 2000 Commonwealth Ave #1705 Brighton MA 02135 Office: The Framingham Heart Study 73 Mount Wayte Ave Framingham MA 01702

**RAMACHANDRAN, VENKATANARAYANA DEEKSHIT,** electrical engineering educator; b. Mysore, India, May 3, 1934; s. K.C. Venkatanarayana Deekshit and Subbamma Deekshit R.; m. Kamala Visweswaraiya, June 12, 1960; 1 child, Ravi P. BS, U. Mysore, 1953; B in Engring., Indian Inst. Sci., Bangalore, 1956, M in Electronics, 1958, PhD, 1965. Registered profl. engr. Sr. research asst. Indian Inst. Sci., 1958-59, lectr., 1959-66; asst. prof. N.S. Tech. Coll., Halifax, Can., 1966-69; prof. elec. engring. Concordia U. (formerly Sir George Williams Univ.), Halifax, Can., 1971—; acting chmn. dept. elec. and computer engring. Montreal, various times; grad. program dir. dept., 1969-84. Adj. prof. U. Windsor, Ont., Can., 1983—, Ecole Tech. Superieure U. Quebec, Montreal, 1989—; mem. program com. Internat. Symposium on Operator Theory of Networks and Systems, 1975; vice chmn. Internat. Symposium on Circuits and Systems IEEE, Montreal, 1984, mem. tech. program com., 1987; internat. coordinator Internat. Conf. on Computers, Systems and Signal Processing, Indian Inst. Sci., 1984. Author papers in profl. jours., over 125 papers presented to confs.; others. Named to Order of Engrs. of Que.; recipient Merit award Concordia Council on Student Life, 1981-82, Outstanding Contbn. award Engring. and Computer Sci. Assn., Concordia U., 1996. Fellow Inst. Electronics and Telecomms. India (edit. bd. jour. 1986), Inst. Engrs. India, Inst. Elec. Engrs. Eng., Engring. Inst. Can. (sec. Montreal chpt. 1979-80, centennial bd. 1983-84), IEEE (Outstanding Engring. Educator award IEEE Can. 2003); mem. Circuits and Systems chpt. IEEE (chmn. Montreal sect. 1978-84), Can. Soc. Elec. Engrs. (editor jour. 1983-85, editor bull. 1981-83), Am. Soc. Engring. Edn. (chmn. awards com. St. Lawrence chpt. 1987-88, Western Elec. Fund award 1983, Myril B. Reed Best Rsch.

Paper award 1984, Outstanding Svc. 1993) Office: Concordia U Faculty of Engring 1455 de Maisonneuve Blvd W Montreal PQ Canada H3G 1M8 Office Phone: 514-848-2424 ext. 3078. Business E-Mail: kamala@ece.concordia.ca.

**RAMADAN, NABIH M.,** pharmaceutical company official, educator; b. Beirut, Feb. 3, 1960; came to U.S., 1985; s. Manih Fawzi Ramadan and Nadia Shaar; m. Cynthia Ann Ramadan, Mar. 26, 1988. BS in Biology and Chemistry, Am. U. of Beirut, Lebanon, 1980, MD, 1985. Resident in neurology U. Cin., Ohio, 1985-88; fellow in cerebrovascular disease Henry Ford Hosp., Detroit, 1988-90, dir. Ambulatory Headache Clinic, 1990-96, dir. Cerebrovascular Diseases Lab., 1990-96; dir. Cin. Headache Ctr., 1996-99; assoc. prof. neurology U. Cin., 1996-99; med. dir. Eli Lilly & Co., Indpls., 1999, rsch. advisor, 1999—. Adj. prof. neurology Ind. U. Med. Ctr., Indpls.

**RAMAGE, JAMES ALFRED,** history professor; b. Paducah, Ky., May 6, 1940; s. Willis Newman and Lora Helen Ramage; m. Judith Ann Winstead, June 6, 1964; 1 child, Andrea Susanne Watkins. BS, Murray State U., Ky., 1965, MA, 1968; PhD, U. Ky., Lexington, 1972. Tchr. history Mehlville H.S., St. Louis, 1965—67; prof. history No. Ky. U., Highland Heights, Ky., 1972—. Author: John Wesley Hunt, 1974, Rebel Raider, 1986 (Freeman award, 1986), Gray Ghost, 1999 (History Book Club selection). Chair Recreation Commn. City of Highland Heights, Ky., 1975—81. With USAF, 1958—62. Named Outstanding Prof., No. Ky. U., 1988; recipient Ky. Gov.s Vol. Activist award, 1978, Regents Prof. award, No. Ky. U., 1994, Acorn award, Ky. Advocates Higher Edn., 2003. Mem.: Ky. Hist. Soc., So. Hist. Assn., Phi Alpha Theta (faculty advisor (No. Ky. U. chpt.) 1985—2004, nat. coun. mem. 2002—03, nat. v.p. 2006—). So. Baptist. Achievements include preservation work on Civil War Battery Hooper honored in James A Ramage Civil War Museum. Avocation: reading. Office: History Dept No Ky Univ One Nunn Dr Highland Heights KY 41099

**RAMAGE, MARTIS DONALD, JR.,** banker; b. Tupelo, Miss., Oct. 6, 1957; s. Martis Donald and Helen Frances (Estes) R. AA, Itawamba Jr. Coll., Fulton, Miss., 1978; BBA in Banking and Fin., U. Miss., 1980; grad., Mid South Sch. of Banking, 1989. Mgmt. trainee Renasant Bank (formerly Peoples Bank & Trust Co.), Tupelo, 1981-82, asst. cashier, 1983-89, asst. v.p., 1989-90, v.p., 1990-93, 1st v.p., 1993-2000, sr. v.p., 2000—02, divsn. v.p., 2002—. Sec. Renasant Corp., 1993-96, v.p., 1996—. Author: Our Ramage Family, 1986, Mississippi Society SAR 1909-1993, Tupelo, Mississippi, Tornado 1936, 1997; co-editor: The Peoples Bank & Trust Co-In Partnership with the Community, 1989; editor N.E. Miss. Hist. Geneal. Soc. Quar. Treas. United Way of Greater Lee County, Tupelo, 1991-2000, sec., 1991-2001, Leadership Lee; pres. Friends of Lee County Libr., 1995-97; bd. dirs. Brice's Battlefield Commn., Inc., 1995—, Tupelo Cmty. Concert, 1998—, Regional Rehab. Ctr., 2003—; trustee Miss. Dept. Archives and History, 1996—; trustee Lee/Itawamba County Libr., 1998—, chmn., 2004—; chmn. Christmas Festival Com., Tupelo, 1990-91; mem. Miss. rev. bd. Nat. Register Hist. Places, 1999-2002. Mem. SAR (trustee 1992-94, pres. Miss. 1991-92, Silver Good Citizenship medal 1990), SCV, Mil. Order of Stars and Bars, Am. Inst. Banking (pres. Tupelo chpt. 1986-87), Ole Miss. Alumni Assn. (bd. dirs. 1991-94), Bank Adm. Inst. (v.p. North Miss. chpt. 1990-94, pres. 1994-95), Tupelo Artist Guild (bd. dirs. 1993-98, sec. 1996-98), Miss. Hist. Soc. (bd. dirs. 1995-97), Itawamba Jr. Coll. Alumni Assn. (pres. 1982-83), Itawamba C.C. Alumni Assn. (bd. 2002—), Itawamba Found. Rehab. Ctr. (bd. dirs. 2003—), Civitan Club, Masons. Home: 4218 Ridgemont Dr Belden MS 38826-9785 Office: Renasant Bank 209 Troy St Tupelo MS 38804-4827 Office Phone: 662-680-1306. Personal E-Mail: martyr@tsixroads.com. Business E-Mail: martyr@renasant.com.

**RAMAKRISHNAN, KADANGODE KRISHNAMOORTHY,** computer science researcher; b. Bangalore, Karnataka, India, Feb. 11, 1954; came to U.S., 1978; s. Kadangode P. and Kanakavalli (Ramakrishnan) Krishnamoorthy; m. Anuradha Ramakrishnan, Feb. 6, 1984; 1 child, Venkat. BEE, Bangalore U., 1976; ME in Automation, Indian Inst. Sci., Bangalore, 1978; MS in Computer Sci., U. Md., 1981, PhD in Computer Sci., 1983. Grad. rsch. asst. U. Md., College Park, 1979-83; prin. engr. Digital Equipment Corp., Littleton, Mass., 1983-92, cons. engr., 1992—. Contbr. articles to profl. jours. Recipient Jawaharlal Nehru award Govt. of India, 1978. Mem. IEEE (editorial bd. 1992—), Assn. Computing Machinery (book display chair sigmetrics conf. 1994—). Avocations: tennis, travel. Office: Digital Equipment Corp LKG1-2/A19 550 King St Littleton MA 01460-1250

**RAMAKRISHNAN, KANNAN,** mechanical engineer; arrived in US, 1996; s. Sivarama Subramanium and Sarasa Ramakrishnan. B in Mech. Engring., Walchand Inst. Tech., Solapur, Maharashtra, India, 1994; MME, Lamar U., 1998, DEng, 2001. Prodn., purchase engr. Walchandnagar Industries Ltd., Pune, Maharashtra, India, 1994—96; rsch. asst. Lamar U., Beaumont, Tex., 1996—98, tchg. fellow, 1998—2001; design engr. GEMCO Port Lavaca, Inc., 2001—. Contbr. scientific papers. Mem.: ASME, ASM Internat. Metallographic Soc., ASM Thermal Spray Soc., Soc. Plastics Engrs., ASM Internat. Material Info. Soc. Avocations: travel, sports, music, winemaking. Office Phone: 361-552-5122. Personal E-Mail: kanna_ramakrishnan@hotmail.com.

**RAMAKRISHNAN, VENKATASWAMY,** civil engineer, educator; b. Coimbatore, India, Feb. 27, 1929; came to U.S., 1969, naturalized, 1981; s. Venkataswamy and Kondammal (Krishnaswamy) R.; m. Vijayalakshmi Unnava, Nov. 7, 1962; children: Aravind, Anand. B.Engring., U. Madras, 1952, D.S.S., 1953; D.I.C. in Hydropower and Concrete Tech, Imperial Coll., London, 1957; PhD, Univ. Coll., U. London, 1960. From lectr. to prof. civil engring., head dept. P.S.G. Coll. Tech., U. Madras, 1952-69; vis. prof. S.D. Sch. Mines and Tech., Rapid City, 1969-70, prof. civil engring., 1970—, dir. concrete tech. research, 1970-71, head grad. div. structural mechanic and concrete tech., 1971—, program coordinator materials engring. and sci. Ph.D. program, 1985-86, disting. prof., 1996—. Emeritus mem. TRB. Author: Ultimate Strength Design for Structural Concrete, 1969; contbr. over 350 articles to profl. jours. Recipient Outstanding Prof. award, S.D. Sch. Mines and Tech., 1980, 1st Rsch. award, 1994; Colombo Plan fellow, 1955—60. Mem. ASCE (vice chmn. constrn. divsn. publs. com. 1974), NSPE, Internat. Assn. Bridge and Structural Engring., Am. Concrete Inst. (chmn. subcom. gen. considerations for founds., chmn. com. 214 on evaluation of strength test results, sec.-treas. Dakota chpt. 1974-79, v.p. 1980, pres. 1981, Robert Philio Rsch. Excellence award), Instn. Hwy. Engrs., Transp. Rsch. Bd. (chmn. com. on admixtures and curing, chmn. com. on mech. properties concrete), Am. Soc. Engring. Edn., Internat. Coun. Gap-Graded Concrete Rsch. and Application, Sigma Xi. Address: 5260 Autumn Place Rapid City SD 57702 Office Phone: 605-394-2403. E-mail: vramakrishnan@rushmore.com. *To me, success is a coin with hard work on one side and perseverance with devotion on the other. No matter what—head or tails—the message is the same: keep on working. Goals in my life were pursuit of truth and beauty. The structures I have created, and my writings based on research have given me greater satisfaction than any wealth, position, or power.*

**RAMAKUMAR, RAMACHANDRA GUPTA,** electrical engineering educator; b. Coimbatore, Tamil Nadu, India, Oct. 17, 1936; came to U.S., 1967; s. Gopalakrishna Ramachandra and Saraswathi (Bai) Gupta; m. Tallam Gokuladevi, June 13, 1963; children—Sanjay, Malini, B.E. U. Madras, 1956; M.Tech., Indian Inst. Tech., 1957; Ph.D., Cornell U., 1962. Registered profl. engr., Okla., Asst. lectr., lectr elec. engring. Coimbatore Inst. Tech., 1957-62, asst. prof., 1962-67; vis. and assoc. prof. Okla. State U., Stillwater, 1967-76, prof. elec. engring., 1976—; dir. engring. energy lab., 1987—; PSO/Albrecht Naeter prof., 1991—; cons. JPL, Pasadena, Calif., 1979-79; cons. UN, UNU, NSF, Kuwait U., others. TCM scholar, 1959-62; NSF grantee, 1978. Fellow IEEE, Power Engring. Soc. (energy devel. subcom., power generation com.), Internat. Solar Energy Soc., Okla. Soc. Profl. Engrs. (outstanding achievement award 1972). Contbr. articles to profl. jours.; patentee in field. Home: 2623 N Husband St Stillwater OK 74075-2611 Office: Okla State Univ 216 Engring South Stillwater OK 74078-5034 Office Phone: 405-744-5157. Business E-Mail: rama.ramakumar@okstate.edu.

**RAMALHO-AHRNDT, MARIA GABRIELA,** art educator; b. Foz Do Arelho, Portugal, June 14, 1965; arrived in Can., 1967, arrived in U.S., 1991; d. Bernardino Maria and Maria Gabriela (Da Silva) Ramalho; m. Timothy James Ahrndt, Aug. 26, 1995; children: Vincent J. Ahrndt, Alexandra Maria Ahrndt. BA, U. Toronto, Can., 1988; MA in Edn., Mankato State U., 1993. Printing asst. Art Svcs. Agy., Toronto, 1988; gallery asst. Wynick/Tuck Gallery, Toronto, 1988, Odon Wagner Gallery, Toronto, 1989-91, Art Gallery Ont., Toronto, 1990-91; art tchr. Washington Elem. Sch., Mankato, Minn., 1993, Spring Lake Park (Minn.) HS, 1994—. Author, illustrator: Bedtime Stories about Zany Creatures, 2002. Mem.: Am. Arts Crafts Coun., Nat. Art Edn. Assn., Nat. Mus. Women in the Arts. Roman Catholic. Avocations: sculpting, stamp-collecting, art history. Office: Spring Lake Park HS 8001 Able St NE Minneapolis MN 55432-2059

**RAMAN, LAKSHMI,** education educator; b. Bangalore, India, June 21, 1969; m. Pradeep Attibele, Aug. 29, 1992. PhD, Ohio State U., Columbus, 2000. Lic. psychologist Ohio. Rsch. specialist U. Mich., Ann Arbor, 2001—06; asst. prof. Oakland U., Rochester, Mich., 2006—. Presenter in field. Contbr. articles to profl. jours.; presenter at prof. confs. Sec. Foxfire Homeowners Assn., Ann Arbor, Mich., 2005—06. Recipient Ruth L. Kirschstein award, NRSA, 2001; NRSA Postdoctoral fellow, NICHD, 2001. Mem.: Cognitive Development Soc., Soc. for Rsch. in Child Devel. Home: 2378 Hickory Point Dr Ann Arbor MI 48105 Personal E-mail: raman@oakland.edu.

**RAMANAN, SUNDARAM V.,** internist, hematologist, oncologist; s. Tarakad Appadoraier Subndaram. MD, MS, Vellore CMC, India, 1959. Prof. medicine U. of Conn., Farmington, 1976—; emeritus attending physician St. Francis Hosp., Hartford, Conn., 1993—. Fellow: ACP (corr.); mem.: Royal Coll. Physicians (Edinburgh). Office: St Francis Hosp 1000 Asylum Ave Ste # 1004 Hartford CT 06105 Office Phone: 860-714-4152.

**RAMANATHAN, RAGULAN,** chemistry researcher; b. Jaffna, Sri Lanka, Sept. 18, 1966; came to U.S. 1984; s. Saravanamuttu and Sakuntala R. BS, U. of Southern Miss., 1988; MS, U. Fla., 1992, PhD, 1994. Tchg. instr. U. of Southern Miss., Hattiesburg, Miss., 1986-88; tchg. asst. U. Fla., Gainesville, Fla., 1989-92, rsch. asst., 1992-94. Office: Univ Fla Chemistry Dept Gainesville FL 32611

**RAMANI, RAJA VENKAT,** engineering educator; b. Madras, India, Aug. 4, 1938; came to U.S., 1966; s. Natesa and Meenakshi (Srinivasan) Rajaraman; m. Geetha V. Chalam, July 9, 1972; children: Deepak, Gautam. BSc with honors, Indian Sch. Mines, Dhanbad, Bihar, 1962, DSc (hon.), 1997; MS, Pa. State U., 1968, PhD, 1970. Registered profl. engr., Pa., 1971; lic. first class mine mgr., 1965. Mining engr., mgr. Andrew Yule & Co., Asansol, West Bengal, India, 1962-66; grad. asst. Pa. State U., University Park, 1966-70, asst. prof., 1970-74, assoc. prof., 1974-78, prof. mining engring., 1978—, chmn. mineral engring. mgmt. sect., 1974—, head dept. mineral engring. 1987-98, George and Anne Deike chair in mining engring., 1997—2001, prof. emeritus, 2001—, Deike chair emeritus, 2001—. Chmn. com. post-disaster survival/rescue NAS, Washington, 1979-81; mem. health rsch. panel NAS Com. on the Rsch. Programs of the U.S. Bur. of Mines, 1994; mem. NAS Com. on Techs. for the Mineral Industries, 2000-01; mem. NAS Com. on Coal Waste Impoundments, 2001-02; mem. NAS Com. on NIOSH programs, 2005—; chmn. Gov.'s Commn. on Mine Voids and Mine Safety, Pa., 2002; cons. UN, UN Devel. Program, Dept. Econ. and Social Devel., N.Y.C., 1983-97, World Bank, 1998-99, Nat. Safety Coun., 2003-; cons., expert panels U.S. Dept. Labor, 1979, 92, 96, HHS, 1977, 92, U.S. Dept. State, 1986, 87, U.S. Dept. Interior, 1995, Dept. Environ. Resources, Commonwealth of Pa., 1990, 92; co-dir. Generic Mineral Tech. Ctr. on Respirable Dust, U.S. Bur. Mines, 1983—. Nat. Mines/Land Reclamation Ctr., 1988—, Std. Oil Ctr. of Excellence on Longwall Tech., 1983-89; presenter in field. Sect. editor, author: Computer Methods for the Eighties, 1979, SME Mining Engineering Handbook, 1992; editor State-of-the-Art in Longwall-Shortwall Mining, 1981, Longwall Thick Seam Mining, 1988, Computers in Mineral Industry, 1994, Internat. Mine Ventilation Congress, 1997. Recipient Disting. Alumni award Indian Sch. Mines, Dhanbad, 1978, Ednl. Excellence award Pitts. Coal Mining Inst., 1986, Environ. Conservation award AIME, N.Y.C., 1990, Howard N. Eavenson award SME/AIME, N.Y.C., 1991, Robert Stefanko Best Paper award, 1993, Coal Divsn. Disting. Svc. award, 1993, Howard L. Hartman award, 1997, Percy H. Nicholls award AIME/ASME Joint Soc., 1994, Mineral Industry Edn. award Am. Inst. Mining Engrs., 1999, The Thornton medal Instn. Mining and Metallurgy, 2000, Erskine Ramsay medal AIME, 2005; Fulbright scholar to Soviet Union Coun. Internat. Exch. of Scholars, Washington,, 1989-90; Henry Krumb lectr. AIME, 1994. Mem. NAE, Internat. Coun. for Application of Computers in the Mineral Industry (chmn. 1984-87, Disting. Achievement award 1989), Soc. Mining, Metallurgy & Exploration, Inc. Found. (pres. 2001-04), Soc. Mining, Metall. and Exploration (Disting. Mem. 1989, pres. 1995), Mine Ventilation Soc. South Africa, Inst. for Ops. Rsch. and Mgmt. Scis. Achievements include research in health, safety, environmental and productivity aspects in underground and surface mining engineering. Home: 285 Oakley Dr State College PA 16803-1349 Office: Dept Mineral Engring Pa State U University Park PA 16802 Office Phone: 814-863-1617. Business E-Mail: RVR@PSU.edu.*

**RAMANUJACHARY, KANDALAM V.,** chemistry professor, researcher; s. Janakiramacharyulu and Padmavathi Kandalam; m. Ramani Vinjamuri, Aug. 22, 1988; children: Pallavi Chary, Pavan Chary, Priya Chary. PhD, Indian Inst. Tech., Madras, India, 1982. Assoc. prof. Rowan U., Glassboro, NJ, 1997—99, prof. chemistry 1999—. Contbr. articles to profl. jours. Mem.: Am. Chem. Soc. Achievements include patents for humidity and pH sensors. Office: Rowan University 201 Mullica Hill Rd Glassboro NJ 08028 Office Phone: 856-256-5451. Office Fax: 856-256-4478.

**RAMAPRASAD, KACKADASAM RAGHAVACHAR,** physical chemist; b. Dec. 8, 1938; came to U.S., 1965, permanent resident, 1971; s. Kackadasam Raghavachar and Saroja (Narasimhachar) R.; m. Rukmani Raghavachari, July 14, 1968; children: Saroja, Venkat. BS in Chemistry (hon.), U. Mysore, Bangalore, 1958; MS in Phys. Chemistry, NYU, 1971; PhD, 1972. Trainee Bhabha Atomic Rsch. Ctr. Tng. Sch., Bombay, India, 1958-59; rsch. asst., jr. sci. officer chemistry divsn., 1959-65; teaching fellow N.Y.C., 1965-71; duPont teaching asst., 1967-68; maitre-asst. dept. de chimie physique U. Geneva, 1972-73; chemist Ecole Poly-Technique Federale de lausanne, Switzerland, 1974; rsch. assoc. mem. profl. rsch. staff dept. chem. engring., 1977-79; sr. scientist Chronar Corp., Princeton, 1979-89, Electron Transfer Techs., Inc., Princeton, 1990-93; staff scientist TRI-Princeton, 1993-96, sr. scientist, 1996-2001, sr. scientist, group leader, 2001—. Contbr. articles to profl. publs. Recipient Founder's Day award, NYU, 1972. Mem. Am. Chem. Soc., Sigma Xi. Office: TRI/Princeton PO Box 625 Princeton NJ 08542-0625

**RAMBERG, WALTER DODD,** architect; b. Charlotte, N.C., Feb. 17, 1932; s. Walter Gustav Charles and Julia Elisabeth (Lineberger) R.; m. Lucinda Jenifer Ballard, Nov. 25, 1961 (dec. 1989); children: Lucinda E.G., Jenny S.F., Julia E.L.; m. Seska Peck Dunne, Sept. 14, 1996. BA, Yale U., 1953, M.Arch., 1956. Fulbright fellow Kyoto (Japan) U., 1956-58; apprentice architect Paul Rudolph, New Haven, 1958-61; project designer Meyer & Ayers, Balt., 1961-63; partner Howe & Ramberg, Washington, 1963-65; prin. Walter Dodd Ramberg (Architect), Washington, 1965—. Prof. architecture Cath. U. Am., 1977—; mem. design adv. panel Balt. Dept. Housing and Community, 1973—; mem. bd. architecture rev. Baltimore County, 1986-89. Designer: N.W. Balt. High Sch. 1963 (P.A. Excellence in Design award); architect: Bridge for Washington Cathedral, 1965 (Excellence in Design award Washington Bd. Trade, AIA), Kidder Guest House, 1965 (1st Honor award Balt. AIA), Azrael House, 1969 (Honor award Balt. AIA), Cutts House, 1973 (Honor award Balt. AIA), Woody House, 1975 (Merit award Balt. AIA), Lineberger Meml. Library, 1976 (Merit award Nat. AIA, ALA); contbr.

articles to profl. publs. Served to lt. USCGR, 1958-59. Mem. AIA (corp.), AAUP, Soc. Archtl. Historians. Clubs: Met. (Washington). Episcopalian. Home: 1651 Belfast Rd Sparks MD 21152-9788 Office: 1830 T St NW Washington DC 20009-7138

**RAMBO, DOMINGO H.,** elementary school educator; b. Marietta, Tex., Apr. 20, 1924; d. Joseph E. and Elvira (Henderson) Johnson; m. Buford Rambo, Oct. 15, 1951; children: Jennifer Joan, George Alford. BA, Huston Tillotson Coll., Austin, Tex., 1951; postgrad., Calif. State U., L.A., Calif. State U., UCLA, Pepperdine U. Cert. elem. tchr., Calif. Tchr. Greenville (Tex.) Ind. Sch. Dist., L.A. Unified Sch. Dist., profl. expert. Co-founder L.A. Bridge Conservatory Performing and Visual Arts, pres., 1992—. Recipient outstanding and merit award for 35-yrs. svc. L.A. Unified Sch. Dist.; named to Wall of Tolerance, Montgomery, Ala. Mem. NEA, Calif. Tchrs. Assn., UTLA, Phi Delta Kappa.

**RAMBO, HELEN MARIE,** librarian; b. Hutchinson, Kans., Jan. 29, 1927; d. Lowell Merwin and Laura Elizabeth (Ball) R. BA in History, N.W. Nazarene Coll., 1949; M in Librarianship, U. Wash., 1957. Tchr. Emmett (Idaho) High Sch., 1950-52; tchr., libr. Merrill (Oreg.) High Sch., 1952-53, Bly (Oreg.) High Sch., 1953-54; sch. libr. Miller Jr. High Sch., Aberdeen, Wash., 1954-57; catalog libr. N.W. Nazarene U., Nampa, Idaho, 1957—94, emeritus faculty, 1994—. Instnl. rep. N.W. Nazarene U., 1970-94, AAUW, 1970-94. Bd. dirs. Nampa Pub. Libr. Trustees, 1971-85. Mem. AAUW, ALA, Idaho Libr. Assn. (pres. 1979-80). Avocations: reading, travel, crocheting, embroidery. Office: NW Nazarene U Riley Libr Nampa ID 83686

**RAMBO, SYLVIA H.,** federal judge; b. Royersford, Pa., Apr. 17, 1936; d. Granville A. and Hilda E. (Leonhardt) R.; m. George F. Douglas, Jr., Aug. 1, 1970. BA, Dickinson Coll., 1958; JD, Dickinson Sch Law, 1962; LLD (hon.), Wilson Coll., 1980, Dickinson Sch. Law, 1993, Dickinson Coll., 1994, Shippensburg U., 1996, Widener U., 1999. Bar: Pa. 1962. Atty. trust dept. Bank of Del., Wilmington, 1962-63; pvt. practice Carlisle, 1963-76; from public defender to chief public defender Cumberland County, Pa., 1974-76; judge Ct. Common Pleas, Cumberland County, 1976-78, U.S. Dist. Ct. (mid. dist.) Pa., Harrisburg, 1979—, chief judge, 1992-99; federal judge U.S. Dist. Ct., Harrisburg, 2000—. Asst. prof., adj. prof. Dickinson Sch. Law, 1974—76; mem. Jud. Conf. Com. on Adminstrn. of Magistrate Judges Sys., 1996—2002. Bd. dirs. Dickinson Sch. Law., Pa. State U., bd. govs., 2000—05, mem. bd. counselors, 2005—. Mem. Pa. Bar Assn. (mem. task force legal svcs. to needy 2000-03, mem. third cir. com. devel. model criminal jury infrastructures 2004—), Phi Alpha Delta. Democrat. Presbyterian. Office: US Dist Ct Federal Bldg PO Box 868 Harrisburg PA 17108-0868 Office Phone: 717-221-3960.

**RAMCHARAN, BERTRAND,** former international organization official; LLD, London Sch. Econ. and polit. Sci.; diploma in Internat. Law, Hague Acad. of Internat. Law. Adviser peace negotiators in the Yugoslavia conflict, UN; dir. peace keeping oper. UN in Yugoslavia; chief speech writer Sec.-Gen.; spl. asst. Ctr. for Human Rights; dir. studies Hague Acad. Internat. Law; adj. prof. of internat. human rights Columbia U.; mem. Permanent Ct. Arbitration; commr. Internat. Commn. Jurists; dep. high commr. for human rights UN, 1998—2003, acting high commr. for human rights, 2003—04; chancellor U. Guyana; vis. prof., Internat. Law Lund U., Sweden. Carr Fellow, JFK Sch. Govt Harvard U., Cambridge, Mass., 2004—; sr. fellow Ralph Bunche Inst. Internat. Studies. Author of over 15 books. Office: Carr Ctr for Human Rights Policy JFK Sch Govt 79 JFK St Cambridge MA 02138

**RAMDAS, JAGADEESH,** physician; arrived in U.S., 1995; s. Ramdas and Sharada Shenoy; children: Ganesh, Maya. MBBS, Calicut Med. Coll., 1989, MD, 1994. Bd. Cert. Pediats. and Oncology Am. Bd. Pediats. Fellow pediat. hematology/oncology LSU Med. Ctr., New Orleans, 1997, pediat. resident, 1998; pediat. hematology/oncology fellowship LSU, Tulang U., New Orleans, 1999—2002; pediat. hematologist/oncologist Geisinger Med. Ctr., Danville, Pa., 2002—; pediat. oncologist Jefferson Med. Coll., Phila., 2003—. Mem.: Am. Soc. Pediat. Hematolgy/Oncology (investigator 2002—), Am. Soc. Hematology (investigator 2002—), Children's Oncology Group (investigator 2002—). Office: Divsn Pediat Hematology/Oncology 100 N Academy Ave Danville PA 17821 Office Phone: 570-271-6848. E-mail: jramdas@geisinger.edu.

**RAMENSKAYA, LUDMILA MIKAEL,** chemical engineer, researcher; b. Ivanovo, Russia, Nov. 9, 1953; d. Mikael Mikael Krasnov and Anastasiya Ivan Krasnova; m. Ergchiy Vladimir Ramenskiy (div.); 1 child, Alexander Ramenskiy. Grad., Inst. Chemistry, Ivanovo, Russia, 1976, postgrad., 1982—85. Engr. Inst. Chemistry, Ivanovo, Russia, 1976—82, 1985—87; rsch. officer Inst. Solution Chemistry, Ivanovo, Russia, 1987—. Contbr. articles to profl. jours. Home: Gromoloya st 16/00-24 153002 Ivanoto Russia Office: Inst Solution Chemistry Abademicheskaya 1 153045 Ivanovo Russia Office Phone: 8-1932 33-62-64. E-mail: lmr@isc-rol.ra.

**RAMER, BRUCE M.,** lawyer; b. Teaneck, N.J., Aug. 2, 1933; s. Sidney and Anne S. (Strassman) R.; children: Gregg B., Marc K., Neal I. BA, Princeton U., 1955; LLB, Harvard U., 1958. Bar: Calif. 1963, N.J. 1958. Assoc., Morrison, Lloyd & Griggs, Hackensack, N.J., 1959-60; ptnr. Gang, Tyre, Ramer & Brown, Inc., L.A., 1963—. Exec. dir. Entertainment Law Inst., Law Ctr. of U. So. Calif.; bd. of councilors Law Ctr. U. So. Calif.; chmn., nat. bd. govs. Am. Jewish Com., 1995-98, nat. v.p., 1982-88, pres., 1998—, L.A. chpt., 1980-83, chair Western region, 1984-86, cmty. svc. award, 1987, nat. pres., 1998—, adv. bd. Skirball Inst. on Am. Values, 1998—; chmn. Asia Pacific Rim Inst., 1989-98; trustee Loyola Marymount U., L.A. Children's Mus., 1986-89; vice chair United Way, 1991-93, corp. bd. dirs., 1981-93, chair coun. pres. 1989-90, mem. cmty. issues coun., 1989-90, chair discretionary fund distbn. com., 1987-89; bd. dirs., chair Geffen Playhouse, 1995-98, founding chair, 1998—; bd. dirs. L.A. Urban League, 1987-93, 96—, Jewish Fedn. Coun. of Greater L.A. (mem. Cmty. Rels. com., bd. dirs., exec. com.), Jewish TV Network, Sta. KCET-TV; mem., bd. dirs. Rebuild L.A., 1992-96; mem. bd. govs. Calif. Cmty. Found., 1988-98; recipient Ann. Brotherhood award NCCJs, 1990; mem. Fellows of Am. Bar Found.; mem. econ. strategy panel State Calif., 1997—; bd. dirs. Shoah Visual History Found., Righteous Persons Found., L.A. 2012 Bid Com. for the So. Calif. Olympic Games; bd. dirs. Jewish Fedn. Coun. Greater L.A., mem. exec. com., cmty. rels. com. Pvt. U.S. Army, 1958-59, 2d lt., 1961-62. Mem. ABA (mem. spl. com. jud. ind.), L.A. County Bar Assn., Calif. Bar Assn., Beverly Hills Bar Assn. (Exec. Dirs. award 1988, Entertainment Lawyer of Yr. award 1996), L.A. Copyright Soc. (pres. 1974-75), Calif. Copyright Conf. (pres. 1973-74), Princeton Club (pres. 1975-78). Office: Gang Tyre Ramer & Brown Inc 132 S Rodeo Dr Beverly Hills CA 90212-2415

**RAMER, HAL REED,** academic administrator; b. Kenton, Tenn., June 8, 1923; s. Claude Orion and Dixie Clayton (Carroll) R. BS, George Peabody Coll., 1947; MSW, U. Tenn., 1952; PhD, Ohio State U., 1963. Asst. dean men Ohio State U., Columbus, 1953-58, dir. internat. house, 1958-60, staff asst. to pres., 1960-62; asst. commr. State Dept. Edn., Nashville, 1963-70; founding pres. Vol. State C.C., Gallatin, Tenn., 1970—2003, pres. emeritus, 2003—. Bd. dirs. Sumner Regional Health Sys., Inc. Com. mem. March of Dimes, Gallatin; trustee Nashville United Way, 1970, Hiwassee Coll., 2001; bd. advisors Aquinas Coll., Nashville, 1967—; former chmn. Tenn. Fulbright-Hays Sch. Commn.; bd. visitors U. Tenn. Sch. Social Work; YMCA. With U.S. Army Air Corps, 1943—45. Recipient Distinctive Svc. award Ohio State U., 1970, Outstanding Leader award Vanderbilt U. chpt. Phi Delta Kappa, 1987, Gov.'s Svc. award State of Tenn. 1993, Sertoma Club Svc. to Mankind award, 1995-96, Disting. Alumnus award Peabody Coll., 1996, Disting. Svc. award Tenn. Bd. Regents, 1997, Svc. award Am. Assn. Cmty. Col., 1999, Otis Floyd Jr. award for excellence Tenn. Coll. Pub. Rels. Assn., 1999, Lifetime Achievement award Peabody Coll. of Vanderbill U., 2003; named Rotarian of the Yr., 1979; Paul Harris fellow Rotary Internat., 1981. Mem. Am. Legion, Coun. Pres. C.Cs. (chmn. state Tenn. 1988-89), Tenn. Coll. Assn. (pres.

1985-86), Nat. Alumni Assn. Peabody Coll. (pres. 1970-71, trustee), Tenn. Acad. Sci., Tenn. and Sumner County Hist. Socs. (bd. dirs.), English Speaking Union Internat. (Nashville chpt.), So. Assn. Colls. and Schs., Univ. Club Nashville, Gallatin and Hendersonville C. of C., St. Thomas Aquinas Soc., Torch Club, Alpha Tau Omega, Kappa Phi Kappa, Alpha Phi Omega, Phi Delta Kappa. Methodist. Avocations: antiques, antique cars, photography. Home: 120 Abbottsford Nashville TN 37215-2440

**RAMER, JAMES LEROY,** civil engineer; b. Marshalltown, Iowa, Dec. 7, 1935; s. LeRoy Frederick and Irene (Wengert) Ramer; m. Jacqueline L. Orr, Dec. 15, 1957; children: Sarah T., Robert H., Eric A., Susan L. Student, U. Iowa, Iowa City, 1953-57; MCE, Washington U., St. Louis, 1976, MA in Polit. Sci., 1978; postgrad., U. Mo., 1984—. Registered profl. engr., land surveyor. Civil and constrn. engr. U.S. Army C.E., Tulsa, 1960-63; civil and relocations engr. U.S. State Dept., Del Rio, Tex., 1964; project engr. H.B. Zachary Co., San Antonio, 1965-66; civil and constrn. engr. U.S. Army C.E., St. Louis, 1967-76, tech. advisor for planning and nat. hydropower coord., 1976-78; project mgr. for EPA constrn. grants Milw., 1978-80; chief arch. and engring. HUD, Indpls., 1980-81; civil design and pavements engr. Whiteman AFB, Mo., 1982-86; project mgr. maintenance, 1993—; soil and pavements engr. Hdqrs. Mil. Airlift Command, Scott AFB, Ill., 1986-88. Project mgr. AF-1 maintenance hangar; cattle and grain farmer, 1982—; pvt. practice civil-mech. engr., constrn. mgmt., estimating, cost analysis, cash flow, project scheduling, expert witness, profl. land surveying, Fortuna, Mo., 1988—2001; chief constrn. inspector divsn. design and constrn. State of Mo., 1992—93; project engr. Mil. Housing, 2001—; adj. faculty civil engring. Washington U., 1968—78, U. Wis., Milw., 1978—80, Ga. Mil. Coll., Whiteman AFB, Longview Coll., Kansas City; adj. rsch. engr. U. Mo., Columbia, 1985—86; project engr., quality control officer Korte Constrn. Co. Author (tech. writing operation and maintenance manuals,); fin. reports and environ. control plans, designs & builds tech. and indsl. models. Mem.: AAUP, NSPE, ASCE, Soc. Am. Mil. Engrs., Optimists Internat. Lutheran. Achievements include patents for in diverse art, 9 copyrights; development of solar waterstill, deep shaft hydropower concept. Home: 11147 Angel Rd Fortuna MO 65034-2167 Office Phone: 660-337-6444. Business E-Mail: jlramer@iland.net.

**RAMER, LAWRENCE JEROME,** corporation executive; b. Bayonne, NJ, July 29, 1928; s. Sidney and Anne (Strassman) R.; m. Ina Lee Brown, June 30, 1957; children: Stephanie Beryl, Susan Meredith, Douglas Strassman. BA in Econs, Lafayette Coll., 1950; MBA, Harvard U., 1957; LLD (hon.), Lafayette Coll., 1992. Sales rep., then v.p. United Sheet Metal Co., Bayonne, 1953-55; with Am. Cement Corp., 1957-64; v.p. mktg. div. Riverside Cement Co., 1960-62, v.p. mktg. parent co., 1962-64; vice chmn. bd., chief exec. officer Clavier Corp., NYC, 1965-66; exec. v.p., vice chmn. bd. Pacific Western Industries, LA, 1966-70; pres., chief exec. officer Nat. Portland Cement Co. Fla., 1975-89; chmn. bd. Sutro Partners, Inc., LA, 1977-89, Somerset Mgmt. Group, 1975-92, Luminall Paints Inc., LA, 1972-95; chmn. bd., CEO Bruning Paint Co., Balt., 1979—2000; chmn. bd., chief exec. officer Pacific Coast Cement Co., LA, 1979-90; pres., CEO Ramer Equities, Inc., 1990—2000, chmn., 2000—; chmn. bd. Scott Paint Co., Sarasota, Fla., 2000—. Chmn. Lee and Lawrence J. Ramer Family Found., 1986—; bd. dirs. The Music Ctr., LA, Canyon Ranch, Tucson; bd. dirs. Ctr. Theatre Group-Mark Taper Athmanson Theatres, LA, pres. and chmn., 1987-97. Mem. Coun. on Fgn. Rels., NYC; chmn. bd. trustees Lafayette Coll., Easton, Pa., 1992—2001, bd. trustees, 1992—2001, Helen Keller Internat., NYC; chmn. bd. trustees Calif. Inst. Arts, Valencia, Calif., 1995—2006; nat. bd. govs. Am. Jewish Com., NY, assoc. treas., trustee NY; trustee Facing History and Ourselves; bd. dirs. LA World Affairs Coun., Pacific Coun. Internat. Policy, 2004; bd. govs. Hebrew Union Coll.; trustee Leo Baeck Inst., NY. Office: Ramer Equities Inc 10900 Wilshire Blvd Ste 550 Los Angeles CA 90024-6501 Office Phone: 310-209-0442. Personal E-mail: lj.ramer@verizon.net.

**RAMETTE, RICHARD WALES,** chemistry professor; b. Hartford, Conn., Oct. 9, 1927; s. Joel Edward and Grace Margaret (Wales) R.; m. Lenora Kathryn Kelleher, Aug., 21, 1949; children: Cheryl Lee, James Edward, John Richard, David Joel, William Michael. BA, Wesleyan U., Middletown, Conn., 1950; PhD, U. Minn., 1954. Prof. chemistry Carleton Coll., Northfield, Minn. 1954-90, Laurence M. Gould prof. chemistry, 1971-90, prof. emeritus, 1990—. Sci. advisor FDA, Mpls., 1969-80. Author: Chemical Equilibrium and Analysis, 1981. Asst. scoutmaster Boy Scouts Am., Northfield, 1968-73; calligraphy instr. Northfield Arts Guild, 1974-80; sec. Unitarian Universalist Congregation Green Valley, 1998-2001, pres., 2001-2002. Recipient Chemistry Teaching award Mfg. Chemists, 1966, Analytical Chemistry Teaching award Am. Chem. Soc., 1991, Disting. Alumnus award Wesleyan U., 1995. Mem.: Am. Chem. Soc. (Analytical Chemistry Tchg. award, 50 yr. mem. award 2002). Home: 765 W Fountain Creek Dr Green Valley AZ 85614-3272 Personal E-mail: rramette@carleton.edu.

**RAMEY, CARL ROBERT,** lawyer; b. Binghamton, N.Y., Feb. 15, 1941; s. Clinton W. and Hester May (Wisdom) R.; m. Maryan Sitzenkopf, Aug. 11, 1962 (div. Sept. 1987); children: Mark Alan, Christian David; m. Karen Reichard, Nov. 28, 1987. AB, Marietta Coll., 1962; MA, Mich. State U., 1964; JD, George Washington U., 1967. Bar: D.C. 1968, U.S. Dist. Ct. D.C. 1968, U.S. Ct. Appeals (D.C., 2d, 3d, 4th, 5th, 7th and 9th cirs.), U.S. Supreme Ct. 1972, Md. 1999. Assoc. McKenna, Wilkinson & Kittner, Washington, 1967-71, ptnr., 1971-86, Wiley, Rein & Fielding, Washington, 1986—. Contbr. articles to profl. jours., chpt. to Copyright Law Symposium, 1969; editorial staff George Washington Law Rev., 1965-67. Recipient First Prize award Nat. Nathan Burkan Meml. Writing Competition, ASCAP, 1969. Mem. ABA, Fed. Communications Bar Assn. (treas. 1977-78, co-chair editl. adv. bd. Fed. Comms. Law Jour. 1993-96), D.C. Bar Assn., Md. Bar Assn. Republican. Episcopalian. Avocations: skiing, tennis, boating, biking. Office: Wiley Rein & Fielding 1776 K St NW Washington DC 20006-2304 Home: 409 Rehoboth Ave Apt 23 Rehoboth Beach DE 19971 3112

**RAMEY, CECIL EDWARD, JR.,** lawyer; b. Shreveport, La., Nov. 9, 1923; s. Cecil Edward and Blanche (Gwin) R.; m. Betty Loper, June 15, 1945; children— Martha L., L. Christine, Stephen E. BS summa cum laude, Centenary Coll., 1943; LLB, Yale U., 1949; postgrad., Tulane U., 1950-51. Bar: Wis. 1949, La. 1951. Assoc. Miller, Mack & Fairchild, Milw., 1949-50; mem. faculty Tulane U., 1950-54; assoc. Hargrove, Guyton, Van Hook and Hargrove, Shreveport, 1954-56, ptnr., 1956-63, Hargrove, Guyton, Van Hook and Ramey, Shreveport, 1963-73, Hargrove, Guyton, Ramey and Barlow, Shreveport, 1973-89, of counsel, 1989-94, Barlow and Hardtner, L.C., Shreveport, 1994-2001, Lemle Kelleher Barlow and Hardtner, Shreveport, 2001—03, Lemle & Kelleher LLP, Shreveport, 2003—05; ret., 2005. Adj. prof. Centenary Coll., 1992—98. Former chmn. Citizens Capital Improvements com. City of Shreveport; former mem. governing bd. Shreveport YMCA; former chmn. bd. trustees Broadmoor Meth. Ch., Shreveport, chmn. bd. stewards; former bd. dirs., former chmn. Shreveport-Bossier Found.; trustee Centenary Coll. With AC, U.S. Army, 1943-46. Named Shreveport's Outstanding Young Man of Yr., 1956, Mr. Shreveport, 1968; recipient Clyde E. Fant Meml. award community service United Way, 1979 Fellow Am. Coll. Trust and Estate Counsel; mem. ABA, La. Bar Assn., Shreveport Bar Assn. (pres. 1970), La. Law Inst., Shreveport C. of C. (pres. 1974), Centenary Coll. Alumni Assn. (past pres.), Shreveport Club, Order of Coif, Phi Delta Phi, Kappa Sigma. Clubs: Shreveport. Home: 139 Oscar Ln Shreveport LA 71105-3566

**RAMEY, DENNY L.,** bar association executive director; b. Portsmouth, Ohio, Feb. 22, 1947; s. Howard Leroy and Norma Wylodine (Richards) R.; m. Jeannine Gayle Dunmyer, Sept. 24, 1971 (div. Nov. 1991); children: Elizabeth Michelle, Brian Michael. BBA, Ohio U., 1970; MBA, Capital U., 1976. Cert. assn. exec. Adminstrv. mgr. Transit Warehouse div. Elston Richards Storage Co., Columbus, Ohio, 1972-79; mgr. continuing profl. edn. Ohio Soc. CPA's, Columbus, 1973-79; exec. dir. Engrs. Found. of Ohio, Columbus, 1979-80; asst. exec. Ohio State Bar Assn., Columbus, 1980-86, exec. dir., sec., treas., 1986—. Treas., exec. com., bd. dirs. Ohio Bar Liability Ins. Co., Columbus, 1986—; treas. Ohio State Bar Found., 1986—; treas. Ohio Legal Ctr. Ins., Columbus, 1988-91; sec. Ohio Printing Co., Ltd., 1991; v.p. Osbanet, Inc.,

1993—; chmn. Lawriter LLC, 2000—; bd. dirs. OSBA.com, LLC. Mem.: Ohio Soc. Assn. Execs., Am. Soc. Assn. Execs., Nat. Assn. Bar Execs., Scioto Country Club. Methodist. Avocations: golf, sports, music, art. Office: Ohio State Bar Assn 1700 Lake Shore Dr PO Box 16562 Columbus OH 43216-6562 Office Phone: 614-487-4405. Business E-Mail: dramey@ohiobar.org.

**RAMEY, EUDORA MALOIS,** minister; b. Maywood, Ill., Oct. 26, 1923; d. Cleonus and Ora Helen Garner; m. Edward F Ramey, July 27, 1947; children: Jonathan, RoseMary, Paul, Student, Herzl Jr. Coll., Chgo., Peter's Bus. Coll., Master's Sewing Coll., Vennard Bible Coll., Moody Bible Inst. Ordained minister African Episcopal Ch., 1951. Mem. Dist. 9 Bd. Edn., McKinley Sch., Chgo., 1966—75; counselor aide Bd. Edn./Whitney Young Magnet Sch., Chgo., 1975—80; implementor Job Club/Pres.'s Office/Employment Tng., Chgo., 1980—92. Advisor Garfield Pk. Conservatory, Chgo., 1991—, bd. dirs., 1996—. Mem. Chgo. Urban League, 1943—68, PUSH (People United to Serve Humanity), Chgo., 1970—91; ordained local elder/min. St. Stephen AME Ch., Chgo., 1951—; mem. NAACP, Chgo., 1943—68. Recipient Trailblazer for Women in Ministry award, 4th Dist. of the AME Ch., 2001, Cert. of Honor, Internat. Way of Life /City of Chgo., 1999, Chgo. Sr. Citizen's Hall of Fame, 1997. Avocations: Scrabble, Bingo, reading, checkers, crossword puzzles. Personal E-mail: rev.eudora1026@sbc.global.net.

**RAMIREZ, AGUSTIN A (GUS RAMIREZ),** auto parts manufacturing company executive; b. Puerto Rico; BS in aerospace engring., Ga. Inst. Tech., 1968, MS, 1969; MBA, Harvard U., 1974. With Pratt & Whitney; v.p., gen. mgr. HUSCO, 1984—85, organized mgmt. to purchase, 1985; chmn., CEO HUSCO Internat., 1985—. Named to Acad. Disting. Engring. Alumni, Ga. Inst. Tech., 2001. Office: HUSCO Internat W239 N218 Pewaukee Rd Waukesha WI 53188 Office Phone: 262-513-4200.*

**RAMIREZ, AINISSA,** materials scientist; BSc, Brown U.; MS, PhD, Stanford U. Rschr., scientist Hewlett Packard Lab., Bell Lab., Lucent Tech., sci. curriculum developer pub. sch.; current asst. prof. mech. engring. Yale U. Named one of 100 Top Young Innovators, MIT's Tech. Review, 2003. Office: Yale Univ Mech Engring Dept PO Box 208284 New Haven CT 06520

**RAMIREZ, ARAMIS,** professional baseball player; b. Santo Domingo, Dominican Republic, June 25, 1978; Third baseman Pittsburgh Pirates, 1998—2003, Chicago Cubs, 2003—. Named to Nat. League All-Star Team, 2005. Office: Chicago Cubs 1060 W Addison St Chicago IL 60613*

**RAMIREZ, EVANGELINE ROSE,** elementary school educator; d. Alfredo and Rose Ramirez. BS in Criminal Justice, U. Tex., El Paso, 1980, MPA, 1987. Tchr. Desert View Mid. Sch., El Paso, 2001—05. Named Tchr. of Yr., Desert View Mid. Sch., 1999, 2004, Outstanding Tchr., Tex. Mis. Sch. Assn., 2004; named to Cheerleader Hall Fame, City El Paso, 2003. Mem.: Coun. Social Studies, Tex. Classroom Tchrs. Assn.

**RAMÍREZ, FELIPE J.,** musician, composer, artist, photographer; b. Madrid; s. Felipe Ramirez Plaza and Lourdes Esteban Montilla. M, So. Meth. U., Dallas, 1998—2000, Artist Cert. Diploma. Artist-in-residence Figaro Acad. Music, Irving, Tex., 2003—, Dallas, 2003—. Musician: (piano performances) Musical Contribution (Musician of Yr., 2003); photograph, Peñiscola; poetry Missing Love, Am. at Millenium, 2000. Founder Neighborhood Crime Watch, Dallas. Recipient Best Spanish Pianist award, Iturbi Internat. Piano Competition, First Prize award, Melilla Nat. Competition, Spain, Best Interpreter of Spanish Music award, Ferrol Internat. Competition.

**RAMIREZ, JANICE L.,** assistant school superintendent; b. Dodge City, Kans., July 16, 1947; d. Chris William and Lois (Moore) Langvardt; 1 child, Jessica. BS, Emporia State U., 1969, MA, 1970; PhD, Kans. State U., 1982. Div. prin. Highland Park High Sch./Topeka (Kans.) pub. schs.; prin. Topeka pub. schs., Mesa (Ariz.) pub. schs., asst. supt. Mem. mid. level task force Ariz. Dept. Edn. Contbr. articles to profl. jours. Bd. dirs. Maricopa County Sports Commn.; chair merit sys. bd. City of Mesa. Recipient Kamelot award; named one of Top 100 Bus. Women in Ariz., Today's Ariz. Woman Success Mag., 1996—. Mem. Am. Assn. Sch. Pers. Adminstrs., Ariz. Sch. Pers. Adminstrs. Assn., Nat. Assn. Ednl. Negotiators, Ariz. Sch. Adminstrs. Assn., Phi Delta Kappa. Office: 63 E Main St # 101 Mesa AZ 85201-7204 Office Phone: 480-472-0412. E-mail: jlramire@mpsaz.org.

**RAMIREZ, LEO ARMANDO, SR.,** mathematics educator; Math. tchr. McAllen (Tex.) High Sch., 1985—; founder, owner Ram Materials, Inc., McAllen, Tex. Named Hero in Edn., Reader's Digest, 1992, Tex. State Math. Tchr. of Yr., 1993, Disney's Am. Teacher award finalist, 1994, Teacher award Honorable Mention, USA Today, 1999, HEB Excellence award finalist, 2004; recipient Denius Univ. Interscholastic League Sponsors Excellence award, 1991, Tandy Corp. Scholar award, 1995. Mem.: Tex. Math and Sci. Coaches Assn. (Numerous Coach of Yr. award), Univ. Interscholastic League. Achievements include has written more Number Sense, Calculator, and Mathematics tests for invitational tournaments and more workbooks/practice tests than any person in the history of University Interscholastic League. Office: Ram Inc Materials 2908 Flamingo Mcallen TX 78504 Office Phone: 956-682-5185. Office Fax: 956-682-7281. Business E-Mail: toywiz127@aol.com.

**RAMIREZ, MANUEL ARISTIDES (MANNY RAMIREZ),** professional baseball player; b. Santo Domingo, Dominican Republic, May 30, 1972; m. Juliana Ramirez. Grad. high sch., N.Y.C. Outfielder Cleve. Indians, 1993—2000, Boston Red Sox, 2001—. Named World Series MVP, 2004; named to The Sporting News Am. League Silver Slugger team, 1995, Am. League All-Star team, 1993, 1995, 1998, Am. League All-Star Team, 2005; recipient Players Choice award for Am. League Outstanding Player, 1999, Am. League Batting Title, 2002, Silver Slugger award, MLB, 2005. Achievements include led the American League in RBIs, 1999, home runs (43), 2004; being a member of World Series Champion Boston Red Sox, 2004. Office: Boston Red Sox Fenway Park 4 Yawkey Way Boston MA 02215*

**RAMIREZ, MARI CARMEN,** curator; b. San Juan, PR, 1955; m. Hector Olea. M in art history, PhD in art history, U. Chgo. Dir. Mus. Anthropology, History, and Art U. PR, Rio Piedras; curator L.Am. art Jack S. Blanton Mus. Art, U. Tex., Austin, 1989—2001; Worthman Curator L.Am. Art Mus. Fine Arts, Houston, 2001—; dir. Internat. Ctr. for the Arts of the Americas, 2001—. Adj. lectr. art dept. U. Tex., Austin. Editor: (books) El Taller Torres-Garcia: The School of the South and Its Legacy, 1992, Collecting L.Am. Art for the 21st Century, 2002, Questioning the Line: Gego in Context, 2003; co-author (with Hector Olea): Inverted Utopias: Avant-Garde Art in L.Am., 2004; co-curator Re-Aligning Vision: Alternative Currents in South American Drawing, 1997, co-curator (with Hector Olea) (exhibitions) Inverted Utopias: Avant-Garde Art in L.Am., 2004, co-curator (with Beverly Adams) Encounters/Displacements: Alfredo Jaar, Luis Camnitzer, Cildo Meireles, curator Cantos Paralelos: Visual Parody in Contemporary Argentinean Art, Global Conceptualism: Points of Origin (L.Am. sect.). Named one of 25 Most Influential Hispanics, Time Mag., 2005; recipient Peter Norton Family Found. Award for Curatorial Excellence, Ann. award for curatorial excellence, Ctr. for Curatorial Studies, Bard Coll., 2005; Getty Curatorial Residence Fellowship. Office: Mus Fine Arts PO Box 6826 Houston TX 77265-6826

**RAMIREZ, MARIA EUGENIA,** primary school educator; b. Chihuahua, Mexico, Sept. 14, 1960; d. Federico Barrio and Luz Ramirez; m. Alfonso Ramirez, Dec. 8, 1983; children: Gabriela, Javier Alfonso. BS in Med. Tech., U. Tex., El Paso, 1983, MEd in Bilingual Edn., 1990. Cert. tchr. pre K-8 Tex. Tchr. bilingual kindergarten Ysleta Ind. Sch. Dist., El Paso, 1989—2000; tchr. dual lang. kindergarten El Paso Ind. Sch. Dist., 2000—. Mem.: Assn. for Tchrs. and Profl. Educators. Roman Catholic.

**RAMIREZ, MARIA FIORINI,** financial consultant; b. Naples, Italy, Jan. 1, 1948; came to U.S., 1961; d. Fernando and Clelia Ambrosio Fiorini; m.

George M. Ramirez, 1973. BBA, Pace U., 1972, postgrad., 1974-76. Analyst Meinhard-CIT Comml. Fin., N.Y.C., 1967-68; credit analyst Am. Express Internat. Bank, N.Y.C., 1968-72; credit mgr. Banca Nazionale del Lavoro, N.Y.C., 1972-73; credit mgr., asst. v.p. Merrill Lynch G.S.I., 1973-74, economist, 1974—81, v.p., sr. money market economist Merrill Lynch Econs. Inc., 1981-84; sr. v.p., sr. money market economist Becker Paribas Inc., N.Y.C., 1984; corp. first v.p., money market economist Drexel Burnham Lambert Inc., N.Y.C., 1984-86, mng. dir., chief money market economist, 1986—90; pres. Maria Ramirez Capital Cons. Inc. (subs. Hancock Freedom), N.Y.C., 1990—92; pres., CEO Maria Fiorini Ramirez, Inc., 1992—. Bd. dirs. Statewide Savings Bank, 1989—2000, Arlington Capital, 1991—2000, Security Benefit Life, 1996—98, Independence Community Bank, 2000—06, Schroder Hedge Funds, 2004—, AMF funds, 2005—, Sovereign Bancorp, Inc., 2006—; mem. investment policy com. & product review com. Edward Jones & Co., 1996—. Mem. advisory bd. Pace U. Lunblin Sch. Bus., 1997—; trustee Notre Dame H.S., 2001, Pace U., 2002—. Recipient Lubin Alumni Achievement award, Pace U., 2001, Metro Internat. Fulbright award for Contributing to Internat. Understanding, 2004, Ellis I. Medal of Honor, 2004. Mem.: The Econ. Club NY. Roman Catholic. Office: 675 3rd Ave New York NY 10017*

**RAMIREZ, MARIO EFRAIN,** physician; b. Roma, Tex., Apr. 3, 1926; s. Efren M. and Carmen (Hinojosa) R.; m. Sarah B. Aycock, Nov. 25, 1949; children: Mario, Patricia Ann, Norman Michael, Jaime Eduardo, Roberto Luis. Student, U. Tex., 1942—45; MD, U. Tenn., 1948. Diplomate Am. Bd. Family Physicians. Intern Shreveport Charity Hosp., La., 1949, resident, practice medicine specializing in family practice; pvt. family practice Roma, 1950—75, Rio Grande City, Tex., 1975—93; owner, administr. Ramirez Meml. Hosp., Roma, 1958—75. Assoc. med. dir. South Tex. Blue Cross Blue Shield Tex., McAllen, 1993-95 County judge Starr County, Rio Grande City, 1969-78; chmn. South Tex. Devel. Coun., 1975-76, Tri-County Cmty. Action Coun., 1971-78; mem. coordinated bd. Tex. Colls. and Univs., 1979-85; mem. devel. bd. U. Tex., 1986—; presdl. appointee bd. regents Uniformed Svcs. U. Tex. Health Scis., 1985-92; mem. bd. regents U. Tex. Sys., 1989-95, vice chmn. bd., 1991-92 Recipient Spl. citation Surgeon Gen., 1967, Disting. Alumnus award U. Tex., 1975, 78, Achievement award Lab World, 1978, Presdl. citation U. Tex., 1979, Outstanding Alumnus award U. Tenn., 1991, Mirabeau B. Lamar medal Assn. Tex. Colls. and Univs., 1997; named Family Dr. of Yr., Good Housekeeping mag. and Am. Acad. Family Physicians, 1978, Border Texan of the Yr., 1995; honoree Founder's Day for contbns. to higher edn. U. Tex. Pan Am., 1989; honored by elem. sch. named Dr. Mario E. Ramirez elem. sch., Rio Grande City, Tex., 2006. Fellow Am. Acad. Family Physicians; mem. AMA (vice chmn. com. health care of poor 1971-75, Benjamin Rush Bicentennial award 1976, Coun. Med. Svcs. 1985-94), Tex. Med. Assn. (chmn. com. health care of poor 1971, Disting. Svc. award 1972, pres. 1979-80), Tex. Acad. Family Physicians (v.p. 1973, pres. 1975, Disting. Svc. award 1967, Outstanding Leadership award 1975-76, v.p. Valley chpt. 1960-61, pres. 1961-62), Hidalgo-Starr Counties Med. Soc. (pres. 1964), Lions, K.C. Rotary, Alhambra Club Address: 212 W Pine Ridge Ln Mcallen TX 78503-3129 Personal E-mail: mramirezmd@aol.com.

**RAMIREZ, MARY CATHERINE,** retired secondary school educator; b. McLeansboro, Ill., Feb. 16, 1921; d. George Washington and Mary Margaret (Lane) Tousley; m. John Ramirez, Oct. 30, 1948 (dec. 1975). BS, Ctrl. U., Edmond, Okla., 1942; MA, U. Okla., 1945. Tchr. Bradley (Okla.) High Sch., 1942-43, McLeansboro (Ill.) High Sch., 1943-46, No. Okla. Jr. Coll., Tonkawa, Okla., 1946-47, Draughon Bus. Coll., Springfield, Mo., 1947-48, VA Hosp., Springfield, Mo., 1948-52, Madison Sch., 1952-63, Madison pub. sch., 1963-85; tchr. ESL Poland, 1995. Tchr. English (summer), Poland, 1994. Mem. AAUW (publicity chmn. Madison br. 1954-60)., NEA, Madison Civics Club. Avocations: travel, photography, coin and stamp collecting, needlecrafts. Home: 971 Wellington Ct Nekoosa WI 54457-9040

**RAMIREZ, MONICA E.,** education educator, consultant; b. New York, NY, Nov. 27, 1952; d. Luis Ramirez de Arellano and Margarete Brendel; m. Neil Allen, Aug. 17, 2002; children: Luis Preiss, Suellen Melzer-Drinnen. BA, MS, U. Munich, 1979; EdS, Novasout Eastern, 1989; PhD, Columbia Pacific U., 1992. Assoc. prof. Fla. Atlantic U., Boca Raton, 1994—97; prof. geology Aims Coll., Greeley, Colo., 2000—; assoc. prof. Colo. State U. at Pueblo, 2004—. Stormwater adv. bd. City of Greeley, 2003—; tchr. edn. bd. Colo. State U., 2004—05; geology state chmn. Aims Coll., 2001—04. Contbr. articles to jours.; lang. editor Ctrl. European Sci. Jour., 2002—. Nominee Fla. Governor's award, Fla. Dept. Environ. Edn., 1993; recipient grant, NSF, 2000—04;, Math and Sci. Initiative, Colo. Commn., 2004—05. Avocations: rock climbing, mountain climbing. Office: Colo State U 2200 Bonforte Blvd Pueblo CO 81001 Business E-Mail: monica.ramirez@colostate-pueblo.edu.

**RAMIREZ, NOLA MARIE,** librarian; b. Painesville, Ohio, July 25, 1953; d. Ruth Alice Young; m. Robert Cisneros Ramirez, Dec. 20, 1983; 1 child, Geoffrey Michael Ross. Attended, West Valley Jr. Coll., San Jose, Calif. Vol. Merced County Librr., Gustine, Calif., 1988—90, libr. asst., 1990—92, branch mgr., 1992—. Co-leader Girl Scouts Am., 1998—. Avocation: reading. Home: 263 Laurel Ave Gustine CA 95322 Office: Merced County Libr Gustine Branch 205 Sixth St Gustine CA 95322 Office Phone: 209-854-3013. Personal E-mail: nolar55@hotmail.com.

**RAMIREZ, RAUL,** academic administrator; s. Julio and Carolina Ramirez; m. Sonya Annie Hohm, May 18, 1985; 1 child, John Julio. MSc, U. Tex., El Paso, 1975; EdD, N.Mex State U., 1996. Campus exec. officer Dona Ana CC, Las Cruces, N.Mex., 1999—2004; pres. east campus Pima CC, Tucson, 2004— Home: 5400 E Williams Blvd Tucson AZ 05007 Offc: Pima Community Coll 8181 E Irvington Rd Tucson AZ 85709 Business E-Mail: raul.ramirez@pima.edu.

**RAMIREZ, SARA,** actress; b. Mazatlan, Mexico, Aug. 31, 1976; Actress (Broadway plays) The Capeman, 1998, The Gershwins' Fascinating Rhythm, 1999, A Class Act, 2001, Dreamgirls, 2001, Monty Python's Spamalot, 2005 (Tony award, best performance by featured actress in a musical, 2005), Outer Critics Circle award, outstanding featured actress in a musical, 2005), (off-Broadway plays) The Vagina Monologues, (films) You've Got Mail, 1998, actress (voice) UnJammer Lammy, 1999, actress PaRappa the Rapper 2, 2001, Spider-Man, 2002, Washington Heights, 2002, Chicago, 2002, (TV series) Baseball Wives, 2002, (guest appearance) Law & Order SVU, As the World Turns, 2002, NYPD Blue, 2004, Grey's Anatomy, 2006—. Office: Cornerstone Talent Agency 37 W 20th St Ste 1108 New York NY 10011-3713*

**RAMIREZ, STEVAN G.,** consumer products company executive; BS in Bus. Mgmt., Univ. Redlands, Calif.; MBA, Univ. Rochester. Various positions to customer svc. v.p. Xerox Corp., 1972—2000; v.p., worldwide quality, supply chain, consumer imaging Eastman Kodak Co., 2000—01, chief quality officer, v.p., 2001; gen. mgr. consumer care Health Group, 2006—. Mgmt. sponsor Kodak Hispanic Orgn. for Leadership, Advancement (HOLA); steering com. chair United Way Latino Leadership Devel. Program. Named one of 50 Most Important Hispanics in Tech. and Bus., Hispanic Engineer Info. Tech. mag., 2003, 2004, 2005. Office: Chief Quality Officer Eastman Kodak 343 State St Rochester NY 14650

**RAMIREZ, TED L.,** lawyer; b. San Antonio, Aug. 16, 1952; BA cum laude, Southwestern Adventist Coll., 1974; JD, Ohio State Univ., 1976. Bar: Ohio 1977, US Tax Ct. 1978. Ptnr. Arter & Hadden, LLP; ptnr., co-chair health care practice Venable LLP, Washington, 2003—. Adj. faculty Columbia Union Coll., Moritz Coll. Law, Ohio State Univ. Contbr. articles profl. journals. Legal affairs com. Loma Linda Univ. and Medical Ctr.; Gen. Conf., exec.com. Seventh-Day Adventists. Mem.: Am. Health Lawyers Assn., Ohio State Bar Assn., Dayton (Ohio) Bar Assn., Columbus (Ohio) Bar Assn., 2004—05. Office: Venable LLP 575 Seventh St NW Washington DC 20004 Office Phone: 202-344-4622. Office Fax: 202-344-8300. Business E-Mail: tramirez@venable.com.

**RAMIREZ, TINA,** artistic director; b. Caracas, Venezuela; d. Gloria Maria Cestero and Jose Ramirez Gaonita. Studied dance with Lola Bravo, Alexandra Danilova, Anna Sokolow. Toured with Federico Rey Dance Co.; founder, artistic dir. Ballet Hispanico, NYC, 1970—. Panelist NEA N.Y. Sate Coun. on Arts; mem. advisory panel N.Y.C. Dept. Cultural Affairs; bd. dirs Dance Theater Workshop. Appearances (Broadway plays) Kismet, Lute Song, (TV series) Man of La Mancha. Bd. mem. The New 42nd Street, Inc. Named one of ten people of yr., AARP Mag., 2004; recipient Arts and Culture Honor award, Mayor of NYC, 1983, Ethnic New Yorker award, NYC, 1986, Gov.'s Arts award, NY State Gov. Mario Cuomo, 1987, honoree Nat. Puerto Rican Forum, Hispanic Inst. for Performing Arts, Hispanic Heritage Award, 1999, Dance Magazine Award, 2002, Nat. Medal of Arts, Nat. Endowment for the Arts, 2005. Office: Ballet Hispanico 167 W 89th St New York NY 10024-1901*

**RAMIREZ-LLUCH, NORMAN FELIPE,** orthopedic surgeon; b. Mayaguez, PR, Jan. 11, 1963; s. Norman Ramirez and Gloria Lluch; m. Sonia Vazquez, Apr. 2, 1993; children: Nicole Ramirez, Adriana Ramirez. MD, U. PR, San Juan, 1988. Lic. PR, 1993. Pediatric orthopaedist Hosp. La Concepcion, San German, PR, 2003—. Mem. Synthes Chest Wall Deformity Study Group. Mem.: SRS, PR Orthop. Soc., Mexican Orthop. Pediat. Soc., Am. Acad. Orthop. Surgeons, Pediat. Orthop. Soc. N.Am. Home: Box 6847 Mayaguez PR 00681 Office: Carr # 2 Km 1734 San Vicente de Paul San German PR

**RAMIREZ-MIRELES, FERNANDO,** electrical engineer; s. Fernando Ramirez Matuk and Maria Elia Mireles Tabares; m. Gina Miroslava Guerrero Barja; children: Tania Fernanda Ramirez Guerrero, Thalia Miroslava Ramirez Guerrero. BSc in Electronics Comm., Met. Autonomous U., Mexico City; MScEE, Ctr. for Rsch. and Advanced Studies of Nat. Politechnic Inst., Mexico City; PhDEE, U. So. Calif. Intern Mex. Tel. Co., Mexico City, Distrito Federal, 1987—88; rschr. Ctr. for Rsch. and Advanced Studies Nat. Politechnic Inst., Mexico City, 1988—92; rsch. asst. U. So. Calif., L.A., 1996—98; summer intern Torrey Sci. Corp., San Diego, 1997; mem. tech. staff Glenayre/Wireless Access, Santa Clara, Calif., 1998—99; comm. sys. engr. Aware, Inc., Lafayette, Calif., 1999—2001; sr. comm. sys. engr. Ikanos Comms., Fremont, Calif., 2001—03; prof. Inst. Tech Autonomo, Mexico, 2003—. Cons. Nat. Bank Mex., Mexico City, 1991; invited spkr. at tech. confs. Referee: profl. jours.; contbr. articles to profl. jours. and confs. Named Candidate to Nat. Rschr., Nat. Sys. Rschrs., Mex., 1993—94; named one of Best Students of Mex., Best Students of Mex. Orgn., 1989; recipient Fulbright Scholarship, Fulbright-Garcia Robles Commn., 1992—97, Universitarian Merit medal, Met. Autonomous Univ., Mex., 1987, Honorific Mention, IV Ericsson's Nat. Prize of Sci. and Tech., Mex., 1990. Mem.: IEEE (sr.), Soc. Hispanic Profl. Engrs., Tau Beta Pi. Achievements include research in field of DSL communications. Avocation: travel. Office: Inst Tech Autonomo Rio Hondo 1 Caolniatizapan Mexico Office Phone: +525 55 628 4000 ext. 3620. Personal E-mail: fernandomireles@yahoo.com. Business E-Mail: ramirezm@ieee.org.

**RAMIREZ-RIVERA, JOSE,** physician; b. Mayaguez, PR, June 26, 1929; s. Jesus Ramirez and Nieves Rivera; m. Leila Suner, May 14, 1971; children: Frederico, Steven, Sally, Juliette, Natasha, Leila. BA, Johns Hopkins U., 1949; MD, Yale U., 1953. Diplomate Am Bd Internal Med, re-certified 1974. Intern U. Md. Hosp., 1953-54; resident in medicine Univ. Hosp., Balt., 1954-55, fellow in hematology, 1958-59, resident, 1959; staff physician VA Hosp., Balt., 1960-67, assoc. chief of staff, 1962-68; asst. in medicine Johns Hopkins U., 1960-67, instr. in medicine, 1967-68; asst. prof. medicine U. Md., 1961-68; assoc. prof. Duke U., Durham, NC, 1968-70; dir. med. edn. and clin. investigation Western Region P.R., 1970-80; chief medicine Mayaguez (P.R.) Med. Ctr., 1971-82. Prof med Univ PR, San Juan, 1974—, dir univ med servs Med Sci Campus, 1982—86; prof med Univ Cent del Caribe, 1998—; dir Rincon Rural Health Project, 1975—82; assoc chief staff educ VA Med Ctr, San Juan, 1990—92; dir clin investigation La Concepcion Hosp, San German, 1996—. Contbr. articles to med. jours.; author books of Puerto Rican Legends. Bd dirs Soc Educ Suroeste. With USPHS, 1955—57. Decorated Comendador Imperial Orden Hispanica de Carlos V; named author of Yr., PR Med. Soc. Western Sect., 1975, 1981. Master: ACP (pres. PR chpt. 1986—88, Blaine Brower Traveling Scholar 1967, Laureate award 2005); fellow: Coll. Chest Physicians, Royal Soc. Med (London); mem.: Imperial Orden Hispanica de Carlos V, Puerto Rican Fedn. Bioethics (bd. dirs. 1999—2002, pres. 2002—), Soc. Autores Puertorriguenos, PR Lung Assn. (bd. dirs. 1975—80), Casa España (bd. dirs. 1998—), Alliance Francaise PR (v.p. 1995—96, pres. 1996—2000, bd. dirs. 2006), PEN Club. Roman Catholic. Achievements include creating a technique of lung lavage for alveolar proteinosis. Avocations: classical music, literature. Office Phone: 787-793-6576. Personal E-mail: ramirj@hotmail.com.

**RAMIS, HAROLD ALLEN,** film director, screenwriter, actor; b. Chgo., Nov. 21, 1944; s. Nathan and Ruth (Cokee) R.; m. Anne Jean Plotkin, July 2, 1987 (div.) 1984; 1 child, Violet; m. Erica Mann May 7, 1989; children: Julian, Daniel. BA, Washington U., St. Louis, 1966, ArtsD (hon.), 1993. Assoc. editor Playboy mag., 1968-70; actor, writer Second City, Chgo., 1970-73, Nat. Lampoon Radio Hour, Lampoon Show, 1974-75; actor, head writer SCTV, 1977-78; producer, head writer Rodney Dangerfield Show, ABC-TV, 1982. Screenwriter (with Douglas Kenny and Chris Miller) National Lampoon's Animal House, 1978, (with Janice Allen, Len Blum and Dan Goldberg) Meatballs, 1979, (with Douglas Kenny, Brian Doyle-Murray) Caddyshack, 1980, (with Len Blum and Dan Goldberg) Stripes, 1981, (with Dan Aykroyd) Ghostbusters, 1984, (with Brian Doyle-Murray) Club Paradise, 1986; co-screenwriter (with Peter Torokvei) Armed and Dangerous, 1986; writer (with Dan Akroyd) Ghostbusters II, 1989, Rover Dangerfield, 1991; dir. Stuart Saves His Family, 1995, The Ice Harvest, 2005; dir., prodr. Multiplicity, 1996, Bedazzled, 2000; dir., writer: Caddyshack, 1980, National Lampoon's Vacation, 1983, Club Paradise, 1986, Analyze This, 1999, Analyze That, 2002; writer, dir. prodr. Groundhog Day, 1993; exec. prodr. The First $20 Million is Always the Hardest, 2002; exec. prodr., co-screenwriter (with Rodney Dangerfield) Back to School, 1986; film appearances include: Stripes, 1981, Ghostbusters, 1984, Baby Boom, 1987, Stealing Home, 1988, Ghostbusters II, 1989, As Good As It Gets, 1997, Orange County. Mem. AFTRA, SAG, Writers Guild Am., Dirs. Guild Am.

**RAMJEE, RAMACHANDRAN,** telecommunications industry executive, computer scientist; s. V. and Vatsala Ramjee; m. Priya Ravi, May 1, 2000; children: Rahul Ramachandran, Ramana Ramachandran. BS in Computer Sci., Indian Inst. Tech., 1992; MS, U. Mass., 1997; PhD, U. Mass, 1997. Mem. tech. staff Bell Labs. Lucent Technologies, Murray Hill, NJ, 1996—2005, tech. mgr. Bell Labs., 2005—. Adj. faculty Dept. Elec. Engring. Columbia U., N.Y., 2003—04. Contbr. over 50 articles to profl. jours. Recipient Best Paper award, Internat. Subscriber Loop Conf., 1996; fellow, AT&T, 1995—96. Mem.: IEEE (sr.; editor Transactions on Mobile Computing, editor Wireless Comms., guest editor Jour. Selected Areas in Comm.), Assn. Computing Machinery. Achievements include 27 patents in field. Office Phone: 908-582-2034.

**RAMKRISHNA, DORAISWAMI,** chemical engineering educator, researcher; b. Trichur, Kerala, India, Oct. 29, 1938; came to U.S., 1974; s. M.R. and Ponnu (Raman) Doraiswami; married, 1966; children: Sriram, Arvind. B in Chem. Engring., Bombay U., 1960; PhD in Chem. Engring., U. Minn., 1965, DSc (hon.), 2004. From asst. to assoc. prof. chem. engring. Indian Inst. Tech., Kanpur, 1967-75, prof., 1975-76; prof. chem. engring. Purdue U., West Lafayette, Ind., 1976—; Harry Creighton Peffer disting. prof., 1994—. Vis. assoc. prof. U. Wis., Madison, 1974-75; vis. prof. U. Minn., Mpls., 1975-76, George T. Piercy disting. vis. prof., 1988; Kane vis. prof. dept. chem. tech. Bombay U., 1983; Melchor vis. prof. U. Notre Dame, Ind., 1994. Author: (with Neal R. Amundson) Linear Operator Methods in Chemical Engineering, 1985, Population Balances, 2000; contbr. over 175 papers to profl. jours. Named Disting. Engring. alumnus Bombay U., 1994. Fellow Am. Inst. Med. and Biol. Engring.; mem. AIChE (Alpha Chi Sigma award 1987, RH Wilhelm award in Chem. Reaction Engring., 1998, Thomas Baron award, 2004), Am.

Chem. Soc. (Sr. Humboldt award 2001). Democrat. Hindu. Achievements include application of operator theory, population balances and stochastic methods to numerous chemical engineering problems. Home: 3517 Woodwind Pl West Lafayette IN 47906-8861 Office: Purdue U Sch Chem Engring Northwestern Ave West Lafayette IN 47907 Office Phone: 765-494-4066. Business E-Mail: ramkrish@ecn.purdue.edu.

**RAMLER, SIEGFRIED,** foundation administrator; b. Vienna, Oct. 30, 1924; s. Lazar and Eugenia Ramler; m. Piilani A. Ahuna, Dec. 1948 (dec. July 2003); children: David K., Dita L., Laurence K., Malia R.; m. Kiyoko Koizumi, Dec. 1, 2003. Diplôme supérieur, U. Paris, 1958; MA, U. Hawaii, 1961. Interpreter Internat. Mil. Tribunal, Nuremberg, Germany, 1945-46, chief interpreting br., 1946-49; chair fgn. lang. dept. Punahou Sch., Honolulu, 1951-71, dir. instnl. svcs., 1971-91, dir. World Internat. Ctr., 1990-95; exec. dir. Found. Study in Hawaii and Abroad, Honolulu, 1969-90. Sr. adj. fellow East-West Ctr., 1995—; pres. adv. bd. Pacific Basin Consortium, Hawaii, 1997-02. Contbr. articles to profl. publs. Vice chair, sec., bd. dirs Crown Prince Akihito Scholarship Found., 1989—; trustee St. Francis Sch., Honolulu, 1996—. Decorated Order of the Palmes Académiques, Ordre National du Mérite (France); Order of the Sacred Treasure (Japan); recipient medal Freedom Found., 1958. Mem. ASCD, Internat./Global Edn. Com. (chair nat. adv. com. 1987-93), Japan-Am. Soc. Hawaii (pres. 1986-87, program chmn. 1975-94, Alliance Française of Hawaii (pres. and founder 1961, bd. dirs 1992-2001, regent 2001-), World Assn. Internat. Studies (bd. dirs. 2000—). Avocations: running, travel, swimming. Home: 921 Maunawili Cir Kailua HI 96734-4620 Office: East West Ctr 1777 E West Rd Honolulu HI 96848 Fax: (808) 944-7070. E-mail: ramlers001@hawaii.rr.net.

**RAMM, DOUGLAS ROBERT,** psychologist; b. New Haven, Dec. 11, 1949; s. Robert Frederick and Gladys (Torgrimson) R.; m. Barbara Stephens, Aug. 10, 1974; children: Jennifer, Jessica. BA, Ithaca Coll., 1972; MA, Duquesne U., 1974, PhD, 1979. Diplomate Am. Bd. Profl. Psychology; bd. cert. clin. psychologist Am. Bd. Profl. Psychology. Staff psychologist Westmoreland Hosp., Greensburg, Pa., 1976-79, chief clin. psychologist, dir. child & adolescent psychiat., 1979-82; pvt. practice Greensburg, Pa., 1980—. Pres. Ethics Inc., Ctr. for Sci. Study of Values and Morality, 1995-98; cons. U. Pitts., Pa. Bur. Vocat. Rehab.; Westmoreland County Ct. of Common Pleas; past pres. Mental Health Assn. Westmoreland County. Author: Clinically Formulated Principles of Morality, 1996, Consider the Scientific Study of Morality, 1998, The Formula for Happiness, 2004, Principles for Achieving Emotional Well-Being, 2005. Mem. APA, ASCD, Am. Philos. Assn., Pa. Psychol. Assn., Acad. Clin. Psychology, Soc. Personality Assessment, Nat. Acad. Neuropsychologists, Nat. Register Health Svc. Providers in Psychology, Am. Coll. Forensic Examiners (diplomate), Soc. Bus. Ethics, Rotary Club. Methodist. Office: 225 Humphrey Rd Greensburg PA 15601-4571 Office Phone: 724-832-9096. Personal E-mail: plato1211@aol.com.

**RAMMING, MICHAEL ALEXANDER,** retired school system administrator; b. St. Louis, Feb. 4, 1940; s. William Alexander and Emily Louise (Reingruber) Ramming; m. Susan Ray Oliver, July 9, 1962; children: Michael Murray, Todd Alexander. BS, Centenary Coll., 1963; MA, Washington U., St. Louis, 1968. Cert. administr. secondary schs. Mo. Tchr., coach Ladue Sch. Dist., St. Louis, 1963-88, administr., 1988—2002; ret., 2002. Adj. prof. Lindenwood U., 2002—; cons. Ladue Sch. Dist., St. Louis, 2002—. Vol. Sr. Olympics, St. Louis, 1992, 1993. Mem.: Mo. Interscholastic Athletic Administrs. Assn. (25 Yr. Svc. award), Nat. Interscholastic Athletic Adminstrs., Mo. Assn. Secondary Sch. Prins., Nat. Assn. Secondary Sch. Prins. Avocations: tennis, walking, travel. Home: 18128 Dawns Trail Wildwood MO 63005 Office: Ladue Horton Watkins High Sch 1201 S Warson Rd Saint Louis MO 63124-1266 Personal E-mail: mikeramming@earthlink.net. *As I look back I feel that participation in sports as a player, coach, and fan provided me with a wealth of leadership, community building, daring, sharing, and the ability to accept success and failure.*

**RAMO, SIMON,** retired engineering executive; b. Salt Lake City, May 7, 1913; s. Benjamin and Clara (Trestman) Ramo; m. Virgina Smith, July 25, 1937; children: James Brian, Alan Martin. BS, U. Utah, 1933, DSc (hon.), 1961; PhD, Calif. Inst. Tech., 1936; DEng (hon.), Case Western Res. U., 1960, U. Mich., 1966, Poly. Inst. NY, 1971; DSc (hon.), Union Coll., 1963, Worcester Polytechnic Inst., 1968, U. Akron, 1969, Cleve. State U., 1976; LLD (hon.), Carnegie-Mellon U., 1970, U. So. Calif., 1972, Gonzaga U., 1983, Occidental Coll., 1984, Claremont U., 1985. With Gen. Electric Co., 1936—46; v.p. mgr. Hughes Aircraft Co., 1946—53; with Ramo-Woolridge Corp., 1953—58; dir. U.S. Intercontinental Ballistic Missile Program, 1954—58, TRW Inc., 1954—85, exec. v.p., 1958—61, vice chmn. bd., 1961—78, chmn. exec. com., 1969—78, cons., 1978—; pres. The Bunker-Ramo Corp., 1964—66; chmn. bd. TRW-Fujitsu Co., 1980—83. Vis. prof. mgmt. sci. Calif. Inst. Tech., 1978—; Regents lectr. UCLA, 1981—82, U. Calif. at Santa Cruz, 1978—79; chmn. Ctr. for Study Am. Experience, U. So. Calif., 1978—80; Faculty fellow John F. Kennedy Sch. Govt., Harvard U., 1980—84; mem. White House Energy Rsch. and Devel. Adv. Coun., 1973—75; chmn. Pres.'s Com. on Sci. and Tech., 1976—77; bd. advisors for sci. and tech. Repu. of China, 1981—84; chmn. bd. Aetna, Jacobs & Ramo Venture Capital, 1987—90, Allenwood Ventures, Inc., 1987—. Author: The Business of Science, 1988, other sci., engring. and mgmt. books, (non-fiction) Meetings, Meetings and More Meetings, 2005. Life trustee Calif. Inst. Tech., Nat. Symphony Orch. Assn., 1973—83; trustee emeritus Calif. State U.; bd. govs., pres. Performing Arts Coun. Mus. Ctr. LA, 1976—77; co-chair bd. overseers Keck Sch. Medicine, U. So. Calif., 1999—; bd. dirs. W. M. Keck Found., 1983—, LA World Affairs Coun., 1973—85, Mus. Ctr. Found., LA, LA Philharm. Assn., 1981—84. Named to Bus. Hall of Fame, 1984; recipient IAS, 1956, award, Am. Inst. Elec. Engrs., 1959, Am. Iron and Steel Inst., 1968, Medal of Achievement, AEA, 1970, Disting. Svc. medal, Armed Forces Comm. and Electronics Assn., 1970, medal of achievement, WEMA, 1970, Kayan medal, Columbia U., 1972, award, Am. Cons. Engrs. Coun., 1974, Nat. Medal of Sci., 1976, 1979, medal, Franklin Inst., 1978, awards, U. So. Calif., 1979, Pres. Medal Sci., 1981, UCLA medal, 1982, Presdl. Medal of Freedom, 1983, Aesculapian award, UCLA, 1984, Durand medal, AAIA, 1984, John Fritz medal, 1986, henry Townley Heald award, Ill. Inst. Tech., 1988, Nat. Engring. award, Am. Assn. Engring. Socs., 1988, Franklin-Jefferson medal, 1988, Howard Hughes meml. award, 1989, Air Force Space and Missile Pioneers award, 1989, Pioneer award, Internat. Coun. on Sys. Engring., 1997, Disting. pub. Svc. medal, NASA, 1999, Lifetime Achievement trophy, Smithsonian Inst., 1999, John F. Kennedy Astronautics award, Am. Astronautical Soc., 2000, John R. Alison award for indsl. leadership, Air Force Assn., 2000, Presdl. Medallion, U. So. Calif., 2002, Founders award, USC Thornton Sch. of Music, 2003. Fellow: IEEE (Electronic Achievement award 1953, Golden Omega award 1975, Founders medal 1980, Centennial medal 1984), Am. Acad. Polit. Sci., Am. Acad. Arts and Scis.; mem.: NAS, Nat. Acad. Engring. (founder, coun. mem. Bueche award), Internat. Acad. Astronautics, Pacific Coun. Internat. Policy, Coun. Fgn. Rels., Inst. advancement Engring., Am. Philos. Soc., Am. Physical. Soc., Theta Tau (Hall of Fame laureate), Eta Kappa Nu (eminent mem. award 1966). Office: 9200 W Sunset Blvd Ste 801 Los Angeles CA 90069-3603

**RAMO, VIRGINIA M. SMITH,** civic worker; b. Yonkers, NY; d. Abraham Harold and Freda (Kasnetz) Smith; m. Simon Ramo; children: James Brian, Alan Martin. BS in Edn., U. So. Calif., DHL (hon.), 1978. Nat. co-chmn., am. giving U. So. Calif., 1968-70, vice chmn., trustee, 1971—, co-chmn. bd. councilors Sch. Performing Arts, 1975-76, co-chmn. bd. councilors Schs. Med. and Engring. Vice-chmn. bd. overseers Hebrew Union Coll., 1972-75; bd. dirs. The Muses of Calif. Mus. Sci. and Industry, UCLA Affiliates, Estelle Doheny Eye Found., U. So. Calif. Sch. Medicine; mem. adv. coun. L.A. County Heart Assn., chmn. com. to endow Chair in cardiology at U. So. Calif.; vice chmn., bd. dirs. Friends of Libr. U. So. Calif.; bd. dirs., nat. pres. Achievement Rewards for Coll. Scientists Found., 1975-77; bd. dirs. Les Dames L.A., Cmty. TV Soc.; bd. dirs., v.p. Founders L.A. Music Ctr.; v.p. L.A. Music Ctr. Opera Assn.; v.p. corp. bd. United Way; v.p. Blue Ribbon-400 Performing Arts Coun.; chmn. com. to endow chair in gerontology U. So. Calif.; vice chmn. campaign Doheny Eye Inst,. 1986; co-chair, bd.

overseers Keck Sch. Medicine U. So. Calif., 1999—. Recipient Svc. award Friends of Librs., 1974, Nat. Cmty. Svc. award Alpha Epsilon Phi, 1975, Disting. Svc. award Am. Heart Assn., 1978, Svc. award U. So. Calif., Spl. award U. So. Calif. Music Alumni Assn., 1979, Life Achievement award Mannequins of L.A. Assistance League, 1979, Woman of Yr. award Pan Hellenic Assn., 1981, Disting. Svc. award U. So. Calif. Sch. Medicine, 1981, U. So. Calif. Town and Gown Recognition award, 1986, Asa V. Call Achievement award U. So. Calif., 1986, Phi Kappa Phi scholarship award U. So. Calif., 1986, Vision award Luminaires of Doheny Eye Inst., 1994, Presdl. medallion U. So. Calif., 2002, USC Thornton Sch. of Music Founder's award, 2003. Mem. UCLA Med. Aux., U. So. Calif. Pres.'s Cir., Commerce Assocs. U. So. Calif., Cedars of Lebanon Hosp. Women's Guild (dir. 1967-68), Blue Key, Skull and Dagger.

**RAMOS, ALBERT A.,** electrical engineer; b. L.A., Feb. 28, 1927; s. Jesus D. and Carmen F. (Fontes) R.; B.S. in Elec. Engring., U. So. Calif., 1950, M.S. in Systems Mgmt., 1972; P.h.D., U.S. Internat. U., 1975; m. Joan C. Pailing, Sept. 23, 1950; children—Albert A., Richard R., James J., Katherine. With guided missile test group Hughes Aircraft Co., 1950-60; with TRW DSG, 1960-91, sr. staff engr. Norton AFB, San Bernardino, Calif., 1969-91, ret., 1991. Served with USNR, 1945-46. Registered profl. engr., Calif. Mem. IEEE, NSPE, Air Force Assn., Mexican-Am. Engring. Soc., Mexican-Am. Profl. Mgmt. Assn. (mem. administering commn. dept. community svcs.), Sigma Phi Delta, Eta Kappa Nu, Tau Beta Pi. Home: 8937 Napoli Dr Las Vegas NV 89117-1182

**RAMOS, JAMIE,** information scientist; s. David and Sue Ramos; m. Crystal Ramos, July 10, 1999; children: Alyssa, Andrew. Micro tech. Ind. U., Kokomo, 1998—2000; instrnl. systems coord. Kokomo-Ctr. Schs., 2000—. Office: Kokomo-Center Schools 2501 S Berkley Kokomo IN 46902 Office Phone: 765-455-8095. Office Fax: 765-455-8098. Business E-Mail: jdramos@kokomoschools.com.

**RAMOS, JOHN C., JR.,** protective services official, educator; s. John C. and Helen Barbara Ramos; m. Kathryn Elizabeth Fisher, July 16, 1967; children: John C. III, Joeseph Michael, Amanda Ann. Grad. high sch., Munster, IN. Indiana Law Enforcement Academy Basic Course: Ind. Law Enforcement Tng. Bd. 1990, Basic SWAT Team Tactics: Muncie Police Dept. 1996, Sub-machinegun Instructor: Singleton Internat. 1997, Advanced Handgun, Shotgun, Machinegun and High Risk Entry: Singleton Internat. 1999, Diversionary Devices & Less Lethal Munitions: Tng. Resource Group, Inc. 1999, High Risk Entry: HSS Internat. 2001, GSG-9 Tactics: HSS Internat. 2001, Basic SWAT Tactics & Operation: Lake County Sheriffs Police 2001, SWAT Training: US Dept. of Justice Fed. Bur. of Investigation 2002, Managing Civil Actions in Threat Incidents Command Course: US Dept. of Homeland Security 2003, Instructor Development: Ind. Law Enforcement Tng. Bd. 1995, Police Rifle & Carbine: NW Ind. Law Enforcement Acad. 2002, Firearms Instructor: Ind. Law Enforcement Tng. Bd. 1996, Firearms Training Systems: NW Ind. Law Enforcement Tng. Bd. 1994, Hostage Negotiator Seminar: NW Ind. Law Enforcement Tng. Bd. 1993, Police Officer Survival Tactics: NW Traffic Inst. 1989, Street Survival: Calibre Press 1989; Haz-Mat Operations East Chgo. Fire Dept., 2003, ASP Tactical Baton Instructor Armament Systems and Procedures, Inc., 1992, Sexual Assault Awareness FBI, 1989. Profl. motocrosser National #127, 1981—83; part time police office Cedar Lake Police Dept., Ind., 1987—89; police officer East Chicago Police Dept., 1989—. Dept. instr. East Chicago Police Dept., 1995—. Author: The Book of Room Domination and Assault Techniques, The Book of Cop Rules and Patrol Tactics. Recipient 2nd Pl. Expert Duty Class, State FOP Elkhart, 1989, 5th Pl. B Class, Ind. Law Enforcement Acad. League, 1990, Mr. VCO, East Chgo. Police Dept., 1990, 1st Pl. Sharpshooter Team, Ill. Police Combat Assn., 1990, 2nd Pl. Marksman, Ill. Police Combat League, 1990, Outstanding Performance, Lake County Task Force Against Drunk Driving, 1991, Outstanding Dedication and Svc., Am. Legion Post 369. Mem.: Nat. Tactical Officers Assn. Conservative. Penticostal. Avocations: bicycling, shooting, gaming. Office: East Chgo Police Dept 2301 E Columbus Dr East Chicago IN 46312 Office Phone: 219-680-7122. Personal E-mail: reeper351@prodigy.net.

**RAMOS, JORGE,** newscaster; b. Mexico City, Mar. 16, 1958; arrived in U.S., 1983; 2 children. Grad. in comm., Ibero-Am. Univ., Mexico City; M in internat. studies, Univ. Miami. News reporter Univision, LA, 1984—86; host Mundo Latino, Univision TV prog., 1986; anchorman Noticiero Univision, 1986—. Founder Wake Up Reading book club, 2002—. Author: (autobiography) No Borders: a Journalist's Search for Home, Behind the Mask, The Other Face of America, What I Saw, Hunting the Lion, The Latino Wave, Dying to Cross; contbr. weekly column, NY Times Syndicate. Named one of Ten Most Admired Latinos, Latino Leaders mag., 2004, 25 Most Influential Hispanics, Time Mag., 2005; recipient Maria Moors Cabot award, Columbia Univ., 2001, Ruben Salazar award, Nat. Council La Raza, 2002, Ron Brown award, Nat. Child Labor Com., 2002, David Brinkley award for Journalistic Excellence, Barry Univ., 2003, 8 Emmy awards, Nat. Acad. Television Arts & Sci. Office: Univision Communications Ste 3050 1999 Ave of the Stars Los Angeles CA 90067 Studio: WNJU-TV Noticiero 47 6th Fl 2200 Fletcher Ave Fort Lee NJ 07024 Office Phone: 201-969-9447. Office Fax: 201-969-4120. E-mail: jramos@univision.net, jorge.ramos@nbcuni.com.*

**RAMOS, JOSE A.,** engineering educator; b. San Juan, P.R., Apr. 29, 1957; s. Luis R. and Lydia Ramos. BSCE, U. P.R., Mayaguez, 1987; MSCE, Ga. Inst. Tech., 1979, PhD, 1985. Registered profl. engr., P.R. Rsch. engr. United Techs. Optical Systems, West Palm Beach, Fla., 1986—90; postdoctoral fellow Katholieke U. Leuven, Belgium, 1990—93; cons. Sci. Studies Co., Palm Beach Gardens, Fla., 1993—95; assoc. prof. elec. engring. Ind. U./Purdue U., Indpls., 1995—2002; assoc. prof. U. Miami, Coral Gables, Fla., 2000—02. Vis. summer rsch. scholar U. Montpellier II, France, 1998—2000. Contbr. articles to profl. jours. Ford Found. fellow, 1983—85. Mem.: IEEE (assoc.; faculty advisor 1997—2003), Soc. Indsl. and Applied Math. (assoc.). Office: Ind U Purdue U 723 W Michigan St SL 164 - E Indianapolis IN 46202 Office Phone: 317-274-0044. Business E-Mail: jaramos@iupui.edu.

**RAMOS, PAUL-JOHN,** composer, writer; b. Bronx, N.Y., Mar. 11, 1978; s. John and Paula Veronica Ramos. BS in English, Oneonta State Coll., 2000. Columnist Yonkers (N.Y.) Tribune, 2002—. Composer: (chamber music) String Trio in G Minor, (orchestral music) Elegy. Mem.: U.S. Harness Writers Assn. Protestant. Avocations: publishing, internet design. Home: 180 W Post Rd White Plains NY 10606

**RAMOS, VICTOR JOSE,** computer company executive, educator; b. Fajardo, PR, Aug. 20, 1966; s. Victor Manuel and Alicia (Ortiz) Ramos; m. Brunilda Pinero, June 16, 1986; children: Victor Javier, Victor Jose, Jean Victor, Ross Victor, Victoria Maria. MS in Info. Sys. Admin., Interamerican U., San Juan, PR, 2000. Sr. is analyst Quality Improvement Prof Rsch., San Juan, 1999—2001; csv project leader Caribbean Validation Svcs., Caguas, PR, 2001—02; automation, csv cons. Day & Zimmermann, Guaynabo, PR, 2002—04, Compliance Integration Solution, Manati, PR, 2005—. Prof. Met. U., San Juan, 2001—06. Sgt. Puerto Rico NG, 1986—2002. Decorated 3rd Army Achievement Medal Army N.G. Avocations: tennis, swimming. Home: PO Box 4101 Puerto Real PR 00740-4101 Office: Dival Cons Group & Assoc Inc Gettysburg St #T7 Park Gardens San Juan PR 00927 Office Phone: 787-312-6955. Personal E-mail: vj_ramos@yahoo.com.

**RAMOS-CANO, HAZEL BALATERO,** caterer, chef, innkeeper, restaurateur, entrepreneur; b. Davao City, Mindanao, Philippines, Sept. 2, 1936; came to U. S., 1960. d. Mauricio C. and Felicidad (Balatero) Ramos; m. William Harold Snyder, Feb. 17, 1964 (div. 1981); children: John Byron, Snyder, Jennifer Ruth; m. Nelson Allen Blue, May 30, 1986 (div. 1990); m. A. Richard Cano, June 25, 1994. BA in Social Work, U. Philippines, Quezon City, 1958; MA in Sociology, Pa. State U., 1963, postgrad., 1966—67. Cert. exec. chef, Am. Culinary Fedn. Faculty, tng. staff Peace Corps Philippine

Project, University Park, Pa., 1961-63; sociology instr. Albright Coll., Reading, Pa., 1963-64; rsch. asst. Meth. Ch. U.S.A., State College, Pa., 1965-66; rsch. asst. dept. child devel. & family rels. Pa. State U., University Park, 1966-67; exec. dir. Presbyn. Urban Coun. Raleigh Halifax Ct. Child Care and Family Svc. Ctr., 1973-79; early childhood educator Learning Together, Inc., Raleigh, NC, 1982-83; loan mortgage specialist Raleigh Savs. & Loan, 1983-84; restaurant owner, mgr. Hazel's on Hargett, Raleigh, 1985-86; admissions coord., social worker Brian Corp. Nursing Home, Raleigh, 1986-88; food svc. dir., 1989-90; regional dir. La Petite Acad., Raleigh, 1989-90; asst. food svc. mgr. Granville Towers, Chapel Hill, NC, 1990-92; mgr. trainee Child Nutrition Svcs. Wake County Pub. Sch. Sys., Raleigh, 1993-94; food svc. dir. S.W. Va. 4-H Ednl. Conf. Ctr., Abingdon, 1994-95; caterer, owner The Eclectic Chef's Catering, 1995—; innkeeper, owner Love House Bed and Breakfast, 1996—; pres. Ramos-Cano Inc., 1996—; owner Withers Hardware Restaurant, Abingdon, 2002—; pres. Ramos-Cano Mgmt. Svcs., LLC, 2002—; owner The Frame Shop, Abingdon, 2004—. Cooking instr. Wake Cmty. Tech. Coll., Raleigh, 1986-92; freelance caterer, 1964-95; chair Internat. Cooking Demonstrations Raleigh Internat. Festival, 1990-93. Pres. Wake County Day Care United Coun., 1974-75, NC Assn. Edn. Young Children (Raleigh chpt.), 1975-76; bd. mem. Project Enlightenment Wake County Pub. Schs., 1976-77; various positions Pines of Carolina Girl Scout Council, 1976-85; chmn. Philippine Health and Medical Aid Com., Phil-Am Assn. Raleigh 1985-88 (publicity chmn.); elder Trinity Presbyn. Ch., Raleigh, 1979-81, bd. deacons, 1993-94; elder, session mem. Sinking Spring Presbyn. Ch., 1997—; treas. Abingdon Newcomers Club, 1997—, Presbyn. Women, Sinking Spring Presbyn. Ch., Abingdon, 1999—; master gardener Va. Tech. Master Gardeners Program, 1998—. Rockefeller grant Rockefeller Found., 1958-59; recipient Ramon Magsaysay Presdl. award Philippine Leadership Youth Movement, 1957; Gov.'s Cert. Appreciation State NC, 1990. Raleigh Mayor's award Quality Childcare Svcs., 1990, award for keeping hist. Abington beautiful Abington Kiwanis Club, 1997 Mem. Am. Culinary Fedn., Presby. Women, Raleigh, Historian 1975-76), Penn State Dames (pres. 1968-69). Democrat. Office: Victoria & Albert Inn 224 Oak Hill St Abingdon VA 24210 also: The Love House Bed and Breakfast 210 E Valley St Abingdon VA 24210 also: Withers Hardware Restaurant 260 W Main St Abingdon VA 24210 also: The Frame Shop 115 Charwood Dr Abingdon VA 24210 also: Somethyme Bistro 115 Charwood Dr Abingdon VA 24210 Office Phone: 276-628-1111. E-mail: v&ainn@naxs.com, rcano@naxs.com.

**RAMOS-RINZE, JORGE RAFAEL,** computer scientist; b. Guatemala, Jan. 14, 1972; arrived in U.S., 2001; s. Jorge Rafael Ramos and Trudy Rinze; m. Maria del Pilar del Busto; 1 child, Isabella del Pilar Ramos. MS in Computer Sci., Purdue U., 2003, postgrad. Rsch. asst. Purdue U., West Lafayette, Ind., 2003—. Recipient Gold medal. Nat. Sci. Olympics, Guatemala, 1998; fellow, Purdue U., 2003—05; scholar, Fulbright Found., 2001—03. Mem.: Upsilon Pi Epsilon (treas. 2003—05).

**RAMPACHER, HERMANN HANS,** writer, consultant; b. Ulm, Germany, Dec. 29, 1934; s. Hermann Alexander and Pauline Katharine (Milch) R.; m. Ursel Hanna Brand; 1 child, Carsten. BS, Coll. Stuttgart, 1954, MSc in Physics, 1962; Dr.rer.nat., U. Munich, 1968. Charter IT profl. Brit. Computer Soc. Rsch. asst. Max Planck Gesellschaft, Munich, 1965-68; asst. prof. U. Tuebingen, 1968-70; systems engr. IBM Deutschland, Stuttgart, 1970-79; rschr. GMD German Nat. Rsch. Ctr. for Info. Tech., Bonn, 1979-81; chief exec. German Informatics Soc., Bonn, 1982-99; mng. dir. German Info. Acad. GmbH (DIA), 1997-2000; ptnr. DLGI Ltd. Bd. dirs. Internat. Conf. and Rsch. Ctr. for Computer Sci., Castle Dagstuhl, 1995-99; founder Coun. European Profl. Informatics Socs Fellow Brit. Computer Soc. (chartered info. tech. profl.); mem. Max-Planck Gesellschaft, German Soc. Philosophy, Gesellschaft Deutscher Naturforscher und Aerzte. Avocations: normative theories, history. Office: DLGI Wissenschaftszentrum Ahrstr D-53175 Bonn Germany Fax: 49 0 228 302-161. E-mail: hrampacher@dlgi.de.

**RAMPE, DAVID,** editor; Asst. fgn. editor, weekend New York Times. Office: New York Times 229 W 43d St New York NY 10036 Office Phone: 212-556-7415. Office Fax: 212-556-7278.*

**RAMPE, KEVIN M.,** real estate developer; b. 1966; m. Christine Rampe; children: William, Matthew. BA cum laude, Union Coll.; JD magna cum laude, Albany U.; grad. in Sr. Exec. Program, Harvard U.; LLD (hon.), Union Coll., 2004. Litig. assoc. Shearman & Stearling, 1992—96; first asst. counsel Gov. Pataki's Office, 1996—99; from dep. supt. and gen. counsel to first dep. supt. ins. Dept. N.Y. State Ins. Dept., 1999—2004, first dep. supt., COO, 2004—05; exec. v.p., gen. counsel Lower Manhattan Devel. Corp, NYC, 2002—03; pres. Lower Manhattan Devel. Corp., NYC, 2003—05, chmn., 2006—. Named one of 40 Under 40, Crain's NY Bus., 2005. Office: Lower Manhattan Development Corp One Liberty Plaza 20th Fl New York NY 10006*

**RAMPERSAD, PEGGY A. SNELLINGS,** sociologist, consultant; b. Fredericksburg, Va., Jan. 12, 1933; d. George Daniel and Virginia Riley (Bowler) Snellings; m. Oliver Ronald Rampersad, Mar. 19, 1955; 1 child, Gita. BA, Mary Washington Coll., Fredericksburg, 1953; student, Sch. Art Inst. Chgo., 1953—55; MA, U. Chgo., 1965, PhD, 1978. Grad. admissions counselor U. Chgo., 1954—57, adviser fgn. students, 1958, dir. admissions Grad. Sch. Bus., 1958—63, rsch. project specialist, 1970—78, pers. mgr., 1979—80, mgr. orgnl. devel., 1980—82, adminstr. dept. econs., 1983—95; cons. PSR Consulting, Chgo., 1995—. Cons. North Ctrl. Assn. Colls. and Secondary Schs., Chgo., 1964—70, Orchestral Assn. Chgo. Symphony Orch., 1982, Chgo. Ctr. Decision Rsch., 1982, Harvard U., 1993—97. Exhibitions include Va. Mus. Fine Arts, Art Inst. Chgo.; others; editor: North Ctrl. Assn. Quar., 1972; contbr. articles to profl. jours. Grad. fellow, U. Chgo. 1960. (17 Mem AAUW, Am. Acad. Polit. and Social Sci., Am. Econ. Assn., Art Inst. Chgo. (assoc.), Pi Lambda Theta (past pres.). Episcopalian. Avocations: painting, drawing, opera, reading, walking. Home and Office: 28 Seneca Ter Fredericksburg VA 22401-1115

**RAMPERSAUD LUNDY, SHERYLL,** special education educator; b. Portsmouth, Va., Dec. 30, 1947; d. Rebecca Greene and Freddie Lee Drake; children: Vincent Earle Rampersaud, Sean Derrik Rampersaud, Sharon Antoinette Rampersaud. BS in Acctg., Norfolk State U., 1971—74, Advanced Studies Tchr. Certification, 2000—01. Spl. Educator Emotional Disturbance and Specific Learning Disabilities Va. Bd. Edn., 2002. Fire rates clk. Geico, Friendship Heights, Md., 1968—70; staff acct. Peat, Marwick, Mitchell CPAs, Washington, 1974—76; asst. internal auditor Howard U., Washington, 1976—80; pension acct./ cons. Qualified Pension Consultants/ Compdesign Inc., Bethesda, Md., 1983—98, Thomas F. Barrett, Inc., Bethesda, 1998—99; spl. edn. tchr. The Pines Residential Treatment Ctr., Portsmouth, Va., 2000—. Dir. Sankofa Cultural and Learning Ctr., Inc., Portsmouth, 1999—. Chief officer John F. Kennedy Poling Sta., Portsmouth, 1999—2001. Mem. Christian Ch. Home: 3204 Gwin St Portsmouth VA 23704 Office: The Pines Residential Treatment Center 825 Crawford Pky Portsmouth VA 23070 Office Phone: 757-391-6588. Personal E-mail: srampersaud@cox.net. E-mail: sheryl.rampersaud@absfirst.com.

**RAMPHAL, JULIE FRANCES,** retired secondary school educator; b. Sioux Falls, SD, Jan. 31, 1944; d. Shelton Russell and Frances Pauline (Hospers) Tilgner; m. Cecil Edward Ramphal, Aug. 29, 1976 (dec. Apr. 2000); stepchildren: Richard Andre, Rani. BA in English, Macalester Coll., 1966; MS in Ednl. Computing, Pepperdine U., 1985. Secondary tchr. Glendora Unified Sch. Dist., Calif., 1966—69, Tustin Unified Sch. Dist., Calif., 1969—2000. Ednl. cons. instr. Nat. U., Irvine, Calif., 1987; mentor tchr. Tustin Unified Sch. Dist., Calif., 1995—97; workshop leader Orange County Dept. of Edn., Costa Mesa, Calif., 1998. Workshop presenter Computer Using Educators (CUE) State Confs.; Palm Springs, Calif., 1988—95. Recipient Exemplary Achievement in the field of Ednl. Tech., Ednl. Computing Alumni of Pepperdine U., 1992, grant, Women's Action Alliance of NYC, 1991—93, Mentor Tchr. in Tech., Tustin Unified Sch. Dist., 1995—97; grant, Calif.

Academic Partnership Program, 1992. Mem.: Am. Assn. of U. Women (v.p. membership 2004—06). Avocations: swimming, singing, gardening, piano, travel. Home: 20141 Crown Reef Lane Huntington Beach CA 92646 Personal E-mail: julieps23@aol.com.

**RAMPHELE, MAMPHELA A.,** international organization administrator, physician, former academic administrator; b. Dec. 28, 1947; Diploma in tropical health and hygiene and pub. health, U. Witwatersrand; B.Com. in Adminstrn., U. South Africa; MD, U. Natal, 1972; PhD in Social Anthropology, U. Cape Town. Sr. rsch. officer U. Cape Town, South Africa, 1986—91, dep. vice chancellor, 1991—95, vice chancellor, 1996—2000; mng. dir. human devel. World Bank, Washington, 2000—. Immediate past chmn. bd. trustees Ind. Devel. Trust; adv. bd. World Bank Econ. Devel. Inst. Contbr. articles to profl. jours.; author: Across Boundaries, A Life, A Bed Called Home, Restoring the Land. Student activist Black Consciousness Movement; trustee Rockefeller Found. Recipient of numerous nat. and internat. awards including 17 hon. doctorates, awards for svc. to cmty., Kilby award, 2003. Mem.: Inst. of Medicine of NAS. Office: The World Bank 1818 H St NW Washington DC 20433*

**RAMPONE, CHRISTIE P.,** professional soccer player; b. Broward County, Fla., June 24, 1975; m. Chris Rampone, Nov. 9, 2001. BS in spl. edn., Monmouth U., N.J., 1997. Mem. N.Y. Power, WUSA, 2001—; soccer player, defender U.S. Women's Nat. Team, 1997, mem. World Cup championship team, 1999. Founding player N.Y. Power, WUSA, 2001. Named First Team All-Mid-Atlantic Region, 1995, 1996, Player of Yr., N.E. Conf., 1995, 1996.

**RAMSAUR, ALLAN FIELDS,** legal association administrator, lobbyist; b. Rocky Mount, N.C., Dec. 30, 1951; s. Carl Hamilton and Celestine (Fields) R.; m. Jimmie Lynn Brewer, Sept. 2, 1972; children: Katherine Celeste, Benjamin Allan. BA in Polit. Sci., Lambuth U., 1974; JD, U. Tenn., 1977. Bar: Tenn. 1977. Staff atty. Tenn. Dept. Mental Health, Nashville, 1977—80; dir. Tenn. Assn. Legal Svcs., Nashville, 1980—86; campaign dir. Steve Cobb, Nashville, 1986; exec. dir. Nashville Bar Assn., 1986—98, Tenn. Bar Assn., 1999—. Pres. Woodland-in-Waverly Neighborhood Assn., Nashville, 1985; bd. dirs. SAGA, Nashville, 1984-86, Bethlehem Ctr., Nashville, 1990-96 (sec. 1992, v.p. 1994-95). Recipient Leadership Nashville award, 1988. Mem. ABA (liaison to standing com. on legal aid and indigent defendants 1984-86, spl. com. on prepaid legal svcs. 1988-89, standing com. on lawyer referral and info. svc. 1990-92), Nat. Assn. Bar Execs. (chair edn. com.), Tenn. Bar Assn. (pres. young lawyers divsn. 1985-86), Nat. Legal Aid and Defender Assn. (chmn. legis com. 1984-86), Tenn. Soc. Assn. Execs. (pres. 2000). Democrat. Methodist. Home: 1417 Beddington Park Nashville TN 37215-5815 Office Phone: 615-383-7421. Business E-Mail: aramsaur@tnbar.org.

**RAMSAY, DAVID LESLIE,** physician, dermatologist, medical educator; b. Rochester, NY, Apr. 25, 1943; s. Joseph Walter and Jean (Eastwood) R. AB in English with honors, Ind. U., 1965, MD, 1969; MEd, U. Ill., 1973. Diplomate Am. Bd. Dermatology. Assoc. faculty mem. Ind. U., Indpls., 1965-69; intern in medicine George Washington U. Med. Ctr., 1969-70; resident in dermatology NYU Med. Ctr., 1970-73; dir. dermatology residency tng. Nat. Naval Med. Ctr., Bethesda, Md., 1973-75; asst. prof. medicine Georgetown U., Washington, 1974-75; asst. prof. dermatology NYU, 1974-78, assoc. prof. dermatology, 1978-95, prof. dermatology, 1995—2003, clin. prof. dermatology, 2003—, senator, 1986-94, pres. faculty coun., 1988-90, dir. ednl. affairs dermatology, 1975—2002, dir. cutaneous lymphoma sect., 1975—. Author: Simulations in Dermatology, 1974; contbg. author: Adolescent Dermatology, Basic Mechanisms of Physiologic and Aberrant Lymphoproliferation in the Skin, Hematology and Oncology Clinics in North America; sr. editor: Jour. of Drugs in Dermatology, 2003-; contbr. more than 25 articles to profl. jours. Pres., bd. dirs. One Fifth Ave. Apt. Corp., N.Y.C., 1978-88; trustee Bklyn. Acad. Music, 1989—, chmn. visual arts com., chmn. edn. com; bd. dirs. Cutaneous Lymphoma Found., 2003—. Lt. comdr. USN, 1973-75. NIH fellow U. Ill., 1972-73. Fellow ACP, Internat. Soc. Cutaneous Lymphomas, Am. Acad. Dermatology; mem. Am. Dermatologic Assn. Roman Catholic. Avocations: collecting visual art, swimming, reading. Home: One Fifth Ave New York NY 10003 Office: NYU Med Ctr 530 5th Ave New York NY 10036-5101 E-mail: DRamsay1@nuc.rr.com.

**RAMSAY, DONALD ALLAN,** physical chemist; b. London, July 11, 1922; s. Norman and Thirza Elizabeth (Beckley) Ramsay; m. Nancy Brayshaw, June 8, 1946 (dec. July 25, 1998); children: Shirley Margaret, Wendy Kathleen, Catharine Jean, Linda Mary; m. Marjorie Craven Findlay, Apr. 13, 2000. BA, Cambridge U., Eng., 1943, MA, PhD, Cambridge U., Eng., 1947, ScD, 1976; D honoris causa, U. Reims, France, 1969; Filosofie hedersdoktor, U. Stockholm, Sweden, 1982. With divsn. chemistry Nat. Rsch. Coun. Can., Ottawa, 1947-49, with divsn. physics, 1949-75; with Herzberg Inst. Astrophysics, 1975-87, sr. research officer, 1961-68, prin. research officer, 1968-87, guest worker, 1987—2001, Steacie Inst. Molecular Scis., rschr. emeritus, 2002—. Vis. prof. U. Minn., 1964, U. Orsay, 1966, U. Stockholm, 1967, 71, 74, U. Calif., Irvine, 1970, U. Sao Paulo, 1972, 78, U. Bologna (Italy), 1973, U. We. Australia, 1976, Australian Nat. U., 1976, East China Normal U., Shanghai, 1987, Tex. Christian U., 1988, U. Wuppertal, Germany, 1988, U. Canterbury, Christchurch, New Zealand, 1991, 96, U. Ulm, Germany, 1992, Germany, 96, Germany, 97. Editor: (with J. Hinze) Selected Works of Robert S. Mulliken, 1975; contbr. articles to profl. jours. Recipient commemorative medal for 125th anniversary Confederation Can., 1992, Alexander von Humboldt Rsch. award, 1993-95; decorated Queen Elizabeth Silver Jubilee medal. Fellow: Chem. Inst. Can. (Chem. Inst. Can. medal 1992), Am. Phys. Soc., Royal Soc. London, Royal Soc. Can. (life; treas. 1976—79, pres. 1981-91, Centennial medal 1982); mem.: Order of Can. Mem. United Ch. of Canada (organist 1951-91). Club: Leander (Henley-on-Thames, Eng.). Achievements include research in molecular spectra and molecular structure. Home: 400 Laurier Ave E Apt 11 Ottawa ON Canada K1N 8Y2 Office: Nat Rsch Coun 100 Sussex Dr Ottawa ON Canada K1A 0R6 E-mail: donald.ramsay@nrc.ca.

**RAMSAY, J. RUSSELL,** psychologist; s. J. Roger and Mary Ann Ramsay; m. Amy D. Bozzuto; children: Abigail G., Brynn A. BA in Psychology, U. Miami, 1988; MS in Clin. Psychology, Pacific Grad. Sch. Psychology, 1994, PhD in Clin. Psychology, 1995. Instr. U. Pa. Sch. Medicine, Phila. 1997—2000, asst. prof. psychology in psychiatry, 2001—. Ad hoc reviewer Jour. Psychotherapy Integration, 1999, 2004; editl. cons. Oxford U. Press, 2003. Mem. editl. bd. Jour. Attention Disorders, 2005—; contbr. chapters to books, articles to profl. jours. Fellow, Ctr. Cognitive Therapy, Phila., 1995—96; Henry King Stanford scholar, U. Miami, 1984—88. Fellow: Pa. Psychol. Assn.; mem.: APA, Internat. Assn. Cognitive Psychotherapy, Psi Chi, Golden Key Honor Soc. Avocations: soccer, exercise, reading.

**RAMSAY, KARIN KINSEY,** publisher, educator; b. Brownwood, Tex., Aug. 10, 1930; d. Kirby Luther and Ina Rebecca (Wood) Kinsey; m. Jack Cummins Ramsay Jr., Aug. 31, 1951; children: Annetta Jean, Robin Andrew. BA, Trinity U., 1951. Cert. assoc. ch. edn., 1980. Youth coord. Covenant Presbyn. Ch., Carrollton, Tex., 1961-76; ch. edn. Northminster Presbyn. Ch., Dallas, 1976-80, Univ. Presbyn. Ch., Chapel Hill, N.C., 1987-90, Oak Grove Presbyn. Ch., Bloomington, Minn., 1990-93; coord. ecum. ministry Flood Relief for Iowa, Des Moines, 1993; program coord. 1st Presbyn. Ch., Green Bay, Wis., 1994—98; owner, sole proprietor Hist. Resources Press, Corinth and Denton, Tex., 1994—. Dir. Godspell tour Covenant Presbyn. Ch., 1972-75; mem. Presbytery Consultation on Sabbath, Dallas, 1977-82, Presbytery Exams. Com. Dallas, 1979-81; clk. coun. New Hope Presbytery, Rocky Mount, NC, 1989-90; creator, dir. Thee Holy Fools mime/musical group and This Is Me retreats. Author: Ramsay's Resources, 1983—; co-author: Walking In the Dark, 2006; pub., editor: Patton's Ill-Fated Raid, 2002, Angel Kisses and My Beating Heart, 2004; contbr. articles to profl. jours. Design cons. Brookhaven Hosp. Chapel, Dallas, 1977-78; elder Presbyn. Ch. U.S.A., 1982—; coord. Lifeline Emergency Response, Dallas, 1982-84. Mem. Internat. Platform Assn., Small Publisher's Assn. of N. Am.,Pub. Marketing Assoc., Writer's League of Tex. Office Phone: 940-321-1066. *Yesterday*

*taught me the lessons which made today possible. Today is the challenging link between yesterday and tomorrow. Tomorrow is an opportunity built on the foundation of today. Today is special.*

**RAMSAY, MICHAEL,** communications company executive; BSEE, U. Edinburgh, Scotland. Sr. v.p., gen. mgr. visual systems group Silicon Graphics, Inc., 1991—94, pres. Silicon Studio, Inc, 1994—96, sr. v.p. Silicon Desktop Group, 1996—97; CEO TiVo Inc., 1997—2005, chmn., 1997—. Bd. dir. Netflix. Office: TiVo Inc 2160 Gold St Alviso CA 95002-2160*

**RAMSAY, WILLIAM CHARLES,** writer, composer; b. N.Y.C., Nov. 6, 1930; s. Claude Barnett and Myrtle Marie (Scott) Ramsay; m. Jane Coutant Evans, July 7, 1997; children from previous marriage: Alice, John, Carol Ramsay Scott, David. BA in English Lit., U. Colo., 1952; MA in Physics, UCLA, 1957, PhD in Physics, 1962. NFS postdoctoral fellow U. Calif., San Diego, 1962-64, asst. prof. Santa Barbara, 1964-67; tech. mgr. Sys. Assocs., Inc., Long Beach, Calif., 1967-72; sr. environ. economist U.S. AEC, Bethesda, Md., 1972-75; tech. adviser U.S. Nuc. Regulatory Agy., Washington, 1975-76; sr. fellow Resources for the Future, Washington, 1976-83, Ctr. Strategic and Internat. Studies, Washington, 1983-85; sr. staff officer NAS, Washington, 1985-86; Cons. Vols. Tech. Assistance, Arlington, Va., 1987—90, Arlington, 1998—, Internat. Resources Group, Washington, 1991. Author: (book) Unpaid Costs of Electrical Energy, 1979, Bioenergy and Economic Development, 1985, (plays) Agamemnon, 2000; co-author: (book) Managing the Environment, 1972, Energy in America's Future, 1979; composer: Glory Road, The Hawk, Genesis, Spring Dawn. Bd. diro. Opera Santa Barbara. Buenos Aires Conv. fellow, 1952, NSF fellow, 1962, NATO scholar, 1960, 1962. Mem.: Internat. Assn. Energy Economists, Am. Astron. Soc., Am. Phys. Soc. Avocation: piano. Home and Office: 115 Summit Ln Santa Barbara CA 93108-2323 E-mail: ram556@cox.net.

**RAMSBY, MARK DELIVAN,** lighting designer, consultant; b. Portland, Oreg., Nov. 20, 1947; s. Marshall Delivan and Verna Pansy (Culver) R.; married; children: Aaron Delivan, Venessa Mercedes. Student, Portland State U., Oreg., 1966-67. With C.E.D., Portland, 1970-75; minority ptnr. The Light Source, Portland, 1975-78, pres., 1978-87; prin. Illume Lighting Design, Portland, 1987-90; ptnr. Ramsby, Dupuy & Seats, Inc., Portland, 1990-91; dir. lighting design PAE Cons. Engrs., Inc., Portland, 1991—2001; dir. design LUMA, Portland, 2001—. Pvt. practice cons. Portland, 1979—. Recipient Top 100 Outstanding Achievement award Metalux Lighting, 1981-85, 100% award, 1985, Edwin F. Guth award of merit, 1990, 95, 96, 99, 2001, 03, Edison award of excellence, 1990, Edwin F. Guth award of excellence, 1993, 94, Paul Waterbury award of Merit, 1995. Mem. Illuminating Engring. Soc. Am. (sec.-treas. Oreg. sect. 1978-79, Oreg. sect. pres. 2002-03, Oreg. Section and Regional and Internat. awards 1989, 90, 93, 94, Lighting Design awards), Internat. Assn. Lighting Designers. Lutheran. Avocations: lighting design, historical restoration, fly fishing, downhill skiing. Office: LUMA 808 SW 3d Ave Ste 450 Portland OR 97204-2426 Office Phone: 503-226-3905.

**RAMSDEN, VIRGINIA ANN,** retired music educator; b. Wellsville, N.Y., Feb. 28, 1937; d. Orville Lester and Marie Louella Knox; m. Lawrence Earl Ramsden. BS in Music Edn., SUNY, Fredonia, 1960, MEd, 1960; postgrad., Boston U., 1961; MA in Music Edn., NYU, 1964. Violinist Erie Philharmonic Orch., 1956—60, Huntington Symphony Orch., 1961—64; tchr. music Lindenhurst Pub. Schs., NY, 1961—68; soloist, concert master Islip Symphony and Chamber Orch., NY, 1970—79; tchr. music Islip Pub. Schs., 1976—84; violinist Internat. Performing Art Trio, L.I., 1979—88; tchr. music Schem Pub. Schs., Holbrook, NY, 1984—88, Commack Pub. Schs., NY, 1988—2000; artist-in-residence, publicity dir. Islip P.R.O.-Arts, 1983—2000. Spkr. L.I. Arts Edn. Assembly, 1979; cons., Islip. Columnist: Suffolk County News, 1980, columnist, publicity dir.: L.I. String Festival Assn., Islip Task Force, 1979—80. Vol. Islip Art Tour. Mem.: L.I. String Tchrs. Assn., Suffolk County Music Educators Assn. Avocations: walking, reading, attending concerts and ballets, travel. Home: 1618 Spur Dr S Islip NY 11751-1214

**RAMSER, WANDA TENE,** librarian, educator; b. Atlanta, Ga., June 4, 1951; d. Galen Eugene Ramser and Christine Elizabeth Owen; children: Catherine Nicole Hannabach, David Richmond Hannabach. BA in History, U. Calif., Santa Barbara, 1973; MLS in Libr. and Info. Sci., UCLA, 1976, MLS in L.Am. Studies, 1977. With UCLA L.Am. Ctr., 1973—78; literacy coord. County of L.A. Libr., 1978—83; assoc. faculty South Orange County C.C. Dist., Mission Viejo, 1986, 2002—03, 2005—; with City of Oceanside (Calif.) Libr., 2001—. Chancellors assoc. UCLA, 1993—. Mem.: NOW, ALA (affiliate to Latinos and Spanish spkg., pres. San Diego chpt.), AAUW, Calif. Libr. Assn. (pres. svcs. to Latinos roundtable), UCLA Women Philanthropy, Habitat for Humanity, Mex. Am. Nat. Assn., Palomar Libr. Assn. (pres.). Address: UCLA Alumni Assn PO Box 1484 Beverly Hills CA 90213-1484 Business E-Mail: wanda.ramser@uclalumni.net.

**RAMSEUR, T. MICHAEL,** social worker; b. Princeton, N.J., Aug. 18, 1947; s. Thomas Michael and Suzanne T. Ramseur; life ptnr. Annette D. N/A; 1 child, Georgia Anne Bennett-Ramseur. Degree, Trinity Coll., Hartford, Conn., 1970; MSW, Simmons Sch. of Social Work, Boston, 1991. LCSW Mass., 1993. Dir. of social svcs. Baldpate Hosp., Georgetown, Mass., 1999—. Illustration in The New Yorker, Picture for Strange Love, flash films, Vortex and The Ghost of the Witch Judge; author: The Eye of Danvers, 2004, (CD) The Haunted Palace, 2004. Mem.: NASW (assoc.). Home: 11 Riverside Dr Newbury MA 01951 Office: Baldpate Hospital 83 Baldpate Road Georgetown MA 01833 Office Phone: 978-352-2131. Office Fax: 978-352-6755. Personal E-mail: mramseur@yahoo.com.

**RAMSEY, ARDETH JANE,** retired elementary school educator; b. Sumner, Iowa, Apr. 30, 1933; d. Herbert Carl and Cordella (Griese) Seehase; m. Richard Keith Ramsey, June 1, 1955; children: William Robert, Thomas Edward, Patricia Eileen. BA, Upper Iowa U., 1965. Cert. Tchr. Iowa. Tchr. Arlington (Iowa) Cmty. Schs., 1952-55, Rialto (Calif.) Cmty. Schs., 1955-56, Bellevue (Iowa) Cmty. Schs., 1958-59, Starmont Cmty. Schs., Arlington, 1961-68, Oelwein (Iowa) Cmty. Schs., 1970-76, Vinton (Iowa) Cmty. Schs., 1976—94, head reading dept., 1990—94; reading cons. West Elem. Sch., Vinton, 1982—94, reading recovery tchr., 1993—94; ret., 1994. Mem. Vinton Edn. Assn. (sec. 1984-85), P.E.O. (pres. chpt. HG 2001-02), Early Arts Study Club (pres. 2000-01), Alpha Delta Kappa (pres. 1990-92), Delta Kappa Gamma (sec. 1982-84), Mentor Lit. Club (sec., 2005-06), Bethlehem Lutheran Women (sec. 2000-06). Republican. Avocations: antiques, children's literature. Home: 1502 Washington Dr Vinton IA 52349-1654

**RAMSEY, CHARLES EUGENE,** sociologist, educator; b. Paragon, Ind., Apr. 24, 1923; s. Sarcefield Dodson and Stella (Goss) R.; m. Alberta Mae Jordan, July 19, 1943; children— James D., Charles W., Jane E., Suzanne. BS, Ind. State Tchrs. Coll., 1947; MS, U. Wis., 1950, PhD, 1952. Faculty U. Wis., 1951-52, U. Minn., 1952-54, Cornell U., 1954-62, Colo. State U., 1962-65; prof. sociology U. Minn., Mpls., 1965-77; chmn. dept. sociology U. Tex., Arlington, 1977-83. Vis. prof. Inter-Am. Instn. Agrl. Sci., Costa Rica, 1961, Exptl. Sta., U. P.R., 1961-62; research cons. to various univs., agys. Author: (with Lowry Nelson and Cooley Verner) Community Structure and Change, 1960, (with David Gottlieb) The American Adolescent, 1965, Understanding the Deprived Child, S.R.A., 1967, Problems of Youth, 1967, (with D.J. McCarty) The School Managers: Power and Conflict in American Public Education, 1971, (with William A. Stacey) Social Statistics, 1992; also articles. Achievements include developing and testing theory of variations in community power structure, types of sch. bds., and roles of sch. supt.; developed method of comparative measurement of level of living for different countries. Home: 1102 De Pauw Dr Arlington TX 76012-5339 Office: U Tex Dept Sociology Arlington TX 76004

**RAMSEY, CHARLES H.,** police chief; B in Criminal Justice, M in Criminal Justice, Lewis U.; grad., FBI Nat. Acad., Nat. Exec. Inst. Cadet Chgo. Police Dept., 1968, police officer, 1971, promoted through the to commdr. of patrol, detectives and narcotics units, dept. supt. bur. staff svcs., 1994; chief police Met. Police Dept., Washington, 1998—. Spkr. in field; adj. faculty mem. Northwestern U. Traffic Inst. Sch. Police and Command, Lewis U. Recipient Gary P. Hayes award, Police Exec. Rsch. Forum, 1994, Robert Lamb Humanitarian award, Nat. Orgn. Black Law Enforcement Exec., 2001, Civil Rights award, Internat. Assn. Chiefs of Police, 2001. Office: Govt of DC John A Wilson Bldg 1350 Pennsylvania Ave NW Washington DC 20004

RAMSEY, DAVID SELMER, retired health facility administrator; b. Mpls., Feb. 19, 1931; s. Selmer A. and Esther D. (Dahl) R.; m. Betty Seiler, May 15, 1953; children— Scott, Stewart, Thomas BS, U. Mich., 1953, MS in Microbiology, 1954, M.H.A., 1962. Research asst. Detroit Inst. Cancer Research, 1954-60; asst. administr. Harper Hosp., Detroit, 1962-68, assoc. administr., 1968-72; exec. v.p. Iowa Meth. Med. Ctr., Des Moines, 1972-83, pres., 1983-93, Iowa Health Sys., 1993-95, Fine Wood Designs, 1996—. Avocations: golf, tennis, photography. Home: 18710 Poco Rio Dr Rio Verde AZ 85263-7108

RAMSEY, DORIS THERESA, elementary school educator; b. N.Y.C., Aug. 22, 1933; d. Alfonso Henry and Grace Elizabeth Ramsey. BA in sociology, Lehman Coll., 1973—76; MA in spl. edn., CUNY, City College, 1977—81, MA in reading, 1981—84. Billing clk. Simon & Schuster Publishers, NYC, 1952—65; acctg. clk. Princeton U. Store, NJ, 1965—68; edn. asst. NYC Bd. Edn., 1968—78, tchr., 1978—95; ret. Author: (book) Journey of the Ramsey Moores, 1995; actor: (cmty. theater group) The Hadley Players. Mem. Schemburg Ctr. for Rsch. in Black Culture, Met. Mus. Art. Mem.: Assn. of Black Educators, Alliance of Ret. Americans, Smithsonian Inst., Getty Mus. Avocations: music, travel. Home: 3010 Yates Ave Apt 4H Bronx NY 10469

RAMSEY, FORREST GLADSTONE, JR., retired engineering company executive; b. Wichita, Kans., Oct. 25, 1930; s. Forrest Gladstone and Anastasia Ruth (Linot) R.; m. Gwendolyn Moreton, June 22, 1953 (div. Jan. 1982); children: Deborah Jenkins, Rebecca Johnson, Susan Klopp, Diane Hayes, Forrest G. III, Mark, Kenneth; m. Carmen Bergen, Apr. 30, 1988. BS in engring., U.S. Naval Acad., 1952; postgrad., Wichita State U., 1957-58, U. Colo., 1958-64. Commd. ensign USN, 1952, res., 1957; planner, engr. Boeing Corp., Wichita, Kans., 1957-58; engr., logistician Martin-Marietta, Denver, 1959-65; div. dir. Computer Scis., Washington, 1965-73; program dir. Systems Cons., Washington, 1973-76; CEO Am. Sys. Corp., Washington, 1976-92, chmn., bd. dirs., 1992-97; ret., 1997. Mem. Profl. Svcs. Coun. (vice chmn. 1990), Naval Submarine League (bd. dirs. 1982-90). Roman Catholic. Home: 1700 Stony Brook Rd Bedford VA 24523 Personal E-mail: forrest.ramsey@1952.usna.com.

RAMSEY, FRANK ALLEN, veterinarian, retired army officer; b. Rocksprings, Tex., May 1, 1929; s. Reynolds Allen and June (Burdette) R.; m. Lucette C. Reboul, Jan. 1958; children: Randal R., Ramsay A.; m. 2d, Mary Lou Cain, June 1991. D.V.M., Tex. A & M U., 1954; grad., U.S. Army Command and Gen. Staff Coll., 1965, U.S. Army War Coll., 1972. Commd. 1st. lt. U.S. Army Vet. Corps, 1955, advanced through grades to brig. gen., 1980; chief vet. service Ft. Leonard Wood, Mo., 1958-61; acad. vet. U.S. Mil. Acad., West Point, NY, 1962-64; vet. staff officer U.S. Army Combat Devel. Command Med. Service, Ft. Sam Houston, Tex., 1965-67; asst. chief profl. programming and planning br. Office Surgeon Gen., Washington, 1967-68, chief profl. programming and planning br., 1968-71, chief food inspection policy office, 1972-73, sr. vet. staff officer, 1973-77; asst. chief of staff Vet. Service, 7th Med. Command, Army Europe and 7th Army, Heidelberg, W. Ger., 1977-80; asst. for vet. services to surgeon gen. and chief U.S. Army Vet. Corps, Hdqrs. Dept. Army, Washington, 1980-85; ret., 1985. Decorated Army Commendation medal, Legion of Merit with oak leaf cluster, D.S.M. Mem. AVMA, Assn. Fed. Veterinarians, Assn. Mil. Surgeons U.S., Assn. Equine Practitioners, Am. Assn. Food Hygiene Veterinarians, Conf. Pub. Health Veterinarians, Tex. Vet. Med. Assn. Lodges: Masons (32 degree). Presbyterian. Home: 8 El Norte Cir Uvalde TX 78801-4021

RAMSEY, INEZ LINN, librarian, educator; b. Martins Ferry, Ohio, Mar. 25, 1938; d. George and Leona (Smith) Linn; m. Jackson Eugene Ramsey, Apr. 22, 1961; children: John Earl, James Leonard. BA in History, SUNY, Buffalo, 1971, MLS, 1972; EdD in Audiovisual Edn., U. Va., 1980. Libr. Iroquois Ctrl. H.S., Elma, N.Y., 1971-73, Lucy Simms Elem. Sch., Harrisonburg, Va., 1973-75; instr. James Madison U., Harrisonburg, 1975-80, asst. prof., 1980-85, assoc. prof., 1985-91, prof., 1991-98; ret., 1998. Mem. Va. State Library Bd., Richmond, 1975-80; cons. in field. Author (with Jackson E. Ramsey) Budgeting Basics, Library Planning and Budgeti;g; contbr. to Ency., articles to profl. jours.; project developer Internet Sch. Libr. Media Ctr.; project dir. Oral (tape) History Black Community in Harrisonburg, 1977-78; storyteller, puppeteer. Recipient Pierian Press's Libr. Hi Tech (periodical) award, 1998; rsch. grantee James Madison U., Harrisonburg, 1981, Commonwealth Ctr. State Va., 1989. Mem. ALA, Am. Assn. Sch. Librs., Assn. Edn. Comm. Tech. (exec. bd. DSMS 1989-98, DSMT Meritorious Svc. award 1998), Va. Ednl. Media Assn. (sec. 1981-83, citation 1983, pres. 1985-86, Educator of Yr. award 1984-85, Meritorious Svc. award 1987-88), Phi Beta Kappa (pres. Shenandoah chpt. 1980-81), Beta Phi Mu, Phi Delta Kappa. Home: 3215 S Torrey Pines Dr Las Vegas NV 89146-6529 Personal E-mail: inezramsey@cox.net.

RAMSEY, IRA CLAYTON, retired petroleum industry executive; b. Quitman, Ga., May 13, 1931; s. James Redding and Ruth Frances (Treadaway) R.; m. Marianne Vinzant, Dec. 23, 1962; children: Clayton Hamilton, Robin Leigh. BBA, U. Ga., Atlanta, 1954; LLB, Atlanta Law Sch., 1950; postgrad., U. Tex., 1968, U. Pitts., 1973. With Plantation Pipe Line Co., Atlanta, 1948-96, asst. sec., 1967-70, treas., contr., 1970-90, v.p. fin., 1990-96. Life trustee Ga. Found. for Ind. Colls.; trustee emeritus KingsBridge Retirement Ctr., Inc. Baptist. Home: 780 Wesley Oak Rd NW Atlanta GA 30328-4738

RAMSEY, JACKSON EUGENE, management educator; b. Cin., Dec. 20, 1938; s. Leonard Pershing and Edna Willa (Blakeman) R.; m. Inez Mae Linn, Apr. 22, 1961; children: John Earl, James Leonard. BS in Metallurgical Engring., U. Cin., 1961; MBA, SUNY, Buffalo, 1969, PhD, 1975. Registered profl. engr., Va., Ohio. Welding engr. Gen. Electric Co., Cin., 1961-62, Westinghouse-Bettis Lab., Pitts., 1962-66; mgr. prodn. ctrl. Columbus-McKinnon Corp., Buffalo, 1966-71; asst. prof. mgmt. SUNY, Buffalo, 1971-73; prof. mgmt. James Madison U., Harrisonburg, Va., 1973—. Cons. in field. Author: R D Strategic Decision Criteria, 1986, Handbook for Professional Managers, 1985, Budgeting Basics, 1985, Library Planning and Budgeting, 1986; contbr. articles to profl. jours. Vice chmn. Harrisonburg Reps., 1974-78, chmn., 1978-86; vice chmn. 6th dist. Rep. com., 1984-94. Served with USMCR, 1956-62. Named Outstanding Young Scholar, Xerox Corp., 1976. Mem. Acad. Mgmt., Am. Inst. Decision Scis., Inst. Mgmt. Sci., Am. Soc. Metals, Nat. Soc. Profl. Engrs. Baptist. Home: 3215 S Torrey Pines Dr Las Vegas NV 89146-6529 Office: James Madison U Coll Intergrated Sci & Tech Harrisonburg VA 22807-0001 Office Phone: 702-251-0589. E-mail: jackramsey@cox.net.

RAMSEY, JAROLD WILLIAM, literature and language professor, writer; b. Bend, Oreg., Sept. 1, 1937; s. Augustus S. and Wilma E. Ramsey; m. Dorothy Ann Quinn, Aug. 16, 1959; children: Kate, Sophia, John. BA with honors, U. Oreg., 1959; Ph. D., U. Wash., 1966. Acting instr. U. Wash., Seattle, 1963-65; asst. prof. English U. Rochester, NY, 1965-70, assoc. prof. NY, 1970-81, prof. NY, 1981-97; prof. emeritus, 1997—; dir. undergrad. rsch. U. Rochester, NY, 1990-96. Vis. prof. English U. Victoria, B.C., Can., 1974, 75-76; dir. NEH summer seminars on Indian lit., 1985, 88. Author: The Space Between Us, 1970, Love in an Earthquake, 1973 (Lillian Fairchild award 1973), Dermographia, 1982, Reading the Fire, 1983, rev. edit., 1999, Hand-shadows, 1989, (play) Coyote Goes Upriver, premier 1985, (cantata) (with Samuel Adler) The Lodge of Shadows, premiere 1988; editor: Coyote Was Going There, 1977, Nehalem Tillamook Tales, 1990, The Stories We Tell: Oregon Folk Literature (with Suzi Jones), 1994, New Era: Reflections on the Human and Natural History of Central Oregon, 2003, (with Dorothy

Ramsey) The Piper of Cloone: Father Keegan and the Early Gaelic Revival, 2005. Recipient Don Walker award Western Am. Lit., 1979, Borestone Mount Found. Best Poems award, 1972, 75, 76; Helen Bullis prize, 1984, Poetry prize Quar. Rev., 1989; Alumni Achievement award U. Oreg. Alumni Assn., 1990; Nat. Endowment Arts writing grantee, 1974, 76; Ingram Merrill Found. writing grantee, 1976 Mem.: MLA (chair com. on lits. and langs. of Am. 1991—92), Assn. Study Am. Indian Lit. (pres. 1981), Phi Beta Kappa. Democrat. Home: 5884 NW Highway 26 Madras OR 97741-9543 E-mail: jwr1937@madras.net.

RAMSEY, JOHN ARTHUR, lawyer; b. Apr. 1, 1942; s. Wilbert Lewis and Lillian (Anderson) R.; m. Nikki Ann Ramsey, Feb. 9, 1943; children: John William, Bret Anderson, Heather Nichole. AB, San Diego State U., 1965; JD, Calif. Western Sch. Law, 1969. Bar: Colo. 1969, Tex. 1978. Assoc. Henry, Cockrell, Quinn & Creighton, 1969-72; atty. Texaco Inc., 1972-80; asst. to pres. Texaco U.S.A., 1980-81, asst. to divsn. v.p. Houston, 1981-82, divsn. atty. Denver, 1982-88; ptnr. Holland & Hart, 1989—. Editor-in-chief: Calif. Western Law Rev., 1969. Bd. dirs. Selective Svc., Englewood, Colo., 1972-76; chmn. coun. Bethany Luth. Ch., Englewood, 1976; mem. exec. bd. Denver Area coun. Boy Scouts Am., 1999—. Mem. ABA (vice-chmn. oil, natural gas exploration and prodn. com. sect. natural resource law 1983-88, chmn. 1989, coun. sect. natural resources, energy and environ. law 1990-93). Republican. Office: Holland & Hart 8390 E Crescent Pkwy Ste 400 Greenwood Village CO 80111-2822 Office Phone: 303-290-1600.

RAMSEY, LLOYD HAMILTON, medical educator; b. Lexington, Ky., June 10, 1921; s. James Chandler and Hattie O. (Frisbee) R.; m. June Clarke Byars, June 22, 1948 (dec. Aug. 1981); children: Anne C., Robert B., Craig H., Frances C.; m. Marie Luise Erickson, Oct. 12, 1983 BS, U. Ky., 1942; MD, Wash. U., St. Louis, 1950. Diplomate Am. Bd. Internal Medicine. Mem. faculty Vanderbilt U., Nashville, 1953—, prof. medicine, dir. continuing med. edn., 1978-91, prof. medicine emeritus, 1991—. Maj. inf. U.S. Army, 1942-46, PTO. Office: Vanderbilt U Emeritus Med Faculty Office 209 Oxford House 1313 21st Ave S Nashville TN 37232-2425*

RAMSEY, MARGIE, librarian; b. Bay City, Tex., Aug. 29, 1921; d. Cyrus Otis Lansford and Myra Lenore Ferrell; m. Joe Bryan Ramsey, July 29, 1945; children: Ronald Lansford, Kevin Bryan. BA in Libr. Sci., Tex. State U., 1942. Cert. tchr., Tex. Libr. Talco (Tex.) Ind. Sch. Dist., 1942-44; sec. Consolidated Aircraft, San Diego, summer 1943; bookkeeper Lockheed Aircraft, Dallas, 1944; libr. Dallas Pub. Libr., 1944-45; sec. Steck Co., Austin, Tex., 1946-48; libr. U. Tex., Austin, 1948-51. Author, poet: Vol. libr. Hyde Park United Meth., Austin, 1963-2002, Leander (Tex.) Ind. Sch. Dist., 1982-92, Aspen Ridge Lodge, Los Alamos, N.Mex.; mem. The Internat. Libr. of Poetry. Named Outstanding Vol., Nat. Assn. Ptnrs. in Edn., Kraft-Disney, 1989. Fellow AAUW. Democrat. Avocations: teaching, camping, computers, reading, collecting rare books. Home: 1010 Sombrillo Ct # 313 Los Alamos NM 87544 E-mail: laraishere8321@aol.com.

RAMSEY, MICHAEL W., lawyer; b. Galveston, Tex., Feb. 18, 1940; s. V.V. Ramsey; married; 2 children. BA, So. Meth. U., 1962, JD, 1965. Bar: 1965. With Richard Haynes & Assoc., 1965—72; ptnr. Ramsey & Tyson, 1972—85; pvt. practice, 1985—. Named Criminal Def. Lawyer of the Year, Tex. State Bar Assn., 1999. Office: Law Office of Michael Ramsey 2120 Welch St Houston TX 77019

RAMSEY, NATALIE D., lawyer; b. Greeneville, Tenn., Dec. 6, 1959; d. William Trent and Nancy Elizabeth (Maupin) Ramsey. BS, U. Del., 1981; JD, Villanova U., 1984. Bar: Pa. 1984, US Dist. Ct. (ea. dist.) Pa., US Ct. Appeals (3d and 11th cirs.), US Supreme Ct. 2004. Assoc. Montgomery, McCracken, Walker & Rhoads, LLP, Phila., 1985-93; ptnr. Montgomery, McCracken, Walker & Rhoads, Phila., 1993—, chair bankruptcy and reorgn. group, 1997—. Dir. Consumer Bankruptcy Advocacy Project, 1998—; chair Ea. Dist. Pa. Bankruptcy Conf., 2005—06. Contbr. articles to profl. jours. Pres. bd. dirs. Delaware County Habitat for Humanity, 1997—2002. Mem.: Turnaround Mgmt. Assn., Comml. Law League. Presbyterian. Avocations: travel, reading. Office: Montgomery McCracken Walker & Rhoads LLP 123 S Broad St Ste 2538 Philadelphia PA 19109-1099

RAMSEY, NORMAN F., physicist, researcher; b. Washington, Aug. 27, 1915; s. Norman F. and Minna (Bauer) Ramsey; m. Elinor Jameson, June 3, 1940 (dec. Dec. 1983); children: Margaret, Patricia, Janet, Winifred; m. Ellie Welch, May 11, 1985. AB, Columbia U., 1935; BA, Cambridge U., Eng., 1937, MA, 1941, DSc, 1954; PhD, Columbia U., 1940; MA (hon.), Harvard U., 1947; DSc (hon.), Case Western Res. U., 1968, Middlebury Coll., 1969, Oxford U., Eng., 1973, DCL (hon.), 1990; DSc (hon.), Rockefeller U., 1986, U. Chgo., 1989, U. Sussex, 1990, U. Houston, 1991, Carleton Coll., 1991, Lake Forest Coll., 1992, U. Mich., 1993, Phila. Coll. Pharmacy & Sci., 1995, Colby Coll., 1998, Harvard U., Cambridge, Mass., 2006. Kellett fellow Columbia U., 1935—37, Tyndall fellow, 1938—39; Carnegie fellow Carnegie Inst. Washington, 1939—40; assoc. U. Ill., 1940—42; asst. prof. Columbia U., 1942—46; assoc. MIT Radiation Lab., 1940—43; cons. Nat. Def. Research Com., 1940—45; expert cons. sec. of war, 1942—45; group leader, asso. div. head Los Alamos Lab., 1943—45; assoc. prof. Columbia U., 1945—47; head physics dept. Brookhaven Nat. Lab. of AEC, 1946—47; assoc. prof. physics Harvard U., 1947—50, prof. physics, 1950—66, Higgins prof. physics, 1966—86, Higgins prof. emeritus, 1986—. Sr. fellow Harvard Soc. Fellows, 1970—; Eastman prof. Oxford U., 1973—74; Luce prof. cosmology Mt. Holyoke Coll., 1982—83; prof. U. Va., 1983—84; dir. Harvard Nuc. Lab., 1948—50, 1952—53, Varian Assocs., 1963—66; mem. Air Forces Sci. Adv. Com., 1947—54; sci. advisor NATO, 1958—59; mem. Dept. Def. Panel Atomic Energy; exec. com. Cambridge Electron Accelerator; gen. adv. com. AEC. Author: Nuclear Moments and Statistics, 1953, Nuclear Two Body Problems, 1953, Molecular Beams, 1956, 1985, Quick Calculus, 1965, Spectroscopy with Coherent Radiation, 1998; contbr. articles Phys. Rev., other sci. jours. on nuclear physics, molecular beam experiments, radar, nuclear magnetic moments, radiofrequency spectroscopy, masers, nucleon scattering. Trustee Assoc. Univs., Inc., Brookhaven Nat. Lab., Carnegie Endowment Internat. Peace, 1962—85, Rockefeller U., 1977—90; pres. Univs. Rsch. Assocs., Inc., 1966—72, 1973—81, pres. emeritus, 1981—. Recipient Presdl. Order of Merit for radar devel. work, 1947, award, E.O. Lawrence and AEC, 1960, Columbia award for excellence in sci., 1980, medal of honor, IEEE, 1983, Rabi prize, 1985, Monte Ferst award, 1985, Compton medal, 1985, Rumford premium, 1985, Oersted medal, 1988, Nat. medal of sci., 1988, Nobel prize for Physics, 1989, Pupin medal, Columbia Engring. Sch. Alumni Assn., 1992, Sci. for Peace prize, 1992, Einstein medal, 1993, Vannevar Bush award, 1995, Svc. award, PTTL, 2005; fellow Guggenheim, Harvard U., 1954—55. Fellow: Am. Phys. Soc. (coun. 1956—60, pres. 1978—79, Davisson-Germer prize 1974), Am. Acad. Sci.; mem.: AAAS (chmn. physics sect. 1977), NAS, Am. Inst. Physics (chmn. bd. govs. 1980—87), Am. Philos. Assn., French Acad. Sci., Sigma Xi, Phi Beta Kappa (senator 1979—88, v.p. 1982—85). Home: 24 Monmouth Ct Brookline MA 02446-5634 Office: Harvard U Lyman Physics Lab Cambridge MA 02138 Office Phone: 617-495-2864,

RAMSEY, PAUL GLENN, dean, internist; b. Pitts., 1949; MD, Harvard U., 1975. Diplomate Am. Bd. Internal Medicine. Intern Cambridge Hosp., 1975-76; resident in medicine Mass. Gen. Hosp., Boston 1976-78, U. Wash., Seattle, 1980-81, fellow infectious diseases, 1978-80, prof., 1991—, chmn. dept. medicine, 1992-97; physician-in-chief U. Wash. Med. Ctr., 1992-97; v.p. for med. affairs, dean Sch. Medicine U. Wash. Seattle, 1997—. Mem.: Inst. Medicine, AAAS, Assn. Am. Physicians, Am. Fedn. Clin. Rsch, ACP. Office: U Wash Sch Medicine PO Box 356350 Seattle WA 98195-6350

RAMSEY, SALLY ANN SEITZ, retired state official; b. Columbus, Ohio, Feb. 15, 1931; d. Albert Blazier and Mildred (Dodson) Seitz; m. Edward Lewis Ramsey, Apr. 11, 1953 (div. 1982); children: Edward Lewis, Sylvia Ann Mitchell. BA, Ohio State U., 1952, MA, 1955, postgrad., 1963-66; postgrad. St. Mary Coll.-Xavier, Kans., 1962. Rsch. engr., then sr. rsch. engr.

N.Am. Aviation, Inc., Columbus, Ohio, and Downey, Calif., 1962-67; legis. intern State of Ohio, 1964-65; rsch. and info. officer Ohio Dept. Urban Affairs, Columbus, 1967-68; adminstrv. specialist Ohio Dept. Devel., Columbus, 1968; assoc. planner, then sr. planner Div. State Planning, Fla. Dept. Adminstrn., Tallahassee, 1968-76; econ. analysis supr., then econ. analyst Fla. Dept. Commerce, 1976-93; ret., 1993; congl. campaign cons., 1966. U.S. Econ. Devel. Adminstrn. fellow, 1978-79. Mem. ASPA, DAR., Fla. Econs. Club, Kappa Kappa Gamma, Pi Sigma Alpha. Episcopalian. Home: 2963 Golden Eagle Dr E Tallahassee FL 32312-4056

RAMSEYER, J. MARK, law educator; b. 1954; BA, Goshen Coll., 1976; AM, Mich. U., 1978; JD, Harvard U., 1982. Bar: Ill. 1983. Law clk. to Hon. S. Breyer U.S. Ct. Appeals (1st cir.), Boston, 1982-83; assoc. Sidley & Austin, Chgo., 1983-85; acting prof. UCLA, 1986-89, prof., 1989-92, U. Chgo. Law Sch., 1992-98; Mitsubishi prof. of Japanese Legal Studies Harvard U., Cambridge, Mass., 1998—. Office: Harvard U Sch of Law Cambridge MA 02138

RAMSEY-GOLDMAN, ROSALIND, physician; b. N.Y.C., Mar. 22, 1954; d. Abraham L. and Miriam (Colen) Goldman; m. Glenn Ramsey, June 29,1 975; children: Ethan Ramsey, Caitlin Ramsey. BA, Case We. Res. U., 1975, MD, 1978; MPH, U. Pitts., 1988, DPH, 1992. Med. resident U. Rochester, NY, 1978—81; chief resident Rochester Gen. Hosp., 1981—82; staff physician U. Health Svc., Rochester, 1982—83; rheumatology fellow U. Pitts., 1983—86, instr. medicine, 1986—87, asst. prof., 1987—91, co-dir. Lupus Treatment and Diagnostic Ctr., 1987—91; asst. prof. medicine Northwestern U., Chgo., 1991—96, assoc. prof. medicine, 1996—2001, prof. medicine, 2001—. Dir. Chgo. Lupus Registry, Northwestern U., Chgo., 1991—; chairperson Systemic Lupus Internat. Collaborating Clinics Group, 2003—; program dir. Gen. Clin. Rsch. Ctr. at NCRR/NIH, 2005—. Contbr. rsch. articles to profl. jours. Recipient Finkelstein award Hershey (Pa.) Med. Ctr., 1986. Fellow ACP, Am. Coll. Rheumatology; mem. Soc. for Epidemiologic Rsch., Ctrl. Soc. Clin. Rsch. Office: Northwestern U Feinberg Sch Medicine McGaw Pavilion 240 E Huron Ste M-300 Chicago IL 60611 Office Phone: 312-503-8003. Business E-mail: rgramsey@northwestern.edu.

RAMSTAD, JAMES, congressman, lawyer; b. Jamestown, ND, May 6, 1946; s. Marvin Joseph and Della Mae (Fode) Ramstad. BA, U. Minn., 1968; JD with honors, George Washington U., 1973. Bar: ND 1973, DC 1973, Minn. 1979, admitted to practice: US Supreme Ct. 1976. Adminstrv. asst. to LL Duxbury Minn. Ho. Reps., 1969, spl. asst. to Congressman Tom Kleppe, 1970; pvt. practice law Jamestown, 1973, Washington, 1974—78, Mpls., 1978—90; asst. campaign mgr. for Congressman William E. Frenzel US Ho. Reps., 1978; mem. Minn. Senate, 1981—90, asst. minority leader, 1983—87; mem. US Congress from 3rd Minn. dist., 1991—. Adj. prof. Am. U., Washington, 1975—78. Bd. dir. D.A.R.E., Minn., Children's Heart Fund, Lake Country Food Bank; mem. C. of C., Twin West, Wayzata, North Metro. 1st lt. USAR, 1968—74. Named Representative of Yr., Nat. Assn. of Police Organizations, 1997, 2000, Legislator of Yr., Nat. Assn. of Alcoholism and Drug Addiction Counselors, 1998, Nat. Mental Health Assn., 1999; recipient Fulbright Disting. Pub. Service award. Mem.: Hennepin County Bar Assn., ND Bar Assn., DC Bar Assn., Minn. Bar Assn., Minn. Prayer Breakfast Com., Plymouth Lions Club, U. Minn. Alumni Assn., Am. Legion, Phi Delta Theta, Phi Beta Kappa. Republican. Office: US Ho Reps 103 Cannon Ho Office Bldg Washington DC 20515-2303

RAMUS, JOSEPH S., marine biologist; b. Grosse Pointe Farms, Mich., May 7, 1940; married; three children. BA, U. Calif., Berkeley, 1963, PhD in Botany, 1968. From asst. prof. to assoc. prof. biology Yale U., New Haven, 1968-78; from assoc. prof. to prof., asst. dir. marine lab. Duke U., Beaufort, NC, 1978-90, dir. marine lab., 1990-99, prof. marine lab., biological oceanography, coastal system sci. and policy divsn., 1999—. Mem. AAUP, Am. Soc. Limnology & Oceanography, Phycol. Soc. Am., Am. Geophys. Union. Office: Duke U Marine Lab Marine Lab BRL 220 135 Duke Marine Lab Rd Beaufort NC 28516 also: Duke U Marine Lab Piver's Island Beaufort NC 28516

RAN, SHULAMIT, composer; b. Tel Aviv, Oct. 21, 1949; U.S. m. Abraham Lotan, 1986. Studied composition with, Paul Ben-Haim, Norman Dello, Joio, Ralph Shapey; student, Mannes Coll. Music, N.Y.C., 1963—67. With dept. music U. Chgo., 1973—, William H. Colvin prof. music; composer-in-residence Chgo. Symphony Orch., 1990—97, Lyric Opera of Chgo., 1994—97. Compositions include 10 Children's Scenes, 1967, Structures, 1968, 7 Japanese Love Poems, 1968, Hatzvi Israel Eulogy, 1969, O the Chimneys, 1969, Concert Piece for piano and orch., 1970, 3 Fantasy Pieces for Cello and Piano, 1972, Ensembles for 17, 1975, Double Vision, 1976, Hyperbolae for Piano, 1976, For an Actor: Monologue for Clarinet, 1978, Apprehensions, 1979, Private Game, 1979, Fantasy-Variations for Cello, 1980, A Prayer, 1982, Verticals for piano, 1982, String Quartet No. 1, 1984, (for woodwind quintet) Concerto da Camera I, 1985, Amichai Songs, 1985, Concerto for Orchestra, 1986, (for clarinet, string quartet and piano) Concerto da Camera II, 1987, East Wind, 1987, String Quartet No. 2, 1988—89, Symphony, 1989—90, Mirage, 1990, Inscriptions for solo violin, 1991, Chicago Skyline for brass and percussion, 1991, Legends for orch., 1992—93, Invocation, 1994, Yearning for violin and string orch., 1995, (opera) Between Two Worlds (The Dybbuk), 1995—97, Soliloquy, 1997, Vessels of Courage and Hope for orch., 1998, (flute concerto) Voices, 2000, Three Scenes for solo clarinet, 2000, Supplications for chorus and orch., 2002, Violin Concerto, 2003, commd. pieces include for Am. Composers Orch., Phila. Orch., Chgo. Symphony, Balt. Symphony, Chamber Soc. of Lincoln Ctr., Mendelssohn String quartet, Da Capo Chamber Players, Sta. WFMT, Lyric Opera Chgo., composer and soloist for 1st performances Capariccio, 1963, Symphonic Poem, 1967, Concert Piece, 1971. Named Guggenheim fellow, 1977, 1990; recipient Acad. Inst. Arts and Letters award, 1989, Pulitzer prize for music, 1991, Friedheim award for orchestral music, Kennedy Ctr., 1992. Office: U Chgo Dept Music 1010 E 59th St Chicago IL 60637-1512

RANALD, MARGARET LOFTUS, English literature educator, author; b. Auckland, New Zealand, Sept. 5, 1927; came to U.S., 1952; d. Leonard R. and Geraldine (McGrath) Loftus; m. Ralph Arthur Ranald, Feb. 26, 1955; 1 child, Caroline Margaret. AB, U. New Zealand, 1949, MA honors, 1951; MA, UCLA, 1954, PhD, 1958. Jr. asst. Dept. Prime Min. Govt. New Zealand, Wellington, 1944—52; asst. to sec. Princeton U., NJ, 1956—57; from instr. to asst. prof. Temple U., Phila., 1957—61; from asst. prof. to prof. CUNY, N.Y.C., 1961—. Assoc. bibliographer MLA, N.Y.C., 1958—; mem. assoc. faculty, mem. adv. com. Columbia U., N.Y.C., 1976—; vis. prof. UCLA, 1970-85, 98, tchg. asst., 1953-55. Author: The Eugene O'Neill Companion, 1984, Shakespeare and his Social Context, 1987, John Webster, 1989; assoc. editor (book series): International Bibliography of Theatre, 1985—. Fulbright fellow, 1952-54; sr. fellow Folger Shakespeare Libr., 1970-72. Mem. MLA, Am. Soc. Theatre Rsch. (exec. sec., v.p. 1976-83), Eugene O'Neill Soc. (coun., pres. 1996-2000, Gold Medallist), Shakespeare Soc. Am. (former rsch. asst.), Princeton Club N.Y. Avocations: music, drama, theatrical history, travel. Office: CUNY Dept of Eng 65-30 Kissena Blvd Flushing NY 11367 Office Phone: 212-595-6711.

RANALD, RALPH ARTHUR, former government official, educator; b. N.Y.C., Nov. 25, 1930; s. Josef A. and Pearl R.; m. Margaret Florence Loftus, Feb. 26, 1955; 1 dau., Caroline. AB, UCLA, 1952, MA, 1954; AM, Princeton U., 1958; postgrad., Harvard U., 1961—62, postgrad., 1976—77, postgrad., 1999—2000; grad., Exec. Program Nat. and Internat. Security, 1978; PhD, Princeton U., 1962; JD, Fordham U., 1997. Bar: N.Y., U.S. Supreme Ct. 2000. Tchg. asst. UCLA, 1952—54; fellow, rsch. asst. Princeton U., NJ, 1956—59; asst. prof. Fordham U. Grad. Sch., N.Y.C., 1959—65; asst. dean acad. affairs, prof. Coll. Arts and Scis. NYU, 1965—69; prof. CUNY, 1969—; spl. policy asst. HEW, Washington, 1968—69, Office of Mgmt. and Budget, 1976—77; sr. cons. U.S. Dept. Def., 1969—70, 1977—78; mem. staffs Dept. Def. and Army Gen. Staff U.S. Govt. Long Com., 1989, U.S. Dept. Def., 1995—96. Vis. prof. and cons. univs. including U. So. Calif., summers 1968-74, Calif.

State U., UCLA, summers 1985, 98; vis. scholar Harvard Law Sch., 1999—2003. Author: Management Development in Government, 1979, George Orwell, 1965; contbr. reports, articles to publs. in law, govt. and edn. Treas. N.Y. State Com. for Pub. Higher Edn., 1975-78, mem. com., 1970—. 1st lt. U.S. Army, 1953-56, to col., 1977-78, res., 1978—. Recipient U.S. Legion of Merit, 1983; sr. fellow Am. Soc. Pub. Adminstrn. (selection com. for fellows, 1970-74); mem. Res. Officers Assn. U.S. (life), Harvard U. Law Sch. Assn., Assn. of Princeton U. Grad. Alumni, U.S. Army War Coll. Alumni Assn., John F. Kennedy Sch. of Govt. Alumni Assn., Princeton Club of N.Y., Army and Navy Club, Phi Beta Kappa. Home and Office: 239 Central Park W Ste 7E New York NY 10024-6038

**RANCK, EDNA RUNNELS,** academic administrator, researcher; b. Waterville, Maine, Aug. 24, 1935; d. Everett Elias and Edna May (King) Runnels; m. James Gilmour Ranck, June 30, 1971 (dec. May 1979); children: Matthew, Christopher, Joshua Duggan; m. Martin Fleischer, Apr. 19, 1982; stepchildren: Christina, Laura. BA cum laude, Fla. State U., Tallahassee, 1957; MDiv magna cum laude, Drew U. Theol. Sch., Madison, NJ, 1971; MEd in Edn. Adminstrn., 1978; EdD in Curriculum and Tchg., Columbia U., NYC, 1986. Dir. Collinsville Child Care Ctr., Morristown, NJ, 1971-78; exec. dir. Children's Svcs. Morris County, Morristown, 1980-84; co-mgr. NJ Child Care Clearinghouse, Trenton, NJ; coord. NJ Child Care Adv. Coun., Trenton, 1987-92; dir. NJ Office Child Care Devel., Trenton, 1992; child care coord. NJ Dept. Human Svcs., Trenton, 1992-98, Nat. Assn. Child Care Resource & Referral Agys., Washington, 1998—2002, Westover Consultants, Inc., Bethesda, Md., 2002—. Adj. faculty Kean U. NJ, Union, 1983; dir. Sprout House Presch., Chatham, NJ, 1984-87; mem. Morris County Human Svcs. Adv. Coun., Morristown, NJ, 1986-87; spkr. in field. Author: Dodge Foundation Project, 1984, Young Children, 1987, Our History, Our Vision: A History of the National Association of Child Care Rsource and Referral Agencies, 1997, monthly Policy Perspectives column, 2000-02; contbr. chapters to books, articles to profl. jours. Exec. bd. Drew U. Alumni Assn. Theol. Sch., 1986-92; active Drew U. Alumni Study Commn., 1993, Non-Govt. Orgn. rep. to UN Internat. Fedn. Educative Cmtys., 1992-99; mem. history/archives panel Nat. Assn. for Edn. of Young Children, 1999-2001. Recipient Volpe Commitment in Child Care award, NJ Child Care Assn., 1991, Essex C.C. Early Childhood award, 1997, Aletha Wright award for Excellence in Early Edn., 1998. Mem. Internat. Assn. Presch. Edn. N.Am. (bd. dirs.), Child Care Action Campaign Panel, Acad. Child and Youth Care Workers, Nat. Assn. Regulatory Adminstrn. (bd. dirs. 2000-05), World Orgn. Presch. Edn. (bd. dirs. 2000—, pres.-elect, 2006), Nat. Assn. Edn. Young Children (moderator history seminar 2002—), Tchrs. Coll. Columbia U. Washington Alumni Assn. (co-chmn.), GCH Found. (sec./treas. bd. dirs. 2004—), Phi Beta Kappa, Pi Sigma Alpha, Sigma Delta Pi. Republican. United Methodist. Avocations: writing, travel, clothing design, art collecting, walking. Home: 4447 MacArthur Blvd NW Washington DC 20007-2564 Personal E-mail: edna.ranck@verizon.net.

**RANCK, JAMES BYRNE, JR.,** neuroscience researcher, educator; b. Frederick, Md., Aug. 17, 1930; s. James Byrne and Dorothy Irene (Schwieger) R.; m. Helen Haukeness, June 9, 1961; 1 child, Mary Haukeness. BA, Haverford Coll., 1952; MD, Columbia U., 1955. Intern U. Chgo. Clinics, 1955-56; scientist NIH, Bethesda, Md., 1956-58; postdoctoral fellow Dept. Physiology U. Washington, Seattle, 1959-61, instr., 1961-62; from asst. prof. to prof. U. Mich., Ann Arbor, 1962-75; prof. SUNY Health Sci. Ctr., Bklyn., 1975—2005, disting. tchg. prof., 2005—. Home: 100 Bank St New York NY 10014-2123 Office: SUNY Dept Physiology 450 Clarkson Ave Brooklyn NY 11203-2056 Office Phone: 718-270-1600. E-mail: jranck@downstate.edu.

**RAND, A. BARRY,** financial services executive; m. Donna (Rand); children: Christopher and Allison. BA, Am. Univ.; MBA, Stanford U., M in Mgmt. sci.; various degrees (hon.). Exec. v.p. worldwide ops. Xerox Corp., until 1999; chmn. bd. dirs., CEO, Avis Group Holdings, Inc., Garden City, NY, 1999—2001; chmn., CEO Equitant Corp., 2003—. Bd. dirs. AT&T Wireless, Abbott Laboratories, Agilent Technologies, Equitant Corp., Aspect Communications Corp. Bd. dir. Urban Family Inst.; Garth Fagan Dance Theater; bd. trustees Howard U.; mem. adv. coun. Stanford U. Grad. Sch. Bus. Recipient Image Award NAACP, 1993; inducted into Nat. Sales Hall of Fame, 1993; Stanford Sloan fellow, Stanford U. Office: Equitant Corp Stamford Ctr Six Landmark Sq, 4th Fl Stamford CT 06901-2792

**RAND, CALVIN GORDON,** art educator, educational consultant; b. Buffalo, May 15, 1929; s. George Franklin and Isabel (Williams) R.; m. Patricia Clemens Andrew, Aug. 18, 1951; children: Robin, Melissa, Jennifer, Lucinda, Elizabeth BA, Princeton U., 1951; MA, Columbia U., 1954; LHD (hon.), York U., Can., 1984. Head history dept. Riverdale Sch., N.Y.C., 1955-60; lectr. philosophy SUNY-Buffalo, 1961-68, acting dir. cultural affairs, 1968-71; founder, pres. The Niagara Inst., Niagara-on-the-Lake, Canada, 1971-79; pres. Am. Acad. in Rome, N.Y.C., 1980-84; intl. producer, theatre and film cons., N.Y.C., 1985-90. Founding chmn., dir. Shaw Festival Theatre, Niagara-on-the-Lake, 1964-78,. bd. govs., 1979—; trustee Playwrights Horizons Theatre, N.Y.C., 1982-92; bd. dirs. Arts in Edn. Inst.; mem. N.Y. State Coun. on Arts, 1978-82, Arts Coun. Western N.Y. 1987-93; chmn. World Ency. Contemporary Theater; chmn. arts coun. SUNY, Buffalo, 1987-94, adj. prof. theater, 1988—. Contbr. articles to profl. jours. Bd. dirs. Burchfield-Penney Art Ctr., Buffalo, 1991—, vice-chair, 1999—; bd. dirs. Irish Classical Theater, 1993—, pres., 1998-2004; trustee Albright-Knox Gallery, Buffalo, 1976-80, 84-88, 90-94. Recipient spl. citation Ont. Arts Coun., 1976, Fellowship Fund award Niagara Inst., 1980, Centennial Arts award Nichols Sch., 1992, Red Jacket award, Erie County Hist. Soc., 2000; named Man of Yr., Can. World Affairs, 1976, Buffalo Courier Express, 1976, Arts Patron of Yr., Western N.Y. Arts Coun. and C. of C., 1989; Disting Non-Alumni, SUNY, Buffalo, Man of Yr., 1997, YMCA of Western NY, 1999; Visitor Coll. fellow York U. Mem. Princeton Club, Saturn Club. Office Phone: 716-883-2942.

**RAND, DUNCAN DAWSON,** retired librarian; b. Biggar, Sask., Can., Oct. 28, 1940; s. Dawson Ellis and Elizabeth Edna (Gabie) R.; m. Nancy Jean Daugherty, Sept. 7, 1963; children: Jacqueline Nancy, Duncan Dawson, Thomas Nelson, John David, Jennifer Nancy. BA, U. Sask., 1963; B.L.S., McGill U., 1964. Young adult librarian Regina Pub. Library, Sask., 1964-65; coordinator library services Regina Separate Sch. Bd., 1965-68; asst. chief librarian Regina Pub. Library, 1968-71; dep. dir. London Pub. Library and Art Mus., 1971-73, acting dir., 1973-74; chief librarian Lethbridge Pub. Library, Alta., 1974-2000, ret. Alta., 2001. Dir. So. Alta. Art Gallery, Alberta Libr., 1996—. Editor: Sask. Geneal. Soc. Bull, 1968-71. Vice pres. Alta. council Boy Scouts. Mem. Libr. Assn. Alta (dir., pres. 1986-87), Can. Libr. Assn. (dir.), Can. Assn. Pub. Librs. (chair 1976-77), Sask. Geneal. Soc. (pres.), Assn. Profl. Librs. of Lethbridge (chmn. 1982-84), So. Alta. Regional Info. Network (chmn. 1996-2000), Samaritans (pres. 1998-2001), Allied Arts Coun. (bd. dirs. 1993-98), Southern Alberta Regional Info. Network (chmn.), Rotary, Ipalosh (archivist, sec. 1980-94). Office: 810 5th Ave S Lethbridge AB Canada T1J 4C4

**RAND, JOELLA MAE,** retired nursing educator, counselor; b. Akron, Ohio, July 9, 1932; d. Harry S. and Elizabeth May (Miller) Halberg; m. Martin Rand (dec.); children: Craig, Debbi Stark. BSN, U. Akron, 1961, MEd in Guidance, 1968; PhD in Higher Edn. Adminstrn., Syracuse U., 1981. Staff nurse Akron Gen. Hosp., 1953-54; staff-head nurse-instr. Summit County Receiving, Cuyahoga Falls, Ohio, 1954-56; head nurse psychiat. unit Akron Gen. Hosp., 1956-57; instr. psychiatric nursing Summit County Receiving, Cuyahoga Falls, 1957-61; head nurse, in-service instr. Willard (N.Y.) State Hosp., 1961-62; asst. prof. Alfred (N.Y.) U., 1962-76, assoc. prof., assoc. dean, 1976-78, acting dean, 1978-79, dean, 1979-90, dean coll. profl. studies, 1990-91, prof. counseling, 1991-2000; ret. 2000. Cons. N.Y. State Regents Program for Non-Collegiate Sponsored Instrn., 1984; cons. collegiate programs N.Y. State Dept. Edn., 1985, Elmira Coll., 1991, U. Rochester, 1992-93; accreditation visitor Nat. League for Nursing, 1984-92; ednl. cons. Willard Psychiat. Hosp., 1992-93; mem. profl. practice exam. subcom. Regents Coll., 1990-95. Vol. Williard Drug Treatment Ctr., 1997—, bd. dirs.; Romulus Zoning Bd., 2002—; vol. Red Cross, 2003—, co-capt. disaster team,

2004—05; bd. dirs. Five Point Correctional Facility, Willard Drug Treatment Ctr. Recipient Tchg. Excellence award Alfred U., 1977, Mary E. Gladwin Outstanding Alumni award Akron U. Coll. Nursing, 1983, Alfred Alumni Friends award, 1989, Grand Marshall commencement Alfred U., 1993, Vol. of Yr. award Willard Drug Treatment Ctr., 1999, Cert. Appreciation, Seneca County Cmty. Svcs. Bd., 2005. Mem.: ACA (NAR rep. 2000—04, co-capt. disaster team Red Cross-Finger Lakes chpt. 2003—05, pres. NYCA 2005, Seneca County Med. Reserve Corps. 2005—), Genesee Valley Edn. Com. (chair 1984—86), Western N.Y. League Nursing (bd. dirs. 1991—93), Genesee Regional Consortium (v.p.), N.Y. State Coun. of Deans (treas. 1984—88), N.Y. State Counseling Assn. (v.p.-elect profl. svcs. 1995—96, v.p. profl. svcs. 1996—98, 1999—2000, pres. 2005—06), Sigma Theta Tau (treas. Alfred chpt. 1984—85). Avocations: boating, fishing, public speaking in areas of family and child abuse. E-mail: drand@rochester.rr.com.

**RAND, KATHY SUE,** public relations consultant, public relations executive; b. Miami Beach, Fla., Feb. 24, 1945; d. William R. and Rose (Lasser) R.; m. Peter C. Ritsos, Feb. 19, 1982. BA, Mich. State U., 1965; MBA, Northwestern U., 1980. Asst. editor Lyons & Carnahan, Chgo., 1967-68; mng. editor Cahners Pub. Co., Chgo., 1968-71; pub. rels. writer Super Market Inst., Chgo., 1972-73; account supr. Pub. Communications Inc., Chgo., 1973-77; divisional mgr. pub. rels. Quaker Oats Co., Chgo., 1977-82; exec. v.p., dep. gen. mgr. Golin/Harris Communications, Chgo., 1982-90; exec. v.p. Lesnik Pub. Rels., Northbrook, Ill., 1990-91; mng. dir. Manning, Selvage & Lee, Chgo., 1991—2002; public rels. cons., 2002—. Dir. midwest region NOW, 1972-74; mem. Kellogg Alumni Adv. Bd.; bd. dirs. Jr. Achievement of Chgo. Mem. Pub. Rels. Soc. Am. (Silver Anvil award 1986, 87), Pub. Club Chgo. (Golden Trumpet awards 1982-87, 90, 94, 95, 97, 98, 99, 00), Vet. Feminists of Am. (bd. dirs., v.p. pub. rels.), Northwestern Club Chgo., Kellog Alumni Club, Beta Gamma Sigma. Home: 400 Riverwoods Rd Lake Forest IL 60045-2547 Personal E-mail: ksrand@aol.com.

**RAND, LAWRENCE ANTHONY,** investor, finance company executive; b. Bklyn., Nov. 19, 1942; s. Gerald M. and Elaine Shirley Rand; m. Madelon L., July 4, 1942; children: Allan, Joshua, Emily. AB with honors, Brown U., 1964; MA, NYU, 1965, PhD, 1998. Lectr. NYU, 1967, CUNY, 1968; analyst CIA, Langley, Va., 1967-68; account supr. Ruder & Finn Inc., N.Y.C., 1968-71; co-founder, sr. v.p. Kekst & Co., N.Y.C., 1971—, also bd. dirs. Chmn., bd. dirs. ALS Assn., L.A., 1987-92. Chmn. ethics com. Village Rye Brook, NY, 1993—2000, village trustee, 2000—02, mayor, 2004—; bd. dirs. U.S. Tennis Assn. Tennis and Edn. Found. Mem. Brown U. Club, Bailiwick Club (Greenwich, Conn.). Office: Kekst & Co 437 Madison Ave 19th Fl New York NY 10022-7195 Office Phone: 212-521-4800. Personal E-mail: lar@kekst.com.

**RAND, LEON,** academic administrator; b. Boston, Oct. 8, 1930; s. Max B. and Ricka (Muscanto) Rakisky; m. Marian L. Newton, Aug. 29, 1959; children: Debra Ruth, Paul Martin, Marta Leah. BS, Northeastern U., 1953; MA, U. Tex., 1956, PhD, 1958. Postdoctoral fellow Purdue U., 1958-59; asst. prof. to prof. U. Detroit, 1959-68; prof., chmn. dept. chemistry Youngstown (Ohio) State U., 1968-74, dean grad. studies and research, 1974-81, acting acad. v.p., 1980; vice chancellor acad. affairs U. N.C., Pembroke, 1981—85; chancellor Ind. U.S.E., New Albany, 1986-96; chancellor emeritus Ind. U. 1996—, prof. emeritus, 1999—; spl. asst. to chancellor IUPUI, 1996-98. Bd. dirs. Floyd Meml. Hosp., New Albany, 1987—90, Jewish Hosp., Louisville, 1991—96. Bd. dirs., mem. exec. com. Louisville (Ind.) area chpt. ARC; docent Indpls. Mus. Art, 1998—. Mem.: Metroversity (bd. dirs.), Am. Inst. Chemists, Am. Chem. Soc., Sigma Xi, Phi Kappa Phi. Home: 1785 Arrowwood Dr Carmel IN 46033-9019 E-mail: LRand7658@sbcglobal.net.

**RAND, PETER,** writer, editor, educator; b. San Francisco, Feb. 23, 1942; s. Christopher T.E. Rand and Margaret Aldrich Demott; m. Bliss I. Rand, Dec. 19, 1976; 1 child, James. Student, U. Calif., Berkeley; MA, Johns Hopkins U., 1975. Adv. fiction editor Antaeus, NYC, 1970-73; editor Washington Monthly, 1974-75; instr. Columbia U., NYC, 1976-91; preceptor Harvard U., Cambridge, Mass., 1997-98, Boston U., 1999—. Freelance editor, Belmont, Mass., 1994—. Author: Firestorm, 1969, The Time of the Emergency, 1977, The Private Rich, 1984, Gold from Heaven, 1988, China Hands, 1995; editor: Deng Xiaoping, Chronicle of an Empire (by Ruan Ming), 1994, Scarlet Memorial, Tales of Cannibalism in Modern China (by Zheng Yi), 1996, Tiananmen Follies (by Dai Qing), 2004. Trustee Belmont Citizens Forum, 1999—2002. Grantee Creative Artists Performing Svc., NYC, 1977. Mem. PEN, J.K. Fairbank Ctr. for East Asian Rsch. (affiliate), Tavern Club (sec.). Avocation: tennis. Home: 35 Falmouth St Belmont MA 02478 Business E-mail: prand@bu.edu. E-mail: inuirand@aol.com.

**RAND, ROBERT STEPHEN,** electrical engineer, physicist, statistician; b. Worcester, Mass., Nov. 10, 1953; s. Raymond Stephen and Dorothy May Rand; m. Maria Elisa Rand; 1 child, Christine Allie. PhD in Engring. Physics, U. Va., Charlottesville, 2001. Scientist U.S Army ERDC, Alexandria, Va., 1977—2006; project scientist NGA, Reston, Va., 2006—. Mem.: SPIE, IEEE-Geosci. and Remote Sensing Soc., Sigma Xi. Achievements include research in hyperspectral imagery, remote sensing, pattern recognition, and biologically plausible neurodynamical processing. Business E-mail: robert.s.rand@erdc.usace.army.mil.

**RAND, ROBERT WHEELER,** neurosurgeon, educator; b. L.A., Jan. 28, 1923; s. Carl W. and Catherine (Humphrey) R.; m. Helen L. Pierce, Dec. 17, 1949; children: Carl W., Richard P. Student, Harvard U., 1940-42, UCLA, 1942-44; MD, U. So. Calif., 1947; MS, U. Mich., 1951, PhD in Anatomy, 1952; JD, U. West L.A., 1974. Intern, resident in neurosurgery U. Mich., Ann Arbor, 1947/54; from instr. to prof. neurol. surgery UCLA, 1953-89; assoc. med. dir. John Wayne Cancer Inst., Santa Monica, Calif., 1989—. Expert witness malpractice cases Superior Ct. Author: Spinal Cord Tumors in Childhood, 1960, Microneurosurgery, 3d edit.; 1985; contbr. articles to profl. jours.; inventor neuropledgets, thermomagnetic surgery coil system, microballoon for aneurysm occlusion, Malcolm-Rand graphite cranial frame, cobalt scalpel. Lt. comdr. USNR, 1943-46, 54-56. Recipient Profl. award UCLA, 1973. Fellow ACS; mem. AMA, Calif. Med. Assn., L.A. County Med. Assn., Am. Surg. Assn., Internat. Coll. Surgeons, Am. Assn. Neurol. Surgeons, Am. Assn. Neurol. Surgeons, Soc. Neurol. Surgeons, Western Neurosurg. Soc., L.A. Country Club. Office: John Wayne Cancer Inst St John's Hosp 2200 Santa Monica Blvd Santa Monica CA 90404-2302

**RAND, WILLIAM,** lawyer, retired judge; b. NYC, Oct. 11, 1926; s. William and Barbara (Burr) R.; married; children: Alicia, Carley Coudert, William Coudert, Paula Burr. AB, Harvard U., 1948; LLB, Columbia U., 1951. Bar: N.Y. 1951, U.S. Dist. Ct. N.Y. 1951, U.S. Supreme Ct., 1958, U.S. Ct. Appeals (2d cir.) 1961, U.S. Ct. Appeals (4th cir.) 1985, U.S. Ct. Appeals (3rd cir.) 2004. Asst. dist. atty. New York County, 1954-59; asst. counsel to gov. of State of N.Y., 1959-60; assoc. Coudert Bros., N.Y.C., 1961-62, ptnr., 1963-98; justice N.Y. State Supreme Ct., 1962. Justice Village of Cove Neck, Oyster Bay, N.Y., 1974-98. Mem. exec. com. New York County Reps., 1968-72. Served with USN, 1944-46, PTO. Mem.: Racquet and Tennis Club (N.Y.C.), Piping Rock Club (Locust Valley, N.Y.). Home: 73 Cove Neck Rd Oyster Bay NY 11771-1821 Office: Coudert Bros Fl 43 1114 Avenue of the Americas New York NY 10036-7710 Office Phone: 212-626-4433. E-mail: randw@coudert.com.

**RANDA, JAMES PAUL,** physicist, electrical engineer; b. Chgo., Jan. 26, 1947; s. John Joseph and Catherine Anne (Baier) R.; m. Susan Bulmann, June 12, 1980; 1 child, David. BS, Ill. Benedictine Coll., 1969; MS, U. Ill., 1970, PhD, 1974. Vis. asst. prof. Tex. A&M U., College Station, 1974-75; postdoctoral fellow U. Manchester, Eng., 1975-78; asst. prof. U. Colo., Boulder, 1978-83; physicist, sr. project leader Nat. Inst. of Stds. and Tech., Boulder, 1983—. Lectr. physics dept. U. Colo., Boulder, 1985-89; lectr., cons. Productivity and Stds Bd., Singapore, 2001. U.S. rep. to working group on radiofrequency quantities Internat. Com. of Weights and Measures, Sevres, France, 1999—, chmn., 2002—. Editor: Quantum Flavordynamics, Quantum

Chromodynamics, and Unified Field Theories, 1980; contbr. articles to profl. jours. Recipient Bronze medal, U.S. Dept. Commerce, 1992, 1999, award for best paper, IEEE Transactions on Electromagnetic Compatibility, 1992. Mem. IEEE, MTT Soc., EMC Soc. (tech. com., chair 1990-94), Am. Phys. Soc., Automated RF Techniques Group, Geoscience and Remote Sensing Soc. of IEEE. Avocations: reading, hiking, gardening, writing. Office: NIST 818-01 325 Broadway Boulder CO 80305-3328 Business E-Mail: randa@boulder.nist.gov.

**RANDALL, ANTHONY SHIELDS,** environmental scientist, military officer; b. Springfield, Mo., Apr. 16, 1966; s. Shiela Francis Robles, adopted s. Gene Bertram and Barbara Randall; children: Matthew Anthony, Hallie Marie Randall-Davidson. BS in Edn., Mo. State U., 1988, MS in Edn., 1990; PhD, Okla. State U., 1993. Registered environmental mgr. Nat. Registry Environl. Profls., Ill., 1997. Instr. Tulsa Jr. Coll., 1993—95; hydrogeologist Ozark Underground Lab., Protem, Mo., 1994; environ. scientist, team leader Dynamac, Inc., Topeka, 1995—98; pollution prevention mgr. Adj. General's Dept., Topeka, 1998—2000; environ. program mgr. Kans. Army N.G., Topeka, 2000—, comdr., 102d mil. history detachment, 2004—06; ops. officer Kans. Army N.G. State Surgeon, 2006—. Cons. Randall Geoconsulting, Tulsa, 1994—95. Col. Hon. Order of Ky. Colonels, Louisville; past pres. EPA Region VII Pollution Prevention Roundtable, Kansas City, Mo. Decorated Army Commendation medal U.S. Army, Army Achievement medal, Meritorious Svc. medal, La. Commendation medal State of La.; recipient Environ. Security award, Dept. of the Navy, 2001, Dept. of the Army, 2003, Pollution Prevention award, Kans. Dept. of Health and Environ., 1998, EPA Region 7, 1998, Kans. Meritorious Svc. Ribbon, State of Kans. 2000, Achievement award (Heritage Painting), N.G. Bur., 2001—02, Environ. Security award, Dept. of Def., 2001, N.G. Bur., 2003, Dept. of Def., 2003. Mem.: Kans. Acad. Sci., N.G. Assn. of the U.S., Assn. Mil. Engrs., Assn. Mil. Surgeons U.S., Phi Kappa Phi. Conservative. Methodist. Achievements include research in Located new locations of endangered species (cavefish) in southwest Missouri; origination and formation mechanisms of playas on the High Plains of Oklahoma. Avocations: travel, Tae Kwon Do, hiking, camping. Office: Kansas Army Nat Guard 131 SW 27th St Topeka KS 66611-1159 Personal E-mail: soldier42us@yahoo.com.

**RANDALL, BEATRICE JANET,** retired secondary school educator; b. Everett, Wash., Sept. 4, 1944; d. Bert Kermit and Una Mamie (Cushman) Wangerin; m. Charles Vern Randall, Sept. 12, 1964; children: William Eugene, Vern Aaron Charles. AA, Everett Community Coll., 1962-64; BA in Edn., Western Wash. U., 1966, MA, 1972. Cert. tchr., counselor. Tchr. Sedro Woolley (Wash.) Sch. Dist., 1966-67, Arlington (Wash.) Sch. Dist., 1967—68, 1984—2000, Mukilteo (Wash.) Sch. Dist., 1968-70; ret. Coach various sports Post Middle Sch. and Arlington High Sch., Wash., 1984-94. Airport commr. City of Arlington, 1978-82; commr. Snohomish County Mental Health Bd., 1980-82; city council mem. City of Arlington, 1982-2002, mayor pro-tem, pres. of coun., 1992-2002; mem. Snohomish County Solid Waste Adv. Com., 1988-2002. Pacific N.W. Master's shot-put champion, 1986-88, Master's discus champion, 1986-87, javelin, 1988—, triple jump record holder, 1988, Citizen of Yr. award City of Arlington, 2002. Mem. Wash. Edn. Assn., NEA, Arlington Garden Club (master gardener). Democrat. Methodist. Avocations: gardening, quilting, writing, track and field officiating. Home: 427 S French Ave Arlington WA 98223-1618

**RANDALL, CLAIRE,** retired religious organization administrator; b. Dallas, Oct. 15, 1919; d. Arthur Godfrey and Annie Laua (Fulton) Randall. AA, Schreiner Coll., 1948; BA, Scarritt Coll., 1950; DD (hon.), Berkeley Sem., Yale U., 1974; LHD (hon.), Austin Coll., 1982; LLD (hon.), Notre Dame U., 1984. Assoc. missionary edn. Bd. World Missions Presbyn. Ch., U.S., Nashville, 1949-57, dir. art Gen. Coun. Atlanta, 1957-61; dir. Christian World Mission, program dir., assoc. dir. Ch. Women United, N.Y.C., 1962-73; gen. sec. Nat. Coun. Ch. of Christ U.S.A., NYC, 1974-84; nat. pres. Ch. Women United, NYC, 1988-92; ret., 1992. Mem. Nat. Commn. Internat. Women's Yr., 1975—77, Martin Luther King Jr. Fed. Holiday Commn., 1985. Recipient Woman of Yr. in Religion award, Heritage Soc., 1977, Empire State woman of Yr. in Religion award, State of NY, 1984, medal Order of St. Vladimir, Russian Orthodox Ch., 1984. Democrat. Episcopalian. Avocations: golf, swimming, painting, reading, music. Home: 9965 W Royal Oak Rd # 1214 Sun City AZ 85351-6116

**RANDALL, CLIFFORD WENDELL,** civil engineer, educator; b. Somerset, Ky., May 1, 1936; s. William Lesbert and Geneva (James) R.; m. Phyllis Amis, Aug. 15, 1959; children: Andrew Amis, William Otis. BSCE, U. Ky., 1959, MS in Sanitary Engring., 1963; PhD in Environ. Health Engring., U. Tex., 1966. Asst. prof. civil engring. U. Tex., Arlington, 1965-68; mem. faculty Va. Poly. Inst. and State U., 1968—2001, civil engring., 1972-81, Charles Lunsford prof., 1981—2001; vis. prof. U. Cape Town, South Africa, 1983; chmn. environ. engring. and scis. program Va. Poly. Inst. and State U., 1979-97, Charles Lunsford prof. emeritus, 2001—. Lectr. Shanghai Archtl. and Mcpl. Engring. Inst., Wuhan Tech. U., 1987; dir. Occoquan Watershed Monitoring Program, 1971-2001; mem. Occoquan watershed monitoring subcom. Va. State Water Control Bd., 1971—, chair, 1971-85, 2001-, vice chair, 1986-2001; mem. U.S. nat. com. Internat. Water Quality, 1976-88, chair 1986-88, mem. 1992 IAWQ Biennial Conf. Com., chair conf. arrangements, Washington; tng. grant cons. EPA, 1970-71; cons. to industry, 1969—; WHO cons. to Nat. Environ. Engring. Rsch. Inst. India, 1983-83 Va. gov. appointee sci. and tech. adv. com. Chesapeake Bay Program; mem. sci. and tech. adv. com. Chesapeake Bay Program, 1984-2006, chmn. 1993-97; mem. nitrogen tech. adv. com. N.Y.C. Dept. Environ. Protection, 1994—; mem. blue ribbon panel wastewater treatment City of Atlanta, 1997-2001. Author tech. papers in field; co-author; Biological Process Design for Wastewater Treatment, 1980, Stormwater Management in Urbanizing Areas, 1983, Design and Retrofit of Wastewater Treatment Plants for Biological Nutrient Removal, 1992. Troop com. chmn. local Boy Scouts Am., 1978-84, chmn. dist. Camporee com., 1977; camp pres. Gideons Internat., 1976-78, 80, 95-97, state cabinet mem., 1985-88; vice moderator Highlands Bapt. Assn., 1980-81, moderator, 1982-83; mem. bd. deacons Blacksburg Bapt. Ch., 1971-74, 79-82, chmn., 1974. Lt. U.S. Coast and Godetic Survey, 1959-62. Ford Found. fellow, 1964-65; recipient citation Engring. News-Record, 1988, Disting. Svc. award U.S. nat. com. Internat. Assn. Water Quality, 1989, Salute to Excellence Gov. of Md., 1994, Alumni Pub. Svc. award Va. Tech., 1996, Mathias medal for sci. excellence Chesapeake Rsch. Consortium and the Sea Grant Offices of Md. and Va., 1996, Dean's award Excellence Pub. Svc., Va. Tech. Engring., 1997; named Conservationist of Yr. Chesapeake Bay Found., 1986; AEC trainee U. Tex., 1963-65. Mem. ASCE (hon. water resources mgmt. com. 1977, environ. engring. rsch. coun. 1989-90, svc. award 1978, 80, meritorious tech. paper award 1969), Am. Water Works Assn. (cert. recognition for acad. excellence 1980, 89), Water Environ. Fedn. (bd. dirs. 1981-84, Morgan cert. of merit for full scale rsch. 1982, Bedell award 1983, svc. award 1984, Gordon M. Fair medal for excellence in engring. edn. 1998), Internat. Water Assn. (governing bd. 1986-88, USA rep. on sci. and tech. com. 1994-98, mem. nutrient removal specialist group mgmt. com. 1990-2002, chmn. 1994-98), Va. Water Environment Assn. (v.p. 1974-75, pres. 1975-76), Assn. Environ. Engring. Profs. (sec.-treas. 1979-80, bd. dirs. 1978-80, 93-97, v.p. 1994-95, pres. 1995-96, past pres. 1996-97). Home: 1302 Crestview Dr Blacksburg VA 24060-5609 Office: Va Poly Inst & State U Dept Civil Engring 330 Norris Hall Blacksburg VA 24061 Office Phone: 540-231-6018. Business E-Mail: cliff@vt.edu.

**RANDALL, DAVID JOHN,** physiologist, zoologist, educator; b. London, Eng., Sept. 15, 1938; arrived in Hong Kong 2000; BSc, U. Southampton, 1960, PhD, 1963, FRSC, 1981. From asst. to assoc. prof. U. B.C., 1963-73, prof. zoology, 1973—2006, assoc. dean grad. studies, 1990-96, 2000; head biology and chemistry U. Hong Kong, 2000—05; univ. grants coun. mem. Hong Kong Govt. Spl. Adminstrv. Region, 2003; ret., 2006. Vis. lectr. Bristol U., 1968-69; vis. sci. Marine Labs U. Tex., 1970, Zool. Sta., Naples, Italy, 1973; NATO vis. sci. Acadia U., 1975, Marine Lab U. Tex., 1977; chief sci. Alpha Helix Amazon Expedition, 1976; mem. adv. bd. J. Comp Physiology, 1977-92, J. Exp. Biol., 1981-84; chmn. animal biol. comt.

Nat. Res. Coun., Can., 1974; vis. prof. U. Nairobi, 1988, George Washington U., 1988-89, City U. Hong Kong, 1997; concurrent prof. Nanjing U., China, 1993—; external examiner U. Singapore, 1990-91, 2000-02; mem. UGC, Hong Kong, 2001-03. Assoc. editor: Marine Behavior Physiology. Recipient Award of Excellence Am. Fisheries Soc., 1994. Fellow Royal Soc. Can.; mem. Can. Soc. Zoologists (Fry medal 1993), Soc. Exp. Biologists.

**RANDALL, DOUGLAS D.,** biochemist, educator; b. Cheyenne, Wyo. BS, SD State U., 1965; PhD, Mich. State U., 1970. With U. Mo.-Columbia, 1971—, prof. emeritus biochemistry, dir. interdisciplinary program on plant biochemistry-physiology. Past officer, chair bd. trustees Am. Soc. Plant Biologists; bd. dirs. Nat. Sci. Bd., 2002—; mem. Great Barrier Reef Photorespiration Expdn. Nat. Sci. Found., 1973. Mem. editl. bd. Plant Physiology, Annual Reviews Plant Physiology and Plant Molecular Biology, Protein Expression and Purification, Biochemical Archives, Current Topics in Plant Biochemistry and Physiology; contbr. articles to profl. jours. Mem.: Am. Chemical Soc., Am. Soc. Biol. Chemistry. Achievements include research in plant metabolism, signal transduction, regulation of plant enzymes and understanding the metabolic interations between photosynthesis, photorespiration and respiration. Office: U Mo Columbia Biochemistry Dept 117 Schweitzer Hall Office 213 Columbia MO 65211 Office Phone: 573-882-4847. Office Fax: 573-882-5635. Business E-Mail: randalld@missouri.edu.*

**RANDALL, FRANCES,** technical writer; b. Frederick, Md., Oct. 6, 1924; d. George Birely and Ruth Carty Delaplaine; m. Myron William Randall, Apr. 10, 1949; children: George Elliott, Myron William Jr., Ruth Ann Randall, Eleanor Jane Randall Luttrell. BA, Hood Coll., 1945; MS, Johns Hopkins U., 1947; DHL (hon.), Hood Coll., 2006. Chemist U.S. Army Lab., Frederick, Md., 1947—49; writer-historian Frederick News-Post, 1965—. Chmn. bd. dirs. The Randall Family LLC, 2001—. Author: Mirror on Frederick, 1998, More Reflections on the History of Frederick, 2005 Bd. dir. Cmty. Found. Frederick County, 1988-96, Braddock Hts. Cmty. Assn., Penn Laurel coun. Girl Scouts U.S. Recipient Cmty. Svc. award, Ch. Transfiguration, Braddock Heights, Md., 1999, Thanks Badge, Penn Laurel Girl Scout Coun., 1988, Alumnae Achievement award Hood Coll., 1998, Woman of Distinction award Penn Laurel coun. Girl Scouts U.S.A., 2000, Families Plus! Cmty. Svc. award, 2004. Mem. DAR (Woman of Yr. in History, 2005), Hood Coll. Alumnae Assn. (pres., sec.), Frederick Woman's Civic Club (publicity chair, pres.), Hist Soc. Frederick County (bd. dir. 2005-) Avocations: swimming, biking, photography, travel, music. Home: 6301 Jefferson Blvd Frederick MD 21703-5809

**RANDALL, FRANCIS BALLARD,** retired historian, educator, writer; b. NYC, Dec. 17, 1931; s. John Herman, Jr. and Mercedes (Moritz) R.; m. Laura Regina Rosenbaum, June 11, 1957; children: David R., Ariane R. BA, Amherst Coll., 1952; MA, Columbia, 1954, PhD, 1960. Instr. history Amherst Coll., 1956-59; from instr. to asst. prof. history Columbia, 1959-61, vis. prof., 1967-68; humanities faculty Sarah Lawrence Coll., Bronxville, NY, 1961—2002, chmn., 1985—89, 1998—2001, trustee, 1971-76. Author: (with others) Essays in Russian and Soviet History, 1963, Stalin's Russia, an Historical Reconsideration, 1965, N.G. Chernyshevskii, 1967, Vissarion Belinskii, 1987, History Papers: A Teaching Life, 2000. Freedom rider civil disobedience to racism, 1961, war draft resistance arrests, 1967, 70. Fulbright fellow for study in India, 1965, Wye fellow, 1986. Mem.: AAUP (chpt. chmn. 1966—69), Am. Assn. for Advancement Slavic Studies, Am. Hist. Assn., Sigma Xi, Phi Beta Kappa. Home: 425 Riverside Dr Apt 10I New York NY 10025-7730

**RANDALL, JESSY,** curator, writer; b. Hornell, NY, Dec. 25, 1969; d. Katherine Cronk Randall; m. Ross Gresham, May 27, 2000; children: William Randall Gresham, Celia Randall Gresham. AB, Columbia U., 1992; MLS, U. NC-Chapel Hill, 1994. Rare book cataloger Glenn Horowitz, Bookseller, Inc., N.Y.C., 1994—96; reference libr. and curator women's studies collection Libr. Co. Phila., 1996—2000; curator spl. collections Colo. Coll., Colo. Springs, 2001—. Co-author: Slumber Party at the Aquarium, 2004, Because Mona is in the Psychiatric Hospital, 2005; occasional guest editor: online poetry jour. Snakeskin, 2001—06. Office: Special Collections Colorado Coll 1021 North Cascade Ave Colorado Springs CO 80903 Office Phone: 719-389-6668. Business E-Mail: jrandall@coloradocollege.edu.

**RANDALL, KAREN W.,** film company executive; BA cum laude, Vassar Coll., 1973; JD, UCLA, 1976. Ptnr. Wyman Bautzer Kuchel & Silbert, 1976; mng. ptnr. Katten Muchin & Zavi, LA; sr. v.p., gen. counsel Universal Studios, 1996—2000; exec. v.p., gen. counsel Vivendi Universal Entertainment, Universal City, Calif., 2000—. Bd. mem. United Internat. Pictures, Hollywood Sign Trust, Hollywood Canteen Found. Named to, YWCA Acad. Women Achievers, The Am. Lawyer's 1995 edit. of "Forty-Five Under 45"; recipient Women of Distinction award, Hollywood C. of C., Pursuit of Justice award, Calif. Women's Law Ctr., Corp. Leadership award, Big Sisters L.A. Mem.: Motion Picture Assn. Am. (Universal's liaison, bd. dirs., mem. spl. policy group), Am. Corp. Counsel Assn. (nat. bd. dirs.). Office: Vivendi Universal Entertainment 100 Universal City Plaza Universal City CA 91608-1002

**RANDALL, KARL W.,** air transportation executive, lawyer; b. Mount Pleasant, Mich., Feb. 12, 1951; s. Herbert J. and Wilma E. (Worstell) R.; m. Natalie Kilmer Randall, Dec. 17, 1971; children: Adam B., Kara J. AA, Mich. Christian Coll., Rochester, 1971; BA, Oakland U., Rochester, 1977; JD, Wayne State U. Law Sch., Detroit, 1981. Bar: Mich., 1981, U.S. Dist. Ct., 1981, U.S. Ct. Appeals, 1983; cert. airport mgr., Mich., 1993. Quality contr. Staley SNO BOL Corp., Pontiac, Mich., 1971-72; engring. tech. Oakland Co. Drain Comm., Pontiac, 1972-83; sr. asst. corp. counsel Oakland County Corp. Counsel, Pontiac, 1983-93; mgr. aviation Oakland County Internat. Airport, Waterford, Mich., 1993—. Dir. Integrity Jour., Mt. Pleasant, 1980-98, Oakland County Coord. Child Care Coun., Waterford, 1992-97. Author, editor: (religious jour.) Integrity, 1982, 94-95. Mem. Rep. Com. Oakland County, 1988—, Exec. Club Oakland County, 1993—. Mem. Mich. Assn. Airport Execs. (exec., pres., 2005—), Langsford Men's Chorus. Republican. Mem. Ch. of Christ. Avocations: physical fitness, motorcycling, jogging, golf, piano. Office: Oakland County Internat Airport 6500 Highland Rd Waterford MI 48327-1607 Office Phone: 248-666-3900. E-mail: randallk@co.oakland.mi.us.

**RANDALL, KAY TEMPLE,** accountant, retired real estate agent; b. Chattanooga, Sept. 23, 1952; d. James H. Temple and Hortense N. (Dailey) Goodner; m. Gary F. Goodner, Feb. 9, 1968 (div. July 1972); 1 child, Jeffrey F. Goodner; m. Rodney B. Randall, Oct. 3, 1987. Student, Chattanooga State Coll., 1970-77, 82-83, Am. Inst. Banking, 1977-79. Lic. real estate agt., Tenn. ret.; notary public, Tenn. Ins. rep. Colonial Life Accident and Health, Columbia, SC, 1980-82; real estate appraiser, agt. Chattanooga, 1983-88; acct. Mr. Transmission of Chattanooga, Inc., 1987—; real estate agt. Chattanooga, 1989—. Adminstry. asst. to legal profession, Chattanooga, 1972-75. Adv. bd. United Meth. Ch., Chattanooga, 1979-82, tchr., 1979-83; fellow coun. br. YMCA, Chattanooga, 1977-97. Fellow Walden's Club. Republican. Episcopalian. Avocation: collecting art. Home: 1858 Rivergate Ter Soddy Daisy TN 37379-5947 Office: Mr Transmission of Chattanooga Inc PO Box 1395 Soddy Daisy TN 37384-1395 E-mail: rodkayj@aol.com.

**RANDALL, KENNETH C.,** dean, law educator; JD, Hofstra U., 1981; MA, Yale U., 1982, Columbia U., 1989, PhD, 1988. Practice law Simpson Thacher & Bartlett, N.Y.C., 1982-84; with faculty U. Ala. Sch. Law, Tuscaloosa, 1985—, vice dean, 1989-93, dean, 1993—. Author-book on international law; contbr. articles to law jours. and revs. W. Bayard Cutting Jr. fellow of internat. law Columbia U. Sch. Law, 1984-85. Office: U Ala Law Sch PO Box 870382 Tuscaloosa AL 35487-0001 Office Phone: 205-348-5117. E-mail: kcrandal@law.ua.edu.

**RANDALL, LILIAN MARIA CHARLOTTE,** museum curator; b. Berlin, Feb. 1, 1931; came to U.S., 1938; d. Frederick Henry and Elizabeth Agnes (Ziegler) Cramer; m. Richard Harding Randall, Apr. 11, 1953; children: Christopher, Julia, Katharine. BA cum laude, Mount Holyoke Coll., 1950; MA, Radcliffe Coll., 1951, PhD, 1955; LHD (hon.), Towson State U., 1993; D of Arts (hon.), Mt. Holyoke Coll., 1998. Asst. dir. Md. State Arts Coun., 1972-73; curator manuscripts and rare books Walters Art Gallery, Balt., 1974-85, rsch. curator manuscripts, 1985-95; rsch. cons., 1995-97. Vis. lectr. dept. art history Johns Hopkins U., 1964-68; hon. vis. lectr. U. Mich., Ann Arbor; lectr. in field; bd. dirs. Digital Scriptorium: Electronic Access to Medieval Manuscripts; advisor Union Manuscript Computer Catalogue, 1996—. Author: Images in the Margins of Gothic Manuscripts, 1966; co-editor: Gatherings in Honor of Dorothy Miner, 1974, The Diary of George A. Lucas: An American Art Agent in Paris, 1909-1957, 1979, Illuminated Manuscripts: Masterpieces in Miniature, 1984, Medieval and Renaissance Manuscripts in the Walters Art Gallery, Vol. I, France, 875-1420, 1989, Vol. II, France, 1420-1540, 1992, Vol. III, Belgium, 1250-1530, 1997; contbr. articles to profl. jours. Mem. Williston Libr. com., 1988-89; reviewer, panelist NEH, 1980. Grantee AAUW, 1953-54, ACLS, 1960, 65, Bunting Inst., 1961-63, Ford Found., 1967-68, Am. Philos. Soc., 1971, NEA, 1975, Samuel H. Kress Found., 1979, 81-84, NEH, 1977-84, 89-95; grantee publ. subsidy Md. State Arts Coun., 1972, Mcpl. Art Soc. Balt., 1972, Andrew W. Mellon Found., 1988, Getty Grant program, 1990-92, NEA Mus. program, 1992-93; recipient Festschrift, Walters Art Gallery, ed. Elizabeth Burin, 1996, Sesquicentennial award Mount Holyoke Coll., 1987. Fellow Medieval Acad. Am. (libr. preservation com., various coms. 1985-87, 90-93, 2004—); mem. Internat. Ctr. Medieval Art (bd. dir. 1978-82, 96-99, mem. com. 2004—), Coll. Art Assn. (Arthur Kingsley Porter prize 1957), Balt. Bibliophiles (bd. dir. 1966-80, pres. 1980-83), Pyramid Atlantic (bd. dir. 1985-88), Mus. Fine Arts Boston (vis. com. Art of Europe dept. 2002-2006, adv. bd. Manuscripta 2004—), Grolier Club, Phi Beta Kappa. Home: 370 Adams St Milton MA 02186-4233 Personal E-mail: lmcrand@ix.netcom.com.

**RANDALL, LINDA LEA,** biochemist, educator; b. Montclair, N.J., Aug. 7, 1946; d. Lowell Neal and Helen (Watts) Randall; m. Gerald Lee Hazelbauer, Aug. 29, 1970. BS, Colo. State U., 1968; PhD, U. Wis., 1971. Postdoctoral fellow Inst. Pasteur, Paris, 1971—73; asst. prof. Uppsala (Sweden) U., 1975—81; assoc. prof. Wash. State U., Pullman, 1981—83, prof. biochemistry, 1983—2000; Wurdock prof. biochemistry U. Mo., Columbia, 2000—. Guest scientist Wallenberg Lab. Uppsala U., 1973—75; mem. study sect. NIH, 1984—88. Contbr. articles to profl. jours.; co-editor: (book) Virus Receptors Part I, 1980; mem. editl. bd.: Jour. Bacteriology, 1982—96. Recipient Eli Lilly award in Microbiology and Immunology, 1984, Faculty Excellence Award in Rsch., Wash. State U., 1988, Parke-Davis award, 1995. Fellow: AAAS, Am. Acad. Arts and Scis., Am. Acad. Microbiology; mem.: NAS, Protein Soc., Am. Soc. Biol. Chemists, Am. Microbiological Soc. Avocation: dance. Office: Univ Mo Dept Biochemistry 117 Schweitzer Hall Columbia MO 65211 Office Phone: 573-884-4160.

**RANDALL, LISA,** physics professor; BA in Physics, Harvard U., 1983, PhD in Particle Physics, 1987. Rschr. Smithsonian Astrophysical Observatory, 1981, IBM, 1982, Bell Labs, 1983; teaching asst. physics Harvard U., 1984; physics tutor Adams House, 1984—87; president's fellow U. Calif., Berkeley, 1987—87; postdoctoral fellow Lawrence Berkeley Lab., 1989—90; junior fellow Harvard Soc. of Fellows, 1990—91; asst. prof. physics MIT, 1991—95, assoc. prof. physics, 1995—98; prof. physics Princeton U., 1998—2000, MIT, 1998—2001, Harvard U., 2001—; fellow Radcliffe Inst. Fellow, 2002; chair Radcliffe Inst. Cosmology & Theoretical Astrophysics Cluster, 2003. Assoc. editor Nuclear Physics, 1999—; editor Annual Review of Nuclear & Particle Sci., 1997—; Jour. of High Energy Physics, 1997—98, 2000—. Author: Warped Passages: Unraveling the Mysteries of the Univers's Hidden Dimensions, 2005. Recipient Young Investigator award, NSF, 1992, Premio Caterina Tomassoni e Felice Pietro Chisesi award, U. Rome, 2003; grantee Alfred P. Sloan Found. Rsch. Fellowship, 1992, Bell Labs Graduate Rsch. Fellowship for Women. Fellow: AAAS, Am. Acad. Arts & Sciences. Office: Harvard U Physics Dept 17 Oxford St Cambridge MA 02138*

**RANDALL, LYNN ELLEN,** librarian; b. Chgo., Oct. 10, 1951; d. Ward W. and Hazel A. R. BA, King's Coll., 1970; MA, Seton Hall U., 1973; MLS, Rutgers U., 1978. Libr. asst. Newark Coll. Engring, Newark, 1970-75; libr. dir. N.E. Bible Coll., Essex Fells, N.J., 1975-81; reference libr. Seton Hall U., South Orange, N.J., 1983-85; dir. libr. svc. Berkeley Coll., NJ, 1985-89; with Caldwell Coll., NJ 1989—2006, exec. dir. libr. svcs.; dir. human resources Am.'s Keswick, Whiting, NJ, 2006—. Reference libr., instr. Morris (N.J.) County Coll., 1981-83; panelist/facilitator Middle States Self-Study Inst., 1996, 97, 2004. 05; Evaluator, Middle States, 1994-. Mem. N.J. Libr. Assn. (pres. 1996-97), Am. Libr. Assn. Office: America's Keswick 601 Route 530 Whiting NJ 08759 Office Phone: 973-618-3304. E-mail: lrandall@caldwell.edu.

**RANDALL, MARILYN MAE,** writer; d. Dice A. and Margaret L. Hartman; m. Charles D. Randall, Aug. 24, 1991; children: Philip E. Marechal, Cheryl L. Pitman. BA magna cum laude, Trinity Coll., Washington, 1988. Registrar Va. Theol. Sem., 1974—87; bus. mgr. St. Margaret's Episcopal Ch., 1987—89; bus. owner, 1989—95. Vis. author/lectr. various elem. and mid. schs., Tenn., 2002—; featured lectr./workshop presenter Christian Writers' Conf., Memphis, 2002, Ea. Tenn. State U. Celebration Books and Authors, 2004; featured local author Fall for the Book George Mason U., 2004; workshop presenter; contest judge Life Press, 2006. Author: (children's books) Southern Christmas, 2001, Wishes for Christmas, 2002, Wellington's Windows, 2003, The Three Wives of Hero the Second, 2004, The Meanie, 2006, A Marine Salute (endorsed by USMC and Young Marine Orgn.); editor: The Forty Days of Lent; composer, lyricist: Angel with an Attitude, 2004. Pres. Good Samaritan chpt. Daus. of the King, Knoxville, 1998—2004. Mem.: Alpha Sigma Lambda, Phi Beta Kappa. Episcopalian. Avocations: composing, poetry. Home: 1550 Scenic View Dr Loudon TN 37774 Personal E-mail: mmrcdr@bellsouth.net.

**RANDALL, NEIL WARREN,** gastroenterologist; b. White Plains, N.Y., Mar. 24, 1957; s. Leroy Bruce and Libby Cynthia (Brandt) R.; m. Linda Ilene Zell, Oct. 31, 1992. BA, U. Va., 1978; MD, U. Md., 1983. Diplomate Am. Bd. Internal Medicine with subspecialty in gastroenterology, geriat. Resident in internal medicine Ochsner Clinic, New Orleans, 1983-86; fellow in gastroenterology Tufts U., Boston, 1986-88; staff gastroenterologist Cleve. Clinic Fla., Fort Lauderdale, 1988-92, Geisinger Clinic, Danville, Pa., 1992-97, Pa. State Geisinger Health Sys., Danville, 1997-98; med. dir. gastrointestinal endoscopy Geisinger Health Sys., 1999-2000; gastroenterologist Gastroenterology Group of Naples, 2001—. Fellow ACP, Am. Coll. Gastroenterology; mem. Am. Soc for Gastroent. Endoscopy. Avocations: theater, travel, wine. Office: Gasterenterology Group of Naples 1064 Goodlette-Frank Rd Naples FL 34102-5449 Office Phone: 239-649-1186.

**RANDALL, PETER,** retired plastic surgeon; b. Phila., Mar. 29, 1923; s. Alexander and Edith Tilghman (Kneedler) R.; m. Rose Gordon Johnson, May 1, 1948; children: Deborah K., Peter G., Julia B., Susanna T. BA, Princeton U., 1944; MD, Johns Hopkins U. 1946; MS (hon.), U. Pa., 1969. Diplomate Am. Bd. Plastic Surgery. Intern Union Meml. Hosp., Balt., 1946—47; asst. resident in surgery Hosp. of U. of Pa., Phila., 1949—50; fellow in plastic surgery Barnes Hosp.-St. Louis Childrens Hosp., 1950—52, resident in plastic surgery, 1952—53; asst. instr. plastic surgery Washington U., St. Louis, 1950—53; from asst. prof. to assoc. prof. plastic surgery U. Pa. Hosp., Phila., 1953—69, prof. plastic surgery, 1969—92, emeritus prof. plastic surgery, 1992—; chief div. plastic surgery sch. medicine U. Pa., Phila., 1979—87; ret., 1994. Sr. surgeon Children's Hosp. Phila., 1965—. Contbr. articles to profl. jours. Pres. Plastic Surgery Edn. Found., 1972-73. Lt. (j.g.) USNR, 1947-49. Fellow: ACS (bd. govs., chmn. 1982—84), 1st v.p. 1985—86), Am. Assn. Plastic Surgeons (hon. Clinician of Yr. award 1987, disting fellow 1994); mem.: AMA, Am. Cleft Palate Assn. (Pres. 1965—66, Honors award 1986), Plastic Surgery Rsch. Coun. (founder, chmn. 1964—65), Phila. Acad. Surgery, Phila. County Med. Soc., Northea. Soc.

Plastic Surgery (founder), Am. Surg. Assn., Coll. Physicians of Phila., Am. Soc. Plastic Surgeons (pres. 1978—79, Spl. Achievement award 1987), Am. Bd. Plastic Surgery (vice-chmn. 1976—77), Am. Cleft Palate Ednl. Found. (founder, pres. 1972—73), Robert H. Ivy Soc. (founder, pres. 1966—67), Halsted Soc., others, Sigma Xi.

**RANDALL, RICHARD J.,** academic administrator; BA, U. Maine, 1966, MA, 1967, LLD, 2004. Instr. sociology U. Maine at Augusta, 1967, asst. prof., assoc. prof., prof., dir. student affairs, 1968—71, dean student affairs and ednl. svcs., 1971—78, acting dean, 1984—85, dean, 1985—87, provost, 1989—93, provost, v.p. academic affairs, 1993—2001, interim assoc. provost, 2005, interim pres., 2005—06, pres., 2006—. Office: U Maine at Augusta Off of Pres 46 University Dr Augusta ME 04330-9410 Office Phone: 207-621-3403. Office Fax: 207-621-3496. E-mail: rrandall@maine.edu.*

**RANDALL, RICHARD RAINIER,** geographer; b. Toledo, July 21, 1925; s. Robert Henry and Maree (Gard) R.; m. Patricia Lee Spencer, June 9, 1962; children: Allison Maree, Susan Rebecca, Richard Rainier Jr. BA, George Washington U., 1949, MA, 1950; PhD, Clark U., 1955. Fulbright scholar Graz U., Austria, 1953—54; Geog. analyst CIA, Washington, 1955-61; Washington rep. Rand McNally & Co., Washington, 1961-72; owner Randall Assocs., Washington, 1972-73; exec. sec. U.S. Bd. Geog. Names, Washington, 1973-93; geographer Def. Mapping Agy., Washington, 1973-93; ret., 1993; cons. on geog. names, 1993—. Convenor UN Working Group on Undersea and Maritime Feature Names, 1975-84; mem., prin. U.S. tech. advisor U.S. and U.K. Conf. on Geog. Names, 1976, 79, 81, 84, 86, 88, 92; dep. head U.S. del. UN Conf. on Geog. Names, 1977, head, 1982, 87, 92; 1st v.p. of 6th UN Conf. 92; prin. U.S. expert UN Group Experts on Geog. Names, 1975, 77, 79, 82, 84, 86, 87, 89, 92; pres. com. on geog. terminology Pan Am. Inst. Geography and History, 1973-77, pres. working group on geog. names and gazetters, 1981-94. Author: Place Names: How they Define the World—And More, 2001; contbr. articles to profl. jours.; inventor flexible fishhook V.p. North Cleveland Park Citizens Assn., Washington, 1968. With U.S. Army, 1943-46, ETO. Decorated ETO ribbon with 4 battle stars, Bronze Star, Combat Infantryman's badge, others. Mem. Am. Congress on Surveying and Mapping (dir. cartography divsn. 1973-75, dir. press rels. 1961-72, program dir. cartography divsn. ann. meeting 1967), Am. Geog. Soc., Assn. Am. Geographers (chmn. Mid-Atlantic divsn. 1978, dir. press rels. ann. conf. 1968), Am. Names Soc., Am. Austrian Soc. (v.p. 1955-57), Explorers Club (Washington group steering com.), Cosmos Club. Republican.

**RANDALL, ROBERT L(EE),** ecological economist; b. Aberdeen, SD, Dec. 28, 1936; s. Harry Eugene and Juanita Alice (Barstow) Randall. MS in Phys. Chemistry, U. Chgo., 1960, MBA, 1963. Market devel. chemist E.I. du Pont de Nemours & Co., Inc., Wilmington, Del., 1963-65; chem. economist Battelle Meml. Inst., Columbus, Ohio, 1965-68; mgr. market and econ. rsch. Kennecott Copper Corp., N.Y.C., 1968-74, economist, 1974-79, dir. new bus. venture devel., 1979-81; pres., mng. dir. R.L. Randall Assocs., Inc., 1981—; economist U.S. Internat. Trade Commn., Washington, 1983—. Founder, pres., exec. dir. RainForest ReGeneration Inst., 1986—, ind. internat. press corr., 1997—, indsl. panel policy rev. of effect of regulation on innovation and U.S.-internat. competition U.S. Dept. Commerce, 1980-81; participant preparatory com. UN Conf. on Environ. and Devel., Rio de Janeiro, 1991; del. observer internat. negotiating com. UN Framework Conv. on Climate Change, 1991—. Contbg. author: Computer Methods for the 80's; sect. lead author, editor: World Energy Assessment, 2000; pub. reviewer intergovtl. panel on climate change Third Assessment Report; addresser 4th Internat. Greenhouse Gas Tech. conf., Interlaken, Switzerland, 1998; contbr. articles to profl. jours. Mem. Gay Activists Alliance, N.Y.C., 1971-75, chmn. state and fed. legislation com., 1975. Mem. AAAS (organizer ann. meeting, Tropical Forest Regeneration Symposium), AIME (econ. coun., mineral econ. subsect.), Internat. Soc. Ecol. Health, Internat. Soc. Ecol. Economists, Am. Econ. Assn., Am. Statis. Assn., Am. Chem. Soc., Soc. Mining Engrs., Chemists Club of N.Y.C., Metall. Soc., N.Y. Acad. Scis., Nat. Econs. Club Washington (sec., reporter), Assn. Environ. and Resource Economists, Marine Biol. Assn. (Plymouth, Eng.), Wanderbirds Hiking Club (hike leader, treas.), Capital Hiking Club (hike leader, Washington). Home: 1727 Massachusetts Ave NW Washington DC 20036-2153 Office: US Internat Trade Com 500 E St SW Washington DC 20436-0003 E-mail: randall@usitc.gov. *Like thousands of organizations around the world, The RainForest ReGeneration Institute is trying to find a practical and effective way forward, through United Nations-sponsored treaty negotiations, appropriate national actions, and imaginative project work, on the ground, in local communities. Tropical rainforests must have recognizable community value if they are to be viable. Global value is not enough for the conservation of the tropical rainforests. Ultimate wisdom does not reside in any individual or organization. All must work together through every available forum and mechanism, and to create new modalities where those presently in existence are inadequate or ineffective.*

**RANDALL, ROGER DAVID,** publishing executive; b. St. Charles, Minn., Dec. 24, 1953; s. Curtis Clark and Virginia Mae (Tollefson) Randall; m. Mary Barnard, Aug. 25, 1979; children: Sara Louise, Clark Robinson. BA, Morningside Coll., 1976. Advt. dir. Nutra-Flo Chem. Co., Kay Dee Feed Co., Sioux City, Iowa, 1976-78; agrl. account svc. Lewis & Gilman, Phila., 1978-80, Creswell, Munsell, Fultz & Zirbel, Cedar Rapids, Iowa, 1980-81, Richardson, Myers & Donofrio, Inc., Balt., 1981-84; mktg. mgr. Farm Jour., Inc., Phila., 1984-85, v.p., 1986-89, v.p., pub., 1989-95, pres., 1995-99, CEO, 1999-2000, also bd. dirs.; pres., CEO AgWeb.com, 1999-2001; exec. v.p. Miller Meester, Inc., 2001—03. Mem. bus. adv. com. Nat. Assn. Conser. Dist. Bd. dirs. Planned Parenthood Sioux City, 1977-78, Iowa Planned Parenthood Fedn., 1978, Sioux City Pub. Mus., 1977-78; trustee Old 1st Reformed Ch., 1994-95. Recipient Disting. Alumni award, Morningside Coll., 1997. Mem. Nat. Agri-Mktg. Assn. (pres. Chesapeake chpt. 1984, nat. awards agri. excellence 1988, exec. com. 1990-92, sec.-treas. 1992-93), Queen Village Neighbors Assn. (dir., treas. 1987-90, pres. 1994-95), Preservation Alliance of Minn. (dir., vice chair, commn. com. co-chair, chair 2005) Mem. United Ch. Of Christ. Home: 4270 Norwood Ln N Minneapolis MN 55442 E-mail: rrandall112953@msn.com

**RANDALL, SUSAN,** education educator; b. Gastonia, NC, Oct. 24, 1965; m. Robert Randall, June 9, 1962; children: Robert Alexander, Thomas Micah, John Houston Lattimore, Thomas Micah. AS, Cleve. Cmty. Coll., Shelby, NC, 1991; BS, Gardner-Webb Coll., Boiling Springs, NC, 1988. Adminstr. Greg Randall Custom Woodworking, LLC, Kings Mountain, NC, 1996—; adj. faculty Cleve. Cmty. Coll., Shelby, NC, 2001. Youth adv. coun. Christ Covenant Ch., Shelby, NC, 2006. Office: Greg Randall Custom Woodworking LLC 905 Stoney Point Rd Kings Mountain NC 28086 Office Phone: 704-484-2033. Home Fax: 704-484-2026; Office Fax: 704-484-2026. Personal E-mail: randalls@cleveland.cc.nc.us. E-mail: info@grcw.com

**RANDALL, WILLIAM SEYMOUR,** leasing company executive; b. Champaign, Ill., July 5, 1933; s. Glenn S. and Audrey H. (Honnold) R.; m. Sharon Larsen; children: Steve, Cathy, Mike, Jennifer. BS, Ind. State U., 1959. Controller Amana Refrigeration Co., Iowa, 1966-70; div. controller Trane Co., Clarksville, Tenn., 1970-74, corporate controller La Crosse, Wis., 1974-79; v.p., chief fin. officer Sta-Rite Industries, Milw., 1979-82; owner Profl. Staff Resources, Inc., Milw., 1982—. Served with AUS, 1953-55. Mem. Financial Execs. Inst. Republican. Home: 13365 Tulane St Brookfield WI 53005-7141 Office: 14430 W Bluemound Rd Ste 103 Milwaukee WI 53226 Office Phone: 414-778-5100. E-mail: wmrandall@msn.com.

**RANDAZZO, GARY WAYNE,** newspaper executive; b. Georgetown, Tex., Sept. 23, 1947; s. Frank Birchmans and Edna Earle (Forbis) R.; m. Joyce Sue McNorton, Oct. 7, 1966; children: Gary Wayne Jr., Vanessa Rene, Michael Jason, Daniel Paul. BBA, U. Tex., 1974; MBA, Tex. A&I U., 1976. Instr. Del Mar Coll., Corpus Christi, 1974—76; bus. mgr. Corpus Christi Caller-Times, 1976—81; pres., pub. Huntsville Item, Tex., 1981—83; pres. Am. Property Data, Houston, 1984—87; gen. mgr. Health Care News, Houston, 1987—89;

sr. v.p. sales and mktg. Houston Chronicle, 1989—2002; exec. v.p., gen. mgr. San Francisco Chronicle, 2002—05; pres. G.W. News Corp., 2005—. Chmn., bd. dirs. Leadership Houston; bd. dirs. Downtown Houston Assn., treas.; bd. dirs. Better Bus. Bur.; chmn. Big Bros./Big Sisters; mem. adv. coun. San Francisco Unified Sch. Dist. Mem. Kiwanis (bd. dirs.). Home: 8306 Glenn Elm Dr Spring TX 77379 Office Phone: 832-717-0604. Business E-Mail: garyrandazzo@sbcglobal.net.

**RANDAZZO, MARISA REDDY,** psychologist; d. Hilary Phillip and Susan Hilborn Reddy; m. Robert Salvatore Randazzo, May 15, 2004. BA in Psychology and Religion, Williams Coll., 1989; MA in Psychology, PhD in Psychology, Princeton U., 1995. Chief rsch. psychologist US Secret Svc., Washington, 1996—2004; sr. expert Bus. Intelligence Advisors, Boston, 2004—06; pres. Threat Assessment Resources Internat., Boston, 2006—. Editl. bd. Jour. Threat Assessment, 2001—. Recipient Bicentennial Medal Recipient, Williams Coll., 2005; fellow, Soc. Psychol. Study Social Issues, Washington, 1995—96. Mem.: APA, Am. Psychology-Law Soc. (program chair 1998—2000). Achievements include research in American school shooters; preventing violence in schools. Office Phone: 775-424-6685. Personal E-Mail: marisa_randazzo@yahoo.com.

**RANDEL, DON MICHAEL,** foundation administrator, former academic administrator, musicologist; m. Carol Randel; children: Amy Elizabeth Keating, Julia, Emily Catherine Pershing, Sally Randel Eggert. AB magna cum laude, Princeton U., 1962, MFA in Music, 1964, PhD in Music, 1967. Asst. prof., dept. fine arts Syracuse U., 1966—68; asst. prof. music Cornell U., Ithaca, NY, 1968—71, assoc. prof. music, 1971—75, chair dept. music, 1971—76, prof. music, 1975—2000, vice provost, 1978—79, assoc. dean Coll. Arts and Scis., 1989—91, Given Found. prof. musicology, 1990—2000, Harold Tanner dean Coll. Arts and Scis., 1991—95, provost, 1995—2000; pres. U. Chgo., 2000—06, Andrew W. Mellon Found., NYC, 2006—. V.p. Am. Musicological Soc., 1977—78; mem. adv. com. dept. music Princeton U., 1987—99; mem. Penn Nat. Commn. Soc., Culture and Cmty., 1996—99; bd. govenors Argonne Nat. Lab., 2000—; bd. trustees Chgo. Symphony Orch. Assn., 2001—06; bd. dirs. Chgo. Coun. Fgn. Relations, 2001, CNA Fin. Corp., 2002—; bd. mem. Lyric Opera Chgo., 2004—06. Editor: New Harvard Dictionary of Music, 1986, Harvard Biographical Dictionary of Music, 1996, Harvard Concise Dictionary of Music and Musicians, 1999, The Harvard Dictionary of Music, 2003; mem. editl. bd. advisors Ency. Britannica, editor-in-chief Jour. Am. Musicological Soc., 1972—74. Bd. mem. Internet2, 2004—. Recipient Fulbright award; Hon. Woodrow Wilson fellow, Danforth Grad. fellow, 1962—66. Fellow: Am. Acad. Arts and Scis.; mem.: Am. Assn. Advancement Sci., Modern Language Assn., Am. Musicological Soc., Am. Philos. Soc. Office: Andrew W Mellon Found 140 E 62nd St New York NY 10021

**RANDELL, CORTES W.,** news service executive; b. Washington, 1935; m. Joan. V. (Wirz) 1968; children: Cortes John, Christina Alexis. BSME, U. Va., 1959; student, Darden Sch., U. Va., 1962. Engr. Gen. Electric, N.Y., 1959-61, Internat. Telephone & Telegraph, Chgo., 1962-64; pres. Nat. Student Mktg., N.Y., 1964-71; cons. and trustee Washington Trust, 1972-84; pres. Federal News Svc., Washington, 1985—2002; mcht. banker, 2002—. Author: Taking the Stand, Testimony of Oliver North, 1987, The National Press Club's Best Contemporary Speakers, 1995. Mem. Nat. Press Club, Yale Club. Avocations: ballooning, boating. Office: 9017 Swift Creek Rd Fairfax Station VA 22039-2815 Office Phone: 703-685-4828. E-mail: cort.randell@cox.net.

**RANDELS, DAVID GEORGE,** retired secondary school educator; b. Bryan, Ohio, Feb. 6, 1943; s. George D. and Doris L. Randels; 1 child, Kellie R. BS in Edn., Bowling Green State U., 1965, MusM, 1971. Instr., counselor Culver (Ind.) Mil. Acad., 1962-67; instr. music Port Clinton (Ohio) City Schs., 1965—2004; ret., 2004. Tchr., drummer various jazz bands, 1960—; drummer Jamie Wight New Orleans Joymakers, 1980—. Musician (drummer): (albums) 6 recordings. Named Outstanding Bandsman, Bowling Green State U., 1965; recipient John Phillips Sousa Band award, Bryan HS, 1961, Dist. Svc. award, Ottawa County, Ohio, 2004, Mayor's Svc. award, Port Clinton, Ohio, 2004. Mem.: Music Educators Nat. Conf., Port Clinton Fedn. Tchrs. (Lifetime Achievement award 1984), U.S. Capital Hist. Soc., Nat. Sch. Orch. Assn. (Disting. Svc. award 1994), Port Clinton Model R.R. Club (pres. 1965), Elks, Phi Kappa Psi, Phi Delta Kappa, Kappa Kappa Psi. Democrat. Avocations: model railroading, music, antique cars, camping, fishing. Home: PO Box 182 Port Clinton OH 43452-1901 Office: 8060 W Mud Creek Rd Oak Harbor OH 43449-9642 Office Phone: 419-898-2442. Business E-Mail: davidrandels@cnos.net.

**RANDHAWA, BIKKAR SINGH,** retired psychologist, retired educator; b. Jullundur, India, June 14, 1933; came to Can., 1961, naturalized, 1966; s. Pritam S. and Sawaran K. (Basakhi) R.; m. Leona Emily Bujnowski, Oct. 8, 1966; children: Jason, Lisa. BA in Math., Panjab U., India, 1954, BT in Edn., 1955, MA in History, 1959; BEd, U. Alta., Can., 1963; MEd in Measurement and Evaluation, U. Toronto, 1967, PhD, 1969. Tchr. secondary sch. math., Panjab, 1955-61; asst. headmaster, then headmaster, 1955-61; tchr. h.s. math. and sci. Camrose County, Canada, 1961—64, Beaver County, 1964—65, Edmonton (Alta.) Pub. Schs., 1965-67; tutor in math. for social sci. Ont. Inst. Studies in Edn., Toronto, 1968-69; mem. faculty U. Sask., Saskatoon, Canada, 1969—76, 1977—, prof. ednl. psychology, 1977-2000, prof. emeritus, 2000—, asst. dean rsch. and field svcs., 1982-87. Prof., coord. Visual Scholars' Program, U. Iowa, 1976-77; adj. prof. edu. psychology, U. Alta., 2002-; cons. in field. Contbr. articles to profl. jours. Treas. St. Albert Crime Stoppers, 2002—05. Fellow APA, Am. Psychol. Soc. (charter), Can. Psychol. Assn.; mem. Can. Ednl. Rsch. Assn. (pres. 1997-99), Can. Soc. Study Edn., St. Albert Rotary Club (treas. 2003-05), Phi Delta Kappa (pres. Saskatoon chpt. 1971, 85). Home: 14 Harwood Dr Saint Albert AB Canada T8N 5V3 Office Phone: 780-419-2549. Personal E-mail: randy.randhawa@shaw.ca.

**RANDI, JAMES (RANDALL JAMES HAMILTON ZWINGE),** magician, educator; b. Toronto, Aug. 7, 1928; naturalized U.S. citizen, 1987; s. George Randall and Marie Alice (Paradis) Zwinge. Student, Oakwood Collegiate Inst., Toronto, 1940-45; LittD (hon.), U. Indpls., 1995. Internationally known conjuror, lectr., author, investigator. Regent's lectr. UCLA, 1984; skeptical lectr. on paranormal subjects. Author: The Magic of Uri Geller, 1975 (with Bert Sugar) Houdini, His Life and Art, 1978, Flim-Flam, 1982, Test Your ESP Potential, 1983, The Faith Healers, 1987, The Magic World of the Amazing Randi, 1989, The Mask of Nostradamus, 1990, James Randi: Psychic Investigator, 1991, Conjuring, 1992, An Encyclopedia of Claims, Frauds, and Hoaxes of the Occult and Supernatural, 1995 (English, Chinese, French, Italian, German, Japanese, Korean, Norwegian, Punjabi, Polish and Spanish edits.); host TV spls. Recipient Blackstone award Internat. Platform Assn., 1983, 87, Forum award Am. Phys. Soc., 1988, Nat. Consumer Svc. award Nat. Coun. Against Health Fraud, 1988, Gold medal U. Ghent, Belgium, 1989, Humanist Disting. Svc. award Am. Humanist Assn., 1990, medal with golden wreath Hungarian Soc. for Dissemination of Scientific Knowledge, 1992; MacArthur Found. fellow, 1986, Spl. fellow Acad. Magical Arts and Scis., 1987; inducted into Soc. Am. Magicians Hall of Fame, 1988. Founding fellow Com. for Scientific Investigation of Claims of the Paranormal (exec. bd. dirs. 1973-91). Achievements include performing at White House, 1974. Home: 12000 NW 8th St Fort Lauderdale FL 33325-1406 Office: James Randi Ednl Found 201 SE 12th St Fort Lauderdale FL 33316-1815 Office Phone: 954-467-1112. Personal E-mail: randi@randi.org. *We are well into the third millennium with quack medicine, "Creation Science," faith "healing" and other pseudo-scientific matters heedlessly and increasingly embraced by the public, and major TV programs feature performers who claim to "speak to the dead." These con artists, feeding on the grief and vulnerability of their victims, are ignored, even tolerated, by our state and federal agencies. TV "magazine" shows promote belief in superstition by failing to properly research their subjects, and thereby serve their audiences poorly. Medieval notions and an anti-science movement threaten our very survival. We must reach out to our youth and develop in them a respect and understanding for real science. Acceptance of "politically correct" and "faith-based" standards, and of unquestioning belief in obviously crackpot theories, have brought us to a crisis in education. We need to adopt higher standards for our young people in respect to critical thinking, and encourage them to question the claims of the quacks and scam artists. The one-million dollar prize offered by my Foundation for proof of any paranormal power is still unclaimed. Why?.*

**RANDICH, STEVEN J.,** financial services company executive; BS in computer sci., No. Ill. U.; MBA, U. Chgo. Mgr. KPMG Peat Marwick; joined IBM, 1989; mng. prin. IBM Global Services; exec. v.p., chief info. officer Chgo. Stock Exch.; exec. v.p., chief tech. officer NASDAQ Stock Market Inc., 2000—01, exec. v.p. ops. and tech., chief info. officer, 2001—05; chief info. officer, corp. and investment banking Citigroup, 2005—. Named one of Premier 100 IT Leaders, Computerworld, 2005. Office: Citigroup Inc 399 Park Ave New York NY 10043*

**RANDINELLI, TRACEY ANNE,** magazine editor; b. Morristown, N.J., Apr. 6, 1963; d. Andrew R. and Patricia Ann (Brenner) Randinelli. BA in Comm., U. Del., 1985. Copywriter Macy's N.J., Newark, 1985-86; editl. asst. Globe Comms. Corp., N.Y.C., 1986-87; from asst. editor to assoc. editor Scholastic Math and DynaMath Mags. Scholastic, Inc., N.Y.C., 1987-89, editor Scholastic Math Mag., 1989-95; mng. editor Zig Zag Mag. Games Pub. Group, N.Y.C., 1995; sr. editor Contact Kids Mag./ Sesame Workshop, N.Y.C., 1996-2001; freelance writer, 2001—02; sr. editor Pearson Learning Group, 2002—04, supervising editor, 2004—. Mem. Soc. Children's Book Writers, Ednl. Press Assn. Am. (Disting. Achievement award feature articles divsn. 1991, 95, coverdesign 1996, how-to feature divsn. 1998, 99). E-mail: pen4kidz@aol.com.

**RANDLE, BERNADETTE,** musician, composer, graphics designer; b. St. Louis, Jan. 8, 1947; d. William George Randle and Louise Robinmae Randle-Ware. BA summa cum laude, Concordia U. Wis., 1993; MA, Lindenwood U., 1994. Dir. employment programs YMCA of Greater St. Louis, 1980—83; freelance studio musician Platinum Chess Record, Englewood, NJ, 1983—86; office clk. Def. Contract Audit Agy. & HUD, St. Louis, 1986—87; mktg. specialist Tailored Software Corp., Maryland Heights, Mo., 1987—89; graphic illustrator The Bionetics Corp., St. Louis, 1989—97; concept developer/tech. writer Bus. Blueprints, St. Louis, 1997—2000; composer, arranger ReMembered/The Gozz Ensemble; creative dir. Prosit Media Group; min. music Third United Presbyn. Ch., St. Louis. Mktg. cons. The Enterprise Found., St. Louis, 2002—03. Author: (short story) Chicken Soup for the Surviving Soul; pianist, arranger, composer numerous recs., 1974—. Vol. counselor CanSurmount, St. Louis, 1991—96; vol. visitor Am. Heartland Hospice, St. Louis, 1994. Grantee, Mo. Arts Coun., 1991. Mem.: Broadcast Music Inc., Mensa, Sigma Phi Omega. Avocations: reading religious histories, surfing the web, collecting baseball caps and kaleidoscopes. Office: Prosit Media Group 11621 Olive Street Rd Creve Coeur MO 63141 Personal E-mail: bernadettrandle@sbcglobal.net.

**RANDLE, PETER,** communications company executive; b. Warwickshire, Eng., Apr. 16, 1951; BSc with honors, London U., 1973; MSc, Queen's U., Can., 1975; Doktorand, Max-Planck-Institut, Heidelberg, Germany, 1975—78. Chartered chemist 1976, chartered engr. 1990, chartered mathematician 1996, cert. qualified tchr. status U.K., 1979. Mng. dir. Global ICT Consultancy Ltd.; mitarbeiter Max-Planck-Institut, Heidelberg, Germany, 1975—78; head computing Std. Telephones & Cables/ITT Inc., 1982-84; dir. computing and order processing Micro Bus. Sys. plc, 1985-86; ptnr., prin. Nova Consultancy, England, 1980-92. IP adviser Coun. European Profl. Info. Socs. (CEPIS), 1997—, EURIM, 1996—99, electronic working groups including Health Informatics, World Health Orgn. (WHO) and G8-Standards with IEEE WWW best practice; chartered scientist, IT practitioner in field, 2004. Contbr. reports to nat. govts. and G8 summit report; contbr. articles to profl. jours. Recipient Chartered IT Practitioner, 2004, Chartered Scientist award, 2004; grantee, Royal Soc. Medicine, 2004. Fellow Royal Soc. Medicine (disting. scientist); mem. Inst. Math. and Its Applications, IEEE, Inst. of Dirs. of U.K., Brit. Computer Soc. (chmn. intellectual property com. 1990-91, 96-98, mem. pornography task force, profl. and pub. affairs bd. 1996-98), Inst. of Mgmt. of U.K., Royal Soc. Chemistry of U.K. (life), Computer Soc. of IEEE, Gesellschaft für Informatik e.V. (Bonn), EURIM (various working parties 1996-99), N.Y. Acad. Scis., Can. Info. Processing Soc. Avocations: music, languages, travel, walking, cooking. Home: 9 Coppice Ct Broadwey Dorset DT3 5SA England Office Phone: +44 7050 26 2850. Business E-Mail: peter_randle@computer.org.

**RANDLE, RODGER A.,** human relations professor, political science professor; b. Oct. 26, 1943; BA, U. Okla., 1967; LLB, U. Tulsa, 1978. Bar: Okla. 1978. Mem. Okla. Ho. of Reps., 1971-72, Okla. Senate, 1973-88; mayor City of Tulsa, 1988-92; pres. U. Ctr., Tulsa, 1992-96, Rogers U., 1996-98; prof. human rels. U. Okla., Tulsa, 1999—. Hon. Brit. consul State of Okla. Chmn. bd. dirs. Sister Cities Internat., 1998-00. Home: 1395 E 26th St Tulsa OK 74114-2733 Office: U Okla 4502 E 41st St Tulsa OK 74135 Office Phone: 918-660-3495. Personal E-mail: rarandle@gmail.com.

**RANDLETT, MARY WILLIS,** photographer; b. Seattle, May 5, 1924; d. Cecil Durand and Elizabeth (Bayley) Willis; m. Herbert B. Randlett, Oct. 19, 1950 (div.); children: Robert, Mary Ann, Peter, Susan. BA, Whitman Coll., Walla Walla, Wash., 1947. Freelance photographer, 1949—. One-woman shows include Seattle Sci. Ctr., 1971, Western Wash. State U., 1971, Seattle Art Mus., 1971, Art Gallery Greater Victoria, 1972, Alaska State Mus., 1972, State Capitol Mus., 1983, Whatcom Mus. History and Art, Bellingham, Wash., 1986, Janet Huston Gallery, LaConner, Wash., 1990, Gov.'s Gallery, Office of Gov., Olympia, Wash., 1991, Stonington Gallery, Seattle, 1992, Valley Mus. Art, LaConner, 1992, Grad. Sch. Design Dept. Landscape Arch. Harvard U., Cambridge, Mass., 1996, Mus. N.W. Art, LaConner, 1998, Mary Randlett Portraits in the Arts Cmty., Wright Exhbn. Space, Seattle, 2002—03, Safco Plaza, Seattle and Richmond, Wash., 2003, Seattle's One Percent for Art, 2004, Walla Walla CC, 2004, Wash. State Libr., Olympia, 2005, others, exhibited in group shows at Am. Soc. Mag. Photographers, 1970, Whatcom Mus., Bellingham, Henry Gallery, Seattle, 1971, 1974, Royal Photg. Soc., 1979, Heard Mus., Phoenix, 1979, State Capitol Mus., Olympia, Wash., 1983, 1984, 1988, 1989, 1993, Santa Fe Ctr. for Photography, 1987, Tacoma Art Mus., 1989, Helen Day Art Ctr., Stowe, Vt., 1989, Valley Mus. N.W. Art, LaConner, 1991, 1994, 1996—98, Allen Libr. U. Wash., Seattle, 1991, Wing Luke Asian Mus., 1991, Cheney Cowles Mus., Spokane, 1991, 1998, Security Pacific Gallery, Seattle, 1992, Benham Gallery, 1993, Stonington Gallery, 1993, 1998, Rainier Club, Seattle, 1994, Port Angeles (Wash.) Fine Arts Ctr., 1994, Mus. History and Industry, Seattle, 1994, Whatcom Mus., Bellingham, 1994, Pacific N.W. Annual Bellevue Art Mus., Wash., 1995, Skagit Valley Hist. Mus., LaConner, 1995, Seattle Art Mus., 1996, 98, Kirkland (Wash.) Arts Ctr., 1997, Bainbridge Arts and Crafts, Bainbridge Island, Wash., 1997, Lucia Douglas Gallery, Bellingham, 1997, Anchorage Mus. History & Art, 1997, Burke Mus. Natural History and Culture, Seattle, 1998, Henderson House, Turnwater, Wash., 1998, Whatcom Arco Exhibit Gallery, Bellingham, 1998, Sea First Gallery, Seattle, 1998, 1999, Citizens Cultural Ctr., Fujinomita, Japan, 1999, Mus. Am. Indian, N.Y.C., 1999, Cheney Cowels Mus., Spokane, 1999, J. Paul Horiuchi Seattle Asian Art Mus., 2000, Mus. NW Art, 2000, Seattle Art Mus., 2002, Whitney Mus. Am. Art, N.Y.C., 2002, High Mus., Atlanta, 2002, Mus. NW Art, 2003, Seattle Art Mus., 2003, Tacoma Art Mus., 2003, Whatcom Mus., 2003, MONA, La Conner, Wash., 2004, Lucia Douglas Gallery, Bellingham, Wash., 2005, U. Wash. Press, Seattle, 2005, U. Portland, Oreg., 2006, and numerous others, Represented in permanent collections Met. Mus., Nat. Collection of Fine Arts, Nat. Portrait Gallery, Washington State Libr., Manuscript divsn. U. Wash., Pacific Northwest Bell, Seattle, Swedish Med. Ctr., Whatcom Mus., Bellingham, Henry Gallery, Seattle, Wash. State Capitol Mus., Olympia, Phillips Collection, Wash.; works appeared in books The Master and His Fish (Roderick Haig-Brown), 1982, Theodore Roethke: The Journey to I and Otherwide (Neal Bowers), 1982, Mountain in the Clouds (Bruce Brown), 1982, Masonry in Architecture (Louis Redstone), 1982, Writings and Reflections from the World of Roderick Haig-Brown, 1982, Pike Place Market (Alice Shorett and Murray Morgan), 1982, The Dancing Blanket, (Cheryl Samuel), 1982, Collected Poems of Theodore Roethke, 1982, Spires of Form (Victor Scheffer), 1983, Assault on Mount Helicon (Mary Barnard), 1983, New as a Wave (Eve Triem), 1983, Sketchbook: A Memoir of the '30's and the Northwest School (William Cumming), 1983, Good Intentions (Jane Adams), 1985, Blackbirds of the Americas (Gordon Orians and Tony Angell), 1985, Historic Preservation in Seattle (Larry Kreisman), 1985, Down Town Seattle Walking Tours (Mary Randlett and Carol Tobin), 1986, Seattle, the Seattle Book, 1986, When Orchids Were Flowers (Kate Knap Johnson), 1986, Jacob Lawrence, American Painter, (Ellen Wheat), 1986, Manic Power: Robert Lowell and His Circle (Jeffrey Meyers), 1987, The Isamu Noguchi Garden Museum (Isamu Noguchi), 1987, Washington's Audacious State Capitol an its Builders (Norman Johnston), 1988, The Bloedel Reserve: Gardens in the Forest (Lawrence Kreisman), 1988, Washingtonians: A Biographical Portrait of the State on the Occasion of its Centennial, 1988, Directory of Literary Biography: Canadian Writers 1920-59, 2d series, 1989, Crafts of America, 1989, The Lone Tree Tragedy (Bruce Brown), 1989, Northwest Coast Handbook of North American Indians, 1990, Dancing on the Rim of the World, 1990, Openings, Original Essays by Contemporary Soviet and American Writers (eds. Robert Atwan, Valeri Vinokurov), 1990, George Tsutakawa (Martha Kingsbury), 1990, Contemporary American Poetry (ed. Al Polin Jr.), 1991, Natural History of Puget Sound Country (Arthur Kruckberg), 1991, Bones (Joyce Thompson), 1991, Cebu (Peter Basho), 1991, Catalogue of Historic Preservation Publications, 1992, Art in Seattle's Public Places (James Rupp), 1992, The Olympic Rainforest (Ruth Kirk with Jerry Franklin), 1992, Steelhead Fly Fishing (Trey Combs), 1992, Illustrated Guidelines for Rehabilitation Historic Buildings, 1993, A History of African American Artists (Bearden and Henderson), 1994, Childrens Literature Review Vol. 1, 1994, Invisible Gardens: The Search for Modernism the American Landscape (Walker and Simo), 1994, Seeing Seattle (Roger Sale), 1994, Reaching Home (Jay and Matson), 1994, Redesigning the American Lawn: A Search for Environmental Harmony (Gordone Geballe, Diana Balmari and F. Herbert Bormann), 1995, Reaching Home: Pacific Salmon, Pacific People (Foves, Jay and Matson), 1995, Carl F. Gould: A Life in Architecture and the Arts (T. William Booth and William H. Wuksib), 1995, Destination Zero (Sam Hamill), 1996, Market Sketchbook, 25th Anniversary Edition, 1996, Spririts of the Ordinary, 1997, Instrument of Change: Jim Schoppert 1947-1992, 1997, Looking for Edulabee Dix (Joann Ridley), 1997, Jack Lenor Larsen: A Memoir, 1998, Museo Nacional Centro de Arte Reina (Mark Tobey), 1998, Fountains Splash, and Spectacle: Water and Design from the Renaissance to Present (ed. Marilyn Symmes), 1998, Ghost Dancing (Anna Linzer), 1998, The Flower in the Skull (Kathleen Alcala), 1998, This Great Unknowing: Last Poems (Denise Levertov), 1999, Building Washington (Paul Dorpat, Genevier McCoy), 1999, The Wright Collection, Seattle Art Museum, 1999, Made to Last: Historic Preservation in Seattle and King County (Larry Kreisman), 1999, Isamu Noguchi: A Study of Space (Ana Maria Torres), 2000, The Tiger Iris (Joan Swift), 2000, The Eighth Lively Art (Wesley Wehr), 2000, All Powers Necessary and Convenient (Mark F. Jenkins), 2000, Ice Breakers: Alaska's Most Innovative Artists (Julie Decker), 2000, Over the Line: The Life and Art of Jacob Lawrence (Peter Nesbett and Michelle Dubois), 2000, Iridescent Light: The Emergence of Northwest Art (Delores Tarzan Ament), 2001, Messages from Frank's Landing, 2000, Leo Kenney: A Retrospective, 2000, Building for Learning: Seattle Public Schools History 1860-2000, 2001, Geology and Plant Life, 2001, and numerous others; works also appeared in newspapers and mags., book, Maritime Seattle, 2002, Picture Bainbridge Island: A Pictorial History, Distant Corner, 2003, Child of the Oemulgee. Passing the Three Gates, 2003, Northwest Mythologies, The Interactions of Mark Tobey, Morris Graves, Kenneth Callahan and Guy Anderson, 2003, The Accidental Collector, Art, Fossils, Friendships, 2004, Isamu Noguchi and Sky Viewing Sculpture, 2004, A San Juan Island's Journal, 2004, Poems From Ish River Country, 2004, American Knees, 2005, Groundswell: Constructing the Contemporary Landscape, 2005. Recipient Wash. State Gov.'s award for spl. commendation for contbns. in field of photography, 1983, Individual Artist award, King County Arts Commn., 1989, Lifetime Achievement award, Artist Trust, 2001, Matrix Table, Seattle Women of Achievement, 1999, Nancy Blankenship Pryor award, 2001, Alumnus of Merit award, Whitman Coll, 2003, History Maker's award, Mus. History and Industry, 2003; grantee, Nat. Endowment for Arts, 1976, Allied Arts Found., 2000. Mem. AIA (hon.), Am. Soc. Mag. Photographers. Home: PO Box 11238 Olympia WA 98508-1238 Office Phone: 360-352-1716.

**RANDMAN, BARRY I.,** real estate developer; b. Cin., Apr. 1, 1958; s. David I. and Marilyn June (Garfinkel) F. BBA in Fin., U. Denver, 1980. With acctg. dept. Rookwood Pottery & Celestial Restaurants, Cin., 1976-80; asst. to pres., head mktg. and real estate branching Great Am. Banks Inc., Miami, 1980-83; pres. Tower Mgmt. Inc., Cin., 1983-85, bd. dirs.; pres. Ohio Jet Svcs. Inc., Cin., 1983-85; v.p. Home State Fin. Svcs. Inc., Cin., 1984-85; pres. East Hill Devel. Corp., Cin., 1985—, B.I.R. Properties Inc., Cin., 1985—. Pres. Golden Devel. Corp., 1988-91, SRB Food Corp., 1988-92, Scarborough Devel. Corp., 1989, Redmont Devel Corp., 1990—, Eastridge, Inc., 1993-99, 613 Race LLC, Hale Justis, LLC, 1999—, Middleton-Ludlow LLC, 2004, Butterfield Pl. Devel., LLC, 2002—, Bulluck Terr. Devel. LLC, Gilbert Ave. Devel. LLC. Mem. Jewish Welfare Fund, Cin., 1980. Avocations: skiing, tennis, gardening. Home: 9 Hill and Hollow Ln Cincinnati OH 45208-3357 Office: 2321 Kemper Ln Cincinnati OH 45206-2610 Office Phone: 513-751-9700. E-mail: brand1111@aol.com.

**RANDO, JOHN,** theater director; MA, UCLA. Asst. dir. Old Globe Theater, San Diego, Acting Co., NY. Dir.: (plays) The Dinner Party, 2000, A Thousand Clowns, 2001, Urinetown, 2001 (Tony award, best direction of a musical, 2002), Dance of the Vampires, 2002, My Beautiful Goddamn City, 2003, Miami, 2005, The Wedding Singer, 2006, The Underpants, 2006, Of Thee I Sing, 2006, Pig Farm, 2006. Mailing: c/o Geffen Playhouse 10886 Le Conte Ave Los Angeles CA 90024*

**RANDOLPH, A. RAYMOND (ARTHUR RAYMOND RANDOLPH),** federal judge; b. Riverside, N.J., Nov. 1, 1943; m. Eileen J. O'Connor, May 18, 1984; children: John Trevor, Cynthia Lee. BS, Drexel U., 1966; JD summa cum laude, U. Pa., 1969. Bar: Calif. 1970, D.C. 1973, U.S. Supreme Ct. 1973. Law clk. to Hon. Henry J. Friendly U.S. Ct. Appeals (2d cir.), N.Y.C., 1969—70; asst. to solicitor gen. U.S. Dept. Justice, Washington, 1970—73, dep. solicitor gen., 1975—77; ptnr. Sharp, Randolph & Green, Washington, 1977—83, Randolph & Truitt, Washington, 1983—87, Pepper, Hamilton & Scheetz, Washington, 1987—90; judge U.S. Ct. Appeals (D.C. cir.), Washington, 1990—. Spl. asst. atty. gen. State of Mont., 1983—90, State of N.Mex., 1985—90, State of Utah, 1986—90; adv. panel Fed. Cts. Study Com., 1989—90; spl. counsel Com. on Stds. Ofcl. Conduct, U.S. Ho. of Reps., 1979—80; adj. prof. Georgetown U. Law Ctr., 1974—78; exec. sec. Atty. Gen.'s Com. on Reform of Fed. Jud. Sys., 1975—77; com. on fed. rules evidence U.S. Justice Dept., 1972; chmn. Com. on Govtl. Structures, McLean, Va., 1973—74; adj. prof. law sch. George Mason U., 1992, disting. prof., 1999—; com. codes conduct Jud. Conf. U.S., 1992—95, chmn., 1995—98. Recipient Spl. Achievement award, U.S. Dept. Justice, 1971, James Wilson Disting. Alumnus award, U. Pa. Law Sch., 2004, Drexel 100 award, Drexel U., 2005. Mem.: D.C. Bar Assn., Calif. Bar Assn., Am. Law Inst., Order of Coif. Office: US Court of Appeals 333 Constitution Ave NW Washington DC 20001-2866*

**RANDOLPH, CARL LOWELL,** chemicals executive; b. Pasadena, Calif., May 30, 1922; s. Carl L. and Lulu (McBride) R.; m. Jane Taber, June 25, 1943; children: Margaret, Stephen. BA, Whittier Coll., 1943; MS, U. So. Calif., 1947, PhD, 1949; LLD, Whittier Coll., 1982; D in Pub. Svc. (hon.), U. Alaska, 1983. Prin. chemist Aerojet-Gen. Corp., 1949-57; v.p. U.S. Borax Rsch. Corp., Anaheim, Calif., 1957-63; asst. to pres. U.S. Borax & Chem. Corp., L.A., 1963-66, v.p., 1966-68, exec. v.p., 1968-69, pres., 1969-86, vice chmn., 1983-87. Trustee, chmn. bd. Whittier Coll., emeritus, 1969—; bd. dirs., chmn. Ind. Colls. So. Calif., 1982—. Lt. (j.g.) USNR, 1944-46. Mem.: Phi Beta Kappa, Sigma Xi. Home: 3836 Bay Ln Anacortes WA 98221-8413

**RANDOLPH, DAVID,** conductor; b. NYC, Dec. 21, 1914; s. Morris and Elsie (Goodman) R.; m. Mildred Greenberg, July 18, 1948. BS, CCNY, 1936; MA, Tchrs. Coll., Columbia U., 1942; LHD (hon.), Saint Peter's Coll., Jersey City, 2006; DFA (hon.), CUNY, 2006. Music specialist OWI, N.Y.C., 1943-47. Adj. prof. music NYU, 1948-85, Mostly Mozart course, 1976-85; lectr. Town Hall, N.Y.C., 1955-60, Columbia U., 1957, Cosmopolitan Club, N.Y.C., 1962-63; pre-concert lectr. N.Y. Philharm., Avery Fisher Hall, 1964-86,Cleve. Orch., 1981, Vienna Symphony Orch., 1988; tchr. conducting Dalcroze Sch., 1948-49; music commentator Little Orch. Soc. Concerts and Broadcasts, 1950-62, Met. Opera Intermission Broadcasts, 1951, 52; intermission commentator Lewisohn Stadium Concert Broadcasts, 1952-58; vis. prof. music SUNY, New Paltz, 1970-72, Fordham U., 1972-73; lectr. New Sch. for Social Rsch., 1973-90, IBM, N.Y.C., 1978-86, Beethoven Soc., 1977, 83; prof. music Montclair State Coll., Upper Montclair, N.J., 1973-87; guest condr. Rockland County (N.Y.) Ann. Choral Festival, 1972, 73; adviser film Music to Live By, mem. N.J. Arts Coun., 1967-70; mem. music com. Gov. N.J.'s Commn. to Study Arts, 1965; honored guest Handel Festival, Halle, Germany, 1991. Condr. Randolph Singers, 1944-62 (appeared on NBC Today and Tonight Shows), concerts Town Hall, NYC, Carnegie Recital Hall, recs. for Columbia, Concert Hall Soc., Esoteric Records, Vanguard, Westminster Records, The Triumphs of Oriana, 1953, Monteverdi's Lagrime d'amante, Satie's Mass for the Poor, CRI, 13 Modern American Madrigals composed for the Randolph Singers, condr. United Choral Soc., LI, NY, 1961-86, NJ Ballet Orch., 1977, 83, Masterwork Chamber Orch., 1982-83, Philharmonia Orch. in Brahms' Requiem, Barbican Ctr., London, 1988, Barge Concert, NYC, 1987, 89; guest condr., Conn. Symphony Orch., 1961; condr. concert tour Spain with Am. choruses and Radio TV Orch. of Moscow, 1992; music annotator, CBS, NYC, 1947-48; choral seminar leader Mohonk Mountain House, 1986-95; music dir., condr. Masterwork Chorus and Orch., 1955-93, St. Cecilia Chorus and Orch., NYC, 1965—; performances at Carnegie Hall, Avery Fisher Hall, Lincoln Ctr., Kennedy Ctr. including Brahms' Requiem, Schicksalslied, Nänie, Gesang der Parzen, Mozart's Requiem, C Minor Mass, Vesperae de Confessore, Beethoven's Missa Solemnis, Symphony No. 9, Mass in C Major, Choral Fantasy, Bach's Mass in B Minor, St. John Passion, St. Matthew Passion, Christmas Oratorio, Magnificat, Haydn's St. Cecilia Mass, Theresienmesse, Paukenmesse, Lord Nelson Mass, The Creation, Heiligmesse, Schöpfungsmesse, Michael Haydn's Requiem, Bruckner's Mass in E Minor, Requiem, Vaughan Williams' A Sea Symphony, Dona Nobis Pacem, Mass in G Minor, Hodie, Verdi's Requiem, Four Sacred Pieces, Honegger's King David, Elgar's The Music Makers, Corigliano's Fern Hill, Salieri's Mass in D, Purcell's The Fairy Queen, Mendelssohn's Elijah, Die erste Walpurgisnacht, Lobgesang, Lauda Sion, Poulenc's Gloria, Rutter's Gloria, Dvorak's Requiem, Te Deum, Kodaly's Te Deum, Berlioz' Requiem, Messe solennelle, Cherubini's Requiem, Schubert's Masses 5 and 6, Stabat Mater, Vivaldi's Gloria, Dixit Dominus, Zelenka's Missa Dei Patris, Gounod's St. Cecilia Mass, Handel's Solomon, Israel in Egypt, Judas Maccabaeus, Dixit Dominus and 172 complete performances of Handel's Messiah, Orff's Carmina Burana, Saint-Saëns' Requiem, Puccini's Messa di Gloria, Zimmermann's Psalmkonzert, Finzi's For St. Cecilia, In Terra Pax, Rachmaninoff's The Bells, others; broadcaster: David Randolph Concerts, WNYC and radio stas. of Nat. Assn. Ednl. Broadcasters, 1946-79, Young Audience telecasts, CBS-TV, 1958-59, series of candid rehearsals of Bach's Mass in B minor, PBS, 1967; host: weekly broadcasts Lincoln Ctr. Spotlight, Sta. WQXR, NYC, 1966-67; regular guest critic First Hearing program Sta. WQXR, NYC, and 68 other stas., 1986-95; author: This Is Music, 1964, 98, numerous album jacket notes; A New Music Made with a Machine, Horizon Magazine, 1959; editor: David Randolph Choral Series; writer, narrator: Instruments of the Orchestra, 1958, compact disc 1995, Stereo Review's Guide to Understanding Music, 1973; music critic, High Fidelity Mag., 1952-57; composer: A Song for Humanity, 1968, Andante for Strings, 1937, Edward, 1937; contbg. author: NY Times Guide to Listening Pleasure, 1968; analyzed Mendelssohn's Symphony No. 3 on records for Book of Month Club. Recipient 1st award for edn. by radio Ohio State Inst., 1948, 50, 51, Sylvania TV award, 1959, Disting. Alumni award Columbia U., 1982, cert. of appreciation Mayor of City of N.Y. at Carnegie Hall, 1991, Townsend Harris medal CCNY, 1996, Lifetime Achievement award Carnegie Hall, MidAmerica Prodns., 2000; St. Cecilia Chorus endowed David Randolph Disting. Artist-in-Residence Program at New Sch. in N.Y., 1996. Home: 420 E 86th St Apt 4-c New York NY 10028-6456 Office Phone: 212-744-1444.

**RANDOLPH, DONALD PHILLIP,** nurse anesthetist; b. Cedar Rapids, Iowa, Jan. 24, 1957; s. Eugene George Randolph and Shirley Jean Mathieson. B, Mt. Marty Coll., 1981; PhD in Religion, U. Calif., 2002. Cert. nurse anesthetist, Am. Assn. Nurse Anesthetists, 1981. Staff nurse anesthetist Tucson Anesthesia, 1981—89, Mayo Clinic, Scottsdale, 1989—94; nurse anesthetist pvt. practice, 1995—. Coord. and polit. action coord. A.B.A.T.E. Mesa, Ariz., 2000—02: Mem.: League Am. Bicyclists (effective cycling instr. 1986—), Sportbike Riders Assn., Motorcycle Riders Found.; Am. Brotherhood Aimed Toward Edn. (life), Am. Motorcyclist Assn. (life; field rep. 2001—03), Modified Motorcycle Assn. (life), Harley Owner's Group (life). Independent-Republican. Christian. Avocations: motorcycle rights, bicycle education. Personal E-mail: dprcrna@sprintmail.com.

**RANDOLPH, JENNINGS, JR., (JAY RANDOLPH),** sportscaster; b. Cumberland, Md., Sept. 19, 1934; s. Jennings and Mary Katherine (Babb) R.; m. Sue Henderson, May 28, 1966; children: Jennings, Brian Robert, Rebecca Sue. Student, George Washington U., 1952—54, student, 1957—58; BA, Salem Coll., W.Va., 1963. Sports and promotion dir. Sta. WHAR, Clarksburg, W.Va., 1958-61; sportscaster Sta. KLIF, Dallas, 1963-66; Sta. KMOX, St. Louis, 1966-68; with Sta. KSDK-TV, St. Louis, 1968—, sports dir., 1968-88, spl. sports corr., 1988—, also on nationally televised broadcasts for various sports events including Sr. PGA tour; TV announcer Fla. Marlins Baseball Club, Ft. Lauderdale, 1993—2002; announcer PGA Tour Classic on Golf Channel, 2002—; staff KFNS Radio, St. Louis, 2002—. Interviewer analyst Champions Tour on Golf Channel and CNBC; broadcaster coll. basketball ESPN regional TV; TV announcer St. Louis Cardinals, 1970-87, Cin. Reds., 1988; mem. NBC's broadcast staff for 1988 Olympics, Seoul, Korea and 1992 Summer Games, Barcelona, Spain; host The Golf Show. Trustee Salem Coll., 1976-89. With U.S. Army, 1954-56. Named to Boys and Girls Clubs of Am. Hall of Fame, 1990, Tex. Radio Hall Fame, 2005; named Champion, Southern Conf. Golf, 1958 Mem. Nat. Assn. Sportscasters, Delta Tau Delta (Disting. Alumni award 2006) Achievements include being an amateur golf champion. Home: 12021 Charter Oakpky Saint Louis MO 63146

**RANDOLPH, JESSE See CASTILE, RAND**

**RANDOLPH, JUDSON GRAVES,** pediatric surgeon; b. Macon, Ga., July 19, 1927; s. Milton Fitz and Abigail Theresa (Graves) R.; m. Susan Comfort Adams, June 14, 1952; children: Somers, Garrett, Judson, Adam, Comfort, m. Joyce Dunn, Oct. 11, 2003. BA, Vanderbilt U., 1950, MD, 1953. Intern in surgery U. Rochester, NY, 1953-54; asst. resident in pathology Vanderbilt U., 1954-55; asst. resident, then sr. resident in surgery Mass. Gen. Hosp., Boston, 1956-58; asst. resident in surgery Children's Hosp., Boston, 1955-56, sr. resident, then chief resident, 1958-61, asst. surgeon, 1961-63; teaching fellow to instr. surgery Med. Sch. Harvard U., 1960-63; jr. assoc. in surgery Peter Bent Brigham Hosp., Boston, 1961-63; surgeon-in-chief Children's Hosp., Washington, 1964-91; mem. faculty Med. Sch. George Washington U., 1964-91, prof. surgery and child health, 1968-91; prof. surgery Meharry Med. Coll., 1992-96. Cons. Nat. Naval Med. Ctr., NIH, Walter Reed Army Med. Ctr.; trustee Vanderbilt U., 1980—. Editor: Pediatric Surgery, 3d edit., 2 vols, 1979, 4th edit., 2 vols., 1985, The Injured Child, 1980; mem. editl. bd. Surgery, 1978-92; contbr. numerous articles to med. jours. With USNR, 1945-46, PTO. Mem. ACS (exec. com. surg. sect. 1974-75), AMA, Am. Acad. Pediats. (chmn. exec. com. surg. sect. 1974-75), Am. Assn. Thoracic Surgery, Am. Pediat. Surg. Assn. (gov. 1980—, pres. 1984), Washington Acad. Surgery (pres. 1989), Soc. U. Surgeons, Am. Surg. Assn., So. Surg. Assn., Am. Bd. Surgery (bd. dirs. 1973-79, diplomate), Alpha Omega Alpha (faculty), Cosmos Club (Washington), Belle Meade Club. Methodist. Office Phone: 615-383-3757. Personal E-mail: jrpedsurg@aol.com.

**RANDOLPH, LEONARD MCELROY, JR.,** career officer; b. Washington, Sept. 22, 1943; s. Leonard McElroy and Jessie Marshall (Stockton) R.; m. Linda Fleming Raney, Aug. 1, 1987; children: Nathaniel Randolph, Brion Randolph, Holly Tocknell, Chad Muterspaw, Judd Muterspaw. BS in Biology, Marietta (Ohio) Coll., 1965; MS in Microbiology, Howard U., Washington, 1967; MD, Meharry Med. Coll., Nashville, 1972; DHL (hon.), Meharry Med. Coll., 2001. Diplomate Am. Bd. Surgery, Am. Bd. Med. Mgmt., Am. Coll. Physician Execs.; cert. physician exec. Grad. tchg. asst. Howard U., Washington, 1966-67; rsch. microbiologist Georgetown U., Washington, 1966-67; chemistry tchr. Ballou H.S., Washington, 1967-68; commd. 2d lt. USAF, 1968, advanced through grades to maj. gen., 1998, intern Keesler AFB, Miss., 1972-73, resident, 1973-77, gen. surgeon Bergstrom AFB, Tex., 1977-78, chief gen. surgery, 1978-80, chief surg. svcs., 1980-83, attending surgeon Wright-Patterson AFB, Ohio, 1983-84, dir. med. edn., 1984-85, chief med. officer Minot AFB, ND, 1985-86, hosp. cmdr. George AFB, Calif., 1988-90, dep. command surgeon HQ Tactical Air Command Langley AFB, Va., 1990-91, forward command surgeon Desert Storm Riyadh, Saudi Arabia, 1990-91, med. ctr. comdr. Travis AFB, Calif., 1994-97; asst. prof. surgery Wright State U. Sch. Medicine, Dayton, Ohio, 1983-88; command surgeon U.S. Ctrl. Command, MacDill AFB, Fla., 1991-94, U.S. Transp. Command and Air Mobility Command, Scott AFB, Ill., 1997-99. Lead agt. DOD Health Svc. Region 10, 1994-97; spec. asst. to USAF Surg. Gen., 1999, dep. surgeon gen., 1999-2001; dep. exec. dir. Tricare Mgmt. Activity, Office of Under Sec. Def., Washington, 2001-03; assoc. prof. surgery U. Calif. Davis Sch. Medicine, 1995-97; assoc. prof. mil. medicine and emergency medicine Uniformed Svcs. U. of Health Scis., 1995—; acting dep. asst. sec. def. Health Plan Adminstrn., TRICARE Mgmt. Activity, 2003—04, COO, 2003-04; v.p. med. ops. Cath. Healthcare West, 2003-05; sr. v.p. and chief med. officer, Mercy Health Ptnrs., 2005-. Contbr. articles to profl. jours. Bd. trustees Marietta Coll., 2001—. Decorated Def. Superior Svc. medal for Operation Restore Hope, Legion of Merit Operation Desert Storm, Disting. Svc. medal USAF; selected for Boys State (Georgetown U.); recipient Excellence award Fed. Healthcare Execs., 1997, Disting. Alumni of Yr. award Nat. Assn. for Equal Opportunity in Higher Edn., 1999, Disting. Alumnus award Marietta Coll. Alumni Assn., 2000, Exceptional Svc. award Uniformed Svcs. U. of the Health Scis., 2003; named to Hall of Excellence, Ohio Found. Ind. Colls., 2003. Fellow ACS (bd. govs. 1996—2002), Am. Coll. Physician Execs. (disting. pres. 2000-2001), Am. Acad. Med. Adminstrs. (hon.); mem. Soc. Air Force Clin. Surgeons (bd. govs. 1996-2002), Soc. Med. Adminstrs., Soc. Med. Cons to Armed Forces, Assn. Mil. Surgeons of the U.S., Air Force Assn. (life), Christian Med. Assn., Aerospace Med. Assn., Alpha Omega Alpha, Beta Kappa Chi, Beta Beta Beta. Avocations: reading, sports, writing. Office: Mercy Health Partners 4600 McAuley Pl 6th Fl Cincinnati OH 45242-4745 Office Phone: 513-981-6347. Office Fax: 513-981-6133. Business E-mail: lmrandolph@health-partners.org. E-mail: caprand@aol.com.

**RANDOLPH, LYNN MOORE,** artist; b. NYC, Dec. 19, 1938; d. Cecil Howard and Dorothy (Didenhover) M.; m. Robert Raymond Randolph, June 5, 1959 (div. June, 1975); children: Robert Cean, Grayson Moore; m. William Simon, July 22, 1986 (dec. June 2000); m. Michael Berryhill, Sept. 14, 2005. BFA, U. Tex., 1961. Pres. Houston chpt. Nat. Women's Caucus for Art, 1979-80. regional v.p., 1982-85, nat. adv. bd. 1986-88, co-chair ann. 1988 ann. conf.; lectr. and conf. participant to art and women's groups, 1980—; set designer, Space, Dance Theater, Houston, 1977, Main St. Theater, 1982; coord. Art Under Duress, El Salvador, Lawndale Art and Performance Ctr., Houston. One-woman shows include Graham Gallery, Houston, 1984, 86, 91, Mary Ingraham Bunting Inst., Cambridge, Mass., 1990, Lynn Goode Gallery, Houston, 1995, U. Tex. Health Sci. Ctr., 1997, Ariz. State U., 1998, Joan Wich Gallery, Houston, 2003, Joan Wich Gallery, 2006; exhibited in group shows at Contemporary Arts Mus., Houston, 1978-79, 90, 500 Exposition Gallery, Dallas, 1980, Ga. State U. Gallery, 1982, Mus. Fine Arts, Houston, 1986, Aspen (Colo.) Art Mus., 1987, Nat. Mus. Women in Art, Washington, 1988, San Antonio Mus. Art, 1989, Sewell Gallery, Rice U., 1993, Diverse Works, Houston, 1994; works in pub. collections at Ariz. State U., Tempe, The Menil Collection, Houston, San Antonio Mus. of Art, Mary Ingraham Bunting Inst., Cambridge, Houston Mus. Fine Arts, others. Organizer Houston Area Artist's Call Against U.S. Intervention in Ctrl. Am., 1984. Summer fellow Yaddo, Saratoga Springs, NY, 1987, Mary Ingraham Bunting Inst. fellow, Radcliffe Coll., 1989-90. Mem. The Ilusas (women's drum corps), Artists Bd. Lawndale Art and Performance Ctr., Houston. Home: 1803 Banks St Houston TX 77098-5403 Office Phone: 713-528-0909.

**RANDOLPH, MICHAEL K.,** state supreme court justice; b. 1946; m. Kathy Webb; 3 children. BA in Bus. Administration, Rollins Coll., Winter Park, Fla., 1972; JD, U. Miss. Sch. of Law, 1974. Atty. Ross, King and Randolph, Biloxi, 1975—76, Bryan, Nelson, Allen, Schroder and Randolph, Hattiesburg, 1976—2004; justice Miss. Supreme Ct., 2004—. Former mem. Nat. Coal Council. Mem. adv. bd. Hattiesburg Salvation Army; former pres. Hattiesburg Civic Assn.; mem. Hattiesburg Area Development Partnership; mem. bd. dirs. William Carey Coll., Boys and Girls Club of Hattiesburg, Hattiesburg Girls Shelter. Air traffic controller U.S. Army, atty., Judge Advocate General Corps USN. Mem.: ABA, Fifth Federal Circuit Bar Assn., Miss. Bar Assn. (Com. on Continuing Legal Ed. 1975—76), S. Central Miss. Bar Assn. (pres. 1986). Office: Miss Supreme Ct PO Box 117 Jackson MS 39205

**RANDOLPH, ROBERT DEWITT,** lawyer; b. Sligo, Pa., Mar. 6, 1929; s. DeWitt Lyman and Hazel Irene (McCall) R.; m. Betty Ann McElhattan, May 8, 1953 (dec. Aug. 1979); children: Douglas, Andrew; m. Susan Denise Hopkins, Oct. 15, 1988 BA, Westminster Coll., 1951; LLB, Harvard U., 1957. Bar: Ohio 1958, Pa. 1960, U.S. Supreme Ct. 1981. Assoc. Buckingham, Doolittle & Burroughs, Akron, Ohio, 1957-59, Rose, Houston, Cooper & Schmidt, Pitts., 1959-60, 61-65; fgn. svc. officer U.S. Dept. State, Washington, 1960-61; ptnr. Houston, Cooper, Spear & German, Pitts., 1965-70, Randolph & O'Connor, Pitts., 1970-74, Buchanan Ingersoll P.C., Pitts., 1974-93. Pres. Assn. Retarded Citizens Allegheny, Pitts., 1990-92; mem. Allegheny County Mental Health/Mental Retardation Bd., 2002-. With U.S. Army, 1951—54. Mem. St. Clair Country Club. Democrat. Presbyterian. Avocations: golf, skiing. Home: 750 Washington Rd Pittsburgh PA 15228-2051

**RANDOLPH, ROBERT LEE,** economist, educator; b. East St. Louis, Ill., Jan. 2, 1926; s. John Andrew and Willye (Smith) R.; m. Patricia Smith, June 13, 1954 (div. 1986); 1 dau., Heather Elizabeth. AB, DePauw U., Greencastle, Ind., 1948; MS, U. Ill., Urbana, 1954, PhD, 1958; postdoctoral student, Case Western Res. U., 1960, U. Mich., 1962. From instr. to assoc. prof. econs. Springfield (Mass.) Coll., 1958-65, chmn. dept., 1960-63, dir. eve. and summer schs., 1960-64; dep. exec. dir. Equal Employment Opportunity Commn., Washington, 1967-68; dep. assoc. dir. Job Corps, 1965-67; exec. v.p. Chgo. State U., 1969-73; pres. Westfield (Mass.) Coll., 1973-79; vice-chancellor Mass. State Coll. System, 1979-81; pres. Ala. State U., 1981-83; prof. econs. U. Montevallo, Ala., 1983-86; pres. Randolph Assocs., Birmingham, Ala., Boston, 1983-91, Hyannis, Mass., 1991—, State C.C., East St. Louis, Ill., 1993-95. Mem. Cape Cod Commn., Barnstable, Mass., 1996—; cons. to industry. Author articles, monographs. Vice pres. Springfield Urban League, 1962-66; bd. dirs. Wesson Hosp., Springfield, Holyoke (Mass.) Hosp., Sickle-Cell Anemia Found.; mem. Cape Cod Commn., 1996—. Served to lt. (j.g.) USNR, 1943-45, 50-51. Decorated Bronze Star; recipient Danforth Found. award, 1943; Republic Steel Found. award, 1961; Vice Pres.'s award excellence pub. service U.S. Govt., 1967; Outstanding Alumni award Lincoln High Sch., E. St. Louis, 1973, Alumni Svc. award U. Ill., 1990, DePauw U., 1991; Navy V-12 scholar, 1943-45; State of Ill. scholar, 1952-56; Bailey fellow, 1957-58, Carnegie fellow, 1962. Mem. Am. Assn. State Colls. and Univs. (chmn. personnel com. 1974-75), Am. Assn. Polit. and Social Scis., Am. Econ. Assn., Phi Delta Kappa, Alpha Phi Omega, Kappa Alpha Psi. Clubs: Quandrangle (Chgo.), Barnstable Yacht Club (Cape Cod). Office: 3225 Main St Barnstable MA 02630-1105

**RANDOLPH, VIRGELLA,** retired federal official; d. Russell and Catherine (Smith) Snowden; m. Alphonso L. Randolph, 1960; children: Victor, Pebble, Deborah. At, D.C. C.C., 1976, Georgetown U. Clk. typist census bur. US

Dept. Commerce, Suitland, Md., 1955—56; clk. typist to dep. chief fed. acquisition and assistance divsn. Nat. Bur. Stds. (now Nat. Inst. Sci. Tech.) U.S. Dept. Commerce, Gaithersburg, 1956—87; ret. Vol. Providence Hosp., 1987; past mem., pres. We Chick, Inc.; past mem. The Musical Choraleers; past mem., v.p. The Stereophonic Chorale; deaconess Greater First Baptist Ch., Washington, 2004—; mem. Gospel Chorus, Pres., v.p., fin. sec.; mem. Fellowship Choir; co-chair Elevator Ministry. Recipient Bronze medal, U.S. Dept. Commerce, 1974. Mem.: Choir Dirs. and Organists Guils, Hampton U. Annual Minister's Conf. Democrat. Baptist. Achievements include development of in-house procurement training program for Nat. Bur. Stds; subject of Black History Week at Nat. Bur. Stds. for accomplishments. Avocations: flower arranging, singing, writing. Personal E-mail: virgella7@aol.com.

**RANDOLPH, WILLIE LARRY,** professional baseball manager; b. Holy Hill, S.C., July 6, 1954; m. Gretchen Randolph; children: Taniesha, Chantre, Ciara, Andre. Baseball player Pitts. Pirates, 1975—76, N.Y. Yankees, 1976—88, Dodgers, 1989—90, Oakland A's, 1990, Milw. Brewers, 1991, N.Y. Mets, 1992; assn. age. mgr. N.Y. Yankees, Bronx, 1993, 3d base coach, 1993—2003, bench coach, 2004; mgr. N.Y. Mets, 2004—. Named Dodgers' most valuable player Anaheim/L.A. chpt. BBWAA, 1989; named to MLB All-Star game 1976, 1977, 1980, 1981, 1987, 1989 Office: c/o NY Mets 123 01 Roosevelt Ave Flushing NY 11368*

**RANDT, CLARK THORP, JR.,** ambassador, lawyer; b. Cleve., Nov. 24, 1945; s. Clark Thorp and Mary-Louise (Mitchell) R.; m. Sarah Talcott, Nov. 3, 1979; children: Clark Thorp III, Paull Mitchell, Clare Talcott. BA, Yale U., 1968; JD, U. Mich., 1975; People's Republic China law diploma, U. East Asia, 1988. Bar: NY 1976, Hong Kong 1992. Assoc. Milbank, Tweed, Hadley & McCloy, N.Y.C., Hong Kong and Tokyo, 1975-82; 1st sec., comml. attache Am. Embassy, Beijing, 1982-84; ptnr. Heller, Ehrman, White & McAuliffe, San Francisco and Hong Kong, 1985-87, Gibson, Dunn and Crutcher, Hong Kong, 1987—91, Shearman & Sterling, Hong Kong, 1991—2001; US amb. to China US Dept. State, 2001—. Legal advisor Nat. Coun. US-China Trade, 1974. Contbr. articles to profl. jours. and books. Mem. nat. steering com. George Bush for Pres., 1988; vice chmn. Reps. Abroad Com., Hong Kong, 1988-93; chmn. George Bush for Pres., Hong Kong, 1998-00. With USAF, 1968-72. Recipient Disting. Svc. medal U.S. Dept. Commerce, 1984. Mem. ABA, N.Y. Bar Assn., Hong Kong Bar Assn., Am. Soc. Internat. Law, Am. C. of C. in Hong Kong (v.p., gov.), Yale Club (pres. 1987-95), Am. Club in Hong Hong, Ladies Recreation Club. Office: 7300 Beijing Pl Washington DC 20521-7300 also: US Embassy 3 Xiu Shui Bei Jie Beijing 100600 China Office Phone: 86 10 6532 3831.*

**RANEY, MIRIAM DAY,** actress; b. Florence, SC, Sept. 30, 1922; d. Lewis Griffith and Iola Lewis (Edwards) Day; m. Robert William Raney, Mar. 31, 1946 (div. Sept. 1976); children: Robert William Jr., Miriam, Kevin, Paige, Megan. BSM in Voice, Music Edn., U. N.C., Greensboro, 1943; student, Julliard Sch. Music, 1942—43; BA in Music History and Lit., U. Ark., Little Rock, 1981; cert., Adam Roarke Film Actors Lab., Irving, Tex., 1989. Singing chorus N.Y.C. Ctr. Opera Co., 1943-44; understudy, singing chorus Oklahoma, Theater Guild, N.Y.C., 1944-45; ingenue lead Connecticut Yankee, Geosan Subway Cir., N.Y.C., 1945; understudy, singing chorus Up In Central Park, Michael Todd, N.Y.C., 1945-46. Beauty cons. Mary Kay Cosmetics, Inc., Dallas, 1993—96. Author: Ark Women in Music, 1982; composer, lyricist: songs The Bend and the Willow, 1982, Ballad of Petit Jean, 1983; actor: (plays) Hedda Gabler, 1990, Time of Your Life, 1991, Our Town, 1991, Evening with Women II, 1991; (TV series) Unsolved Mysteries, 1988; (films) Killing Time with Aunt Olene, 1988, commls. and tng. films, 1987—99; reviewer: Ency. of Ark. History, 2005—06; print model, Little Rock, Memphis, Ft. Worth, 1988—98. Sec. sr. adult coun. Pulaski Heights United Meth. Ch., 2004—05. Named Illustrious Alumna, U. NC, Greensboro, 1945; recipient Thanks Badge, Girl Scouts USA, Oachita Coun., Little Rock, 1962. Mem.: AAUW (mem. Little Rock br. legis. com., mem. program com. 1973—79, cultural interest rep. 1975—77, 1996—98, state rep. cultural interests 1976—78), Ctrl. Ark. Guild Organists (pres. student chpt. 1977—80), Mus. Coterie. Democrat. Avocations: birdwatching, gardening, reading, movies. Home: 25 Valley Forge Dr Little Rock AR 72212-2613 Personal E-mail: mimraney@comcast.net.

**RANGARAJU, PRASADA RAO,** engineering educator, researcher; s. Narasimha Rao and Padmavathy Rangaraju; m. Himabindu Rangaraju; children: Nikhil, Rahul. B.Tech., J.N.T. U., Hyderabad, India, 1991; MS, Iowa State U., 1993; PhD, Purdue U., West Lafayette, Ind., 1997. Registered profl. engr., Minn., 1999. Sr. rsch. engr. Minn. Dept. of Transp., St. Paul, 1998—2001; asst. prof. Clemson U., Clemson, SC, 2001—. Contbr. articles to profl. jours. Mem.: ASTM, Am. Concrete Inst., Transp. Rsch. Bd. Office: Clemson U Rm 220 Lowry Hall Dept of Civil Engg Clemson SC 29634 Office Phone: 864-656-1241. E-mail: prangar@clemson.edu.

**RANGASWAMY, KULUMANI M.,** mathematician, educator; b. Tiruchendurai, India, July 8, 1938; s. Kulumani Meenakshisundaram and Suganthi Kunthalambal; m. Sarah Saraswathy R. Ayer; 1 child, Satish R. Ayer. BA, U. Madras, India, 1958, MSc, 1960, PhD, 1964. Lectr. math. Panjab U., Chandigarh, India, 1964—66; instr. math. U. Ill., Urbana-Champaign, Ill., 1966—67; asst. prof. U. Miami, Miami, Fla., 1967—68; reader math. Madurai U., India, 1968—72; sr. rsch. fellow Australian Nat. U., Canberra, A.C.T., Australia, 1972—76; assoc. prof., head Dept. Math. U. Papua New Guinea, Port Moresby, 1976—79; prof. math. U. Tex., El Paso, Tex., 1979—80, U. Nev., Las Vegas, 1980—83, U. Colo., Colo. Springs, 1983—, chmn. Dept. Math., 1983—95, interim dean engring., 1995—96, assoc. dean, engring., 1998—2002, chmn. mech. engring., 1999—2000. Vis. rsch. fellow Australian Nat. U., Canberra, Australia, 1965. Editor: Comms. in Algebra; contbr. over 65 articles to profl. jours. Recipient Chancellor award, U. Colo., 1998; fellow, NRC, Italy, 1994, 1997; grantee, U. Wuerzburg, Germany, 1993, South African Sci. Found., 1996. Mem.: Indian Math. Soc. (life), Am. Math. Soc. (life). Achievements include research in new discoveries in the theory of abelian groups and rings. Avocations: hiking, travel, yoga, meditation. Office: University of Colorado Colorado Springs 1420 Austin Bluffs Parkway PO Box7150 Colorado Springs CO 80933-7150 Personal E-mail: ranga@uccs.edu.

**RANGEL, CHARLES BERNARD,** congressman; b. NYC, June 11, 1930; s. Ralph and Blanche (Wharton) Rangel; m. Alma Carter, July 26, 1964; children: Steven, Alicia. BS, NYU, 1957; JD, St. John's U. Sch. Law, 1960; LLD (hon.), Wagner Coll., 1982, Atlanta U., 1983, St. John's U., 1988, Mt. Sinai Sch. Medicine, 1988, NYU, 1988, Howard. U., 1988, Hofstra U., 1989. Bar: NY 1960. Counsel NYC Housing and Redevelopment Bd.; asst. US atty. So. dist. NY US Dept. Justice, 1961-62; mem. NY State Assembly, 1966-70, US Congress from 15th NY dist., 1971—, ranking minority mem. ways and means com., chmn. bd. Dem. Congl. Campaign Com., dean NY State Congl. Del. Chmn. Congl. Narcotics Abuse and Control Caucus US Congress, mem. Congl. Black Caucus; co-chair African Trade and Investment Caucus, Congressional Glaucoma Caucus; mem. Congressional Human Rights Caucus. With U.S. Army, 1948—52, Korea. Decorated Bronze Star, Purple Heart; named one of Most Influential Black Americans, Ebony Mag., 2006; recipient Korean Presdl. citations, Henry F. Scheig Nat. Pub. Svc. award, Aid Jssn. Luths., 1987, Excellence in Pub. Svc. award, Am. Acad. Pediat., 1988, Marcus Garvey Lifetime Achievement award, Inst. Caribbean Studies, 1995, Edmund S. Muskie Disting. Pub. Svc. award, Ctr. Nat. Policy, 2002. Mem.: NY State Bar Assn., Nat. Assn. State Legislators, 369th Vets. Assn., NAACP. Democrat. Roman Catholic. Office: US Ho Reps 2354 Rayburn Ho Ofc Bldg Washington DC 20515-0001 Office Phone: 202-225-4365.*

**RANGER, MARK J.,** music educator; b. Farmington, Maine, May 6, 1972; s. Eugene A. and Meredith P. Ranger; m. Jennifer D. Byrnes, July 1, 1995; children: Malia, Natalie. BS in music edn., U. Southern Maine, 1994. Cert. tchg. State of Maine. Music educator Richmond Sch. Dep., Richmond, Maine, 1994—96, Maine Sch. Adminstrv. Dist. #75, Bowdoinham, Maine, 1994—96, Maine Sch. Adminstrv. Dist. #54, Skowhegan, Maine, 1996—;

educator, applied faculty U. Maine, Farmington, Maine, 2002—. Freelance profl. percussionist and adjudicator, Maine, 1994—. Mem.: Music Educator's Nat. Conf., Maine Music Educator's Assn. E-mail: rangers@gwi.net.

**RANGOS, ALEXANDER W.,** waste management enironmental services administrator; Student, U. Pitt.; pres., COO, Chambers Devel. Co., 1994—. Vice chmn. USA Waste Service Inc., Pittsburgh, PA, 1994—. Office: USA Waste Service Inc 10700 Frankstown Rd Pittsburgh PA 15235-3039

**RANIS, GUSTAV,** economist, educator; b. Darmstadt, Germany, Oct. 24, 1929; s. Max and Bettina (Goldschmidt) R.; m. Ray Lee Finkelstein, June 15, 1958; children: Michael Bruce, Alan Jonathan, Bettina Suzanne. BA summa cum laude, Brandeis U., 1952, hon. degree, 1982; MA, Yale U., 1953, PhD, 1956. Asst. adminstr. program and cultural AID/Dept. of State, 1965-67; dir. Econ. Growth Ctr. Yale U., New Haven, 1967-75, prof. econs., 1964—81, Frank Altschul prof. internat. econs., 1981—2005, Frank Altschul prof. emeritus internat. econs., 2005—, dir. Ctr. Internat. and Area Studies, 1996—2004. Ford Found. vis. prof. U. De Los Andes, Bogota, Colombia, 1976-77; Ford Found. vis. prof. Colegio de Mex., 1971-72; fellow Inst. for Advanced Study, Berlin, 1993-94; cons. World Bank, AID, Ford Found., ILO, FAO, Inter-Am. Devel. Bank. Author: (with John Fei) Development of the Labor Surplus Economy: Theory and Policy, 1964,; (with Fei and Shirley Kuo) Growth with Equity: The Taiwan Case, 1979; (with Keijiro Otsuka and Gary Saxonhouse) Comparative Technology Choice in Development, 1988; (with F. Stewart and E. Angeles-Reyes) Linkages in Developing Economies: A Philippine Study, 1990; (with S.A. Mahmood) Political Economy of Development Policy Change, 1992; (with John C. H. Fei) Growth and Development from an Evolutionary Perspective, 1997, Globalization and the Nation State, 2006; editor: Taiwan: From Developing to Mature Economy, 1992, En Route to Modern Economic Growth: Latin America in the 1990s, 1994, Japan and the U.S. in the Developing World, 1997,; co-editor: The State of Development Economics, 1988, Science and Technology: Lessons for Development Policy, 1990; mem. editl. bd. Jour. Internat. Devel., 1995—, Oxford Devel. Studies, 1996—, Internat. Econ. Jour., 2005-. Trustee Brandeis U., 1967-93, chmn. acad. affairs com., 1986-93. Social Sci. Rsch. Coun. fellow, Japan, 1955-56, Carnegie scholar, 2004-. Mem. Am. Econ. Assn., Coun. Fgn. Rels., Overseas Devel. Coun. (mem. adv. com.) Home: 7 Mulberry Rd Woodbridge CT 06525-1716 Office: Econ Growth Ctr Yale 27 Hillhouse Ave New Haven CT 06520 Office Phone: 203-432-3632. Business E-Mail: gustav.ranis@yale.edu.

**RANISESKI, JEAN,** psychology professor; PhD, U. of Houston, 1997. Psychology lectr. U. of Houston, 1992—; psychology and sociology prof. Alvin C.C., Tex., 1993—. Chair profl. devel. com. Alvin C.C., 1999—. Recipient Gt. Tchr. award. Office: Alvin C C 3110 Mustang Rd Alvin TX 77511 Office Phone: 281-756-3733. Business E-Mail: jraniseski@alvincollege.edu.

**RANJAN, RAHUL,** engineer, researcher; b. Ranchi, Jharakhand, India, June 28, 1980; arrived in US, 2004; s. Rajendra Prasad and Asha Chaudhary. BTech, Indian Inst. Tech., Kharagpur, 2002; MS, Wayne State U., Detroit, 2006. Rsch. engr. CDOT, New Delhi, 2002—04; high speed circuit design engr. Altera Corp., San Jose, Calif., 2006—. Author (and co-author): jour. articles and conf. papers. Recipient GRA award, Wayne State U., 2004, Outstanding Grad./Profl. Leadership award, 2005; Thomas C. Rumble Fellow, 2005. Mem.: SPIE, IEEE, ASHA, Sillicon Valley, Calif. Achievements include development of Video Image Fusion using Fuzzy and Neuro Fuzzy Logic; research in Image Fusion using Subtractive Clustering Approach; Fuzzy Applications. Avocations: reading, travel. Office Phone: 408-544-8190. Personal E-Mail: rahulr@wayne.edu. Business E-Mail: rranjan@altera.com.

**RANJAN, VIVEK,** physicist, researcher; b. Patna, Bihar, India, June 29, 1973; arrived in U.S., 2002; s. Devendra and Chandrakala Prasad. MSc, Patna U., 1996; PhD, Indian Inst. Tech., Kampur, India, 2001. Jr. rschr. Coun. Sci. Indsl. Rsch., India, 1999; rsch. scholar Inst. Electronics, Microelectronics and Nanotechnology, Lille, France, 2001—02, U. Ark., Fayetteville, 2002—, N.C. State U., Raleigh, 2005—. Referee Materials Rsch. Bull. Coord. outreach program NSF, 2004. Mem.: Material Rsch. Soc. (reviewer, writer 2003—), Am. Phys. Soc., Indian Physics Tchrs. Assn. (life; editor 2000), Indian Physics Assn. (life). Achievements include research in state-of-the-art first principles density functional theory; total energy and linear response theory; tight-binding computer codes. Avocations: photography, reading, philosophy, sports. Office: NC State U 851 Main Campus Dr Parnters III Rm 120F Raleigh NC 27695 Office Phone: 919-513-0613.

**RANK, EVERETT GEORGE,** federal agency administrator; b. Fresno, Calif., Dec. 1, 1921; s. Everett George and Evelyn Lydia (Dawson) R.; m. Evelyn Ingeborg Karschen, Apr. 30, 1948; children— Patricia, Judy, Ginny Student pub. sch., Clovis, Calif. Farmer, Fresno, 1946-81; chmn. Fresno County Agrl. Stblzn. and Conservation Service, 1959-69, Calif. Agrl. Stblzn. and Conservation Service, Berkeley, 1969-73; western regional dir. Agrl. Stblzn. and Conservation Service, Dept. Agr., Washington, 1974-76, adminstr., 1981-86. Pres. Clovis Unified Sch. Bd., 1959-72; bd. govs. U. Calif.- Fresno, 1977-81. Served with USN, 1941-45, PTO Mem. Masons (32 degreer), Shriners. Republican. Baptist. Avocation: golf. Home: 11868 Old Friant Rd Fresno CA 93720-9701

**RANKAITIS, SUSAN,** artist; b. Cambridge, Mass., Sept. 10, 1949; d. Alfred Edward and Isabel (Shimkus) Rankaitis; m. Robbert Flick, June 5, 1976. BFA in Painting, U. Ill., 1971; MFA in Visual Arts, U. So. Calif., 1977. Rsch. asst., art dir. Plato Lab., U. Ill., Urbana, 1971-75; art instr. Orange Coast Coll., Costa Mesa, 1977-83, chair dept. art Chapman Coll., Orange, Calif., 1983-90; Fletcher Jones chair art Scripps Coll., Claremont, Calif., 1990—. Represented by Robert Mann Gallery, N.Y.C.; overview panelist visual arts Nat. Endowment for Arts, 1983, 84; selector Bingham Ednl. Trust, 1997—2002; scholar-in-residence Borchard Found., Missillac, France, 2004; artist-in-residence Europos Parkus, 2005. One-woman shows include LA County Mus. Art, 1983, Internat. Mus. Photography, George Eastman House, 1983, Gallery Min. Tokyo, 1988, Ruth Bloom Gallery, Santa Monica, 1989, 90, 92, Schneider Mus., Portland, Ore., 1990; Ctr. Creative Photography, 1991, Robert Mann Gallery, NYC, 1994, 97, Mus. Contemporary Photography, Chgo., 1994, Mus. Photographic Arts, 2000, Europos Parkas, Vilnius, 2005; represented in permanent collections MOCA, LA, U. N.Mex Art, Ctr. Creative Photography, Mus. Contemporary Photography, Chgo., Santa Barbara Mus. Art, LA County Mus. Art, Mpls. Inst. Arts, St. Louis Art Mus., San Francisco Mus. Modern Art, Art Inst. Chgo., Mus. Modern Art, Lodz, Poland, Princeton U. Art Mus., Stanford U. Art Mus., Contemporary Art Mus., Honolulu, Mus. Contemporary Photography, Art Inst. Chgo., St. Louis Art Mus., others. Active art auction Venice Family Clinic, 1980-2005. Recipient Graves award in Humanities, 1985; fellow NEA, 1980, 88, US, France, 1989, Agnes Bourne fellow Djerassi Found., 1989, Award in the Visual Arts, Flintridge Found., 2004; Durfee Chinese/Am. grantee, 2000-2001, Cultural Affairs grantee City L.A., 2001, grantee Mellon Found., 2005, 06; Borchard Found. scholar-in-residence, France, 2004. Mem. Coll. Art Assn., LA County Mus. Art, Santa Monica Mus. Art, Mus. Contemporary Art. Home: 3117 N Lansbury Ave Claremont CA 91711-4146 Office Phone: 909-607-4439. Business E-Mail: srankait@scrippscollege.edu.

**RANKER, DENNIS W.,** social studies educator; s. Kenneth and Susan Ranker. BA in Polit. Sci., U. Pitts.; diploma in social studies edn., Duquesne U., Pitts. Social studies educator Grove City (Pa.) HS. Avocations: golf, music, reading, sports. Office: Grove City HS 511 Highland Ave Grove City PA 16127 Business E-Mail: ranker@grovecity.k12.pa.us.

**RANKIN, ALEX C.,** management executive; B in Commerce, BA in Psychology, MBA. With Agra Industries, Ltd., 1976-94; pres., CEO Nex-Cycle, Inc., Irving, Tex., 1994—. Office: Nexcycle 26021 Business Center Dr Redlands CA 92374-4553 E-mail: arankin@nexcycle.com.

**RANKIN, ALFRED MARSHALL, JR.,** manufacturing executive; b. Cleve., Oct. 8, 1941; s. Alfred Marshall and Clara Louise (Taplin) R.; m. Victoire Conley Griffin, June 3, 1967; children: Helen P., Clara T. BA in Econs. magna cum laude, Yale U., 1963, JD, 1966. Mgmt. cons. McKinsey & Co., Inc., Cleve., 1970-73; with Eaton Corp., Cleve., 1974-81, pres. materials handling group, 1981-83, pres. indsl. group, 1984-86, exec. v.p., 1986, vice chmn., chief oper. officer, 1986-89; pres., COO NACCO Industries, Inc., Cleve., 1989-91, pres., CEO, 1991-94, also bd. dirs., chmn., pres., CEO, 1994—; bd. dirs. The Goodrich Corp., Vanguard Group. Former pres., trustee Hathaway Brown Sch.; trustee U. Hosps. Health Sys., Cleve., Mus. Arts Assn., Univ. Circle, Inc., Cleve. Mus. Art, John Huntington Art Trust, Greater Cleve. Partnership; dir., exec. com. mem. Nat. Assn. Manufacturers; past chairperson The Cleve. Found. Mem. Ohio Bar Assn. Clubs: Chagrin Valley Hunt, Union, Tavern, Pepper Pike, Kirtland Country (Cleve.); Rolling Rock (Ligonier, Pa.); Met. (Washington). Republican. Office: NACCO Industries Inc 5875 Landerbrook Dr Ste 300 Mayfield Heights OH 44124*

**RANKIN, CLYDE EVAN, III,** lawyer; b. Phila., July 3, 1950; s. Clyde Evan, Jr. and Mary E. (Peluso) R.; m. Camille Cozzone, Aug. 24, 1997; AB, Princeton U., 1972; JD, Columbia U., 1975; postgrad. Hague Acad. Internat. Law, 1975. Bar: NY 1976, NJ 1976, DC 1978, U.S. Supreme Ct. 1980. Law clk. to Judge Dudley B. Bonsal US Dist. Ct. So. Dist. NY, 1975-77; assoc. Debevoise, Plimpton, Lyons & Gates, NYC, 1977-79; assoc. Coudert Bros., NYC, 1979-83, ptnr., Corp. & Fin. Practice, 1984-2005, chmn., 2005; ptnr. Baker & McKenzie LLP, NYC, 2005—. Trustee Rensselaerville (NY) Inst., 1989-, chmn. 2001-; mem. Coun. on Fgn. Rels., 1996—, bd. vis. Columbia U. Law Sch., 1991-; chmn. alumni coun. Princeton U., 2003-05. Stone scholar, 1974. Mem. ABA, Assn. Bar City NY, NY State Bar Assn., DC Bar Assn., NJ Bar Assn. Roman Catholic. Amateur Comedy Club (NYC). Contbr. articles to profl. jours. Office: Baker & McKenzie LLP 1114 Ave of Americas New York NY 10036-7703 Office Phone: 212-626-4740. Office Fax: 212-310-1639. Business E-Mail: clyde.e.rankin@bakernet.com.

**RANKIN, DOUGLAS HOUSTON,** finance executive; b. Lancaster, Pa., June 4, 1945; s. Lynn Boyd and Jessie Marrianne (Hirst) R.; m. Mary Wendell Pearce, Aug. 2, 1969; children: Benjamin Rusk, Amanda Marie. BSEdn in Psychology, N. Tex. State U., 1970. Draftsman Tex. Highway Dept., Amarillo, Tex., 1963-65; supr. Tex. Instruments, Dallas, 1965-70; office mgr. Tech. Fastener Co., Dallas, 1970-72; adminstrv. asst. Burke Concrete Accessories, Dallas, 1972-74; pres., founder Boyd Houston Co., Inc., Garland, Tex., 1974—. Mem. Nat. Small Bus. Adminstrn. Republican. Methodist. Avocation: travel.

**RANKIN, EDWARD ANTHONY,** orthopedist, surgeon; b. Holly Springs, Miss., July 6, 1940; s. Edgar Everett and Robbie Lee Rankin; m. Frances Espy, June 8, 1965; children: Tony(dec.), Marc Espy. BS, Lincoln U., 1961; MD, Meharry Med. Coll., 1965. Cert. Am. Bd. Orthop. Surgery. Pvt. practice Epps Gladden Rankin, Washington, 1973—87; prof. surgery Howard U., Washington, 1988—; ptnr. Rankin Diagnostic Ctr., Washington, 1988—. Pres. Ea. Orthop. Assn., 2002—03; sec. Am. Acad. Orthop. Surgeons 2001—04, second v.p., 2006—; pres. med. staff Providence Hosp., Washington, 2003—05. Editor-in-chief: Am. Acad. Orthop. Surgery Bulletin, 2001—. Gov.-at-large Am. Coll. Surgeons; bd. dirs. Blue Cross Blue Shield, 1985—88, Meharry Med. Coll., Nashville, 1990—2000. Am. Acad. Orthop. Surgeons, 1996—98, 2001—04. Maj. U.S. Army, 1965—73. Named to Hall of Fame, Lincoln U., Jefferson City, Mo.; recipient Disting. Svc. award, 33 deg. Masons, 2002, Cmty. Svc. award, DC Med. Soc., 2004. Mem.: Daus. Charity, Sigma Phi Phi. Catholic. Avocations: travel, golf, reading, music. Office: 1160 Norman St NE Washington DC 20017

**RANKIN, JAMES,** finance company executive; b. Morris Plains, N.J., Jan. 25, 1957; s. Bernard James and Carol Joyce (Cooper) R.; m. Rebecca R. Samuel, May 11, 1989. BS, U. Calif., Davis, 1980; postgrad., U. Calif., Berkeley, 1981-83; MBA, Harvard U., 1986. Asst. v.p. Wells Fargo Bank, San Francisco, 1979-88; v.p. T. Rowe Price, L.A., 1988-93; v.p., chmn. oper. com. Founders Asset Mgmt., Denver, 1993-98; v.p. customer support FOLIOfn Investments, LLC, Vienna, Va., 1999-2000; sr. mng. dir. product mgmt. EquiServe, Jersey City, 2000—03; assoc. dir. Pacific Alternative Asset Mgmt. Co., Irvine, Calif., 2004—. Mem. Harvard Bus. Sch. Club of So. Calif. Avocations: skiing, bicycling, travel. Office: Pacific Alternative Asset Mgmt Co 1920 Main St Irvine CA 92614 Home: 120 Sidney Bay Dr Newport Coast CA 92657-2112 Office Phone: 949-261-4937. E-mail: rankinjp@yahoo.com.

**RANKIN, JAMES WINTON,** lawyer; b. Norfolk, Va., Sept. 9, 1943; s. Winton Blair and Edith (Griffin) R.; m. Donna Lee Carpenter, June 25, 1966 (dec.); children— Thomas James, William Joseph, Elizabeth Jeanne; m. JoAnne Katherine Murray, Feb. 11, 1978. AB magna cum laude, Oberlin Coll., 1965; JD cum laude, U. Chgo., 1968. Bar: Ill. 1968, U.S. Dist. Ct. (no. dist.) Ill. 1969, U.S. Ct. Appeals (7th cir.) 1971, U.S. Ct. Appeals (5th cir.) 1979, U.S. Supreme Ct. 1975, Calif. 1986. Law clk. U.S. Dist. Ct. (no. dist.) Ill., 1968-69; assoc. Kirkland & Ellis, Chgo., 1969-73, ptnr., 1973—. Fellow Am. Bar Found.; mem. ABA, Order of Coif, Mid-Am. Club, Univ. Club, Mich. Shores Club, Kenilworth Club, Ephriam Yacht Club. Presbyterian. Home: 633 Kenilworth Ave Kenilworth IL 60043-1070 Office: Kirkland & Ellis 200 E Randolph St Fl 54 Chicago IL 60601-6636

**RANKIN, ROBERT ARTHUR,** journalist; b. Richmond, Va., May 31, 1949; s. Arthur Norton and Martha Louise (Rountree) Rankin; m. Janis Johnson, May 11, 1979 (div. May 2001); 1 child, Benjamin John; m. Judy A. Stromberg, Apr. 9, 2005. BA in Polit. Sci., Randolph Macon Coll., 1971; MA in Govt., U. Va., 1974; Walter Bagehot fellowship, Columbia U., 1978-79. Reporter Richmond News Leader, Va., 1972-75; reporter Congl. Quar., Washington, 1975-78; editorial writer Miami Herald, Fla., 1980-85; Phila. Inquirer, 1985-87; nat. corr. Washington bur. Knight Ridder Newspapers, 1987-99, govt. and politics editor Washington, 2000—. V.p. Civic Assn. Hollin Hills, Alexandria, Va., 1991—92. Co-recipient Pulitzer prize for editl. writing, 1983; recipient Olive Br. award, NYU Ctr. War, Peace and News Media, 1990, 1st prize, Va. Press Assn., 1974, Best Editl. award, Phila. chpt. Sigma Delta Chi, 1987. Mem.: Nat. Press Club, White House Corr. Assn. (bd. govs. 1996—98). Office: Knight Ridder Newspapers 700 12th St NW Ste 1000 Washington DC 20005-3994 Business E-Mail: rrankin@krwashington.com.

**RANKIN, SCOTT DAVID,** artist, educator; b. Newark, Mar. 21, 1954; s. Clymont J. and Jean L. (Lane) R.; m. Linda K. Piemonte, Sept. 3, 1989 (div. Apr. 2000); m. Stephanie Volz, Apr. 23, 2005. BFA, Tyler Sch. of Art, Phila., 1976; MFA, UCLA, 1980. Asst. prof. U. Iowa, Iowa City, 1985-86, U. Chgo., 1986-94; assoc. prof. Ill. State U., Normal, 1994—2005, prof., 2005—. Video cons. Math. Edn. Rsch. Project, LA, 1991—93, 3d internat. math. and sci. study UCLA dept. psychology, 1994—95, 1998—99. Prodr., dir.: (videotapes) Fugue, 1985, This and that (version 1), 1987, (version 2), 1990, The Pure, 1993, Wire, 1998, Flow, 2000, Central, 2001, Path, 2003, Piccadilly, 2004. Regional media arts fellow, Nat. Endowment for Arts, 1984, visual artists fellow, Ill. Arts Coun., 1989, 1990, Nat. Endowment for Arts, 1990, 1993. Office Phone: 309-438-8090. Business E-Mail: sdranki@ilstu.edu.

**RANKIN, WILLIAM LEE,** air transportation scientist; b. Marshalltown, Iowa, June 15, 1947; m. Lori Fumi Nakahara, Feb. 21, 2004. PhD, Wash. State U., 1972—76. Sr. rsch. scientist Battelle Seattle Rsch. Ctr., 1976—86; tech. fellow-human factors specialist The Boeing Co., Seattle, 1986—. Mem. Soc. for Indsl. Orgnl. Psychology (assoc.). Avocations: gardening, backpacking. Home: 2315 W Viewmont Way W Seattle WA 98199 Office: The Boeing Company PO Box 3707 MC 2J-10 Seattle WA 98124-2207 Office Phone: 206-766-3602. Office Fax: 206-662-3672. Business E-Mail: william.l.rankin@boeing.com.

**RANKIN, WILLIAM PARKMAN,** communications educator, academic administrator; b. Boston, Feb. 6, 1917; s. George William and Bertha W. (Clowe) Rankin; m. Ruth E. Gerard, Sept. 12, 1942; children: Douglas W.,

Joan W. BS, Syracuse U., 1941; MBA, NYU, 1949, PhD, 1979. Sales exec. Redbook mag., N.Y.C., 1945-49, This Week mag., N.Y.C., 1949-55, adminstrv. exec., 1955-60, v.p., 1957-60, v.p., dir. advt. sales, sales devel. dir., 1960-63, exec. v.p.; gen. exec. newspaper divsn. Time Inc., N.Y.C., 1969-70; gen. mgr. feature svc. Newsweek Inc., N.Y.C., 1970-74, fin. and ins. advt. mgr., 1974-81; prof., asst. to dir. Walter Cronkite Sch. Journalism & Telecom., Ariz. State U., Tempe, 1981-98, prof. emeritus, 1998—, also bd. dirs. Lectr. Syracuse U., NYU, N.Y.C., Berkeley Sch. Author: Selling Retail Advertising, 1944, The Technique of Selling Magazine Advertising, 1949, Business Management of Consumer Magazines, 1980, 2d edit., 1984, The Practice of Newspaper Management, 1986. Mem.: Dutch Treat Club (N.Y.C.). Home: 2625 E Southern Ave Cottage 18 Tempe AZ 85282-7615 Office: Ariz State U Walter Cronkite Sch Journalism and Mass Communication Tempe AZ 85287-1305

**RANN, ROBERT KENNEDY,** humanities educator; b. Detroit, Mich., Oct. 2, 1953; s. Robert Earle and Mary Ann Rann; m. Satoko Yamakawa; children: Jennifer Nishio, Evan Kentaro. PhD. U. Mich., 1987. Assoc. prof. humanities Madonna U., Livonia, Mich., 1987—. Editor: Japanese Studies Across the Curriculum, 1992. Recipient Fulbright-Hays Doctoral Dissertation award, 1984, Japan Found. Doctoral Dissertation fellowship, 1984, Nat. Endowment for Humanities Dist. Tchg., 2003—05. Mem.: Assn. for Asian Studies.

**RANNEBERGER, MICHAEL E.,** ambassador; BA, Tonson State U.; MA, U. Va., 1973. Angola desk officer Bur. African affairs US Dept. State, under sec. political affairs, 1981—84, spl asst. to under sec., 1984—85, dep. chief of mission Office US amb. to Mozambique, 1986—89, dep. chief of mission Office US amb. to Paraguay, 1989—92, dep. dir. Office Ctrl. Am. and Panamanian Affairs, Bur. We. Hemisphere Affairs, 1992—94, dep. chief of mission Office US amb. to Somalia, 1994, dep. prin. officer Office US amb. to Kenya, 1994—95, coord. Cuban affairs, 1995—99, US amb. to Mali, 1999—2002, spl adv. Office Sudan Programs Group, under sec. polit. affairs, prin. dep. asst. sec. Bur. African Affairs, under sec. polit. affairs, sr. rep. Sudan Programs Group, US amb. to Kenya Nairobi, 2006—. Office: 8900 Nairobi Pl Washington DC 20521*

**RANNEY, CARLETON DAVID,** retired plant pathologist; b. Jackson, Minn., Jan. 23, 1928; s. Carleton Oran and Ada Elizabeth (Harriman) R.; m. Mary Kathryn Ransleben, July 16, 1949; children: David Clayton, Mary Elizabeth. AA, Chaffey Jr. Coll., Ontario, Calif., 1952; BS, Tex. A&M U., 1954, MS, 1955, PhD, 1959. Plant pathologist Crops Rsch. Divsn. Agrl. Rsch. Svc. USDA, College Station, Tex., 1955-58, Stoneville, Miss., 1958-70, investigations leader Beltsville, Md., 1970-72; area dir. Ala. No. Miss. area Agrl. Rsch. Svc. USDA, Starkville, Miss., 1973-78, area dir. Delta States area Stoneville, Miss., 1978-84, area dir. Mid-South area, 1984-87; asst. dir. Miss. Agrl. and Forestry Exptl. Stas., Stoneville, 1987-94, head Delta Rsch. and Ext. Ctr., 1987-94, emeritus plant pathologist, 1994—. Adj. prof. agronomy Miss. State U., 1970-94; sr. exec. sec. USDA, Stoneville, 1984-87; adv. bd. Belt Wide Meetings Nat. Cotton Coun., Memphis, 1987-96. Contbr. articles to profl. jours. Sect. advisor SE2 Order of Arrow, Boy Scouts Am., Miss. and West Tenn., 1973-83; pres. Delta Area coun. Boy Scouts Am., Clarksdale, Miss., 1990-91, Eagle Scout; v.p. Leland Habitat for Humanity, 1995-2000, bd. dirs. 2000—. Served with USAAC, 1946-49. Recipient Silver Beaver Boy Scouts Am., 1981, Disting. Svc. Order of Arrow Boy Scouts Am., 1983, Superior Svc. award USDA, 1981, Cert. of Merit USDA, 1983. Mem. Agron. Soc. Am., Nat. Cotton Disease Coun. (sec. 1959-60, chmn. 1961-62), Lions (pres. Leland club 1995-96), Sigma Xi, Alpha Zeta, Phi Kappa Phi. Methodist. Achievements include development of fungicide control seedling diseases; definition of relationship of microclimate to boll rot of cotton; development of non-mercurial seed treatments. Office: Delta Rsch & Ext Ctr PO Box 226 Stoneville MS 38776-0226 E-mail: rs2dk49@tecinfo.net.

**RANNEY, GEORGE A., JR.,** lawyer; b. Chgo., Apr. 11, 1940; BA magna cum laude, Harvard U., 1962; JD, U. Chgo., 1966. Bar: Ill. 1966. Law clk. to Hon. Carl McGowan U.S. Ct. Appeals, Washington, 1966-67; dep. dir. Bur. Budget, State of Ill., 1969-73; counsel, v.p. Inland Steel Co., 1973-86; ptnr. Mayer, Brown & Platt, Chgo. Mem. Commn. Uniform State Laws, Campaign for RTA 1969-73; chmn. State Task Force on Future Ill., 1978-80; lectr. U. Chgo., 1975-79; CEO, chmn. Chgo. Met. 2020. Editor-in-chief U. Chgo. Law Rev., 1966-67. Mem. ABA, Chgo. Bar Assn. Office: Mayer Brown & Platt 190 S La Salle St Ste 3900 Chicago IL 60603-3410 Office Phone: 312-701-7360. Office Fax: 312-706-8191.*

**RANNEY, HELEN MARGARET,** retired internist, hematologist, educator; b. Summer Hill, NY, Apr. 12, 1920; d. Arthur C. and Alesia (Toolan) Ranney. AB, Barnard Coll., 1941; MD, Columbia U., 1947; ScD, U. S.C., 1979, SUNY, Buffalo, 1996. Diplomate Am. Bd. Internal Medicine. Intern Presbyn. Hosp., N.Y.C., 1947—48, resident, 1948—50, asst. physician, 1954—60; practice medicine specializing in internal medicine, hematology N.Y.C., 1954—70; instr. Coll. Phys. and Surg. Columbia, N.Y.C., 1954—60; from assoc. prof. to prof. medicine Albert Einstein Coll. Medicine, N.Y.C., 1960—70; prof. medicine SUNY, Buffalo, 1970—73, U. Calif., San Diego, 1973—90, chmn. dept. medicine, 1973—86, Disting. physician vet. adminstr., 1986—91; cons. Alliance Pharm. Corp., San Diego, 1991—2004; ret., 2004. Master: ACP; fellow: AAAS; mem.: NAS, Am. Acad. Arts and Scis., Am. Assn. Physicians, Harvey Soc., Am. Soc. Hematology, Am. Soc. for Clin. Investigation, Inst. Medicine, Alpha Omega Alpha, Sigma Xi, Phi Beta Kappa. Personal E-Mail: hranney@ucsd.edu.

**RANNEY, JOSEPH AUSTIN,** lawyer; b. Urbana, Ill., May 19, 1952; s. Joseph Austin and Elizabeth (Mackay) R.; m. Rebecca S. Rice, Sept. 5, 1982; 1 child, Emily M. BA, U. Chgo., 1972; JD, Yale U., 1978. Bar: Wis. 1978, U.S. Dist. Ct. (ea. dist. 1978, we. dist. 1988) Wis., U.S. Ct. Appeals (7th cir.) 1995, U.S. Ct. Appeals (fed. cir.) 2000. Assoc. Gibbs, Roper, Loots & Williams, Milw., 1978-81, Trowbridge, Planert & Schaefer, Green Bay, Wis., 1981-88, Ross & Stevens, S.C., Madison, Wis., 1988-90, ptnr., 1990-94, DeWitt Ross & Stevens S.C., Madison, Wis., 1995—. Dir., pres. Legal Svcs. of Northeastern Wis., Green Bay, 1982-88; adj. prof. Marquette Law Sch., Milw., Wis., 2000—. Author: Trusting Nothing to Providence: A History of Wisconsin's Legal System, 1999, In the Wake of Slvery: Civil War, Civil Rights and the Reconstruction of Southern Law, 2006; contbr. articles to profl. law refs. Chmn. Brown County Dem. Party, Green Bay, 1984-86, Wis. 8th Congl. Dist., Dem. Party, 1986-88. With U.S. Army, 1972-75. Recipient Charles Dunn Author award Wis. State Bar, 1993. Office: DeWitt Ross & Stevens SC Two E Mifflin St Madison WI 53703 Home: 595 Fargo Tr Middleton WI 53562 Office Phone: 608-255-8891. E-mail: jar@dewittross.net.

**RANONE, JOHN LOUIS,** school board executive; b. NYC, July 7, 1940; s. Michael Nicholas and Josephine Clara (Iannone) R.; m. Carolyn Margaret Smith, June 13, 1964; children: Michelle Mary, Margaret Anne. AA in data processing, Fairleigh Dickinson, 1960; BA in Elem. Edn., Jersey City State Coll., 1964; AA/Classroom Renaissance, Montclair State Coll., 1969; MA in Adminstrn., Monmouth Coll., 1974. Tchr. elem. sch., adminstr., svc edn., classroom renaissance. Teaching prin. Hollie M. Davis Sch., River Edge, N.J., 1972-77; prin. Lincoln Sch., Ridgefield Park (N.J.) Bd. Edn., 1977-89; dir. curriculum and instruction Ridgefield Park Bd. Edn., 1989—. Cons., lectr. N.J. State Dept. Edn., Trenton, 1974—; chmn. N.J. State Adv. Council, Trenton, 1976—; lectr. Jersey City State Coll., 1979—; rep. U.S. Council for Individually Guided Edn., Atlanta, 1979-87; bd. trustees for teacher edn. Felician Coll. Trustee River Edge Pub. Libr., 1978-85. Recipient Outstanding Svc. award, Cath. Youth Orgn., Newark, 1965, Bergen County Outstanding Tchr. award, PTA, 1971, Child Assault Prevention award, N.J. State Dept. Edn., 1988, Halls Motor Co. scholarship, Jersey City, N.J., 1958-59; named to Edn. at the Met., Met. Opera Co., N.Y.C., Workshop Series I, 1988. Mem. Assn. Supervision and Curriculum Devel., Prins. and Suprs. Assn., River Edge Edn. Assn. (pres. 1974-76, v.p. 1972-74), Ridgefield Park Adminstr. Assn. (treas. 1981-98), River Edge Dem. Club, Friends of the Libr. Roman Catholic. Avocations: travel, reading, ceramic, collector. Home: 5 Oakmont Ln Jackson NJ 08527-3988 Office Phone: 201-819-8649.

**RANSEL, DAVID LORIMER,** history professor; b. Gary, Ind., Feb. 20, 1939; s. Joseph A. and Patricia (Lorimer) R.; m. Therese Holma; children: Shairstin, Annaliisa. BA, Coe Coll., 1961; MA, Northwestern U., 1962; PhD, Yale U., 1969. Instr. Tollare Folkhogskola, Boo, Sweden, 1959-60; asst. instr. Yale U., New Haven, 1966-67; instr. U. Ill., Urbana, 1967-69, asst. prof., 1969-73, assoc. prof., 1973-81, prof., 1981-85, Ind. U. Bloomington, 1985—, Robert F. Byrnes prof. history, 2001—, dir. Russian and East European Inst., 1995—; co-dir. European Union Ctr., 2005—. Author: The Politics of Catherinian Russia, 1975, Mothers of Misery, 1988, Village Mothers: Three Generations of Change in Russia and Tataria, 2000; editor: The Family in Imperial Russia, 1978, Imperial Russia: New Histories for the Empire, 1998, Polish Encounters, Russian Identity, 2005; editor/translator: Village Life in Late Tsarist Russia, 1993; editor Slavic Rev., Urbana, 1980-85, Am. Hist. Rev., Bloomington, 1985-95; bd. editors The History of the Family: An International Quarterly, Historisk Tidskrift, Forum for Anthropology and Culture, Kritika: Explorations in Russian and Eurasian History, Jour. Modern History, 2005—. Guggenheim fellow, 1989-90, Wilson fellow, 1989-90, NEH fellow, 1998-99; Fulbright-Hays grantee, 1979, 90, Irex grantee, 1990, 93. Mem. Am. Hist. Assn. (mem. gov. coun. 1985-95, mem. fin. com. 1980-85, chmn. com. on status of women 1991-93, v.p., pres.-elect 2003, pres. 2004-05, immediate past pres. 2005), Irex (program com. 1995-99). Avocations: classical guitar, sailing, running. Office: Ind Univ Russian/East European Inst 565 Ballantine Hall Bloomington IN 47401-5017 Office Phone: 812-855-7309. Business E-mail: ransel@indiana.edu.

**RANSOHOFF, RICHARD MILTON,** neurologist, researcher; b. Cin., Aug. 18, 1946; s. Jerry Nathan and Sue (Westheimer) R.; m. Margaret Seidler, Mar. 26, 1988; children: Amy Julia, Lena Jane. BA, Bard Coll., 1968; MD, Case Western Reserve U., 1978. Diplomate Am. Bd. Psychiatry and Neurology, Am. Bd. Internal Medicine. Resident in internal medicine Mt. Sinai Hosp., Cleve., 1978-81; resident in neurology The Cleve. Clinic Found., 1981-83, chief resident in neurology, 1983-84, mem. assoc. staff in neurology, 1984-93, mem. asst. staff in molecular biology Rsch. Inst., 1989-94, mem. staff neurology dept., 1993—, mem. staff in molecular biology Lerner Rsch. Inst., 1994—97, mem. staff in neuroscis. Lerner Rsch. Inst., 1994—; prof. dept. med. virology, immunology and molecular genetics Ohio State U. Health Sci. Ctr., Cleve. Clinic Found., 1997—2001; postdoctoral fellow in molecular biology Case Western Reserve U., Cleve., 1984-89; adj. prof. Case Med. Sch., Dept. Pathology, 2004—; dir. Neuroinflammation Rsch. Ctr., Cleve. Clinic Found., 2005—. Mem. neurology C study sect., Washington, 1995—98; cons. Rsch. Ctr. for AIDS Dementia, Johns Hopkins U., 1998—2002; mem. clin. adv. bd. LeukoSite, Inc., Cambridge, Mass., 1998—2000; project dir. Nat. Inst. Neurol. Diseases and Stroke, Washington, 1999—; mem. sci. adv. bd. ChemoCentryx, Santa Clara, Calif., 2001—; cons. Ctr. Neurobiology & Neurodegeneration U. Nebr. Med. Ctr.; external adv. European Union Project on Brain Inflammation, 2004—06. Co-author: Transcriptional Regulation in the Interferon System, 1997; co-editor: Cytokines in the CNS, 1996, 2d edit., 2005; editor: Chemokines in the CNS, 2002; sect. editor: Jour. Immunology, 2002—05, editl. bd.: Jour. of Neuroimmunology, 1998—, Ency. Neurol. Scis., 2003, mem. editl. adv. bd.: Trends in Immunology; mem. editl. adv. bd. Nature Review Immunology, 2005—; contbr. more than 190 articles to profl. jours. Chair profl. adv. com. Nat. Multiple Sclerosis Soc., N.E. Ohio, 1985-95, trustee, 1985-97, mem. med. adv. bd. Nat. Multiple Sclerosis Soc., N.Y.C. 1996—, chmn. peer rev. com. B, 2003—; mem. corp. Hathaway Brown Sch., Shaker Heights, Ohio; ad hoc reviewer Charles Dana Fund, N.Y.C., Wellcome Trust, U.K. Grantee NIH, Washington, 1988—, Harry Weaver Neurosci. scholar Nat. Multiple Sclerosis Soc., N.Y.C., 1987-92; recipient Physicians Rsch. Tng. award Am. Cancer Soc., N.Y.C., 1984-86, Clin. Investigator Devel. award Nat. Inst. Neurol. and Communicative Diseases and Stroke, Washington, 1988-93, John and Samuel Bard award for Sci. and Medicine, 2002. Mem.: Assn. Am. Physicians, Am. Assn. Immunologists, Am. Assn. Neurology, Am. Neurol. Assn. (mem. sci. program com. 1996—98). Office: Lerner Rsch Inst NC-30 Cleve Clinic Found 9500 Euclid Ave Cleveland OH 44195-0001 Office Phone: 216-444-8939. E-mail: ransohr@ccf.org.

**RANSOM, ANGELA DAWN,** nurse; b. Provo, Utah, Sept. 30, 1978; d. Samuel Elmer and Glenda Lou Trevenen; m. Michael Todd Ransom. A, Utah Valley State Coll., Orem, 2002; B, U. ND, Grand Forks, 2006. RN ND, Ala., CCRN. Lic. practical nurse LDS Hosp., Salt Lake City, 1999—2002; RN Altru Hosp., Grand Forks, 2002—. Mem.: Am. Assn. Critical Care Nurses.

**RANSOM, JAMES W.,** Native American tribal leader; AAS in civil tech., SUNY Canton Coll. Tech.; BS in civil engring., Clarkson U., Potsdam, NY. Dir. environment program St. Regis Band of Mohawk Indians, 1978—90, now chief. Office: St Regis Bank of Mohawk Indians 412 State Rt 37 Akwesasne NY 13655*

**RANSOM, MARGARET PALMQUIST,** public relations executive; b. Davenport, Iowa, Aug. 13, 1935; d. Herman Philip and Margaret (Burchell) Palmquist; m. David Duane Ransom, July 16, 1960; 1 child, David Burke. BA in Speech and English, Augustana Coll., 1957. Tchr. speech and english Beloit (Wis.) High Sch., 1957-59; tchr. English Lake Forest (Ill.) High Sch., 1959-60, Warren High Sch., Gurnee, Ill., 1960-62, 64-66; asst. to dean Grad. Sch. Bowling Green (Ohio) State U., 1963; freelance writer Coll. Bd. Examinations, 1966; market rsch. analyst Kitchens of Sara Lee, Deerfield, Ill., 1972-74; pub. affairs mgr. Sara Lee Bakery, Deerfield, 1975-89; sr. cons. Ransom Pub. Svc. Cons., Libertyville, Ill., 1990-94; cons. Olsten Staffing Svcs., Chgo., 1994-96, Kelly Svcs. Chgo. Region, 1996—. Judge nat. competitions Pub. Rels. Soc. Am., 1986-89; spkr. on motivation and orgn.; chmn. employer coun. Ill. Dept. Employment Security, 1995-96; cons. Kelly Svcs., 1996-98. Bd. dirs. Early Childhood Adv. Coun., Northeastern Ill. State U., 1989-91; mem. Main St. Libertyville com., 1990-92; creator Job Market Place '96, Lake County; ct.-appts. spl. advocate, 2003; adult Christian edn. vol. coord. HOpe EPC, 2004—. Recipient Ill. Citizens Svc. medal, 1993. Mem. AAUW, Bus. and Profl. Women Lake County, Mortar Bd. Avocations: computers, reading, art. This is the day the Lord has made. Let us rejoice and be glad.

**RANSOM, MICHAEL T.,** counselor; b. Fullerton, Calif., Apr. 15, 1975; s. Gary D. and Carol S. Ransom; m. Angela D. Ransom, Jan. 18, 2002. BS magna cum laude, Westminster Coll., 1998—2003; doctoral student, U. ND, MA, 2003, grad. tchg. asst., 2003—05. Undergraduate tchg. asst. Westminster Coll., Salt Lake City, 1999—2000; grad. rsch. assisstant U. of ND, Dept. of Counseling, Grand Forks, ND, 2002—; psychiat. technician McKay-Dee Hosp. Ctr., Ogden, Utah, 2002. Mem.: Clin. Neuropsychology, Divsn. 40 of APA, Student Mem., APA Student Affiliate, APA of Grad. Students (APAGS), Psi Chi - The Nat. Honor Soc. in Psychology (vice-president 2001—02), Beta Beta Beta - The Nat. Honor Soc. in Biology. Office: University of North Dakota Dept of Counseling PO Box 8255 c/o Michael Ransom Grand Forks ND 58202

**RANSOM, TASHA ELANA,** news production assistant; b. Evanston, Ill., Aug. 24, 1973; d. Vincent Allen and Mary Geraldine Ransom. BS, Drake U., Des Moines, 1995; postgrad., Valparaiso U., Ind., 1996—97; MA, Columbia Coll., Chgo., 2002. Law clk. Vickie Pasley & Assocs., Chgo., 1992, 1994; product mgr. Zachs Investment & Rsch., Chgo., 1996; law clk. Hoeppner Wagner & Evans, Valparaiso, Ind., 1997—98; intern Lawyers for the Creative Arts, Chgo., 1999—2000; asst. Linda S. Mensch P.C., Chgo., 1999—2001; intern, prodn. cmty. affairs Fox News Chgo., 2000—01, asst. to news dir., 2001—. Recipient Alumni of the Yr., Outstanding Contbn. in the African Am. Cmty., Youth Action Ministry, 2002; Chuck Suber scholarship, Columbia Coll., 2001—02. Mem.: Nat. Assn. Black Journalists, Phi Alpha Delta, Delta Sigma Pi.

**RANSOME, ERNEST LESLIE, III,** retail executive; b. Riverton, NJ; s. Percy A. and Clarice (Frishmuth) R.; m. Nancy Ellis Clark, Aug. 16, 1947 (div. Jan. 1984); children: Leslie Ransome Hudson, Elizabeth Ransome, Jane Ransome Bromley; m. Myradean Alcott, Feb. 12, 1984. AB in Econs.,

Princeton U., 1947; LLD, U. St. Andrews, Scotland, 2001. Ins. exec. Johnson & Higgins, Phila., 1947-48; asst. to dean Princeton (N.J.) U., 1948-50; asst. treas. Giles & Ransome, Bensalem, Pa., 1950-55, v.p. adminstrn., 1955-69, exec. v.p., 1969-82, vice chmn., 1982-88, chmn. bd., 1988—; v.p. Ransome Airlines, Bensalem, Pa., 1966-86. With Mannington Mills, Salem, N.J., chmn., 1991-92. Mem. Zoning Bd. Borough of Riverton, N.J., 1965-69; bd. trustees Riverton Library, 1959-79; campaign chmn. Zurbrugg Hosp., Riverside, N.J., 1971. 2d lt. USMC, 1944-46. Mem. Pine Valley Golf Club (pres. 1977-88, chmn. 1988-2001), Royal and Ancient Golf Club (St. Andrews, Scotland). Republican. Episcopalian. Avocation: golf.

**RANTS, CAROLYN JEAN,** academic administrator, educator; b. Hastings, Nebr., Oct. 3, 1936; d. John Leon and Christine (Helzer) Halloran; m. Marvin L. Rants, June 1, 1957 (div. July 1984); children: Christopher Charles, Douglas John. Student, Hastings Coll., 1954—56; BS, U. Omaha, 1960; EdM, U. Nebr., 1968; EdD, U. S.D., 1982. Elem. sch. tchr. Ogallala (Nebr.) Cmty. Sch., 1956-58, Omaha Pub. Schs., 1958-62, Hastings Pub. Schs., 1960-64, Grosse Pointe (Mich.) Cmty. Schs., 1964-67; asst. prof., instr. Morningside Coll., Sioux City, Iowa, 1974-82, dean for student devel., 1982-84, v.p. for student affairs, 1984-94, interim v.p. for acad. affairs, 1992-94, v.p. enrollment and student svcs., 1994-96, v.p. adminstrn., 1996-99; exec. dir. enrollment svcs. Western Iowa Tech C.C., 1999—, dean of students, 2000—. Pres. New Perspectives, Inc., 1999—2000. New agy. com., chmn. fund distbn. and resource deployment com. United Way, Sioux City, 1987-94, co-chair, United Way Day of Caring, 1996; active Iowa Civil Rights Commn., 1989-97; bd. dirs. Leadership Sioux City, 1988-93, pres., 1992-93; bd. dirs. Siouxland Y, Sioux City, 1985-90, pres., 1988; bd. dirs. Girls, Inc., 1995-2000, Sioux City Symphony, 2001—, Red Cross, 2002—; mem. Vision 2020 Cmty. Planning Task Force, 1990-92; pres. bd. dirs. Siouxland Youth Chorus, 2001—, treas., 2002-05; mem. Vision Iowa Bd., 2005—. Mem. Iowa Women in Ednl. Leadership (pres. Sioux City chpt. 1986), Nat. Assn. Student Pers. Adminstrs.(region IV-E adv. bd.), Nat. Assn. for Women Deans, Adminstrs. and Counselors, Iowa Student Pers. Adminstr. (chmn. profl. devel. Iowa chpt. 1988-89, pres. 1991-92, Outstanding Svc. award 1992, Disting. Svc. award 1994), AAUW (corp. rep., coll./univ. rep. 1994-96), P.E.O. (pres. Sioux City chpt., Tri-State Women's Bus. Conf. (treas., planning com. Sioux City chpt. 1987-89), Quota Club (com. chmn. Sioux City 1987-89, v.p. 1992-94, pres. 1994-95, Siouxland Woman of Yr. award 1988), Sertoma (officer, bd. govs., regional dir.), Omicron Delta Kappa (faculty dir. province X 1996-99), Delta Kappa Gamma (state 1st v.p. 1993-95, state pres. 1995-97, internat. com. 1998-2000, 2002-04, N.W. regional dir. 2004—), Phi Delta Kappa (pres. 1988-89, Excellence in Leadership award 1998, Spl. Commendation Bessie Gabbard award 2001). Republican. Methodist. Avocations: handbells, cross-stitching. Home: 2904 S Cedar St # 4 Sioux City IA 51106-4246 Office: Western Iowa Tech Comm Coll PO Box 5199 4647 Stone Ave Sioux City IA 51102-5199 E-mail: rantsc@witcc.com, cjrants@willinet.net.

**RANU, HARCHARAN SINGH,** biomedical scientist, administrator, orthopaedic biomechanics educator; b. Lyallpur, India; came to U.S., 1976; s. Jodh Singh and Harnam Kaur R. BSc, De Montfort U., Eng., 1963; MSc, U. Surrey, Guilford, Eng., 1967, Cambridge (Eng.) U., 1972; PhD, Middlesex Hosp. Med. Sch. and U. Westminster, London, 1975; diploma, MIT, 1984. Chartered engr., scientist, Eng. Med. scientist Nat. Inst. Med. Rsch. of the Med. Rsch. Coun., London, 1967-70; rsch. fellow Middlesex Hosp. Med. Sch. and Poly. of Cen. London, 1971-76; rsch. scientist Plastics Rsch. Assn. of Great Britain, Shawbury, Eng., 1977; asst. prof. Wayne State U., Detroit, 1977-81; prof. biomed. engring./orthopaedic biomechanics biomaterials La. Tech. U., Ruston, 1982—; prof., chmn. dept. biomechanics N.Y. Coll. Osteo. Medicine, Old Westbury, 1989-93; dir. tng. Renbak R&D Ctr., 1983-85; mem. La. Tech. U. Libr. Com., 1983-85; chmn. design competition Assn. Biomed. Engrs.; mem. steering com. So. Biomed. Engring. Confs., 1983—; chmn. tech. in health care conf. U. Cambridge, 1985; chmn. Internat. Symposium on Bioengring., Calcutta, India, 1985; dir. orthopaedic biomechanics rsch. labs., staff Nassau County Med. Ctr., Long Island, 1989—; prof., exec. asst. to pres., and dir. doctoral program Life U., Marietta, Ga., 1993—; pres. Am. Orthop. Biomechanics Rsch. Inst., Atlanta, 1997—. Biomed. engring. faculty com. La. Tech. U., faculty com., rsch. awards com., grad. studies com., grad. faculty, acad. bd. dirs; vis. scientist Dryburn Hosp., Durham, Eng., 1985-87, cons., 1988—; vis. prof. U Istanbul, 1982, Lab. de Recherch Orthopediques, Paris, 1985—, Kings Coll. Med. Sch. U. London, 1989—, Indian Inst. Tech., New Delhi, Postgrad Inst. Med. Edn. and Rsch., Chandigarh, India, 1989—, Polytech. Ctrl. London, 1991—, U. Buenos Aires, Pontific Cath. U. Chile, Fed. U. Rio de Janeiro; adj. prof. Coll. Physicians and Surgeons Columbia U., NYC, 1988—, Inst. Biol. Physics USSR Acad. Sci., Moscow, 1990, NY Coll. Podiatric Medicine, 1991—, CUNY, 1992—; cons. Lincoln Gen. Hosp., Ruston, La., 1982-85, La. State U. Med. Ctr., Shreveport, 1982—, St. Luke's and Roosevelt Hosp. Ctr., NY, 1988—, Foot Clinics N., 1991—, Vets. Affairs Med. Ctr., NY, 1992—, others; media resource svc. Inst. Pub. Info., NY, 1989—; med. scientist, cons. NATO, 1982—; presenter, lectr. in field; external examiner for doctoral candidates All India Inst. Med. Scis., New Delhi, Indian Inst. Tech., New Delhi, Banaras Hindu U., Varanasi, India, 1994— Author: Rheological Behavior of Articular Cartilage Under Tensile Loads, 1967, Effects of Ionizing Radiation on the Mechanical Properties of Skin, 1975, Effects of Fractionated Doses of X-irradiation on the Mechanical Properties of Skin--A Long Term Study, 1980, Effects of Ionizing Radiation on the Structure & Physical Properties of the Skin, 1983, 3-D Model of Vertebra for Spinal Surgery, 1985, Application of Carbon Fibers in Orthopaedic Surgery, 1985, Relation Between Metal Corrision & Electrical Polarization, 1989, The Distribution of Stresses in the Human Lumbar Spine, 1989, Medical Devices & Orthopaedic Implants in the United States, 1989, Spinal Surgery by Modeling, 1989, Multipoint Determination of Pressure-Volume Curves in Human Intervertebral Discs, 1993, Evaluation of Volume-Pressure Relationship in Lumbar Discs Using Model and Experimental Studies, 1994, A Mechanism of Laser Nuclectomy, 1994, Microminiaturization in Laser Surgery in Vivo Intradiscal Pressure Measurements in Lumbar Intervertebral Discs, 1994, An Experimental and Mathematical Simulation of Fracture of Human Bone Due to Jumping, 1994; editor The Lower Extremity, 1993—; guest editor IEEE Engring. in Medicine & Biology, 1991; mem. editl. bd. Med. Instrumentation, 1988—, Jour. Biomed. Instrumentation & Tech., 1988—, Jour. Med. Engring. & Tech., 1989—, Jour. Med. Design & Material, 1990—, Jour. Long-Term Effects Med. Implants, 1991—, Biomed. Sci. & Tech., 1991—; reviewer Jour. Biomechanics, 1981—, Clin. Biomechanics, 1984—, Jour. Biomed. Engring., 1981, Phys. Therapy, 1990—, IEEE Biomed. Transactions, 1991—, Jour. Engring. in Medicine, 1989—; contbr. articles to profl. jours. Faculty advisor India Students Assn. Wayne State U., 1980. Recipient Edwin Tate award U. Surrey, 1968, Third Internat. Olympic Com. World Congress On Sprots Scis. award, Atlanta, 1995; numerous rsch. grants. Fellow ASME (bioengring. com. 1990—, award L.I. chpt. 1991), Biol. Engring. Soc. (London, President's prize 1984), Instn. Mech. Engrs. (chmn. revv. bd. for corp. memberships, James Clayton awards 1974-76), Inst. Physics and Engring. in Medicine; mem. AAAS, Am. Soc. Biomechanics (edn. com. 1990—), Orthopaedic Rsch. Soc., Am. Coll. Sports Medicine, Biomed. Engring. Soc., India Assn., India Assn. North La., Sci. Coun. Eng. (chartered scientist). Sikh. Achievements include research in microfracture simulation of human vertebrae under compressive loading, lasercotomy of the human nucleus pulposus and its effect on the intradiscal pressure, pressure-volume relation in human intervertebral discs, in vitro and in vivo intradiscal pressure measurements before and after lasercotomy of the human nucleus pulposus, gait analysis of a diabetic foot, bioengineering in the millennium, bioengineering-building the future of biology and medicine, bioengineering the cutting edge of biology and medicine in the millennium, in vivo micro-fracture simulation in Indian Olympic field hockey players, relief from low-back pain in sports by infusion of saline into the human nucleus pulposus and establishing the pressure-volume relationship, clinical applications of bioinstrumentation for better health, fifth IOC World Congress on sports sciences, micro-fracture simulation in tennis players, human gait analysis normal and pathological, simulation of micro-fracture injury in female gymnasts-an in vivo study, pattern recognition in human gait, identification of ethnicity from human gait; micro-fracture injury simulation in pole-vaulting and female gymnasts; 3-D simulation of drop in intradiscal pressure in spinal discs due to laserectomy; Ranu's principle and laserectomy to relieve low

back pain; Ranu's cumulative gait effect phenomenon, invivo micro-fracture simulation in skiers; 3-D foot pressure measurements in normal and diabetic persons; normal and abnormal gait of successive steps with miniature triaxial load cells. Office: Life Univ Sch Grad Studies Marietta GA 30060 Personal E-mail: drhsranu@yahoo.com.

**RANUM, OREST ALLEN,** historian, educator; b. Lyle, Minn., Feb. 18, 1933; s. Luther George and Nada (Chaffee) R.; m. Patricia McGroder, July 4, 1955; children— Kristin, Marcus BA, Macalester Coll., St. Paul, 1955; MA, U. Minn., 1957, PhD, 1961. Asst. prof. U. So. Calif., 1960-61; asst. prof. Columbia U., N.Y.C., 1961-63, assoc. prof., 1963-69; prof. history Johns Hopkins U., Balt., 1969-99; ret., 1999. Mem., chmn. GRE Ednl. Testing Service, Princeton, 1973-78 Author: Richelieu and Councilors, 1963, Paris, Age of Absolutism, 1968, revised and expanded edit., 2002, Artisans of Glory, 1981, The Fronde, 1993, Paris in the Age of Absolutism, 2002. Recipient Bronze medal City of Tours, France, 1980. Mem. Am. Hist. Assn., Soc. French Hist. Studies, Inst. de France (corr.), Académie des Sciences Morales et Politiques (Paris; corr. 1989), Société de l'Histoire de France, Collège de France (internat. chair 1994-95). Home: 208 Ridgewood Rd Baltimore MD 21210-2539 Office: History Dept Johns Hopkins U Baltimore MD 21218 Office Phone: 410-516-7575. E-mail: orestranum@cs.com.

**RANZAN, DAVID ALDRICH,** archivist; b. East Stroudsburg, Pa., Feb. 21, 1973; s. William Theodore Ranzan and Audrey Dorothy (Meier) Ranzan; m. Kelly Gene Smith, May 31, 2002. BA in History, East Stroudsburg U., 2000, MA in History, 2002; MLIS, Rutgers U., 2006. Grad. asst. Papers of War Dept., 1784-1800, East Stroudsburg, Pa., 1999—2000, asst. editor, 2004—05; documentary editor Thomas A. Edison Papers, Piscataway, NJ, 2000—; cons. The Hist. Speedwell, Morristown, 2004—; archivist Rutgers U. Archives, New Brunswick, 2005—. Co-editor: Thomas A. Edison Papers, A Selective Microfilm Edition: Part V (1911-1919), Sussex County (N.J.) Marriage and Obituary Dates (1814-1903). Fellow, NHPRC, 2001. Mem.: ALA, Assn. Documentary Editing, NJ. Libr. Assn., Soc. Am. Archivist, Phi Alpha Theta. Home: PO Box 334 Saylorsburg PA 18353 Office: Thomas A Edison Papers 44 Rd 3 Piscataway NJ 08854-8049 Office Phone: 732-445-8511 ext. 18. Office Fax: 732-445-8512.

**RAO, ANJANA,** immunologist, educator; MS in Physics, Osmania U., Hyderabad, India; PhD in Biophysics, Harvard U. Postdoctoral rschr. Harvard Med. Sch. and Dana-Farber Cancer Inst.; prof. pathology Dana Farber Cancer Inst., Harvard Med. Sch.; sr. investigator CBR Inst. Biomedical Rsch. Contbr. articles to profl. jours. Recipient Am. Assn. Immunologists-Huang Found. Meritorious Career award, 2000. Office: Harvard Med Sch Dept Pathology CBR Inst Biomedical Rsch 200 Longwood Ave Rm 152 Boston MA 02115 E-mail: arao@cbr.med.harvard.edu.*

**RAO, DABEERU C. (D.C. RAO),** epidemiologist, educator; b. Apr. 6, 1946; came to U.S., 1972; naturalized. s. Ramarao Patnaik and Venkataratnam (Raghupatruni) R.; m. Sarada Patnaik, 1974; children: Ravi, Lakshmi. BS in Stats., Indian Statis. Inst., Calcutta, 1967, MS, 1968, PhD, 1971. Rsch. fellow U. Sheffield, England, 1971-72; asst. geneticist U. Hawaii, Honolulu, 1972-78, assoc. geneticist, 1978-80; dir. divsn. biostats. Washington U. Med. Sch., 1980—, assoc. prof. St. Louis, 1980-82, prof. depts. biostats., psychiatry and genetics, 1982—. Adj. prof. math., 1982—. Author: A Source Book for Linkage in Man, 1979, Methods in Genetic Epidemiology, 1983, Genetic Epidemiology of Coronary Heart Disease, 1984; editor-in-chief Genetic Epidemiology jour., 1984-91; contbr. over 400 articles to profl. jours. Grantee NIH, 1978—; Telugu Assn. N.Am. Mem. Am. Statis. Assn., Am. Soc. Human Genetics, Internat. Genetic Epidemiology Soc. (pres. 1996), Behavior Genetics Assn., Soc. Epidemiol. Rsch., Biomed. soc. Office: Washington U Sch Medicine Divsn Biostats Box 8067 660 S Euclid Ave Saint Louis MO 63110-1010 E-mail: rao@wubios.wustl.edu.

**RAO, K.V.R. MOHAN** See KOTTAMASU, MOHAN

**RAO, MAHADEV,** pharmacologist, researcher, molecular biologist; s. Radha Bai and Gopalakrishna Bhat; m. Shanthalaxmi Thada, Apr. 24, 2002. B in Pharmacy, Mangalore U., 1992, PhD in Pharm. sci., 1999. Asst. prof. & head Mangalore U., Nanthoor, Karnataka, India, 1999—2000, rsch. assoc. Manipal, Karnataka, India; postdoctoral rsch. assoc. dept. oncology Lombardi Cancer Ctr., Georgetown U. Med. Ctr., Washington, 2003—. Recipient Travel Bursary award, Simon Wolf Charitable found., UK, 1998; Fogarty Internat. fellow, NIH, 2000-02, Rsch. Assoc. fellow, Dept. of Atomic Energy, India, 1995-1999, Jr. Rsch. fellow, U. Grants Commn., India, 1993-95. Mem.: Am. Assn. Pharm. Scientists (assoc.), Indian Pharm. Assn. (life). Achievements include discovery of novel tRNAs and cDNAS and publ. several papers. Home: 258 Congressional Ln #103 Rockville MD 20852 Office: Georgetown U 3970 Reservoir Rd NW Washington DC 20057-1468 Personal E-mail: raom999@yahoo.com. E-mail: mr262@georgetown.edu.

**RAO, NANNAPANENI NARAYANA,** electrical engineer; b. Kakumanu, Andhra Pradesh, India; m. Sarojini Jonnalagadda, June 10, 1955; children: Vanaja, Durgaprasad, Hariprasad. BSc in Physics, U. Madras, India, 1952; DMIT in Electronics, Madras Inst. Tech., 1955; MSEE, U. Wash., 1960-64, acting asst. prof., 1964-65; asst. prof. elec. engring. U. Ill., Urbana, 1965-69, asso. prof., 1969-75, prof., 1975—; Edward C. Jordan prof., 2003—, assoc. head elec. and computer engring., 1987—. Cons. Fakultas Teknik, Univ. Indonesia, Jakarta, 1985-86, 87. Author: Basic Electromagnetics with Applications, 1972, Elements of Engineering Electromagnetics, 6th edit., 2004; contbr. numerous articles to profl. jours. Recipient Engring. award Telugu Assn. N.Am., 1983, Excellence in Edn. award, 1999, Fakultas Teknik award Universitas Indonesia, 1986. Fellow IEEE (Undergrad. Teaching award 1994); mem. Am. Soc. Engring. Edn. (AT&T Found. award for excellence in instrn. engring. students 1991), Internat. Union Radio Sci. (U.S. Commn. G). Achievements include contributions to engineering education in the United States and abroad. Home: 2509 S Lynn St Urbana IL 61801-6841 Office: U Ill Dept Elec & Computer Engring 1406 W Green St Urbana IL 61801-2918 E-mail: rao@ece.uiuc.edu.

**RAO, POTARAZU KRISHNA,** environmental consultant; b. Andhra Pradesh, India, Mar. 26, 1930; s. Satyanarayana and Annapooma (Mullapudi) Rao; m. Rukmani Krutiviniti, Aug. 5, 1954; children: Ramanarayan, Sreedhar. BS, Andhra U., 1950, MS, 1952, Fla. State U., 1957; PhD, NYU, 1968. Meteorologist Can. Meteorol. Svc., Montreal, Canada, 1960-61; rsch. phys. scientist Nat. Oceanic and Atmospheric Adminstrn./Nat. Environ. Satellite Data and Info. Svc., Washington, 1961-74, chief atmospheric energetics br., acting dir., 1976-80, chief satellite applications lab., 1980-86, dir. office of rsch. and applications, 1986-96; chief scientist for satellite and info. svcs. Nat. Oceanic and Atmospheric Adminstrn., Washington, 1996—2002; program dir., weather modification NSF, Washington, 1971-72; advisor on satellite programs World Meteorological Orgn., Geneva, 1974-76; cons. TRW, ITT. Bd. dirs. Climate and Global Change Program Nat. Oceanic and Atmospheric Adminstrn., Washington; mem. adv. bd. Coop. Inst. for Rsch. in Atmospheres, Ft. Collins, 1986—. Editor: Weather Satellites, 1990; contbr. articles to profl. jours. Founder, trustee Sri Siva Vishnu Temple, Lanham, Md. Fellow: N.Y. Acad. Scis., Royal Meteorol. Soc. U.K., Am. Meteorol. Soc. Hindu. Avocations: tennis, photography. Home: 15824 Buena Vista Dr Rockville MD 20855-2658 E-mail: potarazukrao@netscape.net.

**RAO, RAMA KRISHNA R.,** pharmaceutical company executive; b. Tanuku, Andhra Province, India, Nov. 20, 1955; came to U.S., 1990; s. R.R. and Satyavani R. (Gudipati) R.; m. Kavitha Advikolanu, May 19, 1996. B in Tech., Indian Inst. Tech., Delhi, 1977; postgrad. diploma in mgmt., Indian Inst. Mgmt., Calcutta, 1981; MBA, INSEAD, Fontainebleu, France, 1989. Asst. mgr. Metal Box India, Calcutta, 1977-84; exec. asst. to gen. mgr. Bank of Bahrain & Kuwait, Bahrain, 1985-88; fin. assoc. Eli Lilly, Geneva, credit and customer svc. mgr., 1993-94, fin. mgr. Africa, 1994-95; mgr. (global treasury) Gems Eli Lilly, Brussels, 1995-97; fin. advisor corp. fin. and investment banking Lilly Corp. Ctr., Indpls., 1998-99; CFO, fin. mgr. PC/NS Lilly USA, Indpls., 1999—2001; fin. dir. intercontinental region Novartis Oncology Bus. Unit, East Hanover, NJ, 2001—04; CFO, v.p. fin. Novartis Can., Dorval, Canada, 2004—. Alumni mem. panel for INSEAD interviews, Belgium, U.S., 1995-99. Contbr. journalist Students' Newsletter, IIT, Delhi, co-editor Students' Newsletter, I.I.M., Calcutta, INSEAD, Fontainebleu, France. Vol. Samaritans/Befrienders, Bahrain, 1987, 88; donor of blood Red Cross/Crescent, India, Belgium, U.S., Bahrain, 1974-97. Recipient First prize Nat. Young Mgrs. Competition, All India Mgmt. Assn., 1983. Mem. AMA, Assn. Investment Mgmt. and Rsch., Inst. Mgmt. Accts. Hindu. Avocations: travel, military history, foreign policy. Office Phone: 514-633-7859. Business E-Mail: rama.rao@novartis.com.

**RAO, SADASIVA MADIRAJU,** engineering educator; b. Hyderabad, Andhra Pradesh, India, June 16, 1951; s. Sitarama Rao and Rangamma Madiraju; m. Kalyani Madiraju Gurazada, Nov. 14, 1986; children: Yeshaswi Madiraju, Siri Madiraju. B of Engring., Osmania U., Hyderabad, India, 1974; M of Engring., Indian Inst. Sci., Bangalore, 1976; PhD, U. Miss., Oxford, 1980. Asst. prof. Rochester Inst. Tech., NY, 1980—85; sr. scientist Osmania U., Hyderabad, Andhra Pradesh, India, 1985—87; prof. Auburn U., Ala., 1988—. Vis. assoc. prof. U. Houston, 1987—88. Home: 894 Tulane Road Auburn AL 36830 Office: Department of E&CE Auburn University 200 Broun Hall Auburn AL 36849 Office Phone: 334-844-1876. Home Fax: 334-844-1809; Office Fax: 334-844-1809. Business E-Mail: rao@eng.auburn.edu.

**RAO, SRIKUMAR SRINIVAS,** marketing educator; b. Bombay, Apr. 11, 1951; came to U.S., 1972; s. Hassan K. S. and Jaya S. Rao (Jayamma) R.; m. Meenakshi S., June 26, 1981; children: Gowri S., Gautam S. BS, St. Stephen's Coll., Delhi, India, 1970; MBA, Indian Inst. Mgmt., Ahmedabad, 1972; MPhil in Mktg., Columbia U., 1980, PhD in Mktg., 1982. Assoc. dir. mktg. rsch. Data Resources, Inc., Lexington, Mass., 1978-80; asst. prof. mktg. Baruch Coll., NYC, 1983-85; assoc. prof. mktg. LI U., Brookville, NY, 1985—, chmn. mktg. dept., 1991—; Louis and Johanna Vorzimer prof. mktg.; adj. prof. Columbia Bus. Sch., NYC, 2000—; London Sch. Bus. Sr. cons. Continental Group; spl. ass. to pres. Warner Communications, Inc.; cons. in field; seminar leader in field. Author: Are You Ready To Succeed? Unconventional Strategies for Achieving Personal Mastery in Business and Life, 2006; contbg. editor Forbes mag. Mem.: Am. Soc. Journalists and Authors, South Asian Journalists Assn., MENSA. Avocations: tennis, squash, karate, chess. Home: 25 Shirley Ct Commack NY 11725-4112 Office: Long Island U 302 Roth Hall Greenvale NY 11548 Office Phone: 516-864-3146. E-mail: srikumarsrao@cs.com.

**RAO, SUDHAKAR,** aerospace engineer, researcher; b. Tenali, Andhra Pradesh, India, July 15, 1951; arrived in US, 1996, naturalized, 2004; s. Baparao and Hymavathi Krothapalli; m. Rajani Krothapalli, Apr. 30, 1978; 1 child, Neha. BE, JNT U., Warangal, India, 1974; ME, Indian Inst. Tech., Kharaghpur, 1976; PhD, Indian Inst. Tech., Madras, 1980. Tech. officer Electronic Corp. India Ltd., Hyderabad, Andhra Pradesh, India, 1976—77; sr. sci. officer Electronic and Radar Devel. Establishment, Bangalore, Karnataka, India, 1980—81; postdoctoral rsch. fellow U. Trondheim, Norway, 1981—82; rsch. assoc. U. Man., Winnipeg, Canada, 1982—83; staff scientist Spar Aerospace Ltd., Ste-Anne-de-Bellevue, Que., Canada, 1983—96; chief scientist Boeing Satellite Sys., El Segundo, Calif., 1996—2003; divsn. fellow Lockheed Martin Comml. Space Sys., Newtown, Pa., 2003—. Mem. intellectual property rev. bd. Lockheed Martin. Contbr. articles to profl. jours. Sponsored eye camps Rotary Club India, Vijayawada, Andhra Pradesh, 2005—06. Recipient Boeing's Spl. Invention award, 2002, Lockheed Martin's Key Inventor award, 2005; NTNF Postdoctoral fellow, Norwegian Coun. Sci. and Indsl. Rsch., 1981, 1982. Fellow: IEEE (Benjamin Franklin Key award 2006, Fellow award 2006). Republican. Hindu. Achievements include patents for advanced payloads for satellite communications; patents pending for satellite payloads; development of radiation templates for interferences analysis of various satellite systems. Avocations: tennis, basketball. Home: 125 Livery Dr Churchville PA 18966 Office: Lockheed Martin Comml Space Sys 100 Campus Dr Newtown PA 18940 Office Phone: 215-497-2265. Personal E-mail: skraoks@yahoo.com.

**RAO, VITTAL SRIRANGAM,** electrical engineering educator; b. Inumpamula, India, June 8, 1944; came to U.S., 1981; s. Rangaiah Srirangam and Lakshmamma (Immadi) R.; m. Vijaya Morishetti, Feb. 28, 1965; children: Asha, Ajay. M of Tech., Indian Inst. Tech., 1972, PhD, 1975. Asst. prof. Indian Inst. of Tech., New Delhi, India, 1975-79; vis. prof. T.U., Halifax, N.S., Can., 1980-81; assoc. prof. U. Mo., Rolla, 1981-88, prof., 1988—; dir. Intelligent Systems Ctr., Rolla, 1991—. Cons. Delco Remy, Anderson, Ind., 1985-87, Allison Gas Turbines, Indpls., 1986-87, U.S. Army Picatinny Arsenal, N.J., 1988-91. Contbr. articles to profl. jours. including Suboptimal/Near Optimal Control, Reduced Order Modeling Techniques, Robust Control, Large Space Structures, Smart Structures. Fellow AIAA (assoc.); mem. IEEE (sr., subsect. 1981-88, Centennial medal 1984). Achievements include devel. of reduced order modeling techniques for large space structures, interdisciplinary approach for control of smart structures and structural health monitoring. Home: 501 Oak Knoll Rd Rolla MO 65401-4727 Office: U Mo Intelligent Systems Ctr Rolla MO 65401

**RAOUAFI, NOUR-EDDINE,** astrophysicist, researcher; D, U. Paris XI, Orsay, 2000. Rschr. Max-Planck-Inst. Solar Sys. Rsch., Katlenburg-Lindau, Niedersachsen, Germany, 2002—05; rsch. assoc. Nat. Solar Obs., Tucson, 2005—. Achievements include research in coronal heating and solar wind acceleration. Office Phone: +1-520-891-0461.

**RAOUFI, AZADEH,** music educator; arrived in U.S., 1998; d. Mohammad Sadogh Raoufi and Fatemeh (Mali) Fakoor-Sevvom. B in Piano and Computer Sci., U. Iowa, 2004, postgrad., 2005—. Tchr. English Shokoh, Mashad, 1995—98; with Tech. Ctr., Iowa City, 2001—02; with internal med. rsch. lab. U. Iowa, Iowa City, 2001—02; piano tchr. West Music, Iowa City, 2002—. Mem.: Iowa City Ind. Piano Tchrs. (v.p.), Iowa Music Tchr. Assn. (pub. rels. person 2004—), Music Tchr. Nat. Assn., Phi Theta Kappa. E-mail: azadeh-raoufi@uiowa.edu.

**RAPACZYNSKI, ANDRZEJ,** law educator; b. 1947; PhD, Columbia U., 1974; JD, Yale U., 1982. Bar: NY 1984. Asst. prof. philosohy Yale U., New Haven, 1974-79; asst. prof. Columbia U., NYC, 1982-86, prof. law, 1986—, Daniel G. Ross prof. law. Vis. scholar Heidelberg U. Starnberg, Germany, 1976; vis. assoc. prof. philosophy Princeton U., 1977—78; vis. prof. Yale U., 1999—2000. Mem. Am. Soc. Polit. and Legal Philosophy. Office: Columbia U Sch Law 435 W 116th St New York NY 10027-7297 Office Phone: 212-854-3421. Office Fax: 212-854-7946. E-mail: andrap@law.columbia.edu.

**RAPADAS, LEONARDO M.,** prosecutor, lawyer; b. 1960; BS, Pacific Univ.; JD, Williamette Univ. Coll of Law. Pros. Guam Atty. Gen. office, 1989—97, chief pros., 1997—99; US Atty. dist. Guam & Mariana Islands US Dept. Justice, Saipan, 2003—. Office: US Attys Office Sirena Plz Ste 500 108 Hernan Cortez PO Box 500377 Saipan MP 96950-0377*

**RAPER, CHARLES ALBERT,** retired management consultant; b. Charleston, W.Va., Aug. 18, 1926; s. Kenneth B. and Louise (Williams) R.; m. Margaret Ann Weers, Dec. 26, 1947; children: Kathleen, Josephine, Charles. Student, Okla. State U., 1945; BS, U. Ill., 1949. Sales mgr. Meyer Furnace Co., Peoria, Ill., 1949-54; v.p. mktg. Master Consol., Inc., Dayton, Ohio, 1954-61; mgmt. cons. McKinsey & Co., Inc., Chgo., 1961-67; v.p. mktg. Gen. Portland Inc., Dallas, 1967-69, pres., as dir., 1969-75; v.p., gen. mgr. Scholl Inc., Chgo., 1975-81; pres. Oxford Group of Sara Lee, 1981-84; mgmt. cons. McKinsey & Co., 1984—. Vice-chmn. devel. bd. U. Tex., Dallas; exec. bd. Circle 10 coun. Boy Scouts Am.; Svc. Corp. of Ret. Execs. counselor. With

USN, 1944-46. Mem. Dallas C. of C. (chmn. bd. dirs. 1974—), Sales Execs. Club, Cherokee Country Club, Chattooga Club, Atlanta Mallet Club (pres.), Phi Gamma Delta. Methodist. Home: 3750 Peachtree Rd Apt 482 Atlanta GA 30319

**RAPER, WILLIAM BURKETTE,** retired college president; b. nr. Wilson, N.C., Sept. 10, 1927; s. William Cecil and Beulah Maybelle (Davis) R.; m. Rose Mallard, Aug. 19, 1951; children: Olivia, Kristie, Burkette, Elizabeth, Stephen (dec.), Laura. AB, Duke U., 1947, MDiv, 1951; MS (Kellogg fellow), Fla. State U., 1962; LLD, Atlantic Christian Coll. (now Barton Coll.), 1960. Ordained to ministry Free Will Baptist Ch., 1946; pastor Hull Rd. Free Will Bapt. Ch., Snow Hill, NC, 1951-55; pres. Mt. Olive (N.C.) Coll., 1954-95, ret. pres. emeritus, 1995. Dir. Wachovia Bank and Trust Co., 1979-97; promotional dir. Free Will Bapt. State Conv. N.C., 1953-54; pres. council Ch.-Related Colls. N.C., 1966-67; mem. N.C. Edn. Assistance Authority, 1972-76; sec. Ind. Coll. Fund of N.C., 1976-78; Mem. N.C. Gov.'s Com. on Hwy. Traffic Safety, 1968; regional coordinator U.S. Office Edn. Program with Developing Instns., 1968-70; dir. Edn. Professions Devel. Act Grant for Strengthening Devel. in Pvt. Two-Year Colls., 1970-72; trustee N.C. Coll. Found., 1977-94; adv. com. Ind. Coll. Presidents, U. N.C. Pres. N.C. Found. Christian Ministries, 2005. Recipient Disting. Service award Mt. Olive Jr. C. of C., 1961; named N.C. Young Man of Year, 1961 Mem. Am. Assn. Community and Jr. Colls. (commn. on legislation 1963-66, cons. 1968-71, chmn. commn. on student personnel 1970-71), N.C. Assn. Ind. Colls. and Univs. (exec. com. 1967-70, 76-77, 83-85), N.C. Assn. Colls. and Univs. (pres. 1969-70), Masons. Democrat. Office: Mt Olive Coll Office of Pres Emeritus Mount Olive NC 28365 Office Phone: 919-658-5250. E-mail: wraper@moc.edu.

**RAPHAEL, ALBERT ASH, JR.,** retired lawyer; b. NYC, June 4, 1925; s. Albert Ash and Clare (Schindler) R.; m. Dorothy Buck, Oct. 7, 1960; 1 child, Bruce William. AB, Yale U., 1947; LL.D., Harvard U., 1950. Bar: N.Y. 1950, Vt. 1972. Mem. firm Gallett, Hilborn & Raphael, N.Y.C., 1950-60, Alter, Lefevre, Raphael, Lowry, and Gould, N.Y.C., 1960-78; pvt.practice Waitsfield, Vt., 1972—86; pvt. practice, 1995—2002; ptnr. Raphael and Ware, Waitsfield, 1986-95; ret., 2002. Dir. various real estate cos. Mem. bd. zoning appeals, Waitsfield, 1974-83, selectman, 1976-82, chmn. bd. selectmen, 1981-82 Mem. Waitsfield Planning Commn., 1996-2003. Served with F.A. AUS, 1943-46. Mem. Vt. Bar Assn., Assn. of Bar of City of N.Y. Home: PO Box 113 Warren VT 05674-0113 Personal E-mail: aar@madriver.com.

**RAPHAEL, AMY BETH,** director; b. Hartford, Conn., Mar. 24, 1975; d. Michael A. and Anita Z. Raphael. BA in Psychology, Wake Forest U., 1997; MS in Counselor Edn., The U. N.C., Greensboro, N.C., 2000; PhD in Counseling and Student Pers. Svcs., U. Ga., 2005. Cert. counselor Nat. Bd. Cert. Counselors, 2000. Asst. dir. career resources and tech. Coll. Holy Cross, Worcester, Mass., 2000—02; instr., grad. asst. U. Ga., Athens, Ga., 2002—05; dir. career planning and placement svcs. Barry U., Miami Shores, Fla., 2005—. Distance career counselor ReadyMinds, N.Y., 2000—. Contbr. articles to profl. jours. Grantee, So. Assoc. Coll. Student Affairs, 2004. Mem.: Nat. Assn. Colls. and Employers, So. Assn. Colls. and Employers, Nat. Assn. Student Personnel Adminstrs. Office: Barry University Career Services 11300 NE 2nd Avenue Miami Shores FL 33161 Office Phone: 305-899-3956. Office Fax: 305-899-4009.

**RAPHAEL, JAY E.,** theater educator, director, actor; b. NYC; s. Harry Arlen Raphael and Stella Bernice Stuart. BA, Bklyn. Coll., 1964; MA, Northwestern U., Evanston, Ill., 1965; PhD, Mich. State U., East Lansing, 1971. Prof., actor, dir. prodr., 1971—. Recipient Disting. Contbn. Theatre award, Mich. State U., 1990; grantee, NEH, 1980; Dees Coun. Tchg. fellow, U. Utah, 2001. Mem.: Soc. Stage Dirs. and Choreographers, Screen Actors Guild, Actors Equity. Office: Theatre Arts and Dance Dept U Ark Little Rock 2801 S Univ Ave Little Rock AR 72204 Office Phone: 501-569-8350. Office Fax: 501-569-8355.

**RAPHAEL, LOUISE ARAKELIAN,** mathematician, educator; b. NYC, Oct. 24, 1937; d. Aristakes and Antionette (Sudbeaz) Arakelian; m. Robert Barnett Raphael, June 12, 1966 (div. 1985); children: Therese Denise, Marc Philippe. BS in Math., St. John's U., 1959; MS in Math., Cath. U., Washington, 1962; PhD in Math, Cath. U., 1967. Asst. prof. math. Howard U., Washington, 1966-70, vis. prof., 1981-82, assoc. prof., 1982-86, prof., 1986—; assoc. prof. Clark Coll., Atlanta, 1971-79, prof., 1979-82. Vis. assoc. prof. MIT, Cambridge, 1977-78, vis. prof., 1989-90; vis. mem. Courant Inst. Math. Scis., NYU, 1996-97; vis. scholar Cornell U., 2004. Contbr. over 40 rsch. articles to profl. jours. Program dir. NSF, Washington, 1986—88; acting adminstrv. officer Conf. Bd. Math. Scis., 1985—86. Grantee NSF, 1975-76, 79-81, 89-91, Army Rsch. Office, 1981-89, Air Force Sci. Rsch., 1981-82, 91-95, Nat. Security Agy., 1994-96. Mem.: Soc. Indsl. and Applied Math., Math. Assn. Am. (1st v.p. 1996—98, chmn. minorities in math. task force 1988), Am. Math. Soc. (coun. 2001—04, com. mem.), Sigma Xi. Democrat. Roman Catholic. Office: Howard U Dept Math Washington DC 20059-0001

**RAPHAELSON, JOEL,** retired advertising agency executive; b. NYC, Sept. 27, 1928; s. Samson and Dorothy (Wegman) R.; m. Mary Kathryn Hartigan, Aug. 20, 1960; children: Matthew, Katherine, Paul. BA, Harvard U., 1949. Copywriter Macy's, N.Y.C., 1950-51, BBDO, N.Y.C., 1953-58; with Ogilvy & Mather, Inc., N.Y.C., 1958-94, sr. v.p. dir., 1966-75, mem. exec. com., 1970-75; creative cons. Ogilvy & Mather, Inc., Europe, 1975-76; exec. creative dir. Ogilvy & Mather, Inc., Chgo., 1976—82; sr. v.p. internat. creative svcs. Ogilvy & Mather Worldwide, 1982-92, spl. assignments as editor, writer, speechwriter, cons., 1993-94, ret., 1995. Lectr. Am. Assn. Advt. Agys., other bus orgns, writers groups, cons. Author (with Kenneth Roman) How To Write Better, 1978, Writing That Works, 1981, rev. expanded edit., 1992, 00; editor The Unpublished David Ogilvy, 1986, Viewpoint (co. jour.), 1983-94; contbr. Harvard Bus. Rev., other bus. publs. Cons. Lyric Opera Chgo., 1983-2005, Exec. Svc. Corps, Chgo.; dir. Santa for the Very Poor, 1988— Home: 20 E Cedar St Apt 8A Chicago IL 60611-5115 Personal E-mail: joelr28@aol.com.

**RAPIN, ISABELLE,** physician; b. Lausanne, Switzerland, Dec. 4, 1927; d. Rene and Mary Coe (Reeves) R.; m. Harold Oaklander, Apr. 5, 1959; children: Anne Louise, Christine, Stephen, Peter. Physician's Diploma. Faculte de Medicine, U. Lausanne, 1952, Doctorate in Medicine, 1955. Diplomate Am. Bd. Psychiatry and Neurology. Intern in pediatrics N.Y. U. Bellevue Med. Center, 1953-54; resident in neurology Neurol. Inst. of N.Y., Columbia-Presbyn. Med. Center, 1954-57, fellow in child neurology, 1957-58; mem. faculty Albert Einstein Coll. Medicine, Bronx, NY, 1958—, prof. neurology and pediatrics, 1972—; attending neurologist and child neurologist Einstein Affiliated Hosps., Bronx. Mem. Nat. Adv. Neurol. and Communicative Disorders and Stroke Coun., NIH, 1984-88. Contbr. chpts. to books, articles to med. jours. Recipient award Conf. Ednl. Adminstrs. Serving the Deaf, 1988. Fellow: Am. Acad. Neurology (exec. bd. 1995—99); mem.: AAAS, Assn. for Rsch. in Nervous and Mental Diseases (v.p. 1986), Internat. Neuropsychology Soc., Am. Neurol. Assn. (hon.; v.p. 1982—83), Child Neurology Soc. (Hower award 1987), Internat. Child Neurology Assn. (sec.-gen. 1978-92, v.p. 1982—86), Frank R. Ford lectr. 1990). Office: Albert Einstein Coll Medicine K807 1300 Morris Park Ave Bronx NY 10461-1101

**RAPINI, RONALD PETER,** dermatology educator; b. Akron, Ohio, Feb. 15, 1954; s. Vincent Thomas and Joann Irene (Tufexis) R.; m. Mary Jo Beigel, June 16, 1979; children: Brianna Marie, Sarina Elizabeth. BS in Biology, U. Akron, 1975; MD, Ohio State U., 1978. Diplomate Am. Bd. Dermatology (bd. dirs. 1996-2004, pres. 2004), Am. Bd. Dermatopathology. Assoc. prof. U. Tex. Med. Sch., Houston, 1983-93; prof. and chair dermatology dept. Tex. Tech. U., Lubbock, 1994—2002; prof., chair dept. dermatology U. Tex. Med. Sch., Houston, 2002—; MD Anderson Cancer Ctr., Houston, 2002—. Author (with K.G. Gross and H.K. Steinman): Mohs Surgery, 1999; author (with J. Bolognia and J. Jorizzo) Dermatology, 2003; author: Practical Dermatopathology, 2005, of over 150 other publications. Fellow Am. Acad. Dermatol-

ogy, Am. Soc. Dermatol. Surgery (bd. dir. 1995-98), Soc. Investigative Dermatology; mem. AMA, Am. Soc. Dermatopathology (pres. 1998-99), Am. Soc. Mohs Surgery (pres. 2003), Internat. Soc. Dermatopathology, Tex. Dermatol. Soc. (pres. 2006—). Avocations: tennis, entomology, piano. Office: U TEx Med Sch 6655 Travis St 980 Houston TX 77030-0001 Office Phone: 713-745-1113.

**RAPOPORT, ANATOL,** humanities educator, biophysicist; b. Lozovaya, Russia, May 22, 1911; emigrated to U.S., 1922, naturalized, 1928; s. Boris and Adel (Rapoport) R.; m. Gwen Goodrich, Jan. 29, 1949; children: Anya, Alexander, Charles Anthony. PhD, U. Chgo., 1941; DHL, U. Western Mich., 1971; LLD, U. Toronto, 1986; DS, Royal Mil. Coll. Can., 1995; Ehrendoktor, U. Bern, Switzerland, 1995. Faculty dept. math. Ill. Inst. Tech., 1946-47; com. math. biology U. Chgo., 1947-54; fellow Ctr. Advanced Study Behavioral Scis., Stanford, 1954-55; asso. prof. Mental Health Research Inst., prof. math. biology U. Mich., 1955-70; prof. psychology and math. U. Toronto, 1970-80; dir. Inst. for Advanced Studies, Vienna, 1980-83; prof. peace studies U. Toronto, 1984—. Author: Science and the Goals of Man, 1950, Operational Philosophy, 1953, Fights, Games, and Debates, 1960, Strategy and Conscience, 1964, Prisoner's Dilemma, 1965, Two-Person Game Theory, 1966, N Person Game Theory, 1970, The Big Two, 1971, Conflict in Man Made Environment, 1974, Semantics, 1975, The 2 x 2 Game, 1976, Mathematische Methoden in den Sozialwissenschaften, 1980, Mathematical Models in the Social and Behavioral Sciences, 1983, General System Theory, 1986, The Origins of Violence, 1989, Decision Theory and Decision Behavior, 1989, Canada and the World, 1992, Peace: An Idea Whose Time Has Come, 1992, Gewissheiten und Zweifel, 1994, Uverennost' i Somnenia, 1999, Certainties and Doubts, 2000, Skating on Thin Ice, 2002; editor: General Systems, 1956—77. Served to capt. USAAF, 1942-46. Fellow Am. Acad. Arts and Scis.; mem. Am. Math. Soc., Internat. Soc. Gen. Semantics (pres. 1953-55), Canadian Peace Research and Edn. Assn. (pres. 1972-75), Soc. for Gen. Systems Research (pres. 1965-66), Sci. for Peace (pres. 1984-86) Home: 38 Wychwood Park Toronto ON Canada M6G 2V5

**RAPOPORT, BERNARD ROBERT,** lawyer; b. NYC, Jan. 18, 1919; s. Max and Rose (Gerard) R.; m. Robyrta Wechter, May 31, 1959; 1 son: Michael. AB, Cornell U., 1939, JD, 1941. Bar: NY 1941, Fed. Ct. (so. dist.) 1946. Assoc. firm Proskauer, Rose, Goetz, Mendelsohn, NYC, 1941-50; gen. counsel M. Lowenstein Corp., NYC, 1950-86; dir., treas., sec. Leon Lowenstein Found. Capt. Signal Corps, U.S. Army, 1942-45. Mem. ABA, Assn. of Bar of City of N.Y. Address: 910 5th Ave New York NY 10021-4155 Office Phone: 212-486-7119.

**RAPOPORT, DAVID E.,** lawyer; b. Chgo., May 27, 1956; s. Morris H. and Ruth (Teckteil) R.; m. Andrea Gail Albun; children: Alyson Faith, Steven Andrew. BS in Fin., No. Ill. U., 1978; JD with high honors, Ill. Inst. Tech., 1981; cert. trial work, Lawyers Postgrad. Inst., Chgo., 1984; cert. civil trial specialist, Nat. Bd. Trial Advy., 1991. Bar: Ill. 1981, Wis. 1995, U.S. Dist. Ct. (no. dist.) Ill. 1981, U.S. Dist. Ct. (trial bar no. dist.) Ill. 1983, U.S. Dist. Ct. (so. and ctrl. dists.) Ill., U.S. Ct. Appeals (7th cir.) 1983, U.S. Ct. Appeals (4th cir.) 1996, U.S. Dist. Ct. (ea. dist.) Wis. 2000 U.S. Supreme Ct. 2000. Assoc., ptnr. Katz, Friedman, Schur & Eagle, Chgo., 1981-90, of counsel, 1990—; ptnr. Baizer & Rapoport, Chgo., Highland Park, Ill., 1990-95; founder, pres. Rapoport Law Offices, P.C., 1995—. Instr. legal writing Ill. Inst. Tech.-Kent Coll. Law, Chgo., 1981, guest lectr., 1985-2004; instr. Ill. Inst. CLE, 1995; arbitrator Million Dollar Advs. Forum, 1995—; state coord. Nat. Bd. Trial Advocacy; lead trial counsel, mem. plaintiff's steering com. In Air Disaster at Charlotte Douglas Airport, 1994; mem. lead counsel com. In Air Disaster at Morrisville, N.C., 1994; lead trial counsel, In The Air Disaster at Sioux Gateway Airport, 1989. Contbr. articles to various law jours. and pubs., chapters to books. Bd. dirs. Injury Prevention Works, 1999—. Fellow Roscoe Pound Found., Law Pilots Bar Assn.; mem. ABA, ATLA (sustaining mem.), Ill. Bar Assn., Ill. Trial Lawyers Assn., Trial Lawyers for Pub. Justice, Chgo.-Kent Law Sch. Alumni Assn. (bd. dirs. 2004—). Democrat. Jewish. Avocations: water-skiing, skiing, snowboarding, handball, sailing. Office: Rapoport Law Offices PC 20 N Clark St Ste 3500 Chicago IL 60602-2801 Office Phone: 312-327-9880. Business E-Mail: drapoport@ropoportlaw.com.

**RAPOPORT, JUDITH,** psychiatrist; b. NYC, July 12, 1933; d. Louis and Minna (Enteen) Livant; m. Stanley Rapoport, June 25, 1961; children: Stuart, Erik. BA, Swarthmore Coll., 1955; MD, Harvard U., 1959. Lic. psychiatrist. Cons., child psychiatrist NIMH/St. Elizabeth's Hosp., Washington, 1969—72; clin. asst. prof. Georgetown U. Med. Sch., Washington, 1972—82, clin. assoc. prof., 1982—85, clin. prof. psychiat., 1985—; med. officer biol. psychiatry br. NIMH, Bethesda, Md., 1979—82, chief, child psychiatry lab. of clin. scis., 1982—84, chief, child psychiatry div. intramural rsch. programs, 1984—; prof. psychiatry George Washington U. Sch. Med., Washington, 1979—; prof. pediat. Georgetown U., Washington, 1985—. Cons. in field. Author: (non-fiction) The Boy Who Couldn't Stop Washing, 1989 (best seller literary guild selection, 1989), Childhood Obsessive Compulsive Disorder, 1989. Recipient Scolnick award, MIT, 2005. Fellow: Am. Acad. Arts & Scis., Am. Acad. Child Psychiatry, Am. Psychiat. Assn.; mem.: Inst. Medicine, D.C. Psychiat. Assn. Home: 3010 44th Pl NW Washington DC 20016-3557 Office: NIMH Rm 3N202 10 Center Dr Bldg 10 Bethesda MD 20892-0001 Office Phone: 301-496-6081. Business E-Mail: rapoport@helix.nih.gov.

**RAPOPORT, MILES S.,** former state official; m. Sandra Luciano; children: Jeff, Ross. BA in Polit. sci., N.Y. U., 1971. Exec. dir. Conn. Citizen Action Group, 1979-84; mem. Conn. Ho. of Reps., asst. majority leader, 1987-92, house chmn. govt. adminstrn. and elections com., mem. fin., revenue and bonding com.; sec. of state State of Conn., 1994-98; exec. dir. Democracy Works, Hartford, Conn., 1999—2001. Office: President Demos 5th Fl 220 Fifth Ave New York NY 10001

**RAPOPORT, NANCY B.,** law educator; b. Bryan, Tex., June 29, 1960; m. Jeffrey D. Van Niel, Oct. 13, 1996. BA summa cum laude (hon.), Rice U., 1982; JD, Stanford Law Sch., 1985. Bar: Calif. 1987, U.S. Dist. Cts. (no., ea., ctrl., and so. dists.) Calif. 1987, U.S. Ct. Appeals (9th cir.) 1987, Ohio 1993, Nebr. 1999, U.S. Dist. Ct. (no. dist.) Tex. 2003. Jud. clk. Hon. Joseph T. Sneed, U.S. Ct. Appeals (9th cir.), San Francisco, 1985—86; assoc. bus.dept. of bankruptcy and workouts group Morrison & Foerster, San Francisco, 1986—91; asst. prof. Ohio State U. Coll. Law, Columbus, 1991—95, tenured assoc. prof., 1995—98, assoc. dean student affairs, 1996—98, prof., 1998; dean, prof. law U. Nebr. Coll. Law, Lincoln, 1998—2000, U. Houston Law Ctr., 2000—. Invited spkr., panelist, and presenter in field. Co-editor (with Bala G. Dharan): Enron: Corporate Fiascos and Their Implications, 2004. Bd. trustees Law Sch. Admissions Coun., 2001—04; bd. dirs. ADL Southwest Regional Bd., Houston Area Women's Ctr. Named Outstanding Prof. of Yr., Ohio State U. Coll. Law, 1997; recipient Rice U. Dist. Alumna award. Fellow: Am. Coll. Bankruptcy, Am. Bar Found., Houston Bar Found. (selection com. Best Article award 2000—); mem.: ABA (task force atty. discipline 2005—, commn. loan repayment and forgiveness), Assn. Am. Law Sch.'s Profl. Develop. Com., Ohio State Bar Assn. (legal edn. com. 1997—98), Am. Bankruptcy Inst. (law sch. com. 1994—), Bar Assn. San Francisco, Nat. Assn. Coll. and U. Attys., Nebr. State Bar Assn. (Named Legal Pioneer for Women in Law (first women to serve as dean of Nebr. Law Sch. 1999—), Houston Bar Assn., Am. Law Inst. Avocations: ballroom dancing, Latin dancing, black and white photography, blues music. Office: U Houston Law Ctr 100 Law Ctr Houston TX 77204-6060 Office Phone: 713-743-2100. Business E-Mail: nrapoport@uh.edu.

**RAPOPORT, RONALD JON,** journalist; b. Detroit, Aug. 14, 1940; s. Daniel B. and Shirley G.; m. Joan Zucker, Sept. 2, 1968; children— Rebecca, Julie. BA, Stanford U., 1962; MS, Columbia U., 1963. Reporter Mpls. Star, 1963-65; assoc. editor Stanford U., 1965-66; sports reporter AP, N.Y.C., and San Francisco, 1966-70, Los Angeles Times, 1970-77; sports columnist Chgo. Sun-Times, 1977-88, Los Angeles Daily News, 1988-95; sports commentator Weekend Edit. Nat. Pub. Radio, 1986—; dep. sports editor Chgo. Sun-Times, 1996-98, sports columnist, 1998—2006. Author: (with Chip Oliver) High for the Game, 1971; (with Stan Love) Love in the NBA, 1975, (with Jim McGregor) Called for Travelling, 1979; editor: A Kind of Grace: A Treasury of Sportswriting by Women, 1994; (with Betty Garrett) Betty Garrett and Other Songs, 1998, See How She Runs: Marion Jones and the Making of a Champion, 2000, The Immortal Bobby: Bobby Jones and the Golden Age of Golf, 2005, (with Eddie Einhorn) How March Became Madness: How the NCAA Tournament Became the Greatest Sporting Event in America, 2006. Served with U.S. Army Res., 1963. Personal E-mail: rjrapoport@ameritech.net.

**RAPOPORT, SANDRA E.,** lawyer, consultant; b. N.Y.C., Dec. 5, 1951; d. Gabriel and Rebecca Sharon; m. Samuel Rapoport, June 21, 1973; children: Benjamin, Ezra, Sarah. BS, Cornell U., 1973; JD, St. John's U., N.Y.C., 1976. Bar: N.Y. 1976, U.S. Dist. Ct. (so. and ea. dists.) N.Y. 1976. Law clk. Ladas, parry, Von Gehr, et al, N.Y.C., 1973-76, N.Y. Civil Liberties Union, N.Y.C., 1974-75; assoc. law dept. Am. Jewish Com., N.Y.C., 1976-77; corp. counsel divsn. gen. litigation City of N.Y., N.Y.C., 1977-80; assoc. Seyfarth, Shaw, Fairweather, et al, N.Y.C., 1980-84; cons. William M. Mercer divsn. Marsh & McClennan), N.Y.C., 1984-89; pvt. practice law N.Y.C., 1989—99. Co-author: The Passions of the Matriarchs, 2005. Office: 535 E 86th St New York NY 10028-7533

**RAPP, ADAM,** writer, playwright; b. Chgo. Grad., Clarke Coll., Dubuque, Iowa. Artist-in-residence Vassar Coll., Dartmouth Coll.; playwright-in-residence The Juilliard Sch.; resident playwright Edge Theater Co., NYC. Author: (plays) Gompers, Ghosts in the Cottonwoods, 1996, Dreams of the Salthrose, Trueblinka, 1997, Faster, Finer Noble Gases, 2001, Stone Cold Dead Serious, Blackbird, Animals and Plants, 2001, Nocturne, 2001, Red Light Winter, 2005 (OBIE award spl. citation, Village Voice, 2006), cagelove, 2006, (young adult novels) Missing the Piano, 1994, The Buffalo Tree, The Copper Elephant, 1999, Little Chicago, 2002, 33 Snowfish, 2003, Under the Wolf, Under the Dog, 2004, (adult novels) The Year of Endless Sorrows, 2005; writer & dir. (films) Winter Passing, 2005. Recipient Princess Grace award for playwrighting, 1999, Roger L. Stevens award, Kennedy Ctr. Fund for New Am. Plays, 2000, Helen Merrill award for emerging playwrights, 2001, Elliot Norton award, Le Compte de Nuoy awards, Lincoln Ctr.; Herbert & Patricia Brodkin Scholarship, 1997, Camargo Found. fellowship, Cassis, France. Office: Resident Playwright Edge Theater Co 880 Third Ave 16th Floor New York NY 10022 Office Phone: 212-350-7223. Office Fax: 212-350-7295.*

**RAPP, GEORGE ROBERT (RIP RAPP),** geology and archeology educator; b. Toledo, Sept. 19, 1930; s. George Robert and Gladys Mae (Warner) R.; m. Jeannette Messner, June 15, 1956; children: Kathryn, Karen. BA, U. Minn., 1952; PhD, Pa. State U., 1960. Asst. then assoc. prof. S.D. Sch. Mines, Rapid City, 1957-65; assoc. prof. U. Minn., 1965-75, prof. geology and archeology Duluth, 1975-95, dean Coll. Letters and Sci., 1975-84, dean Coll. Sci. and Engring., 1984-89, dir. Archeometry Lab., 1975—2004, Regents' prof. geoarchaeology, 1995—2003, emeritus 2003—. Prof. Ctr. for Ancient Studies, U. Minn., Mpls., 1970-93, prof. interdisciplinary archaeol. studies, 1993—; cons. USIA, Westinghouse Corp., Exxon Corp., Ford Found. Author, editor: Excavations at Nichoria, 1978, Troy: Archeological Geology, 1982, Archeological Geology, 1985, Excavations at Tel Michal, 1989, Encyclopedia of Minerals, 1989, Phytolith Systematics, 1992, Geoarchaeology, 1998, Artifact Copper Sources, 2000, Archaeomineralogy, 2002; mem. editl. bd. Jour. Field Archeology, 1976-85, Jour. Archeol. Sci., 1977-79, Geoarcheology Jour., 1984-92, Am. Jour. Archeology, 1985-92. NSF postdoctoral fellow, 1963-64, Fulbright-Hayes sr. rsch. fellow, 1972-73. Fellow AAAS (chmn. sect. E, 1987-88, nat. coun. 1992-95), Geol. Soc. Am. (Archeol. Geology award 1983), Mineral. Soc. Am.; mem. Nat. Assn. Geology Tchrs. (pres. 1986-89), Soc. for Archeol. Sci. (pres. 1983-84), Assn. Field Archeology (pres. 1979-81), Archaeol. Inst. Am. (Pomerance medal 1988), Sigma Xi (bd. dirs. 1990-98). Avocations: classical music, exercise, nutrition. Office: U Minn-Duluth Dept Geol Scis Duluth MN 55812 Office Phone: 218-726-7629. Business E-Mail: grapp@d.umn.edu.

**RAPP, ROBERT ANTHONY,** metallurgical engineering educator; b. Lafayette, Ind., Feb. 21, 1934; s. Frank J. and Goldie M. (Royer) R.; m. Heidi B. Sartorius, June 3, 1960; children: Kathleen Rapp Raynaud, Thomas, Stephen, Stephanie Rapp Surface. BSMetE, Purdue U., 1956; MSMetE, Carnegie Inst. Tech., 1959, PhDMetE, 1960; D (hon.), Inst. Polytech., Toulouse, France, 1995. Asst. prof. metall. engring. Ohio State U., Columbus, 1963—66, 1966—69, prof., 1969—, M.G. Fontana prof., 1988—95, prof., 1989—95, disting. univ. prof. emeritus, 1995—. Vis. prof. Ecole Nat. Superior d'Electrochimie, Grenoble, France, 1972-73, U. Paris-Sud, Orsay, 1985-86, Ecole Nat. Superior de Chimie, Toulouse, France, 1985-86, U. New South Wales, Australia, 1987; Acta/Scripta Metallurgica lectr., 1991; rsch. metallurgist WPAFB, Ohio, 1960-63. Editor: Techniques of Metals Research, vol. IV, 1982, High Temperature Corrosion, 1984; translator Metallic Corrosion (Kaesche), 1986; bd. rev. jour. Oxid. Metals; contbr. 265 publs. and numerous articles to profl. jours. First lt. USAF, 1960—63, Wright-Patterson AFB. Decorated chevalier des Palmes Academiques; recipient Disting. Engring. Alumnus award Purdue U., 1988, B.F. Goodrich Collegiate Inventor's award, 1991, 92, Ulrick Evans award Brit. Inst. Corrosion, 1992; Guggenheim fellow, 1972; Fulbright scholar Max Planck Inst. Phys. Chemistry, 1959-60, Linford award for Disting. Tchg., The Electrochem. Soc., 1998. Fellow: Nat. Assn. Corrosion Engrs. (W.R. Whitney award 1986), Electrochem. Soc. (HTM Divsn. Outstanding Achievement award 1992, Linford Tchr. award 1998, Olin Palladium award 2005), Mining Metals and Materials Soc. (R.F. Mehl medal 2000, Educator award 2003), Am. Soc. Metals Internat. (Zay Jeffries lectr. 2006, B. Stoughton award 1968, Howe gold medal 1974, Gold medal 2000); mem.: Nat. Acad. Engring., French Soc. Metals and Materials (hon.). Lutheran. Achievements include patents for About Twenty Patents. Avocations: gardening, golf, travel. Home: 1379 Southport Dr Columbus OH 43235-7649 Office Phone: 614-292-6178. E-mail: rrapp001@columbus.rr.com, rapp.4@osu.edu.

**RAPP, ROBERT NEIL,** lawyer; b. Erie, Pa., Sept. 10, 1947; m. Sally K. Meder; 1 child: Jeffrey David. BA, Case Western Res. U., 1969, JD, 1972; MBA, Cleve. State U., 1989. Bar: Ohio 1972, U.S. dist. Ct. (no. dist.) Ohio 1973, U.S. Ct. Appeals (6th crct.) 1981, U.S. Supreme Ct. 1980. Assoc. Metzenbaum, Gaines & Stern, Co., L.P.A., Cleve., 1972-75; prin. Calfee, Halter & Griswold, Cleve., 1975—. Adj. prof. law Case Western Res. U., 1975—78, Cleve.-Marshall Coll. Law, Cleve. State U., 1976—82; practitioner-in-residence Cornell U. Law Sch., 1993; mem. legal adv. bd. Nat. Assn. Securities Dealers, 1992—96; mem. market ops. rev. com. Nasdaq Stock Market, 1996—; arbitrator, practitioner mediator Nat. Futures Assn. Author: Blue Sky Regulation, 2d edit., 2003; contbr. numerous articles to law jours. Mem. ABA (sect. bus. law: mem. com. fed. regulation of securities, subcom. broker-dealer regulation, sect. litigation: mem. com. securities litigation), Am. Arbitration Assn. (securities arbitrator, mem. comml. adv. coun. Cleve. region), Ohio State Bar Assn. (elected mem. coun. dels. 1976-82, corp. law com. 1980—), Cleve. Bar Assn. (chmn. young lawyers sect. 1976-77), assoc. mem. cert. grievance com., sect. securities law: exec. coun. 1980-85, chmn. govt. liaison com. 1980-81). Office: Calfee Halter & Griswold LLP 1400 McDonald Investment Ct Cleveland OH 44114-2688

**RAPP, STEPHEN JOHN,** international prosecutor; b. Waterloo, Iowa, Jan. 26, 1949; s. Spurgeon John and Beverly (Leckington) R.; m. Donna J.E. Maier, 1981; children: Alexander, Stephanie. AB cum laude, Harvard U., 1971; JD with honors, Drake U., 1973. Bar: Iowa 1974, U.S. Dist. Ct. (no. and so. dists.) Iowa 1978, U.S. Ct. Appeals (8th cir.) 1979, U.S. Supreme Ct. 1979. Rsch. asst. Office of U.S. Senator Birch Bayh, Ind., 1970; community program asst. HUD, Chgo., 1971; mem. Iowa Ho. Reps., 1972-74, 79-83, Coun. to Majority Caucus, Iowa Ho. Reps., 1975; staff dir., counsel subcom. on juvenile delinquency U.S. Senate, Washington, 1977-78; prosec. Rapp & Gilliam, Waterloo, 1979-83; pvt. practice Waterloo, 1983-93; U.S. atty. U.S. Dist. Ct. (no. dist.) Iowa, 1993—2001; sr. prosecuting atty. U.N. Internat. Crime Tribunal Rwanda, 2001—05, chief prosecutions, 2005—. Del., mem. com. Dem. Nat. Conv., 1976, 80, 84, 88, 92; mem. Dem. Nat. Adv. Com. on

Econ., 1982-84, chmn. Black Hawk Dem. Com., 1986-91; mem. Iowa Dem. Com., 1990-93, chair 2d C.D. Dem. Com., 1991-93. Mem. ABA, Iowa Bar Assn., Order of Coif. Methodist. Home: 219 Highland Blvd Waterloo IA 50703-4229 Office: S-460 UN-ICTR PO Box 6016 Arusha Tanzania Office Phone: 212-963-2850 x5033. E-mail: rapp@un.org.

**RAPPAPORT, CHARLES OWEN,** lawyer; b. NYC, May 15, 1950; s. Edward and Edith (Novick) R.; m. Valerie B. Ackerman, Oct. 11, 1987; children: Emily Randle, Sarah Elisabeth. BA, Columbia U., 1972; JD, NYU, 1975. Bar: N.Y. 1976. Assoc. Simpson, Thacher & Bartlett LLP, N.Y.C., 1975—82, ptnr., 1982. Home: 26 N Moore St Apt 4W New York NY 10013-2436 Office: Simpson Thacher & Bartlett LLP 425 Lexington Ave 14th Fl New York NY 10017-3954 E-mail: corappaport@stblaw.com.

**RAPPAPORT, IRVING S.,** entrepreneur, lawyer, consultant; s. Melvin Rappaport and Minette Grober; children: Steven, Matthew, Diana Robinson, David. BSEE, Wash. U., St. Louis, 1962; JD (hons.), George Wash. U. Law Sch., Washington, DC, 1966; MBA, Boston Univ. Grad. Sch. Mgmt., 1969. Bar: Mo. State Bar 1966, Ct. of Appeals for the Fed. Circuit 1966, US Supreme Ct. 2005, registered: US Patent & Trademark Office (patent atty.) 1966, Can. Intellectual Property Office (patent agent) 1980. Patent examiner US Patent & Trademark Office, Washington, 1962—63; 1st lt. US Army, Ft. Meade, Md., 1963—65; patent agt. RCA, Washington, 1965—66, Philpitt, Steininger & Priddy, Washington, 1965; patent and trademark atty. Raytheon Co., Lexington, Mass., 1966—70, Schiller & Pandiscio, Waltham, Mass., 1970—71; asst. gen. counsel for patents, asst. sec. Medtronic, Inc., Mpls., 1971—77; corp. sec., gen. counsel Renal Sys., Inc., Mpls., 1977—78; chief patent counsel Data Gen. Corp., Westboro, Mass., 1978—82; assoc. gen. counsel for intellectual property and licensing Bally Mfg., Chgo., 1982—84, Apple Computer, Inc., Cupertino, Calif., 1984—90; intellectual property cons. Intel Corp., Santa Clara, Calif., 1990—91; v.p., assoc. gen. counsel for intellectual property and licensing Nat. Semiconductor Corp., Santa Clara, 1991—93; founder, dir. and v.p. intellectual property Aurigin Sys., Inc., Cupertino, 1993—2002; v.p. intellectual property licensing bus. Symyx Technologies, Inc., Sunnyvale, Calif., 2002—03; intellectual property lawyer and cons. Irving S. Rappaport, Palo Alto, Calif., 2003—; co-founder, mng. dir. IP Checkups, LLC, Berkeley, Calif., 2004—. Sec. Minn. Patent & Trademark Law Assoc., Mpls., 1977—78; mem. bd. dirs. Aurigin Sys., Inc., Cupertino, Calif., 1993—2002; bd. of advisors Intellectual Property Innovations, Charlotte, NC, 2004—, Altitude Capital Ptnrs., NYC, 2006—; mng. dir. Telemaze LLC, Los Altos, Calif., 2005—; strategic advisors bd. PatentCafe.com, Inc., Yuba City, Calif., 2006—. Author over 60 articles and presentations on intellectual property matters. First lt. Army Sec. Agy. U.S. Army, 1963—65. Recipient Svc. to U.S. Gov't. on Trade Related IP Matters, 3 U.S. Secretaries of Commerce & 3 U.S. Trade Rep., 1987—94. Mem.: Ill. State Bar, Minn. State Bar, Mass. State Bar, Minn. Patent & Trademark Law Assn. (sec. 1977—78), Boston Patent Law Assn., Am. Intellectual Property Law Assn., Licensing Execs. Soc., ABA. Achievements include having 18 US patents. Avocations: jogging, bicycling, tennis, squash. Office Phone: 650-321-7024 publish. Business E-Mail: isport1@yahoo.com.

**RAPPAPORT, JAMES WYANT,** lawyer, real estate developer; b. Boston, May 9, 1956; s. Jerome Lyle and Nancy (Vahey) R.; m. Cecelia Catherine Ewald; children: James, Jessica, Joshua. BS in Econs., Wharton, U. Pa., 1977; JD, Boston U., 1980. Assoc. Law Offices of Alan Jacobs, Boston, 1980-81; atty. Rappaport and Rakov, Boston, 1981-93; ptnr. Rappaport, Aserkoff & Rappaport, Boston, 1994-2000, New Boston Fund Inc, 2000—. Gen. ptnr. Charles River Park, Boston, 1982-2001; prin. New Boston Funds, 1992—; pres. Charles River Properties, Ltd, 1986-93, Charles River Hawaii Devel. Corp., 1987-90; chmn. Park Transit Displays, 1992-2000, Silent Sys., Inc., 1994-98; dir. Jillians Holding Co., 1998—. Class chmn. Roxbury Latin Sch., 1978-95; vice chmn. Rep. 3d ward, Boston, 1978-83, chmn., 1988-89; mem. Young Eagle sect. Rep. Nat. Com., Boston, 1985-88, Rep. state fin. com., Boston, 1985—, Concord (Mass.) Rep. Town Com., 1985-87, 1989—; bd. dirs. Mass. Taxpayers Com.; Needham, Mass., 1984-91, chmn., 1988-91; gen. ptnr. Charles River Hawaii L.P., Kauai, 1986-89; Rep. candidate U.S. Senate, 1990; chmn. Mass. Rep. Party, 1992-97; mem. Rep. Nat. Com., 1992-97; bd. dirs. Jewish Vocat. Svcs., Jewish Community Rels. Coun., Dana Farber Cancer Inst., 1998—, Children's Hosp., 2000—; mem. fin. com. Rep. Nat. Com., 1992-2000. Mem. ABA, Mass. Bar Assn., Vt. Bar Assn., Boston Bar Assn., Greater Boston Real Estate Bd., King David Soc. (chmn. 1999—). Jewish. Avocations: hiking, golf. E-mail: jwrappinc@aol.com.

**RAPPAPORT, LAWRENCE,** plant physiology and horticulture educator; b. NYC, May 28, 1928; s. Aaron and Elsie R.; m. Norma, Nov. 21, 1953; children: Meryl, Debra Kramer, Craig. BS in Horticulture, U. Idaho, 1950; MS in Horticulture, Mich. State Coll., 1951; PhD in Horticulture, Mich. State U., 1956. Lectr. U. Calif., Davis, 1956-67, jr. olericulturist, dept. vegetable crops, 1956-58, asst. olericulturist, 1958-63, assoc. olericulturist, 1963-67, prof., 1968—, prof. emeritus, 1991—, dir. plant growth lab., 1975-78, chairperson dept. vegetable crops, 1978-84. Vis. scientist Calif. Inst. Tech., 1958; co-dir. Horticulture Subproject, Calif./Egypt project, 1978-82. Contbr. articles to profl. jours. 1st pres. Davis Human Rels. Coun., 1964-66; v.p. Jewish Fedn. Sacramento, 1969; pres. Jewish Fellowship, Davis, 1985-89; founder, 1st dir. Hillel Counselership at Davis, 1965-76. Decorated Bronze star; Guggenheim Found. fellow, 1963, Fulbright fellow, 1964, USPHS Spl. fellow, 1970, Am. Soc. Horticulture Sci. fellow, 1987, Sir Frederick McMaster fellow, 1991. Achievements include discovery of evidence for gibberellin-binding protein in plants; evidence for the signal hypothesis operating in plants, positive evidence for phytochrome-mediated gibberellin metabolism and stem growth; isolation of somaclonal variants of celery bearing stable resistance to Fusarium oxysporum f. sp. apii. Home: 637 Elmwood Dr Davis CA 95616-3514 Office: Dept Plant Environ Sci One Shields Ave Davis CA 95616 Business E-Mail: lrappaport@ucdavis.edu.

**RAPPAPORT, LINDA ELLEN,** lawyer; b. Freeport, NY, Jan. 12, 1952; d. William Jay and Marcia Ann (Wiland) Rappaport; m. Leonard Chazen, June 1, 1980; 1 child, Matthew Ross Chazen. BA, Wesleyan U., Middletown, Conn., 1974; JD, NYU, 1977. Bar: N.Y. 1977. Law clk. Chief Judge James S. Holden U.S. Dist. Ct. Vt., Rutland, 1978; assoc. Shearman & Sterling, NYC, 1979—85, ptnr., 1986—, elected mem. policy com., 1995—, mem. exec. group, 2005—. Bd. dirs. NY Women's Found., NYC, 1995—2001, AIESEC Internat., NYC, 1994—2000; bd. govs. Mannes Coll. Music, 2004—; bd. dirs. Legal Aid Soc. N.Y., 2005—, exec. com., 2005—. Fellow: Am. Coll. Employee Benefits Coun.; mem. Bar Assn. City of N.Y. (employee benefits com. 1986—, employment law com. 1986—). Office: Shearman & Sterling 599 Lexington Ave Fl 13 New York NY 10022-6069 E-mail: lrappaport@shearman.com.

**RAPPAPORT, LISA N.,** psychologist; b. NYC; d. Judith and Bob Rappaport; m. Darren Jay Friedman, Apr. 2, 2005. PhD, Fordham U. Lic. psychologist NY, 1998. Asst. prof. pediat. Albert Einstein Coll. Medicine, Bronx, NY, 2000—; pvt. practice NYC. Mem.: Internat. Dyslexia Assn., Learning Disabilities Assn., APA (mem. NY state divsn.), Smart Kids with Learning Disabilites (profl. adv. bd. 2000). Office: Albert Einstein Coll Medicine 1165 Morris Park Ave Bronx NY 10461 Office Phone: 718-430-8600 6404. Personal E-mail: shrinkrapp@gmail.com.

**RAPPAPORT, MARTIN PAUL,** internist, nephrologist, educator; b. Bronx, N.Y., Apr. 25, 1943; s. Joseph and Anne (Kramer) R.; m. Bethany Ann Mitchell; children: Karen, Steven; stepchildren: Aaron Cole, Kevin Cole. BS, Tulane U., 1957, MD, 1960. Diplomate Am. Bd. Internal Medicine, Nat. Bd. Med. Examiners. Intern Charity Hosp. of La., New Orleans, 1960-61, resident in internal medicine, 1961-64; pvt. practice internal medicine and nephrology, Seabrook, Tex., 1968-72, Webster, Tex., 1972-98; internist Univ. Med. Group, Houston, 1998; mem. courtesy staff Mainland Ctr. Hosp. (formerly Galveston County Meml. Hosp.), Texas City, 1968-96, Bapt. Meml. System, 1969-72, 88-98; mem. staff Clear Lake Regional Med. Ctr., 1972-98; cons. staff St. Mary's Hosp., 1973-79; cons. nephrology St. John's Hosp., Nassau Bay, Tex.;

fellow in nephrology Northwestern U. Med. Sch., Chgo., 1967—68; clin. asst. prof. in medicine and nephrology U. Tex., Galveston, 1969—; part-time physician dept. family medicine outpatient clinics U. Tex. Med. Br., Galveston, 2000; locum tenens, 2000—. Lectr. emergency med. technician cours e, 1974-76; adviser on respiratory therapy program Alvin (Tex.) Jr. Coll., 1976-82; cons. nephrology USPHS, 1979-80. Served to capt. M.C. U.S. Army, 1961-67. Fellow ACP, Am. Coll. Chest Physicians; mem. Internat., Am. Socs. Nephrology, So. Med. Assn., Tex. Med. Assn., Tex. Soc. Internal Medicine (bd. govs. 1994-96), Am. Soc. Artificial Internal Organs, Tex. Acad. Internal Medicine, Harris County Med. Soc., Am. Geriatrics Soc., Bay Area Heart Assn., Clear Lake C. of C., Conroe Rotary Club, Rotary, Phi Delta Epsilon, Alpha Epsilon Pi, Tulane Alumni Assn. Home: 15913 Malibu W Willis TX 77318-6784 Personal E-mail: mrappapo@msn.com.

**RAPPAPORT, MICHAEL PAUL,** columnist; b. San Diego, Dec. 11, 1949; s. Norman Lewis and Yvonne Naomi Rappaport; m. Leslie Ann Rappaport, Apr. 19, 1975 (div. May 1982); m. Nicole Jacqueline Rappaport, Nov. 2, 1992; children: Pauline Nicole Borderies, Virgile Georges Borderies. AS, No. Va. C.C., Annandale, 1976; BS, George Mason U., 1981. Asst. sports editor Alexandria (Va.) Gazette, 1979-81, Gastonia (N.C.) Gazette, 1982-83; sportswriter Anderson (S.C.) Ind. Mail, 1983-84, St. Louis Globe Dem., 1984-86; sports editor, columnist Greeley (Colo.) Tribune, 1986-88; sportswriter, columnist Reno Gazette Jour., 1988-90; sportswriter Inland Valley Daily Bull., Ontario, Calif., 1990-96, metro columnist, 1996—. Co-author: (e-book) The Woman in the Box, 2000; creator website mikerappaport.com, 2000. Recipient Sweepstakes Writing award Soc. Profl. Journalists Inland Calif. Chpt., 1997, Writing award for best local column, 2001-; named Sportswriter of Yr., South Atlantic League, 1982, 83. Mem. Nat. Soc. Newspaper Columnists, Nat. Press Club, Greater L.A. Press Club, Sigma Phi Epsilon (life, chpt. pres. 1981). Roman Catholic. Avocations: reading, golf, films, rotisserie baseball. Home: 1234 Fernside Dr La Canada Flintridge CA 91011 Office: 2041 E 4th St Ontario CA 91764-2605 Office Phone: 909-483-9395. E-mail: m_rappaport@earthlink.net.

**RAPPAPORT, NORMAN HARVEY,** plastic surgeon; b. Phila., Apr. 23, 1947; s. Herbert and Ruth Rappaport; m. Deborah Ann Finn, Oct. 2, 1982; children: Jonathan David, Betsy, William. BA, LaSalle Coll., 1969; DDS, Temple U., 1972; MD, Hahnemann Med. Coll., 1975. Diplomate Am. Bd. Plastic Surgery. Resident in gen. surgery Abington (Pa.) Meml. Hosp., 1975-78; fellow in hand surgery U. Pa., Phila., 1978; resident in plastic surgery Baylor Coll. Medicine, Houston, 1978-80; clin. assoc. prof. surgery Baylor Coll. Surgery, Houston, 1994—. Contbr. articles to profl. jours. Fellow: ACS; mem.: AMA, Houston Surg. Soc. (pres. 2001), Tex. Soc. Plastic Surgeons, Tex. Med. Assn., N.Am. Burn Soc., Houston Soc. Plastic Surgeons (pres. 2002), Harris County Med. Soc., Am. Assn. Hand Surgeons, Am. Assn. Plastic Surgeons, Am. Soc. for Aesthetic Plastic Surgery, Am. Soc. Plastic Surgeons (bd. dirs. 1998—2000), Plastic Surgery Ednl. Found. (bd. dirs. 1994—2000), Am. Soc. Maxillofacial Surgeons (pres. 2000), Omicron Kappa Upsilon. Office: 6560 Fannin St Ste 1812 Houston TX 77030-2775 Office Phone: 713-790-4500. E-mail: nhr@hcps.cc.

**RAPPAPORT, RICHARD J.,** lawyer; b. Chgo., Aug. 13, 1943; m. Roberta Rappaport; children: Michael, Barbara. BS, Loyola U., 1965, JD cum laude, 1967. Bar: Ill. 1967, Fla. 1993, US Dist. Ct. No. Dist. Ill. 1967, US Ct. Appeals 7th Cir. 1978, 10th Cir. 1978, 6th Cir. 1986, 4th Cir. 1988, 11th Cir. 1997, 8th Cir. 2000, US Tax Ct. 1988, US Supreme Ct. 1979. Trial atty. antitrust divsn. US Dept. Justice, Washington, 1967-69; ptnr. Ross & Hardies (merged with McGuireWoods LLP in 2003), Chgo., McGuireWoods LLP, Chgo., 2003—, co-mng. ptnr. Chgo. office, 2003—04. Bd. dirs. Am. Assn. for Klinefelter Syndrome Info. & Support; bd. mem. Loyola U. Sch. Law Inst. Consumer Antitrust Studies. Fellow: Am. Bar Found.; mem.: ABA, Lawyers Club of City of Chgo., Chgo. Bar Assn. (mem. judicial evaluation com.). Office: McGuireWoods LLP Ste 4100 77 W Wacker Dr Chicago IL 60601-1815 Office Phone: 312-750-8618. Office Fax: 312-920-3696. Business E-Mail: rrappaport@mcguirewoods.com.

**RAPPAPORT, STUART RAMON,** lawyer; b. Detroit, Apr. 13, 1935; s. Reuben and Zella (Golechen) R.; m. Anne M. Plotnick; children: Douglas, Erica Rappaport Witt. BA in History, U. Mich., 1956; JD, Harvard U., 1959. Bar: Calif. 1962. Trial lawyer, chief trials, bur. chief, chief. asst. pub. defender L.A. County Pub. Defender's Office, L.A., 1962-87; pub. defender Santa Clara County, San Jose, Calif., 1987-95; pvt. practice, 1995—. Mem. standing adv. com. on criminal law Jud. Coun. Calif., San Francisco, 1993—; mem. discipline evaluation com. State Bar of Calif. Contbr. articles to profl. jours. Recipient Lifetime Achievement award Calif. Attys. for Criminal Justice. Mem. Calif. Pub. Defenders Asn. (pres. 1982-83, Lifetime Achievement award), L.A. County Pub. Defenders Assn. (pres.). Democrat. Jewish. Home: 4500 Bloomfield Rd Sebastopol CA 95472 Business E-Mail: sturap@mcn.org.

**RAPPEPORT, IRA J.,** lawyer; b. Phila., Jan. 13, 1954; BA with honors, Washington U., 1975; JD with honors, Villanova U., 1978. Bar: Calif. 1978. Assoc. Pillstory Madison & Sutro, 1978-83, Memel, Jacobs, Pietro & Gersh, 1983-85, ptnr., 1985-87, McDermott, Will & Emery, LA, 1987—. Mng. editor Villanova Law Rev., 1977-78. Recipient Scribes award Villanova Sch. Law, 1978. Mem. Am. Acad. Hosp. Attys., L.A. County Bar Assn. (mem. healthcare law sect.), Beverly Hills Bar Assn. (mem. healthcare law sect.), Century City Bar Assn. (mem. healthcare law sect.), Nat. Health Lawyers Assn., Calif. Soc. Healthcare Attys. Office: McDermott Will & Emery 2049 Century Park E Fl 34 Los Angeles CA 90067-3101

**RAPSON, RICHARD (RIP RAPSON),** foundation administrator; b. Bonn, Fed. Republic Germany, Mar. 16, 1952; came to U.S., 1954. s. Ralph E. and Mary Christine (Dolan) R.; m. Gail M. Johnson, Aug. 19, 1989. BA, Pomona Coll., 1974; JD, Columbia U., 1981. Legis. asst. to U.S. Rep. Donald M. Fraser US Congress, Washington, 1974-78; assoc. Leonard, Street & Deinard, Mpls., 1981-86, ptnr., 1987-89; dep. mayor City of Mpls., 1989—93; sr. fellow Design Ctr. for Am. Urban Landscape U. Minn.; pres. McKnight Found., Mpls., 1999—2005, The Kresge Found, Troy, Mich., 2005—. Counsel Harriet Tubman Women's Shelter, Mpls., 1987-89, Coffee House Press., Mpls., 1986-89. Trustee, Mpls. Pub. Library, 1983, pres. bd.; bd. dirs. Mpls. Bd. Estimate and Taxation, 1985-88, Mpls. Youth Coordinating Bd., Mpls., 1986-89. Recipient Sigurd Olsen award for outstanding vol. svc. to environment, Sierra Club Northstar Chpt. Mem. ABA, Minn. Bar Assn., Hennepin County Bar Assn. Democrat. Avocations: art collecting, running, tennis, literature. Office: The Kresge Found 3215 W Big Beaver Rd Troy MI 48084 Business E-Mail: rrapson@kresge.org.

**RARICK, PHILIP JOSEPH,** lawyer, retired state supreme court justice; b. Troy, Ill., Nov. 10, 1940; s. Philip J. and Mary (Buckman) R.; m. Janet N. Arnovitz, Feb. 1, 1963; 1 child, Philip J. IV. BA, So. Ill. U., 1962; JD, St. Louis U., 1966. Bar: Ill. 1966, U.S. Dist. Ct. Ill. 1966. Twp. atty. Collinsville & Jarvis, Collinsville, Ill., 1966-75; asst. state's atty. Madison County, Edwardsville, Ill., 1966-75; city atty. City of Collinsville, 1967-75; cir. judge Third Jud. Cir., Edwardsville, 1975-88; presiding judge Criminal Div. in Madison County, Ill., 1982—85; chief cir. judge Third Jud. Cir., Edwardsville, 1985-87; presiding judge Criminal Div. in Madison County, Ill., 1987—88; elected judge Appellate Ct., Fifth Dist., Ill., 1988; judge indsl. commn. divsn. Ill. Appellate Ct., 1988—2002; elected judge, retained Appellate Ct., Fifth Dist., Ill., 1998; justice Ill. Supreme Ct., 2002—04; with Callis, Papa, Hale, Szewczyk, Rongey & Danzinger, PC, Granite City, Ill., 2004—. Mem. exec. com. Ill. Jud. Conf. Springfield, 1985—2000, chmn. complex litigation com., 1988—2000, mem. Industrial Comm. Div. of the complex litigation com., 1992-2002, Ill. Cts. Commn. State of Ill., Springfield, 1992—99. Chmn. (manual) Illinois Manual for Complex Litigation. Mem. Ill. State Bar Assn., Ill. Judges Assn. (dir. 1977—82), Madison County Bar Assn., Tri-City Bar Assn. Office: Callis Papa Hale Szewczyk Rongey & Danzinger PC 1326 Niedringhaus Ave Granite City IL 62040 Office Phone: 618-452-1323.

**RARIDON, RICHARD JAY,** retired computer scientist; b. Newton, Iowa, Oct. 25, 1931; s. Jack Allison and Letha Helen (Woods) R.; m. Mona Marie Herndon, May 28, 1956; children— Susan Gayle, Ann Chaney. BA, Grinnell Coll., 1953; MA, Vanderbilt U., 1955, PhD, 1959. Assoc. prof. phys. sci. Memphis State U., 1958-62; rsch. scientist Oak Ridge Nat. Lab., 1962-92; cons. ORNL, 1992—2004. Environ. specialist Coop. Sci. Edn. Center, Oak Ridge, 1971-72 Contbr. articles to profl. jours. Radiol. Physics fellow AEC, 1953-55 Fellow AAAS, Tenn. Acad. Sci. (pres. 1971); mem. Assn. Acads. Sci. (sec.-treas. 1972-76, pres. 1977), Sigma Xi. Home: 111 Columbia Dr Oak Ridge TN 37830-7720 Personal E-mail: raridon@hotmail.com.

**RASCHE, ROBERT HAROLD,** banker, retired economics educator; b. New Haven, June 29, 1941; s. Harold A. and Elsa (Bloomquist) R.; m. Dorothy Anita Bensen, Dec. 28, 1963; children: Jeanette Dorothy, Karl Robert. BA, Yale U., 1963; A.M., U. Mich., 1965, PhD, 1966. Asst. prof. U Pa., Phila., 1966-72; assoc. prof. econs. Mich. State U. East Lansing, 1972-75, prof., 1975-98, prof. emeritus, 1999—; sr. v.p., dir. rsch. St. Louis Fed. Res. Bank, 1999—. Vis. scholar St. Louis Fed. Res., 1971-72, 76-77, 94-98, San Francisco Fed. Rsch. Bank, 1985, Bank of Japan, Tokyo, 1990; disting. vis. prof. econs. Ariz. State U., Tempe, 1986; rsch. assoc. Nat. Bur. Econ. Rsch., Cambridge, Mass., 1982-91; mem. Mich. Gov. Coun. Econ. Advisers, 1992-96; mem. Shadow Open Market Com., 1973-98. Mem. Am. Econs. Assn. Lutheran. Home: 14531 Radcliffeborough Ct Chesterfield MO 63017-5626 Office: Fed Res Bank St Louis Rsch Divsn PO Box 442 Saint Louis MO 63166-0442 Business E-mail: rasche@msu.edu.

**RASCOE, PAUL STEPHEN,** librarian, researcher; b. Corpus Christi, Tex., July 7, 1954; s. Stephen Thomas and Barbara Jean (Butler) R. BA, U. Tex., Arlington, 1975, U. Tex., Austin, 1976, M Libr. Info. Sci., 1983; MA, U. London, 1977. Govt. documents and electronic info. svcs. libr. U. Tex., Austin, 1985-96, libr., 1978-85, libr. govt. documents maps and electronic info. svcs., 1996—. Dir. rsch. Weissmann Travel Reports, Austin, 1990-96. Avocation: travel. Office: U Tex Austin Documents Collection Gen Librs PCL 2-400 Austin TX 78713-7330 Office Phone: 512-495-4262.

**RASENOW, BENJAMIN THEODORE,** engineering educator; b. Berkeley, Calif., June 30, 1962; s. Brian Kashchenoff and Charlotte Ada Steinzig, Donald Steinzig (Stepfather); m. Sabina Jo Rachman, Sept. 28, 1998; 1 child, Sasha Duncan. BSME, San Francisco State U., 1995. Cert. Control Sys. Engr., Calif. Dept. Consumer Affairs. Asst. engr. East Bay Mcpl. Utility Dist., Oakland, Calif., 1997—2005, assoc. control sys. engr., 2005—. Instr. San Francisco (Calif.) State U., 1999—. Mem.: IEEE (assoc.), ISA (assoc.), AFSCME (assoc.), Earth Ecology Club Campoindo HS (assoc.; alternative energy commr. 1978—80), Shotokan Karate of Am. (assoc.; treas. 1980—82). Office: E Bay Mcpl Utility Dist 375 11th St Oakland CA 94610 Office Phone: 510-287-2045. Home Fax: 510-444-9876. Business E-mail: brasenow@ebmud.com.

**RASGON, NATALIE LUZINA,** psychiatrist; b. Odessa, Russia, Sept. 9, 1957; came to U.S., 1990, citizen; d. Lev Lazarevich and Nadejda Abramovna (Vainstein) Luzin; m. Dave Rasgon, Sept. 1, 1989; 1 child, Alexander. MD, Odessa Med. Inst., 1980; cert. proficiency in sci. English. Ctrl. Inst. Postgrad. Med. Edn., Moscow, 1987; cert. path. physiology, Acad. Med. Sci., U.S.S.R., 1987; PhD in Ob-Gyn. and Path. Psychiatry, Ctr. Inst. Postgrad. Med. Edn., U.S.S.R., 1988; PhD, Acad. Med. Sci., U.S.S.R., 1989. Cert. Med. Bd. Calif. Physician and Surgeon. Intern in ob-gyn. Nicolaev (U.S.S.R.) Delivery Hosp., 1980-81; intern in psychiatry Harbor - UCLA Med. Ctr., Torrance, 1992-93; psychiatric resident Cedars - Sinai Med. Ctr., L.A., 1993-96, chief psychiatric resident, 1994-95; attending physician Ctr. Hosp. of Black Sea Shipping Co., Odessa, 1983-84; asst. prof. Odessa Med. Inst., 1983-84, Moscow Ctrl. Inst. for Postgrad. Studies, 1988-89; asst. prof. dept. ob-gyn. UCLA, 1996—, clin. instr. Neuropsychiat. Inst., 1996—. Cons. Nat. Com. of Psychiatry, Moscow, 1984-89; sci. sec. Pharmacologies Com., Ministry of Health, Moscow, 1988-89; Astra Merk fellow 6th U.S. Psychiatric and Mental Health Congress, San Diego, 1993; Janssen clin. scholar 7th U.S. Psychiatric and Mental Health Congress, Washington, 1994; rsch. fellow Neurobiology Neuro-Psychiatric Inst., UCLA Med. Sch., 1995-96. Contbr. articles to profl. jours.; patentee in field. Recipient Leo Rigler M.D. award for acad. achievement Cedars-Sinai Med. Ctr., L.A., 1995. Mem. AMA, Am. Psychiatric Assn., N.Y. Acad. Scis., Internat. Soc. Psychosomatic Obstetrics and Gynecology, Am. Soc. Psychosomatic Obstetrics and Gynecology, So. Calif. Psychiatric Soc. (mem. internat. med. grads. com. 1993—). Democrat. Achievements include contributions to the physiology of cyclic pelvic pain; patents (with other) in Improved Method of Mitochondrial Destruction; (with others) in Method of Dysmenorrhea Treatment; (with others) in Substance for Reduction of Side Effects During Physical Medicine Treatment Invention; (with others) in invention of Method of Dysmenorrhea Treatment. Office: UCLA Neuropsychiatric Inst 760 Westwood Plz Los Angeles CA 90095-8353

**RASHAD, PHYLICIA,** actress, singer, dancer; b. Houston; m. Ahmad Rashad; children: William Bowles, Condola Phylea. Grad. magna cum laude, Howard U., N.Y. Mem. Negro Ensemble Co.; founder Phylicia Rashad and Co., 1990. Actor: (plays) The Cherry Orchard, 1973, Zora, 1981, A Raisin in the Sun, 1984, Gem of the Ocean, 2005, (Off-Broadway) The Duplex, 1972, Zooman and the Sign, 1980—81, Weep Not for Me, 1981, In an Upstate Motel, 1981, Puppetplay, 1983, Sons and Fathers of Sons, 1983; (Broadway plays) Ain't Supposed to Die a Natural Death, 1971, The Wiz, 1975, Dreamgirls, 1981, Into the Woods, 1988, Jelly's Last Jam, 1992—93, A Raisin in the Sun, 2004 (Tony award best actress in a play, 2004, Drama Desk award best actress in a play, 2004), Bernarda Alba, 2006, (films) The Broad Coalition, 1972, The Wiz, 1978, Once Upon a Time When We Were Colored, 1995, Free of Eden, 1999, Loving Jezebel, 1999, The Visit, 2000; (TV films) We're Fighting Back, 1981, Uncle Tom's Cabin, 1987 (Cable ACE award nom. best sup. actress, 1987), False Witness, 1989, Polly, 1989, Polly: Comin Home, 1990, Jailbirds, 1991, Hallelujah, 1993, David's Mother, 1994, The Possession of Michael D., 1995, The Babysitters Seduction, 1996, Free of Eden, 1999, The Old Settler, 2001, Murder, She Wrote: The Last Free Man, 2001; (TV series) One Life to Live, 1983—84, The Cosby Show, 1984—92 (NAACP Image award best actress, 1987, Emmy award nom. best actress, 1985, 1986), Santa Barbara, 1985, Cosby, 1996—2000, (voice) Little Bill, 1999—; (TV guest appearances) The Love Boat, 1985, A Different World, 1988—90, Blossom, 1991, Touched by an Angel, 1994, 2002, The Cosby Mysteries, 1994, In the House, 1995, Bull, 2001. Recipient Theatre Artist award, Nat. Corp. Theatre Fund, 2006.*

**RASHBAUM, WILLIAM K.,** journalist; Reporter The New York Times. Author: (articles) In Some Countries They Arrest Corrupt Judges!, 2002, Terror Officials Work to Assess Subway Threat, 2005. Office: The New York Times 229 W 43rd St New York NY 10036*

**RASHEED, JEROME NAJEE See NAJEE**

**RASHID, MUHAMMAD HARUNUR,** electrical engineering educator; b. Comilla, Bangladesh, Feb. 15, 1945; came to U.S., 1980; s. Sultan Ahmed and Sultana (Begum) R.; m. Fatema Begum, Aug. 14, 1970; children: Fa-eza, Farzana, Hasan. BSEE, U. of Dhaka, Bangladesh, 1967; MSc, U. Birmingham, England, 1971, PhD, 1976. Registered profl. engr., Ont., Can. Instrument control engr. Eastern Refinery, Ltd., Bangladesh, 1968-70; sr. devel. engr. Brush Elec. Machines, Ltd., England, 1974-76; rsch. engr. Lucas Group Rsch. Ctr., England, 1976—77; lectr. Higher Inst. Electronics, Malta, 1977-79, Libya, 1979-80; asst. prof. U. Conn., 1980-81; assoc. prof. Concordia U., Montreal, 1981-85; prof. Purdue U. Calumet, Hammond, Ind., 1985-89; prof., chmn. Purdue U., Ft. Wayne, Ind., 1989—97; prof. electrical and computer engring. U. Fla., 1997—, dir. joint engring. prog., 1997— . Cons. Ngee Ann Poly., Singapore, 1974-95; external examiner U. Hong Kong, 1987-89. Author: Power Electronics, 1993, SPICE for Power Electronics, 1993, SPICE

for Circuits and Electronics, 1995; co-author: (with others) Electromechanics and Electrical Machinery, 1986. Mem. IEE (fellow 1985, Meritorious Achievement award, 2002). Office: U Fla 11000 Univ Pkwy Pensacola FL 32514-5750

**RASHID, MUSHFIQUR M,** statistician; s. Abul Abdur and Abeda Rashid; m. Nazrin Joarder, Sept. 3, 1981; children: Naim U., Shafique A., Alma A., Raheem A. BA with honors, Rajshahi U., Bangladesh, 1976; MSc in math., Carleton U., Can., 1984; PhD, Ohio State U., 1988. Lectr., asst. prof. Rajshahi U., Bangladesh, 1977—81; asst. prof. SUNY, Albany, NY, 1988—92, Worcester Poly. Inst., Mass., 1992—96; math. statistician Divsn. of Biometrcs II/CDER/FDA, Rockville, Md., 1996—. Reviewer NIH, Bethesda, Md., NSF, Arlington, Va., 1988—; referee Jour. of the Am. Statis. Assn., Alexandria, Va., 1988—. Author: (encyclopedia article) Encyclopedia of Biopharmaceutical Statistics (Recognized as an Internat. Expert, 2000). Pres. Bangladesh Students' Assn., Ohio State U., Columbus, 1986—87. Recipient Excellent Reviewer award, Divsn. of Biostatistics/CDER/FDA, 2000; Merit scholarship, Bangladesh Govt., 1970-1976. Mem.: Am. Statis. Assn., Phi Kappa Phi. Achievements include research in small area estimation; non-inferiority trials; robust analysis of cross-over designs; repeated measures designs; mixed models. Avocations: gardening, travel, swimming. Office: Divsn Biometrics II/CDER/FDA HFD-715 5600 Fishers Ln Rockville MD 20857 Office Phone: 301-827-3121.

**RASI, HUMBERTO MARIO,** editor, educator; b. Buenos Aires, Mar. 23, 1935; came to US, 1962, naturalized, 1968; s. Mario and Gertrudis Frida (Heyde) R.; m. Julia Cuchma, Feb. 28, 1957; children: Leroy Mario, Sylvia Beatrice. BA, Instituto Superior del Profesorado, Buenos Aires, 1960; MA, San Jose State U., 1966; PhD, Stanford U., 1971; D honoris causa, U. Peruana Union, Peru, 1999, U. Adventista del Plata, Argentina, 2001, U. Montemorelos, Mex., 2003. Ordained to ministry Seventh-day Adventist Ch., 1980. Mem. faculty Instituto Florida, Buenos Aires, 1957-61; asst. editor Pacific Press Publ. Assn., Mountain View, Calif., 1962-66; asst. prof., assoc. prof. modern langs. Andrews U., 1969-76, prof., dean Sch. Grad. Studies, 1976-78; chief editor internat. publs. Pacific Press Publ. Assn., 1978-83, v.p. editorial devel., 1984-86; assoc. world dir. edn. Gen. Conf. Seventh-day Adventists, Silver Spring, Md., 1987-90, world dir. edn., 1990—2002; ret., 2002. Exec. dir. Inst. for Christian Teaching, 1987—. Author: The Life of Jesus, 3 vols., 1984—85; contbg. editor: Handbook of L.Am. Studies, Libr. of Congress, 1972—82; editor: Comentario Biblico Adventista, 7 vols., 1978—90; co-editor: Meeting the Secular Mind, 1985; founder, editor-in-chief: Coll. and Univ. Dialogue, 1989—; compiler: Christ in the Classroom, 33 vols., 1991—; contbr. articles on modern Hispanic lit., cultural issues, and religious trends. Exec. sec. Found. Adventist Edn., 2005-; NEH postdoctoral fellow Johns Hopkins U., 1975-76. Personal E-mail: h.rasi@adelphia.net.

**RASIC-STEBEN, STEPHANIE ANN,** secondary school educator; d. Phillip J. Rasic; m. Jay C. Steben, Sept. 11, 1993. BA in English, Seattle U., 1989. Cert. educator Wash. State, 1990. Substitute tchr. Highline Sch. Dist., Wash., 1990—93; tchr. lang. arts and psychology tchr. Seattle Sch. Dist., 1993—. Emergency worker Shoreline Fire Dept., Wash., 2005—06. Recipient Sch. Letter in Sailing, Seattle U., 1988. Mem.: APA. Office: West Seattle High School 3000 California Ave SW Seattle WA 98116 Office Phone: 206-252-8889.

**RASIN, RUDOLPH STEPHEN,** corporate financial executive; b. Newark, July 5, 1930; m. Joy Kennedy Peterkin, Apr. 11, 1959; children: Rudolph Stephen, James Stenning, Jennifer Shaw Denniston. BA, Rutgers U., 1953; postgrad., Columbia U., 1958-59. Mgr. Miles Labs., Inc., 1959-61; devel. mgr. Gen. Foods Corp., White Plains, NY, 1961-62; asst. to pres., chmn. Morton Internat. Inc., Chgo., 1962-72; pres. Rasin Corp., Chgo., 1971—, Alliance Brands, LLC. Bd. dirs. Facets Media. Bd. dirs. Geneva Lakes Conservancy, Gatherings Waters Land Trust, Poetry Found. With USAF, 1954—56. Mem. Hinsdale Golf Club, Mid Am. Club (Chgo.), Lake Geneva Country Club, Williams Coll. Club (N.Y.C.), Casino Club (Chgo.), Chgo. Club. Mem. United Ch. of Christ. Office: Alliance Brands LLC 21 S Clark St Chicago IL 60603 Office Phone: 312-236-8453.

**RASINARIU, CONSTANTIN,** physics professor; PhD, U. Ill., Chgo., 1999. Prof. physics Columbia Coll., Chgo., 1999—, acting chmn. Dept. Sci. and Math., 2006—. Office: Columbia College Chicago 600 S Michigan Ave Chicago IL 60605 Office Phone: 312-344-7515. Business E-mail: crasinariu@colum.edu.

**RASKA, KAREL FRANTISEK JULIAN, JR.,** pathologist, virologist, educator; b. Prague, Czech Republic, May 26, 1939; arrived in U.S., 1965; s. Karel Raska and Helena (Heller) Raskova; m. Jana Dostalova, Feb. 18, 1960; children: Karel III, Francis. MD, Charles U., Prague, 1962; PhD in Biochemistry, Czechoslovak Acad. Scis., Prague, 1965. Diplomate Am. Bd. Pathology (anatomic and clin., immunopathology). Fellow Yale U. Sch. Medicine, New Haven, 1965—66; assoc. Waksman Inst. Microbiology, New Brunswick, NJ, 1966—67; scientist Czech Acad. Sci., Prague, 1967—68; prof. microbiology and pathology Rutgers Med. Sch., Piscataway, NJ, 1968—82; profl. pathology, lab. medicine, microbiology U. Medicine and Dentistry-Robert Wood Johnson Med. Sch., New Brunswick, 1982—; prof., chmn. dept. lab medicine and pathology U. Medicine and Dentistry NJ Med. Sch., Newark, 1989—92; chmn. dept. lab medicine and pathology St. Peter's U. Hosp., New Brunswick, 1992—. Cons. Newark Beth Israel Med. Ctr., Newark, 1991—2001, E. Orange (NJ) VA Med. Ctr., 1991—; vis. prof. Charles U. Med. Sch., Prague, 1993—94; prof. path. and lab. medicine Drexel U., Coll. Medicine, Phila., 2005—. Contbr. articles to profl. jours., chapters to books. Trustee N.J. Organ Sharing Network, Springfield, 1991—2000; pres. Czechoslovak Soc. for Arts and Scis. In Am., 2000—. Lt. Czechoslovak Air Force, 1962—63. Grantee, NIH, 1975—93, Damon Runyon-Walter Winchell Cancer Rsch. Fund, 1975, NJ Commn. Cancer Rsch., 1985—86, 1994—95. Mem.: Learned Soc. of the Czech. Republic, Am. Soc. Cell Biologists, Am. Soc. Virology, NJ Soc. Pathology, Assn. Univ. Pathologists, Internat. Acad. Pathology, Am. Assn. Cancer Rsch., Am. Soc. Clin. Immunology, Am. Assn. Immunology, Am. Soc. Investigative Pathology. Avocations: skiing, boating. Office: St Peters Univ Hosp Dept Lab Medicine & Pathology 254 Easton Ave New Brunswick NJ 08901 Office Phone: 732-745-8504. Personal E-mail: jkraskamd@aol.com.

**RASKAR, RAMESH,** computer scientist; BS in Electronics & Telecom., Govt. Coll. Engring., Pune, India, 1991; MS in Computer Sci., U. Iowa, 1995; PhD in Computer Sci., U. NC, Chapel Hill, 2000. Rsch. scientist Mitsubishi Electric Rsch. Labs., 2000—. Contbr. articles to profl. jours. Named one of Top 100 Young Innovators, MIT Tech. Review, 2004; recipient Global Indus Technovator award, 2003. Mem.: IEEE, Assn. for Computing Machinery. Office: Mitsubishi Electric Rsch Labs 201 Broadway Cambridge MA 02139

**RASKIN, FRED CHARLES,** retired transportation and utility holding company executive, educator; b. N.Y.C., Sept. 11, 1948; s. Harry and Isabel Raskin; m. Lorraine Mary Sabourin, Apr. 25, 1974; children: Elizabeth Harris, Alexander Eastwood. BS, Syracuse U., 1970; JD, NYU, 1973. Bar: R.I. 1973, Mass. 1974; CPA, Ohio. Assoc. counsel Fleet Nat. Bank, Providence, 1973-75, Bank of Boston, 1975-78; asst. gen. counsel Eastern Enterprises, Boston, 1978-79, treas., 1979-81, v.p., treas., 1981-84; sr. v.p. fin. Eastern Assoc. Coal Co., Pitts., 1984-87; exec. v.p. Midland Enterprises, Inc., Cin., 1987-90, pres., 1991-98; pres., COO Eastern Enterprises, Weston, Mass., 1998-2000; CEO Woods Hole, Martha's Vineyard and Nantucket Steamship Authority, 2002—04; ret., 2004. Lectr. Boston U., 2001—; adj. prof. Merrimack Coll., 2005-. Trustee Boston Heart Found. Personal E-mail: derfniksar@comcast.net.

**RASKIN, MICHAEL A.,** retail executive, director; b. N.J., Feb. 26, 1925; s. Harry and Elizabeth Rose (Furstenberg) R.; m. Mary Bonetta Whalen, June 12, 1948; children: Robin Raskin Crowell, Hillary Raskin Maass, Mary Allison Sullivan. AB, Pa. State Coll., 1947; MBA, Columbia U., 1948. With Abraham & Straus, 1949-65; successively mdse. v.p., dir. stores, sr. v.p.

Abercrombie & Fitch, N.Y.C., 1966-68; exec. v.p. Dayton's div. Dayton Hudson Corp.; pres. Jos. Magnin Co., San Francisco, 1978—. Chmn., CEO, bd. dirs. Imnar Corp., San Francisco, Info. Please; chmn. More Investments; chmn. exec. com. Acajoe Internat.; bd. dirs. Fortune Almac, Canterbury Cuisine, Cultural Devel. Assocs., HELP Inc., Express Yourself Through Art, Inc., Munsingwear, Inc., B&B Acceptance Corp. Bd. dirs. Amyotrophic Lateral Sclerosis Assn.

**RASKIND, LEO JOSEPH,** law educator; b. Newark, Nov. 2, 1919; s. Isaac and Fannie (Michelson) R.; m. Mollie Gordon, June 14, 1948; children— Carol Inge, John Richard. AB, UCLA, 1942; MA, U. Wash., 1949; PhD (Fulbright fellow), London Sch. Econs., 1952; LL.B., Yale, 1955. Faculty Stanford Law Sch., 1955-56; lectr., research asso. Yale Law Sch., 1956-58; faculty Vanderbilt Law Sch., 1958-64, Ohio State U. Coll. of Law, 1964-70, U. Minn., 1970-90, emeritus 1991—. Counsel Am. Econ. Assn., 1979—88; vis. tchr. NYU, 1964, 83, U. Tex., 1964, U. Utah, 1967, So. Meth. U., 1973, U. N.C., 1978, Lyon III, 1984, Kiel U., 1988; vis. prof. Bklyn. Law Sch., 2003—04, Coll. Law, U. Tenn., Knoxville, 1994, Law Sch., U. Calif., Davis, 1995, U. Minn., 1998, Bklyn. Law Sch., 1998—. Co-author: Casebook Corporate Taxation, 1978, Casebook Antitrust Law, 2001; mem. adv. bd. BNA jour. Served to capt. AUS, 1942-46. Mem. Am. Law Inst. Office: U Minn Law Ctr 229 19th Ave S Minneapolis MN 55455 Office Phone: 612-625-2317. Personal E-mail: ljraskind@aol.com.

**RASKY, HARRY,** producer, director, writer; b. Toronto, Ont., Can., May 9, 1928; emigrated to U.S., 1955; s. Louis Leib and Pearl (Krazner) R.; m. Ruth Arlene Werkhoven, Mar. 21, 1965; children: Holly Laura, Adam Louis. BA, U. Toronto, 1949, LLD, 1984. Reporter No. Daily News, Kirkland Lake, Ont., 1949; news editor-producer Sta. CHUM, Toronto, 1950, Sta. CKEY, 1951-52; co-founder new documentary dept. CBC, 1952-55; assoc. editor Saturday Night Mag., 1955; producer-dir-writer Columbia Broadcasting Corp., 1955-60, NBC-TV, N.Y.C., 1960-61, ABC-TV, N.Y.C., 1963-69, CBC-TV, Toronto, 1971-78; pres. Harry Rasky Prodns., N.Y.C. and Toronto, 1971—, Maragall Prodns., Toronto, 1978—. Guest lectr. film and TV at various univs., colls.; lectr. U. Toronto, York U. Creator (films) Raskymentary (Emmy 1978, 86, San Francisco Film Festival 1978, Grand prize N.Y. TV-Film Festival 1978, Jerusalem medal 1975), Travels Through Life with Leacock, 1976, Arthur Miller on Home Ground, 1979, (TV films) Hall of Kings (Emmy, 1965), prodr., dir., writer (films) Next Year in Jerusalem, 1973, The Wit and World of G. Bernard Shaw, 1974, Tennessee Williams South, 1975, (films) Homage to Chagall-The Colours of Love, 1977 (200 internat. prizes including Oscar nomination Emmy, 1986), Stratasphere, The Mystery of Henry Moore, Karsh: The Searching Eye, (plays) Tiger Tale, 1978, Christopher Plummer: King of Players, 1988, The War Against the Indians, 1992 (Humanities prize, Great Plains Film Festival, Lincoln, Nebr., Golden Hugo award Chgo. Film Festival), Prophecy, 1994 (Golden Angel, honored by Smithsonian, Jerusalem Found.), William Hutt: A Fortunate Man, 1997; author: (memoirs) Nobody Swings on Sunday-The Many Lives of Harry Rasky, 1980, Tennessee Williams a Portrait in Laughter and Lamentation, 1986, Karsh: The Searching Eye, 1986, To Mend the World, 1987, Stratas: An Affectionate Tribute, 1988, Book 2001: The Song of Leonard Cohen, The Great Teacher, 1989, Robertson-Davies-The Magic Season, 1989; author (19 hour retrospective of films including documentaries) Rasky's Gallery: Poets, Painters, Singers and Saints, CBC, 1988, The War Against the Indians, 1993 (12 Internat. awards, adopted Huron Nation title Keeper of the Flame, The Three Harrys, 1999), Modigliani Body & Soul, 2005. Mem. YMCA; mem. adv. coun. Univ. Coll./U. Toronto. Decorated Order of Can.; recipient honors City of Venice, Italy, 1970, Golden Eagle, Grand prize N.Y. Intenat. TV and Film Festival of N.Y., 1977, Cert. of Merit, Acad. Motion Picture Arts and Scis., 1984, Red Ribbon, Am. Assn. Film and Video, N.Y.C., 1988, Blue Ribbon, Am. Film Festival, Emmy award, 1990, Moscow award for cultural contbn. to 20th Century USSR, 1991, Retrospective of Films, 1990, Golden Hugo award Chgo. Film Festival, 1993; named Best Non-Fiction Dir., Dirs. Guild Am., N.Y.C. and L.A., 1988, hon. Mayor N.Y.C., 1977, City of Toronto, 1979; Harry Rasky Day named in his honor, City of Toronto, 1988; Moscow Film Festival honoree, 1991; adopted by Huron Indians, named Keeper of the Spirit, adopted by Ojibway Tribe, named Mountain Eagle; presented to Her Royal Majesty Queen Elizabeth, 2002. Mem. Writers Guild Am. (best non-fiction dir. 1986), Dirs. Guild Am., Writers Union Can., Am., Acad. TV Arts and Scis., Assn. Can. TV and Radio Artists, Producers Assn. Can., Acad. Motion Picture Arts and Scis., Overseas Press Club, Acad. of Can. TV and Film Can. (lifetime achievement award 1992), PEN (Toronto), Nat. Arts Club. Jewish. Avocations: swimming, lecturing. Home: 15 Gregory Ave Toronto ON Canada M4W 2X7 Office: care CBC Box 500 Terminal A Toronto ON Canada M5W 1E6 Office Phone: 416-205-6867. E-mail: harryrasky@cbc.ca. *I have tried to find the positive forces in life and out of them create works of art of a lasting nature with the idea of improving the lives of others. This, plus the adventure of passing on the tradition of my father and his, is my life.*

**RASMUS, JOHN CHARLES,** trade association administrator, lawyer; b. Rochester, NY, Dec. 27, 1941; s. Harold Charles and Myrtle Leota (Dybevik) R.; m. Elaine Green Reeves, Mar. 19, 1982; children: Kristin, Stuart, Karin. AB, Cornell U., 1963; JD, U. Va., 1966. Bar: Va. 1970, U.S. Supreme Ct. 1974. Spl. agt. Def. Dept., Washington, 1966-70; v.p., adminstrv. officer, legis. rsch. counsel U.S. League Savs. Instns., Washington, 1970-83; asst. to exec. v.p. Nat. Assn. Fed. Credit Unions, 1983-84; sr. fed. adminstrv. counsel, mgr. regulatory & trust affairs Am. Bankers Assn., 1985—. Bd. trustees The Appraisal Found. Mem. ABA, FBA (disting. svc. award 1980, 82, past chmn. long range planning com., past chmn. coun. fin. instns. and economy), Univ. Club, Exchequer Club, Masons. Office: Am Bankers Assn 1120 Connecticut Ave NW Washington DC 20036 Home: 3302 Alabama Ave Alexandria VA 22305-1734 Office Phone: 202-663-5333. Business E-mail: jrasmus@aba.com.

**RASMUSON, BRENT J.,** photographer, small business owner; b. Logan, Utah, Nov. 28, 1950; s. Eleroy West and Fae (Jacobsen) Rasmuson; m. Tess Bullen, Sept. 30, 1981 (div. Jan. 2003); children: John, Mark, Lisa. Grad. auto repair and painting sch., Utah State U. Pre-press supr., ptnr. Herald Printing Co., Logan, 1969—80; profl. drummer, 1971-75; owner, builder auto racing engines Valley Automotive Specialties, 1971-76; exec. sec. Herald Printing Co., 1980—89; owner Brent Rasmuson Photography, Logan, 1986—, Temple Picture Classics, Logan, 1996—. Author photo prints of LDS temples: Logan, 1987, 95, 98, 2000, 04, Manti, 1989, 2000, Jordan River, 1989, 96, 98, 2000, Provo, 1990, 2001, Mesa, Ariz., 1990, 96, Boise, Idaho, 1990, 96, 2000, Salt Lake Temple, 1990, 96, 2001, 04, Idaho Falls, 1991, 94, 2000, St. George, 1991, 93, 2000, Portland, Oreg., 1991, 96, 97, 2000, LA, 1991, 96, 97, 2000, Las Vegas, Nev., 1991, Seattle, 1992, Oakland, Calif., 1993, 94, Ogden, 1992, 2001, Bountiful, 2002, Mt. Timpanogos, 2002; author photo print: Statue of Angel Moroni, 2002; author photos used to make neckties and watch dials of LDS temples: Salt Lake, Manti, Logan, LA, Oakland, Seattle, Las Vegas, Mesa, Portland, St. George, Jordan River, scenic tie Mammoth Hot Springs in Yellowstone Park, 1995; landscape scenic photographs featured in Best of Photography Ann., 1987-89; also in calendars and book covers; author photo print of Harris Rsch., Inc. Internat. Hdqrs. (recipient 1st prize nat. archtl. photo competition); designer several bus. logos. Mem.: Internat. Freelance Photographers Orgn., Assoc. Photographers, Internat. Platform Assn., Nat. Air and Space Soc., Nat. Trust Hist. Preservation. Republican. Mem. Lds Ch. Avocations: automobiles, travel, reading, coin collecting/numismatics, stamp collecting/philately. Home and office: 66 W 100 N Logan UT 84321-4506 Office Phone: 435-755-0668. Personal E-mail: bjr021@msn.com.

**RASMUSON, EDWARD BERNARD,** banker; b. Aug. 27, 1940; s. Elmer Edwin and Lile Vivian Rasmuson; m. Cathryn Elaine Robertson, Sept. 11, 1969; children: Natasha Ann, Laura Lile, David Edward. BA, Harvard U., 1962. Mgmt. trainee Brown Brothers Harriman, 1963, Chem. NY, 1964; asst. cashier Nat. Bank Alaska, Anchorage, 1964—66, asst. v.p., chmn. bd., 1968—73, pres., 1973—85, chmn. bd. dirs., 1986—2001; chmn. adv. bd. Wells Fargo Bank, Anchorage, 2001—02. Bd. regents U. Alaska, 1975—89; mem. Rasmuson Found., 1973—; past trustee Sheldon Jackson Coll.; past pres. Anchorage United Way; Hon. Consul of Sweden State of Alaska. Mem.:

World Bus. Coun., Young Pres.'s Orgn., Harvard Club (N.Y.C.), Rainier Club, Seattle Yacht Club, Wash. Athletic Club, Metropolitan Club, Pioneers Club Am., Explorers Club, Elks, Rotary. Office: Wells Fargo K3212-051 PO Box 196127 Anchorage AK 99519 Office Phone: 907-265-2927. Personal E-mail: erasmuson@gei.net.

**RASMUSSEN, FREDERICK TATUM,** lawyer; b. Madison, Wis., Feb. 21, 1943; s. Aaron Frederick and Besse Carol (Tatum) R.; children: Wendy, Frederick, Lauren. BA, UCLA, 1965; JD, U. Wis., 1974. Bar: Wash. 1974, U.S. Dist. Ct. (ea. and we. dists.) Wash. 1974, U.S. Ct. Appeals (9th cir.) 1986, U.S. Supreme Ct. 1987. Ptnr. Stokes Lawrence, Seattle, 1996—. Lt. comdr. USCG, 1966-69. Mem. ABA, Wash. State Bar Assn., Seattle-King County Bar Assn., Order of Coif. Office: Stokes Lawrence 800 5th Ave Ste 4000 Seattle WA 98104-3179 Office Phone: 206-626-6000.

**RASMUSSEN, HARRY PAUL,** horticulture and landscape educator; b. Tremonton, Utah, July 18, 1939; s. Peter Y. and Lorna (Nielsen) R.; m. Mary Jane Dalley, Sept. 4, 1959; children: Randy Paul, Lorianne, Trent Dalley, Rachelle. AS, Coll. of So. Utah, 1959; BS, Utah State U., 1961; MS, Mich. State U., 1962, PhD, 1965. Rsch. scientist Conn. Agr. Expt. Sta., New Haven, 1965-66; rschr., instr. Mich. State U., East Lansing, 1966-81; chmn. dept. horticulture and landscape architecture Wash. State U., Pullman, 1981-88; dir. Utah Agrl. Expt. Sta. Utah State U., 1988—. Assoc. v.p. Utah State U., Logan, 1992-99, 2002—. Contbr. articles to profl. jours., chpts. to books. Mem. bd. control YMCA, Lansing, Mich., 1976; mem. coun. Boy Scouts Am., Lansing, 1980; stake pres. Ch. of Jesus Christ of Latter Day Saints, Lansing, 1973-81. NDEA fellow, 1961-65. Fellow Am. Soc. Horticulture Sci.; mem. AAAS, Scanning Electron Microscopy (chmn. plant sect. 1976-83, chmn. exptl. sta. com. on orgn. and policy 1996-97). Home: 1949 N 950 E Logan UT 84341-1813 Office: Utah State U 225 Agr Sci Bldg Logan UT 84322-0001

**RASMUSSEN, JOHN OSCAR,** nuclear research scientist; b. St. Petersburg, Fla., Aug. 8, 1926; s. John Oscar and Hazel R.; m. Louise Brooks, Aug. 27, 1950; children: Nancy, Jane, David, Stephen. BS, Calif. Inst. Tech., 1948; PhD, U. Calif. at Berkeley, 1952; MA (hon.), Yale U., 1969. Mem. faculty dept. chemistry U. Calif., Berkeley, 1952-68, 73-91, prof. chemistry, 1971-91, ret., 1991, mem. research staff, 1952-68; sr. rsch. assoc. Lawrence Berkeley Nat. Lab., 1972—. Prof. chemistry Yale U. 1969-73; assoc. dir. Yale Heavy Ion Accelerator Lab., 1970-73; vis. research prof. Nobel Inst. Physics, Stockholm, 1953; vis. prof. Inst. Nuclear Sci. U. Tokyo, 1974, Fudan U., Shanghai, 1979, hon. prof., 1984. Contbr. articles to profl. jours. Served with USN, 1944-46. Recipient E.O. Lawrence Meml. award AEC, 1967; NSF sr. postdoctoral fellow Niels Bohr Inst., Copenhagen, 1961-62, NORDITA fellow, 1979, Guggenheim Meml. fellow, 1973, Alexander von Humboldt sr. rsch. fellow Tech. U. Munich, 1991. Fellow Am. Phys. Soc.; mem. Am. Chem. Soc. (Nuclear Applications in Chemistry award 1976), Fedn. Am. Scientists (chmn. 1969). Office: Lawrence Berkeley Nat Lab MS 70 319 Berkeley CA 94720-0001

**RASMUSSEN, KERRIE L.,** theater educator; b. Brigham City, Utah, Mar. 21, 1962; d. Eugene McLaws and Sharon B. Rasmussen. BFA, Idaho State U., Pocatello, 1985; MA, U. N.Mex., Albuquerque, 1988; postgrad., U. N.Mex., 1998. Drama tchr. Albuquerque Acad., 1998—99, West Mesa HS, Albuquerque, 1999—. Mem.: Edul. Theater Assn., Order Ea. Star. Avocations: karate (3d deg. black belt), poetry, stage managing, short stories. Office: West Mesa HS 6701 Fortuna Rd NW Albuquerque NM 87121

**RASMUSSEN, ROBERT DEE,** retired real estate appraiser; b. Lincoln, Kans., Dec. 24, 1936; s. Sam and Kristena (Andersen) R.; m. Beverly Bert Rowden, Mar. 22, 1959; children: Robert Denis, Kay Lynn. B Gen. Edn., U. Nebr., 1965; MA, Ariz. State U., 1970. Cert. gen. real estate appraiser, U. Nebr., 1965; MA, Ariz. State U., 1970. Cert. gen. real estate appraiser, Fla. Commd. USAF, 1957, advanced through grades to col., 1978, fighter pilot various locations, 1956-75, comdr. 59th Tactical Fighter Squadron Eglin AFB, Fla., 1975-77, chief Europe/Nato Plans Washington, 1978-80, vice-comdr. 474th Tactical Fighter Wing Nellis AFB, Nev., 1980-81; chief of plans U.S. European Command Joint Chiefs of Staff, Stuttgart, Germany, 1981-84; dir. joint matters Hdqrs. Tactical Air Command USAF, Langley AFB, Va., 1984-86, ret., 1986; appraiser, cons. Appraisal House Inc., Ft. Walton Beach, Fla., 1987-94; gen. appraiser Niceville, Fla., 1994-2000; ret., 2000. Dir. US Power Squadrons, Ft. Walton Beach, 1988-90. Decorated Defense Superior Svc. Medal, Legion of Merit, D.F.C. Mem. Ret. Officers Assn., Am. Assn. Ind. Investors, Porsche Club Am. (v.p. Germany region 1983-84, pres. North Fla. region 1989, 97, dir. 1988-94), Mid-Bay Rotary Club (charter, dir. 1995-96). Avocations: boating, fishing, sports cars. Home: 2421 Duncan Dr Niceville FL 32578-2915

**RASMUSSEN, TERESA J.,** lawyer, insurance company executive; b. Fergus Falls, Minn., Oct. 9, 1956; BS magna cum laude, Moorhead State Univ., 1981; JD, Univ. N. Dak., 1984. CPA 1981; bar: Colo. 1984, Minn. 1986. Trial atty., tax div. US Dept. Justice, Washington, 1984—86; assoc. Oppenheimer Wolff & Donnelly, Mpls., 1986—89; exec. v.p. & gen. counsel Northeast Securities Corp., Mpls., 1989—90; various legal positions up to v.p. & gen. counsel, IDS Life Ins. subsidiary Am. Express Fin. Corp., 1990—2005; sr. v.p., gen. counsel & sec. Thrivent Fin. for Lutherans, Mpls., 2005—. Mem.: ABA, Minn. State Bar Assn., Hennepin County Bar Assn. Office: Thrivent Financial for Lutherans 625 4th Ave S Minneapolis MN 55415-1624

**RASMUSSEN, THOMAS VAL, JR.,** lawyer, small business owner; b. Salt Lake City, Aug. 11, 1954; s. Thomas Val and Georgia (Smedley) R.; m. Donita Gubler, Aug. 15, 1978; children: James, Katherine, Kristin. BA magna cum laude, U. Utah, 1978, JD, 1981. Bar: Utah 1981, U.S. Dist. Ct. Utah 1981, U.S. Supreme Ct. 1985, U.S. Ct. Appeals (10th cir.) 1999. Atty. Salt Lake Legal Defender Assn., Salt Lake City, 1981-83, Utah Power and Light Co., Salt Lake City, 1983-89; of counsel Hatch, Morton & Skeen, Salt Lake City, 1989-90; ptnr. Morton, Skeen & Rasmussen, Salt Lake City, 1991-94, Skeen & Rasmussen, Salt Lake City, 1994-97; pvt. practice, Salt Lake City, 1997—. Co-owner, developer Handi Self-Storage, Kaysville, Utah, 1984-93; instr. bus. law Brigham Young U., Salt Lake City, 1988-90. Adminstrv. editor Jour. Contemporary Law, 1980-81, Jour. Energy Law and Policy, 1980-81. Missionary Ch. of Jesus Christ of Latter-Day Sts., Brazil, 1973-75. Mem. Utah, Salt Lake County Bar Assns., Intermountain Miniature Horse Club (pres. 1989, 2d v.p. 1990), Phi Eta Sigma, Phi Kappa Phi, Beta Gamma Sigma. Avocations: tennis, scuba diving, showing horses, travel, collecting art. Home: 3094 Whitewater Dr Salt Lake City UT 84121-1561 Office: 4659 Highland Dr Salt Lake City UT 84117-5137 Office Phone: 801-484-3000.

**RASOR, DINA LYNN,** journalist, private investigator; b. Downey, Calif., Mar. 21, 1956; d. Ned Shaurer and Genevieve Mercia (Eads) R.; m. Thomas Taylor Lawson, Oct. 4, 1980. BA in Polit. Sci., U. Calif., Berkeley, 1978. Editorial asst. ABC News, Washington, 1978-79; researcher Pres.'s Commn. on Coal, Washington, 1979; legis. asst. Nat. Taxpayers Union, Washington, 1979-81; founder, dir. Project on Mil. Procurement, Washington, 1981-89; investigative reporter Lawson-Rasor Assocs., El Cerrito, Calif., 1990-92; pres., CEO, investigator Bauman & Rasor Group, El Cerrito, Calif., 1993—. Author: The Pentagon Underground, 1985; editor: More Bucks, Less Bang, 1983; contbr. articles to profl. jours. Recipient Sigma Delta Chi Outstanding Leadership award Soc. Profl. Journalists, 1986; named to register Esquire Mag., 1986, Nat. Jour., 1986. Mem. United Ch. Christ. Office Phone: 510-235-5021.

**RASPBERRY, BRENDA,** pre-school educator; d. Vera Raspberry. Student, Ind. U.; diploma in Early Childhood Edn. and Sign Lang., Monterey Pennisula Coll., Calif., 1988; diploma in elem. behavior mgmt., Chapman Coll., Calif., 1980; diploma in child devel. and care, Cabrillo Coll., Calif., 1997; diploma in computer bus. and data entry, Regional Occupl. Program, Calif., 1999; diploma in early childhood ed. devel., Hartnell Coll., 2000. Cert. parent educator. Interpreter for deaf Montery County Interpreting Svcs., Salinas, Calif., 1996—; interpreter Fin. Adminstrv. Secretarial and Transl.

Svc., Salinas, Calif., 1998; assistance to adminstrs., sec. Montery County Broadcasting, Inc., Salinas, Calif., 1998—99; ct. apptd. spl. advocate Monterrey County. Actor: (plays) Yesterday and Today. Pub. rels. Mayor Richard G. Hatcher, Gary, Ind., 1974; spl. adv. Monterey County. Avocations: writing, painting.

**RASPBERRY, WILLIAM JAMES,** journalist; b. Okolona, Miss., Oct. 12, 1935; s. James Lee and Willie Mae (Tucker) R.; m. Sondra Patricia Dodson, Nov. 12, 1966; children—Patricia D., Angela D., Mark J. BS in History, Ind. Central Coll., 1958, LHD, 1973. Reporter-editor Indpls. Recorder, 1956-60; reporter-editor Washington Post, 1962-65, urban affairs columnist, 1966—2005; instr. journalism Howard U., 1971-73; prof. pub. policy Duke U., Durham, NC, 1995—. Lectr. on race relations and pub. edn. Mem. Pulitzer Prize Bd., 1979-86 TV commentator, Sta. WTTG, Washington, 1973-75, TV discussion panelist, Sta. WRC-TV, Washington, 1974-75; Contbr. articles on race relations and pub. edn. to popular mags; author, Looking Backward at US, 1991. Bd. visitors U. Md. Sch. Journalism, 1985—; bd. advisors Poynter Inst. for Media Studies, 1984-94. With US Army, 1960-62. Recipient Pulitzer Prize for commentary, 1994; Elijah Parish Lovejoy Fellowship, 1999; Lifetime Achievement Award, Nat Assn Black Journalists, 1994. Mem. Nat. Press Club, Capital Press Club, Kappa Alpha Psi. Clubs: Gridiron. Home: 1301 Iris St NW Washington DC 20012-1434 Office Phone: 919-613-7388. E-mail: wr3@duke.edu.

**RASPINO, LOUIS A.,** energy executive; b. 1953; Various positions to sr. v.p. fin., adminstrn., CFO La. Land & Exploration Co. (merged with Burlington), 1978—97; sr. v.p. Burlington Resources, 1997—98; v.p., fin. Halliburton Co., 1999—2000; exec. v.p., CFO, COO JRL Enterprises Inc., 2000—01; sr. v.p., fin., CFO Grant Prideco Inc., Houston, 2001—03; exec. v.p., CFO Pride Internat. Inc., Houston, 2003—05, pres., CEO, dir., 2005—. Office: Pride Internat Inc 5847 San Felipe Houston TX 77057 Office Phone: 713-789-1400.

**RASSBACH, HERBERT DAVID,** marketing executive; b. Glen Ridge, NJ, Mar. 23, 1944; s. Merrill Augustus and Ruth Bruce (Sims) Rassbach. BS, Del. State Coll., 1971; MBA, Drexel U., 1979. Prodn. planning mgr. Standard Brands Chem. Industries, Edison, NJ, 1971-74; order fulfillment mgr. P Q Corp., Valley Forge, Pa., 1974-77, mkt. devel. project mgr., 1977-82; market mgr. Willson Safety Products, Reading, Pa., 1983-85; pres. HDR Group, mktg. and mgmt. cons., Wayne, Pa., 1986—. Guest speaker Wharton Sch. U. Pa., 1988, Temple U., Phila., 1989, Wharton Club, 1995. Media comms. bd. Upper Merion Twp., 1989, vice-chmn., 1990, 1992—2004, chmn., 1991, 2005—, ex-officio mem. Citizens Police Adv. Bd., 2005—, committeeman, 1977. Mem. Drexel U. Alumni Assn. (v.p. Montgomery County chpt. 1988-91), Alpha Kappa Mu, Delta Mu Delta. Avocations: golf, tennis, running, travel, american history. Home: 635 Mallard Rd Wayne PA 19087-2346 Office: HDR Group PO Box 2164 Southeastern PA 19399-2164 Office Phone: 610-964-8555. Business E-Mail: hdrassbach@hdrgroup.com.

**RASSEL, RICHARD EDWARD,** lawyer; b. Toledo, Ohio, Jan. 10, 1942; s. Richard Edward and Madonna Mary (Tuohy) R.; m. Elizabeth Ann Frederick, Dec. 5, 1967 (dec. June 1977); children: Richard III, Elizabeth; m. Dawn Ann Lynch, Sept. 17, 1983; children: Lauren, Brian. BA, U. Notre Dame, 1964; JD, U. Mich., 1966; cert. judge advocate, USN Judge Advocate Sch., 1967. Law clk. Mich. Ct. Appeals, Detroit, 1966-70; shareholder, v.p. Butzel Long, Detroit, 1970-94, chmn., CEO, 1994—2006, dir. global client rels., 2006—. Bd. dirs. Robertson-Jamieson Corp., Birmingham, Mich., WTVS-Channel 56. Pres. Birmingham Cmty. House; bd. advisors U. Detroit Mercy Grad. Sch. Bus.; bd. dirs. Detroit Legal News, Detroit Police Athletic League, Internat. Visitors Coun., William Beaumont Hosp.; chair meta. affairs coalition Oakland U. Coll. Arts and Scis.; past pres., past bd. dirs. Rosa Parks Scholarship Found.; trustee Seed Found. Lt. USNR, 1967-69. Mem. ABA (vice chmn. media and law com.), State Bar of Mich. (chmn. multidisciplinary practice law com.), Am. Coll. Trial Lawyers, Birmingham Athletic Club, Detroit Athletic Club, Otsego Ski Club, Village Club. Office: Butzel Long 150 W Jefferson Ave Ste 900 Detroit MI 48226-4416 E-mail: rassel@butzel.com.*

**RASSIDAKIS, GEORGE Z.,** pathologist, researcher; b. Athens, Greece, Jan. 12, 1968; s. Zacharias M Rassidakis and Ioanna A Vardava. MD, PhD, U. Patras, Greece, 1992. Pathologist Greek Min. of Health, Greece, 1997. Resident in pathology U. of Athens, Athens, Greece, 1992—96; clin. fellow in cytopathology Sotiria Gen. and Chest Dis. Hosp., Athens, Greece, 1996—97; attending pathologist 401 Army Hosp., Athens, Greece, 1998—99; rschr. in hematopathology MD Anderson Cancer Ctr., Houston, 2000—. Rsch. fellow Karolinska Hosp., Stockholm, 1998—98; asst. prof. in hematopathology MD Anderson Cancer Ctr., Houston, 2004—. Author: scientific articles (medical journals) Mechanisms of Lymphomagenesis and Prognostic Implications. Scholar ICRETT fellowship, UICC, 1997, Alexander S. Onassis Found. Scholarship, Alexander S. Onassis Found., 2000—02. Mem.: Am. Assn. for Cancer Rsch., Am. Soc. of Hematology, US and Can. Acad. of Pathology. Achievements include research in Lymphoma Biology And Prognosis. Office: MD Anderson Cancer Ctr 1515 Holcombe Blvd Houston TX 77030 E-mail: gzrassidakis@mail.mdanderson.org.

**RASSMAN, JOEL H.,** home construction company executive; b. NYC, May 16, 1945; BBA, CUNY, 1967. CPA, N.Y. Ptnr. Ernst & Young (formerly Kenneth Leventhal & Co.), N.Y.C., 1967-84; exec. v.p., CFO, bd. dirs. Toll Bros., Inc., Huntingdon Valley, Pa., 1984—. Mem. AICPA, N.Y. State Soc. CPA's.

**RASSMAN, WILLIAM R.,** plastic surgeon; BS in Biology, L.I. U., 1962; MD, Med. Coll. Va., 1966. Diplomate Am. Bd. Surgery, lic. Calif., Fla., N.Y., Hawaii, Va., Pa., Ill., Nev., Ga., N.C., Wash., Colo., Md., N.J. Intern U. Minn., 1966—67; fellow in cardiovascular surgery Cornell Med. Ctr., 1968—69, resident in orthop. surgery, 1967—69; resident in gen. vascular surgery Dartmouth Med. Ctr., 1971—73; founder, mng. ptnr. N.E. Kingdom Surg. Assocs., 1973—79; staff surgeon, bus. advisor Hilo Med. Group, 1979—83; pres. Bosley Med. Group, 1988—90; CEO IntelliMED Corp., 1984—; pres., founder RW2 Med. Group, 2001—; founder, pres. Maven Technologies, 2001—, New Hair Inst. Med. Group, L.A., 1991—. Cons. IBM, Hosp. Corp. Am., Control Data Corp., E.I. DuPont; lectr. in field. Achievements include patents for hair transplant harvesting device and method for its use; development of and design of heart valves, intra-aortic balloon pump and balloon technology, safety chamber for intra-aortic balloon; and design pulsatile assistance device; design of sophisticated commercial point of transaction clinical information systems for surgery; software scheduling system with application in real time. Office: 9911 W Pico Blvd Ste 301 Los Angeles CA 90035

**RASTETTER, WILIAM H.,** biotechnology company executive; BS in Chemistry, MIT; MA, Harvard U., PhD in Chemistry. Faculty MIT, Cambridge, Mass., 1975—82; scientist/rschr. biocatalysis and chem. scis. groups Genentech, 1982—84, dir. corp. ventures, 1984—86; pres. & CEO IDEC Pharms. Corp., San Diego, 1986—2002, CFO, 1988—93; dir. IDEC Pharms. Corp. (now Biogen IDEC), 1986—; chmn. bd. dirs. IDEC Pharms. Corp., 1996—2002; CEO Biogen IDEC, 2002—03, exec. chmn., 2003—. Bd. dir. Argonaut Technologies, Inc., Illumina, Inc.; mem. Calif. Healthcare Inst.; R.B. Woodward vis. scholar, dept. chem. and chem. biology Harvard U. Office: Biogen IDEC 5200 Research Pl San Diego CA 92122 also: Biogen IDEC 14 Cambridge Ctr Cambridge MA 02142

**RASTOGI, ANIL KUMAR,** health products executive; b. India, July 13, 1942; came to U.S., 1990, naturalized, 1978; s. R.S. and K.V. Rastogi; m. Anjali Capur, Mar. 18, 1970; children: Priya, Sonya. BS with honors, Lucknow U., 1963, MS, 1964; PhD in Polymer Sci., McGill U., 1969. From staff to dir. corp. diversification profucts Owens-Corning Tech. Ctr., Granville, Ohio, 1969—87; v.p. Mead Imaging, Miamisburg, Ohio, 1987-89; pres. Mead Cycolor Divsn., Dayton, Ohio, 1989-92; v.p., gen. mgr.infusion

systems div. Pharmacia Deltec, Inc., St. Paul, 1992-93, exec. v.p., 1993-94; COO SIMS Deltec, Inc., St. Paul, 1994-95; pres., COO Sabratek Corp., Niles, Ill., 1995—98; pres., CEO NOMOS Corp., Sewickley, Pa., 1998—2002; v.p. entrepeneurship and tech. commercialization Drexel U., Phila., 2002—05; pvt. investor Reston, Va., 2005—. Mem. adv. bd. Central Ohio Tech. Coll.; lectr., cons. in field. 8 bus. and tech. publs.; patentee in field. Bd. dirs. Licking County Family Services Assn.; bd. dirs. Tech. Alliance of Central Ohio; v.p. local United Way; bd. dirs. and treas. Columbus Bus. Tech. Ctr.; mem. Overview Adv. Com. Strategic Hwy. Research Program. Fellow NRC Can., 1966-69 Mem. AAAS, Am. Mgmt. Assn., Am. Chem. Soc., Soc. Plastics Engrs., Comml. Devel. Assn., Med. Alley (bd. dirs.), Health Ind. Mfrs. Assn., Nat. Infusion Therapy Alliance (bd. dirs.), Toastmasters (past pres.), Rotary, Sigma Xi. Home and Office: 1584 Regatta Lane Reston VA 20194

**RASULO, JAMES A.,** theme park executive; Grad. in Econs., Columbia U., 1978; MA in Econs., U. Chgo., 1982. MBA, 1984. Exch. rate/interest rate forecaster Chase Manhattan Bank; mgr. corp. planning Marriott Corp.; from dir. to sr. v.p. corp. strategic planning Walt Disney Co., Lake Buena Vista, Fla., 1986—93, sr. v.p. corp. alliances, 1993—95; exec. v.p. Euro Disney S.C.A., Paris, 1998—2000, also pres., COO, 1999—2000, chmn., CEO, 2000—02; pres. Walt Disney Pks. and Resorts Worldwide Walt Disney Co., Lake Buena Vista, Fla., 2002—. Mem.: Am. C. of C. (France), Columbia U. Club France. Office: Walt Disney Co 1375 N Buena Vista Dr Lake Buena Vista FL 32830-8402

**RATCHEV, BORIS A,** management consultant; b. Sofia, Bulgaria, July 16, 1969; s. Anton Slavov and Blaga Borisova Ratchev; m. Leticia G. Ratchev, Mar. 22, 1996. BSc, U. of Wis., 1990—93, MSc, 1993—95, Stanford U., 2000—05. Summer intern-analyst Siemens Power Sys. Control Divsn., Mpls., 1995; sr. reliability engr. Altera Corp., San Jose, Calif., 1996—2000, sr. software engineer-architect, 2000—05; mgmt. cons. PRTM, Mountain View, Calif., 2005—. Grad. fellowship, U. of Wisconsin-Madison, 1993. Mem.: IEEE (life). Achievements include patents for technology mapping technique for fracturable logic; novel method of using randomly generated; techniques for automated sweeping of parameters in computer aided design to achieve optimum performance and resource usage. Avocations: skiing, soccer, reading, travel. Home: 992 Belmont Terrace #9 Sunnyvale CA 94086

**RATCHFORD, MELINDA EUDY,** education educator; b. Kannapolis, N.C., Feb. 22, 1948; adopted d. Hauty William and Mary Effie Hathcock Eudy; m. Don Ratchford, June 18, 1977. BS in edn. and social scis., Appalachian State U., Boone, N.C., 1969; MS in libr. sci., U. N.C., Greensboro, 1973; sixth yr. degree in curriculum and supervision, Appalachian State U., Boone, N.C., 1979; EdD in ednl. adminstrn. and supervision, U. N.C., Chapel Hill, 1990; AS in applied sci. paralegal tech., Gaston Coll., Dallas, N.C., 1999. Jr. high and h.s. history and english tchr. N.C. Pub. Schs., 1969—76, libr., 1976—85; tchr. resource ctr. founder and coord. Gaston County Schs., Gastonia, NC, 1985—88, dir., media and libr. systems, 1990—93, instrnl. support, 1995—2000; asst. prof. of edn. Belmont Abbey Coll., NC, 2000—, interim chmn. Dept. Edn. Ednl. cons. Multi-Ednl. Resources, Inc., Belmont, NC, 2000—. Pres. Gaston County AIDS Coun., Gastonia, NC, 1996—2000. Named Faculty Tchr. of Yr., Belmont Abbey Coll., 2001—02; recipient Odyssey Project, New Am. Schools Devel. Corp., 1991—93. Mem.: N.C. Assn. Sch. Libres. (pres. 1995—2001), N.C. Assn. Educators (N.C. State Sch. Press Award 1982, 1985, 1986, 1988), N.C. Edn. Assn. (life First Union Non-Teaching Educator of the Yr. 1998). Liberal. Presbyterian. Avocations: reading, Titanic historian. Home: 1000 Tomshire Dr Gastonia NC 28056 Office: Belmont Abbey Coll 100 Belmont Mt Holly Rd Belmont NC 28012 Office Phone: 704-825-6846. Office Fax: 704-825-6222. Personal E-mail: mratch@bellsouth.net. Business E-Mail: melindaratchford@bac.edu.

**RATCHFORD MERCHANT, BETTY JO,** retired elementary school educator; b. Huntsville, Ala., Feb. 9, 1937; d. Howard Clyde and Margaret (Kyle) Wikle; m. McClellan Ratchford, 1960 (div.); children: McClellan III, Margaret Lee, Rosalyn Hampton; m. Curtis Merchant, 1992. BS, Auburn U.; MEd, Ala. A&M U., 1998. Cert. tchr. elem. Tchr. elem. Gilbert Sch., Atlanta, Madison County Sch. Sys., Huntsville, Ala., Riverton Elem. Sch., Mt. Carmel Elem. Sch., 2003. Named Tchr. of Yr. for Madison County, 1992. Mem. NEA, AAUW, Ala. Edn. Assn., Environ. Edn. Assn. Ala., Madison County Edn. Assn. Episcopalian. Avocations: poetry, singing, reading, painting, rock climbing. Home: 11033 Everest Cr Huntsville AL 35803

**RATCHYE, BOYD HAVENS,** lawyer; b. Helena, Mont., June 10, 1938; s. John Frederick and Leanora (Boyd) R.; m. Jean P. Cunningham, Sept. 1, 1962 (div. Oct. 1985); children: Ellen C., Stephen B.; m. Susan Light, May 21, 1994. BA cum laude, Harvard U., 1960, JD, 1963. Bar: Minn. 1964, U.S. Dist. Ct. (Minn. 1964, ND 1993), U.S. Ct. Appeals (8th cir.) 1967, U.S. Supreme Ct. 1972, U.S. Ct. Appeals (fed. cir.) 1983. Law clk. to justice J.C. Otis Supreme Ct. Minn., St. Paul, 1963-64; assoc. Erickson, Popham, Haik & Schnobrich, Mpls., 1964-65; assoc. to ptnr. Doherty, Rumble & Butler, P.A., St. Paul, 1966—99; shareholder, civil litig. Bassford Remele, Mpls., 1999—. Adj. prof. William Mitchell Coll. of Law, 1975-94. Chmn., bd. dir. Yellowstone Assn. Named a Minn. Super Lawyer, Mpls St. Paul Mag. & Minn. Law & Politics mag., 2000—06; named one of Best Lawyers in Am., 1986—2006. Mem. ABA, Am. Bd. Trial Advocates (pres. Minn. chpt. 1990-91), Minn. State Bar Assn., Minn. Def. Lawyers Assn., Hennepin County Bar Assn., Harvard Radcliffe Club Minn., Inns of Ct. (Warren Burger chpt., pres. 1999-2000, counselor 2000-01). Episcopalian. Avocations: rowing, running, cross country skiing, scuba diving, snorkeling. Office: Bassford Remele Ste 3800 33 S 6th St Minneapolis MN 55402 Office Phone: 612-376-1604. Office Fax: 612-333-8829. Business E-Mail: boydr@bassford.com.

**RATCLIFF, CARTER GOODRICH,** writer, critic, poet; b. Seattle, Aug. 20, 1941; s. Francis Kenneth and Marian Elizabeth (Carter) R.; m. Phyllis Derfner, Jan. 28, 1976. BA, U. Chgo., 1963. Dir. poetry workshop St. Mark's Poetry Project, N.Y.C., 1969-70; editorial assoc. Artnews, N.Y.C., 1969-72; advisory editor Art Internat., Lugano, Switzerland, 1970-75; instr. modern and contemporary art and art theory The Sch. of Visual Arts, N.Y.C., 1972-83; instr. modern and contemporary art Phila. Coll. of Art, 1973; instr. art history NYU Sch. of Continuing Edn., 1973-75; contbg. editor Saturday Review, N.Y.C., 1980-82, Art in America, N.Y.C., 1976—; mem. editorial adv. com. Sculpture, Washington, 1992—. Vis. prof. post-war Am. art SUNY, Purchase, 1983-84, Pratt Inst., Bkyn., 1984-85, Hunter Coll., CUNY, 1985-89, 95-99, 2002; lectr. in field. Author: (books, poetry) Fever Coast, 1973, Give Me Tomorrow, 1983; (books) John Singer Sargent, 1982, Andy Warhol, 1983, Robert Longo, 1985, Komar and Melamid, 1989, Gilbert and George: The Singing Sculpture, 1993, The Fate of a Gesture: Jackson Pollock and Post War American Art, 1996, paperback edit., 1998, Out of the Box: The Reinvention of Art, 1965-1975, 2001; (essays) Joseph Cornell, 1980, Willem de Kooning: The North Atlantic Light, 1983, Roy Lichtenstein, 1989, Barnett Newman, 1991, Gilbert & George, 1993, Ellsworth Kelly, 1996, Francis Bacon, 1998, William Blake, 2001, Barnett Newman, 2002, Georgia O' Keeffe, 2003, Alex Katz, 2005; contbg. editor Art in America, 1976—, Art on Paper, 2001—, Sculpture Mag., 2001—; mem. editl. bd. Sculpture Mag., 1992—; contbr. over 500 articles on art to mags. and catalogs. Recipient of the Frank Jewett Mather award for art criticism Coll. Art Assn., 1987; Poets Found. grantee, 1969, NEA Arts Critics grantee, 1972, 76; Guggenheim fellow, 1976. Home and Office: 373 Red Top Rd Highland NY 12528 E-mail: ratcliff1@earthlink.net.

**RATCLIFF, DONALD EARL,** minister, educator; s. Clarence Earl and Lois Anna R.; m. Brenda Sue Campbell. BA, Spring Arbor Coll., 1973; MA, Mich. State U., 1975; EdS, U. Ga., 1986, PhD, 1995. Ordained to ministry Christian Nation Ch., 1978. Asst. prof. Circleville Bible Coll., 1975—78; tchr. adminstr., dean of men Christian Union Bible Sch., Roseau, Dominica, W.I., 1978-79; dir. Christian edn. Vinton Bapt. Ch., Ohio, 1981-82; interim pastor Mt. Pleasant Bapt. Ch., Toccoa, Ga., 1983-84; assoc. prof. Toccoa Falls (Ga.) Coll., 1982—2001, Biola U., La Mirada, Calif., 2001—04; prof. Vanguard U., Costa Mesa, Calif., 2004—. Spkr. in field. Author: Using Psychology in the

Church, 1984, Handbook of Preschool Religious Education, 1988, Handbook of Youth Ministry, 1991, Introduction to Psychology and Counseling, 1991, Handbook of Children's Religious Education, 1992, The Complete Guide to Religious Education Volunteers, 1993, Bruised and Broken, 1992, Child-Rearing and Personality Development, 1993, Handbook of Family Religious Education, 1995, Raising Your Child From Birth to Age Twelve, 1999, Children's Spirituality, 2004; contbr. articles to profl. jours. Mem. Nat. Assn. Profs. Christian Edn., Christian Assn. Psychol. Studies. Office: Vanguard Univ Dept Psychology 55 Fair Dr Costa Mesa CA 92626 Office Phone: 714-556-3610 306. Business E-Mail: dratcliff@vanguard.edu. *Children are perhaps the most undervalued treasure of the church. They are the key to both short-term and long-term growth of the church; they are the church of the future.*

**RATCLIFFE, DAVID M.,** utilities executive; b. Tifton, Ga. BS in Biology, Valdosta State U., 1970; JD, Woodrow Wilson Coll. Law, 1975. Bar: Ga. Biologist Ga. Power, 1971; v.p. fuel svcs. So. Co. Svcs., 1986—89, exec. v.p., 1989—91, pres., CEO Miss. Power, 1991—95, sr. v.p. external affairs, 1995—98, exec. v.p., treas., CFO Ga. Power, 1998—99, CEO Ga. Power, 1999—2003, chmn., pres, CEO, 2004—. Bd. dirs. Edison Electric Inst., CSX Transp., Ga. Rsch. Alliance, Ctrl. Atlanta Progress, Ga. Partnership for Excellence in Edn., chair, 2001—04; bd. dirs. Fed. Res. Bank Atlanta, chair, 2004. Trustee Woodruff Arts Ctr.; mem. adv. bd. Salvation Army. Mem.: Metro Atlanta C. of C. (chair econ. devel.), Ga. Bar Assn. Office: Southern Co 270 Peachtree St NW Atlanta GA 30303*

**RATH, ALAN T.,** sculptor; b. Cin., Nov. 25, 1959; s. George and Carolyn R. BSEE, MIT, 1982. One-man exhbns include San Jose (Calif.) Art Mus., 1990, Dorothy Goldeen Gallery, Santa Monica, Calif., 1990, 92, Walker Art Ctr., Mpls., 1991, Mus. Contemporary Art, Chgo., 1991, Carl Solway Gallery, Cin., 1991, Inst. Contemporary Mus., Honolulu, 1992, Ctr. Fine Art, Miami, Fla., 1992, Galerie Hans Mayer, Dusseldorf, Germany, 1992, Hiroshima (Japan) City Mus. Contemporary Art, 1994, Worcester (Mass.) Art Mus., 1994, John Weber Gallery, N.Y.C., 1994, Haines Gallery, San Francisco, 1995, 96, 98, Contemporary Art Mus., Houston, 1995, Aspen Art Mus., Colo., 1996, Dorfman Projects, N.Y.C., 1998, Yerba Buena Ctr. for the Arts, San Francisco, 1998, Site Santa Fe (N.Mex.), 1998, Mus. of Art, Austin, Tex., 1999, Scottsdale Mus. of Contemporary Art, 1999; group exhbns include Visiona, Zurich, 1989, Ars Electronica, Linz, Austria, 1989, L.A. Contemporary Exhbns., 1989, Mus. Folkwang, Essen, Germany, 1989, Cite des Arts et des Nouvelles Technologies, Montreal, 1990, Stadtmuseum Siegburg, Siegburg, Germany, 1990, San Francisco Mus. Modern Art, 1990, 95, 98, Denver ArtMus., 1991, Whitney Am. Art, N.Y.C., 1991, Alvar Alto Mus., Jyvaskyla, Finland, 1992, Internat. Ctr. Photography, N.Y.C., 1992, Padigilione d'Arte Contemporanea, Ferrara, Italy, 1992, John Weber Gallery, N.Y.C., 1993, Spiral Art Ctr., Tokyo, 1994, Aldrich Mus. of Contemporary Art, Ridgefield, Conn., 1995, Otso Gallery, Espo Finland, 1996, LaLonja, Palma de Malloren, Spain, 1996, Kunsthalle, Vienna, 1998, L.A. Mus. Contemporary Art, 1999, Taipei ICA, Taiwan, 2001, Bienal de Valencia, Spain, 2001. Grantee NEA, 1988; Guggenheim fellow, 1994. Office: IKON 830 E 15th St Oakland CA 94606-3631

**RATH, HOWARD GRANT, JR.,** lawyer; b. L.A., Sept. 2, 1931; s. Howard Grant and Helen (Cowell) R.; m. Peyton McComb, Sept. 13, 1958 (dec. Apr. 1984); children: Parthenia Peyton, Francis Cowell; m. Dorothy Moser, Aug. 29, 1986. BS, U. Calif., 1953; JD, U. So. Calif., 1958. Bar: Calif. 1959, U.S. Dist. Ct. (cen. dist.) Calif., 1959, U.S. Ct. Claims 1974, U.S. Tax Ct. 1960. Assoc. O'Melveny & Myers, L.A., 1959-66; tax counsel, dir. tax adminstrn., asst. treas. Northrop Corp. L.A., 1966-74; sr. tax ptnr. Macdonald, Halsted & Laybourne, L.A., 1974-86, Hill & Weiss, L.A., 1986-90; ptnr. Lewis Brisbois Bisgaard & Smith, L.A., 1990—; dir. Rath Packing Co., Waterloo, Iowa, 1966-81. 1st lt. U.S. Army, 1953-55. Mem. State Bar Calif., L.A. County Bar Assn., L.A. Yacht Club, The Athenaeum, Order of Coif, Phi Beta Kappa. Republican. Episcopalian. Office: Lewis Brisbois Bisgaard & Smith 221 N Figueroa St Ste 1200 Los Angeles CA 90012-2646 Business E-Mail: rath@lbbslaw.com.

**RATH, JOSEPH F.,** psychologist, researcher, educator; s. Joseph Francis Rath and Giovanna Maria Pizzella. MEd, Columbia U., N.Y.C., 1992; PhD, Fordham U., N.Y.C., 2000. Lic. psychologist N.Y., 2001. Adj. lectr. CUNY, NYC, 1992—94; adj. asst. prof. of psychology and edn. Columbia U., NYC, 2001—03; rsch. scientist NYU Sch. Medicine, NYC, 1996—2005, clinical asst. prof., 2005—; staff psychologist Rusk Inst. Rehab. Medicine, NYC, 2005—. Contbr. articles to profl. jours. Fellow Rehab. Rsch. fellow, NIH, 1993—94. Mem.: APA. Office: New York University School of Medicine 400 East 34th St RR515 New York NY 10016 Business E-Mail: joseph.rath@nyumc.org.

**RATH, NIGAM P.,** research scientist, educator; s. Satybadi and Urmila Rath; m. Suchitra Misra, Mar. 19, 1963; 1 child, Niharika. PhD, Okla. State U., Stillwater, 1986. Rsch. assoc. U. Notre Dame, Ind., 1986—87, asst. faculty fellow, 1987—89; rsch. asst. prof. U. Mo., St. Louis, 1989—96, rsch. assoc. prof., 1996—2004, rsch. prof., 2004—. Cons. EMT Assocs., Enchino, Calif., 1999—2006, Novus Internat., St. Louis, 2003—06, Chemir, U.S. Mem. Commr. City of Maryland Heights, 2001. Mem.: Am. Crystallography Assn. (assoc.). Office: U Mo St Louis Dept Chemistry 8001 Natural Bridge Rd Saint Louis MO 63121 Office Phone: 314-516-5333. E-mail: rathn@umsl.edu.

**RATH, THOMAS DAVID,** lawyer, retired prosecutor; b. East Orange, N.J., June 1, 1945; s. Harvey and Helen R.; m. Christine Casey, Dec. 18, 1971; children— Erin, Timothy. AB, Dartmouth Coll. 1967; JD, Georgetown U. 1971. Bar: N.J. 1971, N.H. 1972, U.S. Supreme Ct. 1978. Law clk. Judge Clarkson Fisher, U.S. Dist. Ct. N.J., 1971-72; atty. criminal div. Office of Atty. Gen., NH, 1972-73; asst. atty. gen., 1973-76, dep. atty. gen., 1976-78, atty. gen., 1978-80; ptnr. Orr & Reno, P.A., Concord, NH, 1980-87, Rath & Young, P.A., Concord, 1987-91; founding ptnr. Rath, Young, Pignatelli & Oyer, P.A., Concord, 1991—. Polit. analyst WHDH-TV, Boston, WGBH Pub. TV, Boston, WENH, N.H. Pub. TV, WBUR-Boston Radio; chief strategist Alexander for Pres.; vice chmn. of bd. Primary Bank, 1995-97; pres. Play Ball, N.H., 1994—; commentator, polit. analyst WMUR-TV and Yankee Network; bd. dirs. Assoc. Grocers New England, Chubb Am. Fund. Host State of the State, Yankee Cable Network; co-host Close-Up, WMUR-TV. Chmn. campaign Warren B. Rudman for U.S. Senate, 1980, 86; bd. overseers Aquinas House, Dartmouth Coll., com. on trustees Rockefeller Ctr. Bd. Visitors; bd. oversers Dartmouth Med. Sch.; nat. dir. Baker Exploratory Com., 1986-87; sec. bd. trustees Concord Hosp.; treas. N.H. Rep. party, 1981-93; trustee DWC, 1981-87, chmn., 1982-86; mem. Baker Exploratory Com., 1986-87; trustee Concord Hosp., 1980-86; sr. nat. com. Duke for Pres.; del. Rep. Nat. Conv., 1984, 88, 92, rules com., 1988, 92, N.H. committeeman, 1996—; Rep. nat. committeeman State of N.H., 1996; bd. dirs. New Eng. Coun.; 1997. Mem. Nat. Assn. Attys. Gen. (vice-chmn. Eastern region, vice chmn. standing com. on energy), N.H. Bar Assn. (spl. Pres. award 1992). Clubs: Dartmouth Coll. (v.p. Merrimack County). Roman Catholic. Office: Rath Young and Pignatelli One Capital Plaza PO Box 1500 Concord NH 03302-1500 Business E-Mail: tdr@rathlaw.com.

**RATHA, DILIP,** economist, consultant; PhD in Econs., Indian Statis. Inst., New Delhi, 1987. Asia economist Indosuez W.I. Carr Securities, Singapore, 1995—98; sr. economist World Bank, Washington, 1998—. Asst. prof. Indian Inst. Mgmt., Ahmedabad, 1989—90. Editor: Remittances: Development Impact and Future Prospects. Achievements include first to reveal the global significance of migrant remittances - a key discovery in the field of migration and development; research in estimated the size of South-South FDI flows, first to reveal the emergence of the south as a major source of capital flows to the south; predicted shadow ratings for developing countries that do not have sovereign ratings from major rating agencies. Business E-Mail: dratha@worldbank.org

**RATHBONE, PETER B.,** art appraiser; BA in Art History, Boston U. Dir. Am. paintings, drawings and sculpture dept. Sotheby's, NYC, 1976—. Office: Sotheby's 1334 York Ave New York NY 10021 Office Phone: 212-606-7280. Office Fax: 212-606-7039. Business E-Mail: peter.rathbone@sothebys.com.

**RATHER, DAN,** news correspondent, former network news anchor; b. Wharton, Tex., Oct. 31, 1931; m. Jean Goebel, 1957; children: Dawn Robin, Daniel Martin. BA in Journalism, Sam Houston State Tchrs. Coll., Huntsville, Tex., 1953; student, U. Houston, South Tex. Sch. Law. Instr. journalism Sam Houston State Coll.; reporter AP, Huntsville, Tex., 1950, UPI, 1950—52, Houston Chronicle, 1954—55; news writer, reporter, news dir. KTRH Radio, Houston, 1956; dir. news and pub. affairs KHOU (CBS TV affiliate), Houston, 1959—61; chief southwestern bur. CBS, Dallas, 1961—64, White House corr., 1963, 1966—74, chief London bureau, 1965—66, war corr. Vietnam, 1966; anchor, corr. CBS Reports, 1974—75; corr., co-editor 60 Minutes, 1975—81; anchor Dan Rather Reporting, CBS Radio Network, 1977—2005; anchor, mng. editor CBS Evening News with Dan Rather, 1981—2005; anchor 48 Hours, 1988—2002; corr. 60 Minutes II, 1998—2006. Co-editor show Who's Who, CBS-TV, 1977; anchored numerous CBS News spl. programs. Author: (with Gary Gates) The Palace Guard, 1974, (with Mickey Herskowitz) The Camera Never Blinks, 1977, (with Peter Wyden) Memoirs, I Remember, 1991, The Camera Never Blinks Twice: The Further Adventures of a Television Journalist, 1994, The American Dream, 2001; editor Our Times, 1994. Recipient ten Emmy awards, George Foster Peabody award, 2005; honors include dedication of Dan Rather Comm. Bldg., classroom facility Sam Houston State U., Huntsville, Tex. Office: CBS 60 Minutes 524 W 57th St New York NY 10019-2924

**RATHER, LUCIA PORCHER JOHNSON,** library administrator; b. Durham, N.C., Sept. 12, 1934; d. Cecil Slayton and Lucia Lockwood (Porcher) Johnson; m. John Carson Rather, July 11, 1964; children: Susan Wright, Bruce Carson. Student, Westhampton Coll., 1951-53; AB in History, U. N.C., 1955, MS in Library Sci., 1957; PhD in History, George Washington U., 1994. Cataloger Library of Congress, Washington, 1957-64, bibliographer, 1964-66, systems analyst, 1966-70; group head MARC Devel. Office, 1970-73, asst. chief, 1973-76, acting chief, 1976-77, dir. for cataloging, 1976-91. Chmn. standing com. on cataloguing Internat. Fedn. Library Assns., 1976-81; sec. Working Group on Content Designators, 1972-77; chmn. Working Group on Corp. Headings, 1978-79, Internat. ISBD Rev. Com., 1981-87. Co-author: the MARC II Format, 1968. Recipient Libr. Congress Disting. Svc. award, 1991, Disting. Alumnus award U. N.C. Sch. Libr. and Info. Sci., 1992. Mem. ALA (Margaret Mann award 1985, Melvil Dewey award 1991), Phi Beta Kappa. Democrat. Presbyterian. Home: 438 Heron Point Chestertown MD 21620-1680

**RATHJE, JAMES LEE,** broker; b. Davenport, Iowa, Nov. 23, 1947; s. Gilbert L. and Wanda L. (Henning) R.; m. Karen L. Mangels, May 15, 1980. BBA with high distinction, U. Iowa, 1970, MBA, 1972. Plant acct. Container Corp. Am., Wilmington, Del., 1972-73; portfolio mgr. Davenport Bank and Trust, 1973-76; investment broker Loewi and Co., Davenport, 1976-78; fin. cons. A.G. Edwards and Sons, Inc., Davenport, 1978—. With USAR, 1970-76. Republican. Lutheran. Avocations: basketball, baseball, golf, bicycling. Home: 3861 Parkdale Dr Bettendorf IA 52722-1974

**RATHKE, BARBARA JOANNE ANDREWS,** art educator; b. Carroll, Iowa; d. Wayne Henry and Bernice Marie Andrews; m. Jerome William Rathke, Aug. 31, 1968; children: Benjamin Jerome, Joseph Andrews. BA, North Ctrl. Coll., 1986. Cert. tchr., Ill. Art tchr. Dist. 68, Edgewood Sch., Woodridge, Ill., 1987—. Program chmn. Faithful Circle Quilters, Downers Grove, Ill., 1986; coord. quilt rsch. days Early Am. Mus., Mahomet, Ill., 1988; mem. PTO, Woodridge, 1971—. Recipient Diane Duvigneaud Sr. Art award North Ctrl. Coll., 1986; named to Pres.'s List for Acad. Achievement, North Ctrl. Coll., 1984, 2003. Mem. NEA, Nat. Art Edn. Assn., Am. Quilters Soc., Ill. Art Assn., Woodridge Edn. Assn. Avocations: quiltmaking, gardening with hist. roses and native perennials. Office: Edgewood Sch 7900 Woodridge Dr Woodridge IL 60517-3824

**RATHKE, SHEILA WELLS,** marketing professional, consultant; b. Columbia, S.C., Aug. 9, 1943; d. Walter John and Betty Marie (McLaughlin) Wells; m. David Bray Rathke, Sept. 1966 (dec. 1997); 1 child, Erinn Michele. BA summa cum laude, U. Pitts., 1976, postgrad., 1976-77. Loan coord. Equibank, Pitts., 1961-65; office mgr. U.S. Steel Corp., Pitts., 1966-70; various account and mgmt. positions Burson-Marsteller, Pitts., 1977-87, exec. v.p., gen. mgr., 1987-94, CEO Can. ops. Toronto, Montreal, Ottawa, Vancouver, 1994-95; sr. v.p., dir. corp. devel. Young and Rubicam, Inc., N.Y.C., 1995-99, COO, 1999-2000; asst. provost strategic and program devel. U. Pitts., 2000—. Instr. Slippery Rock Coll., Pitts., 1984-85; adviser Exec. Report Mag., Pitts., 1986-88, A Better Chance, N.Y.C., 1996-2000, N.Y. Philharm., 1997-99. Trustee U. Pitts., 1976-80, mem. alumni bd., 1990-94; trustee Robert Morris Coll., 1992-95; bd. dirs. Near Rehab. Ctr., 1987-93, Freewheelers, 1989-92, Pitts. Hist. Soc., River City Brass Band, Quantam Theatre, 2003-. Named Disting. Alumnus, U. Pitts., 1992, Legacy Laureate, 2000. Mem. Female Execs. Am., Am. Assn. Assn. Advt. Agys. (chair ea. region 1994-95), Pitts. Advt. Club (bd. dirs. 1988-91, pres. 1990), Alpha Sigma Lambda (chapter). Avocations: skiing, reading, gardening, travel, photography. Home: 1819 Sarah St Apt 2 Pittsburgh PA 15203 Office: U Pitts Cathedral of Learning Pittsburgh PA 15260- E-mail: sheilarathke@msn.com.

**RATHMAN, WILLIAM ERNEST,** retired lawyer, minister; b. Middletown, Ohio, Jan. 10, 1927; s. Ernest Daniel and Marguerite (Sebald) R.; m. Constance Schedler, Nov. 28, 1958; children: Marchie, William E. Jr. Grad. Phillips Exeter Acad., 1944; BA, Kenyon Coll., 1948; postgrad., Harvard U., 1950, Ohio State U. Coll. of Law, 1951, United Theol. Seminary, Dayton, Ohio, 1975. Bar: Ohio 1952, ordained to ministry Episc. Ch., 1975. Pvt. practice law, Middletown, Ohio, 1952-78; sr. ptnr. Rathman, Elliott & Boyd, Middletown, 1979-84, Rathman, Combs, Schaefer, Valen & Kaup, Middletown, 1985-88, Rathman, Combs, Schaefer & Kaup, Middletown, 1989-95, ret., 1995—. Spl. counsel to County of Butler, 1956-64, City of Middletown, 1965-66, Ohio Atty. Gen., 1967-69; acting judge Middletown Mcpl. Ct., 1969-74. Pres. Middletown Community Found., 1972-76, Middletown Chamber Found., 1977-80, Butler County Park Commn., 1986-90; trustee-at-large Ohio Found. of Ind. Colls., Columbus, 1972-90; trustee, mem. exec. com. Middletown United Way, 1963-90; trustee Middleton Req. Hosp. Found., 1986-90; bd. advt. bd. Middletown campus Miami U., 1984-90. With USN, 1944-46, capt. USAF, 1959, comdr. Am. Legion, 1965. Named Exec. Yr., Middletown chpt. Nat. Secs. Assn., 1969; recipient Outstanding Community Svc. award Middletown post Am. Legion, 1975, Outstanding Svc. award Parstoral Counselling Svc., 1983, Vol. of Yr. award Middletown Area United Way, 1986. Fellow Am. Coll. Trust and Estate Counsel; mem. ABA (estate tax com. 1966-69), Ohio Bar Assn. (coun. del. 1980-93), Butler County Bar Assn. (pres. 1980), Middletown Bar Assn. (pres. 1967), Fed. Bar Assn. (pres. Cin. chpt. 1975), Middletown Bar Found. (trustee 1992-96, Ohio Supreme Ct. bd. commrs. on grievances and discipline 1996-99), Masons (master 1959-60, 33d deg.), Scottish Rite Valley of Cin. (treas. 1986, chmn. bd. 1990), Sea Pines Country Club. Episcopalian. Home (Summer): 501 Thorn Hill Ln Middletown OH 45042-3750 Home: 1924 S Beach Club Hilton Head Island SC 29928-3750 Personal E-mail: crathman@aol.com.

**RATHMANN, GEORGE BLATZ,** genetic engineering company executive; b. Milw., Dec. 25, 1927; s. Louis and Edna Lorle (Blatz) R.; m. Frances Joy Anderson, June 24, 1950; children: James, Margaret, Laura, Sally, Richard. BS in Phys. Chemistry, Northwestern U., 1948; MS, Princeton U., 1950, PhD in Phys. Chemistry, 1952. With 3M Co., St. Paul, 1951-72, various positions including rsch. chemist, rsch. dir., group tech. dir., mng. X-ray products; with Litton Med. Systems, Des Plaines, Ill., 1972-75; v.p. R & D diagnostics div. Abbott Labs., North Chicago, Ill., 1975-80; pres., chief exec. officer Amgen Inc., Thousand Oaks, Calif., 1980-88, chmn. Newbury Park, Calif., 1980—90, chmn. emeritus; founder, chmn. ICOS Corp., 1990-2000; pres & CEO Hyseq, Inc., Sunnyvale, Calif., 2000—01, chmn., 2000—; chmn. bd. dir. ZymoGenetics Inc., Seattle, 2000—05. Bd. dirs. ZymoGenetics Inc., Seattle.

Mem. NAE, AAAS, Am. Chem. Soc., Indsl. Biotech. Assn. (bd. dirs.), Nat. Sci. and Tech. Medals Found. (bd. dir., pres.), Phi Beta Kappa, Sigma Xi. Office: Hyseq Inc 201 Industrial Rd # 310 San Carlos CA 94070-6211

**RATHMANN, PEGGY,** writer, illustrator; b. St. Paul; BA in Psychology, U. Minn.; student, Am. Acad. Chgo., Atelier Lack, Mpls., Otis Parsons Sch. Design, L.A. Author: Ruby the Copycat (Most Promising New Author Cuffie award Pubs. Weekly 1991), Good Night, Gorilla (ALA Notable Children's Book 1994), Officer Buckle and Gloria (Caldecott medal 1996), Ten Minutes Till Bedtime, 1998 (ALA Notable Children's Book 1998), The Day The Babies Crawled Away, 2003; illustrator: Bootsie Barker Bites, 1992. Office: Penguin Putnam Inc 345 Hudson St Fl 15 New York NY 10014-4502

**RATHNAU, HEATHER HEARN,** music educator, writer; b. San Antonio, Tex., Mar. 8, 1958; d. Claude Adam Hearn, Jr. and Mildred Ruby Damron; m. Ronald Alan Rathnau, Aug. 1, 1981; children: Mallory Dawn. MusB magna cum laude, Baylor U., 1980, MusM, 1982. Pvt. music and voice tchr., Houston, 1984—; prin., owner Theory Time, Mo. City, Tex., 1996—. Guest instr. Schmitt Music Expo, 1999, Mpls., 2005; lectr. in field. Author: Theory Time, 1996, 2002. Mem.: Music Tchrs. Nat. Assn., Tex. Music Tchrs. Assn., Forum Music Tchrs. Assn. (pres. 1992—94), Nat. Piano Tchrs. Guild (adjudicator 1990—2005), Houston (Tex.) Music Tchrs. Assn. (v.p. 1989—90), Music Tchrs. Nat. Conf., Houston (Tex.) Fedn. Music Clubs, Mu Phi Epsilon. Republican. Baptist. Avocations: travel, reading, gardening. Home: 6639 Sutters Creek Trail Missouri City TX 77459

**RATHOD, MULCHAND,** mechanical engineering educator; b. Pathri, India, Mar. 3, 1945; came to U.S., 1970, naturalized, 1981; s. Shamjibhai Laljibhai and Ramaben Rathod; m. Damayanti Thakor, Aug. 15, 1970; children: Prerana, Falgun, Sejal. BS in Mech. Engring., Sardar Patel U., India, 1970; MS, Miss. State U., 1972, PhD, 1975. Rsch. grad. asst. Miss. State U., 1970-75; cons. engr. Bowron & Butler, Jackson, Miss., 1975-76; asst. prof. Tuskegee Inst., Ala., 1976-78; assoc. prof., coord. MET program SUNY, Binghamton, 1979-87; prof. Wayne State U., Detroit, 1987—, dir. engring. tech. divsn., 1987—2003. Cons. Interpine, Hattiesburg, Miss., 1977-79, Jet Propulsion Lab., 1980-83, IBM Corp., 1982-85; pres. Shiv-Parvati, Inc. 1982—. Contbr. articles to profl. jours.; patentee in field. Den leader Boy Scouts Am., Vestal, N.Y., 1983-84. Recipient award NASA, 1981; grantee SUNY Found., 1984, Dept. Energy, 1978, GM, 1988-92, UAW Chrysler, 1990-91, Hudson-Webber Found., 1991-92, Ford, 1992-93, Kellogg Found., 1993-94, SME Found., 1994, Mich. Dept. Edn., 1994, NSF, 1995-2001. Fellow: ASME (cert. of appreciation 1982—89, 1991—2005, Dedicated Svc. award 1995, Ben C. Sparks medal 1998, BMW award 2001); mem.: ASHRAE, Profl. Order Engring. Tech., N.Y. State Engring. Tech. Assn., Am. Soc. Engring. Edn. (reviewer), India Assn. Miss. State U. (pres. 1972-73), Tau Beta Pi, Tau Alpha Phi (founder, faculty advisor 1989—), Pi Tau Sigma. Home: 1042 Woods Ln Grosse Pointe Woods MI 48236-1157 Office: Wayne State U Div Engring Tech Detroit MI 48202

**RATI, ROBERT DEAN,** retired data processing executive; b. Pittsburg, Kans., Jan. 8, 1939; s. Steve Julius Rati and Dorothy Bill (Rodebush) McWilliams; m. Margaret Fort Henry, June 7, 1969; children: Susan Margaret, Robert Henry. BA, U. Kans., 1961; MA, Northeastern U., Boston, 1970; MBA, Columbia U., 1973. Systems engr. IBM Corp., Boston, 1965-72; mgr. mgmt. services Arthur Young and Co., N.Y.C., 1973-75; mgr. client systems Touche Ross and Co., N.Y.C., 1975-76; mgr. systems and programs Walker Mfg. div. Tenneco, Racine, Wis., 1976-78; mgr. data processing Schwitzer div. Household Internat., Indpls., 1979-87; mgr. mgmt. info. systems Nat. Machinery Co., Tiffin, Ohio, 1988-90; pres. Dunhill Profl. Search of Carmel (Ind.), 1990-97; mgr. Muncie MIS Power Transformer div. Asea Brown Boveri, Muncie, Ind., 1991-94; dir. info. svcs. State Lottery Commn. Ind., Indpls., 1995-97; mgmt. cons. Aerotek-Maxim Group, Indpls., 1998-2000; project mgr. corp. info. tech. AT&T (formerly SBC Comms.), Indpls., 2000—05; ret., 2005. Contbr. articles to fraternal orgs. publs. Mem. Rep. Com., Ramsey, N.J., 1972-74; treas. Rep. Club Ramsey, 1972-79, vice chmn. Swimming Pool Commn., Ramsey, 1972-74; bd. dirs., exec. com. Near Eastside Multi-Svc. Ctr., Indpls., 1984-87; fin. com. Carmel (Ind.) United Meth. Ch., 1984-87, adminstrv. bd., 1987-90. Lt. (j.g.) USN, 1961-64. Recipient Regional Mgrs. award, IBM Corp., 1967. Mem. SAR (pres. 1979), Soc. Ind. Pioneers (pres. 1996-98), Huguenot Soc. Ind. (pres. 1985-89), S.R. in State of Ill. (pres. 1980-82), Ind. Soc. Colonial Wars (gov. 1995-98), Gen. Soc. Sons of the Revolution (chmn. awards com. 1983-91, Gen. Pres. Commendation award 1985, 91), Pi Mu Epsilon. Republican. Avocations: genealogy, home computer. Home: 4919 Regency Pl Carmel IN 46033-5959

**RATICK, RANDIE H.,** music educator, elementary school educator; b. Ellenville, N.Y., Apr. 14, 1956; d. Saul and Rose Finkelstein; m. Lawrence Richard Ratick, Oct. 1, 1983; 1 child, Benjamin. BFA, SUNY, Buffalo, 1978, MFA, 1979. Cert. tchr. Music tchr. Circleville (N.Y.) Mid. Sch., 1979-85, Hagan Elem. Sch., Poughkeepsie, NY, 1985—. Music coord. k-5 Spackenkill Union Free Sch. Dist. Grantee, Cmty. Found. Dutchess County, 1992—93, Mid-Hudson Tchrs. Ctr., 2001, 2002, Dutchess County Arts Coun., 2001, 2002, 2003, 2004. Mem.: Dutchess County Music Educators Assn. (exec. bd.), Music Educators Nat. Conf., N.Y. State Sch. Music Assn. Avocations: reading, crafts. Home: 454 N Elting Corners Rd Highland NY 12528 Office Phone: 845-463-7840.

**RATILAL, PURNIMA,** acoustician; b. Singapore, July 29, 1971; d. Ratilal Chandulal and Pushpaben Ratilal. BSc, Nat. U. Singapore, 1994, MS, MIT, Cambridge, Mass., 2002. Rsch. scientist DSO Nat. Labs., Singapore, 1994—98; rsch. asst. MIT, Cambridge, 1998—2002, postdoctoral assoc., 2002—04; asst. prof. Northeastern U., Boston, 2004—., DSO Nat. Labs. grad. scholar, 1998-2002, postdoc. awardee, Office of Naval Rsch., 2002—04. Mem.: Acoustical Soc. Am. (assoc.; underwater acoustics tech. com. 2004—, Bruce Lindsay award 2006). Achievements include patents pending for ocean acoustics waveguide remote sensing technology for imaging marine life; research in long range remote sensing of marine life. Office: Northeastern U 409 Dana Research Center Boston MA 02115 Office Phone: 617-373-8458. Office Fax: 617-373-8627. E-mail: purnima@alum.mit.edu.

**RATKOWSKI, DONALD J.,** mechanical engineer, consultant; b. Cleve., July 29, 1938; m. Joyce Ellen Kotlarczyk, July 15, 1961; children: Rhonda, Tamyra, Cheryl, Randall. Student, Ariz. State U.; AAS, Alliance Coll., 1959, DSc (hon.), 1986. Sr. project engr. semiconductor products div. Motorola, 1960-70, 75-77; v.p. engring. Danker & Wohlk, 1970-75; founder, pres. Paragon Optical Inc., 1976-90; assoc. v.p. Pilkinton Vision Care, 1987-90, cons., 1990-91; pres. DJR Resources Inc., Paradise Valley, Ariz., 1990—. Mem. adv. bd. Am. Sec. Com., 1988-89; mem. steering com. Optometry Coll., Marcinkowski Acad. Medicine, Poland, 1989-91; founder Rigid Gas Permeable Lens Inst., 1985; speaker Nat. Contact Lens Examiners, 1984-91. Contbr. articles to profl. jours.; patentee in field. Sustaining mem. Rep. Nat. Com., 1983-90; mem. U.S. Congl. Adv. Bd., 1990. Recipient Alumnus of Yr. award Alliance Coll., 1985. Mem. Opticians Assn. Am. (assoc. mem. adv. coun. 1987-88), Contact Lens Soc. Am. (bd. dirs. 1986-88, founder scholarship program 1988, hon. chmn. steering com. edn. fund 1989-91), Contact Lens Mfrs. Assn. (chmn. external communication com. 1981-90, bd. dirs. 1982-84, Trailblazer award 1987, program chmn. 1989-90, Leonardo DaVinci award 1990), Ariz. Soc. Plastic Engrs. bd. dirs. 1976-78, 83, v.p. 1980-81, pres. 1981-82), Sigma Tau Gamma (Outstanding Alumni award 1985). Home and Office: DJR Resources Inc 8105 N 47th St Paradise Valley AZ 85253

**RATLIFF, BEN,** music critic; Contbr. Coda mag., Option, Village Voice; popular music critic NY Times, NYC. Author: The New York Times Essential Library: Jazz: A Critic's Guide to the 100 Most Important Recordings, 2002. Office: NY Times Culture Desk 229 W 43rd St New York NY 10036 Office Phone: 212-556-4922. Office Fax: 212-556-1516.*

**RATLIFF, JOY,** music educator, singer; d. John Barton Ratliff Jr. and Vera Ratliff; children: Oskar Barton Hillebrandt, Vera Vanessa Hillebrandt. MusB, Southeastern La. U., 1968; MusM, Northwestern U., Evenston, Ill., 1969; Dr. Mus. Arts, U. of Md., 1997. Assoc. prof. of music/voice Marshall U., Huntington, W.Va., 1993—2002; asst. prof. of music/voice Southeastern La. U., Hammond, La., 2002—05, assoc. prof. of music/voice, 2005—. Singer mezzo-soprano/trouser roles Opera, Annina/LaTraviata. Mem.: Nat. Assn. of Tchrs. of Singing. Office: Southeastern Louisiana University Department of Music Box 10815 Hammond LA 70402 Office Phone: 985-549-2366. Office Fax: 985-549-2892. Personal E-mail: jratliff@selu.edu.

**RATLIFF, KIMBERLEE MICHELLE,** counselor; b. Harrison, Ark., June 27, 1975; d. Henry Wendell Roberts and Janice Marie Watkins; m. Maurice Cortez Ratliff, July 29, 1995; 1 child, Baylen Maurice. MEd in Sch. Counseling, Campbell U., Buies Creek, N.C., 2000. Cert. counselor Nat. Bd. for Cert. Counselors, 2003, trauma and loss in children school specialist TLC Inst., 2002. Sch. counselor Cumberland County Schs., Fayetteville, NC, 1998—2004, Prince William County Schs., Woodbridge, Va., 2004—. Counseling curriculum revision team Prince William County Schs., 2004, sch. counseling curriculum manual revision team, 05. Vol. coord. Nat. Race to Stop the Silence: Stop Child Sexual Abuse, Washington, 2004—06; mem. disaster response team ARC, Woodbridge, 2005; team capt. and vol. Leukemia & Lymphoma Soc., Alexandria, Va., 2004—06; coach Girls on the Run, Fairfax, Va., 2005—06. Recipient Team Recognition Award for Counseling Curriculum Devel., Prince William County Schs., 2005, Presdl. Vol. Svc. Silver award, Presdl. Vol. Svc., 2006. Mem.: Va. Sch. Counselor Assn. (assoc.), Va. Counseling Assn. (assoc.), ACA (assoc.), Chi Sigma Iota (assoc.; pres. 2005—06). Avocations: running marathons and half-marathons, travel. Personal E-mail: kimratbay@hotmail.com.

**RATLIFF, LOUIS JACKSON, JR.,** mathematics professor; b. Cedar Rapids, Iowa, Sept. 1, 1931; s. Louis Jackson and Ruth Sara (Sidlinger) R.; m. Georgia Lee Smith, May 9, 1996. BA, State U. Iowa, 1953, MA, 1958, PhD, 1961. Lectr. Ind. U., Bloomington, 1961-63, U. Calif., Riverside, 1963-64, asst. prof. math., 1964-67, assoc. prof., 1967-69, prof., 1969—. Author: Chain Conjectures in Ring Theory, 1978; assoc. editor Procs. of AMS, 1987-92, Comm. in Algebra, 1990-95; contbr. articles to profl. jours. 1st lt. USAF, 1953-57. NSF fellow, 1960-62, grantee, 1965-69, 71-88; recipient Disting. Teaching award, U. Calif.-Riverside, 1983. Mem. Am. Math. Soc., Phi Beta Kappa. Democrat. Seventh Day Adventist. Home: 22344 San Joaquin Dr W Sun City CA 92587-7849 Office: U Calif Dept Math Riverside CA 92521-0001 Office Phone: 951-827-5024. Business E-Mail: ratliff@math.ucr.edu.

**RATLIFF, ROBERT J.,** retired farm equipment manufacturing executive; With Internat. Harvester Co., Chgo., 26 years; pres. Uniroyal Tire Co. Worldwide, Troy, Mich.; pres. & CEO Deutz-Allis, Duluth, Ga., 1988-90; co-founder AGCO Corp., Duluth, Ga., 1990, pres., CEO, 1990—96, CEO, 1997—99, chmn., pres., CEO, 2002—04 chmn., 2004—06. Mem. exec. com. NAM.*

**RATLIFF, THOMAS ASBURY, JR.,** retired engineer; b. Phila., May 5, 1919; s. Thomas Asbury and Edna Dorothy (Overman) R.; m. Lucy Lila Graydon, Aug. 15, 1942; children: Deborah Ratliff Miller, Anne Ratliff Naberhaus. Test technician GE, Cin., 1951; quality engr. Am. Standard Corp., Cin., 1951-54, asst. dir. rsch., 1956-58; chief inspector Gruen Watch Co., Cin., 1954-58; cons. Hyde Engring. Co., Cin., 1958-60, Badgett & Smith, Inc., Cin., 1963-67; sales mgr. Lehmann Corp., Cin., 1960-63; purchasing mgr. Access Corp., Cin., 1967-70; pres. Ratliff & Assoc., Inc., Cin., 1970-96; ret., 1996. Adj. prof. engring. U. Cin., 1998-2000. Author: Basic Statistics for Lab Workers, 1992, The Laboratory Quality Assurance System, 1993, 3d edit., 2003. Col. U.S. Army, 1940-72. Fellow Am. Soc. for Quality (various coms.). Republican. Mem. Soc. of Friends. Avocation: collecting model cannons. Home: 755 Greenville Ave Cincinnati OH 45246-4608 Personal E-mail: tarqc@aol.com.

**RATLIFF, WILLIAM,** former state senator, former lieutenant governor, civil engineer; b. Aug. 16, 1936; BS in Civil engring., U. Tex., 1960. City mgr., Copperas Cove, Tex.; pvt. practice civil engr. Mt. Pleasant, Tex.; mem. Tex. Senate Dist. 1, 1989—2003, chair fin. com., mem. edn. com., mem. adminstrn. com.; mem. internat. rels., trade and tech. com.; lt. gov. of Tex., 2000—; Dist. 1 State Senator Tex., 2003—04. Pres. Mt. Pleasant Indsl. Found.; mem. exec. com. N.E. Tex. Econ. Devel. Dist., Inc.; Sunday sch. tchr.; lay reader; chair fin. com.; bd. trustees Tennison Meml. United Meth. Ch.; Sgt. USAR. Recipient Outstanding State Leader Award, 2001, John F Kennedy Profile in Courage award, John F. Kennedy Libr. Found., 2005. Mem. Am. Consulting Engr. Coun. (past pres.). Republican.

**RATNATHICAM, CHUTTA,** transportation executive; b. Colombo, Sri Lanka; married; 3 children. Grad., Royal Coll., Sri Lanka, 1967; MBA, U. Portland, 1973; grad. in bus. adminstrn., Columbia U. Corp. auditor CNF Transp. Inc., Palo Alto, Calif., 1977-78, various positions, 1978-91, v.p. Emery Subs., 1991-97; sr. v.p., CFO CNF Inc., Palo Alto, Calif., 1997—2000, 2001—; interim CEO Menlo Worldwide Forwarding, 2000—01. Mem. Am. Inst. Cert. Mgmt. Accts., Sri Lanka Inst. Chartered Accts., Fin. Execs. Inst. (San Francisco chpt.).

**RATNER, BRUCE C.,** professional sports team executive, real estate developer; b. Cleve., Jan. 23, 1945; children: Rebecca, Elizabeth. BA cum laude, Harvard U., 1967; JD, Columbia U., 1970. Dir. Model Cities Program, head Consumer Protection Divsn NYC, 1970—73, commr. consumer affairs, 1978—82; prof. law NYU, 1974—78; pres., CEO Forest City Ratner Cos., N.Y.C., 1982—; owner N.J. Nets, 2004—. Trustee Bklyn. (N.Y) Acad. Music, 1989, chmn., 1992—2001; bd. dirs. Mus. Jewish Heritage, Met. Mus. Art, City Pks. Found., Internat. Rescue Com., Bklyn. C. of C., N.Y.C. Partnership. Named The Top N.Y.C. Exec., Crain's N.Y. Bus., 1992; named one of N.Y.'s Most Influential Business Leaders, 2002; recipient N.Y. State Gov.'s Arts award, 1994. Office: Forest City Ratner Cos 1 Metrotech Ctr N Brooklyn NY 11201*

**RATNER, BUDDY DENNIS,** biomedical engineer, educator; b. Bklyn., Jan. 19, 1947; s. Philip and Ruth Ratner; m. Cheryl Cromer; 1 child, Daniel Martin. BS in Chemistry, Bklyn. Coll., 1967; PhD in Polymer Chemistry, Bklyn. Poly. U., 1972. From fellow to prof. U. Wash., Seattle, 1972—86, prof., 1986—, Darland prof. bioengring., 2005—. Dir. U. Wash. Engineered Biomaterials NSF Engring. Ctr.; founder Asemblon, Inc., Healionics, Inc. Editor: Surface Characterization of Biomaterials, 1989, Plasmas and Polymers, 1994-99, Biomaterials Science: An Introduction to Materials in Medicine, 2d edit., 2004, Characterization of Polymeric Biomaterials, 1997; mem. editl. bds. 9 jours. and book series; editor Jour. Undergrad. Rsch. in Bioengring., 1998—; contbr. over 300 articles to profl. jours. Recipient Faculty Achievement/Outstanding Rsch. award, Burlington Resources Found., 1990, Perkin Elmer Phys. Electronics award for excellence in surface sci. Fellow Internat. Acad. Med. and Biol. Engring., Am. Inst. Med. Biol. Engring. (founder, pres. 2002-03), Am. Vacuum Soc. (Medard Welsh medal 2002); mem. AAAS, AIChE (C.M.A. Stine award 1998), Nat. Acad. Engring., Am. Chem. Soc., Internat. Soc. Contact Lens Rsch., Materials Rsch. Soc., Soc. for Biomaterials (pres. 1991-92, Clemson award 1989, fellow 1994, Founders award 2004, C.W. Hall award 2006), Biomed. Engring. Soc. Achievements include patents in field. Office Phone: 206-685-1005. E-mail: ratner@uweb.engr.washington.edu.

**RATNER, CARL JOSEPH,** opera stage director, baritone; b. Memphis, Tenn., Sept. 17, 1957; MusB, Oberlin Conservatory of Music, 1980; MA, Northeastern Ill. U., 1999; DM, Northwestern U., 2005. Intern Juilliard Sch., N.Y.C., 1980-81, N.Y.C. Opera, 1981-82; asst. dir. Lyric Opera Chgo., 1982-84; prodn. asst. San Francisco Opera, 1985-86; asst. dir. Metropolitan Opera, N.Y.C., 1989-91; artistic dir. Chamber Opera Chgo., 1985-93, Chgo. Opera Theater, 1994-99; opera dir. Western Mich. U., 2001—. Home: 3440 N

---

Lake Shore Dr Apt 9D Chicago IL 60657-2848 Office: Western Michigan Univ Sch Music Dalton Ctr Kalamazoo MI 49008-5434 Office Phone: 269-387-4706, 773-454-4919. Personal E-mail: carlratner@aol.com.

**RATNER, DAVID LOUIS,** retired law educator; b. London, Sept. 2, 1931; AB magna cum laude, Harvard U., 1952, LLB magna cum laude, 1955. Bar: N.Y. 1955. Assoc. Sullivan & Cromwell, N.Y.C., 1955-64; assoc. prof. Cornell Law Sch., Ithaca, NY, 1964-68, prof., 1968-82; prof. law U. San Francisco Law Sch., 1982-99, dean, 1982-99, prof. emeritus, 1999—. Exec. asst. to chmn. SEC, Washington, 1966-68; chief counsel Securities Industry Study, Senate Banking Com., Washington, 1971-73; vis. prof. Stanford (Calif.) U., 1974, Ariz. State U., Tempe, 1974, U. San Francisco, 1980, Georgetown U., Washington, 1989-90, U. Calif., Hastings, San Francisco, 1992, U. Ariz., 2004; mem. Larkspur (Calif.) Planning Commn., 1992-2004. Author: Institutional Investors: Teaching Materials, 1978, Securities Regulation: Cases and Materials, 6th edit., 2002, Securities Regulation in a Nutshell, 8th edit., 2005. Fulbright scholar Monash U., Australia, 1981. Mem. Cosmos Club (Washington), Harvard Club of San Francisco (pres. 1999-2000), Phi Beta Kappa. Home and Office: 84 Polhemus Way Larkspur CA 94939-1928 E-mail: dlratner@aol.com.

**RATNER, ELLEN FAITH,** news analyst, news correspondent, writer; b. Cleve., Aug. 28, 1951; d. Harry Ratner and Anne Spott. BA, Goddard Coll., 1974; EdM, Harvard U., 1978. Coord. women's svcs. Homophile Comty. Health Svc., Boston, 1971-73; co-dir., co-founder Boundaries Therapy Ctr., Acton, Mass., 1973-86; dir. psychiat. day treatment program South Shore Mental Health Ctr., Quincy, Mass., 1974-81; v.p. rsch., devel. and svc., dir. ARC Rsch. Found. Addiction Recovery Corp., Rockville, Mass., 1986-90; health care cons., dir. Found. for Addiction Rsch., 1990-94; White House reporter, bur. chief Talk Radio News Svc., Washington, 1991—, chief polit. corr., news analyst; polit. analyst FOX News Channel, 1997—; Washington bur. chief, polit. editor Talkers Mag., 1996—; CEO Coll. Media News Co. Tchr. Curry Coll., Milton, Mass., 1979-80; cons. program devel. Addiction Recovery Corp., 1984-86; developer, planner The Art's in Mileau Treatment of Phychiatric Outpatients, Quincy, 1980, New Eng.'s first conf. on Chem. Dependency and AIDS, 1988. Author: The Other Side of the Family: A Book for Recovery from Abuse, Incest and Neglect, 1990, 101 Ways to Get Your Progressive Issues on Talk Radio, 1997; mem. adv. bd. The Counselor Mag., 1987-90; appeared on nat. TV and radio shows including C-SPAN, The Oprah Winfrey Show, CNN, Nat. Empowerment TV, others; co-host (radio) Washington Reality Check, Good Day USA, New World Chronicle; polit. corr, Talk Radio Countdown Show; prodr. Talk Daily. Bd. trustees, mem. exec. com., vis. com. presdl. search com. Goddard Col., Plainfield, Vt. 1977-81; bd. trustees Samaritan Coll., L.A., 1988-90; bd. dirs. Nat. Lesbian and Gay Health Found., Washington, 1985-92, pres., exec. com., program com., program chair; v.p. Harry Ratner Human Svcs. Fund, Cleve., 1991—; mem. adv. bd. Women of Washington, Inc., 1992—; bd. dirs. Theater Chamber Players, Kennedy Ctr., Washington, 1988-91, An Uncommon Legacy Found., N.Y.C., 1993—, The Ctr. for Spiritual Enlightment, Falls Church, Va., 1994—. Recipient Comty. Svc. award Lesbian and Gay Counseling Svc., Boston, 1985, The Addams-Brown award Nat. Lesbian and Gay Health Found., 1993. Mem. Nat. Assn. Radio Talk Show Hosts, Mass. Assn. Day treatment Adminstrs. (chair regulations and standards com. 1979-81), Lily Dale Assembly. Democrat. Jewish. Avocation: writing works on spiritualism. Office: Talk Radio News Svc 2514 Mill Rd NW Washington DC 20007-2950 Address: FOX News Channel 1211 Avenue of the Americas New York NY 10036

**RATNER, GAYLE,** special education educator; b. Bronx, NY; BS, SUNY, Plattsburgh, 1991, MS in Edn., 1993. Cert. spl. edn. grades K-12 and elem. edn. grades N-6. Spl. edn. tchr. Chazy (N.Y.) Ctrl. Rural Sch., 1991—. Asst. chief reader N.Y. State Tchr. Cert. Examinations, mem. students with disabilities content adv. com.; instr. N.Y. State United Tchrs. Effective Tchg. Program, 1999—, mentor coord.; mem. policy bd. North Country Tchr. Resource Ctr.; new tchr. mentor coord. Chazy Ctrl. Rural Sch. Mem.: N.Y. State United Tchrs., Chazy Tchrs. Assn. (pres. 1995—2005, newsletter editor 2003—), Nat. Bd. Profl. Tchg. Stds. (spl. edn. and elem. edn. com. 2005—, bd. dirs.). Office: Chazy Ctrl Rural Sch 609 Route 191 Chazy NY 12921

**RATNER, GERALD,** lawyer; b. Chgo., Dec. 17, 1913; s. Peter I. and Sarah (Soreson) R.; m. Eunice Payton, June 18, 1948. PhB, U. Chgo., 1935, JD cum laude, 1937. Bar: Ill. 1937. Since practiced in, Chgo.; sr. ptnr. Gould & Ratner and predecessor firm, 1949—. Officer Henry Crown & Co., CC Industries, Inc., Material Svc. Corp., Freeman United Coal Mining Co., Mineral and Land Resources Corp.; lectr., writer on real estate law. Capt. U.S. Army, 1942—46. Gerald Ratner Athletics Ctr. named in his honor, U. Chgo.; recipient Disting. Svc. medal U. Chgo., 2005 Mem. ABA, Ill. Bar Assn., Chgo. Bar Assn., Order of Coif, Phi Beta Kappa. Home: 180 E Pearson St Apt 6205 Chicago IL 60611-2191 Office: 222 N La Salle St Ste 800 Chicago IL 60601-1086 Office Phone: 312-236-3003. Business E-Mail: gratner@gouldratner.com.

**RATNER, HANK J.,** broadcast executive; BA, Emory U., JD with distinction. Assoc. Sullivan & Cromwell; asst. gen. counsel Cablevision Sys. Corp., Bethpage, NY, 1987—88; vice chmn. Rainbow Media, Cablevision Sys. Corp. Office: Cablevision Systems Corp 1111 Stewart Ave Bethpage NY 11714-3581

**RATNER, JAMES,** real estate developer; m. Susan Ratner; 2 children. BA, Columbia U.; MBA, Harvard U. Former loan officer Citibank, N.Y.C.; with Nasher Co., Dallas, 1971—76; chmn., CEO Forest City Commercial Group, Cleve., 1976—; pres. devel. divsn. Forest City Enterprises, Cleve., 1978—. Bd. mem. Cleve. Museum of Art, Urban Land Inst., Playhouse Square Found. Office: Forest City Mgmt Terminal Tower 50 Public Sq Ste 1100 Cleveland OH 44113-2267*

**RATNER, MARCIA,** research scientist; b. Hartford, Conn., June 24, 1960; d. William and Gertrude Chorches Ratner. BA in Psychology, Boston U., 1995, PhD, 2004. Project mgr. dept. neurology Boston U., 1998—2004; rsch. assoc. in neurology Boston U. Sch. Medicine, 1998—, instr. toxicology and forensic toxicology, 2000—, rsch. assoc. pharm., 2004—. CEO, v.p. Chem. Safety Net, Inc., 2002—04; counselor Specialized Housing, Brookline, Mass., 1995—2004. Mem.: N.Y. Acad. Sci., Am. Conf. Govt. Indsl. Hygiene, Soc. Occupl. Environ. Health, Soc. Occupl. Health, Soc. for Neurosci., Mass. Neuropsychol. Soc., Am. Acad. Clin. Toxicology, Internat. Neurotoxicol. Assns., Combined Jewish Philanthropies, Psi Chi, Alpha Phi Omega. Jewish. Avocations: horseback riding, guitar, running, skiing. Office: Boston U Sch Medicine L-603 715 Albany St Boston MA 02118-2526 E-mail: marcia@bu.edu.

**RATNER, MICHAEL D.,** lawyer; b. June 13, 1943; s. Harry and Anne (Spott) Ratner. BA, Brandeis U., 1966; JD magna cum laude, Columbia U., 1971. Bar: N.Y. 1971, U.S. Supreme Ct. 1983. Law clk. U.S. Dist. Ct. (so. dist.), N.Y.C., 1971-72; prof. NYU Law Sch., N.Y.C., 1973-74; atty. Ctr. for Constl. Rights, N.Y.C., 1978-85, legal dir., 1985-90. Adj. prof. Yale Law Sch., New Haven, 1990—95, lectr., 2000; spl. counsel for human rights Govt. of Haiti, 1996; lectr. Columbia Law Sch., N.Y.C., 1999—. Author: International Human Rights Litigation in U.S. Courts, 1997, Che Guevara and the FBI, 1997, The Pinochet Papers: The Case of Augusto Pinochet Ugarte in Spain and Britain, 2000; co-author (with Barbara Olshansky & Jennie Green): Against War with Iraq, 2003; co-author: (with Ellen Ray) Guantanamo: What the World Should Know, 2004; contbr. articles to profl. jours.; co-author: Disappeared in America, 2005. Recipient Medal of excellence Columbia Law Sch., 2004, John Minor Wisdom pro bono award ABA, 2006, Brandeis Alumni award, 2006; named Trial Lawyer of Yr., Trial Lawyers for the Pub. Interest; Skelly Wright fellow Yale Law Sch., 2000. Hon. fellow U. Pa. Law Sch., 2005. Mem. Nat. Lawyers Guild (pres. 1982-83). Office Phone: 212-614-6429. E-mail: mratner@igc.org.

---

**RATO Y FIGAREDO, RODRIGO,** international banking official; b. Madrid, Mar. 18, 1949; married; 3 children. Law degree, Madrid Complutense U., 1971; MBA, U. Calif., Berkeley, 1974; PhD in Economics, Universidad Complutense, 2003. Mem. Nat. Exec. Com. of AP, 1979-86; co-founder Econ. Commn. of AP, 1979; spokesman for the econ., 1984-86; asst. gen. sec. AP, 1983-86; mem. Parliament for Cádiz in the 2d Legislature; v.p. of def. and security commn. NATO, 1987, 88, mem. spl. com. for strategy and control of armaments, 1988; asst. gen. sec. IXth Party Congress; nat. mem. Parliament for Madrid, 1982—2004; spokesman for Grupo Parlamentario Popular Parliament in the IVth and Vth Legislatures; mem. Parliament in the VIth Legislatures; vice gen. sec. of Partido Popular XIIth Nat. Congress, 1996—; 2d v.p. of govt. Ministry Econs. and Fin, Madrid, 1996—2000; 2nd v.p. of govt. and min. of the economy, 2000—04; mng. dir., chmn. Internat. Monetary Fund, 2004—. Bd. gov. Internat. Monetary Fund, World Bank, Inter-Am. Development Bank, European Investment Bank, European Bank for Reconstruction and Develop.; regularly attends the European Union's Economics and Fin. Ministers mtgs.; represented the European Union at the Group of Seven Fin. Min. meeting, Ottawa, Canada, 2002; in charge of fgn. trade relations for the Govt. of Spain; represented Spain at the World Trade Orgn. Min. meetings, Doha, Qatar, 01, Cancún, Mexico, 03. Office: IMF 700 19th St NW Washington DC 20431*

**RATTI, CARLO FILIPPO,** architect, researcher; b. Turin, Italy, Jan. 7, 1971; s. Giuseppe Enrico Ratti and Anna Chiara Frisa. MSc Civil Engring., Poly. Inst. Turin, 1995; MSc, Ecole Nationale des Ponts et Chaussées, Paris, 1995; PhD, U. Cambridge, Eng., 2002, MPhil, 1996. Registered arch., U.K.; engr., Italy, France. Dir. archtl. firm Carlo Ratti Associati, Turin, 2002—; dir. MIT SENSEable City Lab., Cambridge, Mass., 2002—. Co-designer SandScape (Ars Electronica Exhbn., Lintz, Austria, 2002); contbr. articles to profl. publs., newspapers. Founder Coll. Milan, 2000—; pres. Comitato Valdo Fusi, Turin, 2005; mem. Associazione Effetto-T, Turin. Aspen for the New Leadership fellow, Aspen Inst. Italy, 2000—, Fulbright scholar, Fulbright Commn., 2001—02. Achievements include patents in field. Office: Mit 77 Massachusetts Ave Cambridge MA 02139 Home Fax: 0039-011-8393218; Office Fax: 617-258-8081.

**RATTIE, KEITH O.,** gas industry executive; Sr. v.p. The Coastal Corp., 1996—2001; pres. Questar Corp., 2001—, CEO, 2002—, chmn., 2003—. Dir. Zions First Nat. Bank, Interstate Natural Gas Assoc. of Am., Gas Technology Institute, United Way of Salt Lake, U. Wyo. Energy Resources Coun. Mem.: Salt Lake C. of C. (chmn.). Office: c/o Questar 180 E 100 S Salt Lake City UT 84145

**RATTINER, DANIEL STEVEN,** communications executive; b. N.Y.C., Aug. 15, 1939; s. A. Alan and Jeanette Brody Rattiner; children: Maya, Adam, David, Gabriel. BA, U. Rochester, N.Y., 1961; postgrad., Harvard U., Cambridge, Mass., 1961—64. Editor, pub. Davis Papers, Bridgehampton, NY, 1960—. Columnist Our Town, N.Y.C., NY, 1992—94; commentator WQXR, N.Y.C., NY, 1994—2000. Author: Albert Einstein's Summer Vacation, 1980, Loose Change in the New World, 1981, The Eat All You Want and Still Lose Weight Cookbook, 1985, Who's Here (The Heart of The Hamptons), 1995, Dan's Shorts, 2000, Valet Parking, 2002. Bd. dirs. Bridgehampton Child Care Ctr., NY, 2004—06, Music Festival of the Hamptons, NY, 1991—2006, Cancer Care of the Hamptons, NY, 2004—06. Recipient Pride of N.Y. award, 2000, L.I. Coalition for Fair Broadcasting, 2002. Mem.: Harvard Club of N.Y. Home: 28 Three Mile Harbor Hog Creek Rd East Hampton NY 11937 Office: Dan's Papers 2221 Montauk Hwy Bridgehampton NY 11932 Office Phone: 631-537-0500. Office Fax: 631-537-1686.

**RATTMAN, WILLIAM JOHN,** electronics and electro-optic engineer; b. Springfield, Mass., Nov. 16, 1933; s. Frank William and Sylvia Mary (Berry) R.; m. Jayne Winona Crockett, Aug. 19, 1954; children: Joy Diane, Beth Jayne, Amy Catherine. BSEE, U. Mass, 1955; MSEE, Northeastern U., 1961. Sr. engr. Raytheon Co., Bedford, Mass., 1955-63; prin. engr., 1967-72; engring. specialist Sylvania Applied Rsch. Lab., Waltham, Mass., 1963-67; mgr. R&D Electro Signal Lab., Inc., Rockland, Mass., 1972-86. Cons. electronics, electro-optics to mfg. firms. Patentee optical depth finder, contrast detector, low drive power wideband optical modulator, laser ablative printing system, photoelectric smoke detector, self diagnostic smoke detector. Co-chmn. Town of Needham United Way Campaign, 1973. Mem. Soc. Photo-Optical Instrumentation Egnrs., S. Yarmouth Hist. soc. (pres. 1974-75). Home and Office: 303 Bellingrath Terr Deland FL 32724 Office Phone: 386-736-3232. E-mail: wrattman@cfl.rr.com.

**RATTNER, STEVEN LAWRENCE,** investment banker; b. N.Y.C., July 5, 1952; s. George Seymour and Selma Ann (Silberman) R.; m. P. Maureen White, June 22, 1986; children: Rebecca White, Daniel Irvin, David William, James Brennan. AB in Econs. with honors, Brown U., 1974. Asst. to James Reston, corr. N.Y. Times, Washington, N.Y.C., London, 1974-82; assoc., v.p. Lehman Bros. Kuhn Loeb, NYC, 1982-84; assoc., v.p., prin., mng. dir., head communications group Morgan Stanley & Co., NYC, 1984-89; mng. dir., head comms. group Lazard Fréres & Co., LLC, NYC, 1989-97; dep. chief exec., dep. chmn., 1998—2000; mng. prin. Quadrangle Group LLC, NYC, 2000—. Dir. Falcon Cable Holding Group, 1993—. Contbr. articles to various publs. including N.Y. Times, Wall St. Jour., L.A. Times, Fin. Times. Trustee Brookings Instn., 1998—, Met. Mus. Art, 1996—; trustee Ednl. Broadcasting Corp., 1990—, vice chmn., 1994-98, chmn., 1998-2006; fellow & chmn. budget & fin. com. Brown Univ.; dir. N.Y.C. Outward Bound Ctr., 1990—; past trustee Mus. TV & Radio. Harvey Baker fellow Brown U. 1974, Poynter fellow Yale, 1979. Mem. Coun. Fgn. Rels., Royal Inst. for Internat. Affairs (assoc.). Office: Quadrangle Group LLC 375 Park Ave New York NY 10152*

**RATUM, CECILIA BANGLOY,** retired psychologist; b. Jones, Isabela, Philippines, Feb. 1, 1935; arrived in U.S., 1968, naturalized, 1963. d. Federico Reyes and Vivina Pastor Bangloy; m. Pablo Agpaoa Ratum, Apr. 21, 1958; children: Nympha, Locelia. Psychology program, U. San Francisco 1980—81; MA in Elem. Counseling, San Francisco State U., 1975; grad. program, Philippine Normal U., 1963, BS in Elem. Edn., 1955. Cert. tchr. Ilocos Norte Normal Sch., Philippines, 1953, nat. cert. sch. psychologist 1989. Instr. Philippine Wesleyan Coll., Cabanatuan, Philippines, 1955—56; critic tchr. Philippine Women's U., Manila, 1956—57; head tchr., classroom tchr. Philippine Pub. Schs., Jones, 1957—60, dist. guidance coord., 1960—68; filing clk. Pacific Telephone, San Francisco, 1968—69; substitute tchr. San Francisco Unified Sch. Dist., 1969—70, counselor, 1970—78, tchr., 1978—79, counselor, 1979—81, psychologist, 1981—98; ret., 1998—2002; psychologist San Francisco Unified Sch. Dist., 2002—04; ret., 2004. Team leader for sch. pschologist San Francisco Unified Sch. Dist., 1984—86, supr. sch. psychology intern, 1993—96, cadre leader for sch. psychologists, 1997—98. Mem. JCC, San Francisco. Mem.: Calif. Ret. Tchrs. Assn. (San Francisco Divsn.), Sixty Plus San Francisco U. Beta Chpt., Internat. Dyslexia Assn., Calif. Assn. Sch. Psychologists, Nat. Assn. Sch. Psychologists, San Francisco State U. Alumni Assn. (life), San Francisco State U. Osher Learning Inst. (life). Avocations: reading, writing, music, writing. Home: 168 Lowell St San Francisco CA 94112-4307 Personal E-mail: ratum5f@sbcglobal.net.

**RATZENBERGER, JOHN DESZO,** actor, writer, film director; b. Bridgeport, Conn., Apr. 6, 1947; s. Dezso Alexander and Bertha (Grohowski) R.; m. Elizabeth Georgia Stiny, Sep. 9, 1984 (div. May 27, 2004); children: James John, Nina Katherine. Grad. high sch., Bridgeport, Conn.; Doctorate, Sacred Heart U., 1992. Actor, writer, dir. own theater troupe Sal's Meat Market, 1971-75; touring actor Europe, 1971-81. Pres., founder Eco-Pack Industries, Kent, Wash. Appeared in plays Curse of the Starving Class, The Connection; films include The Ritz, 1974, Toy Story (voice), 1995, That Darn Cat, 1997, Yanks, Ragtime, Motel Hell, Superman I, II, A Bridge Too Far, Firefox, The Empire Strikes Back, Protocol, Gandhi, Outland, One Night Stand, Bad Day on the Block, That Darn Cat, (voice) A Bug's Life, Toy Story 2 (voice), 1999, Tic Tock, 2000, Monsters, Inc., 2001, Finding Nemo (voice), 2003, The Incredibles (voice), 2004, All In, 2005, Something New, 2006, (voice) Cars, 2006, (TV films) How I Spent My Summer, 1990, Camp Cucamonga, 1990,

Dog's Best Friend, 1997, The Pennsylvania Miners' Story, 2002; TV performances include Songs of a Sourdough, The Good Soldier, (series) Cheers, 1982-1993; co-author TV plays: Friends in Space, 1978, Scalped, 1979. Recipient cash award Arts Council of Great Britain Mem. AFTRA, SAG, Writers Guild Am. Dirs. Guild, Am. Farmland Trust, Brit. Actors Equity Assn., Greenpeace, Wilderness Soc., Nat. Resources Def. Coun., Sierra Club (San Francisco). Avocations: sailing, reading, woodworking.*

RATZLAFF, RUBEN MENNO, theology studies educator, minister; b. Burrton, Kans., Jan. 8, 1917; s. Henry and Julia (Foth) R.; m. Frances Irene King, Sept. 7, 1941; children: Keith Lowell, Paul Dennis, Mark Henry, Loren Lee; m. Doris Carr Arneson, Aug. 1, 1992; m. Marian McCuistion, June 10, 2006. BA, Johnson Bible Coll., 1940; BD, Butler U., 1955, MA, 1959. Ordained to ministry Chs. of Christ, 1938. Min. Pleasant Hill Christian Ch., Hall, Ind., 1948-50, Christian Ch., Clermont, Ind., 1950-55, Kennard, Ind., 1955-59; prof. San Jose (Calif.) Christian Coll., 1959-98, prof. emeritus, 1998—. Ann. vis. lectr. Springdale Coll., Selly Oak Colls., Birmingham, Eng., 1985-97; vis. lectr. Zimbabwe Christian Coll., Harare, 1995, Philippine Coll. Ministry, Baguio City, 1998. Author: Ezra Nehemiah, 1982; contbr. articles to profl. jours. Recipient Hebrew award Hebrew Synagogue, 1950. Mem. Theta Phi. Home: 5425 Denver St SE Apt 4 Turner OR 97392 Personal E-mail: rubenotprof@juno.com. *What amazes me most is that God the Almighty sends His Son to knock at our door, and wait with His hat in His hand while we decide whether to follow Him.*

RAU, DAVID EDWARD, real estate consultant; b. Lincoln, Nebr., Sept. 27, 1956; s. Leo George and Anne Marie (Pavel) R.; divorced; children: Andrew David, Peter Nicholas, Victoria Anne. BBA, U. Ariz., 1978. CPA, Ariz., N.Mex.; cert. real estate sales, Ariz. Sr. KPMG, Albuquerque, 1978-82, supervising sr. Phoenix, 1982-83; asst. treas. Kroy Inc., Scottsdale, Ariz., 1983-85; acct. Zolondek & Blumenthal, Phoenix, 1985; v.p., controller Del Webb Corp., Phoenix, 1985—2002. Bd. dirs. Ariz. Tax Rsch. Assn. Chmn. Phoenix chpt. walk Juvenile Diabetes Found., 1990, pres. 1992, 93, 94; mem. Ariz. Town Hall; advisor Phoenix Sky Harbour Ctr. Tech. Adv. Panel, 1987; treas. Drugs Don's Work in Ariz., 1994—. Mem. Ariz. Soc. CPAs, Albuquerque Jaycees (treas. 1981-82), Nat. Assn. Real Estate Cos. (tax com.), Ariz. C. of C. (bd. dirs.), Beta Alpha Psi. Republican. Roman Catholic. Avocations: skiing, fishing. E-mail: drau52611@aol.com.

RAU, LEE ARTHUR, lawyer; b. Mpls., July 22, 1940; s. Arthur W. and Selma A. (Lund) R.; m. Janice R. Childress, June 27, 1964; children: Brendan D., Patrick C., Brian T. BSB, U. Minn., 1962; JD, UCLA, 1965. Bar: Calif. 1966, DC 1972, Va. 1986, US Dist. Ct 1973, US Dist. Ct. (ea. dist.) Va. 1988, US Ct. Mil. Appeals 1966, US Ct. Appeals (DC cir.) 1972, US Ct. Appeals (3d cir.) 1975, US Ct. Appeals (6th cir.) 1980, US Ct. Appeals (4th cir.) 1988, US Supreme Ct. 1971. Trial atty. evaluation sect. antitrust div. US Dept. Justice, Washington, 1965-66, appellate sect., 1970-72; assoc. Reed Smith Shaw & McClay, Washington, 1972-74, ptnr., 1975—2002; commr. Fairfax County Redevel. and Housing Authority, 2002—. Former mem. constl. and adminstrv. law adv. com. Nat. Chamber Litigation Ctr. Inc.; sec., bd. dirs. Old Dominion Land Co., Inc. Contbr. articles to profl. jours. Sec. bd. dris. Reston Found., 1982-93; bd. dirs. Reston Interfaith Inc., 1973-89, pres, 1984-88; bd. dirs. Greater Reston Arts Ctr., 1988-96, pres., 1989-91, sec., 1991-95; mem. Washington Dulles Task Force, 1982-91; mem. exec. com. and ops. com. Fairfax-Falls Ch. United Way, mem. regional coun., 1988-92. Capt. JAGC, U.S. Army, 1966-70. Named Restonian of Yr., 1990; decorated Commendation with oak leaf cluster; recipient Best of Reston award. Mem.: D.C. Bar Assn. (past chmn. energy study group). Democrat. Lutheran. Home: 11654 Mediterranean Ct Reston VA 20190-3401 Personal E-mail: leerau@comcast.net.

RAU, MAGDA, ophthalmologist; b. Zlin, Czechoslovakia, Aug. 31, 1952; arrived in Germany, 1982; d. Jaromir Broul and Vera Broulova; m. Hans-Konrad Pfeiffer, Dec. 26, 2001; m. Čestmir Mičán, Dec. 20, 1975 (div. 1992); 1 child, Čestmir Mičán; m. Björn Rau, Dec. 23, 1996 (div. 1998). Degree, Coll., Frydlant, Czechoslovakia, 1970; med. diploma, Palacky U., Olomouc, 1976; ophthalmologist diploma, Prag, Czechoslovakia, 1980, Munich, 1984. Intern Residency Hosp., Frydek-Mistek, Czech Republic, 1976—82; ophthalmologist Prof. Dr. Dausch Eye Dept., Amberg, Germany, 1983—85; practice owner Furth Im Wald, 1985—; day clinic owner Tagesklinik, Cham, 1995—; chief ophthalmologist Hosp., 1995—; pvt. clinic owner Privatklinik Rau, 2000—. Contbr. articles to profl. jours. including multifokal IO Lenses, LASEK, LASEK-Viscodissection; author: (interactive CD-ROM) ICRS (Intrastromal Corneal Ring Segments), 1999, 2001. Mem. Albert Schweizer Stiftung Lambarene, 1996. Mem.: European Soc. Cataract and Refractive Surgery, Internat. Soc. Refractive Surgery, Internat. Soc. Cataract and Refractive Surgery. Roman Catholic. Avocations: tennis, horseback riding, skiing, skating. Home: Aepflet 24 93437 Furth Germany Office: Ophtalmologist Practice Von Mueller Str 12 93437 Furth Germany

RAU, RALPH RONALD, retired physicist; b. Tacoma, Sept. 1, 1920; s. Ralph Campbell and Ida (Montgall) R.; m. Maryjane Uhrlaub, June 2, 1944; children: Whitney Leslie, Little Elise. BS in Physics, Coll. Puget Sound, 1941; MS in Physics, Calif. Inst. Tech., 1943, PhD in Physics, 1948; LHD (hon.), U. Puget Sound, 2002. Asst. prof. physics Princeton U., 1947-56; Fulbright research prof. physics Ecole Polytechnique, Paris, 1954-55; physicist Brookhaven Nat. Lab., Upton, NY, 1956-66, chmn. dept. physics, 1966-70, assoc. dir. for high energy physics, 1970-81. Adj. prof. U. Wyo.; vis. prof. MIT, 1984-88; staff scientist Desy Lab., Hamburg, Fed. Republic Germany, 1984-85. Trustee U. Puget Sound, 1978-84 Named Alumnus Cum Laude U. Puget Sound, 1960. Recipient Alexander von Humboldt U.S. br. Scientist award 1988. Mem. Am. Phys. Soc. Office: Brookhaven Nat Lab Upton NY 11973

RAUB, DONALD WILMER, minister, author; b. Quakertown, Pa., Dec. 24, 1931; s. Harvey Wilmer and Estella Martha (Bleam) R.; m. Dolores Jean Kern, Oct. 20, 1951; children: Diane, Donald, Deborah, Devlyn. DRE, Evang. Bible Sem., Lake Worth, Fla., 1987, ThD, 1999. Ordained minister Evang. Ch. Alliance, 1951. Evangelist Evang. Ch. Alliance, Bradley, Ill., 1951-58; pastor Troy (Ohio) Gospel Tabernacle, 1959-60; writer and photographer Quakertown (Pa.) Free Press, 1963-73; pastor East Rockhill Chapel, 1965—; with Merck & Co., West Point, Pa., 1968-94; ret., 1994. Advisor Lebanon (Pa.) Gospel Assn., 1992-94; lectr. in field. Author: I, Being of Sound Mind, 1988, 2d edit., 1989, Unusual Experiences and Special Moments, 1990, The Value of Christian Holiness, 1992; inventor fin. game: Independence, 1976; patentee in field; contbr. articles to profl. jours. Bd. dirs. Transylvania Bible Sch. (now Biblical Life Inst.), Freeport, Pa., 1957—, North Penn Symphony Orch. Soc., Lansdale, Pa., 1980-90; v.p. Transylvania, Inc., 1994-97, chmn. bd. dirs., 1997-2003. Mem. Songwriters of N.Am. (founder). Republican. Avocation: horticulture. Address: PO Box 224 Tylersport PA 18971-0224

RAUCH, ARTHUR IRVING, management consultant; b. NYC, Sept. 18, 1933; s. David and Miriam (Frankel) R.; m. Roxane M. Spiller, Aug. 19, 1962 (div. 1977); children: David S., Janine B.; m. Lynn R. Saidenberg, Oct. 11, 1987. BA magna cum laude, Dartmouth Coll., 1954, MS, 1955. Chartered fin. analyst. Security analyst Lionel D. Edie & Co., N.Y.C., 1959-64; group dir. rsch. Eastman Dillon, Union Securities & Co., N.Y.C., 1964-68; v.p., sr. analyst Laird, Inc., N.Y.C., 1968-69, dir. rsch., 1969-71, sr. v.p., 1970-73; ptnr. Oppenheimer & Co., N.Y.C., 1973-77; v.p. corp. devel. Rorer Group, Inc., Ft. Washington, Pa., 1977-84; v.p. corp. fin. Arnhold & S. Bleichroeder, Inc., N.Y.C., 1984-88; cons. corp. devel. ICN Pharms., Inc., N.Y.C., 1988-89. Mem. investment com. Dartmouth Rsch. 1969-73. Exec. com. Dartmouth Class of 1954, 1968-79, 94-2004. Lt. (j.g.) USNR, 1956-59. Rufus Choate scholar Dartmouth Coll., 1951. Mem. NY Soc. Security Analysts, Assn. Corp. Growth, Fin. Analysts Fedn. (corp. fin. com.), Phi Beta Kappa. Home and Office: 115 Central Park W Apt 9D New York NY 10023-4153 Personal E-mail: arauch@rcn.com.

RAUCH, ERIC, biology educator; s. Duane T. Rauch and Ellen M. Schoettelkotte; m. Heidi Leanne Hancher; 1 child, Madysen. BS, Marian Coll., Indpls., 1995. Tchr., basketball coach Tri-West HS, Lizton, Ind., 1992—. Named Indpls. Star Coach of Yr., 2006. Office: 7883 N State Rd 39 Lizton IN 46149

RAUCH, GEORGE WASHINGTON, lawyer, director; b. Marion, Ind., July 18, 1919; s. George W. and Emma Asenath (Nolen) R.; m. Audrey M. Cranfield, Feb. 28, 1943 (div.); children: George Washington III, Nancy Lynn, Jane Nolen; m. Dorothy D. Farlow, June 26, 1970. BS, Ind. U., 1941; LL.B., U. Va., 1947. Bar: Ind. 1948, Ill. 1957, Mass. and Fla. 1972. Practice law Batton, Harker and Rauch (and predecessor firms), Marion, Ind., 1948-57; v.p., gen. counsel The Greyhound Corp., Chgo., 1957-61; mem. firm Hubachek & Kelly Ltd. and predecessor firms, Chgo., 1961-82; pres. Hubachek & Kelly Ltd., 1972-80; of counsel firm Chapman and Cutler, Chgo., 1982-95; gen. counsel Household Internat., 1967-78, dir., 1967-92, mem. fin. com., 1969-92, exec. com., 1972-92; dir. Edwards Engring. Corp., Constrn. Materials Co., Indsl. Air & Hydraulics Co., 1976-90, Burch Co., 1972-97, pres., 1975-97; dir. 1242 Lake Shore Dr. Corp., 1971-83, pres., 1973-74. Mem. Nat. Conf. Commrs. on Uniform Laws, 1955-57. Served as aviator USNR, 1941-45; lt. comdr. Mem. Raven Soc., Sankaty Head Golf Club (Nantucket, Mass.), Casino Club (Nantucket), Beach Club (Palm Beach, Fla.), Masons, Shriners, Phi Delta Phi, Delta Tau Delta. Home: 83 Baxter Rd PO Box 149 Siasconset MA 02564

RAUCH, IRMENGARD, linguist, educator; b. Dayton, Ohio, Apr. 17, 1933; d. Konrad and Elsa (Knott) R.; m. Gerald F. Carr, June 12, 1965; children: Christopher, Gregory. Student, Nat. U. Mex., summer 1954, BS with honors, U. Dayton, 1955; MA, Ohio State U., 1957; postgrad. (Fulbright fellow), U. Munich, Fed. Republic Germany, 1957-58; PhD, U. Mich., 1962. Instr. German and linguistics U. Wis., Madison, 1962-63, asst. prof., 1963-66; assoc. prof. German U. Pitts., 1966-68; assoc. prof. German and linguistics U. Ill., Urbana, 1968-72, prof., 1972-79, U. Calif., Berkeley, 1979—. Author: The Old High German Diphthongization: A Description of a Phonemic Change, 1967, The Old Saxon Language: Grammar, Epic Narrative, Linguistic Interference, 1992, Semiotic Insights: The Data Do the Talking, 1998, The Gothic Language: Genetic Provenance and Typology, Readings, 2002; editor (with others): Approaches in Linguistic Methodology, 1967; editor: Spanish edit., 1974, Der Heliand, 1974, Linguistic Method: Essays in Honor of Herbert Penzl, 1979, The Signifying Animal: The Grammar of Language and Experience, 1980, Language Change, 1983, The Semiotic Bridge: Trends from California, 1990, On Germanic Linguistics: Issues and Methods, 1992, Insights in Germanic Linguistics I: Methodology in Transition, 1995, Across the Oceans: Studies from East to West in Honor of Richard K. Seymour, 1995, Insights in Germanic Linguistics II: Classic and Contemporary, 1996, Synthesis in Diversity: Semiotics Around the World, 1997, New Insights in Germanic Linguistics I, 1999, II, 2001, III, 2002; editor of three series: Berkeley Insights in Linguistics and Semiotics, Berkeley Models of Grammars, Studies in Old Germanic Languages and Literatures; founder, co-editor Interdisciplinary Jour. for Germanic Linguistics and Semiotic Analysis; contbr. articles to profl. jours. Named outstanding woman on campus U. Ill. Sta. WILL, 1975; recipient Disting. Alumnus award U. Dayton, 1985; research grantee U. Wis., summer 1966, U. Ill., 1975-79, Eastern Ill. U., 1976, Nat. Endowment Humanities, 1978, U. Calif., Berkeley, 1979—; travel grantee NSF, Linguistics Soc. Am., 1972; Guggenheim fellow, 1982-83; IBM Distributed Acad. Computing Environment, 1986; NEH grantee, 1988; Festschrift: Interdigitations: Essays for Irmengard Rauch, 1999. Mem. Linguistics Soc. Am., MLA, Am. Assn. Tchrs. German (hon.), Society for Germanic Philogy, Philogical Assn. of the West Coast, Phonetics Assn., Semiotic Soc. Am. (pres. 1982-83), Semiotic Circle of Calif. (founder), Internat. Assn. for Semiotic Studies (pres., dir. 5th congress 1994), Alpha Sigma Tau, Delta Phi Alpha. Home: 862 Camden Ct Benicia CA 94510-3633 Office: U Calif Dept German Berkeley CA 94720-0001

RAUCH, JAMES E., economics professor; b. Trenton, NJ, Jan. 18, 1959; s. Harry E. and Helen F. Rauch; m. Doris E. Bittar, June 16, 1984; children: Joseph Benjamin Bittar, Gabriel James Bittar. BA, Princeton U., 1980; PhD, Yale U., New Haven, Conn., 1985. Rsch. assoc. Nat. Bur. Econ. Rsch., Cambridge, Mass., 1993—; asst. prof. econs. U. Calif., La Jolla, 1986—92, assoc. prof. econs., 1992—98, prof. econs., 1998—. Prin. investigator NSF, 1990—2002. Author: Leading Issues in Economic Development, 7th edit., 2000, Networks and Markets, 2001, 8th edit., 2005; co-editor Jour. Internat. Econs., Netherlands, 2001. Vis. Ind. scholar, Russell Sage Found., 1995—96. Mem.: Am. Econ. Assn. Home: 3026 Granada Ave San Diego CA 92104 Office: Dept Econs U Calif San Diego La Jolla CA 92093-0508 Office Phone: 858-534-2405. Office Fax: 858-534-7040. E-mail: jrauch@ucsd.edu.

RAUCH, JOHN KEISER, JR., architect; b. Phila., Oct. 23, 1930; s. John Keiser and Marjorie (Gretz) R.; m. Carol Pfaff, Mar. 11, 1953 (div. June 1978); children: John David, Charles Daniel, Kathryn Mari, Peter, Carol Anne; m. Carol A. McConochie, Jan. 10, 1981. Student, Wesleyan U., Middletown, Conn., 1948-51; BArch., U. Pa., 1957; grad. cert. program, Pa. Acad. Fine Arts, 2001. Draftsman Cope & Lippincott, Phila., 1957-60; architect Venturi and Short, Phila., 1960-64; partner Venturi and Rauch (Architects and Planners), Phila., 1964-79, Venturi, Rauch and Scott Brown, 1980-82, v.p., mng. prin., 1982-87, mgmt. cons., mediator, arbitrator, 1988-96; instr. U. Pa. Grad. Sch. Fine Arts, 1966-78, 89. Lectr. dept. architecture Princeton (N.J.) U., 1990-94. Trustee Found. for Architecture, 1977-84, mem. adv. com., 1994-2002; treas. Phila. Rehab., Inc., 1984-94; pres. Reading Terminal Market Pres. Fund, 1988-93, bd. dirs., 1994-2001; bd. dirs. United Cerebral Palsy Assn., 1988-91. Recipient Good Neighbor award Mellon/PSFS Bank, 1992. Fellow AIA (emeritus; Firm award 1983, John Harbeson Disting Svc. Phila. Chpt. award 1992); mem. Pa. Soc. Architects. Democrat. Home: 620 Oate House Ln Philadelphia PA 19118-4303

RAUCH, PAUL DAVID, television producer; b. Jersey City, N.J. s. Harry and Ruth (Reyman) R.; children— Stacie Jennifer, Tyler Meade. Classical music corr. Yomiuri Shimbun, 1956-58; corr. Voice of Am., 1958; Supr. prodn. TV programs CBS-TV, 1958-59; supr. prodn. TV programs Procter & Gamble Co., 1960-70; v.p. in charge daytime and east coast primetime programming CBS-TV, 1970-72; exec. producer Another World, others NBC-TV, 1972-82; exec. TV producer Twentieth Century Fox, 1982-83; executive producer One Life To Live ABC-TV, 1983-91; exec. producer Santa Barbara NBC-TV, 1991-93; exec. producer 919 Fifth Ave CBS, 1994-95; producer Lover's Knot (feature film), 1995-96; developer Columbia-Tristar TV, FOX TV, USA cable TV, 1994-96; exec. producer Guiding Light CBS, 1996—. Exec. prodr., Run The Wild Fields (Showtime feature film, Emmy award 2001), 1999. Served with AUS, 1956-58 Recipient Emmy award Nat. Acad. TV Arts and Scis., 1975, 76, Emmy award nomination for Another World, NBC-TV, 1976-77, NBC Bicentennial Special, Rachel Jackson, 1976.

RAUCHER, HERMAN, screenwriter, novelist; b. Bklyn., Apr. 13, 1928; s. Benjamin Brooks and Sophie (Weinshank) R.; m. Mary Kathryn Martinet, Apr. 20, 1960; children: Jacqueline Leigh, Jennifer Brooke. BS, NYU, 1949. Asst. trade ad mgr. 20th Century Fox Films, N.Y.C. and Los Angeles, 1950-54; copy dir. Walt Disney Studios, N.Y.C., 1954-55; copy supr. Calkins & Holden Advt., N.Y.C., 1955-57; copy dir., v.p., dir. Reach McClinton Advt., N.Y.C., 1957-63; v.p., creative dir. Maxon Advt., N.Y.C., 1963-64; creative supr. Gardner Advt., N.Y.C., 1964-65; v.p. advt., cons. Benton & Bowles Advt., N.Y.C., 1965-67; freelance novelist, screenwriter, 1967—; pres. Bearfilm Prodns., 1971-96. Author: (novels and screenplays) Watermelon Man, 1970, Summer of '42 (nominated Acad. award for best original screenplay 1971, Writers Guild award nomination, Photoplay award), Ode to Billy Joe, 1975, A Glimpse of Tiger, 1972, (novel) Maynard's House, 1979, (screenplays) Sweet November, 1968, The Other Side of Midnight, 1977, Class of 44, 1972, Hieronymus Merkin (Best Original Screenplay award Writers Guild of Great Britain 1969), There Should Have Been Castles, 1978, Ginger, 1995, ARA/Froom, 2001 also various dramas appearing on TV in Alcoa Hour, Studio One, Matinee Theatre, Goodyear Playhouse, (TV mini-series under pseudonym) Master of the Game, 1984, (TV pilot)

Remember When, 1974; playwright: Harold, 1962, Two Weeks Somewhere Else, 1967, Red Lights and Dragons, 1996, Kitty Hawk (musical), 2000; contbg. editor Greenwich Time; contbr. to book revs. to N.Y. Times. Served with U.S. Army, 1950-52. Mem. Writers Guild Am., Authors League Am., Am. Film Inst., Dramatists Guild, Acad. of Motion Picture Arts and Scis.

RAUCKHORST, WILLIAM HERMAN, physics professor, academic administrator; b. Covington, Ky., Sept. 9, 1940; m. A. Elaine Kroger, June 20, 1964; children: Cynthia, Jane, Julie. BA summa cum laude, Thomas More Coll., Crestview Hills, Ky., 1962; PhD in Physics, U. Cin., 1967. From asst. prof. to assoc. prof. Bellarmine Coll., Louisville, 1967-72; assoc. prof. Sangamon State U., Springfield, Ill., 1972-76; program mgr. U.S. Dept. Energy/ERDA, Washington, 1976-78; head coll./univ. programs sect. Argonne (Ill.) Nat. Lab., 1978-85; sr. program dir. NSF, Washington, 1990-92; prof. physics, assoc. provost Miami U., Oxford, Ohio, 1985—. Home: 129 Country Club Dr Oxford OH 45056-9002 Office: Miami U 107 Roudebush Hall Oxford OH 45056 Business E-Mail: rauckhwh@muohio.edu.

RAUE, JORG EMIL, electrical engineer; b. Stettin, Germany, June 13, 1936; came to U.S., 1952; s. Ludwig and Liselotte (Barth) R.; m. Anke Volkmann, June 29, 1957; children: Monika Kay, Jennifer Faye. BSEE, Milw. Sch. Engring., 1961; MSEE, Marquette U., 1965, PhDEE, 1968. Mem. faculty Milw. Sch. Engring., 1961-68, chmn. dept., 1968-69; research engr. TRW Systems, Redondo Beach, Calif., 1969-76, mgr. dept., 1976-79; sr. research scientist TRW Electronic Systems, Rendondo Beach, advanced systems mgr., 1980-93; tech. cons. Calif., 1993—; chmn. dept. elec. engring. Calif. Poly. State U., San Luis Opispo, 1979-80. Mem. faculty Marquette U., Milw., 1968-69, Loyola U., L.A., 1970-72, U. So. Calif., L.A., 1983—. Contbr. articles to profl. jours. Served with U.S. Army, 1955-58. Recipient Disting. Tchr. award Milw. Sch. Engring., 1968; named Outstanding Alumnus Milw. Sch. Engring., 1985. Fellow IEEE; mem. Microwave Soc. of IEEE (sec. adminstrn. com. 1985—), Sigma Xi. Avocations: tennis, bicycling, flying, bridge. Home and Office: 28813 Rothrock Dr Palos Verdes Estates CA 90275-3060

RAUH, CARL STEPHEN, lawyer; b. Washington, Dec. 14, 1940; s. Joseph L. and Olie (Westheimer) R. AB, Columbia U., 1962; LL.B., U. Pa., 1965; LL.M., Georgetown U., 1968. Bar: D.C. 1966, U.S. Supreme Ct. 1969. Asst. U.S. atty. for D.C., 1966-69; atty. Dep. Atty Gen.'s Office Dept. Justice, Washington, 1969-71; 1st asst. atty. gen. U.S. VI., 1971-73; prin. asst. U.S. atty. for D.C., 1974-79; U.S. atty. for D.C., 1979; ptnr. Dunnells, Duvall, Bennett & Porter, Washington, 1980-90, Skadden, Arps, Slate, Meagher & Flom, Washington, 1990—. Mem. D.C. Jud. Nomination Commn., 1985-90. Recipient Dir.'s award Dept. Justice, 1976; Atty. Gen.'s Disting. Service award, 1980 Fellow Am. Coll. Trial Lawyers; mem. ABA, D.C. Bar Assn., Nat. Assn. Former U.S. Attys., Asst. U.S. Attys. Assn. (Harold J. Sullivan award 1980). Office: 1440 New York Ave NW Washington DC 20005-2111 Office Phone: 202-371-7000.

RAUH, LINDA ANN, rehabilitation services professional, counselor; d. John Matthew and Edna Ruth (Price) Rauh. MA in Counseling Edn., Kean U., 1997. Cert. counselor Nat. Bd. for Cert. Counselors, clin. hypnotherapist Md., psychosocial rehab. practitioner Md., marriage and family therapist N.J., lic. profl. counselor. Sr. counselor Bridgeway Rehab. Svcs., Inc., Elizabeth, NJ, 1999—2001, dir. staff devel. and quality improvement, 2001—. Clinician SERV Behavioral Healthcare, Elizabeth, 1997—99. Counselor Ctr. for Hope Hospice, Linden, NJ, 1996—97. Mem.: Am. Mental Health Counselors Assn., N.J. Counseling Assn. (Grad. Student of Yr. award 1997). Avocations: guitar, reading, swimming. Office: Bridgeway Rehab Svcs Inc 615 N Broad St Elizabeth NJ 07208 Office Phone: 908-355-7886. Office Fax: 908-355-6668. Personal E-mail: msrauh@comcast.net. E-mail: linda.rauh@bridgewayinc.com

RAUL, ALAN CHARLES, lawyer; b. Bronx, NY, Sept. 9, 1954; s. Eugene and Eduarda (Müller-Mañas) R.; m. Mary Tinsley, Jan. 30, 1988; children: Caroline Tinsley, William Eduardo Tinsley, Alexander Tinsley. AB magna cum laude, Harvard U., 1975, MPA, 1977; JD, Yale U., 1980. Bar: N.Y. 1982, D.C. 1982, U.S. Ct. Appeals (D.C. cir.) 1982, U.S. Supreme Ct. 1988. Law clk. to judge U.S. Ct. Appeals (D.C. cir.), Washington, 1980-81; assoc. Debevoise & Plimpton, N.Y.C., 1981-86; White House assoc. counsel Pres. Reagan, Washington, 1986-88; gen. counsel Office Mgmt. and Budget, Washington, 1988-89, USDA, Washington, 1989-93; prin. Beveridge & Diamond P.C., Washington, 1993-97; ptnr. Sidley Austin LLP, Washington, 1997—. Vice chair Privacy and Civil Liberties Oversight Bd., 2006. Author: (book) Privacy and the Digital State, 2001. Co-chair, co-founder Lawyers Have Heart; chmn. bd. USDA Grad. Sch., 1991-93; bd. dirs. Nation's Capital affiliate Am. Heart Assn., 1993-97, 2003—, Greater Washington region, 2002—; treas., dir. Citizens Assn. Georgetown, 1993-97; mem. Nat. Policy Forum's Environ. Policy Coun.; mem. adv. coun. Atlantic Legal Found., 2001—. Recipient Disting. Achievement award Am. Heart Assn., 1991, Vol. of Yr. award, 1993, Lifetime Achievement award, 1999. Mem. ABA (chmn. com. on nat. security and internat. law 1990-92, coun. sect. internat. law and practice 1992-98, standing com. on election law 1995-99, sect. internat. law and practice govt. affairs officer 1996-98, coun. sect. adminstrv. law and regulatory practice 2004—), Assn. of Bar of City of N.Y. (chmn. subcom. on Cen. Am. issues 1985, mem. com. on inter-Am. affairs 1983), Federalist Soc. (mem. nat. practitioners adv. coun., chair environ. and property rights practice group 1996-99), Coun. on Fgn. Rels. Office: Sidley Austin LLP 1501 K St NW Washington DC 20005 Office Phone: 202-736-8477. E-mail: araul@sidley.com.

RAULINAITIS, PRANAS ALGIS, electronics executive, consultant; b. Kaunas, Lithuania, May 13, 1927; came to U.S., 1954, naturalized, 1960; s. Pranas Viktoras and Paulina (Gervaite) R.; m. Angele Staugaityte, Oct. 4, 1952; 1 son, Pranas Darius. With Commonwealth Rys. of Australia, Melbourne, 1949-53; asst. to fin. acct. Kitchen & Sons, Pty. Ltd., Melbourne, 1953-54; v.p. photo divsn. Interphoto Corp., L.A., 1954-71; sr. v.p. fin., sec. Craig Corp., L.A., 1971-87; pres. PAR Enterprises, Burbank, Calif., 1987—. Adviser Ministry Fgn. Affairs Republic of Lithuania, 1992; asst. sec. M & F Corp. Enterprises, Ltd., Chgo., 2004—. Former pres. Lithuanian Am. Coun., Inc. of Calif.; bd. dirs. Lithuanian-Am. Assns.; founder, former dir., v.p. Baltic Am. Freedom League; former mem. Am. Soc. Internat. Law. Home and Office: PAR Enterprises 1501 W Riverside Dr Burbank CA 91506-3027 Personal E-mail: raulalgis@juno.com.

RAULLERSON, CALVIN HENRY, political scientist, consultant; b. Utica, N.Y., Dec. 18, 1920; s. Calvin Thomas and Cora (White) R.; m. Olive Lewis, Dec. 1, 1956; children: Kevin Greer, Cheryl Harp, Earl Henry. AB, Lincoln U., Pa., 1943; M.P.A., NYU, 1949; postgrad., Harvard, 1947, Harvard Bus. Sch., 1979. Instr. polit. sci. Lincoln U., 1946, 49; editor, dir. research Christian E. Burckell Assocs., Yonkers, N.Y., 1950-52; asst. to exec. dir. United Negro Coll. Fund, 1952-57, dir. edited. services, 1957-61; dir. African programs Am. Soc. African Culture, Lagos, Nigeria, 1961-64, exec. dir. N.Y.C., 1964-66; chief Peace Corps, East and So. Africa, 1966-69; dir. Kenya, 1969-71; Africa regional dir., 1971-73; exec. asst. to dean Sch. Medicine, asst. to pres. for internat. programs, spl. cons. research and devel., exec. dir. Internat. Ctr. for Arid and Semi-Arid Lands, Tex. Tech U., 1973-78; asst. prof. health orgn. mgmt., Health Scis. Ctr. Tex. Tech U., 1973-78; asst. adminstr. Bur. Pvt. Devel. Cooperation, AID, 1978-81; v.p. African Am. Inst., 1981-84; assoc. Keene, Monk Assocs., Middleburg, Va., 1985-86; dir. internat. programs One Am., Inc., 1987-88; pres. internat. group LABAT Anderson, 1988-94; v.p. internat. group Gardner Kamya Inc., Washington, 1994-95; sr. project mgr. Labat-Anderson Inc., McLean, Va., 1995—, ret., 2000-. Mgmt. cons. Mgmt. Devel. Consortium, Phelps Stokes Fund, 1973-75; Mem. information resources com. group on bus. affairs assn. Am. Med. Colls.; mem. adv. com. on desertification AAAS, 1976-78; mem. Career Ministers Selection Bd., Dept. State, 1980; U.S. del. U.N. Conf. Desertification Nairobi, 1977; chmn. U.S. del. Com. on Food Aid and Agriculture, World Food Program, Rome, 1980; research analyst Pres.'s Com. on Fair Employment Practices, 1944; treas. U.S. planning com. 1st World Festival Negro Art, Dakar,

1965-66; del. Internat. Conf. on African History, U. Ibadan (Nigeria), 1962, Internat. Conf. on African Affairs, U. Ghana, 1963. Assoc. editor: Who's Who in the United Nations, 1952; Contbr. to: Negro Yearbook, 1952. Mem. nat. adv. com. Peace Corps, 1986-89; trustee African Wildlife Found., 1992—, chmn. strategic planning com., 1993-95. Rockefeller travel grantee East and Central Africa, 1960; Woodrow Wilson scholar, 1978-79 Mem. Harvard Club (Washington). Nat. Press Club. Home: 5823 Bradley Blvd Bethesda MD 20814-1104 E-mail: olrchr@msn.com.

RAUM, MARY BETH, performing arts educator; b. Takoma Park, Md., Oct. 14, 1957; d. Lawrence Arthur and Catherine Tompkins Raum. BS cum laude, U. Md., 1979; M in Adminstrv. Sci. magna cum laude, Johns Hopkins U., 1979; PhD summa cum laude, U. Wash., 1992. Administr. Johns Hopkins U./APL, Laurel, Md., 1976—82; adj. faculty/tech. mgmt U. Md. Open Univ., College Park, 1980—84; cons. Lawrence A. Raum & Assocs., Inc., Tacoma, 1982—92; doctoral rsch. assoc. George Washington U., Washington, 1983; asst. prof. orgnl. leadership Chapman U., Bangor, Wash., 1984—2005; adj. grad. faculty City U., Silverdale, Wash., 1986—88; corps de ballet/instr. Pacific Regional Ballet, Bremerton, Wash., 1996—2004; doctoral rsch. assoc. U. Wash., Seattle; ballet instr. MK Ballet Studio, Bremerton, Wash.; adj. faculty Pacific U., Dept. Econs., 2005; nat. security decision making prof. Naval War Coll., 2006—. Ballet mistress Pacific Regional Ballet, Bremerton, Wash., 2002—. Classical dance pointe, Raymonda (High Second Pl. Regional Dance Competition, 2002), character dance, Untitled (Internat. Dance Competition Sterling Silver Champion, 2001), classical ballet pointe, Raymonda (Dance Magic Regional High Score 2nd Pl., 2002), Spanish character dance, Voz de la Referencia (Regional 1st Pl. & Championship High Score Adult Trophy, 2002)., NSF grantee, 1985. Mem.: Soc. Judgement and Decision Making, European Assn. Decision Making, Women in Internat. Security, Women in Aviation Internat., Phi Kappa Phi. Methodist. Avocation: free lance writer. Office: Naval War Coll 686 Cushing Rd Newport RI 02840 Personal E-mail: maryraumphd@aol.com. Business E-mail: mary.raum@nwc.navy.mil.

RAUP, DAVID MALCOLM, paleontology educator; b. Boston, Apr. 24, 1933; s. Hugh Miller and Lucy (Gibson) R.; m. Susan Creer Shepard, Aug. 25, 1956; 1 son, Mitchell D.; m. Judith T. Yamamoto, May 30, 1987. BS, U. Chgo., 1953; MA, Harvard U., 1955, PhD, 1957. Instr. Calif. Inst. Tech., 1956-57; mem. faculty Johns Hopkins U., 1957-65, assoc. prof., 1963-65; mem. faculty U. Rochester, 1965-78, prof. geology, 1966-78, chmn. dept. geol. scis., 1968-71, dir. Center for Evolution and Paleobiology, 1977-78; curator geology, chmn. dept. geology Field Mus. Natural History, Chgo., 1978-80, dean of sci., 1980-82; prof. geophys. sci. U. Chgo., 1980-95, chmn. dept., 1982-85, Sewell L. Avery disting. service prof., 1984-95; prof. emeritus, Sewell L. Avery disting. svc. prof. emeritus, 1995—. Geologist U.S. Geol. Survey, part-time, 1959-77; vis. prof. U. Tubingen, Germany, 1965, 72 Author: (with S. Stanley) Principles of Paleontology, 1971, 78, The Nemesis Affair, 1986, 2d edit., 1999, Extinction: Bad Genes of Bad Luck?, 1991; editor: (with B. Kummel) Handbook of Paleontological Techniques, 1965; contbr. articles to profl. jours. Recipient Best Paper award Jour. Paleontology, 1966; Schuchert award Paleontol. Soc., 1973; grantee Calif. Rsch. Corp., 1955-56, Am. Assn. Petroleum Geologists, 1957, Am. Philos. Soc., 1957, NSF, 1960-66, 75-81, Chem. Soc., 1965-71, NASA, 1983-95. Mem. AAAS, Am. Acad. Arts and Scis., Nat. Acad. Sci., Paleontol. Soc. (pres. 1976-77, medal 1997), Am. Soc. Naturalists (v.p. 1983), Am. Philos. Soc. Home: 423 Johnson Dr Washington Island WI 54246-9753 Personal E-mail: draup@itol.com.

RAUSCH, PAUL MATTHEW, financial executive; b. Lafayette, Ind., Dec. 14, 1953; s. Richard Leo and Vernice Ruth R. Student, Purdue U., 1976. County supr. Farmers Home Adminstrn., Richmond and Falmouth, Ky., 1979-87; loan officer spl. accounts team Farm Credit Svcs., LaPorte, Ind., 1987; br. mgr. Nat. Mortgage Corp., Merrillville, Ind., 1987-89; collection mgr. Greentree Acceptance, Lexington, Ky., 1989; county supr. Farmers Home Adminstrn., Springfield and Alamosa, Colo., 1990-96; v.p. Hershey (Nebr.) State Bank, 1996-98; fin. svcs. mgr. Coop. Fin. Assn. for Elsie, Chappell and Stapleton, Nebr., 1998-2000; econ. devel. fin. specialist West Ctrl. Nebr. Devel. Dist., Ogallala, 2001—05; exec. dir. Nat. Children's Found., 2003—; v.p. comml. and agrl. lending Sunflower Bank, Monte Vista, Colo., 2005—. Pres. rural devel. Madison County, Richmond, 1980-85; bd. dirs. Mosca-Hooper Soil Conservation Dist., 1993-94, San Luis Valley Rural Devel. Coun., Alamosa, 1993-94, Nat. Children's Found., Hooper, Colo., 1993-2003; mem. Monte Vista Econ. Devel. Recipient Dedication to Cmty. award Madison County, Richmond, 1983; named Ky. Col., Richmond, 1985. Mem. Nat. Parks and Conservation Assn., Am. Soc. Farm Mgrs. and Rural Appraisers, Nature Conservancy, Wilderness Soc., Sierra Club (agr. com. 1987-94), Kiwanis (bd. dirs. 1980-85). Avocations: music collecting, antiques and art collecting, studebaker vehicle restoration, hunting, farming. Home: 9531 Lane 9N Mosca CO 81146 Office: 104 Adams St Monte Vista CO 81144 Office Phone: 719-852-5901. Business E-mail: paulr@sunflowerbank.com.

RAUSCHENBERG, BRADFORD LEE, museum program director; b. Atlanta, Sept. 11, 1940; BS in Archaeology and Biology, Ga. State Coll., 1963; MA in History, Wake Forest U., 1995. Archaeologist Ga. Hist. Commn., 1963-64; site supr., asst. Stanley South. State Archaeologist of N.C., 1964-66; antiquarian, asst. Dir. Restoration Old Salem, Inc., Winston-Salem, NC, 1966-73; asst. to dir. Mus. Early So. Decorative Arts, Winston-Salem, 1973-76, rsch. fellow, 1976-87, dir. rsch., 1987-93, Mus. Early So. Decorative Arts and Old Salem, Inc., Winston-Salem, 1993—, sr. fellow emeritus. Cons., lectr. in field. Author: British Regional Carving (1600-1640), and Furniture (1600-1800), 1984, Wachovia Historical Society: 1895-1995, 1995, Charleston Furniture, 1680-1820, 3 vols., 2003. With USCG, 1964-72. Recipient Halifax Resolves award, 1986; grantee NEH, 1972-81, Kaufman Americana Found., 1981-82. Mem. Am. Ceramic Circle (granter), Orgn. Am. Historians, No. Ceramic Soc., So. Hist. Assn., Friends of Swiss Ceramic Circle, Regional Furniture Soc., Furniture History Soc., Soc. Hist. Archaeology, Soc. Post-Medieval Archaeology, Soc. Historians Early Am. Republic. Address: 221 Harmon Ct Winston Salem NC 27106-4613 Office: Mus Early So Decorative Arts PO Box 10310 Winston Salem NC 27108-0310 E-mail: k4blr@triad.rr.com.

RAUSCHENBERG, ROBERT, artist; b. Port Arthur, Tex., Oct. 22, 1925; m. Susan Weil, 1950 (div. 1952); 1 child, Christopher. Student, U. Tex., Kansas City Art Inst., Academie Julian, Paris, Black Mountain Coll., N.C., Art Students League, N.Y.C.; LHD (hon.), Grinnell Coll., 1967; DFA (hon.), U. So. Fla., 1976. Neuropsychiat. tech. Calif. Naval Hosps. Founder Overseas Culture Interchange traveling exhbn., 1985—. One-man shows include Parsons Gallery, N.Y.C., 1951, Stable Gallery, 1953, White Chapel Art Gallery, London, 1964, Galerie Ileana Sonnabend, Paris, 1971, 1972, 1973, Leo Castelli Gallery, N.Y.C., 1972, 1973, Ace Gallery, L.A., 1973, Nat. Collection Fine Arts, Smithsonian Inst., Washington, 1976, Mus. Modern Art, N.Y.C., 1977, Albright Knox Gallery, 1977, Art Inst. Chgo., 1977, San Francisco Mus. Modern Art, 1977, Vancouver Art Gallery, 1978, Staatliche Kunsthalle, Berlin, 1980, Kunstalle, Düsseldorf, 1980, Louisiana Mus., Copenhagen, 1980, Stadelsches Kunstinst., Frankfurt, 1981, Tate Galery, London, 1981, Städtische Galerie im Lembacchaus, Munich, 1981, Phoenix Art Mus., 1982, G.H. Dalsheimer Gallery, Balt., 1983, Castelli Graphics, 1984, Galerie Bayeler, Basle, 1984, Juan March, Madrid, 1985, L.A. County Mus. Art, 1987, Inst. Contemporary Art, London, 1987, Galerie Alfred Kren, Cologne, 1988—89, Tretyakov Gallery, Moscow, 1989, Nat. Art Gallery, Kuala Lumpur, Malaysia, 1990, Mus. Contemporary Art, L.A., 1995—97, Pace Wilder Stein Gallery, N.Y.C., 1996, L.A., 1996—97, Guggenheim Mus., 1998, others, exhibited in group shows at Sao Paulo Biennial, 1959, Exposition Internat. Surrealisme, Paris, 1959—60, Mus. Modern Art, 1959, Guggenheim Mus., 1961, 1992, Mus. South Tex., Corpus Christi, 1974, N.Y. Collection in Stockholm, 1972, Whitney Mus. Am. Art, N.Y.C., 1972, 1973, Garage Show, Rome, 1973, Automme Festival d'Artes, Paris, 1973, N.Y. Cultural Ctr., 1973. Represented in permanent collections Albright-Knox Art Gallery, Whitney Mus. am. Art, Wadsworth Atheneum, Tate Gallery, Mus. Modern Art, Neue Galerie Aachen, Germany, Hirshhorn Mus., Moderna

Museet, Stockholm, others, prin. works include electronic sculpture Soundings, prin. works include painting Tut-Scape; set and costume designer, lighting expert, stage mgr. Merce Cunningham Dance Co., 1964; choreographer others. With USMC, 1947—48. Recipient 1st Prize, Internat. Exhbn. Prints Gallery Modern Art, Ljubljana, Yugoslavia, 1963, Venice Biennale, 1964, Corcoran Biennal Contemporary Am. Painters, 1965, Skowhegan Sch. Painting and Sculpture medal, 1982, Grammy award, 1984. Mem.: NAD (assoc.), Am. Acad. and Inst. Arts and Letters. Gallery: Pace Wildenstein Gallery 32 E 57th St New York NY 10022-2513

RAUSCHENBUSCH, STEPHANIE, artist, educator, poet; b. Washington, July 27, 1942; d. Stephen and Josephine Burns Raushenbush; m. Joseph Marchant Hayman, Dec. 29, 1984; m. Louis R. Rowan, June 20, 1964 (div. June 20, 1979); 1 child, Quentin Rowan. BA magna cum laude, Radcliffe Coll., Cambridge, Mass., 1964; MA summa cum laude, Columbia U., NYC, 1966. Treas. Noho Gallery, NYC, 1999—. One-woman shows include Noho Gallery, NYC, 1983, 1987, 1989, 1991, 1993, 1995, 1997, 1999, 2002, 2005, exhibited in group shows at Woodstock (NY) Guild, 1986, Art and the Law traveling exhibit, 1988—1889, Biennale d'Arte Contemporanea, Florence, 2001, in pvt. collections; author: (book of poetry) The Heart's Ice Thaws, 1999; contbr. poetry to lit. jours.; exhibitions include, 1986—90, 2003. Trustee Friends Sem., NYC, 1998—2001. Fellow, Woodrow Wilson Found., 1964—65; grantee Kent fellowship grad. studies, Danforth Found., 1966—70. Mem.: N.Y. Soc. Women Artists (pres. 2006—), Women's Caucus for Art, Catherine Lorillard Wolfe Art Club. Democrat. Mem. Soc. Of Friends. Avocation: gardening. Home: 46 Sherman St Brooklyn NY 11215

RAUSEN, AARON REUBEN, pediatric hematologist, oncologist; b. Jersey City, June 30, 1931; s. David and Ruth (Schwartz) R.; m. Emalou Watkins, Apr. 7, 1968; children: David, Susan, Elisabeth. Degree, Dartmouth Coll., 1950; MD, SUNY, Bklyn., 1954. Intern, then resident in pediatrics Bellevue Hosp. Ctr., N.Y.C., 1954-56; chief resident in pediatrics Mt. Sinai Hosp., N.Y.C., 1958-59; asst. assoc. and attending pediatrician, 1961-81; fellow in hematology Children's Hosp. and Harvard Med. Sch., Boston, 1959-61; chief of pediatrics City Hosp. Ctr., Elmhurst, N.Y., 1964-72; dir. pediatrics Beth Israel Med. Ctr., N.Y.C., 1972-81; dir. pediatric oncology NYU Med. Ctr., N.Y.C., 1981-97; prof. pediatrics NYU Sch. Medicine, N.Y.C., 1981—. Prof. pediat. Mt. Sinai Sch. Medicine, N.Y.C., 1971—81, professorial lectr., 1981—; dir. Stephen D. Hassenfeld Children's Ctr. for Cancer and Blood Disorders, N.Y.C., 1990—97, founding dir., 1997—; cons. Lenox Hill Hosp., N.Y.C., 1981—; vis. prof. Dartmouth Med. Sch., Hanover, NH, 1984—86; prin. investigator Children's Oncology Group, 1999—2005; vis. staff pediat. Greenwich (Conn.) Hosp., 2005—; attending pediat. Stamford (Conn.) Hosp., 2005—. Contbr. articles to profl. jours. Bd. dirs. N.Y.C. chpt. Am. Cancer Soc., 1984-1996, Nat. Childhood Cancer Found., 1992—, Children's Oncology Soc. N.Y., 1993—, Ovarian Cancer Rsch. Fund, 1994-99. Capt. Med. Corps, U.S. Army, 1956-58. Fellow Am. Acad. Pediatrics; mem. Am. Pediatric Soc., Am. Soc. Hematology, Am. Soc. Clin. Oncology, Am. Assn. Cancer Rsch., Am. Soc. Pediatric Hematology-Oncology, N.Y. Pediatric Soc. (pres. 1974), Yale Club N.Y.C., Phi Beta Kappa, Alpha Omega Alpha. Office: 317 E 34th St Fl 8 New York NY 10016-4974 Office Phone: 212-263-7144. Personal E-mail: aaron.rausen@nyumc.org.

RAUSHENBUSH, WALTER BRANDEIS, retired law educator; b. Madison, Wis., June 13, 1928; s. Paul A. and Elizabeth (Brandeis) R.; m. Marylu de Watteville, May 3, 1956; children: Lorraine Elizabeth, Richard Walter, Carla de Watteville, Paul Brandeis. AB magna cum laude in Govt., Harvard U., 1950; JD with high honors, U. Wis., 1953. Bar: Wis. 1953. Ptnr. LaFollette, Sinykin & Doyle, Madison, 1956-58; mem. faculty U. Wis., Madison, 1958—, prof. law, 1966-95, prof. emeritus, 1995—; vis. prof. law U. San Diego, 1992—94, 1996—; project dir. real estate transfer study Am. Bar Found., 1967-72. Trustee nat. Law Sch. Admission Coun., 1968-70, 72-95, chmn. pre-law com., 1970-74, chmn. svcs. com., 1976-78, pres., 1980-82; legal advisor Madison Citizens Fair Housing, 1961-63, Wis. Citizens Family Planning, 1965-73; real property drafting com. Multistate Bar Exam., 1986-2002. Author: Wisconsin Construction Lien Law, 1974, (with others) Wisconsin Real Estate Law, 1984, 4th edit., 1994, Brown on Personal Property, 3d edit., 1975, Real Estate Transactions Cases and Materials, 1997. With USAF, 1953-56, col. Res. ret. Mem. ABA, State Bar Wis., Order of Coif, Stage Harbor Yacht Club (Chatham, Mass.), Cape Cod Nat. Golf Club (Harwich, Mass.), Phi Beta Kappa, Phi Delta Phi (province pres. 1963-75). Presbyterian (Elder). Home: Unit 908 1730 Avenida Del Mundo Coronado CA 92118-3026

RAUSHER, DAVID BENJAMIN, internist, gastroenterologist; b. Bklyn., Sept. 15, 1952; s. Herbert and Shirley Ruth R.; m. Judy A. Steinlauf, Aug. 8, 1976; children: Scott, Michael, Steven. BA, Hamilton Coll., 1973; MD, SUNY, Bklyn., 1977. Diplomate Am. Bd. Internal Medicine, Am. Bd. Gastroenterology. Resident Emory U. Hosps., Atlanta, 1977-80, fellow in gastroenterology, 1980-82; pres. Atlanta Ctr. for Gastroenterology, Decatur, Ga., 1982—; med. dir. Atlanta Endoscopy Ctr., Decatur, 1994—. Chmn. diagnostic treatment ctr. DeKalb Med. Ctr., Decatur, Ga., 1985—, co-chief gastroenterology, 1995-97, chief sect. gastroenterology, 1998—. Fellow: Am. Gastroenterology Assn., Am. Coll. Gastroenterology. Office Phone: 404-296-1986.

RAUSSER, GORDON C(LYDE), agricultural and resource economics educator; b. Lodi, Calif., July 21, 1943; s. Elmer A. and Doyve Ester (Meyers) R.; children: Sloan, Stephanie, Paige. BS summa cum laude, Calif. State U., 1965; MS with highest honors, U. Calif., Davis, 1968, PhD with highest honors, 1971. Prof. econs. and agrl. econs. U. Calif., Davis, 1969-74; vis. prof. U. Chgo., 1972-74; prof. econs. and stats. Iowa State U., 1974-75; prof. bus. adminstrn. Harvard U., 1975-78; prof., chmn. dept. agrl. and resource econs. U. Calif., Berkeley, 1979-85, 93-94, Robert Gordon Sproul disting. prof., 1985—, dean nat. resources, 1994-2000; dir. Giannini Found., Berkeley, 1984-86. Vis. prof. Hebrew U. and Ben-Gurion U., Israel, 1978; Ford Found. vis. prof., Argentina, 72; spl. coms. and sr. economist Coun. Econ. Advisors, 1986—87; chief economist AID, 1988—90; advisor econ. rsch. svc. USDA, 1978—80, 1986—88, Agr. Can., 1977—79, Bur. Agrl. Econs., Australia, 1987, U.S. Office Mgmt. and Budget, 1986; mem., chmn. planning com. Sch. Bus. Adminstrn. U. Calif., Berkeley, 1986—87, mem. adv. com. Agrl. Issues Ctr., 1984—85, mem. planning com. Agrl. and Natural Resources Program, 1986, mem. econs. programs evaluation com., 1987—88; mem. Citrus Planning Commn., Brazil, 1984; pres. Inst. for Policy Reform, Washington, 1989—94; prin., founder Law & Econ. Cons. Group, Berkeley, Washington, Chgo., NYC, 1990—2000; sr. cons. Charles River Assocs., 2000—. Author: Macroeconomic Environment for U.S. Agricultural Policy, Alternative Agricultural and Food Policies and the 1985 Farm Bill, The Emergence of Market Economies in Eastern Europe, New Directions in Econometric Modeling and Forecasting, Dynamics of Agricultural Systems: Economic Prediction and Control, Quantitative Methods in Agricultural Economics, GATT Negotiations and the Political Economy of Policy Reform; co-editor: Handbook of Agricultural Economics, Vol. 2A, 2002, Vol. 2B, 2002, Vol. 1A, 2001, Vol. 1B, 2001; editor Decision-Making in Business and Economics, 1977-79, Am. Jour. Agrl. Econs., 1983-86. Mem. western nutrition ctr. coordinating com. USDA, 1980-83; mem. Arab-Am. Coun. for Cultural and Econ. Exch., 1979-81; bd. dirs. Giannini Found. Agrl. Econs., 1979-84, mem. exec. com., 1982-84; mem. planning com. Berkeley Food Coop., 1980-83, planning com. for food policy Resources for the Future, 1984-85; mem. adv. com. Calif. State Dept. Agr., 1982-84; bd. dirs. Am. Agrl. Econs. Awards. Grantee USDA, NSF, World Bank, Chgo. Merc. Exch., U.S. Bur. Mines; Fulbright scholar, Australia, 1987; Sr. fellow Resources for Future, 1984-85. Fellow: AAAS, Am. Agrl. Econs. Assn. (outstanding enduring rsch. contbn. com. 1982—84, outstanding PhD dissertation com. 1974—76, chmn. outstanding article com. 1983—86, rsch. awards of merit 1976, 1978, 1980, 1982, 1986, 1989, 1992, Pub. Enduring quality award 1993, rsch. awards of merit 1993, Disting. Policy Contbn. award 1993, rsch. awards of merit 1994, 2000, 2001), Am. Statis. Assn.; mem.: Coll. Natural Resources Citation, Western Agrl. Econ. Assn. (Best Pub. Rsch. award 1978, Outstanding Pub. Rsch. award 1994), Ops. Rsch. Soc., Math. Assn. Am.,

Econometric Soc., Am. Acad. Polit. and Social Sci., Am. Econ. Assn., Commonwealth Club (dir. agr. study group 1983—84), Alpha Zeta, Alpha Gamma Rho. Home: 661 San Luis Rd Berkeley CA 94707-1725 Office: U Calif Berkeley ARE 207 Giannini Hall Berkeley CA 94720-3310 Business E-Mail: rausser@are.berkeley.edu.

RAUT, LAKSHMI KANTA, economist, educator; s. Gajendra Nath and Janaki Bala Raut; 1 child, Han Abhik Tran. BSc in Stats. with honors, Calcutta U., Kolkata, India, 1972; M. Stat, Indian Statis. Inst., Kolkata, India, 1978; PhD, MA in Econs., Yale U., New Haven, Conn., 1985. Cons. The World Bank, New Delhi, 1983—84, rschr. Washington, 1984—86; postdoctoral fellow U. Chgo., 1986—87; asst. prof. U. Calif. San Diego, La Jolla, 1987—95; assoc. prof. U. Hawaii Manoa, Honolulu, 1995—98; rsch. assoc. U. of Chgo., Chicago, Ill., 1998—99; vis. fellow Yale U., New Haven, 1999—2000; assoc. professor Calif. State U., Fullerton, 2000—05; economist Social Security Adminstrn., Washington, 2005—. Editor: (book) Trade, Growth and Development: Essays in Honor of Professor T.N. Srinivasan; author: Theory of Games and its Applications to Economics and Politics, numerous rsch. articles in field. Office: Social Security Administration 500 E St SW 9th Fl Washington DC 20254 Office Phone: 202-358-6513.

RAUTENSTRAUCH, GARY M., marketing executive; BBA, Miami U., 1975; MBA, NYU. Exec. v.p. technology Baker & Taylor, Inc., exec. v.p. distribution, COO, pres., CEO, 2001—03; CEO Blackwell's Book Svcs., 2005—06; pres., CEO Advanced Mktg. Svcs., Inc., 2006—. Office: Advanced Mktg Svcs Inc 5880 Oberlin Dr Ste 400 San Diego CA 92121 Office Phone: 858-457-2500, 858-452-2237.*

RAUTIOLA, NORMAN A., small business owner, manufacturing executive; b. Hancock, Mich., Aug. 6, 1932; s. Arnold and Irene Rautiola; m. Sarah-Binah Rautiola, Dec. 5, 1997; children: Jeffrey, Jordan, Leijona, Niikolas, Ari. BS in metal engring., Mich. Tech. U., 1954; MBA, George Wash. U., 1960. Engring. officer U.S. Air Force, Hamilton AFB, Calif., 1954—56; sr. patent examiner U.S. Paten Office, Wash., DC, 1957—60; patent devel. mgr. Tex. Instruments, Dallas, 1960—65; asst. to president Bunker Ramo Corp., Canoga Park, Calif., 1965—66; dir., corp. devel. Sparton Corp., Jackson, Mich., 1966—68; pres. Nartron Corp., Reed City, Mich., 1968—; founder, chmn. Smart Power Sys. Inc., Sylvan Lake, Mich., 1986—. Dir. Smart Power Sys. Inc., Sylvan Lake, Mich., 1985—, Nartron Corp., Reed City, Mich., 1968—; chmn. Nonometal LLC, Birmingham, Mich., 2004—. Bd. of control Mich. Tech. U., Houghton, Mich., 2002—. Cpt. USAF, 1954—60. Mem.: IEEE (sr.). Office: Nartron Corp 5000 N US 131 Reed City MI 49677 Office Phone: 231-832-5525. Business E-mail: hhuber@nartron.com.

RAUWERDINK, WILLIAM JAY, accountant; b. Sheboygan, Wis., Mar. 3, 1950; s. Harvard M. and Dorothy M. (Duenk) R.; m. Ann Catherine Geske, July 14, 1979; 1 child, Margaret Allene. BBA, U. Wis., 1972; MBA, Harvard U., 1974. CPA, N.Y., Mich., Mass. Ptnr. Deloitte & Touche, Detroit, 1978—93; exec. v.p., CFO, treas., sec. The MEDSTAT Group, Inc., Ann Arbor, Mich., 1994—96, Lason, Inc., Troy, Mich., 1996—2000; exec. v.p., CFO, treas. Hotwire.com, San Francisco, 2001; interim pres., CFO, Gyricon, LLC, Ann Arbor, 2002—04; mng. dir. BAM Investments, LLC, West Bloomfield, Mich., 2005—. Bd. dirs. Trinity Health Svcs., Novi, Mich. Mem. Wis. Bus. Alumni Assn. (bd. dirs. 1980-89, 92—), pres. 1984-85), Harvard Club (Boston). Mailing: 5382 Pembrooke Crossing Ct West Bloomfield MI 48322

RAVAL, ALPAN, computational biologist, mathematics professor; b. Bhavnagar, Gujarat, India, July 19, 1968; s. Piyush and Daksha Raval; m. Sonal Majeethia, June 21, 1997; 1 child, Adi. MS, Indian Inst. Tech., Kanpur, 1990; PhD, U. Md., 1996. Postdoctoral assoc. gravitational physics U. Wis., Milw., 1996—2000; postdoctoral fellow, bioinformatics Keck Grad. Inst., Claremont, Calif., 2000—02, asst. prof. computational biology, 2002—; asst. prof. math. Claremont (Calif.) Grad. U., 2002—. Dir. computational sci. Claremont Grad. U., 2002—. Contbr. articles to profl. jours. Fellow, Can. Inst. Theoretical Astrophysics, 1996—. Office: Keck Grad Inst 535 Watson Dr Claremont CA 91711 Personal E-mail: araval@kgi.edu.

RAVECHÉ, HAROLD JOSEPH, academic administrator; b. NYC, Mar. 18, 1943; s. Harold Edward Raveche and Helen Patricia (DeVincent) Gravino; m. Elizabeth Marie Scott, Jan. 26, 1974; children— John Vincent, Justin Blaise, Bernice Helen, Elizabeth Ann. BA in Chemistry, Hofstra U., 1963; PhD in Phys. Chemistry, U. Calif.-San Diego, 1968. NRC postdoctoral assoc. Nat. Bur. Standards, Gaithersburg, Md., 1968-70, research chemist, 1970-78, chief thermophysics div., 1978-85; dean Sch. of Sci., prof. chemistry Rensselaer Poly. Inst., Troy, NY, 1985-88; pres. Stevens Inst. Tech., Hoboken, NJ, 1988—. Bd. dirs. Nat. West N.J. and Bancorp, Atlantic Energy Inc.; commr. of sci. and tech., N.J. Editor: Perspectives in Statistical Physics, 1980; contbr. articles to profl. jours. Pres. Potomac Highlands Citizens Assn., Md., 1978-80 Recipient Disting. Young Scientist of Yr. award Md. Acad. Scis., 1975, U.S. Sr. Exec. Service award Nat. Bur. Standards, 1983, Equal Employment Opportunity award Nat. Bur. Standards, 1984 Mem. AAAS (commn. on sci. edn. 1972-75), Am. Phys. Soc. (adv. council 1975-78), Soc. for Indsl. and Applied Math. (adv. bd. conf. on large-scale computational problems 1984-88), Am. Chem. Soc., Sigma Xi Roman Catholic. Avocations: hiking, swimming, skiing, music, theater. Office: Stevens Inst Tech Office of Pres Castle Point On Hudson Hoboken NJ 07030 E-mail: hraveche@stevens.edu.*

RAVEN, ABBE, broadcast executive; b. New York, 1953; 1 child. BA in Theater, U. Buffalo, 1974; MA in Cinema and Theater, Hunter Coll. Prodn. mgr., stage mgr. Manhattan Theater Club, Bklyn. Acad. Music, N.Y.C.; mgr. prodn. Hearst/ABC Video Svcs.; dir. prodn. svcs. A&E TV Networks, 1984-88, sr. v.p. prodn., 1988—95; sr. v.p. programming and prodn. The History Channel and HTV Prodns., 1995-97; sr. v.p. programming The History Channel, 1997—2000, gen. mgr., exec. v.p., 2000—02, A&E Network-USA, pres., 2004—05; pres., CEO A&E Television Networks, 2005—. Instr. various ednl. instns. Active Competition Com. CableACE Awards, chair 12 Ann. Ceremonies; active coms. focusing on violence in TV. Named to Hunter Coll. Hall of Fame; recipient U. Buffalo Alumni award, National History Day Org. Corp. Leadership Award, 2000. Mem. NATAS, Women in Cable, Am. Women in Radio and TV, PROMAX, Nat. Acad. Cable Programming. Office: A&E TV Networks The Hearst Corp 235 E 45th St 9th Fl New York NY 10017-3305*

RAVEN, BERTRAM H(ERBERT), psychology professor; b. Youngstown, Ohio, Sept. 26, 1926; s. Morris and Lillian R.; m. Celia Cutler, Jan. 21, 1961; children: Michelle G., Jonathan H. BA in psychology summa cum laude with great distinction, Ohio State U., 1949, MA in psychology, 1950; PhD in social psychology, U. Mich., 1953. Rsch. assoc. Rsch. Ctr. for Group Dynamics, Ann Arbor, Mich., 1952-54; lectr. psychology U. Mich., Ann Arbor, 1953-54; vis. prof. U. Nijmegen, U. Utrecht, Netherlands, 1954-55; psychologist RAND Corp., Santa Monica, Calif., 1955-56; prof. UCLA, 1956—, chair dept. psychology, 1983-88, prof. emeritus 1991—. Vis. prof. Hebrew U., Jerusalem, 1962-63, U. Wash., Seattle, 1965, U. Hawaii, Honolulu, 1968, London Sch. Econs. and Polit. Sci., 1969-70; external examiner U. of the W.I., Trinidad and Jamaica, 1980—, rsch. assoc. Psychol. Rsch. Ctr., 1993—; participant Internat. Expert Conf. on Health Psychology, Tilburg, Netherlands, 1986; cons., expert witness in field, 1979—; mem. internat. adv. bd. Acad. Freedom, Bar-Ilan U., 2005—; mem. sci. bd. Kurt Lewin Ctr. Psychol. Rsch. Kazimierza Wielkiego U., Poland. Author: (with others) People in Groups, 1976, Discovering Psychology, 1977, Social Psychology, 1983, Social Psychology: People in Groups (Chinese edit.), 1994; editor: (with others) Contemporary Health Services, 1982, Policy Studies Rev. Ann., 1980; editor: Jour. Social Issues, 1969-74; mem. editl. bd. Jour. of Criminology and Social Psychology, 2001-, Revista de Psicologia de la Salud, 1995-; mem. adv. bd. Jour. Entrepreneurship, 2004-; contbr. articles to profl. jours. Co-dir. Tng. Program in Health Psychology, UCLA, 1979-88; cons. WHO, Manila, 1985-86; cons., expert witness various Calif. cts., 1978—. Guggenheim fellow, Israel, 1962-63; Fulbright scholar Netherlands, 1954-55, Israel, 1962-63, Britain, 1969-70; recipient Citation from L.A. City Coun., 1966, Rsch. on Soc. power by Calif. Sch. of profl. psychology, L.A., 1991; NATO sr. fellow, Italy, 1989. Fellow APA (chair bd. social and ethical responsibility 1978-82, ethics com. 2003—), Am. Psychol. Soc., Soc. for Psychol. Study of Social Issues (pres. 1973-74, coun. 1995-97, Kurt Lewin award 1998), Soc. for Personality and Social Psychology; mem. AAAS, Am. Sociol. Assn., Internat. Assn. Applied Psychology, Soc. Exptl. Social Psychology, Assn. Advancement of Psychology (founding, bd. dirs. 1974-81), Internat. Soc. Polit. Psychology (governing coun. 1996-98), Interam. Psychol. Soc., Am. Psychology-Law Soc., Psychologists for Social Responsibility. Democrat. Jewish. Avocations: guitar, travel, international studies. Home: 2212 Camden Ave Los Angeles CA 90064-1906 Office: UCLA Dept Psychology Los Angeles CA 90095-1563 Office Phone: 310-825-2296. Business E-Mail: raven@ucla.edu.

**RAVEN, FRANCIS HARVEY,** mechanical engineer, educator; b. Erie, Pa., July 29, 1928; s. Frederick James and Eleanor Elizabeth (Sopp) R.; m. Therese Mary Strobel, June 21, 1952; children: Betty, Ann Raven McCarthy, Paul, Cydne, John, Anne, Mary Raven Mansmann, Cathy, Linda. BS in Math., Gannon U., Erie, Pa., 1948; BSME, Pa. State U., University Park, 1950, MSME, 1951; PhD, Cornell U., Ithaca, N.Y., 1958. Design engr. Hamilton Standard div. United Techns., Hartford, Conn., 1951-54; instr. Cornell U., Ithaca, N.Y., 1954-58; asst. prof. mech. engring. U. Notre Dame, 1958-62, assoc. prof., 1962-66, prof., 1966—. Cons. microprocessor and computer control of robots and mech. systems; devel. Vector Loop Method (first analytical method for the design of mechanisms and cam systems.). Author: Automatic Control Engineering, 1961, 5th edit., 1995, Mathematics of Engineering Systems, 1966, Engineering Mechanics, 1973; pub. McGraw-Hill Book Co. Mem. ASME, Am. Soc. for Engring. Edn. (AT&T Teaching award 1968-69), Sigma Xi. Roman Catholic. Office Phone: 574-631-7381. Business E-Mail: fraven@nd.edu.

**RAVEN, LUISA ANTONIA,** psychotherapist, nurse; b. N.Y.C., Sept. 25, 1939; d. Joseph A. and Mary Louise (Swann) R. BSN, St. Louis U., 1976; BA in Edn., Caldwell Coll., NJ, 1970; MSN, Columbia U., 1982. RN, N.J. Joined Order Sisters of St. Joseph of Peace, Roman Cath. Ch., 1962. Pvt. practice nurse psychotherapist, Englewood Cliffs, N.J.; instr. nursing Felician Coll., Lodi, N.J.; clin. specialist psychiat. nursing Greystone Park (N.J.) Psychiat. Hosp.; staff nurse med./surg. psychiat. unit St. Mary's Hosp., Passaic, NJ. Adj. faculty Bergen C.C., Paramus, N.J. Mem. N.J. Nurses Assn. (Psychiat. Nurse of Yr. award 1984), Sigma Theta Tau, Alpha Sigma Nu. Home: 5 Oakdale Manor Apt B18 Suffern NY 10901-5700 Office Phone: 201-871-2266.

**RAVEN, PATRICIA ELAINE (PENNY RAVEN),** real estate broker, developer, columnist, gas industry executive; b. Oakland, Calif., Apr. 27, 1943; d. Allen James and Patricia Elaine (McClure) Nichelini; m. Larry Joseph Raven June 15, 1963; children: Laurence Tagge Allen, Corbyn Lance. Student, U. So. Calif., 1961—62, U. Calif., Fresno 1962—63, Fresno City Coll., 1973. Model, Fresno Calif., 1960—; owner, operator Del Mar Motel and apts., Fresno, 1963—64; owner R Pantry Markets, 1965—72, v.p., 1968—72; owner Holy Cow Meat Markets, Fresno, 1965—72; real estate salesman, developer, 1973; real estate broker, owner The Raven Co., Fresno, 1974—; v.p. Raven Devel., Inc., 1980—; owner Raven Alcohol Distillery, 1979—89; pres. Am. Gasohol, Inc., 1980—; spl. events com. Royal Cruise Line, 1986. Columnist: Party Line, Fresno Bee, 1978—87, Central Valley Homes & Lifestyles, 2003—, contbg. editor Fresno Mag., 2003—; actress: (TV miniseries) Fresno, 1986; co-author: National Handbook on Toll Roads, 1977; actress: (films) Pretty Woman, 1989; Princess Diaries 2, 2004; contbg. editor: Fresno Weekly, 2001—02. Pres. Fresno Cancer League, 1972—73; Jackson Sch. PTA, 1980—82; hon mem. Fresno Zool. Soc.; commr. Fresno County Hist. Landmarks and Records Commn., 2005—; Democratic candidate for lt. gov. Calif., 1978; Fresno County Dem. ctrl. com. alt., 1977; bd. dirs. Women's Symphony League, 1973—74; pres. Huntington Blvd. Homeowners Hist. Assn., 1987—97, officer, 1997—. Named Betty Crocker Homemaker of Tomorrow, 1961; recipient Mayor's award, 1976, Hon. Svc. award, Jackson Sch. PTA, 1982, Appreciation award, United Cerebral Palsy Assn., 1982—86, Fresno Zool. Soc., 1982, Calif. State Senate, 1983, San Joaquin chpt. Assn. Gen. Contractors, 1983, Holland Sch., 1984, Huntington Blvd. Neighbors, 1985, proclamation in her honor, City of Fresno, 1985, others, San Joaquin Valley's Most Fashionable award, 1984, Appreciation award, Huntington Blvd. Neighbors, 1986, hon. mayor, City of Fresno, 1986. Roman Catholic. Home: 3504 E Huntington Blvd Fresno CA 93702-3224

**RAVENAL, EARL CEDRIC,** international relations educator, writer; b. NYC, Mar. 29, 1931; s. Alan M. and Mildred S. (Sherman) R.; m. Carol Bird Myers, May 26, 1956; children: Cornelia Jane, John Brodhead, Rebecca Eliza. BA, Harvard U., 1952; postgrad., U. Cambridge, Eng., 1952-53; M.M.P. diploma, Harvard Bus. Sch., 1958; MA, Johns Hopkins U., 1971, PhD, 1975. Treas. Elbe File & Binder Co., Inc., Fall River, Mass., 1955-64, pres., 1965-67; dir. Asian div. systems analysis Office Sec. Def., Washington, 1967-69; prof. internat. relations Johns Hopkins U. Sch. Advanced Internat. Studies, Washington, 1973-78, Georgetown U. Sch. Fgn. Service, Washington, 1976—. Bd. advisors Ctr. for Def. Info., Washington, 1971-97, Ctr. for Study Conflict, 1983—; bd. dirs. Critical Rev. Author: (with others) Peace with China?, 1971, (with others) Atlantis Lost, 1976, Never Again, 1979, Toward World Security, 1978, Strategic Disengagement and World Peace, 1979, NATO's Unremarked Demise, 1979, Defining Def., 1984, NATO: The Tides of Discontent, 1985, Large-Scale Foreign Policy Change, 1989, Designing Defense, 1991, Defending America in an Uncontrollable World, 2002; contbg. editor Inquiry Mag., 1976-85, Critical Rev., 1987—; contbr. articles to profl. jours Advisor Democratic Prendl. Campaign, 1977, advisor Jerry Brown Presdl. Campaign, 1976, Libertarian Presdl. Campaigns, 1980, 84. Served with JAGC U.S. Army, 1953-55. Henry fellow U. Cambridge, 1952-53; mem. faculty Salzburg Seminar in Am. Studies, 1977; fellow Bellagio Ctr. Rockefeller Found., 1975, Woodrow Wilson Internat. Ctr. for Scholars, 1973, Washington Ctr. of Fgn. Policy Research, 1974; sr. fellow Cato Inst., 1985-91, 97—. Mem. Council Fgn. Relations, Am. Polit. Sci. Assn., Internat. Inst. Strategic Studies, Fed. Am. Scientists, Internat. Studies Assn. Clubs: Cosmos (Washington); Fed. City (Washington); Harvard (N.Y.C.); Signet (Cambridge, Mass.); Tred Avon Yacht (Oxford, Md.). Libertarian. Home and Office: 4439 Cathedral Ave NW Washington DC 20016-3562

**RAVENAL, JOHN B.,** curator; BA in art history, Wesleyan U., 1982; MA in art history, Columbia U., 1987, MPhil in art history, 1990. Rschr. in contemporary art Wadsworth Atheneum, Hartford, Conn., 1982—85; asst. curator 20th-century art Phila. Mus. Art, 1991—97, assoc. curator 20th-century art, 1997—98; curator of modern and contemporary art Va. Mus. Fine Arts, Richmond, 1998—. Curator (exhibitions) robert lazzarini, Va. Mus. Fine Arts, 2003—04 (Award for Best Exhbn. of Digital Art, Assn. Independent Art Critics/USA, 2005). Office: Va Mus Fine Arts 200 N Blvd Richmond VA 23220-4007 Office Phone: 804-340-1606.

**RAVENEL, SHANNON,** book publishing professional; b. Charlotte, NC, Aug. 13, 1938; d. Elias Prioleau and Harriett Shannon (Steedman) R.; m. Dale Purves, May 25, 1968; children: Sara Blake, Harriett. BA, Hollins Coll., 1960. Mktg. asst., sch. dept. Holt, Rinehart & Winston, Inc., NYC, 1960-61; editl. asst. Houghton Mifflin Co., Boston, 1961-64, editor, 1964—70; editl. cons. pvt. practice, St. Louis, 1973-90; sr. editor, co-founder Algonquin Books of Chapel Hill, NC, 1982-91, editl. dir., 1992-2000; dir. Algonquin imprint Shannon Ravenel Books, 2001—. Series editor: Best American Short Stories, 1978-90; editor: Best American Short Stories of the Eighties, 1990, New Stories From the South, 1986-2005 Recipient Disting. Achievement award Coun. Lit. Mags. & Presses, NYC, 1990, R. Hunt Parker Meml. award for contbns. to the lit. of N.C., 2004. Mem. PEN Am. Ctr. Democrat. Office: Algonquin Books of Chapel Hill PO Box 2225 Chapel Hill NC 27515-2225 Business E-Mail: shannonr@algonquin.com.

**RAVENELL, KENNETH W.,** lawyer; b. Cross, SC, May 9, 1959; BA cum laude, SC State Coll., 1981; JD, U. Md., 1985. Bar: Md. 1985, U.S. Dist. Ct. (Md. dist.) 1990, U.S. Dist. Ct. (DC dist.). Asst. editor U. Md. Law Forum, 1983—84; asst. states atty. Balt., 1985—88; ptnr. Schulman, Treem, Kaminkov, Gilden & Ravenell P.A., Balt. Mem. jud. nominating. com. Trial Courts; instr. bar exam tutorial program U. Md., 1987—90. Named one of Balt.'s Top Lawyers, Balt. Mag., 2003, Top Criminal Lawyers in Balt., 2004. Mem.: Fed. Bar Assn., Am. Bar Assn. Balt. City, Md. Criminal Def. Attys. Assn., Monumental Bar Assn., Md. State Bar Assn. Office: Schulman Treem Kaminkow Gilden & Ravenell PA The Balt Inner Harbor World Trade Ctr 401 E Pratt St Ste 1800 Baltimore MD 21202-3004 Office Phone: 410-659-0111. Office Fax: 410-332-0866. E-mail: dness@stkgrlaw.com.

**RAVENHOLT, REIMERT THOROLF,** epidemiologist, researcher; b. Milltown, Wis., Mar. 9, 1925; s. Ansgar Benedikt and Kristine Henriette (Petersen) R.; divorced; children: Janna, Mark, Lisa, Dane; m. Betty Butler Howell, Sept. 26, 1981. BS, U. Minn., 1948, MB, 1951, MD, 1952; MPH, U. Calif., Berkeley, 1956. Bd. cert. preventive medicine. Intern USPHS Hosp., San Francisco, 1951-52; epidemic intelligence service officer USPHS Communicable Disease Ctr., Atlanta, 1952-54; dir. epidemiology and communicable disease div. Seattle-King County Health Dept., 1954-61; epidemiology cons. European area USPHS, Paris, 1961-63; assoc. prof. preventive medicine U. Wash. Med. Sch., Seattle, 1963-66; dir. Office of Population, AID, Washington, 1966-79, World Health Surveys, Ctrs. for Disease Control, 1980-82; asst. dir. epidemiology and research Nat. Inst. Drug Abuse, Rockville, Md., 1982-84; chief epidemiology br. FDA, Rockville, Md., 1984-87; dir. World Health Surveys, Inc., Seattle, 1987-93; pres Population Health Imperatives, Seattle, 1993—. Author/designer website Adventures in Epidemiology. Served with USPHS, 1951-54, 61-63. Recipient Disting Honor award AID, 1973, Hugh Moore Meml. award IPPF and Population Crisis Com., 1974. Fellow Am. Coll. Epidemiology, APHA (Carl Schultz award 1978), mem. Am. Coun. on Sci. and Health (bd. dirs.); mem. Cosmos Club (Washington). Independent. Achievements include discovery of cause of Meriwether Lewis' death of progressive neurosyphilis. Home: 3156 E Laurelhurst Dr NE Seattle WA 98105-5333 Office Phone: 206-525-8479. E-mail: ravenrt@oz.net.

**RAVENSTAHL, LUKE R.,** mayor; b. Pitts., Pa., Feb. 6, 1980; s. Robert P. and Cindy Ravenstahl; m. Erin Lynn Feith, July 2004. Attended, Mercyhurst Coll., U. Pitts.; BBA with honors, Washington and Jefferson Coll., 2002. Account mgr. for courier svc.; mem., Coun. Dist. 1 Pitts. City Coun., 2004—05, pres., 2005—06; mayor City of Pitts., 2006—. Bd. mem. City of Pitts. Mcpl. Pension Fund. Bd. pres. Neighborhood Enterprises; mem. Allegheney County Democratic Com., 1998—2004; bd. mem. Fireman's Relief and Pension Fund, Comprehensive Mcpl. Pension Trust Fund., Pitts. Cultural Trust, Sports and Exhbn. Authority, Carnegie Libr.; bd. trustee Carnegie Mellon U.; mem. adv. bd. North Catholic HS; mem. Northside Cmty. Develop. Fund, City-County Summit Com. of Pub. Works, Parks, and Facilities. Office: Rm 512 City County Bldg 414 Grant St Pittsburgh PA 15219 Office Phone: 412-255-2626. Office Fax: 412-255-2687. Business E-Mail: mayorcompl@city.pittsburgh.pa.us.*

**RAVETCH, IRVING,** screenwriter; b. Newark, Nov. 14, 1920; s. I. Shalom and Sylvia (Shapiro) R.; m. Harriet Frank Jr., Nov. 24, 1946. BA, UCLA, 1941. Screenwriter: (films) (with La Cava) Living in a Big Way, 1947, The Outriders, 1950, Vengeance Valley, 1951; (with Harriet Frank, Jr.) The Long, Hot Summer, 1958, The Sound and the Fury, 1959, Home from the Hill, 1959, The Dark at the Top of the Stairs, 1960, House of Cards, 1969, The Cowboys, 1972, Conrack, 1974, The Spikes Gang, 1974, Norma Rae, 1979 (Academy award nomination best adapted screenplay 1979), Murphy's Romance, 1985, Stanley and Iris, 1990; writer, prodr.: (with Frank) Hud, 1963 (Academy award nomination best adapted screenplay 1963, N.Y. Film Critics Circle award best screenplay 1963), Hombre, 1967, The Reivers, 1969; story: (with Frank) Ten Wanted Men, 1955. Recipient N.Y. Film Critics award, 1963, Writers' Guild Am. award, 1988; Oscar nomination for Hud, Acad. Motion Picture Arts and Scis., 1963, Norma Rae, 1979.

**RAVETCH, JEFFREY VICTOR,** molecular biologist, immunologist, educator; s. Sylvia and Paul H. Ravetch; m. Wendy Evans Joseph, Oct. 27, 2001. Grad., Yale U., New Haven; PhD in Genetics, Rockefeller U.; MD, Cornell U. Postdoctoral rschr. NIH; mem. faculty Meml. Sloan-Kettering Cancer Ctr. and Cornell Med. Coll., 1982; Theresa and Eugene M. Lang prof. Rockefeller U., NYC. Mem. sci. adv. bd. Cancer Rsch. Inst., Irvington Inst. Med. Rsch., Damon Runyon Found.; co-founder, dir. MacroGenics, Rockville, Md., 2000—. Contbr. articles to profl. jours. Named a Pew Scholar, 1985. Fellow: NAS. Office: Leonard Wagner Lab Molecular Genetics and Immunology Rockefeller U 1230 York Ave New York NY 10021 E-mail: ravetch@rockefeller.edu.*

**RAVICHANDRAN, PASALA SANKARAN,** cardiologist, thoracic surgeon, educator; b. Madras, India, June 29, 1955; arrived in US, 1989; s. Pasala Subramanyann and Maha Lakshmi Sankaran; m. Cheryl Ravi Smith, Dec. 24, 1992; 2 children. MBBS, Madras Med. Coll., India, 1977. Diplomate Am. Bd. Hosp. Physicians. Rotating resident medicine, surgery Gov. Gen. Hosp., Madras, India, 1978—79; resident gen. surgery, cardiovascular, thoracic surgery, 1979—80; clin. faculty, cardiac, gen. surgery resident program, chief cardiothoracic surgery VA Med. Ctr., 1994—; assoc. prof. cardiothoracic surgery, 1999—; assoc. prof., dir. heart transplant ast. device program, asst. chief cardiothoracic surgery Oreg. Health and Scis. U., Portland, 1999—; registrar cardiovascular, thoracic surgery Freeman Hosp., Newcastle, England, 1981—82; SHO accident, emergency Tynemouth Infirmary, North Shields, 1982; SHO gen. surgery Preston Hosp. North Shields, 1982 83; SHO cardiothoracic surgery Wythenshawe Hosp., Manchester, England, 1983—84; Killingbeck Hosp., Leeds, England, 1984—85; registrar cardiovascular, thoracic surgery Gen. Infirmary, Leeds, 1985—87; sr. registrar cardiovascular, thoracic surgery, 1987—89; Bristol Royal Infirmary, England, 1989; clin. fellow cardiovascular, thoracic surgery St. Vincent's Hosp., Portland, Oreg., 1990—91; cardiac surgery fellow Barnes Hosp., Wash. U., St. Louis, 1991—92; sr. resident surgery St. Louis (Mo.) U. Hosp., 1992—93; cardiac rsch. fellow VA Rsch. Found., Portland, 1993—94; instr. Leeds (England) U., 1985—89. Vis. lectr. various U., India. Contbr. articles various profl. jours., scientific papers. Vol. Organ Donation Collaborative; prin. investigator Multicenter Rsch. Project. Recipient Gold medal in anatomy, VNC Rao, 1975, Kini Meml. prize in orthopedic surgery. Fellow: ACS, Am. Coll. Cardiology, Royal Coll. Surgeons; mem.: AMA (sec. 2005—), Western Thoracic Surgical Assn., Gen. Med. Coun., British Med. Assn., Royal Coll. Physicians and Surgeons, Internat. Soc. Heart And Lung Transplantation, Am. Coll. Cardiology, St. Louis U. Alumni Assn. Avocations: skiing, snowshoeing. Office: Oreg Health Scis U Divsn Cardiothoracic Surgery 3183 SW Sam Jackson Rd L353 Portland OR 97201 also: VA Med Ctr Surgery Dept P8CT 3710 SW U S Vet Hosp Rd Portland OR 97201 Office Phone: 503-494-7820.

**RAVINA, BERNARD MAYER,** neurologist; b. Queens, NY, Mar. 22, 1967; s. Oscar and Ruth Ravina; m. Joanna Ravina; children: Sam, Sophie, Leo. BA, Columbia U., 1989; MD, Johns Hopkins U., 1995. Program dir. Nat. Inst. Neurol. Disorders and Stroke, Bethesda, Md., 2001—05; assoc. prof. movement disorders U. Rochester, NY, 2005—. Contbr. articles to profl. jours.; mem. edit. bd.: Clin. Neuropharmacology. Mem. Dystonia Med. Rsch. Found., 2006, Friedreich Ataxia Rsch. Alliance. Mem.: Movement Disorders Soc., Am. Acad. Neurology, Phi Beta Kappa. Office: University of Rochester 1351 Mt Hope Ave Ste 223 Rochester NY 14620 Office Phone: 585-275-7430. Home Fax: 585-276-1870; Office Fax: 585-276-1870. Business E-Mail: bernard.ravina@ctcc.rochester.edu.

**RAVINSKY, ANTHONY,** music educator; s. Tony and Anna Ravinsky. MusB, Crane Sch. Music, 2003. Carpenter N.Y. Stage and Film, Poughkeepsie, 2002—04; choral dir. Cornwall (N.Y.) Ctrl. H.S., 2003—. Mem.: N.Y. State Theater Educators Assn., Music Educators Nat. Conf., Am. Choral Dir. Assn.

**RAVIPRAKASH, KANAKATTE,** molecular biologist; PhD, Indian Inst. Sci., Bangalore, 1985. Head molecular biology divsn., viral diseases dept. Naval Med. Rsch. Ctr., Silver Spring, Md., 1991—; rsch. assoc. prof. dept. medicine Uniformed Svcs. U. of Health Scis., Bethesda, Md., 1992—. Contbr. articles to profl. jours. Rsch. fellow, Cancer Rsch. Inst., NYC, 1988—91. Office Phone: 301-319-7454.

**RAVISHANKARA, AKKIHEBAL R.,** chemist; PhD, U. Fla., 1975. Chief atmospheric chem. kinetics group NOAA, Boulder, Colo. Adj. prof. dept. chemistry U. Colo., Boulder; postdoctoral rsch. assoc. U. Md., 1976. Named Robertson Meml. lectr., NAS, 1999. Office: DSRC Rm 1A123 325 Broadway Boulder CO 80305-3328

**RAWITCH, DIANE SILVERS,** historian, educator, writer, government official; b. Houston, July 1, 1938; d. Walter Cracker and Ann Celia (Katz) Silvers; m. Richard Ravitch, June 26, 1960 (div. 1986); children: Joseph, Steven (dec.), Michael. BA, Wellesley Coll., 1960; PhD, Columbia U., 1975; LHD (hon.), Williams Coll., 1984, Reed Coll., 1985, Amherst Coll., 1986, SUNY, 1988, Ramapo Coll., 1990, St. Joseph's Coll., N.Y., 1991, Middlebury Coll., 1997, Union Coll., 1998. Adj. asst. prof. Tchrs. Coll., Columbia U., N.Y.C., 1975-78, assoc. prof., 1978-83, adj. prof., 1983-91; asst. sec. office ednl. rsch. and improvement U.S. Dept. Edn., Washington, 1991-93, counselor to the sec. edn., 1991-93. Vis. fellow Brookings Instn., Washington, 1993-94, non-resident sr. fellow, 1994-, editor papers on edn. policy, 1997-05, Brown chair in edn. policy, 1997-05; rsch. prof. NYU, 1994-; mem. Nat. Assessment Governing Bd., 1997-04; com. on edn. policy Nat. Acad. Scis., 2003 05; mem. Koret task force Hoover Instn., 1999-, sr. fellow, 2005-. Author: The Great School Wars, 1974, The Revisionists Revised, 1977, The Troubled Crusade, 1983, The Schools We Deserve, 1985, National Standards in American Education, A Citizens Guide, 1995, Left Back, 2000, The Language Police, 2003; author: (with others) Educating an Urban People, 1981; author: The School and the City, 1983, Against Mediocrity, 1984, Challenges to the Humanities, 1985, What Do Our 17 Year Olds Know?, 1987; editor: The American Reader, 1990; co-editor: The Democracy Reader, 1992, New Schools for a New Century, 1997, City Schools, 2000, Making Good Citizens, 2001, Kid Stuff, 2003, Forgotten Heroes of American Education, 2006, The English Reader, 2006; editor: Learning from the Past, 1995, Debating the Future of American Education, 1995. Chair Ednl. Excellence Network, 1988—91, 1994—96; trustee Nat. Humanities Ctr., 1999—2000, N.Y. Pub. Libr., N.Y.C., 1981—87, hon. life trustee, 1988—; trustee N.Y. Coun. on Humanities, 1996—; mem. Landmarks Preservation Commn., Southold, NY, 2000—02; bd. dirs. Woodrow Wilson Nat. Fellowship Found., 1987—91, Coun. Basic Edn., 1989—91, Thomas B. Fordham Found., 1998—, New Am. Found., 2000—, Albert Shanker Inst., 2002—, Core Knowledge Found., 2003—, Hunt Inst. Ednl. Policy and Leadership, 2002—. Recipient Disting. Svc. award NY Acad. Pub. Edn., 1994, Alumnae Achievement award Wellesley Coll., 1989, Uncommon Book award Hoover Instn., 2004, John Dewey award United Fedn. Tchrs., 2005, Gaudium award Breukelein Inst., 2005, Pub. Svc. award Am. Jewish Hist. Soc., 2006; Guggenheim fellow, 1977-78; Phi Beta Kappa vis. scholar. Mem. Nat. Acad. Edn., Am. Acad. Arts and Scis., Soc. Am. Historians, N.Y. Hist. Soc. (trustee 1995-98), PEN Internat. Office: NYU 82 Wash Sq E New York NY 10003-6644

**RAVIV, GABRIEL,** medical products executive; BS, Hebrew U., Jerusalem, Israel, 1973; MSEE, Northwestern U., PhD in Elec. Engring. and Computer Sci. From officer to pres., CEO Bio-Logic Sys. Corp., Mundelein, Ill., 1979—81, pres., 1981—99, CEO, 1981—; bd. dir. Adj. prof. Northwestern U. Office: Bio Logic Systems Corp 1 Bio Logic Plaza Mundelein IL 60060

**RAWAL, DARSHAN LAL,** civil engineer, structural engineer, consultant; b. India, Nov. 12, 1934; arrived in U.S., 1966; s. Sodagar Mal and Kaushalya Devi Rawal; m. Raj Kumari, Dec. 5, 1956; children: Upma, Bela, Neeru. BSCE, M.U. Aligarh, U.P. India, 1957; MSCE, Utah State U., 1967; M in Engring. Adminstrn., Ill. Inst. Technology, Chgo., 1977. Registered profl. engr., Ill.; structural engr., Ill. Sr. civil engr. Ill. Dept. of Transp., 1967-73; sr. structural engr. Sargent & Lundy, Chgo., 1974-86, Brown & Root, Lombard, Ill., 1979-81, Stone & Webster Engring. Corp., N.Y.C., 1986—87; sr. engr. Ambitech Engring. Corp., Downers Grove, Ill., 1988—99, John Brown Engrs. & Constructor's, Chgo., 1991—94. Pres. Hindu Soc., Chgo., 1971—72, chmn. bd. trustees Medinah, Ill., 1994—97. Mem.: ASCE (life). Hindu. Achievements include civil/structural design and preparation of civil/structural drawings related to fossil/nuclear power plants, highways/bridges, petro chemical, steel industries and automobile dealership buildings. Home: 2078 Audubon Dr Glendale Heights IL 60139-1808 Personal E-mail: drawal1@yahoo.com.

**RAWAT, KULDEEP S.,** engineering educator; b. New Delhi, Nov. 4, 1975; arrived in U.S., 2000; s. Anand Singh and Laxmi Rawat. BSEE, Bombay U., 1997; MS in Computer Sci., U. La., Lafayette, 2001, MS in Computer Engring., 2003, PhD in Computer Engring., 2005. Rsch. assoc. Procter & Gamble R&D, Thane, India, 1997—99; rsch./grad. asst. U. La., 2000—03, adj. prof., 2003—04; asst. prof. Elizabeth City (NC) State U., 2004—. Cons., reviewer La. Bd. Regents, Baton Rouge, 2004—05; presenter at confs. in field. Contbr. articles to profl. jours. Mem.: IEEE, Am. Soc. Engring. Edn., IEEE Computer Soc., Nat. Assn. Indsl. Tech. (reviewer jour. 2006—). Achievements include research in low power VLSI design; video processing/compression, reconfigurable computing; VLSI for signal processing; design of data acquisition systems for control applications. Avocations: racquetball, tennis, cooking, road trips, travel. Office: Elizabeth City State U 1704 Weeksville Rd Elizabeth City NC 27909

**RAWDEN, DAVID,** financial services company executive; CFO, Peregine, Southfield, Mich., until 1999; prin. Jay Alix & Assocs., Southfield, 1999—. Office: Jay Alix and Associates 2000 Town Ctr Ste 2400 Southfield MI 48075-1250

**RAWITCH, ALLEN BARRY,** medical educator, academic administrator; b. Chgo., Dec. 29, 1940; s. Sam and Jean Rawitch; m. Patricia Nan Rawitch, July 21, 1962; children: Bruce, David. BS in Chemistry, UCLA, 1963, PhD in Biol. Chemistry, 1967. Rsch. fellow U. Ill., Urbana, 1967-69; asst. prof. Kent (Ohio) State U., 1969-73, assoc. prof., 1973-75, U. Kans. Med. Ctr., Kansas City, 1975-80, prof., 1980—, asst. dean student affairs, 1999-2000, vice chancellor acad. affairs, dean grad. studies, 2000—, chmn. biochemistry and molecular biology, 2002—03. Vice chair biochemistry U. Kans. Med. Ctr., 1977-95, chair edn. coun., 1995-99 Editor Med. Biochemistry Question Bank, 1985-94; contbr. articles to profl. jours. Res. police officer capt. Overland Park Police Dept., 1979—. Rsch. grant NIH, 1971-2000, NSF, 1970, Am. Heart Assn., 1998-2002. Mem. Am. Soc. for Biochemistry and Molecular Biology, The Protein Soc., Am. Thyroid Assn., Sigma Xi. Avocations: amateur radio, woodworking, target shooting. Office: Office Acad Affairs U Kans Med Ctr 3901 Rainbow Blvd Kansas City KS 66160-0001 Office Phone: 913-588-1258. Business E-Mail: arawitch@kumc.edu.

**RAWITCH, ROBERT JOE,** journalist, educator; b. LA, Oct. 11, 1945; s. Sam and Jean (Reifman) R.; m. Cynthia Z. Knee, Oct. 27, 1968; children: Dana Leigh, Jeremy Aaron, Joshua Eric. BA in Journalism, Calif. State U. Northridge, 1967; MS in Journalism, Northwestern U., 1968. Reporter L.A. Times, 1968-80, asst. metro. editor, 1980-82, editor Valley sect., 1982-83, suburban editor, 1983-89, exec. editor Valley and Ventura County edits., 1989-93; dir. editl. ops. Valley and Ventura County edits., 1993-95; sr. v.p. Winner and Assocs., 1996—. Lectr. Calif. State U., Northridge, 1971-83, 95-96, 03-. Co-author: Adat Ari El, The First Fifty Years, 1988. Chmn. Calif. Freedom of Info. Com., 1978-79; pres. Calif. First Amendment coalition, 1991-93; bd. dirs. Temple Adat Ari El, 1987-92, Calif. State U. Northridge Found., 1999-, Univ. Corp., 2000-. Recipient Greater L.A. Press Club award, 1973, 75, 79, L.A. Jewish Youth of Yr. award United Jewish Fund, 1963, Clarence Darrow Found. award, 1979, Heitz award outstanding vol. Calif. State U. Northridge, 2003. Mem. Soc. Profl. Journalists (nat. bd. dirs.

1979-82), Calif. Soc. Newspaper Editors (pres. 1995-96), Medill Alumni Assn. (bd. dirs. 1994-2000), CSUN Journalism Alumni Assn. (bd. dirs. 2002—). Office: Winner & Assocs 16501 Ventura Blvd Encino CA 91436-2007 Office Phone: 818-385-1900. Business E-Mail: brawitch@winnr.com.

**RAWL, ARTHUR JULIAN (LORD OF CURSONS)**, retail executive, consultant, accountant, writer; b. Boston, July 6, 1942; s. Philip and Evelyn (Rosoff) R.; m. Karen Lee Werby, June 4, 1967; 1 child, Kristen Alexandra. BBA, Boston U., 1967, postgrad, 1972-74; DBA, St. George's U., 2000. CPA, Mass., N.Y., La. Audit mgr. Touche Ross & Co., Boston, 1967-77, N.Y.C., 1977-79, ptnr., 1979, Newark, 1980-88, N.Y.C., 1988-89, Deloite & Touche, N.Y.C., 1989-90; exec. v.p., CFO Hanlin Group, Inc., Linden, NJ, 1990-94, United Auto Group, Inc., NYC, 1994-97; pres., CEO, bd. dirs. Brazil Internat. Motors, Brazil Am. Auto Group, São Paulo, 1999—2003; chmn., CEO Auto Alliance, Englewood, NJ, 2003—, Rawl & Assocs., Miami, Fla., 2003—. Bd. dirs. BiakalInterPlast (USSR), Kuperwood Enterprises, Hanlin Group, Inc., Quipp, Inc., 2004—; mem. adj. faculty Boston U., 1971-75. Contbr. articles to profl. journals, mags. and trade publs. Mem. Newton Upper Falls (Mass.) Hist. Commn., 1977; bd. dirs. Sherburne Scholarship Fund Boston U., 1977-80; mem. Englewood (N.J.) Planning Bd., 1981-83; trustee Englewood Bd. Edn., 1983-85, 89-93, pres., 1991-92; trustee, treas. exec. com. Englewood Econ. Devel. Corp., 1986-89; fin. and compensation com. Dwight Englewood Sch., 1985-90; mem. parent devel. com. Mt. Holyoke Coll., 1991-94; chmn. Brit. Meml. Garden Trust, 2003—. Served to 2d class petty officer USN, 1960-63. Fellow AICPA, Mass. Soc. CPAs, N.Y. Soc. CPAs; mem. VFW, Am. Legion, Navy League U.S., N.J. Hist. Soc. (bd. govs., exec. com., nominating com., treas. 1987-99), St. George's Soc. N.Y. (treas. exec. com. 1998-2005), H.M. Sovereign Order of St. John, Coll. Arms Found. (v.p. 2001—), The Most Venerable Order of the Hosp. of St. John of Jerusalem, Most Excellent Order of the Brit. Empire, Univ. Club, Essex Club, Sloane Club (London). Home: 1581 Brickell Ave Ste 1003 Miami FL 33129 E-mail: a.rawl@att.net.

**RAWLINGS, GREGORY OWEN**, science educator, consultant; b. Roswell, N.Mex., Jan. 29, 1951; s. Vernon Keith and Mildred Mary Rawlings; m. Virginia Lee Murphy, Oct. 25, 1985; 1 child, Stephanie Janiece. BS, U. of Kans., 1973. Cert. edn. Kans. State Dept. of Edn. Intermediate sci. tchr. Unified Sch. Dist. #497, Lawrence, Kans., 1973—78, Unified Sch. Dist. #305, Salina, Kans., 1978—82; asst. mgr., cashier supr. Wal-Mart #558, Salina, 1983—84; account rep. Burroughs Computer Corp., Rochester, NY, 1984—85; tchr. 8th grade earth sci. and algebra Unified Sch. Dist. 469, Lansing, Kans., 1986—. Resource person Harvard-Smithsonian Ctr. for Astrophysics - Project ESTEEM. Mem. Dist. Site Coun., Lansing, 1995—2002, Dist. Steering Com., Lansing, 1986—94; mem. blue ribbon adv. bd. ShareNet Pan Ednl. Inst., Independence, Mo., 1989—93. Mem.: NEA, Kans. Nat. Edn. Assn. (adminstrv. bd. dirs. 2003—04), Nat. Sci. Tchrs. Assn. Home: 210 Jayhawk Ct Lansing KS 66043-1811 Office: USD 509 - Lansing Mid Sch 509 Ida Lansing KS 66043-1522 Personal E-mail: vrawlings@csiweb.com.

**RAWLINGS, HUNTER RIPLEY, III**, classicist, former academic administrator; b. Norfolk, Va., Dec. 14, 1944; m. Elizabeth Trapnell Rawlings; 4 children. BA, Haverford Coll., 1966; PhD Classics, Princeton U., 1970. Asst. prof. U. Colo., Boulder, 1970—75, assoc. prof., 1975—80, prof. classics, 1980—88, v.p. acad. affairs, rsch., dean System Grad. Sch., 1984—88; pres. U. Iowa, 1988—95, Cornell U., Ithaca, NY, 1995—2003, prof. greek classics, 1995—, pres. emeritus, 2003—, interim pres., 2005—06. Chair Iowa Commn. Fgn. Lang. Studies and Internat. Edn., 1988—91; bd. dirs. Tokpkins County Trust Co.; bd. dirs. Brookhaven Sci. Assocs. Author: The Structure of Thucydides' History, 1981; editor-in-chief: Classical Jour., 1977—83; contbr. articles to profl. jours. Norwest Bank Iowa N.A., 1988—95. Fellow, Ctr. Hellenic Studies, 1975—76. Fellow: Am. Acad. Arts and Scis.; mem.: Nat. Fgn. Lang. Ctr. (mem. nat. adv. bd. 1995—), Am. Coun. Edn. (bd. dirs. 1994—97), Assn. Am. Univs. (exec. com. 1990—92). Home: 54 Woodard RD Newfield NY 14867-9267 Office: Cornell U Dept Classics 120 Goldwin Smith Hall Ithaca NY 14853-3201*

**RAWLINGS, PAUL C.**, retired government official; b. Cave City, Ark., June 21, 1928; s. Otha A. and Leona (King) R.; m. Catherine Terral, 1951 (div. 1970); children: William A., Rebecca, Neal; m. Erma Martin, June 20, 1971 (div. Jan. 1997). Grad., Little Rock Jr. Coll.; LL.B., Ark. Law Sch., 1950. Bar: Ark. 1950. Practiced in Little Rock, 1950, 52-73; adminstrv. law judge Office Hearings and Appeals, Social Security Adminstrn., HEW, Hattiesburg, Miss., 1973-92; ret. adminstrv. law judge sr. status, 1992; partner firm Terral, Rawlings, Matthews & Purtle, until 1973. Asst. atty. gen., Ark., 1955-56 Bd. dirs. Ark. Enterprises for Blind, Partel Ark. del. White House Conf. on Aging, 1995. Served with AUS, 1950-52 Mem. Ark. Bar Assn., Law Sci. Acad. Methodist (past chmn. bd. adminstrn., trustee). Club: Lion (past pres.). Home: 100 # 14 Swinging Bridge Dr Heber Springs AR 72543-8717

**RAWLINS, DONALD RAY**, lawyer; b. Dyersburg, Tenn., Apr. 28, 1965; s. Dal M. and Rebecca S. Rawlins. BBA, U. Memphis, 1987; JD, Am. U., 1990. Bar: Tenn., 1990. V.p., asst. gen. counsel, asst. sec. AutoZone, Inc., Memphis, 1990—2004; asst. gen. counsel Thomas & Betts Corp., Memphis, 2004—05, asst. sec., 2004—05, chief compliance officer, 2004—05. Vice chmn. Memphis Landmarks Commn., 2004—05. Recipient Best Brief award ATLA, 1990. Republican. Methodist. Home: 102 Savannah Dr Matthews NC 28105

**RAWLINS, V. LANE**, academic administrator; b. Rigby, Idaho, Nov. 30, 1937; m. Mary Jo Rawlins, three children. BA in Economics, Brigham Young U., 1963; PhD in Economics, U of Calif., Berkeley, 1969. Faculty Wash. State U., Pullman, 1968-86, chair. economics, 1977-82, vice provost, 1982—86; vice chancellor, academic affairs U. of Alabama, 1986-91; pres. Memphis St. U., Memphis, 1991-00, Wash. State U., Pullman, 2000—. Office: Washington State U Office Pres PO Box 641048 Pullman WA 99164-1048 E-mail: rawlins@wsu.edu.*

**RAWLINS, W. SCOTT**, art educator; b. New Brunswick, NJ, Oct. 28, 1954; s. Stokes Sheldon and Hazel Mae Rawlins. BA in Biology, Earlham Coll., Richmond, Ind., 1976; MA in Tchr. in Museum Edn., George Washington U., Washington, 1981; MFA in Med. Illustration, U. Mich., Ann Arbor, 1989. Cert. EMT. Asst. curator natural sci. Children's Mus., Indpls., 1978—79; ednl. cons., exhibit designer Trailside Mus. and Sci. Ctr., Mountainside, NJ, 1981—82; dir. edn. Calvert Marine Mus., Solomons, Md., 1982—86; curator natural sci. Pub. Mus. Grand Rapids, Mich., 1990—94; from asst. prof. to assoc. prof., chair fine arts dept. Aquinas U., Glenside, Pa., 1994—. Adj. prof. Kendall Coll. Art and Design, Grand Rapids, 1990—94; contractor Nat. Mus. Natural History, Washington, 1981—82. Contbg. author: The Guild Handbook of Scientific Illustration, 2003. Canvasser Move On, Pa., 2004. Mem.: Am. Assn. Museums, Guild Natural Sci. Illustrators (bd. dirs., dir. edn., Members' Choice award 2002), Am. Soc. Bot. Artists (bd. dirs., pres.). Phi Kappa Phi. Office: Arcadia U Dept Fine Arts 450 S Easton Rd Glenside PA 19038

**RAWLINSON, HELEN ANN**, librarian; b. Columbia, S.C., Mar. 30, 1948; d. Alfred Harris and Mary Taylor (Moon) R. BA, U. S.C., 1970; MLS, Emory U., 1972. Asst. children's librarian Greenville (S.C.) County Library, 1972-74, br. supr., 1974-76, asst. head extension div., 1976-78; children's room librarian Richland County Pub. Library, 1978-81, sr. adult services librarian, 1981-82, chief adult services, 1982-85, dep. dir., 1985—. Mem. adv. com. S.C. Pre-White House Conf. on Libr. and Info. Svcs., chmn. program com. Recipient Outstanding S.C. Librarian award by S.C. Library Assn., 1998. Mem. ALA, S.E. Libr. Assn., S.C. Libr. Assn. (2d v.p. 1987-89, editl. com. 1993, chmn. pub. libr. sect. 1995), U. S.C. Thomas Cooper Soc. (bd. dirs., v.p., pres.-elect, pres.). Baptist. Home: 1316 Guignard Ave West Columbia SC 29169-6137 Office: Richland County Pub Libr 1431 Assembly St Columbia SC 29201-3101 Office Phone: 803-799-9084. E-mail: harawlin@richland.lib.sc.us.

**RAWLINSON, JOHNNIE BLAKENEY**, federal judge; b. Concord, N.C., Dec. 16, 1952; BS in Psychology summa cum laude, NC A&T State U., 1974; JD, U. of Pacific, 1979. Private practice, Las Vegas, 1979—80; staff atty. Nevada Legal Services, 1980; from dep. dist. atty. to asst. dist. atty. Clark County Dist. Atty.'s Office, 1980—98; judge U.S. Dist. Ct. Nev., 1998—2000, U.S. Ct. Appeals (9th cir.), 2000—. Office: 333 Las Vegas Blvd S Rm 7072 Las Vegas NV 89101

**RAWLINSON, JOSEPH ELI**, foundation administrator, lawyer; b. Delta, Utah, May 9, 1915; s. Eli Wilford and Dora Pearl (Day) Rawlinson; m. Elaine Millicent Andersen, June 2, 1947; children: James, Joleine, Nancy, Rex, Anina, Cheryl, Mark, Lisa, David. BS, U. Utah, 1936; JD, Loyola U., 1958. CPA Calif.; bar: Calif. 1959. Agt. IRS, Wichita, Kans., 1938—52; acct. Serene Koster, Barbour, Calif., 1952—62; pvt. practice Calif., 1959; pres., CEO Fritz B. Burns Found., Burbank, Calif., 1980—. Recipient Silver medal, Am. Inst. Accts., 1942. Office: Fritz B Burns Found 4001 W Alameda Ave Ste 203 Burbank CA 91505-4338 Business E-Mail: josepheli@sbcglobal.net.

**RAWLINSON, NORA**, publishing executive; Dir. collection devel. County Public Libr., Balt.; editor Libr. Jour.; editor in chief Pubs. Weekly, NYC, 1992—2004; v.p. libr. svcs. Time Warner Book Group, NYC, 2005—. Office: Book Group Time Warner 1271 Ave of the Americas New York NY 10020

**RAWLS, FRANK MACKLIN**, lawyer; b. Suffolk, Va., Aug. 24, 1952; s. John Lewis and Mary Helen (Macklin) R.; m. Sally Hallum Blanchard, June 26, 1976; children: Matthew Christopher, John Stephen, Michael Andrew. BA in History cum laude, Hampden Sydney Coll., 1974; JD, U. Va., 1977. Bar: Va. 1977, U.S. Dist. Ct. (ea. dist.) Va. 1977, U.S. Ct. Appeals (4th cir.) 1977. Assoc. Rawls, Habel & Rawls, Suffolk, 1977-78, ptnr., 1978-91, Ferguson & Rawls, Suffolk, 1991-94, Ferguson, Rawls, MacDonald, Overton & Grissom PC, Suffolk, 1996-98, Ferguson, Rawls, MacDonald & Overton PC, Suffolk, 1999—2002, Ferguson, Rawls & Raines, P.C., 2002—. Sec., Suffolk Title Ltd., 1986-95; bd. dirs. Secure Title, Inc. Deacon Westminster Reformed Presbyn. Ch., Suffolk, 1979-83, elder, clk. of session, 1983-91, 94-99, elder, 2004—; chmn. bd. dirs. Suffolk Crime Line, 1982-90, Suffolk Cheer Fund, 1982—, Covenant Christian Schs., Suffolk, 1982-84; bd. dirs. Norfolk Christian Schs., 1990-2004, v.p., 1998-99, pres., 1999-2004; pres. Parent Tchr. Fellowship, 1995-97, vice-chmn. steering com. for capital campaign, 1996-98, v.p., 1997-98; adv. bd. dirs. Salvation Army, Suffolk, 1977-95, chmn., 1989-90; chmn. Suffolk Com. on Affordable Housing, 1989-90; bd. dirs. Suffolk YMCA, 1988-90, Suffolk Youth Athletic Assn., 1999-2000. Mem. ATLA, Suffolk Bar Assn. (past pres.), Va. State Bar, Va. Bar Assn., Christian Legal Soc., Va. Trial Lawyers Assn., Suffolk Bar Assn. Office Phone: 757-539-1036. Business E-Mail: frawls@frrlaw.com.

**RAWN, WILLIAM LEETE, III**, architect; b. Berkeley, Calif., Aug. 8, 1943; s. William Leete Jr. and Betsy (Blanckenburg) R. BA, Yale U., 1965; JD, Harvard U., 1969; MArch, MIT, 1979. Bar: D.C. 1969. Assoc. Arent, Fox, Kintner, Plotkin & Kahn, Washington, 1969-71; asst. to pres. U. Mass., Boston, 1971-73, asst. chancellor phys. planning, 1973-75; architect Davis Brody & Assocs., N.Y.C., 1979-83, William Rawn Assocs., Boston, 1983—. Vis. prof. urban design Harvard U. Grad. Sch. Design, 1993, 94. Designer serigraphs, 1971-79; contbr. articles to profl. jours., newspapers. Mem. Boston Civic Design Com., 1990; Inst. Contemporary Art, Boston, 1994. Recipient Urban Design citation Progressive Architecture, U. Va./City of Charlottesville Urban Plan, 1995. Fellow AIA (hon., Nat. AIA Award of Excellence, 1993, 7 Nat. AIA Honor Awards in Arch. 1994, 95, 96, 00 (2 awards), 04, 05, Louis Sullivan award 1995); mem. Boston Soc. Architects (55 regional and local AIA design awards 1985-96), DC Bar Assn., Yale Club of NYC, Harvard Club (Boston). Office: William Rawn Assocs Archs Inc 101 Tremont St Ste 204 Boston MA 02108-5004

**RAWNSLEY, HOWARD MELODY**, pathologist, educator; b. Long Branch, NJ, Nov. 20, 1925; s. Walter A. and Elizabeth (Melody) R.; m. B. Eileen Fiddes, Sept. 5, 1967; children: Virgilia Ingram, Elizabeth Sue. AB, Haverford Coll., 1949; MD, U. Pa., 1952. Diplomate Am. Bd. Pathology (trustee 1988-96). Intern Hosp. U. Pa., 1952-53, resident, 1953-57; practice medicine, specializing in pathology Phila., 1957-75; mem. Wm. Pepper Lab., U. Pa., 1957-75, asst. dir., 1960-68, dir., 1968-75; assoc. dir. Clin. Research Ctr., 1962-67, acting dir., 1969— 70, asst. prof. pathology and medicine, 1960-65, assoc. prof., 1965-69, prof., 1969-75; prof. pathology Dartmouth Hitchcock Med. Ctr., Hanover, NH, 1975-95, chmn. dept., 1980-87, sr. v.p. med. affairs, 1987-94. Cons. VA Hosp.; mem. exec. com. Am. Bd. Med. Spltys., 1998-2001. Chmn. bd. dirs. New Eng. Blood Svcs. ARC, 1996—2000, 2002—05. With U.S. Army, 1944—46. Woodward fellow in chemistry, 1953-55 Mem. AMA, ARC (biomed. svcs. com. 1990-92), Pathology Soc. Phila. (pres.), Coll. Am. Pathologists (bd. govs. 1985-93), Coll. Am. Pathologists Found. (bd. dirs. 2003-), Am. Soc. Clin. Pathology (Disting. Svc. award 1995). Personal E-Mail: hrawn@valley.net.

**RAWSKI, EVELYN SAKAKIDA**, history professor; b. Honolulu, Feb. 2, 1939; d. Evan T. and Teruko (Watase) Sakakida; m. Thomas G. Rawski, Dec. 16, 1967. BA, Cornell U., 1961; MA, Radcliffe Coll., 1962; PhD, Harvard U., 1968. Asst. prof. History U. Pitts., 1967-72, assoc. prof., 1973-79, prof. history, 1980—; univ. prof., 1996—. Author: Agricultural Change and the Peasant Economy of South China, 1972, Education and Popular Literacy in Ch'ing China, 1979, The Last Emperors: A Social History of Qing Imperial Institutions, 1998; co-author: Chinese Society in the Eighteenth Century, 1987, Worshiping the Ancestors: Chinese Commemorative Portraits, 2001; co-editor: Popular Culture in Late Imperial and Modern China, 1985, Death Ritual in Late Imperial and Modern China, 1988, Harmony and Counterpoint: Chinese Music in Ritual Context, 1996. Grantee Am. Coun. Learned Socs., 1973-74; NEH fellow, 1979-80, Chinese Studies fellow Am. Coun. Learned Socs./Social Sci. Rsch. Coun., 1989, Guggenheim fellow, 1990, Woodrow Wilson Internat. Ctr. fellow 1992-93, NEH fellow, 2006—. Mem.: Assn. Asian Studies (China-Inner Asia coun., bd. dirs. 1976—79, v.p. 1994—95, pres. 1995—96). Home: 5317 Westminster Pl Pittsburgh PA 15232-2120 Office: U Pitts Dept History Pittsburgh PA 15260 Office Phone: 412-648-7458. Business E-Mail: esrx@pitt.edu.

**RAWSKI, FREDERICK**, lawyer; BA in Psychology, Coll. William and Mary, 1992; MA in Anthropology, SUNY, 1995; JD, NYU, 2002. Bar: NY State Bar Assn. 2003. Lectr., rschr. SUNY, Buffalo, 1993—98; field coord. Carter Ctr., Dili, 1999; human rights officer UN Transitional Adminstrn. East Timor, Dili, 2000—01; student asst. dist. atty. NY County Dist. Attorney's Office, NYC, 2001—02; litig. assoc. Stroock & Stroock & Lavan LLP, NYC, 2002—; law clk. UN Internat. Criminal Tribunal for Rwanda, Arusha, Tanzania, 2002. Election monitor/deployment advance staff Nat. Dem. Inst. Internat. Affairs, Jakarta, Indonesia, 1999; cons. East Timor Commn. for Reception, Truth and Reconciliation, Dili, 2004; rsch. intern Human Rights Watch Asia, NYC. Contbr. articles to jour., chapters to books. Bd. advisors Am. Coll. Program, U. Fribourg, Switzerland, 2004. Fellow Marion White Grad. Fellowship, SUNY, 1993-1997; grantee Global Law Sch. Clerkship Grant, NYU Sch. Law, 2002. Mem.: Assn. Polit. and Legal Anthropology, Am. Anthropology Assn., Am. Soc. Internat. Law. Office: Stroock & Stroock & Lavan LLP 180 Maiden Ln New York NY 10038-4982 Office Phone: 212-806-6236. Office Fax: 212-806-9236. E-mail: frawski@stroock.com.

**RAWSON, CLAUDE JULIEN**, literature and language professor; b. Shanghai, Feb. 8, 1935; came to U.S., 1985; m. Judith Ann Hammond, July 14, 1959; children: Hugh, Tim, Mark, Harriet, Annabel. BA, Oxford (Eng.) U., 1955, MA, BLitt, 1959. English lectr. U. Newcastle, Eng., 1957-65; from lectr. to prof., chmn. dept. U. Warwick, Coventry, Eng., 1965-85, hon. prof., 1986—; George Sherburn prof. English U. Ill., Urbana, 1985-86; George M. Bodman prof. English Yale U., New Haven, Conn., 1986-96, Maynard Mack prof. English, 1996—. Vis. prof. U. Pa., Phila., 1973, U. Calif., Berkeley, 1980; chmn. Yale Boswell Papers, 1990—2001; del. for lang. and lit. Oxford U. Press, NY, 2001—05; mem. ednl. adv. bd. John Simon Guggenheim Meml. Found., 2005—. Author: Henry Fielding and the Augustan Ideal, 1972, 2d

edit., 1991, Gulliver and the Gentle Reader, 1973, 2d edit., 1991, The Character of Swift's Satire, 1983, Order from Confusion Sprung, 1985, 2d edit., 1992, (with F.P. Lock) Collected Poems of Thomas Parnell, 1989, Satire and Sentiment 1660-1830, 1994, 2d edit., 2000, (with H. B. Nisbet) Cambridge History of Literary Criticism, vol. 4: The Eighteenth Century, 1997, God, Gulliver, and Genocide, 2001, 2d edit. 2002, Basic Writings of Jonathan Swift, 2002; editor: Modern Lang. Rev. and Yearbook of English Studies, London, 1974-88; gen. editor: Cambridge (Eng.) History of Literary Criticism, 1983—, Unwin Critical Libr., London, 1974—, Blackwell Critical Biographies, 1985—, Cambridge Edition of the Works of Jonathan Swift, 2001— Recipient Cert. of Merit for Disting. Svc. Conf. of Editors of Learned Jours., 1988; Andrew Mellon fellow Clark and Huntington Libr., 1980, 90, Guggenheim fellow, 1991-92, Sr. Faculty fellow Yale U., 1991-92; NEH grantee, 1991. Fellow Am. Acad. Arts and Scis.; mem. Modern Humanities Rsch. Assn. (life mem., com. mem. 1974-88), Internat. Soc. 18th Century Studies, Am. Soc. for 18th Century Studies, Brit. Soc. for 18th Century Studies (pres. 1973-74), Grolier Club. Office: Yale U Dept English PO Box 208302 New Haven CT 06520-8302

**RAWSON, JAMES RULON YOUNG**, chemist; b. Boston, July 28, 1943; s. Rulon Wells and Jane (Young) R.; m. Judy Macdonald, Aug. 15, 1970; children: Donald, David. BS, Cornell U., Ithaca, N.Y., 1965; PhD, Northwestern U., Evanston, Ill., 1969. Postdoctoral fellow U. Chgo., 1969-72; asst. prof. U. Ga., Athens, 1972-78, assoc. prof., 1978-83, prof., 1983-84; rsch. scientist Standard Oil, Cleve., 1984-85, sr. scientist, 1985-89, sr. rsch. assoc., 1989-93; microbiologist BP Am. R&D, Cleve., 1988-93; chemist Gen. Electric Global Rsch., Niskayuna, NY, 1994—. Mem. Water Quality Sci. Adv. Bd., 1999-2003, NSF Internat. Standards Commn., 1999—. Mem. editl. bd. Jour. Biol. Chemistry, 1989-91. Lic. whitewater raft guide, 2000—. Grantee NIH, 1967, 72, NSF, 1973-84, USDA, 1980-84. Mem. Am. Chem. Soc. Office: Gen Electric Global Rsch One Research Cir Niskayuna NY 12309 Personal E-mail: rawsonjim@aol.com. Business E-Mail: rawson@crd.ge.com.

**RAWSON, JIM CHARLES**, finance company executive; b. Houston, Apr. 20, 1947; s. Charles Manly and Georgie (Kearse) R.; m. Linda Eidman, Arp. 12, 1968; children: John Erich, Susan Margaret. BBA, Tex. Christian U., 1969. CPA, Tex. Acctg. clk. Tenneco, Inc., Houston, 1969—71, Projects Am. Corp., Houston, 1971—74, chief mgr., 1974—77, v.p., gen. mgr., 1977—82, pres., 1982—. Recipient Gold award, Am. Land Devel. Assn., 1983, Silver award, 1983, Bronze award, 1985. Mem. AICPA, Tex. Soc. CPA's (Houston chpt.), Sports Car Club Am. Methodist. Avocations: sports car racing, salt water fishing. Office: Projects Am Corp 6124 Beverlyhill St Houston TX 77057-6610

**RAWSON, JOHN ELTON**, neonatologist, medical educator; b. Okolona, Miss., Jan. 31, 1938; s. Elton Phlemuel and Marjorie Morgan Jones Rawson; m. Mary Crouch Rawson, June 23, 1962; children: Katherine Asbury Rawson Kronzer, Edwin Lauderdale. BS in Chemistry, Millsaps Coll., 1960; MD, U. Miss., 1965. Diplomate Am. Bd. Pediat., Am. Bd. Neonatology and Perinatal Medicine; lic. physician, Miss. Clin. assoc. prof. pediat. U. Miss. Sch. Medicine, Jackson, 1972—; attending neonatologist, chief newborn medicine Ctrl. Miss. Med. Ctr., Jackson, 1978—; attending neonatologist Miss. Bapt. Med. Ctr., Jackson, 1982—. Chmn. bd. dirs. Health Choice of Miss., Jackson, 1991-98, Integrity Health Plan, Inc., Jackson, 1995-98, State Watch, Inc., Jackson, 1988-96; chief of staff Meth. Healthcare, Inc., Jackson, 1994-95. Editor: Newborn Ventilation, 1976. State chmn. March of Dimes, Jackson, 1972-82; mem. vestry St. James Episcopal Ch., Jackson, 1975-78; trustee St. Andrew's Day Sch., Madison, Miss., 1978-89, Meth. Lebouner Found., Memphis, 1991-2000. Capt. USAF, 1968-70. Mem. Rotary (Paul Harris fellow 1984). Office: Ctrl Miss Med Ctr 1850 Chadwick Dr Jackson MS 39204 Home: 632 Lake Cavalier Rd Madison MS 39110-7155 Office Phone: 601-376-1370. Personal E-mail: jackrawson@hotmail.com.

**RAWSON, RACHEL L.**, lawyer; BA magna cum laude, Kenyon Coll., 1987; JD, Columbia U., 1990. Bar: N.Y. 1991, Ohio 1995. With Jones Day, Cleve., 1992—, ptnr., 2003—. Mem.: ABA (bus. law sect.), Cleve. Bar Assn. (banking and bus. law sect.). Office: Jones Day North Point 901 Lakeside Ave Cleveland OH 44114-1190

**RAWSON, RICHARD J.**, telecommunications industry executive, lawyer; b. Florham Park, N.J., Nov. 22, 1952; BS, Notre Dame U.; JD, Rutgers U. Formerly with Sullivan & Cromwell, N.Y.C. and Washington; various positions with Law Divsn. AT&T, 1984—96, sr. v.p., gen. counsel, 1995, Lucent Technologies, Murray Hill, NJ, 1996—. Mem. ABA, Am. Corp. Counsel Assn.

**RAWSON, ROBERT H., JR.**, lawyer; b. Washington, Oct. 18, 1944; AB, Princeton U., 1966; MA, Oxford U., Eng., 1968; JD, Harvard U., 1971. Bar: Ohio 1971, D.C. 1972. Ptnr. Jones, Day, Reavis & Pogue, Cleve.; ptnr.-in-charge Jones Day, Cleve. Rhodes scholar. Mem.: ABA, Bar Assn. of DC, Cleve. Bar Assn., Ohio State Bar Assn., Phi Beta Kappa. Office: Jones Day Reavis & Pogue North Point 901 Lakeside Ave E Cleveland OH 44114-1190 Office Phone: 216-586-3939. Office Fax: 216-579-0212. Business E-Mail: rrawson@jonesday.com.

**RAY, ALBERT**, physician, educator; b. NYC, Aug. 8, 1948; s. Herman and Stella (Meritz) R.; m. Cheryl Antecol, Oct. 8, 1977; children: Heather, Erin, Samantha. BA, Bklyn. Coll., 1969; MD, Cath. U. Louvain, Belgium, 1976. Diplomate Am. Bd. Family Practice, Can. Coll. Family Physicians. Intern Meml. U. of Nfld., St. John's, Can., 1976; resident McGill U., Montreal, 1978; family physician SCPMG, San Diego, 1978—. Clin. prof. U. Calif., San Diego, 1978—; cmty. faculty UCLA, USD, U. Calif., Davis, USC; clerkship cmty. adv. bd. U. Calif., San Diego, 1995—; pres. profl. staff Kaiser Found. Hosp.; bd. dirs. So. Calif. Permanente Med Group; asst. chief family medicine Kaiser Permanente, San Diego; physician coord. health promotion and preventive care Kaiser Permanente, 2004-2005. Author: Lecons d'Histologie, 1973; contbr. to profl. jours. Program chair adult edn. Congregation Beth Israel, 1995; bd. dirs. Temple Emanuel, San Diego, 1990, Agy. for Jewish Edn.; expert reviewer Med. Bd. Calif., 1995; spl. med. cons. Calif. Dept. of Corps., 1996; hon. chmn. physician's adv. bd. Nat. Rep. Congl. Com. Named Family Physician of Yr., Calif. Acad. Family Physicians, 2002. Fellow: Am. Acad. Family Physicians; mem.: Calif. Acad. Family Physicians, San Diego Acad. Family Physicians, San Diego County Med. Soc. (councilor 2002—03, treas. 2004—05, pres.-elect 2005—06), Calif. Med. Assn. (ho. of dels.), AMA (alt. del.). Avocations: golf, tennis, travel, antiques, gardening. Office: Kaiser Permanente 4405 Vandever Ave San Diego CA 92120-3315 Office Phone: 619-516-7400.

**RAY, AMRIT**, pharmaceuticals strategist, company executive; s. N.K. Ray. BS with honors, U. Edinburgh, MD; MBA, Dartmouth Coll. Physician Full Registration Gen. Med. Coun., U.K.; Fellow Chartered Mgmt. Inst., U.K. Bus. strategy cons. McKinsey & Co., Inc., London; cardiology resident physician Edinburgh Royal Infirmary, Edinburgh, Scotland, England; med. rsch. collaborator Mayo Clinic, Rochester, Minn.; tropical medicine rschr. All-India Inst. Med. Sciences, New Delhi; med. rsch. collaborator Veterans Assn. Med. Ctr., Roanoke, Va.; strategic mgmt. group Pfizer, Inc., New London, Conn., 2002—. Strategy cons. Dartmouth-Hitchcock Med. Ctr., NH, Polaroid Corp., Mass., Pfizer Global Rsch. & Devel., Groton, Conn.; worldwide med. team leader Pfizer, Inc., NYC, 2004—. Exec. coach to the dir. Garde Theater and Arts Ctr., New London, Conn.; exec. coach to CEO Women's Comm. for Refugee Women and Children, NY. Recipient Myre-Sim award, Royal Coll. Physicians, U.K., 1997, Global Healthcare Practice - Top 5 Bus. Plan, McKinsey & Co., Inc., 1998, Reuben Cohen award, Dartmouth Coll., 2000, Top 100 Most Inspiring People in Life Scis. Pharma Voice award, 2005, Faculty Medicine Rsch. award, U. Edinburgh, Med. Rsch. award, Med. Rsch. Coun. U.K.; Breast Cancer Rsch. scholar, Zeneca Pharms. Mem.: No.

New Eng. Soc. Healthcare Risk Mgmt., Internat. Pharm. Fedn., Am. Soc. Pharmacology and Exptl. Therapeutics, Am. Mgmt. Assn., Brit. Med. Assn., Tuck Biotechnology & Healthcare Soc. (pres.).

**RAY, AMY,** vocalist, guitarist; b. Decatur, Ga., Apr. 12, 1964; BA, Emory U., 1986. Vocalist, guitarist Saliers & Ray, 1980-83, Indigo Girls, 1983—; signed to Epic Records, 1988—2006, Hollywood Records, 2006—. Founder, pres. Daemon Records, Decatur, Ga., 1990—. Musician: (albums) Stag, 2001, Prom, 2005; musician: (with Emily Saliers) Early 45, 1985, Strange Fire, 1987, Indigo Girls, 1989 (Grammy Award for Best Contemporary Folk Album, 1990), Nomads Indians Saints, 1990, Back On the Bus, Y'All, 1991, Rites of Passage, 1992, Swamp Ophelia, 1994, 1200 Curfews, 1995, Shaming of the Sun, 1997, Come On Now Social, 1999, Retrospective, 2000, Become You, 2002, All That We Let In, 2004, Rarities, 2005, Despite Our Differences, 2006, (songs) Closer to Fine, 1989, Hammer and Nail, 1990, Galileo, 1992, Least Complicated, 1994, Shame on You, 1997; appears in (films) Boys on the Side, 1995, Join the Resistance: Fall in Love, 2003, (documentaries) Trudell, 2005, Wordplay, 2006. Nominee Best New Artist, Grammy Awards, 1990; named one of Greatest Women of Rock'n'Roll, VH1. Office: c/o Russell Carter Artist Mgmt Ste 755 315 W Ponce de Leon Ave Decatur GA 30030 Office Phone: 404-377-9900. E-mail: igfan@rcam.com.*

**RAY, ANNETTE D.,** executive secretary; b. Decatur, Ind., Mar. 24, 1950; d. Gilbert O. and Florence L. Hoffman; m. Richard M. Ray, Nov. 28, 1975 (dec. June 1999); children: Michelle Ann, Ellen Marie, Laura Leigh, David Richard, Ruth Anne. AA, Concordia Jr. Coll., Ann Arbor, Mich., 1970; BS, Concordia Tchrs. Coll., Seward, Nebr., 1972; attended, Ctrl. Fla. C.C., Ocala, 1974. Lic. real estate, Ind.; lic. tchr., Ind., Fla. Elem. tchr. St. John's Luth., Ocala, 1972-74; mgr. apt. complex Victoria Sq. Apts., Ft. Wayne, Ind., 1974-75; substitute tchr. East Allen County Schs., Allen County, Ind., 1976-79, Circut A Luth. Schs., Adams and Allen County, Ind., 1977-81; corp. sec., treas., office mgr. Heritage Wire Die, Monroeville, Ind., 1987—. Co-author, co-editor: 1928-1988 A Remembrance, 1988, Coming to America--32 Families 1597-1997; author, collator Madison Township portion 2005 Allen County History, 1990-2000. Vol. Monroeville C. of C., 1987—, Concerned Area Residents Quality Edn., Allen County, 1990—, Am. Cancer Soc., Allen County, 1991—, chairperson Celebrity Bagger Day, 1995, 96; bd. dirs. Hoagland (Ind.) Hist. Soc., 1985—, sec. 2002; bd. dirs. Hoagland Area Advancement Assn., 1999—, sec. 2003; contbr. 2005 Allen County (Ind.) History. Lutheran. Avocations: remodeling old homes, reading, genealogy, gardening, floral arranging. Home: 16901 Berning Rd Hoagland IN 46745-9753 Office: Heritage Wire Die Inc 19819 Monroeville Rd Monroeville IN 46743-9113 E-mail: heritagewiredie@yahoo.com, annetteray9@aol.com.

**RAY, BILLY JOHN, JR.,** music educator; b. Puyallup, Wash., Apr. 9, 1964; s. Billy John, Sr. and Leone Dorothy Ray; m. Claudette Ann Laycock, Mar. 31, 1990; children: Jazmyn, Kierstyn. BA in Edn., Ctrl. Wash. U., 1987. Instrumental music tchr. Ellensburg (Wash.) Sch. Dist., 1987—88, Endicott (Wash.) Sch. Dist., 1988—2006; athletic dir. Endicott-St. John Mid. Sch., 2006—. Mid. sch. football asst. coach Endicott-St. John Mid. Sch., 1993—95, mid. sch. football head coach, 1996—; baseball asst. coach St. John (Wash.)-Endicott HS, 1996—97, softball asst. coach, 1997—2002, mid. sch. asst. coach baseball, 2003—06. Mem.: Southeast Wash. Music Educators Assn. (pres. 2004—06), Wash. Interscholastic Activities Assn. mem. music com. 1997—2003), Wash. Music Educators Assn. Home: 104 E St Endicott WA 99125 Office: Endicott Sch Dist 308 School Dr Endicott WA 99125 E-mail: bray@endicott.wednet.edu.

**RAY, BRADLEY STEPHEN,** petroleum geologist; b. Ada, Okla., Feb. 15, 1957; s. Walter Lloyd and Betty Louise (McCurley) R. BS in Geology, Baylor U., 1980; MS in Geology, U. Tex., 1985. Cert. geologist. Asst. geologist Hunt Oil Co., Dallas, 1978, geologist, 1979-81; ind. oil and gas producer Dallas, 1981—. Chmn. adv. bd. Geol. Info. Libr. Dallas, 1988-94, Criswell Coll., 1990-92; chmn. The Habitats Project, 1993—; mem. Peoples Info. Network. Mem. Am. Assn. Petroleum Geologists, Ind. Petroleum Assn. Am., Soc. Ind. Profl. Earth Scientists, Dallas Geol. Soc., Tex. Ind. Producers and Royalty Owners, Okla. Ind. Petroleum Assn., Geol. Soc. Am., Computer Oriented Geol. Soc., Nat. Stripper Well Assn., Energy Club, Oklahoma City Geol. Soc., Colbert-Tracht Club. Republican. Baptist. Home: 4925 Greenville Ave Ste 1348 Dallas TX 75206-4021 Office: 1348 One Energy Sq Dallas TX 75206

**RAY, CARLOS See NORRIS, CHUCK**

**RAY, CAROL RENEÉ,** allied health professional; b. Petersburg, Va. d. Frederick Chester Ray and Brenda Ray-Moore. BSc, Spelman Coll., 1987; MSc, N.C. Agrl. and Tech. State U., 1995; PhD, U. Nebr.-Lincoln, 2003. Tutor coord. U. Nebr., Lincoln, Nebr., 2000, prin. investigator, 1998—2003; instr. chemistry Fayetteville Tech. C.C., 2002; TV tutor comcast U. Md. - Ea. Shore, Princess Anne, 2004, coord. allied health project, 2005—. Adj. faculty Sojouriner Douglass Coll., Salisbury, Md., 2004—; cons. Nebr. Divsn. on Aging., 1998. Contbr. articles to profl. jours. Nominee Avon scholarship, 1984; Chemistry Scholarship, Spelman Coll., 1984. Mem.: Phi Upsilon Omicron Nat. Honor Soc. Avocations: flute, reading, tennis, writing. Personal E-mail: carol2004_500@hotmail.com.

**RAY, CHARLES AARON,** ambassador; b. Center, Tex., July 5, 1945; m. Myung Wook Soe, Nov. 3, 1973; children: David Edward, Denise Ellen, Gayle Denene, Jason Andre. BSBA, Benedictine Coll., 1972; MS in Sys. Mgmt., U. So. Calif., 1981; MS in Nat. Security Strategy, Nat. War Coll., 1997. Commd. 2d lt. U.S. Army, 1965, advanced through grades to maj., ret., 1982; consular officer U.S. Consulate Gen., Guangzhou, China, 1983-84, [illegible line] China, 1985-87; dept. administ'v. sect. Chiang-mai, Thailand, 1988-91; spl. asst. to dir. Office Det. Trade Controls, Washington, 1991-93; dep. chief of mission Am. Embassy, Freetown, Sierra Leone, 1993-96; detailed to Nat. War Coll., Washington, 1996-97, Nat. Fgn. Affairs Tng. Ctr., Arlington, Va., 1997-98; consul gen. U.S. Consulate Gen., Ho Chi Minh City, Vietnam, 1998-2001; sr. seminar Nat. Fgn. Affairs Tng. Ctr., 2001—02; US amb. to Cambodia US Dept. State, Phnom Penh, Cambodia, 2002—. Editl. cartoonist Spring Lake News, 1975-79; contbr. articles to Asia Mag., 1974-79; editor Mag. Psyop Digest, 1976-78; exec. editor Def. Trade News, 1992-93. Avocations: golf, taekwondo, softball, tennis, painting, poetry.

**RAY, CHARLES ALBERT,** photojournalist; b. Franklin County, Tenn., Feb. 9, 1928; s. Sherman Peaturney and Sona Arlena Ray; m. Betty Heringa, Dec. 10, 1950 (div. June 1965); m. Deborah Freshwater, Apr. 7, 1972 (div. Apr. 1980); m. Theresa Ann Bailey, Dec. 20, 1997; children: David Charles, Thomas Wesley. Student, Grand Rapids Jr. Coll., Mich., 1951—53, Bay City Jr. Coll., 1956—61. News cinematographer Sta. WWTV-TV, Cadillac, Mich., 1953—54, Sta. KWWL-TV, Waterloo, Iowa, 1955, Sta. WNEM-TV, Bay City, 1956—61, Sta. WGN-TV, Chgo., 1961—65, NBC News, Chgo., 1965—87; ret., 1987. Author: The Life of a Network Newsreel Cameraman, 2001; exhibitions include Charles Ray Photo Archives, Florida Gulf Coast U., 2002. Named Chgo. Cameraman of Yr., 1963, 1965, 1967; recipient numerous news awards. Mem.: Internat. Cinematographers Guild Local 600, Chgo. Press Photographers Assn., Nat. Press Photographers Assn. (News Film award). Avocations: photography, reading, writing, fishing. Home: PO Box 1167 Sanibel FL 33957-1167

**RAY, CHARLES DEAN,** neurosurgeon, spine surgeon, bioengineer, inventor; b. Americus, Ga., Aug. 1, 1927; s. Oliver Tinsley and Katherine (Broadfield) R.; children: Bruce, Marlene. AB, Emory U., 1950; MS, U. Miami, 1952; MD, Med. Coll. Ga., 1956. Diplomate Am. Bd. Neurol. Surgery, Am. Bd. Spine Surgery. Intern Bapt. Meml. Hosp., Memphis, 1956-57; resident, rsch. assoc. neurosurgery U. Tenn. Hosp., Memphis, 1957-62; fellow, rsch. assoc. Mayo Clinic and Found., Rochester, Minn., 1962-64; asst. prof. neurosurgery, lectr. bioengring. Johns Hopkins U. Med. Sch., Balt., 1964-68; chief dept. engring. F. Hoffmann-LaRoche, Basel,

Switzerland, 1968-73; clin. assoc. prof. medicine U. Minn., Mpls., 1973; practice medicine specializing in neurosurgery Norfolk, Williamsburg, Va., 1973—. Lectr. U. Basel (Switzerland), 1968—73; dir. emeritus Inst. Low Back and Neck Care; med. dir. The Spine Program Ea. Va. Med. Sch., Norfolk, Va.; pres. Am. Coll. Spine Surgery; mem. staff Sentara Hosps., Norfolk; chmn. bd. pres. Cedar Devel. Corp., Cedar Surg., Inc., 1985—; v.p. med. rsch. Medtronic, Inc., Mpls., 1972—79; bd. dirs. Herman Miller, Inc.; chmn. emeritus, med. dir. Raymedia, Inc., Mpls.; cons. in field; adj. prof. orthopedics Ain Shams U., Cairo, 2002—, U. Colo., Denver, 2002—. Author: Principles of Engineering Applied to Medicine, 1964, Medical Engineering, 1974, Lumbar Spine Surgery, 1988; contbr. over 360 articles to profl. publs. Chmn. com. materials and devices World Fedn. Neurosurg. Socs., 1977—, Cosmos Club, 1976—; vestry St. Martin's Episcopal Ch., Wayzata, Minn., 1976-79. With USN, 1945-49. Named Disting. Alumnus, Med. Coll. Ga., 1999; recipient Gold award for Best Med. Device Design of Yr. R&D 100, 2000. Fellow: ACS, Royal Soc. Health, Am. Coll. Spine Surgery (pres.); mem.: ASTM, AMA (sr.), IEEE (sr.), Internat. Spine Arthroplasty Soc. (pres.), N.Am. Spine Soc. (past pres., chmn., Wiltse award 1999), Internat. Orgn. Standardization, Pan-Am. Med. Assn. (life), Am. Assn. Neurol. Surgeons (sr.), Internat. Soc. Stereotaxic and Functional Neurosurgery, Internat. Fedn. Med. Biol. Engring., West Germany Armed Forces Med. Soc., Congress Neurol. Surgeons, Mpls. Club, Sigma Xi. Achievements include over 50 U.S. patents and over 100 foreign patents. Home and Office: 4320 Via Presada Santa Barbara CA 93110 Office Phone: 805-964-7026. Personal E-mail: inveray@aol.com.

**RAY, CHARLES KENDALL,** retired university dean; b. Boise City, Okla., Mar. 15, 1928; s. Volney Holt and Mamie (Burton) R.; m. Doris Derby, Aug. 26, 1951. BA, U. Colo., 1951; MA, Columbia, 1955, Ed.D., 1959. Teaching prin. Bur. Indian Affairs, Savoonga, Alaska, 1951-54; mem. faculty U. Alaska, 1957-93, prof. edn., 1960-93, dean Sch. Behavioral Scis. and Edn., 1961-80, dir. summer sessions, 1980-93. Author: A Program of Education for Alaska Natives, 1959, Alaskan Native Secondary School Dropouts, 1961. Mem. N.E.A., Phi Delta Kappa. Home: 2000 1st Ave Apt 2204 Seattle WA 98121-2171

**RAY, CREAD L., JR.,** retired judge; b. Waskom, Tex., Mar. 10, 1931; s. Cread L. and Antonia (Hardesty) Ray; m. Janet Watson Keller, Aug. 12, 1977; children: Sue Ann(dec.), Robert E., Glenn L., David B., Marcie Lynn, Anne Marie. BBA, Tex. A&M U., 1952; JD, U. Tex., 1957; LHD (hon.), Wiley Coll., Marshall, Tex., 1980. Bar: Tex. 1957. Pvt. practice law, Marshall, 1957-59; judge Harrison County, 1959-61; justice 6th dist. Ct. Civil Appeals, Texarkana, 1970-80, Supreme Ct. Tex., Austin, 1980-90; ret., 1990; prin. C.L Ray, Austin, 1991—. Prin. C. L. Ray, Austin, 1991—; pres., CEO White Oil, Inc. Past pres. Marshall Jaycees, Marshall C. of C.; active Boy Scouts Am.; mem. Tex. Ho. of Reps., 1966—70; trustee Wiley Coll. Lt. col. USAF, 1952—54, Korea. Recipient awards, Boy Scouts Am. Mem.: N.E. Tex. Bar Assn. (past pres.), State Bar Tex., Tex. Aggies, Rotary. Democrat. Methodist. Home and Office: 604 Beardsley Ln Austin TX 78746-4929 Office Phone: 512-328-9238. Personal E-mail: clray4523@hotmail.com. E-mail: judgeclray@aol.com, judgeclray@msn.com.

**RAY, DOUGLAS KENT,** newspaper executive; Pres., CEO Daily Herald/Sunday Herald, Arlington Heights, Ill., 1970—. Named Pubisher of Yr., Editor & Publisher, 2006. Office: Daily Herald/Sunday Herald Paddock Publs PO Box 280 Arlington Heights IL 60006-0280

**RAY, EDWARD JOHN,** economics professor, academic administrator; b. Jackson Heights, NY, Sept. 10, 1944; s. Thomas Paul and Cecelia Francis (Hiney) R.; m. Virginia Beth Phelps, June 14, 1969; children: Stephanie Elizabeth, Katherine Rebecca, Michael Edward. BA, CUNY, 1966; MA, Stanford U., 1969, PhD, 1971. Asst. prof. econs. Ohio State U., Columbus, 1970-74, assoc. prof., 1974-77, prof., 1977—, chmn. dept. econs., 1976-92, assoc. provost acad. affairs Office Acad. Affairs, 1992-93, sr. vice provost, chief info. officer Office Acad. Affairs, 1993-98, acting sr. v.p. and provost, 1997-98, exec. v.p., provost, 1998—2003; pres. Oreg. State U., 2003—. Cons. Dept. Labor, 1974-76, Dept. Commerce, 1977. AID, Office Tech. Assessment, winter 1982 Contbr. articles to profl. jours. Active Upper Arlington Civic Assn., Columbus, 1983—. Mem. Am. Econs. Assn., Phi Beta Kappa Home: 3700 SW Brooklane Dr Corvallis OR 97333 Office: Office of Pres Oreg State U Corvallis OR 97331-2128

**RAY, ELISE,** gymnast; b. Tallahassee, Feb. 6, 1982; d. Bill and Ellen Ray. Mem. U.S. Gymnastics Team, 1996-2001, U.S. Olympic Team, 2000. Recipient 1st team Internat. Team Championships, 1997; 1st pl. uneven bars, John Hancock U.S. Gymnastics Championships, 1998; 1st pl. fixed bars, John Hancock U.S. Gymnastics Championships, 1999; 1st pl. All Around uneven bars, John Hancock U.S. Gymastics Championships, 2000; 1st pl. All Around vault, uneven bars, fixed bars, Aussie Haircare Gymnastics Invitational, 2000; 1st team All-Around Champion, Sr. Pacific Alliance Championship, New Zealand, 2000, All-Around Champion, NCAA Championships, 2001, 1st pl. balance beam, NCAA Championships, 2002. Mem. Hill's Angels Club. Avocations: shopping, arts and crafts, movies, family. Address: Womens Gymnastics 1000 S State St Ann Arbor MI 48109

**RAY, FRANK ALLEN,** lawyer; b. Lafayette, Ind., Jan. 30, 1949; s. Dale Allen and Merry Ann (Fleming) R.; m. Carol Ann Olmutz, Oct. 1, 1982; children: Erica Fleming, Robert Allen. BA, Ohio State U., 1970, JD, 1973. Bar: Ohio 1973, U.S. Dist. Ct. (so. dist.) Ohio 1975, U.S. Supreme Ct. 1976, U.S. Tax Ct. 1977, U.S. Ct. Appeals (6th cir.) 1977, U.S. Dist. Ct. (no. dist.) Ohio 1980, U.S. Dist. Ct. (ea. dist.) Mich. 1983, U.S. Ct. Appeals (1st cir.) 1986; cert. civil trial adv. Nat. Bd. Trial Advocacy. Asst. pros. atty. Franklin County Ohio, 1973 75, chief civil counsel 1976—70, [illegible] project Nat. Dist. Attys. Assn., Washington, 1975-76; assoc. Brownfield, Kosydar, Bowen, Bally & Sturtz, Columbus, Ohio, 1978, Michael F. Colley Co., L.P.A., Columbus, 1979-83; pres. Frank A. Ray Co., L.P.A., Columbus, 1983—93, Columbus, 2000—05, Ray & Todaro Co., LPA, Columbus, 1993-94, Ray, Todaro & Alton Co., L.P.A., Columbus, 1994-96, Ray, Todaro, Alton & Kirstein Co., L.P.A., Columbus, 1996, Ray, Alton & Kirstein Co., L.P.A., Columbus, 1996—98; sr. ptnr. Ray & Alton, L.L.P., Columbus, 1998—2000; ptnr. Chester, Willcox & Saxbe, LLP, 2006—; adj. prof. Moritz Coll. of Law, Ohio State U., 2003—. Mem. seminar faculty Nat. Dist. Attys., Houston, 1975-77; mem. nat. conf. faculty Fed. Jud. Ctr., Washington, 1976-77; bd. editors Man. for Complex Litigation, Fed. Jud. Ctr., 1999—2004; bd. mem. bar examiners Ohio Supreme Ct., 1992-95, mem. rules adv. com., 1995-99. Editor: Economic Crime Digest, 1975-76; co-author: Personal Injury Litigation Practice in Ohio, 1988, 91. Mem. fin. com. Franklin County Rep. Orgn., Columbus, 1979-84, 2005—; trustee Ohio State U. Coll. Humanities Alumni Soc., 1991-93, Nat. Coun. Ohio State U. Coll. Law Alumni Assn., 1998—; mem. Legal Aid Soc. of Columbus Capital Campaign Fund Cabinet, 1998. Capt. inf. U.S. Army, 1976. Named to Ten Outstanding Young Citizens of Columbus, Columbus Jaycees, 1976; recipient Nat. award of Distinctive Svc., Nat. Dist. Attys. Assn., 1977, Worthy Adversary award Ohio Assn. Civil Trial Attys., 2005. Fellow: Ohio Acad. Trial Lawyers (pres. 1989—90, Pres.'s award 1986), Ohio State Bar Found., Roscoe Pound Found., Am. Coll. Trial Lawyers, Internat. Soc. Barristers, Columbus Bar Found. (trustee 2003—); mem.: ATLA (state del. 1990—92), Franklin County Trial Lawyers Assn. (pres. 1987—88, Pres.'s award 1990), Ohio State Bar Assn. (com. negligence law 1990—97, mem. com. jury instrns. 2002—), Friend of Legal Edn. award 2005), Million Dollar Advs. Forum, Columbus Bar Assn. (pres. 2001—02, Profl. award 1992), Am. Bd. Trial Advs. (pres. Ohio Chpt. 2004), Inns of Ct. (pres. Judge Robert M. Duncan chpt. 1993—94). Presbyterian. Home: 2030 Tremont Rd Columbus OH 43221-4330 Office: Ste 1000 65 E State St Columbus OH 43215 Office Phone: 614-221-7791. Business E-Mail: fray@cwslaw.com

**RAY, GENE WELLS,** industrial executive; b. Murray, Ky., Apr. 23, 1938; s. Terry Lee and Loreen (Lovett) R.; m. Becky Huie, Mar. 5, 1956 (dec. 1976); m. Taffin Ray; children: Don Dickerson, Kathy Pratt, Nancy Solomon. BS in Math., Physics and Chemistry, Murray State U., 1956; MS in Physics, U.

Tenn., 1962, PhD in Theoretical Physics, 1965. With tech. staff Aerospace Corp., San Bernardino, Calif., 1965-68; mgr. strategic div. USAF (OA), Washington, 1968-70; scientist, sr. v.p., systems group mgr. Sci. Applications Inc., La Jolla, Calif., 1970-81, also bd. dirs.; pres., chief exec. officer Titan Systems Inc., San Diego, 1981-85, CEO, 1985—, CEO, pres., assoc. prof. Carson Newman Coll., Tenn., 1964-65. Inventor mass flow meter. 1st lt. USAR, 1963-68. Republican. Avocations: tennis, wine collecting. Home: PO Box 2464 Rancho Santa Fe CA 92067-2464 Office: Titan Corp 3033 Science Park Rd San Diego CA 92121-1199

**RAY, GILBERT T.,** lawyer; b. Mansfield, Ohio, Sept. 18, 1944; s. Robert Lee Ray and Renatha (Gigill) Ray; m. Valerie J. Reynolds, June 14, 1969; children: Tanika, Tarlin. BA, Ashland Coll., 1966; MBA, U. Toledo, 1968; JD, Howard U., 1972. Assoc. O'Melveny & Myers, L.A., 1972-79, ptnr., 1980-2000, ret. ptnr., 2000—. Bd. dirs Sierra Monolithics, Inc., IHOP Corp., Watson, Wyatt & Co., Advance Auto Parts, Automobile Club of So. Calif., Haynes Found., DiamondRock Hospitality, Inc., Seasons Series Fund, SunAmerica Series Trust. Mem. The Calif. Club, L.A. Country Club. Democrat. Office: 400 S Hope St Ste 1900 Los Angeles CA 90071-2899

**RAY, GLENN,** art association administrator; Exec. dir. Assn. for the Advancement of Arts Edn., Cin. Office: Assoc For The Advancement Of Arts Edu 1223 Central Pkwy # 100 Cincinnati OH 45214-2812 Office Phone: 513-721-2223.

**RAY, HUGH MASSEY, JR.,** lawyer; b. Vicksburg, Miss., Feb. 1, 1943; s. Hugh Massey and Lollie Landon (Powell) R.; m. Carroll Robertson, Sept. 7, 2002; children: Hugh, Hallie. BA, Vanderbilt U., 1965, JD, 1967. Bar: Tex. 1967, U.S. Dist. Ct. (so. dist.) Tex. 1967, U.S. Dist.Ct. (we. dist.) La. 1979, U.S. Dist. Ct. (we. dist.) Tex. 1979, U.S. Dist Ct. (no. dist.) Tex. 1980, U.S. Ct. Appeals 1st, 5th, 9th, 11th cirs.) 1982, U.S. Dist. Ct. (no. dist.) Calif. 1989, N.Y. 1992; cert. Tex. Bd. Legal Specialization. Asst. U.S. atty. So. Dist. Tex., 1967-68; assoc. Andrews & Kurth, Houston, 1968-77, ptnr., Bankruptcy Dept., 1977—. Lectr. Ctrl. and Ea. European Law Initiative, Vilnius, Lithuania, 1996. Co-author: Bankruptcy Investing, 1992, Creditor's Rights in Texas, vol. 1 & 2, 1998; contbr. articles to profl. jours. Mem.: ABA (chmn. real property practice com. 1975—77, chmn. cont. legal edn. com. young lawyers divsn. 1976—78, vice-chmn. 1979, chmn. oil and gas subcom. bus. bankruptcy com. 1985—89, chmn. executory contracts subcom. 1989—93, chmn. bus. bankruptcy com. 1993—96, chmn. com. on trust indentures and indenture trustees 1995—97, mem. standing com. on jud. selection, tenure and compensation 1996—97, chmn. ad hoc com. on bankruptcy ct. structure 1996—2001, mem. bus. law sect. 1997—2001, chair energy com. 2001—), South Tex. Coll. Law (trustee 2003—), Houston Symphony Orch. (governing trustee 2004—), Am. Coll. Bankruptcy., Am. Law Inst., Tex. Bar Assn. (chmn. bankruptcy com. 1985—88), Houston Bar Assn., River Oaks Country Club, Houston Country Club. Episcopalian. Office: Andrews & Kurth 600 Travis St Ste 4200 Houston TX 77002-2910 Office Fax: 713-238-7225. Business E-Mail: hray@andrewskurth.com.

**RAY, HUGH MASSEY, III,** lawyer; b. Houston, June 25, 1970; s. Hugh Massey and Florence Hargrove Ray; m. Katheryn Elaine Shaffer, June 19, 1993; children: James Henry, Mary Carol. BA, Vanderbilt U., Nashville, 1992; MDiv, JD, Vanderbilt U., 1996. Cert.: Tex. Bd. of Legal Specialization (bus. bankruptcy law) 2005. Shareholder Weycer, Kaplan, Pulaski & Zuber, P.C., Houston, 2001—. Mem. State Bar of Tex. Disciplinary Rules Com., Austin, 2000—; barrister of Davis-Foltz Inn of Ct. Am. Inns of Ct., Houston, 2004—. Patron Houston Symphony, 2004; mem. St. Martin's Episc. Ch., Houston, 1993—2006. Mem.: ABA (young lawyer divsn. profl. devel. team 2005—, editl. bd. young lawyers mag. 2004—05), Am. Law Inst., Houston Bar Assn. (CLE com. 2006—), Coll. of State Bar Tex., The Briar Club, The Houston Club, Lambda Chi Alpha (rush chmn. 1990—92). Avocations: running, hunting. Home: 4414 Ingersoll Houston TX 77027 Office: Weycer Kaplan Pulaski & Zuber PC 11 greenway Plz Ste 1400 Houston TX 77046 Office Phone: 713-341-1158. Office Fax: 713-961-5341. E-mail: hray@wkpz.com

**RAY, JANE ZIMRUDE,** retired machine shop executive; b. Strawn, Tex., May 9, 1937; d. M.A. and Susie Matilda (Kitchens) Wooton; m. Earl Vernon Ray, Oct. 19, 1956; children: Marcus Vernon, Martha Ruth Ray O'Grady, Douglas Wayne, Patricia Ann. Grad., Stephenville (Tex.) High Sch., 1955. Bookkeeper Ray's Texaco Svc. Ctr., Ft. Worth, Tex., 1967-74, Ray's Repair & Mfg., Ft. Worth, Tex., 1974-79, pres., 1979-80, Cisco, Tex., 1980-92. Sunday sch. tchr., Cisco, Tex., 1983-92, sub. tchr., 1992—; mem. Civic League of Cisco, 1990—; instr. Community Svc. course Cisco Jr. Coll., 1991.

**RAY, JOHN WALKER,** otolaryngologist, educator, broadcast commentator; b. Columbus, Ohio, Jan. 12, 1936; s. Kenneth Clark and Hope (Walker) R.; m. Susanne Gettings, July 15, 1961; children: Nancy Ann, Susan Christy. AB magna cum laude, Marietta Coll., 1956; MD cum laude, Ohio State U., 1960; postgrad., Temple U., 1964, Mt. Sinai Hosp., Columbia U., 1964, 66, Northwestern U., 1967, 71, U. Ill., 1968, U. Ind., 1969, Tulane U., 1969. Diplomate Am. Bd. Otolaryngology. Intern Ohio State U. Hosps., Columbus, 1960-61, clin. rsch. trainee NIH, 1963-65, resident dept. otolaryngology, 1963-65, 66-67, resident dept. surgery, 1965-66, instr. dept. otolaryngology, 1966-67, 70-75, clin. asst. prof., 1975-82, clin. assoc. prof., 1982-92, clin. prof., 1992-2000, clin. prof. emeritus, 2000—; hon. staff, past chief of staff Good Samaritan Hosp., Zanesville, Ohio, 1967—, Bethesda Hosp., Zanesville, 1967—. Hon. active staff Meml. Hosp., Marietta, Ohio, 1992—; [illegible line] ..., 1982 ... Contbr. articles to profl. jours., collaborator with surg. motion picture: Laryngectomy and Neck Dissection, 1964. Past pres. Muskingum chpt. Am. Cancer Soc. Capt. USAF, 1961-63. Recipient Barrauquer Meml. award, 1965; named to Order of Ky. Col., 1966, Muskingum County Country Music Hall of Fame. Fellow ACS, Am. Soc. Otolaryn. Allergy, Am. Acad. Otolaryngology-Head and Neck Surgery (past gov.), Am. Acad. Facial Plastic and Reconstructive Surgery; mem. AMA, Nat. Assn. Physician Broadcasters, Muskingum County Acad. Medicine (past pres.), Ohio Med. Assn., Columbus Ophthalmol. and Otolaryn. Soc. (past pres.), Ohio Soc. Otolaryngology (past pres.), Am. Soc. Contemporary Medicine and Surgery, Acad. Radio and TV Health Commentators, Fraternal Order of Police Assocs., Internat. Bluegrass Music Assn., Phi Beta Kappa, Alpha Omega Alpha, Beta Beta Beta, Alpha Tau Omega, Alpha Kappa Kappa. Presbyterian. Home: 1245 East Dr Zanesville OH 43701-1445

**RAY, MARILYN ANNE,** nursing educator, researcher; b. Hamilton, Ont., Can., Jan. 24, 1938; d. Arthur William Anthony and Elvera Caroline (Montag) Ray; m. James L. Droesbeke, Aug. 18, 1979 (dec. Nov. 2001). Diploma, St. Joseph's Hosp. Sch. Nursing, Hamilton, 1958; BSN, U. Colo. Denver, 1968, MSN, 1969; MA in Anthropology, McMaster U., 1978; PhD of Nursing, U. Utah, 1981; HD (hon.), Nev. State Coll., 2005. RN Fla., cert. advanced nursing adminstr., transcultural nurse, CTN. Instr. sch. nursing U. San Francisco, 1970—72; asst. prof. sch. nursing McMaster U., 1973—76; asst. prof. U. Colo., 1984—87; Christine E. Lynn eminent scholar sch. nursing Fla. Atlantic U., Boca Raton, 1989—94, prof. sch. nursing, 1995—; Yingling vis. scholar Va. Commonwealth U., Richmond, Va., 1994—95; prof. Va. Commonwealth U. Sch. Nursing, 2003—2004, adj. prof., 2004—05, prof. emeritus, 2006—. Vis. prof. U. Colo., 1989—2004, Alta. Heritage Found. U., 2005—. Contbr. articles to profl. jours. Col. USAF, 1967—99. Recipient Leininger award, 1989; Transcultural Nursing scholar, 2005. Mem.: ANA, Space Nursing Soc. (charter), Aerospace Human Factors Assn. (charter), Coll. Nurses Ont., Transcultural Nursing Soc. (cert., mem. editl. bd. jour.), Am. Anthrop. Assn., Sigma Theta Tau. Business E-Mail: mray@fau.edu.

**RAY, NELDA HOWTON,** financial consultant; Grad., U. Montevallo, Ala., 1962. Fin. cons. Merrill Lynch, Tuscaloosa, Ala. Mem.: Rotary Internat. (local and dist. officer). Home: 4704 Oneida Ave Northport AL 35473-1431 Office: Merrill Lynch 302 Merchants Walk Ste 100 Tuscaloosa AL 35406-2214

**RAY, PAUL SUKHAMAY,** engineering educator, researcher; b. Bengal, India, Feb. 1, 1933; arrived in U.S., 1974; s. Suresh Chandra and Radha Rani Ray; m. Sudha Karmakar, Apr. 29, 1961; children: Steve S., Sumit S. B in Mech. Engring. with first class honors, Jadavpur U., Calcutta, India, 1956; M in Mech. Engring., Indian Inst. Tech., Kharagpur, India, 1961; MBA in Mgmt., Golden Gate U., 1978; PhD in Indsl. Engring., U. Okla., 1988. Registered profl. engr., Tex., chartered engr., Engring. Coun., London; cert. safety profl. Bd. Cert. Safety Profls. Sr. indsl. engr. Hindustan Motors Ltd., India, 1960—63; sr. asst. Union Carbide (I) Ltd., India, 1963—72; mgr. mgmt. svcs. Hindustan Copper Ltd., India, 1972—74; project plan-scheduling engr. Bechtel Corp., San Francisco, 1974—87; asst. prof. U. Ala., Tuscaloosa, 1989—95, assoc. prof., 1995—2005, prof., 2005—. Presenter in field. Mem. editl. bd. Internat. Jour. Indsl. Engring., Theory, Applications and Practice; contbr. chapters to books, articles to profl. jours. Recipient Outstanding advisor Departmental Hon. award Ala. chpt. Alpha Pi Mu, Coordinating Coun. Student Orgns. U. Ala., 2004—05; Gordon fellow, U. Okla., 1985, recipient numerous rsch. grants. Mem.: Campus Safety Assn., Nat. Safety Coun., Sys. Safety Soc. (Educator of the Yr.), Human Factors and Ergonomics Soc. (newsletter editor indsl. ergonomics tech. group 1990—91), Internat. Soc. Occupl. Ergonomics & Safety (pres. elect 2002—03, pres. 2003—04), Am. Soc. Safety Engrs. (Safety Rsch. award 1999), Inst. Indsl. Engrs. (sr.; v.p. publ. Ala. chpt. 1988—89, 2d v.p. Birmingham chpt. 1992—93, sec. 1994—95, bd. dirs. 1995—96), Alpha Pi Mu. Achievements include patents pending for. Avocations: travel, TV, reading. Home: 3 Highland Manor Dr Tuscaloosa AL 35406 Office: Univ Ala Tuscaloosa Dept Indsl Engring PO Box 870288 Tuscaloosa AL 35487 Office Phone: 205-348-1603. E-mail: pray@coe.eng.ua.edu.

**RAY, RACHAEL,** chef, television personality; b. Cape Cod, Mass., Aug. 25, 1968; m. John Cusimano, Sept. 24, 2005. Student, Pace Univ. Mgr. fresh foods dept. Macy's Marketplace, NY; store mgr., buyer Agata & Valentina, NY; mgr., pub and rest. Sagamore Resort, Lake George, NY; food buyer Cowan & Lobel, Albany; editor-in-chief Everyday with Rachael Ray mag., 2005—. Author: 30-Minute Meals, 1998, Veggie Meals, 2001, Comfort Foods, 2001, 30-Minute Meals 2, 2003, Get Togethers: Rachael Ray 30 Minute Meals, 2003, Cooking 'Round the Clock: Rachael Ray's 30-Minute Meals, 2004, Cooking Rocks!: Rachael Ray's 30-Minute Meals for Kids, 2004, 30-Minute Get Real Meals: Eat Healthy Without Going to Extremes, 2005 (Quills award-cookbook, 2005), Comfort Food: Rachael Ray's Top 30 30-Minute Meals, 2005, Rachael Ray 365: No Repeats, 2005, Express Lane Meals, 2006; host 30 Minute Meals, Food Network, 2002—, $40 A Day, 2004—, Inside Dish, 2004—, Rachael Ray's Tasty Travels, 2005—, (syndicated talk show) The Rachel Ray Show, 2006—; guest appearances Pyramid, 2003, The Tony Danza Show, 2004, Live With Regis and Kelly, 2004, 2005, Sidewalks Entertainment, 2004, Good Day Live, 2004, The View, 2005, Isaac Mizrahi, 2005, Tonight Show with Jay Leno, 2005, Late Show with David Letterman, 2005, Oprah Winfrey Show, 2005, 2006. Named one of 100 Sexiest Women, FHM-US Mag., 2004, 100 Most Influential People, Time Mag., 2006.*

**RAY, RAYMOND B.,** federal judge; b. 1943; BA, U. South Fla., 1965; JD, U. Fla., 1971. Bar: Fla. Asst. U.S. atty. Dept. Justice, So. Dist. Fla., Miami, 1971-74; bankruptcy judge U.S. Bankruptcy Ct. (so. dist.) Fla., Ft. Lauderdale, 1993—. Comdr. USNR, 1961—85. Office: US Courthouse Rm 306 299 E Broward Blvd Fort Lauderdale FL 33301-1944 Office Phone: 954-769-5761. Business E-Mail: bettyrobaina@flsb.uscourts.gov.

**RAY, REBECCA ANN,** elementary school educator; b. Albuquerque, N. Mex., Jan. 7, 1950; d. Thomas Walter and Margaret (Phillips) Dailey; m. Ronnie Leslie Ray, June 30, 1973; children: Ronette Lewise, Lance Micheas. BS in Edn., U. N. Mex., 1977, MA in Elem. Edn., 1998. Tchr's asst. Laguna (N. Mex.) Elem. Sch., 1970-77, classroom tchr., 1977—. Sponsor Laguna Elem. Md. Sch. Cultural Dance Group. Mem. NSTA, Math Sci. Tchrs. (Tribal Coalition), Soc. for Advancement Chicanos and Native Am. in Sci. (edn. com.), Nat. Coun. Tchrs. Math. Democrat. Roman Catholic. Home: PO Box 1406 Paguate NM 87040-1406 Office: Laguna Elem Sch PO Box 191 Laguna NM 87026-0191 E-mail: bigsunlady@hotmail.com.

**RAY, ROBERT WILLIAM,** lawyer; b. Frankfurt, Germany, Apr. 4, 1960; s. Robert Luman and Margaret Ann (Bangs) R.; m. Kristen Jane Morsches, Aug. 4, 1984; children: Caroline Margaret, William Charles, Edward Francis. AB magna cum laude, Princeton U., l982; JD cum laude, Washington and Lee U., 1985. Bar: N.Y. 1986, Va. 1986, D.C. 1986, U.S. Dist. Ct. (so. and ea. dists.) N.Y. 1986, U.S. Ct. Appeals (2nd and 4th Cirs.) l987. Assoc. Brown & Wood, N.Y.C., 1985-87; law clk. to judge US Ct. Appeals (2nd Cir.), Uniondale, 1987-89; asst. U.S. atty. (so. dist.) N.Y. US Dept. Justice, N.Y.C., 1989—95; ptnr. Pitney Hardin LLP, NJ, 2002—05, Kelley Drye & Warren LLP, N.Y.C., 2005—. Dep. ind. counsel investigation of former sec. agrl. Michael Espy US Dept. Justice, 1995—99, sr. litigation counsel Whitewater Investigation, 1999, ind. counsel of Whitewater & Monica Lewinsky investigations, 1999—2002. Recipient Community Svc. award Rotary Internat., l978. Mem. ABA, Assn. of Bar of City of N.Y., Univ. Cottage Club (Princeton). Roman Catholic. Office: Kelley Drye & Warren LLP 200 Kimball Dr Parsippany NJ 07054 E-mail: rray@kelleydrye.com.

**RAY, RONALD DUDLEY,** lawyer; b. Hazard, Ky., Oct. 30, 1942; BA in Psychology and English, Centre Coll., 1964; JD magna cum laude, U. Louisville, 1971. Assoc. Greenebaum, Doll & McDonald, 1971-75, ptnr., 1975-84, 85-86, Ray & Morris, Louisville, 1986-89; mng. ptnr. Ronald Ray Attys., Louisville, 1990—; dep. asst. sec. def. Pentagon, Washington, 1984-85. Adj. prof. law U. Louisville Sch. Law, 1972-80; commrr. Presdl. Comm. on Assignment Women in Mil., 1992. Author: Military Necessity & Homosexuality, 1993; sr. legal editor: Personnel Policy Manual, Bank Supervisory Policies, The Bank Employee Handbook, 1985-86; mil. historian. State fin. chmn. Nat. Fin. Com. for George Bush for Pres.; chmn. Vietnam Vets. Leadership Program in Ky., 1982-85, Ky. Vietnam Vets. Meml. Fund, 1985-91; trustee Marine Corps Command and Staff Found., 1985-92; mem. exec. com. State Cen. Com., Ky. Rep. Party, 1986-90; mem. Am. Battle Monuments Commn., 1990-94; chmn. Vets. for Bush in Ky., 2000; mem. Nat. Com. Vets. for Bush, 2000; spokesman Coalition of Am. Vets., 1999—, chmn., 1999—; spl. coun. Naval Aviation Found., 1994—. With USMC, 1964-69; col. USMCR (ret.). Decorated Silver Star medal with gold star, Bronze Star medal, Purple Heart, Vietnamese Cross of Gallantry, Vietnamese Honor Medal; recipient Nat. Eagle award Nat. Guard Assn., 1985. Mem. Naval Inst. (life), Marine Corps Res. Officers' Assn. Home: Halls Hill Farm 3317 Halls Hill Rd Crestwood KY 40014-9523 Office Phone: 502-241-5552. Personal E-mail: colray@aye.net.

**RAY, RUTH ALICE YANCEY,** retired rancher, real estate developer; b. Birmingham, Ala., July 26, 1931; d. John Grayson and Ruth Ethel (Lutman) Yancey; (div. July 1986); children: Virginia Ruth, John Edward, William Arthur. Student, Fla. State U., 1949-50; BS, Appalachian State U., 1954; postgrad., Stetson U., 1966-67, Appalachian State U., 1962-63, Stetson U., 1964-67. Tchr. pub. schs., Nenana, Alaska, 1955-56; tchr. 1st Christian Ch., Clermont, Fla., 1965-67, Lake County Sch. Bd., Clermont, 1969-70; rancher Rays' Ranch, Clermont, 1963-97; pvt. real estate developer Clermont, 1990—; substitute tchr. Buncombe County Asheville City Sch. Sys., 1999—; tchr. Marion County Sch. Bd., 2006—. Chmn. Clermont Planning and Zoning Commn., 1973-81; mem. Heart of Fla. Girl Scout Coun., 1988—, life mem. Ctr. Fla. Girl Scout Coun.; life mem. Friends of Cooper Mem. Libr.; South Lake Art League; assoc. Sisters of St. Mary. Named Conservation Farmer of Yr., State of Fla., 1982. Mem. Lake County Farm Bur. (bd. dirs. 1977-81), Lake County Cattlemen's Assn. (v.p. 1979-81), Lake County Farmer's Home Adminstrn. (bd. dirs. 1984-88, 1990—, chmn. 1985, 88, 90-91), Nat. Cutting Horse Assn. (life), Am. Quarter Horse Assn., Am. Paint Horse Assn., E.S.A. Internat., Daus. of King (pres., sec.), St. Bridcats Guild, Sigma Kappa. Republican. Episcopalian (sr. warden, eucharistic min.). Avocations: needlepoint, fishing, hiking, reading. Home: 3001 SE Lake Weir Ave Apt 1101 Ocala FL 34471-6778

**RAY, SIBA PRASAD,** materials scientist, ceramics scientist; b. Dinhata, India, Jan. 4, 1944; came to U.S., 1969; s. Nilmony P. and Bina Pani Ray; m. Lipika Ray, May 28, 1977; children: Sourav, Leena. B of Engring., Calcutta (India) U., 1964; MS, Columbia U., 1970, D of Engring. Sci., 1974. Sci. officer Bhabha Atomic Rsch. Ctr., Bombay, 1964-68; rsch. assoc. Pa. State U., University Park, 1974-76; scientist Alcoa Labs., Alcoa Ctr., Pa., 1977-78, sr. scientist, 1978-82, sci. assoc. Alcoa Center, Pa., 1982-91, sr. sci. assoc., 1991-98; program mgr. materials devel. NGAP, Alcoa, Alcoa Center, 1999—. Cons. Alcoa Separations Tech., Warrendale, Pa., 1991, Electro Metallurgy and Electrochemistry Cons., New Kensington, Pa., 1992. Contbr. articles to Jour. Solid State Chemistry, J. Am. Ceramic Soc., Light Metals, Bull. Am. Ceramic Soc. Pres. Bengali Assn. Pitts., 1988. Mem. The Metall. Soc., Am. Ceramic Soc., Sigma Xi. Achievements include 52 patents in the area of inert elctrodes, ceramic composites and reaction sintering. Home: 6007 Pilgrim Ct Murrysville PA 15668-8533 Office: Alcoa Labs Alcoa Tech Ctr Alcoa Center PA 15069 Personal E-mail: sray12@alltel.net.

**RAY, SUSAN ELAINE,** principal; b. Huntington, W.Va. d. Emory Joseph and Frances Fulkerson Ray. BS, Fla. State U., Tallahassee, 1974, MS in Edn., 1976; MS in Edn. Adminstrn., Coll. New Rochelle, N.Y., 2003; post grad., St. Johns U. Cert. tchr. N.Y., Fla., admistr. N.Y., Fla. Tchr. Longwood Ctrl. Schs., Middle Island, NY, 1979—85; instr. Elon Coll., NC, 1986—87; tchr. Riverside H.S., Durham, 1988—2000; instr. edn. Kamuzu Coll., Lilogwe, Malawi, 2000; asst. prin. Lake Grove (N.Y.) Sch., 2001—02, Copiague Mid. Sch., 2003—04; prin. The Broach Sch., St. Petersburg, Fla., 2005—. Staff developer Tchg. Children of Poverty and Tng. New Tchrs., Copiague, NY, 2003—04; dir. The Broach Sch., St. Petersburg, Fla., 2005—. Youth coach U.S. Volleyball Assn., Durham, NC, 1988—99; site dir. Internat. Spl. Olympics, 1999; active Tchrs. Africa Fellowship, 2000—01. Named Durham County Tchr. of Yr., 1998, State Volleyball Coach of Yr., N.C. H.S. Athletic Assn., 1998; recipient Outstanding Achievement in Edn award, Duke U., 1998. Mem.: ASCD, Phi Delta Kappa.

**RAY, VIRGINIA H. S.,** columnist, writer; b. Chgo., Aug. 4, 1931; d. Russell Horton and Cora Virginia Stafford; m. Wilson K. Ray, Nov. 8, 1952 (dec. Oct. 14, 2000); 1 child, Virginia Ray Bouchillon. Writer, reporter South Bend (Ind.) Tribune, 1953—58; freelance writer Lausanne, Switzerland, 1963—68, Tokyo, 1973—79; freelance writer, corr. York County Coast Star, Kennebank, Maine, 1989—2002, Biddeford (Maine) Jour. Tribune, 1990—. Newsletter editor Jr. League Pitts., 1969—70, Tokyo Am. Club, 1974—78; founder libr., Fox Chapel, 1st Internat. Fair, Japan, 1974. Active Pitts. Jr. League, 1958—73; chmn. Three Rivers Art Festival, Pitts., 1962; active Kennebankport Hist. Soc., 1990. Mem.: Portland Jr. League, Brick Store Mus. Republican. Avocations: reading, history, travel, tennis. Home: #15 Pt Arundel PO 1144 Kennebunkport ME 04046-1144 Office Phone: 207-967-4227. Personal E-mail: vsr@gwi.net.

**RAY, WILLIAM JACKSON,** psychologist; b. Birmingham, Ala., Sept. 3, 1945; s. Norman M. and Mary K. Agnew; m. Judith Mebane, Aug. 22, 1987; children from previous marriage: Adam, Lauren. BA, Eckerd Coll., 1967; MA, Vanderbilt U., 1969, PhD, 1971; Fellow in med. psychology, Langley Porter Neuropsychiat. Inst., U. Calif. Med. Center, San Francisco, 1971-72. Prof., dir. clin. psychology tng. program Pa. State U., 1972—, dir. clin. trng., 1991-97. Author: (with R.M. Stern) Biofeedback, 1977, (with others) Evaluation of Clinical Biofeedback, 1979, (with R.M. Stern and C.M. Davis) Psychophysiological Recording, 1980, 2d edit. (with R.M. Stern and K. Quigley), 2000, Methods Toward a Science of Behavior and Experience, 1981, 8th edit., 2006, (with E. Susman & L. Feajous) Emotion, Cognition, Health and Development in Children and Adolescents, 1992, (with L. Michelson) Handbook of Dissociation, 1996 (Cornelia Wilbur award ISSD); series editor: Plenum Series in Behavioral Psychophysiology and Medicine. Recipient Nat. Media award Am. Psychol. Found., 1976, 78, Rsch. award Best Empirical Paper, Soc. Clin. Experimental Hypnosis. Mem. AAAS, APA, APS, Soc. Psychophysiol. Rsch. Office: Dept Psychology Pa State U University Park PA 16802 Office Phone: 814-863-1726. Business E-Mail: wjr@psu.edu.

**RAYBURN, BOYD DALE,** artist; b. Carriere, Miss., May 12, 1942; s. Sammual Boyd and Irene Rayburn; m. Mamie Joe Rayburn, Jan. 14, 1948; children: Brandon, Glen, Cory, Todd. BA in Fine Arts, U. So. Miss., 1964; MFA, U. Miss., Oxford, 1970. Tchr. Ga. Southwestern Coll., Americus, 1971—72, La. State U., Shreveport, 1980—82; full time studio artist Rayburn Studio, Roswell, Ga., 1982—. Represented in permanent collections De Cordova Mus., Lincoln, Mass., Yale U. Art Gallery, New Orleans Mus. Art, Miss. Mus. Art, Emory U. Mus. Art, High Mus. Art. Recipient 1st Pl. Printmaking, Coconut Grove Arts Festival, 2003, Merit award, Winter Pk. Festival Art, 2003, Award of Distinction, New Orleans Coun. Art-Fresh Festival, 2003, 1st Pl. Printmaking, Coconut Grove Arts Festival, 2005. Mem.: Nat. Assn. Ind. Artist (assoc.; bd. mem. 1995—98). Avocations: fishing, travel. Home: 1538 Jones Rd Roswell GA 30075 Studio: Rayburn Studio 1538 Jones Rd Roswell GA 30075 Office Phone: 770-998-3453. Personal E-mail: dale@dalerayburn.com.

**RAYBURN, CAROLE ANN (MARY AIDA),** psychologist, researcher, writer, consultant; b. Washington, Feb. 14, 1938; d. Carl Frederick and Mary Helen (Milkie) Miller; m. Ronald Allen Rayburn (dec. Apr. 1970). BA in Psychology, Am. U., 1961; MA in Clin. Psychology, George Washington U., 1965; PhD in Edn. Psychology, Cath. U. Am., 1969; MDiv in Ministry, Andrews U., 1980. Lic. psychologist, Md. Psychometrician Columbian Prep. Sch., Washington, 1963; clin. psychologist Spring Grove State Hosp., Catonsville, Md., 1966—68; pvt. practice, 1969, 1971—; staff clin. psychologist Instl. Care Svcs. Divsn. D.C. Children's Ctr., Laurel, Md., 1970—78; psychologist Md. Dept. Vocat. Rehab., 1973—74; psychometrician Montgomery County Pub. Schs., 1981—85. Lectr. Strayer Coll., Washington, 1969-70; forensic psychology expert witness, 1973—; guest lectr. Andrews U., Berrien Springs, Mich., 1976, Hood Coll, Frederick, Md., 1986-88; instr. Johns Hopkins U., 1986, 88-89; adj. faculty Profl. Sch. Psychology Studies, San Diego, 1987; adj. asst. prof. Loyola Coll., Columbia, Md., 1987; cons. Julia Brown Montessori Schs., 1972, 78, 82—, VA Ctr., 1978, 91-93. Editor: (with M.J. Meadow) A Time to Weep and a Time to Sing, 1985; contbg. author: Montessori: Her Method and the Movement (What You Need to Know), 1973, Drugs, Alcohol and Women: A National Forum Source Book, 1975, The Other Side of the Couch: Faith of the Psychotherapist, 1981, Clinical Handbook of Pastoral Counseling, 1985, An Encyclopedic Dictionary of Pastoral Care and Counseling, 1990, Religion Personality and Mental Health, 1993; co-editor (with Violet Franks) Springer Focus on Women series; author copyrighted inventories Religious Occupational and Stress Questionnaire, 1986, Organizational Relationships Survey, 1987, Attitudes Toward Children Inventory, 1987, State-Trait Morality Inventory, 1987, Body Awareness and Sexual Intimacy Comfort Scale (BASICS), 1993, Inventory in Religiousness, 1996, Inventory on Spirituality, 1997, Sports, Exercise, Leadership and Friendship Questionnaire, 1997, Peacefulness Inventory, Life Choices Inventory, 1998, Inventory on the Supreme and Work, 1999, Children's and Adolescents' Peace Inventory, 2002, Inventory on Well-Being, 2004, TEACH: Traumatic Experiences and Children's and Adolescents' Health, 2005, Creative Personality Inventory, 2005, Intuition Inventory, 2005, Health and Traumatic Experiences in Adults, 2005, Inventory on Religiousness, Children's Version, 2005; cons. editor Profl. Psychology, 1980-83; assoc. editor Jour. Pastoral Counseling, 1985-90, guest editor, 1988; coproposer (with Lee Richmond) The Theory and Field of Theobiology: interfacing of theology and the sciences, 1998; mem. editl. bd. Internat. Jour. Ethics (Nova Sci.), 2004—; contbr. numerous articles to profl. jours. Bd. dirs. Psychologists Ethical Treatment of Animals, 1998-2000. Recipient Svc. award Coun. for Advancement Psychol. Professions and Scis., 1975, cert. D.C. Dept. Human Resources, 1975, 76, cert. recognition D.C. Psychol. Assn., 1976, 1985; AAUW rsch. grantee, 1983. Fellow: APA (editl. bd. Jour. Child Clin. Psychology 1978—82, divsn. Psychology women chair task force on women and religion 1980—81, chair equal opportunity affirmative action divsn. clin. psychology 1980—82, clin. psychology women's sect. 1984—86, divsn. psychology issues in grad. edn. and clin. tng. 1988—, program chair 1991—94, pres. divsns. psychology of religion 1995—96, gen. psych. divsn. liaison to commn. internat. rels. 2004—, fellow, divsn. on internat. psychology, divsn. psychology of religion, psychology of women, clin. psychology, cons. psychology, gen. psychology, psychotherapy, state assn. affairs, divsn. media psychology, divsn. family psychology, Mentoring award divsn. clin. psychology, sect. of clin. psychology of women 1997, divsn. psychology of religion 1997, William C. Bier rsch. award divsn. psychology of religion 2000), Md. Psychol. Assn. (editor newsletter 1975—76, chair ins. com. 1981—83, pres. 1984—85, exec. adv. com. 1985—, chpt. recognition 1978), Am. Assn. Applied & Preventive Psychology (sec. 1992—93, chair fellows com. 1992—93), Am. Orthopsychiat. Assn.; mem.: Md. Assn. Counseling and Devel., Md. Asn. Measurement and Evaluation (pres. 2005—), Balt. Assn. Cons. Psychologists (pres. 1991—92), Assn. Practicing Psychologists Montgomery-Prince George's Counties (pres. 1986—88, editor newsletter 1990—, treas. 1996—98), Internat. Soc. Polit. Psychology, Psi Chi (hon.). Achievements include research in stress in religious professionals, women and stress, women and religion, pastoral counseling, state-trait morality inventory, leadership, mentoring, clergy stress, psychotherapy, children, body image; intimacy, peacefulness, spirituality, life choices, religiousness, well-being, work, traumatic experiences and health, creative personality, intuition. Address: 1200 Morningside Dr Silver Spring MD 20904-3149 Personal E-mail: valentinecarole@copper.net.

**RAYBURN, DAVID B.,** manufacturing executive; b. Gallipolis, Ohio, May 24, 1948; BS, Pa. State Univ., 1970; MBA, Xavier Univ., 1979. Mgmt. positions through dir. mfg. Rockwell Internat., 1970—91; v.p., gen. mgr. heavy duty & indsl. div. Modine Mfg. Co., Racine, Wis., 1991—93, v.p., gen. mgr. automotive div., 1993—94, group v.p. highway products, 1994—98, exec. v.p., 1998—2002, pres., COO, 2002—03, pres., CEO, 2003—, bd. dir., 2003—. Bd. dir. Marshall & Illsley Bank, Twin Disc, Jason Holdings Inc. RAMAC. Mem.: Soc. Automotive Engineers. Office: Modine Mfg Co 1500 DeKoven Ave Racine WI 53403*

**RAYBURN, WENDELL GILBERT, SR.,** educational consultant; b. Detroit, May 20, 1929; s. Charles Jefferson and Grace Victoria (Winston) R.; m. Gloria Ann Myers, Aug. 19; children: Rhonda Renee, Wendell Gilbert; 1 stepson, Mark K. Williams. BA, Eastern Mich. U., 1951; MA, U. Mich., 1952; Ed.D., Wayne State U., Detroit, 1972. Tchr., adminstr. Detroit public schs., 1954-68; from asst. dir. to dir. spl. projects U. Detroit, 1968-72, asso. dean acad. support programs, 1972-74; dean Univ. Coll., U. Louisville, 1974-80; pres. Savannah (Ga.) State Coll., 1980-88, Lincoln U., Jefferson City, Mo., 1988-97; v.p. fin. Am. Assn. State Colls. and Univs., Washington, 1997—2001; v.p., sec., treas., sr. assoc. Penson Associates, Chevy Chase, Md. Chmn. adv. com. Office for Advancement of Pub. Black Colls., 1989-97. Trustee Candler Gen. Hosp., 1982-85, Telfair Acad. Arts, 1980-87; bd. dirs. Candler Health Svcs., 1985-88, YMCA Blue Ridge Assembly, 1986-88, Internat. Food and Agrl. Devel. and Econ. Cooperation, 1988-94, Meml. Cmty. Hosp., Jefferson City, 1988-94, United Way Mo., 1989-97, No. Capital Punishment Resource Ctr., 1990-95, Stephens Coll., Columbia, Mo., 1993-97, Capital Regional Med. Ctr., 1994-97; campaign chmn. Jefferson City Area United Way, 1994-95. With AUS, 1952-59. Decorated Commendation medal with pendant; recipient Disting. Alumni award Wayne State U., 1993, Whitney M. Young Jr. award Lincoln Found., 1980, Disting. Citizens award City of Louisville, 1980. Mem. Mo. Bar Assn. (foresight com.), Am. Assn. Higher Edn., Am. Assn. State Colls. and Univs. (bd. dirs. 1988—, chmn. 1992-93), Nat. Assn. State Univs. and Land Grant Colls., Nat. Assn. for Equal Opportunity in Higher Edn., Coun. on Pub. Higher Edn. for Mo. (chmn. 1991-93), Coun. of 1890 Colls. and Univs., Jefferson City C. of C. (bd. dirs. 1988-97), Rotary (bd. dirs. Jefferson City 1989-96, pres. 1994-95), Kappa Alpha Psi, Sigma Pi Phi. Episcopalian. Mailing: Penson Associates Apt 1735 4701 Willard Ave Chevy Chase MD 20815-4632

**RAYCHOUDHURY, SAMIR,** biology professor, researcher; b. India, Nov. 1954; m. Krishna Raychoudhury, 1985; children: Parag, Abir. BSc, B.C. Agrl. U., 1977, MSc, 1984; PhD, Griffith U., 1989. Assoc. prof. Benedict Coll., Columbia, SC, 2002—, dir. R&D, 2002—. Editor: Frontiers in Bioscience Spl. Issues. Recipient Disting. Faculty award, Benedict Coll., 2002—03, Govs. Disting. Prof., S.C. Commn. Higher Edn., 2004; grantee, NIH, 2001—. Mem.: Am. Soc. of Andrology (chmn. minority affairs com. 2001—04), S.C. Acad. of Sci., The Soc. for the Study of Reproduction. Achievements include research in reproductive toxicology. Office: Benedict College 1600 Harden Street Columbia SC 29204 Office Phone: 803-255-1781. Business E-Mail: raychoudhurys@benedict.edu.

**RAYFIELD, ELLIOT JAMES,** medical educator; b. Phila., May 6, 1942; s. Joseph and Rachel Evelyn (Aisenstein) Rayfield. AB, U. Pa., 1963; MD, Jefferson Med. Coll., 1967. Assoc. prof. medicine Mt. Sinai Sch. Medicine, N.Y.C., 1974—77, assoc. prof. medicine, 1977—82, prof. medicine, 1982—88, clin. prof. medicine, 1988—. Mem. med. adv. bd. Mirro Islet, San Diego, 2001—05. Author (with C. Soelmani): (book) Diabetes - Beating the Cure, 1992. Maj. U.S. Army, 1971—73. Recipient Recognition award, Endocrine Soc. Devel. Com., 2004, 1st Profl. Edn. Sci. award, N.Y. Downstate Affiliate, Rsch. Career R&D award, NIH, 1975—80, Disting. Rsch. award, Dept. Medicine, Mt. Sinai Sch. Medicine, 1985. Fellow: ACP, Am. Assn. Clin. Endocrinology (charter); mem.: Mt. Sinai Alumni Assn. (v.p. 2005—07), Am. Diabetes Assn. (1st Profl. Edn. Sci. award N.Y. downstate affiliate 1989), Am. Soc. Clin. Investigation (pres. N.Y. downstate affiliate 1993—94), Alpha Omega Alpha. Avocation: running. Office: 1150 Park Ave New York NY 10028

**RAYHILL, STEPHEN CORRIGAN,** surgeon; s. Philip Anthony and Julia Mary Rayhill; m. Maureen Kinney, Sept. 24, 1999; children: Corrigan Rose, Maisie Grace. BA, Middlebury Coll., 1978; MD, Columbia U., 1987. Resident in surgery Stanford (Calif.) U., 1987—94, chief resident, 1993—94; asst. prof. surgery and urology U. Iowa, Iowa City, 1997—2004; assoc. prof. surgery and urology Oreg. Health Scis. U. Sch. Medicine, Portland, 2004—. Transplant fellow, U. Wis., 1994—97. Am. Heart Assn. Postdoctoral fellow, Stanford U., 1989—91. Fellow: ACS. Avocations: skiing, surfing, biking, music. Office: OHSU Sch Medicine Mail Code L590 3181 SW Sam Jackson Park Blvd Portland OR 97239-3098 Office Phone: 503-494-2744. Business E-Mail: rayhills@ohsu.edu.

**RAYLE, HEATHER LYNNETTE,** chemist; b. Greensboro, NC, June 10, 1968; d. Donald Lee and Sharon Sue R. BS in Chemistry with high distinction, Pa. State U., 1989; PhD in Chemistry, UCLA, 1994; MBA, Lehigh U., 2001. Sr. scientist Rohm & Haas Co., Spring House, Pa., 1994-98, rsch. sect. mgr., 1998-99, mgr. tech. planning, 1999-2000, bus. devel. mgr. Phoenix, 2001—03, mktg. dir., 2003—05, dir. slurry technology, 2006—. Bd. dirs. Rohm & Haas Tech. Comty. Orgn., Spring House, Pa., 1997-2000, chair 1999, Pa. State U. Coll. Sci., alumni bd., 2001—, treas., 2005—. Braddock scholarship, Pa. State U. Coll. of Sci., 1985-89; fellow NSF, 1989-92, fellow UCLA, 1989-94; recipient Otto Haas award for Scientific Achievement, 1998. Mem. Am. Chem. Soc., Phi Beta Kappa. Achievements include development of commerical processes to manufacture agricultural chemicals and their intermediates; commercial marketing and technology management of consumables for semiconductor processing. Office: Rohm and Haas Electronic Materials 451 Bellevue Rd Newark DE 19713 E-mail: hrayle@rohmhaas.com.

**RAYLESBERG, ALAN IRA,** lawyer; b. NYC, Dec. 6, 1950; s. Daniel David and Sally Doris (Mantell) Raylesberg; m. Caren Thea Coven, Nov. 20, 1983; children: Lisa Maris, Jason Todd. BA, NYU, 1972; JD cum laude, Boston U., 1975. Bar: N.Y.1976, US Dist. Ct. (so. dist.) NY 1976, US Dist. Ct. (ea. dist.) NY 1978, US Tax Ct. 1981, US Ct. Appeals (2d and 5th cirs.) 1982, US Ct. Appeals (1st cir.) 1986, US Ct. Appeals (9th cir.) 1996, US Ct. Appeals (fed. cir.) 2004. Assoc. Orans, Elsen & Polstein, NYC, 1975-77, Guggenheimer & Untermyer, NYC, 1977-83, ptnr., 1983-85, Rosenman & Colin, NYC, 1985—2002, co-head comml. litig. group, 1998-99, chmn. litig. dept., 1999—2002; ptnr., sect. head litig. group Vinson & Elkins, NYC, 2002—04; ptnr. Chadbourne & Parke, NYC, 2004—, head comml. litig.

group, 2006—. Adj. instr. NY Law Sch., 1980—83; instr. Nat. Inst. Trial Advocacy; mem. adv. group commI. divsn., mem. mediation panel NY State Supreme Ct.; mem. arbitration panel US Dist. Ct. (ea. dist.) NY; mem. CPR Inst. Dispute Resolution Panel Disting. Neutrals, NYC; judge Nat. Moot Ct. Competition, 1980—. Author: Case Evaluation, Commercial Litigation in New York State Courts, 2005. Bd. dirs. Fund Modern Cts., 1994—. Fellow: NY Bar Found.; mem.: ABA, NY Coun. Def. Lawyers (legal and compliance divsn.), Securities Industry Assn. NY State Bar Assn. (ho. dels. 1996—2000), NY County Lawyers Assn. Found. (bd. dirs. 1998—2003), NY County Lawyers Assn. (bd. dirs. 1995—98, 1999—2002, mem. fed. ct. com. 1988—, mem. appellate ct. com. 1990—, co-chmn. appellate ct. com. 1992—93, chair appellate ct. com. 1993—96), Assn. Bar City NY, Fed. Bar Coun., Town Club New Castle (mem. exec. com. 1987—91). Democrat. Jewish. Office: Chadbourne & Parke 30 Rockefeller Plz New York NY 10112 Office Phone: 212-408-5198. Personal E-mail: alan.raylesberg@verizon.net. Business E-Mail: araylesberg@chadbourne.com.

**RAYMAN, RUSSELL BARRY,** physician; b. Toledo, Ohio, Jan. 13, 1936; m. Ludy Rayman; children: Joseph, David, Ariel. MD, U. Mich., 1961. Diplomate Am. Bd. Family Practice, Am. Bd. Aerospace Medicine. Intern Jackson Meml. Hosp., Miami, Fla., 1961-62; commd. 2d lt. USAF, 1962, advanced through grades to col., 1989; resident in aerospace medicine Brooks AFB, Tex., 1969-72; mgr. operational medicine Lockheed, Washington, 1989-92; exec. dir. Aerospace Med. Assn., Alexandria, Va., 1992—. Author: Clinical Aviation Medicine, 4th edit., 2006. Decorated numerous mil. awards. Office: Aerospace Med Assn 320 S Henry St Alexandria VA 22314-3524

**RAYMER, JOHN DAVID,** literature and language professor; b. Elkhart, Ind., July 9, 1948; m. Kathleen Russell, June 24, 2006; children: Thomas, Carolyn Mary MacEachran, Janet Theresa, Thomas Joseph, Mariah Trench. BA, Wittenberg U., Springfield, Ohio, 1970; MA, Nat. U. Ireland, Dublin, 1971; PhD, Ohio U., Athens, 1975; postdoctoral, Purdue U., West Lafayette, Ind. Asst. prof. English Purdue U., Calumet, Ind., 1976—80; ins. agt. C.M. Alliance Group Inc., South Bend, Ind., 1980—90; adj. asst. prof. Ind. U., South Bend, 1989—94; assoc. prof. English Holy Cross Coll., Notre Dame, Ind., 1990—. Chair faculty forum Holy Cross Coll., Notre Dame, 1991—93, homework tutoring campus coord., 1994—2006, co-founder, dir. homework tutoring program, 1995—, acad. affairs faculty rep., 1997—98, chair promotions and retention com., 2005—; mem. Ind. Middle Grades Reading Network, 1993—, Nat. Scholastic Hon. Middle Grades Reading Network; adv. editor Collegiate Press, 1995—2004; mentee Midwest Tech. Tchg. Acad., Chgo., 2000—01. Contbg. editor: The Hole in Me Since the Day You Died, 2005. Leader student groups South Bend Walk for Hospice; sr. warden St. Michael and All Angels Episcopal Ch., South Bend, Ind., 2004—; founding mem. English Connection; former bd. mem., Big Brothers/Big Sisters, South Bend. Named Outstanding Mentoree of U. Notre Dame bound students, 2005; recipient Outstanding Cmty.-Coll. Collaboration award, Coll. Compact, Miami Beach, Fla., 1998, Attendance award, Kiwanis Internat., 2003, 2004, George Hixson award, 2004, Outstanding Young Men of Am. award. Mem.: Internat. Reading Assn., Knute Rockne Kiwanis Club, Phi Kappa Phi. Democrat. Episcopalian. Avocations: travel, swimming, canoeing, hiking, reading. Home: 1613 E Madison St South Bend IN 46617 Office: Holy Cross Coll 54515 State Rd 933 Notre Dame IN 46556-0308 Office Phone: 574-239-8385.

**RAYMOND, BRUCE ALLEN,** medical association administrator; b. Aberdeen, S.D., Dec. 8, 1924; s. Samuel A. and Pearl (Blackstone) R.; m. Virginia Stratton, Apr. 2, 1948 (div. 1969); children: Judith Ann, Jaqueline Marie, Bruce Allen Jr., Brian Andrew; m. Jane Molnar, Nov. 15, 1969; children: Douglas A., Andrew D., Colin K. BS, Leland Stanford U., U.S.D., 1945; MD, Washington U., St. Louis, 1949. Diplomate Am. Bd. Surgery, Am. Bd. Thoracic Surgery. Intern U. Ored. Med. Sch. Hosps., Portland, 1949-50; resident in surgery Walter Reed Gen. Hosp., Washington, 1953-57, resident in thoracic surgery, 1957-59, asst. chief thoracic surgery, 1959-60; chief thoracic and cardiovascular surgery Letterman Gen. Hosp., San Francisco, 1960-64, Fitzsimmons Gen. Hosp., Denver, 1967-69, chief dept. surgery, 1969-71; pvt. practice surgery Warwick, R.I., 1975-86; sr. med. dir. Health Care Compare Corp., Downers Grove, Ill., 1986—89, Equicor Corp. Healthcare Mgmt., Pitts., 1989—90; med. dir. The Health Plan of the Upper Ohio Valley, 1996—2003. Asst. clin. prof. U. Colo., 1967-71; assoc. clin. prof. surgery Northwestern U., Chgo., 1973-80; mem. staff Kent County Med. Mem. Hosp., Warwick, 1975-86, Miriam hosp., Providence, 1975-86; cons. in field. Contbr. articles to profl. jours. Elder, Prebyn. Ch.; various offices, bd. dirs. Boy Scouts Am., R.I., Pa., and Ill. Col.M.C. U.S. Army, 1949-72. Decorated Legion of Merit. Fellow ACS, Am. Coll. Cardiology, Am. Coll. Chest Physicians; mem. Soc. Thoracic Surgeons, Pan Pacific Surg. Assn., Am. Heart Assn., AMA, Am. Assn. Med. Instrumentation, Am. Acad. Med. Dirs., Uniformed Svcs. Univ. Surg. Assocs., New Eng. Vascular Soc. Republican. Avocation: downhill skiing. Home: 218 Salem Dr Upper Saint Clair PA 15241-2226 E-mail: braymond66@adelphia.net.

**RAYMOND, DAVID WALKER,** lawyer; b. Chelsea, Mass., Aug. 23, 1945; s. John Walker and Jane (Beck) R.; m. Sandra Sue Broadwater, Aug. 12, 1967 (div.); m. Margaret Byrd Payne, May 25, 1974; children: Pamela Payne, Russell Wyatt. BA, Gettysburg Coll., 1967; JD, Temple U., 1970. Bar: Pa. 1970, D.C. 1971, Ill. 1975, U.S. Dist. Ct. (no. dist.) Ill. 1981, U.S. Supreme Ct. 1974. Govtl. affairs atty. Sears, Roebuck and Co., Washington, 1970-74, atty. Sears Hdqrs. law dept. Chgo., 1974-80, asst. gen. counsel advt., trademarks and customs, 1981-84, asst. gen. counsel adminstrn., 1984-86, mgr. planning and analysis corp. planning dept., 1986-89, sr. corp. counsel pub. policy corp. law dept., 1989-90; assoc. gen. counsel litigation and adminstrn. law dept. Sears Mdse. Group, 1990-92, dep. gen. counsel, 1992-93, v.p., gen. counsel, 1993-95: v.p. law Sears Roebuck and Co. 1996-97 of counsel Winston & Strawn, Washington, 1996-2001; v.p., gen. counsel C-NAV Systems, Inc., Gettysburg, Pa., 2001—03. Mem. staff Temple Law Quar., 1968—69; editor: Temple Law Quar., 1969—70. Trustee No. Ill. U., 1996—98; bd. dirs. Christopher Newport U., 1999—2003; bd. fellows Gettysburg Coll., 1999—2003; bd. dirs. ATO House Corp., 1997—, pres., 2004—. Mem.: ABA, Phi Alpha Delta. Presbyterian.

**RAYMOND, DOROTHY SARNOFF,** communications consultant, former actress, former singer; b. N.Y.C.; d. Jacob and Belle (Roossin) S.; m. Milton Harold Raymond, Mar. 15, 1957. BA, Cornell U., 1935. Cons. 5 adminstrns., over 12 years; cons. 5 adminstrns. U.S. Dept. State; founder, chmn. Dorothy Sarnoff Speech Dynamics and Communications Svcs. Inc. subs. Ogilvy & Mather, N.Y.C., 1975—2000. Lectr., cons. nat. and internat. orgns., 1975—. Appeared in Broadway plays: Rosalinda, 1942, Magdalena, 1948, The King and I, 1951, My Darling Aida, 1953; debut in opera as Marguerite in Faust, Phila. Opera, 1942; leading roles with N.Y.C., Phila., L.A. and San Francisco Civic Light, New Orleans, St. Louis Mcpl., Salt Lake City operas include La Boheme, Tosca, Tales of Hoffmann, Carmen, Merry Widow, Fleidermaus, Pagliacci, New Moon, Chocolate Soldier, Great Waltz, Vagabond King; soprano soloist with various symphony orchs., soloist and guest on numerous TV programs incl. Ed Sullivan Shows, 1951—; author: Speech Can Change Your Life, 1970, Make the Most of Your Best, 1981, Never Be Nervous Again, 1988, contbr. articles to profl. jours. and mags. Mem. spl. med. adv. bd. N.Y. Cornell Hosp. Recipient Gold Medal of Honor award for disting. svc. to humanity Nat. Inst. Social Scis.; named Woman of Achievement Albert Einstein Med. Coll. Mem. Women's Forum, Women in Communication, Mortar Bd., Tower Club (Cornell U. chpt.), Lotos Club, N.Y. Hosp. Med. Adv. Bd. Home: 150 E 69th St New York NY 10021-5704

**RAYMOND, GEORGE MARC,** city planner, educator; b. Odessa, Russia, Jan. 1, 1919; came to U.S., 1937, naturalized, 1942; s. Mark J. and Rachelle (Schneiderman) R.; m. Kathleen E. Waid, Oct. 3, 1942 (div. Mar. 1978); 1 dau., Valerie M.; m. Lois Jean Gainsboro, Mar. 26, 1979. BArch, Columbia, 1946. Planning dir. Harrison, Ballard & Allen, Inc., N.Y.C., 1952-54; founder, pres. Raymond, Parish, Pine & Weiner, Inc., 1954-83; pres. George M. Raymond Assocs., 1983—; prof. planning, chmn. dept. city and regional planning Pratt Inst., Bklyn., 1959-75; founder, dir. Pratt Ctr. for Community

Improvement, Bklyn., 1963-70. Lectr. planning Columbia U., 1955-58; lectr. planning and urban renewal New Sch. Social Rsch., 1967-72; pres. Assn. Collegiate Sch. Planning, 1968-69; chmn. Westchester County Housing Implementation Commn., 1992-93. Editor: Pratt Planning Papers, 1963-73, (with Astrid Monson) Pratt Guide to Housing, Planning and Urban Renewal for New Yorkers, 1965. V.p. Citizens Housing and Planning Coun. N.Y.C., 1967-86, N.Y. Assn. Environ. Profls., 1977-79; pres. Westchester Citizens Housing Coun., 1964-66, Met. Com. on Planning, 1950-51; founder, pres. Friends of Music Concerts, 1954-57, Spoken Arts Soc., 1966-67; past 1st v.p. Federated Conservationists Westchester County; past dir. Nat. Housing Conf., Phipps Houses, Wave Hill, Settlement Housing Fund; chmn. Westchester County Housing Opportunity Commn., 1994—; land use adv. com. N.Y. State Legis. Commn. on Rural Resources, 1992-98. Fellow: Am. Inst. Cert. Planners; mem.: Am. Planning Assn. (pres. NY met. chpt. 1983—85), Am. Soc. Cons. Planners (pres. 1968—70). Home: 192 Locust Ln Irvington NY 10533-2315 Office: 101 Executive Blvd Elmsford NY 10523-1316

**RAYMOND, JACK,** journalist, public relations executive, foundation administrator; b. Lodz, Poland, Oct. 6, 1918; s. Harry and Anna (Lange) R.; m. Gertrude Silverman, Oct. 6, 1946; children: David Alan, Judith. Student, CCNY, 1939. Sports writer N.Y. World-Telegram, 1934-38; ct. reporter, city editor, columnist N.Y. Daily North Side News, 1938-40; Corr. N.Y. Times, 1940-66, Berlin, 1946-47, Frankfurt, 1947-49, Bonn, 1949-52, Balkans, Belgrade, 1952-56, Moscow, 1956, Pentagon corr. Washington, 1956-66; pub. rels. exec., pres. Thomas J. Deegan Co., Washington and N.Y.C., 1966-67; v.p. Bryan Publs., N.Y.C., 1970-74; founding pres. Internat. Inst. for Environ. and Devel., 1970—73; pres. Dialog divsn. J. Walter Thompson Co., 1973-75; pres. Jack Raymond & Co., Inc., NYC, 1975—87, chmn., 1987—92; pres. JR Cons. Svc., Inc., 1987-96; acting comm. dir. Commonwealth Fund, 1987. Book reviewer The Villager, N.Y.C., 1970-74; cons. UN Conf. on Human Environment, 1972, Aspen Inst. Humanistic Studies, HABITAT, UN Conf. Human Settlements; adv. com. Ctr. for Environ. Info. UN Assn. U.S., 1975-78; mem. Rumanian-U.S. econ. coun. U.S. C. of C., 1973-75; project dir. 1987 Workshop Internat. Environ. Bur. Internat. C. of C.; cons. INFORM, 1989, Rene Dubos Ctr. for Human Environments, 1989-2000; adv. bd. Volvo Journalists Retreat Duke U., 1992; internat. adv. bd. Ctr. for Social Policy in Mid-East, 1983-91; exec. bd. Ency. of Environment. Author: How to Serve and Get Ahead in the Armed Forces, 1963, reissued as Your Military Obligations and Opportunities, 1964, Power at Pentagon, 1964, Robert O. Anderson: Oil Man/Environmentalist, 1988; co-author: This is Germany, 1950; editor U.S. Army Camp Upton Nooz, 1942-43; combat corr. Stars and Stripes, news editor Naples and Rome edits., mng. editor Marseilles edit.; combat corr., war editor, editor Stars and Stripes mag. Paris edit., combat corr., news editor Frankfurt edit., 1943-45; contbr. articles to profl. jours. Trustee N.Y. Urban League, 1969-72; bd. dirs. Internat. Inst. Environ. Affairs, N.Y.C., 1970-74, pres., 1970-73; bd. dirs. Internat. Inst. Environment and Devel., London, 1974-89, mem. adv. coun., 1978-82, mem. exec. com., 1982-89; bd. dirs. Epoch B. Found., La Jolla, Calif., acting pres., 1977-85; trustee Moroccan-Am. Found., 1982-88; bd. overseers Heller Grad. Sch., Brandeis U., 1981-88; founding assoc. John J. McCloy Internat. Ctr., N.Y.C., 1986, bd. dirs., 1987-99; mem. adv. bd. Ctr. for East-West Dynamics, 1992-95, Volvo JNLSTS Retreat, Williamsburg, Va., 1992; With U.S. Army, 1942-45. Decorated 5 Battle Stars, Bronze Star, Purple Heart. Mem. Coun. on Fgn. Rels. Clubs: Overseas Press Am. (N.Y.C.) (pres. 1972-76), Country Assn. (N.Y.C.), Nat. Press (Washington). Office: 340 E 57th St New York NY 10022

**RAYMOND, JASON,** geneticist, microbiologist; b. Phoenix, May 6, 1975; s. Mark Raymond and Shelley Howell; m. Kristy LoVecchio, Oct. 23, 2004. BS in Biophysics, Southwestern Okla. State U., Weatherford, BA in Chemistry, 1998; PhD in Biochemistry, Ariz. State U., Tempe, 2003. E. O. Lawrence fellow Lawrence Livermore (Calif.) Nat. Lab, 2004—. Contbr. scientific papers to profl. jours. Mem.: AAAS (assoc.), Sigma Pi Sigma (life). Independent. Home: 1426 Steel Creek Dr Patterson CA 95363 Office: Lawrence Livermore Nat Lab 7000 East Ave Livermore CA 94551 Office Phone: 925-423-6507. Office Fax: 925-422-2099. Personal E-mail: jay.raymond@gmail.com.

**RAYMOND, KAY E. (KAY ENGELMANN RAYMOND),** Spanish language educator, consultant; b. Cin., Feb. 1, 1939; d. Gerson Silas and Pauline Coleman (Early) Engelmann; m. Ralph Raymond II, Feb. 1, 1964 (div. Nov. 1977); 1 child, Jenifer Kay Raymond-Judy. AB magna cum laude, Radcliffe Coll., 1961; MA, Brown U., 1964; PhD, Ind. U., 1983. Lectr. Boston U., 1965—68, Assumption Coll., Worcester, 1965—67; instr. Regis Coll., Weston, 1967—71; assoc. instr. Ind. U., Bloomington, 1972—83; lectr. Emporia (Kans.) State U., 1983—84; asst. prof. U. Ala., Huntsville, 1984—89, Sam Houston State U., Huntsville, 1989—94, assoc. prof., 1995—, coord. fgn. langs., 1995—98. Adv. fgn. lang. program Sam Houston State U., Huntsville, Tex., 2004—. Advisor Internat. Hispanic assn., Sam Houston State U., 1990—; vol. translator City of Huntsville, 1993-98. Named Top Prof Sam Houston State U. Bapt. Student Ministry, 1996, Outstanding Advisor Internat. Hispanic Assn., 1996-97, Sammy award Sam Houston State U. Student Activities, 2003. Mem.: Tex. Fgn. Lang. Assn., Tex. Assn. Coll. and Univ. Lang. Suprs., Harvard Univ. Club Houston (schs. and scholarship com. 1997—), Sigma Delta Pi, Pi Delta Phi, Phi Sigma Iota. Home: 3464 Youpon Ln Huntsville TX 77340-8920 Office: Sam Houston State U Dept Fgn Langs PO Box 2147 Huntsville TX 77341-2147 Office Phone: 936-294-1444. Business E-Mail: fol_ker@shsu.edu.

**RAYMOND, KENNETH NORMAN,** chemistry professor, researcher; b. Astoria, Oreg., Jan. 7, 1942; s. George Norman and Helen May (Dunn) R.; m. Jane Galbraith Shull, June 19, 1965 (div. 1976); children: Mary Katherine, Alan Norman; m. Darlene Gabriele Bernhardt, June 19, 1977; children: Gabriella Petra, Christopher Norman. BA, Reed Coll., 1964; PhD, Northwestern U., 1968. Asst. prof. chemistry U. Calif.-Berkeley, 1967-74, assoc. prof., 1974-78, prof., 1978—; vice chmn. dept. U. Calif. Berkeley, 1982-84, 1999—2000, chmn., 1993-96; faculty sr. scientist Lawrence Berkeley Lab., 1996—; dir. Seaborg Ctr., 2002—. Mem. study sect. NIH, 1983—86, 2006—; adv. com. NSF, 1985—87; co-chmn. bd. chem. scis. & tech. NRC, 2000—; co-founder Lumiphore, Inc., 2001. Editor: Bioinorganic Chemistry II, 1977; assoc. editor Biology of Metals, 1987-91; editl. bd. Inorganic Chemistry, 1976-86, Accounts Chem. Rsch., 1982-90, Inorganica Chemica Acta f-Block Elements, 1984-90, Jour. Coordination Chemistry, 1981-2003, Jour. Inorganic and Nuclear Chemistry, 1974-81, Jour. Am. Chem. Soc., 1983-95, Topics in Current Chemistry, 1981-97, Metals in Biology, 1993—, Jour. Supramolecular Chemistry, 1992—, Jour. Biol. Inorganic Chemistry, 1996-2004, Procs. NAS USA, 2002-04, Accts. Chem. Rsch., 2005—; U.S. editl. advisor Springer-Verlag in Chemistry, 1972-91; 14 patents in field; contbr. articles to profl. jours.; author more than 400 papers. Alfred P. Sloan rsch. fellow, 1971-73; Miller rsch. prof., 1977-78, 96; Guggenheim Fellow, 1980-81; recipient E.O. Lawrence award Dept. Energy, 1984, Humboldt Rsch. award for U.S. Scientists, 1992, 2000, Alfred R. Bader award Am. Chem. Soc., 1994, Vollum award Reed Coll., 2002, Izatt/Christensen award, 2005. Mem. NAS, Am. Acad. Arts and Scis., Am. Chem. Soc. (chair divsn. inorganic chemistry 1996), Am. Crystallographic Soc., Sigma Xi. Democrat. Achievements include patents in field. Office: U Calif Berkeley Dept Chemistry Berkeley CA 94720-1460 E-Mail: raymond@socrates.berkeley.edu.

**RAYMOND, LEE R.,** retired oil company executive; b. Watertown, S.D., Aug. 13, 1938; m. Charlene Raymond. BSChemE, U. Wis., 1960; PhD ChemE, U. Minn., 1963. Joined Exxon Corp., Tulsa, Okla., 1963; various positions Exxon Co. USA and Creole Petroleum Corp., Houston and Caracas, Venezuela, 1963—72; mgr. planning Exxon Internat. Co., N.Y.C., 1972—75; v.p. Lago Oil, Aruba, 1975—76, pres., dir., 1976—79; pres. Exxon Nuc. Co., Bellevue, Wash., 1979—81; exec. v.p. Exxon Enterprises Inc., N.Y.C., 1981—83; pres., dir. Esso Inter-Am. Inc., Coral Gables, Fla., 1983—84; sr. v.p., dir. Exxon Corp., N.Y.C., 1984—86, pres., dir., 1987—93, chmn., CEO, 1993—99, pres., chmn., 1999; chmn., CEO Exxon Mobil Corp., Irving, Tex., 1999—2006. Bd. dirs. J.P. Morgan and Co., Inc., N.Y.C., 1987—; co-chmn. corp. governance and nominating com., mem. compensation and mgmt. develop.

com.; bd. dirs. Morgan Guaranty Trust Co. of N.Y., N.Y.C.; bd. dirs., mem. exec. and policy coms. Am. Petroleum Inst.; mem. Emergency Com. for Am. Trade, President's Export Coun. Bd. dirs. United Negro Coll. Fund, 1991—; mem. adv. bd. Project Shelter Pro-Am, Sect. Energy; trustee Wis. Alumni Rsch. Found., 1987—; bd. dirs., hon. trustee bus. coun. Internat. Understanding, Inc.; mem. innovations in medicine leadership coun. U. Tex. Southwestern Med. Ctr.; ptnr. emeritus N.Y. Partnership; vice chmn., bd. trustee Am. Enterprise Inst., Washington; mem. Dallas Citizens Coun., U. Wis. Found., Am. Coun. on Germany, Dallas Com. Fgn. Rels., Coun. on Fgn. Rels., Emergency Com. for Am. Trade, Singapore-US Bus. Coun., Trilateral Commn. Mem.: Am. Inst. Chem. Engrs. (mem. exec. com. of the 21st Century Campaign), Trilateral Commn., Occupl. Physicians Scholarship Fund (chmn. fundraising campaign 1995), Am. Soc. Engring. Edn. (nat. adv. coun.), Singapore-U.S. Bus. Coun., Coun. Fgn. Rels., Nat. Petroleum Coun. (mem. nom. and natural gas coms.), Bus. Roundtable (mem. policy com., security task force, taxation task force, govt. rels. working group), Bus. Coun., NAE.*

**RAYMOND, LISA,** professional tennis player; b. Norristown, Pa., Aug. 10, 1973; d. Ted and Nancy Raymond. Student, U. Fla. Profl. tennis player WTA Tour, 1993—. Mem. U.S. Fed Cup Team, 1997—98, 2000, 2002—03. Recipient 1 Career singles title, 42 Career Doubles Titles, WTA Tour; winner U.S. Open, 1996, 2002, Wimbledon, 1999, Australian Open Grand Slam doubles, 2000, Wimbledon, 2001, U.S. Open Grand Slam doubles, 2001, WTA Doubles Championship, 2001, Mixed Doubles Roland Garros, 2003; named NCAA Singles Champion, 1992, 93. Avocations: shopping, hanging out with friends, watching television, football, volleyball. Office: US Tennis Assn 70 W Red Oak Ln White Plains NY 10604 3602

**RAYMOND, PATRICIA,** gastroenterologist, medical educator; MD, Med. Coll. Va., 1986. Intern, resident Vanderbilt U., Nashville, 1986—89; fellow in gastroenterology U. Miss. Med. Ctr., 1989—90, Med. Coll. Va., 1990—92; pvt. practice gastroenterology Chesapeake, Va., 1992—. Author: (book) Don't Jettison Medicine: Resuscitate Your Passion For The Career You Loved, 2004, Colonoscopy: It'll Crack You Up, 2004; spkr. in field. Fellow: ACP, Am. Coll. Gastroenterology. Office: Rx For Sanity 613 River Strand Ste 200 Chesapeake VA 23320 Office Phone: 757-547-2673. Business E-Mail: plraymond@rxforsanity.com.

**RAYMOND, RICHARD GERARD, JR.,** lawyer; b. Detroit, Jan. 1, 1959; s. Richard G. Raymond Sr. and Mary Jo (Bradley) Raymond; m. Holly Lyn Russell, Aug. 4, 1984; 3 children. BS in chemistry, U. Mich., 1981; JD, U. Detroit, 1986. Bar: Mich. 1986, US Dist. Ct. Ea. Dist. Mich. 1986. Indsl. chemist Product-Sol Inc., Birmingham, Mich., 1982-83; assoc. Johnson & Valentine, Detroit, 1986—89; asst. gen. counsel Fruehauf Trailer Corp., 1989; assoc. gen. counsel, asst. sec. Gen. Automotive Corp.; corp. counsel Am. Axle & Mfg. Holdings Inc., 1995—2000, gen. counsel, 2000—. Mem. ABA, Mich. Bar Assn., Detroit Bar Assn., Am. Chem. Soc. Roman Catholic. Office: Am Axle & Mfg Holdings Inc 1840 Holbrook Ave Detroit MI 48212

**RAYMOND, TIMOTHY MICHAEL,** engineering educator; b. Pa. BSChemE, Bucknell U., Lewisburg, Pa., 1997; PhD in Chem. Engring., Carnegie Mellon U., Pitts., 2002. Asst. prof. chem. engring. Bucknell U., Lewisburg, 2002—. Office: Bucknell U Chem Engring Dept Lewisburg PA 17837 Office Phone: 570-577-3192. Office Fax: 570-577-1141. Business E-Mail: traymond@bucknell.edu.

**RAYMOND, URAL WAYNE,** retired retail executive; b. Missoula, Mont., May 20, 1944; s. Ural Daniel and Fayetta Arilla Raymond. Student, U. N.C., 1969-70, U. Mont., 1962-66, 93-94. Enlisted man U.S. Army, 1966-69, 70-89; advanced through grades to master sgt. U.S. Army, 1985; ret., 1989; advt. mgr. Sears & Roebuck, Missoula, 1993-99; ret., 1999. Chmn. western dist. Am. Legion Baseball, Missoula, 1997—; pres. Friends of the Libr., Missoula, 1997-99. With U.S. Army, 1966-69. Decorated Bronze Star. Mem. Nev. Internat. Lic. Plate Soc. (treas. state br. 1998—). Democrat. Evangelical. Avocations: collecting license plates, collecting flags, baseball, collecting stamps, collecting coins.

**RAYMOND, USHER, IV, (USHER),** vocalist, actor; b. Chattanooga, Tenn., Oct. 14, 1978; s. Jonnetta Patton and Usher Raymond. Co-owner Cleve. Cavaliers NBA team. Singer: (albums) Usher, 1994, My Way, 1997 (Soul Train award Best R&B/Soul Single for "You Make Me Wanna", 1998), 8701, 2001 (Grammy award Best Male R&B Vocal Performance, 2001, 2002, Platinum 7 times), Confessions, 2004 (MTV Video Music award Best Dance Video for song "Yeah!", 2004, MTV Video Music award Best Male Video for the song "Yeah!", 2004, Am. Music Award Favorite Album Pop or Rock, 2004, Am. Music Award Favorite Album Soul/Rhythm & Blues Music, 2004, Billboard 200 Album of Yr., 2004, Hot 100 Single of the Yr.: "Yeah!", Billboard Music Awards, 2004, Hot 100 Airplay Single of Yr.: "Yeah!", Billboard Music Awards, 2004, Mainstream Top 40 Single of Yr: "Yeah!", Billboard Music Awards, 2004, R&B/Hip Hop Album of Yr., Billboard Music Awards, 2004), In the Mix soundtrack, 2005; actor: (films) The Faculty, 1998, She's All That, 1999, Light It Up, 1999, Texas Rangers, 2001, In the Mix, 2005; (TV films) Geppetto, 2000; (TV series) Moesha, 1997—98, The Bold and the Beautiful, 1998, (TV guest appearances) The Famous Jett Jackson, 2000, Sabrina the Teenage Witch, 2002, The Twilight Zone, 2002, American Dreams, 2002, 7th Heaven, 2002, Soul Food, 2003; (Broadway plays) Chicago, 2006—. Named Artist of Yr., Billboard Music Awards, 1998, 2004, Mainstream Top 40 Artist of Yr., 2004, Hot 100 Artist of Yr., 2004, Billboard 200 Artist of Yr., 2004, Artist of Yr., Radio Music Awards, 2004; recipient Pop Music award, ASCAP, 2003, Favorite Male Artist award Pop or Rock, Am. Music Awards, 2004, Favorite Male Artist award Soul/Rhythm & Blues Music, 2004, R&B/Hip Hop Artist of Yr., Billboard Music Awards, 2004, R&B/Hip-Hop Albums Artist of Yr., 2004, Male Entertainer of Yr., World Music Awards, 2005. Achievements include First place on the Star Search TV talent series, 1992. Mailing: c/o JPat Mgmt 3996 Pleasantdale Rd # 104A Atlanta GA 30340*

**RAYMS-KELLER, ALFREDO,** molecular scientist; s. Gustavo O. Ramos and Ligia B. Yepez; m. Diane Marie Keller, Sept. 27, 1987; children: Roderick K., William A., Gabrielle M. PhD, Case Western Res. U., 1990; MA, Naval War Coll., 2005. Cert. Acquisition, Tech. Workforce, Dept. of Navy. Head, chem. biol. sci., tech. br. Naval Surface Warfare Ctr. Dalgren Divsn., Va., 2002—04, sr. scientist, 2005—. Rsch. prof. molecular microbiology, toxicology Colo. State U., Fort Collins, 1990—2000; scientist Naval Surface Warfare Ctr. Dalgren Divsn., 2000—01, head, biotechnology sect., 2001—02. Contbr. articles various profl. jours. Grantee Rsch. Funds, Epa, Darpa, Onr, 2000, 2001, 2002, 2003, 2004, 2005, 2006. Mem.: USA Moodok Kwan Karate (assoc.). Achievements include patents for method of producing dimethyl dinitro butane and patents; patents pending for microtags for detection and identification of materials. Office: Naval Surface Warfare Ctr Dahlgren Divsn 17320 Dahlgren Rd Dahlgren VA Personal E-mail: raymskeller@adelphia.net.

**RAYMUND, STEVEN A.,** computer company executive; b. Van Nuys, Calif., Nov. 16, 1955; s. Edward C. and Annette Leah Raymund. BS in Economics, U. Oreg., 1978; MA in Internat. Polit., Georgetown U. Sch. Fgn. Svc., 1980. With Manufacturers Hanover Corp., NYC, 1980—81; ops. mgr. Tech Data Corp., 1981—84, COO, 1984—86, CEO, 1986—2006, chmn., 1991—2006, non-exec. chmn., 2006—. Bd. dir. Jabil Circuit. Named Entrepreneur of the Yr., Arthur Young Entrepreneurial Services, 1988; named one of 25 Most Influential Executives in the PC Industry, Computer Reseller News, 1989—2004; named to Industry Hall of Fame, 1999. Office: Tech Data Corp 5350 Tech Data Dr Clearwater FL 33760-3122*

**RAYNAULD, ANDRE,** economist, educator; b. Quebec, Can., Oct. 20, 1927; s. Léopold and Blanche (Gauthier) R.; m. Michelle Nolin, Oct. 15, 1951; children: Francoy, Olivier, Dominique, Isabelle. BA cum laude, U. Montreal, 1948, MA in Indsl. Rels. magna cum laude, 1951; D. in Econs., U. Paris, 1954; D. in Econs. (hon.), U. Ottawa, 1976, U. Sherbrooke, 1976.

Mem. faculty U. Montreal, 1954-71, founder, dir. Ctr. Econ. Research and Devel., 1970-72; vis. prof. U. Toronto, 1962-63; chmn. Economic Council Can., Ottawa, 1971-76; mem. Que. Nat. Assembly, Montreal, 1976-80; prof. U. Montreal, 1980-93, prof. emeritus, 1993—. Exec. com. Can. Social Sci. Rsch. Coun., 1961-63, 64-65; pres. Inst. Canadien Affaires Publiques, 1961-62; bd. govs. Can. Labour Coll., 1962-66; dir., exec. com. CBC, 1964-67; trustee CBC Pension Fund, 1967-70; pres. Soc. Canadienne de Sci. Economique, 1967-69; mem. Royal Commn. Bilingualism and Biculturalism, 1969-70, Can. Coun. Urban and Regional Rsch., 1971, Quebec Coun. Planning and Devel., 1971; chmn. com. inquiry French-lang. tchr.-tng. Western provinces Dept. Sec. State, 1971; mem. interfutures study group OECD, Paris, 1976-78; mem. bd. Inst. Rsch. Pub. Policy, 1980—; rsch. fellow Devel. Ctr. OECD, Paris, 1986—; invited prof. College de France, Paris, 1987. Author: Economic Growth in Quebec, 1961, The Canadian Economic System, 1967., La propriete des entreprises au Quebec, 1974, Institutions Economiques Canadiennes, 2d edition, 1977, Le financement des exportations, 1979, Government Assistance to Export Financing, 1984, The External Financing of Tunisia's Imports, OECD, 1988, Financing Exports to Developing Countries, OECD, 1992; co-editor: Economic Integration in Europe and North America, 1992, Labour Standards and International Competitiveness, 1998; co-author: L'Etat Providence des Entreprises, 1999; editor Can. Jour. Econs., 1965-70. Recipient am. award des Diplomes de l'U. de Montreal, 1994; apptd. Officer of Order of Can., 1986; fellow Walter Levy Coun. on Fgn. Rels., Boston, 1977. Fellow Royal Soc. Can.; mem. Can. Econs. Assn. (pres. 1983-84), Am. Econs. Assn., Atlantic Econ. Soc. (disting. assoc.). Liberal. Roman Catholic. Home: 4820 Roslyn St Montreal PQ Canada H3W 2L2

**RAYNER, ARNO ALFRED,** investment company executive, consultant; b. San Francisco, Sept. 23, 1928; BS in Econs., U. Calif., Berkeley, 1949, MBA, 1954. Security analyst Bank of Calif., San Francisco, 1950—54; various positions to sr. v.p. Indsl. Indemnity, San Francisco, 1954—74; v.p. internat. svcs. Bechtel Group, San Francisco, 1975—76; pres. Rayner & Haynor, Mill Valley, Calif., 1977—99, chmn. bd., 1999—; pres. Raynor Found. Recipient Investment prof. of the Yr., San Francisco Bond Club, 1999, Disting. Citizen of the Yr., Marin Coun. Boy Scouts of Am., 2000. Mem.: Security Analysts (San Francisco) (life). Home: 7 Venado Dr Belvedere Tiburon CA 94920-1625 E-mail: arnorayner@aol.com.

**RAYNER, KEITH,** psychology professor, researcher; b. Dover, England, June 20, 1943; s. William T. and Olive Rayner; m. Susan K. Knight, Dec. 16, 1966; children: Ashley A. Fairgrieve, Jonathan K. BS, U. Utah, Salt Lake City, 1968, MS, 1970; PhD, Cornell U., Ithaca, N.Y., 1974. Asst. prof. U. Rochester, NY, 1973—78; disting. prof. U. Mass., Amherst, Mass., 1978—. Recipient Outstanding Scientist award, Soc. Sci. Study Reading. Fellow: APA (editor 1990—96, 2004—), Assn. Psychol. Sci.; mem.: Psychonomic Soc. (chmn. governing bd. 2000—01). Office: University of Massachusetts 433 Tobin Hall Amherst MA 01003 Office Phone: 413-545-2175. Office Fax: 413-545-0996. Business E-mail: rayner@psych.umass.edu.

**RAYNER, VICTORIA LEIGH,** medical educator, consultant; b. Sacramento, Mar. 6, 1954; d. Harold Edward Rayner and Angela Jane Allitore; m. Vallucci Rayner, July 20, 1997. BA, Coll. of Marin, 1974; AA in Bus. Studies, Highline CC, Seattle, 1976. Lic. post-secondary instr. Calif., 1995, continuing edn. instr. Calif. Bd. of Registered Nursing, 1996. Founder and pres. Bay Area Skin Assn., San Francisco, 1981; founder and dir. Ctr. Appearance and Esteem, 1987; founder Camouflage Therapy Clinic, dept. dermatology San Francisco Gen. Hosp., 1987, clin. assoc. Camouflage Therapy Clinic, 1991—; clin. assoc. Alta Bates Hosp., Berkeley; founder Rayner Inst. Career Advancement, Washington; owner Creative Career Bldg. Inst. Contbg. mem. and presenter U. Calif. Arts and Lectrs., San Francisco, 1988—; adv. bd. Dermascope, Sunnyvale, Tex., 1990—, Les Nouvelle Esthetique, Coral Gables, Fla., 1990—; adv. com. rsch. divsn. Almay Cosmetics, Oxford, NC, 1992—93; cons. and rep. Nat. Assn. Women in Bus., mem. public rels. com., 1993—95; founder Women's Forum for Discussion Group, San Francisco, 1996; spokesperson Fibroid Ctr. Wash. Med. Ctr.; lectr. on med. esthetics; presenter to physicians, hosps. and clinics. Author: Clin. Cosmetology; A Med. Approach to Aesthetic Procedures, 1993, A Survival Guide for Today's Career Woman, 1994; columnist Skin Inc. Mag.; contbr. chapters to books. Hon. chmn. Bus. Adv. Coun., Washington, 2005; leader medical esthetics trng. and care Task Force Legis. Reform of Patients' Rights, Sacramento, 1993—95; bd. dirs Alissa Ann Ruch Burn Found., San Francisco, 1991—93. Recipient For Those Who Care Vol. award, KRON-TV, 1989, Merit award, Commn. on Status of Women of City and County of San Francisco, 1993, Contribn. to Cosmetology, Internat. Congress of Esthetics, 2003. Mem.: NAFE, Am. Med. Women Assn. (author online distance edn. course 2006), Nat. Cosmetology Esthetic Assn., Am. Soc. Plastic Surgery Skin Care Specialists, Dermatology Nursing Assn. Independent. Roman Catholic. Achievements include development of long distance learning programs in esthetic procedures; women over forty, reentry career devel. programs; four outpatient cosmetic rehabilitation clinics for women and children. Avocations: interior design, cooking, reading, painting. Office: Rayner Inst for Career Advancement #300 1201 Penn Ave NW Washington DC 20004 Office Phone: 202-667-9596. Fax: 202-667-6297. Personal E-mail: victoriarayner@hotmail.com.

**RAYNER, WILLIAM ALEXANDER,** retired newspaper editor, author; b. Winnipeg, Man., Can., Nov. 7, 1929; s. William and Annie Mitchell (McDonald) R.; divorced; 1 child, Robert William. Student Can. schs. Sports editor Trail Times, B.C., 1954-55; sportswriter Victoria (B.C.) Times, 1955-57, Vancouver (B.C.) Herald, 1957; copy editor, reporter Montreal (Que.) Star, 1957-58; asst. sports editor Vancouver Sun, 1958-62, copy editor, then slotman, 1962-74, news editor, 1974-83, systems mgr., 1983-88, ret., 1988; copy editor Toronto Globe & Mail, 1962. Author: Vancouver Sun Style Guide, 1976, Images of History - Twentieth Century British Columbia Through the Front Pages, 1997, British Columbia's Premiers in Profile-The Good, The Bad and the Transient, 2000, Scandal! 130 Years of Damnable Deeds in Canada's Lotus Land, 2001, The Canadian Journey - Provacative Glimpses into Canada's Past, 2006. Dir. B.C. Newspaper Found. Mem. Writers Union Can. Personal E-mail: wrayner@telus.net.

**RAYNOLDS, DAVID ROBERT,** buffalo breeder, writer; b. N.Y., Feb. 15, 1928; s. Robert Frederick and Marguerite Evelyn (Gerdau) R.; m. May (Kean) Raynolds, May 12, 1951; children: Robert, Linda, Martha, Laura, David A.F. AB, Dartmouth Coll., 1949; MA, Wesleyan U., Middletown, Conn., 1955; predoctoral, Johns Hopkins Sch. Advanced Internat. Studies, Washington, 1956; grad., Nat. War Coll., Washington, 1973. Account exec. R.H. Morris Assoc., Newtown, Conn., 1949-50; fgn. svc. officer Dept. of State, Washington, 1956-76; pres. Ranch Rangers, Inc., Lander, Wyo., 1976—. Pres. Nat. Buffalo Assn., Ft. Pierre, S.D., 1987-88. Author: Rapid Development in Small Economies (Praeger); contbr. articles to profl. jours. Trustee, bd. dirs. Liberty Hall Found.; dir. Leader Corp.; mem. steering com. Wyo. Bus. Alliance; chmn. bd. govs. Mus. of the Am. West. With U.S. Army, 1950—53. Recipient Meritorious Svc. Award, Dept. of State, Washington, 1966. Mem. The Explorers Club, Dacor Assn., Fremont County Farm Bur., Fgn. Svc. Assn., Am. Legion, Rotary, Elks. Republican. Episcopalian. Avocation: travel. Office: Table Mountain Group PO Box 1310 Lander WY 82520-1310

**RAYNOR, BRUCE S.,** labor union administrator; m. Joan Raynor; children: Alvin Carter, Kudjo Sogadzi, Candice, Robin Sydney. Grad., Cornell U., 1972. Edn. dir. edn. dept. Textile Workers Union Am., 1973, edn. dir., 1974; so. regional dir., internat. v.p. Amalgamated Clothing and Textile Workers Union, 1981, exec. v.p., 1993, Union Needletrades, Indusl., and Textile Employees, 1995, sec.-treas., 1998, pres., 2001—. Mem. bd. trustees N.Y. State Statutory Affairs Com. Cornell U., 1989; v.p. AFL-CIO, mem. exec. bd. Pres. The Sidney Hillman Found.; bd. trustees Cornell U., adv. bd., Sch. Indsl. and Labor Rels. Recipient Groat award for disting. alumni, Sch. Indsl. and Labor Rels., Cornell U., 1999. Mem.: Cornell Sch Indsl. and Labor Rels. (mem adv. com). Office: 275 7th Ave Fl 11 New York NY 10001-6708*

**RAYNOR, EILEEN MARGOLIES,** otolaryngologist, educator; b. N.Y.C., Feb. 11, 1965; d. Allan Fred and Noemi (Schmerz) Margolies; m. Dewey Lee Raynor, Jr., Nov. 9, 1991; children: Stephanie Dianne, Logan Foster. AB in Chemistry, Duke U., 1987; MD, U. N.C., 1993. Cert. Am. Bd. Otolaryngology. Resident otolaryngology Med. Coll. Ga., Augusta, 1993—98; asst. prof. otolaryngology U. Fla., Jacksonville, 1998—2006, assoc. prof., 2006—. Cons. Medimetrics Corp., Jacksonville, Fla., 1999—; med. dir. Pediat. Hearing Program, Jacksonville, 2000—; mem. Cleft Palate Team Childrens Med. Svcs., Jacksonville, 2000—. Contbr. articles to profl. jours., chapters to books. Recipient Nat. Leadership award, Rep. Nat. Com., 2003; Deafness Rsch. Found. rsch. grantee, 1991. Fellow: Am. Acad. Otolaryngology (cmty., acad. rels. com. 2002—); mem.: AMA, Assn. for Rsch. in Otolaryngology, Triological Soc. (James Harrell award So. sect. 1997), Am. Acad. Facial Plastic Surgery, Duke Alumni Club (bd. dirs. 2000—). Avocations: cooking, skiing, photography, jewelry design. Home: 1031 River Oaks Rd Jacksonville FL 32207 Office: U Fla Jacksonville 653-2 W 8th St Jacksonville FL 32209 Office Phone: 904-244-3498. E-mail: eileen.raynor@jax.ufl.edu.

**RAYNOR, RICHARD BENJAMIN,** neurosurgeon, educator; b. NYC, Aug. 16, 1928; s. Murray and Mildred (Pitt) R.; m. Barbara Golob; children: Geoffrey, Michele. BSME, U. Mich., 1950; MD, U. Vt., 1955. Diplomate Am. Bd. Neurol. Surgery. Intern Mt. Sinai, N.Y.C., 1955-56; residency Neurol. Inst. Presbyn. Hosp., N.Y.C., 1956-57, Nat. Hosp., London, 1957; residency neurosurgery Neurol. Inst. Presbyn. Hosp., 1958-62; assoc. in neurosurgery Coll. Physicians and Surgeons Columbia U., N.Y.C., 1965-77; clin. assoc. prof. NYU, N.Y.C., 1977-2000, clin. prof., 1984—. Pvt. practice neurosurgery, N.Y.C., 1965—. Cons. editor Spine; contbr. over 50 articles to profl. jours., chpts. to books. Served as capt. U.S. Army, 1962-64. Fellow Am. Coll. Surgeons; mem. Cervical Spine Research Soc. (pres. 1986-87), Am. Assn. Neurol. Surgeons, Congress Neurol. Surgeons. Clubs: University (N.Y.C.). Avocations: skiing, squash. Office: 112 E 74th St New York NY 10021-3535 Office Phone: 212-535-1255.

**RAYNOVICH, GEORGE, JR.,** retired lawyer; b. Pitts., Dec. 30, 1931; s. George Sr. and Zora (Mamula) R.; m. Mary Ann Senay, July 11, 1953; children: George III, Andrew. BS, U. Pitts., 1957; JD, Duquesne U., 1961. Bar: Pa. 1962, U.S. Dist. Ct. (we. dist.) Pa. 1962, U.S. Patent and Trademark Office 1962, U.S. Supreme Ct. 1966, U.S. Ct. Appeals (fed. cir.) 1986. Patent agt. Consolidation Coal Co., Library, Pa., 1959-62; ptnr. Stone & Raynovich, Pitts., 1962-75; atty. Wheeling-Pitts. Steel Corp., Pitts., 1975-77, gen. counsel, sec., 1978-85, v.p., 1980-85; sr. atty. Buchanan Ingersol P.C., Pitts., 1986-88, 89-96; ptnr. Price & Raynovich, Pitts., 1988-89; of counsel Gorr Moser Dell and Loughney, Pitts., 1997-2000, Paul A. Beck and Assocs., Pitts., 2001—04; ret., 2004. Councilman Borough of Baldwin, Allegheny County, Pa., 1972-75, govt. study commr., 1973. 1st lt. USAF, 1952-56. Mem. Allegheny County Bar Assn., Pitts. Intellectual Property Law Assn., Acad. Trial Lawyers Allegheny County. Democrat. Roman Catholic. Mem. Serbian Orthodox Ch. Home: 335 Jean Dr Pittsburgh PA 15236-2511

**RAYSON, EDWIN HOPE,** lawyer; b. Earlville, Ill., Jan. 13, 1923; s. Edwin H. and Lillian (Astley) R.; m. Evelyn Sherry Kirkland, Oct. 1, 1983; children: Jane Rayson Young, Edwin Hope III, G. Scott. AB, U. Tenn., 1944, LL.B., 1948. Bar: Tenn. 1948. Pvt. practice, Knoxville, 1948—; ptnr. Kramer Rayson LLP, 1949—. Lectr. labor law U. Tenn. Coll. Law, 1951-71 Served to lt. (j.g.) USNR, 1944-46. Mem. Order of Coif, Sigma Chi, Omicron Delta Kappa. Home: 501 River Rd Loudon TN 37774-5583 Office: 25th Fl 1st Tennesse Plaza Knoxville TN 37901 Office Phone: 865-525-5134. Business E-mail: ehrayson@kramer-rayson.com.

**RAYSON, GARY DONN,** chemistry educator; b. Oklahoma City, Okla., Apr. 27, 1957; s. Ralph LeRoy and Muriel Rayson; m. Jenny Ruth Moorer, June 18, 1988. BS, Baker U., 1979; PhD, U. Tex., Austin, 1983. Teaching asst. U. Tex., Austin, 1979-80, rsch. asst., 1980-83; rsch. assoc. Ind. U., Bloomington, 1983-86; asst. prof. N.Mex. State U., Las Cruces, 1986-93, assoc. prof., 1993—2005, prof., 2005—. Inventor in field. Mem. Am. Chem. Soc., Soc. Applied Spectroscopy, Optical Soc. Am. Republican. Methodist. Avocations: photography, camping, hiking,. Office: NM State U PO Box 30001 # 3C Las Cruces NM 88003-8001 Business E-mail: garayson@nmsu.edu.

**RAYSON, GLENDON ENNES,** internist, preventive medicine specialist, writer; b. Oak Park, Ill., Dec. 2, 1915; s. Ennes Charles and Beatrice Margaret (Rowland) R. AB, U. Rochester, 1939; MD, U. Ill., Chgo., 1948; MPH, Johns Hopkins U., 1965; MA, Northwestern U., 1965. Diplomate Am. Bd. Internal Medicine, Am. Bd. Preventive Medicine, Am. Bd. Forensic Medicine, Am. Bd. Forensic Examiners. Resident in internal medicine Presbyn.-St. Luke's Hosp., Chgo., 1953-56; physician-in-charge Contagious Disease Hosp., Chgo., 1956-58, asst. med. supt., 1958-64; rsch. assoc. Sch. Hygiene and Pub. Health Johns Hopkins U., Balt., 1966-71; internist Johns Hopkins Hosp., 1971-82, Columbia Free State Health Plan, Balt., 1984-91; pvt. practice Balt. 1984—; with Neurodiagnostics Assocs., 1990—2001. Attending internist emergency rm. South Balt. Gen. Hosp., 1982-84; asst. prof. health sci. U. Ill., Chgo., 1958-64; fellow in gastroenterology and endocrinology Presbyn.-St. Luke's Hosp., 1956-58. Contbr. articles to med. jours., chpt. to book. Vol. physician, Vietnam, 1968, 7l, 72, 73; mem. Citizens Amb. Program Delegation to Vietnam, 1993. Capt. M.C., USAF, l95l-53. Fellow: Am. Geriatrics Soc., Am. Col. Preventive Medicine; mem.: APHA, ACP-ASIM, AMA. Avocations: poetry, writing, composing songs. Home: 337 Poplar Point Rd Perryville MD 21903-1803 Office: 218 N Charles St Apt 1407 Baltimore MD 21201-4024

**RAYWARD, WARDEN BOYD,** librarian, educator; b. Inverell, NSW, Australia, June 24, 1939; s. Warden and Ellie Rayward. BA, U. Sydney, 1960; diploma in libr., U. NSW, 1964; MS in L.S., U. Ill., 1965; PhD, U. Chgo., 1973. Asst. state library, NSW, 1961-64; research librarian planning and devel. NSW, 1970; lectr. Sch. Librarianship U. NSW, Sydney, 1971-72, head sch. info., Libr. and Archive Studies, 1986-92, prof., 1986-00, dean Faculty Profl. Studies, 1993-96, prof. emeritus, 2000—; asst. prof. U. Western Ont., 1973-74, Grad. Library Sch. U. Chgo., 1975-77, assoc. prof., 1978-80, prof., 1980-86; dean U. Chgo. Grad. Library Sch., 1980-86; rsch. prof. U. Ill., Champaign, 2000—, prof., 2004—. Cons. NEH, 1976-79, U.S. Dept. Edn., 1981; bd. govs. Charles Stuart U., 1994-96; bd. dirs. Internat. House-U. NSW, 1992-97; George A. Miller vis. prof. U. Ill., 1997-98; Leverhulme Trust vis. prof. Leed Met. U., 2002; vis. prof. Leeds Met. U., 2004—. Author: The Universe of Information: The Work of Paul Otlet for Documentation and International Organization, 1975 (also transl. Russian and Spanish), Hasta la documentacion electronica, 2002; editor: The Variety of Librarianship: Essays in Honour of John Wallace Metcalfe, 1976, The Public Library: Circumstances and Prospects, 1978, Library Quar., 1975-79, Library History in Context, 1988, Libraries and Life in a Changing World: the Metcalfe Years 1920-1970, 1993; editor, translator: International Organization and the Dissemination of Knowledge: Selected Papers of Paul Otlet, 1990; editor Confronting the Future, University Libraries in the Next Decade, 1992, Developing a Profession in Librarianship in Australia: Travel Diaries and Other Papers of John Wallace Metcalfe, 1996, Aware and Responsible: Papers of The Nordic-International Colloquium (Scarlid), 2004; mem. editl. bd. World Book of Encyclopedia, 1990-97; co-editor: History and Heritage of Scientific and Technological Information Systems, 2004; contbr. articles to profl. jours. Coun. on Library Resources fellow, 1978, vis. fellow U. Coll. London, 1986, 90, Mortenson fellow U. Ill., 1992-93, Garfield fellow in hist. sci. lit., 2000. Mem.: ALA, Union Internat. Assocs., Am. Soc. Info. Sci. (Rsch. award 2004), Australian Libr. and Info. Assn. (hon.). Office: U Ill Grad Sch Libr and Info Scis 501 E Daniel St Champaign IL 61820-6211 Office Phone: 217-244-9741. Business E-mail: wrayward@uiuc.edu.

**RAZ, AMIR,** neuroscientist, educator; m. Deborah Karen Steinberger. BSc, Farleigh Dickinson U., Teaneck, N.J., 1988; MSc, Yale U., New Haven, Conn., 1990; PhD, Hebrew U., Jerusalem,Israel, 1999. Prof. Cornell U.,

NYC, Columbia U., NYC, 2002—. Capt. Israeli AF. Recipient, Soc. of Clin. and Exptl. Hypnosis, 2002. Avocation: magic. Office: Columbia U 1051 Riverside Dr New York NY 10322 Home: 200 W 79th St Apt 3D New York NY 10024

**RAZ, HILDA,** editor-in-chief, language educator; b. Rochester, N.Y., May 4, 1938; d. Franklyn Emmanuel and Dolly (Horwich) R.; m. Frederick M. Link, June 9, 1957 (div. 1969); children: John Franklin Link, Aaron Link; m. Dale Nordyke, Oct. 4, 1980. BA, Boston U., 1960. Asst. dir. Planned Parenthood League of Mass., Boston, 1960-62; edit. asst. Prairie Schooner, Lincoln, Nebr., 1970-74, contbg. editor, 1974-77, assoc. editor, 1977-87, acting editor, 1981-83, 85, poetry editor, 1980-87, editor-in-chief, 1987—; prof. dept English U. Nebr., Lincoln, 1990—. Luschei endowed lectr., reader, panelist in field; participant many workshops, symposia, confs.; panelist creativity arts com. NEA, 2000, PEN, 2004; judge Kenyon Rev., 1990, Ill. Art Coun./NEA fellowships, 1987; bd. govs. Ctr. for Great Plains Studies, U. Nebr., 1989-95. Author: The Bone Dish, 1997, What Is Good, 1997, Divine Honors, 1998, Trans, 2001, What Becomes You, 2007; editor: Best of Prairie Schooner: Fiction and Poetry, 2001, Best of Prairie Schooner: Essays, 2000, Living on the Margins, 1999, other books; editor Nebr. Humanist, 1990. Pres. Assoc. Writing Programs, bd. dirs., 1988-89, ex-officio pres., 1989-90, v.p., 1987-88; bd. dirs. Nebr. Libr. Heritage Assn., 1988-91; mem. Mayor's Blue Ribbon Com. on Arts, 1985-88; bd. dirs. Planned Parenthood League Nebr., 1978-83, sec. bd. dirs., 1979-80, chair long-term planning com., 1980-81, 81-82. Recipient Literary Heritage award, Mayor's Art award, Lincoln, 1988, 2002, ORCA award, 2002, May Sartm award, NE Poetry Club, 2004; Bread Loaf scholar editors, 1974, poetry, 1985; Robert Frost Fellow, 1988, 89, Mag. Panel fellow, 1993, 94. Avocation: gardening. Home: 960 S Cotner Blvd Lincoln NE 68510-4926 Office: Univ of Nebraska Lincoln Prairie Schooner 201 Andrews Hall Lincoln NE 68588-0334 Office Phone: 402-472-1812. E-mail: HRaz1@unl.edu.

**RAZ, JOSEPH,** philosophy educator, law educator; b. Haifa, Israel, Mar. 21, 1939; arrived in Great Britain, 1970; M in Juris summa cum laude, Hebrew U., Jerusalem, 1963; PhD, Oxford (Eng.) U., 1967; Doctorate (hon.), Cath. U., Brussels, 1993. Lectr. then sr. lectr. depts. law and philosophy Hebrew U., Jerusalem, 1967-72; fellow, tutor in law Balliol Coll., Oxford, 1972-85, fellow, 1985—2006; prof. philosophy of law Oxford U., 1985—2006, rsch. prof., 2006—; prof. law Columbia U., NYC, 2002—. Prof. law Columbia U., NYC, 2002—. Author: (book) Practical Reason and Norms, 1975, The Authority of Law, 1979, The Concept of a Legal Sys., 1970—80, The Morality of Freedom, 1986, Practical Reason and Norms, 2d edit., 1990, Ethics in the Pub. Domain, 1995, Engaging Reason, 2000, Value, Respect and Attachment, 2001, The Practice of Value, 2003. Recipient The W.J.M. Mackenzie Book prize The Polit. Studies Assn. of the U.K., 1987, The Elaine and David Spitz Book prize The Conf. for the Study of Political Though, 1988, Internat. Hector Fix-Zamndio prize Legal Rsch. UNAM, Mexico City, 2005. Fellow Brit. Acad.; mem. Am. Acad. Arts and Scis. (fgn. hon.). Office: Balliol Coll Broad St Oxford OX1 3BJ England also: Columbia Law Sch 435 W 116th St New York NY 10027 Office Phone: 212-845-5191. E-mail: raz@law.columbia.edu.

**RAZA, ASIM,** psychiatrist; b. Rawalpindi, Pakistan, Apr. 27, 1958; s. Kamal and Sughra Raza. FSc, Sir Syed Sch. and Coll., Rawalpindi, 1975; BSc, B Medicine and Surgery, Rawalpindi Med. Coll., 1983. Diplomate Am. Bd. Psychiatry and Neurology. Intern dept. medicine Rawalpindi Gen. Hosp., 1983; med. officer dept. medicine Cantonment Gen. Hosp., Rawalpindi, 1984—91, med. officer outpatient dept., 1991—92; resident dept. psychiatry U. Mo. Sch. Medicine, Kansas City, 1993—97, chief resident dept. psychiatry, 1996—97; mem. staff Counseling Assocs., Inc., Conway, Ark., 1998—. Cons. in field; mem. spkrs. bur. Pfizer Inc., Wyelt Pharms. Treas. Residents Assn. Western Mo., Kansas City, 1994—95, v.p., 1995—96, pres., 1996—97. Recipient Psychiatry Resident of Yr. award, Pfizer, 1997; fellow, Eli Lilly, 1994. Fellow: Am. Psychiat. Assn. (Wyeth Ayerst Resident Reporter 1996, mem.-in-tng. rep. Western Mo. br. 1996—97); mem.: Ark. Psychiat. Soc. Home: 1801 Champlin Dr 112 Little Rock AR 72223 Office Phone: 501-336-8300. Personal E-mail: selfless@sbcglobal.net.

**RAZIANO, AMANDA,** environmental scientist; d. Adam and Paula Gonzalez; m. Todd Raziano, Mar. 25, 2005. BA, U. Wash., 2001. Environ. health scientist Agy. Toxic Substances Disease Registry, Atlanta, 2001—03; cons. Delta Air Lines, Atlanta, 2004—04; environ. health policy analyst Assn. State and Territorial Health Officials, Washington, 2005—. Fellow Agy. Toxic Substances Disease Registry, Atlanta, 2001; rsch. asst. Environ. Def., Washington, 2004—05, ERG/EPA, Washington, 2005—. Grad. Merit scholarship, George Wash. U., 2004. Mem.: APHA, Nat. Environ. Health Assn.

**RAZZANO, FRANK CHARLES,** lawyer; b. Bklyn., Feb. 25, 1948; s. Pasquale Anthony and Agnes Mary (Borgia) R.; m. Stephanie Anne Lucas, Jan. 10, 1970; children: Joseph, Francis, Catherine. BA, St. Louis U., 1969; JD, Georgetown U., 1972. Bar: N.Y. 1973, U.S. Dist. Ct. (so. dist.) N.Y. 1973, U.S. Dist. Ct. (es. dist.) N.Y. 1973, N.J. 1976, D.C. 1981, Va. 1984, U.S. Dist. Ct. N.J. 1976, U.S. Dist. Ct. Md. 1977, U.S. Dist. Ct. (no. dist.) Calif. 1981, U.S. Dist. Ct. D.C. 1982, U.S. Dist. Ct. (ea. dist.) Va. 1989, U.S. Dist. Ct. (we. dist.) Va. 1990, U.S. Ct. Appeals (2d cir.) 1973, U.S. Ct. Appeals (3d cir.) 1975, U.S. Ct. Appeals (D.C. and 5th cirs.) 1983, U.S. Ct. Appeals (4th cir.) 1984, U.S. Ct. Appeals (6th cir.) 1990, U.S. Ct. Appeals (8th and 9th cirs.) 2000, U.S. Supreme Ct. 1976. Assoc. Shea & Gould, N.Y.C., 1972-75; asst. U.S. atty. Dist. of N.J., Newark, 1975-78; asst. chief trial atty. SEC, Washington, 1978-82; ptnr. Shea & Gould, Washington, 1982-94, mng. ptnr., 1991-92; ptnr. Camhy Karlinsky Stein Razzano & Rubin, Washington, 1994-96, Dickstein, Shapiro LLP, Washington, 1996—. Lectr. in field; adv. bd. Securities Litigation Reform Act Reporter, Securities Regulation Law Jour.; adj. prof. law U. Md. Sch. Law. Civil law editor Rico Law Reporter; hon. adv. com. Jour. Internat. Law and Practice, Detroit Coll. Law; contbr. articles to legal jours. Scoutmaster Vienna coun. Boy Scouts Am., 1984. Recipient spl. achievement award Justice Dept., 1977, spl. commendation, 1978, Outstanding Achievement award Detroit Coll. of Law, 1993. Mem. ABA (chmn. criminal law com., secs. law 1996-98), Va. Bar, D.C. Bar (chmn. litigation sect. 1987-89, vice-chmn. coun. sects. 1988-89), Assn. Securities & Exch. Commn. Alumni (pres. 1993-95), Phi Beta Kappa, Eta Sigma Phi. Roman Catholic. Home: 1713 Paisley Blue Ct Vienna VA 22182-2326 Office Phone: 202-420-2291. Business E-mail: razzanof@dicksteinshapiro.com.

**RAZZANO, PASQUALE ANGELO,** lawyer; b. Bklyn., Apr. 3, 1943; s. Pasquale Anthony and Agnes Mary (Borgia) R.; m. Maryann Walker, Jan. 29, 1966; children: Elizabeth, Pasquale, Susan, ChristyAnn. BSCE, Poly. Inst. Bklyn., 1964; student law, NYU, 1964-66; JD, Georgetown U., 1969. Bar: Va. 1969, N.Y. 1970, U.S. Ct. Appeals (2d, 3d, 7th, 9th and fed. cirs.), U.S. Supreme Ct., U.S. Dist. Ct. (so., ea. and western dists.) N.Y., U.S. Dist. Ct. (we. dist.) Tex., U.S. Dist. Ct. Hawaii, U.S. Dist. Ct. Conn. Examiner U.S. Patent Office, 1966-69; assoc. Curtis, Morris & Safford, P.C., 1969-71, ptnr., 1971-91, Fitzpatrick, Cella, Harper & Scinto, 1991—. Guest lectr. U.S. Trademark Assn., Am. Intellectual Property Law Assn., Practicing Law Inst., NYU Law Ctr., ABA, N.Y. Intellectual Property Law Assn. Mem. bd. editors Licensing Jour., 1986—; mem. bd. editors Trademark Reporter, 1987—, book rev. editor, 1989-91; pub. articles editor, 1991-94, domestic articles editor, 1992-93, 95, editor-in-chief 1996-98. Rep. committeeman Rockland County. Recipient Robert Ridgeway award, 1964. Mem.: FBA (chmn. patent law com. 1999—2002, bd. govs. 2002—), ABA (guest lectr.), Columban Laws Assn., Bar Assn. City N.Y., Italian Am. Bar Assn., Va. Bar Assn., N.Y. Coun. Bar Leaders (exec. coun. 1993—94), N.Y. Bar Assn., Am. Intellectual Property Law Assn., Internat. Trademark Assn. (bd. dirs. 1996—99), Licensing Exec. Soc. (chmn. N.Y. chpt. 1996—99), N.Y. Intellectual Property Law Assn. (bd. dirs. 1985—93, sec. 1988—91, pres. 1994—95), Shorehaven Golf Club (bd. dirs. 2005—), Minute Man Yacht Club, N.Y. Athletic Club. Republican. Roman Catholic. Address: 21 Covlee Dr Westport CT 06880-6407 also: 14 Deerwood Trl Lake Placid NY 12946-1834 Office Phone: 212-218-2253. Business E-mail: prazzano@fchs.com.

**RAZZOUK, BASSEM IBRAHIM,** hematologist, oncologist; b. Afisdeek, Lebanon, Aug. 13, 1964; US, 1990; s. Ibrahim M. and Lamia C. Razzouk; m. Jacky F. Farah, Sept. 7, 1997; children: Lamya Celina, Ralph Bassem, Carla Janet, Nour Grace. BSc, Am. U. Beirut, Lebanon, 1983, MD, 1987. Diplomate in pediat. Am. Bd. Pediat., 1992, in hematology and oncology Am. Bd. of Pediat., 1996. Internship, residency Am. U. Beirut, 1987—90; resident to chief resident SUNY Health Sci. Ctr., Syracuse, 1990—92; fellowship in pediat. St. Jude Children's Rsch. Hosp., Memphis, 1992—95; attending pediatrician Boaz-Albertville Med. Ctr., Ala., 1995—98; asst. St. Jude Children's Rsch. Hosp., 1998—2004, assoc., 2004—. Med. dir., Mid. East and Telemedicine Programs St. Jude Children's Rsch. Hosp., 1998—, chmn. clin. protocol sci. rev. and monitoring com., 2004—. Contbr. articles to profl. jours. Fellow: Am. Acad. Pediat.; mem.: Am. Soc. Hematology. Achievements include research in new agents for relapsed leukemia, prognostic factors in pediatric leukemia. Home: 1948 Autumndale Cove Cordova TN 38016 Office: St Jude Children's Research Hospital 332 North Lauderdale Memphis TN 38105 Office Phone: 901-495-3940. Office Fax: 901-495-3122. Business E-Mail: bassem.razzouk@stjude.org.

**RE, EDWARD DOMENIC,** law educator, retired judge; b. Santa Marina, Italy, Oct. 14, 1920; s. Anthony and Marina (Maetta) R.; m. Margaret A. Corcoran, June 3, 1950; children: Mary Ann, Anthony John, Marina, Edward, Victor, Margaret, Matthew, Joseph, Mary Elizabeth, Mary Joan, Mary Ellen, Nancy Madeleine. BS cum laude, St. John's U., 1941, LLB summa cum laude, 1943, LLD (hon.), 1968; JSD, NYU, 1950; DPed (hon.), Aquila, Italy, 1960; LLD (hon.), St. Mary's Coll., Notre Dame, Ind., 1968, Maryville Coll., St. Louis, 1969, N.Y. Law Sch., 1976, Bklyn. Coll., CUNY, 1978, Nova U., 1980, Roger Williams Coll., 1982, Dickinson Sch. Law, 1983, Seton Hall U., 1984, Stetson U., 1990, William Mitchell Coll. Law, 1992, St. Francis Coll. Bklyn., 1993; L.I.D (hon.), St. Thomas U., Miami, 2003; LHD (hon.), DePaul U., 1980, Coll. S.I., CUNY, 1981, Pace U., 1985, Am. U. Rome, 1995; DCS (hon.), U. Verona, 1987; JD (hon.), U. Bologna, 1988, U. Urbino, 1994. Bar: N.Y. 1943. Apptd. faculty St. John's U., Jamaica, NY, 1947, prof. law, 1951—69, adj. prof. law, 1969—80, Disting. prof., 1980—2002, Disting. prof. emeritus, 2003—; vis. prof. Georgetown U. Sch. Law, 1962—67; adj. prof. law N.Y. Law Sch., 1972—82, Martin disting. vis. prof., 1982—90; spl. hearing officer U.S. Dept. Justice, 1956—61; chmn. Fgn. Claims Settlement Commn. of U.S., 1961—68; asst. sec. ednl. and cultural affairs U.S. Dept. State, 1968—69; judge U.S. Customs Ct. (now U.S. Ct. Internat. Trade), N.Y.C., 1969—91; chief judge U.S. Ct. Internat. Trade, N.Y.C., 1977—91, chief judge emeritus, 1991—. Mem. Jud. Conf. U.S., 1986-91, adv. com. on appellate rules, 1976-88, com. on internat. jud. rels., 1994-97; chmn. adv. com. on experimentation in the law Fed. Jud. Ctr., 1978-81; mem. bd. higher edn. City of N.Y., 1958-69, emeritus, 1969—; Jackson lectr. Nat. Coll. State Trial Judges, U. Nev., 1970. Author: Foreign Confiscations in Anglo-American Law, 1951, Selected Essays on Equity, 1955, (chpt., freedom in internat. soc.) Concept of Freedom, 1955, Cases and Materials on Equitable Remedies, 1975; co-author (with Joseph R. Re): Cases and Materials on Remedies, 1982, 6th edit., 2005, Law Students' Manual on Legal Writing and Oral Argument, 1991, Brief Writing and Oral Argument,9t edit, 2005, 9th edit., 2005; co-author (with Lester D. Orfield) Cases and Materials on International Law, 1965; co-author: (with Zechariah Chafee Jr.) Cases and Materials on Equity, 1967; contbr. articles to legal jours. Served with USAAF, 1943-47; col. JAGD, ret. Decorated Grand Cross Order of Merit Italy; recipient Am. Bill of Rights citation; Morgenstern Found. Interfaith award; USAF commendation medal; Distinguished service award Bklyn. Jr. C. of C., 1956 Mem. ABA (ho. of dels. 1976-78, chmn. sect. internat. and comparative law 1965-67), Am. Fgn. Law Assn. (pres. 1971-73), Am. Law Inst., Fed. Bar Coun. (pres. 1973-74), Am. Soc. Comparative Law (pres. 1969-91), Am. Justinian Soc. Jurists (pres. 1974-76), Internat. Assn. Jurists: Italy-USA (pres. 1991—), Internat. Assn. Judges (prin. rep. to UN 1993-), Scribes Am. Soc. Writers on Legal Subjects (pres. 1978). Home and Office: 305 B 147th St Neponsit NY 11694 Office Phone: 718-474-3775.

**RÉ, PAUL BARTLETT,** artist, writer; b. Albuquerque, Apr. 18, 1950; s. Ernest Ré and Helen Alice Bartlett. BSc in Physics with honors, Calif. Inst. Tech., Pasadena, 1972. Artist and writer, N.Mex., 1972—; dir. Paul Ré Collection and Archives, Albuquerque, 1994—. Mem. artist adv. bd. Mus. Am. Folk Art Access to Art Program, N.Y.C., NY, 1987—94. Permanent exhibit, Paul Ré Collection and Sculpture Garden, Jonson Gallery, U. N.Mex., one-man shows include Triangle Gallery, San Francisco, 1974, 1975, Jonson Gallery, U. N.Mex., 1978, J.B. Speed Mus., 1985, Albuquerque Mus., 1986, Wichita Mus., 1986, ABEC Ctr., Can., 1989, Sumter Gallery, S.C., 1990, Colo. Springs Mus., 1990, Jonson Gallery, U. N.Mex., 2001, Karpeles Mus., 2002; subject: (documentaries) Touchable Art by Paul Ré, 1990; author: Touchable Art: A Book for the Blind and Sighted, 1983, The Dance of the Pencil: Serene Art by Paul Ré, 1993; contbr. chapters to books (Rolex award, Geneva, 1990), articles on art to profl. jours.; traveling exhibit, Touchable Art, 1981—. Named to The Paul Bartlett Ré Peace prize, U. N.Mex.; recipient Legion of Honor, United Cultural Convention, 2005, Lifetime Achievement award; grantee, Wurlitzer Found., 1982, 1984. Mem.: Nature Conservancy, Caltech Alumni Assn. Avocations: guitar, bicycling, Escherian puns, walking. Office: Paul Ré Archives 10533 Sierra Bonita Ave NE Albuquerque NM 87111 Office Phone: 505-298-0290.

**REA, ANN W.,** librarian; b. Jefferson City, Mo., Aug. 3, 1944; d. William H. and Ruby (Fogleman) Webb; m. Glen N. Rea, Sept. 28, 1974; children: Sarah, Rebecca. BA, U. Mo., 1966; MLS, U. Ky., Louisville, 1968. Libr. St. Charles (Mo.) County Libr., 1967-71; libr. adult svcs. Paterson (N.J.) Free Pub. Libr., 1971-74; libr. Beal Coll. Libr., Bangor, Maine, 1983—. Mem ALA, Maine Libr. Assn.(scholarship and loan com.). Office: Beal Coll Libr 99 Farm Rd Bangor ME 04401 Office Phone: 207-947-4591.

**REA, ANNE E.,** lawyer; b. 1959; AB, Brown U., 1981; JD, U. Cgho., 1984. Bar: Ill. 1984. With Sidley Austin Brown & Wood, Chgo., 1984—, ptnr., 1992—. Selected as one of 15 Rising Stars You Won't Want to Oppose in Ct., Ill. Legal Times. Mem.: ABA, Leadership Greater Chgo., Chgo. Bar Assn., Ill. State Bar Assn. Office: Sidley Austin Brown and Wood Bank One Plz 10 S Dearborn St Chicago IL 60603

**REA, EVAN ANDREW,** curator; b. Washington, Feb. 21, 1979; s. Sam W.P. and Jane Harwood Rea. BA, St. Mary's Coll. of Md., St. Mary's City, 2001; MA, U. of Md., Catonsville, 2005. Head rowing coach U. of Charleston, Charleston, W.Va., 2001—02; curator of edn. and interpretation Balt. and Ohio RR Mus., Balt., 2005—. Mem.: Masters Rowing Assn., U.S. Rowing Assn., Phi Alpha Theta. Episcopalian. Avocation: competitive rowing. Office: Baltimore & Ohio Railroad Museum 901 West Pratt St Baltimore MD 21223 Office Phone: 410-752-2490.

**REA, ROGER UHL,** chemistry educator, consultant; b. Newton, Kans., Aug. 26, 1944; s. Harold Hugh and Elinor Lucile (Uhl) R.; m. Elizabeth Agnes Woerdeman. BS, Kans. State U., 1966; MNS, U. S.D., 1973. Cert. tchr., Nebr. Chemistry tchr. Omaha Pub. Schs., 1966—2000. Cons. Kiewit Constrn., Omaha, 1973; planner asst. Waccmaw Planning Ctr., Georgetown, S.C., 1974, driving instr. Dual Driving Sch., Omaha, 1979; computer programmer Merrill Pub. Co., Columbus, Ohio, 1983-89. Reviewer Jour. Chem. Edn., 1984-94; author chemistry and physics software. Pres. Omaha Edn. Assn., 1984-85; v.p. OEA Sr. Citizens Inc., Omaha, 1983-84; del. Douglas County Rep. Conv., Omaha, 1980—; treas. Educators Credit Union, Omaha, 1978-99; vice chmn. of First Nebr. Educators Credit Union, Omaha, 1999-2004, chmn., 2004—, trustee Omaha Schs. Employees Retirement System, 1987-94, 2000—, trustee of Nebr. Pub. Employee Retirement Sys., 2003—; mem. exec. com. Nebr. Christa McAuliffe Prize, Lincoln, 1987—. Recipient Tchr. of Yr. award Nebr. Dept. Edn., 1989, Cooper Found. Award for Excellence in Teaching, 1988. Mem. NEA (del. 1981—), Am. Chem. Soc. (high sch. exams. com. 1973-91), Nat. Sci. Tchrs. Assn. (Presdl. award for excellence 1985, grantee 1983), Nebr. State Edn. Assn. (chmn. tchr. welfare and svcs. commn. 1988-94, bd. dirs. 1993-99),trustee of Educators Health Alliance BC/BS Group, 1997—, Nebr. Acad. Scis., Nebr. Assn. Tchrs. Sci., Omaha Edn. Assn. (pres. 1984-85, trustee 1982-86), Nebr. Profl.

**Practices Commn.** (vice chmn. 1992-93, chmn. 1993-94). Republican. Avocations: piano, gardening, sports car rallies, photography, astronomy. Office: Omaha NW High Sch 8204 Crown Point Ave Omaha NE 68134-1922

**READ, IAN C.,** pharmaceutical executive; BSChemE, London U. Imperial Coll., 1974. Cert. Chartered Acct., Inst. Chartered Accts. of Eng. and Wales, 1978. Operational auditor Pfizer, Inc., 1978, CFO Pfizer Mex. to country mgr. Brazil, pres. Internat. Pharms. Grp. L.Am./Can., 1996, exec. v.p. Europe/Can., 2000, v.p., 2001—, exec. v.p. Africa/Mid. East, 2004, exec. v.p. L.Am., 2006, pres. worldwide pharm. ops. Pfizer rep. internat. sect. exec. com. Pharm. Rsch. and Mfrs. Am. Office: Pfizer Inc 235 E 42nd St New York NY 10017*

**READ, SISTER JOEL,** academic administrator; BS in Edn., Alverno Coll., 1948; MA in History, Fordham U., 1951; degree (hon.), Lakeland Coll., 1972, Wittenburg U., 1976, Marymount Manhattan Coll., 1978, DePaul U., 1985, Northland Coll., 1986, SUNY, 1986, Lawrence U., 1997, Marquette U., 2003. Former prof., chmn. history dept. Alverno Coll., Milw., pres., 1968—2003. Past pres. Am. Assn. for Higher Edn., 1976-77; mem. coun. NEH, 1977-84; bd. dirs. Ednl. Testing Svc., 1987-93, Neylan Commn., 1985-90; past pres. Wis. Assn. Ind. Colls. and Univs.; mem. Commn. on Status of Edn. for Women, 1971-76, Am. Assn. Colls., 1971-77. Bd. dirs. Jr. Achievement, 1991-2003, State of Wis. Coll. Savs. Bd., 2000-03, Greater Milw. Com., Wis. Found. Ind. Colls., 1990-99, Women's Philanthropy Inst., 1997-2000, Wis. Women Higher Edn. Leadership, 1997-2000; bd. dirs. YMCA, 1989-2003, trustee, 2003—; mem. Profl. Dimensions. First recipient Anne Roe award Harvard U. Grad. Sch. Edn., 1980; recipient Morris T. Keaton award, Coun. for Adult and Experiential Learning, 1992; recipient Jean B. Harris award, Rotary; Paul Harris fellow, Rotary. Fellow Am. Acad. Arts and Scis., Wis. Acad. Arts and Scis. Office: Alverno Coll Office of Pres PO Box 343922 Milwaukee WI 53234-3922 E-mail: joel.read@alverno.edu.

**READ, JOHN CONYERS,** non-profit company executive; b. NYC, May 21, 1947; s. Edward Cameron Kirk and Louise (Geary) R.; m. Alexandra Gould, Mar. 30, 1968; children: Cameron Kirk, Trevor Conyers, Alexandra. AB, Harvard, 1969, MBA, 1971; LHD (hon.), Centenary Coll., 2004. Ops. rsch. analyst HEW, Washington, 1971-72; exec. asst. to dir. Cost of Living Council, Washington, 1973; chief econ. adviser to Gov. Mass., 1974; exec. asst., counselor to sec. labor Washington, 1975; asst. sec. labor for employment standards, 1976—77; dir. corp. employee rels., pers. Cummins Engine Co., Columbus, Ind., 1977-80, plant mgr., 1980-85; v.p. Midrange Engines, 1986-90; v.p., gen. mgr. engine group Donaldson Co., Inc., Mpls., 1990-92; exec. v.p., 1992-94; ptnr. Hidden Creek Industries, Mpls., 1996—2000; pres., CEO Heavy Duty Holdings, Mpls., 1997-2000; pres. Read Ptnrs. Inc., Mpls., 2001—02; pres., CEO Outward Bound USA, Garrison, NY, 2002—. Cons. nat. productivity and energy policies; chmn. NAM Task Force on Wage and Price Policies, 1978-80; bd. dirs. MAC Equipment Co., Active Leasing Co., Summer Search. Contbr. articles to newspapers and mags. Trustee Summer Search, Nat. Ctr. Occupl. Readjustment, 1984-87; trustee NC Outward Bound Sch., dir., 1995—, chmn., 1997-2000; chmn. Charleston Pvt. Industry Coun., 1985; plant closing task force US Dept. Labor, 1986, mfg. task force NRC, 1989, critical industries task force Def. Dept., 1989 Mem. Nat. Assn. Mfrs. (bd. dirs., chair employee rels. com. 1993-95). Home: 111 Marlborough Rd Briarcliff Manor NY 10510 E-mail: jread@outwardbound.org.

**READ, MICHAEL OSCAR,** editor, consultant; b. Amarillo, Tex., July 11, 1942; s. Harold Eugene and Madeline (Welch) R.; m. Jill Kay Vanderby, July 6, 1963 (div. Apr. 1967); 1 child, Rebecca Anne; m. Fawn Dale Barby, Apr. 10, 1977; 1 child, Nathan Michael. AA in Chemistry, Amarillo Coll., 1962; BA in Journalism, Tex. Tech. U., 1965. News editor Olton Enterprise, Tex., 1963—64; reporter, photographer Lubbock Avalanche-Jour., Tex., 1964—67, copy editor, 1967—70, city editor, 1970—72; copy editor Houston Post, 1972—74, sys. editor, 1974—89, dir. news tech., 1989—95; coord. electronic media content Houston Chronicle, 1995—2000, editor web ops. and devel., 2000—. Bd. dirs. Shell Employees Fed. Credit Union, Houston, vice chmn., 2002—, supervisory com., 1996-2001; tchr. Let's Compute!, Stafford, Tex., 1985—; cons. Newspaper Pub. Sys., Stafford, 1989—; mem. joint Newspaper Assn. Am.-Internat. Press, Telecommn. Coun. Com. Wire Svc. Stds.; mem. adv. bd. Found. for Am. Comms. FACSNET; mem. adv. com. Sch. of Mass Comm., Tex. Tech U., chmn., 2001-04 Author weekly newspaper column, 1977—. Vol. United Way, Houston, 1973—; bd. dirs. Meadows (Tex.) Cmty. Improvement Assn., 1985-95, Meadows Utility Dist., 1988-93, Meadows Econ. Devel. Corp., 1994-99. Named among Outstanding Alumni, Tex. Tech U. Sch. Mass Comms., 2001; Eldon Durrett scholar, 1961-65. Mem. Am. MENSA, Am. Philatelic Soc., Am. 1st Day Cov. Soc. (life), U.S. Chess Fedn. (life), Soc. Profl. Journalists (conv. com. 1989-90), Press Club of Houston. Avocations: stamp collecting/philately, photography, gardening. Office: Houston Chronicle 801 Texas St Houston TX 77002-2996 Office Phone: 713-362-2905. E-mail: mike.read@chron.com.

**READ, PIERS PAUL,** author; b. Beaconsfield, Eng., Mar. 7, 1941; s. Herbert Edward and Margaret (Ludwig) R.; m. Emily Albertine Boothby, July 29, 1967; children: Albert Nathaniel, Martha Marianna, William Edward, Beatrice Mary. BA, St. John's Coll., Cambridge U., 1962, MA, 1963. Sub-editor Times Lit. Supplement, 1963-64. Adj. prof. writing Columbia U., 1980; lit. panel mem. Arts Coun. Gt. Britain, 1974-76; gov. Cardinal Manning Boys Sch., 1985; chmn. Cath. Writers Guild, 1993-97. Author: (novels) Game in Heaven with Tussy Marx, 1966, The Junkers, 1968 (Sir Geoffrey Faber Meml. prize, 1969), Monk Dawson, 1970 (Somerset Maugham award, Hawthornden prize, 1970), The Professor's Daughter, 1971, The Upstart, 1973, Polonaise, 1976, A Married Man, 1980, The Villa Golitsyn, 1982, The Free Frenchman, 1986, A Season in the West, 1988 (James Tait Black Meml. prize), On the Third Day, 1990, The Patriot, 1995, Knights of the Cross, 1997, (non-fiction) Alive: The Story of the Andes Survivors, 1974 (Thomas More medal), The Train Robbers, 1978, Ablaze: The Heroes and Victims of Chernobyl, 1993, The Patriot, 1996, (songs) Knights of the Cross, 1997, The Templars, 1999, The Gospel of St. John: The Story of the Son of God, 1999, Alice in Exile, 2001, Alec Guiness: The Authorised Biography, 2003, Hell and Other Destinations, 2006, (TV plays) Coincidence, The Family Firm, The House of Highburgh Hill. Mem. Brit. bd. of Aid to Church in Need, 1988. Ford Found. fellow, 1963-64; Harkness fellow, 1967-68 Fellow Royal Soc. Lit.; mem. Soc. Authors (com. mgmt. 1972-74), Internat. Contemporary Arts (com. mgmt. 1972-74) Roman Catholic. Address: 50 Portland Rd W11 4LG London England E-mail: piersread@dial.pipex.com.

**READ, RICHARD EATON,** newspaper reporter; b. St. Andrews, Scotland, Sept. 3, 1957; s. Arthur H. and Katharine (Eaton) R.; m. Kim R. Kunkle, July 26, 1986; 1 child, Nehalem Kunkle-Read. BA in English, Amherst Coll., 1980; postgrad., Harvard U., 1996—97; LHD (hon.), Williamette U., 2003. Press sec. Mass. Commn. on State and County Bldgs., 1980; staff writer The Oregonian, 1981-86; fellow The Henry Luce Found./The Nation, Bangkok, 1986-87; freelance writer Tokyo, 1987-89; Asia bur. chief The Oregonian, Tokyo, 1989-94; sec., 1st dir., 1st v.p. Fgn. Corrs. Club of Japan, 1990-93; internat. bus. writer The Oregonian, Portland, 1994-99, sr. writer internat. affairs, 1999—. 1st v.p. bd. dirs. The Internat. Sch., Portland, 2002—. Recipient Pulitzer prize for explanatory reporting, 1999, Overseas Press Club award for bus. reporting from abroad, 1999, Scripps Howard Found. award for bus. reporting, 1999, Blethen award for enterprise reporting Pacific Northwest Newspaper Assn., 1999, 2001, Pacific Northwest Soc. Prof. Journalists first place award for local issues, 2001, 05, bus. 1998, 2004, spot news 1997, edn. 1990, Oreg. Gov.'s award for achievement in internat. bus., 2000, Pulitzer prize for pub. svc., 2001, Unity award in media investigative reporting, Lincoln U., 2001, Blethen award, 2001, Bruce Baer award, 2001, Media Leadership award Am. Immigration Lawyers Assn., 2001; named Internat. Citizen of Yr. 1999 World Affairs Coun. Oreg., named Internat. Citizen of Yr. 2002 Oreg. Assn. Consuls Eisenhower Exch. fellow, Peru, 1997; Nieman fellow, 1996-97; U. Md. CASE fellow, 2002.

**READ, ROBERT ALLEN,** music educator; b. Pottstown, Pa., Dec. 16, 1958; s. Kenneth Edward Read; m. Ruth Ann Radakovic, Nov. 17, 1984; children: Brian William, Stephanie Lynne, Rachel Ann. B of Edn., Ind. U. Pa., 1980; MEd in Music, U. Pa., 1990. Dir. marching Churchill Area H.S., Pitts., 1980—82, Gateway Sr. H.S., Monroeville, 1982—. Marching activities cons. Casavant Cavalcade, Indiana, Pa., 1976—; marching band drill cons., prodn. design pvt. practice, Harrison City. Mem.: Nat. Band Assn., Pa. Music Educators Assn., Music Educators Nat. Conf., Phi Mu Alpha (sec. 1978—79). Achievements include development of Curriculum/National Standards adaptability. Home: 127 Cold Springs Lane Harrison City PA 15636 Office: Gateway Senior High School 3000 Gateway Campus Boulevard Monroeville PA 15146 Office Phone: 412-373-5751. Personal E-mail: read5@comcast.net. E-mail: rread@gator.gasd.k12.pa.us.

**READ, SUSAN PHILLIPS,** state appeals court judge; b. Gallipolis, Ohio, June 27, 1947; d. Gomer Wesley and Elizabeth Molineaux Phillips; m. Howard John Read. BA summa cum laude, Ohio Wesleyan U., 1969; JD Floyd R. Mechem Prize Scholar, U. Chgo., 1972. Bar: NY 1974. Legal intern US Atomic Energy Commn., 1972—73; asst. counsel SUNY, 1974—77; in-house counsel GE Co., 1977—88, chief environ. counsel, 1980—85; ptnr. Bond, Schoeneck & King, Albany, NY, 1988—94; dep. counsel to Gov. Pataki, 1995—97; judge (confirmed for an unexpired term in 1998 and full term in 1999) NY Ct. of Claims, 1998—2003, presiding judge, 1999; assoc. judge NY State Ct. Appeals, Schenectady, 2003—. Mem.: Phi Beta Kappa. Office: NY State Ct Appeals 20 Eagle St Albany NY 12207-1095*

**READ, TONY JOHN,** management consultant; BSc, Loughborough U., Leicestershire, UK, 1981; MBA, Kingston U., London, 1989; MEd, Vanderbuilt U., Nashville, 1997; PhD, Nova Southeastern U., Miami, 2005. V.p. IT Nortel Networks, Maidenhead, 1992—2000, Nashville, 1992—2000, Miami, 1992—2000; CIO sr. v.p. IT CCI, Miami, 2000—01; sr. v.p. T & O, Toronto, Canada, 2001—02, CIBC, Toronto, 2001—02; mng. ptnr. Read Assoc., Toronto, Canada, 2003—. Contbr. articles, various pubs. and confs. Recipient Upsilon Pi Epsilon, Hon. Soc. Computer Sci. Office Phone: 905 342 2713. Personal E-mail: tread@readassociates.net.

**READ, VIRGINIA HALL,** retired biochemistry professor; b. Louisville, Miss., Oct. 15, 1937; d. Angus R. and Hassie (Bowie) Hall; m. Dale Gilbert Read Sr., Mar. 5, 1960; children: Laura Read Sprabery, Dale Gilbert Jr., Eva Read Warden. BS, U. Miss., 1959; MS, U. Miss., Jackson, 1962, PhD, 1964. Instr. biochemistry U. Miss., Jackson, 1965-66, asst. prof. biochemistry, 1966-68, 70-74, assoc. prof. biochemistry, 1974-2000, assoc prof. pathology, 1979-2000; asst. prof. medicine U. Ala., Birmingham, 1968-70. Contbr. articles to Jour. Clin. Investigation, Jour. Clin. Endocrinology and Metabolism, Nature, Biochem. Pharmacology. Grantee U.S. Pub. Health Svc., 1960-62, fellow, 1968-70. Mem. Am. Assn. Clin. Chemistry, Acad. Clin. Biochemistry, Endocrine Soc., Sigma Xi. United Methodist. Personal E-mail: dread@was.net.

**READ, WILLIAM TIM,** musician; s. William Alexander and Emily Sanford Read; m. Carol Gerjon. Diploma, Juilliard Sch. Music. Soloist, N.Y.C.; artist-in-residence U. Calif., Santa Cruz. Grantee, Martha Baird Rockefeller. Mem.: Musician Local N.Y. 802, Chamber Mus. Am. Home: 145 W 71 St New York NY 10023 Office Phone: 212-362-4375. Personal E-mail: wmtimread@aol.com.*

**READE, CLAIRE ELIZABETH,** lawyer; b. Waltham, Mass., June 2, 1952; d. Kemp Brownell and Suzanne Helen (Dorntge) R.; m. Earl Phillip Steinberg, Nov. 22, 1980; children: Evan Samuel, Emma Miriam. BA, Conn. Wesleyan U., 1973; JD, Harvard U., 1979; MA in Law and Diplomacy, Tufts U., 1979. Bar: Mass. 1980, D.C. 1983. Sheldon fellow Harvard U., Cambridge, Mass. and Republic of China, 1979-80; assoc. Ropes & Gray, Boston, 1980-82, Arnold & Porter, Washington, 1982-86, ptnr. internat. law, chmn. Hiring Com., 1987—2006; chief counsel China trade enforcement Office U.S. Trade Rep., Washington, 2006—. Exec. editor: International Trade Policy: The Lawyer's Perspective, 1985; contbr. articles to profl. jours. Mem. ABA (co-chair internat. trade com.), DC Bar Assn., Coun. on Foreign Rels. Office: US Trade Rep 600 17th St NW Washington DC 20508

**READER, GEORGE G.,** retired internal-public health medicine educator; b. Bklyn., 1919; m. Helen Brown, May 23, 1942; 4 children. BA in Animal Biology, Cornell U., Ithaca, N.Y., 1940; MD, Cornell U., N.Y.C., 1943; ScD (hon.), Drew U., 1988. Intern in medicine N.Y. Hosp., N.Y.C., 1944-45, resident and fellow in medicine, 1946—50, resident in hematology, 1950—51; instr. medicine Cornell U. Med. Ctr., 1951—52, from asst. prof. to prof., 1952—89, emeritus prof. medicine, 1989—, Livingston Farrand prof. pub. health, 1989—. Former advisor Social Security Adminstrn.; former chmn. human ecology study sect. NIH; former chmn. tech. com. on tng. White House Conf. on Aging; former cons. OEO, Office Sec. of HEW, Health Svcs. and Mental Health Adminstrn.; head transition task force health adv. coun. N.Y. State Dept. Health, 1974—84; former chmn. N.Y. State Task Force on Health of Sch. Age Child and Health Manpower; rep. Cornell U. Med. Ctr. in Health Planning for N.Y.C.; mem. master plan com. N.Y.C. Hosp. Coun. Mem. N.Y.C. Mayor's Organized Task Force for Health Planning; mem. local planning bd. representing N.Y. Hosp., Health Sys. Agy., N.Y.C. Scholar Regents scholar, Cornell U. 1940. Mem.: AOA, Inst. of Medicine (sr.), Skulls.

**READER, JOSEPH,** physicist; b. Chgo., Dec. 1, 1934; BS, Purdue U., 1956, MS, 1957; PhD in Physics, U. Calif., 1962. Rsch. assoc. physics Argonne Nat. Lab., 1962-63; staff physicist Nat. Inst. Standards and Tech., Gaithersburg, Md., 1963-99, group leader atomic spectroscopy group, 1999. Recipient of Gold medal Dept. Commerce, 1989. Fellow Am. Phys. Soc., Optical Soc. Am. (William F. Meggers award 1992). Achievements include research in experimental atomic physics, optical spectroscopy, hyperfine structure, electronic structure of highly ionized atoms, wavelength standards, and ionization energies of atoms and ions. Office: Natl Inst Of Stds & Tech Gaithersburg MD 20899-8422

**READING, ANTHONY JOHN,** retired psychiatrist, educator; b. Sydney, Australia, Sept. 10, 1933; s. Abe Stanley and Esma Daisy R.; m. Elisabeth Ann Hoffman, July 27, 1975; children: Wendy Virginia Elisabeth, Sarah Alexandra Jane. M.B., B.S. U. Sydney, 1956; M.P.H., Johns Hopkins U., 1961, Sc.D., 1964. Intern Sydney Hosp., 1957-58; resident in psychiatry Johns Hopkins Hosp., Balt., 1965-68; asst. prof. psychiatry and medicine Johns Hopkins U. Sch. Medicine, Balt., 1968-73, assoc. prof. psychiatry, 1973-75, dir. psychiat. liaison service, 1974-75; dir. comprehensive alcoholism program Johns Hopkins Hosp., 1972-75; prof. U. South Fla. Coll. Medicine, 1975—2006, chmn. dept. psychiatry and behavioral medicine, 1975—2002, assoc. dean, 1993-96; med. dir. Bay Med. Behavioral Health Ctr., Panama City, Fla., 2001—05; ret., 2006. Mem.: AAAS. Home: 3202 Magnolia Islands Blvd Panama City Beach FL 32408-7176 Business E-Mail: tonytoo@comcast.net.

**READING, JAMES EDWARD,** transportation executive; b. Milw., June 26, 1924; s. James Edwards and Helen Marie (Boehm) R.; m. Ada Irene Kelly, May 24, 1944; children: Wendy Irene, James David, Christopher Kelly, Mary Katherine, Kevin Sinclair. Student, San Diego State U., 1942, Ga. Inst. Tech., 1944. With Union-Tribune Pub. Co., San Diego, 1942-59, dist. mgr., 1953-58, circulation promotion mgr., 1958-59; adminstrv. asst. to v.p. Copley Newspapers, La Jolla, Calif., 1959-60; dir. advt. and pub. rels. San Diego Transit System, 1960-67; dir. mktg. Calif. Motor Express, 1967-68; asst. to exec. v.p. Am. Transit Assn., Washington, 1968; v.p. Nat. City Mgmt. Co.; resident mgr. Regional Transit Service, Rochester, N.Y., 1968-74; asst. gen. mgr. ops. Regional Transit Dist., Denver, 1974-77; gen. mgr. Central Ohio Transit Authority, Columbus, 1977-85; dir. Santa Clara County Transp. Agy., San Jose, Calif., 1985-90; ind. cons. San Diego, 1990—. Lectr. field. Treas. Contg. Edn. Ctr., Rancho Bernardo. With ETO U.S. Army, 1943—46. Named Public Relations Man of Yr. Public Relations Club, San Diego, 1962;

recipient Urban Mass Transp. Adminstrs. award for outstanding pub. service, 1980, 82; charter mem. Herbert Hoover H.S. Achievement Hall of Fame, San Diego, 1998; named to Rancho Bernardo Hall of Fame, 2000. Mem. Am. Pub. Transit Assn. (bd. dirs., past v.p., elected Hall of Fame 1995), Am. Legion, Rotary Club Rancho Bernardo (past pres.), Press Club of Rancho Bernardo (past pres.), Rancho Bernardo Spirit of Fourth (past pres., treas.), Tau Kappa Epsilon. Republican. Roman Catholic. Home: 11728 Caminito Corriente San Diego CA 92128-4548

**READY, ROBERT JAMES,** finance company executive; b. Bridgeport, Conn., June 26, 1952; s. John Edward and Anne (Salata) R.; m. Margaret S. Neale, Aug. 23, 1975; children: Carolyn, Christopher and Steven (twins). AS, Housatonic Community Coll., 1972; BS, Babson Coll., 1974. CLU; chartered fin. cons.; registered fin. cons.; cert. ins. cons; cert. retirement cons.; cert. retirement adminstr. Agt. John Hancock Mut. Life Ins. Co., Hamden, Conn., 1975-77; broker Beardsley, Brown & Bassett Inc., Bridgeport, Conn., 1977-80; agt. Aetna Life and Casualty Ins. Co., Trumbull, Conn., 1980-83; v.p. Crestview Fin. Services Inc., Westport, Conn., 1983-2000, Crestview Securities Inc., Westport, Conn., 1983-2000, Crestview Investment Advisors Inc., Westport, Conn., 1983-2000; sr. v.p. ins. RDM Ins. Svcs. Inc., Westport, Conn., 2000—. Mem. Nat. Assn. Life Underwriters, Conn. Assn. Life Underwriters, Bridgeport Life Underwriters (bd. dirs. 1977), New Haven County CLU and Chartered Fin. Cons., Soc. of Fin. Svc. Profls. (Fairfield county chpt.). Roman Catholic. Avocations: golf, tennis, softball. Office: RDM Financial Group Inc 1555 Post Rd E Westport CT 06880-5602 Office Phone: 203-255-0222. E-mail: bready@rdmfinancial.com

**REAGAN, BETTYE JEAN,** artist; b. Oviedo, Fla., Jan. 27, 1934; d. Andrew and Mary Alice (Powell) Aulin; m. Joel Edwin McGill, Sept. 16, 1952 (dec. July 15, 1956); children: Daniel Lee, Kathleen Ann; m. Donald Thomas Reagan, Mar. 30, 1957; children: Debbie Lynn, Julie Karin, Andrew Scott, Patrick Kelley. Grad., Oviedo (Fla.) High Sch., 1951; student, Arrowmont Arts and Crafts Sch., 1993—96. Co-chmn. 1st St. Gallery, Sanford, Fla., 1986. One-woman shows include G. Sander Fine Art Gallery, Daytona Beach, Fla., 1986, 1987, Artist Hand Gallery, Oviedo, 1983, two-person shows, Ormond Beach (Fla.) Meml. Mus., 1987, 1998, 1st St. Gallery, Sanford, Fla., 1992, exhibited in group shows at Maitland (Fla.) Rotary Art Festival, 1991, St. Johns River Art Festival, 1994, Heathrow Festival of the Arts, 2001, Winter Park Sidewalk Art Festival, 2000, one-woman shows include Ormond Meml. Art Mus., Ormond Beach, 1998, Hope Barton Fine Arts, Clermont, 2001, Steinway Piano Gallery, 2003. Recipient 2nd Place, Maitland Art Festival, 1995, Award of Distinction, Deland (Fla.) Fall Festival of Art, 1995, 1st Place, Beaux Arts 45th Annual Festival Art, 1996, Cert. of Recognition for leadership and role model, Fla. Ho. of Reps., 2001, Poster Artist, Five Fla. Art Festivals, 1991—2002. Mem.: Sanford Seminole C. of C. (chmn. cultural arts com.), Portrait Soc. Am., Pastel Soc. Am. Republican. Baptist. Avocations: tennis, swimming, beach. Home: 2636 Reagan Tr Lake Mary FL 32746 Office: Reagan Studios 2636 Reagan Tr Lake Mary FL 32746 Office Phone: 407-322-8177. E-mail: donbetreagan@aol.com.

**REAGAN, BRILLA JANE,** principal; d. James Robert and Clara Jane Magee; m. Tony Reagan. Postgrad., Angelo State U., 1973—2004. Cert. tchr. Tex. Tchr. Winters (Tex.) Ind. Sch. Dist., 1973—2002, prin., 2002—. Office: Winters Ind Sch Dist 603 N Heights Winters TX 79567 Office Phone: 325-754-5577. Office Fax: 325-754-4686.

**REAGAN, GARY DON,** state legislator, lawyer; b. Amarillo, Tex., Aug. 23, 1941; s. Hester and Lois Irene (Marcum) R.; m. Nedra Ann Nash, Sept. 12, 1964; children: Marc Kristi, Kari, Brent. BA, Stanford U., 1963, JD, 1965. Bar: N.Mex. 1965, U.S. Dist. Ct. N.Mex. 1965, U.S. Supreme Ct. 1986. Assoc. Smith & Ransom, Albuquerque, 1965—67; ptnr. Smith, Ransom, Deaton & Reagan, Albuquerque, 1967—68, Williams, Johnson, Houston, Reagan & Porter, Hobbs, 1968—77, Williams, Johnson, Reagan, Porter & Love, Hobbs, 1977—82; pvt. practice Hobbs, 1982—; city atty. City of Hobbs, 1978—80, 1997—2004, City of Eunice, N.Mex., 1980—2004; mem. N.Mex. State Senate, 1993—96. Instr. N.Mex. Jr. Coll. and Coll. of S.W., Hobbs, 1978-84; N.Mex. commr. Nat. Conf. Commrs. Uniform State Laws, 1993-96; adv. mem. N.Mex. Constl. Revision Commn., 1993-95. Mayor City of Hobbs, 1972-73, 76-77, city commr., 1970-78; pres., dir. Jr. Achievement of Hobbs, 1974-85; pres., trustee Landsun Homes, Inc., Carlsbad, N.Mex., 1972-84; trustee Lydia Patterson Inst., El Paso, Tex., 1972-84, N.Mex. Conf. United Meth. Ch., 1988—, Coll. S.W. Hobbs, 1989-2001 Mem. ABA, State Bar N.Mex. (comm. 1989-96, v.p. 1992-93, pres. 1994-95), Lea County Bar Assn. (pres. 1976-77), Hobbs C. of C. (pres. 1989-90), Rotary (pres. Hobbs 1985-86), Hobbs Tennis Club (pres. 1974-75). Home: 200 E Eagle Dr Hobbs NM 88240-5323 Office: 1819 N Turner Ste G Hobbs NM 88240-3834 Office Phone: 505-397-6551. Business E-Mail: lglregan@nm.net.

**REAGAN, HARRY EDWIN, III,** lawyer; b. Wichita, Kans., Sept. 9, 1940; s. Harry E. II and Mary Elizabeth (O'Steen) R.; m. Marvene R. Rogers, June 17, 1965; children: Kathleen, Leigh, Mairen. BS, U. Pa., 1962, JD, 1965. Bar: Pa. 1965, U.S. Dist. Ct. (ea. dist.) Pa. 1965, U.S. Ct. Appeals (3d cir.) 1965. From assoc. to ptnr. Morgan, Lewis & Bockius, Phila., 1965-98. Chmn. Northhampton Twp. Planning Commn., Bucks County, Pa., 1974-79; mem. Warwick Twp. Planning Commn., 1980-95, chmn., 1994; supr. Warwick Twp., 1996-98; mem. San Miguel County (Colo.) Open Space Commn., 1998—, chmn., 2001-05; mem. Town of Telluride Open Space Commn., 1999-2002, San Miguel County Planning Commn., 2002—. Mem. ABA (labor sect.), Pa. Bar Assn. (labor sect.), Phila. Bar Assn. (labor sect.), Indsl. Rels. Assn. (pres. Phila. chpt. 1990-91). Republican. Presbyterian. Avocations: rugby, skiing, raising horses, bicycling. Home and Office: Box 190 Norwood CO 81423

**REAGAN, JOSEPH BERNARD,** retired aerospace executive, management consultant; b. Somerville, Mass., Nov. 26, 1934; s. Joseph B. and Helen Lowry R.; m. Dorothy Hughes; children: Patrick, Michael, Kevin, Kathleen, Brian, John, Maureen. BS in Physics, Boston Coll., 1956, MS in Physics, 1959; PhD in Space Sci., Stanford U., 1975; postgrad. exec. mgmt., Pa. State U., State College, 1981. Staff scientist, rsch. scientist, sr. scientist, scientist Lockheed Rsch. & Devel. Div., Palo Alto, Calif., 1959-75, mgr., 1975-84, dir., 1984-86, dep. gen. mgr., 1986-88, v.p., asst. gen. mgr., 1988-90; v.p. gen. mgr. Lockheed Missile and Space Co., 1991-96. Contbr. articles to profl. jours. Bd. dirs. SM&A, Newport Beach, Calif. Capt. U.S. Army, 1956-64. Recipient Career Achievement in Sci. award Boston Coll. Alumni Assn., 1993. Fellow AIAA (outstanding engr. San Francisco chpt. 1988); mem. Am. Geophys. Union, Nat. Acad. of Engring., Nat. Rsch. Coun. Republican. Roman Catholic. Avocation: computer and woodworking hobbies. Home and Office: 13554 Mandarin Way Saratoga CA 95070-4847 Personal E-mail: jbr733@comcast.net.

**REAGAN, LAWRENCE PAUL, JR.,** engineering executive, consultant; b. Honolulu, Nov. 5, 1957; s. Lawrence Paul Sr. and Laura Louise (Sears) R.; m. Ann Marie Decker, Apr. 15, 1989; children: Lawrence P. III, Andrew Scott, Kelly Rene, Ryan Joshua. BS in Mech. & Aerospace Engring., Ill. Inst. Tech., Chgo., 1979; MS in Acquisition & Contract Mgmt., West Coast U., Santa Barbara, Calif., 1986; advanced cert. in Chinese/Soviet/Middle East/North Africa studies, Nat. Cryptological Sch., 1992. Cert. Air Force Acquisition Level 3. Product engr. R.G. Ray Corp., Schaumburg, Ill., 1978—80; launch integration mgr. USAF Hqrs. Space Divsn., L.A. AFB, 1980—84; chief Titan program mgmt. USAF Aerospace Sys. Ctr., Vandenberg AFB, Calif., 1984—89; chief joint comm. br. USAF Pentagon, Washington, 1989—91; sr. sys. engr. Dynamics Rsch. Corp., Arlington, Va., 1992—96, dir. Md. ops. California, Md., 1996—97; fed. programs mgr. Info. Builders, Inc., Arlington, 1997—98, dir. fed. programs, 1998—2003; v.p. PRICE Systems LLC, Arlington, 2003—. CEO Jacob's Well, Inc., Lexington Park, Md., 1993—. Contbr. papers to profl. publs. Officer USAF, 1979—92. Named Outstanding Young Engr., Air Force Assn. Mem. AIAA, Soc. Logistics Engring., Air Force Assn., Armed Forces Comms. Electronics Assn., Govt. Electronic Industry Assn. (bd. dirs.), Industry Adv. Coun. Ptnr. Program Avocations: boating,

---

water sports, reading, photography. Home: PO Box 22 Lusby MD 20657-0022 Office: PRICE Systems LLC 1700 N Moore St Ste 1100 Arlington VA 22209 Office Phone: 703-740-0078. Business E-Mail: larry.reagan@pricesystems.com.

**REAGAN, NANCY DAVIS (ANNE FRANCIS ROBBINS),** former First Lady of the United States, volunteer; b. NYC, July 6, 1921; d. Kenneth and Edith (Luckett) Robbins, Loyal Davis (Stepfather); m. Ronald Reagan, Mar. 4, 1952 (dec. June 5, 2004); children: Patricia Ann, Ronald Prescott stepchildren: Maureen(dec.), Michael. BA in Theatre, Smith Coll., 1943; LLD (hon.), Pepperdine U., 1983; LHD (hon.), Georgetown U., 1987. Sales clk. Marshall Fields Dept. Store, Chgo.; First Lady of The U.S. Washington, 1981—89. Contract actress, MGM, 1949-56; films include Portrait of Jennie, 1948, East Side, West Side, 1949, Doctor and the Girl, 1949, Shadow on the Wall, 1950, The Next Voice You Hear, 1950, Night into Morning, 1951, It's a Big Country, 1951, Shadow in the Sky, 1952, Talk About a Stranger, 1952, Donovan's Brain, 1953, Hellcats of the Navy, 1957, Crash Landing, 1958, You Can't Hurry Love, 1988, Lunar: Silver Star Story, 1992; TV credits include Schlitz Playhouse of Stars, 1951, Climax, 1954, General Electric Theater, 1953, Zane Grey Theater, 1956, The Tall Man, 1960, 87th Precint, 1961, Wagon Train, 1957, Different Strokes, 1978, Dynasty, 1981; Broadway: Lute Song, 1946; formerly author syndicated column on prisoner-of-war and missing-in-action soldiers and their families; author: Nancy, 1980; (with Jane Wilkie) To Love a Child, 1982, (with William Novak) My Turn: The Memoirs of Nancy Reagan, 1989. Civic worker, visited wounded Viet Nam vets., sr. citizens, hosps. and schs. for physically and emotionally handicapped children, active in furthering foster grandparents for handicapped children program; hon. nat. chmn. Aid to Adoption of Spl. Kids, 1977; spl. interest in fighting alcohol and drug abuse among youth: hosted first ladies from around the world for 2d Internat. Drug Conf., 1985; hon. chmn. Just Say No Found., Nat. Fedn. of Parents for Drug-Free Youth, Nat. Child Watch Campaign, President's Com. on the Arts and Humanities, Wolf Trap Found. bd. of trustees, Nat. Trust for Historic Preservation, Cystic Fibrosis Found., Nat. Republican Women's Club; hon. pres. Girl Scouts of Am. Named one of Ten Most Admired Am. Women, Good Housekeeping mag., ranking #1 in poll, 1984, 85, 86; Woman of Yr. Los Angeles Times, 1977; permanent mem. Hall of Fame of Ten Best Dressed Women in U.S.; recipient humanitarian awards from Am. Camping Assn., Nat. Council on Alcoholism, United Cerebral Palsy Assn., Internat. Ctr. for Disabled; Boys Town Father Flanagan award; 1986 Kiwanis World Service medal; Variety Clubs Internat. Lifeline award; numerous awards for her role in fight against drug abuse. Republican. Presbyterian.*

**REAGINS-LILLY, SONCIA RAE,** dean; d. Leonard Garrett and Sarah Elizabeth Reagins; m. Leslie Kyle Lilly, Aug. 7, 1993; children: Kyle Austin Lilly, Kennedy Elizabeth Lilly. BA, U. Calif., Irvine, 1986; MA, Calif. State U., San Bernardino, 1991; D, U. So. Calif., L.A., 1999. Cert. pupil pers. svcs. Calif. State U., 1991. Asst. vice chancellor student affairs adminstrn. UCLA, 2000—06; sr. assoc. v.p.dean students U. Tex., Austin, 2006—. founder women's resource and adult re-entry ctr. Calif. State U., 1993—, founder multicultural ctr., 1993—; strategic planning cons. U. Calif., San Diego, 2002, prin. investigator, L.A., 2002—06; strategic planning cons. Calif. Poly. State U., San Luis Obispo, 2004, Concerned Parents Alliance, Inc, San Diego, 2005—06. Grantee, Ed Fund, UCLA, 2003—06, AmeriCorps, 2003—06. Fellow: U. Calif. Mgmt. Inst.; mem.: Assn. Coll. Unions Internat., Nat. Assn. Student Pers. Adminstrs., Alpha Kappa Alpha. Home: 2867 Malcolm Ave Los Angeles CA 90064 Office Phone: 310-206-1605.

**REALS ELLIG, JANICE,** marketing professional, human resources specialist; b. NYC, May 14, 1946; d. Otto Peter and Anne (Briganti) Astolfi; m. Paul T. Reals, 1971 (div.); m. Bruce Robert Ellig, July 16, 1994; 1 child, Meredith Evans. BBA, U. Iowa, 1968; MA, Rider Coll., Princeton, N.J., 1978. Dir. Shareholders Mgmt., L.A., 1968—71; v.p. human resources Cooper Med. Ctr., NJ, 1971—80; dir. human resources Pfizer, N.Y.C., 1980—86; v.p. human resources Citibank, 1986—91; sr. v.p. mktg., human resources, adminstrn. Ambac Fin. Group, 1991—2000; prin. Heidrick & Struggles, 2000; pres., owner Gould, McCoy, Chadick, Ellig, 2000—. Chmn. bd. Women's Econ. Roundtable, N.Y.C., 1997—98. Author: What Every Successful Woman Knows, 2001. Bd. dirs. Fountain House, N.Y.C., Nat. Exec. Svc. Corp., N.Y.C., 2000-03, YMCA of N.Y., 2004—; bd. dirs. U. Iowa Found., 2003—, pres. club, 2000—; dir. adv. coun. Bus. Sch., U. Iowa, Iowa City, 1998-2004; bd. dirs. Women in the State and House, Washington, 1998-2006; mem. bus. com. Met. Mus. Art, N.Y.C., 1994—; bd. mem. Women's Forum, N.Y.C., 2004—; mem. adv. coun. Children's Aid Soc., N.Y.C., 1995-97; mem. leadership cir. Women's Campaign Fund, N.Y.C., 1990—2003. Named Woman of Yr., Rhinelander's Children Ctr./Children's Aid Soc., 1999, Woman of Excellence award TV Channel 21, 2002. Mem. Fin. Women's Assn., Econ. Club N.Y.C. Republican. Avocations: writing, gourmet cooking, reading, travel, tennis. Home: Apt 12G 10 Gracie Sq New York NY 10028-7052 Office: Gould McCoy Chadick Ellig 300 Park Ave New York NY 10022 Office Phone: 212-688-8671. Business E-Mail: jrellig@gmcsearch.com.

**REAM, JAMES B. (JIM REAM),** air transportation executive; married; 1 child. MBA, Northwestern Univ. Mng. dir. fin. planning Am. Airlines Inc.; v.p. fin. Continental Airlines, 1994—96; exec. v.p., COO Continental Micronesia Inc., Guam, 1996, pres., COO Guam, 1996—98; sr. v.p. Asia Continental Airlines, 1998—99; pres. ExpressJet, 1999—; CEO Express Jet, 2002—. Office: ExpressJet 1600 Smith St HQSCE Houston TX 77002 Office Phone: 713-324-4722. Office Fax: 713-324-4716.*

**REAMAN, GREGORY HAROLD,** pediatric hematologist, oncologist; b. Akron, Ohio, Sept. 9, 1947; s. Harold J. and Margaret U. (D'Alfonso) R.; m. Susan J. Pristo, Sept. 7, 1974; children: Emily Margaret, Sarah Elizabeth. BS in Biology, U. Detroit, 1969; MD, Loyola U., Chgo., 1973. Diplomate Nat. Bd. Med. Examiners, Am. Bd. Pediats. with subspecialty in pediat. hematology and oncology. Pediatric intern Loyola U. Med. Ctr., 1973-74; resident in pediatrics Montreal Children's Hosp., McGill U., 1974-76; clin. assoc. pediatric oncology br. Nat. Cancer Inst., NIH, Bethesda, Md., 1976-78, investigator pediatric oncology br., 1978-79; assoc. dept. hematology/oncology, attending physician Children's Nat. Med. Ctr., Washington, 1979—, chmn. dept. hematology/oncology, 1985—2003, dir. med. spl. svcs., 1995—99, exec. dir. Ctr. for Cancer and Blood Disorders, 1999—2002; asst. prof. pediats. Sch. Medicine and Health Scis. George Washington U., 1979—82, assoc. prof. pediats., 1982—87, prof. pediats., 1987—. Assoc. chmn. Children's Cancer Group; strategic planning com. Children's Oncology Svcs. of Met. Washington; exec. v.p. for sci. and med. affairs Nat. Childhood Cancer Found./Children's Oncology Group, chmn. bd. dir., 2000-; mem. oncologic drugs adv. com., FDA, 2002—. Mem. editl. bd. Cancer Data Query, Nat. Cancer Inst., Jour. Clin. Oncology, Am. Jour. Pediat. Hematology Oncology, Cancer, The Oncologist; reviewer Blood, Jour. Clin. Oncology; assoc. editor: Cancer, 1990-2000; contbr. articles to profl. publs. Trustee Nat. Childhood Cancer Found., Arcadia, Calif.; bd. dirs. Am. Cancer Soc., Atlanta; trustee, family patient care and profl. edn. coms. Leukemia Soc. Am. Lt. comdr. USPHS, 1976-79, Res., 1979—. Folger Summer scholar Am. Cancer Soc.; recipient Spl. Fellowship Rsch. award Leukemia Soc. Am., 1980-82; grantee DHHS, Nat. Cancer Inst., 1987—. Mem. Soc. Pediat. Rsch., Am. Soc. Hematology, Am. Pediat. Soc., Am. Fedn. Clin. Rsch., Am. Soc. Clin. Oncology, Am. Assn. Cancer Rsch., Am. Soc. Pediat. Hematology/Oncology, Children's Oncology Group. Washington Blood Club, Alpha Omega Alpha. Democrat. Roman Catholic. Home: 7306 Brennon Ln Chevy Chase MD 20815-4064 Office: Children's Nat Med Ctr 111 Michigan Ave NW Washington DC 20010-2916 Office Phone: 240-235-2220. Business E-Mail: greaman@childrensoncologygroup.org.*

**REAMS, BERNARD DINSMORE, JR.,** law educator; b. Lynchburg, Va., Aug. 17, 1943; s. Bernard Dinsmore and Martha Eloise (Hickman) Reams; m. Rosemarie Bridget Boyle, Oct. 26, 1968 (dec. Oct. 1996); children: Andrew Dennet, Adriane Bevin; m. Lee Anne Oberhofer, Apr. 19, 2003. BA, Lynchburg Coll., 1965; MS, Drexel U., 1966; JD, U. Kans., 1972; PhD, St.

---

Louis U., 1983. Bar: Kans. 1973, Mo. 1986, N.Y. 1996, Tex. 2002. Instr., asst. libr. Rutgers U., 1966—69; asst. prof. law, libr. U. Kans., Lawrence, 1969—74; mem. faculty law sch. Washington U., St. Louis, 1974—95, prof. law, 1976—95, prof. tech. mgmt., 1990—95, libr., 1974—76, acting dean univ. libraries, 1987—88; prof. law, assoc. dean, dir. Law Libr. St. John's U. Sch. Law, Jamaica, NY, 1995—97, assoc. dean acad. affairs, 1997—99, prof., dir. law libr. and info. tech. St. Mary's U., San Antonio, 2000—03, prof. law, 2000. Vis. fellow Max-Planck Inst., Hamburg, 1995, 97-98, 2001; vis. prof. law Seton Hall U., 1998-2000, Inst. World Legal Problems, Innsbruck, Austria, 2002, 05-06. Author: Law For The Businessman, 1974, Reader in Law Librarianship, 1976, Federal Price and Wage Control Programs 1917-1979: Legis. Histories and Laws, 1980, Education of the Handicapped: Laws, Legislative Histories, and Administrative Documents, 1983, Internal Revenue Acts of the United States: The Revenue Act of 1954 with Legislative Histories and Congressional Documents, 1983, Congress and the Courts: A Legislative History 1978-1984, 1984, University-Industry Research Partnerships: The Major Issues in Research and Development Agreements, 1986, Deficit Control and the Gramm-Rudman-Hollings Act, 1986, The Semiconductor Chip and the Law: A Legislative History of the Semiconductor Chip Protection Act of 1984, 1986, American International Law Cases, 2d series, 1986, Technology Transfer Law: The Export Administration Acts of the U.S., 1987, Insider Trading and the Law: A Legislative History of the Insider Trading Sanctions Act, 1989, Insider Trading and Securities Fraud, 1989, The Health Care Quality Improvement Act of 1989: A Legislative History of P.L. No. 99-660, 1990, The National Organ Transplant Act of 1984: A Legislative History of P.L. No. 98-507, 1990, A Legislative History of Individuals with Disabilities Education Act, 1994, Federal Legislative Histories: An Annotated Bibliography and Index to Officially Published Sources, 1994, Electronic Contracting Law, 1996, Health Care Reform, 1994, The American Experience: Clinton and Congress, 1997, The Omnibus Anti-Crime Act, 1997, The Law of E-SIGN: A Legislative History of the Electronic Signature in Global and National Commerce Act, 2001; co-author: Segregation and the Fourteenth Amendment in the States, 1975, Historic Preservation Law: An Annotated Bibliography, 1976, Congress and the Courts: A Legislative History 1787-1977, 1978, Federal Consumer Protection Laws, Rules and Regulations, 1979, A Guide and Analytical Index to the Internal Revenue Acts of the U.S., 1909-1950, 1979, The Numerical Lists and Schedule of Volumes of the U.S. Congressional Serial Set: 73d Congress through the 96th Congress, 1984, Human Experimentation: Federal Laws, Legislative Histories, Regulations and Related Documents, 1985, American Legal Literature: A Guide to Selected Legal Resources, 1985, U.S.A. Patriot Act: A Legislative History, 2002, Supplement, 2005, Intelligence Reform: A Legislative History of the Intelligence Reform and Terrorism Prevention Act, 2006. Trustees Quincy Found. for Med. Rsch. Charitable Trust, San Francisco; bd. dirs. San Antonio Lighthouse for Blind Fellow Am. Bar Found.; recipient Thornton award for excellence Lynchburg Coll., 1986, Joseph L. Andrews Bibliog. award, 1995; named to Hon. Order Ky. Cols., 1992; named Admiral Tex. Navy, 2005. Mem. ABA, ALA, Am. Law Inst., Am. Soc. Law and Medicine, Nat. Health Lawyers Assn., Am. Assn. Higher Edn., Spl. Librs. Assn., Internat. Assn. Law Libr. Coll. and Univ. Attys., Order of Coif, Phi Beta Kappa, Sigma Xi, Beta Phi Mu, Phi Delta Phi, Phi Delta Epsilon, Kappa Delta Pi, Pi Lambda Theta. Office: St Marys U Sch Law One Camino Santa Maria San Antonio TX 78228 Office Phone: 210-431-5030. E-mail: breams@stmarytx.edu.

**REAMS, PATRICIA LYNN,** retired elementary school educator; b. Fresno, Calif., Dec. 10, 1938; d. Chris H. and Marjorie Lois (nee Maul) Pedersen; m. William Everett Harvey (dec.); m. George William Reams, Nov. 10, 1972; children: Holly, Richard, George, Susan, Kristin. AA, Colo. Women's Coll., 1958; BA, San Jose State U., Calif., 1960. Cert. tchg. life diploma 1966. Tchr. Salinas Sch. Dist., Calif., 1960—61, Cupertino Sch. Dist., Calif., 1961—63, Spreckels Sch. Dist., Salinas, 1963—68, Alisal Sch. Dist., Salinas, 1971—74, Kingsburg Charter Sch., Calif., 1987—2002. BITSA trainer Fresno County Sch., Kingsburg, 1996—98. Pink lady, women's aux. local hosp., Salinas, Calif., 1972—83, Boulder City, Nev., 1984—87; adv. Rainbow Girls, Salinas, 1980—83; sec. PTA, Boulder City, 1984—86; brownie leader, 1985—86; Girl Scout leader, 1986—87; sec. Kingsburg HS Music Boosters, 1992—94; classroom vol. Lincoln Sch., Kingsburg, 2002—06. Recipient Grand Cross of Color award, Rainbow Girls, 1983. Mem.: PEO (pres. 2004—06), Ladies Oriental Shrine. Republican. Avocations: reading, gardening, travel. E-mail: plreams@sbcglobal.net.

**REAMY, MICHAELIN,** marriage and family therapist, educator, consultant; b. N.Y.C., Feb. 20, 1938; d. Judson Reamy and Eleanor Stevens (McMichael) R.; m. James Donald Cowie, Aug. 29, 1959; children: Jennifer D., James J., David K., Laura S.; m. Richard Ward Stephenson, Aug. 31, 1979. B.S. with Distinction in Human Ecology, Cornell U., 1960; M.S.W., U. Ga., 1979; student of Carolyn Myss and Norm Shealy, cert. program in intuition and energy medicine. Cert. primordial sound meditation instr. with Deepak Chopra, 1996. Tchr. swimming, Conn., E. Africa, Lebanon, 1968-75; social work intern, grad. asst., Atlanta, 1978-79; dir. social services, assoc. dir. and coordinator family therapy adult treatment program Brawner Psychiat. Inst., Atlanta, 1980-82; dir. extramural tng., marriage and family therapist Atlanta Inst. Family Studies, 1982-87; Perspective Ctr. for Psychotherapy, 1988-98; Natural Color & Design, 1988—. Mem. Atlanta Com. Children, 1983-85; instr. Water Safety ARC, 1957—. Recipient DAR Citizen award, 1956; YMCA Service Award, White Plains, N.Y., 1958. Diplomate NASW; mem. Nat. Assn. Social Workers, Am. Assn. Marriage and Family Therapy (com. on supervision), Cornell U. Human Ecology Alumni Assn., Mortar Bd., Omicron Nu, Phi Kappa Phi. Contbr. articles to profl. jours. Kappa Phi. Contbr. articles to profl. jours. Home and Office: Natural Color & Design 11 Garzas Trail Carmel CA 93923 Address: PO Box 190 Apalachicola FL 32329-0190 Office Phone: 831-624-4294.

**REARDEN, CAROLE ANN,** clinical pathologist, educator; b. Belleville, Ont., Can., June 11, 1946; d. Joseph Brady and Honora Patricia (O'Halloran) R. BSc, McGill U., 1969, MSc, MDCM, 1971. Diplomate Am. Bd. Pathology, Am. Bd. Immunohematology and Blood Banking, Am. Bd. Histocompatibility and Immunogenetics. Resident and fellow Children's Meml. Hosp., Chgo., 1971-73; resident in pediatrics U. Calif., San Diego, 1974, resident then fellow, 1975-79, asst. prof. pathology, 1979-86, dir. histocompatability and immunogenetics lab., 1979-94, assoc. prof., 1986-92, prof., 1992—, head divsn. lab. medicine, 1989-94; dir. med. ctr. U. Calif. Thornton Hosp. Clin. Labs., San Diego, 1993—. Prin. investigator devel. monoclonal antibodies to erythroid antigens, recombinant autoantigens; dir. lab. exam. com. Am. Bd. Histocompatibility and Immunogenetics. Contbr. articles to profl. jours.; patentee autoantigen prodt. Mem. Mayor's Task Force on AIDS, San Diego, 1983. Recipient Young Investigator Rsch. award NIH, 1979; grantee U. Calif. Cancer Rsch. Coordinating Com., 1982, NIH, 1983; scholar Nat. Blood Found. Mem. Am. Soc. Investigative Pathology, Am. Soc. Hematology, Am. Assn. Blood Banks (com. organ transplantation and tissue typing 1982-87, tech. com. 13 and 14 edit. tech. manual 1996-2002). Office: U Calif San Diego Dept Pathology 0612 9500 Gilman Dr La Jolla CA 92093-0612 E-mail: arearden@ucsd.edu.

**REARDON, FRANK EMOND,** lawyer; b. Providence, May 22, 1953; s. J. Clarke and Dorothy (Emond) R.; m. Deborah Walsh, Sept. 30, 1978; children: Kathleen Elizabeth, Brendan Francis, William James, Sean Patrick. BA, Holy Cross Coll., Worcester, Mass., 1975; JD, Suffolk U., 1978; MS, Harvard U., 1981. Bar: Mass. 1978, R.I. 1978, U.S. Dist. Ct. Mass. 1980, U.S. Dist. Ct. R.I. 1980, U.S. Supreme Ct. 1986. Counsel Nat. Assn. Govtl. Employment and Internat. Brotherhood Police Officers, Cranston, R.I., 1978-81; asst. gen. counsel Brigham and Women's Hosp., Boston, 1981-84; litigation counsel Risk Mgmt. Found. Harvard Med. Instns., Cambridge, Mass., 1984-87; ptnr. Hassan and Reardon, Boston, 1987—. Bd. dirs. St. Monica's Nursing Home, 1984-89, Med. Area Fed. Credit Unon, 1984-89; clk., trustee Deaconness Glover Hosp., Needham, Mass.; ethics com. Boston Children's Hosp., 1993-96. Contbr. articles to profl. jours. Chmn. fin. com. Town of Needham, Mass.; mem. pres.'s council Coll. Holy Cross, 1985—. Beuilacqua scholar, 1978. Mem. ABA, Mass. Bar Assn. (chmn. health law sect. 1987—), Assn.

Trial Lawyers Am., Am. Soc. Law and Medicine (cmty. rep. children's hosp. ethics com.). Democrat. Roman Catholic. Avocations: tennis, sailing, golf, writing. Home: 44 Sargent St Needham MA 02492-3434 Office: Hassan & Reardon 535 Boylston St Boston MA 02116-3720

**REARDON, GEORGE MARTIN,** lawyer; b. Detroit, Aug. 7, 1947; BS in bus., Fla. U., 1972; JD, U. Fla., Gainesville, 1975. Bar: Fla. 1976, US Ct. Appeals 5th Cir. 1976, US Dist. Ct. Mid., No., So. Districts Fla. 1976, Tex. 1992, US Dist. Ct. So. Dist. Tex. 1992, Mich. 1999. V.p., gen. counsel Charles Stedman & Co. Inc., 1976—82; v.p., asst. gen. counsel Snelling & Snelling, Inc., 1983—90; v.p., gen. counsel, corp. sec. The Talent Tree Corp., 1990-94; atty. pvt. practice, Houston, 1994-98; sr. v.p., gen. counsel Kelly Services Inc., Troy, Mich., 1998. Served Adj. Gen. Corps U.S. Army, 1970—72, Vietnam.

**REARDON, MICHAEL J.,** finance company executive; Mng. dir. high yield leverage fin. Salomon Smith Barney, NYC, 1994—96; mng. dir. fin. planning and analysis Travelers Group, 1996—98; mng. dir. Strategy and Bus. Devel. Group Citigroup, 1999—2002, chief adminstrn. officer Consumer Fin. and Consumer Assets Div., 2000—02, CFO Consumer Assets Div., 2000—04; acting CFO Student Loan Corp., Stamford, Conn., 2004, CEO, 2004—, pres., 2005—, chmn., 2006—. Office: Student Loan Corp 750 Washington Blvd Stamford CT 06901

**REARDON, NANCY ANNE,** food products executive; b. Little Falls, NY, Sept. 19, 1952; d. Warren Joseph and Elizabeth Owen (Tiel) Reardon; m. Steven Jonathan Sayer, Aug. 28, 1976; children: Scott Jason, Kathryn Anne. BS in Psychology, Union Coll., 1974; MS in Social Psychology, Syracuse U., 1978. With GE Co., N.Y.C., 1979-85, Avon Products Inc., N.Y.C., 1985-89, Am. Express, N.Y.C., 1989-91; sr. v.p. human resources Duracell Internat., Inc., Bethel, Conn., 1991-97; sr. v.p. corp. affairs & human resources Borden Inc., Columbus, Ohio, 1997—2004; sr. v.p., chief human resources and comm. officer Campbell Soup Co., Camden, NJ, 2004—. Bd. dir. Warnaco Group Inc. 2006-; adv. bd. mem. Catalyst, 1995. Mem. Human Resource Planning Soc. (bd. dirs. 1991-94, treas. 1992-93), N.Y. Human Resource Planners (bd. dirs., pres. 1989-91), Sr. Pers. Execs. Forum, Nat. Fgn. Trade Coun. (bd. dirs. 1995), Soc. Human Resource Mgmt., Phila. Women's Forum. Avocation: skiing. Office: Campbell Soup Co 1 Campbell Pl Camden NJ 08103-1799

**REARDON, ROBERT IGNATIUS, JR.,** lawyer; b. N.Y.C., Nov. 28, 1945; s. Robert I. and Mildred (Lomax) R.; m. Lise Hofffman; children: Colleen Brooke, Kelly Elizabeth. BS in Econs., Boston Coll., 1967; JD, Fordham U., 1970. Bar: Conn. 1970, U.S. Dist. Ct. Conn. 1974, U.S. Ct. Mil. Appeals 1971, U.S. Ct. Appeals (2d cir.) 1974, U.S. Supreme Ct. 1974, U.S. Ct. Claims 1986. Ptnr. Shapiro & Reardon, P.C., New London, Conn., 1973-83; pres. Reardon Law Firm P.C., New London, 1983—. State trial referee Conn. Superior Ct., 1985—. Chmn. Bd. Fin. Town of Waterford, Conn., 1974-79; mem. Bd. Edn. Town of East Lyme, Conn., 1981-84; trustee Eugene O'Neill Meml. Theater, Inc., 1978-84; active Conn. Commn. Pub. Trust, 1998-2000. Served as capt. USMC, 1970-73. Recipient Disting. Alumnus award, Fordham Law Sch., 2004. Mem. ABA (award of achievement young lawyers sect. 1975), ATLA (bd. dirs. 1998—), Conn. Trial Lawyers Assn. (pres. 1997-98), Conn. Bar Assn. (bd. govs. 1979-81, ho. of dels. 1975-79), New London County Bar Assn. (mem. exec. com. 1975-79)Fordham Law Sch. (Dist. Alumnus award, 2004) Office: 160 Hempstead St New London CT 06320-5638 Office Phone: 860-442-0444. Personal E-mail: reardonlaw@aol.com.

**REASON, ELIZABETH M.,** health facility administrator; b. Lansing, Mich., July 31, 1966; d. James F. and Pauline R. McClure; m. Gary M. Reason, July 29, 1989; children: James A. Jr., Aaron R., Hannah E., Caleb O. BA, We. Mich. U., Kalamazoo, Mich., 2001. Cert. healthcare access mgr. Nat. Assn. Healthcare Access Mgmt., 2005. With admitting and billing St Joseph Mercy Health Sys., Ann Arbor, Mich., 1997—99, Sparrow Health Sys., Lansing, 1999—2001; asst. mgr. admitting Ingham Regional Med. Ctr., Lansing, 2002—. Edn. chair Mich. Alliance of Healthcare Access Professionals, Mich., 2005—; adj. faculty Davenport U., Lansing, 2004—06. Mem.: Mich. Alliance Healthcare Access Profls. (educator 2005—06). Republican. Bapt. Avocations: gardening, reading. Home: 220 Winifred Ave Lansing MI 48917 Office Phone: 517-377-8473. Personal E-mail: elizabeth.reason@davenport.edu.

**REASON, J. PAUL,** naval officer; b. Washington, Mar. 22, 1941; s. Joseph Henry and Bernice (Chism) R.; m. Dianne Lillian Fowler, June 12, 1965; children: Rebecca, Joseph. BS, U.S. Naval Acad., 1965; MS, USN Postgrad. Sch., 1970. Cert. nuclear propulsion engr. Commd. ens. USN, 1965, advanced through grades to adm., 1996; naval aide to pres. The White Ho., Washington, 1976-79; exec. officer USS Miss., 1979-81; comdg. officer USS Coontz, 1981-83, USS Bainbridge, 1983-86; comdr. Naval Base, Seattle, 1986-88, Cruiser-Destroyer Group 1, 1988-90, Naval Surface Force Atlantic, 1991-94; dep. chief naval ops. plans, policy and ops. Dept. Navy, Washington, 1994-96; comdr.-in-chief U.S. Atlantic Fleet, 1996-99; retired, 1999; v.p. Syntek, Inc., Arlington, Va., 1999-2000; pres. Metro Machine Corp., Norfolk, Va., 2000—. Bd. dirs. Wal-Mart Stores Inc., 2000—06, Amgen, 2001—, Norfolk Southern Corp., 2002—. Decorated DSM, Legion of Merit, other mil. awards. Achievements include the first African-American in naval history to achieve the rank of four-star admiral. Avocations: fishing, tennis. Address: 201 W Tazewell St Apt 319 Norfolk VA 23510-1319*

**REASONER, HARRY MAX,** lawyer; b. San Marcos, Tex., July 15, 1939; s. Harry Edward and Joyce Majorie (Barrett) Reasoner; m. Elizabeth Macey Hodges, Apr. 15, 1963; children: Barrett Hodges, Elizabeth Macey Reasoner Stokes. BA summa cum laude in Philosophy, Rice U., 1960; JD with hons., U. Tex., 1962; postgrad., U. London, 1962—63. Bar: Tex., DC, NY. Law clk. U.S. Ct. Appeals (2d cir.), 1963—64; assoc. Vinson & Elkins, Houston, 1964—69, ptnr., 1970—, mng. ptnr., 1992—2001, ex-officio mem. Mgmt. Com. Vis. prof. U. Tex. Sch. Law, 1971, Rice U., 1976, U. Houston Sch. Law, 1977; chair adv. group U.S. Dist. Ct. (so. dist.) Tex.; mem. adv. com. Supreme Ct. Tex. Author (with Charles Alan Wright): Procedure: The Handmaid of Justice, 1965; mem. editl. bd.: Nat. Law Jour., 2004—. Trustee U. Tex. Law Sch. Found., Ctr. Am. and Internat. Law, Baylor Coll. Medicine; chair Tex. Higher Edn. Coordinating Bd., 1991; chair Houston A+ Challenge, Houston, 1997—; bd. dirs. Supreme Ct. of U.S. Bd. Hist. Soc, 2000—. Named Disting. Alumnus, U. Tex., 1997, U. Tex. Sch. Law, 1998, Rice U., 2003; recipient Professionalism award, US Court Appeals, Fifth Circuit, Am. Inns Court Found., 2004; fellow, Rotary Found., 1962—63. Fellow: Tex. Bar Found., ABA Found., Internat. Soc. Barristers, Am. Coll. Trial Lawyers, Internat. Acad. Trial Lawyers (bd. dirs. 2005—06); mem.: ABA (chmn. antitrust sect. 1989—90), Am. Bd. Trial Advocates, Philos. Soc. Tex., Houston Philos. Soc., Am. Law Inst., Assn. Bar City of NY, Houston Bar Assn., Century Assn. N.Y.C., U.S. Hist. Soc., Chancellors, Cosmos Club (DC), Phi Delta Phi, Phi Beta Kappa. Office: Vinson & Elkins First City Tower 1001 Fannin St, Ste 2300 Houston TX 77002-6760 Office Phone: 713-758-2358.

**REASONER, WILLIS IRL, III,** lawyer; b. Hamilton, Ohio, Dec. 24, 1951; s. W. Irl Jr. and Nancy Jane (Mitchell) R.; m. Lana Jean Mayes, Apr. 19, 1975 (div. Sept. 1985); 1 child, Erica M.; m. Joan Marie Mogil, Dec. 30, 1985; children: Scott, Sally. BA in History, Ind. U., 1974; JD cum laude, U. S.C. 1978. Bar: Ohio 1978, U.S. Dist. Ct. (so. dist.) Ohio 1978, U.S. Dist. Ct. (no. dist.) Ohio 1979, U.S. Ct. Appeals (6th cir.) 1988, U.S. Ct. Appeals (1st cir.) 1991, U.S. Ct. Appeals (7th cir.) 1999. Assoc. Porter, Wright, Morris & Arthur, Columbus, Ohio, 1978-83; ptnr. Baker & Hostetler, Columbus, 1983-94, Habash, Reasoner & Frazier, 1994—. Mem. ABA, Ohio Bar Assn., Columbus Bar Assn. Home: 4005 Redford Ct New Albany OH 43054-9500 Office: Habash, Reasoner & Frazier 471 E Broad St Ste 800 Columbus OH 43215-3854 Office Phone: 614-221-9400. E-mail: jreasoner@hrf-law.com.

**REATEGUI, LISA J.,** lawyer; b. 1966; BA magna cum laude, Princeton U., 1988; MA in Latin Am. Studies, Stanford U., 1990; JD magna cum laude, Northwestern U., 1995. Atty. Sidley Austin Brown & Wood, Chgo., 1995—2003, ptnr., 2003—. Chmn. major gifts fund raising Princeton U.; mem. women's bd. The Field Mus., mem. young profl.'s bd. Mem.: ABA, Chgo. (Ill.) Bar Assn. Office: Sidley Austin Brown & Wood Bank One Plz 10 South Dearborn St Chicago IL 60603

**REATH, GEORGE, JR.,** lawyer, mediator, arbitrator; b. Phila., Mar. 14, 1939; s. George and Isabel Duer (West) Reath; m. Ann B. Rowland, 1990; children from previous marriage: Eric(dec.), Amanda. BA, Williams Coll., 1961; LLB, Harvard U., 1964. Bar: Pa. 1965, U.S. Dist. Ct. (ea. dist.) Pa. 1966, U.S. Ct. Appeals (3d cir.) 1996. Assoc. Dechert Price & Rhoads, Phila., 1964-70, Brussels, 1971-74; atty. Pennwalt Corp., Phila., 1974-78, mgr. legal dept., asst. sec., 1978-87, sr. v.p. law, sec., 1987-89; sr. v.p., gen. counsel, sec. Elf Atochem N.Am., Inc. (formerly Pennwalt Corp.), Phila., 1990-92; sr. v.p., gen counsel, sec. Legal Triage Svcs., Inc., Phila., 1993-98; sr. v.p., gen. counsel, sec. Triage Mediation Svcs., Inc., Phila., 1999—. Trustee Children's Hosp., Phila., 1971—2003, sec., 1980—81, vice chmn., 1984—97, trustee emeritus, 2003; bd. mgrs. Phila. City Inst. Libr., 1974—, treas., 1981—88, pres., 1989—99; bd. dirs. Phila. Festival Theatre New Plays, 1983—94, Ctrl. Phila. Devel. Corp., 1987—93, Bach Festival Phila., 1990—98, v.p., 1992—93; bd. dirs. Citizens Crim Commn. Delaware Valley, 1st vice chmn., 1992—94, chmn., 1994—96, exec. com., 1996—; bd. trustees Episcopal Cmty. Svcs., 1999—, treas., 2000—06. Mem.: ABA, Assn. Conflict Resolution, Am. Corp. Counsel Assn., Phila. Bar Assn., Pa. Bar Assn., Penn Club, Winter Harbor Yacht Club, Penllyn Club, Phi Beta Kappa. Office Phone: 215-235-7711. Business E-mail: gr@triagemediation.com. E-mail: greath@comcast.net.

**REAVES, CHARLES DURHAM,** investment company executive, lawyer; b. Florence, S.C., June 1, 1935; s. Howard Meacham and Kathleen (Durham) R.; m. Gretchen Wuerdeman, May 4, 1963; 1 son, Mark Charles. BA magna cum laude, Furman U., 1956; LLB, U. Ala., 1961; LLM, Georgetown U., 1966; MBA, Emory U., 1981. Bar: Ala. 1961, Mass. 1967, D.C. 1970. Legal adv. to chmn. FTC, Washington, 1963-67; sec., assoc. counsel Paul Revere Life Ins. Co., Worcester, Mass., 1967-70; v.p., sec., gen. counsel Saunders Leasing System, Inc., Washington, 1970-74, Birmingham, Ala., 1974-80, sr. v.p. fin., sec., 1981-86; pres. Southeastern Asset Mgmt. Funds Trust, Memphis, 1986-93; exec. v.p., gen. counsel, chief compliance officer Longleaf Ptnrs. Funds, 1993—2002; of counsel Armstrong Allen PLLC, 2002—. Bd. trustees Memphis Opera, 1993—. Capt. USAR, 1961-63. Decorated Army Commendation medal. Mem. ABA, FBA, Mass. Bar Assn., D.C. Bar Assn., Ala. Bar Assn., Tenn. Bar Assn., Ala. Assn. Corp. Counsel (pres. 1981-82), Fin. Execs. Inst. (dir. 1983-84), Rotary, The Club (Birmingham), Westwood Country Club (Vienna, Va.), Econ. Club of Memphis (dir. 1993-96, 2004), Southwind Country Club (Memphis). Office: Brinkley Plaza Ste 700 80 Monroe Ave Memphis TN 38103 E-mail: creaves@armstrongallen.com.

**REAVES, JOSEPH SHANE,** protective services official; b. Raliegh, N.C., Oct. 12, 1976; s. Herbert Melvin Reaves and Loretta Larue Phelps; 1 child, David Micheal. B, Columbus U., Ohio, 2002. Fire controlman USN, Norfolk, Va., 1999—. Athlete Ironman Triathalon, Kona, Hawaii, 2001—04. With USN, 2000—05. Decorated Meritorious Mast Commdg. Officer. Liberal. Achievements include Enlisted Surface Warfare Specialist. Home: 142 Spring Ave Danville VA 24541

**REAVES, MELVIN JUNIOR,** retired small business owner; b. Benson, NC, May 4, 1919; s. Edgar Washington and Bess Ann (Rowsey) Reaves; m. Cynthia Thomas, Nov. 18, 1937; children: Sherwood, Sharon, Dennis, Jackie. Owner Reaves Music Co., Odessa, Tex., San Angelo, Tex., House Beautiful, Odessa, Tex., Austin Piano Co., Austin P&O Inc., Seguin (Tex.) Piano Co., Mel Reaves Realty, Austin, Tex. Author: West Texas - 1947, 2006, What Color Blue, 2006, Romance in Prose and Poems, 2006, Writer's Aid, 2006. Mem. C. of C., Odessa, Tex. With USN, WWII. Mem.: DAV, VFW, Am. Legion, Lions Club. Presbyterian. Home: 512 Green Valley Dr Unit A Bastrop TX 78602-6873 Personal E-mail: melreaves@academicplanet.com.

**REAVES, MICHAELA CRAWFORD,** history professor; d. Alvin Clegg and Mary Henry Crawford; m. James Alan Reaves, May 21, 1988; children: David James, Katherine Rose. BA, Calif. Luth. U., 1979; MA, Calif. State U., Northridge, 1987; PhD, U. Calif., Santa Barbara, 1996. Assoc. prof. Calif. Luth. U., Thousand Oaks, Calif., 1987—. Contbr. chapters to books Wilma Pearl Mankiller; author: (periodical) Cephas Little Bard: Soldier, Pioneer, Doctor. Mem.: Org. of Am. Historians (assoc.), Am. Hist. Assn. (assoc.), Phi Kappa Phi. Roman Catholic. Avocations: reading, gardening, camping. Office: Calif Luth U 60 West Olsen Rd Thousand Oaks CA 91360 Personal E-mail: reaves@clunet.edu.

**REAVES, RAY DONALD,** civil engineer; b. Jacksonville, Ala., Aug. 6, 1935; s. William Ozzie and Josephine (Jackson) R.; m. Annette Baird, Dec. 18, 1959; children: Tanya Ann Walker, Ronald Ray. BS in Civil Engring., Auburn (Ala.) U., 1960; MBA, U. Utah, 1976; postgrad., U. Mo., Kansas City. Registered profl. engr., Okla.; diplomate Am. Acad. Environ. Engrs. Commd. 2d lt. USAF, 1961, advanced through grades to col., 1981; comdt. Airlift Ops. Sch., Scott AFB, Ill., 1980-82; dep. base comdr. Little Rock AFB, 1982-83; base comdr. Kunsan Air Base, Korea, 1983-84, Tinker AFB, Oklahoma City, 1984-85; dir. environ. mgr. Oklahoma City Air Logistics Ctr. Tinker AFB, 1985-89, ret. USAF, 1989; mgr. environ. engrng. Oklahoma County, Oklahoma City, 1989-95, Okla. county engr., 1995—. Bus. Tech. Delegation Citizen to Citizen ambassador to Russia and Ukraine, 1992. Mem. ASCE, NSPE, Okla. Soc. Profl. Engrs. (citizen ambassador to Russia and Ukraine 1992), Midwest City C. of C., Rotary, Masons, Shriners. Avocations: golf, boating, tinkering.

**REAVIS, CHARLES BENTON,** choir director, educator; b. Salisbury, N.C., Nov. 20, 1946; s. James Clyde and Mildred Benton Reavis; m. Muriel Marjorie Roberts, July 4, 1949; children: Christopher Benton, Heather Reavis Fullerton. M of Secondary Edn., Salisbury U., 1978. Cert. advanced profl. Md., 1985. Tchr. Daniels Jr. HS, Raleigh, NC, 1969—71, Carneige Jr. HS, Raleigh, 1971—73, James M. Bennett HS, Salisbury, Md., 1973—; choir dir. St. Stephen's United Meth. Ch., Delmar, Del., 1973—. Mem. state curriculum task force Md. State Dept. Edn., Balti., 1986—88. Coun. mem. St. Stephen's United Meth. Ch., 1973. Mem.: NEA (life). Office Phone: 410-677-5141.

**REAVLEY, THOMAS MORROW,** federal judge; b. Quitman, Tex., June 21, 1921; s. Thomas Mark and Mattie (Morrow) Reavley; m. Florence Montgomery Wilson, July 24, 1943 (dec.); children: Thomas Wilson, Marian, Paul Stewart, Margaret; m. Carolyn Dineen King, Aug. 27, 2004. BA, U. Tex., 1942; JD, Harvard U., 1948; LLD, Austin Coll., 1974, Southwestern U., 1977, Tex. Wesleyan, 1982; LLM, U. Va., 1983; LLD, Pepperdine U., 1993. Bar: Tex. 1948. Asst. dist. atty., Dallas, 1948—49; mem. Bell & Reavley, Nacogdoches, Tex., 1949—51; county atty. Nacogdoches, Tex., 1951; with Collins, Garrison, Renfro & Zeleskey, 1951—52; mem. Fisher, Tonahill & Reavley, Jasper, Tex., 1952—55; sec. state Tex., 1955—57; mem. Powell, Rauhut, McGinnis & Reavley, Austin, Tex., 1957—64; dist. judge Austin, Tex., 1964—68; justice Tex. Supreme Ct., 1968—77; counsel Scott & Douglass, 1977—79; judge U.S. Ct. Appeals (5th cir.), Austin, Tex., 1979—90, sr. judge, 1990—. Lectr. Baylor U. Law Sch., 1976—94; adj. prof. U. Tex. Law Sch., 1958—59, 1978—79, 1988—95, South Tex. Sch. Law, Pepperdine Law Sch., 1990, Tex. Tech. Law Sch., 2003; mem. Am. Bar Assn., Am Bar Found., Tex. Bar Assn, Am. Law Inst., Am. Judicature Soc. Chancellor S.W. Tex. conf. United Meth. Ch., 1972—. Lt. USNR, 1943—45. Mem.: Masons (33 degree). Office: US Ct Appeals Rm 11009 515 Rusk St Houston TX 77002-2605 Office Phone: 713-250-5185.*

**REAY, STEFANIE,** application developer, educator; d. Rick and Ruth Lagerquist; m. Brent Reay, Feb. 14, 2004; children: Katelynn, Adrianna. BS in Math. and Stats., U. Conn., Storrs, 1999, MS in Stats., 2001. Lectr. U. Conn., Storrs, 1999—; analyst CentrPort, Westport, Conn., 2001; portfolio rev. analyst People's Bank Credit Card Divsn., Bridgeport, Conn., 2002—03, sr. quantitative analyst, 2003; analyst The Student Loan Corp., Pittsford, NY, 2004—. Adj. lectr. U. New Haven, 2002—. Mem. Am. Statis. Assn. Avocation: volleyball. Personal E-mail: stefanie_reay@hotmail.com.

**REAY-JONES, FRANCIS PETER FORTNUM,** entomologist, researcher; b. Oxford, England, May 23, 1978; arrived in U.S., 2002; s. Nigel S. and Georgea Reay-Jones. BS in Organism Biology, U. Bordeaux 1, 1999; MS in Plant Tech., U. d'Angers, 2001; PhD in Entomology, La. State U., 2005. Grad. rsch. asst. C.I.R.A.D, St-Denis-de-la-Réunion, France, 2001, La. State U., Baton Rouge, 2002—05, post-doctoral rsch. assoc., 2005, Tex. A&M U., Beaumont, Tex., 2006—. Contbr. articles to profl. jours. Co-chair movie com. Internat. Cultural Ctr. La. State U., 2002—03. Recipient L.D. Newsom Outstanding PhD Student award, La. State U., 2004; Sigma Xi grantee, 2004. Mem.: Am. Soc. Sugar Cane Technologists (D.T. Loupe Best Paper Presentation award 2005), La. Plant Protection Assn., Entomol. Soc. Am. (Robert T. Gast Best Rsch. Presentation PhD Student award S.E. br. 2004). Avocations: movies, travel. Office: Texas A&M University 1509 Aggie Drive Beaumont TX 77713 Office Phone: 409-752-2741. Office Fax: 409-752-5560. Business E-Mail: freayj1@lsu.edu.

**REBACK, RICHARD NEAL,** lawyer; b. Knoxville, Tenn., Feb. 9, 1954; s. Theodore and Delores (Robinson) R.; m. Kathryn Ann Gellens, Aug. 7, 1980; children: Jessica, Joshua, Matthew. BA magna cum laude, Duke U., 1976; JD with honors, U. Tex, 1979. Bar: Tex. 1980, U.S. Ct. Appeals (5th cir.) 1980, D.C. 1981, U.S. Ct. Appeals (D.C. cir.). Law clk. to assoc. judge U.S. Ct. Appeals (5th cir.), Austin, Tex., 1979-80; assoc. Wilmer, Cutler & Pickering, Washington, 1981-83, Swidler & Berlin, Washington, 1984-87; asst. U.S. atty. Washington, 1987-95; chief of staff, counselor to Insp. Gen. U.S. Dept. Interior, Washington, 1995-99; counsel insp. gen. U.S. Dept. State, Washington, 1999—2003; counsel inspector gen. U.S. Homeland Security, 2003—. Bd. dirs. Child Devel. Ctr.; mem. Ballston Ptnrship., Arlington, Va., 1986-89. Note editor: Tex. Law Rev., 1978-79. Mem. Ballston-Va. Sq. Civic Assn., Arlington, 1985-89, Am. Israel Pub. Affairs Com., Washington, 1984—; pres. Vernon Sq. Assn., Arlington, 1986-89; commr. Montgomery County Ethics Commn., 2000—, chair 2005—. Mem. ABA, D.C. Bar Assn., Tex. Bar Assn., Pi Sigma Alpha, Phi Eta Sigma. Democrat. Jewish. Avocations: athletics, civic and political activities. Home: 11209 Korman Dr Potomac MD 20854-2049 Office Phone: 202-254-4100.

**REBAY, LUCIANO,** language educator, literary critic; b. Milan, Apr. 23, 1928; came to U.S., 1955; s. Angelo and Pierina (Doniselli) R.; m. Martha Virginia Krauss, Aug. 2, 1952; children: Alexandra, Ilaria. Maturita classica Liceo Manzoni, Milan, 1946; Licence es lettres, U. Aix-en-Provence, France, 1951; PhD, Columbia U., 1960. Instr. Italian Columbia U., N.Y.C., 1957-60, asst. prof., 1960-63; assoc. prof., 1963-65, prof., 1965-73, Giuseppe Ungaretti prof. Italian lit., 1973—, chmn. Italian Dept., 1970-73; dir. Ctr. Italian Studies, 1985-88. Cons. to scholarly jours.; mem. Nat. Bd. Translators, Columbia U. Transl. Ctr. Author: Le origini della poesia di Giuseppe Ungaretti, 1962, Invitation to Italian Poetry, 1969, Alberto Moravia, 1970, Giuseppe Ungaretti, Gli scritti egiziani, 1909-1912, 1980, Montale, Clizia e l'America, 1982, Montale per amico, 1994, Montale: del dire e del non dire, 1998; editor: Giuseppe Ungaretti, Saggi e interventi, 1974, Jean Paulhan-Giuseppe Ungaretti, Correspondance, 1921-68, 1989. Guggenheim fellow, 1966-67; Am. Council Learned Socs. fellow, 1970-71; NEH fellow, 1980-81; Am. Philos. Soc. research grantee, 1970, 75 Mem. MLA, Am. Assn. Tchrs. of Italian, Associazione Internazionale per gli Studi di Lingua e Letteratura Italiana

**REBEIZ, CONSTANTIN ANIS,** plant biochemist, educator, lab administrator, foundation administrator; b. Beirut, July 11, 1936; arrived in U.S., 1959, naturalized, 1975; s. Anis C. and Valentine A. (Choueyri) Rebeiz; m. Conness Carole Louise, Aug. 18, 1962; children: Paul A., Natalie, Mark J. BS, Am. U., Beirut, 1959; MS, U. Calif., Davis, 1960, PhD, 1965. Dir. dept. biol. scis. Agrl. Rsch. Inst., Beirut, 1965—69; rsch. assoc. biology U. Calif., Davis, 1969—71; assoc. prof. biochem. and plant physiology U. Ill., Urbana-Champaign, 1972—76, prof., 1976—2005, dir. Lab. Plant Biochemistry and Photobiology, 1973—2005, prof. emeritus, 2005—; dir. Rebeiz Found. for Basic Rsch., Champaign, 2005—. Adj. prof. U. Limerick, Ireland, 2003. Contbr. articles to profl. jours. Bd. dirs. Rebeiz Found. for Basic Rsch. Named one of 100 Outstanding Innovators, Sci. Digest, 1984—85; recipient Beckman Rsch. award, 1982, 1985, Funk award, 1985, Sr. Rsch. award, U. Ill., 1994, Presdl. Green Chemistry Challenge award, 1999, Outstanding Sci. Achievement award, Faculty of Agrl. and Food Sci., Am. U. Beirut, 2002; grantee John P. Trebellas Rsch. Endowment, 1986, A.C. and C.C. Rebeiz Endowment for basic rsch., 2000. Mem.: AAAS, Lebanese Assn. Advancement Scis. (exec. com. 1967—69). Achievements include research in pathway of chlorophyll biosynthesis; chloroplast development; bioengineering of photosynthetic reactors; first to biosynthesis of chlorophyll in vitro; duplication of greening process of plants in test tube; development of demonstration of operation of multibranched chlorophyll biosynthetic pathway in nature; formulation of a blue-print chloroplast bioengineering in green plants aimed at improving plant productivity; formulation and design of laser herbicides, insecticides and cancer chemotherapeutic agents. Home: 2209 Edgewater Pl Champaign IL 61822 Office: Rebeiz Found Basic Rsch 2209 Edgewater Pl Champaign IL 61822 Office Phone: 217-377-9147. Business E-Mail: crebeiz@uiuc.edu. *Meaningful scientific discoveries are those that help humans achieve a better understanding of themselves, of their environment or of the universe at large, as well as those that contribute to the betterment of the human spiritual, psychological and physical condition.*

**REBENACK, JOHN HENRY,** retired librarian; b. Wilkinsburg, Pa., Feb. 10, 1918; s. Charles Lewis and Carrie (Fielding) R.; m. Dorothy Merle Treat, Oct. 31, 1942 (dec. Apr. 1971); children: Charles Edwin, Christine (Mrs. Clair N. Hayes III); m. Frances Strabley Krieger, May 6, 1972. AB, U. Pitts., 1942; BS in L.S, Carnegie Library Sch., 1947. Reference asst. Carnegie Library, Pitts., 1947-50; librarian Salem (Ohio) Pub. Library, 1950-53, Elyria (Ohio) Library, 1953-57; asst. librarian Akron (Ohio) Public Library, 1957-65, asso. librarian, 1965-67, librarian-dir., 1967-80. Dir. U.S. Book Exchange, Inc., 1972 Mem. United Community Council, Citizens' Com. Pub. Welfare, 1965-66, chmn. group work and recreation div., 1963-66, v.p., 1967-68, pres. conf. of execs., 1975-76; mem. steering com., planning div. United Way; mem. Akron Mayor's Task Force on Human Relations, 1962; mem. library com. President's Com. on Employment of Handicapped, 1967-80, chmn., 1973-80, mem. sch. library manpower adv. com., 1967-73; mem. coll. adv. com. U. Akron, 1972-85; mem. adv. council on fed. programs State Library of Ohio, 1975-79; Bd. visitors Grad. Sch. Library and Info. Sci., U. Pitts., 1968-74; mem. exec. bd. Gt. Trail council Boy Scouts Am., 1977-80; bd. dirs. Summit County unit Am. Cancer Soc., 1976—, pres. 1979-81; bd. dirs. Ohio div., 1981-91, chmn. pub. relations div., 1984-91, mem. 1988-91. With AUS, 1942-45. Recipient Newton D. Baker citation, 1968 Mem. ALA (chmn. personnel adminstrv. sect. 1966-67, chmn. bldgs. and equipment sect. 1971-73, chmn. legislation assembly 1976-77), Ohio Library Assn. (exec. bd. 1957-60, chmn. adult edn. round table 1963, chmn. legis. com. 1965-66, 70-72, 76-80, pres. 1966-67, Librarian of Year 1979, named to Hall of Fame 1989), Carnegie Library Sch. Assn. (pres. 1961-63), U. Pitts. Grad. Sch. Library and Info. Sci. Alumni Assn. (exec. com. 1978-79, Disting. Alumnus award 1980), Am. Assn. UN (v.p. Akron chpt. 1960), Kiwanis Internat. Found. (Tablet of Honor 1997, George F. Hixson fellow 1998), Torch Club (pres. 1968-69), Kiwanis (pres. Akron 1978-79, Man of Yr. 2004), Beta Phi Mu. Congregationalist. Home: 2095 Brookshire Rd Akron OH 44313-5323

**REBER, DAVID JAMES,** lawyer; b. Las Vegas, Nev., Mar. 1, 1944; s. James Rice and Helen Ruth (Cusick) R.; m. Jacqueline Yee, Aug. 31, 1968; children: Emily, Brad, Cecily. BA, Occidental Coll., L.A., 1965; JD, Harvard U., 1968.

Bar: Calif. 1969, Hawaii 1975, U.S. Dist. Ct. Hawaii, U.S. Ct. Appeals (9th cir.), U.S. Supreme Ct. Asst. prof. law U. Iowa, Iowa City, 1968-70; assoc. Sheppard Mullin Richter & Hampton, L.A., 1970-75, Goodsill Anderson Quinn & Stifel, Honolulu, 1975-76, ptnr., 1976—. Bd. dirs. Enterprise Honolulu; bd. dirs., pres. Legal Aid Soc. Hawaii. Mem. ABA (bus. and pub. utilities sects.), Hawaii Bar Assn. Avocations: golf, tennis, softball, travel. Office: Goodsill Anderson Et Al 1099 Alakea St Ste 1800 Honolulu HI 96813-4511 Office Phone: 808-547-5611. E-mail: dreber@goodsill.com.

REBER, JEFFREY STEPHEN, psychology professor; b. Anaheim, Calif., Apr. 18, 1970; s. Philip Reed and Betty Jane Reber; m. Angela Kathryn Moody, Aug. 8, 1992; children: Brooklyn Elise, Dylan Jeffrey, Carson James, Madison Grace. BS, Brigham Young U., 1994, MS, 1999, PhD, 2000. Instr. Brigham Young U., Provo, Utah, 1996—2000; asst. prof. psychology U. West Ga., Carrollton, 2000—05, learning cmty. coord., 2004—, assoc. prof. psychology, 2005—. Mem. instl. rev. bd. Inner Harbor, Douglasville, Ga., 2001—; ad hoc reviewer Wiley Pub., Thomson Wadsworth, Pastoral Scis. Editor, author (book) Critical Thinking About Psychology: Hidden Assumptions and Plausible Alternatives, 2005 (William James award nominee, 2005); author: New Ideas in Psychchology, Theory and Psychology. Judge West Ga. Regional Sci. and Engring. Fair, Carrollton, 2002—04, Ga. Commin. Holocaust Ann. Art and Writing Contest, Atlanta, 2004; bishop LDS Ch., Carrollton, 2002—. Recipient Student Rsch. award, Am. Psychol. Soc. Student Caucus, 1999, Disting. Svc. award, Office Disabilities, 2001, 2003. Mem.: APA, Ga. Psychol. Assn. Acad. Affairs Com., Soc. Theoretical and Philos. Psychology (program chair 2000—01, membership chmn. 2005—), Golden Key Nat. Honor Soc. Mem. Lds Ch. Avocations: surfing, tennis, volleyball, travel, guitar. Office: U W Georgia 1601 Maple St Carrollton GA 30118 Office Phone: 678-839-0614. Office Fax: 678-839-0611. Business E-Mail: jreber@westga.edu.

REBER, VERA BLINN, history professor; b. Hong Kong, May 23, 1941; d. Calvin H. and Audrie E. Reber; m. John L. Offner, June 20, 1979; 1 child, Stella Susannah Reber Offner. BA, U. Hisgts., 1963; MA, U. Wis., 1967, PhD, 1972. With Peace Corps, Costa Rica, 1963—65; asst. prof. history Shippensburg U., Pa., 1970—72, assoc. prof. history, 1972—78, prof. history, 1978—. Author: British Mercantile Houses in Buenos Aires 1810-1880, 1979; contbr. articles to profl. jours. Pres. APSCUF, Shippensburg, 1977—78; judge History Day, 1994—2006. Mem.: Conf. L.Am. Hhistory, am. Hist. Assn., World History Assn. Avocation: travel. Home: 314 E King St Shippensburg PA 17257 Office: Shippensburg U Dept History Shippensburg PA 17257 Office Phone: 717-477-1736. Business E-Mail: vbrebe@ship.edu.

REBERT, JEPHREY LEE, urban planner, musician; b. Carlisle, Pa., June 10, 1959; s. John Alton and Mary Anna (Feeman) R. BS, Pa. State U., 1982. Residential appraiser County of York, Pa., 1984-85; phys. and environ. planner York County Planning Commn., 1985-87, transp. planner, 1987-93, sr. transp. planner, 1993—. Musician, prodr.: audiotape Peace of Mind (Loose Cannons), 1995; musician: (CD) Colonial Pagoda (Namaste), 1997, Smoke Signals (Anderson's Tool Shed), 2004. Alumni mem. Pa. State Blue Band; treas., bd. dirs. Ctr. for Ind. Living Opportunities; mem. Susquehanna Regional Transp. Partnership; ptnr. York Rescue Mission. Mem.: ASCE, Inst. Transp. Engrs., Am. Planning Assn., Phi Mu Alpha Sinphonia (Alpha Zeta chpt., alumnus). Avocations: anthropology, racquet sports, coin collecting/numismatics. Home: 59 N Lehman St York PA 17403-1116 Office: York County Planning Commn 100 W Market St York PA 17401-1332 E-mail: zoombangi@aol.com.

REBHUN, JOSEPH, allergist, immunologist, medical educator; b. Przemysl, Poland, Oct. 7, 1921; came to U.S., 1950; s. Baruch and Serel R.; m. Maria Birkenhejm, Aug. 10, 1945; children: Lillian Friedland, Richard B.R., Donald. MD, U. Innsbruck, austria, 1950; MS in Medicine, Northwestern U., 1954. Diplomate Am. Bd. Allergy and Immunology. Intern Barnert Meml. Hosp., Patterson, NJ; resident in internal medicine Tompkins County Meml. Hosp. and Cornell U., NY, 1951-52; fellow in allergy Northwestern U. Med. Sch./Chidlren's Meml. Hosp., Chgo., 1952-54; fellow instr. Northwestern U. Med. Sch., 1954; asst. clin. prof. medicine Loma Linda U., 1957-93; clin. prof. medicine U. So. Calif., L.A., 1965-91, ret., 1998. Chief allergy Chgo. Eye, Ear, Nose and Throat Hosp., 1953-55; cons. Pacific State Hosp., Spadra Pomona Valley Cmty. Hosp., Pomona Casa Colina Hosp. Author: SOS, 1946, The Cry of Democracy for Help, God and Man in Two Worlds, 1985, The Embers of Michael, 1993, Crisis of Morality and Reaction to the Holocaust, 1998, Leap to Life: Triumph Over Nazi Evil, 2000, Why Me?, 2004; contbr. numerous articles to med. jours. Pres. Am. Congress Jews from Poland, 1969—70. Capt. U.S. Mil., San Francisco, capt. med. reserve corps., L.A. Recipient honors City and County of L.A., L.A. Office Dist. Atty., Senate of State of Calif., all 1985. Fellow Am. Acad. Allergy (rsch. coun. 1960-65), Am. Coll. Allergy, Assn. Clin. Allergy and Immunology; mem. West Coast Allergy Soc., Calif. Allergy Assn., L.A. Soc. Allergy, L.A. Med. Assn., Calif. Med. Assn. Personal E-mail: joerebhun@yahoo.com.

REBMANN, TERRI, director; b. St. Louis, Aug. 18, 1970; d. Charles and Sandra Jones; m. Craig Rebmann, Mar. 8, 1996; children: Kevin, Alexis. BSN, Truman State U., Kirksville, Mo., 1992; MSN, U. Mo., Columbia, 1996; PhD, St. Louis U., 2006. Cert. infection control Cert. Bd. Infection Control and Epidemiology, 2000. RN, U.S. commd. officer U.S. Nat. Ctr. for Fed. Prisoners, Springfield, Mo., 1989—93; RN Harry S. Truman VA Hosp., Columbia, Mo., 1993—95; clin. rsch. coord. AIDS Project of the Ozarks, Springfield, 1996; patient services supr. Reproductive Health Svcs., Planned Parenthood, St. Louis, 1996—97; infection control specialist Inst. for Biosecurity, St. Louis U., Sch. Pub. Health, St. Louis, 2000—05, assoc. dir. for curricular affairs, 2005—. Infection control cons. Planned Parenthood, St. Louis, 2005—. Contbg. editor: Briefings on Infection Control, HCPro, 2003—06; contbr. chapters to books, articles to profl. jours. Lt. j.g. USPHS, 1989—93. Recipient George Wash. Carver award, Truman State U., 1988, Nat. Collegiate Nursing award, 1991, Quality Leadership award, Barnes Jewish Hosp., 1999, 2000; Grace Devitt Nursing Writing Found. scholar, Truman State U., 1992, Anne Zimmerman/Am. Nurses Found. scholar, Am. Nurses Found., 2005. Mem.: APIC (treas. 2002—04, chair emergency preparedness com. 2004—06), Sigma Theta Tau. Office: Institute for Biosecurity St Louis U Ste 300 3545 Lafayette Saint Louis MO 63104 Office Phone: 314-977-8260. Office Fax: 314-977-1674. Personal E-mail: rebmannt@slu.edu.

REBOLLO-LOPEZ, FRANCISCO, judge; b. San Juan, PR, Aug. 5, 1938; BA, U. PR, 1959, JD, 1963. Asst. dist atty. San Juan, PR, 1966; asst. prosecutor US Dist. Ct. of PR; judge PR Superior Ct., 1973—77; atty. priv. practice, 1977—82; justice PR Supreme Ct., San Juan, 1982—. Office: Supreme Court PO Box 2392 San Juan PR 00902-2392*

REBOUL, JOHN W., lawyer; b. NYC, Nov. 12, 1937; AB, Harvard Univ., 1959, LLB, 1963; Doctorat de l'Universite, Faculte de Droit et Sciences Economiques, Univ. Paris, 1964. Bar: NY 1965. Founding ptnr. Reboul Mac Murray Hewitt & Maynard, N.Y.C., 1973—2003; ptnr. corp. dept. & co-head internat. practice group Ropes & Gray, N.Y.C., 2003—. Mem.: ABA, Assn. Bar City of N.Y., Internat. Law Assn. (Am. branch), Union Internationale des Avocats. Office: Ropes & Gray 45 Rockefeller Plz New York NY 10111-0087 Office Phone: 212-841-5705. Office Fax: 212-841-5725. Business E-Mail: jreboul@ropesgray.com.

REBSTOCK, THEODORE LYNN, chemist, educator, retired research scientist; b. Elkhart, Ind., June 24, 1925; s. Adolph Rebstock and Redna Dunkelberger; m. Barbara Jean Lee, Nov. 30, 1957; children: David Lynn, Donald Lee. BA, North Ctrl. Coll., Naperville, Ill., 1949; MS, Mich. State U., 1951, PhD, 1956. Instr. rsch. Mich. State U., East Lansing, 1951—56, asst. prof. agrl. chemistry, 1956—59, vis. prof., 1965; assoc. prof. chemistry Westmar Coll., Le Mars, Iowa, 1959—66, prof. chemistry, 1966—83, chmn. chemistry dept., 1963—83; mgr. R&D Lab. Harkers, Inc., Le Mars, Iowa,

1984—90; ret., 1990. Dir. divsn. natural scis. Westmar Coll., Le Mars, Iowa, 1970. Contbr. articles to profl. jours. Fellow: AAAS; mem.: Am. Chem. Soc., Kiwanis Club (pres. 1993), Sigma Xi. Methodist. Avocations: golf, bowling, gardening, woodworking. Home: 1026 Sixth Ave SE Le Mars IA 51031

REBUELTA, AVELINO LUIS, public administration educator; b. June 22, 1944; MPA, Am. U., Washington, 1982; M in Ednl. Adminstrn., U. Tex., Edinburg, 1999. Prof. Universidad Nacional Autonoma De Mexico, Mexico City, 1962—, Instituto Politecnico Nacional, Mexico City, 1962—, Universidad Pedagogica Nacional, Mexico City, 1982—. Home: 701 Hibiscus Ave Apt 5 Mcallen TX 78501-1858 Office Phone: 956-630-6417. E-mail: al_rebuelta@hotmail.com.

RECCHI, MARK, professional hockey player; b. Kamloops, BC, Can., Feb. 1, 1968; Right wing Pitts. Penguins, 1988—92, 2004—06, 2006—, Phila. Flyers, 1992—95, 1999—2004, Montreal Canadiens, 1995—99, Carolina Hurricanes, 2006. Named Most Valuable Player, All-Star Game, 1997; named to NHL All-Star Game, 1991, 1993, 1994, 1997, 2000. Achievements include being a member of Stanley Cup Champion Pitts. Penguins, 1991, Carolina Hurricanes, 2006. Office: c/o Pittsburgh Penguins 66 Mario Lemieux Pl Pittsburgh PA 15219*

RECCHIUTI, JOHN LOUIS, history professor; s. John Louis and Maryann Recchiuti; m. Amy Louise Baldwin, June 13, 1998; children: John III, Elizabeth. PhD, Columbia U., 1992. Lectr. Columbia U., N.Y.C., 1985—91; adj. NYU., N.Y.C., 1986—89; prof. Mt. Union Coll., Alliance, Ohio, 1998—. Dir. Am. studies Mt. Union Coll., 2005—. Author: Civic Engagement: Social Science and Progressive-Era Reform in New York City. Mem.: Am. Studies Assn., Orgn. Am. Historians, Am. Hist. Assn. Office Phone: 330-823-3276. Personal E-mail: jlr234@gmail.com.

RECH, LINDSAY FAITH, writer; b. Phila., Mar. 30, 1978; d. Ivan Blaine and Hillary-Sue Resnick; m. Scott Rech, Oct. 21, 2000. BFA in Theater and English, Rider U., 2000. Writing tutor Rider U., Lawrenceville, NJ, 2000; columnist Pennington (NJ) Post, 2000—01; freelance reporter, theater critic Times Pub. Newspapers, Inc., Yardley, Pa., 2000, asst. editor, 2000—02; author Red Dress Ink, N.Y.C., 2003—; editl. quality control specialist Law Sch. Admission Coun., Newtown, Pa., 2005—. Spkr. Northampton Writers Group, Richboro, Pa., 2003. Columnist: A Different Voice, 2000—01; author: Losing It, 2003, Joyride, 2004. Acad. achievement scholar, presdl. scholar, Rider U., 1996—2000, Clayton Family scholar, 1997—2000. Mem.: Authors Guild, Phi Beta Kappa, Sigma Tau Delta, Alpha Lambda Delta. Jewish. Avocations: vegetarianism, 80's pop culture. Personal E-mail: lindsay@lindsayfaithrech.com.

RECHARD, PAUL ALBERT, retired civil engineering company executive, consultant; b. Laramie, Wyo., June 4, 1927; s. Ottis H. and Mary R. (Bird) R.; m. Mary Lou Roper, June 26, 1949; children: Robert Paul, Karen Ann. BS, U. Wyo., 1948, MS, 1949, CE, 1955. Registered land surveyor, Wyo.; registered profl. engr., Wyo.; cert. profl. hydrologist Am. Inst. Hydrology. Hydraulic engr. U.S. Bur. Reclamation, Cody, Wyo. and Billings, Mont., 1949-54; dir. water resources Natural Resource Bd., Cheyenne, Wyo., 1954-58; prin. hydraulic engr. Upper Colorado River Commn., Salt Lake City, 1958-64; dir. Water Resources Rsch. Inst. U. Wyo., Laramie, 1964-81, mem. faculty dept. civil engring., 1964-82, prof., 1964-82; pres. Western Water Cons., Laramie, 1980-2001, Hydrology Assocs., Laramie, 1978-80; ret. Western Water Consults., Inc., 2001. Owner Paul A. Rechard, P.E., Laramie, 1964-1978, 2001-. Editor: Compacts, Treaties and Court Decrees Affecting Wyoming Water, 1956; contbr. articles to tech. publs. Pres., Thayer Sch. PTA, Laramie, 1965; mem. Laramie City Planning Commn., 1974-80. Served with USNR, 1945-46. Recipient Wyo. Eminent Engr. award Tau Beta Pi, 1993; named Disting. Alumnus U. Wyo., 1998; named Outstanding Engr. Wyo. Engring. Soc., 1999. Fellow ASCE (life mem., pres. Wyo. sect. 1968); mem. NSPE (life), Am. Geophys. Union, Wyo. Engring. Soc. (pres. 1976, hon.), U.S. Com. on Irrigation and Drainage, Lions (pres. Laramie 1968), Masons, Sigma Xi (pres. Wyo. chpt. 1973), Phi Kappa Phi (pres. Wyo. chpt. 1969), Gamma Sigma Delta, Sigma Tau (pres. Wyo. chpt. 1948, selected Wyo. Eminent Engr. 1993). Republican. Presbyterian. Home and office: 316 Stuart St Laramie WY 82070-4866 Office Phone: 307-745-7477. Personal E-mail: prechard@msn.com.

RECHY, JOHN FRANCISCO, writer; b. El Paso, Tex. s. Roberto Sixto and Guadalupe (Flores) R. BA, U. Tex., El Paso; student, New Sch. Social Research. Instr. creative writing UCLA, Occidental Coll., U. So. Calif. Author: City of Night, 1963, Numbers, 1967, This Day's Death, 1969, The Vampires, 1971, The Fourth Angel, 1973, The Sexual Outlaw, 1977, Rushes, 1979, Bodies and Souls, 1983, Marilyn's Daughter, 1988, The Miraculous Day of Amalia Gómez, 1991, Our Lady of Babylon, 1996, The Coming of the Night, 1999, The Life and Adventures of Lyle Clemens, 2003, Outlaw: The Life and Careers of John Rechy, 2004; (essays) Beneath the Skin, 2004; (plays) Momma As She Became-Not As She Was, 1968, Rushes, 1978, Tigers Wild, 1986; (CD-Rom) Mysteries and Desire: Exploring the Worlds of John Rechy, 2000; contbr.: short stories and articles to Tex. Observer, The Nation, Village Voice, London mag., Saturday Rev., N.Y. Times Book Rev., L.A. Times, San Francisco Chronicle Books, Washington Post Book World, Phila. Inquirer, Contemporary Fiction, Big Table, others; also anthologies Chicano Voices, Black Humor, Urban Reader, Evergreen Rev. Reader, New Am. Story, The Moderns, Rediscoveries, Men on Men, others; trans.: stories and articles for Tex. Quar., Evergreen Rev. Served with AUS. Recipient Lifetime Achievement award PEN-USA, 1997, Pub. Triangle's William Whitehead award for lifetime achievement in lit., 1999, Longview Found. award for short story The Fabulous Wedding of Miss Destiny, 1960, Golden Nugget Outstanding Alumni award U. Tex El Paso, 2001; Nat. Endowment for Arts grantee, 1976. Fellow L.A. Inst. Humanities; mem. Authors Guild, Tex. Inst. Letters, PEN, Nat. Writers Union.

RECK, ANDREW JOSEPH, philosopher; b. New Orleans, Oct. 29, 1927; s. Andrew Gervais and Katie (Mangiaracina) R.; m. Elizabeth Lassiter Torre, June 17, 1987. BA, Tulane U., 1947, MA, 1949; postgrad., U. St. Andrews, Scotland, 1952—53; PhD, Yale U., 1954; student, U. Paris, 1962, student, 1964. Instr. English U. Conn., 1949-50; instr. philosophy Yale U., 1951-52, 55-58; faculty Tulane U., 1958—2003, prof. philosophy, 1964—2003, chmn. dept., 1969-89, dir. Master Liberal Arts program, 1984—2003, ret., 2003. Thomasfest lectr. Xavier U., Cin., 1970; Suarez Centy Sigma Hill Coll., 1971; Niebuhr lectr. Elmhurst (Ill.) Coll., 1976; vis. prof. Fordham U., 1979; vis. scholar Hastings Ctr. U. N.Y., 1981; Woodruff lectr. Emory U., 1982; Fairchild lectr. U. So. Miss., 1982, 87; Matchette Found. lectr. Cath. U. Am., 1991, 95; Sr. Scholar Inst. Humane Studies, Menlo Park, Calif., 1982; vis. scholar Poynter Ctr., Ind. U., Bloomington, 1983; Tulane U. faculty rep. to bd. adminstrs. Tulane Ednl. Fund., 1988-91. Author: Recent American Philosophy, 1964, Introduction to William James, 1967, New American Philosophers, 1968, Speculative Philosophy, 1972; co-author: Die Philosophie des 18. Jahrhunderts I, 2004; editor: George Herbert Mead Selected Writings, 1964, 2d edit., 1981, Knowledge and Value, 1972, (with T. Horvath, T. Krittek and S. Grean) American Philosophers' Ideas of Ultimate Reality and Meaning, 1993; co-editor Ultimate Reality and Meaning, Interdisciplinary Studies in the Philosophy of Understanding, 1990-2005; mem. adv. editl. bd. Internat. Jour. World Peace, Trans. Charles Peirce Soc., Santayana edit. So. Jour. Philosophy, Library of Living Philosophers; editor History of Philosophy Quar., 1993-98. Served with AUS, 1953-55. Howard fellow, 1962-63, Liberty Fund grantee, 1982, Newcomb fellow, 1991-93; Fulbright scholar, 1952-53; Am. Coun. Learned Socs. grantee, 1961-62, Am. Philos. Soc. grantee, 1972, Huntington Libr. grantee, 1973, La. Ednl. Quality State Found. grantee, 1994-96, U.S. Info. Agy. grantee, Brazil, 1993. Mem.: La. Endowment for Humanities (bd. dirs 1990—96), Internat. Soc. for Study of Human Ideas of Ultimate Reality and Meaning (bd. dirs. 1989—2005, treas. 2001—03, sec., treas. 2003—05), Charles S. Peirce Soc. (sec., treas. 1985—86, v.p. 1986—87, pres. 1987—88), Soc. Advancement Am. Philosophy (exec. com. 1980—82, pres.-elect 1997—98, pres. 1998—2000, exec. com. 2001—03, chair nominating com. 2002—04), Metaphys. Soc. Am. (councillor

1971—75, pres. 1977—78, program com. 1989—90, chair program com. 1995—96), Coun. for Internat. Rsch. Scholars (philosophy screening com. 1974—77), Am. Coun. Learned Socs. (Am. studies adv. com. 1972—76), So. Soc. Philosophy and Psychology (treas. 1968—71, pres. 1976—77), Southwestern Philos. Soc. (exec. com. 1965—69, v.p. 1971—72, pres. 1972—73), Am. Philos. Assn. (program com. ea. divsns. 1969, nominating com. western divsn. 1975—76, 1981—82, adv. com. to program com. ea. divsn. 1994—97, chair ad hoc com. on history 1996—2004), Tulane U. Emeritus Club (Outstanding Grad. of Class of 1947 award 1997), Omicron Delta Kappa, Alpha Sigma Lambda (hon. Theta chpt. of La.), Phi Beta Kappa (pres. Alpha of La. 1966—67). Home: 6125 Patton St New Orleans LA 70118-5832 Personal E-mail: ereck@cox.net.

RECK, ELIZABETH TORRE, social worker, educator; b. Winston-Salem, N.C., June 17, 1931; d. Vernon Clark and Mary (Pfohl) Lassiter; m. Mottram Peter Torre, Aug. 13, 1957 (dec.); m. Andrew Joseph Reck, June 17, 1987. Student, Wellesley Coll., Mass., 1948-49; BA, Duke U., 1952; MRE, Union Theol. Sem., 1957; MSW, Tulane U., 1966, PhD, 1972. Cert. social worker, La. Field dir. undergrad. admissions Duke U., Durham, NC, 1952—53; head tchr. primary dept. Riverside Ch., N.Y.C., 1957—60; instr. Sch. Social Work Tulane U., New Orleans, 1966—72, assoc. prof., 1972—2000, coord. Indsl. Social Work Program, 1982—88, mem. faculty senate, 1972—88, prof. emeritus, 2000—. Non-govtl. orgn. rep. UNICEF, World Fedn. Mental Health, 1957—; cons. to v.p. cmty. affairs WETA, Washington, 1979; cons. Office Spl. Symposia and Seminars, Smithsonian Instn., Washington, 1979-86; treas. N.Y. Jr. League, 1961-62, v.p., 1962-63; bd. dirs. Cmty. Vol. Svcs., New Orleans, 1965-68; mem. profl. adv. com. Project Pre-Kindergarten, Orleans Paris Sch. Bd., New Orleans, 1967-69; mem. adv. bd. DePaul Cmty. Mental Health Ctr., New Orleans, 1971-72; mem. citizens adv. com. Orleans Parish Juvenile Ct., New Orleans, 1970-73; mem. Coun. on Social Work Edn. Task Force on Prevention, 1981-87; mem. New Orleans Women's Coalition Task Force on Employers and Working Parents, 1985-90; mem. med. social svcs. subcom. Mayor's Adv. Com. on Domestic Violence, 1995-96; v.p. Torre Realty Bd., 1996—. Grantee NIMH, Summer Inst. grantee Nat. Endowment Humanities, 1982; Newcomb Coll. fellow, 1999-2002. Mem. AAUW (Tulane Corp. rep. 1990-2000), NASW (bd. dir. La. chpt. 1987-89), AAUP (treas. Tulane chpt. 1984-86, 88-91, exec. com. 1991-95, v.p. New Orleans chpt. 1996), Coun. Social Work Edn., Am. Orthopsychiat. Assn. (life), Tulane U. Women's Assn. (v.p. 1996-97, pres. 1997-98, bd. mem. 2006-), Phi Beta Kappa (Tulane chpt. exec. com. 1990-2002, pres. Tulane chpt. 1991, regional sec. 1994—2002). Personal E-mail: ereck@cox.net.

RECKER, PATRICIA BULLION, secondary school educator; b. San Antonio, Tex., May 29, 1953; d. Richard Wood and Vera Williams Bullion; m. Steven Isadore Recker, Aug. 20, 1983; children: Noah James, Samantha Jo. AS in biology, San Antonio Coll., 1971—73; BS in biology, Southwest Tex. State U., 1973—75; MS in biology, Incarnate Word Coll., 1977—79; PhD, Bowling Green State U., 1980—82. Cert. Nat. cert. in Biology Sci. Tchrs. Assn., 1990. Chemistry/biology tchr. Meml. H.S., San Antonio, 1975—77; instr. zoology Incarnate Word Coll., San Antonio, 1979—80; instr. anatomy Owens Tech. Inst., Toledo, 1983; biology tchr. Upward Bound, San Antonio, 2000—02, John Jay H.S., San Antonio, 1984—. Recipient Subaru Nat. Sci. Tchg. award, 2001. Mem.: Tex. Assn. of Biology Teachers, Nat. Sci. Tchr. Assn., Nat. Assn. Biology Teachers. Avocation: travel. Home: 112 Miller Cove La Vernia TX 78121 Office: John Jay H S 7611 Marbach Rd San Antonio TX 78227 Personal E-mail: jay187@nisd.net.

RECKERS, PHILIP MERLE, accountant, educator; b. Quincy, Ill., May 1, 1946; s. Merle Joseph and Frances Adelaide (Friye) R.; m. Patricia Anne Polchinski, May 12, 1979; children: Brian, Colleen, Ashley. BS, Quincy Coll., 1968; MBA, Washington U., St. Louis, 1972; PhD, U. Ill., 1978. Asst. prof. U. Md., College Park, 1976—80; assoc. prof. Ariz. State U., Tempe, 1980—83, prof. acctg. and bus., 1983—; dir. Sch. Accountancy, 1993—2002; dir. rsch. Ctr. for Advancing Bus. through Info. Tech., 2002—05. Assoc. editor: Advances in Acctg., 1985—93, mem. editl. bd.: Auditing, 1987—2003, Behavioral Rsch. in Acctg., 1992—2002, Internat. Jour. Auditing, 1999—2006; editor: Advanes in Acctg., 1994—; contbr. articles to profl. jours. With U.S. Army, 1970—72, Vietnam. Auditing rsch. grantee, Peat Marwick Found., 1976, 1985, 1989, 1990, 1991, tax rsch. grantee, Ernst and Young Found., 1991. Mem. Am. Acctg. Assn. (v.p. 2006—, Innovations in Acctg. Edn. award 2003, Edn. Rsch. grant 1982), Fedn. Schs. Accountancy (pres. 2002, Joseph Silvoso Lifetime Achievement award 2006), AICPA (pre-cert. edn. exec. com.), Acctg. Programs Leadership Group (v.p. 2005—) Roman Catholic. Home: 7461 S Rita Ln 4-779 Tempe AZ 85283 Office: Ariz State U Sch Accountancy Ba 301D Tempe AZ 85287 Office Phone: 480-965-2283. Business E-Mail: philip.reckers@asu.edu.

RECKFORD, JONATHAN THOMAS MORE, nonprofit organization administrator; b. Chapel Hill, NC; s. Kenneth and Mary (Stevens) Reckford; m. Ashley Louise Richards, June 9, 1990; 3 children. BA in polit. sci., U. NC, Chapel Hill, 1984; MBA, Stanford U., 1989. Fin. analyst Goldman, Sachs & Co., 1984—86; mgr. svc. group strategy and bus. devel. Host Marriott Corp.; mgr. bus. planning The Walt Disney Co., 1991—92, mktg. mgr. Disney Vacation Club, 1993, dir. fin. and bus. planning Disney's Am., 1994, dir. bus. planning and devel. Disney Design and Devel., 1994—95; v.p. Circuit City Stores, Inc., 1995—97, sr. v.p. corp. planning and comm., 1997—99; pres. mall stores divsn. The Musicland Group, Inc., 1999—2000, pres. stores, 2000—02; exec. pastor Christ Presbyn. Ch. of Edina, Minn., 2003—05; CEO Habitat for Humanity Internat., Inc., Americus, Ga., 2005—. Henry Luce Found. Scholarship for Young Am. Leaders. Office: Habitat for Humanity Internat Inc 121 Habitat St Americus GA 31709-3498 Office Phone: 229-924-6935.

RECKHOW, KENNETH HOWLAND, conservationist, educator; b. San Francisco, Feb. 7, 1948; s. Alan Harding and Barbara (Howland) R.; m. Ellen Jo Waldman, June 21, 1975; children: Sarah, Michael. SB, Cornell U., 1971; SM, Harvard U., 1972, PhD, 1977. Asst. prof. Mich. State U., East Lansing, 1977-80; prof. Duke U., Durham, N.C., 1980—. Dir. Water Resources Rsch. Inst., NCSU, Raleigh, 1996—. Author: Engineering Approaches for Lake Management, 1983; contbr. articles to profl. jours. Mem. N.Am. Lake Mgmt. Soc. (pres., 1995), N.C. Water Resources Assn. (pres. 1994). Avocation: distance running. Home: 11 Pine Top Pl Durham NC 27705-1990 E-mail: Reckhow@Duke.edu.

RECKLINE, SIGMUND JOSEPH, publishing executive, editor; b. Balt., Oct. 29, 1956; s. Sigmund Joseph Reckline and Regina Ann DeBarry; m. Marilyn Louise Windes, May 2000; children: Clarissa Irene, Sigmund Joseph III, William Joseph, Quinten Christopher. BA in Liberal Arts, W.Va. U., 2002; BS in Applied Sci., Siena Heights U. 2002; MBA, U. Notre Dame, 2002; PhD in Bus. Adminstrn., Madison U., 2003; postgrad, Capella U., 2006, U. Md. Ordained Ch. of Spiritual Humanism. I&C technician Va. Electric Power Co., 1981—82; tech. writer, technician Nuc. Support Svcs., 1982, 1986—88; field engr. Johnson Controls, 1983—84; tech. writer Butler Svc. Group, 1984—85; field engr. Westinghouse Instrument Svc. Co., 1985—86; ops. mgr. Chesapeake Internat., 1988—91; sys. engr. Peak Tech. Svcs., 1991—92; tech. editor GTS/Duratek, Rockhill, SC, 1992—97; engring. mgr. Duke Engring and Svcs., Bridgman, 1997—99, Estes Group, Bridgman, Mich., 1999—2000; aux. operator CMS Energy, Covert, Mich., 2000—02; online instr., instr. Siena Heights U., Adrian, Mich., 2002—05; with Global Transitions Pub., Baroda, Mich., 2005—. Founder Environ. Cancer Res. Inst., Baroda, Mich. Co-author: America Rewired. Mem. Berrien County Cancer Ctr., Bridgman 2002; amb. Am. Cancer Soc., Kalamazoo, 2005; pres. South Potomac Forest Property Owners Assn., Springfield, W.Va., 1986—88; comdr. Antioch Commandery Knights Templar, 2000; hereditary chief Clan Recklein, 1990—. Sgt. USAF, 1981—87. Mem.: Am. Coll. Heraldry, Royal Order Scotland (life), St. Andrews Soc. Balt. (life), Phi Theta Kappa (disting. prof. 2004), Alpha Sigma Lambda. Republican. Presbyterian. Avocations: writing, genealogy, collecting swords, jewelry design. Office: Global Transitions Pub PO Box 41 Baroda MI 49101 Office Phone: 269-369-9897. E-mail: reckline@hotmail.com.

**RECKOWSKY, MICHAEL J.,** academic administrator; s. Allen D. Reckowsky and Shirley J. Jones; m. Constance L. Albrecht, May 4, 1996; children: Ryan M., Robert A. BA in Polit. Sci., Purdue U., West Lafayette, Ind., 1995. Mem. roll of attys. Clk. of Courts, State of Ind., Indpls., 1996—97; devel. assoc. advancement office Purdue U., West Lafayette, 1997—2000, adminstrv. dir. food sci., 2000—. Mem. task force Ind. Dept. of Health, Food Protection Task Force, 2003—. Author: (publ.) Preparing for Bioterrorism Through Simulation; co-creator (copyright for computer data) Food Defense Simulation. Chmn. 7th Dist. Young Reps., Ind., 1997—98, Tippecanoe County Young Reps., Lafayette, 1995—97; campaign mgr. Pool for Congress, Lafayette, 1995—96; mem. Imagination Sta., Lafayette, Ind., 2006—. Recipient Jack McCord award, Tippecanoe Young Reps., 1997, Ill. Ea. Star scholarship, Ea. Star, 1990. Mem.: Inst. of Food Technologists, Antique and Classic Boat Soc. (sec. 2004—06). Evangelical Covenant. Avocations: sailing, boating, woodworking. Office: Purdue U Dept Food Sci 745 Agriculture Mall Dr West Lafayette IN 47907 Office Phone: 765-494-6303. Office Fax: 765-494-7953. E-mail: mreckowsky@purdue.edu.

**RECORD, PHILLIP JULIUS,** journalist; b. Fort Worth, Jan. 12, 1929; s. Phillip Cross and Frances Virginia (McElwee) R.; m. Patricia Ann Edwards, Sept. 29, 1954; children: Christopher Phillip, Gregory Edwards, Timothy James. BA in Journalism, U. Notre Dame, 1950. Gen. reporter Lubbock Avalanche-Jour., Tex., 1950-54; copy editor, reporter Fort Worth Star-Telegram, 1954-67, asst. city editor, 1967-68, city editor evening edit., 1968-76, mng. editor, 1976-80, assoc. exec. editor, 1980-91, spl. asst. to pub., ombudsman, 1991-97, columnist, 1997—2001. Mem. mass comms. com. Tex. Tech. U., 1971—2000, chmn., 1990—92, bd. dirs., 1992—; journalism profl. in residence Tex. Christian U., 1999—. Mem. Friends of Ft. Worth Pub. Libr.; bd. visitors Tex. Christian U.; conciliation/arbitration bd. Cath. Diocese of Ft. Worth, 1994—; chair, 1996—; publs. adv. com., 1982—; bd. dirs. Tarrant County Mental Health Assn., 1990—95; dir. Freedom Info. Found., Tex., 1987—93; bd. dirs. Depression Connection Team, 1999—, Cassata H.S., 2006—; founding mem. Ft. Worth Theatre. With U.S. Army, 1950—52. Recipient Ethics award Tex. Christian U., 1991, others for reporting, photography and headline writing; named to Tex. Tech U. Mass Comms. Hall of Fame. Mem. ABA (nat. commn. on pub. understanding about law 1984-90, commn. on partnership programs 1990-93), Investigative Reporters and Editors Inc., Soc. Profl. Journalists (pres. 1983-84, bd. dirs. Found. 1980-2001, v.p. Found., 1991-94, bd. chair 1994-01, Wells Key 1991), Creative Thinking Assn., Orgn. News Ombudsmen (dir. 1994-98, v.p. 1995-96, pres. 1996-97). Avocation: tennis. Office: 6144 Walla Ave Fort Worth TX 76133 *As a journalist, I strive to be a servant of the truth and a servant of the people. As a follower of Jesus, I try to live my life as he would. But, being human, I fail frequently. But I try and I care. I think that makes me OK in God's eyes.*

**RECORD, WILLIAM JOHN,** librarian; b. N.Y.C., June 21, 1931; s. William and Betty (Collins) R.; m. Betty Lowrey, Oct. 7, 1950; children: Linda, William John, Jr., Michael, John. BA, George Peabody Coll. for Tchrs., 1961; MLS, Pratt Inst., 1965. Cert. pub. librarian, N.Y. State. Cataloger N.Y. Pub. Library, N.Y.C., 1963-66; cataloger Coll. Dentistry, NYU, 1966-67; achivist Sch. Medicine, NYU, 1967-68; librarian Milton Helpern Libr. Legal Medicine, N.Y.C., 1969-70, Fordham Hosp., Bronx, N.Y., 1973-76, Misericordia Hosp., Bronx, 1976-81, asst. Vol. Surg. Contraception, N.Y.C., 1981-97, ret., 1997. Periodicals librarian Met. Hosp., N.Y.C., 1971-72. Editor Odyssey, pres. parents group phase III, Odyssey House, N.Y.C., 1970. With U.S. Army, 1947-58, Korea. Mem. Assn. for Population/Family Planning Libraries Internat. (pres. 1987-88), Med. Library Assn. Home: 437 E 80th St Apt 26 New York NY 10021-0611

**RECTOR, DONNA LYNN,** writer, photographer, vocalist; b. Warrenton, Va., July 8, 1959; d. Allen Leon and Elizabeth Ann (Godfrey) R. Freelance photographer, journalist, calligrapher, writer, Culpeper, Va., 1985—; corr. Culpeper (Va.) Star Exponent, Culpeper News, Culpeper, Va., 1987-95. Pub. info. coord. Va. Dept. Transp., Culpeper, 1988-89; advisor CommonHealth, 1989; cons. in field. Editor: Va. Dept. Transp. Newsletter, 1989; columnist, photographer: Va.'s Music Line, The Corridor; blues vocalist, 1996—; pub.: Stylus newsletter; columnist: Corridor Mag., Rock and Read Mag., SHAKE! Mag. Vol. Svcs. to Abused Families, Culpeper, 1987-92; vol. art instr. Culpeper County Sch. Vis. Artisan Program; vol. Culpeper Renaissance Downtown Assn.; canvasser United Way, 1987-88; coord. fundraisers & major charity events, pub. rels. coord. for charity and community orgns.; spl. events/fund raiser coord. Nat. Multiple Sclerosis Soc., Blue Ridge chpt., 1990-91; coord., publicist Culpeper Music Festival, 2004-05. Recipient First Place awd. for Poetry, Germanna Community Coll., 1988, 92, 98, Bus. and Profl. Women's Assn. Young Career Woman of Yr. award, Spl. Svc. award Va. Dept. Transp., 1989, Cert. Appreciation Blue Ridge chpt. Nat. Multiple Sclerosis Soc., 1991, Piedmont United Way Gold award, 1993, Cert. Appreciation, Vocat. Indsl. Clubs Am., 1993, Cert. Appreciation Culpeper Downtown Renaissance Inc., 1990, Cert. Recognition for exceptional contribution to Va. employee suggestion program Gov. George Allen, Va., 1994, Top Hat award Windmore Found. for Arts, 1999, Mem. Phi Theta Kappa, Alpha Beta Gamma. Avocations: writing, singing, photography, public relations, music. Home: PO Box 822 Culpeper VA 22701-0822 Personal E-mail: donnalynnrector@yahoo.com, drectorrecords@yahoo.com.

**RECTOR, JOHN MICHAEL,** pharmaceutical association executive, lawyer; b. Seattle, Aug. 15, 1943; s. Michael Robert and Bernice Jane (Allison) R.; m. Carmen De Ortiz, 1994; children: Christian Phillip, Ciera Rose, Zachary Ryan M. U. Calif., Berkeley, 1966; JD, U. Calif., Hastings, 1969; PharmD (hon.), Ark. State Bd. Pharmacy, 1991. Bar: Calif. 1970, U.S. Supreme Ct. 1974. Trial atty. civil rights divsn. Dept. Justice, 1969-71; dep. chief counsel judiciary com. U.S. Senate, 1971-73; counsel to Sen. Birch Bayh, 1971-77, chief counsel, staff dir., 1973-77; confirmed by U.S. Senate as assoc. adminstr. to Law Enforcement Assistance Adminstrn. and adminstr. of Office Juvenile Justice Dept. Justice, 1977-79; spl. counsel to U.S. Atty. Gen., 1979-80; dir. govt. affairs Nat. Assn. Retail Druggists, Washington, 1980-85; sr. v.p. govt. affairs, gen. counsel Nat. Cmty. Pharmacists Assn., 1986—2005, sr. v.p., gen. counsel, 2006—. Chmn. adv. bd. Nat. Juvenile Law Ctr., 1973-77; mem. Hew panel Drug Use and Criminal Behavior, 1974-77; cons. panel Nat. Commn. Protection Human Subjects of Biomed. and Behavioral Rsch., 1975-76; chmn. U.S. Interdepartmental Coun. Juvenile Justice, 1977-79; mem. bd. com. civil rights and liberties Am. Dem. Action, 1976-80, Pres.'s Com. Mental Health-Justice Group, 1978; com. youth citizenship ABA, 1978-84; mem. Pharm. Industry Adv. Com.; treas. polit. action com. Nat. Pharmacists Assn., 1981; exec. dir. Retail Druggist Legal Legis. Def. Fund, 1985-2005, founder, chmn. Washington Pharmacy Industry Forum; owner Second Genesis Mem. editl. bd. Managed Care Law; contbr. articles to profl. jours. Mem. exec. com. small bus. and fin. couns. Dem. Nat. Com., 1988-92; dir. Dem. Leadership Coun.'s Network, 1989-92, bd. advisers, 1992-94, Clinton-Gore Washington Bus. adv. com.; bd. dirs. Small Bus. Legis. Coun., 1987—, sec., 1999, treas., 2000, chmn. elect, 2001, chmn. 2002; bd. dirs. Nat. Bus. Coalition for Fair Competition, 1984—; policy advisor Presdl. campaigns; active Reagan for Pres. Task Force on Criminal Justice, Germanna Found. Perry E. Towne scholar, 1966-67; recipient Children's Express Juvenile Justice award, 1981, John W. Dargavel medal, 2003, J. Leon Lascoff Meml. award, 2004. Mem. ABA, ATLA, Calif. Bar Assn., Nat. Health Lawyers Assn., Am. Soc. Assn. Execs. (govt. affairs sect.), Washington Coun. Lawyers, Assn. Former Sr. Senate Aides, Vinifera Wine Growers Assn. Va. (life), Health R Us, Am. League of Lobbyists, Theta Chi Libertarian. Avocations: antiques, books and documents. Office: Nat Cmty Pharmacists Assn 100 Daingerfield Rd Alexandria VA 22314-2885 Business E-Mail: john.rector@ncpanet.org.

**RECTOR, M. EUGENE,** community pharmacist; b. Sequin, Tex., Aug. 16, 1950; m. Marcia A. Rector, May 15, 1982. AA, Blinn Coll., 1970; BS in Pharmacy, U. Tex., Austin, 1972; BA in Philosophy, U. Tex., Dallas, 1982, MS in Mgmt. and Adminstrn. Scis., 1985; PharmD, Broadmore U., Belize City, Belize, 1998. Staff pharmacist Baylor U. Med. Ctr., Dallas, 1973-81, Presbyn. Hosp., Dallas, 1981-86; dir. pharmacy Madison St. Joseph Health Ctr., Madisonville, Tex., 1986—2001; pharmacist Walgreens #4999; 2001—.

Fellow Am. Coll. Apothecaries (assoc.); mem. Am. Soc. Health-Sys. Pharmacists, Tex. Soc. Health-Sys. Pharmacists, Lions Club, Masons (Vickery Lodge 1351, Rogers Prairie Lodge 540 past master), Shriners. Republican. Methodist. Avocations: hunting, ranching. Home: 16584 Fm 3 S Normangee TX 77871-3511 Office Phone: 936-291-6764. Personal E-mail: gener@txcyber.com.

**RECTOR, PHILLIP ALAN,** minister, musician; b. Greenville, S.C., Oct. 12, 1960; s. John Marion and Doris May Rector; m. Melonie Ruth Rust, Dec. 13, 1986; children: Kelsey Elaine, Madeline Leigh. M in Ch. Music, So. Bapt. Theol. Sem., 1993; MusB in Edn., Mars Hill Coll., 1986; cert. Orff Schulwerk, U. Ky., 2001. Band dir. Statesville (N.C.) City Sch., 1986—90; min. music Ballardsville Bapt. Ch., Crestwood, Ky., 1990—93, Wytheville (Va.) Bapt. Ch., 1994—98, Lexington Ave. Bapt. Ch., Danville, Ky., 1998—2003, First Bapt. Ch., Lexington, NC, 2003—. Dir. Chautauqua Festival Choir, Wytheville, 1995—96; choral condr. summer music camp Henry County Bapt. Assn., Martinsville, Va., 1996; orch. condr. summer music camp Va. Bapt. Gen. Assn., Lynchburg, 2002. Actor: (community theater) Oliver Twist, 2001; dir.: (choir) The Journey Home, 2004; musician: Messiah-Handel. Mem. Wilderness Trace YMCA, Harrodsburg, Ky., 2002—03, Crossroads Shelter, Inc., Wytheville, Va., 1997—98. Named Tchr. of Yr., Statesville Mid. Sch., 1988—89; Dr. and Mrs. Joy Gentile Music scholar, Mars Hill Coll., 1984—85, Joe DeNardo Music scholar, 1985. D-Liberal. Protestant. Avocations: motorcycling, golf, racquetball, photography, fishing. Office: First Baptist Ch 201 W Third Ave Lexington NC 27292 Office Phone: 336-249-9158. Office Fax: 336-249-4762. E-mail: phil@fbclex.org.

**RECTOR, SUSAN DARNELL,** lawyer; b. Wilmington, Del., Feb. 14, 1959; d. W. Thomas and Barbara Joan (Shafer) Darnell; m. Neil Kenyon Rector, Aug. 7, 1982. BA in Econs., Wake Forest U., Winston-Salem, N.C., 1981; JD, U. N.C., Chapel Hill, 1984. Bar: Ohio 1984. Lawyer Ohio Legislative Svc. Commn., Columbus, Ohio, 1984-87; assoc. Schottenstein, Zox & Dunn, Columbus, Ohio, 1987-93, ptnr., 1993—. Bd. trustees Firstlink, Inc., 1990-95, v.p., 1993, pres., 1994; apt. to Ohio Small Bus. and Entrepreneurship Coun., 1991-95; bd. dirs. The Wilds. Contbr. articles to profl. jours. Mem. allocation com. United Way, Columbus, 1990-96, campaign cabinet, 1991, co-chair planning, evaluation and allocation com., 1993-94, bd. trustees, 1996-05, chair health vision coun., 1996-99; trustee Columbus Zool. Park Assn., 2001—, v.p., 2003-04, pres. 2005-06; chmn. devel. com., 2001-03, chmn. zoo fund, 2000; bd. dir., sec., treas. Cmty. Rsch. Ptnrs., 2000-03. Named Harry S. Truman scholar, Truman Scholarship Fund., 1979, named one of 10 Outstanding Young Citizens, Columbus Jaycees, 1993, 40 under 40, Bus. (Columbus); grad. Columbus Area Leadership program; Best Lawyers in Am., 2003, 04, 05. Fellow Am. Bar Found.; mem. Ohio Bar Assn., Columbus Bar Assn. (Cmty. Svc. award 1997), Columbus Bar Found. (trustee 1995—2004, pres. 2003), Women Lawyers of Franklin County, Jr. League of Columbus (bd. trustees, sec. 1989-90, 95-98, pres. 1997-98), Columbus Club, Columbus Met. Club, Columbus Women's Network (Cmty. Leader award), Mortar Bd., Phi Beta Kappa, Omicron Delta Kappa. Home: 67 E Deshler Ave Columbus OH 43206-2655 Office: Schottenstein Zox & Dunn 250 West Street Columbus OH 43215 Office Phone: 614-462-2219. Business E-Mail: srector@szd.com.

**RECUPERO, PATRICIA RYAN,** hospital president, psychiatrist, lawyer, health facility executive; m. Joseph Recupero. AB, SUNY, 1969; JD, Boston Coll., 1973; MD, Brown U., 1985. Bar: Mass. 1973, RI 1974, Fed. Bar: Dist. of Mass. 1975, Dist. of RI 1975; diplomate Am. Bd. Psychiatry and Neurology, 1990, cert. in Forensic Psychiatry RI, 1994. Assoc. dir. edn./tng. dept. psychiatry and human behavior Brown U., Providence, 1989—94, assoc. dir. edn./tng., 2005—, clin. prof. psychiatry, 1989—91, clin. asst. prof. psychiatry, 1991—2000; asst. prof. medicine Tufts U., 1995—98; vice chair, dept. psychiatry St. Elizabeth's Med. Ctr., Boston, 1995—97, clin. svcs., 1995—97, dir. residency tng. psychiatry, 1996—97; dir. managed care Butler Hosp., Providence, 1990—95, dir. alcohol/drug inpatient svcs., 1991—94, chief forensic psychiatry, 1994—95, med. dir. med. adminstrn., 1997—98, v.p. systems integration/managed care, assoc. med. dir., med. adminstrn., 1998—98, exec. v.p., 1998—98, pres., CEO, 1999—; exec. v.p. behavioral health Care New Eng., Providence, 1999—; clin. assoc. prof. psychiatry Brown U., 2000—05, clin. prof. psychiatry, 2005—. Mem. resource utilization com. Health Advantage, 1993—95; mem. contract for competency to stand trial evaluation program RI Dept. Mental Health Retardation and Hospitals, 1993—95; mem. utilization mgmt. com. Blue Chip RI, 1995—98; forensic evaluations Dept. Disabled Persons Protection Commn., 1995—; ind. med. evaluations Northwestern Ins. Co., 1995—; spl. master RI Supreme Ct., 1996; gender equity/sexual harrassment officer Brown U. Program in Medicine (Office of Women in Medicine), 1997—98; chairperson Butler Hosp. Profl. Lecture Series; mem., ho. delegates RI Bar Assn., 1976—77, mem., confidential assistance com., 1992—95; chair, bylaws revision com. RI Psychiat. Soc., 1989—90, deputy legis. rep., 1989—94, sec./treas., 1991—95, pres. elect., 1995—97, pres., 1997—99, dep. rep. to apa assembly dist. branches, 1999—2003, assembly rep., 2003—, 1997—2000; addiction psychiatry splty. com. Am. Acad. Psychiatry and the Law, 1997—2005, edn. com., 1999—2004, chair, gender issues com., 2000—03, geriatric psychiatry com., 2000, councillor, 1994—; coun. on psychiatry and law corr. mem. Am. Psychiat. Assn., 1994—, mem. com. on quality indicators, 2000—02, chair, workgroup on cyber medicine, 2000—, assembly liaison to coun. psychiatry and law, 2000—02, guttmacher award com. mem., 2003—, task force to rev. guidelines on seclusion/restraint mem., 2003—, coun. on psychiatry and law mem., 2003—; bd. mem. Nat. Assn. Psychiat. Health Systems, 2002—, planning com. mem., 2002—, third v.p., 2003—, membership com., 2003—, exec. com., 2003, pres. elect, 04, pres. 05. Author: (newsletter) e-Health: Enhanced Treatment or Legal Quagmire?; Women in Forensic Psychiatry; contbr. numerous presentations in field, articles to profl. jours., chapters to books. Parole bd. mem. Parole Bd. State of RI, RI, 1993—98; bd. mem. RI Coalition Against Domestic Violence, 1994—95, mem., 1993—98; merit selection panel US Dist. Ct., Dist. of RI, 1998; forensic psychiatry com. on re-cert. Am. Bd.Psychiatry/Neurology, 2000—03; governor's coun. on mental health RI State, 1998—2001; corp. mem. Blue Cross/Blue Shield of RI, 1999—2003; bd. mem. Nurse Assn./Care New Eng., 1999—2003. Recipient Ann. Exemplary Psychiatrist Award, Nat. Alliance for the Mentally Ill, 2000, Teaching Recognition award, Brown U. Sch. Med., 2001. Fellow: Am. Psychiat. Assn. (disting.); mem.: Internat. Acad. Law and Mental Health, RI Med. Women's Assn., RI Med. Soc., Assn. Women Psychiatrists, Mental Health Assn. of RI, Alliance for the Mentally Ill. Office: Butler Hosp 345 Blackstone Blvd Providence RI 02906

**RECUPERO-FAIELLA, ANNA ANTONIETTA,** poet; b. Boston, Nov. 22, 1966; d. Vittorio and Anna Maria Recupero; m. Mark Stephan James Faiella, May 30, 1998; 1 child, Dante Vincenzo Faiella. Cert. early edn., Wheelock Coll. Tchr. N. Bennet St. Sch., Boston, 1981-87; clk. Post Office, Boston, 1988—. Art coord. N. Bennett Sch., Boston, 1985-87; acting extra films and commls. Author: A View From the Edge, 1992, Dusting Off Dreams, 1994, Echoes From the Silence, 1995, Treasure the Moment, 1996, Whispers, 1996, Sensations, 1997; co-author: Distinguished Poets of Amercia, 1993, Outstanding Poets of 1994, 1994, Treasured Poems of America, 1995, Treasured Poems of America, 1996, Best Poems of the 90's, 1996, Best Poems of '97, 1997, Ten Years of Excellence, 1998. Co-author Wall of Tolerance, 2003. Recipient Internat. Writer Yr. award, Internat. Biographical Ctr., 2003, Outstanding Writer award, Internat. Soc. Poetry, 2004, Outstanding Achievement in amateur photography award, Internat. Soc. Photographers, 2004; Mass. State Gen. scholar, 1985. Mem. Internat. Soc. Poets (disting. mem. adv. com. 1994), Nat. Mus. Women Arts, Point of Pines Assn. Democrat. Roman Catholic. Avocations: painting, writing poems, travel, nascar racing, comedy. Home: 40 Bickford Ave Revere MA 02151-1723

**REDA, JAMES FRANCIS,** business consultant; b. Bklyn., Aug. 27, 1953; s. Ralph Charles and Evelyn Susan (Buchan) R.; m. Susan Rosemary Hisnay, June 10, 1982 (div. dec. 1993); 1 child, Jennifer Beryl; m. Deborah Linda Grannis, July 4, 1994; children: Jennifer Rose, James Francis Jr., Linda

Victoria. BS in Indsl. Engring., Columbia U., 1981; MS in Mgmt., MIT, 1983. 1st class lic., FCC; lic. internat. fin. analyst. Indsl. engr. IBM Corp., Bklyn., 1980, East Fishkill, NY, 1981; process engr. Hewlett-Packard Co., Andover, Mass., 1982; bus. mgr. Wang Labs., Inc., Lowell, Mass., 1983-85; sr. product mgr. Honeywell Fed. Systems, Inc., McLean, Va., 1985-87; assoc. cons. Touche Ross & Co., N.Y.C., 1987; v.p., cons. The Bachelder Group, N.Y.C., 1987-96; cons. Buck Cons., N.Y.C., 1996-97, Hewitt Assocs., Atlanta, 1997-99; sr. mgr. Arthur Andersen LLP, Atlanta, 1999-2000; prin., regional practice leader Buck Cons., Inc., Atlanta, 2000—03; mng. dir. James F. Reda & Assocs., LLC, N.Y.C., 2003—. Campaign advisor Friends of Vincent Gentile, Bklyn., 1994. With USN, 1971-77; lt. comdr. USCGR. Mem. Internat. Inst. Indsl. Engrs. (sr. mem., chpt. pres. 1979-81, Walter Rautenstrauch award 1981), Res. Officers Assn. (Top Grad. award 1983), N.Y. Soc. Security Analysts (mem. com. corp. governance), CFA Inst., Soc. Corporate Governance Profls., World at Work, U.S. Naval Inst., Armed Forces Comms. Assn., Ret. Officers Assn., Nat. Assn. Stock Plan Profls., Nat. Assn. Corp. Dirs., Naval War Coll. Found., Am. Legion, Tau Beta Pi, Alpha Pi Mu. Republican. Methodist. Avocations: spectator sports, exercise, travel, history, current events. Office: 1500 Broadway 9th Fl New York NY 10036-4055 Home: 5 Howard Dr Princeton Junction NJ 08550-2150 Office Phone: 646-367-4466. Personal E-mail: jfreda@jfreda.com.

**REDBORD, KELLEY PAGLIAI,** dermatologist; d. Larry Pagliai and Carlene Braun; m. Ari Redbord. MD, Johns Hopkins U., Balt., 2002. Dermatology resident U. of Cin., 2002—. Fellow Procedural Dermatology, ACGME.

**REDBURN, TOM,** newspaper editor; BA in sociology, Pomona Coll., 1972. With OSHA, U.S. Dept. Labor, 1972—73; editor & reporter The Washington Monthly, 1974—75, Environ. Action, 1975—76; reporter & chief econ. correspondent LA Times, 1977—90; internat. econ. correspondent Internat. Herald Tribune, 1991—93; reporter NY Times, 1993—94, editor, Bus. Day sect., 1994—97, asst. bus. editor, 1997—2003, tech. editor, 2003—04, dep. bus. editor, 2004—. Named to Athletic Hall of Fame, Pomona Coll., 1992. Office: New York Times 229 W 43d St New York NY 10036 Office Phone: 212-556-1548. Business E-Mail: redburn@nytimes.com.

**REDD, KENNETH ERIC,** statistician, researcher; b. Boston, June 17, 1965; s. Phyllis and Charles William Redd. BA, Tufts U., Medford, Mass., 1983—87; MA, U. Minn., Mpls., 1987—89. Analyst in social legislation Congl. Rsch. Svc., Washington, 1989—91; rsch. assoc. Pa. Higher Edn. Assistance Agy., Harrisburg, 1991—94; rsch. and policy analyst Nat. Assn. of Ind. Colls. and Univs., Washington, 1994—96; rsch. assoc. Am. Assn. State Colls. and Univs., Washington, 1997—98; sr. rsch. assoc. Sallie Mae, Inc., Washington, 1998—99; dir. of higher edn. rsch. USA Group Found., Indpls., 1999—2000; dir. of rsch. and policy analysis Nat. Assn. of Student Fin. Aid Administrs., Washington, 2000—. Bd. dirs. Sallie Mae Fund, Reston, Va., 2003—. Contbr. articles to profl. jours., chapters to books. Recipient Governor's Award for Outstanding Cmty. Svc., Office of Gov. Michael S. Dukakis, 1985, Commendation for Outstanding Svc., Social Security Adminstrn., 1985; fellow, Assn. for Pub. Policy Analysis and Mgmt., 1986, Nat. Ctr. for Pub. Policy and Higher Edn., 2001—02. Mem.: Toastmasters. Home: 7290 Mandan Rd Greenbelt MD 20770 Office: Nat Assn Student Fin Aid Adminstrs 1129 20th St NW Ste 400 Washington DC 20036 Office Phone: 202-785-0453. Office Fax: 202-785-1487. E-mail: reddk@nasfaa.org, kredd31@comcast.net.

**REDD, MICHAEL,** professional basketball player; b. Aug. 24, 1979; Attended, Ohio State Univ. Basketball player Milw. Bucks, 2001—. Named to All-American Team Hon. Mention, 2000—01, NBA All-Star Team, 2004. Office: Milwaukee Bucks 1001 N Fourth St Milwaukee WI 53203*

**REDD, SCOTT (JOHN SCOTT REDD),** federal official, retired military officer; b. Sidney, Iowa, Sept. 10, 1944; m. Donna Ford; children: Anne, Scott Jr., Adam. BSc in Math. and Physics, U.S. Naval Acad., 1966; postgrad. studies, Uruguay; MS in Ops. Analysis, Naval Post Grad. Sch.; postgrad. studies for Sr. Execs., MIT; grad., Armed Forces Staff Coll. Commd. ensign USN, 1966, advanced through grades to rear admiral, 1994, ret., 1998; mem. staff Sec. Defense, Washington; naval officer 5 operational commands USN destroyers and frigates; acting dep. chief naval ops. for plans, policy and ops. USN, Washington; comdr. US Naval Forces, US Ctrl. Command US Dept. Def., 1991—96; commdr. Fifth Fleet USN, 1995; dir. strategic plans and policy The Joint Staff, Washington, 1996—98; chmn., pres., CEO NetSchools Corp., Atlanta, 1999—2002; COO, dep. adminstr. Civilian Provisional Authority, Baghdad, Iraq, 2003—04; dir. Nat. Counterterrorism Ctr. Office Nat. Intelligence, Washington, 2005—. Pres. Naval Acad. Class, 1966; exec. dir. Commn. on the Intelligence Capabilities of the US Regarding Weapons of Mass Destruction, 2004-05 Decorated Order Bahrain 1st degree, Legion of Merit (2 awards), Disting. Svc. medal (2 awards), Meritorious Svc. medal (2 awards), Navy Commendation medal (2 awards). Mem. U.S. Naval Acad. Alumni Assn. (past bd. dirs.) Avocation: amateur radio.

**REDD, TERESA M.,** English language educator; b. Balt., Sept. 21, 1954; d. Mary and Rudolph Redd; 1 child, Tarik Donaldson. BA, Princeton U., 1976; MA, Howard U., 1982; PhD, U. Md., 1987. Writer-editor Time-Life Books, Alexandria, Va., 1976—79; from instr. to assoc. prof. dept. English Howard U., Washington, 1983—2003, dir. ctr. for excellence in tchg., learning, and assessment, 2003—. Bd. of cons. Nat. Network of Writing Across the Curriculum Programs, 1998—; editl. bd. Coll. Composition and Comm. jour., 1999—2001, Written Comm. jour., 1994—2003. Author: (book) A Teacher's Introduction to African American English: What a Writing Teacher Should Know, editor: Revelations: An Anthology of Expository Essays by and about Blacks. Recipient Tchg. Excellence award, Academic Affairs, Howard U., 1994, Phi Beta Kappa, Princeton U., 1976, Phi Delta Kappa, U. of Md., Coll. Pk., 1987, Sigma Tau Delta, 1988; fellow PEW Humanities Fellowship, PEW Charitable Trusts, 1985, 1986. Mem.: Am. Ednl. Rsch. Assn., Nat. Coun. of Tchrs. of English (ccc exec. com. 1995—98), Phi Delta Kappa, Phi Beta Kappa (pres., v.p., treas. 1996—2005). Office: CETLA Howard University 2301 Georgia Ave NW Ste 244 Washington DC 20059

**REDDEL, CARL WALTER,** academic administrator; b. Gurley, Neb., May 31, 1937; s. Walter Julius and Friedora Regina (Sorge) R.; m. Colette Marie Antoinette Mansuy, Oct. 26, 1963; children: Eric, Damien. BSED, Drake U., 1959; MA in Russian Studies, Syracuse U., 1962; PhD in Russian History, Ind. U., 1973, cert. Russian Studies, 1973. Lectr. U. Md., Toul-Rosieres, France, 1963-66; instr. U.S.A.F. Acad., Colorado Springs, Colo., 1967-68, 71-72, from asst. prof. to assoc. prof., 1972—80; from assoc. prof. to prof., head dept. history, fellow U. Edinburgh, 1980—82; pres., CEO, Eisenhower World Affairs Inst., 1999—2000; pub. svc. fellow Gettysburg (Pa.) Coll., 2000-01; cons. coord. Dwight D. Eisenhower Meml. Commn., Washington, 2001—02, exec. dir. 2002—. Nat. coord., regional World History Assn. Phila., 1990-95; bd. editors, mem. Joun. Slavic Mil., London, 1988—; series editor Military Hist. Symposium Series, Colorado Springs, 1993-2001. Editor: Transformation in Russian and Soviet Military History, 1990; contbr. articles to profl. jours. Mem. Rotary Internat., 1994—. Served to brig. gen. U.S. Air Force, 1962-99. Recipient Young Faculty exch. Internat. Rsch. Exchs. Bd., Moscow State U., 1975; Woodrow Wilson fellow, 1959-60, Danforth Found. fellow, 1959-61. Mem.: World History Assn., Am. Assn. Advancement of Slavic Studies, Am. Hist. Assn., Phi Alpha Theta. Lutheran. Home: 420 7th St NW Apt 800 Washington DC 20004-2214 Office: 1629 K St NW Ste 801 Washington DC 20006-3837 Office Phone: 202-296-0005. Business E-Mail: creddel@eisenhowermemorial.org.

**REDDEN, JAMES ANTHONY,** federal judge; b. Springfield, Mass., Mar. 13, 1929; s. James A. and Alma (Cheek) R.; m. Joan Ida Johnson, July 13, 1950; children: James A., William F. Student, Boston U., 1951; LL.B., Boston Coll., 1954. Bar: Mass. 1954, Oreg., 1955. Pvt. practice, Mass., 1954-55; title examiner Title & Trust Ins. Co., Oreg., 1955; claims adjuster Allstate Ins. Co., 1956; mem. firm Collins, Redden, Ferris & Velure, Medford, Oreg., 1957-73;

treas. Oreg., 1973-77; atty. gen., 1977-80; U.S. dist. judge, now sr. judge U.S. Dist. Ct. Oreg., Portland, 1980—. Chmn. Oreg. Pub. Employee Relations Bd.; mem. Oreg. Ho. of Reps., 1963-69, minority leader, 1967-69. With AUS, 1946-48. Mem. ABA, Mass. Bar Assn., Oreg. State Bar. Office: US Dist Ct 1527 US Courthouse 1000 SW 3d Ave Portland OR 97204-2902 Office Phone: 503-326-8370.

**REDDEN, LAWRENCE DREW,** lawyer; b. Tallassee, Ala., Dec. 16, 1922; s. A. Drew and Berta (Baker) R.; m. Christine U. Cunningham, Dec. 20, 1943. AB, U. Ala., 1943, LL.B., 1949. Bar: Ala. bar 1949. Since practiced in, Birmingham; asst. U.S. atty. No. Dist. Ala., 1949-52; partner firm Rogers, Howard, Redden & Mills, 1952-79, Redden, Mills & Clark, 1979—; Civilian aide for Ala. to sec. army, 1965-69. Mem. Ala. Democratic Exec. Com., 1966-74 Editor-in-chief: Ala. Law Rev, 1948. Trustee Ala. Law Sch. Found.; adv. council Cumberland Law Sch. Served with AUS, 1943-46; maj. gen. ret. Decorated D.S.M.; recipient Outstanding Civilian Service medal Dept. Army, 1970 Fellow Am. Coll. Trial Lawyers, Internat. Soc. Barristers; mem. ABA, Am. Judicature Soc., Ala. Bar Assn. (pres. 1972-73), Birmingham Bar Assn. (past pres.), Ala. Law Inst. (mem. coun.), U. Ala. Law Sch. Alumni Assn. (past pres.), Phi Beta Kappa, Alpha Tau Omega, Omicron Delta Kappa. Baptist. Home: 2513 Beaumont Cir Birmingham AL 35216-1301 Office Phone: 205-322-0457. Business E-Mail: ldr@rmclaw.com.

**REDDEN, PERSEFINI KORE ANNE,** protective services official; b. Santa Monica, Calif., Nov. 17, 1968; d. Donlee M. and MaryAnn E. Salisbury; m. Michael F. Redden, May 14, 1970; 1 stepchild, Myranda K. BS in Biology, Ariz. State U., 2006. Firefighter, paramedic Rural, Metro Fire Dept., Yuma, Ariz., 1989—99, compliance officer Scottsdale, 2000—04, asst. fire chief, 2004—. Bd. mem. YMCA Scottsdale, Paradise Valley Br., 2005—06. Named Firefighter Yr., 1990—91. Mem.: Ariz. Fire Chiefs Assn., Internat. Assn. Fire Chiefs. Conservative. Roman Catholic. Office: Rural/Metro Fire Dept 4141 N Granite Reef Rd Scottsdale AZ 85251 Office Phone: 482-627-6024. Business E-Mail: kore_redden@rmetro.com.

**REDDEN, ROGER DUFFEY,** lawyer; b. Washington, Dec. 19, 1932; s. Layman J. and Elizabeth (Duffey) R.; m. Gretchen Sause, July 14, 1962 AB, Yale Coll., 1954; LLB, U. Md., 1957. Bar: Md. 1958, U.S. Dist. Ct. Md. 1958, U.S. Ct. Appeals (4th cir.) 1958, U.S. Supreme Ct. 1965. Law clk. to judge U.S. Ct. Appeals (4th cir.), 1957-58; assoc. Smith, Somerville & Case, Balt., 1959-63, ptnr., 1965-68; asst. atty. gen. State of Md., 1964-65; ptnr. DLA Piper Rudnick Gray Cary, Balt., 1969—97, ptnr. emeritus, 1998—. Bd. dirs. Peoples Water Svc. Co.; draftsman Md. State Dept. Legis. Reference, 1958; counsel Md. Savs. and Loan Study Commn., 1960-61; mem. Gov.'s Commn. to revise testamentary laws of Md., 1965-70; mem. standing com. on rules of practice and procedure Md. Ct. Appeals, 1969-73, 88-91, Md. code revision com., 1970—, Appellate Jud. Nominating Commn., 1975-79, Commn. to study Md. Tax Ct., 1978-79, Gov.'s Task Force on Energy, 1991-95; chmn. Task Force on Permits Simplification, 1979-81. Editor (in chief): (Univ. law rev.) Md. Law Rev., 1956—57; contbr. articles to legal jours. With U.S. Army, 1958-59, 61-62. Fellow Am. Bar Found., Md. Bar Found.; mem. Md. State Bar Assn. (chmn. probate and estate law sect. 1966-68, chmn. long range planning com. 1972-73, chmn. com. on laws 1988-89, council sect. adminstrv. law 1980-82, council sect. bus. law 1978-81), Balt. City Bar Assn. (chmn. com. on continuing legal edn. 1976-77, chmn. com. on judiciary 1978-79, chmn. com. on by-laws 1981-82), ABA, Jud. Conf. U.S. Ct. Appeals for 4th Cir. (conf. study com. 1982-83) Democrat. Episcopalian. Office: DLA Piper Rudnick Gray Cary 6225 Smith Ave Baltimore MD 21209-3600

**REDDEN, TAYLOR TILGHMAN,** musician; b. Swarthmore, Pa., Mar. 2, 1946; s. O. Tilghman Redden and Virginia Dare (Martin) Martin-Redden. Artist diploma, Phila. Conservatory of Music, 1965; BA, Phila. Music Acad., 1967, BFA in Music, 1967. Artist, tchr. Phila. Settlement Music Schs. 1968—70; prof. piano Bryn Mawr Conservatory of Music, Bryn Mawr, Pa., 1971—. Mem.: Music Tchrs. N. Am., U. of Arts Alumni Assn. Home: 539 Cornell Ave Swarthmore PA 19081

**REDDER, THOMAS,** consumer products company executive; V.p. info. systems Newsday, 1986—95; v.p., chief info. officer Del Laboratories, 1996—. Named one of Premier 100 IT Leaders, Computerworld, 2005. Office: Del Laboratories PO Box 9357 726 Reckson Plz Uniondale NY 11553 Office Phone: 516-844-2020.*

**REDDICK, BRYAN DEWITT,** language educator, academic administrator; b. Austin, Tex., Feb. 4, 1942; s. DeWitt Carter and Marjorie Alice (Bryan) R.; m. Sheila Ann Farrell, Oct. 3, 1970; children: Bridget Louise, George William. BA, U. Iowa, 1964; MA, Syracuse U., 1966; PhD, U. Calif., Davis, 1969. Fulbright teaching fellow U. Lyon, France, 1969-70; Maitre de Confs. U. Grenoble, France, 1970-71; asst. prof. English Am. U., Washington, 1971-75; prof. Olivet (Mich.) Coll., 1980-86, assoc. dean, 1981-82, acad. v.p., 1982-86, Elmira Coll., NY, 1986—. Author: Student Journalist and Effective Writing Style, 1976; editor: Mass Media and the School, 1984. Contbr. articles to profl. jours. Chmn. Olivet Planning Commn., Mich., 1978; mem. Sch./Community Adv. Coun., 1986-89; mem. exec. com. Sullivan Coun. BSA, 1988-92; trustee Chemung Valley History Mus., 1992—. NDEA fellow, 1966-69. Mem. Phi Beta Kappa. Home: 85 Decker Pkwy W Elmira NY 14905-2303 Office: Elmira Coll 1 Park Pl Elmira NY 14901-2085 E-mail: breddick@elmira.edu.

**REDDICK, CATHERINE ANNE (CAT REDDICK),** Olympic athlete; b. Richmond, Va., Feb. 10, 1982; Majoring in comm., U. N.C., 2000—. Mem. Under-16 Nat. Team, 1998, Under-18 Nat. Team, 1998—99, capt., 2000; mem. Under-21 Nat. Team, 2003; soccer player, defender U.S. Women's Nat. Team, 2000—; mem. U.S. Olympic Soccer Team, Athens, 2004. Co-recipient U-18 Soccer Gold medal, Pan Am. Games, 1999, Nordic Cup, Denmark, 2000, 2001, 2002, 2003; named Defensive MVP, NCAA Final Four, 2000, Freshman All-Am. Team, NSCAA, 2000, Second Team All-Am., 2001, First Team All-Am., 2002; named to First Team All-ACC, 2002. Achievements include being a member of gold medal winning US Women's Soccer Team, Athens Olympic Games, 2004. Office: US Soccer Fedn 1801 S Prairie Ave Chicago IL 60616

**REDDICK, C.N. (FRANK)LIN, III,** lawyer; b. Quantico, Va. BA with high honors, Calif. State Univ., San Jose, 1977; JD, Univ. Calif., 1980. Bar: Calif. 1980. Mng. ptnr., chair, corp. practice group Troop Steuber Pasich Reddick & Tobey LLP, LA; ptnr., chair corp. and securities practice group and mem. mgmt. com. Akin Gump Strauss Hauer & Feld LLP, LA, 2001—. Bd. dir. VCA Antech Inc., LA, 2002—. Mem. Hastings Law Jour., 1978—79, note and comment editor, 1979—80. Mem.: ABA, Thurston Soc., Order of Coif. Office: Akin Gump Strauss Hauer & Feld LLP Ste 2400 2029 Century Pk E Los Angeles CA 90067-3012 Office Phone: 310-728-3204. Office Fax: 310-229-1001. Business E-Mail: freddick@akingump.com.

**REDDICLIFFE, STEVEN,** television critic; m. Constance Reddicliffe; children: Rebecca, Anna, James (triplets). BS in Journalism, Northwestern U., 1975. Assoc. editor Self Mag., 1988—89; mng. editor US Mag., 1988; founding sr. editor Entertainment Weekly, 1989—92; editor-in-chief Parenting Mag., 1992—95; TV Guide, NYC, 1995—2002; mag. devel. Reader's Digest, Pleasantville, NY, 2003; TV critic Miami Herald, Balt. News Am., Dallas Times Herald, NY Times, 2004—. Office: TV critic NY Times 229 W 43rd St New York NY 10036*

**REDDIN, GEORGE,** religious organization administrator; Dir. Lifeword Broadcast Ministries, Conway, Ark., 1986. Office: Lifeword Broadcast Ministries PO Box 6 Conway AR 72033-0006 Office Phone: 501-329-6891. E-mail: george@lifeword.org.

**REDDING, BOBBIE NEWMAN,** lawyer; b. Guilford County, NC, Mar. 30, 1935; d. John J. Newman and Flora Pearl (Kirkman) Brower; m. Marshall S. Redding, June 2, 1957 (div. 1982); children: Joan Lucile, Rebecca Marie

Redding Greene. Student, U. N.C., Greensboro, 1952-54; BA in Edn., U. N.C., 1956, MSLS, 1957; JD, Campbell U., 1985. Bar: N.C. 1986. Staff atty. Lumbee River Legal Svcs., Fayetteville, NC, 1986-88, Cumberland County Dept. Social Svcs., Fayetteville, 1988—. Local adv. coun. Legal Aid N.C. Mem. ABA, N.C. Bar Assn., N.C. Assn. Social Svcs. Attys., N.C. State Bar Assn., N.C. Guardianship Assn. (bd. dirs.), Cumberland County Bar, Twelth Judicial Bar Home: Box F Unit 106 1100 Clarendon St Fayetteville NC 28305-4800 Office: Cumberland County DSS 1225 Ramsey St Fayetteville NC 28301 Office Phone: 910-677-2667. Business E-Mail: lg2@ccdssnc.com.

**REDDING, EVELYN A.,** dean; b. Gulfport, Miss., Mar. 13, 1945; d. Arthur Edward and Rebecca (Morris) R. BSN, U. Ala., 1967; MS, Fla. State U., 1971; EdD, Okla. State U., 1974; cert. PNP, Tex. Women's U., 1974; MSN, Wichita State U., 1980. Psychiat. nurse Camp Ponderosa, Mentone, Ala., 1967; dir. health svcs. Community Action Agy., Head Start, Dadeville, Ala., 1967-68; pediatric nurse All Children's Hosp., St. Petersburg, Fla., 1968-69; instr. A&M U. Sch. Nursing, Tallahassee, 1969-71; coord. mater and child health Western Ky. U., Bowling Green, 1971-72; dir. grad. program U. Tex. Health Sci. Ctr., Houston, 1974-78; prof., assoc. dean Coll. Nursing U. Tulsa, 1978-81; dean, prof. Coll. Nursing U. Southwestern La., Lafayette, 1981-97, prof., 1997—. Presenter in field. Contbr. articles to profl. jours. Policy adv. bd. Northwest Fla. Family Planning Project, 1969-71, Nurses Coalition for Action in Politics; mem. exec. com. Hospice of Acadiana, 1982-85, pres., bd. dirs., 1984; cons. big Bend Comprehensive Svcs. Clinic, Tallahassee, 1970-71; cons. family planning nurse practitioner program Planned Parenthood Ctr., Houston, 1975-78; cons. grad. edn., nurse clinician program Madigan Army Med. Ctr., Washington, 1975; pres. Dirs. Nursing Edn. and Nursing Svc. Acadiana, 1982-83; docent intern Gilcrease Mus.; chair Tulsa Area Dirs. Nursing Svc. and Nursing Edn. Mem. AAUW (cultural affairs and community com.), ANA, Nat. League for Nursing, ANA Coun. Nurse Researchers, Soc. for Rsch. Nursing Edn., La. State Nurses Assn. (program com. dist. IV 1986), Okla. Nurses Assn. (nurse edn. com. dist. 2 1978-79, by-laws com. 1978-80), Tex. Nurses Assn. (chairperson task force for profl. self-determination 1976-78), Coun. Adminstrs. Nursing Edn. La. (presenter 1987-88), Sigma Theta Tau, Omicron Nu. Avocations: bike riding, reading, fishing, yard work. Office: U Southwestern La Coll Nursing PO Box 42490 Lafayette LA 70504-0001 Home: 14336 Dalton Rd Kaplan LA 70548-6729

**REDDING, KIMBERLY ANN,** history professor; b. Pitts., Dec. 20, 1968; d. Keith Lee Kussmaul and Carol Faust Cowan; m. Frank Winship Redding, Oct. 23, 1993; children: Morgan, Thomas, William. BA, Goucher Coll., 1991; MA, U. NC, 1995, PhD, 2001. Tchg. asst. Heinrich Hertz Schule, Berlin, 1991—92, U. NC, Chapel Hill, 1993—95, writing tutor, 1996—2000; asst. prof. hist. Carroll Coll., Waukesha, Wis., 2001—. Author: Growing Up in Hitler's Shadow, 2004. Mem.: Cold War Hist. Soc. (bd. mem. midwest chpt. 2004—), Am. Hist. Soc. (Fritz Stern prize 2001). Avocations: cooking, music. Office: Carroll Coll 100 NE Ave Waukesha WI 53186 Office Phone: 262-650-4894.

**REDDING, ROBERT ELLSWORTH,** lawyer; b. South Bend, Ind., Mar. 23, 1919; s. Harry Ellsworth and Lorraine (Livengood) R.; m. Blanche Breisch, Apr. 14, 1941 (div.); children: Rosemary, Robert Ellsworth Jr., Douglas; m. a. Virginia Boender Korn, July 22, 1972 (dec. Aug. 2004). AB, Ohio State U., 1940; LLB, JD, Georgetown U., 1946. Bar: DC 1946, Md. 1949, US Supreme Ct. 1951. Legal asst. to judge U.S. Tax Ct., Wash., 1947—48; legal asst. to mem. CAB, Washington, 1949-51; mem. Bradshaw Shearin Redding & Thomas, Silver Spring, Md., 1951-59; v.p., gen. counsel Transp. Assn. Am., Washington, 1960-69; dir. Office Facilitation Dept. Transp., 1970-76; sole law practice Washington, Md., 1976—2006. Sec. Cert. Claims Profl. Accreditation Council, Washington, 1981-85; chief judge Appeal Tax Ct., Rockville, Md., 1953-55; internat. cons., G.E. Co., 1977; cons. Ford Motor Co., 1978-79; dir. fed. affairs Shippers Nat. Freight Claim Council, Washington, 1979-89; cons. UN Devel. Program, NYC, 1980-81, Montgomery County, Md. Office of Inspector Gen., 1997-2004; Washington counsel Japan Airlines. Author: Community Planning for Air Transportation, 1960; Washington editor Handling and Shipping mag., 1976—81, dir. Olney Jazz Troupe, 2005—. Pres. Allied Civic Group (50 assns.), Silver Spring, 1956-58; chmn. rsch. com. Md. Rep. Com., 1965-70; chmn. fin. adv. com. to county coun., Montgomery County Taxpayers League, 1994-97. 2d lt. US Army, 1943-46. Mem.: Assn. Intelligence Officers, Univ. Club (bd. govs.), Washington), 33 Degree Scottish Rite Mason, Phi Beta Kappa, Phi Alpha Delta (supreme justice 1966—68, exec. v.p. Pub. Svc. Ctr. 1984—91). Achievements include while dir. Office Facilitation Dept. Transp., principal negotiator of bilateral transport agreements with U.S.S.R., Canada and U.K; chairman, U.S. delegation attending 13 U.N. transportation conferences, also U.S. delegate to similar conferences in Chile, Africa, Thailand and World Bank. Home: 9105 Falls Chapel Way Potomac MD 20854-2452 E-mail: robredding@comcast.net.

**REDDING, ROGERS WALKER,** physics professor, academic administrator; b. Louisville, July 15, 1942; s. George Walker and Carolyn Lorraine (Rogers) R.; m. Jennie Ruth Fincher, Sept. 6, 1966 (div.); children: Jeffrey Walker, Jonathan Hull; m. Shirley Rubrecht, Aug. 24, 1991. BS, Georgia Tech., 1965; PhD, Vanderbilt U., 1969. Rsch. assoc. Nat. Bur. Standards, Washington, 1969-70; from asst. prof. to assoc. prof. North Tex. State U. (name now U. North Tex.), Denton, 1970-78, prof. physics, 1978-94, dept. chmn., 1980-87, dir. Tex. Acad. Math. and Sci., 1987-89, assoc. dean arts and scis., 1990-94; prof. physics, dean Coll. Arts and Scis. No. Ky. U., Highland Heights, 1994—, v.p. acad. affairs, provost. Disting. vis. prof. USAF Acad., 1989-90. Author: Exploring Physics, 1984; contbr. articles to profl. jours. Mem. Am. Phys. Soc., Am. Assn. Physics Tchrs., AAAS, Optical Soc. Am. Lodges: Kiwanis. Democrat. Avocations: handball, jogging, referee college football, little league coach. E-mail: redding@nku.edu.

**REDDINGTON, MARY JANE,** retired secondary school educator; b. New Rochelle, N.Y., July 21, 1923; d. Gordon William and Katharine Regina (Coleman) Kann; m. John Martin Reddington, Oct. 11, 1947; children: Terence, Martha, Robert. BA cum laude, Coll. New Rochelle, 1945; postgrad., Columbia U., 1947—49; MA, Hunter Coll., 1954; PhD (hon.), Iona Coll., 1996. Tchr. St. Gabriel's H.S., New Rochelle, NY, 1945—51, Albert Leonard Jr. H.S., New Rochelle, NY, 1960—81; dir. devel. The Ursuline Sch., New Rochelle, NY, 1981—88; ret., 1988. Active Bd. Edn., New Rochelle, 1983—, v.p., 1985—87, pres., 1987—89, Colburn Meml. Home; active New Rochelle Pub. Libr. Found. Bd., New Rochelle Cmty. Svcs. Bd.; vol. Sound Shore Med. Ctr.; bd. dirs. United Way New Rochelle, 1972—, pres., 1979—82, campaign chair, 1976—82; trustee Coll. New Rochelle, 1967—73; lector Holy Family Ch.; active Holy Family Ch. Ladies Guild. Named to Westchester County Hall of Fame, 2005; recipient Gold Key award, Columbia Scholastic Press Assn., 1976, Ursula Laurus citation, Coll. New Rochelle, 1962, St. Angela Merici medal, 1970, citation, United Way New Rochelle, 1970—82, Spl. Recognition award, 1986, 2001, St. Angela award, The Ursuline Sch., 1977, Nat. Cmty. Svc. award, AARP, 1994, Loyal Svc. and Dedication award, Colburn Home, 1992, Cmty. Salute honoree, New Rochelle Pub. Libr. Found., 1999, Cmty. Svc. award, New Rochelle YMCA, 2001, honoree, Sr. Pers. Placement Bur., 2002, Interreligious Coun. of New Rochelle, 2002, Meals-On-Wheels of New Rochelle, 2003, New Rochelle Fund for Ednl. Excellence, 2004, Marie Vitt award, Sound Share Med. Ctr., 2005. Mem.: Bus. and Profl. Women's Club New Rochelle (past pres., Woman of Yr. 1979), So. Westchester Ret. Tchrs. Assn. (co-pres.), Coll. New Rochelle Alumnae Assn. (past pres.), Ladies of Charity (past pres.), Cath. Women's Club Westchester (founder, past pres.), Woman's Club New Rochelle (pres.), LWV, Alpha Delta Kappa (past pres.). Roman Catholic. Avocations: travel, reading, antiques, writing, cross country skiing. Home: 56 Wykagyl Terr New Rochelle NY 10804

**REDDY, DANIEL JOSEPH,** vascular surgeon; b. Jackson, Mich., June 2, 1947; s. Martin Joseph and Phyllis Watson Reddy; m. Diane Marie D'Angelo; children: Caitlin Marie, Daniel Martin. BS, Georgetown U., 1969; MD, U. Mich., 1973. Diplomate in gen. surgery and vascular surgery Am. Bd. Surgery. Sr. staff vascular surgeon Henry Ford Hosp., Detroit, 1979—, chief

of vascular surgery, 1997—, dir. vascular surgery fellowship tng. program, 1997—, d. emerick szilagyi chair in vascular surgery, 2002—. Mem. bd. govs. Henry Ford Med. Group, Detroit, 1995—2002. Author numerous papers, exhibits, movies, abstracts. V.p. Christus Medicus, Metro Detroit, 1999—. Ignatius Academic scholar, Georgetown U., 1965—69, Traveling Pub. Health fellow to Yugoslavia, Am. Assn. Med. Colls., 1973. Fellow: ACS (Fredrick Coller award 1975); mem.: Ctrl. Surg. Assn., Western Surg. Assn., Soc. Vascular Surgery. Independent. Roman Catholic. Achievements include patents for Reddy Treadle Asssessing Arterial Systems. Avocation: ice hockey. Office: Henry Ford Hosp 2799 W Grand Blvd Detroit MI 48202 E-mail: dreddy1@hfhs.org.

**REDDY, GERARD ANTHONY,** consumer banker; b. N.Y.C., Sept. 25, 1958; s. Warren and Julia (O'Reilly) R.; m. Lorraine (Bush), Feb. 20, 1994; 1 child, Katelyn Grace. BA in English Writing and Comm. Media, Queens Coll., 1981. Rsch. analyst John Blair and Co., N.Y.C., 1981—82, Katz Ind. TV Sales, N.Y.C., 1982—83; sr. rsch. analyst Seltel, N.Y.C., 1983—84; sales presentation writer Capital Cities ABC TV Sales, N.Y.C., 1984—86; client svc. exec. A.C. Nielsen Co., N.Y.C., 1986—87; rsch. mgr. off network programming MCA-TV, N.Y.C., 1987—88; mgr. corp. tng. and instrn. Dale Carnegie Tng., N.Y.C., 1989—96, major accounts bus. mgr., 1996—97; tng. supr. Americhoice Inc., Newark, 1998; sr. tng. specialist The Dreyfus Corp., Uniondale, NY, 1999—2000; fin. advisor Am. Express Fin. Advisors, Inc., Mitchel Field, NY, 2000—03, para planner, 2004—05; consumer banker J.P. Morgan Chase, Gt. Neck, NY, 2003—04; tng. specialist Wm. Fin. Svcs., Inc., Uniondale, NY, 2005—. Mgr. Little League Our Lady Miraculous Medal, Ridgewood, N.Y., 1993-94; campaigned for Rudolph Guliani for Mayor, N.Y.C., Ridgewood, 1994. Avocations: script writing, motorcycling, meditation, jogging. Home: 3 Smith St East Rockaway NY 11518-1716 Office: Wm Fin Svcs Inc Reckson Plz 11th Fl E Tower Uniondale NY 11556-0125 Business E-Mail: GerardAReddy/jpmchase@jpmchase.com. E-mail: gerard.reddy@wamu.net.

**REDDY, J. N.,** mechanical engineering educator; b. Warangal, AP, India, Aug. 12, 1945; m. Aruna Reddy; children: Anita, Anil. BE in Mech. Engring., Osmania U., 1968; MS in Mech. Engring, Okla. State U., 1970; PhD in Engring. Mechanics, U. Ala., 1973. Rsch. scientist Lockheed Missiles & Space Co., 1974-75; asst. prof. U. Okla., 1975-78, assoc. prof., 1978-80; prof. mech. engring. Va. Poly. Inst. and State U., Blacksburg, Va., 1980-85, Clifton G. Garvin prof., 1986-92; Oscar S. Wyatt Jr. chair Tex. A&M U., College Station, 1992—, Univ. Disting. prof., 1998—. Author: Energy Principles and Variational Methods in Applied Mechanics, 1984, 2nd edit., 2002, Applied Functional Analysis and Variational Methods in Engineering, 1986, An Introduction to the Finite Element Method, 2d edit., 1993, Mechanics of Laminated Composite Plates and Shells: Theory and Analysis, 2d edit., 2004, Theory and Analysis of Elastic Plates, 1999, An Introduction to Nonlinear Finite Element Analysis, 2004, (with others) Variational Methods in Theoretical Mechanics, 1976, A Mathematical Theory of Finite Elements, 1976, Advanced Engineering Analysis, 1982, Finite Element Analysis of Composite Laminates, 1992, The Finite Element Method in Heat Transfer and Fluid Dynamics, 1994, 2d edit., 2001, Practical Analysis of Laminated Composite Structures, 1995; editor-in-chief Mechanics of Advanced Materials and Structures, Internat. Jour. Computational Methods Engring. Sci. Mechanics, Internat. Jour. Structural Stability and Dynamics; mem. editl. bd. Jour. Applied Mechanics, Internat. Jour. Numerical Methods in Engring., Internat. Jour. Numerical Methods in Fluids, others; contbr. over 300 papers to profl. jours. Recipient Ralph R. Teetor Edn. award Soc. Automotive Engrs., 1976, Technical Achievement award NAE, 1995, Archie Higdon Disting. Educator award Am. Soc. Engring. Edn., 1997. Fellow ASME (Worcester Reed Warner medal 1992, Charles Russ Richards Meml. award 1995), ASCE (Walter L. Huber Civil Engring Rsch. prize 1983, Nathan M. Newmark medal 1998), AIAA (assoc.), Am. Acad. Mechanics, Aeronautical Soc. India, U.S. Assn. Computational Mechanics (Computational Solid Mechanics award 2003), Internat. Assn. Computational Mechanics, Am. Soc. Composites (Excellence in the Field of Composite award 2000, Outstanding Rsch. award 2004). Office: Texas A&M Univ Dept Mech Engring College Station TX 77843-3123 Fax: 979-862-3989. Office Phone: 979-862-2417. Business E-Mail: jmreddy@tamu.edu.

**REDDY, KAMBHAM RAJA,** botanist, educator; b. Ambuvari Palli, India, July 1, 1953; s. Kambi Kambham and Ammannamma (Reddy) R.; m. Anasuya Reddy; 1 son, Sasank. BSc in Biology, S.V. U., Tirupati, India, 1975, MSc in Botany, 1977, PhD in Botany, 1984. Curator in botany S.V. U., 1977-88; prof. plant physiology Miss. State U., 1991—. Editor: Climate Change and Global Crop Productivity, 2000; contbg. author: Climate Change and Agriculture: Analysis of Potential International Impacts, 1995; contbr. articles to profl. jour., chpt. to books. Recipient Career Rsch. award, So. Br. Am. Soc. Agronomy and Assn. Agrl. Scientists Indian Origin, 2004. Fellow Agronomy Soc. Am.; mem. Crop Sci. Soc. Am., Biol. Sys. Simulation Work Group, Gamma Sigma Delta (Rsch. award of merit 1995). Achievements include development of new theories and concepts in plant growth regulation and incorporated into a cotton simulation model GOSSYM, used by cotton producers, consultants and rschr. across the cotton belt; extensive contributions to the field of climate change, environmental plant physiology, ethnobotany, remote sensing and crop simulation modeling. Home: 505 Banyan Rd Starkville MS 39759-4348 Office: Mississippi State U Box 9555 Mississippi State MS 39762-9555 Office Phone: 662-325-9463.

**REDDY, KRISHNA NARAYANA,** artist, educator; b. Chittoor, India, July 15, 1925; s. Narayana B. and Laksmamma Reddy; m. Judith Blum, June 30, 1967; 1 child, Aparna. Diploma in Fine Arts, Internat. U. Santiniketan, India, 1947; cert. in Fine Arts, Slade Sch. Fine Arts, U. London, 1952; student of Zadkine in sculpture, Academie Grande Chaumière, Paris, 1952—55; student of Marino Marini in sculpture, Academia di Belle Arti di Brera, Milan, 1956—57; specialist in Gravure, Internat. Ctr. for Graphics, Atelier 17, Paris, 1953—55; DLitt (hon.), S.V. Univ., India, 1984. Asst. dir. Internat. Ctr. for Graphics, Atelier 17, Paris, 1957—64, prof., co-dir., 1964—76; from prof. art to prof. emeritus NYU, NYC, 1977—2001, prof. emeritus art and art edn., 2001—. Dir. dept. art Coll. Fine Arts, Kalakshetra, Madras, India, 1947—49; lectr. art Arundale Montessori Tchrs. Tng. Ctr., 1948—49; vis. prof. Am. U., 1964; prof. U. Calif., Davis, 1970—71, U. Wis., Madison, 1973; guest prof. Yale U. Summer Sch. Music and Art, 1973; Andrew Mellon vis. prof. Cooper Union Sch. Art and Arch., 1977; vis. prof. Yale U. Summer Sch. Music and Art, 1978, Kala Inst. Graphics, Berkeley, Calif., 1979, U. Calif., Santa Cruz, 1979. Author: Intaglio Simultaneous Color Printmaking: Significance of Materials and Processes, 1989, New Ways of Colour Printmaking, 1997; retrospective exhbns., Bronx Mus. Arts, 1981-82, Indian Council for Cultural Relations, Ministry of Culture and India Nat. Acad. Fine Arts, 1984-85, Museo del Palacio de Bellas Artes, Mexico City, 1988-89. Recipient Gagan-Abani Puraskar Nat. award Viswa-Bharati, 1983, Printmaker Emeritus award So. Graphics Coun. of Am., 2000; named Featured Guest Artist-Printmaker at the Northwest Print Coun. Ann. Meeting, 1985; Title of Padma Shree awarded by Pres. of India, 1972. Home: 80 Wooster St New York NY 10012-4347 Personal E-mail: jreddy5@nyc.rr.com.

**REDDY, NEELIMA G.,** gastroenterologist, researcher; b. India; m. Mahesh Basireddy; children: Abhay, Akshay. Attended, St. Francis Coll. for Women, India, 1992; MD, Gandhi Med. Coll., India, 1998. Grad. Ednl. Commn. Foreign Med. Graduates, 2000, cert. ACLS provider 2001, ACLS instr. 2003, BLS provider 2001. Med. officer Gandhi Med. Coll., Secunderabad, India, 1997—98; resident med. officer Heritage Hosp., Hyderabad, India, 1998—2000; rschr. Weill Med. Coll. Cornell U., N.Y.C., 2000; resident physician internal medicine U. Ala., Birmingham, 2001—04, ACLS instr., 2004, fellow gastroenterology, 2004—. Resident Gandhi Med. Coll., Hyderabad, 1995—98; med. officer Nat. Pulse Polio Eradication Program, Hyderabad, 1995—98; rural health clinic med. officer Gandhi Med. Coll., Hyderabad, 1997—98. Author (rsch. publ. in hepatology) Use of Granulocyte Colony Stimulating Factor (GCSF) For Interferon Induced Neutropenia in Patients with Chronic Hepatitis C Infection, (rsch. publ. in gastroenterology ACP Nat. Conf., 2003) The Prevalence of Antinuclear Antibody in Patients with

NAFLD (Digestive Diseases Week Travel award, 2003; author, presenter unusual clin. case of Chylothorax and Chylous ascites in Lupus (Travel award for Digestive Diseases Week, 2003), unusual clin. case complications in Kaposi's Sarcoma (Travel award for So. Soc. Gen. Internal Medicine, New Orleans, 2003), (nat. rsch. poster presentation) The Intrazonal Distribution of Steatosis in Chronic Hepatitis C and the Impact of Hepatic Steatosis on Fibrosis and Necroinflammatory Activity (Travel award So. Soc. Gen. Internal Medicine, 2003), (internat. conf. rsch. poster) Prevalence and Titer Distribution of Autoantibodies in Patients with Nonalcoholic Fatty Liver Disease (Travel award Nat. Am. Coll. Physicans, Travel award Digestive Diseases Week, 2003). Recipient award, Nat. Talent Search, 1991, Resident Scholar Travel award, Am. Assn. Study Liver Disease, 2001, GI Cancer Symposium Travel award, 2004, Astrazeneca Travel award, GI Fellows Conf., 2004. Mem.: Assn. Physicians of Indian Origin, Jefferson County Med. Soc., Am. Coll. Physicans (assoc.), Gandhi Med. Coll. Alumni. Personal E-mail: neelima_greddy@yahoo.com.

**REDDY, RANGA VALLELA,** anesthesiologist; b. India, Jan. 1, 1946; came to US, 1976; MS in Gen. Surgery, Kurool Med. Coll., 1970. Residency, gen. surgery Kurnool Gen. Hosp., Kurnool, India, 1971—74; med. superintendent St. Raphael's Hosp., Giddalur, India, 1975—76; physician St. John Hosp., Yonkers, NY, 1976-77; resident, anesthesiology dept. SUNY Health Sci. Ctr., Brooklyn, NY, 1977—79, asst. prof., 1979—82; attending anesthesiologist, asst. prof. St. Louis U. Med. Ctr., St. Louis, 1979—82; attending anesthesiologist Veteran Hosp. Med. Ctr., St. Louis, 1979—82; clinical assoc. prof. So. Ill. U. Sch. of Med., 1982—; attending anesthesiologist Meml. Med. Ctr., Springfield, Ill., 1982—, chmn. dept. anesthesiology, 1996—98. Pres. AAPI, 1997-98. Mem. AMA, Am. Surg. Assn., Internat. Anesthesia Rsch. Soc., Ill. Med. Assn., Ill. Surg. Assn., Am. Assn. Physicians of Indian Origin (pres. 1997-98). E-mail: rankris@aol.com.

**REDDY, THIKKAVARAPU RAMACHANDRA,** electrical engineer; b. Nellore, India, June 4, 1944; came to the U.S., 1979; s. Thikkavarapu Kota and Saraswathi T. (Sivareddy) R.; m. Padmavathi Reddy Kakuturu Thikkavarapu, Aug. 17, 1973; children: Lavanya T., Samatha T. BSEE, Osmania U., 1968, PhD in Bus. Adminstrn., 2005; diploma in Computer Sci., Coll. Engring., Madras, India, 1978. Cert. profl. engr., chartered engr. Supervising engr. APSE Bd., Hyderabad, India, 1969—79; engr. elec. design Sargent & Lundy, Chgo., 1979—80; engr. Bechtel Corp., San Francisco, 1980—82, supr. Athens, Ala., 1989—92; sr. project engr. EGS, Inc., Huntsville, Ala., 1983—84; sr. start-up engr. Gilbert Commonwealth Co., Reading, Pa., 1984—86; cons. Quantum Resources, Decatur, Ala., 1986—87; prin. engr. Ebasco Svcs. Inc., N.Y.C., 1987—89; pres. LSP Internat. Inc., Huntsville, 1992—, LASA Internat., Huntsville, 1992—; project engr. Sargent & Lundy, Chgo., 1997—. Guest lectr. gen. interest and wide range of engring. issues. Author: Qualification of Electrical Distribution Components, 1984, Thermal Aging Techniques of Organic Materials, 1984, and others; contbr. articles to profl. jours.; guest lectr. on wide range of engring. issues. Mem. NSPE (Outstanding Profl. award 1991, Profl. Engr. of Yr. award 1996), IEEE (sr.; Meritorious Svc. award 1985), Commonwealth Engrs. Coun., Project Mgmt. Inst., Am. Telugu Assn. (life), Telugu Assn. N.Am. (life), Internat. Platform Assn., Soc. Fire Protection Egrs. (profl.), C. of C. Avocations: journalism, ping pong/table tennis, anthropology, archaeology, classic and modern art, literature. Home and Office: 392 N Summit Ave Apt 101 Gaithersburg MD 20877-3107 Personal E-mail: trr2020@yahoo.com.

**REDDY, VADIYALA MOHAN,** cardiothoracic surgeon; m. Anita Reddy. MD, Kakatiya Med. Coll., Warangal, India, 1983. Resident Delhi U., New Delhi, 1986, 1989; sr. resident, pediatric cardiac surgery Children's Hosp., Boston, 1991; fellow Miami Children's Hosp., Fla., 1992, U. Calif., San Francisco, 1992; dir., pediatric cardiac surgery U. Calif, San Francisco, 1992—2001, assoc. prof., 1992—2001; divsn. chief, pediatric cardiothoracic surgery Cardiothoracic Surgery Clinic, Lucile Packard Children's Hosp. at Stanford U. Med. Ctr., Palo Alto, Calif., 2001—; assoc. prof., cardiothoracic surgery Stanford U. Sch. Medicine, Stanford, Calif., 2001—. Contbr. articles to profl. publs. Mem.: Soc. Thoracic Surgeons, Am. Heart Assn., Am. Assn. for Thoracic Surgeons. Office: Cardiothoracic Surgery 300 Pasteur Dr CVRB MC 5407 Stanford CA 94305 Address: Lucile Packard Childrens Hosp 725 Welsh Rd Palo Alto CA 94304 Office Phone: 650-724-2925, 650-497-8000. Fax: 650-724-0707. Office Phone: 415-476-3501. Fax: 415-476-9678; Office Fax: 650-725-3846. Business E-Mail: vmreddy@stanford.edu.

**REDDY, VENKAT NARSIMHA,** ophthalmologist, researcher; b. Hyderabad, India, Nov. 4, 1922; came to U.S., 1947; s. Malla and Manik (Devi) R.; m. Alvira M. DeMello, Dec. 10, 1955; children: Vinay Neville, Marlita Alvira. BSc, U. Madras, 1945; MS, PhD, Fordham U., 1952. Rsch. assoc. Coll. of Physicians and Surgeons Columbia U., N.Y.C., 1952-56, Banting and Best Inst., Toronto, Can., 1956; ass. and assoc. prof. ophthalmology Kresge Eye Inst. Wayne State U., Detroit, 1957-68; prof., biomed. scis., asst. dir. Eye Rsch. Inst. Oakland U., Rochester, Mich., 1968-75, prof., dir., 1975-98, Disting. prof. biomed. scis., dir., 1996-98; prof. ophthalmology Kellogg Eye Ctr. U. Mich., Ann Arbor, 1998—. Mem. study sect. NIH, Bethesda, 1966-70, nat. adv. eye coun., 1982-87, mem. bd. sci. counselors Nat. Eye Inst., 1977-81 Mem. editl. bd. Investigative Ophthalmology and Visual Scis., 1969-72, 78-88, Ophthalmic Research, 1978-90, Experimental Eye Research, 1985-2000; contbr. articles to profl. jours. Recipient Friendenwald award Assn. Rsch. in Ophthalmology, 1979, Rsch. award Cataract Rsch. Found., 1987, Merit award Nat. Eye Inst., 1989; named Scientist of Yr. State of Mich., 1991, Disting. Faculty Mem. Mich. Assn. Governing Bds. State Univs., 1994. Mem. AAAS, Internat. Soc. Eye Rsch., The Biochem. Soc., Assn. Rsch. in Vision and Ophthalmology (pres. 1985), Am. Soc. for Biochemistry and Molecular Biology, Soc. Free Radicals, Oxygen Soc. Sigma Xi. Achievements include research on cataract etiology, intraocular fluids dynamics relating to glaucoma, cell biology of lens, ciliary body and retinal pigment epithelium, cell differentiation. Office: U Mich Kellogg Eye Ctr 1000 Wall St Ann Arbor MI 48105-1912 Office Phone: 734-763-7246. Business E-Mail: venreddy@med.umich.edu.

**REDFEARN, PAUL L., III,** lawyer; b. Camp Cook, Calif., Oct. 1, 1951; s. Paul Leslie Jr. and Alice Ruby Redfearn; children: Ashley, Lauren; m. Denise Jean Davis, July 24, 1993. BS, S.W. Mo. State U., 1973; JD, Oklahoma City U., 1976. Bar: Mo. 1977, U.S. Dist. Ct. (we. and ea. dists.) Mo., U.S. Dist. Ct. Kans., U.S. Dist. Ct. N.D., U.S. Dist. Ct. Mont., U.S. Ct. Appeal (8th and 11th cirs.); bd. cert. civil trial advocate. Assoc. Sheridan, Sanders & Simpson, P.C., 1977-79, William H. Pickett, P.C., 1979-84; ptnr. The Redfearn Law Firm, P.C., Kansas City, Mo., 1984—. Mem. bd. dirs. treas. Lawyers Encouraging Acad. Performance (LEAP), treas.; lectr. and presenter in field. Contbr. chpts. to books. Bd. govs. S.W. Mo. State U., 1998-2003; instr. Ross T. Roberts Inn of Ct. Program, Kansas City. Mo. Named Best of the Bar, Business Jour., 2003. Mem. ABA, ATLA, Mo. Bar Assn., Mo. Assn. Trial Attys. (bd. govs. 1986-94, exec. com. 1990—, pres. 1992), Am. Bd. Trial Advocates (charter, pres. chpt. 1996-97), Trial Lawyers for Pub. Justice, Kansas City Met. Bar Assn., East Jackson County Bar Assn., Millon Dollar Advocates Forum. Democrat. Avocation: tennis. Office: The Redfearn Law Firm PC 1125 Grand Blvd Ste 1 805 Kansas City MO 64106-2518 Office Phone: 816-421-5301. Business E-Mail: predfearn@redfearnlawfirm.com.

**REDFERN, JOHN D.,** manufacturing executive; b. 1935; Grad., Queen's U., Kingston, Ont., 1958; DEng. honoris causa (hon.), Carleton U., 1992. With Lafarge Can. Inc. (formerly Can. Cement Lafarge Ltd.), Montreal, 1977—, pres., CEO, 1977—84, chmn., 1985—; chmn. bd. parent co. Lafarge Corp., Reston, Va., 1985—88, vice chmn., 1989—96. Office: Lafarge Can Inc 606 Cathcart Ste 800 Montreal PQ Canada H3B 1L7 Office Phone: 514-861-2581. Business E-Mail: john.redfern@lafarge-na.com.

**REDFIELD, CAROL ANN LUCKHARDT,** computer scientist, educator; b. Greencastle, Ind., July 19, 1958; d. Robert Luckhardt and Helen Kinoshta; m. Josiah Beckley Redfield, Mar. 17, 1990 BS Edn., U. Mich., 1980, MS Math, 1982, MS Computer & Controls, 1982, PhD Computer Sci. & Engring., 1989. Cert. secondary tchr. Tchg. asst. U. Mich., Ann Arbor, 1979—87; rsch.

engr. Southwest Rsch. Inst., San Antonio, 1987—94; sr. scientist Mei Tech. Corp., San Antonio, 1995—98; asst. prof. St. Mary's U., San Antonio, 1998—2003, assoc. prof., 2003—; dir. Grad. Program, 2004—. Chair Internat. Space Devel. Conf., San Antonio, 1991 Author: AI and Game Playing, 1986; editor, author: Intelligent Tutoring Systems, 1991, 98; editor: 1991 ISDC Procs., 1991, AI in Education, 2001 Dir. Internet team Landmark Edn.; founder Radiance Acad. West Charter Sch Mem. AAAI, Nat. Space Soc., San Antonio Space Soc. (pres. 1988—) Quaker. Avocations: science fiction, games, ultimate frisbee. Home: 609 Ridge View Dr San Antonio TX 78253-5348 Office: St Marys U 1 Camino Santa Maria St San Antonio TX 78228-8524 Office Phone: 210-436-3298. Business E-Mail: CRedfield@stmarytx.edu.

**REDFIELD, PAMELA A.,** state legislator; b. Chgo., Aug. 11, 1948; m. Jerry Redfield; 6 children. BS in Edn., U. Nebr., 1969. Mem. Nebr. Legislature 12th dist., Lincoln, 1998—. Mem. Ralston Bd. Edn. 1992-1998. Coun. State Govt.; Nat. Conf. State Legislatures; Am. Legis. Exch. Conf.; Nat. Coun. Ins. Legislators Mem.: Am. Legis. Exch. conf., Nat. Conf. State Legis., Nat. Coun. Ins. State Legis. Office: State Capitol Dist 12 Rm 1404 PO Box 94604 Lincoln NE 68509-4604

**REDFIELD, ROBERT R.,** virologist, medical educator; b. Chgo., 1951; BS, Georgetown U., 1973; MD, Georgetown U. Sch. Med., 1977; degree (hon.), N.Y. Med. Coll. Intern Walter Reed Army Med. Ctr, 1977—78, resident in med., 1978—80, fellow infectious diseases, 1980—82, fellow tropical med., 1982; project dir. HIV immunotherapy Walter Reed Army Inst. Rsch., chief dept. retroviral rsch.; project dir. HIV vaccine devel. for treatment and prevention Military Med. Consortium for Applied Retroviral Rsch., Dept. Def.; co-founder, assoc. dir. Inst. Human Virology U. Md., Baltimore, dir. clin. care & rsch. div. Inst. Human Virology; prof. med., immunology, microbiology, dept. infectious disease U. Md. Sch. Med.; dir. adult HIV program U. Md. Med. Mem. adv. bd. Fogarty Internat. Ctr.; mem. AIDS rsch. adv. coun. NIH. Bd. dirs. The Pendulum Project. Recipient Lifetime Science award, Inst. Advanced Studies in Immunology and Aging, Highest Achievement in Clinical Virology award, Ortho Diagnostic Systems Inc., Physician Recognition award, Surgeon Gen., multiple medals in virology, U.S. Army. Achievements include being the first to demonstrate the heterosexual transmission of the HIV virus; development of the first clinical staging system, now used around the world; originated efforts to examine viral replication and viral load at all of stages of disease. Office: Inst Human Virology 725 W Lombard St Baltimore MD 21201

**REDFORD, DONALD BRUCE,** historian, archaeologist; b. Toronto, Ont., Can., Sept. 2, 1934; s. Cyril Fitzjames and Kathleen Beryl (Coe) R.; m. Susan Pirritano, Jan. 30, 1982; children: Alexander, Aksel; children by previous marriage: Christopher, Philip. BA, U. Toronto, 1957, MA, 1958; PhD, Brown U., 1965. Lectr. Brown U., 1960-61; lectr. U. Toronto, 1961-64, asst. prof. Egyptian history and language, 1965-67, asso. prof., 1967-69, prof., 1969-98; site supr. Brit. Sch. Archaeol. Excavations, Jerusalem, 1964-67; dir. Soc. Study Egyptian Antiquities Expdn. to, Karnak, Egypt, 1970-72, Akhenaten Temple Project, Luxor, Egypt, 1972—; research assoc. Univ. Museum, U. Pa., Royal Ont. Mus.; prof. classics Pa. State U., 1998—. Vis. prof. Ben Gurion U., Beersheva, Israel, 1986, U. Pa., 1995-96; dir. excavations Mendes and Ted Kedwa, Egypt, 1991—. Author: History and Chronology of the Egyptian 18th Dynasty, 1967, A Study of the Biblical Joseph Story, 1970, Papyrus and Tablet, 1973, The Akhenaten Temple Project, vol. I, 1977, Akhenaten, the Heretic King, 1984; Annals, King-Lists and Daybooks, 1986, The Akhenaten Temple Project, vol. II, 1988, Egypt, Canaan and Israel in Ancient Times, 1992, The Wars in Syria and Palestine of Thutmose III, 2003; From Slave to Pharaoh: The Black Experience of Ancient Egypt, 2003. Killam grantee, 1975-79; Smithsonian Fgn. Currency grantee, 1973-76, 1979, Social Scis. Humanities Research Council Can. grantee, 1980—. Fellow Royal Soc. Can. Achievements include discovering Temple of Akhenaten at Luxor, 1976. Office: CAMS Weaver Bldg State College PA 16803 also: Pa State U Dept Classics & Mediterranean Studies 108 Weaver Bldg University Park PA 16802-5500 Business E-Mail: dbr3@psu.edu.

**REDFORD, ROBERT (CHARLES ROBERT REDFORD),** actor, film director; b. Santa Monica, Calif., Aug. 18, 1937; s. Charles Robert and Martha Redford; m. Lola Van Wegenen, Sept. 12, 1958 (div. 1985); children: Shauna, Jamie, Amy. Student, U. Colo., Pratt Inst. Design, Am. Acad. Dramatic Arts; LHD (hon.), U. Colo., 1987; D (hon.), U. Mass., 1990. Owner ski resort Sundance, Provo, Utah. Stage appearances include: Tall Story, The Highest Tree, Sunday in New York, Barefoot in the Park; Films include: (actor) War Hunt, 1961, Situation Hopeless But Not Serious, 1965, Inside Daisy Clover, 1965, The Chase, 1966, This Property Is Condemned, 1966, Barefoot in the Park, 1967, Butch Cassidy and the Sundance Kid, 1969, Tell Them Willie Boy is Here, 1969, Little Fauss and Big Halsey, 1970, The Hot Rock, 1972, Jeremiah Johnson, 1972, The Way We Were, 1973, The Sting, 1973 (Academy award nominee), The Great Gatsby, 1974, The Great Waldo Pepper, 1975, Three Days of the Condor, 1975, A Bridge Too Far, 1977, The Electric Horseman, 1979, Brubaker, 1980, The Natural, 1984, Out of Africa, 1985, Legal Eagles, 1986, Havana, 1990, Sneakers, 1992, Indecent Proposal, 1993, Up Close and Personal, 1996, Anthem, 1997, Enredando sombras, 1998, Forever Hollywood, 1999, Spy Game, 2001, The Last Castle, 2001, The Clearing, 2004, An Unfinished Life, 2005; actor, exec. prodr. Downhill Racer, 1969, The Candidate, 1972, All The President's Men, 1976; exec. prodr. Promised Land, 1988, Some Girls, 1988, She's the One, 1996, The Dark Wind, 1991, Slums of Beverly Hills, 1998, How to Kill Your Neighbor's Dog, 2000; exec. prodr., narrator Yosemite: The Fate of Heaven, 1989, Incident at Oglala, 1992 (TV) Independent's Day, 1998, Visions of Grace: Robert Redford and 'The Horse Whisperer' 1998 (Audience award); dir. Ordinary People, 1980 (Academy and Golden Globe Awards, Best Director), Quiz Show, 1994; dir., prodr. The Milagro Beanfield War, 1988, A River Runs Through It, 1993 (narrator); prodr. A Civil Action, 1998, The Legend of Bagger Vance, 2000. Founder, pres. The Sundance Inst., 1981—. Named Officer of French Ordre des Arts et des Lettres; named one of 100 Sexiest Stars in film history, Esquire mag., 1994; recipient Audubon medal, 1989, Dartmouth Film Soc. award, 1990, Cecil B. Demille Golden Globe Award for Lifetime Achievement, 1994, Screen Actors Guild Award for Life Achievement, 1996, hon. award, Acad. Awards, 2002, Kennedy Ctr. Honor, John F. Kennedy Ctr. for Performing Arts, 2005. Mem.: Land Trust of Napa County (mem. adv. com.). Office: 1223 Wilshire Blvd # 412 Santa Monica CA 90403-5400 also: Creative Artists Agy c/o David O'Conner 9830 Wilshire Blvd Beverly Hills CA 90212-1804*

**REDGRAVE, LYNN,** actress; b. London, Mar. 8, 1943; d. Michael Scudemore and Rachel (Kempson) R.; m. John Clark, Apr. 2, 1967 (div. Dec. 22, 2000); children: Benjamin, Kelly, Annabel. Ed., Queensgate Sch., London, Central Sch. Speech and Drama. Stage debut as Helena in Midsummer Night's Dream, 1962; theatrical appearances include The Tulip Tree, Andorra, Hayfever, Much Ado About Nothing, Mother Courage, Love for Love, Zoo, Zoo, Widdershins Zoo, Edinburgh Festival, 1969, The Two of Us, London, 1970, Slag, London, 1971, A Better Place, Dublin, 1972, Born Yesterday, Greenwich, 1973, Hellzapoppin, N.Y., 1976, California Suite, 1977, Twelfth Night, Stratford Conn. Shakespeare Festival, 1978, The King and I, St. Louis, 1983, Les Liaisons Dangereuses, L.A., 1989, The Cherry Orchard, L.A., 1990, Three Sisters, London, 1990, Notebook of Trigorin, U.S., 1996; Broadway appearances include Black Comedy, 1967, My Fat Friend, 1974, Mrs. Warren's Profession (Tony award nomination), 1975, Knock, Knock, 1976, St. Joan, 1977, Sister Mary Ignatius Explains It All, 1985, Aren't We All?, 1985, Sweet Sue, 1987, A Little Hotel on the Side, 1992, The Masterbuilder, 1992, Shakespeare For My Father (Tony and Drama Desk nominations, Elliot Norton award 1993), 1993, also nat. tour, 1996, West End, 1996, Moon over Buffalo, 1996, The Mandrake Root, 2001, Noises Off, 2001, The Constant Wife, 2005; writer, performer (solo show) Nightingale, 2005; film appearances include Tom Jones, Girl With Green Eyes, Georgy Girl (Recipient N.Y. Film Critics award, Golden Globe award, Oscar nomination for best actress 1967), The Deadly Affair, Smashing Time, The Virgin Soldiers, Last of the Mobile Hotshots, Don't Turn the Other Cheek, Every

Little Crook and Nanny, Everything You Always Wanted to Know About Sex, The National Health, The Happy Hooker, The Big Bus, Sunday Lovers, Morgan Stuart's Coming Home, Getting It Right, Shine, 1996, Gods and Monsters, 1998 (Recipient Golden Globe award for best performance by an actress in a supporting role in a motion picture 1998), Strike, 1998, The Annihilation of Fish, 1999, The Simian Line, 2000, The Next Best Thing, 2000, How to Kill Your Neighbor's Dog, 2000, My Kingdom, 2001, Unconditional Love, 2001 (voice) The Wild Thornberrys Movie, 2002, Hansel & Gretel, 2002, Anita and Me, 2002, Charlie's War, 2003, Peter Pan, 2003, Kinsey, 2004, The White Countess, 2005; TV appearances include: The Turn of the Screw, Centennial, 1978, The Muppets, Gauguin the Savage, Beggarman Thief, The Seduction of Miss Leona, Rehearsal for Murder, 1982, Walking On Air, The Fainthearted Feminist (BBC-TV), 1984, My Two Loves, 1986, The Old Reliable, 1988, Jury Duty 1989, Whatever Happened to Baby Jane, 1990, Fighting Back (BBC-TV), 1992, Calling the Shots (Masterpiece Theatre), 1993, Toothless, 1997, Indefensible: The Truth About Edward Brannigan, 1997, Different, 1999, White Lies, 1998, A Season for Miracles, 1999, AFI's 100 Years...100 Stars, 1999, Varian's War, 2000, Lion of Oz and the Badge of Courage (voice), 2000; guest appearances include Carol Burnett Show, Evening at the Improv and Steve Martin's Best show Ever, Circus of the Stars, The Nanny, 1999, Richard & Judy, 2005, The Heaven and Earth Show, 2005; co-host nat. TV syndication Not for Women Only, 1977—79; nat., TV spokesperson Weightwatchers, 1984-92; TV series include House Calls, 1981, Teachers Only, 1982, Chicken Soup, 1989; Rude Awakening, 1998, albums: Make Mine Manhattan, 1978, Cole Porter Revisited, 1979; video: (for children) Meet Your Animal Friends, Off We Go, Off We Go Again: audio book readings include, Pride and Prejudice, The Shell Seekers, The Blue Bedroom, The Anastasia Syndrome, The Women in His Life, Snow In April, Gone With The Wind, 1994, The World of Philosophy, 1996; author: This is Living, 1990, Shakespeare For My Father, 1993; text by: Journal: A Mother and Daughter's Recovery from Breast Cancer. Named Runner-up Actress, All Am. Favorites, Box Office Barometer 1975; recipient Sarah Siddons award as Chgo.'s best stage actress of 1976, 94, Order of Brit. Empire, 2001. Mem. The Players (pres. 1994). Office: Apt 2CB 205 W 57th St New York NY 10019-2198*

**REDGRAVE, MARTYN ROBERT,** retail executive; BA in Economics, Princeton U.; MBA in Finance, N.Y.U. CPA Minn. Various fin. and gen. mgmt. positions PepsiCo, 1980—90; exec. v.p. fin., CFO Kentucky Fried Chicken Corp., 1990—94; CFO, exec. v.p Carlson Cos. Inc., Mpls., 1994—2005; exec. v.p., chief admin. officer Limited Brands, Inc., Columbus, Ohio, 2005—. Vol. United Way. Office: Limited Brands Inc 3 Limited Pkwy Columbus OH 43216

**REDGRAVE, VANESSA,** actress; b. London, Jan. 30, 1937; d. Michael and Rachel (Kempson) Redgrave; m. Tony Richardson, Apr. 29, 1962 (div. 1967); children: Joely Kim, Natasha; 1 child, Carlo. Student, Central Sch. Speech and Drama, London, 1955-57. First stage appearances include: Reluctant Debutante, Frincton Summer Theater, 1957, Come On Jeeves, Arts Theater, Cambridge, 1957, A Touch of the Sun, Saville Theater, London, 1958, Major Barbara, Royal Court, 1958, Mother Goose, Leatherhead, 1958; Prin. theatrical roles include Helena in Midsummer Night's Dream, 1959, Stella in Tiger and the Horse, 1960, Katerina in The Taming of the Shrew, 1961, Rosalind in As You Like It, 1962, Imogene in Cymbeline, 1962, Nina in The Seagull, 1969, Miss Brodie in The Prime of Miss Jean Brodie, 1966, Cato Street, 1971, Threepenny Opera, 1972, Twelfth Night, 1972, Antony and Cleopatra, 1973, Design for Living, 1973, Macbeth, 1975, Lady from the Sea, 1976, 78, 79, The Aspern Papers, 1984 (Laurence Olivier award for actress of yr. in a revival, 1985), The Seagull, 1969, 85, Chekhov's Women, 1985, The Taming of the Shrew, Ghosts, 1986, Touch of the Poet, 1988, Orpheus Descending, 1989, A Madhouse in Goa, 1989, Chekov's Women, 1989, Three Sisters, 1990, When She Danced, 1991, Heartbreak House, 1991, Maybe, 1993, Brecht in Hollywood, 1994, Vita and Virginia, 1994, Long Days Journey Into Night, 2003 (Tony award for best actress, 2003); films include Behind The Mask, 1958, A Man For All Seasons, 1966, Morgan: A Suitable Case for Treatment, 1966 (Best Actress award, Cannes Film Festival, 1966), Blow-Up, 1966, Red And Blue, 1967, Camelot, 1967, The Sailor from Gibralter, 1967, Isadora, 1968 (Best Actress award, Cannes Film Festival, 1969), The Charge of the Light Brigade, 1968, The Seagull, 1968, A Quiet Place in the Country, 1969, Oh! What a Lovely War, 1969, Daniel Deronda, 1969, Dropout, 1969, The Trojan Women, 1970, The Devils, 1970, The Holiday, 1971, Mary, Queen of Scots, 1971, Murder on the Orient Express, 1974, Winter Rates, 1974, 7 per cent solution, 1975, Julia, 1977 (Academy award for best supporting actress, 1978, Golden Globe award for best supporting actress, 1978), Agatha, 1978, Yanks, 1978, Bear Island, 1979, Playing for Time, 1980, My Body My Child, 1981, Wagner, 1981, The Bostonians, 1983 (Best Actress Nat. Film Critics, Best Actress New Delhi Internat. Film Festival), Wetherby, 1985, Steaming, 1985, Prick Up Your Ears, 1987, Comrades, 1987, Consuming Passions, 1988, Diceria dell'Untore, 1989, The Ballad of the Sad Café, 1990, Young Catherine, 1990, Howard's End, 1992, Crime and Punishment, 1993, The House of the Spirits, 1994, Mother's Boys, 1994, A Month by the Lake, 1995, Little Odessa, 1995, Mission Impossible, 1996, For The Love Of Tyler, 1996, Smilla's Sense of Snow, 1996, Deep Impact, 1998, Celebrity, 1998, Lulu on the Bridge, 1998, Uninvited, 1999, Toscano, 1999, A Rumor of Angels, 1999, Mirka, 1999, An Interesting State, 1999, If These Walls Could Talk 2, 1999, The Cradle Will Rock, 1999, Girl, Interrupted, 1999, A Rumor of Angels, 2000, Crime and Punishment, 2000, The 3 Kings, 2000, The Pledge, 2001, Crime and Punishment, 2002, Good Boy!, 2003, The Fever, 2004, Short Order, 2005, The Keeper: The Legend of Omar Khayyam, 2005, The White Countess, 2005; TV movies and miniseries appearances include Playing for Time, 1980 (Emmy award for outstanding lead actress in a limited series or spl., 1981), Anne White and the Seven Dwarfs, 1983, Three Sovereigns for Sarah, 1985, Peter the Great, 1986, Second Serve, 1986 (Emmy award, Golden Globe award), A Man for All Seasons, 1988, Young Catherine, 1990, Whatever Happened to Baby Jane, 1990, The Three Sisters, 1990, When She Danced, 1991, Playing for Time (Emmy award, TV Times award), The Wall, 1992, Heartbreak House, 1992, Great Moments In Aviation, 1993, Down Came A Blackbird, 1994, The Young Indiana Jones Chronicles, 1992, If These Walls Could Talk 2, 2000 (Emmy award for outstanding supporting actress in a miniseries or movie, 2000, Golden Globe award for best supporting actress in a series, mini-series or motion picture made for TV, 2001, Screen Actors Guild award for best supporting actress in a TV movie or miniseries, 2001) The Gathering Storm, 2002, The Locket, 2002, Byron, 2003; Author: Pussies and Tigers, 1964, (autobiography) Vanessa, 1991, Vanessa Redgrave: An Autobiography, 1994. Bd. govs. Central Sch. Speech and Drama, 1963—. Decorated comdr. Order Brit. Empire; recipient 4 times Drama award Evening Standard, 1961-91, Best Actress award, Variety Club, Gt. Brit., 1961, 66, Best Actress award, Brit. Guild TV Producers and Dirs., 1966, Variety Club of Great Britain award, 1992, Laurence Olivier award Actress of the Yr. in a Revival for A Touch of the Poet; fellow Brit. Film Inst., 1988.*

**REDHEAD, RUTH WILLARD,** foreign language educator; b. Burlington, Vt., Dec. 6, 1924; d. Maxwell Van Buren and Blanche Kate (Wimble) Willard; m. Robert Sidney Redhead, Jan. 27, 1959. BEd. U. Vt., 1945, MA, 1954; PhD, U. Minn., 1971. Tchr. Marshfield (Vt.) H.S., 1945-47, West Lebanon (N.H.) H.S., 1947-50; instr. Lincoln (Ill.) Coll., 1951-55, Ft. Hays (Kans.) State Coll., 1956-59; prof. French S.D. State U., Brookings, 1962-93. Author: Themes and Images in the Fictional Works of Mme. de Lafayette, 1990. Named disting. prof. Bd. Regents S.D., 1991, disting. prof. emeritus, 1993; Officier des Palmes académiques, French Min. Edn., Paris, 1991 Mem. MLA, Am. Soc. French Acad. Palms, Am. Assn. Tchrs. French (S.D. chpt. treas. 1990-92), Soc. St. Simon. Home: 210 W Grant St Apt 619 Minneapolis MN 55403-2246

**REDICK, J.J. (JONATHAN CLAY REDICK),** college basketball player; b. Cookeville, Tenn., June 24, 1984; s. Ken and Jeanie. BA in History, Duke Univ., 2006. Coll. basketball player Duke Univ. Blue Devils, 2002—06. Recipient Sullivan award for Top Amateur Athlete, 2005, John Wooden award, 2006. Achievements include all-ACC Freshman Team honoree,

2002-2003; named Rupp Nat. Player Yr., 2004-2006, also unanimous First Team all-America coaches selection, First Team All-American AP, USBWA, NABC, ESPN.com, Sporting News, Baketball News, ACC Player Yr; eclipsed record for all-time ACC Leading Career Scorer, 2006; drafted 11th in NBA draft by Orlando Magic, 2006. Office: Orlando Magic 8701 Maitland Summit Blvd Orlando FL 32810*

**REDING, JOHN ANTHONY, JR.,** lawyer; b. Orange, Calif., May 26, 1944; AB, U. Calif., Berkeley, 1966, JD, 1969. Bar: Calif. 1970, U.S. Dist. Ct. (no. ctrl., ea. and so. dists.) Calif., U.S. Claims Ct., U.S. Supreme Ct. Formerly mem. Crosby, Heafey, Roach & May P.C., Oakland, Calif.; ptnr. Paul, Hastings, Janofsky & Walker, LLP, San Francisco, global chmn. litig. dept. Mem. ABA (sects. on litigation, intellectual property, and natural resources, energy and environ. law, coms. on bus. torts, internat. law, trial practice and torts and insurance), Am. Intellectual Property Law Assn., State Bar Calif. (sect. on litigation), Bar Assn. San Francisco, Assn. Bus. Trial Lawyers. Office: Paul Hastings Janofsky & Walker LLP 55 Second St 24th Floor San Francisco CA 94105-3441 Office Phone: 415-856-7004. Office Fax: 415-865-7104. Business E-Mail: jackreding@paulhastings.com.

**REDISH, EDWARD FREDERICK,** physicist, researcher; b. N.Y.C., Apr. 1, 1942; s. Jules and Sylvia Redish; m. Janice Copen, June 18, 1967; children: A. David, Deborah. AB, Princeton U., 1963; PhD, MIT, 1968. CTP fellow U. Md., College Park, 1968-70, from asst. prof. to assoc. prof., 1970-79, prof., 1979—, chmn. dept. phys. astronomy, 1982-85. Vis. scholar U. Calif., Berkeley, 1999-00; vis. prof. Ind. U., Bloomington, 1985-86, U. Wash., Seattle, 1992-93; vis. fgn. collaborator CEN, Saclay, France, 1973-74; co-dir. Md. U. Project in Physics and Ednl. Tech., 1983-93, Comprehensive Unified Physics Learning Environment, 1989-96; mem. Nuclear Sci. Adv. Com., Dept. of Energy/NSF, 1987-90; mem. program adv. com. Ind. U. Cyclotron Facility, 1985-89, chmn., 1986-89; mem. Internat. Commn. on Physics Edn., 1993-2002, sec., 1999-2002. Author: Teaching Physics with the Physics Suite, 2003, (textbook) Understanding Physics, 2003, (software) Orbits, 1989, The M.U.P.P.E.T. Utilities, 1994, The Comprehensive Unified Physics Learning Environment, 1994; editor: (conf. procs.) Computers in Physics Instrn., 1990, Internat. Conf. Undergrad. Physics Edn., 1997, Internat. Summ. Sch. Phys. Edn. Res., 2004, Jour. Physics Edn. Rsch. Supplement to Am. Jour. Physics., 1999—2004. Named Sr. Resident Rsch. Assoc., NAS-NRC, 1977-78; recipient Inst. medal Ctrl. Rsch. Inst. for Physics, 1979, Leo Schubert award Wash. Acad. Sci., 1988, Educator award Md. Assn. Higher Edn., 1989, Glover award Dickinson Coll., 1991, Forman award Vanderbilt U., 1996, NSF Disting. Tchg. scholar, 2005; Lilly fellow U. Md., 2005, Dist. Scholar Tchr., 2006—. Fellow AAAS, Am. Phys. Soc. (mem. com. edn. 2004—, chair 2005), Wash. Acad. Sci.; mem. Am. Assn. Physics Tchrs. (Robert A. Millikan medal 1998). Office: U Md Dept Physics College Park MD 20742-4111

**REDISH, MARTIN HARRIS,** legal educator; b. Lynbrook, NY, Aug. 16, 1945; m. Caren Beverly Redish; 1 child, Jessica. AB, U. Pa., 1967; JD magna cum laude, Harvard U., 1970. Bar: NY 1971, US Dist. Ct. (so. dist.) NY 1971, US Ct. Appeals (2d cir.) 1971, US Ct. Appeals (7th cir.) 1973. Law clk. Honorable J. Joseph Smith US Ct. Appeals (2d cir.), 1970—71; assoc. Proskauer, Rose, Goetz & Mendelsohn, NYC, 1971—73; asst. prof. Northwestern U. Sch. Law, Chgo., 1973—76, assoc. prof., 1976—78, prof., 1978—90, Louis and Harriet Ancel prof. law and pub. policy, 1990—. Vis. assoc. prof. law Cornell U., 1977, Stanford U., 1977; vis. prof. law U. Mich., 1987—88; mem. 7th Cir. Rules Adv. Com.; cons. U.S. Senate Jud. Com. Author: Federal Jurisdiction: Tensions in the Allocation of Judicial Power, 1980, Federal Courts: Cases, Comments and Questions, 1983, Freedom of Expression: A Critical Analysis, 1984, The Constitution as Political Structure, 1995, Money Talks: Speech, Economic Power and the Values of Democracy, 2001; co-author: Constitutional Law: Principles and Policy, 1987, Civil Procedure: A Modern Approach, 1989, Understanding Federal Court Jurisdiction, 1999; contbr. articles to profl. jours. Mem. Am. Coll. Trial Lawyers, Am. Law Inst. Office: Northwestern U Sch Law 357 E Chicago Ave Chicago IL 60611-3059 Office Phone: 312-503-8545. E-mail: m-redish@law.northwestern.edu.

**REDLENER, IRWIN ELLIOT,** health facility administrator, educator; b. Bklyn., 1944; MD, U. Miami, 1969; DSc (hon.), Hunter Coll. Intern Columbia Presbyterian Med. Ctr, 1969—70; resident Colo. Med. Ctr, 1970—71, Jackson Meml. Hosp, 1973—74; dir. VISTA Health ctr., Ark., 1971—73; dir. grants, med. dir. USA for Africa, Hands Across Am., 1986—87; pres, founder Children's Health Fund, NYC, 1987—2003; pres. Children's Hosp. Montefiore Med. Ctr., dir. child health network and cmty. pediatrics; dir. Nat. Ctr. Disaster Preparedness Columbia U., 2003—, assoc. dean, prof. clin. pub. health and pediats. Mailman Sch. Pub. Health, 2006—. Former chmn. Nat. Adv. Coun. on Nat. Health Svc. Corps.; vice chmn. health profl. rev. group. The White House Task Force on Nat. Health Care Reform, 1993; spkr. in field. Office: Childrens Health Fund 215 W 125 th St New York NY 10027 Office Phone: 212-535-9400. Office Fax: 212-535-7488. E-mail: ir2110@columbia.edu.

**REDLICH, NORMAN,** lawyer, educator; b. N.Y.C., Nov. 12, 1925; s. Milton and Pauline (Durst) R.; m. Evelyn Jane Grobow, June 3, 1951; children: Margaret Bonny-Claire, Carrie Ann, Edward Grobow. AB, Williams Coll., 1947, LLD (hon.), 1976; LLB, Yale U., 1950; LLM, NYU, 1955; LLD (hon.), John Marshall Law Sch., 1990. Bar: N.Y. 1951. Practiced in N.Y.C., 1951-59; assoc. prof. law NYU, 1960-62, prof. law, 1962-74, assoc. dean Sch. Law, 1974-75, dean Sch. Law, 1975-88, dean emeritus, 1992—, Judge Edward Weinfeld prof. law, 1982—; counsel Wachtell, Lipton, Rosen & Katz, N.Y.C., 1988—. Editor-in-chief Tax Law Rev., 1960-66; mem. adv. com. Inst. Fed. Taxation, 1963-68; exec. asst. corp. counsel, N.Y.C., 1966-68, 1st asst. corp. counsel, 1970-72, corp. counsel, 1972-74; asst. counsel Pres. Commn. on Assassination Pres. Kennedy, 1963-64; mem. com. on admissions and grievances U.S. 2d Circuit Ct. Appeals, 1978—, chmn., 1978-87. Author: Professional Responsibility: A Problem Approach, 1976, Constitutional Law, Cases and Materials, 1983, rev. edit., 1996, 2001, Understanding Constitutional Law, 1995, rev. edit., 1999; contbr. articles in field. Chmn. commn. on law and social action Am. Jewish Congress, 1978—, chmn. governing coun., 1996; mem. Borough Pres.'s Planning Bd. Number 2, 1959-70, counsel N.Y Com. to Abolish Capital Punishment, 1958-77; mem. N.Y.C. Bd. Edn., 1969; mem. bd. overseers Jewish Theol. Sem., 1973—; trustee Law Ctr. Found. of NYU, 1975—, Freedom House, 1976-86, Vt. Law Sch., 1977-99, 2003—, Practicing Law Inst., 1980-99; trustee Lawyers Com. for Civil Rights Under Law, 1976—, co-chmn., 1979-81; bd. dirs. Legal Aid Soc. 1983-88, NAACP Legal Def. Fund, 1985—, Greenwich House, 1987—. Decorated Combat Infantryman's Badge. Mem. ABA (coun. legal edn. and admissions to bar 1981—), vice chmn. 1987-88, chmn. 1989-90, equal opportunities in legal profession 1986-92, ho. of dels. 1991—), Assn. of Bar of City of N.Y. (exec. com. 1975-79, professionalism com. 1988-92), com. on capital punishment 1998—). Office: 51 W 52nd St Fl 30 New York NY 10019-6119

**REDMAN, BARBARA KLUG,** nursing educator; b. Mitchell, SD; d. Harlan Lyle and Darlien Grace (Bock) Klug; m. Robert S. Redman, Sept. 14, 1958; 1 child, Melissa Darlien. BS, S.D. State U., 1958; MEd, U. Minn., 1959, PhD, 1964; LHD (hon.), Georgetown U., 1988; DSc (hon.), U. Colo., 1991; M in Bioethics, U. Pa., 2004, MBE, 2004. RN. Asst. prof. U. Wash., Seattle, 1964-69; assoc. dean U. Minn., Mpls., 1969-75; dean Sch. Nursing U. Colo., Denver, 1975-78; VA scholar VA Cen. Office, Washington, 1978-81; postdoctoral fellow Johns Hopkins U., Balt., 1982-83; exec. dir. Am. Assn. Colls. Nursing, Washington, 1983-89, ANA, Washington, 1989-93; prof. nursing Johns Hopkins U., Balt., 1993-95; dean, prof. Sch. Nursing U. Conn., Storrs, 1995-98; dean Coll. Nursing Wayne State U., Detroit. Vis. fellow Kennedy Inst. Ethics, Georgetown U., 1993-94; fellow in med. ethics Harvard Med. Sch., 1994-95. 2004—; vis. scholar U. Pa. Ctr. for Bioethics, 2004—. Author: Practice of Patient Education, 1968—; contbr. articles to profl. jours. Bd. dirs. Friends of Nat. Libr. of Medicine, Washington, 1987—. Recipient Disting.

---

Alumnus award S.D. State U., 1975, Outstanding Achievement award U. Minn., 1989. Fellow Am. Acad. Nursing. Home: 12425 Bobbink Ct Potomac MD 20854-3005 Office: Wayne State U 5557 Cass Ave Detroit MI 48202-3615

**REDMAN, CLARENCE OWEN,** lawyer; b. Joliet, Ill., Nov. 23, 1942; s. Harold F. and Edith L. (Read) R.; m. Barbara Ann Pawlan, Jan. 26, 1964 (div.); children: Scott, Steven; m. 2d, Carla J. Rozycki, Sept. 24, 1983. BS, U. Ill., 1964, JD, 1966, MA, 1967. Bar: Ill. 1966, U.S. Dist. Ct. (ea. dist.) Ill. 1967, U.S. Ct. Appeals (7th cir.) 1973, U.S. Ct. Appeals (4th cir.) 1982, U.S. Supreme Ct. 1975. Assoc. Keck, Mahin & Cate, Chgo., 1969-73, ptnr., corp. ptnr., 1973—, CEO, 1986-97; of counsel Lord, Bissell & Brook, Chgo., 1997—. Spl. asst. atty. gen. Ill., 1975-8; bd. dirs. AMCOL Internat. Corp. Mem. bd. visitors U. Ill. Coll. of Law, 1991-95. Capt. U.S. Army, 1967-69. Decorated Bronze Star. Mem. Ill. State Bar Assn. (chmn. young lawyers sect. 1977-78, del. assembly 1978-81, 84-87), Seventh Cir. Bar Assn. Office: Lord Bissell & Brook 111 South Wacker Dr Chicago IL 60606

**REDMAN, ERIC,** lawyer; b. Seattle, June 3, 1948; s. M. Chandler and Marjorie Jane (Sachs) R.; children: Ian Michael, Graham James, Jing, Amanda; m. Heather Bell, 1996. AB, Harvard U., 1970, JD, 1975; BA, Oxford U., 1972, MA, 1980. Bar: Wash. 1975, U.S. Dist. Ct. (we. dist.) Wash. 1975, D.C. 1979, U.S. Ct. Appeals (9th cir.) 1981, U.S. Supreme Ct. 1983. Asst. U.S. senator W.G. Magnuson, Washington and Seattle, 1968-71, 74-75; assoc. Preston, Thorgrimson et al, Seattle, 1975-78, ptnr., 1979-82, Heller, Ehrman, White & McAuliffe, Seattle, 1983—. Author: Dance of Legislation, 1973; also book revs., articles. Office: Heller Ehrman LLP 701 5th Ave Ste 6100 Seattle WA 98104-7098 Office Phone: 206-389-6000. E-mail: eric.redman@hellerehrman.com.

**REDMAN, ROBERT SHELTON,** pathologist, dentist; b. Fargo, N.D., Aug. 1, 1935; s. Kenneth and Elizabeth Francis (McMillan) R.; m. Barbara Darlien Klug, Sept. 14, 1958; 1 child, Melissa Darlien Redman Johnson. Student, S.D. State U., 1953-55; BS, DDS, U. Minn., 1959, MSD, 1963; PhD, U. Wash., 1969. Cert. Am. Bd. Oral and Maxillofacial Pathology. Clin. asst. prof. sch. dentistry U. Minn., Mpls., 1963-64, assoc. prof., 1969-75; assoc. prof. sch. dentistry U. Colo., Denver, 1975-78; staff dentist, chief oral pathology rsch. lab. Dept. VA Med. Ctr., Denver, 1975-78, Washington, 1978—. Clin. assoc. prof. Balt. Coll. Dental Surgery U. Md., 1989—; cons. Children's Orthop. Hosp., Seattle, 1966-69; program specialist in oral biology Dept. VA, Washington, 1982-86; adj. scientist Nat. Inst. Dental and Craniofacial Rsch., NIH, 1997—. Contbr. 14 chpts. to books, over 100 articles to profl. jours.; mem. editl. bd. Jour. Dental Rsch., 1995-98, Biotech. and Histochemistry, 2000—; bd. reviewers Anatomical Record, 2004—. Mem. Biol. Stain Commn., 1999—, bd. trustees, 2002-2005. Capt. U.S. Army, 1959-61. Recipient Carl A. Schlack award Assn. Mil. Surgeons US, 1997. Fellow Am. Acad. Oral and Maxillofacial Pathology; mem. ADA, Am. Assn. Anatomists, Internat. Assn. Dental Rsch. (program chmn. salivary rsch. group 1982-86, sec.-treas. 1995, 2001, Salivary Rschr. of the Yr., salivary rsch. Group 2001), Soc. for In Vitro Biology, Omicron Kappa Upsilon. Presbyterian. Achievements include discovery and naming of an unique minor salivary gland in the rat; documentation of the relationship between weaning and maturation of salivary glands, of mitotic division of well-differentiated salivary gland cells of all types, including acinar, ductal and myoepithelial cells, of constant cell cycle length and very low rate of apoptosis in salivary glands during development and into maturity; determination of mode of inheritance of benign migratory glossitis, co-developer method to maintain salivary gland acinar cells in culture and several cell lines of these cells, documentation of head and neck cancer in smad 4 deficient mice. Office: Dept VA Med Ctr (151-I) Oral Pathology Rsch Lab 50 Irving St NW Washington DC 20422-0001

**REDMAN, TIMOTHY PAUL,** language educator, writer; b. Elmhurst, Ill., June 26, 1950; s. William Charles and Eileen Marie (Keenan) Redman. BA, Loyola U., Chgo., 1973; MA, U. Chgo., 1974, PhD, 1987. Instr. Loyola U., Rome, 1977, Ill. Inst. Tech., Chgo., 1980-84; lectr. English dept. Loyola U., Chgo., 1982-84, DePaul U., 1982—84; lectr. U. Wis., Parkside, 1984-85; instr. Ohio State U., Lima, 1985-87, asst. prof., 1987-89, U. Tex., Dallas, 1989-91, assoc. prof., 1991-98, prof., 1998—, assoc. dean, coll. master, 1991-92. Editor: Official Rules of Chess, 3d edit., 1987; author: Ezra Pound and Italian Fascism, 1991. Whiting fellow, 1981—82, NEH fellow, 1992—93. Mem.: MLA, U.S. Chess Trust (v.p.), PEN U.S.A. (pres. Tex. chpt.), Nat. Coun. Tchrs. English, U.S. Chess Fedn. (past pres.), World Chess Fedn. (gen. sec. Chess schs. com.), Roman Catholic. Office: U Tex Dallas Sch Arts & Humanities JO31 PO Box 830688 Richardson TX 75083-0688: US Chess Fedn PO Box 3967 Crossville TN 38557 Office Phone: 972-883-2775. Business E-Mail: redman@utdallas.edu.

**REDMAN, WILLIAM WALTER, JR.,** realtor; b. Statesville, NC, Oct. 15, 1933; s. William Walter and Mildred (Huie) R.; m. Elizabeth Ann Wilhelm, Dec. 28, 1956; children: Lisa Dawn, Kathryn Marlene, Adrienne Ann. Student, U. So. Calif., 1966; BS, Embry-Riddle Aeronat. U., 1972; postgrad., Jud. Coll., 1987. Enlisted U.S. Army, 1954, advanced through grades to lt. col., 1974, ret., 1974; dir. pub. rels. Northwestern State Bank, Statesville, 1974-76; pres. Redman Realty, Statesville, 1976-92; mem. N.C. Senate from 26th Dist., 1978-87, minority leader, 1986-87; commr. pub. utilities State of N.C., 1987-95; chmn. N.C. Utilities Commn., 1995—2001. Exec. dir. N.C. Telecom. Industry Assn.; exec. v.p. carolina Vus. Telephone Membership Assn.; mem. exec. com., vice chmn. com. on adminstrn., comm. Nat. Assn. Regulatory Utility Commrs.; chmn. bd. dirs. Nat. Regulatory Rsch. Inst., Ohio State U., 1993; mem. exec. com. Southeastern Assn. Regulatory Utilities Commrs.; past trustee Gardner-Webb Coll.; mem. bd. advisors Sch. Bus. Pub. Utility Regulatory Bd., N.Mex. State U.; dir. N.C. Solar Ctr.; past mem. N.C. Energy Policy Coun., N.C. Tax Rev. Bd.; bd. dirs. N.C. Child Advocay Inst., 1997, Assn. Excs. N.C. 1997—. Decorated DFC with oak leaf cluster, Bronze Star medal with two oak leaf clusters, Air medal with sixteen oak leaf clusters, Meritorious Svc. medal; recipient Valand award NC Mental Assns.; named to Inf. Officers Sch. Hall of Fame, Ft. Benning Ga., Disting. Mem. Regt., U.S. Transp. Corps, 1990; recipient 2 Long Leaf Pine award State of NC, 1987, 94. Mem. VFW (life), Ret. Officers Assn. (life), Nat. Assn. Adminstrv. Law Judges, Vietnam Helicopter Pilots Assn., Army Otter-Caribou Assn., Army Aviation Am. Assn., 1st Cavalry Divsn. Assn. (life), Am. Legion (life), Raleigh Exec. Club. Republican. Baptist. Address: 1320 Royalty Cir Statesville NC 28625-8230

**REDMANN, JOHN WILLIAM,** lawyer, consultant, school system administrator; b. New Orleans, Sept. 10, 1963; s. William Vincent and Ana Maria (Macouzet) R. BA in Psychology, BA in French, Loyola U. of the South, 1986, JD, 1989. Bar: La. 1990, U.S. Dist. Ct. (ea. dist.) La. 1990; cert. notary pub., La. Litigation law clk. Orleans Sewerage and Water Bd., New Orleans, 1989—90; law clk. to Hon. Judge Connolly Orleans Civil Dist. Ct., New Orleans, 1990—92; assoc. Exnicios & Nungesser, New Orleans, 1992—94; prin. Law Offices of John W. Redmann, New Orleans, 1994—. V.p., gen counsel Meridian Group, LLC, New Orleans, 1999—, 5 Lights, LLC, 2000—; v.p. L'Ecole Maternelle, 1998, also bd. dirs.; charter mem. alumni com. Loyola Law Sch. Moot Ct., 1991-96, chmn. 1980's decade ann. fund campaign. Chmn. 1995 Loyola Law Ann. Fund Campaign, New Orleans; charter mem./officer Lawyers Against Crime, Inc., New Orleans, 1995—. Mem. ATLA (traumatic brain injury litigation group 1997-2000), Nat. Inst. Trial Advocacy (diplomate), La. Trial Lawyers Assn. (leadership and membership coms. 1994-96) La. Bar Assn. (treas. Bench and Bar sect. 2001—), La. Bar Found., A.P. Tureaud Am. Inns. of Ct., Assn. of New Orleans Trial Lawyers, Supreme Ct. of La. Hist. Soc. (charter), So. Trial Lawyers Assn. (bd. dirs. 1998-2000), La. Hispanic C. of C. (bd. dirs., sec. 1999, gen. counsel 1999-2005, 1st v.p. 1999-2003), Young Leadership Counsel, Bards Bohemia (exec. bd. 1998-99, 2001—), Celtic Club of New Orleans (pres. 1997-98). Roman Catholic. Avocations: travel, foreign languages. Office: Law Office John W Redmann PLC 9701 Lake Forest Blvd Ste 103 New Orleans LA

---

70127-5403 Home: 5407 Macarthur Blvd New Orleans LA 70131-5313 Office Phone: 504-245-1995, 800-240-1995. Business E-Mail: advice@redmannlaw.com. E-mail: john@redmannlaw.com.

**REDMON, LARRY ALLEN,** agronomist, educator; s. Billy Lee and Edith Bernice Redmon; m. Yvonne Louise Redmon; children: Rebecca Anne Flint, Monica Louise Randolph. BS in Agronomy, Stephen F. Austin State U., 1987, MS in Agr., 1989; PhD, Tex. A&M U., College Station, 1989—92. Cert. Grassland Profl. Am. Forage & Grassland Coun., U.S., 2006. Asst. prof. Okla. State U., Stillwater, 1994—99; prof. Tex. A&M U., 1999—. Recipient Outstanding State Ext. Specialist, Okla. Assn. Ext. Agr. Agents, 1996, Outstanding Tchr., Coll. Agrl. Scis. & Natural Resources, Okla. State U. Student Agrl. Coun., 1997—98, Early Career award for Tech. Transfer, Am. Soc. Agronomy, So. Br., 2002, award in Excellence, Vice Chancellor for Agr., Tex. A&M U., 2004. Mem.: Soc. Range Mgmt. (assoc. editor 2002—04), Am. Forage and Grassland Coun. (bd. dirs. 2000—03), Crop Sci. Soc. Am., Am. Soc. Agronomy (bd. dirs. 2002—05). Office Phone: 979-845-2425.

**REDMOND, ANDREA,** executive recruiter; b. Glen Ellyn, Ill., Feb. 21, 1956; m. Bill Ferguson; 1 child, Duke. BS, No. Ill. Univ.; MBA, George Williams Coll. Asst. v.p. First Nat. Bank of Chgo., 1981—86; with Russell Reynolds Assoc., Chgo., 1986—, mng. dir., co-head, CEO/bd. services practice, 1994—. Mutual fund bd. mem. Fischer, Francis, Trees & Watts. Co-author (with Charles A. Tribbett III): Business Evolves, Leadership Endures, 2004. Bd. dir. Y-Me Breast Cancer Orgn., Chgo. Children's Meml. Hosp. Named one of 100 Most Influential Women, Crain's Chgo. Bus., 2004. Mem.: Chgo. Econ. Forum, Chgo. Club, Executives Club. Office: Russell Reynolds Assoc Inc Ste 2900 200 S Wacker Dr Chicago IL 60606-5802 Office Phone: 312-993-0704. Office Fax: 312-876-1919. Business E-Mail: aredmond@russellreynolds.com.

**REDMOND, ARTHUR J.,** insurance company executive; BBA, MBA, U. Wis. Mng. dir. global consumer insights and market info. Citibank, 1997—99; exec. dir. global consumer insights office Ford Motor Co., 1999—2002; sr. v.p., strategic mktg. Aetna Inc., 2002—05. Bd. trustees Mktg. Sci. Inst. Mem.: U.S. Census Adv. Com., Am. Mktg. Assn., European Soc. of Mktg. and Rsch.

**REDMOND, DAVID DUDLEY,** lawyer; b. Hartford, Conn., May 12, 1944; s. Robert LaVere and Dorothy Iva (Mylchreest) R.; m. Eugenia Blount Scott, Aug. 24, 1968; children: R. Scott, Sarah D. BA, Washington and Lee U., 1966, LLB, 1969. Bar: Va. 1970, U.S. Dist. Ct. (ea. dist.) Va. 1972, U.S. Ct. Appeals (4th cir.) 1972. Ptnr. Christian & Barton LLP, Richmond, Va., 1972—. Mem. editl. bd. Washington and Lee U. Law Rev., 1968—69. Chmn. bd. trustees St. Joseph's Villa, 2004—. Capt. U.S. Army, 1970—71. Decorated Bronze Star; named to Washington and Lee U. Athletic Hall of Fame. Mem.: Richmond Bar Assn. (exec. com. 1980), Va. Bar Assn., Va. State Bar, Washington and Lee Law Alumni Assn. (bd. dirs. 1993—2002, pres. 1995—96), Washington and Lee U. Alumni Assn. (pres. Richmond chpt. 1980—82, bd. dirs. 1997—99, 2003—, exec. com. 2005—), Omicron Delta Kappa. Office: Mutual Bldg Ste 1200 Richmond VA 23219 Office Phone: 804-697-4102. Business E-Mail: dredmond@cblaw.com.

**REDMOND, DONALD EUGENE, JR.,** neuroscientist, educator; b. San Antonio, June 17, 1939; s. Donald Eugene and Viola (Kellum) R.; m. Patricia Welder (Robinson), Dec. 22, 1972; one child Andy J. BA, So. Meth. U., 1961; MD, Baylor U., 1968; MAH, Yale U., 1987. Diplomate Am. Bd. Psychiatry and Neurology. With Lab. of Clin. Sci., NIMH, Bethesda, Md., 1973-74; asst. prof. psychiatry Yale U., New Haven, 1974-77; assoc. chief clin. neurol. sci. unit Conn. Mental Health Ctr., New Haven, 1974-87; assoc. prof. psychiatry Yale U., New Haven, 1978-87; pres. St. Kitts Bio Med. Rsch. Found., St. Kitts, West Indies, 1983—, Axion Rsch. Found., Hamden, Conn., 1985—; prof. psychiatry, dir. neurol. behavior lab. Yale U., New Haven, 1987—, dir. neurol. transplant program for neurol. diseases, 1987—; prof. neurol. surgery, 1993—; with Yale Univ., New Haven, 1993. Contbr. articles to profl. jour.; patentee in field. With USPHS, 1972-74. Recipient Rsch. Scientist Award NIMH, 1980-2001; Found. Fund Prize, Am. Psychiatric Assoc., 1981; grantee NIMH, 1974-91; Nat. Inst. Neurol. Diseases and Stroke, 1986—; others. Mem.: Internat. Soc. Motor Disturbances, Am. Soc. Neural Transplantation and Repair (coun. mem. 1994—98, pres. 2002), Am. Coll. Neuropsychopharmacology (fellow 2002—03). Office: Neurobehavior Lab 300 George St Ste 8107 New Haven CT 06511-6624 Business E-Mail: gene.redmond@yale.edu.

**REDMOND, JOHN,** oncologist; b. Tampa, Fla., July 21, 1944; s. John and Sara (Lee) R.; married; 1 child, Geoff. BS, West Point Acad., 1966; MD, Emory U., 1974. Diplomate Nat. Bd. Med. Examiners, Am. Bd. Internal Medicine. Chief hematology and oncology Walter Reed Meml. Hosp., Washington, 1987-90; dir. Rosenfeld Cancer Ctr. Abington (Pa.) Meml. Hosp., 1990—. Fellow ACP; mem. AMA, Am. Soc. Hematology, Am. Soc. Clin. Oncology, Am. Assn. Cancer Rsch., Phila. Coll. Physicians, Am. Assn. Cancer Edn., Pa. Med. Soc., Am. Cancer Soc. Avocation: bicycling. Office: Abington Meml Hosp 1200 Old York Rd Abington PA 19001-3788 E-mail: redhoarse@aol.com.

**REDMOND, JOHN ANDREW,** elementary school educator; b. Balt., June 18, 1970; d. James Albert and Lynn Taylor (Chambers) R. BA in Geography, U. Md., Balt., 1988—. Library page Calvert County Pub. Libr., Prince Frederick, Md., 1987-88; playground supr. Chesapeake Beach Town Hall, Md., 1988; substitute tchr. Calver County Pub. Schs., Prince Frederick, 1988—, Paul Douglass Tchr. scholar, 1988. Mem. Future Tchrs. of Md. (state exec. bd., pres. 1990—), U. Md. At Balt. Future Educators Club (pres. 1990—), Ambassadors Club (pres. 1990—). Republican. Methodist. Avocations: swimming, sailing, gardening, community service. Home: 2060 Clearview Dr Owings MD 20736-4000

**REDMOND, MICHAEL R.,** ophthalmologist; b. Sterling, Ill. MD, St. Louis U., 1968. Diplomate Am. Bd. Ophthalmology. Intern St. Louis U. Group Hosps., 1968—69, resident ophthalmology, 1971—74; fellow pediat. ophthalmology U. Iowa Hosps.-Clinics, Iowa City, 1974—75; ophthalmologist Ophthalmology Group Practice, Pensacola, Fla., 1975—. Attending physician West Fla. Hosp., Pensacola, Sacred Heart Hosp., Pensacola. Mem.: AMA, Fla. Soc. Ophthalmology, Fla. Med. Assn., Am. Acad. Pediat., Am. Assn. for Pediat. Ophthalmology and Stiabesmas, Am. Coll. Surgery, Am. Acad. Ophthalmology (bd. dirs. 1999—99, pres. 2003—, chmn., vice chmn. coun.). Office: 8333 N Davis Hwy Pensacola FL 32514-6050 Office Phone: 850-474-8436. Business E-Mail: michael.redmond@medicalcenterclinic.com.

**REDMONT, BERNARD SIDNEY,** dean, communications educator; b. NYC, Nov. 8, 1918; s. Morris Abraham and Bessie (Kamerman) R.; m. Joan Rothenberg, Mar. 12, 1940; children: Dennis Foster, Jane Carol. BA, CCNY, 1938; M.J., Columbia U., 1939; D.H.L., Fla. Internat. U., 1980. Reporter, book reviewer Bklyn. Daily Eagle, 1936-38; free lance corr. Europe, 1939, Mexico City, 1939-40; telegraph editor, editorial writer Herkimer (N.Y.) Evening Telegram, 1941-42; newswriter U.S. Office of Inter-Am. Affairs (Washington shortwave radio newscasts to Latin Am.), 1942-43, dir. News div., 1944-46; staff corr., bur. chief U.S. News & World Report, Buenos Aires and Paris, 1946-51; columnist Continental Daily Mail, Paris, 1951-53; chief corr. English Lang. World News Service Agence France-Presse, Paris, 1953-65; European corr. Paris news bur. chief Westinghouse Broadcasting Co., Paris, 1961-76; corr., bur. chief CBS News, Moscow, 1976-79, corr. Paris, 1979-81; prof. journalism, dir. broadcast journalism program, dean Boston U. Coll. Communication, 1982-86, dean emeritus, prof. journalism, 1986—, mem. adv. bd. Latin Am. journalism program, 1989—. Cons. Exec. Svc. Corps. of New Eng., 1991—, Internat. Exec. Svc. Corps, 1992—. Author: Risks Worth Taking: The Odyssey of a Foreign Correspondent, Univ. Press of Am., 1992, Friendly Moderation, 1997. Served with USMCR, 1943-44. Decorated Purple Heart, chevalier Legion of Honor (France); recipient award for advancement of journalism Columbia U., 1986, Townsend

Harris medal for life achievement, 1991, Yankee Quill award for disting. contbns. to betterment of journalism, 1995; Pulitzer travel fellow; named to Commns. Hall of Fame CCNY, 2002 Mem. Overseas Press Club (award best radio reporting from abroad 1968, 73), Soc. Profl. Journalists, Nat. Press Club, Anglo-American Press Assn. of Paris (pres. 1961, treas. 1970-73, sec. 1974-76) Unitarian Universalist. *Life has more meaning when it affirms, with grace, the Yang and the Yin, reconciling opposites--independence, yet cooperative effort and community caring; courage and hard work, yet moderation and generosity; hatred of injustice, yet kindness,fairness and compassion.*

**REDNAM, KRISHNA RAO VENKATA,** ophthalmologist; b. Visakhapatnam, India, Aug. 1, 1949; MD, Andhra Med. Coll., 1971. Diplomate Am. Bd. Ophthalmology. Internist King George Hosp., Visakhapatnam, 1971-73, res. ophthamology, 1973-76; resident in surgery Jewish Hosp. and Med. Ctr., Bklyn., 1976-77; fellow in glaucoma Eye and Ear Infirmary, 1977-79; fellowship retina & citreous Ill. Eye and Ear Infirmary, Chgo., 1979-82; active staff St. Josephs Hosp., Kirkwood, Mo., 1983—; courtesy staff St. Lukes Hosp., Chesterfield, Mo., 1983—, Alexian Bros., St. Louis, Mo., 1984—; Lutheran Med. Ctr., St. Louis, Mo., 1985—; Courtesy staff St. Anthony Med. Ctr., St. Louis, 1985—; assoc. Depaul Med. Ctr., Bridgeton, Mo., 1985—; staff Out Patient Surg. Ctr., St. Louis, 1986—; assoc. St. Marys Eye Ctr., St. Louis, Mo., 1987—, 1988—; courtesy staff Christian Hosp., St. Louis, Mo., 1993—; provisional staff Mo. Bapt. Hosp., St. Louis, Mo., 1995—. Fellow ACS, Am. Acad. Ophthalmology, Internat. Coll. Surgeons; mem. AMA, Am. Assn. Ophthalmology. Office: St Louis Eye Clinic 4530 Hampton Ave Saint Louis MO 63109-2238 also: St Louis Eye Clinic 135 W Adams Ave Kirkwood MO 63122-4043 Office Phone: 314-821-2002.

**REDO, DAVID LUCIEN,** investment company executive; b. Lakewood, Ohio, Sept. 1, 1937; s. Joseph L. and Florence M. (Morse) R.; m. Judy L. Ijams, Aug. 4, 1962; children: Jenny, Mark. BSEE, U. Calif., Berkeley, 1961; MBA, U. Santa Clara, Calif., 1967. Registered investment advisor. Asst. engring. mgr. AT&T, N.Y.C., 1968-71; pension fund mgr. Pacific Telephone, San Francisco, 1971-77; mng. dir. Fremont Group (formerly Bechtel Investments Inc.), San Francisco, 1977—2002; chmn., CEO Fremont Investment Advisors, Inc., San Francisco, 1986—2000; prin., portfolio mgr. Wetherby Asset Mgmt., San Francisco, 2003—. Bd dirs. Sit/Kim Internat Investments; mem. adv. bd. Callan Assocs.; chmn. emeritus Fremont Mutual Funds, 2000—03, chmn., CEO, 1988—2000. Common. investment com. U. Calif. Found., 1988—2001; mem. bd. advisors Sentinel Pension Inst., 1978—2001; trustee U. Calif., Berkeley, 1988—2001, trustee emeritus, 2001—. Mem.: Internat. Assn. Fin. Planners. Avocations: golf, travel, reading, walking. Office: Wetherby Asset Mgmt 3rd Fl 417 Montgomery San Francisco CA 94104

**REDO, S(AVERIO) FRANK,** retired surgeon; b. Bklyn., Dec. 28, 1920; s. Frank and Maria (Guida) R.; m. Maria Lappano, June 27, 1948; children: Philip, Martha. BS, Queens Coll., 1942; MD, Cornell U., 1950. Diplomate Am. Bd. Thoracic Surgery, Am. Bd. Surgery (pediatric surgery). Intern in surgery NY Hosp., NYC, 1950-51, asst. resident surgeon, 1951-56, resident surgeon, 1956-57, asst. attending surgeon, 1958-60, attending surgeon, 1960-66, surgeon in charge pediatric surgery, 1960, attending surgeon, 1966—; practice medicine specializing in surgery; clin. asso. prof. surgery Cornell U. Med. Coll., 1963-72, prof., 1972—2006; ret. Author: Surgery in the Ambulatory Child, 1961, Principles of Surgery in the First Six Months of Life, 1976, Atlas of Surgery in the First Six Months of Life, 1977; contbr. articles to profl. jours.; patentee in field. Served to capt. USAAF, 1942-46. Fellow ACS, Am. Coll. Chest Physicians; mem. Harvey Soc., Pan Am. Med. Assn., Soc. Univ. Surgeons, Am. Acad. Pediatrics, Am. Fedn. for Clin. Research, Internat. Cardiovascular Soc., Am. Surg. Assn., Am. Assn. Thoracic Surgery, Soc. for Surgery Alimentary Tract, Am. Soc. Artificial Internat. Organs, Am. Acad. Pediatrics, Assn. Advancement Med. Instrumentation, Soc. Thoracic Surgeons, Internat. Soc. Surgery, NY Gastroent. Soc., NY Acad. Sci., NY Cardiovascular Soc., NY Acad. Medicine, NY Soc. Thoracic Surgery, NY Pediatric Soc., Med. Soc. County NY, Queens Coll. Alumni Assn. (gov. 1962—), Sigma Xi. Home: 435 E 70th St New York NY 10021-5342 Personal E-mail: sfredo1@aol.com. *My life is based on the principles of doing as much for others as possible and doing no harm; to offer advice only when asked; to apply myself unstintingly, but not selfishly, to my work; to learn from my mistakes; to strive for perfection; and to always have a project and a dream.*

**REDPATH, JOHN SLONEKER, JR.,** lawyer, publishing executive; b. Temple, Tex., Mar. 14, 1944; BA, Princeton U., 1966; JD, U. Mich., 1973; LLM, NYU, 1978. Bar: U.S. Dist. Ct. (so. dist.) N.Y. 1975. Assoc. Dewey, Ballantine, Bushby, Palmer & Wood, N.Y.C., 1974-78; assoc. counsel film programming Home Box Office, Inc., N.Y.C., 1978-79, chief counsel programming, 1979-80, asst. gen. counsel, 1980-81, v.p., gen. counsel, 1981-83, sr. v.p., gen. counsel, 1983-94, exec. v.p., gen. counsel, 1994—2002; sr. v.p., gen. counsel Time Inc., N.Y.C., 2003—. Lt. USNR, 1966-69. Mem. ABA, N.Y. State Bar Assn., Assn. Bar City N.Y. Office: Time Inc 1271 Ave of the Americas New York NY 10020 Business E-Mail: john_redpath@timeinc.com.*

**REDSHAW, JAMES DOUGLAS,** neurologist; b. Montreal, Aug. 5, 1952; s. Robert Leslie Redshaw and Dorothy Ann Levine; m. Evelyn Lee Downs, Dec. 28, 1979; children: Jeffrey Devin, Timothy Douglas. BSc in Biology, Laurentian U., 1975; PhD in Med. Sci., McMaster U., 1980; MD, U. Calgary, 1986. Postdoctoral fellow Alta. Heritage Found. for Med. Rsch., Calgary, 1980-86; med. resident internal medicine U. Calgary Med. Sch., 1986-87; resident in neurology U. Western Ont., London, 1987-89; clin. fellow in neurology U. Alta., Edmonton, 1989-91; neurologist Boise (Idaho) Neurol. Cons., 1991—. Mem. med. staff St. Alphonsus Med. Ctr./St. Lukes Med. Ctr., Boise, 1991—, chmn. dept. neurology/neurosurgery, Boise, 1997-99. Contbr. articles to profl. jours. Mem. profl. adv. bd. Epilepsy Found. Idaho, Boise, 1991—. Mem. Am. Acad. neurology, Idaho Med. Assn., Idaho Neurol. Inst. (bd. dirs. 1994-2000), Nat. Stroke Assn. Avocations: photography, skiing, water-skiing. Home: 4155 W Quail Ridge Dr Boise ID 83703 Office: Boise Neurol Cons 999 N Curtis Rd Ste 506 Boise ID 83706

**REDSTONE, SHARI E.,** amusement company executive; 3 children. JD, Boston U., 1978, M in Tax Law, 1980. Lawyer, Boston area, 1978-93; v.p. corp. planning and devel. Nat. Amusements, Dedham, to 1994, exec. v.p. 1994—2000, pres., also bd. dir., 2000—. Mem. exec. com. Boston U. Sch. Law; bd. dir. Midway Home Entertainment, 2004, Viacom, Global Hyatt Corp., LaSalle Bank Corp., The Marmon Group; chmn., CEO Rising Star Media, CineBridge Ventures, Inc.; co-chmn., co-CEO MovieTickets.com; bd. dir., chair governance com. William Wrigley Jr. Co., 1994—2005. Bd. dir. Jewish Philanthropies; bd. overseers Harvard U., 2002—, co-chair com. on Allston; bd. dir., exec. com. Nat. Assn. Theatre Owners; trustee, Dana Farber Cancer Inst. Tufts U.; mem. adv. com. Tufts Hillel. Named one of 50 Women to Watch, Wall St. Jour., 2005. Office: 200 Elm St Dedham MA 02026-4536*

**REDSTONE, SUMNER MURRAY,** broadcast executive, lawyer; b. Boston, May 27, 1923; s. Michael and Belle (Ostrovsky) R.; children: Brent Dale, Shari Ellin. BA, Harvard U., 1944, LLB, 1947; LLD (hon.), Boston U., 1994; LHD (hon.), N.Y. Inst. Tech., 1996. Bar: Mass. 1947, U.S. Ct. Appeals (1st cir.) 1948, U.S. Ct. Appeals (8th cir.) 1950, U.S. Ct. Appeals (9th cir.) 1948, D.C. 1951, U.S. Supreme Ct. 1952. Law sec. U.S. Ct. Appeals (9th Cir.), San Francisco, 1947-48; instr. law and labor mgmt. U. San Francisco, 1947; spl. asst. to atty. gen. US Dept. Justice, Washington, 1948-51; ptnr. Ford, Bergson, Adams, Borkland & Redstone, Washington, 1951-54; CEO Nat. Amusements Inc., Dedham, Mass., 1967—, pres., 1967—99, chmn. bd., 1986—, CBS Corp., 2006—, Viacom, Inc., NYC, 1987—2006, CEO, 1996—2006, exec. chmn. bd., 2006—. Prof. Boston U. Law Sch., 1982, 85-86; bd. dirs., adv. coun. TV Acad. Arts and Scis. Found.; vis. prof. Brandeis U., Waltham, Mass.; lectr. Harvard Law Sch., Cambridge, Mass.; Judge on Kennedy Libr. Found., (sel. comm. John F. Kennedy Profile in Courage award); bd. trustee Mus. TV and Radio; past pres. Theatre Owners Am. Chmn. met. divsn. NE

---

Combined Jewish Philanthropies, Boston, 1963; mem. exec. bd. Combined Jewish Philanthropies of Greater Boston, chmn. metropolitan divsn.; mem. corp. New Eng. Med. Ctr., 1967—, Mass. Gen. Hosp. Corp.; trustee Children's Cancer Rsch. Found.; founding trustee Am. Cancer Soc.; chmn. Am. Cancer Crusade, State of Mass., 1984-86; Art Lending Libr.; sponsor Boston Mus. Sci.; chmn. Jimmy Fund Found., 1960; v.p. mem. exec. com. Will Rogers Meml. Fund; hon. chmn. Will Rodgers Motion Picture Pioneers Found.; bd. dirs. Boston Arts Festival; bd. overseers Dana Farber Cancer Ctr., Boston Mus. Fine Arts; mem. presdl. adv. com. on arts John F. Kennedy Libr. Found., also judge ann. John F. Kennedy Profile in Courage Award com.; chmn. Corp. Commn. on Edn. Tech., 1996—, presdl. apptd. chmn., 1996. 1st lt. AUS, 1943-45. Decorated Army Commendation medal; named 1 of 10 Outstanding Young Men in New Eng., Boston Jr. C. of C., 1958; recipient William J. German Human Rels. award Am. Jewish Com. Entertainment/Comm. Divsn., 1977, Silver Shingle award Boston U. Law Sch., 1985, Variety New Eng. Humanitarian award, 1989, Golden Plate award Am. Acad. Achievement, 1993, 32d Ann. Salute to Excellence Program, 1993, Bus. Excellence award U. So. Calif. Sch. Bus. Adminstrn., 1994, The Stephen S. Wise award The Am. Jewish Congress, 1994, Man of Yr. award MIPCOM, the Internat. Film and Programme Market for TV, Video, Cable and Satellite, 1994, The Legends in Leadership award Emory U., 1995, Allan K. Jonas Lifetime Achievement award Am. Cancer Soc., 1995, Humanitarian award Variety Club Internat., 1995, Expeditioner's award N.Y.C. Outward Bound Ctr., 1996, Patron Arts award Songwriter's Hall Fame, 1996, Vision 21 award N.Y. Inst. Tech., 1996, Trustees award NATAS, 1997, Ripple of Hope award Robert F. Kennedy Meml., 1998, Humanitarian award Nat. Conf. Christians and Jews, 1998; named Communicator of Yr., B'nai B'rith Comm./Cinema Lodge, 1980, Man of Yr., Entertainment Industries Divsn. of UJA Fedn., 1988, Pioneer of Yr., Motion Picture Pioneers, 1991, Grad. of Yr., Boston Latin Sch., 1989, Honoree 7th ann. fundraiser Montefiore Med. Ctr., 1995, Hall of Fame award Broadcasting and Cable mag., 1995; named one of Forbes Richest Americans, 2006. Mem. ABA, Nat. Assn. Theatre Owners (chmn. bd. dirs. 1965-66, exec. comm. 1995—), Theatre Owners Am. (asst. pres. 1960-63, pres. 1964-65), Motion Picture Pioneers (bd. dirs.), Boston Bar Assn., Mass. Bar Assn., Harvard Law Sch. Assn., Am. Judicature Soc., Masons, Union. Club, Harvard Club. Home: 200 Elm St Dedham MA 02027-9126 Office: Nat Amusements Inc PO Box 9126 Dedham MA 02027-9126 also: Viacom Inc 1515 Broadway New York NY 10036 also: CBS Corp 51 W 52nd St New York NY 10019-6188*

**REDWAY, JONATHAN,** lawyer; b. Washington, Mar. 9, 1960; s. Jim Redway and Tilda Kaufmann; m. Linn Kaiser, June 3, 1998; children: Ethan Parker, Eliza Parker. BA, Roanoke Coll., 1982; LLM, George Wash. U., 1989. Ptnr. Burns, Doane, Swecker & Mathis, LLP, Alexandria, Va., 1998—2004, White, Redway & Brown, LLP, Alexandria, 2004—. Editor: Trademark Law Reporter, 2003—03; contbr. articles to profl. jours. Office: White Redway & Brown LLP 1217 King St Alexandria VA 22314 Office Phone: 703-299-0035. E-mail: jon@wrb-ip.com.

**REDWINE, ROBERT PAGE,** physicist, researcher; b. Raleigh, N.C., Dec. 3, 1947; s. Robert Word and Hazel Virginia (Greer) R.; m. Jacqueline Nina Hewitt, Nov. 22, 1986; children: Keith Hewitt, Jonathan Hewitt. AB, Cornell U., 1969; PhD, Northwestern U., 1973. Rsch. assoc. Los Alamos (N.Mex.) Nat. Lab, 1973-77, staff sci., 1977-79; rsch. assoc. U. Berne, Switzerland, 1974-75; asst. prof. physics MIT, Cambridge, Mass., 1979-82, assoc. prof., 1982-89, prof., 1989—, dir. lab. nuclear sci., 1992-2000, dean for undergrad. edn., 2000—05. Contbr. articles to profl. jours. Fellow AAAS, Am. Phys. Soc. Office: MIT Bldg 26-453 Cambridge MA 02139

**REEB, W. SUZANNE,** retired elementary and middle school educator and nurse; b. Glascow, Ky., Jan. 14, 1932; d. Arthur Henry and Wilma (Kolb) R. BA, Asbury Coll., 1955; assoc. BS, Henry Ford C.C., 1960. Tchr. ctrl. elem. sch. grade 2 Fairborn (Ohio) City Schs., 1960-61, tchr. south elem. grade 5, 1961-65; tchr. social studies Lake Wales (Fla.) H.S., Polk County Sch. Bd., 1965-67; tchr. phys. edn. Avon Park (Fla.) Elem. Sch., Highlands County Sch. Bd., 1967-68, tchr. 5th and 6th grades, 1968-71, tchr. 7th and 8th grade Avon Park Mid. Sch., 1971—2000. Basketball coach Avon Park Mid. Sch., 1973-81, nat. jr. honor soc. peer tutor program, 1990-92, nat. geography bee coach, 1992-95, dept. chmn., team chmn., sch. improvement com. chmn., others, 1966-2000; mem. Polk coun. social studies Polk Edn. Assn., 1964-66. Vol. sch. nurse Avon Park Mid. Sch., 1971-93. Mem. NEA, Nat. Coun. for the Social Studies, Highlands County Coun. for the Social Studies, Highlands County Edn. Assn. Home: 2022 N Scenic Hwy Babson Park FL 33827-9798 Personal E-mail: flmug-z@juno.com.

**REECE, E. ALBERT,** dean, obstetrician, gynecologist, perinatologist; b. Spanishtown, Jamaica, Jan. 3, 1950; came to U.S., 1969; s. Wilfred Anderson Reece and Daisy Lucinda (Price) Reece Batten; m. Sharon Andrea Blake, July 28, 1974; children: Kelie, Brynne, Sharon-Andrea II. BS with honors, L.I. U., 1973; MD, NYU, 1978; PhD in Biochemistry, U. West Indies; MBA, Fox Sch. Bus. Mgmt., Temple U.; ob/gyn specialty diploma, Columbia U., 1982; maternal-fetal subspecialty diploma, Yale U., 1984. Diplomate Am. Bd. Ob-Gyn.; bd. cert. maternal-fetal medicine. Intern, resident Columbia U., Presbyn. Med. Ctr., N.Y.C., 1978-82; maternal-fetal medicine fellow Yale U. Sch. Medicine, 1982-84, asst. prof. ob-gyn New Haven, 1984-87, assoc. prof. ob-gyn, 1987-90; Abraham Roth prof., chmn. obstetrics, Gynecology and reproductive sciences Temple U. Sch. Medicine, Phila., 1991—2001; vice chancellor, dean, v.p. for med. sciences U. of Arkansas for Med. Sciences, Coll. of Med., Little Rock, 2002—. Elected IOM (chair pediatrics, obstetrics & gynecology, 2003 ), NAS, 1998. Co editor Diabetes Mellitus in Pregnancy Principles and Practice, 1st edit., 1988, 2nd edit., 1995, Medicine of the Fetus and Mother, 1992, 2nd edit., 1999, A Study Guide for Medicine of the Fetus and Mother, 1992, A Handbook of Medicine of the Fetus and Mother, 1995; co-author: Fundamentals in Obstetric and Gynecologic Ultrasonography, 1993; contbr. articles, abstract to profl. jours. in excess of 400. Mem. sci. adv. com. March of Dimes, 1993—; mem. sci. adv. bd. NIH-DC Infant Mortality Initiative, 1993—; mem. adv. com. Nat. Inst. Child Health and Human Diseases, NIH, 1994—; trustee Reading Rehab. Hosp., 1992—; mem. bioeffects com. AIUM, 1992-95. Grantee March of Dimes, 1985-87, Friedman Found., 1990-92, William Penn Found., 1989-93, Am. Diabetes Assn., 1991-93, NIH, 1992—; named one of Top 100 Black Physicians in Am., Black Enterprise Mag., 2001. Fellow Am. Coll. Ob-Gyn., Coll. Physicians Phila.; mem. Am. Diabetes Assn. (coun. on diabetes in pregnancy), Am. Inst. Ultrasound in Medicine, Hellenic Perinatal Soc. Greece (hon.), Nat. Med. Assn. (exec. com. 1987-88, chmn. ob-gyn. sect. 1991-93), NAS Inst. Medicine ((in conjunction with NRC) mem. adv. com., Human Embryonic Stem Cell Rsch., 2006-), New Haven Obstet. Soc., Soc. for Gynecol. Investigation, Soc. Perinatal Obstetricians (leader diabetes spl. interest 1992-94, bd. mem. 1995—), Phila. Perinatal Soc. (program chair 1993—), Phila. Obstet. Soc. (mem. coun. 1992-94). Seventh-Day Adventist. Office: Univ Ark for Med Sciences 4301 W Markham Slot 550 Little Rock AR 72205*

**REECE, GREGORY PAUL,** plastic surgeon, educator; b. Lake Charles, La., Aug. 16, 1957; s. John Paul Reece and Mary Agnes Robicheaux; m. Kelley Baldwin; children: John, Kelley. BS, McNeese State U., 1978; MD, La. State U., 1982. Intern U. Hosp. Jacksonville, Fla., 1982—83, gen. surgery resident 1983—87; plastic surgery resident Health Sci. Ctr., Houston, 1987—89; microsurgery fellow U. Tex. M.D. Anderson Cancer Ctr., Houston, 1989—90, asst. prof. plastic surgery, 1990—95, assoc. prof. plastic surgery, 1995—2002, prof., 2002—. Assoc. prof. plastic surgery U. Tex. Health Sci. Ctr., Houston; clin. prof. Baylor Coll. Medicine, Houston; assoc. mem. U. Tex. Ctr. Biomed. Engring., Houston. Contbr. web chpts. to profl. sites, articles to profl. jours. Grantee, Plastic Surgery Ednl. Found., 1999, NIH, 1999. Fellow: ACS; mem.: Tissue Engring. Soc., Am. Soc. Plastic Surgeons. Avocations: hiking, camping. Office: MD Anderson Cancer Ctr Dept Plastic Surgery Box 443 1515 Holcombe Blvd Houston TX 77030-4009 E-mail: greece@mdanderson.org.

---

**REECE, KARYN LYNN,** small business owner, consultant; b. Niagara Falls, N.Y., Apr. 14, 1967; d. George John and Eleanor Roberta (O'Donnell) R. BS in Bus., Empire State Coll., 1996. Lic. stockbroker and fin. cons., N.Y. Stockbroker B.C. Fin., Buffalo, 1989; ins. agt. Mutual of Omaha, Buffalo, 1989-90; fin. cons. Cook Fin. Group, Buffalo, 1990—; ind. fin. cons., 1992—. Mem. Women Everywhere. Republican. Avocations: drawing, aerobics, figure skating. Business E-Mail: mediainsights@adelphia.net.

**REECE, MAYNARD FRED,** artist, writer; b. Arnolds Park, Iowa, Apr. 26, 1920; s. Waldo H. and Inez V. (Latson) R.; m. June Carman, Apr. 7, 1946; children: Mark A., Brad D. Privately educated. Artist Meredith Pub. Co., Des Moines, 1938-40; artist, asst., mus. dir. Iowa Dept. History and Archives, Des Moines, 1940-50. Artist: Fish and Fishing, 1963, Waterfowl of Iowa, 1943; watercolor Trout, Saturday Evening Post (award of Distinctive Merit 1962); watercolors 73 Fish, Life mag. (cert. of merit 1955); print of Water's Edge Canada Geese for Am. Artist Collection, Am. Artist Mag., 1985; author, artist: The Waterfowl Art of Maynard Reece, 1985, The Upland Bird Art of Maynard Reece, 1997. Chmn. Gov.'s Com. Conservation of Outdoor Resource, 1963-64; trustee Iowa Natural Heritage Found., Des Moines, 1979—; hon. trustee Ducks Unltd., Inc., 1983—; trustee J.N. "Ding" Darling Conservation Found., Inc., Des Moines, 1962—. Served with AUS, 1943-45. Recipient awards for duck stamps and others Dept. Interior, 1948, 51, 59, 69, 71; recipient award Govt. Bermuda, 1963, award Iowa Conservation Commn., 1972, 77, 80, 81, award Fish and Game Commn., Little Rock, 1982, 88, award Tex. Parks and Wild Life Dept., 1983, award Nat. Fish & Wildlife Found., 1988, award Wash. State Dept. Wildlife, 1989, award Idaho Dept. Fish & Game, 1998, 4 awards Ill. Dept. of Natural Resources, 1997-2000; named Artist of Yr. Ducks Unltd. Inc., 1973; chosen Master Artist 1989, Leigh Yawkey Woodson Art Mus., Wausau, Wis., 1989. Mem. Nat. Audubon Soc., Nat. Wildlife Fedn., Izaak Walton League Am. (hon. pres. 1974-75). Home and Office: 5315 Robertson Dr Des Moines IA 50312-2133

**REECE, RICHARD KENT,** finance executive; b. Feb. 13, 1956; s. Robert Keith and Shirley (Fly) R.; m. Sonya Rebecca Branum, July 29, 1978; children: Emily, Eric, Ellen. BS in Acctg., Auburn U., 1978. CPA, Tex. Ptnr. Ernst & Young, Houston, 1978-93; v.p. fin., treas., CFO Belden Inc., St. Louis, 1993—2005; sr. v.p., CFO Acuity Brands, Inc., Atlanta, 2005—. Bd. dirs. Tex. Accts. & Lawyers for Arts, Houston, 1990-93, North Harriss County YMCA, Houston, 1991-93. Mem. AICPA, Nat. Investors Rels. Assn., Tex. Soc. CPAs. Office: Acuity Brands Inc 1170 Peachtree St NE Ste 2400 Atlanta GA 30309-7676 Office Phone: 404-853-1400.*

**REECE, SHEILA MARLENE,** health facility administrator, writer; b. Evansville, Ind., Sept. 3, 1965; d. Ralph Samuel and Marie Annette (Seitz) Truelove; m. Larry A. Reece, Sept. 2, 1995 (div. May 13, 2003); children: Brett M. Cargal, Bailey E. Cargal, Kathryn A., Trevor A. AS in Nursing, Vincennes U., Ind., 1986. RN Ind., 1986. Staff nurse Good Samaritan Hosp., Vincennes, Ind., 1986—92; Jasper Meml. Hosp. and Healthcare, Ind., 1992—99; dir. nursing Chandler Healthcare, Ind., 2000—01; med. staff mgr. Beverly Corp., Newburgh, Ind., 2001—04. Author: (children's book) A Pig For Kate. Vol. Dream Ctr., Evansville, Ind., 2003; youth leader United Meth. Ch., Loogootee, Ind., 1993—96. Achievements include invention of Temper Tamer. Personal E-mail: book_baby2002@hotmail.com.

**REECE, TERRY ALLEN,** travel company executive, Internet company executive; b. Texarkana, Ark., Jan. 2, 1958; s. Pendon and Mary Ella Reece; m. Julia Ruth Coleman, July 2, 2001; 5 children. Student, Cear Valley Coll.; cert. in bus. mgmt., Tex. Wesleyan U. Founder, chmn., pres., CEO Reece Enterprises, Detroit. Mem.: NAACP, Nat. Libr. Poetry, Tex. Writer's Assn., Internat. Poets Soc., Fellowship Christian Athletes (life). Address: 17175 Avon Ave Detroit MI 48219 E-mail: warrior_75210@yahoo.com.

**REECE, THOMAS L.,** manufacturing executive; BA, Western Mich. Univ., 1964. Office mgr., Ronnigen-Petter Divsn. Dover Corp., 1965—71, pres., Ronnigen-Petter Divsn., 1971, corp. pres., COO, 1993—94, CEO, 1994—2005, chmn., 1999—. Recipient Disting. Alumni award, Western Mich. Univ. Alumni Assn., 1998. Mem.: Nat. Assn. Manufacturers (bd. dir. 2005—). Office: Dover Corp 280 Park Ave New York NY 10017-1216*

**REECE, WANDA G.,** space station training engineer, writer; b. Tuscaloosa, Ala., June 21, 1956; d. James Elton and Mattie Lou (Keating) R. BA, U. Ala., Tuscaloosa, 1977; MA, U. Ala., 1981. News corr. Birmingham (Ala.) Post-Herald, The New York Times, N.Y.C.; assoc. editor Kentron Internat., Houston, Pickens County (Ala.) Herald, Sumter County (Ala.) Jour.; Spacelab tng. engr. and tng. adminstr. Teledyne Brown Engring., Huntsville, Ala.; engine ops. engr. Tec-Masters, Inc., Huntsville. Contbr. numerous news and feature articles to profl. jours. Recipient Scripps-Howard Found. award, 1981, 1st place writer's contest Randall House Pubrs., 1982, Internat. Cultural Diploma of Honor, 1990, Huntsville/Madison County Conv. and Visitors Bur. award, 1995; first recipient of Paul "Bear" Bryant Acad. scholar U. Ala., 1974. Assoc. fellow AIAA (first woman chmn. of Ala./Miss. sect., chmn. AIAA/ASTD tng. and simulation com'l., missile and space reunion com., spl. citation award 1990, Martin Schilling award 1990, Engr. of Yr. 1988, Profl. of Yr. 1992, Ala./Miss. sect.); mem. NAFE, Nat. Space Soc., Am. Soc. Tng. and Devel., Soc. Profl. Journalists, Internat. Soc. Logistics, Kappa Tau Alpha, Sigma Delta Chi.

**REED, ADAM VICTOR,** psychologist, engineer, information scientist; b. Jan. 11, 1946; s. Henry Kenneth and Eva (Tenenbaum) Reed; m. Barbara Irene Birnbaum, 1982 (div. 2000); 1 child, Halina Brooke. BSEE, MIT, 1967, MS in Biology, MSEE, 1970; PhD, U. Oreg., 1974. Rsch. programmer Artificial Intelligence Lab., MIT, Cambridge, 1965; rsch. engr. Hewlett Packard Co., Palo Alto, Calif., 1966-67; mem. rsch. staff Riverside Rsch. Inst., NYC, 1970-71; postdoctoral fellow, adj. asst. prof. Rockefeller U., NYC, 1974-78; asst. prof., vis. psychology New Sch. Social Rsch., NYC, 1977-82; mem. tech. staff Bell Labs., 1981—99; from assoc. prof. to prof. Calif. State U., LA, 2000—06, prof. Info. Sys., 2006—. Peer rev. referee NSF, others. Contbr. articles to profl. jours. in sci. and tech. adv. Llbertarian v.p. candidate Tonie Nathan, 1972; mem. Marlboro Twp. Bd. Edn., N.J., 1994-97. NDEA Title IV fellow, 1967-70, NSF fellow, 1970-73, NIMH Rsch. Svc. fellow, 1974-77. Mem. IEEE, APA, AAAS, Soc. Engring. Psychologists, Assn. Computing Machinery, Am. Soc. Cybernetics, N.Y. Acad. Sci., Sigma Xi, Tau Beta Pi, Eta Kappa Nu. Achievements include patents in field; first implementation of steepest descent, first statistically adaptive user interface, first switch-based facsimile server, first commercially deployed autonomous expert system; research on experimental psychology-response signals method. Business E-Mail: areed2@calstatela.edu.

**REED, ALFRED DOUGLAS,** retired academic administrator; b. Bristol, Tenn., July 18, 1928; s. Roy Theodore and Elizabeth Brown (Tuft) R.; m. Emily Joyce Freeman, Mar. 18, 1950 (dec. March 2005); children: Roy Frederick, Robert Douglas, David Clark, Timothy Wayne, Joseph William AB, Erskine Coll., 1949. Reporter Citizen-Times, Asheville, NC, 1949—51, city editor, 1953—60, mng. editor, 1962—63, assoc. editor, 1963—66, capital corr., 1959—66; asst. editor Presbyn. Jour., Weaverville, NC, 1951—52; assoc. editor Shelby Daily Star, NC, 1961—62; dir. pub. info. We. Carolina U., Cullowhee, NC, 1966—96, asst. to chancellor, 1996—2002. Cons. Devel. Office, East Carolina U. Greenville, 1980; bd. dirs. Wachovia Bank, Sylva, N.C., 1969-2003. Author: Prologue, 1968, Decade of Development, 1984; exec. editor: Western, The Mag. of Western Carolina University (1990-96. Mem. Asheville City Bd. Edn., 1958-62; vice chmn. bd. dirs. Sta. WCQS FM, We. N.C. Pub. Radio Inc., Asheville, 1978-88; bd. dirs. exec. com. chmn. Cherokee Hist. Assn., 1985-2004, We. N.C. Assn. Cmtys., 1985-2001, Jackson County Fund of N.C. Cmty. Found., 1991-93; mem. Hunter Libr. Adv. Bd., 1991-98, Pack Pl. Adv. Coun., Asheville, 1991-95. Recipient Paul A. Reid Disting. Svc. award We. Carolina U., 1980, Disting. Svc. award, 1996. Mem. Pub. Rels. Assn. We. N.C. (bd. dirs. 1988-98, treas. 1966-86), Coll. News Assn. Carolinas (bd. dirs. 1968-71, 80-82), Smoky Mountain Host Assn. (bd. dirs., 1st v.p. 1994-96, pres. 1996-98), Great Smoky Mountains

Assn. (bd. dirs. 1998-2002). Democrat. Presbyterian. Avocations: travel, stamps, gardening. Home: 931 University Heights Rd Cullowhee NC 28723-6953 Personal E-mail: douglasreed@earthlink.net.

**REED, ANGELICA DENISE,** sculptor, writer, illustrator; b. Murfreesboro, Tenn., Dec. 16, 1955; d. Keith Kenyon and Lester Faye (Todd) Reed; m. David Earl Myers, Apr. 19, 1975 (dec. Mar. 1978); m. John Gregory Bettis, May 11, 1979. Student, Mid. Tenn. State U., 1973-75, 77-78, UCLA, 1981-82, Venice Sculpture Studio, 1983-85, Brucchion Sch. of Art, Culver City, Calif., 1987-90. Artist-in-residence Reed Studio and Gallery, Venice, Calif., 1990-95, The Jerry Solomon Gallery, L.A., 1997, Belle Art Galleries, Inc. at Bel Age Hotel, West Hollywood, Calif., 2000—. Cons. Sweet Harmony Music, Sunset Beach, Calif., 1978-83, Bettis Paradise Music, Sunset Beach, 1978-85, John Bettis Music, L.A., 1983—, John Bettis Property Mgmt., L.A., 1986—. Fundraiser Children's Hosp./Santa Monica Bay Aux., 1991, Nat. Acad. Songwriters, 1985, SEA Environ. Assn., Bonaventure Hotel, L.A., 1990, 91; mem. L.A. com. P.E.T.A. People for the Ethical Treatment of Animals, 1992; vol. St. John Hosp., 1998. Avocations: gymnastics, scuba diving, travel, ballet. Home and Office: 2251 Mid Tenn Blvd Murfreesboro TN 37130 E-mail: angelicadenise@comcast.net.

**REED, ANNE F. THOMSON,** management consultant; BA, Goucher Coll., 1973; MPA, Harvard U., 1981. Devel. rschr. Office of Alumni Devel. Vanderbilt U., Nashville, 1973—74; jr. cmty. planner Nashville City Planning Commn., 1974—76; staff asst. to asst. dean for adminstrn. Kennedy Sch. Harvard U., Cambridge, Mass., 1976—77, registrar, admissions officer John F. Kennedy Sch. Govt., 1977—80; presdl. mgmt. intern Dept. Navy, Washington, 1981—83, budget analyst for Naval Sea Sys. Command, 1983—86, numerous mgmt. positions Office Comptroller, 1986—93; dep. asst. sec. agr. for adminstrn. USDA, Washington, 1993—96, chief info. officer, 1997—2000; v.p. govt. global industry group EDS, 2000—02, pres. State and Local Govt., 2002—03; pres. Aquisition Solutions, Inc., 2003—. Office Phone: 703-253-6309.

**REED, AUSTIN F.,** lawyer; b. Waterbury, Conn., Aug. 4, 1951; m. Mary Cincotta, Dec. 22, 1971; children: George, Patricia, Edward, John. AB in economics and polit. sci., Boston Coll., 1973; JD, U. Fla., 1975. Bar: Fla. 1976, Conn. 1982, Va. 1997. Atty. Fla. Pub. Employee Rels. Commn., 1976-77; sr. atty. Jack Eckerd Corp., 1977-81; assoc. Cummings & Lockwood, Stamford, Conn., 1981-87; asst. gen. counsel Pittston Co., Greenwich, Conn., 1987-89, v.p., gen. counsel The Brink's Inc. subid. Darien, Conn., 1989-93; (Pittston Co. renamed The Brink's Co in 2003); v.p., gen. counsel, sec. The Brink's Co., Richmond, Va., 1994—. Office: The Brink's Co 1801 Bayberry Ct PO Box 18100 Richmond VA 23226-8100

**REED, BERENICE ANNE,** cultural organization administrator, educator, artist; b. Memphis; d. Glenn Andrew and Berenice Marie (Kallaher) R. BFA, St. Mary-of-the-Woods Coll., Ind., 1955; MFA in Painting and Art History, Istituto Pio XII, Villa Schifanoia, Florence, Italy, 1964. Cert. art tchr. Tenn. Comml. artist Memphis Pub. Co., 1955—56; arts adminstr., educator pub. and pvt. instns., Washington, Memphis, 1957—70; arts adminstr. Nat. Park Svc., 1970—73; mem. staff U.S. Dept. Energy, Washington, 1973—81, U.S. Dept. Commerce, Washington, 1983—84, Exec. Office of Pres., Office of Mgmt. and Budget, Washington, 1985; with fin. mgmt. svc. U.S. Treasury Dept., Washington, 1985—2004. Ind. art history rschr. Nat. Gallery of Art, Ctr. Advanced Study in Visual Arts, Washington, 1998—; cons. on art and architecture in recreation AIA, 1972-73; artist-in-residence St. Mary-of-the-Woods Coll., Ind., 1965; guest lectr. instr. Nat. Sch. Fine Arts, Tegucigalpa, Honduras, 1968; exec. com. Parks, Arts and Leisure Project, Washington, 1972-73; rschr. art projects Washington, 1981-83. Developer (video) In Your Interest, 1992; TV interviewer art. Fin. Skylink satellite programs, 1996-98. Advisor Royal Oak Found.; bd. dirs. Am. Irish Bicentennial Com., 1974—76. Recipient various awards for painting; installed as Dama of Merit, Sacred Mil. Constantinian Order of St. George, Naples, 1997, awarded Star, 2001, installed as Dama, Order of St. Maurice and St. Lazarus, 2000; named one of 150 Women Who Made A Difference in 150 years of St. Agnes Acad., 2001. Mem. Soc. Woman Geographers, Nat. Soc. Arts and Letters, Ctr. Advanced Study in Visual Arts, Art Barn Assn. (bd. dir. 1973-83), Patrons Arts in the Vatican Mus., Irish Georgian Soc. Roman Catholic. Avocations: photography, performing arts. Home: PO Box 34253 Bethesda MD 20827-0253

**REED, BETTY JAMERSON,** historian, educator; b. East Flat Rock, NC, July 27, 1937; d. Floyd Wesley and Ella Mae (Case) Jamerson; m. William Alonzo Reed, July 24, 1971; children: Floyd Allan, Sara-Ann Reed Sizemore, David Andrew. BA, Bryan Coll., Dayton, Tenn., 1959; MA in Edn., Western Carolina U., 1969, EdD, 2000. Tchr. NC Pub. Schs., 1960—99; adj. instr. Blue Ridge C.C., Brevard, NC, 1975—2005; instr. continuing edn. Brevard Coll., 2000—04, adj. supr. student tchrs., 2000—04. Trainer NC Tchr. Acad., 1993—2003; instr. Brevard Coll., 2004, Blue Ridge C.C., 2004—06. Author: The Brevard Rosenwald School, 2004 (cert. of commendation Am. Assn. State and Local History, 2005). Vol. interpreter, tutor El Centro Comunitario, Brevard, 2003—05; literacy instr. ESL Literacy Coun., Brevard, 2004—05; mem. Human Rels. Coun., Brevard, 2001—06, Abandoned Cemeteries Commn., Brevard, 2004—06. Named Outstanding Young Educator NC NC Jaycees, 1971; recipient Gov.'s award Excellence in Tchg., Gov.'s NC, 1991, cert. of appreciation, Transylvania County Citizens Improvement Orgn., 2001. Mem.: NEA, Appalachian Studies Assn., Orgn. Am. Historians, Buncombe Hist. Soc., Anderson County Hist. Soc., Transylvania County Hist. Soc., Nat. Trust Historic Preservation.

**REED, CAREY S.,** chemistry professor; BA in Chemistry and Math, Hiram Coll., Ohio, 1991; PhD in Chemistry, Pa. State U., University Park, 1996. Asst. prof. chemistry Pa. State U., Altoona, 1997—. Office: Pa State Univ 3000 Ivyside Park Altoona PA 16601 Office Phone: 814-949-5752. Business E-Mail: csr4@psu.edu.

**REED, CHARLES BASS,** chief academic administrator; b. Harrisburg, Pa., Sept. 29, 1941; s. Samuel Ross and Elizabeth (Johnson) R.; m. Catherine A. Sayers, Aug. 22, 1964; children: Charles Jr., Susan Allison. BS, George Washington U., 1963, MS, 1964, EdD, 1970; postgrad. Summer Inst. for Chief State Sch. Officers, Harvard U. Grad Sch. Edn., 1977; D of Pub. Svc. (hon.), George Washington U., 1987; LLD (hon.), Stetson U., 1987; LHD (hon.), St. Thomas U., 1988; LittD (hon.), Waynesburg Coll., 1990; LHD, Fla. State Univ., 1997; d of the U. (hon.), British Open U., 2000. From asst. prof. to assoc. prof. George Washington U., Washington, 1963—70; asst. dir. Nat. Performance-Based Tchr. Edn. Project, Am. Assn. Colls. for Tchr. Edn., Washington, 1970—71; assoc. for planning and coordination Fla. Dept. Edn., Tallahassee, 1971—79, dir. Office Ednl. Planning, Budgeting, and Evaluation, 1975—79; edn. policy coord. Exec. Office of Gov., Tallahassee, 1979—80, dir. legis. affairs, 1980—81, dep. chief of staff, 1981—84, chief of staff, 1984—85; chancellor State Univ. System Fla., Tallahassee, 1985—98, State U. Sys., Long Beach, 1988—. Mem. Nat. Commn. on H.S. Sr. Yr., Pres. Leadership Group, Higher Edn. Ctr. for Alcohol and Other Drug Prevention, Coll. Edn. Nat. Bd., Policy Bd., EdVoice; mem. Rand Edn. Adv. Bd; bd. dirs. Nat. Ctr. for Ednl. Accountability, Mem. Coun. for Advancement and Support of Edn., Coun. on Fgn. Rels., Bus.-Higher Edn. Forum. Disting. fellow,Fullbright Commn. 50th Anniversary, Peru, 1996, Lamar R. Plunkett Award, So. Regional Edn. Bd., 2001. Mem. Am. Assn. State Colls. and Univs., Am. Assn. for Higher Edn., Am. Coun. on Edn., Assn. Governing Bds. of Univs. and Colls., Nat. Assn. State Univs. and Land-Grant Colls., Nat. Assn. Sys. Heads, Internat. Assn. Univ. Presidents, Hispanic Assn. Colls. and Univs. Democrat. Roman Catholic. Office: Calif State U Office Chancellor 401 Golden Shore St Fl 6 Long Beach CA 90802-4210 E-mail: creed@calstate.edu

**REED, CLAUDE BRINTON,** systems engineer; s. Raymond Oscar and Ethel Logan Reed; m. Judith Ann Reed (div. Oct. 23, 1998); children: Steven Douglas, Kimberly Ann Blackwell, Michael Thomas; m. Rachel Ann Reed, Feb. 13, 2000. BS, Purdue U., W. Lafayette, Ind., 1963—67, MS, 1967—69, PhD, 1969—76. Engr. Westinghouse Bettis, W. Mifflin, Pa., 1973—77; sr.

engr. Argonne Nat. Lab., Ill., 1977—. Contbr. chapters to books. Achievements include research in liquid metal magnetohydr; contributions to liquid metal magnetohydrodynamics for magnetic fusion applications, alkali metal technology for the Rare Isotope Accelerator applications, materials and corrosion, and high-power laser material. Avocation: race cars. Office: Argonne Nat Lab 9700 S Cass Ave Argonne IL 60439 Business E-Mail: cbreed@anl.gov.

**REED, DAPHNE STEVENSON,** artist; b. Hartford, Conn. d. Edward McMurtry and Adele (Vaughan) Stevenson; m. Bruce Penttinen, 2001; children: Bonnie, Laurie, Rory. BA, Am. U.; MFA, U. Mass., 1969. Rschr. author, editor, publisher, artist, Amherst, Mass., 1965—; instr., theatre dir. Mt. Holyoke Coll., South Hadley, Mass., 1970-72; tchr., adminstr., theatre dir. Hampshire Coll. and Amherst Coll., 1972-77; staff asst. Five Colls., Inc., Amherst, 1977-83; adminstr. U. Mass., Amherst, 1977-85; freelance editor, writer, artist, English lang. cons. Amherst, 1986—93; writer, pub. Owl Pub., 1993—2006. Broadcaster Radio Reading Svcs. Western New Eng., Springfield, Mass., 1982-88; cons. in field. One woman show Artwork, 1994; author/dir. (plays) I Woman, 1970, This Thing Called Freedom, 1972; author The Secret World of Angels, 1999; editor Owl Angels Jour., 2000—Organizer Pioneer Valley (Mass.) chpt. P-FLAG, 1985, leader, 1994—, editor Owl Angels Jour. newsletter, 2001—; founding charter mem. Com. on Race Rels., Amherst, 1970-73. Arts Coun. grantee, Amherst, 1987. Mem. Internat. Women's Writing Guild, Ednl. Theatre Assn., Mothers Against War (organizer 2002). Democrat. Congregationalist. Avocations: theater, literature, writing, painting, metaphysical and political research. Home: 305 Middle St Amherst MA 01002-3016 Office Phone: 413-253-3354. Personal E-mail: owlangels@aol.com.

**REED, DAVID GEORGE,** entrepreneur; b. Alameda, Calif., July 19, 1945; s. David Francis and Anna Amelia Vangeline (Paulson) R.; m. Marianne Louise Watson, Apr. 7, 1971 (div. June 1975); m. Michele Ann Hock, June 28, 1989; 1 child, Casey Christine Michele. AA in Bus. Adminstrn., Diablo Valley Coll., Pleasant Hill, Calif., 1965; BA in Design and Industry, San Francisco State U., 1967, MBA in Mktg., 1969; cert. res. police officer, Los Medanos Coll., Pittsburg, Calif., 1977. Owner Western Furs, Ltd., Walnut Creek, Calif., 1963-72; mgmt. cons. Controlled Interval Scheduling, Rolling Hills Estates, Calif., 1972-73; owner Dave Reed's Texaco, Concord, Calif., 1973-76; mgmt. cons. Mgmt. Scheduling Systems, Houston, 1974-76, Thomas-Ross Assocs., Mercer Island, Wash., 1972-82; plant mgr. Bonner Packing, Morgan Hill, Calif., 1981; mfg. engr. Systron Donner, Concord, 1982-84, Beckman Instruments, San Ramon, Calif., 1984-90; owner Dave Reed & Co. Water Ski Sch., White Water Rafting, Chiloquin, Oreg., 1987—, Dave Reed & Co., design, market, mfg. Contender boats, Chiloquin, Oreg., 1976—. Lectr. wildlife mgmt. Dave Reed & Co., Chiloquin, 1965—, lectr. mgmt. seminars, 1982—; coach Japanese Water Ski Team, Bluff Water Ski Club, Tokyo, 1984; fin. mgr. Japanese investors Dave Reed & Co., Chiloquin, 1986—, design and supply solar electric power sys., 1994—. Res. dep. sheriff Contra Costa County Sheriff's Dept., Martinez, Calif., 1977-80. With U.S. Army, 1965-71, Vietnam. Recipient Gold medal internat. freestyle wrestling Sr. Olympics, Fullerton, Calif., 1983. Mem. Am. Water Ski Assn. (Calif. state water ski champion 1977, 86, western region water ski champion 1977, silver medal nat. water ski championships 1977), Bay Area Tournament Assn. (chmn. 1968—), Diablo Water Ski Club (bd. dirs. 1968—). Republican. Avocations: water-skiing, skiing, surfing, camping, fly fishing. Home: PO Box 336 Chiloquin OR 97624-0336

**REED, DAVID PATRICK,** information scientist; b. Portsmouth, Va., Jan. 30, 1952; s. Sherman Clark and Bernice Lois (Maul) R.; m. Lynn Susan Schwartz, June 10, 1973 (div. Mar. 1979); 1 child, Colin Alexander; m. Jessica Amy Kenn, Sept. 4, 1983; children: Katherine Anne, Carly Diana. BS, MIT, 1973, SM, 1975, Degree in Elec. Engring., 1976, PhD, 1978. Asst. prof. computer sci. and engring. MIT, Cambridge, 1978-84, lectr., 1984-86; chief scientist Software Arts, Wellesley, Mass., 1983-84, v.p. R&D, 1984-85; v.p. R&D, chief scientist Lotus Devel., Cambridge, 1985-92; sr. scientist Interval Rsch. Corp., 1992-96; pvt. practice, 1996—; mem. adv. bd. Vanguard, 1991—. Fellow Diamond Tech. Ptnrs. Exch. program, 1997—; vis. scientist MIT Media Lab., 2001-02; adj. prof. MIT Media Lab., 2003—; mem. tech. adv. coun., FCC, 2003-2004. Contbr. articles to profl. jours. Recipient Tchg. award MIT Elec. Engring. Dept., 1975, Tech. award World Tech. Network Comms., 2004, IP3 award Pub. Knowledge, 2005; fellow Hewlett-Packard Labs., 2003—. Mem. IEEE, Assn. Computing Machinery, Computer Soc., Sigma Xi. Democrat. Achievements include multiple US patents.

**REED, DIANE MARIE,** retired psychologist; b. Joplin, Mo., Jan. 11, 1934; d. William Marion and Olive Francis (Smith) Kinney; m. William J. Shotton; children: Wendy Robison, Douglas Funkhouser. Student, Art Ctr. Coll., L.A. 1951-54; BS, U. Oreg., 1976, MS, 1977, PhD, 1981. Lic. psychologist. Illustrator J.L. Hudson Co., Detroit, 1954-56; designer, stylist N.Y.C., 1960-70; designer, owner Decor To You, Inc., Stamford, Conn., 1970-76; founder, exec. dir. Alcohol Counseling and Edn. Svcs., Inc., Eugene, Oreg., 1981-86, clin. supr., 1986, Christian Family Svcs., Eugene, 1986-87; pvt. practice Eugene, 1985-94; co-founder Reed Consulting, Bend, Oreg., 1995—2000; pvt. practice Bend, Oreg., 2000—04; ret., 2005. Evaluator Vocat. Rehab. Div., Eugene, 1982—; alcohol and drug evaluator and commitment examiner Oreg. Mental Health Div., 1981—86. Named Disting. Alumnus, Ctrl. Oreg. region U. Oreg. Coll. Edn., 2003. Mem.: AAUW, APA, Ctr. Ore. Psychological Assn. (pres. elect), Lane County Psychol. Assn. (pres. 1989—90), Oreg. Psychol. Assn., U. Oreg. Nat. Alumni, Ctrl. Oreg. Llama Assn. (pres. 1999—2000), Bend C. of C., Sunriver Area C. of C. (bd. dirs. 1997—98), Sunriver Women's Club (comm. chair), Toastmasters Internat., Rotary (pres. 1997—98, Rotarian Yr. 1996—97, 1997—98). Avocations: photography, skiing, hiking, backpacking.

**REED, DONNA MARIE,** editor; b. Dayton, Ohio, Mar. 29, 1950; d. Andrew Levi and Golda Mabel (Branham) Tatman; m. Donald Ray Newsome, May 12, 1973 (div. Sept. 1985); 1 child, Amanda Marie; m. James A. Reed, Sept. 26, 1987. BA, Morehead State U., 1973, MA, 1974. Junior high sch. tchr. English, 1974; part-time corr. Tampa Tribune, Fla., 1974—75, reporter, bur. chief, asst. suburban editor, suburban editor, asst. metro editor, state editor, dep. mng. editor, mng. editor Fla.; dir. comm. Hillsborough County Schs., Tampa, 1990-96. Bd. dirs. Tampa Edn. Channel; com. mem. Hillsborough Edn. Found., Tampa, 1990—. Recipient Sunshine Medallion award Sunshine State Sch. PR Assn., 1991-96, Prin.'s award Armwood H.S., 1994-95. Mem. Fla. Press Assn., Fla. Soc. Newspaper Editors, Hillsborough Assn. Sch. Adminstrs. (Pub. Rels. award 1991, 95), Plant City Little League, Delta Gamma Alumni Assn. Baptist. Avocations: reading, needlecrafts, sports, bike riding. Office: Tampa Tribune 202 S Parker St Tampa FL 33606-2395

**REED, EDWARD CORNELIUS, JR.,** federal judge; b. Mason, Nev., July 8, 1924; s. Edward Cornelius Sr. and Evelyn (Walker) R.; m. Sally Torrance, June 14, 1952; children: Edward T., William W., John A., Mary E. BA, U. Nev., 1949; JD, Harvard U., 1952. Bar: Nev. 1952, U.S. Dist Ct. Nev. 1957, U.S. Supreme Ct. 1974. Atty. Arthur Andersen & Co., 1952-53; spl. dep. atty. gen. State of Nev., 1967-79; judge U.S. Dist. Ct. Nev., Reno, 1979—, chief judge, now sr. judge. Former vol. atty. Girl Scouts Am., Sierra Nevada Council, U. Nev., Nev. Agrl. Found., Nev. State Sch. Adminstrs. Assn., Nev. Congress of Parents and Teachers; mem. Washoe County Sch. Bd., 1956-72, pres. 1959, 63, 69; chmn. Gov.'s Sch. Survey Com., 1958-61; mem. Washoe County Bd. Tax Equalization, 1957-58, Washoe County Annexation Commn., 1968-72, Washoe County Personnel Com., 1973-77, chmn. 1973; mem. citizens adv. com. Washoe County Sch. Bond Issue, 1977-78, Sun Valley, Nev., Swimming Pool Com., 1978, Washoe County Blue Ribbon Task Force Com. on Growth, Nev. PTA (life); chmn. profl. TV studio, 1978; bd. dirs. Reno Silver Sox, 1962-65. Served as staff sgt. U.S. Army, 1943-46, ETO, PTO. Mem. ABA (jud. adminstrn. sect.), Nev. State Bar Assn. (adminstrv. com. dist. 5, 1967-79, lien law com. 1965-78, chmn. 1965-72, probate law

com. 1963-66, tax law com. 1962-65), Am. Judicature Soc. Democrat. Baptist. Named in his honor Edward C. Reed H.S., Sparks, Nev., 1972. Office: US Dist Ct 400 S Virginia St Ste 606 Reno NV 89501-2182 Office Phone: 775-686-5919.

**REED, ELLEN BETH,** librarian; b. Albany, Calif., Aug. 1942; d. Howard Ben Reed and Lillian Margaret Vanlandingham; life ptnr. Rita Bea Miller. BS, Moorhead State Coll., Minn., 1960—64; MA in Theatre, U. of Denver, 1979—81, MA in Librarianship and Info. Mgmt., 1984—85. English teacher, drama dir. Pine River (Minn.) HS, 1965—67; with Strawhat Theatre, Moorhead, 1966—66; english-speech instr., dir. of theatre Milbank (SD) HS, 1967—79; artistic & mng. dir. Pied Pipers Theatre, Inc, Milbank, 1968—70; grad. tchg. asst. theatre dept. U. Denver, 1979—81; asst. to the dir. Picketwire Players, Lajunta, Colo., 1979—79; stack maintenance unit dept. head Penrose Libr., U. of Denver, 1981—85; with Las Vegas-Clark County Libr. Dist., 1985—; stage mgr. Actor's Repertory Theatre, Las Vegas, 1991—91; sr. libr., spl. collections Clark County Libr., Las Vegas, 1996—2003, reference dept. head, 2003—. Exec. sec. Alpha Lambda Epsilon, Moorhead, Minn., 1961—64, Pine River Edn. Assn., Minn., United States, 1965—67; past pres. Las Vegas-Clark County Libr. Dist. Staff Assn., 1981—92; trustee Sumi Laetz Found., Las Vegas, 1995—; conduct workshops statewide on the subject of nonprofit funding Clark County Libr., 1996—2004, compiler of Nev. funding directory, 1996—. Dir.: (stage plays) various productions including The Diary of Anne Frank, The Crucible, Hello Dolly, The Fantastiks, Antigone, and over 50 more, Including Barefoot in the Park, Cinderella, Bye-Bye Birdie, Including Medea, Stephen Vincent Benet's Stories of America, School for Scandal; (stage play) The Lady Patriot: A Story of Abigail Adams (Gov. & Bicentennial Commn. Medal for Outstanding Svc., 1976), (author, producer) (video) A New World Of Books (Cert. of Recognition, Libr. Dist. Bd. of Trustees, 1994); author (compiler): (bibliography) An Annotated Bibliography Of The Nev. Collection At The Clark County Libr. (LVCCLD Bd. of Trustees Incentive Award, 1996), Mem.: Teamsters local #14 LVCCLD (shop steward). Avocations: cross country skiing, horseback riding, swimming, reading, fishing. Office: Clark County Libr 1401 East Flamingo Las Vegas NV 89119

**REED, FRANCES BOOGHER,** writer, actress; b. Marion, Ky., May 29, 1938; d. Charles Boogher and Evelyn Shelby (Roberts) R.; m. José Joaquín Solís, June 1, 1957 (div. Sept. 1964); children: Julie, Michael Charles; m. Arnold Haslund, Jan. 30, 1965 (div. May 1967); 1 child, Elizabeth Evelyn Marie; 1 adopted child, Leni Ellis. BA in English and Spanish, U. Houston, 1960; MPH, U. P.R., 1970. Tchr. English as 2d lang. Author: A Dream With Storms, 1979, Thoughts, Feelings and Dreams, 1985, Black Mexican Necklace, 1990, TOEIC Test Guide, 1997, Miguel's Aztec Calendar, 1997, (with Koji Shimada) From Chocolate Bars to CEO, A MacArthur's Kid, 2000, (with Francisco Diaz Infante M.) Pockets and Jingles: Something for His Pockets, 2000, Love Blooms in Mazatlan, 2004; co-artist (with Francisco Diaz Infante M.) Art Works Gallery, Hilton Head, SC, Museo de Arte, Mazatlan, Mex.; ghostwriter: Life On the Run; actress (television shows) General Hospital, Rescue-911, others, also movies. Mem. Am. Pub. Health Assn., Screen Actors' Guild, Mensa, Phi Kappa Phi. Democrat. Methodist. Avocations: teaching, dance, reading. Home: 239 Beach City Rd Apt 2113 Hilton Head Island SC 29926-4713 Office Phone: 843-689-9258. E-mail: ML888888@aol.com.

**REED, FRANK METCALF,** bank executive, director; b. Seattle, Dec. 22, 1912; s. Frank Ivan and Pauline B. (Hovey) R.; m. Maxine Vivian McGary, June 11, 1937; children: Pauline Reed, Frank Metcalf. Student, U. Alaska, 1931-32; BA, U. Wash., 1937. V.p. Anchorage Light and Power Co., 1937-42; pres. Alaska Electric & Equipment Co., Anchorage, 1946-50; sec., mgr. Turnagain, Inc., Anchorage, 1950-56; mgr. Gen. Credit Corp., Anchorage, 1957; br. mgr. Alaska SBA, Anchorage, 1958-60; sr. v.p. First Interstate Bank of Alaska, Anchorage, 1960-87, also dir., corp. sec. Dir. First Interstate Corp. of Alaska, First Nat. Bank of Fairbanks; pres., dir. Anchorage Broadcasters, Inc.; past pres., chmn. Microfast Software Corp.; dir., treas. R.M.R., Inc.; dir. Anchorage Light and Power Co., Turnagain, Inc., Alaska Fish and Farm, Inc., Life Ins. Co. Alaska. Pres., Anchorage Federated Charities, Inc., 1953-54; mem. adv. bd. Salvation Army, 1948-58; mem. Alaska adv. bd. Hugh O'Brian Youth Found., 1987-91; trustee Anchor Age Endowment Fund, 1988-96, chmn., 1991; mem. City of Anchorage Planning Commn., 1956; mem. City of Anchorage Coun., 1956-57; police commr. Territory of Alaska, 1957-58; chmn. City Charter Commn., 1958; mem. exec. com. Greater Anchorage, Inc., 1955-65; mem. Sch. Bd., 1961-64; mem. Gov.'s Investment adv. com., 197-72; mem. Alaska State Bd. Edn.; mem. citizens adv. com. Alaska Meth. U.; chmn. Anchorage Charter Commn., 1975; chmn. bldg. fund dr. Cmty. YMCA, 1976 dir., 1976-97, hon. dir. 1998—; sec.-treas. Breakthrough, 1976-78; bd. dirs. Alaska Treatment Ctr., 1980-87, pres. 1985-86; trustee Marston Found., Inc., 1978, exec. dir. 1988. Served as lt. USNR, 1942-46. Elected to Hall of Fame, Alaska Press Club, 1969; named Outstanding Alaskan of Yr. Alaska C. of C., 1976, Alaskan of Yr., 1990, Outstanding Vol. in Philanthropy Alaska chpt. Nat. Soc. Fundraising Execs., 1991; laureate Jr. Achievement's Alaska Bus. Hall of Fame, 2000. Mem.: Alaska Bankers Assns. (pres. 1970—71), Nat. Assn. State Bds. Edn. (sec.-treas. 1969—70), Am. Inst. Banking Am. (exec. coun. 1971—72), Navy League (pres. Anchorage coun. 1961—62), Pioneers of Alaska, Anchorage C. of C. (presl 1966—67 dir.), San Francisco Tennis Club, Tower Club (life), Elks (life), Lions (life; sec. Anchorage 1953—54, pres. 1962—63, dir. 1988, treas. 2002—04, Melvin Jones fellow 2000). Home: 1361 W 12th Ave Anchorage AK 99501-4235 Personal E-mail: freed@acsalaska.net.

**REED, GALEN K.,** music educator; s. Harold Elias and Barbara Keener Reed. BS in music edn., Millersville U., 1976—81. Instructional II Penna. Dept of Edn., 1981. Tchr. Ephrata Area Sch. Dist., Ephrata, Pa., 1983—. Mem.: Am. String Teachers Assn. Christian. Avocations: nature, music. Office: Ephrata Area Sch Dist 803 Oak Blvd Ephrata PA 17522 Office Phone: 717-721-1130. E-mail: g_reed@easdpa.org

**REED, GEORGE FORD, JR.,** investment executive; b. Hollywood, Calif., Dec. 26, 1946; s. George Ford and Mary Anita Reed; B.A. in Econs. with honors, U. So. Calif., 1969, M.A., 1971; m. Kathryn Nixon, 1969. Analyst planning and research Larwin Group, Beverly Hills, Calif., 1971-72; with Automobile Club So. Calif., Los Angeles, 1972-76, supr. mgmt. info., research and devel., 1973-74, mgr. fin. and market analysis, 1975-81, group mgr. fin. analysis and forecasting, 1981-86; pres. Reed Asset Mgmt. Co., Inc., Los Angeles, 1986—; instr. bus. and econs. Los Angeles Community Coll. Mem. population task force Los Angeles C. of C., 1974; mem. Gov. Calif. Statewide Econ. Summit Conf., 1974. Served with U.S. Army, 1969. Mem. Assn. Corp. Real Estate Execs., Fin. Execs. Inst., Nat. Assn. Bus. Economists, Western Regional Sci. Assn., Am. Mgmt. Assn., Am. Fin. Assn., Calif. Planners Assn., Rotary Internat., Omicron Delta Epsilon. Home: 1001 S Westgate Ave Los Angeles CA 90049-5905

**REED, GLEN ALFRED,** lawyer; b. Memphis, Sept. 24, 1951; s. Thomas Henry and Evelyn Merle (Roddy) Reed; m. Edith Jean Renick, June 17, 1972; children: Adam Christopher, Alec Benjamin. BA, U. Tenn., 1972; JD, Yale U., 1976. Bar: Ga. 1976. Project dir. Tenn. Rsch. Coordinating Unit, Knoxville, 1972-73; assoc. Alston Miller & Gaines, Atlanta, 1976-77, Bordurant Miller Hishon & Stephenson, Atlanta, 1978-81, prin., 1981-85, King & Spalding, Atlanta, 1985—. Author: (book) Practical Hospital Law, 1979. Gen. counsel Assn. Retarded Citizens, Atlanta, 1979—, bd. dirs., 1986—2006, pres., 1992—96; mem. adv. bd. CARE Atlanta, 1992—, chmn., 1994—99; v.p. Ga. Network People with Devel. Disabilities, 1991—92; legal advisor Ga. Gov.'s Commn. on Healthcare, 1994; bd. dirs. Ga. Partnership for Caring, 1999—2002, Ga. Comm. Support and Solutions, 2000—, vice chmn., 2005—; bd. dirs. Healthcare Ethics Consortium Ga., 2002—04, MedShare Internat., 1999—, chmn., 2005—; bd. dirs. Ctrl. Health Ctr., 1989—95, Vis. Nurse Health Sys., 1992—, chmn., 1996—99; mem. dean's coun. Sch. Pub. Health Emory U., Atlanta, 1998—. Mem.: ABA, Ga. Acad. Hosp. Attys. (pres. 1981—82), Am. Health Lawyers Assn. (bd. dirs. 1997—2000, pres.

1998—99), Am. Acad. Hosp. Attys. (bd. dirs. 1991—97, pres.-elect 1997), Ga. Bar Assn., Phi Beta Kappa. Methodist. Office: King & Spalding 191 Peachtree St NE Ste 40 Atlanta GA 30303-1740 Office phone: 404-572-3393. Business E-mail: gareed@kslaw.com.

**REED, GLENN W.,** lawyer; b. Melrose Park, Ill., Jan. 18, 1953; AB summa cum laude, Dartmouth Coll., 1975; JD cum laude, Harvard U., 1978. Bar: Ill. 1978, U.S. Dist. Ct. Ill. (No. dist.). With Gardner, Carton & Douglas, Chgo., 1978—99, ptnr., 1985—99; exec. v.p., gen. counsel UICI, North Richland Hills, Tex., 1999—, dir., 2001—. Mem. exec. com. bd. dirs. UICI, mem. privacy com., mem. investment com.; dir., v.p. MEGA Life and Health Ins. Co., Mid-West Nat. Life Ins. Co., Tenn., Chesapeake Life Ins. Co., Fidelity First Ins. Co.; dir. Pepper Companies, Inc., Chgo., 1990—, Peoples Bankcorp, Inc., Arlington Heights, Ill., 1999—. Mem.: Ill. State Bar Assn. Office: UICI 9151 Grapevine Hwy North Richland Hills TX 76180 Office Phone: 817-255-5200. Office Fax: 817-255-5394.

**REED, H. OWEN,** retired music educator; b. Odessa, Mo., 1910; m. Esther M. Reed (dec.); children: Sara Jo Ferrar, Carol Ann Wetters; m. Mary L. Arwood, 1982. Student, U. Mo., 1929—33; MusB in Music Composition, La. State U., 1934, MusM in Music Composition, 1936, BA in French, 1937; PhD in Music Composition, U. Rochester, 1939. Educator Mich. State U., 1939—76, chmn. theory and composition, 1939—67, acting head, Sch. Music, 1957—58, chmn. music composition, Sch. Music, 1967—76, prof. emeritus, 1976—; ret., 1976. Physics educator Army Spec. Tng. Program, 1943—44; guest prof. Mont. State U., 1950, Gettysburg Coll., Pa., 1969, U. Pacific, Stockton, Calif., 1983; founding mem. Geriatric Six Plus One Jazz Ensemble. Author: 9 books on music theory and composition; composer: variety of works for orchestra, band, voices, opera, and chamber music; guest conductor: various conducting engagements, asst. conductor, arranger: The La. Kings Brass Ensemble, second trumpet: Lansing Symphony Orchestra, band leader: The Missourians Jazz Ensemble; composer: (orchestral works) Evangeline, 1938, Symphony No. 1, 1939, Overture, 1940, Symphonic Dance, 1942, Concerto for Cello and Orchestra, 1949, Overture for Strings, 1961, La Fiesta Mexicana, 1964, The Turning Mind, 1968, Ut Re Mi, 1979;: Christmas Eve, 2001, Song of Acapulco, 2001, (winds and percussion) Spiritual, 1947, Missouri Shindig, 1951, Theme and Variations, 1954, Renascence, 1958;: Che-Ba-Kun-Ah, 1959, The Touch of the Earth, 1971, For the Unfortunate, 1972, Ut Re Mi, 1980, The Awakening of the Ents, 1985, La Fiesta Mexicana, 1986, Of Loth Lorien, 1987, The Heart of the Morn, 1987, Frolicking Winds, 2006, The Song of Acapulco, 2001, (chamber work) Piano Sonata, 1934, String Quartet, 1937, The Passing of John Blackfeather, 1945, Scherzo for Clarinet & Piano, 1947, Three Nationalities, 1947, Dusk, 1947, Wondrous Love, 1948, Mountain Meditation, 1948, Nocturne, 1953, Symphonic Dance, 1954, Christmas Eve, 1954, The Song of Acapulco, 1954, Earth-Trapped, 1960, El Muchacho, 1962, 1965, El Son De La Negra, 1975, Give the Fiddler a Dram, 1976, Fanfare for Remembrance, 1986, Make a Joyful Noise, 2005, (choral works) Two Tongue Twisters, 1950, Close Beside the Winding Cedar, 1957, Ripley Ferry, 1958, Proud Chieftains, 1958, A Tabernacle for the Sun, 1963, Lord God of Sea, 1963, Rejoice! Rejoice!, 1977, Make a Joyful Noise, 2004, (stage works) The Masque of Red Death, 1936, Michigan Dream, 1955, Earth Trapped, 1960; author: A Workbook in the Fundamentals of Music, 1947, Basic Music, 1954, Basic Music Workbook, 1954, Composition Analysis Chart, 2004; co-author (with Paul Harder): Basic Contrapuntal Technique, Basic Contrapuntal Technique Workbook, 1964; co-author: (with Joel T. Leach) Scoring for Percussion and the Instruments of the Percussion Section, 1969; co-author: (with Robert G. Sidnell) The Materials of Music Composition, 1978. Recipient Composers Press Symphonic award for Concerto for Cello and Orchestra, 1949, Disting. $1000 award, Mich. State U., 1962, Recognition and Honors for Scholarly Contbns. and Publ. of La Fiesta Mexicana, 1999, award for Psalm of Praise, Basic Contrapuntal Techniques, Belwin Mills Pub., 2004, Libr. Pub. award for sound recording of Awakening of the Ents, La Fiesta Mexicana, For the Unfortunate, and Missouri Shindig, 2005, Citation for Disting. Contbns. in Arts, George Romney and Greater Mich. Found., 1963, Neil A. Kjos Meml. award for For The Unfortunate, 1975, various ann. awards, ASCAP, 1978—; award of Merit, Youth Arts Festival, 1978, Hon. Mention for Rejoice! Rejoice!, Brown U. Choral Composition Competition, 1978, Nat. Arts Assoc. award, Sigma Alpha Iota, 1983, First Place award for Butterfly Girl and Mirage Boy, Bklyn. Coll. Chamber Opera Competition, 1985, Edwin Franco Goldman Meml. Citation for conspicuous svc. in interest of bands and band music in Am., Am. Bandmasters Assn., 1994; fellow for Creative Work in Musical Composition, Guggenheim, 1948—49; Resident Fellowship, Huntington Hartford Found., Pacific Palisades, Calif., 1960, Helene Wurlitzer Found., Taos, N.Mex. 1967. Mem.: Nat. Assn. Composers (mem. nat. coun.), Am. Music Ctr., ASCAP, Music Tchrs. Nat. Assn. (chmn. theory composition section), Mich. Sch. Band and Orchestra Assn. (hon.), Phi Mu Alpha Sinfonia (Orpheus award, Gamma Epsilon chpt. 1976).

**REED, HELEN SKUGGEDAL,** law librarian, musician; b. Halifax, N.S., Can., June 19, 1948; came to U.S., 1971; d. Johan Martin Skuggedal and Anna Gurine (Ringdal) Burns; m. Robert Douglas Reed, Aug. 14, 1971 (div. 1996); 1 child, Eric Douglas Reed. BA with honors, Dalhousie U., Halifax, 1969; MM, U. Mich., 1971. Libr. Hochstein Sch. Music, Rochester, 1972-75; organist Neu Chapel U. Evansville, 1976-83; acting archivist U. So. Ind., Evansville, 1978-80; organist Washington Ave. Presbyn., Evansville, 1984-90; prin. harpsichordist Evansville Philharm., 1984—; law libr. William H. Miller Law Libr., Evansville, 1985—. Archival cons. Evansville Mus. of Arts and Scis., 1984-85; exec. bd. mem. Four Rivers area Libr. Svcs. Authority, Evansville, 1988-91; bd. dirs., mem. adv. coun. Ind. Coop. Libr. Svcs. Authority, 1995-2000; adj. instr. U. Evansville, 2004—. Recitalist Royal Can. Coll. of Organists Conv., 1973; artist-fellow Bach Aria Festival and Inst., 1992. Founding mem. Evansville Chamber Orch., 1981—; organist Eastminster Presbyn. Ch., Evansville, 1991—; Quinter Nova Scotia Talent Trust, 1969-70. Mem. Am. Assn. Law Librs., Am. Guild Organists (Evansville chpt. exec. 1982-91, 94—), Evansville Area Librs. Consortium, Friends of UE Music (sec., treas. 1988-91), Ohio Regional Assn. Law Librs., Midwestern Hist. Keyboard Soc. (dir. at large 2004—), Evansville Philharmonic Youth Orch. (mem. adv. coun.). Home: 1435 Brookside Dr Evansville IN 47714-2043 Office: William H Miller Law Libr 825 Sycamore St Ste 207 Evansville IN 47708-1849 Office Phone: 812-435-5175. Personal E-mail: hsr@evansville.net.

**REED, HOWIE,** music educator, minister; s. Howie and Rita Reed; children: Howie, Julia, Janelle. A in Liberal Arts, Berger C.C., 1982; BS in Edn., William Paterson U., 1986; M in Adminstrn., Montelair U., 2000. Tchr. Wallkill Valley H.S., Hamburg, NJ, 1976—87, Parsippany (N.J.) Troy Hills H.S., 1987—. Music minister St. Monica's Roman Catholic Ch., Sussex, NJ, 1996—; ceo Colon Records, Franklin, NJ, 1992. Author: Grow Younger with Howie Reed, singer albums. Mem.: NRA, MENC. Address: 82 Berlin Rd Parsippany NJ 07054-3281

**REED, JAMES C., JR.,** lawyer; b. 1945; BS, Abilene Christian U., 1967; JD, Methodist U., 1970. Asst. gen. counsel Tesoro Petroleum Corp., San Antonio, 1982—90, v.p., asst. gen. counsel, asst. sec., 1990—93, v.p., gen. counsel, sec., 1993—94, sr. v.p., gen. counsel, sec., 1994—95, exec. v.p., gen. counsel, sec., 1995—2005; ret., 2005.

**REED, JAMES ELDIN,** historian, consultant, educator; b. Walla Walla, Wash., Mar. 13, 1945; s. Eldin Wallace and Mary Ellen (White) R.; m. Deborah Jean Addis, Apr. 14, 1983. AB, Ripon Coll., 1967; AM, Harvard U., 1968, MTS, 1971, PhD, 1976. Cert. mgmt. cons., 1984-89. Tchg. fellow Harvard U., Cambridge, Mass., 1972-77, dir. summer writing program, 1977-78; founder, pres., chmn. Addis & Reed Cons., Boston, 1977—; pub. ARC Publs., Boston, 1999—99; sr. rsch. fellow Ctr. on Internat. Governance Innovation, 2004—05. Vis. scholar Harvard U., 1992-94, 96—; rsch. assoc. North Pacific program Fletcher Sch. Law and Diplomacy, Medford, Mass., 1994-96; v.p., pres. Assn. Mgmt. Cons., Boston, 1985-89; founder, bd. dirs. Nat. Coun. Pub. History, Washington, 1980-83; vis. prof., Fulbright Disting. chair U. Waterloo, 2004-05; participant internat. confs.;

cons. in field. Author: The Missionary Mind and American East Asia Policy, 1983, China On Our Minds, 2006; contbg. author: Enhancing Global Governance, 2002; editor: American Canada Watch, 1995-99; contbr. numerous articles, papers, and revs. to profl. publs., Christian Sci. Monitor, Boston Globe, Toronto Globe and Mail, others. Cons. House Agr. Com. Washington, 1978, House Judiciary Com., 1999-2000, invited witness Senate Judiciary Com., 1990, Ontario Coun. on Grad. Studies, 1999-2000; legis. dir. Asbestos Victims Campaign, Boston, 1987-90. Woodrow Wilson fellow, 1967-68, Harvard Grad. Prize fellow, 1967-68, fellow Newberry Libr., Chgo., 1965, Ctr. for Internat. Affairs, Harvard U., 1993-94, James Luther Adams Soc., Harvard Div. Sch., 2001—; Fulbright Found. scholar, 2004-05. Mem. Am. Hist. Assn., Am. Acad. Religion, Can. Inst. Internat. Affairs (mem. Boston br. 1998—), Fulbright Assn. (bd. dirs. Mass. chpt. 2006—), Boston Athenaeum, Harvard Club Boston, Phi Beta Kappa. Home: 25 Holly Ln Brookline MA 02467-2156 Office: Addis & Reed Cons PO Box 85 Chestnut Hill MA 02467 Office Phone: 617-232-3378. Business E-mail: jjmreed@post.harvard.edu.

**REED, JAMES MICHAEL,** music educator, singer; b. Little Rock, Ariz., June 22, 1944; s. Carl T. and Laura B. Reed; m. Helen L. Reed, Aug. 26, 1965; children: Darren, Bradley. BA, Point Loma Nazarene U. (formerly Pasadena Coll.), San Diego, 1962—67. Minister music Olive Knolls Nazarine Ch., Bakersfield, Calif., 1967—96; tchr. Beardsley Sch. Dist., 1967—; football offical KCOA, 1968—2004; owner RSV Quartet, 1985—. Mem. alumni bd. Point Loma Nazarene U., 1985—90. Recipient CTA of Yr., Calif. Tchrs. Assn., 1998, Tchr. of Yr. award, County of Kern, 2000, Jim Reed Day award, Mayor Bakersfield, 2006. Mem.: We. States Gospel Music Assn. (v.p. 2005), Beardsley Tchrs. Assn. (pres. 1989—91), Kern County Officials Assn. (pres. 1985—87) Home: 12606 Gila River Dr Bakersfield CA 93312

**REED, JAMES WESLEY,** social historian, educator; b. New Orleans, Oct. 17, 1944; married. BA, U. New Orleans, 1967; AM, Harvard U., 1968, PhD, 1974. Research fellow in history Schlesinger Library, 1973-75; prof. history Rutgers U., New Brunswick, NJ, 1975—; dean Rutgers Coll., Rutgers U., New Brunswick, 1985-94. Author: From Private Vice to Public Virtue: The Birth Control Movement and American Society Since 1830, 1978. Office: Rutgers U Dept History Van Dyck Hall Rm 118 New Brunswick NJ 08901 E-mail: reed@history.rutgers.edu.

**REED, JAMES WHITFIELD,** internist, educator, endocrinologist; b. Pahokee, Fla., Nov. 1, 1935; s. Thomas Reed and Chineater (Grey) Whitfield; married; children: David M., Robert A., Mary I., Katherine E. BS, W.Va. State Coll., 1954; MD, Howard U., 1963. Diplomate Am. Bd. Internal Medicine, Am. Bd. Endocrinology and Metabolism; cert. specialist Am. Soc. Hypertension. Commd. U.S. Army, 1963, advanced through grades to col.; 1981; postdoctoral rsch. fellow U. Calif. Med. Ctr., San Francisco, 1969—71; resident in internal medicine Madigan Army Med. Ctr., Tacoma, 1966—69, chief endocrinology and metabolism, 1971—76, chief dept. clin. rsch., 1976—78; chief dept. medicine Eisenhower Army Med. Ctr., Augusta, Ga., 1978-81; assoc. prof. internal medicine edn. for FP program U. Tex., Dallas, 1981—84; prof. medicine Morehouse Sch. Medicine, Atlanta, 1985—, chmn. dept., 1985—92, chmn. grad. med. edn., 1992—96, activity chmn.; 1986—88, dir. internal medicine residency, 1992—98, dir. Clin. Rsch. Ctr., 1998—2000, assoc. chair and prof. medicine, 1992—, chief endocrinology, 1992—, chief of medicine svc. at Grady. Dir. endocrinology, fellowship Madigan Army Med. Ctr., 1976-78; dir., chief medicine and program dir. internal medicine residency program Eisenhower Army Med. Ctr., 1978-81, chmn. directorate of clin. investigation, 1978-81, dir. endocrinology fellowship program; med. cons. Tuskgee (Ala.) VA Hosp., 1985—; mem. nat. high blood pressure com. NHLBI/NIH, Nat. Diabetes Mellitus Adv. Coun., Nat. Diabetes Adv. Bd., NHLBI working Com. on Hypertension and Diabetes; chmn. Sub Com. Special Population and Situations, chmn. subcom., mem. exec. com. Joint Nat. Commn. for Detection Evaluation and Treatment of High Blood Pressure; mem. diabetes epidemic action coun. Am. Diabetes Assn. Author: Black Man's Guide to Good Health, 1994, rev. edit., 2000, High Blood Pressure: The Black Man and Woman's Guide to Living with Hypertension, 2002, Living with Diabetes: A Guide for Patients and Parents, 2005; contbr. articles to profl. jours. Med. advisor, chmn. March of Dimes, Pierce County, Tacoma, 1976-78; pres. Charles Drew Sickle Cell and Health Bd., Tacoma, 1976-78; mem. task force on cardiovascular risk reduction Am. Heart Assn. Decorated Legion of Merit; recipient Disting. Alumni award Nat. Assn. for Equal Opportunity in Higher Edn., 1988, Nat. Alumnus of Yr. award W.Va. State Coll.; 1987; inducted into ROTC Hall of Fame, W.Va. State Coll., 1987. Master ACP; fellow Am. Coll. Clin. Endocrinologists; mem. Assn. Profs. Medicine, Endocrine Soc., Internat. Soc. Hypertension in Blacks (v.p. 1986-92, pres. 1992—2001, Lifetime Achievement award), Assn. Program Dirs. in Internal Medicine, Am. Heart Assn. (task force on cardiovasc. risk), Alpha Phi Alpha. Democrat. Avocations: bowling, skiing. Home: 380 Mcgill Pl NE Atlanta GA 30312-1069 Office: Morehous Schole Medicine 202 Rotherhithe Ln Nw Marietta GA 30066-3492 Office Phone: 404-756-5788. Business E-mail: jreed@msm.edu. *One cannot control the circumstance of one's birth, but with keen alertness and honest hard work there are no limits to what one can achieve. So hitch your wagon to a star and never lose sight of it.*

**REED, JANE GARSON,** entrepreneur; b. Cleve., Jan. 11, 1948; d. Joseph John Guzowski and Irene Sophie (Dominic) Garson; children: Craig Michael, Kevin Matthew. BBA magna cum laude, Baldwin Wallace Coll., 1977; MBA in Mgmt., Case Western Res. U., 1983; postgrad., Case State U., 1991-97. CPA, Ohio. Sr. asst. acct. Deloitte, Haskins & Sells, Cleve., 1977-78; sr. corp. auditor White Motor Corp., Beachwood, Ohio, 1979-81; instr. acctg. Cuyahoga C.C., Parma, Ohio, 1981-82; ind. contractor State of Wash., Olympia, 1982-84; dir. fin. Nonprofit SNF, Cleveland Heights, Ohio, 1985-86; controller Proprietary SNF, Akron, Ohio, 1986-87; lectr. mgmt. acctg. U. Akron, 1987-88; asst. prof. Baldwin-Wallace Coll., Berea, Ohio, 1989-94; pres. Athena Music, Inc., 2002—. Lectr. advocacy and health policy change Cleve. State U., 2001—02. Asst. editor Ohio CPA Jour., 1997-99; editor CPA Advisor, 2003-05 Chair Trinity (Marymount) H.S. Reunion Com., 1990-91; vice-chair Com. for Advanced Edn. in Brunswick, 1995-96; mem. acctg. curriculum adv. com. Lorain County C.C.; bd. dirs. Greater Cleve. Brain Injury Coalition, 1997-2000; mem. Ohio Brain Injury Assn., 1996—, 2d v.p., 1999-2001. Mem. AICPA, Ohio Soc. CPAs (editl. bd. jour. com. 1992-95, task force on implementing quality edn. 1992-94, assurance svcs. com. 1998-2000, adv. coun. M.A.P. sect. 1999-2000), Inst. Mgmt. Accts. (faculty advisor to Baldwin-Wallace student chpt. 1990-94), Am. Soc. Women Accts. (pres. 1993-94), Medina County Writers Group (treas. 1998-2003), Delta Mu Delta. Methodist. Avocation: amateur radio. Home: 1254 Hadcock Rd Brunswick OH 44212-3018 Office Phone: 330-225-1488. Personal E-mail: janreeed@adelphia.net. Business E-mail: jane@thunderechodrums.com.

**REED, JANET,** dance educator, choreographer; b. Shelby, Tenn., Feb. 22, 1955; d. Robert and Mary Evelyn Reed; 1 child, Malik Isaiah Griffin. BS in Phys. Edn., SUNY, Brockport, 1977; MA in Theatre and Dance, U. Buffalo, 1997. Artistic dir. Buffalo City Ballet Co., 1988—; asst. prof. dance State U. Coll. at Buffalo, 1993—. Dir. Janet Reed and Dancers, Buffalo, 1998—. Choreographer (contemporary African dance) Standing on Shaky Ground: yet, she dances with abandon against the turbulent sea, dancer, costume designer I-Woman-I, Mask. Fellow, N.Y. Found. for the Arts, 2002; grantee, N.Y. State Coun. on the Arts, 1991, Barbara Demming Meml. Fund for Women, 1993. Republican. Avocations: travel, sewing, costume design, reading. Office: SUNY at Buffalo 1300 Elmwood Ave Buffalo NY 14222-1095 Personal E-mail: janetreeddancer@aol.com. E-mail: reedj5420usa@netscape.net.

**REED, JEAN T.,** retired archivist; b. Northampton, Mass., Apr. 7, 1937; d. Gifford Hoag and Marjorie Blossom Towle; m. Charles M. Reed, Sept. 20, 1963; 1 child, Laura Reed Goodson. BA in English, Earlham Coll., 1959; MA, U. Chgo., 1966; MA in Libr. and Info. Sci., U. SC, 2005. History prof. Hampton Inst., 1964—66; asst. prof. Old Dominion Coll., Newport, Va., 1967—68; English tchr. Ablemarle H.S., Charlottesville, Va., 1968—69; libr. asst. U. Va., 1969—70; adj. prof. Va. Polytechnical Inst., 1978—86, U. Md.,

1981—82; children's libr. asst. Rowan Pub. Libr., Salisbury, NC, 1988—92; libr. asst. Queens U. Charlotte, Charlotte, NC, 1993—2000, archival specialist, 2000—02, grant writer NC, 2002—05. Edn. com. chmn., bd. dirs. League of Women Voters, Charlotte, NC, 1995—2002; chief judge, polling sta. Bd. Elections, 2005—. Recipient Cert. Appreciation, League of Women Voters, 1999, Cert. of Distinction in French, Oxford Polytechnic Inst., 1976. Mem.: SC Archival Assn., Soc. NC Archivists, Soc. Am. Archivists. Democrat. Avocations: reading, writing.

**REED, JOAN-MARIE,** special education educator; b. St. Paul, Sept. 8, 1960; d. William Martin Reed and Diana-Marie (Miller) Reed Moss. BA, U. Minn., 1982, BS, 1983; MEd, Tex. Woman's U., 1986. Cert. tchr., Tex. Tchr. emotionally disturbed Birdville Ind. Sch. Dist., Ft. Worth, 1984-86, Goose Creek Ind. Sch. Dist., Baytown, Tex., 1986-92, ctr. leader, 1992-93, dept. chairperson, 1987-91; tchr. emotionally disturbed Conroe (Tex.) Ind. Sch. Dist., 1993-94, Willis (Tex.) Ind. Sch. Dist., 1994-95, Jefferson County (Colo.) Pub. Schs., 1995—. Co-editor: New Teacher Handbook, 1986—87, Behavior Improvement Program Handbook, 1987—88, Student Teacher Supervisor, 1997, Intern Supervisor, 2005—. Mem. NEA, Coun. for Exceptional Children. Congregationalist. Avocations: reading, cooking, travel, running. Office: Sobesky Acad Adolescent Day Treatment Program 2001 Hoyt St Lakewood CO 80215 Business E-Mail: jmreed@jeffco.k12.co.us.

**REED, JOANN A.,** corporate financial executive; Dir. fin. planning & analysis, then v.p. controller PAID subsidiary Medco Health Solutions, Franklin Lakes, NJ, 1988—92, sr. v.p. fin., 1992—, CFO, 2002—. Office: Medco Health Solutions 100 Parsons Pond Dr Franklin Lakes NJ 07417*

**REED, JOHN ALTON,** lawyer; b. Washington, June 29, 1931; s. John Alton and Emma Powers (Ball) R.; m. Louisa Wardman, June 6, 1953; children: Donna, Joanne, Deborah. AB, Duke U., 1954, LLB, 1956. Bar: Fla. 1956. Assoc. Fowler-White, Tampa, Fla., 1956-57; ptnr. Rush, Reed & Marshall, Orlando, Fla., 1957-67; judge Fla. 4th Dist. Ct. Appeal, 1967-73, chief judge, 1971-73; judge U.S. Dist. Ct. for Middle Dist. Fla., Orlando, 1973-84; ptnr., chmn. dept. litigation Lowndes, Drosdick, Doster, Kantor & Reed, Orlando, 1985-99. Com. on standard civil jury instructions Fla. Supreme Ct., 1986-90. Bd. visitors Duke U. Law Sch., 1983—. Mem. ABA, Fla. Bar Assn., Orange County Bar Assn. Republican. Episcopalian. Office: PO Box 2809 215 N Eola Dr Orlando FL 32802 Home: 1600 US Hwy 64 W 203 Sapphire NC 28774-9513 Office Phone: 407-843-4600.

**REED, JOHN C.,** physician, researcher; b. NYC, Oct. 11, 1958; s. Anthony J. and Patricia A. (Brown) R.; m. Martha Walker, June 7, 1986; children: Hunter Ashley, Tyler Austin. BA in Biochemistry, U. Va., 1980; MD, PhD, U. Pa., 1986. Resident, pathology and lab. medicine Hosp. U. of Pa., Phila., 1986-90; asst. dir. lab. molecular diagnosis U. Pa., Phila., 1990—; postdoctoral rsch. fellow, molecular biology Wistar Inst., Phila., 1986-88; asst. prof. U. Pa., Phila., 1990—92, dir., Lab. for Molecular Diagnosis; joined Burnham Inst., La Jolla, Calif., 1992—, scientific dir., 1995—2002, dep. dir., NCI-sponsored Cancer Ctr., 1994—2002, interim dir., NCI-sponsored Cancer Ctr., 2002, pres., CEO, 2002—, current bd. trustee. Mem. grant rev. com. Am. Cancer Soc., Atlanta, 1990—; cons. Genta, Inc., La Jolla, Calif., 1991—; adj. prof. U. Calif.-San Diego, San Diego State U.; advisor nat. Cancer Inst., Am. Cancer Soc., Am. Assn. for Cancer Rsch.; advisor and cons. to numerous biotechnology and pharm. cos.; sci. co-founder, scientific adv. bd., (current) bd. dir. IDUN Pharm., Inc.; sci. co-founder, sci. adv. bd. GMP/Diagnostics; current bd. dir. ISIS Pharm., Inc. (also sci. adv. bd.), STRATAGENE, Inc. (also sci. adv. bd.), and BIOCOM; sci. adv. bds. Abbott Lab.. Bristol-Myers-Squibb, Genta, Structural Bioinformatics, Genome Biosciences, Entropia, global Life-sciences Information Tech. initiative. Author 50 book chpts.; contbr. over 600 articles to profl. jours.; serves on editl. bds. of over 12 scientific jours. Leukemia Soc. Am. fellow, 1988-91, recipient scholar award, 1991—, Rsch. award Am. Cancer Soc., 1989—; grantee NIH, Nat. Cancer, Inst., Am. Cancer Soc., Leukemia Soc. Am., CaP-CURE, ABC2, and the Susan B. Komen Breast Cancer Found. Mem. AAAS, Am. Soc. Cancer Rsch., Am. Soc. Human Genetics, Am. Assn. Immunology. Republican. Episcopalian. Achievements include patent for DNA therapeutic strategy for treating cancer; research on cancer causing genes (oncogenes), on mechanism of action of immunomodulator Interleukin 2; his inventions have resulted in over 40 US Patents or Patent applications, and have spawn drug-discovery programs at several biopharmaceutical cos.; pioneer in delineating the fundamental mechanisms that regulate programmed cell death; has the distinction of having published more papers on programmed cell death (known as "apoptosis") during the past decade than any other scientist worldwide; recognized by the Institute for Scientific Information as the world's most cited scientist in all areas of research from 1997-99. Office: Burnham Inst 10901 N Torrey Pines Rd La Jolla CA 92037 Fax: 858-646-3199. Office Phone: 858-646-3132. Business E-Mail: president@burnham.org.

**REED, JOHN FRANCIS (JACK REED),** senator; b. Providence, Nov. 12, 1949; s. Joseph Anthony and Mary Louise (Monahan) R.; m. Julia Hart. BS in Engring., US Mil. Acad., 1971; MA in Pub. Policy, Harvard U., 1973, JD cum laude, 1982. Bar: DC 1982, RI 1983. Commd. 2d. lt. US Army, 1971, served with 82d Airborne Div., 1973-77; asst. prof. US Mil. Acad., West Point, NY, 1977-79; resigned US Army, 1979; assoc. Sutherland, Asbill & Brennan, Washington, 1982-83, Edwards & Angell, Providence, 1983-89; mem. RI Senate, 1984-90, 102nd-104th Congresses from 2d R.I. dist., 1991—97; US Senator from RI, 1997—. Mem. com. armed services US Senate, com. banking, housing, and urban affairs, com. health, edn., labor and pensions, joint econ. com. Author: (with others) American National Security 1981, served to Major U.S. Army, 1967—79. Recipient Disting. Legis. award United Way Southeastern New Eng., 1988, Disting. Svc. award AARP, 1989, John Fogarty award, 1990, Crystal Apple award Am. Assn. Sch. Librarians, 1994, Excellence in Public Svc. award Am. Acad. Pediatrics, 1998, Excellence in Immunization award Nat. Partnership for Immunization, 2001, Congressional Leadership award Coalition to Stop Gun Violence and Edn. Fund to Stop Gun Violence, 2002, Nat. Excellence in Public Health award Assn. State and Territorial Health Officials, 2002, Joan Gallagher Legis. award Mass. Sch. Libr. Media Assn., 2003. Mem. ABA, RI Bar Assn., DC Bar Assn., Environ. and Energy Study Inst., Phi Kappa Phi. Democrat. Roman Catholic. Avocations: reading, hiking. Office: US Senate 728 Hart Senate Ofc Bldg Washington DC 20510-0001 also: District Office Ste 200 201 Hillside Rd Cranston RI 02920 Office Phone: 202-224-4642, 401-943-3100. Office Fax: 202-224-4680, 401-464-6837.*

**REED, JOHN HATHAWAY,** former ambassador; b. Fort Fairfield, Maine, Jan. 5, 1921; s. Walter and Eva Ruth (Seeley) R.; m. Cora Mitchell Davison, Mar. 24, 1944; children—Cheryl, Ruth. BS, U. Maine, 1942, LL.D. (hon.), 1960, Ricker Coll.; grad., Harvard Naval Supply Sch., 1944. Officer Reed Farms, Inc., Fort Fairfield, Maine, 1948-98; pres. Aroostook Raceway, Inc., 1958-59; adv. com. Fort Fairfield br. No. Nat. Bank of Presque Isle; mem. Nat. Transp. Safety Bd., Washington, 1967-75, chmn., 1969-75; ambassador to Sri Lanka Colombo, 1975-77; dir. govt. rels. Assoc. Builders & Contractors, Inc., Washington, 1978-81; ambassador to Sri Lanka and Republic of Maldives, 1982-85; cons. Dept. State, 1985-90; pvt. practice cons. Washington, 1990—. Chmn. Nat. Govs. Conf. Rep., 1966; rep. Fort Fairfield to Maine Legislature, 1954-56; mem. Senate, 1957-59, pres., 1959-60; gov. State of Maine, 1960-67. Pres. bd. Community Gen. Hosp., Fort Fairfield, 1952-54, No. Maine Fair, 1953-59; trustee Ricker Coll., 1953-60, Oak Grove Sch., Vassalboro, Maine; bd. advisors Coll. of Democracy, 1986—, chmn., 1991-2000. Served to lt. (j.g.) USNR, 1942-46. Mem. Am. Fgn. Svc. Assn., Coun. Am. Ambassadors, Soc. Aerospace Execs. Inc. (bd. dirs. 1987-99, pres. 1988-91), Nat. Inst. Former Govs. (bd. dirs. 1992—), Am. Legion, VFW, Grange, Maine Assn. Agrl. Fairs (pres. 1956), Mil. Order of Carabao, Capitol Hill Club, Driving Club (Ft. Fairfield) (pres. 1950-53), Aeroclub of Washington, Internat. Aviation Club, Rotary, Masons, KP, Anah Temple Shrine. Republican. Congregationalist. Office: 410 O St SW Washington DC 20024-2239

**REED, JOHN SHEDD,** former railway executive; b. Chgo., June 9, 1917; s. Kersey Coates and Helen May (Shedd) R.; m. Marjorie Lindsay, May 4, 1946; children: Ginevra, Keith, Helen, Peter, John Shedd Jr. Student, Chgo. Latin Sch., Hotchkiss Sch.; BS in Indsl. Adminstrn., Yale U., 1939; grad., Advanced Mgmt. Program, Harvard U., 1955. With A.T. & S.F. Ry., 1939-83; test dept. asst., successively spl. rep. to gen. supt. transp. Chgo.; transp. insp. Amarillo, Tex.; trainmaster Slaton, Tex., Pueblo, Colo.; supt. Mo. div., Marceline, Mo.; asst. to v.p. Chgo., 1957-59; exec. asst. to pres., 1957-59; v.p. finance, 1959-64; v.p. exec. dept., 1964-66; pres., 1967-78; chief exec. officer, 1968-82; chmn. bd., 1973-83. Pres. Santa Fe Industries, Inc., 1968-78, chmn. bd. dirs., CEO Santa Fe So. Pacific Corp., 1987, chmn., 1987-88. Dir. Nat. Merit Scholarship Corp., 1996, past chmn.; trustee Shedd Aquarium, Chgo., 1996, past pres.; vice chmn., dir. Alliance Francaise de Chicago. With USNR, 1940-45. Mem. Chgo. Club, Old Elm Club, Shoreacres Club, Onwentsia Club (Lake Forest).

**REED, JOHN SHEPARD,** former stock exchange executive; b. Chgo., Feb. 7, 1939; divorced; 4 children; m. Cindy McCarthy, 1994. BA, Washington and Jefferson Coll., 1961; BS, MIT, 1961; MS, Sloan Sch. MIT, 1965. With Citicorp/Citibank, 1965—2000, chmn., CEO, 1984-98; co-chmn. CitiGroup, Inc., N.Y.C., 1998—2000; interim chmn. NY Stock Exch., NYC, 2003—05, interim CEO, 2003—04; Robert S. Hatfield Fellow, Econ. Edn. Cornell Univ., Ithaca, 1998; sr. visiting fellow Princeton Univ., Bendheim Ctr. for Finance, 2002. Bd. dirs. Citicorp/Citibank, 1975-2000, Altria Group (formerly Philip Morris Inc.), 1975-, Monsanto Co.; mem. Bus. Coun.; mem. policy com., Bus. Roundtable; chmn. Coalition of Svc. Inds., svcs. policy adv. com. to the U.S. Trade Rep. Mem. bd. MIT, Meml. Sloan-Kettering Cancer Ctr., Rand Corp., Spencer Found., Am. Mus. Nat. History. Served with C.E. U.S. Army, Korea, 1962-64.

**REED, JOHN WESLEY,** lawyer, educator; b. Independence, Mo., Dec. 11, 1918; s. Novus H. and Lilian (Houchens) R.; m. Imogene Fay Vonada, Oct. 5, 1946 (div. 1958); m. Dorothy Elaine Floyd, Mar. 5, 1961; children: Alison A., John M. (dec.), Mary V., Randolph F., Suzanne M. AB, William Jewell Coll., 1939, LLD, 1995; LLB, Cornell U., 1942; LLM, Columbia U., 1949, JSD, 1957. Bar: Mo. 1942, Mich. 1953. Assoc. Stinson, Mag, Thomson, McEvers & Fizzell, Kansas City, Mo., 1942-46; assoc. prof. law U. Okla., 1946-49; assoc. prof. U. Mich., 1949-53, prof., 1953-64, 68-75, Thomas M. Cooley prof., 1985-87, Thomas M. Cooley prof. emeritus, 1987—; dean, prof. U. Colo., 1964-68, Wayne State U., Detroit, 1987-92, prof. emeritus, 1992—. Vis. prof. NYU, 1949, U. Chgo., 1960, Yale U., 1963-64, Harvard U., 1982, U. San Diego, 1993; dir. Inst. Continuing Legal Edn., 1968-73; reporter Mich. Rules of Evidence Com., 1975-78, 83-84; mem. faculty Salzburg Sem., 1962, chmn., 1964. Author: (with W.W. Blume) Pleading and Joinder, 1952; (with others) Introduction to Law and Equity, 1953, Advocacy Course Handbook series, 1963-81; editor in chief Cornell Law Quar., 1941-42; contbr. articles to profl. jours. Pres. bd. mgrs. of mins. and missionaries benefit bd. Am. Bapt. Chs. U.S.A., 1967-74, 82-85, 88-94; mem. com. visitors JAG Sch., 1971-76; trustee Kalamazoo Coll., 1954-64, 68-70. Recipient Harrison Tweed award Assn. Continuing Legal Edn. Adminstrs., 1983, Samuel E. Gates award Am. Coll. Trial Lawyers, 1985, Roberts P. Hudson award State Bar Mich., 1989. Fellow Internat. Soc. Barristers (editor jour. 1980—); mem. ABA (mem. coun. litigation sect.), Assn. Am. Law Schs. (mem. exec. com. 1965-67), Am. Acad. Jud. Edn. (v.p. 1978-80), Colo. Bar Assn. (mem. bd. govs. 1964-68), Mich. Supreme Ct. Hist. Soc. (bd. dirs. 1991—), Sci. Club Mich., Order of Coif. Office: U Mich Sch Law Ann Arbor MI 48109-1215 Office Phone: 734-763-0165. E-mail: reedj@umich.edu.

**REED, JOSEPH WAYNE,** American studies educator, artist; b. St. Petersburg, Fla., May 31, 1932; s. Joseph Wayne and Gertrude (Cain) R.; m. Kit Craig, Dec. 10, 1955; children: Joseph McKean, John Craig, Katherine Hyde Maruyama. BA, Yale U., 1954, MA, 1958, PhD, 1961. Lectr. asst. Yale Libr., 1956-57; instr. English Wesleyan U., Middletown, Conn., 1960-61, assoc. prof., 1967-71, prof., 1971—, chmn. dept., 1971-73, 75-76, 85-86, prof. English and Am. studies, 1987—2004; prof. emeritus, 2004—. Vis. lectr. Yale U., New Haven, 1974; lectr. U.S. dept. State and USIS, Can., India, Nepal, 1974; coord. cultural exch., New Delhi, Bombay, 1992; coord. music and writing workshop U. Va., Georgetown U.; lectr. U. Essex, GB, 2005. Author: English Biography in the Early Nineteenth Century, 1966; Faulkner, 1973, Three American Originals: John Ford, William Faulkner, Charles Ives, 1984, American Scenarios, 1989; editor: Barbara Bodichon's American Diary, 1972, (with W.S. Lewis) Horace Walpole's Family Correspondence, 1975, (with F.A. Pottle) Boswell, Laird of Auchinleck, 1977, 2d edit., 1994; one-man shows include Portal Gallery, London, 1971, USIS Libr., New Delhi, 1974, 92, Addison/Ripley Gallery, Washington, 1987, 92, 95, 98, Sterling Meml. Libr., Yale U., 2004; sculptor Johnson Medal of the Johnsonians, 1984, Elizabethan Medal, Yale Elizabethan Club, 1986, Daniel Patrick Moynihan Medal, Citizens Com., N.Y., 1999, Vincent Scully Medal, Nat. Bldg. Mus., Wash., Freeman Medal, Wesleyan U., 1999, Moynihan plaque, D.P. Moynihan Courthouse, N.Y.C., 2000. Chmn. Wesleyan Sesquicentennial, 1982; chmn. bd. trustees Yale Libr. Assocs., 1984-2000, hon. trustee, 2000—. Lt. (j.g.) USNR, 1954-56. Mem. Elizabethan Club, The Johnsonians (chmn. 1988). Democrat. Episcopalian. Home: 45 Lawn Ave Middletown CT 06457-3135

**REED, KATHLYN LOUISE,** occupational therapist, educator; b. Detroit, June 2, 1940; d. Herbert C. and Jessie R. (Krehbiel) R. BS in Occupl. Therapy, U. Kans., 1964; MA, Western Mich. U., 1966; PhD, U. Wash., 1973; MLIS, U. Okla., 1987. Occupl. therapist in psychiatry Kans. U. Med. Ctr., Kansas City, 1964-65; instr. occupl. therapy U. Wash., Seattle, 1967-70; assoc. prof. dept. occupl. therapy U. Okla. Health Scis. Ctr., Oklahoma City, 1973-77, prof., 1978-85, chmn. dept. occupl. therapy, 1973-85; libr. edn. info. svcs. Houston Acad. Medicine Tex. Med. Ctr. Libr., 1988-97. Cons. Okla. State Dept. Health, 1976-77, Children's Convalescent Ctr., Oklahoma City, 1977-80, Oklahoma City Pub. Schs., 1980-81; vis. scholars program Tex. Woman's U., 1991-94; adj. prof. Sch. Occupl. Therapy, 1992-97, vis. prof., 1997-2006, assoc. prof., 2006—; prof. Houston Acad. Author: (with Sharon Sanderson) Concepts of Occupational Therapy, 1980, 4th edit., 1999, Models of Practice in Occupational Therapy, 1983, Quick Reference to Occupational Therapy, 1991, 2d edit., 2000, (with Julie Pauls) Quick Reference to Physical Therapy, 1996, 2d edit., 2004; (with S. Cunningham) Internet Guide for Rehabilitation Professionals, 1997; (with Sally Pore) Quick Reference to Speech-Language Pathology, 1999. Vol. crisis counselor Open Door Clinic, Seattle, 1968-72; mem. exec. bd. Seattle Mental Health Inst., 1971-72; Mem. Citizen Participation Liaison Coun., Seattle, 1970-72. Recipient Award of Merit, Can. Assn. Occupl. Therapists, 1988. Fellow: Am. Occupl. Therapy Assn. (Merit award 1983, Slagle lectr. award 1985, Svc. award 1985, 2001); mem.: Soc. for the Study of Occupations, Tex. Occupl. Therapy Found. (pres. 1998—), Neuro-Devel. Treatment Assn., Assn. Advancement Rehab. Tech., Am. Occupl. Therapy Found., Med. Libr. Assn. (Rittenhouse award 1987, Acad. Health Info. Professions), Tex. Occupl. Therapy Assn. (Roster of Merit award 2002, Disting. Svc. award 2004), Okla. Occupl. Therapy Assn. (pres. 1974—76), Coun. Exceptional Children, World Fedn. Occupl. Therapists, N.Am. Riding for Handicapped Assn., Sigma Kappa (Colby award 1994), Pi Theta Epsilon. Democrat. Home: 6699 De Moss Dr Houston TX 77074-5003 Personal E-mail: klreed3@juno.com.

**REED, LEON SAMUEL,** photographer, writer; b. Warren, Ohio, July 6, 1949; s. Walter Charles and Lois Avaleene (Botroff) R.; m. Margaret Smith, Dec. 27, 1975 (div.); m. Lois S. Lembo, Aug. 5, 1997; children: Samuel, Stephen, Catherine. BA in Econs. and Journalism, Antioch Coll., Yellow Springs, Ohio, 1971. Project dir. Coun. on Econ. Priorities, N.Y.C. and Washington, 1970-75; sr. mem. profl. staff Joint Com. on Def. Prodn., U.S. Congress, Washington, 1975-77; mem. profl. staff Com. on Banking, Housing and Urban Affairs, U.S. Senate, Washington, 1977-81; analyst TASC, 1981-82; mgr. contingency planning, 1982-85, mgr. instl. resources dept., 1985-91, dir. indsl. and mfg. scis. divsn., 1991-97; rsch. staff Inst. Def. Analyses, 1998—2003; freelance writer, photographer, 2000—; rsch. asst. George Mason U., 2004—; tchr. Woodbridge H.S., 2005—. Author: Military Maneuvers, 1975, Resource Management: A Historical Perspective, 1988;

co-author: Guide to Corporations, 1973, Report of the National Critical Technologies Panel, 1991; contbr. Strategic Survey, 1981-82, The American Defense Mobilization Infrastructure, 1983; corr. Potomac Almanac; author numerous congressional and exec. br. reports, also mag. and jour. articles. Del. White House Conf. on Youth, 1971; writer, photographer Md. Soccer News, 1996—2005; pres. Randolph Civic Assn., 1978—80; v.p. North Bethesda Congress of Citizens Assns., 1983—84, pres., 1984—86; v.p. Md. State Youth Soccer Assn., 1998—2005; bd. dirs. Coun. on Econ. Priorities, 1971—73, Montgomery Soccer, Inc., 1994—, pres., 2001—06. Named to Warren HS Alumni Hall of Fame, 1997.

**REED, LOWELL A., JR.,** federal judge; b. Westchester, Pa., 1930; BBA, U. Wis., 1952; JD, Temple U., 1958. Bar: Pa. 1959, U.S. Dist. Ct. (ea. dist.) Pa. 1961, U.S. Ct. Appeals (3d cir.) 1962, U.S. Supreme Ct. 1970. Corp. trial counsel PMA Group, Phila., 1958-63; assoc. Rawle & Henderson, Phila., 1963-65, gen. ptnr., 1966-88; judge U.S. Dist Ct., Phila., 1988-99; sr. judge U.S. Dist. Ct., Phila., 1999—. Lectr. law Temple U., 1965-81, faculty Acad. Advocacy, 1988—, Pa. Bar Inst., 1972—. Contbr. articles to profl. jours. Elder Abington (Pa.) Presbyn. Ch.; past. mem. Pa. Senate Select Com. Med. Malpractice; past pres., bd. dirs. Rydal Meadowbrook Civic Assn.; bd. dirs. Abington Sch. Bd., 1971, World Affairs Coun. Phila. 1983-88; trustee Abington Health Care Corp., 1983-88, 90-93. Lt. Comdr. USNR, 1952-57. Recipient Alumni Achievement award Temple U. 1988, Cert. of Honor, 2001, A. Sherman Christensen award Am. Inns. of Ct. Found., 2003. Mem. ABA, Phila. Bar Assn. (chmn. medico legal com. 1975, constl. bicentennial com. 1986-87, commn. on jud. selection and retention 1983-87), Temple Am. Inn of Ct. (pres. 1990-93, master of bench 1990—), Am. Judicature Soc., Temple U. Law Alumni Assn. (exec. com. 1987-90, 99—), Hist. Soc. U.S. Supreme Ct., Hist. Soc. U.S. Dist. Ct. Ea. Dist. Pa. Republican. Office: US Dist Ct US Courthouse Independence Mall W Philadelphia PA 19106

**REED, M. SCOTT,** accounting company executive; CFO Grant Thornton LLP, Chgo., 1997-99, CEO, 1999-2000. Office: Grant Thornton LLP 175 W Jackson Blvd #20 Chicago IL 60604-3033

**REED, MARC C.,** human resources specialist, communications executive; B in Bus. Adminstrn., State U. NY. Mem. human resources staff GTE World Hqtrs., 1986—87; various human resources exec. positions including dir. human resources GTE Wireless, 1987—97, v.p. human resources, 1997—2004, Verizon Wireless, NYC, exec. v.p. human resources, 2004—. Office: Verizon Comm Inc 1095 Avenue of the Americas New York NY 10036 Office Phone: 212-395-2121. Office Fax: 212-869-3265.

**REED, MARY CAROLYN CAMBLIN,** retired music educator, retired county official; b. North Platte, Nebr., June 22, 1938; d. Brick and Evelyn Camblin; m. Paul E. Reed, Dec. 20, 1960. BA, U. No. Colo., 1960; MA, Calif. State U., 1964; PhD in Ednl. Adminstrn., U. So. Calif., 1976. Cert. administr. Calif., 1970. Music educator Rowland Unified Sch. Dist, Rowland Heights, Calif., 1960—67; tchr and writer instrnl. TV LA (Calif.) County Office Edn.; asst. to supt. and chief dep. supt. LA (Calif.) County Office of Edn., 1976—79; adminstr. Regional Ednl. TV Adv. Coun., LA, 1979—82; ednl. tech. unit adminstr. Calif. State Dept. Edn., Sacramento, 1982—83; dir. media svcs. Sacramento (Calif.) County Office Edn., 1983—94, dir. ednl. media, 1993—94; mng. cons. Northern Calif. Media/Tech. Consortium, 1994—2004, Ctrl. Calif. Ednl. Tech. Consortium, 1994—2004. Cons. music series PBS Sta. WETA, Washington, 1974—76; bd. dirs. LA (Calif.) Music Ctr., AMAN Folk Dance group, LA, 1975—77, PBS Sta. KQED, San Francisco, 1989—95. Musician: Am. Flute Orch., 2001, 2002, Internat. Flute Orch., 2004—, Sacramento (Calif.) Symphonic Band, 1995, 2003, Camellia City Flut Choir, 2000—. Recipient Outstanding Alumnus, U. of No. Colo. 1983. Mem.: Calif. Music Educators Assn. (pres. 1976—78), Cosumnes Cmty. Orch, West Sacramento Orch. (prin. flutist 1990—). Office Phone: 916-928-9332.

**REED, MICHAEL HAYWOOD,** lawyer; b. Phila., Jan. 17, 1949; s. Soloman Taylor and Vivian (Haywood) Reed; m. Yalta Gilmore, Aug. 12, 1978; children: Alexandra Haywood, Michael Harward Jr. BA in Polit. Sci., Temple U., 1969; JD, Yale U., 1972. Bar: Pa. 1972, U.S. Dist. Ct. (ea. dist.) Pa. 1972, U.S. Dist. Ct. (ea. dist.) Mich. 1982, U.S. Supreme Ct. 1982, U.S. Ct. Appeals (3d cir.) 1985. Assoc. Pepper, Hamilton & Scheetz, Phila., 1972-80; ptnr., corp. restructuring, bankruptcy practice Pepper Hamilton LLP (formerly Pepper, Hamilton & Scheetz), Phila., 1980—. Co-adj. prof. law Rutgers U., Camden, NJ, 1983, 85; adj. prof. sch. law Temple U., Phila., 1989; mem. Pa. Judicial Inquiry and Rev. Bd., 1990-93; chair Ea. Dist. Pa. Bankruptcy Conf., 1997-98; mem. Presdl. Adv. Coun. on Diversity in the Profession, 2006—; spkr. in field. Contbr. articles to profl. jours. Advisor Post 913 Law Explorers, Phila., 1974-84; trustee Acad. Natural Scis., Phila., 1988—, Episcopal Hosp., Phila., 1986-98; mem. bd. advisors Pub. Interest Law Ctr., Phila., 1992—; mem. Com. Seventy, Phila., 1981—. Recipient cert. of honor Alumnus of Yr. Coll. of Arts and Scis. Temple U., 1995, Award of Excellence, Thurgood Marshall Scholarship Fund, Inc., 2003, J. Austin Norris award, Barristers Assn. Phila., 2005. Fellow Am. Coll. Bankruptcy; mem. ABA (chmn. subcom. labor and employment law, bus bankruptcy com. sect. bus. law 1991-97, chmn. subcom. on labor and employment law 1997-02, subcom. on avoiding powers 2002-05, subcom. bankruptcy coms. 2005-, ho. of dels. 2002-, bd. govs. 2005-06), Nat. Bar Assn. Am. Law Inst., Am. Bankruptcy Inst., Pa. Bar Assn. (mem. ho. of dels. 1999-01, chmn. minority bar com. 1988-90, mem. bd. govs. 1993-96, co-chair 1994, v.p. 2002-03, pres.-elect 2003, pres. 2004-05, ann. meeting, Spl. Achievement award 1989, Cert. of Honor award 1995), Barristers Assn. Phila. (1st v.p. 1974-76), Phila. Bar Assn. (chair profl. guidance com. 1986), Yale Club (Phila.), Alpha Phi Alpha, Sigma Pi Phi. Democrat. Baptist. Avocations: racquetball, films, theater, biking, piano. Office: Pepper Hamilton LLP 3000 Two Logan Sq 18th and Arch Streets Philadelphia PA 19103-2799 Office Phone: 215-981-4416. Office Fax: 215-981-4750. Business E-Mail: reedm@pepperlaw.com.

**REED, MICHAEL JOHN,** dentist, dean, oral biology educator; b. Wednesbury, Eng., Dec. 25, 1940; came to U.S., 1967, naturalized, 1972; s. Harry Ernest and Ida Veva (Heywood) R.; m. Pamela Twycross, July 4, 1965 (div. Feb. 1976); children: Justine Marianne, Helena Clare; m. Ingrid Liepins, Sept. 8, 1978; children: Kathryn Anne, Matthew Harrison. BS with honors, U. Durham, Eng., 1963; B in Dental Surgery, U. Newcastle-Upon-Tyne, Eng., 1967; PhD, SUNY, Buffalo, 1971. Lic. dentist U.K.Y., Miss. Instr. oral biology SUNY, Buffalo, 1971-72, asst. prof. oral biology, 1972-77, assoc. prof., 1977-79; asst. dean Sch. Dentistry, U. Miss., Jackson, 1980-85, assoc. dean, 1985; dean; dir. oral biology Sch. Dentistry, U. Mo., Kansas City, 1985—. Cons. Nat. Inst. Dental Rsch., Washington, 1975-85. Contbr. numerous articles to profl. jours. Recipient rsch. career devel. award NIH, 1975-80. Fellow Acad. Dentistry Internat., Internat. Coll. Dentists, Am. Coll. Dentists; mem. ADA (cons. 1982—, joint com. on nat. dental exam., 1988-93, chair 1992-93), Am. Assn. Dental Schs. (sect. chair 1985-86, chmn. schs. coun. of deans, 1992-93, pres. 1997-98), Am. Assn. Dental Rsch. (councillor 1974-76), Fedn. Dentaire Internat., Am. Assn. for Microbiology, Mid-Am. Masters Club, Omicron Kappa Upsilon. Episcopalian. Avocations: running, European current affairs. Office: U Mo-Kansas City Sch Dentistry 650 E 25th St Kansas City MO 64108-2716 Office Phone: 816-235-2010. Office Fax: 816-235-2157. Business E-Mail: reedm@umkc.edu.*

**REED, MICHAEL ROBERT,** agricultural economist; b. Lawrence, Kans., July 11, 1953; s. Robert Stanley and Marian Lucille (Karr) R.; m. Patricia Gail Gurtler, Mar. 16, 1973; children: Laura Gail, Brian Michael. BS, Kans. State U., 1974; MS, Iowa State U., 1976, PhD, 1979. Asst. prof. U. Ky., Lexington, 1978-83, assoc. prof., 1983-89; prof., 1989—; exec. dir. Ctr. for Export Devel., 1988-95; dir. office of internat. affairs U. Ky., Lexington 1994-98, dir. office of internat. programs for agr., 1998—. Cons. USDA, 1994-97, 02—, US AID, Washington, 1983-86, 99-01, 04-. Author: (textbook) International Trade in Agricultural Products, 2000; mem. editl. bd. So. Jour. of Agrl. Econs., 1983-84, 87-88, TVA, 1982-85, Fed. Crop Ins. Corp., 1985-87, USDA, 1986-2003, 2005—; recipient Outstanding Jour. Article award Soc. Farm

Mgrs. and Rural Appraisers, 1986, Jour. Agrl. and Applied Econs., 2002 Mem. Am. Agrl. Econs. Assn., So. Agrl. Econs. Assn., Gamma Sigma Delta. Home: 2216 Bonhaven Rd Lexington KY 40515-1150 Office: U Ky Dept Agrl Econs 308 Barnhart Bldg Lexington KY 40546-0001 Office Phone: 859-257-7259. Business E-Mail: mrreed@uky.edu.

**REED, MIRIAM BELL,** legislative staff member; b. NYC, May 31, 1930; d. Samuel Dennis and Miriam Wilkes Bell; m. John Grady Reed, May 1, 1954; children: Roberta, Christine, Karen, Laura, Margaret, Abigail, Elisabeth. BA, Mount Holyoke Coll., 1952. Asst. to adminstrv. asst. Rep. Harlan Hagan, Washington, 1953-54; asst. to econ. prof. Littauer Sch. Pub. Adminstrn., Cambridge, Mass., 1954; producer, treas. Video Ed Prodns., Inc., Hyattsville, Md., 1974-90; Singapore testing coord. Malaysian Am. Commn. on Ednl. Exch., Singapore, 1991-92; legis. aide Del. Constance A. Morella, Annapolis, Md., 1978-86; legis. asst. Hon. Constance A. Morella, Washington, 1987-90, 92, 94-97; staff Friends of Connie Morella for Congress, 1999-2000. Cons. Acad. Arrangements Abroad, NYC, 1974-99. Rsch. and writing of ednl. hist. videotapes, 1974-90 (Pratt Libr. award 1986). V.p., pres. bd. LWV, Bronxville, NY, 1957-74; mem. Montgomery County Commn. on the Humanities, 1985-88; mem. Montgomery County Com. to Celebrate Md.'s 350th Birthday. Mem. Montgomery County Hist. Soc. (dir. 1998-2001), C&O Canal Assn. (info. officer 2000, 02, 2004-06). Avocations: swimming, hiking, backpacking. Home: 8221 Burning Tree Rd Bethesda MD 20817-2908 Personal E-mail: mreed8221@aol.com.

**REED, R. DOUGLAS,** music educator; b. Cheboygan, Mich., Apr. 17, 1947; s. Robert G. and Marian L. Reed; 1 child, Eric Douglas. MusB in Organ Performance, U. Mich., 1969, MusM in Organ Performance, 1971; cert. in Performance, U. Rochester, 1974, MusD in Performance and Lit., 1975. Prof. music U. Evansville, Ind., 1975—. Organist The Luth. Ch. Our Redeemer, Evansville, 1975—78; organist, dir. music First Presbyn. Ch., Evansville, 1980—88; prin. organist Cathedral Immaculate Conception, Memphis, 2001—02; cons. in field. Musician: Organ Concerts in United States, Europe, and Japan, William Albright: The King of Instruments, (albums) William Albright: Music for Organ and Harpsichord, Eastman American Music Series, Vol. 3, Douglas Reed Plays the C.B. Fisk Organ, Op. 98, Douglas Reed Plays the Taylor & Boody Organ, In Memoriam William Albright Douglas Reed Plays the C.B. Fisk Organ, Op. 110; author: (chapter) North American Organ Music after 1800 for Cambridge Companion to the Organ; contbr. articles to profl. jours. Recipient The Sadelle and Sidney Berger award, U. Evansville, 1998; grantee, The Mesker Trust Fund Evansville, Ind., 1978, U. Evansville, 1985, Ind. Arts Commn. and NEA, 1987, Friends U. Evansville Music, 1991, 2000, 2005. Mem.: Westfield Ctr. Early Keyboard Studies, Organ Hist. Soc., Am. Guild Organists (dean 1998—2001), Phi Kappa Phi, Pi Kappa Lamda. Avocations: travel, reading, photography. Office: University of Evansville 1800 Lincoln Avenue Evansville IN 47722 Office Phone: 812-488-2877. Business E-Mail: dr5@evansville.edu.

**REED, RALPH EUGENE, JR.,** political consultant, former political organization administrator; b. Portsmouth, Va., June 24, 1961; s. Ralph Sr. and Marcy R.; m. Jo Anne Young, 1987; children: Brittany, Ralph III, Christopher, Nicole. BA in History, U. Ga., 1985; Ph.D in Am. History, Emory U., 1991. Exec. dir. Christian Coalition, Chesapeake, Va., 1989-97; founder, pres. Century Strategies, Strategies Cons. Co., Duluth, Ga., 1997—; chmn. Ga. Republican Party, 2001—03; southeast regional campaign chmn. George Bush re-election campaign, 2003—04. Founder Students for Am., Raleigh, N.C., 1984; lobbyist; spkr. in field. Author: Politically Incorrect: The Emerging Faith Factor in American Politics, 1994, After the Revolution: How the Christian Coalition is Impacting America, 1995, Active Faith: How Christians Are Changing the Face of American Politics, 1996. Office: Century Strategies 3235 Satellite Blvd Ste 575 Duluth GA 30096-9017

**REED, RAYMOND DERYL,** architect; b. Alturas, Calif., Mar. 29, 1930; s. Russell Jacob and Nita Ferne (Wilcox) R.; m. Patricia Reinerth, Apr. 30, 1954; children— Kathryn, Russell, Ann, Andrea. B.Arch., Tulane U., 1953; M.Arch., Harvard U., 1958. Chmn. architecture and interior design dept. U. Southwestern La., 1958-64; head dept. architecture Iowa State U., 1964-70, dir. grad. research in architecture, 1970-73; mem. faculty Tex. A&M U., 1973—, prof. architecture, 1973—96, dean Coll. Architecture and Environ. Design, 1973-80, prof. emeritus, 1996—. Dir. Internat. Ctr. for Cybernetics and Informatics, 1990. Author: Sustainable Architecture, 1988, rev. edit, 1990; contbr. numerous articles on energy conservation and post petroleum architecture to research projects. Served with USNR, 1953-58. Mem. AIA, Nat. Council Archtl. Registration Bds., Am. Collegiate Schs. Architecture, Tex. Soc. Architects, La. Architects Soc. Home: 1601 Wolf Pen Ct College Station TX 77840-3169 Office Phone: 979-492-4858. Personal E-mail: rayreed@verizon.net.

**REED, ROBERT ALLEN,** elementary school educator; b. Springfield, Mo., May 10, 1965; s. Gary Allen and Edith Marie Reed; m. Sharon Kay Renshaw, June 21, 1986; children: Grant Taylor, Chandler Cameron. BS in Music Edn., Southwest Mo. State U., 1987; M in Ednl. Adminstrn., Evangel. U., 2006. Music specialist Springfield Pub. Schs., Mo., 1988—. Artistic dir. Boys Choir Springfield, 2000—05. Contemporary worship leader First & Calvary Presbyn., Springfield, 2004—05; cmty. theatre Springfield Little Theatre, 1995—2003. Mem.: Mo. Choral Dirs. Assn., Am. Choral Dirs. Assn., Music Educators Nat. Conf. Avocations: travel, theater. Home: 3762 N Mill Rd Springfield MO 65803 Office: Springfield Pub Schs 940 N Jefferson Springfield MO 65802

**REED, ROBERT JAMES, JR.,** painter, art educator; b. 1938; BS, Morgan State Coll., Balt., 1958; BFA, Yale U., 1960, MFA, 1962; DFA (hon.), Mpls. Coll. Art and Design, 2001. Mem. faculty Skidmore Coll., Mpls. Coll. Art and Design, head Found. Studies Divsn., 1964; mem. painting faculty Yale U., New Haven, 1969—, former head grad. studies in painting/printmaking, now dir. undergraduate studies in art. Dir. art divsn. Yale Summer Sch. Music and Art, 1970—75; mem. faculty summer program Pont-Aven Sch. Contemporary Art, France, 2005. Group exhibitions, Albright-Knox Art Gallery, Hirshhorn Mus. and Sculpture Garden, Mpls. Inst. Arts, Walker Art Ctr., Whitney Mus. Am. Art, Yale U. Art Gallery, solo exhibitions, Bayly Mus., Va., Washburn Gallery, NY, Whitney Mus. Am. Art, Represented in permanent collections, Bayly Mus., Va., Hirshhorn Mus. and Sculpture Garden, Walker Art Ctr., Whitney Mus. Am. Art, Yale U. Art Gallery. Recipient Disting. Tchg. of Art Award, Coll. Art Assn., 2004, grantee Nat. Endowment for the Arts, 1980; Yaddo Fellow. Office: Yale U Sch Art Holcombe T Green Jr Hall 1156 Chapel St New Haven CT 06520

**REED, ROD A.,** music educator, director; MusB in Edn., We. Ill. U., Macomb Ill., 1987. Dir. band John T. Hoggard H.S., Wilmington, NC, 1998—. Office Phone: 910-350-2072. Personal E-mail: redsled65@hotmail.com.

**REED, SALLY GARDNER,** cultural organization administrator; BA in English, Colo. State U., 1979; MLS, No. Ill. U., 1981. Dir. North Hampton (H.H.) Pub. Libr., 1981-85, Ilsley Pub. Libr., Middlebury, Vt., 1985-93, Ames (Iowa) Pub. Libr., 1993-95; dir. librs. Norfolk (Va.) Pub. Libr., 1995—2001; exec. dir. Friends of Librs. USA, Phila., 2001—. Author: Small Libraries: A Handbook for Successful Management, 1991, 2d edit., 2002, Saving Your Library: A Guide to Getting, Using and Keeping the Power You Need, 1992, Library Volunteers: Worth the Effort!, 1994; editor: Creating the Future: Essays on the Future of Librarianship in an Age of Great Change, 1996, Speaking Out: Voices in Celebration of Intellectual Freedom, 1999, Making the Case for Your Library, 2001, 101+ Great Ideas for Libraries and Friends, 2004; contbr. articles to profl. jours. Bd. dirs. Sheldon Art History Mus., Middlebury, 1988-93, United Way Story County, Ames, 1994-95; mem. cabinet United Way Norfolk, 1996-97, chair city campaign, 1997. Recipient Recognition award Tidewater Area Minority Libr. Network, 1997, Am. Libr. Assoc. Herb & Virginia White award for Promoting Librarianship, 2000. Mem. ALA (chpt. coun. 1989-93, adv. com. office libr. outreach svcs.

1993-94, nat. libr. week com. 1993-95, presdl. com. pub. awareness 1994-96, councilor at large 1995-99, chair membership com. 1996, resolutions com. 1997, exec. dir. 1997-2001, chair pub. awareness com. 2004-06). Office: Friends Libraries USA 1420 Walnut Ste 450 Philadelphia PA 19102 Office Phone: 215-790-1674. Business E-Mail: sreed@folusa.org.

**REED, SAM,** state official; b. Portland, Oreg. m. Margie Reed, 1963; children: David, Kristen. BA, MA, Wash. State U. Cert. profl. elections officer. Exec. dir. Gov. Evans' Urban Affairs Coun.; Thurston County auditor; asst. sec. of state State of Wash.; dir. State Constl. Reform Commn.; sec. of state State of Wash., 2001—. Bd. mem. Fed. Election Commn. Voting System; internat. election observer, Rwanda, Uganda; mem. Wash. State Archives Adv. Com., Americorps Adv. Coun., Wash. State Election Admin. & Cert. Bd. Recipient Gov.'s Disting. Vol. award, Thurston County Citizen of the Year Disting. Svc. award. Mem.: Mainstream Reps. of Wash., Wash. State Assn. County Auditors, Olympia Kiwanis. Republican. Avocations: running, piano, arts, tennis. Office: Office Sec of State Legislative Bldg 2nd Floor PO Box 40220 Olympia WA 98504 Office Phone: 360-902-4151. Office Fax: 360-586-5629. E-mail: sreed@secstate.wa.gov.*

**REED, SCOTT C.,** music educator, writer; b. Chgo., Aug. 28, 1957; s. Vernon C. Reed and Betty M. Ryan. MusB, U. of So. Calif., 1981. Adj. prof. Gov.'s State U., U. Pk., Ill., 1989—95, Prairie State Coll., Chgo. Heights, Ill., 1994—2005. Author: Getting Into Guitar Improvising: A Systematic Approach To Soloing, 2002, Getting Into Guitar Styles, 2005. Fellow, NEA, 1992—93. Office: Prairie State College 202 South Halsted Chicago Heights IL 60411

**REED, SHERMAN KENNEDY,** chemicals executive, consultant; b. Chgo., Apr. 11, 1919; s. Frank Hynes and Helen Louise (Kennedy) R.; m. Octavia Bailey, Oct. 11, 1943; children: Martin Bailey, Holly Anne Johnson, Julie Marie Reed. BS with honors, Ill., 1940; PhD, Cornell U., 1949. Asst. instr. chemistry Cornell U., 1940-43; asst. rsch. scientist Manhattan Project, N.Y.C., 1942-46; asst. prof. Bucknell U., Lewisburg, Pa., 1946-50; with FMC Corp., 1950—, mgr., asst. dir. rsch., 1950-60, divisional dir. rsch. and devel., ctrl. rsch. dir., 1960-76, v.p., 1976-82, cons. Chgo., 1983—; dir. Avicon, Inc., 1970-82; pres., dir. FMC Gold Corp.; mng. dir. COGAS Devel. Co., 1975—; dir. Indsl. Rsch. Inst., N.Y.C., Franklin Inst., Phila., 1975-83; chmn. bd. Franklin Rsch. Ctr., Phila., 1976-83. Fellow Am. Inst. Chemists; mem. AAAS, Am. Chem. Soc., Assn. Rsch. Dirs. (pres. 1973), Vero Beach Country Club, Union League Club (Phila.), Nassau Club (Princeton, N.J.). Republican. Home and Office: 2300 Indian Creek Blvd W #C211 Vero Beach FL 32966-2400 Personal E-mail: shermankreed@aol.com, shermankreed@bellsouth.net.

**REED, SUELLEN KINDER,** school system administrator; BA in History, Polit. Sci. and Secondary Edn., Hanover Coll., 1967; MA in Elem. Edn. and History, Ball State U., 1970, EdD in Adminstrn. and Supervision, LLD (hon.), 1997; EdD (hon.), Vincennes U., 1996; LittD (hon.), U. Indpls., 1997; LHD (hon.), St. Joseph Coll., 1999, Hanover Coll., 2003; postgrad., Fla. Atlantic U., U. Scranton, Purdue U., Earlham Coll., Ind. U., Ind. State U., U. So. Ind., Butler U., U. Alaska, U. Va. at Edinburgh (Scotland) U., Oxford (Eng.) U. Lic. supt., life lic. in elem. edn., U.S. history, world history, govt., adminstrn. and supervision and endorsement in edn. for gifted and talented K-12, Ind.; lic. adminstr., U.S. history, world history, govt., middle sch. lang. arts, social studies, elem. edn., gifted edn., Fla. Tchr. 5th and 6th grades Rushville (Ind.) Consol. Sch. Corp., 1967-70; tchr. Shelbyville (Ind.) High Sch., 1970-71; tchr. 6th, 7th and 8th grade social studies, curriculum Broward County (Fla.) Sch. Corp., 1971-76; tchr. Rushville Jr. High Sch., 1976-77; asst. prin. Rushville Elem. Sch., 1977-79; prin. Frazee Elem. Sch., Connersville, Ind., 1979-87; asst. supt. Rushville Consolidated Schs., 1987-90, supt., 1991-93; supt. pub. instrn., chairperson bd. edn., CEO dept. edn. State of Indiana, Indpls., 1993—. Pres. N. Ctrl. Regional Edn. Lab., Oak Brook, Ill., 1993—97, Oak Brook, 2002; mem. The Ctr. on Congress Outstanding Tchr. Award Selection Com. Contbr. articles to profl. jours. Bd. trustees Hanover Coll., Commn. Drug-Free Ind., Ind. Commn. Cmty. Svc., Ind. Higher Edn. Telecom. Sys., Ctr. Agrl. Sci. Heritage; hon. mem. Rush County Cmty. Found.; alumni bd. Ball State U. Tchrs. Coll., 1999-; bd. dirs. Nat. Children's Film Festival; trustee, mem. New Salem United Meth. Ch.; bd. dirs. Ind. Historic Landmarks Found., Agy. for Instrnl. Tech., Project Lead the Way, Virtual H.S., 2003—; bd. visitors Ind. U.; hon. bd. mem. Indpls. Zool. Soc. Named Outstanding Sch. Edn. Alumnus, Ball State U., 1994, Govt. Leader Yr., Ind. C. of C., 2001; recipient Pres. award, Ind. Assn. Sch. Prins., 1996, Achievement award, Ind. Network Women Adminstrs., 1996, Alumni award, Hanover Coll., 1997, Legis. award, Ind. Assn. for the Edn. Young Children, 1998, Pres. award, Ind. Middle Level Edn. Assn., 2001, Elizabeth Heywood Wyman award for alumnae, Alpha Omicron Pi, 2001, Friend Youth award, Ind. Sch. Counselors, 2001, Hoosier Heritage Civic Leadership award, 2002, Turn Off the Violence award, Ind. Crime Prevention Coalition, 2002, Ind. Sch. Safety Leadership award, 2002, Citizen's award, Ind. Libr. Fedn., Counselor's award, Assn. for Ind. Media Educators. Mem. ASCD (nat. and ind. chpts.), Internat. Reading Assn., Nat. Coun. for Accreditation Tchr. Edn. (mem. exec. bd.), Nat. Assn. Elem. and Mid. Sch. Prins. (assoc.), Nat. Assn. Gifted Children (nat. adv. bd.), Internat. Tech. Edn. Assn. (mem. adv. com.), Ind. Assn. Pub. Sch. Supts., Ind. Assn. Elem. and Mid. Sch. Prins. (assoc.), Women's Coun. on Literacy for the Ind. Literacy Found., Rose Hulman Inst. Tech., Network Woman Adminstrs., Indpls. Zoo, Indpls. Art Mus., Indpls. Bd. Assocs., Bus. and Profl. Women of Rushville, Connersville Area Reading Coun., Smithsonian, Rushville Rotary Club, Monday Cir., K-12 Compact Learning and Citizenship (chairwoman), Edn. Commn. States (commr., mem. exec. com. 1994-98, 2002—), Council Chief State Sch. Officers (pres.-elect., 2000-01, pres., 2001-02, v.p., 2002-03), Ind. Hist. Soc., Ind. State Mus., Conner Prairie Farm, Order of Ea. Star (Andersonville chpt.), Delta Kappa Gamma (past pres.), Phi Lambda Theta, Phi Delta Kappa (Comicl Prairie). Office: Superintendent Edn Dept 229 State House Indianapolis IN 46204-2798

**REED, TRAVIS DEAN,** public relations executive; b. Trinity, Tex., Sept. 27, 1930; s. Travis and Alma (Rains) R.; m. Caroline M. McDonald, June 15, 1957; children: Anne Reed Adams, Lisa Reed Lettau. Student, Tex. A&M U., 1948-51, U. Houston, 1951-53. Reporter Houston Post, 1951-53; Washington Bur. corr. McGraw-Hill Pub. Co., 1955-61, Boston Herald-Traveler, 1961-62; with Newhouse News Svc., Washington, 1962-79, chief corr., 1964-67, editor, 1967-79; pub. rels. cons. Washington, 1979—. 1st lt. U.S. Army, 1953-55. Mem. Nat. Press Club, Gridiron Club, Army and Navy Club. Home: 37277 Branchriver Rd Purcellville VA 20132-1922 Office: T Dean Reed Co PO Box 65276 Washington DC 20035

**REED, VASTINA KATHRYN (TINA REED),** child and adolescent psychotherapist; b. Chgo., Mar. 5, 1960; d. Alvin Hillard and Ruth Gwendolyn (Thomas) R.; 1 child, Alvin J. BA in Human Svcs. magna cum laude, Nat.-Louis U., Chgo., 1988; MA, Ill. Sch. Profl. Psychology, 1991; tng. cert., Appelbaum Inst. Child Devel.; cert. family devel. specialist, U. Iowa, 2002; fashion cons. of Evangelist Audey Donson, Good Shepherd Grace Min., 2002—. Notary pub. Ill., lic. profl. counselor Ill., child and adolescent psychotherapist, nat. cert. counselor NBCC. Tchr. early childhood edn. Kendall Coll. Lab. Sch., Evanston, Ill., 1983-85, Rogers Park Children's Learning Ctr., Chgo., 1983-85; child life therapist Mt. Sinai Hosp., Chgo., 1988; child psychotherapist Nicholas Barnes Therapeutic Day Sch., Chgo., 1989-90; preschl. instr. YMCA, 1999-2000; crisis line counselor Washington Security Corp., 2000—02; family support specialist Maywood (Ill.) Head Start, 2000—03; health care rep. Care Entrée, 2002—03; mental health svc. coord. Head Start Chgo. Dept. Children & Youth Svcs., 2005—. Den leader Boy Scouts Am., Chgo., 1989-92, scoutmaster, 1992-2000, merit badge counselor, 1999—, troop advisor for Order of the Arrow, 1999—; co-labourers Christ Ministry; editor, mem. praise and worship team Christ Outreach Deliverance Ctr. Ministry, 2001—; mem. Ill. Notary Public. Recipient Cub Scouter award Boy Scouts Am., 1990, Scoutmaster award of merit, 1993, 94, Scouters Vet. award, 1994, Scouters Tng. award, 1995, Scoutmasters Key award, 1996, Okpik Cold Weather Camping cert., 1994-95,

Outstanding Women of 20th Century medal, 2000, Boy Scout Woodbadge Tng. award, 2001. Mem. APA, Nat. Orgn. for Human Svc. Edn., Order of the Arrow, Charles F. Menninger Soc. (patron), Phi Theta Kappa, Kappa Delta Pi. Democrat. Pentecostal. Avocations: camping, films, singing, music. Home: 1872 S Millard Ave Chicago IL 60623-2542 Office Phone: 773-921-8674. Personal E-mail: treed2010@aol.com.

**REED, W. ALLEN,** automotive executive; b. Nashville, Apr. 4, 1947; B in Engring., Auburn U., 1970; M in Bus. Adminstrn., Ga. State U., 1975. Cert. Chartered Fin. Analyst. Asst. treas. Delta Airlines, 1981—84; staff v.p., pres. investment mgmt. co. Hughes Aircraft Co., Hughes Investment Mgmt. Co., 1984—91; v.p., treas. Hughes Aircraft, 1991, Hughes Elecronics, 1992; chmn. HIMCO, 1984—92; v.p. GM, 1994—; pres., CEO GM Asset Mgmt., 1994—. Mem. investment adv. com. N.Y. State Retirement Sys.; mem. editl. bd. Morgan Stanley Capital Internat.; bd. dirs. GMAC, GMAC Ins. Holdings, iShares, Inc., Temple-Inland Inds. Office: GM Asset Mgmt 767 Fifth Ave 15th Fl New York NY 10153

**REED, W. FRANKLIN,** lawyer; b. Louisville, Dec. 30, 1946; s. William Ferguson and Stella Elizabeth (Richardson) R.; m. Sharon Ann Coss, June 16, 1973; children: Jonathan Franklin, William Brian, Carrie Ann. BA, Williams Coll., 1968; JD, Columbia U., 1971. Bar: N.Y. 1972, U.S. Dist. Ct. (so. dist.) N.Y. 1975, U.S. Ct. Appeals (2d cir.) 1975, Pa. 1982, U.S. Dist. Ct. (we. dist.) 1983. Assoc. Milbank, Tweed, Hadley & McCloy, N.Y.C., 1971-82, Reed Smith Shaw & McClay, Pitts., 1982-83; ptnr. Reed, Smith, Shaw & McClay, Pitts., 1984—. Mem. instnl. devel. com. The Pitts. Cultural Trust; bd. dirs. Steel Industry Heritage Corp. Mem. ABA, Pa. Bar Assn., Allegheny Bar Assn, Carnegie 100, Williams Coll. Alumni Soc. W. Pa. (sec. 1983—), Rivers Club (Pitts.), St. Clair Country Club (Upper St. Clair, Pa.), Duquesne Club (Pitts.), Phi Beta Kappa. Democrat. Presbyterian. Avocations: fishing, golf. Home: 525 Miranda Dr Pittsburgh PA 15241-2039 Office: Reed Smith LLP 435 6th Ave Pittsburgh PA 15219-1886 E-mail: wreed@reedsmith.com

**REED, WALLACE ALLISON,** anesthesiologist; b. Covina, Calif., May 19, 1916; s. Wallace Allison and Mary Julia (Birdsall) Reed; m. Maria Eva Wiemers, Jan. 20, 1938; children: Ellen E., Barbara R., Wallace J., Michael E., Kathryn L., Vikki T. AB, UCLA, 1937; postgrad., U. Cologne, 1937-38, U. Freiburg, 1938-39; MD, U. So. Calif., 1944. Diplomate Am. Bd. Anesthesiology. Intern Santa Fe Coast Lines Hosp., Los Angeles, 1943—44; resident Precept Sanders-Valley Forge Hosp., 1944—46, Los Angeles County Gen. Hosp., 1946-47; asst. to head dept. anesthesiology Precept Dillon-Los Angeles County Gen. Hosp., 1946-47; clin. instr. surgery U. So. Calif. Sch. Medicine, 1946-47; practice medicine, specializing in anesthesiology Phoenix, 1948-89; ret., 1989. Hon. staff mem. Good Samaritan Hosp., St. Joseph Hosp., Maricopa County Gen. Hosp.; mem. hon. staff Children's Hosp.; co-founder John L. Ford, M.D., Surgicenter, 1970; vice pres. Maricopa Found. for Med. Care, 1970-74, pres., 1975-76; mem. House Ways and Means Adv. Com.; adv. coun. Nat. Health Inst., 1975-76; mem. accreditation coun. for ambulatory health care Joint Commn. on Accreditation of Hosps., 1975-79; vice-chmn. Accreditation Assn. for Ambulatory Health Care, 1979-81, pres., 1981-83; mem. panel for study Nat. Health Ins., Congl. GAO; chmn. bd. Alterna Care Corp., 1984-87, now chmn. bd. emeritus; mem. adv. bd. Kino Inst., 1994-95. Bd. dirs. South Phoenix Montessori Sch., pres. bd., 1971—75; bd. dirs. Alzheimer's Assn., Greater Phoenix chpt., 1998—2000, co-v.p., 2000; co-chmn. med. and sci. adv. com. Desert S.W. chpt. Alzheimer's Assn. 2004—05; bd. dirs. Ctrl. Ariz. Health Sys. Agy., 1975—78; exec. dir. Surgictr. of Phoenix, 1987—97. Capt. M.C. AUS, 1944—46. Recipient Pinal award Ariz. Psychiat. Soc., 1967-68, Gerard B. Lambert Merit award for innovative ideas that improve patient care; John L. Ford M.D., 1972; recipient spirit of philanthropy award Alzheimer's Assn., 1996, Samba Disting. Svc. award, 2000; Disting. Svc. award Ariz. Soc. Anesthesiology, 2003. Fellow: Am. Coll. Anesthesiologists; mem.: AMA, Alzheimer's Assn. (co-chmn. med. and sci. adv. com. Desert S.W. chpt. 2004—05, co-v.p. Greater Phoenix (Ariz.) chpt. 2000), Soc. for Advancement Geriatric Anesthesia (charter mem.), Guedel Assn. (pres. 1972), Am. Assn. Founds. for Med. Care (dir. 1970—74), Central Ariz. Physicians Svc. Assn. (pres. 1982—83), Maricopa County Med. Soc. (pres. 1964, dir., Salsbury medal 1967, 1971, Thomas Dooley medal 1970), Internat. Assn. Amb. Surgery (hon.), Soc. for Ambulatory Anesthesia (bd. dirs. 1985—87), Federated Amb. Surgery Assn. (pres. 1974—75, dir.), Acad. Anesthesiology (dir. 1966—72, pres. 1969), Ariz., Maricopa County Socs. Anesthesiologists, Am. Soc. Anesthesiologists, WarMer Rsch. Found., Seed Money for Growth Found. (pres. 1984—). Methodist. Home: 4716 N Dromedary Rd Phoenix AZ 85018-2939 Office: 1040 E Mcdowell Rd Phoenix AZ 85006-2622 Office Phone: 602-258-1521. Personal E-mail: somnus4@cox.net.

**REED, WALTER GEORGE, JR.,** retired osteopath; b. Ardmore, Okla., Sept. 10, 1928; s. Walter George and Lillian Dorene (Gee) Reed; children: Jay Walter, David George, Kimberly Sue. BA, Phillips U., 1955; DO, Kansas City U. Medicine and Biosci., 1959. Intern Des Moines Gen. Hosp., 1959—60; pvt. practice Oklahoma City, 1960-63, Atoka, Okla., 1963-80; flight surgeon USAF, Omaha, 1980-84, Lubbock, Tex., 1984-86; chief med. officer Army Health Clinic, McAlester, Okla., 1986-96; ret. USAF, 1996. Mayor City of Atoka, 1969—75; v.p. Atoka Bd. Edn., 1970—75. Lt. col. USAF, 1980—86. Mem.: Assn. Mil. Surgeons U.S., Okla. Osteo. Assn. (life), Assn. Mil. Osteo. Physicians and Surgeons (life), Ret. Officers Assn. (life), Air Force Assn. (life), Masons (32d degree). Avocations: flying, hunting, computers, plate collecting. Home: 9921 N 110th East Ave Owasso OK 74055-4358 Address: PO Box 119 Owasso OK 74055-0119 Office: Slim Care Owasso OK 74055 also: Slim Care Tulsa OK 74135

**REED, WILLIAM R., JR.,** bank executive; Chmn. Nat. Bank of Commerce; vice chmn. Nat. Commerce Bancorporation; COO Nat. Commerce Fin. Corp. 2000—03, pres., CEO, 2003—04; vice chmn. SunTrust Banks Inc., Atlanta, 2004—. Office: SunTrust Banks Inc 303 Peachtree St NE Atlanta GA 30308 Mailing: SunTrust Banks Inc PO Box 4418 Atlanta GA 30308-4418*

**REEDE, JOAN YVONNE,** academic administrator, medical educator, pediatrician; b. Boston, 1953; 1 child, Loretta Jackson. BS, Brown U., 1977; MD, Mt. Sinai Sch. Med., 1980; MPH, Harvard Sch. Pub. Health, 1990, MS in Health Policy and Mgmt, 1992. Intern Johns Hopkins Hosp., Baltimore, 1980—81, pediat. resident, 1981—83; child psychology fellow Children's Hosp., Boston, 1986—88; med. dir. Cmty. Health Ctr., Boston, Commonwealth of Mass. Dept. Youth Services; dean diversity and cmty. partnership Harvard Med. Sch., 2002—, dir. minority faculty devel. program, faculty dir. cmty. outreach programs, assoc. prof. med.; asst. prof. maternal and child health Harvard Sch. Pub. Health; asst. in health policy Mass. Gen. Hosp. Founder Biomedical Sci. Careers Program, 1991; mem. bd. govs. Warren Grant Magnuson Clin. Ctr.; mem. adv. com. on minority health US Dept. Health and Human Services, 2000—, mem. adv. com. on genetics, health and soc., 2002—; bd. dirs. Mass. Tech. Park. Corp. Named a Ctr. for Disease Control and Prevention/U. Calif. Public Health Leadership Inst. Scholar; recipient Boston NAACP Health award, 1986, Community Service award, Epilepsy Assn. Mass., 1993, Exemplary Models Adminstrv. Leadership award, Am. Assn. U. Adminstrs., 1996. Achievements include being included in the Changing the Face of Medicine exhibit honoring women physicians. Office: Harvard Med Sch 25 Shattuck St Rm 152 Boston MA 02115

**REEDER, CHARLES BENTON,** retired economic consultant; b. Columbus, Ohio, Oct. 31, 1922; s. Charles Wells and Lydia (Morrow) R.; m. Carol Lincoln, June 25, 1949 (div. June 1972); 1 son, Charles; m. Beverly Lawrence, Nov. 11, 1972; adopted children: Keith, Sue. BS, Ohio State U., 1945, PhD, 1951; MBA, Harvard U., 1947. Econ. analyst Cleve. Elec. Illuminating Co., 1947-48; instr. Ohio State U., Columbus, 1948-51; econ. analyst, asst. economist Armstrong Cork. Co., Lancaster, Pa., 1951-55; assoc. economist E. I. DuPont de Nemours & Co., Inc., Wilmington, Del., 1955-70; chief economist E.I. DuPont de Nemours & Co., Inc., Wilmington, Del., 1970-85; pres. Charles Reeder Assocs., 1986-99. Bd. dirs. DP Am. Growth Fund, Amsterdam, The Netherlands. Author: The Sobering Seventies, 1981. Bd. dirs. Greater Wilmington Devel. Coun., 1963-84; treas. Del. Coun. on

Econ. Edn., 1958-85, Bank of Del., Wilmington 1975-92. 1st lt. Q.M.C., AUS, 1943-46. Recipient Silbert award Sterling Nat. Bank of N.Y., 1982 Fellow Nat. Assn. Bus. Economists (pres. 1966-67); mem. Nat. Bur. Econ. Research (past bd. dirs.) Clubs: Wilmington, Greenville Country. Presbyterian. Home: 1001 Kensington Ln Greenville DE 19807-2539 E-mail: cbrecon@aol.com.

**REEDER, F. ROBERT,** lawyer; b. Brigham City, Utah, Jan. 23, 1943; s. Frank O. and Helen H. (Heninger) R.; m. Joannie Anderson, May 4, 1967; children: David, Kristina, Adam. JD, U. Utah, 1967. Bar: Utah 1967, U.S. Ct. Appeals (10th cir.) 1967, U.S. Ct. Appeals (D.C. and 5th cirs.) 1979, U.S. Ct. Mil. Appeals 1968, U.S. Supreme Ct. 1972. Shareholder Parsons, Behle & Latimer, Salt Lake City, 1968—, bd. dirs., 1974—92. Bd. dirs. Holy Cross Found., 1981-90, chmn., 1987-90; bd. dirs. Holy Cross Hosp., 1990-93, treas., 1986-87, vice chmn., 1987-93; bd. dirs. Holy Cross Health Svcs. Utah, 1993-94, treas., 1993-94; bd. dirs. Salt Lake Regional Med. Ctr., 1995—, vice chmn., 1995-2000, chmn., 2000—; trustee Univ. Hosp. Found.; hon. col. Salt Lake City Police, Salt Lake County Sheriff; bd. dirs. Utah Hosp. and Health Sys. Assn., 2005—, This is the Place Found. Served with USAR, 1967-73. Mem. ABA, Utah Hosp. Health Sys. Assn. (bd. dirs. 2006—), Utah State Bar, Salt Lake County Bar (ethics adv. com. 1989-94), Cottonwood Country Club (bd. dirs. 1978-82, 83-86, pres. 1981-82), The Country Club (Salt Lake), Rotary Office: Parsons Behle & Latimer PO Box 45898 Salt Lake City UT 84145-0898 Office Phone: 801-536-6769. Business E-Mail: bobreeder@parsonsbehle.com.

**REEDER, HUBERT,** elementary school educator; b. Plainfield, NJ, Mar. 17, 1948; s. Henry M. Reeder Sr. and Algaelee Reeder. BS, Rutgers U., 1988. Supr. Arthur Young and Co., Newark, 1976—86; accounts payable Coopers Lybrand, Newark, 1986—92; youth team coord. East Orange YMCA, NJ, 1992—94; substitute tchr. Plainfield Bd. of Edn., NJ, 1994—; resident poet Plainfield Pub. Lib., 1997—; fitness specialist Plainfield YMCA, 2001—, recreation specialist, 2001—. Author: (various) works of poetry, 1999—2002. Named Man of Year, African Am. Group, 1989; recipient Golden Poet award, World of Poetry, 1989. Fellow: Internat. Biog. Org., Am. Biog. Inst.; mem.: Acad. of Am. Poets. Avocations: road racing, basketball, bicycling. Home: P O Box 1132 Plainfield NJ 07062

**REEDER, JAMES ARTHUR,** lawyer; b. Baton Rouge, June 29, 1933; s. James Brown and Grace (Britt) R.; m. Mary Leone Guthrie, Dec. 30, 1958; children: Mary Virginia, James Jr., Elizabeth Colby. BA, Washington and Lee U., Lexington, Va., 1955; LLB, U. Tex., 1960; JD, La. State U., 1961. Ptnr. Booth, Lockard, Jack et al, Shreveport, La., 1961-72; pres. and mgng. ptnr. Shreveport Broadcasting Co., 1972-86; CEO, mng. gen. ptnr. Radio USA Limited, Houston, 1986-89; pres. SW subsidiaries Sun Group, Inc., Houston, 1990-92; atty. Patton & Boggs, LLP, Washington, 1991-94; ptnr. Patton, Boggs LLP, Washington, 1994—. Dir. ABC Radio Sta. Affiliates adv. bd., N.Y.C., 1978-84. Dir. Boys Country, Houston, 1986-90; pres. Holiday in Dixie, Shreveport, 1968; chmn. Ambassadors Club, Shreveport, 1979. 1st lt. U.S. Army, 1955-57. Named La. Outstanding Young Man, La. Jaycees, 1969. Mem. ABA (bd. dirs. young lawyers sect. 1967-68, Gavel awards com. 1980), La. Bar Assn. (pres. young lawyers sect. 1966, La. Outstanding Young Lawyer award 1968), D.C. Bar Assn., Tex. Bar Assn., Nat. Assn. Broadcasters, Houston Country Club, Allegro Club (Houston). Roman Catholic.

**REEDER, JOE ROBERT,** lawyer, former federal official; b. Tacoma, Nov. 28, 1947; s. William Thomas and Marilyn Ruth (Parker) R.; m. Katharine Randolph Boyce, Jan. 1, 1983; children: Rachael Anne, Aubrilyn, Julia, Kelsey. BS, U.S. Mil. Acad., West Point, N.Y., 1970; JD, U. Tex., 1975; LLM, Georgetown U., 1981. Bar: Tex. 1975, D.C. 1979, U.S. Dist. Ct. (so. dist.) Tex 1975, U.S. Ct. Appeals (5th cir.) 1989, U.S. Ct. Claims 1979, U.S. Dist. Ct. D.C. 1982, U.S. Ct. Appeals (Fed. cir.) 1984, U.S. Supreme Ct. 1988, U.S. Ct. Appeals (4th cir.) 1988, Md. 1989, U.S. Dist. Ct. (Md. dist) 1989, U.S. Dist. Ct. (no. dist.) Tex. 1991, U.S. Dist. Ct. (so. dist.) Tex. 1991. Commd. 2d lt. U.S. Army, 1970, advanced through grades to maj., 1985; law clk. to presiding justice U.S. Dist. Ct. (so. dist.) Tex., 1976; trial atty. litigation div. U.S. Army, Pentagon, DC, 1976-78, trial atty. contract appeals div., 1978-79; assoc. Patton, Boggs & Blow, Washington, 1979-82, ptnr., 1983-93; under sec. of U.S. Army U.S. Dept. Def., Washington, 1993; chmn. bd. Panama Canal Commn., 1994; now shareholder-in-charge Mid-Atlantic Region, bd. dir. Greenberg Traurig LLP, Washington. Mem. ABA (assoc. editor pub. contract law jour. 1985-93), ATLA, Am. Law Inst., Fed. Bar Assn., D.C. Bar Assn., Tex. Bar Assn., Bar Assn. 5th Fed. Circuit, Bd. Contract Appeals Bar Assn., Rotary. Episcopalian. Office: Greenberg Traurig LLP Ste 500 800 Connecticut Ave NW Washington DC 20006-2709 Office Phone: 202-331-3125. Office Fax: 202-331-3101. Business E-Mail: reederj@gtlaw.com.

**REEDER, ROBERT HARRY,** retired lawyer; b. Topeka, Dec. 3, 1930; s. William Harry and Florence Mae (Cochran) R. AB Washburn U., 1952, JD, 1960. Bar: U.S. Dist. Ct. Kans. 1960, Kans. 1960, U.S. Supreme Ct. 1968. Rsch. asst. Kans. Legis. Council Rsch. Dept., Topeka, 1955-60; asst. counsel Traffic Inst., Northwestern U., Evanston, Ill., 1960-67, gen. counsel, 1967-92; exec. dir. Nat. Com. on Uniform Traffic Laws and Ordinances, Evanston, 1982-90; ret. Co-author: Vehicle Traffic Law, 1974; The Evidence Handbook, 1980. Author: Interpretation of Implied Consent by the Courts, 1972. Served with U.S. Army, 1952-54. Mem. Com. Alcohol and Other Drugs (chmn. 1973-75). Republican. Methodist.

**REEDY, FRANCES STARR,** music educator, cellist; b. Walla Walla, Wash., Jan. 26, 1948; d. Oliver Calmar and Lucie Margaret (Starr) R.; 1 child, Alejandro Miguel. MusB in Music Edn., Oberlin Conservatory, 1970; MusM in Cello, U. Ill., 1976. Camp counselor, unit leader Midland Empire coun. Girl Scouts U.S.A., Billings, Mont., 1966-69; vol. Nat. Ctr. Arts, Peace Corps, El Salvador, 1970-73; tchr. cello and violin Nat. Acad. Arts, Champaign, Ill., 1975-86, coord. music studies, 1976-77; tchr. cello and violin Conservatory Cen. Ill., Champaign, 1986—, trustee, 1986—88. Cellist Champaign-Urbana Symphony, 1977—; instr. Suzuki Inst., U. Louisville, 1990. Contbr. articles to mus. jours. Bd. dirs. Champaign County Youth Symphony, 1985-89; bishop's warden Chapel of St. John the Divine, Champaign, 1980, 82-83, chmn. stewardship, 1984-94, vestrywoman, 1985-86, 88-89, also former mem. bishop's com., chalice bearer, mem. choir. Recipient Exec. Com. award for Outstanding Svc., The Conservatory of Ctrl. Ill., 1994. Mem. Am. String Tchrs. Assn., Suzuki Assn. Ams., Music Educators Nat. Conf., Pi Kappa Lambda. Episcopalian. Avocation: backpacking. Home: 901 E Michigan Ave Urbana IL 61801-5274 Office: Conservatory Cen Ill 113 S Walnut St Champaign IL 61820-4927 Office Phone: 217-356-9812.

**REEDY, HARRY LEE,** financial services executive; b. Lebanon, Pa., Dec. 25, 1945; s. Harry Lee and Charlotte (Weedmark) R.; m. Linda Bartley, Nov. 7, 1970; children: Jennifer Beth, Sara Emily. BS in Indsl Engring., Pa. State U., 1967; MBA, U. Conn., 1977. Cert. Six Sigma Master Black Belt 2006. Mgmt. asst. Bell Telephone Pa., Phila., 1967-70; field engring. rep. Travelers Cos., Hartford, Conn., 1971-72, ops. analyst, 1972-76, supervising ops. analyst, 1976-79, sr. mgmt. cons., 1979-83, adminstr. consumer affairs, 1983-85, dir. consumer affairs, 1985-90; dir. corp. customer svc. John Hancock Fin. Svcs., Boston, 1990-91, dir. Ctr. for Quality, 1991-96; asst. v.p. quality State U. Boston, 1997—98, v.p., dir. quality, 1998—. Mem. consumer affairs com. Ins. Info. Inst., N.Y.C., 1988-90. Contbr. articles to trade pubs. Participant Leadership Greater Hartford, 1985; bd. dirs., treas. Woodland Manor Condominium Assn., Manchester, Conn., 1986-87; bd. mgrs. Auburn Ct. Condominium Assn., 2001-04; bd. examiners Malcolm Baldridge Nat. Quality award, 1995-2000, sr. examiner, 1997-2000, panel of judges, 2002-05, chmn., 2003-05; sr. examiner Mass. State Quality award, 1995-99, judge, 1999; judge New Hampshire Quality Award, 2002. With U.S. Army, 1968-70 Fellow Ins. Consumer Affairs Exch. (1975-87, v.p. 1987-88, pres. 1988-90), Soc. Consumer Affairs Profls. (v.p. New Eng. Chpt. 1991-92); mem. Am. Coun. Life Ins. (consumer affairs com. 1987), Am. Soc. Quality Control, Am. productivity & Quality Ctr., Internat. Benchmarking Clearing House, Strategic Planning Inst., Mass. Coun. Quality (bd. dirs. 1998—, treas. exec. com. 1999-2001), Benchmarking Coun., Assn. Quality and Participation, Beta Gamma Sigma. Democrat. Avocations: photography, racquetball, swimming, reading, Karate (black belt). Home: 3 Auburn Ct # 2 Brookline MA 02446-6302 Office Phone: 617-662-7030. Business E-Mail: hlreedy@statestreet.com.

**REEDY-DEWEY, MADELINE ANNE,** retired occupational therapist; b. Milw., Jan. 25, 1954; d. Samuel Smith and Louise Rita (Thomas) Reedy; m. Craig D. Dewey, Sept. 28, 1989. BS in Occupl. Therapy, U. Wis., Milw., 1978. Registered occupl. therapist Wis. Dir. occupl. therapy Hillhaven, Shorewood, Wis., 1978-83; Colonial Manor, Glendale, Wis., 1983-85; Saturday/on-call occupl. therapist Northwest Gen. Hosp., Milw., 1981-84; chief occupl. therapist Silver Spring Convalescent Ctr., Glendale, 1985-86; dir. occupl. therapy Colonia Manor, Glendale, 1986-91; rehab. clin. cons. Therapy Mgmt. Inc. Facilities, various locations, 1991-92; cons./instr. in edn. program W.H. Carter, U. Milw., 1994-95; instr. med. terminology and anatomy/physiology Concordia U., Mequon, Wis., 1996; ret., 1996. Clin. supr. practicum students occupl. therapy program U. Wis., Milw. Area Tech. Coll., 1978—83; bd. dirs. Toner Tech Cartridge Svcs., Inc., Panama City, Fla. Vol. Gulf Coast Cmty. Hosp., Panama City, 1985, St. Michael's Hosp., Milw., 1994, St. Francis Children's Ctr., Milw., 1996, Humane Soc. Bay County, Fla., 2000—01, Vocat. Rehab., Panama City, 2001. Mem.: Wis. Occupl. Therapy Assn., Am. Occupl. Therapy Assn. Roman Catholic. Avocations: gardening, cooking. Home: 314 Massalina Dr Panama City FL 32401 E-mail: cdeweybc@att.net.

**REEG, GLORIA D.,** investment consultant; b. Bellevue, Iowa, Mar. 30, 1951; d. Robert J. and Darlene A. (Schenk) Reeg; m. Steven D. Given, Feb. 27, 1982; children: Alexander, Elisabeth. BS, U. Wis., Platteville, 1971; MMgmt., Northwestern U., 1982. Editor Scott, Foresman & Co., Glenview, Ill., 1972-73; actuary, statistician Kemper Ins. Co., Long Grove, Ill., 1974-75; assoc. TPF&C, Chgo., 1975-81; prin. William M. Mercer, Chgo., 1981-88, Ennis, Knupp & Assocs., Chgo., 1989—92; mng. dir. global consulting Russell Investment Group, 1992—2000; exec. dir. then pres. Principal Capital Income Investors, 2000—05. Trustee Casey Family Programs. Office: Casey Family Programs 1300 Dexter Ave N Seattle WA 98109-3542*

**REEHER, JAMES IRWIN,** minister; b. Sharon, Pa., Dec. 6, 1948; s. James William and Lillian (Irwin) R.; m. Marian Powell, Oct. 25, 1969; children: Elizabeth Margret, James Michael. BA, U. Tampa, 1975; MDiv, Emory U., 1978; DD, Boston U., 1989. Ordained to ministry United Ch., 1978. Min. Christ United Meth. Ch., Tampa, Fla., 1972-75, Lamar United Meth. Ch., Barnesville, Fla., 1975-78, 1st United Meth. Ch., Seffner, Fla., 1986-90; asst. min. Grace United Meth. Ch., Venice, Fla., 1978-79; founding min. 1st United Meth. Ch., Sarasota, Fla., 1980-86; min. Forest Hills United Meth. Ch., Tampa, 1990—. Del. bd. ordained ministry Tampa Dist., 1987—; dell. stewardship com. Fla. United Meth. Conf., 1986; bd. dirs. Jim Russo Prison Ministries, Bradenton, Fla., 1990—; chmn. anti-gambling campaign Fla. United Meth. Conf., 1986; v.p. Shade and Fresh Water, Inc. Founding chmn. East Hillsborough Orgn., Seffner, 1988; bd. dirs. Life Enrichment Sr. Ctr., Tampa, 1990—; founder Family Hall of Fame. Recipient Outstanding Religious Leader award Sarasota Jaycees, 1985. Mem. Assn. for Clin. Pastoral Edn., Alban Inst., North Tampa Ministerial Assn., West Orange Ministerial Assn. Democrat. Office: First United Meth Ch 125 Lakeview Dr Winter Garden FL 34787 Home: 10370 Frankie Lane Dr Saint James City FL 33956-3233

**REEP, EDWARD ARNOLD,** artist; b. Bklyn., May 10, 1918; s. Joseph and Elsie (Abramson) R.; m. Karen Patricia Stevens, Dec. 9, 1942; children— Susan Kay, Cristine Elyse, Janine J., Mitchell Jules. Student, Art Center Coll. Design, 1936-41. Instr. painting and drawing Art Center Coll. Design, Los Angeles, 1946-50, Chouinard Art Inst., Los Angeles, 1950-69; prof. painting, chmn. dept., artist in residence E. Carolina U., 1970-85, prof. emeritus, 1985—. Cons. editor Van Nostrand Reinhold Pub. Co.; ofcl. war artist-corr. WWII, Africa and Italy. Author: The Content of Watercolor, 1968, A Combat Artist in World War II, 1987; shows include Whitney Mus. Am. Art Ann., N.Y.C., 1946-48, Los Angeles County Mus. Ann., 1946-60, Corcoran Gallery Art Biennial, Washington, 1949, Nat. Gallery Art, Washington, 1945, They Drew Fire, 2000, Mus. Modern Art, N.Y.C.; represented in permanent collections Los Angeles County Mus., U.S. War Dept., Grunwald Graphic Arts Collection, UCLA, Nat. Mus. Am. Art, Washington, Lytton Collection, Los Angeles, State of Calif. Collection, Sacramento. Guggenheim fellow, 1945-46; Nat. Endowment for Arts grantee, 1975 Mem. AAUP, Nat. Water-color Soc. (past pres., Lifetime Achievement award 2002), Watercolor USA Honor Soc. (lifetime achievement gold medal 1997). Democrat. Home: 9021 Crowningshield Dr Bakersfield CA 93311-1901 *I once was consumed by the desire to become an artist. I had set goals for myself I no longer can recall what they may have been; I go along painting as well or as inventively as I can. Never have I sacrificed living life as I feel I must for my art. My work is a reflection of my life—experiences real and imagined.*

**REES, CLIFFORD HARCOURT, JR., (TED REES),** consulting company executive, retired trade association administrator, retired military officer; b. Newport News, Va., Dec. 11, 1936; s. Clifford Harcourt Sr. and Mary Evelyn (Brooks) R.; m. Joan Elizabeth Mittong, July 26, 1958; children— Clifford Harcourt III, Steven M., Daniel B., William B. BS in Fgn. Svc., Georgetown U., 1958; MS in Polit. Sci., Auburn U., 1969; grad., Air War Coll. Montgomery, Ala., 1978; grad. program for sr. exec. in nat. and internat. security, JFK Sch. Govt., Harvard U. Commd. 2d lt. U.S. Air Force, 1958; advanced through grades to lt. gen., 1988; comdr. 421st Tactical Fighter Squadron, Udorn Royal Thai AFB, 1974-75; chief, house liaison office U.S. Ho. Reps., Washington, 1978-80; asst. col. assignments Randolph AFB, 1980-82; vice-comdr. Air Force Manpower and Personnel Ctr., 1982; dep. dir. legis. liaison Office Sec. Air Force, 1982-84, dir. legis. liaison, 1984-86; comdr. USAF Air Defense Weapons Ctr., Tyndall AFB, Fla., 1986-88; vice comdr. in chief USAF in Europe, Ramstein AB, Federal Republic of Germany, 1988-92, ret., 1992; founder, pres. Rees Group Cons., 1992—; pres. Air Conditioning and Refrigeration Inst., Arlington, Va., 1992—2002. U.S. rep. to v.p. Internat. Coun. Mil. Sports, Brussels, 1982-94; dir. bd. dirs. Armed Forces Benefit Assn. Investment Mgmt. Co., 1996—. Decorated D.S.M. with one oak leaf cluster, DFC with one oak leaf cluster, Legion of Merit with one oak leaf cluster, Meritorious Svc. medal with one oak leaf cluster, Air medal with 11 oak leaf clusters, Das Grosse Verdienstkreuz Mit Stern, Fed. Republic Germany; named comdr. Order of Meritorious Svc. Internat. Mil. Sports Coun., 1993, Order of the Sword, U.S. Air Forces in Europe, 1992. Mem. Delta Phi Epsilon (v.p. membership 1957-58, nat. pres. 1984-86) Methodist. Home: 52 Stoneykirk Dr Pinehurst NC 28374 E-mail: ted@thereesgroup.com.

**REES, ELAINE,** chemistry educator; b. Springhill, La., Feb. 23, 1956; d. Jimmie Dale and Lillie Serena Jackson; m. Dwane Rees, Aug. 1, 1980; children: Kristin Lynne, Kameka Anne, Kameron Michael. BS, La. Tech., Ruston, 1978; MS, Ctrl. Mo. State U., Warrensburg, 1994. Gen. sci. tchr. Plaquemine Jr. High, La., 1978—80; sci. tchr. Vandalia (Mo.) Far HS, 1980—90; chemistry tchr. Ft. Osage H.S., Independence, Mo., 1991—. Mem.: Mo. State Tchrs. Assn. Avocations: gardening, sewing, travel. Home: 316 SE 2d St Blue Springs MO 64014 Office: Ft Osage HS 2101 N Twyman Independence MO 64098 Business E-Mail: erees@fortosage.net.

**REES, FRANK WILLIAM, JR.,** architect; b. Rochester, N.Y., June 5, 1943; s. Frank William and Elizabeth R. (Miller) R.; m. Joan Mary Keevers, Apr. 1, 1967; children: Michelle, Christopher. BS in Architecture, U. Okla., 1970; postgrad., Harvard U., Boston, 1979, 90; OPM, Harvard U., 1990; DArch, U. Hawaii, 2001. Registered architect, 39 states & D.C.; cert. Nat. Coun. Archtl. Registration Bds.; registered interior designer. Sales mgr. Sta. KFOM, Oklahoma City, 1967-70; project architect Benham-Blair & Affiliates, Okla-homa City, 1970-75; pres., CEO, founder Rees Assocs., Inc., Oklahoma City, 1975—. Pres., chmn. bd. Weatherscan Radio Network, Oklahoma City, 1973-78; chmn. bd. Weatherscan Internat., Oklahoma City, 1972-78; pres. Frontier Communications, Oklahoma City, 1980-84; chmn. architecture bd. U. Okla., Norman, 1988-91; bd. dirs. Century, Inc., Oklahoma City. Past pres.

Lake Hefner Trails, Oklahoma City, Hosp. Hospitality House, Oklahoma City, Oklahoma City Beautiful; mem. Leadership Oklahoma City. Mem. AIA, Am. Assn. Hosp. Architects, Am. Healthcare Assn., Tex. Hosp. Assn., World Pres. Orgn. (chmn. 1997-98), Assisted Living Fedn. of Am., Am. Assn. Homes and Svcs. for the Agig. Home: 1104 Stone Gate Dr Irving TX 75063-4676 also: 1801 N Lamar St Ste 600 Dallas TX 75202-1711

**REES, FRED JOSEPH,** music educator; b. Mar. 7, 1949; BMus, SUNY, Potsdam, 1971; Dr. Mus. Arts, U. So. Calif., L.A., 1977. Assoc. prin. bassist Orch. Sinfonica, San Juan, P.R., 1977-78; lectr. music U. Queensland, Brisbane, 1978-86; assoc. prof. music NYU, N.Y.C., 1986-91; prof. music, assoc. dir. Sch. Music U. No. Iowa, Cedar Falls, 1991-99; head grad. program Ind. U. Sch. Music at IUPUI, Indpls., 1999—. Home: 8423 Sandpiper Ct Indianapolis IN 46256-1639 Office: Ind U Sch Music 535 W Michigan St IT 389 Indianapolis IN 46202-3108 Office Phone: 317-274-4610. Business E-Mail: frees@iupui.edu.

**REES, JAMES CONWAY, IV,** historic site administrator; b. Richmond, Va., May 5, 1952; BA, Coll. William & Mary, 1974; MPA, George Washington U., 1978. Reporter, photographer Newport News Daily-Press, 1974; coord. radio and television programming The Coll. William & Mary, 1974-78; mng. editor The William & Mary Mag., 1978-82; promotions dir. Va. Shakespeare Festival, 1980; dir. annual giving and pub. info. The Coll. William & Mary, 1978-80, dir. annual support and corp. rels., 1980-81, dir. capital support, 1981-82; asst. dir. devel. Nat. Trust Historic Preservation, 1982-83, assoc. dir. devel., 1983; dir. devel. and comms. Historic Mount Vernon, 1983-85, assoc. dir., 1985-94, exec. dir., 1994—. Bd. dirs. Va. Shakespeare Festival, Washington Area chpt. William and Mary Alumni Soc. Mem. Nat. Trust for Historic Preservation, Friends of the Nat. Symphony, WETA Pub. TV; bd. dirs. Va. Shakespeare Festival, Nt. Parks and History Found. Mem. Am. Film Inst., Va. Assn. Mus. (pres. 1991-94), William and Mary Alumni Soc. (bd. dirs. Washington area chpt.). Methodist. Home: 710 A St NE Washington DC 20002-6032 Office: Mount Vernon Ladies Assn Mount Vernon VA 22121

**REES, LANE CHARLES,** industrial relations consultant; b. Longview, Tex., June 23, 1951; s. Holly Elias and Charlene Elizabeth (Quin) R.; m. Brenda Faye Anderson, July 1, 1978; children: Brian Andrew, Lauren Catherine. BBA in Mgmt. magna cum laude, Tex. A&M U., 1973, MEd in Ednl. Adminstrn., 1978. Pers. rep. Tex. A&M U., College Station, 1973—77; v.p. Brazos Gen. Svcs., Bryan, Tex., 1977—78; successively pers. office supr., wage and salary adminstr., employee rels. rep., sr. employee rels. rep. ARCO, various cities, Tex., 1979—83, from sr. employee rels. rep. to employee rels. dir. Anchorage and Kuparuk, Alaska, 1983—87, dir. employee rels. Prudhoe Bay, Alaska, 1987—90, dir. human resources dept. engring., 1990—94; sr. human rels. advisor Algeria and engring. exploration Arco Internat. Oil and Gas, Plano, Tex., 1994—99; pres. Human Resources Solutions, Inc., Dallas/Santa Rosa Beach, Tex., 1999—. Ptnr. Rees and Assocs., Anchorage, Tex., Fla., 1978—. Mem. editl. staff Conf. Leadership, 1978. Vice chmn. Rep. Party of Alaska, 1993-94, chair, 1994; vice-chmn. Walton Co. GOP exec. com., 1999-2005; mem. ctrl. com. State of Alaska, 1990-94; chmn. utility regulatory commn. municipality of Anchorage, 1989-91; mem. com. sec. United Meth. Com. Commn., Nashville, 1988-97; evangelism chmn., mem. adv. coun. St. John United Meth. Ch., Anchorage, 1986-91, chmn. adminstrv. bd., 1991-93; trustee Nat. Found. Evangelism, Lake Junalukssa, NC, 1988—; exec. coun., 1995—, chmn. 2002—; conf. lay leader Ala. Missionary Conf.-Meth. Ch., 1992-94; chmn. evangelism and mem. adminstrv. bd. 1st United Meth. Ch., Allen, Tex., 1995-97; mem. adminstrv. bd. Suncreek (Tex.) United Meth. Ch., 1997-99, adv. bd. Freeport United Meth. Ch., lay del. to ann. conf., 1995-2001; active Port Washington United Meth. Ch., 2001—, mem. ch. coun. 2003—, del. ann. conf., 2004—; mem. internat. bd. George Bush Ctr., Tex. A&M U., 1996—; bd. dirs. Walton County C. of C., 1999—2005, interim pres., CEO, 2005; bd. dirs. Fla. Assn. Counties, 2002-04, Fla. Assn. Counties Trust, 2001-04, vice chair, 2002-04; comm. Walton County, 2000-04; vice chair Walton Bd. County Commrs., 2000-01, chair, 2001-02; mem. adv. bd. Walton Tourist Devel. Coun., 2001-04; mem. adv. coun. U. West Fla. Coll. Bus., 2002—. Recipient Denman award Alaska Missionary Conf. United Meth. Ch., 1989, Legis. citation State of Alaska, 1989. Mem. Acad. Mgmt., Tex. A&M U. Assn. Former Students (nat. councilman 1987-91, bd. dirs. 1996—), Am. Numis. Assn., Alaska Soc. SAR (pres. 1989-90, trustee Nat. Soc. 1991-94, Silver Good Citizenship award 1989), Phi Eta Sigma, Phi Kappa Phi, Sigma Iota Epsilon (pres. 1972-73), Beta Gamma Sigma. Avocations: golf, racquetball, reading, travel, coin collecting/numismatics. Home: 323 Lakeview Dr Santa Rosa Beach FL 32459-6604 Office Phone: 850-231-0735. Personal E-mail: solutionhr@aol.com.

**REES, MARTIN JOHN,** astronomy educator; b. York, Eng., June 23, 1942; s. Reginald and Joan (Bett) R. MA, PhD, Cambridge (Eng.) U., 1967; DSc (hon.), Sussex (Eng.) U., 1990, Leicester (Eng.) U., 1993, Uppsala (Sweden) U., 1995, Keele (Eng.) U., 1995, Newcastle (Eng.) U., 1995, Copenhagen U., 1995, Toronto (Can.) U., 1997, Durham (Eng.) U., 1999, Oxford (Eng.) U., 2000. Rsch. fellow Calif. Tech. Inst., 1968; vis. rsch. fellow Inst. for Advanced Study, Princeton, NJ, 1969, 82, 96, 97; vis. scientist Harvard U., Cambridge, Mass., 1972, 87-90; Regents fellow Smithsonian Instn., 1984-87; prof. Sussex U., 1972-73; Plumian prof. astronomy Cambridge U., 1973-91; dir. Inst. Astronomy, Cambridge, 1977-91; rsch. prof. Royal Soc. Cambridge U., England, 1992—2003, prof. cosmology and astrophysics, 2002—; master Trinity Coll., Cambridge, 2004—; astronomer royal, 1995—2005. Fellow King's Coll., Cambridge U., England, 1969—2003; hon. fellow Trinity Coll., 1995—, Jesus Coll., 1996—, Cardiff U., Wales, 1998, Darwin Coll., 2004—; vis. prof. Harvard U., Princeton U., Calif. Tech., Imperial Coll., London, Leicester U., hon. prof.; bd. trustees Brit. Mus., 1996—2002, Nat. Endowment for Sci., Tech. and Arts, 1998—2001, Inst. for Advanced Study, Princeton, 1998—, Kennedy Meml. Trust, England, 1999—2004, Inst. for Pub. Policy Rsch., 2001—, Nat. Mus. of Sci. and Tech., 2003—. Author: (with M.C. Begelman) Gravity's Fatal Attraction, 1995, Perspectives in Astrophysical Cosmology, 1995, Before the Beginning, 1997, Just Six Numbers, 1999, Our Cosmic Habitat, 2001, Our Final Century?, 2003. Decorated officer Order of Arts and Letters (France); recipient Heinemann prize, Am. Inst. Physics, 1984, Gold medal, Royal Astron. Soc., 1987, Balzan prize, 1989, Robinson prize, 1990, Bruce medal, 1993, Sci. Writing award, Am. Inst. Physics, 1996, Bower award, Franklin Inst., 1998, Rossi prize, AAS, 2000, Cosmology prize, Gruber Found., 2001, Einstein award, World Sci. Coun., 2003, Craford prize, Royal Swedish Acad., 2005, Niels Bohr prize, UNESCO, 2005; created knight bachelor, 1992, created life peer, 2005. Fellow AAAS, Royal Soc. London (pres. 2005-, Henry Norris Russell lectureship, 2004), Royal Netherlands Acad. Arts and Scis., Indian Acad. Scis. (hon.), Russian Acad. Scis. (hon.), Swedish Acad. Scis., Am. Philosophy Soc.; mem. NAS (fgn. assoc.), Pontifical Acad. Scis., Academia Europea, Inst. Physics (Eng.) (Guthrie prize 1994—), Royal Astron. Soc. (pres. 1992-94), Brit. Assn. Advancement Sci. (pres. 1994-95), Norwegian Acad. Sci., Acad. Lincei (Rome), Finnish Acad. Arts and Sci. Anglican. Office: Inst Astronomy Cambridge England CB3 0HA also: Trinity Coll Cambridge CB2 1TQ England

**REES, NINA SHOKRAII,** federal agency administrator; b. Iran; BS in Psychology, Va. Polytech and State U., 1989; MS in Internat. Transactions, George Mason U., 1991. Mem. staff Rep. Porter Goss, Washington, 1990—92; policy analyst Ams. for Tax Reform, Washington, 1992—93; dir. outreach programs Inst. for Justice, Washington, 1993—97; chief edn. analyst The Heritage Found., Washington, 1997—2000; with Bush/Cheney transition team, 2000—01; aide to v.p. U.S. Govt., Washington, 2001—02; asst. deputy sec. Innovation and Improvement US Dept. Edn., 2002—. Contbr. commentaries in newspapers, TV, radio on ednl. issues, 1995. Education adviser to Bush Campaign, Phila., 2000; contbr. to Rep. platform in edn. area Rep. Paty, 2000. Recipient Rita Ricardo Campbell award, Heritage Found., 1999. Office: US Dept Edn 400 Maryland Ave SW Rm 4W317 Washington DC 20202 Office Phone: 202-205-4500. Business E-Mail: nina.rees@ed.gov.

**REES, NORMA S.,** academic administrator; b. NYC, Dec. 27, 1929; d. Benjamin and Lottie (Schwartz) D.; m. Raymond R. Rees, Mar. 19, 1960; children— Evan Lloyd, Raymond Arthur BA, Queens Coll., 1952; Ma, Bklyn. Coll., 1954; PhD, NYU, 1959; D of Arts and Letters honoris causa, John F. Kennedy U., 2001. Cert. speech-language pathology, audiology. Prof. communicative disorders Hunter Coll., NYC, 1967-72; exec. officer, speech and hearing scis. grad. sch. CUNY, NYC, 1972-74, assoc. dean for grad. studies, 1974-76, dean grad. studies, 1976-82; vice chancellor for acad. affairs U. Wis., Milw., 1982-85, from 1986, acting chancellor, 1985-86; vice chancellor for acad. policy and planning Mass. Bd. Regents for Higher Edn., Boston, 1987-90; pres. Calif. State U. East Bay, Hayward, 1990—. Chmn. Commn. Recognition of Postsecondary Accreditation, 1994-96; mem. adv. com. quality and integrity U.S. Dept. Edn., commn. on internat. edn. Coun. on Higher Edn. Accreditation, 2003—. Contbr. articles to profl. jours. Trustee Citizens Govtl. Rsch. Bur., Milw., 1985-87; active Task Force on Wis. World Trade Ctr., 1985-87; bd. dirs. Am. Assn. State Colls. and Univs., 1995-97, Coun. of Postsecondary Accreditation, Washington, 1985-94, Greater Boston YWCA, 1987-90; mem. Calif. Sch. to Career Coun.; bd. dir. Econ. Devel. Alliance for Bus., Alameda County, 1995—; sec. edn. Nat. Adv. Com. Institutional Quality and Integrity, 1998-2002; bd. dirs. Bay Area World Trade Ctr., 2001—, Alameda County Health Care Found., 2002-. Fellow Am. Speech-Lang-Hearing Assn. (honors); mem. Am. Coun. Edn. (com. internat. edn. 1991-93), Am. Assn. Colls. and Univs. (chair task force on quality assessment 1991-92), Nat. Assn. State Univs. and Land Grant Colls. (exec. com. divsn. urban affairs 1985-87, com. accreditation 1987-90), Hayward C. of C. (bd. dirs. 1995-98), Oakland C. of C. (bd. dirs. 1997-2004). Office: Calif State Univ East Bay 25800 Carlos Bee Blvd Hayward CA 94542-3001 Office Phone: 510-885-3877. E-mail: norma.rees@csueastbay.edu.

**REES, RAYMOND F.,** military officer; b. Pendleton, Oreg., Sept. 29, 1944; s. Raymond Emmett and Lorna Doone (Gemmell) R.; m. Karen Kristine Young, Nov. 1966 (div. Mar. 1974); children: Raymond Gordon, Christian Frederick; m. Mary Len Middleton, Dec. 30, 1977; 1 child, Carrie Evelyn. BS, U.S. Mil. Acad., 1966; JD, U. Oreg., 1976. Commd. 2d lt. U.S. Army, 1966; platoon leader, troop exec. officer, co. comdr. 2d Armored Cavalry Regiment, Bamberg, Fed. Republic Germany; troop comdr. 2-17 Cavalry 101 Airborn divsn., Camp Eagle, Vietnam, 1969; troop exec. officer 1-17 Cavalry 82 Airborn divsn., Ft. Bragg, N.C., 1972; resigned U.S. Army, 1973; with Oreg. Army Nat. Guard, 1973—, advanced through grades to maj. gen., 1990; asst. ops. officer Infantry Brigade; co. comdr. 2d Battalion, 162d Infantry, Corvallis, Oreg.; with 116th Armored Calvary Regiment, 1976-87; comdr. 116th cavalry regiment, adjutant gen. Oreg. Army Nat. Guard, 1987-91; dir. Army N.G., 1991-92; vice chief N.G. Bur., Washington, 1992-94; adjutant gen. Oreg. N.G., 1994-99; vice chief N.G. Bur., Washington, 1999—2002, acting chief, 2002—03; chief of staff Hdqrs. NORAD and U.S. No. Command, 2003—05. Decorated Bronze Star, Legion of Merit, D.S.M., Def. Disting. Svc. medal. Mem. VFW, Adjutant Gen. Assn. U.S., Nat. Guart Assn. U.S., Assn. of U.S. Army, Oreg. Nat. Guard Assn., U.S Armor Assn., Oreg. Bar Assn., Am. Legion, Mil. Order World Wars, West Point Soc. Oreg., 101st Airborne Div. Assn., 116th Armored Cavalry Assn., 41st Infantry Div. Assn., Elks.

**REES, THOMAS DYNEVOR,** lawyer; b. S.I., N.Y., Sept. 25, 1949; s. Thomas and Caroline (Bridgman) Rees; m. Josephine Stephanie Madej, Apr. 8, 1978; 1 child, Thomas D. III. AB in Polit. Sci., Stanford U., 1971; JD, U. Pa., 1975. Bar: N.Y. 1976, Pa. 1977, U.S. Supreme Ct. 1982. Assoc. Lovejoy, Wasson, Lundgren & Ashton, N.Y.C., 1975-77, Morgan, Lewis & Bockius, Phila., 1977-81; dep. assoc. counsel Office of Gov. of Pa., Harrisburg, 1981-85; counsel High, Swartz, Roberts & Seidel, Norristown, Pa., 1985-86, ptnr., 1987—. CLE course planner, author, faculty mem. Pa. Bar Inst., 1990—; employment panel arbitrator Am. Arbitration Assn., Phila., 1991—. Contbr. Solicitor Upper Merion Twp., King of Prussia, Pa., 1987—88, 1990—95, Abington Twp., Pa., 1986—87; pres. Gladwyne Civic Assn., Pa., 1995—97. Mem.: ABA, Montgomery County Bar Assn. (co-chair employment law com. 1996—2000), Pa. Bar Assn. (chair mcpl. law sect. 1993—95), King of Prussia C. of C. (solicitor 1996—, v.p., gen. counsel 1999—). Republican. Episco-palian. Office: High Swartz Roberts & Seidel LLP 40 E Airy St Norristown PA 19401-4803 Office Phone: 610-275-0700. E-mail: trees@highswartz.com.

**REESE, ALBERT LESLIE, JR.,** financial executive; b. Birmingham, Ala., June 20, 1949; s. Albert Leslie and Carolyn (Evans) R.; m. Caryl Reese. BBA, Tex. A&M U., 1971; MBA, U. Houston, 1977. CPA, Ala.; Tex. Officer Capital Bank, Houston, 1971-75; auditor Peat Marwick Mitchell, Houston, 1975-77; ptnr. Arnold, Reese, Swenson, Houston, 1977-79; CFO Plumb Oil Co., Houston, 1979-86; v.p. Harbert Corp. and Subsidiaries, Birmingham, Ala., 1983-90; pres. Corp. Fin. Mgmt., Birmingham, 1990—2000; CFO Controlled Environ Sys., Birmingham, 1993—96; CFO, treas. ATP Oil & Gas, Houston, 1991—. Adv. dir. ATP Oil & Gas, Houston, 1992—, Baxter & Korge, Inc., Houston, 1977—; advisor N.R.T., Inc., Nashville, 1990—. Mem., com. vol. Houston Livestock Show, 1983—; mem. vol. Birmingham Mus. Art, 1986—; founder, pres. ACR Found., Houston, 2000—. Capt. U.S. Army, 1971-79. Mem. AICPA. Office: ATP Oil & Gas Corp 4600 Post Oak Pl Ste 200 Houston TX 77027 Office Phone: 713-622-3311.

**REESE, ALFRED GEORGE,** retired army civilian logistics specialist; b. Granville, N.D., Apr. 5, 1934; s. Ferdinand Emil and Iola May (Boulds) R.; m. Donna Mae Berger, 1955 (div. 1972); children: Rick, Denise, Roxanna; m. Nelda Cecilia Pena, May 31, 1985; children: Nancy, Joyce, Alfred, Jeffrey, Jessica, James, Alicia. AS, Humphreys Coll., 1963; BS, U. State of N.Y., Albany, 1983; MPA, U. Colo., Colorado Springs, 1985; postgrad., Ga. State U., 1987-88; PhD, Columbia Pacific U., 1994. Inspector, mechanic Sharp Army Depot, Lathrop, Calif., 1958-66; equipment specialist various stations U.S. Army Aviation Systems Command, 1966-84, supervisory equipment specialist Atlanta, 1984-88, supervisory logistics specialist St. Louis, 1988-93; ret. Civil Svc., 1993. Mem. com. Boy Scouts Am., Fed. Republic Germany, 1979-81. With USAF, 1953-57. Mem. Army Aviation Assn. Assn. (USAEUR Dept. Army Civilian of Yr. 1980, 81), Acad. Polit. Sci., Am. Soc. for Pub. Adminstrn., Nat. Rifle Assn. Avocations: golf, skiing, photography, painting. Home: 1590 Fairmount Dr Florissant MO 63033-2645

**REESE, ANGELA BROOKE,** elementary school educator; b. Salt Lake City, June 26, 1976; d. Michael Paul and Carol Robertson Nielsen; m. Kevin Gordon Reese, Mar. 20, 2004; 1 child, Katherine Lola. BA, Brigham Young U., 1999; MEd, Portland State U., Oreg., 2004. 4th grade tchr. Nebo Sch. Dist., Springville, Utah, 1998—99; 6th grade tchr. Estacada (Oreg.) Sch. Dist., 1999—2000, 1st grade tchr., 2000—01; 3d grade tchr. David Douglas Sch. Dist., Portland, 2003—. Pres. LDS Relief Soc., Portland, 2001—04. Mem.: Internat. Reading Assn. Republican. Avocations: sewing, scrapbooks, hiking, travel, reading. E-mail: reeseangela@hotmail.com.

**REESE, ANNETTE EVELYN,** music educator; b. Waynesville, NC, Sept. 23, 1958; d. James F. and Shirley Sharpe Robertson; m. Mark A. Reese, Nov. 22, 1980; children: Caitlan Annette, Sarah Anne. MusB Edn., Mars Hill Coll., 1980; MEd, Belmont Abbey Coll., 1996. Cert. music educator K12. Elem. music specialist Marlboro County Schs., Bennettsville, SC, 1980—81; choral dir. North Gaston H.S., Dallas, NC, 1981—85; dir. of bands East Gaston High/Stanley Mid. Sch., Mt. Holly/Stanley, NC, 1985—95, Belmont Mid. Sch., Belmont, NC, 1995—98, Olympic High/Kennedy Mid. Sch., Charlotte, NC, 1998—. Pres. NC Bandmasters Assn., Charlotte, NC, 2000—, South Ctrl. Dist. Bandmasters, NCBA, Charlotte, NC, 1996—98; sec. NC Band-masters Assn., Charlotte, NC, 1998—2000; band sect. chair, exec. bd. mem. NC Music Educators Assn., Raleigh, NC, 2004—. Contbr. articles to profl. jours. Troop leader Pioneer Girl Scout Coun., GSUSA, Gastonia, NC, 1996—2002. Mem.: NEA, N.C. Assn. Educators, Music Educators Nat. Conf., N.C. Bandmasters Assn. (pres. 2000—02, Excellence award 1996), N.C. Music Educators Assn. (band sect. chair 2000—02), Delta Omicron Profl. Music Frat. Mem. Evangelical Lutheran Ch. Of America. Avocations: needlework, music, travel. Office: SW Mid Sch 13624 Steele Creek Rd Charlotte NC 28273

**REESE, C. RICHARD,** data processing executive; BS, MS in Ceramic Engring., Clemson Univ.; MBA, Harvard Univ. Former cons.; former pres., dir. PRISM Internat. trade assn.; lectr. Harvard Bus. Sch.; pres. Iron Mountain Inc., Boston, 1981, CEO, 1981—, also chmn., 1995—. Recipient New England Entrepreneur of Yr., Ernst & Young, 2003. Office: Iron Mountain 745 Atlantic Ave Boston MA 02111 Office Phone: 617-535-4766.*

**REESE, CHARLES EDGAR,** columnist; b. Washington, Ga., Jan. 29, 1937; s. Edgar Ernest and Neoma (Moody) R.; m. Gretchen Elise Krughoff, May 16, 1965 (div. July 1984); children: Benjamin, Alice, Theodore. PhD (hon.), Webber Coll., 1989. Caption writer Planet Newspictures Ltd., London, 1956-57; reporter Pensacola (Fla.) News-Jour., 1957-67; account exec. Dodson, Craddock & Born, Pensacola, 1967-69, Fry, Hammond & Born, Pensacola, 1971-72; chief bur. media svcs. State of Fla. Dept. of Commerce, Tallahassee, 1969-71; asst. metro editor Orlando Sentinel, 1972-75, asst. to pub., 1975-78, columnist, mem. editorial bd., 1978—. Author: Great Gods of the Potomac, Common Sense for the 80s. Active Hist. Commn., Pensacola, 1968; bd. dirs. Holocaust Meml., Orlando, 1985-90. With USAR, 1959-65. Named Best Columnist, Fla. Press Club, 1984, Fla. Soc. Newspaper Editors. Mem. SCV. Avocations: pistol shooting, hunting, sketching. Office: Orlando Sentinel 633 N Orange Ave Orlando FL 32801-1349 Address: King Features Syndicate 235 E 45th St New York NY 10017

**REESE, CHARLES WOODROW, JR.,** lawyer, real estate developer; b. San Antonio, June 21, 1944; s. Charles Woodrow and Mary Ruth (Gott) R.; m. Jill Fritschi, Aug. 10, 1979; children: Clarissa, Alexandra. BA cum laude, Washington and Lee U., 1966; JD, U. Calif., Berkeley, 1969. Bar: Calif. 1970, U.S. Sup. Ct. 1994. Staff assoc. McCutchen, Doyle, Brown & Enersen, San Francisco, 1969-75; asst. atty. Kaiser Industries Corp., Oakland, Calif., 1975-78; asst. gen. csl. Kaiser Cement Corp., Oakland, 1978-86; mng. dir. Reese Interests, Houston, 1978—; mng. trustee Clotilde deMartini Trusts, San Francisco, 1977-; prin Lempres & Wulfsberg PC, Oakland, 1986-98; exec. v.p. Wulfsberg Reese & Sykes PC, 1998-2002; pres., CFO Wulsberg Reese Colvig & Firstman PC, 2002—. Hon. trustee Orinda Found., 1976—; bd. dirs. Planned Parenthood Alameda/San Francisco, 1981-83, Brown and Caldwell, Walnut Creek, 1987-, PLA Holdings, Inc., Port Costa, 1991-2000. Robert E. Lee Rsch. scholar, 1965-66. Mem. State Bar Calif., ABA, Bar Assn. San Francisco, Alameda County Bar Assn. (coms.), Omicron Delta Upsilon, Pacific Union Club (San Francisco), Orinda (Calif.) Country Club. Republican. Episcopalian. Home: 89 La Salle Piedmont CA 94611 Office: 300 Lakeside Dr 24th Fl Oakland CA 94612-3534 E-mail: creese@wulfslaw.com.

**REESE, CYNTHIA DENE,** psychologist, educator, quality assurance professional, risk management consultant; b. Milledgeville, Ga., July 19, 1958; d. Robert Weyman, Sr. and Sara Powers (Neal) Reese. BS in Criminal Justice Adminstrn., Ga. Coll. & State U., Milledgeville, 1994; MA in Psychology, Ga. Sch. Profl. Psychologists, Atlanta, 1998; doctoral candidate, N. Ctrl. U., Prescott, Ariz., 2002—. Investigator, social svcs. supr. Dept. of Family and Children Svcs., Ga.; program dir. Ga. Children's Home, Macon, 1998—2001; state clinical dir. Nat. Mentor Healthcare, Inc., Macon, 2001—; adj. prof. Macon State Coll., 2000—. Clin. cons. Ga. Children's Home, Macon, 1998—99; legal child abuse cons. Recipient Excellence award, Houston County Dist. Atty., 1994, Houston County Sheriff's Office, 1994, Houston County Dept. Family and Child Svcs., 1994. Mem.: Nat. Assn. Forensic Counselors, Am. Soc. Trial Cons. Avocations: physical fitness, travel. Home: 1175 Chisholm Trail Macon GA 31220 Office: The Mentor Network 2987 Clairmont Rd Atlanta GA 30329 Office Phone: 478-737-2466. E-mail: samanthatreese@yahoo.com.

**REESE, DELLA (DELOREESE PATRICIA EARLY),** singer, actress; b. Detroit, July 6, 1931; d. Richard and Nellie Early; m. Vermont Adolphus Bon Taliaferro (div.); m. Leroy Basil Gray (div.); m. Franklin Thomas Lett, Jr. Student, Wayne U. Ordained to ministry Ch. Understanding Principles for Better Living Inc., April, 1987. Choir singer, 1938—, with Mahalia Jackson troupe, 1945-49, Erskine Hawkins, N.Y.C.; solo artist, 1957—; organized gospel group at Wayne U.; appearances include: (radio shows) with Robert Q. Lewis; (TV series) Della, 1969, The Voyage of the Yes, 1972, Twice in a Lifetime, 1974, Cop on the Beat, 1975, Chico and the Man, 1974, 76-78, Nightmare in Badham County, 1976 (Emmy nomination), Roots: The Next Generation, 1979, It Takes Two, 1982, Charlie & Co., 1985, 86, The Kid Who Loved Christmas, 1990, The Royal Family, 1991, You Must Remember This, 1992, Touched By an Angel, 1994-2003, A Match Made in Heaven, 1997, Miracle in the Woods, 1997, Emma's Wish, 1998, The Secret Path, 1999, Having Our Say: The Delany Sisters' First 100 Years, 1999; spl. appearances with Jackie Gleason, Ed Sullivan, McCloud, 1971, Sanford and Son, 1972, Welcome Back, Kotter, 1975, The A-Team, 1983, Night Court, 1984, MacGyver, 1985, Designing Women, 1986, L.A. Law, 1986, Married People, 1990, Dream On, 1990, Picket Fences, 1992, Promised Land, 1996, Anya's Bell, 1999, The Moving of Sophia Myles, 2000; guest host The Tonight Show; actress (films) Let's Rock, 1958, Psychic Killer, 1975, Harlem Nights, 1989, A Thin Line Between Love and Hate, 1996, (voice) Dinosaur, 2000, Beauty Shop, 2005, (plays) Same Time Next Year, Ain't Misbehavin, Blues in the Night, The Last Minstrel Show; recs. for Jubilee, RCA Victor Records, ABC Paramount Records, Jazz Ala Carte, AIR Co. (Grammy nomination 1987); author: Angels Along the Way, 1997, (voice) Dinosaur, 2000. Voted Most Promising Singer of Yr. 1957; recipient Image awards, 1996, 98-2000, Star on Walk of Fame, 1994. Office: William Morris Agy c/o Jeff Kolodny 151 S El Camino Dr Beverly Hills CA 90212-2775

**REESE, EVAN CHARLES, JR.,** orthopedist; b. Washington, June 29, 1942; s. Evan Charles Reese and Barbara Cross; m. Rosemary Burr, Sept. 2, 1965; children: Abigail Leigh, Evan C. III, Timothy C. BA, Princeton U., 1963; MD, U. Pa., 1967. Lic. N.J., Pa. Orthop. surgeon Easton (Pa.) Orthop. Group, 1972—. Pres. Easton Hosp. Med. Staff, 1988—90. Bd. dirs. Am. Cancer Soc., Bethlehem, Pa., 1990. Named to Notre Dame H.S. Hall of Fame, Easton, 2004. Fellow: Am. Acad. Orthop. Surgeons, Am. Coll. Surgeons; mem.: AMA, U.S. Golf Assn., Rotary. Republican. Episcopalian. Avocations: golf, birdwatching, fishing. Home: 3570 Westwood Dr Easton PA 18045 Office: Easton Orthop Group 2005 Fairview Ave Easton PA 18042

**REESE, FRANCIS EDWARD,** retired chemical company executive, consultant; b. Monaca, Pa., Nov. 3, 1919; s. Francis Edward and Vivian Iris (Hancuff) R.; m. Katherine Mary McBrien, June 29, 1946; 1 son, Francis Edward III. BS in Chem. Engring, Purdue U., 1941. Registered profl. engr., Pa. From rsch. engr. Plastics Divsn. to sr. v.p. Monsanto Co., 1941—79, sr. v.p., 1979-84. Pres. FTR Assocs., Inc., 1993-2005; mem. engring. found. adv. coun. U. Tex. Fellow AAAS, Am. Inst. Chem. Engrs.; mem. Am. Chem. Soc., Nat. Soc. Profl. Engrs., Soc. Chem. Industry, Tau Beta Pi, Phi Lambda Upsilon. Home: Rydal Park 271W 1515 The Fairway Rydal PA 19046-1435 Personal E-mail: FTRAssoc@aol.com.

**REESE, HARRY EDWIN, JR.,** electronics executive; b. Balt., Oct. 27, 1928; s. Harry Edwin and Margery Lee (Stroud) R.; m. Elizabeth Syra Pfeiffer, Oct. 15, 1955; children: Clifford Owen, Susan Syra, Peter Eyre. BSEE, Tufts U., 1950; MS in Stats., Villanova U., 1960. Engr. Philco Corp., Phila., 1950-54; project engr. Burroughs Corp., Paoli, Pa., 1956-59, dept. mgr., 1959-65, GE Co., King of Prussia, Pa., 1965-69; group staff mgr. Burroughs Corp., Paoli, Pa., 1969-75, gen. mgr. Plainfield, NJ, 1975-82, corp. staff dir. Detroit, 1982-83; v.p. quality assurance Am. Electronic Labs., Inc., Lansdale, Pa., 1984—90, ret., 1990. Chmn. Charlestown Twp. Planning Commn., Pa., 1973-75. With U.S. Army, 1954-56. Fellow IEEE (life, pres. Reliability Soc. 1969-70, gen. chmn. Rams symposium 1968, chmn. bd. 1969, Centennial medal 1984); mem. Nat. Mgmt. Assn. (life, chmn. formation com. Am. Electronics Labs. chpt. 1985, Leadership award 1973, 86), Lake Hopatcong Yacht Club (commodore 2000-01), Masons, Rotary (Paul Harris fellow, treas.). Republican. Episcopalian. Avocations: carpentry, architecture, boating, antiques, travel. Home: 17 Bass Rock Rd Hopatcong NJ 07843-1901

**REESE, HAYNE WARING,** psychologist, educator; b. Comanche, Tex., Jan. 14, 1931; s. Tom F. and Marion (Waring) R.; m. Patsy Atwood, Aug. 24, 1957 (div. Apr. 1967); children: Anne, William, Margaret; m. Nancy Mann, Dec. 16, 1967; 1 child, Bradley. Student, So. Meth. U., 1949-50; BA, U. Tex., 1953, MA, 1955; PhD, U. Iowa, 1958. Asst. prof. U. Buffalo, 1958-62; assoc. prof. SUNY-Buffalo, 1962-66, prof., 1966-67, U. Kans., Lawrence, 1967-70; Centennial prof. psychology W.Va. U., Morgantown, 1970-2000, dir. grad. tng. in life-span devel. psychology, 1973-2000, Centennial prof. emeritus, 2000—. Mem. initial rev. groups div. research grants NIH, Washington, 1969-71, 74-78, 79-84; vis. prof. SUNY, Buffalo, 1970, U. Iowa, 1972, U. Hawaii, 1975, S.W. China Normal U., 1997, 2000. Author: Perception of Stimulus Relations, 1968, Basic Learning Processes in Childhood, 1976; co-author: Life-Span Developmental Psychology, 1977, 1988, Child Development, 1979; editor: Advances in Child Development and Behavior, 26 vols., 1969-2001; co-editor: Life-Span Developmental Psychology, 8 vols., 1973-97; assoc. editor: Jour. Exptl. Child Psychology, 1975-83, editor, 1983-97, mem. editl. bd. 1965-74, 98-2000. Served with U.S. Army, 1954. Fellow AAAS, Am. Psychol. Soc.; mem. Soc. for Rsch. in Child Devel., Psychonomic Soc., Assn. for Behavior Analysis, Internat. Soc. for Study Behavioral Devel. Personal E-mail: haynereese@aol.com.

**REESE, JOHN ROBERT,** lawyer; b. Salt Lake City, Nov. 3, 1939; s. Robert McCann and Glade (Stauffer) R.; m. Francesca Marroquin Gardner, Sept. 5, 1964 (div.); children: Jennifer Marie, Justine Francesca; m. Robin Ann Gunsul, June 18, 1988. BA, Harvard U., 1962; LLB, Stanford U., 1965. Bar: Calif. 1966, U.S. Dist. Ct. (no. dist.) Calif. 1966, U.S. Ct. Appeals (9th cir.) 1966, U.S. Dist. Ct. (ctrl. dist.) Calif. 1974, U.S. Supreme Ct. 1976, U.S. Dist. Ct. (ea. dist.) Calif. 1977, U.S. Ct. Appeals (6th cir.) 1982, U.S. Ct. Appeals (8th cir.) 1985, U.S. Ct. Appeals (10th cir.) 1992, U.S. Ct. Appeals (Fed. cir.) 1994. Assoc. McCutchen, Doyle, Brown & Enersen, San Francisco, 1965—74, ptnr., 1974—2002, Bingham McCutchen, San Francisco, 2002—. Adj. asst. prof. law Hastings Coll. of Law, 1991; lectr. U. Calif., Berkeley, 1987, Berkeley, 92. Mem. editl. and adv. bds.: Antitrust Bull., Jour. Reprints for Antitrust Law and Econs., 1981—99. Bd. dirs. Friends of San Francisco Pub. Libr., 1981-87; bd. vis. Stanford U. Law Sch., 1983-86. Capt. U.S. Army, 1966-68. Decorated Bronze Star. Mem. ABA, Am. Acad. Appellate Lawyers, State Bar Calif., San Francisco Bar Assn., U.S. Supreme Ct. Hist. Soc., Ninth Jud. Cir. Hist. Soc., Calif. Acad. Appellate Lawyers, Order of Coif. Avocation: gardening. Home: 9 Morning Sun Dr Petaluma CA 94952-4780 Office: Bingham McCutchen 3 Embarcadero Ctr San Francisco CA 94111-4003 Office Phone: 415-393-2225. Business E-Mail: john.reese@bingham.com.

**REESE, LYMON CLIFTON,** civil engineering educator; b. Murfreesboro, Ark., Apr. 27, 1917; s. Samuel Wesley and Nancy Elizabeth (Daniels) R.; m. Eva Lee Jett, May 28, 1948; children: Sally Reese Melant, John, Nancy. BS, U. Tex. at Austin, 1949, MS, 1950; PhD, U. Calif. at Berkeley, 1955; D in Civil Engring. (hon.), Inst. Bucharest, Romania, 1994. Diplomate: Registered profl. engr., Tex. Internat. Boundary Commn., San Benito, Tex., 1939-41; surveyor U.S. Naval Constrn. Bns., U.S., Aleutian Islands, Okinawa, 1942-45; field engr. Assoc. Contractors & Engrs., Houston, 1945; draftsman Phillips Petroleum Co., Austin, 1946-48; research engr. U. Tex., Austin, 1948-50; asst. prof. civil engring. Miss. State Coll., 1950-51, 53-55; asst. prof. U. Tex., Austin, 1955-57, assoc. prof., 1957-64, prof., 1964—, chmn. dept., 1965-72, Taylor prof. engring., 1972-81, assoc. dean engring. for program planning, 1972-79, Nasser I. Al-Rashid Chair, 1981-84; prin. Ensoft, Inc., 1985—, Lymon C. Reese Assocs. Contbr. articles to profl. jours. Recipient Thomas Middlebrooks award ASCE, 1958; Joe J. King Profl. Engring. Achievement award, 1977, Offshore Tech. Conf. Disting. Achievement award for Individuals, 1985, Disting. grad. Coll. of Engring., U. Tex., Austin., 1985. Mem. ASCE (Karl Terzaghi lectr. 1976 Terzaghi award, 1983, Tex. sect. award of Hon. 1985, hon. mem. 1984—), Nat. Acad. Engring. Baptist (deacon). Office: U Tex Dept Civil Engring Austin TX 78712-1104 Home: 11503 April Dr Austin TX 78753-2903 Office Phone: 512-244-6464 ext. 113. Personal E-mail: lymonreese@aol.com.

**REESE, POKEY,** professional baseball player; b. Columbia, S.C., June 10, 1973; Player Cin. Reds, 1997—2001, Pittsburgh Pirates, 2002—03, Boston Red Sox, 2004, Seattle Mariners, 2005—. Recipient Nat. League Golden Glove Award, 1999—2000. Achievements include being a member of World Series Champion Boston Red Sox, 2004. Office: c/o Seattle Mariners 1250 1st Ave South Seattle WA 98134

**REESE, ROBERT M.,** retired lawyer; AB, Harvard U., 1972; JD, Georgetown U., 1976. Bar: Pa. 1976, D.C. 1977. Asst. counsel, staff asst. Ways & Means Com. U.S. House of Reps., 1975-76; assoc. Reed, Smith Shaw & McClay, 1976-78; counsel Hershey Foods Corp., 1978-79, staff counsel, 1979-82, sr. counsel, 1982-87, v.p., gen. counsel, 1993-98, sr. v.p., gen. counsel, sec., 1999—2004, retired, 2004.

**REESE, STUART HARRY,** insurance company executive; b. Richmond, Va., May 3, 1955; s. Allison and Virginia (Saul) R.; m. Elizabeth Garr, Aug. 21, 1976; children: Katharine, Elizabeth, Jillian, Thomas. BA, Gettysburg (Pa.) Coll., 1977; MBA, Dartmouth Coll., 1979. Securities analyst investment pvt. placements Aetna, Hartford, Conn., 1979-81, sr. securities analyst dept. fin. guaranty, 1981-82, dir. treas. investment planning, 1982-83, sr. investment officer, 1983-84, asst. v.p., 1984-85, mng. dir., 1985-89, v.p., mng. dir. capital markets, 1989—93; various sr. mgmt. positions, including chmn. & CEO Babson Capital Mgmt. subsidiary, Mass. Mutual Fin. Group, Springfield, Mass., 1993—99, exec. v.p. & chief investment officer, 1999—2005, pres & CFO 2005—. Mem. investment com. Vis. Nurses Assn., Simsbury, Conn., 1991—. Mem. Hartford Soc. Fin. Analysts (v.p. bd. 1991—). Office: Mass Mutual Financial Group 1295 State St Springfield MA 01111*

**REESE, TRACY,** fashion designer; b. Detroit; Degree, Parsons Sch. Design, 1984. Design asst. to Martine Sitbon Arlequin Paris, 1984-87; designer with Marc Jacobs Perry Ellis Portfolio; design dir. Magaschoni, Inc., 1990—95; launched own label Tracy Reese, 1987—89, 1997—, Plenty by Tracy Reese, 1998—, Plenty by Tracy Reese Home. Office: care of Factory PR 580 Broadway Ste 602 New York NY 10012*

**REESE, WILLIAM ALBERT, III,** clinical neuropsychologist; b. Tabor, Iowa, Nov. 23, 1932; s. William Albert and Mary-Evelyn Hope (Lundeen) R.; m. Barbara Diane Windermere, Dec. 22, 1954 (dec. Jan. 1995); children: Judy, Diane William IV, Sandra-Siobhan, Debra-Anne, Robert-Gregory, Barbara-Joanne; m. Ruth Alice Moller, Sept 12, 1996. BA, U. Wash. Reed Coll., 1955; MEd, U. Ariz., 1964, PhD, 1981; postgrad., Fielding Inst. Clin. Neuropsychology, 2000. Diplomate Am. Bd. Christian Psychology, Am. Bd. Forensic Neuropsychology, Am. Coll. Advanced Practice Psychologists, Prescribing Psychologists Register; cert. in clin. neuropsychology. Clin. psychology cons. Nogales Pub. Schs., Nogales-Tucson, Ariz., 1971-79; clin. psychologist Astra-Found., NYC, 1979-86, chief psychology svc., neuropsychiatry, 1980-89; chief psychologist Family Support Ctr. Cmty.-Family Exception mem. Svcs., Sonoita, Ariz., 1986-89, Psychol. Svc. Ctr. Mount Tabor, Iowa, 1989-95, Calif. Ctr. Health and Wellness, 1995—; clin. psychologist Calif. Dept. Corrections, 1997—. Dir. religious Marriage and Family Life Wilderness Ctr., Berchtesgaden, Germany, 1981-82; exec. sec. Astra Ednl. Found. 1975-79, bd. dirs, 1979—, EEO officer, 1978—. Author: Developing a Scale of Human Values for Adults of Diverse Cultural Backgrounds, 1981, rev. edit., 1988. Served with USAF, 1967-71, Vietnam. Decorated Bronze Star; fellow in cons. psychology and holistic medicine Clin. Svcs. Found., Ariz., 1979—. Fellow Am. Psychol. Soc., Am. Coll. Forensic Examiners, Clin. Neuropsychiatry and Neuropsychology, 1998; mem. APA, ACA, Internat. Neuropsychol. Assn., Calif. Psychol. Assn., Iowa Psychol. Assn., KC, Los Padres Wilderness Ctr., Outdoor Club, Sierra Club, Skyline Estates Golf and Country Club (Tucson). Office: AstraWorldMedicineUSA com 798 Lighthouse Ave Ste 323 Monterey CA 93940-1010 Office Phone: 877-845-8950.

**REESE, WILLIAM LEWIS,** philosophy educator; b. Jefferson City, Mo., Feb. 15, 1921; s. William Lewis and Lillian Amelia (Fisher) R.; m. Louise Weeks, June 11, 1945; children: Claudia, Patricia, William Lewis III. AB, Drury Coll., 1942; B.D., U. Chgo., 1945, PhD, 1947; postdoctoral, Yale U., 1955-56. Asst. prof. philosophy Drake U., 1947-49, asso. prof. philosophy, 1949-57, head dept., 1954-57; asso. prof. philosophy Grinnell Coll., 1957-60; vis. prof. philosophy Iowa State U., 1958; prof. philosophy, chmn. dept. U. Del., Newark, 1960-67, dir. seminar in philosophy of sci., 1960-66, H. Rodney Sharp prof. philosophy, 1965-67; prof. philosophy SUNY-Albany, 1967-99, chmn. dept., 1968-74, 84, prof. philosophy emeritus, rsch. prof. philosophy, 1999—. Tully Cleon Knoles lectr. U. Pacific, 1962; del. U.S. Nat. Commn. for UNESCO, 1963; gen. mem. 4th East-West Philosophers Conf., 1964 Author, contbr.: Studies in C.S. Peirce, 1952, (with Charles Hartshorne) Philosophers Speak of God, 1953, 2d edit., 2000, The Ascent from Below, 1959, 2d edit., 2000, (with Eugene Freeman) Process and Divinity, 1964, Dictionary of Philosophy and Religion: Eastern and Western Thought, 1980, 3d edit., 1999, Freedom, 2000, Values, 2000; gen. editor: Philosophy of Science, The Delaware Seminar, vols. 1, 2, 1963, vol. 3, 1967; editor: Philosophy and World Religions: The Reader's Adviser, vol. 4, 1988, Fundamental Issues in Philosophy Series, 2 vols., 2000; editl. bd.: State of N.Y. Press, 1968-78; contbr. articles to profl. jours Recipient Ford Found. Study award Argentina, 1967; Fulbright lectr. Argentina, summer 1971; Inst. Humanistic Studies fellow, 1977— Mem.: AAUP, Metaphysical Soc. Am. (sec. 1962—65, treas. 1962—65), Am. Philos. Assn. Mem. Christian Ch. (Disciples Of Christ). Home: Font Grove Rd Slingerlands NY 12159 Office: SUNY Dept Philosophy Albany NY 12222-0001 Personal E-mail: reesewl@aol.com. *To have before one always the realistic sense that if one has been successful in one way one has failed in others, and that one's failures surely outnumber one's successes.*

**REES-JONES, TREVOR D.,** oil industry executive; b. Dallas, Tex., 1950; married; 2 children. BA, Darmouth Coll.; JD, So. Methodist U. Sch. Law, 1978. Atty. Thompson & Knight, Dallas, 1978—84; oil & gas investor, 1984—93; founder Chief Oil & Gas LLC (sold to Devon Energy), 1994—2006; founder, pres. & CEO Chief Operating LLC, Dallas, 2006—. Named one of 400 Richest Americans, Forbes, 2006. Office: Chief Operating LLC Ste 600 8111 Preston Rd Dallas TX 75225 Office Phone: 214-265-9590. Office Fax: 214-265-9593.*

**REEVES, ALAN M.,** automotive company executive; Pres. Spalding Ford-Lincoln-Mercury, Inc., Griffin, Ga., 1982, Spalding Automotive Group, Griffin, 1982—. Recipient Award Black Enterprise, 1991. Office: Spalding Ford O Box 819 Experiment GA 30212-0819

**REEVES, BARBARA ANN,** lawyer; b. Buffalo, Mar. 29, 1949; d. Prentice W. and Doris Reeves; m. Richard C. Neal; children: Timothy R. Neal, Stephen S. Neal (dec.), Robert S. Neal, Richard R. Neal. Student, Wellesley Coll., Mass., 1967-68; BA (NSF fellow, Lehman fellow), New Coll., Sarasota, Fla., 1970; JD cum laude, Harvard U., 1973. Bar: Calif. 1973, D.C. 1977. Law clk. U.S. Ct. Appeals, 9th Circuit, Portland, Oreg., 1973—74; assoc. firm Munger, Tolles and Rickershauser, L.A., 1977—78; trial atty. spl. trial sect. Dept. Justice (Antitrust div.), 1974—75; spl. asst. to asst. atty. gen. Antitrust div. Dept. Justice, Washington, 1976—77; chief antitrust div. L.A. field office, 1978—81; ptnr. Morrison & Foerster, L.A., 1981—94, Fried, Frank, Harris, Shriver & Jacobson, L.A., 1995—97, Paul, Hastings, Janofsky & Walker, L.A., 1997—99; assoc. gen. counsel So. Calif. Edison, 1999—2004, v.p. shared svcs., 2004—06; mediator, arbitrator JAMS, 2006—. Mem. exec. com. state bar conf. of dels. L.A. Delegation, 1982-91; del. 9th Cir. Jud. Conf., 1984-88; mem. Fed. Ct. Magistrate Selection Com., 1989; bd. dirs. Pub. Counsel, 1988-92, Western Ctr. Law and Poverty, 1992-98; lectr. in field. Editor: Federal Criminal Litigation, 1994; contbg. author: World Antitrust Law, 1995; contbr. articles to profl. jours. Mem. ABA (litigation sect., antitrust sect.), Fed. Bar Assn. (officer 1998—), Assn. Bus. Trial Lawyers (officer 1997—), Am. Arbitration Assn. (arbitrator, mediator, mem. adv. panel large complex case program), L.A. County Bar Assn. (antitrust sect. officer 1980-81, litigation sect. officer 1988-93 trustee 1990-92, chair alternative dispute resolution sec. 1992-95, L.A. County Ct. ADR com.). Home: 1410 Hillcrest Ave Pasadena CA 91106-4503 Office: 46th Fl 707 Wilshire Blvd Los Angeles CA 90017 Office Phone: 213-620-1133. Business E-Mail: breeves@jamsadr.com.

**REEVES, DANIEL EDWARD,** former professional football coach; b. Rome, Ga., Jan. 19, 1944; m. Pam Reeves; children: Dana, Laura, Lee. Grad., U. S.C. Running back Dallas Cowboys, NFL, 1965-72, player-coach, 1970-71, asst. coach, 1972, 74-80; head coach Denver Broncos, NFL, 1981-92, also v.p.; head coach N.Y. Giants, 1993-96, Atlanta Falcons, 1997—2003. Recipient NFL Coach of the Year award, 1984, 1989, 1991, 1993, 1998; named to S.C. Hall Fame.

**REEVES, DIANNE,** singer; b. Detroit, 1956; Student, U. Colo., 1970s. Performed with trumpeteer Clark Terry; recorded sessions with Lenny White, Stanley Turrentine, Alphonso Johnson, 1970s; performer with Night Flight, 1970s, Sergio Mendes tour, 1981, Harry Belafonte, 1983-86; toured as trio with Billy Childs, 1986; rec. artist: (albums) Welcome to My Love, 1982, For Every Heart, 1986, Dianne Reeves, 1987, Never Too Far, 1989, I Remember, 1990, Art and Survival, 1993, Quiet After the Storm, 1994, The Grand Encounter, 1996, That Day..., 1997, Bridges, 1999, In the Moment: Live in Concert, 2000, The Calling, 2001, A Little Moonlight, 2003, Christmas Time is Here, 2004, Good Night and Good Luck motion picture soundtrack, 2005; actress (films) Good Night and Good Luck, 2005. Recipient Best Jazz Vocal Album for The Calling, Grammy Awards, 2001, Best Jazz Vocal Album for A Little Moonlight, 2003, Best Jazz Vocal Album for Good Night and Good Luck, 2006. Office: Blue Note Records 150 5th Ave New York NY 10011 Office Phone: 212-786-8600.*

**REEVES, JAMES N.,** lawyer; b. Albert Lea, Minn., Oct. 14, 1945; AB, Dartmouth Coll., 1967; student, George Washington U.; JD, U. Minn., 1970. Bar: Minn. 1970, Alaska 1972, U.S. Ct. Appeals (9th cir.), U.S. Supreme Ct. Law clk. U.S. Dist. Ct. Minn., 1970-71; asst. atty. gen. State of Alaska, 1971-78; mem. Bogle & Gates (now Dorsey & Whitney), Anchorage; ptnr.-in-charge, Anchorage; mem. trial dept., environ. and natural resources practice groups Dorsey & Whitney LLP, Anchorage. Sr. fellow East-West Ctr., Honolulu, 1977. Mem. ABA, Alaska Bar Assn. Office: Dorsey & Whitney 1031 W 4th Ave Ste 600 Anchorage AK 99501-5907 Office Phone: 907-276-4557. Office Fax: 907-276-4152. Business E-Mail: reeves.jim@dorsey.com.

**REEVES, JENNIFER TODD,** filmmaker; b. Colombo, Sri Lanka, 1971; MFA, U. Calif., San Diego. Founder Sparky Pictures, Inc., NYC, 2000—. Vis. asst. prof. film and electronic arts Yale U., New Haven; part-time tchr. Bard Coll. Milton Avery Sch. Arts, Cooper Union, Millennium Film Workshop. Filmmaker (prin. works) The Girl's Nervy, 1995, Chronic, 1996, Darling Internat. (with MM Serra), 1999 (Cinematography award, Cinetexas Film Festival, 2000), Fear of Blushing, 2001, The Time We Killed, 2004 (FIPRESCI Critics prize, Berlin Film Festival, Outstanding Artistic Achievement, OUTFEST, Best NY, NY Narrative Feature, Tribeca Film Festival), Shadows Choose Their Horrors, We Are Going Home (Film Co-op award, Ann Arbor Film Festival, 1999, Juror's Citation, Black Maria Film Festival, 1999), (group shows) Toronto Film Festival, Kill Your Timid Notion: Dundee Contemporary Arts Festival, Whitney Biennial: Day for Night, Whitney Mus. Am. Art, 2006. Recipient Princess Grace award, 2000; grantee Jacob K. Javits fellowship, 1997—2001, Andrea Frank Found. grant, 1999. Office: Sparky Pictures Inc PO Box 136 Planetarium Sta New York NY 10024*

**REEVES, JOAN HUTCHINS,** painter; b. Seattle, June 22, 1932; d. John Marvin and Bess Irene (Sowler) Hutchins; m. George Catherwood Reeves, Sept. 5, 1953; children: David Alan, John Michael. Exhibitions include Whatcom Mus. History and Art. Mem. Art Stall Gallery Coop. (chmn. 1986-89), Nat. Mus. Women in the Arts (charter), N.W. Watercolor Soc.

(signature mem., exhbn. chmn. 1986, Purchase award 1988), Women Painters of Wash. (membership chmn. 1986-88, Transparent Watecolor award 1985, 86, 90, Best of Show 1989, 2001, Purchase award, 2004), Mont. Watercolor Soc. (signature mem.), Watercolor West (signature mem.), San Diego Watercolor Soc. (signature mem.) Avocation: travel. Home: 3901 Fremont Ave N Seattle WA 98103-7756

**REEVES, JOHN DRUMMOND,** retired English language professional, writer; b. Troy, NY, Dec. 8, 1914; s. Robert Brockway and Emma Caroline (Mausert) R.; m. Mary Markwick Moore, Sept. 1, 1951. AB, Williams Coll., Williamstown, Mass., 1937; AM, Columbia U., 1941. Instr. in Eng. Irving Sch., Tarrytown, N.Y., 1937-40, Horace Mann Sch., N.Y.C., 1940-41, 46-47; asst. prof. of classics and Eng. Whitman Coll., Walla Walla, Wash., 1956-62; assoc. prof. English Millikin U., Decatur, Ill., 1962-65; lectr. in Eng. Hofstra U., Hempstead, N.Y., 1965-73, ret., 1973. Author: Windows on Melville, 2001; contbr. articles to profl. jours. Lt. USNR, 1941-45, PTO. Mem. AAUP, Coll. Eng. Assn., Am. Coun. Learned Soc. (reg. assoc. 1957-59), Walla Walla Archaeol. Assn. (pres. 1959-62), SR (Conn. state chpt.), Masons. Home: 20 Devonwood Dr Apt 161 Farmington CT 06032-1422

**REEVES, KATHLEEN WALKER,** English language educator; b. Mt. Pleasant, Mich., Dec. 7, 1950; d. John J. and Gladys M. W.; m. Daniel H. Reeves, Mar. 10, 1972; children: Sheila, Michael. BA, Ctrl. Mich. U., 1973, MA, 1984. English tchr. Shepherd (Mich.) High Sch., 1973-76, Chippewa Hills High Sch., Remus, Mich., 1978-79, Onekama (Mich.) High. Sch., 1983-86, Seaholm High Sch., Birmingham, Mich., 1986—. Bd. dirs. Nat. Bd. Profl. Tchg. Stds.

**REEVES, KEANU,** actor; b. Beirut, Sept. 2, 1964; s. Samuel Nowlin Reeves and Patricia Taylor. Stage appearances: Wolf Boy (debut), For Adults Only, Romeo and Juliet; films: Flying, 1986, Youngblood, 1986, River's Edge, 1987, Permanent Record, 1988, The Night Before, 1988, The Prince of Pennsylvania, 1988, Dangerous Liaisons, 1988, Bill and Ted's Excellent Adventure, 1989, Parenthood, 1989, I Love You to Death, 1990, Tune in Tomorrow, 1990, Bill and Ted's Bogus Journey, 1991, Point Break, 1991, My Own Private Idaho, 1991, Bram Stoker's Dracula, 1992, Much Ado About Nothing, 1993, Little Buddha, 1994, Even' Cowgirls Get the Blues, 1994, Speed, 1994, Johnny Mnemonic, 1995, A Walk in the Clouds, 1995, Feeling Minnesota, 1996, Chain Reaction, 1996, Devil's Advocate, 1997, The Last Time I Committed Suicide, 1997, The Matrix, 1999, The Replacements, 2000, The Watcher, 2000, The Gift, 2000, Hard Ball, 2001, Sweet November, 2001, The Matrix Reloaded, 2003, The Matrix Revolutions, 2003, Something's Gotta Give, 2003, Thumbsucker, 2005, Constantine, 2005, A Scanner Darkly, 2006, The Lake House, 2006 (with Sandra Bullock Movie-Choice Liplock, Teen Choice Awards, 2006); TV films: Letting Go, 1985, Act of Vengeance, 1986, Young Again, 1986, Babes in Toyland, 1986, Under the Influence, 1986, Brotherhood of Justice, 1986, Life Under Water, 1989, Children Remember the Holocaust, 1995, (narrator) The Great Warning, 2003. Named one of 50 Most Powerful People in Hollywood, Premiere mag., 2006. Office: Creative Artists Agy care Kevin Houvane 9830 Wilshire Blvd Beverly Hills CA 90212-1825*

**REEVES, LUCY MARY,** retired elementary school educator; b. Pewamo, Mich., July 2, 1932; d. Lavaldin Edgar and Marian S. (Lee) Hull; m. Walter Emery Reeves, Jan. 21, 1922. BS, Western Mich. U., Kalamazoo, 1965; postgrad., Western Mich. U., 1965-75. Tchr. Country Sch. One Room, Matherton, Mich., 1956-57, Ionia, Mich., 1957-58, Belding, Mich., 1958-62, Saranac, Mich., Belding, 1965, Belding Area Schs., 1965—89; ret., 1989. Vol. Frederick Meijers Garden, Grand Rapids, Point Man Internat. Ministries, Shiloh Cmty. Ch., United Meml. Health Ctr., Shiloh Cmty. Ch.; vol. United Meml. Health Ctr., Greenville. Mem. NEA, Mich. Edn. Assn., Belding Area Edn., Profl. Businesswomen's Assn. Avocations: computers, reading, travel, sewing.

**REEVES, MICHAEL SPENCER,** investment company executive; b. Memphis, Mar. 13, 1967; s. Rodger Clifton and Betty Lou Reeves; m. Julie Mackle Mackle; children: Spencer J.M., Kathleen Kohl, Vivian Asbridge. BA, U. South, Sewanee, Tenn., 1985—89; MBA, Duke U., Durham, NC, 1993—95. Vp New South Capital Mgmt., Inc., Memphis, 1995—2004; sr. mng. dir. Third Ave. Mgmt., LLC, NYC, 2004—06; mng. dir. Lapides Asset Mgmt., LLC, Greenwich, Conn., 2006—. Mem.: AIMSE, Assn. Investment Mgmt. Sales Executives, CFA Inst. Office: Lapides Asset Mgmt LLC 500 W Putnam Ave Greenwich CT 06830

**REEVES, NANCY RAPP,** elementary school educator; BS, Ohio State U., 1991; MA in Tchg., Mary Groves Coll., 2001. Cert. tchr., Ohio. Social studies tchr. East Clinton Mid. Sch., Lees Creek, Ohio, 1991—. Recipient Outstanding Educator award, East Clinton Sch., 2001, 2003, Martha Holden Jennings scholar award, 2005. Mem. Pi Lambda Theta, Phi Kappa Phi, Golden Key Soc. Home: 3816 Bloomingburg New Holland Rd New Holland OH 43145-9611 Office Phone: 937-584-9267.

**REEVES, RALPH BERNARD, III,** publishing executive; b. Raleigh, NC, Apr. 2, 1947; s. Ralph Bernard Reeves Jr. and Frances Rhoda (Campbell) M.; m. Caroline Holton Green, Apr. 24, 1971 (div. 1986); children: Ralph B. IV, Daniel MacQuarrie; m. Katherine Drewry Reid, June 20, 1998. AB in History, U. NC, 1970. Field coord. FMI Mgmt. Group, Raleigh, NC, 1972-76; gen. mgr., v.p. The Leader Newspaper, Rsch. Triangle Pk., NC, 1977-78; pres., pub., founder Spectator Pubs. Inc., Raleigh, 1978-98, Triad Bus., Greensboro, NC, 1986-88, Triangle Bus., Raleigh, 1985-91, Spectator Pub., NC Architect, 1981-84; pres. Reeves Media, 1998—; pub., editor Raleigh Metro Mag., 1999—. Editor: Mr. Spectator, 1978—88; author: (monthly column) My Usual Charming Self in Metro Mag. 1st v.p. Mordecai Square Hist. Soc., Raleigh, 1980—83; pres. Hilltop Home, 1982—84; coun. mem. NC Mus. Art; founder Raleigh Internat. Spy Conf.; chmn. Downtown Adv. Com., 1983—85; bus. adv. com. NC Sec. of State, Raleigh, 1992—; bd. dirs. NC State U. Friends of Libr., Carolina Ballet. Gov's. Bus. award in the Arts and Humanities, 1986, Benjamin Fine award, 1991, AABP award Triangle Bus., 1st place award Feature Writing, 1991. Mem. Assn. Former Intelligence Officers (assoc.), Fifty Group, English Speaking Union (past pres. RTP br. 1988—), Carolina Co. Club, Sphinx Club. Episcopalian. Avocations: golf, history, travel. Home: 3066 Granville Dr Raleigh NC 27609 Office Phone: 919-831-0999. E-mail: reevesmedia@msn.com.

**REEVES, RICHARD,** writer, historian; b. NYC, Nov. 28, 1936; s. Furman W. and Dorothy (Forshay) R.; m. Carol A. Wiegand, June 1, 1959 (div. 1971); m. Catherine E. O'Neill, July 28, 1979; children: Cynthia Ann, Jeffrey Richard, Colin O'Neill, Conor O'Neill, Fiona O'Neill. ME, Stevens Inst. Tech., 1960. Engr. Ingersoll-Rand Co., Phillipsburg, NJ, 1960-61; editor Phillipsburg Free Press, 1961-63; reporter Newark News, 1963-65, NY Herald Tribune, 1965-66; chief polit. corr. NY Times, 1966-71; editor NY, 1971-77; lectr. Hunter Coll., 1969-70, Columbia U., 1971-72; nat. editor, columnist Esquire, 1977-79; chief corr. Frontline, PBS, 1981—84; syndicated columnist, 1979—. Regents prof. polit. sci. UCLA, 1992-93, vis. prof. Annenburg Sch. for Comm., 1998; host "Sunday" NBC-TV, 1972-75, "American Journey" PBS-TV, 1983. Author: A Ford, Not a Lincoln, 1975, Old Faces of 1976, 1976, Convention, 1977, Jet Lag: The Running Commentary of a Bi-coastal Reporter, 1981, American Journey: Travelling with Tocqueuille in Search of Democracy in America, 1982 (Christopher Book award 1983), The Reagan Detour: Conservative Revolutionary, 1985, A Passage to Peshawar: Pakistan Between the Hindu Kush and the Arabian Sea, 1985, President Kennedy: Profile of Power, 1993 (PEN Non-Fiction Book of Year, Time mag., Book of the Year, Wash. Monthly 1993), Running in Place: How Bill Clinton Disappointed America, 1996, Do the Media Govern?: Politicians, Voters, and Reporters in America, 1997, Family Travels: Around the World in 30 (or So) Days, 1997, What the People Know: Freedom and the Press, 1998,

Richard Nixon: Alone in the White House, 2002, President Reagan: The Triumph of Imagination, 2006. Recipient Emmy award, 1980, Columbia-Peabody award, 1984, Carey McWilliams award, Am. Polit. Science Assn., 1998. E-mail: rr@richardreeves.com.

**REEVES, ROY FRANKLIN,** mathematician, engineer, educator; b. Warrensberg, Mo., July 8, 1922; s. Archie R. and Lucie P. (Jahn) R.; m. Priscilla L. LaVanway, Mar. 17, 1951; children: Dennis, James, Terrence, Sandra, Timothy. BEE, U. Colo., 1947; PhD, Iowa State U., 1951. Instr. Iowa State U., Ames, 1948-51; prof. Ohio State U., Columbus, 1951-81, Otterbein Coll., Columbus, 1981—91. Contbr. approximately 20 articles to profl. jours. Mem. Assn. for Computing Machinery, Am. Math. Soc., Math. Assn. Am. Office: Dept Math Sci Otterbein Coll Westerville OH 43081 Home: 204 Kendal Dr Granville OH 43023 Business E-Mail: reeves.3@osu.edu.

**REEVY-MANNING, GRETCHEN MARIA,** psychologist, educator; b. Cortland, NY, Oct. 17, 1964; d. William Robert and Carole May Reevy; m. Todd Royal Manning. AB in Psychology, U. N.C., 1986; PhD in Psychology, U. Calif., Berkeley, 1994. Lectr. psychology dept. Dominican Coll., San Rafael, Calif., 1993—98; lectr. U. Calif., Davis, 1994, Profl. Sch. Psychology, San Francisco, 1995; lectr. psychology dept. Calif. State U., East Bay, 1994—. Grantee, Rand Corp., 1993. Mem.: APA, Soc. for Psychological Study of Social Issues, Am. Psychol. Soc., Western Psychol. Assn., Phi Beta Kappa, Psi Chi. Avocations: swimming, reading, running. Office: Calif State Univ Psychology Dept Hayward CA 94542 Office Phone: 510-885-3421. Business E-Mail: gretchen.reevy@csueastbay.edu.

**REFAAT, TAMER F.,** electrical engineer, researcher; s. Fawzi Ibrahim Refaat and Zeinab Helmi; m. Rehab Hafez; 1 child, Mostafa Tamer. BS, Alexandria U., 1991, MS, 1995; PhD, Old Dominion U., 2000. Tchg. asst. and lectr. Elec. Engring. Dept., Faculty of Engring., Alexandria U., Alexandria, Egypt, 1991—95; rsch. asst. Phys. Electronics Rsch. Lab., Elec. and Computer Engring. Dept., Old Dominion U., Norfolk, Va., 1996, Elec. and Computer Engring. Dept., Old Dominion U., 1996—99; on-site contr. NASA Langley Rsch. Ctr., Hampton, Va., 1996—99; sr. lidar and instrumentation engr., Sci. and Engring. Svcs. Inc., Burtonsville, Md., 2000—01; rsch. elec. engr., Sci. and Tech. Corp., Hampton, Va., 2001—; on-site contr. NASA Langley Rsch. Ctr., Hampton, Va., 2001—06; sr. rsch. scientist Applied Rsch. Ctr. Old Dominion U., Norfolk, Va., 2006—. Contbr. articles to profl. jours. Mem.: Optical Soc. of Am. (corr.), The Internat. Soc. for Optical Engring. (corr.), IEEE (corr.). Moslem. Achievements include design of advanced atmospheric water vapor differential absorption lidar (DIAL) detection system; characterization of optical detectors. Office: NASA Langley Research Center 5 North Dryden St MS468 Hampton VA 23681 Office Phone: 757-864-1540. Personal E-mail: tamer.refaat@hotmail.com. E-mail: fn.t.f.refaat@larc.nasa.gov.

**REFAI, SHAHID,** history professor; b. Baroda, Gujarat, India, Dec. 17, 1936; s. Zainulabedin Badruddin and Afzal Banu R.; m. Shama Banu Nagamia, May 19, 1963 (div. Mar. 1998); children: Irfan, Saba, Farah, Aslam; m. Sartaj Banu Kazi, Aug. 16, 1998. BA magna cum laude, MS U., Baroda, India, 1959, MA summa cum laude, 1962; PhD, Cambridge U., 1968. Asst. prof. Cen. Wash. U., Ellensburg, 1971-77; assoc. prof. Coll. St. Rose, Albany, NY, 1977-82, 84-88, prof. of history, 1988—. Vis. lectr. UCLA, 1969-70, U. Calif. Berkeley, 1971; adj. assoc. prof. Cen. Wash. U., Ellensburg, 1983-84; pres. N.Y. Conf. on Asian Studies, New Paltz, N.Y., 1999-2001, chmn. 2000. Contbr. essays to profl. publs. Gen. sec. Tri-City India Assn., Albany, 1985-88, bd. dirs., 1988-91; organizer and coord. Sunday Urdu Sch. of Albany, 1990-95; judge Nat. History Day, Inc., Seattle, 1984; panelist Assn. for Asian Studies, U. Mich., Ann Arbor. Recipient Lady Mountbatton award Cambridge, 1967, scholarship Bombay-Cambridge Soc., 1964-66, others. Avocations: rare book collecting, computers, indian music, videography. E-mail: refais@mail.strose.edu.

**REFO, PATRICIA LEE,** lawyer; b. Alexandria, Va., Dec. 31, 1958; m. Don Bivens; 1 child, Andrew stepchildren: Jody, Lisa. BA with high honors and high distinction, U. Mich., 1980, JD cum laude, 1983. Bar: Ill. 1983, US Dist. Ct. No. Dist. Ill. 1983, US Ct. Appeals 7th cir. 1988, US Ct. Appeals 11th cir. 1989, US Ct. Appeals 5th cir. 1993, Ariz. 1996, US Dist. Ct. Ariz. 1997, US Ct. Appeals 9th cir. 1998, US Tax Ct. Assoc. Jenner & Block, Chgo., 1983—90, ptnr., 1990—96, Snell & Wilmer LLP, Phoenix, 1996—. Mem. faculty Nat. Inst. Trial Advocacy, 1989—; adv. com. on fed. rules of evidence, US Jud. Conf. 2000—; mem. bd. advisors Comml. Lending Liability News, 1989-, Nat. Law Jour., 2005—; lectr. ALI/ABA and Practicing Law Inst. Chancellor Episcopal Parish of St. Barnabas on the Desert, 1999—; bd. dirs. Ariz. Academic Decathlon Assn., 1997—2001, bd. advisors, 2001—; bd. dirs. Ariz. Found. for Women, 1999—2005; dir. Greater Phoenix C. of C., 2005—. Fellow: Ariz. Found. for Legal Services and Edn., Am. Bar Found.; mem.: ABA (sec. sect. litig. 1994—98, exec. com. sect. litig. 1994—, ho. delegates 1998—2001, standing com. on membership 2000—03, chmn. sect. litig. 2003—04, chair Am. Jury Project 2004—05, ho. delegates 2005—). Office: Snell & Wilmer LLP One Arizona Ctr Phoenix AZ 85004-2202

**REGALMUTO, NANCY MARIE,** small business owner, consultant; b. Bay Shore, N.Y., Aug. 24, 1956; d. Antonio J. Jr. and Agnes C. (Dietz) R. Student, SUNY, Stony Brook. Sales mgr. Fire, Inc., Hempstead, NY, 1976-78; sports handicapper Red Hot Sport, J. Dine Sports, Diamond Sports, Hicksville, NY, 1978—; small bus. owner, pres. Synergy (vitamin/nutritional product mfr. and distributor), Bellport, NY, 1981—. Cons. on medicine, fin., past life, bus. readings, hypnosis, substance abuse, archeology, law enforcement investigations, family, counseling, inter-species comm., animal therapy, psychic surgery, healing 1989—; lectr. in field, specializing in holistic remedies and therapies, 1989-91. Columnist Daily Racing Form, 1989-91; appeared on numerous TV programs, worldwide radio, mags., newspapers. Lectr., seminar leader, written about in numerous books. Min. Universal Life Ch., 1996, 97, Ch. of Inner Wisdom, 1996, 97. Mem. NAFE, Internat. Platform Assn., Horse Protection Assn., Therapeutic Riding for the Handicapped, World Wildlife Fedn. Office: 18 Woodland Park Rd Bellport NY 11713-2315

**REGAN, DAVID,** neuroscientist; b. Scarborough, Eng., May 5, 1935; arrived in Can., 1976; m. Marian Pauline Marsh, Aug. 15, 1959; children: Douglas Lawrence, Howard Michael BSc, London U., 1957, MSc, 1958, PhD, 1964, DSc, 1974. Lectr. physics London U., 1960-65; reader neurosci. Keele U. England, 1965-75; prof. psychology Dalhousie U., Canada, 1976-80, prof. physiology, 1980-84, assoc. prof. medicine, 1978-84, prof. medicine, 1984-87, prof. ophthalmology, 1980-87, prof. otolaryngology, 1980-84, Killam rsch. prof., 1978-82; prof. engring. Rutgers U., 1985-86; prof. psychology York U., 1987—2003, prof. biology; prof. ophthalmology U. Toronto, Ont., Canada, 1987—. Retained inventor Wilkinson-Graviner Group, Eng., 1970-75; cons. Westinghouse, Pitts., 1980-86; co-dir. human performance in space lab. Inst. for Space and Terrestrial Sci., York U., 1989-2002, disting. rsch. prof., 1991-93, emeritus 1993—; indsl. rsch. chair aviation vision Natural Sci. and Engring. Rsch. Coun. Can./Can. Aviation Electronics, 1993-2003; Spinoza profl. U. Amsterdam, The Netherlands, 1999. Author: Human Evoked Potentials, 1972, Human Brain Electrophysiology, 1989, Human Perception of Objects, 2000; editor: Spatial Vision, 1989, Binocular Vision, 1989, Vision Research, 1992; contbr. over 250 articles to profl. jours.; holder 8 patents. Recipient Forman prize for med. rsch., 1983, Prentice medal, 1990, Sir J.W. Dawson Medal, Royal Soc. Can., 1997, award of excellence Nat. Sci. and Engring. Rsch. Coun. Can., 2000, Proctor medal, 2000, Queen Elizabeth II medal, 2002, Hebb medal, 2003; rsch. grantee NIH, NRC, Air Force Office Sci. Rsch., Nat. Scis. and Engring. Rsch. Coun. Can., Med. Rsch. Coun.; mem. Order of Can., 2001; Killam fellow, 1990. Fellow: Optical Soc. Am., Royal Soc. Can.; mem.: Netherlands Royal Acad. (fgn.), Am. Acad. Optometry, Royal Coll. Sci. (London) (assoc.), Assn. Rsch. in Vision and Ophthalmology, Soc. Clin. Electroretinography, Exptl. Psychology Soc. Avocations: cricket, walking, modern european history. Office: York U Dept Psychology 4700 Keele St North York ON Canada M3J 1P3 Business E-Mail: dregan@yorku.ca.

**REGAN, DONALD H.,** lawyer, educator; b. 1944, A.B., Harvard U., 1963; LLB., U. Va., 1966; BPh. (Rhodes scholar), Oxford (Eng.) U., 1968; PhD., U. Mich., 1980. Asst. prof. U. Mich., Ann Arbor, 1968-71, assoc. prof., 1972-73, prof., 1974-83, prof. law and philosophy, 1983—, William W. Bishop Prof. law, 1991—. Guggenheim fellow, 1985, Nat. Humanities Ctr. fellow, 1989; recipient Matchette prize Am. Philos. Assn., 1981. Author: Utilitarianism and Co-operation, 1980; editor U. Va. Law Review, 1966. Mem. Am. Acad. Arts and Scis. Office: U Mich Law Sch 343 Hutchins Hall 625 S State St Ann Arbor MI 48109-1215 Office Fax: 734-763-0269, 734-763-9375. E-mail: donregan@umich.edu.

**REGAN, ELIZABETH ANNE,** bail bond agent; b. Portland, Oreg. d. David H. and Carmen M. (Nazario) Regan. AA, Clark Coll., Wash. Bail bond agt. Metro Bail Bonds, 1998—2002. Mem.: Profl. Bail Agts. of U.S., Wash. Bail Assn. Home: 612 W Evergreen Blvd Vancouver WA 98660 Office: A-1 Bail Bonds 612 W Evergeeen Blvd Vancouver WA 98660 Office Phone: 360-574-7415.

**REGAN, ELLEN FRANCES (MRS. WALSTON SHEPARD BROWN),** ophthalmologist, educator; b. Boston, Feb. 1, 1919; d. Edward Francis and Margaret (Moynihan) R.; m. Walston Shepard Brown, Aug. 13, 1955. AB, Wellesley Coll., 1940; MD, Yale U., 1943. Intern Boston City Hosp., 1944; asst. resident, resident Inst. Ophthalmology, Presbyn. Hosp., NYC, 1944-47, asst. ophthalmologist, 1947-56, asst. attending ophthalmologist, 1956-84; instr. ophthalmology Columbia Coll. Physicians and Surgeons, 1947-55, assoc. ophthalmology, 1955-67, asst. clin. prof., 1967-84; ret., 1984. Mem. AMA, Am. Ophthal. Soc., Am. Acad. Ophthalmology, NY Acad. Medicine, NY State Med. Soc., Mass. Med. Soc., River Club, Tuxedo Club. Home: PO Box 632 Tuxedo Park NY 10987-0632

**REGAN, GEOFF,** Canadian government official; b. Windsor, N.S., Can., Nov. 22, 1959; m. Kelly Regan; 3 children. BA, St. Francis Xavier U.; LLB, Dalhousie U. Mem. Can. Parliament, 1993—, parliamentary sec. to the leader of the govt. in the House of Commons, 2001—03; min. fisheries and oceans Govt. Can., Ottawa, Ont., Canada, 2003—. Office: House of Commons Ottawa ON Canada K1A 0A6 also: Fisheries and Oceans Centennial Towers Ste 1570 200 Kent St Ottawa ON Canada K1A 0E6 Office Phone: 613-992-3474.

**REGAN, JUDITH TERRANCE,** publishing executive; b. Leominster, Mass., Aug. 17, 1953; d. Leo James and Rita Ann (Impresica) Regan; children: Patrick, Lara. BA, Vassar Coll., 1975. Reporter Nat. Enquirer; sr. editor, v.p. Simon & Schuster, N.Y.C., 1989—94; pres., pub. Regan Books imprint of HarperCollins, N.Y.C., 1994—. TV prodr. Entertainment Tonight, N.Y.C., Geraldo, N.Y.C.; prodr. 20th Century Fox Films, Fox TV; anchor Full Disclosure, Fox TV; host Judith Regan Tonight, Fox News Channel. Editor, pub. (books) The Way Things Ought to Be (Rush Limbaugh), 1992, Rogue Warrior (Richard Marcinko), 1992, She's Come Undone (Wally Lamb), 1992, Shampoo Planet and Life After God (Douglas Coupland), 1992, Private Parts, Miss America (Howard Stern), 1993, Judge Robert Bork, Slouching Towards Gomorrah, 1993, I Can't Believe I Said That (Kathie Lee Gifford), 1994, Microserfs, 1996, Shabby Chic (Rachel Ashwell), 1996, The Zone (Dr. Barry Sears), 1996, Brain Lock (Dr. Jeffrey Schwartz), 1997, Wicked, 1997, Confessions of an Ugly Stepsister (Gregory Maguire), 1997—2000, Girlfriend in A Coma, 1998, I Know This Much is True, 1998, Marilu Henner's Total health Makeover, 1998, Story (Robert McKee), 1998, Have a Nice Day, Mick Foley (Mankind), 1999, The Rock Says, 2000, and others, —; exec. prodr.: (TV series) Growing Up Gotti, 2004—. Office: Regan Books 10 E 53rd St New York NY 10022-5244

**REGAN, MICHAEL PATRICK,** lawyer; b. Bklyn., Feb. 22, 1941; s. Cornelius Francis and Marguerite (Cann) Regan; m. Susan Ann Light, July 13, 1974; children: Michael Patrick, Brian Christopher, Mark Dennis. BA in English, U. Notre Dame, 1963; LLB, Union U., Albany, 1967, JD, 1968. Bar: N.Y. 1967, Va. 1975. Assoc. Medwin & McMahon, Albany, NY, 1967—69; asst. dist. atty. Albany County, NY, 1969; corp. atty. Mohasco Corp., Amsterdam, NY, 1969—74; asst. gen. consel Dan River, Inc., Danville, Va., 1975, assoc. gen. counsel, 1981—88, acting gen. counsel, asst. sec., 1988, gen. counsel, asst. sec., 1989; assoc. gen. counsel, asst. sec. Dan River Svc. Corp. of Va., Danville, 1984—88; gen. counsel Wunda Weve Carpets, Inc., Greenville, SC, 1990—93; pvt. practice Danville, 1990—. Clarinetist, saxophonist Tightsqueeze Philharm. Band, 1981—; active Danville Symphony Orch., 1991—, prin., 1997—2005; leader The DanceNotes, 1986—; active Starmont Swing Band, 1999—; sec. DanPac Polit. Action Com., 1976—89. Fellow Paul Harris fellow, Rotary Internat. Mem.: ABA, ATLA, Va. Trial Lawyers Assn., Danville Bar Assn., Va. Bar Assn., N.Y. State Bar Assn. Republican. Roman Catholic. Home: 236 Cambridge Cir Danville VA 24541-5233 Office: 703 Patton St Danville VA 24541-1905

**REGAN, NOELLE KRISTIN,** middle school educator; d. Jeff and Melodee Blevins; m. Gary Regan, May 30, 1999. BA, Wheaton Coll., Ill., 1997; MA in Curriculum and Instrn., U. Phoenix, 2005. Cert. adm. area. Tchr. 7th grade social studies and reading Fox Creek Jr. High, Bullhead City, Ariz., 1997—, head girls interscholastic basketball coach, intramural girls volleyball coach, 1998—. Social studies com. chair Fox Creek Jr. High, 2003—, team leader, 2005—. Named WalMart Tchr. of the Yr., Bullhead City, 2005—06. Republican. Office: Fox Creek Jr High 3101 Desert Sky Blvd Bullhead City AZ 86442 Office Phone: 928-704-2500. E-mail: nregan@bullheadschools.com.

**REGAN, PAUL JEROME, JR.,** manufacturing company executive, consultant; b. Ithaca, N.Y., Mar. 13, 1940; s. Paul Jerome and Mildred (Dempsey) R.; m. Barbara Ann Easton, Feb. 4, 1962 (dec. Nov. 1996); children: Paul J. III, Timothy Andrew, Allison Ann; m. Susan Margaret Mulcair, Sept. 7, 2002. BS, Cornell U., 1962, MBA, 1965. Pers. asst. Corning (N.Y.) Glass Works, 1963, pers. mgr. Corning and State College, 1964-68, dept. mfg. State College, 1968-70, personnel devel. cons. Corning, 1970-72, prodn. supt. Wilmington, N.C., 1972-74, devel. mgr. Corning, 1974-77, corp. dir., 1977-83, v.p.h. human resources, 1983-86; sr. v.p. Corning Inc., Corning, 1986-93; ret. Mem. adv. bd. Cornell U., Ithaca, N.Y., 1970-82, lectr., 1977—; founding mem. Human Resource Planning Soc., 1974-93; dir. Corning Can. Inc., Toronto, 1983-93. Contbr. articles to books and profl. jours. including Human Resource Planning Soc. jour.; expert comment on exec. compensation and succession including Wall St. Jour., N.Y. Times, Bus. Week, Forbes. Mem. exec. bd. Thousand Islands Assn., Gananoque, Ont., Can., 1988—, pres., 1999—2001; chmn. Blue Ribbon Fund, Corning Hosp., 1989-93; mem. Rep. Nat. Com., Washington, 1984—; dir. State College C. of C., 1967-73, Half Moon Bay Found., dir. Friends of the 1000 Islands Mus., Inc., 2000—; chair Museums of 1000 Islands, Inc., 2002—; chmn. Historic Thousand Islands Village Found., 1998—. Johnson Soc. fellow Cornell U., 1991; named Ky. Col., State of Ky., 1984, Adm. Thousand Islands Navy, 1999. Mem. Am. Compensation Assn. (regional chair 1978-81), Am. Acad. Polit. and Social Sci., Heron Soc. (life.), Cornell Club, Nat. Mus. Am. Indian (charter, membership com. 1991—), Antique Boat Mus., Canadian Antique Boat Trust(dir. 2004—), Save the River Com. (adv. 1982—), Menninger Found. (patron), Trust for Historic Preservation, Delta Phi (past pres.). Avocations: antique wooden boats, decoys, photographs, Inuit art, poetry.

**REGAN, PETER FRANCIS, III,** physician, medical educator; b. Bklyn., Nov. 11, 1924; s. Peter Francis Jr. and Veronica (Tierney) R.; m. Laurette Patricia O'Connor, June 18, 1949; children: Peter, Stephen, William, Elizabeth, John, Carol. MD, Cornell U., Ithaca, N.Y., 1949. Diplomate Am. Bd. Psychiatry and Neurology, Nat. Bd. Med. Examiners. Intern in medicine N.Y. Hosp., 1949-50; asst. resident psychiatry Payne Whitney Psychiat. Clinic, 1950, 53-54, resident, 1954-56; asst. prof. psychiatry Cornell U. Med. Coll., 1956-58; prof., head dept. psychiatry U. Fla. Coll. Medicine, chief psychiat. svc. Univ. Teaching Hosp., 1958-64; prof. psychiatry SUNY, Buffalo, 1964-84, v.p. health affairs, 1964-67, exec. v.p. univ., 1967-69, exec. v.p., acting pres. univ., 1969-70, vice chancellor acad. programs, 1970-71; assoc.

chief staff for edn. Buffalo VA Med. Ctr., 1979-84; prof. psychiatry U. Tex. Health Sci. Ctr., San Antonio, 1984-87, assoc. dean Sch. Medicine, 1986-87; assoc. chief staff for edn. San Antonio VA Med. Ctr., 1984-86, chief staff, 1986-87; dep. assoc. chief med. dir. for acad. affairs VA Cen. Office, Washington, 1987-88, assoc. chief med. dir. for acad. affairs, 1988-92; prof. emeritus / sen. cons. dept. psychiatry SUNY, Buffalo, 1992—; interim chair dept. psychiatry Med. U. S.C., 2001—02. Project dir. Ctr. for Ednl. Rsch. and Innovation, OECD, 1972-74. Author: (with F. Flach) Chemotherapy in Emotional Disorders, 1960, (With E. Pattishall) Behavioral Science Contributions to Psychiatry, 1960; contbr. articles to profl. jours. Capt. M.C. AUS, 1951-52. Fellow Am. Psychiat. Assn., Am. Coll. Psychiatrists (bd. regents 1986-95, 2d v.p. 1988, 1st v.p. 1989, pres.-elect 1990, pres. 1991); mem. AMA, Alpha Omega Alpha.

**REGAN, RICHARD FELIX,** secondary school educator, musician, conductor; b. Potsdam, NY, May 17, 1969; s. Philip James and Linda Levison Regan; m. Nicole Caroline Cook, July 24, 1993; 1 child, Sean Patrick. MusB in Music Edn., SUNY, Potsdam, 1991; M in Trombone Performance, Fla. State U., 1993. Cert. music tchr. NY. Music tchr. Herkimer (NY) HS, 1993—97, Monroe-Woodbury HS, Central Valley, NY, 1997—. Artistic dir. wind ensemble OCMEA, Central Valley, NY, 2004—, conductor; conductor chamber ensemble Lincoln Ctr., NYC, 2000; guest condr. in field. Musician (prin. trombone): Greater Newburgh Symphony Orch., 2000—. Democrat. Avocations: golf, travel, fine dining, scotch tasting and collecting. Home: 457 Burlingham Rd Bloomingburg NY 12721 Office: Monroe-Woodbury High Sch 155 Dunderberg Rd Central Valley NY 10917 Office Phone: 845-460-7000 ext 7657. Personal E-mail: rregan@earthlink.net.

**REGAN, ROBERT CHARLES,** English language educator; b. Indpls., Mar. 13, 1930; s. Francis Bernard and Alma Ophelia (McBride) R.; m. Katherine Jeanclos, Aug. 11, 1989; children by previous marriage: Christopher, Alison, Amelia. BA, Centenary Coll., 1951; MA, Harvard U., 1952; PhD, U. Calif., Berkeley, 1965. Instr. English, Centenary Coll., 1956-57; asst. prof. English, U. Va., 1963-67; Fulbright-Hays lectr. Am. civilization U. Montpellier, France, 1967-68; assoc. prof. English, U. Pa., Phila., 1968-82, prof., 1982-2000, undergrad. chmn. dept. English, 1978-80, 81-83, 89-90, dir. Penn-in-London program, prof. emeritus, 2000—. Lectr. Internat. Communications Agy., Morocco, Algeria, Jordan, 1980, Main Line Sch. Night, Radnor, Pa., 2001—; vis. prof. King's Coll., London, 1983-84 Author: Unpromising Heroes; Mark Twain and His Characters, 1966, Poe: A Collection of Critical Essays, 1967; mng. editor: Am. Quar., 1969-72; mem. editl. bd. Mark Twain Papers, U. Calif., Berkeley, 1997-2001; contbr. articles to lit. jours. Served with USNR, 1952-56, 61-62. Woodrow Wilson fellow, 1962-63; Am. Philos. Soc. research grantee, 1970 Mem. Univ. Mews Assn. (pres. 1999-2001), Faculty Club U. Pa. (bd. govs. 1997-2001). Democrat. Episcopalian. Office: U Pa Dept English Philadelphia PA 19104 E-mail: robertregan@earthlink.net.

**REGAN, WILLIAM JOSEPH, JR.,** energy company executive; b. Bronx, NY, Mar. 7, 1946; s. William Joseph and Eleanor F. (Malone) R.; m. Mary Lee Wynn; children—Katrina Lee, Thomas Wynn, James William BS, U.S. Air Force Acad., 1967; MBA, U. Wis.-Madison, 1969, PhD, 1972. Asst. prof. Wayne State U., Detroit, 1971-75; with Nat. Bank Detroit, 1975-77; sr. bus. planner Am. Natural Resources Co., Detroit, 1977-78, dir. fin. planning, 1978-82, v.p., treas., 1982-85; v.p. corp. fin. United Svcs. Automobile Assn., San Antonio, 1986-88, sr. v.p., treas., 1988-95; v.p., treas. Entergy Corp., New Orleans, 1995-99; CFO Calif. Ind. Sys. Operator Corp., Folsom, Calif., 1999—. Home: 15181 De La Pena Cir Rancho Murieta CA 95683-9798 Office: 151 Blue Ravine Rd Folsom CA 95630 E-mail: wregan37@earthlink.net.

**REGAN GOSSAGE, MURIEL,** librarian; b. NYC, July 15, 1930; d. William and Matilda (Riebel) Blome; m. Robert Regan, 1966 (div. 1976); 1 child, Jeanne Booth; m. Wayne Gossage, 2003. BA, Hunter Coll., N.Y.C., 1950; MLS, Columbia U., 1952; MBA, Pace U., N.Y.C., 1982. Post libr. US Army, Okinawa, 1952-53; researcher P.F. Collier, N.Y.C., 1953-57; asst. libr. to libr. Rockefeller Found., N.Y.C., 1957-67; dep. chief libr. Manhattan Community Coll., N.Y.C., 1967-68; libr. Booz Allen & Hamilton, N.Y.C., 1968-69, Rockefeller Found., N.Y.C., 1969-82; prin. Gossage Regan Assocs., Inc., N.Y.C., 1980-95; pub. svcs. libr. Carlsbad (N.Mex.) Pub. Libr., 1995-2000. Dir. N.Y. Met. Reference and Rsch. Libr. Agy., 1988-95, Coun. Nat. Libr. and Info. Assns., 1991-95; cons. Librs. Info. Ctrs., Gossage Sager Assocs., 2001—. Elder First Presbyn. Ch. of Carlsbad, 1997-99, Stephan min., 2000—, deacon, 2002-03. Mem. Spl. Librs. Assn. (pres. 1989-90), Archons of Colophon. Avocations: cats, reading, playing piano, travel. Home: 702 Lakeside Dr Carlsbad NM 88220-5209 Personal E-mail: murielregan@zianet.com.

**REGAN-STANTON, CHRISTA MARIA,** artist; b. Stuttgart, Germany, Dec. 30, 1930; arrived in U.S., 1952; d. Friedrich Wilhelm and Anna Katharina (Schiller) Hohnhausen; m. James Allen Stanton (dec.); m. James Dale Regan, Apr. 27, 1955 (div. 1983); children: Jessica Ute, Jeffrey William. M Interpretive Dance, Tanzmeister Sch. Vock, Stuttgart, Germany, 1950. Tchr. Christa Studio Dance, Stuttgart, Germany, Athens, Ohio, 1952—54, Miami U., 1955—56; mgr. Treehouse Gallery, Oak Ridge, Tenn., 1983—95; studio potter Oak Ridge, Tenn. Bd. dirs. Upstairs Gallery, Oak Ridge, Tenn.; show dir. Foothills Craft Guild, Oak Ridge, Tenn., 1985. Recipient Honorable Mention award, Oak Ridge Mus. Fine Arts, 1982, First Place award, 1983, Second Place award, 1985. Mem.: Nat Mus. Women in Arts, Southern Highland Crafts Guild, Tenn. Arts and Crafts Assn., Am. Craft Coun., Foothills Craft Guild. Home: 119 Cooper Cir Oak Ridge TN 37830-7156

**REGAZZI, JOHN JAMES, III,** dean, publishing executive; b. Bklyn., June 8 1948; s. John James Jr. and Theresa Cecil (Finn) R.; m. Marie Louise Paola, May 30, 1971; children: John James IV, Thomas Paul, Michael Rees. BS, St. John's U., Queens, N.Y., 1970; MA, U. Iowa, 1972; MS, Columbia U., 1974; PhD, Rutgers U., 1983. Systems mgr. No. Ill. U., De Kalb, Ill., 1974-76; dir. pub. Found. Ctr., NYC, 1976-79; assoc. prof. Rutgers U., New Brunswick, NJ, 1979-81; v.p. The H.W. Wilson Co., NYC, 1981-88; pres., chief exec. officer Engring. Info., Inc., NYC, 1988-99; CEO, pres. Elsevier Inc. NYC, 1999—2005; dean LI U. Coll. Info. and Computer Sci., Brookville, 2005—. Chmn. Article Express Internat., 1992-94; bd. dirs. ICSTI, NTIS, NFAIS, AAP/PSP, CAB Internat.; adj. prof. SUNY, Albany, Columbia U., Rutgers U. Author: Guide to Periodicals in Religion, 1974. Mem. AAAS, IEEE, ALA, Am. Assn. Pubs. (bd. dirs. N.Y.C. chpt. 1987-88), Nat. Info. Standards Orgn. (vice chmn. 1989-90), Nat. Fedn. of Abstracting and Info. Svcs. (bd. dirs. 1980-81, 88, 2004), Assn. Computing Machinery, N.Y. Acad. Sci. Avocation: cycling. Office: LI U Coll Info & Computer Sci 720 Northern Blvd Greenvale NY 11548 Office Phone: 516-299-4109. Business E-mail: john.regazzi@liu.edu.

**REGEL, TERESA DIAMOND,** elementary school educator; d. Frank Wesley and Delphine Margaret Kaminski; children: Jonathan F., Kristal D. BA, U. Wis., Eau Claire, 1971; M in profl. edni. devel., U. Wis., La Cross, 1991. Adminstrv. lic. Edgewood Coll., Wis., 2003. Retail mgmt. Fish Bldg. Supply, Baraboo, Wis., 1973—79, Country Market, Lake Delton, Wis., 1979—93; bus. owner Fishin' Hut, Lake Delton, Wis., 1978—81; elem. tchr. Wis. Dells. Sch. Dist., 1993—; second grade tchr. Lake Delton (Wis.) Elem., 1995—. Mem.: Wis. Reading Assn. Avocations: reading, cooking, sewing.

**REGELBRUGGE, ROGER RAFAEL,** steel company executive; b. Eeklo, Belgium, May 22, 1930; arrived in U.S., 1953, naturalized, 1961; s. Victor and Rachel (Roesbeke) Regelbrugge; m. Dorcas Merchant; children: Anita, Marc, Laurie, Jon, Craig, Kurt, Christiane, Lauren, Lauren, Roger Rafael Jr. BSME, State Tech. Coll., Ghent, 1951; BS in Indsl. Engring, Gen. Motors Inst., Flint, Mich., 1955; MSME, Mich. State U., 1964. Supr. product engring. dept. Gen. Motors Corp., Antwerp, 1955—58; chief devel. engr., then gen. mgr. Airmaster div. Hayes Industries Inc., Jackson, Mich., 1958—66; with Koehring Co., 1966—74, group v.p. internat. ops. Milw., 1969—74; exec. v.p. Korf Industries, Inc., Charlotte, NC, 1974—77, chmn.; chmn., pres., CEO

Georgetown Industries, Inc. (formerly Korf Industries, Inc.), 1977—95; chmn., CEO GS Industries Inc. (formerly Georgetown Industries), 1995—97, chmn., 1997—2001. Mem. adv. coun. Coll. Engring. U. Notre Dame; trustee Belmont (N.C.) Abbey Coll. Mem.: Am. Soc. Automotive Engrs., ASME, Georgetown Club, Carmel Country Club. Roman Catholic.

**REGENSTEIN, JOE M.,** food scientist, educator; b. Bklyn., Sept. 22, 1943; s. Alfred B. and Fannie (Kleinmeyer) Regenstein; m. Carrie Ellen Forsheit, June 12, 1966; children: Elliot Michael, Scott Lewis. BA in Chemistry, Cornell U., Ithaca, NY, 1965, MS in Dairy Chemistry, 1966; PhD in Biophysics, Brandeis U., Waltham, Mass., 1973. Postdoctoral Children Biomed. Ctr., Boston, 1973—74; asst. prof. Cornell U., 1974—80, assoc. prof., 1980—87, prof., 1987—. Gen. ptnr. C&J Assoc., Ithaca, 1990—2006; mem. animal welfare com. Food Mktg. Inst./Nat. Coun. Chain Restaurants, Washington, 2001—06; advisor Jewish Vegetarians of North Am., Humane Farm Animal Care. Columnist: Kashrus Mag., 1986—2002; author: (book) Food Protein Chemistry, 1984, Introduction to Fish Technology, 1991, (internet article) The Kosher and Halmal Food Laws, 2003. Congl. fellow U.S. Senate, 1996—97. Recipient Elizabeth Strer Humanitarian award, Inst. Food Technologists, 2000, Multicultural Diversity award, Cornell Coll. Agr. and Life Scis., 2003; fellow, Inst. Food Technologists, 1995; guest fellow, New Zealand Inst. Food Sci. and Tech., 1983. Mem.: Am. Meat Source Assn., Atlantic Fisheries Tech. Conf., Inst. Food Technologists (mem. exec. com. 1993—96). Conservative. Jewish. Avocations: deltiology, jogging, birdwatching. Office: Cornell Univ Dept Food Sci Stocking Hall Ithaca NY 14853 Business E-Mail: jmr9@cornell.edu.

**REGENSTREIF, HERBERT,** lawyer; b. NYC, May 13, 1935; s. Max and Jeannette (Hacker) R.; m. Patricia Friedman, Dec. 20, 1967 (div. July 1968); m. Charlotte Lois Levy, Dec. 11, 1980 (div. Sept. 2002); 1 child, Cara Rachael. BA, Hobart Coll., 1957; JD, N.Y. Law Sch., 1960; MS, Pratt Inst., 1985. Bar: N.Y. 1961, Ky. 1985, U.S. Dist. Ct. (ea. and so. dists.) N.Y. 1962, U.S. Dist. Ct. (ea. dist.) Ky. 1998, U.S. Tax Ct. 1967, U.S. Ct. Appeals (2d cir.) 1962, U.S. Supreme Ct. 1967. Ptnr. Fried & Regenstreif, P.C., Mineola, N.Y., 1963—; reservist atty. Fed. Emergency Mgmt. Agy., 1998-99. Cons. in field; arbitrator Dist. Ct., Nassau County, N.Y., 1989—, NYC Civil Ct., 1984-86; sec.-treas. Sta. WAHY-FM, Inc., 1998-2000. Contbr. articles to profl. jours. County committeeman Dem. Com., Queens County, N.Y., 1978-79. Mem. Bar Assn. Nassau County, Ky. Bar Assn., Am. Judges Assn., Phi Delta Phi, Beta Phi Mu, Harvard Club of N.Y. (gov. 1968-69). Office Phone: 516-294-6442.

**REGENSTREIF, S(AMUEL) PETER,** political scientist, educator; b. Montreal, Que., Can., Sept. 9, 1936; s. Albert Benjamin and Miriam Lillian (Issenman) R.; children: Anne Erica, Mitchell Chester, Jeffrey Gershon, Gail Aviva. BA, McGill U., 1957; PhD, Cornell U., 1963. Mem. faculty U. Rochester, 1961—, prof. polit. sci., 1971—; coordinator Can. studies program, 1967—. Editl. cons. Toronto Star, 1968-82, Chgo. Sun-Times, 1988-89; polit. cons. Bunting Warburg, Toronto, 1973-90, Coopers & Lybrand, Ltd., 1981-89, Loewen, Ondaatje, McCutcheon, 1991-94; prin. Policy Concepts Inc., Toronto; broadcaster CKO Radio Network, 1983-89; pvt. polit. cons. Author: The Diefenbaker Interlude: Parties and Voting in Canada, 1965; syndicated columnist: Toronto Star, 1963-82; contbr. articles to profl. jours. Served to lt. Canadian Army, 1957. Ford. Found. fellow, 1960; Can. Council fellow, 1960, 65; Canadian Royal Commn. on Bilingualism and Biculturalism grantee, 1964-66; recipient Edward Peck Curtis award U. Rochester, 1979 Mem. AAAS, Am. Polit. Sci. Assn., Can. Polit. Sci. Assn., Assn. Can. Studies in U.S., Phi Beta Kappa. Jewish. Home: 438C Browncroft Blvd Rochester NY 14609 Office: Univ Rochester Dept Polit Sci Rochester NY 14627 Office Phone: 585-275-5466. Business E-Mail: peter.regenstreif@rochester.edu.

**REGER, LAWRENCE LEE,** trade association administrator; b. Lincoln, Nebr., June 23, 1939; s. Lawrence John and Bertha (Hergenrader) R. Student, U. Nebr., 1961; LL.B., Vanderbilt U., 1964. Bar: NY 1964. Assn. firm Crosby, Guenzel & Binning, Lincoln, 1964-70; gen. counsel Nat. Endowment Arts, 1970-72, dir. program devel. and coordination, 1972-78; dir. Am. Assn. Mus., Washington, 1978-86; pres. Heritage Preservation, Washington, 1988—. Mem. visual arts com. U. Del., 1995—; mem. cultural property adv. com. USIA, 1996—2000; mem. bd. trustees St. Petersburg Internat. Preservation Ctr., 1996—; bd. dirs. Peck Stacpoole Found. Chmn. Nat. Humanities Alliance, 1982-86; bd. dirs. Nat. Musical Arts, 1990—. Recipient Forbes medal Am. Inst. Conservation, 2000, Alumni Achievement award Hixon-Leid Coll. Fine and Performing Arts, U. Nebr., 2004. Home: 5010 Garfield St NW Washington DC 20016-3469 Office: Heritage Preservation 1012 14th St NW Ste 1200 Washington DC 20005 Office Phone: 202-233-0800.

**REGER, ROBERT J., JR.,** lawyer; b. Buffalo, June 6, 1948; BA summa cum laude, Fordham U., 1970; JD, U. Va., 1973. Bar: NY 1974. Ptnr. Thelen Reid & Priest LLP, NYC, mem. exec. com. Mem.: ABA, Phi Beta Kappa. Office: Thelen Reid & Priest LLP 875 Third Ave New York NY 10022-2001 Office Phone: 212-603-2204. Office Fax: 212-603-2001. Business E-Mail: rreger@thelenreid.com.

**REGES, MARIANNA ALICE,** marketing executive; b. Budapest, Hungary, Mar. 23, 1947; arrived in U.S., 1956, naturalized, 1963; d. Otto H. and Alice M. Reges; children: Rebecca, Charles III. AAS with honors, Fashion Inst. Tech., N.Y.C., 1967; BBA magna cum laude, Baruch Coll., 1971, MBA in Stats., 1978. Media rsch. analyst Doyle, Dane, Bernbach advt., N.Y.C., 1967—70; rsch. supr. Sta. WCBS-TV, N.Y.C., 1970—71; rsch. mgr. Woman's Day mag., N.Y.C., 1971—72; asst. media dir. Benton & Bowles advt., N.Y.C., 1972—75; mgr. rsch. and sales devel. NBC Radio N.Y.C. 1975—77; dir. rsch. mgr. Zill-Davis Pub. Co., N.Y.C., 1977—84; media mgr. Bristol-Myers Squibb Co., 1984—2001, Procter & Gamble Co., 2001—. Mem. Spanish Radio Adv. Coun., N.Y.C., 1986—88, Pan-European TV Audience Rsch. Mgmt. Com., 1988—. Mem. advisor Baruch Coll. Advt. Soc., 1975—; active First Presbyn. Ch., N.Y.C. Mem.: Advt. Rsch. Found., Radio and TV Rsch. Coun., Media Rsch. Dirs. Assn., Am. Advt. Fedn., Am. Mktg. Assn., Anthroposophical Soc., Nature Conservancy, Baruch Alumni Assn., Gilda's Club, Beta Gamma Sigma. Home: 626 E 20th St New York NY 10009-1509 Personal E-mail: marianna10009@hotmail.com.

**REGEV, ARIE,** gastroenterologist, researcher, hepatologist; b. Haifa, Israel, Oct. 6, 1959; s. Shimon Rushansky and Rivka Halperin; m. Anat Ackerman, Aug. 24, 1982; children: Ayelet, Guy, Omer. MD, Hebrew U. and Hadassah, Jerusalem, 1987. Cert. in medicine Israel 1992, in gastroenterology Israel 1987. Resident, internal medicine Rabin Med. Ctr., Petach-Tikva, Israel, 1988—92, attending physician, 1992—94, fellow in gastroenterology, 1994—96, assoc. chief of medicine, 1996—98; fellow hepatology U. of Miami, Jackson Meml. Hosp., Miami, Fla., 1998—99, fellow transplant hepatology, 1999—2000; attending physician Jackson Meml. Hosp., U. of Miami, 2001—05; asst. prof. medicine U. Miami Sch. Medicine, 2005—. Contbr. articles to profl. jours., chpts. to books. Recipient Outstanding Tutor award, Sackler Sch. of Medicine, Tel-Aviv U., 1988, Student Tchg. award, Sackler Sch. of Medicine, U. Miami Sch. Medicine, 2004—05, REGAL award for rsch. excellence in GI and Liver, 2005. Mem.: Am. Coll. of Gastroenterology, Am. Assn. for the Study of Liver, Gastroent. Assn., Israel Med. Assn. Office: Univ Miami Divsn Hepatology 1500 NW 12th Ave Ste 1101 Miami FL 33136 Business E-Mail: aregev@med.miami.edu.

**REGGIO, VITO ANTHONY,** retired management consultant; b. Rochester, N.Y., Dec. 17, 1929; s. Salvatore and Carrie Angela (LoRe) R.; m. Mary Ann Dolores Pippie, Sept. 28, 1957; children: Salvatore, Angela. BS, Purdue U., 1952; postgrad. sch. modern langs., Middlebury Coll., 1948; postgrad. fellowship, U. Ky., U. Tenn. and U. Ala., 1952-53. Jr. engr. Rochester (N.Y.) Gas and Electric Co., 1950; designer/drafter Globe Constn. Co., Rochester, 1951; rsch. analyst Commonwealth of Ky., Frankfort, 1952; orgn. & methods analyst, then wage adminstrn. specialist USN Dept. Indsl. Rels., Indpls.,

1955-56; cons. mgmt. engr. to project mgr. to account exec. Bus. Rsch. Corp., Chgo., 1956-60; sr. cons. econ. feasibilities Ebasco Svcs., Inc., Chgo., 1960-63, dir. pers. mgmt. cons. dept., 1970-77; regional mgr., orgn. and pers. mgmt. svcs. EBS Mgmt. Cons., Chgo., 1963-65, nat. dir. orgn. and pers. mgmt. svcs., 1965-70; pres., bd. dirs. Reggio and Assocs., Inc., Chgo., 1977—2005; mng. dir. Pay Data Svc., 1977—2005, ret., 2005. Bd. dirs. Pay Data Svcs., Chgo. Contbr. papers to profl. publs. With U.S. Army, 1953-55. Named Solco Cultural Soc. fellow, Rochester, N.Y., 1948. Mem. Am. Compensation Assn., Am. Mgmt. Assn., Chgo. Compensation Assn., Soc. Human Resources Profls., Soc. Human Resources Mgmt., Human Resources Mgmt. Assn. Chgo., Western Soc. Engrs. Office: Reggio and Assocs Inc 441 South Sixth Ave La Grange IL 60525-2439

**REGIER, BRYAN L.,** music educator; b. Topeka, Kans., Sept. 20, 1970; s. Russell L. and Nancy A. Regier; m. Kelly L. Hitt, Dec. 20, 2003. BS, Tabor Coll., 1992; MS, U. Nebr., Kearney, 2000. Grade 5-12 instrumental music tchr. Rushville (Nebr.) H.S., 1994—96; K-12 music, vocal tchr. Arcadia (Nebr.) H.S., 1996—98; grades 5-12 instr. music Bridgeport (Nebr.) H.S., 1998—2000; grades 6-12 instr. music McCook (Nebr.) H.S., 2000—. Bd. dirs. S.W. Nebr. Music Theatre Assn., McCook, 2000—, McCook Arts Coun. Mem.: Nebr. State Bandmasters Assn., Nebr. Music Educators Assn., Masons. Republican. Mennonite. Avocations: trap shooting, golf, music, gardening. Home: PO Box 97 Indianola NE 69034 Office: McCook HS 600 W 7th Mc Cook NE 69001

**REGIER, DARCY JOHN,** professional sports team executive; b. Swift Current, Sask., Can., Nov. 27, 1956; came to U.S., 1979; m. John Melvin and Helen (Neufeld) Regier; m. Katherine Opyr, June 30, 1979; children: Jonathan, Justin, Jarrett. Student, U. Lethbridge (Alta., Can.), 1980-85. Head coach Indpls. Checkers, 1984-85; dir. hockey adminstrn. NY Islanders, Uniondale, 1985-89, asst. coach, 1989-91, Hartford Whalers, 1991—92; gen. v.p. Buffalo Sabres, 1997—. Mem. all-star team Cen. Hockey League, 1983. Mem. Profl. Hockey Players Assn. (chmn. exec. com. 1980-83). Avocations: bicycling, video productions on sports. Office: Buffalo Sabres HSBC Arena One Seymour H Knox III Plz Buffalo NY 14203-3096*

**REGISTER, ANNETTE ROWAN,** literature educator; b. Doctors Inlet, Fla., Apr. 5, 1931; d. Ernest Ambors and Frances Perlena (Monroe) R.; Henry Ira Register, Oc. 31, 1954; 1 child, Andrew Henry. RN, Greenville Gen. Hosp. Sch. of Nursing, Greenville, 1948-51; BS, Tex. Woman's U., Denton, 1954; MEd, U. Fla., Gainesville, 1959; SEd, Fla. State U., 1983; student, U. West Fla., Okaloosa Walton C.C. Instrn. dir. nursing edn. Alachua Gen. Hosp., Gainesville, Fla., 1955-57; pub. sch. tchr. Okaloosa County, Ft. Walton Beach, Fla., 1966-93. V.p., Internat. Tng. in Communication Ft. Walton Beach, Fla.; active Inst. Sr. Profls. Okaloosa Walton C.C. Pres. Okaloosa Reading Coun., 1976—80; mem. Okaloosa Walton C.C. Symphony Guild, 1998—; pres. United Meth. Women, Ft. Walton Beach, Fla., 1985—87; dist. v.p. Mem. Fla. C. of C. (amb. 1996—), Phi Delta Kappa (1st v.p.). Methodist. Avocations: crafts, painting, sketching, travel. Office: Okaloosa County Sch Bd 10 Lowery Pl SE Fort Walton Beach FL 32548 Office Phone: 850-243-2250. Personal E-mail: registerannette@yahoo.com.

**REGISTER, KAREN,** microbiologist, researcher; b. Manchester, NH, Jan. 20, 1959; m. James Register. PhD, U. NC, Chapel Hill, 1986. Cert. med. technologist Am. Soc. Clin. Pathologists, 1981. Rsch. microbiologist USDA, Ames, Iowa, 1990—. Mem.: Am. Soc. Microbiology. Office Phone: 515-663-7200.

**REGNERY, ALFRED SCATTERGOOD,** publishing executive; b. Chgo., Nov. 21, 1942; s. Henry and Eleanor (Scattergood) R.; m. Christina Sparrow, Nov. 29, 1969; children: George M., Louise S., Alfred W., Charles H. BA, Beloit Coll., 1965; JD, U. Wis., 1971. Bar: Wis. 1971, D.C. 1987. Pvt. practice law, Madison, Wis., 1971-78; minority counsel Senate Judiciary Com., Washington, 1978-81; dep. asst. atty. gen. land and natural resources div. Dept. Justice, Washington, 1981-82; adminstr. Office of Juvenile Justice and Delinquency Prevention, 1982-86; pres., chief exec. officer Regnery Pub. Inc., Washington, 1986—2003; publisher The Am. Spectator, Arlington, Va., 2003—. Counsel Keller and Heckman, Washington; bd. dirs. Eagle Pub., Inc., Washington. Bd. dirs. Found. for Am. Studies, Washington; trustee Intercollegiate Studies Inst., Wilmington, Del., Inst. World Politics, Washington; bd. dirs. Am. Fgn. Policy Coun., Washington, Jamestown Found. Served with USCG, 1966-67. Office: The American Spectator 1611 N Kent St Arlington VA 22209 Office Phone: 703-807-2011.

**REGNERY, RUSSELL LAWRENCE,** microbiologist; b. Palo Alto, Calif., May 27, 1950; s. David Cook and Dorothy May Regnery; m. Helen Sears, Apr. 22, 1943; children: Donna Maria Toepfer, Roslynn. PhD, Australian Nat. U., Canberra, 1976. Supervisory rsch. microbiologist Ctrs. Disease Control & Prevention, Atlanta, 1978—. Achievements include research in Characterization of agents of human disease including Rickettsial agents, members of the bacterial genus Bartonella, and orthopoxvirus agents. Avocations: photography, observing the natural environment, woodworking. Office Phone: 404-639-1080.

**REGNI, JOHN F.,** academic administrator, career military officer; BS in Biology, USAF Acad., 1973; MS in Systems Mgmt., St. Mary's U., 1981; attended, Air Command and Staff Coll., Maxwell AFB, 1984, Air War College, 1990, Nat. Defense U., Fort Lesley J. McNair, 1997. Commd. 2d lt. USAF, 1973, advanced through grades to lt. gen., 2004; pers. officer Ogden Air Logistics Ctr., Hill AFB, Utah, 1973-76; chief, pers. utilization 40th Tactical Group, Aviano AB, Italy, 1976-78; chief force analysis and asst., col. assignments Air Force Manpower and Pers. Cu., Randolph AFB, Tex., 1978-81; asst. exec., dep. chief of staff for manpower and pers. Hdqrs. USAF, The Pentagon, Washington, 1981-83; asst. chief of staff Hdqrs. Air Tng. Command, Randolph AFB, Tex., 1984-87; base comdr. 3380th Air Base Group, Keesler AFB, Miss., 1987-89; base comdr. 8th Combat Support Group, Kunsan AB, Republic of Korea, 1990-91; dir. manpower, pers. and support Hdqrs. U.S. Pacific Command, Camp H.M. Smith, Hawaii, 1991-94; dir. pers. Hdqrs. Air Mobility Command, Scott AFB, Ill., 1994-96; dir. mil. pers. policy, dep. chief of staff for pers. Hdqrs. USAF, the Pentagon, Washington, 1996-98, dir. pers. resources, dep. chief of staff for pers., 1998—2000; dir. Air Force Pers. Ops. Agy., Washington, 1998-2000, maj. gen., 2000; comdr. 2nd Air Force, Keesler AFB, Miss., 2000—04, Air Univ., Maxwell AFB, Ala., 2004—05; supt. USAF Acad., Colorado Springs, 2005—. Decorated Legion of Merit, Air Force Commendation Medal, Meritorious Svc. Medal with silver oak leaf cluster, Defense Superior Svc. Medal, Disting. Svc. Medal with oak leaf cluster. Office: Supt 2304 Cadet Dr, Ste 342 U S A F Academy CO 80840-5001*

**REGNIER, JAMES,** retired state supreme court justice; b. Aurora, Ill., July 22, 1944; m. Linda Regnier; 3 children. BS, Marquette U., 1966; JD, U. Ill., 1973. Judicial Fellow ACTL, Internat. Soc. Barristers; completed atty. mediator tng., Atty.-Mediator Tng. Inst., Dallas, 1993. Lawyer pvt. practice, Rochelle, Ill., 1973-78; co-founder, ptnr. Regnier, Lewis and Boland, Great Falls, Mont., 1979-91; lawyer pvt. practice, Missoula, Mont., 1991-97; justice Mont. Supreme Ct., Helena, 1997—2004. Appt. Mont. Supreme Ct. Commn. on Civil Jury Instrn.; appt. lawyer-rep. to 9th Cir. Judicial Confs., 1987, 88, 89, chair Mont. lawyer delegation, 1989; lectr. U. Mont. Sch. Law, numerous continuing legal edn. seminars. Contbr. Mont. Pattern Jury Instrns. for Civil Cases, 1985. Co-founder Mont. Am. Bd. Trial Advocates, 1989—. Officer USN. Office: PO Box 203001 Helena MT 59620-3001 Office Phone: 406-444-5494.

**REGO, CESAR,** science educator, researcher; b. Porto, Portugal, Apr. 9, 1963; s. Julio and Amelia Rego; 1 child, Bruno. PhD, U. of Versailles, 1996. Assoc. prof. Universidade Portucalense, Porto, Portugal, 1991—99, U. of Miss., Oxford, 1999—; invited prof. Instituto Superior Tecnico (IST-UTL), Lisbon, Portugal, 1996—98; asst. prof. Faculdade de Ciencias (FCUL), Lisbon, Portugal, 1998—99. Recipient IFORS-Lisbon Best Internat. Paper,

IFORS/APDIO, Best Master Thesis, Portuguese Ops. Rsch. Soc.; PhD Scholarship, JNICT, Portugal, Rsch. Grant, Office of Naval Rsch. Mem.: INFORMS (assoc.). Home: 405 Whitney Oxford MS 38655 Office: University of Mississippi Oxford MS 38677 E-mail: crego@bus.olemiss.edu.

**REGO, SIMON ALEXANDER,** psychologist; s. Joseph A.V. and Barbara D. Rego; m. Katherine Lynn Muller, May 15, 2003. BSc with honors, Queen's U., Kingston, Ont., Can., 1994; MA, CUNY, NYC, 1995; M of Psychology, Rutgers U., Piscataway, NJ, 1999, PsyD, 2001. Cert. cognitive therapist Acad. Cognitive Therapy, 2004. Open clinic coord. Ctr. for the Treatment and Study of Anxiety, U. Pa., Phila., 2001—03; clin. and rsch. coord. Anxiety and Depression Clinic Montefiore Med. Ctr., Bronx, NY, 2003—04, assoc. dir psychology tng., 2004—; asst. prof. psychiatry and behavioral scis. Albert Einstein Coll. Medicine, Bronx, 2004—. Mem. instl. rev. bd. for the protection of human subjects Montefiore Med. Ctr., Bronx, 2004—; clin. supr. Ferkauf Grad. Sch. Psychology, Yeshiva U., Bronx, 2004—; Psychol. Clinic, Grad. Sch. Applied and Profl. Psychology, Rutgers U., Piscataway, 2004—; mem. instl. rev. bd. Biomedical Rsch. Alliance NY, Great Neck, NY, 2005—. Sect. editor: the clinical psychologist Internet Update. Recipient GSAPP Scholars award, Grad. Sch. Applied and Profl. Psychology, 1996, Robert S. Morrow prize for Excellence in the Grad. Forensic Psychology Program, John Jay Coll. Criminal Justice, 1996, Dean's award for Contbn. to Student Life, Grad. Sch. Applied and Profl. Psychology, 1998, 1999, 2000, Robert D. Weitz award, 2002. Mem.: APA, Assn. for Behavioral and Cognitive Therapies (chair profl. issues com. 2004—, spl. interest group insomnia and other sleep disorders, spl. interest group anxiety disorders), Can. Psychol. Assn. (sect. on clin. psychology), NY State Psychol. Assn., Obsessive-Compulsive Found., APA Soc. Clin. Psychology, APA Soc. for a Sci. Clin. Psychology, Internat. Assn. for Cognitive Psychotherapy. Office: Montefiore Medical Center 111 E 210th St Klau 1 Bronx NY 10467 Office Phone: 718-920-7667. Office Fax: 718-920-6538. Business E-Mail: srego@montefiore.org.

**REGULA, RALPH STRAUS,** congressman, lawyer; b. Beach City, Ohio, Dec. 3, 1924; s. O.F. and Orpha (Walter) Regula; m. Mary Rogusky, Aug. 5, 1950; children: Martha, David, Richard. BA, Mt. Union Coll., 1948, LLD, 1981; LLB, William McKinley Sch. Law, 1952; LLD, Malone Coll., 1976. Bar: Ohio 1952. Sch. adminstr. Stark County Bd. Edn., 1948-55; lawyer Navarre, 1952—; mem. Ohio State Ho. Reps., 1965-66, Ohio State Senate, 1967-72, US Congress from 16th Ohio dist., 1973—, mem. appropriations com., chmn. labor, health and human svcs., edn. and related agencies subcommittee; ptnr. Regula Bros. Mem. Pres.'s Commn. Fin. Structures and Regulation, 1970-71. Mem. Ohio Bd. Edn., 1960-64; hon. mem. adv. bd. Walsh Coll., Canton, Ohio; trustee Mt. Union Coll., Alliance, Ohio, Stark County Hist. Soc., Stark County Wilderness Soc. With USNR, 1944—46. Named Outstanding Young Man of Yr. Canton Jr. C. of C., 1957, Legis. Conservationist of Yr. Ohio League Sportsmen, 1969; recipient Cmty. Svc. award Navarre Kiwanis Club, 1963, Meritorious Svc. in Conservation award Canton Audubon Assn., 1965, Ohio Conservation award Gov. James Rhodes, 1969, J. Sterling Morton award Nat. Arbor Day Found., 2000, Sheldon Colemon Great Outdoors award Am. Recreation Coaltion, 2000, Award for Legis. Excellence, Nat. Assn. Mfrs., 2001, Legislator of Yr., Assn. Home Appliances Mfrs., 2001, Pick and Gavel award, Am. State Geologists, 2001, Spirit of Enterprise award, US C.of C., 2001, Vanguard award North County Trail Assn., 2001, Thomas Jefferson award, Food Distributors Internat., 2002, Disting. Cmty. Health Champion award, Nat. Assn. Cmty. Health Ctrs., 2002, Nat. Ednl. Svc. award Am. Assn. CC, 2002, Policy Maker of Yr. award, Assn. Corp. Travel Execs., 2002-03, Pub. Svc. award Creutzfeldt-Jacob Disease Found., 2003, Benjamin Franklin Pub.Policy award Nat. Assn. Mutual Ins. Cos., 2003, Crystal Apple award Affiliate Assembly of the Am. Assn. Sch. Librarians, 2003, Disting. Legis. award, Nat. Devel. & Rsch. Insts., Inc. 2003, Congl. Am. Spirit Medallion, Nat. D-Day Mus., 2004 Republican. Episcopalian. Office: US Ho Reps 2306 Rayburn Ho Office Bldg Washington DC 20515-3516 Office Phone: 202-225-3876.

**REH, SHEILA NATKINS,** humanities educator; b. New York, NY, Apr. 7, 1926; d. Benjamin F. Natkins and Bertha North; m. William S. Reh, Nov. 25, 1944 (dec. Dec. 21, 1969); 1 child, Virginia A. BA-English, NYU -Wash. Sq. Coll., New York, NY, 1942—45; MS-education, Wagner Coll., Staten Island, N Y, 1964—65. Tchr. Bd. of Ed., New York, NY, 1964—89. Actor: (acting) Emerson Little Theatre-Staten Island. Bd. of directors, exec. comm. Snug Harbor Cultural Ctr., Staten Island, NY, 1993—96, lead docent-dept. of ed., 2005—, co-chair b ook fair, 1996—98. Recipient, N ew York State Assembly, 1998, Vol. of the Yr., Snug Harbor Cultural Ctr., 2001, Vol. Of The Week, SI Advance, 2001 (Year of the Volunteer-UN). Avocations: tennis, drama.

**REHA, ROSE KRIVISKY,** retired finance educator; b. N.Y.C., Dec. 17, 1920; d. Boris and Freda (Gerstein) Krivisky; m. Rudolph John Reha, Apr. 11, 1941; children: Irene Gale, Phyllis BS Bus. and Music Edn., Ind. State U., 1965; MA Bus. and Psychology, U. Minn., 1967, PhD Ednl. Psychology and Counseling, 1971. With U.S. and State Civil Svc., 1941—63; tchr. pub. schs., Minn., 1965—66; tchg. assoc., instr. U. Minn., Mpls., 1966—68, 1968—85; prof. coll. bus. St. Cloud State U., Minn., 1968—85, prof. emeritus, 1985—, chmn. bus. edn. & office adminstrn. dept., 1982—83. Advisor Small Bus. Inst., 1972-85, SBA, 1972-85; ct. advocate for women in distress St. Cloud Women's Shelter, 1986-89; adj. prof. profl. and bus. comm. Fla. Atlantic U., Boca Raton, 1989-90; substitute tchr. Broward County, 1990—; tutor (reading) Lauderdale, Fla., 1990-92; moderator, counselor Posnack Jewish Cmty. Ctr., Davie, Fla.; lectr. comm. Soref Jewish Cmty. Ctr. Continuing Edn. for sr. groups, Sunrise, Fla., 1994—; cons., lectr. in field; small bus. cons. Small Bus. Inst. Coll. Bus. St. Cloud State U. Minn.; reviewer bus. comm. and consumer edn. textbooks Contbr. articles to profl. jours Camp dir. Girl Scouts U.S., 1960-62; active various cmty. fund drives; sec., mem. relicensure rev. Com. Minn. Bd. Tchg. Continuing Edn., 1984-85 Recipient Achievement award St. Cloud State U., 1985, St. Cloud State U. Rsch. and Faculty Improvement grantee, 1973, 78, 83 Mem. NEA, ACA (cert.), Am. Vocat. Assn. (cert.), Am. Mental Health Counselors Assn. (cert.), Minn. Econ. Assn., Minn. Women of Higher Edn., Minn. Edn. Assn. (pres. women's caucus 1981-83, award 1983), St. Cloud U. Faculty Assembly (pres. 1975), St. Cloud State U. Grad. Coun. (chmn. 1983-85), Fifty-five-plus Sr. Group (moderator 1994-97), Pi Omega Pi, Phi Chi Theta, Delta Pi Epsilon, Delta Kappa Gamma Jewish. Home: 6501 Woodlake Dr Apt 304 Minneapolis MN 55423-1393 Office Phone: 612-866-0544.

**REHAK, JAMES RICHARD,** orthodontist; b. Chgo., Jan. 2, 1938; s. James Joseph and Lydia Ann (Thomas) R.; m. Joann Marie Tabbert, Oct. 15, 1969; 1 child, Suzanne Therese. BS, U. Ill., 1960, DDS cum laude, 1962, MS, 1967, cert. in orthodontics, 1965. Pvt. practice dentistry, Chgo., 1962-63; pvt. practice orthodontics Chgo., Arlington Heights, Ill., Cape Coral, Naples, Fla. Asst. prof. U. Ill. Coll. Dentistry, 1966-68. Pres. bd. trustees St. Ann Sch. Foun.; chmn. bd. dirs. St. John Neumann H.S.; organizer, dir. 1st Nat. Bank, Naples; trustee Catholic Cultural Ctr., Washington. Served to capt. U.S. Army Res., 1962-69. Kellogg Found. fellow, 1958; recipient Blessed Edmund Rice medal, Christian Bros., 1996 Fellow Royal Soc. Health; mem. ADA, Ill. Dental Assn., Chgo. Dental Soc., Fla. Dental Assn., West Coast Dental Soc., Collier County Dental Assn., Am. Assn. Orthodontists, Am. Lingual Orthodontists, Fedn. Dentaire Internationale, Psi Omega, Omicron Kappa Upsilon.

**REHBEIN, EDWARD ANDREW,** minister, geologist, consultant; b. Aug. 13, 1947; s. Edward Louis and Marjorie Ann (Simshaw) R.; m. Phyllis Jean Boyer, June 23, 1973; children: Matthew Louis, Angela Mae. BS in Geology, Calif. Inst. Tech., 1969. Geologist U. S. Forest Svcs., Elkins, W.Va. 1972—74, U.S. Geol. Survey, Billings, Mont., 1974—76; coal geologist W.Va. Geologic Survey, Morgantown, 1977; cons. Morgantown, 1978; geologist Allied Corp., Beckley, W.Va., 1979; sr. exploration geologist Kerr-McGee Corp., Beckley, W.Va., 1980—82, regional mgr. exploration Reno, 1983—85, exploration geologist Oklahoma City, 1985—88; assoc. min. Ch. of Christ, Beckley, 1989—90, min., 1990—; pres. M&R Compart Sales and Svc., Inc., Beckley, 1989—90. Author: Rememberich God's Word, 1991, Overcome by the Cross, 2003; contbr. articles. Mem.: Am. Assn.

Petroleum Geologists, Shotokan Karate Am. Office: N Beckley Ch of Christ PO Box 951 Beckley WV 25802-0951 Personal E-mail: rehbein321@hotmail.com. *So God created man in his own image. (Genesis 1:27). Search the Scriptures, find the full meaning of this, and your life will never be the same.*

**REHBERG, DENNIS R.,** congressman; b. Billings, Mont., Oct. 5, 1955; m. Janice Rehberg; 3 children. Student, Mont. State U., 1974; BA in Pub. Adminstrn. and Polit. Sci., Wash. State U., Pullman, 1977. Tchr. gymnastics, Billings, Mont., 1973—74; with Green Giant Co., Dayton, Wash., 1975—76, Ramada Inn, Billings, 1977; ditch digger Lockrem Constrn., Billings, 1977; real estate salesman Billings, 1977—79; legis. aide Staffs of State Senator Bill Mathers and State Senator Sonny Lockrem, 1977; legis. asst. Staff of US Rep. Ron Marlenee, Mont., 1979—82; mgr. Rehberg Ranch, Billings, 1982—2000; mem. Mont. State Ho. Reps. from Dist. 88, 1985—89; state dir. Staff of US Senator Conrad Burns, Mont., 1989—91; lt. gov. Mont., 1991—97; mem. US Congress from Mont. at large, 2001—, mem. appropriations com. Named Champion of Small Bus., Small Bus. Survival Com., 2001, 2002, Hero of the Taxpayer, Americans for Tax Reform, 2002; recipient Guardian of Senior's Rights award, 60 Plus Assn., 2002, Presdl. award, Leadership, Nat. Farmers Union, 2003. Republican. Episc. Office: US Ho Reps 516 Cannon Ho Office Bldg Washington DC 20515-2601 Office Phone: 202-225-3211.*

**REHDER, JON,** social studies educator; b. Cottonwood, Idaho, July 9, 1978; s. Jim and Sally Rehder; m. Renee Arnzen, June 9, 2004; 1 child, Aliah. BS in Secondary Edn., Lewis-Clark State Coll., 2004. Cert. secondary edn. Idaho. Social studies tchr. Meridian (Idaho) Sch. Dist., 2004—. Boys basketball coach. Home: 3260 S Pompei Ave Meridian ID 83642

**REHG, JENNIFER,** anthropology educator; b. St. Louis; m. David Rasmussen. BA in Anthropology, Wash. U., St. Louis, 1995; MA in Anthropology, U. Ill., Urbana-Champaign, 2003, PhD, 2003. Instr. U. Ill., Urbana-Champaign, 1999, So. Ill. U., Edwardsville, 2003—04, asst. prof., 2004—. George A. Beslow fellow, 1999—2000, Dissertation Travel grantee, 1998—99, Tinker grantee, Ctr. for Latin Am. and Caribbean Studies, 1998. Mem.: Animal Behavior Soc., Am. Assn. Phys. Anthropologists, Am. Soc. Primatologists, Internat. Primatological Soc. Office: So Ill U Edwardsville Box 1451 Edwardsville IL 62026 Office Phone: 618-650-3843. E-mail: jrehg@siue.edu.

**REHG, KENNETH LEE,** linguistics educator; b. East St. Louis, Ill., Nov. 21, 1939; s. Theophil Albert and Kathryn Louise (George) R.; m. Kimi Miyagi; 1 child, Laura Le'olani. BA, U. Ill., 1962; MA, So. Ill. U., 1965; PhD, U. Hawaii, 1986. Tng. officer Internat. Ctr. for Lang. Studies, Washington, 1966-67; lang. officer U.S. Peace Corp, Saipan, Micronesia, 1967-70; asst. rschr. Social Sci. Rsch. Inst. U. Hawaii, Honolulu, 1974-83, assoc. prof., 1984—. Cons. Micronesian govt., 1973-76, 97, 2000, 2003, 2004, Samoa Dept. Edn., Pago Pago, 1978, U.S. Geol. Survey, Menlo Park, Calif., 1979-81, Japan Nat. Mus. Ethnology, Osaka, 1986; participant Fulbright-Hays Study Group, Ea. Indonesia, 1991. Author: Ponapean Reference Grammar, 1981; co-author: Kitail Lokaiahn Pohnpei, 1969, Ponapean-English Dictionary, 1979; co-editor: Issues in Austronesian Morphology; mng. editor: jour. Oceanic Linguistics; contbr. papers to profl. publs. Rsch. fellow U. Hawaii, 1981-82; recipient Excellence in Teaching award Hawaii Tchrs. ESL, 1984, Mortar Bd., 1990, Presdl. Citation for meritorious tchg., 1996. Mem. Linguistic Soc. Am., Linguistic Soc. Hawaii. Office: U Hawaii Dept Linguistics Moore Hall 569 1890 E West Rd Honolulu HI 96822-2318 Office Phone: 808-956-3277. E-mail: rehg@hawaii.edu.

**REHM, CAROLYN AGNES,** pediatrician, educator; b. Queens, NY, Mar. 2, 1952; d. Donald Edward and Agnes Catherine Schanck; m. Steven Thomas Rehm, Oct. 4, 1980; children: Catherine, Tim, Emily. BS, Coll. Mt. St. Vincent, 1974; MD, Columbia U., 1978. Diplomate Am. Bd. Pediats. Intern Johns Hopkins Hosp., Balt., 1978—79, resident, 1979—81; pediatrician Bel Air Clinic, Bowie, Md., 1981—83; pvt. practice pediatrician Huntington, NY, 1983—94; mem. staff pediats. United Cerebral Palsy, Roosevelt, NY, 1994—99; tchr. sci. St. Dominic H.S., Oyster Bay, NY, 1999—2005; prof. Molloy Coll., 2005—. Tchr. sci. Coll. Mt. St. Vincent, Riverdale, NY, 2003—04; dir. Am. Health and Safety Inst., Oyster Bay, NY; moderator student amb. cmty. svc. St. Dominic HS, Oyster Bay, 1999—2005; medical dir. Mill Need Sch. Deaf, NY, 2005—. Author: The Flowerpot Bunnies, 2004. Leader Girl Scouts Am., N.Y., 1986—2005, Boy Scouts Am. N.Y., 1989—94; com. Cath. girl scouts Girl Scouts Am., N.Y., 1999—2004. Recipient Humanitarian award, Columbia Coll. Physicians and Surgeons, 1978, N.Y., 1978, St. Anne award, Girl Scouts, St. Elizabeth award, Outstanding Svc. award, 2000. Fellow: Am. Acad. Pediats.; mem.: Children with Disabilities Am. Roman Catholic. Home: 28 Shamrock Ct Syosset NY 11791

**REHM, LYNN PAUL,** psychologist, educator; b. Chgo., May 20, 1941; s. Stanley Franklin and Bernice Agnes (Stiebler) R.; m. Susan Hanson Higginbotham, Feb. 28, 1964; children: Elizabeth Susan, Sarah Ann. BA, U. So. Calif., 1963; MA, U. Wis., 1966, PhD, 1970. Asst. prof. neuropsychiat. inst. UCLA, 1968-70; assoc. prof. U. Pitts., 1970-79; prof. U. Houston, 1979—. Bd. dirs. Coun. Dirs. Clin. Psychology, 1986—88, 2000—04, chair, 1987—88; chair licensing exam. com. Assn. State and Provincial Psychology Bds., 1995—2005. Editor: Behavior Therapy for Depression, 1981, (with others) Psychology Research, Public Policy and Practice, 1985. Fellow APA (chair bd. ednl. affairs 1993-94, pres. divsn. 1997); mem. Assn. for Advancement Behavior Therapy, Soc. for Psychotherapy Rsch., Soc. for Rsch. in Psychopathology, Tex. Psychol. Assn. (pres. 1994), Houston Psychol. Assn. (pres.), Soc. Sci. of Clin. Psychology (pres 1989), Internat. Soc. Clin. Psychology (pres 2002), Phi Beta Kappa. Avocations: reading, gardening. Office: U Houston Dept Psychology Houston TX 77204-5022 Office Phone: 713-743-8606. Business E-Mail: lprehm@uh.edu.

**REHM, PATRICE KOCH,** radiologist, educator; b. DeSoto, Mo., Nov. 23, 1954; d. James Clarence and Eleanor (Koch) R. BA in Chemistry, U. Mo., 1977; MD, Yale U., 1981. Diplomate Am. Bd. Radiology, Am. Bd. Nuclear Medicine. Intern in medicine Waterbury (Conn.) Hosp., 1981-82; resident in radiology Yale New Haven Hosp., 1982-83, 84-85, fellow in neuroradiology 1985-86, fellow in nuclear medicine, 1986-87; resident in radiology SUNY Upstate Med. Ctr., Syracuse, 1983-84; clin. assoc. Cleve. Clinic, 1987-88, staff physician, 1988-89, Presbyn. Hosp., Charlotte, N.C., 1989-91, Georgetown U. Med. Ctr., Washington, 1992—; assoc. prof. radiology, dir. nuc. medicine U. Va. Health System, Charlottesville, Va. Fellow Am. Coll. Radiology (dir. nuc. medicine), Radiologic Soc. N.Am., Soc. Nuclear Medicine. Office: U Va Health System PO Box 800170 Charlottesville VA 22908

**REHM, SUSAN,** physician; BS, U. Nebr., 1975; MD, U. Nebr., Omaha, 1978. Diplomate Am. Bd. Internal Medicine with subspecialty in infectious disease. Resident in internal medicine The Cleve. Clinic Found., 1978—81, fellow in infectious diseases, 1981—83, assoc. chief of staff, 1997—. Clin. assoc. prof. Ohio State U., Columbus. Mem.: AMA, ACP, Am. Coll. Physician Execs., Infectious Diseases Soc. Am., Am. Soc. Microbiology, Nat. Found. for Infectious Diseases (med. dir.). Office: The Cleveland Clinic 9500 Euclid Ave Cleveland OH 44195

**REHM, SUSAN J.,** social services professional; b. Yorktown, Va., May 17, 1945; d. Gilbert F. and Jeradean Dolly (Field) R. BA, U. Redlands, 1967; MSW, San Diego State U., 1969. Diplomate in clin. social work; lic. social worker, Calif.; cert. tchr., Calif. Dir. clin. social work home health care and child devel. depts. UCLA Med. Ctr.; dir. social work svcs. Mercy Hosp. and Med. Ctr., San Diego, Calif.; lectr. Sch. Social Work San Diego State U.; exec. dir. Family Svc. Agy., Santa Barbara, Calif. Named state scholar, Calif.,

1963-67, U.S. Children's Bur. Fellow, 1968-69. Mem. NASW, Family Svc. Am. (exec. coun.), Santa Barbara Sunrise Rotary, Nat. Found. Infectious Diseases (pres.). Office: Family Svc Agy 123 W Gutierrez St Santa Barbara CA 93101-3424

**REHMAN, SAIFUR,** web site design company executive; b. Lahore, Pakistan, Sept. 9, 1965; s. Mohammad Makhdoom and Naseem Akhtar; m. Sana Rehman. BSBA, Ctrl. Mo. State Univ., 1993; MS in MIS, U. Balt., 1995. Analyst Accenture (formerly Andersen Consulting), Washington, 1996—97; sr. assoc. IBM (formerly PricewaterhouseCoopers), Fairfax, Va., 1997—99; mgr. Midwest Consulting Group, Kansas City, Mo., 1999—2000; dir. KPMG Consulting Inc., Mountain View, Calif., 2000—; chmn., CEO WebBiz Inc., Palo Alto, Calif., 2001—. Mem.: Am. Soc. Quality, Data Processing Mgmt. Assn., Soc. Info. Mgmt., Project Mgmt. Inst., Delta Sigma Pi. Office: WebBiz Inc P O Box 61034 Palo Alto CA 94306 E-mail: info@irisfirm.com.

**REHMUS, CHARLES MARTIN,** arbitrator; b. Ann Arbor, Mich., June 27, 1926; s. Paul A. and Amy D. (Martin) R.; m. Carolyn Brown, Dec. 21, 1948 (div. July 1982); children—Paul, James, Jon, David; m. Laura Carlson, Sept. 4, 1982 AB, Kenyon Coll., 1947; MA, Stanford U., 1951, PhD, 1955. Commr. Fed. Mediation and Conciliation Service, San Francisco, 1952-58; staff dir. Presdl. R.R. Commn., Washington, 1959-61; prof. polit. sci. U. Mich., Ann Arbor, 1962-80, dir. Inst. Labor and Indsl. Relations, 1962-76; chmn. Mich. Employment Relations Commn., Detroit, 1976-80; dean N.Y. State Sch. Indsl. and Labor Relations, Cornell U., Ithaca, 1980-86; prof. law U. San Diego, 1988-97. Author: Final-Offer Arbitration, 1975, The Railway Labor Act at Fifty, 1977, Labor and American Politics, 1967, rev. edit., 1978, The National Mediation Board, 1984, Emergency Strikes Revisited, 1990. Chmn. 4 Presdl. emergency bds. at various times. Served to lt. USNR, 1943-45; PTO Mem. Internat. Inst. Labor Studies (bd. govs. 1984-92), Indsl. Rels. Rsch. Assn. (exec. bd. 1984-88), Nat. Acad. Arbitrators (bd. govs. 1979-82, v.p. 1993-95). Home: 18755 W Bernardo Dr Apt 1027 San Diego CA 92127-3011

**REHNKE, MARY ANN,** academic administrator; b. Faribault, Minn., Jan. 23, 1945; d. Wesley Arthur and Sarah Frances (Smith) Rehnke; m. Charles Orin Willis, Apr. 18, 1924. BA in English, Cornell Coll., 1967; MA in English, U. Chgo., 1968, PhD in Lit., 1974; MS in Ednl Adminstrn., U. Wis., 1975; Cert. of Completion, Shalem Inst. for Spiritual Formation. Head resident Elizabeth Waters Hall, U. Wis., Madison, 1970-73; asst. prof. English No. Ky. U., Highland Heights, 1973-82, acad. adminstr., 1976-77, dir. summer sessions, 1977-80; dir. conf. planning Am. Assn. Higher Edn., Washington, 1980-82; assoc. dean for faculty relations and acad. programs Coll. St. Catherine, St. Paul, 1982-83; assoc. dean of coll. Daemen Coll., Buffalo, 1983-85; v.p. programs Council of Ind. Colls., Washington, 1986—. Mem. planning com. nat. identification program Am. Council Edn., Washington, 1978-85; mem. program com. Nat. Conf. Women Student Leaders and Women of Distinction, Washington, 1985-88. Author: Women in Higher Education Administration: A Brief Guide for Conference Planners, 1982, Guide to Spiritual Retreats in the Washington, D.C. Area, 1997; editor: Creating Career Programs in a Liberal Arts Context, 1987; editor newsletter N. Ctrl. Regional Women's Studies, 1978-80. Vestry mem Ch. of St. Clement, Alexandria, Va., 1982, vice chair search com., 1986-87. Named one of Outstanding Young Women Am., 1976. Mem.: Nat. Women's Studies Assn., Jane Austen Soc., Soc. Values in Higher Edn., N.Am. Assn. Summer Sessions (rsch. chair 1979—80), Am. Assn. Higher Edn. (coord. nat. conf. roundtable 1982—86), Phi Beta Kappa, Phi Delta Kappa. Democrat. Episcopalian. Office Phone: 202-466-7230.

**REHNQUIST, JANET,** lawyer, former federal agency administrator; b. Phoenix, May 4, 1957; d. William and Margery (Peck) Rehnquist. BA, U. Va., 1979; JD, U. Va. Law School, 1985. Assoc. atty. The White House, Washington, 1990—93; asst. U.S. atty. (ea. dist.) Va. US Dept. Justice, Washington; insp. gen. US Dept. HHS, Washington, 2001—03; ptnr. Venable LLP, Washington, 2003—, co-chair Wash. Health Care practice. Counsel U.S. Senate Permanent Subcom. on Investigations. Office: Venable LLP 575 7th St NW Washington DC 20004 Office Phone: 202-344-8241. Office Fax: 202-344-8300. E-mail: jrehnquist@venable.com.

**REHR, DAVID K.,** broadcast association executive; BS, St. Johns U., 1981; MA, George Mason U., 1989, PhD. Exec. asst. to US Rep Vin Weber U.S. Ho. of Reps., mem. staff com. small bus., dir. fed. govt. rels.; dir. Nat. Fedn. Independent Businesses; pres. govt. affairs Nat. Beer Wholesalers Assn., Inc., sr. v.p.; pres., CEO Nat. Assn. Broadcasters, 2005—. Office: Nat Assn Broadcasters 1771 N St NW Washington DC 20036-2891 Office Phone: 202-429-5300. Office Fax: 202-429-4199. E-mail: irc@nab.org.*

**REHTH, ANN,** counselor; b. Pennyan, N.Y., May 28, 1942; d. J. Allen and Jean Eleanor (Stanhope) Henderson; children: Nikki, Douglas, Scott. BA, U. South Fla., 1983; MS, Nova U., 1994. Cert. tchr., ESL tchr. Tchr. Venice H.S., Fla., 1984—94; mental health counselor Meridian Behavioral, Gainsville, Fla., 1994—98, YMCA, Sarasota, Fla., 1998—2001; tchr. Gulf Coast Marine Inst., Venice, 2000—01; tchr. ESOL and reading North Port H.S., Fla., 2001—. Dir. intervention program for children and teens Meridian Behavioral, Gainsville, Fla., 1994—98; cons. to schs. for abuse and crisis intervention YMCA, Venice, Fla., 1999—2001. Mem.: STESOL, Fla. Reading Assn., Sarasota Reading Council. Avocations: reading, volunteering, walking. Personal E-mail: annrehth@comcast.net.

**REIBEL, KURT,** physicist, researcher; b. Vienna, May 23, 1926; came to U.S., 1938; s. Michael and Regina (Pak) R.; m. Eleanor Elvira Mannino, June 10, 1954; children—Leah, Michael, David BA, Temple U., 1954; MS, U. Pa., 1956, PhD, 1959. Jr. research assoc. in physics Brookhaven Nat. Lab., 1957-59; research assoc. U. Pa., Phila., 1959-61; asst. prof. Ohio State U., Columbus, 1961-64, assoc. prof., 1964-70, prof. physics, 1970-92, prof. emeritus, 1992—. Vis. scientist CERN, Geneva, Switzerland, 1968-69, 75-76 Author research papers on nuclear and elementary particle physics NSF fellow, 1954-56 Mem. Am. Phys. Soc., AAUP, Fedn. Am. Scientists, Union Concerned Scientists, Sigma Xi Jewish. Office: Ohio State U Dept Physics 191 West Woodruff Ave Columbus OH 43210-1117

**REIBER, PAUL L.,** state supreme court chief justice; b. Pitts., June 20, 1947; BA, Hampden-Sydney Coll., Va., 1970; JD, Suffolk Law Sch., 1974. Prtnr. Reiber, Kenlan, Schwiebert and Facey, 1984—2003; town moderator Chittenden, 1985—; justice Vt. Supreme Ct., 2003—04, chief justice, 2004—. Former mem. Vt. Jud. Nomination Bd. Mem.: ABA, Vt. Bar Assn. Avocations: bicycling, reading. Office: Vt Supreme Ct 109 State St Montpelier VT 05609-0701*

**REIBOLD, DOROTHY ANN,** accountant, researcher; b. Leigh, Nebr., Feb. 22, 1922; d. Herman Ludwig Marty and Frances Jane Harvey; m. Wayne Henry Reibold, Mar. 27, 1947; children: Lillie Frances, Marty John. BEd, Wayne State Tchrs., 1945. Tchr., prin. Nenzel Sch., Nebr., 1941-42; tchr. Cozad Sch., Nebr., 1942-43; sec. Burroughs Adding Machine, Omaha, 1943-44; tchr. Lyons Pub. Sch., Nebr., 1945-47; office mgr. Yoelin Bros. Wholesale, Denver, 1947-52; freelance bookkeeper Henderson, Colo., 1960-00; bookkeeper Hazeltine Heights Water, Henderson, 1964—2003; dir. sch. lunch program Zion Luth. Sch., Brighton, Colo., 1969—78; dir. Hazeltine Heights Water, 1982-00. Author: Ecklin Family Story, 1988, Life of Matthias Harvye, 1998. Mem.: DAR. Republican. Lutheran. Avocations: genealogy, travel. Home and office: 8181 E 104th Ave Henderson CO 80640-9049 Personal E-mail: dotareibold@earthlink.net.

**REICH, ABRAHAM CHARLES,** lawyer; b. Waterbury, Conn., Apr. 17, 1949; s. Samuel and Esther (Gurvitz) Reich; m. Sherri Engelman, Aug. 15, 1971; children: Spencer, Alexander. BA, U. Conn., 1971; JD, Temple U., 1974. Bar: Pa. 1974, U.S. Supreme Ct. 1979. Assoc. Fox Rothschild LLP, Phila., 1974-81, ptnr., 1981—, mng. ptnr., 2001—05, co-chair, 2005—. Chair lawyers adv. com. U.S. Ct. Appeals (3d cir.), 1998. Fellow: Am. Coll. Trial Lawyers; mem.: ABA (ho. of dels. 1997—2002, 2004—), Phila. Bar Assn.

(chair profl. responsibility com. 1983—84, chair bench-bar com. 1985, chair profl. guidance com. 1987—88, bd. govs. 1987—89, chair bd. govs. 1989, chancellor 1995, del. ABA 1996—2000). Home: 2224 Mount Vernon St Philadelphia PA 19130-3115 Office: Fox Rothschild LLP 2000 Market St Ste 10 Philadelphia PA 19103-3231 Office Phone: 215-299-2090. Business E-Mail: areich@foxrothschild.com.

**REICH, ALLAN J.,** lawyer; b. Chgo., July 9, 1948; s. H. Robert and Sonya (Minsky) R.; m. Lynne Susan Roth, May 23, 1971; children: Allison, Marissa, Scott. BA, Cornell U., 1970; JD cum laude, U. Mich., 1973. Bar: Ill. 1973, U.S. Dist. Ct. (no. dist.) Ill. 1973. Ptnr. McDermott, Will & Emery, Chgo., 1973-93; vice chmn. D'Ancona & Pflaum LLC, Chgo., 2000—2003; ptnr. Seyfarth Shaw LLP, Chgo., 2003—. Trustee Oakmark Family of Mutual Funds, 1994—. V.p., mem. exec. com. Coun. for Jewish Elderly, 1989—97; mem. men's coun. Mus. Contemporary Art, Chgo., 1988—89; mem. Chgo. exec. bd. Am. Jewish Com., 1989—, nat. bd. govs.; mem. met. Chgo. bd. Am. Heart Assn.; bd. dirs. Young Men's Jewish Coun., Chgo., 1974—84, Coun. for Jewish Elderly, 1986—97. Fellow: Am. Bar Found.; mem.: ABA, Chgo. Bar Assn., Econ. Club Chgo., Northmoor Country Club (Highland Park, Ill.), Standard Club (Chgo.). Home: 936 Skokie Ridge Dr Glencoe IL 60022-1434 Office: Seyfarth Shaw LLP 131 S Dearborn St Ste 2400 Chicago IL 60603 Office Phone: 312-460-5650. Business E-mail: areich@seyfarth.com.

**REICH, BERNARD,** political science professor; b. Bklyn., Dec. 5, 1941; s. Moe and Rosalyn (Hartglass) R.; m. Madelyn Sue Ingber, June 16, 1963; children— Barry, Norman, Michael, Jennifer BA cum laude with spl. honors, CCNY, 1961; MA, U. Va., 1963, PhD, 1964. Asst. prof. polit. sci. and internat. affairs George Washington U., Washington, 1964-70, assoc. prof., 1970-76, prof., 1976—, chmn. dept. polit. sci., 1976-82, 88-91. Vis. prof. U. Va., 1969, 94, Sch. Advanced Internat. Studies Johns Hopkins U., 1978-80; vis. rsch. assoc. Tel Aviv U., 1971-72. Author: Quest for Peace: United States-Israel Relations and the Arab-Israeli Conflict, 1977, The U.S. and Israel: Influence in the Special Relationship, 1984, Israel: Land of Tradition and Conflict, 1985, 1993, Historical Dictionary of Israel, 1992, Securing the Covenant: United States-Israel Relations After the Cold War, 1995, A Brief History of Israel, 2005, A Brief History of Isreal, 2005; co-author, co-editor: Government and Politics of the Middle East and North Africa, 1980, 1986, 1995, 2002, Israel Faces the Future, 1986, The Powers in the Middle East, 1987, Israeli National Security Policy: Political Actors and Perspectives, 1988, Political Leaders of the Contemporary Middle East and North Africa: A Biographical Dictionary, 1990; co-author: Israeli Politics in the 1990's: Key Domestic and Foreign Policy Factors, 1991; co-editor: Israeli Politics in the 1990's Key Domestic and Foreign Policy Factors, 1991, Arab-Israeli Conflict and Conciliation: A Documentary History, 1995, An Historical Encyclopedia of the Arab-Israeli Conflict, 1996; editor, co-author: Handbook of Political Science Research on the Middle East and North Africa, 1998; co-author, co-editor: Government and Politics of the Middle East and North Africa, 2002, Israel Faces the Future, 1986, The Powers in the Middle East, 1987, Israeli National Security Policy: Political Actors and Perspectives, 1988, Political Leaders of the Contemporary Middle East and North Africa: A Biographical Dictionary, 1990; co-author: United States Foreign Policy and the Middle East/North Africa: A Bibliography of Twentieth-Century Research, 1990, Asian States' Relations with the Middle East and North Africa: A Bibliography, 1950-93, 1994, U.S. Foreign Relations with the Middle East and North Africa: A Bibliography, 1998, 1999, Political Dictionary of Israel, 2000; mem. adv. bd. editors Middle East Jour., 1977—, Terrorism, 1987—93, Jour. Israel Affairs, 1994—, Fgn. Svc. Jour., 1987—90, contbr. articles to profl. jours. Bd. govs. Middle East Inst. Fulbright research scholar, UAR, 1965; NSF postdoctoral fellow, 1971-72 Mem.: Phi Beta Kappa. Home: 13800 Turnmore Rd Silver Spring MD 20906-2134 Office: George Washington U Dept Polit Sci Washington DC 20052-0001 Office Phone: 202-994-6716. Business E-Mail: breich@gwu.edu.

**REICH, BERNARD,** communications engineer; b. N.Y.C., Jan. 7, 1926; s. Adolph and Rose (Gluck) R.; m. Sylvia Greenberg, June 15, 1947; children: Robin Reich Murphy, Richard. BS in Physics, CCNY, 1948; MSc, Rutgers U., 2002. Electronic engr., supervisory electronic engr. U.S. Army Electronics R & D Command, Ft. Monmouth, N.J., 1948-81; unit mgr. Semcor, Farmingdale, N.J., 1981-88; telecommunications engr. Telos Corp., Shrewsbury, N.J., 1988-99, retired, 1999. Chmn. spl. working group on semicondrs. and microelectronics NATO, Brussels, 1959-80, chmn. group experts on electronic parts, 1972-80; adv. editor Microelectronics and Reliability, 1970—. Contbr. over 100 articles to tech. jours.; patentee in field. Mem. Juvenile Conf. Com., Ocean Twp., N.J., 1964—; mem. Manor at Wayside Condominium Assn., Ocean Twp., 1990-91. Sgt. U.S. Army, 1945-46, ETO. Recipient decoration for meritorious civilian svc. U.S. Army Electronics R & D Command, 1981. Fellow IEEE (chartered), IEE (Eng.). Avocation: walking. Home: 45 Gimbel Pl Ocean NJ 07712-2565

**REICH, DAVID LEE,** library director; b. Orlando, Fla., Nov. 25, 1930; s. P.F. and Opal Katherine (Wood) Reichelderfer; m. Kathleen Johanna Weichel, Aug. 2, 1954 (div. Sept. 1964); 1 son, Robert Weichel. PhB magna cum laude, U. Detroit, 1961; AM in LS, U. Mich., 1963. Tchr. English Jefferson Davis Jr. Sch., San Antonio, 1961-62; dir. engring. library Radiation Inc., Melbourne, Fla., 1963-64; asst. to dir. libraries Miami-Dade Jr. Coll., Miami, Fla., 1964-65; dir. learning resources Monroe County C.C., Monroe, Mich., 1965-68; dep. dir. Dallas Pub. Library, 1968-73; dep. chief librarian Chgo. Pub. Library, 1973-74, commr., 1975-78; dir. Bd. Libr. Commrs., Commonwealth of Mass., Boston, 1978-80; exec. sec. New Eng. Libr. Bd., Augusta, Maine, 1980-82, vice chmn., 1979-80; dir. Lakeland (Fla.) Pub. Libr., 1983-99, ret., 1999; exec. sec. Fla. Archivists, 1999—2001, ret. 2001. Libr. cons. Macomb County C.C., Warren, Mich., 1967; chmn. adv. com. to libr. tech. asst. program El Centro Coll., Dallas, 1969-71; mem. inter-task working group Goals for Dallas, 1968-70, mem. Dallas Area Libr. planning coun., 1970-73; mem. adv. coun. dept. libr. sci. No. Ill. U., 1975-78; v.p., pres.-elect Tampa Bay Libr. Consortium, 1985-86, pres., 1986-87. Co-author: The Public Library in Non-traditional Education, 1974; editor The Villas II News, 1999—; contbr. articles to library jours. Bd. dirs. The Villas II Homeowners Assn., 1994-96, 98-2001; mem. steering com. Friends of Tampa Bay Libr. Consortium, 2000—. Sgt. U.S. Army, 1952-55. Recipient Disting. Alumnus award U. Mich., 1978; William B. Calkins Found. scholar Orlando, 1963; Carnegie L.S. Endowment scholar, 1963. Mem. ALA (coun.-at-large 1968-72, 75-79), S.E. Libr. Assn., Fla. Libr. Assn. (sec.-treas. coll. and spl. librs. divsn. 1965, steering com. mcpl. librs. caucus 1983-84, chmn. 1984-85, exec. bd. 1984-87), Soc. Fla. Archivists (exec. bd. 1994-96, sec. 1996-97, exec. sec. 1999-2001, treas. 2000-01), Fla. Pub. Libr. Assn. (pres. 1987-88, exec. bd. 1988-89, 94-95, pres. emeritus 1996-98, editor newsletter 1992-93, 96-97, chmn. libr. adminstrn. divsn. 1992, friends and trustees divsn. 1993, 95), Soc. Automotive Historians, Alumni Assn. U. Mich. (pres. Libr. Sch. alumni 1973), Nat. Soc. SAR, Polk Sr. Games (bd. dirs., 2004-). Home: 4011 Heron Ave Lakeland FL 33813-1123 E-mail: dreich@tampabay.rr.com.

**REICH, HERB,** editor; b. N.Y.C. s. Herman S. and Hattie (Davis) R.; m. Gerri Toog, Aug. 7, 1960; children: Amanda Suri, Elizabeth Jo. BA, Bklyn. Coll., 1950; MA, Bklyn. Coll. and Kings County Hosp., 1951; postgrad., Columbia U., 1951-54. Author sketches and lyrics Tamiment Revues (Pa.), 1951; staff writer NBC-TV, N.Y.C. and Los Angeles, 1955-57; research coordinator Inst. for Motivational Research, Croton-on-Hudson, NY, 1958-59; research dir. Scientist and Engr. Technol. Inst., N.Y.C., 1960-64; mng. editor SETI Pubs. Inc., N.Y.C., 1961-64; sr. editor Odyssey Press, N.Y.C., 1964-65; editorial dir. Profl. and Tech. Programs Inc., N.Y.C., 1966-72; dir. Behavioral Sci. Book Service, N.Y.C., 1966-72; dir. behavioral scis. program Basic Books Inc., N.Y.C., 1973-79; editor Microelectronics. div. John Wiley & Sons Inc., N.Y.C., 1979-87, sr. editor profl. and trade divsn., 1987-95; pres. H&G Reich, Cons., Hastings Hdsn., NY, 1980—. Publ., rsch., advt. and polit. cons.; rschr., statistician, rsch. cons. Am. Found. for Blind, Pepsi Cola Co., Nowland and Co., Comms. and Media Rsch. Svcs. Mng. editor: Odyssey Science Library Ency. of Engring., Signs and Symbols, 1965, Dictionary of Physics and Mathematics Abbreviations, Signs and Symbols, 1965, Dictionary of Electronics Abbreviations, Signs and Symbols, 1965, Dictionary of Comput-

ers and Control Systems Abbreviations, Signs and Symbols, 1965; contbr. Random House Dictionary of the English Language, 1967, rev. edit., 1987, The Greatest Revue Sketches, 1982, Ency. of Psychology, 2d edit., 1994, Corsini Encyclopedia of Psychology and Behavioral Scienses, 2001; TV writer: Broadway Open House, 1951, Olsen and Johnson Show, 1951, Milton Berle Texaco Star Theatre, 1952, All-Star Revue, 1952, Mel Torme Show, 1952, Eddie Cantor Show, 1953, Red Buttons Show, 1954, Summer Colgate Show, 1954, Jerry Lester Show, 1954, Jan Murray Time, 1955, Howdy Doody Show, 1955-56, Tonight Show, 1956, NBC Comedy Hour, 1956, Wayne and Schuster Hour, 1957. Co-founder, vice chmn. Mt. Vernon United for Better Edn., N.Y., 1970-73; mem. Westchester County Democratic Com., 1972-76; exec. com. Mt. Vernon Dem. City Com., 1973-76; mem. supt.'s adv. com. Hastings Schs., Hastings-on-Hudson, N.Y., 1981-82. Recipient Gold award of excellence for radio advt. Advt. Club of Westchester, 1980; recipient Gold and Bronze awards of excellence for radio advt. Advt. Club of Westchester, 1981 Mem. AAAS, APA, Alpha Phi Omega. Office: 127 Mount Hope Blvd Hastings On Hudson NY 10706 Office Phone: 914-478-4042. Personal E-mail: hgreich@aol.com.

**REICH, JILL,** dean; B.A., Regis College; PhD in Psychology, Dartmouth Coll. Fmr. dept. chair, assoc. dean Grad. school Loyola; fmr. dean of faculty Trinity College; fmr. exec. dir. of education American Psychology Assoc.; prof., dept. of psychology Bates Coll., v.p. of academic affairs, dean of faculty Lewiston, Maine, 2000—. Office: Bates Coll Lane Hall Rm 120A 2 Andrews Rd Lewiston ME 04240

**REICH, JOHN M.,** federal agency administrator; BS, So. Ill. U., 1961; MBA, U. South Fla.; graduate, Sch. Banking of South, La. State U. Cmty. banker, Ill., Fla.; pres., CEO Nat. Bank Sarasota, Fla.; staff mem. for US Senator Connie Mack, 1988—2000, chief of staff, 1998—2000; bd. dirs. FDIC, 2001—, acting chmn., 2001, vice chmn., 2002—05; dir. Office of Thrift Supervision, Washington, 2005—. Chmn. bd. dir. Sarasota Family YMCA, Fla. Office: Office of Thrift Supervision 1700 G St NW Washington DC 20552 Office Phone: 202-898-3888.

**REICH, LAURENCE,** lawyer; b. Jersey City, Jan. 22, 1931; s. Victor and Miriam (Gross) R.; m. Doris Rita Diamond, Oct. 21, 1965 (dec. Apr. 15, 2002). BA, U. Chgo., 1951, JD, 1953. Bar: N.J. 1954, N.Y. 1982, U.S. Dist. Ct. N.J. 1954, U.S. ct. appeals (3rd cir.) 1958, U.S. Supreme ct. 1963, U.S. Tax Ct. 1971, U.S. Dist. Ct. (so. dist.) N.Y. 1982, U.S. Ct. Appeals (2nd cir.) 1987. From mem. firm to sr. counsel McElroy, Deutsch, Mulvaney & Carpenter, LLP (formerly Carpenter, Bennett & Morrissey), Newark, 1957—2003. Mem. Bur. Nat. Affairs Tax Adv. bd., 1972—; lectr. in field. Author: N.J. Corporation Law and Practice; contbr. articles to profl. jours. With U.S. Army, 1955-57. Fellow Am. Coll. Tax Counsel, Am. Bar Found.; mem. ABA (com. chmn. sect. taxation 1972-74, 85-86, mem. coun. 1991-94), N.J. Bar Assn. (chmn. taxation sect. 1975-76), Assn. Fed. Bar State N.J. (v.p. 1982-94, bd. trustees 1994-99), Essex County Bar Assn. Office Phone: 973-565-2003. Business E-Mail: lreich@mdmc-law.com.

**REICH, MICHAEL,** economics professor; b. Poland, Oct. 18, 1945; came to U.S., 1949; s. Melvin and Betty (Mandelbaum) R.; children: Rachel, Gabriel. BA, Swarthmore Coll., 1966; PhD, Harvard U., 1974. Asst. prof. Boston U., 1971-74, U. Calif., Berkeley, 1974-81, acting assoc. prof., 1981-82, assoc. prof., 1982-89, prof., 1989—. Rsch. dir. Nat. Ctr. for the Workplace, 1993-96, Inst. Labor and Employment, 2001-04; dir. Inst. Indsl. Rels., 2004-. Author: Segmented Work, Divided Workers, 1982, Racial Inequality, 1981, The Capitalist System, 1986, Social Structures of Accumulation, 1994, Work and Pay in the U.S. and Japan, 1997; editor: Indsl. Rels. Jour., 1986-94; contbr. articles to profl. jours. Mem. Am. Econ. Assn., Indsl. Rels. Rsch. Assn., Phi Beta Kappa, Sigma Xi. Office: Dept of Econs U Calif 611 Evans Hl Berkeley CA 94720-0001

**REICH, OTTO JUAN,** political analyst, business consultant; b. Havana, Cuba, Oct. 16, 1945; came to U.S., 1960; s. Walter and Graciela Maria (Fleites) R.; m. Connie Lynn Dillinger, Apr. 19, 1975; children: Adrienne Michelle, Natalie Lauren BA, U. N.C., Chapel Hill, 1966; MA, Georgetown U., 1973; grad., Officers Candidate Sch., U.S. Army, 1967. Civil affairs officer U.S. Army, Panama, 1967-69; staff asst. U.S. Ho. Reps., Washington, 1970-71; v.p. Cormorant Enterprises, Miami, Fla., 1972-73; internat. rep. Fla. Dept. Commerce, Coral Gables, 1973-75; community devel. coordinator City of Miami, Fla., 1975-76; dir. Washington ops. Council of the Americas, 1976-81; asst. adminstr. U.S. AID, Washington, 1981-83; spl. adv. for pub. diplomacy to sec. state with rank of ambassador U.S. Dept. State, Washington, 1983-86, ambassador to Venezuela, Caracas, 1986-89; sr. assoc. Ctr. for Strategic and Internat. Studies, Washington, 1989—2002; asst. sec. for We. Hemisphere Affairs U.S. Dept. State, 2002—03; spl. envoy to Latin Amer., 2003—04. Ptnr. Brock Group, 1990-96; mem. alt. U.S. rep. UN Human Rights Commn., Geneva, 1991-92. Lt. U.S. Army, 1966-69. Decorated Order of Liberator grand cordon class (Venezuela); recipient Superior Honor award U.S. State Dept., 1986-89, 91, Exemplary Svc. award U.S. State Dept., 1988. Mem. Coun. Am. Ambs., Nat. Leadership Coun. (vice chmn.), Ctr. for Strategic and Internat. Studies.

**REICH, RICHARD ALLEN,** bank executive; b. Rhinelander, Wis., Mar. 12, 1962; s. John E. and Alma Louise (Post) R. BBA, U. Wis., 1984; MBA, NYU, 1989. CPA, Okla. Staff acct., cons. Deloitte, Haskins and Sells, NYC, 1984-86; fin. analyst Salomon Bros., Inc., NYC, 1986-89; treasury mgr. Citibank-US Card Products Group, NYC, 1989-92; with Bankers Trust Corp., NYC, 1992-93; v.p., dir. risk mgmt. Nikko Securities Internat., Inc., NYC, 1993-95, CDC Capital, Inc., NYC, 1995-99; dir. risk mgmt. and control OGE Energy Corp., Oklahoma City, 1999—2005; sr. v.p. corp. fin, BancFirst Corp, Oklahoma City, 2005—. investment mgr. Wis. Eastern Scholarship Fund, 1996-2001. Mem. AICPA, Okla. State Soc. CPA, Okla. Soc. Security Analysts, CFA Inst., U. Wis. Alumni Assn. NY (sec. 1989-91, v.p. 1991-92, pres. 1992-95). Avocations: golf, skiing. Home: 12300 E 2nd St Arcadia OK 73007-8103 Office: BancFirst Corp 101 N Broadway Ste 900 Oklahoma City OK 73102-8405 Office Phone: 405-218-4126. Personal E-mail: richard_a_reich@yahoo.com.

**REICH, ROBERT BERNARD,** political economics educator, former secretary of labor; b. Scranton, Pa., June 24, 1946; s. Edwin Saul and Mildred Dorf (Freshman) R.; m. Clare Dalton, July 7, 1973. BA, Dartmouth Coll., 1968, MA (hon.), 1988; MA, Oxford (Eng.) U., 1970; JD, Yale U., 1973. Asst. solicitor gen. U.S. Dept. Justice, Washington, 1974-76; dir. policy planning FTC, Washington, 1976-81; mem. faculty John F. Kennedy Sch. Govt. Harvard U., Cambridge, Mass., 1981-92; sec. U.S Dept. of Labor, Washington, 1993-97; Maurice B. Hexter prof. econ. and social policy Brandeis U. Heller Grad. Sch., 1997—; vis. prof. Goldman Sch. of Pub. Policy, U. Calif., Berkeley, 2004, 2005. Chmn. biotech. sect. U.S. Office Tech. Assessment, Washington, 1990-91. Author: The Next American Frontier, 1983, Tales of a New America, 1987, The Work of Nations, 1991, Locked in the Cabinet, 1997, The Future of Success, 2001, I'll Be Short: Essentials for a Decent Working Society, 2002, Reason: Why Liberals Will Win the Battle for America, 2004; co-author: The Power of Public Ideas, 1987; contbg. editor The New Republic, Washington, 1982-93; co-founder, nat. editor, chmn. editl. bd. The Am. Prospect, 1990—; playwright Public Exposure, 2005. Mem. governing bd. Common Cause, Washington, 1981-85; bd. dirs. Bus. Enterprise Trust, Palo Alto, Calif., 1989-93; trustee Dartmouth Coll., Hanover, N.H., 1989-93. Rhodes scholar, 1968; recipient Louis Brownlow award ASPA, 1983.

**REICH, ROBERT SIGMUND,** landscape architect; b. N.Y.C., Mar. 22, 1913; s. Ulysses S. and Adele G. R.; m. Helen Elizabeth Adams, May, 1945; children: Barbara, Betsy, Bob, Bill. BS, Cornell U., 1934, PhD, 1941; postgrad., U. So. Calif., 1951. Instr. landscape design Cornell U., 1936-39, 40-41; instr. landscape design U. Conn., 1939-40; Inst. Land Design La. State U., 1941-46, asst. prof. landscape architecture, 1946-49, asso. prof., 1949-60, prof., 1960—, Alumni prof., 1967—, head dept. landscape architecture,

1964-79, dir. Sch. Landscape Architecture, 1979-83; prof. Landscape Architecture, 1992—. Instr. Shrivenham (Eng.) Am. U., 1946, Biarritz (France) Am. U., 1947; vis. lectr. Tulane U., 1958-67; judge, instr. Nat. Council Garden Clubs, 1956—; mem. task force on parks, recreation and tourism Goals for La. Program; mem. com. to establish Chicot State Park Arboretum, Ville Plate, La., 1964, mem. steering com., 1964-75; examiner La. Bd. Examination for Landscape Architects, 1957-77 Co-author: Landscape and You, 1953. Mem. com. to establish Univ/Parish Beautification Commn., 1961-82; mem. area and facilities com. Baton Rouge Recreation and Pk. Commn., 1957-83; bd. dirs. Hubbard Edn. Trust, Weston, Mass., 1967—; adv. com. Friends of Frederick Law Olmsted Papers, 1983-95. With U.S. Army, 1942-45; in charge alter arrangements U. United Meth. Ch., 1945—. Recipient Tchg. award of merit Gamma Sigma Delta, 1963, Baton Rouge Green Individual Honor award, 1996. Fellow Am. Soc. Landscape Architects (trustee 1968-71, 83-86, 3d v.p. 1971-73, Medal 1992); mem. AIA (hon.), S.W. Park and Recreation Tng. Inst. (dir. 1975-77, award of merit 1968), Phi Kappa Phi, Pi Alpha xi, Omicron Delta Kappa, Sigma Lambda Alpha. Home: 333 E Boyd Dr Baton Rouge LA 70808-4507 Office: La State U Sch Landscape Architecture Coll Design Bldg Baton Rouge LA 70803-0001 E-mail: doc@reichassociates.net.

**REICH, STANLEY BENJAMIN,** radiologist, medical educator; b. NYC, Feb. 20, 1921; s. Harry Max Reich and Bessie Bangel; m. Adele Axelrod, Dec. 15, 1944; children: Linda, James, Judi. AB, Cornell U., 1941; MD, NYU, 1944. Diplomate Am. Bd. Radiology, Am. Bd. Nuclear Medicine. Intern Bellevue Hosp., N.Y.C., 1944-45, resident in radiology, 1946-49; asst. prof. NYU/Bellevue Hosp., N.Y.C., 1949-50; clin. prof. radiology U. Calif., San Francisco, 1952-72, 77—; prof. radiology U. Colo., Denver, 1972-77, U. Calif. Davis, Sacramento, 1977—; chief radiology No. Calif. VA Clinics, Martinez, 1979-84. Contbr. articles to profl. jours. Pres. Concordia-Argonaut Club, San Francisco, 1963-65; cons. Travis AFB, Fairfield, Calif., 1977—; Exec. Svc. Corps., San Francisco, 1997—. Lt. (sr.) USN, 1944-47, 50-52. Fellow Am. Coll. Radiology; mem. Am. Soc. Thoracic Radiology (sec. 1967), Am. Radium Soc. Avocations: travel, photography. Home: 2 Abbott Way Piedmont CA 94618-2610 Personal E-mail: asreich@att.net.

**REICH, STEVE,** composer; b. NYC, Oct. 3, 1936; m. Beryl Korot; children: Ezra, Michael. Studies in percussion with Roland Kohloff, 1950—53; BA in Philosophy with honors, Cornell U., 1957; studies in composition with Hall Overton, 1957—58; studies with Bergsma and Persichetti, Julliard Sch. Music, 1958—61; MA in Music, Mills Coll., 1963; studies in drumming, Inst. for African Studies, U. Ghana, 1970; student, Am. Soc. for Ea. Arts, Seattle and Berkeley, 1973—74, Cantillation of Hebrew Scriptures, N.Y.C. and Jerusalem, 1976—77; D (hon.), Calif. Inst. Arts, 2000. Organized ensemble Steve Reich and Musicians, 1966; performed throughout the world, 1971—; recs. with various cos. including Columbia Records, Deutsche Grammophon, Nonesuch, Disques Shandar, Hungaraton, Angel, ECM, Phillips, Virgin Classics, Argo. Regents lectr. U. Calif., Berkeley, 2000. Composer, performer: (albums) Come Out, 1967, It's Gonna Rain, 1969, Violin Phase, 1969, Four Organs, 1970, Phase Patterns, 1970, Drumming, 1971, Four Organs, 1973, Six Pianos, 1973, Music for Mallet Instruments, Voices, and Organ, 1973, Music for Eighteen Musicians, 1978 (Grammy award 1999), Octet, 1980, Music for a Large Ensemble, 1980,Tehillim, 1982, The Desert Music, 1984, Sextet, 1986, Six Marimbas, 1986, Electric Counterpoint, 1987, Different Trains, 1988 (Grammy award 1989), The Four Sections, 1987, The Cave, 1994, City Life, 1995, Proverb, 1996, Triple Quartet, 1999, Three Tales, 2002, others; recordings include (10 CD boxed set) Steve Reich Works: 1965-1995; composer: Vermont Counterpoint, Variations for Winds, Strings and Keyboards, Eight Lines for Chamber Orchestra, Piano Phase, Clapping Music, Pendulum Music, Music for Pieces of Wood, Nagoya Marimbas, other works performed by major orchs. and ensembles; commd. to compose for Holland Festival, 1978, Radio Frankfurt, 1979, San Francisco Symphony, 1980, Rothko Chapel, 1981, West German Radio, Cologne, 1984, Fromm Music Found., 1985, Richard Stoltzman, 1985, Bklyn. Acad. Music, 1987, Kronos Quartet, 1988, St. Louis Sympnony, 1987, (with Beryl Korot) The Cave video opera commd. by Vienna Festival, Holland Festival, Festival d'Automne à Paris, Theatre de la Monnaie, Brussels, Hebbel Theatre, Berlin, South Bank Centre/Serious Speakout, London and the Brooklyn Acad. Music, Next Wave Festival, 1993; 4-concert retrospective Lincoln Ctr. Festival, N.Y.C., 1999, video opera (with Beryl Korot) Three Tales, commd. by Vienna Festival, Barbican Ctr., London, SPoleto Festival, Bklyn. Acad. Music, Music Strassbourg, Hebbel Theater, Berlin. Recipient Kousseivitzky Found. award, 1981, 2002, Schuman prize Columbia U., 2000, Praemium Imperiale award (Music), Japan Art Assn., 2006; named Composer of Yr., Musical Am., 2000; Rockefeller Found. grantee 1975, 78, 81, 90, Nat. Endowment for the Arts grantee, 1974, 76, 91, N.Y. State Coun. on the Arts grantee, 1974; Guggenheim fellow, 1978, Montgomery fellow Dartmouth Coll., 2000; elected to Am. Acad. Arts and Letters, 1994, Bayerische Akademie der Schönen Künst, 1995; named Commr. dans l'Ordre des Arts et des Lettres, 1999. Office: c/o Boosey & Hawkes Inc 35 E 21st St New York NY 10010-6212

**REICH, WALTER,** psychiatrist, museum director, educator; b. Rzeszów, Poland, July 6, 1943; came to U.S., 1947; s. Simon and Anna (Nussbaum) R.; m. Tova Rachel Weiss, June 10, 1965; children: Daniel S., David E., Rebecca Z. AB, Columbia U., 1965; MD, NYU, 1970; cert. in Psychiatry, Yale U., 1975. Diplomate Am. Bd. Med. Examiners, Am. Bd. Psychiatry and Neurology. Fellow, asst. instr. psychiatry Yale U., New Haven, 1971-73, lectr., 1973—; assoc. rsch. psychiatrist NIMH, Bethesda, Md., 1973-75; psychiatrist The Pres.'s Biomed. Panel, Washington, 1975-76; dir. advanced studies NIMH, Rockville, Md., 1976-86, sr. rsch. psychiatrist, 1976-94; rsch. prof. psychiatry Uniformed Svcs. U. Health Scis., Bethesda, 1986-88, prof. psychiatry, 1988—; sr. rsch. assoc., then sr. scholar Woodrow Wilson Internat. Ctr. Scholars, Washington, 1988, dir. project on health, sci. and pub. policy, 1992-95; prof. psychiatry and behavioral scis. George Washington U., 1995—, Yitzhak Rabin Meml. Prof. of Internat. Affairs, Ethics and Human Behavior, 1998—. Dir. U.S. Holocaust Meml. Mus., Washington, 1995-98; chmn. program in med. and biolog. scis. Washington Sch. Psychiatry, 1975-85; rsch. assoc. Forum on Psychiatry and the Humanities. Author: A Stranger in My House: Jews and Arabs in the West Bank, 1984, author (with others) How to Beat Jet Lag, 1993; editor: Origins of Terrorism: Psychologies, Ideologies, Theologies, World Views; contbr. numerous articles to profl. jours. Nat. co-chmn. Com. Concerned Scientists, NYC, 1995—. Capt. USPHS, 1973-94. Kennan Inst. Advanced Russian Studies fellow, 1982-83; Lustman fellow Davenport Coll. Yale U., 1984, 91—; recipient Adminstr.'s award for meritorious achievement Alcohol, Drug Abuse, and Mental Health Adminstrn., 1978; David J. Fish meml. lectr. Brown U., 1984, Albert Kahn meml. lectr. Boston, U., Muriel Gardiner lectr. Yale U., 1994, Solomon A. Berson Medical Alumni Achievement award, 1994; decorated Order of Military Medical Merit U.S. Army, 1991, Outstanding Svc. medal, 1992, Holocaust Humanitarian award Holocaust Meml. Mus., 1999, AAAS award for Sci. Freedom and Responsibility, 2003, Human Rights Award Am. Psychiatric Assn., 2004. Fellow Am. Psychiat. Assn. (disting., com. human rights, task force on terrorism, Spl. Presidential Commendation 1998); mem. AMA, AAAS (com. sci. freedom and responsibility). Home: 200 Primrose St Chevy Chase MD 20815-3323 Office: Elliott Sch Internat Affairs Rm 501K Geo Wash Univ 1957 E Street NW Washington DC 20052 Office Phone: 202-994-5075. Business E-Mail: wreich@gwu.edu.

**REICHARD, GARY WARREN,** academic administrator, historian, educator; b. Phila., Nov. 23, 1943; s. David Carl and Gabrielle Rosalind (Doane) R.; m. Marcia Ann King, Aug. 7, 1965 (div. 1978); children: Jennifer D., James J. BA, Coll. of Wooster (Ohio), 1965; MA, Vanderbilt U., Nashville, 1966; postgrad., Ohio U., 1966-67; PhD, Cornell U., 1971. Instr. history Coll. of Wooster, 1967-69; asst. prof. to assoc. prof. history, chmn. dept. Ohio State U., Columbus, 1971-82; assoc. prof. history and dir. univ. honors program U. Del., Newark, 1983-85; assoc. vice chancellor for acad. affairs, assoc. prof. hist. U. Md. System, Adelphi, 1985-89; prof. history and dean undergrad. studies Fla. Atlantic U., Boca Raton, Fla., 1989-92, chmn. dept. history, 1992-94; assoc. vice pres. acad. affairs Calif. State U., Long Beach, 1994—2002, provost, sr. v.p. acad. affairs, 2002—06; exec. vice chancellor, chief acad. officer Calif. State U. System, 2006—. Assoc. editor Ency. of Am. Legislative System; reviewer numerous comml. and univ. presses; author: The Reaffirmation of Republicanism, 1975, Politics as Usual, 1988, 2d edit., 2004; co-author: America: Changing Times, 1979, 2d edit., 1982; co-editor: Reshaping America, 1982, American Choices, 1986, American Issues, 1988, 3d edit., 2002; contbr. articles to profl. jours. Moody rsch. grantee Lyndon B. Johnson found., 1977, Harry S. Truman Libr. Inst. rsch. grantee, 1979, Congl. Leadership rsch. grantee, 1981, Carl Albert Congl. rsch. grantee, 1993, Minn. Hist. Soc. grantee, 1993. Mem. AAUP, Am. Hist. Assn., So. Hist. Assn., Orgn. Am. Historians, Immigration Hist. Soc., Phi Beta Kappa, Phi Kappa Phi. Office: Calif State U Long Beach Office of Chancellor 401 Golden Shore Long Beach CA 90802 Office Phone: 562-951-4170. Business E-Mail: greichard@calstate.edu.

**REICHARD, ROBERT ROSS,** pathologist; b. Dec. 18, 1970; m. Kaari Reichard. MS, U. Louisville, 1991; MD, U. Louisville Sch. Medicine, 1998. Cert. Anatomic Pathology, Neuropathology. Resident, neuropathology U. Tex. Southwestern Health Sciences, Dallas, 1998—2002, intern, pathology, 1999; resident, anatomic pathology Stanford U., 2002—03; fellow, forensic pathology U. N.Mex., 2003—04, asst. prof. pathology, 2004—. Achievements include swimming the English Channel from England to France in 12 hours and 23 minutes on August 16, 2006. Office: Pathology Dept MSCOB 4640 1 University of New Mexico Albuquerque NM 87131*

**REICHARDT, PAUL BERNARD,** academic administrator, chemist, educator; b. St. Louis, Aug. 15, 1943; s. Bernard George and Elaine Charlotte (Schmudde) R.; m. Cordelia Morris (Hufnagel), Apr. 27, 1968; children: Laura, Rebecca, Daniel. BS, Davidson Coll., 1965; PhD in Organic chemistry, U. Wis., 1969. Post doctoral rsch. assoc. Yale U., New Haven, 1969-71, instr., 1971; asst. prof. Ohio State U., Columbus, 1971-72; asst. prof. chemistry U. Alaska, Fairbanks, 1972-75, assoc. prof. chemistry, 1975-81, prof. chemistry, 1981—, dean coll. natural sci., 1991-96, dean coll. sci., engring. and math., 1996-98, provost, 1998—. Head dept. chemistry, U. Alaska, Fairbanks, 1978-82, 88-90; interim dean coll. natural sci., 1990-91; interim provost, 1993-94; interim dir. U. Alaska Mus., 1992-93; NASCU commr. on colleges and universities, 2003-; mem. Gov. Sci. and Engring. Adv. Com., 1986-90; Alaska 2000 Sci. Standards Com., 1992-93. Contbg. articles to profl. jour.; chpts. to books and monographs. Named one of Outstanding Young Men of Am., Jaycees, 1980; recipient Inspirational Tchr. Award, U. Alaska, Fairbanks Alumni Assn., 1982. Mem. AAAS; Am. Chem. Soc.; Phi Beta Kappa; Sigma Xi (pres. local chpt. 1994-95); Phi Kappa Phi. Presbyterian. Avocations: fishing, camping, hiking. Office: U Alaska Office Provost Signers Hall Fairbanks AK 99775-7580 Office Phone: 907-474-7096. Business E-Mail: fnpbr@uaf.edu.

**REICHBACH, GUSTIN LEWIS,** state supreme court justice; b. Bklyn., Oct. 9, 1946; s. Herman and Lee (Klein) R.; m. Ellen Meyers, Oct. 24, 1984; 1 child, Hope Isadora. BA in Polit. Sci. with high honors (hon.), SUNY, Buffalo, 1967; JD, Columbia U., 1970. Bar: N.Y. 1972, U.S. Dist. Ct. (ea. and so. dists.) N.Y. 1972, Calif. 1975, U.S. Dist. Ct. (ea. and no. dists.) Calif. 1975, U.S. Supreme Ct. 1984. Pvt. practice, NY, 1972-92; Calif., 1975-90; judge Civil Ct. City of N.Y., Bklyn., 1991-98; justice Supreme Ct. N.Y. Bklyn., 1998—; internat. judge UN Interim Mission in Kosovo, 2003; permanent internat. judge Supreme Ct. of Kosovo, 2003—04. Counsel to commr. Calif. Agrl. Labor Rels. Bd., Sacramento, 1975-76. Co-author: The Bust Book, 1970, (Grove Press, NY); Litigating Electronic Surveillance Claims in Criminal Cases, 1977. (Lakes Law Books, S.F.) Recipient David Michael award N.Y. State Bar Assn., 1992. Mem. Phi Beta Kappa. Office: Supreme Ct State NY 320 Jay St Brooklyn NY 11201 Office Phone: 347-295-1845. E-mail: greichba@courts.state.ny.us.

**REICHBLUM, AUDREY ROSENTHAL,** public relations executive, publishing executive; b. Pitts., June 28, 1935; d. Emanuel Nathan and Willa (Handmacher) Rosenthal; m. M. Charles Reichblum, Jan. 25, 1956; children: Robert Nathan, William Mark. Student, Bennington Coll., 1952-53; BS, Carnegie Mellon U., 1956. Founder, creator, chmn. Pitts. Children's Mus., 1970-73; mag. writer Pitts. Mag., 1978; dir. pub. rels. Pitts. Pub. Theater, 1978-79; pres. arPR audrey reichblum PUB. RELS. inc., Pitts., 1980—, arpr, inc., 1996—; pub. "Knowledge in a Nutshell" Series, 1996—99, "The Edible Game A Smart Cookie", 1996—, "Sweet Smarts The Candy With A Brain", 2004, Pub. rels. cons., bd. mem. Pitts. Planned Parenthood, 1980-84, United Jewish Fedn., Bus. and Profl. Women, Pitts., 1980-85, Pitts. City Theater, 1985-94, Pa. Coun. on Aging, 1996—; chmn. Villa de Marillac Nursing, 1999, Vincencian Collaborative Svcs. Bd.; syndicator The Dr. Knowledge Show. Recipient Gold Cindy award Info. Film Producers Am., 1982, award of excellence Internat. Assn. Bus. Communicators, Pitts., 1986, Matrix award for Three Rivers Arts Festival, Lifetime Achievement award NAWBO-YWCA, Y-Tribute to Women in Comms. award, 1998. Mem. Pub. Rels. Soc. Am. (accredited; award of merit 1983, G. Victor Barkman award for excellence 1984, 1st place award Race For The Cure), Women in Comm. (Matrix-sales promotion award 1987), Nat. Assn. Women Bus. Owners (Life Time Achievement award 1995). Office: 1420 Centre Ave Ste 2213 Pittsburgh PA 15219-3536

**REICHE, FRANK PERLEY,** lawyer, former federal commissioner; b. Hartford, Conn., May 8, 1929; s. Karl Augustus and LaFetra (Perley) R.; m. Janet Taylor, Sept. 26, 1953; children: Cynthia Reiche Schumacker, Dean S. AB, Williams Coll., 1951; LLB, Columbia U., 1959; MA, George Washington U., 1959; LLM in Taxation, NYU, 1966. Bar: N.J. 1960, D.C. 1981. Assoc. Stryker, Tams & Dill, Newark, 1959-61, Smith, Stratton, Wise & Heher, Princeton, NJ, 1962-64, ptnr., 1964-79; commr. Fed. Election Commn., Washington, 1979-85. chmn., 1982; ptnr. Kazenbach, Gildea & Rudner, Lawrenceville, NJ, 1986-93; pvt. practice law Princeton, 1993-97; of counsel Schragger, Lavine & Nagy, West Trenton, NJ, 1997-2000, Archer & Greiner, Princeton, 2001—. Trustee Westminster Choir Coll., Princeton, 1974-86, Ctr. Theol. Inquiry, Princeton, 1991-97, Wells Coll., Aurora, N.Y., 1994-2003; mem. planned giving com. Williams Coll., Williamstown, Mass., 1973-87, nat. chmn. planned giving, 1983-87; dir., Ctr. Responsive Politics, Washington, 2002—. Lt. USN, 1952-56. Mem. ABA, D.C. Bar Assn., N.J. Bar Assn., Am. Coll. Trust and Estate Counsel (N.J. state chair 1995-2000, bd. regents 2001—). Clubs: Washington Golf and Country, Capitol Hill. Republican. Presbyterian.

**REICHEK, MORTON ARTHUR,** retired magazine editor, writer; b. N.Y.C., Nov. 2, 1924; s. Meyer and Katherine (Rabinowitz) R.; m. Sybil Green, June 13, 1953; children: Amy, Marjorie (dec.), James. BS, NYU, 1948; postgrad., Am. U., 1948-50. Press officer, editor U.S. Fish & Wildlife Svc., Washington, 1948-49, U.S. Br. Labor Statistics, Washington, 1949-51, U.S. Nat. Prodn. Authority, Washington, 1951-52; Washington corr. McGraw-Hill Publs., 1952-63, Newhouse Newspapers, 1963-65; assoc. editor Forbes, N.Y.C., 1965-66, Bus. Week, N.Y.C., 1966-76, sr. editor, writer, 1978—89; dir. editl. svcs. Gulf & Western. Industries, Inc., N.Y.C., 1976-78. U.S. rep. NATO journalist program US Dept. State, France, 1957; adj. lectr. Columbia U. Graduate Sch. Journalism, N.Y.C., 1981. Contbr. articles to N.Y. Times Mag., New Republic, others. Staff sgt. U.S. Army, 1943-46, China-Burma-India. Journalist fellow Carnegie-Mellon U. Grad. Sch. Indsl. Adminstrn., 1979; grantee NEH, 1980. Avocations: computers, music. Home: 1 Worchester Dr Concordia Monroe Township NJ 08831-4723 Home (Winter): The Cascades 6975 Lismore Ave Boynton Beach FL 33437-6441 E-mail: iankev@att.net.

**REICHEL, WALTER EMIL,** advertising executive; b. Irvington, N.J., Dec. 12, 1935; s. Walter Edwin and Flora Mania (Pfister) R.; m. Priscilla Tedesco, Feb. 1, 1969; 1 son, Bradley Joseph. BA, Columbia U., 1959; MA., NYU, 1971, M Philosophy, 1989, postgrad., 1989—. With Benton & Bowles, N.Y.C., 1959-67 v.p., 1965-67, asso. media dir., 1965-67; with Ted Bates & Co., Inc. N.Y.C., 1967-87; sr. v.p. Ted Bates & Co., Inc., N.Y.C., 1973-82, exec. dir. media and programs, 1974-82, exec. v.p., 1982-87, dir.; cons.

---

1987-91; mng. ptnr. A.S. Link Inc., N.Y.C., 1991-2000; sr. v.p., dir. client svcs. KSL Media, 2000—01; prof. advt. and comm. Fashion Inst. of Tech., 2002—. Home and Office: 449 1/2 Henry St Brooklyn NY 11231-3011 E-mail: aslreichel@aol.com.

**REICHENBACH, LINDA LOUISE,** mathematician, educator, language educator; b. Joliet, Ill., Dec. 3, 1946; d. Frank James and Mary Lavonne Kachelhoffer; m. Michael Joseph Reichenbach, July 19, 1969; children: Heidi Marie, Brian Joseph. BS in Math. with honors, Ill. State U., 1968; MS with honors, U. St. Francis, Joliet, Ill., 1997. Tchr. math Joliet Cath. Acad., Ill.; tchr. math. Lockport Twp. H.S., Ill.; tchr. math Oswego Cmty. H.S., Ill.; chair dept. math. Aurora Ctrl. Cath. H.S., Ill.; ret., 2006. Inclusive tchr. REI Level One Tng., Ill., 1997—98; dir. program for acad. excellence Aurora Ctrl. Cath. H.S., Ill.; mem. Diocesan-wide math. assessment com. Joliet Diocese, Ill.; local, regional and state sci. fair judge, Ill., 1988—2005. Mem. Cantigny VFW Ladies Aux., 1968—, Trailways Coun., Ill. Girl Scouts Am. Named Tchr. of Yr., Aurora Ctrl. Cath. H.S., 2002; recipient Nat. Appreciation award for svc., Girl Scouts of Am. Mem.: Math. Assn. Am., Nat. Cath. Educators Assn., Ill. Coun. Tchrs. Math., Nat. Coun. Tchrs. Math., ASCD. Avocations: writing, antique cars, gardening, sewing, art. Home: 219 N Willow Dr E Plainfield IL 60544*

**REICHERT, CHRISTINE EDWARDS,** academic administrator; b. St. Joseph, Mich., May 25, 1949; d. Jerome Calvin Patterson and Jane Edna Wohl; children: Jennifer Elizabeth, Rachel Ariana. Degree in English lit., Baldwin-Wallace Coll., 1985, U. Toledo, 1998. Bureau chief The Morning Journal, Lorain, Ohio, 1987—99, regional editor, 1988—89, reporter, 1985—87; instr. U. Toledo, Monroe County, Toledo, 1997—99; dir. acad. svcs. Lourdes Coll., Sylvania, Ohio, 1999—, dir. of retention, 2004—05. Parlimentary Lourdes Coll., Sylvania, Ohio, 2002—05; chair Policy and Procedure Ctr., Sylvania, Ohio, 2003—05. Contbr. articles to profl. jours. Recipient Outstanding Tchg. award, U. Toledo, 1998. Mem.: AAUW, Nat. Coll. Learning Ctr. Assn., Coll. Reading Learning Assn., Nat. Tutoring Assn., Modern Lang. Assn. Avocations: art, music, theater, reading. Office: Lourdes Coll 6832 Convent Blvd Toledo OH 43615 Office Phone: 419-824-3759. Business E-Mail: creichert@lourdes.edu.

**REICHERT, DAVID,** lawyer; b. Cin., Nov. 23, 1929; s. Victor E. and Louise F. Reichert; m. Marilyn Frankel, May 31, 1959; children— James G., Steven F., William M. B.A, Bowling Green State U., 1951; JD, U. Cin., 1954. Bar: Ohio 1954, U.S. Supreme Ct. 1963. Ptnr. firm Porter, Wright, Morris & Arthur, formerly sr. ptnr. Reichert, Strauss & Reed and predecessors, Cin. Dir. numerous corps. Monthly columnist: Scrap Age mag., 1966-74; bd. editors: U. Cin. Law Rev, 1953-54. Pres. brotherhood Rockdale Temple, Cin., 1960-61, temple treas., 1973-75, v.p., 1975-79, pres., 1979-81; mem. Amberley Village Planning Commn. & Zoning Bd. Appeals, 1972-79, Ohio Solid Waste Adv. Group, 1974; treas. Contemporary Arts Ctr., Cin., 1973-75, pres., 1976-77, trustee, 1982-88; trustee Cin. Art Mus., 1978-93, v.p., 1992-93, chmn. vis. com. for contemporary art, 1990-92; trustee Jewish Publ. Soc., 1980-86, Cin. Sculpture Coun., 1984-87; mem. acquisitions com. Miami U. Art Mus., 1982-85. Mem. Cin. Print and Drawing Cir. (pres. 1974-76), The Literary Club (sec. 1988-91, v.p. 1991-92, pres. 1992-93), Losantiville Country Club (bd. govs. 1985-92, sec. 1986-90, pres. 1990-92), ISRI 20th Century Club (hon. 1998), Omicron Delta Kappa, Sigma Tau Delta, Phi Delta Phi, Zeta Beta Tau. Office: Porter Wright Morris & Arthur 250 E 5th St Ste 2200 Cincinnati OH 45202-5118

**REICHERT, DAVID G. (DAVE REICHERT),** congressman; b. Detroit Lakes, Minn., Aug. 29, 1950; m. Julie Reichert; 3 children. AA, Concordia Lutheran Coll., Portland, Oreg., 1970. Police officer Sheriff's Office King County, Wash., 1972—97, sheriff Wash., 1997—2004; mem. US Congress from 8th Wash. dist., 2005—, mem. sci. com., mem. transp. and infrastructure com., vice chmn. Coast Guard and maritime transp. subcommittee, mem. homeland security com., chmn. emergency preparedness, sci. and tech. Author: Chasing the Devil: My Twenty Year Quest to Capture the Green River Killer, 2004. Co-chmn. Wash. State Partners in Crisis; mem. adv. bd. Criminal Justice Coun., King County, Wash., Domestic Violence Coun., King County, Wash. Served in Res. USAF, 1971—76, served in USAF, 1976. Named Sheriff of Yr., Nat. Sheriffs Assn., 2004; recipient Champion of Freedom award, Wash. Policy Ctr., 2 Medal of Valor awards, King County, Wash. Sheriff's Office. Mem.: Wash. Assn. Sheriffs & Police Chiefs (mem. exec. bd.), Wash. State Sheriffs Assn. (past pres.). Republican. Lutheran. Office: US Ho Reps 1223 Longworth Ho Office Bldg Washington DC 20515-4708 Office Phone: 202-225-7761.*

**REICHERT, LEO EDMUND, JR.,** biochemist, department chairman, endocrinologist; b. N.Y.C., Jan. 9, 1932; s. Leo and Anne (Holsten) R.; m. Gerda Sihler, July 20, 1957; children: Leo, Christine, Linda, Andrew. BS, Manhattan Coll., N.Y.C., 1955; PhD, Loyola U., Chgo., 1960. Asst. prof. biochemistry Emory U. Med. Sch., Atlanta, 1960-66, assoc. prof., 1966-72, prof., 1972-79; prof., chmn. dept. biochemistry Albany (N.Y.) Med. Coll., 1979-88, prof. biochemistry and molecular biology, 1988-99; dir. Tucker Endocrine Rsch. Inst., LLC, Atlanta, 2000—. Dir. human and animal hormone isolation lab. (NIH), Emory U. Med. Sch., 1960-75; mem. med. adv. bd. Nat. Pituitary Agy., 1971-74; com. on glycoprotein hormones Nat. Hormone and Pituitary Program, 1968-86; mem. reproductive biology study sect. NIH, 1971-75; mem. adv. panel on cellular physiology NSF, 1983-86, divsn. of integrative and neuro biology, 1992; mem. WHO Expert Adv. Panel on Biol. Standardization, 1984—, Nat. Bd. Med. Examiners, Part I, 1989-91. *Dr. Reichert developed methods for purification of a variety of hormones from human pituitary glands. This made possible use of these hormones in treatment of clinical problems related to human growth and fertility. His studies also facilitated development of techniques for quantitative measurement of pituitary hormones in trace amounts in human blood, an analysis basic to diagnosis in most areas of contemporary clinical endocrinology. Related studies with farm animal pituitary glands contributed significantly to improved fertility and growth of such commercially important food species as cow, sheep, and pig. Students and Fellows trained by Dr. Reichert have achieved prominent positions in academics, industry, and clinical teaching and research.* Mem. editl. bd. Endocrinology, 1967-75, Molecular and Cellular Endocrinology, 1977-83, 90-94, Biology of Reproduction, 1968-70, 86-90, Andrology, 1983-86, Molecular Andrology, 1989-99; contbr. more than 275 articles to profl. jours.; patentee in field. With USMC, 1949—52. Listed among 75 endocrinologists, 1000 scientists most cited, 1965-78. Mem.: Soc. for Study of Reprodn., Andrology Soc. (coun. 1983—87), Endocrine Soc. (ethics adv. com. 2000—01, Ayerst award 1970), Am. Soc. Biol. Chemists. Home: 1974 Mountain Creek Dr Stone Mountain GA 30087-1018 Office Phone: 770-491-8436. Personal E-mail: lerjr@aol.com.

**REICHERTZ, PETER STUART,** lawyer; b. Dallas, Sept. 28, 1950; s. Paul Peter and Clara Stuart (Robinson) Reichertz. AB, Brown U., 1972; JD with honors, George Washington U., 1975. Bar: DC 1976, U.S. Supreme Ct. 1984. Atty. US Rlwy. Assn., Washington, 1975-78; assoc. McMurray & Pendergast, Washington, 1978-79, Hamel, Park, McCabe & Saunders, Washington, 1979-81, ptnr., 1981-83, McMurray & Pendergast, 1983; assoc. Arent Fox Kintner Plotkin & Kahn, Washington, 1983-86, ptnr., 1987—2002, Sonnenschein Nath & Rosenthal LLP, Washington, 2002—, head food and drug law group, 2002—. Mem.: ABA, Internat. Trademark Assn., Fed. Cir. Bar Assn. Office: Sonnenschein Nath & Rosenthal LLP Ste 600, E Tower 1301 K St NW Washington DC 20005 Office Phone: 202-408-9222. Office Fax: 202-408-6399. Business E-Mail: preichertz@sonnenschein.com.

**REICHGOTT, MICHAEL JOEL,** medical educator, dean, physician; b. Newark, July 26, 1940; s. Leo and Gertrude (Millman) R.; m. Lynn Gay Haar, Dec. 22, 1962; children: Jay Howard, Seth Alan, Douglas Jordan. AB, Gettysburg (Pa.) Coll., 1961; MD, Albert Einstein Coll. Medicine, 1965; PhD, U. Calif., San Francisco, 1973. Diplomate Am. Bd. Internal Medicine. Fellow in clin. pharmacology U. Calif., 1969-72; asst. prof. medicine U. Pa., Phila., 1973-81, assoc. prof., 1981-84, Albert Einstein Coll. Medicine, Bronx, N.Y., 1984-94, prof., 1994—, assoc. dean of students and grad. med. edn., 1989-99,

---

assoc. dean clin. affairs and grad. med. edn., 1999—; med. dir. Bronx Mcpl. Hosp. Ctr., 1984-89. Mem. Liaison Com. on Med. Edn., 2002—; presenter in field. Contbr. articles to profl. jours. V.p. Larchmont (N.Y.) Temple, 1990-92, pres., 1992-94. Maj. M.C., U.S. Army, 1967-69, Vietnam. Fellow ACP (com.); mem. Assn. Am. Med. Colls. (com. 1990—), N.Y. Acad. Medicine, Phila. Acad. Medicine, Soc. for Gen. Internal Medicine (com.). Avocations: camping, gardening, print collector. Office: Albert Einstein Coll of Medicine 1300 Morris Park Ave Bronx NY 10461-1926

**REICHGOTT JUNGE, EMBER DARLENE,** retired senator, lawyer, writer, broadcast commentator, radio personality; b. Detroit, Aug. 22, 1953; d. Norbert Arnold and Diane (Pinrich) Reichgott; m. Michael Junge. BA summa cum laude, St. Olaf Coll., Minn., 1974; JD, Duke U., 1977; MBA, U. St. Thomas, 1991. Bar: Minn. 1977, D.C. 1978. Assoc. Larkin, Hoffman, Daly & Lindgren, Bloomington, Minn., 1977-84; counsel Control Data Corp., Bloomington, Minn., 1984-86; ptnr. The Gen. Counsel, Ltd., 1987—; mem. Minn. State Senate, 1983-2000, chmn. legis. com. on econ. status of women, 1984-86, vice chmn. senate edn. com., 1987-88, senate majority whip, 1990-94, chmn. property tax divsn. senate tax com., 1991-92, chmn. senate judiciary com., 1993-94, senate asst. majority leader, 1995-2000, chmn. spl. subcom. on ethical conduct. Dem. endorsed candidate Minn. Atty. Gen., 1998; instr. polit. sci. St. Olaf Coll., Northfield, Minn., 1993; bd. dirs. Citizens Ind. Bank, St. Louis Park, Minn. Host cable TV monthly series Legis. Report, 1985-92. State co-chair Clinton/Gore Presdl. Campaign, Minn. Dem. Farmer-Labor Party, 1992, 1996; del. Nat. Dem. Conv., 1984, 1992, 1996; pres. Minn. Women's Polit. Caucus, 2002—04; trustee, bd. dirs. N.W. YMCA, New Hope, Minn., 1983—88, United Way Mpls., 1989—, Greater Mpls. ARC, 1988—2004, chair, 2001—03. Recipient Woman of Yr. award North Hennepin Bus. and Profl. Women, 1983, award for contbn. to human svcs. Minn. Social Svcs. Assn., 1983, Clean Air award Minn. Lung Assn., 1988, Disting. Svc. award Mpls. Jaycees, 1984, Minn. Dept. Human Rights award, 1989, Myra Bradwell award Minn. Women Lawyers, 1993, Disting. Alumnae award Lake Conf. Schs., 1993, Disting. Alumnae award St. Olaf Coll., 1998, awards for leadership Am. Lung Assn., 1999, Am. Heart Assn., 1997, Everyday Hero award Up with People, 1995, Unsung Hero award United Way of Mpls., 1999, 1st recipient of award named in her honor for prevention of sexual assault, 2000; charter inductee Robbinsdale H.S. Hall of Fame, 2000; author of Minn. charter sch. law, winner of "2000 Innovations in Am. Govt. award" Harvard U. and Ford Found., others; named One of ten Outstanding Young Minnesotans, Minn. Jaycees, 1984, Policy Adv. of Yr., NAWBO, 1988, Woman of Achievement, Twin West C. of C., 1989, Marvelous Minn. Woman, 1993; youngest woman ever elected to Minn. Senate, 1983. Mem. Minn. Bar Assn. (bd. govs. 1992-96, Pro Bono Publico Atty. award 1990), Hennepin County Bar Assn., Corp. Counsel Assn. (v.p. 1989-96). Home: 7701 48th Ave N Minneapolis MN 55428-4515 Home Fax: 763-536-1447. Personal E-mail: emberrj@visi.com.

**REICHL, RUTH MOLLY,** editor-in-chief; b. NYC, Jan. 16, 1948; d. Ernst and Miriam and (Brudno) R.; m. Douglas Wilder Hollis, Sept. 5, 1970 (div. 1985); m. Michael Singer, 1985; 1 child, Nicholas Singer. BA, U. Mich., 1968, MA in history of art, 1970. Chef, co-owner The Swallow Restaurant, Berkeley, Calif., 1974—77; food writer, editor New West mag., San Francisco, 1977—84; editor restaurant column LA Times, 1984-93, food editor, 1990-93; restaurant critic NY Times, 1993-99; editor-in-chief Gourmet Mag., 1999—. Lectr. in field. Author: Mmmm: A Feastiary, 1972, The Contest Book, 1977, Tender at the Bone: Growing Up at the Table, 1998, Comfort Me with Apples: More Adventures at the Table, 2001; editor: Modern Library Food Series, 2000—, Endless Feasts: Sixty Years of Writing from Gourmet, 2002, Remembrance of Things Paris, 2004, The Gourmet Cookbook, 2004, Garlic and Sapphires, 2005, Tanner Lectures on Human Values, 2005. Recipient James Beard Award for journalism, 1994, James Beard Award for restaurant criticism, 1996, 1998. Office: 4 Times Sq New York NY 10036-6518 Business E-Mail: ruth.reichl@gourmet.com.

**REICHLEY, A. JAMES,** political scientist; b. St. Clair, Pa., Mar. 3, 1929; s. Grant G. and Mary (Thompson) R.; m. Mary Donohue, Apr. 15, 1961; children: Douglas G., Richard J., Susan M. BA, U. Pa., 1950; MA, Harvard U., 1956. Reporter Pottsville (Pa.) Republican, 1951-61; legis. asst. Senator Kenneth Keating, Washington, 1961-62; legis. sec. Gov. William Scranton, Harrisburg, Pa., 1962-67; polit. editor Fortune, N.Y.C., 1967-76; spl. asst. Pres. Gerald Ford, Washington, 1976; sr. fellow Brookings Instn., Washington, 1977-91, Georgetown U., Washington, 1992—2003. Author: Conservatives in an Age of Change, 1981, Religion in American Public Life, 1985 (Benchmark award 1986), The Life of the Parties, 1992, rev. edit., 2000, The Values Connection, 2001, Faith in Politics, 2002; others; editor: Elections American Style, 1987; contbr. articles to profl. jours. Served with U.S. Army, 1951-53. Congl. fellow, 1959. Mem. Am. Polit. Sci. Assn., Cosmos Club. Republican. Presbyterian. Home: 11912 Gregerscroft Rd Potomac MD 20854-2145 E-mail: j.reichley@worldnet.att.net.

**REICHLIN, SEYMOUR,** endocrinologist, educator; b. N.Y.C., May 31, 1924; s. Henry and Celia (Rosen) R.; m. Elinor Thurman Dameshek, June 24, 1951; children: Seth David, Douglas James, Ann Elise. Student, CCNY, 1940-41; AB, Antioch Coll., 1945; MD, Washington U., St. Louis, 1948; PhD, U. London, 1954. Intern N.Y. Hosp., 1948-49; asst. resident Barnes Hosp., St. Louis, 1949-50, N.Y. Hosp., 1950-51; chief resident Barnes Hosp., 1951-52; research fellow physiology dept. Maudsley Hosp., London, Eng., 1952-54; instr. psychiatry Washington U., 1954-55, asst. prof. psychiatry and medicine, 1955-60; assoc. prof. medicine U. Rochester, 1960-66, prof., 1966-69; prof., head dept. med. and pediatric spltys. Sch. Medicine U. Conn., 1969-71, prof., head dept. physiology, 1971-72; prof. medicine Tufts U., 1972-97, prof. emeritus, 1997—; rsch. prof. U. Ariz., 1994-2003. Sr. physician New Eng. Med. Ctr., 1972-93, sr. endocrinologist, 1993-96; mem. endocrinology study sect. NIH, 1966-70; mem. adv. panel FDA, 1977-79; mem. coun. Nat. Inst. Kidney, Diabetes, Digestive Diseases, 1987-90. Mem. editl. bd. Endocrinology, 1969-74, New Eng. Jour. Medicine, 1976-79, Jour. Psychoneuroendocrinology, 1979-83, Brain, Behavior and Immunity, 1990—; contbr. articles to profl. jours., also monographs. Bd. dirs. Founds. Fund, New Haven, 1968-70; med. adv. bd. Med. Found., Boston, adv. bd. MacArthur Found., 1988. Served with AUS, 1943-44. Commonwealth Fund fellow, 1952-54, Lowell M. Palmer fellow, 1954-56. Master ACP-Am. Soc. Internal Medicine (award 2002); fellow AAAS, Am. Acad. Arts and Scis.; mem. Ctrl. Soc. Clin. Rsch., Am. Soc. Clin. Investigation, Assn. Am. Physicians, Am. Physiol. Soc., Endocrine Soc. (Eli Lilly award 1972, Disting. Leadership awrad 1986, pres. 1975-76), Brit. Soc. Endocrinology, Am. Psychosomatic Soc., Am. Thyroid Assn., Internat. Brain Orgn., Assn. for Rsch. in Nervous and Mental Disease (pres. 1976), Pituitary Soc. (pres. 1994-95), Sigma Xi, Alpha Omega Alpha. Home: X-9 Ranch 6480 South Upper Valley Rd Vail AZ 85641 E-mail: reichlin@dakotacom.net.

**REICHMAN, JOEL H.,** retail executive; With The GAP, San Francisco, 1971-76, Slak Shak Inc., Boston, 1971-76, Designs, Inc., 1976—, exec. v.p., 1985-93, dir., 1987, pres., COO Chestnut Hill, Mass., 1993-94; pres., CEO, 1994—. Home: Designs Inc 555 Turnpike St Canton MA 02021-2724

**REICHMAN, LEE BRODERSOHN,** physician; b. NYC, June 25, 1938; s. Theodore and Elinore (Brodersohn) R.; m. Rose Ehrinpreis, Oct. 9, 1965; children: Daniel Mark, Deborah Gar. AB, Oberlin Coll., Ohio, 1960; MD, NYU, 1964; MPH, Johns Hopkins U., Balt., 1971. Intern Bellevue Hosp., I Med. Divsn., N.Y.C., 1964-65, resident, 1967-68; Harlem Hosp. Ctr., N.Y.C., 1968-69, fellow in pulmonary medicine, 1969-70; dir. Bur. Tb, Bur. Chronic Disease, N.Y.C. Health Dept., 1971-73, asst. commr. health, 1973-74; assoc. prof. medicine U. Medicine and Dentistry N.J. Med. Sch., Newark, 1974-78; prof. medicine N.J. Med. Sch., Newark, 1978—, prof. preventive medicine, cmty. health, 1993—; dir. pulmonary div. U. Medicine and Dentistry N.J.-N.J. Med. Sch. Univ. Hosp., 1974-92; founding exec. dir. N.J. Med. Sch. Nat. Tb Ctr., 1993—2006, N.J. Med. Sch. Global Tubercular Inst., 2006—. Cons. CDC, Atlanta, 1970—; prin. investigator pulmonary complications of HIV infection NHLBI, 1987—95; prin. investigator Model Tb Ctr. CDC, 1993—2003, prin. investigator Nat. Tb Trials Consortium, 1994—99, adv.

coun. for elimination of Tb, 2002—; prin. investigator Regional Tng. & Med. Conv. Ctr. CDC, 2003—. Editor: Tuberculosis-A Comprehensive International Approach, 2d edit., 2000; author: Timebomb-The Global Epidemic of Multi-Drug Resistant Tuberculosis, 2002; contbr. articles to profl. jours. Bd. dirs. Art Ctr. No. N.J., 1979-86; chmn. N.J. Commn. on Smoking of Health, 1986-87; mem. N.J. TB Adv. Coun., 1976—, chmn. 1991—; chair Nat. Coalition for Elimination of Tb, 1992—2004; mem. N.J. Clean Air Coun., 1987. With USPHS, 1965-67. Recipient Nat. Heart Lung and Blood Inst., Pulmonary Acad. career award, 1975-80, Preventive Pulmonary Acad. career award, 1987-92, Tb Acad. career award, 1993—98, 1st prize trade category Am. Med. Writers Assn., 2002, Solomon A. Berson Med. Alumni Achievement award NYU, 2003. Fellow ACP, Am. Coll. Chest Physicians (gov. 1984-90, pres. N.J. chpt. 1982-84, Simon Rodbard Meml. lectr. 2000); mem. Am. Thoracic Soc. (hon. life), Internat. Union Against Tb and Lung Disease (exec. com. 1982-92, vice chair exec. com. 1989-91, N.Am. Region Disting. Svc. award 2001), Am. Lung Assn. (hon. life, nat. bd. dirs. 1980-94, pres. elect 1991-92, pres. 1992-93, past pres. 1993-94, Will Ross medalist 1999), N.J. Thoracic Soc. (pres. 1982-84), Am. Lung Assn. N.J. (hon. life, bd. dirs. 1976—86, pres. 1984-86), Global Alliance for Tb Drug Devel. (pres.) Office: PO Box 1709 225 Warren St Newark NJ 07101-1709 Office Phone: 973-972-3270. E-mail: reichmlb@umdnj.edu.

**REICHMANIS, ELSA,** chemist; b. Melbourne, Victoria, Australia, Dec. 9, 1953; arrived in U.S., 1962; d. Peteris and Nina (Meiers) R.; m. Francis Joseph Purcell, June 2, 1979; children: Patrick William, Elizabeth Anne, Edward Andrew, Thomas Alexander. BS in Chemistry, Syracuse U., 1972, PhD in Chemistry, 1975. Postdoctoral intern Syracuse (N.Y.) U., 1975-76, Chaim Weizmann rsch. fellow, 1976-78; mem. tech. staff AT&T Bell Labs., Murray Hill, NJ, 1978-84, supr. radiation sensitive materials and applications, 1984-94, head organic and polymer materials, 1994-95; head polymer and organic materials Lucent Techs., Bell Labs., New Providence, NJ, 1996—2000, dir. materials rsch., 2001—. Panel on advanced materials. Japanese Tech. Evaluation Prog., NSF, Washington, 1986, com. to survey materials. rsch. opportunities and needs for electronic industry Nat. Rsch. Coun., 1986, Nat. Materials Adv. Bd., 1993-98, U.S. Nat. Com. for Internat. Union for Pure and Applied Chemistry, 1996-2001. Editor: The Effects of Radiation on High Tech Polymers, 1989, Polymers in Microlithography, 1989, Irradiation of Polymer Materials, 1993, Microelectronics Technology: Polymers for Advanced Imaging and Packaging, 1995, Micro and Nano Patterning Polymers, 1998; patentee in field; assoc. editor Chemistry of Materials, 1996—; contbr. numerous articles to profl. jours. Recipient Soc. Women Engrs. Achievement award, 1993, Engring. Materials award ASM, 1996, Arents Pioneer medal Syracuse U., 2001. Fellow: AAAS; mem.: IEEE, Soc. Women Engrs., Am. Phys. Soc., Soc. for Photo-optical Instrs., Soc. Chem. Industry (Perkin medal 2001), Am. Chem. Soc. (mem.-at-large 1986—90, sec. 1991—92, polymer materials sci. and engring. divsn. 1991—, vice chair 1993, chair-elect 1994, chmn. 1995, pres.-elect 2002, pres. 2003, award in applied polymer sci. 1999), Nat. Acad. Engring. (elected mem.). Avocations: music, reading, needlepoint.

**REICHMANN, PÉTER IVÁN,** mathematics professor; b. Budapest, Hungary, Feb. 10, 1942; came to U.S., 1959; s. Rezső Rudolf and Margit (Grünberger) R. BSEE, Ill. Inst. Tech., 1967, MS in Math., 1973, PhD in Math., 1986; BFA in Visual Comm. cum laude, Am. Internat. U. Online, 2006. Elec. engr. Zenith Military and Motorola Comm. and Govt. divsns., various cities, 1967—69; instr. math. and elec. engring. depts. Chgo. Tech. Coll., 1973—74; asst. prof. of math. Cath. U. Am., Washington, 1987—89; ind. distbr. Brain Garden Co., American Fork, Utah, 2001—; instr. math. Star Sch. Technol. U., Laguna, N.Mex., 2004—; chief mathematician Psitronics Group Sys. Internat., 2002—. Grantee NASA, 1982. Achievements include research on the introduction of a novel geometry for individual cell for negative Poisson's ratio foam and computing its volume. Home and Office: 1305 Coloma Way Roseville CA 95661-4604 E-mail: pireichmann@hotmail.com, pireichmann@msn.com.

**REICHS, KERRY E.,** lawyer; b. Bethesda, Md., Nov. 17, 1970; BA, Oberlin Coll., 1993; MA in Pub. Policy, Duke U., 2000, JD, 2000. Bar: DC, NC. Assoc. Arent Fox Kintner Plotkin & Kahn PLLC, Washington, Sonnenschein Nath & Rosenthal LLP, Washington. Office: Sonnenschein Nath & Rosenthal LLP Ste 600, E Tower 1301 K St NW Washington DC 20005 Office Phone: 202-408-9145. Office Fax: 202-408-6399. Business E-Mail: kreichs@sonnenschein.com.

**REICIN, RONALD IAN,** lawyer; b. Chgo., Dec. 11, 1942; s. Frank Edward and Abranita (Rome) R.; m. Alyta Friedland, May 23, 1965; children: Eric, Kael. BBA, U. Mich., 1964, MBA, 1967, JD cum laude, 1967. Bar: Ill. 1967, U.S. Tax Ct. 1967; CPA, Ill. Mem. staff Price Waterhouse & Co., Chgo., 1966; ptnr. Jenner & Block, Chgo., 1967—. Bd. dirs. Nat. Kidney Found., Ill., 1978-2003, v.p., 1992-95, pres., 1995-98, life trustee, 2004—; bd. dirs. Ruth Page Found., 1985—, v.p., 1990—; bd. dirs. Scoliosis Assn. Chgo., 1981-90, Kohl Children's Mus., 1991-95, River North Chgo. Dance Co., 1999—. Mem.: Ill. State Bar Assn., Chgo. Mortgage Attys. Assn., Chgo. Bar Assn., ABA, Lawyers Club (Chgo.), Exec. Club, Beta Alpha Psi, Beta Gamma Sigma, Phi Kappa Phi. Office: Jenner & Block LLP 1 E IBM Plz Fl 38 Chicago IL 60611-3586 Office Phone: 312-923-2687. Personal E-mail: rreicin@jenner.com.

**REID, ANDY,** professional football coach; b. LA, Mar. 19, 1958; m. Tammy Reid; 5 children. Student, Brigham Young Univ., 1979—81. Coach BYU, 1982, San Francisco state, 1983—85; head coach Northern Arizona, 1986, Texas-El Paso, 1987—88; asst. coach U. Mo., Columbia, 1989—91, Green Bay Packers, 1992-99, head coach Philadelphia Eagles, 2000—. Named NFL Coach of the Yr., 2002. Achievements include asst. coach Super Bowl XXXI Champion Green Bay Packers, 1997. Office: Philadelphia Eagles Nova Care Complex 1 Nova Care Way Philadelphia PA 19145-5298*

**REID, ANTONIO (L.A. REID),** music company executive; 1 child, Aaron. With musical group The Deele; co-founder La Face Records, 1989; pres., CEO Arista Records, NYC, 2000—04; chmn. Island Def Jam Music Group, 2004—. Songwriter with Kenny Edmonds, also occasionally with Darryl Simmons. Songs include Girlfriend, 1987, Rock Steady, 1987, Two Occasions, 1987, Don't Be Cruel, 1988, Love Saw It, 1988, Lover In Me, 1988, Every Little Step, 1988 (Grammy award nomination for R&B Song of Yr. 1989), Dial My Heart, 1988, Way You Love Me, 1988, Secret Rendezvous, 1988, Superwoman, 1988, Roses Are Red, 1988, Can't Stop, 1989, My Kinda Girl, 1989, It's No Crime, 1989, On Our Own, 1989, Ready or Not, 1989, Tender Lover, 1989, Giving You the Benefit, 1990, I'm Your Baby Tonight, 1990, Shock Dat Monkey, 1992, End of the Road, 1996. Recipient three Grammy awards; named one of Most Influential Black Americans, Ebony mag., 2006 Office: Island Def Jam Music Group 825 8th Ave, 28th fl New York NY 10019*

**REID, CHARLES ADAMS, III,** lawyer; b. Plainfield, N.J., Apr. 21, 1947; s. Charles Adams Jr. and Gertrude C. (Egan) R.; m. Teresa Keenan, May 1, 1974. BA, Colgate U., 1969; JD, Columbia U., 1974. Bar: N.Y. 1974, N.J. 1976, U.S. Ct. Appeals (3d cir.) 1983, U.S. Ct. Appeals (fed. cir.) 1989, U.S. Ct. Appeals (2d cir.) 1991, U.S. Ct. Appeals (9th cir.) 2002, Calif. 2002. Law clk. to hon. John R. Bartels U.S. Dist. Ct. (ea. dist.) N.Y., Bklyn., 1974-75; assoc. Coudert Bros., N.Y., 1975-77, Shanley & Fisher, Newark, 1977-82, ptnr. Newark and Morristown, N.J., 1983-99, Drinker Biddle & Reath LLP, Florham Park, NJ, 1999—. Mem. planning bd. Peapack-Gladstone, N.J., 1984-88, chmn., 1987-88; bd. dirs. Morris Ctr. YMCA, Cedar Knolls, N.J., 1986-93. Served with U.S. Army, 1970-72, Vietnam. Mem. ABA (litigation sect.), N.J. Bar Assn., Morris County Bar Assn., Essex County Bar Assn., Calif. State Bar, Park Avenue Club (Florham Park). Home: PO Box 716 Gladstone NJ 07934 Office: Drinker Biddle & Reath LLP 500 Campus Dr Florham Park NJ 07932-1047 Office Phone: 973-360-1100, 415-591-7500. Business E-Mail: Charles.Reid@dbr.com.

**REID, DAVID G.,** lawyer; b. NYC, Oct. 28, 1948; s. Donald D. and Charlotte A. (Marois) Reid. BA, McGill U., Montreal, 1970; JD, Boston U., 1973. Bar: Vt. 1973, U.S. Dist. Ct. Vt. 1973, Mass. 1977, U.S. Supreme Ct. 1978, U.S. Ct. Appeals (2d cir.) 1978, U.S. Dist. Ct. Mass. 1991. Pub. defender Orleans, Caledonia, Essex counties, St. Johnsbury, Vt., 1973-75, Bennington (Vt.) County, 1975-79, Windham County, Brattleboro, Vt., 1979-89; ptnr. Reid & Rodgers, Brattleboro, 1989—. Office: Reid & Rodgers 47 Williston St Brattleboro VT 05301-3202 Office Phone: 802-257-7887. E-mail: reidrodg@sover.net.

**REID, DEBRA ANN,** history professor; b. Chester, Ill., July 2, 1960; d. Harry Glenn and Francis Surman Reid. BS, S.E. Mo. State U., 1982; MA, SUNY, Oneonta, 1987, Baylor U., 1996; PhD, Tex. A&M U., 2000. Site adminstr. Washburn-Norlands Living History Ctr., Livermore Falls, Maine, 1983—85; interpreter Old World Wis., Eagle, 1985; dir. ednl. svcs. Montgomery County Hist. Soc., Dayton, Ohio, 1987; ops. mgr. Farmers' Mus., Inc., Cooperstown, NY, 1988—93; collections specialist Henry Ford Mus., Dearborn, Mich., 1993; curator Gov. Bill and Vara Daniel Hist. Village, Baylor U., Waco, Tex., 1993—97; rsch. asst. Tex. Edn. Agy., Austin, 1997—99; assoc. prof. Ea. Ill. U., Charleston, 1999—. Reviewer Inst. of Mus. Svcs. Gen. Oper. Support Grants, Washington, 1991—94, Mus. Assessment Program - Am. Assn. of Museums, Washington, 1992—2001; advisor to the bd. Friends of Chrisholm Hist. Farmstead, Trenton, Ohio, 2000—; humanities scholar Between Fences exhibit Mus. on Main St. - Smithsonian Instn./Ill. Humanities Coun., 2004—06; adj. assoc. prof. U. Ill., Champaign-Urbana. Author (contbr.): (book) Texas Social Studies Framework, K-12: Research and Resources for Designing a Social Studies Curriculum; editor: (conf. procs.) Assn. for Living History, Farm and Agrl. Museums; curator (exhbn.) Citizen Gregg: Charleston Born, California Bound (cinematographer Gregg Toland), 2004, Folk Art at the Tarble Arts Ctr., 2006—. Vol. Charleston-Mattoon Shaped Note Singers, Ill., 2004—; Ground Squirrels Vintage Baseball Club, Decatur, Ill., 2004—; chair libr. com. First Mennonite Ch., Urbana, Ill., 2003—04. Recipient Huguenot Soc. History award, Cooperstown Grad. Program in History Mus. Studies, 1987, Arthur H. Mattingly Hist. Preservation award to disting. alumni, S.E. Mo. State U., 1996; grantee, Ill. Humanities Coun., 2004, 2005; Summer fellowship in material culture studies, Hist. Deerfield, Inc., 1981, Nurse Found. fellowship, 1986, Nat. Endowment for the Arts fellowship, 1986, grant, NEH, 1994, Ottis Lock Rsch. grant, East Tex. Hist. Assn., 1999, Grad. Rsch. fellowship, Tex. A&M U., 1999, Grad. Student scholarship, Women's Faculty Network, Tex. A&M U., 1999-2000, Mus. Exhibit and Ednl. Programs grant, Ill. Assn. of Museums, 2004. Mem.: Orgn. of Am. Historians, Am. Hist. Assn., Cooperstown Grad. Assn. (treas. 1990—93), Assn. Internationale Des Musées D'Agriculture (N.Am. rep. to presidium 2004—), Am. Assn. for State and Local History (conf. program com. 2004, 2005), Agrl. History Soc. (Edwards Award selection com. 2003), Rural Women's Studies Assn. (treas. 1997—), Midwest Open Air Museums Coordinating Coun. (treas. 2000—), Nat. Coun. on Pub. History, So. Hist. Assn., Vernacular Architecture Forum, Assn. for Living History, Farm and Agrl. Museums (publs. chair 1996—2006, John T. Schlebecker award for excellence 2000), Phi Kappa Phi, Phi Alpha Theta, Delta Kappa Gamma. D-Liberal. Roman Catholic. Avocations: walking, knitting, reading, traveling.

**REID, DONNA JOYCE,** small business owner; b. Springfield, Tenn., June 25, 1954; d. Leonard Earl Reid and Joyce (Robertson) Kirby; m. Kenneth Bruce Sadler, June 26, 1976 (div. Apr. 1980); m. John Christopher Moulton, Oct. 18, 1987 (div. Dec. 1992); m. Peter Leatherland, Apr. 3, 1993. Student, Austin Peay State U., Clarksville, Tenn., 1972-75. Show writer, producer WTVF-TV (CBS affiliate), Nashville, 1977-83, promotion producer, 1983-85, on-air promotion mgr., 1985-86; gen. mgr. Steadi-Film Corp., Nashville, 1986-90; co-owner Options Internat., Nashville, 1990—2003, Shanti's, Inc., Hermitage, 2003—. Big sister Buddies of Nashville, 1981-87. Named to Honorable Order of Ky. Cols. John Y. Brown, Gov., 1980; recipient Significant Svc. award ARC, 1982, Clara Barton Communications award, 1983. Mem. NAFE, Nat. Assn. TV Arts and Scis., Nat. Film Inst., Nat. Assn. Broadcasters, Internat. Platform Assn., Am. Soc. Prevention of Cruelty to Animals, Humane Soc. U.S. Methodist. Avocations: reading, outdoor sports, travel. Office: Shantis Inc 4715 Andrew Jackson Pkwy Hermitage TN 37076 Office Phone: 615-391-4144. Personal E-mail: donnaoptionspj@aol.com.

**REID, E. LEWIS,** lawyer; Grad., Princeton U.; JD, Harvard Law Sch. Former minority counsel U.S. Senate Interior Comm.; former gen. counsel Calif. Endowment, exec. dir., 1999—2001; founding ptnr. Marron, Reid, LLP. Former pres., trustee Am. Trust for Wolfson Coll.; adv. dir. U.S. Acad. Ctr. for Nonprofit Mgmt.; chmn., pres. Am. Soc. for Royal Botanic Gardens, Joseph Banks Soc.; mem. legal adv. comm. Counsel on Environmental Quality; lecturer U. Calif., Berkeley. Bd. dirs. Calif. Endowment, 2000—, Sonoma Land Trust, Larry Hillblom Found., CSR Am.; adv. dir. Am. Land Conservancy. Office: Calif Endowment 1000 N Alameda St Los Angeles CA 90012*

**REID, EDWARD SNOVER, III,** lawyer; b. Detroit, Mar. 24, 1930; s. Edward S. Jr. and Margaret (Overington) Reid; m. Carroll Grylls, Dec. 30, 1953; children: Carroll Reid Highet, Richard Gerveys, Jenny Reid McTigue, Margaret Reid Boyer. BA, Yale U., 1951; LL.B. magna cum laude (Sheldon fellow), Harvard U., 1956. Bar: Mich. 1957, N.Y. 1958, D.C. 1982, Gaikokuho jimu-bengoshi, Tokyo 1991-96. Asso. Davis, Polk & Wardwell, N.Y.C., 1957-64, partner, 1964-95, sr. counsel, 1996—; dir. Gen. Mills, Inc., 1974-89. Mem. N.Y.C. Bd. Higher Edn., 1971—73; trustee Bklyn. Inst. Arts and Scis., 1966—93, chmn., 1974—79; trustee Bklyn. Mus. Art, 1973—93, 1994—; bd. dirs. Bklyn. Bot. Garden Corp., 1977—92, 1996—, Bargemusic Ltd., 1990—93. Active duty USMCR, 1951—53. Mem. ABA, N.Y. State Bar Assn., Assn. of Bar of City of N.Y., Am. Law Inst., Internat. Bar Assn., Heights Casino Club, Rembrandt Club, Century Assn. Club, Yale Club, Quogue Beach Club, Shinnecock Yacht Club, Quogue Field Club. Home: PO Box 39 Quogue NY 11959-0039 Office: Davis Polk & Wardwell 450 Lexington Ave New York NY 10017-3982 E-mail: ereid@dpw.com.

**REID, FRANCES EVELYN KROLL,** freelance/self-employed cinematographer, film director, communications executive; b. Oakland, Calif., Mar. 25, 1944; d. William Farnham and Marion Storm (Teller) Kroll. BA, U. Oreg., 1966. Tchr. secondary sch., Los Angeles, 1968-69; sound recordist Churchill Films, Los Angeles, 1971; freelance sound recordist Los Angeles, 1972-75; freelance dir., prodr., 1975—; freelance cinematographer Berkeley, Calif., 1978—; dir. Iris Films, Berkeley, 1977—; lectr. U. Calif. Grad. Sch. Journalism, 2005. Vol. Peace Corps, Malawi, Africa, 1969-70. Producer/dir. Long Night's Journey Into Day, 2000 (Grand Jury award Sundance 2000, Acad. award nominee 2001); dir. (film) In The Best Interests of the Children, 1977 (Blue Ribbon Am. Film Festival 1978), The Changer: A Record of the Times, 1991, The Faces of AIDS, 1992, Skin Deep, 1995, Talking About Race, 1994, Straight from the Heart, 1994 (Acad. award nominee 1995); cinematographer: (film) Times of Harvey Milk, 1984 (Oscar 1985), Living with AIDS, 1986 (Student Acad. award 1987), Common Threads: Stories from the Quilt, 1989 (Oscar award 1990), Complaints of a Dutiful Daughter, 1994 (Acad. award nominee 1995). Mem. Film Arts Found., Assn. Ind. Video and Filmmakers, Acad. Motion Picture Arts and Scis. Office: Iris Films 2600 10th St Berkeley CA 94710-2522 Office Phone: 510-845-5414.

**REID, GEORGE WILLIS,** college president; b. Herford, N.C., June 1, 1945; m. Mae Freeman-Reid; six children. AB in History with honors, 1967, MA in History with honors, 1968, PhD in History with honors, 1974. Dean U. Coll. at N.C. Cen. U., Durham, 1986; v.p. for acad. affairs Savannah (Ga.) State Coll.; dean Univ. Coll., assoc. v.p. U.Cin.; sr. v.p. Benedict Coll., 1991; pres. Ky. State U., Frankfort, 1998—2002; COO Porter Educational & Communications, Inc. Spkr./cons. in field. Author numerous books, articles, papers in field. Named to Outstanding Young Men of Am., 1978. Office: Ky State U 400 E Main St Frankfort KY 40601-2334 Business E-Mail: gwreid@gwmail.kysu.edu.

**REID, GERALDINE WOLD (GERALDINE REID SKJERVOLD),** artist; b. Apr. 11, 1944; d. Alden Elroy and Verna (Kocinski) Wold BA in Fine Art, Calif. State U., Sacramento, 1972, MFA, 1975; postgrad., Ind. U. - Purdue U. Instr. dental aux. edn. U. Minn., 1966-70, anthropol. rsch. asst. 1976-78; mng. editor Nat. Arts Guide, Chgo., 1978-80; freelance artist Chgo., 1981-94; pres. Chgo. Art Emerging Inc., 1983-85; graphic artist Reid Design & Illustration, Chgo., 1981-94; dir. show coordination Circle Fine Art, Chgo., 1981. Instr. comm. art and design Alexandria Tech. Coll., Minn., 1994—; seminar lectr., 1977, 86; lectr., art and math. Dept. Math. U. Ill., 1987—88; guest lectr. women's art history AAUW, Alexandria, 1997; lectr. on drawing approaches, 2005. One-woman shows include Artists' Coop. Gallery, Santa Fe, 1976, Artlink, Ft. Wayne, Ind., 1979, 84—, D.E.O. Fine Arts, Inc., Chgo., 1982-83, Union League Gallery, Chgo., 1989, Brodsky Gallery, 1993, Second Floor Gallery, Cen. Square, Glenwood, Minn., 1999, Ann Bickle Heritage House, Glenwood, 2000, Pope County Mus., Glenwood, 2004, Pope Art, Ter. Mill, Minn., 2005; group exhbns. include Crocker Art Mus., Sacramento, 1975, Ft. Wayne Mus. Art, 1978, Artists Guild Chgo., 1982, Charles A. Wustum Mus., Racine, Wis., 1983, Limelight, Chgo., 1986, 87, 88, Neville-Sargent Gallery, 1986, 87, Beacon Street Hull House Gallery, 1988, McDonalds Corp., Chgo., 1988, Prairie Ave. Gallery, Chgo., 1990, Peace Mus., Chgo., 1990, Hyde Park Art Ctr., Chgo., 1990, Lettuce Entertain You Enterprises, Inc., 1990, Olive Tree Gallery, Daley Coll., Chgo., 1991, Crown Ctr. Gallery, Loyola U., Chgo., 1992, Agora Syndicate, Inc., 1992, Kieffer-Nolde/TIC, 1992, Flora '92, 1992, Chgo. Bot. Garden, 1992, Open Spectrum, David Adler Cultural Ctr., 1994, August House Studio, Chgo., 1994—; Upper West Gallery, Alexandria Tech. Coll., Minn., 1995, Plains Art Mus., Fargo, N.D., 1997, Regional Art Exhibit, New York Mills, Minn., 1997, Runestone Mus., Alexandria, 1997-98, Art on the Plains, 3d Ann. Regional Exhbn., Plains Art Mus., Fargo, 31st Ann. Fergus Falls Cmty. Coll. Invitational Art Show, Fergus Falls, Minn., 2002, 03, Pope County Artists Exhibit, Lake Region Arts Coun. Gallery, Fergus Falls, Minn., 2002, Prairie Renaissance Cultural Alliance Gallery, Morris, Minn., 2002-03, Celebration of Lake Region Arts Coun., Fergus Falls, 2002-2003, Fergus Falls C.C. Ann. Invitational, 2003, New York Mills (Minn.) Ann. Regional Exhbn., 2003, Minn. State Cmty. & Tech. Coll., Fergus Falls, 2004, Minn. State Colls. and Univs., 2005-06, Wind and Water exhibit, Lakes Region Arts Coun. Gallery, Fergus Falls, Minn., 2006; contbr. artwork to 2 ann. 1994 calendars; artwork selected for inclusion in Alex Tech Coll. greeting card suite, 2005. Mem. New York Mills Cultural Ctr., Mpls. Art Inst., Am. Inst. Graphic Arts, Mpls. Inst. Arts, Glacial Ridge Artists. Business E-Mail: gerrir@alextech.edu.

**REID, HARRY MASON,** senator; b. Searchlight, Nev., Dec. 2, 1939; s. Harry and Inez Jaynes Reid; m. Landra Joy Gould; children— Lana, Rory, Leif, Josh, Key AS, Southern Utah State U., 1959; BS in Hist. and Polit. Sci., Utah State U., 1961; JD, George Washington U., 1964; LLD (hon.), U. So. Utah, 1984. Bar: Nev. Bar 1963. Police officer US Capitol, Washington, 1961—64; city atty. City of Henderson, Henderson, Nev., 1964—66; mem. Nev. State Assembly, 1969—70; lt. gov. State of Nev., 1971—75; chmn. Nev. Gaming Commn., 1977—81; US rep. from Nev. Washington, 1983—87; US Senator from Nev., 1987—; minority whip US Senate, 1998—2001, 2002—03, majority whip, 2001—02, asst. minority leader, 2003—04, minority leader, 2004—. Mem. select cm. intelligence US Senate, mem. com. appropriations; vice chmn. US Senate Commn. Art. Author: Searchlight: The Camp that Didn't Fail, 1998. Bd. dirs. Am. Cancer Soc., Legal Aid Soc., Young Men's Christian Assn.; bd. trustees So. Nev. Meml. Hosp., 1967—69. Recipient Humanitarian award, Nat. Asthma Ctr. and Nat. Jewish Hosp., 1984, Public Svc. award, Am. Found. Suicide Prevention, 1999, Friend of Zion award, The Jerusalem Fund, 2000, MLA award disting. public svc., 2002, Award of Merit, The Military Coalition, 2002, Arthur T. Marix award, Military Officers Assn. Am., 2003, Disting. Svc. award, Am. Public Works Assn., 2003, Inspirational Leadership award, Military Order of Purple Heart, 2003, Nat. Landscape Conservation Sys. Champion award, NLCS Coalition, 2004, Pick and Gravel award, Am. Am. State Geologists, 2004, TechNet Founders Cir. award, 2005. Mem.: Nev. Athletic Commn., Nat. Conf. Lt. Governors, Am. Bd. Trial Advocates, Clark County Bar Assn., Nev. Bar Assn., ABA. Democrat. Ch. Latter-Day Saints. Office: US Senate 528 Hart Senate Office Bldg Washington DC 20510-0001 also: Lloyd D George Bldg Ste 8016 333 Las Vegas Blvd South Las Vegas NV 89101 Office Phone: 202-224-3542, 702-388-5020. Office Fax: 202-224-7327, 702-388-5030.*

**REID, HELEN VERONICA,** dean; b. Reading, Eng., Sept. 25, 1956; d. Alan A. and Teresa H. (Thatcher) Ware; m. Gary B. Reid, May 29, 1976; children: Robert, Jennifer, Kristen. BA in Biology, U. Tex., 1976; BSN, U. Tex., Arlington, 1978; MSN, Tex. Women's U., 1983; EdD, U. North Tex., 2000. CCRN, 1980, cert. CPR instr. Asst. nurse coord., staff nurse, float pool nurse Parkland Meml. Hosp., Dallas, 1979—83, float pool nurse, 1987—93; instr. Trinity Valley C.C., Kaufman, Tex., 1983—86, leader freshman team, 1986—90, dean health occupations, 1990—. Mem.: Tex. Assn. Deans and Dirs. for Profl. Nursing Programs (treas. 2005—), Tex. C.C. Tchrs. Assn., Nat. Orgn. ADN (pub. rels. dir. 1998—2002), Tex. Orgn. for ADN (sec. 1988—92, nominating com. chair 1995—96, pres.-elect 2002—03, pres. 2003—05, past pres. 2005—06), Tex. Assn. Vocat. Nurse Educators, Phi Kappa Phi, Sigma Theta Tau. Office Phone: 972-932-4309. Business E-Mail: reid@tvcc.edu.

**REID, INEZ SMITH,** lawyer, educator, judge; b. New Orleans, Apr. 7, 1937; d. Sidney Randall Dickerson and Beatrice Virginia (Bundy) Smith. BA, Tufts U., 1959; LLB, Yale U., 1962; MA, UCLA, 1963; PhD, Columbia U., 1968; LLM in Jud. Process, U. Va., 2004. Bar: Calif. 1963, N.Y. 1972, D.C. 1980. Assoc. prof. Barnard Coll. Columbia U., N.Y.C., 1972-76; gen. counsel youth divsn. State of N.Y., 1976-77; dep. gen. counsel HEW, Washington, 1977-79; inspector gen. EPA, Washington, 1979-81; chief legis. and opinions, dep. corp. counsel Office of Corp. Counsel, Washington, 1981-83; corp. counsel D.C. 1983-85, counsel Hogan & Hartson, Perlis & Dubuc, Washington, 1986-90, ptnr., 1990-91; counsel Graham & James, 1991-93, Lewis, White & Clay, P.C., 1994-95; assoc. judge D.C. Ct. Appeals, 1995—. William J. Maier, Jr. vis. prof. law W.Va. U. Coll. Law, Morgantown, 1985-86. Contbr. articles to profl. jours. and publs. Trustee emeritus Lancaster Sem., Pa., 2002—; bd. dirs. Homeland Ministries bd. United Ch. of Christ, N.Y., 1978—83, vice chmn., 1981—83; chmn. bd. govs. Antioch Law Sch., Washington, 1979—81; chmn. bd. trustees Antioch U., Yellow Springs, Ohio, 1981—82; trustee Tufts U., Medford, Mass., 1988—98, trustee emeritus, 1999—; trustee Lancaster (Pa.) Sem., 1988—2001; bd. govs. D.C. Sch. Law, 1990—96, chmn., 1991—95. Recipient Emily Gregory award Barnard Coll., 1976, Arthur Morgan award Antioch U., 1982, Service award United Ch. of Christ, 1983, Disting. Service (Profl. Life) award Tufts U. Alumni Assn., 1988. Office: DC Ct Appeals 500 Indiana Ave NW Fl 6 Washington DC 20001-2138

**REID, IVONNE FIGUEROA,** language educator; b. Santiago, Chile, May 25, 1938; d. Hector Francisco Figueroa and Uberlinda Eulogia Cristi; m. Roderic Eugene Reid, June 13, 1963; children: David Alan, Nancy Gail. B in English, U. Chile, 1960; MS in Edn., U. So. Calif., 1963, PhD in Edn., 1972. Rschr. Inst. Statistical Rsch. U. Chile, 1959—63; prof. statistics Family Edn. Inst. Cath. U., Santiago, Chile, 1960—61; rsch. assoc. in evaluation U. S.C. Art in Elem. Edn. Rsch. Project, 1975—80; intermediate sch. tchr. Montebello Unified Sch. Dist., Bell Gardens, 1981—89, h.s. Spanish tchr. 1989—99, literacy facilitator, 1999—2002, cons., 2002—05; vol. cons., 2005—. Presenter Calif. Edn. Rsch. Assn., 1972, 77, 78, Calif. Assn. of Bilingual Edn. Assn., 1997; Fulbright scholarship, Dept. State, U. So. Calif., 1961—62. Mem.: Montebello Teachers Assn., Calif. Teachers Assn., Nat. Edn. Assn., Calif. Assn. Bilingual Edn., Am. Ednl. Rsch. Assn. Avocations: travel, music, art, reading. Home: 11102 Orange Dr Whittier CA 90606 Personal E-mail: ivonnereid@earthlink.net.

**REID, JAMES EDWARD,** lawyer; b. Balt. Aug. 8, 1951; s. Edward Kessinger and Jane Kathryn (Fraver) R.; m. Linda Susan Peterson, Sept. 14, 1979; children: Edward Kessinger, Griffin Arthur, Andrew James. BA in Classics U. of Syracuse U., 1973, JD, 1978. Bar: N.Y. 1978, U.S. Ct. Mil. Appeals 1979, U.S. Dist. Ct. (no. dist.) N.Y. 1980, U.S. Ct. Appeals (2d cir.) 1979, U.S. Supreme Ct. 1983, U.S. Dist. Ct. (we. dist.) N.Y. 1988. Assoc. firm Davoli &

McMahon, Syracuse, N.Y., 1979-82; ptnr. Greene & Reid, LLP, Syracuse, 1982—; instr. civil practice and litigation paralegal program Syracuse U., 1984-87; adj. prof. advanced trial practice Syracuse U., 1987—. Author: Service of Process Desk Reference Manual, 1984, Legal Implications of Fire Apparatus Color Selection-Its Impact on Liability Consideration, 1987, Jury Instructions in the Civil Law Suit, 1987, Handling the Plaintiff's Personal Injury Case, 1989, Uninsured MVAIC and Underinsured Claims and Problems under New York Law: What They Are and How to Avoid Them, 1992, Personal Injury Chapter: General Practice, 1998. Life mem. bd. visitors Syracuse U. Coll. Law; bd. trustess Utica Coll., 2002—; mem million dollar avocates forum Am. Bd. Trial Advocates. Maj. USMC, 1972-86. Mem. Onondaga County Bar Assn. (chmn. legis. com. 1983—, bd. dirs. 1985-87), N.Y. State Bar Assn. (chmn.-elect gen. practice sect. 1989, ho. of dels. 1990-92), Upstate Trial Lawyers Assn. (pres. 1988-90, 1997—, N.Y. State Trial Lawyers Assn. (bd. dirs. 1987-88, 1997—, asst. dist. atty. Wayne County, N.Y. 1992—), Order of Barristers, Phi Delta Phi. Republican. Roman Catholic. E-mail: jereid@greenereid.com. also: 330 East Ave Newark NY 14513-1743 Office Phone: 315-492-9665. E-mail: jreid@greenereid.com.

**REID, JOHN MITCHELL (JACK REID),** biomedical engineer, researcher, consultant; b. Mpls., June 8, 1926; s. Robert Sherman and Meryl (Mitchell) R.; m. Virginia Montgomery, Dec. 31, 1949 (div.); children: Donald, Kathryn, Richard; m. Shadi Wang, June 30, 1983. BS, U. Minn., 1950, MS, 1957; PhD, U. Pa., 1965. Engring. assoc. U. Minn., Mpls., 1950-54; rsch. engr. St. Barnabas Hosp., Mpls., 1954-57; assoc. U. Pa., Phila., 1957-66; rsch. asst. prof. U. Wash., Seattle, 1966-72; rsch. engr. Providence Hosp., 1972-74; dir. bioengring. Inst. of Applied Physiology & Medicine, 1973-81; Calhoun prof. Drexel U., Phila., 1981-94; prof. emeritus, rsch. prof., 1994—. Adj. prof. radiology Thomas Jefferson Med. Sch., Phila., 1982—; affiliate prof. U. Washington, 1995—; cons. Inst. Applied Physiology and Medicine, Seattle. Contbr. numerous articles to profl. jours.; 5 U.S. patents on devel. of ultrasonic med. imaging. Scoutmaster Boy Scouts Am., Mpls., 1955-57, Phila., 1960-65, cub and scoutmaster, Seattle, 1965-70. With USN, 1944—46. Recipient Pioneer award U. Vascular Technologists, 1994; grantee NIH; Professorship in his named established at Drexel U. Sch. Biomed. Engring. and Health Sys., Phila., 2004. Fellow IEEE, Am. Inst. Ultrasound in Medicine (bd. govs., Pioneer award), Acoustical Soc. Am., Engring. in Medicine and Biology Soc. (Lifetime Achievement award 1993), Am. Inst. Med. and Biol. Engrs.; mem. World Fedn. Ultrasound in Medicine and Biology (hon.). Home: 16711 254th Ave SE Issaquah WA 98027-6973 Business E-Mail: jmreid@u.washington.edu.

**REID, JOHN PHILLIP,** law educator; b. Weehawken, N.J., May 17, 1930; s. Thomas Francis and Teresa Elizabeth (Murphy) R. BSS., Georgetown U., 1952; LLB, Harvard U., 1955; MA, U. N.H., 1957; LLM, NYU, 1959, JSD, 1962. Bar: N.H. 1955. Law clk. U.S. Dist. Ct. N.H., 1956; instr. NYU, N.Y.C., 1960-62, asst. prof. law, 1962-64, assoc. prof., 1964-65, prof. Sch. Law, 1966—2003, prof. emeritus, 2003—. Author: Chief Justice: The Judicial World of Charles Doe, 1967, A Law of Blood: The Primitive Law of the Cherokee Nation, 1970, In a Defiant Stance, 1977, In a Rebellious Spirit, 1979, Law for the Elephant: Property and Social Behavior on the Overland Trail, 1980, In Defiance of the Law, 1981, Constitutional History of the American Revolution: The Authority of Rights, 1986, Constitutional History of the American Revolution: The Authority to Tax, 1987, The Concept of Liberty in the Age of the American Revolution, 1988, The Concept of Representation in the Age of the American Revolution, 1989, Constitutional History of the American Revolution: The Authority to Legislate, 1991, Constitutional History of the American Revolution: The Authority of Law, 1993, Policing the Elephant: Crime, Punishment, and Social Behavior on the Overland Trail, 1997, Patterns of Vengeance: Crosscultural Homicide in the North American Fur Trade, 1999, Contested Empire: Peter Skene Ogden and the Snake River Expeditions, 2002, Controlling the Law: Legal Politics in Early National New Hampshire, 2004, Rule of Law: The Jurisprudence of Liberty in the Seventeenth and Eighteenth Centuries, 2004, The Ancient Constitution and the Origins of Anglo-American Liberty, 2005. Fellow Guggenheim Found., 1980, Huntington Library-NEH, 1980, 84; hon. fellow Am. Soc. Legal History, 1986. Fellow Am. Acad. Arts and Scis. Republican. Roman Catholic. Office: NYU Law Sch 40 Washington Sq S New York NY 10012-1099 Office Phone: 212-998-6230. Business E-mail: john.reid@nyu.edu.

**REID, KAREN DENISE,** aerospace transportation executive, writer; b. Memphis, Jan. 17, 1961; d. L.C. and Shirley (Spencer) Reid. BS in Edn., Memphis State U., 1992; postgrad., Strayer U., 2006—. Journeyman trainee Memphis Pub. Co., 1977—2000; exec. sec., treas., trustee Raleigh Ch., Memphis, 1985—94; acctg. clk. Nat. Hardwood Lumber Assn., Memphis, 1996—98; customer svc. agt. Pinnacle Airlines divsn. Northwest Airlines, Memphis, 1998—; owner K.K's Express Boutique, 1998—. Author: From Mistress to Ministry, 2003, (manual) Strageic Management Survival Kit for Church Leaders, 2004. Bd. dirs., CEO Twin Ministries, 2000—; pres. Twin Ministries Singles Fellowship, 2004. Avocations: travel, bowling, writing. Home and Office: Twin Ministries PO Box 752613 Memphis TN 38175 Office Phone: 901-634-2667. Personal E-mail: thetwinministries@yahoo.com.

**REID, KATHERINE LEE,** retired museum director, curator; BA magna cum laude, Vassar Coll.; MFA, Harvard U., 1966; studied at, Institut d'Art et Archaeologie, Sorbonne, Paris. Curator Toledo Mus Art, Ohio, David and Alfred Smart Mus., U. Chgo., Ackland Art Mus., U. NC, Chapel Hill; asst. dir. Art Inst. Chgo., 1982—86, dep. dir., 1986—91; dir. Va. Mus. Fine Arts, 1991—2000, Cleve. Mus. Art, 2000—05. Chair vis. com. Frances Lehman Loeb Art Ctr., Vassar Coll. Bd. mem. Van Gogh Mus., Amsterdam, Nat. Conf. Cmty. and Justice. Mem.: Am. Fedn. of Arts, Am. Assn. Mus., Am. Assn. Mus. Dirs. (pres. 2000—01, past mem. bd. trustees).*

**REID, KATHERINE LOUISE,** artist, educator, writer; b. Port Arthur, Tex., Mar. 25, 1941; d. Clifton Commodore and Helen Ross (Moore) Reid. BA, Baylor U., 1963; postgrad. in design and illustration, Kans. City Art Inst., 1964; MEd, U. Houston, 1973; cert. supervision, U. Houston-Clear Lake City, 1980; postgrad., San Jacinto Coll., 1982. Litho reprodn. artist Hallmark Cards, Kansas City, Mo., 1963-64; tchr. art high sch. Pasadena (Tex.) Ind. Sch. Dist., 1964-71, supr. art, gifted and talented and photography, 1977-85, supr. art and photography InterAct, 1985-90, instrnl. specialist, 1990-2000, photography and art, 1990-93, instrnl. specialist in art and spl. programs, 1993-96, rsch. planning, data disaggregation, 1996-2000; internet tchr. recruiter, 2001—02; mural artist Old Car Barn, Edna, Tex., 2000—. 4 MAT learning styles trainer DuPont Leadership Devel. Process Trainer, Selective Rsch., Inst., tchr. perceiver specialist, performance quality sys. trainer, coop. learning trainer, outcome based edn. trainer, integrated unit devel. and authentic assessment trainer Greater Gulf Coast Adminstr. Assessment Project, Assessor, 1990-2000; head crafts, asst. dir., dir. summer, winter discovery program-ski camp Cheley Colo. Camps, Denver, Estes Park, 1967-75; awards com. John Austin Cheley Found., 1990-92; staff artist, media workshop Tex. Edn. Agy., Austin, 1961; art enrichment tchr. Port Arthur Ind. Sch. Dist. (Tex.), 1961; head crafts Camp Waluta, Silsbee, Tex., 1960; mem. Tex. Edn. Agy., Art Leadership Inst., 1989-90, Tracking Rsch. Com., 1991, Core Strategic Planning Team, 1992-2000, Outcome Based Edn. Dist. Planning Com., 1991-92, Quality Sys. Improvement Team, 1991-92, Outcome Based Edn. Com. Exit Outcomes, 1991; Region IV data disk trainer, 1998-2000, target teach coord., 1993-2000, multiple intelligence trainer, 1997-2000, data disaggregation trainer, 1997-2000, supt.'s rsch. com., 1999. Author: Through Their Eyes, 1989. Mem. Friends of Fine Arts-Baylor U., Waco, Tex., 1981—, Scholastic Art Awards Regional Bd., Houston, 1978-84; bd. dirs. Houston Coun. Student Art Awards, Inc., 1984-90, Pasadena Ind. Sch. Dist. Edn. Found., 2005—; mem. Baylor U. Endowed Scholarship Soc., Baylor U. Old Main Scholarship Soc. Recipient Baylor U. Endowed scholarship Baylor U. Old Main Soc., 2005—; named Outstanding Secondary Educator of Am., 1975, Tex. Art Educator of Yr., 1985, Outstanding Vol. City of Pasadena, 2004. Mem. ASCD, Tex. ASCD, Tex. Art Edn. Assn. (rep. editor newsletter 1982-85, chmn. supervision divsn. 1982-83, v.p. membership

1978-80, chmn. pub. info. com., regional chmn. youth art month 1980-82; regional chmn. membership com. 1976-78, pres. elect 1986, sec. 1991-93, Disting. Fellows award 2004), Tex. Alliance for Arts Edn. (bd. vice chmn. 1984-86, treas. 1988-90), Nat. Art Edn. Assn. (conv. com. 1977, 85), Tex. Assn. Sch. Adminstrs., Houston Art Edn. Assn. (sec. 1969), Tex. Ret. Tchrs. Assn. (Dist. IV historian 2001-03), Pasadena Area Ret. Sch. Employees (parliamentarian 2002-04), Baylor U. Endowed Scholarship Soc., Delta Kappa Gamma (2d v.p. 1984-86, pres. 2002-2004, state leadership devel. for chpt. pres. com., 2003-2005, state banner com., 2004, State Leadership Seminar 2005, area III coord. 2005—, Internat. Golden Gift Leadership Seminar 2006). Baptist. Achievements include patents for pet car seat. Home: 106 Ravenhead Dr Houston TX 77034-1520 Personal E-mail: klreid@academicplanet.com.

**REID, LANGHORNE, III,** merchant banker; b. Dallas, Apr. 3, 1950; s. Langhorne Jr. and Mary Anne (Beasley) R.; m. Sally Wolf, Dec. 26, 1972 (div. Aug. 1977); m. Eve Catherine Murphy, Sept. 6, 1986 (div. 1996); 1 child, Claire Hart Reid; m. Vera Anderson Reid, 1999. BA in Psychology, U. Tex., 1972, JD, 1975; MBA, U. Pa., 1977. Bar: Tex. 1975. V.p. Dillon, Read & Co., Inc., N.Y.C., 1977-82; mng. dir. Drexel Burnham Lambert Inc., N.Y.C., 1982-87; co-dir. mergers and acquisitions Paine Webber Group, N.Y.C., 1987-89; ptnr. Gordon Investment Inc., N.Y.C., 1989-93; pres. Beacon Advisors, Inc., Dallas, 1993-99. Bd. dirs. Windmill Holdings; pres. Partnership Svcs., 1992-93; chmn. Cedco Sys., Inc., 1997—, Amtex Holdings, Inc., 1996—, Garland Broadcast Investors, Inc., 1997—, Pogesa SA, 2002-. Trustee, treas. Animal Med. Ctr., N.Y.C., 1981—; trustee St. Mark's Sch. of Tex., 2002-. Mem. Tex. Bar Assn. Home: 4109 Windsor Pkwy Dallas TX 75205-1670 Office: Arcady Capital Inc Ste 330 100 Highland Park Village Dallas TX 75205-2726

**REID, LAURETTA GLASPER,** retired principal; b. Balt., Sept. 6, 1931; BS, Coppin State Coll., 1953; MA, Columbia U., 1957; postgrad., Peabody Consevatory of Music, 1962; MS, Johns Hopkins U., 1980. Cert. elem. and middle sch. supr., prin., Md. Asst. prin., edn. specialist, master tchr. Balt. City Pub. Schs., prin. Recipient Senator's Cert. of Merit Tenure; Gov's. Citation. Mem. NAFE, ASCD, Nat. Assn. Elem. Sch. Prins., Md. Assn. Elem. Sch. Prins., Assn. of Tchr. Educators, Phi Delta Kappa. Office: 6405 Laurel Dr Baltimore MD 21207-6326

**REID, LORENE FRANCES,** middle school educator; b. St. Louis, May 28, 1946; d. Frank Bernard and Marcella Marie (Froechtenigt) Niemeyer; m. Patrick Joseph Reid, Aug. 11, 1967; 1 child, Christina Marie. BA in Spanish, Maryville U., 1968; MEd in Secondary Edn., U. Mo., St. Louis, 1990; PhD in Edn., St. Louis U., 1995; MA in English, S.E. Mo. State U., 1996. Cert. Spanish, social studies, ESL tchr., reading specialist K-12, sch. psychologist, Mo.; cert. early adolescence/English lang. arts Nat. Bd. for Profl. Tchg. Stds. Spanish tchr. Rosary H.S., Spanish Lake, Mo., 1968-69, Taylor Sch., Clayton, Mo., 1969-70, Roosevelt H.S., St. Louis, 1988-89, Cleve. Jr. Naval Acad., St. Louis, 1989-90, Thomas Dunn Meml. Adult Edn., St. Louis, 1992-95; social studies tchr. St. Luke's Sch., Richmond Heights, Mo., 1981-88; ESL tchr. Grant Mid. Sch., St. Louis, 1990-92, Fanning Mid. Sch., St. Louis, 1992-98; tchr. leader Mid. Sch. Initiative, 1998-99; Schs. for Thought coord. MEGA Magnet Cluster, St. Louis, 1999-2000; psychol. examiner Student Support Svcs.-Gifted and Talented, St. Louis, 2000—03, sch. psychologist, 2003—04; sch. psychologist/psychol. examiner Ft. Zumwalt Sch. Dist., 2004—. Adj. prof. U. Mo.-St. Louis, 2000—; tutor Sylvan Learning Ctr., Crestwood, Mo., 1990-92; mem. St. Louis Ednl. Leadership Inst., 1994-97. Mem. Cmty. Leadership Program for Tchrs., St. Louis, 1993-94. Recipient Emerson Electric Excellence in Teaching award, 1994; named Tchr. of Yr., St. Louis Pub. Schs., 1994-95; named as one of 60 tchrs. recognized by Disney Channel Salutes the Am. Tchr., 1995-96. Mem. ASCD, Tchrs. English to Spkrs. of Other Langs., Nat. Coun. Tchrs. English, Midam. Tchs. English to Spkrs. of Other Langs., Internat. Reading Assn., Nat. Assn. Sch. Psychologists, Mo. Assn. Sch. Psychologists, Phi Delta Kappa. Home: 12208 Applerock Dr O Fallon MO 63368 Personal E-mail: lorenereid@sbcglobal.net.

**REID, MARGARET ELIZABETH,** elementary school educator, secondary school educator; b. Tampa, Fla., Feb. 8, 1934; d. James Byron and Zella Mae (Thompson) Bruce; m. Arthur M. Reid Jr., Dec. 28, 1955 (div. Dec. 1982); children: Laura Jean, Nancy Ann. BS in Edn., SUNY, Potsdam, 1956; postgrad., SUNY, Stony Brook, 1975—78; MS in Spl. Edn., L.I. U., 1979, postgrad., 1989—. Cert. spl. edn. tchr. N.Y. Tchr. Harborfields Sch. Dist., Greenlawn, NY, 1956—61; tchr. Project Able Three Village Sch. Dist., Stony Brook, 1971—72; substitute tchr. Smithtown Sch. Dist., NY, 1972—75, substitute tchr. spl. edn., 1972—75; substitute tchr. Shoreham Sch. Dist., NY, 1974—76, Mt. Sinai Sch. Dist., NY, 1974—79, Middle Island Sch. Dist, NY, 1974—79; tchr. resource rm. Hempstead Sch. Dist., NY, 1979—96. Tchr. rep. spl. edn. com. Hempstead Sch. Dist., 1985—. Mem. N.Y. Pub. Interest Rsch. Group, N.Y.C. 1987—, Citizens Campaign for the Environment, 1988—, Arthur Murray Sch. Dance (V.I.P. Hon. Student award 2002). NSF grantee Stevens Inst. Tech., 1959. Mem. N.Y. Assn. for Learning Disabled, Hempstead Classroom Tchrs. Assn., Coun. for Exceptional Children, N.Y. Branch Orton Dyslexia Soc., Kappa Delta Pi Republican. Methodist. Avocations: music, art, drama. Home: 64 Walter Ave Hauppauge NY 11788-3425

**REID, ORIEN,** former medical association administrator; b. Oct. 1945; BA, Clark Coll., Atlanta. MSW. Anchor WCAU-TV, Phila., 1979—98; chmn., bd. dirs. Alzheimer's Assn.'s Nat. Bd. Dirs., 1999—2002. Former mem. bd. govs. Nat. Acad. Television Arts and Scis.; former pres. Phila. Consumer Coun. Recipient Best Investigative Reporting, Phila. Press Assn., Excellence in Journalism award, Inst. Food Technologists.

**REID, ROBERT LELON,** engineering educator; b. Detroit, May 20, 1942; s. Lelon Reid and Verna Beulah (Custer) Menkes; m. Judy Elaine Nestell, July 21, 1962; children: Robert James, Bonnie Kay, Matthew Lelon. ASE, Mott C.C., Flint, Mich., 1961; BChemE, U. Mich., 1963; MME, So. Meth. U., 1966, PhDME, 1969. Registered profl. engr., Tenn., Tex., Wis. Asst. rsch. engr. Atlantic Richfield Co., Dallas, 1966-65; assoc. staff engr. Linde Divsn., Union Carbide Corp., Tonawanda, NY, 1966-68; from asst. to assoc. prof. U. Tenn., Knoxville, 1966-75; assoc. prof. Cleve. State U., 1975-77; from assoc. to full prof. U. Tenn., Knoxville, 1977-82; prof., chmn. U. Tex., El Paso, 1982-87; dean Coll. Engring., Marquette U., Milw., 1987-98, prof. mech. engring., 1998-2001; dean emeritus, 2001. Summer prof. NASA Marshall Space Ctr., Huntsville, Ala., 1970, EXXON Prodn. Rsch., Houston, 1972, 73, NASA Lewis Space Ctr., Cleve., 1966. Oak Ridge Nat. Lab., 1974-75, TVA, 1978, 79, State of Calif., Sacramento, 1985, Tex. Higher Edn. Coordinating Bd., Austin, 1987. Contbr. articles 100 articles on heat transfer and solar energy. Grantee NSF, DOE, TVA, NASA, DOI, 1976-87; named Engr. of Yr. Engring. Socs. El Paso, 1986. Fellow ASME (Centennial medallion 1980, chmn. cryogenics com. 1977-81, chmn. solar energy divsn. 1983-84, chmn. Rio Grande sect. 1985-87, John Yellott award, 1997, Dedicated Svc. award 1998); mem. ASHRAE, Engrs. and Scientists Milw. (bd. dirs. 1988-93, v.p. 1989-90, pres. 1991-92), Wis. Assn. Rsch. Mgmt. (pres. 1996-97). Lutheran. Avocations: travel, classic car restoration. Business E-Mail: bobreid@umich.edu.

**REID, RUST ENDICOTT,** lawyer; b. N.Y.C., Dec. 31, 1931; s. Thorburn and Mary (Newhall) R.; m. Jeanne Inge, Aug. 5, 1955; children: Dorothy, Elizabeth, Margaret, Mary. BA, U. Va., 1954, LLB, 1960. Bar: Tex. 1960, Va. 1960. Bd. cert. in estate planning, probate. Assoc. Thompson & Knight, Dallas, 1960-65, ptnr., 1965—; lectr. SW Grad. Sch. Banking, Dallas, 1978-88; adj. prof. So. Meth. U., Dallas, 1980-86. Contbg. author: Texas Estate Administration, 1975. Trustee Child Care, Dallas, 1968-72, pres. 1970-72, Hockaday Sch., Dallas, 1972-82 (chmn. 1976-78), Texas coun. Girl Scouts U.S., 1982-83; trustee Vis. Nurse Assn., Dallas, 1984—, treas. 1986-89, v.p. 1989-91, pres., 1991-93; pres. Dallas Estate Planning Coun., 1988-89; trustee Dallas Children's Advocacy Center (v.p. 1993—). Lt. (j.g.)

USNR, 1954-57. Fellow Am. Trust and Estate Counsel; mem. Tex. Bar Found. Presbyterian. Office: Thompson & Knight 1700 Pacific 1700 Pacific 3300 Dallas TX 75201 Home: 6715 Golf Dr Dallas TX 75205-1213 Office Phone: 214-969-1483.

**REID, SUE TITUS,** law educator; b. Bryan, Tex., Nov. 13, 1939; d. Andrew Jackson Jr. and Lorraine (Wylie) Titus. BS with honors, Tex. Woman's U., 1960; MA, U. Mo., 1962, PhD, 1965; JD, U. Iowa, 1972. Bar: Iowa 1972, U.S. Ct. Appeals (D.C. Cir.) 1978, U.S. Supreme Ct. 1978. From instr. to assoc. prof. sociology Cornell Coll., Mt. Vernon, Iowa, 1963-72; assoc. prof., chmn. dept. sociology Coe Coll., Cedar Rapids, Iowa, 1972-74; assoc. prof. law. U. Wash., Seattle, 1974-76; exec. assoc. Am. Sociol. Assn., Washington, 1976-77; prof. law U. Tulsa, 1978-88; dean, prof. Sch. Criminology, Fla. State U., Tallahassee, 1988-90; prof. pub. adminstrn. and policy Fla. State U., 1990—. Acting chmn. dept. sociology Cornell Coll., 1965-66; vis. assoc. prof. sociology U. Nebr., Lincoln, 1970; vis. disting. prof. law and sociology U. Tulsa, 1977-78, assoc. dean 1979-81; vis. prof. law U. San Diego, 1981-82; mem. People-to-People Crime Prevention Del. to People's Republic of China, 1982; George Beto Vis. Disting. Prof. criminal justice Sam Houston U., Huntsville, Tex., 1984-85; lecture/study tour of Criminal Justice systems of 10 European countries, 1985; cons. Evaluation Policy Rsch. Assocs., Inc., Milw., 1976-77, Nat. Inst. Corrections, Idaho Dept. Corrections, 1984, Am. Correctional Inst., Price-Waterhouse. Author (with others): Bibliographies on Role Methodology and Propositions Volume D - Studies in the Role of the Public School Teacher, 1962, The Correctional System: An Introduction, 1981, Crime and Criminology, 11th edit., 2006; author: Criminal Law, 6th edit., 2004, Criminal Justice, 7th edit., 2006; editor (with David Lyon): Population Crisis: An Interdisciplinary Perspective, 1972; contbr. articles to profl. jours. Recipient Disting. Alumni award Tex. Woman's U., 1979; named One of Okla. Young Leaders of 80's Oklahoma Monthly, 1980. Mem. ABA, Am. Soc. Criminology, Acad. Criminal Justice Scis., Soc. Criminal Jus. Assn. Avocations: walking, reading, cooking, skiing. Office: Fla State Univ Dept Pub Adminstrn Tallahassee FL 32306 Personal E-mail: suetreid@adelphia.net.

**REID, SUSAN L.,** conductor; b. Charlottesville, Va., Apr. 4, 1958; d. L. Leon and Jane S. Reid, Roseann B. Reid. BM, Westminster Choir Coll., 1980; MS, Okla. State U., 1987; MMus, U. Surrey, Guildford, Eng., 1990; DMA, Ariz. State U., 1995; Cert., Royal Coll. of Church Music, Croydon, Eng., 1980. Tchg. asst. U. Surrey, Guildford, England, 1989—90, Ariz. State U., Tempe, 1990—94; dir. of music First United Meth. Ch., Edwardsville, Ill., 1980—83, First Christian Ch., Stillwater, Okla., 1983—89; faculty assoc. in music Ariz. State U., Tempe, 1990—95; dir. of choral activities S.D. Sch. of Mines and Tech., Rapid City, SD, 1995—2000, James Madison U., Harrisonburg, Va., 2000—. Prin. owner Integrated Conducting Inc. Bd. dirs., U.S. corr. Internat. Fedn. Choral Music.

**REID, S.W.,** language educator; b. Neptune, N.J., Nov. 24, 1943; s. Sidney Webb and Mary Cook (Bennett) R.; m. Judith Wright, Aug. 22, 1969; 1 child, Laura. BA, Duke U., 1965; MA, U. Va., 1966, PhD, 1972. Grad. tchg. fellow U. Va., Charlottesville, 1968-70; asst. prof. English, Kent (Ohio) State U., 1970-75, assoc. prof., 1975-84, prof., 1984—, dir. Inst. Bibliography and Editing, 1985—. Vis. fellow Clare Hall, Cambridge (Eng.) U., 1992-93, life mem., 1993—. Textual editor Bicentennial Edition of Charles Brockden Brown, 6 vols., 1977-87; editor-in-chief: (Cambridge edits. of Joseph Conrad) The Secret Agent, 1990, Almayer's Folly, 1994, Notes on Life and Letters, 2004. NDEA fellow U. Va., 1965-68; Rsch. grantee NEH, 1977-84. Office: Kent State University Inst Bibliography-Editing 1118 Library Kent OH 44242-0001 Office Phone: 330-672-2092.

**REID, TARA,** actress; b. Wyckoff, NJ, Nov. 8, 1975; Owner prodn. co. Hi Happy Films. Actor: (TV series) Child's Play, 1982, Saved by the Bell: The New Class, 1994; (TV films) What We Did That Night, 1999; (films) A Return to Salem's Lot, 1987, The Big Lebowski, 1998, Girl, 1998, I Woke Up Early the Day I Died, 1998, Urban Legend, 1998, Cruel Intentions, 1999, Around the Fire, 1999, American Pie, 1999, Body Shots, 1999, Dr. T and the Women, 2000, Just Visiting, 2001, Josie and the Pussycats, 2001, American Pie 2, 2001, Van Wilder, 2002, Devil's Pond, 2003, My Boss's Daughter, 2003, Knots, 2004, Alone in the Dark, 2005; TV appearances include: California Dreams, 1996; G vs E, 2000; Scrubs, 2003—05; host Taradise, E! TV, 2005.

**REID, WILLIAM HILL,** mathematics professor; b. Oakland, Calif., Sept. 10, 1926; s. William Macdonald and Edna Caroline (Hill) R.; m. Elizabeth Mary Kidner, May 26, 1962; 1 child, Margaret Frances. BS, U. Calif., Berkeley, 1949, MS, 1951; PhD, Cambridge U., Eng., 1955, ScD (hon.), 1968; AM (hon.), Brown U., 1961. Lectr. Johns Hopkins U., Balt., 1955-56; NSF fellow Yerkes Observatory, Williams Bay, Wis., 1957-58; asst. prof. Brown U., Providence, 1958-61, assoc. prof., 1961-63, U. Chgo., 1963-65, prof., 1965-89, prof. emeritus, 1989—; prof. Ind. U.-Purdue U., Indianapolis, 1989—. Cons. research labs. Gen. Motors Corp., Warren, Mich., 1960-73. Author (with P.G. Drazin): Hydrodynamic Stability, 1981; author: 2d edit., 2004; contbr. articles to profl. jours. Served with U.S. Mcht. Marine, 1945-47; with AUS, 1954-56. Fulbright Rsch. scholar, Australian Nat. U., 1964—65. Fellow Am. Phys. Soc., Cambridge Philos. Soc.; mem. Am. Math. Soc., Am. Meteorol. Soc., Sigma Xi. Office: Ind U-Purdue U Dept Math Scis 402 N Blackford St Indianapolis IN 46202-3216 Home: 10900 Lightship Ct Fishers IN 46038-2651

**REID, WILLIAM JAMES,** mining executive; b. Cowdenbeath, Scotland, Jan. 18, 1941; arrived in U.S., 1968; s. William and Sheila (Davidson) Reid; m. Thelma Rear, Sept. 27, 1969; children: Judith, Robert. Nat. cert. Mining Engring, Ashington County Tech. Coll., Northumberland, Eng., 1961. Student apprentice Brit. Coal, England, 1958-63; sales engr. Huwood Ltd., England, 1964-68; mining engr. Huwood-Irwin Co., Irwin, Pa., 1968-71, mgr. mining sales, 1971-74, gen. sales mgr., 1974-77, v.p. 1977-79; internat. sales dir. Huwood Ltd., England, 1979-81; exec. v.p. Am. Longwall Mining Corp., Abingdon, Va., 1981-83, pres., 1983-95, Am. Longwall Face Conveyors Inc., Abingdon, 1993-95, Internat. Longwall Cons., Abingdon, 1996-98, Internat. Entertainment Assocs., 1996-98; v.p. mktg. Long Airdox Co., Blacksburg, Va., 1998-99; pres. Eimco LLC, Bluefield, W.Va., 1999-2001, Internat. Longwall Cons., Bluefield, 2001—. Apptd. to Nat. Coal Coun. by Sec. Energy, 1994—; dir. Ea. Coal Coun., 1994—2002. Editor (mng.): Coal Leader, 2001—04; editor: (mng., pub.) Coal News, 2004—. Trustee Sullins Acad., Bristol, Va., 1984. Recipient Overseas medal, Brit. Instn. Mining Engrs., 1992. Mem.: AIME (treas. 1978), Nat. Mining Assn. (bd. govs. mfrs. divsn. 1991—96, 1999—2001), N. Eng. Inst. Mining and Mech. Engrs. (assoc.), Greater Irwin Area C. of C. (bd. dirs. 1977). Presbyterian. Avocations: travel, tennis, wine tasting. Home and Office: Coal News Inc 106 Tamarack St Bluefield WV 24701-4573 Office Phone: 304-327-6777. Personal E-mail: billreid007@comcast.net.

**REID, WILLIAM R.,** agricultural studies educator; b. Morristown, N.J., Jan. 21, 1956; s. Roger A. and Helen L. Reid; m. Brenda L Olcott, June 11, 1977; children: Catherine G., Sarah J., Michael W. BS in Hort. Sci., Rutgers U., New Brunswick, N.J., 1978; MS in Soil Sci., N.C. State U., 1980; PhD in Entomology, Okla. State U., 1993. Rsch. and ext. specialist Kans. State U., Chetopa, 1981—. Contbr. articles to profl. jours. Grantee Nut Tree Ext. in Mo., U. of Mo. 1996—. Mem.: Am. Phytopathol. Soc., Am. Pomological Soc., Entomol. Soc. of Am., Am. Soc. for Hort. Sci., Kans. Nut Growers Assn. (life; sec./treas. 1983—), No. Nut Growers Assn. (life). Achievements include research in Development of new pecan cultivars and novel production techniques. Office: Pecan Experiment Field PO Box 247 Chetopa KS 67336-0247 Office Phone: 620-597-2972. E-mail: wreid@ksu.edu.

**REID-ANDERSON, JAMES,** diagnostic equipment company executive; BS in Commerce with honors, U. Birmingham, Eng.; MBA, Rutgers U. Exec. level positions with Pepsico Inc., Grand Met. PLC, Mobil Oil Corp.; COO chief adminstrv. officer Wilson Sporting Goods, Chgo., 1994-96; exec. v.p., CFO Dade Behring, Deerfield, Ill., 1996-97, exec. v.p., CFO, chief adminstrv.

officer, 1997-99, pres., COO, 1999—2000, pres., CEO, 2000—, chmn., 2002—. Fellow Chartered Assn. Cert. Accts. Office: Dade Behring Corp Hdqrs 1717 Deerfield Rd Deerfield IL 60015-3977*

**REIDENBERG, MARCUS MILTON,** physician, educator; b. Phila., Jan. 3, 1934; m. June Wilson, July 14, 1957; children: Bruce, Joel, Julie. Student, Cornell U., 1951-54; MD, Temple U., 1958. Diplomate Am. Bd. Internal Medicine. Intern Community Gen. Hosp., Reading, Pa., 1958-59; resident Temple U. Hosp., Phila., 1962-65; from instr. to assoc. prof. Temple U. Med. Sch., Phila., 1962-75; assoc. prof. Cornell U. Med. Coll., N.Y.C., 1975-76, prof. pharmacology, head div. clin. pharmacology, 1976—, prof. medicine, 1980—, prof. pub. health, 2002—, acting assoc. dean, 1981-82, asst. dean, 1988—; attending physician N.Y. Hosp., 1980—. Vis. physician Rockefeller U. Hosp., N.Y.C., 1980—; mem. project adv. group FDA, Rockville, Md., 1977-82; vice chmn. Joint Commn. on Prescription Drug Use, Washington, 1977-80; mem. study sect. NIH, Bethesda, Md., 1980-86; del. U.S. Pharmacopeal Conv., 1975-80. Author: Renal Function and Drug Action, 1971; editor: various books, Clin. Pharmacology and Therapeutics, 1985—2001; contbr. articles to profl. jours. Served to lt. M.C., USNR, 1960-62. Recipient Research Career Devel. award NIH, 1970, Julius Sturmer award Phila. Coll. Pharmacy and Sci., 1982. Fellow ACP; mem. Am. Soc. Clin. Investigations, Assn. Am. Physicians, Am. Soc. Clin. Pharmacology and Therapeutics (pres. 1984-85, Rawls Palmer award 1981), Am. Soc. Pharmacology and Expll. Therapeutics (award 1983, Harry Gold award 1999), Internat. Union Pharmacology (vice chmn. sect. clin. pharmacology 1984-87, chmn. 1987-89), World Health Organization Expert Com. on the Selection and Use of Essential Drugs, 1989, 93, 94, 95, 2002, 03, 05 (chmn. essential drugs com. 2003, 05). Office: Cornell U Med Coll Dept Clin Pharmacology 1300 York Ave New York NY 10021-4805 Office Phone: 212-746-6227.

**REIDER, SHIRLEY ANN,** travel company executive; b. Coldwater, Mich., Feb. 21, 1930; d. James J. and Ruth Gray; m. Lee P. Bowman, 1992 (dec.); m. Jack L. Reider, Nov. 13, 1999. AS Bus., Western Mich. U., Kalamazoo, 1949. Co-owner Manzanita Decorative Wood, Potrero, Calif., 1961—2004; travel agt. Great Escape, La Mesa, Calif., 1980—2003; co-owner Laser Engraving, Potrero, Calif., 2002—. Author: (Book) Highway 94 History, 2000, Potrero Roots: A Back Country Heritage, 2004. Highway Planning Group, 1992—; philanthropist proceeds from Highway 94 History go to Hwy. 94 Club, from Potrero Roots go to Friends of Potrero Libr. Mem.: VFW, Highway 94 Club, Friends of Potrero Libr., Kiwanis. Avocations: painting, photography, travel. Home: 1558 Round Potrero Rd Potrero CA 91963 E-mail: jack@aabol.com.

**REIDY, CAROLYN KROLL,** publisher; b. Washington, May 2, 1949; d. Henry August and Mildred Josephine (Mencke) Kroll; m. Stephen Kroll Reidy, Dec. 28, 1974. BA, Middlebury Coll., 1971; MA, Ind. U., 1974, PhD, 1982. Various positions to mgr. subs. rights Random House, Inc., NYC, 1975-83, assoc. pub., 1987-88; dir. subs. rights William Morrow & Co., NYC, 1983-85; v.p., assoc. pub. Vintage Books, NYC, 1985-87, pub., 1987-88, Anchor Books, Doubleday & Co., NYC, 1988; pres., pub. Avon Books, NYC, 1988-92; pres., pub. trade divsn. Simon & Schuster, NYC, 1992—2001, pres. adult publ. divsn., 2001—. Bd. dirs. NAMES Project, 1994—98, Literacy Partners, Inc., 2000—, Nat. Book Found., 2001—. Mem.: NY Women in Comm. (recipient Matrix award 2003). Pubs. Lunch Club. Office: Simon & Schuster 1230 Avenue Of The Americas New York NY 10020-1586 Business E-Mail: carolyn.reidy@simonandschuster.com

**REIDY, DANIEL EDWARD,** lawyer; b. Chgo., Nov. 21, 1949; s. Francis W. and Ann E. (Harrington) R.; m. Elizabeth Gamble. Aug. 21, 1971; children: David, Patrick, Kevin, Jean. BA in Polit. sci., cm laude, Loyola U., 1971; JD magna cum laude, U. Mich., 1974. Bar: Ill. 1974, US Dist. Ct. (no. dist.) Ill. 1974, US Supreme Ct., Ill., 1974, US Ct. Appeals (7th cir.) 1975, US Ct. Appeals (11th cir.) 1992, US Ct. Appeals (fed. cir.) 1994, US Dist. Ct. (ctrl. dist.) Ill. 1995, US Dist. Ct. (so. dist.) Ill. 2002, US Ct. Appeals (1st cir.), 2004. Law clk. to Hon. Walter J. Cummings U.S. Ct. Appeals (7th cir.), Chgo., 1974-75; asst. US Atty.'s Office, Chgo., 1975—85; first asst. US atty. No. Dist. of Ill., Chgo., 1985—87; ptnr. Jones Day, Chgo., 1987—. Litig. group coord., Chgo. & nat. chair, Corp. Criminal Investigation Practice; mem. commn. adminstrn. justice Ill. Supreme Ct., Chgo., 1992-93. Fellow Internat. Acad. Trial Lawyers, Am. Coll. Trial Lawyers; mem. ABA, Fed. Bar Assn., Chgo. Bar Assn.(sec. 2001-2005), Chgo. Coun. Lawyers, Chgo. Inn Ct. Office: Jones Day 77 W Wacker Ste 3500 Chicago IL 60601-1692 Office Phone: 312-782-3939. Business E-Mail: dereidy@jonesday.com.

**REIDY, THOMAS MICHAEL,** financial executive; b. Elmira, N.Y., Dec. 22, 1951; s. Bernard Thomas and Betty Pauline Reidy; m. Rosemarie Stella, June 12, 1982; 1 child, Carla. AS, Corning C.C., 1971; BA, St. John Fisher Coll., 1973; Cert. in Exec. Leadership, Cornell U. Cert. fin. planner. Exec. br. dir. YMCA, Rochester, N.Y., 1975-84; fin. planner IDS/Am. Express, Rochester, 1984-86; pres., CEO TMR Adv. Group, Rochester, 1986-95; divsn. mgr. Waddall & Reed, Rochester, 1995-98; pres. Morgan & Alexander Ltd., Rochester, 1998—. Pres. CPA/Bus. Forum, Rochester, 1988—90; prin. Sandler Sales Inst., Pittsford, NY, 2002—. Author: (tng. manual) The NOW Client System, 1996, The True Wealth Revolution, 1999, Quality Life Management System, 1999, Winning and Losing It, 2005. Recipient Outstanding Young Man Am. Jaycees, 1979, Businessman of Yr. Nat. Rep. Congrl. Com., 2003. Mem. Rotary Club, C. of C. Profl. Sales Soc. (bd. dirs. 1988-89). Office Phone: 585-249-9189. Business E-Mail: tom@thomasreidy.com.

**REIF, DAVID (FRANK DAVID REIF),** artist, educator; b. Cin., Dec. 14, 1941; s. Carl A. and Rachel L. (Clifton) R.; m. Ilona Jekabsons, July 30, 1966; 1 child. Megan Elizabeth. BFA, Art Inst. Chgo., 1968, MFA, Yale U., 1970. Asst. prof. art U. Wyo., Laramie, 1970-74, assoc. prof., 1974-81, U. Mich., Ann Arbor, 1980-81; prof. U. Wyo., Laramie, 1981—2004, acting head dept. art, 1986—87, Disting. prof. emeritus, 2004—; prin., owner Reif Artworks & Design Consulting, Laramie, Wyo., 2005—. Selection cons. Ucross Found. Residency Program, Wyo., 1983—; exhibit juror Artwest Nat., Jackson, Wyo., 1986; panelist Colo. State U., Ft. Collins, 1981; lectr. U. Mich.; 1980; apptd. Wyo. Arts Coun., 1993-96; vis. artist lectr. Colo. State U., 1996; vis. artist Colo. State U. Ft. Collins, 1996; 3-D juror art exhbn. Colo. State Fair, Pueblo, 2001. One-man shows include U. Wyo. Art Mus., 1993, Dorsky Galleries, NYC, 1980, No. Ariz. U., 1977, 87, U. Mich., 1980-81, One West Ctr. Contemporary Art, Ft. Collins, 1991, West Wyo. C.C., Rock Springs, 1999, Casper Coll. Goldstein Gallery, 2003; exhibited in group shows at First, Second and Third Wyo. Biennial Tour, 1984-88, U.S. Olympics Art Exhbn., LA, 1984, Miss. Mus. Art and NEA Tour, 1981-83, LA Invitational Sculpture Tour Exhbn., 1991-92, Nicolaysen Art Mus., Casper, Wyo., 1994, Jackson Hole Ctr. Arts, Wyo., 2006, Gene Siskel Film Ctr. Gall, Art Inst. Chgo., 2006. Apptd. chair Wyo. Arts Coun., 1995-96. With USAR, 1963-69. Recipient F.D. Pardee award Yale U., 1970; Best Sculpture award Joslyn Art Mus. Omaha, 1978; grantee Nat. Endowment Arts, 1978-79, Wyo. Basic Rsch., 1983-84, 86-87; Tchg. Excellence grantee U. Wyo., 1996-97. Mem. Coll. Art Assn., Internat. Sculpture Ctr. Democrat. Home: 3340 Aspen Ln Laramie WY 82070-5702 Office: U Wyo Dept Art PO Box 3138 Laramie WY 82071-3138 Office Phone: 307-745-3110.

**REIF, L. RAFAEL,** academic administrator, engineering educator; m. Christine Reif; children: Jessica, Blake. BS, Universidad de Carabobo, Venezuela, 1973; MS, Stanford U., 1975, PhD, 1979. Asst. prof. Universidad Simon Bolivar, Caracas, Venezuela, 1973—74; faculty mem. MIT, Cambridge, 1980—, Maseeh Professor of Emerging Tech., dir. Microsystems Tech. Labs., 1990—99, assoc. head electrical engring., 1999—2004, head Dept. Electrical Engring. and Computer Sci., 2004—05, provost, 2005—. Recipient US Presdl. Young Investigator Award, 1984, Aristotle Award, Semiconductor Rsch. Corp., 2000. Fellow: IEEE; mem. Am. Physical Soc., Electrochemical Soc., Tau Beta Pi. Office: MIT Rm 38-403 77 Massachusetts Ave Cambridge MA 02139-4307 Office Phone: 617-253-4601. E-mail: reif@mtl.mit.edu.

**REIF COHEN, JESSICA,** broadcast executive; m. Bob Cohen; children: AJ, Marisa Rachel. BS in Mktg., NYU, MBA in Fin. and Internat. Bus. Securities analyst, mng. dir. Oppenheimer & Co. Inc.; securities analyst First Boston Corp., Credit Lyonnais, Arnhold & S. Bleichroeder; mng. dir. and sr. media & entertainment analyst Merrill Lynch & Co., 1994, first v.p. rsch., media and global securities. Mem.: Nat. Assn. Television Program Execs., Mus. Television and Radio, Internat. Radio and Television Soc., Media and Entertainment Analysts NY, Beta Gamma Sigma. Office: Merrill Lynch & Co 4 World Financial Ctr New York NY 10080*

**REIFEL WERNER, MELODY ANN,** academic administrator; b. Cheboygan, Mich., Mar. 19, 1957; d. Robert Thomas Johnson and Delight Lou Fagan, William Joseph Fagan (Stepfather); m. Thomas Joseph Werner, Apr. 2, 2004; children: Thomas Joseph Reifel, Anthony John Reifel. EdD, Ea. Mich. U., 2006. Assoc. athletics dir., sr. woman adminstr. Ea. Mich. U., Ypsilanti, 2002—04, dir. compliance, 2004—. Asst. athletics dir. Ea. Mich. U., 1999—2002. Voting mem. Chelsea Edn. Found., Mich., 1992—95. Mem.: Nat. Assn. Collegiate Women Athletics Administrs. Office: Ea Mich U 200 Pierce Hall Ypsilanti MI 48197 Office Phone: 734-487-2327. Home Fax: 734-487-3064; Office Fax: 734-487-3064. Business E-Mail: melody.reifel@emich.edu.

**REIFF, LAURA FOOTE,** lawyer; b. Goldsboro, NC, July 21, 1964; BA in Legal Inst., Econ., Govt., Am. Univ., 1986; JD with honors, George Washington Univ., 1989. Bar: Md. 1989, DC 1990, US Ct. of Internat. Trade. Shareholder, co-chair bus. immigration group Greenberg Traurig LLP, McLean, Va. Co-recipient Outstanding Young Lawyers award, Am. Immigration Law Assn., 1996; recipient Albert Arent Pro Bono award for Cmty. Svc., 1991. Mem.: ABA, Fed. Bar Assn., DC Bar Assn., Md. Bar Assn., Am. Immigration Law Found., Am. Immigration Lawyers Assn. Office: Greenberg Traurig LLP 12th Fl 1750 Tysons Blvd Mc Lean VA 22102-4202 Office Phone: 703-749-1372. Office Fax: 703-714-8372. Business E-Mail: reiffl@gtlaw.com.

**REIFF, PATRICIA HOFER,** space physicist, educator; b. Oklahoma City, Mar. 14, 1950; d. William Henry and Maxine Ruth (Hoffer) R.; m. Thomas Westfall Hill, July 4, 1976; children: Andrea Hofer Hill, Adam Reiff Hill, Amelia Reiff Hill. Student, Wellesley Coll., 1967-68; BS, Okla. State U., 1971; MS, Rice U., 1974, PhD, 1975. Cert. secondary tchr., Okla., Tex. Resident rsch. assoc. Marshall Space Flight Ctr., Huntsville, Ala., 1975-76; rsch. assoc. space physics and astronomy dept. Rice U., Houston, 1975, asst. prof. space physics and astronomy dept., 1978-81, asst. chmn. space physics and astronomy dept., 1979-85, assoc. rsch. sci., 1981-87, sr. rsch. scientist, 1987-90. Adj. asst. prof. Rice U., 1976-78, disting. faculty fellow, 1990-92, prof. 1992—, chmn. dept. space physics and astronomy, 1996-99, dir. Rice Space Inst., 1999—; mem. sci. team Atmosphere Explorer Mission, Dynamics Explorer Mission; co-investigator Global Geospace Sci. Mission, ESA/Cluster Mission, IMAGE Mission; prin. investigator The Public Connection NASA, Mus. Tchg. Planet Earth Immersive Earth; cons. Houston Mus. Natural Sci., 1986—; adv. com. on atmospheric scis. NSF, Washington, 1988-92; mem. stategic implementation study panel NASA, Washington, 1989-91; mem. space sci. adv. com. NASA, 1993-98, mem. space sta. utilization subcom., 1995-98; mem. adv. com. Los Alamos Non-Proliferation Divsn., 1998-2001; univ. rep. U. Space Rsch. Assn., Washington, 1993—, chair Coun. of Instns., 2001-04; exec. com. George Observatory, Houston, 1989-92, others. Designer Cockrell Sundial/Solar Telescope, 1989; editor EOS (sci. newspaper), 1986-89; contbr. articles to profl. jours. Trustee, Citizens' Environ. Coalition, Houston, 1978-98, pres. 1980-85, adv. com. 1998-2000; mem. air quality com. Houston/Galveston Area Coun., 1980-83, Green Ribbon Com., City of Houston, 1981-83; active coms. Macedonia United Meth. Ch., 1988—. Named rsch. fellow NAS/NRC., 1975, an Outstanding Young Woman Am., 1977, '80, to Houston's Women on the Move, 1990; named Outstanding Aerospace Educator, Women in Aerospace, 1999; NASA grantee 1993, 94, 95, 98, 99; recipient NASA Group Achievement award. Fellow Am. Geophys. Union (fin. com. 1980-82, editor search com. 1992, pub. edn. com.); mem. Cosmos Club, Wellesley Club, Internat. Union of Geodesy and Geophysics (del. 1975, 81, 83, 89, 91, 93, 95, chair working group 2F, 1991-95). Avocations: organic gardening, beef ranching, scouting. Office: Rice U Dept Physics and Astronomy 6100 S Main St Houston TX 77251 Business E-Mail: reiff@rice.edu.

**REIFFEL, LEONARD,** physicist, consultant; b. Chgo., Sept. 30, 1927; s. Carl and Sophie (Miller) R.; m. Judith Eve Blumenthal, 1952 (div. 1962); children— Evan Carl, David Lee; m. Nancy L. Jeffers, 1971. B.Sc., Ill. Inst. Tech., 1947, M.Sc., 1948, PhD, 1953. Physicist Perkin-Elmer Corp., Conn., 1948; engring. physicist U. Chgo. Inst. Nuclear Studies, 1948-49; with Ill. Inst. Tech. Research Inst., Chgo., 1949-65, dir. physics research, 1956-63, v.p., 1963-65; cons. to Apollo program NASA Hdqrs., 1965-70; pvt. practice cons., 1970—; tech. dir. manned space flight expts. bd. NASA, 1966-68; chmn. bd. Instructional Dynamics, Inc., 1966-81, Interand Corp., 1969-91, Telestrator Industries, Inc., 1970-73; sci. editor Sta. WBBM-CBS radio, Chgo.; sci. cons./commentator WBBM-TV, 1971-72; host Backyard Safari, 1971-73; sci. feature broadcaster WEEI-CBS radio, Boston, 1965-75; syndicated newspaper columnist World Book Ency. Sci. Service, Inc. (later Universal Sci. News, Inc.), 1966-72, Los Angeles Times Syndicate, 1972-76; sci. cons. CBS Network, 1967-71; chmn., CEO Exelar Corp., Chgo., 1991—; chmn. bd., pres., CEO Ameraine Corp., Chgo., 1992-95; bd. overseers Armour Coll., bd. advisors engring. depts. Ill. Inst. Tech., 1995—; founder, chmn. Luxelar Corp., 2001—; founder Exelar Med. Corp., 2004, chmn., CTO, 2004—; founder, chmn., CTO Iron Mount Corp., 2005—. Cons. Korean Govt. on establishment atomic energy rsch. program; mem. adv. com. isotope and radiation devel. AEC; com. rsch. reactors NAS, 1958-64; cons. U.S. Army, 1976—; chmn. Reiffel Technologies, LLC; mem. advanced tech. adv. com. Children's Mem. Rsch. Ctr. Chgo., 2005-. Author: (book) The Contaminant, 1979; author numerous sci. papers; patentee in field. Bd. dirs. Student Competitions on Relevant Engring. Named Outstanding Young Man of Year Chgo. Jr. C. of C., 1954, 61; recipient Merit award Chgo. Tech. Socs., 1968, Peabody award, 1968, IR-100 award Telestrator CBS Chalkboard, 1970, award Aviation Writers Assn., 1971, IR-100 award, 1972, 73, 85, Disting. Alumni Achievement award Ill. Inst. Tech., 1974, Third Annual High Tech Entrepreneur award, 1986, Emmy award, 2004; named to Hall of Fame IIT, 1984. Fellow Am. Phys. Soc.; mem. AAAS, Chgo. Literary Club, Sigma Xi, Tau Beta Pi, Eta Kappa Nu. Achievements include being responsible for world's 1st indsl. nuclear reactor, 1956. Home: 602 W Deming Pl Chicago IL 60614-2618 Office Phone: 773-871-0171. Personal E-mail: lreiffel@aol.com.

**REIFLER, STEWART,** lawyer; b. Poughkeepsie, N.Y., May 5, 1954; s. Aaron and Sally Reifler; m. Sheryl Louise Perry, Sept. 19, 1982; 1 child, Jonathan Perry. Student, McGill U., 1972—75; BA, Bard Coll., 1979; JD magna cum laude, NY Law Sch., 1992. Bar: N.Y. 1992, Conn. 1992, US Tax Ct. 1992, U.S. Supreme Ct. 2004. Assoc. Law Offices of Joseph E. Bachelder, N.Y.C., 1992—95; Weil, Gotshal & Manges, 1995—98; ptnr. Pricewaterhouse-Coopers, 1998—2001; ptnr., shareholder, head N.Y. exec. compensation group Vedder, Price, Kaufman & Kammholz, 2001—. Steering com. mem., exec. compensation AICPA. Co-author: Compensation Committee Handbook, 2d edit., 2004; contbr. articles to profl. jours. Trustee Westport Pub. Libr., Conn. Recipient Outstanding Editl. Contbn., NY Law Sch. Law Rev., 1991, Law Rev., NY Law Sch., Am. Jurisprudence award, 1991. Mem.: ABA, N.Y. State Bar Assn., Conn. State Bar Assn., Assn. of Bar of City of N.Y., WorldatWork, Nat. Assn. Stock Plan Profls., Minuteman Yacht Club, The Sky Club. Home: 8 Brightfield Ln Westport CT 06880 Office: Vedder Price Kaufman & Kammholz 805 Third Ave New York NY 10022 Office Phone: 212-407-7700. E-mail: sreifler@vedderprice.com.

**REIFSNIDER, KENNETH LEONARD,** metallurgist, educator; b. Balt., Feb. 19, 1940; s. David Leonard and Daisy Pearl (Hess) R.; m. Loretta Lieb, June 15, 1963; children: Eric Scott, Jason Miles. BA, Western Md. Coll., 1963; BS in Engring., Johns Hopkins U., 1963, MS in Engring., 1965, PhD, 1968. Jr. instr. Johns Hopkins U., Balt., 1966-67; asst. prof. Va. Poly. Inst. and State U., Blacksburg, 1968-72, chmn. materials engring. sci. Ph.D. program,

1974-92, assoc. prof., 1972-75, prof., 1975-83, Reynolds Metals prof. engring. sci. and mechanics, 1983-90, Alexander Giacco prof., 1990—2002; chmn. adminstrn. bd. Ctr. Composite Materials and Structures, 1984, 1994-97; Pratt and Whitney Chair prof. design and reliability U. Conn., 2002—; dir. Conn. Global Fuel Cell Ctr., Storrs. Dir. Va. Inst. for Material Systems, 1988-2001, Conn. Global Fuel Cell Ctr., 2004—; assoc. provost for interdisciplinary programs, 1996-2001; engr. Lawrence Livermore Nat. Lab., 1981; mem. Nat. M aterials Adv. Bd., 1996—; cons. in materials sci. NATO, 1969, 75. Editor in chief Internat. Jour. of Fatigue; assoc editor Internat. Jour. of Fuel Cell Science and Technology, 2003—; editor, co-editor, author books, book chpts., articles for profl. publs. Mem. troop 44 com. Boy Scouts Am. Blacksburg, Va. Recipient Va. Acad. Sci. J. Shelton Horsley award, 1978, Va. Poly Inst. Alumni award, 1982, Disting. Rsch. award Am. Soc. Composites, 1992. Fellow ASTM (founder Jour. of Composites Tech. and Rsch., vice chmn. standing com. on publs., award of merit 1982); mem. ASME, NAE, Coun. on Engring. Home: 13 Quail Run Rd Storrs Mansfield CT 06268-2768 Office: Conn Global Fuel Cell Ctr 44 Weaver Rd, Unit 5233 Storrs Mansfield CT 06269-5233 also: 262 United Technologies Bldg 191 Auditorium Rd, Unit 3139 Storrs Mansfield CT 06269-3139 Office Phone: 860-486-5360, 860-486-3139. Office Fax: 860-486-8378, 860-486-5088. E-mail: reifsnid@engr.uconn.edu.*

**REIG, JUNE WILSON,** scriptwriter, television director, television producer; b. Schenectady, N.Y., June 1, 1933; d. Wallace John and Lillian Lucy (Gay) Wilson; m. Robert Maxwell, Nov. 26, 1969. BA summa cum laude, N.Y. State U., 1954; MA in Dramatic Arts, NYU, 1962. Instr. NYU, N.Y.C., 1962—67; prodr., dir. NYU Theater, N.Y.C., 1963—67; dir.-prodr., writer news and pub. affairs NBC TV Network, N.Y.C., 1963—67; dir., writer, prodr. divsn. entertainment NBC-TV Network, N.Y.C., 1967—73; pres. Bunny/Chord Prodns., N.Y.C., 1972—97. Author: (book) Dairy of the Boy King Tut-Ankh-Amen, Charles Scribner's Sons, 1978; writer: (music spl.) The Heart of Christmas with Skitch Henderson, Robert Shaw Chorale and NBC Symphony, 1965; An Afternoon at Tanglewood with Erich Leinsdorf and the Boston Symphony Orch. (Peabody award); writer, dir. (with Johnny Carson) (TV spl.) Stuart Little, 1966 (Peabody award, Prix Jeunesse); writer The Reluctant Dragon, 1968 (Brotherhood award); writer, dir. prodr. (with Burl Ives) Rabbit Hill, 1966 (ALA award); writer, dir., prodr. Bill Cosby As I See It, 1970 (Ohio State award); A Day with Bill Cosby, 1971; Jennifer & Me, 1972; prodr., writer (with Edward Villella and Joanne Woodward) Little Women, the ballet, 1976; prodr., writer (with Orson Welles) Tut, the Boy King, 1978 (Peabody award); writer, dir., prodr.: (TV series) Watch Your Child - The Me Too Show, 1973 (Action for Children's TV Achievement award); films in permanent collections Mus. Broadcasting, N.Y.C. Nominee Emmy award, 1966, 1976; recipient Christopher award. Mem.: NATAS, Dirs. Guild Am., Writers Guild Am., Audubon Soc., NYU Alumni Assn., Internat. Soc. Animal Rights, Friends of Animals, Alan Devoe Bird Club (Old Chatham, N.Y.). Avocations: photography, music, animals. Office: care Howard Comart 450 7th Ave Ste 1701 New York NY 10123-1701 *Whether I am working on a teleplay or book, I write about things I believe children are interested in: feelings, aspirations, caring, animals, loving. As I see it, too much of the fare for young people gives them a distorted view of how much violence there is in the world, and I want to counteract that impression. I want to write about things that create a sense of worth, warm security, and an absence of unnecessary anxiety. When I do write about the darker things that happen in life, it is to help the young person understand himself and the world a little better.*

**REILEY, JORGE ALBERTO,** neurologist; b. Arequipa, Peru, Sept. 27, 1958; arrived in U.S., 1988; s. Octavio Rene and Dora Luz Reiley; m. Susan Zecchin, Apr. 8, 1989; children: Giulianna, Jordan, Andrew, Alexander. MD, U. Carabobo, Valencia, Venezuela, 1986. Diplomate Am. Bd. Psychiatry and Neurology, cert. in acupuncture N.Y., diplomate Am. Acad. Pain Mgmt. Pgy-1 internal medicine Cath. Med. Ctr., Jamaica, NY, 1993—94; resident to chief resident dept. neurology SUNY Health Sci. Ctr., Bklyn., 1994—97, clin. neurophysiology fellow, 1997—98; attending dept. neurology Queens Hosp. Ctr., Jamaica, 1998—2000; staff neurologist Comprehensive Care N.Y., Hewlett, NY, 1998—2000; attending dept. neurology Peninsula Hosp., Far Rockaway, NY, 1998—2000, St. Johns Episcopal Hosp., Far Rockaway, 1998—2000; staff neurologist ARCE Med., Woodside, NY, 2000, Village Med. and Rehab., Huntington, NY, 2000, S. Shore Neurol. Assn., Southampton, NY, 2000—02; pres. East End Neurol., East Hampton, NY, 2002—, Cutchogue, NY, 2002—, Ctr. Moriches, NY, 2002—; attending dept. neurol. South Hampton Hosp., NY, 2002—, Ctrl. Suffolk Hosp., Riverhead, NY, 2002—, Ea. LI Hosp., Greenport, NY, 2002—. Decorated Medal of Honor Venezulan Armed Forces; named Neurology Del., Com. Interns and Residents, 1997—98. Mem.: Am. Acad. Pain Mgmt., Am. Acad. Neurology. Roman Catholic. Avocations: tennis, travel, theater. Office: East End Neurol PO Box 716 32645 Main Rd Cutchogue NY 11935

**REILEY, T(HOMAS) PHILLIP,** systems analyst, consultant; b. Ft. Lewis, Wash., May 5, 1950; s. Thomas Phillip and Anne Marie (Russick) R. BSc in Biophysics, Pa. State U., 1973; postgrad. in Bus. Adminstrn., Rutgers U.; MBA, NYU, 1991. Cert. prodn. and inventory mgmt., cert. integrated resource mgmt. Inventory supr. Leland Tube Co., South Plainfield, NJ, 1973-76; prodn. inventory control supr. Bomar Crystal Co., Middlesex, NJ, 1976-79; prodn. control mgr. Codi Semiconductor Inc., Linden, NJ, 1979-81; mfg. systems analyst Western Union Info. Systems, Mahwah, NJ, 1981-85; bus. analyst Nabisco Brands Biscuit Divsn., Parsippany, NJ, 1985-91, sr. systems analyst, 1991-94, tech. advisor 1994-97; applications cons. SAP Am., Morristown, NJ, 1997—, Newton Sq., Pa. Mem. Am. Prodn. and Inventory Control Soc. (past chmn. ednl. com. Raritan Valley chpt.), NY Acad. Sci., Conn. Logistics Mgmt., Am. Inst. Mgmt. Accts., Mensa. Republican. Home: 1308 Centennial Ave #111 Piscataway NJ 08854 Office Phone: 610-661-7603. Business E-Mail: phillip.reiley@sap.com, preiley@world.std.com.

**REILING, HENRY BERNARD,** business educator; b. Richmond, Ky., Feb. 5, 1938; s. Henry Bernard and Lucille Frances (Fowler) R.; m. Carol-Lina Maria Schuetz, June 4, 1962; children: Christina Lucille Reiling Breiter, Maria Hays, Carol-Lena Alexis Reiling Lessans. BA, Northwestern U., 1960; MBA, Harvard U., 1962; JD, Columbia U., 1965. Bar: N.Y. 1965. Mem. faculty Columbia U. Bus. Sch., 1965-76, prof., 1974-76; vis. prof. Stanford U. Bus. Sch., 1974-75; vis. assoc. prof. Harvard U. Bus. Sch., 1972-73, prof., 1976—, Eli Goldston prof. bus. adminstrn., 1978—2005, Baker Found. prof., 2005—. Contbr. articles to profl. jours. Trustee Riverside Ch., NYC, 1976-77; bd. advisors Northwestern U. Coll. Arts and Scis., 1989—; alumni regent, 1997-, alumni trustee, 2004- Recipient Alumnus Merit award, Northwestern U., 1996, Svc. award, 2002. Mem. ABA, N.Y. Bar Assn., Bar Assn. City N.Y., Am. Fin. Assn., Fin. Mgmt. Assn., Nat. Tax Assn., Tax Inst. Am., Union Club (N.Y.C.), The Country Club (Chestnut Hill, Mass.), Beta Gamma Sigma. Home: 28 Meriam St Lexington MA 02420-3618 Office: Harvard U Bus Sch Boston MA 02163

**REILING, WALTER ANTHONY, JR.,** surgeon; b. Dayton, Ohio, July 22, 1939; s. Walter Anthony and Eva Dorothy Reiling; m. Suzanne Jane Geyer, July 22, 1961; children: Walter Anthony, Elizabeth S.(dec.), Mary Anne, Joseph C., Jennifer E. BS, U. Dayton, Ohio, 1961; MD, Harvard U., Boston, 1965. Diplomate Am. Bd. Surgery. Intern Boston City Hosp. Harvard Surg. Svc., 1965—66, surg. resident, 1966—70; instr. surgery Harvard U., Boston, 1969—71; clin. prof. surgery Wright State U., Dayton, 1971—; pvt. practice Gem City Surg. Assocs., Dayton, 1970—. Bd. dirs. OHA Ins. Solutions, Columbus, 2004—, Premier Health Ptnrs., Dayton, 1996—2003. Mem. Ohio Bd. Regents, 2005—; treas. Physicians Charitable Trust, Dayton, 1995—; bd. dirs. Wright Health Found., 2000—05. Fellow: ACS (del. 1988—); mem.: AMA, Ohio State Med. Assn. (pres. 1992—93), Ohio Hosp. Assn. (bd. dirs. 1996—2003). Republican. Roman Catholic. Avocations: amateur radio, fishing, boating, water sports. Home: 1431 Ridgefield Way Centerville OH 45459 Office: Gem City Surgical Associates 9000 N Main St Ste 233 Dayton OH 45415

**REILLEY, DENNEN,** research agency administrator, educator; b. Greenwich, Conn., Mar. 1, 1937; s. Philip Francis and Florence Rita (Junkersfield) R.; m. Margaret Randall, Dougherty, Dec. 26, 1976; children: Philip F., Christopher J., Diane L., Elizabeth S., Katherine M. BSS, Fairfield U., 1959; MEd, U. Hartford, 1965; postgrad., U. Conn., 1965-70, CAGS, 1970. Tchr. New Britain (Conn.) Pub. Schs., 1960-65; tchr., adminstr. West Hartford (Conn.) Pub. Schs., 1965-69, 72-73; mem. faculty Central Conn. State Coll., New Britain, 1969-72; dir. field svcs. Edn. Devel. Ctr., Newton, Mass., 1973-82; sr. assoc., CEO Applied Rsch. Assocs., Sharon, Mass., 1980—. Adj. faculty U. Wyo., U. Minn.; cons. Am. Humane Assn., Edn. Devel. Ctr.; particip. Intl. Wannsee Conf., Berlin, Germany, 2002. Author: Training Program for Animal Care and Control Professionals, Sources: A Resource Guide to Funding Assistance for Parenting Programs, Education for Parenthood Conference Report; the Tri-State Parenting Collaborative, (with Jan Mokros) Summary of Exploring Childhood Evaluation Findings, The Animal Welfare Board of Directors, Total Quality Management: Implications for Animal Care and Control Professionals, Management Perspectives for Animal Care and Control Professionals, Board Perspectives for Nonprofit Organizations, Long Range Planning for Nonprofit Organizations; contbr. articles to profl. jours. Mem. New Britain Rep. town com., 1961-65; conductor mgmt. seminars nationally Not-for-profit orgns., 1982—. Recipient Rosemary Ames award Am. Humane Assn., 1983. Mem. Nat. Coun. Social Studies (conv. spkr. 1963-79, curriculum com. 1974-77, field svcs. bd. 1977-80), Conn. Coun. Social Studies (pres. 1965-66), NEA (life), ASCD, Am. Humane Assn., HSUS (conv. spkr. 1980-94, cons. 1994—). Office: 57 Brook Rd Sharon MA 02067-1415

**REILLEY, DENNIS H.,** chemicals executive; m. Cindy Reilley; children: Jason, Michael. BS in Fin, Okla. State U., 1975. With Conoco, 1974-80, mgr. adminstrn. surface transp. Houston, 1980-81, exec. asst. to pres. petroleum ops., 1981-83, gen. mgr. planning and adminstrn. N.Am. mktg., 1983-84; v.p. ops. Kayo Oil Co., Chattanooga, 1984-87; pres., mng. dir. Conoco, 1987-89; dir. ops. white pigment and mineral products divsn. DuPont, 1989-91, v.p., gen. mgr. white pigment and mineral products, 1991-95, v.p., gen. mgr. specialty chems., 1995-96, v.p., gen. mgr. Lycra/Terathane, 1996-97, sr. v.p., 1997-99, exec. v.p., COO, 1999-2000; chmn., pres., CEO Praxair, Danbury, Conn., 2000—06, chmn., CEO, 2006—. Mem. electricity adv. bd. U.S Dept. Energy; past chmn. Am. Chemistry Council; bd. dir. Entergy Corp., Marathon Oil Co. Bd. mem. Conservation Fund. Address: Praxair Inc 39 Old Ridgebury Rd Danbury CT 06810-5103*

**REILLEY, JAMES CLARK,** artist, cartoonist, small business owner; b. Detroit, Nov. 4, 1919; s. James Aloyisus and Lillian May (Cole) R.; m. Beatrice C. Clemente, May 10, 1952 (dec.); children: James A. (dec.), Anthony Francis, Beatrice Anita. Grad., Art Inst. of Pitts., 1948. Artist Banner Advt., Phila., 1948-49; layout artist Lit Bros. Dept. Store, Phila., 1949; comic book illustrator Jim Prentice, LI, 1950; artist DuPont Co., Wilmington, Del., 1950-59; artist/owner Jim Reilley Studio, Wilmington, 1959-94; ret. Link trainer instr.; jazz harmonica soloist various radio programs and shows, Chanutefield, Ill., Walla-Walla, Wash. Cartoon series, This is the Life, Hornepipe. Sgt. USAAF, 1942-45. Inducted to Penns Grove H.S. Personal Achievement Hall of Fame, 1990. Roman Catholic. Avocations: fishing, music, sports. Home: 110 N Broad St Penns Grove NJ 08069-1269

**REILLEY, MARGARET RANDALL,** secondary school educator; b. Atlanta, Feb. 7, 1948; d. Guy Randall and Margaret Olivia (Ross) Dougherty; m. Dennen Reilley, Dec. 27, 1975; stepchildren: Philip F., Christopher J., Diane L. Reilley Waitkus, Elizabeth S. Reilley-Matthews, Katherine M. Reilley Lawn. BA in History, Stanford U., 1970; MA in Edn., Tufts U., 1971. Cert. tchr., adminstr., Mass. Tchr. social studies Norwood HS, Mass., 1971—. Founder, chmn. Norwood Law-Related Edn. Adv. Com., 1987-90; vice chmn. law related edn. com. Mass. Bar Assn., Boston, 1989-93; trainer Nat. Inst. for Citizen Edn. in the Law, Washington, 1990—; cons., reviewer Street Law, 4th edit., 1990-91; bd. dirs. Mass. Assn. for Law-Related Edn., 1990-98; mentor for new tchrs., 2000-; particip. Intl. Wannsee Conf., Berlin, Germany, 2002; bd. dirs. Harriet Goldin Found. Contbr. articles to legal jours. Recipient Horace Mann award Norwood Pub. Schs., 1989, Sch.-Cmty. Bar Partnership award ABA, 1990, Law-Related Edn. Tchr. of Yr. award Mass. Assn. for Law-Related Edn., 1990, Excellence in Tchg. award Harriet Goldin Found., 1993, Superior Tchr. of Law-Related Edn. award Norfolk County Bar Assn., 1994, Mass. Team Dist. Team fellow, 1996—, edn./rsch. fellow, JFK Libr. Mem. Nat. Coun. for Social Studies, Mass. Coun. for Social Studies (bd. dirs. 1993-95), South Shore Coun. for Social Studies (pres. 1993-95) Delta Kappa Gamma, Alpha Iota (pres. 1990-92), Harriet Goldin Found. (bd. dirs., 2002—). Avocations: walking, travel, gardening. Office: Norwood Pub Schs Nichols St Norwood MA 02062

**REILLEY, SEAN PATRICK,** psychology professor, consultant; s. Michael Charles and June Carol Reilley; m. Autumn Reilley, July 7, 2001. BA, U. Cin., 1995, MA, 1999, PhD, 2002. Lic. psychologist KY Bd. Examiners of Psychology, 2004. Asst. prof. Morehead State U., Ky., 2002—. Clin. cons. Univ. Counseling Ctr., Morehead, 2004—. Contbr. scientific papers, articles to profl. jours. Grantee, Ky. NSF Exptl. Program to Stimulate Competitive Rsch., 2003, Rsch. and Creative Prodn. Com. Morehead State U., 2003, Ctr. Tchg. and Learning, 2004, Inst. Regional Analysis and Pub. Policy, 2004, 2005. Mem.: APA, Ky. Psychol. Assn., Ky. Acad. Sci. (sec psychology sect. 2004, chair 2005), Midwestern Psychol. Assn., Am. Psychol. Soc. Office: Morehead State U Dept Psychology 601 Ginger Hall 150 University Blvd Morehead KY 40351 Office Phone: 606-783-2985. Home Fax: 606-783-5077; Office Fax: 606-783-5077. Personal E-mail: s.reilley@morehead-st.edu.

**REILLY, ANNE HUEDEPOHL,** university educator, researcher; b. Chgo., Sept. 16, 1957; d. E. Bradley and Lynne (Swanson) Huedepohl; m. John J. Reilly, Aug. 12, 1978; children: Kristine Anne, Meghan Lynne, Caroline Hannah. BA in Econs. and Bus. Adminstrn. summa cum laude, Knox Coll., 1978; MBA in Finance, U. Iowa, 1980; PhD in Organizational Behavior, Northwestern U., 1989. Banking officer spl. industries Cont. Ill. Nat. Bank, Chgo., 1980-82; asst. v.p. corp. banking Lloyds Bank Internat., Chgo., 1983-84; lectr. bus. adminstrn. U. Iowa, 1979-80; teaching asst. Northwestern U., Evanston, 1987; asst. prof. mgmt. Loyola U., Chgo., 1988-95, assoc. prof. mgmt., 1995—2000, prof. mgmt., 2000—. Presented numerous papers in field; contbr. articles to profl. jours. including Jour. Orgnl. Behavior, Acad. Mgmt. Jour., Sloan Mgmt. Rev., Orgn. Sci., Indsl. Crisis Quar., Jour. Mgmt. Studies, Jour. Vocat. Behavior, Jour. Mgmt. Edn.; book and textbook reviewer. Bd. trustees Knox Coll., Galesburg, Ill., 2000—. Rsch. grantee Northwestern U. Banking Rsch. Ctr., 1987, 88, Nat. Ctr. for Mgmt. R&D, Can., 1989-90, Employee Relocation Coun., 1989-90, Loyola U. Summer Rsch., 1990, Abbott Labs., 1997-99. Mem. Acad. Mgmt., Orgnl. Behavior Teaching Soc., Phi Beta Kappa, Beta Gamma Sigma, Phi Beta Delta. Democrat. Lutheran. Avocations: travel, reading, swimming. Office: Loyola U Chgo 820 N Michigan Ave Chicago IL 60611-2147 Business E-mail: areilly@luc.edu.

**REILLY, CHARLES EDMUND, JR.,** communications executive; b. Phila., Nov. 4, 1928; s. Charles Edmund, Sr. and Kathryn (McHugh) Reilly; m. Joan Emily Hunter; children from previous marriage: Lynn, Susan, Kathryn, Charles III. BS in Bus., St. Joseph's U., Phila., 1950; postgrad., U. Pa., 1955; MA in Liberal Studies, Villanova U., 2002. Med. rep. Stuart Pharms., Phila., 1954-56; mgr. newsstand promotion TV Guide Mag., Radnor, Pa., 1956—64, rep. ea. coast NYC, 1959—63; asst. to v.p., dir. corp. relations Young & Rubicam Inc., N.Y.C., 1964-66; exec. dir. Nat. Cath. Office for Radio-TV. N.Y.C., 1966-71; exec. v.p. Patrick Carr Assocs., N.Y.C., 1971-72; corp. exec. J. Walter Thompson, N.Y.C., 1972-74; v.p. Ogilvy and Mather, N.Y.C., 1975-76; founder In-Person Communications Inc., N.Y.C., 1976—. Cons. Pontifical Commn. Social Commn., Vatican City, 1968—71; adj. assoc. prof. St. John's U., N.Y.C., 1971—72; mem. vis. com. Loyola U., New Orleans, 1987—. Author: You Speak.They Listen, 1984, You and A Life of Reilly, 1987, Special Delivery, 1988, Korea 1950-1953--The War That Never Was, 2000, others; newspaper columnist Suburban and Wayne, 1991—, Main Line Life, 1994—. Lt. col. Valley Forge Mil. Coll., 1995—2003. 1st lt. U.S. Army,

1950—53. Named to Hall of Fame, Inf. Sch., Ft. Benning, Ga., 1996. Mem.: St. Davids Golf Club (Wayne, Pa.), Princeton Club (N.Y.C.) (former mem.), Merion Cricket Club (Haverford, Pa.), Union League (Phila.) (former mem.). Republican. Personal E-mail: crinperson@aol.com.

**REILLY, DANIEL PATRICK,** retired bishop; b. Providence, May 12, 1928; s. Francis E. and Mary (Burns) R. Student, Our Lady of Providence Sem., 1943—48, Grand Seminaire, St. Brieuc, France, 1948—53, Harvard U., 1954—55, Boston Coll., 1955—56; D (hon.), Providence Coll., St. Michael's Coll., Holy Apostles Coll. and Sem., Salve Regina Coll., Our Lady of Providence Coll., Sacred Heart U., Assumption Coll., 1995, Anna Maria Coll., 1995, Holy Cross Coll., 1996. Ordained priest Roman Cath. Ch., 1953. Asst. pastor Cathedral Saints Peter and Paul, Providence, 1953—54; asst. chancellor Diocese of Providence, 1954—56, sec. to bishop, 1956—64; became monsignor, 1964; chancellor Diocese of Providence, 1964—72, adminstr., 1971—72, vicar gen., 1972—75; consecrated bishop, 1975; bishop Norwich, Conn., 1975—94; Conn. state chaplain K.C., 1976—94; Episcopal moderator Nat. Cath. Cemetery Corp., 1977—87; bishop of Worcester Mass., 1994—2004. Ad hoc mem. to aid ch. in Ea. Europe, adminstrv. com. mem. NCCB/U.S. Cath. Conf., 1976—86, 1992—; pro-life com. mem. NCCB, 1989—92, chmn. 10th anniversary peace pastoral com., 1992—93, chmn. internat. policy com., 1993; mem. Priestly Life and Ministry Commn., 1991—94; past pres. New Eng. Consultation Ch. Leaders; drafting com. mem. U.S. Cath. Conf. Pastoral Letter on Peace, 1983, mem. com. on econs.; active Holy See Pontifical Coun.-Cor Unum, 1984—89. Trustee Cath. Mut. Relief Soc., Omaha, 1979—, St. John's Sem., Brighton, Mass., 1987—, Am. Coll., Louvain, Belgium, St. Mary's Sem., Balt.; bd. Cath. Relief Svcs. Cath. Relief Svcs., 1978—86; mem. fin. and budget com. U.S. Cath. Conf. U.S. Cath. Conf., 1985—87; chancellor Holy Apostles Coll. and Sem., Cromwell, Conn., 1982—94; pres. Conn. Interfaith Housing, 1975—94; cons. Pontifical Coun. Justice and Peace, 1995; bd. dirs. United Way Southeastern Conn., 1976—94, Conn. Drug and Adv. Coun., 1978—80. Mem.: KC (R.I. state chaplain 1964—75), Rotary. Roman Catholic. Office: St Paul Cathedral Rectory 38 High St Worcester MA 01609 Office Phone: 508-799-4193. Personal E-mail: vocdir@aol.com. Business E-Mail: breilly@worcesterdiocese.org. *If you would make a true success of your life for time and for eternity, never forget that it will be achieved by your willingness to make countless efforts that will be known only to God.*

**REILLY, DAVID HENRY,** retired university dean; b. Paterson, NJ, Nov. 7, 1936; s. David Henry and Ethel Taylor (Alt) R.; m. Jean Lockwood, July 2, 1960; children— David Scott, Chris Robert, Sandra Jean. BA, U. Vt., 1959; Ed.M., Rutgers U., 1962, Ed.D, 1965. Diplomate: Am. Bd. Profl. Psychology. Remedial reading instr. Drake Sch. of N.J. Neuro-Psychiat. Inst., Princeton, 1959-62, jr. fellow psychol. services at inst., summer 1962-63; research asst. N.J. Bur. Research Neurology and Psychiatry; also sch. psychologist Woodbridge (N.J.) sch. system, 1962-63; clin. psychologist, then research asso. N.J. Bur. Research Neurology and Psychiatry, 1963-64, 65; sch. and research psychologist Woodbridge sch. system, 1964-65; post doctoral fellow clin. child psychology Devereux Found., Devon, Pa., 1965-66; mem. faculty U. N.C., Chapel Hill, 1966-74, prof. psychology, 1974—, chmn. dept. sch. psychology program, 1966-74; dean U. N.C. (Sch. Edn.), Greensboro, 1974-86; dean Coll. of Grad. and Profl. Studies The Citadel, Charleston, 1992—. Mem. N.C. Bd. Examiners Practicing Psychologists, 1973—, treas., 1975, chmn., 1976 Contbr. articles to profl. jours. Research grantee NIMH, 1963; Fulbright Vis. scholar Republic of Cyprus, 1986-87, USSR, 1990. Fellow APA; mem. Am. Acad. Sch. Psychology (pres.-elect 1996-97, pres. 1997-98), Southeastern Psychol. Assn., N.C. Psychol. Assn. (pres. 1980-81), N.C. Assn. Coll. Tchr. Edn. (pres. 1981), N.C. Sch. Psychology Assn. (pres. 1976-77), S.C. Grad. Deans Assn. (pres. 1998-99). Home: 3311-Seven Lakes W Seven Lakes NC 27376 Personal E-mail: skipreilly@aol.com.

**REILLY, DAVID N. (NICK REILLY),** automotive executive; b. Wales, 1949; Diploma, U. Cambridge, 1971. Gen. ops. mgr. GM Svc. Parts Ops., 1984—86, dir. mfg., 1986—87; v.p. ops. GM, Isuzu, IBC, Luton, England, 1987—90; dir. mfg. Vauxhall Port Plant, Ellesmere, 1990—94; v.p. GM Europe, Zurich, Switzerland, 1994—96; chmn. mng. dir. Vauxhall Motors, 1996—2001; v.p. GM Corp., 1997—; v.p. sales, mktg. GM Europe, 2001—02; pres., CEO GE Daewoo Auto and Tech. Co., Republic of Korea, 2002—06; pres. GM Asia Pacific divsn, 2006—. Mem. Asia Pacific Strategy Bd. GM. Recipient Cmdr. Order British Empire, 2000. Mem.: Soc. Motor Mfgs. and Traders (pres. 2001—02). Office: GM Corp 300 Rennaissance Ctr Detroit MI 48265*

**REILLY, EDWARD ARTHUR,** lawyer; b. N.Y.C., Dec. 17, 1943; s. Edward Arthur and Anna Marguerite (Sautter) R.; children: M. Teresa, Edward A. AB, Princeton U., 1965; JD, Duke U., 1968. Bar: NY 1969, NC 1971, Fla. 1979, Conn. 1983. Asst. dean law sch. Duke U., 1970-72; assoc. Shearman & Sterling, NYC, 1972-80, ptnr., 1980-87, Harlow, Reilly, Derr & Stark, Rsch. Triangle Park, NC, 1988-90; counsel Morris & McVeigh, NYC, 1991-93, ptnr., 1993—. Pres. Am. Friends Paris Opera Ballet, Inc.; sec. Camille and Henry Dreyfus Found., Inc.; sec. Owen Cheatham Found. Decorated Knight of Order of Arts and Letters, French Govt.-Ministry of Culture and Communs., 1992. Fellow Am. Coll. Trust & Estate Counsel; mem. NY State Bar Assn., Fla. Bar Assn., Conn. Bar Assn. Episcopalian. Office: Morris & McVeigh 767 3rd Ave New York NY 10017-2023 Home: 5 Old Field Pl Norwalk CT 06853-1116

**REILLY, EDWARD FRANCIS, JR.,** federal agency administrator, former state senator; b. Leavenworth, Kans., Mar. 24, 1937; s. Edward F. and Marian C. (Sullivan) R. BA, U. Kans., 1961. V.P. Reilly & Sons, Inc., Leavenworth, 1967-92; pres. Yllier Lake Estates, Inc., Easton, Kans., 1965-89; mem. Kans. Ho. Reps., 1963-64, Kans. State Senate, 1964-92, asst. majority leader, 1977-80, vice-chmn. govtl. orgn., chmn. ins. subcom., chmn. fed. and state affairs com.; mem. U.S. Parole Commn., U.S. Dept. Justice, 1992—, chmn., 1992—97, 2001—. Commr. Nat. Commn. on Accreditation of Law Enforcement Agys., 1982-96; adv. mem. Am. Justice Inst. fed. and state prisons; mem. cmty. liaison com. U.S. Penitentiary Lansing, Kans. Commr. ex officio U.S. Sentencing Commn., Washington; del. to Rep. Nat. Conv., Miami Beach, Fla., 1968; chmn. Leavenworth County Radio Free Europe Fund, 1972; bd. dirs. St. John's Hosp., Leavenworth, 1970-79, sec.; bd. dirs. Leavenworth Assn. for Handicapped, 1968-69, ARC, Leavenworth chpt., Kans. Blue Cross/Blue Shield, 1969-72; apptd. by Pres. Reagan Nat. Hwy. Safety Adv. Com.; active Trinity Nat. Leadership Roundtable, Cath. Campaign Am., Kans. Adv. Bd. Juvenile Offenders, Nat. Com. Cmty. Corrections. Recipient Cmty. Leaders of Am., 1971, 85, 86, Hallpac Pub. Svc. award, 1988, Am. Police Hall of Fame award, 1990, Good Samaritan award Order of Michael the Arch Angel Police Legion, 1990, Commendation award mayor and city commn. of Leavenworth, Kans., 1990, Carnegie Hero Fund Commn. award and medallion, 1991, Silver Angel award Kans. Cath. Conf., 1992; named Outstanding Young Men of Am., 1965-76. Mem. Nat. Criminal Justice Assn., Nat. Inst. Corrections (adv. bd.), Advisory Bd., Dept. of Philosophy, Catholic Univ. of America, Am. Paroling Authorities Internat., Am. Correctional Assn., Am. Probation and Paroling Assn., Leavenworth C. of C. (hon. dir. 1970-73), No. Assn. Chiefs Police, Assn. U.S. Army (Henry Leavenworth award 1960), Kansas City (Kans.) C. of C., Leavenworth Hist. Soc. (dir. 1968-73), John Carroll Soc., Native Sons of Kansas City, Ancient Order of Hibernians, U.S. Supreme Ct. Hist. Soc., Kiwanis (dir. 1969-70, Connelly award 1991, Legion of Honor award 1996), K.C., Elks, Eagles, Order of Malta, Equestrian Order Holy Sepulchre Jerusalem, Sacred Military Constantinian Order of Saint George. Republican. Roman Catholic. Office: US Parole Commn 5550 Friendship Blvd Ste 420 Chevy Chase MD 20815-7201

**REILLY, EDWARD T., JR.,** advertising executive; b. NYC, Oct. 21, 1946; s. Edward Thomas and Dorothy (Comba) R.; m. Susan M. Brooke, June 28, 1969; children: Kristen, Gregg. BBA, St. Francis Coll., N.Y.C., 1968. Editor-in-chief Gregg div. McGraw Hill Book Co., N.Y.C., 1974-76; controller CTB, Monterey, Calif., 1976-78; gen. mgr. Instructo, Palli, Pa., 1978-79; group v.p. for Europe, Africa, Mideast McGraw Hill UK Ltd., Maidenhead, U.K., 1980-83; exec. v.p. McGraw-Hill Internat. Book Co., N.Y.C., 1983-84;

sr. v.p. fin., planning and adminstrn. McGraw-Hill Broadcasting Co., N.Y.C., 1985-86, exec. v.p., chief operating officer, 1986-87, pres., 1987—; CEO Big Flower Holdings, 1997-2000. Mem. corp. adv. council Nat. Council La Raza; mem. local carriage task force Nat. Assn. Broadcasters; mem. adv. com. on local excellence in TV programming Mus. of Broadcasting; bd. dirs. Internat. Radio and TV Found., Nat. Assoc. of Broadcasters, 1990-94, TV Bur. of Advt., 1988-95, 1990-93, assoc. of Max Svc. TV, 1987—, chmn. 1994—, Gov.- ABC TV network affiliates assoc., chmn. gov. rel., 1993-95. Chmn. Monterey County Overall Econ. Devel. Com., Monterey, Calif., 1977; bd. govs. Carmel Unified Sch. Dist. (Calif.), 1977. Fellow Inst. Dirs. Great Britain Office: Big Flower Holdings Inc 345 Park /ave New York NY 10154-0004

**REILLY, FRANK KELLY,** business educator; b. Chgo., Dec. 30, 1935; s. Clarence Raymond and Mary Josephine (Ruckrigel) R.; m. Therese Adele Bourke, Aug. 2, 1958; children: Frank Kelly III, Clarence Raymond II, Therese B., Edgar B. BBA, U. Notre Dame, 1957; MBA, Northwestern U., 1961, U. Chgo., 1964, PhD, 1968; LLD (hon.), St. Michael's Coll., 1991. CFA. Trader Goldman Sachs & Co., Chgo., 1958-59; security analyst Tech. Fund, Chgo., 1959-62; asst. prof. U. Kans., Lawrence, 1965-68, assoc. prof., 1968-72; prof. bus., assoc. dir. divsn. bus. and econ. rsch. U. Wyo., Laramie, 1972-75; prof. fin. U. Ill., Champaign-Urbana, 1975-81; Bernard J. Hank prof. U. Notre Dame, Ind., 1981—, dean Mendoza Coll. Bus. Ind., 1981-87. Bd. dirs., chmn. Brinson Funds, Assn. Investment Mgmt. and Rsch.; past chmn. Inst. Chartered Fin. Analysts; past chmn. bd. dirs. NIBCO Corp.; bd. dirs. Internat. Bd. CFPs, Discover Bank, Ft. Dearborn Income Securities, Battery Park High Yield Fund., Morgan Stanley Trust Fed. Savs. Bank (FSB). Author: Investment Analysis and Portfolio Management, 1979, 8th edit., 2006, Investments, 1982, 7th edit., 2006; co-editor: Ethics and the Investment Industry, 1989; editor: Readings and Issues in Investments, 1975, High Yield Bonds: Analysis and Risk Assessment, 1990; assoc. editor Fin. Mgmt., 1977-82, Quar. Rev. Econs. and Bus, 1979-87, Fin. Rev., 1979-87, 92—, Jour. Fin. Edn., 1981—, Jour. Applied Bus. Rsch., 1986—, Fin. Svcs. Rev., 1989-96, Internat. Rev. Econs. and Fin., 1992—, European Jour. Fin., 1994—, Arthur J. Schmidt Found. fellow, 1962-65; U. Chgo. fellow, 1963-65; recipient faculty award U. Notre Dame, 1999. Fellow Fin. Mgmt. Assn. (pres. 1983-84, chmn. 1985-91, bd. dirs.); mem. Midwest Bus. Adminstrn. Assn. (pres. 1974-75), Am. Fin. Assn., Western Fin. Assn. (exec. com. 1973-75), Ea. Fin. Assn. (exec. com. 1979-84, pres. 1982-83), Midwest Fin. Assn. (pres. 1993-94), Fin. Analysts Fedn., Acad. Fin. Svcs. (pres. 1990-91), Inst. Chartered Fin. Analysts (coun. of examiners, rsch. and edn. com., edn. steering com.), Internat. Assoc. Fin. Planners (edn. resource com., bd. dirs.), Assn. of Investment Mgmt. and Rsch. (C. Stewart Sheppard award 1991, Daniel J. Forrestal III Leadership award for profl. ethics 2001), Investments Analysts Soc. Chgo. (bd. dirs. 1988-89), Beta Gamma Sigma. Roman Catholic. Office: U Notre Dame Mendoza Coll Bus Notre Dame IN 46556-5646 Business E-Mail: reilly.1@nd.edu. *Any success I have enjoyed is due to the talents God has given me and my belief that I have an obligation to maximize the output from those talents by hard work, while never forgetting that my family comes first because they have always provided me with the love and support necessary for success and happiness.*

**REILLY, JILL MARLENE,** school system administrator; b. Chgo., Jan. 27, 1951; d. Jack Louis and Leah M. Cappels; m. Patrick Duane Reilly, May 29, 1971; children: Elizabeth M. Brama, Joseph D., Heather von Mering. BA in English, U. Cin., 1974; MA in Curriculum, U. Minn., 1985; D in Edn. Leadership, U. St. Thomas, St. Paul, 1992. Co-ptnr. Featherstone-Reilly Ednl. Cons., Apple Valley, Minn., 1984-95; mentor program coord. Intermediate Sch. Dist. # 917, Apple Valley, 1985-93; sr. cons. Honeywell, Inc., Mpls., 1993-95; adj. asst. prof. St. Mary's U., Mpls., 1994—; pres. Acad. Holy Angels, Richfield, Minn., 1995—. Author: Mentorship: The Essential Guide for Schools and Business, 1992; co-author: College Comes Sooner Than You Think, 1987. Bd. dirs. guidance div. Nat. Assn. Gifted Children, Mpls., 1988-93; bd. dirs., chair elect Minn. Coun. Gifted and Talented, Mpls., 1991-94. Office: Acad Holy Angels 6600 Nicollet Ave Richfield MN 55423-2498 Office Phone: 612-798-2611. E-mail: jreilly@ahastars.org.

**REILLY, JOHN C.,** actor; b. Chgo., May 24, 1965; m. Alison Dickey, 1992; 2 children. BFA, DePaul U., 1987. Actor: (films) Casualties of War, 1989, We're No Angels, 1989, Days of Thunder, 1990, State of Grace, 1990, Shadows and Fog, 1992, Out on a Limb, 1992, Hoffa, 1992, What's Eating Gilbert Grape, 1993, The River Wild, 1994, Georgia, 1995, Dolores Claiborne, 1995, Hard Eight, 1996, Boys, 1996, Boogie Nights, 1997, The Thin Red Line, 1998, Never Been Kissed, 1999, For Love of the Game, 1999, Magnolia, 1999 (Nat. Bd. Rev. award for Best Ensemble, 1999), The Settlement, 1999, The Perfect Storm, 2000, The Anniversary Party, 2001, Frank's Book, 2001, The Good Girl, 2002, Gangs of New York, 2002 (Las Vegas Film Critics Award for Best Supporting Actor, 2003), Chicago, 2002 (Golden Globe for Best Supporting Actor, Acad. award nomination for Best Actor, Las Vegas Film Critics Award for Best Supporting Actor, 2003), The Hours, 2002 (Las Vegas Film Critics Award for Best Supporting Actor, 2003), Anger Management, 2003, Piggie, 2003, Criminal, 2004, The Aviator, 2004, Are You the Favorite Person of Anybody?, 2005, Dark Water, 2005, A Prairie Home Companion, 2006, Talladega Nights: The Ballad of Ricky Bobby, 2006; (plays) True West, 2000 (Spl. Outer Critics Cir. Award, 2000), Streetcar Named Desire, 2005. Roman Catholic.*

**REILLY, JOHN J.,** lawyer; b. N.Y.C., 1942; AB, Fordham U., 1964, LLB, 1967. Bar: N.Y. 1968, D.C. 1968, U.S. Ct. Appeals DC 1968, U.S. Supreme Ct. 1971, U.S. Dist. Ct. (So. and Ea. Dist. NY) 1971, U.S. Ct. Appeals (2nd Cir.) 1971, U.S. Ct. Appeals (9th Cir.) 1974, U.S. Ct. Internat. Trade 1988, U.S. Dist. Ct. (Dist. Ore.) 1988, U.S. Ct. Appeals (3rd Cir.) 1995. Mem. Haight, Gardner, Poor & Havens, N.Y.C.; ptnr. Holland & Knight LLP, NYC, mem. dir. com. Speaker in field: dir. Ireland-U.S. Coun. for Commerce & Industry, Inc. Mem. Fordham Law Review, 1965-67, notes editor, 1966-67; contbr. articles to profl. jours. Capt. USMCR, 1967-71; served in Republic of Vietnam, 1968 & 1969. Mem. ABA (litigation sect., chair, maritime com. pub. utility, comm. and transportation law sect.), Internat. Bar Assn., Fed. Bar Coun., N.Y. State Bar Assn., N.Y. County Lawyers Assn. (chair admiralty law com. 1980-82), London Maritime Arbitrators Assn. Office: Holland & Knight LLP 195 Broadway 24th Fl New York NY 10007 Office Phone: 212-513-3488.

**REILLY, KATHLEEN C.,** director, retired secondary school educator; b. Bridgeport, Conn., Mar. 24, 1937; d. John J. and Lillian (Higgins) Collins; m. Donald Reilly, Aug. 21, 1988; children: Robert L., John, Maura Williams. BS, Boston U., 1958; MA in Teaching, Manhattanville Coll., Purchase, N.Y., 1973; postgrad., Teachers Coll. Columbia U., 1983; CAS, Wesleyan U., 1985. Cert. permanent-English tchr., grades 7-12, N.Y. English tchr. Sch. of Holy Child, Rye, NY, Edgemont High Sch., Scarsdale, NY; ret., 2000; dir. of tng. Tri-State Consortium. Adj. prof. Hofstra U., Hempstead, N.Y., 1991. Grantee Am. Studies Consortium, NEH, SUNY Tchr. Rsch., 1991, Nat. Coun. Tchrs. English, 1990.; recipient Scarsdale-Westchester Phi Beta Kappa award, N.Y. State Educator of Excellence award, 1996; named Edgemont High Sch. Tchr. Yr.; finalist N.Y. State Tchr. of Yr. Mem. Nat. Coun. Tchrs. of English (tchr. researcher grant). Home: 211 Newtown Tpke Wilton CT 06897-4713

**REILLY, KENNETH JAMES,** lawyer; b. Elizabeth, N.J., Jan. 19, 1949; s. James Arthur and Lucille (Vernon) R.; m. Mary Jane Stanley, Mar. 17, 1973; children: Lauren V., Kristopher L., Peter D. Bra, Trinity U., 1970; JD, U. Tex., 1973. Bar: Colo. 1973, Kans. 1974, U.S. Dist. Ct. Kans. 1974, U.S. Supreme Ct. 1978, Mo. 1990, U.S. Dist. Ct. (we. dist) Mo. 1990. Assoc. Boddington & Brown, Kansas City, Kans., 1974-90, McDowell, Rice & Smith, Overland Park, Kans., 1990-95, Shook, Hardy & Bacon, Kansas City, Mo., 1995—, assoc. to mng. ptnr. Miami, Fla., 1998—. Office: Shook Hardy & Bacon LLP 201 S Biscayne Blvd Ste 2400 Miami FL 33131-4313 Office Fax: 305-358-7470. E-mail: kreilly@shb.com.

**REILLY, KEVIN DENIS,** computer scientist, educator; s. Brian Augustine and Dorothy Evelyn Reilly; m. Jo Ann Grace Caniglia, Feb. 4, 1961; children: Martin Louis, Dennis Patrick(dec.), Ann Marie(dec.), Eileen Marie, Shannon Denise Ray. BS summa cum laude, Creighton U., 1959; MS, U. of Nebr., 1962; PhD, U. of Chgo., 1966. Tchr. U.Calif., L.A., 1966—70; sr. lectr. U. of So. Calif., L.A., 1968—70; prof. U. Ala., Birmingham, Ala., 1970—. Spkr. in field; cons. in field. Contbr. over 250 articles to profl. jours. Judge various sci. fairs, Birmingham; participant in ecumenical dialogs Greek Orthodox-Cath. Discussion Group, Birmingham. Fellow, Woodrow Wilson Found., 1959, NIH, 1962—66, Mobusho fellow, Ministry of Internat. Trade and Industry, Japan, 1989; grantee, NSF, 1966—70, U.S. Office of Edn., 1968—70, NIH, 1972—77, 1977—78, US Army, 1987—90, NSF, 1993, NIH, 1998—2000, 2000—. Mem.: IEEE, Soc. for Modeling and Simulation, European Acad. Sci., Assn. for Computing Machinery. Independent. Roman Catholic. Avocations: travel, philosophy, history, poetry. Home: 304 N Burbank Dr Bluff Park AL 35226-1608 Office: U Ala Birmingham University Station Birmingham AL 35294-1170 E-mail: reilly@cis.uab.edu.

**REILLY, KEVIN P.,** academic administrator; BA, U. Notre Dame, 1971; MA, U. Minn., 1974, PhD in English, 1979. Teaching asst. dept. English U. Minn., Mpls., 1974-79, asst. to dir. undergrad. study dept. English, 1976-77; coord. project on ednl. advisement in the work setting N.Y. State Bd. Regents, 1979-80, dir. Teaching and Beyond project, 1983-84, dir. nat. program non-coll. sponsored instrn., 1979-84, dir. div. coll. and univ. evaluation, 1984-92; assoc. provost for acad. programs, sec. of the univ. SUNY Sys., Albany, 1992—96; also sr. fellow in univ./sch. rels. SUNY Systems, Albany, 1992—96; provost, vice-chancellor U. Wis.-ext., 1996—2000, chancellor, 2000—04, U. Wis. System, Madison, 2004—. Mem. vis. del. Am. educators to rev. sch. system in No. Ireland, 1990; lectr. and presenter in field. Editor: (with Carol Wolfe) A Guide to Educational Programs in Noncollegiate Organizations, 1983, (with Sheila Murdick) Teaching and Beyond: Nonacademic Career Programs for Ph.D.'s, 1984; contbr. numerous articles to profl. jours. Tutor, Literacy Vols. of Am., Schenectady, 1988-90. Recipient Mgmt. Performance award N.Y. State, 1989, 90; recipient fellowships at U. Minn. Mem. MLA, Am. Assn. for Higher Edn., Am. Conf. for Irish Studies, Am. Ednl. Rsch. Assn., Assn. for Continuing Higher Edn., Irish Am. Cultural Inst. Office: U Wis System 1720 Van Hise Hall 1220 Linden Dr Madison WI 53706-1557 E-mail: kreilly@uwsa.edu.*

**REILLY, MICHAEL ATLEE,** finance company executive, venture capital investor; b. Ft. Worth, Dec. 10, 1948; s. Thomas William and Alma Margaret (Cox) R.; m. Beverly Ann Yates, Dec. 27, 1974; children: Atlee Michael, Asher Yates, Anson Marcus, Austin Thomas, Axton Carter. BA, U. Tex., 1971. Ptnr. Michael A. Reilly Co., Dallas, 1971—80; pres., CEO Ryan Cos., Arlington, Tex., 1980—90, Reilly Bros., Arlington, 1990—. Trustee Childrens Trust Fund State of Tex; vice chmn. Troy Aikman Found. Mem.: Urban Land Inst. Office: Reilly Bros Property Co 1017 So F M Rd 5 Aledo TX 76008-5169

**REILLY, NANCY (ANNE CAULFIELD REILLY),** painter; b. Bryn Mawr, Pa., Mar. 29, 1927; d. Ralph Caulfield and Claire Helena (Roesch) Goodman; m. Donald Elliott Reilly, May 14, 1949; children: Kevin Caulfield, William Stockbridge, Peter Elliott. Studies with Samuel E. Brown, Westport, Conn., 1955-63; studies with Mimi Jennewein, Larchmont, N.Y., 1964-65. Lectr., demonstrator portrait painting Bridgeport (Conn.) Art League, Milford (Conn.) Art League, Pen and Brush Club, New Haven, Conn. Classic Arts Assn., Allied Artists Am., Kent (Conn.) Art Assn., SCAN, Newtown, Conn. Exhibited in group shows at Nat. Acad. Design, N.Y.C., 1964, 1965, 1969, 1970, Stamford (Conn.), 1965, Wadsworth Antheum, Hartford, Conn., 1966, 1972, Nat. Acad. Arts and Letters, N.Y.C., 1971, Mus. Sci. and Industry, Bridgeport, 1972, Salmagundi Club, N.Y.C., Nat. Arts Club, Butler Inst. Am Art, Youngstown, Ohio, 2001, New Britain (Conn.) Mus. Am. Art, 2001, exhibitions include invitational travelling exhbn. Allied Artists Am., 2003—05; included in slide collection Smithsonian Instn., Washington, U. Conn. Health Ctr., Farmington. Vol. artist rehab. unit Norwalk Hosp., 1984—95. Recipient Gold medal for oil painting, Catherine Lorillard Wolfe Art Club, 1965, Silver medal for oil painting, Nat. Arts Club, 1969, George Height award for portrait, 1969, Blanche Farr award, 1991. Fellow: Am. Artists Profl. League (Claude Parsons Meml. award 2003, Leila Gardin Sawyer Meml. award 2005); mem.: Conn. Pastel Soc. (signature, Honors award 2003, 2004, J.D. Altobello Meml. award), Artists' Fellowship N.Y., Kent Art Assn. (Best in Show 1991, Conrad C. Aymar award for oil 1993, Mabel Rowe Aiken award for oil 1995, Frances B. Townley award for portrait 1998, 1999), Hudson Valley Art Assn. (Bronze medal for oil painting 1981, Thora M. Jensen Portrait award 1989, 2005), Pastel Soc. Am. (CPS award 2005), Nat. Arts Club (Silver medal for oil painting 1969, Bruce Stevenson award for portrait 1971, 1988, 1991, First prize 106th Annual Exhibiting Artist Mems. Exhbn. 2005), Allied Artists Am. (bd. dirs. 1991—99, participant in travelling exhbn. 2003—05), New Haven Paint and Clay Club (Merit award 1992, 1997). Home: 9 Marilane Westport CT 06880-1008

**REILLY, RICHARD R.,** lawyer; b. Montclair, NJ, Dec. 22, 1951; BA, Rutgers U., 1973; JD, Fordham U., 1980; LLM, NYU, 1984. Bar: NJ 1980, NY 1981, US Dist. Ct. (NJ dist.) 1980. Ptnr., head Global Employment & Employee Benefits practice Coudert Bros. LLP, NYC. Mem.: ABA, NY State Bar Assn. Office: Coudert Bros LLP 1114 Ave of the Americas New York NY 10036 Office Fax: 212-626-4468, 212-626-4120. Business E-Mail: reillyr@coudert.com.

**REILLY, ROBERT FREDERICK,** investment banker; b. NYC, Oct. 3, 1953; s. James R. and Marie (Griebel) Reilly; m. Janet H. Steiner, Apr. 16, 1975; children: Ashley Lauren, Brandon Christopher, Cameron Courtney. BA in Econs., Columbia U., 1975 MBA in Fin., 1976 CPA Ohio, Ill., nat'l. acct., CFA, cert. real estate appraiser, rev. appraiser, gen. appraiser Ill., Va., Utah, Oreg., N.Y., bus. appraiser, accredited bus. valuator. Sr. cons. Booz, Allen & Hamilton, Cin., 1975-76; dir. corp. planning Huffy Corp., Dayton, Ohio, 1976-81; v.p. Arthur D. Little Valuation, Inc., Chgo., 1981-85; ptnr., nat. dir. valuation svcs. Deloitte & Touche, Chgo., 1985-91; mng. dir. Willamette Mgmt. Assocs., Chgo., 1991—. Adj. prof. acctg. U. Dayton Grad. Sch. Bus., 1977—81; adj. prof. econs. Elmhurst Coll., Ill., 1982—87; adj. prof. fin. Ill. Inst. Tech. Grad. Sch. Bus., Chgo., 1985—91; adj. prof. taxation U. Chgo. Grad. Sch. Bus., 1985—87. Co-author: (book) Valuing Small Businesses and Professional Practices, 1993, 4th edit., 2000, Business Valuation Video Course, 1993, Valuing a Business, 1995, Valuing Accounting Practices, 1997, Valuing Professional Practices--A Practitioner's Approach, 1997, Valuing Intangible Assets, 1998, Handbook of Advanced Business Valuation, 1999, Handbook of Business Valuation and Intellectual Property Analysis, 2004, Guide to ESOP Valuation, 2005; editor; columnist: Ohio CPA Jour., 1984—86, 1991—2001, Small Bus. Taxation, 1989—90, Bus. Valuation Rev., 1990—99, Jour. Real Estate Acctg. and Taxation, 1991—93, Jour. Property Taxation Mgmt., 1993—, Jour. Am. Bankruptcy Inst., 1993—, Valuation Strategies, 2003—; co-editor: (book) Financial Valuation-Valuation of Business and Business Interests, 1997; contbr. articles to profl. jours. Mem.: AICPA (mem. ABV exam. com. 2002—), Appraisal Inst., Nat. Assn. Bus. Economists, Am. Econ. Assn., Am. Bankruptcy Inst., Inst. CFAs, Chgo. Soc. Investment Analysts, Bus. Valuation Assn., Accreditation Coun. Accountancy (accredited fed. income taxation), Ohio Soc. CPAs (chpt. dir. 1978—81), Ill. Soc. CPAs, Inst. Property Taxation, Inst. Cert. Mgmt. Accts. (chpt. dir. 1976—), Nat. Assn. Real Estate Appraisers, Am. Soc. Appraisers (mem. bd. examiners 1985—89), Inst. Bus. Appraisers (life). Home: 310 Algonquin Rd Barrington IL 60010-6109 Office: 8600 W Bryn Mawr Ave Chicago IL 60631-3579

**REILLY, ROBERT JOSEPH,** counselor; b. Spokane, Wash., Mar. 7, 1936; s. John Francis and Vivian Helen (White) R.; m. Joan Steiner, June 20, 1960; children: Sean Michael, Patrick Joseph, Bridget Colleen. BA in Psychology, Seattle U., 1985; postgrad., Infantry Officer Candidate Sch., Ft. Benning, 1960, EOAC, Ft. Belvoir, 1968, Leadership Inst. Seattle/City U., 1991—92. Ordained Congl. Ch. Practical Theology, 1992. Enlisted U.S. Army, 1953, advanced through grades to maj., 1981, served in Republic of Korea,

1961-62, Vietnam, 1966-67, 69-70, ret., 1981; counseling supr. Schick Shadel Hosp., Seattle, 1984-89; dir. Canyon Counseling, Puyallup, Wash., 1987-92, 95—; social worker Wash. State Employee Adv. Svc., Olympia, 1992-99. Exec. v.p. Coll. Therapeutic Hypnosis, Puyallup, 1989-94; mem. adj. faculty Pierce Coll., Tacoma, 1991-92; mem. Wash. State Chem. Dependency Counselor Cert. Bd., sec., 1995—. Editor: The Update, 2003—05. Ombudsman Officer of Asst. Sec. of Def. Res. Affairs; mem. vestry St. Luke's Episcopal Ch., Wenatchee, 2003—06; pres. Irish Cultural Club, Tacoma, 1983—85, 1993—94; sec. Tacoma chpt. Ret. Officers Assn., 1983—87, pres., 1993—96, bd. dirs., 1982—97, Tacoma Mus. Playhouse Theater Co., 1997—2000, adv. bd., 2000—06, Friends of the Ctrl. Highlands, Vietnam, 1999—2005. Decorated Vietnamese Cross of Gallantry with silver star, Bronze Star with oak leaf cluster, Meritorious Svc. medal, Army Commendation medal with 2 oak leaf clusters; recipient Nobel Fredspris, United Peacekeeping Forces, 1988; named Profl. of Yr. Chem. Dependency Profls. Wash., 1994. Mem.: Assn. Addiction Profls., The Ret. Enlisted Assn. (pres. Wehatchee chpt. 2001—02, chaplain 2002—, editor Appleland 86er), Mil. Officers Assn. Am., Nat. 4th Inf. Divsn. Assn. (sec.-treas. NW chpt. 1993—2003, chpt. pres. 2002—03, nat. svc. officer 2004—), Army Engrs. Assn., Nat. Assn. Tobacco Addiction Counselors, Am. Congress Hypnotist Examiners, Nat. Assn. Alcohol and Drug Abuse Counselors (del. Russia and Czech Republic 1996), Nat. Guild Hypnotists, Nat. Bd. Hypnotherapy and Hypnotic Anesthesiology (pres. Wash. chpt. 1991—94, v.p. 1995—97, Mem. of Yr. 1994), Internat. Conf. War Vet. Mins., La Soc. des Quarante Hommes et Huit Chevaux (Aumonier 2001—04, chef de gare 2004—05), Wash. West Home Owners Assn. (pres. 2001—02). Avocations: symphony music, theater. E-mail: joans.bob@charter.net.

**REILLY, THOMAS F.,** state attorney general; b. Springfield, Mass. m. Ruth Reilly; 3 children. BA, Am. Internat. Coll., 1964; JD, Boston Coll., 1970. Atty. Civil Rights divsn. Atty. Gen.'s Office; dist. atty. Middlesex County Dist. Atty. Office, 1991—99; atty. gen. State of Mass., Springfield, 1999—. Founder The Cmty. Based Justice Program. Democrat. Office: Office Atty General One Ashburton Pl Boston MA 02108-1698 also: 436 Dwight St Springfield MA 01103 also: One Exchange Place Worcester MA 01608*

**REILLY, WILLIAM KANE,** former government official, educator, lawyer, conservationist; b. Decatur, Ill., Jan. 26, 1940; s. George P. and Margaret (Kane) M.; m. Elizabeth Buxton; children: Katherine, Megan. BA in History, Yale U., 1962; JD, Harvard U., 1965; MS in Urban Planning, Columbia U., 1971. Bar: Ill., Mass. 1965. Atty. firm Ross & Hardies, Chgo., 1965; assoc. dir. Urban Policy Center, Urban Am., Inc., also Nat. Urban Coalition, Washington, 1969-70; sr. staff mem. Pres.'s Council Environ. Quality, 1970-72; exec. dir. Task Force Land Use and Urban Growth, 1972-73; pres. Conservation Found., Washington, 1973-89, World Wildlife Fund, Washington, 1985-89; adminstr. U.S. EPA, Washington, 1989-93; Payne vis. prof. Stanford U., 1993-94, vis. prof., 1994-97; CEO Aqua Internat. Ptnrs., Tex. Pacific Group, San Francisco, 1997—. Chmn. Natural Resources Coun. Am., 1982-83; head U.S. del. Earth Summit, 1992; head U.S. del. to negotiate Amendments to Montreal Protocol on the Ozone Layer, 1990, 92; bd. dirs. E.I. DuPont de Nemours and Co., Am. Acad. in Rome, Evergreen Holdings, Inc., Ionics Inc., Nat. Geog. Soc., World Wildlife Fund, Presidio Trust; mem. internat. adv. bd., Lafarge; chair adv. bd. Goldman Sch. Pub. Policy U. Calif. at Berkeley. Editor: The Use of Land, 1973, Environment Strategy America, 1994-96; author articles in field, chpts. in books. Served to capt., CIC U.S. Army, 1966-67; bd. dirs. David and Lucile Packard Found. Mem.: University (Washington), Univ. (N.Y.C.). Office: Aqua Internat Ptnrs 345 California St Ste 1770 San Francisco CA 94104-2606*

**REILLY, WILLIAM THOMAS,** lawyer; b. Passaic, N.J., Feb. 25, 1949; s. Thomas Edwin and Edna May (Dorritie) R.; m. Sheila Mary Brogan, Aug. 1, 1981; children: Kathleen Anne, Brendan Thomas, Timothy John. BS, Boston Coll., 1971; JD, Harvard U., 1974. Bar: N.J. 1974, U.S. Dist. Ct. N.J. 1974, U.S. Supreme Ct. 1979, U.S. Ct. Appeals (3rd cir.) 1984, U.S. Ct. Claims, 1996, U.S. Ct. Appeals (fed. cir.) 1997. Assoc. McCarter & English LLP, Newark, 1974-81; ptnr., 1982—. Trustee Internat Hosps. Med. Ctr., Newark, 1983-89, One-to-One/N.J., Inc., 1990-97, chmn., 1993-97. Mem. ABA, N.J. State Bar Assn., Harvard Law Sch. Assn., Eastward Ho Country Club. Avocation: golf. Home: 302 Kensington Dr Ridgewood NJ 07450-1822 Office: McCarter & English LLP Four Gateway Ctr 100 Mulberry St Newark NJ 07102-4004 Office Phone: 973-622-4444. Business E-Mail: wreilly@mccarter.com.

**REIMAN, DONALD HENRY,** language educator; b. Erie, Pa., May 17, 1934; s. Henry Ward and Mildred Abbie (Pearce) R.; m. Mary (Warner), 1958 (div. 1974); one child, Laurel Elizabeth Reiman Henneman; m. Hélène (Liberman) Dworzan, Oct. 3, 1975. BA, Coll. of Wooster, 1956; MA, U. Ill., 1957, PhD, 1960; LittD., Coll. of Wooster, 1981. Instr. English, Duke U., Durham, NC, 1960—62, asst. prof., 1962—64; assoc. prof. U. Wis., Milw., 1964—65; adj. assoc. prof. grad. program in English City Univ. of N.Y., 1967—68; adj. prof. Columbia U., N.Y.C., 1969—70; sr. rsch. assoc. in English, 1970—73; vis. prof. St. John's U., Jamaica, NY, 1974—75; editor Shelley and His Cir., Carl H. Pforzheimer Libr., N.Y.C., 1965—86, N.Y. Pub. Libr., 1986—92; with Carl and Lily Pforzheimer Found., 1992—. Vis. lectr. U. Ill., 1963; vis. prof. U. Wash., Seattle, 1981, N.Y. U., 1992; Lyell reader in bibliography Oxford U., 1988-89; adj. prof. English, U. Del., 1992—; cons. Harvard U. Press, Yale U. Press, Princeton U. Press, Johns Hopkins U. Press, Garland Pub., Inc., W.W. Norton, Oxford U. Press, others. Author: Shelley's The Triumph of Life, A Critical Study, 1965, 2d edit., 1979, Percy Bysshe Shelley, 1969, 2d edit., 1990, (with D.D. Fischer) Byron on the Continent, 1974, English Romantic Poetry, 1800-1835, 1979, Romantic Texts and Contexts, 1987, Intervals of Inspiration: The Skeptical Tradition in the Psychology of Romanticism, 1988, The Study of Modern Manuscripts, 1993; editor: Shelley and His Circle, Vols. V-VI, 1973, Vols. VII-VIII, 1986, (with D.D. Fischer) IX-X, 2002, The Romantics Reviewed: Contemporary Reviews of English Romantic Writers, 9 vols., 1972, (with S.B. Powers) Shelley's Poetry and Prose: A Norton Critical Edit., 1977, (with Neil Fraistat) 2nd rev. edit., 2002, The Romantic Context: Poetry, 128 vols., 1976-79, (with M.C. Jaye and B.T. Bennett) The Evidence of the Imagination, 1978; gen. editor: Manuscripts of the Younger Romantics, 1985-98; I The Esdaile Notebook: A Facsimile, 1985, II The Mask of Anarchy: Facsimiles, 1985, III Hellas, 1985, V The Harvard Shelley Poetic Manuscripts, 1991; (with M. O'Neill) VIII Fair-Copy Manuscripts of Shelley's Poems, 1997; editor-in-chief: The Bodleian Shelley Manuscripts, 1986-99, I Peter Bell The Third and the Triumph of Life, 1986, VII Shelley's Last Notebook and Other MSS, 1990, (with M.J. Neth) XVI The Hellas Notebook, 1994, (with N. Fraistat) The Complete Poetry of Percy Bysshe Shelley Vol. I, 2000, Vol. II, 2004; mem. editl. com. adv. bd. Keats Shelley Jour., 1968-73, Milton and the Romantics, 1975-80, Studies in Romanticism, 1977—, Romanticism Past and Present, 1980-86, Text, 1981—, Nineteenth Century Literature, 1986—, Nineteenth Century Contexts, 1987-90; co-founder, editor (with others) Romantic Circles. Website; contbr. articles to encyclopedias, books, and profl. journals. Active in Common Cause. Am. Coun. Learned Soc. Fellow, 1963-64, Wesleyan Ctr. Advanced Studies Fellow, 1963-64, NEH Fellow, 1978; grantee Am. Coun. Humanities Rsch. Assn. (life), Wordsworth Coleridge Assn. Am. (founder), Byron Soc. (Am. com. 1973—, treas. 1999-2002, pres. 2003-05), Keats Shelley Assn. Am. (bd. dirs., treas. 1973-91, v.p. 1991-2005, Disting. Scholar Award 1987), Soc. Textual Scholarship (exec. com. 1981-93, pres. 2005-06), Charles Lamb Soc., Assn. Documentary Editing, N.Am. Soc. Study of Romanticism. Democrat. Presbyterian. E-mail: dhreiman@udel.edu.

**REIMANN, ARLINE LYNN,** artist; b. St. Louis, Nov. 25, 1937; d. Albert Robbins and Bess (Kagan) Miner; m. Hans Reimann, Feb. 24, 1957; 1 child, Robert. BA, Rutgers U., N.J., 1974; MA, Montclair State U., N.J., 1980. Exhibited in group shows at Hunterdon Art Ctr., Clinton, NJ, 1982, 96, Galeria San Jeronimo, San Juan, P.R., 1987, Nat. Artists Club, NYC, 1988, 90—, Interch. Ctr., NYC, Butler Inst. Am. Art, Youngstown, Ohio, 1989, 395 West Broadway Gallery, NYC, 1994, 420 West Broadway Gallery, Soho, NY, 1995, Lever House Gallery, NYC, 1995, Art Ctr. Municipality of Athens,

Greece, 1996, West Beth Gallery, Montclair in Manhattan, NYC, 1996, ISE Art Found. NYC, 1996, Soc. Am. Graphic Artists, New Rochelle, NY, 1997, Gallery Art 54, NYC, 1997, Jane Voorhees Zimmerli Art Mus., New Brunswick, NJ, 1998-99, Old Print Shop, NYC, 2004, Art Students League of NY, NYC, 2005, Worldwide Feminist Expo, Balt., 2000, Nat. Assn. Women Artists, UN, 2002, Salmagondi Club, NYC, 2005, Ringling Mus. Sch. Art, Sarasota, Fla., 2006, Goggleworks Ctr. Arts, Reading, Pa., 2006, Venezulan Consulate, NYC, 2006, Salmagundi Club, NYC, 2006; represented in permanent collections at Jane Voorhees Zimmerli Art Mus., New Brunswick, NJ, Newark Pub. Libr. Fine Print Collection, Newark, Montclair (NJ) State U., Bailey Matthews Mus., Sanibel, Fla., Black Hills Inst., Hill City, SD. Recipient Best in Show award Salute to Women in Arts, Lincoln Ctr., N.Y.C., 1981, Hon. mention award Nat. Juried Exhbn. Small Works Montclair State U., N.J., 1995. Aida Whedon Meml. award Nat. Assn. Women Artists, 1996. Mem. Nat. Assn. Women Artists (bd. dirs., chair traveling print exhbn. 1984-89, printmaking jury 1987-89, 95-97), Audubon Artists (bd. dirs., rec. sec. 1991-97), Soc. Am. Graphic Artists, Phi Beta Kappa. Home: 546 Hillrise Pl Walnut Creek CA 94598-4064

**REIMANN, MATHIAS W.,** law educator; Grad., U. Freiburg Law Sch.; LLM, U. Mich., 1983. Hessel E. Yntema Prof. Law U. Mich. Law Sch., Ann Arbor. Contbr. articles to law jours. Office: U Mich Law Sch 334 Hutchins Hall 625 S State St Ann Arbor MI 48109-1215 Office Phone: 734-763-6331. Office Fax: 734-763-9375.

**REIMER, DENNIS J.,** retired career military officer; b. Medford, Okla., July 12, 1939; m. Mary Jo Powers; 2 children. BS, U.S. Mil. Acad., 1962; MS, Shippensburg State Coll. Gen. U.S. Army, Ft. McPherson, Ga., chief of staff Washington, 1995—99; ret., 1999; dir. Nat. Meml. Inst. for Prevention of Terrorism, Oklahoma City, 2000—. Bd. mem. Plato Learning Inc., Minn. Decorated Def. Disting. Svc. medal, Disting. Svc. medal, two Legions of Merit, Disting. Flying Cross, six Bronze Star medals, Purple Heart, Combat Infantryman badge, Parachutist badge, Aircraft Crewman badge, Ranger Tab; recipient Nat. Vets. award, 1999. Office: Nat Meml Inst for Prevention of Terrorism Chief of Staff PO Box 889 Oklahoma City OK 73101-0889

**REIMSCHUESSEL, RENATE,** pathologist; b. Wolfen, East Germany, Apr. 14, 1953; children: Victoria Martha Reimschuessel Myers, Kathleen Anna Reimschuessel Myers. BA cum laude, U. Pa., 1975, VMD, 1981; PhD, U. Md., 1989. Veterinarian Delaware Valley Animal Hosp., Fairless Hills, Pa., 1981-86; rsch. assoc. dept. pathology U. Md. Sch. Medicine, Balt., 1986-89, vet. pathologist ctrl. animal facility, 1987-88, asst. prof., dir. Aquatic Pathobiology Ctr., 1990—96, assoc. prof., dir. Aquatic Pathobiology Ctr., 1996—99; sci. dir. AIP environ. lab. Assocs. in Pathology PA, Balt. 1990—99; sr. rsch. biologist FDA, Laurel, Md., 1999—. Q.A. mgr. Ctr. for Vaccine Devel., U. Md., Balt., 1991; coun. Sch. Medicine, mem. Instl. Animal Care and Use Com., 1991-99; faculty U. Md. System, 1991—, toxicology program, 1993—; aquacultural reviewer Office Tech. Assessment, Congress of US, 1993, 94; vet.cons. Md. Aquaculture Assn., 1993-95; mem. aquatic animal health com. Md. Dept. Agr., 1995—; presenter in field. Author: (with others) Normal Histology of the Teleost: A Laboratory Guide, 1993, Fish Medicine, 1993, Necropsy Examination of Fish, 1988; author (monthly column) The Windmill Vet., 1990-92; contbr. numerous articles to profl. sci. jours. Bd. dirs. Holland Hill Improvement Assn., 1987-92, v.p., 1990-92; active Ann. Cmty. Food Dr., 1986-91, Ann. Cmty. Yard Sale, 1986-91. Md. fellow UMAB, 1988-89, 89-90; Recipient Faculty Devel. award Pharm. Mfrs. Assn., 1991-93; Prin. investigator numerous grants. Mem. AAAS, ASTM, Am. Fisheries Soc., Am. Vet. Med. Assn., Assn. for Women Vets, Avian Vets., Chesapeake Soc. for Electron Microscopy, Internat. Assn. Aquatic Animal Medicine, Mid-Atlantic Assn. Avian Vets., Soc. Environ. Toxicology and Chemistry, Wildlife Disease Assn. Office Phone: 301-210-4024.

**REIN, BERT WALTER,** lawyer; b. Bklyn., Feb. 7, 1941; s. Moe and Florence (Fishman) Rein; m. Jennifer Christine Bulson, July 11, 1966 (dec. Mar. 1989); children: Joanna, Benjamin, Samantha; m. Barbara Jean Kahn, Oct. 18, 1992. BA, Amherst Coll., 1961; LLB, Harvard U., 1964. Bar: DC 1965, U.S. Dist. Ct. DC 1965, U.S. Ct. Appeals (DC cir.) 1968, U.S. Ct. Appeals (2d cir.) 1973, U.S. Ct. Appeals (8th cir.) 1974, U.S. Ct. Appeals (4th cir.) 1976, U.S. Ct. Appeals (11th cir.) 1982, U.S. Supreme Ct. 1982. Law clk. to Justice John M. Harlan U.S. Supreme Ct., Washington, 1966-67; assoc. Kirkland & Ellis, Washington, 1967-69, ptnr., 1973-83; U.S. Dept. State, Washington, 1969-70, dep. asst. sec., 1970-73; ptnr. Wiley, Rein & Fielding, Washington, 1983—. Bd. dirs. Nat. Chamber Litig. Ctr.; advisor com. U.S.C. of C., 1986—90; bd. dirs. Nat. Chamber Litig. Ctr.; advisor Reagan Dept. Justice Transition, Washington, 1980; mem. adv. com. U.S. Sentencing Commn., 1988—89; edn. gen. counsel Cmty. Learning and Info. Network, 1992—. Contbr. articles to profl. jours. Mem. capitol area adv. bd. Salvation Army. Capt. USAR, 1964—68. Mem.: ABA, Internat. Trade Commn. Trial Lawyers Assn. (pres. 1990—91), Am. Law Inst., Aviation Club. Republican. Jewish. Home: 6423 Shadow Rd Chevy Chase MD 20815-6613 Office: Wiley Rein & Fielding 1776 K St NW Washington DC 20006-2304 Office Phone: 202-719-7080. Business E-Mail: brein@wrf.com.

**REIN, CATHERINE AMELIA,** insurance company executive, lawyer; b. Lebanon, Pa., Feb. 7, 1943; d. John and Esther (Scott) Shultz. BA summa cum laude, Pa. State U., 1965; JD magna cum laude, NYU, 1968. Bar: NY 1968, US Supreme Ct. 1971. Assoc. Dewey, Ballantine, Bushby, Palmer & Wood, NYC, 1968-74; with Continental Grp., Stamford, Conn., 1974-85, sec., sr. atty., 1976-77, v.p., gen. counsel, 1980-85; sec., asst. gen. counsel Continental Ill. Nat'l. Corp., 1978-80; v.p. human resources Met. Life Ins. Co., NYC, 1985-88, sr. v.p. human resources, 1988-89, exec. v.p. corp. and profl. svcs. dept., 1989—98, sr. exec., v.p. bus. svcs. and corp. svcs., 1998-99; pres., CEO Met. Life Auto and Home, Warwick, RI, 1999—2004; sr. exec. v.p., chief adminstrv. officer Met. Life Inc., 2004—. Bd. dirs. Bank of NY, First Energy Corpn. Trustee NYU Sch. Law Found. Mem.: ABA, Assn. Bar City of NY. Episcopalian. Avocations: decorating, restoration, cooking. Office: Met Life Inc One Metlife Plz 27 01 Queens Plz North Long Island City NY 11101

**REIN, CHRISTOPHER M.,** military officer; b. Panama City, Fla., Nov. 6, 1970; s. Charles Richard and Marilyn McWhorter Rein; m. Beth Aline Daze, Jan. 6, 2001. BS in Naval Arch. and Marine Engring., MIT, 1992; MA in History, La. State U., 2001. Commd. ensign USN, 1992—2001, advanced through grades to naval flight officer; lt. col. USAF, 1992—, advanced through grades to navigator, 2001—; asst. prof. ops. 116 EACCS, RAF Aksotici, Cyprus, 2003. Mem.: KC. Democrat. Roman Catholic. Avocations: hunting, reenacting. Office Phone: 719-333-2316. Business E-Mail: christopher.rein@usafa.af.mil.

**REIN, DAVID B.,** economist, researcher; b. N.Y.C., Oct. 22, 1970; s. Joel M. and Judith Grace Rein; m. Maria Angelou McHugh, June 26, 2001; 1 child, Anna A. PhD, Ga. Inst. Tech., 2003. Rsch. assoc. Ga. State U., Atlanta, 1999—2003; rsch. economist RTI Internat., Atlanta, 2003—. Fellow U.S. Ctrs. for Disease Control and Prevention, Atlanta, 1997—99. Author peer-reviewed sci. articles. Recipient William H. Read award, Ga. Inst. Tech., Sch. of Pub. Policy, 1999, Faculty award, 2003; fellow ORISE Fellowship, Ctrs. for Disease Control and Prevention, 1997-1999; grantee Health Services Dissertation Rsch. grant, Agy. for Healthcare Rsch. and Quality, 2002. Mem.: Am. Evaluation Assn., APHA. Avocations: cross-country skiing, biking, reading, music. Office: RTI International 2951 Flowers Rd Ste 119 Atlanta GA 30341 E-mail: drein@rti.org.

**REIN, JEFFREY A.,** retail executive; b. Feb. 28, 1952; BS in Acctg., U. Ariz., 1974, BS in Pharmacy, 1980. Asst. mgr. Walgreen Co., Deerfield, Ill., 1982—84, store mgr. 1984—90, dist. mgr. 1990—96, divisional v.p., treas., 1996—2000, v.p. mktg. systems svcs., 2000—01, exec. v.p. mktg., 2001—03, COO, 2003—06, pres., 2003—, CEO, 2006—. Office: Walgreen Co 200 Wilmot Rd Deerfield IL 60015*

**REINALDA, DAVID ANTHONY,** elementary school educator; b. Lynwood, Calif., May 17, 1966; s. Robert Aarlen and Marie Antoinette (Presicci) R. AA, Riverside (Calif.) City Coll., 1989; BA, Calif. State U., San Bernardino, 1992; cert. elem. tchr., U. Calif., Riverside, 1994. Instrnl. aide Jurupa Unified Sch. Dist., Riverside, 1985, 89-93, substitute tchr., 1993—; day care worker Our Lady of Perpetual Help, 1988-89; substitute tchr. Riverside Unified Sch. Dist., 1996—; adult edn. tchr. Jurupa Unified Sch. Dist., 1999—. Vol. aide Jurupa Unified Sch. Dist., 1989-91; home tutor, 1987-89. Author: ABC, What's at School for Me, 1997; author children's stories Stone Soup, 1981. Little League coach, Riverside, 1980-82, scorekeeper, 1982-84; Sunday sch. tchr. supr. Hope Cmty. Ch., Riverside, 1988-98. Winner 1st pl. Lions Club speech contest, 1984; named Christian Youth of Yr. Kiwanis Club, 1985, Outstanding Young Man Am., 1992, 96. Mem. Phi Lambda Omega. Democrat. Mem. Christian Reformed Ch. Avocations: bowling, dance, writing, acting.

**REINBOLD, ERIC,** social studies educator; s. Richard and Patricia Reinbold; m. Jennifer L. Reinbold, Oct. 21, 2005. BS in Edn., Elizabethtown Coll., Pa., 1993; MA in History, U. Del., Newark, 1995. Tchr. social studies Hertford County H.S., Ahoskie, NC, 1995—96, Saucon Valley H.S., Hellertown, Pa., 1996—99, Coun. Rock North H.S., Newtown, Pa., 1999—. Office Phone: 215-944-1300. E-mail: ereinbold9@yahoo.com.

**REINECKE, MANFRED G.,** chemistry professor; b. Milw., May 19, 1935; s. Fritz Wilhelm and Erna (Rittmeyer) R.; m. Marlene Zwisler, June 15, 1957; children: Kurt, Kryn, Claire. BS in Chemistry, U. Wis., 1956; PhD in Organic Chemistry, U. Calif., 1960. Asst. prof. U. Calif., Riverside, 1959-64, Tex. Christian U., Ft. Worth, 1964-68, assoc. prof., 1968-73; vis. prof. U. Tubingen, Fed. Republic of Germany, 1971-72; prof. Tex. Christian U., Ft. Worth, 1973—; vis. prof. U. British Columbia, Vancouver, Can., 1987. Chmn. health professions adv. com. Tex. Christian U., 1974-91; mem. sci. adv. bd. Univera Pharm., Inc., 1996-2002; cons. in field. Contbr. more than 85 articles on natural product, organic chemistry and chem. edn. to profl. jours. Recipient W.T. Doherty award Ft. Worth, Dallas sect. Am. Chem. Soc., 1984; NSF Tchg.fellow, 1971-72, NAS fellow, 1979, 90. Mem. Am. Chem. Soc. (chmn. Ft. Worth, Dallas sect. 1976), So. Assn. Advisors Health Professions (bd. dirs. 1986-89), Alpha Epsilon Delta (dir. SW region 1985-2002). Office: Tex Christian Univ Dept of Chemistry PO Box 298860 Fort Worth TX 76129-0001 E-mail: m.reinecke@tcu.edu.

**REINECKE, WILLIAM T.,** conductor, educator; b. New Rochelle, N.Y., Oct. 12, 1959; s. Betty Baltz and Ralph James Reinecke. BS, Lebanon Valley Coll., 1980; M in Music Edn., U. S.C., 1986. Profl. edn. cert. Va. Dir. bands Fieldale-Collinsville (Va.) HS, 1980—84, asst. wrestling coach, 1982—84; dir. bands Apopka (Fla.) HS, 1986—. Guest dir. FBA Dist. 19 Honors Jazz Band, 1999, Orange County Pub. Schs. Honor Jazz Band, Orlando, Fla., 2001. Conductor: Boyertown Alumni Marching Unit Spring Concert, 2002—03. Mem.: Fla. Bandmasters Assn. (dist. sec. 2000—01, mem. adjudication com. 2001, guest dir. dist. 19 jazz band 1999, dist. chmn.). Home: 517 Oakcrest St Altamonte Springs FL 32714 Office: Apopka HS 555 W Martin St Apopka FL 32712 E-mail: reinecw@ocps.net.

**REINEMUND, STEVEN S.,** food products executive; b. Queens, N.Y., Apr. 6, 1948; s. Ott and Dora (Kramer) R.; m. Gail Timbers, Dec. 14, 1974; children: Steven S. Jr., Jonathan Craig. BS in Naval Sci., U.S. Naval Acad., 1970; MBA, U. Va., 1978. Commd. 2d lt. USMC, 1970, advanced through grades to capt., 1974, resigned, 1975; mktg. rep. IBM Corp., 1975-76; v.p., gen. mgr. Marriott-Roy Rogers, 1978-84; sr. v.p., field operator Pizza Hut, Inc., Wichita, Kans., 1984-86, exec. v.p., 1986, pres., CEO, 1986—92, Frito-Lay N.Am., 1992—96; pres., CEO Frito-Lay, 1996—99; pres., COO PepsiCo, 1999—2001, chmn., CEO, 2001—. Bd. dirs. Bank IV, Wichita. Sec., treas. bd. dirs. U. Va., Darden Sch. Alumni Assn. Named one of Outstanding Young Men Am. Mem. Wichita Area C. of C. (bd. dirs.). Republican. Presbyterian. Presbyterian. Avocations: tennis, running. Office: PepsiCo 700 Anderson Hill Rd Purchase NY 10577*

**REINER, CARL,** director, actor, writer; b. Bronx, N.Y., Mar. 20, 1922; s. Irving and Bessie (Mathias) R.; m. Estelle Lebost, Dec. 24, 1943; children: Robert, Sylvia A., Lucas. Student, Sch. Fgn. Service, Georgetown U., 1943. Appeared on Broadway and with road co.: Call Me Mister, 1947-48; on Broadway in:Inside U.S.A, 1948-49, Alive and Kicking, 1950; TV actor, 1950—; appeared: Your Show of Shows, 1950-54, Caesar's Hour, 1954-58 (Emmy award 1956, 57); master ceremonies: Keep Talking, 1958-59; writer-actor: Dinah Shore Show, 1960; producer, writer: The Dick Van Dyke Show (Emmy awards as writer 1962, 63, 64, as producer 1965, 66), The New Dick Van Dyke Show, Enter Laughing, written 1958, directed 1967, The Comics, 1968; dir.: (films) Enter Laughing, The Comic, 1967, The Comic, 1969, Where's Poppa, 1970, Oh, God!, 1977, The One and Only, 1978, The Jerk, 1979, Dead Men Don't Wear Plaid, 1982, The Man With Two Brains, 1983, All of Me, 1984, Summer Rental, 1985, Summer School, 1987, Bert Rigby, You're a Fool, 1989, Sibling Rivalry, 1990, Fatal Instinct, 1993; appeared in: movie Happy Anniversary, 1959, The Gazebo, 1960, Gidget Goes Hawaiian, 1961, It's a Mad, Mad, Mad, Mad World, 1963, The Russians Are Coming, 1966, The End, 1978, Dead Men Don't Wear Plaid, 1982, (TV movies) Danny Kaye: A Legacy of Laughter, 1996, The Right to Remain Silent, 1996, The Slums of Beverly Hills, 1998, The Adventures of Rocky and Bullwinkle, 2000, Oceans Eleven, 2001, The Majestic, 2001, Good Boy!, 2003, Oceans Twelve, 2004; writer, dir.: Something Different, 1967; writer: Sid Caesar, Imogene Coca, Carl Reiner, Howard Morris Special (Emmy award, 1967); producer: TV series Good Heavens, 1976 (recipient Emmy award 1957, 58, 62, 63); Author: (novels) Enter Laughing, 1958, All Kinds of Love, 1993, Continue Laughing, 1995, NNNNN, 2005; (memoir) My Anecdotal Life, 2003; short stories: (screenplay) The Thrill of It All; (with Mel Brooks) albums The 2000 Year Old Man, The 2001 Year Old Man, The 2013 Year Old Man; exec. producer: film Heaven Help Us, 1985, The Man with Two Brains, 1983. Served with AUS, 1942-46. Recipient Guest Actor in a Comedy Series Emmy award for Mad About You, 1995, Mark Twain Prize for Am. Humor, Kennedy Center, 1999. Achievements include receiving the greatest number of Emmys (12) for any individual. Office: care George Shapiro Shapiro-West 141 S El Camino Dr Ste 205 Beverly Hills CA 90212-2718*

**REINER, GARY M.,** diversified technology and services company executive; BA, Harvard U., 1979. Mgmt. Rsch. analyst Boston Consulting Group, 1980—86, ptnr., 1986—91; v.p. corp. bus. devel. GE, Fairfield, Conn., 1991-96, sr. v.p., chief info. officer, 1996—. Office: GE 3135 Easton Tpke Fairfield CT 06431-0002

**REINER, ROB,** film director, actor; b. Bronx, NY, Mar. 6, 1947; s. Carl and Estelle (Lebost) R.; m. Penny Marshall, 1971 (div. 1979), m. Michele Singer, May 19, 1989; 3 children. Student, UCLA. Co-founder Castle Rock Entertainment, Beverly Hills, Calif. Actor: (TV series) All In the Family, 1971-78 (Emmy award 1974, 78), (TV movies) Thursday's Game, 1974 (films) Enter Laughing, 1967, Halls of Anger, 1970, Summertree, 1971, The Jerk, 1979, This is Spinal Tap, 1984, Throw Momma From the Train, 1987, Postcards From the Edge, 1990, The Spirit of '76, 1990, Sleepless in Seattle, 1993, Bullets Over Broadway, 1994, Mixed Nuts, 1994, Bye Bye, Love, 1995, First Wives Club, 1996, Mad Dog Time, 1996, I Am Your Child (TV), 1997, Primary Colors, 1998, EDtv, 1999, The Muse, 1999, The Story of Us, 1999, (voice) The Majestic, 2001, Dickie Roberts: Former Child Star, 2003, (voice) Everyone's Hero, 2006, (theatre) The Roast, 1980; actor, writer: (films) Halls of Anger, 1970, Where's Poppa?, 1970, Summertree, 1971, Fire Sale, 1971; actor, co-writer, prodr. (TV) More Than Friends, 1978, Million Dollar Infield, 1982; actor, co-writer, dir. (films) This Is Spinal Tap, 1984; dir: (films) The Sure Thing, 1985, Stand By Me, 1986, Rumor Has It, 2005; dir. prodr. (films) The Princess Bride, 1987, When Harry Met Sally, 1989, Misery, 1990, A Few Good Men, 1992, North, 1994, The American President, 1995, Ghosts of Mississippi, 1996, The Story of Us, 1999, Alex & Emma, 2003; co-creator

(TV series) The Super, 1972; co-creator, actor (TV series) Free Country, 1977-78. Mem. SAG, AFTRA, Dir. Guild Am., Writers Guild Am. Office: Castle Rock Entertainment 335 N Maple Dr Ste 135 Beverly Hills CA 90210-3867*

**REINER, THOMAS KARL,** manufacturing executive, engineering scientist; b. Budapest, Hungary, Dec. 29, 1931; came to U.S., 1959; s. Pál and Jozefa (Keller) R.; m. Joyce Kramer (div.); children: Paul A., Reneé K. Hedsand; m. Eleanor Ruth Aldridge (div.); m. Bonnie Sherman, 1995. Diploma optics trade sch., Budapest, 1952; MSME, Tech. U., Budapest, 1955; postgrad., London Coll., 1958, U. Pitts., Carnegie Inst. Tech., 1964.; PhD, U. Wexford, England, 2001. Shift charge engr. Power Sta., Hungary, 1954-56; test engr. Blaw-Knox Co., London, 1956-57; sr. engr. Eubank & Ptnrs., London, 1957-59; rsch. engr. Pitts. Plate Glass Co., 1959-60, product mgr. Copes-Vulcan divsn., 1960-62; chief engr. J.W. Fecker divsn. Am. Optical Co., 1962-66; product mgr. Carco Electronics, Calif., 1966-68; chief engr. Fairchild Camera Space and Def. Divsn., Calif., 1968-70; dir. engring. Templeton, Kenly & Co., 1970-72; gen. mgr. Foremark Corp., Calif., 1972-74; owner Kinetron, Inc., Calif., 1974-76, GRW, Inc., Calif., 1977-97; pres. Renmark-Pacific Corp., Calif., 1998—2003; chief engring. scientist Integrated Def. Sys., The Boeing Co., Calif., 2004—. Adj. prof. math. Tech. U., Budapest, 1951-54. Pres. Peacock Ridge Homeowners Assn., Calif. Lt. Hungarian Army, 1951-57. Mem. Internat. Soc. Weighing and Measurements. Achievements include patents for concrete post tensioning device, air bearing and slave connector for Satellite Attitude Control Space Simulator; synchronization of hydraulic jacking systems to raise the Freemont Street Bridge in one piece; bending of automotive side windows; invention of a tug/barge latching system, membrane type PANCAKE loadcells, ultra low profile industrial scales, air cargo direct loading device. Home: 14110 Valley Vista Blvd Sherman Oaks CA 91423 Office Phone: 310-367-9997. Personal E-mail: t-reiner@pacbell.net.

**REINERT, JAMES A.,** entomology educator; b. Enid, Okla., Jan. 26, 1944; s. Andrew J. and Emma Reinert; m. Anita Irwin; children: Travis J., Gina N., Mindy K., Melanie B., Gregory W., Teresa J. BS, Okla. State U., 1966; MS, Clemson U., 1968, PhD, 1970. Asst. state entomologist U. Md., College Park, 1970; asst. prof. entomology to prof. entomology Ft. Lauderdale Rsch. and Edn. Ctr., U. Fla., 1970-84; resident dir., prof. entomology Tex. A&M Univ. Sys., Dallas, 1984-94, prof. entomology, 1994—2003, prof. entomology, Tex. agrl. experiment sta. faculty fellow, 2004—, regents fellow, 1994—. Contbr. over 420 articles to profl. jours. Grantee, NDEA, 1968. Mem. Inter-Turfgrass Soc., Entomol. Soc. Am. (S.W. br. sec.-treas. 1998, pres. 2000, chair sec. sect. F 2005, award in urban entomology 2002), So. Nurserymen's Assn. (Porter Henegar Meml. award 1982), Fla. Entomol. Soc. (v.p. 1983, pres. 1984, Entomologist of Yr. 1985), Fla. State Hort. Soc. (v.p. 1982), S.C. Entomol. Soc. (J.H. Cochran award 2002, Rsch. Ctr. Adminstrs. Soc. (v.p. 1994, state rep. 1991-92, sec. 1993), Dallas Agr. Club (bd. dirs. 1989, v.p. 1990, pres. 1991). Roman Catholic. Home: 3805 Covinton Ln Plano TX 75023-7731 Office: Tex A&M Univ Rsch and Ext Ctr 17360 Coit Rd Dallas TX 75252-6599 Business E-Mail: j-reinert@tamu.edu.

**REINERT, NORBERT FREDERICK,** lawyer, retired chemicals executive; b. Hamilton, Ohio, Apr. 12, 1928; s. Fred F. and Jennie A. R.; m. Ida Elizabeth Barickman, Jan. 26, 1956; children: Matthew W., Paul H. B.Ch.E., Ohio State U., 1951; LL.B., Cleve.-Marshall Law Sch., 1959. Bar: Ohio 1959, D.C. 1961. Patent agt. Standard of Ohio, Cleve., 1957-59, patent lawyer, 1959-60, E.I. duPont de Nemours & Co., Wilmington, Del., 1960-91, dir. investor relations, 1981-84, mng. counsel, 1985-91; v.p., gen. counsel Endo Labs, Inc. subs. DuPont, Garden City, NY, 1971-73, exec. v.p., 1973-77, pres., 1977-81; pvt. practice patent law, 1991—2002. Served with Chem. Corps AUS, 1955-56. Mem. Am. Patent Law Assn., Tau Beta Pi. Republican. Roman Catholic. Home: PO Box 311 Mendenhall PA 19357-0311

**REINERTSEN, NORMAN,** retired air transportation executive; b. Bklyn., Mar. 27, 1934; s. Berthin and Malene Katherine (Dahl) R.; m. Elizabeth T. O'Shea, Aug. 30, 1958 (dec. 2003); children: Michael, Christopher, Katherine. BEE, CCNY, 1960; postgrad., Harvard U., 1982. Registered profl. engr., Calif. Various positions Grumman Aerospace Corp., 1960-75; gen. mgr. Grumman Aerospace Corp. (Great River ops.), 1975-77; v.p. automotive Grumman Allied Industries, Melville, NY, 1977-83, sr. v.p. vehicle div., 1983-94; sr. v.p. Olson Bodies, Inc., 1977-79; exec. v.p. Grumman Flexible, Delaware, Ohio, 1979-82; pres. Grumman Olson, Mellville, 1983-85; sr. v.p. Vehicle div. Grumman Allied, 1985-87; v.p. quality ops. Grumman Aircraft Sys. div. Northrop Grumman, 1987-94; ret., 1994. With U.S. Army, 1955-57. Mem. Air Force Assn., Northport Yacht Club. Home: 7 Oleander Dr Northport NY 11768-3438

**REINFELD, GEORGE,** retired communications educator; b. Newark, Dec. 24, 1927; s. Abe and Grace Reinfeld; children: Larry, Grace Lubin. BA, Montclair State Tchrs. Coll., 1950, MA, 1954. Tchr. Westwood (NJ) HS, 1950—54, North Arlington (NJ) HS, 1954—56; prof. Glassboro (NJ) State Coll., 1956—2002, founder dept. comms. Contbr. numerous articles to profl. publs. With Air Corp USN, 1945—46. Avocations: piano, backgammon, reading. Home: 16 Monroe Ave Pitman NJ 08071-1563

**REINGLASS, MICHELLE ANNETTE,** lawyer; b. LA, Dec. 9, 1954; d. Darwin and Shirley (Steiner) R. Student, U. Calif., Irvine, 1972-75; BSL, Western State U., 1977; JD, Western State U., Coll. Law, 1978. Bar: Calif. 1979, U.S. Dist. Ct. (ctrl. dist.) Calif. 1979, U.S. Ct. Appeals (9th cir.) 1981, U.S. Dist. Ct. (so. dist.) Calif. 1990. Pvt. practice employee litig., Laguna Hills, Calif., 1979—. Instr. Calif. Continuing Edn. of Bar, 1990—, Western State Coll., 1991, Rutter Group, 1994—; chmn. magistrate selection com. U.S. Dist. Ct. (ctrl. dist.) Calif., LA, 1991, 93-95, com. mem., 1997, lawyer rep. to 9th cir. jud. conf.; lectr. in field. Contbr. articles to profl. jours. Pres., bd. dirs. Child or Parental Emergency Svcs., Santa Ana, Calif., 1982-92; bd. dirs. Pub. Law Ctr., Santa Ana, Coalition for Justice, Working Wardrobes; mem. exec. com. and cast CHOC Follies. Recipient Jurisprudence award Anti-Defamation League, 1997; named to Western State U. Hall of Fame, 1993; named one of Top 100 Most Influential Lawyers in Calif., LA Daily Jour., 2001; one of Top 30 Female Litigators in Calif., LA Daily Jour., 2002; one of Top 50 Female Litigators, LA Daily Jour., 2003-04; named to Super Lawyers, LA Mag., 2004, 05. Mem. State Bar Calif., Am. Bus. Trial Lawyers (bd. dirs.), Orange County Bar Assn. (del. to state conv. 1980-94, bd. dirs. 1983-94, chmn. bus. litigation sect. 1989, sec. 1990, treas. 1991, pres.-elect 1992, pres. 1993), Calif. Employee Lawyers Assn. (com. mem., chair elect)Orange County Trial Lawyers Assn. (bd. dirs. 1987-89, Bus. Trial Lawyer of Yr. award 1995, Employee Trial Lawyer of Yr. award 2004), Orange County Women Lawyers (Lawyer of Yr. award 1996), Vols. in Parole (chmn. adv. com. 1990-91), Peter Elliot Inns Ct. (master), Am. Bd. of Trial Advocates. Avocations: distance running, skiing. Office: 23161 Mill Creek Dr Ste 170 Laguna Hills CA 92653-1650 E-mail: michelle@reinglasslaw.com

**REINGOLD, ARTHUR LAWRENCE,** epidemiologist, educator; b. Chgo., Oct. 31, 1948; married AB, U. Chgo., 1970, MD, 1976. Diplomate Am. Bd. Internal Medicine. Resident in internal medicine Mount Auburn Hosp., Cambridge, Mass., 1976-78; instr. dept. medicine (epidemiology) U. Conn., Hartford, 1979; epidemic intelligence svc. officer Conn. State Dept. Health Svcs., Hartford, 1979-80; epidemic intelligence svc. officer spl. pathogens br., bacterial diseases divsn. Ctr. Disease Control, Atlanta, 1980-81, resident in preventive medicine, 1980-82, asst. chief respiratory & spl. pathogens epidemiology br. Ctr. Infectious Disease, 1981-85, liaison officer, 1985-87; vis. lectr. dept. biomed. and environ. health scis. (epidemiology) U. Calif., Berkeley, 1985-87, prof. epidemiology, 1987—, head epidemiology program 1990—, prof. dept. epidemiology & biostatistics San Francisco, 1989—, clin. prof. dept. medicine, 1991—; dir. UCB-UCSF Fogarty Internat. AIDS Training Program; co-dir. Calif. Emerging Infections Program. Cons. in field. Contbr. articles to profl. jours. Fellow Am. Coll. Epidemiology, Infectious Disease Soc. Am.; mem. ACP, Am. Epidemiological Soc., Am. Soc. Micro-

biology, Soc. Epidemiologic Rsch., Sigma Xi, Inst. Medicine. Office: UC Berkeley Sch Pub Health 140 Warren Hall 7360 Berkeley CA 94720-7360 Office Phone: 510-642-0327. Office Fax: 510-643-5163. E-mail: reingold@berkeley.edu.*

**REINGOLD, DAVID AMI,** sociologist, educator; b. Chgo., Oct. 30, 1968; s. Haim and Badonna Reingold. BA in Sociology and Social Welfare, U. Wis., 1990; MA in Sociology, U. Chgo., 1992, PhD in Sociology, 1996. Asst. prof. Ind. U., Bloomington, 1997—2003, assoc. prof., 2003—; dir. rsch. and policy devel. corp. for Nat. and Cmty. Svc., Washington, 2002—04; dir. pub. affairs and doctoral pub. policy programs Ind. U. Sch. Pub. and Environ. Affairs, 2006—. Rsch. assoc. Ctr. for the Study of Urban Inequality, Chgo., 1990—94; program assoc. Govs. Task Force on Human Svcs. Reform, Chgo., 1993; rsch. assoc. Dept. Children and Family Svcs., Chgo., 1996; field assoc. Rockefeller Inst. Govt., Albany, NY, 1996—98. Contbr. articles to profl. jours. Family self sufficiency com. Bloomington Housing Authority, 1997—2002, chmn. family self-sufficiency com., 1998—2002; housing commr. Bloomington Housing Authority Bd., 1999—2002, vice chmn., 2000—02; task force for disadvantaged youth White House, 2002—03; chmn. Ind. Commn. on Cmty. Svc. and Volunteerism, 2005—; pres. bd. dirs. South Ctrl. Ind. Cmty. Action Program, 2006—. Fellow fellowship on race, poverty and social policy, NSF/U. Chgo., 1992—96; grantee rsch. grantee, Ind. Family Social Svcs. Adminstrn., The Joyce Found., Ind. Twp. Assn., 1998—2000, The Joyce Found., 2001—02; scholar Century scholar, U. Chgo., 1990—92. Mem.: Assn. for Pub. Policy Analysis and Mgmt. (policy com. 2003—), Urban Affairs Assn., Am. Sociol. Assn. Office: Ind Univ, Sch Pub & Environ Affairs 1315 E 10th St Bloomington IN 47405 Office Phone: 812-855-5971. E-mail: reingold@indiana.edu.

**REINGOLD, PAUL D.,** law educator, lawyer; b. 1951; BA, Amherst Coll., 1973; JD, Boston U., 1977. Bar: Mich. 1977. Sr. staff atty. legal svcs S.E. Mich., Ann Arbor, 1977-82; asst. city atty. City of Ann Arbor, 1982-83; clin. asst. prof. U. Mich. Law Sch., Ann Arbor, 1983-89, clin. prof., dir. clin. law program, 1989—. Vis. prof. law, Japan, Spain; vis. clin. prof. Boston Coll. Law Sch. Recipient L. Hart Wright teaching award. Mem.: Inst. of Continuing Legal Edn. (mem. exec. com.). Office: U Mich Law Sch 362 Legal Rsch 625 S State St Ann Arbor MI 48109-1215 Office Phone: 734-763-4319. Office Fax: 734-764-4702. E-mail: pdr@umich.edu.

**REINHARD, CHRISTOPHER JOHN,** merchant banker, venture capitalist, biotechnologist, director; b. Bridgeport, Conn., Nov. 11, 1953; s. Warren John and Marian Louise (Dutter) R.; m. Maureen Francis, Sept. 24, 1977; 1 child, Griffin John. BS, Babson Coll., 1976, MBA, 1977. Sr. fin. analyst Gen. Motors Corp., Detroit and N.Y.C., 1977-81; asst. sec. Wheelabrator-Frye Inc., NH, 1981-83; asst. sec., asst. treas. The Signal Cos., Inc., La Jolla, Calif., 1983-86; mng. dir., v.p. The Henley Group, Inc., La Jolla, 1986-90; mng. dir. Fisher Sci. Group, Inc., La Jolla, 1986-90; mng. dir., v.p. Wheelabrator Tech. Inc., Henley Mfg. Corp., 1987-90; founder, pres. Colony Group Inc., Rancho Santa Fe, 1990—, Reinhard Assocs., Rancho Santa Fe, 1990-95; founder, v.p., CFO Advanced Access, Inc., San Diego, 1995-97. Pres. Direct Feedback, Inc., 1990, Dairy Queen Ventures, 1990-94, Winsor Sport Fencing, 1993—; CEO, founder, pres. Collateral Therapeutics Inc., 1995-2005; gen. ptnr. Cabrillo Ventures, 1995-96; founder, pres. ihumon, 2000—; exec. chmn. Artes Med., Inc., 2004—; chmn., CEO, founder Cardium Therapeutics Inc., 2003—. Mem. Boston Athenaeum, N.Y. Athletic Club, San Diego Polo Club, Rancho Santa Fe Polo Club. Office: Cardium Therapeutics 3611 Valley Ctr Dr Ste 525 San Diego CA 92130 Office Phone: 858-436-1000.

**REINHARD, DIANE L.,** retired university president; B in elem. edn., U. Wis., M in ednl. psychology; PhD ednl. evaluation, Ohio State U. Faculty mem., assoc. dean, acting dean U. of Oreg.; prof., dept. of ednl. psychology W.Va. U., dean, coll. of human resources and edn., acting pres.; pres. Clarion U., 1990—2003; interim pres. Ind. U. of Pa., 2004—05; ret., 2005.

**REINHARD, JOAO PEDRO,** chemicals company executive; b. Sao Paulo, Brazil, Aug. 4, 1945; BA, MBA, Escola de Administracao de Empresas da Fundacao Vargas, Sao Paulo, Brazil, 1967. Fin. planning supr. Squibb do Brazil, Sao Paulo, 1968; credit mgr. Dow Quimica, Sao Paulo, 1970-72; fin. asst. Dow Latin Am., Miami, Fla., 1973; treas. Latin Am. Dow Lepetit Latin Am., Miami, Fla., 1974-76; corp. fin. planning mgr. The Dow Chem. Co., Midland, Mich., 1976-77; fin. dir. Dow Quimica S.Am., Sao Paulo, Brazil, 1978-80; treas. Dow Chem. Europe, Horgen, Switzerland, 1981-85; mng. dir. Dow Italy, Milan, 1985-87; v.p. Dow Europe, Horgen, Switzerland, 1985-87; treas. The Dow Chem. Co., Midland, Mich., 1988—, exec. v.p., CFO, 1995—. Bd. dirs. Royal Bank of Canada, Dow Corning Corp., Sigma-Aldrich Corp., Coca-Cola Co., Liana Ltd., Midland, Mich., Dorinco Reinsurance Co., Midland, Dow Chem. Internat. BV, Midland, DCOMCO Inc., Midland, Dow Chm. Inter-Am. Ltd., Midland, Dow Chem. Internat. Inc. (Panama), Midland,, Dow Chem. Internat. Ltd., Midland, Midland Engine Property Corp., Dow Chem. Overseas Capital N.V., Midland, Bank Mendes Gans nv, Amsterdam, The Netherlands. Mem. Fin. Execs. Inst., Fin. Mgmt. Assn., Nat. Assn. Corp. Treasurers, Corp. Fin. Inst. Office: The Dow Chemical Co 2030 Dow Ctr Midland MI 48674-0001 E-mail: preinhard@dow.com.

**REINHARD, KEITH LEON,** advertising executive; b. Berne, Ind., Jan. 20, 1935; s. Herman L. and Agnes V. R.; m. Rose-Lee Simons, Nov. 7, 1976; children: Rachel, Elizabeth; children by previous marriage: Christopher, Timothy, Matthew, Geoffrey, Jacqueline. Student public schs., Berne. Comml. artist Kling Studios, Chgo., 1954-56; mgr. tech. comm. dept. Magnavox Co., Ft. Wayne, Ind., 1957-60; creative/account exec. Biddle Co., Bloomington, Ill., 1961-63; jr. copywriter Needham, Harper & Steers, Chgo., 1964; named creative dir., 1975, pres., 1980, chmn., 1982; chmn., CEO DDB Needham Worldwide & DDB Worldwide Inc., 1986—2001; chmn. DDB Worldwide Inc., 2001—06, chmn. emeritus, 2006—. Episcopalian. Office: DDB Worldwide Inc 437 Madison Ave New York NY 10022-7001*

**REINHARD, KENNETH EDWARD,** psychologist; b. Bklyn., Mar. 12, 1953; s. Edward Leo and Theresa Reinhard. BS in Psychology magna cum laude (hons.), CCNY, 1975; MA, LIU, 1977, PhD, 1979. Diplomate in clin. psychology Am. Bd. Profl. Psychology. Dir. F.D.R. Anxiety Disorders Clinic, Montrose, N.Y., 1984—; staff clin. psychologist Roosevelt VA Hosp., Montrose, 1979—, Ctr. Applied Clin. Rsch., N.Y.C., 1979-81; pvt. practice Yorktown Heights, N.Y., 1981—. Mem. aux. med. staff No. Westchester Med. Ctr., Mt. Kisco, N.Y. Contbr. articles to profl. jours. Mem. APA, ABPP, AGPA, EGPS, N.Y. Soc. Clin. Psychologists, Westchester Psychol. Assn., Phi Beta Kappa. Home: 17 Dailey Dr Croton On Hudson NY 10520-3536 Office Phone: 914-737-4400 2773. Personal E-mail: kenneth.reinhard@va.gov. Business E-Mail: kennethreinhard@med.va.gov.

**REINHARD, PHILIP G.,** federal judge; b. LaSalle, Ill., Jan. 12, 1941; s. Godfrey and Ruth R.; married Virginia Reinhard; children: Bruce, Brian, David, Philip. BA, U. Ill., Champaign, 1962, JD, 1964. Asst. state atty. Winnebago County, 1964-67; atty. Hyer, Gill & Brown, 1967-68; state atty. Winnebago County, 1968-76; judge 17th Jud. Cir., 1976-80, Appellate Ct., 1980-92, U.S. Dist. Ct. (no. dist.) Ill., 1992—. Mem. Am. Acad. Jud. Edn., Winnebago County Bar Assn. Office: US Courthouse 211 S Court St Rockford IL 61101-1219 Office Phone: 815-987-4480.

**REINHARDT, BENJAMIN MAX,** lawyer, arbitrator, mediator; b. N.Y.C., Dec. 29, 1917; s. Meyer and Miriam (Fischer) R.; children: Dennis, Dixie, Sara, Shawn; m. Rosa Reinhardt. BA, Harvard U., 1940; JD magna cum laude, Southwestern U., L.A., 1956. Bar: Calif. 1956, U.S. Supreme Ct. 1960. Pvt. practice, Van Nuys, Calif., 1957-87, Palm Desert, Calif., 1987—. Chief legal counsel Northridge (Calif.) Hosp. Found., 1965-75; calif. Psychol. Assn., San Francisco, 1965-70; tchr. law Los Angeles County Bd. Edn., L.A., 1965-73; instr. law U. So. Calif., L.A., 1963-69, Coll. of Desert, Palm Desert, Calif., 1992-94; arbitrator Superior Ct. Calif., Palm Springs, 1994—; atty. Sr. T.V., Indian Wells, Calif., 1992—. Mem. Palm Desert Police Adv. Com., 1993-98; mem. adv. bd. Ret. Sr. Vol. Program, Palm Desert, 1994-96; instr.

law Elderhostel, Indian Wells, Calif., 1993-98. Capt. U.S. Army, 1941-46. Mem. State Bar Calif., Desert Bar Assn. Republican. Avocations: golf, reading. Office: Palm Desert Greens 38-101 Story Creek Dr Palm Desert CA 92260-8617 Fax: 760-346-0936. E-mail: reino81@earthlink.net.

**REINHARDT, DANIEL SARGENT,** lawyer; b. Orange, NJ, Jan. 27, 1949; s. Warren Irwin and Winifred Ruth (Sargent) R.; m. Elizabeth Ann Johnson, June 11, 1982; 1 child, Meredith Alexandra. BA, Duke U., 1971; JD, Georgetown U., 1974. Bar: Ga. 1975, U.S. Dist. Ct. (no. dist.) Ga. 1975, U.S. Ct. Appeals (5th and 11th cirs.) 1981, U.S. Dist. Ct. (so. dist.) Ga. 1984, U.S. Dist. Ct. (mid. dist.) Ga. 1985, U.S. Ct. Appeals (4th cir.) 1985. Assoc. Troutman Sanders LLP, Atlanta, 1974—79, ptnr., 1980—, mem. exec. com. Dep. asst. atty. gen. State of Ga., 1975-79. Named a Super Lawyer, Atlanta Mag., 2004. Mem. ABA, Ga. Bar Assn., Atlanta Bar Assn., fellow, Am. Coll. Trial Lawyers, Lawyers Club. Avocation: sports. Office: Troutman Sanders LLP 600 Peachtree St Atlanta GA 30308-2265 Office Phone: 404-885-3206. Office Fax: 404-885-3900. Business E-Mail: daniel.reinhardt@troutmansanders.com.

**REINHARDT, GEORGE ROBERT,** lawyer; b. Tifton, Ga., Mar. 1, 1954; BBA magna cum laude, U. Ga., 1975; JD, U. Va., 1978. Bar: Ga. 1979. Atty. Reinhardt, Whitley, Wilmot, Summerlin & Pittman, PC, Tifton, Ga. Mem.: Tifton Bar Assn., State Bar Ga. (bd. govs. 1992—, state disciplinary bd. review panel 1993—98, chmn. 1996—98, fin. com. 1996—, program com. 1998—, exec. com. 1998—, chair fin. com. 1999—2000, treas. 2000—01, pres.-elect 2003—, pres. 2004), Sphinx Soc. Office: Reinhardt Whitley Wilmot et al PO Drawer 1287 1001 N Central St Tifton GA 31794

**REINHARDT, JOHN EDWARD,** former international affairs specialist; b. Glade Spring, Va., Mar. 8, 1920; s. Edward Vinton and Alice (Miller) R.; m. Carolyn Lillian Daves, Sept. 2, 1947; children: Sharman W. Reinhardt Lancefield, Alice N., Carolyn C. Reinhardt Fenstermaker. AB, Knoxville Coll., 1939; MS, U. Wis., 1947, PhD, 1950. Prof. English Va. State Coll., Petersburg, 1950-56; cultural affairs officer USIS, Manila, 1956-58; dir. Am. Cultural Ctr., Kyoto, Japan, 1958-63; cultural attache USIS, Tehran, Iran, 1963-66; dep. asst. dir. Office East Asia and Pacific, USIA, Washington, 1966-68, 70-71, asst. dir. Office for Africa, 1968-70; ambassador to Nigeria, 1971-75; asst. sec. state for pub. affairs, 1975-77; dir. USIA, Washington, 1977-78, U.S. Internat. Communication Agy., Washington, 1978-81; acting dir. Smithsonian Mus. African Art, Washington, 1981-83; asst. sec. for history and art Smithsonian Instn., Washington, 1983-84, dir. directorate internat. activities, 1984-87; prof. polit. sci. U. Vt., Burlington, 1987-90, prof. emeritus, 1990—. Served as officer AUS, 1942-46. Mem. MLA, Am. Fgn. Svc. Assn. (v.p. 1969-71). Clubs: Cosmos. Methodist. E-mail: john.reinhardt3@verizon.net.

**REINHARDT, JOHN W.,** dean, dental educator; b. Nashville, Ill. m. Claudia Reinhardt. B in biology, Ill. Wesleyan U., 1971; DDS, Loyola U., 1975; MS in operative dentistry, U. Iowa, 1979; MPH in health services rsch., Harvard U., 1988. Diplomate Am. Bd. Operative Dentistry. With US Army Dental Corps; asst. prof. U. Iowa Coll. Dentistry, 1980—84, assoc. prof., 1984—90, head dept. operative dentistry, 1988—2000, prof., 1990—2000; dean U. Nebr. Med. Ctr. Coll. Dentistry, 2000—, prof. dept. adult restorative dentistry, 2000—. Rschr. in field; cons. NIH, ADA, US Navy, Am. Dental Edn. Assn., Consortium Operative Dentistry Educators, Internat. Assn. Dental Rsch., others.; chair Children's Amalgam Trial Data and Safety Monitoring Bd. Nat. Inst. Dental and Craniofacial Rsch., 1997—; mem. bd. dirs. Friends of the Nat. Inst. of Dental and Craniofacial Rsch., 2005—. Contbr. articles to profl. pubs., scientific papers, chapters to books. Fellow: Internat. Coll. Dentists, Am. Coll. Dentists; mem.: ADA, Am. Bd. Operative Dentistry, Acad. Operative Dentistry (pres. 1997, chair. bd. dirs. founder's fund 2000—Award of Excellence 2002). Office: U Nebr Med Ctr Coll Dentistry 40th and Holdrege Streets Box 830740 Lincoln NE 68583-1301 Office Phone: 402-472-1344. Office Fax: 402-472-6681. Business E-Mail: jreinhardt@unmc.edu.*

**REINHARDT, STEPHEN ROY,** federal judge; b. NYC, Mar. 27, 1931; s. Gottfried and Silvia (Hanlon) Reinhardt; children: Mark, Justin, Dana. BA cum laude, Pomona Coll., 1951; LLB, Yale, 1954. Bar: Calif. 1958. Law clk. to Hon. Luther W. Youngdahl U.S. Dist. Ct., Washington, 1956—57; atty. O'Melveny & Myers, L.A., 1957—59; ptnr. Fogel Julber Reinhardt Rothschild & Feldman LC, L.A., 1959—80; judge U.S. Ct. Appeals (9th cir.), L.A., 1980—. Adj. prof. Loyola Law Sch., LA, 1988—90. Pres. LA Recreation and Parks Commn., 1974—75; active Coliseum Commn., 1974—75, LA Police Commn., 1974—78, pres., 1978—80; sec., exec. organizing com. LA Olympics, 1980—84; exec. com. Dem. Nat. Com., 1969—72; nat. Dem. committeeman State of Calif., 1976—80; bd. dirs. Amateur Athletic Found. L.A, 1984—92. 1st lt. USAF, 1954—56. Mem.: ABA (labor law coun. 1975—77), Calif. Bar Assn., LA County Bar Assn. Office Phone: 213-894-3639.*

**REINHARDT, WILLIAM PARKER,** chemical physicist, educator; b. San Francisco, May 22, 1942; s. William Oscar and Elizabeth Ellen (Parker) R.; m. Katrina Hawley Currens, Mar. 14, 1979; children: James William, Alexander Hawley. BS in Basic Chemistry, U. Calif., Berkeley, 1964; AM in Chemistry, Harvard U., 1966, PhD in Chem. Physics, 1968; MA (hon.), U. Pa., 1985. Instr. chemistry Harvard U., 1967-69, asst. prof. chemistry, 1969-72, assoc. prof., 1972-74; prof. U. Colo., Boulder, 1974-84, chmn. dept. chemistry, 1977-80; prof. chemistry U. Pa., Phila., 1984-91, chmn. dept., 1985-88, D. Michael Crow prof., 1987-91; prof. chemistry U.Wash., Seattle, 1991—, assoc. chmn. undergrad. program, 1993-96. Adj. prof. physics U. Wash., Seattle, 1998—; vis. fellow Joint Inst. for Lab. Astrophysics of Nat. Bur. Stds. and U. Colo. 1972-74, fellow, 1974-81; dir. Telluride Summer Rsch. Ctr., 1986-89, treas., 1989-93; com. on atomic, molecular and optical scis. NRC, 1988-90; sub com. Internat. Union Pure and Applied Physics, Atomic Molecular Physics, 2002—; vis. scientist Nat. Inst. Stds. and Tech., summers 1993—, Harvard-MIT Ctr. Ultra-Cold Atoms, 2005; vis. prof. chemistry U. Paris VI, 1991, U. Melbourne, Australia, 1997, Harvard U., 1998, Davidson lectr. U. Kans., 2000; Kohler lectr. U. Calif., Riverside, 2002; R.S. Berry pub. lectr. Telluride, Colo., 2004, Bertman Meml. lectr. Wesleyan U., Middletown, Conn., 2005. Mem. editl. bd. Phys. Rev. A., 1979-81, 05-, Chem. Physics, 1985-94, Jour. Chem. Physics, 1987-89, Jour. Physics B. (U.K.), 1992-2004, Internat. Jour. Quantum Chemistry, 1994-2001, Digital Libr. of Math. Functions, 1999-; rschr. theoretical chem. physics, theoretical atomic and molecular physics for numerous publs Recipient Camille and Henry Dreyfus Tchr. Scholar award, 1972; Alfred P. Sloan fellow, 1972; J.S. Guggenheim Meml. fellow, 1978; Coun. on Rsch. and Creative Work faculty fellow, 1978; Wismore fellow U. Melbourne (Australia), 1997; J.W. Fulbright sr. scholar, Australia, 1997. Fellow AAAS, Am. Phys. Soc. (vice chmn. div. atomic, molecular and optical physics 1985-86); mem. Am. Chem. Soc., Sigma Xi (nat. lectr. 1980-82), Phi Lambda Upsilon (Fresenius award 1977), Phi Beta Kappa (vis. scholar 2002-03, disting. fellow lectr., 2004-). Office: U Wash Dept Chemistry Box 351700 Seattle WA 98195-1700 Office Phone: 206-543-0578. Business E-Mail: rein@chem.washington.edu.

**REINHART, ANNE CHRISTINE,** special education educator, consultant; b. Detroit, Mar. 9, 1950; m. Charles Reinhart; children: Kim Meredith, Theodore Justin. BS, Ea. Mich. U., 1972; MA, U. Detroit, 1977. Cert. spl. edn., Mich. Spl. edn. tchr. for emotionally impaired State of Mich. Hosp., Pontiac, Berkley (Mich.) Sch. Dist, 1976—. Co-chair ASSET (support group for gifted and talented students), Birmingham, Mich., 1996-98; com. mem. Mich. Dept. of Edn., Office of Spl. Edn.; participant Mich Pilot Study grant Quality Assurance Rev., 2000-03. Grantee, Dept. Spl. Edn., Mich., 2000—03. Mem. Kappa Delta Pi. Avocation: writing. Home: 25925 Romany Way Franklin MI 48025-1909

**REINHART, CHARLES LAWRENCE,** performing company executive; b. Summit, N.J., Dec. 5, 1930; s. Albert and Rose Belle (Goldstein) R.; m. Molly Moore, Jan. (div. 1974); children: Taylor, Adam; m. Stephanie Reinhart,

July, 1987; 1 child, Ariane; m. Patricia Reinhart, 1953 (div. 1962); 1 child, Scott. BA, Rutgers U., 1952; postgrad., U. Copenhagen, 1955-56; DFA (hon.), Duke U., 2003. Pres. Am. Dance Festival, Durham, NC, 1968—, co-dir., 1993—2002; co-artistic dir. for dance Kennedy Ctr., Washington, 1996—2002, artistic dir. for dance, 2002—04. Mem. dance panel Guggenheim Found., 1973-85; producer numerous NYC dance events including City Ctr. Spring Dance Festival, 1969-73, dance seasons at Anta Theater & City Ctr. for Music and Drama, 1968-73, Dance Repertory Season at Billy Rose Theatre, 1969; developer, nat. coord. NEA Dance Touring Program, 1967-78, NEA Artists-in-Schs. program, 1970-81; organizer cultural presentation program U.S. Dept. State, 1966; mem. adv. com. Asia Soc. Performing Arts program, 1970; dir. Jacob's Pillow Dance Festival, 1974; bd. dirs. Theatre Devel. Fund, Anglo-Am. Contemporary Dance Found., Internat. Theatre Inst., Japan Soc. Performing Arts Com.; co-exec. prodr. PBS Series Free to Dance: The African American Presence in Modern Dance, 2001 (Emmy award, 2001). Cpl. U.S. Army, 1952-53, Korea. Decorated officer Order Arts and Letters comdr. Order Arts and Letters (France); recipient Morrison award, 1985, Dance/USA Honors for lifetime achievement in dance, 1994, Capezio Dance award, 1996, Diaghilev award, 1997, Dance Notation Bur. Svc. award, 1999, Dance Mag. award, 2003. Office: Am Dance Festival 1697 Broadway Rm 900 New York NY 10019 Office Phone: 212-586-1925. E-mail: clr@americandancefestival.org.

**REINHART, DIETRICH THOMAS,** academic administrator, social studies educator; b. Mpls., May 17, 1949; s. Donald Irving and Eleanor Therese (Noonan) R. BA in History, St. John's U., Collegeville, Minn., 1971; AM in History, Brown U., 1976, PhD in History, 1984. Benedictine monk St. John's Abbey, 1971—; prof. history St. John's U., 1981—, dean of the coll., 1988-91, pres., 1991—. Dir. liturgy St. John's Abbey, 1983-88. Bd. dirs. Minn. Pvt. Coll. Coun., 1991—, George A. MacPherson Fund, 1991—, Hill Monastic Manuscript Library, 1991—, Inst. for Ecumenical and Cultural Rsch., 1991—, First Am. Nat. Bank St. Cloud, 1992—; bd. overseers St. John's Prep. Sch., 1990—. Home: St Johns Abbey Collegeville MN 56321 Office: St John's U Office of Pres Collegeville MN 56321

**REINHART, JOHN BELVIN,** retired child and adolescent psychiatrist, educator; b. Merrill, Wis., Dec. 22, 1917; s. Dabney Belvin and Ann (Toomey) R.; m. Helen Elsen Reinhart, Jan. 3, 1949; children: Peter, Catherine, Ann, John, Frederick, Andrew. BA, Duke U., 1939; MD, Bowman Gray Sch. Medicine, Winston-Salem, N.C., 1943. Diplomate Am. Bd. Pediatrics, Am. Bd. Psychiatry in child and adolescent psychiatry. Instr pediatrics Bowman Gray Sch. Medicine, Winston-Salem, 1950-52; asst. prof., assoc. prof., prof. pediatrics and psychiatry U. Pitts. Sch. Medicine, 1956-83, emeritus prof. pediatrics, 1983—; clin. prof. psychiatry Bowman Gray Sch. Medicine, Winston-Salem, 1986-99, ret., 1999—. Co-Author: A Baby's First Year, 1956. Capt. M.C. AUS, 1946-48. Roman Catholic. Avocations: reading, golf, tennis, travel. Home: 34 Hunters Ln Hendersonville NC 28791-1665

**REINHART, KELLEE CONNELY,** journalist; b. Kearney, Nebr., Dec. 15, 1951; d. Vaughn Eugene and Mary Jo (Mullen) Connely; m. Stephen Wayne Reinhart, June 15, 1974; children: Keegan Connely, Channing Mullen. BA, U. Ala., 1972, MS, 1974. Advt. copywriter Stas. WTBC-AM, WUOA-FM, 1970-72; asst. mgr. Ala. Press Assn., 1972-74; asst. to the editor Antique Monthly mag., 1974-75, mng. editor, 1975-77; editorial dir. Antique Monthly and Horizons mags., 1977-89; dir. univ. rels. U. Ala. Sys., Tuscaloosa, 1989—2004, vice chancellor for sys. rels., 2004—. Editor: Wild Birds of America: The Art of Basil Ede, 1991, Centennial Memories, Millennial Hopes, 2000, The People's City, 2003. Bd. dirs. Ala. Humanities Found.; bd. dirs. Ala. Writers Forum, pres., 1999—2001. Recipient Druids Arts award, 1995, Betsy Plank Disting. Communicator award U. Ala., 2006. Mem. Soc. Profl. Journalists, Am. Soc. Mag. Editors, Newcomen Soc. U.S., Art Table, XXI/U. Ala. Women's Hon. Soc. Office: 401 Queen City Ave Tuscaloosa AL 35401-1551 Business E-Mail: kreinhar@uasystem.ua.edu.

**REINHART, PETER SARGENT,** lawyer; b. Mineola, N.Y., May 17, 1950; s. Charles Woodham and Martha Way (Sargent) R.; m. Susan Stockwell, Aug. 29, 1970 (div. Jan. 2001). BA, Franklin and Marshall Coll., 1971; JD, Rutgers U., 1975. Bar: N.J. 1975. Atty. Pillsbury and Russell, Atlantic Highlands, NJ, 1975-78; corp. counsel K. Hovnanian Enterprises, Inc., Red Bank, NJ, 1978-81, sr. v.p., gen. counsel, 1981—; also bd. dirs. Inst. Multi-Family Housing, Plainsboro, N.J., 1989-90. Trustee, mem. editorial bd. Housing N.J. mag., 1991—. Trustee Community Assns. Inst., Arlington, Va., pres. N.J. chpt., 1988; trustee Assn. for Children of N.J., Newark, 1988-93, Keep Middlesex Moving, New Brunswick, 1990-93, Bayshore Cmty. Hosp., Holmdel, N.J., 1992-01, v.p., 1995, chmn., 1997, Meridian Hosp. Corp., 2002-; chmn. Jersey Shore Partnership, 2003-; pres. Greater Red Bank Jaycees, 1978-79, Atlantic Highlands Rep. Club, 1978; v.p. Monmouth coun. Boy Scouts Am., Oakhurst, N.J., 1987-94, pres., 1994-95; v.p. Garden State Games, Edison, N.J., 1991-94; mem. Coun. Affordable Housing, Trenton, N.J., 1993-2004. Named to Community Assns. Inst. Hall of Fame, 1988; named Jaycee of Yr. Greater Red Bank Jaycees, 1977. Mem. N.J. State Bar Assn., N.J. Shore Builders Assn. (pres. 1989-90, Builder of Yr. 1987, Hall of Fame 1991), Nat. Assn. Indsl. and Office Parks (bd. dirs. 1996-99), N.J. Builders Assn. (v.p. 1992-94, pres. 1995-96, Builder of Yr. award 1995, Shore Athletic Club (Oakhurst), Ea. Monmouth C. of C. (trustee 1992-98, Vol. of Yr. 1995). Avocations: road racing, marathon running, golf. Office: Hovnanian Enterprises Inc PO Box 500 110 West Front St Red Bank NJ 07701-5902

**REINHART, ROBERT ROUNTREE, JR.,** lawyer; b. Chgo., Oct. 21, 1947; s. Robert Rountree and Ruth (Duncan) R.; m. Elizabeth Aileen Plews, July 26, 1969; children: Andrea Jean, Jessica Elizabeth, Rebecca Jill. BA, Northwestern U., 1968, JD, U. Mich., 1971. Bar: Ill. 1971, Mich. 1972, Minn. 1973, U.S. Supreme Ct. 1976. Law clk. to judge U.S. Dist. Ct. (we. dist.) Mich., Grand Rapids, 1971-73; assoc. Oppenheimer Wolff & Donnelly, Mpls., 1973-77, ptnr., 1978-96, chair labor and employment bus. group, 1985-92; ptnr. Dorsey & Whitney, Mpls., 1996—, chair labor and employment practice group, 2000—. Co-chmn. Upper Midwest Employment Law Inst., Mpls., 1984—; gen. counsel Minn. Empoyment Law Coun., 1990—. Mem. ABA (labor and employment, civil litigation sects.), Minn. Bar Assn. Office: Dorsey & Whitney Ste 1500 50 S 6th St Minneapolis MN 55402-1498 Office Phone: 612-340-7835. Office Fax: 612-340-2868. E-mail: reinhart.robert@dorseylaw.com.

**REINHARZ, JEHUDA,** academic administrator, history educator; b. Haifa, Israel, Aug. 1, 1944; came to U.S., 1961; s. Fred and Anita (Weigler) R.; m. Shulamit Rothschild, Nov. 26, 1967; children— Yael, Naomi BS, Columbia U., 1967; BRE, Jewish Theol. Sem., 1967; MA, Harvard U., 1968; PhD, Brandeis U., 1972; LHD (hon.), Hebrew Union Coll., 1995; DHL (hon.), Jewish Theol. Sem. Am., 1996, Fairfield U., 1999. Prof. modern Jewish history U. Mich., Ann Arbor, 1972—82; Richard Koret prof. modern Jewish history Brandeis U., Waltham, Mass., 1982—84; dir. Tauber Inst. Study of European Jewry, 1984—94; provost, sr. v.p. for acad. affairs Brandeis U., Waltham, Mass., 1992—94; pres. Brandeis U., Waltham, Mass., 1994—. Mem. internat. acad. bd. Annenberg Rsch. Inst., 1986-90; bd. dirs. Yad Chaim Weizmann, 1990-2000, Internat. Editl. Bd. Pardès, 1996—; pres. Israel Prize, 1990, Akiba award, Am.-Jewish Com., 1996. Author: Fatherland or Promised Land: The Dilemma of the German Jew 1893-1914, 1975, Chaim Weizmann: The Making of a Zionist Leader, 1985 (Present Tense Literary award 1985, Kenneth B. Smilen Literary award 1985, Nat. Jewish Book award 1986, Shazar prize in history Israel, 1988), (in Hebrew) Hashomer Hazair in Germany, 1931-39, 1989, Chaim Weizmann: The Making of a Statesman, 1993 (Nat. Jewish Book award 1994); also numerous articles in French, German, Hebrew and English; co-author: Zionism and the Creation of a New Society, 1998, 2d edit., 2000, The Era of Political Zionism, 2000; gen. editor: Studies in Jewish History, 1984, European Jewish History, 1985; co-editor: The Jew in the Modern World, 1980, 2d edit. 1995, Mystics, Philosophers and Politicians, 1982, Israel in the Middle East 1948-83, 1984, The Jewish Response to German Culture, 1985, The Jews of Poland Between Two World

Wars, 1989, The Impact of Western Nationalisms, 1992, Zionism and Religion, Hebrew edit., 1994, Essential Papers on Zionism, 1996; editor: The Letters and Papers of Chaim Weizmann, 1918-20, 1977, Dokumente zur Geschichte des deutschen Zionismus 1882-1933, 1981, Living with Anti-semitism, 1987. Bd. govs. United Israel Appeal/Jewish Agy., 1994, 2000; bd. dirs., mem. exec. com. Am. Joint Distbn. Com., 1994-2002; mem. acad. com. U.S. Holocaust Mus., 1990-2003, mem. com. on conscience nat. adv. forum, 1996—; mem. Presdl. Adv. Commn. on Holocaust Assets in U.S., 1998-2000; mem. Common. on Israel-Diaspora Rels., 1996-97; trustee Am. Hebrew Acad., Greensboro, N.C., 2000—. Recipient Akiba award, Am. Jewish Com., 1996. Fellow Leo Baeck Inst., Royal Hist. Soc., Am. Acad. Jewish Rsch., Am. Acad. Arts and Scis.; mem. Yad Vashem Inst. (adv. bd. 1983), Nat. Coun. Shazar Ctr., Assn. for Jewish Studies (sec. 1986-88, treas./sec., 1989-88), Coun. on Fgn. Rels. Home: 66 Beaumont Ave Newton MA 02460-2331 Office: Office Of The Pres Irving Enclave 113 415 South St # Ms100 Waltham MA 02453-9110 E-mail: jreinharz@brandeis.edu.*

**REINHERZ, HELEN ZARSKY,** social worker, researcher; b. Boston, Aug. 4, 1923; d. Zachary and Anna (Cohen) Zarsky; m. Samuel E. Reinherz, Aug. 29, 1943; 1 son, Ellis. AB magna cum laude, Wheaton Coll., 1944; MS, Simmons Coll., 1946; S.M., Harvard U., 1962, Sc.D., 1965. Social worker Newton Family Service, Mass., 1946-49, Mass. Gen. Hosp., Boston, 1949-51; supr. psychiat. social work State Hosp., Waltham, Mass., 1958-61; faculty mem. Simmons Coll., Boston, 1965—, prof. methods rsch., 1972—, dir. research Sch. Social Work, 1968-93, dir. PhD program, 1993-96. Prin. investigator Identifying Children at Risk, 1976—84, Adaption in Adolescence, 1987—93, Adult Rsch. Project, 1998—2001, Early Adulthood Rsch. Project, 1993—97, Simmons Longitudinal Study, 2001—, Study Adolescent Drug Abuse, 1971—73; rsch. cons. Dept. Mental Health, 1970—80; chmn. Gov.'s Adv. Coun. on Mental Health and Retardation, 1972; mem. adv. com. Mental Health Manpower fed. Govt., 1980—82. Author (with H. Wechsler, D. Dobbins): Social Work Research in the Human Services, 1976; author: (with M. Heywood, J. Camp) A Community Response to Drug Abuse, 1976; cons., assoc. editor: Jour. Prevention, 1980—91, mem. fed. adv. com.: Rsch. in Prevention Rev., 1984—87, editl. bd.: Jour. Early Adolescence, cons. editor: NASW Jour.; contbr. articles to profl. jours. Recipient Maida H. Solomon award, Simmons Coll. Alumni, 1961, Disting. Career award, Soc. Social Work and Rsch., 2005, Rsch. Achievement award, NASW, 2005, grantee, Grant Found., 1963, Med. Found., 1967—69, NIMH, 1975—84, 1987—; NIH tng. fellow, 1961—65. Fellow Am. Orthopsychiat. Assn.; mem. Acad. Cert. Social Workers, Am. Pub. Health Assn., Coun. Social Work Edn., Harvard Sch. Pub. Health Alumni Assn. (sec.-treas. 1965-68), Phi Beta Kappa, Delta Omega. Home: 17 Corey Rd Malden MA 02148-1116 Office: Simmons Sch Social Work 300 The Fenway Boston MA 02115 Business E-Mail: helen.reinherz@simmons.edu, reinherz@simmons.edu. *As a teacher and researcher my efforts have been directed towards encouraging students to formulate the right questions about human problems as a first step to understanding and change.*

**REINHOLD, KARIN,** mathematics professor; PhD, Ohio State U., Columbus, OH. Assoc. prof. U. Albany, SUNY, NY, 1992—. Contbr. scientific papers. Recipient Excellence in Tchg. Award, SUNY - Chancellor. Office: U Albany State U NY 1400 Washington Ave Albany NY 12222 Office Phone: 518-442-4641.

**REINHOLD, RICHARD LAWRENCE,** lawyer; b. Buffalo, Feb. 24, 1951; s. Richard J. and Ann J. R.; m. Beth Stacey Grossman, May 11, 1991; children: Elizabeth Jane, Eleanor Terese, Rebecca Hope. AB, Cornell U., 1973; JD, SUNY, Buffalo, 1976. Bar: NY 1977, Fla. 1977. With office of tax legis. counsel US Dept. Treasury, Washington, 1982-84; ptnr., chair tax dept. Willkie Farr & Gallagher LLP, NYC. Adj. faculty Sch. Law NYU. Contbr. articles to profl. jours. Bd. dirs. NYU Internat. Tax Program; mem. dean's adv. coun. sch. of law SUNY, Buffalo. Fellow Am. Coll. Tax Counsel; mem. ABA, NY State Bar Assn. (chair tax sect. 1996-97, mem exec. com. 1985-), Internat. Fiscal Assn., Tax Forum, Tax Club, Am. Alpine Club. Office: Willkie Farr & Gallagher 787 Seventh Ave New York NY 10019-6099 Office Phone: 212-728-8292. Office Fax: 212-728-9292. E-mail: rreinhold@willkie.com.

**REINHOLD, SANDRA LYNNE,** psychologist; d. John David Reinhold and Carol Ann Hertel, Paula Joy Reinhold (Stepmother). BA in Psychology, Ohio Wesleyan U., 1995; MA in Clin. Psychology, U. Hartford, 1998; D in Psychology, Chgo. Sch. Profl. Psychology, 2002. Lic. psychologist N.Y., 2003. Dir. Dialectical Behavior Therapy Program Child & Adolescent Treatment Svcs., Buffalo, 2002—. Tchr. Buffalo (N.Y.) State Coll., 2005—, SUNY, Buffalo. Mem.: APA, Psychol. Assn. We. N.Y., N.Y. State Psychol. Assn., Psi Chi (life), Delta Zeta (life; corr. sec., social chair, historian). Achievements include development of treatment program for suicidal and self-injurious teens. Office: Child & Adolescent Treatment Services 3350 Main Street Buffalo NY 14214 Office Phone: 716-835-4011. Business E-Mail: sreinhold@catswny.org.

**REINICHE, DOMINIQUE,** food products executive; b. July 13, 1955; MBA, ESSEC Bus. Sch. Asst. prod. mgr. Procter & Gamble, 1978—81, prod. mgr., 1981—83, assoc. advt. mgr., 1983—86; mktg., strategy mgr. Kraft Jacobs Suchard, 1986—92; mktg. mgr. Coca-Cola Enterprises, 1992—94, comml., operational mktg. mgr., 1994—97, asst. CEO, 1997—98, chmn., CEO, 1998—2002; vice chmn. Coca-Cola Enterprises-Europe Group, 2002—03, chmn., 2003—. Exec. bd. Medef; adv. bd. ING Direct; bd. dir. ECR Europ; chmn. Union des Annonceurs; first vice chmn. Union of European Soft Drinks Associations; supervisory bd. AXA Group. Recipient Legion d'Honneur, 2002.*

**REINIKE, IRMA,** retired writer, artist, poet, lyricist; b. White Harbor, Long Beach, Miss., Oct. 20, 1927; d. Chester Henry and Edna Claire (Latille) Reinike; children: Harvey Franklin Linn Shows Jr., George David Shows, Thelam Jewell Shows Hoffman. Student, St. Mary's Dominican Coll.; grad., North Light Art Sch., Cin., 1996, 97, 99. Freelance writer, student Famous Writers Sch., Westport, Conn., 1965—69; editor Seabee Courier US Naval Contrn. Battalion Ctr., Gulfport, 1969—71; adminstr. US Army Corps. Engrs.; ret., 1994. Author: Mystery, 1940—41, Long Beach Movie Personality, 1949, My Beach, 1990, Thelma, 1991, (poetry) My Lady of Medjugorje, 1987—88, Irma Reinike Poetry-Book 1, 2002, I Love My Flag, 2000, numerous poems; columnist Round the Town, Long Beach, Miss., 1963—66, The Illustrated Press, Irma Reinike's Personality Parade, New Orleans, 1952; composer: (songs) See You Tomorrow, 1995—96, Days of Love, 1997, The Blue of Your Eyes, 1997, I Am An American, 2006, others, (stage play) Ethel Chichester, Peg O' My Heart, Kaye Hamilton, Stage Door, 1949, Song, Dance Dixieland Minstrel and Variety Artists, 1950—52, Charity Performer, Le Petit Theatre de Vieux Carre' Sunday Salon, 1996, Destruction by Hurricane Camille, Times Picayune, 1970; Introduction Camille Book-Hurricane, 1969, Ten Acres, 1970—71, Sunrise Lake Ponchartrain, Represented in permanent collections Nat. D-Day Museum, exhibitions include St. Thomas Parish, Long Beach, Miss., Baton Rouge Gallery, Le Petite Theatre, New Orleans, Mandeville, La., City Long Beach, Miss., 2005, many others. Mem. La. Libr. Found. New Orleans Friends Pub. Libr., 1994—96; charter mem. World War II Monument Meml., Washington; mem. Nat. Rep. Senatorial Com., 1994—97, Nat. Rep. Congl. Com., 2000. Named Honored Author, La. Libr. Assn., 1994, 1996, La. State Libr., 1995, Friends Fest New Orleans Pub. Libr., 1994—96, Patron, Le Petit Theatre de Vieux Carre, 1996. Mem.: New Orleans Mus. Art. Republican. Roman Catholic. Avocations: fine arts, songwriting, poetry, lyricist, philosophy.

**REININGHAUS, RUTH,** retired artist; b. NYC, Oct. 4, 1922; d. Emil William and Pauline Rosa (Lazarik) R.; m. George H. Morales, Feb. 20, 1944; children: George James, Robert Charles; m. Allan Joseph Smith, May 28, 1960. Student, Hunter Coll., NYU, Nat. Acad. of Design, 1960-61, Frank Reilly Sch. of Art, 1963, Art Students League, 1964, 68; studied oil painting, with Robert Beverly Hale and Robert Philips, with Morton Roberts and Frank Reilly, Robert Maione, with Rudy Colao. Instr. art Banker's Trust, N.Y.C., 1971-77, 79-99, Kittredge Club for Women, N.Y.C., 1967-77, Bankers Trust

Co., 1971-98. Exhibited in group shows at Berkshire Art Mus., 1970s, Hammer Galleries, Inc., N.Y.C., 1974, Far Gallery, N.Y.C., 1974, Mufalli Gallery, N.Y. and Fla., 1983-90, Pen and Brush Club, 1985—, Petrucci Gallery, Saugerties, N.Y., 1988-94, Pastel Soc. Am., 1988—, John Lane Gallery, Rhinebeck, N.Y., 1992-97, Regianni Gallery, N.Y.C., 1994, Catherine Lorillard Wolfe Club, Salmagundi Club, Allied Artists Am., Heidi Newhoff Gallery, N.Y.C., Hudson Valley Art Assn., Knickerbocker Artists, N.Y.C., Pen & Brush Club Inc., Pastel Soc. Am., Heritage Mus.; represented in permanent collections at US Navy Art, US Coast Guard Art Program, Hon. Murtogh D. Guinness, Salmagundi Club; contbr. to popular mags. Active Navy Art Coop. and Liaison, Coast Guard Art Program. Recipient 3d prize in Oils, Murray Hill Art Show, 1959, 69; Washington Sq. Outdoor Art Exhibit scholar Nat. Acad., 1962, Frank Reilly Sch. Art, 1963, NYU, 1963, Talens award, 1963, Robert Lehman award, 1968, Richtone Artists award, 1968, Baker Brush award, 1969, Silver medal award ART Spirit Found., 2006; Salmagundi scholar, 1969; subject NBC TV show You Are an Artist, 1950s. Fellow: Hudson Valley Art Assn. (Claude Parson's Meml. award 1974), Am. Artists Profl. League (Claude Parsons Meml. award 1974, 2d prize oils 1992, 3d prize pastel 1993, Pres. award 1994, Hon. Mention award 2004); mem.: Navy Art Coop. and Liaison, Knickerbocker Artists (Flora B. Giffuni PSA Pres.' award 1990), Oil Pastel Assn. (Pen and Brush award 1987, Strathmore award 1989, Pen and Brush award 1990, Salmagundi Club award 1991), Allied Artists Am. (assoc.), Washington Sq. Outdoor Art Assn. (bd. dirs. 1983—90), Nat. Arts Club (Reciprocal) Artists Fellowship, Soc. Illustrators (hon. 1983—87), Pastel Soc. Am. (bd. dirs. 1988—90, J. Giffuni purchase award 1988, Pastel Soc. of West Coast award 1991), Coast Guard Art Program, Salmagundi Club N.Y. (pres. 1983—87, curator 1989—97, 2003—04 Philip Isenberg award 1974, Salmagundi Club prize 1985, Franklin B. Williams Fund prize 1987, Tom Picard award 1987, Mortimer E. Freehof award 1988, John N. Lewis award 1988—89, Medal of Honor 1989, Philip Isenberg award 1989—90, Helen S. Coes award 1990, Flora B. Giffuni Pres. award 1990, Thomas Moran award 1990, Samuel T. Shaw award 1990, Alphaeus Cole Meml. award 1991, Salmagundi award 1991, Alice B. McReynolds Meml. award 1991, Philip Isenberg award 1992, 1995, Harry Ballinger Meml. award 2000—01, Philip Isenberg award 2001, Jane Impastato award 2003, 1st prize John N. Lewis award 2004, John N. Lewis award 2004, Best in Show award 2004, Mortimer Freehof award 2005), Pen and Brush Club (Helen Slotman award 1986, OPA Internat. award 1987, Gene Alden Walker award 1988, Pen and Brush Solo award 1992, Margaret Sussman award 1996, 1998, Merit award 2000), Catharine Lorillard Wolfe Art Club (bd. dirs. 1987—97, Anna Hyatt Huntington award 1978, Coun. Am. Artists award 1985, Pastel award 1992, Still Life award 1993, 1st prize 2001), Alpha Delta Pi. Lutheran. Avocations: travel, technical illustration, oil, pastel and watercolor painting, collecting antique music boxes and watches. Home: 222 E 93rd St Apt 26A New York NY 10128-3758 Personal E-mail: reininghaus@netzero.com.

**REINISCH, JUNE MACHOVER**, psychologist, educator; b. NYC, Feb. 2, 1943; d. Mann Barnett and Lillian (Machover) R. BS cum laude, NYU, 1966; MA, Columbia U., 1970, PhD with distinction, 1976. Asst. prof. psychology Rutgers U., New Brunswick, N.J., 1975-80, assoc. prof. psychology New Brunswick, N.J., 1980-82, adj. assoc. prof. psychiatry, 1981-82; prof. psychology Ind. U., Bloomington, 1982-93, dir. Kinsey Inst. Rsch. in Sex, Gender, and Reprodn., 1982-93; prof. clin. psychology Sch. Medicine, Indpls., 1983-93; dir. emeritus Kinsey Inst., 1993—. Dir., prin. investigator Prenatal Devel. Projects, Copenhagen, 1976—; sr. rsch. fellow, trustee The Kinsey Inst., 1993—; pres. R2 Sci. Comms., Inc., Ind., NY, 1985—; vis. sr. rschr. Inst. of Preventive Medicine, Copenhagen Health Svcs., Kommune-hospitalet, Copenhagen, 1994—; cons. SUNY; sr. cons. Mus. of Sex, NYC, 1998, dir. acquisitions and new exhbns., 2003-, v.p. sci. affairs, 2003; exec. dir. Health and Sci. Adv. Bd., 2004—. Author: The Kinsey Institute New Report on Sex, 1990, 94, pub. 8 fgn. edits.; editor, contbr. books Kinsey Inst. series; syndicated newspaper columnist: The Kinsey Report; contbr. rsch. reports, revs., articles to profl. jours.; appeared on TV shows including PBS, BBC, ABC and NBC sci. spls., Discovery, ABC Science Specials, 20/20, Oprah Winfrey, Geraldo Rivera, Charles Grodin, Montel Williams, Sally Jessy Rafael, Good Morning Am., Today Show, CBS This Morning; guest host TV shows including CBC Real Personal, TalkLive, also fgn. appearances. Founders day scholar NYU, 1966; NIMH trainee, 1971-74; NIMH grantee, 1978-80, Ford Found. grantee, 1973-75, Nat. Inst. Edn. grantee, 1973-74, Erikson Ednl. Found. grantee, 1973-74, grantee Nat. Inst. Child Health and Human Devel., 1981-88, Nat. Inst. on Drug Abuse, 1989-95; recipient Morton Prince award Am. Psychopath. Assn., 1976, medal for 9th Dr. S.T. Huang-Chan Meml. Lectr. in anatomy Hong Kong U., 1988, Dr. Richard J. Cross award Robert Wood Johnson Med. Sch., 1991, Award First Internat. Conf. on Orgasm, New Delhi, 1991, Disting. Alumnae award Tchrs. Coll. Columbia U., 1992, award for su contbn. Profl. al Conocimiento dela Sexualidad Humana, Assn. Mexicana de Sexologia, Mexico City, 1996; named Regents lectr. UCLA, 1999. Fellow AAAS, APA, Am. Psychol. Soc., Soc. for Sci. Study Sex; mem. Internat. Acad. Sex Rsch. (charter), Internat. Women's Forum, Women's Forum. Inc., Internat. Soc. Psychoneuroendocrinology, Internat. Soc. Rsch. Aggression, Internat. Soc. Devel. Psychobiology, Am. Assn. Sex Educators, Counselors and Therapists, Sigma Xi. Office: SUNY HSCB PBL Box 120 450 Clarkson Ave Brooklyn NY 11203-2056 also: The Kinsey Inst Prenatal Devel Project Ind U Bloomington IN 47405 Business E-mail: jreinisch@museumofsex.com. E-mail: DrReinisch@aol.com.

**REINISH, GLORIA BROOKS**, electrical engineer, educator; b. Bklyn., July 23, 1925; d. Julius Benjamin and Celia Glickman Brooks; m. Martin David Reinish, 1948; children: Nancy Reinish Passow, Julie Brook Askins, James Charles. BSEE, Columbia U., NY, 1945, MSEE, 1948, D of Engring Sci. in Bioengineering, 1974. Mem. tech. staff Bell Telephone Lab., NYC, 1945—46; project. engr. Sperry Gyroscope Co., Lake Success, 1946-51; prof. elec. engring Fairleigh Dickinson U., Teaneck, NJ, 1962—. Chair elec. engring. dept. Fairleigh Dickinson U., 1975—78, chair bioengring. program; cons. Medical Devices Panel FDA, 1976—86; dir. Matrix Instruments, Orangeburgh, NY, 1980—85. Contbr. numerous articles to profl. jours. Grantee Project Kaleidoscope grant, 2001. Fellow: Soc. Women Engrs.; mem.: Inst. Elec. & Electronic Engrs. (life), Tau Beta Pi (Women's Badge 1945), Sigma Xi (Project Kaleidoscope grant 2001). Achievements include patents for a new method of precision ranging; research in electrical stimulation of bone growth; being first woman to earn an engineering degree from Columbia University. Avocations: tennis, golf, piano, bridge, crossword puzzles. Office: Fairleigh Dickinson Univ 1000 River Rd Teaneck NJ 07666

**REINKE, DORIS MARIE**, retired elementary school educator; b. Racine, Wis., Jan. 12, 1922; d. Otto William Reinke and Louise Amelia Goehring. BS, U. Wis., 1943, MS, 1967. Tchr. kindergarten Elkhorn Area Sch. Sys., Wis., 1943—69, prin. bldg., 1968—70, dir. summer sch., 1974—75, tchr. grade 2, 1970—84, chmn. primary dept., 1967—84, administrv. asst., supervising tchr., 1957—83, student tchr., 1984, ret., 1984; tchr. oriented experience Program Area Sch. Sys., Elkhorn, 1966. Pres. Elkhorn Edn. Assn., 1949-50; rep. dist. State Kindergarten Conf., Oshkosh, Wis., 1966; participant early edn. conf. State Early Edn. Conf., Eagle River, Wis., 1968; Univ. of Covenant Harbor Elderhostel, 1997, 98; established Doris M. Reinke Resource Ctr., 2002. Author: Doris' Corner newsletter Walworth County Geneal. Soc., 1992—; author: (with Charlotte and William Gates) Guide to Beckwith's History of Walworth County, 2000; author: Images of America-Elkhorn, 2004; contbr. weekly newspaper column Webster Notes, 1989, monthly column in The Week, 1991. Chmn. Sch. Centennial, Elkhorn, 1987; mem. Elkhorn Hist. Preservation Com., 1991—; chmn. Sesquicentennial com., 1997—; dir. Webster House Mus., 1991—; mem. Walworth County Sesquicentennial Com., 1997—98; mem. sesquicentennial com. Walworth County Fair, 1998—; archivist Sugar Creek Luth. Ch., 1992—, mem. ch. coun., 2003, sec., 2005; choir mem. Luth. Ch., 1995—2001; del. dist. constn. conv. Evang. Luth. Ch. Am., Beloit, Wis., 1987; com. mem. Luth. Ch., Elkhorn, 1987 sec., 2005; RSVP Vol. Food Pantry, Elkhorn, 1985—2002, bd. dirs., 1985—88, 1995—. Recipient Wis. Edn. Rsch., West Bend, Wis., 1966, Outstanding Elem. Tchrs., Wash., 1973, Wis. Dept. Edn., Madison, 1980, Local History award State Hist. Soc. Wis., 1993, Outstanding Sr. Citizen award Walworth County Fair, 1999, Cmty. Svc. award Masons, 2000, Disting. Svc. award

Rotary, 2004; named one of 50 Who Matter, Janesville Gazette, 2006, Vol. of Yr., Walworth County Ret. Educators Assn., 2006. Mem.: Walworth County Ret. Tchrs. Assn. (v.p. 1988, pres. 1991), Nat. Ret. Tchrs. Assn., Walworth County Geneal. Soc. (bd. dirs. 1991—92), Walworth County Hist. Soc. (treas. 1985—89, v.p. 1990—91, pres. 1991—96, v.p. 1999—2000, pres. 2000—05), Elkhorn Women's Club (sec. 1999—2000, v.p. 2003, pres. 2005—), Alpha Delta Kappa (state pres. 1968—70, 1976—78, chpt. pres. 2002—03). Avocations: reading, baseball, bird watching, travel. Home: 516 N Wisconsin St Elkhorn WI 53121-1119 Office Phone: 262-723-4248. Personal E-mail: walcohistory@elknet.net.

**REINKE, RALPH LOUIS**, retired academic administrator; b. Elmhurst, Ill., June 22, 1927; s. Louis Fred and Malinda Marie (Beckmann) R.; m. Lois Hermine Borneman, Aug. 28, 1948 (dec. Mar. 1984); children: Janice Reinke Eisenloeffell, Stephan, Sharon Reinke Holaway; m. Carole Louise Rediehs, June 14, 1986 Student, U. Ill., 1945—46; BS, Concordia U., River Forest, Ill., 1949; MA, Northwestern U., 1952; postgrad, U. Chgo., 1956—63; LittD, Concordia Sem., 1972. Prin. St. John Elem. Sch., Houston, 1949-56; assoc. prof. psychology and edn. Concordia U., River Forest, Ill., 1956-68, CEO, 2003—04; pres., chief exec. officer Concordia Pub. House, St. Louis, 1968-86; pres. Concordia U., Seward, Nebr., 1986—90; ret., 1990; CEO Concordia U., Ill., 2002—04. Author: Christian Spelling Series, 2d edit, 1971. Mem. sch. bd. selecting com., Oak Park, Ill., 1965-67, chmn. lit. commn. Mo. Synod Luth. Ch., 1967-69; bd. dirs. Concordia U., 1992-2004, chair, 1999-2002. With USNR, 1944-46. Mem. Protestant Ch. Owned Pubs. Assn. (dir. 1969-84, pres. 1982-84), St. Louis Printing Assn. (bd. dirs. 1975-77), Am. Assn. Indsl. Mgmt. (bd. dirs. 1981-85), Assn. Ind. Colls. and Univs. of Nebr. (pres. 1988-89), Luth. Edn. Assn. (pres. 1967-69), Rotary, Phi Delta Kappa. Lutheran. Personal E-mail: rlreinke@aol.com. *Life is a most precious and finite gift of God to man. Those who would lead must make a commitment to devote their full energies and intellects to the improvement of the quality of life of their fellowmen. In the highest sense, leadership is the integrity to heed the quiet voice of conscience from within in the quest of that quality.*

**REINKE, WILLIAM JOHN**, lawyer; b. South Bend, Ind., Aug. 7, 1930; s. William August and Eva Marie (Hein) R.; m. Sue Carol Colvin, 1951 (div. 1988); children: Sally Sue Taelman, William A., Andrew J.; m. Elizabeth Beck Lockwood, 1991. AB cum laude, Wabash Coll., 1952; JD, U. Chgo., 1955. Bar: Ind. 1955. Assoc. Barnes & Thornburg and predecessors, South Bend, Ind., 1957-61, ptnr., 1961—, of counsel, 1996—, former chmn. compensation com. Chmn. compensation com. Barnes & Thornburg and predecessors, mem. mgmt. com. Trustee Stanley Clark Sch., 1969-80, pres., 1977-80; life mem. adv. bd. Salvation Army, 1973—, pres., 1990-92; bd. dirs. NABE Mich. chpt., 1990-94, pres. 1993-94, Isaac Walton League, 1970-81; bd. dirs. United Way, 1979-81; pres. South Bend Round Table, 1963-65; trustee First Meth. Ch., 1976-70; bd. dirs. So. Bend Civic Theatre, 1997-2003. Served with U.S. Army, 1955-57. Recipient Outstanding Local Pres. award Ind. Jaycees, 1960-61, Boss of Yr. award, 1979, South Bend Outstanding Young Man award, 1961. Mem. ABA, Ind. State Bar Assn., St. Joseph County Bar Assn., Ind. Bar Found. (patron fellow), Am. Judicature Soc., Summit Club (founders com.), Rotary (bd. dirs. 1970-73, pres. 74-97). Home: 51795 Waterton Square Cir Granger IN 46530-8317 Office: Barnes & Thornburg 1st Source Bank Ctr 100 N Michigan St Ste 600 South Bend IN 46601-1632

**REINKER, MARY STEFANICH**, musician, music educator; b. Joliet, Ill., Aug. 12, 1947; d. Anthony Edward and Mary Vidmar Stefanich; m. Myron Edward Reinker, Oct. 20, 1984; children: Meryt Antonia Reinker Dean, Molly Elizabeth. MusB, U. St. Francis, Joliet, IL, 1969; MusM, Roosevelt U., Chicago, Ill., 1971. Teaching Certificate Chgo. Bd. of Edn., 1972. Organist St. John's Ch., Joliet, Ill., 1958—65; tchr. Chgo. Pub. Schools, 1971—84; pianist/organist St. Edward's Ch., Dana Point, Calif., 1989—94, Gloria Dei Ch., Dana Point, Calif., 1985—89, St. Frances Cabrini Ch., Littleton, Colo., 1994—, St. Mary's Ch., Littleton, Colo., 2004—; private piano instr. Laguna Beach & Dana Point, 1984—94; founder/dir. Forte Acad. of Music, Littleton, Colo., 1997—, Centennial, Colo., 2004—; organist St. Mary's Chamber Orchestra, 2005—. Clinician & pedagogy advisor Colo. State Music Teachers Assn., Colo., 1996—, Forte Acad. of Music, Littleton, Colo., 1997—. Musician: (performance) Requiem by John Rutter; musician: (organist/pianist) St. Peter's Basilica, Rome, Salzburg Music Festival (Medal, 2002), St. Mark's Cathedral, Notre Dame, Chartres; organist (performance) Cathedrals of Madrid and Barcelona. Vol. St. Frances Cabrini Ch., Littleton, Colo., 1994—2004; vol. for local retirement and nursing homes Littleton, Colo., 1995—2004. Scholar Ill. State Scholarship, State of Ill., 1965. Mem.: Music Teachers Assn. of Calif., Colo. State Music Teachers Assn., Music Teachers Nat. Assn., Delta Mu Theta Music Honor Soc. Avocations: horse-back riding, travel, reading. Office: Forte Acad Music 10143 W Chatfield Ave Ste 15 Littleton CO 80127 Office Phone: 303-948-9221 ext. 305. Personal E-mail: maryreinker@qwest.net. Business E-mail: forteacademy@att.net.

**REINKING, ANN H.**, dancer, actress; b. Seattle, Nov. 10, 1949; d. Walter Floyd and Francis Holmes (Harrison) R.; m. Larry Small, 1970; m. Herbert A. Allen; Aug. 25, 1982; (stepchildren): Leslie, Christie, Herbert, Charlie. Student public schs. Guest instr. NYU, Duke U., Durham, N.C., Rutgers, N.J., Harvard, Cambridge, Mass.; choreographer Pal Joey, Goodman Theater, Chgo., 1988. Broadway appearances include Coco, 1970, Wild and Wonderful, 1972, Pippin, 1973, Over Here, 1974, Goodtime Charlie, 1975, Chicago, 1977, A Chorus Line, 1976, Dancin', 1978, Sweet Charity, 1986-87; TV appearances include Ellery Queen, Doug Henning: Magic on Broadway, 1982, Parade of Stars, 1983, American Treasury, 1985, Salute to Jules Styne, Broadway Salutes Washington, An Introduction to the Dance Gala of the Stars; film appearances include Movie, Movie, 1978, All That Jazz, 1979-80, Annie, 1982, Micki and Maude, 1984; play Ann Reinking...Music Moves Me, 1984; actor, choreographer Broadway shows: Chicago, 1996 (Tony award 1997), Annie Get Your Gun, 1999 (Tony award 1999), Fosse, 2001; choreographer Broadway shows: Annie Get Your Gun, 1999, Look of Love, 2003 Recipient Clarence Derwent award, 1974, Outer Critics Circle award, 1974, Theatre World award, 1974, Dance Educators Am. award, 1979, Harkness Dance award, 1979, two Tony award nominations, Tony award for Choregraphy, 1997; Ford Found. scholar, 1964-66; Robert Joffery scholar, 1967; Harkness scholar; Nat. Dance Educators award. Mem. Actors Equity, AFTRA, Stage Actors Guild. Avocations: horseback riding, skiing, swimming, hiking. also: Steps Contemporary & Classical Dance 2121 Broadway Fl 3 New York NY 10023-1786

**REINL, HARRY CHARLES**, economist, researcher; b. Muttersdorf, Suden, Germany, Nov. 13, 1932; arrived in U.S., 1946; s. Carl and Angela (Plass) Reinl. BS. Fordham U., 1953; MA, George Washington U., 1968; cert. in career English, USDA, Washington, 1966; HHD, London Inst. Applied Rsch., 1992; PhD, Brownell U., 1993. Head market rsch. Timex Mfg., Waterbury, Conn., 1955-58; jr. observer Sperry-Rand Corp., NYC, 1958-62; labor economist manpower adminstrn. US Dept. Labor, Washington, 1962-68; labor economist Office Pers. Mgmt. US Civil Svc. Commn., Washington, 1968—. Mgr. NY br. Willmark Svc., NYC, 1971; prof. rsch. Haute Ecole Rsch. Alliance Universelle pour la Paix par la Connaissance, Paris, 1992; rsch. bd. advs. Am. Biog. Inst., Raleigh, NC, 1991—. mem. adv. coun. Internat. Biog. Ctr., Cambridge, England, 1992. Author (on microfilm): The Story of My Life, 1984. Founding mem. Nat. Campaign Tolerance, Montgomery, Ala., 2004; with Willmental health testing VA Med. Ctr., Washington, 1989—; charter mem. Nat. D-Day Mus., New Orleans, 2004—; mem. Diesen Ranch, Santa Barbara, Calif., 2005—; founder Colonial Williamsburg, Va.; mem. Found. for Nat. Archives, Washington, 2005; founder Martin Luther King Jr. Nat. Meml., Washington, 2005; life mem. Rep. Nat. Com., Washington, 1979—; mem. Rep. Nat. Senatorial Com., Washington, 1990, adv. mem., 2006; founding mem. Wold Peace and Diplomacy Forum, Cambridge, 2003; host NYC com. Rep. Nat. Conv., 2004; team mem. Bush-Cheney 2004; inner cir. co-chair inaugural festivities Rep. Nat. Party, 2005; mem. George Bush Presdl. Libr. Found., Tex. A&M U., College Station. Decorated Knight Templar Bur. Internat.; recipient John Edgar Hoover Meml. award, Police Assn., 1983, HIR citation of Leadership, Rep. Nat. Conv., 1996, medal of Freedom, Rep. Nat. Senatorial Inner Cir., 1999, Order of Merit, Nat. Rep.

Congl. Com., 2006; fellow, AA, 1988—. Mem.: World War II Soc., London Diplomatic Acad., Academic Coun., NY Acad. Scis., George Mason U. Mercatus Ctr. (contbr.), Family Immigration History Ctr. Ellis Island, Collegiate Network, Inc. (hon. sponsor), Pres.'s Club, Fordham Univ. Club Washington. Mem. Lds Coll. Home: 2425 Mount Vernon Ave Alexandria VA 22301-1347

**REINMAN, GLENN D.**, computer scientist, educator; b. Miami, Fla., Sept. 1, 1974; s. Raymond Rodney and Helene Reinman; m. Terry Soossani Reinman, July 7, 2002. BS in Computer Sci. and Engring., MIT, Cambridge, 1996; MS in Computer Sci., U. Calif., San Diego, 1999, PhD in Computer Sci., 2001. Prof. dept. computer sci. UCLA, L.A., 2001—. Contbr. articles to profl. jours. Recipient TA Excellence award, U. Calif. San Diego, 1996—97, CAREER Award, NSF, 2001—06, Excellence in Tchg. award, Northrop Grumman, 2004; grantee ITR: Reconfigurable Fabric, NSF, 2002—05; Microarchitectural Evaluation with Phys. Planning grantee, U. Calif. Micro, 2003—04. Mem.: IEEE. Achievements include patents pending for. Office: UCLA Computer Science Dept 4731 D Boelter Hall Los Angeles CA 90095 Business E-Mail: reinman@cs.ucla.edu.

**REINOEHL, RICHARD LOUIS**, social services administrator, scholar; b. Omaha, Oct. 11, 1944; s. Louis Lawrence and Frances Margaret (Robinson) R.; 1 child, Joy Margaret Iroff-Reinoehl. BS in Sociology, Portland State U., 1970; MSW, U. Minn., Duluth, 1977; postgrad., Cornell U., 1984-88. Acting dir. Vanguard Group Homes, Virginia, Minn., 1976-77; dir. Minn. Chippewa Tribe Group Home, Duluth, 1978, Human Devel. Consortium, Minn., N.Y., Ohio, 1978—; coord. NE Ohio Green Libertarian Party's Vote Recount Observation Teams, 2004. Faculty Social Work Program U. Wis., Superior, 1981-84, Bohecker Coll., 2005—; adv. bd. Computers in Social Svcs. Network, 1982-85; mem. Com. on Internat. Social Welfare Edn., 1982-86, Am. Evaluation Assn., 1986-89; affiliate scholar Oberlin Coll., 1991—; artist-in-residence Ohio Arts Coun., 1996-97. Editor: Computer Literacy in Human Services Education, 1990, Computer Literacy in Human Services, 1990, Men of Achievement, 16th edit., 1993; mem. editl. bd. Computers in Human Svcs., 1983-96, 99, Jour. Technology in Human Svcs., 1999—; assoc. editor book rev., 1996-99; contbr. numerous articles to profl. jours. Mem. Legis. Task Force Regional Alcoholism Bd., 1972-73, Assn. Drug Abuse, Prevention and Treatment, 1973-74, Minn. Pub. Health Assn., 1976-78, Minn. Social Svc. Assn., 1976-83, Wis. Coun. Social Work Edn., 1983-84, N.Y. State Coun. Family Rels., 1986-89, Nat. Coun. Family Rels., 1986-89; exec. bd. Duluth Community Action Program, 1982-83; Dem. precinct chair, Portland, Oreg., 1972-74; precinct vice-chair Dem. Farmer-Labor Party, Duluth, 1979-81, chair, 1981-83, 2d vice-chair exec. bd., 1981-83; mem. Zoning Appeals Bd., New Russia Twp., Ohio, 1996—; mem. art edn. com. Fireland Assn. Visual Arts, 1996-99; mem. land use planning com. New Russia Twp., Ohio, 1998—; chair Lorain County Comprehensive Plan Growth Mgmt. Com., 1999—; mem. Smart Devel. Coalition of Lorain County, 1998—, Lorain County Multi-Modal Transp. Planning Steering Com., 2000—, airport subcom., 2000—, roadways sub-com., 2000—, transit subcom., 2000—, info. tech. sub-com., 2000—; field spl. projects field coord., nat. coord. rural issues Kucinich for Pres. campaign, 2003-; chmn. Smart Devel. Coalition Lorain County, 1996-98, Lorain County Growth Mgmt. Com., mem. Environ. Sub-Com., 1997-98; mem. Lorain County Multi-Modal Transp. Plan Steering Com., sub-coms. transit, roadways, airports, rail, and info. tech., 1999-2001, New Russia Township Zoning Bd. Appeals, 1995-2000, New Russia Township Land Use Planning Com., 1996-98; N.E. Ohio coord. Green/Libertarian vote recount obs. teams, 2004; coord. Ohio Voters Reform, 2005—. Mem. NASW (exec. com., chair program com. Arrowhead Region Minn. chpt., 1980-81, co-chair task force on computers in social work, 1981-82), Acad. Cert. Social Workers, Cornell U. Sailing Club (pres. 1990). Avocations: canoeing, antique volkswagens, wilderness hiking. Office: Human Devel Consortium Inc 46180 Butternut Ridge Rd Oberlin OH 44074-9778 Office Phone: 440-315-0121. Business E-Mail: Richard.Reinoehl@oberlin.edu. *It's noteworthy that the most sought-after items in a society cannot be bought or sold. Included are wisdom, respect, generosity, truthfulness, and the love of family and friends.*

**REINOLD, CHRISTY DIANE**, school counselor, consultant; b. Neodasha, Kans., July 21, 1942; d. Ernest Sherman and Faye Etta (Herbert) Wild; m. William Owen Reinold, Dec. 20, 1964; children: Elizabeth, Rebecca. BA Edn., Calif. State U., Fresno, 1964, MA in Edn. and Psychology, 1964. Cert. counselor, Family Wellness instr.; lic. mental health counselor, Fla. Tchr. Clovis (Calif.) Unified Sch. Dist., 1965-66, Santa Clara (Calif.) Unified Sch. Dist., 1966-67, Inst. Internat. Chateaubriand, Cannes, France, 1968-69; tchr., vice prin. Internat. Sch., Sliema, Malta, 1969-70; elem. sch. counselor Duval City Schs., Jacksonville, Fla., 1977-82, Lodi (Calif.) Unified Sch. Dist., 1982—2004. Cons. Calif. Dept. Edn.; mem. Calif. Commn. on Tchr. Credentialing, Sacramento, 1986—2004, mem. adv. panel, 1998—2004; mem. stds. rev. com. Nat. Bd. Cert. Sch. Counselors, 2002—04. Co-author: The Best for Our Kids; Counseling in the 21st Century; contbr. articles. Chmn. bd. dirs. Oak Crest Child Care Ctr., Jacksonville, 1979-81. Named Anne Upton Sch. Counselor of Yr. for Calif., Calif. Sch. Counselor's Assn., 1995; named to H.B. McDaniel Hall of Fame, Stanford U., 2003; recipient H.B. McDaniel Individual award, 1986, James Saum Legis. award, Calif. Sch. Counselor's Assn., 1991, Donald Hayes Lifetime Achievement award, Assn. Calif. Sch. Counselors, 2002. Mem.: AAUW (3rd v.p. 1974, 1st v.p. 1980, by-laws chmn. 1990, chmn. pub. policy 1991—93, pres. 1993), Lodi Pupil Pers. Assn. (pres. 1986—87), Calif. Alliance Pupil Svcs. Orgns. (bd. dirs. 1988—95), Fla. Sch. Counselors Assn., Calif. Assn. Counseling and Devel., Calif. Sch. Counselor Assn. (legis. chmn. 1985—90, pres. 1991), Am. Sch. Counselor Assn. (govt. rels. specialist 1993—94). Republican. Avocations: history, travel, politics. Home: 1772 Le Bec Ct Lodi CA 95240 Personal E-mail: creinold@earthlink.net.

**REINSCH, WILLIAM ALAN**, association executive, educator; b. Evanston, Ill., Jan. 15, 1946; s. Bert and Kathleen (Penn) R.; m. Susan Polley Reinsch, Jan. 3, 1970; children: Andrew, Christian. BA, Johns Hopkins U., 1968; MA in Internat. Rels., Johns Hopkins U.-Sch. Advanced Internat. Studies, 1969. Legis. asst. Congressman Gilbert Gude, Washington, 1973-76; Congressman Richard Ottinger, Washington, 1976; chief legis. asst. Senator John Heinz, Washington, 1977-91; legis. asst. Senator John D. Rockefeller IV, Washington, 1991-93; cons., under sec. for export administrn. Dept. Commerce, Washington, 1994-2001; pres. Nat. Fgn. Trade Coun., Washington, 2001—; mem. U.S.-China Econ. and Security Rev. Commn., 2001—. Tchr. Landon Sch., Bethesda, Md., 1968-73; acting staff dir. Environ. Study Conf. U.S. Ho. Reps., 1976. Contbr. articles to profl. jours. Pres. St. Mark Elderly Housing Corp., Rockville, Md.; bd. dirs. Middle East Inst. Mem. Phi Beta Kappa, Omicron Delta Kappa, Alpha Delta Phi. Democrat. Presbyterian. Office: Nat Fgn Trade Coun 1625 K St NW Ste 200 Washington DC 20006 E-mail: breinsch@nftc.org.

**REINSDORF, JERRY MICHAEL**, professional sports team executive, real estate company executive, accountant, lawyer; b. Bklyn., Feb. 25, 1936; s. Max and Marion (Smith) Reinsdorf; m. Martyl F. Rifkin, Dec. 29, 1956; children: David Jason, Susan Janeen, Michael Andrew, Jonathan Milton. BA, George Washington U., 1957; JD, Northwestern U., 1960. CPA Ill., registered mortgage underwriter; bar: DC, Ill. 60; cert. specialist real estate securities, rev. appraiser. Atty. staff regional counsel IRS, Chgo., 1960-64; assoc. law firm Chapman & Cutler, 1964—68; ptnr. Altman, Kurlander & Weiss, 1968—74; of counsel firm Katten, Muchin, Gitles, Zavis, Pearl & Galler, 1974—79; gen. ptnr. Carlyle Real Estate Ltd. Partnerships, 1971—72; chmn. bd. Balcor Co., 1973—87; mng. ptnr. TBC Films, 1975—83; chmn. Chgo. White Sox, 1981—; Chgo. Bulls Basketball Team, 1985—; ptnr. Bojer Fin., 1987—. Lectr. John Marshall Law Sch., 1966—68; bd. overseers Inst. for Civil Justice, 1996—98; lectr. in real estate, sports and taxation. Author (with L. Herbert Schneider): Uses of Life Insurance in Qualified Employee Benefit Plans, 1970. Chmn. Chgo. region bd. Anti-Defamation League, 1986—2001; mem., trustee Ill. Inst. Tech., 1991—96; mem. Ill. Commn. on African-Am. Males, 1992—; bd. dirs. Chgo. Youth Success Found., 1992—, Corp. for Supportive Housing, 1995—; nat. trustee Northwestern U., 1993—2005, bd.

govs., 1993—2005, Hugh O'Brian Youth Found.; mem. internat. adv. bd. Barrow Neurol. Found., 1996—97; active Chgo. Baseball Cancer Charities, 1994, 1998; bd. trustees Equity Office Properties, 1997—2004. Named to B'nai B'rith Nat. Jewish Am. Sports Hall of Fame, 1994, Chgo. Sports Hall of Fame, 1997; recipient Hallmark award, Chgo. Baseball Cancer Charities, 1986, Corp. Superstar award, Ill. chpt. Cystic Fibrosis Found., 1988, portsman of Yr. award, 1994, Chicagoan of Yr. award, Chgo. Park Dist., 1990, Kellogg Excellence award, 1991, Cmty. Hero award, Interfaith Organizing Project, 1991, Operation Push Bridgebuilder award, 1992, Alumni Merit award, Northwestern U., 1992, Ellis Island Medal of Honor award, Nat. Ethnic Coalition of Orgns., 1993, Lifetime Achievement award, March of Dimes, 1994, Hallmark Hall of Fame Civic award, Ind. Sports Charities, 1994, Am. Spirit award, USAF, 1995, Alpha Epsilon Pi Arthur and Simiteich Outstanding Alumnus award, 1995, Order of Lincoln, 1997, Mayor's medal Hon., 1997, Bklyn. Businessman of Yr., 1997, Guardian of Children award, Jewish Coun. for Youth Svc., 1998, Amb. award, Keshet, 2005. Mem.: FBA, ABA, Nat. Sports Lawyers Assn., Chgo. Bar Assn., Ill. Bar Assn., Northwestern U. Law Sch. Alumni Assn. (bd. dirs.), Order of Coif, Comml. Club Chgo., Omega Tau Rho. Achievements include owner, MLB World Series Champions, 2005. Office: Chgo White Sox 333 W 35th St Chicago IL 60616-3651 Office Phone: 312-674-5200.

**REINSDORF, JUDITH A.,** lawyer; b. 1963; BA in Polit. Sci., magna cum laude, U. Rochester; JD, Cornell U. Bar: NY 1990. With Crowell & Morling, Washington; asst. gen. counsel to chief legal counsel Monsanto Co.; v.p., assoc. gen. counsel Pharmacia Corp., 2000—03; v.p., corp. sec. Tyco Internat. Ltd., Princeton, NJ, 2003—04; v.p., gen. counsel, corp. sec. C.R. Bard, Inc., Murray Hill, NJ, 2004—. Mem.: ABA. Office: CR Bard Inc 730 Central Ave New Providence NJ 07974

**REINSEL, JOSEPH THOMAS,** art educator, artist; b. Fairfax City, Va., July 11, 1971; s. Robert David and Bernice Theresa Reinsel; m. Maureen Jude Reinsel, Apr. 18, 1975. B in Music Composition, Radford U., Va., 1994, MA in Music Composition and Tech., 1998; MFA in Electronic Arts, Rensselaer Poly. Inst., Troy, NY, 2002. Video and sound performance, From the Center Out, public art installation, URBANtells:URBANtraces, video sound performance, Leaves, digital prints, Resonation Series, sound performance, Collapse/Redefine. Grantee, Harvestworks Digital Media Ctr., 2002—03. Mem.: Coll. Art Assn. (assoc.). Office: University of Maryland Baltimore County FA 111A 1000 Hilltop Circle Baltimore MD 21250 Office Phone: 410-455-2581. Office Fax: 410-455-1053. E-mail: jreinsel@umbc.edu.

**REINSTEIN, JOEL,** lawyer; b. N.Y.C., July 23, 1946; s. Louis and Ruth Shukovsky; children: Lesli, Louis, Mindy. BSE, U. Pa., 1968; JD cum laude, U. Fla., 1971; LLM in Taxation, NYU, 1974. Bar: 1971, U.S. Tax Ct. 1973, U.S. Dist. Ct. (so. dist.) Fla. 1976. Atty., office of chief counsel IRS, 1971-74; ptnr. Capp, Reinstein, Kopelowitz and Atlas, P.A., Ft. Lauderdale, Fla., 1975-85; dir., ptnr. Greenberg, Traurig, Hoffman, Lipoff, Rosen & Quentel, P.A., Ft. Lauderdale, 1985-92; gen. counsel Internat. Magnetic Imaging, Inc., Boca Raton, Fla., 1992-94; prin. Law Offices of Joel Reinstein P.A., Boca Raton, 1993—. Lectr. Advanced Pension Planning, Am. Soc. C.L.U.s; lectr. in field. Mem. editl. bd. Fla. Law Rev. 1970-71; contbr. articles to profl. jours. Mem. Fla. Bar Assn. (tax sect.), ABA (tax sect.), Order of Coif, Phi Delta Pi. Office: 925 S Federal Hwy Ste 325 Boca Raton FL 33432 Office Phone: 561-393-6714. E-mail: joel@reinsteinlaw.com.

**REINSTEIN, ROBERT J.,** dean, law educator; b. Balt., Mar. 17, 1945; m. Mary Taylor Aspinwall; children: Ellen, Thomas. BS in Engring. Physics with distinction, Cornell U., 1965; JD cum laude, Harvard U., 1968. Bar: Md. 1969, Pa. 1982, U.S. Supreme Ct. 1971. Law clk. to Hon. Frank A. Kaufman U.S. Dist. Ct. Md., 1968-69; from asst. prof. to assoc. prof. Sch. Law Temple U., Phila., 1969-73, prof. Sch. Law, 1973—; sr. atty. appellate sect. Civil Rights Divsn., U.S Dept. Justice, 1977-78, chief litigation sect., 1979-80; chief legal officer Temple U., 1982-89, dean Sch. Law, 1989—. Vis. prof. law Hastings Coll. Law, San Francisco, 1975, Georgetown U., 1978-79; cons. atty. NAACP Spl. Contbn. Fund, 1970-77. Contbr. articles to profl. jours. Chair civil rights com. B'nai Brith Anti-Defamation League, Phila. Recipient Friendship Award, People's Rep. China, 2002. Mem. ABA, Pa. Bar Assn. Office: Temple U Sch Law 1719 N Broad St Philadelphia PA 19122-6002 E-mail: robert.reinstein@temple.edu.

**REINTHALER, RICHARD WALTER,** lawyer; b. NY, Feb. 27, 1949; s. Walter F. and Maureen C. (Tully) R.; m. Mary E. Maloney, Aug. 8, 1970; children: Brian, Scott, Amy. BA in Govt. magna cum laude, U. Notre Dame, 1970, JD summa cum laude, 1973. Bar: N.Y. 1974, U.S. Dist. Ct. (so. and ea. dists.) N.Y. 1974, U.S. Ct. Appeals (2d cir.) 1974, U.S. Ct. Appeals (9th cir.) 1976, U.S. Supreme Ct., 1977, U.S. Ct. Appeals (5th cir.) 1978, U.S. Ct. Appeals (11th cir.) 1981, U.S. Ct. Appeals (1st cir.) 2004, U.S. Ct. Appeals (3d cir.) 2005. Assoc. White & Case, N.Y.C., 1973—81, ptnr., 1981—95, Dewey Ballantine LLP, N.Y.C., 1995—, co-chmn. litigation dept., 2002—03. Mem. adv. group U.S. Dist. Ct. (ea. dist.) N.Y., 1992-2004, chairperson subgroup on ethics, 1993-2004. Contbr. articles to profl. jours. Served to 1st lt. U.S. Army, 1974. Fellow Am. Bar Found.; mem. ABA (2d cir. chmn. discovery com. 1982-87, program coord. 1986, ann. meeting litigation sect., vice chmn. com. on fed. procedure 1988-89, co-chmn. com. on profl. responsibility 1989-92, vice chmn. securities litigation com. 1993-94, vice chair Hong Kong meeting 1995, co-chair energy litigation com. 1996-97, co-chair antitrust litigation com. 1997-2000, mem. Ethics 2000 task force 1999-2000), N.Y State Bar Assn. Assn. of Bar of City of N.Y. (comm. com. to enhance diversity in the profession 1990-95, mem. Orison S. Marden Meml. Lectrs. com. 1994-2000, chair 1997-2000, spl. com. on mergers, acquisitions and corp. control contests 1995-2002); Scarsdale Golf Club (Hartsdale, N.Y., bd. govs. 1994—2003, pres. 2002-2003), Capital Hill Club (Washington). Republican. Roman Catholic. Avocations: golf, tennis. Office: Dewey Ballantine LLP 1301 Avenue Of The Americas New York NY 10019-6022 Office Phone: 212-259-6090.

**REINTZEL, WARREN ANDREW,** trust company executive; b. Phila., Jan. 4, 1945; s. Warren H. and Lorna (Geibel) R.; m. Susan Rodgers, Dec. 20, 1969; children: Lisa S., Kurt W. BA with high honors, U. Del., 1967; MA in History, Rutgers U., 1968; JD, U. Pa., 1971. Trust adminstrn. trainee First Pa. Bank, Phila., 1971, trust adminstr., 1972-73, trust officer, 1973-79, sr. trust officer, 1979-81; v.p. Provident Nat. Bank, Phila., 1981-86; v.p., head trust adminstrn. dept. Glenmede Trust Co., Phila., 1986—, sr. v.p., 1994—. Trustee Wanamaker Inst., Phila., 1986—, 1st v.p., 1995-2000, pres., 2000-; trustee Meml. Fund, Luth. Ch. of our Saviour, Haddonfield, N.J., 1989-2000, Haddonfield Hist. Soc., 1997—, Haddonfield Cmty. Found., 1998-. Mem. Phila. Bar Assn., Phila. Fin. Assn. (treas. bd. trustees 1987-89), Phila. Estate Planning Coun. (trustee 1991, sec. 1994-95, treas. 1995-96, v.p. 1996-97, pres. 1997-98), Corp. Fiduciaries Assn. Phila. (mem. personal trust com. 1986-89, pres. 1996-98), Phi Beta Kappa. Republican. Office: Glenmede Trust Co 1650 Market St Ste 1200 Philadelphia PA 19103-7391 E-mail: warren_reintzel@glenmede.com.

**REIS, DON,** publishing executive; b. NYC, Nov. 19, 1927; m. Barbara Weinberg, 1949; children: Robert, Richard. AB, Princeton U., 1947; MA, NYU, 1955. Rsch. editor Bantam Books, 1952-55, edn. editor, 1955-66; editor-in-chief Washington Square Press Divsn. Simon & Schuster, 1966-68; v.p., editorial dir. Edn. Directions Inc., Westport, Conn., 1968-85; mng. editor Barron's Edn. Series, 1985-87; gen. and ednl. editor Barron's, 1987-93, sr. cons. editor, 1993-99; editorial dir. Reis Assocs., Forest Hills, NY, 1993—. Author (with A. Butman and D. Sohn) Paperback Books in the Schools, 1962; editor The Collected Essays of Aldous Huxley, 1958. Home and Office: 57 Summer St Forest Hills NY 11375-6035 Personal E-mail: reis@att.net, donjreis@yahoo.com.

**REIS, LESLIE ANN,** law educator, lawyer; b. Plainfield, N.J., Apr. 21, 1958; BS cum laude, Syracuse Univ., 1981; JD, John Marshall Law Sch., Chgo., 1996. Bar: Ill. 1996. Broadcast journalist, 1981—96; legal fellow Reporters Com. for Freedom of the Press, 1996—97; adj. prof. John Marshall Law Sch., 1997—; dir. Ctr. for Info. Tech. & Privacy Law, John Marshall Law Sch., 1997—. Contbr. articles to prof. jour. Mem. Fed. Info. Security & Privacy Adv. Bd. Mem.: Am. Judicature Soc. (past dir., Ctr. for Judicial Independence). Office: Center for Information Technology and Privacy Law John Marshall Law School 315 S Plymouth Ct Chicago IL 60604

**REIS, SIGNO TADEU,** research scientist, consultant; b. Sao Paulo, Brazil, Jan. 22, 1962; s. Joaquim Nicolau and Nair Oliveira Reis; m. Marcia Maria Oliveira, Apr. 29, 2004; 1 child, Joana Oliveira. PhD, U. Sao Paulo, 1999. With Energy and Nuc. Inst., Sao Paulo, 1996—2001; asst. rschr. U. Mo. Rolla, 2002—. Mem.: Am. Ceramic Soc. (assoc.; glass ceramic divsn. 2003—05). Achievements include patents pending for glass and glass-ceramic sealant compositions. Office: Univ Mo Rolla Materials Sci and Engring 302 Straumanis Hall 1870 Miner Cir Rolla MO 65409-1170 Office Phone: 573-341-7094. Office Fax: 573-341-2071. Business E-Mail: reis@umr.edu.

**REISBERG, BARRY,** geriatric psychiatrist, neuropsychopharmacologist; b. Bklyn., Dec. 3, 1947; s. Harry and Claire (Cohen) R.; m. Rosalie DePaola, Feb. 23, 1974 (dec. Oct. 1975); m. Nancy A. Minich, May 7, 1988. BA, CUNY, Bklyn., 1968; MD, N.Y. Med. Coll., 1972. Diplomate Am. Bd. Psychiatry and Neurology, Am. Bd. Geriatric Psychiatry. Intern N.Y. Med. Coll./Met. Hosp., N.Y.C., 1972-75, resident in psychiatry, 1972-75; fellow dept. psychiatry Middlesex Hosp. Med. Sch. U. London, 1975; staff psychiatrist Franklin D. Roosevelt VA Hosp., Montrose, NY, 1975-78; staff psychiatrist Neuropsychopharmacology Rsch. Unit NYU Med. Ctr., N.Y.C., 1978-80, asst. attending psychiatrist, 1978—2001, attending psychiatrist, 2002—, clin. dir. William and Sylvia Silberstein Aging and Dementia Rsch. Ctr., 1978—. Adj. prof. Ctr. for Studies in Aging McGill U., Montreal, Que., 1993—; clin. instr. dept. psychiatry N.Y. Med. Coll., Valhalla, 1975—78; asst. prof. NYU Sch. Medicine, N.Y.C., 1978—84, assoc. prof., 1984—90, prof., 1990—; rsch. collaborator, vis. clinician Brookhaven Nat. Labs., Upton, NY, 1979—90; dir. clin. core NIMH Clin. Rsch. Ctr., 1989—93, Nat. Inst. Aging Alzheimer's Disease Ctr., 1990—; dir. Zachary and Elizabeth M. Fisher Alzheimer's Disease Edn. and Resources Program NYU Sch. Medicine, 1995—; med. and sci. adv. bd. Alzheimer's Assn., Chgo., 1993—97; med. and sci. panel Alzheimer's Disease Internat., 1997—; cons. psychiatrist N.Y. VA Hosp., 1980—89; chmn. work group WHO, Copenhagen, 1984; mem. aging sect. NIH, 1986—90; vis. prof. Palmerston North Postgrad. Med. Soc., New Zealand, 1991; rsch. adv. bd. WHO Project on Alzheimer's Disease, 1995; Bayer vis. prof. St. Louis U. Sch. Medicine, 1999; vis. prof. Georgetown U. Med. Ctr., 2004; vis. prof. in geriatrics Stony Brook U. Health Scis. Ctr., 2005. *Our studies have demonstrated that Alzheimer's disease recapitulates normal human development inversely in terms of cognition, functioning, neurological reflexes and in other ways. These findings, termed retrogenesis, appear to represent a new mechanism of disease. Retrogenesis implies that a better understanding of Alzheimer's disease can improve understanding of normal human development and behavior, and conversely, improved knowledge of human development can enhance understanding and treatment of Alzheimer's disease.* Author: Brain Failure, 1981; editor: Alzheimer's Disease, 1983; editor: (with others) Diagnosis and Treatment of Senile Dementia, 1989; guest editor Drug Devel. Rsch., Internat. Psychogeriat., mem. editl. bd. Jour. Am. Aging Assn., 1985—2004, Alzheimer's Disease and Associated Disorders, 1985—2004, Jour. Geriat. Psychiatry and Neurology, 1986—, Am. Jour. Alzheimer's Disease, 1986—, Internat. Psychogeriat., 1989—96, Am. Jour. Geriat. Psychiatry, 1992—2001, Rsch. and Practice in Alzheimer's Disease, 1999—, Middle East Jour. of Age and Aging, 2004—, Polish Jour. Geriatric Psychiatry, 2005—; contbr. over 250 articles to med. and sci. jours. and books. Recipient Home Care award Vis. Nurse Svc. NY, 1985, Disting. Svc. award, Internat. Psychogeriatric Assn., 2001, Ann. Barry Reisberg Lectr. award Hearthstone Alzheimer's Family Found., 2002-, Lifetime Achievement award Alzheimer's Assn. and 9th Internat. Conf. on Alzheimer's Disease and Related Disorders, 2004; fellow NSF, 1963, Coun. on Internat. Ednl. Exch.-Japan Soc., Tokyo, 1968; grantee NIH, 1979-85, 87-2003, 90-95, NIMH, 1983-85, Adminstrn. on Aging, 1998-2003. Fellow: Am. Aging Assn. (bd. dris. 1990—92), Am. Psychiat. Assn.; mem.: Am. Coll. Neuropsychopharmacology, Alzheimer's and Related Disorders Soc. India (hon.), Am. Assn. Geriat. Psychiatry (sec. 1991—92, bd. dirs. 1992—96), Internat. Psychogeriat. Assn. (bd. dirs. 1985—93, treas. 1993—95, pres.-elect 1995—97, pres. 1997—99, Disting. Svc. award 2001). Achievements include patents for assessment of dementia; patents in field. Office: NYU Sch Medicine William and Sylvia Silberstein Aging and Dementia Rsch Ctr 550 1st Ave New York NY 10016-6402 Office Phone: 212-263-8550. Business E-Mail: barry.reisberg@med.nyu.edu.

**REISBERG, LEON ELTON,** education educator; b. Dallas, Sept. 1, 1949; s. Morris Abraham and Gertrude (Turner) R.; m. Iris Fudell, July 3, 1973 (div. 1986); children: Joshua Fudell, Leah Fudell; m. Donna Brodigan, July 11, 1993. BS in Edn., U. Tex., Austin, 1971; MEd, U. Ark., Fayetteville, 1972; EdD, U. Kans., Lawrence, 1981. Tchr. Oklahoma City Sch. Dist., 1972-75, Putnam City Sch. Dist., Oklahoma City, 1975-78, U. Kans. Med. Ctr., Kansas City, 1978-79; asst. prof. Pacific Luth. U., Tacoma, 1981-88; tchr. Tacoma (Wash.) Sch. Dist., 1989-90; assoc. prof. edn. Pacific Luth. U., 1988-94, chmn. dept. spl. edn. Tacoma, 1986-93, chmn. profl. edn. adv. bd., 1992-94, assoc. dean sch. edn., 1993-98, prof., 1995—, assoc. dean info. resources, 1999, dean info. resources, 2000—01. Project dir., Consulting Spl. Edn. Personnel Tng. Project, Tacoma, 1983-86; chmn. Profl. Edn. Adv. Bd. Cons. editor Learning Disability Quar., 1981-89, Acad. Therapy, 1988-90, Intervention, 1990—; contbr. articles to profl. publs. Bd. trustees First Pres. for Children; pres. Temple Beth El, 2002—04. Mem. Coun. Exceptional Children, Coun. Learning Disabilities (Pacific Rim region rep. 1993-96), Assn. Trainer Spl. Edn. Pers. (chmn. 1991), Phi Kappa Phi. Democrat. Jewish. Office: Pacific Luth U Sch Edn Tacoma WA 98447-0001 Office Phone: 253-535-7280. Business E-Mail: reisberg@plu.edu. *Personal philosophy: Research and professional interests in promoting the inclusion of students with disabilities in regular classrooms.*

**REISCHAUER, ROBERT D.,** research organization executive; AB, Harvard U., 1963; MIA, Columbia U., 1966, PhD, 1971. Spl. asst. to dir., dep. dir., asst. dir. human resources and cmty. devel. Congl. Budget Office, 1975-81, dir., 1989-95; sr. v.p. Urban Inst., 1981-86, pres., 2000—; chmn. bd. trustees MDRC (formerly Manpower Devel. Rsch. Corp.), 1999—2000; vice chair payment adv. commn. Medicare, 2001—06. Author: (with Henry J. Aaron) Countdown to Reform: The Great Social Security Debate, 2001 (revised and updated); editor: Setting National Priorities: Budget Choices for the Next Century, 1997; co-editor: Medicare: Preparing for the Challenges of the 21st Century, 1998, Setting National Priorities: The 2000 Election and Beyond, 1999; contbr. articles to profl. jours., chpts. to books. Sr. Fellow econ. studies Brookings Inst., 1970-75, 86-89, 95-2000. Office: Urban Inst 2100 M St NW Washington DC 20037 Office Phone: 202-261-5400. Business E-Mail: rreischa@ui.urban.org.

**REISER, BRIAN SYDNEY,** economist, statistician; b. Bklyn., Feb. 28, 1937; s. Eugene N. and Ruth (Cohen) R. BA, Syracuse U., 1961; postgrad. Am. U., 1962, U.S. Dept. Agr. Grad. Sch., 1963. Econ. statistician Bur. of Census, Washington, 1962-69, 1979-88; economist, econ. statistician IRS, Washington, 1969-79; econ. cons., 1988—; econ. sec. Govt. Economists, 1980-81, adv. com., 1982, dir., 1984-85. Vice pres. Springfield Stamp Club, Va., 1982. Mem. Am. Econ. Assn., Am. Topical Assn., Am. Philatelic Soc., Am. Numismatic Assn., Am. Polit. Items Collectors, Masons, Shriners.

**REISER, MORTON FRANCIS,** psychiatrist, educator; b. Cin., Aug. 22, 1919; s. Sigmund and Mary (Roth) R.; m. Lynn B. Whisnant, Dec. 19, 1976; children: David E., Barbara, Linda. BS, U. Cin., 1940, MD, 1943; grad., N.Y. Psychoanalytic Inst., 1960. Diplomate Am. Bd. Psychiatry and Neurology. Intern King's County Hosp., Bklyn., 1944; resident Cin. Gen. Hosp.,

1944-49; practice medicine, specializing in psychiatry Cin., 1947-52, Washington, 1954-55, N.Y.C., 1955-69; mem. faculty Cin. Gen. Hosp., also U. Cin. Coll. Medicine, 1949-52, Washington Sch. Psychiatry, 1953-55; faculty Albert Einstein Coll. Medicine, Yeshiva U., N.Y.C., 1955-69, prof. psychiatry, 1958-69, dir. research dept. psychiatry, 1958-65; chief div. psychiatry Montefiore Hosp. and Med. Center, N.Y.C., 1965-69; chmn. dept. psychiatry Yale Med. Sch., 1969—, prof., 1969-78, chmn. dept., 1969-86, Charles B.G. Murphy prof., 1978-86, Albert E. Kent prof., 1986-90, Albert E. Kent prof. emeritus, 1990—. Cons. Walter Reed Army Inst. Research, 1957-58, WHO, 1963; mem. clin. program projects rev. com. NIMH, 1970—, chmn., 1973-74. Author: (with H. Leigh) The Patient: Biological, Psychological, and Social Dimensions of Medical Practice, 1980, Mind, Brain, Body: Toward a Convergence of Psychoanalysis and Neurobiology, 1984; (with H. Leigh) The Patient, 3d edit., 1992; Memory in Mind and Brain: What Dream Imagery Reveals, 1990; editor: American Handbook of Psychiatry, vol. IV, 1975; editor in chief Psychosomatic Medicine, 1962-72; mem. editorial bd. AMA Archives of Gen. Psychiatry, 1961-71, (with H. Leigh) Psychiatry Medicine and Primary Care, 1978; contbr. articles to profl. jours. and books. Fellow Am. Coll. Psychiatrists, Am. Psychiat. Assn. (Seymour Vestermark award 1986); mem. Am. Soc. Clin. Investigation, Am. Psychosomatic Soc. (pres. 1960-61), Am. Fedn. Clin. Research, Am. Assn. Chairmen Depts. Psychiatry (exec. com. 1971—, pres. 1975-76), Acad. Behavioral Medicine Research (exec. council 1978), Am. Psychoanalytic Assn. (pres.-elect 1980-82, pres. 1982-84), Internat. Psycho-Analytical Assn., Assn. Psychophysiol. Study of Sleep, Internat. Coll. Psychosomatic Medicine (pres. 1975), Psychiat. Research Soc., A. Graeme Mitchell Undergrad. Pediatric Soc., Benjamin Rush Soc., Kapaport-Klein Study Group, World Psychiat. Assn. (organizing com. sect. psychosomatic medicine 1967), Sigma Xi, Phi Eta Sigma, Pi Kappa Epsilon, Alpha Omega Alpha. Home: PO Box 187039 Hamden CT 06518-7017 Personal E-mail: mdmreiser@comcast.net.

**REISER, RICHARD SCOTT,** lawyer; b. Chester, S.D., Apr. 8, 1946; s. Kinney S. and Edna E. (Sweet) R.; m. Mary Lynn Durrie, Aug. 24, 1968; children: Todd S., Sally A. BS, U. Nebr., 1968, JD, 1972. Bar: Iowa 1972, Nebr. 1972, U.S. Dist. Ct. Nebr. 1972, U.S. Ct. Appeals (8th cir.) 1989. Assoc. Nelson & Harding, Omaha, 1972-75, ptnr., 1975-84; dir. Gross & Welch, P.C., Omaha, 1984-92; v.p., gen. counsel Werner Enterprises, Inc., Omaha, 1993—96, exec. v.p., gen. counsel, 1996—. Com. mem. Nebr. Transp. Efficiency Task Force, Lincoln, 1995. Bd. dirs., treas. Fontenelle Forest Assn., Omaha, 1988-94; pres. 2d lt. USAR, 1968-74. Mem. Am. Corp. Counsel Assn., Transp. Lawyers Assn., Omaha Bar Assn. (bd. dirs., exec. com.), Nebr. State Bar Assn. (mem. task force on civil justice sys. 1994-95), Iowa State Bar Assn, Nebr. State Hwy. (comm Dist.2, 2001-), Nebr. Trucking Assn. (bd. dir., sec., 2003-), Am. Trucking Assn. (bd. dir., 1999-). Democrat. Presbyterian. Avocations: bicycling, hunting, skiing, motorcycling.

**REISERT, CHARLES EDWARD, JR.,** realtor; b. New Albany, Ind., Apr. 5, 1941; s. Charles Edward, Jr. and Jane W. (Wilcox) Reisert; m. Mary Lynn Nunemacher, Nov. 9, 1963; children: Perry G., Heidi L. BS in Edn. Ind. U., 1963, MA, 1968. Tchr. Ind. Pub. Schs., 1963-67; mgr. Ind. Bell Tel. Co., Indpls., 1967-70; trust officer Ind. Nat. Bank, Indpls., 1970-72; ptnr. R.F.R. Prodns. Inc., Zionsville; dir. Wichita (Kans.) Art Assn., 1972-73; mng. ptnr. Century 21 Realty Group-Reisert, Jeffersonville, Ind., 1973—. Mem. Ind. Real Estate Commn., 1982—90, pres. Ind., 1990; past pres. Clark County Youth Shelter; bd. dirs., past pres. United Way Clark County; bd. dirs. New Hope, Inc., Sagamore of Wabash; mem. Leadership So. Ind., Leadership Louisville; v.p. Clark County Redevel. Commn.; pres. Jeffersonville Housing Authority; trustee, past pres. Clark Meml. Hosp. Found. Recipient Pinnacle award, Sales Mgmt. and Mktg. Assn. Louisville, Servant Leader award, Leadership So. Ind., 2006. Mem.: Realtors Nat. Mktg. Inst., Ind. Assn. Realtor, Nat. Assn. Realtors, So. Ind. Realtors Assn. (past pres., past bd. dirs., Realtor of Yr. 1983, Realtor Hall of Fame 1998), So. Ind. C. of C. (Profl. Person of Yr. 1990), Rotary (past pres., Paul Harris fellow). Roman Catholic. Home: 14 Abby Chase Jeffersonville IN 47130-9762 Office: Century 21 Realty Group-Reisort 1302 E 10th St Jeffersonville IN 47130-4299 Office Phone: 812-285-5000.

**REISING, RICHARD P.,** lawyer; BA, Stanford U.; JD, U. Mo. Bar: Ill. 1970. Asst. gen. counsel, sec. Archer-Daniels-Midland Co., Decatur, Ill., v.p., sec., gen. counsel, 1991-97, sr. v.p., 1997—. Office: Archer-Daniels-Midland Co 4666 E Faries Pky Decatur IL 62526-5666

**REISINGER, RONALD BUSCH (BARON OF INNERYNE, LAIRD OF ASCOG CASTLE, LAIRD OF EILEAN NA BEITHE),** bank executive; b. N.Y.C., Jan. 4, 1943; s. Walter Chalmers and Osa-Lisa Bernadotte (Pearson) Reisinger; m. Carolyn Gall, Dec. 17, 1989; children: Christopher, Hope, Abigail, William, Timothy. Pres., CEO The Reisinger Corp. LLC, Grand Haven, Mich., 1990—. Advisor The Kingdom of Biffeche, Biffeche City, 1965—97; v.p. Central Highland Park Assn., Grand Haven, Mich., 1971—. Decorated knight Grand Cross Order of the Great White Leopard The Kingdom of Biffeche, knight Grand Cross Order of the Palm, knight Grand Cross of The Military Order the Sword of St. Michael, knight G.C. of the Most Illustrious Order of the Raven, knight Grand Crescent the Order of the Crescent, knight Grand Cross of the Order of The Elephant, knight of Saint Germain Scotland's House of Stuart, knight Grand Cross and Grand Prior for N.Am. the Order of The Holy Trinity Ukraine, comdr. the Military and Hospitaller Order of St. Lazarus of Jerusalem Duc de Brissac, knight of Moravian Order St. Wrastislav and St. Columba. Mem.: Celtic Soc., Monarchist League, Traveler's Century Club, Circumnavigators Club, Carlouel Yacht Club, Royal Yacht Club of Biffeche, Bayou Club, Atlanta Polo Club, Spring Lake Country Club, St. Louis Country Club, Kyles of Bute Angling Club (hon.), Convention of the Baronage of Scotland (life). Home: 9441 Beachberry Pl Pinellas Park FL 33782 Office: The Barony of Inneryne Ascog Castle Argylle Tighnabruaich PA21 2BY Scotland Personal E-mail: rreisin1@tampabay.rr.com.

**REISLER, HELEN BARBARA,** public relations executive; b. N.Y.C., June 21; d. George and Elizabeth Lois (Schultz) Gottesman; m. Melvin Reisler, June 5, 1955; children: Susan O'Brien, Karen Reisler, Keith James. BS in Edn., NYU, 1954; MS in Edn. and Reading, L.I. U., 1978. Elem. tchr., N.Y.C., 1954-78; instr. grad. sch., adj. lectr. L.I. U., Bklyn., 1978; acct. exec. N.Y. Yellow Pages, Inc., N.Y.C., 1979, personnel mgr., 1979, adminstrv. dir., 1980-83, v.p. personnel, 1983-84, v.p. adminstrn./personnel, 1984-85, also dir.; staff specialist sales and market support Southwestern Bell Publs., 1985-88; N.Y. mgr. pub. rels. and recruitment N.Y. Yellow Pages/Mast Advt. and Publs., Inc. of Southwe. Bell, 1988; cons. human resources devel. and product promotion, 1989—. Recruiter N.E. Region, N.Y. area cmty. rels. rep.; moderator weekly cable TV show New York Business Forum, N.Y.C., 1983-85. Founder Firefighters Vacation com., 2001—02; bd. dirs. Park Slope Geriatric Ctr., 2002—, Heritage Hills Condo. Assn., 2000—. Named Ptnr. in Edn., N.Y.C. Bd. Edn., 1984, Heritage Hills Theatre Group, 2004, Golden Poets Award; Paul Harris award, 2002, 03, 05. Mem. Internat. Assn. Sales and Mktg. Exec. (bd. dir. 1993, 94), UN Assn., Sales Execs. Club NY (bd. dirs., reception, membership and mem. rels. coms., chmn. youth edn., v.p. 1987-88, chmn. internal com. 1989), Execs. Assn. Greater NY (chmn. com. Sec. Day), Heritage Hills Country Club Westchester (bd. dir. 2000—), Sales Exec. Club (v.p.), NY Rotary (chmn. environ. com. 1991—, bd. liaison to pub. rels. and membership coms. 1994—, interviewing com. scholarship candidates 1993-2003, mentor Japanese amb. scholars, 1992-93, divsn. chmn. cmty. svcs., chmn. pub. rels. com., bd. liaison, 1996-2001, 03, bd. dir., co-chmn. advt. com. chmn. pub. rels. 1996-04, coord. Gift of Life, 2d v.p, bd. dirs. 1999—, 1st v.p., bd. dirs. 1999—, pres. 2001, prodr. cable TV series NY Rotary-A Club That Works, exec. prodr. Gift of Life-A Child's Story, apptd. media liaison to NY 1998—, creator 9/11 disaster fund 2001-02, chmn. 9/11 adv. com. 2001-04, chmn. publicity and pub. rels., dist. leadership com. 2002-04, #7230 dist. gov.-elect, 2004, #7230 dist. gov., 2005—, Paul Harris Soc. fellow 1992, 2001, 03, 05, Disting. Pres. award 2001-02, Pub. Rels. award, 1905 Silver Nickel award 2003, Dist. Centennial Project award, "Response to 9/11", 2004, Global History fellowship, bd. dir. 2003-, 4x Dist. P.R. award,

Svc. Above Self award, Centennial Project award Rotary Zone 32, profiled in 100th hist. edit. The Rotarian Mag. 2005), Dutch Treat Club, 100 Club (bd. dirs. 2006). Office: 47 Plaza St W Brooklyn NY 11217-3905 Personal E-mail: helenbreisler@aol.com.

REISLER, MARC S., lawyer; b. NYC, Nov. 19, 1960; BA, McGill U., 1984; MA, Syracuse U., 1988, JD cum laude, 1988. Bar: NY 1990. Ptnr., co-head Tech. Practice, Corp. Dept. Katten Muchin Zavis Rosenman, NYC. Mem.: Copyright Soc. of USA. Office: Katten Muchin Zavis Rosenman 575 Madison Ave New York NY 10022 Office Phone: 212-940-6456. Office Fax: 212-940-8776. E-mail: marc.reisler@kmzr.com.

REISMAN, ANDREW LOUIS, information technology executive, lawyer; b. Memphis, Tenn., Nov. 24, 1969; s. John Mark and Margo Sue Reisman; m. Polina Shadkin Shadkin, July 27, 1997; 1 child, Elijah Nathaniel. BS, Ill. State U., Normal, Ill., 1990; JD, U. Ill. Coll. of Law, Champaign, Ill., 1993. Bar: Supreme Ct. of Ill. 1993. Jud. clk. Hon. Harlington Wood, Jr., U.S. Ct. of Appeals, 7th Circuit, Springfield, Ill., 1993—94; assoc. Mayer, Brown & Platt, Chgo., 1994—97; gen. counsel Internat. Save the Children Alliance, Geneva, 1997—98; ptnr. Foley & Lardner, Chgo., 1998—2003, Enterprise Law Group, LLP, Chgo., 2003—; pres. Elijah Tech., Ltd., Chgo., 2003—. Pres. Internat. Info. Systems Forensics Assn., Chgo. Chpt., Chgo., 2004—. Dir. Internat. Info. Systems Forensics Assn., Chgo. Chpt., Chgo., 2004. Recipient Outstanding Recent Alumni Award for Pub. Svc., U. Ill. Coll. of Law Recent Alumni Adv. Bd., 2001. Mem.: Assn. Corp. Counsel (Ill. Chgo. chpt. 2005—), Internat. Info. Systems Forensics Assn. (dir. 2005—). Achievements include patents for Self-Generating Elevator Emergency Power Source. Office: Elijah Tech Ltd 70 W Madison St Ste 740 Chicago IL 60602 Home: 395 Brownville Highland Park IL 60035 Office Phone: 866-354-5240. Office Fax: 866-354-5240. Business E-Mail: andy@elijahtechnologies.com.

REISMAN, ELLEN KELLY, lawyer; b. Oct. 24, 1959; BA summa cum laude, Boston Coll., 1981; JD cum laude, U. Chgo., 1984. Bar: DC 1984, US Dist. Ct., DC 1985, Calif. 1996. Assoc. Arnold & Porter LLP, Washington, 1984, ptnr., 1992—99; gen. counsel, v.p. legal divsn. Wyeth-Ayerst Pharmaceuticals, 1999—2001; ptnr., Product Liability Practice Group Arnold & Porter LLP, LA, 2001—. Named one of Top 50 Women Litigators, The Nat. Law Jour., 2001, The Top 45 Under 45, The Am. Lawyer, 2003. Office: Arnold & Porter 777 S Figueroa St 44th Flr Los Angeles CA 90017-2513 Office Phone: 213-243-4111. Office Fax: 213-243-4199.

REISMAN, JUDITH ANN GELERNTER, media communications executive, educator; b. Hillside, NJ, Apr. 11, 1935; MA in Speech Comm., Case Western Res. U., 1976, PhD in Speech Comm., 1980. Faculty dept. anthropology and sociology Haifa U., Israel, 1981—83; rsch. prof. sch. edn. Am. U., Washington, 1983—85; founder, pres. Inst. Media Edn., 1985—. Cons., reviewer grant proposals audio-visual drug programs for youth Dept. Edn., 1987; rsch. design cons. Alcohol and Tobacco Media Analysis in Mainstream Mags., Dept. HHS, 1987—90; cons., field reviewer Drug Free Youth Sch. Candidates Dept. Edn., 1988; lectr., adj. prof. George Mason U., Va., 1990; expert witness Pres.'s Commn. on Assignment of Women in Armed Forces, 1992, U.S. Atty. Commn. on Pornography, 1985—86, U.S. Atty. Gen. Task Force on Domestic Violence, Washington, 1985, Mapplethorpe Trial, Cin., 1990, Australian Parliament, 1992, Ga. State Senate, 1992; nominated to panel on sex harassment in the Air Force U.S. Inspector Gen., 2003; sci. advisor Protective Parents Assn.; subcom. junk sci. Am. Legis. Exchange Coun. Edn. Task Force, 1999—2004. Author: Images of Children, Crime and Violence in Playboy, Penthouse and Hustler, 1989, Kinsey, Sex and Fraud, 1990, Softport Playes Hardball, 1991, Kinsey, Crimes and Consequences, 1998, 2003, Kinsey's Attic, 2006; contbr. preme Ct. cases to profl. jours. Co-recipient Scholastic Mag. awards, Dukane award, 1982; recipient Gold Camera award, 1982, Silver Screen award, 1982, Filmstrip of Yr. award, 1981—82, Silver Plaque award, 1982, Family Svc. Assn. Am. 1st pl. award local TV series, 1974, Best of 1965 award, 1965, Scientist of Yr. for Children award, 1993; U.S. Dept. Justice grantee. Mem.: AAAS, Women in Neurosci., Nat. Black Child Devel. Inst., Soc. Sci. Study Sex, N.Y. Acad. Scis., Internat. Comm. Assn., Am. Statis. Assn., Am. Assn. Composers, Authors and Pubs., Nat. Assn. Scholars. E-mail: jareisman@cox.net.

REISMAN, ROBERT E., allergist, educator; b. Buffalo, Nov. 1, 1932; s. Harry S and Jessie (Goldberg) Reisman; m. Rena Estry, Sept. 5, 1954; children: Jeanne, Linda, Nancy, David. MD, SUNY-Buffalo, 1956; Dr.h.c., U. Montpellier, France, 1982. Diplomate Am. Bd. Internal Medicine, Am. Bd. Allergy and Clin. Immunology. Intern Buffalo Gen. Hosp., 1956-57, resident in medicine, 1957-59; practice medicine specializing in allergy and clin. immunology Buffalo, 1961—; co-dir. Allergy Rsch. Lab., Buffalo Gen. Hosp., 1970—90; clin. prof. pediatrics and medicine SUNY, Buffalo, 1978—. Mem. panel allergenic extracts Bur. Biologists FDA; bd. dirs. Am. Bd. Internal Medicine, 1984—86, Am. Bd. Allergy and Clin. Immunology, 1981—86, chmn., 1985. With U.S. Army, 1968—69. Master: ACP; fellow: Am. Acad. Allergy (pres 1980—81). Home: 113 Carriage Cir Buffalo NY 14221-2163 Office: 295 Essjay Rd Williamsville NY 14221-8216 also: 85 High St Buffalo NY 14203-1149 Office Phone: 716-630-1130. Business E-Mail: rreisman@buffalomedicalgroup.com.

REISMAN, ROSEMARY MOODY CANFIELD, writer, humanities educator; b. Des Moines, Nov. 18, 1927; d. V. Alton and Lois Gloria (Slee) Moody; m. Michael Ellison Canfield, Sept. 6, 1952 (div. May 1961); children: Michael, John Charles, Celia Catherine, Christopher James; m. Maurice Reisman, May 10, 1986 (dec. 1990). BA in English, U. Minn., 1949, MA in English, 1952; PhD in English, La. State U., 1971. Reporter Ames (Iowa) Tribune, summer 1944; writer, actor Sta. WOI Pub. Radio, Ames, 1944-48; dir., writer children's plays Sta. KASI, Ames, 1949; tchg. asst. U. Minn., 1949-52; writer Sta. WOI-TV, Ames, summer 1952; writer, show host Sta. WDGY, Mpls., 1952-54; instr. La. State U., 1961-69, NDEA fellow, 1969-71; asst. prof. English Troy (Ala.) State U., 1971-80, assoc. prof., 1980-90, chairperson dept. English, 1985-90, prof., 1990-94. Honors coun. Troy State U., 1985-94, honors faculty, 1986-94, acad. coun., 1989-92, faculty adv. coun., 1990-92, Rhodes scholar instnl. rep., 1987-91; adj. prof. Charleston So. U., 1996-99, vis. prof., 1999—; humanities scholar Richland County Libr., S.C., 2002—; coord. sr. honors seminar Coll. of Charleston, 1996-98; prodn., writer Perspectives project Ala. ETV, 1977-80; chmn. conf. sessions South Ctrl. Soc. for 18th-Century Studies, 1988, Southeastern Am. Soc. for 18th Century Studies, 1991, 93, workshop Ala. Coun. Tchrs. English, 1987; grant writer, project dir. Ala. Humanities Found., 1980, 89, asst. project dir. summer grad. course, 1990; grant writer, project dir. Ala. Pub. Libr. Sys., 1977-80; presenter, lectr., cons. in field. Author: Perspectives: The Alabama Heritage, 1978; co-author: Contemporary Southern Women Fiction Writers, 1994, Southern Men Fiction Writers, 1998; editor, course writer Coastal C.C., Calif., 2002—; editor advt. adv. bd. Ala. Lit. Rev., 1986-94; mem. editl. bd. Biog. Guide to Ala. Lit., 1985-89; guest editor spl. issue Ala. English F, 1995; contbr. articles to profl. jours. Baldwin County Humanities scholar Ala. Humanities Found., 1983-84. Mem.: AAUW (past br. pres., mem. steering com.), NEA, Thomas Cooper Soc. (bd. dirs. 2001—04), English Spkg. Union (bd. dirs. Charleston 1997—98, pres. 1998—2002, Sourcelist spkr. 1999—2000), Troy State U. Nat. Lit. Assn. (pres. 1990—93), Ala. Edn. Assn., Assn. Coll. English Tchrs. Ala., Assn. Depts. English (state pres. 1986—88), South Atlantic MLA, Soc. of Mary, Confrat. of the Blessed Sacrament, Gamma Beta Phi (nat. pres. 1978—79, cert. of merit 1979), Phi Beta Kappa (del. to nat. triennial coun. 1991, alt. 1994, pres. Low Country Assn. 1996—98, del. 1997, bd. dirs. 1998—2001, alt. del. 2000, bd. dirs. 2003—05, past pres. S.E. Ala. assn.). Anglican. Home and Office: 121 Innisbrook Bend Summerville SC 29483-5084 Personal E-Mail: creisman@bellsouth.net.

REISMAN, SHARYL A., lawyer; b. NYC, 1967; AB magna cum laude, Dartmouth Coll., 1989; JD cum laude, U. Mich., 1992. Bar: Ill. 1992, NY 1998. Ptnr., environmental law Jones Day (formerly Jones,Day, Reavis & Pogue), NYC. Office: Jones Day 222 E 41st St New York NY 10017-6702 Office Phone: 212-326-3939. Office Fax: 212-755-7306. Business E-Mail: sareisman@jonesday.com.

REISMAN, WILLIAM MICHAEL, lawyer, educator; b. 1939; LL.B., Hebrew U., 1963; LL.M., Yale U., 1964, J.S.D., 1965. Bar: Conn. 1964. Assoc. prof. Yale U. Law Sch., New Haven, 1969-72, prof., 1972-82, Hohfeld prof. jurisprudence, 1982-98, McDougal prof. internat. law, 1998—. Mem. Inter-Am. Commn. on Human Rights, 1990—95, chmn., 1994—95; vice-chmn. Policy Scis. Ctr., Inc., 1992—; assoc. Inst. Droit Internat., 1999; pres. Arbitration Tribunal Bank for Internat. Settlements, 2001—; mem. Eritrea-Ethiopia Boundary Commn., 2001—; pres. Anglo-Irish OSPAR Convention Tribunal, 2001—03. Author: Nullity and Revision, 1971, Art of the Possible: Diplomatic Alternatives in Middle East, 1970, Puerto Rico and the International Process, 1974, Folded Lies: Bribery, Crusades and Reforms, 1979, (with Weston) Toward World Order and Human Dignity, 1976, (with McDougal) International Law in Contemporary Perspective, 1981, (with McDougal) International Law Essays, 1981, (with McDougal) Power and Policy in Quest of Law: Essays in Honor of Eugene V. Rostow, 1985, (with Schreiber) Jurisprudence: Understanding and Shaping Law, 1986, (with Willard) International Incidents: The Law that Counts in World Politics, 1988, (with James E. Baker) Regulating Covert Action: Practices, Contexts and Policies of Covert Coercion Abroad in International and American Laqw, 1991, Systems of Control in International Adjudication and Arbitration: Breakdown and Repair, 1992, (with Westerman) Straight Baselines in International Maritime Boundary Delimitation, 1992, (with C. Antoniou) The Laws of War, 1994, The Supervisory Jurisdiction of the International Court of Justice: International Arbitration and International Adjudication, 1997, (with L. Craig W. Park and J. Paulsson) International Commercial Arbitration: Cases, Materials and Notes on the Resolution of International Business Disputes, 1997, Law in Brief Encounters, 1999, Jurisdiction in International Law, 1999, (with M. Arsanjani, S. Wiessner and G. Westerman) International Law in Contemporary Perspective, 2004; editor-in-chief Am. Jour. Internat. Law, 1998-2003, (with R. Doak Bishop and James Crawford) Foreign Investment Disputes: Cases, Materials and Commentary, 2005. Decorated 1st class Order of Bahrain; Fulbright grantee, 1966-67 Mem. Fgn. Policy Assn. (bd. dirs. 1997—), Coun. Fgn. Rels, Am. Soc. of Internat. Law (Manley O. Hudson Medal). Office: Yale U Law Sch PO Box 208215 New Haven CT 06520-8215 Fax: 203-432-7247. E-mail: michael.reisman@yale.edu.

REISMANN, HERBERT, engineer, educator; b. Vienna, Jan. 26, 1926; s. Henrik and Olga (Pokorny) R.; m. Edith Falber, Aug. 14, 1952; children: Sandra Jean, Barbara Anne BS Aero. Engring., Ill. Inst. Tech., 1947, MS, 1949; PhD Engring., U. Colo., 1962. Project engr. Convair, Ft. Worth, 1951—53; prin. structures engr. Republic Aviation Corp., Hicksville, NY, 1954—56; chief engr. sys. analysis, chief solid mechanics Martin Marietta Corp., 1957—64; prof., dir. aerospace engring. SUNY, Buffalo, 1964—2001, prof. emeritus, 2002—. Cons. NASA, Bell Aero Sys. Corp Co-author: Elastokinetics, 1974, Elasticity, 1980; author: Elastic Plates, 1988; contbr. articles to profl. jours Assoc. fellow AIAA (Best Tech. Paper award 1962, Oustanding Aerospace Achievement award 1987); mem. ASME, AAUP, Internat. Assn. Bridge and Structural Engring., Sigma Xi, Tau Beta Pi Home: 71 Chaumont Dr Buffalo NY 14221-3511 Office: SUNY-Buffalo 605 Furnas Hall Buffalo NY 14260-4200 Office Phone: 716-634-5862. Personal E-mail: herreis@msn.com.

REISNER, ANDREW DOUGLAS, psychologist; b. Ithaca, NY, Dec. 28, 1955; s. Gerald Seymour and Estelle Ruth (Siegel) R.; m. Deborah Kay Dermen, Aug. 1, 1981; children: David Aaron, Alyssa Danielle. BA, Allegheny Coll., 1977; MA, Edinboro (Pa.) State U., 1978; D of Psychology, Baylor U., 1987. Lic. psychologist, Ohio. Psychology asst. Tiffin Devel. Mental Health Ctr., 1979—80, Cmty. Counseling Svcs., Galion, Ohio, 1980—83, chief clin. officer, 1990—99; pvt. practice, 1996—99; intern in clin. psychology Mich. State U., East Lansing, 1986—87; postdoctoral tng. in clin. psychology Harding Hosp., Worthington, Ohio, 1987—88; psychologist Ctr. for Individual Family Svcs., Mansfield, Ohio, 1988—90, Appalachian Behavorial Healthcare, Cambridge, Ohio, 1999—. Cons. MedCtrl. Crestline (Ohio) Hosp., 1989-99, Forensic Diagnostic Ctr., Byesville (Ohio), 1999—; mem. adj. faculty Ashland U., 1993-96. Contbr. chpt. to book; contbr. articles to profl. jours. Mem. APA, Ohio Psychol. Assn. Office: Appalachian Behavioral Healthcare 66737 Old 21 Rd Cambridge OH 43725-9298 Office Phone: 740-439-1371. Business E-Mail: reisnera@mh.state.oh.us.

REISNER, LORIN L., lawyer; b. Bklyn., Dec. 30, 1961; s. Ira Aaron and Roberta Goldglit. AB in Politics, Brandeis U., 1983; JD, Harvard U., 1986. Bar: NY 1987, U.S. Dist. Ct. (so. dist.) N.Y. 1987, (ea. dist.) N.Y. 2000, U.S. Ct. Appeals (2d cir.) 1991, (11th cir.) 1995, (4th cir.) 2001, (7th cir.) 2002, U.S. Supreme Ct. 2003. Law clk. to judge U.S. Dist. Ct. (so. dist.) N.Y., NYC, 1986-87; assoc. Debevoise & Plimpton LLP, NYC, 1987-90; asst. U.S. atty. for so dist. N.Y. U.S. Atty.'s Office, NYC, 1990—94; assoc. Debevoise & Plimpton LLP, 1994—96, ptnr., 1996—. Author: (with Bruce P. Keller) Trademark Related Causes of Action and Defenses, 2000; contbr. articles to law revs. and jours. Mem. alumni admissions coun. Brandeis U., 1987—. Mem. ABA, Assn. of Bar of City of N.Y. Democrat. Jewish. Office: Debevoise & Plimpton LLP 919 Third Ave New York NY 10022 Office Phone: 212-909-6191. Office Fax: 212-909-6836. Business E-Mail: llreisner@debevoise.com.

REISS, DALE ANNE, corporate financial executive; b. Sept. 3, 1947; d. Max and Nan (Hart) R.; m. Jerome L. King, Mar. 5, 1978; children: Matthew Reiss, Mitchell, Stacey. BS, Ill. Inst. Tech., 1967; MBA, U. Chgo., 1970. CPA, Fla., Ill., Mich., Mo. Cost acct. First Nat. Bank, Chgo., 1967; asst. contr. City Colls. of Chgo., 1967-71; dir. fin. Chgo. Dept. Pub. Works, 1971-73; prin. Arthur Young & Co., Chgo., 1973-80; sr. v.p., contr. Urban Investment & Devel. Co., Chgo., 1980-85; mng. ptnr. Ernst & Young LLP, Chgo., 1985-98, Ernst & Young, N.Y.C., 1998-99; global dir. real estate, hospitality and constrn. Ernst & Young LLP, N.Y.C., 1999—. Bd. dirs. Ill. Inst. Tech., Urban Land Inst.; adv. bd. Kellogg Real Estate, Northwestern U., U. Chgo. Grad. Sch. of Bus. Mem. AICPA, Fin. Execs. Inst., Pension Real Estate Assn., Chgo. Network (bd. dirs.), Econ. Chgo. Club, Met. Club, Chgo. Yacht Club, NY Athletic Club. Office: Ernst & Young 5 Times Sq 16th Fl New York NY 10036-6530 E-mail: dale.reiss@ey.com.

REISS, GEORGE RUSSELL, JR., physician; b. Phila., Dec. 25, 1928; s. G. Russell Sr. and Mary Ellen (Brogan) R.; m. Rosemarie Theresa Curcillo, Sept. 19, 1959; children: Mary Elizabeth, Stephanie, G. Russell III, Charlene. BA, LaSalle U., 1953; MD, Temple U., 1957. Diplomate Am. Bd. Pediatrics. Intern Misericordia Hosp., Phila., 1957-58; resident pediatrics St. Christopher Hosp. for Children, Phila., 1958-60; pvt. practice Glenside, Pa., 1960—. With USCG, 1946-49. Mem. Montgomery County Med. Soc., Pa. Med. Soc., Am. Acad. Pediatrics, AMA, Am. Assn. Pro-Life Pediatricians. Roman Catholic. Office: 2220 Mount Carmel Ave Glenside PA 19038-4610 Office Phone: 215-884-7861. Personal E-mail: grcreissjr@aol.com.

REISS, HOWARD, chemistry professor; b. NYC, Apr. 5, 1922; s. Isidor and Jean (Goldstein) R.; m. Phyllis Kohn, July 25, 1945; children: Gloria, Steven. AB in Chemistry, NYU, 1943; PhD in Chemistry, Columbia U., 1949. With Manhattan Project, 1944-46; instr., then asst. prof. chemistry Boston U., 1949-51; with Ctrl. Rsch. Labs., Celanese Corp. Am., 1951-52, Edgar C. Bain Lab. Fundamental Rsch., U.S. Steel Corp., 1957, Bell Telephone Labs., 1952-60; assoc. dir., then dir. chemistry div. Atomics Internat., div. N.Am. Aviation, Inc., 1960-62; dir. N.Am. Aviation Sci. Ctr., 1962-67, v.p. co., 1963-67; v.p. rsch. aerospace systems group N.Am. Rockwell Corp., 1967-68; vis. lectr. chemistry U. Calif. at Berkeley, summer 1957; vis. prof. chemistry UCLA, 1961, 62, 64, 67, prof., 1968-91, prof. emeritus, 1991—2003, disting. prof. emeritus, 2003—; vis. prof. U. Louis Pasteur, Strasbourg, France, 1986, U. Pa., 1989; vis. fellow Victoria U., Wellington, New Zealand, 1989. Vis. fellow Princeton (N.J.) Materials Inst., 1996; cons. to chem.-physics program USAF Cambridge Rsch. Labs., 1950-52; mem. editor Procs. Internat. Conf. Nucleation and Interfacial Phenomena, Boston; mem. USAF Office Sci. Rsch. Physics and Chemistry Rsch. Evaluation Groups, 1966—; Oak Ridge Nat. Lab. Reactor Chemistry Adv. Coun., 1966-68; adv. com. math. and phys. scis. NSF, 1970-72, ARPA Materials Rsch. Coun., 1968—; chmn. site rev. com. NRC Associateships Program, Naval Rsch. Lab., 1989. Author: Methods of Thermodynamics, 1965; author articles; editor in field; editor: Progress in Solid State Chemistry, 1962-71, Jour. Statis. Physics, 1968-75, Jour. Colloid Interface Sci; mem. editorial adv. bd. Internat. Jour. Physics and Chemistry of Solids, 1955, Progress in Solid State Chemistry, 1962-73, Jour. Solid State Chemistry, 1969, Jour. Phys. Chemistry, 1970-73, Ency. of Solid State, 1970, Jour. Nonmetals, 1971—, Jour. Colloid and Interface Sci., 1976-79, Langmuir, 1985—. Guggenheim Meml. fellow, 1978; Howard Reiss chair in chemistry and biochemistry established named in his honor, UCLA, 1999. Fellow AAAS, Am. Phys. Soc. (exec. com. div. chem. physics 1966-69); mem. NAS, Am. Chem. Soc. (chmn. phys. chemistry sect. N.J. sect. 1957, Richard C. Tolman medal 1973, Kendall award in colloid and surface chemistry 1980, J.H. Hildebrand award in theoretical and exptl. phys. chemistry of liquids 1991, Van Arkel hon. chair in chemistry U. Leiden, The Netherlands, 1994), Am. Assn. for Aerosol Rsch. (David Sinclair award 1997), Phi Beta Kappa, Sigma Xi, Phi Lambda Upsilon. Office: U Calif Dept Chemistry And Biochemis Los Angeles CA 90095-0001 Office Phone: 310-825-3029. Business E-Mail: reiss@chem.ucla.edu.

REISS, IRA LEONARD, retired sociology educator, writer; b. N.Y.C., Dec. 8, 1925; s. Philip and Dorothy (Jacobs) R.; m. Harriet Marilyn Eisman, Sept. 4, 1955; children: David, Pamela, Joel. BS cum laude, Syracuse U., 1949; MA, Pa. State U., 1951, PhD, 1953. Instr. in sociology Bowdoin Coll., Brunswick, Maine, 1953-55; asst. prof. sociology Coll. William and Mary, Williamsburg, Va., 1955-59; assoc. to full prof. U. Iowa, Iowa City, 1961-69; prof. U. Minn., Mpls., 1969-96, prof. emeritus, 1996—. Rsch. evaluator U.S. Dept. Edn. and Nat. Inst. Child Health and Human Devel., Washington, 1966-78; rsch. dir. Family Study Ctr., U. Minn., 1969-74; ednl. advisor Kimberly-Clark Corp., Neenah, Wis., 1971-75; chair planning com. and bd. dirs. Inst. for Child, Adolescent Sexual Health, 1992-93; vis. prof. Uppsala Univ., Sweden, 1975-76; lectr. in field. Author: Premarital Sexual Standards in America, 1960, The Social Context of Premarital Sexual Permissiveness, 1967, Family Systems in America, 1971, 4th edit., 1988, Journey into Sexuality: An Exploratory Voyage, 1986, An End to Shame: Shaping Our Next Sexual Revolution, 1990, Solving America's Sexual Crises, 1997, At the Dawn of the Sexual Revolution: Reflections on a Dialogue, 2002, An Insider's View of Sexual Science Since Kinsey, 2006; editor: 3 textbooks; contbr. over 150 papers to jours. and textbooks in field. Mem. ACLU, 1948—, Planned Parenthood, 1960—, Nat. Abortion Rights Action League 1975—, Amnesty Internat., 1984—. With U.S. Army, 1944-46, ETO. Mem. Midwest Sociol. Soc. (pres. 1971-72), Am. Sociol. Assn. (chair family sect. 1975-76), Nat. Coun. on Family Rels. (pres. 1979-80, Reuben Hill award 1980, E.W. Burgess award 1984), Polish Acad. Sexual Sci. (hon., Internat. Sexual Sci. award 1989), Soc. for Sci. Study Sex (pres. 1980-81, Disting. Sci. Achievement award 1982, Alfred Kinsey award 1990), Internat. Acad. Sex Rsch. (pres. 1984-85), Am. Assn. Sex Educators, Counselors and Therapists (leadership award 1993). Democrat. Jewish. Home: 5932 Medicine Lake Rd Minneapolis MN 55422-3328 E-Mail: irareiss@comcast.net.

REISS, JEROME, retired lawyer; b. Bklyn., Dec. 7, 1924; s. William and Eva (Marenstein) Reiss; m. Naomi Betty Plutzik, June 15, 1947; children: Bob, Harlan Morgan, Andrea Ellen, Samantha Glynis. BA, Bklyn. Coll., 1948; JD, Harvard U., 1951. Bar: NY 1951, U.S. Dist. Ct. (so. dist.) N.Y. 1954, U.S. Ct. Claims 1960, U.S. Dist. Ct. (ea. dist.) N.Y. 1964, DC 1967, U.S. Dist. Ct. (we. dist.) N.Y. 1979, U.S. Supreme Ct. 1989. Staff atty. civil br. Legal Aid Soc., N.Y.C., 1951—54; asst. corp. counsel City of N.Y., 1954—58; assoc. Max E. Greenberg, 1958-67; sr. ptnr. Max E. Greenberg, Trayman, Cantor, Reiss & Blasky, 1967-80, Max E. Greenberg, Cantor & Reiss, N.Y.C., 1980-88, Thelen, Marrin, Johnson & Bridges, N.Y.C., 1989-97, Thelen, Reid & Priest, 1997-2000, ret., 2003; gen. counsel Kiska Constrn. Co.-USA, Inc., 2004—. Arbitrator Small Claims Ct., 1960—88; bd. adv. Fed. Pub., Inc.; chmn. bd. AMT-Pacific, Israel, 2000—02; former mem. Am. Judges Assn.; rep. various Japanese, British, Turkish, Israeli internat. contractors; lectr. in constrn. field. Contbr. articles to profl. jours., chapters to books. Trustee Brownsville Boys Club Alumni Assn.; gen. counsel Artist Fellowship, Inc. With USAAF, 1943—46. Fellow: Am. Coll. Constrn. Lawyers (founding mem.); mem.: Wash. (DC) Bar Assn., NY Bar Assn., Internat. Bar Assn., Jacob K. Javits Conv. Ctr. Oper. Corp. (bd. dirs.), Mcpl. Assist. Corp. City NY (bd. dirs.), Am. Arbitrators Assn.

REISS, JOHN BARLOW, lawyer; b. London, Aug. 29, 1939; arrived in U.S., 1963; s. James Martin and Margaret Joan (Ping) R.; m. Mary Jean Maudsley, Aug. 6, 1967 (div. 1978); m. Kathleen Strouse, Aug. 2, 1979; 1 child, Juliette Blanche. BA with honors, Exeter U., Devon, Eng., 1961; AM, Washington U., St. Louis, 1966, PhD, 1971; JD, Temple U., 1977. Bar: Pa. 1977, N.J. 1977, U.S. Dist. Ct. N.J. 1977, D.C. 1980, U.S. Supreme Ct. 1981, U.S. Dist. Ct. D.C. 1982. Economist Commonwealth Econ. Com., London, 1962-63; asst. prof. Allegheny Coll., Meadville, Pa., 1967-71; assoc. prof. Stockton State Coll., Pomona, NJ, 1971-75; asst. health commr. State of N.J., Trenton, 1975-79; dir. office of health regulation U.S. Dept. HHS, Washington, 1979-81; assoc. Baker & Hostetler, Washington, 1981-82, Dechert Price & Rhoads, Phila., 1982—93, ptnr., 1986-93, asst. chair health law group, 1984-91, chmn. health law group, 1991-93; ptnr. Saul Ewing LLP, Phila., 1993—, chmn. health law dept., 1995—2002, chmn. health law practice group, 2002—. Mem. editl. bd. Topics in Hosp. Law, 1985-86, Hosp. Legal Forms Manual, 1985-2002, Jour. Health Care Tech., 1984-86; contbr. Hosp. Contracts Manual, 1983-2002; contbr. articles to profl. jours., chpts. to books. Bd. dirs. Gateway Sch. Little Children, Phila., 1986-99; bd. dirs. ECRI Plymouth Meeting, Pa., 1994—, chmn. bd., 2001—; mem. bd. vestry All Saints Ch., Wynnewood, Pa., 1993, 96-2001; treas. The U.B.C. 1871 Found. Pub. Health Svc. fellow, 1979-81, English Speaking Union fellow, 1963-66, Econ. Devel. Adminstr. fellow Washington U., 1966-67. Mem. Nat. Health Lawyers Assn., Phila. Bar Assn., Brit. Am. C. of C. of Greater Phila. (bd. dirs. 1991), Union League Phila., Univ. Barge Club. Brit. Officers Club Phila. (1st v.p. 2003—04, pres. 2005-), Health Care Fin. Mgmt. Assn. (bd. dirs. NJ chpt. 2005-), Phila. Club. Avocations: gardening, house restoring, reading, sculling. Home: 415 Wister Rd Wynnewood PA 19096-1808 Office: Saul Ewing LLP 3800 Centre Sq W Philadelphia PA 19102 Office Phone: 215-972-7124. Business E-Mail: jreiss@saul.com.

REISS, LENORE ANN, language educator, retired secondary school educator; b. Bklyn., Apr. 17, 1936; d. Morris and Alice Shestack; m. Edward Lawrence Reiss, Sept. 13, 1959 (dec. June 5, 2000); children: Stephanie Lynne, Jonathan David. BA cum laude, Boston U., 1957; postgrad., Middlebury Coll., 1956, NYU, 1974—76, U. Miami, 1979. Tchr. Spanish and French Martin Van Buren HS, Queens Village, NY, 1957—59; pvt. tutor N.Y.C., 1960—77; pvt. sch. tchr. Studio on Eleventh St., N.Y.C., 1970—77; tchr. The Livingston Sch., N.Y.C., 1977—78, Chiaravalle Montessori Sch., Evanston, Ill., 1986—87; pvt. tutor Evanston, 1990—95; ret., 1995. Author: White-Robed Recluse: A Study of Emily Dickinson, 1993, Genius of Darkness: A Study of Edgar Allan Poe, 1994, The Good Lady of Nohant: A Study of George Sand, 1995; contbr. poems to jours., articles to profl. jours. Avocations: reading, music, dance, antiques, theater. Home: 2025 Sherman Ave Evanston IL 60201 also: 136 E 76th St New York NY 10021

REISS, PAUL J., academic administrator; b. Lake Placid, NY, Aug. 10, 1930; s. Julian J. and Daisy M. (Smith) R.; m. Rosemary A. Donohue, June 25, 1955; children: Catherine, Paul, Gregory, Mark, Julia, David, Steven, Martha, John. BS, Holy Cross Coll., 1952; MA, Fordham U., 1954; PhD, Harvard U., 1960; LHD (hon.), Showa U., 1994; LLD (hon.), Middlebury Coll., 1996; LHD (hon.), St. Michael's Coll., 2005. Tutor Harvard U., 1954-57; instr., asst. prof. Marquette U., 1957-63, chmn. dept. sociology, 1961-63; assoc. prof. sociology Fordham U., Bronx, NY, 1963-75, prof., 1976-85, chmn. dept. sociology and anthropology, 1964-68; dean Fordham U. (Liberal Arts Coll.), 1968-69, v.p. acad. affairs, 1969-75, exec. v.p., 1975-85; pres. St. Michael's Coll., Colchester, Vt., 1985-96, pres. emeritus, 1996—. Editor: Sociological Analysis: A Journal in the Sociology of Religion, 1961-68; contbr. articles to profl. jours. Cmnr. bd. dir. Julian Reiss Found., Lake Placid, N.Y.; trustee Wadhams Hall Sem. Coll.; bd. dirs., treas. Lake Placid Sinfonietta; chmn. Mercy Care for Adirondacks, Greater Burlington

Indsl. Commn.; mem. Nat. Assn. Ind. Colls. and Univs., Assn. Cath. Colls. and Univs., Lake Placid Vis. Bur., St. Edmund's Retreat; mem. indsl. commn. Greater Burlington. Fellow Am. Sociol. Assn.; mem. Assn. Sociology Religion (pres.), Assn. Vt. Ind. Colls. (pres.), Vt. Higher Edn. Coun. (pres.), Vt. Bus. Roundtable, Vt. World Trade Office (chmn.). Democrat. Roman Catholic. Home: 48 Daisy Way Lake Placid NY 12946 Personal E-mail: proreiss@aol.com.

**REISS, RICHARD,** environmental consultant; b. Abington, Pa., Feb. 9, 1967; s. Richard and Diane Reiss. BS, U. Calif., Santa Barbara, 1989; MS, Northwestern U., 1990; DSc, Harvard U., 1994. Sr. air quality analyst Sonoma Tech., Santa Rosa, Calif., 1994—98; sr. scientist Jellinek, Schwartz & Connolly, Arlington, Va., 1998—2000; v.p. Scis. Internat., Alexandria, Va., 2000—. Chmn. young adults Christ Ch., Alexandria, 2004—05. Walter P. Murphy fellow, Northwestern U., 1989, Leslie Silverman scholar, Harvard U., 1991. Mem.: Soc. Risk Analysis (Chauncey Starr award 2001). Office: Scis Internat 1800 Diagonal Rd Ste 500 Alexandria VA 22314 Office Phone: 703-684-0123. Office Fax: 703-684-2223.

**REISS, ROBERT FRANCIS,** physician; b. Watertown, N.Y., Dec. 11, 1938; s. Ernest Paul and Elizabeth Munk (Clark) R.; m. Giovanna Dora Bassi, Mar. 18, 1964; children: Carroll, Christian, Mark, Dylan. AB, Syracuse U., 1959; MD, U. Bologna, Italy, 1965. Diplomate Am. Bd. Pathology (hematology, transfusion medicine). Dir. lab. hematology and blood bank State U. Hosp., Bklyn., 1975-77; asst. prof. pathology SUNY Downstate Med. Ctr., Bklyn., 1975-77; dir. Hudson Valley Blood Svc., Valhalla, NY, 1978-85; assoc. prof. pathology and medicine N.Y. Med. Coll., Valhalla, 1978-88; med dir N.Y Blood Ctr., N.Y.C., 1985-88; dir. lab. hematology and transfusion medicine Columbia-Presbyn. Med. Ctr., N.Y.C., 1988-98; prof. clin. pathology and clin. medicine Columbia U. Coll. Physicians and Surgeons, N.Y.C., 1988—; v.p. chief med. officer N.Y. Blood Ctr., N.Y.C., 1998—2001. Chmn. steering com. Hudson Valley Blood Resources Assn., Valhalla, 1981-85; chief examiner blood banking N.Y.C. Dept. Health, 1980-86, mem. adv. com. on blood banking, 1988-90; mem. instnl. rev. bd. N.Y. Blood Ctr., N.Y.C., 1991-2001. Editor, co-author: Clinical Laboratory Medicine, 1992; contbr. more than 40 articles to med. jours., chpts. to books. Bd. mgrs. camping plus N.Y. Mission Soc., 1975-78; scout leader Boy Scouts Am., N.Y.C., 1975-80. Col. U.S. Army, 1966-69, USAR, 1988—2005. Fellow Assn. Clin. Scientists (vice chair sect. on hematology and transfusion medicine, 1999—; mem. Am. Assn. Blood Banks (dist. advisor 1982-88, mem. editl. bd. Ann. Clin. Labs. Sci. 1999—), Coun. Hosp. Blood Bank Dirs. Greater N.Y. (bd. dirs. 1989-98), Am. Soc. Hematology. Avocations: travel, running, stamps. Office Phone: 718-446-2739. Business E-Mail: rfr1@columbia.edu.

**REISS, STEVEN,** psychology professor; b. N.Y.C., Apr. 10, 1947; s. Benjamin A. and Margaret (Schmidt) R.; m. Maggi B. Reiss, Sept. 4, 1971; children: Michael, Ben AB magna cum laude, Dartmouth Coll., 1964; PhD in Psychology, Yale U., 1972. Registered psychologist, Ill. Prof. psychology U. Ill.-Chgo., 1972-91; prof. psychology and psychiatry Ohio State U., Columbus, 1991—, dir. Nisonger Ctr., 1991—. Dir. ISDD Mental Health Clinic, Chgo., 1980-91. Author: Who Am I: The 16 Basic Desires, 2000; editor: Psychophropic Medications, 1998; author psychol. tests: Reiss Screen, 1988, Anxiety Sensitivity Index, 1986. ARC Rsch. awardee, 1991, NADD Career awardee, 1998. Fellow APA, Am. Assn. Mental Retardation (bd. dirs. 1987, Svc. award 1987). Office: Ohio State Univ 1581 Dodd Dr Columbus OH 43210-1267 Office Phone: 614-292-2390. E-mail: reiss.7@osu.edu.

**REISS, STEVEN ALAN,** lawyer, educator; b. NYC, Dec. 18, 1951; s. Louis and Ruth (Harrow) R.; m. Mary A. Mattingly; children: Alexandra Mattingly Reiss, Tyler Brennan Reiss. BA, Vassar Coll., 1973; JD, Stanford (Calif.) U., 1976. Bar: N.Y., D.C., Calif. Law clk. to John Minor Wisdom U.S. Ct. Appeals for 5th Cir., New Orleans, 1976-77; law clk. to justice William J. Brennan U.S Supreme Ct., Washington, 1977-78; assoc. Miller, Cassidy, Larroca & Lewin, Washington, 1978-80; vis. prof. Georgetown U. Law Ctr., Washington, 1981; asst. prof. Law Sch., NYU, 1981-83, assoc. prof., 1984-87, prof., 1987-91; ptnr. Weil, Gotshal & Manges, N.Y.C., 1990—. Editor-in-chief White Collar Crime Reporter, 1987-91, contbg. editor, 1991—. Trustee Vassar Coll. Poughkeepsie, N.Y., 1987-82; bd. dirs. NYU Cmty. Fund, 1984-87, Concert Artists Guild, 1991-94, Lyrics Chamber Music Soc., 2000--; gen. counsel Brennan Ctr. for Justice, 1996—; bd. trustees Vols. of Legal Svcs. Mem. N.Y. State Bar Assn., D.C. Bar Assn., Calif. Bar Assn., Assn. of Bar of City of N.Y. (fed. legis. com. 1981-87), 2d Jud. Conf. (reporter 1984—). Home: 25 E 86th St New York NY 10028-0553 Office: Weil Gotshal & Manges 767 5th Ave Fl Concl New York NY 10153-0119 E-mail: steven.riess@weil.com.

**REISS, SUSAN MARIE,** editor, writer; b. Washington, Sept. 14, 1963; m. Paul L. Roney Jr., May 25, 1991. BA in English Lit., U. Va., 1985; MA in English, George Mason U., 1989. Editl. asst. Water Pollution Control Fedn., Alexandria, Va., 1985-87; freelance writer, editor Arlington, Va., 1987-90; staff writer George Mason U., Fairfax, Va., 1988-90, Optical Soc. Am., Washington, 1990-91, news editor, 1991-93, mng. editor, 1993-96; editor On Campus With Women Assn. Am. Colls. and Univs., 1996—2000; freelance writer, editor Arlington, 1996—. Newsletter editor: Arlington County Tennis Assn., 1990-91; contbr. articles to profl. jours. and mags. Mem. Am. Soc. Laser Medicine and Surgery, Nat. Assn. Science Writers, Nat. Press Club, Washington Ind. Writers, D.C. Sci. Writers Assn., Sigma Tau Delta (founding mem. U. Va. chpt.). Avocations: tennis, piano, cross country skiing. Home and Office: 6814 30th Rd N Arlington VA 22213-1602

**REISTER, RAYMOND ALEX,** retired lawyer; b. Sioux City, Iowa, Dec. 22, 1929; s. Harold William and Anne (Eberhardt) R.; m. Ruth Elizabeth Alkema, Oct. 7, 1967 AB, Harvard U., 1952, LLB, 1955. Bar: N.Y. 1956, Minn. 1960. Assoc. Paul, Weiss, Rifkind, Wharton & Garrison, N.Y.C., 1955-56; ptnr. Dorsey & Whitney LLP, Mpls., 1959-92; ret., 1993. Instr. U. Minn. Extension Divsn., 1964-66. Editor (with Larry W. Johnson): Minnesota Probate Administration, 1968. Trustee Mpls. Soc. Fine Arts, 1981-87; mem. exec. coun. Minn. Hist. Soc., 1984-2002; bd. dirs. Mpls. Athenaeum, 1992—, pres., 1998-2001; bd. dirs. Minn. Humanities Commn., 1997—. 1st lt. U.S. Army, 1956-59. Mem. Minn. Bar Assn., Hennepin County Bar Assn. Home: 93 Groveland Ter Minneapolis MN 55403-1142 Office: Dorsey & Whitney LLP Ste 1500 50 South 6th Street Minneapolis MN 55402-1498

**REISTER, RUTH ALKEMA,** lawyer, finance company executive; b. Grand Rapids, Mich., May 30, 1936; d. Henry and Lena (Land) Alkema; m. Raymond A. Reister, Oct. 7, 1967. BA, U. Mich., 1958, JD, 1964; grad. Program in Bus. Adminstrn., Harvard U., 1959, postgrad. Program in Mgmt. Devel., 1976. Bar: Minn., Mich. 1964, U.S. Supreme Ct. 1976. Trust officer Northwestern Nat. Bank, Mpls., 1964-70; asst. counsel, asst. v.p., sec. Fed. Res. Bank, Mpls., 1970-81; asst. sec., bd. govs. Fed. Res. System, 1977; dep. under sec. U.S. Dept. Agr., Washington, 1981-83; pres. First Bank Systems Agrl. Credit Corp., Mpls., 1983-84; pres. Groveland Corp., Mpls., 1986—; dir. Herman Miller, Inc., Zealand, Mich., 1984—. Bd. dirs. United Way, ARC, Jones Harrison Home, Mpls.; bd. dirs., chair Gustavus Adolfus Coll.; chmn. Jones-Harrison Found. Mem. Harvard Bus. Sch. Club Minn., Minn. Women's Econ. Round Table (pres. 1980-81).

**REITAN, DANIEL KINSETH,** electric and computer engineering educator; b. Duluth, Minn., Aug. 13, 1921; s. Conrad Ulfred and Joy Elizabeth R.; m. Marian Anne Stemme, July 18, 1946; children: Debra Leah, Danielle Karen. BSEE, N.D. State U., 1946; MSEE, U. Wis., 1949, PhD, 1952. Registered profl. engr., Wis. Control engr. GE, Schenectady, N.Y, 1946-48; transmission line engr. Gen. Telephone Co., Madison, Wis., 1949-50; mem. faculty Coll. Engring. U. Wis., Madison, 1952-85, prof. elec. and computer engring., 1962-85; cons. Energy Industries, 1985-95; dir. power sys. simulation lab. Coll. Engring. U. Wis., 1968-84, also dir. wind power rsch. Energy Ctr. Coll. Engring. Cons. Nat. Inst. Sci. and Tech. (formerly U.S. Nat. Bur. Stds.); dir. electric network calculator lab. Wis. Utilities, 1959-68. Author: Interstellar Space Travel at Near Light Speed, 1995, The Visual Appearance of Relativ-

istically Moving Objects, 1999; contbr. articles to profl. jours.; patentee in field. With U.S. Army, World War II. Recipient Outstanding Tchr. award Polygon Engring. Council., Gov.'s citation for service to State of Wis. Fellow IEEE (Centennial medal and cert. for outstanding achievement 1984, Centennial medal and cert. dept. ECE U. Wis., 1991, IEEE power Engring., Computer Control Indsl. Applications and Edn. Soc.), Conf. Internat. des Grand Reseaux Electriques a Haute Tension, Am. Soc. Engring. Edn., Wis. Acad. Scis., Am. Wind Energy Assn., The Planetary Soc., Sigma Xi, Tau Delta Pi, Tau Beta Pi, Kappa Mu Epsilon. Republican. Lutheran. Home: 1200 Harwood Dr Apt 322 Fargo ND 58104-6294 *I believe that in one's career professionalism and perseverance are key factors in success. In one's personal life, the family should be the center, but not the circumference, about which all activities revolve.*

**REITAN, HAROLD THEODORE,** management consultant; b. Max, ND, Nov. 3, 1928; s. Walter Rudolph and Anna Helga (Glesne) R.; m. Margaret Lucille Bonsac, Dec. 29, 1954 (div.); children: Eric, Karen, Chris, Jon. BA, St. Olaf Coll., 1950; MA in Social Psychology, U. Fla., 1962, PhD, 1967. Commd. officer USAF, 1951, advanced through grades to col., 1971; comdr. USAF Spl. Treatment Ctr., Lackland, Tex., 1971-74, USAF Corrections and Rehab. Group, Lowry, Colo., 1974-76, USAF Tech. Tng. Wing, 1976-78; ret., 1978; mgr. health svcs. Coors Industries, Golden, Colo., 1978-84, mgr. tng. and orgnl. devel., 1984—89, cons. mgmt. assessment, tng. and devel., 1989—. Contbr. articles to profl. jours. Decorated D.F.C. with oak leaf cluster, Bronze Star, Legion of Merit with oak leaf cluster, Air medal with 5 oak leaf clusters. Mem. APA, Phi Kappa Phi. Republican. Lutheran. Home and Office: 116 S Nome St Aurora CO 80012-1242 Personal E-mail: htr1@earthlink.net.

**REITAN, PAUL HARTMAN,** geologist, educator; b. Kanawha, Iowa, Aug. 18, 1928; s. John Olsen and Anna (Meldahl) R.; m. Reidun Engebretsen, Sept. 28, 1962; children: Kirsten Berit, Eric Hartmann. AB (Salisbury fellow), U. Chgo., 1953; PhD, U. Oslo, Norway, 1959. Instr. U. Ill., Chgo., 1955; geologist U.S. Geol. Survey, 1953-56; state geologist Geol. Survey of Norway, 1956-60; asst. prof. mineralogy Stanford U., 1960-66; mem. faculty SUNY, Buffalo, 1966-98, prof. dept. geology emeritus natural sci. and math., dean, 1975-79. Guest scientist Centre for Geol. Sci., Acad. Sci., Warsaw, Poland, Geol. Survey Prague, Czechoslovakia., Geol. Survey, Norway, Nat. Geophys. Rsch. Inst. and Geol. Survey, India Author: (with Davis and Pestrong) Geology, 1976; contbr. articles to profl. jours. Served with U.S. Army, 1946-49. Fulbright fellow, Norway, 1955-56; NATO sr. fellow in sci., 1972; G. Unger Vetlesen fellow, 1973; Fulbright sr. lectr., India, 1986; Norwegian Marshall Fund grantee, 1986, 93. Fellow AAAS, Geol. Soc. Am., Mineral. Soc. Am.; mem. Internat. Assn. Geochemistry and Cosmochemistry, Royal Norwegian Soc. Scis. and Letters (fgn.), Norsk Geologisk Forening (life), Sigma Xi. Home: 120 Walton Dr Buffalo NY 14226-4556 Office: U Buffalo Dept Geology Buffalo NY 14260-3050 Office Phone: 716-645-6800 3988. E-mail: preitan@buffalo.edu.

**REITAN, RALPH MELDAHL,** clinical neuropsychologist, former educator; b. Beresford, SD, Aug. 29, 1922; s. John O. and Anna (Meldahl) Reitan; m. Lucille Ann Kirsch, Feb. 14, 1952 (dec. July 1985); children: Ellen, Jon, Ann, Richard, Erik. BA, Ctrl. YMCA Coll., Chgo., 1944; PhD, U. Chgo., 1950. Cert. in clin. psychology and clin. neuropsychology Am. Bd. Profl. Psychology. Instr. U. Chgo., 1948-51; asst. prof. Roosevelt U., Chgo., 1950-51; from asst. prof. to prof. Ind. U. Med. Sch., Indpls., 1951-70; prof. U. Wash., Seattle, 1970-77, U. Ariz., Tucson, 1977-86; pres. Reitan Neuropsychology Labs., Tucson, 1981—. Cons. NIH, Bethesda, Md., 1960-71, VA, Washington, 1955-84, NASA, Washington, 1964-66. Author: Traumatic Brain Injury, 1985, Neuropsychological Evaluation of Older Children, 1992, The Halstead-Reitan Neuropsychological Test Battery, 1993, Detection of Malingering and Invalid Test Results, 1998, Mild Head Injury: Intellectual, Cognitive and Emotional Consequences, 2000, also 15 others; contbr. articles to profl. jours. Trustee Easter Seal Rsch. Found., Chgo., 1974-83. With U.S. Army, 1942-43. Fellow APA, Nat. Acad. Neuropsychology; mem. Am. Neurol. Assn., Am. Acad. Neurology (affiliate), Coalition Clin. Neuropsychology Practitioners, Reitan Soc. Avocations: walking, bird watching. Home: 4831 N Via Serenidad Tucson AZ 85718-5715 Office: Reitan Neuropsychology Labs PO Box 66080 Tucson AZ 85728-6080 Office Phone: 520-299-5725. Personal E-mail: reitanlabs@aol.com.

**REITEMEIER, RICHARD JOSEPH,** physician; b. Pueblo, Colo., Jan. 2, 1923; s. Paul John and Ethel Regina (McCarthy) Reitemeier; m. Patricia Claire Mulligan, July 21, 1951; children: Mary Louise, Paul, Joseph, Susan, Robert, Patrick, Daniel. AB, U. Denver, 1944; MD, U. Colo., 1946; MS in Internal Medicine, U. Minn., 1954. Diplomate Am. Bd. Internal Medicine. Intern Corwin Hosp., Pueblo, 1946—47; resident Henry Ford Hosp., Detroit, 1949—50, Mayo Found., Rochester, Minn., 1950—53; cons. internal medicine and gastroenterology Mayo Clinic, Rochester, 1954—87; chmn. dept. internal medicine Mayo Clinic (Mayo Clinic and Mayo Med. Sch.), 1967—74, prof., 1971—; bd. govs. Mayo Clinic, 1970—74. Gov. Am. Bd. Internal Medicine, 1971—79, chmn., 1978—79, rep. to Am. Bd. Med. Specialites, 1977—80, 1983—84, accreditation council grad. med. edn., 1979—85, chmn., 1982—83; governing bd. Am. Bd. Med. Specialties, 1983—86; sci. and med. dir. Ludwig Inst. Cancer Rsch., 1987—88; cons. Kaiser Family Med. Found., 1989—90; med. dir. Phoenix Alliance Inc., 1990—93. Author (with C.G. Moertel): Advanced Gastrointestinal Cancer, Clinical Management and Chemotherapy, 1969; contbr. articles to profl. jours. Trustee Mayo Found., 1970—74, St. Mary's Hosp., Rochester, 1976—82; mem. governing bd. Sisters of Mercy Hosp., St. Louis, 1988—94. With U.S. Army, 1947—49. Recipient Alumni award, U. Colo. Sch. Medicine, Irving Cutter award, Phi Rho Sigma, 1986, Disting. Alumnus award, Mayo Found., 1997. Master: ACP (regent 1979—82, gov. for Minn., 1975—79, pres. 1983—84, Alfred Stengel Meml. award 1990); fellow: AMA, Nat. Bd. Med. Examiners (treas. 1987—89), Am. Assn. Study Liver Disease, Am. Assn. Cancer Rsch., Inst. Medicine, Coun. Med. Splty. Socs., Am. Soc. Clin. Oncology, Am. Fedn. Clin. Rsch., Am. Clin. and Climatol. Assn., Am. Gastroenterol. Assn.; mem.: Alpha Omega Alpha. Republican. Roman Catholic. Office: 200 1st Ave SW Rochester MN 55902-3129

**REITER, GLENN MITCHELL,** lawyer; b. NYC, Feb. 1, 1951; s. Bernard Leon and Helene (Edson) R.; m. Marilyn Beckhorn, Sept. 5, 1976; children: Benjamin, Diana, Julie. BA, Yale U., 1973, JD, 1976. Bar: N.J. 1976, Pa. 1977, D.C. 1978, N.Y. 1979. Law clk. to judge U.S. Ct. Appeals, Phila., 1976-77; assoc. Schnader, Harrison, Segal & Lewis, Phila., 1977-78, Simpson Thacher & Bartlett LLP, N.Y.C., 1978-84, ptnr., 1984—; resident ptnr. London, 1986-90. Mem.: Phi Beta Kappa. Office Phone: 212-455-3358.

**REITER, LUIS,** lawyer; b. Lima, Peru, 1956; BA magna cum laude, U. Miami, 1977, JD, 1980. Bar: Fla. 1980. Ptnr. Squire, Sanders & Dempsey LLP, Miami, co-chmn., Project Fin. Practice Group. Mem.: Fla. Bar, Nat. Assn. Bond Lawyers. Fluent in Spanish. Home: Squire Sanders & Dempsey LLP 200 S Biscyne Blvd Ste 4000 Miami FL 33131 Office Phone: 305-577-7710. Office Fax: 305-577-7001. Business E-Mail: lreiter@ssd.com.

**REITER, MICHAEL A.,** lawyer, educator; b. Pitts., Nov. 15, 1941; BS, U. Wis., 1963, MS, 1964, JD, 1967, PhD, 1969. Bar: Wis. 1967, Ill. 1975, U.S. Supreme Ct. 1975. Ptnr. Holleb & Coff, Chgo., 1987-99, Duane Morris LLP, Chgo., 1999—. Adj. prof. law Northwestern U., Chgo., 1977—99; mem. faculty Nat. Inst. Trial Advocacy, 1980—. Office: Duane Morris LLP 227 W Monroe St Ste 3400 Chicago IL 60606-5098 Office Phone: 312-499-6718.

**REITER, STANLEY,** economist, educator; b. N.Y.C., Apr. 26, 1925; s. Frank and Fanny (Rosenberg) R.; m. Nina Sarah Breger, June 13, 1944; children: Carla Frances, Frank Joseph. AB, Queens Coll., 1947; MA, U. Chgo., 1950, PhD, 1955. Rsch. assoc. Cowles Commn., U. Chgo., 1948-50; mem. faculty Stanford U., 1950-54, Purdue U., 1954-67; prof. econs. and math. Northwestern U., 1967—, now Morrison prof. econs. and decision scis. Kellogg Sch. Mgmt. Dir. Ctr. for Math. Studies in Econs. and Mgmt.

Sci.; cons. in field. Trustee Roycemore Sch., Evanston, Ill., 1969-71, treas., 1970-71. Served with inf. AUS, 1943-45. Decorated Purple Heart. Fellow Econometric Soc., AAAS; mem. Soc. Indsl. and Applied Math., Inst. Mgmt. Scis., Ops. Rsch. Soc. Am., Am. Math. Soc., Math. Assn. Am., Am. Acad. of Arts and Scis. Home: Apt 4B 838 Michigan Ave Evanston IL 60202 Office: Northwestern U Ctr for Math Studies 2001 Sheridan Rd Evanston IL 60208-0814 E-mail: s-reiter@northwestern.edu.

**REITER-PALMON, RONI,** finance educator; d. Michael and Avia Reiter; m. Ophir Palmon, Mar. 1, 1962; children: Shir Palmon, Tomer Palmon. BA, Tel Aviv U., 1987; PhD, George Mason U., Fairfax, Va., 1993. Asst. prof. U. Nebr., Omaha, 1993—99, assoc. prof., 1999—2006, prof., 2006—. Contbg. author: Encyclopedia or Industrial/Organizational Psychology; contbr. articles to profl. jours. Tech. advisor SkillsNET, Waxahachie, Tex., 2005. Mem.: APA, Acad. Mgmt., Soc. Indsl. and Orgnl. Psychology. Office: Univ Nebr 60th and Dodge Omaha NE 68182 Office Phone: 402-554-4810. E-mail: rreiter-palmon@mail.unomaha.edu.

**REITMAN, IVAN,** film director, producer; b. Komarmo, Czechoslovakia, Oct. 27, 1946; came to Can., 1951; s. Leslie and Clara R.; m. Genevieve Robert, Sept. 12, 1976; children: Jason, Catherine, Caroline. MusB, McMaster U., 1969. Judge FOCUS Nissan-Datsun, N.Y.C., 1981-83. Theatrical prodr.: The Magic show, 1974, The National Lampoon Show, 1975, Merlin, 1983 (also dir.); films include: (dir., exec. prodr.) Cannibal Girls, 1973; (prodr.) They Came From Within (aka Shivers), 1975, Death Weekend (aka The House by the Lake), 1977, Blackout, 1978, National Lampoon's Animal House, 1978, Heavy Metal, 1981, Stop! Or My Mom Will Shoot, 1992, Space Jam, 1996, Private Parts, 1996, Father's Day, 1997, Six Days and Seven Nights, 1998, Doomsday Man, 1999, Evolution, 2001; (prodr., dir.) Foxy Lady, 1971, Meatballs, 1979, Stripes, 1981, Ghostbusters, 1984, Legal Eagles, 1986, Twins, 1988, Ghostbusters II, 1989, Kindergarten Cop, 1990, Dave, 1993, Junior, 1994; (exec. prodr.) Rabid, 1976, Spacehunter: Adventures in the Forbidden Zone, 1983, Big Shots, 1987, Casual Sex?, 1988, Feds, 1988, Beethoven, 1992, Beethoven's 2nd, 1993, Commandments, 1996, Road Trip, 2000, Killing Me Softly, 2002, Old School, 2003, Eurotrip, 2004; (dir.) My Super Ex-Girlfriend, 2006; TV series: (prodr., dir.) Delta House, 1978; TV film exec. prodr. The Late Shift, 1996, Fathers Day, 1997. Mem. Dirs. Guild Am. also: Bldg 489 100 University City Plz Universal City CA 91608-1002*

**REITMAN, JERRY IRVING,** advertising agency executive; b. Phila., Jan. 9, 1938; s. Benjamin and Ruth (Eisenberg) R.; m. Monica Birgitta Hall, Oct. 27, 1968; children: Jennifer Sharon, Sarah Beth. BS in Fin., Pa. State U., 1961. Exec. v.p., CEO Brit. Pubs., N.Y.C. and London, 1965-69; pres., pub. Acad. Media, Sherman Oaks, Calif., 1969-73; v.p. Pubs. Clearing House, Port Washington, NY, 1973-78; exec. v.p. Ogilvy & Mather, N.Y.C., 1978-81; with Scali, McCabe, Sloves, Inc., N.Y.C., 1981-86; pres. Scali, McCabe, Sloves Direct, N.Y.C.; chmn. bd. dirs. The Reitman Group, 1986; exec. v.p. The Leo Burnett Co., Chgo., 1986-96; pres., CEO, vice chair Internat. Data Response Corp., Chgo., 1996—. Dir. Scandinavian Airlines Sys. Pub./Distbn. Svcs.; mem. adv. bd. Ill. Dept. Trade and Tourism, 1988—; internat. awards chmn., bd. dirs. John Caples Internat., 1989—; mem. Internat. Direct Mktg. Symposium, Zürich, Switzerland. Author: A Common Sense Approach to Small Business, 1968, Beyond 2000: The Future of Direct Marketing, 1994; contbr. articles to profl. jours. Trustee Locust Valley Libr. Assn., N.Y., 1982—; exec. com. mem. Pub. Hall of Fame, 1987—; bd. govs. Children's Miracle Network, 1992—, vice chmn., chmn. bd. govs., 1998—, 1999-2001; bd. dirs. Children's Meml. Found. Telethon, The Direct Mktg. Ednl. Found., exec. dir., 1996—. Anderson scholar, 1960; recipient Key to City, New Orleans, 1959, Silver Apple award N.Y. Direct Mktg. Club, 1989, Ed Mayer award Ednl. Found., 1996, Charles S. Downs award, 1997. Fellow Psychiat. Re-Edn. Assn.; mem. Am. Mktg. Assn. (at-large mem., 2000, bd. dirs.), Direct Mktg. Assn. (bd. mem. ethics com. 1984), Creative Guild (dir. 1984), Internat. Direct Mktg. Assn. (bd. dirs. 1981-82), Publ. Hall of Fame (exec. com. 1988—), Direct Mktg. Club N.Y. (pres. 1983-84), Beta Gamma Sigma. Avocations: tennis, auto restoration, woodworking. Home and Office: Callahan Group LLC 2204 N Leavitt St Chicago IL 60647-3204 Home (Summer): Ringso 237 Nasbyviken 64061 Stallanholmen Sweden Office Phone: 773-342-1973. Personal E-mail: jireitman@aol.com.

**REITMAN, ROBERT STANLEY,** management consultant, not-for-profit advisor; b. Fairmont, W.Va., Nov. 18, 1933; s. Isadore and Freda A. (Layman) R.; m. Sylvia K. Golden, Dec. 24, 1955; children: Scott Alan, Alayne Louise. BS in Acctg., W.Va. U., 1955; JD, Case Western Res. U., 1958. Bar: Ohio 1958. Mem. firm Burke, Haber & Berick, Cleve., 1958-60, ptnr., 1960-68; exec. v.p., vice chmn. Tranzonic Cos. (formerly AAV Cos.), Pepper Pike, Ohio, 1968-70, pres., vice-chmn., 1970-73, chief exec. officer, pres., vice chmn., 1973-82, pres., chmn., CEO, 1982-98, chmn. emeritus, bd. dirs., 1998—; prin. Riverbend Advisors, 1998—. Mem. bus. adv. com. Mandel Ctr. for non-profit Orgn. Case We. Res. U., 1995-99, vis. com. Weatherhead Sch. of Bus., 1995-03, vis. com. Sch. of Law, 1998-03, chmn. dean's nat. adv. com., Sch. of Law, 1997-98; mem. pvt. banking adv. bd. Key Bank, N.A., 1997—; mem. dean's adv. com. Sch. Medicine, 2004—. Mem. Rep. fin. com., Cuyahoga County, 1968-78; mem. Com. for Econ. Growth for Israel, Cleve., 1977-80, pres., 1978-80; mem. adv. coun. Cleve. Mus. Nat. History, 1982-85, Cleve. Opera, 1977—; del. Coun. of Jewish Fedns., N.Y.C., 1981-97; gen. co-chmn. Jewish Welfare Fund, Cleve., 1975-78, 81-85, gen. vice chmn., 1985-89, gen. chmn., 1989-91; sect. and div. chmn., team capt. United Way Svcs., 1974-97, mem. del. assembly, 1976-85, trustee, 1977-83, 84-90, 91—2000, v.p., 1985-88, chmn. nominating. com., 1988-90, campaign chmn., 1993, chair fund raising planning com., 1994-97, chair bd. trustees, 1997-2000, life trustee, 2000—; mem. employment com. Jewish Vocat. Svc., Cleve., 1974-83; bd. dirs. Capital for Israel, Inc., N.Y.C., 1986-87; nat. vice chmn. United Jewish Appeal, 1987-92, nat. allocations chmn., 1987-90, trustee, 1988-94, chair retirement fund com., 1994-97; trustee B'nai B'rith Hillel Found., 1975-81, Cleve. Jewish News, 1976-79, Ideastream (pub. broadcasting), Cleve., 1976-99, vice chmn. 1986-90, chmn. bd., 1990-97, immediate past chair, 1997-99, chair emeritus, 1999—; trustee, pres. Bus. Volunteerism Coun., 1994-96, chmn. 1996-97; trustee Jewish Cmty. Fedn. Cleve., 1983-98, 1999-03, treas., 1991-94, v.p., 1995-97, life trustee, 2003—; Jewish Edn. Ctr. of Cleve., 1993-96, Cleve. Zool. Soc., 1972—, pres., 1979-87, chmn., 1987-92, chmn. emeritus, 1992—, chmn. JDC-Brookdale Inst. of Gerontology and Human Devel. (Israel), 1995; trustee Am. Jewish Joint Distbn. Com., 1988-96, 97-05, United Israel Appeal, 1987-94, Mt. Sinai Med. Ctr., Cleve., 1976-96, chmn., 1982-85; trustee Cleve. State U. Devel. Found., 1988-91, Greater Cleve. Roundtable, 1995-99, adv. bd., 1999-02, trustee The Wilds, 1995-99, adv. bd., 1999-02, trustee The Mt. Sinai Health Care Foundation, 1995-04, life trustee, 2004—, vice chair 1998-2001, chair, 2001-04; trustee Univ. Hosps. Health Sys., 1999-04, 05-, Univ. Hosps. Cleve., 1999—; trustee, chair Heather Hill, Inc., 2001—; coun. mem. Village of Gates Mills, Ohio, 1997-00, clk., 2000—. Mem. The 50 Club Cleve., Case We. Res. Univ. Sch. of Law Soc. Benchers, Am. Kennel Club (regional del. 1960-75), We. Res. Kennel Club (officer, trustee 1959-75), Beechmont Club (fin. com. 1972-80, house com. 1974), Pepper Pike Club, Union Club, Carambola Golf Club, Masons, Zeta Beta Tau, Tau Epsilon Rho. Avocations: golf, swimming. Office: Riverbend Advisors 2087 Chagrin River Rd Gates Mills OH 44040-9740 Business E-Mail: rsrform@core.com.

**REITNAUER, OTTO CHARLES,** fine arts director; b. Hornell, NY, June 3, 1958; s. Karl Monroe and Ann Lucille Reitnauer; m. Lori Grace Sawtelle, Aug. 1, 1981; children: Jonathan Reuben, Jared Reuel, Joshua David. B sacred music, Bapt. Bible Coll. Pa., 1980; MA in intercultural studies, Columbia Internat. U., 1995. Pastor, music and worship Calvary Ch., Trumbull, Conn., 1998—2001; dir. of fine arts First Presbyn. Day Sch., Macon, Ga., 2001—. Composer: (composition and recording) Piano Reflections, 1988. Music min. various local chs., Macon, Ga., 2002—05. Mitchell Music scholar, Bapt. Bible Coll. of Pa., 1979. Mem.: Ga. Music Educator's Assn. Baptist. Avocations: music, languages, gardening. Home: 4884 Timberlane Dr Macon GA 31210 Office: First Presbn Day Sch 5671 Calvin Dr Macon GA 31210 Office Phone: 478-477-6505 165.

**REITSEMA, HAROLD JAMES,** aerospace engineer; b. Kalamazoo, Jan. 19, 1948; s. Robert Harold and Bernice Jean (Hoogsteen) R.; m. Mary Jo Gunnink, Aug. 6, 1970; children: Ellen Celeste, Laurie Jean. BA, Calvin Coll., 1972; PhD, N.Mex. State U., 1977. Rsch. assoc. U. Ariz., Tucson, 1977-79, sr. rsch. assoc., 1979-82, vis. scientist, 1987—; sr. mem. tech. staff Ball Aerospace, Boulder, Colo., 1982-85, prin. systems engr., 1985-88, program mgr., 1988-89, staff cons., 1989-96, dir., 1996—. Cons. Aerospace Tech., 1987—. Contbr. articles to profl. jours. including Astrophys. Jour., Aston. Jour., Nature, Sci., Icarus. Bd. dirs. EE Barnard Obs., Golden, Colo., 1984-91. Fellow AIAA (assoc. tech. com. chair 1991, Engr. of Yr. Colo. region 1990); mem. Am. Astron. Soc. (planetary sci. com. 1991-94), Internat. Astron. Union. Achievements include discovery of Larissa, fifth satellite of Neptune; co-discovery of Telesto, seventeenth satellite of Saturn; patents for Optically-coupled Shaft Angle Encoder. Home: 4795 Hancock Dr Boulder CO 80303-1103 Office: Ball Aerospace 1600 Commerce St Boulder CO 80301-2734 E-mail: hreitsema@ball.com.

**REITZ, ALLEN BERNARD,** organic chemist; b. Alameda, Calif., Apr. 7, 1956; s. Arnold Benno and Ruth Hazel (Stillings) R.; m. Evelyn June McCullough, Nov. 24, 1978; children: Darryl, Meredith. BA in Biochemistry and Molecular Biology, U. Calif., Santa Barbara, 1977; MS in Chemistry, U. Calif., San Diego, 1979, PhD in Chemistry, 1982. Postdoctoral rsch. fellow McNeil Pharm., Spring House, Pa., 1982-83, rsch. scientist, 1983-84, sr. scientist, 1984-87; prin. scientist Janssen Rsch. Found., Spring House, 1987-89; rsch. fellow R.W. Johnson Pharm. Rsch. Inst., Spring House, 1990-98, sr. rsch. fellow, 1999—. Reviewer Jour. Organic Chemistry, Tetrahedron Letters, Jour. Am. Chem. Soc. Editor: Adv. Med. Chem., Vol. 4, 1997—, (symposium series) Inositol Phosphates and Derivatives, 1991, Current Topics in Medicine of Chemistry, 2001—; contbr. articles to profl. publs., chpt. to books; expert analyst Chemtracts-Organic Chemistry. Recipient Johnson & Johnson Achievement awards, 1990, 97, Philip B. Hofmann Rsch. award, 1994, excellence in sci. award, 1999. Mem. N.Y. Acad. Sci., Am. Chem. Soc., Phila. Organic Chemists Club (sec. 1986-88, chmn. 1996), Sigma Xi. Achievements include patents and patents pending; research on mechanistic synthetic organic chemistry, medicinal chemistry, stereocontrol and conformational analysis. Home: 109 Greenbriar Rd Lansdale PA 19446-1519 Office: Johnson and Johnson PO Box 776 Spring House PA 19477-0779 Office Phone: 215-628-5615. E-mail: areitz@prius.jnj.com.

**REITZ, BRUCE ARNOLD,** cardiac surgeon, educator; b. Seattle, Sept. 14, 1944; BS, Stanford U., 1966; MD, Yale U., 1970. Diplomate: Am. Bd. Surgery, Am. Bd. Thoracic Surgery. Intern Johns Hopkins Hosp., Balt., 1970-71, cardiac surgeon-in-charge, 1982-92; resident Stanford U. Hosp., Calif., 1971-72, 74-78; clin. assoc. Nat. Heart Lung Blood Inst., NIH, Bethesda, Md., 1972-74; asst. prof. Stanford U. Sch. Medicine, 1977-81, assoc. prof., 1981-82; prof. surgery Johns Hopkins U. Sch. Medicine, Balt., 1982-92; prof., chmn. Sch Medicine Stanford (Calif.) U., 1992—2005; prof. Stanford U. Sch. Medicine, 2005—. Developer heart-lung transplant technique, 1981. Office: Stanford U Sch Medicine Dept Cardiothoracic Surgery Stanford CA 94305-5407 Office Phone: 650-725-4497. Business E-Mail: breitz@stanford.edu.

**REITZ, CURTIS RANDALL,** lawyer, educator; b. Reading, Pa. s. Lester S. and Magdalene A. (Crouse) R.; m. Virginia R. Patterson, Dec. 19, 1953 (div.); children— Kevin R., Joanne E., Whitney A.; m. Judith N. Renzulli, Sept. 18, 1983 BA, U. Pa., 1951, LL.B., 1956. Bar: Pa. 1957, U.S. Supreme Ct. 1959. Law clk. to Chief Justice Earl Warren U.S. Supreme Ct., 1956-57; mem. faculty law U. Pa., Phila., 1957—, asst. prof. law, 1957-60, assoc. prof., 1960-63, prof., 1963—, provost, v.p., 1971—73, Algernon Sydney Biddle prof. law, 1985—. Trustee Internat. House Ctr. Phila.; bd. mgrs. Glen Mills Schs., Pa. Served to 1st lt. U.S. Army, 1951-53 Life Mem. Am. Law Inst., Mem., Nat. Conf. Commrs. on Uniform State Laws, Order of Coif Office: U Pa Law Sch 3400 Chestnut St Philadelphia PA 19104-6204 Business E-Mail: creitz@law.upenn.edu.

**REITZAS, JOSHUA T.,** lawyer, venture capitalist; b. Fall River, Mass., July 9, 1974; s. Richard Arthur Reitzas and Donna Lee Haas. BA, Bowdoin Coll., Brunswick, Maine, 1998; JD, Benjamin N. Cardozo Sch. Law, 2001. Bar: NY 2002, NJ 2002, US Dist. Ct. (3d cir.) NJ 2002, US Dist. Ct. (so. dist.) 2005, US Dist. Ct. (ea. dist.) 2005. Assoc. Rockefeller & Co., Inc., NYC, 1999—2000, Bear Stearns & Co., Inc., NYC, 2001—02, Jaffe & Asher LLP, NYC, 2002—. Adv. bd. Beacon Capital LLC, Martinsville, 2004—; founder ModernFetch, Inc., NYC, 2002—. Fundraiser Metrolacrosse, Boston, 2003—04; alumni interviewer Phillips Exeter Acad., Exeter, NH, 2004. Mem.: ABA (assoc.), NY State Bar Assn. (mem. com. atty. professionalism), NY County Bar Assn. (assoc.), Harvard Club Private Equity and Hedge Fund Group. Achievements include patents pending for Business Patent; E-commerce Patent. Office: Jaffe & Asher LLP 600 Third Ave New York NY 10016 Office Phone: 212-687-3000. Office Fax: 212-687-3601. Business E-Mail: jreitzas@jaffeandasher.com.

**REITZFELD, ALAN D.,** lawyer, department chairman; b. Bklyn., Mar. 13, 1951; s. William and Jeanette (Winzelberg) Reitzfeld; m. Lois Carol Goldfinger, June 24, 1973; children: Jordan Lawrence, Stacey Elyse. BA, Syracuse U., 1973; JD, Hofstra U., 1976. Bar: NY 1977, US Dist. Ct. (So. and Ea. Dists. NY), 1977, US Ct. of Internat. Trade, 1978, US Ct. of Military Appeals, 1978, US Dist. Ct. (No. and Western Dists. NY), 1979, US Ct. of Appeals (2nd and 4th Dists.), 1979, US Ct. of Appeals (7th Cir.), 1980, US Supreme Ct., 1980, US Dist. Ct. (Ea. Dist. Wis.), 1988, US Ct. of Appeals (6th Cir.), 1993; 1997, US Ct. of Appeals (8th Cir.), 1997, US Ct. of Appeals (9th Cir.), 2001, US Ct. of Appeals, DC Cir., 2004. Dir. First Yr. Legal Rsch. and Advisement Fellows Program, Hofstra U., 1975—76; assoc. Martin, Van de Walle & Sawyer, Great Neck, NY, 1976—77, Haight, Gardner, Poor & Havens, 1978—86, ptnr. NY, 1986—, Holland & Knight LLP, N.Y., 1997—2006. Chmn. firmwide tech. com. Holland & Knight LLP, N.Y., 2003—, firmwide tech. ptnr., 2006—; lectr. in field; spkr. in field. Mem. Hofstra Law Review, 1974—76, tech. editor, 1975—76; contbr. articles to profl. jours. Mem.: Internat. Tech. Law Assn., Def. Rsch. Inst., Nassau County Bar Assn., Internat. Assn. Def. Counsel, Fed. Bar Coun., Assn. of the Bar City of NY (aeronautical law com. 2002—), Internat. Bar Assn. (vice-chair tech. and e-Commerce law com. 2004—06), NY State Bar Assn. (mem. bus. law sect. exec. com. 1996—2006, chmn. bus. law sect. internet and tech. law com. 1998—2001, del. Ho. of Dels. 2002—06). Office: Holland & Knight LLP 195 Broadway 24th Fl New York NY 10007 Office Phone: 212-513-3400. Business E-Mail: alan.reitzfeld@hklaw.com.

**REIVICH, MARTIN,** neurologist, neuroscientist; b. Phila., Mar. 2, 1933; s. Solomon Reivich and Belle Lagay; children: Jennifer, Karen. BS, U. Pa., 1954, MD, 1958; D (hon.), Semmelweis U. Medicine, 1990. Intern King County Hosp., Seattle, 1958—59; resident Hosp. U. Pa., Phila., 1959—61, Queen Sq. Neurologic Inst., London, 1961—62; rsch. assoc. Nat. Inst. Mental Health, Bethesda, Md., 1964—66; from asst. prof. neurology to prof. emeritus U. Pa., Phila., 1966—99. Mem.: prof. emeritus, 1999—, dir. Cerebrovascular Rsch. Ctr., 1973—. Dir., positron emission tomography ctr. Univ. of Pa., Philadelphia, Pa., 1979—90. Contbr. over 340 articles to profl. jours. Recipient Semmelweis award, 1977, Hugo-Spatz prize, German Soc. Neurology, 1978, Racz Samuel award, Hungarian Physiol. Soc., 1985; fellow, Fulbright Found., 1961; grantee, NIH, 1966—99. Mem.: Am. Neurol. Assn., Am. Acad. Neurology, Internat. Soc. Cerebral Blood Flow and Metabolism (pres. 1997—99, Lifetime Achievement award 2005), Phi Beta Kappa. Achievements include first to develope fluorodeoxyglucose method for measuring cerebral glucose metabolism in man; discovery of subclavian steal syndrome. Avocations: photography, travel, gardening. Office: Hosp of the Univ Pa 36th and Spruce St Philadelphia PA 19104-6063 Office Phone: 215-662-2632. Home Fax: 215-349-5629; Office Fax: 215-349-5629. Personal E-mail: mreivich@mail.med.upenn.edu.

**REJ, ROBERT,** biochemist; Dir. clin. chemistry N.Y. State Dept. Health, Albany, 1987—; assoc. prof. biomedical scis. SUNY, Albany, 1985—. Internat. fellow, Am. Assn. Clin. Chemistry, 1995. Office: NY State Dept Health Wadsworth Ctr Labs & Rsch PO Box 509 Albany NY 12201-0509 Office Phone: 518-474-5101.

**REJAI, MOSTAFA,** political science professor; b. Tehran, Iran, Mar. 11, 1931; came to U.S., 1954; s. Taghi and Forough (Lashgari) R. AA, Pasadena City Coll., 1957; BA, Calif. State U., L.A., 1959, MS, 1961; PhD, UCLA, 1964. Teaching fellow UCLA, 1963-64; asst. prof. polit. sci. Miami U., Oxford, Ohio, 1964-67, assoc. prof., 1967-70, prof., 1970-83, Disting. prof., 1983—. Vis. scholar Ctr. for Internat. Affairs, Harvard U., 1972, Hoover Instn. on War, Revolution and Peace, Stanford U., 1973, Inst. Internat. Studies, Iran, 1974-75; vis. prof. Western Coll., Oxford, 1971, 72. Author: World Miltary Leaders: A Collective and Comparative Analysis, 1996, The Strategy of Political Revolution, 1973, The Comparative Study of Revolutionary Strategy, 1977, Comparative Political Ideologies, 1984; (with Kay Phillips) Leaders of Revolution, 1979, World Revolutionary Leaders, 1983, Loyalists and Revolutionaries: Political Leaders Compared, 1988, Political Ideologies: A Comparative Approach, 1991, 2d edit., 1995, Demythogizing an Elite: American Presidents in Empirical, Comparative, and Historical Perspectives, 1993, World Military Leaders: A Collective and Comparative Analysis, 1996, Leaders and Leadership: An Appraisal of Theory and Research, 1997, The Young George Washington in Psychobiographical Perspective, 2000, Concepts of Leadership in Western Political Thought, 2002; editor, contbr.: Democracy: The Contemporary Theories, 1967, Decline of Ideology?, 1971; editor: Mao Tse-Tung on Revolution and War, 1969, rev. edit., 1970; assoc. editor Jour. Polit. and Mil. Sociology, 1973—; contbr. articles to profl. jours., book chpts. Recipient Outstanding Teaching award Miami U., 1970. Mem. Am. Polit. Sci. Assn. (polit. psychology sect.), Am. Sociol. Assn. (polit. soc. sect.), Internat. Soc. Assn., Internat. Soc. Polit. Psychology, Internat. Studies Assn., Inter-Univ. Seminar on Armed Forces and Soc., Conf. for Study Polit. Thought, Midwest Polit. Sci. Assn., So. Polit. Sci. Assn., Wesetern Polit. Sci. Assn., Pi Gamma Mu, Pi Sigma Alpha. Office: Miami U Dept of Political Science Oxford OH 45056

**REJENT, MARIAN MAGDALEN,** retired pediatrician; b. Toledo, Aug. 12, 1920; d. Casimir Stanley and Magdalen (Szymanowski) R. BS, Mary Manse Coll., 1943; MD, Marquette U., 1946; MPH, U. Mich., 1960. Diplomate Am. Bd. Pediatrics. Intern St. Vincent Med. Ctr., Toledo, 1946-47; resident communicable diseases City Hosp., Cleve., 1947-48; resident pediatrics Childrens Hosp., Akron, Ohio, 1948-50; pvt. practice Toledo, 1950-54; chief div. maternal child health Toledo Bd. Health, 1953-64; dir. pediatrics Maumee Valley Hosp., Toledo, 1964-69; assoc. prof. pediatrics Med. Coll. Ohio, Toledo, 1969-76; med. dir. State Crippled Childrens Program, Columbus, Ohio, 1976-78; attendant pediatrician St. Vincent Med. Ctr., Toledo, 1978-80, 87-99; chief pediatric svcs. Wake County Health Dept., Raleigh, NC, 1980-87; ret. clin. prof. pediatrics Med. Coll. Ohio, 1998; ret., 1999. Exec. com. March of Dimes, 1988-92. Mem. AMA, APHA, Am. Acad. Pediatrics, Am. Med. Women's Assn., Ohio PHA, Ohio State Med. Assn., NW Ohio Pediatric Assn., Acad. Medicine Toledo, Alpha Omega Alpha. Republican. Roman Catholic. Avocations: travel, photography, painting. Home: The Woodlands Apt 401 4030 Indian Rd Toledo OH 43606

**REJESUS, RODERICK MORALLO,** agricultural and applied economist; b. Manila, Aug. 11, 1972; arrived in US, 1993, permanent resident, 2004; s. Romeo Sario and Belen Morallo Rejesus; m. Janina Acain Perez, Feb. 28, 2003; children: Justin Russ Perez, Julianne Reese Perez. BS cum laude in Agrl. Econ., U. Philippines, Los Banos, 1992; MS in Agrl. Econ., Clemson U., SC, 1993—95; PhD in Agrl. Econ., U. Ill., Urbana, 1996—2001. Rsch. tchg. asst. Clemson U., 1993—95; vis. rsch. assoc. Internat. Maize & Wheat Improvement Ctr. (CIMMYT), El Batan, Mexico, 1995; rsch., tchg. asst. U. Ill., 1996—98, rsch. specialist, 1998—2001; asst. prof. agrl. economics Tarleton State U., Stephenville, Tex., 2001—02; asst. prof. Tex. Tech U., Lubbock, 2002—. Cons. Risk Mgmt. Agy., Kansas City, 2003—05. Contbr. articles to profl. jours. Recipient Grad. Fellowship Recognition award, Coll. Agrl., Consumer, & Environ. Scis., U. Ill., 2000, Outstanding Faculty Mem. of Yr., Ag. Econ. Grad. Student Assn., Tex. Tech U., 2003—04, Outstanding Jour. Article award, Jour. Agr. & Applied Econ., 2004. Mem.: Northeastern Agrl. Econ. Assn., Internat. Agrl. Economics Assn., So. Agrl. Economics Assn., Am. Agrl. Economics Assn., Gamma Sigma Delta, Phi Kappa Phi, Pi Gamma Mu, Phi Beta Delta. Avocation: travel. Office: Texas Tech Univ PO Box 42132 Lubbock TX 79409-2132 Office Fax: 806-742-1099. Business E-Mail: roderick.rejesus@ttu.edu.

**REKERS, GEORGE ALAN,** education educator, clinical psychologist; b. Waterloo, Iowa, July 11, 1948; s. Roger Arthur and Helen K Rekers; m. Sharon Lee Chapin, Aug. 26, 1972; children: Steven, Andrew, Matthew, Timothy, Mark, Brandon. BA in psychology, Westmont Coll., 1969; PhD, U. Calif., L.A., 1972; ThD, U. South Africa, 1997; MBA, So. Wesleyan U., 2004. Rsch. fellow/vis. scholar Harvard U., 1972—73; clin. psychology intern Tufts U. Med. Ctr., Boston, 1973—74; asst. rsch. psychologist U. Calif., 1974—77; pres. and CEO (part time) Logos Rsch. Inst., Van Nuys, Calif., 1975—85; assoc. prof. and chief psychologist U. Fla., 1977—80; dept. head and prof. Kans. State U., 1980—85; disting. prof. and chair., med. sch. faculty in psychology U. So. Carolina, 1985—2005, disting. prof. neuropsychiatry and behavioral sci. emeritus, 2005—. Bus. cons. and seminar leader 33 Dynamics Cons., LLC, Columbia, SC, 2003—, chmn., CEO, 2005—; invited lectr. and cons. over 50 universities in Africa, Asia, Europe, Latin Am. and Mid. East, 1986—; chmn., bd. dirs. InterAct Internat. Inc., Columbia, SC, 1994—; invited cons. U.S. Sec. of Health Human Svcs., Wash., DC, 1989; invited expert to testimony U.S. Senate and House of Rep., 1983—91; invited cons. and rev. Office of the Gov. of SC, 1998—2001. Author: (book) Susan Smith: Victim or Murderer, 1996, There's Room at the Top: 33 Dynamics for Managerial Excellence, 2004; editor: (book) Family Building, 1985, Handbook of Child and Adolescent Sexual Problems, 1995; author: over 150 academic jour. articles and textbook chpts. Recipient Sigmund Freud award, Nat. Assn. for Rsch. and Therapy, 2000, Postdoctoral fellowship award, Found. Fund for Rsch. in Psychiatry, Harvard U., 1972—73; Rsch. grants, Nat. Inst. Mental Health, 1973—80. Fellow: Am. Acad. Clin. Psychology; mem.: Univ. Studies Coun. (adv. bd. mem., chmn. 2001—), Nat. Register of Health Service Providers in Psychology. Avocations: piano, organ, charity. Office: Univ South Carolina Dept Neuropsychiatry 3555 Harden St E Columbia SC 29203 Office Phone: 803-434-4250. Business E-Mail: gr@gw.mp.sc.edu.

**RELCH, JOHN,** banker, federal agency administrator; BS, So. Ill. U.; MBA, U. South Fla.; grad., La. State U. Sch. Banking. Pres., CEO Nat. Bank Sarasota, Fla., 1980—89; staff mem. Office Senator Connie Mack, 1990—98, chief staff, 1998—2000; bd. mem. FDIC Bd. Dirs., 2001—, acting chmn., 2001, vice chmn., 2002—. Chmn. bd. dirs. Sarasota Family YMCA. Office: FDIC 500 17th St NW Washington DC 20429-9990

**RELIAS, JOHN ALEXIS,** lawyer; b. Chgo., Apr. 2, 1946; s. Alexis John and Marie Helen (Metos) R.; m. Linda Ann Pontious, Nov. 27, 1971; children: Anne, Alexandra. BA, Northwestern U., Evanston, 1968; LLB, Northwestern U., Chgo., 1972. Bar: Ill., 1972, U.S. Dist. Ct. (no. dist.) Ill. 1972, U.S. Ct. Appeals (9th cir.) 1981, U.S. Ct. Appeals (7th cir.) 1983, U.S. Supreme Ct. 1997. Assoc. Vedder, Price, Kaufman & Kammholz, Chgo., 1972-78, ptnr., 1979-94, Franczek, Sullivan, Mann, Crement, Hein & Relias, Chgo., 1994—. Mem. bd. edn. Wilmette (Ill.) Sch. Dist. 39, 1989-97, 2001—, pres., 1992-93, 1995-96. Mem. Nat. Sch. Attys., Ill. Assn. Sch. Attys., Order of the Coif, Phi Beta Kappa. Greek Orthodox. Home: 2500 Kenilworth Ave Wilmette IL 60091-1337 Office: Franczek Sulian Mann Crement Hein & Relias 300 S Wacker Dr Chicago IL 60606-6680 Office Phone: 312-786-6160. Business E-Mail: jar@franczek.com.

**RELIFORD, JUDY LYNN PETTY,** science educator; b. Louisville, Aug. 31, 1957; d. Elmo N. and Jeanette M. Petty; m. David H. Reliford, Mar. 10, 1978; children: David BRett, Andrew Kyle. AA, Lindsey Wilson Coll.,

Columbia, Ky., 1977; BS, Campbellsville Coll., Ky., 1980; MA, Western Ky. U., Bowling Green, 1988. Cert. tchr. Ky. Tchr. sci. Adair County H.S., Columbia, 1985—, mem. sch.-based decision-making com., 1999—2001. Sunday sch. tchr., ch. sec. Antioch United Meth. Ch., Columbia. Named Tchr. of the Yr., Wal-Mart, Columbia. Mem.: NEA, Adair County Edn. Assn., Ky. Edn. Assn. Methodist. Avocation: farming. Office: Adair County Board of Education 526 Indian Dr Columbia KY 42728

**RELL, M. JODI,** governor; b. Norfolk, Va., June 16, 1946; m. Lou Rell; children: Meredith, Michael. Student, Old Dominion U., Western Conn. State U.; LLD (hon.), Univ. of Hartford, 2001. Mem., dep. minority leader Conn. Ho. Reps., 1984-94; lt. gov. State of Conn., 1995—2004, gov., 2004—. Past vice chmn. Brookfield Rep. Town Com., appt. chair of the Hartford Econ. Devel. Adv. Group, (HEDAG), 1998; trustee YMCA Western Conn.; played a key role in raising funds for the Conn. Firefighters Meml.; estab. the Lt. Gov.'s Comm. on State Mandate Reform, Lt. Gov.'s Conn. Treasures award. Named Melvin Jones Fellow, Lions Club Internat. Found., 2003; recipient Leadership award, Nat. Order of Women Legislators (NOWL), Impact award, Conn. Tech. Coun., 2001, First Kids 2001 Policy Leadership award, Conn. Voices for Children, Arnold Markle Public Service award. Mem. Nat. Order Women Legislators (past nat. pres., former v.p., treas., corr. sec.), Women Execs. in State Govt., Brookfield Rep. Women's Club (past pres.), Brookfield Bus. and Profl. Women's Club, Prison and Jail Overcrowding comm., Governor's Law Enforcement Coun., Yale Corp., State Finance Advisory Com. Republican. Office: Office Gov Exec Chambers 210 Capitol Ave Hartford CT 06106 E-mail: Governor.Rell@po.state.ct.us.*

**RELLE, FERENC MATYAS,** chemist; b. Gyor, Hungary, June 13, 1922; came to U.S., 1951, naturalized, 1956; s. Ferenc and Elizabeth (Netratics) R.; m. Gertrud B. Tubach, Oct. 9, 1946; children: Ferenc, Ava, Attila. BSChemE, MS, Jozsef Nador Poly. U., Budapest, Hungary, 1944. Lab. mgr. Karl Kohn Ltd. Co., Landshut, Germany, 1947-48; resettlement officer Internat. Refugee Orgn., Munich, 1948-51; chemist Farm Bur. Coop. Assn., Columbus, Ohio, 1951-56; indsl. engr. N.Am. Aviation, Inc., Columbus, 1956-57; rsch. chemist Keever Starch Co., Columbus, 1957-65, Ross Labs. divsn. Abbott Labs., Columbus, 1965-70, rsch. scientist, 1970-89; cons. in field. Congl. sci. counselor, 1971—81. Chmn. Columbus and Ctrl. Ohio UNWeek, 1963; pres. Berwick Manor Civic Assn., 1968; trustee Stelios Stelson Found., 1968-69; deacon Brookwood Presbyn. Ch., 1963-65, 92-93, trustee, 1990-91. Decorated knight St. Ladislaus Order, Am. Chem. Soc. (emeritus; alt. councilor 1973, chmn. long range planning com. Columbus sect. 1972-76, 78-80), Am. Assn. Cereal Chemists (life; chmn. Cin. sect. 1974-75), Ohio Acad. Sci., Arpad Acad. (gold medal mem.), Internat. Tech. Inst. (adv. dir. 1977-82), Nat. Intercollegiate Soccer Ofcls. Assn., Am. Hungarian Assn., Hungarian Cultural Assn. (pres. 1978-81), Ohio Soccer Ofcls. Assn., Columbus Mannerchor, Germania Singing and Sport Soc., Civitan (gov. Ohio dist. 1970-71, dist. treas. 1982-83, pres. Ea. Columbus 1963-64, 72-73, gen. sec. for Hungary 1991-92, Ea. European growth mgr. 1993-94, amb. at large 1994—, established 1st Civitan club in Hungary 1991, Ukraine, 1992, Slovakia 1994, Internat. Gov. of Yr. award 1971, Internat. Honor Key 1992, Internat. Found. fellow 2000, master club builder award 1992, various other awards), World Fedn. Hungarian Engrs. Home and Office: 2983 Melford Rd Upper Arlington OH 43221-2822

**RELMAN, ARNOLD SEYMOUR,** physician, educator, editor; b. NYC, June 17, 1923; s. Simon and Rose (Mallach) Relman; m. Harriet Morse Vitkin, June 26, 1953; children: David Arnold, John Peter, Margaret Rose. AB, Cornell U., 1943; MD, Columbia U., 1946; LLD (hon.), U. Pa.; ScD (hon.), Med. Coll. Wis., Union U., Med. Coll. Ohio, CUNY; DMSc (hon.), Brown U.; DLH (hon.), SUNY; LittD (hon.), Temple U. Diplomate Am. Bd. Internal Medicine. House officer New Haven Hosp., Yale, 1946—49; NRC fellow Evans Meml., Mass. Meml. hosps., 1949—50; practice medicine, specializing in internal medicine Boston, 1950—68, Phila., 1968—77; asst. prof., prof. medicine Boston U. Sch. Medicine, 1950—68; dir. Boston U. Med. Services, Boston City Hosp., 1967—68; prof. medicine, chmn. dept. medicine U. Pa.; chief med. services Hosp. of U. Pa., 1968—77; editor New Eng. Jour. Medicine, Boston, 1977—91, editor emeritus, 1991—; sr. physician Brigham and Women's Hosp., Boston, 1977—; prof. medicine and social medicine Harvard Med. Sch., 1977—93, prof. medicine and social medicine emeritus 1993—95, prof. emeritus 1995—. Cons. NIH, USPHS; mem. bd. registration in medicine Commonwealth of Mass., 1995—2001. Editor: Jour. Clin. Investigation, 1962—67; editor: (with F.J. Ingelfinger and M. Finland) Controversy in Internal Medicine, Vol. 1, 1966, Controversy in Internal Medicine, Vol. 2, 1974; contbr. articles to profl. jours. Trustee Columbia U., 1990—96; bd. dirs. Hastings Ctr., 1981—83. Recipient Columbia Alumni Gold medal, 1980, Disting. Svc. award, Am. Coll. Cardiology, 1987, McGovern award, Cosmos Club Washington, 1991, John Peters award, Am. Soc. Nephrology, 1992, George Polk award in journalism, 2003. Master: ACP (John Phillips medal 1985); fellow: Am. Acad. Arts and Scis.; mem.: AMA, Am. Fedn. Clin. Rsch. (past pres.), Am. Soc. Clin. Investigation (past pres.), Inst. of Medicine of NAS (coun. 1979—82), Mass. Med. Soc., Am. Physiol. Soc., Assn. Am. Physicians (coun., pres. 1983—84, Kober medal 1993), Alpha Omega Alpha, Phi Beta Kappa (senator 1991—98). Office: Brigham and Women's Hosp Dept Medicine 181 Longwood Ave Fl 5 Boston MA 02115-5804

**RELWANI, NIRMAL MURLIDHAR (NICK RELWANI),** mechanical engineer; b. Bombay, Aug. 9, 1954; came to the U.S., 1976; m. Prema Vasandani; children: Karuna, Daksh. BS in Mech. Engring., U. Baroda, 1976; student, U. Nebr., 1977-78; MS in Mech. Engring., U. Wis., Milw., 1980. Registered profl engr., Wis., Ill. Rsch. asst. dept. mech. engring. U. Nebr., Lincoln, 1978; design engr. Allis Chalmers Corp., Milw., 1978-80; engring. cons. Bombay, 1980-86; assoc. engr. IIT Rsch. Inst., Chgo., 1986; mech. engr. Gen. Energy Corp., Oak Park, Ill., 1987-89, Arrowhead Environ. Control, Chgo., 1989-90; environ. engr. Ill. Dept. Pub. Health, Bellwood, 1990-92; sr. environ. protection engr. field ops. sect. bur. air Ill. EPA, Maywood, 1992—. Recipient Cert. of appreciation Ill. EPA, 1993, 94. Mem. ASME, ASHRAE (energy conservation award 1991), Assn. Energy Engrs. (sr.). Home: 1806 Marne Rd (River Bend) Bolingbrook IL 60490-4589 Office: Ill EPA 9511 W Harrison St Des Plaines IL 60016 Office Phone: 847-294-4030.

**RELYEA, CARL MILLER,** retired hydrologist; b. Claverack, NY, Dec. 29, 1912; s. Charles Miller Croswell and Edna (Pulver) R.; m. Harriet Watson, Sept. 6, 1946 (dec. Nov. 1982); children: Richard, Deborah, Cornelia. Grad., Inst. Musical Art, 1933; AB, Columbia Coll., 1935; MA, Columbia U., 1938; postgrad., MIT, 1943. Organist, choirmaster Morrow Meml. Ch., Maplewood, NJ, 1937-41; meteorologist Air Corps, Pan Am., Weather Bur., Bermuda, 1946-48, Weather Bur., JFK Internat. Airport, NJ, 1948-50; hydrologist Ohio River Forecast Ctr., Cin., 1950-65, hydrologist-in-charge, 1965-77; ret., 1977; dep. dir. Hamilton County Emergency Mgmt. Agy., Cin., 1979-2000. Contbr. articles to profl. jours. Organist Highland United Meth. Ch., Fort Thomas, Ky., 1962-99, now organist emeritus; clk. of vestry Grace Episcopal Ch., Cin. Capt. U.S. Army Air Corps, 1943-46. Recipient Pub. Svc. cert. Hamilton County Disaster Coun., Cin., 1990. Mem. Ret. Engrs. and Scientists Cin. (chmn. 1984-86), N.Y. Acad. Scis., Columbia U. Club N.Y., Downtown Kiwanis Club. Republican. Avocations: travel, music, organist, home maintenance. Home: 1346 Teakwood Ave Cincinnati OH 45224-2126

**RELYEA, HAROLD CLARENCE,** political scientist, writer; b. Oneida, N.Y., Apr. 5, 1944; s. Clyde Frederick and Pauline Elizabeth R.; children: Jennifer L., Stephen F. AB, Drew U., 1966; PhD, American U., 1971. Specialist in Am. nat. govt. Congrl. Rsch. Svc. Libr. Congress, Washington, 1971—. Author: A Brief History of Emergency Powers in the United States, 1974, The Evolution and Organization of the Federal Intelligence Function: A Brief Overview 1776-1975, 1988, Silencing Silence: National Security Controls and Scientific Communication, 1994; co-author: Presidential Staffing-A Brief Overview, 1978, United States Government Information: Policies and Sources, 2002; editor, contbg. author: The Presidency and Information Policy, 1981, Striking a Balance: National Security and Scientific Freedom, 1985, The Executive Office of the President, 1997; co-editor, contbg. author: Freedom of Information Trends in the Information Age, 1983, United States Government Information Policies: Views and Perspectives, 1989, Comparative Perspectives on E-Government, 2006; bd. editors Presdl. Studies Quar., 1979-99, Govt. Publs. Rev., 1981-83, Transnational Data Report, 1982-89, Jour. Media Law and Practice, 1982-95, Govt. Info. Quar., 1984-, Internat. Jour. E-Govt. Rsch., 2004-, Jour. E-Govt., 2001-; contbr. articles to profl. jours. Mem. adv. bd. Coll. Info. Studies, U. Md., 2004—. Named Expert's Expert on U.S. Freedom Info. Act, The Economist of London, 1981; recipient Exec. Bd. award for superior pub. svc. Am. Soc. Access Profls., 1983, The Best of 1983 award for essay selection Libr. Lit. 14, 1984, Blue Pencil award Nat. Assn. Govt. Communicators, 1984; named to Freedom of Info. Act Hall of Fame, Freedom Forum, 1996. Mem. Pi Sigma Alpha. Office: Libr Congress CRS 101 Independence Ave SE Washington DC 20540-7470

**REMAR, ROBERT BOYLE,** lawyer; b. Boston, Nov. 19, 1948; s. Samuel Roy and Elizabeth Mary (Boyle) R.; m. Victoria A. Greenhood, Nov. 11, 1979; children: Daniel A.G., William B.G. BA, U. Mass., 1970; JD, Boston Coll., 1974. Bar: Ga. 1974, Mass. 1975, U.S. Ct. Appeals (5th cir.) 1978, U.S. Ct. Appeals (11th cir.) 1981, U.S. Ct. Appeals (2d cir.) 1995, U.S. Supreme Ct. 1981. Staff atty. Ga. Legal Svcs. Program, Savannah, 1974-76, Western Mass. Legal Svcs., Greenfield, 1976-77; sr. staff atty. Ga. Legal Svcs. Program, Atlanta, 1977-82; ptnr. Remar & Graettinger, Atlanta, 1983-95, Kirwan, Parks, Chesin & Remar PC, Atlanta, 1993-96, Rogers & Hardin, Atlanta, 1996—. V.p., mem. exec. com., bd. dirs ACLU, N.Y.C., pres. Ga. chpt., 1985-87, gen. counsel, 1980-83; hearing officer Ga. Pub. Svc. Commn., Atlanta, 1985-98; adj. prof. Ga. State U., Atlanta, 1984-98, spl. asst. atty. gen., 1990-2003; bd. experts Lawyers Alert, Boston, 1985-94; bd. dirs. Fed. Defender Program. Mem. Ga. Energy Regulatory Reform Commn., Gov. of Ga., 1980-82, Ga. Consumer Adv. Bd., 1981-82, City Atl. Bd. Ethics, AAA Comml. Panel; pres. Ga. Consumer Ctr. Inc., 1988-91; bd. dirs., exec. com. Ga. Resource Ctr.; v.p Ga Ctr. Law Pub. Inst., 1991-94; bar coun. U.S.D.C. N.D.G., 1996-99. Fellow Am. Coll. Trial Lawyers; mem. ABA (chmn. individual rights access to civil justice com. 1988-99), Ga. Bar Assn. (chmn. individual rights sect. 1981-83, co-chmn. consumer rights and remedies com. 1979-83, chmn. death penalty re. com. 1993—, mem. legis. adv. com. 1994-97, mem. indigent def. com. 2000—), Atlanta Bar Assn., Lawyers Club Atlanta, Lamar Inn of Ct. (master of the bench). Democrat. Avocations: golf, gardening. Home: 1714 Meadowdale Ave NE Atlanta GA 30306-3114 Office: Rogers & Hardin Internat Tower Peachtree Ctr 229 Peachtree St NE Ste 2700 Atlanta GA 30303-1638 Office Phone: 404-420-4031. Business E-Mail: RBR@RH-LAW.COM.

**REMBOLT, JAMES EARL,** lawyer; b. Nov. 13, 1943; s. Earl Lester and Dorothy Elouise (Mehring) Rembolt; m. Marilyn Sue Schmadeke, July 16, 1972; children: Tami Anne, Michelle Sue. BBA, U. Nebr., 1965; MA in Bus. Orgn. and Mgmt., 1967, JD with distinction, 1972. Bar: Nebr. 1972, U.S. Dist. Ct. Nebr. 1972, U.S. Tax Ct. 1978, U.S. Ct. Claims 1978. Pres. Nebr. Moot Ct. Bd., 1972; pilot Nebr. Air Nat. Guard, Lincoln, 1969-74; lecr. legal writing U. Nebr. Coll. Law, 1973-74; ptnr. Rembolt, Ludtke LLP, Lincoln, 1976—. Chmn. bd. trustees YWCA, Lincoln, 1982—83; mem., past pres. Lincoln/Lancaster Sr. Ctrs. Found., Inc., bd. dirs., 1988—90; mem., past chair bd. dirs. Madonna Found., Inc., 1989—91; trustee, past bd. dirs. U.Nebr. Found.; past bd. dirs., pres. Nebr. Continuing Legal Edn., Inc.; bd. elders Eastridge Presbyn. Ch., Lincoln, 1979—82. Fellow: ABA, Nebr. State Bar Found., Am. Coll. Trust and Estate Counsel; mem.: Lincoln Estate Planning Coun. (past pres.), Lincoln Probate Discussion Group (charter mem.), Nebr. State Bar Assn. (pres. 2002—03, ho. of dels.), Lincoln Bar Assn., U. Nebr. Lincoln Coll. Bus. Adminstrn. Alumni Assn. (past pres.). Office: Rembolt Ludtke LLP 1201 Lincoln Mall Ste 102 Lincoln NE 68508-2839 Office Phone: 402-475-5100. E-mail: jrembolt@remboltludtke.com.

**REMEK, ROBERT THOMAS,** music educator, church musician; b. Erie, Pa., Nov. 26, 1960; s. Anthony T. and Mildred E. Remek; m. Mary Jo Schlichte, Dec. 26, 1989. BS in Computer Sci. magna cum laude, Fla. Internat. U., 1990; MusB in Piano Performance magna cum laude, U. Miami, 1983, MusM in Choral Conducting, 1986, D of Musical Arts in Organ Performance, 2002. Dir. music, organist Ch. of St. Martha, Miami Shores, Fla., 1985—89, Immaculate Conception Ch., Hialeah, Fla., 1989—94, Resurrection Cath. Ch., Dania, Fla., 1994—98; adj. prof. Miami Dade Coll., 1994—; dir. music and organist 1st United Meth. Ch. of Miami, 1998—; organ prof., univ. carillonneur U. Miami, Coral Gables, 2000—. Organist Visit of Pope John Paul II, Miami, 1987. Recipient Grad. Sch. award of merit, U. Miami, 2002, Sch. of Music award for outstanding music student, U. Miami Sch. of Music, 1983; Presdl. scholar, U. Miami, 1978—82, grad. fellow, 1984—86. Mem.: AAUP (corr.), Am. Guild English Handbell Ringers (corr.), Am. Guild Organists (assoc.; dean Ft. Lauderdale chpt. 1998—2000, colleague 1990, associateship 1994, choirmaster 1995), Am. Choral Dirs. Assn. (life). Republican. Roman Catholic. Avocations: travel, art galleries, church architecture. Home: 8841 Southern Orchard Rd S Davie FL 33328 Office: 1st United Meth Ch of Miami 400 Biscayne Blvd Miami FL 33132

**REMELE, LEWIS ALBERT, JR.,** lawyer; b. Mpls., Nov. 25, 1948; s. Lewis Albert Sr. and Mary Elizabeth (Ryan) R.; m. Constance Ann Bauser, June 26, 1982; 1 child, Lewis Albert III. BA magna cum laude, Harvard U., 1970; JD cum laude, Creighton U., 1975. Bar: Minn. 1975, U.S. Dist. Ct. Minn. 1976, U.S. Ct. Appeals (8th cir.) 1978, U.S. Supreme Ct. 2004. Law clk. Judge Miles W. Lord, U.S. Dist. Ct., Minn., Mpls., 1975-77; assoc. Simonson & Bartsh, Mpls., 1977-78; ptnr. Rider, Bennett, Egan & Arundel, Mpls., 1978-88; ptnr., gen. & comml. litig., past CEO Bassford, Lockhart, Truesdell & Briggs (now Bassford Remele), Mpls., 1989—. Mem. bd. dir. & vol. atty. Legal Advice Clinics; dir. Pillsbury Neighborhood Svcs; trustee William Mitchell Coll. Law 2001-. Named Minn. Super Lawyer, Mpls. St. Paul mag. & Minn. Law & Politics mag., 2000-04. Fellow Am Bar Found., Am. Bd. Trial Advocates, Am. Coll. Trial Lawyers; mem. ABA, Minn. Bar Assn. (sec. 1992-93, treas. 1993-94, pres. 1995-96), Hennepin County Bar Assn. (pres. 1989-90, sec. 1986-87, treas. 1987-88), Hennepin County Bar Found. (dir. 1986-), Def. Rsch. Inst., Minn. Def. Lawyers Assn., Harvard & Radcliffe Club Minn. (pres. 1984-85). Office: Bassford Remele Ste 3800 33 S 6th St Minneapolis MN 55402 Office Phone: 612-376-1601. Office Fax: 612-333-8829. Business E-Mail: lewr@bassford.com.

**REMENGESAU, THOMAS, JR.,** Palauan government official; b. Koror, Palau, Feb. 28, 1956; married; 4 children. BS in Criminology, Grand Valley State U., 1979; postgrad., Mich. State U., 1979-81. Legal rschr. Fed. Dist. Ct., Saipan, No. Mariana Islands, 1981; health planner, adminstrn. officer Govt. of Palau, 1982; pub. info. officer Palau Nat. Congress, 1983; senator Second & Third Olbiil Era Kelulau, 1984-92; chmn. ways and means com.; v.p., min. adminstrn. rep. Repub. of Palau Nat. Govt., 1992—2000; president of Palau, 2000—. Chmn. Palau/Micronesia Olympic Games Com., 1990, Compact of Free Assn. Transition Commn., 1994; mem. Presdl. Task Force on Polit. Status Negotiations with USA Govt., 1991; chmn. Palau Sports Commn., 1994—, chmn. disaster plan task force, 1996—; Palau rep. Internat. Monetary Fund, 1998—. Office: Office of Pres PO Box 100 Palau PW 96940-0100

**REMER, DEBORAH JANE,** elementary school educator; b. Detroit, Dec. 10, 1953; d. Maynard William and Marie Josephine (Wells) Remer. BS, Mich. State U., 1976, MA in Tchg., 1977. Secondary provisional tchg. cert. Mich., secondary continuing tchg. cert. Mich. Sci. tchr. Walled Lake (Mich.) Mid. Sch., 1977-81; substitute tchr. Utica (Mich) Cmty. Schs., 1981-85; sci. tchr. Kingsbury Sch., Oxford, Mich., 1985-86; sci. tchr., sci. dept. chair Walled Lake Consol. Schs., 1986—. Chair 8th grade sci. fair Walled Lake Mid. Sch., 1987, 1989—, coach sci. competition, 1987—94; mem. K-12 sci. com. Walled Lake Consol. Schs., 1990—. Co-author: Environmental Conservation Program Design, 1996; author: The Joachim Ernest Theodore Remer Family in Michigan, 1980, revised, 1995. Archaeology program presenter, pianist Rochester Mills (Mich.) Mus., 1988—, co-dir. archaeology programs 1989—; tallykeeper Rochester Grangers Vintage Baseball Team. Named winner in conservation, Mich. 4-H Clubs, 1971; recipient Key Club award, 1972, Earl Borden Hist. Preservation award, City of Rochester Hills Hist.

---

Dist. Commn., 1995. Mem.: MADD, NEA, Nat. Trust Hist. Presevation, Oakland County Pioneer and Hist. Soc., Detroit Zool. Soc., Mich. Archeol. Soc., Nat. Wildflower Rsch. Ctr., Archeol. Inst. Am., N.Am. Butterfly Assn., New Eng. Hist. Geneal. Soc., Suffolk County (N.Y.) Hist. and Geneal. Soc., Rochester Avon (Mich.) Hist. Soc. (rec. sec. 1990), Hist. Soc. Mich., Met. Detroit Sci. Tchrs. Assn. (conf. presenter 1993—94), Mich. Sci. Tchrs. Assn. (mem. mid. sch. program com. 1977—81, dir.-at-large 1981, conf. presenter 1993—95), Mich. Earth Sci. Tchrs. Assn., Walled Lake Edn. Assn., Mich. Edn. Assn., Nat. Earth Sci. Tchrs. Assn., Nat. Sci. Tchrs. Assn., Am. Livestock Breeds Conservancy, Mich. Karst Conservancy, Colonial Williamsburg Found., Bat Conservation Internat., Earthwatch, Cranbrook Inst. Sci., Macomb Audubon Soc., Smithsonian Assocs., Founders Soc.-Detroit Inst. Arts, Mich. State U. Alumni Assn., Soc. Preservation Old Mills, Archeol. Conservancy, Alpha Zeta. Republican. Congregationalist. Avocations: archaeology, gardening, reading, music, needlecrafts. Office: Walled Lake Middle Sch 46720 W Pontiac Trl Walled Lake MI 48390-4048 Office Phone: 248-956-2942. Business E-Mail: remerd@walledlake.k12.mi.us.

**REMICK, FORREST JEROME, JR.,** former university official; b. Lock Haven, Pa., Mar. 16, 1931; s. Forrest Jerome Sr. and Ruth Betsy (Saiers) R.; m. Grace Louise Grove, June 7, 1953; children: Beth Ann Remick Gillio, Eric Forrest; m. Soon Ja Cho, Dec. 8, 1995. BSME, Pa. State U., 1955, MSME, 1958, PhD in ME, 1963; diploma, Oak Ridge Sch. Reactor Tech., Tenn., 1956. Engr. Bell Telephone Labs., Whippany, NJ, 1955—56; dir. nuclear reactor facility Pa. State U., University Park, 1959—65, dir. Inst. Sci. Engring., 1967—79, acting dir. Ctr. Air Environ. Studies, 1976—78, dir. intercoll. research programs, 1979—85, asst. v.p. research, grad. studies, 1979—84, assoc. v.p. research, 1985—89; dir. Curtiss Wright Nuclear Research Lab., Quehanna, Pa., 1960—65; chief tng. sect. dept. tech. assistance IAEA, Vienna, 1965—66. Mem. Nat. Nuclear Accrediting Bd., Inst. Nuclear Power Ops., Atlanta, mem. adv. coun., 1995—; mem. Sci. Adv. Com. Idaho Nat. Engring. Lab., Idaho Falls, 1984-89, Reactor Safety Adv. Com., Savannah River Lab., Aiken, S.C., 1986-89, chmn., 1989; mem. Adv. Com. on Reactor Safeguards, Washington, 1982, vice chmn., 1987-88, chmn., 1989; commr. U.S. Nuclear Regulatory Commn., 1989-94, cons., 1994—; bd. dir. Pub. Svc. Enterprise Group, Pub. Svc. Electric and Gas, 1995-2001; mem. adv. bd. Applied Rsch. Lab., Pa. State U., 1994-97. Served to capt. U.S. Army, 1951-52. Named Outstanding Engring. Alumnus, Pa. State U., 1993; recipient Thomas P. Hamrick award for contbns. to tng. of nuclear facility pers., 1995. Fellow Am. Nuclear Soc. (bd. dir. 1995-98, meml. lectr. award 1971, disting. speaker award 1983); mem. ASME, Am. Soc. Engring. Edn., Nuclear Accrediting Bd. Republican. Lutheran. Home and Office: Canterbury Crossing 439 Brandywine Dr State College PA 16801-7984

**REMIEN, NATALIE A.,** lawyer; b. Evanston, Ill., Oct. 25, 1974; BSBA, Univ. Colo., Boulder, 1996; JD, DePaul Univ., Chgo., 1999. Atty. Baker & Enright, Chgo., 1999—2000; assoc. counsel Ty Inc., Westmont, 2000—02; atty. Welsh & Katz Ltd., Chgo., 2002—. Mem.: Nat. Assn.Womens Bus. Owners (com. mem. 2004—05, com. co-chair 2005—06), Profl. Womens Club Chgo. (com. mem. 2006—). Avocations: running, triathlons. Office: Welsh & Katz Ltd 120 S Riverside Plaza 22nd Fl Chicago IL 60606

**REMINE, WILLIAM HERVEY, JR.,** retired surgeon; b. Richmond, Va., Oct. 11, 1918; s. William Hervey and Mabel Leeu (Walthall) ReM.; m. Doris Irene Grumbacher, June 9, 1943; children: William H., Stephen Gordon, Walter James, Gary Craig. BS in Biology, U. Richmond, 1940, D.Sc. (hon.), 1965; MD, Med. Coll. Va., Richmond, 1943; MS in Surgery, U. Minn., Mpls., 1952. Diplomate Am. Bd. Surgery. Intern Doctor's Hosp., Washington, 1944; fellow in surgery Mayo Clinic, Rochester, Minn., 1944-45, 47-52; instr. surgery Mayo Grad. Sch. Medicine, Rochester, Minn., 1954-59, asst. prof. surgery, 1959-65, assoc. prof. surgery, 1965-70, prof. surgery, 1970-83, prof. surgery emeritus, 1983—. Surg. cons. to surgeon gen. U.S. Army, 1965-75; surg. lectr., USSR, 1987, 89, Japan, 1988, 90, Egypt, 1990; lectr. Soviet-Am. seminars, USSR, 1987, 89. Sr. author: Cancer of the Stomach, 1964, Manual of Upper Gastro-intestinal Surgery, 1985; editor: Problems in General Surgery, Surgery of the Biliary Tract, 1986; mem. editorial bd. Rev. Surgery, 1965-75, Jour. Lancet, 1968-77; contbr. 200 articles to profl. jours. Served to capt. U.S. Army, 1945-47 Recipient St. Francis surg. award St. Francis Hosp., Pitts., 1976, Disting. Svc. award Alumni Coun., U. Richmond, 1976, Dist. Alumnus award Mayo Found.; Priestley Soc. Mayo Clinic Surg. Alumni Legacy award, 2004. Mem. ACS, AAAS, Am. Assn. History of Medicine, AMA, Am. Med. Writers Assn., Am. Soc. Colon and Rectal Surgeons, Soc. Surgery Alimentary Tract (v.p. 1983-84), Am. Surg. Assn., Assn. Mil. Surgeons U.S., Internat. Soc. Surgery, Digestive Disease Found., Priestley Soc. (pres. 1968-69, Legacy award 2004), Central Assn. Physicians and Dentists (pres. 1972-73), Central Surg. Assn., Soc. Med. Cons. Armed Forces, Mayo Clinic Surg. Soc. (chmn. 1964-66), Soc. Head and Neck Surgeons, Soc. Surg. Oncology, So. Surg. Assn., Western Surg. Assn. (pres. 1979-80), Minn. State Med. Assn., Minn. Surg. Soc. (pres. 1966-67), Zumbro Valley Med. Soc., Sigma Xi; hon. mem. Colombian Coll. Surgeons, St. Paul Surg. Soc., Flint Surg. Soc., Venezuelan Surg. Soc., Colombian Soc. Gastroenterology, Dallas So. Clin. Soc., Ga. Surg. Soc., Soc. Postgrad. Surgeons Los Angeles County, Japanese Surg. Soc., Argentine Surg. Digestive Soc., Bassanese Surg. Assn. (Italy), Tex. Surg. Soc., Mayo Clinic Surg. Alum Assn., Omicron Delta Kappa, Alpha Omega Alpha, Beta Beta Beta, Kappa Sigma (pres. 1939-40). Methodist. Avocations: hunting, fishing, golf, photography, boating, music. Home: Sawgrass Players Club 8212 Seven Mile Dr Ponte Vedra Beach FL 32082-3129

**REMINGER, RICHARD THOMAS,** lawyer, artist; b. Cleve., Apr. 3, 1931; s. Edwin Carl and Theresa Henrietta (Bookmyer) Reminger; m. Billie Carmen Greer, June 26, 1954; children: Susan Greer, Patricia Allison, Richard Thomas. AB, Case Western Res. U., 1950, JD, Ohio State U., 1957. Bar: Ohio 1957, Pa. 1978, U.S. Supreme Ct. 1961. Pers. and safety dir. Motor Express, Inc., Cleve., 1954-58; founder, mng. ptnr. Reminger & Reminger Co., L.P.A., Cleve., 1958-90. Mem. nat. claims coun. adv. bd. Comml. Union Assurance Co., 1980—90; lectr. transp. law Fenn Coll., 1960—62; lectr. bus. law Case Western Res. U., 1962—64; lectr. products liability U. Wirtschaft at Schloss Gracht, Erfstadt-Liblar, Germany, 1990—91, Bar Assn. City of Hamburg, Germany, 1990; mem. faculty Nat. Inst. Trial Advocacy, 1992. Trustee Cerebral Palsy Assn., 1984—87, Andrew Sch., 1984—94, Meridia Huron Hosp., Cleve., 1978—96, Cleve. Sch. Blind, 1987—88, Intracoastal Health Sys., Palm Beach, Fla., 1992—2000; mem. joint com. Cleve. Acad. Medicine-Greater Cleve. Bar Assn.; v.p. Cleve. Zool. Soc., 1984—87. With AC USNR, 1950—58. Mem.: FBA, ABA (profl. responsiblity com. 1977—90, com. law and medicine), Palm Beach County Bar Assn., Internat. Ins. Law Soc., Am. Coll. Law and Medicine, Maritime Law Assn., Def. Rsch. Inst., Am. Judicature Soc., Ohio Assn. Civil Trial Attys., Soc. Ohio Hosp. Attys., Am. Soc. Hosp. Attys., Cleve. Assn. Civil Trial Attys., Transp. Lawyers Assn., Cleve. Bar Assn. (profl. liability com. 1977—90, chmn. med. legal com. 1978—79), Pa. Bar Assn., Ohio Bar Assn. (coun. dels. 1987—90, internat. law com. 1990—91), Internat. Bar Assn., Fedn. Ins. and Corp. Counsel, 8th Jud. Bar Assn. (life), Internat. Soc. Marine Painters (v.p.), Oil Painters Am., Soc. Four Arts, Cleve.-Marshall Law Alumni Assn. (hon. trustee 1980—), Univ. Club (N.Y.C.), Salmagundi Club (N.Y.C.), Rolling Rock Club (Pa.), Kirtland Country Club (Cleve.), Everglades Club (Fla.), Lost Tree Club (Fla.) (bd. govs. 1991—94), Hermit Club (Cleve.) (pres. 1973—75), Mayfield Country Club (Cleve.) (pres. 1980—82), Case Res. Athletic Club (life). Office: Reminger & Reminger Co LPA 1400 Midland Bldg 101 Prospect Ave W Cleveland OH 44115-1093

**REMINGTON, DEBORAH WILLIAMS,** artist; b. Haddonfield, N.J., June 25, 1935; d. Malcolm Van Dyke and Hazel Irwin (Stewart) R. BFA, San Francisco Art Inst., 1955. Adj. prof. art Cooper Union, N.Y.C., 1973—97, NYU, 1994—98; tchr. Nat. Acad. Design, N.Y.C., 2003, 65. One-woman shows include Dilexi Gallery, San Francisco, 1962, 63, 65, San Francisco Mus. Art, 1964, Bykert Gallery, N.Y.C., 1967, 69, 72, 74, Galerie Darthea Speyer, Paris, 1968, 71, 73, 92, Pyramid Gallery, Washington DC, 1973, 76, zola-Leiberman Gallery, Chgo., 1976, Hamilton Gallery, N.Y.C., 1977, Portland (Oreg.) Ctr. for Visual Arts, 1977, Michael Berger Gallery, Pitts.,

---

1979, Mary Ryan Gallery, N.Y.C., 1982, Ramon Osuna Gallery, Washington D.C., 1983, Newport Harbor Art Mus., 1983, Oakland (Calif.) Mus., 1984, Jack Shainman Gallery, N.Y.C., 1987, Shoshana Wayne Gallery, L.A., 1988, Mitchell Algus Gallery, N.Y.C., 2001; group shows include Whitney Mus. Am. Art, N.Y.C., 1965, 67, 72, San Francisco Mus. Art, 1956, 60, 61, 63, 64, 65, Lausanne Mus., Switz., 1966, Fondation Maeght, St. Paul de Vence, France, 1968, Smithsonian Am. Art Mus., Washington, D.C., 1968, Art Inst., Chgo., 1974, Inst. Contemporary Art, Boston, 1975, Nat. Gallery Modern Art, Lisbon, Portugal, 1981, Toledo Mus. Art, 1975, The 6 Gallery, 1954-57, Natsoulas Gallery, Davis, Calif., 1990, 1st Trienale des Ameriques Maubeuge, France, 1993, Tamarind Inst. Retrospective, 2000, Worcester (Mass.) Art Mus., 2001, San Jose (Calif.) Mus. Art, 2002, numerous others; represented in permanent collections Whitney Mus. Am. Art, Smithsonian Am. Art Mus., Washington, Art Inst., Chgo., Centre d'Art et de Culture Georges Pompidou, Paris, Carnegie Mus., Pitts. Recipient Hassam and Speicher Purchase award Am. Acad. and Inst. Arts and Letters, 1988; NEA fellow, 1979-80; Tamarind Inst. fellow, 1973; Guggenheim fellow, 1984; Pollock-Krasner Found. grantee, 1999. Mem. NAD (Benjamin Altman prize for painting 178th Ann. Exhbn. 2003). Home: 309 W Broadway New York NY 10013-5325 Office Phone: 212-925-3037. Office Fax: 212-426-1711. E-mail: deborahremington@aol.com. *Be aware of yourself, aware of what makes you distinctive from others, and make those individual characteristics part of your work, whatever that may be. Read philosophy. Develop your own. This gives you ballast when the pendulum swings too far in one direction.*

**REMINGTON, MARY,** artist, author; b. Kansas City, Mo., Jan. 15, 1930; d. Edwin Jennings and Mary Pauline (Remington) Anderson; m. Robert Alan Smith, Dec. 14, 1957 (div. 1978); 1 child, Susanah Mara Smith. BA, Ottawa (Kans.) U., 1951; postgrad., U. Kans., 1951, Kansas City Art Inst. Artist animation dept. Walt Disney Prodns., Burbank, Calif., 1954-58; pvt. cartoonist Calif., 1977-92; humor and cartooning tchr. Mira Costa Coll. Extension course, Calif., 1992; tchr. So. Oreg. U., 1993. Freelance cartoonist, caricaturist, Calif. Author: Long Ago Elf, 1968, Crocodiles Have Big Teeth All Day, 1970; one-woman show at Josephine County Main Libr., Grants Pass, Oreg., Adobe Gallery, San Diego County, Rogue Gallery, Medford, Oreg., Grants Pass Art Mus., Stiverhouse Gallery, Grants Pass, 2005, Firehouse Gallery, Grants Pass, Rogue CC, 2005; group exhibitions include Yosemite Mus. Gallery, Okla. Art Workshops 15th Nat. Exhbn., Tulsa, Wiseman Gallery, Grants Pass, Adobe Gallery, San Diego County, others; artist for animated films Lady and the Tramp, Sleeping Beauty. Mem. Grants Pass Art Museum. Avocations: history, reading. Office Phone: 541-899-0211.

**REMINI, LEAH,** actress; b. Bklyn., June 15, 1970; m. Angelo Pagan, July 19, 2003; 1 child, Sofia Bella. Appearances include (TV series) Living Dolls, 1989, Saved By The Bell, 1991, The Man in the Family, 1991, Getting Up and Going Home, 1992, King of Queens, 1999—, (voice) Gabriel Knight: Sins of the Fathers, 1994, (voice) Phantom 2040: The Ghost Who Walks, 1994, The First Time Out, 1995, Glory Daze, 1996, Fired Up, 1997, Follow Your Heart, 1998, also numerous guest appearances, including Head of the Class, 1988, Who's Boss?, 1989, Valerie, 1990, Paradise, 1991, Cheers, 1991 & 1993, Blossom, 1992, Evening Shade, 1993, The Commish, 1994, Renegade, 1994, Diagnosis Murder, 1995, Friends, 1995, NYPD Blue, 1996; TV Movies: Legend of the Lost Tribe, 2002 (voice), Hooves of Fire, 1999 (voice); Films: Follow Your Heart, 1998, Old School, 2003. Office: Gold Marchak & Liedtke 3500 W Olive Ave Ste 1400 Burbank CA 91505-5512

**REMINI, ROBERT VINCENT,** historian; b. NYC, July 17, 1921; s. William Francis and Lauretta (Tierney) R.; m. Ruth Theresa Kuhner, Oct. 9, 1948; children: Elizabeth Mary, Joan Marie, Robert William. BS, Fordham U., 1943; MA, Columbia U., 1947, PhD, 1951; LHD (hon.), Gov.'s State U., 1989; LittD (hon.), Ea. Ky. U., 1992, Fordham U., 1993, Columbia Coll. Chgo., 2000, So. Ill. U., 2004. Prof. History, emeritus prof. U. Ill. Chgo., 1965—, historian, 1997—, U.S. Ho. of Reps., 2005—. Vis. lectr. Columbia U., 1959-60. Author: Martin Van Buren and the Making of the Democratic Party, 1959, The Election of Andrew Jackson, 1963, Andrew Jackson, 1966, Andrew Jackson and the Bank War, 1968, The Revolutionary Age of Andrew Jackson, 1976 (award of merit Friends of Am. Writers), Andrew Jackson and the Course of American Empire, 1767-1821, 1977, Andrew Jackson and the Course of American Freedom, 1822-1832, vol. II, 1981 (George Washington medal of Honor, Freedoms Found.), Andrew Jackson and the Course of American Democracy, 1833-1845, vol. III, 1984 (Nat. Book award for non-fiction 1984, Chgo. Found. for Lit. award 1985, English Speaking Union U.S. Ambassador of Honor award 1985); The Legacy of Andrew Jackson: Essays on Democracy, Indian Removal and Slavery, 1988, The Life of Andrew Jackson (abridgement of 3-vol. biography), 1988 (Carl Sandburg Lit. award for non-fiction 1989), The Jacksonian Era, 1989, Henry Clay: Statesman for the Union, 1991 (award for biography Soc. Midland Authors 1992), The Battle of New Orleans, 1999, Andrew Jackson and His Indian Wars, 2001, (Am. Hist. Assn. award for scholarly dist., 2001, Western Writers of Am. award, 2002, John Hope Franklin Hist. Maker award, Chgo. Hist. Soc., 2003), John Quincy Adams, 2002, Joseph Smith, 2002 (Freedom award Capitol Hist. Soc. 2004), The House: The History of the House of Representatives, 2006; co-author: We the People: A History of the United States, 1975, The Era of Good Feelings and the Age of Jackson, 1816-1841, 1979, The American People: A History, 1981, Andrew Jackson: A Bibliography, 1991; also articles, chpts. in books.; editor: The Decline of Aristocracy in the Politics of New York, 1965, The Presidency of Andrew Jackson, 1967, The Age of Jackson, 1972; spl. editor Am. history, Crowell-Collier Co., 1960-68, 72-73; mem editl. bd. Jour. Am. History, 1969-72; editl. cons. Papers of Andrew Jackson, 1972—. Lt. USNR, 1943—46. Recipient Encaenia award Fordham U., 1963, Silver Circle award U. Ill., Chgo., 1981, Univ. Scholar award, 1986; grantee Am. Coun. Learned Socs., 1964, Am. Philos. Soc., 1966, 80; Guggenheim fellow, 1978-79. Mem. Am. Hist. Assn. (council 1979-82), So. Hist. Assn., Orgn. Am. Historians. Roman Catholic. Office: Univ Ill at Chgo Office of Historian 815 W Van Buren Chicago IL 60607*

**REMKUS, CONNIE ELAINE,** nutritional consultant; d. Charles Edward and Phyllis Mary Remkus. BSBA in Acctg., San Francisco State U., 1986. Registered nutritional cons. Sch. of Nutritional Sci., San Jose. Flight attendant United Air Lines, Chgo., 1966—2002; self-employed property and investment mgr. Chgo., 1973—2003; tax preparer David Nitz & Assocs., San Mateo, Calif., 1975; nutritional cons., ind. distbr. Diamite Corp., San Carlos, Calif., 1988—95; field v.p. Symmetry Direct, Chgo., 1995—. Mem. South Loop Neighbors, Chgo., 2001—05; vol. SPCA, San Mateo, 1984—87. Mem.: Airline Flight Attendants Union (membership chair grievance com. 1967—70), Bus. Networking Internat. (sec. 2001—03, asst. dir., amb. 2002—03). Avocations: travel, real estate, health and wellness. Office Phone: 312-455-2850.

**REMMELE, RICHARD L., JR.,** research scientist; s. Richard L. Remmele, Sr. and Esther Remmele. BS, Oral Roberts U., 1978; MS, Calif. Poly. U., Pomona, 1983; PhD, Ariz. State U., 1988. Postdoctoral fellowship Colo. State U., Fort Collins, 1988—93, Univ. of Colo. Sch. of Pharmacy, Denver, 1993; formulations chemist Immunex Corp., Seattle, 1993—2002; biotherapeutics formulations scientist Amgen, Thousand Oaks, Calif., 2002—. Editor: (rational protein drug design) Current Pharmaceutical Biotechnology; author: (book chpt.) Real-time infrared spectroscopic analysis of lysozyme during lyophilization, Microcalorimetric Approaches to Biopharmaceutical Development; contbr. articles to sci. jours. Recipient DAAD scholarship, Karlsruhe Tech. Inst. of Phys. and Electrochemistry. Mem.: AIChE, Am. Chem. Soc., Am. Assn. of Pharm. Sci., Phi Lambda Upsilon (treas. 1985—86), Alpha Chi Sigma. Achievements include patents for increased recovery of active proteins; Polypeptide Formulation; research in liquid formulation development using differential scanning calorimetry, Real-time in situ monitoring lysozyme during lyophilization using infrared spectroscopy; dehydration stress in the presence of sucrose; designing proteins that work using recombinant technologies, Biophysical characterization of a soluble CD40 ligand (CD154) coiled-coil trimer; low-temperature infrared spectroscopy reveals four stages of water loss during lyophilization of hen egg-white lysozyme. Office: Amgen One Amgen Center Dr Thousand Oaks CA 91320-1799 Office Phone: 805-447-5534. E-mail: remmeler@amgen.com.

**REMNICK, DAVID J.,** journalist, editor-in-chief; b. Hackensack, NJ, Oct. 29, 1958; s. Edward C. and Barbara (Seigel) Remnick; m. Esther B. Fein; children: Alexander, Noah, Natasha. BA in comparative lit., Princeton U., 1981. Reporter The Washington Post, 1982—88, Moscow (Russia) corr., 1988—92; staff writer The New Yorker, NYC, 1992—98, editor, 1998—. Author: (book) Lenin's Tomb: The Last Days of the Soviet Empire, 1993 (Pulitzer Prize for gen. non-fiction, 1994, George Polk award, 1994), Resurrection, 1997, The Devil Problem (and other True Stories), 1997, King of the World: Muhammad Ali and the Rise of an American Hero, 1998, Life Stories: Profiles from The New Yorker, 2000; Reporting: Writings from The New Yorker, 2006. Named Editor of Yr., Advt. Age Mag., 1999; recipient Livingston award, 1991, Helen Bernstein award, N.Y. Pub. Libr., 1994. Fellow: Am. Acad. Arts & Sciences. Office: The New Yorker 4 Times Sq New York NY 10036-6561 Office Phone: 212-286-5774.*

**REMPALA, GRZEGORZ A.,** mathematician, statistician, educator; b. Warsaw, Mar. 19, 1968; s. Jan and Ryszarda Rempala; m. Helena A. Hofmokl, 1991; children: Jas, Antos. PhD, Bowling Green State U., Ohio, 1996. Asst. prof. U. Louisville, Louisville, 1996—2002, assoc. prof., 2002—. Rsch. fellow Inst. Math. and Its Applications, Mpls., 2003—04, Duke U., Durham, NC, 2006—. Author: (articles) Annals of Applied Probability, Proceedings of AMS, Probability Theory and Related Fields. Grantee, NIH, 2005—, NSF, 2006—. Achievements include research in Applied Mathematics and Statistics. Office: Univ Louisville S Third St Louisville KY 40292 Office Phone: 502-852-6826. Business E-Mail: math@louisville.edu.

**REMPT, RODNEY P.,** career military officer, academic administrator; b. Burbank, Calif., June 13, 1945; married. BS, U.S. Naval Acad., 1966; MS in Sys. Analysis, Stanford U.; M.Security and Strategic Studies, Naval War Coll. Commd. ensign USN, advanced through grades to vice admiral; comdr. USS Antelope, Naples, Italy; exec. officer USS Dahlgren; initial project officer MK 41 vertical launch sys. Naval Sea Sys. Command; program coord. AEGIS weapons sys. Chief Naval Officer; adminstrv. asst., aide Vice Chief of Naval Ops.; comdr. USS Callaghan, USS Bunker Hill, Yokosuka, Japan; dir. PCO/PXO dept. Surface Warfare Officers Schs. Command, Newport, R.I.; dir. anti-air warfare requirements divs. Staff of Dep. Chief Naval Ops., Naval Warefare; head surface ships and combat sys. Staff of Chief of Naval Ops.; dir. Theater Air Def., 1994-96, program exec. officer, 1996-98; dep. asst. sec. theater combat sys. USN, Washington, 1998—2001; pres. Naval War Coll., Newport, RI, 2001—03; supt. U.S. Naval Acad., Annapolis, Md., 2003—. Decorated Disting. Svc. medal, Legion of Merit (3 awards), Meritorious Svc. medal (3 awards), Navy Commendation medal with combat V (3 awards). Office: US Naval Academy Office of Superintendent 121 Blake Rd Annapolis MD 21402-5000

**REMSBERG, ELLIS EDWARD,** meteorologist, researcher; b. Buckeystown, Md., Oct. 24, 1943; s. Daniel Ellwood and Elizabeth Louvenia Remsberg; m. Judith Anne Perdue, June 17, 1967; children: Mark Edward, Karen Elizabeth. BSc in Physics, Va. Poly. Inst. (Va. Tech), Blacksburg, Va., 1966; MSc in Meteorology, U. Wis., Madison, 1968, PhD in Meteorology, 1971. Jr. rsch. asst. Nat. Radio Astronomy Obs., Green Bank, W.Va., 1962—65; res. asst. prof.-chemistry Coll. of William & Mary, Williamsburg, Va., 1971—72; res. assoc.-geophysical scis. Old Dominion U., Norfolk, Va., 1972—73; rsch. scientist NASA Langley Rsch. Ctr., Hampton, Va., 1973—; haloe project scientist, 1996—. Co-i. of nimbus 7 lims satellite expt. NASA Langley Rsch. Ctr., Hampton, Va., 1976—84, co-i on timed/saber satellite expt., 1993—. Recipient Exceptional Sci. Achievement medal, NASA, 2000, best paper prize, World Meteorol. Orgn., 2005; Langley Floyd Thompson fellow, 1983. Mem.: Americal Geophys. Union, Am. Meteorol. Soc. Independent. Unitarian-Universalist. Office: NASA Langley Rsch Ctr 2 Langley Blvd Mail Stop 401B Hampton VA 23681 Office Phone: 757-864-5823. Business E-Mail: ellis.e.remsberg@nasa.gov.

**REMSEN, JAMES F., JR.,** biology educator; b. Oceanside, N.Y., Oct. 17, 1964; s. James F. and Ethel M. Remsen; m. Angela G. Pepe, June 25, 2000. AS, Nassau C.C., 1982—84; BS, Hofstra U., 1982—86, MA, 1988—91; PhD, NY U., 1993—2000. Substitute asst. prof. NYC Coll. of Tech., Bklyn., 2001—03, asst. prof., 2003—. Contbr. chapters to books, articles to profl. jours. Com. chair South Shore Audubon Soc., Freeport, NY, 1988—2004, pres., 1992—94, v.p., 1990—92, mem., 1973—2004. Recipient Gladys Mateyko award for Excellence in Biology, NY U. Dept. of Biology, 1999; Grad. Rsch. Tech. Initiative, CUNY, 2004, Grad. Assistantship, NY U., 1993—2000, South Shore Audubon Soc. Scholarship, South Shore Audubon Soc., 1989, Hofstra U. Grad. scholarship, Hofstra U., 1988—89, Hofstra U. Academic scholarship, 1984, NY State Regents scholarship, NY State Bd. of Regents, 1982—86. Mem.: Met. Assn. of Coll. and U. Biologists. Achievements include research in systematics of drosphilidae; systematics of phyllostomid bats; character congruence in systematics; role of developmental programs in evolution. Avocations: birdwatching, films, travel. Office: NYC Coll of Tech 300 Jay St Brooklyn NY 11201 Office Phone: 718-260-5960. E-mail: jremsen@citytech.cuny.edu.

**REMSHARD, JOHN W.,** insurance company executive; BS in Acctg. and English, LaSalle U., MBA in Fin.; degree, Dartmouth Coll. CPA. Acct. Touche Ross; v.p. Fin. Divsn. CIGNA Corp., 1978—95; sr. v.p. Audit Dept. HealthChoice, 1995—96; sr. v.p. WellChoice, N.Y., 1996—, CFO, 1996—. Office: WellChoice 11 West 42nd Street New York NY 10036

**REN, CHIANG H.,** aerospace engineer; b. Taipei, Taiwan, Aug. 3, 1965; arrived in U.S., 1972; m. Kelly Yoon, May 20, 1995; children: Heather Victoria, Gloria Isabel. BSE magna cum laude in Mech. Engring., U. Pa., 1987; MS in Aeronautics and Astronautics, MIT, 1989. Sr. aerospace engr. ANSER, Arlington, Va., 1989—2001; chief tech. officer Kepler Rsch., Inc., Arlington, 2002—. Contbr. numerous articles to profl. jours.; author: (3 books) Christian Mission Series, 2000. Deacon Presbyn. Ch. Recipient Letter of Recognition, Sec. of the Air Force, 2001, Air Force Space Commn. Task Force, 2001. Fellow: AIAA (assoc.); mem.: Internat. Coun. on Systems Engring., Pi Tau Sigma, Tau Beta Pi. Office: Kepler Research Inc 1530 Wilson Blvd #600 Arlington VA 22209 Office Phone: 703-465-4035. Business E-Mail: chiangren@keplerresearch.com.

**REN, JIANHUA,** education educator; d. Shumin (Zhang) and Shanhou Ren; m. Bogdan Bogdanov, Mar. 18, 2006. PhD, Purdue U., West Lafayette, Ind., 1999. Asst. prof. U. of the Pacific, Stockton, Calif., 2002—. Recipient Petroleum Rsch. Fund Type-G grant, Am. Chem. Soc., 2006—. Achievements include research in phys. organic chemistry. Office: Univ of the Pacific 3601 Pacific Ave Stockton CA 95211 Office Phone: 209-946-2393. Office Fax: 209-946-2607. Business E-Mail: jren@pacific.edu.

**REN, JIYU,** library director; b. Pingyuan County, Shandong, China, Apr. 15, 1916; s. Zijiu and Guofang (Song) R.; m. Zhongyun Feng, Sept. 15, 1946; children: Ren Yuan, Ren Zhong. Student, Peking U., 1934-37; BA, Southwest Associated U., Kun Ming, China, 1938; MA, Southwest Associated U., 1939-42. Lectr. philosophy dept. Southwest Associated U., 1946-49; assoc. prof. philosophy dept. Peking U., 1949-56, prof. philosophy dept., 1956-64; dir. Inst. for World Religion Study Chinese Acad. Social Scis., Beijing, 1964—87; dir. Nat. Libr. of China, Beijing, 1987—2005, hon. dir., 2005—. Author: Re-Explanation of Philosophy, 1981; History of Chinese Philosophy, vols. 1-4, 1963-79 (Nat. Excellent Textbook spl. prize 1987), History of Chinese Buddhism, Vols. 1-3, 1984, The Complete Collections of Buddhism, Vols. 1-10 (Zhung Hwa Da Zangjing), 1984-93, History of Chinese Taoism, 1990, rev. edit. 2001, Religion Dictionary, 1981, (100 books) The Historical Knowledge of Chinese Culture Series, 1998; co-editor: Abstracts of Classical Works of Daoism, 1991, Selected Essays of Ren Jiyu, 1991, Ren Jiyu's Essays on Philosophy and Religion, 1996, Relations Between God and

Man, 1998, Great Religion Dictionary, 1998, Great Buddhism Dictionary, 2003, Ren Jiyu's Essays on Zen Buddhism, 2005; mem. editl. bd. Chinese Ency., philosophy vol., 1987. Rep. Nat. People's Congress 1980, 84, 88, 92. Mem. Chinese Religion Soc. (dir.), Chinese Soc. Philosophy History (pres.), Chinese Libr. Soc. (dir.), Chinese Inst. of Tibetan Buddhists. Mem. Communist Party of China. Home: Sanlihe Rd 100045 Beijing China Office: Nat. Libr China 33 Zhongguancun Nandajie Beijing 100081 China Office Phone: (010)-88545072.

**REN, JUN,** science educator, research scientist; b. Beijing, Dec. 24, 1964; s. Deji Ren and Yukun Ma; m. Bonnie Hl Zhao; children: Sidney Y., Dylan Y. PhD, U. Alta., Edmonton, Can., 1994. Prof. U. ND, Grand Forks, 1998—2002, U. Wyo., Laramie, 2002—. Grantee, NIH, 2001—. Mem.: Rsch. Soc. Alcoholism, Am. Diabetes Assn., Am. Heart Assn. Office: U Who 1000 E University Ave Dept 3375 Laramie WY 82071 Office Phone: 307-766-6131.

**REN, WEI,** control systems educator; m. Fei Cheng, Jan. 10, 2002. BS, Hohai U., 1997; MS, Tongji U., 2000; PhD, Brigham Young U., 2004. Rsch. assoc. Brigham Young U., Provo, Utah, 2000—04, U. Md., College Park, 2004—05; asst. prof. Utah State U., Logan, 2005—. Contbr. articles to profl. jours., chapters to books. Taitan scholar, Guanghua scholar. Mem.: AIAA, IEEE. Achievements include research in coordinated control of multiple fully or partially autonomous systems, autonomous control technologies for unmanned air, ground, or underwater vehicles, nonlinear control theory and applications. Office: Utah State U Dept Electrical & Computer Engring Logan UT 84322 Office Phone: 435-797-2831. Home Fax: 435-797-3054; Office Fax: 435-797-3054. Business E-Mail: wren@engineering.usu.edu.

**REN, XING JIAN,** physician; b. Shanghai, June 27, 1961; s. Yun Feng Ren and Xin Yi Zhang; m. Bei Xie, June 27, 1990; 1 child, Oriana Leigh. MD, Shanghai First Med. Coll., 1984. Diplomate internal medicine and geriatric medicine Am. Bd. Internal Medicine. Resident in surgery Shanghai Ruhui Hosp., China, 1984-85; resident Ft. Wayne (Ind.) Med. Edn. Program, 1993-94; resident, intern in medicine Loyola U. of Chgo., Maywood, Ill., 1994-97; fellow in medicine Harvard Med. Sch., Boston, 1997-99; staff physician Scripps Clinic Found., La Jolla, Calif., 1999—; asst. clin. prof. medicine U. Calif. Sch. Medicine, 2003—. Co-author: Virology, 1986; contbr. articles to profl. jours. Fellow Harvard Med. Sch., 1998; recipient 1st prize Nat. Med. Student Competition for Knowledge of Med. Lit., 1983, grad. student scholarship U. N.C., Chapel Hill, scholarship Carolina Biotechnolgoy Ctr., others. Fellow ACP; mem. AMA, Mass. Med. Soc., Am. Geriatrics Soc., Fell. Am. Coll. Physician. Office Phone: 858-268-9500, 858-554-8077.

**RENARD, MEREDITH ANNE,** marketing and advertising professional; b. Newark, Apr. 12, 1952; d. W. Edward and Lois E. (Velthoven) Young; m. Robert W. Renard, Nov. 11, 1995. BA, Caldwell Coll., 1974. Advt., pub. rels. asst. Congoleum Corp., Lawrenceville, NJ, 1974—77; account mgr. Saatchi & Saatchi Compton, N.Y.C., 1977—82; dir. advt., sales promotion Singer Sewing Co., Edison, NJ, 1982—86, dir. product mktg., 1986—88, dir. nat. accounts, 1988—90; sr. mktg. rep. Walt Disney World Co., Lake Buena Vista, Fla., 1990—91; divsn. mktg. rep. Vista Advt., Walt Disney World Co., Lake Buena Vista, Fla., 1991—92; mgr. advt. Walt Disney World Co., Lake Buena Vista, Fla., 1992—94, mgr. Fla. tourist mktg., 1994—97; mgr. spl. events Disney Cruise Vacations, Celebration, Fla., 1997—; mgr. ops. integration Disney Cruise Line, Celebration, Fla., 2000—02, dir. youth activities and ops. integration, 2002—. Contbr. articles to profl. jours. Vol. North Brunswick Dem. Orgn., 1985—87; pub. rels. mgr. Cultural Arts Com., North Brunswick, 1986—87; props chair Adult Drama Group, North Brunswick, 1986—87; mem. mktg. com. Wal Fla. Direct Mktg., 1993—94. Mem.: Ctrl. Fla. Direct Mktg. Assn. (bd. dirs. 1990—92), Fla. Direct Mktg. Assn. Episcopalian. Avocations: cross stitch, reading. Office: Disney Cruise Line 210 Celebration Pl Ste 400 Celebration FL 34747-4978 Office Phone: 407-566-3651.

**RENARD, PAUL STEVEN,** music educator; b. N.Y.C., May 5, 1934; s. Joseph Maurice and Elsie (Wolpow) R. Student, Miami (Fla.) Conservatory, 1947-48, Sch. of Am. Music, 1950-51; cert., Ida Elkan Sch. of Music, 1958. Staff concert organist Hammond Organ Co., N.Y.C., 1950-74; staff organist various TV stas., N.Y.C., 1952-61, King Records and Riverside Records, N.Y.C., 1955-64; staff organist, ednl. dir. Lyon-Healy Music Co., Chgo., 1962-72; founder, dir. Paul Renard's Music Dynamics, Chgo., 1972—. Cons. in field. Co-inventor first electric piano, Wurlitzer Mus. Instruments Co., 1953-54; inventor (software) Paul Renard's Music Dynamics, 1999; author numerous piano and organ texts; contbr. articles to profl. jours. Office: 203 N Wabash Ave Ste 1510 Chicago IL 60601-2415 Office Phone: 312-609-0061.

**RENARD, RONALD LEE,** allergist; b. Chgo., July 31, 1949; s. Robert James and Dorothy Mae (Fruik) R.; m. Maureen Ann Gilmore, Aug. 5, 1972 (div. Mar. 1992); children: Jeffrey, Stephen, Justin, Leigh Ellen; m. Catherine L. Walker, Apr. 1, 1992; children: Morgan, Michal, Luke. Degrees in Lang., U. de Montepellier, France, 1970; BS in French, U. San Francisco, 1971; MD, Creighton U., 1976. Dir. med. ICU, lt. U.S. Army Hosp., Ft. Leonard Wood, Md., 1980-81; dir. respiratory therapy; asst. chief allergy svc. Walter Reed Med. Ctr., Washington, 1981-84; staff allergist Chico (Calif.) Med. Group, 1984-86; allergist pvt. practice Redding, Calif., 1986—. Dir. ACLS program Enloe Hosp., Chico, 1988-91; bd. dirs. Am. Lung Assn. Calif., 1989-91, med. dir. asthma camp, Chico, Redding, 1986-95; asst. prof. medicine USPHS, Bethesda, Md., 1982-84; asst. prof. family medicine U. Calif. Davis Med. Sch., Redding, 1990-94; Shasta County Planning Commr., 1994-95. Contbr. articles to profl. jours. Fellow Am. Acad. Allergy and Immunology, Am. Coll. Allergists; mem. Assn. Mil. Allergists, Calif. Thoracic Soc., Alpha Omega Alpha. Republican. Roman Catholic. Avocations: hunting, biking. Office: 1505 Victor Ave Redding CA 96003 Office Phone: 530-226-5325. Home Fax: 530-246-8856. Personal E-mail: dr@reddingallergy.com.

**RENAUD, BERNADETTE MARIE ELISE,** author; b. Ascot Corner, Que., Can., Apr. 18, 1945; d. Albert and Aline (Audet) R. Diploma, Présentation de Marie, Granby, Que., 1962-64. Librarian asst. Schs. of Waterloo, Que., 1964-67, tchr. primary schs. Que., 1967-70; adminstrv. sec. Assn. Medi-Tech-Sci., Montreal, Que., 1972-76. Author: Emilie La Baignoire A Pattes, 1976 (Can. Coun. Children's Lit. prize, 1976, Assn. Advancement of Scis. and Technics of Documentation award, 1976), 2d edit., 2002, Le Chat de l'Oratoire, 1978, Emilie la baignoire à pattes album, 1978, La maison tête de pioche, 1979, La révolte de la courte pointe, 1979, La dépression de l'ordinateur, 1981, Une boîte Magique Très Embêtante, 1981, La grande question de Tomatelle, 1982, Comment on fait un livre?, 1983, The Cat in the Cathedral, 1983, The Computer Revolts, 1984, (book and movie) Bach et Bottine, 1986 (awards for movie, 19 awards across the world, transl. ino 8 langs., subtitled into 18 langs.), Bach and Broccoli, 1986, (short movie) Quand l'accent devient grave, 1989, (novels) Un Homme Comme Tant d'Autres, tome 1, 1992, tome, II, 1993, tome, III, 1994, Prix Germaine Guévremont, 1995, Gala des Arts du Bas-Richelieu (QC); dir., coord.: Ecrire pour la jeunesse, 1990; author: short stories, adaptations of 8 children's classics, 1977—73, La quête de Kurweena, 1997; dir., coord.: album and CD Le petit violon muet, 1997, Héritiers de l'éternité, 1998, Les Funambules D'un Temps Nouveau, 2001, Les Chemins d'Eve Tome I, 2002, Les Chemins d'Eve Tome II, 2002, Grand Prix du Livre de la Monteregie, 2001, 2002, Émilie, la baignoire à pattes, rééd, 2002, Drôle de nuit pour Miti, 2004, Les gros bisous, 2004, Pas de chouchous, 2004, Les chemins d'Ève Tome III, 2005.

**RENAULD, CYRIL,** chef; b. Brittany, France; Studied at, Les Sorbets, Brittany, France. With Le Villard, Paris, L'Escalier du Palais Royal, Paris, La Villa Lorraine, Belgium, London Hilton; chef Cellar in the Sky, NYC, 1991; exec. chef Bouley, NYC, 1994—96, La Caravelle, NYC, 1996—2000; owner, chef Fleur de Sel, NYC, 2000—. Office: Feur de Sel 5 E 20th St New York NY 10003 Office Phone: 212-460-9100. Office Fax: 212-640-8319.

**RENBAUM, BARRY JEFFREY,** lawyer; b. Balt., Feb. 26, 1948; s. David and Leah (Cohen) R.; m. Carol Barbash, June 22, 1980. BS magna cum laude, Rider U., 1970; postgrad., NYU, 1973; JD, Georgetown U., 1973. Bar: Md. 1973, U.S. Dist. Ct. Md. 1998. Jud. clk. to Hon. John C. Eldridge, Md. Ct. Appeals, 1974-75; asst. pub. defender State of Md., 1975-79; exec. v.p., gen. counsel Custom Savs. Bank, Tmple Fin. Co., Balt., 1980-91; pvt. practice Glyndon, Md., 1991—. Mem. ATLA, Md. Bar Assn., Alpha Epsilon Zeta. Office: Brydonwood Glyndon MD 21071-0326 E-mail: brydonwood@earthlink.net.

**RENDA, LARREE M.,** retail executive; Exec. v.p. retail ops., human resources, pub. affairs, labor and govtl. rels. Safeway, Inc., Pleasanton, Calif., 1999—, joined, 1974. Office: Safeway Inc 5918 Stoneridge Mall Rd Pleasanton CA 94588

**RENDALL, DONALD JAMES, JR.,** lawyer; b. Phila., Jan. 31, 1956; s. Donald James and Mary (Hough) R.; m. Sandra Smallwood, July 28, 1979; children: Samuel, Katherine, Ann. AB summa cum laude, Dartmouth Coll., 1978; JD, Duke U. 1981. Bar: Ill. 1982, U.S. Dist. Ct. (no. dist.) Ill. 1983, U.S. Dist. Ct. Vt. 1984, Vt. 1985, U.S. Ct. Appeals (2d cir.) 1986. Law clk. to Hon. James S. Holden U.S. Dist. Ct. for Vt., Rutland, 1981-82; assoc. Jenner & Block, Chgo., 1982-84; asst. US atty. US Attorney's Office for Dist. Vt., Rutland, Vt., 1984-87; assoc. Sheehey Furlong Rendall & Behm PC, Burlington, Vt., 1987, ptnr., 1988—2002; v.p. & gen. counsel, sec. Green Monster Power Corp., 2002—. Mem. ABA, Vt. Bar Assn.(pres. 2002-03), Chittenden County Bar Assn., Order of Coif, Phi Beta Kappa. Office: Green Mountain Power Corp 163 Acorn Ln Burlington VT 05446-6611 E-mail: rendall@greenmountainpower.bix.

**RENDELL, EDWARD GENE,** governor, retired mayor, lawyer; b. NYC, Jan. 5, 1944; s. Jesse T. and Emma (Sloat) R.; m. Marjorie Osterlund, July 10, 1971; 1 son, Jesse Thompson. BA in Polit. Sci., U. Pa., 1965; JD, Villanova U., 1968. Bar: Pa. 1968, U.S. Supreme Ct. 1981. Asst. dist. atty., chief homicide unit Office Dist. Atty., Phila., 1968-74; dep. spl. prosecutor Phila., 1976; dist. atty., 1978-86; mayor City of Phila., 1992—2000; gov. Commonwealth of Pa., Harrisburg, 2003—. Gen. chmn. Dem. Nat. Com., 1999—2000. 2d lt. USAR, 1968—74. Recipient Man of Yr. award VFW, 1980, Am. Cancer League, 1981, Disting. Pub. Svc. award Pa. County Detectives Assn., 1981. Mem. ABA, Pa. Dist. Attys. Assn. (legis. chmn. 1979—), Phila. Bar Assn., B'nai B'rith, United Jewish Orgns., Jewish War Vets. Democrat. Jewish. Office: Governor's Office Rm 225 Main Capitol Bldg Harrisburg PA 17120 Office Phone: 717-787-2500. Office Fax: 717-772-8284.*

**RENDELL, KENNETH WILLIAM,** rare and historical documents dealer, consultant; b. Boston, May 12, 1943; s. Harry H. and Pauline (Walsh) R.; m. Diana J. Angelo, June 3, 1967 (div. 1985); children: Jeffrey H., Jason J. (dec.); m. Shirley L. McNerney, July 14, 1985; 1 child, Julia Louise. Student, Boston U., 1961-63. Pres. Kingston Galleries, Inc., Somerville, Mass., 1960-67, Kenneth W. Rendell, Inc., Newton, Mass., 1967—, Kenneth W. Rendell, Ltd., London, 1970—, Kenneth W. Rendell Gallery, Inc., NYC, Tokyo, 1985—, Mus. World War II. Bd. dirs. John Wilson Autographs Ltd., London, 1961-75, Charles Ede Gallery Ltd., London, 1976-92; chmn. New England Antiquarian Booksellers Assn., 1975-77; cons. numerous univ. librs., govtl. and media orgns. Author: The Fundamentals of Autograph Collecting, 1976, Tax Appraisals of Manuscript Collections, 1983, Changing Concepts of Value and Rarity, 1985, The Hitler Diaries: Bad Forgeries But a Great Hoax, 1986, The Mormon Conman, Forger and Killer, 1987, Other People's Mail: 30 Years As a Dealer in Historical Documents, 1988, The One Hundred Americans Who Have Made America What it is Today, 1989, The Detection of Forged Historical Letters and Documents, 1990, With Weapons and Wits: Propaganda and Psychological Warfare in World War II, 1991, Forging History: The Detection of Fake Historical Letters and Documents, 1994, History Comes to Life, 1995, The Western Pursuit of the American Dream, 2005; co-editor: Autographs and Manuscripts: A Collector's Manual, 1978 (Outstanding Reference Book award ALA); contbr. numerous articles in field to mags. and profl. jours. Trustee D-Day Mus., New Orleans, 1998, Youth Enrichment Svcs., Boston, 1998, William J. Donovan Meml., N.Y., 1998. Recipient Dept. Justice award, 1991. Fellow Manuscript Soc. (bd. dirs. 1968-74, pres. 1972-74); mem. Assn. Internat. de Bibliophilie Paris, Grolier Club, Army and Navy Club, Am. Antiquarian Soc., Bohemian Club (San Francisco), Appalachian Mountain Club (trustee 2000), Explorers Club, Saville Club (London), Spl. Forces Club (London). Avocation: ski racing. Office: Kenneth W Rendell Inc 46 Eliot St Natick MA 01760-6042 also: 989 Madison Ave New York NY 10021-1825

**RENDELL, MARC S.,** physician, researcher; MD, SUNY, N.Y.C., 1972. Diplomate Am. Bd. Internal Medicine, 1977. Dir. Creighton Diabetes Ctr., Omaha, 1985; med. dir. Rose Salter Med Rsch. Found., Balt., 1999—. Comdr. USPHS, 1973—82. Home: 6201 Underwood Ave Omaha NE 68132 Office: Creighton Diabetes Ctr 601 North 30th St Omaha NE 68131 Personal E-mail: marcrendell@hotmail.com.

**RENDELL, MARJORIE O.,** federal judge; b. 1947; m. Edward G. Rendell, 1971; 1 child, Jesse. BA, U. Pa., 1969; postgrad., Georgetown U., 1970—71; JD, Villanova U., 1973; LLD (hon.), Phila. Coll. Textile and Sci., 1992. Ptnr. Duane, Morris & Heckscher, Phila., 1972—93; judge U.S. Dist. Ct. (ea. dist.) Pa., 1994—97, U.S. Ct. Appeals (3d cir.), Phila., 1997—. Mem. Am. Jud. Soc., Fed. Judges Assn. Asst. to dir. ann. giving Dept. Devel. U. Pa., 1973—78; mem. adv. bd. Chestnut Hill Nat. Bank/East Falls Adv. Bd.; mem. alternative dispute resolution com. mediation divsn. Ea. Dist. Pa. Bankruptcy Conf.; active Acad. Vocal Arts, Market St. East Improvement Assn., Pa.'s Campaign for Choice, Phila. Friends Outward Bound; vice chair Ave. of Arts, Inc.; vice chair bd. trustees Vis. Nurse Assn. Greater Phila.; bd. mem. Alumni Trust, U. Penn. Mem.: ABA, Phila. Bar Found. (bd. dirs.), Phila. Bar Assn. (bd. dirs. young lawyers sect. 1973—78), Pa. Bar Assn., Am. Bankruptcy Inst., Internat. Women's Forum, Forum Exec. Women, Phi Beta Kappa. Office: US Courthouse 601 Market St Rm 21613 Philadelphia PA 19106-1715*

**RENDICH, ANA,** painter, collage artist; arrived in U.S., 1988; d. Ernesto Pedro Rendich and Maria Elena Romero de Rendich; m. Glenn D. Millis, Dec. 31, 1990; children: Sara C. Millis, Amy C. Millis, Sophie A. Millis. Student, Sch. Art U. Salvador, Buenos Aires, 1979—81, Inst. Superior del teatro Colon, 1980—81; master classes with Victor Callegary, Buenos Aires, 1981, Franco Zeffirelli, NYC, 1996. Chief of characterization Met. Opera House, N.Y.C., 1981—. Exhibitions include Cork Gallery Lincoln Ctr., NYC, 2003, 2004, 2005, Brush Strokes Art Gallery, Fredericksburg, Va. Mem.: Nat. Coll. Soc. Roman Catholic. Achievements include being the first South American painter to specialize in miniature painting. Avocations: art, opera. Office: Phone: 540-368-0560. E-mail: ana_rendich@brushstrokesfredericksburg.com.

**RENDINA, SALVATORE N., JR.,** musician; b. N.Y.C. s. Salvatore N., Sr. and Angie T. (Galella) Rendina. Tchr. music Sacred Heart, Bronx, NY, 1972—89, Santa Maria, Bronx, 1972—89, Our Lady Pompeii, N.Y.C., 1982—89; music dir., organist Assumption Ch., Bronx, 1978—86; music dir. St. Raymond's, Bronx, 1989—96, Our Lady Mercy, Deerfield Beach, Fla., 1996—98, St. Brendan, Miami, Fla., 2000—. Dir. Dell'oro Voci, Miami, 2003—. Mem.: Nat. Assn. Pastoral Musicians. Democrat. Roman Catholic.

**RENDINE, MARIA FARESE,** retired secondary school educator; b. Newark, Apr. 15, 1946; d. Louis Rocco and Angela Maria (Nente) Farese; m. Michael Joseph Rendine, 1967 (div. 1993); children: Renee Danielle, Jon Daniel. BA, Montclair State Coll., 1967; postgrad., Wright State U., Dayton, Ohio, U. Va., Falls Ch., George Mason U. Cert. English, speech, pub. speaking, theater arts thcr. Va.; English tchr. Ohio, Fla. Tchr. Bibb County Schs., Macon, Ga.; English, speech tchr., English dept. chair Wayne Township Schs., Dayton, Ohio, 1975; English, drama, speech, photo journalism tchr. Fairfax County Pub. Schs., Va., 1982—2001, chmn. dept. fine arts,

1999—2001, theatre arts tchr. mentor, 2001—04; career switch mentor Old Dominion U., Norfolk, Va., 2005—. Sponsor yearbook Fairfax County Pub. Schs., 1986—94, developed, expanded programs studies poetry, drama, theatre-goers, film study, 1990—95, instrl. content and design cons. HS theatre arts program studies, 2003—04; developer Career I-Search Projects grades 10, 12, 1985—89; critic judge Fairfax County Short Play Festival, 1988, Va. HS League, 2001—03; mem. curriculum revision team Fairfax County Program Studies, 1998—2004. Author: numerous poems; co-author (with Sharon O'Brien): Souls on a Half Shell, 2006. Bd. dirs. Alliance Theatre, 2001—. Named Poet of Merit, Am. Poetry Assn., 1989; recipient Editor's Choice award, Internat. Libr. Poetry, 2004; grantee, Am. Poetry Assn., 1986. Mem.: Theatre Arts Dirs. Assn. (pres. 2000), Journalism Edn. Assn., Ednl. Theatre Assn., English Tchrs. Assn. No. Va., Va. Assn. Tchrs. English, Nat. Coun. Tchrs. English. Home: 4127 Nomis Dr Fairfax VA 22032-1204

**RENDLEN, CHARLES EARNEST, III, (SKETCH RENDLEN),** federal judge, lawyer; b. Hannibal, Mo., Aug. 17, 1950; s. Charles Earnest and Shirley Anne (Raible) R.; m. Susan L. David, Aug. 14, 1976; 1 child, Lindsey D. BS magna cum laude, William Jewell Coll., 1972; JD, U. Mo., 1976. Bar: Mo., U.S. Ct. Claims, U.S. Dist. Ct. (ea. and we. dists.) Mo., U.S. Tax Ct, U.S. Ct. Appeals (8th and Fed. cirs.), U.S. Supreme Ct. Assoc. The Rendlen Law Firm, P.C. (formerly Rendlen, Rendlen, Redington & Bastian, P.C.), Hannibal, Mo., 1976—79, ptnr., 1979—91, mng. ptnr., 1991—2003; US trustee, Reg. 13, Exec. Office US Trustees US Dept. Justice, 2003—06; judge US Bankruptcy Ct. (ea. dist.) Mo., St. Louis, 2006—. Mem. com. for jud. redistricting Mo. Supreme Ct., 1991-92, civil rules com., 1990-92; vice-chmn. worker compensation sect. Mo. Bar, 1992—. Co-author: Hedonics, 1992. Coord. Danforth for Senator, Marion County, 1976, 82, 88; chmn. Marion County Rep. Com., 1976-80, state com. 1992—; field worker Re-Elect the Pres., Mo., 1972; bd. dirs. Mennonite Home Assn., Inc., v.p., 1986—; v.p. bd. dirs. Beth Haven Terrace, Inc., 1986—, Beth Haven Group Homes, 1988—, Beth Haven Mgmt. Svcs., 1986—; bd. dirs. Hannibal Regional Hosp., sec., 1987-89. Mem. Rotary (pres. 1985-86). Avocations: golf, sailing. Office: Thomas F Eagleton US Courthouse 111 S Tenth St Rm 4380 Saint Louis MO 63102

**RENDL-MARCUS, MILDRED,** artist, economist; b. May 30, 1928; d. Julius and Agnes (Hokr) Rendl; m. Edward Marcus, Aug. 10, 1956. BS, NYU, 1948, MBA, 1950; PhD, Radcliffe Coll., 1954. Economist GE, 1953-55, Bigelow-Sanford Carpet Co., Inc., 1956-58; instr. econs. Hunter Coll. CUNY, 1959-60, Columbia U., 1960-61, rschr., 1961-63; sr. economist Nat. Indsl. Conf. Bd., 1963-66; asst. prof. Pace Coll., 1964-66; assoc. prof. Borough of Manhattan C. of C. CUNY, 1966-71, prof., 1972-85. Lectr. econs. CCNY, 1953-58; vis. prof. Fla. Internat. U., 1986; bd. dirs. N.Y.C. Coun. on Econ. Edn.; assoc. mem. Allied Artists Am., Inc., 2004—; cons. in field. Exhibited group shows at in New Canaan Art Show, 1982-85, Am. Soc. Bus. and Behavioral Scis., 1990-96, New Cannan Soc. for Arts Ann., 1983, 85, New Canaan Arts, 1985, Silvermine Galleries, 1986, Stamford Art Assn., 1987, Phoenix Gallery, 1988, N.Y.C., Parkview Point Gallery, 1982-89, Miami Beach, Fla., 1982-89, Art Complex, New Canaan, Miami Beach, 1985—, Lever House, N.Y.C., 1990, Cork Gallery, Lincoln Ctr., N.Y.C., 1990, Women's Caucus for Art, San Antonio, 1990, Artist's Equity, Broome St. Gallery, N.Y.C., 1991, Greater Hartford Architecture Conservancy, 1991, N.H. Arts Ctr., 1997, Just Originals Art Web, Albuquerque, 1999, Ward-Nasse Gallery, N.Y.C., 2000—, Art Complex Gallery, Las Vegas, 2000-, Liliana Fine Art Gallery, Lenox, Mass., 2003—, Artists Gallery, Chelsea, N.Y.C. 2003, Nat. Assn. Women Artists, 2003—, 115-Yr. Anniversary Show, World Trade Ctr., N.Y.C., 2004, Pen and Brush Non-Mem. Show, 2004, Allied Artists of Am., N.Y.C., 2005, Nat. Assn. Women Artists, N.Y.C., 2005, Catherine Lorillard Wolfe Art Club, 2005 (Rendl Drawing award 2006), Audubon Artists, N.Y.C., 2005, Real Art Gallery, Hartford, 2006; author (with E. Marcus) Investment and Development of Tropical Africa, 1959, International Trade and Finance, 1965, Monetary and Banking Theory, 1965, Economics, 1969, Economic Progress and the Developing World, 1970, Economics, 1978, Fine Art with Many Equilibrium Prices, 1995; editor Women in the Arts Found. Newsletter, 1986-92; contbr. articles to profl. jours. Founder Rendl Fund for Slavic Art, Mus. of Modern Art, N.Y.C., 1999—, Harvard U. Art Mus. Fund for Slavic Art, Cambridge, 2000—, Harvard Mus. Natural History, Peabody Mus. Archeology and Ethnology, Rendl Fund for the Conservation of Slavic Artifacts, 2000—, Rendl Fund for the Conservation of the Ware Collection of Blaschka Glass Models of Plants, 2001—; mem. mus. coun. Harvard Mus. Natural History, 2001—; founder Rendl Fund for Czech Art, 2006—. Recipient Merit award Manhattan Arts Internat., 1998, Excellence award 1998, Artist Showcase award Manhattan Arts Internat., 1999; Dean Bernice Brown Cronkhite fellow Radcliffe Coll., 1950-51, Anne Radcliffe Econ. Rsch. Sub-Sahara Africa fellow, 1958-59; fellow Gerontol. Assn. Mem. AAUW, Internat. Schumpeter Econs. Soc. (founding), Met. Econ. Assns. (sec. 1954-56), Indsl. Rels. Rsch. Assn., Women's Econ. Roundtable (program planning com.), N.Y.C. Women in Arts, Allied Social Sci. Assn. (artist 1994), Allied Artists Am. Inc. (assoc.), NYU Grad. Sch. Bus. Adminstrn. Alumni (sec. 1956-58), Radcliffe Club, Women's City Club (art and landmarks com.).

**RENDU, JEAN-MICHEL MARIE,** mining executive; b. Tunis, Tunisia, Feb. 25, 1944; s. Paul C. and Solange M. (Krebs) R.; m. Karla M. Meyer, Aug. 18, 1973; children: Yannick P., Mikaël P. Ingénieur des Mines, Ecole des Mines St. Etienne, France, 1966; MS, Columbia U., 1968, D of Engring. Sci., 1971. Mgr. ops. rsch. Anglovaal, Johannesburg, 1972-76; assoc. prof. U. Wis., Madison, 1976-79; assoc. Golder Assocs., Denver, 1979-84; dir. tech. and sci. systems Newmont Mining Corp., Danbury, Conn., 1984-88; v.p. Newmont Gold Co., Denver, 1988-93, Newmont Mining Corp., Denver, 1993-2001; ind. cons. Denver, 2001—. Author: An Introduction to Geostatistical Methods of Mineral Evaluation, 1978, 81; contbr. tech. papers to profl. jours. Fellow South African Inst. of Mining and Metallurgy (corr. mem. of coun.) Australasian Inst. Mining and Metallurgy; mem. NAE, Soc. Mining, Metallurgy and Exploration (bd. dirs. 1998—, Jackling award 1994, Pres.'s citation 1993, 2004), Sigma Xi. Roman Catholic. E-mail: JMRendu@aol.com.

**RENE, VIDAL,** electrical engineer, educator; s. Oscar Vidal and Amelia Navarro. PhD, U. Calif., Berkeley CA, 2003. Rsch. asst. U. Calif., Berkeley, 1999—2003; asst. prof. Johns Hopkins U., Balt., 2004—. Recipient Eli Jury award, U. Calif., Berkeley, 2003, Sakrison Meml. prize, 2004, Best Paper award, European Conf. Computer Vision, 2004, Career award, NSF, 2005; fellow, NICTA, 2003. Mem.: IEEE. Office: Johns Hopkins University 308B Clark Hall 3400 N Charles St Baltimore MD 21218 Office Phone: 410-516-7306.

**RENEAU, BRENDA,** trade association executive; b. Ft. Hood, Tex. d. Norman L. and Marjorie L. (Shaffer) Fallen; 1 child from previous marriage, Jennifer G. Houghton. Student, U. Okla. Dir. edn. Associated Builders and Contractors Western Okla., Oklahoma City, exec. dir.; commr. of labor OK, Okla. City, 1995—. Contbr. articles to trade pubs. Mem. Okla. Soc. Execs., Okla. State C. of C., Oklahoma City C. of C. Achievements include 1st female exec. dir. of Assoc. Builders and Contractors Western Okla. Address: 200 W Wilshire Blvd Ste A-12 Oklahoma City OK 73116-7756 Office: Dept of Labor 4001 N Lincoln Blvd Oklahoma City OK 73105-5298 Office Phone: 405-528-1500. Business E-Mail: reneau_wynn@oklaosf.state.ok.us.

**RENEE, LISABETH MARY,** small business owner, art designer; b. Bklyn., July 28, 1952; d. Lino P. and Elizabeth M. (Dines) Rivano; m. John S. Witanowski, May 15, 1982. Student, U. Puget Sound, 1972-74; BA in Art, SUNY, Buffalo, 1977; MFA, L.I. U., 1982; EdD, U. Ctrl. Fla., 1996. Cert. art tchr., Fla. Adj. faculty L.I. U., Greenvale, N.Y., 1980-82, Rollins Coll., Winter Park, Fla., 1982; art tchr. Phyllis Wheatley Elem. Sch., Apopka, Fla., 1983-85, McCoy Elem. Sch., Orlando, Fla., 1985-86, Lake Howell H.S., Winter Park, Fla., 1986-93; adj. faculty U. Ctrl. Fla., 1994-95, vis. instr., coord. art edn., 1995-96; gallery dir., prof. West Campus Valencia (Fla.) C.C., 1996-98; owner, designer Nartique, 2002—; dir. Renée Studios, Casselberry, Fla. Adj. faculty Valencia C.C., 1995-96; dir. So. Artists Registry, Winter Park, 1984-87; cons. Fla. Dept. Edn., 1989-90, mem. curriculum writing team for

arts edn. program; mem. com. Fla. Bd. Edn. Task Force for Subject Area Subtest of Fla. Tech. Cert. Exam.; visual arts dir. Very Spl. Arts Ctr. Fla. Fest, 1996; presenter at profl. confs. Author: The Phenomenological Significance of Aesthetic Communion, 1996, Co-operative Art, 1991; editor: Children and the Arts in Florida, 1990. Visual arts dir. Very Spl. Arts Ctrl. Fla. Festival 1995; mem. local Sch. Adv. Coun., Winter Park, 1992. Grantee Found. for Advancement of Cmty. Through Schs., 1991, Divsn. Blind Svcs. Invision, 1995, Tangelo Park Project, 1995; ACE scholar Arts Leadership Inst., 1993-96; recipient Tchr. Merit award Walt Disney World Co., 1990. Mem. NEA, ASCD, Nat. Art Edn. Assn., Fla. Art Edn. Assn. (regional rep. 1989-94), Seminole Coun. for the Arts Assn., Coll. Art Assn., Caucus on Social Theory and Art Edn., Women's Caucus for Art, Phi Kappa Phi, Kappa Delta Pi. Home and Office: Nartique 20 Cobblestone Ct Casselberry FL 32707-5410 Office Phone: 407-921-0257. E-mail: nartiqueinc@yahoo.com.

**RENEHAN, EDWARD JOHN,** writer; b. NYC, Aug. 7, 1956; s. Edward John Renehan and Joan Margaret Salvesen; m. Christa Elizabeth Bartkovich, Aug. 24, 1985; children: William James, Katherine Eleanor. BA in Polit. Sci., SUNY, New Paltz, 1980. Author: John Burroughs: An American Naturalist, 1992, The Secret Six: The True Tale of the Men Who Conspired with John Brown, 1995, The Lion's Pride: Theodore Roosevelt and His Family in Peace and War, 1998, The Kennedys at War, 2002, Dark Genius of Wall Street: The Misunderstood Life of Jay Gould, King of the Robber Barons, 2005; tech. cons. film John Kennedy and PT-109, 2003; contbr. columns to papers; contbr. articles to jours. Dir. So. R.I. Conservation Dist., Warwick, 2000-05; del. R.I. Conservation Com., 2001-05. Mem. PEN, Theodore Roosevelt Assn. (trustee 2000-04), Nat. Arts Club, Hudson River Sloop Clearwater, Inc. (dir. 1976-80), Boston Atheneaum, Pi Sigma Alpha. Avocations: hiking, mountain climbing, sailing. Office: Chris Calhoun/Sterling Lord Literistic 65 Bleecker St New York NY 10012

**RENEHAN, RICHARD WILLIAM,** lawyer; b. Boston, Dec. 30, 1933; s. Francis Xavier and Mary (Sullivan) R.; m. Mary B. Brophy, Feb. 17, 1962; children: Anne M., Joan F., Richard W., Jr., Mark D. BA, Boston Coll., 1955; LLB, Harvard U., 1958. Bar: Mass. 1958, U.S. Dist. Ct. Mass. 1959, U.S. Ct. Appeals (1st cir.) 1964, U.S. Supreme Ct. 1971. Assoc. Peabody, Koufman & Brewer, Boston, 1959-64; ptnr. Hill & Barlow, Boston; dir., profl. liability, securities litig. Goulston & Storrs, Boston. Mem. Gov's Select Com. on Jud. Needs, Boston, 1978-79, Joint Bar Com. on Jud. Appointments, 1979-84, Gov's Jud. Nominating Coun., Boston, 1987-90. Mem. Milton (Mass.) Housing Authority, 1979-86, chmn., 1981-85. Fellow Am. Bar Found, Am. Coll. Trial Lawyers; mem. ABA, Mass. Bar Assn., Boston Bar Assn. (pres. 1985-86). Office: Goulston & Storrs 400 Atlantic Ave Boston MA 02110-3333 Office Phone: 617-574-4024. Office Fax: 617-574-7593. Business E-Mail: rrenehan@goulstonstorrs.com.

**RENEKER, MAXINE HOHMAN,** librarian; b. Chgo., Dec. 2, 1942; d. Roy Max and Helen Anna Christina (Anacker) Hohman; m. David Lee Reneker, June 20, 1964 (dec. Dec. 1999); children: Sarah Roeder, Amy Johannah, Benjamin Congdon. BA, Carleton Coll., 1964; MA, U. Chgo., 1970; DLS, Columbia U., 1992. Asst. reference libr. U. Chgo. Libraries, 1965-66; classics libr. U. Chgo. Libr., 1967-70, asst. head acquisitions, 1970-71, personnel libr., 1971-73; personnel/bus. libr. U. Colo. Libr., Boulder, 1978-80; asst. dir. sci. and engring. div. Columbia U., N.Y.C., 1981-85; assoc. dean of univ. librs. for pub. svcs. Ariz. State U. Libr., Tempe, 1985-89; dir. instrnl. and rsch. svcs. Stanford (Calif.) Univ. Librs., 1989-90; assoc. provost for libr. and info. resources Naval Postgrad. Sch., Monterey, Calif., 1993—2005, prof. emerita, 2005—. Acad. libr. mgmt. intern Coun. on Libr. Resources, 1980-81; chmn. univ. librs. sect. Assn. Coll. and Rsch. Librs., 1989-90. Contbr. articles to profl. jours. Trustee Monterey Pub. Libr. Rsch. grantee Coun. on Library Resources, Columbia U., 1970-71, fellow, 1990-92. Mem. ALA, Am. Soc. Info. Sci., Sherlockian Scion Soc., Phi Beta Kappa, Beta Phi Mu. Home: 740 Dry Creek Rd Monterey CA 93940-4208 E-mail: mreneker@pacbell.net.

**RENFREW, ANDREW COLIN (LORD RENFREW OF KAIMSTHORN),** archaeologist, educator, director; b. July 25, 1937; s. Archibald and Helena Douglas (Savage) R.; m. Jane Margaret Ewbank, Apr. 21, 1965; children: Helena Margaret, Alban Robert, Magnus Archibald. BA, St. John's Coll., Cambridge U., 1962, MA, 1964, PhD, 1965, ScD, 1976. Lectr. archaeology U. Sheffield, 1965-72; prof. U. Southampton, 1972-81; Disney prof. archaeology Cambridge U., 1981—2004; dir. McDonald Inst. Archeol. Rsch., 1990—2004. Vis. lectr. UCLA, 1967; fellow St. John's Coll., 1981-86, hon. fellow 2004—; master Jesus Coll., Cambridge, 1986-97, fellow, 1997-04, hon. fellow, 2004—; George Grant McCurdy lectr. Harvard U., 1977; Patten lectr. Ind. U., 1982; field excavations in Saliagos, 1961-64, Sitagroi, 1968-70, Quaterness, Orkney, 1972-74, Phylakopi, Melos, 1974-76. Author (with J. D. Evans): Excavations at Saliagos Near Antiparos, 1968 in Orkney, 1979; author: Problems in European Prehistory, 1979; author: (with J. M. Wagstaff) An Island Polity, 1982; author: Approaches to Social Archaeology, 1984, The Prehistory of Orkney, 1985, The Archaeology of Cult, 1985, Archaeology and Language, 1987; author: (with G. Daniel) The Idea of Prehistory, 1988; author: The Cycladic Spirit, 1991; author: (with P. Bahn) Archaeology, 1991; author: Loot, Legitimacy and Ownership: The Ethical Crisis in Archaeology, 2000, Figuring It Out, 2003; editor: The Explanation of Culture Change, 1973, British Prehistory, 1974, Transformations: Mathematical Approaches to Culture Change, 1979, Theory and Explanation in Archaeology, 1982; presenter (TV films) The Tree That Put the Clock Back, 1970, Islands Out of Time, 1973, Orkney Underground, 1974, Aphrodite's Other Island, 1977, Bronze Age Blast Off, 1978, Lost Kings of the Desert, 1980, The Emperor's Immortal Army, 1981, City of the Dead, 1982, Who Built Stonehenge, 1986. Trustee Brit. Mus., 1991-01. With RAF, 1956-58. Recipient European Sci. Found. Latsis Prize, 2003, Rivers Meml. medal Royal Anthrop. Inst., 1979, Huxley Meml. medal, 1991, Balzan prize, 2004: named Fgn. Assoc. NAS, 1996; elevated to peerage, 1991. Fellow Brit. Acad., Soc. Antiquaries London, Royal Soc. Edinburgh (hon.), Austrian Acad. Sci., German Archeol. Inst.; mem. Athenaeum. Office: Dept Archaeology Downing St Cambridge CB2 3DZ England also: House of Lords London SW1A 0PW England Office Phone: 01223-333521. Business E-Mail: des25@cam.ac.uk.

**RENFREW, CHARLES BYRON,** lawyer; b. Detroit, Oct. 31, 1928; s. Charles Warren and Louise (McGuire) R.; m. Susan Wheelock, June 28, 1952 (div. June 1984); children: Taylor Allison Ingham, Charles Robin, Todd Wheelock, James Bartlett; m. Barbara Jones Orser, Oct. 6, 1984; 5 stepchildren. AB, Princeton U., 1952; JD, U. Mich., 1956. Bar: Calif. 1956. Assoc. Pillsbury, Madison & Sutro, San Francisco, 1956-65, ptnr., 1965-72, 81-82; U.S. dist. judge No. Dist. Calif., San Francisco, 1972-80; dep. atty. gen. U.S. Washington, 1980-81; instr. U. Calif. Boalt Hall Sch. Law, 1977-80; v.p. law Chevron Corp. (formerly Standard Oil Co. Calif.), San Francisco, 1983-93, also bd. dirs.; ptnr. LeBoeuf, Lamb, Greene & McRae, San Francisco, 1994-97; pvt. practice San Francisco, 1998—. Mem. exec. com. 9th Cir. Jud. Conf., 1976-78, congl. liaison com. 9th Cir. Jud. Council, 1976-79, spl. com. to propose standards for admission to practice in fed. cts. U.S. Jud. Conf., 1976-79; chmn. spl. com. to study problems of discovery Fed. Jud. Ctr., 1978-79; mem. council on role of cts. U.S. Dist. Justice, 1978-83; mem. jud. panel Ctr. for Pub. Resources, 1981—; head U.S. del. to 6th UN Congress on Prevention of Crime and Treatment of Offenders, 1980; co-chmn. San Francisco Lawyers Com. for Urban Affairs, 1971-72, mem., 1983—; bd. dirs. Internat. Hospitality Ctr., 1961-74, pres., 1967-70; mem. adv. bd. Internat. Comparative Law Ctr., Southwestern Legal Found., 1983-93; trustee World Affairs Council No. Calif., 1984-87, 94—, Nat. Jud. Coll., 1985-91, Grace Cathedral, 1986-89. Contbr. articles to profl. jours. Bd. fellow Claremont U., 1986-94; bd. dirs. San Francisco Symphony Found., 1964-80, pres., 1971-72; bd. dirs. Coun. Civic Unity, 1962-73, pres., 1971-72; bd. dirs. Opportunity Through Ownership, 1969-72, Marin County Day Sch., 1972-74, No. Calif. Svc. League, 1975-76, Am. Petroleum Inst., 1984—, Nat. Crime Prevention Coun., 1982—; alumni trustee Princeton U., 1976-80; mem. vis. com. u. chgo. Law Sch., 1977-79, u.Mich. Law Sch., 1977-81; bd. visitors J. Reuben Clark Law Sch., Brigham Young U., 1981-83, Stanford Law Sch., 1983-86; trustee Town Sch. for Boys, 1972-80,pres. 1975-80; gov. San Franscisco Symphony Assn., 1974—; mem. nat. adv. bd. Ctr. for Nat. Policy, 1982—; bd.

dirs. Nat. Coun. Crime and Deliquency, 1981-82,NAACP Legal Def. and Edn. Fund, 1982—; parish chancellor St. Luke's Episcopal Ch., 1968-71, sr. warden, 1974-76; mem. exec. coun. San Francisco Deanery, 1969-70; mem. diocesan coun. Episcopal Diocese of Calif., 1970; chmn. Diocesan Conv., 1977, 78, 79. Served with USN, 1946-48, 1st lt. U.S. Army, 1952-53. Fellow Am. Bar Found.; mem. ABA (coun. mem. sect. antitrust law 19778-82, vice c hmn. sect. antitrust law 1982-83), San Francisco Bar Assn. (past bd. dirs.), Assn. Gen. Counsel, State Bar Calif., Am. Judicature Soc., Am. Coll. Trial Lawyers (pres. 1995-96), Am. Law Inst., Coun. Fgn. Rels., Order of Coif, Phi Beta Kappa, Phi Delta Phi. Office: 710 Sansome St San Francisco CA 94111-1704 Office Phone: 415-397-3933.

**RENFREW, MALCOLM MACKENZIE,** chemist, educator; b. Spokane, Wash., Oct. 12, 1910; s. Earl Edgar and Elsie Pauline (MacKenzie) R.; m. Carol Joy Campbell, June 26, 1938. BS, U. Idaho, 1932, MS, 1934, D.Sc., 1976; PhD, U. Minn., 1938. Asst. physics U. Idaho, 1932-33, Asst. chemistry, 1933-35, U. Minn., 1935-37, duPont fellow, 1937-38; research chemist plastics dept. duPont Co., 1938-44, supr. process devel., 1944-46, supr. product devel., 1946-49; head chem. research dept., research labs. Gen. Mills, Inc., 1949-52, dir. chem. research, 1952-53, dir. chem. research and devel., 1953-54; dir. research and devel. Spencer Kellogg & Sons, Inc., 1954-58; phys. sci. div. head, prof. chemistry U. Idaho, 1959-73, prof., 1973-76, emeritus, 1976—; dir. U. Idaho (Coll. Chem. Cons. Service), 1969-76. On leave as sr. staff assoc. Adv. Coun. Coll. Chemistry, Stanford, 1967-68; mem. materials adv. bd. Nat. Rsch. Coun., 1963-67; exec. v.p. Idaho Rsch. Found., 1977-78, patent dir., 1978-88. Editor: Safety in the Chemical Laboratory, Vol. IV, 1981, (with Peter Ashbrook), Safe Laboratories: Principles and Practices for Design and Remodeling, 1991; safety editor: Jour. Chem. Edn, 1977-91; Contbr. to tech. and trade pubs. on plastics, coatings, safety, chem. edn. Recipient Excellence in Teaching award Chem. Mfrs. Assn., 1977, Outstanding Achievement award U. Minn., 1977; named to U. Idaho Hall of Fame, 1977, Idaho Hall of Fame, 1996. Fellow AAAS, Am. Inst. Chemists; mem. Am. Chem. Soc. (councilor 1948, 59, 67-89, chmn. paint varnish and plastics div. 1949, chmn. chem. mktg. and econs. div. 1958-59, chmn. chem. health and safety div. 1982, James Flack Norris award 1976, Chem. Health and Safety award 1985, Mosher award 1986), Am. Inst. Chem. Engrs., Soc. Chem. Industry, Phi Beta Kappa, Sigma Xi, Phi Kappa Phi, Sigma Pi Sigma, Phi Gamma Delta (disting. Fiji 1986). Presbyterian. Home: 1271 Walenta Dr Moscow ID 83843-2426 Office: U Idaho Coll Sci Dept Chemistry PO Box 442343 Moscow ID 83844-2343 Business E-Mail: renfrew@uidaho.edu.

**RENFRO, CHARLES,** architect, educator; Collaborator Diller & Scofidio, 1997—; ptnr. Diller & Scofidio (now Diller Scofidio & Renfro); adj. asst. prof., arch. Columbia U. Sch. Arch. Works include Blur Bldg. (Progressive Architecture Design award), media pavillion for Swiss EXPO 2002, designed viewing platform for Ground Zero, NYC, Brasserie Restaurant, NY (James Beard Found. award for Best New Restaurant Design), Slither, Gifu, Japan, The American Lawn: Surface of Everyday Life, Canadian Centre for Architecture, Montreal, 1998, (permanent collections) Travelogues, Internat. Arrivals Terminal 4, JFK Airport, NY, (installation) The Desiring Eye: Reviewing the Slow House, Gallery MA, Tokyo, 1992, Master/Slave, Fondation Cartier, Paris, InterClone Hotel, Ataturk Airport for Istanbul Biennial, 1997, (dance collaborations with the Lyon Ballet Opera of France and Charlerol/Danses of Belgium (touring exhbn.) EJM1: Man Walking at Ordinary Speed and EJM2: Inertia, 1998, (web project) Refresh, Dia Art Found., (video installation) Pageant, Johannesburg Biennial & Rotterdam Film Festival, 1997, (permanent installation) X,Y, Kobe, Japan, 1997, (multi-media work for stage in collaboration with Builders Assn.) Jet Lag, 1998 (Obie award for Creative Achievement), (pub. art commn., permanent video marques) Jump Cuts, United Artists Cineplex, San Jose, Calif., (collaborative dance work with Charlerol/Danses) Moving Target, (collaborative theater work with Dumb Type and Hotel Pro Forma) Business Class, Copenhagen Cultural Capital, (interactive video installation) Indigestion, Barbican Art Gallery, London, Walter Phillips Gallery, Banff, Canada, Biennial Nagoya, Japan, 1997, (electronic project) Subtopia, ICC Gallery, Tokyo, 1997, and several others. Office: Diller Scofidio & Renfro 36 Cooper Sq New York NY 10003 Address: Grad Sch Arch Planning and Preservation Columbia U 1172 Amsterdam Ave New York NY 10027 Office Phone: 212-260-7971.

**RENFRO, CHARLES GILLILAND,** economist; b. Paris, Tex., Nov. 23, 1943; s. Charles G. and Virginia Armstrong (Dawsey) R.; m. Patricia Elise Candlin, June 21, 1969; children: Rebecca Elise, James Lawrence. BA, U. of York, Eng., 1966; MSc, London Sch. Econs., U. London, 1968; MA, U. Pa., 1971, PhD, 1976. Rsch. asst. Indsl. Manpower Project London Sch. Econs., 1967-68; rsch. asst. Brookings Instn., Washington, 1968-70; econ. rsch. fellow U. Pa.-Wharton Econometric Forecasting Assocs., Phila., 1970-71; instr. econs. U. Pa., 1971-73; lectr. dept. econs. Swarthmore (Pa.) Coll., 1972-73; rsch. assoc., asst. prof. econs. U. Ky., Lexington, 1973-77, assoc. dir. econ. studies and analysis, 1975-81, dir. ctr. for Applied Econ. Rsch., 1979-81; dir. regional forecasting, chief regional economist Chase Econometric Assocs. Inc., Bala Cynwyd, Pa., 1981-83; pres. C.G. Renfro & Assocs., Bala Cynwyd, 1978—, Alphametrics Corp., Bala Cynwyd, 1984—. Pres Sparks Agribus. Info. Systems, Inc., Bala Cynwyd and Memphis, 1989-92; bd. dirs. Alphametrics Ltd., Cambridge, Eng.; former bd. dirs. Integrated Modelling Applications Ltd., Cambridge, Eng., 1985-90; econ. advisor office budget and mgmt. State of Ohio, 1980, 82-83, permanent subcom. investigations, com. govt. ops. U.S. Senate, 1974-75, State Govt. Pa., 1981-83, environ. protection agy. State of N.J., 1982-83, State of Conn., 1982-83, State of Tex., 1982-83, dept. of taxation State of North Dakota, 1981-83, State of Mo., 1982-83; assoc. dir. Ky. Coun. Econ. Advisors, 1977-79, exec. dir. 1979-81; mem. advisor State of Va., 1982-83, info. systems advisor small bus. subcom. U.S. Ho. Reps., 1979-80; cons. Merrill Lynch Econs. Inc., 1986-87, Data Resources Inc., 1985-90, Wharton Econometric Forecasting Assocs., Inc., 1984-86, Chase Econometric Assocs., 1983, 85-87, Humana, Inc., 1981, Dames & Moore, 1980-81, Gen. Telephone Co., Ky., 1977-81, 1st Security Nat. Bank and Trust Co., 1979-81, Elsevier Sci. Publ. Co., Inc., 1980-87, Townsend-Greenspan & Co., Inc., 1984-86. M & DR Cons. adv. com. Pitagora Spa, Rome, 1990-93, M & DR Cons. Srl, Milan, 1990-93, Ibermetrics S.A., Madrid, 1987—. Author and developer computer software systems, first PC-based comml. econ. forecasting svc., principally MODLER Statis. Info. and Modeling System, 1970, DATAVIEW Statis. Info. System, 1982; author: Computational Econometrics: Its Impact on the Development of Quantitative Economics, 2004; co-author: MODLER BLUE Advanced Econometric Estimation System, 1985-86, MODLER MBA Bus. Decision Support and Forecasting System, (co-author) Wharton PC-Mark 7/MODLER Microcomputer-based Econometric Modelling System and Quar. Model of U.S. Economy, 1984, POWERSTATION, MAESTRO; MODLER systems used worldwide by internat. orgns. such as UN, EEC, govt's, major econ. forecasting firms; editor Rev. of Public Data Use. 1980-84, Jour. Econ. and Social Measurement, 1985—; editl. adv. bd. Computers and the Social Sciences, 1985-87; contbr. articles to profl. jours.; founder, prin. developer Ky. Econ. Info. System, 1973-81; designer, developer Online Retrieval and Computation Lang. for Economists (Oracle), 1976. Mem. Am. Econ. Assn., Am. Statis. Assn., Southeastern Econ. Analysis Conf. (program chmn. 1977, exec. com. 1977-81), Early English Text Soc., Soc. for Econ. Dynamics and Control, Soc. for Computational Econs., Nat. Assn. Bus. Economists, Penn Club (N.Y.C.).

**RENFRO, JOHN M.,** human resources specialist; b. Collinsville, Ill., Dec. 31, 1959; BS, So. Ill. U., 1982. V.p. human resources A.C. Nielson Internat.; v.p. human resources consumer mktg. info. group Asia-Pacific, Latin Am. and Africa ops. Dun & Bradstreet; v.p. human resources and adminstrn. small bus. svcs. divsn. Ameritech, Chgo.; sr. v.p. human resources and adminstrn. Zenith Electronics Corp., Chgo.; v.p. corp. human resources to sr. v.p. human resources Gateway, San Diego, 1998—2002; sr. v.p., chief human resources officer Walt Disney Co., Burbank, Calif., 2002—06; v.p. human resources HP Imaging and Printing Group (IPG) Hewlett-Packard, 2006—. Mem. external adv. bd. coll. bus. adminstrn. So. Ill. U.; bd. dirs. LA Urban League; mem.

external adv. bd. So. Ill. U., Carbondale. Mem. exec. com. United Way, San Diego, mem. Alexis de Tocqueville Soc. Office: HP Imaging and Printing Group 3000 Hanover St Palo Alto CA 94304 Office Phone: 818-560-1000. Office Fax: 818-560-1930.

**RENFRO, NORM,** energy executive; BS in Biology, S.W. Tex. State U.; BS in Chemistry, Corpus Christi State U. With Kerr McGee Corpn., Okla. City, Southwestern Refining Co., Corpus Christi, Tex.; v.p. environ. and safety affairs Valero Energy Corpn., San Antonio, 1997, v.p. health, safety and environ. Office: Valero Energy Corpn 1 Valero Way San Antonio TX 78292-0500*

**RENFRO, PATRICIA ELISE,** library director, academic administrator; b. Nelson, Lancashire, Eng. d. Henry Lawrence and Maud (Thompson) Candlin; m. Charles Gilliland Renfro, June 21, 1969; children: Rebecca Elise, James Lawrence. BA in English and History with honors, U. York, Eng., 1966; acad. postgrad. diploma, U. London, 1968; MA in History, U. Ky., 1981. Libr. asst. Holborn br. London Borough of Camden Pub. Librs., London, 1966-67, sr. asst. libr., 1968-69; dep. acquisitions libr. Folger Shakespeare Libr., Washington, 1969-70; cataloger Libr. Co. of Phila., 1970-72; reference libr. U. Pa. Librs., 1972-73, U. Ky. Librs., 1975-76, head of reference svcs., 1976-78; exec. sec. U. Ky. Libr. Assocs., U. Ky., 1979-80; reference libr. U. Pa., 1982-83, head circulation svcs. Van Pelt Libr., 1983-85, asst. dir. librs. for pub. svcs., 1985-89, assoc. dir. librs., 1989—2000; dep. univ. libr. Columbia U., N.Y.C., 2000—. Mem. programs adv. com. Rsch. Librs. Group, 1991-92; mem. circulation interchange com. NISO 1999-2002; bd. dirs. N.Y. State Higher Edn. Initiative, 2004—. Contbr. articles to profl. jours. Mem. ALA, Assn. Coll. and Rsch. Librs. (rsch. com. 1992-94, ULS program com. 2005).

**RENFRO, WILLIAM LEONARD,** futurist, lawyer, inventor, entrepreneur; b. West Palm Beach, Fla., Sept. 9, 1945; s. Ernest Leonard and One Warren (McAdams) R. BS in Physics, Rensselaer Poly. Inst., 1967, MS in Nuclear Engring., 1972; postgrad., Yale U., 1967-68; JD, U. Conn., 1972. Bar: Conn. 1973, U.S. Ct. Fed. Claims, Fed. Ct. Appeals (D.C. cir.). Physicist Compustion Engring., Windsor Locks, Conn., 1968-69; pvt. practice law, Hartford, Conn., 1973-74; sr. rsch. assoc. The Futures Group, Glastonbury, Conn., 1973-76; analyst futures rsch. Congl. Rsch. Svc., U.S. Congress, Washington, 1976-80; pres. Policy Analysis Co., Inc., Washington, 1980—. Vis. fellow Ark. Inst.; guest lectr. Georgetown U., Brookings Inst., Nat. War Coll.; adj. prof. George Washington U., Indsl. Coll. Armed Forces Nat. Def. U.; mem. nat. foresight network U.S. Congress. Author: (with others) The Futures Research Handbook, 1997, Anticipatory Democracy, 1978, The Public Affairs Handbook, 1983, The Legislative Role of Corporations, 1982, Applying Methods and Techniques of Futures Research, 1983, Future Research and the Straegic Planning Process, 1985, Non-Extrapolative Forecasting in Business, 1988, Futures Research Methodology: The UN Millennium Project, 1999; author: Issue Management in Strategic Planning, 1993, Vision-2020, 1999; editor Futures Rsch. Quar. World Futures Soc., 1980-1991; issues mgmt. editor the Futurist, 1982—. Tech. Analysis and Strategic Mgmt. Mem. long range planning com. United Way; trustee World Tech. Found.; Am. Friends of Romania, 2002—; lic. pastoral vis. lay eucharistic min. Wash. Diocese; Atlantic Coun., 2004—. Mem.: ABA, Washington Choral Ensemble (trustee 2004—), Russian Am. Student Exchange (chmn., founder), Georgetown Hist. Structures Preservation Soc. (chmn., co-founder), People to People Internat., Hartford County Bar Assn., Conn. Bar Assn., Internat. Pub. Rels. Assn., Assn. Former Intelligence Officers, World Futures Soc., Issues Mgmt. Assn. (bd. dirs. 1981—98, v.p. 1986—88, pres. 1988—96), Pub. Rels. Soc. Am., St. Andrews Soc., Clan Hamilton Soc., English Speaking Union (trustee, v.p. internat. programs Washington br.). Episcopalian. Achievements include U.S. and foreign patents.

**RENFROE, OWEN,** television director; Dir.: (TV series) General Hospital, One Life to Live; (films) The Prospector, 1998. Co-recipient Outstanding Directorial Achievement in Daytime Serials for One Life to Live, Directors Guild Am. (DGA), 1991, 2001, Outstanding Drama Series Directing Team for General Hospital, Daytime Emmy Awards, 2004, 2006; recipient Outstanding Directorial Achievement in Daytime Serials for General Hospital, Directors Guild Am. (DGA), 2005. Office: ABC Inc 500 S Buena Vista St Burbank CA 91521-4551 Studio: Prospect Studios 4151 Prospect Ave Los Angeles CA 90027*

**RENFROE, W. DOUGLAS,** musician, conductor, music educator; b. Anderson, Ind., Mar. 7, 1948; s. Walter D. and Mary M. Renfroe; m. Halina K. Gawel, May 26, 1990 (div. May 2001); m. Lorraine Murphy-Renfroe, Apr. 6, 2002; children: Brenna, Sean, James. B in Music Edn., Westminster Choir Coll., 1970; MusM, Cath. U. Am., 1974. Concert artist, tchr. Providence-St. Mgmt. et al, Boston, 1974—88, N.Y.C., 1974—88, NH, 1974—88; v.p. sales and mktg. Brand Svcs./Waste Mgmt., Chgo., 1988—94; concert artist, condr. ES Mgmt., Bristol, NH, 1994—98, Fantasia Mgmt., Sarasota, Fla., 1998—2001, SRO DOLOR, Inc., Ft. Myers, Fla., 2001—. Prof. Edison Coll., Ft. Myers, 1999—; consulting, clinician in field, 1972—; consulting and adv. bd. dir. Lowcountry Theatre, Beaufort, SC, 1976—88; mem. adv. bd. Literacy of Am., Columbia, SC, 1976—86. Author: The Art of German Lieder, 1979; contbr. articles to profl. jours. With USN, 1970—74. Named Outstanding Tchr. Yr., S.C. Bd. Edn., 1978, N.H. Bd. Edn., 1986; named to Outstanding Young Men of Am., 1980. Mem.: Music Tchrs. Nat. Assn. (v.p. 1978—), Am. Legion (life), Rotary Club Internat. (v.p. 1995—2000). Avocations: reading, swimming, golf, travel. Home: 1448 S Brandywine Cir Fort Myers FL 33919 Office: SRO DOLOR Inc PO Box 826 Fort Myers FL 33919

**RENGASWAMY, RAGHUNATHAN,** chemical engineering researcher, educator; b. Madras, Tamilnadu, India, Aug. 15, 1969; s. Rengaswamy Srinivasan and Saroja Rengaswamy; m. Suchitra Veeravalli, June 28, 1998; children: Abhishek Raghunathan, Aadarsh Raghunathan. B in Tech., IIT Madras, India, 1990; PhD, Purdue U., West Lafayette, Ind., 1995. Sr. engr. Asea Brown Boveri, Bangalore, Karnataka, India, 1995; asst. prof. IIT Bombay, Mumbai, Maharashtra, India, 1996—2000; vis. asst. prof. Purdue U., West Lafayette, Ind., 2001; assoc. prof. Clarkson U., Potsdam, NY, 2002—. Cons. Asea Brown Boveri, Bangalore, Karnataka, India, 1996—2002. Author: (20 peer reviewed articles) Chem. Engring. Jours., aiche conf. presentation. Recipient Young Engr. award, Indian NAE, 2000. Mem.: Am. Chem. Soc., AIChE. Achievements include invention of Qualitative trend analysis (QTA) technique while at Purdue University. Home: 401 Swan St Potsdam NY 13676 Office: Clarkson Univ Dept of Chem Engring Potsdam NY 13699-5705 Business E-Mail: raghu@clarkson.edu.

**RENICK, JAMES CARMICHAEL,** educational association administrator, former academic administrator; b. Rockford, Ill., Dec. 8, 1948; s. Constance Renick; m. Peggy Renick; 1 child, Karinda. BA, Ctrl. State U., Ohio, 1970; MSW, Kans. U., 1972; PhD in public adminstrn., Fla. State U., 1980. Cmty. mental health counselor; asst. prof social work U. West Fla., 1975—81; assoc. prof. pub. adminstrn. U. South Fla., 1981—85, asst. to pres., 1983—85; asst. dean adminstrn. U. South Fla., Grad. Sch., 1985—88; founding edn. chair Exec. Fellows Prog. Inst. of Govt., U. South Fla., 1985—88, dir. pub. adminstrn. prog., 1988; assoc. provost & dir. Early Identification Prog. George Mason U., 1989—91, vice provost academic initiative & external affairs, 1991—93; chancellor U. Mich., Dearborn, 1993—99; prof polit. sci. NC A&T State U., 1999—, chancellor, 1999—2006; sr. v.p. programs and rsch. Am. Coun. Edn., Washington, 2006—. Cons. in edn. field nat. and internat.; mem. President's Bd. Adv. on Historically Black Coll. and Univ., NC Bd. of Sci. and Tech., Bus.-Higher Edn. Forum; bd. trustees JSTOR; bd. dirs. Microelectronics Ctr. of NC, Piedmont Triad Ctr. for Adv. Mfg., Piedmont Triad Partnership. Contbr. articles to profl. jours. Mem. James Lawrence Found., Parrin J. Mitchell Found.; mem. hon. edn. coun. Nat. Minority Military Mus. Found.; bd. dirs. Greater Greensboro C. of C; pres. Greensboro Merchants Assn. Named to Donald K. Anthony Achievement Hall of Fame, Ctrl. State U., Ohio, 1993; recipient President's Medallion, U. Mich., Exemplary Award for Pub. Service, Am. Assn. for Higher Edn. Black Caucus. Office: Am Coun Edn One Dupont Circle NW Washington DC 20036 Office Phone: 202-939-9300.*

**RENICK, KYLE,** artistic director; b. St. Louis, Apr. 24, 1948; s. Mark Allen and Annabelle (Myers) R. BA magna cum laude, Tufts U., 1970. Sr. fund acct. New Eng. Mchts. Nat. Bank, Boston, 1970-73; fund acct. Fidelity Mgmt. and Rsch. Corp., Boston, 1973; bus. mgr. Am. Pl. Theatre, N.Y.C., 1973-78; producing dir. WPA Theatre, N.Y.C., 1977-82, artistic dir., 1982—; pres. WPA Prodns., Inc., N.Y.C., 1987—. Trustee Alliance of Resident Theatres-N.Y., 1982-92; cons. N.Y. State Council on Arts, 1982-85, Nat. Endowment for Arts, 1986. Producer Steel Magnolias, 1987, The Lady in Question, 1989; contbr. articles to profl. pubs. Recipient spl. award for outstanding achievement Drama Desk Assn., 1983. Mem.: Neue Bachgesellschaft, Nev. Hist. Soc., Film Music Soc., Wildlife Conservation Soc., The Packard Club, Phi Beta Kappa. Avocations: early music, record collecting, ghost town photography. Home: 2 Bethune St Apt 4B New York NY 10014-1862 E-mail: wpatheatre@msn.com.*

**RENKES, GREGG D.,** former state attorney general; m. Maureen Renkes; 2 children. BA, Vassar Coll.; MS, Yale U.; JD, U. Colo. Bar: Alaska 1987. Law clk., magistrate State Alaska Ct. Sys.; chief of staff, chief counsel to U.S. Senator Frank Murkowski; majority staff dir. U.S. Senate Com. on Energy and Natural Resources, 1995—98; pres. The Renkes Group, Ltd.; atty. gen. State of Alaska, Juneau, 2002—05. Spkr. in field. Contbr. articles to profl. jours. Mem. Campaign to Re-elect Senator Frank Murkowski, 1992, 1998, Murkowski 2002 Alaska Gubernatorial Campaign; active Rep. Nat. Conv. Platform Com., 1996. Republican.

**RENKIS, ALAN ILMARS,** plastics formulating company executive; b. Preili, Latvia, Apr. 16, 1938; arrived in U.S., 1950, naturalized, 1958; s. Joseph and Malvine (Sturitis) R.; m. Inara Balodis, July 15, 1961; children: Martin Alan, Laura Alise. BSChemE, Pa. State U., 1960. Staff product devel. and tech. svc. divsn. Diamond Alkali Co., Painesville, Ohio, 1960-63; tech. dir. G.S. Plastics Co., Cleve., 1963; founder, pres. Thermoclad Co., Erie, Pa., 1963—, Riverside, Calif., 1972-80, Ocala, Fla., 1985—. Developer comml. PVC resins for formulating fluidized bed and electrostatic coating powders; formulations and compounding techniques. Mem. World Pres. Orgn., Soc. Plastic Engrs., Soc. Mfg. Engrs., Am. Latvian Assn., Erie Yacht Club, Kahkwa Club, Sigma Pi, Fraternitas Metropolitana. Home: 214 Crystal Point Dr Erie PA 16505 Office: Thermoclad Co 361 W 11th St Erie PA 16501-1703 Business E-Mail: arenkis@thermoclad.com.

**RENNA, CATHY,** communications executive, activist; Grad., Adelphi U. Vol. Gay and Lesbian Alliance Against Defamation (GLAAD), NY, 1990, dir. regional media and cmty. rels., 1996—2001, news media dir., 2001—04; media rels. dir. Fenton Comm., NY, 2004—. Office: Fenton Comm 260 Fifth Ave Ninth Fl New York NY 10001 Office Phone: 212-584-5000 319. Office Fax: 212-584-5045. E-mail: crenna@fenton.com.

**RENNE, PAUL A.,** lawyer; b. Mpls., Nov. 2, 1930; AB, Univ. Minn., 1956; JD, Harvard Univ., 1959. Bar: DC 1959, NY 1961, Calif. 1964, US Supreme Ct. 1964. Law clk. Judge Edwin D. Steel, Jr., US Dist Ct. (Del.), 1959—60; assoc. Haight Gardner Poor & Havens, NYC, 1960—61; atty. U.S. Dept. Justice, civil rights div., Washington, 1961—62; asst. U.S. atty. U.S. Dept. Justice, DC dist., 1962—64; sr. counsel, litigation dept. Cooley Godward LLP, San Francisco, 1964—. Adj. prof. Golden Gate Univ.; lectr. Calif. CLE; mediator Assn. San Francisco, US Dist. Ct. Contbr. articles to profl. jours. Pilot USAF, 1951—56. Mem.: ABA, Am. Coll. Trial Lawyers (state chmn., no. Calif.), Am. Arbitration Assn. (mem. com. panel), Bar Assn. San Francisco: Office: Cooley Godward Llp 101 California St Fl 5 San Francisco CA 94111-5800 Office Phone: 415-693-2073. Office Fax: 415-951-3699. Business E-Mail: prenne@cooley.com.

**RENNE, PAUL F.,** retired food products executive; b. Pitts. BS in Acctg., St. Vincent Coll. CPA. With acctg. firm, 1965-73; fin. analyst H.J. Heinz Co., Pittsburgh, Pa., 1973-75, dir. fin. rels., 1975-81, v.p. fin. Heinz Can., 1981-84, corp. treas. Heinz World Hdqrs., 1984-86, v.p. treas., 1986-1996, v.p. fin., treas., 1989—, CFO, 1996—2001, sr. v.p. fin. to exec. v.p., 1997—2001, spl. advisor, fin., 2002.

**RENNER, ANDREW IHOR,** surgeon; b. Buenos Aires, Aug. 1, 1951; came to U.S., 1956; s. Vladimir and Emelia R.; m. Cristina Sasyk, Apr. 17, 1982. MD, Albert Einstein Coll. Medicine, 1975. Diplomate Am. Bd. Surgery. Pvt. practice gen. surgery, Burbank, Calif.; chief of staff Providence-St. Joseph Med. Ctr., 2005, 2006. Chmn. dept. surgery St. Joseph Hosp., Burbank, 1995-97, vice chief of staff Providence St. Joseph Med. Ctr., Burbank, 2003-04, chief of staff, 2005-06. Fellow ACS, Internat. Coll. Surgeons; mem. Am. Soc. Gen. Surgeons, L.A. Surg. Soc. Office: 2701 W Alameda Ave Ste 300 Burbank CA 91505-4408 Office Phone: 818-843-1492. Office Fax: 818-843-5283.

**RENNER, WILLIAM SCOTT,** retired military officer; b. Washington, Pa., Apr. 26, 1935; s. Albert Conrad and Ruth Estel (Tombaugh) Renner; m. Sara Elisabeth Donahue, Apr. 4, 1959; children: Michael Paul, Mandy Jane. BA in Finance, Pa. State U., State College, 1958; grad., Naval War Coll., Newport, RI, 1973. Comd. ensign USNR, 1958; rose to capt. US Navy, 1980; anti-submarine pilot HS-9, Quonset Point, RI, 1959—63; flight instr. HS-1, Key West, Fla., 1963—66, 1968—70, Jacksonville, Fla., 1973—74; asst. navigator USS Independence CV-62, Norfolk, Va., 1966—68; ASW pilot and ops. officer HS-5, Quonset Point, 1970—72; commanding officer HS-15, Jacksonville, 1974—76; enlisted rating coord. Chief of Naval Pers., Washington, 1976—79; head ASW manpower and tng. Chief of Naval Ops., Washington, 1979—82; commanding officer US Naval Support Facility Diego Garcia, Indian Ocean, 1982—83; dir. adminstrn. Naval Mil. Pers. Command, Washington, 1983—86; commander program support divsn. Def. Logistics Agy., Washington, 1986—90; ret. US Navy, 1990. Mem. mil. adv. bd. Pa. Senator Piccola, Harrisburg, 1996—. Constrn. leader Habitat for Humanity, Harrisburg, 1996—; pres. Kensington PUD, Harrisburg, 2004—. Recipient Winged S award, Sikorsky Aircraft, 1961, 1975—76, Meritorious Svc. award, Sec. of Navy, 1982, 1989, Legion of Merit, 1983, Def. Superior Svc. medal, Sec. of Def., 1990, Humanitarian award, Habitat for Humanity of Greater Harrisburg, 2002. Mem.: Mil. Officers of Am. Assn., Navy Helicopter Assn., Pi Kappa Alpha (Beta Alpha social chmn.). Republican. Avocations: woodworking, gardening, travel. Home: 4309 S Victoria Way Harrisburg PA 17112 E-mail: salscroren@aol.com.

**RENNERT, IRA LEON,** manufacturing executive; b. 1934; married; 3 children. BA. Bklyn. Coll., 1954; MBA, NYU, 1956. Credit analyst M. Lowenstein Corp., NYC, 1956-57; salesman Underwood Corp., NYC, 1957-58; registered rep. Francis I. Dupont & Co., NYC, 1958-60; established I.L. Rennert & Co., Inc. (formerly Rubin, Rennert & Co., Inc.), NYC, 1960-64; cons. NYC, 1964-75; pres. Consolidated Sewing Machine Corp., NYC, 1975—; pres., CEO, chmn. Renco Grp., Inc., NYC, 1980—; CEO WCI Steel Inc., Warren, Ohio, 1988—. Chmn. bd. Am. Gen. Corp., South Bend, Ind., 1992. Named one of 400 Richest Ams., Forbes mag., 2006. Office: Renco Grp 30 Rockefeller Plz New York NY 10112*

**RENNERT, OWEN MURRAY,** pediatrician, geneticist, educator; b. NYC, Aug. 8, 1938; s. David Rennert and Frieda (Weinsteiner) Sommer; m. Sandra Serota, Mar. 22, 1964; children: Laura, Rachel, Ian. BS, BA, U. Chgo., 1957, MD, 1961, MS in Biochemistry, 1963. Diplomate Am. Bd. Pediatrics, Am. Bd. Genetics, Am. Bd. Med. Genetics. Assoc. prof. pediatrics U. Fla. Coll. Medicine, Gainesville, 1968—70, assoc. prof. biochemistry, 1970—71, head instl. divsn. genetics, endocrinology and metabolism, 1970—78, prof. pediatrics, biochemistry and neurosci., 1971-78; prof. biochemistry, prof. and head dept. pediatrics U. Okla., Oklahoma City, 1977-88; chief pediatrics svc. and head genetics, sect. endocrinology and metabolism Okla. Children's Mem. Hosp.; Oklahoma City, 1977-88; prof., chmn. dept. pediatrics Georgetown U. Sch. Medicine, Washington, 1988-98, prof. dept. biochemistry and molecular biology, 1995—98, prof. emeritus, 1998—2000; spl. asst. to dir. ctr. rsch. mothers and children Nat. Inst. Child Health Human Devel., NIH, Bethesda, Md., 1998—2000, dir. Ctr. Rsch. Mothers and Children, 2000, sci.

dir. divsn. intramural rsch., 2000—. Co-author: Metabolism of Trace Metals in Man: Developmental Biology and Genetic Implications (2 vols.), 1984; contbr. articles to profl. jours. Bd. dirs. Children's Med. Rsch., Oklahoma City, 1984-88. Served to sr. surgeon USPHS, 1964-66. Named Clin. Scientist of Yr., Am. Assn. Clin. Scientists, 1978. Mem. Am. Pediatric Soc., Am. Acad. Pediatrics, Soc. Pediatric Research, Am. Coll. Clin. Nutrition, Biochem. Soc., Am. Soc. Molecular Biology and Biochemistry, Am. Coll. Med. Genetics, Am. Soc. Human Genetics. Office: NICHD/NIH Divsn Intramural Rsch 31 Center Dr Bldg 31 Rm 2A46 Bethesda MD 20892-2425 Office Phone: 301-594-5984. Business E-Mail: rennerto@mail.nih.gov.

**RENNEY, TOM,** professional hockey coach; m. Glenda Renney; children: Jessica, Jamie. Head coach Kamloops Blazers (WHL), 1991—93, Team Can., 1993—96, Vancouver Canucks, 1996—97; v.p. hockey Can. Nat. Team, 1998—99, head coach, v.p., 1999—2000; dir. player pers. NY Rangers, 2000—02, asst. coach, 2003—04, v.p. player devel., 2003—, head coach, 2004—. Head coach Team Canada, Lillehammer Olympic Games, 1992. Office: c/o NY Rangers 2 Pennsylvania Plaza New York NY 10121*

**RENNICK, JOHN H.,** psychiatrist, director; b. El Paso, Tex., July 23, 1948; s. Charles F. and Patricia N. Rennick; m. Judith C. Rand, June 28, 1975; children: Theresa M., Marcus J., Julia C., Angela R. BS Magna Cum Laude, U. Ariz., 1970; MD, U. Tex. Med. Sch., 1974. Diplomate Practice Am. Bd. Family Practice, 1979, Am. Bd. Psychiatry/Neurology, 1984, Geriatric Psychiatry Am. Bd. Psychiatry/Neurology, 1996. Physician Nat. Health Svc. Corps, Spring City, Tenn., 1975—77; resident psychiatry U. Tex. Health Sci. Ctr. Med. Sch., 1978—81; pvt. practice psychiatry Psychiat. Assocs., Las Cruces, N.Mex., 1982—90; staff psychiatrist U.S. Army 34th Gen. Hosp., Augsburg, Bavaria, Germany, 1990—92; sr. staff psychiatrist Scott & White Clinic and Hosp., Temple, Tex., 1992—94; staff psychiatrist Hutchinson Area Health Care, Minn., 1994—97, Hartshorn Health Svc., Colo. State U., Ft. Collins 1997—99; med./clinical dir. Larimer Ctr. for Mental Health, Ft. Collins, 1999—2002, 2004—; staff psychiatrist Mountain Crest Hosp., Ft. Collins, 2002—03. Chief resident psychiatry U. Tex. Health Sci. Ctr. Med. Sch., San Antonio, 1980—81, asst. prof. psychiatry, 1981—82; chmn. bd. Mesilla Valley Hospice, Las Cruces, 1984—86; chief of staff Meml. Med. Ctr. Hosp., Las Cruces, 1986—87; asst. prof. psychiatry Tex. A & M U. Sys. Health Sci. Ctr., Temple, Tex., 1992—94; clin. affiliate faculty U. Colo. Health Sci. Ctr. Med. Sch., Denver, 1999—. Chmn. bd. Boy Scout Troop 246, Hutchinson, Minn., 1995—97; mem. Rotary Club, Ft. Collins, 1999—2002. Maj. USAR, 1999—. Recipient Eagle Scout award, Boy Scouts Am., 1963, Key, Phi Kappa Phi, 1970, Woodbadge award, Boy Scouts Am., 1997; fellow, Am. Acad. Family Practitioners, 1979. Fellow: Am. Psychiat. Assn. (Falk Fellow 1980), Am. Psychiat. Assn. (Disting. Fellow 2002); mem.: Sigma Xi. Office: 2001 S Shields Bldg K Fort Collins CO 80526 Office Phone: 970-494-4200.

**RENNIE, JOHN,** soccer coach; b. Sept. 22, 1944; Head soccer coach Duke U., Durham, N.C. Office: Duke Univ Cameren Indoor Stadium PO Box 90555 Durham NC 27708-0555

**RENNIE, JOHN,** editor-in-chief; b. 1959; BS in Biology, Yale U., 1981. With Harvard Med. Sch.; sci. writer various publs.; mem. bd. editors Sci. Am., 1989—94, editor-in-chief, 1994—. Am. Presents, 1998—. TV appearances include ABC World News Hour, ABC News Overnight, The Newshour with Jim Lehrer, Fox News Channel, Entertainment Tonight, Science Friday (National Public Radio), CBS Early Show; contbr. articles to profl. publications including The Economist, The New York Times, Longevity. Recipient Sagan award, Coun. Sci. Soc. Presidents, Navigator award, Potomac Inst. Policy Studies. Avocation: Karate. Office: Sci Am 415 Madison Ave New York NY 10017-1111 Office Phone: 212-754-0550. Business E-Mail: editors@sciam.com.*

**RENNIE, PAUL STEVEN,** research scientist, surgeon; b. Toronto, Ont., Can., Feb. 9, 1946; m. Carol Andrews, 1968; 1 child, Jan. BSc, U. Western Ont., 1969; PhD in Biochemistry, U. Alta., Can., 1973. Rsch. assoc. U. Alta., 1975-76, asst. prof. medicine, 1976-79, assoc. prof., 1979; rsch. scientist B.C. Cancer Agy., Canada, 1979-92, dir. rsch., 1992-97; prof. surgery U. B.C., 1986—, dir. prostate rsch. lab., 1998—. Med. Rsch. Coun. rsch. fellow Imperial Cancer Rsch. Fund, 1973-75; rsch. scholar Nat. Cancer Inst. Can., 1976-79. Achievements include research on biochemical control of growth in androgen responsive organs and neoplasms; genetic markers in prostate cancer. Office: Prostate Ctr Jack Bell Rsch Ctr 2660 Oak St Vancouver BC Canada V6H 3Z6 Business E-Mail: prennie@interchange.ubc.ca.

**RENNINGER, MARY KAREN,** retired librarian; b. Pitts., Apr. 30, 1945; d. Jack Burnell and Jane (Hammerly) Gunderman; m. Norman Christian Renninger, Sept. 3, 1965 (div. 1980); 1 child, David Christian. BA, U. Md., 1969, MA, 1972, M.L.S., 1975. Tchr. English West Carteret High Sch., Morehead City, NC, 1969-70; instr. in English U. Md., College Park, 1970-72; head network services Nat. Libr. Svc., Libr. of Congress, Washington, 1974-78, asst. for network support, 1978-80; mem. fed. women's program com. Libr. of Congress, Washington, 1978-80; chief libr. divsn. Dept. Vets. Affairs, Washington, 1980-90; chief serial and govt. pubs. divsn. Libr. of Congress, Washington, 1991—2006, mem. fed. com., 1980-90, mem. exec. adv. bd., 1985-90; ret., 2006. Mem. USBE pers. subcom., 1982-84; bd. regents Nat. Libr. of Medicine, 1986-90, mem. outreach panel, 1988-89; fed. libr. task force for 1990 White House Conf. on Librs., 1986-90; liaison to The White House Conf. Med. Libr. Assn., 1989-90. Recipient Meritorious Svc. award Libr. of Congress, 1974, Spl. Achievement award, 1976, Performance award VA, ann. 1982-89, Adminstr.'s Commendation, 1985, Spl. Contbn. award, 1986. Mem. ALA (Govt. Documents Roundtable), Libr. Tech. Assn., Med. Libr. Assn. (govt. rels. com. 1985—), DC Libr. Assn., Soc. Applied Learning Tech., Med. Interactive Videodisc Consortium, Govt. Documents Roundtable, Knowledge Utilization Soc., Nat. Multimedia Assn. Am., US Tennis Assn., Phi Beta Kappa, Alpha Lambda Delta, Beta Phi Mu. Home: 840 College Pky Rockville MD 20850-1931 Personal E-Mail: KarenRenniger@comcast.net.

**RENO, JANET,** former United States attorney general; b. Miami, Fla., July 21, 1938; d. Henry and Jane (Wood) R. AB in Chemistry, Cornell U., 1960; LL.B., Harvard U., 1963. Bar: Fla. 1963. Assoc. Brigham & Brigham, 1963-67; ptnr. Lewis & Reno, 1967-71; staff dir. judiciary com. Fla. Ho. of Reps., Tallahassee, 1971-72; cons. Fla. Senate Criminal Justice Com. for Revision Fla.'s Criminal Code, spring 1973; adminstrv. asst. state atty. 11th Jud. Circuit Fla., Miami, 1973-76, state atty., 1978-93; ptnr. Steel Hector and Davis, Miami, 1976-78; US atty. gen. Dept. Justice, Washington, 1993-2001. Mem. jud. nominating commn. 11th Jud. Circuit Fla., 1976-78; chmn. Fla. Gov.'s Council for Prosecution Organized Crime, 1979-80. Recipient Women First award YWCA, 1993. National Women's Hall of Fame, 2000. Mem. ABA (Inst. Jud. Adminstrn. Juvenile Justice Standards Commn. 1973-76), Am. Law Inst., Am. Judicature Soc. (Herbert Harley award 1981), Dade County Bar Assn., (Fla. Pros. Atty.'s Assn. (pres. 1984-86). Democrat.

**RENO, JOHN F.,** foundation administrator; b. Peoria, Ill., June 15, 1939; s. John Henkle and Alice Hanna (Findley) R.; m. Suzanne McKnight, Apr. 18, 1964; children: David, Anne. AB, Dartmouth Coll., 1961; MBA, Northwestern U., 1963. Ptnr. G.H. Walker & Co., Boston, 1964-74; divsn. pres. Dynatech Cryomedical Co., Barnardville, Mass., 1974-79; corp. v.p. Dynatech Corp., Burlington, 1979-82, group v.p., 1982-87, pres., COO, 1987-93, pres., CEO, 1993-99, chmn., 1996-99, Reno Family Found., Winchester, Mass., 1999—. Bd. dirs. Millipre Corp., Bedford, Mass. Trustee, chmn. Boston Mus. of Sci., 1992—; bd. dirs. CEOs for Fundamental Change in Edn., Cambridge, Mass.; dir. WGBH Pub. TV, 1999— Named Entrepreneur of Yr., Inc. mag., 1995. Avocations: painting, writing. Office: Reno Family Found 63 Shore Rd Ste 33 Winchester MA 01890-2828

**RENO, OTTIE WAYNE,** former judge; b. Pike County, Ohio, Apr. 7, 1929; s. Eli Enos and Arbannah Belle (Jones) Reno; m. Janet Gay McCann, May 22, 1947; children: Jennifer Lynn, Lorna Victoria, Ottie Wayne II. A in Bus. Adminstrn., Franklin U., 1949; LLB, Franklin Law Sch., 1953; JD, Capital U., 1966; grad. Coll. Juvenile Justice, U. Nev., 1973. Bar: Ohio 1953. Practiced in Pike County; recorder Pike County, 1957-73, common pleas judge probate and juvenile divsn., 1973-79. Author: Story of Horseshoes, 1963, Pitching Championship Horseshoes, 1971; 2d rev. edit., 1975; author: The American Directory of Horseshoe Pitching, 1983, Ohio vs. Smith, Murder, 1990, Reno and Apsaalooka Survive Custer, 1996. Del. Dem. Nat. Conv., 1972, 1996; mem. Camp Creek precinct Dem. Ctrl. Com., 1956—72, 1983—90, 1999—2002; sec. Pike County Dem. Exec. Com., 1971—72, 1983—90, 1983—87, chmn., 1971—72, 1988—90; mem. Ohio Dem. Ctrl. Com., 1969—70; Dem. candidate 6th Ohio dist. U.S. Ho. of Reps., 1966; Dem. candidate 88th Ohio dist. Ohio Ho. of Reps., 1992; pres. Scioto Valley Local Sch. Dist., 1962—66. Named to Nat. Horseshoe Pitchers Hall of Fame, 1978; recipient Disting. Svc. award, Ohio Youth Commn., 1974, 6 Outstanding Jud. Svc. awards, Ohio Supreme Ct., 17 times Ala. horseshoe pitching champion. Mem.: Pike County Bar Assn., Nat. Coun.Juvenile Ct. Judges, Ohio Bar Assn., Am. Legion. Mem. Ch. Of Christ In Christian Union. Home: 148 Reno Rd Lucasville OH 45648-9580

**RENO, ROGER,** lawyer; b. Rockford, Ill., May 16, 1924; s. Guy B. and Hazel (Kinnear) R.; m. Janice Marie Odelius, May 17, 1952 (dec. Aug. 2005); children: Susan Marie, Sheri Jan Reno-Rudolph, Michael Guy. Student, Kenyon Coll., 1943-44, Yale U., 1944, U. Wis., 1946; AB, Carleton Coll., 1947; LL.B., Yale U., 1950. Bar: Ill. 1950. Practiced in Rockford, 1950; assoc. firm Reno, Zahm, Folgate, Lindberg & Powell, 1950-56, partner, 1956-84; of counsel Reno & Zahm LLC, 1984—. Chmn. Amcore Fin. Inc., 1982-95; atty. Rockford Bd. Edn., 1955-64. Past pres., bd. dirs. Childrens Home Rockford; trustee Swedish-Am. Hosp. Assn., 1967-77, Keith Country Day Sch. Served to 1st It. USAAF, 1943-46. Mem. ABA, Ill. Bar Assn., Winnebago County Bar Assn. (pres. 1979-80) Clubs: Forest Hills Country (Rockford). Methodist. Home: 2515 Chickadee Trl Rockford IL 61107 Office: Reno & Zahm LLC Amcore Fin Plaza Rockford IL 61104 Office Fax: 815-961-7723.

**RENO, RUSSELL RONALD, JR.,** lawyer; b. Gary, Ind., Nov. 28, 1933; s. Russell Ronald Sr. and Katherine Narcissus (White) R.; m. Mary Ellen Klock, Jan. 30, 1956 (dec. June 5, 2004); children: Mary Hall, Russell III, William, Elizabeth. AB, Haverford Coll., 1954; JD, U. Pa., 1957. Bar: Md. 1957, D.C. 1983. Assoc. Venable, Baetjer & Howard, Balt., 1958-66, ptnr., 1966—; asst. atty. gen. State of Md., Balt., 1962-64. Author: Maryland Real Estate Law-Practice, 1983. Bd. dirs. Balt. Choral Arts Soc., 1966—; trustee Goucher Coll., Balt., 1978-98, trustee emeritus, 1998—; chancellor Episcopal Diocese of Md., Balt., 1985—; bd. mgrs. Haverford Coll., 1990-2002. Fellow Am. Bar Found., Md. Bar Found.; mem. ABA, Md. State Bar Assn., Am. Coll. Real Estate Lawyers, Hamilton St. Club, Wednesday Law Club. Home: 224 Grindall St Baltimore MD 21230 Office: Venable Baetjer & Howard 2 Hopkins Plz Ste 2100 Baltimore MD 21201-2982 Office Phone: 410-244-7480. E-mail: rrreno@venable.com.

**RENOUF, ANNE,** corporate financial executive, consultant; b. N.Y.C., Apr. 3, 1937; Diploma, Emma Willard Sch., 1954; student, Inst. World Affairs, 1957; AB magna cum laude, honors in Anthropology, Columbia U., 1959; MA, Yale U., 1962, PhD, 1966; JD with honors, Am. U., 1978; postgrad., Duke U. Asst. prof. U. N.C., Chapel Hill, 1966-71; sr. profl. cons. U.S. Govt., Washington, 1972-75; pvt. practice fin. cons. Washington, 1976—; vis. assoc. prof. George Washington U. Sch. Bus. Adminstrn., Washington, 1983-84; gen. ptnr., v.p. Tech. Mgmt. Corp., Montgomeryville, Pa., 1986-88; chmn. Pivot, Inc., 1988—90; founding prin. SaraTech Fin. Inc., 1990-92; pvt. practice fin. cons. Founding dir., chmn. bd., CFO/bd. treas. Initiatives in Industry, Inc., 1996-02; corp. dir.; dir. fin. devel. Ctr. for Space and Advanced Tech., 1990; cons. The Brookings Instn., Washington, 1966, U.S. Dept. State, Washington, 1967, World Bank, 1992—; mem. Pres.'s Commn. Grad. Edn., 1967-68, Nat. Chamber Found. Task Force on Space Commercialization, Washington, 1983-86; vis. scholar Carnegie Endowment for Internat. Peace, N.Y.C., 1968-69; fellow U.S. Dept. State, EUR/RPE, 1967; northeastern dir. Va. Advanced Tech. Assn., 1984-88; fin. and tech. spkr.; mem. Coun. on Competitiveness, 1998—2003, Tech. Coun. Washington, 1998—; mem. Greater Washington Bd. Trade, The Potomac Conf., 1999-2001; mem. The World Bank, The Global Devel. Network, 1998 —. Contbr. articles on tech. commercialization and to profl. jours. Co-chair, charter mem. U.S./China Capital Cities Coun., Washington, 1985-95; advisor Greater Washington D.C. Bd. Trade, 1985-86, Internat. Red Cross, 1987-90; mem. Mayor's Adv. Coun. on Trade and Investment, 1987-91; mem. adv. coun. Ctr. for Internat. Bus. Edn. U. Alaska, Fairbanks, 1990-91, co-chmn. World Trade Day, 1989; bd. dirs. Nat. Symphony Orch., 1990-99, Greater Washington Met. Boys and Girls Clubs, 1992-2000; dir. Initiatives in Industry, Inc., 1996-02. Recipient citation, Washington D.C. Mayor's Office, 1986; Woodrow Wilson fellow, 1958, Bushnell fellow, Yale U., 1964, Hon. Officer-Faculty fellow, U.S. Dept. State, 1967. Fellow Washington Acad. Scis.; mem. Am. Soc. Internat. Law, Internat. Forum U.S. C. of C., Internat. Energy Seminar-Johns Hopkins Sch. for Advanced Internat. Study, Corcoran Gallery of Art (nat. coun.), Washington Internat. Trade Assn., Assn. for Corp. Growth, Phi Beta Kappa. Office Phone: 202-965-3000, 202-530-5285. Business E-Mail: arenouf@indevone.com.

**RENOUF, EDDA,** artist; b. Mexico City, June 17, 1943; d. Edward and Catharine Smith; m. Alain Middleton, Sept. 20, 1977; 1 child, Mélisande. BA, Sarah Lawrence Coll., 1965; M.F.A., Columbia U., 1971. One-woman shows include Yvon Lambert Gallery, Paris, 1972, 1974, 1976, 1978, 1980, 1982, 1984, 1993, Konrad Fischer Gallery, Dusseldorf, Germany, 1974, 1979, Blum-Helman Gallery, N.Y.C., 1978, 1980, 1982, 1985, 1987, 1989, U. Mich. Mus. Art, 1995, Elisabeth Kaufmann Gallery, Basel, Switzerland, 1994, 1996, Galerie Sollertis, Toulouse, France, 1994, 1996, 1998, Staatliche Kunsthalle Karlsruhe, Germany, 1997, Galerie Hubert Winter, Vienna, Austria, 1998, Galerie Liesbeth Lips, Rotterdam, 1998, 2001, Helman Gallery, N.Y.C., 2001—02, Joseph Helman Gallery, 2002, Nat. Mus. Women in the Arts, Washington, D.C., 2004, Brenan U. Galleries, Gainesville, Ga., 2004, Arnaud Lefebvre Gallery, Paris, 2006, New Arts Gallery, Litchfield, Conn., 2006; exhibited in group shows at Mus. Modern Art, N.Y.C., 1973, 1990, 1998, Stedelijk Mus., Amsterdam, 1974, 8th Paris Biennale, 1973, Whitney Mus. Am. Art, N.Y.C., 1979, 1985, Centre Georges Pompidou, Paris, 1979, 2002, Met. Mus. Art, N.Y.C., 1982, Serpentine Gallery, 1984, Galerie Denise René, Paris, 1985, Tel Aviv Mus., 1986, 1998, Mus. Fridericianum, Kassel, Germany, 1988, Mus. d'Art Moderne de Lille, France, 1992, Bibliothèque Nationale, Paris, 1992, Nat. Gallery Art, Washington, 1993—94, Harvard U. Straus Gallery, 1996, Yokohama (Japan) Mus. Art, 1998, Yale U. Art Gallery, 1998, Cabinet des Estampes et des Dessins, Liege, Belgium, 1999, Brit. Mus., London, 2000, 2004, Corcoran Gallery, Washington, 2001, Neue Galerie, Graz, Austria, 2001—02, Ctr. Georges, Pompidou, Paris, 2002, Riva Yares Gallery, Santa Fe, N.Mex., 2004, Brit. Mus., London, 2004, Staatliche Kunsthalle, Karlsruhe, Germany, 2004, New Arts Gallery, Litchfield, Conn., 2005, Addison Gallery Am. Art, Andover, Mass., 2005, Represented in permanent collections Mus. Modern Art, Whitney Mus. Am. Art, Met. Mus. Art, Centre Georges Pompidou, Paris, Chgo. Art Inst., Mus. of Contemporary Art, Chgo., Phila. Art Mus., Yale U. Art Gallery, Neuberger Mus., Australian Nat. Gallery, Cin. Mus. Art, St. Louis Art Mus., Tel Aviv Mus., La. Mus., Denmark, Walker Art Ctr., Washington, BibliotequeNationale Paris, Brit. Mus., London, Bklyn. Mus. Art, Dallas Mus. Fine Art, Detroit Mus. Art, Mus. Contemporary Art, L.A., High Mus., Atlanta, Corcoran Gallery, Washington, Staatliche Kunsthalle, Karlsruhe, Nat. Gallery Art, Washington, Kunstmuseum Winterthur, Switzerland, Neue Galerie, Graz, Nat. Mus. of Women in the Arts, Washington. Nat. Endowment Arts grantee, 1976-77, Pollock-Krasner Found. Inc. grantee, 1990-91, Ctr. Nat. Arts Plastiques grantee, 1996. Address: 37 rue Volta 75003 Paris France Office Phone: 01-42-78-3649.

**RENOUF, HAROLD AUGUSTUS,** retired transportation executive; b. Sandy Point, Nfld., Can., June 15, 1917; s. John Robert and Louisa Maud (LeRoux) R.; m. Janet Dorothy Munro, June 16, 1942; children: Janet Dorothy, Ann Louise Petley-Jones, John Robert, Susan Elizabeth Thompson. B.Commerce, Dalhousie U., 1938, LL.D. (hon.), 1981. N.S.C.A., Halifax, 1942 C.M.A., 1950. With H.R. Doane and Co., Halifax, N.S., Can., 1938-75, ptnr., 1942-75, ptnr. in charge New Glasgow, N.S., Can., 1947-62, ptnr. in charge mgmt. svcs. Halifax, 1963-67, chmn., 1967-75; bd. dirs. Associated Acctg. Firms Internat., 1971-75; commr. Anti-Inflation Bd. Ottawa, Ont., 1975-77, chmn., 1977-79, Petroleum Monitoring Agy., Ottawa, 1980-82, VIA Rail Can. Inc. Montreal, Que., 1982-85; pres. Fundy Industries Ltd., Halifax, 1990-94; ret., 1996. Cons. to N.S. Provincial Mcpl. Fact-Finding Com., 1967-70; pres. Can. Inst. Chartered Accts., 1974-75. Contbr. articles to profl. publs. Chmn. adv. commn. Dalhousie U. Grad. Sch. Bus. Adminstrn., 1978-86. Recipient Queen's medal, Queen's Golden Jubilee medal, 2002, Commemorative medal for 125th anniversary of Can. Confedn., 1992; decorated officer Order of Can.; named to Acctg. Hall of Fame St. Mary's Univ., N.S., 1993. Fellow Inst. Chartered Accts. N.S. (pres. 1948); mem. Can. Inst. Chartered Accts. (pres. 1974-75), Can. Tax Found. (gov. 1969-71), Soc. Mgmt. Accts. N.S., Dalhousie U. Alumni Assn. (hon. chmn. 1987-89), Halifax Club, Saraguay Club (treas. 1972-75), Waegwaltic Club. Liberal. Mem. United Ch. Can. Avocations: boating, fishing. Home: 6369 Coburg Rd Apt 1605 Halifax NS Canada B3H 4J7

**RENOUX, ANDRÉ,** physicist, researcher; b. Courbevoie, France, Oct. 27, 1937; s. Robert and Jeanne (Noël) R.; divorced; children: Vincent, Nathalie. Lic. Sci., Faculty Scis. Paris, 1958, D 3d cycle, 1961, D, 1965. Asst. Faculty Scis., Paris 1959—61, master asst., 1961—66; prof. faculty scis. U. Tunis, Tunisia, 1966—69, U. Brest, France, 1969—80; prof. U. Paris, 1980—2003, dir. lab. phys. aérosols et transfert des contaminations, 1980—, dir. DESS (3d cycle) sci. des aérosols-génie de l'Aérocontamination, 1981—2003, prof. emeritus, 2003—. Gen. chmn. European Aerosol Conf., Blois, France, 1994; del. Internat. Coun. for Engring. and Tech., UNESCO, 2000-; adminstr. Maisons Maternelles, 2005-. Author: (with D. Boulaud, Lavoisier, Ed.) Les Aérosols, Physique et Métrologie, 1998; mem. editl. bd. Idojaras, 1979—, Pollution Atmospherique, 1979-2003, Aerosol Sci. & Tech., 1992-2000, Revue Salles Propres, 2000-02; contbr. over 300 articles to profl. jours. Gen. sec. Syndicat d'initiative, Brest, 1973-77; mem. Coms. Com. Univs., France, 1973-77. Mem. Am Assn. Advancement Rsch., N.Y. Acad. Scis., Com. Regional Anti-Pollution Brest (pres. 1973-80), Soc. France for Nuclear Energy idFNE (pres. 1987-91), Am. Assn. Aerosol Rsch., Gesellschaft Aerosolforschung, Hungarian Meteorol. soc. (hon.), French Aerosol. Rsch. Assn. (pres. 1983-2000, hon. pres. 2000—), European Aerosol Assembly (co-founder, pres. 1998-2000), Office Professionnel de qualification des Entreprises de l'Ultrapropreté (pres. 1995—), Chevalier des Dames du vin et de la Table, Ordre de l'Echarpe. Avocations: tennis, opera, photography. Home: 11 Sq de L'eau Vive 94000 Creteil France Office: Univ Paris XII Lab Phys Aérosols Ave Gal de Gaulle 94000 Creteil France Office Phone: 33-6-84211880. Business E-Mail: renoux.andre@numericable.fr.

**RENSBERGER, BOYCE,** science journalism fellowship program administrator; b. 1942; BS in Zoology and Journalism, U. Miami; MS in Mental Health Comm., Syracuse U. Sci. editor Detroit Free Press, 1966—71, NY Times, 1971—79, Washington Post, 1984—88; dir. Knight Sci. Journalism Fellowship program Mass. Inst. Tech., Cambridge, 1998—. Co-dir. summer sci.writing fellowships program Marine Biol. Lab, Woods Hole, Mass. Head writer: TV series 3-2-1 Contact; author: (book) How the World Works: A Guide to Science's Greatest Discoveries, 1977, The Cult of the Wild, 1986, Instant Biology: From Single Cells to Human Beings, and Beyond, 1996, Life Itself: Exploring the Realm of the Living Cell, 1997. Alicia Patterson Fellow, 1973—74. Mem.: AAAS (sr. editor Science Mag. 1981—84, chmn. com. on pub. understanding sci. and tech., two-time sci. writing award recipient). Office: Knight Sci Journalism Fellowships Mass Inst Tech 77 Massachusetts Ave E32-311 Cambridge MA 02139-4307 E-mail: boyce@mit.edu.

**RENSHAW, AMANDA FRANCES,** retired physicist, nuclear engineer; b. Wheelwright, Ky., Dec. 10, 1934; d. Taft and Mamie Nell (Russell) Wilson; divorced; children: Linda, Michael, Billy. BS in Physics, Antioch Coll., 1972; MS in Physics, U. Tenn., 1982, MS in Nuclear Engring., 1991. Rsch. asst. U. Mich., Ann Arbor, 1970-71; teaching asst. Antioch Coll., Yellow Springs, Ohio, 1971-72; physicist GE, Schenectady, N.Y., 1972-74, Union Carbide Corp., Oak Ridge, Tenn., 1974-79; rsch. assoc. Oak Ridge Nat. Lab., 1979-91, mgr. strategic planning, 1991-92, liaison for environ. scis., 1993-96; ret., 1996. Asst. to counselor for sci. and tech. Am. Embassy, Moscow, 1990; asst. to dir. nat. acid precipitation assessment program Office of Pres. U.S., 1993-94. Contbr. articles to profl. jours. Mem. AAUW, Am. Nuclear Soc. (Oak Ridge chpt.), Soc. Black Physicists Avocations: reading, travel. Home: 1850 Cherokee Bluff Dr Knoxville TN 37920-2215

**RENSHAW, JEAN REHKOP,** management educator, consultant; b. Canoga Park, Calif., Oct. 15, 1936; d. Al H. and Ada E. (Heins) Rehkop; m. William B. Renshaw (div. 1985); children: Blair, Jeannine, Alan. BS, UCLA, 1959, MS, 1972, PhD, 1974. Economist The RAND Corp., Santa Monica, Calif.; prof. U. So. Pacific, Suva, Fiji, U. Hawaii, Honolulu; prof., chair bus. dept. Ea. Oreg. State Coll., La Grande; prof. mgmt. Pepperdine U., L.A. Cons. AJR Internat. Assocs., San Diego, 1979—; monitor New Zealand Qualification Auth., Wellington, 1989—. Author: Japanese Women Managers, 1996, Kimono in the Boardroom, 1999, Korea's Unrecognized Scandal: The Absence of Women Managers, 2005; contbr. chpt. to book, articles to profl. jours. Cons. Hawaii State, Honolulu, 1990-94. Fulbright sr. rsch. scholar Tokyo, 1990-93. Mem. Womencare, Assn. Asian Studies, Soc. Ind. Scholars. Avocations: sailing, painting. E-mail: arenshaw@pacbell.net.

**RENSHLER, ROSEMARY P.,** retired music educator; d. Charles Allen and Rose Mae Plyley; children: Kevin, Kara, Kristin. MusB in Edn., Capital U., 1961; MA in Music Edn., The Ohio State U., 1979; student, Pa. State U., 1981, Milliken U., 1982, Heidelberg Coll., 1987—88, Otterbein Coll., 1995. Dir. gen. music, choir Clinton Jr. H.S., Columbus, Ohio, 1961—63, Johnson Pk. Jr. H.S., Columbus, 1972—73, Eastmoor Jr. H.S. and Mid. Sch., Columbus, 1973—81; dir. vocal music Northland H.S., Columbus, 1981—; ret., 2004. Dir. choir Oakland Pk. United Meth. Ch., Columbus, 1961—72, Epworth United Meth. Ch., Columbus, 1980—88; dir. music Nat. Rep. Glee Club, Columbus, 1989—2006, Aladdin Shrine Chanters, Columbus, 2000—06. Mem. fin. com. Epworth United Meth. Ch., Columbus, mem. com. membership, head usher, mgr. kitchen, cook. Recipient 34 Yr. Svc. award, Columbus (Ohio) Pub. Schs., 2005. Mem.: NEA, Am. Choral Dirs. Assn., Music Educators Nat. Conf., Ohio Educators Assn., Tri-M Internat. Music Hon. Soc. (life; adv. 2002—05). Methodist. Avocations: crafts, dance, gardening, cooking. Home: 1687 Riverbirch Dr Columbus OH 43229

**RENSLOW, CHARLES GEORGE,** entrepreneur; b. Chgo., Aug. 26, 1929; Student, Wright U., Northwestern U. Pub. Kris Studio, 1950—79; owner GoldCoast Leather Bar, 1958—93; pub. Gay Life Newspaper, 1979—85; prodr. Internat. Mr. Leather, Inc., 1979—; owner Chgo. Eagle Leather Bar, 1997—. Pres. Leather Archives and Mus., 1994—. Charter mem. City Chgo. Gay/Lesbian Hall of Fame, 1991; participant Internat. Gay/Lesbian Assn. Found. AIDS Rsch., 2002—; mem. Nat. Trust Historic Preservation, 2002—, Nat. Orgn. Women, 2002—; mem. Dem. Nat. Com., 2002—; mem. adv. bd. (O'Brien) 43d Ward Dem. Party; mem. adv. bd. (Orbach) 46th Ward Dem. Party; organizer Second Harvest, 1st Dist. Wide Masonic Food Dr., 1997, Masonic Children's Home, Franzen Circus fundraiser, 1995; bd. dirs. Nat. Gay and Lesbian Task Force, 2005—; charitable fundraiser Gay Rights Nat. Lobby, 1979—85. Named Humanitarian of Yr., 1977, Pantheon Bus. Person of Yr., Leather Jour., 1996, Leather Man of Century, 2000; named to Hall of Fame, Gay Chgo. mag., 1982; recipient Chgo. Gay/lesbian CC, Cmty. Svc. award, 1997, Lodge Builder's award, Hesperia Masonic Lodge AF & AM, 1999, award, Min. of Canadian Heritage, City of San Francisco, 1993, Cmty. Builder award, Masonic Lodge #411, 2004. Mem.: Internat. Lesbian and Gay

Assn. Home: 4535 N Beacon Chicago IL 60640 Office: Renslow Family Enter 5015 N Clark St Chicago IL 60640 Fax: 773-878-5184. Office Phone: 773-878-6360. Personal E-mail: chuck@chuckrenslow.com.

**RENSTROM, LISA,** environmental organization administrator; married; 2 children. Chair Ctrl. Piedmont Group; exec. dir. Voices and Choices; held leadership positions various orgns. including WTVI Pub. TV, Charlotte, NC, Mus. of Life and the Environment, Raptor Ctr., Riverkeep Found.; bd. dirs. Sierra Club, San Francisco, 2001—, pres. 2005—. Office: Sierra Club Nat Hdqs 85 Second St 2d Fl San Francisco CA 94105 Office Phone: 415-977-5500.

**RENT, CLYDA STOKES,** academic administrator; b. Jacksonville, Fla., Mar. 1, 1942; d. Clyde Parker Stokes Sr. and Edna Mae (Edwards) Shuemake; m. George Seymour Rent, Aug. 12, 1966; 1 child, Cason Rent Lynley. BA, Fla. State U., 1964, MA, 1966, PhD, 1968; LHD (hon.), Judson Coll., 1993. Asst. prof. Western Carolina U., Cullowhee, NC, 1968-70, Queens Coll., Charlotte, NC, 1972-74, dept. chair, 1974-78, dean Grad. Sch. and New Coll. 1979-84, v.p. for Grad. Sch. and New Coll., 1984-85, v.p. acad. affairs, 1985-87, v.p. cmty. affairs, 1987-89; pres. Miss. U. for Women, Columbus, 1989—2001; disting. prof. sociology Miss. State U. Mem. adv. bd. Nat. Women's Hall of Fame; cons. Coll. Eb. N.Y.C., 1983-89; sci. cons. N.C. Alcohol Rsch. Authority, Chapel Hill, 1976-89; bd. mem. So. Growth Policies Bd., 1992-94; adv. bd. Nat. Women's Hall of Fame, Trustmark Nat. Bank, 1991-97; rotating chair Miss. Instns. Higher Learning Pres. Coun., 1990-91; commn. govtl. rels. Am. Coun. Edn., 1990-93; mem. adv. bd, Entergy/Miss 1994 97, Freedom Forum 1st Amendment Ctr., 1996-2001; mem. Miss. adv. bd. Trustmark Nat. Bank, 1991-97; mem. Mary Baker Eddy Adv. Group, 2000—; mem. ACE Commn. on Women in Higher Edn., 1999—. Mem. editl. bd. Planning for Higher Education, 1995; contbr. articles to profl. jours.; speeches pub. in Vital Speeches; mem. editl. bds. acad. jours. Trustee N.C. Performing Arts Ctr., Charlotte, 1988-89, Charlotte County Day Sch., 1987-89; bd. visitors Johnson C. Smith U., Charlotte, 1985-89; exec. com. bd. dirs. United Way Allocations and Rev., Charlotte, 1982-88; bd. advisors Charlotte Mecklenburg Hosp. Authority, 1985-89; bd. dirs. Jr. Achievement, Charlotte, 1983-89, Miss. Humanities Coun., Miss. Inst. Arts and Letters, Miss. Symphony, Miss. Econ. Coun.; chair Leadership Miss. and Collegiate Miss.; chmn. bd. dirs. Charlotte/Mecklenburg Arts and Sci. Coun., 1987-88; Danforth assoc. Danforth Found., St. Louis, 1976-88, Leadership Am., 1989; mem. golden triangle adv. bd. Bapt. Meml. Hosp., 1999—; pres. So. Univs. Conf., 1994-95; mem. commn. govt. rels. Am. Coun. Edn., 1990-93; mem. alumni bd. First United Meth. Ch., 1996—. Recipient Grad. Made Good award Fla. State U., 1990, medal of excellence Miss. U. for Women, 1995, Women Who Make a Difference award IWF, 2000; named Prof. of Yr., Queens Coll., 1979, One of 10 Most Admired Women Mgrs. in Am., Working Women mag., 1993, One of 1000 Women of the 90's, Mirabella mag., 1994; Ford Found. grantee, 1981; Paul Harris fellow, 1992; OWHE fellow, 1999—. Mem. Am. Assn. State Colls. and Univs. (bd. dirs. 1994-96, 99), Sociol. Soc., So. Assn. Colls. and Schs. (mem. commn. on colls. 1996-98), N.C. Assn. Colls. and Univs. (exec. com. 1988-89), N.C. Assn. Acad. Officers (sec.-treas. 1987-88), Soc. Internat. Bus. Fellows, Miss. Assn. Colls. (pres. 1992), Newcomen Soc. U.S., Internat. Women's Forum, Univ. Club, Rotary. Achievements include 1st female pres. of Miss. U. for Women (1st pub. coll. for women in Am.).

**RENTER, LOIS IRENE HUTSON,** retired librarian; b. Lowden, Iowa, Oct. 23, 1929; d. Thomas E. and Lulu Mae (Barlean) Hutson; m. Karl A. Renter, Jan. 3, 1948; children: Susan Elizabeth, Rebecca Jean, Karl Geoffrey. BA cum laude, Cornell Coll., 1965; MA, U. Iowa, 1968. Tchr. Spanish Mt. Vernon High Sch., 1965-67; head libr. Am. Coll. Testing Program, Iowa City, Iowa, 1968-89, ret., 1989. Vis. instr. U. Iowa Sch. Library Sci., 1972-82. Mem. Phi Beta Kappa. Methodist. Home: 1308 Brendel Hill Dr NW Cedar Rapids IA 52405-1566 E-Mail: thisislois@mchsi.com.

**RENTERIA, EDGAR,** professional baseball player; b. Barranquila, Columbia, Aug. 7, 1975; Short stop Fla. Marlins, 1996—98, St. Louis Cardinals, 1999—2004, Boston Red Sox, 2005, Atlanta Braves, 2005—. Named to NL All-Star Team, 1998; recipient NL Gold Glove award, MLB, 2002—03, NL All-Star Team, 2000, 2003, 2004. Achievements include named to series champion, 1998. Office: Turner Field 755 Hank Aaron Dr Atlanta GA 30315*

**RENTON, HOLLINGS C.,** health products executive; BS Maths., Colo. State U.; MBA, U. Mich. Pres., COO Cetus Corp., 1981—91; pres., Chiron Corp., 1991—92; chmn., pres., CEO Onyx Pharms. Inc., Emeryville, Calif., 1993—. Office: Onyx Pharms Inc 2100 Powell St Emeryville CA 94608

**RENTOUMIS, ANN MASTROIANNI,** psychotherapist; b. New Haven, Apr. 27, 1928; d. Luigi Mastroianni and Marian Dallas; m. George Rentoumis, June 27, 1959; children: Michael, Mary, Anne. BA in Psychology, Vassar Coll., 1949; postgrad., Boston U. Med. Sch., 1949-50; MS in Social Work, Columbia U., 1952. Diplomate Am. Bd. Social Work, Am. Psychotherapy Assn.; lic. cert. social worker; lic. marriage and family therapist. Child and adolescent therapist Bklyn. Psychiat., 1952-55; family therapist Community Svc. Soc., N.Y.C., 1955-58; psychotherapist Bleuler Psychotherapy Ctr., L.I., N.Y., 1958-60, Adolescent Psychiat. Clinic, Tex. Children's Hosp., Houston, 1975-76; pvt. practice Houston, 1976-77, Lauderdale Psychiat. Group, Ft. Lauderdale, Fla., 1978-90, Pompano Beach, Fla., 1990-93, Ft. Lauderdale, 1993—. Bd. dirs. Envirodyne, Inc., 1989—2000. Pres. Pine Crest Sch. Mothers Club, 1985-86; v.p. Opera Soc., 1987-88, bd. dirs. 1998, parliamentarian 2000-01, parliamentarian 2006—; bd. govs., v.p. exec. bd. Fla. Philharm. Orch., 1988-91, bd. dirs., 1990-2003; pres. Ft. Lauderdale Philharm. Soc., 2003—; bd. dirs. Goodwill Ambassadors, 2003—. Recipient Golden Rule award J.C. Penney Co., 1990; named Woman of Yr., Am. Cancer Soc., 1989, Woman of Style and Substance, Ft. Lauderdale Philharm. Soc., 1998. Fellow Am. Psychotherapy Assn., Am. Orthopsychiat. Assn.; mem. Am. Assn. Marriage and Family Therapists, Am. Group Therapy Assn., Royal Dames of Cancer Rsch., Inc. (trustee 2006-, dir. 2006), Harbor Beach Surf Club (v.p. 1986-90). Avocations: piano, tennis, swimming. Home: 2200 S Oeean Ln Ph 6 Fort Lauderdale FL 33316-3836 Office: 1326 SE 3d Ave Fort Lauderdale FL 33316-1260 Office Phone: 954-767-0048.

**RENUART, VICTOR E., JR.,** career military officer; BS in Prodn. and Indsl. Mgmt., Ind. U., 1971; MA in Psychology, Troy State U., 1975; Disting. grad., Squadron Officer Sch., Maxwell AFB, Ala., 1977; Grad., Air Command & Staff Coll., 1979, Army War Coll., 1992, Sr. Officers in Nat. Security Program, 1997. Commd. 2d lt. USAF, 1973, advanced through grades to lt. gen., 2004; instr., pilot Craig AFB, 1973-76; instr. aerospace studies U. Notre Dame, South Bend, Ind., 1976-79; A-10 instr. pilot, flight comdr. to ops. officer 81st Tactical Fighter Wing, RAF Bentwaters, Eng., 1980-84; ops. inspector Office of the Inspector Gen. Hdqrs. USAF Europe, Ramstein AB, West Germany, 1984-85, exec. officer to inspector gen., 1985-86; chief wing inspections 23rd Tactical Fighter Wing, England AFB, La., 1986-91, ops. officer to comdr., 1986-91, dir. assignments, 1992-93; comdr. support group Allied Air Forces Ctrl. Europe, England AFB, 1993-94, asst. chief of staff ops., sr. U.S. rep., 1994-95; dir. ops. plans NATO Combined Air Ops. Ctr. 5th Allied Tactical AF, Vicenza, Italy, 1994-95; asst. dir. ops. Hdqrs. USAF Europe, Ramstein, Germany, 1995-96; comdr. 52nd Fighter Wing, Spangdahlem AB, Germany, 1996-98, 347th Wing, Moody AFB, Ga., 1998—2000; comdr. Joint Task Force-Southwest Asia, comdr. 9th Air & Space Expeditionary Task Force-Southwest Asia US Ctrl. Command, Riyadh, Saudi Arabia, 2000—01; dir. ops. (J-3) US Ctrl Command, MacDill AFB, Fla., 2001—03; vice comdr. Pacific Air Forces, Hickam AFB, Hawaii, 2003—05; dir. strategic plans & policy Joint Staff, Washington, 2005—06; sr. mil. asst. to sec. US Dept. Def., Washington, 2006—. Decorated Def. Disting. Svc. medal with oak leaf cluster, Disting. Svc. medal, Def Superior Svc. medal with oak leaf cluster, Meritorious Svc. medal with four oak leaf clusters, Aerial Achievement medal with three oak leaf clusters, Air Force

Commendation medal with oak leaf cluster, Air Force Achievement medal with oak leaf cluster, Legion of Merit with oak leaf cluster, Air medal with two oak leaf clusters. Office: US Dept Def Office Sec 1000 Def Pentagon Washington DC 20301*

**RENWICK, EDWARD S.,** lawyer; b. LA, May 10, 1934; AB, Stanford U., 1956, LLB, 1958. Bar: Calif. 1959, U.S. Dist. Ct. (cen. dist.) Calif. 1959, U.S. Ct. Appeals (9th cir.) 1963, U.S. Dist. Ct. (so. dist.) Calif. 1973, U.S. Dist. Ct. (no. dist.) Calif. 1977, U.S. Dist. Ct. (ea. dist.) Calif. 1981, U.S. Supreme Ct. 1985. Ptnr. Hanna and Morton LLP, L.A. Mem., bd. vis. Stanford Law Sch., 1967-69; mem. environ. and natural resources adv. bd. Stanford Law Sch. Bd. dirs. Calif. Supreme Ct. Hist. Soc. Fellow Am. Coll. Trial Lawyers, Am. Bar Found.; mem. ABA (mem. sect. on litigation, antitrust law, bus. law, chmn. sect. of nat. resources, energy and environ. law 1987-88, mem. at large coord. group energy law 1989-92, sect. rep. coord. group energy law 1995-97, Calif. del. legal com., interstate oil compact com.), Calif. Arboretum Assn. (trustee 1986-92), L.A. County Bar Assn. (chmn. natural resources law sect. 1974-75), The State Bar of Calif., Chancery Club (pres. 1992-93), Phi Delta Phi. Office: Hanna and Morton LLP 444 S Flower St Ste 1500 Los Angeles CA 90071-2922 E-mail: erenwick@hanmor.com.

**RENWICK, GLENN M.,** insurance company executive; b. May 22, 1955; B in Mathematics & Economics, U. Canterbury, Christchurch, New Zealand; MS in Engring., U. Fla., Gainesville, 1978. Joined Progressive Corp., 1986—, former chief info. officer, 1998—2000; CEO, ins. ops. and bus. tech. process leader Progressive Casualty Ins. Co., 1998—2000, pres., chmn., CEO 2000—04; CEO ins. ops. Progressive Corp., 2000, pres., CEO, 2001—. Bd. dirs. Fiserv Inc. Office: Progressive Corp 6300 Wilson Mills Rd Cleveland OH 44143*

**RENYI, THOMAS A.,** bank executive; b. 1946; m. Elizabeth Renyi; children: Christopher, Caroline, Timothy. BA in Bus. Adminstrn., Rutgers U., 1967, MBA, 1968. With The Bank of N.Y., Inc., 1971—; pres., COO, dir. parent holding co., 1992—; vice chmn., dir. The Bank of N.Y., Inc., 1992-98, chmn., CEO, 1998—. Mem. Fin. Services Roundtable; chmn. BITS; bd. dirs. Public Svc. Enterprise Group, The Clearing House; pres. Fed. Advisory Coun. Fed. Reserve Bd. Trustee Rutgers U., Bates Coll.; bd. dirs. United Way NY, Lincoln Ctr. Performing Arts; bd. managers NY Botanical Gardens; bd. dirs. World Trade Ctr. Meml. Found. First lt. M.I. U.S. Army, 1968—70, Vietnam.*

**RENZETTI, PHYLLIS JEAN,** retired technical editor; b. Kingman, Ind., Feb. 3, 1925; d. Claude and Helen (Duchene) A.; divorced; 1 child, Jeanne. BA, Wheaton (Ill.) Coll., 1947; MA, Columbia U., 1950; PhD, Ind. U., 1961. Tchr. Wheaton Coll., 1948-49; tech. editor U.S. Geol. Survey, Reston, Va., Menlo Park, Calif., 1963-94, ret., 1994. Mem. AAAS, Paleontological Soc. Home: 3266 Hanover Dr Lafayette IN 47909-3852

**RENZI, RICK,** congressman; b. Ft. Monmouth, NJ, June 11, 1958; s. Gene Renzi; m. Roberta Renzi; 12 children. BS in Criminal Justice, No. Ariz. U., 1980; JD, Cath. U., 2001. Former owner real-estate investment firm, insurance co.; with US Dept. of Defense; mem. U.S. Congress from 1st Ariz. dist., 2003—, mem. fin. svc. com., permanent select com. on intelligence, resources com.; mem. subcom. on capital markets, insurance, and govt. sponsored enterprises, subcom. on fin. inst. and consumer credit, subcom. on housing. Republican. Office: US Ho Reps 418 Cannon Ho Office Bldg Washington DC 20515-0301

**REOCK, ERNEST C., JR.,** retired social studies educator, director; b. Belleville, N.J., Oct. 13, 1924; s. Ernest C. and Helen Rutan (Evans) R.; m. Jeanne Elizabeth Thomason, Jan. 25, 1953; children: Michael, Thomas, Kathleen. BS, Swarthmore Coll., 1945; AB, Rutgers U., 1948, MA, 1950, PhD, 1959. Rsch. assoc. bur. govt. rsch. Rutgers U., New Brunswick, N.J., 1950-59, asst. prof., dir., 1960-63, assoc. prof., dir., 1963-68, prof., dir., 1968-92. Cons. N.J. Constnl. Conv., New Brunswick, 1966, N.J. State and Local Revenue and Expenditure Commns., 1986-88. Author: Handbook for New Jersey Assessors, 1962, School Budget Caps in New Jersey, 1981 (Govtl. Rsch. Assn. award, 1983), Unfinished Business: The New Jersey Constitutional Conv. of 1966, 2003; editor: New Jersey Legislative District Data Book, 1972—92. Chmn. Middlesex County Charter Study Commn., New Brunswick, 1973—74; cons. State Apportionment Commn., 1981, 1991, 2001, various mcpl. charter commns., 1965—; mem. NJ Property Tax Conv. Task Force, 2004. Lt. USN, 1943—46, lt. USN, 1951—53. Recipient Gov.'s award for Pub. Svc., 1997. Mem.: Am. Soc. Pub. Adminstrn. (Pub. Adminstr. Yr. 1982), Am. Ednl. Fin. Assn. Avocations: sailing, swimming. Home: 7 Kendall Rd Kendall Park NJ 08824-1010 Office: Rutgers U Ctr Govt Svcs 33 Livingston Ave New Brunswick NJ 08901-1900 Office Phone: 732-932-3640 633.

**REPHAN, JACK,** lawyer; b. Little Rock, Mar. 16, 1932; s. Henry and Mildred (Frank) R.; m. Arlene Clark, June 23, 1957; children: Amy Carol, James Clark. BS in Commerce, 1954; LLB, U. Va., 1959. Bar: Va. 1959, D.C. 1961. Assoc. Kanter & Kanter, Norfolk, Va., 1959-60; law clk. to Judge Sam E. Whitaker, U.S. Ct. Claims, Washington, 1960-62; assoc. Pierson, Ball & Dowd, Washington, 1962-64; ptnr. Danzansky, Dickey, Tydings, Quint & Gordon, Washington, 1964-77; mem. Braude, Margulies, Sacks & Rephan, Washington, 1977-87; ptnr. Porter, Wright, Morris & Arthur, Washington, 1987-88; Sadur, Pelland & Rubinstein, Washington, 1988-93; counsel Hofheimer Nusbaum P.C., Norfolk, Va., 1993-00; principal Rephan Lassiter PLC, Norfolk, 2001—. Mem. Nat. Panel Arbitrators Am. Arbitration Assn., Nat. Panel Mediators Am. Arbitration Assn., NASD Bd. Arbitrators; lectr. joint com. continuing legal edn. State Bar Va. Contbr. articles to legal jours. Pres. Patrick Henry PTA, Alexandria, Va., 1968-69, Linkhorn Bay Condominium Assn., 2000—; treas. John Adams Mid. Sch. PTA, Alexandria, 1970-71; pres. Seminary Ridge Citizens Assn., 1976-77; Dem. candidate for Alexandria City Com., 1969. 1st lt. AUS, 1955-57. Mem. ABA (chmn. subcom. on procurement of jud. remedies pub. contract sect. 1973-74), Va. Bar Assn. (govt. sect. constrn. law 1979-81, 1991—, vice chmn. 1980-81, chmn. 1981-82), D.C. Bar Assn., Assoc. Gen. Contractors, Hampton Roads Utility and Heavy Contractors Assn. (gen. counsel), Cavalier Golf and Yacht Club, Kiwanis (pres. Landmark Club 1969). Home: 1276 Laskin Rd Ste 402 Virginia Beach VA 23451-5272 Office: 500 E Main St Ste 1200 Norfolk VA 23510 Office Phone: 757-274-0045. Business E-Mail: jrephan@rephanlassiter.com.

**REPINE, JOHN EDWARD,** internist, educator; b. Rock Island, Ill., Dec. 26, 1944; married, 1969, 88; 6 children. BS, U. Wis., 1967; MD, U. Minn., 1971. Instr., then assoc. prof. internal medicine U. Minn., Mpls., 1974-79; asst. dir divsn. exptl. medicine Webb-Waring Inst. Biomedical Rsch., Denver, 1979-89; prof. medicine, pres. and dir. Webb-Waring Inst. Cancer, Aging & Antioxidant Rsch., Denver, 1989—; prof. medicine U. Colo., Denver, 1979—, James J. Waring prof. medicine, 1996—, prof. pediatrics, 1981-96. Mem. rsch. com., co-chmn. steering com. Aspen Lung Conf., 1980, chmn., 1981; assoc. dean for student advocacy Nat. Heart and Lung Inst., 1990—; Young Pulmonary Investigator grantee Nat. Heart & Lung Inst., 1974-75; recipient Basil O'Connor Starter Rsch. award Nat. Found. March of Dimes, 1975-77. Mem. AAAS, Am. Assn. Immunologists, Am. Soc. Clin. Investigation, Am. Heart Assn. (established investigator award 1976-81), Am. Thoracic Soc., Assn. Am. Physicians. Achievements include research in role of phagocytes and oxygen radicals in lung injury and host defense (ARDS). Office: Webb Waring Inst Cancer Aging & Antioxidant Rsch Box C322 4200 E 9th Ave Denver CO 80220-3706

**REPINSKI, SARA,** library director; d. Stephen Charles and Sharon Ann Gilles; m. Jeffrey Lawrence Repinski, Dec. 10, 1998. BS in History and Art, U. Wis., La Crosse, 1998; MLIS, U. S.C., 2002. Libr. dir. So. Meth. Coll., Orangeburg, SC, 2002—. Mem. accreditation team Transnat. Assn. Christian Colls. and Schs., Lynchburg, Va., 2002—. Mem.: SC Libr. Assn., Assn. Christian Librs., Civil War Preservation Trust. Avocations: scrapbooks, music, Green Bay Packer football.

**REPLOGLE, DAVID ROBERT,** publishing executive; b. Chgo., Feb. 24, 1931; s. Homer Mock and Helen (Fluke) R.; m. Jeanne Lonnquist, Nov. 4, 1954; children: William T., Bruce R., Stewart D., James M., John B. AB, Dartmouth Coll., 1953; postgrad., Princeton U., 1957-58. V.p., gen. mgr. Doubleday & Co., Inc., N.Y.C., 1958-70; pres., chmn. bd. G. & C. Merriam Co., Springfield, Mass., 1970-75; pres. Praeger Publishers, N.Y.C., 1970-75; exec. v.p., dir. Houghton Mifflin Co., Boston, 1975-91; pres. DR&A Inc., Cohasset, Mass., 1992—; pres., publ. Hot House Press, Cohasset. Dir. L.I. Replogle Found., Chgo., 1982—; trustee South Shore Health and Ednl. Found, 2000—. Served to lt. USNR, 1953-57. Mem. Cohasset Golf Club, Plantation Golf and Country Club. Home: 84 Gammons Rd Cohasset MA 02025-1406 Office: David Replogle & Assocs 760 CJ Cushing Hwy Cohasset MA 02025-2124 Office Phone: 781-383-8360. Personal E-mail: drreplogle@aol.com.

**REPLOGLE, ROBERT LEE,** cardiovascular surgeon, thoracic surgeon; b. Ottumwa, Iowa, Sept. 30, 1931; s. Ralph Ruby and Edith Dorothy (Swartz) R.; m. Carol A. Heeschen, Aug. 24, 1958; children: Robert E., Jennifer Bremer, Edith Sheffer. MD cum laude, Harvard U., 1960; DSc (hon.), Cornell Coll., 1972. Diplomate Am. Bd. Surgery, Am. Bd. Thoracic Surgery, Am. Bd. Pediat. Surgery. Intern in surgery U. Minn. Hosp., 1960-61; asst. resident in surgery Peter Bent Brigham Hosp., Boston, 1961-63, Mass. Gen. Hosp., Boston, 1965-66; sr. resident in surgery Children's Hosp. Med. Ctr., Boston, 1966; asst. in surgery Children's Hosp. Med. Ctr. and Harvard Med. Sch., Boston, 1966-67; asst. prof. surgery Pritzker Sch. Medicine U. Chgo., 1967-70, assoc. prof. surgery and head, sect. pediat. surgery, 1970-73, prof. surgery and head, sect. pediat. surgery, 1973-74, prof. surgery and head, sect. cardiac surgery, 1973-80, prof. surgery, sect. cardiac surgery, 1973-90; med. dir. cardiac surgery unit Ingalls Meml. Hosp., 1989-98; chief divsn. cardiac surgery Columbus Hosp., Chgo., 1987-97; pres. CTS Net Inc., Chgo., 1998—. Vis. prof. Albany Med. Coll., 1974, Dalhousie Sch. of Medicine, Halifax, 1975, Walter Reed Army Med. Ctr., 1978, U. Miami Med. Sch., 1992, Philippine Heart Ctr. for Asia March, 1979, Health Inst. Japan, Tokyo, 1982, Creighton Med. Sch., 1988, Brooke Army Med. Ctr., 1993, U. Heidelberg, 1995, Kerkoff Clinic/Max Planct Inst., Bad Nanheim, Germany, 1995, German Heart Ctr., Munich, 1995, Peter Bent Brigham Hosp. Harvard Med. Sch., 1996; mem. surgery and bioengring. study sect. HHS, NIH, 1979-83; mem. ad hoc adv. com. bypass angioplasty revascularization investigation, NIH, 1993-94; mem. subcom. on quality N.Y. State Dept. Health, 1989-96, mem. subcom. on resources and facilities, 1993—, mem. cardiac adv. com., 1989—; pres. Ctsnet.org, Inc., 1999—. Author: (with others) Microcirculation, Perfusion, and Transplantation of Organs, 1970, The Critically Ill Child, 1972, Surgical Clinics in North America, 1976, Biprosthetic Cardiac Valves, 1979, Year Book of Nuclear Medicine, 1981, among others; mem. editl. bd. Jour. Cardiac Surgery, 1982-99; contbr. more than 125 articles to profl. jours. With USN, 1951-54. Recipient Merit award Philippine Heart ctr. for Asia, Manila, 1985, Friendship award Shanghai Chest Hosp., 1987. Mem. AMA (diagnostic and therapeutic tech. assessment panel 1995—, ho. of dels. 1992—, joint rev. com. on ednl. programs for physicians assts. 1979-84), ACS (com. on allied health pers. 1979-84, chmn. 1983-84, com. on med. motion pictures 1979-85, com. on membership 1988—, residency rev. com. for thoracic surgery of the accreditation com. for grad. med. edn. 1992-95, 96—), Ill. State Med. Soc., Chgo. Med. Soc., Am. Surg. Assn., European Assn. for Cardiothoracic Surgery, Soc. for Acad. Surgery, Am. Heart Assn. (adv. coun. cardiovasc. surgery 1968-71), Soc. Univ. Surgeons, Internat. Cardiovasc. Soc., Societe Internationale de Chirurgie (N.Am. chpt.), Am. Assn. for Thoracic Surgery (del. AMA 1992—, com. on soc. responsibility 1991—), Soc. Thoracic Surgeons (program com. 1978-81, chmn. 1981, com. on medico-legal affairs, chmn. 1985-88, ad hoc fin. adv. com. 1987-89, ad hoc exhibitors adv. com. 1988-89, ad hoc com. on social responsibility 1992-95, ad hoc database liaison com. 1993-94, database liaison com. 1994—, ad hoc com. on physician-specific mortality for cardiac surgery 1993-96, stds. and ethics com. 1984-88, treas. 1986-92, exec. com. 1986—, pres.-elect. 1995-96, pres. 1996-97, rep. to the coun. of med. specialty socs. 1990—, annals of thoracic surgery liaison com. 1992—, com. on grad. edn. in thoracic surgery 1992—, com. on major issues in thoracic surgery 1993, chmn. 1994, 95, pres.-elect coun. med. splty. socs 1997-98, pres. coun. med. specialty socs. 1998-99), Coun. of Med. Specialty Socs., German Cardiac Surgery Soc. (hon. mem.). Avocations: wine collecting, photography, travel. Address: CTS Net Inc 1160 E 56th St Chicago IL 60637-1541

**REPMAN, JUDITH LAVINE,** educator; b. Martinez, Calif., May 16, 1954; d. Alvin Joseph and Marion (Holston) LaVine; m. Duane Arthur Repman, Jan. 3, 1975; 1 child, James Alvin. BA, La. State U., 1974, MLS, 1976, PhD, 1989. Media specialist Cornerstone Acad., Baton Rouge, 1983-86; research asst. La. State U., Baton Rouge, 1986-89; asst. prof., dir. Learning Resources Ctr. Tex. Tech U., Lubbock, Tex., 1989—. Tex. La. Assn. for Ednl. Communications & Technology, Baton Rouge, 1987-88. Recipient Eleanor Oleson Doctoral Fellowship La. State U., 1987-89, LAECT Scholarship, 1987. Mem. AASL, Am. Ednl. Rsch. Assn., Assn. for Ednl. Communications and Tech., Internat. Soc. Tech. in Edn., ALA, Tex. Libr. Assn., Tex. Assn. Sch. Librs., Tex. Assn. Ednl. Tech., Tex. Computer Educators Assn. Presbyterian. Home: 13 Greenwood Ave Statesboro GA 30458-5032 Office: Tex Tech U PO Box 41071 Lubbock TX 79409-1071

**REPP, JOAN MERCEDES,** retired librarian; b. N.Y.C., Oct. 24, 1930; d. Paul Francis and Anna Crescentia (Stock) McIntyre; m. Victor E. Repp, Sept. 3, 1949; children: Anna, James. BS, State Tchrs. Coll., Oswego, N.Y., 1951; MEd, U. Md., 1954; AMLS, U. Mich., 1974. Cert. elem. educator. Tchr. Arlington County (Va.) Schs., 1951-57, Perrysburg (Ohio) Pub. Schs., 1968-69; from instr. English and libr. to head cataloging dept. Bowling Green (Ohio) State U., 1972-82, chmn. access svc., 1983-87, dir. access svcs., 1987-91; ret., 1991. Cons. State Libr. Ohio, Columbus, 1980—83, Ohionet Instrn. and Tng. Coun., 1983—87; workshop dir. N.W. Libr. Dist., North Ctrl. Libr. Consortium, Ohio Ednl. Libr. and Media Assn., Dade County Libr. Assn., 1984, 577 Foundation, Perrysburg, Ohio, 1998; mem. Ohio Libr. Info. Sys./Ohio Bd. Regents, 1988—91. Contbr. articles to profl. jours. Svc. unit dir. Girl Scouts Am., Toledo, 1963—67; mem. Environ. Health Coun. Ohio and Mich., 1964; cons. Ronald McDonald House, Toledo, 1987; docent Toledo Zoo, 1998—; trustee Maumee Sch. Found., 2000—, Victor E. Repp Charitable Trust, 2000—. Mem. AAUP, ALA, Acad. Libr. Assn. Ohio, Assn. Coll. and Rsch. Librs., Libr. Adminstrn. and Mgmt. Assn., Resources and Tech. Svcs. Assn., Mensa, Beta Phi Mu, Kappa Delta Pi.

**REPPERT, DAVID THOMAS,** controller; b. Reading, Pa., Mar. 10, 1961; s. John Erwin and Margaret Marie Reppert. BS in Acctg., Pa. State U., 1983; MPH in Health Policy and Mgmt., Columbia U., 1996. Supr. fin. reporting Clin. Practices U. Pa., Phila., 1990—2000; acctg. mgr. Temple Physicians Inc., Elkins Park, Pa., 2000—04, controller, 2004—. Mem. Old First Ref. United Ch. of Christ; moderator Phila. Assn. United Ch. of Christ, 2005—.

**REPPERT, RICHARD LEVI,** lawyer; b. Phila., Nov. 6, 1948; s. William Downing and Angela R. (Schmid) R.; m. Faith Simpson, Dec. 30, 1972 (div. Aug. 1992); 1 child, Richard Jacob; m. Jeanette T. deHaven, Apr. 10, 1994. BA, Lehigh U., 1970; JD, Villanova U., 1974. Bar: Ohio 1974, U.S. Dist. Ct. (no. dist.) Ohio 1974, Pa. 1993. Assoc. Thompson, Hine and Flory, Cleve., 1974-82, ptnr., 1982-89, Jones Day, Cleve., 1989—. Mem. ABA, Am. Coll. Real Estate Lawyers, Ohio State Bar Assn., Cleve. Bar Assn. Office: Jones Day North Point 901 Lakeside Ave Cleveland OH 44114-1190 E-mail: rreppert@jonesday.com.

**REPPERT, SIBLEY PUTNAM,** lawyer; b. Lancaster, Pa., July 4, 1945; s. Reppert Miller Charles and Charlotte Putnam Reppert; m. Christine Ann Vezetinski, May 10, 1980; children: Victoria Charlotte, Catherine Abigail Burke. BA summa cum laude with highest honors, Wesleyan U., 1967; BPhil, Oxford U., Eng., 1969; JD, Harvard U., 1975. Bar: Mass. 1975. Thr. Posternak, Blankstein & Lund, Boston, 1990—94, Herrick & Smith, Boston, 1994—95, Goodwin Procter & Hoar, Boston, 1995—2000, Samuels, Gauthier, Stevens & Reppert, Boston, 1995—98; pres., CEO LawRisk, Inc., Boston, 1998—2000, Incogno Corp., Boston, 2000—02; ptnr. Lahive &

Cockfield, LLP, Boston, 2002—. Dir. Coalition for Buzzards Bay, Marion, Mass., 1990—94. Lt. USN, 1969—72. Keasbey fellow, Keasbey Meml. Found., 1967—69, Hon. fellow, Woodrow Wilson Found., 1967. Mem.: ABA, New Bedford Yacht Club (dir. 2000—). Avocations: sailing, rowing. Home: PO Box 14 Westport Point MA 02791 Office: Lahive & Cockfield LLP 28 State St Boston MA 02109 Office Phone: 617-227-7400. Office Fax: 617-742-4214. Business E-Mail: spr@lahive.com.

**REPPERT, STEVEN MARION,** pediatrician, research scientist, educator; b. Sioux City, Iowa, Sept. 4, 1946; s. Ray Fred and Norma Grace (Coppock) R.; m. Mary Alice Herman, Dec. 28, 1968; children: Jason Steven, Katherine Mary, Christina Marie. BS, U. Nebr., Lincoln, 1973; MD with distinction, U. Nebr., Omaha, 1973; MA (hon.), Harvard U., 1993. Diplomate Nat. Bd. Med. Examiners. Intern Mass. Gen. Hosp., Boston, 1973-74, resident in pediatrics, 1974-76, asst. in pediatrics, 1979-80, asst. pediatrician, 1980-85, dir. lab devel. chronobiology, 1983-2001, assoc. pediatrician, 1985-2000, pediatrician, 2000-2001. Clin. assoc. NIH, Bethesda, Md., 1976-79; instr. pediatrics Harvard Med. Sch., Boston, 1979-81, asst. prof., 1981-85, assoc. prof., 1985-93, prof., 1993—, Higgins family prof. neurosci., 2001—; vis. scientist Lab. Molecular Neurobiology, Mass. Gen. Hosp., 1989-90; prof., chair dept. neurobiology U. Mass. Med. Sch., 2001—. Editor: Development of Circadian Rhythmicity and Photoperiodism in Mammals, 1989; co-editor: Suprachiasmatic Nucleus: The Mind's Clock, 1991; mem. editl. bd. Neuron, 1997—; contbr. articles to sci. jours., chpt. to books. Mem. adv. com. Charles H. Hood Found., 1993-98. Recipient E. Mead Johnson award, 1989, NIH Merit award, 1992; Regents scholar U. nebr., 1971; Pfizer Labs. Med. scholar, 1971; Charles King Trust rsch. fellow, 1981-83; grantee NIH, 1981—, Nat. Found./March of Dimes, 1981-88. Mem. Am. Pediatric Soc., Am. Physiol. Soc., Am. Soc. for Clin. Investigation, Endocrine Soc., Soc. for Pediatric Rsch., Soc. for Neurosci., Soc. for Rsch. on Biol. Rhythms (adv. com.), Am. Heart Assn. (established investigator 1985-90), Lepidopterists Soc., Cambridge Entomol. Club, Alpha Omega Alpha. Democrat. Office: Mass Gen Hosp 32 Fruit St Boston MA 02114-2620

**REPPUCCI, NICHOLAS DICKON,** psychologist, educator; b. Boston, May 1, 1941; s. Nicholas Ralph and Bertha Elizabeth (Williams) R.; m. Christine Marlow Onufrock, Sept. 10, 1967; children: Nicholas Jason, Jonathan Dickon, Anna Jin Marlow Chapman. BA with honors, U. N.C., 1962; MA, Harvard U., 1964, PhD, 1968. Lectr., rsch. assoc. Harvard U., Cambridge, Mass., 1967-68; from asst. prof. to assoc prof. Yale U., New Haven, 1968-76; prof. psychology U. Va., Charlottesville, 1976—, dir. grad. studies in psychology, 1984-95, 97-98. Originator biennial conf. on community rsch. and action, 1986. Author: (with J. Haugaard) Sexual Abuse of Children, 1988; (with P. Britner and J. Woolard) Preventing Child Abuse and Neglect Through Parent Education, 1997; editor: (with J. Haugaard) Prevention in Community Mental Health Practice; (with E. Mulvey, L. Weithorn and J. Monahan) Mental Health, Law and Children, 1984; assoc. editor Law and Human Behavior, 1986-96, mem. editl. bd., 1996—; mem. editl. bd. Am. Jour. Cmty. Psychology, 1974-83, 88-91; contbr. articles to profl. jours., chpts. in books. Adv. bd. on prevention Va. Dept. Mental Health, Mental Retardation and Substance Abuse Svcs., Richmond, 1986-92. Recipient Disting. Scholar in psychology award Va. Assn. Social Sci., 1991, Outstanding Psychology Tchg. award, U. Va., 2005. Fellow APA (chmn. task force on pub. policy 1980-84), Am. Psychol. Soc., Soc. for Cmty. Rsch. and Action (pres. 1986, Disting. Contbn. award in theory and rsch. 1998, Inaugural award for ednl. mentoring 1999), Phi Beta Kappa. Office: U Va Dept Psychology PO Box 400400 Charlottesville VA 22904-4400 Office Phone: 434-924-0662. E-mail: ndr@virginia.edu.

**REPPY, JOHN DAVID, JR.,** physicist, educator; b. Lakewood, NJ, Feb. 16, 1931; s. John David, Sr. and Alice Evelyn (Johnson) R.; m. Judith Belle Voris, Aug. 29, 1959; children— John, David, Mary BA, U. Conn., 1954, MS, 1956; PhD, Yale U., 1961. Asst. prof. physics Yale U., New Haven, 1962-66; assoc. prof. physics Cornell U., Ithaca, NY, 1966-69, prof., 1969-87, John L. Wetherill prof. physics, 1987—. Vis. scientist AT&T Bell Labs, Summit, NJ, 1983; vis. prof. physics MIT, Cambridge, Mass., 1984 Recipient Fritz London Meml. Low Temperature Physics award, 1981; NASA Distinguished Pub. Svc. Medal, 2000; NSF fellow, 1961-62; Guggenheim fellow, 1972-73, 79-80; Fulbright-Hays spl. fellow, 1978; U.K. Sci. Rsch. Council sr. research fellow, 1979-80. Fellow AAAS, Am. Physics Soc., Inst. Physics (U.K.), Am. Acad. Arts and Sci.; NY Acad. Sci. mem. NAS. Clubs: Appalachian Mountain (Boston); Am. Alpine. Democrat. Home: 493 Ellis Hollow Creek Rd Ithaca NY 14850-9623 Office: Cornell U Dept Physics 614A Clark Hall Ithaca NY 14853-2501 Office Fax: 607-255-6428. E-mail: reppy@ccmr.cornell.edu.*

**RESCH, JOSEPH ANTHONY,** neurologist; b. Milw., Apr. 29, 1914; s. Frank and Elizabeth (Zetsch) R.; m. Rose Catherine Ritz, May 25, 1939; children— Rose, Frank, Catherine. Student, Milw. State Tchrs. Coll., 1931-34; BS, U. Wis., Madison, 1936, MD, 1938. Intern St. Francis Hosp., LaCrosse, Wis., 1938-39; gen. practice medicine Holmen, Wis., 1939-40; med. fellow in neurology U. Minn., 1946-48, clin. instr. neurology, 1948-51, clin. asst. prof., 1951-55, clin. assoc. prof., 1955-62, assoc. prof., 1962-65, prof., 1965-84, prof. emeritus, 1984—, head dept. neurology, 1976-82, asst. v.p. health sci., 1970-79, prof. lab. medicine and pathology, 1979-84; practice medicine specializing in neurology Mpls., 1948-62. Contbr. articles and abstracts to profl. jours., chpts. to books. Served to lt. col. M.C. U.S. Army, 1940-46; col. Med. Res. 1946-53. Mem. Hennepin County Med. Soc., Minn. Med. Assn., AMA, Minn. Soc. Neurol. Scis., Am. Acad. Neurology, Am. Neurol. Assn., Am. Assn. Neuropathologists, Am. Clin. Neurophysiol. Soc., Am. Epilepsy Soc. Home: 1609 Pleasant St Apt 307 Lauderdale MN 55108

**RESCHER, NICHOLAS,** philosopher, author, educator; b. Hagen, Westphalia, Germany, July 15, 1928; came to U.S., 1938, naturalized, 1944; s. Erwin Hans and Meta Anna Rescher; m. Dorothy Henle, Feb. 10, 1968; children: Mark, Owen, Catherine; 1 child from previous marriage, Elizabeth. BS in Math., Queens Coll., 1949; PhD, Princeton U., 1951; LHD (hon.), Loyola U., Chgo., 1970, Lehigh U., 1993; Dr. honoris causa (hon.), U. Córdoba, Argentina, 1992, U. Constance, Germany, 1995; DS (hon.), CUNY, 1999; PhD (hon.), Fern U., Hagen, 2001; Dr.rer.pol.hc, Helsinki, 2006. Instr. philosophy Princeton (N.J.) U., 1951-52; mathematician RAND Corp., 1954-56; assoc. prof. philosophy Lehigh U., Bethlehem, Pa., 1957-61; univ. prof. philosophy U. Pitts., 1961—, chmn. Ctr. for Philosophy of Sci., 1988—; Trustee St. Edmunds Acad., Pitts., 1980-85; nonresident mem. Corpus Christi Coll., Oxford; disting. vis. lectr. Oxford, Salamanca, Munich, Konstanz; cons. in field. Author: The Coherence Theory of Truth, 1973, Methodological Pragmatism, 1977, Scientific Progress, 1978, The Limits of Science, 1985, Luck, 1995, Predicting the Future, 1997, Complexity, 1998, Nature and Understanding, 2000, Paradoxes, 2000, Philosophical Reasoning, 2001, Fairness, 2002, Epistemic Logic, 2004, Epistometrics, 2006; exec. editor Am. Philos. Quar., 1964—; mem. editl. bd. 15 jours.; contbr. over 250 articles to profl. jours. Sec. gen. Internat. Union History and Philosophy of Sci., UNESCO, 1969-72. With USMC, 1952-54. Recipient Alexander von Humboldt Humanities prize, 1983; fellow Ford Found., 1959-60, Guggenheim Found., 1970-71. Mem. Am. Philos. Assn. (past pres.), Am. Cath. Philos. Assn. (past pres.), Am. Metaphys. Soc. (past pres.), Royal Asiatic Soc., Royal Soc. Can., G.W. Leibniz Soc. Am. (past pres.), C.S. Peirce Soc. (past pres.), Inst. Internat. de Philosophie, Academie Internat. de Philosophie des Scis., Acad. Europaea. Roman Catholic. Avocation: reading history and biography. Home: 1033 Milton Ave Pittsburgh PA 15218 Office: U Pitts Dept Philosophy 1012 Cathedral Pittsburgh PA 15260 Office Phone: 412-624-5950. Business E-Mail: rescher@pitt.edu.

**RESCHKE, MICHAEL W.,** real estate company officer; b. Chgo., Nov. 29, 1955; s. Don J. and Vera R. (Helmer) R.; children: Michael W. Jr., Tiffanie G., Taylor N. BS summa cum laude with univ. honors, No. Ill. U., 1977; JD summa cum laude, U. Ill., 1980. Bar: Ill. 1980; CPA, Ill. Assoc. Winston & Strawn, Chgo., 1980-82; pres., CEO The Prime Group, Inc., Chgo., 1981, chmn. bd. dirs., CEO, 1981—. Mem. Chgo. Devel. Coun., 1987—. Mem.

ABA, Ill. Bar Assn., Urban Land Inst., Chgo. Econ. Club, Real Estate Roundtable (dir.), Order of Coif, Phi Delta Phi, Beta Alpha Psi. Business E-Mail: mreschke@primegroupinc.com.*

**RESCHLY, DANIEL J.,** education educator, psychologist; b. Wayland, Iowa, Dec. 30, 1943; married; 3 children. BS, Iowa State U., 1966; MA, U. Iowa, 1968; PhD, U. Oreg., 1971. Lic. sch. psychologist Iowa, Oreg., Ariz.; nat. cert. sch. psychologist, cert. secondary edn. educator Iowa. Sch. psychologist Louisa County Schs., Wapello, Iowa, 1967–69; dir. summer head start program Louisa County, Iowa, 1969; sch. psychology intern Albina Youth Opportunity Ctr. and Portland (Oreg.) Pub. Schs., 1970–71; asst. prof. U. Ariz., Tucson, 1971–75; assoc. prof., prof., disting. prof., dir. Sch. Psychology Program Iowa State U., 1975–98, interim assoc. dean Coll. Edn., 1996–98, dir. Rsch. Inst. for Studies in Edn., 1996–98; prof. edn. and psychology, chair dept. spl. edn. Vanderbilt U., Nashville, 1998—. Presenter in field. Contbr. chapters to books, articles to profl. jours. Fellow: APA, Am. Psychol. Soc.; mem.: Tenn. Assn. Sch. Psychologists, Internat. Sch. Psychology Assn., Am. Assn. Applied and Preventive Psychology, Coun. for Exceptional Children, Am. Assn. on Mental Retardation, Am. Ednl. Rsch. Assn., Iowa Acad. Edn. (charter), Nat. Assn. Sch. Psychologists (pres., editor Sch. Psychology Rev., chair grad. program approval, Lifetime Achievement award, three Disting. Svc. awards). Office: Vanderbilt Univ Box 328 Peabody Coll Nashville TN 37203-5701

**RESCIGNO, RICHARD JOSEPH,** editor; b. NYC, Apr. 13, 1946; s. Vincent James and Rose (Sofia) R.; m. Carol Sue Conyne, Apr. 22, 1978; children: Timothy, Daniel. BA in English Lit., Fairleigh Dickinson U., 1967; MS in Journalism, Columbia U., 1968. Reporter The Hudson Dispatch, Union City, NJ, 1967; reporter, copy editor The Bergen Record, Hackensack, NJ, 1971-75; reporter, copy editor, asst. city editor Newsday, Melville, NY, 1975-81; news editor, asst. mng. editor, mng. editor Barron's, The Dow Jones Bus. and Fin. Weekly, N.Y.C., 1981—; mng. editor, 1987—. With U.S. Army, 1968-70. Avocations: foreign languages, travel, sports. Office: Barron's 200 Liberty St New York NY 10281-1003 Business E-Mail: rich.rescigno@barrons.com.

**RESCINITI, JOHN WILLIAM,** music educator, protective services official; b. Morristown, NJ, Oct. 26, 1969; s. Joseph John and Eleanor Jane Resciniti; m. Kristina Leigh Craig, Nov. 29, 2002. BS in Jazz and Comml. Music, Hofstra U., 1992, MS in Edn., 1993. Cert. music tchr. NJ. Dir. bands Rutherford (NJ) H.S., 1994—96, Battin and McAullife Mid. Schs., Elizabeth, NJ, 1996—97, Belleville (NJ) Mid. Sch. and Sch. No. 9, 1997—. Freelance musician, Parsippany, NJ, 1990—. Firefighter Mt. Tabor Vol. Fire Dept., Parsippany, 1988—. Mem.: Music Educators Nat. Conf. (assoc.). Libertarian. Avocations: digital production, camping, off highway vehicles, music. Office: Belleville Mid Sch 279 Washington Ave Belleville NJ 07109 Office Phone: 973-751-3533. Business E-Mail: john.resciniti@belleville.k12.nj.us.

**RESCOE, MICHAEL E.,** computer company executive; b. 1953; BA, Tulane U.; MBA, U. Tex. Sr. v.p. corp. fin. Kidder, Peabody & Co.; sr. mng. dir. Bear, Stearns & Co. Inc.; CFO, ENSERCH Corp., Dallas, until 1997; sr. v.p., CFO, PG&E Corp., San Francisco, from 1997; now v.p. fin. 3Com Corp., Santa Clara, Calif.

**RESCORLA, ROBERT ARTHUR,** psychology professor; b. Pitts., May 9, 1940; s. Arthur R. and Mildred J. (Jenkins) Rescorla; m. Shirley Steele; children: Eric, Michael. BA, Swarthmore Coll., 1962; PhD, U. Pa., 1966; MA, Yale U., 1974; PhD (hon.), Ghent U., Belgium, 2006. Successively asst. prof., assoc. prof., prof. Yale U., New Haven, 1966—80; prof. psychology U. Pa., Phila., 1981—. James Skinner prof. sci., 1986—2000, Christopher Browne disting. prof. psychology, 2000—, dean of coll. Sch. Arts and Scis., 1994—97. Author: Pavlovian Second-Order Conditioning, 1980; editor: Animal Learning and Behavior, 1995—97; contbr. articles to profl. jours. Recipient Ira Abrams Tchg. award, 1999, Horsley Grant award, Pavlovian Soc., 2005. Mem.: AAAS (pres. sect. J., psychology 1988—89), NAS, APA (pres. divsn. 3 1985, Disting. Sci.Contbn. award 1986), Psychonomic Soc. (mem. governing bd. 1979—85, chmn. publ. bd. 1985), Ea. Psychol. Assn. (bd. dirs. 1983—86, pres. 1986—87, Warren medal 1991), Soc. Exptl. Psychologists, Am. Psychol. Soc. (William James fellow). Office: U Pa Dept Psychology 3720 Walnut St Philadelphia PA 19104-3604

**RESEK, ROBERT WILLIAM,** economist; b. Berwyn, Ill., July 2, 1935; s. Ephraim Frederick and Ruth Elizabeth (Rummele) R.; m. Lois Doll, July 9, 1960; 1 child, Richard Alden. BA, U. Ill., 1957; AM, Harvard U., 1960, PhD, 1961. Asst. prof. econs. U. Ill., Urbana, 1961-65, assoc. prof., 1965-70, prof., 1970—2005, prof. emeritus, 2005—; vis. scholar MIT, Cambridge, 1967-68; dir. Bur. Econ. and Bus. Rsch., 1977-89, acting v.p. for acad. affairs, 1987-89, v.p. for acad. affairs, 1989—94, v.p. emeritus, 1995—; prof. Inst. Govt. and Pub. Affairs, 1994—2005, prof. emeritus, 2005—. Tchg. fellow Harvard U., 1959-61; vis. prof. U. Colo., 1967, 74-76, 82, Kyoto (Japan) U., 1976; cons. GM, 1964-66, U.S. Congress Joint Econ. Com., 1978-80, ABA, 1980-82; vis. scholar UCLA, 1994-95; co-dir. Midwest Economy: Issues and Policy, Midwest Govs. Conf., 1981; bd. dirs. Midwest U. Consortium Internat. Activities, 1989-94, v.p., 1991-94; mem. Ill. Gov.'s Econ. Policy Coun., 1999-2003. Co-author: Environmental Contamination by Lead and Other Heavy Metals–Synthesis and Modeling, 1978, Special Topics in Mathematics for Economists, 1976, A Comparative Cost Study of Staff Panel and Participating Attorney Panel Prepaid Legal Service Plans, 1981, Illinois Higher Education: Building the Economy, Shaping Society, 2000; editor: Illinois Economic Outlook, 1982-87, Illinois Economic Statistics, 1981, Economic Edge, 1996-2004; co-editor: The Midwest Economy: Issues and Policy, 1982, Frontiers of Business and Economic Research Management, 1983, Illinois Statistical Abstract, 1987, 2002-04. Mem. econ. com. Assn. Univ. Bur. and Econ. Rsch., 1977-89, v.p., 1978-82, pres., 1982-83. Woodrow Wilson fellow, 1957; Social Sci. Rsch. Coun. grantee, 1964; NSF fellow, 1967-69, grantee, 1974-77; U.S. Dept. State scholar, Japan, 1976; grantee Ill. Bd. Higher Edn., 1998-99. Mem. Econometric Soc., Beta Gamma Sigma, Phi Kappa Phi. Home: 201 E Holmes St Urbana IL 61801-6612 Office: Univ Ill 211 IGPA 1007 W Nevada St Urbana IL 61801-3812 Business E-Mail: resek@uiuc.edu.

**RESHCHIKOV, MICHAEL A.,** physics professor, researcher; b. Leningrad, Russia, June 11, 1959; s. Alexander Pavlovich Reshchikov and Oktyabrina Grigorievna Reshchikova; m. Elena Nikolaevna Petrova, Nov. 25, 1983; children: Paul, Alexander. MSEE, St. Petersburg Poly. Inst., St. Petersburg, Russia, 1976—82; PhD in physics, Ioffe Physico-Technical Inst., St. Petersburg, Russia, 1982—89. Rsch. scientist Ioffe Physico-Technical Inst., St. Petersburg, Russia 1982—97, Northwestern U., Evanston, Ill., 1997—99, Dept. of Elec. Engring., Va. Commonwealth U., 1999—2004; asst. prof. Dept. of Physics, Va. Commonwealth U., 2004—. Contbr. more than 100 articles to profl. jours. Mem.: Va. Acad. Scis., Am. Phys. Soc., Materials Rsch. Soc. (assoc.). Achievements include research in deep defects in semiconductors, mostly by luminescence methods. Identification of point defects in GaN, GaAs, InSb, Ge. Avocations: swimming, diving, reading. Office: Dept Physics Virginia Commonwealth Univ 1020 West Main St Richmond VA 23284 Office Phone: 804-828-1613. Office Fax: 804-828-7073. Business E-Mail: mreshchi@vcu.edu.

**RESHOTKO, ELI,** aerospace engineer, educator; b. NYC, Nov. 18, 1930; s. Max and Sarah (Kalisky) R.; m. Adina Venit, June 7, 1953; children: Deborah Naomi, Miriam Ruth. BS, Cooper Union, 1950; MS, Cornell U., 1951; PhD, Calif. Inst. Tech., 1960. Aero. research engr. NASA-Lewis Flight Propulsion Lab., Cleve., 1951-56, head fluid mechanics sect., 1956-57; head high temperature plasma sect. NASA-Lewis Research Center, 1960-61, chief plasma physics br., 1961-64; assoc. prof. engring. Case Inst. Tech., Cleve., 1964-66, prof., 1966-87; prof. engring. Case Western Res. U., Cleve., 1966-88, chmn. dept. fluid thermal and aerospace scis., 1970-76, chmn. dept. mech. and aerospace engring., 1976-79, Kent H. Smith prof. engring., 1989-98, Kent H. Smith prof. emeritus, 1999—. Susman vis. prof. dept. aero.

engring. Technion-Israel Inst. Tech., Haifa, Israel, 1969-70; cons. Inst. Def. Analyses, Dynamics Tech. Inc.,Wyle Labs.; adv. com. fluid dynamics NASA, 1961-64; aero. adv. com. NASA, 1980-87, chmn. adv. subcom. on aerodynamics, 1983-85; chmn. U.S. Boundary Layer Transition Study Group, NASA/USAF, 1970—2001, steering com., 2001-; U.S. mem. fluid dynamics panel AGARD-NATO, 1981-88; chmn. steering com. Symposium on Engring. Aspects of Magneto-hydro-dynamics, 1966, Case-NASA Inst. for Computational Mechanics in Propulsion, 1985-92, USRA/NASA ICASE Sci. Coun., 1992; Joseph Wunsch lectr. Technion-Israel Inst. Tech., 1990 Contbr. articles to tech. jours. Chmn. bd. govs. Cleve. Coll. Jewish Studies, 1981-84; bd. govs. Technion-Israel Inst. Tech., Haifa, Israel, 1999-2005; mem. NRC Air Force Studies bd., 2000-06 Guggenheim fellow Calif. Inst. Tech., 1957-59. Fellow ASME, AAAS, AIAA (Fluid and Plasma Dynamics award 1980, Dryden lectr. in rsch. 1994), Am. Phys. Soc. (vice-chmn. divsn. fluid dynamics 1998, chair-elect 1999, chair 2000, Otto Laporte award in fluid dynamics 1999), Am. Acad. Mechanics (pres. 1986-87); mem. NAE, Ohio Sci. and Engring. Roundtable, Sigma Xi, Tau Beta Pi, Pi Tau Sigma. Home: 1200 Humboldt St Apt 601 Denver CO 80218-2454

**RESIKA, PAUL,** artist; b. N.Y.C., Aug. 15, 1928; Student, Sol Wilson, NYC, 1940—44, Hans Hofmann Sch., 1945—47, Sch. Venice, Italy, 1950—52, Sch. Venice, Rome, 1953. Adj. prof. art Cooper Union, 1966-78; instr. Art Students League, 1968-69; faculty Skowhagen Sch. Painting and Sculpture, 1973, 76; chmn. M.F.A. program Parsons Sch. Design, 1978-89. Dartmouth Coll. 1972 Artist in Residence. One-man shows include George Dix Gallery, NYC, 1948, Peridot Gallery, 1965, 1967, 1968, 1969, 1970, Washburn Gallery, 1971, 1973, Hopkins Ctr. Dartmouth Coll., 1972, Graham Gallery, 1976, 1979, 1981, 1983, 1985, Longpoint Gallery, Provincetown, Mass., 1979, 1981, 1989, 1992, 1995, 25-yr. survey Artists Choice Mus., 1985, Merideth Long Gallery, Houston, 1986, 1997, 2005, Walker-Kornbluth Gallery, Fair Lawn, N.J., 1986, 1995, 1997, Crane Kalman Gallery, London, 1986, Graham/Modern Gallery, 1987—88, 1990, Salander-O'Reilly Galleries, NYC, 1993, 1994, 1995, 1999, 2001, 2002, 2005, Benucci, Rome, 2005, Vered Gallery, East Hampton, N.Y., 1995, 2003, 2004, Gerald Peters Gallery, Santa Fe, 1996, Provincetown Art Assn. and Mus., 1997, Lori Bookstein Gallery, N.Y.C., 1998, 2001, Berta Walker Gallery, Provincetown, 1998, 2001, 2003, Provincetown, Mass., 2004, 2005, Bertha Walker Gallery, 2005, 2006, Lizan Tops Gallery, East Hampton, N.Y., 1998, Hackett Freedman, San Francisco, 1998, Hackett-Freedman, 1999, 2000, 2002, 2006, Metta Galleria, Madrid, 2000, Camino Real Gallery, Boca Raton, Fla., 2003, Benucci Gallery, Rome, 2005, Lori Bookstein Gallery, 2006, Represented in permanent collections Nat. Mus. Am. Art, Washington, Muson-Williams-Proctor Inst. Mus. Art, Utica, N.Y., U. Nebr. Art Gallery, Indpls. Mus. Art, Chase Manhattan Bank, N.Y.C., Neuberger Mus., SUNY, Purchase, U. Wyo., Laramie, Met. Mus. Art, N.Y., Colby Coll., NAD, Owensboro (Ky.) Mus. Art, U. Ariz., William Benton Mus. Art, Hood Mus., Dartmouth Coll., Hanover, N.H., Tucson Mus. Art, Crackow Mus. Art, Poland, Parish Art Mus., Southampton, N.Y., Heckscher Mus., Huntington, N.Y., Mills Coll. Mus. Oakland, Calif., Meml. Art Gallery, Rochester, Whitney Mus., NYC, Mus. Modern Art, also pvt. collections. Recipient award Am. Acad. Arts and Letters, 1977; Altman prize NAD, 1982, 91, 97, 2003, Obrig prize, 1996; Louis Comfort Tiffany grantee, 1959, Ingram Merrill grantee, 1969; John Simon Guggenheim Meml. fellow, 1984. Mem. NAD, Am. Acad. Arts and Letters. Office: Salander Oreilly Galleries 22 E 71st St New York NY 10021-4975

**RESING, MARYLORETTO RACHEL,** guidance counseling administrator, elementary school educator, pastoral counselor; b. Covington, Ky., Jan. 27, 1949; d. Raymond Anthony and Carole Mary (Glover) Seifert; m. John Joseph Resing, Sept. 6, 1969; children: Jayne Carole, Matthew Raymond-Albert, Markus John, Joseph Thomas; foster child Betty. BA, Thomas More Coll., Crestview Hills, Ky., 1984; MEd, Xavier U., Cin., 1989; M of Religious Studies, Athenaeum, Cin., 1994; MA in Counseling Agency, 2004. Cert. elem. tchr. Ky., elem. and secondary guidance counselor Ky., rank 1 specialist counseling edn. 1996, nat. bd. cert. counselor 2001, nat. cert. counselor 2002, lic. profl. clin. assoc. 2005. Tchr. St. Joseph Sch. Diocese of Covington, Crescent Springs, Ky., 1969-70, tchr. St. Cecelia Sch. Independence, Ky., 1984-85, tchr. Covington Cath. H.S. Park Hills, Ky., 1985-90, dir. religious edn. St. Therese Parish Southgate, Ky., 1990-95; guidance counselor Kenton County Sch., Taylor Mill, Ky., 1995-96; dir. religious edn. St. Agnes Parish Diocese of Covington, Park Hills, 1995-96; tchr., dir. alternative coop. edn. program Covington Ind. Sch., 1997-99; counselor Holmes Jr. H.S., 2000—. Mem. Covington Diocesan Family Life Bd., Erlanger, Ky., 1994-96; initiator, chair Religious Edn. Group, Erlanger, 1991-96. Contbr. to mag. and diocesan newspaper. Active Boy Scouts Am., Independence, Ky., 1983—; bd. dirs. YMCA, Independence, 1986-92; mem. Greater Cin. NCCJ, 1985-90; chair St. Cecilia Sch. Bd., Independence, 1985-89; mem. La Leche League No. Ky., 1970-80, leader, 1976-80; bd. dirs. Nat. Assn. Parish Coords. and Dirs. of Religious Edn., 1997. Mem.: Ky. Counseling Assn. (bd. dirs. 2002—, v.p. exec. bd. 2005—06, pres. elect 2006—), Ky. Sch. Counselor Assn., Covington Edn. Assn. (rep. 1999—, v.p. 2005—06), No. Ky. Counseling Assn. (v.p. 2002—03, 2004—05, pres. 2005—06), Am. Counseling Assn., Ky. Edn. Assn., Dirs. of Religious Edn. Support Group, Phi Delta Kappa. Roman Catholic. Avocations: antiques, gardening, reading.

**RESKIN, BARBARA F.,** sociologist; b. St. Paul; Student, Reed Coll., Portland, Oreg.; BA in Sociology, U. Wash., 1968, MA in Sociology, 1970, PhD in Sociology, 1973. Acting asst. prof. sociology U. Calif., Davis, 1972—73; asst. to assoc. prof. sociology Indiana U., Bloomington, 1973—83; prof. sociology and women's studies U. Mich., Ann Arbor, 1983—85; prof. sociology, dir. grad. studies U. Ill., Urbana, 1985—91; prof. sociology Ohio State U., 1991—97, Harvard U., 1997—2002; S. Frank Miyamoto prof. sociology U. Wash., 2002—. Study dir. com. women's employment and related social issues Nat. Rsch. Coun./NAS, Washington, 1981—82; vis. scholar Stanford U. Inst. Rsch. Women and Gender, 1987; fellow Ctr. Advanced Study in Behavioral Scis., 1987—88; chair dept. sociology Ohio State U., 1993—95. Contbr. articles to profl. jours., chapters to books; assoc. editor: Am. Sociol. Rev., 1979—81, Rsch. in Social Stratification and Mobility, 1988—, Work and Occupations, 1995—; author: Sex Differences in the Profl. Life Chances of Chemists, 1980, Realities of Affirmative Action, 1998; editor: Sex Segregation in the Workplace: Trends, Explanations, Remedies, 1984; co-author: Women's Work, Men's Work: Sex Segregation on the Job, 1986, Job Queues, Gender Queues: Explaining Women's Inroads into Male Occupations, 1990, Women and Men at Work, 1994, Mng. Work and Family: Nonstandard Work Arrangements Among Mgrs. and Profls., 1997, Nonstandard Work, Substandard Jobs: Flexible Work Arrangements in the U.S., 1997; adv. editor: Gender & Soc., 1986—88, assoc. editor:, 1990—93, mem. editl. bd.: Social Forces, 1992—95, Gender, Work and Orgns., 1993—. Recipient SWS Mentorship award, Sociologists for Women in Soc., 1998. Fellow: NAS, Am. Acad. Arts and Scis.; mem.: Sociol. Rsch. Assn., Am. Sociol. Assn. (chair sect. on occupations, orgns. and work 1997—98, pres. 2001—02, v.p. 1990—91, Disting. Scholar award, sect. on sex and gender 1995). Office: Dept Sociology U Wash Box 353340 Seattle WA 98195-3340 E-mail: reskin@u.washington.edu.*

**RESNECK-SANNES, HELEN,** psychologist; b. Marion, Ind., Dec. 14, 1947; d. William and Charlotte Resneck; m. Larry David Sannes, June 20, 1976; children: Aaron Sannes, Myrrhia. PhD, U. Wis., Madison, 1974. Lic. psychologist Bd. of Med. Quality Assurance, 1975. Pvt. psychotherapy practice Helen Resneck-Sannes, Ph.D., Santa Cruz, Calif., 1977—; tchr. trainer Internat. Inst. for Bioenergetic Analysis, N.Y.C., 1997—. Asst. prof. Antioch Coll., Monterey, Calif., 1977—77; prof. U. Calif., Santa Cruz, 1989; presenter in field. Author: (memoir) Father's Rooms, 2004; contbr. articles to profl. jours. Recipient medal, Phi Kappa Phi Hon. Soc., 1969; Work study grant, Western Interstate Commn. for Higher Edn., 1968, fellowship, NIMH, 1970-1974, grant to establish a women's therapy ctr., Wis. Psychol. Assn., 1972. Mem.: APA, Monterey Bay Psychol. Assn., Calif. Psychol. Assn., Internat. Inst. for Bioenergetic Analysis (bd. of trustees 2002—03, co-editor jour. 2003). Home and Office: 216 Suburbia Ave Santa Cruz CA 95062 Office Phone: 831-426-2768. Personal E-mail: helenrs@aol.com.

**RESNIC, BURTON S.,** lawyer; s. Samuel and Theresa Babe Resnic; m. Marjoie C. Meyer, July 1, 1961; children: Laura J. Brounstein, Joanne H. Lippman. BA, Washington St. Louis, 1950; LLB, Harvard U., Cambridge, Mass. Bar: Mass. 1954, D.C. 1954. Ptnr. Resnic, Beauregard, Waite & Driscoll, Holyoke, Mass., 1955—. Spkr. in field, 1975—2005. Contbr. articles to profl. jours. Del. Rep. Nat. Conv., 1976, 1980. With U.S. Army, 1953—55. Recipient Recognition for Successful Major Capital Campaign, Holyoke Hosp., 1986—87. Avocations: golf, tennis, skiing. Home: 20 Longfellow Rd Holyoke MA 01040 Office: Resnic Beauegard Waite & Driscoll 330 Whitney Ave Ste 400 Holyoke MA 01040 Office Phone: 413-536-0653. Office Fax: 413-536-4074. Business E-Mail: kstdenis@rbwd.com.

**RESNICK, ALICE ROBIE,** state supreme court justice; b. Erie, Pa., Aug. 21, 1939; d. Adam Joseph and Alice Suzanne (Spizarny) Robie; m. Melvin L. Resnick, Mar. 20, 1970 PhB, Siena Heights Coll., 1961; JD, U. Detroit, 1964; LLD (hon.), Heidelberg Coll., 1999, U. Akron, 1994. Bar: Ohio 1964, Mich. 1965, U.S. Supreme Ct. 1970. Atty. priv. practice, 1964—75; asst. county prosecutor Lucas County Prosecutor's Office, Toledo, 1964-75, trial atty., 1965-75; judge Toledo Mcpl. Ct., 1976-83, 6th Dist. Ct. Appeals, State of Ohio, Toledo, 1983-88; instr. U. Toledo, 1968-69; justice Ohio Supreme Ct., 1988—. Co-chairperson Ohio State Gender Fairness Task Force. Trustee Siena Heights Coll., Adrian, Mich., 1982—; organizer Crime Stopper Inc., Toledo, 1981—; mem. Mayor's Drug Coun.; bd. dirs. Guest House Inc. Named to Ohio Women's Hall of Fame, 1995; recipient Gertrude W. Donahey award, Ohio Democratic Party, 1999, Woman of Toledo award, St. Vincent Mercy Medical Ctr., 1999. Mem. ABA, Toledo Bar Assn., Lucas County Bar Assn., Ohio State Bar Assn. (Nettie Cronise Lutes award 1995), Nat. Assn. Women Judges (Making A Difference award 1996), Am. Judicature Soc., Toledo Women's Bar Assn., Ohio State Women's Bar Assn. (Alice Robie Resnick Outstanding Lawyer award 1998), Toledo Mus. Art, Internat. Inst. Toledo. Roman Catholic. Office: Ohio Supreme Ct 65 S Front St Columbus OH 43215*

**RESNICK, DONALD IRA,** lawyer; b. Chgo., July 19, 1950; s. Roland S. and Marilyn B. (Weiss) R.; m. Jill Allison White, July 3, 1977; children: Daniel, Allison. BS with high honors, U. Ill., 1972; JD, Harvard U., 1975. Bar: Ill. 1975, U.S. Dist. Ct. (no. dist.) Ill. 1975. Assoc. Arvey, Hodes, Costello & Burman, Chgo., 1975-80, ptnr., 1981-83; sr. ptnr. Nagelberg & Resnick, Chgo., 1983-89, Levenstein & Resnick, Chgo., 1989-91; chmn. real estate dept. Jenner & Block, Chgo., 1992—. Mem. mgmt. com. Jenner & Block, Chgo. Home: 651 Greenwood Blvd (Highland Park, Ill.) Club. Office: Jenner & Block 1 E Ibm Plz Fl 4000 Chicago IL 60611-7603 E-mail: dresnick@jenner.com.

**RESNICK, IDRIAN NAVARRE,** foundation administrator; b. Wichita, Kans., Apr. 24, 1936; s. Herbert and Virginiae Miriam (Goldsmith) Speer; m. Jane Letham Riley (div. 1980); children: Michael Mosi, David Shaka; m. Kathleen Margaret Pelich (div. 1993); m. Louise LaMontagne, 1996. BA, Clark U., 1958; MA, Boston U., 1961, PhD, 1966. Lectr. dept. econs. Boston U., 1962-63; asst. prof. econs. Howard U., Washington, 1963-64; lectr. econs. U. Dar es Salaam, Tanzania, 1964-67; vis. prof. econs. Princeton (N.J.) U., 1967-68; asst. prof. econs. Columbia U., N.Y.C., 1968-70; sr. economist Ministry Econ. Planning, Dar es Salaam, 1970-72; exec. dir. Econ. Devel. Bur., New Haven, 1974-81; pres. Resnick Devel. Services, New Haven, 1982—; exec. dir. Assn. Am. Indian Affairs, N.Y.C., 1985-89, Action for Corp. Accountability, New Haven, 1991-94; fiction writer, 1995—; lectr. ESL, 1997—. Prof. Cornell U., Ithaca, N.Y., 1982-84; cons. Govt. of Nicaragua, Managua, 1979-81, Govt. of the Netherlands, The Hague, 1977, Govt. of Somalia, Mogodishu, 1985. Author: The Long Transition: Building Socialism in Tanzania, 1981, Controlling Consulting, 1989; editor: Tanzania: Revolution by Education, 1968; video producer (in the Lakota lang.) AIDS, 1989; contbr. articles to profl. jours. Organizer Namibia Com., New Haven, 1977-79, Conn. Task Force on Cen. Am., 1985; mem. Pledge of Resistance, U.S., 1985-89; vol. adviser AIDS Interfaith Network, New Haven, 1990. Nat. Edn. scholar U.S. Govt., 1959-62; Albert Schweitzer Resh fellow Columbia U., 1969-70. Avocations: chess, theater, travel, tennis, golf. Home: 16 Old Pawson Rd Branford CT 06405-5117 Office Fax: 203-481-4802.

**RESNICK, IRVEN MICHAEL,** philosophy educator; b. Rochester, NY, Nov. 22, 1952; s. William Resnick and Mary Eskenazi; m. Elizabeth Anne Scofield, May 28, 1989; children: Austin Scofield, Matthew Scofield, Ariel Resnick. BA, Tulane U., 1974; MA, Cath. U. Am., 1980; PhD, U. Va., 1983. Asst. prof. La. State U., Baton Rouge, 1987-90; prof. Dept. Philosophy and Religion U. Tenn., Chattanooga, 1990—. Chair of excellence in Judaic studies; sr. assoc. Oxford Ctr. for Hebrew and Jewish Studies, 2003—. Author: Divine Power and Possibility in St. Peter Damian's De Divina Omnipotentia, 1992, Two Theological Treatises of Odo of Tournai, 1994; co-author, translator: Albertus Magnus On Animals, 1999, An Annotated Bibliography of Albert the Great (1900-2000), 2004, The Letters of Peter Damian, 121-150, 2004, The Letters of Peter Damian, 151-180, 2005 Jerusalem Trust fellow Oxford Ctr. for Hebrew Std., Yarnton, Eng., 1995, corr. fellow Ingeborg Rennert Ctr., Bar-Ilan U., Israel, 1996, C.G. Found. Jerusalem Project, Bar-Ilan U., 1996. Mem.: Assn. for Jewish Studies, Soc. for Medieval and Renaissance Philosophy, Oxford Ctr. for Hebrew and Jewish Studies (sr.). Home: 204 Slayton St Signal Mountain TN 37377-2285 Office: U Tenn Chattanooga 615 Mccallie Ave Chattanooga TN 37403-2504 Office Phone: 423-425-4446. E-mail: Irven-Resnick@utc.edu.

**RESNICK, JEFFREY I.,** plastic surgeon; b. Jersey City, Mar. 2, 1954; s. Victor and Regina (Bistritz) R.; m. Michele Gail Zinger, July 12, 1981; children: Andrew Gregory, Daniel Zachary. BS, Yale U., 1975; MD, U. Pa., 1980. Diplomate Am. Bd. Surgery, Am. Bd. Plastic Surgery. Resident in surgery Mass. Gen. Hosp., Boston, 1980—85; resident in plastic surgery, 1985—87; asst. clin. prof. plastic surgery UCLA, 1987—, fellow in craniofacial surgery, 1987—88; full time asst. prof. clin. surgery U. So. Calif. Med. Sch., 1990—98—. Contbr. articles to profl. jours. Surgeon Interplast, Vietnam, Nepal, Myanmar. Mem. Am. Assn. Plastic Surgeons., Am. Soc. Plastic Surgeons, Am. Soc. Maxillofacial Surgeons, Am. Cleft Palate-Craniofacial Assn., Plastic Surgery Ednl. Found., Sigma Xi, Alpha Omega Alpha. Office: 1301 20th St Ste 470 Santa Monica CA 90404-2082 Office Phone: 310-315-0222. Business E-Mail: jresnick@ucla.edu.

**RESNICK, KENNETH,** photography director; b. NYC, May 11, 1934; s. Reuben and Helen (Edelson) R.; m. Marijke Koch, Aug. 1960 (div. Aug. 1974); children: Sonya, Paul, Karen; m. Karen louise Matthesius, July 23, 1977; children: Margaret Rose, Charles Andrew. Student, Trinity Coll., 1952—56. Dir. photography Ga. Ctr., U. Ga., Athens, 1960-61; cameraman, editor Milner and Fenwick, Inc., Balt., 1961-63; film maker US Info. Agy., Washington, 1963-66; producer Nat. Ednl. TV, NYC, 1965; cameraman, asst. cameraman NBC-TV, Washington, 1967-68; chief photographer Md. Ctr. for Pub. Broadcasting Sta. WMPB-TV, Owings Mills, 1969; cameraman, asst. dir. BF&J Prodns., Balt., 1969-72; news film cameraman Sta. WTTG-TV, Metromedia Prodns., Washington, 1972-78; producer, videographer Cable News Network, Atlanta, 1981-82; video producer Wang Labs., Inc., Lowell, Mass., 1986-90; freelance dir. photography. Instr. Md. Inst. Coll. of Art, Balt., 1968-73; guest lectr. Goucher Coll, Towsen, Md., 1969-70, Caselton (Vt.) State Coll., 1985; conf. participant Arts and Scis., Morgan State Coll, Balt., 1966. Co-produced, co-directed, cinematographer Sunday on the River, 1962 (Bronze medal, Silver Gondola award humanitarian idealism in film Venice Internat. Documentary Film Festival 1962, An Outstanding Film of Yr. Brit. Film Inst. and London Film Festival 1962, Golden Eagle award Council Internat. Nontheatrical Events 1962, 63, work inducted in the Mus. Modern Art Film Archives 1991); produced, directed, photographed Men, Marble and Machines, 1984 (Bronze medal Internat. Film and TV Festival of NYC 1984, Golden Eagle award, 1984 Chris plaque Columbus Film Festival 1985, Emmy award 1987); photographed Now and in the Future (Silver Plaque INTER-COM 1988); producer, dir., photographer A Celebration of Architecture (Gold Camera award, 3 Silver Screen awards, U.S. Indsl. Film and Video Festival 1989, Gold CINDY award, Rose Layos Green Meml. award 1989, Chris award Columbus Film Festival 1989, Silver Plaque INTERCOM, 1989, 2

Silver Medals Internat. Film & TV Festival N.Y. 1990, Golden Eagle award 1990). Mem. World Wildlife Found., Wilderness Soc., Nature Conservancy. Recipient First Prize Gen. News Class award, 1973, Spot News Class award, 1976, 78, White House News Photographer's Assn., First Place Spot News award Nat. Press Photographer's Assn., 1978, Emmy news film photography Washington Chpt. Nat. Acad. TV Arts and Scis., Inc., 1978. Mem. Internat. Photographers of Motion Picture and TV Industries (local 600), Sierra Club. Democrat. Unitarian Universalist. Home: 73 Washington St Concord NH 03301-4172

RESNICK, KIRSTEN FAY MARKUSON, history professor; b. Torrance, Calif., Aug. 22; d. Daniel Maxwell Bluck and Miriam Priscilla (Anne) Sheridan; m. William David Crook, Mar. 11, 2000; children: Micah James Resnick Crook, Kira Danielle Resnick Crook. Student, CULA, 1980—81; BA, U. Calif., Santa Barbara, 1985, MA, 1994; adult edn. credential, Calif. State U. Dominguez Hills, Carson, 1998. Cert. adult edn. tchr. Calif. Tchr. various elem and HS, Mombasa, Kenya, 1981—91; tchr. asst. black studies U. Calif., Santa Barbara, 1991, tchg. asst. history of western civilization, 1992—94; tchr. Met. Sch. Ctr., LA, 1997—2000, County Clerical Cert. Program, LA, 1998—2001; adj. prof. history Coll. of Canyons, Santa Clarita, Calif., 2001—, El Camino Coll., Torrance, Calif., 2002—. Spkr. in field; tchr. adults various vol. orgns., 1980—; cons. to home-schooling families. Author written/oral expression curriculum. Advisor homeless adolescents, Hollywood, Calif., 1986—88; presch. tchr. El Segundo, 2002—; vol. tsunami relief orgn., El Segundo, Calif., 2002—. Recipient Achievement award, Nat. Assn. Counties, 2000, award, 14th Ann. Productivity and Quality Awards Projects, LA County, 2000. Mem.: Orgn. Am. Historians, Western Assn. Women Educators. Avocations: wedding coordinating, collecting vintage clothing.

RESNICK, LYNDA, corporate financial executive; Co-owner, vice chmn. Franklin Mint; co-owner Roll Internat. Chmn. Teleflora. Chmn. mktg. com. Conservation Internat.; bd. dirs. Assn. for Cure of Cancer of the Prostate, CaP CURE, Milken Family Found.; mem. exec. com., trustee, chmn. acquisitions com. L.A. County Mus. Art; mem. com. on sculpture and decorative arts Met. Mus. Art; trustee Phila. Mus. Art. Recipient Gold Effie award, 1983; named one of Top 50 U.S. Women Bus. Owners. Working Women, #1 L.A.-based woman Bus. Owner, L.A. bus. Jour., one of top 100 U.S. art collectors Art & Antiques mag. Office: Roll Internat Corp 11444 W Olympic Blvd Los Angeles CA 90064-1549

RESNICK, MARTIN I., urologist, educator; b. Bklyn., Jan. 12, 1943; s. Daniel and Bertha (Becker) R.; m. Victoria Klein, July 4, 1965; children: Andrew Howard, Jeffrey Scott. BA, Alfred U., N.Y., 1964; MD, Bowman Gray Sch. Medicine, Winston-Salem, N.C., 1969; MS, Northwestern U., Evanston, Ill., 1973. Diplomate Am. Bd. Urology. Instr. urology Northwestern U., Chgo., 1974-75, Bowman Gray Sch. Medicine, 1974-77, asst. prof., 1977-79, assoc. prof., 1979-81; prof., chmn. dept. urology Case Western Res. U., Cleve., 1981—, prof. oncology, 1987—. NIH awardee. Mem. Am. Urol. Assn. (pres. 2003-04), Am. Bd. Urology (pres. 2002-03), Alpha Omega Alpha. Jewish. Avocation: running. Office: 11100 Euclid Ave Cleveland OH 44106-5046 Office Phone: 216-844-3011. Business E-mail: martin.resnick@case.edu.

RESNICK, MYRON J., retired insurance company executive, lawyer; b. Louisville, July 13, 1931; s. Harry C. and Sybil G. (Glick) R.; m. Alicia M. Ward, Dec. 16, 1967; children— Hugh, Clay, David. BS in Econs., U. Pa., 1953; JD, U. Mich., 1956. Various positions Allstate Ins. Co., Northbrook, Ill., 1959-88, sr. v.p., treas. bd. dirs., 1959-95; chmn. bd. Federated Ins. Co. Ltd. (UK), Sale, Cheshire, England, 1979-81; ret., 1995. Dir. Allstate Ins. Co. Ltd. (U.K.), Sale; pres. Allstate Investment Mgmt. Co.; mem. adj. faculty John Marshall Law Sch., Chgo., 1996-98. Chmn. Chgo. exec. com. Anti-Defamation League, 1975—; bd. dirs Chgo. Urban League, 1987-2001, St. Scholastica High Sch., Chgo., 1977-79; trustee George Williams Coll., Downers Grove, Ill., 1981-93, chmn. bd. trustees, 1991-93; trustee Aurora U., 1993—; bd. advisors Inst. Law and Econs. U. Pa., 1994— With U.S. Army, 1956-58. Mem. ABA, Chgo. Bar Assn., Ill. Bar Assn., Assn. Life Ins. Counsel, Chgo. Mortgage Attys. Assn. (bd. dirs. 1965-75), Reform Club (London). E-mail: amresnick@aol.com.

RESNICK, RHODA BRODOWSKY, psychotherapist; b. Mar. 22, 1930; d. Isador and Rose (Wasserman) Brodowsky; m. Jack H. Resnick, May 21, 1950; children: Steven E., Caryn B. BS, CCNY, 1951; MS, Queens Coll., 1973; postgrad., Hunter Coll. Tchr. N.Y.C. Bd. Edn., 1960—80, guidance counselor, 1980—; psychotherapist L.I. Cons. Ctr., 1973—77; priv. practice psychotherapy, 1975—. Fellow, L.I. Inst. Mental Health, 1975. Mem.: PGA, United Fedn. Tchrs., Am. Pers. and Guidance Assn., PGA Hole in One Club, Am. Contract Bridge League (Bronze life). Home: 340 E 64th St New York NY 10021-7503 E-mail: xrojac@hotmail.com.

RESNICK, ROBERT, physicist, researcher; b. Balt., Jan. 11, 1923; s. Abraham and Anna (Dubin) R.; m. Mildred Saltzman, Oct. 14, 1945; children— Trudy, Abby, Regina. AB, Johns Hopkins U., 1943, PhD (Pres.'s Fund scholar 1946-49), 1949. Physicist NACA, Cleve., 1944-46; asst. prof., assoc. prof. physics U. Pitts., 1949-56; assoc. prof., prof. physics Rensselaer Poly. Inst., Troy, NY, 1956-93; prof. emeritus, 1993—; chmn. interdisciplinary sci. curriculum Rensselaer Poly. Inst., Troy, NY, 1973-88, Edward P. Hamilton Disting. prof. sci., 1975-93; hon. research fellow Harvard U., 1964-65; Fulbright prof. Peru, 1971. Hon. vis. prof. Peoples Republic of China, 1981, 85; mem. Commn. on Coll. Physics, 1960-68; commencement speaker Rensselaer Poly. Inst., 1993; mem. U.S. adv. bd. Quantum Joint USSR/USA sci. mag., 1989-93. Author: A Manual for Laboratory Physics, 1954, (with D. Halliday) Physics, 1960, 3d edit., 1978, 4th edit., 1991, 5th edit., 2000, (with Halliday and Krane) extended version, 1986, 2d edit. extended version, 1991, 3rd edit., 2000, 5th edit., 2003, (with Halliday and Krane) Introduction to Special Relativity, 1968, (with R. Eisberg) Notes on Quantum Theory, 1968, Notes on Modern Physics, 1969, Quantum Physics of Atoms, Molecules, Solids, Nuclei and Particles, 1974, 2d edit., 1985, (with D. Halliday) Fundamentals of Physics, 1970, 5th edit., 1996, extended version, 1988, 2d edit., 1993, 3rd edit., 1996, 4th edit., 1999, (with J. Walker and D. Halliday) 7th edit., 2004, (with others) Student Study Guide for Physics, 1970, 6th edit., 2001, Basic Concepts in Relativity and Early Quantum Theory, 1972, 2d edit., 1985, Basic Concepts in Relativity, 1991; author: (with others) Sourcebook for Programmable Calculators, 1978, (with E. Derringh) Solutions to Physics Problems, 1980, 5th edit., 1996, (with K. Brownstein) Tests for Physics, 1987, (with J. Walker and D. Halliday) CD Physics, 1993, 3rd edit., 2000; books translated into numerous fgn. langs; So You Want to Write a Textbook, 1999 (video); mem. adv. ed., project staff: Physical Science for Non-Scientists, 1964-68, pub., 1968; co-dir.: Project Physics Demonstration Experiments, 1962-70; pub. project, 1970, Workshop on Apparatus for College Physics, 1964-65, 66, Videotapes in Physics Instruction, 1975-78; dir. Physics Demonstration and Laboratory Apparatus Workshop, 1960-61; adv. editor: John Wiley & Sons, Inc., 1967-89, Macmillan Pubs., 1990-94. Recipient Disting. Svc. citation Am. Assn. Physics Tchrs., 1967, Hans Christian Oersted medal, 1974, Disting. Alumnae award Johns Hopkins U., 2005; named to Hall of Fame, Balt. City Coll., 1989, Rensselaer Poly. Inst., 2003; Robert Resnick Ctr. for Physics established at Rensselaer Poly. Inst., 1993, Robert Resnick Ann. Sci. Lectr. series endowed, 1993. Fellow AAAS, Am. Phys. Soc.; mem. AAUP, Am. Assn. Physics Tchrs. (v.p. 1986, pres.-elect 1987, pres. 1988), Am. Soc. Engring. Edn., Am. Inst. Physics (governing bd. 1987-90, mem. coun. Ctr. for History of Physics 1997—), Philosophic Soc. South Fla. (exec. bd. 1997-2000), Textbook Author Assn. (coun. 1990-93), Phi Beta Kappa, Sigma Xi. Achievements include rsch. publs. in aerodynamics, nuclear physics, atomic physics, upper atmosphere physics, history of physics, physics edn. Home: 5757 Bartlett St Pittsburgh PA 15217 E-mail: resnir@aol.com.

RESNICK, SCOTT N., real estate company executive; s. Burton P. Resnick. Grad., NYU. With Sonnenblick-Goldman Co.; joined Jack Resnick & Sons Inc., NYC, 1989, named v.p., 1991, mng. dir., exec. mng. dir. leasing & mgmt., 1995—2000, pres & COO, 2000—. Dir. comml. bd. Realty Adv. Bd.

on Labor Rels. Inc. Bd. trustees Whitney Mus. Am. Art, NYC, The Phipps Housing Group; bd. dirs. Grand Ctrl. Partnership. Mem.: Real Estate Bd. NY (bd. governors). Office: Jack Resnick & Sons Inc 110 E 59th St New York NY 10022 Office Phone: 212-421-1300. Office Fax: 212-758-2948.

RESNICK, STEWART ALLEN, diversified company executive; b. Jersey City, Dec. 24, 1936; s. David and Yetta (Goldmaker) R.; children from previous marriage: Jeffrey Brian, Ilene Sue, William Jay; m. Lynda Rae Harris, Nov. 26, 1972; children: Jonathan Charles Sinay, Jason Daniel Sinay. BS, UCLA, 1959, LLB, 1962. Co-chmn., CEO, pres. Roll Internat. Corp., LA; chmn., CEO The Franklin Mint, Aston, Pa., 1985—; co-chmn., CEO Teleflora, LA; pres. Paramount Farms, Inc., LA; other subsidiaries of Roll Internat. Corp. include Paramount Citrus, Fiji Water, POM Wonderful. Bd. trustees J. Paul Getty Trust, LA, 2005—; mem. bd. Caltech, Bard Coll., Conservation Internat. Avocation: health and fitness related activities. Office: Roll Internat Corp 10th Fl 11444 W Olympic Blvd Los Angeles CA 90064 Office Phone: 310-966-5700. Office Fax: 310-914-4747.*

RESNICOW, NORMAN JAKOB, lawyer; b. N.Y.C., July 23, 1947; s. Herbert and Melly (Engelberg) R.; m. Barbara Jane Roses, June 14, 1970; children: Daniel Ilan, Joel Ethan. BA summa cum laude, Yale U., 1969, JD, 1972. Bar: N.Y. 1973, U.S. Dist. Ct. (so. and ea. dists.) N.Y. 1973. Assoc. Baker & McKenzie, N.Y.C., 1972-79, ptnr., 1979-98, Piper, Marbury Rudnick & Wolff, N.Y.C., 1998-2000, Fox Horan & Camerini, N.Y.C., 2000—. Term mem. Council Fgn. Relations, N.Y.C., 1976-81; exec. com., vice chair, v.p., treas., bd. dirs. Hebrew Immigrant Aid Soc., N.Y.C., 1981—; mem. nat. young leadership cabinet United Jewish Appeal, N.Y.C., 1978-83. Recipient Young Leadership award United Jewish Appeal-Fedn. Jewish Philanthrophies, 1978. Mem. ABA (corp. bus. and banking law, internat. law sects.), Assn. of Bar of City of N.Y. (internat. trade com. 1987-89, com. nuclear law and tech. 1992-98), N.Y. State Bar Assn. (internat. law com. 1985-87, internat. employement law com. 1997—), Phi Beta Kappa. Democrat. Avocation: international political relations. Office: Fox Horan & Camerini LLP 825 Third Ave New York NY 10022 Home: 71 Washington PL Apt 1A New York NY 10011-9184 E-mail: njresnicow@foxlex.com.

RESNIK, HARVEY LEWIS PAUL, psychiatrist; b. Buffalo, Apr. 6, 1930; s. Samuel and Celia (Greenberg) R.; m. Audrey Ruth Frey, Aug. 30, 1964 (dec. 1993); children: Rebecca Gabrielle, Henry Seth Maccabee, Jessica Ruth. BA magna cum laude, U. Buffalo, 1951; MD, Columbia, 1955; grad., Phila. Psychoanalytic Inst., 1967. Diplomate: Am. Bd. Psychiatry and Neurology. Intern Phila. Gen. Hosp., 1955-56, resident in surgery, 1956-57; resident in psychiatry Jackson Meml. Hosp., Miami, Fla., 1959-61; fellow U. Pa. Hosp., 1961-62, mem. staff, 1962-67; instr. Sch. Medicine, U. Pa., 1962-66; instr. med. hypnosis Sch. Medicine, U. Pa. (Grad. Sch. Medicine), 1963-65; clin. dir. psychiatry E. J. Meyer Meml. Hosp., Buffalo, 1967, dir. psychiatry, 1968; from assoc. prof. to prof., dep. chair Sch. Medicine, SUNY at Buffalo, 1968—70; chief Nat. Center for Studies of Suicide Prevention, NIMH, 1969-74, chief mental health emergencies sect., 1974-76; with Reproductive Biology Rsch. Found., St. Louis, 1971; clin. prof. psychiatry and behavioral sci. Sch. Medicine, George Washington U., 1969—2002, prof. emeritus clin. psychiatry and behavioral scis., 2002—; dir. Human Behavior Found., 1975—; lectr. Sch. Medicine, Johns Hopkins, Balt., 1969-74; adj. lectr. Johns Hopkins U. Sch. Pub. Health, Balt., 1981-82. Prof. cmty. health Fed. City Coll., 1971-75; med. dir. Johns Hopkins U. Compulsive Gambling Ctr., 1981-83; med. dir. alcohol and substance abuse program, College Park, 1986-2000; vis. prof. Katholieke U., Leuven, Belgium, 1986-93; cons. to Sec.-Gen. Ministry of Health, Belgium, 1986-90, NATO fellow, 1986-87; cons. various hosps. and orgns., Medicare, Pa. Blue Shield, 1984-96, Trailblazer Health, 1996-99, Blue Cross/Blue Shield S.C., 1999; sr. attending Suburban Hosp., Bethesda, Md., 1976—, psychiatry chair, 2006—. Author: Suicidal Behaviors: Diagnosis and Management, 1968, 2d edit., 1994, (with M. E. Wolfgang) Treatment of the Sexual Offender, 1971, Sexual Behaviors: Social, Clinical and Legal Aspects, 1972, (with B. Hathorne) Suicide Prevention in the Seventies, 1973, (with H.L. Ruben) Emergency Psychiatric Care, 1974, (with others) The Prediction of Suicide, 1974, Emergency and Disaster Management, 1976; (with J.T. Mitchell) Emergency Response to Crisis, 1981; Editor: Bull. Suicidology, 1969-74; Contbr. (with others) articles on hypnosis, sexual offenders, marriage and sexual dysfunction treatment, suicide, death and dying, emergency psychiatric care. Mem. Addictions Adv. Bd. Prince Georges County, 1980-85. Served to capt. USAF, 1957-59, ETO-Middle East; capt. USNR; ret. Decorated officer Order of Crown (Belgium). Fellow Am. Coll. Mental Health Adminstrs. (life), Am. Coll. Psychiatrists (life), Am. Psychiat. Assn. (life); mem. Med-Chi of Md., Prince Georges County Med. Soc. (co-chair joint com. with Bar Assn. 1996-2001), Montgomery County Med. Soc., Washington Psychiatry Soc., Am. Acad. Psychiatry and Law (suicidology com. 1998-2000), Phila. Psychoanalytic Soc., NIH Alumni Assn., Columbia U. Med. Alumni Assn. (bd. dirs. 1993-95), Cosmos Club (Washington), Phi Beta Kappa, Beta Sigma Rho (grand vice warden 1963). Jewish. Office: 4209 Bradley Ln Chevy Chase MD 20815-5234 Office Phone: 301-294-8324.

RESNIK, JUDITH, law educator; b. Bryn Mawr, 1972; JD, NYU, 1975. Orrin B. Evans prof. law U. So. Calif., 1989—97; Arthur Liman prof. law Yale U., New Haven, 1997—. Vis. prof. Harvard U., Yale U., U. Chgo., 1988—90, NYU, 1996—97; founding dir. Arthur Liman Pub. Interest Program and Fund. Co-author: Adjudication and Its Alternatives: An Introduction to Procedure, 2003; author: The Processes of Law: Understanding Courts and Their Alternatives, 2004; contbr. articles to law jours. Recipient Florence K. Murray Service Award, Internat. Assn. Women Judges, 1993, USC Assocs. Award for Creativity in Rsch., 1994. Fellow: Am. Philos. Soc.; mem.: ABA (Margaret Brent Award 1998), Am. Acad. of Arts and Scis. Internat. Assn. of Women Judges (mem. Bd. of Managerial Trustees), Am. Assn. Law Schs. (chair Sect. on Civil Procedure 1991, liaison to ABA Commn. on Women 2000—04, chair Sect. on Civil Procedure 2003). Office: Yale Law Sch PO Box 208215 New Haven CT 06520 E-mail: judith.resnik@yale.edu.

RESNIK, ROBERT, medical educator; b. New Haven, Dec. 7, 1938; s. Nathan Alfred and Elsie (Hershman) R.; m. Lauren Brahms, Oct. 29, 1966; children: Andrew Scott, Jamie Layne. BA, Yale U., 1960; MD, Case Western Res. U., 1965. Intern in internal medicine Mt. Sinai Hosp., Cleve., 1965-66; resident in ob-gyn. Yale U. Sch. Medicine, 1966-70; asst. prof. Sch. Medicine U. Calif., San Diego, 1974-78, assoc. prof., 1978-82, prof. reproductive medicine, 1982—, chmn. dept., 1982-95, dean clin. affairs, 1988-90, dean admissions, 1995—2003. Cons. Nat. Heart, Lung and Blood Inst. NIH, Washington, 1987; mem. exec. com. Coun. Residency Edn. Ob-Gyn, Washington, 1988-94, residency rev. com., 1988-94. Editor: (textbook) Maternal-Fetal Medicine: Principles and Practice, 1984, 5th edit., 2004; contbr. numerous articles to profl. jours. Major U.S. Army, 1970-72. Recipient Lifetime Achievement award, Soc. Maternal Fetal Medicine, 2004; Rsch. grantee, Nat. Found., NIH. Fellow: Royal Coll. Obstet. Gynecologists (ad eundem), N.W. Obstet. Gynecological Soc., Pacific Coast Obstet. and Gynecol. Soc., Am. Coll. Ob-Gyn. (vice chmn. obs. practice com. 1998—2000), New England Obstet. Gynecological Soc.; mem.: San Diego Gynecol. Soc. (pres. 1982), Am. Gynecologic and Obstet. Soc. (treas. 2003—), Perinatal Rsch. Soc. (pres. 1985), Soc. Gynecologic Investigation (coun. 1983—88), Yale Club, Am. Gynecol. Club (pres. 2002—03). Office: UCSD Med Ctr 200 W Arbor Dr 8433 San Diego CA 92103-8433 Business E-Mail: rresnik@ucsd.edu.

RESO, ANTHONY, geologist, educator, earth resources economist; b. London, Eng., Aug. 10, 1931; arrived in U.S., 1940, naturalized, 1952; AB, Columbia Coll., 1954; MA, Columbia U., 1955; postgrad., U. Cin., 1956—57; PhD, Rice U., 1960; postgrad., Grad. Sch. Bus. U. Houston, 1964—68. Instr. geology Queens Coll., Flushing, NY, 1954; geologist Atlantic Richfield Corp., Midland, Tex., 1955—56; asst. prof. geology and curator invertebrate paleontology Pratt Mus., Amherst Coll., Mass. 1959—62; staff rsch. geologist Tenneco Oil Co., Houston, 1962—86; mgr. geol. Peak Prodn. Co., Houston, 1986—, v.p., 1988—2000. Cons. in geol.

rsch. Tenn. Gas and Oil Co., 1960—61; lectr. U. Houston, 1962—65; vis. prof. Rice U., 1980; mem. bd. advisers Gulf Univs. Rsch. Corp., Galveston, Tex., 1967—75, chmn., 1968—69. Contbr. articles to profl. jours. Grantee Rsch., Eastman Fund, 1962, NSF fellow, 1958—59. Fellow: AAAS, Geol. Soc. Am. (com. investments 1984—95, chmn. 1993—95, budget com. 1993—95, found. trustee 1999—2004, Rsch. grantee 1958, Disting. Svc. award 1996); mem.: English-Speaking Union U.S. (dir. Houston br. 1978—, v.p. 1982—88, mem. scholarship com. 1988—97, chmn. 1991—97, pres. 1997—98), Houston Geol. Soc. (v.p. 1973—75, pres. 1975—76, chmn. constn. revision com. 1981, Disting. Svc. award 1985), Paleontol. Rsch. Instn., Am. Assn. Petroleum Geologists (life; com. convs. 1977—83, gen. chmn. nat. conv. 1979, chmn. 1980—83, com. investments 1982—88, chmn. com. group ins. 1986—88, treas. 1986—88, found. trustee assoc. 1991, Rsch. grantee 1958, 1959, Disting. Svc. award 1985), SEPM Soc. for Sedimentary Geology (com. investments 1990—2004, chmn. 1992—95, treas. SEPM Found. 1997—2003, Disting. Svc. award 2003), Paleontol. Soc., Varsity C Club, Beta Theta Pi, Sigma Gamma Epsilon, Sigma Xi. Episcopalian. Home: 1805 Brun St Houston TX 77019-5712 Office: care Peak Prodn Co PO Box 130785 Houston TX 77219-0785 E-mail: aresogeo@swbell.net.

RESOR, RANDOLPH RICHARDSON, transportation consultant; b. White Plains, N.Y., Sept. 3, 1952; s. Robert Reuben and Julie Houston (Harper) R.; m. Carol Diane Wahl, June 8, 1991; children: Joy Patricia, Robert Randolph. BA, U. Chgo., 1975. Spl. asst. exec. dept. Assn. Am. RRS., Washington, 1977-78; analyst maintenance of way U.S. Railway Assn., Washington, 1978-80; mem. profl. staff Dynatrend, Inc., Arlington, Va., 1980; sr. systems analyst Advanced Tech., Inc., McLean, Va., 1981; project mgr. Met. Transp. Authority, N.Y.C., 1982-84; asst. dir. planning N.Y.C. Transit Authority, Bklyn., 1984-87; dir. costing and pricing Zeta-Tech. Assocs., Inc., Cherry Hill, N.J., 1987-92, v.p. costing and econ. analysis, 1992—. Contbr. articles to profl. jours. Recipient Rail Transp. award ASME, 1992, Special Act award, FRA, 2001. Mem. Transp. Rsch. Forum (Cost Analysis Rsch. award, 1992), Rotary Internat. Republican. Methodist. Avocations: bicycling, rowing, hist. rsch. Office: Zeta-Tech Assocs Inc 900 Kings Hwy N Ste 208 Cherry Hill NJ 08034-1516 Office Phone: 856-779-7795. Business E-Mail: resor@zetatech.com.

RESOR, STANLEY ROGERS, retired lawyer; b. N.Y.C., Dec. 5, 1917; s. Stanley Burnet and Helen (Lansdowne) Resor; m. Jane Lawler Pillsbury, Apr. 4, 1942 (dec.); children: Stanley R., Charles P., John L., Edmund L., William B., James P., Thomas S.; m. Louise Mead Walker, May 1, 1999. BA, Yale U., 1939, LLB, 1946. Bar: N.Y. 1947. From assoc. to ptnr. Debevoise & Plimpton, N.Y.C., 1946-65, 71-73, 79-87, of counsel, 1988-90; undersec. Dept. Army, 1965, sec., 1965-71, amb. negotiations Mut. and Balanced Force Reductions in Ctrl. Europe, 1973-78; undersec. policy Dept. Def., 1978-79; ret., 1990. Fellow Yale Corp., 1979—86. Served to maj. U.S. Army, 1942—45. Decorated Silver Star US Army, Bronze Star, Puple Heart; recipient George C. Marshall award, Assn. U.S. Army, 1974, Sylvanus Thayer award, Assn. Graduates U.S. Mil. Acad., 1984. Mem.: ABA, Internat. Inst. Strategic Studies, Lawyers Alliance World Security, Coun. Fgn. Rels., Arms Control Assn. (chmn. bd. dirs. 1994—2000), Atlantic Coun., Assn. Bar City of N.Y., UN Assn. U.S.A. Republican. Episcopalian. Home: 809 Weed St New Canaan CT 06840-4023

RESPELIERS, PATRICK J., lawyer; s. John Joseph and Lucille Ann Respeliers; m. Monica Jeanne Demma, May 29, 1987; children: Emily, Madeline, John Patrick. BSBA in Acctg., Creighton U., Omaha, 1984; JD, So. Meth. U., Dallas, 1987. Bar: Tex. 1987, Mo. 1996. Assoc. Akin Gump Strauss Hauer & Feld, Dallas, 1987-95; ptnr. Stinson Morrison Hecker LLP, Kansas City, Mo., 1995—. Mem.: aba, Mo. Bar Assn., Tex. Bar Assn. Avocations: remodeling, woodworking, reading, cycling. Office: Stinson Morrison Hecker LLP 1201 Walnut Kansas City MO 64106

RESS, CHARLES WILLIAM, management consultant; b. Columbus, Ohio, Aug. 6, 1933; s. George Leonard and Martha (Lake) R.; m. Virginia M. Beck, Aug. 28, 1954; children: Beverly Beck, Suzanne E., Charles W. Jr., Linda Perrins Foxworth, Jennifer Laurel Brulé. BS, Miami U., 1955; MA in Psychology, Rutgers U., 1969. Buyer The Higbee Co., Cleve., 1956-59; asst. to gen. mdse. mgr. The Halle Bros. Co., Cleve., 1959-64; research dir. The Associated Mdse. Corp., N.Y.C., 1964-73; v.p. Mgmt. Horizons, Columbus, 1973-76; founder, chmn. bd. C.W. Ress & Assoc., Inc., Columbus, 1976-90; gen. mgr. Levi Strauss & Co., Columbus, 1990-94, mgmt. cons., 1994—. Lectr. in field. Author: Future Trends in Retailing, 1983, Trans National Retailing, 1988, Retailing 2000, 1991; contbr. articles to profl. jours. Republican. Avocations: cooking, wine tasting. Office: 3860 Lyon Dr Columbus OH 43220-4907 Office Phone: 614-457-8885. E-mail: ressandress@wowway.com.

RESSA, GREGORY JOHN, lawyer; b. Rockville Centre, N.Y., Oct. 3, 1962; s. Ames D. and Roslyn Maguire Ressa; 1 child, Margo Avallone. BA, Tufts U., 1984; JD, Fordham U., 1987. Bar: N.Y. 1987. Ptnr. Simpson Thacher & Bartlett, N.Y.C., 1987—. Mem.: Assn. Bar City N.Y. Office: Simpson Thacher & Bartlett 425 Lexington Ave Fl 15 New York NY 10017-3954 Office Phone: 212-455-7430. Office Fax: 212-455-2502. Business E-Mail: gressa@stblaw.com.

RESSEL, TERESA MULLETT, federal agency administrator; BS in Engring., MS in Engring., U. Del.; MBA, Rensselaer Poly. Inst., 1990. V.p., chief compliance officer Kaiser Found. Health Plan, Inc., Kaiser Found. Hosps., Inc.; prin. dep. asst. sec. for mgmt. and budget U.S. Dept. Treasury, Washington, 2001—02, asst. sec. for mgmt. and CFO, 2003—. Recipient Presdl. Citation for Outstanding Alumni Achievement, U. Del., 1996, Disting. Svc. award, Dept. Treasury, 2003. Office: US Dept of the Treasury 1500 Pennsylvania Ave NW Washington DC 20220

RESSING, THOMAS GARRETT, lawyer; s. Clinton P. and Georgiana (Quackenbush) R.; m. Sharon Ressing, July 19, 1980; 1 child, Garrett L. BS, Muskingum Coll., New Concord, Ohio, 1963; JD, Ohio No. U., Ada, 1966. Bar: Ohio 1966, U.S. Supreme Ct. 1972, U.S. Dist. Ct. Ohio 1973. Pvt. practice, Mount Vernon, Ohio, 1966—. Active YMCA. Mem. C. of C., Rotary. Presbyterian. Office: 10 E Vine St Mount Vernon OH 43050-3226 Office Phone: 740-397-0711. Personal E-mail: tgressing@hotmail.com.

RESSLER, PETER D., executive recruiter; b. Bklyn., 1955; m. Monika Mitchell Ressler, 1992; 3 children. Cert. firefighter N.Y., 1st level hazardous materials specialist 2004. CEO RMG Search Inc., N.Y.C. Lectr. in field. Contbr. articles to profl. jours. Mem.: SBA, Norris County C. of C. Avocations: boating, fishing, Karate. Office: RMG Search Inc 1123Broadway Ste 1117 New York NY 10010

RESSOM, HABTOM W., education educator; b. Addis Ababa, Ethiopia; PhD, U. Kaiserslautern, Germany, 1999. Asst. prof. U. oMaine, Orono, 1999—2004, Georgetown U., Washington, 2004—. Office Phone: 202-687-2283.

RESTANI, JANE A., federal judge; b. San Francisco, Feb. 27, 1948; d. Roy J. and Emilia C. Restani. BA, U. Calif., Berkeley, 1969; JD, U. Calif., Davis, 1973. Bar: Calif. 1973. Trial atty. U.S. Dept. Justice, Washington, 1973-76, asst. chief comml. litigation sect., 1976-80, dir. comml. litigation sect., 1980-83; judge U.S. Ct. Internat. Trade, N.Y.C., 1983—2003, chief judge, 2003—. Mem. Order of Coif. Office: US Ct Internat Trade 1 Federal Plz New York NY 10278-0001

RESTIVO, CHARLES L., academic administrator; BS, Rutgers U.; MS, Steven Inst.; Teachs: MBA, Rutgers U. Pres. DeVry Inst. Tech., Dallas; exec. v.p. & dir. Wade Coll.; pres. Ill. Inst. Art-Chgo.; 2002—. Office: Office of Pres Illinois Institute Art 350 North Orleans St Ste 136 Chicago IL 60654-1593

**RESTIVO, JAMES JOHN, JR.,** lawyer; b. Pitts. s. James J. and Dorothy (Ardolino) R.; m. Gail Sharon Hackenburg, July 11, 1970; 4 children. BA in History, U. Pa., 1968; JD, Georgetown U., 1971. Bar: Pa. 1971, U.S. Dist. Ct. (we. and ea. dists.) Pa. 1971, U.S. Ct. Appeals (3d cir.) 1971, U.S. Supreme Ct. 1979. Ptnr. Reed Smith, Pitts., 1979—; head litig. dept. Reed, Smith, Shaw & McClay, Pitts., 1986-97. Mem. editl. staff Georgetown Law Rev., 1970-71. Bd. dirs. Rebuilding Together-Greater Pitts., Pitts. Regional Alliance. Fellow Am. Coll. Trial Lawyers; mem. Acad. Trial Lawyers Allegheny County, Allegheny County Bar Assn., Pa. Economy League (We. divsn.), Def. Rsch. Inst. Home: 209 Deer Meadow Dr Pittsburgh PA 15241-2253 Office: Reed Smith 435 6th Ave Ste 2 Pittsburgh PA 15219-1886 Office Phone: 412-288-3122. Business E-Mail: jrestivo@reedsmith.com.

**RESTON, ROCKY RUSSELL,** anesthesiologist, engineer, educator; b. Cheyenne, Wyo., Sept. 8, 1962; s. Russell Turrefiel and Beverly Elaine Reston. BSEE, USAF Acad., 1984; PhD, Air Force Inst. Tech., 1993; MD, Uniformed Svcs. U. Health Scis, 1998. Cert. board cert. Am. Bd. of Anesthesiology, 2003. Commd. 2d lt. USAF, 1984, advanced through grades to lt. col., 2005; instrumentation engr. 4484th Test Squadron, Tyndall AFB, Fla., 1984-87; electronics device processing engr. Wright Labs., Wright Patterson AFB, Ohio, 1992-94; resident in internal medicine Wilford Hall Med. Ctr., Lackland AFB, Tex., 1998-99, resident in anesthesiology, 1999—2002; assoc. prof. tech. and mgmt. U. Md., College Park, 1996—; staff anesthesiologist Wright Patterson Med. Ctr., Ohio, 2002—03; chmn. anesthesia dept. Wright-Patterson Med. Ctr., Ohio, 2003—. Presenter in field. Contbr. articles to profl. jours.; patentee in field. Mem. IEEE, Am. Soc. Anesthesiologists, USAF Acad. Assn. Grads, Eta Kappa Nu (treas. 1988-89), Tau Beta Pi. Address: 2726 Greenridge Cir Beavercreek OH 45431 Office: 88 SGOS/SGC5 4881 Sugar Maple Dr Wright Patterson Afb OH 45433 E-mail: Rocky_R@msn.com.

**RESTREPO, RUBEN DARIO,** physician, educator; b. Medellin, Antioquia, Colombia, June 6, 1963; s. Jose Ignacio Restrepo and Maria Alma Panesso; m. Lorena Maria Fernandez, Dec. 1, 2002; children: Andrea, Natalia, Simon Usuga. MD, Universidad Pontificia Bolivariana, Medellin, Colombia, 1987; BS, Ga. State U., Atla., 1994. Primary care physician Comedal, Medellin, 1988—90; pediatric outreach program coord. St. Joseph's Hosp., Atla. 1991—92; pediatric ICU therapist Children's Healthcare of Atla., 1994—2005; clin. instr. Ga. State U., Atla., 1997—98, adj. faculty, 1998—99, asst. prof., 1999—2005; assoc. prof. U. Tex. Health Sci. Ctr., San Antonio, 2005—. Contbr. chapters to books, articles to profl. jours. Usher St. Matthew Cath. Ch., San Antonio, 2005—06; bd. mem. and vol. Habitat for Humanity, San Antonio; bd. mem. Office of Family Concerns, Atlanta, 1995—2002. Recipient Respiratory Therapy award, Am. Lung Assn., 1992, Academic Excellence award, Ga. State U., 1994, Berneice Castella Allied Health Aging Rsch. award, U. Tex. Health Sci. Ctr. San Antonio, 2006—; scholar James Ancil Lewis award, Ga. Soc. for Respiratory Care, 1992. Mem.: Am. Assn. for Respiratory Care, Am. Thoracic Soc., Am. Coll. Chest Physicians, Lambda Beta Soc. Catholic. Achievements include development of Educational CD. Avocations: travel, sports, computer technology. Office: Univ TexHealth Scis Ctr 7703 Floyd Curl Dr San Antonio TX 78229 Office Phone: 210-567-8858. Business E-Mail: restrepor@uthscsa.edu.

**RESWICK, JAMES BIGELOW,** former government official, biomedical engineer; b. Ellwood City, Pa., Apr. 16, 1922; s. Maurice and Katherine (Parker) R.; children: James Bigelow, David Parker (dec.), Pamela Reswick; m. Irmtraud Orthlies Hoelzerkopf, Dec., 27, 1973. SBME, MIT, 1943, SM, 1948, ScD, 1952; DEng (hon.), Rose Poly. Inst., 1968. Asst. prof., then assoc. prof., head machine design and graphics div. MIT, 1948-59; Leonard Case prof. engring., dir. Engring. Design Ctr., Case Western Res. U., 1959-70; prof. biomed. engring. and orthopaedics U. So. Calif., also dir. of rsch. dept. orthopaedics, 1970-80; assoc. dir. tech. Nat. Inst. Handicapped Rsch., U.S. Dept. Edn.; dir. VA Rehab. R & D Evaluation Unit VA Med. Ctr., Washington, 1984-88; rsch. scis. Nat. Inst. on Disability and Rehab. Rsch. U.S. Dept. Edn., Washington, 1989—94; ret., 1994; acting dir. Nat. Inst. Disability and Rehab. Rsch., Washington, 1989-91. Engring. cons. on automatic control, product devel., automation and bio-med. engring. Mem. com. prosthetics R & D Nat. Acad. Scis., 1962-; chmn. design and devel. com.; mem. bd. rev. Army R & D Office, 1965-; mem. applied physiology and biomed. engring. study sect. NIH, 1972-. Author: (with C.K. Taft) Introduction to Dynamic Systems, 1967; also articles.; Editor: (with F.T. Hambrecht) Functional Electrical Stimulation, 1977; series on engring. design, 1963-; inventor, patentee in field. Chmn. Mayor's Commn. for Urban Transp., Cleve., 1969. Served to lt. (j.g.) USNR, 1943-46, PTO. Decorated officer Yugoslav Flag with golden wreath medal (Yugoslavia), 1990; recipient Product Engring. Master Designer award, 1969, Isabelle and Leonard H. Goldenson award United Cerebral Palsy Assn., 1973; NSR sr. postdoctoral fellow Imperial Coll., London, 1957. Fellow IEEE, Am. Inst. Med. and Biological Engring. (founder); mem. ASME (honor award for best paper 1956, sr. mem.), Am. Soc. Engring. Edn., Instrument Soc. Am., Biomed. Engring. Soc. (sr. mem., pres. 1973, dir.), Am. Acad. Orthopedic Surgeons (assoc.), Inst. Medicine of NAS, NAE, Internat. Soc. Orthotics and Prosthetics, Orthopaedics Rsch. Soc., Rehab. Engring. Soc. N.Am. (founding pres.), Sigma XI. Home: 1834 Calf Mountain Rd PO Box 549 Crozet VA 22932 Personal E-mail: jimreswick@ntelos.net.

**RETALLACK, GREGORY JOHN,** geologist, educator; b. Hobart, Australia, Nov. 8, 1951; arrived in U.S., 1977; s. Kenneth John Retallack and Moira Wynn (Dean) Gollan; m. Diane Alice Retallack, May 31, 1981; children: Nicholas John, Jeremy Douglas. BA, Macquarie U., Sydney, 1973; BSc with honors, U. New Eng., 1974, PhD, 1978. Vis. asst. prof. No. Ill. U., DeKalb, 1977—78; vis. scholar Ind. U., Bloomington, 1978—81; asst. prof. U. Oreg., Eugene, 1981—86, assoc. prof., 1986—92, prof., 1992—. Author: Late Eocene and Oligocene Paleosols from Badlands National Park, South Dakota, 1983, Soils of the Past, 1990, 2d edit. 2001, Miocene Paleosols and Ape Habitats in Pakistan and Kenya, 1991, Colour Guide to Paleosols, 1997; contbr. articles to profl. jours. Grantee, NSF, 1979—, Wenner-Gren Found., 1983. Fellow: AAAS, Geol. Soc. Am.; mem.: Soc. Econ. Paleontologists and Mineralogists, Oreg. Acad. Sci. (pres. 1986), Paleontology Soc. (pres. Pacific sect. 1986), Bot. Soc. Am., Geol. Soc. Australia, Sigma Xi (pres. U. Oreg. chpt. 1983—84). Home: 2715 Elinor St Eugene OR 97403-2513 Office Phone: 541-346-4558. Business E-Mail: gregr@uoregon.edu.

**RETALLICK, MICHAEL S.,** agricultural studies educator, director; b. Lancaster, Wis., Jan. 27, 1971; s. Steven F. and Jaquelyn J. Retallick; m. Dawn M. Johnson, July 27, 1991; children: Danielle Marie, Alex Michael. PhD in Agrl. Edn., Iowa State U., 2005. Cert. C.C. tchr. Agrl. edn. instr. Maquoketa (Iowa) Cmty. Schools, 1993—2001; coord. academic advising Iowa State U., Ames, 2001—03, coord. undergraduate programs, 2003—06, sci. with practice co-coordinator, 2005—06, asst. prof. agrl. edn., 2006—, dir. undergrad. edn., 2006—, dir. sci. with practice, 2006—. T-ball and soccer coach Story City (Iowa) Recreation Dept., 2004—05; adv. com. mem. Indian Hills C.C., Centerville, Iowa, 2005—06, Des Moines Area C.C., Ankeny, Iowa, 2003—06. Named Sam Walton Bus. Leader of the Yr., Maquoketa Area C. of C., 1999; recipient Rsch. Excellence award, Iowa State U., 2005, Exceptional Support Recognition award, 2005, Friends of Agr. Outstanding Pub. Svc. award, Maquoketa Area C. of C. and Maquoketa Rotary, 2000. Mem.: N.Am. Colls. and Tchrs. Agr., Iowa Assn. Agrl. Educators (v.p. 1999—2000, Outstanding Young Mem.), Am. Assn. Agrl. Educators, Am. Edn. Rsch. Assn., Assn. Career and Tech. Edn. Rsch., Acad. of Career and Tech. Tchr. Edn., US Assn. Small Bus. and Entrepreneurship, Nat. FFA Alumni (life Hall of Fame 2001), Iowa FFA Alumni (life), Gamma Sigma Delta. Office: Iowa State U 206 Curtiss Hall Ames IA 50011 Office Phone: 515-294-4810. Office Fax: 515-294-0530. Personal E-mail: rplace@iowatelecom.net. Business E-Mail: msr@iastate.edu.

**RETHORE, BERNARD GABRIEL,** retired manufacturing and mining company executive; b. May 22, 1941; s. Francis Joseph and Katharine Eunice (MacDwyer) Rethore; m. Marilyn Irene Watt, Dec. 1, 1962 (div. Apr. 2002); children: Bernard Michael, Tara Jean, Kevin Watt, Alexandra Marie, Rebecca Ann, Christopher Philip, Abigail Lyn. BA, Yale U., 1962; MBA, U. Pa., 1967.

Assoc. McKinsey & Co., Inc., Washington, 1967—73, sr. assoc., 1973; v.p. gen. mgr. Greer div. Microdot, Inc., Darien, Conn., 1973—77, v.p. ops. connector group, 1977—78, pres. bus. devel. group, 1978—82, pres. fastening sys. and sealing devices groups, 1982—84; pres. Microdot Industries, Darien, Conn., 1984—87, pres., CEO, 1988; pres. Microdot Europe Ltd., Darien, Conn., 1984—88; sr. v.p. Phelps Dodge Corp., Phoenix, 1989—95; group exec. Phelps Dodge Industries, Phoenix, 1989—90, pres., 1990—95; pres., CEO, bd. dirs. BW/IP Internat., Inc., Long Beach, Calif., 1995—97, chmn., 1997; CEO, chmn. bd. dirs. Flowserve Corp., Dallas, 1997—2000, chmn. emeritus, 2000—; chmn. McDyre & Spendley, Ltd., 2000—. Bd. dirs. Belden, Inc., Dover Corp., Walter Industries, Inc., Mueller Water Products, Inc.; cons. U.S. Govt., UN; mem. Thunderbird Global Bus. Coun., Garvin Sch. Internat. Mgmt., 1990—, chmn., 1991—94; dean's adv. bd. Wharton Sch. Bus., U. Pa., 1972—80. Elected mem. bd. fin. Town of Westport, Conn. 1986-90; trustee Ballet Ariz., 1989-95, vice chmn., 1991-95, Franciscan Renewal Ctr., 2005-; bd. dirs. Boys Hope of Phoenix, 1989-95; trustee Phoenix Country Day Sch., 1992-2003, Thunderbird, Garvin Sch. Internat. Mgmt., 1994—, vice chmn., 2004—. Served to capt., inf. AUS, 1962-65. Decorated Bronze Star. Mem. Nat. Assn. Mfrs. (bd. dirs. 1994-95, 96-99), Yale Club (N.Y.C.), Union League (Chgo.), Nat. Assn. Corp. Dirs. (blue ribbon com. on bd. role in strategic plan 2000), Gainey Ranch Club (Scottsdale, Ariz.). Home: 7010 East Avenida El Alba Paradise Valley AZ 85253 Office: McDyre & Spendley Ltd Ste 300 7702 E Doubletree Ranch Rd Scottsdale AZ 85258

**RETIF, THOMAS NEWTON,** music educator; b. Baton Rouge, La., May 16, 1942; s. Alfred J. Sr. and Tommie Alene (Hutchinson) R. Mus.B., La. State U., 1964; Mus. M., U. Tex., 1968; Mus.D., Southwestern Bapt. Theol. Sem., 1980. With Tarrant County Jr. Coll., Fort Worth, 1968-75, U. Tex., Arlington, 1975-76, Southwestern Bapt. Theol. Sem., Fort Worth, 1976-80, Hardin Simmons U., Abilene, Tex., 1980-81; prof. Brewton-Parker Coll., Mount Vernon, Ga., 1981—; profl. singer Santa Fe Opera Co., N. Mex., 1964-65; dir. Ohoopee Council Arts, Vidalia, Ga., 1982—; massed ringing conductor and handbell workshop clinician. Chmn. bd. dirs. Schola Cantorium of Tex., Fort Worth, 1976-77, Franklinia Theater, condr. Baron Ringers; music dir., faculty advisor Alumni Baron Ringers. Mem. Nat. Assn. Tchrs. Singing treas. Ga. chpt., chmn. rules com., SE regular repertiore com.), Am. Musicological Soc., Am. Guild English Handbell Ringers (chmn.-elect area IV), GA. Music Tchrs. Assn. (music tchr.), Coll. Music Soc. Republican. Episcopalian.

**RETTIE, DWIGHT FAY,** retired political science educator, writer; b. New Haven, Conn., Mar. 27, 1930; s. James Cardno and Lois (Morris) Rettie; m. Karen Ross, Aug. 4, 1984; children: Stuart, Catherine, Thomas, Jeffery. BA, Yale U., 1952; MA, U. Calif., Berkeley, 1955; cert. leadership tng., George Washington U., 1959; cert. def. mgmt. sys. course, U.S. Naval Postgrad. Sch., 1964. Various positions Dept. of Interior, Washington, 1957-65; program dir. Dept. Housing and Urban Devel., Washington, 1965-71; exec. dir. Nat. Recreation and Park Assn., Arlington, Va., 1971-75; exec. Nat. Park Svc., Washington, 1975-81, chief office policy devel., 1981-86; instr. Carteret C.C., Morehead City, N.C., 1995-98; vis. prof. East Carolina U., Greenville, NC, 1998—2001. Dir. Arlington Telecomm. Inc., Va., 1973-79; cons. Nat. Parks and Conservation Assn., 1995-96. Author: Our National Park System: Caring for America's Greatest Natural and Historic Treasures, 1995. Mem. nat. coun. Boy Scouts Am., 1958-62; chmn. Arlington County Pub. Utilities Commn., 1967-73; mem. U.S. Bd. Geographic Names, Washington, 1981-86; pres. bd. No. Va. Regional Park Authority, Fairfax, Va., 1973-81. Staff sgt. U.S. Army, 1952-54. Democrat. Mem. Unitarian Ch. Avocations: sailing, teaching, writing. Home: 415 Hardy Rd Newport NC 28570 Business E-Mail: tarwathie@clis.com.

**RETTIG, HELEN B.,** construction executive; b. BishKek, Kyrgyzstan, Nov. 15, 1967; arrived in U.S., 1996; d. Pavil Borovikov and Natalie George; m. Terry Rettig, Mar. 12, 1996; 1 child, Bill B. BS in Constrn. Engring. with distinction, U. Kyrgyzstan, BishKek, 1990; MBA in Constrn. Mgmt. with distinction, Keller Grad. Sch. of Bus. Mgmt., Atlanta, 2004. Cert. constrn. engr., Kyrgyzstan Ministry of Constrn. Constrn. engr. Ministry of Constrn., BishKek, 1990—96; CEO Am. Dream Constrn., Inc., Alpharetta, Ga., 1996—. Youth leader Boy Scouts of Am., Alpharetta, 2003—. Mem.: Nat. Assn. of Homebuilders, Greater Atlanta Homebuilders Assn., Conventlant Homebuilders Assn. (Ga. Systems Homebuilder of the Yr. 2004). Avocations: swimming, travel, camping, reading. Home: 5035 Kimball Bridge Rd Alpharetta GA 30005-5649 Office: Am Dream Constrn Inc 5035 Kimball Bridge Rd Alpharetta GA 30005-5649 Office Phone: 770-664-6900. Personal E-mail: helenrettig@comcast.net.

**RETTIG, PAM,** literature educator; b. Williston, ND, Mar. 11, 1964; d. Vincent Gregory and Agnes Caroline Rettig. BS, Minot State U., 1986; MS in edml. psychology, U. of Mary, 1994. Tchr. Burke Ctrl. Sch., Lignite, ND, 1986—89; tchr., prin. Manning Sch., Bismarck, ND, 1989—92; reading specialist Bismarck Pub. Sch., Bismarck, ND, 1992—; adj. prof. U. of Mary, Bismarck, 1998—. Internat. tchr. trainer Internat. Reading Assn., Newark, 2004—; trainer of assessors Nat. Bd. of Tchg. Certification, Clemson, SC, 2004; ednl. cons. U. of Mary, Bismarck, 2000—. Co-author: ND Lang. Arts Standards, 1996—2000. Recipient Milken award, Milken Family Found., 2000, Constance McCullough award, Internat. Reading Assn., 2004; Fulbright scholar, Fulbright Meml. Fund Found., 2001. Mem.: South Ctrl. Reading Assn., ND Reading Assn. Office: Bismarck Public School 1227 N 35th St Bismarck ND 58504 Office Phone: 701-224-1784 x 119. Office Fax: 701-250-1172. Business E-Mail: pam_rettig@educ8.org.

**RETZ, WILLIAM ANDREW,** naval consultant, retired naval officer; b. Blauvelt NY June 3, 1940; s. Andrew Mcmillan and Katherine (Deyoe) R.; m. Julia Irene Patterson, Sept. 23, 1989; children: Andrew, Gregory, Mark, Alyse Reavis, Mark Rogers. Student, Tex. A&M U., 1957; BS in Mech. Engring., U. N.Mex., 1963; MS, George Washington U., 1971; grad., Naval War Coll., 1972. Commd. ensign USN, 1963, advanced through grades to rear adm., 1991, patrol officer river div. 511 Vietnam, 1968-69, flag sec. to comdr. Amphibious Group Two Norfolk, Va., 1972-74, exec. officer USS Ainsworth, 1974-76, commanding officer USS Stump, 1980-82, commodore Destroyer Squadron 22, 1985-87, dep. for ops. U.S. Cen. Command Tampa, Fla., 1987-90; comdr. Naval Base Pearl Harbor, 1992-94, Naval Surface Group Mid. Pacific, 1992-94; commanded and closed Naval Base Phila., 1994-95; ret. USN, 1995; v.p. govt. svcs Aramark Corr., Phila., 1996-99; ind. cons., 1999; CEO Nofire Techs., Inc., 2000—03; exec. dir. Am. Competitiveness Inst., Phila., 2003—05; ind. cons. Retz & Assoc., 2005—; with Def. Solutions, Washington, 2005—. Active Episcopal Ch.; chmn. coun. Texona Tech. Enterprise, Denison Devel. Found.; adv. bd. U. Tex., Dallas; bd. dirs. St. Luke's Sch.; chmn. coun. Texoma Tech. Enterprise, Denision Devel. Found.; mem. indsl. adv. bd. U. Tex., Dallas. Decorated Disting. Svc. medal, Legion of Merit, Def. Disting. Svc. medal, Meritorious Svc. medal, Bronze Star, Purple Heart. Mem. Surface Navy Assn., Nat. Def. Indsl. Assn. Avocations: gardening, sailing. Office: Def Solutions 1725 Ist NW Ste 300 Washington DC 20006 Personal E-mail: retzw@comcast.net.

**RETZER, KENNETH ALBERT,** mathematics professor, entrepreneur; b. Jacksonville, Ill., Nov. 6, 1933; s. Samuel Stark and Cora Edith (Martin) R.; m. Dorcas Anne Schroeder, Apr. 18, 1954 (dec. Aug. 4, 1990); children: Martin Wayne, Kent Arnold, Sheryl Kaye; m. Wei Dong, Feb. 14, 1991; children: Roger Dong Retzer, Kenneth Samuel Retzer. AB, Ill. Coll., 1954; MEd, U. Ill., 1957, PhD, 1969. Cert. tchr., Ill., 1954-57; cert. sch. adminstrn. Ill., 1957—. Tchr. Saunemin (Ill.) Twp. High Sch., 1954-58, asst. supt., 1955-58; prof. math. Ill. State U., Normal, 1959-89, Abilene (Tex.) Christian U., 1989—97; tv. bd. dirs. DR Global Enterprises, DBA Cafe China, DBA DR Gifts and Accessories, 1995—2000; v.p.; bd. dir. WD Mgmt. LLC, DBA Gary's Pizza, 2002—06. Asst. chmn. math. dept. Ill. State U., Normal, 1969-71; vis. prof. U. Ga., Athens, 1973, Tex. A&M U., College Station, 1984, U. Hawaii-Maui, Kahului, 1990, 91; cons. Arabian Am. Oil Co., Dhahran, Saudi Arabia, 1984, Ill. State Bd. Edn., Springfield, 1983-88; rsch. fellow U. Western Sydney, Australia, 1993; lectr. Zhejiang U., Hangzhou,

China, Northwest Normal U., Lanzhou, China, Gansu Edn. U., Lanzhou, Lanzhou Normal U., Zhangye Normal U., China, summer 1994. Contbr. articles to profl. jours. in the U.S., Can., China. Mem. NEA, AAUP, Nat. Coun. Tchrs. Math., Sch. Sci. and Math. Assn., Math. Assn. Am., Rsch. Coun. on Diagnostic and Prescriptive Math., Ill. Coun. Tchrs. Math. (Max Beberman award 1988), Tex. Coun. Tchrs. Math., Big County Coun. Tchrs. Math., Ill. Assn. Higher Edn., Pi Mu Epsilon, Phi Delta Kappa. Mem. Church of Christ. Avocations: travel, photography, reading, Christian studies, learning. Home: 31 Rue Maison St Abilene TX 79605-4710

**RETZER, MARY ELIZABETH HELM,** retired librarian; b. Balt. d. Francis Leslie C. and Edna (Smith) Helm; m. William Raymond Retzer, June 28, 1945; children: Lesley Elizabeth, April Christine. BA, Western Md. Coll., Westminster, 1940; MA, Columbia U., N.Y.C., 1946; postgrad., George Washington U., 1941, Ind. U., 1952, U. Ill., 1958-59, Ill. State U., Normal, 1964-66, Bradley U., Peoria, Ill., 1968; PhD, Western Colo. U., 1972. Faculty Rockville Bd. Edn., Md., 1940-47, elem. supr. Md., 1945-47; staff Peoria Pub. Libr., 1957-63, reference libr., 1961-63; cons., organizer libr. Bergan High Sch., 1964-67; condr. libr. sci. course in reference Bradley U., 1966-83. Libr. Hines Elem. Sch., 1963-66, Roosevelt Jr. H.S., 1966-69; head media ctr. Manual H.S., Peoria, Ill., 1969-83. Instr. water safety courses ARC, 1938-93; pres. Entre Nous, 1949-51; pres. women's bd. Salvation Army, 1952-54; pres. Peoria Nursery Sch. Assn., 1953-54; mem. legis. action com. Ill. Congress PTA, 1955-56; mem. Crippled Children's Adv. Com., Peoria, 1957-60; active various community drives; women's adv. bd. Peoria Jr. Star, 1970-73; vol. Sarasota Internat. Airport, 1990-98. Mem. AAUW (life), NEA, ALA (life), Ill. Edn. Assn. (life), Peoria Edn. Assn. (life), Ill. Libr. Assn. (life), Valley Librs. Assn. (pres. 1971-72), Ill. Assn. Media in Edn. (cert. com. 1973-80), Ill. Audiovisual Assn., Internat. Platform Assn., Order Ea. Star (life), Ill. State U. Adminstrs. Club, Willowknolls Country Club, Sarasota Yacht Club, Ladies Oriental Shrine. Republican. Presbyterian. Home: 3240 Lake Pointe Blvd Unit 101 Sarasota FL 34231

**RETZLOFF, DAVID GEORGE,** engineering educator; s. John Joseph Retzloff and Ruth Retzloff Georgia; m. Betty Jean Burks, May 5, 2001; 1 child, Lauren Brooke. PhD, U. Pitts., 1967. Rsch. engr. Exxon, Baytown, Tex., 1973—75; assoc. prof. U. Mo., Columbia, 1975—. Cons. AT&T, Lee's Summit, Mo., 1984—90. Mem.: Am. Math. Soc. Home: 801 Hulen Drive Columbia MO 65203 Office: University of Missouri-Columbia W2026 Lafferre Hall Columbia MO 65211 Office Phone: 573-882-4036. Home Fax: 573-884-4940; Office Fax: 573-884-4940. Business E-Mail: retzloffd@missouri.edu.

**REUBEN, ALVIN BERNARD,** communications and entertainment executive; b. Harrisburg, Pa., Aug. 11, 1940; s. Maurice and Lillian (Katzef) R.; m. Barbara Ann Harrison, Mar. 18, 1968; 1 dau., Mindee Jill. BS in Commerce, Rider U., 1962. Buyer Pomeroy's div. Allied Stores Corp., Harrisburg, 1962-67; sales rep. Random House, Inc., N.Y.C., 1967-74; dir. mktg. Ballantine Books, Inc. (div. Random House), N.Y.C., 1974-76; v.p. sales Simon & Schuster, N.Y.C., 1976-79, sr. v.p. sales Pocket Books div., 1979-81, sr. v.p. mktg., 1981-82, press. ref. and promotional pub. group, 1982-83, exec. v.p. electronic pub. div., 1983-85; exec. v.p. Prentice Hall div. Simon & Schuster, 1985-86; sr. v.p. mktg., sales and distbn. Vestron, Inc., 1986-89; sr. v.p. St. Martin's Press, N.Y.C., 1989-91; sr. v.p. sales, mktg. Sony Music Video, N.Y.C., 1991-92; sr. v.p. spl. markets Sony Music, N.Y.C., 1992-95; sr.v.p. video and interactive sales and distbn. BMG Entertainment, 1995-97; pres. BMG Video, 1997-99. Instr. edn. in pub. program, grad. program SUNY. With USAFR, 1963-69. Mem. Tau Kappa Epsilon. Home and Office: 5 Tyler Ln Bluffton SC 29909-5028 Personal E-mail: alreubenschh@aol.com.

**REUBEN, DON HAROLD,** lawyer; b. Chgo., Sept. 13, 1928; s. Michael B. and Sally (Colucci) R.; m. Evelyn Long, Aug. 27, 1948 (div.); children: Hope Reuben Boland, Michael Barrett, Timothy Don, Jeffrey Long, Howard Ellis; m. Jeannette Hurley Haywood, Dec. 13, 1971; stepchildren: Harris Hurley Haywood, Edward Gregory Haywood. BS, Northwestern U., 1949, JD, 1952. Bar: Ill. 1952, Calif. 1996, U.S. Supreme Ct. 1957. With firm Kirkland & Ellis, Chgo., 1952-78, sr. ptnr., Reuben & Proctor, Chgo., 1978-86, Isham, Lincoln & Beale, Chgo., 1986-88; sr. counsel Winston & Strawn, Chgo., 1988-94; of counsel Altheimer & Gray, Chgo., 1994—2003, Kane & Carbonara Ltd., Chgo., 2003—. Spl. asst. atty. gen. State of Ill., 1963—64, 1969, 84; gen. counsel Tribune Co., 1965—88, Chgo. Bears Football Club, 1965—88, Cath. Archdiocese of Chgo., 1975—88; counsel spl. session Ill. Ho. of Reps., 1964, for Ill. treas. for congl., state legis. and jud. reapportionment, 1963; spl. fed. ct. master, 1968—70; mem. citizens adv. bd. to sheriff County of Cook, 1962—66, jury instrn. com., 1963—73; past mem. pub. rules com. Ill. Supreme Ct., 1963—73; past mem. pub. rels. com. Nat. Conf. State Trial Judges; com. study caseflow mgmt. in law divsn. Cook County Cir. Ct., 1979—88; adv. implementation com. U.S. Dist. Ct. No. Dist. Ill., 1981—82; mem. Chgo. Better Sch. Com., 1968—69, Chgo. Crime Commn., 1970—80; supervisory panel Fed. Defender Program, 1971—78; sec. gen. counsel, chair audit com. Palm Springs Air Mus., 1998—. Bd. dirs. Lincoln Pk. Zool. Soc., 1972—84; trustee Northwestern U., 1977—; mem. vis. com. U. Chgo. Law Sch., 1976—79; bd. dirs. Blood Bank of the Desert, 1999—2004, vice-chmn., 2003—04; chmn. gen. plan adv. com. City of Rancho Mirage, 1994—; dir., sec. Friends of the Animal Campos, 2004—. Recipient Northwestern U. Law Sch. Alumni Merit award, 2002. Fellow: Am. Bar Found., Internat. Acad. Trial Lawyers; mem.: ABA (standing com. on fed. judiciary 1973—79, standing com. on jud. selection, tenure and compensation 1982—85), Desert Bar Assn., Calif. Bar Assn., Am. Arbitration Assn. (nat. panel arbitrators 1998—), Am. Coll. Trial Lawyers (Rule 23 com. 1975—82, judiciary com. 1987—91), Am. Law Inst., Chgo. Bar Assn. (chmn. subcom. propriety and regulation of contingent fees cvil com. 1966—69, standing com. on media liaison 1980—82, com. on profl. into. 1980—82), Ill. Bar Assn., Mission Hills Country Club, Casino Club, Mid-Am. Club, Com. of 25 Palm Springs, Chgo. Club, Tamarisk Country Club (hon.), Order of Coif, Beta Gamma Sigma, Beta Alpha Psi, Phi Eta Sigma. Office: 1100 Glendon Ave 10th fl Los Angeles CA 90024 also: 74-900 Hwy 111 Ste 2I Indian Wells CA 92210 Office Phone: 760-324-0619, 312-726-2322. Personal E-mail: dreuben456@aol.com.

**REUBEN, GLORIA,** actress, singer; b. Toronto, Ont., June 9, 1964; m. Wayne Isaak, 1999. T.V. and movie actress; backup singer and dancer Tina Turner's World Tour, 2000. Actress (films) Immediate Family, 1989, Wild Orchid II: Two Shades of Blue, 1992, The Waiter, 1993, Time Cop, 1994, Nick of Time, 1995, David and Lola, 1999, Macbeth in Manhattan, 1999, Bad Faith, 2000, Pilgrim, 2000, Happy Here and Now, 2002, Kettle of Fish, 2005, The Sentinel, 2006, (TV films) The Day They Came to Arrest the Book, 1987, Shadowhunter, 1993, Percy & Thunder, 1993, Confessions: Two Faces of Evil, 1994, Dead Air, 1994, Johnny's Girl, 1995, Indiscreet, 1998, Sara, 1999, Deep in My Heart, 1999, Sole Survivor, 2000, The Agency, 2001, Feast of All Saints, 2001, Little John, 2002, Salem Witch Trials, 2002, host (TV series) Polka Dot Door, 1985, actress ER, 1995, The Agency, 2001—02, actress, composer, prodr. 1-800-Missing, 2003—04, appearances in Alfred Hitchcock Presents, 1987, 21 Jump Street, 1988, The Flash, 1990—91, Silk Stalkings, 1993, Homicide: Life on the Street, 1995, The District, 2002, Law & Order: Special Victims Unit, 2002, Numb3rs, 2005, actress (plays) Stuff Happens, 2005, A Nervous Smile, 2006; singer: (albums) Just for You, 2004; back-up singer Twenty Four Seven, Tina Turner's World Tour, 2000. Recipient SAG Awards, 1998, 99, Q Award, 1997, 98; named one of 50 Most Beautiful People in World, People mag., 1996. Mailing: c/o Elise Konialian/ Untitled Mgmt Floor 3 23 East 22nd St New York NY 10010 Office Phone: 212-777-1214.*

**REUBER, GRANT LOUIS,** banking insurance company executive; b. Mildmay, Ont., Can., Nov. 23, 1927; s. Jacob Daniel and Gertrude Catherine (Wahl) R.; m. Margaret Louise Julia Summerhayes, Oct. 21, 1951 (dec. Feb. 1998); children: Rebecca, Barbara, Mary. BA, U. Western Ont., 1950; AM, Harvard U., 1954, PhD, 1957; LLD (hon.), Wilfred Laurier U., 1983, Simon Fraser U., 1985, U. Western Ont., 1985, McMaster U., 1994; postgrad., Cambridge U., 1954-55. Mem. research dept. Bank Can., Ottawa, 1950-52;

mem. Can. Dept. Finance, Ottawa, 1955-57; asst. prof. econ. U. Western Ont., London, 1957-59; assoc. prof., 1959-62; prof., head dept., 1963-69, 1963-69; mem. bd. govs. U. Western Ont., London, 1974-78, acad. v.p.; provost, 1975-78, chancellor, 1988-92; sr. v.p., chief economist Bank of Montreal, Que., Canada, 1978-79; exec. v.p., 1980-81, dep. chmn., dep. chief exec. officer, 1981-83, dir., mem. exec. com., 1981-89, pres., chief operating officer, 1983-87, dep. chmn., 1987-89; dep. minister fin. Can., 1979-80; chmn. Can. Deposit Ins. Corp., 1993-99; sr. adv., dir. Sussex Circle, 1999—. Staff mem. Royal Commn. Banking and Fin., Toronto, 1962—63; chmn. Ont. Econ. Coun., 1973—78; cons. Can. Internat. Devel. Agy., 1968—69; hon. rsch. assoc. in econs. Harvard U., 1968—69; mem. devel. ctr. OECD, 1969—73; lectr. U. Chgo. Sch. Bus., 1992—93. Author: Private Foreign Investment in Development, 1973, Canada's Political Economy, 1980; contbr. articles. Bd. dirs. Can. Merit Scholarship Found., 1994—2000; bd. govs. Royal Ont. Mus., 2000—02; chmn. Can. Ditchley Found., 1981—. Decorated officer Order of Can. Fellow: Royal Soc. Can. Office Phone: 416-867-3614.

**REUBISH, GARY RICHARD,** English language educator; b. Breckenridge, Minn., Jan. 6, 1946; s. Irving Earl and Genevieve Loretta (Miller) R. AA, N.D. State Coll. Sci., Wahpeton, 1969; BS, Valley City State Coll., 1971. Cert. tchr., N.D. Tchr. English Wolford Pub. Sch., ND, 1971-72, Lake Benton Pub. Sch., Minn., 1972-76, Wahpeton Pub. Sch., ND, 1976—2001. With USAF, 1965-71. Mem. N.D. Edn. Assn. Home: PO Box 181 Wahpeton ND 58074-0181

**REUM, JAMES MICHAEL,** lawyer; b. Oak Park, Ill., Nov. 1, 1946; s. Walter John and Lucy (Bellegay) R. BA cum laude, Harvard U., 1968, JD cum laude, 1972. Bar: N.Y. 1973, D.C. 1974, U.S. Dist. Ct. (so. dist.) N.Y. 1974, Ill. 1979, U.S. Dist. Ct. (no. dist.) Ill. 1982. Assoc. Davis Polk & Wardwell, N.Y.C., 1973-78; assoc. Minority Counsel Com. on Judiciary U.S. Ho. of Reps., Washington, 1977; ptnr. Hopkins & Sutter, Chgo., 1979-93, Winston & Strawn, Chgo., 1994—. Midwest advance rep. Nat. Reagan Bush Com., 1980; nominee commr. Securities and Exchange Comm., Pres. Bush, 1992; mem. fin. com. G.W. Bush, 2000; mem. Lawyers for Bush, 2004. Served to SP4 USAR, 1969—75. Recipient Harvard U. Honorary Nat. Scholarship, 1964-72. Mem.: Monte Carlo Country Club (Monaco), Univ. Club (NYC), Racquet Club Chgo. Republican. Home: 12 E Scott St Chicago IL 60610-2320 Office: Winston & Strawn 35 W Wacker Dr Ste 4200 Chicago IL 60601-1695 Office Phone: 312-558-5644. E-mail: jreum@winston.com.

**REUM, W. ROBERT,** manufacturing executive; b. Oak Park, Ill., July 22, 1942; m. Sharon Milliken. BA, Yale U., 1964; JD, U. Mich., 1967; MBA, Harvard U., 1969. Dir. investment analysis City Investing Co., N.Y.C., 1969-72; v.p. corp fin. Mich. Nat. Corp., Bloomfield Hills, Mich., 1972-78; v.p., treas. White Motor Corp., Cleve., 1978-79; v.p. fin., CFO, Lamson & Sessions, Cleve., 1980-82, The Interlake Corp., Oak Brook, Ill., 1982-88, exec. v.p., 1988-90, chmn., pres., CEO, 1991-99, Amsted Industries Inc., Chgo., 2001—, also bd. dirs. Lindberg Corp. Contbr. articles to Harvard Bus. Rev. Bd. dirs. Morton Arboretum, Lisle, Ill.; trustee Elgin (Ill.) Acad. Mem. Chgo. Golf Club, Chgo. Club, Rolling Rock Club (Ligonier, Pa.). Office: AMSTED Industries Inc 205 N Michigan Ave 44th Fl Chicago IL 60601*

**REUPKE, WILLIAM ALBERT,** engineer; b. Chgo., Jan. 22, 1940; BA, Northwestern U., 1961; AM, Ind. U., 1967; MS, Ga. Inst. Tech., 1973, PhD, 1977. Gen. physicist NASA, Cleve., 1963-64; staff physicist Aerospace Rsch. Applications Ctr., Bloomington, Ind., 1965-67; rsch. engr. Lockheed Missiles and Space Co., Sunnyvale, Calif., 1967-68; engring. physicist Stanford (Calif.) Linear Accelerator Ctr., 1968-71; staff mem. Los Alamos (N.Mex.) Nat. Lab., 1977-82; sr. engr. Computer Scis. Corp., Lanham-Seabrook, Md., 1983-95, Sci. Applications Internat. Corp., Seabrook, Md., 1996—2006, QSS Group, Inc., Lanham, 2006—. Recipient Group Achievement award NASA, 1987, 91, 93, 2001, Dr. Robert H. Goddard Hist. Essay award Nat. Space Club, 1991. Fellow Brit. Interplanetary Soc.; mem. AIAA (sr.), Am. Phys. Soc. Achievements include development of new method of adjusting neutron cross sections to improve fit of measured and calculated reaction rates in nuclear fusion integral experiments and application of that method to show that a neutron cross section important for fusion energy production is significantly smaller than was previously believed. Office: QSS Group Inc 4500 Forbes Blvd Ste 200 Lanham MD 20706 Business E-Mail: reupke@mailaps.org.

**REUTER, FRANK THEODORE,** historian, educator; b. Kankakee, Ill., Mar. 18, 1926; s. Frank Theodore and Evelyn Marie (Scott) R.; m. Kathleen Ann Pester, June 16, 1951; children: Mark, Stephen, Christopher, Ann, Katherine. BS, U. Ill., 1950, MA, 1959, PhD, 1960. Instr. West Liberty (W. Va.) State Coll., 1960-62; asst. prof. Texas Christian U., Fort Worth, 1962-66, assoc. prof., 1966-71; prof. history Tex. Christian U., 1971-92, dean Grad. Sch., 1970-75, chmn. dept. history, 1980-83, prof. emeritus, 1992—. Vis. prof. Pázmány Péter Cath. U., Budapest, Hungary, 1999. Author: West Liberty State College: The First 125 Years, 1963, Catholic Influence on American Colonial Policies, 1898-1904, 1967, Trials and Triumphs: George Washington's Foreign Policy, 1983; co-author: Injured Honor: The Chesapeake-Leopard Affair, 1996. Served with USNR, 1944-46. U. Durham Rsch. fellow, 1991. Mem. Orgn. Am. Historians, Am. Hist. Assn., Soc. Historians Early Republic, Soc. Historians Am. Fgn. Relations, Phi Beta Kappa, Phi Alpha Theta. Roman Catholic. Home: 3617 Winifred Dr Fort Worth TX 76133-2126 Office: Tex Christian U Dept History Fort Worth TX 76129-0001 Office Phone: 817-257-7288. E-mail: rfkreuter@sbcglobal.net.

**REUTER, STEWART RALSTON,** retired radiologist; b. Detroit, Feb. 14, 1934; s. Carl H. and Grace M. R.; m. Marianne (Ahfeldt), June 6, 1966. BA, Ohio Wesleyan U., 1955; MD, Case Western Res. U., 1959; JD, U. San Francisco, 1980. Diplomate: Am. Bd. Radiology, Am. Bd. Legal Medicine. Bar: Tex., 1981. Intern U. Calif., San Francisco, 1959—60, resident in radiology, 1960—63; instr. radiology Stanford U., Calif., 1963—64; asst. prof. U. Mich., Ann Arbor, 1964—69; assoc. prof. U. Calif., San Diego, 1969—72; prof. U. Mich., Ann Arbor, 1972—76, U. Calif., San Francisco and Davis, 1976—80; prof., chmn. dept. radiology Health Sci. Ctr., U Tex., San Antonio, 1980—2001, prof. emeritus, 2001. Co-author: Gastrointestinal Radiology, 3d edit., 1986; mem. editorial bd. Am. Jour. Roentgenology, 1975-91, Iatrogenics, 1990-93; contbr. articles to profl. journals. Picker Fellow, 1964-66. Fellow: Soc. Interventional Radiologists (pres. 1978, Gold medal 2004), Am. Coll. Legal Medicine (bd. gov. 1985—91, 1992—94, sec. 1994, pres. elect 1995, pres. 1996), Am. Heart Assn., Am. Coll. Radiology (councillor 1996—99, fellow emeritus 2000); mem.: Am. Roentgen Ray Soc., Assn., Soc. Gastrointestinal Radiologists, Tex. Radiol. Assn. (trustee 1989—92, pres. 1994, trustee 1995—98, Gold medal 2000), Assn. Univ. Radiologists, Am. Bd. Legal Medicine, Tex. Bar Assn. Home: 3923 Morgans Creek San Antonio TX 78230-1945 Office: U Tex Health Sci Ctr Dept Radiology 7703 Floyd Curl Dr San Antonio TX 78284-6200 Business E-Mail: reuter@uthscsa.edu.

**REUTHER, DAVID LOUIS,** retired children's book publisher, writer; b. Detroit, Nov. 2, 1946; s. Roy Louis and Fania (Sonkin) R.; m. Margaret Alexander Miller, July 21, 1973; children: Katherine Anna, Jacob Alexander. BA with honors, U. Mich., 1968. Tchr. Lewis-Wadhams Sch., Westport, NY, 1969-71; asst. dir. Children's Book Coun., N.Y.C., 1971-73; editor children's books Macmillan Pub. Co., N.Y.C., 1973-76; sr. editor Four Winds Press-Scholastic Inc., N.Y.C., 1976-82; sr. v.p., pub. Morrow Jr. Books, N.Y.C., 1982-98; co-founder Baseball Ink, Inc., 1986-90; pub. Lothrop Lee & Shepard, N.Y.C., 1996-98, Beech Tree Books, N.Y.C., 1997-98; pres., pub. SeaStar Books, N.Y.C., 1999—2002, North-South Books, N.Y.C., 1999—2002. Chmn. Am. Children's Book Coun. Author: (with Roy Doty) Fun To Go, A Take-Along Activity Book, 1982, Save-the-Animals Activity Book, 1982, (with John Thorn and Pete Palmer) The Hidden Game of Baseball, 1984, Total Baseball, 1989, The Whole Baseball Catalog, 1990, Total Baseball II, 1991; editor: (with John Thorn) The Armchair Quarterback, 1982, The Armchair Aviator, 1983, The Armchair Mountaineer, 1984, The Armchair Book of Baseball, 1985, The Armchair Angler, 1986, The Armchair

Book of Baseball II, 1987, The Armchair Traveler, 1988. Bd. dirs. Smith House Family Book Ctr. Mem.: NSTA (children's book coun. joint com. 1982—85), ALA (co-chmn. children's book coun. joint com. 2000—02), Champlain Valley Film Soc. (pres. bd. dirs.), Am. Bookseller Assn. (childrens book coun. joint com. 1990—93). Home: Box 337 Willsboro NY 12996

**REUTHER, RONALD THEODORE,** museum director; b. Dec. 29, 1929; s. Frederick and Grace (Roehll) R.; m. Mary B. Howard, 1956; children: Catherine Virginia, Paul Douglas, Jon Frederick, Victoria Grace. BA, U. Calif., 1951, postgrad., 1953, U. Ariz., 1952. Mgr. Micke Grove Zoo, 1957-62; gen. curator Cleve. Zoo, 1958-62, asst. dir., 1964-66; dir. Indpls. Zoo, 1962-64, San Francisco Zoo, 1966-73; pres., exec. dir. Phila. Zoo, 1973-78; dir. corp. devel. Exploratorium, San Francisco, 1980-81; founder, pres. Western Aerospace Mus., Oakland, Calif., 1980—88, exec. dir., 1995-99; field rep. Bell & Howell Edn. Corp./DeVry Inst. Tech., 1983-88; exec. dir. Whale Ctr., Oakland, 1988-89; cons. Sierra Acad. Aeronautics, Oakland, 1989-92; lectr. Golden State U., San Francisco, 1992. Co-founder Pt. Reyes Bird Obs., Calif., 1968-70; v.p. Del. Valley Mus. Coun., 1976-78. Author zoo guidebooks, Wings Over San Francisco Bay, 1997. Mem. exec. com. Greater Phila. Cultural Alliance, 1976-78; owner, moderator internet Amelia Earhart Rsch. Discussion Group, 2000-03. 1st lt. USAF, 1953-57; with USARNG, 1958-66; lt. col. USAR, 1966-81, ret. Mem. The Explorers Club (chmn. No. Calif. chpt. 1990-95), Tamalpais Conservation Club (life mem.), Aero Club No. Calif. (bd. dirs. 2004-), Ox-5 Pioneers (bd. govs. Golden Gate chpt. 1996—, editor newsletter), Silver Wings Frat. (pres. No. Calif. chpt. 2003—). E-mail: reuther@comcast.net.

**REUTHINGER, GEORGEANNE,** special education educator; b. Laredo, Tex., Mar. 10, 1952; d. George and Maria Josefina (Elizondo) Ramon; m. David Lawrence Reuthinger, Apr. 5, 1952; 1 child, David L. Jr. AA in Music and Drama, Laredo Jr. Coll., 1972; BS in Speech and Drama Edn., Tex. A&I U., 1974, MS in Edn., 1978; postgrad., Tes. A&M Internat. U. Lic. speech therapist, Tex.; cert. speech therapist, ednl. diagnostician, profl. supervision. Speech and drama tchr. Laredo ISD Martin High Sch., 1974; supr., diagnostician spl. edn. program Laredo ISD Martin H.S., 1992-96, Cigarra H.S., Nixon H.S., 1998—; speech therapist Laredo ISD, 1974-78, ednl. diagnostician, 1978-92; sales assoc. Country Wide Real Estate, Laredo, 1997—; cons. in spl. edn. United Ind. and Laredo Ind. Sch. Dists., 1997-98. Founding mem., lead actress in bilingual theatrical touring co. Tex. A&I U., 1974. Active in fundraising for charities Women's City Club, Boy Scouts Am.; judge UIL Acad. & Fine Arts events, Spl. Olympics. Scholar Art League, 1970, Tex. A&I Alumni, 1972-74; recipient awards U.S. Army, 1973, USO Shows, 1973-74. Mem. Tex. Speech and Hearing Assn. (legis. network 1992-97), Coun. for Exceptional Children (lobbyist 1995, sec. Laredo chpt. 1975), Valley Coun. Adminstrs. and Suprs. in Spl. Edn., ASCD, Tex. Coun. Adminstrs. and Suprs. in Spl. Edn., Delta Kappa Gamma (sec. Alpha Nu chpt. 1977-78). Avocations: directing and acting in theatrical productions, singing in community choirs, special olympics volunteering and judging. Home: 206 Granada Dr Laredo TX 78041-2615 Office: Country Wide Real Estate 1303 Calle Del Norte Ste 6 Laredo TX 78041-6041 also: Laredo Ind Sch Dist 1702 Houston St Laredo TX 78040-4906

**REUTIMAN, ROBERT WILLIAM, JR.,** lawyer; b. Mpls., June 4, 1944; s. Robert William and Elsbeth Bertha (Doering) R.; m. Virginia Lee Traxler, June 25, 1983; children: Robert James, Joseph Lee. BA magna cum laude, U. Minn., 1966, JD, 1969. Bar: Minn. 1969, U.S. Ct. Mil. Appeals 1969, U.S. Dist. Ct. Minn. 1973, U.S. Ct. Appeals (8th cir.) 1976, U.S. Tax. Ct. 1979. Mem. Armstrong, Phleger, Reutiman & Vinokour, Ltd., Wayzata, Minn., 1973-76; ptnr. Phleger & Reutiman, Wayzata, 1976-81; pvt. practice Wayzata, 1981—. Chmn. Spring Pk. Planning Commn., 1978; city ct. judge, Hopkins and Minnetonka, Minn. Capt. U.S. Army, 1969-73. Decorated Army Commendation medal. Mem. ABA, Minn. Bar Assn., Hennepin County Bar Assn., Phi Beta Kappa. Lutheran. Avocations: fishing, gardening. Home: 11610 3rd Ave N Plymouth MN 55441-5919 Office: PO Box 367 Wayzata MN 55391 Office Phone: 952-473-7328. Business E-Mail: billreutiman@lycos.com.

**REUTTER, EBERHARD EDMUND, JR.,** education and law educator; b. Balt., May 28, 1924; s. Eberhard Edmund and Irene Louise (Loewer) R.; m. Bettie Marie Lytle, Aug. 16, 1947; 1 son, Mark Douglas. BA, Johns Hopkins U., 1944; MA, Columbia U., 1948, PhD, 1950. Dir., Tokyo Army Edn. Program Sch., 1945-47; head math. dept. Barnard Sch., N.Y.C., 1947-49; mem. faculty Tchrs. Coll., Columbia U., 1950—, prof., 1957-96, prof. emeritus, 1996—. Vis. prof. U. Alaska, 1960, 66, U. P.R., 1954, U. So. Calif., 1960; speaker, cons. Coordinator spl. edn. projects NAACP Legal Def. Fund, 1965-68 Author: The School Administrator and Subversive Activities, 1951, Schools and the Law, 5th edit., 1981, (with W.S. Elsbree) Staff Personnel in the Public Schools, 1954, (with R.R. Hamilton) Legal Aspects of School Board Operation, 1958, (with W.S. Elsbree) Principles of Staff Personnel Administration in Public Schools, 1959, (with L.O. Garber) The Yearbook of School Law, 1967, 68, 69, 70, Legal Aspects of Control of Student Activities by Public School Authorities, 1970, The Law of Public Education, 4th edit., 1994, The Courts and Student Conduct, 1975, The Supreme Court's Impact on Public Education, 1982; also articles, chpts. in books. Chmn. citizens adv. com. Emerson (N.J.) Bd. Edn., 1954-57. Served from pvt. to 1st lt. inf. AUS, 1943-46. Recipient Marion A. McGhehey award for outstanding service in field edn. law, 1986. Mem. NEA, AAUP, Nat. Orgn. Legal Problems of Edn. (pres. 1967), Am. Assn. Sch. Adminstrs., Am. Assn. Sch. Pers. Adminstrs., Internat. Pers. Mgmt. Assn., Phi Beta Kappa, Kappa Delta Pi, Phi Delta Kappa. Home: 316 Grand Blvd Emerson NJ 07630-1157 Office: Columbia Univ Tchrs Coll New York NY 10027

**REUTTY, MICHELE MARIE,** library director; b. Passaic, N.J., Oct. 17, 1949; d. Charles Hugo and Jean Cammarano Reutty; children: David Lavern Walters Jr., Jennifer Walters McCoy, Cristian Michael Maiullo. AA, Bergen County C.C., Paramus, N.J., 1979; B in English, Montclair State Coll., 1987; MLS, Rutgers U., 1989. Cert. ESL tutor Bergen County Coop. Libr. Systems/N.J., 1989. Reference libr. Elmwood Pk. (N.J.) Pub. Libr., 1987—88; asst. dir. Cresskill (N.J.) Pub. Libr., 1988—89; libr. dir. Free Pub. Libr. Hasbrouck Heights, NJ, 1989—. Editor-in-chief, contbg. author: history book Remembering the Past, Looking Toward the Future, 1996. Sec. Kelley Found., New Brunswick, NJ, 2005—. Named Citizen of the Yr., Mayor and Coun., Hasbrouck Heights, 1992; fellow Snowbird Leadership Inst., Salt Lake City, Utah, Rutgers U., 1991. Mem.: ALA (assoc.), Rutgers Sch. Communication, Info. and Libr. Studies (mem. exec. bd. 2006—07), NJ Libr. Assn. (assoc.; second v.p./chair adminstrn. and mgmt. com. 2004—05, v.p., pres.-elect 2006—07), Kiwanis Hasbrouck Heights/Teterboro (assoc.). Democrat. Roman Catholic. Avocations: creative writing, motorcycling, pysanky writing. Home: 189 Lincoln Ave Elmwood Park NJ 07407 Office: Free Public Library of Hasbrouck Heights 320 Boulevard Hasbrouck Heights NJ 07604 Office Phone: 201-288-0488. Office Fax: 201-288-5467. Business E-Mail: reutty@bccls.org. E-mail: xlibris@optonline.net.

**REVAK, FRANCIS CHARLES,** priest, educator; b. Philadelphia, Pa., Jan. 28, 1914; s. Joseph J. and Emma E. Revak. BA, St. Charles Sem., Overbrook, PA, 1939; ME, Lehigh U., Bethlehem, PA, 1968; MA, St. Charles Sem., Overbrook, PA, 1974. Ordained Catholic Priest Diocese of Phila., 1940. Priest Parish Ministry, 1940—67; theology and lang. educator Allentown Ctrl. Cath. H.S., Allentown, Pa., 1967—2002. Moderator, chaplain Allentown Ctrl. Cath. H.S. Football Team, Allentown, Pa., 1990—90. Roman Catholic. Avocations: state and world news, walking, bicycling, reading. Office: Allentown Central Catholic High School 301 N Fourth Street Allentown PA 18102-3098 E-mail: altlcchs@ptd.net.

**REVAN, DAVID R.,** language educator; b. Tryon, NC, Aug. 31, 1953; s. Demastrice L. and Betly L. Revan; m. D. Lawson, Sept. 1, 1971; 1 child, Alison C. AA, Sotby Meth., SC, 1973; BA, Berry Coll., Ga., 1975; MA, U. Tenn., Knoxville, 1976, Converse Coll., Spartansburg, SC, 1981. Tchr. A. S. Clark Jr. HS, Cordele, Ga., 1977—78, Lehitlock Jr. HS, Spartansburg,

1994—96; AP English tchr. Paul M. Dorman HS, Roebuck, SC, 1996—. Mem.: NEA, SC Assn. Educators. Avocations: reading, hiking, volleyball. Office: Paul M Dorman HS 1050 Cavalier Way Roebuck SC 29376-3364

**REVEAL, ERNEST IRA, III,** retired lawyer; b. Chgo., Oct. 19, 1948; s. Ernest Ira Jr. and Hazel (Holt) R.; m. Katherine Trennerry, Nov. 24, 1979; children: Genevieve, Adrienne, Danielle. BA, Cornell U., 1970; JD cum laude, U. Mich., 1973. Bar: Minn. 1973, U.S. Dist. Ct. Minn. 1973, U.S. Ct. Appeals (8th cir.) 1974, U.S. Dist. Ct. S.D. 1976, U.S. Ct. Claims 1976, U.S. Ct. Appeals (7th cir.) 1984, U.S. Dist. Ct. (ctrl. dist.) Calif. 1991, U.S. Ct. Appeals (9th cir.) 1991, U.S. Supreme Ct., 1991, U.S. Cir. Ct. Appeals (fed. cir.)2001. Assoc. Robins, Kaplan, Miller & Ciresi, Mpls., 1973—79, ptnr., 1979—2002, mediator, arbitrator, 2003—; atty. settlement officer US Dist. Ct. Author: Public Sector Labor Law, 1983. Pro tem mem. Civil Svc. Commn., St. Paul, 1976; chmn. regional adv. com. So. Calif. Pub. Radio. Mem. ABA, Minn. Bar Assn. (past chair labor law and employment law sect.), Calif. State Bar Assn. (adv., past exec. com., antitrust and unfair competition sect.), Cornell Club of Minn. (past pres.), LA Theatre Works (bd. dirs.). Democrat. Presbyterian. Avocations: history, travel. Office Phone: 949-589-1276. Personal E-mail: ernest.reveal@cox.net.

**REVEL, JEAN-PAUL,** biology professor; b. Strasbourg, France, Dec. 7, 1930; arrived in U.S., 1953; s. Gaston Benjamin and Suzanne (Neher) Revel; m. Helen Ruth Bowser, July 27, 1957 (div. 1986); children: David, Daniel Neher, Steven Robert; m. Galina Avdeeva Moller, Dec. 24, 1986 (dec. 2004); 1 stepchild, Karen (dec.). BS, U. Strasbourg, 1949; PhD, Harvard U., 1957. Rsch. fellow Cornell U. Med. Sch., N.Y.C., 1958-59; from instr. to prof. Harvard Med. Sch., Boston, 1959-71; prof. Calif. Inst. Tech., Pasadena, 1971—, AB Ruddock chair in biology, 1978—2006, dean of students, 1996—2005, emeritus, 2006—. Mem. sch. advisors bd. Nat. Insts. Aging, Balt., 1977-80; mem. ad hoc adv. biology NSF, Washington, 1982-83; mem. Nat. High Voltage Microscopy Adv. Group, Bethesda, Md., 1983, Nat. Rsch. Resources Adv. Coun., 1986-90. Author: (with E.D. Hay) Fine Structure of Developing Avian Cornea, 1969, over 150 publs., 1952-99; editor: Cell Shape and Surface Architecture, 1977, Science of Biological Specimen Preparation, 1986; mem. editl. bd. Jour. Cell Biology, 1969-72, Internat. Rev. Cytology, 1970, Cell and Tissue Rsch., 1979—, Molecular and Cell Biology, 1983-91; editor in chief Jour. Microscopy Soc. Am., 1994-96. Fellow AAAS (leader biol. scis. sect. 1991-92, Gordon conf. cell adhesion); mem. Am. Soc. Cell Biology (pres. 1972-73), Electron Micros. Soc. Am. (pres. 1988, Disting. Scientist award 1993), Soc. Devel. Biology. Avocations: watercolors, photography. Office: Calif Inst Tech # 156-29 Pasadena CA 91125-0001 Office Phone: 626-395-4986. Business E-Mail: revelj@caltech.edu.

**REVELEY, WALTER TAYLOR, III,** dean, law educator; b. Churchville, Va., Jan. 6, 1943; s. Walter Taylor and Marie (Eason) R.; m. Helen Bond, Dec. 18, 1971; children: Walter Taylor IV, George Everett Bond, Nelson Martin Eason, Helen Lanier. AB, Princeton U., 1965; JD, U. Va., 1968. Bar: Va. 1970, D.C. 1976. Asst. prof. law U. Ala., 1968-69; law clk. to Justice Brennan U.S Supreme Ct., Washington, 1969-70; fellow Woodrow Wilson Internat. Ctr. for Scholars, 1972-73; internat. affairs fellow Coun. on Fgn. Rels., N.Y.C., 1972-73; assoc. Hunton & Williams, Richmond, Va., 1970-76, ptnr., 1976-98, mng. ptnr., 1982-91, cons., 1998—; dean William and Mary Law Sch., 1998—, law prof. Lectr. Coll. William and Mary Law Sch., 1978—80; cons. in field. Author: War Powers of the President and Congress: Who Holds the Arrows and Olive Branch, 1981; mem. editl. bd. Va. Law Rev., 1966-68; contbr. articles to profl. jours. Trustee Princeton U., 1986-90, 91-2001, Presbyn. Ch. (U.S.A.) Found., 1991-97, Va. Hist. Soc., 1991-96, 2003—, Union Theol. Sem., 1992-2000, Andrew W. Mellon Found., 1994—, JSTOR, 1995—, Va. Mus. Fine Arts, 1995-2005, pres. 1996-99, St. Christopher's Sch., 1996-01, 2004—, Carnegie Endowment for Internat. Peace, 1999—; bd. dirs. Fan Dist. Assn., Richmond, Inc., 1976-80, pres., 1979-80; bd. dirs. Richmond Symphony, 1980-92, pres., 1988-90, pres. symphony coun., 1994-99; bd. dirs. Presbyn. Outlook Found., 1985-2003, 2004-, pres., 1992-95; bd. dirs. Va. Mus. Found., 1990-99; bd. dirs. New Covenant Trust Co., 1997-99, Va. Found. Humanities, 2001—. Mem. ABA, Va. Bar Assn., D.C. Bar Assn., Am. Bar Found., Va. Bar Found., Princeton Assn. Va. (bd. dirs. 1981—, pres. 1983-85), Va. State Bar (Edn. Lawyers sect. bd. govs. 1992—, chmn. 1992-95), Raven Soc., Phi Beta Kappa, Omicron Delta Kappa. Home: 2314 Monument Ave Richmond VA 23220-2604 Office: William and Mary Law Sch PO Box 8795 Williamsburg VA 23187-8795 Office Phone: 757-221-3790. Business E-Mail: taylor@wm.edu.

**REVELL, BILL,** mayor; b. Flint, Mich., Jan. 5, 1930; s. John Archie and Violet May Revell; m. Sherrie Gail Purvis, Apr. 17, 1950; children: Peggy, Janice. Student in Bus. Mgmt., Kettering U., 1950. Owner Revell GMC Auto Co., Inc., Dyersburg, Tenn., 1956—81; mayor City of Dyersburg, 1980—. Bd. dirs. Nat. League of Cities, Wash., DC, adv. bd. Mayor of Yr. Tenn. Mcpl. League, 1987. Meth. Avocation: running. Home: 840 Lattawoods Dyersburg TN 38024 Office: City of Dyersburg P O Box 1358 Dyersburg TN 38024

**REVELL, HENRY, JR.,** social services administrator, retired education educator; b. Selma, NC, Apr. 13, 1932; s. Henry William Sr. and Flora (Vinson) Revell; m. Carolyn Yvonne L. Revell (dec.); children: Gary, Keith, Kevan Croper. BS, NC A&T State U., Greensboro, 1974. Facilitator, pres. Family Strengths, Greensboro, NC, 1980—; pres., CEO Kent-FJHB, Inc., Selma, NC, 1989—; owner, dir. Revell's Enrichment Ctr., Greensboro, 2002—. State 4-H youth coord. NC A&T State U., Greensboro, 1974—87; program dir. Another Chance Recovery Ctr., Greensboro, 2002—; presenter in field. Pres., bd. dirs. Triad Sickle Cell Reg., Greensboro, 1987—91, Daniel Godfrey Meml. Fund, Greensboro, 1988—; past pres. RH Family Orgn.; deacon Providence Bapt. Ch., Greensboro, 1981—. With U.S. Army, 1956—58. Grantee, Cmty. Found., Greensboro, 2000. Mem.: NACCP (parlimentarian 1990—), Epsilon Sigma Phi (life). Democrat. Baptist. Avocations: baseball, basketball, football, walking, dance. Home: 3316 S Elm-Eugene St Greensboro NC 27406

**REVELLE, DONALD GENE,** manufacturing and health care company executive, consultant; b. Cape Girardeau, Mo., July 16, 1930; s. Lewis W. and Dorothy R.; m. Jo M. Revelle, Aug. 1, 1954; children: Douglas, David, Daniel, Dianne BA, U. Mo., 1952; JD, U. Colo., 1957; grad., Harvard U. Bus. Sch., 1971. Dir. employee relations Westinghouse Corp., Pitts., 1957-65; asst. to v.p. Diebold Corp., 1966; v.p. human resources TRW Corp., Cleve., 1967-84; sr. v.p. human resources Black and Decker Co., Towson, Md., 1984-86; v.p. corp. rels. Montefiore Acad. Med. Ctr., Bronx, 1987-98; pres., CEO Syzygy, Inc., 1998—. Univ. lectr.; cons. Duerba Ship, Blue Cross N.Y., Windsor Hosp., Salvation Army Contbr. articles to profl. jours. Mem. sch. bd. State of N.Y. Lt. USNR, 1952-54 Mem.: ABA (labor law com.), Human Resource Planning Soc., Colo. Bar Assn., MBA Assn. Rotary. Methodist. Home and Office: Syzygy Inc 29903 Baywood Ln Wesley Chapel FL 33543-9744 Office Phone: 813-994-3403.

**RE VELLE, JACK B(OYER),** statistician, consultant; s. Mark A. and Myril (Bubes) Re V.; m. Brenda Lorraine Newcombe, Aug. 2, 1968; 1 child, Karen Alyssa. BSChemE, Purdue U., 1957; MS in Indsl. Engring. and Mgmt., Okla. State U., 1965, PhD in Indsl. Engring. and Mgmt., 1970. Adminstrv. asst. Gen. Dynamics, Ft. Worth 1970-71; cons. engr. Denver, 1971-72; chmn. decision scis. U. Nebr., Omaha, 1972-77; dean Chapman U. Sch. Bus. and Mgmt., Orange, Calif., 1977-79; sr. staff engr. McDonnell Douglas Space Systems, Huntington Beach, Calif., 1979-81; head mfg. tng. and devel. Hughes Aircraft Co., Fullerton, Calif., 1981-82, sr. statistician, 1982-86, corp. mgr. R & D L A, 1986-88, corp. chief statistician, 1988-93; leader continuous improvement Raytheon Missile Systems Co., Tucson, 1994-97; dir. Ctr. for Process Improvement GenCorp Aerojet, Azusa, Calif., 1998-99; consulting statistician Santa Ana, Calif., 1999—. Mem. bd. examiners Malcolm Baldrige nat. quality award Nat. Inst. Stds. and Tech., U.S. Dept. Commerce, Washington, 1990, 93; judge Ariz. Quality Alliance, Phoenix, 1994-96, Rochester Inst. Tech.-USA Today Quality Cup Competition, 1994-2001, Def. Contract Mgmt. Command-Commdrs. Cup, 1995-2000; cons., presenter, lectr. in field. Author: Safety Training Methods, 1980, 2d edit., 1995, The

Two-Day Statistician, 1986, The New Quality Technology, 1988, Policy Deployment, 1993, What Your Quality Guru Never Told You, 2000, Quality Essentials, 2004; (with others) Quest for Quality, 1986, Mechanical Engineers Handbook, 1986, 2d edit., 1998, 3d edit., 2005, Production Handbook, 1987, Handbook of Occupational Safety and Health, 1987, A Quality Revolution in Manufacturing, 1989, Quality Engineering Handbook, 1991; co-author: Quantitative Methods for Managerial Decisions, 1978, The Executive's Handbook on Quality Function Deployment, 1994, From Concept to Customer, 1995, The Quality Function Deployment Handbook, 1998, Manufacturing Handbook of Best Practices, 2001; (software) TQM ToolSchool, 1995, QFD/Pathway, 1998. Bd. dirs. Assn. for Quality and Participation, Cin., 1985-86; mem. adv. bd. dept. indsl. and mech. engring. Calif. Poly. State U., Pomona, 1985-2000; mem. adv. bd. dept. indsl. and sys. engring. Ohio U., Athens, 2000—05; mem. Svc. Corp. Retired Execs., Santa Ana, 2005-. 2d lt. to maj. USAF, 1957—68, served in Japan USAF, 1957—59, served in Vietnam USAF, 1966—67, joint svc. assignment Defense Nuclear Agy., 1967—68, Wash., DC. Recipient Disting. Econs. Devel. award Soc. Mfg. Engrs., 1990, Taguchi Recognition award Am. Supplier Inst., 1991, Akao prize QFD Inst., 1999, Melvin R. Lohmann medal Okla. State U. Coll. Engring., Arch. and Tech., 2006; named to Purdue U. ROTC Hall of Fame, 2006. Fellow Am. Soc. for Quality (co-chair total quality mgmt. com. 1990-92), Inst. Advancement Engring., Inst. Indsl. Engrs. (regional v.p. 1982-84, treas. 1992-93, sr. v.p. 1993-94); mem. Aerospace and Def. Divsns. (dir. 1997-99). Office: The Wizard of Odds A Consulting Statistician Re Velle Solutions LLC PO Box 10315 Santa Ana CA 92711-0315 Office Phone: 714-289-1664. Personal E-mail: cactus_statman@yahoo.com.

**REVELOS, CONSTANTINE NICHOLAS,** law educator, writer; b Middletown, Ohio, Mar. 1, 1938; s. Nicholas George and Efrosine (Aredas) R. AB, Bowdoin Coll., 1961; JD, Duke U., 1965; LLM, U. Calif., Berkeley, 1971. Bar: Ohio 1965, Mich. 1975, U.S. dist. Ct. (so. dist.) Ohio 1967, U.S. Ct. Appeals (6th cir.) 1967, U.S. Supreme Ct. 1968. With sales-svc. dept. Armco Steel Corp., Middletown, 1961-62; asst. prof. law No. Ky. State U., Cin., 1965-67, assoc. prof., dean, 1968-70; prof. law Detroit Coll. Law, East Lansing, Mich., 1971—. Dir. King scholars program, 1996—; arbiter N.Y. Stock Exchange, 1981—, Am. Arbitration Assn; Ctrl. & Eastern European Law Initiative specialist and lectr. Faculty of Law, Babes/Bolyai U., Cluj, Romania, 1994-95; lectr., faculty of law, Vytautus Magnus Univ. Kaunas, Lithuania, 2000. Author: Michigan Business Organizations, 1985. Pres. Sts. Constantine & Helen Greek Orthodox Ch., Middletown, 1967-70; trustee, Annunciation Cathedral, Detroit, 1982-91. Mem. ABA, Ohio Bar Asns., Mich. Bar Assn., Am. Judicature Soc., Am. Arbitration Assn. (arbitrator), N.Y. Stock Exch. (arbitrator), Order Ahepa. Home: 1575 Mojave Ct Okemos MI 48864-3442 Office: Mich State U-DCL 353 Law College Bldg East Lansing MI 48824-1300 Office Phone: 517-432-6882. Business E-Mail: revelos@law.msu.edu.

**REVENKOVA, EKATERINA,** biologist, researcher; b. Moscow, May 22, 1962; arrived in U.S., 2000; d. Vladimir Preobrazhensky and Natalia Alekhina; 1 child, Anton Revenkov. MS in Genetics, Moscow State U., 1984; PhD in Molecular Biology, V.A.Engelhardt Inst. Molecular Biology, Moscow, 1993. Rsch. scientist Ctr. of Bioengineering, Moscow, 1989—94; postdoctoral rsch. fellow Friedrich Miescher Inst., Basel, Switzerland, 1995—99; scientist Basel Inst. for Immunology, 1999—2000; instr. Mt. Sinai Sch. Medicine, N.Y.C., 2001—04, asst. prof., 2004—. Contbr. articles to profl. jours. Mem.: Am. Soc. for Cell Biology. Office: Mount Sinai School of Medicine 1 Gustave L Levy Pl New York NY 10029 Office Phone: 212-659-8248.

**REVENS, JOHN COSGROVE, JR.,** state legislator, lawyer; b. Providence, Jan. 29, 1947; s. John C. and Rita M. (Williams) R.; m. Susan L. Shaw, Aug. 31, 1974; children: Leigh Elizabeth, Marcie Greene, Emily May. AA, C.C. of RI, 1966; BA, Providence Coll., 1969; JD, Suffolk U., 1973. Bar: RI 1973. Mem. RI Ho. of Reps., Providence, 1968-74, sec. house steering com., 1971-74, mem. edn. and welfare com., 1968—78; pres. Revens, Revens & St. Pierre, Warwick, RI, 1977—; mem. RI Senate, Dist. 31, Providence, 1990—. Mem. RI Senate, 1974-89, 1991—, fin. svs., tech. and regulatory issues, mem. jud. and labor coms., 1974, chmn. jud. com. 1980-83, majority whip, 1977-80, Senate majority leader, 1983-89; Senate pres., pro tempore, 1993-95, 2001—; dir. New Eng. Bd. Higher Edn., 1975-83, chmn., 1977-81; chmn. RI Children's Code Commn., 1979-83; bd. dirs. C.C. of RI Found., Vols. of Warwick Schs., RI Acad. Decathlon Assn.; mem. Commn. on Jud. Tenure and Discipline, 1982-84, Family Ct. Bench Bar Com., 1980-82, Women and Infants Hosp. Corp., 1983—; commr. Uniform State Laws, 1982-84. Bd. dirs. Senate Presidents' Forum. Mem. RI Bar Assn., Kent County Bar Assn., Am. Arbitration Assn. (panel of arbitrators 1980-), State Legis. Leaders Found. (pres. senate forum, bd. dirs.), KC. Democrat. Roman Catholic. Office: 946 Centerville Rd Warwick RI 02886-4398

**REVER, GEORGE WRIGHT,** psychiatrist, health facility administrator; b. Balt., May 18, 1928; s. William Benjamin and Amy Blanche (Wright) R.; m. Bridget Valerie Hanley, 1961 (dec. 1988); children: Kurt, Maeve Rever Raedle; m. Ann Roe, Feb. 4, 1994. BS, U. Md., 1950; MD, U. Md., Balt., 1957. Rotating intern Mercy Hosp., Balt., 1957-58; resident psychiatry and neurology VA Hosp., Boston, 1958-60; fellow Harvard Med. Sch., Cambridge, Mass., 1960-64, clin. instr. psychiatry, 1964—2004; psychiatrist divsn. legal medicine Cambridge Ct., 1960-71; psychiatrist Cambridge Ct. Clinic Divsn. of Legal Medicine, Mass., 1960-71; pvt. practice Cohasset, Mass., 1963-90, Easton, Md., 1990-93; psychiatric cons. Travelers Aid Soc., Boston, 1966-74; psychiatrist Eunice Kennedy Shriver Ctr., Waltham, Mass., 1967-90; fellow child psychiatry Mass. Gen. Hosp., Boston, 1960-61, 62-63, fellow community mental health, 1963-64, staff psychiatrist, 1964-90, dir. child psychiatry tng. program neuropsychiatry devel. disabilities sect. 1967-90, and jud. rsch. lab. 1969-71, psychiat. cons. social svc. dept., 1970-74, psychiatrist Chelsea Health Ctr., 1974-77, hon. psychiatrist, 1991—2004; med. dir. Brockton (Mass.) Family and Community Rsch., 1979-90; child and adolescent psychiatrist Wicomico County Health Dept., Salisbury, Md., 1990-91, Queen Anne County Mental Health, Centreville, Md., 1990-92, Talbot County Mental Health, Easton, 1990-92, med. dir., 1992—2002, Regional Mid-Shore Mental Health Svcs., 1994—2005, Caroline County Mental Health Clinic, 2005—, Bay Hundred Behavioral Health Svcs./Choptank Cmty. Health Svcs., 2005—; psychiatric cons. Benedictine Sch., Ridgely, Md., 1990—. Part-time fellow child psychiatry Mass. Gen. Hosp., Boston, 1961-62, James Jackson Putnam Children's Ctr., Roxbury, Mass., 1961-62; cons. Am. Heritage Dictionaries, 1992; fleet surgeon Miles River Yacht Club, 2000—. Editl. cons. The Am. Jour. of Child and Adolescent Psychiatry, 1994—. Sgt. U.S. Army, 1950-52, Korea. Decorated Bronze Star medal; Recipient Talbot County Assn. Retarded Citizens award, 1993. Fellow: Am. Psychiat. Assn. (life Disting.), Am. Coll. Forensic Examiners (life); mem. AMA, Mass. Child Psychology and Psychiatry, Am. Neuropsychiat. Assn., Talbot County Med. Soc., Med. and Chururg. Faculty Md., Md. Psychiat. Soc., Am. Assn. Mental Retardation, Am. Assn. Cmty. Psychiatrists, Am. Acad. Child and Adolscent Psychiatry. Home: 8627 North Bend Cir Easton MD 21601-7327 Business E-Mail: rever@shore.intercom.net.

**REVERDIN, BERNARD J.,** lawyer; b. Baden, Switzerland, June 21, 1919; came to U.S., 1948, naturalized, 1954; s. Jean and Germaine Reverdin; m. Marcelle Coicou Reverdin; children: Caroline Reverdin Flanagan, Brigitte, Nathalie. LLB, U. Geneva, 1942; postgrad., Harvard Law Sch., 1949. Bar: Switzerland 1945, N.Y. 1955. Atty., legal asst. Geneva Govt., 1945-48; assoc. Sullivan & Cromwell, N.Y.C., 1949-51; assoc., ptnr. Lovejoy, Wasson & Ashton, N.Y.C., 1951-84; ptnr., counsel Hunton & Williams, N.Y.C., 1984-88; ptnr. Eaton & Van Winkle, N.Y.C., 1988-97; sr. counsel intern, 1998—. Dir. subs. of European corps. Contbr. articles to profl. jours.; lectr. in field V.p. LCM Found. on European Affairs Inc. Mem. N.Y. State Bar Assn. (chair com. internat. trust and estate 1988-90), Am. Fgn. Law Assn. (past pres.), Consular Law Soc. (past pres.), Internat. Law Assn., Union Internat. des Avocats, Swiss Soc. N.Y., German Am. Law Assn. Office: Eaton & Van Winkle LLP 3 Park Ave Fl 16 New York NY 10016-5902 E-mail: breverdin@evw.com.

**REVERE, FRANCES LEE,** healthcare educator; b. Pensacola, Fla., Apr. 17, 1970; d. Ralph Myron and Patricia Lee Roberts; m. Shaun Michael Revere, May 14, 1994. B Indsl. Engring., Ga. Inst. Tech., Atlanta, 1992; MS, Trinity U., San Antonio, 1997; PhD, U. South Fla., Tampa, 2002. Cons. Sun Health Enterprises, Charlotte, NC, 1992—93; clin. info. specialist Christus Healthcare Sys., Houston, 1993—96; mem. svcs. dir. Humana Health Plans, Houston, 1996—97; exec. dir. Health Help Network, Tampa, Fla., 1997—98; asst. prof. U. Houston Clear Lake, 2001—. Adj. prof. St. Leo (Fla.) Coll., 1998—99, U. Phoenix, Tampa, Fla., 1999; presenter, cons. in field. Contbr. articles to profl. jours.; reviewer: Acad. Info. and Mgmt. Scis. Jour., 2004; author: Supplemental Materials for Quantitative Methods for Management, 9th edit., 2004. Recipient Instnl. Innovations award, Decision Sci. Inst., 2003, Hayhow Best Paper of Yr. award, Jour. Healthcare Mgmt., 2004. Office: U Houston Clear Lake 2700 Bay Area Blvd Box 263 Houston TX 77058

**REVERE, VIRGINIA LEHR,** psychologist; b. Long Branch, NJ; d. Joseph and Essie Lehr; m. Robert B. Revere; children: Elspeth, Andrew, Lisa, Robert Jr. PhB, U. Chgo., 1949, MA, 1959, PhD, 1971. Lic. cons. clin. psychologist, Va. Intern, staff psychologist Ea. Mental Health Reception Ctr., Phila., 1959-61; instr. Trenton (N.J.) State Coll., 1962-63; psychologist Trenton State Hosp., 1964-65, Bucks County Psychiat. Ctr., Phila., 1965-67; assoc. prof. Mansfield (Pa.) State U., 1967-77; clin. rsch. psychologist St. Elizabeth Hosp., Washington, 1977-81, tng. psychology coord., 1981-83, psychologist, 1985-91; child psychologist Cmty. Mental Health Ctr., Washington, 1983-85; pvt. practice Alexandria, Va., 1980—. Cons., lectr. in field. Author: Applied Psychology for Criminal Justice Professionals, 1982; contbr. articles to profl. jours. Recipient Group Merit award St. Elizabeth's Hosp., 1983, Community Svc. award D.C. Psychol. Assn., 1978, Outstanding Educator award, 1972; traineeship NIH, USPHS, Chgo., 1963-65; fellow Family Svcs. Assn., 1958-59. Mem. APA, No. Va. Soc. Clin. Psychologists, Va. Acad. Clin. Psychologists. Office Phone: 703-780-4872. E-mail: rrevere923@aol.com.

**REVES, JOSEPH GERALD (JERRY REVES),** anesthesiology educator, dean; b. Charleston, SC, Aug. 14, 1943; s. George Everett and Frances (Masterson) R.; m. Virginia Cathcart, Jan. 05, 1945; children: Virginia Masterson, Christine Frances, Elizabeth Cathcart. BA, Vanderbilt U., 1965; MD, Medical Coll. S.C., 1969; MS, U. Ala., Birmingham, 1973. Lic. anesthesiologist S.C., Ala., Md., N.C.; Diplomate Am. Coll. Anesthesiology, Am. Bd. Anesthesiology. Rsch. asst., dept. pharmacology Med. Coll. S.C., 1965, 66 (summers); intern U. Ala. Hosp. and Clinics, Birmingham, Ala., 1969-70, resident in anesthesiology, 1970-72; post-doctoral, dept. anesthesia and physiology U. Ala. Med. Sch., 1972; instr., dept anesthesiology U. Ala. Hosp. and Clinics, 1973; dept. tng. staff, anesthesiology Nat. Naval Med. Ctr., Bethesda, Md., 1973-75; clin. instr., dept anesthesiology George Washington U. Sch. Med., Washington, 1973-75; assoc. prof., dept. anesthesiology U. Ala. Hosp. and Clinics, 1975-78; dir., div. anesthesia rsch. U. Ala., 1977-84, prof. anesthesiology, 1978-84; clin. anesthesia coord. UAB Cardiac Transplant Program, Birmingham, 1982-84; prof. anesthesiology, dir. cardiothoracic anesthesia Duke U. Med. Ctr., Durham, NC, 1984-1991; dir. Duke Heart Ctr., Duke Med. Ctr., Durham, NC, 1987-97; interim chmn., dept. anesthesiology Duke U. Med. Ctr., 1990-91, prof. and chmn., dept. anesthesiology, 1991—2001; dean, v.p. for med. affairs Med. U. S.C. Coll. Medicine, Charleston, 2001—. Cons. Hoffman-LaRoche, Somatogen, Abbott/Oximetric. Contbr. to numerous profl. jours., refereed jours., chpts. in books, published scientific reviews, selected abstracts, editorials, films, audio visual presentations, letters, positions and background papers; author: Acute Revascularization of the Infracted Heart, 1987, Common Problems in Cardiac Anesthesia, 1987, Intravenous Anesthesia and Analgesia, 1988, Anesthesiology Clinics of North America, 1988, Anesthesia, 1990, International Anesthesiology Clinics, 1991; Cardiac Anesthesis, Privileges and Practice, 1994; editor: Anesthesia and Analgesia, 1984—, cardiovascular sect. editor 1991—; editorial bd. Society Cardiovascular Anesthesia Monograph Series (chmn. 1986-89), Current Opinion in Anaesthesia 1987—, American Antec Newsletter 1989—; co-editor in chief: Current Opinion in Anaesthiology 1990—. Dir. Clairmont Ave Hist. Preservation Com. 1976-78; Am. Heart Assn. (Durham chpt. pres. 1988-90, com. mem. anesthesiology, radiology and surgery rsch. study com. 1988-91). Grantee NIH 1991—, Janssen Pharmaceutica 1991-92, Anaquest 1989-92, Diprivan Ednl. grant ICI Pharmaceuticals Group 1991-92. Fellow Am. Coll. Cardiology; mem. AMA, Durham County Medical Soc., Internat. Soc. on Oxygen Transport to Tissue, N.C. Soc. Anesthesiologist (edn. com. 1992—), N.C. State Medical Soc., Birmingham Vanderbilt Club (bd. dirs. 1975-80, 1st v.p. 1979, pres. 1980), Southern Med. Assn. (chmn. elect. anesthesiology sect. 1976-77, chmn. 1977-78, chmn. 1988-89), Southern Soc. Anesthesiologists (v.p. 1978-79, pres. elect 1979-80, pres. 1980-81), Soc. Cardiovascular Anesthesiologists (pres. 1979-80), Assn. Univ. Anesthetists (elected to mem. 1980), Assn. Cardiac Anesthesiologists (elected to mem. 1982, pres. 1990), Soc. for Neuroleptanalgesia (bd. dirs. 1988), U. Ala. Birmingham Nat. Alumni Soc. (dist. dir., bd. dirs. 1991-93), Internat. Anesthesia Rsch. Soc. (bd. Trustees 1992—), Am. Soc. Anesthesiologists (com. sub-specialty representation 1980—, subcommittee on clin. circulation 1992—, com. geriatric anesthesia 1992—), Sigma Xi, Alpha Omega Alpha. Achievements include research on effects of age on neurologic response to cardiopulmonary bypass; cerebral blood flow and metabolism during cardiac surgery; automated delivery system of intravenous anesthetic drugs; pathophysiology of cardiopulmonary bypass; redesign of medical education. Office: Med U SC PO Box 250617 96 Jonathan Lucas St Ste 601 Charleston SC 29425 Office Phone: 843-792-2842. Business E-Mail: revesj@musc.edu.

**REVESZ, AKOS GEORGE,** physicist; b. Balassagyarmat, Hungary, July 25, 1927; came to U.S., 1959; s. Eugen and Ilona (Rachler) R.; m. Agnes Ernszt, June 1956 (div. May 1973); 1 child, Tom; m. Kinga M. Lutter, Jan. 10, 1975; 1 child, Paul. Diploma in engring., Tech. U., Budapest, Hungary, 1950, PhD, 1968. Rsch. asst. Tech. U., Budapest, 1947-48; rsch. engr. Iron and Steel Rsch. Inst. Budapest, 1950, Phillips, Eindhoven, The Netherlands, 1950-51; rsch. engr., head dept. Tungsram, Budapest, 1951-53, 56; mem. tech. staff RCA Rsch. Lab., Princeton, N.J., 1959-69; sr. scientist Comsat Labs., Clarksburg, Md., 1969-83; ind. cons. Revesz Assocs., Bethesda, Md., 1984—. Co-author: Field-Effect Transistors, 1966; editor books in field; contbr. over 150 articles to profl. publs.; patentee in field. Mem. Electrochem. Soc. Avocations: reading, classical music, hiking, swimming. Home and Office: 7910 Park Overlook Dr Bethesda MD 20817-2719

**REVESZ, RICHARD LUIS,** dean, law educator; b. Buenos Aires, May 9, 1958; BSE in Civil Engring. summa cum laude, Princeton U., 1979; MS, MIT, 1980; JD, Yale U., 1983. Bar: NY 1986, DC 1986, US Supreme Ct. 1989, US Ct. Appeals DC Cir. 1986, US Dist. Ct. So. Dist. NY 1986. Jud. clerk to Chief Judge Wilfred Feinberg US Ct. Appeals 2nd Cir., NYC, 1983-84; jud. clerk to Justice Thurgood Marshall US Supreme Ct., 1984-85; asst. prof. NYU Sch. Law, 1985-88, assoc. prof., 1988-90, prof., 1990—2001, Lawrence King prof. law, 2001—, dir. Program on Environ. Regulation, 1996—, dean, 2002—. Vis. prof. U. Geneva Sch. Law, 1995, Harvard Law Sch., 1995-96, Yale Law Sch., 2001; Shelby Cullum Davis vis. prof. Grad. Inst. Internat. Studies, Geneva, 1995; vis. prof. pub. & internat. law Princeton U., 2002; pro-bono rep. Natural Resources Def. Coun., 1987; term mem. Coun. Fgn. Rels., 1989-94; cons. Environ. Economics Adv. Com. of Sci. Advisory Bd. EPA, 1998-99; mem., chmn.; cons. dept. tech. coop. for devel. UN, 1980-81, Adminstrv. Conf. of US, 1986-89, 1991-92, Carnegie Commn. Sci., Tech., and Govt., 1989-90; mem. internat. adv. bd. Yearbook European Environ. Law, 1998—. Author: Foundations of Environmental Law and Policy, 1997; editor: Distinctive Practices of the Second Circuit, 1989; co-editor: Analyzing Superfund: Economics, Science and Law, 1995, Environmental Law, the Economy, and Sustainable Development: The United States, the European Union, and the International Community, 2000. Mem. ABA (vice chmn. com. jud. review sect. adminstrv. law 1988-98, chair, 1998—), Am. Law Inst., Assn. Bar City of NY (chmn. com. adminstrv. law 1988-91, sec. com. second century 1986-88, mem. com. environ. law 1986-88), Am. Law and Economics Assn. (bd. dirs. 1998—), Phi Beta Kappa, Sigma Xi, Tau Beta Pi (prize winner). Office: NYU Sch Law Vanderbilt Hall Ste 406 40 Washington Sq S New York NY 10012-1099 Office Phone: 212-998-6000. Office Fax: 212-995-3150. E-mail: richard.revesz@nyu.edu.

**REVILLE, ROBERT T.,** economist; PhD, Brown Univ. Economist RAND Inst. Civil Justice, 1995—99, rsch. dir., 1999—2003, dir., 2003—. Author of books & articles on workers compensation issues. Office: RAND Institute for Civil Justice 1776 Main St PO Box 2138 Santa Monica CA 90407-2138

**REVILLS, ISAIAH,** minister; b. Moultrie, Ga., Aug. 23, 1931; s. William Mack and Irene Revills; m. Ullainee S. Sanders, June 4, 1955; 5 children. DD, LHD, United Christian Coll., Goldborg, N.C., 1995. Marriage counselor, Albany, Ga., 1969—; founder, pastor Evangelical Faith Vision Ministry, Inc., Albany, Ga., 1970—. Author: (book) The Unfolding Vision, 1996, God's Added Blessings, 1998. Mem. Complete Count Com., Albany, Ga., 2000. Avocations: travel, reading, golf, fishing. Home: 1618 Moultrie Rd Albany GA 31705 Office: Evangelical Faith Vision Ministry Inc 1506 S Slappey Blvd Albany GA 31701

**REVIS, DON RAY, JR.,** plastic surgeon; b. Greenwood, SC, Oct. 16, 1966; BS in Zoology, Duke U.; MD, Med. U. S.C., 1992. Cert. Am. Bd. Surgery 1999, Am. Bd. Plastic Surg. 2001, lic. Fla. Founder So. Fla. Plastic Surgery Assocs. Intern, gen. surgery George Washington U. Med. Ctr., Washington, 1992—93, residency, gen. surg., 1993—98; residency, plastic & reconstructive surg. U. Fla., Gainesville, 1998—2000; fellowship, cosmetic surgery Plastic Surgery Assocs., Miami, Fla., 2000. Vol. Interplast, Honduras, Project Senegal, Senegal. Nominee Exec. Com., Candidates and Assocs. Soc., Am. Coll. Surgeons, mem. editl. adv. bd., Obesity Help Magazine, Ethics Com., eMedicine Online Med. Textbook, 2000—, Ho. of Dels., Fla. Med. Assn. 2001; named Disting. Physician, Best Plastic Surgeon and Best Physician, Coral Springs Forum, The Jewish Journal newspapers, Up and Coming Physician of Year, Fla. Med. Bus. Jour., to symposium com., Am. Soc. Aesthetic Plastic Surg. and Aesthetic Soc. Education and Rsch. Found., among America's top surgeons, Consumer Rsch. Coun. of Am., 2001; recipient Physician's Recognition award, Am. Med. Assn., 1998; grantee Rsch. fellow, Nat. Insts. Health, Bethesda, Md., 1995—96. Fellow: ACS; mem.: AMA, Duke U. Alumni Assn., Better Bus. Bureau, Lipoplasty Soc., Wound Healing Soc., Fla. Med. Assn., Internat. Coll. Surgeons, Broward County Med. Assn., Internat. Fedn. Surgery of Obesity, Am. Soc. Bariatric Surgery, Broward County Soc. Plastic Surgeons, Am. Soc. Aesthetic Plastic Surgery, Am. Soc. Plastic Surgeons, Med. Univ. So. Carolina Alumni Assn. (life), Monterey Bay Sea Otter Rsch. and Conservation Program, Nat. Trust Historic Preservation, Iron Dukes, Rotary Club Internat. Achievements include numerous speaking engagements; tv appearances include Healthy Living, 2001, The Maury Povich Show, 2004, Channel 10 News, WPLG, 2004; Author of numerous publications including author of 26 chptrs. of an online medical textbook: emedicine.com. Office: So Fla Plastic Surgery Assocs 2500 N Federal Hwy Ste 301 Fort Lauderdale FL 33305 Office Phone: 954-630-2009.

**REVIS-PYKE, ROBIN LYNN,** director; b. Orlando, Fla., Feb. 16, 1962; d. Ed Revis and Carol Joan Rogers; m. Scott Douglas Pyke; children: Robert Stevin Revis Pyke, Spencer Douglas Pyke, Barrett Harper Pyke. BS in Comm., Trinity Internat. U., Miami; MS in Higher Edn. Adminstrn., Barry U., Miami, post graduate studies in Edn. Preschool tchr. Miami Shores Baptist Ch., 1996—97, fin. asst., 1997—2000; media comm. coord. Archdiocese of Miami, 2000—01; assoc. dir. admission and fin. aid Miami Country Day Sch., Miami, 2001—06; dean of admission Montverde (Fla.) Acad., 2006—. Assoc. editor The Admission Review. Chair Miami Shores Village Fine Arts Commn., Fla., 1997—2002; mem. Philanthropic Educators Orgn., 1999—2002; exec. bd. mem. Shores Performing Arts Theater, Miami Shores, 2002—04; mem. pres. bd. advisors St. Thomas U.; chair Miami Shores Village Mayors Task Force, Fla., 1998—2001. Mem.: Assn. Ind. Sch. Admission Profls., Secondary Sch. Admission Test Bd., Nat. Coun. Measurement in Edn., Nat. Assn. Independent Schs., Am. Ednl. Rsch. Assn. (grad. student coun. camps liaison 2005—), Am. Assn. U. Women, Phi Delta Kappa, Kappa Delta Pi. Republican. Baptist. Avocations: yoga, cooking, reading, boating, snorkeling. Home: 1800 NE 114 St #2005 Miami FL 33181 Office: Miami Country Day Sch 601 NE 107 St Miami FL 33161 E-mail: robin@revispyke.net.

**REVKIN, ANDREW C.,** writer, reporter; married; 2 children. B in Biology, Brown Univ.; M in Journalism, Columbia Univ. Staff writer LA Times; sr. writer Science Digest; sr. editor Discover mag.; reporter New York Times, 1995—. Lectr. on writing and environment; appearances on Today Show, Good Morning America, NPR, CNN; adj. prof. Columbia U. Sch. Journalism, NYC. Author: (books) The Burning Season (Sidney Hillman Foundation Book prize, Robert F. Kennedy Book award, New York Times Notable Book of Yr.), 1990, Global Warming: Understanding the Forecast, 1992. Recipient AAAS Journalism award, 2002, Investigative Reporters & Editors award. Avocations: guitar, songwriting. Office: Environmental Writer New York Times 229 W 43rd St New York NY 10036*

**REVOILE, CHARLES PATRICK,** lawyer; b. Jan. 15, 1934; s. Charles Patrick and Olga Lydia (Zecca) R.; m. Sally Cole Gates, Nov. 8, 1963. BA, U. Md., 1957, LLB, 1960. Bar: Md. 1962, U.S. Dist. Ct. Md. 1962, U.S. Supreme Ct. 1970, U.S. Ct. Claims 1976, U.S. Ct. Appeals (fed. cir.) 1982. Legis. counsel Nat. Canners Assn., Washington, 1960-64; asst. counsel Deco Electronics Inc., Washington, 1964-67; divsn. counsel Westinghouse Electric, Leesburg, Va., 1967-71; v.p., gen. counsel Stanwick Corp., Arlington, Va., 1971-85; sr. v.p., gen. counsel, sec. CACI Internat. Inc., 1985-92, bd. dirs., 1992—, chmn. compensation com., 1995—, exec. com., 1999—, mem. investor rels. com., 2001—, mem. corp. governance com., 2003—. Mem. regional adv. coun. NASD, 1989-92, mem. nominating com., 2004—; lectr., panelist, advisor. Active in Md. Ednl. Found., College Park, 1974-98; assoc. Nat. Symphony Orch. Washington, 1972-93, Smithsonian Instn., 1980-93, Nat. Club Found., 1985-98; lawyer, lobbyist various non-profit orgns., Washington, 1984-98; mem. exec. com. mem. campaign Gallaudet U., 1989-91; chmn. various coms. Kemper Open Championships, 1980-86; exec. com. mem. various coms. Kemper Open Championships. Mem. Md. Bar Assn., Washington Corp. Counsels Assn., Am. Corp. Counsels Assn., Nat. Assn. Corp. Dirs., USGA, Mid. Atlantic Golf Assn. (exec. com. 1989-99, v.p., pres. 1998), Roger Howell Soc. U. Md. Sch. Law (charter), Congl. Country Club (com. chmn. 1966-92, bd. govs. 1987-93, Bethesda, Md.), Ocean Forest Golf Club (Sea Island, Ga.), Sea Island Club (founder), Sea Island Srs. Golf Assn. (pres. 2003). Home: PO Box 31223 Sea Island GA 31561-1223

**REW, KEN E.,** physical education educator, healthcare educator, coach; b. Mt. Pleasant, Iowa, Jan. 4, 1952; s. Orra K. and Norma L. Rew; m. Virginia C. Bender, Aug. 15, 1975; children: Molly E. Rew De Escalera, Bradley K. BS, U. Iowa, Iowa City, 1975. Std. tchg. lic. Iowa. Studyhall supr. and coach Solon Cmty. Schs., Iowa, 1977—78; phys. edn. and health tchr., coach Highland Cmty. Schs., Riverside, Iowa, 1978—. Recruiter host families Katoh Gyoshu Sch., Numazu, Japan, 2000—. Office: Highland Riverside Elem Sch 220 Schnoebelen St Riverside IA 52327 Office Phone: 319-648-2821. E-mail: krew@highland.k12.ia.us.

**REW, LAWRENCE BOYD,** lawyer; b. Eugene, Oreg., June 22, 1936; BA, Whitman Coll., 1958; JD, Willamette U., 1961. Bar: Oreg. 1961. Ptnr., of counsel Corey, Byler, Rew, Lorenzen & Hojem, LLP, Pendleton, Oreg., 1965—2005, ret. 2005. Fellow Am. Bar Found.; mem ABA, Oreg. State Bar Assn. (pres. 2000, Pub. Svc. award 1991, bd. bar examiners 1975-79, bd. govs. 1996-2000). Personal E-mail: lbrew01@yahoo.com.

**REW, WILLIAM EDMUND,** civil engineer; b. Corning, N.Y., Nov. 24, 1923; s. Robert James and Clara (Neal) R.; m. Jean Ella Ohls, Aug. 16, 1947 (dec.); children: Virginia Ann, Robert James, John Edward. BE, Yale U., 1954, M in Engring., 1955. Registered profl. engr., N.Y., Fla., Calif., Ill. Project engr. Texaco & Affiliate, USA and Saudi Arabia, 1955-62; sr. engr. Martin-Marietta Corp., Cape Kennedy, Fla., 1962-63, Chrysler Corp, Cape Kennedy, 1963-65, The Boeing Co., Cape Kennedy, 1965-70; project mgr. Brevard Engring. Co., Cape Canaveral, Fla., 1970-74; city engr. City of Vero

Beach (Fla.), 1974-77; resident engr. Post, Buckley, Schuh & Jernigan, Miami, Fla., 1977-85; mgr. Keith & Schnars, P.A., West Palm Beach, Fla., 1985-90; pvt. practice consulting Lake Placid, Fla., 1990—. Active Rep. Party Highlands County, Fla. 1st lt. U.S. Army, 1942—46, ATO U.S. Army. Scholar of 2d rank, Yale U., 1953, grad. scholar, 1955. Fellow ASCE (chmn. Fla. ann conv. 1971, Engr. of Yr. 1974); mem. NSPE, Soc. Am. Mil. Engrs. (bd. dirs. 1982-83), Fla. Engring Soc. (chpt. pres. 1976), Yale Club, Browning Assn. Club. Episcopalian. Avocations: woodworking, reading. Home: 425 Lake August Dr Lake Placid FL 33852-4031 Mailing: 1308 El Rado St Coral Gables FL 33134 Office Phone: 863-465-3921.

**REWAK, WILLIAM JOHN,** retired academic administrator, clergyman; b. Syracuse, N.Y., Dec. 22, 1933; s. William Alexander and Eldora Venetia (Carroll) R. BA, Gonzaga U., 1957, MA in English, 1958; MA in Theology, Regis Coll., Toronto, Ont., Can., 1965; PhD in English, U. Minn., 1970. Joined S.J., 1951, ordained priest Roman Cath. Ch., 1964. Tchr. English Bellarmine Coll. Prep. Sch., 1958-61; asst. prof. English Santa Clara (Calif.) U., 1970-71, pres., 1976-88; rector Jesuit Community, 1971-76; pres. Spring Hill Coll., Mobile, Ala., 1989-97; ret., 1997. Bd. dirs. Gulf Coast Broadcasting Inc., Badger-Stonewall Ins. Co., Marine Environ. Scis. Consortium. Contbr. articles to theol. and critical jours., poetry, short stories to lit. jours. Bd. dirs. Mobile Bay Area Partnership for Youth, Mercy Med. Ctr.; mem. Ala. Ind. Colls., Coun. for Advancement Pvt. Colls. in Ala.; bd. trustees Loyola U. New Orleans. Mem. MLA, Coll. English Assn., Bienville Club. Democrat. Home and Office: Spring Hill Coll Office of Pres 4000 Dauphin St Mobile AL 36608-1780

**REWCASTLE, NEILL BARRY,** neuropathologist; b. Sunderland, Eng., Dec. 12, 1931; arrived in Can., 1955; s. Albert Alexander and Eva (Coapes) R.; m. Eleanor Elizabeth Barton Boyd, Sept. 27, 1958 (dec. Jan. 1999); 4 children. MB, BChir cum laude, U. St. Andrews, Scotland, 1955; MA, U. Toronto, 1962. Licentiate Med. Coun. Can., 1957; cert. in gen. pathology, 1962, and neuropathology, 1968 Royal Coll. Physicians, Can. Rotating intern Vancouver Gen. Hosp., 1955-56; resident in pathology Shaughnessy Hosp., Vancouver, 1956-57, U. Toronto, Ont., Canada, 1957-60, demonstrator dept. pathology, 1964-65, lectr., acting head divsn. neuropathology, 1965—69, assoc. prof., 1969-70, prof., head divsn. neuropathology, 1970—81; fellow Med. Rsch. Coun. Can., 1960-64; prof., head dept. pathology U. Calgary, Alta., Canada, 1981-91, prof., 1981-2000, prof. emeritus pathology, lab. medicine, clin. neuroscis., 2000—, mem. neurosci. rsch. group, 1982—2003; sr. pathologist Toronto Gen. Hosp., 1970—81. Dir. dept. histopathology Foothills Hosp., Calgary, 1981-91, pathologist, 1981—, cons. neuropathology, 1981—; spl. acad. adv. to dean faculty medicine U. Calgary, 1995-97; presenter in field. Contbr. over 146 articles to profl. jour., chpts. to books. Recipient Queen Elizabeth Silver Jubilee medal, 1977. Fellow: Royal Coll. Physicians (cert. 1968); mem. Can. Assn. Neuropathologists (ret. mem., sec. 1965-69, pres. 1976-79), Am. Assn. Neuropathologists (sr.), Sunshine Coast Power and Sail Squadron (bd. dirs., lt. comdr., exec. officer), Gibsons Curling Club (bd. dirs.) Sunshinre Cost Golf and Country Club. Avocations: gardening, philately, golf, curling. E-mail: rewcastle@telus.net.

**REWOLDT, CHRISTIAN WALTER,** school psychologist, military officer; b. Detroit, Feb. 24, 1958; s. Herbert John Rewoldt and Geraldine Pauline Steffens; m. Noelia Soliz, Aug. 17, 1990; 1 child, Amy Rene. BA, Tex. A&M U., College Station, 1982—85; MA, SW Tex. State U., San Marcos, 1996—99. Nat. cert. sch. psychologist, lic. specialist in sch. psychology Tex. Mil. officer U.S. Army, Fort Bragg, NC, 1985—95; specialist in sch. psychology Del Valle Ind. Sch. Dist., Tex., 1998—2003, Mansfield Ind. Sch. Dist. Mem. So. Poverty Law Ctr., Dem. Nat. Com.; offr. officer Lambda Chi Alpha Frat., Kingsville, Tex., 1984. Capt. U.S. Army, 1979—95. Decorated Nat. Def. Svc. medal., Army Svc. Ribbon, Overseas Ribbon, Airborne Parachutist Badge; recipient Disting. Mil. Grad., Res. Officer Tng. Corps, 1985. Mem.: United Educators Assn., Nat. Assn. Sch. Psychologists, Tex. Assn. Sch. Psychologists (licentiate), Tex. Assn. Spl. Edn. Adminstrs. (assoc.), Lambda Chi Alpha (life). Avocations: musician, sports, travel. Home: 202 Moss Ct Mansfield TX 76063-7588 Office: Mansfield Ind Sch Dist 1016 Magnolia Mansfield TX 76063 Office Phone: 817-229-4328. Office Fax: 817-473-5748. Personal E-mail: crewoldt@netscape.net. Business E-Mail: rewoch@mansfieldisd.org.

**REX, LONNIE ROYCE,** religious organization administrator; b. Caddo, Okla., May 11, 1928; s. Robert Lavern and Lennie Cordy (Gilcrease) R.; m. Betty Louise Sorrells, Apr. 8, 1949; children: Royce DeWayne, Patricia Louise, Debra Kaye. MusB, Oklahoma City U., 1950; DD (hon.), Am. Bible Inst., 1970; LLD (hon.), Wesley Synod, N.Y.C., 1999, Meth. Wesley Synod, Toledo, 1999; LittD, Wesley Synod, 2000. Advt. mgr. Oral Roberts Evang. Assn., Tulsa, 1955-57; bus. mgr. T.L. Osborn Found., Tulsa, 1957-69; gen. mgr. Christian Crusade, Tulsa, 1969-80; sec.-treas. David Livingstone Missionary Found., Tulsa, 1970-80, pres., 1980—. Dep. dir. gen. Internat. Biog. Assn.; bd. dirs. Intra-Ch. Pension Fund, Bethany, Okla.; spkr. internat. confs. Eng., Hungary, Korea, Singapore, Spain, N.Y.C., Congress of Arts and Comms., Oxford U., 1997; invited Pyongyang, North Korea to meet as an NGO with Peace Com. and med. aid, 1996, 97; participant peace conf. Carter Ctr. between North Korea and South Korea, 1997. Author: Never a Child, 1989. Mem. Internat. PHC Loan Fund; bd. dirs. Armand Hammer United World Coll. of Am. West, 1993—; bd. mem. Internat. Humanitarian Centre Russia, Moscow, 2000. Recipient Merit award Korea, 1975, Moran medal Republic of Korea, Humanitarian award Senator Hugh Scott, 1983, Svc. to Mankind award Internat. Biog. Congress, Spain, 1987, Internat. Lions Club award, UN award, medal Gen. Ground Forces USSR, 1990, World Humanitarian Leadership award by M. Susan Savage Mayor of Tulsa, 1998, Roseland Cook Bronze award David Livingstone Found., 1998; knighted in Moscow, 1993; Lonnie Royce Rex Day named in his honor by Gov. Keating of Okla., Jan. 24, 1998. Mem. Knights of Malta (Sword of Svc. 1996), Phi Beta Kappa. Home: 7914 Oxfordshire Dr Spring TX 77379-4668 E-mail: lonnierrex@sbcglobal.net. *In my work among the starving in Ethiopia, I walked into a tent of over 100 mothers, lying on mats, who had given birth during the last three days. It was silent! Morbid silence! That haunting silence lives with me since that moment. I asked why? I was informed the babies did not have the strength to cry. I have given my life to "cry out" for those in need that did not have the strength to "cry".*

**REXFORD, JENNIFER,** communications engineer; BSEE, Princeton U., 1991; MS in Computer Sci. & Engring., U. Mich., 1993, PhD in Computer Sci. & Engring., 1996. Mem. IP network mgmt & performance dept. AT&T Rsch., 1996—. Bd. dirs. Assn. Computing Machinery (ACM) SIGMETRICS, 2003—; mem. tech. adv. bd. Arbor Networks, 2003—; chair Assn. Computing Machinery (ACM) SIGCOMM, 2003—; membership svcs. bd. Assn. Computing Machinery (ACM), 2004—. Contbr. articles to profl. jours. Named one of Top 100 Young Innovators, MIT Tech. Review, 2004. Mem.: IEEE (sr.). Office: AT&T Rsch A139 180 Park Ave Florham Park NJ 07932-0971

**REXNER, ROMULUS,** publishing executive; b. Odessa, Russia, July 16, 1920; came to U.S., 1951; s. Richard Rexner and Nova Norvid; m. Elisabeth Unger, Aug. 22, 1964. BS in Econs. with hons., Univ. London, 1951. Founder, mgr. Pantheon Press, Gen. Enterprises, L.A., 1951-86, Honolulu, 1986—. Author: (book) Planetary Legion, 1961, 4th edit. 2001; pub.: periodical Cosmopolitan Contact, 1962—. Founder Planetary Legion for Peace, 1955. With Brit. Forces WWII. Achievements include patents in field. Office: Pantheon Press Gen Enterprises Planetary Legion PO Box 89300 Honolulu HI 96830-7300

**REY, ANAMARIA,** psychologist; b. La Habana, Cuba; arrived in US, 1960; B in Edn., U. Miami, 1971; M of Edn., U. Fla., 1972; BA in Psychology, Fla. Internat. U., 1989; MS in Clin. Psychology, Nova SE U., 1994, D in Psychology, 1997. Cert. Spanish Second Lang. La. State U., 1979, lic. psychologist 1998. Intern in psychology Citrus Health Network, 1996—97; resident in psychology Citrus Health Network Cmty. Menal Health Ctr., Hialeah, Fla., 1997—98; incl. practice Dade Psychiatric Assocs., Fla., 1998—; psychologist Devel. Evaluation Ctr., Mt. Sinai Med. Ctr., 1998—2001,

Behavorial Medicine-Oncology Hematology Group, Fla., 2001—04, Miami-Date County Pub. Schs., 2004—. Spanish tchr. of non-native spkrs. St. Phillip's Sch., 1990—91; tchg. asst. Nova SE U., 1992—96; adj. instr. St. Thomas U., 1999, Fla. Internat. U., 2002—; presenter in field and conducted numerous workshops in career related subjects. Crisis counselor vol. The Phone Crisis Intervention Line, Baton Rouge, 1974—75; parent counselor vol. Neonatal ICU Women's Hosp., 0194—1985; vol. Miami Mental Health Ctr. Alzheimer Day Treatment Program, 1995; group co-therapist Miami Dade Domestic Violence Program, 1993. Recipient Outstanding Acad. Achievement Psychology award, Fla. Internat. U., JFK Cmty. award. Mem.: APA, Kappa Delta Pi, Phi Kappa Phi, Psi Chi. Achievements include research in children's concept of death and loss; components of effective therapeutic programs for Spanish speaking parents of SED children; Dandy Walker Syndrome.

**REY, MARK E.,** federal agency administrator; b. Canton, Ohio; BS in Wildlife Mgmt., U. Mich., BS in Forestry, MS in Natural Resources Policy and Adminstrn. Staff asst. bur. land mgmt. U.S. Dept. of Interior's, 1974—75; various positions Am. Paper Inst./Nat. Forest Products Assn., 1976—84; v.p. pub. forestry programs Nat. Forest Products Assn., 1984—89; exec. dir. Am. Forest Resource Alliance, 1989—92; v.p. forest resources Am. Forest and Paper Assn., 1992—94; staff mem. U.S. Senate Com. on Energy and Natural Resources, 1995—2001; under sec. for natural resources and environ. USDA, Washington, 2001—.

**REY, ROBERT M.,** plastic surgeon; b. São Paolo, Brazil; arrived in US, 1974; m. Hayley Rey; children: Sydney, Robby. BA in Chemistry, Ariz. State U., 1983; M in Health Policy, Harvard U., 1990; MD, Tufts U. Sch. Medicine, 1990. Diplomate Nat. Bd. Med. Examiners. Resident, gen. surgery Harbor-UCLA Med. Ctr., 1995; resident, plastic surgery U. Tenn. Med. Ctr., 1997; aesthetic and breast reconstruction fellowship Harvard Med. Sch., 1998; private practice Beverly Hills, Calif. Former health policy writer Office of the US Surgeon General. Contbr. articles to med. and plastic surgery jours.; cons. (films) Seven, featured on Dr. 90210, 2004—, featured in CBS, WB, E! Channel, Elle Mag. and fgn. media. Recipient Am. Assn. Clin. Anatomist Student award for original anatomy and biomechanics rsch., Southeastern Soc. Plastic Surgeons Resident's award. Mem.: AMA, SAG. Avocations: Eagle Scout, martial arts. Office: 436 North Bedford Dr Ste 304 Beverly Hills CA 90210 Office Phone: 310-205-3107. Office Fax: 310-205-8822.*

**REYELTS, PAUL C.,** chemical company executive; MBA; Harvard U. V.p. corp. fin. dept. Piper, Jaffray & Hopwood; sr. v.p. fin., CFO Valspar Corp., Mpls. Office: Valspar Corp 1101 Third St South Minneapolis MN 55415

**REYER, STEVEN E.,** engineering educator; s. Elliott and Jean Reyer; m. Linda Philipps, May 21, 1989. BSEE, U. of Wis., Milw., 1972, MSEE, 1973; ABD, U. of Ill., Urbana, 1975; PhD, Marquette U., 1978. Registered profl. engr., Wis. Asst. prof. elec. engring U. Wis., 1978—84; prof. elec. engring. Milw. Sch. Engring., 1984—. Cons. numerous cos. Contbr. articles to tech. publs., photographs to contests (numerous nat. photo contest awards). Recipient univ. fellowship, U. of Ill., 1973—75, F. R. Bacon fellowship, Marquette U., 1977—78, rsch. grant, ANR Pipeline Co., 1988, 1991, 3M Co., 1988, 1990, 1992, 1993, fellow F. R. Bacon fellowship, U. Wis.-Milw., 1972—73. Mem.: ASEE, IEEE (dir. Milw. sect. 1981—84), Mensa, Sigma Xi, Phi Eta Sigma, Phi Kappa Phi, Eta Kappa Nu, Tau Beta Pi. Achievements include development of First FM Stereo Radio Transmitter based on Digital Signal Processing. Avocation: photography. Office: Milw Sch Engring 1025 N Broadway Milwaukee WI 53202 Office Phone: 414-277-7347. E-mail: reyer@msoe.edu.

**REYES, CZARINA SUZANNE,** mathematics educator; d. Suzanne Paulette Reynolds. BA in Math., So. Meth. U., 1998, MA, 2001; attended in Higher Edn., U. N. Tex. Cert. tchr. Tex., 1999. Math. tchr. Creekview HS, Carrollton, Tex., 1999—2000; faculty math. Dallas County C.C. Dist.-Brookhaven Coll., Farmers Branch, Tex., 2000—. Recipient LENs award Focusin Excellence, Brookhaven Coll., 2006. Mem.: AAUW, Tex. C. C. Tchrs. Assn., Math. Assn. Am., Nat. Scholars, Phi Theta Kappa (Outstanding Student Honor Soc. 2004). Office: Brookhaven Coll 3939 Valley View Ln Farmers Branch TX 75244 Office Phone: 972-860-4338. Office Fax: 972-860-4151. Business E-Mail: creyes@dcccd.edu.

**REYES, GEORGE,** information technology executive; BA in acctg., U. South Fla.; MBA, Santa Clara U. Various fin. roles Sun Microsystems Inc., Santa Clara, Calif., 1994—2001; interim CFO ONI Systems, 2002; CFO Google Inc., Mountain View, Calif., 2002—. Dir. Symantec Corp., BEA Systems Inc., Chordiant Software. Office: Google Inc 1600 Amphitheatre Pky Mountain View CA 94043 Office Phone: 650-623-4000. Office Fax: 650-618-1499.

**REYES, GUILLERMO AUGUSTO,** playwright, educator; s. Guillermo Enrique Reyes and Maria Graciela Caceres. MFA, U. Calif., San Diego, 1987—90. Lit. mgr. Bilingual Found. of Arts, LA, 1992—96; head playwriting program Ariz. State U., Tempe, Ariz., 1996—. Author: (plays) Men on the Verge of a His-Panic Breakdown (Ovation award, 1994), A Southern Christmas (Nat. Hispanic Playwrights award, 1997), Men on the Verge of a His-panic Breakdown (NY Outer Critics Cir. award, 1997), Deporting the Divas (Drama-Logue Critics award, 1996), Men on the Verge 2 (Portland Critics award, 2006), Miss Consuelo (Phoenix AriZoni award for original play prodn., 2002), Sunrise at Monticello (Prodn.-Playwrights Theater NJ award, 2005), The Suspects (Prodn.-Guthrie Theater Mpls. award, 2005); artistic dir. Teatro Bravo, Bilingual Theater Phoenix, 2000—06. Recipient Best Prodn. award, AriZoni Theater Arts Orgn. Phoenix, 2002—05; fellow Creative Writing Fellowship, Va. G. Piper Ctr. Creative Writing, 2006; grantee Phoenix Arts Commn. Project grant, Phoenix Arts Commn., 2002—06. Office: Ariz State U Box 872002 Tempe AZ 85287 Home Fax: 480-965-5351; Office Fax: 480-965-5351. Business E-Mail: reyes1@asu.edu.

**REYES, J. CHRISTOPHER,** food products distribution executive; BS in Finance, U. Maryland, 1975. Co-founder, CEO Reyes Holdings, Lake Forest, Ill., 1976—. Bd. dirs. Fortune Brands Inc., Wintrust Financial Corp., 1991—, Allstate Corp., Tribune Co., 2005—. Bd. dirs. Lyric Opera of Chgo., Mus. Sci. and Industry, Northwestern Meml. Found., U. Notre Dame. Mem.: Old Elm, Onwentsia. Office: Reyes Holdings LLC 9500 W Bryn Mawr Ave Ste 700 Rosemont IL 60018 Office Fax: (847) 604-9972.*

**REYES, JOSE,** professional baseball player; b. Villa Gonzalez, Dominican Republic, June 11, 1983; s. Jose Manuel and Rosa Reyes. Shortstop NY Mets, 2003—. Office: New York Mets Shea Stadium 123-01 Roosevelt Ave Flushing NY 11368-1699

**REYES, JOSE OCTAVIO,** food products executive; BSChE, U. Autónoma de Mex.; MBA, Inst. Tech. Superior Studies, Monterrey, Mex. Devel. mgr., strategic planning mgr., corp. devel. asst. dir., mktg. asst. dir. Mex. Divsn. The Coca-Cola Co., 1980—87, region mktg. dir., 1987, brand mgr. Diet Coke and Sprite, 1987—90, divsn. mktg. mgr. Brazil, 1990—93, mktg. and ops. v.p. dep. divsn. pres. Mex. divsn., 1993—96, pres. North Latin Am. Divsn., 1996—2002, pres., COO Coca-Cola Latin Am., corp. exec. v.p., 2002—. Office: The Coca-Cola Co PO Box 1734 Atlanta GA 30301

**REYES, JUDY,** actress; b. NYC, Nov. 5, 1968; m. Edwin M. Figueroa. Founding mem. Labyrinth Theatre Co., NYC. Actor: (films) Jack & His Friends, 1992, Lena's Dreams, 1997, No Exit, 1998, Godzilla, 1998, Bringing Out the Dead, 1999, King of the Jungle, 2000, Home Invaders, 2001, Washington Heights, 2002, King of the Corner, 2004, Dirty, 2005; (TV films) The Prosecutors, 1996, Mind Prey, 1999, WW3, 2001, It's a Very Merry Muppet Christmas Movie, 2002, Our House, 2006; (TV series) Oz, 1999, Scrubs, 2001—; (documentaries) Pieces of Courage: In Search of My Cultural Heroes, 2003; (plays) Some Girls, 2006; exec. prodr.: (films)

Moment to Moment, 2003; actor, co-prodr. (films) Taino, 2001, actor, prodr. Glow Ropes: The Rise & Fall of a Bar Mitzvah Emcee, 2005. Recipient Am. Latin Media Arts (ALMA) award for Outstanding Actress in a TV Series, Nat. Coun. La Raza, 2006.*

**REYES, LUIS A.,** federal agency administrator; BS, U. Puerto Rico, MS in nuclear engring.; grad., Fed. Exec. Inst.; attended, Harvard U. John F. Kennedy Sch. Govt. Lic. Engr. With Argonne Nat. Lab., Experimental Breeder Reactor II facility, Idaho Engring. Lab.; reactor inspector, region II Nuclear Regulatory Commn., Geln Ellyn, Ill., 1978, first sr. resident inspector Ohio, sect. chief, region III, Divsn. of Reactor Projects and Divsn. of Reactor Safety, dep. dir. & dir., Divsn. of Reactor Projects Atlanta, 1986, dep. regional adminstr. region II, 1992, regional adminstr., 1997, exec. dir. ops., 2004—. Special asst. to undersecretary Office of Energy, Sci., and Environment, Dept. of Energy, 2001—02. Recipient Presidential Meritorious Rank Award, 1991, 1999, 2003, 2004. Office: US Nuclear Regulatory Commn One White Flint N 11555 Rockville Pike Rockville MD 20852

**REYES, M. JUDE,** food products distribution executive; Bachelor's in economics, Wofford College, NC. Principal Reyes Holdings LLC, Lake Forest, Ill. Bd. mem., officer Premium Distributors, Va., bd. mem., DC, Chicago Beverage Sys., Harbor Distributing, Zema Foods, Martin Brower Co.; bd. dirs. Building One Svcs. Corp., Nat. Rehabilitation Hosp. Mem.: Miller Brewing Company Distributors Adv. Panel, VA Beer Wholesalers Assn., Nat. Beer Wholesalers Assn., Young President's Orgn.

**REYES, SILVESTRE,** congressman; b. Canutillo, Tex., Nov. 10, 1944; m. Carolina Gaytan; children: Monica, Rebecca, Silvestre Jr. Student, U. Tex., Austin, 1964—65, U. Tex., El Paso, 1965—66; AA, El Paso CC, 1976. Agt. US Immigration and Naturalization Svc. Border Patrol, 1969, asst. regional commr. Dallas, sector chief, 1984-95; mem. US Congress from 16th Tex. Dist., 1997—; mem. armed svcs. com., ranking mem. strategic forces subcommittee, mem. permanent select com. on intelligence, mem. vets. affairs com., founder Missing and Exploited Children's Caucus. Served in U.S. Army, 1966—68, Vietnam. Recipient Moving Forward award, El Paso Hispanic C. of C., Presdl. award, Outstanding Svc., Mex. Am. Bar Assn., Outstanding Leadership award, Hispanic Assn. Colls. and Univs., Disting. Cmty. Health Defender award, Nat. Assn. Cmty. Health Ctr., Chmn.'s award, US Hispanic C. of C., Govt. Bus. Adv. of Yr. award, Pres.'s award, League of United Latin Am. Citizens, Govt. Hispanic Bus. Adv. of Yr. award, Tex. Assn. Mex. Am. Cs. of C., Border Health Hero award, Pan Am. Health Orgn., Susan. G. Hadden Pioneer award, Alliance for Pub. Tech., Nat. Congl. award, Nat. Pks. Conservation Assn., L. Medel Rivers award, Legis. Excellence, Air Force Sgts. Assn., Century Coun. Congl. award, Elected Ofcl. of Yr. award, Rio Grande Coun. Govts. Democrat. Office: US Ho Reps 2433 Rayburn Ho Office Bldg Washington DC 20515 Office Phone: 202-225-4831.*

**REYES, SUSANA,** nuclear engineer; b. Madrid, Spain, June 18, 1974; arrived in US, 1999; d. Eduardo Reyes and Hortensia Suarez. MSci Power Engring., UPM, Madrid, 1998; PhD Indsl. Engring., UNED, Madrid, 2001. Cert. Project Mgmt. and Sys. Engring., UCLA, Calif. 2001. Grad. student term employee LLNL, Livermore, Calif., 1999—2001, nuc. engr., 2001—. Vice-chair, chair elect No. Calif. Sect., Am. Nuc. Soc., Calif., 2004—; exec. com. officer Fusion Energy Divsn., Am. Nuc. Soc., 2002—. Contbr. scientific papers pub. to profl. jour. (Extraordinary Doctorate Award UNED, Madrid, 2001, Best Student Paper, ANS Topical of Fusion Energy Meeting, Pk. City, Utah, 2000). Vol. outreach activities and sci. fairs expand your horizons, llnl's discover sci. Sat. Recipient LLNL PAT/FEP spot award, LLNL PAT directorate, Fusion Energy Program, 2003; scholar Waste Mgmt. summer course, Universidad Internacional Menendez Pelayo, 1998, PhD courses, Ministerio de Educacion y Ciencia de Espana, 1999-2001. Mem.: Spanish Nuc. Soc., Am. Nuc. Soc., Asociacion de Espanoles del Silicon Valley. Achievements include research in Designed new methodology employing a set of state-of-the-art computer codes and data libraries for safety analysis of IFE power plants. Office: Lawrence Livermore Nat Lab 7000 East Ave L-641 Livermore CA 94550 Office Phone: 925-424-5684. Business E-Mail: reyes20@llnl.gov.

**REYES, VICTOR H.,** lawyer; b. Mexico, Apr. 28, 1964; BA Polit. Sci., Loyola Univ., 1987; JD, DePaul Univ., 1990. Bar: Ill. 1990. Asst. to Mayor City of Chgo., 1989—95, dir. Mayor's Off. Intergovernmental Affairs, 1995—2002; shareholder, governmental and adminstrv. law dept. Greenberg Traurig LLP, Chgo., 2002—. Bd. dir. Park Fed. Savings. Bd. dir. Rehabilitation Inst. Chgo.; bd. overseers Chgo-Kent Coll. of Law. Mem.: Ill. Inst. Technology (bd. trustees). Office: Greenberg Traurig LLP Ste 2500 77 W Wacker Dr Chicago IL 60601-1732 Office Phone: 312-456-8400. Office Fax: 312-456-8435. Business E-Mail: reyesv@gtlaw.com.

**REYES-CUBIDES, WILLIAM,** language educator, researcher, writer, actor; b. Bogotá, Colombia, Dec. 21, 1969; arrived in US, 1992; s. Alvaro Reyes and Patricia Cubides. BA, Nat. Pedagogical U., Bogotá, 1990; MA in Applied Linguistics, Nat. U., Bogotá, 1992; postgrad. in PhD program, Boston Coll., 1999—. Fgn. langs. lectr. Goucher Coll., Towson, Md., 1995—96, Towson U., Towson, Md., 1996—99; Romance langs. tchg. fellow Boston Coll., Chestnut Hill, Mass., 1999—; lectr. Spanish and fgn. langs. MIT, 2005—; asst. prof. cultural studies U. Mass., Lowell, 2005—. Editor-in-chief Romance Rev., Boston, 2000—02; conf. dir. Internat. Congress on Romance Studies, Boston, 2000—02. Scriptwriter: pedagogic video Impresiones, 2002. Dir. Colombia's March for Peace, Boston, 1999. Recipient Donald J. White Tchg. Excellence award, Boston, 2003; grantee U.S. Dept. Edn. 2003. Fellow: Internat. Alliance of Tchr.-Scholars; mem.: ACTFL, MLA, L.Am. Studies Assn., Romance Langs. Grad. Assn. (pres. Boston 2002—04). Office: MIT 77 Massachusetts Ave 14N-426 Cambridge MA 02139 Business E-Mail: reyescw@mit.edu.

**REYES ROBBINS, ANN MARIE,** lawyer, researcher, educator, former magistrate judge; b. Los Angeles, Calif., Mar. 9, 1966; d. Raymond Alexander and Flora (Sanchez) Reyes; m. Jeffrey Warren Schroeder, Sept. 20, 1986 (div. July 22, 1997); 1 child, Andrew Nicholas Reyes Schroeder; m. Bruce Anthony Robbins, Nov. 7, 1997. BA in Am. Lit. and Bus. minor with honors, U. So. Calif., LA, 1994; attending, U. So. Calif., 2005—; JD, U. Mich., Ann Arbor, 1998; AA in Social and Behavioral Scis., Mt. San Antonio Coll., Walnut, Calif., 2004, AA in Fine Arts and Humanities, 2004, AA in Lang. Arts and Communication, 2005. Bar: Ind. 1999, US Dist. Ct. (so and no. dists.) Ind. 1999, cert.: Ind. Jud. Ctr. (probation officer) 1998, Ind. (domestic rels. mediator) 1998, Ind. Appellate Ct. (family law specialist) 2002. Edn. track liaison, title IV-E waiver coord. Allen Superior Ct. Family Rels. Divsn., Fort Wayne, Ind., 1998, asst. chief juvenile probation officer, adminstrv. divsn., 1999—99; assoc. atty. Avery & Van Gilder, Fort Wayne, Ind., 1999—2000; assoc. atty., jr. ptnr. Blume Connelly Jordan & Stucky, LLP, Fort Wayne, Ind., 2000—01, ptnr., 2002; magistrate judge Allen Superior Ct. Family Rels. Divsn., Fort Wayne, Ind., 2003; family law specialist Mallor, Clendening, Grodner & Bohrer LLP, Bloomington, Ind., 2003—04; tchr. Elite Edl. Inst., Rowland Heights, Calif., 2004—05; st. pub. adminstrv. analyst, dept. social welfare Children and Families Rsch. Consortium, Inter-U. Consortium Social Work Schs., U. So. Calif., LA, 2006—; rsch. asst., ctr. rsch. crime and social control U. So. Calif., 2006—. Trial atty. Allen County Divsn. Children and Family Svcs., Ft. Wayne, 1999—2000; continuing legal edn. tchr., Ind., 2000—04; gen. counsel Allen County Apptd. Spl. Advs., 2001—02; com. mem. Ind. 3rd Dist. Pro Bono Commn., Fort Wayne, 2002—03; lectr. in field; cons. in field. Latino/Hispanic liaison Allen County Dem. Party, Fort Wayne, Ind., 2001, vice chair, 2002; bd. dirs. Assn. Hispanic Profls. Edn., LA, 1992—95, vice chair fin., 1994—95; v.p. League of United Latin Am. Citizens, Fort Wayne, Ind., 1999—2000; bd. dirs. United Hispanic Am., LA, 1992—95, vice chair fin., 1994—95; v.p. League of United Latin Am. Citizens, Fort Wayne, Ind., 1999—2000; bd. dirs. United Hispanic Am., Fort Wayne, 1999—2001, Ind. Minority Health Coalition, 2001—02, Vol. Lawyers Program, Fort Wayne, 2002—04; pres. Allen County Minority Health Coalition, Fort Wayne, 2001—02; mem. parent adv. com. Diabetech, Inc., Dallas, 2003—. Fellow Kellogg/Bergstom Child Welfare Law Summer Fellow, U. Mich. Law Sch., 1997, Mexican Am. Legal Def. and Edn. Fund, Pub. Interest Law Initiative (PILI), 1997, Hispanic Lawyers Assn., 1997; scholar Juan Luis Tienda scholarship, U. Mich. Law Sch., 1996. Fellow: Ind.

Bar Found.; mem.: Soc. Social Work and Rsch., Coun. Social Work Edn., Nat. Ct. Apptd. Spl. Advs., Nat. Assn. of Counsel for Children, Ind. State Bar Assn. (civil rights of children, Latino affairs, diversity profession coms.), Allen County Bar Assn. (women lawyers sect. co-chair 2000), Hispanic Nat. Bar Assn., U. Mich. Alumni Assn., UCLA Anderson Sch. Mgmt. Riordan Fellows Alumni Assn., U. So. Calif. Mexican Am. Alumni Assn. Office: University Southern California Ctr Research Crime and Social Control AHF B61 University Pk Los Angeles CA 90089-0375 Office Phone: 213-740-4285. Office Fax: 213-740-8077. Personal E-Mail: childlaw@sbcglobal.net. Business E-Mail: reyesrob@usc.edu.

**REY-HERNANDEZ, CESAR A.,** school system administrator; BA, MA Polit Sc. and Internat. Rels., Nat. Autonomous U., Mex., PhD in Sociology. Sec. edn. PR Dept. Edn., San Juan, 2001—. Office: Puerto Rico Dept Edn PO Box 190759 San Juan PR 00919-0759

**REYNA, CLAUDIO,** professional soccer player; b. Springfield, NJ, July 20, 1973; m. Danielle Egan, 1997; 2 children. Student, U. Va. Midfielder Bayer Leverkusen, Germany, 1994—97, VfL Wolfsburg, Germany, 1997—99, Glasgow Rangers, Scotland, 1999—2000, Sunderland FC, England, 2001—03, Manchester City FC, England, 2003—. 109 caps, 8 goals U.S. Nat. Soccer Team, 1994—, capt., 1999—; mem. U.S. World Cup Team, 1994, 98, 2002, 06. Named Nat. H.S. Player of the Yr., Parade Mag., 1989—90, N.J. H.S. Player of the Yr., 1990, Gatorade H.S. Player of the Yr., 1990, Freshman of Yr., Soccer Am., 1991, 3-time first-team All-Am., Nat. Soccer Coaches Assn. Am., 1991—93; recipient Player of Yr. award, Mo. Athletic Club, 1992, 1993. Office: US Soccer Fedn 1801 S Prairie Ave Chicago IL 60616-1319*

**REYNA, MAGDALENA BESSY,** writer; b. San Luis, Santiago, Cuba, July 22, 1942; d. Ruben and Maria de Reyna. BA magna cum laude, Mount Holyoke Coll., 1970; MA, U. Conn., 1972, JD, 1982. Asst. reporter jud. decisions Office of the Reporter of Jud. Decisions, State Conn., Hartford, 1986—2002; freelance writer, 2002—. Former faculty mem. child devel. and family rels., U. Conn., Storrs; former staff mem. New Haven Legal Assistance; freelance translator Spanish-English langs.; invited poet Second Sunken Garden Poetry Festival, Farmington, Conn., 1992. Author: Terrarium, 1975, She Remembers, 1997, (poems) Battlefield of Your Body, 2005, poetry and short stories, —; editor: Taller Literario, 1986—87, El Extra Cultural arts' page El Extra News, 1996—2000, Latin Arte News, 2000—; opinion columnist: Hartford Courant. Founder, facilitator The Poetry Exch.; organizer, prodr. Sisters of the Americas, 1986; adv. bd. mem., tv presenter Adelante; former adv. bd. mem. The Pump House Gallery, City of Hartford Pk. and Recreation Dept., 1994-96; bd. mem. Hartford Stage SueNo Adv. Com., Hartford, 1996, Catalyst Endowment of the Hartford Found. for Pub. Giving, 1998-2003, Conn. Ctr. for the Book, Hartford Pub. Libr., 1998-2003; mentor for poetry winning students Sunken Garden Poetry Festival H.S. Competition, 1995—; mentor for student poets Young Writers' Inst., Hartford, 1995—; master-tchg. artist Conn. Commn. on the Arts, Hartford, 1997—. Named Fgn. fellow, Mt. Holyoke Coll., South Hadley, Mass. and Inst. Internat. Edn., N.Y., 1968—70, UNESCO fellow, U. Conn., 1977, Reginald Smith Cmty.-Lawyer fellow, 1983, Artist fellow in fiction, Conn. Commn. on the Arts, 1990, Latina Citizen of Yr., State of Conn. Commn. Latino and Puerto Rican Affairs, 2001; recipient 1st prize Joseph E. Brodine Poetry Competition, Conn. Poetry Soc., 1996; grantee, Greater Hartford Arts Coun., 1996. Democrat. Avocations: reading, movies, concerts. Office: Latin Arte News PO Box 9341 Bolton CT 06043-9341

**REYNALES, BARBARA WALLACE,** literature educator; b. Wallace, Idaho, Nov. 13, 1927; d. Harold Turk and Irene Leona (Hughes) W.; m. C. H. Reynales. AB in English, U. So. Calif., 1949; MA in English, Calif. State U., Long Beach, 1969. Adj. prof. Long Beach (Calif.) City Coll., 1962-63, 70-71, 74-91, Calif. State U., Long Beach, 1969-76, 89-90. Edit. cons. Nat. Scientific Svcs., Seal Beach, Calif., 1970—. Calif. State U. grantee. Mem. Calif. Tchrs. Assn., Phi Delta Gamma (nat. editor 1978-80), Pi Lambda Theta. Home: PO Box 2547 Seal Beach CA 90740-1547

**REYNIK, ROBERT JOHN,** materials scientist, consultant, science educator; b. Bayonne, N.J., Dec. 25, 1932; m. Georgiana M. Walker, Apr. 12, 1959; children: Michael, Christopher, Jonathan, Katherine, Steven, Kevin. BS in Math. and Physics, U. Detroit, 1956; MSEE, U. Cin., 1960, PhD in Phys. Chemistry, 1963. Rsch. assoc. Sch. Metall. Engring. U. Pa., Phila., 1963-64, asst. prof., 1964-67; assoc. prof. Drexel U., Phila., 1967-70; assoc. dir. engring. materials program NSF, Washington, 1970-71, dir. engring. materials program, 1971-74, dir. metallurgy program, 1974-82, head metallurgy, polymers, ceramics and electronic materials, 1983-90, head office spl. programs in materials, 1990-94, sr. staff scientist divsn. materials rsch. Arlington, Va., 1994-96; exec. sec. and cognizant program dir. US-USSR Internat. Agreement in Sci. and Tech., Washington, 1974-79; NSF liaison rep. Nat. Materials Adv. Bd., Washington, 1985-91; math. and phys. sci. directorate coord. Integration of Rsch. and Edn., 1996-97; sr. scientist Office of Sci. and Tech. Infrastructure, 1997-98, sr. staff scientist divsn. materials rsch., 1998-99, grantsmanship cons., 1999—. Dir. electrometallurgy and materials, corrosion, program US-USSR internat. agreement sci. and tech., 1974-80; mem. First U.S. Metall. Del. People's Republic China, 1978;bd. dirs. 1980-81; vis. prof. materials sci. and engring. U. Pa., 1982-83; tech. coord. Sci. & Tech. Ctrs. in Materials Sci. & Engring., 1990-94; co-chair Fed. Coord. Coun. for Sci., Engring. and Tech. joint com. edn. and tng. Office of Sci. and Tech. Policy, 1992-93; co-chair task group edn. and tng. Aeronautics Materials and mfg. Tech. Working Groups Nat. Sci. and Tech. coun., Office of Vice Pres. of U.S., 1994; tech. mgr. rsch. grants mfg. devel. and mfg. Tech. Reinvestment Project, Fed. Govt. 1994-96 Fellow Am. Soc. Materials Internat. (mem.-at-large materials sci. coun. 1990-96, mem.-at-large materials sci. tech. sector coun. 1993-96, fed. affairs com. 1996-99, gold medal selection com.); mem. AAAS, AIME (chmn. govt. pub. affairs com. 1994-96), Am. Chem. Soc., Am. Assn. Engring. Socs. (honors and awards com.), The Metals, Minerals and Materials Soc. (mem. and chmn. tech. coms., Leadership award 2004), Materials Rsch. Soc., Sigma Xi (past chpt. pres., exec. counselor), Tau Beta Pi. Fax: 856-428-2186. E-mail: r.reynik@worldnet.att.net.

**REYNOLDS, ALBERT BARNETT,** nuclear engineer, educator; b. Lebanon, Tenn., Feb. 1, 1931; s. George Lazenby and Marion (Barnett) R.; m. Helen Buck, Sept. 6, 1954; children— Albert Jr., Charlotte, Marion Student, U. of South, 1948-51; S.B. in Physics, MIT, 1953, S.M. in Nuclear Engring., 1955, Sc.D. in Chem. Engring., 1959. Physicist-mgr. Gen. Electric Co., San Jose, Calif., 1959-68; prof. nuclear engring. U. Va., Charlottesville, 1968-96, chmn. dept. nuclear engring. and engring. physics, 1991-92, prof. emeritus, 1996—. Cons. NRC, Washington, 1970-84, U.S. Dept. Energy, 1987-89 Author: Bluebells and Nuclear Energy, 1996; co-author: Fast Breeder Reactors, 1981; contbr. numerous articles to profl. jours. Fellow Am. Nuclear Soc. (exec. com. div. nuclear reactor safety 1980-83, chair Va. sect. 1986-87); mem. ASME, IEEE, Am. Soc. Engring. Edn., Sigma Xi, Tau Beta Pi Achievements include research in liquid metal reactor safety, electric cable aging. Home: 2228 Shepherds Ridge Rd Charlottesville VA 22901-0674 Personal E-Mail: hareyn@aol.com.

**REYNOLDS, BARBARA C.,** retired mental health educator, dean; b. Syracuse, N.Y. d. Robert J. Clark; m. George L. Reynolds, June 9, 1962 (dec.); children: George L. III, Katherine C.; m. George Barnard, Apr. 17, 2004. BSN, Syracuse U., 1952; MPH, U. Minn., 1968, PhD, 1990. Asst. prof. U. Cin., 1968-75; ind. human resources cons. Cin., 1975-76; asst. prof. sch. pub. health U. Minn., 1976-82; asst. prof. Vanderbilt U., Nashville, 1986-90, N.Y. Med. Ctr. Sch. Nursing, 1964—69, Coll. Mt. St. Joseph, 1973—75; dean sch. nursing Tenn. Tech. U., Cookeville, 1991-98. Contbr. articles to profl. jours. Mem. Leadership Putnam Alumni Assn. (pres. 1995-96), Rotary (Cookeville chpt., bd. dirs.), Sigma Theta Tau, Phi Kappa Phi. Home: 1750 Heathrow Dr Cookeville TN 38506

**REYNOLDS, BRUCE GRAHLMANN,** physicist; b. Fort Myers, Fla., Jan. 16, 1937; s. Alva August and Ann (Frantz) R.; m. Dee Ring, Dec. 19, 1961; children: Bruce Jr., Jennifer. BS in Physics, Fla. State U., 1961, MS in Physics, 1963, PhD in Physics, 1966. Asst. prof. physics Fla. State U., Tallahassee, 1966-68, Ohio U., Athens, 1968-71; staff physicist Martin Marietta Corp., Orlando, 1971-74, Argonne (Ill.) Nat. Lab., 1974-81; staff scientist Bell Telephone Labs., Napierville, Ill., 1980-81; CEO Omega Svcs., Mount Dora, Fla., 1981—. Contbr. articles to profl. jours. Mem. Am. Phys. Soc., Sigma Pi Sigma. Home: 3521 Calgary Ln Mount Dora FL 32757-2309 Office: Omega Svcs PO Box 1231 Tavares FL 32778-1231 Office Phone: 352-383-7571. Personal E-Mail: bgromega@cs.com.

**REYNOLDS, BURT,** actor, film director; b. Waycross, Ga., Feb. 11, 1936; s. Burt R.; m. Judy Carne (div. 1965); m. Loni Anderson, Apr. 29, 1988 (div. 1994). Ed., Fla. State U., Palm Beach Jr. Coll. Owner ranch, Jupiter, Fla. Actor numerous stage prodns. including The Rainmaker; movie appearances include: Angel Baby, 1961, Armored Command, 1961, Operation CIA, 1965, Navajo Joe, 1967, Impasse, 1969, 100 Rifles, 1969, Sam Whiskey, 1969, Skullduggery, 1970, Shark, 1970, Deliverance, 1972, Fuzz, 1972, Everything You've Always Wanted to Know about Sex But Were Afraid to Ask, 1972, Shamus, 1973, The Man Who Loved Cat Dancing, 1973, White Lightning, 1973, The Longest Yard, 1974, At Long Last Love, 1975, W.W. and the Dixie Dance Kings, 1975, Hustle, 1975, Lucky Lady, 1975, Silent Movie, 1976, Nickelodeon, 1976, Smokey and the Bandit, 1977, Semi-Tough, 1977, Hooper, 1978, Starting Over, 1979, Rough Cut, 1980, Smokey and the Bandit II, 1980, Cannonball Run, 1981, Paternity, 1981, The Best Little Whorehouse in Texas, 1982, Best Friends, 1982, Stroker Ace, 1983, The Man Who Loved Women, 1983, City Heat, 1984, Cannonball Run II, 1984, Stick, 1985, Uphill All The Way, 1986, Rent A Cop, 1987, Heat, 1987, Malone, 1987, Switching Channels, 1988, Physical Evidence, 1989, Breaking In, 1989, Modern Love, 1990, Cop and a Half, 1993, also voice in All Dogs Go To Heaven, 1989, The Maddening, 1996, Striptease, 1996, Ravin, 1996, Mad Dog Time, 1996, Frankenstein and Me, 1996, Citizen Ruth, 1996, Meet Wally Sparks, 1997, Crazy Six, 1997, Boogie Nights, 1997, Raven, 1997, Waterproof, 1998, Mystery Alaska, 1998, The Hunter's Moon, 1998, Without a Paddle, 2004, The Librarians, 2004, Grilled, 2005, Forget About It, 2005, The Longest Yard, 2005, The Dukes of Hazzard, 2005; dir., actor: Gator, 1976, The End, 1978, Sharkey's Machine, 1981; TV appearances include: M Squad, 1959, Alfred Hitchcock Presents, 1960, Zane Grey Theater, 1961, Route 66, 1962, Perry Mason, 1962, The Twilight Zone, 1963, Branded, 1965, Flipper, 1965, Twelve O'Clock High, 1965, The Carol Burnett Show, 1967, The FBI, 1968, Love American Style, 1970, The Golden Girls, 1986, Dolly, 1987, Beverly Hills, 90210, 1993, The Larry Sanders Show, 1993, Hope & Gloria, 1995, Cybill, 1995, (voice) King of the Hill, 1997, The X Files, 2002, Hollywood Squares, 2002, Ed, 2003, Dinner for Five, 2004, The King of Queens, 2005; regular appearances on Gunsmoke, 1962-65; star series Hawk, 1966, Dan August, 1970-71, B.L. Stryker, 1989, ABC Saturday Mystery Movie, 1988, Evening Shade, 1990-94, (TV movie) The Cherokee Kid, 1996. Recipient Emmy award as Outstanding Lead Actor in a Comedy Series ("Evening Shade") Nat. Acad. TV Arts and Scis., 1991. Mem. Dirs. Guild Am. Office: Jeffrey Lane & Assocs 8380 Melrose Ave Ste 206 Los Angeles CA 90069-5498

**REYNOLDS, C. LEWIS, JR.,** materials scientist, educator; b. Roanoke, Va., Dec. 16, 1948; s. Claude Lewis and Lois Anne Reynolds; m. Judith Ann Grenko, May 11, 2002; children: Karen Marie, Brian Lewis, Kristin Marie. BS, Va. Mil. Inst., Lexington, Va., 1970; MS, PhD, U. Va., Charlottesville, Va., 1974. Sr. scientist U. Va., Charlottesville, 1974—75; rsch. assoc. physics U. Ill., Urbana, Ill., 1975—77; sr. project engr. Union Carbide Corp., Indpls., 1977—80; disting. mem. tech. staff AT&T Bell Labs., Reading, Pa., 1980—92, disting. mem. tech. staff Agere/Lucent Breinigsville, Pa., 1992—2002; rsch. prof. N.C. State U., Raleigh, NC, 2003—, tchg. asst. prof., 2004—. Contbr. more than 120 articles to profl. jours. Mem.: IEEE, Am. Assn. Physics Tchrs., Materials Rsch. Soc., Am. Phys. Soc., Sigma Xi. Independent. Methodist. Achievements include 8 patents in field. Avocations: reading, running, hiking. Office: NC State Univ Dept Materials Sci Engring 911 Partners Way Raleigh NC 27695-7907 Office Phone: 919-515-7623. Home Fax: 919-515-7724; Office Fax: 019-515-7724. Business E-Mail: lew_reynolds@ncsu.edu.

**REYNOLDS, CLARK WINTON,** economist, educator; b. Chgo., Mar. 13, 1934; m. Nydia O'Connor Viales; children: Rebecca, C. Winton III, Matthew, Camila. AB, Claremont (Calif.) Men's Coll., 1956; student, MIT, 1956-57, 58; student divinity sch., Harvard U., 1957-58; MA, U. Calif., Berkeley, 1961, PhD in Econs., 1962. Asst. prof. Occidental Coll., L.A., 1961-62; from asst. to assoc. prof. dept. edn. and econ. growth Yale U., New Haven, 1962-67; sr. fellow The Brookings Inst., Washington, 1975-76; prof. econs., prin. investigator, founding dir. Americas program Stanford (Calif.) U., prof. emeritus econs., 1996—. Vis. prof. Nat. U. Mex., Chapingo, 1966, El Colegio de Mex., Mexico City, 1964, 65, 79, Hopkins-Nanjing Ctr. for Chinese and Am. Studies, Nanjing, China, 1999-2002, China Europe Internat. Bus. Sch., Shanghai, 2002, 03; vis. lectr. in econs. Stockholm U. Econs., 1968; fellow St. Antony's Coll., Oxford, 1975; vis. rsch. scholar Internat. Inst. for Applied Systems Analysis, Laxenburg, Austria, 1978; Fulbright chair in internat. econs. U. Viterbo, Italy, 2001. Author: The Mexican Economy, 1970, The New Reorganization: How Globalization Reorders the Three Worlds of Development, 2006; co-author: Essays on the Chilean Economy, 1965, (with C. Tello) U.S.-Mexican Relations: Economic and Social Aspects, Las Relaciones Mexico Estados Unidos, 1983, Dynamics of North American Trade, 1991, North American Labor Market Interdependence, 1992, Open Regionalism in the Andes, 1996, The New Regionalism: How Globalization Reorders the Three Worlds of Development, 2004. Founding dir. Monticello West Found., 1980-2003. Woodrow Wilson Found. fellow, 1956-57, Rockefeller Found. fellow, 1957-58, Doherty Found. fellow, 1960-61, Inst. Internat. Studies fellow Stanford U., 1990-2000; grantee Social Sci. Rsch. Coun., Ford Found., Hewlett Found., Rockefeller Found., Mellon Found., MacArthur Found., Tinker Found. Mem. Am. Econ. Assn. E-mail: reynolds@stanford.edu.

**REYNOLDS, CRAIG W.,** research scientist; PhD. Dir. office sci. ops. Nat. Cancer Inst.; project officer SAIC Frederick, Inc., Data Mgmt. Svcs. Inc., Wilson Info. Svcs. Corp.; assoc. dir. Nat. Cancer Inst. at Frederick, Frederick, Md., 2002—. With NCI-Frederick's ednl. outreach program. Achievements include research in the development and production of vaccines for treatment of patients with leukemia and myeloma. Office: NCI-Frederick Bldg 427 Rm 1 PO Box B Frederick MD 21702-1201 Business E-Mail: reynoldsc@ncifcrf.gov.*

**REYNOLDS, DAVID SPENCER,** humanities educator, writer; b. Providence, Aug. 30, 1948; s. Paul Ripley and Adelaide (Koch) R.; m. Suzanne Nalbantian, July 23, 1983; 1 child, Aline Elizabeth. BA, Amherst (Mass.) Coll., 1970; PhD, U. Calif., Berkeley, 1979. Asst. prof. Northwestern U., Evanston, Ill., 1980-83; vis. prof. Barnard Coll., N.Y.C., 1983-84; assoc. prof. Rutgers U., Camden, N.J., 1986-89; prof. Dept. English Baruch Coll. and Grad. Sch. CUNY, N.Y.C., 1996-99, disting. prof. dept. of English, 1996—. Author: Faith in Fiction: The Emergence of Religious Literature in America, 1981, Beneath the American Renaissance: The Subversive Imagination in the Age of Emerson and Melville, 1988 (Christian Gauss award 1988), Walt Whitman's America: A Cultural Biography, 1995 (Bancroft award 1996), A Historical Guide to Walt Whitman, 1999, Walt Whitman, 2005, John Brown, Abolitionist, 2005, The Man Who Killed Slavery, Sparked The Civil War, and Seeded Civil Rights, 2005. Recipient Christian Gauss award Phi Beta Kappa, Washington, 1988, Bancroft award Columbia U., N.Y.C., 1996, Ambassador Book award English-Speaking Union, N.Y.C., 1996. Fellow: Am. Antiquarian Soc., Soc. Am. Historians. Avocations: musical performance (singing, playing guitar and piano), tennis, swimming. Office: English Dept Baruch Coll 17 Lexington Ave New York NY 10010-5518 Office Phone: 646-312-3942. E-mail: rey.sn@juno.com.

**REYNOLDS, DEBBIE (MARY FRANCES REYNOLDS),** actress; b. El Paso, Tex., Apr. 1, 1932; m. Eddie Fisher, Sept. 26, 1955 (div. 1959); children— Carrie, Todd; m. Harry Karl, Nov., 1960 (div. 1973); m. Richard Hamlett (div. May 1996). Active high sch. plays; screen debut Daughter of Rosie O'Grady; motion pictures include: June Bride, 1948, The Daughter of Rosie O'Grady, 1950, Three Little Words, 1950, Two Weeks With Love, 1950, Mr. Imperium, 1951, Singin' in the Rain, 1952, Skirts Ahoy!, 1952, I Love Melvin, 1953, The Affairs of Dobie Gillis, 1953, Give a Girl a Break, 1953, Susan Slept Here, 1954, Athena, 1954, Hit the Deck, 1955, The Tender Trap, 1955, The Catered Affair, 1956, Bundle of Joy, 1956, Tammy and the Bachelor, 1957, This Happy Feeling, 1958, The Mating Game, 1959, Say One For Me, 1959, It Started With a Kiss, 1959, The Gazebo, 1959, The Rat Race, 1960, Pepe, 1960, The Pleasure of His Company, 1961, The Second Time Around, 1961, How the West Was Won, 1962, My Six Loves, 1963, Mary, Mary, 1963, The Unsinkable Molly Brown, 1964, Goodbye Charlie, 1964, The Singing Nun, 1966, Divorce American Style, 1967, How Sweet It Is!, 1968, What's the Matter with Helen?, 1971, Charlotte's Web, (voice only) 1973, That's Entertainment!, 1974, The Bodyguard, 1992, Heaven and Earth, 1993, (with Albert Brooks) Mother, 1996, That's Entertainment III, 1994, In & Out, 1996, Zack and Reba, 1998; star TV program The Debbie Reynolds Show, 1969; star Broadway show Irene, 1973-74, Annie Get Your Gun, Los Angeles, San Francisco, 1977, Woman of the Year, 1984, The Unsinkable Molly Brown, 1989-90 (nat. tour); author: If I Knew Then, 1963, Debbie-My Life, 1988; creator exercise video Do It Debbie's Way, 1984; recurring role (TV series) Will and Grace; actress (TV movies) Perry Mason, 1989, Battling for Babies, 1991, Halloweentown, 1998, The Christmas Wish, 1998, A Gift of Love, 1999 (Emmy nominee), Virtual Mom, 1999, These Old Broads, 2001, Return to Halloweentown, 2001, Connie and Carla, 2003, Halloweentown High, 2004. Named Miss Burbank, 1948 Office: Debbie Reynolds Studios care Margie Duncan 6514 Lankershim Blvd North Hollywood CA 91606-2409 Office Phone: 818-985-3193.

**REYNOLDS, DEVALYN L.,** mathematician, educator; b. Tenn. d. Larry and Emma Reynolds. BS in Math., U. Tenn., Martin, 2003. Tchg. asst., tutor math lab. U. Tenn., 2001—03; instr. math. Dyersburg State C.C., 2003—. Mem.: Nat. Assn. Devel. Edn. Avocations: travel, sports.

**REYNOLDS, DONALD MARTIN,** art historian, foundation administrator, educator; b. Kansas City, Mo., Jan. 11, 1931; s. James Martin and Mary Helen (Hughes) Reynolds; m. Nancy Zlobik, June 5, 1970. Student, Amarillo Coll., 1949-51; BA, Assumption Sem., San Antonio, 1955, Columbia U., 1968, MA, 1970, PhD, 1975. Announcer Sta. KGNC Radio/TV, Amarillo, Tex., 1949-51; account exec. Monte Rosenwald & Assocs., Amarillo, 1957-59; copy writer, account rep., account supr. J. Walter Thompson, N.Y.C., C.Am., 1959-61; mgr. Ctrl. Am., Young & Rubicam Advt., N.Y.C., Panama, 1961-62; advt. mgr., mktg. dir. Colgate-Palmolive Co. Western Hemisphere Divsn., 1962-64; founder, dir. Image, Internat. Mktg. Agy., N.Y.C., 1964-66; mus. educator in charge Dept. Pub. Edn. Met. Mus. Art, 1977-79; curator pks. Dept. Pks. and Recreation, N.Y.C., 1986-88; founder, coord. Ann. Symposium Pub. Monuments, N.Y.C., 1991—; founder, dir. Monuments Conservancy, Inc., N.Y.C., 1992—. Adj. prof. art history Columbia U., NYC, 1970—, Fairfield (Conn.) U., 1981—; adj. asst. prof. Hunter Coll., 1972—81; asst. prof. Coll. Mt. St. Vincent, 1973—77, Manhattan Coll., 1973—77; cons. Corps of Discovery monument Kemper Found., Kansas City, Mo., 2000; designer sculpture program Our Mother of Africa Chapel, Nat. Shrine of the Immaculate Conception, Nat. Black Cath. Congress, Washington, 2001. Author: (book) The Ideal Sculpture of Hiram Powers, 1977, The Architecture of New York City: Histories and Views of Important Structures, Sites, and Symbols, 1984, The Architecture of New York City: Histories and Views of Important Structures, Sites, and Symbols, rev. edit., 1994, Nineteenth-Century Art, 1985, Manhattan Architecture, 1988, Monuments and Masterpieces: Histories and Views of Public Sculpture in New York City, 1988, Nineteenth Century Architecture, 1992, Masters of American Sculpture, The Figurative Tradition from American Renaissance to the Millennium, 1993; editor, compiler: book The Impact of Non-European Civilizations on the Art of the West: Selected Lectures of Rudolf Wittkower, 1989; co-author: MacMillan Ency. Archs., 1982. With U.S. Army, 1952—61. Mem.: Authors Guild, Coll. Art Assn., Nat. Sculpture Soc.

**REYNOLDS, DORIS ELIZABETH,** management consultant, poet; b. Nashville, Apr. 16, 1944; children: James Jr., Tony Antonio. BA, Coby Coll., 1990; cert., U. Tenn., Nashville, 2000. Cert. med. terminologist St. Thomas Hosp. Edn. Mgmt. supr. St. Thomas Hosp., Nashville, 1979—90, patient transfer liaison, 1985—90, supr., 1972, 1976. Spkr. in field of people mgmt. Author (under the pseudonym Dynasty): (poetry) Internat. Soc. Poets, 2003 (Cup, 2003). Recipient Cert. of Achievement, Tenn. Hosp. Assn., 1978, George W. Gore honor for outstanding scholarship and acad. excellence, Tenn. State U., 2002. Mem.: Internat. Soc. Poets. Home: 2006 15th Ave N Nashville TN 37208

**REYNOLDS, EDGAR L.,** telecommunications industry executive; b. Ala. BS in Elec. Engring., Auburn U.; MBA, U. Ala. Pres. BellSouth Wireless, Inc., BellSouth Mobility DCS, Am. Cellular Comm. Corp., BellSouth Mobility; pres., network opers. Cingular Wireless, Atlanta, 2001—. Office: Cingular Wireless Glenridge Highlands Two 5655 Glenridge Connector Atlanta GA 30342

**REYNOLDS, EDWIN WILFRED, JR.,** retired secondary education educator; b. Englewood, N.J., Mar. 23, 1937; s. Edwin W. and Ellen H. (Hueber) R.; m. Sharon Policastro, Feb. 12, 1983, BA cum laude, Fairleigh Dickinson U, 1961, MA magna cum laude, 1966; postgrad., NYU, 1964-65, Seton Hall U., 1970-71, Montclair State Coll., 1972-73. Cert. social studies tchr., supr., tchr. psychology, N.J. Supr. installation Western Electric Co., N.Y.C., 1961-65; tchr. social studies Teaneck (N.J.) High Sch., 1965-92, chmn. dept. social studies, 1968-71; supr. social studies Teaneck Secondary Schs., 1971-80, supr. grades K-12, 1980-92, supr. bus. edn. grades 7-12, 1984-92, ret., 1992. Pres. bd. dirs. Global Learning, Inc., 1992-97; sr. state cons. in Holocaust Edn., N.J.; curriculum coord. Ctr. for Holocaust/Genocide Studies, Ramapo Coll.; guest lectr. Kean Coll.; coord. M.A.T. program Fairleigh Dickinson U., 1969-71; mem. planning com. N.E. Regional Social Studies Conf., mem. steering com. Mid-Atlantic Conf.; mem. N.J. Dept. Edn. Social Studies Adv. Com., N.J. Gov.'s Adv. Coun. for Holocaust Edn. in the Pub. Schs.; cons. world history Scott Foresman Pub. Co. Author curriculum devel. and learning guides, 1973-92; co-editor: Holocaust and Genocide: A Search for Conscience. V.p., newsletter editor Pike County Hist. Soc.; elder Presbyn. Ch. U.S. With USN, 1955-57. Recipient Human Rights Award Temple Beth Tikvah, 1985, Brotherhood Award B'nai B'rith No. and Pascack Valleys, 1986, Daniel Roselle Lectr. award Mid. States Coun. for Social Studies, 1988. Mem. ASCD, Nat. Coun. for Social Studies (former bd. dirs.), N.J. Coun. for Social Studies (bd. dirs., past pres.), Greater Bergen County (N.J.) Coun. for Social Studies (bd. dirs., past pres.), Nat. Social Studies Suprs. Assn. (bd. dirs., past pres.), Assn. Ednl. Suprs. (bd. dirs., past pres.), Am. Hist. Assn., Pike County Hist. Soc. (pres. 1998-99), Phi Delta Kappa, Phi Omega Epsilon. Home: PO Box 626 Milford PA 18337-0626

**REYNOLDS, ERNEST WEST,** retired internist, educator; b. Bristow, Okla., May 11, 1920; s. Ernest West and Florence (Brown) R. BS, U. Okla., 1942, MD, 1946, MS, 1952. Diplomate: Am. Bd. Internal Medicine. Intern Boston City Hosp., 1946-47; resident Grady Meml. Hosp., Atlanta, 1949-50; practice medicine Tulsa, Okla., 1953-54; prof. medicine U Mich., 1965-72; prof. medicine, dir. cardiology U. Wis., 1972-90, prof. emeritus, 1991—. Dir. Kellogg Found. Comprehensive Coronary Care Project, 1967-72; chmn. NIH Cardiovascular Study Sect. A, 1972-73 Mem. editorial bd.: Am. Heart Jour; Contbr. articles to profl. jours. Served to capt. AUS, 1947-49. Mem. Am. Heart Assn. (fellow coun. clin. cardiology), Ctrl. Soc. Clin. Rsch. Home: 17 Red Maple Trl Madison WI 53717-1515 Personal E-Mail: ernest_reynolds@yahoo.com. *In the academic environment, research oriented toward the solution of human problems is more productive in career* *advancement than the pursuit of applications of new technology. In the private sector applied research which solves real problems rather than copies or improves existing technology is met with surprising sales success and few failures.*

**REYNOLDS, FRANK MILLER,** retired government agency administrator; b. Tulsa, Jan. 8, 1917; s. Frank Miller and Grace (Shields) R.; m. Barbara G. MacWilliams, Dec. 7, 1946; children: Susan G., Ellen M., Frank M. AB, LL.B., U. Okla., 1939; LL.M., George Washington U., 1942; BS, Georgetown Sch. Fgn. Service, 1946. Bar: Okla. 1940. Mem. firm Flippo & Reynolds, Tulsa, 1940; elec. engr. Bur. Ships, Dept. of Navy, 1942-43; with Office Gen. Counsel, Dept. of Navy, 1946; chief negotiator, dep. dir. contract div. Office Naval Research, 1947-54; dep. dir., dir. resources div. Office Asst. Sec. Def., 1954-57; asst. sec. Inst. for Defense Analyses, 1957-61; sec., treas. Logistics Management Inst., Washington, 1961-65, v.p., 1966-76; dir. adminstrv. affairs Uniformed Services U. Health Scis., Bethesda, Md., 1976-78, dir. resource mgmt., 1978-82, exec. sec. bd. regents, 1978-83; dir. patient relations Sibley Meml. Hosp., 1983-84, cons., 1984-87. Professorial lectr. mgmt. research George Washington U. Sch. Engring., 1956—; cons. Nat. Exec. Service Corps., United Srs. Health Coop., 1984—. Served with radio divsn. Naval Research Lab., 1944-46. Mem. Okla. Bar Assn., Congl. Country Club, Delta Upsilon. Personal E-mail: frank17re@verizon.net.

**REYNOLDS, FREDRIC G.,** broadcast executive; b. Miami, Fla. married; 4 children. BBA in Fin., U. Miami, 1972. CPA. Tax cons., staff auditor Touche Ross & Co., from 1972, prin.; v.p. fin. Burger King Internat. divsn. Pillsbury Co.; various positions to sr. v.p. and CFO Frito-Lay unit PepsiCo Foods Internat., 1981-94, CFO KFC, Pepsi-Cola Internat., Pizza Hut units; exec. v.p., CFO, Westinghouse Elec. Corp., 1994-96; CFO, CBS Inc., N.Y.C., 1996—97; exec. v.p., CFO CBS Corp., N.Y.C., 1997-2000, 2005—, Viacom, N.Y.C., 2000—01; pres., CEO Viacom Television Stations Group, 2001—05; pres., COO CFO Evercore Partners Inc., 2005.

**REYNOLDS, GEORGE ANTHONY, JR.,** engineering executive; b. Columbia, S.C., May 5, 1961; s., George Anthony and Flora Mae (La Coste) R.; m. Katherine Alison Albea, Apr. 14, 1984; children: Amanda Kate, William Anthony. BSME, Clemson U., 1983; postgrad., U. Ala., Huntsville, 1985. Design engr. Motorola, Plantation, Fla., 1983-85; sr. engr. Chrysler, Huntsville, Ala., 1985-88; prin. engr. NCR, Liberty, S.C., 1988-91, project leader, 1991-94; mgr. mech. engring. Sensormatic Electronics, Boca Raton, Fla., 1994-96, dir. product engring., 1996-98, dir. active products, 1998-2000, v.p. hard tag and product line engring., 2000—02; v.p. electronic article surveillance Tyco Internat., Boca Raton, Fla., 2002, v.p. radio frequency identification, 2002—05; v.p. worldwide sales and mktg., radio frequency identification Avery Dennison, Atlanta and Clinton, SC, 2006—. Mem. editl. quality audit panel Electronic Packaging & Prodn. Mag., N.Y.C., 1992. Advisor Clemson U. Mech. Engring. Endowment Fund; elder, mem. edul. dir. search com., chair Christian edn. com., nominating com., chair stewardship campaign 1st Presbyn. Ch., Delray Beach, Fla.; pres. Seagate Neighborhood Assn., 1996-97; team mgr. Caloosa Park Girls Fast Pitch Softball League.; mem. adv. bd. ID World, Rome. Italy, 2005. Finalist S. Fla. Up and Comers award, 1997. Mem. ASME (life), NRA (life; Legion of Honor), Jack E. Pro/Engr. User Group (pres. 1992-93), S. Fla. Clemson Alumni Club, Nature Conservancy, Nat. Wildlife Fedn., Ducks Unltd., Fla. Sheriff's Assn. (life), Fla. Wildlife Fedn., Billfish Found., Tau Beta Pi, Phi Kappa Phi, Alpha Tau Omega (alumni adv. bd. Eta Pi chpt. 1993-94). Republican. Presbyterian. Avocations: genealogy, hunting, fishing. Office: Avery Dennison RFID Co Atlanta Tech Ctr 4350 Avery Dr Flowery Branch GA 30542 Office Phone: 770-967-5750. Business E-Mail: george.a.reynolds@excite.com.

**REYNOLDS, GLENN HARLAN,** law educator; b. Birmingham, Ala., Aug. 27, 1960; s. Charles Harlan Reynolds and Glenda Lorraine (Teal) Childress; m. Helen S. BA, U. Tenn., 1982; JD, Yale U., 1985. Bar: Tenn. 1985, D.C. 1986. Law clk. U.S. Ct. Appeals, Nashville, 1985-86; assoc. Dewey, Ballantine, Bushby, Palmer & Wood, Washington, 1986-89; assoc. prof. law U. Tenn., Knoxville, 1989-96, prof., 1996—. Author: Outer Space: Problems of Law and Policy, 1989, 97, The Appearance of Impropriety: How the Ethics Wars Have Undermined American Government, Business and Society, 1997; co-author with Peter W. Morgan, An Army of Davis:How Markets and Technology Empower Ordinary People to Beat Big Media, Big Government, Business and Society, 1997; supervising exec. editor, Pajamas Media; contbg. editor, TechCentralStation.com; maintains blog site, Instapundit.com; co-founder (record co.) WonderDog Records. Recipient Outstanding Svc. award Space Cause, Washington, 1990; nominee WIRED mag. RAVE award, 2005. Mem. AAAS, Nat. Space Soc. (chair legis. com. 1989-93, CEO 1994-95, Space Pioneer award 1991). Avocation: music. Office: U Tenn 1505 Cumberland Ave Knoxville TN 37916-3199*

**REYNOLDS, HELEN ELIZABETH,** management consultant; b. Minerva, N.Y., Aug. 30, 1925; d. Henry James and Margurite Catherine (Gallagher) McNally; m. Theodore Laurence Reynolds, Feb. 27, 1948; children: Laurence McBride, David Scott, William Herbert. BA, SUNY, Albany, 1967; MA, Union Coll., Schenectady, N.Y., 1971. Cert. realtor Realtors Inst., N.Y. Owner, mgr. Schafer Studio, Schenectady, 1970—73; co-owner, v.p. Reynolds Chalmers Inc., Schenectady, 1971—97; program coord. Schenectady County, 1980—81; adminstr. Wellspring House Albany, NY, 1981—94; pres. HR Mgmt. Cons., Port Charlotte, Fla., 1994—2002; ret. Cons., examiner N.Y. State Civil Svc., Albany, 1971—81; mem. adv. com. SBA, Washington, 1978—80. Planning bd. Town of Niskayuna, NY, 1977—81, town councilwoman, 1986—94; co-chair Great N.E. Festival Mohawk River, 1989—90; bd. dirs. HAVEN, Schenectady YWCA; mem. N.Y. State Commn. Capital Region, 1994—98, Acad. Women Achievement, Schenectady, 1994; pres. Photo Arts Group Charlotte County, 1998—2003, Buena Vista Property Owners Assn., Port Charlotte, 1998—2003; bd. mem. Charlotte Symphony Orch. Named Woman Vision, 1986—87, Today's Woman, Schenectady YWCA, 1987. Mem.: Assn. Adminstrs. Ind. Housing, Charlotte County Art Guild, Union Coll. Alumni Assn., Charlotte Symphony League (pres.), Antique and Classic Boat Soc. (bd. dirs. 1974—89, Disting. Svc. award 1979), Charlotte Harbor Yacht Club, Zonta (pres. 1981—82). Avocations: photography, reading, golf, skiing, canoeing. Home and Office: 104 Leland St SW Port Charlotte FL 33952-9131

**REYNOLDS, HERBERT HAL,** university administrator; b. Frankston, Tex., Mar. 20, 1930; s. Herbert Joseph and Ava Nell (Taylor) R.; m. Joy Myrla Copeland, June 17, 1950; children: Kevin Hal, Kent Andrew, Rhonda Sheryl. BS, Trinity U., 1952; MS, Baylor U., 1958, PhD, 1961; ScD (hon.), Seinan Gakuin U., Japan, 1990, Baylor Coll. Dentistry, 1993; PhD (hon.), Yonok Coll., Thailand, 2000. Entered USAF, 1948, advanced through grades to col., 1966; with Aeromed. Lab., Alamogordo, N.Mex., 1961—68, Air Force Human Resources Lab., San Antonio, 1968; ret., 1968; exec. v.p. Baylor U., Waco, Tex., 1969—81, pres., 1981—95, chancellor, 1995—2000, pres. emeritus, 2000—. Vis. fellow, scholar Cambridge U., 1994-97. Contbr. articles to profl. jours. Mem.: Sigma Xi, Phi Beta Kappa, Omicron Delta Kappa, Alpha Chi. Office: Baylor U Office of Pres Emeritus Waco TX 76798 Office Phone: 254-710-1311. E-mail: president_emeritus@baylor.edu.

**REYNOLDS, HERBERT YOUNG,** internist; b. Richmond, Va., Aug. 20, 1939; s. George Audney and Pearle Maupin (Young) R.; m. Anne Browning Leavell, July 11, 1964; children: Nancy, George, William Stuart. BA in English, U. Va., 1961, MD, 1965; MA (hon.), Yale U., 1979. Diplomate Am. Bd. Internal Medicine. Intern NY Hosp., med. Allergy and Immunology. Intern NY Hosp. Cornell Med. Ctr., N.Y.C., 1965—66, asst physician, fellow in medicine 1966—67; clin. assoc., lab. clin. investigation Nat. Inst. Allergy, Infectious Diseases, NIH, Bethesda, Md., 1967—70, clin. assoc., lab. clin. investigation, 1968—69; chief resident, instr. medicine U. Hosp. U. Wash., Seattle, 1970—71; sr. investigator, lab. clin. investigation Nat. Inst. Allergy, Infectious Diseases, NIH, Bethesda, 1971—76; assoc. prof. internal medicine, head pulmonary divsn. Yale U. Sch. Medicine, New Haven, 1976—79, prof., 1979—88; J. Lloyd Huck prof. medicine, chmn. dept. Pa. State U., Milton S. Hershey Med. Ctr., 1988—2002; assoc. chmn. divsn. medicine Pa. State

Geisinger Health Sys., 1997—2000, chief medicine ops. Hershey Med. Ctr. Region, 1997—2000; med. officer Lung Biology and Disease program, divsn. lung diseases NHLBI/NIH, Bethesda, 2002—; prof. medicine emeritus Pa. State U. Coll. Medicine, 2002—. Adj. prof. medicine Uniformed Svcs. U. Health Scis., Bethesda, 2003—; mem. exec. com. Coll. Medicine Pa. State U.-Hershey Med. Ctr., 1988-2002, exec. bd. U. Hosp., 1988-2002, fin. bd. acad. enrichment fun, 1988-95, dean's adv. com., 1988-97, diversity task force, 1995-2002, physicians faculty practice plan exec. com. 1996-97, human resources team leader, 2000-02; dept. chair rep. Milton S. Hershey Med. Ctr. Bd., 2000-2002; cons. in infectious diseases Nat. Naval Med. Ctr., NIH, Bethesda, 1971-76, clin. rsch. com., 1971-76, chmn., 1974-76, pulmonary disease adv. com. divsn. of lung diseases NHLBI, 1978-82, sci. counselors bd., 1984-88, data and safety monitoring bd. registry of patients with deficiency of Alpha-1 Antitrypsin, 1989-96. Mem. editl. bd. Lung, 1978-2005, Am. Jour. Medicine, 1979-89, Jour. Clin. Investigation, 1980-86, Am. Rev. Respiratory Diseases, 1980-87, Jour. Applied Physiology, 1981-89, Resident Physician, 1981-95; contbr. more than 300 articles to profl. jours. and med. textbooks. Parent com. Troop 1 Boy Scouts Am., Madison, 1979-82; bd. dirs. Neighborhood Music Sch., Guilford, Conn., 1978-87; Music at Gretna, 1994-2002; bd. dirs. Harrisburg Symphony, 1996-2000; active All Saints Episc. Ch., Hershey; pulmonary infections com. Cystic Fibrosis Found., Bethesda, 1980-86; mem. coun. sci. advisors Parker B. Francis Found., Kansas City, Kans., 1983-87; internat. com. World Orgn. for Sarcoidosis and other Granulomatous Disorders, 1987-95; bd. dirs., mem. coun. Am. Lung Assn., 1989-93, bd. govs. 1990-93, com. mem., 1990-93; coach Guilford Soccer League, 1985-88; vol. Mercy Health Clinic, Germantown, Md., 2003—. Surgeon USPHS, 1967-70. John Edward Nobel fellow, 1961-65; named Outstanding Med. Specialist in USA, Town and Country Mag., 1989, 97, The Best Med. Specialists, Town & Country mag., 1995, One of 400 Best Drs. in U.S. Good Housekeeping Mag., 1991, Best Drs. in Am., 2005-2006. Fellow ACP (coun. subsplty. socs. 1989-2000, gov. Pa. Ea. Region 1, 2000-02), Am. Coll. Chest Physicians (program com. 1978-84), Infectious Disease Soc. Am., Coll. Physicians Phila.; mem. Am. Thoracic Soc. (sec.-treas. 1987-88, bd. dirs. 1989-93, v.p. 1988-89, pres. 1991-92), Am. Soc. Clin. Investigation, Assn. Am. Physicians, Am. Assn. Immunologists, Am. Fedn. Clin. Rsch., Am. Clin. and Climatol. Assoc., v.p. 2001-02, pres. 2002-03), Acad. Medicine Wash., Interurban Clin. Club (emeritus 1989), Hershey Country Club, Farmington Country Club, Raven Soc., Phi Beta Kappa, Alpha Omega Alpha, Omicron Delta Kappa. Republican. Avocations: tennis, violin. Home: 226 E Caracas Ave Hershey PA 17033-1309 Office: NHLBI/NIH Divsn Lung Diseases 6701 Rockledge Dr Rm 10112 Bethesda MD 20892-7952 Office Phone: 301-435-0218. Business E-Mail: reynoldh@nhlbi.nih.gov.

**REYNOLDS, JAMES,** management consultant; s. Richard James and Esther (Nikander) R.; m. Joanne M.J. BA in Econs., NYU, 1965, postgrad., 1965-66. Cons. to pres. Rothrock, Reynolds & Reynolds Inc., NYC, 1966-70; sr. v.p. health, med. divsn. Booz, Allen & Hamilton, NYC, 1970-80; pres. Reynolds & Co. (mgmt. cons.), San Francisco, NYC, Washington, 1981—. Developer Combining Pay for Performance with Gain Sharing to align incentives, ACPE, 2006; bd. dirs. Booz, Allen & Hamilton, 1977-79; chmn. bd. J.X. Reynolds Fine Arts, Ltd., 1979—; lectr. Harvard Sch. Pub. Health; faculty mem. Am. Coll. of Healthcare Execs.; bd. dirs. Health Ctr. Mgmt. Inst., Richmond, Va., 1977; mem. health adv. bd. Hunter Coll., 1980—. Mem. editl. bd. Physicians Fin. News. Recipient NYU Founders award, 1965 Mem. Am. Pub. Health Assn., Am. Mgmt. Assn., Assn. Am. Med. Colls., Am. Hosp. Assn., Hosp. Mgmt. Systems Soc., Hosp. Fin. Mgmt. Assn., Asia Soc., China Inst., Phi Beta Kappa, Guggenheim Mus., Mus. Modern Art, Mus. Natural Hist. Met. Opera Guild (NYC) Episcopalian. Home and Office: Reynolds & Co 333 E 51st St New York NY 10022-6702 Home: 333 E 51st St New York NY 10022-6702 Office Phone: 212-826-1818. Business E-Mail: jreynolds@jxreynolds.com.

**REYNOLDS, JEAN EDWARDS,** publishing executive; b. Saginaw, Mich., Dec. 11, 1941; d. F. Perry and Kathrine (Edwards) R.; m. Cary Wellington, Sept. 10, 1975 (div. 1982); children: Bradley, Abigail, Benjamin; m. Jon Haddon, Nov. 8, 1997. BA, Wells Coll., 1963; postgrad., CCNY, 1965-67. Asst. editor, sr. editor trade book div. Prentice-Hall, Englewood Cliffs, NJ, 1963—66, dir. children's books, 1966—69, McCall Pub. Co., N.Y.C., 1969—71; sr. v.p., editorial dir. Franklin Watts Inc., N.Y.C., 1971—75; pres. Pet Projects Inc., Ridgefield, Conn., 1975—81; editor in chief young people's publs. Grolier Inc., Danbury, Conn., 1981—89; founder, pub., exec. v.p. The Millbrook Press, Brookfield, Conn., 1989—2004; assoc. pub. Lerner Publs., Mpls., 2004—06, exec. editor, 2006—. Bd. dirs. Wellington Leisure Products, Atlanta, Kiper Enterprises, Oswego, N.Y., Jewish Fedn. Greater Danbury; chairperson Conn. Ctr. for the Book, 1991-94. Mem. Bd. of Govs. for Higher Edn., State of Conn., 2004—; pres. Jewish Fedn. Greater Danbury 1991—93, 2003—; bd. dirs. Jewish Home for the Elderly, Fairfield, Conn., 1989—90, 1999, Book Industry Study Group, 1991—98, The Wooster Sch., Danbury, Conn., 1992—, chair headmaster search, 2002—; bd. dirs. Temple Shearith Israel, Ridgefield, Conn., 1994—97, chair Kehila campaign, 2002; bd. dirs. The Children's Book Coun., 1996—2000, vice chair, 1997—98, chair, 1998—99. Mem. ALA, Children's Book Coun., Mensa. Avocations: skiing, sailing, needlecrafts. Home and Office: 33 Corntassle Rd Danbury CT 06811-3208 E-mail: jreynolds@lernerbooks.com.

**REYNOLDS, JEFFREY MICHAEL,** music educator; b. Camden, NJ, Oct. 5, 1971; s. Thomas Leroy and Judith Lynn Reynolds; m. Tammi Sue Murray, July 24, 1993; children: Kaitlyn Elizabeth, Michael Andrew. MusB in Edn., Wingate U., 1995. Dir. bands Anson County Schs., Wadesboro, NC, 1995—96; asst. band dir. Piedmont HS and Mid. Sch., Monroe, NC, 1996—99, Sun Valley Mid. and High Schs., Monroe and Indian Trail, NC, 1999—2000; dir. bands Sun Valley HS, Monroe, 2000—. Pit coord. Union County Performance Ensemble, Monroe, 2001—, condr., 2005—. Sgt. U.S. Army, 2001—06. Mem.: NC Music Educators Assn., Music Educators Nat. Conf. Office: Sun Valley HS Band 5211 Old Charlotte Hwy Monroe NC 28110 Office Phone: 704-296-3020. Business E-Mail: jeff.reynolds@ucps.k12.nc.us.

**REYNOLDS, JEFFREY WARREN,** music educator; b. Tuscaloosa, Ala., Jan. 5, 1961; s. John Edward Reynolds and Betty Francis Rainwater; m. Laura Stone Reynolds, July 30, 2005; children: Jennifer, Dylan, Christian. MusB, Samford U., Birmingham, Ala., 1982; MusM, Southwestern Sem., Ft. Worth, Tex., 1985; D of Mus. Arts, U. Ill., Champaign/Urbana, 1990. Dir. choral activities, coord. of music Brevard C.C., Melbourne, Fla., 1989—97; dir. choral activities U. Ark., Monticello, 1997—98, U. Ala., Birmingham, 1998—, chmn. dept. music, 2000—. Condr. Brevard Symphony Youth Orch., 1993—96; music dir., condr. Internat. Cathedral Music Festival England, 1998—; min. of arts Southside Bapt. Ch., Birmingham, Ala., 2005—. Contbr.: chpt. Maurice Durufle-The Last Impressionist, 2001. Recipient Disting. Educator award, Brevard C.C., 1991, Tchg. Excellence award, Nat. Inst. for Staff and Orgnl. Devel., 1992. Mem.: Music Educators Nat. Conf., Am. Choral Dirs. Assn. (life). Baptist. Avocations: bicycling, kayaking, gardening, cooking, photography. Home: 1575 Oak Park Dr Helena AL 35080 Office: 240 Hulsey Ctr Birmingham AL 35209 Office Fax: 205-975-1931. E-mail: jwr@uab.edu.

**REYNOLDS, JERRY (GERALD A. REYNOLDS),** federal agency administrator; BA, CUNY York Coll.; JD, Boston U. Atty. Schatz & Schatz, Conn., Ribicoff & Kotkin; legal analyst Ctr. Equal Opportunity, 1995—97; pres., legal counsel Ctr. New Black Leadership, 1997—98; sr. regulatory counsel Kansas City Power & Light Co., 1998—2002; asst. sec. civil rights US Dept. Edn., Washington, 2002—04; chairperson US Comm. on Civil Rights, Washington, 2004—. Mem. editl. bd.: Am. Jour. Law and Medicine. Office: US Commn on Civil Rights 624 Ninth St NW Ste 700 Washington DC 20425*

**REYNOLDS, JOAN LORELLE,** music educator; b. Dayton, Ohio, Aug. 23, 1950; d. Robert Charles and Lorelle Hedrick; m. Perry Finis II Reynolds, Oct. 10, 1970; children: Perry Finis III, Robert Miles. BA in Music (hons.),

Wright State U., Dayton, 1990, MusM in music edn., 1999. Lic. Profl. Tchr. Ohio, 1994. Pvt. vocal studio, Dayton, Ohio, 1989—; grad. tchg. asst. dept. of music Wright State U., Dayton, 1992—94, dept. music adj. faculty, 1994—96, faculty assoc. in voice; music tchr. Kettering (Ohio) City Schs., 1996—. Musical dir. Kettering (Ohio) Mid. Sch., 1996—. Dir.(prodr.): (musical) You're a Good Man, Charlie Brown, Schoolhouse Rock Live, Jr., Fiddler on the Roof, Jr., Honk! Junior, American Pop Forever, Annie, Jr. Advisor Muse Machine, Dayton, Ohio, 1996—2006. Grantee Grant, Kettering Ednl. Found., 2000. Mem.: DAR, Nat. Assn. Tchrs. of Singing, Music Educators Nat. Assn. (licentiate), Am. Choral Dirs. Assn. (licentiate). Home: 5007 Rhine Way Centerville OH 45458 Office: Kettering Mid Sch 3000 Glengarry Dr Kettering OH 45420 Office Phone: 937-499-1550. Office Fax: 937-499-1598. Personal E-mail: joanreynolds@woh.rr.com. Business E-Mail: joan.reynolds@kettering.k12.oh.us.

**REYNOLDS, JOCK,** artist, curator, art gallery director; m. Suzanne Hellmuth, 1977; 2 children. BA, Univ. Calif., Santa Cruz, 1969; MFA, Univ. Calif., Davis, 1972. Assoc. prof., dir., grad. program, Center for Experimental and Interdisciplinary Art San Francisco State Univ., 1973—83; co-founder 80 Langton St. (now New Langton Arts), 1975; dir. Washington Project of the Arts, Washington, 1983—89, Addison Gallery of Am. Art, Andover, Mass., 1989—98; Henry J. Heinz II dir. Yale Univ. Art Gallery, New Haven, 1998—; and adj. prof. Yale Univ., New Haven, 1998—. Represented in permanent collections Smithsonian Nat. Mus. of Am. Art., Corcoran Gallery of Art, Walker Art Ctr., Mpls. Inst. of Arts., Univ. Washington Henry Art Gallery. Bd. dir. Williamstown Art Conservation Ctr., Mass. Recipient Fulbright Fellowship. Office: Yale Univ Art Gallery Chapel at High St PO Box 208271 New Haven CT 06520-8271 Office Phone: 203-432-0600.

**REYNOLDS, JOHN FRANCIS,** insurance company executive; b. Escanaba, Mich., Mar. 29, 1921; s. Edward Peter and Lillian (Harris) R.; m. Dorothy Gustafson, May 1, 1946; children; Lois, Margaret, Michael. BS, Mich. State U., 1942. Claims and assoc. surety mgr. Hartford Ins. Co., Escanaba, Mich. and Chgo., 1946-55; asst. v.p., bond mgr. Wolverine Ins. Co., Battle Creek, Mich., 1955-64, v.p. underwriting, 1964-69; Midwest zone underwriting mgr. Transamerica Ins. Co. (Wolverine Ins. Co.), Battle Creek, Mich., 1969-74; pres., gen. mgr. Can. Surety Co. subs. Transamerica Ins. Co. Toronto, Ont., Canada, 1974-75; v.p. midwestern zone mgr. Transamerica Ins. Group, Battle Creek, Mich., 1975-83, pres., chief operating officer Los Angeles, 1983-84, chmn., chief exec. officer, 1984-85; apptd. spl. dep. ins. commr., dep. conservator Cadillac Inc. Co., 1989. Pres. Underwriting Exec. Council Midwest, 1967; dir. Underwriters Adjustment Bur., Toronto, 1974, Underwriters Labs. of Canada, Montreal, 1974; chmn. Mich. Assn. Ins. Cos., Lansing, 1976, Mich. Basic Property Ins. Assn., Detroit, 1973. Commr. City of Battle Creek, 1967-69; dir. Urban League, Battle Creek, 1969, 70, dir. Mich. Ins. Fedn., Lansing, 1975-83. Served to sgt. U.S. Army, 1942-45; New Guinea Roman Catholic. Avocations: golf, fishing. Home: 14037 N Cameo Dr Sun City AZ 85351-2903 Personal E-mail: jreynolds212@cox.net.

**REYNOLDS, JOHN R.,** hospital executive; Joined Hosp. for Special Surgery, NYC, 1985, CFO, 1985—97, co-CEO, 1997—99, pres., CEO, 1999—. Office: Hosp for Special Surgery 535 East 70th St New York NY 10021 Office Phone: 212-606-1000.*

**REYNOLDS, JUDITH AMY,** nutritionist, consultant, animal scientist, educator; d. Jacob Alen and Mary Emeline Lundgren; m. Rodney Roger Reynolds, Aug. 28, 1971; children: Andrea Mary Rickards, James Christopher. AA summa cum laude, Anoka Ramsey CC, 1988; BS summa cum laude, St. Cloud State U., 1990; MS, Tex. A&M U., 1993, PhD, 1997. Cert. Profl. Animal Scientist Am. Registry Profl. Animal Scientists, 1995. Co-owner, mgr. Reynolds Quarter Horses, Palmyra, Mo., 1978—; grad. asst. rschr. Tex. A&M U., College Station, 1990—91, grad. asst. tchr., 1991—95; long term substitute tchr. biology, anatomy physiology, chemistry Princeton and Elk River Pub. Sch. Sys., Minn., 1997—98; divisional equine tech. specialist Archer Daniels Midland Animal Health Nutrition and MoorMan's Inc. Quincy, Ill., 1998—2001; equine nutritionist Archer Daniels Midland Alliance Nutrition Inc., Quincy, 2001—. Asst. prof. William Woods U., Fulton, Mo., 1995—97; assoc. faculty John Woods CC, Quincy, Ill., 2004—; spkr. in field; ofcl. reviewer Nat. Rsch. Coun., Nutrient Requirements of Horses, 2006; mem. Equine Sci. Soc. Nutrition Com., 2006—. Author: (online source) Equine Nutrition in the 21st Century (1st Pl. Online Svc. To Reader, 2003); contbr. articles to profl. jours. Vol. Princeton Pub. Schools, Princeton, Minn., 1983—90; vol. leader; horse sci., horse bowl, horse advancement, vet. sci. Isanti County 4-H, Minn., 1983—90; vol. leader horse judging, market steers, poultry Bryan HS Future Farmers of Am., Tex., 1992—94; vol. horse judge Brazos County, College Station, Tex., 1991—94, Tex. A&M U., College Station, 1991—95; vol. horse bowl team coach Mo. State 4-H, 1996—97; vol. 4-H horse judge Audrain and Calloway Counties, Fulton, Mo., 1996—97. Recipient High Point All Around Horse, Minn. Quarter Horse Assn., 1980, Two Register of Merit Horses, Am. Quarter Horse Assn., 1980, 1982, Four High-Point and Res. Performance Gelding awards, Five State Champions, Five Res. State Champions, Minn. Quarter Horse Assn., 1980-1983, One Performance Horse Qualified, Outstanding Horses of World, World Equine Rsch. Inst., 1983; Mensa scholarship, Am. Mensa, 1987, Alliss scholarships, Alliss, 1987-1990, Academic scholarships, Anoka Ramsey CC, 1987-1988, St. Cloud State U., 1988-1990. Mem.: Am. Registry Profl. Animal Scientists, Equine Sci. Soc. (nutrition com. 2006—), Am. Quarter Horse Assn., Nat. Reining Horse Assn., Phi Kappa Phi, Psi Chi, Kappa Delta Pi, Phi Theta Kappa, Gamma Sigma Delta. Achievements include development of equine feeds and supplements, SENIORGLO, MOORGLO, PRO-VITA-MIN 20 supplement tubs, FORAGE FIRST horse rewards, MOORGLO Canadian formula, GROSTRONG QuadBLOCK Canadian formula; StaySTRONG metabolic mineral pellets. Avocations: horses, reading, writing, cooking. Office: ADM Alliance Nutrition 1000 N 30th St Quincy IL 62305 Office Fax: 217-222-9060. Business E-Mail: judy_reynolds@admworld.com.

**REYNOLDS, KAREN ANN,** retired elementary school educator; b. Mpls., Jan. 20, 1944; d. Herbert Laverne and Doris Emma (Olson) Hinrichs; m. Kenneth Allen Reynolds, Aug. 2, 1975; stepchildren: Terri Lynn Winberry, Sheri Lee DeMaagd, Robert Scott. BS in Elem. Tchr. Edn. cum laude, So. Oreg. Coll., Ashland, 1966, MS in Elem. Tchr. Edn., 1974. Std. tchg. cert. State of Oreg. Tchr. elem. sch. Riddle (Oreg.) Sch. Dist., 1966—70, Ashland Sch. Dist. # 5, 1970—80; substitute tchr. Coos Bay and North Bend (Oreg.) Sch. Dists., 1981, Williston (N.D.) Sch. Dist., 1982—83; tchr. County and City Schools and pvt. kindergarten, Klamath Falls, Oreg., 1983—90; tchr. elem. sch. Klamath Falls City Schools Dist. 1, Klamath Falls, 1990—98. Dir. Christmas Program Trenton (N.D.) K-12 Sch., 1984. Sunday sch. and Bible sch. tchr. Grace Luth. Ch., Ashland, 1959—65, tchr. confirmation class, 1972—74; children's message presenter Zion Luth. Ch., Klamath Falls, 2000—05, mem. altar guild, altar server, banner artist, 2002—06, asst. to sec., e-mail prayer chain, 2005—06. Named Best Student in a Survey Class in Am. History, Faculty of So. Oreg. Coll., 1964, Best Student in Prins. of Econs. Survey Class, 1965, Best Student in a Survey Course in Geography, Faculty So. Oreg. Coll., 1964, Co-Salutatorian of Graduating Class, Ashland Sr. H.S., 1962; recipient State Bd. Full Tuition scholarship, State of Oreg., 1962—65. Mem.: Ashland Edn. Assn. (mem. salary negotiation team 1972—73), Klamath Falls Edn. Assn. (treas. 1996—98), Riddle Edn. Assn. (v.p. 1967—68, pres. 1968—69, salary negotiations team 1968—69). Lutheran. Avocations: sewing, crafts, digital photographic art works, genealogy, writing.

**REYNOLDS, KEVIN,** film director, writer; b. San Antonio, Jan. 17, 1952; BA, Baylor U.; JD; grad. U. Calif. Sch. Cinema and TV. With TIG Prodns. 1996; former atty. Actor film Into the West, 1992; writer film Red Dawn, 1984; writer, dir. Proof, 1980, Fandango, 1985, Rapa Nui, 1994; dir. The Beast of War, 1988, Robin Hood: Prince of Thieves, 1991, Waterworld, 1995, One Eight Seven, 1997, The Count of Monte Cristo, 2002, Tristan & Isolde, 2006. Office: care William Morris Agy 151 S El Camino Dr Beverly Hills CA 90212-2704*

**REYNOLDS, LEWIS DAYTON,** pastor; b. Charleston, W.Va., July 26, 1937; s. James Shelby and Sybil Catherine (Lanham) R.; m. Ann Kathryn Combs, Aug. 25, 1962; children: John Mark, Daniel Adam. BBA, Marshall U., 1959; BTh, Aurora U., 1961; MDiv, Evang. Theol. Sem., Naperville, Ill., 1962. Ordained to ministry Advent Christian Ch., 1962. Pastor Mendota (Ill.) Advent Christian Ch., Mendota, Ill., 1961-64, Clendenin (W.Va.) Advent Christian Ch., Clendenin, W.Va., 1964-72, New Covenant Fellowship, Penfield, NY, 1972-89; gen. overseer Elim Fellowship, Lima, NY, 1989-97; sr. pastor Faith Christian Fellowship, Clarksburg, W.Va., 1997—2002, Charismatic Episcopal Ch. of the Transfiguration, Sterling, Va., 2002—; dir. Appalachian Highlands mission, eastern province Charismatic Episcopal Ch. 2003—. Mem. Phi Eta Sigma. Republican. Personal E-mail: daytonr@charter.net.

**REYNOLDS, LINDA ANN,** elementary school educator; b. Teheran, Iran, Jan. 1, 1959; d. John Kendrick and Fatemah Nikou Reynolds; 1 adopted child, Derek. BS in Elem. Edn., Auburn U., Ala., 1991, MEd, 1995, Edn. Specialist degree, 2000. LCSW. Med. transcriptionist St. Margaret's Hosp., Montgomery, Ala., 1980—84, Drs. Reynolds, Little and Thomas, Montgomery, 1981—87; typing instr. Riley Coll., Montgomery, 1987—88; tchr. 5th grade Davis Elem. Sch., Montgomery, 1991—92; edn. instr. Fews Elem. Sch., Montgomery, 1995, tchr. 5th grade, 2000—01. Ednl. instr. CAP Program, Montgomery, 1995. Vol. city crime prevention unit Montgomery Police Dept.; vol. Montgomery Area Food Bank; active Rainbow Con. Recipient Tchr. of Yr., 1991—92. Mem.: Chi Sigma Iota. Home: PO Box 153 Coosada AL 36020-0153

**REYNOLDS, LOUISE WEBB,** retired volunteer, director; b. Demopolis, Ala., Feb. 22, 1946; d. John Cox Webb, III and Marie Suttle Webb; m. Peter Michael Reynolds; children: Peter Michael Jr., Angie Marie, John Webb. BS, U Ala., 1968. Exec. dir. The Demopolis City Schs. Found., Inc., Demopolis, Ala., 1994—99; tchr. English Demopolis City Schs., Demopolis, Ala., 1968—69; clerk Demopolis Stock Yards, Demopolis, Ala., 1969—72; coord. media West Ala. Mental Health Ctr., Demopolis, Ala., 1974—78; clerk Reynolds Cattle Co., Forkland, Ala., 1986—90. First female chmn. Bd. Edn., Demopolis, 1988—90, Demopolis City Schs. Bd. Edn., 1992—93; active City of Demopolis Cemetery Bd., 2004—06; mem. bd. dirs. Bd. Edn., Demopolis City Schs., Demopolis, 1985—95; vol. counselor "Save-a-Life" Crisis Pregnancy Ctr., Demopolis, 1990—94; pres. Demopolis Kappa Delta Alumnae, Demopolis, 1990—93; orgnl. pres., first integrated PTA Demopolis Elem. PTA, Demopolis, 1980—81; reorganizational pres. Marengo County chpt. U. Ala. Alumni Assn., Demopolis, 1977—78; orgnl. pres. Marengo County Assn. Brain Damaged Children, Demopolis, 1971—74; vol. coord. The Achievement Ctr. Spl. Children, Demopolis, 1972—74; orgnl. pres. Marengo County chpt. Nat. Assn. Retarded Children, Demopolis, 1972—74; pres. Demopolis Kappa Delta Alumnae, Demopolis, 1976—77; leader Brownie Scout Tombigee Girl Scout Coun., Demopolis, 1979—83; Cub Scout Den Mother Boy Scouts of Am., Prairie Dist., Black Warrior Coun., Demopolis, 1976—79; orgnl. pres. Pastoral Coun., St. Leo's Cath. Ch., Demopolis, 1993—97; orgnl. coord. "RENEW" St. Leo's Cath. Ch., Demopolis, 1983—88; lector. Confraternity Christian Doctrine, St. Leo's Cath. Ch., Demopolis, 1973—93; Eucharistic min., lector St. Leo's Cath. Ch., Demopolis. Recipient Disting. Svc. award, Demopolis Jaycees, 1972, Outstanding Chpt. Devel. award, U. Ala., Nat. Alumni Assn., 1979, Paul Harris Fellow, Rotary, 2003. Mem.: The Reading Club (pres. Demopolis chpt. 1982—83, 2003—04). Roman Catholic. Avocations: painting, travel. Home: 303 West Lyon Demopolis AL 36732

**REYNOLDS, MARIANNE GERALYN,** librarian; b. Cin., Oct. 7, 1954; d. Don A. and Dorothy A. (Gerding) Davis; m. Kevin Reynolds, June 26, 1976. BS summa cum laude, U. Cin., 1976, postgrad., 1987, 89; MLS, U. Ky., 1999. Tchr. elem. St. Catharine Sch., Cin., 1979-82, St. Francis Seraph Sch., Cin., 1982-84, St. John Sch., Cin., 1984—92; reference libr. Pub. Libr. of Cin. and Hamilton County, Ohio, 1999—. Rollman scholar. Mem.: Pub. Libr. Assn., Am. Libr. Assn. Home: 6827 Hillary Dr Cincinnati OH 45239-5525 Office: Pub Libr of Cin and Hamilton County Mag and Newspaper Dept 800 Vine St Cincinnati OH 45202-2071 Office Phone: 513-665-3367.

**REYNOLDS, MARSHALL TRUMAN,** printing company executive; b. Logan, W.Va., Feb. 21, 1937; s. Douglas Vernon and Dorothy Lee (Dingess) R.; m. Shirley Ann Earwood, Mar. 24, 1968; children: Jack Marine, Douglas Vernon. Student, Marshall U., 1956-58. Sales mgr. Chapman Printing Co., Huntington, W.Va., 1960-61, gen. mgr., 1961-64, pres., gen. mgr. Huntington, Parkersburg and Charleston, W.Va., Lexington, Ky., 1964—. Chmn. bd. McCorkle Machine & Engring., Huntington, KYOWVA Corrugated Container, Huntington, Stationers, Inc., Huntington, Charleston, Radisson Hotel, Huntington, Huntington Indsl. Corp., Champion Industries Inc., Am. Babbit Bearing Inc.; bd. dirs Guyan Machinery, Huntington, United Huntington Industries, Persinger Supply Co., Prichard, W.Va., First Guaranty Bank, Hammond, La., Banc One WV Corp., Charleston, W.Va. Bd. dirs. W.Va. Roundtable, Huntington, 1989—, W. Va. Bus. Found., Huntington, 1989—, Boys and Girls Club, Huntington, 1989—, Huntington United Way, 1989—; mem. Gov.'s Task Force on Children, Youth and Families, 1989—; guest lectr. various high schs. on free enterprise. Named Outstanding Small Businessman of Yr., Huntington Jaycees, 1983, Business Man of Yr. Jaycess, 1988. Mem. Huntington C. of C., Western Star Lodge (Guyandotte, W.Va.). Republican. Baptist. Avocation: raising cattle. Home: 1130 13th St Huntington WV 25701-3632 Office: Chapman Printing Co 2450 1st Ave Huntington WV 25703-1218

**REYNOLDS, NANCY REMICK,** writer, researcher, editor; b. San Antonio, July 15, 1938; d. Donald Worthington and Edith (Remick) R.; m. Brian Rushton, June 25, 1983; 1 child: Ehren P. Student, Sch. Am. Ballet, N.Y.C., 1951, student, 1953—61, Juilliard Sch. Music, 1957, Martha Graham Sch. Contemporary Dance, 1959, U. Sorbonne, Paris, 1962; BA in Art History, Columbia U., N.Y.C., 1965; postgrad., Goethe Inst., Prien, 1972, U. Chgo., 1974—77, Sarah Lawrence Coll., Bronxville, N.Y., 1974—77. Dancer NYC Ballet, 1956—61; editor Praeger Pubs., NYC, 1965—71; dir. rsch. book Choreography by George Balanchine: A Catalogue of Works, 1979—82; dir. rsch. pub. TV spl. Balanchine, NY, 1983—84; assoc. editor Internat. Ency. of Dance, 1998; dir. rsch. The George Balanchine Found., NYC, 1994—. Co-pub. Twentieth-Century Dance in Slides, 1978-93. Author: Repertory in Review: Forty Years of the New York City Ballet, 1977 (De la Torre Bueno prize 1977), The Dance Catalog: A Complete Guide to Today's World of Dance, 1979, co-author: In Performance, 1980, Dance Classics, 1991 (rec. for teen age NY Pub. Libr.), No Fixed Points: Dance in the Twentieth Century, 2003; editor: Movement and Metaphor: Four Centuries of Ballet (Lincoln Kirstein), 1970, Dance as a Theatre Art: Source Readings in Dance History from 1581 to the Present (Selma Jeanne Cohen), 1974, School of Classical Dance (V. Kostrovitskaya and A. Pisarev), 1978; contbr. (book) Ballet: Bias and Belief, "Three Pamphlets Collected" and Other Dance Writings of Lincoln Kirstein, 1983; contbr. articles to profl. jours Ford Found. Travel and Study grantee, 1974; Mary Duke Biddle Found. grantee, 1990. Mem. Dance Critics Assn. (pres. 1986-87), Soc. Dance History Scholars, Soc. for Dance Rsch., Am. Soc. for Theatre Rsch., European Assn. Dance Historians, Internat. Fedn. for Theatre Rsch. in affiliation with Societe Internat. des Bibliotheques et Musees des Arts du Spectacle, Phi Beta Kappa. Home: 9 Prospect Park W Brooklyn NY 11215-1758 Office Phone: 718-783-4265.

**REYNOLDS, NICHOLAS S.,** lawyer; b. Grosse Point, Mich., June 16, 1944; BS, Wilkes Coll., 1968; JD with honors, George Washington U., 1971. Bar: Va. 1971, DC 1973. Atty. FTC, 1971—73; ptnr. Winston & Strawn LLP, Washington, 1977—, chmn. energy dept., mem. exec. com. Mem. ABA (chmn. atomic energy com. sect. public utility, comm. and transp. law 1989—). Office: Winston & Strawn 1400 L St NW Ste 800 Washington DC 20005-3502 Office Phone: 202-371-5717. Office Fax: 202-371-5950. E-mail: nreynolds@winston.com.

**REYNOLDS, PATRICIA ELLEN,** artist; b. Apr. 6, 1934; d. Edwin and Anna (Pacewicz) Steeg; m. Carlyle Reynolds, Oct. 4, 1953 (div. 1991); children: Clifford, Stephanie. Student, SUNY, Plattsburg, 1951-52, Moon Bus. Sch., N.Y.C., 1953; studied with Robert Whitney, studied with Mario Cooper. Watercolor painter, Willsboro, N.Y. Condr. workshops in field, mem. art juries. One-woman shows include Gallerie Camille Renaud, Paris, 1979, Hollsworthy Gallery, London, 1980, Ctr. Modern Design, Riyadh, Saudi Arabia, 1981-83, 25 Yr. Retro Art Mus., SUNY, Plattsburgh, Remington Mus., 1996, North Country Cultural Ctr., Plattsburgh, NY, 2005; exhibited in group shows at Schenectady Mus., SUNY, Plattsburgh, St. Lawrence U., Canton, N.Y., Ctr. Music, Drama and Arts, Lake Placid, N.Y., 1980, Audubon Artists Ann., 1980, 94, Fleming Mus. Burlington, Vt., Am. Watercolor Soc., 1982, 87 (Traveling Shows awards, Lena Newcastle award), Salmagundi Club (Gold Medal award), 1983, 88-89, 91-92 (awards 1983, 88), Nat. Works Paper, 1982 (award), Nat. Exhbn. Am. Watercolors, 1983-84, 87 (award), Allied Trusts Exhbn., 1987, 91, 93, Watercolor West, 1988, Mid-West Watercolor Soc., 1983, 89, 92, Nat. Watercolor Soc., 1991. Recipient Best of Show arad No. Vt. Artists, 1970-71, 76, 78-79, Adirondack Art Exhbn. award, 1973, Oustanding Woman award Am. Pen Women, 1975, Benedictine Nat. award, 1975, Lena Newcastle award Am. Watercolor Soc., 1987, Travel Exhbn. award Am. Watercolor Soc., 1987, William Kowalsky Meml. award, 1991, Adirondack Pk. Centennial award, 1992, Multi-Focus award, 1992, Adirondack Art Assn. award, 2003 Mem. Mid-West Watercolor Soc. (Signature Mem. award 1992, North Country award), Allied Artist Am. (assoc.), Nat. Watercolor Soc. (assoc.), Ctrl. N.Y. Watercolor Soc. (signature), Adirondack Art Assn. Office Phone: 518-963-8356.

**REYNOLDS, PAUL DAVIDSON,** social sciences educator; b. Mattoon, Ill., Mar. 5, 1938; s. John Tom and Barbara Barteldes Reynolds; m. Anne-Marie T. Lair, Aug. 5, 1963; children: Christopher Mosdale, Nicole. BS in Engring., U. Kans., 1960; MBA, Stanford U., 1964, MA in Psychology, 1966, PhD in Sociology, 1969. Asst. prof. sociology U. Calif., Riverside, 1968—70; from asst. prof. to prof. sociology U. Minn., Mpls., 1970—90; Coleman Found. chairholder in entrepreneurial studies Marquette U., Milw., 1990—95; Paul T. Babson chairholder in entrepreneurial studies Babson Coll., Wellesley, Mass., 1995—99; prof. entrepreneurship London Bus. Sch., 1999—2004; prof. mgmt. Fla. Internat. U. Miami, 2004—. Author: (monograph) Ethical Dilemmas and Social Science Research, (introductory text) A Primer in Theory Construction; editor: (conference proceedings) Frontiers of Entrepreneurship Research.; contbr. articles to profl. jours. Co-chair of state platform com. Dem. Farmer Labor Polit. Party, Minn., 1986—88. 1st lt. Ordnance Corps U.S. Army, 1963—64. Recipient Internat. Award for Entrepreneurship and Small Bus. Rsch., Swedish Bus. Devel. Agy. & Swedish Found. for Small Bus. Rsch., 2004. Achievements include design and implementation of US Panel Study of Entrepreneurial Dynamics (PSED) and Global Entrepreneurship Monitor (GEM). Home: 600 Grapetree Dr Unit 10FN Key Biscayne FL 33149 Personal E-mail: paulreynolds@earthlink.net.

**REYNOLDS, PAUL L,** lawyer; b. Covington, Ky., May 29, 1961; BS cum laude, No. Ky. U., 1983; JD, U. Ky. Sch. Law, Lexington, KY, 1986. Asst. sec. Fifth Third Bank, sr. v.p.; exec. v.p. Fifth Third Bancorp, Cin., 1990—, gen. counsel, sec., 2002—. Am. Jurisprudence, Constl. Law; Am. Jurisprudence, Corp. Fin. Law. Office: Fifth Third Bancorp 38 Fountain Square Plaza Cincinnati OH 45263

**REYNOLDS, PAULA ROSPUT,** energy executive; b. Newport, RI; m. Stephen P. Reynolds, Oct. 2004. BA with highest honors, Wellesley Coll., 1978. Economist consulting firm, Boston; sr. v.p. Pacific Gas Transmission Co.; pres. CEO Duke Energy No. Am., Houston; pres., COO AGL Resources, Atlanta, pres., CEO, 2000—05, chmn., 2002—05; pres., CEO Safeco Corp., Seattle, 2006—. Bd. dir. AGL Resources, Coca Cola Enterprises, Delta Air Lines. Bd. dir. United Way Met. Atlanta, Ga. Rsch. Alliance, Ga. C. of C., Commerce Club, Atlanta. Named one of 100 Most Powerful Women, Forbes Mag., 2006; named to Ga. State Univ. Bus. Hall Fame, 2004. Mem.: Am. Gas Assn. (bd. dir.). Office: AGL Resources PO Box 4569 Atlanta GA 30302-4569 Office Phone: 404-584-4000.*

**REYNOLDS, PEGGY JEAN,** elementary school educator; b. Gaffney, S.C., Dec. 28, 1940; d. Floyd and Mary Rebecca (Bratton) R. BA, Limestone Coll., 1963; MA in Teaching, Winthrop Coll., 1973. Cert. elem. tchr., S.C. Sec. Limestone Coll., Gaffney, 1963-68; elem. tchr. Cherokee County Sch. Dist. 1, Gaffney, 1968—. Chmn. sch. improvement coun. Goucher Sch., Gaffney, 1989-91, chmn. spelling bee, 1991—. Mem. Cherokee County Edn. Assn., S.C. Edn. Assn., NEA, Cherokee County Reading Coun. Baptist.

**REYNOLDS, PETER JAMES,** physicist; b. N.Y.C., Nov. 19, 1949; s. Rudolph and Lydia Mary (Schanzer) R.; m. Louise Perini, Aug. 7, 1982. AB in Physics, U. Calif., Berkeley, 1971; PhD, MIT, 1979. Rsch. assoc., lectr. Boston U., 1978, asst. rsch. prof., 1979-83; mem. sci. staff Nat. Resource for Computation in Chemistry Lawrence Berkeley Lab., U. Calif., 1980-81, mem. rsch. staff materials and chem. scis. divsn., 1982-88; vis. scientist NEC Fundamental Rsch. Lab., Kawasaki, Japan, 1986; vis. rsch. chemist U. Calif., Berkeley, 1988; adj. assoc. prof. dept. chemistry San Francisco State U., 1988-91; program mgr. Office Naval Rsch., 1988—2003, Army Rsch. Office, 2003—, assoc. dir. head physics, 2004—, divsn. chief, 2006—. Vis. scientist Inst. for Theoretical Physics, Santa Barbara, 1994; rsch. prof. Georgetown U., Washington, 1996—2003; lectr. and rsch. in field of statis., chem. and computational physics and Monte Carlo Methods; program mgr. atomic and molecular physics, laser cooling and trapping, Bose-Einstein condensates, quantum degenaracy, quantum coherence and control, atom lasers, quantum computing. Editor: On Clusters and Clustering: From Atoms to Fractals, 1993; co-author: Monte Carlo Methods in Ab Initio Quantum Chemistry, 1994; contbr. articles to profl jours, also rev articles, book chpts. NATO lectr., NSF fellow, 1971-74, IBM fellow, 1975; Lawrence Berkeley Lab. grantee, 1982-83. Fellow Am. Phys. Soc. (chmn. membership com. 1998, nominating com. Divsn. Computational Physics and Forum on Physics and Soc. 1996-97, exec. com. Divsn. Computational Physics 1992-96, 2002-04, mem. editl. bd. Am. Jour. Physics 2002-04); mem. Materials Rsch. Soc., Optical Soc. Am., N.Y. Acad. Scis., Phi Beta Kappa, Sigma Xi. Business E-Mail: pjr@ohm.nrl.navy.mil.

**REYNOLDS, R. KEVIN,** gynecologic oncologist; MD, U. N.Mex, Albuquerque, 1982. Cert. gynecologic oncology Am. Bd. Obstetrics and Gynecology, 1988, ob-gyn Am. Bd. Obstetrics and Gynecology, 1988. George W. Morley prof. U. Mich., Ann Arbor, 1988—. Chief divsn. gynecologic oncology U. Mich., Ann Arbor, 1998—; dir. gyn oncology fellowship, 1997—. Recipient Tchg. award, U. Mich., 1993, 2004, Coun. on Resident Edn. in Obstetrics and Gynecology, 1997, 2003, Assn. Profs. Gynecology and Obstetrics, 2003. Fellow: ACS, Am. Coll. Obstetricians and Gynecologists; mem.: Soc. Gynecologic Oncologists. Office: U Mich L4000 Women's Hosp Ann Arbor MI 48109-2076 Office Phone: 734-764-9106. Business E-Mail: rkr@umich.edu.

**REYNOLDS, ROBERT,** artist, educator; b. San Luis Obispo, Calif., Mar. 7, 1936; s. Agee Grady and Viola Elizabeth (Curran) R.; m. Sharon Ardelle Bodley, June 17, 1962 (div. 1979); children: Robert Scott, Richard Lance, Jill Elizabeth; m. Patricia Lee Smith, Oct. 5, 1981. BPA with honors, Art Ctr. Coll. Design, L.A., 1963; MA, Calif. Poly. U., 1970. Artist Creative Arts Studio, San Luis Obispo, 1955-56; free-lance artist/illustrator L.A., San Luis Obispo, 1957—; staff artist Calif. Poly. U., San Luis Obispo, 1964—, assoc. prof. architecture 1970-75, prof. art & design, 1980-81, dept. chair art & design, 1984-86, acting head dept. art, 1983-84. Artist Ford Times mag., Dearborn, Mich., 1971-79; instr. Cuesta Coll., San Luis Obispo, 1972-76; artist, tchr., co-founder High Sierra Watercolor Workshop, 1975—, Asilomar Watercolor Workshop, Pacific Grove, Calif., 1980-83; free-lance illustrator for variousi studios, Calif., 1972—; painting instr. Robert Reynolds Workshop, high Sierra, 1973-2002; resident dir. London Study Program Calif. Poly. U., London, 1986, 91; art. acquisitions com. mem. Calif. Poly. State U., 1997—, performing arts adv. com., 1995—, London Study Program Com., 1986—. One-man shows include San Luis Obispo Art Ctr., 1975, Calif. State

U. Hdqrs./Gallery, 1979, Allan Hancock Coll., Santa Maria, Calif., 1981, Olive Tree Gallery, Santa Maria, 1983, Johnson Gallery, 1998-2002, Harbinger Gallery, 1998-99, 02, Elverhoj Mus. Art History, Solvang, Calif. 2004; group shows include Calif. Survey Drawing and Watercolor, Humboldt, 1982, U. Gallery, Calif. Poly. State U., 1985; exhibitions include Florence Biennale Internat. Art Exhbn., Italy, 2003; represented in permanent collections at City of Stockton, Calif., City of San Luis Obispo, Santa Barbara Mus. Natural history, Calif. State U. and CSU Collection, Long Beach, Mid-State Fair Assn., others; works include design of San Luis Obispo bicentennial symbol and coin, design of ofcl. seal County of San Luis Obispo, ofcl. painting 1984 Mozart Festival, San Luis Obispo: designer U.S. Commemorative Postcard Stamp, 1987, Annual Bear Valley Music Festival Poster, Calif., 2004; design (book): Splash9: Best of Watercolor, 2006; author: Painting Nature's Peaceful Places, 1993; executed mural Mus. Nat. History, Calif., 1983; commd. to do poster for Morro Bay Nat. Estuary Program, 2001; book pub.: The Art of Robert Reynolds: Quiet Journey, 2006. Mem. San Luis Obispo Design and Rev. Bd., 1970-73; chmn. San Luis Obispo Glad Design Competition, 1973. With USNR, 1955-63. Recipient Disting. Teaching award Calif. Poly. State U., 1986, Pres. Art award, 1993, Bronze award Nat. Painting Competition Artist mag., 1996, finalist 1999, 2000, Gold medal Art Inst. Calif., 1994, Alumni award Calif. Poly. State U., 2005; Purchase prize IronStone Vineyards Nat Art Competition, 1999; named Calif. Ctrl. Coast Wine Classic Commemorative Artist, 2002; subject of article Ctrl. Coast Mag., 2004. Mem. San Luis Obispo Art Assn. (past pres. 1970-71), Ctrl. Coast Watercolor Soc. (co-founder 1978, pres. 1980-81) Achievements include artwork featured in over 20 art books in the US and England. Personal E-mail: rgreynolds@charter.net.

**REYNOLDS, ROBERT A., JR.,** electric distributor executive; Degree in bus., Stonehill Coll., 1972. Joined Graybar Electric Co., St. Louis, 1972, various mgmt. positions, v.p. comm./data divsn., 1991, pres., CEO, 2000—, chmn., 2001—. Mem.: Nat. Assn. Wholesaler-Distributors (sec., vice chmn. 2002—05, chmn. elect 2005—). Office: Graybar Electric 34 N Meramec Ave Saint Louis MO 63105*

**REYNOLDS, ROBERT EDGAR,** academic administrator; b. Pontiac, Mich., June 3, 1938; s. Arthur James and Jean Lucille (Thompson) R.; m. Barbara Fisher, June 11, 1961 (div. May 1980); children: Jennifer Robin, Lisa Anne; m. Erika Renate Forte, July 25, 1981; children: Timothy William, Julia Renate. BA, Yale U., 1960; MD, Harvard U., 1964; MPH, Johns Hopkins U., 1967, DrPH, 1970. Med. dir. Chonic Disease Hosp., Balt. City Hosps., 1968-70; assoc. prof. medicine and community medicine, assoc. dean Med. Coll. Ga., Augusta, 1970-73; med. dir. hr. hosps. Rush Presbyn. St. Lukes Med. Ctr., Chgo., 1973-81, assoc. prof. internal medicine, prof. preventive medicine, 1973-81, med. dir., 1975-81; assoc. dean, assoc. prof. medicine Johns Hopkins U. Sch. Medicine, Balt., 1981-88; sr. assoc. v.p. for health scis., prof. medicine U. Va. Health Sci. Ctr., Charlottesville, 1988—; prof. health evaluation scis. U. Va., Charlottesville, 1995—, dir. divsn. clin. info., 1997—2000, vice provost for health scis., 1995—99, v.p., chief info. officer, 1999—2006, acting chmn. pub. health sci., 2006—. Sec.-treas. Med. Adminstrs. Conf., 1979-80, pres., 1981. Served to capt. USAR, 1965-73. Fellow ACP, Am. Coll. Preventive Medicine; mem. AMA, Assn. Am. Med. Colls. (assoc., chmn. group on instnl. planning 1988-89), Found. for Health Svcs. Rsch. (nat. adv. com.), Assn. for Health Svc. Rsch., Nat. Libr. Medicine (biomed. rev. com. 1992-95), Computer-based Patient Record Inst. (bd. dirs. 1992—). Office: Univ Va PO Box 800717 108 Cresap Rd Charlottesville VA 22908-0717 Office Fax: 804-924-8437. Business E-Mail: rreynolds@virginia.edu.

**REYNOLDS, ROBERT HUGH,** lawyer; b. St. Louis, Jan. 3, 1937; s. Leslie A. and Rebecca (McWaters) R.; m. Carol Jemison, Apr. 8, 1961; children: Stephen H., Cynthia C., Laura M. BA, Yale U., 1958; JD, Harvard U., 1964. Assoc. Barnes & Thornburg, Indpls., 1964-70, ptnr., 1970—2004, chmn. bus. dept., 1983-91, of counsel, 2005—; chmn. internat. practice group, 1992—2004; vice-chmn. TerraLex, 1996—2003, chmn., 2003—. Co-chmn., editor Comml. Real Estate Financing for Ind. Attys., 1968; vice-chmn., co-editor Advising Ind. Businesses, 1974; chmn., editor Counseling Ind. Businesses, 1981, The Purchase and Sale of a Business, 1987. Bd. dir. Crossroads Am. Coun. Boy Scouts Am., v.p., 1971—75, pres., 1987—89, v.p. Area 4 Ctrl. Region, 1989—92, pres., 1992—93, pres. Ctrl. Region, 1993—96, nat. exec. bd., 1993—; bd. dir. Family Svc. Assn. Indpls., 1974—81, pres., 1978—80; bd. dir. Family Svc. Am., 1979—88, Greater Indpls. Fgn. Trade Zone, 1987—2000, Indpls. Conv. and Visitors Assn., 1989—2000, Indpls. Econ. Devel. Corp., 1983—99, Greater Indpls. Progress Com., 1986—2000, exec. com., vice chmn.; trustee Children's Mus. Indpls., 1988—96, chmn., 1992—94; bd. dir. Indpls. Downtown Inc., chmn., 1996—99; bd. govs. Legacy Fund, 1992—, vice chmn., 2000—03, chmn., 2004—06; bd. dir. Noyes Meml. Found., pres., 2004—; bd. dir. Japan-Am. Soc. Ind., pres., 1994—2005, pres emeritus, 2005—; bd. dir. Ctrl. Ind. Cmty. Found., 2003—; bd. dirs. Indpls. Symphony Orch. Found., 2003—. Named hon. Consul Gen. of Japan, 1999—, hon. trustee, Children's Mus. Indpls.; recipient Silver Buffalo award, Boy Scouts Am., Charles L. Whistler award, Greater Indpls. Progress Com. Fellow Ind. Bar Found., Indpls. Bar Found.; mem. ABA, Ind. Bar Assn. (chmn. corp., banking and bus. law sect. 1981-82, chmn. internat. sect. 1994-96), Internat. Bar Assn., Indpls. Bar Assn., Greater Indpls. C. of C. (bd. dirs., sec. 2000-05, dir. emeritus 2005—), Econ. Club Indpls. (bd. dirs. 1995-2004), Univ. Club, Skyline Club (Indpls.), Kiwanis. Republican. Office: Barnes & Thornburg LLP 11 S Meridian St Indianapolis IN 46204-3535 Office Phone: 317-231-7227. Business E-Mail: rreynolds@btlaw.com.

**REYNOLDS, ROBERT JOEL,** economist, consultant; b. Indpls., May 13, 1944; s. Joel Burr and Betty (Schimpf) R.; m. Lucinda Margaret Lewis, May 27, 1979; children: Joel, Sarah. BSBA in Fin., Northwestern U., Evanston, Ill., 1965, PhD in Econs., 1970. Asst. prof. econs. U. Idaho, Moscow, 1969—73, assoc. prof., 1973—75; asst. dir. sr. economist econ. policy office Dept. Justice, Washington, 1973—81; sr. economist, v.p. ICF Inc., Washington, 1981—87, sr. v.p., 1987—91; exec. v.p., pres. Econsult Corp., Washington, 1991—96; chmn., exec., v.p. Econsult of D.C., Inc., Washington, 1997; chmn. Competition Econs., Inc., Washington, 1997—2004; prin. Brattle Group, 2004—. Vis. assoc. prof. U. Calif., Berkeley, 1976-77, Cornell U., Ithaca, N.Y., 1981. Reviewer: NSF, Rand Jour. of Econs., Internat. Econ. Rev., Internat. Jour. Indsl. Orgn., Jour. Indsl. Econs., Am. Econ. Rev.; mem. editl. bd. Managerial and Decision Econs.; contbr. articles to profl. jours. Recipient Dow Jones award Wall St. Jour., 1965; AT&T grantee, 1971-72, Brookings Instl. grantee, 1968-69; NDEA fellow, 1965-69. Mem. AAAS, IEEE (computer sect.), SIAM, Am. Math. Assn., Am. Econ. Assn., Econometric Soc., Royal Econ. Soc., Am. Statis. Assn., European Assn. for Rsch. in Indsl. Econs., Soc. for the Promotion of Econ. Theory, Math. Assn. Am. Congregationalist. Home: PO Box 59712 Potomac MD 20859-9712 Office: Competition Econs Inc 4800 Montgomery Ln Bethesda MD 20814 Office Phone: 202-955-5050. Personal E-mail: rjrcei@aol.com. Business E-Mail: bob.reynolds@brattle.com.

**REYNOLDS, ROGER LEE,** composer, educator; b. Detroit, July 18, 1934; s. George Arthur and Katherine Adelaide (Butler) Reynolds; m. Karen Jeanne Hill, Apr. 11, 1964; children: Erika Lynn, Wendy Claire. BSE in Physics, U. Mich., 1957, MusB in Music Lit., 1960, MusM in Composition, 1961. Assoc. prof. U. Calif. San Diego, La Jolla, 1969—73, founding dir. Ctr. Music Expt. and Related Rsch., 1972—77, prof., 1973—; George Miller prof. U. Ill., 1971—. Vis. prof. Yale U., New Haven, 1981; sr. rsch. fellow ISAM Bklyn. Coll., 1985; Valentine prof. Amherst (Mass.) Coll., 1988; Rothschild composer in residence Peabody Conservatory of Music, 1992—93; pub. Peters Music Pubs.; mgr. Graham Hayter, Contemporary Music Promotions. Author: MIND MODELS: New Forms of Musical Experience, 1975, A Searcher's Path: A Composer's Ways, 1987, A Jostled Silence: Contemporary Japanese Musical Thought, 1992—93, Form and Method: Composing Music, 2002; first Dolby Digital 5.1 DVD release of custom-designed, multichannel classical compositions: WATERSHED, Mode Records, 1998; contbr. numerous articles and revs. to profl. jours. Mem. bd. govs. Inst. Current World

Affairs; co-founder ONCE festivals, 1960; bd. dirs. Am. Music Ctr., Meet the Composer; bd. dirs. Fromm Found. Harvard U. Named sr. fellow, Inst. Studies in Am. Music, 1985, fellow, Inst. Current World Affairs, Rockefeller Found., Guggenheim Found., Fulbright scholar; recipient Koussevitzky Internat. Rec. Award, 1970, Nat. Inst. Arts and Letters award, 1971, NEA awards, 1975, 1978, 1979, 1986, Pulitzer prize for music, 1989. Office: U Calif San Diego Dept Music 0326 La Jolla CA 92093 Office Phone: 858-534-3230.

REYNOLDS, SALLIE BLACKBURN, artist, volunteer; b. Kansas City, Mo., Feb. 9, 1940; d. Anton and Sallie Churchill (Blackburn) Zajic; m. Jeffrey Calhoun Loker, Mar. 25, 1959 (div. May 1965); children: Toni Lynne Loker, Michael David Loker, Kathryn Lee Loker Simpson; m. Everett Lee Reynolds, Mar. 29, 1969 (dec. Sept. 1992). Student, William Jewell Coll., 1959, BA magna cum laude, 1977; student, U. Mo., Kansas City, 1966-67, Kansas City Art Inst., 1966-70; Cert., Famous Artists Sch., 1965. Cert. tchr., Mo. From clk. to sec. Hdqrs. Strategic Air Command, Offutt AFB, Omaha, 1960-62; sec., wage and hr. law enforcement asst., wage-hr. divsn. U.S. Dept. of Labor, Kansas City, 1963-68, exec. sec. to regional manpower adminstr., 1968-71, spl. asst. to regional exec. com., 1971-72, mgmt. asst. Office of Regional Dir., 1972-73; co-owner Claycomo Skelly Svc. Sta. & Garage, 1970—78; from clk. to sec. air carrier dist. office FAA, Kansas City, 1978-81; from clk. typist procurement and contracts divsn. to sec. regional pers. officer Bur. of Reclamation, U.S. Dept. of Interior, Boulder City, Nev., 1982—84; edtl. asst. divsn. of planning Bur. of Reclamation, Boulder City, 1984-86; substitute tchr.; owner, operator B-Bar-L Wandering Star Ranch (registered angus, polled Herfords and horses, beefalo), Stover, Mo., 1989—. Editor newsletter Laurie Fine Art, 1989-90; designer historic landmark plaque Clay County, Mo.; designer hist. painting for annual Dogwood Festival pageants Camden County, Mo., 1994. Ofcl. commr., sec., corr. Clay County (Mo.) Bicentennial Commn., 1974-76; mem. Ozark Brush and Palette, Inc., Camdenton, Mo., 1987—, editor newsletter, 1988-89; v.p., sec., life mem. Clay County Hist. Soc., 1972—, active Nat. Wildlife Fedn. (guardian of the wild 2004); med. support asst. 509th Med. Group, Whiteman AFB, Mo., 2005-06. Recipient 1st pl. in oil/acrylic painting Nat. Soc. DAR Am. Heritage Contest, 1990, 3d pl., 1991, 1st pl. profl. photography Laurie Fine Art Show, 1990; named one of Top 50 Profl. Artists, Mo. State Fair, 1992. Mem. Nat. Soc. DAR (pub. rels. chmn., rec. sec., archives chmn., corr. sec. Niangua chpt. Camdenton 1987—; Eldon Mo. chpt. 1999—), Nat. Oil and Acrylic Painters Soc., Phi Gamma (fellow of Phi Beta Kappa, Versailles Saddle Club, Mo. Paint Horse Club (sec. 1998). Presbyterian. Avocations: art, history, needle-crafts, music, photography. Home and Office: B-Bar-L Wandering Star Ranch 23688 S 135 Hwy Stover MO 65078

REYNOLDS, SCOTT WALTON, academic administrator; b. Summit, NJ, July 15, 1941; s. Clark Leonard and Shirley (Hill) R.; m. Margaret Ann Johnson, July 5, 1969; children: Jane, Amy, David. BA, Trinity Coll., Hartford, Conn., 1963; MBA, Harvard U., 1965. Mng. dir. corp. staff Bankers Trust Co., N.Y.C., 1967-94; asst. to the pres. St. Peter's Coll., Jersey City, 1994-96, Hartford, Conn., 1996-98; sec., 1998—, interim v.p. fin., treas., 2004—05. Chmn. fund campaign Montclair (N.J.) ARC, 1974; chmn. bus. and fraternal group Montclair Bicentennial Com., 1976; bd. fellows Trinity Coll., 1982-88, trustee, 1992-96, sec., exec. com., 1993-96. 1st lt. U.S. Army, 1965-67. Recipient 150th Anniversary award Trinity Coll., 1978, Alumni medal for Excellence, 1988, Pres.' Leadership medal, 1993. Mem. Montclair Jaycees (treas. 1973), Trinity Coll. Alumni Assn. N.Y. (pres. 1972-73) Clubs: Harvard (N.Y.C.). Episcopalian. Office: Trinity Coll Office of Pres 300 Summit St Hartford CT 06106-3100 Office Phone: 860-297-2093. Business E-Mail: scott.reynolds@trincoll.edu.

REYNOLDS, SHERI, writer; b. Conway, SC, 1967; BA in English, Davidson Coll., 1989; MFA in creative writing, Va. Commonwealth U., 1992. Adj. instr. English Va. Commonwealth U., Richmond, 1992—. Author: Bitterroot Landing, 1994, The Rapture of Canaan, 1996, A Gracious Plenty, 1997. Office: VCU Dept English 900 Park Ave Hibbs Bldg 306 PO Box 842005 Richmond VA 23284-2005

REYNOLDS, STEPHEN PHILIP, utility company executive; b. Berkeley, Calif., Jan. 5, 1948; s. Philip Elmore and Annette (Medefind) R.; m. Sharon Ann Rudd, Sept. 6, 1969; 1 child, Matthew. BA in Econs., U. Calif., Berkeley, 1970; MBA in Prodn. Mgmt., U. Oreg., 1972. Various mktg./rate positions Pacific Gas and Electric Co., San Francisco, 1967-75, sr. rate engr., 1975-77, supervising rate engr., 1977-80, mgr. rate dept., 1980-84, v.p. rates, 1984-87; pres., CEO Pacific Gas Transmission Co. (subs. Pacific Gas and Electric), 1987—98, Reynolds Energy Internat., 1998—2002; chmn., pres., CEO Puget Energy, Bellevue, Wash., 2002—. Bd. dirs. UNOVA Inc., Oregon Steel Mills Inc., InfrastruX Group,. Interstate Gas of Am., Interstate Gas of Am. Found., Assn. of Northwest Gas Utilities. Contbr. numerous articles to trade publs. and profl. symposiums on rate issues. Served with Calif. Army N.G., 1970-76. Mem. Pacific Coast Gas Assn., Nat. Planning Assn. (Canadian-American Com.), Calif. Found. on Environment & Economy, San Francisco World Affairs Coun., San Francisco Engrs. Club, Commonwealth Club, World Trade Club. Office: Puget Energy 10885 NE 4th St PO Box 97034 Bellevue WA 98009-9734

REYNOLDS, TERRY RAY, curator, anthropologist, educator; d. Raymond Roberts and Harriet Pearl Reynolds. BA, U. Colo., 1962; MA, Stanford U., 1965; PhD, U. BC, 1979. Instr. Calif. State U., Northridge, 1965-68, 1972—74; sessional lectr. U. BC, Vancouver, Canada, 1968—69; dir. mus. studies U. Denver, 1989—98; curator N.Mex. State U., Las Cruces, 1998—. Cons., rschr. Boulder, Denver and Las Cruces, 1979—89. Editor A Place as Wild as West Ever Was, 2004. Fellow, Can. Coun., 1969—72. Mem.: Am. Soc. Ethnohistory, Am. Assn. Museums (chair profl. standing com. 1994—98). Avocations: dogs, antiques. Office: NMex State U Mus PO Box 30001 MSC 3564 Las Cruces NM 88003 Office Phone: 505-646-4056. Fax: 505-646-1419. E-mail: tereynol@nmsu.edu.

REYNOLDS, THOMAS A., III, lawyer; b. Evanston, Ill., May 12, 1952; BSBA, Georgetown U., 1974; JD, Emory U., 1977. Bar: Ill. 1977, U.S. Dist. Ct. (no. dist.) Ill. 1978, U.S. Ct. Appeals (7th cir.) 1979, U.S. Dist. Ct. (no. dist. trial bar) Ill. 1983. Asst. pub. defender, Cook County, Ill., 1977—78; asst. atty. gen. Ill., 1981—83; assoc. to ptnr. litigation Winston & Strawn, Chgo., 1983—. Dir. Smurfit-Stone Container Corp. Dir., v.p. Lyric Opera; dir. LINK Unlimited; pres. Brain Rsch. Found.; dir. U. Chgo. Hospitals; ptnr. Chgo. United. Mem.: Comml. Club Chgo. Office: Winston & Strawn LLP 35 W Wacker Dr Ste 4200 Chicago IL 60601-9703 Office Phone: 312-558-5895. Fax: 312-558-5700. E-mail: treynolds@winston.com.

REYNOLDS, THOMAS M., congressman; b. Springville, NY, Sept. 3, 1950; m. Donna Reynolds; 4 children. Student, Kent State U., Ohio, 1968—69. Pres. TM Reynolds Ins. Agy.; mem. to dep. supr. Concord Town Bd., 1974—82; mem. Erie County Legislature, 1982—88, NY State Assembly from Dist. 147, 1988-98, Rep. leader, 1995—98, chmn. minority affordable housing task force; mem. corrections com. N.Y. State Assembly; mem. US Congress from 26th NY dist., 1999—, chmn. Nat. Rep. Congl. Com., mem. ways and means com., mem. ho. adminstrn. com., dep. majority whip. Rank up to sgt. NY Air Nat. Guard, 1970-76; exec. asst. Staff of NY State Assemblyman Ronald Tillis; clk. Erie County Legislature; legis. asst. to minority Rep. leader, 1987; Erie County Rep. chmn., 1990-96. Named a Friend of Law Enforcement, NY State Sheriff's Assn.; named Legislator of Yr., Am. Legis. Exch. Coun., Shooters Com. Polit. Edn.; recipient Golden Apple award, US Apple Assn. Mem. Am. Legion, NRA, Southtown Walleye Assn., Masons. Republican. Presbyterian. Office: US Ho Reps 332 Cannon Ho Office Bldg Washington DC 20515-3226 Office Phone: 202-225-5265.*

REYNOLDS, VALRAE, museum curator; b. San Francisco, Dec. 18, 1944; d. Ralph Stanley and Valberta May (Eversole) R.; m. Richard Lee Huffman, Sept. 14, 1974; children: Elizabeth Anne, Margaret Lee. BA in Fine Arts with honors, U. Calif., Davis, 1966; MA, NYU, 1969. Asst. curator Asian collections Newark Mus., 1969-70, curator Asian collections, 1970—2002, sr. curator Asian collections, 2003—. Cons. SITES Exhbn., 1988; adj. prof. art history Columbia U., 1996; lectr., presenter in field. Author: From the Sacred Realm, Treasures of Tibetan Art from the Newark Museum, 1999; editor: Newark Mus. Quar., 1976, Tibetan Jour., 1976, Asia Soc., 1977, Arts of Asia, 1989, Explore Tibet, 1992; contbr. over 36 articles and revs. to profl. jours.; prodr. multimedia prodns. in field. Grantee NEA, NEH, 1972-74, 82-83, 85-86, 88-91, 89-92, 99, 2003, J. Paul Getty grantee, 1986, 89-91, Travel grantee Asian Cultural Coun., 1989, NEA grantee, 2003-05, Wallace Found. grantee, 2003-05, Freeman Found. grantee, 2003-05. Office: Newark Mus 49 Washington St Newark NJ 07102

REYNOLDS, VIRGINIA EDITH, sociologist, anthropologist, educator, artist; b. Lafayette, Ind., July 3, 1941; d. Ira Hubert and Harriet G. (Robertson) Reynolds; m. Antonio G. Arroyo, 1961 (div. 1974); children: Mary-Jane R. Arroyo Young, Joanne R. Arroyo Shirley. BS with hons. in Sociology, Columbia U., 1965, MA in Sociology, 1967; postgrad., Pa. State U., 1974—84. Rsch. asst. demographic divsn. Population Coun., N.Y.C., 1968; tchr. CUNY Borough Manhattan C.C., N.Y.C., 1969; asst. prof. sociology and anthropology Lycoming Coll., Williamsport, Pa., 1970—75, Indiana U. Pa., 1975—2001; ret. 2001. Mem. exec. com. Assn. for Asian Studies Mid-Atlantic Region, 1997—99; Tai Chi tchr. Exhibited in group shows at Old Courthouse Office Gallery, 2002 (Hon. Mention award, 2002), 2003 (2d Pl. award, 2003), Centennial of the Union Street Sanctuary, 2004, Presbyn. Ch. of Punxsutawney, 2004. Singer Indiana County Singers and Ch. Choir; mem. Indiana County Dem. Com., Pa., 2001—05. Mem.: AAUW (chair nat. conv. 2005), Touchstone Ctr. for Crafts, Indiana (Pa.) Art Assn., Pitts. Ctr. for the Arts. Episcopalian. Avocations: tai chi, community theatre musicals, international folk dancing, chinese painting. Home and Studio: 1699 Church St Indiana PA 15701 Office Phone: 724-349-4952. E-mail: veren77@hotmail.com.

REYNOLDS, WILLIAM BRADFORD, lawyer; b. Bridgeport, Conn., June 21, 1942; s. William Glasgow and Nancy Bradford (DuPont) R.; m. Marguerite Lynn Morgan, June 27, 1964 (div. Feb. 1987); children: William Bradford Jr., Melissa Morgan, Kristina DuPont, Wendy Riker; m. Clare Alice Conroy, Aug. 27, 1987 (div. June 2000); 1 child, Linda Matisan; m. Barbara Lynn Wooster, July 15, 2000; children: Courtney Enright, Brooke Ashley. BA, Yale U., 1964; LLB, Vanderbilt U., 1967. Bar: N.Y. 1968, D.C. 1973, U.S. Supreme Ct. 1971. Assoc. Sullivan and Cromwell, N.Y.C., 1967-70; asst. to Solicitor Gen. U.S. Dept. Justice, Washington, 1970-73; ptnr. Shaw, Pittman, Potts & Trowbridge, Washington, 1973-81; asst. atty. gen. Civil Rights div. U.S. Dept. Justice, Washington, 1981-88, counselor to Atty. Gen., 1987-88; ptnr. Ross & Hardies, 1989-91, Dickstein, Shapiro & Morin, 1991-94, Collier, Shannon, Rill & Scott, 1994-2000, Howrey LLP, Washington, 2000—. Chmn. Archtl. Transp. Barriers Compliance Bd., 1982-84. Editor-in-chief Vanderbilt Law Rev., 1966. Disting. scholar Free Congress Found., 1989-93, Disting. fellow Nat. Legal Ctr. for Pub. Interest, Washington, 1989-90. Mem. ABA, Fed. Bar Assn., D.C. Bar Assn., Order of Coif. Republican. Episcopalian. Office Phone: 202-383-6912. Business E-Mail: reynoldsw@howrey.com.

REYNOLDS, WILLIAM FRANCIS, mathematics professor; b. Boston, Jan. 31, 1930; s. William Leo and Grace Regina (Devlin) R.; m. Pauline Jane Fitzgerald, Aug. 5, 1962; children: Nancy Elizabeth, Jane Anele. AB summa cum laude, Holy Cross Coll., 1950; A.M., Harvard, 1951, PhD, 1954. Instr. Holy Cross Coll., Worcester, Mass., 1954-55; instr. Mass. Inst. Tech., Cambridge. 1955-57; asst. prof. math. Tufts U., Medford, Mass., 1957-60, assoc. prof., 1960-67, prof., 1967-98, Walker prof. math., 1970-98, prof. emeritus, 1998—. Contbr. articles to math. jours. Mem. Am. Math. Soc. Achievements include research on modular and projective representations of finite groups. Home: 3 Preble Gardens Rd Belmont MA 02478-3460 E-mail: wfr@post.harvard.edu.

REYNOLDS, WILLIAM LEROY, lawyer, educator; b. Balt., July 26, 1945; s. Austin Leroy and Doris (Hill) R.; m. Theodora Hoe, Sept. 3, 1966; children: William, Megan, Sarah. AB, Dartmouth Coll., 1967; JD, Harvard U., 1970. Bar: Md. 1972, U.S. Supreme Ct. 1975. Clk. to judge U.S. Dist. Ct. Md., 1970-71; asst. prof. law U. Md., 1971-74, assoc. prof., 1974-77, prof., 1977—; of counsel DLA PiperRudnick LLP, Balt., 1997—. Bd. dirs. Md. Jud. Inst. Author: Judicial Process in a Nutshell, 1980, 3d edit., 2002, Understanding the Conflict of Laws, 1984, 3d edit., 2002, Cases and Materials on Conflict of Laws, 1990, 2d edit.- 2003, The Full Faith and Credit Clause, 2005. Mem. Am. Law Inst., Md. State Bar Assn., Am. Judicature Soc. Clubs: Serjeants' Inn, Wranglers (Balt.); St. Regis Yacht (Paul Smiths, N.Y.), Hamilton St. Office: U Md Sch Law 500 W Baltimore St Baltimore MD 21201-1701 Business E-Mail: wreynolds@law.umaryland.edu.

REYNOLDS, WYNETKA ANN, academic administrator, educator; b. Coffeyville, Kans., Nov. 3, 1937; d. John Ethelbert and Glennie (Beanland) King; m. Thomas H. Kirschbaum; children: Rachel Rebecca, Rex King. BS in Biology-Chemistry, Kans. State Tchrs. Coll., Emporia, 1958; MS in Zoology, U. Iowa, Iowa City, 1960, PhD, 1962; DSc (hon.), Ind. State U., Evansville, 1980; LHD (hon.), McKendree Coll., 1984, U. N.C., Charlotte -1988, U. Judaism, LA, 1989, U. Nebr., Kearney, 1992; DSc (hon.), Ball State U., 1985, Emporia State U., 1987; PhD (hon.), Fu Jen Cath. U., China, 1987; LHD (hon.), Colgate U., 1993, No. Mich. U., 1995. Asst. prof. biology Ball State U., Muncie, Ind., 1962-65; asst. prof. anatomy U. Ill. Coll. Medicine, Chgo., 1965-68, assoc. prof. anatomy, 1968-73, rsch. prof. ob-gyn, 1973—, prof. anatomy, 1973—, acting assoc. dean acad. affairs Coll. Medicine, 1977, assoc. vice chancellor, dean grad. coll., 1977-79; provost, v.p. for acad. affairs, prof. ob-gyn. and anatomy Ohio State U., Columbus, 1979-82; chancellor Calif. State Univ. system, Long Beach, 1982-90, prof. biology, 1982-90; chancellor CUNY, 1990-97; pres. U. Ala., Birmingham, 1997—2002. Clin. prof. ob-gyn. UCLA, 1985—90; bd. dirs. Abbott Labs., Maytag, Owens-Corning, Humana, Inc., Invitrogen, News-Gazette, Champaign, Ill. Contbr. chapters to books, articles to profl. jours.; assoc. editor: Am. Biology Tchr., 1964—67. Trustee Internat. Life Scis. Inst.-Nutrition Found., 1987—2001, S.W. Mus.; mem. nat. adv. bd. Am. Indian Arts, 1992—97; bd. dirs. Lincoln Ctr. Inst., 1993—. Recipient Disting. Alumni award, Kans. State Tchrs. Coll., 1972, Prize award, Ctrl. Assn. Obstetricians and Gynecologists, 1988, Calif. Gov.'s award for Arts Outstanding Individual Arts in Edn., 1989; NSF Predoctoral fellow, 1958—62, Woodrow Wilson Hon. fellow, 1958. Fellow: ACOG; mem.: Soc. Gynecol. Investigation (sec./treas. 1980—83, pres. 1992—93), Perinatal Rsch. Soc., Sigma Xi.

REYNOLDS, Z. PAUL, academic administrator; b. Sandusky, Ohio, May 29, 1967; s. Nancy J. Reynolds. BEd, U. Toledo, 1989; MS in Edn., U. Pa., 1992, EdD, 1997. Asst. mgr. student life U. Pa., Phila., 1990—98; pres. and ceo TechKnow Designs, LLC, Corpus Christi, Tex., 1997; exec. dir. adminstrn. and ops. Carmelo Ruta, Inc., Sandusky, Ohio, 1999—2001; dir. interim mng. Island Express Boatlines, LTD, Sandusky, Ohio, 2002; asst. dir. U. Ctr. and Student Activities Tex. A&M U., Corpus Christi, Tex., 2002—. Soc. adv. bd. Corpus Christi (Tex.) Animal Care Ctr., 2005; mem. human rels. coun. City Sandusky, Ohio, 2000—02. Mem.: Assn. Coll. Unions Internat. (assoc.; various positions 1991). Republican. Roman Catholic. Avocations: computer gaming, fishing, pet care, web designs. Home: 2002 Airline Road 101 Corpus Christi TX 78412 Office: Texas A&M University-Corpus Christi 215 University Center/6300 Ocean Drive Corpus Christi TX 78412 Office Phone: 361-825-5204. Home Fax: 361-825-5201; Office Fax: 361-825-5201. Business E-Mail: paul.reynolds@tamucc.edu.

REYNOLDS COOCH, NANCY D. (MRS. EDWARD W. COOCH JR.), sculptor; b. Greenville, Del., Dec. 28, 1919; d. Eugene Eleuthere and Catherine Dulcinea (Moxham) duPont; m. William Glasgow Reynolds, May 18, 1940 (dec. Jan. 1987); children: Katherine Glasgow Reynolds, William Bradford Reynolds, Mary Parminter Reynolds Savage, Cynthia duPont Reynolds Farris.; m. Edward W. Cooch Jr., Sept 6, 2003. Student, Goldey-Beacom Coll., Wilmington, Del., 1938. One-woman shows include Caldwell Inc., 1975, Nat. Museum of Women in Arts, 1998; exhibited in group shows at Corcoran Gallery, Washington, 1943, Soc. Fine Arts, Wilmington, 1937-38,

40-41, 48, 50, 62, 65, Rehoboth (Del.) Art League, 1963, NAD, N.Y.C., 1964, Pa. Mil. Coll., Chester, 1966, Del. Art Ctr., 1967, Del. Art Mus., Wilmington, Wilmington Art Mus., 1976, Met. Mus. Art, N.Y.C., 1977, Lever House, N.Y.C., 1979, Nat. Mus. Women in the Arts, Washington, 1998; represented in permanent collections Wilmington Trust Co., E.I. duPont de Nemours & Co., Children's Home, Inc., Claymont, Del., Children's Bur., Wilmington, Stephenson Sci. Ctr., Vanderbilt U., Nashville, Lutheran Towers Bldg., Travelers Aid and Family Soc. Bldg., Wilmington, bronze fountain head Longwood Gardens, Kennett Square, Pa., bronze statue Brookgreen Gardens, Murrells Inlet, S.C., bronze sculpture "Veiled Lady", Nat. Mus. Women in Arts, Washington, 1998, bronze sculpture U. Del., Newark, 2001, bronze sculpture Biggs Mus., Dover, Del., 2002; contbr. articles to profl. jours. Organizer vol. svc. Del. chpt. ARC, 1938-39; chmn. Com. for Revision Del. Child Adoption Law, 1950-52; pres., bd. dirs. Children Bur. Del.; pres., trustee Children's Home, Inc.; del., past pres. Gunston Hall Plantation, Lorton, Va.; mem. adv. com. Longwood Gardens, Kennett Sq., Pa.; garden and grounds com. Winterthur (Del.) Mus.; mem. rsch. staff Henry Francis DuPont Winterthur Mus., 1973—88; mem. archtl. com. U. Del., Newark. Recipient Confrerie des Chevaliers du Tastevin Clos de Vougeot-Bourgogne France, 1960; Hort. award Garden Club Am., 1964, medal of Merit, 1976, Dorothy Platt award Garden Club of Phila., 1980, Alumni medal of merit Westover Sch., Middlebury, Conn., Medal of Distinction, U. Del., 1999. Mem. Pa. Hort. Soc., Wilmington Soc. Fine Arts, Mayflower Descs., Del. Hist. Soc., Colonial Dames, League Am. Pen Women, Nat. Trust Hist. Preservation. Garden Club of Wilmington (past pres.), Garden Club of Am. (past asst. zone 4 chmn.), Vicmead Hunt Club, Greenville Country Club, Chevy Chase Club (Washington), Colony Club (N.Y.C.). Episcopalian. Address: PO Box 3919 Greenville DE 19807-0919

REYNOLDSON, WALTER WARD, retired judge, lawyer; b. St. Edward, Nebr., May 17, 1920; s. Walter Scorer and Mabel Matilda (Sallach) Reynoldson; m. Janet Aline Mills, Dec. 24, 1942 (dec. 1986); children: Vicki, Robert; m. Patricia A. Frey, June 3, 1989. BA. State Tchrs. Coll., 1942; JD, U. Iowa, 1948; LLD (hon.), Simpson Coll., 1983, Drake U., 1987. Bar: Iowa 1948. Justice Iowa Supreme Ct., 1971-78, chief justice, 1978-87, sr. judge, 1989-93; of counsel Reynoldson Law Firm, Osceola, Iowa, 1993—. County atty. Clark County, Iowa, 1953—57; adj. prof. law Drake U., 1989—93. Co-author: (book) Trial Handbook, 1969. Pres. Nat. Ctr. State Cts.; trustee Drake U., 1987—2000. With USNR, 1942—46. Recipient Osceola Cmty. Svc. award, 1968. Fellow: Am. Bar Found.; mem.: Am. Coll. Trial Lawyers, Conf. Chief Justices (pres. 1984—85), Acad. Trial Lawyers, Am. Judicature Soc. (bd. dirs. 1983—87, Herbert Harley award 1990), Iowa Bar Assn. (chmn. com. legal edn. and admission to bar 1964—71). Office: Reynoldson Law Firm 200 W Jefferson St Osceola IA 50213-1413

REYNOLDS-SAKOWSKI, DANA RENEE, science educator; b. Centralia, Ill., June 28, 1968; d. David Lavern and Betty Lou (Shelton) Reynolds; m. Jason Bielas Sakowski, Oct. 8, 1994. BS in Edn., U. No. Colo., 1991, MEd in Middle Sch. Edn., 1996. Tchr. life sci. and math. Ken Caryl Mid. Sch., Littleton, Colo., 1991-92; tchr. sci. Moore Mid. Sch., Arvada, Colo., 1992-93, tchr. life sci., 1993—. Mem. Nat. Wildlife Fedn., Colo. Assn. Sci. Tchrs., Colo. Biology Tchrs. Assn., Sierra Club, World Wildlife Fund, Nat. Parks and Conservation Assn., Natural Resources Def. Coun., Audubon Soc., Nature Conservancy. Avocations: camping, poetry, hiking, singing. Office: Mandalay Mid Sch 9651 N Pierce St Westminster CO 80020

REYNOSO, DAVID, chef; Grad., Washburne Trade Sch., Chgo., 1990. Head chef Trattoria Mangia, Kenosha, Wis., Tuttaposto Mediterranean Tavern, Chgo., Spoodles, Orlando, Fla.; opened Padres Restaurant, Verden, Germany; chef of kitchen ops. The Butcher Shop, Boston, B&G Oysters, Boston. Named one of Boston's Rising Stars, StarChefs.com, 2006. Office: The Butcher Shop 552 Tremont St Boston MA 02118 Office Phone: 617-423-4800.*

REYNVAAN, MICHAEL THOMAS, lawyer; b. Bremerton, Wash., Sept. 26, 1953; s. Theodore Thomas Reynvaan and Clara Anne (Malinowski) Reynvaan-Graves; m. Gale Arlene Beegle; children: Amanda, Angela, Matthew. Student, Whitman Coll., 1971-73; BA in Polit. Sci, Lewis and Clark Coll., 1976; JD, U. Puget Sound, 1982. Bar: Wash. 1982, US Dist. Ct. (We. Dist.) Wash. 1983, US Ct. Appeals (9th Cir.) 1983, US Dist. Ct. (Ea. Dist.) Wash. 1985. Mill worker Internat. Telephone & Telegraph/Rayonier Inc., Hoquiam, Wash., 1976-77, 79; legal asst. Bogle & Gates, Seattle, 1979; law clk. to chief justice Wash. State Supreme Ct., Olympia, 1982-83; assoc. Perkins Coie, Seattle, 1983—, ptnr., mem. mgmt. com. & exec. com. Active Alki Found., Seattle, 1988, Leadership Tomorrow, 1988—; campaign treas. Callow for Supreme Ct., Seattle, 1984; del. Kitsap County Dem. Conv. Mem. ABA (YLD labor law com., vice-chair 1988-89, chmn. 1989—), Seattle-King County Bar Assn. (young lawyers div., bd. trustees), Wash. State Bar Assn., Wash. Athletic Club. Episcopalian. Office: Perkins Coie LLP 1201 3rd Ave Fl 40 Seattle WA 98101-3029 Office Phone: 206-359-8469. Office Fax: 206-359-9000. Business E-Mail: mreynvaan@perkinscoie.com

REZA, ALI HAJMOHAMMAD, cardiologist; b. Tehran, Iran, Apr. 14, 1957; came to U.S., 1988; s. Tayeb Hajmohammad and Fakhri (Mohajer) R.; m. Elizabeth Gheisari; children: Tara, Arteen. MD, Nat. U. Iran, Tehran, 1982. Diplomate Am. Bd. Internal Medicine, Am. Cardiovasc., Am. Bd. Interventional Cardiology; bd. cert. nuclear cardiology, bd. cert. in vascular medicine, 2005, endovascular medicine, 2005. Rsch. in pathology Rush Med. Sch., Chgo., 1988-89; resident in internal medicine SUNY, Buffalo, 1989-93, fellow in nephrology, 1992-93; fellow in cardiology Tulane U., New Orleans, 1993-96; pvt. practice, Chalmette, La., 1996—; pvt. practice Oschner Cardiovascular Inst., 2001—. Mem. ACP, AMA, Am. Coll. Cardiology. Moslem. Home: 1804 Octavia St New Orleans LA 70115 Office: 5701 Deerpark Blvd New Orleans LA 70127

REZA, YASMINA, author, playwright; Author: (plays) Conversations After A Burial, 1987 (Moliere award for best author, SACD New Talent award, Johnson Found. award), Winter Crossing, 1990 (Moliere award for best fringe prodn., 1990), The Unexpected Man, Art, 1995 (Moliere award for best author, Olivier award, Evening Standard award, Tony award), (novels) Hammerklavier, 1997, (translator) (Kafka) Metamorphosis (Moliere award for best translation); screenwriter (TV films) See You Tomorrow, Kunst, 1997, (films) Le Pique-nique de Lula Kreutz, 2000.

REZANKA, THOMAS W., lawyer; b. Plainfield, NJ, Mar. 3, 1954; s. William L. and Helen G. Rezanka; m. Karen T. Rezanka, May 21, 1977. BA, Montclair State U., Upper Montclair, N.J., 1976; JD, Stetson U., 1980. Bar: Fla. 1980, U.S. Ct. Appeals (5th and 11th cirs.) 1980. Pvt. practice, Palm Harbor, Fla., 1980—. Presenter Joint Conf. on Law and Aging, Washington, 1995. Columnist Tropical Breeze, 1995-2001, Countryside Cougar, East Lake Eagle, Palm Harbor Panther, 1995-2005, Dunedin Highlander, 2001-05; author: The Catholic Challenge: A Question of Conscience, 2004. Adv. com. Countryside HS, Clearwater, Fla., 1998-99; bd. dirs. Tampa Bay Area Planned Giving Coun., Tampa, 2001. Mem. ABA, Nat. Acad. Elder Law Atty., Fla. Bar Assn. (former mem. legis. drafting com. real property, probate and trust law sect.) exec. coun. elder law sect. 1995-99, faculty counseling your Fla. client seminar for out-of-state atty. 1999, faculty elder law bd. cert. rev. course 1998, editor The Advocate newsletter 1996-97, elder law sect.), Clearwater Bar Assn. (estate planning columnist 1996-97, 2000-01, probate, guardianship and trust practice com.), Pinellas County Estate Planning Coun. (bd. dir. 1995-99). Office: 2672 Westlake Rd Palm Harbor FL 34684 Office Phone: 727-787-3020.

REZBA, PATRICIA LOUISE, middle school educator; b. Red Bud, Ill., Feb. 2, 1951; d. Walker LeVern and Bebe Irlene Joiner; m. Willis Eugene Rezba, Jan. 27, 1972; children: Joshua David, Timothy Alan. BS in Edn., Eastern Ill. U., 1973; MA in English Edn., Olivet Nazarene U., 1984. History tchr. Bourbonnais (Ill.) Elem. Sch. Dist., 1974—. Edn. grantee First of Am., 1990; recipient Ill. Math and Sci. Acad. award of Excellence, 1993. Mem.

Bourbonnais Edn. Assn. (pres. 1992—, Mem. of Yr. 1991). Avocations: reading, watercolor painting, handicrafts. Office: Bourbonnais Upper Grade Ctr 200 John Casey Bourbonnais IL 60914

**REZEK, FRANCISCO,** judge, former supreme court justice; b. Cristina, Brazil, Jan. 18, 1944; s. Elias and Baget Rezek; m. Myreia de Palma Castro, Jan. 14, 1971; children: Adriana, Veronica, Francisco, João Paulo. LLB. U. Minas Gerais, Belo Horizonte, 1966; LLD, U. Paris-Sorbonne, 1970; diploma in law, Oxford U., England, 1979. Atty. Rep. of Brazil, 1972-79, dep. atty. gen., 1979-83, justice Supreme Ct., 1983—90, 1992—97; fgn. min. Dept. State, Brasilia, 1990-92; dean faculty of law U. Brasilia, 1978-79; judge Intl. Ct. of Justice, The Hague, Netherlands, 1997—. Prof., internat. law and constl. law, Univ. Brasilia, 1971-97 (chmn., dept. of law, 1974-76, dean, faculty of social studies, 1978-79); prof., internat. law, Rio Branco (diplomatic) Inst., 1976-97; lecturer, The Hague Acad. of Internat. Law, 1986, Inst. of Internat. Public Law and Internat. Rels., Thessaloniki, 1989; mem., Permanent Ct. of Arbitration, 1987-; chief justice at the High Electoral Ct., Brasilia, 1989. Author: Law of Treaties, 1984, International Law, 1989, 4th edit., 1994, others. Recipient Grand Cross Orders of Brazil, Argentina, Chile, Colombia, Lebanon, Tunisia, Korea, Portugal, Spain, and Italy, 1986-92. Roman Catholic. Office: Internat Ct of Justice Peace Palace 2517 KJ The Hague Netherlands

**REZKALLA, LAURENCE,** internist; b. Asyut, Egypt, Mar. 9, 1958; arrived in U.S., 1990; s. Lamie Rezkalla Rophael and Eniat William Basaly; m. Evette Wadie Kamel, Apr. 15, 1990; children: Paul, Peter, John, Mary. ND, Asyut Med. Sch., 1982; ob-gyn. specialist, Ain Shams Med. Sch., Cairo, 1988. Cert. Am. Bd. Internal Medicine. Intern Asyut U. Hosp., 1983—84; ob gyn resident El-Iman Gen. Hosp., Asyut, 1986—88; ob-gyn. physician Oasis Gen. Hosp., El-Wahat El-Bahria, Egypt, 1989, Sahelsleem (Egypt) Hosp., 1989—91; internal medicine resident Kingsbrook Jewish Med. Ctr., Bklyn., 1995—98; physician St. Barnabas's Hosp., East Elmhurst, NY, 1998—2000, Woodull Hosp., Bklyn., 1999—, N.Y. Meth. Hosp. 2002—, Victory Meml. Hosp., 2004—. Pres. Bay Ridge Med. Svcs., Bklyn., 2001—; mem. exec. com. Kingsbrook Hosp., 1996—2003. Author: (book) 10 Cases of Ob/Gyn, 1988. Leader youth meetings Salvation Soc., Asyut, 1973—81; founder Arab 2000 Inc., Bklyn., 1997—2000; ptnr. Internat. Resource Ctr., Johannesburg, 1997—2000. With med. svcs. Egyptian Army, 1984—86. Scholar Full scholar, Egyptian Govt., Asyut U., 1976. Mem.: ACP, AMA, Egyptian Med. Syndicate, Com. of Internal Residents (del. 1996—97). Avocations: travel, reading, painting. Home: 124 86th St Brooklyn NY 11209 Office: Bay Rige Med Svcs 124 86th St Brooklyn NY 11209 Office Phone: 718-921-1977.

**REZNICK, RICHARD HOWARD,** pediatrician; b. Chgo., Oct. 31, 1939; s. Louis and Mae Reznick; m. Barbara Ann Glantz, June 20, 1965; children: Steven L., Alicia T., Scott M., Stacey R. BS, U. Ill., 1961; MD, Loyola U., Chgo., 1965. Diplomate Am. Bd. Pediatrics. Resident in pediat. Michael Reese Hosp., Chgo., 1966-68; pediatrician USAF, Homestead AFB, Fla., 1968-70; pediatrician pvt. practice Winnetka, Ill., 1970—71, Scottsdale, Ariz., 1971—. Pres. med. staff Phoenix Children's Hosp., 1990-93, bd. dirs. 1990-94. Capt. USAF, 1968-70. Fellow Am. Acad. Pediatrics (treas. Ariz. chpt. 1982-84); mem. AMA, Ariz. Med. Assn., Phoenix Pediatric Soc. (treas. 1976-77), Maricopa County Med. Soc. Avocations: aerobics, bicycling, gardening, classical music, collecting stamps. Office: Papago Buttes Pediatric Ctr 8573 E San Alberto Ste E100 Scottsdale AZ 85258-4318 Office Phone: 480-778-1732.

**REZNICK, STEVEN MICHAEL,** orthopedic surgeon, educator; b. Washington, 1954; 3 children. BS, U. Md., 1975; MD, George Washington U., 1979; MBA, Columbia U., 2000. Diplomate Am. Bd. Orthopedic Surgery. Resident in gen. surgery George Washington U., 1979-81; resident in orthop. surgery U. Mich., Ann Arbor, 1981-84; clin. instr. orthopedic surgery UCLA Sch. Medicine, 1988-94. SV. aviation med. examiner FAA, 1985-87; talk show host KGIL-Radio, L.A., 1987-90. Mem. Calif. Rep. Party, Calif. Rep. Assembly, bd. dirs. Palm Springs chpt., 1996-98. Fellow Internat. Coll. Surgeons, Am. Coll. Surgeons, Am. Acad. Orthopedic Surgeons, Beta Gamma Sigma Honor Soc. Avocation: commercial pilot. Home: PO Box 101 Somers NY 10589 E-mail: smr50@columbia.edu.

**REZNIK, LEONID CARLOVICH,** engineering and information technology educator, researcher; b. St. Petersburg, Russia, Oct. 18, 1955; arrived in Australia, 1992, arrived in U.S., 2001; s. Carl and Ninel (Kaganovich) R.; m. Olga Kuftova, Dec. 6, 1982; 1 child, Dmitry. Diploma in Elec. Engring., St. Petersburg Aircraft Acad., 1978; PhD, St. Petersburg U. Tech., 1983. Engr., programmer, prin. scientist, sr. scientist Rsch. Inst. Electromeasuring Instruments, St. Petersburg, 1978-87; leading scientist Rsch. Inst. Shipbldg. Tech., St. Petersburg, 1987-88, Interguadro, Moscow, 1988-91; sr. lectr., lectr. Victoria U., Melbourne, Australia, 1992—2002; assoc. prof. U. Tex., El Paso, 2002—. Sr. rschr./lectr. High Certifying Commn., Russia, 1986. Author: Fuzzy Controllers, 1997; editor/ Fuzzy System Design, 1998. Mem. IEEE, N.Y. Acad. Sci. and Tech. Avocations: detective stories, swimming. Office: U Tex Computer Sci El Paso TX 79968-0518

**REZNIK, MYKHAILO B.,** ambassador; b. Dec. 5, 1950; m. Irina Reznik; 1 child. Grad., Kyiv Trade and Econ. U., 1972, Acad. of Nat. Econ. of Ukraine, 1977; grad., Sr. Exec. Program, Stanford U. Bus. Sch., 1992. Gen. dir. State Trade Procurement Com., Ukraine, 1973—82, v.p., 1982—86, pres., 1986—88; chmn. State Fgn. Trade Assn., UkrTechMashImpex, Ukraine, 1988—92; first dep.min. of fgn econ rels and trade Ukraine, 1992—93; head Trade and Econ Mission of Ukranian Embassy, Washington, 1994—97; Ukranian amb. to Korea, 1997—2001, to China, 2001—03, to the U.S., 2003—. Office: Embassy of Ukraine 3350 M St NW Washington DC 20007

**REZNIKOV, VLADIMIR LVOVICH,** historian, playwright; b. Donetzk, Ukraine, May 26, 1937; s. Lev Davidovich Reznikov and Sofia Semyonovna Baskina; m. Natalya Klueva, Nov. 4, 1994; children: Lev, Michael, Sonya. MS in History, Moscow State Pedagogic U., 1962; PhD in History, Russain Acad. Scis., 1972; MS in Screenplay Writing (hon.), State Inst. Cinematography, Moscow, 1973. Sci. editor Oriental Book Publishers, Moscow, 1962—69; dept. editor Asia and Africa Today, Moscow, 1977—81; sr. rsch. fellow Inst. Oriental Studies of Russian Acad. of Scis., Moscow, 1969—97, 1981—97; freelance playwright scholar of art history, 1997—. Author: (screenplays) Encounter, 1971, Forgive me, Vietnam, 1971, Personal Case, 1971, Nature and Society, 1980, (screen play) Voice of the Centuries, 1975, Use of Isotope Control Devices in Automatization of Production Processes, 1975, (books) Policy of Caeser's Germany in Oceania, 1975; editor: India - Country and People, 1967 (Hon. Diploma Geog. Soc. of USSR, 1973). Mem.: Journalist Soc. of Russia, Am. Taekwondo Assn. (2d Degree Black belt). Avocation: Tae Kwon Do. Personal E-mail: nklueva@yahoo.com.

**REZNOR, TRENT,** musician; b. Mercer, Pa., May 17, 1965; Albums include Pretty Hate Machine, 1989, Broken, 1992, The Downward Spiral, 1994, Further Down the Spiral, 1995, The Fragile, 1999, Things Falling Apart, 2000, With Teeth, 2005. (co-prodr. (albums) Get Your Gunn, 1994, Portrait of an Am. Family, 1994, Prick, 1995, Smells Like Children, 1995, Antichrist Superstar, 1995, Sweet Dreams, 1997, The Beautiful People, 1997, Tourniquet, 1997, Voyeurs 2, 1998, It Dreams, 2004; composer, writer, actor video Broken, 1992, film Lost Highway, 1996; composer film Natural Born Killers, 1994; performer Woodstock '94. Grammy Award, Best Metal Performance, 1992, 1995; named Most Vital Artist in Music, Spin Mag., 1997, One of Most Influential Americans, Time Mag., 1997. Office: Interscope Geffen A&M Records 2220 Colorado Ave Santa Monica CA 90404*

**REZYKOWSKI, CATHERINE R.,** secondary school educator; b. Sayre, Pa., July 28, 1958; d. William Samuel and Jean Elisabeth Davis; m. Stanley Stephen Rezykowski, July 24, 1982; children: Stacy Marie, Anthony Joseph, Steven William. BS, Wilkes U., 1980. Tchr., band dir. Elk Lake Sch., Dimock, Pa., 1980—. Condr. 2 county band festivals; pianist weddings, square dance

band. Organist Dimock Cmty. Ch., 1995—2005, choir dir., 1995—2005. Republican. Methodist. Avocations: gardening, watching son's baseball and basketball games. Home: PO Box 4 Dimock PA 18816

**RHAMES, VING (IRVING),** actor; b. NYC, May 12, 1961; m. Valerie Scott, 1994 (div. 1999); m. Deborah Reed, Dec. 25, 2000; children: Tiffany, Rainbow, Freedom. Grad., Julliard Sch. Drama. Actor (Broadway plays) The Winter Boys, 1984; (films) Native Son, 1986, Patty Hearst, 1988, Casualties of War, 1989, The Long Walk Home, 1990, Jacob's Ladder, 1990, Flight of the Intruder, 1991, Homicide, 1991, Stop! Or My Mom Will Shoot, 1992, The People Under the Stairs, 1992, Dave, 1993, The Saint of Fort Washington, 1993, Bound By Honor Blood In Blood Out, 1993, Pulp Fiction, 1994, Drop Squad, 1994, Kiss of Death, 1995, Ed McBain's 87th Precinct, 1995, Mission: Impossible, 1996, Striptease, 1996, Con Air, 1997, Rosewood, 1997, Dangerous Ground, 1997, The Split, 1998, Out of Sight, 1998, Body Count, 1998, Entrapment, 1999, Bringing Out the Dead, 1999, Mission Impossible II, 2000, (voice) Final Fantasy: The Spirits Within, 2001, Baby Boy, 2001, Lilo & Stitch (voice only), 2002, Dark Blue, 2002, Undisputed, 2002, (voice) Stitch! The Movie, 2003, Back in the Day, 2004, Dawn of the Dead, 2004; (TV films) Go Tell It On the Mountain, 1985, Rising Son, 1990, When You Remember Me, 1990, Amerique en otage L', 1991, Terror on Track 9, 1992, Deadly Whispers, 1995, Don King: Only in America, 1997 (Golden Globe for best performance by an actor in a mini-series or motion picture made for TV 1998), American Tragedy, 2000, Holiday Heart, 2000, Little John, 2002, RFK, 2002, Sins of the Father, 2002; (TV series) Another World, 1986, Men, 1989, UC: Undercover, 2001; TV appearances include Miami Vice, 1985, 87, Crime Story, 1986, Tour of Duty, 1987, Spenser: For Hire, 1988, The Equalizer, 1989, ER, 1994, 95, 96, New York Undercover, 1995, The District, 2002, 03, The Adventures of Jimmy Neutron: Boy Genius, 2003. Office: William Morris Agy 151 S El Camino Dr Beverly Hills CA 90212-2775

**RHEA, JERRY DWAINE,** consumer lending director; b. Knoxville, Tenn., Dec. 11, 1950; s. Paul Edward and Pearl (Cornett) R.; m. Lamara Hurt, Aug. 22, 1973; children: Kathryn, Jerry. BS in Acctg., Tenn. Wesleyan Coll., Athens, 1973. Corp. credit adminstr. G.E. Capital, Stamford, Conn., 1973-88; exec. v.p., consumer lending officer, dir. Chase Fin., Cleve., 1988-97; exec. v.p. ops. So. Pacific Funding Corp., Lake Oswego, Oreg., 1997-98; pres. Financial Ptnrs., Portland, Oreg., 1998—. Avocations: photography, boating.

**RHEAMS, ANNIE ELIZABETH,** education educator; b. Lake Providence, La. d. Curtis Kleinpeter Sr. and Annie Augusta (Webb) Kleinpeter; 1 child, Darryl Jemall Rheams. BA, Grambling (La.) U., 1971; MS, Ala. A&M U., 1975; PhD, U. Wis., Milw., 1989. Cert. tchr. in exceptional edn., adminstrn. Tchr. Ala. A&M U., Normal, 1971-79; adminstr., 1977-79; acad. specialist U. Wis., Milw., 1979-82, Parkside, 1982-84; tchr. diagnostician, adminstr. Milw. Schs., 1984-89; asst. dept. edn. Marquette U., Milw., 1989-96; asst. prin. North Divsn. H.S., Milw., 1996—, Marshall H.S., Milw., 1997—99, tchr. exceptional edn. cognitively disabled, consumer math., 1999—, adminstr., asst. prin., 1999. Career counselor Madison County Career Counseling Svcs., Huntsville, 1975; adj. prof. Oakwood (Ala.) SDA Coll., 1975-78; tchr. Gateway to Engring. Program, Milw., 1984-88; cons. pub. schs./Wee Care Day Care, Milw., 1992-96; condr. workshops in field. Author: P.A.C.E.: A Thematic Approach to Developing Essential Experiences, 1996. Voter registrar/poll watcher NAACP, Lake Providence, 1966; v.p. Work for Wis. Inc., Milw., 1993-94, Messmer H.S. Bd., Milw., 1990-94; com. chmn. Citizen's Rev. Bd., Milw., 1980-82, Met. Milw. Alliance Black Sch. Educators, 1994-95. Assoc. fellow Ctr. for Great Plains Studies, U. Nebr.-Lincoln, 1995; named Outstanding Tchr. Educator, Am. Assn. for Coll. Tchr. Educators Directory, 1995. Mem. Zonta Internat., Alpha Kappa Alpha, Phi Delta Kappa. Avocations: tennis, sewing, ceramics, horseback riding, biking. Home: PO Box 90681 Milwaukee WI 53209-0611 Office Phone: 414-902-8497. Office Fax: 414-902-8315. Business E-Mail: rheams@hotmail.com.

**RHEAULT, KEITH W.,** school system administrator; m. Denise Rheault; 4 children. BS, ND State U., 1976, MS in Agrl. Edn., 1980; PhD in Agrl. Edn., Iowa State U., 1985. With Nev. Dept. Edn., 1986—, agriculture edn. cons., state FFA adv., asst. dir. to dir. Office of Occupational and Continuing Edn., dep. supt. for Instructional, Rsch. and Evaluative Svcs., supt. pub. instrn., 2004—. Adj. prof. Agrl. Engring. Dept. Iowa State U. Officer USAR, 1977—85. Office: Nev Dept Edn 700 E Fifth St Carson City NV 89701-5096 Office Phone: 775-687-9200. Office Fax: 775-687-5660. E-mail: krheault@doe.nv.gov.

**RHEE, HONGJOO,** materials scientist; s. Hang-Chull Rhee and In-Kyung Chung; m. Hyeona Lim, Dec. 14, 2005. PhD. Mich. State U., East Lansing, 2005. Rsch./tchg. asst. Inha U., Incheon, Republic of Korea, 1991—93; rsch. staff Kia Steel Co. Ltd., Kunsan, Republic of Korea, 1992—95, asst. mgr., 1996—98; rsch. staff Inha U., Incheon, Republic of Korea, 1998—99; rsch. asst. Mich. State U., East Lansing, 2000—04, tchg. asst., 2004, rsch. assoc., 2005; post-doctoral assoc. Ctr. for Advanced Vehicular Systems, Starkville, Miss., 2006—. Contbr. articles to profl. jours. Achievements include 3 Korean patents; patents pending for Materials and preparation of high strength gear steel; Ingot casting technology using heat sink material. Office Phone: 662-325-9221.

**RHEE, JEONG-EUN,** education educator; b. Seoul, Korea, Apr. 20, 1969; d. Choonyoun Rhee and Haechung Lee; m. Seung-keon Kwak, Apr. 20, 1991; 1 child, Bethia Juhyun Kwak. BA, Ewha Women's U., Seoul, Korea, 1991; MA, W.Va. U., 1994; PhD, The Ohio State U., 2002. Asst. prof. St. Cloud State U., St.Cloud, Minn., 2002—04, LI U. C.W. Post, Brookville, NY, 2004—. Tchr. preparation edn. program - human rels. requirement reviewer Minn. Dept. of Children, Families and Learning, Mpls., 2002—04. Recipient Hayes Forum Grad Symposium 1st prize in edn. Ohio State U. Grad. Schl., 2000; Earl Anderson Meml. scholar, Ohio State U. Sch. Edn., 1999, Rolfes and Heldt Meml. scholar, 2000, Dai-Ho Chun scholar, 2001, U. Village Lodge scholar, 2001, Critical Difference of Women Profl. Devel. grantee, Ohio State U., 2001. Mem.: Am. Ednl. Rsch. Assn. Office: Long Island University CW Post 720 Northern Blvd Brookville NY 11548 Office Phone: 516-299-2372. Office Fax: 516-299-3312. Business E-Mail: jeong-eun.rhee@liu.ed.

**RHEE, MOOWEON,** business educator; arrived in U.S., 1997; s. Seoung-Bae Rhee and Young-Ja Han; m. Mihyang Ahn, Dec. 24, 1995; children: Yoojin, Jennifer. BBA, Yonsei U., Seoul, 1991, MBA, 1993; PhD, Stanford U., 2003. Air traffic contr. Korean Army, Wontong, Republic of Korea, 1993—95; rsch. assoc. POSCO, Seoul, 1995—96; instr. Seoul Nat. U. Tech., 1997; rsch. asst. UCLA, L.A., 1997, Stanford (Calif.) U., 1998—2003; co-dir. Stanford Project on Entrepreneurial Edn., Stanford, 2003; asst. prof. U. Hawaii, Honolulu, 2004—. Cons. Hyundai Semicondr., San Jose, 2001, F-Net, Seoul, 2002, Hyundai Motors Am., L.A., 2003. Contbr. articles to profl. jours. Recipient Student Writing Competition award, IRRA, 1999, William Miller award, Stanford U., 1999. Mem.: Am. Sociol. Assn., Acad. Mgmt. (Most Pub. Pact Paper award 2003). Office: U Hawaii 2404 Maile Way Honolulu HI 96822

**RHEE, SOKWOO,** mechanical engineer; BS in Mech. Engring., Seoul Nat. U., Korea, 1995; MS in Mech. Engring., MIT, 1997, PhD in Mech. Engring., 2000. Postdoctoral rschr. MIT, 2000—02; chief tech. officer Millennial Net, Inc., 2000—. Contbr. articles to profl. jours. Named one of Top 100 Young Innovators, MIT Tech. Review, 2004; recipient Douglas H. Annin award, Instrumentation, Systems, and Automation Soc., 2004. Achievements include 4 US patents issued or pending. Office: Millennial Net Inc 2 Fourth Ave Burlington MA 01803

**RHEE, SOO-YON,** information scientist; d. Haeyoung Rhee and Yunho Chang; m. Hanhwe Kim, Feb. 14, 1963; 1 child, Paul Taewan Kim. BS in Biology, Korea U., Seoul, 1990; MSIS, U. Pitts., 1997. Sun Certified Java Programmer Sun Microsystem, Calif., 1998. Software engr. BZ Web Corp., Hayward, Calif., 1999—2001; software developer, dept. infectious diseases Sch. Medicine, Stanford U., Calif., 2001—06, lab dir., dept. infectious

diseases, 2006—. Contbr. articles to profl. jours. Roman Catholic. Achievements include setting up and maintaining the Stanford HIV Drug Resistance Database to assist scientists designing new HIV-1 drugs, and clinical investigators studying HIV-1 drug resistance tests; identified and researched multidrug resistant isolates in patients receiving treatment with the majority of available RT and protease inhibitors; research in links between HIV-1 genotypes and treatments, between genotypes and phenotypes, and genotypes, treatments and virologic outcomes; development of web-based tools for presenting data from the Stanford HIV Drug Resistance Database. Office: Stanford Univ Medical Center S-16 300 Pasteur Dr Stanford CA 94305 Office Phone: 650-736-0911. Business E-Mail: syrhee@stanford.edu.

**RHEIN, ARTHUR,** computer company executive; V.p. mktg. Harvey Electronics, 1983—86; sr. v.p. mktg. Pioneer, 1986; from v.p. mktg. to pres. CEO Agilysys, Inc., Mayfield Heights, Ohio, 1986—2002, pres., 2002—, CEO, 2002—, chmn. bd. 2003—. Office: Agilysys Inc 6065 Parkland Blvd Mayfield Heights OH 44124

**RHEIN, JOHN HANCOCK WILLING, III,** publishing executive; b. Richmond, Va., Aug. 8, 1931; s. John Hancock Willing Jr. and Margaret (Packard) R.; m. Phyllis Betz, June 13, 1953; children: Susan Rhein Dubowski, Deborah B., John Hancock Willing IV. BA, Hobart Coll., 1953. With rsch. dept. Benton & Bowles Advt., N.Y.C., 1957; sales mgmt. asst. to pub. Forbes Mag., N.Y.C., 1957-71; sr. v.p., assoc. pub. Fin. Mag., N.Y.C., 1971-73, Fin. World Mag., N.Y.C., 1973-81; pres. Nat. Bus. Confs., N.Y.C., 1975-81; sr. v.p. dir. sales and mktg. Sat. Rev. Mag., N.Y.C., 1980-81, View Mag., N.Y.C., 1980-81; pub. Equities Mag. (formerly OTC Rev.), N.Y.C., 1981 93; CEO Am. Depository Receipt Assn., 1993—2005. Pub. Capitalist-Forum.com, 2000—05; chmn. bd. W.R. Keegan Corp., Focus the Nat. H.S. News Mag., 1994—; pres. The Investor Intelligence Group, Garden City, NY, 1981—; dir. Top Tier Writers, Inc., 2000—03; mng. dir. Green Rhino Pixelbooks, 2003—, Creative Resources Adv. and Pub. Rels., 1995—. Office: Investor Intelligence Group 96 10th St Garden City NY 11530-1560 Personal E-mail: John_Rhein3@yahoo.com

**RHEINFRANK, SALLY LYMAN,** volunteer; b. Boston, Mar. 23, 1941; d. J. Robert and Charlotte Cox (Litchfield) Lyman; m. Lamson Rheinfrank, Jr., June 15, 1963; children: Caroline Adams, Virginia Lamson, Emily Lyman, Lydia Spitzer. BA, Vassar Coll., 1963. Asst. to dir. admissions Oberlin Coll., 1963; substitute tchr. jr. and sr. high schs., Michigan City, Ind., 1963-65; arts program aid Western Mo. Mental Health Ctr., Kansas City, 1965-67; with Am. Field Svc., 1966—73; regional coord. area bd. dirs. Ams. Abroad Program, 1975. Sec. Mo. Rep. Theatre, 1987—91; mem. exec. com. fin. com., planning and devel. com., chair capital campaign, 1990—93; bd. dirs. parents guild St. Paul's Episcopal Parish Day Sch., 1970—79, co-chmn. sch. capital campaign, 1978—79, mem., v.p. bd. trustees, chmn. scholarship fund, 1975—81; mem. admissions com. Sunset Hill Sch., 1977—78, chmn., exec. bd. mem. parents assn., 1978—79, mem. student svcs. com., 1979—80, sec. parents assn., 1980—81, mem. parents awareness com., 1980—81; bd. trustees, mem. various coms. Pembroke Hill Sch., 1986—93; curriculum chair Pembroke Hills Sch., 1987—88, devel. chair, 1989—91, exec., v.p. bd., 1989—93, mem. exec. com. new head, 1990; mem. bd. trustees Vassar Coll., 1987—99, chair acad. affairs com., 1989—99, mem. nominating com., bldg. and grounds com., devel. com., exec. com., personel com., 1989—99, nat. co-chair 8200 capital campaign, 1993—96, co-chair leadership gifts for 40th reunion, 2001—02; chair Vassar Coll. Pyramid Soc., 2005—09. Mem. Rockhill Homes Assn. (bd. dirs.), Neebish Pioneer Assn. (pres., bd. dirs. 1982—), Mo. Repertory Theatre, Inc. (sec. 1984-87, bd. trustees 1980—, mem. various coms.), Friends of Chamber Music (bd. dirs., v.p. 1983—), Met. Performing Arts Found. (bd. dirs. 1984—), Vassar Club Kansas City (v.p. 1968-70, pres. 1970-72, alumni admissions rep. 1976-83, scholarship project chmn. 1984—). Episcopalian. Avocations: reading, gardening, art, travel, sports.

**RHEINGOLD, HOWARD,** technology writer, virtual community expert; Founding exec. editor HotWired, 1994; founder, CEO Electric Minds Inc. (aquired by Durand Communications), San Francisco, 1996—97; founder, cons. Rheingold Assocs. Syndicated columnist; speaker for course, Toward a Literacy of Cooperation Stanford U., 2005. Author: Tools for Thought, 1984, (revised edition 2000), Virtual Reality, 1991, The Virtual Community, 1993, Smart Mobs: The Next Social Revolution, 2002; co-author: Higher Creativity, 1984, Talking Tech, 1982, The Cognitive Connections, 1986, Excursions to the Far Side of the Mind: A Book of Memes, 1988, Higher Creativity, Exploring the World of Lucid Dreaming, 1990, They Have A Word For It: A Lighthearted Lexicon of Untranslatable Words and Phrases, 1988; editor: The Whole Earth Review; editor in chief: The Millenium Whole Earth Catalog, 1994. Recipient Independent Press award for online cultural coverage, Utne mag., 2003. Achievements include smart mobs blog has become one of the top 200 of the 8 million blogs tracked by Technorati. Business E-Mail: howard@rheingold.com.*

**RHEINS, CARL JEFFREY,** historian, director; b. Cin., Sept. 17, 1945; s. Joseph Melvin and Gertrude (Mandell) R.; m. Brenda Dale Gevertz, July 8, 1979; children: Jason Gabriel, Jaclyn Gail. BS with distinction, U. Wis., 1967; MA, SUNY, Albany, 1970; PhD, SUNY, Stony Brook, 1978. Lectr. Judaic studies SUNY, Stony Brook, 1974-78, asst. to provost, 1978-80, 81-86; dir. acad. affairs Nat. Found. Jewish Culture, NYC, 1980-81; asst. dean Adelphi U., Garden City, NY, 1986-87, assoc. dean, 1987, exec. asst. to pres., 1987-90, dean student life and devel., 1990-92; v.p. student life and devel., 1992-97, v.p. external affairs and comty. rels., 1997—99; exec. dir., CEO Yivo Inst. for Jewish Rsch., NYC, 1999—. Bd. dirs. Coalition on Higher Edn., Jewish Cmty. Rels. Coun., NYC; Delegate (NGO) Vilinus Internat. Forum on Holocaust-Era Looted Cultural Assets, 2000. Contbg. author: Yearbook of the Leo Baeck Inst., 1978, 80, 81; an editor Jewish Almanac, 1980 (Am. Jewish Congress, NYC, 1986-87, 1st v-p. Suffolk County, NY, 1985-87; bd. govs. LI region Am. Jewish Com., NY, 1984-85; judge Nat. Jewish Book Awards, 1993, 94, 05-06. Summer fellow NEH, 1987; recipient Frank Cassell Meml. award, 1994. Mem. Garden City C of C. (bd. dirs. 1997—99), Phi Kappa Phi, Phi Alpha Theta, Alpha Epsilon Pi. Home: 424 West End Ave New York NY 10024 Office: YIVO Inst 15 W 16th St New York NY 10011-6301 Office Phone: 212-294-6126. Business E-Mail: crheins@yivo.cjh.org.

**RHEINSTEIN, PETER HOWARD,** healthcare company executive, physician, lawyer; b. Cleve., Sept. 7, 1943; s. Franz Joseph Rheinstein and Hede Henrietta (Neheimer) Rheinstein Lerner; m. Miriam Ruth Weissman, Feb. 22, 1969; 1 child, Jason Edward. BA with high honors, Mich. State U., 1963, MS, 1964; MD, Johns Hopkins U., 1967; JD, U. Md., 1972. Bar: Md. 1973, D.C. 1980, U.S. Supreme Ct. 2000; diplomate Am. Bd. Family Practice; cert. added qualifications in geriatric medicine. Intern USPHS Hosp., San Francisco, 1967-68; resident in internal medicine USPHS Hosp. (now Homewood Hosp. Ctr.), Balt., 1968-70, lt., 1967—68, lt. comdr., 1968—70; instr. internal medicine U. Md., Balt., 1970-73; med. dir. extended care facilities CHC Corp., Balt., 1972-74; dir. drug advt. and labeling divsn. FDA, Rockville, Md., 1974-82, acting dep. dir. Office Drugs, 1982-83, acting dir. Office Drugs, 1983-84, dir. Office Drug Stds., 1984-90, dir. medicine staff Office Health Affairs, 1990-99; sr. v.p. for med. and clin. affairs Cell Works, Inc., Balt., 1999—2004; pres. Severn Health Solutions, 2000—. Bd. dirs. Marnac, Inc., Dallas, 2003-; chmn. FDA Bur. Drugs Com. on Advanced Sci. Edn., 1978-86, Rsch. in Human Subjects Com., 1990-92; adj. prof. forensic medicine George Washington U., 1974-76; WHO cons. on drug regulation Nat. Inst. for Control Pharm. and Biol. Products, China, 1981-90; advisor on essential drugs WHO, 1985-90; FDA del. to U.S. Pharmacopeial Conv., 1985-90, coord. com. for assessment and transfer of tech. NIH, 1990-98, mem. health care fin. adminstrn. tech. adv. com., 1990-98, Nat. Adv. Coun. on Healthcare Policy, Rsch. and Evaluation, 1990-99, Healthy People 2000/2010 Steering Com., 1990-99, US Preventive Svcs. Task Force, 1990-96, CDC Nat. Task Force on Cmty. Preventive Svcs., 1996-99, Nat. Task Force on CME Industry/Provider Collaboration, 1992—, ann. meeting chmn., 2003, com. com. chmn., 2002-05, US Adopted Names Coun. Rev. Bd., 2004-05, US Adopted Names Coun., 2006—; cons. in legal medicine and regulatory affairs, 1999—

Co-author: Human Organ Transplantation, 1987; spl. editl. advisor Good Housekeeping Guide to Medicine and Drugs, 1977-80; mem. editl. bd. Legal Aspects Med. Practice, 1981-89, Drug Info. Jour., 1982-86, 91-95; pub. Discovery Medicine, 2001-; contbr. articles to profl. jours. V.p. Intercultural Friends Found., 1998—. Recipient Commendable Svc. award, FDA, 1981, Group award of merit, 1983, 1988, Group Commendable Svc. award, 1989, 1992—93, 1995, 1999, Commr.'s Spl. citation, 1993; NIH Nat. Cancer Inst. SBIR grant, 2001. Fellow: Am. Acad. Family Physicians, Am. Coll. Legal Medicine (bd. govs. 1983—93, chmn. fin. com. 1985—88, chmn. publs. com. 1988—93, chmn. fin. com. 1990—91, treas. 1985—88, asd. coun. 1993—95, treas. 1990—91, Pres.'s awards 1985, 1986, 1989—91, 1993, Gold medal 2003); mem.: APHA, AMA (life; ho. of dels. 2002—), ABA, Acad. Medicine Wash., Math. Assn. Am., Md. Bar Assn., Johns Hopkins Med. and Surg. Assn., Balt. City Med. Soc., Soc. Indsl. and Applied Math. (life), Md. State Med. Soc., Fed. Bar Assn. (chmn. food and drug com. 1976—79, Disting. Svc. award 1977), Drug Info. Assn. (bd. dirs. 1982—90, pres. 1984—85, v.p. 1986—87, pres. 1988—89, chmn. ann. meeting 1991, steering com. mem. 1991—2004, chmn. ann. meeting 1994, Outstanding Svc. award 1990), Am. Bd. Legal Medicine (treas. 2003—), Am. Acad. Pharm. Phys. (trustee 1999—2003, pres. Washington-Balt. chpt. 1999—2003, v.p. AMA rels. 1999—), FDA Alumni Assn., Johns Hopkins U. Alumni Assn. (life), U. Md. Alumni Assn. (life), Mensa (life), Fed. Exec. Inst. Alumni Assn. (life), Mich. State U. Alumni Assn. (life), Mich. State U. Honors Coll. Alumni Assn. (bd. dirs. 1998—2001, pres. 2000—01), Annapolis Yacht Club, Chartwell Golf and Country Club, Delta Theta Phi (life). Achievements include development of precedents for FDA regulation of prescription drug promotion, initiated FDA's first patient medication information program; implemented Drug Price Competition and Patent Term Restoration Act of 1984, authored medication goals for Healthy People 2000 and 2010. Avocations: boating, exercise, real estate. Home and Office: 621 Holly Ridge Rd Severna Park MD 21146-3520 Office Phone: 410-647-9500. E-mail: phr@jhu.edu.

**RHENEY, SUSAN O.,** paper company executive; MBA, Harvard Univ. CPA. Public acctg. auditor Deloitte & Touche; prin. Sterling Group LP (parent co., Mail-Well), 1992—2001; dir. Mail-Well, 1993—97; interim chmn. Cenveo (formerly Mail-Well), 2005—. Bd. dir. Genesis Energy LP, Cenveo, 2003—. Office: Cenveo Ste 400 8310 S Valley Hwy Englewood CO 80112-5806 Office Phone: 303-790-8023. Office Fax: 303-566-7466.

**RHETT, HASKELL EMERY SMITH,** educational association administrator; b. Evanston, Ill., Aug. 29, 1936; s. Haskell Smith and Eunice Campbell (Emery) R.; m. Roberta Teel Oliver, Sept. 9, 1961 (div. 1973); children: Kathryn Emery, Cecily Coffin; m. Anita Leone, May 30, 1983 (div. 1993); m. Janet Lee Rollings, Nov. 15, 1997. Diploma, Gov. Dummer Acad., 1954; AB, Hamilton Coll., 1958; MA, Cornell U., 1967, PhD, 1968. Asst. to the pres. Hamilton Coll., Clinton, NY, 1961-64; rsch. asst. Cornell U., Ithaca, NY, 1964-66; rsch. assoc. U. London, 1966-67; dir. program devel. Ednl. Testing Svc., Princeton, NJ, 1967-73; asst. chancellor N.J. Dept. Higher Edn., Trenton, 1973-85; v.p. The Coll. Bd., N.Y.C., 1985-90; pres. The Woodrow Wilson Nat. Fellowship Found., Princeton, 1990-97, pres. emeritus, 1997—. Author: Going to College in New Jersey, 1978; contbg. author: Government's Role in Supporting College Savings, 1990. Commr. N.J. Pub. Broadcasting Authority, Trenton, 1983-85; mem. Nat. Task Force on Student Aid Problems, Washington, 1974-75; mem. Gov.'s Adv. Panel on Higher Edn. Restructuring, State of N.J., 1994; trustee Dominican U. of Calif., San Rafael, Calif. 1990-99, 01—; William Alexander Procter Found., 1998-2002; del. Dem. Nat. Conv., Miami, 1972; sr. warden Trinity Episcopal Ch., Princeton, 1988-92, vestryman, 1979-82, 87-88, 2001—04; dep. Gen. Conv., Detroit, 1988, Phoenix, 1991; mem. standing com. Episcopal Diocese of N.J., 1992-97; trustee The Coll. of N.J., 1992-97, vice-chmn., 1995-97, chmn., 1997; trustee Gov. Dummer Acad., Mass., 1993—; Heartland Edn. Comty., Ohio, 1992-97, Forums Inst. for Pub. Policy, N.J., 1999—; treas., 2000-2005, chmn., 2005—; bd. dirs. Reach the World, Inc., N.Y.C., 1998-01, Trenton After Sch. Program, 1999-93, 2001-04. Lt. USNR, 1958—61, Heavy Attack Squadron 5 (VAH-5), USS Forrestal. Nat. Def. fellow U.S. Govt., 1966-67, Eliot-Winant fellow Brit.-Am. Assocs., 1982, fellow Kennedy Sch. Harvard U., 1985, Wilson Coll., Princeton U., 1993-97. Mem. Nat. Assn. State Scholarship and Grant Programs (pres. 1976-78), Princeton Officers Soc., Springdale Golf Club. Avocations: travel, tennis, golf, sailing, classic automobiles. Home: 80 Province Line Rd Skillman NJ 08558-1102 Personal E-mail: hrhett@patmedia.net.

**RHEW, PERRY JAMES,** federal judge; BS in Psychology/Biology, Southeast Mo. State U., Cape Girardeau, 1980; JD, UMKC Sch. Law, Kansas City, 1983. Lic. Mo., 1983. Pub. defender State of Mo., Kennett, 1983-84; asst. prosecuting atty. Dunklin County, Kennett, Mo., 1985-86; prosecuting atty., 1986-90; adjunct prof. Bus. Law Southeast Mo. State U., Cape Girardeau, 1987-89; assoc. circuit judge 35th Judicial Circuit, Kennett, Mo., 1990; US adminstrv. law judge Social Security Adminstrn., Cleve., 1997—2005; mng. adminstrv. law judge Office of Medicare Hearings and Appeals, US Dept. Health & Human Services, Cleve., 2005, acting chief adminstrv. law judge, 2005—06, chief U.S. adminstrv. law judge, 2006—. Bd. dirs. Family Counseling Ctr., Kennett, Mo., 1986-90, Stapleton Detoxification Ctr., Kennett, Mo., 1986-90, Ctr. for Family Resources, Malden, Mo., 1986-90, Cmty. Caring Counsel, Kennett, Mo., 1993-2005. Author: eight published plays. Elected prosecuting atty., 1986, elected assoc. circuit judge, Dunklin Co. Mo., Kennett, 1990, 94. Recipient Young Alumni Merit award Southeast Mo. State U., Cape Girardeau, Mo., 1993, Denman Dist. Evangelism award United Meth. Ch., 1993. Mem. Mo. Bar Assn., Dunklin County Bar, Lions Club Internat. Mem. United Meth. Ch. Avocations: writing, composer, singing, cooking. Office: Cleveland Regional Office of Medicare Hearings & Appeals 200 Public Sq PB Tower Suite 1300 Cleveland OH 44112 Office Phone: 216-615-4000. Office Fax: 216-615-4115.

**RHIM, JOHNG SIK,** physician, medical researcher; b. Kwang Ju, Korea, July 24, 1930; came to U.S., 1958; s. Hac Woon and Moo Duc (Choi) R.; m. Mary Margaret Lytle, Aug. 24, 1962; children: Jonathan, Christopher, Peter, Andrew, Michael, Kathleen. MD, Seoul (Korea) Nat. U., 1957. Intern Seoul Nat. U. Hosp., 1958; rsch. fellow Children's Hosp. Rsch. Found., Cin., 1958-60, Baylor U. Coll. Medicine, Houston, 1961; rsch. assoc. Grad. Sch. Pub. Health, U. Pitts., 1962, La. State U. Acad. Medicine, New Orleans, 1962-64; vis. scientist Nat. Inst. Allergy and Infectious Diseases, NIH, Bethesda, Md., 1964-66; project dir. cancer rsch. Microbiol. Assocs., Bethesda, Md., 1966-78; sr. investigator Nat. Cancer Inst., NIH, Bethesda, 1978-98; assoc. dir., prof. surgery Ctr. Prostate Disease Rsch., Uniformed Svcs. U. of the Health Sci., Bethesda, 1999—; rsch. prof. dept. surgery Uniformed Svcs. U. Health Scis., Bethesda, 2000—. Adj. prof. Georgetown U. Med. Ctr., Washington, 1988—. Editor: Neoplastic Transformation in Human Cell Culture, 1991, 1995, 1999, 2003; mem. editl. bd.: Internat. Jour. Oncology Prostate Cancer and Prostate Disease, Cancer Therapy; contbr. articles to profl. jours., chapters to books. Mem. AAAS, AMA, Am. Assn. Cancer Rsch., Am. Soc. Virology, Soc. Exptl. Biology and Medicine, Internat. Assn. Leukemia Rsch. Achievements include patents in field. Home: 11455 S Glen Rd Potomac MD 20854-1851 Office: CPDR Dept Surgery Uniformed Svcs Univ Health 4301 Jones Bridge Rd Bethesda MD 20814-4712 Office Phone: 301-319-8223. Business E-Mail: jrhim@cpdr.org.

**RHIMES, SHONDA,** producer, director, writer; b. Chgo., Jan. 13, 1970; 1 adopted child, Harper. BA in English, Dartmouth U., 1991; MFA, U. So. Calif., 1994. Dir., writer: (films) Blossoms and Veils, 1998; writer Crossroads, 2002; The Princess Diaries 2: Royal Engagement, 2004; exec. prodr., writer: (TV series) Grey's Anatomy, 2005—. Office: c/o ABC TV 500 S Buena Vista St Burbank CA 91521-4551*

**RHIND, JAMES THOMAS,** lawyer; b. Chgo., July 21, 1922; s. John Gray and Eleanor (Bradley) R.; m. Laura Haney Campbell, Apr. 19, 1958; children: Constance Rhind Robey, James Campbell, David Scott. Student, Hamilton Coll., 1940-42; AB cum laude, Ohio State U., 1944; LL.B. cum laude, Harvard U., 1950. Bar: Ill. bar 1950. Japanese translator U.S. War Dept., Tokyo, 1946-47; congl. liaison Fgn. Operations Adminstrn., Washington,

1954; atty. Bell, Boyd & Lloyd, Chgo., 1950-53, 55—, ptnr., 1958-92, chmn. exec. com., 1976—88, of counsel, 1993—. Bd. dirs Kewaunee Scientific Corp., Statesville, NC. Commr. Gen. Assembly United Presbn. Ch., 1963; life trustee Ravinia Festival Assn., Hamilton Coll., Clinton, N.Y., U. Chgo.; Northwestern Univ. Assocs.; chmn. Cook County Young Republican Orgn., 1957; Ill. Young Rep. nat. committeeman, 1957-58; v.p., mem. bd. govs. United Rep. Fund Ill., 1965-84; pres. Ill. Childrens Home and Aid Soc., 1971-73, life trustee; bd. dirs. E.J. Dalton Youth Center, 1966- 69; governing mem. Chgo. Symphony Orch., Chgo.; mem. Ill. Arts Council, 1971-75; mem. exec. com. div. Met. Mission and Ch. Extension Bd., Chgo. Presbytery, 1966-68; trustee Presbyn. Homes, W. Clement and Jessie V. Stone Found., U. Chgo. Hosps. Served with M.I. AUS, 1943-46. Mem. ABA, Ill. Bar Assn., Chgo. Bar Assn. (bd. mgrs. 1967-69), Fed. Bar Assn., Chgo. Coun. on Fgn. Rels., Japan Am. Soc. Chgo., Lawyers Club Chgo., Phi Beta Kappa, Sigma Phi. Clubs: Chicago, Glen View (Ill.), Commercial (Chgo.), Mid-Day Club (Chgo.), Economic (Chgo.). Home: 830 Normandy Ln Glenview IL 60025- 3210 Office: Bell Boyd & Lloyd 3 First National Plz 70 W Madison St Ste 3200 Chicago IL 60602-4244 Office Phone: 312-372-1121. Business E-Mail: jrhind@bellboyd.com.

**RHINESMITH, STEPHEN HEADLEY,** management consultant; b. Mineola, N.Y., Dec. 13, 1942; s. Homer Kern and Winifred Headley (Long) Rhinesmith; m. Kathleen Alys Law, Aug. 28, 1965; children: Christopher Law, Colin Headley. BA (Baker scholar), Wesleyan U., 1965; M in Pub. and Internat. Affairs, (Heinz fellow), U. Pitts., 1966, PhD (NDEA fellow), 1972. Dir. internat. svcs. McBer and Co., Cambridge, Mass., 1969-71; pres. AFS Intercultural Programs, N.Y.C., 1972-80, 87-89, Holland Am. Cruises, N.Y.C., 1980-82, Moran, Stahl, Boyer, N.Y.C., 1982-84, Rhinesmith & Assocs. Inc., West Chatham, Mass., 1984—; ptnr. CDR Internat., 1998—, Mercer Delta Con., 2004—. Named amb., coord. Pres.'s U.S.-Soviet Exch. Initiative, 1986—87; chmn. dept. orgnl. sociology Moscow State U. 1991—96. Author: (book) Bring Home the World: A Management Guide to Community Leaders of International Programs, 1975, 1985, A Manager's Guide to Globalization: Six Skills for Success in a Changing World, 2d edit., 1996. Mem.: ASTD (chair 1994), Eastward Ho! Country Club, Met. Club (Washington). Home and Office: 23 Pine Ln North Chatham MA 02650-1035 E-mail: SHRglobal@aol.com.

**RHINEWINE, JOSEPH P.,** psychologist; s. Max and Sylvia Rhinewine; m. Katherine Evans Kane, May 4, 2004. BA, Oberlin Coll., Ohio, 1992; MA, Kent State U., 1999, PhD, 2004. Psychologist Children's Farm Home, Corvallis, Oreg., 2002—06; pvt. practice Lake Oswego, Oreg., 2006—. Recipient Sci. Directorate Travel award, APA, 1998. Mem.: APA. Jewish. Avocations: music, meditation, languages. Office: One Centerpointe Dr Ste 110 Lake Oswego OR 97035 Office Phone: 503-977-0400. Personal E-mail: jpenr@yahoo.com. Business E-Mail: drjoe.rhinewine@yahoo.com.

**RHOAD, RICHARD E.,** healthcare executive; s. John E. and Florice F. Rhoad; m. Marlaine J. Walker; children: Scott R., Bradley R., Nicholas W. BS, Ind. U.; MBA, U. Notre Dame. Cert. mem. Am. Coll. Med. Practice Execs., 1995, diplomate Am. Coll. Healthcare Execs., 1995. Sales mgmt. Xerox Corp., Los Angeles, Calif., 1971—82; exec. v.p. and gen. mgr. North Am. Van Lines, Fort Wayne, Ind., 1982—91; healthcare exec. mgmt. Allied Profl. Services, LLC, 1991—2001; CEO Ft. Wayne Orthopaedics, Fort Wayne, Ind., 2001—04; CFO Family and Social Svcs. Adminstrn., State of Ind., Indpls., 2005—. Dir. Luth. Hosp., Fort Wayne, Ind. Author: (refereed literature) Strategic Approach to the Income Statement (award Inst. Mgmt. Accts., 2002); contbr. articles Mgmt. Acctg. Quar. Trustee U. St. Francis; coun. mem. Trinity English Luth. Ch.; bd. mem. Early Childhood Alliance, Anthony Wayne Svcs. Mem.: Gulf Harbour Yact & Country Club (corr.), Ft. Wayne Country Club (corr.). R-Conservative. Lutheran. Office: Family and Social Svcs Adminstrn State of Indiana 402 W Washington St Indianapolis IN 46204 Office Phone: 317-233-4451. Business E-Mail: richard.rhoad@fssa.in.gov.

**RHOADES, M. STEPHEN,** career officer; m. Vivian Rhoades; children: Whitney, Jessica, Hunter, Taylor. B in Engring., U. Fla., 1973, M in Engring., 1980; grad., U.S. Army Command Coll., Indsl. Coll. Armed Forces, Nat. Def. U. Commd. U.S. Army Corps Engrs., 1973, advanced through grades to col., platoon leader, bn. staff officer, co. comdr., TUSEG area engr. Incirlik, Turkey, with hdqrs. USAREUR, exec. officer 39th Engr. Bn., brigade ops. officer 136th Engr. Brigade, brigade exec. officer 136th Engr. Brigade, comdr. 3d Engr. Bn., 24th Inf. Divsn., with dept. Army Staff, Office Chief Engrs., comdr. Engr. Brigade, 1st Inf. Divsn., chief of staff U.S. Army Engr. Ctr. Ft. Leonard Wood, Va., 1997—99; CEO The Board of Commissioners of the Metropolitan District Commission, 2003—.

**RHOADES, MARYE FRANCES,** paralegal; b. Ft. Defiance, Va., Jan. 29, 1937; d. Silas Caswell Sr. and Mary Ann Frances (James) Rhodes; m. Minter James Rowe, May 1964 (div. 1968); children: Margaret Frances Omar, James Robert Rowe; m. Robert Charles Rhoades Jr., July 25, 1980. Student, Mountain State U., 1956-58, 68, U. Charleston, 1962-63, 74, 89, Antioch U., 1972-73; grad., Mike Tyree Sch. Real Estate, 1984, Evans Coll. Legal Studies, 1990. Educator Nicholas County Sch. Sys., Summersville, W.Va., 1958-61; edit. staff, columnist, staff writer, photographer Beckley Newspapers Corp., 1962-76; educator Raleigh County Bd. Edn., Beckley, W.Va., 1967-68; exec. editor, columnist Local News Jour., Whitesville, W.Va., 1976-77; libr. bookmobile, asst. ref. libr., outreach coord. Raleigh County Pub. Libr., Beckley, 1977-78; agt. Combined Ins. Co., Chgo., 1978-79; legal sec., paralegal W.Va. Legal Svcs. Inc., Beckley, 1979-82; paralegal Appalachian Rsch and Defense Fund Inc., Beckley, 1982-83; exec. dir., owner Rhoades and Rowe, Beckley, 1983—85; paralegal patient advocate Comty. Health Sys. Inc., Beckley, 1986-96; pvt. practice Beckley, 1996—. Contbr. articles to mags. State bd. dirs., pub. rel. LWV, Beckley; pub. rels., various coms. Raleigh County Dem. Women, Beckley; sec., pub. rels. Orchard Valley Women's Club, Crab Orchard, W.Va.; trustee Fraternal Order Eagles; pub. rels., various coms. Loyal Order Moose, Beckley, Beckley Profl. Bus. Women; com. mem. Nat. Coalition to Save the New River; sales rep. So. U.S. Rep. to U.S. Mil. Acad., West Point, N.Y.; active Am. Legion Aux., Mullens, W.Va. Mem. NEA, Classroom Tchrs. Assn., Nat. Paralegal Assn., Nat. Fedn. Paralegals Assn., Nat. Ind. Paralegals Assn., Nat. Com. Save Soc., Soc. Medicare, Nat. Legal Aid and Def. Assn., Nat. Orgn. Social Security Claimants Reps., State Soc. Sec. Task Force, Nat. Vets. Legal Svcs. Project Inc., W.Va. U. Alumni Assn., Community AIDS Edn. Com., W.Va. Edn. Assn., Am. Disability Repr. Specs. Assn. Democrat. Mem. Ch. of God. Avocations: creative arts and music, walking, nascar, doll collecting, writing. Home: PO Box 2173 Beckley WV 25802 Office: Benefit Services PO Box 7265 Beckley WV 25802 Office Phone: 304-252-8431. Office Fax: 304-252-1098. E-mail: tv65000@charter.net.

**RHOADES, RODNEY ALLEN,** physiologist, educator; b. Greenville, Ohio, Jan. 5, 1939; s. John H. and Floris L. Rhoades; m. Judith Ann Brown, Aug. 6, 1961; children: Annelisa, Kirsten. BS, Miami U., 1961; MS, 1963; PhD, Ohio State U., 1966. Asst. prof. Pa. State U. College, 1966-72, assoc. prof., 1972-75; rsch. scientist NIH, Bethesda, Md., 1975-76; prof. Ind. U. Sch. Medicine, Indpls., 1976-81, 81—, chmn., 1981—2003. Dir. Indpls. Ctr. for Advanced Rsch. Author: Physiology, 1984; contbr. articles to profl. jours. Fellow NASA, 1964-66; recipient Rsch. Career Devel. award NIH, 1975-80. Mem. Am. Physiol. Soc, AHA, Am. Thoracic Soc., Biophysics Soc., Sigma Xi. Home: 1768 Spruce Dr Carmel IN 46033-9025 Office: Ind U Sch Medicine 635 Barnhill Dr Indianapolis IN 46202-5126

**RHOADS, B. ERIC,** entrepreneur, artist; b. Fort Wayne, Ind., Aug. 30, 1954; s. D. Dean and Eugenia Irene Rhoads; m. Laurie Lynn Graham, May 13, 1994; children: Rotha Grace, Brady Graham, Berkeley Dean. Student, Harvard Bus. Sch., Boston, 1980, Northwestern Kellog Inst., Des Plains, Ill., 1981, U. Notre Dame, South Bend, Ind., 1982, Stanford U., Palo Alto, Calif., 1997. Cert. radio sales mgr. Radio Advt. Bur., 1989, radio mktg. com. Radio Advt. Bur., 1987. With WYYY Radio, Popke Broadcasting, Kalamazoo, 1971—73; air personality Y100 Radio WHYI Heftel Broadcasting, Fort

Lauderdale, Fla., 1973—74, WIFF Radio, Auburn, Ind., 1974, Y100 WHYI Heftel Broadcasting, Fort Lauderdale, 1974—75; pres., photographer Moments Preserved Photography, 1974—77; air personality, asst. program dir. 96X WMJX Bartel Broadcasting, Miami, Fla., 1975—77; air personality WQAM Storer Broadcasting, 1977—78; program dir., air personality K104 KIOY Willson Broadcasting, Fresno, Calif., 1978—79; pres. New World Comm., Fort Lauderdale, 1979—82; pres., CEO Eqivox Broadcasting, Salt Lake City, 1981—86; pres. BlimpBoard Promotional Products, 1984—86; pres., CEO Streamline Comm., Inc., North Palm Beach, Fla., 1986—89; pub. Radio Ink Mag., Palm Beach, Fla., 1986—2006; pres., CEO Streamline Pub., Inc., West Palm Beach, Fla., 1986—, Radio Ctrl., Inc., San Francisco, 1999—2003; pub. Digital Media Mag., Palm Beach, 1999—2004, Plein Air Mag., 2004—05; pub., chmn. Fine Art Connoisseur Mag., 2004—; painter Mountains Edge Fine Art, Santa Fe, 2006—. Steering com. Mus. of Broadcast Comm., Chgo., 1998—. Author: (book) Blast From the Past: Radio's First 75 Years. Bd. mem. Bayliss Broadcast Scholarship Found., NYC, 2000—, WAY FM Media Group, Colorado Springs, Colo., 1996—. Recipient Furthering Causes of Women in Radio award, KATZ Radio Group Womens Conf., 2005. Mem.: Calif. Art Club (assoc.). Avocations: oil painting, art research, photography. Home and Office: Streamline Pub Inc 224 Datura St Ste 1015 West Palm Beach FL 33401 Office Phone: 561-655-8778. E-mail: eric@fineartconnoisseur.com.

**RHOADS, GEORGE GRANT,** medical epidemiologist; b. Phila., Feb. 11, 1940; s. Jonathan Evans and Teresa (Folin) R.; m. Frances Ann Secker, June 5, 1965; children: Thomas C., James E. MD, Harvard U., 1965; MPH, U. Hawaii, 1970. Intern Hosp. of U. Pa., Phila., 1965-66, resident in internal medicine, 1966-68; resident in preventive medicine U. Hawaii Sch. Pub. Health, 1968-71; epidemiologist Japan-Hawaii Cancer Study, Honolulu, 1974-75; assoc. prof. U. Hawaii, Honolulu, 1974-79, chair dept. pub. health sci., 1978-81, dir. gen. preventive medicine, 1978-81, prof. pub. health, 1979-82; chief epidemiology br. Nat. Inst. Child Health and Human Devel./NIH, Bethesda, Md., 1982-89; prof., dir. grad program in pub. health U. Medicine and Dentistry N.J.-Robert Wood Johnson Med. Sch., Piscataway, 1989-2000; assoc. dean UMDNJ Sch. Pub. Health, 2000—. Contbr. more than 180 articles on the epidemiology of non-infectious diseases to profl. jours. Recipient Dirs. award NIH, 1987, EEO award NICHD, 1984. Fellow Am. Coll. Physicians; mem. Am. Epidemiol. Soc. Mem. Soc. Of Friends. Achievements include research on the protective effect of high density Lipoprotein in the blood against development of heart attacks. Office: 683 Hoes Lane West Piscataway NJ 08854

**RHOADS, GERALDINE EMELINE,** editor, consultant; b. Phila., Jan. 29, 1914; d. Lawrence Dry and Alice Fegley (Rice) R. AB, Bryn Mawr Coll., 1935. Publicity asst. Bryn Mawr (Pa.) Coll., 1935-37; asst. Internat. Students House, Phila., 1937-39; mng. editor The Woman mag., N.Y.C., 1939-42; editor Life Story mag., 1942-45, Today's Woman mag., N.Y.C., 1945-52, Today's Family Mag., N.Y.C., 1952-53; lectr. Columbia U., 1954-56; assoc. editor Readers Digest, 1954-55; producer NBC, 1955-56; assoc. editor Ladies Home Jour., 1956-62, mng. editor, 1962-63; exec. editor McCall's mag., 1963-66; editor Woman's Day mag., 1966-82, editorial dir., 1982-84, Woman-an's Day Resource Center, 1984-89; v.p. Woman's Day mag., 1972—84, CBS Consumer Publs., 1977-84; cons. Woman's Day, N.Y.C., 1989-91. Editorial cons., dir. Nat. Mag. Awards, 1991-94. Author: (with others) Woman's Day Help Book, 1988. Mem. journalism awards com. James Beard Found., 1993-2001. Recipient award for profl. achievement Diet Workshop Internat., 1977; Elizabeth Cutter Morrow award YWCA Salute to Women in Bus., 1977; Recipient Econ. Equity award Women's Equity Action League, 1982; March of Dimes Women Editor's citation, 1982 Mem.: Women's Forum (bd. dirs. 1985—87), Advt. Women in N.Y. (bd. govs. 1983—85, 2d v.p. 1985—87, 1st v.p. 1987—89, bd. dirs. 1989—90, Pres.'s award 1987), N.Y. Women in Comm. (Matrix award 1975), Am. Soc. Mag. Editors (chmn. exec. com. 1971—73), Fashion Group (bd. govs. 1977—79, chmn. bd. govs. 1978—80, bd. dirs. Found. 1980—81, treas. bd. govs. 1983—85, bd. govs. 1987—88), Nat. Press Club (dir.), Bryn Mawr Coll. Alumni Assn. (bd. dirs. 1989—94), Turtle Bay Assn. (bd. dirs. 1989—92), Literacy Vols. of N.Y.C. (bd. dirs. 1986—93), YWCA Acad. Women Achievers, Bryn Mawr Club of N.Y.C. (bd. dirs. 1994—2000), Women's City Club of N.Y. (bd. dirs. 1994—2000), chair comm. 2001—04, Honoree of Yr. 2004). Home: 185 W End Ave Apt 21A New York NY 10023-5548 Personal E-mail: rhoadsge@aol.com.

**RHOADS, JAMES BERTON,** archivist, consultant, federal official, educator; b. Sioux City, Iowa, Sept. 17, 1928; s. James Harrison and Mary (Keenan) R.; m. S. Angela Handy, Aug. 12, 1947; children: Cynthia Patrice Neven, James Berton, Marcia Marie MacKellar. Student, Southwestern Jr. Coll., 1946-47, Union Coll., Lincoln, Neb., 1947-48; BA, U. Calif.-Berkeley, 1950, MA, 1952; PhD, Am. U., 1965. With GSA-Nat. Archives and Records Service, Washington, 1952-79, asst. archivist for civil archives, 1965, dept. archivist U.S., 1966-68, archivist U.S., 1968-79; chmn. Nat. Archives Trust Fund Bd., 1968-79; chmn. adminstrv. com. Fed. Register, 1968-79; chmn. Nat. Hist. Publs. and Records Commn., 1968-79; mem. Fed. Council on Arts and Humanities, 1970-79; pres. Rhoads Assos. Internat., 1980-84; dir. grad. program in archives and records mgmt. Western Wash. U., Bellingham, 1984-94, prof. history, 1987-94, dir. Ctr. for Pacific N.W. studies, 1994-97; prof. emeritus, 1994—. Trustee Woodrow Wilson Internat. Center for Scholars, 1969-79; v.p. Intergovtl. Coun. UNESCO Info. Program, 1977-79; mem. adv. bd. Wash. State Hist. Records, 1990-97. Recipient Meritorious and Disting. Service awards GSA, 1966, 68, 79 Fellow Soc. Am. Archivists (pres. 1974-75); mem. Internat. Coun. Archives (pres. 1976-79), Am. Antiquarian Soc., Am. Coun. Learned Socs. (com. Soviet-Am. archival coop. 1986-91), Mass. Hist. Soc. (corr.), Wash. State Hist. Soc. (trustee 1986-95), Acad. Cert. Archivists (pres. 1992-94).

**RHOADS, JONATHAN EVANS, JR.,** surgeon, medical educator; b. Phila., Sept. 20, 1938; s. Jonathan Evans and Teresa Folin Rhoads; m. Julia Gleason, Apr. 2, 1967; children: Mary Teresa, Ruth Anne, Margaret Paxson. BA, Haverford Coll., 1960; MD, Harvard U., 1964. Diplomate Am. Bd. Surgery, Am. Bd. Thoracic Surgery. Rotating intern Cin. Gen. HOsp., 1964-65; resident in surgery U. Cin., 1965-69, resident in thoracic surgery 1971-72, chief resident in surgery, 1972-73; asst. prof. surgery Med. Coll. Pa., Phila., 1974-77, assoc. prof. surgery, 1977-85, clin. assoc. prof. surgery, 1985—. Residency program dir. York (Pa.) Hosp., 1985-91, chmn. surgery, 1985-97; clin. prof. surgery U. Pa., Phila., 1986—, Pa. State U., Hershey, 1987—. Sch. com. mem. Germantown Friends Sch., Phila., 1979-90, 2000—; bd. mgrs. Haverford (Pa.) Coll., 1994—. Lt. comdr. USPHS, 1969-71. Fellow ACS (bd. govs. 1998—), S.E. Surg. Congress (trustee 1995-2000); mem. Pa. Med. Soc. (spkr. ho. dels. 1989-93, v.p. 1993-94, pres.-elect 1994-95, pres. 1995-96), Phi Beta Kappa. Mem. Soc. Of Friends. Avocation: chess. Office: Wellspan Surgical Assocs Apple Hill Medical Ctr 25 Monument Rd Ste 120 York PA 17403*

**RHOADS, MARK B.,** lawyer; b. Mar. 1, 1959; BA, Coll. William and Mary, 1981; JD, U. Richmond, 1985. Bar: Pa. 1985, Va. 1988, US Dist. Ct. Ea. Dist. Pa. 1985, US Dist. Ct. Ea. Dist. Va. 1988. With Montgomery McCracken Walker & Rhoads, Pa., 1985—88, McCandlish Holton (formerly Mezzullo McCandlish), Richmond, Va., 1988—2003; ptnr., practice group leader bus. immigration group Reed Smith LLP, Richmond, Va., 2003—. Editor: US Immigration Law Handbook, A Guide for Foreign Business. Office: Reed Smith LLP Riverfront Plz - West Tower 901 E Byrd St, Ste 1700 Richmond VA 23219-4068 Office Phone: 804-344-3422. Office Fax: 804-344-3410. Business E-Mail: mrhoads@reedsmith.com.

**RHOADS, MICHAEL DENNIS,** sales executive; b. Vinton, Iowa, June 25, 1949; s. Lloyd and Marilyn Mae (Appleton) Rhoads. BS in Indsl. Edn., Iowa State U., 1973; MBA, York Coll. of Pa., 1984. Order detailer, sales rep. Fisher Controls Inc., Marshalltown, Iowa, 1973-75; inside sales engr. Proconex, King of Prussia, Pa., 1975-79, outside sales engr. York, Pa., 1979-85, br. mgr., 1985-87, v.p. process instrumentation sales King of Prussia, Pa., 1987-90, v.p., sales mgr., 1990—, sr. v.p., 1992—2005, COO, 2005—. Instr. Continuing Adult Edn., Marshalltown, 1973—75. Youth group leader Meth. Ch., Center

Square, Pa., 1977—79. With USN, 1968—70, Vietnam. Mem.: VFW, Instrument Soc. Am. (v.p. 1984—86, pres. 1986—87, Best Sect. Pres. award 1987, Old Shoe award 1990), Am. Legion. Lutheran. Avocations: woodworking, carpentry, hunting, boating, sailing. Home: 205 Claremont Ln Downingtown PA 19335-1563 Office: Proconex 101 Enterprise Dr Royersford PA 19468 Personal E-mail: mrhoads835@aol.com. Business E-Mail: mike.rhoads@proconexdirect.com.

**RHOADS, STEVEN ERIC**, political science professor; b. Abington, Pa., May 12, 1939; s. John Reginald and Barbara Ann (Dugan) Rhoads; m. Diana Cabanis Akers, May 17, 1944; children: Christopher, Nicholas, John. BA, Princeton U., 1961; MPA, Cornell U., 1965, PhD, 1972. Mem. staff Office Mgmt. and Budget, Washington, 1965—66; asst. prof. dept. politics U. Va., Charlottesville, 1970—76, assoc. prof., 1977—86, prof., 1986—. Author: Policy Analysis in the Federal Aviation Administration, 1974, Valuing Life: Public Policy Dilemmas, 1980, The Economist's View of the World: Government, Markets and Public Policy, 1985, Incomparable Worth: Pay Equity Meets the Market, 1993, Taking Sex Differences Seriously, 2004; contbr. articles to profl. jours. Lt. (j.g.) USN, 1961—63. Fellow Woodrow Wilson Inst. Ednl. Affairs, Bradley Found., Olin Found. Mem.: Assn. Pub. Policy and Mgmt., Am. Polit. Sci. Assn. Home: 3190 Dundee Rd Earlysville VA 22936-9621 Office: U Va Dept Politics Cabell Hall 232 Charlottesville VA 22903 Office Phone: 434-924-7866.

**RHODA, JANICE TUCKER**, writer, educator, musician; b. Lynn, Mass., Mar. 24, 1955; d. Robert Samuel and Cecilia Mary Ann (DiTroia) Tucker; m. David Michael Cleary, Jan. 21, 2001. BMus, New Eng. Conservatory Music, Boston, 1989; Suzuki Tchr. Tng., Ithaca Coll., NY, 1980—81 Pvt. violin tchr., 1975—; violin tchr. Wakefield Pub. Schs., 1979—80, Newton Pub. Schs., 1979—81, All-Newton Music Sch., 1980—84, McGill U., 1982, 1983, Boston Ctr. for Adult Edn., 1992—95, 1997—98, New Eng. Conservatory of Music, Boston, 2000, Cambridge Ctr. for Adult Edn., Mass., 2003—; dir. tchr. Suzuki program Longy Sch. Music, Cambridge, Mass., 1980—87, Brookline Music Sch., Mass., 1992—94; clinician The ABCs of Strings, 1998—, Royal Conservatory Music, Toronto, 2004, 2005, Vancouver (Can.) Acad. Music, 2004—. Author: (book series) The ABCs of Strings; concertmistress North-Eastern Dist. Orch., 1972—73, Mass. All-State Orch., 1972; actor: (DVD) The ABCs of Violin for the Absolute Beginner, 2006. Mem.: Nat. Assn. for Music Edn., Am. String Tchrs. Assn., Suzuki Assn. of Ams., Mu Phi Epsilon. Office: The ABCs of Strings PO Box 400428 Cambridge MA 02140 Office Phone: 888-846-5460. Personal E-mail: abcsofstrings@comcast.net.

**RHODE, ALFRED SHIMON**, finance educator; b. Vienna, July 31, 1928; came to U.S., 1940, naturalized, 1949; s. Aron and Olga (Schwarz) Rothkirch; m. Phyllis Mazur, Dec. 28, 1959; children: Yael, Tamar, Yvette, Liane. BCE, CUNY, 1950; MEA, George Washington U., 1959; PhD, Am. U., 1973. Registered profl. engr., Md. Engr. Bur. of Reclamation, Sacramento, 1950—52; various engring. positions U.S. Govt., 1954—63; head logistics rsch. Navy Supply Sys. Command, Washington, 1963—68; head support forces, manpower and logistics br. Navy Program Planning Office, Washington, 1968—75; sr. v.p. nat. security analysis and warfare support group Info. Spectrum, Inc., Arlington, Va., 1976—89, cons., 1989—92; professorial lectr. George Washington U., Washington, 1969—75; adj. faculty Sch. Mgmt. George Mason U., Fairfax, Va., 1990—2002; adj. faculty Sch. Bus. Adminstrn. Georgetown U., Washington, 1998—. Exec. dir. Montgomery County Retail Security and Loss Prevention Assn. Contbr. articles to profl. jours. Capt. USAF, 1952-54. Congl. fellow, 1962. Fellow Mil. Ops. Rsch. Soc. (1st v.p., dir.); mem. Inst. Ops. Rsch. and Mgmt. Scis. (chmn. mil. applications sect.), Washington Inst. for Rsch. and the Mgmt. Scis. Home: 8305 Fox Run Potomac MD 20854-2576 E-mail: arhode@comcast.net.

**RHODE, DEBORAH LYNN**, law educator; b. Jan. 29, 1952; BA, Yale U., 1974, JD, 1977. Bar: D.C. 1977, Calif. 1981. Law clk. to judge U.S. Ct. Appeals (2d cir.), N.Y.C., 1977-78; law clk. to Hon. Justice Thurgood Marshall U.S. Supreme Ct., Washington, 1978-79; asst. prof. law Stanford U., Calif., 1979-82, assoc. prof. Calif., 1982-85, prof. Calif., 1985—; dir. Inst. for Rsch. on Women and Gender, 1986-90, Keck Ctr. of Legal Ethics and The Legal Profession, 1994—2003; sr. counsel jud. com. Ho. of Reps., Washington, 1998. Trustee Yale U., 1983-89; pres. Assn. Am. Law Schs., 1998; Ernest W. McFarland prof. Stanford Law Sch., 1997—; sr. counsel com. on the jud. U.S. Ho. of Reps., 1998; dir. Stanford Ctr. on Ethics. Author: Justice and Gender, 1989, (with Geoffrey Hazard) the Legal Profession: Responsibility and Regulation, 3d edit., 1993, (with Annette Lawson) The Politics of Pregnancy: Adolescent Sexuality and Public Policy, 1993, (with David Luban) Legal Ethics, 2005, 4th edit., 2004, Speaking of Sex, 1997, Professional Responsibility: Ethics by the Pervasive Method, 1998, In the Interests of Justice, 2000 (with Geoffrey Hazard, Jr.) Professional Responsibility and Regulation, 2002; editor: Theoretical Perspectives on Sexual Difference, 1990, Ethics in Practice, 2000, The Difference Difference Makes: Women and Leadership, 2002, Access to Justice, 2004, Pro Bono in Principle and in Practice, 2005, (with Katherine Bartlett) Gender and Law, 2005, (with Carol Sanger) Gender and Rights, 2005, Moral Leadership: The Theory and Practice of Power, Judgement and Policy, 2006, In Pursuit of Justice: Scholars, Status, and Academic Culture, 2006; contbr. articles to profl. jours. Mem.: ABA (chmn. commn. on women 2000—02). Office: Stanford U Law Sch Crown Quadrangle Stanford CA 94305

**RHODE, EDWARD ALBERT**, veterinary medicine educator, veterinary cardiologist; b. Amsterdam, NY, July 25, 1926; s. Edward A. and Katherine (Webb) R.; m. Dolores Bangert, 1955; children: David E., Peter R., Paul W., Robert M., Catherine E. DVM, Cornell U., 1947. Diplomate Am. Coll. Veterinary Internal Medicine. Prof. emeritus vet. medicine U. Calif. Davis 1964—, chmn. dept. vet. medicine, 1968-71; assoc. dean internatl. vet. medicine. Stanford U. Sch. Vet. Medicine, Davis, 1971-81, dean, 1982-91. Mem. AAAS, Nat. Acad. Practices, Am. Coll. Vet. Internal Medicine, Am. Vet. Medicine Assn., Basic Sci. Coun., Am. Heart Assn., Am. Acad. Vet. Cardiology, Am. Physiol. Soc., Calif. Vet. Medicine Assn. Office: U Calif Sch Vet Med Davis CA 95616 E-mail: earhode@ucdavis.edu.

**RHODES, ALAN CHARLES**, minister; b. Plattsburgh, N.Y., July 25, 1951; s. Charles Oliver and Lillian Mary (Cromie) R.; m. Holly C. Craver, June 14, 1975 (div. June 1987); m. Nancy Lichtenhan, June 18, 1988. BA, Lycoming Coll., Williamsport, Pa., 1973; MDiv, Boston U., 1976; DMin, Bangor (Maine) Theol. Sem., 1997. Ordained to ministry United Meth. Ch. as deacon, 1974, as elder, 1977. Assoc. pastor Shenendehowa United Meth. Ch., Clifton Park, N.Y., 1976-79; pastor Ft. Plain (N.Y.) and Freysbush United Meth. Chs., 1979-83, St. Paul's United Meth. Ch., Castleton-on-Hudson, N.Y., 1983-87, Grace United Meth. Ch., Ravena, N.Y., 1987-98, North Main St. United Meth. Ch., Gloversville, N.Y., 1998—2002, Mechanicville (N.Y.) United Meth. Ch., 2002—. Trustee Troy Ann. Conf., 1993—; bd. dirs. Captain Youth and Family Svcs., Inc. Founder, former co-chair R.C.S. Task Force Against Domestic Violence; bd. dirs. Mechanicville (N.Y.) Cmty. Ctr. Mem.: Rotary Club (pres. Champlain Canal 2004—05). Republican. Home: 148 S 2d Ave Mechanicville NY 12118-2200 Office: Mechanicville United Meth Ch 7 N Main St PO Box 429 Mechanicville NY 12118-2200 Office Phone: 518-664-3095. Personal E-mail: arhodes1@nycap.rr.com.

**RHODES, ALICE GRAHAM**, lawyer, not-for-profit developer, consultant; b. Phila., June 15, 1941; d. Peter Graham III and Fannie Isadora (Bennett) Graham; m. Charles Milton Rhodes, Oct. 14, 1971 (div. Apr. 21, 1997); children: Helen, Carla, Shauna. BS, East Stroudsburg U., Pa., 1962; MS, U. Pa., 1966, LLB, 1969, JD, 1970, cert. program exec. adminstrn., 2004. Bar: N.Y. 1970, U.S. Dist. Ct. (so. and ea. dists.) N.Y. 1971, U.S. Ct. Appeals (2d cir.) 1971, Ky. 1983, U.S. Dist. Ct. (ea. dist.) Ky. 1985. Staff atty. Harlem Assertion Rights, Mobilization for Youth Office Econ. Opportunity, N.Y.C., 1969-70, coord. Cmty. Action Legal Svcs., 1972-97; assoc. dir. in charge of civil representation HUD Model Cities Cmty. Law Offices, N.Y.C., 1972-73; resource assoc. Commn. on Edn. & Employment of Women, N.C. Dept. Adminstrn., Raleigh, 1975; mgr. policies and procedures Div. for Youth, N.C.

Dept. Human Resources, Raleigh, 1976; in-house counsel, petroleum transactional atty. Ashland, Inc. (formerly Ashland Oil, Inc.), 1980-82; corp. atty. core group Ashland, Inc., 1985-87, 88-91; mem. Ashland City Commn. Human Rights, 1993-99; mem. bd. regents Ea. Ky. U., 1994—2000; asst. county atty. Jefferson County, 1999—2000; atty.-advisor EEOC, 2001. Mem. Property Valuation Appeals Commn., Greenup County, 1994, Pub. Members Foreign Svc.; cons. pub. mem. selection and performance stds. review bd. Fgn. Svc., U.S. Dept. State, 1995, Fgn. Agrl. Svc. USDA, 1997; prison program planner, cons. N.Y. City Dept. Corrections, 1971; lectr. N.Y.C. Corrections Acad., Riker's, 1971; lectr. juvenile justice N.C. Law Enforcement Acad., Salemburg, 1976. Driver Meals on Wheels, 1983—91; vol. Am. Heart Assn., 1982—91; mem. adv. com. task force post secondary edn. Gov. of Ky.; mem. Ky. Gov.'s Conf. on Postsecondary Edn., 1999; active Global Interdependence Ctr. U. Pa., 2003—; bd. dirs. exec. com. Boyd County Dem. Women, 1996—2000; mem. missionary soc., scholarship com. St. Matthew AME Ch.; bd. dirs. YWCA Ashland, 1983—84, Ashland Heritage Pk. Commn., 1983—85, Negro Baseball Hall of History; bd. dirs., budget com. United Way, Greenup County, Ky., 1988—92; bd. dirs. Franciscan Sisters of the Poor, Ky. Health Sys. Inc., 1996—99; mem. presdl. search com. Ea. Ky. U., 1997—98. Recipient Cmty. Svc. award Queens Community Corp., N.Y.C., 1972, Ashland C.C. 1986, Cmty. Svc. award NAACP, Ky.; NSF fellow, 1964, 65; faculty friends of Penn scholar U. Pa. Law Sch., 1966-69, Reginald Heber Smith postgrad. law and cmty. econs. devel. fellow, 1969-71; named to Hon. Order of Ky. Cols., 1989. Fellow Ky. Bar Found.; mem. NAFE, AAUW (bd. dirs. Phila. chpt. 1963-65), NAACP (life), N.Y. Bar, Ky. Bar Assn. (mem. edn. law, corp. house counsel, law sects.), Pilot Club (exec. bd. Ashland 1983), Links, Inc., Penn Club (charter mem.), Assn. Gov. Bds. Colls. and Univs., Fgn. Svc. USA (pub. mem.), Global Interdependence Ctr., Pyramid Club of Phila., U. Pa. Edn. Alumni Assn. (bd. dirs.), SC Club. Democrat. Avocations: interior decorating, sports, dance, gourmet cooking, gardening. Address: 658 N 65th St Philadelphia PA 19151

**RHODES, ALLEN FRANKLIN**, engineering executive; b. Estherville, Oct. 3, 1924; m. Carol Haisler, 1962; children: James Fleming, Stephen Haisler. BSME, Villanova U., 1947; ML, U. Houston, 1950. Reg. profl. engr., Tex. Asst. dir. engring. adminstrn. Hughes Tool Co., Houston, 1947-52; pres. McEvoy Co., Houston, 1952-63; v.p. engring. & rsch. Rockwell Mfg. Co., Pitts., 1963-70; v.p. corp. planning & devel. ACF Industries, N.Y.C., 1971-73; pres., CEO McEvoy Oilfield Equipment Co., Houston, 1974-79; exec. v.p., CEO Goldrus Marine Drilling, Houston, 1979-82; pres., CEO Warren Oilfield Svc., Houston, 1981-82, Anglo Energy, Inc., 1983-86, Gripper Inc., Houston, 1987-90; v.p., CFO Hydrotech Sys. Inc., Houston, 1991; cons. Allen F. Rhodes, Bus. Advisor & Consulting Engr., Houston, 1991—, Silver Fox Advisors, 1986—. Chmn. Com. Dept. Transp. Gas Pipeln Safety Std., 1969-73; dir. Keystone Internat., 1980-97, Triten Corp., 1980—, Rawson-Koenig, 1986-98, S.W. Rsch. Inst., 1989—, Tex. Microsystem, 1989-92, Houston Humane Soc., 1999—; adj. prof. mech. engring. U. Houston, 2001-. Dir. T&B Lehman Animal Shelter, Inc., 2002—; Dir. Dime Box Hist. Soc., 1988—2003. Lt. USN, 1943—46. Recipient Charles Russ Richards Meml. award, 1987, Howard Conley medal Am. Nat. Std. Inst., 1980. Fellow ASME (past nat. pres., Robert Henry Thurston award 1978), Inst. Mech. Engrs. (Gt. Britain); mem. Nat. Acad. Engring., Soc. Petroleum Engrs., Am. Petroleum Inst. Achievements include holding twenty-two US patents for equipment relating to oilfield drilling and completion. Avocations: sailing, history. Home and Office: 8720 Memorial Dr Houston TX 77024-7011 E-mail: afrhodes@houston.rr.com.

**RHODES, ARTHUR DELANO**, benefits administrator; b. Philadelphia, Miss., Nov. 26, 1960; s. A.D. and Mary (McNair) R.; m. Angela Marie Jolly, May 21, 1988. AA, Miss. Delta Jr. Coll., Moorhead, 1980; BA in Polit. Sci., Millsaps Coll., 1982; JD, U. Miss., 1985. Bar: Miss. 1985, U.S. Dist. Ct. (no. and so. dist.) Miss. 1985. Intern asst. dist. atty. Dist. Atty's Office, Hernando, Miss., 1985; counsel Child Support Unit, Dept. of Human Svcs., Brookhaven, Miss., 1985-87; assoc. Prewitt & Bradley, Jackson, Miss., 1987-88; chief of staff Congressman Mike Parker, Washington, 1988-98; pres., CEO The Benefits Bd., Inc., Cleveland, Tenn., 1999—. Republican. Mem. Ch. Of God. Avocations: travel, reading. Home: 2014 Woodchase Way NE Cleveland TN 37311-1461 Office: The Benefits Bd PO Box 4608 Cleveland TN 37320-4608 Office Phone: 423-478-7131. Business E-Mail: artrhodes@benefitsboard.com.

**RHODES, BETTY FLEMING**, rehabilitation services professional, nurse; b. Franklin, Pa., Nov. 28, 1920; d. John and Twyla Odella (Callen) Fleming; m. Donald Muir Cain, Dec. 31, 1952 (div.); m. Lee Chester Rhodes, June 23, 1962 (dec. Apr. 1997). RN, Allegheny Gen. Hosp., Pitts., 1942. Lic. phys. therapist, Pa. Phys. therapist Office of D.T. Watson, Pitts., 1947, Ky. Soc. for Crippled Children, Louisville, 1947-51, St. Anthony Hosp., Louisville, 1953-78. Nurse U.S. Army, 1943-45; capt. Army Nurse Corps, 1951-52. Decorated Bronze Star. Mem. Am. Phys Therapy Assn. (pres. Ky. chpt.). Roman Catholic. Home: Providence Retirement Home 4915 Charleston Rd Apt 312 New Albany IN 47150

**RHODES, DAVID**, academic administrator; s. Silas H. Rhodes. BA in philosophy, Wesleyan Coll.; attended, Columbia U. Pres. Sch. Visual Arts, NYC, 1978—. Mem.: Commn. Higher Edn. Middle States Assn. Coll. & Sch. (appointment 2003—04), Regants Adv. Coun. Instl. Accreditation, Commn. Higher Edn., Assn. Proprietary Coll. (bd. trustees 1989—, chmn. fed. affairs com. 1989—). Office: School of Visual Arts Office of the Dean 209 East 23 St New York NY 10010*

**RHODES, DEBORAH J.**, prosecutor; BA with high honors, Wheaton Coll.; JD with honors, Rutgers U. Law clk. to Hon. J. William Ditter U.S. Dist Ct. (ea. dist.) Pa; mem. Organized Crime & Racketeering sect., Phila. Strike Force U.S. Dept. Justice, Phila., asst. U.S. atty. San Diego, 1990—2004, counselor to asst. atty. gen., criminal divsn. Washington, 2004—05; Us atty. (so. dist.) Ala. US Dept. Justice, Ala., 2005—. Ex-officio commr. U.S. Sentencing Commn., 2003— Editor (in chief): Rutgers Law Jour. Office: US Attys Office Southern District of Alabama 63 S Royal St Ste 600 Mobile AL 36602*

**RHODES, DONALD ROBERT**, musicologist, educator, retired electrical engineer; b. Detroit, Dec. 31, 1923; s. Donald Eber and Edna Mae (Fulmer) R.; children: Joyce R. Holbert, Jane E., Roger C., Diane R. Herran. BEE, Ohio State U., 1945, MEE, 1948, PhD, 1953. Research assoc. Ohio State U., Columbus, 1945-54; research engr. Cornell Aero. Lab., Buffalo, 1954-57; head basic research dept. Radiation, Inc., Orlando, Fla., 1957-61, sr. scientist Melbourne, Fla., 1961-66; Univ. prof. N.C. State U., Raleigh, 1966-94, univ. prof. emeritus, 1994—. Author: Introduction to Monopulse, 1959, 2d edit., 1980, Synthesis of Planar Antenna Sources, 1974, A Reactance Theorem, 1977. Co-founder Central Fla. Community Orch., Winter Park, 1961, pres., 1961-62. Recipient Benjamin G. Lamme medal Ohio State U., 1975; Eminent Engr. award Tau Beta Pi, 1976; named to N.C. State U. Acad. Outstanding Tchrs., 1980. Fellow AAAS, IEEE (Distn. T. Bolljahn award 1963, pres. Antennas and Propagation Soc. 1969); mem. Am. Musicological Soc. Home: Apt 101 625 Centennial Pkwy Raleigh NC 27606-3255 Office: PO Box 7911 Raleigh NC 27695-7911

**RHODES, DORIS CHANEY**, freelance/self-employed secondary school educator; b. Ft. Worth, Sept. 10, 1942; d. R. C. and Louis (Churchill) Chaney; m. Larry Williams, Jan. 19, 1969 (div. 1975); m. King Rhodes, 1981. BS, Bishop Coll., 1968; MS, Calif. State U., Hayward, 1975. Cert. tchr. Tex., Calif. Tchr. Dallas Ind. Sch., 1968—69, Kansas City (Kans.) Schs., 1969—70; project dir., counsellor Oakland (Calif.) Sch. Dist., 1974—75, tchr., resource, 1970—73, sch. adminstr., 1975—80; owner Opportunities Unltd., Plano, Tex., 1980—. Bd. dirs. Boys and Girls Club, Collin County, Tex., 1998, Goodwill Industries, Oakland, 1978. Recipient Excellence in Field of Bus. award, Dallas Met. Bus. and Profl. Womens Club, 1982. Avocations: reading, writing, art, music, travel. Office: Opportunities Unltd Ste 267-153 1900 Preston Rd Plano TX 75093

**RHODES, ERIC FOSTER**, employee relations consultant, writer; b. Luray, Va., Feb. 5, 1927; s. Wallace Keith and Bertha (Foster) R.; m. Barbara Ellen Henson, Oct. 19, 1946; children: Roxanne Jane, Laurel Lee (dec.); m. Lorraine Endresen, July 29, 1972; m. Daisy Chun, May 31, 1980; m. Barbara Rhodes, Oct. 19, 2004. AA, George Washington U., 1949, AB, 1950, MA, 1952, EdD, 1967. Tchr. high sch., Arlington, Va., 1950-52; counselor Washington Lee High Sch., Arlington, Va., 1952-53; dir. publs., 1953-54, chmn. dept. English, 1954-55; exec. sec. Arlington Edn. Assn., Arlington, Va., 1952-53, Montgomery County (Md.) Edn. Assn., Rockville, Md., 1955-57; lectr. edn. George Washington U., Washington, 1955-60, 65-70; salary cons. NEA, Washington, 1957-58, asst. dir. membership div., 1958-60; dir. N.Y. regional office, N.Y.C., 1960-64; ednl. cons. Ednl. Rsch. Svcs., White Plains, N.Y., 1964-65; pres. Ednl. Svc. Bur., Inc., Arlington, Va., 1965-72, chmn. bd., 1972-80; pres. Negotiations Consultation Svcs., Inc., Arlington, 1969-80, Eastern States Advt. Inc., Arlington, 1970-79, EFR Corp., Arlington, 1972-90; exec. dir. Assn. Negotiators and Contract Adminstrs., 1981-89; area coord. U.S. Legal Protection Co., 1989-95; pres. Employee Futures Rsch., New Port Richey, Fla., 1996—, Waterfront Util Real Estate, New Port Richey, Fla., 1988-92, Inst. for Negotiations Tng., New Port Richey, 1989-95, Asset Protection Co., 1991—; asst. supt. for adminstrn. Brighton Schs., Rochester, N.Y., 1983-88; owner Frederick Foster Galleries, Arlington, 1974-80. Cons. Va. Dept. Community Colls., Richmond, 1965-77; vice chancellor Va. Community Coll. System, 1970-71; employee rels. ofcl. City of Orlando, 1980-83; lectr. edn. Frostburg (Md.) State Coll., 1967 Author: Negotiating Salaries, 41 Ways to Cut Budget Costs, Making Good Things Happen Through Negotiation; editor: Inside Negotiations, Wages and Benefits, Employers' Negotiating Service. Mem. Civil Rights Commn., Franklin Twp., N.J., 1962-64; mem. Sr. victim assistance team Colorado Springs Police Dept., 1997-2003; mem. Franklin Twp. Bd. Edn., 1964-65; mem. adv. bd. Keep Am. Beautiful, 1964-75, nat. chmn., 1968; bd. dirs., v.p. Unitarian-Universalist Ch., Tarpon Springs, Fla., 1990-95, pres., 1994-95, bd. dirs. dir. summer programs, 2005—; mem. Land Devel. Rev. Bd., New Port Richey, Fla., 2005—. With U.S. Army, 1945-47. Mem. Am. Assn. Sch. Adminstrs., Internat. Assn. Sch. Bus. Ofcls., NEA, Edn. Press Assn., Nat. Assn. Ednl. Negotiators (exec. dir. 1971-81), Am. Arbitration Assn. (labor arbitrator), Indsl. Rels. Rsch. Assn., United C. of C. of Pasco County (sec., treas. 1989-90, exec. dir. 1990-91), Am. Legion, Fed. Schoolmen's Club, N.Y. Schoolmen's Club, Lions (v.p. N.Y.C. club 1964-65), Kiwanis (pres. West Pasco club 1991-93, treas. 2004-06), Order of St. John of Jerusalem, Phi Delta Kappa (chpt. pres. 1959-60). Home: 5547 Richey Dr New Port Richey FL 34652 Office: PO Box 1178 New Port Richey FL 34656 Office Phone: 727-849-9484. E-mail: ericrhodes@netzero.com.

**RHODES, FRANK HAROLD TREVOR**, academic administrator, geologist; b. Warwickshire, Eng., Oct. 29, 1926; came to U.S., 1968, naturalized, 1976; s. Harold Cecil and Gladys (Ford) R.; m. Rosa Carlson, Aug. 16, 1952; children: Jennifer, Catherine, Penelope, Deborah. BSc, U. Birmingham, 1948, PhD, 1950, DSc, 1963; LLD (hon.), Wooster Coll., 1976, Nazareth Coll. Rochester, 1979, Skidmore Coll., 1989, U. Mich., 1990, Clemson U., 1991, Dartmouth Coll., 1993, U. Birmingham, Eng., 1999, Fla. Internat. U., 2000, Trinity Coll., U. Dublin, 2001; LHD (hon.), Colgate U., 1980, Johns Hopkins U., 1982, Wagner Coll., 1982, Hope Coll., 1982, Rensselaer Poly Inst., 1982, LeMoyne Coll., 1984, Pace U., 1986, Alaska Pacific U., 1987; LHD, Hamilton Coll., 1987; LHD (hon.), SUNY, 1992, Canisius Coll., 1994, Ithaca Coll., 1995, Fla. Atlantic U., 1996, Coll. St. Rose, 2002; DSc (hon.), U. Wales, Eng., 1981, Fla. Atlantic U., 1996, Bucknell U., 1985, U. Ill., 1986, Reed Coll., 1988, Elmira Coll., 1989, U. Southampton, Eng., 1989, U. Sydney, Australia, 1995, U. Durham, Eng., 1995, Millsaps Coll., 1996; DLitt (hon.), U. Nev., 1982; EdD (hon.), Ohio State U., 1992; D Univ. (hon.), U. Stirling, Eng., 1994; LHD (hon.), U. NC, 2003. Post-doctoral fellow, Fulbright scholar U. Ill., 1950-51, vis. lectr. geology, summers 1951, 52; lectr. geology U. Durham, 1951-54; asst. prof. U. Ill., 1954-55, assoc. prof., 1955-56; dir. U. Ill. Field Sta., Wyo., 1956; prof. geology, head geology dept. U. Wales, Swansea, 1956-68, dean faculty of sci., 1967-68; prof. geology and mineralogy Coll. Lit., Sci. and Arts, U. Mich., 1968-77, dean, 1971-74, v.p. for acad. affairs, 1974-77; pres., prof. geology Cornell U., Ithaca, NY, 1977-95, pres emeritus, 1995—. Gurley lectr. Cornell U., 1960; Bownocker lectr. Ohio State U., 1966; Case lectr. U. Mich., 1976; Jefferson lectr. U. Calif., Berkeley, 1996; dir. NSF, Am. Geol. Inst., summer field inst., 1963; Australian vice-chancellors' visitor to Australian univs., 1964; vis. fellow Clare Hall, Cambridge, 1982; Bye fellow Robinson Coll., Cambridge, 1986-87; Am. Fulbright Disting. fellow, Kuwait, 1987, scholar in residence, Bellagio study and conf. ctr., 1995. Author: The Evolution of Life, 1962, 2d edit., 1976, Fossils, 1963, Geology, 1972, Evolution, 1974, Language of the Earth, 1981, Creation of the Future: The Role of the American University, 2001; author numerous articles and monographs on sci. and edn.; editor, contbr.: Successful Fund Raising for Higher Edn., 1997. Trustee Carnegie Found. for Advancement Tchg., 1978-86, vice chmn., 1983-85, chmn. 1985-86; trustee The Freedom Forum, 1983-93, Com. for Econ. Devel., 1984-93; prin. Washington Adv. Group, 1997—; bd. dirs. KMI Continental, Inc., 1985-86, Tompkins County Trust Co., 1984-98, Gen. Electric Co., 1984-2002, NBC, 1986-2002, H. John Heinz III Ctr. Sci., Econs. & Environ., 1996-98, Am. Coun. on Edn., 1983-88, vice chair, 1985-86, chair, 1986-88, The Johnson Found., 2000—, Atlantic Philanthropies, 1995—, chmn., 2000—; bd. dirs. Goldman Sachs Found., 2000—; bd. overseers Meml. Sloan-Kettering Cancer Ctr., 1979-91, Koç U., Turkey, 1996—; chmn. adv. bd. Freedom Forum Media Studies Ctr., 1984-93; mem. Nat. Sci. Bd., 1987-98, chair, 1994-96, Internat. Exec. Svc. Corps Coun., 1984-95; v.p. Dyson Charitable Trust, 1996-98; bd. mem. The Johnson Found., 2000—. Recipient Clark Kerr medal U. Calif., Berkeley, 1995, Reginald Wilson Diversity Leadership award Am. Coun. Edn., 2003; Sr. Vis. Rsch. fellow NSF, 1965-66; scholar U. Calif., Berkeley, 1995. Fellow Am. Acad. Arts and Scis., Geol. Soc. London (coun. 1963-66, Bigsby medal 1967); mem. Am. Philos. Soc. (pres. 2000-2005), Palaeontol. Assn. (v.p. 1963-68), Brit. Assn. Advancement Sci., Geol. Soc. Am., Am. Assn. Petroleum Geologists, Soc. Econ. Paleontologists and Mineralogists, Phi Beta Kappa. Office: Cornell U Office of President Emeritus 3104 Snee Hall Ithaca NY 14853-1504 Office Phone: 607-255-6233.

**RHODES, KARREN**, public information officer; b. Calif., 1947; 2 children. Diploma in Journalism, U. Utah, 1984. Journalist, Salt Lake City, 1983—85, UPI, Cheyenne, Wyo., 1985—86, Green River (Wyo.) Star, 1986—88; pub. info. officer Nev. Dept. Employment Security, Carson City, 1989—94, Nev. Dept. Employment, Tng. and Rehab., Carson City, 1994—. Trustee Carson Access Found., Carson City, 1996—2001; fundraising chair Mound House Bus. Assn. Recipient Vol. of Yr. award, Dept. of Utah Gov.'s Office, Salt Lake City, 1984, Best of Nat. Collegiate Photography award, 1984. Mem.: Soc. Profl. Journalists. Avocations: photography, graphic design, writing, travel, mentoring.

**RHODES, LAWRENCE**, artistic director; b. Mt. Hope, W.Va., Nov. 24, 1939; Studied with Violette Armand. Joined Ballet Russe de Monte Carlo, 1958-60; from dancer to prin. dancer Joffrey Ballet, N.Y.C., 1960-64; prin. dancer Harkness Ballet, 1964-68, dir. prin. dancer, 1968-70; prin. dancer Dutch Nat. Ballet, 1970-72; dir. prin. ballet tchr. Pa. Ballet, N.Y.C., 1973—75; free-lance master ballet tchr., coach. Danced with Makarova, Hayden and Fracci, danced for Butler, Joffrey, Ailey, Lubovitch, Harkavy, Nault, Van Dantzig and Mac Donald, featured dancer (TV films) A Dancer's Vocabulary, PBS's Dance Am. series, CBS's Camera Three. Office Phone: 212-799-5000 x 255. E-mail: llrhodes@worldnet.att.net.

**RHODES, LINDA**, pharmaceutical executive; d. Warren Louis and Josie Rhodes; m. Boaz Roan. Dec. 24, 1984; 1 child, Adam Rhodes-Rogan. BA, Sarah Lawrence Coll., Bronxville, N.Y., 1970; VMD summa cum laude, U. Pa., Phila., 1978; PhD, Cornell U., Ithaca, N.Y., 1988. Lic. veterinarian NY, Calif., 1978. Bovine veterinarian pvt. practice, Logan, Utah, 1978—80; instr. Cornell U., Ithaca, 1983—84; rschr. Sterling Winthrop Pharm. Co., Albany,

NY, 1988—90; rsch. fellow, sr. rsch. fellow Merck Rsch. Labs., Rahway, NJ, 1990—98; dir. Merial, Ltd, Iselin, NJ, 1998—2001; founding ptnr. Alchera-Bio, Metuchen, NJ, 2001—. Dir. Immucell, Portland, Maine, 2005—, Alliance for Contraception in Cats and Dogs, Portland, Oreg., 2006—. V.p. Alumnae/i Assn, Sarah Lawrence Coll., Bronxville, NY, 2002—05. Recipient Black Belt, Jhoon Rhee Tae Kwon Do Assn., 2003; grantee, NIH fellow, 1985—88. Mem.: AVMA, NY Acad. of Sci. Office: AlcheraBio 69 Pearl St Metuchen NJ 08840 Office Phone: 732-205-0192. E-mail: lrhodes@alcherabio.com.

**RHODES, LINDA JANE,** psychiatrist; b. San Antonio, May 23, 1950; d. George Vernon and Lucy Agnes (O'Dowd) R. BA, Trinity U., 1972; MD, U. Tex. Med. Br., 1975. Diplomate Am. Bd. Pediat.; bd. certified, Am. Bd. Psychiatry and Neurology. Resident in pediat. U. Tex. Med. Br., Galveston, 1975-78; fellow in ambulatory pediat. U. Tex. Health Sci. Ctr., Houston, 1978-80, asst. prof. psychiatry San Antonio, 1995—, resident in psychiatry, 1990-92, child and adolescent psychiatrist, fellow in biol. psychiatry, 1992-95; pediatrician Kelsey Seybold Clinic, P.A., Houston, 1980-95. Pediat. rep. Tex. Lay Midwifery Bd. Tex. Dept. Health, Austin, 1994-95. Active San Antonio Conservation Soc., San Antonio Herb Soc., Nat. Trust for Hist. Preservation, San Antonio Mus. Assn., Trinity U. Assocs., 1992-95, Witte Mus. Assn.; patron McNay Art Inst.; bd. dirs. Tex. Found. for Psychiatric Edn. & Rsch., 1997—, sec., 1998-99, treas., 1999-2004. Fellow Am. Acad. Pediat.; mem. Am. Psychiat. Assn., Am. Acad. Child and Adolescent Psychiatry (gifts and endowments com.), Ambulatory Pediat. Assn., Tex. Pediat. Soc., Tex. Soc. Psychiat. Physicians, Tex. Acad. Child and Adolescent Psychiatry, Am. Med. Women's Assn., Am. Soc. Clin. Psychopharmacology, Tex. Med. Assn. (com. on child and adolescent health), AMA, Bexar County Psychait. Soc. (sec. 2000-2001, pres. 2002-2003, past pres. 2003-2004).

**RHODES, MICHAEL E.,** biologist, educator; b. Greensburg, Pa., June 1, 1971; s. Edward C. and Gloria L. Rhodes; m. Lee Ann Kosakowski, Oct. 11, 1997; children: Katelyn Frances, Justin Michael. BS, St. Vincent Coll., Latrobe, Pa., 1993; MS, Duquesne U., Pitts., 1995; PhD, Duquesne U., 1997. Part-time assoc. prof. Duquesne U., Pitts., 1997—2006; rsch. asst. prof. Allegheny-Singer Rsch. Inst., Allegheny Gen. Hosp., Pitts., 1997—2005; part-time assoc. prof. Carlow Coll., Pitts., 1995—2005; asst. prof. of biology St. Vincent Coll., Latrobe, Pa., 2005—. Contbr. articles to profl. jours. Recipient Best Prof. award, Nat. Cmty. Pharmacy Assn., 1998, Internat. Jr. Investigator award, Internat. Coll. of Geriatric Psychoneuropharmacology, 2003; grantee, Royal Soc. Of Edinburgh, 1999, Commonwealth Of Pa. Tobacco Settlement Fund, 2004—06, Allegheny Gen. Aux. Grant Program, 2002—04; Rafaelsen fellow, Collegium Internat. Neuropsychopharmacologi-cum, 2002. Mem.: Internat. Coll. of Geriatric of Psychoneuropharmacology (assoc.), Soc. for Neurosci. (assoc.), Am. Soc. of Pharmacology and Exptl. Therapeutics (assoc.). Independent. Methodist. Achievements include patents for for novel memory-enhancing drugs in 1997. Avocations: fishing, golf, woodcarving. Office: Saint Vincent College 300 Fraser Purchase Rd Latrobe PA 15650 Office Phone: 724-805-2360. E-mail: michael.rhodes@email.stvincent.edu.

**RHODES, PETER EDWARD,** label company executive; b. Rochester, NY, Sept. 25, 1942; s. Robert A. and Anne (Ward) R.; m. Cassandra Durkee, May 26, 1962 (div. Sept. 1991); children: Tamara, Amy, Brian; m. Nancy Lewis, Aug. 16, 2002. BS, Rochester Inst. Tech., 1964, MBA, 1970. With Touche Ross & Co., Rochester, 1962-69, sr. auditor, to 1969; with Xerox Co., Rochester, 1969, Fay's Drug Co., Inc., Liverpool, NY, 1970-87, exec. v.p., 1974-87, also dir.; pres. Syracuse Label Co., Inc., Liverpool, 1987—2002, 2002—, also bd. dirs. Bd. dirs. Byrne Dairy Inc. Mem.: AICPA, NY State Soc. CPAs, Bellevue Country Club.

**RHODES, RAMONA LAGIERS,** medical educator, researcher; d. Jim and Linda Rhodes. BS, Xavier U. La., New Orleans, 1996; MD, U. Ark., Little Rock, 2000]; MPH, Brown U., Providence, R.I., 2006. Diplomate Am. Bd. Internal Medicine, 2003, lic. RI, 2006. Intern/resident Case Western Res. U./MetroHealth Med. Ctr., 2000—03; geriatric medicine fellow Brown U./Rhode Island Hosp., Providence, 2003—06; postdoctoral rsch. fellow Brown U. Ctr. Gerontology and Health Care Rsch., Providence, 2004—06; asst. prof. medicine Brown Med. Sch., Providence, 2006—. Assoc. med. dir. Home and Hospice Care of R.I., Providence, 2006—, mem. diversity task force, 2006—; mem. fellowship exec. com. Brown Med. Sch., divsn. Geriat., Providence. Author: (book chpt.) The Elderly Female Patient; co-author (book chpt.) Pain Management in the Geriatric Patient, (article) Jour. Palliative Medicine, (review) Medicine and Health Rhode Island. Recipient James and Susan Carter Humanitarian award, Dept. Internal Medicine, MetroHealth Med. Ctr., 2003, Haffenreffer award in Fellowship Excellence, R.I. Hosp., Grad. Med. Edn., 2006, Chancellor's List, Nat. Leadership and Academic Affairs, 2004—06, Tannenbaum Scholarship, U. Ark. for Med. SciS., 1996-2000; grantee, Agy. for Healthcare Rsch. and Quality, 2004—06. Mem.: Am. Acad. Hospice and Palliative Medicine, Am. Geriat. Soc., Nat. Med. Assn., Delta Sigma Theta Sorority, Inc. (mentor 2005). Baptist. Avocations: piano, singing, tennis, travel. Office: Brown Univ Ctr for Gerontology 2 Stimson Ave Box GS-311 Providence RI 02912

**RHODES, RANDI,** radio personality; b. Bklyn. d. Loretta; m. Jim Robert-son, 1994 (div. 2004). Jobs at Radio Stations, Seminole, Tex., Mobile, Ala., NY, Dallas, Milw.; former sec., waitress, trucker and US Air Force aircraft mechanic; public relations job then weekend disc jockey WSHE, Coast 97.3 FM, 1987—92; radio talk show host WIOD AM, Miami, Fla., 1992—94, WJNO, West Palm Beach, Fla., 1994—2004, The Randi Rhodes Show, Air Am. Radio, NYC, 2004—. With USAF, 1977. Named Most Outstanding Woman in the Air Force, 1979; recipient Am. Women in Radio and Television award. Mailing: care Carmen Shamwell 4th Fl 641 Sixth Ave New York NY 10019 Office: Air America Radio 641 Avenue Of The Americas Fl 4 New York NY 10011-2038 E-mail: rrhodes@airamericaradio.com.

**RHODES, RAYMOND EARL,** professional sports team executive; b. Mexia, Tex., Oct. 20, 1950; Student, Tex. Christian. Asst. def. backs coach San Francisco 49ers/NFL, 1981-82, def. backs coach, 1982-91; def. coord. Green Bay Packers NFL, 1992-93, San Francisco 49ers/NFL, 1994, asst. def. backs coach, 1981-82, def. backs coach, 1982-91; def. coord. Green Bay Packers NFL, 1992-93, San Francisco 49ers/NFL, 1994; head coach Phila. Eagles, 1995-99, Green Bay Packers, 1999-2000; defensive coord. Washington Redskins, 2000—. Named Named NFL Coach of the Yr., The Sporting News, 1995.

**RHODES, RICHARD (LEE),** writer; b. Kansas City, Kans., July 4, 1937; s. Arthur and Georgia Saphronia (Collier) R.; children: Timothy James, Katherine Hampton; m. Ginger Kay Untrif, Oct. 3, 1993. BA cum laude, Yale U., 1959; LHD (hon.), Westminster Coll., Fulton, Mo., 1988. Author: The Inland Ground, 1970, The Ungodly, 1973, The Ozarks, 1974, Holy Secrets, 1978, Looking for America, 1979, The Last Safari, 1980, Sons of Earth, 1981, The Making of the Atomic Bomb, 1986, Farm, 1989, A Hole in the World, 1990, Making Love, 1992, Nuclear Renewal, 1993, How to Write, 1995, Dark Sun, 1995, (with Ginger Rhodes) Trying to Get Some Dignity, 1996, Deadly Feasts, 1997, Visions of Technology, 1999, Why They Kill, 1999, Masters of Death, 2002, John James Audubon: The Making of an American, 2004. Trustee Andrew Drumm Inst., Independence, Mo., 1991-, Atomic Heritage Found., DC, 2004-, Cypress Found., DC, 2005-. Recipient Nat. Book Critics Cir. award for nonfiction, Nat. Book award for nonfiction, 1987, Pulitzer prize, 1988; Guggenheim fellow, 1974-75, fellow Nat. Endowment for Arts, 1978-79, Ford Found., 1981-83, Sloan Found., 1985, 89, 91, 92, 2002-, MacArthur Found., 1990-91. Office: c/o Janklow & Nesbit Assoc 445 Park Ave New York NY 10022-2606

**RHODES, ROSAMOND,** medical educator, philosophy educator; b. N.Y.C., N.Y., Mar. 19, 1946; d. Michael S. and Helen Rhodes; m. Joe Robert Fitschen, Nov. 0, 1992; children: Keli Ann Rosenberg, David Gabriel Rosenberg. PhD, CUNY, N.Y.C., 1990. Prof. med. edn. Mt. Sinai Sch. Medicine, NYC,

---

1988—; prof. philosophy The Grad. Ctr., CUNY, NYC, 1998—. Editor, newsletter on philosophy and medicine Am. Philosophic Assn., Newark, 1990—; mem. Wadsworth Ctr. working group in bioethics N.Y. Dept. Health, Albany, 2005—. Editor: (book, edited collection) Physician Assisted Suicide: Expanding the Debate, Medicine and Social Justice: Essays on the Distribu-tion of Health Care, The Blackwell Guide to Medical Ethics. Recipient Spl. Recognition award for Achievement in Med. Edn., The Mt. Sinai Alumni, 2005. Mem.: Internat. Hobbes Assn. (founding mem. 2004—2006), Am. Soc. for Bioethics And Humanities (bd. 2005—06), Am. Philos. Assn. (ex officion 1990—2006, com. on philosophy and medicine). Office: Mount Sinai School of Medicine One Gustave Levy Pl New York NY 10029 Office Phone: 212-241-3757. Office Fax: 212-241-5028. E-mail: rosamond.rhodes@mssm.edu.

**RHODES, SAMUEL,** violist, educator; b. Long Beach, N.Y., Feb. 13, 1941; s. Bernard and Martha (Ephraim) R.; m. Hiroko Yajima, Dec. 30, 1968; children— Amy, Harumi. BA, Queen's Coll., 1963; MFA, Princeton U., 1967; D.F.A. (hon.), Mich. State U., 1984; MusD (hon.), Jacksonville U., 1986, San Francisco Conservatory, 1996. Mem. faculty Juilliard Sch., N.Y.C., 1969—, Mich. State U., East Lansing, 1977-85, SUNY-Purchase, 1982-86; violist Marlboro Festival, 1960-68, 78-81, 91—, Galimir String Quartet, 1961-68, Juilliard String Quartet, 1969—; mem. faculty Tanglewood Music Ctr., 1988—. Office: Juilliard Sch Music Lincoln Ctr New York NY 10023

**RHODES, STANLEY WILLIAMS,** retired secondary school educator; b. Syracuse, N.Y., Oct. 30, 1938; s. Foster Twitchell and Josephine Birdsall (Williams) R.; m. Hilda Tylston Wright; children: Robin E., Ellen T., Heather W. BA, Amherst Coll., 1960; M in Sci. Edn., Syracuse U., 1961; cert. in advanced study, Fairfield U., 1979; Nat. Sci. Found. insts., Rutgers U., 1963, 65, 66. Cert. tchr., supr. Sci. tchr. Lewis S. Mills Regional Sch., Harwington, Conn., 1961-66; physics, sci. tchr. Staples High Sch., Westport, Conn., 1966-72, physics, sci. tchr., asst. headmaster, 1972-80, adminstrv. asst., 1980-81, sci. and tech. edn. div. coord., 1981-98, sci. divsn. coord., 1998-2000, physics tchr., 2000—05; ret., 2005. Instr. NSF Summer Inst., U. Mass., 1968-69; tchr. Westport Summer Sch., 1977-85, 88, asst. prin., 1986, 87; mem. Staples Governing Bd., 1971-97, Tritown Sci. Com., Westport, Wilton, Weston, Conn., 1985-92, Staples Collaborative Team, 2001-02, 04-05; cooperating mentor tchr. Conn. Dept. Edn., Hartford, 1989, 90; mem. Westport Tech Com., 1991-2001; mem. Westport Restructuring Com., 1992-93. Developer course in phys. sci., Unified Sci. Workshop, 1972-93; partici-pant Engring. Concepts Curriculum Project, 1966-77. Vol. Mark Twain Libr. Art Show, 1978-79; mem. Redding Elem. Sch. Budget Com., 1975-77; host family, interviewer Redding/Easton Am. Fgn. Svc., 1985-87; participant Barlow Parent Coll. Panel, 1988, 89, Staples PTA Coll. Forum, 1992; mem. Redding Rep. Town Com., 1992—; mem. chmn. Westport Group, Urban Coalition Task Force, 1970; mem. Westport Think Tank, 1987-90. Mem. NEA, Am. Assoc. Physics Tchrs., Conn. Edn. Assn., Conn. Assn. Physics Tchrs., Conn. Sci. Suprs. Assn., Conn. Ret. Tchrs. Assn., Nat. Sci. Tchrs. Assn. Republican. Mem. Ch. of Christ. Congregational. Avocation: U.S. stamp and coin collecting. Home: 5 Archers Ln West Redding CT 06896-2214 E-mail: stanrhodes@aol.com.

**RHODES, STEPHEN MICHAEL,** poultry company executive; b. Harri-sonburg, Va., Mar. 12, 1949; s. Trovilla Geil and Ogretta (Dove) R.; m. Judy Ann Higgs, June 19, 1971; children: Jeremy, Meridith. AA, Shenandoah Coll., 1969; BA in Biology, Madison Coll., 1971. Mgr. quality control Rocco Farm Foods, Inc., Edinburg, Va., 1971-95, wastewater/environ. mgr., 1996—. V.p., bd. dirs. Plains Youth Baseball League, Va., 1989-91, coach 1984-90; coach pony league, 1991; 1st lt., pres. Broadway Emergency Squad, 1971-77; chmn. coun. on Ministries Sunset Dr. United Meth. Ch., Broadway, 1991, 94-96, 99—, vice chmn., 1997-98; mem. PPR com., 1994-95; coach Timber-ville Midget League Football, 1985-89; bd. dirs. Community Pk. Bd., Broadway, 1984-86; mem. Rockingham County Recreation Commn., 1990-97; pres. Broadway H.S. Athletic Booster Club, 1994-96, v.p., 1996-97. Mem. Va. Poultry Industry Lab. (chmn. bd. dirs. 1983, 87), Southeastern Poultry and Egg Fedn. (sci. adv. com. 1983-91). Avocations: hunting, fishing, swimming. Home: 199 3rd St Broadway VA 22815-9511 Office: Rocco Farm Foods Inc 19992 Senedo Rd Edinburg VA 22824-3172

**RHODES, THOMAS WILLARD,** lawyer; b. Lynchburg, Va., Mar. 9, 1946; s. Howard W. and Ruth R.; m. Ann Bloodworth, May 31, 1975; children: Mildred, Andrew. AB, Davidson (N.C.) Coll., 1968; JD, U. Va., 1971. Bar: Ga. 1971. Assoc. Smith, Gambrell & Russell and predecessor firms, Atlanta, 1971-76, ptnr., 1976—. Dir., pres. Atlanta Vol. Lawyers Found., 1984-89; dir. Fed. Defender Program, Atlanta, 1988-92, 2003—, pres., 1991-92. Contbr. profl. jours. and textbooks; editor: Nonprofit News. Capt. USAR, 1968—72. Recipient Heiner award Atlanta Vol. Lawyers Found., 1989, Anderson Lecture award Am. Acad. Facial Plastic and Reconstructive Surgery, 2004. Fellow Am. Law Inst.; mem. ABA, Ga. Bar Assn. (past chmn. antitrust law sect.). Office: Smith Gambrell & Russell Promenade II 1230 Peachtree St NE Ste 3100 Atlanta GA 30309-3592

**RHODES, WILLIAM C., III,** automotive executive; B in acctg., Univ. Tenn.; MBA, Univ. Memphis. CPA. With Ernst & Young, 1988—94, Autozone Inc., Memphis, 1994—, v.p., 1997—99, sr. v.p., 1999—2002, exec. v.p., 2002—05, pres., CEO, 2005—. Bd. mem. Memphis Tomorrow; treas. Nat. Civil Rights Mus.; mem. partners bd. FedEx Inst. Tech. Office: Autozone Inc 123 S Front St Memphis TN 38103*

**RHODES, WILLIAM REGINALD,** banker; b. NYC, Aug. 15, 1935; s. Edward R. and Elsie Rhodes; divorced; 1 child, Elizabeth. BA in History, Brown U., 1957, degree (hon.), 2005. Joined Citibank, 1957, served in several sr. positions in Latin Am. and Caribbean, 1957—77; from sr. officer internat. banking group-L.Am. and Caribbean to vice-chmn. Citibank, N.Am., NYC, 1977—2001, chmn., 2003—, pres., CEO, 2005—; sr. vice chmn. Citibank, 2001—03, Citigroup, Inc., 1999—; chmn., CEO Citicorp Holdings, Inc., 2003—, pres., 2005—. First vice chmn. Inst. Internat. Fin.; mem. Met. Mus. Bus. Com., U.S.-Russia Bus. Coun.; past chmn. adv. com. Export-Import Bank of US; past chmn. U.S. sect. Venezuela-U.S. Bus. Coun.; founding mem. U.S. Nat. Adv. Coun. to the Internat. Mgmt. Ctr., Budapest; active U.S.-Egyptian Pres. Coun.; bd. dirs. ConocoPhillips, Pvt. Export Funding Corp. Chmn. Northfield-Mt. Hermon Sch., Hong Kong-U.S. Bus. Coun.; bd. dirs., gov., trustee NY and Presbyn. Hosp.; bd. overseers Watson Inst. for Internat. Studies, Brown U.; active Lincoln Ctr. Corporate Leadership Com.; vice-chmn. Metropolitan Mus. Art Bus. Com. and chmn. com.; bd. dirs. Africa-Am. Inst.; vice chmn. bd. Nat. Com. on U.S.-China Rels.; hon. chmn., Sister City Program of City of NY. Decorated comdr. and grand officer Nat. Order of the So. Cross (Brazil); officer Legion of Honor (France); Orden de Mayo (Argentina); officer Order Francisco Miranda 1st and 3rd classes, Order Merito en el Trabajo 1st class (Venezuela); Order of Diplomatic Svc., Heung-In medal, Korea; comdr. Order of Distinction (Jamaica); recipient Am.'s award, 1997, African Bus. Devel. award African Am. Inst., 1998, Banker's Lifetime Achievment award Arab Bankers Assn. N.Am., 1999, Stephen P. Duggan award for Internat. Understanding, Inst. for Internat. Edn., 1999, William I. Spencer award NY Blood Ctr., 1999. Mem. Americas Soc. (chmn. bd. dirs.), Coun. of Ams. (chmn. bd. dirs.), Bankers Assn. Fin. and Trade (past pres., Banker of Yr. award 2004), Coun. Fgn. Rels., Venezuelan-Am. C. of C. (past pres.), Fgn. Policy Assn. (bd. dirs.). Avocations: jogging, swimming, archaeology, reading. Office: Citigroup Inc 399 Park Ave New York NY 10043-0001*

**RHODY, RONALD EDWARD,** bank executive, communications execu-tive; b. Frankfort, Ky., Jan. 27, 1932; s. James B. and Mary M. (Clark) R.; m. Patricia Schupp, Apr. 23, 1955; children: Leslie K., Mary M., Virginia K., Ronald C. Student, Georgetown Coll., Ky., 1950-52, U. Ky., 1953-55. Pub. rels. dir. Kaiser Aluminum & Chem. Corp., Ravenswood, W.Va., 1959-62, N.Y.C., 1962-67, corp. v.p. Oakland, Calif., 1967-83; sr. v.p. corp comm Bank of Am. NT&SA, San Francisco, 1983—, exec. v.p., 1992-94; CEO Rhody, Inc., 1994—. Author: The CEO's Playbook, 1999, Wordson Thing, 2006; contbr. articles to profl. jours. Founding chmn. adv. bd. San Francisco

---

Acad. Named Pub. Rels. Profl. of Yr., Pub. Rels. News, 1981; recipient Hall of Fame award Page Soc., 1997. Fellow Pub. Rels. Soc. Am.; mem. Pub. Rels. Soc. Am. (accredited, pres.'s adv. coun. Rex Harlow award), Internat. Assn. Bus. Communicators (Gold Quill award 1980), Pub. Rels. Roundtable San Francisco (mem. bd. govs., awards 1980, 85). Home: 2725 Pontiac Dr Walnut Creek CA 94598-4437 Office: Rhody Inc 2725 Pontiac Dr Walnut Creek CA 94598-4437 E-mail: ron.rhody@att.net.

**RHONE, ELVIE SUE,** educational administrator; b. La., Oct. 06; d. Henry and Clara (McWright) Turner; m. Samuel Rhone, Apr. 24, 1964; children: Debra Lynn, Nedra Lanae. BS, So. U., Baton Rouge, 1962; MEd, Loyola U., Chgo., 1974; MS, Chgo. State U., 1986; EdD, Nova Southeastern U., Ft. Lauderdale, Fla., 1993. Lic. adminstr., supr., guidance, counseling and math. Instr. Cook County Sch. Nursing, Chgo., 1963-65; cons. supr. Cook County Dept. Pub. Aid, Chgo., 1965-66; tchr. Chgo. Pub. Schs., 1966-76, resource tchr., 1976-88, counselor, asst. prin., 1989-94, adminstr. Ctr. Office Ctr., 1994—. Cons. math. textbook Houghton Mifflin Co., Dallas, 1987. Candidate for alt. del. to nat. conv., Chgo., 1980; bd. dirs. Cmty. Mental Health Coun., Inc.; mem. Referral Counselors Real Estate Connection. Recipient Outstand-ing Svc. award nat. legislation Nat. Cmty. Edn. Assn.; named Outstanding Educator PTA, Chgo., 1987; grantee Ill. State Bd. Edn., Springfield, 1992-94. Mem. ASCD, Nat. Sch. Bd., Assn. for Counselors, Chgo. Area Reading Assn. Phi Delta Kappa (Educator of Yr. 1994). Avocations: writing, gardening, travel, reading. Home: 7027 S Bennett Ave Chicago IL 60649-2007 Office Phone: 773-779-7300. Personal E-mail: phd612@aol.com.

**RHONE, SYLVIA MARIE MILLER,** recording industry executive; b. Phila., Mar. 11, 1952; BS in Econs. (hon.), U. Pa., 1974; Degree (hon.), Adelphi U., LHD (hon.), 1996. Comml. lending trainee Bankers Trust Co., NYC; sec. Buddha Records, 1974, nat. promotion coord., Bareback Records; regional promotions mgr. ABC Records, 1976—78, Ariola Records, 1978—79; N.E. regional promotions mgr./special markets Elektra Records, 1980—83, dir. mktg./special markets, 1983—85; dir. nat. black music promotion Atlantic Records, NYC, 1985—88, v.p., gen. mgr. black music ops., 1988—89, sr. v.p., gen. mgr. black music ops., 1989—90; CEO, co-pres. EastWest Records America, NYC, 1990—91; chmn., CEO EastWest/Atco Records, NYC, 1991—94; chair/CEO Elektra Entertainment, NYC, 1994—2004; exec. v.p. Universal Records, 2004—06; pres. Motown Records, 2004—06, Universal Motown Records, 2006—. Mem., bd. dirs. Alvin Ailey Am. Dance Theatre, The RIAA, Rock n' Roll Hall of Fame, Jazz at Lincoln Ctr., R&B Found., Studio Mus. of Harlem; bd. dirs. NARAS. Alumni trustee U. Pa., 2001—. Named an Most Influential Black Americans, Ebony mag., 2006; recipient Whitney M. Young Svc. Award, Boy Scouts of Am., 1992, New Music Seminar Joel Webber Prize for Excellence in Music and Bus. award, 1993, Sony Soul of Am. Music Excellence Award, 1993, Legacy Life Mem. award, Nat. Coun. of Negro Women, 1995, Urban Network Exec. Yr. Award, 1995, Herbert H. Wright award, Nat. Assn. Market Developers, 1995, Studio Mus. Corp. award, 1996, Creative Spirit Award, Black Alumni of Pratt Inst., Echo Awards, Trumpet Awards, Turner Broad-casting, 2004. Achievements include became 1st African American and first woman chairman and CEO of a major record company, 1994. Office: Univeral Motown Records 1755 Broadway # 6 New York NY 10019*

**RHOTEN, KENNETH DALE,** writer; b. Hammond, Ind., Dec. 28, 1950; s. James Edward and Helen Louise (Wasson) R.; m. Virginia Haynie (div.); m. Linda Robin Damron (div.); m. Josephine Meese (dec.). Grad. H.S., New Carlisle, Ind. Draftsman Hahn, Inc., Evansville, Ind., 1973—75; laborer Inland Steel Works, Ind., 1975; draftsman N.W. Ind. Regional Planning Com., Highland, 1975—76; draftsman, artist graphic sys. divsn. Rockwell Internat., Cicero, Ill., 1977—78; designer Roper Outdoor Products (in cooperation with Espo Engring.), Bradley, Ill., 1978—79; draftsman Fedders Corp., Effingham, Ill., 1982—83; freelance writer, inventor, 1983—. Author: editor: Dark Twist of Fate, 1995, 3d edit., 2003, Dark Twist of Fate and Other Works, 1999; author: A Voice From Beyond, 1999, The Complete Works of Kenneth D. Rhoten, 1999, Mathematical Equivalents, 2006; composer pub. songs; pat-entee automatic brewing apparatus, 1984. Candidate state rep. State of Ill.-Rep. Party, 1986. Achievements include successful redevelopment of the Edison storage cell and development of new secondary cell; deduced mechanism of Bessler's wheel and constructed model; development of mechanical advantage gravity motors. Home and Office: PO Box 225 Stoy IL 62464-0225

**RHOTON, ALBERT LOREN, JR.,** neurosurgeon, educator; b. Nov. 18, 1932; s. Albert Loren and Hazel Arnette (Van Cleve) R.; m. Joyce L. Moldenhauer, June 23, 1957; children: Eric L., Albert J., Alice S., Laural A. BS, Ohio State U., 1954; MD cum laude, Washington U., St. Louis, 1959. Diplomate Am. Bd. Neurol. Surgery (bd dirs. 1985-91, vice-chmn. 1991). Intern Columbia Presbyn. Med. Ctr., N.Y.C., 1959; resident in neurol. surgery Barnes Hosp., St. Louis, 1961-65; cons. neurol. surgery Mayo Clinic, Rochester, Minn., 1965-72; chief divsn. neurol. surgery U. Fla., Gainesville, 1972-80, R.D. Keene prof., 1980—, chmn. dept. neurol. surgery, 1980-2000, chmn. emeritus, 2000—. Developer microsurg. tng. ctr.; hon. v.p. World Congress of Neurosurgery, 2005-; hon. prof. Beijing (China) Capital U., 2005—; lectr. in field. Author: The Orbit and Sellar Region: Microsurgical Anatomy and Operative Approaches, 1996, Cranial Anatomy and Surgical Approaches, 2003, Millenium issue Neurosurgery, 25th Anniversary issue; designed more than 200 microsurgery instruments; mem. editl. bd. Neuro-surgery, Jour. Microsurgery, Surg. Neurology, Jour. Fla. Med. Assn., Am. Jour. Otology, Skull Base Surgery; contbr. articles to profl. jours. Bd. dirs. Neurosurgery Edn. and Rsch. Found. Recipient Disting. Faculty award, U. Fla., 1981, Alumni Achievement award, Washington U. Sch. Medicine, 1985, Jones award for outstanding spl. med. exhibit of yr., Am. Assn. med. Illustrators, 1969, Jameison medal, Neurosurg. soc. Australasia, 1997, Out-standing Achievement award, World Congress of Skull Base Surgery, 2000, medal of honor, World Fedn. Neurosurg. Socs., 2001, medal, Neurosurg. Soc. Am., 2001, endowed professorship named in his honor, U. Fla., Lifetime Achievement award, Wall of Fame Honoree, Honorary Alumnus award, 2001, medal of honor, Neurosurg. Soc. of Am., 2001, Bucy award, U. Chgo., 2002; grantee NIH, VA, Am. Heart Assn. Mem. ACS (bd. govs. 1978-84), AMA (Billings Bronze medal 1969), Congress Neurol. Surgeons (pres. 1978, Exceptional and Disting. Svc. award 2004, honored guest 1993), Nat. Found. Brain Rsch. (bd. dirs. 1990-94), Nat. Coalition for Rsch. in Neurol. Disorders (bd. dirs. 1990-94), Neurol. Soc. Am. (medal 2001), Internat. Congress Meningiomas (hon. pres. 2000), Neurosurg. Soc. Brazil (hon., honored guest 2004), Neurosurg. Soc. Japan (hon., Honored guest 2002), Neurosurg. Soc. Mex. (hon.), Neurosurg. Soc. Can. (hon.), Neurosurg. Soc. Uruguay (hon.), Neurosurg. Soc. Venezuela (hon.), Neurosurg. Soc. Turkey (hon.), Neurosurg. Soc. Tex. (hon.), Neurosurg. Soc. Okla. (hon.), Neurosurg. Soc. Wis. (hon.), Neurosurg. Soc. Ga. (hon.), Neurosurg. Soc. Rocky Mountain (hon.), Neu-rosurg. Soc. China (hon.), Neurosurg Soc. Argentina (hon.), Latin Am. Neurosurg. Soc. (hon.), Neurosurg. Soc. Chili (hon.), Fla. Neurosurg. Soc. (pres. 1978), Am. Neurol. Surgeons (chmn. vascular sect., treas. 1983-86, v.p. 1987-88, pres. 1989-90, exec. com. 1993, Cushing medal 1998), Soc. Neurol. Surgeons (treas. 1975-81, pres. 1993), So. Neurol. Soc. (v.p. 1976), Alachua County Med. Soc. (exec. com. 1978), Fla. Med. Assn., Am. Surg. Assn., Soc. Univ. Neurosurgeons, Am. Heart Assn. (stroke coun. Outstanding Achievement award 1971), N.Am. Skull Base Soc. (pres. 1993-94, honored guest 2001, Lifetime Achievement award 2005), Am. Acad. Neurol. Surgery, Acoustic Neuroma Assn. (med. adv. bd. 1983-2000, chmn. 1992-2001, chmn. emeritus 2001—), Trigeminal Neurol. Assn. (med. advisor bd. 1992—), Hemifacial Spasm Assn. (med. adv. bd. 2002—), Internat. Interdisciplinary Congress on Craniofacial and Skull Base Surgery (pres. 1996-97), Internat. Soc. Neurosurg. Tech. and Instrument Invention (pres. 1997—), Japanese Skull Base Soc. (hon. pres. 2000), Internat. Soc. for Microsurgery Anatomy (hon. pres. 2002, 04), World Fedn. Neurosurg. Soc. (hon. v.p. 2005—). Achievements include fundraising for 11 endowed chairs at University of Florida. Home: 2505 NW 22d Ave Gainesville FL 32605-3819 Office: U Fla Dept Neurosurgery PO Box 100265 100 S Newell Dr Gainesville FL 32610 Office Phone: 352-392-2548. Business E-Mail: rhoton@neurosurgery.ufl.edu.

**RHYMER, SCOTT CAMPBELL,** writer, historian; b. Easton, Pa., Aug. 8, 1966; s. Vernon Case Rhymer and Anne Thomson; m. Debra Gail Love, Sept. 20, 1967. BA in History and Polit. Sci., U. N.Mex, 1995; MA in History, N.Mex State U., 2005. Freelance writer, Albuquerque, 2000—05. Author: (novel) Cawnpore, The Bank, (historical roleplaying game) Victoriana, The Smoke, Faulkner's Guide. Specialist U.S. Army, 1995—99. Mem.: Phi Alpha Theta (assoc.). Libertarian. Avocations: marksmanship, cooking, motorcycling.

**RHYNE, JAMES JENNINGS,** condensed matter physicist; b. Oklahoma City, Nov. 14, 1938; s. Jennings Jefferson and Clyde Margaret (Russell) R.; m. Susan Margaret Watson, May 26, 1990; children: Nancy Marie, Edward Paxton. BS in Physics (Dry) R.; m. Rosemarie Kennedy, July 11, 1959; Physics, Iowa State U., 1965. Rsch. scientist Naval Ordnance Lab., White Oak, Md., 1965-75; rsch. physicist Nat. Inst. of Stds. and Tech., Gaithersburg, Md., 1975-90; prof. physics U. Mo., Columbia, 1991—2003, dir. Rsch. Reactor Ctr., 1991-96; dep. group leader Lujan Ctr., Los Alamos Nat. Lab., 2003—. Adv. editor Jour. of Magnetism and Mag. Materials, 1990—; editl. bd. Jour. Applied Physics, 1986-89; co-editor Physica. Fellow: Neutron Scattering Soc. Am. (pres. 1999—2002), Am. Phys. Soc. Office Phone: 505-665-0071. Personal E-mail: jrhyne@los-alamos.net. Business E-mail: rhyne@lanl.gov.

**RHYNE, SIDNEY WHITE,** retired lawyer; b. Charlotte, N.C., Apr. 2, 1931; s. Sidney White and Ruth (Dry) R.; m. Rosemarie Kennedy, July 11, 1959; children: Patricia Ruth, Kendall Sidney, Randall Sylvanus. AB, Roanoke Coll., 1952; LLB, U. Pa., 1955; LLM, Georgetown U., 1961. Bar: Pa. 1955, D.C. 1957, U.S. Supreme Ct. 1959, Md. 1987. Assoc. Rhyne, Mullin, Connor and Rhyne, Washington, 1957—60; mem. Mullin, Rhyne, Emmons and Topel, Washington, 1961—97; individual practice law Washington, 1997—2005; ret., 2005. Lectr. law ctr. Georgetown U., Washington, 1964-70. Pres. Legal Aid Soc. of D.C., 1976-78, trustee, 1968-80, pres. coun., 1991—; trustee Luth. Theol. Sem. at Phila., 1988-93, pres. coun., 1993—. With U.S. Army, 1955-57. Prettyman fellow Georgetown U., 1960-61. Fellow Am. Bar Found. (life); mem. ABA (house delegates 1972-73, 75, 76-78, 98-2001), Bar Assn. D.C. (bd. dirs. 1969-73, 92-94, 98-2002, trustee Found., v.p. 1990-91, presdl. award 2000-2001), Fed. Comm. Bar Assn. (exec. com. 1988-96, treas. 1991-92, Disting. Svc. award 1992, pres. 1994-95). Independent. Lutheran. Office Phone: 202-244-6248. E-mail: swrhyne@abanet.org.

**RHYS-MEYERS, JONATHAN,** actor; b. Dublin, July 27, 1977; Actor: (films) A Man of No Importance, 1994, Michael Collins, 1996, Lengua asesina, La, 1996, The Disappearance of Finbar, 1996, The Maker, 1997, Telling Lies in America, 1997, Velvet Goldmine, 1998, The Governess, 1998, B. Monkey, 1998, The Loss of Sexual Innocence, 1999, Ride with the Devil, 1999, Titus, 1999, Happy Now, 2001, Prozac Nation, 2001, Tangled, 2001, Bend It Like Beckham, 2002, The Tesseract, 2003, Octane, 2003, I'll Sleep When I'm Dead, 2003, The Emperor's Wife, 2003, Vanity Fair, 2004, Alexander, 2004, Match Point, 2005; (TV films) Samson and Delilah, 1996, The Tribe, 1998, The Lion in Winter, 2003; (TV miniseries) Gormenghast, 2000, Elvis, 2005 (Golden Globe award for Best Actor in a Mini-Series or Motion Picture Made for TV, Hollywood Fgn. Press, 2006). Office: c/o United Talent Agency, Inc 9560 Wilshire Blvd Beverly Hills CA 90212*

**RIAL, JOSÉ ANTONIO,** geophysicist, educator; b. Santa Cruz, Canary Islands, Spain, Nov. 8, 1945; s. Jose Antonio and Clorinda Rial; m. Omaira Cruz, May 15, 1973; 1 child, Michelle Alexandra. MS, U. Mich., 1975; PhD, Calif. Inst. Tech., 1979. Geophysicist Woodward-Clyde Cons., Pasadena, Calif., 1980—82; asst. prof. U. NC, Chapel Hill, 1985—90, assoc. prof., 1990—95, prof., 1995—. Chair, environ. sci. curriculum U. NC, 2003—; adj. prof. U. Calif., Santa Cruz, 1982—85. Contbr. scientific papers. Fellow, CIRES, U. Colo., Boulder, 2005; grantee, NSF, 1980—2006, US Dept. Energy, 1983—2006, US Geol. Survey, 1985—90. Fellow: AAAS; mem.: Am. Geophys. Union. Achievements include first to discover the effect of frequency modulation in the climate variability of the Pleistocene. Avocations: travel, painting. Office: U NC Mitchell Hall CB#3315 Chapel Hill NC 27599-3315 Office Phone: 919-966-4553. Business E-mail: jar@email.unc.edu.

**RIAL, JOSEPH J.,** theater educator, set designer; s. Megan Kay and Daniel Linus Rial; m. Jonel Ann-Claire Langenfeld, Aug. 8, 1995; 1 child, Jacob Daniel. MFA, Ill. State U., Bloomington, 2001. Prof. scenic and lighting design SUNY, Oswego, 2001—. Freelance designer, Hawaii, 1987—95. Theatre stage design, Macbeth (Kennedy Ctr. Am. Coll. Theatre Festival Fellowship, 1993), The Diary of Ann Frank, The 1940's Radio Hour, A Midsummer Night's Dream, The Secret Garden, The Importance of Being Earnest, The Real Inspector Hound, Infinity's House, Little Shop of Horrors. Mem.: U.S. Inst. of Theatre Tech. Achievements include development of Sculpting techniques using tape and other non-traditional media. Office: SUNY Oswego Rt 104 Oswego NY 13126 Office Phone: 315-312-2147.

**RIASANOVSKY, NICHOLAS VALENTINE,** retired historian, educator; b. Harbin, China, Dec. 21, 1923; arrived in U.S., 1938, naturalized, 1943; m. Arlene Ruth Schlegel, Feb. 15, 1955; children: John, Nicholas, Maria. BA, U. Oreg., 1942; AM, Harvard U., 1947; DPhil, Oxford U., Eng., 1949. Mem. faculty U. Iowa, 1949-57, U. Calif., Berkeley, 1957—, prof. history, 1961—; Sidney Hellman Ehrman prof. European history, 1969—2003, ret., 2003. Vis. rsch. prof. USSR Acad. Scis., Moscow, 1969, Moscow and Leningrad, 1974, 79. Author: Russia and the West in the Teaching of the Slavophiles: A Study of Romantic Ideology, 1952, Nicholas I and Official Nationality in Russia, 1825-1855, 1959, A History of Russia, 1963, 7th edit. (with Prof. Mark Steinberg), 2005, The Teaching of Charles Fourier, 1969, A Parting of Ways: Government and the Educated Public in Russia, 1801-1855, 1976, The Image of Peter the Great in Russian History and Thought, 1985, The Emergence of Romanticism, 1992, Collected Writings 1947-94, 1993, Russian Identities, a Historical Survey, 2005; co-editor: California Slavic Studies, 1960—; editl. bd. Russian rev., Zarubezhnaia Periodicheskaia Pechat' na Russkom Iazyke, Simvol; contbr. articles to profl. jours. Trustee Nat. Coun. Soviet and East European Rsch., 1978—82; mem. Kennan Inst. Acad. Coun., 1986—89. 2d lt. AUS, 1943—46. Decorated Bronze Star; recipient Silver medal Commonwealth Club Calif., 1964; Rhodes scholar, 1947-49; Fulbright grantee, 1954-55, 74, 79; Guggenheim fellow, 1969; sr. fellow NEH, 1975; Fulbright sr. scholar, sr. fellow Ctr. Advanced Studies in Behavioral Scis., 1984-85; sr. fellow Woodrow Wilson Internat. Ctr. for Scholars, 1989-90. Mem. Am. Assn. Advancement Slavic Studies (pres. 1973-76, Disting. Contbr. award 1993), Am. Hist. Assn. (award for Scholarly Distinction 1995), Am. Acad. Arts and Scis.

**RIBA, SHIRLEY,** artist; d. Arthur Roy and Idell Carolina Riba. BFA, Calif. Coll. of Arts & Crafts, Oakland, 1977. Sales/dept. display Gumps Oriental Antique Dept., San Francisco, 1979—90; owner ARTRIBA, Laporte, Colo., 1995—. Exhibitions include Corcoran Sch. Art, Washington, D.C., 1977—78, Calif. Coll. of Arts & Crafts, San Francisco, 1977, E.B. Crocker Kingsley, Sacramento, 1979, Gump's Gallery, San Francisco, 1979—90, 1981, 1986, Represented in permanent collections Bohemian Found., Calif., prin. works include Mural After Parrish, 2002, represented in pvt. collections. Home: PO Box 800 Laporte CO 80535 Office Phone: 970-221-2023.

**RIBARY, URS,** neuroscientist, educator; b. Lucerne, Switzerland, Nov. 24, 1955; came to U.S., 1988; s. Max and Hilde (Brunner) Ribary; m. Evelyne Dahinden, July 11, 1986; 1 child, Samanta R. MS, U. Tech., Zurich, Switzerland, 1981, DSc, 1985. Rsch. asst. professor NYU Med. Ctr., NYC, 1988—93, dir. ctr. for neuromagnetism, 1989—2005, assoc. prof., 1993—. Vis. assoc. prof. Simon Fraser U., Can., 1986-88. Cons. (Time Life series) The Brain, 1990; contbr. articles to profl. jours. Co-founder, chmn. Samanta S. Ribary Found. Inc. Mem. AAAS, Am. Soc. Neurosci., N.Y. Acad. Scis., European Neurosci. Assn., Soc. Cognitive Neuroscience. Achievements include rsch. on using functional brain imaging techniques, to study quantal sequences of coherent thalamo-cortical activity in humans during normal cognitive processing, and its alterations in neurological and neuropsychiatric patients. Office: 21 Walnut Pl Closter NJ 07624 Business E-Mail: urs.ribary@med.nyu.edu.

**RIBBANS, GEOFFREY WILFRID,** language educator; b. London, Apr. 15, 1927; came to U.S. 1978; s. Wilfrid Henry and Rose Matilda (Burton)R.; m. Magdalena Willmann, Apr. 21, 1956; children: Madeleine Elizabeth, Helen Margaret, Peter John. BA with 1st class hons., Kings Coll., U. London, 1948, MA, 1953. Asst. lectr. U. Sheffield, Eng., 1954-56, lectr., 1956-61, sr. lectr. Spanish, 1961-63; Gilmour prof. Spanish U. Liverpool, Eng., 1963-78; vis. Mellon prof. Spanish U. Pitts., 1970-71; Wm. R. Kenan Jr. U. prof. Spanish Brown U., Providence, 1978-99, chmn. dept., 1981-84, prof. emeritus, 1999—. Editor Bull. Hispanic Studies, 1964-78; vis. prof. U. Salamanca, Spain, 1995. Author: Catalunya i Valencia al Segle XVIII, 1955, 2d edit., 1993, Niebla y Soledad: Aspectos de Unamuno y Machado, 1971, Galdós: Fortunata y Jacinta, 1977 (Spanish transl. 1988); editor: Antonio Machado, Soledades, Galerias, Otros Poemas, 1984, revised 16th edit., 2000, Campos de Castilla, 1989, 13th edit., 2003, History and Fiction in Galdós's Narratives, 1993, 2d edit., 1995, Conflicts and Conciliations: The Evolution of Galdós's "Fortunata y Jacinta", 1997. Decorated La Encomienda de la Orden de Isabel la Catolica Spain; recipient prize for excellence in Galdos studies, Las Palmas, 1997, Batista i Roca prize, Barcelona, 2000; Hispanic studies in his honour, Liverpool, 1992, Symposium on Modernism and Modernity in his honor, Brown U., 1998. Mem. MLA, Internat. Assn. Hispanists (v.p. 1974-80), Internat. Assn. Galdós Scholars (pres. 1988-89), N.Am. Catalan Soc. (hon.). Office: Brown U Dept Hispanic Studies PO Box 1961 Providence RI 02912-1961 Business E-Mail: Geoffrey_ribbans@brown.edu.

**RIBBLE, JOHN CHARLES,** medical educator; b. Paris, Tex., July 26, 1931; s. Elbert Alfred and Dorothy (Pyeatt) R.; m. Anne Blythe Hoerner; 1 stepchild Helen Blythe Strate Kielty. MD, U. Tex., 1955. Diplomate Am. Bd. Internal Medicine. Asst. prof. medicine Cornell U., N.Y.C., 1962-66, assoc. prof. pediatrics, 1966-78, assoc. dean, 1974-78. Med. Scis., U. Tex., Houston, 1978-86, dean, 1986-95; vis. scholar The Health Inst. New Eng. Med. Ctr., Boston, 1995-96; prof. medicine U. Tex., Houston, 1996—. Mem. Nat. Adv. Coun. Gen. Med. Scis. NIH, Bethesda, Md., 1988-91. Episcopalian. Home: 6200 Willers Way Houston TX 77057-2808 Office: U Tex Med Sch 6431 Fannin St Houston TX 77030-1501 Office Phone: 713-500-6709. E-mail: jribble@houston.rr.com.

**RIBBLE, RONALD GEORGE,** psychologist, educator, writer, behavioral consultant; b. West Reading, Pa., May 7, 1937; s. Jeremiah George and Mildred Sarah (Folk) Ribble; m. Catalina Valenzuela Torres, Sept. 30, 1961; children: Christina, Timothy, Kenneth. BSEE cum laude, U. Mo., 1968, MSEE, 1969, MA, 1985, PhD, 1986. Bd. cert. forensic examiner, diplomate in behavioral sci. Am. Bd. Psychol. Spltys., Am. Coll. Forensic Examiners; cert. in homeland security. Enlisted USAF, 1956-60, advance through grades to lt. col., 1976—81; rsch. dir. Coping Resources, Inc., Columbia, Mo., 1986; pres., co-owner Towers and Rushing Ltd. (Pubs. and Psychol. Cons., Troubadour 1997-2001), San Antonio, 1986—; referral devel. Laughlin Pavilion Psychiat. Hosp., Kirksville, Mo., 1987; program dir. Psychiat. Insts. of Am., Iowa Falls, Iowa, 1987-88; lead psychotherapist Gasconade County Counseling Ctr., Hermann, Mo., 1988; sr. lectr. U. Tex., San Antonio, 1989—2002; lectr. Trinity U., San Antonio, 1995-96; assessment clinician Afton Oaks Psychiat. Hosp., San Antonio, 1989-91; ret. from tchg., 2002. Faculty cons. Edn. Testing Svc., 1997; psychologist Olmos Psychol. Svcs., Inc., San Antonio, 1991—93; vol. assessor Holmgreen Children's Shelter, San Antonio, 1992—93; founder Ruth Bohn Weissman Scholarship in Creative Writing U. Tex., San Antonio, 1994—2004; co-sponor Lyric Recovery Festival, Carnegie Hall, 2000; condr. seminars, revs. for maj. publs. *Since his USAF retirement in 1981, Dr Ribble has signficantly broadened his educational background, knowledge, experience, and constructive involvement in the fields of behavioral analysis, education, literary arts, and international relations. As a consequence, he has been recognized by several organizations as a meaningful contributor to the understanding of complex human relations and endeavors. He is one of a very small percentage of university faculty members across America to be continuously recognized over a ten-year period by dean's list students as the one teacher who had the single greatest influence on their academic career and/or their personal life. Besides his on-going leadership roles in the WPDF and The Jefferson Council, Dr. Ribble is active as a behavioral consultant in Special Security matters.* Author: (book) Apples, Weeds, and Doggie Poo, 1995, Dont' Eat the Snake!, 1999; contbr. essays to psychol. refernce books, poetry to anthologies periodicals, lyrics to popular music; interviewer: celebrities in performing and lit. arts, 1995—, columnist: Feelings, 1993—97; pub. access TV appearances, 1991—. Founding cabinet mem. World Peace and Diplomacy Forum; vol. announcer pub. radio sta., Colombia, 1993; vol. Cath. Family and Children's Svc., San Antonio, 1989—91; chpt. advisor Rational Recovery Program for Alcoholics, San Antonio, 1991—92; mem. Pres. Leadership Cir., 1994—2002; contbg. mem. Dem. Nat. Com., 1983—; Presdl. Congl. Task Force, 1994; del. Boone County (Mo.) Dem. Conv., 1984. Recipient Roberts Meml. prize in Poetry, 1995, DaVinci Diamond award, 2004, Internat. Peace prize, United Cultural Conv., U.S.A., 2002, Am. medal Hon., 2004. Fellow: Am. Coll. Forensic Examiners; mem.: ACLU, Internat. Found. for Protection Officers, Internat. Soc. Genetic Genealogists, MENSA, Am. Psychol. Soc., World Affairs Coun. San Antonio, London Diplomatic Acad., Academic Coun., Internat. Soc. Polit. Psychology, Human Behavior and Evolution Soc., Acad. Polit. Sci., Soc. for the Psychol. Study of Social Issues, The Jefferson Coun. (founder, dir. 2002), Physicians for Social Responsibility (leadership cir.), So. Poverty Law Ctr. (leadership coun. for tchg. tolerance), Soc. Profl. Journalists, Interfaith Alliance, Mil. Officers Assn., Air Force Assn., Internat. Platform Assn. (Poetry award 1995). Independent. Deist. Avocations: running and fishing, poetry, singing, public speaking. Home: 14023 N Hills Village Dr San Antonio TX 78249-2534 Address: Towers and Rushing Ltd San Antonio TX 78249 Office Phone: 210-690-5557. Business E-Mail: ronribble@hsa.net.

**RIBEIRO, FRANK HENRY,** bank executive, financial consultant; b. Kowloon, Hong Kong, July 1, 1949; arrived in U.S., 1958; s. Henry Agusto and Agatha Marie (Rodriques) Ribeiro; m. Margaret Ann Mitchell, July 23, 1988. BA, Calif. State U, Northridge, 1973; M in Pub. and Internat. Affairs, Princeton U., 1976. Cons. Omega Rsch. Assocs., Northridge, 1973; economist Fed. Power Commn., San Francisco, 1974; economist dept. state U.S. Embassy, London, 1975; fin. analyst Exxon Corp., N.Y.C., 1976-81; mgr. swaps Marine Midland Bank, N.Y.C., 1982-83; v.p., dir. Bank Am., N.Y.C., 1983-89; v.p., mgr. corp. fin. ABN-AMRO Bank N.V. (formerly Algemene Bank Nederlands, N.V.), N.Y.C., 1989-92; cons., trainer Fin. Dirs., Inc., N.Y.C., 1993-96; pres Paradigm Strategy Group, 1996—. Cons. UN, N.Y.C., Malaysia, Thailand, 1984—85; bd. dirs. Mark Degarmo Dance Co. Coauthor: Handbook of International Corporate Finance, 1988; contbr. articles to profl. jours. Mem.: Internat. Swap Dealers Assn., N.Y.C. Folk Dance Found. (program coord. 1982—86). Office: c/o DEM 4582E Kingwood Dr Kingwood TX 77345-2600 Office Phone: 520-615-7948. Business E-Mail: fr@paradigmtraining.com.

**RICAPITO, JOSEPH VIRGIL (GIUSEPPE RICAPITO),** literature educator; b. Giovinazzo, Bari, Italy, Oct. 30, 1933; came to U.S., 1935; s. Frank and Filomena (Cervone) R.; m. Carolyn Sue Kitchen, Apr. 7, 1958; children: Frank Peyton, Maria Avadna. BA, CUNY, Bklyn., 1955; MA, U. Iowa, 1956; PhD in Romance Langs., U. Calif., L.A., 1966. From instr. to asst. prof. Pomona Coll., Claremont, Calif., 1962-70; from assoc. prof. to prof. Ind. U., Bloomington, Ind., 1970-80; prof. La. State U., Baton Rouge, 1980—, chmn. dept., 1980-85. Joseph Yenni disting. prof. Italian Studies, 1999. Author: Bibliografia Razonada y anotada, 1980; editor: La Vida de Laz de Tormes, 1976; translator: Dialogue of Mercury and Charon, 1986, Cervantes's Novelas ejemplares: Between History and Creativity, 1996. Pres. Greater Baton Rouge Am.-Italian Assn., 1984-85. With U.S. Army, 1957-59. Grantee NEH, 1981; named Knight Order of Merit, Republic of Italy, 1988, Knight Order of Queen Isabel, Govt. of Spain, 1990; named Disting. Rsch. Master La. State U., 2001, Cervantes Lectr., Fordham U., 2004. Mem. MLA, Renaissance Soc. Am., Am. Comparative Lit. Assn., Am. Assn. Tchrs. Spanish and Portuguese, Cervantes Soc. Am. Avocations: music, photography, films. Office: La State U 309 Hodges Hall Baton Rouge LA 70803-0001 Office Phone: 225-578-6616. Business E-Mail: ricapito@lsu.edu.

**RICARD, JOHN H.,** bishop, educator; b. Baton Rouge, Feb. 29, 1940; s. Maceo and Albanie (St. Amant) R. BA, St. Joseph Sem., 1962, MA, 1968; MS, Tulane U., 1970. Ordained priest Roman Cath. Ch., 1968. Pastor Holy Redeemer Ch., Washington, 1972—75, Holy Comforter Ch., Washington, 1975—84; ordained titular bishop of Rucuma, 1984; aux. bishop Balt., 1984—97; assoc. prof. Cath. U. Am., Washington, 1973—; bishop of Pensacola-Tallahassee Fla., 1997—. Mem. priest's senate Archdiocese of Washington, 1974—, mem. sch. bd., 1976—. Pres. Cath. Relief Svcs. USCC, 1995—; mem. Pontifical Coun., COR UNUM, 1996—; Chmn. Com. on Social Devel. and World Peace, Domestic Social Devel., 1992—95. Mem.: Secretariat of Black Caths. Office: PO Drawer 17329 Pensacola FL 32522-7329

**RICARD, VIRGINIA BELLE,** adult education educator; b. Denver, Nov. 27, 1927; d. Raymond and Loraine Hill; m. W. Kenneth Ricard, Apr. 6, 1953 (dec.); 1 child, Valerie. BS in Chemistry, Marymount Coll. Kans., Salina, 1949; MEd, Colo. State U., Ft. Collins, 1972, MEd in Adult Edn., 1973; PhD, Union Inst. and Univ., Cin., 1978. Med. tech. N.Y. Hosp., N.Y.C., 1950—53; rschr. Colo. State U., Ft. Collins, 1971—73, program coord., 1973—75, program devel. specialist, 1978—80; eval. specialist, cons. Model Edn. Program, DHEW, Denver, 1976—78; pvt. cons. Ft. Collins, Colo., 1980—2002; affiliate faculty mem. Regis U., Denver, 2000—. Author: Developing Intercultural Communication Skills, 1993, contbr. articles to profl. jours. Chair, family selection com. Habitat for Humanity, Ft. Collins, 1988—90; lifetime mem. Girl Scouts USA, first v.p., 1990—93; bd. dirs. Larimer County Food Distbn. Ctr., Ft. Collins, 1995—98, Care, Inc., Ft. Collins, 1996—2002. Recipient Disting. Alumni Award, Marymount Coll. Kans., 1985. Mem.: Colo. Assn. for Continuing and Adult Edn., No. Colo. Weavers Guild, Am. Assn. Adult and Continuing Edn., Phi Kappa Phi. Avocations: art, travel, music, genealogy. Home: 1826 Indian Meadows Ln Fort Collins CO 80525-1421 Office Phone: 970-493-1922.

**RICARDO-CAMPBELL, RITA,** economist, educator; b. Boston, Mar. 16, 1920; d. David and Elizabeth (Jones) Ricardo; m. Wesley Glenn Campbell, Sept. 15, 1946; children: Barbara Lee, Diane Rita, Nancy Elizabeth. BS, Simmons Coll., 1941; MA, Harvard U., 1945, PhD, 1946. Instr. Harvard U., Cambridge, Mass., 1946—48; asst. prof. Tufts U., Medford, Mass., 1948—51; labor economist U.S. Wage Stabilization Bd., 1951—53; economist Ways and Means Com. U.S. Ho. of Reps., 1954—55; economist, 1957—60; prof. San Jose (Calif.) State U., 1960—61; sr. fellow Hoover Instn. on War, Revolution, and Peace, Stanford, Calif., 1968—95, sr. fellow emerita, 1995—. Lectr. health Stanford U. Med. Sch., 1973—78; bd. dirs. Watkins-Johnson Co., Palo Alto, Calif., Gillette Co., Boston; mgmt. bd. Samaritan Med. Ctr., San Jose. Author: Voluntary Health Insurance in the U.S., 1960, Economics of Health and Public Policy, 1971, Food Safety Regulation: Use and Limitations of Cost-Benefit Analysis, 1974, Drug Lag: Federal Government Decision Making, 1976, Social Security: Promise and Reality, 1977, The Economics and Politics of Health, 1982, 2d edit., 1985, Resisting Hostile Takeovers: The Gillette Company, 1997, Chinese transl., 2004; co-editor: Below-Replacement Fertility in Industrial Societies, 1987, Issues in Contemporary Retirement, 1988; contbr. articles to profl. jours. Mem. Western Interstate Commn. for Higher Edn. Calif., 1967-75, chmn., 1970-71; mem. Pres. Nixon's Adv. Coun. on Status of Women, 1969-76; mem. Pres. Ford's Adv. Coun. on Status of Women, 1976-79; mem. task force on taxation Pres.'s Coun. on Environ. Quality, 1970-72; mem. Pres.'s Com. Health Svcs. Industry, 1971-73, FDA Nat. Adv. Drug Com., 1972-75; mem. Pres. Reagan's Econ. Policy Adv. Bd., 1981-90, Pres. Reagan's Nat. Coun. on Humanities, 1982-89, Pres. Reagan's Nat. Medal of Sci. com., 1988-91, Pres. Bush's Nat. Medal of Sci. com., 1991-94; bd. dirs. Ind. Colls. No. Calif., 1971-87; mem. com. assessment of safety, benefits, risks Citizens Commn. Sci., Law and Food, Rockefeller U., 1973-75; mem. adv. com. Ctr. Health Policy Rsch., Am. Enterprise Inst. Pub. Policy Rsch., Washington, 1974-80; mem. adv. coun. on social security Quadrennial Health and Human Svcs., 1974-75; bd. dirs. Simmons Coll., Boston, 1975-80; mem. adv. coun. bd. assocs. Stanford Librs., 1975-78; mem. coun. SRI Internat., Menlo Park, Calif., 1977-90. Mem. Am. Econ. Assn., Mont Pelerin Soc. (bd. dirs 1988-92, v.p. 1992-94), Harvard Grad. Soc. (coun. 1991-94), Phi Beta Kappa. Home: Classic Residence Hyatt 620 Sand Hill Rd Apt 308D Palo Alto CA 94304 Office: Stanford U Hoover Instn Stanford CA 94305-6010 Office Phone: 650-723-2074. Personal E-mail: ricardocampbell@sbcglobal.net.

**RICART, FRED,** automotive company executive; Owner Ricart Automotive, Columbus, Ohio. Office: Ricart Automotive Rte 33 and Hamilton Rd Columbus OH 43227-1342

**RICCARDI, VINCENT MICHAEL,** pediatrician, educator, entrepreneur; b. Bklyn., Oct. 14, 1940; s. Gabriel John and Frances Mary (Novak) R.; m. Susan Leona Bogda, July 27, 1967; children: Angela M., Ursula M., Mikah F. AB, UCLA, 1962; MD, Georgetown U., 1966; MBA, U. LaVerne, 1993. Intern, resident in medicine U. Pitts., 1966-68; fellow in genetics Harvard Med. Sch., Boston, 1968-70, 72; asst. prof. medicine U. Colo. Med. Ctr., Denver, 1973-75; assoc. prof. medicine, pediatrics Med. Coll. Wis., Milw., 1975-77; prof. medicine, pediatrics Baylor Coll. Medicine, Houston, 1977-90; med. dir. The Genetics Inst., Pasadena, Calif., 1990-92; clin. prof. pediatrics UCLA, 1991—; founder, CEO Am. Med. Consumers, La Crescenta, 1992. Dir. The Neurofibromatosis Inst., La Crescenta, Calif., 1985—. Author: Genetic Approach to Human Disease, 1977, Communication and Counseling in Health Care, 1983, Neurofibromatosis, 1986, rev. edit., 1992, 99. Maj. U.S. Army, 1970-71. Fellow ACP, AAAS, Am. Coll. Med. Genetics; mem. Am. Soc. Human Genetics, Am. Coll. Physician Execs. Avocations: creative writing, acting. Office: Am Med Consumers 5415 Briggs Ave La Crescenta CA 91214-2205 Office Phone: 818-957-3508. Business E-Mail: riccardi@medcomsumer.com.

**RICCARDS, MICHAEL PATRICK,** academic administrator; b. Hillside, N.J., Oct. 2, 1944; s. Patrick and Margaret (Finelli) Riccards; m. Barbara Dunlop, June 6, 1970; children: Patrick, Catherine, Abigail. BA, Rutgers U., 1966, MA, 1967, MPhil, 1969, PhD, 1970. Spl. asst. to chancellor Dept. Higher Edn., Trenton, NJ, 1969-70; from asst. prof. to assoc. prof. SUNY, Buffalo, 1970-77; dean U. Mass., Boston, 1977-82; provost Hunter Coll. CUNY, NY, 1982—83, prof., 1982-86; pres. St. John's Coll., Santa Fe, 1986-89, Shepherd Coll., Shepherdstown, W.Va., 1989-95, Fitchburg (Mass.) State Coll., 1995—2002; pub. policy scholar-in-residence Coll. Bd., Washington, 2002—; exec. dir. Hall Inst. Pub. Policy, Trenton, NJ, 2005—. Mem. joint commn. tchr. preparation, 1999—2000. Author: (book) The Making of the American Citizenry, 1973, A Republic, If You Can Keep It, 1987, The Ferocious Engine of Democracy, 2 vols., 1995, 2002, Vicars of Christ, 1998, The Presidency and the Middle Kingdom, 2000, The Odes of DiMaggio, 2001, The Papacy and the End of Christendom, 2003, The Myth of American Miseducation, 2005, The State of the Garden State, 2006. Chmn. N.Mex. Endowment Humanities, 1989; trustee Albuquerque Acad., 1988—; mem. Coun. Humanities W.Va., Nat. Skills Stds. Bd., 1993—98; mem. nat. adv. com. Ctr. Study Presidency, 1987—89. Fulbright fellow, 1973, Huntington Libr. fellow, 1974, NEH fellow, Princeton U., 1976—77. Home: 32 Kingston Blvd Hamilton NJ 08690 Office: Hall Inst Pub Policy 130 W State St Trenton NJ 08630

**RICCI, CHRISTINA,** actress; b. Santa Monica, Calif., Feb. 12, 1980; Appeared in films Mermaids, 1990, The Hard Way, 1991, The Addams Family, 1991, The Cemetery Club, 1993, Addams Family Values, 1993, Casper, 1995, Now and Then, 1995, Gold Diggers: The Secret of Bear Mountain, 1995, Bastard Out of Carolina, 1996, The Last of the High Kings, 1996, That Darn Cat, 1996, Ice Storm, 1997, Little Red Riding Hood, 1997, Souvenir (voice) 1998, Pecker, 1999, I Woke Up Early When I Died, 1998, Fear and Loathing in Las Vegas, 1998, Desert Blue, 1998, Buffalo 66, 1998,

The Opposite of Sex, 1998, Small Soldiers (voice only), 1998, Souvenir (voice only), 1998, 200 Cigarettes, 1999, No Vacancy, 1999, Sleepy Hollow, 1999, Bless the Child, 2000, The Man Who Cried, 2000, All Over the Guy, 2001, Prozac Nation (also co-prodr.), 2001, The Laramie Project, 2002, Pumpkin (also prodr.), 2002, Miranda, 2002, The Gathering, 2002, Anything Else, 2003, I Love Your Work, 2003, Monster, 2003, Cursed, 2005; TV appearances include H.E.L.P., 1990, The Simpsons (voice only), 1996, Ally McBeal, 2002, Malcolm in the Middle, 2002, Joey, 2005, Grey's Anatomy, 2006. Office: ICM 8942 Wilshire Blvd Beverly Hills CA 90211-1934*

**RICCIARDI, J.P.,** professional sports team executive; m. Diane Ricciardi; 2 children. Baseball coach minor league N.Y. Yankees, 1982—84, Milw. (Minn.) Brewers, 1985; from scout to dir. player pers. Oakland (Calif.) Athletics, 1986—99, dir. player pers., 1999—2001; sr. v.p. Toronto (Can.) Blue Jays, 2001—, gen. mgr., 2001—. Office: 1 Blue Jays Way Ste 3200 Toronto ON Canada M5V 1J1

**RICCIARDI, LAWRENCE R.,** lawyer; BA, Fordham U., 1962; JD, Columbia U., 1965; course in executive program, Stamford U., 1978. Bar: N.Y. 1967. Assoc. Gilbert, Segall & Young, 1965-69; counsel Overseas Pvt. Invest Corp/US Dept. State Internat. Devel., 1969-73; internat. counsel Am. Express, 1973-75; gen. counsel Internat. Banking Corp., 1975-77, Travel Related Svcs., 1977-89; exec. v.p., gen. counsel RJR Nabisco, Inc., N.Y.C., 1989-93, pres., 1993-1995; sr. v.p. & gen. council IBM, Armonk, 1995—2002; sr. advisor Jones Day, Washington, 2006—. Trustee Andrew W. Mellon Found. Mem. Assn. of Bar of City of N.Y.*

**RICCIARDI, LOUIS MICHAEL,** brokerage house executive; b. Worcester, Mass., 1959; s. Michael Joseph and Mary Theresa Ricciardi; m. Cynthia Anne Booth. BA, Bridgewater State Coll., 1981. Account exec. Shearson/Am. Express, Brockton, Mass., 1981-83; sr. v.p. Thomson McKinnon, Taunton, Mass., 1983-87; sr. v.p. Morgan Stanley Dean Witter, Taunton, Mass., 1988—2002, UBS Paine Webber, Taunton, 2002—. Bd. corporators Bristol County Savs. Bank, Taunton, Mass., 1985—, bd. trustees, 1992—; trustee Taunton Devel. Corp., 1994—, v.p., treas. 1995—. Weekly investment columnist, 1983-2004. Bd. corporators Morton Hosp., Taunton, 1987—, trustee, 1994—, treas., 2002—; pres. Heart of Taunton (Mass.) Revitalization Corp., 1988-89, 2004—; trustee Bridgewater (Mass.) State Coll., 1989-99, 2004—, chmn. 1990-94, 2006—; trustee Bridgewater Found., 1989—, chmn. 1996-2004; bd. dirs. Taunton Boys & Girls Club, 1999—. Recipient Rondileau award for Outstanding Profl. Achievement and Cmty. Svc., 1999, Disting. Svc. award Bridgewater State Coll., 2002, Good Scout award Boy Scouts Am., 2003. Mem. Taunton Rotary Club (Paul Harris fellow 2000, pres. 1991-92), Bridgewater Coll. Alumni Assn. (treas. 1992-95). Avocations: guitar, coin collecting/numismatics, baseball, community service, Coca Cola Memorabilia. Home: PO Box 228 Taunton MA 02780-0228

**RICCIARDI, RICHARD,** military officer; BS, Downstate Med. Ctr., Bklyn., 1980; MS, U. Md., Balt., 1991; student, Uniformed Svcs. U., Bethesda, Md., 2003—. Lic. nurse practitioner, PNCB/ANCC, 1983. Commd. lt. U.S. Army, advanced through grades to col.; with Uniformed Svcs. U., Bethesda, Md., 2003—. Grantee, TriService Nursing Rsch. Program, 2005—06. Office: Uniformed Services University 4301 Jones Bridge Road Bethesda MD 20814 Office Phone: 301-295-3019. Business E-Mail: rricciardi@usuhs.mil.

**RICCIARDI, SALVATORE,** wholesale distribution executive; Pres., CEO Purity Wholesale Grocers, Boca Raton, Fla. Office: Purity Wholesale Grocers Ste 100 5400 Broken Sound Blvd NW Boca Raton FL 33487-3511*

**RICCIARDI, STEVEN DREW,** protective services official; s. Joseph N. Ricciardi and Carole V. Cargill, Janice Ricciardi (Stepmother) and Richmond Cargill (Stepfather); m. Carolyn Coughlin, Oct. 26, 1985; children: William Joseph, John Michael, Drew N. BS in Adminstrn. Justice, Roger Williams U., 1982; MS in Adminstrn. Justice, Salve Regina U., 1986. Police officer Newport (RI) Police Dept., 1981—87; spl. agt. US Secret Svc., Buffalo, 1987—91, Chicago, 1991—94, Washington, 1994—98, asst. spl. agt. in charge, 1998—2000, insp., 2001—03, spl. agt. in charge Boston, 2003—. Prin. fed. ofcl. Dept. Homeland Security, Boston, 2004—. Coach youth hockey. Sgt. USMC, 1978—84. Recipient Life Saving Award, Am. Legion, RI, 1984, award for excellence, Dept. Homeland Security, 2004, Disting. Law Enforcement Agy. award, Mass. Italian Am. Police Officers Assn., 2005. Mem.: Greater Boston Fed. Exec. Bd. (assoc.; law enforcement liaison 2004). Avocations: golf, boating. Office Phone: 617-565-5640.

**RICCIARDONE, FRANCIS JOSEPH, JR.,** ambassador; b. Boston; m. Marie Dunn Ricciardone; 2 children. BS summa cum laude, Dartmouth Coll., 1973. Tchr., Iran, 1976—78; with US Fgn. Svc., 1978—, with Bur. Intelligence and Rsch. Washington, sr. mgmt. positions under dir. gen., chief civilian observer unit Multinational Force and Observers in Egypt Sinai Desert, 1989—91, polit. advisor to U.S. and Turkish commanding gens. Operation Provide Comfort; dep. chief of mission and charge d'affaires US Embassy, Ankara, Turkey, 1995—99; spl. coord. for transition of Iraq US Dept. State, Washington, 1999—2001, US amb. to Philippines and Palau Manila, 2002—05, US amb. to Egypt Cairo, 2005—. Office: American Embassy 7700 Cairo Pl Washington DC 20521-7700 also: American Embassy Garden City 8 Kamal El Din Salah St Cairo Egypt*

**RICCINI, KENNETH A.,** government agency administrator; BS in economics and stats., Pa. State U.; MBA, U. Md. Chief computer services divsn. and telecommunications office US Census Bur. Office: US Census Bur 4700 Silver Hill Rd Washington DC 20233-0001*

**RICCITIELLO, JOHN S.,** former interactive software/gaming executive; venture capitalist; Pres., CEO Wilson Sporting Goods Co.; pres., CEO bakery divsn. Sara Lee Corp.; pres., COO Electronic Arts, Redwood City, Calif., 1997—2004; co-founder Elevation Partners, Menlo Park, Calif., 2004—.

**RICCO, DONNA,** fashion designer; Pres. Donna Ricco Inc., N.Y.C. Office: Donna Ricco Inc 253 W 35th St Fl 9 New York NY 10001-1907*

**RICCO, EDWARD ROBERT,** lawyer; b. Teaneck, NJ, Jan. 17, 1950; s. Leopold Joseph and Rose May (Lotito) R.; m. Mary Ann Sweeney, Feb. 2, 1974; children: Alanna Catherine, Susanna Maria. BS, Stevens Inst. Tech., 1971; MA, Columbia U., 1973; JD, U. N.M., 1980. Bar: N.Mex. 1980, U.S. Dist. Ct. N.Mex. 1980, U.S. Ct. Appeals (10th cir.) 1981, U.S. Supreme Ct. 1984, U.S. Ct. Appeals (D.C. cir.) 1992, U.S. Ct. Appeals (9th cir.) 2004. Law clk. to chief judge U.S. Dist. Ct., Albuquerque, 1980-81; assoc. Rodey, Dickason, Sloan, Akin & Robb P.A., Albuquerque, 1981-87, ptnr., 1987—. Mem. com. uniform jury instructions in civil cases N.Mex. Supreme Ct., Albuquerque, 1986-98, mem. com. rules of appellate procedure, 1999-2004; adj. prof. law U. N.Mex. Lead articles editor Natural Resources Jour. 1979-80. Served to capt. USAF, 1973-77. Mem. ABA (sect. antitrust law, sect. litigation), Am. Acad. Appellate Lawyers, Albuquerque Bar Assn., State Bar Assn. N.Mex. (chmn. health law sect. 1987-88, chmn. appellate practice sect. 1997-98). Office: Rodey Dickason Sloan et al PO Box 1888 201 3rd St NW Ste 2200 Albuquerque NM 87103-1888 Office Phone: 505-765-5900. Business E-Mail: ericco@rodey.com.

**RICCOBONO, RICHARD M.,** federal agency administrator; b. Bklyn., Sept. 15, 1957; Grad., SUNY, Albany; JD, Western New Eng. Sch. Law; postgrad., Boston U. With Deloitte & Touche, Fed. Home Loan Bank Boston, Office of Thrift Supervision, Washington, 1989—, regional dep. dir., 1990-98, dep. dir., 1998—2005, acting dir., 2005; dir. FDIC, Washington, 2005; exec. v.p., COO Fed. Home Loan Bank of Seattle, 2005—. Office: Fed Home Loan Bank 1501 4th Ave Ste 1900 Seattle WA 98101-1693

**RICE, ANNE,** writer; b. New Orleans, Oct. 14, 1941; d. Howard and Katherine (Allen) O'Brien; m. Stan Rice, Oct. 14, 1961 (dec. Dec. 9, 2002); children: Michele (dec. Aug. 5, 1972), Christopher. Student, Tex. Woman's U., 1959-60; BA, San Francisco State Coll., 1964, MA, 1971. Author: Interview with the Vampire, 1976, The Feast of all Saints, 1980, Cry to Heaven, 1982, The Vampire Lestat, 1985, The Queen of the Damned, 1988, The Mummy or Ramses the Damned, 1989, The Witching Hour, 1990 (TV series, 2002), Tale of the Body Thief, 1992, Lasher, 1993, Taltos, 1994, Memnoch the Devil, 1995, Servant of the Bones, 1996, Violin, 1998, The Vampire Armand, 1998, Pandora: New Tales of the Vampires, 1998, Vittorio the Vampire, 1999, Merrick, 2000, Blood and Gold, 2001, The Master of Rampling Gate, 2002, Blackwood Farm, 2002, Blood Canticle, 2003, Christ the Lord: Out of Egypt, 2005; (as A.N. Roquelaure) The Claiming of Sleeping Beauty, 1983, Beauty's Punishment, 1984, Beauty's Release: The Continued Erotic Adventures of Sleeping Beauty, 1985 (as Anne Rampling) Exit to Eden, 1985, Belinda, 1986; screenwriter: Interview with a Vampire, 1994.

**RICE, CHARLES LANE,** surgeon, educator; b. Atlanta, May 22, 1945; s. Marion Jennings and Molly Black (Moore) R.; m. Lynn Carol Inscoe, Dec. 27, 1968 (div. 1976); m. Judith Josephine Bousha, July 9, 1977; children: Aaron Nicholas, Patrick Marion. AB, U. Ga., 1964; MD, Med. Coll. Ga., 1968. Commd. ensign USN, 1966, advanced through grades to comdr., 1976, ret., 1977; intern Bowman Gray Sch. Medicine, Winston-Salem, NC, 1968-69; resident Nat. Naval Med. Ctr., Bethesda, Md., 1969-73; asst. prof. surgery U. Chgo., 1977-80, assoc. prof. surgery, 1980-84; dir. intensive care unit Michael Reese Hosp., Chgo., 1977-84; prof., vice chmn. dept. surgery U. Wash., Seattle, 1985-92; surgeon-in-chief Harborview Med. Ctr., Seattle, 1985-92; Dr. Lee Hudson-Robert R. Penn prof., chmn., divsn. gen. surgery U. Tex. Southwestern Med. Ctr., Dallas, 1992-93; prof. surgery U. Ill., Chgo., 1993—2005, prof. physiology and biophysics, 1996—2005, vice dean Coll. Medicine, 1994-99, vice chancellor health affairs, 1999—2004; prof. surgery, pres. Uniformed Svcs. U. of Health Scis., Bethesda, Md., 2005—. Robert Wood Johnson Health Policy fellow, 1992; legis. asst. to U.S. senator Tom Daschle, 1991-92. Assoc. editor Jour. of Surg. Rsch., 1983-90; contbr. articles to profl. jours. Rep. Accrediting Coun. Grad. Med. Edn., chair elect, 2001—02, chair, 2002—04. Capt. USNR, 1989—2003. Decorated Legion of Merit. Fellow ACS (gov. 1992-98, vice chmn. com. on trauma 1992-93), Am. Surg. Assn., Am. Assn. for Surgery of Trauma (com. chair 1989-91); mem. Soc. Univ. Surgeons, Am. Physiol. Soc., Shock Soc. (pres. 1991-92), Ctrl. Surg. Assn., Pacific Coast Surg. Assn. Democrat. Episcopalian. Office: Uniformed Svcs U Health Sci Office of Pres 4301 Jones Bridge Rd Bethesda MD 20814-4799 Office Phone: 301-295-3013. Business E-Mail: crice@usuhs.edu.

**RICE, CHRISTINA LYNN BOCHTLER,** literature and language educator; d. Stanley Edwin and Roberta Christina Bochtler; m. Tyson Willis Rice, Jan. 1, 2005; 1 child, Alayna Grace; 1 child, Caleb James Hinners. BA in English, Buena Vista Coll., Storm Lake, Iowa, 1993; tchg. cert., Buena Vista U., 2002. Residential coord. Faith Hope & Charity, Storm Lake, 1993—2002; lang. arts tchr. Albert City Truesdale Sch., Iowa, 2002—04, Washington HS, Cherokee, Iowa, 2004—. Mem.: NEA. Office: Washington HS 600 Bluff St Cherokee IA 51012 Office Phone: 712-225-6755. E-mail: cbochtler@cherokee.k12.ia.us.

**RICE, CLARE I.,** electronics company executive; b. Rice Lake, Wis., Nov. 3, 1918; s. Chris Nilson and Josephine (Haug) R.; m. Virginia M. Bateman; children: Karen Rice, Carol Rice Brannon, David Alan; m. Barbara Carlson Denniston, 2002. BSEE, U. Wis., 1943; BS in Law, St. Paul Coll. Law, 1950; DEngring, Rose-Hulman Inst. Tech., 1979. Registered profl. engr., Minn., D.C. Supr. aircraft radio engring. Northwest Airlines, Inc., Mpls., 1946-51; staff engr. Aero. Radio, Inc., Washington, 1951-53; aviation sales mgr., gen. mgr. Bendix Avionics Divsn., Balt., 1953-62; pres. Sunbeam Electronics, Inc., Ft. Lauderdale, Fla., 1962-66; v.p. Nova U., Ft. Lauderdale, 1966-68; asst. v.p., v.p., sr. v.p. Collins Radio Co., pres. Collins Avionics group Rockwell Internat. Corp., Cedar Rapids, Iowa, 1968-83. Dir. Rockwell-Collins Internat., Inc., Dallas. Chmn. United Way, Cedar Rapids, 1973-74; trustee Coe Coll., 1979-83. Hoover Presdl. Libr.; eminent fellow Wisdom Hall of Fame; bd. dirs. St. Luke's Hosp., 1976-82, Mchts. Nat. Bank, 1977-83; chmn. Mcpl. Airport Commn., Cedar Rapids, 1980-84; charter mem. Aviation Hall of Fame; capt. Hon. Dep. Sheriffs Assn., 1987—; pres. Sales and Mktg. Execs. Balt., 1960-61, Cmty. Assn. Bernardo Heights, 1988-91; dir. Rancho Bernardo Cmty. Found. Lt. comdr. USNR, 1943-46. Recipient Disting. Svc. citation U. Wis., 1979, 84; Pioneer award Milw. Sch. Engring., 1981. Sr. mem. IEEE; mem. Iowa Mfrs. Assn. (bd. dirs 1975-81), Gen. Aviation Mfrs. Assn. (dir. 1970-81, chmn. 1979), U. Wis. Alumni Assn. (chmn. 1981-82, pres. 1980-81, Disting. Svc. award 1984). Clubs: Wings (N.Y.C.); Nat. Aviation (Washington); Rancho Bernardo Heights Country. Lodges: Royal Order of Jesters (dir. 1979). Republican. Presbyterian. Home: The Remington Club 16925 Hierba Dr # 219 San Diego CA 92128

**RICE, CONDOLEEZZA,** secretary of state, former national security advisor; b. Birmingham, Ala., Nov. 14, 1954; d. John Wesley and Angelena Ray Rice. BA cum laude, U. Denver, 1974, PhD, 1981; MA, U. Notre Dame, 1975; PhD (hon.), Morehouse Coll., 1991, U. Ala., 1994, U. Notre Dame, 1995, Nat. Def. U., 2002, Miss. Coll. Sch. of Law, 2003, U. Louisville, 2004, Mich. St. U., 2004; degree (hon.), Boston Coll., 2006. Intern, Bur. of Ednl. & Cultural Affairs US Dept. State, Washington, 1977; intern Rand Corp., Santa Monica, Calif., 1978; polit. sci. cons. Stanford U., 1980-81, asst. prof. polit. sci., 1981—87, assoc. prof., 1987—93, prof., 1993—99; provost Stanford U., 1993-99; spl. asst. to dir. of the Joint Chiefs of Staff U.S. Dept. Def., Washington, 1986; spl. asst. to Pres. for nat. security affairs NSC, 1989-91, dir. to sr. dir. Soviet & East European Affairs, 1989—91; sr. fellow Hoover Inst., Stanford, Calif., 1991—93; nat. security cons. George W. Bush presdl. campaign, 2000; asst. to the Pres. for nat. security affairs NSC, Washington, 2001—05; sec. US Dept. State, Washington, 2005—. Cons. ABC News, Washington; mem. spl. advisory panel to comdr. and chief strategic air commd.; mem. gov. ind. advisory redistricting the state of Calif.; mem. U.S. Delegation to 2+4 Talks on German Unification; former mem. bd. dirs. Chevron Corp., Charles Schwab Corp., Internat. Advisory Coun. of J.P. Morgan, William & Flora Hewlett Found., U. Notre Dame. Author: Uncertain Allegiance: The Soviet Union and the Czechoslovak Army, 1984; co-author (with Alexander Dallin): The Gorbachev Era, 1986; co-author: (with Philip Zelikow) Germany Unified and Europe Transformed, 1995. Ex officio trustee Nat. Gallery Art. Named one of Most Influential People, Time mag., 2005, 100 Most Influential People, 2006, 100 Most Powerful Women, Forbes mag., 2005—06, The 10 Most Fascinating People of 2005, Barbara Walters Special, Most Influential Black Americans, Ebony mag., 2006; recipient Sch. of Humanities and Scis. Dean's award for Disting. Tchg., Stanford U., 1993, Walter J. Gores award for Excellence in Tchg., 1984, Pres. award, NAACP Image Awards, 2002. Mem. Coun. Fgn. Rels. Republican. Office: US Dept State 2201 C St NW Washington DC 20520 Office Phone: 202-647-4000.*

**RICE, CONSTANCE LAMAY,** lawyer; b. 1956; BA, Radcliffe Coll.; JD, NYU. Bar: 1984. Law clk. to Honorable Damon Keith, US 6th Circuit Ct. Appeals, 1984—86; atty. to co-dir. LA office NAACP Legal Def. and Edn. Fund; ptnr., civil rights law English, Munger and Rice, LA. Co-dir., co-founder Advancement Project, LA; bd. dirs. Public Inst. Calif., Pub. Radio Station KPCC. Named one of State's Top 100 Most Influential Calif. Attys., Calif. Law Bus. Jour., 2000, Am. Top Black Lawyers, Black Enterprise Mag., 2003; recipient Peace prize, Calif. Wellness Found., 2001, John Anson Ford Humanaturaab award, LA County, 2002. Office: English Munger and Rice Ste 800 1545 Wilshire Blvd Los Angeles CA 90001 Office Phone: 213-989-1300.

**RICE, DALE R.,** education educator; b. New Castle, Pa., Aug. 6, 1948; s. Paul Richard and Charlotte Mae Rice; m. Judy B. Rice, Aug. 6, 1984; children: Brandon Dale, Kristen Leigh, Courtney Alletta; m. Luann Moser Rice, June 10, 1972 (div. Nov. 4, 1983). BS, Pa. State U., State College, PA, 1966—70, MEd, 1970—73; PhD, Ohio State, Columbus, OH, 1974—77. Educator Bethel Pk. City Schools, Bethel Park, Pa., 1970—74; rsch. asst. Ohio State U., Columbus, Ohio, 1974—77; lectr. East Carolina U., Green-

ville, NC, 1977—80; asst. prof. U. of So. Ala., Mobile, Ala., 1980—86; assoc. prof. Auburn U., Auburn, Ala., 1986—89; educator Gwinnett County Schools, Lawrenceville, Ga., 1989—. Article reviewer Sch. Sci. & Math Jour., 1980—88; ednl. cons. Ednl. Jour., 1987—89. Author: (book) Life Science, Earth Science, Energy from Fossil Fuels. Avocation: landscaping. Personal E-mail: dale.rice@att.net.

**RICE, DAVID H.,** medical products executive; V.p., chief info. officer Siemens Med. Solutions Inc., Malvern, Pa. Named one of Premier 100 IT Leaders, Computerworld, 2005. Office: Siemens Med Solutions Inc 51 Valley Stream Pkwy Malvern PA 19355-1406*

**RICE, DAVID LEE,** university president emeritus; b. New Market, Ind., Apr. 1, 1929; s. Elmer J. and Katie (Tate) R.; m. Betty Jane Fordice, Sept. 10, 1950; children: Patricia Denise Rice Dawson, Michael Alan. BS, Purdue U., 1951, MS, 1956, PhD, 1958; degree (hon.), U. Evansville, 1994, U. So. Ind., 1995; LHD, U. Evansville, 1994; LLD, U. So. Ind., 1995. Dir. prof. research Ball State U., Muncie, Ind., 1958-66; v.p. Coop. Ednl. Research Lab., Inc., Indpls., 1965-67; research coordinator, bur. research HEW, Washington; dean campus Ind. State U., Evansville, 1967-71, pres. campus, 1971-85; pres. U. So. Ind., Evansville, 1985-94, pres. emeritus, 1994—. Adminstrv. asst. Gov.'s Com. on Post High Sch. Orgn. Contbr. articles to profl. jours. Past mem. State Citizens Adv. Bd. Title XX Social Security Act; bd. dirs., past pres. bd. commrs. Evansville Housing Auth.; pres. Leadership Evansville, 1978-79; bd. dirs., past pres. S.W. Ind. Pub. TV, 1972—; chair Indian Pub. Broadcasting Sts., 1990-93; bd. dirs. Villages Inc.; mem. Buffalo Trace Coun. Boy Scouts Am., 1963—, New Harmony Commn., 1989-94; chair So. Ind. Rural Devel. Project., Inc.; bd. trustees Rapp Granary-Owen Found.; bd. dirs. So. Ind. Higher Edn. Inc., U. So. Ind. Found. With inf. U.S. Army, 1951-53. Decorated Bronze Star, Combat Infantryman's Badge; recipient Svc. to Others award Salvation Army, 1974, Citizen of Yr. award Westside Civitan Club, 1972, Boss of Yr. award Am. Bus. Women's Assn., 1976, Disting. Citizen of Yr. award Ivy Tech State Coll., 1994; David L. Rice Libr./U. So. Ind. named in his honor, 1994. Mem. DAR (medal of honor for cmty. svc. 1998), Am. Assn. Higher Edn., Am. Ednl. Rsch. Assn., Am. Assn. State Colls. and Univs., Nat. Soc. Study Edn., Met. Evansville C. of C. (dir.), Evansville Kennel Club, Rotary (civic award Evansville club 1985, life), Alpha Kappa Psi, Alpha Zeta, Phi Delta Kappa. Methodist. Home: 1223 S Main St New Harmony IN 47631 Office: Neef Lesueur House 404 Church St New Harmony IN 47631

**RICE, DENIS TIMLIN,** lawyer; b. Milw., July 11, 1932; s. Cyrus Francis and Kathleen (Timlin) R.; children: James Connelly, Tracy Ellen. AB, Princeton U., 1954; JD, U. Mich., 1959. Bar: Calif. 1960. Practiced in, San Francisco, 1959—; assoc. firm Pillsbury, Madison & Sutro, 1959-61, Howard & Prim, 1961-63; prin. firm Howard, Rice, Nemerovski, Canady, Falk & Rabkin, 1964—. Bd. dirs. Anabas, Inc.; chmn., mng. com. San Francisco Inst. Fin. Svcs., 1983—92. Councilman, City of Tiburon, Calif., 1968-72, mayor, 1970-72; dir. Marin County Transit Dist., 1970-72, 77-81, chmn., 1979-81; supr. Marin County, 1977-81, chmn., 1979-80; commr. Marin Housing Authority, 1977-81; mem. San Francisco Bay Conservation and Devel. Commn., 1977-83; bd. dirs. Planning and Conservation League, 1981-2006, Marin Symphony, 1984-92, Marin Theatre Co., 1987-97, Marin Conservation League, 1995-2000, Digital Village Found., 1995—, pres., 1997—; mem. Met. Transp. Commn., 1980-83; mem. bd. visitors U. Mich. Law Sch. 1st lt. AUS, 1955-57. Recipient Freedom Found. medal, 1956 Fellow Am. Bar Found.; mem. ABA (fed. regulation of securities com., chair Asia-Pacific Bus. Law Com., chmn. subcom. on internat. venture law), State Bar Calif. (editor 1978-80, vice chair sect. bus. law 1978-80, chair com. adminstrn. justice 1997-98, chair com. cyberspace law 1997-2001), San Francisco Bar Assn., Am. Judicature Soc., Internat. Tech. Law Assn. (bd. dirs. 1995—), Internat. Property Law Assn., South End Rowing Club, Tiburon Peninsula Club, Pacific Union Club, Olympic Club, Order of Coif, Phi Beta Kappa, Phi Delta Phi. Office: 3 Embarcadero Ctr Ste 700 San Francisco CA 94111-4003 Office Phone: 415-434-1600. Business E-Mail: drice@hrice.com.

**RICE, DERICA,** pharmaceutical company executive; b. 1965; m. Robin Rice; 3 children. Grad., GMI Engring. and Mgmt. Inst., 1988; MBA, Ind. U. Joined Eli Lilly and Co., 1990, internat. treasury assoc., 1990—92, dir. fin. Can., 1995—97, exec. dir. fin. European ops., 1997—99, gen. mgr. UK affiliate, 1999—2003, mem. Diversity Leadership Coun., v.p., controller Indpls., 2003—06, sr. v.p., CFO, 2006—. Office: Eli Lilly and Co Lilly Corp Ctr Indianapolis IN 46285

**RICE, DONALD B.,** biotechnology company executive; Asst. dir. Office of Mgmt. and Budget The White House, Washington; pres., CEO The RAND Corp., 1972—89; sec. Air Force U.S. Dept. Def., Washington, 1989—93; pres., COO, dir. Teledyne, Inc., 1993—96; pres., CEO, dir. UroGenesys, Inc., 1997—; dir. Scios, Inc., Sunnyvale, Calif., 1997—, chmn. bd., 1998—. Bd. dirs. Wells Fargo & Co., Vulcan Materials Co., Unocal Corp., Amgen, Inc.

**RICE, DONALD BLESSING,** biotechnology executive, former federal official; b. Frederick, Md., June 4, 1939; s. Donald Blessing and Mary Celia (Santangelo) R.; m. Susan Fitzgerald, Aug. 25, 1962; children: Donald Blessing III, Joseph John, Matthew Fitzgerald. BSChemE, U. Notre Dame, 1961, DEng (hon.), 1975; MS in Indsl. Mgmt., Purdue U., 1962, PhD in Econs., 1965, D (hon.) in Mgmt., 1985; LLD (hon.), Pepperdine U., 1989; LHD (hon.), West Coast U., 1993; D in Pub. Policy (hon.), Rand Grad. Sch., 1995. Dir. cost analysis Office Sec. Def., Washington, 1967-69, dep. asst. sec. def. resource analysis, 1969-70; asst. dir. Office Mgmt. and Budget, Exec. Office Pres., 1970-72; pres., CEO The Rand Corp., Calif., 1972-89; sec. USAF, 1989-93; pres., COO Teledyne, Inc., L.A., 1993-96; chmn. Scios, Inc., Sunnyvale, Calif., 1998—2003; pres., CEO Agensys, Inc., Santa Monica, Calif., 1996—. Bd. dirs. Vulcan Materials Co., Wells Fargo & Co., Chevron Corp., Amgen Inc.; mem. nat. adv. com. oceans and atmosphere Dept. Commerce, 1972-75; mem. Nat. Sci. Bd., 1974-86; mem. adv. coun. Coll. Engring., U. Notre Dame, 1974-88; chmn. Nat. Commn. Supplies and Shortages, 1975-77; mem. adv. panel Office Tech. Assessment, 1976-79; mem. Def. Sci. Bd., 1977-83; sr. cons., 1984-88; dir. for sec. def. and Pres. Def. Resource Mgmt. Study, 1977-79; mem. U.S. Commn. Nat. Security/21st Century, 1998-2001; trustee RAND, 2001-, chmn. grad. sch. bd. govs., 1999—. Author articles. Served to capt. AUS, 1965-67. Recipient Sec. Def. Meritorious Civilian Svc. medal, 1970, Def. Exceptional Civilian Svc. medal, 1993, Forrestal award, 1992; Ford Found. fellow, 1962-65. Fellow AAAS, Nat. Acad. of Pub. Adminstrn.; mem. Inst. Mgmt. Scis. (past pres.), Tau Beta Pi. Office: Agensys Inc 1545 17th St Santa Monica CA 90404 Office Phone: 310-820-8029 ext. 210. Business E-Mail: drice@agensys.com.

**RICE, DONALD SANDS,** lawyer; b. Bronxville, NY, Mar. 25, 1940; s. Anton Henry and Lydia Phipps (Sands) R.; m. Edgenie Higgins, Aug. 27, 1966; children: Alice Higgins, Edgenie Rice Thomas. AB magna cum laude, Harvard U., 1961, LLB/JD cum laude, 1964; LLM in Taxation, NYU, 1965. Bar: NY 1964, US Ct. Claims 1965, US Supreme Ct. 1981. Law clk. judge US Ct. Claims, 1965-67; assoc. Barrett, Smith, Schapiro & Simon, NYC, 1967-71; ptnr. Barrett, Smith, Schapiro, Simon & Armstrong, NYC, 1971-86; vice chmn. bd. Bowery Savs. Bank, NYC, 1986-88; ptnr. Chadbourne & Parke, NYC, 1988-96; mng. dir., prin. Ravitch Rice & Co. LLC, NYC, 1996—; ptnr. Rice & Ravitch LLP, NYC, 1996—. Bd. dirs. B-Line, LLC; chmn. Yaddo, 1987; co-chmn. Russian-Am. Banking Law Working Group, 1991—99; v.p., treas., bd. dirs. Soviet Bus. Comml. Law Edn. Found., 1991—96; mem. nat. com. Am. fgn. policy study group dels. to China, Taiwan, 1996, 2000—01; roundtable US China Policy Cross-Strait Rels., 1996—; nat. com. Am. for Pol. Ctrl. Asia Project, 2004—; real estate adv. bd. NY State Comptr., 1987—93; bd. advisors Am.-Russian Investment Forum, 1999—2002; lectr. in field. Contbr. articles to profl. jours. Trustee Nat. Com. Am. Fgn. Policy, 1994—, sr. v.p., 1996—; trustee Chapin Sch., 1980—91, v.p., 1989—91; trustee Marimed Found., 1984—97, Hackley Sch., 1974—81, St. Philip's Episcopal Ch., Mattapoisett, Mass., 1987—, Old Dartmouth Hist. Soc.-New Bedford Whaling Mus., 2006—; pres. Quadequina Co./Mattapoisett Casino, 2001—04; mem. adv. bd. Shorenstein Ctr. on Press, Politics and Pub. Policy, JFK Sch. Govt., Harvard U., 2003—; bd. dirs.

African Med. Rsch. Found., 1978—2002. Mem. Coun. Fgn. Rels., NY State Bar Assn., Assn. Bar City NY, Century Assn., Harvard Club NY, NY Yacht Club, Bay Club, Beverly Yacht Club, Mattapoisett Casino. Home: 1120 Fifth Ave New York NY 10128-0144 Office: Ravitch Rice & Co LLC 610 5th Ave Rm 420 New York NY 10020-2403 Office Phone: 212-218-7880. Personal E-mail: ravricellc@aol.com.

**RICE, DOROTHY PECHMAN (MRS. JOHN DONALD RICE),** medical economist; b. Bklyn., June 11, 1922; d. Gershon and Lena (Schiff) Pechman; m. John Donald Rice, Apr. 3, 1943; children: Kenneth D., Donald B., Thomas H. Student, Bklyn. Coll., 1938—39; BA, U. Wis., 1941; DSc (hon.), Coll. Medicine and Dentistry N.J., 1979. With hosp., and med. facilities USPHS, Washington, 1960—61; med. econs. studies Social Security Adminstrn., 1962—63; health econs. br. Community Health Svc., USPHS, 1964—65; chief health ins. rsch. br. Social Security Adminstrn., 1966—72, dep. asst. commr. for rsch. and statistics, 1972—75; dir. Nat. Ctr. for Health Stats., Rockville, Md., 1976—82; prof. Inst. Health & Aging U. Calif., San Francisco, 1982—94, prof. emeritus, 1994—. Developer, mgr. nationwide health info. svcs.; expert on aging, health care costs, disability, and cost-of-illness. Contbr. articles to profl. jours. Recipient Social Security Adminstrn. citation, 1968, Disting. Svc. medal, HEW, 1974, Jack C. Massey Found. award, 1978, UCSF medal, 2002. Fellow: Am. Statis. Assn.; mem.: LWV, APHA (domestic award for excellence 1978, Sedgwick Meml. medal 1988), Assn. Health Svc. Rsch. (President's award 1988), Inst. Medicine. Home: 13895 Campus Dr Oakland CA 94605-3831 Office: U Calif Sch Nursing Calif San Francisco CA 94143-0646 Office Phone: 415-476-2771. Business E-Mail: dorothy.rice@ucsf.edu.

**RICE, EARL CLIFTON,** retired mathematics educator; b. Edmond, Okla., Aug. 28, 1915; s. Ernest Clifton and Bertha Tillie (Rieckhoff) R.; m. Alyce Loree McConnell; children: Margaret Earlene, Loren Lynwood. BA in Math., Ctrl. State Tchrs. Coll., 1937; MA, George Peabody Coll. Tchrs., 1948, PhD, 1957. Tchr. math. and Spanish Dustin Pub. Schs., Okla., 1937—38, Marlow Pub. Schs., Okla., 1940—42, 1945—46; instr. math. Peabody Coll., Nashville, 1948—49; asst. prof. math. Ark. A&M Coll., Monticello, 1952—53; prof. math. U. Ctrl. Okla., Edmond, 1953—81, math. lectr., 1981—94; ret., 1994. Dir. NSF Insts. in Math. and Sci. for Tchrs. U. Ctrl. Okla., 1959-63, chmn. dept. math., statistics and computing, 1970-71. Author: Test of Generalizing Ability, 1956. Sgt. U.S. Army, 1942-45. Mem. Math. Assn. Am., Nat. Coun. Tchrs. Math., Okla. Edn. Assn., NEA, Am. Legion, Rotary (pres. Edmond chpt. 1972-73), Kappa Delta Pi (pres. 1948), Phi Delta Kappa. Avocations: fishing, ping pong/table tennis, hunting. Home: 808 Myrtle Dr Edmond OK 73034-4639

**RICE, EDWARD PERRY,** secondary school educator; b. Brookline, Mass., Oct. 18, 1947; s. Albert and Ruthe Irene Rice; m. Cheryl Rose Leavitt, June 30, 1974 (div. Apr. 2000); 1 child, Meisha. BA, Northeastern U., 1971; MS Edn., U. So. Maine, 1975. Instr. Journalism dept. U. Maine, Orono, 1987—89; asst. prof. comm. studies Doane Coll., Crete, Nebr., 1989—93; editor Winchester Town Crier, Mass., 1994—96; mng. editor Penobscot Bay Press, Stonington, Maine, 1997—98; tchr. English Katahdin H.S., Sherman Station, Maine, 1998—99; tchr. English, coach cross country Forest Hills H.S., Jackman, Maine, 1999—2001; meeting facilitator Amicus, Bangor, Maine, 2002—04; adj. instr. Ea. Maine C.C., 2004—. Theater critic Portland Press Herald/Maine Sunday Telegram, 1972—77; theater/film critic Maine Pub. Broadcasting-Radio, Orono, 1980—84; theatre critic Maine Times, Topsham, 1984—89; adj. instr. U. Maine, Orono, 2006—. Author: Baseball's First Indian, Louis Sockalexis: Penobscot Legend, Cleveland Indian, 2003; editor: If They Could Only Hear Me, 2005. With U.S. Nat. Guard, Air Nat. Guard, USAR, 1971—93. Decorated Keith L. Ware award, 1st Pl. Dept. Army, Thomas Jefferson award, 2d Pl. Dept. Def.; recipient Cmty. Support award, Cancer Care Maine, 2002, Eugene O'Neill fellow, Nat. Com. for Performing Arts, 1976. Independent. Jewish. Achievements include founded and organized for over 20 years the annual Terry Fox 5-K Run in Bangor, Maine; co-founder Angel Fund, supporting rsch. efforts to find a cure for Lou Gehrig's disease. Avocations: art, baseball history, reading, running, golf. Home: Apt 3 64 Mill St Orono ME 04473

**RICE, FERILL JEANE,** writer; b. Hemingford, Nebr., July 4, 1926; d. Derrick and Helen Agnes (Moffatt) Dalton; m. Otis LaVerne Rice, Mar. 7, 1946; children: LaVeria June McMichael, Larry L. Student, U. Omaha, 1961. Dir. jr. and sr. choral Ch., Tabor, Iowa, 1952-66; tchr. Fox Valley Tech. Inst., Appleton, Wis., 1970-77; activity dir. Family Heritage Nursing Home, Appleton, Wis., 1972-75; dir. activity Peabody Manor, Appleton, Wis., 1975-76. Editor: Moffatt and Related Families, 1981; asst. editor (mag.) Yester-Year, 1975-76; contbr. articles to profl jours. Chmn. edn. Am. Cancer Soc., Fremont County, 1962-64; founder, 1st pres. Mothers Club Nishna Valley chpt. Demolay for Boys. Mem. DAR, Heisey Collectors Am., Iowa Fedn. Women's Clubs (Fremont county chmn. 1964, 65, 66, 67, 7th dist. chmn. libr. svcs. 1966-67), Tabor Women's Club (pres. 1962, 63, 64), Jr. Legion Aux. (founder, 1st dir. 1951-52), Fenton Art Glass Collectors Am. (co-founder 1977, sec., editor newsletter 1976-86, editor/sec. 1988-93, pres./editor 1993-95, treas. 1995-96, pres. 2000-01), Mayflower Soc., John Howland Soc., Ross County Ohio Geneal. Soc., Dallas County Mo. Geneal. Soc., Imperial Collectors Am., Clay County (Ind.) Geneal. Soc., Fenton Finders of Wis. (chpt. #1 pres. 1988-90). Republican. Methodist: Lodges: Order Ea. Star (worthy matron 1956, 64), Rainbow for Girls (bd. dirs. 1964), Internat. Order Job's Daus. (honored queen 1945). Home: 302 Pheasant Run Kaukauna WI 54130-1802 Office Phone: 920-991-9072 x 414.

**RICE, FUHRMAN D. (RUNT RICE),** retired paper company executive; b. June 12, 1927; s. Robert Fulton and Carrie Ann (Whitaker) R.; m. Marie Muybon, 1961; 1 child, Kathleen Ann. Forest ranger Ala. Forestry Commn., Marshall County, 1951-74; procurement agent Paperboard Divsn. Mead Corp., Stevenson, Ala., 1974-91. Pres. Grant Conservation Club, 1964-73; chmn. Marshall County Rep. Exec. Com., Ala., 1995-99; bd. dirs. Ala. Wildlife Fedn., 1961-77 (Conservationist of Yr. 1970); mem. Boy Scouts of Am. (Dist. Scouters award 1964, Silver Beaver award 1974); v.p. soc. Ala. Retirees, Guntersville, 1999, Alder Springs Cmty. Assn., Marshall County, 1999, 2003; mem. Alder Springs Vol. Fire Dept. Home: 831 Ham Rd Albertville AL 35951-4321 E-mail: runt@hiwaay.net.

**RICE, GARY RUSSELL,** retired special education educator; b. Franklin, Pa., Oct. 11, 1951; s. Robert Russell and Della Elizabeth Rice. Grad. cum laude, Cleve. State U., 1973. Cert. polit. sci. tchr., learning disabilities, behavioral disorders, Ohio. Substitute tchr. Lakewood, Rocky River, Westlake (Ohio) Schs., 1973—77; instr. West Side Inst. Tech., Cleve., 1977—78; spl. edn. tchr. Parma (Ohio) City Sch. Dist., 1978—2005, ret., 2005. Learning disabilities tutor, Lakewood, 1974-75; guitar cons. Rock and Roll Hall of Fame and Mus., Cleve. Asst. scoutmaster, leader Boy Scouts Am., Cleve.; former Sunday sch. tchr. local chs., Lakewood; author, columnist, spkr. to various groups on Exceptional Children, the Holocaust and Native Americans; charter mem. U.S. Holocaust Meml. Mus. Recipient Outstanding Spl. Educator award Parma PTA Spl. Edn. com., 1985, Thanks to Tchrs. award Sta. TV-8 WJW, Cleve., 2001, dist. award of merit Boy Scouts Am., 1997, Daniel Carter Beard Masonic Scouter award, 2005. Mem. Parma Edn. Assn., Cleve. Fedn. Musicians, DeMolay (active Legion of Honor 1996), Masons, Shriners. Avocations: music, photography.

**RICE, JAMES BRIGGS, JR.,** lawyer; b. Kansas City, Mo., Dec. 31, 1940; s. James Briggs and Oma J. (Smoyer) R.; m. Carolyn Ryan, Aug. 11, 1963 (div.); children: James Briggs III, Cynthia L.; m. Beverly Sue, Oct. 24, 1980. AB, U. Mo., 1962, JD, 1965. Bar: Mo. 1965, U.S. Dist. Ct. (we. dist.) Mo. 1968. Assoc., Rogers, Field & Gentry, Kansas City, 1967-72; ptnr. Wesner, Wesner & Rice, Sedalia, Mo., 1972-75, Rice & Romines, Sedalia, 1975-80; pvt. practice, Sedalia, 1980—; atty. Sedalia Area Devel. Corp., 1976-79. Chmn., Police Pers. Bd., Sedalia, 1976. Served as capt. U.S. Army, 1965-67; Vietnam. Mem. ABA, Mo. Bar Assn., Pettis County Bar Assn. (pres. 1975)., Am. Judicature Soc., Mo. Assn. Trial Atty.'s, VFW, Vietnam Vets. of Pettis

County. Republican. Methodist. Lodges: Kiwanis (pres. 1975), Noon-day Optimist, Masons, Shriners. Office: 701 S Ohio Ave Sedalia MO 65301-4415 Home: 1940 Ashwood Cir Sedalia MO 65301-9296

**RICE, JERRY ALLEN,** educational consultant; b. Marion, Ohio, Oct. 4, 1942; s. Archie Adam and Doris Ruthella Rice; m. Maria Contento; children: Tamara S. Nelson, Jacob Starmer, Jonathan T. Starmer. AB, Asbury Coll., 1964; MS, Ohio State U., 1969; EdD, SUNY, Albany, 1982. Cert. sci. tchr. Ohio, NY. Sci. tchr. Burgin (Ky.) Ctrl. Schs., 1964—65, Bexley (Ohio) City Schs., 1965—69, Burnt Hills (NY) Consol. Sch. Dist., 1969—74; ednl. rschr. SUNY, Albany, 1975—87; ednl. planner, evaluator Albany (NY) Bd. Coop. Ednl. Svcs., 1977—83; asst. supt. curriculum Homer (NY) Consol. Sch. Dist. 1983—98; asst. prof. adminstrn. SUNY, Cortland, 1999—2005; ednl. cons. Syracuse (NY) U., 1999—. Pres. Assoc. Comprehensive Edn., NY, 1978—80. Author: Response to Levine, 2005. Mem.: ACE, ASCD (sec. NY state), Nat. Coun. Tchrs. Math., Rotary (local bd. dirs.). Avocations: woodcarving, reading, music, computers.

**RICE, JERRY LEE,** retired professional football player; b. Starkville, Miss., Oct. 13, 1962; s. Joe Nathan and Eddie Rice; m. Jackie Rice; children: Jaqui, Jerry Jr. Student, Miss. Valley State U., 1981—84. Wide receiver San Francisco 49ers, 1985—2000, Oakland Raiders, 2001—04, Seattle Seahawks, 2004—05, Denver Broncos, 2005. Celebrity dancer Dancing With the Stars, 2006. Named MVP, NFL, 1987, Super Bowl XXIII, 1989, AP/NFL/Sports Illustrated Offensive Player of Yr., 1993; named to Sporting News Coll. All-Am. team, 1984, Pro Bowl team, 1986—96, 1998, 2002; recipient Pro Bowl MVP, 1995. Achievements include holds NFL career records for most touchdowns, receptions, touchdown receptions; having the most consecutive games with one or more touchdowns (13), 1987; holds the NFL single-season record for most touchdown receptions (22), 1987; shares NFL single-game record for most touchdown receptions (5), 1990; holds NFL record of 274 consecutive games with a reception, 1985-2004; led NFL in receptions, 1990, 1996; led NFL in recieving touchdowns, 1986, 1987, 1989-1991, 1993; led NFL in recieving yards, 1986, 1989, 1990, 1993-1995; being a member of SuperBowl XIX, XXIII, XXIV, XXIX Champion San Francisco 49ers.*

**RICE, JERRY MERCER,** biochemist, consultant, pathologist; b. Washington, Oct. 3, 1940; s. John Earle Rice and Leona (Mercer) Greiner; m. Mary Jane Janocha, Jan. 10, 1978; children: Stacey Lynn, Stephen Mark. BA, Wesleyan U., 1962; PhD, Harvard U., 1966. Commd. officer USPHS, 1966, ret., 1996; rsch. scientist Nat Cancer Inst., Bethesda, Md., 1966-81, chief Lab. of Comparative Carcinogenesis Frederick, Md., 1981-94, 96, assoc. dir. Frederick Cancer Rsch. and Devel. Ctr., 1994-95, acting dir. divsn. cancer etiology, 1994-95, ret., 1996; sr. scientist WHO, 1996—2002, ret., 2002; chief unit of carcinogen identification and evaluation Internat. Agy. for Rsch. on Cancer, Lyons, France, 1996—2002, cons. in toxicology, 2003—; Disting. prof. dept. oncology Georgetown U., Washington, 2003—. Editor: Perinatal Carcinogenesis, 1979; co-editor: Organ and Species Specificity in Chemical Carcinogenesis, 1983, Perinatal and Multigeneration Carcinogenesis, 1989, The Use of Short and Medium Term Tests for Carcinogens and Data on Genetic Effects in Carcinogenic Hazard Evaluation, 1999, Species Differences in Thyroid, Kidney and Urinary Bladder Carcinogenesis, 1999, Mech. of Carcinogenesis-contributions of molecular epidemiology, 2004,; contbr. rsch. articles and revs. in mechanisms of chem. carcinogenesis to profl. jours.; dir. emeritus IARC monographs on the evaluation of carcinogenic risks to humans. Mem. Internat. Soc. Differentiation (emeritus), Soc. Toxicology, European Assn. Cancer Rsch., Am. Assn. Cancer Rsch. (emeritus), Phi Beta Kappa, Sigma Xi. Avocations: viticulture, tropical orchids. Home: 3213 Coquelin Ter Bethesda MD 20815-4840 Personal E-mail: jmricewas@aol.com. Business E-Mail: jr332@georgetown.edu.

**RICE, JIM,** state supreme court justice; b. Ramore Air Force Base, Ont., Canada, Nov. 15, 1957; (parents Am. citizens); BA in Polit. Sci., Mont. State U., 1979; JD U. Mont., 1982. Former firefighter Mont. Dept. of Natural Resources & Conservation; former legal intern Missoula City Atty. Office, Lewis and Clark County Atty. Office; former pub. defender Lewis and Clark County; mem. Mont. House Reps., 1989—95, house majority whip, 1993; ptnr. Jackson & Rice, Helena, Mont., 1985—2001; assoc. justice Mont. Supreme Ct., 2001—. Active in Montana Hope Project, Kiwanis; mem. Governor's Council on Food and Nutrition. Recipient Thomas McHugh Disting. Community Service award, Helena Jaycees, 1993. Mem.: Mont. Bar Assn. Office: Justice Bldg Rm 323 PO Box 203003 Helena MT 59620-3003*

**RICE, JOHN G.,** diversified technology and services executive; BA in Econs., Hamilton Coll. Mem. fin. mgmt. program GE, 1978-81, mem. corp. audit staff, 1981-84; mgr. materials GE Appliances, 1984-86, mgr. quality control prodn. engring. and materials ops., 1986-87; pres. GEM Products, Inc., Garden Grove, Calif., 1987-90; gen. mgr. material resources GE Appliances, 1990-92; pres., COO Camco, Inc., Canada, 1992-94; head corp. audit staff GE, 1994-95; pres. GE Plastics Pacific, Singapore, 1995-97; pres., CEO GE Transp. Sys., Erie, Pa., 1997—2000, GE Energy, Fairfield, Conn., 2000—05; vice chmn., pres., CEO GE Industrial, Fairfield, Conn., 2005—06, GE Infrastructure, Fairfield, Conn., 2006—. Chmn. U.S. Energy Assn. Trans. elect Metro Atlanta C. of C.; trustee Hamilton Coll., Woodruff Arts Ctr., Walker Sch.; mem. advt. bd. Ga. Tech. Univ.; dir. Emory Healthcare. Mailing: General Electric Co 3135 Easton Tpke Fairfield CT 06828*

**RICE, JOHN S.,** lawyer; b. Evanston, Ill., Apr. 15, 1938; BA, Roosevelt U., 1962; JD cum laude, Northwestern U., 1967. Bar: Ill. 1967, Tex. 1978. Shareholder Jenkens & Gilchrist, P.C., Dallas, firm leader ERISA practice group. Mem.: ABA, Dallas Pension Soc., Chgo. Bar Assn., Dallas Bar Assn., Ill. State Bar Assn., Tex. State Bar Assn. Office: Jenkens & Gilchrist PC Ste 3200 1445 Ross Ave Dallas TX 75202-2799 Office Phone: 214-855-4327. Office Fax: 214-855-4300. Business E-Mail: jrice@jenkens.com.

**RICE, JOHN THOMAS,** architecture educator; b. New London, Conn., Feb. 4, 1931; s. Clarence Benjamin and Emily (Gudal) R. BS in Engring., U. Conn., 1952, MSME, Newark Coll. Engring., 1954; D.Sc. in Engring., Columbia U., 1962. Registered profl. engr., N.Y. Test equipment designer propeller div. Curtiss-Wright Corp., Caldwell, NJ, 1952-54; stress analyst Wright Aeronautical div. Curtiss-Wright Corp., Woodridge, NJ, 1954-59; chief structural mechanics Gen. Dynamics/Electric Boat, Groton, Conn., 1962-64; asst. prof. mech. engring. Pratt Inst., Bklyn., 1964-66, assoc. prof., 1966-74, prof., 1974—, chmn. dept. mech. engring., 1981-90. Mem. ASME (chmn. mech. engring. dept. heads com. region II 1987-89, chmn. profl. devel. region II 1989-93, mem. exec. com. met. sect. 1990—, vice chmn. 1991-92, chmn. 1992-93, sec. region II 1993-96, treas. met. sect. 1999—), Pi Tau Sigma, Tau Beta Pi. Office: Pratt Inst Dept of Architecture 200 Willoughby Ave Brooklyn NY 11205-3899

**RICE, JON RICHARD,** health facility administrator, physician; b. Grand Forks, N.D., July 10, 1946; s. Harry Frazer and Marian (Lund) R.; m. Roberta Jane Lindbergh, June 7, 1969; children: Kristen, Jennifer. BA, U. N.D., 1969, BS, 1970; MD, U. Tex., San Antonio, 1972; MS in Health Adminstrn., U. Colo., 1991. Intern U.S. Naval Hosp., San Diego, 1972-73; resident U. N.D. Sch. Medicine, Minot, 1975-77; physician Valley Med., Grand Forks, 1977-93; state health officer N.D. Dept. Health, Bismarck, 1993-97; dir. managed care Blue Cross Blue Shield of N.D., Fargo, 1997—. Contbg. author: Pilots, Personality and Performance. Lt. USN, 1972-75. Recipient Outstanding Vol. award Dakota Heart Assn., 1989, YMCA, 1992, Outstanding Health Care Provider Grand Forks C. of C., 1992, Award of Excellence N.D. Hosp. Assn., 1995. Mem. AMA, Am. Acad. Family Physicians, Am. Coll. Physician Execs., Alpha Omega Alpha. Office: Blue Cross Blue Shield ND 4510 13th Ave S Fargo ND 58121-0002 E-mail: jon_rice_1999@yahoo.com, jon.rice@noridian.com.

**RICE, JOSEPH ALBERT,** retired bank executive; b. Cranford, NJ, Oct. 11, 1924; s. Louis A. and Elizabeth J. (Michael) R.; m. Katharine Wolfe, Sept. 11, 1948; children: Walter, Carol, Philip, Alan. B in Aero. Engring., Rensselaer

Poly. Inst., 1948; M in Indsl. Engring., NYU, 1952, MA, 1968. With Grumman Aircraft Engring. Corp., 1948-53, IBM, NYC, 1953-65, mgr. ops., real estate, constrn. divsns., 1963-65; dep. group exec. N.Am. comml. telecom. group, pres. telecom. divsn. ITT, NYC, 1965-67; sr. v.p. Irving Trust Co., NYC, 1967-69, exec. v.p., 1969-72, sr. exec. v.p., 1972-73, vice chmn., 1973-74, pres., 1974-83, chmn., 1984-88, ret., 1988. Exec. v.p. Irving Bank Corp., 1971-74, vice chmn., 1974-75, pres., 1975-83, chmn. bd., CEO, 1984-88. Chmn., trustee John Simon Guggenheim Meml. Found., 1997-2006; trustee Blanton-Peale Inst., 1989-2006, Hist. Hudson Valley, 1998-2006, vice chmn., 1998-2006. Mem. Coun. Fgn. Rels., NY Acad. Scis., Univ. Club, Links, Sky Club.

**RICE, JOSEPH LEE, III,** lawyer; b. Bklyn., Feb. 24, 1932; s. Joseph Lee Jr. and Frances (Plunkett) R.; m. Franci Blassberg, Jan. 4, 1992; children: Kimberley, Daniel, Lee Ann. BA, Williams Coll., Williamstown, Mass., 1954; LLB, Harvard U., 1960. Assoc. Sullivan & Cromwell, N.Y.C., 1960-66; v.p. Laird Inc. N.Y.C., 1966-68, McDonnell & Co., N.Y.C., 1968-69; founding ptnr. Gibbons, Green & Rice, N.Y.C., 1969-78; founder, chmn. Clayton, Dubilier & Rice, Inc., N.Y.C., 1978—. Trustee, Williams Coll., 1988-92. Lt. USMC, 1954-57. Mem. Maidstone Club, The Links Club, River Club. Office: Clayton Dubilier & Rice Inc 375 Park Ave New York NY 10152-0002 E-mail: jrice@cdr-inc.com.

**RICE, JOY KATHARINE,** psychologist, education educator; d. Joseph Theodore and Margaret Sophia (Bednarik) Straka; m. David Gordon Rice, Ill., 1960; MS, U. Wis., 1962, MS, 1964, PhD, 1967. Lic. clin. psychologist. USPHS predoctoral fellow dept. psychiatry Med. Sch. U. Wis., Madison, 1964-65, asst. dir. Counseling Ctr., 1966-74, dir. Office Continuing Edn. Svcs., 1972-78, prof. ednl. policy studies and women's studies, 1974-95, clin. prof. psychiatry, 1995—; pvt. practice psychology Psychiat. Svcs., S.C., Madison, 1967—. Mem. State Wis. Ednl. Approval Bd., Madison, 1972—73; mem. Adult Edn. Commn. U.S. Office Career Edn., Washington, 1978; co-chmn. Wis. Lt. Gov.'s Task Force on Women and Depression, 2005—. Author: Living Through Divorce, A Developmental Approach to Divorce Therapy, 1985, 2d edit., 1989; mem. editl. bd. Lifelong Learning, 1979—86; cons. editor: Psychology Women Quar., 1986—88, assoc. editor: 1989—94, cons. editor: Handbook of Adult and Continuing Education, 1989, Encyclopedia of Women and Gender, 2001, Handbook of Girls' and Women's Psychological Health, 2005; contbr. articles to profl. jours. Pres. Big Bros. Big Sisters Dane County, 2002, bd. dirs.; co-chair Wis. Lt. Gov.'s Task Force on Women and Depression, 2005—06. Recipient Disting. Achievement award, Ednl. Press Assn. Am., 1992, John Fritschler Jr. award for Disting. Achievement, 2004; Knapp fellow, U. Wis., Madison, 1960—62, Tchg. fellow, 1962—63. Fellow: APA (exec. bd. psychology women divsn. 1994—; internat. psychology divsn. 1998—, exec. bd. 1998—, chair internat. com. women 2000—02, chair com. internat. rels. psychology 2005, divsn. pres. 2006, Disting. Leadership award 2000—02); mem.: Am. Assn. Continuing and Adult Edn. (Meritorious Svc. award 1978—80, 1982), Internat. Coun. Psychologists (bd. dir. 1998—2001, sec. 2002—04, bd. dir. 2004—), Nat. Assn. Women Edn. (editl. bd. jour. 1984—88, cons. editor Initiatives 1988—91), TEMPO Internat. (bd. dir., sec. 2000—03, 2006—), Rotary, Phi Delta Kappa. Avocations: interior decorating, painting, gardening, travel. Home: 4230 Waban Hl Madison WI 53711-3711 Office: 2727 Marshall Ct Madison WI 53705-2255 Office Phone: 608-238-9354.

**RICE, JULIAN CASAVANT,** lawyer; b. Miami, Fla., Dec. 31, 1923; s. Sylvan J. and Maybelle (Casavant) R.; m. Dorothy Mae Haynes, Feb. 14, 1958; children: Scott B., Craig M. (dec.), Julianne C., Linda D., Janette M. Student, U. San Francisco, 1941-43; JD cum laude, Gonzaga U., 1950. Bar: Wash. 1950, Alaska 1959, U.S. Tax Ct. 1988. Pvt. practice law, Spokane, 1950-56, Fairbanks, Alaska, 1959—; prin. Law Office Julian C. Rice (and predecessor firms), Fairbanks, 1959. Salcha, Alaska, 1999. Founder, gen. counsel Mt. McKinley Mut. Savs. Bank, Fairbanks, 1965-99, chmn. bd., 1979-80; v.p., bd. dirs., gen. counsel Skimmers, Inc., Anchorage, 1966-67; gen. counsel Alaska Carriers Assn., Anchorage, 1960-71, Alaska Transp. Conf., 1960-67. Mayor City of Fairbanks, 1970-72. Served to maj. USNG and USAR, 1943-58. Decorated Bronze Star, Combat Infantryman's Badge. Fellow Am. Bar Found. (life); mem. ABA, Wash. State Bar Assn. (50-Yr. mem. award 2000), Alaska Bar Assn., Transp. Lawyers Assn., Alternative Dispute Resolution Com., Am. Arbitration Assn. (mem. transp. commıl., transp. panel), Spokane Exch. Club (pres. 1956). Home and Office: 10104 Salcha Dr Salcha AK 99714-9624 E-mail: j.c.rice@att.net.

**RICE, KENNER CRALLE,** medicinal chemist; s. Kenner Cralle Jr. and Annie Grace Rice. BS, Va. Mil. Inst., 1961; PhD, Ga. Inst. Tech., 1966. Sr. scientist Ciba-Geigy Corp., Summit, 1969—72; sr. staff fellow NIH, Bethesda, Md., 1972—76, rsch. chemist, 1977—86; chief sect. drug design and synthesis Nat. Inst. Diabetes, Digestive and Kidney Diseases, Bethesda, Md., 1987—88; chief lab. medicinal chemistry NIDDK, NIH, Bethesda, Md., 1989—. Adj. prof. pharmacology U. Md., Balt., 1985—; mem. Fed. Sr. Exec. Svc., Bethesda, 1989—98, Fed. Sr. Biomed. Rsch. Svc., 1998—; affiliate prof. Va. Commonwealth U., Richmond, 1995—; vis. prof. pharmacology U. Ill., Peoria, 1995—; adj. prof. medicinal chemistry Comprehensive Drug Rsch. Ctr. U. Miami, 1995—. Author (with others): Pharmacological Reviews, 1987; editor: NIDA Research Monograph 96, 1990; contbr. more than 500 rsch. papers to profl. jours. Capt. U.S. Army, 1966—68. Recipient Internat. Sato Meml. award, Japanese Pharm. Soc., 1983, Rsch. Achievement award, Am. Pharm. Assn., 1987, Hillebrand prize, Chem. Soc. Washington, 1986, Divsn. Medicinal Chemistry award, Am. Chem. Soc., 1996, Rsch. Achievement award, Am. Assn. Pharm. Scientists, 1998, Chem. Pioneer award, Am. Inst. Chemists, 2000, Nathan B. Eddy award, Coll. Problems of Drug Dependence, 2001, Fellow: Coll. on Problems of Drug Dependence (bd. dirs. 1988—92, 1997—2001); mem.: Am. Coll. Neuropsychopharmacology, Cosmos Club. Achievements include 42 patents in organic chemical synthesis and pharmacology of drugs of abuse; development of NIH opiate total synthesis as first practical synthesis of opium alkaloids and derivatives as narcotics and narcotic antagonists. Office: NIH NIDDK Lab Medicinal Chemistry Bldg 8 Rm B1-23 Bethesda MD 20892 E-mail: kr21f@nih.gov.

**RICE, LACY L., JR.,** lawyer; b. Martinsburg, W.Va., Dec. 29, 1931; s. Lacy Isaac and Anna (Thorn) R.; m. Linda Watkins, Mar. 2, 1957; children: Anne W., Lacy I. III, William T. BA, Princeton U., 1953; LLB, U. Va., 1956. Bar: W.Va. 1956, U.S. Dist. Ct. (No. Dist.) W.Va. 1956, U.S. Cir. Ct. Appeals (3rd and 4th circs.) 1968, W.Va. Supreme Ct. Appeals. Ptnr. Lacy I. Rice Sr. law firm & Rice, Hannis & Rice & successors, Martinsburg, 1956-89; sr. ptnr. Bowles, Rice, McDavid, Graff & Love LLP, Martinsburg, 1989—. Pres. Old Nat. Bank of Martinsburg, 1978, chmn. bd.; chmn. One Valley Bank-East N.A.; vice chmn. One Valley Bancorp, Inc.; pres. Suburban Nat. Bank Martinsburg; past chmn., CEO Moutaineer Bankshares of W.Va., Inc.; bd. dir. Bell Atlantic W.Va., Continental Brick Co. Sec. bd. dirs. State Coll. Sys. W.Va.; dir., past pres. W.Va. C. of C., W.Va. U. Found., W.Va. Edn. Found. Mem. W.Va. Bar Assn. (pres. 1984-85); W.Va. Golf Assn.(dir., treas.) Home: 600 N Tennessee Ave Martinsburg WV 25401-9281 Office: Bowles Rice McDavid Graff & Love LLP PO Drawer 1419 101 S Quenn St Martinsburg WV 25401-1419*

**RICE, LEONARD S.,** lawyer; b. 1950; AB, Ripon Coll., 1972; JD, William Mitchell Coll., 1981. Bar: Minn. 1981. Ptnr., chair, public fin. group Dorsey & Whitney LLP, Mpls. Editor: Law Rev. Served to 1st lt. Airborne-Ranger U.S. Army, 1972—75. Mem.: ABA, Hennepin Co. Bar Assn., Minn. State Bar Assn.

**RICE, LESTER,** electronics company executive; b. Detroit, Feb. 23, 1927; s. Carvel Lester and Irene R.; m. Barbara Helen Winston, June 27, 1957; children— Scott W., Jody I., Jeffrey C., Judy A., Timohty D. BS.E.E., U. Mich., 1951. Gen. sales mgr. Westinghouse Semicondr. Div., Youngwood, Pa., 1951-68; pres. Airco Speer Elec. div. Airco Inc., Bradford, Pa., 1968-80; vice chmn., dir. KOA Speer Electronics, Inc., Bradford, 1980-98; chmn. KOA Europe GMBH, 1998—; vice chmn. KOA Speer Electronics Inc., Bradford,

Pa., 2001—. Bd. dirs. DeFond No. Am. Inc.; chmn. bd. Lester Rice, Inc., Bradford, 1980—. Adv. bd. U. Pitts. With USN, 1945-46. Mem. IEEE, Electronics Industries Assn. (bd. govs.), Am. Legion, Masons. Republican. Home: 2 Vista Avenue Ext Bradford PA 16701-2759 Office: PO Box 547 Bradford PA 16701-0547 Business E-Mail: lrice@koaspeer.com.

**RICE, LINDA JOHNSON,** publishing executive; b. Chgo., Mar. 22, 1958; d. John J. and Eunice Johnson; m. Andre Rice, 1984, 1 child, Alexa Christine; m. Mel Farr Sr. BA Journalism, Univ. Southern Calif., L.A., 1980; MBA, Northwestern Univ., Evanston, Ill., 1987. With Johnson Pub. Co., 1980—, past v.p. and asst. to pub., COO, 1987—2002; pres. Johnson Pub. Co., Inc., Chgo., 1987—; CEO, 2002—; pres. Fashion Fair Cosmetics, Ill., 1987—. Named one of 100 Most Powerful Women in Chgo., Chgo. Sun-Times, Chicago's 40 Under 40, Crain's Chgo. Bus.; recipient Women of Power award, Nat. Urban League, Trumpet award, Turner Broadcasting, Alumni Merit award, Univ. So. Calif., Alumni of the Year award, Kellogg Grad. Sch. Mgmt.,stern University. Mem.: Exec. Club Chgo., Econ. Club Chgo., Young Presidents Orgn., Nat. Assn. Black Journalists, Fashion Group Internat., Comml. Club Chgo. Office: Johnson Pub Co Inc 820 S Michigan Ave Chicago IL 60605-2191*

**RICE, LOIS DICKSON,** retired computer company executive; b. Portland, Maine, Feb. 28, 1933; d. David A. and Mary D. Dickson; m. Alfred B. Fitt, Jan. 7, 1978 (dec. 1992); children: Susan, John Rice. AB magna cum laude, Radcliffe Coll., 1954; postgrad. (Woodrow Wilson fellow), Columbia U., 1954-55; LLD (hon.), Brown U., 1981, Bowdoin Coll., 1984. Dir. counseling services Nat. Scholarship Service and Fund for Negro Students, N.Y.C., 1955-59; with The Coll. Bd., N.Y.C. and Washington, 1959-81, v.p. Washington, 1973-81; sr. v.p. govt. affairs Control Data Corp., 1981-91. Guest scholar The Brookings Inst., Washington, 1991—; bd. dirs. McGraw Hill, Inc., 1987—2003, Internat. Multifoods, 1991—2003, UNUM/Provident Corp., 1992—2003; overseer Tuck Sch. Mgmt. Dartmouth Coll., 1990—94; mem. Pres.'s Fgn. Intelligence Adv. Bd., 1993—2001; trustee George Washington U., 1992—98, trustee Mgmt. Leadership for Tomorrow, 1994—; trustee CNA Educ. Found., Harry Frank Guggenheim Found., 1994—. Contbr. articles on edn. to profl. publs.; editor: Student Loans: Problems and Policy Alternatives, 1977. Mem. adv. bd. to dir. NSF, 1981—89, chair, 1986—89; mem. Gov.'s Commn. on Future of Postsecondary Edn. in N.Y. State, 1976—77, Carnegie Coun. on Higher Edn., 1975—80; trustee Radcliffe Coll., 1969—75, Stephens Coll., Mo., 1976—78, Beauvoir Sch., Washington, 1970—76, Children's TV Workshop, 1970—73; bd. dirs. Potomac Inst., 1977—92, German Marshall Fund, 1984—94, Joint Ctr. Polit. and Econ. Studies, 1991—94, Reading is Fundamental, 1991—2004. Recipient Disting. Service award HEW, 1977 Mem. Cosmos Club, Phi Beta Kappa. Episcopalian. Home: 2332 Massachusetts Ave NW Washington DC 20008 Office: The Brookings Instn 1775 Massachusetts Ave NW Washington DC 20036-2103

**RICE, LUANNE,** writer; b. 1955; B of humane letters, Conn. Coll., 1977, degree (hon.), 2002. Author: Angels All Over Town, 1985, Crazy in Love, 1988, Stone Heart, 1990, Secrets of Paris, 1991, Blue Moon, 1994, Home Fires, 1996, Cloud Nine, 2000, Follow The Stars Home, 2001, Firefly Beach, 2001, Dream Country, 2002, Summer Light, 2002, True Blue, 2002, Safe Harbor, 2003, The Secret Hour, 2003, The Perfect Summer, 2003, Dance With Me, 2004, Summer's Child, 2005. Mailing: c/o Andrea Cirillo Jane Rotrosen Agency 318 E 51st St New York NY 10022

**RICE, MARY ESTHER,** biologist; b. Washington, Aug. 3, 1926; d. Daniel Gibbons and Florence Catharine (Pyles) R. AB, Drew U., 1947; MA, Oberlin Coll., 1949; PhD, U. Wash., 1966. Instr. biology Drew U., Madison, NJ, 1949-50; rsch. assoc. Columbia U., N.Y.C., 1950-53; rsch. asst. NIH, Bethesda, Md., 1953-61; curator invertebrate zoology and dir. Smithsonian Marine Sta., Smithsonian Instn., Washington, 1966—2002, sr. rsch. scientist emeritus, 2002—. Mem. adv. panel on systematic biology NSF, Washington, 1977-78; mem. com. on marine invertebrates Nat. Acad. Sci., 1976-81; mem. overseers com. on biology Harvard U., Cambridge, Mass., 1982-88. Assoc. editor Jour. Morphology, Ann Arbor, Mich., 1985-91, Invertebrate Biology, 1995—; editor: (with M. Todorovic) Biology of Sipuncula and Echiura, 1975, 2nd vol., 1976, (with F.S. Chia) Settlement and Metamorphosis of Marine Invertebrate Larvae, 1978, (with F.W. Harrison) Microscopic Anatomy of Invertebrates, Vol. 12, 1993; contbr. articles to profl. jours. Recipient Drew U. Alumni Achievement award in sci., 1980. Fellow AAAS; mem. Am. Soc. Zoologists (pres. 1979), Am. Microsopical Soc. (pres. 1999), Phi Beta Kappa. Office: Smithsonian Marine Sta 701 Seaway Dr Fort Pierce FL 34949-3140

**RICE, MICHAEL V.,** voice educator; b. Greenville, S.C., Apr. 30; s. Juanita H. and Clifford G. Rice. MusB, Furman U., S.C., 1975; MusM (Candidate), Northwestern U., Ill., 1976. Cert. State Dept. Edn. S.C. Voice tchr. Fine Arts Ctr., Greenville, SC, 1981—. Musician: (accompanist) Greenville Chorale. Grantee Individual Artist grant, Met. Arts Coun., 1990, 1991. Mem.: Nat. Assn. of Tchrs. of Singing, Music Club of Greenville (hon.), Phi Sigma Iota (life), Phi Mu Alpha Sinfonia (life Bachelor Sinfonian award 1975). Avocations: travel, language. Home: 101 Ridge Rd #5 Greenville SC 29607 Office: Fine Arts Ctr 1613 W Washington St Greenville SC 29601 Office Phone: 864-241-3327. Office Fax: 864-241-3502. Personal E-mail: mvrsc@aol.com.

**RICE, NANCY E.,** state supreme court justice; b. Denver, June 2, 1950; 1 child. BA cum laude, Tufts U., 1972; JD, U. Utah, 1975. Law clerk U.S. Dist. Ct. of Colo., 1975-76, dep. state pub. defender, appellate divn., 1976-77; asst. U.S. atty. Dist. of Colo., 1977-87; dep. chief civil divn. U.S. Attorney's Office, 1985-88; judge Denver Dist. Ct., 1988-98; justice Colo. Supreme Ct., 1998—. Adjunct prof. law, trial advocacy U. Colo. Sch. of Law, 1987—. Contbr. articles to profl. jours. Mem. Denver Bar Assn. (Judicial Excellence award 1993), Colo. Bar Assn. (bd. govs. 1990-92, exec. coun., 1991-92), Women's Bar Assn., Rhone-Brackett Inn of Ct. (master 1993-97), Women Judges Assn. (co-chair nat. com. 1990). Office: Colo Supreme Ct Colo State Jud Bldg 2 E 14th Ave Fl 4 Denver CO 80203-2115*

**RICE, NORMAN B.,** bank executive, former mayor; b. Denver, May 4, 1943; m. Constance Rice; 1 child, Mian. BA in Comm., U. Wash., MPA. Past mgr. corp. contbns. and soc. policy Rainier Nat. Bank; past dir. govt. svcs. Puget Sound Coun. Govts.; past asst. dir. Seattle Urban League; past reporter KIXI Radio; past editor, writer KOMO TV; with govt. City of Seattle, 1978—, city councilman, 1978-89, mayor, 1990-97; pres., chief exec. officer Fed. Home Loan Bank of Seattle, 1999—. Pres. U.S. Conf. of Mayors, 1995; bd. dirs. Safeco Corp. Office: Fed Home Loan Bank 1501 4th Ave Ste 1900 Seattle WA 98101-1693

**RICE, PAMELA ANN,** marriage and family therapist; d. Charles Jefferson Rice, and Helen Ann (Larsen) Rice. B. of Bibl. Studies, Friends Internat. Christian U., 1983, M. of Bibl. Counseling, 1985, Dr. of Ministry, 1988; MA in Marriage, Family, Child Counseling, Calif. Christian Inst., 1991. Lic. marriage and family therapist Calif., 2000. Program dir. clin. psychiat. unit Van Nuys Cmty. Hosp., Calif., 1991—93; self-employed marriage and family therapist L.A., 2000—. Pastoral staff tng. counselor Vineyard Christian Fellowship, Santa Monica, 1981—86; exec. dir. Homes Of Hope, Holland, 1987—89; adminstrv. com. City of Santa Monica, 1987—89; case mgr. clin. psychiat. unit Buena Pk. Cmty. Hosp., Calif., 1988—91; exec. dir. Mental Health Rehab. Facility, Palmdale, Calif. Recipient Outstanding Achievement award, City of Santa Monica, 1989. Mem.: EMDRIAN (assoc.), Calif. Assn. Marriage and Family Therapists (assoc.). Born-Again Christian. Achievements include receiving a commendation from President Ronald Reagan for the development of the Homes of Hope outreach. Avocations: skiing, travel, decorating, poetry. Office: 1460 7th St Se 306 Santa Monica CA 90401 Office Phone: 310-553-2203.

**RICE, PATRICIA JANE,** journalist; b. St. Louis, Oct. 20, 1942; d. Canice T. and Jane Elizabeth Tobin) R. BA, Maryville Coll., 1964; postgrad., St. Louis U., 1965, 66. Copywriter Wohl Co., St. Louis, 1964-67; free-lance journalist Paris, 1967; copywriter D'Arcy Advt. Co., St. Louis, 1968; feature writer, columnist St. Louis Post, 1969-94, religion editor, 1994—2004, South reporter, 2004—05; freelance writer, 2005—. Moderator Rutgers U./Eagleton Ctr. Women in Politics Conf., 1980, 82, 84; lectr. in field. Author: City House, 1968, The Eclectic Shopper, 1973, A Catholic Funeral, 2005; co-author: In the Running: The New Political Woman, 1981 V.p. The St. Louis Forum, 1997-2002; bd. dirs. Leadership St. Louis, 1985-90. Recipient Quest award Mo. Press Women's, 1998; Knight Ctr. fellow U. Md., College Park, 1996, 2004. Mem. Journalism Found. Met. St. Louis (pres. 1984-91), St. Louis Newspaper Guild (treas. 1977-87), Soc. Profl. Journalists. Avocations: gardening, skiing. Office: Rice Assoc 1221 Locust St Ste 800 Saint Louis MO 63103 Office Phone: 314-241-8000.

**RICE, PATRICIA OPPENHEIM LEVIN,** special education educator, consultant; b. Detroit, Apr. 5, 1932; d. Royal A. and Elsa (Freeman) Oppenheim; m. Charles L. Levin, Feb. 21, 1956 (div. Dec. 1981); children: Arthur David, Amy Ragen, Fredrick Stuart; m. Howard T. Rice, Dec. 16, 1990 (div. Apr. 1994). AB in History, U. Mich., 1954, PhD, 1981; MEd, Marygrove Coll., 1973. Cert. elem. tchr., Mich. Tchr. reading and learning disabled, cons., Detroit Pub. Schs., 1967-76; assoc. prof., coord. spl. edn., Marygrove Coll., 1976-86; adj. prof. Oakland U., 1987-90, U. Miami, 1989-95; edn. curriculum cons. Lady Elizabeth Sch., Jávea (Alicante) Spain, 1988-91; v.p. Machpelah Non-profit Cemetery Bd., Ferndale, Mich., 1978-87, co-pres., 1987—; adv. bd. Eton Acad., Birmingham, Mich., 1991-93; workshop presenter Dade City Schs., 1992-97; presenter in field. Mem. Mich. regional bd. ORT, 1965-68; mil. affairs and youth svcs. S.E. Mich. chpt. ARC Bd., 1973-79; v.p. exec. bd. Women's Aux. Children's Hosp. Mich., 1968-73; bd. dirs. women's com. United Cmty. Svcs., 1968-73; judge Dade County Schs. for Tchr. Grants, 1996—2004; bd. dirs. Detroit Grand Opera Assn., 1970-75; com. chair morning of music benefits Detroit Symphony Orch.; torch drive area chmn. United Found., 1967-70; benefactor Fla. Grand Opera, 1990-2001, grand benefactor, 2002—, guild exec. bd., 1992-, v.p., 1998-99, co-pres. 2000-02, chair, found. bd. dirs., 2000-01; guild exec. bd. Miami City Ballet, 1996-2000, Choreographers Cir., 1990-; chair Lincoln Rd. Walk, 1996, co-chair All Star Luncheon, 1996, Ball Com., 1992; active Diabetes Rsch. Inst. & Found. Love & Hope Com., Fla. Concert Assn. Cresendo Soc., 1993-97, Villa Maria Angel, 1996—, v.p. angel bd. 1998—2005, found. bd. dirs. 2000—; v.p. Miami Children's Hosp., 2004-05, co-pres., 2005—; panel judge Dade County Cultural Affairs Coun., 2002-04; v.p., amb. Mt. Sinai Hosp. Alzheimer's Bd. Mem. NAACP (life), Navy League, Greater Miami Social Register, Citizens Interested in the Arts (charter, grant chair, exec. bd. 1997—), Williams Island Club, Turnberry Isle Golf Club (signature), Miami Shores Country Club, Surf Club, Phi Delta Kappa, Pi Lambda Theta.

**RICE, PAUL JACKSON,** lawyer, educator; b. East St. Louis, Ill., July 15, 1938; s. Ray Jackson and Mary Margaret (Campbell) Rice; m. Carole Jeanne Valentine, June 6, 1959; children: Rebecca Jeanne Ross, Melissa Ann Hansen, Paul Jackson Jr. BA, U. Mo., 1960, JD, 1962; LLM Northwestern U., 1970, student, Command and Gen. Staff Coll., 1974-75, Army War Coll., 1982-83. Bar: Mo. 1962, Ill. 1969, U.S. Dist. Ct. (no. dist.) Ill. 1970, U.S. Supreme Ct. 1972, U.S. Ct. Appeals (DC cir.) 1991, DC 1993, U.S. Dist. Ct. DC 2000. Commd. 1st lt. U.S. Army, 1962, advanced through grades to col., 1980; asst. judge advocate 4th Armored Div., Goeppingen, Germany, 1966-69; dep. staff judge advocate 1st Cavalry Div., Vietnam, 1970-71; inst., instr. Judge Adv. Gen. Sch., Charlottesville, Va., 1971-74, commdt., dean, 1985-88; br. chief Gen. Law Br., Pentagon, 1975-78; chief adminstrv. law div. Office Judge Adv. Gen., Pentagon, Washington, 1978-79; staff judge adv. 1st Inf. Div., Ft. Riley, Kans., 1979-82; V Corps U.S. Army, Frankfurt, Germany, 1983-85, USA-CAC, Ft. Leavenworth, Kans., 1989-90; faculty Indsl. Coll. Armed Forces, 1988-89; chief counsel Nat. Hwy. Traffic Safety Adminstrn., Washington, 1990-93; ptnr. Arent Fox PLLC, Washington, 1993—. Contbr. articles to profl. jours. Recipient Granted Legal Svc. award, State of Hessen, Germany, 1985, cert. of merit, U. Mo. Alumni Assn., 1987. Mem.: Ctr. Law and Nat. Security, Mo. Bar Assn., Lion Tamers, Phi Delta Phi. Methodist. Avocations: writing, reading, golf. Home: 7835 Vervain Ct Springfield VA 22152-3107 Office: Arent Fox PLLC 1050 Connecticut Ave NW Washington DC 20036-5339 Office Phone: 202-857-6009. Business E-Mail: ricepj@arentfox.com.

**RICE, REBECCA KYNOCH,** writer, consultant, language educator; b. Pittsfield, Mass., June 13, 1954; d. John Hamilton and Nancy Anne (Kynoch) Rice; m. Leonard Charles Feldstein, Oct. 17, 1981 (dec. Dec. 1984); m. Branford Martin Smith, Aug. 14, 1993; 1 child, Oliver Van Santvoord Smith. BA, Sarah Lawrence Coll., 1977; MA, Fairleigh Dickinson U., 1980; MFA, George Mason U., 1996. English tchr. Newark Acad., Livingston, NJ, 1977-79; staff writer, editor Am. Internat Group, N.Y.C., 1983-85; instr. English George Mason U., Fairfax, Va., 1990-92; mng. editor Green Mountains Rev., Johnson, Vt., 1993-94; freelance writer Johnson, 1994—. Instr. Lone Ridge Writers Group, Redding, Conn., 1998—; grants and publicity mgr. Vt. Studio Ctr., Johnson, 2004—. Author: A Time to Mourn: One Woman's Journey through Widowhood, 1990; contbr. articles to publs. Woodrow Wilson fellow, 1977. Mem.: Authors Guild. Avocation: tennis. Home: PO Box 157 Ober Hill Rd Johnson VT 05656 Office Phone: 802-635-2727.

**RICE, REGINA KELLY,** marketing executive; b. Yonkers, NY, July 11, 1955; d. Howard Adrian and Lucy Virginia (Butler) Kelly; m. Mark Christopher Rice, Sept. 11, 1981; children: Amanda Kelly, Jaime Brannen. BS in Cmty. Nutrition, Cornell U., 1978. Account exec. J. Walter Thompson Co., N.Y.C., 1978—79; sr. account exec. Ketchum, MacLeod & Grove, N.Y.C., 1979—80; supr. Burson Marstellar, Hong Kong, 1981—83; v.p., dep. dir. food and beverage unit, creative dir. N.Y. office Hill and Knowlton, N.Y.C., 1983—91; mktg. cons. Rice & Rohr, N.Y.C., 1991—93; sr. v.p., dir. consumer mktg. practice Manning, Selvage & Lee, N.Y.C., 1993—97, sr. v.p. global tng. dir., 1999—; chief inspiration officer, dir. corp. devel. Internat. Pub. Rels. Assn., 1999—2001. Writer Fast and Healthy Mag., 1991-2000. Mem. Pub. Rels. Soc. Am. Roman Catholic. Avocation: collecting Provence pottery. Home: 31 Wrangler Ln Bell Canyon CA 91307 Office: Manning Selvage & Lee 6500 Wilshire Blvd Los Angeles CA 90048-4920 Office Phone: 323-866-6023.

**RICE, RICHARD LEE,** retired architect; b. Raleigh, N.C., May 4, 1919; s. Robert Edward Lee and Grace Lucille (Betts) R.; m. Cora Belle Stegall. Apr. 12, 1946; children— Richard Lee, Westwood Carter, David Sinclair. BS in Archtl. Engring., N.C. State U., 1941; grad., U.S. Army Command and Gen. Staff Coll., 1961. Assoc. Cooper-Shumaker, Architects, Raleigh, 1946-47; prin. Richard L. Rice, Architects, Raleigh, 1947-48; assoc. Cooper, Haskins & Rice and predecessor firm, Raleigh, 1948-52, ptnr., 1953-54, Haskins & Rice, Architects, Raleigh, 1954-85; prin. Haskins, Rice, Savage & Pearce, Architects, Raleigh, 1985-91, pres., 1985-91. V.p. N.C. Design Found., 1973; pres. N.C. Archtl. Found., 1975; mem. Raleigh Arts Commn., 1978-82, Raleigh Hist. Properties Commn., 1990-92, Raleigh Hist. Dists. Commn., 1991-92. Archtl. works include renovations, Raleigh Meml. Auditorium, 1964, 78, 91 (SE Regional AIA award of merit 1964), Auditorium, 4 high schs. and 13 elem. schs., Raleigh Civic Ctr., stack additoin Wilson Libr. U. N.C., Chapel Hill, 1977, Reidsville, N.C. Jr. High Sch.; assoc. architect Raleigh Radisson Hotel, 1980, One Hanover Sq. Office Bldg., 1985, Two Hannover Sq. Office Bldg., 1990, additions and renovations to Raleigh Meml. Auditorium, 1989, 3 indsl. plants, 7 bldgs., Wake Tech. C.C., '50 chs. Pres. Wake County (N.C.) Hist. Soc., 1973-74; mem. N.C. Gov.'s Com. for Facilities for Physically Handicapped, 1970-73; arbitrator Am. Arbitration Assn. With inf. and C.E. U.S. Army, 1941-46, ETO; col. USAR; ret. Decorated Silver Star.; Legion of Merit; Bronze Star; Purple Heart. Fellow AIA (pres. N.C. chpt. 1970, Disting. Svc. award N.C. chpt. 1975); mem. Raleigh Council Architects (pres. 1950), Nat. Trust for Hist. Preservation, N.C. State Art Soc., Ret. Officers Assn. U.S.

**RICE, RICK BLACKBURN,** application developer, systems analyst; b. Louisville, Sept. 17, 1954; s. Blackburn M. and Alice Jane (Walker) R.; m. Peijuan Miao, June 23, 1989; children: Richard J., Franklin W. BA in Psychology, U. Mich., 1978; MS in Computer Systems Mgmt., U. Md., 1997. Mem. computing staff Hughes Aircraft Co., El Segundo, Calif., 1980-84; programmer, analyst Candle Corp., L.A., 1984-86; sr. programmer, analyst Computer Assocs., L.A., 1986-88; fgn. expert Shaanxi Inst. Fin. and Econs., Xi'an, People's Republic of China, 1989-90; sr. programmer, analyst Disclosure, Inc., Bethesda, Md., 1988-96; info. sys. specialist IBM, Gaithersburg, Md., 1996—97; sr. programmer analyst Sci. Applications Internat. Corp., Falls Church, Va., 1998—2003. Avocation: sinology. Home: 714 Sligo Ave # 210 Silver Spring MD 20910 E-mail: rick_rice@hotmail.com.

**RICE, RONALD JAMES,** hospital administrator; b. Springfield, Mo., Feb. 5, 1944; s. Glen Elwood and Alice Jeanett (Robinson) R. BSBA, Cen. Mo. State U., 1966, MABA, 1969, Specialist, 1972. Lic. nursing home adminstr.; lic. risk mgr. Unit mgr. Bapt. Med. Ctr., Kansas City, Mo., 1970-71; dir. unit mgmt. Ind. Health Ctr., Independence, Mo., 1971-72; adminstrv. officer Meth. Hosp., Jacksonville, Fla., 1972-73; dir. personnel, 1973-74; assoc. adminstr. Humana Hosp. Orange Park (Fla.), 1974-77; adminstr. Cathedral Rehab. Hosp., Jacksonville, 1977-79, Marion County Gen. Hosp., Hamilton, Ala., 1979-80, Nassau Gen. Hosp., Fernandina Beach, Fla., 1980-85, Reception Med. Ctr., Lake Butler, Fla., 1985-91; regional adminstr. health svcs. Dept. Corrections, Gainesville, Fla., 1991—; sr. health svc. adminstr. Columbia Correctional Instn., 1999—2006. Cons. Clay Meml. Hosp., Green Cove Springs, Fla., 1976-77; Allied Health Care, Jacksonville, 1989. Mem. Polit. Action Com., Fla. Hosp. Assn., 1990, Coun. on Crime and Delinquency, Gainesville, 1990, Human Resources Com., Orlando, 1991; active Orange Park Presbyn. Ch. With U.S. Army, 1967-69. Decorated Army Commendation medal. Fellow Am. Coll. Health Care Execs.; mem. Am. acad. Med. Adminstrs., Am. Coll. Health Care Adminstrs., Am. Soc. Personnel Adminstrs., Fla. Hosp. Assn., Rotary (pres. 1984-86). Democrat. Avocations: boating, collecting model cars, antique juke box collecting, reading. Home: 1744 Horton Dr Orange Park FL 32073-2757 Personal E-mail: ricerjq45@aol.com

**RICE, RUTH ELAINE,** music educator; d. Lester Ira and Martha Elizabeth Long; m. Frank Lambert Rice, June 21, 1969; children: Suzanne, Kevin, Lauren. BS in Music Edn., Lebanon Valley Coll., 1968; MS in Edn., Johns Hopkins U., 1980. Tchr. music Lower Dauphin Jr. H.S., Hummelstown, Pa., 1968—69; tchr. music K-6 Northwood Elem. Sch., Balt., 1969—73; tchr. Commonwealth Am. Sch. K-8, Lausanne, Switzerland, 1974—76, Yates Elem. Sch., Schenectady, NY, 1990—97; tchr. elem. music Elsmere Elem., Bethlehem, NY, 1992—95; tchr. Farnsworth Mid. Sch., Guilderland, NY, 1995—96; tchr. mid. sch. gen. choral Van Antwerp Mid. Sch., Niskayuna, NY, 1996—. Co-author: (music jour.) Teaching Music, 2002. Music dir. Bethlehem Luth. Ch., Delmar, NY, 1982—. Mem.: N.Y. State Sch. Music Assn. (accompanist). Lutheran. Avocations: travel, reading, movies. Home: 5 Darroch Rd Delmar NY 12054 Office: Van Antwerp Middle Sch Storey Ave Schenectady NY 12309 E-mail: singasong123@hotmail.com.

**RICE, STEPHEN GARY,** medical educator, pediatrician, sports medicine physician; b. Bklyn., Dec. 21, 1945; s. Abraham S. and Anne (Shelling) R.; m. Hilary Jo Turett, May 10, 1987; children: Adam, Bryan. AB, Columbia Coll., 1967; MD, PhD, NYU, 1974; MPH, U. Wash., 1983. Diplomate in pediat. and sports medicine Am. Bd. Pediat. Intern, resident Children's Hosp. and U. Wash., Seattle, 1974-77; faculty mem. sports medicine U. Wash., Seattle, 1977-96; program dir. primary care sports medicine fellowship Jersey Shore Univ. Med. Ctr., Neptune, NJ, 1996—; clin. assoc. prof. pediat. Robert Wood Johnson Med. Sch. U. Medicine and Dentistry N.J., New Brunswick, 1999—. Developer, dir. Athletic Health Care Sys., 1978—; cons. in field. Author: Athletic Health Care System, 1988. Team physician U. Wash., 1977-81. Fellow: Am. Coll. Sports Medicine (sec. Greater NY regional chpt. 1997—2002, chmn. health and sci. policy com. 2000—, chmn. liaison com. 2002—04), Am. Acad. Pediat. (chmn. sports medicine com. NJ chpt. 1999—, chmn. govt. affairs com. NJ chpt. 2000—03, 2005—06, sec.-editor NJ chpt. 2002—04, treas. NJ chpt. 2004—06, v.p.-elect NJ chpt. 2006—, sports medicine and fitness com. 2003—); mem.: AAHPERD, Med. Soc. NJ, Am. Med. Soc. Sports Medicine, Nat. Strength and Conditioning Assn. Avocations: sports, cooking, gardening, gilbert & sullivan, chess. Home: 6 Wildflower Ct Manalapan NJ 07726-2861 Office: Jersey Shore Univ Med Ctr Dept Pediat PO Box 397 Neptune NJ 07754-0397 Office Phone: 732-776-2384. Business E-Mail: srice@meridianhealth.com.

**RICE, STUART ALAN,** chemist, educator; b. N.Y.C., Jan. 6, 1932; s. Harry L. and Helen (Rayfield) Rice; m. Marian Ruth Coopersmith, June 1, 1952 (dec. June 1994); children: Barbara, Janet; m. Ruth O'Brien, Sept. 27, 1997; 1 child, David Lawrence. BS, Bklyn. Coll., 1952; MA, Harvard, 1954, PhD, 1955. Jr. fellow Harvard, 1955—57; faculty U. Chgo., 1957—60, prof. chemistry, 1960—69, Louis Block prof. phys. scis., 1969—77, chmn. dept. chemistry, 1971—76, Frank P. Hixon disting. service prof., 1977—, dean phys. scis. 1981—95, dir. Inst. Study Metals, 1957—59; Newton Abraham prof. Oxford U., 1999—2000. Mem. Nat. Sci. Bd., 1980—86. Author: Polyelectrolyte Solutions, 1961, Statistical Mechanics of Simple Liquids, 1965, Physical Chemistry, 1980, 2d edit, 2000, Optical Control of Molecular Dynamics, 2000; contbr. articles to profl. jours. Named Falk-Plautt lectr., Columbia U., 1964, Riley lectr., Notre Dame U., 1964, U. lectr. chemistry, U. Western Ont., 1970, Seaver lectr., U. Soc. Calif, 1972, Noyes lectr., U. Tex., 1975, Foster lectr., SUNY, 1976, Frank T. Gucker lectr., Ind. U., 1976, Fairchild lectr., Calif. Inst. Tech., 1979, Baker lectr., Cornell U., 1985—86, Centenary lectr., Royal Soc. Chemistry, 1986—87, Nat. lectr., Phi Beta Kappa, 1994—95, Kennedy lectr., Washington U., 2002, Noyes lectr., U. Oreg., 2002; recipient Centennial medal, Harvard U., 1997, Nat. Medal of Sci., 1999, Hirschfelder award for Theoretical Chemistry, 2002; fellow, Guggenheim, 1960—61, Sr. Postdoctoral fellow, NSF, 1965—66, USPHS Spl. Postdoctoral fellow, U. Copenhagen, 1970—71. Fellow: Royal Irish Acad. Scis., Am. Philos. Soc.; mem.: AAAS, Danish Acad. Sci. and Letters, N.Y. Acad. Scis. (A. Cressy Morrison prize 1955), Faraday Soc. (Marlowe medal 1963), Am. Phys. Soc., Am. Acad. Sci. (Hirschfelder award for theoret. chemistry 2002, Willis Lamb medal 2004), Nat. Acad. Sci., Am. Chem. Soc. (Pure Chemistry award 1963, Leo Hendrik Baekland award 1971, Peter Debye award 1985, Hildebrand award 1987). Office Phone: 773-702-7199. Business E-Mail: s-rice@uchicago.edu.

**RICE, SUE ANN,** retired dean, psychologist; b. Ponca City, Okla., Sept. 17, 1934; d. Alfred and Helen (Revard) R. BS in Edn., U. Okla., 1956; MA. Cath. U., 1970, PhD, 1988. Ensign USN, 1956, advanced through grades to comdr., 1973; ednl. svcs. officer 9th Naval Dist., Great Lakes, Ill., 1956-58; adminstr. asst. staff. comdr. in-chief Pacific Fleet, Honolulu, 1958-61; head dir. Naval Air Sta., Lemoore, Calif., 1961-63; instr., acad. dir. Women Officers' Sch., Newport, R.I., 1963-66; head. chg. Naval Command Systems Support Activity, Washington, 1966-70; head, ops. support sec. staff, comdr.-in-chief Lant, Norfolk, Va., 1970-74; sr. U.S. rep. NATO, subgroup 5 prep. JCS, Washington, 1974-77; ret. USN, 1977; head vocation office Archdiocese of Washington, 1977-78; cons. Notre Dame Inst., Arlington, Va., 1989-97, dean of students, 1990-95; ret. 1995. Lectr. Cath. U. Am., Washington, 1983-84; bd. dirs. Villa Cortona Apostolic Ctr., Bethesda, 1984-94. Tech. reviewer Personnel Administration, 1990; editor (newsletter) Vocation News, 1978. Conoco scholarship Continental Oil Co., 1952-56; recipient Meritorious Svc. medal Pres. of U.S., 1977, rsch. grant Cath. U., Sigma Xi, 1986. Mem.: Lay Women's Assn. (internat. v.p., nat. v.p.), Cath. War Vets. (nat. membership task force com., nat. youth act com., vets. affairs com., nat. co-chmn. pub. rels. com.), Gamma Phi Beta, Kappa Delta Pi. Roman Catholic. Avocations: travel, music, gardening, woodworking. Home: PO Box 2742 Ponca City OK 74602-2742

**RICE, SUSAN ELIZABETH,** foreign policy analyst, former federal agency administrator; m. Ian Cameron; children: John D. Rice-Cameron, H. Maris Rice-Cameron. BA in History, Stanford U., 1986; MPhil, Oxford U., 1988, DPhil, 1990. Mngmt. cons. McKinsey and Co., Toronto, Ont., Canada, 1991-93; dir. internat. orgns. and peacekeeping NSC, Washington, 1993-95, spl. asst. to the Pres., sr. dir. African affairs, 1995-97; asst. sec. state African affairs US Dept. State, Washington, 1997—2001; mng. dir., prin. Intellibridge Internat., Washington, 2001—02; sr. fellow fgn. policy The Brookings Instn., Washington, 2002—. Fgn. policy aide Dem. Pres. Campaign, Boston, 1988 Harry S. Truman scholar, 1984, Rhodes scholar, 1986; recipient Walter Frewen Lord prize, Royal Commonwealth Soc., 1990, Assn. prize, Chatham House-British Internat. Studies, 1992, Samuel Nelson Drew Meml. award, NSC, 2000. Mem. Phi Beta Kappa. Office: The Brookings Instn 1775 Massachusetts Ave NW Washington DC 20036

**RICE, THOMAS CHARLES,** lawyer; b. NYC, Jan. 18, 1956; s. Thomas P. and Laura T. (Hage) R.; m. Cheryl A. Christman, Sept. 15, 1984; children: Thomas Christman, Matthew David. BA in math. magna cum laude, St. John's U., 1978, JD, 1981. Bar: US Dist. Ct. (so. dist.) NY, US Dist Ct. (we. dist.) NY, US Dist. Ct. (no. dist.) NY, US Dist. Ct. (so. dist.) Tex., US Dist. Ct. Colo., US Dist Ct. (no. dist.) Okla., US Ct. Appeals (2nd cir.) (U.S. Ct. Apeals), US Ct. Appeals (3rd cir.), US Ct. Appeals (5th cir.). Assoc. Simpson Thacher & Bartlett, N.Y.C., 1981-88, ptnr., 1989—, mem. exec. com. Contbr. articles to profl. jours. Mem. ABA (litigation sect.), N.Y. State Bar Assn., Assn. Bar City of N.Y. (Judiciary Comm.) Office: Simpson Thacher & Bartlett 425 Lexington Ave Fl 15 New York NY 10017-3954 Office Phone: 212-455-3040. Office Fax: 212-455-2502. Business E-Mail: trice@stblaw.com.

**RICE, THOMAS HOWARD,** healthcare educator; b. Washington, Apr. 21, 1954; s. John Donald and Dorothy Pechman R.; m. Katherine Anne Desmond, Oct. 21, 1953; children: Clara, Daniel. BA, U. N.C., 1976; MA, U. Calif., Berkeley, 1979, PhD, 1982. Sr. health economist SRI Internat., Menlo Park, Calif., 1979—83; assoc. prof. U.N.C. Sch. Pub. Health, Chapel Hill, 1983—91; prof. UCLA Sch. Pub. Health, 1991—, vice chancellor for academic personnel, 2006—. Chmn. bd. dir. Acad. Health, Washington, 2005—06; editor Med. Care Rsch. and Rev., Thousand Oaks, Calif., 1994—2000; chair Dept. Health Svcs., UCLA Sch. of Pub. Health, 1996—2000. Author: Economics of Health Reconsidered, 2003; editor: Changing the U.S. Health Care System, 2006. Recipient Young Investigator of the Yr. award, Assn. Health Svcs. Rsch., 1988, Thompson prize, Assn. U. Programs in Health Adminstrn., 1992, Article of the Yr. award, Health Svcs. Rsch., 1998. Office: UCLA Sch Pub Health 650 S Young Dr Los Angeles CA 90095 Office Phone: 310-206-1824, 310-206-9345. Business E-Mail: trice@ucla.edu, trice@conet.ucla.edu.

**RICE, SIR TIMOTHY MILES BINDON,** lyricist; b. Amersham, Eng., Nov. 10, 1944; s. Hugh Gordon and Joan Odette (Bawden) Rice; m. Jane McIntosh, Aug. 19, 1974; children: Eva Jane Florence, Donald Alexander Hugh. Student, Lancing Coll., Sussex, 1958—62. Solicitor's articled clk. Pettit & Westlake, London, 1963—66; mgmt. trainee E.M.I. Records Manchester Sq., London, 1966—68; record prodr. Norrie Paramor Orgn., London, 1968—69; ind. writer, record producer London, 1969—; broadcaster BBC Radio and TV, Ind. TV, England, 1973—; formed label EP Records with Elaine Paige, 1981. Founder, dir. GRRR Books, 1978—, Pavilion Books, 1981—97; mem. of pop group Aardvarks, 1961—63, Whang and the Cheviots. Host (TV) Friday Night Saturday Morning, Musical Triangles, Disco; lyricist for: Marvin Hamlisch, Rick Wakeman, Vangelis, Paul McCartney, Mike Batt, Francis Lai, John Barry, Freddie Mercury, Richard Kerr, Graham Gouldman, lyricist stage musicals (with music by Andrew Lloyd Weber: Joseph and the Amazing Technicolor Dreamcoat, 1968, Joseph and the Amazing Technicolor Dreamcoat, rev., 1973 (Tony award nominations best book of musical and best original score, 1982, Grammy award nomination best cast show album, 1982), Jesus Christ Superstar, 1970 (Grammy award nomination album of the year, 1971, Tony award nomination best original score, 1972), lyricist: The Likes of Us, 1965, Evita, 1976, rev., 1978 (Tony awards best book of musical and best original score, 1980, Grammy award best cast show album, 1980), Heathcliff, 1995, Cricket, 1986, King David, 1997, Aida, 1998, Andrew Lloyd Webber: Masterpiece, 2002, Mickey's Philhar Magic, 2003, Michelle Kwan: Princess on Ice, Michelle Kwan Skates to Disney's Greatest Hits, Aladdin on Ice, Stuart Little, The Road to El Dorado, Connie and Carla, 2004, lyricist for film musicals (with music by Elton John): The Lion King, 1994, lyricist with music by Stephen Oliver: Blondel, 1983, lyricist with music by Benny Andersson and Björn Ulvaeus: Chess, 1984, rev., 1986, 1988, 1995—96, 2002, lyricist with music by Michel Berger: Tycoon, 1992, lyricist with music by Alan Menken: Beauty and the Beast, 1994, lyricist for film musicals (with music by Menken): Aladdin, 1992, lyricist for songs (from Aladdin, with Menken): A Whole New World, 1992 (Academy award best original song, 1992, Grammy award song of the year, 1993), lyricist for songs from The Lion King with John: Can You Feel the Love Tonight, 1994 (Academy award best original song, 1994), Circle of Life, 1994 (Academy award nomination best original song, 1994), Hakuna Matata, 1994 (Academy award nomination best original song, 1994); prodr.: (stage musical) Anything Goes, 1989; author: Heartaches Cricketers' Almanack (yearly), 1975—; script for 15 part series on the hisotry of Western Pop Music; author: (with others) The Guiness Book of British Hit Singles, 1977, The Guiness Book of Hits of the Seventies, 1980, Treasures of Lord's, 1989, The Complete Eurovision Song Contest Companion, 1998; editor: Lord Taverners Sticky Wicket Book, 1980; actor: Joseph and the Amazing Technicolor Dreamcoat, The Survivor, 1980, Three More Men in a Boat, 1982, Cricket, 1986. Chmn. Stars Orgn. for Spastics, 1983—85, Shaftesbury Ave. Centenary Com., 1984—86, Found. for Sport and the Arts, 1991—; pres. Lord's Taverners 1988—90, 2000; bd. dir. The Really Useful Group, 1986—88. Inducted Songwriters Hall of Fame, 1999, as a Disney Legend, Walt Disney Studios Park, Paris, 2002; knighted, 1994; recipient 12 Ivor Novello awards. Mem.: Music Industry Forum (mem. 1998—), Garrick, Saints and Sinners Club, Heartaches Cricket Club (mem. 1973—), Marylebone Cricket Club (mem. 1969—, pres. 2002—03). Mailing: Attn: Michael Sissons PFD Drury House 34-43 Russell St London WC2B 5HA England

**RICE, WALTER HERBERT,** federal judge; b. Pitts., May 27, 1937; s. Harry D. and Elizabeth L. (Braemer) R.; m. Bonnie Rice; children: Michael, Hilary, Harry, Courtney Elizabeth. BA, Northwestern U., 1958; JD, MBA, Columbia U., 1962; LLD (hon.), U. Dayton, 1991; DHL (hon.), Wright State U., 2000. Bar: Ohio 1963. Asst. county prosecutor, Montgomery County, Ohio, 1964-66; assoc. Gallon & Miller, Dayton, Ohio, 1966-69; 1st asst. Montgomery County Prosecutor's Office, 1969; judge Dayton Mcpl. Ct., 1970-71, Montgomery County Ct. Common Pleas, 1971-80, U.S. Dist. Ct. (so. dist.) Ohio, 1980—, chief judge, 1996—2003. Adj. prof. U. Dayton Law Sch., 1976—, bd. visitors, 1976—; chmn. Montgomery County Supervisory Coun. on Crime and Deliquency, 1972-74; vice chmn. bd. dirs. Pretrial Release, Inc., 1975-79; trustee Wright Dunbar, Inc. Author papers in field. Pres. Dayton Area Coun. on Alcoholism and Drug Abuse, 1971-73; chmn. bd. trustees Stillwater Health Ctr., Dayton, 1976-79, Family Svc. Assn. Dayton, 1978-80; chmn. RTA in 2000 Com., 2003 Com. Designed To Bring Nat. Park to Dayton To Honor Wright Bros. and Birth of Aviation; chmn. Martin Luther King Jr. Meml. Com., Dayton Aviation Heritage Commn.; trustee Montgomery County Vol. Lawyers Project, Miami Valley Cultural Alliance, Barbara Jordan Com. Racial Justice; co-chmn., Dayton Dialogue on Race Rels.; founding trustee Aviation Heritage Found., Inc.; former bd. mem. Sinclair C.C., U.S. Air & Trade Show. Recipient Excellent Jud. Service award, Ohio Supreme Ct., 1976, 77, Outstanding Jud. Service award, 1973, 74, 76, Man of Yr. award Disting. Service Awards Council, Dayton, 1977, Outstanding Jurist in Ohio award Ohio Acad. Trial Lawyers, 1986, Pub. Ofcl. of Yr. award Ohio region of Nat. Assn. Social Workers, 1992, Humanitarian award NCCJ, 1993, City Mgr.'s Cmty. Svc. award City of Dayton, 1994, Paul Laurence Dunbar Humanitarian award, 1996, Pres.' award NAACP, 1996, greater Dayton Peace Bridge (civil rights) Hall of Fame, Mark of Excellence award Nat. Forum Black Pub. Adminstrs., 2001, Conservation Svc. award U.S. Dept. Interior,

2002, Marie Kendrick Fair Housing award Dayton Area Bd. Realtors, 2003, Tom Joyner Hardest Workin Civil Rights Activist award Wilberforce U., 2003. Mem. Dayton Bar Assn., Fed. Judges Assn., Carl D. Kessler Inn of Ct. (founder, former chmn.).

**RICE, WAYNE,** artist, educator, small business owner; b. Chgo., Ill., Jan. 13, 1950; s. Raymond and Genevieve (Kocol) Rice; 1 child, Conor Raymond. Student, U. Calif. Berkeley, 1970, Nothern Ill. U., 1971; BA in art studio, U. N. Mex., 1980; cert. in Tchg., U. Colo., 1988. Cert. tchr. cert. K-12 U. Colo. 1987. Graphic artist Webb-Pantaleoni Design, Taos, N.Mex., 1980—81; art dir. Artlines Inc., Taos, 1981—84; graphic designer Westview Press Inc., Boulder, Colo., 1985—87; designer, mus. educator Mus. of N. Mex., Office of Statewide Programs and Edn., Santa Fe, 1989—92; curator of edn. Mus. of N. Mex., Palace of Gov., Santa Fe, 1992; creative dir., owner Design Arts, 1984—; visual info. specialist The Imagination Team, U.S. Dept. of Interior, Bur. Land Mgmt., Anasazi Heritage Ctr., Dolores, Colo., 1992—. Cons. Design Arts, Boulder, Colo., 1986—2005; staff designer, edn. divsn. Mus. of N.Mex., Santa Fe, 1989—91; curator of edn. Mus. of N.Mex., Palace of the Gov. Mus., Santa Fe, 1991—92. Numerous group shows including, exhibited in group shows at Internat. Art Competition, L.A., Calif., 1984, Palo Alto (Calif.) Cultural Ctr., 1986, Gallery at the Rep, Santa Fe, N.Mex., 1989, Richmond (Calif.) Art Ctr., 1997, Ctr. Visual Arts, Chautauqua, N.Y., 2000, Mus. Contemporary Art, Ft. Collins, Colo., 2004, one-man shows include Harwood Found. U. N.Mex., Taos, N.Mex., 1981, The Bridge Gallery Boulder (Colo.) Pub. Libr., 1985, Art and Crafts Cooperative, 1986, Tybie Davis Satin Gallery Santa Fe (N.Mex.) Pub. Libr., 1992, Centennial Savings Bank, Durango, Colo., 1996, prin. works include mural Four Corners Child Advocacy Ctr., Cortez, Colo., mural Neonatal Intensive Care Unit Holy Cross Hosp., Taos, N.Mex., Represented in permanent collections City Cortez Pub. Libr., Taos (N.Mex.) Coutny Assn. Retarded Citizens. Finalist Nat. Forest Sys. Stamp Contest, USDA, 1992; recipient Design award, N. Mex. Route 66 Assn., Shadow Ridge Corp., Town of Taos Adminstrn., Leopold's Records, U. Calif., Artist-in-residence, Nat. Pk. Svc., USDA Forest Svc., Colo., Wy., N. Mex., Silver award, Nat. Assn. Interpretation, 2005; grantee, N.Mex. Arts Divsn., 1982, 1983. Mem.: Toastmasters Internat., Am. Chess Assn. Avocations: visual arts, writing, hiking, walking, bicycling. Mailing: PO Box 746 Dolores CO 81323 Personal E-mail: desarts@gmail.com.

**RICE, WILLIAM EDWARD,** journalist; b. Albany, N.Y., July 26, 1938; s. Harry Edward, Jr. and Elizabeth (Lally) R.; m. Carol Timmon, June 3, 1978 (div.); m. Jill Van Cleave, Aug. 20, 1983. BA in History, U. Va., 1960; MS with honors, Columbia U., 1963. Reporter, editorial writer, critic Washington Post, 1963-69; student LeCordon Bleu, Paris, 1969-70; dir. L'Ecole de Cuisine, Bethesda, Md., 1971-72; freelance writer, restaurant critic Washingtonian Mag., 1971-72; exec. food editor Washington Post, 1972-80; editor-in-chief Food and Wine Mag., N.Y.C., 1980-85; food and wine columnist Chgo. Tribune, 1986—2003. Dining in columnist Gentlemen's Quarterly, 1987-89; chmn. restaurant awards com. James Beard Found., 1993-2003, chmn. who's who food and beverage in Am. com., 2005—. Author: Feasts of Wine and Food, 1986, Steak Lovers Cookbook, 1997; editor: (with others) Where to Eat in America, 1978, 2d edit., 1980, 3d edit., 1987. Served with USN, 1960-62. Recipient Vesta award as outstanding newspaper food editor, 1979, Ordre du Merite Agricole (France), 1983 Home: 655 W Buena Ave Chicago IL 60613-2201 Office Phone: 773-975-6685. Personal E-mail: wricechicago@yahoo.com.

**RICE, WINSTON EDWARD,** lawyer; b. Shreveport, La., Feb. 22, 1946; s. Winston Churchill and Margaret (Coughlin) R.; m. Barbara Reily Gay, Apr. 16, 1977; 1 child, Andrew Hynes; children by previous marriage: Winston Hobson, Christian MacTaggart. Student, Centenary Coll. La., 1967; JD, La. State U., 1971. Bar: La. 1971, Colo. 1990, Tex. 1992. Cons. geologist, Gulfport, Miss., 1968-70; ptnr. Phelps, Dunbar, New Orleans, 1971-88; sr. ptnr. Rice, Fowler, New Orleans, Houston, Miami, Fla., London and Bogota, 1988-2000; gen. mgr. Winston Edw. Rice LLC, Covington, La., 2000—. Instr. law La. State U., Baton Rouge, 1970-71. Assoc. editor La. Law Rev., 1970-71. Asst. rector Christ Ch., Covington, La., 2005—. Mem.: Trucking Industry Def. Assn., Ctr. Transp. Law and Policy, Soc. Ins. Trainers and Educators, Assn. Average Adjusters (U.K.), Assn. Average Adjusters U.S., Maritime Law Assn. U.S. (chmn. subcom. on offshore exploration and devel. 1985—88, vice chmn. com. internat. law of the sea 1988—91, chmn. 1991—95, membership sec. 1998—2002), Com. Maritime Internat. (titulary mem.), Fedn. Ins. and Corp. Counsel, La. Assn. Def. Counsel, New Orleans Assn. Def. Counsel, Can. Transp. Lawyers Assn., New Orleans Bar Assn., Tex. State Bar, Colo. State Bar Assn., La. Bar Assn., Stratford Club, Boston Club, Mariners Club (treas. 1974—75, 1978—79, sec. 1975—76, v.p. 1976—77, pres. 1977—78), Kappa Alpha, Phi Kappa Phi, Phi Delta Phi, Order of Coif. Republican. Episcopalian. Office: 527 E Boston St Ste 201 Covington LA 70433 Office Phone: 985-893-8949. Business E-Mail: rice@ricellc.com.

**RICH, ADRIENNE,** poet; b. Balt., May 16, 1929; d. Arnold Rice and Helen Elizabeth (Jones) R.; m. Alfred H. Conrad (dec. 1970); children: David, Paul, Jacob. AB, Radcliffe Coll., 1951; LittD (hon.), Wheaton Coll., 1967, Smith Coll., 1979, Brandeis U., 1987, Coll. Wooster, Ohio, 1988, CCNY, Harvard U., 1990, Swarthmore Coll., 1992. Tchr. workshop YM-WHA Poetry Ctr., N.Y.C., 1966-67; vis. lectr. Swarthmore Coll., 1967-69; adj. prof. writing divsn. Columbia U., 1967-69; lectr. CCNY, 1968-70, instr., 1970-71, asst. prof. English, 1971-72, 74-75; Fannie Hurst vis. prof. creative lit. Brandeis U., 1972-73; prof. English Douglass Coll., Rutgers U., 1976-79; Clark lectr., disting. vis. prof. Scripps Coll., 1983-84; A.D. White prof.-at-large Cornell U., 1981-87; disting. vis. prof. San Jose State U., 1984-85; prof. English and feminist studies Stanford U., 1986-93. Marjorie Kovler vis. lectr. U. Chgo., 1989. Author: Collected Early Poems, 1950-1970, 1993, Diving into the Wreck, 1973, The Dream of a Common Language, 1978, A Wild Patience Has Taken Me This Far, 1981, Your Native Land, Your Life, 1986, Time's Power, 1989, An Atlas of the Difficult World, 1991, Dark Fields of the Republic, 1995, Midnight Salvage, 1999, Fox, 2001, The Fact of a Doorframe: Selected Poems 1950-2001, 2002, The School Among the Ruins, 2004 (Nat. Book Critics Cir. prize poetry, 2005); (prose) Of Woman Born: Motherhood as Experience and Institution, 1976, 10th anniversary edit., 1986, On Lies, Secrets and Silence, 1979, Blood, Bread and Poetry, 1986, What Is Found There: Notebooks on Poetry and Politics, 1993, 2d edit., 2003, Arts of the Possible: Essays and Conversations, 2001; editor: Muriel Rukeyser, Selected Poems 2004. Mem. nat. adv. bd. Nat. Writers Union, Rosenberg Fund for Children. Recipient Yale Series of Younger Poets award, 1951, Nat. Inst. Arts and Letters award in poetry, 1961, Eunice Tietjens Meml. prize, 1968, Shelley Meml. award, 1971, Nat. Book award, 1974, Fund for Human Dignity award Nat. Gay Task Force, 1981, Ruth Lilly Poetry prize, 1986, Brandeis U. Creative Arts medal for Poetry, 1987, Nat. Poetry Assn. award, 1989, Elmer Holmes Bobst award arts and letters NYU, 1989, MacArthur fellowship, 1994-99, Dorothea Tanning award Acad. Am. Poets, 1996, others; chancellor Acad. Am. Poets, 1999-2001, Lannan Found. Lifetime Achievement award, 1999, Bollingen prize, 2003, Nat. Found. Jewish Culture award, 2003, Nat. Book Award medal for Disting. Contribution, Nat. Book Found., 2006. Mem. PEN, Nat. Writers Union, A Jewish Voice for Peace. Office: c/o W W Norton Co 500 5th Ave New York NY 10110-0002

**RICH, ALAN,** film critic, writer; b. Boston, June 17, 1924; s. Edward and Helen (Hirshberg) R. AB, Harvard, 1945; MA, U. Calif-Berkeley, 1952. Alfred Hertz Meml. Traveling fellow in music, Vienna, Austria, 1952-53; Asst. music critic Boston Herald, 1944-45, N.Y. Sun, 1947-48; contbr. Am. Record Guide, 1947-61, Saturday Rev., 1952-53, Mus. Am., 1955-61, Mus. Quar., 1957-58; tchr. music U. Calif. at Berkeley, 1950-58; program and music dir. Pacifica Found., FM radio, 1953-61; asst. music critic N.Y. Times, 1961-63; chief music critic, editor N.Y. Herald Tribune, 1963-66; music critic, editor N.Y. World Jour. Tribune, 1966-67; contbg. editor Time mag., 1967-68; music and drama critic, arts editor N.Y. mag., 1968-81, contbg. editor, 1981-83; music critic, arts editor Calif. (formerly New West mag.), 1979-83, contbg. editor, 1983-85; gen. editor Newsweek mag., N.Y.C., 1983-87; music critic L.A. Herald Examiner, 1987-89, L.A. Daily News, 1989-92, L.A.

Weekly, 1992—. Tchr. New Sch. for Social Rsch., 1972-75, 77-79, U. So. Calif. Sch. Journalism, 1980-82, Calif. Inst. Art, 1982-94, UCLA, 1990-91; artist-in-residence Davis Ctr. for Performing Arts CUNY, 1975-76. Author: Careers and Opportunities in Music, 1964, Music: Mirror of the Arts, 1969, Listeners Guides to Classical Music, Opera, Jazz, 3 vols., 1980, The Lincoln Center Story, 1984, Play-by-Play: Bach, Mozart, Beethoven, Tchaikovsky, 4 vols., 1995, American Pioneers, 1995, So I've Heard: Notes of a Migrating Music Critic, 2006; author: (interactive CD-ROM computer programs): Schubert's Trout Quintet, 1991, So I've Heard: Bach and Before, 1992, So I've Heard: The Classical Ideal, 1993, So I've Heard: Beethoven and Beyond, 1993; contbr. articles to entertainment mags. Recipient Deems Taylor award ASCAP, 1970, 73, 74 Mem. Music Critics Circle N.Y. (sec. 1961-63, chmn. 1963-64), N.Y. Drama Critics Circle, Am. Theatre Critics Assn., Music Critics Assn., PEN. Home: 2925 Greenfield Ave Los Angeles CA 90064-4019 Office Phone: 310-475-5102. Office Fax: 310-695-0115. Personal E-mail: alanrich1@mac.com.

**RICH, ANDREA LOUISE,** museum administrator; BA, UCLA, 1965, MA, 1966, PhD, 1968. Asst. prof. comms. studies UCLA, L.A., 1976, asst. dir. office learning resources, 1976, acting dir. Media Ctr., 1977, dir. office of instructional devel., 1978-80, asst. vice chancellor office of instructional devel., 1980-86, asst. exec. vice chancellor, 1986-87, vice chancellor acad. adminstrn., 1987-91, exec. vice chancellor, 1991-95; pres., CEO L.A. County Mus. of Art, 1995—, pres., Wallis Annenberg dir., 2003—. Office: LA County Mus Art 5905 Wilshire Blvd Los Angeles CA 90036-4597

**RICH, BRADFORD WHITMAN,** retired insurance executive, lawyer; b. Winchester, Mass., May 11, 1947; m. Linda Lee Beebe, May 31, 1969; children: Heather, Eric. AB with honors, Denison U., 1969; JD with honors, George Washington U., 1972. Bar: Va. 1972, Pa. 1978. Staff asst., domestic council US Govt., White House, 1971-73; staff judge adv. USAF, Washington, Tucson, 1973-77; assoc. gen. counsel, v.p. litigation counsel, pres. INAPRO Ins. Co. of N. Am., Phila., 1977-83; sr. officer Guardian Royal Exchange, 1983-86; sr. v.p., litigation counsel Crum & Forster Corp., Morristown, NJ, 1987—91; exec. v.p., gen. counsel Ace Ltd., Hamilton, Bermuda, 1991—95; sr. v.p., gen. counsel, sec. United Svcs. Automobile Assn. (USAA), San Antonio, 1995—2003, exec. v.p., gen. counsel, sec., 2003—04, ret., 2004—. Bd. dirs. Talbot, Bird & Co., Inc., NYC; lectr. legal profl., ins. orgns. Served to capt. USAF, 1973-77. Mem. ABA, Internat. Assn. Ins. Counsel, Fedn. Ins. Counsel, Va. Bar Assn., Pa. Bar Assn. Republican. Presbyterian.

**RICH, CLAYTON,** retired academic administrator, educator; b. NYC, May 21, 1924; s. Clayton Eugene and Leonore (Elliot) R.; m. Mary Bell Hodgkinson, Dec. 19, 1953 (div. May 1974); 1 son, Clayton Greig; m. Rosalind Morgan-Jones, Apr. 6, 1987. Grad., Putney Sch., 1942; student, Swarthmore Coll., 1942-44; MD, Cornell U., 1948. Diplomate Am. Bd. Internal Medicine. Intern Albany Hosp., NY, 1948-49, asst. resident, 1950-51; rsch. asst. Cornell U. Med. Coll., 1949-50; asst. Rockefeller U., 1953-58, asst. prof., 1958-60; asst. prof. medicine U. Wash. Sch. Medicine, 1960-62, assoc. prof., 1962-67, prof., 1967-71, assoc. dean, 1968-71; chief radioisotope service VA Hosp., Seattle, 1960-70, assoc. chief staff, 1962-71, chief of staff, 1968-70; v.p. med. affairs, dean Sch. Medicine; prof. medicine Stanford U., 1971-79, Carl and Elizabeth Naumann prof., 1977-79; chief staff Stanford U. Hosp., 1971-77, CEO, 1977—79. Sr. scholar Inst. Medicine, Nat. Acad. Sci., Washington, 1979-80; Mem. gen. medicine B study sect. NIH, 1969-73, chmn., 1972-73; mem. spl. med. adv. group VA, 1977-81; provost U. Okla. Health Scis. Ctr., Oklahoma City, 1980-92—, v.p. for healh scis., 1983-92; also exec. dean, prof. U. Okla. Coll. Medicine, 1980-83, emeritus Regents prof. and provost U. Okla., 1993—. Editorial bd.: Calcified Tissue Research, 1966-72, Clin. Orthopedics, 1967-72, Jour. Clin. Endocrinology and Metabolism, 1971-72; Contbr. numerous articles to med. jours. Bd. dirs. Children's Hosp. at Stanford, Stanford U. Hosp., 1974-79; chmn. Gordon Research Conf. Chemistry, Physiology and Structure of Bones and Teeth, 1967; bd. dirs. Okla. Med. Research Found.; bd. dirs. Leadership Oklahoma City, 1981-92, v.p., 1985-92; bd. dirs. Okla. Blood Inst., 1982-92, Oklahoma City chpt. ARC, 1983-92. Lt. USNR, 1951-53. Fellow ACP, AAAS; mem. Assn. Am. Physicians, Western Assn. Physicians, Am. Soc. Mineral and Bone Research (adv. bd. 1977-80), Am. Soc. Clin. Investigation, Assn. Am. Med. Colls. (exec. council 1975-79), Inst. of Medicine, Western Soc. Clin. Research (v.p. 1967-68), Endocrine Soc., Assn. Acad. Health Ctrs. (bd. dirs. 1984-88, chmn. 1987-88), Sigma Xi, Alpha Omega Alpha. Home: 13450 64th Ter NE Kirkland WA 98034-1656 Personal E-mail: claytrich@aol.com.

**RICH, DANIEL HULBERT,** chemistry professor; b. Fairmont, Minn., Dec. 12, 1942; married, 1964; 2 children. BS, U. Minn., 1964; PhD in Organic Chemistry, Cornell U., 1968. Rsch. assoc. organic chemist Cornell U., 1968; rsch. chemist Dow Chem. Co., 1968—69; rsch. assoc., organic chemist Stanford U., 1969—70; asst. prof. pharm. chemistry U. Wis., Madison, 1970—75, assoc. prof., 1975—81, prof. dept. med. chemistry, 1981—, prof. dept. organic chemistry, 1988—, Ralph F. Hirschmann prof. medicinal and organic chemistry, 1994—. Cons. bioorganic natural product study sect., NIH, 1981-85, chmn., 1985. Recipient H.I. Romnes award, 1980, Vincent du Vigneaud award, 1990, Hitchings award for innovative methods in drug design, 1992, Alexander von Humboldt award, 1993, E. Volwiler award Am. Assn. Colls. Pharmacy, 1995, Outstanding Achievement award U. Minn., 2004; fellow NIH, 1968. Fellow AAAS, Am. Chem. Soc. (Ralph F. Hirschmann award in peptide chemistry 1993, divsn. medicinal chemistry award 1991, A.C. Cope scholar 1999, E. Smissman award, 2005), Am. Assn. Pharm. Sci. (rsch. achievement award 1992), Am. Assn. Coll. Pharmacy (Volwiler award 1995), Am. Peptide Soc. (R.B. Merrifield award 1999). Achievements include research in synthesis in peptides and hormones, inhibition of peptide receptors and proteases, characterization, synthesis and mechanisms of action of peptide natural products. Office: U Wis Dept Med Chemistry 7100 Rennebohm Hall 777 Highland Ave Madison WI 53705-2222

**RICH, DAVID BARRY,** financial executive, accountant, entertainer, publishing executive; b. Bronx, NY, July 3, 1952; s. Steven and Gizella (Kornfeld) R.; m. Beverly Hayag, Dec. 6, 1995; 1 child, Suzanne Stephanie. BS in Health Adminstrn., Ithaca Coll., 1976; postgrad. in acctg., Bryant and Stratton Coll., Buffalo, l977. Office. mgr. Rubin Gorewitz, CPA, N.Y.C., 1977-78; auditor State of Ariz., Phoenix, 1979-83; internal auditor City of Phoenix, 1983-84; sales use tax auditor City of Mesa (Ariz.), 1984-98; pub. Technology TnT, 2003—. Pres. Clovis Acctg. Inc., Mesa, 1980-94; rep. H.D. Vest Investment Inc., Irving, Tex., 1984-94; owner D.B. Rich Enterprises Import/Export Internet Sales, Chandler, 1992-2005; stage name Barry Rich, Stand-up Comedy, 1994-2005 Treas., bd. dirs. Missing Mutts Inc., Tempe, Ariz., 1986-88. With USAF, l971-76. Fellow Nat. Assn. Tax Preparers; mem. Toastmasters (treas. Mesa 1986-87), Phi Beta Kappa. Office Phone: 602-741-6640. Business E-Mail: d.rich@technologytnt.com. *The world is one big neighborhood and we are all neighbors. If we will survive as a planet we must work together as friends. We must treat all people as our equals.*

**RICH, DOROTHY KOVITZ,** educational association administrator, writer; BA in Journalism and Psychology, Wayne U.; MA, Columbia U.; EdD, Catholic U. Founder, pres. The Home and Sch. Inst., Inc., Washington, 1964—. Adv. coun. Nat. Health Edn. Consortium; adv. com. Ctr. for Workplace Prep. and Quality Edn. U.S.C. of C.; mem. readiness to learn task force U.S. Dept. Edn., urban edn. team Coun. Gt. City Schs.; legislative nat. initiatives including work on Family/Sch. Partnership Act, 1989, Improving America's Edn. Act, 1994; formulator New Partnerships for Student Achievement program, 1987; creator MegaSkills Edn. Ctr. The Home and Sch. Inst. Inc., 1990; designer MegaSkills Leader Tng. for Parent Workshops, 1988, MegaSkills Essentials for the Classroom, 1991, Learning and Working program for sch.-to-work initiatives, 1996, Career Megaskills, 1999, New MegaSkills Bond Tchr./Parent Partnership, 1994, Career MegaSkills materials and tng., 1998, Adult MegaSkills for Profl. Growth, 1999, MegaSkills Behavior Mgmt. Kit, 2002; developer NEA/MegaSkills nat. mentor tng. initiative, 2000-06, MegaSkills for the Job, 2002, Adult MegaSkills and MegaSkills for Teachers, 2002-06, MegaSkills for Teachers Video Programs, 2003, edn. columns Knight Ridder News Svc., 2004-06. Author: MegaSkills in School in Life: The Best Gift You Can Give Your Child, 1988, rev. edit., 1992, What Do We Say? What Do We Do? Vital Solutions for Children's Educationsl Success, 1997, MegaSkills, 3d edit., 1997, 18 tng. books, MegaSkills: Building Children's Achievement for the Information Age, new and expanced edit., 1998, Improving Student Teaching through MegaSkills, All Around the House (early childhood literacy curriculum), 2005, The MegaSkills Way to Reading for Preschool, 2005, New MegaSkills Infancy/Toddler Curriculum, 2006, New Megaskill Respect, 2006; TV appearances include The Learning Channel, NBC Today Show, Good Morning Am.: subject of videos nat. ednl. programs in Thailand, Singapore and China: Families and Schools: Teaming for Success, Survival Guide for Today's Parents. Recipient Am. Woman Leader award, Citation U.S. Dept. Edn., Nat. Gov.'s Assn., Alumni Achievement award in edn. Cath. U., 1992, Golden Apple award for MegaSkills Tchrs. Coll., Columbia U., 1996; grantee John D. and Catherine T. MacArthur Found.; named Washingtonian of Yr., ADv. Bd. of McNeil-Lehrer NewsHour, 2004. Mem. Nat. Press Club. Office: MegaSkills Edn Ctr Home and Sch Inst Inc 1500 Massachusetts Ave NW Washington DC 20005-1821 Office Phone: 202-466-3633. Business E-Mail: edstaff@megaskills.org.

**RICH, EUGENE CARROLL,** internist; b. Belleville, Ill., Mar. 6, 1951; s. Carol and Clara G. Rich; m. Elaine Stapf, Sept. 30, 1978; children: Edward, Patrick. BA in Philosophy and Chemistry, U. Miss., 1973; MD, Washington U., St. Louis, Mo., 1977. Diplomate Am. Bd. Internal Medicine. Resident U. Minn. Hosps., Mpls., 1977-80: chief resident in internal medicine St. Paul Ramsey Med. Ctr., 1980-81, fellow in gen. internal medicine, 1981-82, chief sect. gen. internal medicine, 1988-89; internal medicine U. Minn., Mpls., 1980-83; asst. prof. U. Minn. Sch. Medicine and Pub. Health, Mpls., 1983-89, asst. prof. divsn. health scis. rsch. and policy, 1987-89; chief divsn. gen. internal medicine and geriatrics U. Ky. Coll. Medicine, Lexington, 1989, assoc. prof. medicine, 1989-94, prof. medicine 1994—96, assoc. chair clin. affairs, dept. internal medicine, 1993; prof., chair dept. medicine Creighton U. Sch. Medicine, Omaha, 1996—, Tenet Healthcare Endowed chair, 1998—; dir., Ctr. for Practice Improvement and Outcomes Rsch. Creighton U. Med. Ctr.; med. dir. UniNet, Nebr. Cons. Health Resource Svc. Adminstrn., Rockville, Md., Health Care Fin. Adminstrn.; bd. dir. Nat. Fund for Med. Edn.; mem. Step III com., Nat. Bd. Med. Examiners Contbr. articles to profl. jours.; editl. review group chair in health care adminstrn. and health policy, Doody Publishing Rep., State DFL Conv., 1988. USPHS primary care policy fellow, 1991, Robert Wood Johnson Health Policy Fellow, IOM, 2006. Fellow ACP; mem. Am. Geriatric Soc., Ctrl. Soc. for Clin. Rsch., Soc. of Med. Decisionmaking, Soc. Gen. Internal Medicine, Assn. Professors of Medicine, Primary Care Fellowship Soc. Democrat. Presbyterian. Avocations: hiking, camping, reading. Office: Creighton U Med Ctr Sch Medicine Dept Medicine 601 N 30th S Ste 5850 Omaha NE 68131*

**RICH, FRANK HART,** journalist, writer; b. Washington, June 2, 1949; s. Frank Hart Rich and Helene Bernice (Aaronson) Fisher; m. Alexandra Rachelle Witchel 1991; children from previous marriage: Nathaniel Howard, Simon Hart. BA in Am. History and Lit. with honors, Harvard U., 1971. Co-editor Richmond (Va.) Mercury, 1972-73; sr. editor, film critic New Times mag., NYC, 1973-75; film critic NY Post, NYC, 1975-77; film and TV critic Time mag., NYC, 1977-80; chief drama critic NY Times, NYC, 1980-93; columnist NY Times Sunday Mag., NYC, 1993; Op-Ed columnist NY Times, NYC, 1994—2003, 2005—, assoc. editor, columnist, 2003—05. Author: (with others) The Theatre Art of Boris Aronson, 1987, Hot Seat: Theater Criticism for the New York Times 1980-93, 1998, Ghost Light, 2000, The Greatest Story Ever Told, 2006. Assoc. fellow Jonathan Edwards Coll., Yale U., 1998—; recipient George Polk award for commentary, 2006. Office: The NY Times 229 W 43rd St New York NY 10036-3959

**RICH, FREDERIC CARL,** lawyer; b. Elizabeth City, NC, 1956; AB, Princeton U., 1977; JD, U. Va., 1981. Bar: NY 1982. Ptnr., head global project fin. group Sullivan & Cromwell, NYC, 1981—, now co-mng. ptnr. corp. practice group. Chmn. Scenic Hudson; bd. dir. Boscobel Restoration, Inc., Hudson River Found. Sci. and Rsch., Inc., Scenic Hudson, Inc., Friends of Palisades Interstate Pk. Commn., Inc. Keasby fellow King's Coll., Cambridge, Eng., 1978. Office: Sullivan & Cromwell 125 Broad St Fl 28 New York NY 10004-2489 Office Phone: 212-558-4000. Office Fax: 212-558-3588.

**RICH, HARRY EARL,** corporate financial executive; b. Wichita, Kans., Mar. 5, 1940; s. Hubert E. and Lorene (Sadler) R.; m. Elfreda Elizabeth Babcock, Aug. 8, 1964; children: Lisa G., Carey E., Ashley H. BA, Harvard U., 1962, MBA, 1968. Pres. instrumentation divsn. Baxter Travenol, Deerfield, Ill., 1977-78; group v.p. Mallinckrodt, Inc., St. Louis, 1978-83; sr. v.p., chief fin. officer Brown Group, Inc., St. Louis, 1983-88, exec. v.p., chief fin. officer, 1988-00, also bd. dirs. Gen. Am. Capital Co. divsn. GenAm. Bd. dirs. Repertory Theatre, 1984-90, 1998—, pres. bd. dirs.,1988-90; treas., v.p. Fair Found., 1985-88; bd. trustees Mary Inst., 1986-90, Mary Inst./St. Louis Country Day Sch., 1990-97, chmn., 1995-97. Lt. USN, 1962-66. Avocations: tennis, jogging, sailing. Home: 101 Fair Oaks Saint Louis MO 63124-1579

**RICH, JEFFREY A.,** computer company executive; BA, U. Mich., 1982. Asst. v.p. Interfirst Bank Dallas, 1982-86; v.p. Citibank, 1986-89; sr. v.p., CFO Affiliated Computer Svcs., Inc., Dallas, 1989-95, COO, 1995—2001, pres., 1995—2002, CEO, 1999—. Dir. Pegasus Solutions Inc. Dir. US C. of C., Edn. is Freedom Found.; mem. Young President's Orgn., Dallas Citizen's Coun.; bd. gov. Dallas Symphony Orchestra.

**RICH, JOHN HUBBARD, JR.,** news correspondent; b. Cape Elizabeth, Maine, Aug. 5, 1917; s. John Hubbard Rich and Alma Estella Glidden Rich; m. Doris Lee Halstead, Sept. 2, 1954; children: Barb, John III, Whitney, Nathaniel. AB, Bowdoin Coll., 1939, LittD (hon.), 1974. News reporter Daily Kennabec Jour., Augusta, Maine, 1939—40, Portland (Maine) Press Herald, 1941—42; reporter, fgn. corr. Internat. News Svc., Tokyo, 1945—50; fgn. corr. NBC News, Tokyo, 1950—54; fellowship Coun. on Fgn. Rels., N.Y.C., 1954—55. Maj. USMCR, 1943—45, PTO. Decorated Bronze star; recipient Peabody award, 1974. Mem.: Tokyo Fgn. Corrs. Club, Overseas Press Club (award 1974), Sigma Delta Chi. Avocations: tennis, sailing. Home: 13 Rocky Point Ln Cape Elizabeth ME 04107

**RICH, JOHN MARTIN,** humanities educator, researcher; b. Tuscaloosa, Ala., Dec. 14, 1931; s. Emanuel Morris and Bertha (Rose) R.; m. Martha Elaine Schur, June 6, 1955 (div. June 1966); children— Jeffrey Brian, Suzanne Elon; m. Joyce Ann Stegemoller, Aug. 28, 1967 (div. Mar. 1985); m. Audrey Faye Arnold, Aug. 1, 1987. BA, U. Ala., 1954, MA, 1955; PhD, Ohio State U., 1958. Grad. asst. Ohio State U., Columbus, 1955, asst. instr. edn., 1956-58; asst. prof. U. Tenn.-Martin, 1958-60; assoc. prof. edn. Coll. SUNY-Oneonta, 1960-61; from asst. prof. to assoc. prof. Iowa State U., Ames, 1961-66; assoc. prof. social and philos. studies U. Ky., Lexington, 1966-69; prof. cultural founds. edn. U. Tex., Austin, 1969-96, prof. emeritus, 1996—, chmn. dept. cultural founds. edn., 1969-75. Vis. lectr. Nat. Kaohsiung (Taiwan) Normal U., 1993. Author: (books) Education and Human Values, 1968, Humanistic Foundations of Education, 1971, Portuguese translation, 1975, Korean translation, 1985, Challenge and Response, 1974, New Directions in Educational Policy, 1974, Discipline and Authority in School and Family, 1982, Professional Ethics in Education, 1984, Innovative School Discipline, 1985, Foundations of Education, 1992; co-author: Theories of Moral Development, 1985 (named an Outstanding Book of 1985-86 Choice mag.), 2d edit., 1994, Korean translation, 1999, Helping and Intervention, 1988, Competition in Education, 1992, The Success Ethic, Education, and the American Dream, 1996, Korean translation, 1998; editor: Readings in the Philosophy of Education, 1966, 2d edit., 1972, Conflict and Decision, 1972, Innovations in Education, 6th edit., 1992; co-editor, editl. adv. bd. Ednl. Studies,1970-74, 77-80, 89-91; bd. contbg. editors Rev. Edn., 1977-85; editl. bd. Focus on Learning, 1980-84, Educational Foundations 1985-91; bd. cons. Jour. Rsch. and Devel. in Edn., 1982-96, Ednl. Theory, 1991-95; contbr. articles to profl. jours., U.S., Can., Eng., Australia. Recipient Faculty

Research Assignment award Univ. Research Inst., Austin, Tex., 1983-84; vis. scholar U. London, 1977; Univ. Research Inst. grantee, 1981-82, 84-85 Mem. North Central Philosophy of Edn. Soc. (pres. 1966-67), Ohio Valley Philosophy of Edn. Soc. (pres. 1967-68), Philosophy of Edn. Soc. (elec. bd. 1967-68, 80-82, Cert. Significant Svc.), Am. Ednl. Studies Assn. (exec. council 1972-74, pres. 1975-76) Home: 1801 Lavaca St Apt 8M Austin TX 78701-1312 Office: U Tex Edn Bldg 406 Austin TX 78712 E-mail: john1931@webtv.net.

**RICH, JOHN TOWNSEND,** lawyer; b. Lansing, Mich., Mar. 10, 1943; s. Townsend and Jean (Trembley) R.; m. Charlotte Pia Mahon, Nov. 25, 1978; children: Anna-Sophie, Lucia Danforth. BA, Harvard U., 1965, postgrad., 1965-66; LLB, Yale U., 1969; postgrad., U. Coll., Oxford, Eng., 1969-70. Bar: N.Y. 1970, D.C. 1972. Law clk. to Hon. David L. Bazelon U.S. Ct.Appeals D.C. Cir., 1970-71; law clk. to Hon. Harry A. Blackmun U.S. Supreme Ct., Washington, 1971-72; assoc. Shea & Gardner, Washington, 1972-76, ptnr., 1976—2004, Goodwin Procter LLP, Washington, 2004—. Adj. prof. Georgetown U. Law Ctr., 1972-75; spl. master U.S. Dist. Ct. for No. Dist. Tex., 1985-88. Home: 6309 Kenhowe Dr Bethesda MD 20817-5419 Office: Goodwin Procter LLP 901 NY Ave NW Washington DC 20001 Business E-Mail: jrich@goodwinprocter.com.

**RICH, LAURA,** columnist; Grad., DePauw Univ. Writer Adweek mag., Inside Media mag.; sr. writer Industry Standard mag.; contbg. editor fastcompany.com; columnist New York Times. Author: The Accidental Zillionaire: Demystifying Paul Allen, 2003; contbr. articles to Entertainment Weekly, Hollywood Reporter. Mailing: New York Times 229 W 43d St New York NY 10036 Office Phone: 212-389-5369. Business E-Mail: lrich@inc.com.*

**RICH, MARC DAVID,** commodities trader; b. Antwerp, Belgium, Dec. 18, 1934; arrived in US, 1941; s. David Rich and Paula Rich-Wang; m. Denise Eisenberg, Oct. 1966 (div. 1992); children: Ilona, Gabrielle(dec.), Danielle. With Philipps Bros., NYC, 1954—64, Phibro office mgr. Madrid, 1964—74; co-founder Marc Rich + Co AG (name changed to Glencore Internat., 1994), Zug, Switzerland, 1974—97, Marc Rich + Co Holding AG, Zug, Switzerland, 1987. Co-founder Rich Foundations; chmn. Marc Rich Found. Edn., Culture & Welfare, Gabrielle Rich Found. Leukemia Rsch., Swiss Found. for the Doron Prize. Named one of 400 Richest Americans, Forbes, 2000—, World's Richest People, 2001—, The Famous 15: America's Most Fascinating Tycoons, 2001. Office: Glencore Internat AG Baarermattstrasse 3 CH-6340 Baar Switzerland Office Phone: 41-41-709-2000. Office Fax: 41-41-709-3000. E-mail: info@glencore.com.*

**RICH, MARVIN P.,** health association executive; Formerly with CalFed Bank, Carter Hawley Hale Stores, Inc., Dart Industry; former exec. v.p., fin. and info. svcs. Wellpoint Health Networks/Blue Cross of Calif.; exec. v.p. strategic planning, fin. and adminstrn. K-Mart, Troy, Mich., 1994-98; CEO, exec. v.p. Oxford Health, Norwalk, Conn., 1998—99; pres., CEO CareInsight, 2000; pres. WebMD, Elmwood Park, NJ, 2000—01; exec. v.p., fin. and ops. Health Net, inc., Woodland Hills, Calif., 2002—. Office: Health Net Life Insurance Co 21281 Burbank Blvd Woodland Hills CA 91367-6607

**RICH, MICHAEL DAVID,** think-tank executive, lawyer; b. LA, Jan. 23, 1953; s. Ben Robert and Faye (Mayer) R.; m. Debra Paige Granfield, Jan. 12, 1980; children: Matthew, William. AB, U. Calif., Berkeley, 1973; JD, UCLA, 1976. Bar: Calif., 1976. Extern law clk. to judge U.S. Dist. Ct., Boston, 1975; staff mem. RAND, Santa Monica, Calif., 1976—85, dir. resource mgmt. program, 1980—85, dep. v.p., 1986, v.p. nat. security rsch. and dir. Nat. Def. Rsch. Inst., 1986—93, sr. v.p., 1993—95, exec. v.p., 1995—. Co-chmn. bd. overseers Rand-Qatar Policy Inst., 2003—. Author numerous classified and unclassified reports and articles. Bd. dirs. WISE Sr. Svcs., Coun. for Aid to Edn. (chmn. 1996-2005); mem. bd. councillors UCLA Found., 2000—; fin. oversight com., Santa Monica-Malibu Unified Sch. Dist., 2000-04; bd. advisers Santa Monica-UCLA Med. Ctr.; chmn. bd. trustees The Comm. Inst., 2003—. Mem. Coun. Fgn. Rels., Internat. Inst. Strategic Studies (governing coun. 2001—, chmn. bd. trustees, IISS-U.S., 2004—) Office: RAND PO Box 2138 1776 Main St Santa Monica CA 90407-2138 Office Phone: 310-451-6934. E-mail: mrich@rand.org.

**RICH, MICHAEL W,** physician, researcher; s. James G and Beryle V Rich; m. Victoria Weisbard, Feb. 21, 1953; children: Sarah, Daniel, Elizabeth, Madeline, Caroline, Jessica. MD, U. Ill., 1979. Diplomate Am. Bd. Internal Medicine, 1982. Asst. prof. medicine Wash. U. Sch. Medicine, Saint Louis Mo., 1987—93, assoc. prof. medicine, 1993—. Fellow: Am. Coll. Cardiology, Soc. Geriatric Cardiology (pres. 1997—98); mem.: Am. Geriatrics Soc. Office: Washington U Sch Medicine 660 S Euclid Ave Box 8086 Saint Louis MO 63110 Office Phone: 314-454-8146.

**RICH, NANCY JEAN,** lawyer; b. Chgo., June 11, 1959; d. John Keith and Phyllis Vallerie (Delaney) R. AB with honors, Loyola U., Chgo., 1981, JD, 1984. Bar: Ill. 1984, U.S. Dist. Ct. (no. dist.) Ill. 1984. Asst. atty. gen. environ. control div. Ill. Atty. Gen.'s Office, Chgo., 1984-87; assoc. Isham, Lincoln & Beale, Chgo., 1987-88, Sidley & Austin, Chgo., 1988-89, Bell, Boyd & Lloyd, Chgo., 1989-91, ptnr, 1992, Katten Muchin Zavis Rosenman, Chgo. Bd. dirs. Pub. Interest Law Initiative. Contbr. to Loyola Consumer Law Reporter, 1991. Adminstrv. asst. Hartigan for Atty. Gen. Campaign, Chgo., 1982; bd. dirs. Suburban Area Agy. on Aging, 1990-2004, pres. bd. dirs., 1999-2001, chmn. resource devel. com., 1991—. Mem. ABA, Ill. Bar Assn., Chgo. Bar Assn. (environ. law com.). Office: Katten Muchin Zavis Rosenman 525 W Monroe St Chicago IL 60661 Office Phone: 312-902-5536. Office Fax: 312-577-8676. Business E-Mail: nancy.rich@kattenlaw.com. E-mail: nancy.rich@kmzr.com.

**RICH, NORMAN S.,** food service executive; From mem. staff to pres., CEO Weis Markets, Sunbury, Pa., 1964—2002, pres., 2002—, CEO, 2002—. Dir. Food Mktg. Inst.; bd. trustees Evang. Cmty. Hosp.; bd. dirs. Weis Markets. Office: Weis Markets 1000 S Second St Sunbury PA 17801*

**RICH, PHILIP DEWEY,** publishing executive; b. Nashua, N.H., Feb. 1, 1940; s. John Parker and Olive Frances (Hussey) R.; m. Leslie Ann Burke, June 14, 1974 (div. 1982). AB magna cum laude, Harvard U., 1961; MA, NYU, 1962; postgrad., Princeton U., 1962. Editor Houghton Mifflin Co., Boston, 1964-73; asst. mng. editor UpCountry Mag. Berkshire Eagle, Pittsfield, Mass., 1976-77; editor Book Creations Inc., Canaan, NY, 1977-80, editor-in-chief, 1980-91, v.p., exec. editor, 1991-92; cons. editor Berkshire Ho. Publs., Lee, Mass., 1992-93, mng. editor, 1993-96, mng. editor and prodn. editor, 1996-99, editl. dir., prodn. dir., 1999—2003; editl. cons. Pittsfield, Mass., 2003—. Office: 18 Boylston St Pittsfield MA 01201-6748 Office Phone: 413-443-1737. Personal E-mail: prich@bcn.net.

**RICH, R(OBERT) BRUCE,** lawyer; b. N.Y.C., Oct. 28, 1949; s. John J. and Sylvia (Berkenblit) R.; m. Melissa Jo Saxe; children— Megan, Alexander. A.B., Dartmouth Coll., 1970; J.D., U. Pa., 1973. Bar: N.Y. 1974, U.S. Dist. Ct. (so. and ea. dists.) N.Y. 1974, U.S. Ct. Appeals (2d cir.) 1980, U.S. Supreme Ct. 1980, U.S. Ct. Appeals (D.C. cir.) 1985. Assoc. firm Weil, Gotshal & Manges, N.Y.C., 1973-81, ptnr., 1981-. Mem. bd. overseers U. Pa. Law Sch., 2002-, bd. dirs. Expeditionary Leaning Outward Bound, 2002-, Appleseed Found., 2003-. Contbg. author: Cultivating the Wasteland: Can Cable Put the Vision Back in TV?, 1983, The International Libel Handbook, 1995. Contbr. articles to profl. jours.; co-editor: Business and Legal Guide to Online-Internet Law, 1997. Mem. ABA (antitrust law sect., forum com. on communications law), Assn. Bar City N.Y. (com. on trade regulation 1982-85, communications law com. 1985-88), Phi Beta Kappa. Office: Weil Gotshal & Manges 767 5th Ave Fl Concl New York NY 10153-0119

**RICH, ROBERT E., JR.,** frozen foods company executive; b. 1941; s. Robert E. Rich Sr. and Janet Rich; m. Mindy Rich. BA, Williams Coll., 1963; MBA, U. Rochester, 1969; Ph.D (hon.), St. Bonaventure U., Niagra U., Johnson & Wales U. Pres. Rich Products Corp., Buffalo, 1978—, chmn.,

2006—. Co-founder Western NY United Against Drug & Alcohol Abuse, Inc., 1986; chmn. Nat. Grocery Mfrs. Assn., 1999—, Students in Free Enterprise, 2003—06, Nat. Frozen & Refrigerated Foods Assn., 2006—. Author: Fish Fights: A Hall of Fame Quest, 2001, The Fishing Club, 2006. Named a Diplomat, Nat. Restaurant Assn., 2000; named Citizen of the Yr., Buffalo News, 1983, Buffalo/Niagra Frontier Sales & Mktg. Exec. of the Yr., 1984, Exec. of the Yr., Am. Assn., 1986, Triple-A Exec. of the Yr., The Sporting News, 1988, Exec. of the Yr., Refrigerated & Frozen Foods mag., 1996; named to, Nat. Frozen Food Inst. Hall of Fame, 1996, Buffalo Baseball Hall of Fame, S. Fla. Fishing Hall of Fame, 1999, Greater Buffalo Sports Hall of Fame, Nat. Restaurant Assn. Ednl. Found. Coll. Diplomats, 2000; recipient Peter Medaille medal, Outstanding alumni award, U. Rochester. Office: Rich Products Corp One Robert Rich Way Buffalo NY 14213*

**RICH, ROBERT EDWARD,** lawyer; b. Corbin, Ky., Feb. 4, 1944; s. Edward Bluch and Marjorie Brooks (Wentworth) R.; m. Janet Sue Shearer, May 14, 1966; children: Susan M., Christopher R., David E., Sarah M. AB, U. Ky., 1966; JD, Harvard U., 1969. Bar: Ohio 1970. Jud. clk. U.S. Ct. Appeals for 6th Cir., Louisville, 1969-70; assoc. Taft, Stettinius & Hollister, Cin., 1970, ptnr., 1978—. Pres. Lighthouse Youth Svcs., Cin., 1985, Ky. YMCA Youth Assn., Frankfort, 2001; mem. exec. bd. Ky. Hist. Soc.; pres. Cin. Bar Found., 1991. Mem. ABA, Cin. Bar Assn. Republican, Presbyterian. Home: 215 Hilltop Ln Wyoming OH 45215-4121 Office: 1800 US Bank Tower 425 Walnut St Cincinnati OH 45202-3923 Office Phone: 513-381-2838. E-mail: rich@taftlaw.com.

**RICH, ROBERT F.,** law educator, political science professor; married; 3 children. BA in Govt. with honors, Oberlin Coll., 1971; student, Free U. of Berlin, 1971-72; MA in Polit. Scis., U. Chgo., 1973, PhD in Polit. Scis., 1975. Project dir., asst. rsch. scientist Ctr. for Rsch. on Utilization Sci. Knowledge, Inst. Social Rsch., U. Mich., lectr. dept. polit. sci., 1975-76; asst. prof. politics and pub. affairs Princeton U., 1976-82, coord. domestic and urban policy field Woodrow Wilson Sch., 1976-82; assoc. prof. polit. sci., pub. policy and mgmt. Sch. Urban and Pub. Affairs, Carnegie-Mellon U., 1982-86; prof. polit. sci. law, health resources mgmt., med. humanities and social svcs., cmty. health, prof. Inst. Environ. Studies U. Ill., Urbana, 1986—2003, dir. Inst. Govt. and Publ. Affairs, 1986-97, acting head med. humanities and social scis. program Urbana-Champaign, 1988-90, prof. law and polit. sci., health resources mgmt., 1996—, prof. law Urbana-Champaign; fellow Johns Hopkins U. Ctr. for Study of Am. Govt., Washington, 1993-95; Mercator prof. Humboldt U., Berlin, 2002—03. Cons. U.S. Dept. Health and Human Svcs., Carnegie-Mellon U., 1986—, MacArthur Found., NIMH, 1988-89, Food, Drug and Law Inst., HHS, 1989, Am. Career Soc., 1996-97; disting. lectr. German Marshall Fund, Hamburg, Germany, 1997. Author: Social Science Information and Public Policy Making: The Interaction Between Bureaucratic Politics and the Use of Survey Data, 1981; co-author: Government Information Management: A Counter-Report of the Commission on Federal Paperwork, 1980; editor: Translating Evaluation into Policy, 1979, The Knowledge Cycle, 1981, Knowledge, Creation, Diffusion, Utilization, 1979-88, 88-91; co-editor: Competitive Approaches to Health Policy Reform, 1993, Health Policy, Federalism and the Role of the American States, 1996; assoc. editor Society, 1984-88, Evaluation Rev., 1985-89; mem. editl. bd. Policy Studies Rev. Series, 1980-83, Evaluation and Change, 1979-82, Law and Human Behavior, 1983-87; contbr. articles to profl. jours., book chpts. Recipient Emil Limbach Teaching award Carnegie-Mellon U., Sch. Urban and Pub. Affairs, 1985; fellow German Acad. Exch. Program, Fed. Republic Germany, 1971-72, Nat. Opinion Rsch. Ctr. fellow, 1972-73, German Govt. fellow, 1974, Russel Sage Found. Rsch. fellow, 1974-75; vis. scholar Hastings Ctr. for Society, Ethics and Life Scis., 1982. Mem. APA (task force on victims of crime and violence 1982-84), Soc. for Traumatic Stress Studies (bd. dirs. 1980—), World Fedn. for Mental Health (chmn. com. on mental health needs of victims 1985—, vice chmn. 1981-83, Robert F. Rich rsch. ann. award established in his honor, sci. com. on mental health needs of victims 1983), Howard R. Davis Soc. for Knowledge Utilization and Planned Change (pres. 1986-89), Polit. Sci. 400, Policy Studies Assn. (Aaron Wildausky award 1994), Phi Beta Kappa, Sigma Xi, Phi Kappa Phi. Office: U Ill Inst Govt & Pub Affairs 1007 W Nevada St # 204 Urbana IL 61801-3812 also: 815 W Van Buren St Chicago IL 60607-3506 Office Phone: 217-244-8550. Business E-Mail: rrich@law.uluc.edu.

**RICH, ROBERT REGIER,** physician, medical educator, immunologist; b. Newton, Kans., Mar. 7, 1941; s. Eldon Stahly and Margaret Joy (Regier) R.; m. Susan Jepsen Solliday, Mar. 22, 1974; children from previous marriage: Kenneth Eldon, Cathryn Louise; 1 stepchild, Lynn Solliday Todorov. AB, Oberlin Coll., 1962; MD, U. Kans., 1966. Diplomate Am. Bd. Internal Medicine (bd. dirs. 1990-93), Am. Bd. Allergy and Immunology (bd. dirs. 1987-93, chmn. 1991); cert. spl. qualification Diagnostic Lab. Immunology. Intern, resident in internal medicine U. Wash., Seattle, 1966-68; clin. asso., chief clin. asso., sr. staff fellow NIH, Bethesda, Md., 1968-71; research asso. Harvard Med. Sch., Boston, 1971-73; asst. in medicine Peter Bent Brigham Hosp., 1972-73; asst. prof., assoc. prof. microbiology, immunology and internal medicine Baylor Coll. Medicine, Houston, 1973-78, prof., 1978-95, Disting. Svc. prof., 1995—2002, head immunology sect., 1978-98, chief clin. immunology, 1979-91, v.p., dean rsch., 1990-98; exec. assoc. dean, prof. medicine & microbiology/immunology Emory U. Sch. Medicine, 1998—2004; sr. v.p. for medicine, dean Sch. Medicine U. Ala., Birmingham, 2004—. Investigator Howard Hughes Med. Inst., Bethesda, Md., 1977-91; mem. immunobiology study sect. NIH, 1977-81; mem. transplantation biology and immunology com. Nat. Inst. Allergy and Infectious Disease, 1982-86, chmn., 1984-86; mem. nat. rsch. com., 1984-89, chmn., 1986-89, ho. of dels., 1985-91, Blue Ribbon com. on rsch. 2000-01; mem. rsch. adv. com. Nat. Multiple Sclerosis Soc., 1989-94, chmn., 1993-94; adv. panel on rsch. Assn. Am. Med. Coll., 1990—, shared responsibility advocacy com., 1997-98; chmn. ctrs. working group Nat. Inst. Arthritis Musculoskeletal Skin Diseases, 1996-97; mem. nat. human rsch. protections adv. com., dept. health and human svcs., 2000-02; vice chmn. UAB Health Sys., 2004—, bd. dirs.; bd. dirs. Ctr. Infectious Diseases Rsch., Zambia. Associate editor: Jour. Immunology, 1978-82, sect. editor, 1991-96, deputy editor, 1997-2002, editor-in-chief, 2003—; assoc. editor: Jour. Infectious Diseases, 1984-88; adv. editor: Jour. Exptl. Medicine, 1980-84; mem. editl. bd. Jour. Clin. Immunology, 1989-96, Clin. and Exptl. Immunology, 1995-2000; editor-in-chief Clin. Immunology: Principles and Practice, 1996, 2d edit., 2001; contbr. articles to profl. jours. With USPHS, 1968—70. Recipient Rsch. Career Devel. award, NIH, 1975—77, Merit award, 1987. Fellow ACP, Am. Acad. Allergy, Asthma, and Immunology (chmn. basic and clin. immunology interest sect. 1992-93, chmn. profl. edn. com. 1996-98, v.p. 2001-2002), Infectious Diseases Soc. Am.; mem. AMA, AAAS, Am. Bd. Internal Medicine (diplomate, bd. dirs. 1990-93), Am. Bd. Allergy and Immunology (diplomate, bd. dirs. 1987-93), Assn. Am. Physicians, Am. Soc. Clin. Investigation, Am. Assn. Immunologists (chmn. pub. affairs com. 1994-2000, Disting. Svc. award 1999), Am. Assn. Investigative Pathology, Am. Soc. Microbiologists, Am. Fedn. Med. Rsch., Am. Clin. Climatological Assn. (councillor 2001-05), Fedn. Am. Socs. for Exptl. Biology (bd. dirs. 1998-2003, pres. and chmn. bd. dirs. 2001-02), Clin. Immunology Soc. (coun. 1990-96, pres. 1995), Nat. Assn. Biomed. Rsch. (bd. dirs. 2002-05), Assn. for Assessment and Accreditation of Lab. Animal Care Internat. (trustee 2003-05), Alpha Omega Alpha, Sigma Xi. Office: Univ Ala Birmingham Sch Medicine 1530 3d Ave S Birmingham AL 35294-3412 Business E-Mail: rrich@uab.edu.

**RICH, ROBERT STEPHEN,** lawyer; b. NYC, Apr. 30, 1938; s. Maurice H. and Natalie (Priess) R.; m. Myra N. Lakoff, May 31, 1964; children: David, Rebecca, Sarah. AB, Cornell U., 1959; JD, Yale U., 1963. Bar: NY 1964, Colo. 1973, U.S. Tax Ct. 1966, U.S. Supreme Ct. 1967, U.S. Ct. Claims 1968, U.S. Dist. Ct. (so. dist.) N.Y. 1965, U.S. Dist. Ct. (ea. dist.) N.Y. 1965, U.S. Dist. Ct. Colo. 1980, U.S. Ct. Appeals (10th cir.) 1978; conseil juridique, Paris, 1968. Assoc. Shearman & Sterling, N.Y.C., Paris, London, 1963-72; ptnr. Davis, Graham & Stubbs, Denver, 1973—. Adj. faculty U. Denver Law Sch., 1977—; mem. adv. bd. U. Denver Ann. Tax Inst., 1985—, global bus. and culture divsn., U. Denver, 1992—, Denver World Affairs Coun., 1993—;

mem. Colo. Internat. Trade Coun., 1985—; mem. Rocky Mt. Dist. Export Coun., US Dept. Commerce, 1993—; tax adv. com. US Senator Hank Brown; bd. dirs. Clos du Val Wine Co. Ltd., Danskin Cattle Co., Ouray Ranch, Areti Wines, Ltd., Taltarni Vineyards, Christy Sports, others. Contbr. articles to profl. jours. Actor, musician N.Y. Shakespeare Festival, 1960; sponsor Am. Tax Policy Inst., 1991—; adv. bd. Middle Park Land Trust, Granby, Colo., 2003—; pres. So. Boulder Park Ecol. Assn., 1999—; sec. Bhutan Found.; sec., treas. Citizens for Arts to Zoo; bd. dirs. Alliance Francaise, 1977—, Copper Valley Assn., Denver Internat. Film Festival, 1978—79, Anschutz Family Found.; trustee, sec. Denver Art Mus., 1982—; pres., bd. dirs. Ouray Ranch, Granby, Colo., 2001—; bd. dirs. Aspen Music Festival and Sch., 2004—. Capt. U.S. Army, 1959—60. Fellow Am. Coll. Tax. Coun. (bd. regents 10th cir. 1992—), Soc. Fellows Aspen Inst.; mem. ABA, Internat. Bar Assn., Colo. Bar Assn., NY State Bar Assn., Assn. Bar City of NY, Asia-Pacific Lawyers Assn., Union Internat. des Avocats, Internat. Fiscal Assn. (pres. Rocky Mt. br. 1992—, US regional v.p. 1988—), Japan-Am. Soc. Colo. (bd. dirs. 1989—, pres. 1991-93), Confrerie des Chevaliers du Tastevin, Rocky Mt. Wine and Food Soc., Meadowood Club, Denver Club, City Club Denver, Mile High Club, Cactus Club Denver, Yale Club, Denver Tennis Club. Office: Cherry Creek Sta PO Box 61429 Denver CO 80206-8429 also: Antelope Co 555 17th St Ste 2400 Denver CO 80202-3941 Office Phone: 303-299-1230. Personal E-mail: robertrich@compuserve.com. Business E-Mail: robertrich@aya.yale.edu.

**RICH, RONALD LEE,** chemistry professor; b. Washington, Ill., Mar. 29, 1927; s. Rufus Joseph and Lillian May (Lantz) Rich; m. Elaine Horner Sommers, June 14, 1953; children: Jonathan Joseph, Andrew Forrester, Miriam Sommers, Mark Monroe. BS in Math. and Chemistry, Bluffton Coll., 1948; PhD in Chemistry, U. Chgo., 1953. Rsch. fellow Harvard U., Cambridge, Mass., 1963-64; prof. chemistry Bethel Coll., North Newton, Kans., 1964-66, Internat. Christian U., Tokyo, 1966-79; dean acad. affairs Bluffton (Ohio) Coll., 1979-80, scholar in residence, 1981—. Vis. prof. Stanford (Calif.) U., 1974, U. Ill., Urbana, 1975, U. Oreg., Eugene, 1984; electrochemical engr. N.C. State U., Raleigh, 1989—90. Author: Periodic Correlations, 1965; co-author: Chemical English (for Japanese), 1969, 2 vols., 1976; contbr. articles to profl. jours. Mem.: Lima Astron. Soc. (pres. 1995—97). Achievements include a general way to predict boiling points; a qualitative analysis scheme whose groups fit in the periodic chart. Home and Office: 112 S Spring St Bluffton OH 45817-1112

**RICH, S. JUDITH,** public relations executive; b. Chgo., Apr. 14; d. Irwin M. and Sarah I. (Sandock) R. BA, U. Ill., 1960. Staff writer, reporter Economist Newspapers, Chgo., 1960—61; asst. dir. pub. rels. and communications Coun. Profit Sharing Industries, Chgo., 1961—62; dir. advt. and pub. rels. Chgo. Indsl. Dist., 1962—63; account exec., account supr., v.p., sr. v.p., exec. v.p. and nat. creative dir. Edelman Pub. Rels. Worldwide, Chgo., 1963—85; exec. v.p., dir. Ketchum Pub. Rels. Worldwide, Chgo., 1985—89, exec. v.p., exec. creative dir. USA, 1990—97, exec. v.p., chief creative officer worldwide, 1998—2001; pres. Rich Rels A Creativity Consultancy, Chgo., 2002—. Frequent spkr. on creativity and brainstorming; workshop facilitator. Contbr. articles to popular mags. Mem. pub. rels. adv. bd. U. Chgo. Grad Sch. Bus., Roosevelt U., Chgo., DePaul U., Chgo., Gov.'s State U. Recipient Pub. Rels. All-Star award for Creativity, Inside PR mag., 1999. Mem. Pub. Rels. Soc. Am. (Silver Anvil award, judge Silver Anvil awards), Counselors Acad. of Pub. Rels. Soc. Am. (exec. bd.), Chgo. Publicity Club (8 Golden Trumpet awards). Avocations: theater, swimming, bicycling, racquetball. Office: Rich Rels A Creativity Consultancy Ste 2603 2500 N Lakeview Ave Chicago IL 60614

**RICH, SHARON LEE,** financial planner; b. Houston, Sept. 7, 1956; d. Hershel Maurice and Hilda R.; children: Mariah, Sophie. BA, Cornell U., 1977; MAT, U. Chgo., 1978; diploma in fin. planning, Boston U., 1985; EdD, Harvard U., 1986. Registered investment advisor, Mass. High sch. tchr. Clear Lake High Sch., Houston, 1978-80; rschr. Harvard U., Cambridge, Mass., 1981-86; fin. planner, pres. Womoney, Belmont, Mass., 1984—. Instr. Cambridge Ctr. for Adult Edn. Co-author: The Challenges of Wealth, 1988; co-editor: Women's Experience and Education, 1985. Conf. organizer Haymarket People's Fund, Jamaica Plain, Mass., 1988—96; spkr. Pub. Edn. Svcs., Boston, 1984—; organizer, mem. The Consortium, Boston, 1991—99; referral for battered women B'nai Brith Women's Connection Card, Boston, 1991—95; co-founder Pride Planners; treas. Beth El Temple Ctr., Belmont, 1999—2001, trustee, 1999—, chair social action com., budget com.; bd. dirs. Boston Women's Fund, 1988—90, Arsenal Ctr. for the Arts, 2004—06. Named One of Ams. Top Fin. Advisors, Worth Mag., 1994, 96. Mem.: Nat. Assn. Personal Fin. Advisors, Fin. Planners Assn. Avocation: parenting. Office: Womoney 76 Townsend Rd Belmont MA 02478-3435 Business E-Mail: sharon.rich@womoney.com.

**RICH, TARA SCHILLARI,** lawyer; b. Teaneck, NJ, Oct. 22, 1975; d. Frank and Theresa Schillari. BA, Cath. U. Am., 1997; JD, Seton Hall U., 1999. Bar: NJ 1999, U.S. Dist. Ct. (fed. dist.) NJ 1999. Law clk. Judge Lyons-Union County, Elizabeth, NJ, 1999—2000; assoc. Shapiro & Croland, Hackensack, 2000—. Named a NJ Rising Star, 2006. Mem.: ABA, Bergen County Bar Assn., N.J. State Bar Assn. Roman Catholic. Avocations: reading, travel, exercise, home decorating. Office: Shapiro & Croland 411 Hackensack Ave Hackensack NJ 07601 Office Phone: 201-488-3900. E-mail: tschillaririch@shapiro-croland.com.

**RICH, WALTER GEORGE,** railroad transportation executive; b. Oneonta, N.Y., Jan. 9, 1946; s. George C. and Dorretta (Gregg) R.; m. Karine Schmook, July 14, 1990; children: Derik, Stephanie. BA, Syracuse (N.Y.) U., 1968, JD, 1971. Gen. mgr. Delaware Otsego Corp., Oneonta, 1966-68, v.p., gen. mgr., 1968-71, chmn., pres., CEO Cooperstown, NY, 1971— N Y Susquehanna & Western Rwy., Cooperstown, NY, 1980—. Bd. dir. Delaware Otsego Corp., Cooperstown, Security Mut. Life Ins. Co. of N.Y., Energy East Corp., Crucible Materials; mem. N.Y. Pub. Transp. Safety Bd., 1993—; chmn. bd. dirs. Am.Shortline and Regional R.R. Assn., 1999—2004; bd. dirs. Crucible Materials, 2005—. Commr. of elections Delaware County, 1971-78; mem. N.Y. Gov. George Pataki's transition team, 1994; bd. dirs. N.Y. Bus. Devel. Corp., 1995—. Mem. Nat. Rwy. Hist. Soc., Lexington Group in Transp., Ft. Orange Club (Albany), Union League Club (Phila.), Met. Club (N.Y.C.), Binghamton (N.Y.) Club. Episcopalian. Republican. Home: One Lake St Cooperstown NY 13326-1016 Office: NY Susquehanna & Western Rwy 1 Railroad Ave Cooperstown NY 13326-1110 Office Phone: 607-547-2555. E-mail: wrich@nysw.com.

**RICH, WILLIS FRANK, JR.,** banker; b. Ft. Dodge, Iowa, July 26, 1919; s. Willis Frank and Agnes Reed (Paterson) R.; m. Jo Ann Rockwell, Apr. 12, 1947; children: Ronald Rockwell, Roxanne, Andrew Paterson. BA, Princeton U., 1941. Credit analyst Northwestern Nat. Bank, Mpls., 1947-52, asst. cashier, 1952-55, asst. v.p., 1955, v.p., 1955-57; pres. N.W. Nat. Bank, Bloomington-Richfield, Minn., 1952-58, v.p., cashier, 1957-60, v.p. div. A, 1960-68, sr. v.p. nat. and internat. divs., 1968-73, exec. v.p. Mpls., 1973-81, vice chmn. bd. dirs., chief credit officer, 1981-84; fin. cons., 1984—. Dir. Advance Acceptance Corp., 1985-2000. Pres. Viking coun. Boy Scouts Am., 1970-71, trustee found., 1971-86; mem. exec. bd. Minn. Cmty. Rsch. Coun., 1969-77; dir. Minn. Zoo, 1987-95; trustee St. Martin's Found., 1986-90; vestry mem. St. Martin's-By-The-Lake Ch. With AUS, 1941-46. Decorated Bronze Star. Mem. Robert Morris Assocs. (nat. pres. 1977-78), Mpls. Suburban Gyro Club. Clubs: Woodhill, Swan Lake Country. Episcopalian. Home: 378 Waycliffe N Wayzata MN 55391-1390 Personal E-mail: WFRJR@msn.com.

**RICHARD, ALISON FETTES,** anthropology educator; b. Great Britain, Mar. 1, 1948; BA, Cambridge U. 1969; PhD, London U., 1973; PhD (hon.), U. Peking, 2004. Asst. prof. anthropology Yale U., New Haven, 1972-76, assoc. prof. anthropology, 1976-85, prof. anthropology, 1985—2003, provost, 1994—2002, Franklin Muzzy Crosby prof., 1998—2002, prof. emeritus, 2003—; vice-chancellor Univ., Cambridge, 2003—. Dir. Yale Peabody Mus. Natural History, 1990-94. Bd. dir. Yale-New Haven Health Svc., 1994-2002,

World Wildlife Fund, 1995-2004. Decorated officer Nat. Order Madagascar. Mem. Am. Primatological Soc., Am. Assn. Phys. Anthropologists, Am. Anthrop. Assn., Brit. Ecol. Soc., Primate Soc. Gt. Britain, Zool. Soc. London, Cambridge Philosophical Soc. Office: Office of the Vice Chancellor Univ of Cambridge The Old Schools CB2 1TN Cambridge England Office Phone: 44 1223 332290. E-mail: v-c@admin.cam.ac.uk.

**RICHARD, CANDACE L.,** music educator; d. James S. and Nelda M. (Northrup) Terrill; m. Loren D. Richard, July 20, 1974; children: Christopher L., Colby A. MusB in Edn., Emporia State U., 1970; MusM, Kans. State U., 1993. Cert. tchr. Kans. Vocal music tchr. Unified Sch. Dist. 322, Onaga, Kans., 1970—73, Unified Sch. Dist. 457, Garden City, Kans., 1973—76; vocal and instrumental music tchr. Trinity Cath. HS, Hutchinson, Kans., 1982—84; applied vocal music instr. Cloud County CC, Concordia, Kans., 1985—2000; vocal music tchr. Unified Sch. Dist. 333, Concordia, 1990—2000, Unified Sch. Dist. 480, Liberal, Kans., 2000—. Choral clinician, adjudicator, Kans. Bd. dirs. Cmty. Concert Assn., Concordia, 1987—2000, Liberal, 2000—04, Live on Stage II, 2000—. Mem.: NEA, Music Edn. Nat. Conf., Seward County Hist. Soc., DAR, PEO, Delta Kappa Gamma. Lutheran. Avocation: genealogy.

**RICHARD, EDWARD H.,** manufacturing executive, retired municipal official; b. Mar. 15, 1937; s. Henry and Ida Richard. BA, Antioch Coll., 1959. Pres., chmn., bd. dirs. Magnetics Internat. Inc., Maple Heights, Ohio, 1967-86; exec. v.p. Stearns Magnetics S.A., Brussels, Belgium, 1974-77; prin. Edward H. Richard & Assocs., Cleve., 1967-96; pres., treas. David Round & Son, Inc., Cleve. Chmn. Cleve. dist. adv. council Small Bus. Adminstrn., 1975-79; past nat. adv. council Dept. Treasury; cons. and advisor in field; del. world trade fairs. Former trustee Regional Econ. Devel. Coun., Met. Cleve. Jobs. Coun., Cleve. Devel. Found., Cleve. BBB; former trustee Hiram House, Antioch U., former treas., 1972-77; N.E. Ohio Regional Sewer Dist., Greater Cleve. Domed Stadium Corp., Greater Cleve. Conv. and Visitor Bur.; former trustee, vice-chmn. Cleve. Ctr. Econ. Edn.; former pres. Bratenahl Condominium Assn.; chmn. fin. com. Bratenahl Bd. Edn., 1971-75; trustee, chmn. nominating com.; exec. com. La Jolla Playhouse; CFO Mainly Mozart Festival, 1998—; CFO, chmn. bd. orch. rels. com., exec. com., fin. com., trustee San Diego Symphony Orch.

**RICHARD, ELLEN,** theater executive; b. Bridgeport, Conn., Dec. 12, 1957; d. Laurent and Anne (Markham) R. Bus. mgr. Atlas Scenic Studio, Bridgeport, 1977-82; theater mgr. Stamford (Conn.) Ctr. for Arts, 1980-83; bus. mgr. Westport (Conn.) Country Playhouse, 1982-84; gen. mgr. Roundabout Theatre Co. Inc., N.Y.C., 1983—; dir. design and constrn. Am. Airlines Theatre, Studio 54, Harold and Mirium Steinberg Ctr. Theatre, Laurel Pels Theatre, various Broadway Theatres. Dir. design and constrn. Am. Airlines Theatre, Studio 54, Harold and Miriam Steinberg Ctr. for Theatre, Laura Pels Theatre, Broadway theatres. Mng. dir.: (Broadway plays) A View From the Bridge, 1997-98 (Tony award Revival of a Play 1998), Cabaret, 1998-2004 (Tony award Revival of a Musical 1998), The Deep Blue Sea, 1998, Side Man, 1998-99 (Tony award Best Play 1999), Little Me, 1998-1999, Death of a Salesman, 1999, The Lion in Winter, 1999, The Rainmaker, 1999-2000, Uncle Vanya, 2000, The Man Who Came to Dinner, 2000, Betrayal, 2000-01, Design for Living, 2001, Major Barbara, 2001, The Women, 2001-02, An Almost Holy Picture, 2002, The Crucible, 2002, The Man Who Had All the Luck, 2002, An Evening with Mario Cantone, 2002, The Boys from Syracuse, 2002, Tartuffe, 2003, A Day in the Death of Joe Egg, 2003, As Long As We Both Shall Laugh, 2003, Nine, 2003 (Tony award Best Revival of a Musical, 2003), The Look of Love, 2003, "MASTER HAROLD"...and the boys, 2003, Big River, 2003, The Caretaker, 2003-04, Twentieth Century, 2004, Assassins, 2004 (Tony award Best Revival of a Musical, 2004); prodr.: Sideman, 1999 (Tony award New Play). Mem. NY Cycling Club. Avocations: bicycling, antiques, art, sailing. Office: 203 Brewster St Bridgeport CT 06605-3112 Personal E-mail: ellrch2@aol.com.

**RICHARD, HOWARD M.,** lawyer; b. Oak Park, Ill., Sept. 20, 1944; BA, Cornell U., 1965; LLB, Harvard U., 1968. Bar: Ill. 1968. Ptnr. Katten Muchin Rosenman, Chgo. Bd. editors Harvard Law Rev., 1967-68. Mem. ABA (sect. real property, probate and trust law), Chgo. Bar Assn. Office: Katten Muchin Rosenman 525 W Monroe St Ste 1900 Chicago IL 60661-3693 Office Phone: 312-902-5219. Office Fax: 312-577-8670. E-mail: howard.richard@kattenlaw.com.

**RICHARD, JEAN-FRANCOIS,** education educator, consultant; b. Uccle, Belgium, Feb. 10, 1943; s. Marcel Richard and Anne De Brouwer; m. Colette Dubois, Sept. 2, 1967; children: Oliver M., Tanguy C. PhD in Econs., Cath. U. of Louvain, Belgium, 1973. Lic. Physics Cath. U. of Louvain (Belgium), 1965. Vis. lectr. London Sch. of Econs., 1973—74; assoc. prof. Cath. U. of Louvain, Belgium, 1973—78, prof., 1978—88; vis. Belgian prof. U. of London, London, 1984—85; prof. Duke U., Durham, NC, 1988—91, U. of Pitts., 1991—98; univ. prof. U. Pitts., 1998—. Assoc. editor Econometrica, Evanston, Ill., 1979—84; asst. editor Rev. of Econ. Studies, Oxford, England, 1982—85; rsch. dir. Ctr. for Ops. Rsch. & Econometrics, Louvain-la-Neuve, Belgium, 1983—86; assoc. editor Jour. of Econometrics, Amsterdam, Netherlands, 1990—93; chmn. dept. of econs. U. of Pitts., 2000—. Author: Posterior And Predictive Densities For Simultaneous Equation Models, 1973, Bayesian inference in dynamic econometric models, 1999; contbr. articles to profl. jours. Pres. Royal Automobile Club Jr., Brussels, 1964—66; cub scout leader Brussels, 1958—61. Instr. Royal Cadet Sch., 1962—63, Brussel, Belgium. Recipient Chevalier, Ordre de Leopold (Belgium), 1989, Marschack Lectr., Econometric Soc., 1999, Auger lectr., Societe Canadienne d'economie, 1999; grantee Rsch. Grants, NSF, 1987—, Rsch. Grant, Pew Charitable Trust, 1988—90, Ford Found., 1989—91; W. Hallam Tuck Fellow, Belgian Am. Edul. Found., 1968. Fellow: Econometric Soc., mem. Am. Stat. Assn. Roman Catholic. Achievements include research in weak exogeneity, encompassing, importance sampling, empirical auction models, Monte Carlo simulation, constrained strategic equilibrium, GDP forecasting. Avocations: model train collecting, stamp collecting/philately, jogging, bicycling, skying. Home: 4107 Bigelow Blvd Pittsburgh PA 15213-1407 Office: Pitts U WWPH Bouquet St Pittsburgh PA 15260 Office Phone: 1-412-648-1750. Office Fax: 1-412-648-7038. Personal E-mail: fantin+@pitt.edu.

**RICHARD, LOREN DRU,** bank executive; b. Ellsworth, Kans., Feb. 12, 1947; s. Loren Clarence and Drucilla Ruth Richard; m. Candace Leigh Terrill, July 20, 1974; children: Christopher Loren, Colby Alexander. BS, Kans. State U., Manhattan, 1970. HS agr. instr., Garden City, Kans., 1972—75; field rep. Evans Grain Co., Garden City, 1975—76; asst. v.p. Fidelity State Bank, Garden City, 1977—80; agr. loan officer Hutchinson Nat. Bank, Kans., 1980—84; sr. v.p. UMB Bank, Concordia, Kans., 1984—2000, Cmty. Bank, Liberal, Kans., 2000—. Pres. Kans. Bankers Assn. Bank Agr. Reps., 1984—85; chmn. agr. com. Kans. Bankers Assn., 1984—85; mem. adv. bd. UMB, Concordia, 1998—2000. Chmn. agr. com. C. of C., Liberal, 2003—04; v.p. Crossroads Ctr., Liberal, 2005—06; chmn. Luth. Ch. Coun., Liberal, 2005—06. 1st lt. U.S. Army, 1970—72. Mem.: Kans. Agr. Bankers, Am. Quarter Horse Assn., Lions (Liberal club 2006, pres. Concord Club 1988). Office: The Cmty Bank Liberal KS 67905 Office Phone: 620-624-6898. Office Fax: 620-624-2381. E-mail: dru@communitybankliberal.com.

**RICHARD, ROBERT CARTER,** psychologist; b. Waterloo, Iowa, Apr. 4, 1938; s. Quentin Leroy and Adeline Pauline (Halverson) R.; m. Shirley Ruth Jones, Aug. 25, 1962 (div. Mar. 1999); children: David, John; m. Jacqueline J. Mendes, Feb. 19, 2000; stepchildren: Julianna Mendes, Katherine Mendes BA Wheaton (Ill.) Coll., 1960; BD, Fuller Theol. Sem., 1963, PhD, 1973; STM, Andover Newton Theol. Sch., 1964. Ordained to ministry Am. Bapt. Conv., 1963; lic. psychologist, Calif. Pastor Peninsula Bapt. Ch., Gig Harbor, Wash., 1965-68; marriage and family counselor Glendale (Calif.) Family Svc., 1970-71; psychol. asst. Oakland and Pleasant Hill, Calif., 1972—73; psychologist Rafa Counseling Ctr., Pleasant Hlll, 1974—2006; ret. Mem. faculty John F. Kennedy U., Orinda, Calif., 1975-78; adj. faculty mem. New Coll., Berkeley, Calif. 1986; mem. dean's adv. coun. Sch. Psychology, Fuller Theol. Sem., 2005—; co-founder, bd. dirs. New Directions Counseling Ctr.,

1974-81; rschr. assertiveness tng., lay counselor tng., psychotherapy and religious experience, treatment of adults abused as children. Author: (with Deacon Anderson) The Way Back: A Christian's Journey to Mental Wholeness, 1989; contbr. articles to profl. publs. Recipient Integration of Psychology and Theology award, 1973. Mem.: APA, Christian Assn. Psychol. Studies, Contra Costa Psychol. Assn. (past pres.), Calif. Psychol. Assn. Republican. Avocations: boating, astronomy, photography, art, tennis. Office: Rafa Counseling Ctr 101 Gregory Ln Ste 33 Pleasant Hill CA 94523-4915 Office Phone: 925-827-9876. E-mail: robertcrichard@cs.com.

**RICHARD, STELLA MARIE SCHWARZ,** veterinary science professor; b. Phila., Feb. 15, 1967; m. Richard. AS, Colo. Mountain Coll., Colenwood Springs, 1990; BS, Ariz. State U., Tempe, 1992; M in Zoology, Ariz. State U., 1994; MEd, Assumption Coll., Worcester, Mass., 1999. Prof. Becker Coll., Worcester, 1994—. Mem. adv. bd. vet. tech. Tufts U., Grafton, Mass. Contbr. articles to profl. jours. Mem.: AALAS, AVTE, IACUC, Gt. Ape Soc. Avocation: outdoor activities. Office: Baker Coll 61 Sever St Worcester MA 01609 Office Phone: 508-791-9241 ext 505. E-mail: srichard@beckercollege.edu.

**RICHARD, VIRGINIA RYNNE,** lawyer; b. Mt. Vernon, N.Y., Aug. 6, 1943; m. Peter L. Richard. BA, Manhattanville Coll., 1965; LLB, NYU, 1969. Bar: N.Y. 1969, Colo. 1973, U.S. Supreme Ct. 1992. Pvt. practice, Denver, 1973-75; assoc. Kane, Dalsimer, Sullivan, N.Y.C., 1970-72, 76-82, ptnr., 1982—99, Winston & Strawn LLP, N.Y.C., 1999—, mem. exec. com., chair IP practice group. Chmn. trademark appeals com. Fed. Cir. Bar Assn., 1991-93; spkr. in field. Mem. editl. bd. Trademark Reporter, 1988-89; contbr. articles to profl. jours. Mem. ABA, Internat. Trademark Assn., U.S. Trademark Assn. (trademark reporter, mem. editorial bd., chmn. subcom. 1982-87), N.Y. Patent, Trademark and Copyright Lawyers Assn., NY Intellectual Property Law Assn. (chair copyright law com. 1994-96). Office: Winston & Strawn LLP 200 Park Ave New York NY 10166-4193 Office Phone: 212-294-4639. Office Fax: 212-294-4700. Business E-Mail: vrichard@winston.com.

**RICHARDS, ANN,** actress, educator, poet; b. Sydney; came to U.S., 1942; d. Mortimer Delaforce and Marion Bradshaw (Dive) Richards; m. Edmond J. Angelo, Feb. 4, 1949 (dec. Mar. 1983); children: Christopher E., Mark R., Juliet M.; m. Paul M. Kramer, Feb. 14, 1987 (dec. Aug. 1996). Student, Stotts Coll., 1936-37, Studio Sch. of Drama, 1936-38. Actress Cinesound Studio, Australia, 1936-42, Metro-Goldwyn Mayer, 1942-45, Hall Wallis-Paramount, 1945-47, R.K.O., 1947, Eagle-Lion Studios, 1947-48, Edmond Angelo Prodns., 1953, Anthony Buckley Prodns., Australia, 1995. Poetry reader with Robert Pinsky's nat. program Lib. of Congress Bicentennial Project, 1999. Author: The Grieving Senses, 1971, Odyssey for Edmond, 1996, New Poems-Old Themes, 1997; contbr. poetry to anthology Poetry From the Art, 1999; actress films including An American Romance, Love Letters, The Searching Wind, Badman's Territory, Sorry, Wrong Number, Lost Honeymoon, Breakdown, Don't Call Me Girlie, Celluloid Heroes, 1994-95; appearances TV program, film, and tape maker Australia, Time Life Assocs., 1977. Vice pres. Tchr. Rememberance Day Found., 1952—; internat. chmn. Apple of Gold Edn. awards, 1953—. Recipient meritorious svc. citation Govs. of Great Britain, U.S., New Zealand, Australia, 1939-46, Star Pattern award Inst. Profl. Direction, 1951, Cert. of Appreciation award Literacy is Reading Program, 1997, Edward Dean Mus., 1996. Mem. AAUW, Nat. Mus. Women in Arts, San Gorgonio Poets Soc., San Gorgonio Artists Soc., Zeta Phi Eta (v.p. nat. coun. 1970-73).

**RICHARDS, ANN ADAIR,** psychologist; b. Tulsa, Okla., Jan. 28, 1949; d. William Jenkins and Virginia Ann (Daniels) Richards; 1 child, Desiree Ann Perkins. BS in bus. edn., U. Okla., 1970; BA in theatre arts, U. No. Colo., 1983, MA in agy. counseling, 1985, EdS, 2002. Nationally Certified School Psychologist, lic. Professional Counselor Colo. Regulatory Bd. Workshop coord. Rocky Mtn. Planned Parenthood, Denver, 1977—79; para profl., remedial reading Denver Pub. Schools, 1979—80; generalist clinician Centennial Mental Health Ctr., 1986—95; children and family therapist No. Range Behavior Health, Greely, Colo., 1995—99; pvt. practice Greely, 1999—2000; sch. psychologist intern Northeast Bd. Cooperative Ednl. Svcs., Haxton, Colo., 2000—01; sch. psychologist East Ctrl. Bd. Cooperative Ednl. Svcs., Limon, Colo., 2001—. Mem. crisis response team Colo. Soc. Sch. Psychologists, 2004—; crisis response coord. East Ctrl. Bd. Cooperative Ednl. Svcs., 2001—; chair and vice chair Logan County Sexual Assault Team, Sterling, Colo., 1989—95. Spl. olympics vol. Sterling H.S., 1992—94; bd. mem. Yuma Cmty. Resource Ctr., Yuma, Colo., 1986—88; bdm. mem. Help for Abused Ptnrs., Sterling, Colo., 1989—95, sec., 1989—95; com. mem. Arts Picnic, Greeley, Colo., 1983. Recipient Women of the Yr., Beta Sigma Phi Social Svc. Sorority, 2000, Scholarship, Am. Assn. of U. Women; Circle Key Alumni grant, Kappa Kappa Gamma Found., 1994, 1995, Mildred Guch Scholarship, U. No. Colo., 1984—85. Mem.: Colo. Soc. Sch. Psychologists, Nat. Assn. Sch. Psychologist. Democrat. Luth. Avocations: weightlifting, aerobics, movies, reading, interior decorating. Home: 15400 CR L Box 180 Woodrow CO 80757 Office: East Ctrl Bd Ednl Svcs 820 2d St Limon CO 80828

**RICHARDS, AUSTIN AMES,** physicist, artist; s. Peter Ames Richards and Virginia Rotan Youngren, William Thomas Harvey Youngren (Stepfather) and Caroline Frick Richards; m. Victoria Charters, Apr. 14, 2006. PhD, U. Calif. Berkeley, 1995. Prin. scientist Wyatt Tech. Corp., Santa Barbara, Calif., 1998—99; sr. rsch. scientist FLIR Systems, Indigo Ops., Goleta, 1999—. Adj. prof. Brooks Inst. Photography, Santa Barbara, Calif., 2004—. Author: (non-fiction book) Alien Vision: Exploring the Electromagnetic Spectrum with Imaging Technology (Book Pub. by SPIE Optical Engring. Press as a tech. monograph, 2001). Libertarian. Achievements include patents pending for Extending dynamic range of NIR/SWIR infrared cameras.

**RICHARDS, BERNARD,** investment company executive; b. NYC, July 12, 1927; s. Charles and Sadie (Rubin) R.; m. Arlene Kaye, Dec. 23, 1948; children: Carol Leslie, Patricia Ellen, Lori Gale. BBA, Baruch Coll., 1949. CPA, NY. Acct. Eisner & Lubin, N.Y.C., 1949-53, S.D. Leidesdorf, N.Y.C., 1953-56; from contr. to treas. to v.p. fin. to pres. Slattery Group Inc., N.Y.C., 1956-87; pres. Slattery Investors Corp., N.Y.C., 1988—; chmn. bd. dirs. Slattery Assocs., Inc., N.Y.C., 1968-87. Trustee Temple Sinai, Roslyn, NY, 1969-89; bd. dirs. Variety Boys Club, Queens, NY, 1972-96; bd. dirs. NYC Indsl. Devel. Bd., 1973-76; bd. dirs. Baruch Coll. Fund, NYC, 1975—, pres., 1996-98. Recipient Heavy Constrn. award United Jewish Appeal, 1980, Pres.'s medal Baruch Coll., 1989; named Oustanding Alumnus of Yr. Baruch Coll., 1979, Man of Yr. United Jewish Appeal, 1980, March of Dimes, 1983, Man of Yr. Baruch Coll. Fund, 1972; Wood fellow Baruch Coll., 1979. Mem. AICPA, N.Y. State Soc. CPAs, Moles, Beavers (bd. dirs. 1982-96), Shelter Rock Tennis Club. Republican. Jewish. Avocations: tennis, travel, bicycling, swimming, hiking. Home: 18 Applegreen Dr Old Westbury NY 11568-1203 Office: Slattery Investors Corp 1 Hollow Ln Ste 311 New Hyde Park NY 11042-1215

**RICHARDS, BILL ARTHUR,** artist, educator; b. Bklyn., Sept. 19, 1944; s. Donald F. and Mildred (Pedersen) R.; m. Judith Fonda Olch, May 2, 1971. BFA, Pratt Inst., 1966; MA, U. Iowa, 1968; MFA, U. N.Mex., 1970. Instr. Sch Visual Arts, NYC, 1977-79, Parsons Sch. Design, 1986-99. Ad. asst. prof. art SUNY, Purchase, 1977—78; adj. asst. prof. fine arts Pratt Inst., Bklyn., 1999—. One-man shows include Irwin Tuttle Gallery, Dallas, 1973, Nancy Hoffman Gallery, N.Y.C., 1980, 85, 89, 96, 2003, Allen R. Hite Inst., U. Louisville, 1983, Moravian Coll., Pa., 1985, Union County Coll., Cranford, N.J., 1986. Fellow NEA, 1977-78, Creative Artists Pub. Svc. Program, 1975-76. Home: Apt 2B 575 Avenue Of The Americas New York NY 10011-2029

**RICHARDS, BRAD,** professional hockey player; b. Murray Harbour, Prince Edward Island, May 2, 1980; Player Rimouski Oceanic (QMJHL), 1998—2000, Tampa Bay Lightning, 2000—. Player Team Can., World

Championships, 2001; mem. Team Can., World Cup of Hockey, 2004. Named to, NHL All-Rookie Team, 2000; recipient Conn Smythe Trophy, 2004, Lady Byng Trophy, 2004. Achievements include being a member of Stanley Cup Champion Tampa Bay Lightning, 2004; being a member of World Cup Champion Team Canada, 2004. Office: c/o Tampa Bay Lightning 401 Channelside Dr Tampa FL 33602

**RICHARDS, BRIAN F.,** lawyer; b. Oaklawn, Ill., Jan. 23, 1967; BS, U. Ill., 1989; JD, U. Va., 1992. Bar: Ill. 1992. Ptnr., co-chair Mergers and Acquisitions Practice Katten Muchin Zavis Rosenman, Chgo. Office: Katten Muchin Zavis Rosenman 525 W Monroe St Chicago IL 60661 Office Phone: 312-902-5234. Office Fax: 312-577-8764. E-mail: brian.richards@kmzr.com.

**RICHARDS, CARLYLE EDWARD,** lawyer; b. Deadwood, S.D., July 21, 1935; BA, Northwestern U., 1957; LLB, U. S.D., 1960. Bar: S.D. 1960. Law clk. to judge U.S. Dist. Ct., 1960-61; pvt. practice Aberdeen, SD, 1961—; U.S. magistrate, 1971-2000. Mem. S.D. Bar Assn., Brown County Bar Assn. Office: 222 Midwest Bldg Aberdeen SD 57401 Address: PO Box 114 Aberdeen SD 57402-0114

**RICHARDS, CARMELEETE A.,** computer company executive, network administrator, consultant; b. Springport, Ind., Feb. 8, 1948; d. Gordon K. and Virginia Christine (New) Brown; 1 child, Annasheril. AA in Elem. Edn., No. Okla. Coll., 1969; BS in Edn., Southwestern State Coll., Weatherford, Okla., 1971; postgrad., Ashland (Ohio) Coll., 1981—. U. Phoenix, 1994—; MEd in Instrnl. Design, Am. Intercontinental U., 2004. Cert. tchr. Ohio. 6th grade tchr., Scott City, Kans., 1971; salesperson, customer svc. Jafra Cosmetics, 1979-81; br. asst. mgr. Barclays Am. Fin., Columbus, 1981-84; tng. mgr., ednl. dir. Computer Depot, Columbus, Ohio, 1984-85; corp. trainer, exec. sales Litel Telecommunications, Worthington, Ohio, 1985-87; communications cons. Telemarketing Communications of Columbus, Ohio, 1988-89; corp. computer tng. O/E Learning, Troy, Mich., 1989-98; corp. computer trainer ETOP Cols., Ohio, 1989—; dist. asst. network adminstr. Bexley Sch. Dist., 1998-99; dir. tech., computer instr. MCS, 2001—02; info. tech. specialist, trainer Franklin County Common Pleas Ct., 2002—. Pres. PTA, 1981—82. Recipient Outstanding Participation award Dorothy Carnegie Pub. Speaking; winner Ms. Ohio Beauties of Am. Pageant, 1991. Mem. IEEE, NAFE, Am. Soc. for Tng. and Devel., Columbus Computer Soc., Kappa Delta Pi. Baptist. Avocations: western square dancing, bowling, boating, reading, hiking. Office Phone: 614-462-6792. Personal E-mail: bkar10@yahoo.com.

**RICHARDS, CAROL ANN RUBRIGHT,** retired editor, retired journalist; b. Buffalo, Sept. 24, 1944; d. Jesse Bailey and Emma Amanda (Fisher) Rubright; m. Clay F. Richards, Aug. 12, 1967; children: Elizabeth Amanda, Rebecca Diana. BA, Syracuse U., 1966. Reporter Rochester (N.Y.) Times-Union, 1966; legis. corr. Gannett News Svc., Albany, NY, 1967-73, White House corr. Washington, 1974-76, regional/nat. editor, 1979-84; founding editor USA Today, Arlington, Va., 1982, mem. editl. bd., 1985-87; dep. editor editl. page Newsday, Melville, NY, 1987—2006; ret., 2006. Adj. prof. journalism Hofstra U., Hempstead, NY; freelance editor. Pres. Washington Press Club, 1981-82. Mem: Women's Press Club N.Y. (named to Hall of Honor 2003), Nat. Press Club. Home: 352 Scudder Ave Northport NY 11768-3021 Office: Newsday 235 Pinelawn Rd Melville NY 11747-4250 Office Phone: 631-896-4571. Business E-mail: carol.richards@yahoo.com.

**RICHARDS, CECILE,** healthcare network executive; b. 1958; d. Ann Richards; married; 3 children. Grad., Brown U., 1980. Dep. chief of staff to Rep. Nancy Pelosi US Ho. Reps., Washington; founder, pres. America Votes, Washington, 2003—06; pres. Planned Parenthood Fedn. of Am., Inc., NYC, 2006—. Bd. dirs. NARAL Pro-Choice Am., Planned Parenthood Action Fund; founder, bd. dirs. Tex. Freedom Network, 1995. Democrat. Office: Planned Parenthood Fedn Am Inc 434 W 33rd St New York NY 10001-2601 Office Phone: 212-541-7800. Office Fax: 212-245-1845.*

**RICHARDS, CHRISTINE P.,** transportation services executive; b. Amityville, NY, Jan. 8, 1955; BA magna cum laude, Bucknell U., 1976; JD, Duke U., 1979. Bar: Tenn. 1987, NC 1980. Joined FedEx Corp., 1984, corp. v.p. customer and bus. transactions & gen. counsel FedEx Corp. Services, exec. v.p., gen. counsel, sec., 2005—. Office: FedEx Corp 942 S Shady Grove Rd Memphis TN 38120 Office Phone: 901-818-7500. Office Fax: 901-395-2000.

**RICHARDS, DAVID A.J.,** law educator; b. 1944; AB, Harvard U., 1966, JD, 1971; PhD in Moral and Polit. Philosophy, Oxford U., Eng., 1970. Bar: NY, 1972. Assoc. Cleary, Gottlieb, Steen & Hamilton, NYC, 1971-74; assoc. prof. Fordham U., NYC, 1974-77; vis. assoc. prof. philosophy Barnard Coll., NYC, 1974-77; assoc. prof. law NYU Sch. Law, 1977-79, prof. law, 1979—, Edwin D. Webb prof. law, 1994—. Author: A Theory of Reasons for Action, 1971, The Moral Criticism of Law, 1977, Sex, Drugs, Death and the Law, 1982, Toleration and the Constitution, 1986, Foundations of American Constitutionalism, 1989, Conscience and the Constitution, 1993, Women, Gays and the Constitution, 1998, Italian American: The Racializing of an Ethnic Identity, 1999, Identity and the Case for Gay Rights, 1999, Free Speech and the Politics of Identity, 1999. Rockefeller grantee Austinian Soc. and Ctr. for Study of Law and Soc., Berkeley, Calif., 1974; Knox Meml. Fellow, 1966-68; Humanities Fellow Aspen Inst., 1979. Fellow NYU Soc. Fellows; mem. Soc. for Philosophy and Pub. Affairs (bd. dirs. NY chpt. 1975-76), Am. Soc. Polit. and Legal Philosophy (v.p. 1984), Austinian Soc. (pres. 1974) Clubs: Tuesday Evening. Office: NYU Sch Law Vanderbilt Hall Rm 421 40 Washington Sq S New York NY 10012-1099 Office Phone: 212-998-6251. E-mail: david.richards@nyu.edu.

**RICHARDS, DAVID ALAN,** lawyer; b. Dayton, Ohio, Sept. 21, 1945; s. Charles Vernon and Betty Ann (Macher) R.; m. Marianne Catherine Del Monaco, June 26, 1971; children: Christopher, Courtney. BA summa cum laude, Yale U., 1967, JD, 1972; MA, Cambridge U., Eng., 1969. Bar: N.Y. 1973. Assoc. Paul, Weiss, Rifkind, Wharton & Garrison, N.Y.C., 1972-77, Coudert Bros., N.Y.C., 1977-80, ptnr., 1981-82; ptnr., head real estate group Sidley & Austin, N.Y.C., 1983-2000; ptnr. McCarter & English, N.Y.C., 2001—, mng. ptnr. N.Y. office, 2002—. Gov. Anglo-Am. Real Property Inst. U.S./U.K., 1983-88, chair, 1993; mem. Chgo. Title N.Y. Realty Adv. Bd., 1992—. Co-editor: Kipling and His First Publisher, 2001; co-author: The Commercial Office Lease Handbook, 2003; contbr. articles to profl. jours. Trustee Scarsdale Pub. Libr., 1984-89, pres., 1988-89; co-chair N.Y. Lawyers for Clinton/Gore, 1996. Fellow Am. Bar Found.; mem. ABA (real property, probate and trust sect., coun. 1982-88, chair 1991-92), Am. Coll. Real Estate Lawyers (gov. 1987-93), Assn. of Bar of City of N.Y. (real property com. 1978-80, 84-87), Century Assn., Kipling Soc. (N.Am. rep., v.p. 2005—), Assn. Fellows of Morgan Libr., Shenorock Shore Club (Rye, N.Y.), The Grolier Club (N.Y.C., coun. 2003—, sec. 2006-), Yale Club (N.Y.C.), Yale Libr. Assn. (trustee 2003—). Democrat. Home: 18 Forest Ln Scarsdale NY 10583-6464 Office: McCarter & English 245 Park Ave Fl 27 New York NY 10167 Office Phone: 212-609-6817. E-mail: darichards21@aol.com, drichards@mccarter.com.

**RICHARDS, DAVID GLEYRE,** German language educator; b. July 27, 1935; s. Oliver L. and Lilian Marie (Powell) R.; m. Annegret Horn, Sept. 3, 1959 (div. 1992); 1 child, Stephanie Suzanne; m. Friederike Hensler, Oct. 11, 1997. BA, U. Utah, 1960, MA, 1961; PhD, U. Calif., Berkeley, 1968. Asst. prof. German SUNY, Buffalo, 1968, assoc. prof., 1974—84, prof., 1984—99, chair dept., 1986—92, prof. emeritus, 1999—. Author: Georg Buchners Woyzeck, 1975, George Buchner and the Birth of the Modern Drama, 1976, The Hero's Quest for the Self: An Archetypal Approach to Hesse's Demian and other Novels, 1987; editor: (with H. Schulte) Crisis and Culture in Post-Enlightenment Germany: Essays in Honor of Peter Heller, 1993, Exploring the Divided Self: Hermann Hesse's Steppenwolf and its Critics, 1996, Georg Büchner's Woyzeck: A History of Its Criticism, 2001. SUNY grantee, 1973; NEH grantee, 1977-78, Fulbright Commnr. grantee, 1980. Rsch. Found. of SUNY fellow, 1982. Democrat. Avocation: photography. Personal E-mail: dgrich@nc.rr.com.

**RICHARDS, DENISE,** actress; b. Downers Grove, Ill., Feb. 17, 1971; m. Charlie Sheen, June 15, 2002 (separated 2006); children: Sam, Lola. Former model. Actor: (films) Loaded Weapon 1, 1993, Nowhere, 1997, Starship Troopers, 1997, Wild Things, 1998, Lookin' Italian, 1998, Drop Dead Gorgeous, 1999, The World is Not Enough, 1999, Tail Lights Fade Away, 1999, Valentine, 2001, Good Advice, 2001, Empire, 2002, Undercover Brother, 2002, The Third Wheel, 2002, You Stupid Man, 2002, Love Actually, 2003, Scary Movie 3, 2003; (TV films) 919 5th Avenue, 1995, In the Blink of an Eye, 1996, Pier 66, 1996, (guest appearances): (TV series) Spin City, Melrose Place. Office: 722 Elvira Ave #A Redondo Beach CA 90277*

**RICHARDS, ERIC ALBERT STEPHAN,** lawyer; b. Detroit, Jan. 1, 1965; s. June Hill. BA, Yale Coll., 1986; JD cum laude, Harvard U., 1989. Bar: Calif. 1989, US Ct. Appeals (9th Cir.) 1989, US Dist. Ct. (Ctrl. Dist. Calif.) 1989. With O'Melveny & Myers, LA, 1989—, assoc., ptnr., mem. policy com., mem. project development practice group, mem., 1940 Act Practice group, active with joint venture and corp. combinations. Mem.: LA County Bar Assn., Nat. Bar. Assn., ABA. Office: O'Melveny & Myers LLP 400 S Hope St Los Angeles CA 90071-2899

**RICHARDS, FEMI SOYINKA,** lawyer; b. Pontiac, Mich., Aug. 29, 1971; s. Josephus and Laura Richards; m. Nettie Mahone, Mar. 23, 2002. Master of Pub. Policy, Harvard U., Cambridge, MA, 1997—99; JD, U of Conn. Sch. of Law, Hartford, CT, 1994—97; BA, U. of Mass. - Amherst, Amherst, MA, 1989—94. Connecticut Bar: Conn. 1997, District of Columbia Bar: DC 2002. Assoc. Holland & Knight, LLP, Washington, 2001—; sr. policy analyst Ct. Services and Offender Supervision Agy. for the DC, Washington, 1999—2001. Contbr. journal. Multiculturalism and the Democratic State: Three Frameworks for Social Equity. Public Integrity. Spring 2000. Volume 2. Number 2, journal. Sports and the Socialization of Women. Five College Journal of Law and Society. Spring 1993. Volume 1. Number 2. Recipient Outstanding Performance Award, Ct. Services and Offender Supervision Agy., 2000, Manuel C. Carballo Meml. Prize, John F. Kennedy Sch. of Govt., Harvard U., 1999, Cali Excellence for the Future Award, U. of Conn. Sch. of Law, 1997, Round Robin Moot Ct. Competition Best Brief, Nova Southeastern U. Sch. of Law, 1997, Best Oral Adv., Alva P. Loiselle Moot Ct. Competition, U. of Conn. Sch. of Law, 1995, Academic Achievement Award, U. of Mass., Black Student Union, 1993. Mem.: Acad. of Polit. Sci. (assoc.), ASPA (assoc.), Conn. Bar Assn. (assoc.), DC Bar Assn. (assoc.), ABA (assoc.), Harvard Club of Wash., DC (assoc.), D-Liberal. Avocations: basketball, travel. Home: 98 East Wayne Avenue Silver Spring MD 20901 Office: Holland & Knight LLP 2099 Pennsylvania Avenue NW Washington DC 20006 Personal E-mail: frichards_mpp99@post.harvard.edu. E-mail: fsrichar@hklaw.com.

**RICHARDS, GALE LEE,** communications educator; b. Long Run, W.Va., July 31, 1918; s. Robert Amaziah and Edna Jane (Scott) R.; m. Barbara Lee Neely, Apr. 19, 1944; children: Robin Lee, Wendell Scott, Jeffrey Marshall. BA (Pixley scholar), U. Akron, 1940; MA (C.S. Knight Meml. scholar), U. Ia., 1942, PhD, 1950. Instr. speech U. Akron, 1941-42; asst. prof. speech Drake U., 1947-48; asst. prof. English U. Nev., 1948-52; asst. prof. speech U. Wash., 1952-58; assoc. prof. speech U. So. Calif., 1958-65; prof. communication Ariz. State U., Tempe, 1965—, chmn. dept. speech and theatre, 1965-73. Pub. relations cons. Red Feather campaign United Fund, Los Angeles, 1955-58; mgmt. and tng. cons. various profl. and comml. orgns., 1955— Cons. editor: Western Speech, 1957-61, 62-65, 69-72, Jour. of Communication, 1961-67; Contbr. articles profl. jours. Bd. dirs. Phoenix Little Theatre. Served to lt. USNR, 1942-45, PTO. Recipient Distinguished Alumni award Radio Sta. WSUI, 1942 Mem. We. States Communication Assn. (adminstrv. coun., legis. coun., chair commn. on Am. Parliamentary procedure, 1988, emeritus 1991), Internat. Communication Assn. (adminstrv. coun.), Am. Inst. Parliamentarians, Western States Communication Assn. (2d v.p. 1956, 71, pres. Exec. club 1975, Disting. Svc. award 1989), Ariz. Communication and Drama Assn. (pres. 1967, editor jour. 1984-87), Blue Key, Phi Kappa Phi, Delta Sigma Rho. Democrat. Presbyterian. Home: 614 E Bishop Dr Tempe AZ 85282-2325 E-mail: galeri@imap3.asu.edu.

**RICHARDS, GEORGE ALVAREZ,** psychiatrist, educator; b. La Paz, Bolivia, May 11, 1934; came to U.S., 1952; s. John Joseph and Matilde (Alvarez) R.; m. LaClaire Lissetta Jones, July 26, 1958; children: Leslie Rosario Richards-Yellen, Lia Mercedes Richards Palmiter. BA, Hastings Coll., 1957; MD, U. Autonoma Guadalajara, Jalisco, Mex., 1970. Lic. physician, S.D. Lang. asst. Hastings (Nebr.) Coll., 1953-57; nursing asst. Hastings State Hosp., 1952-57; tchr. lang. and sci. Knoxville (Iowa) Pub. Sch., 1960-65; rotating intern Regina (Sask., Can.) Gen. Hosp., 1970-71; gen. med. officer Dept. Vets. Affairs, Knoxville, 1974; resident psychiatrist Mental Health Inst., Cherokee, Iowa, 1974-77; acting chief, adminstrv. chief, staff psychiatrist Royal C. Johnson Vets. Meml. Hosp., Sioux Falls, S.D., 1977—; asst. prof. psychiatry U. S.D. Sch. Medicine, Sioux Falls, 1977—. Mem. planning and health coms. Multi-Cultural Ctr., Sioux Falls, 1996—; mem. NAACP, Sioux Falls, 1980—. Recipient Exemplary Psychiatrist award Nat. Alliance for Mentally Ill, 1996—. Fellow Interam. Coll. Physicians and Surgeons; mem. AMA (Hispanic Physicians), Am. Psychiat. Assn. (Nancy C. A. Roeske, MD, Cert. of Excellence 1998), S.D. State Med. Assn., S.D. Psychiat. Assn., 7th Dist. Med. Assn. Avocations: languages, mineral, music, reading, jogging. Office: Royal C Johnson Vets Meml Hosp 2501 W 22d St Sioux Falls SD 57117

**RICHARDS, GERALD THOMAS,** lawyer, educator, writer; b. Monrovia, Calif., Mar. 17, 1933; s. Louis Jacquelyn Richards and Inez Vivian (Richardson) Hall; children: Patricia M. Richards Grauf, Laura J., Dag Hammarskjold; m. Mary Lou Richards, Dec. 27, 1986. BS magna cum laude, Lafayette Coll., 1957; MS, Purdue U., 1963; JD, Golden Gate U., 1976. Bar: Calif. 1976, U.S. Dist. Ct. (no. dist.) Calif. 1977, U.S. Patent Office 1981, U.S. Ct. Appeals (9th cir.) 1984, U.S. Supreme Ct. 1984. From computational physicist to asst. lab. counsel Lawrence Livermore Nat. Lab., Calif., 1967—84, asst. lab. counsel, 1984—93; sole practice Livermore, Calif., 1976-78, Oceanside, Calif., 1994-97; emeritus atty. pro bono participant Calif. State Bar, 1998—; staff atty. Contra Costa Sr. Legal Svcs., Concord, 1996—. Constrn. law instr. Contrs. State License Schs., Van Nuys, Calif., 1998; mem. exec. com., policy advisor Fed. Lab. Consortium for Tech. Transfer, 1980-88; panelist, del. White House Conf. on Productivity, Washington, 1983; del. Nat. Conf. on Tech. and Aging, Wingspread, Wis., 1981. Author: (novel) Jimmy, 2003. Commr. Housing Authority, City of Livermore, 1977, vice chair, 1978, chair, 1979; mem. Bd of Administrn. Appeals, City of Antioch, Calif., 2003-2005, Contra Costa Count Adv. Coun. on Aging, 2005—; pres. Housing Choices, Inc., Livermore, 1980-84; bd. dirs. Valley Vol. Ctr., Pleasanton, Calif., 1983, pres., 1984-86; mem. staff Calif. Boys' State Am. Legion, 1996—. Served to maj. U.S. Army, 1959-67 Recipient Engring. award GE, 1956. Mem. ABA, Calif. State Bar (conv. alt. del. 1990-92, del. 2000, mem. com. on sr. lawyers 2002-05), Alameda County Bar Assn., Contra Costa County Bar Assn., Ea. Alameda County Bar Assn. (sec. 1978, bd. dirs. 1991-92, chair lawyers referral com. 1992-93), Los Angeles County Bar Assn., Santa Barbara County Bar Assn., San Diego County Bar Assn., Bar Assn. No. San Diego County, San Francisco Bar Assn., Phi Beta Kappa (No. Calif. chpt. bd. dirs., newsletter chair 2001—), Tau Beta Pi, Sigma Pi Sigma. Home: 1099 Baywood Ln Hercules CA 94547-2739 Personal E-mail: hesiod@calbears.com.

**RICHARDS, HERBERT EAST,** retired minister, commentator; b. Hazleton, Pa. m. Louis Marcey, Jan. 1, 1942; children: Herbert Charles, Marcey Lynn, Robyn Lois, Fredrick East, Mark Allen. AB, Dickinson Coll., 1941; BD, Drew U., 1944; MA, Columbia, 1944; DD, Coll. of Idaho. 1953; postgrad. Union Theol. Sem., 1941-48, Bucknell U., 1943-44. Accredited news reporter Nat. Assn. Broadcasters. Ordained to ministry Methodist Ch., 1944; pastor in Boiling Springs, Pa., 1937-40, West Chester, Pa., 1940-41, Basking Ridge, NJ, 1941-47; mem. faculty Drew U. and Theol. Sem., 1944-51, assoc. prof. homiletics and Christian criticism, chmn. dept., asst. dean, 1947-51; spl. lectr. religion Howard U., 1947; minister 1st Meth. Cathedral, Boise, Idaho, 1951-69, 1st United Meth. Ch., Eugene, Oreg., 1969-78, Tabor Heights

United Meth. Ch., Portland, Oreg., 1978-86, minister emeritus, 1986—. Weekly radio broadcaster Sta. KBOI, Sta. KIDO, 1941—; weekly TV broadcaster CBS, 1945—, ABC, 1969—, NBC, 1973; pres. Inspiration, Inc., TV Found., 1965—, TV Ecology, 1973; producer Life TV series ABC, 1974-85, PBS TV, 1968-85, also BBC, Eng., Suise Romande, Geneva; chmn. Idaho bd. ministerial tng. Meth. Conf., 1954-60, TV, Radio and Film Commn., 1954-62, Oreg. Coun. Public Broadcasting, 1973; del. Idaho Conf. Meth. Gen. Conf., 1956, Jurisdictional Conf., 1956, World Meth. Coun., 1957, 81, World Meth. Conf., 1981, mem. Gen. Conf., 1956-60, Jurisdictional Conf., 1956, 60; meml. chaplain Idaho Supreme Ct., 1960; chaplain Idaho Senate, 1960-68; mem. Task Force on TV and Ch., 1983 Author: In Time of Need, 1986, Faith and the Pursuit of Healing, 1996; contbr. articles to religious publs.; composer: oratorios Prophet Unwiling, 1966, Meet Martin Luther, 1968, Dear Jesus Boy, 1973. Mem. Commn. on Centennial Celebration for Idaho, 1962-63; committeeman Boy Scouts Am.; bd. dirs. Eugene chpt. ARC, 1954-73; trustee Willamette U., Cascade Manor Homes; adv. bd. Medic-Alert Found. Recipient Alumni citation in religious edn. Dickinson Coll., 1948, Golden Plate award Am. Acad. Achievement, 1965, Jason Lee Mass Media TV award, 1983, Disting. Citizen award Idaho Statesman Newspaper, 1964, Disting. Alumnus award Drew U., 1965, disting. Eagle award Boy Scouts Am.; named Clergyman of Yr., Religious Heritage Am., 1964. Mem. AAUP, CAP (chaplain Idaho wing, lt. col.), Am. Acad. Achievement (bd. govs. 1967—), Am. Found. Religion and Psychiatry (charter gov.), Idaho Found. Medicine and Biology (charter), Greater Boise Ministerial Assn. (pres.), Eugene Ministerial Assn. (pres. 1978), Masons (33 degree, editor Pike's Peak Albert That Is), Shriners, Elks, Rotary (editor Key and Cog, pres. dist. 510 Pioneer Club), Kappa Sigma (Grand Master of Beta Pi). Home: 10172 SE 99th Dr West Linn OR 97068 *When a person presses his face against the window pane of life, he becomes as a child waiting for his father's return; simple, trusting and infinitely wiser. In our present time of growth/conflict, such a face-pressing is essential to get us safely from where we are to where we ought to be.*

**RICHARDS, JAY CLAUDE,** photographer, publishing executive, historian; b. Glen Ridge, N.J., Apr. 6, 1954; s. Jacob Tilghman and Joan Louise (Walsh) Richards. Student, Tenn. Wesleyan Coll., Athens, 1972-73. Various positions armed security work, 1973-75; reporter, photographer Press Publs.: The News, Belvidere, NJ, 1977-98; pres. J.C. Richards Assocs., Harmony Twp., NJ, 1980—; owner Poor Richards' Brit. Gun Shop, Harmony Twp., 1976—; freelance ct. reporter The Morning Call, Allentown, Pa., 1986—; reporter The Knowlton News, 1998—2002, NorthWarren News, 2002—04. Photography judge Warren County 4-H, Belvidere, 1990—; press officer Warren County Office Emergency Mgmt, Belvidere, 1989—98; news corresp WRNJ-News, 1991—, NJN Pubs, The News, 2001—02. Author: Penn, Patriots and the Pequest: The History of Pre-Victorian Belvidere, 1716-1845, 1995, Flames Along the Delaware, 1996 (NJ Frontier Guard's Book Award, 1997), Officers and Men of Warren County, N.J. Civil War, 1998, Officers and Men of Warren County in the Civil War, expanded edit., 2005, More Bugles, Battles and Belvidere: Warren County, N.J. Civil War Letters to Home, 1999, Following the Hand of Franklin: Warren County, N.J. and the Search for the North Pole, 2000, Warren, Warriors & The World: Warren County, New Jersey In the Plains Indians Wars & The Spanish-American War 1865-1902, 2002, 1903 Flood Centennial Souvenier Book, 2003, Fighting Fascism for Freedom: Warren County, NJ in World War 2, Book 1, 2006; contbr. art work Hackettstown, NJ "Billy Yank" Civil War Monument, 2001. Mem Hazardous Materials Adv Coun, Warren County, NJ, 1989—98, Joint Emergency Mgmt Coun, Belvidere/White Township, NJ, 1989—98, Warren County Arts Adv Coun, Warren County War Mem Comt, 1997—98; trustee Warren County War Mem Corp, 1999—; consult Harmony NJ Hist Preservation Commn., 2000—; mem Warren County Purple Heart Monument Construction Com., 2000; mem. Statue of Liberty - Ellis Island Found.; participant foreign policy leadership George Washington Univ., 1999, 2003, 2005; Civil War monument project Hackettstown, NJ, 2001; mem. Glamour Photographers Internat., 2003—04. Named hon. mem., Boy Scout Troop 141, Belvidere, 1993; recipient Outstanding Cmty. Svc. award, Am Legion Post 131, 1994. Mem.: Nat Indian Wars Asn, Oxford NJ Hist Soc, US Naval Inst, Sr Army Res Comdrs Asn, Res Officers Asn US, Soc Profl Journalists, Nat Press Photographers Asn, NRA, Forks of the Del. Hist. Arms Soc., Frederick A. Cook Soc., Sigma Delta Chi. Episcopalian. Avocations: gourmet cooking, gardening, herbal medicine, military antiques, making leather and canvas gear for re-enacters. Home and Office: 3110 Belvidere Rd Phillipsburg NJ 08865-9515 E-mail: jayrichards@enter.net.

**RICHARDS, JEFFREY HAMILTON,** English language educator; b. Libertyville, Ill., Dec. 4, 1948; s. Fenton O. and Elizabeth A. (Quantz) R.; m. Stephanie Kay Sugioka, May 7, 1978; children: Aaron Nicholas, Sarah Grace. BA, Yale U., 1971; PhD, U. N.C., 1981. Prof. Lakeland Coll., Sheboygan, Wis., 1979-86, U. N.C., Chapel Hill, 1986-87, N.C. State U., Raleigh, 1987-92, Duke U., Durham, N.C., 1992, Old Dominion U., Norfolk, Va., 1992—. Author: Theater Enough, 1991, Mercy Otis Warren, 1995, Drama Theatre, and Identity in the American New Republic, 2005; editor: Early American Drama, 1997, Eugene O'Neill: Early Plays, 2001; contbr. articles to profl. jours. Mem.: MLA, Soc. Early Americanists. Office: Old Dominion U Dept English Norfolk VA 23529

**RICHARDS, JODY,** state legislator, communications educator, small business owner; b. Columbia, Ky., Feb. 20, 1939; m. Neva Richards; 1 child, Roger. BA in English, Ky. Wesleyan Coll., Owensboro; MA in Journalism, U. Mo., 1962. Mem. faculty in journalism Western Ky. U., from 1962; owner Superior Books, Bowling Green, Ky.; mem. Ky. Ho. of Reps., 1976—, speaker, 1995—; vice chair So. Legislative Conf., 1998—. Mem. adv. bd. dirs. Republic Savs. Bank. Pres. bd. dirs. So. Ky. Fair; bd. dirs. Bowling Green Girls Club, United Way, Warren County (Ky.) Drug Abuse Task Force. Recipient Disting. Svc. award Nat. Art Edn. Assn., 1992. Mem. Bowling Green C. of C., Bowling Green Noon Rotary Club. Office: Ky Ho of Reps State Capitol Rm 309 Frankfort KY 40601

**RICHARDS, JOHN PICKFORD,** musician, educator; b. St. Matthews, Ky., Feb. 27, 1980; s. Robert Manor Richards and Sherrie Pickford. MusB, Eastman Sch. of Music, U. of Rochester, N.Y., 2002; MusM, Eastman Sch. of Music, U. of Rochester, 2004. Founding mem., violist, and fdr. Alarm Will Sound, NY; founding mem. and violist Payton MacDonald Ensemble, JACK Quartet; profl. freelance musician. Musician: (recording) Jeff Manookian: Concertos, Improvisations on Armenian Folk Songs for Viola and Orchestra performed by John Pickford Richards and the Armenian Philharmonic Orchestra, TROY581, Steve Reich: Tehillim and The Desert Music performed by Alarm Will Sound and Ossia, CA21009, Acoustica: Alarm Will Sound performs Aphex Twin, CA21028, (dvd recording) Reich at the Roxy performed by Alarm Will Sound, Sweetspot Productions. Mem.: Chamber Music Am. Office Phone: 717-422-6359.

**RICHARDS, KEITH,** musician; b. Dartford, Kent, Eng., Dec. 18, 1943; s. Bert and Doris Richards; m. Anita Pallenberg; children: Marlon, Angela; m. Patti Hansen, Dec. 18, 1983; children: Theodora, Alexandra. Student, Sidcup Art Sch. Recording artist on label Mindless Records. Lead & rhythm guitarist, vocalist Rolling Stones, 1962—; films include Sympathy for the Devil, 1968, Gimme Shelter, 1970, Ladies and Gentlemen, the Rolling Stones, 1974, Let's Spend the Night Together, 1983, The Magic Years, Vol. 1, 1989, 25X5: The Continuing Adventures of the Rolling Stones, 1989, At the Max, 1991, Rolling Stones: Voodoo Lounge, 1994, The History of Rock 'N' Roll, Vol. 7, 1995, The Rolling Stones Rock 'N' Roll Circus, 1996, Can't You Hear Me Wind Howl? The Life & Music of Robert Johnson, 1997, Rolling Stones: Bridges to Babylon Tour, 1997—98, Forty Licks Tour, 2002—03, film mus. dir. (with Chuck Berry, Eric Clapton and friends) Hail! Hail! Rock & Roll, 1987; composer (with Mick Jagger): numerous songs and albums, 1964; including (albums) The Rolling Stones, Now!, 1964, Aftermath, 1966, Flowers, 1967, Beggars Banquet, 1968, Let It Bleed, 1969, Sticky Fingers, 1971, Hot Rocks, Exile on Main Street, 1972, Goat's Head Soup, 1973, It's Only Rock and Roll, 1974, Metamorphosis, 1975, Black and Blue, 1976, Some Girls, Emotional Rescue, 1980, Tattoo You, 1981, Still Life, 1982,

Under Cover, 1983, Dirty Work, 1986, Steel Wheels, 1989, Flashpoint, 1991, Voodoo Lounge, 1994 (Grammy award Best Rock Album, 1994), Stripped, 1995, Bridges to Babylon, 1997, No Security, 1999, 40 Licks, 2002, Live Licks, 2004, A Bigger Bang, 2005, Rarities 1971-2003, 2005, songs Wild Horses, Angie, Start Me Up, Honky Tonk Woman, Jumpin' Jack Flash, (I Can't Get No) Satisfaction, Before They Make Me Run, Miss You, Happy, Shattered, Paint It Black, Waiting On a Friend, Ruby Tuesday, You Can't Always Get What You Want, Brown Sugar, Tumbling Dice, Faraway Eyes, Mixed Emotions, Rock and a Hard Place, Highwire, Love is Strong, Anybody Seen My Baby; prodr.: Wingless Angels, 1997, (soundtrack album) Hail! Hail! Rock 'N Roll, 1987; solo albums Talk Is Cheap, 1988, Keith Richards & The X-Pensive Winos Live At The Hollywood Palladium, 1991, Main Offender, 1992. Named to Rock and Roll Hall of Fame, 1989; recipient Living Legend award Internat. Rock, Knight Comdr. of Brit. Empire, 2003, Greatest Touring Band of All Time, World Music Awards, 2006.

**RICHARDS, LACLAIRE LISSETTA JONES (MRS. GEORGE A. RICHARDS),** social worker; b. Pine Bluff, Ark. d. Artie William and Geraldine (Adams) Jones; m. George Alvarez Richards, July 26, 1958; children: Leslie Rosario, Lia Mercedes. BA, Nat. Coll. Christian Workers, 1953; MSW, U. Kans., 1956; postgrad, Columbia U., 1960. Diplomate Clin. Social Work, Am. Bd. of Examiners in Clin. Social Work, Nat. Assn. Social Workers; cert. gerontologist. Psychiat., supr., tchg., cmty. orgn., adminstrv., cons. Hastings Regional Ctr., Ingleside, Nebr., 1956-60; supr., cons., adminstrv. VA Hosp., Knoxville, Iowa, 1960-74; field instr. for grad. students U. Mo., 1969-74, 78-90, com. chmn., 1975-77; sr. social worker Mental Health Inst., Cherokee, Iowa, 1974-77; adj. asst. prof. dept. social behavior U. S.D., Cherokee, Iowa, 1974-77, instr. dept. psychiat., 1988-96, Augustina Coll., 1981-86; outpatient social worker VA Med. and Regional Office Ctr., Sioux Falls, SD, 1978-96, med., surg. and intensive care social worker, 1992-96, 1990-92, sur. and intermediate care social worker, 1992-96, EEO counselor. EEO counselor. Mem. Knoxville Juvenile adv. com., 1963-65, 68-70, sec., 1965-66, chmn., 1966-68; sec. Urban Renewal Citizens' adv. com., Knoxville, 1966-68; mem. United Meth. Ch. task force Expt. Styles Ministry and Leadership, 1973-74, adult choir, ch. and society com.; counselor Knoxville Youth Line program; sec. exec. com. Vis. Nurse Assn., 1979-80; canvasser cmty. fund drs., Knoxville; active Cherokee Civil Rights Commn.; bd. dirs., pub. rels., devel. and program devel. cons. YWCA, 1983-85; bd. dirs. Family Svc. Agy., 1989-90, Food Svcs. Ctr., Inc., 1992-96; active SD Symphonic Choir, 1991—, Youth-At-Risk Task Force and Multicultural Ctr. Advocate; deaconess 1st Evang. Free Ch., 1999-2004. Named S.D. Social Worker of Yr., 1983. Mem. NAACP (chmn. edn. com. 1983-85), AAUW (sec. Hastings chpt. 1958-60), Nat. Assn. Social Workers (co-chmn. Nebr. chpt. profl. standards com. 1958-59), Acad. Cert. Social Workers, S.D. Assn. Social Workers (chmn. minority affairs com., v.p. S.E. region 1980, exec. com. 1985-84, mem. social policy and action com.), Nebr. Assn. Social Workers (chmn. 1958-59), Seventh Dist. S.D. Med. Soc. Aux., Coalition on Aging., Nat. Assn. Social Workers (qualified clin. social worker 1991—), Methodist (Sunday Sch. tchr. adult divsn.; mem. commn. on edn.; mem. Core com. for adult edn.; mem. Adult Choir; mem. Social Concerns Work Area). Home: 1701 E Ponderosa Dr Sioux Falls SD 57103-5019

**RICHARDS, LARRY LEONARD,** child and adolescent psychiatrist; b. Garden Grove, Iowa; s. P. P. Richards and Clara Mae Leonard-Richards; m. Mary Anderson; children: Melinda, Jennifer. BS, Simpson Coll., 1960; DO, Kansas City Coll. Osteo. Medicine, 1967. Cert. Adult, Chlid and Adolescent Psychiatry. Gen. residency Mt. Clemens (Mich.) Gen. Hosp., 1967—68; psychiatry resident Kirksville (Mo.) Coll., 1977—80; fellow in child and adolescent psychiatry U. Iowa, Iowa City, 1992—94; child and adolescent psychiatrist Des Moines, 1980—92, Iowa City, 1992—. With USNR. Fellow: APA; mem.: Phi Mu Alpha. Republican. Roman Catholic.

**RICHARDS, LEONARD MARTIN,** investment executive, consultant; b. Phila., June 4, 1935; s. Leonard Martin and Marion Clara (Lang) R.; m. Phyllis Janelle Mowrey, Aug. 26, 1961 (div. Aug. 1978); children: Lisa, David Reed. BS, Pa. State U., 1957; MBA, U. Pa., 1963; MTh, Universal Sem., 1996, ThD, 2000. Asst. to sr. ptnr. Van Cleef, Jordan & Wood, NYC, 1963-68; v.p., portfolio mgr. Bernstein-Macaulay, Inc., NYC, 1968-72; ptnr. G. H. Walker, Laird Co., NYC, 1972-74; v.p., trust officer, mgr. instnl. funds group Republic Bank N.A., Dallas, 1974-77; v.p., sr. investment officer, mem. exec. com. Variable Annuity Life Ins. Co., Houston, 1977-88; v.p., sr. investment officer Am. Gen. Series Portfolio Co., 1985-88; pres. L.M. Richards & Co., Houston, 1982—, asst. bd. dirs.; mem. adv. bd. Trinity Life Ctr., Houston, 1996-2000; pres. Lenan Holdings, Inc., Houston, 2005—. Pres., bd. dirs. Sand Dollar, Inc., Houston, 1985—96; trustee Post Oak Sch., Houston, 1997—99, Universal Sem., 1997—2000, pres., 2001—; mem., bd. dirs. Capital Institutional Services, Dallas, 1991—99; trustee PAIRS Found., Reston, Va., 2004—06; bd. dirs. Houston Chorale, 1988—90. Capt. U.S. Army, 1957—65. Mem. ACFA Inst., Houston Soc. Fin. Analysts, Wharton Club (Houston), Houstonian Club Republican. Avocations: skiing, travel, scuba. Home: 9023 Briar Forest Dr Houston TX 77024-7220 Office: LM Richards & Co 1900 St James Pl Ste 800 Houston TX 77056 Office Phone: 713-961-5243. Business E-Mail: lrichards@enhancementinstitute.com.

**RICHARDS, MARK E.,** plastic surgeon, educator; b. Bethesda, Md., Aug. 5, 1957; s. Edward J. Richards; children: Kira, Ian. BS, Yale U., 1979; MD, U. Md., 1983. Diplomate Am. Bd. Surgery, 1983. Resident in gen. surgery St. Barnabas Med. Ctr., Livingston, NJ, 1984—88; resident in plastic and reconstructive surgery Lahey Clinic Med. Ctr., Boston, 1988—90; cosmetic plastic surgeon Mark E. Richards M.D.P.C., North Bethesda, Md., 1985—. Lectr. in field. Named Top Surgeon, Washingtonian Mag., 2002, 2005, America's Top Surgeon, Consumers Rsch. Coun. of Am., 2002, 2003, 2004, 2005. Mem.: Nat. Capital Soc. of Plastic Surgeons (pres. 1999), Montgomery County Med. fac. (pres. 2000, Chmn. of Yr. 1996, 1997), Office: Mark E Richards MD PC Ste # 912 11300 Rockville Pike North Bethesda MD 20852 Office Phone: 301-468-3458. Business E-Mail: drrichards@drrichards.us.

**RICHARDS, MARTA ALISON,** lawyer; b. Mar. 15, 1952; d. Howard Jay and Mary Dean (Nix) Richards; m. Richard Peter Massony, June 16, 1979 (div. Apr. 1988); 1 child, Richard Peter Massony Jr. Student, Vassar Coll., 1969-70; AB cum laude, Princeton U., 1973; JD, George Washington U., 1976. Bar: La. 1976, U.S. Dist. Ct. (ea. dist.) La. 1976, U.S. Ct. Appeals (5th cir.) 1981, U.S. Supreme Ct. 1988, U.S. Dist. Ct. (mid. dist.) La. 1991. Assoc. Phelps, Dunbar, Marks, Claverie & Sims, New Orleans, 1976-77; assoc. counsel Hibernia Nat. Bank, New Orleans, 1978; assoc. Singer, Hutner, Levine, Seeman & Stuart, New Orleans, 1978-80, Jones, Walker, Waechter, Poltevent, Carrere & Denegre, New Orleans, 1980-84; ptnr. Montgomery, Barnett, Brown, Read, Hammond & Mintz, 1984-86, Montgomery, Richards & Ballin, 1986-89, Gelpi, Sullivan, Carroll and Laborde, 1989; gen. counsel Maison Blanche Inc., Baton Rouge, 1990-92, La. State Bond Commn., 1992-97; pvt. practice, cons., 1998—. Lectr. paralegal inst. U. New Orleans, 1984-89, adj. prof., 1989; of counsel Sanford & Assocs. Law Firm, 2004—. Contbr. articles to legal jours. Treas. alumni coun. Princeton U., 1979-81. Mem. ABA, La. State Bar Assn., New Orleans Bar Assn., Baton Rouge Bar Assn., Nat. Assn. Bond Lawyers, Princeton Alumni Assn. New Orleans (pres. 1982-86), Princeton Alumni Assn. Baton Rouge (pres. 2002—). Episcopalian. Home: 4075 S Ramsey Dr Baton Rouge LA 70808-1653 Office: 5800 One Perkins Pl Ste 5F Baton Rouge LA 70808 Office Phone: 225-761-9600. Business E-Mail: marta73@alumni.princeton.edu. E-mail: mrichards@sanfordlaw.org.

**RICHARDS, MARTIN,** theatrical producer; m. Mary Lea Johnson (dec.). Co-founder Prodr. Circle, 1976—. Prodr. plays including Chicago (11 Tony nominations Best Musical London and L.A.), The Norman Conquests (Outer Critics Circle award), On the Twentieth Century (5 Tony awards), Sweeney Todd (8 Tony awards including Best Musical), Crimes of the Heart (Pulitzer prize), Foxfire, La Cage aux Folles (6 Tony awards including Best Musical), Grand Hotel (5 Tony awards), The Will Rogers Follies (6 Tony awards including Best Musical), Sally Marr... and Her Escorts, Dylan (Obie award), March of the Falsettos (Outer Critics Circle award Best Musical), Mayor, The

Best of Friends, 1971, The Life, films include The Boys From Brazil, 1978, The Shining, 1980, Fort Apache the Bronx, 1981, Chicago, 2002 (Best Picture Academy award, 2003). Trustee Trust for Cultural Resources of City of N.Y. Office: Prodrs Circle 200 W 57th St Ste 1403 New York NY 10019-3211

**RICHARDS, NORMAN BLANCHARD,** lawyer; b. Melrose, Mass., May 27, 1924; s. Henry Edward and Annie Jane (Blanchard) R.; m. Diane Maionchi, July 9, 1977; children— Terri, Jeffrey. BS, Bowdoin Coll., 1945; JD, Stanford U., 1951. Bar: Calif. bar 1951. Mem. firm McCutchen Doyle Brown & Enersen, San Francisco, 1951—, partner, 1960—. Mem. faculty Tulane Admiralty Law Inst., Hastings Coll. Advocacy. Bd. visitors Stanford Law Sch. With USN, 1943-46. Fellow Am. Coll. Trial Lawyers; mem. ABA, Calif. State Bar, San Francisco Bar Assn., Maritime Law Assn. U.S. Home: 85 Platt Ave Sausalito CA 94965-1897 Office: Bingham McCutchen 3 Embarcadero Ctr San Francisco CA 94111-4003 Office Phone: 415-393-2030.

**RICHARDS, PATTY,** secondary school educator; d. Roger Roy and Leola Richards. BS in Edn., U. Ill., Charleston, 1971, MS in Edn., 1973. Tchr. Jerseyville HS, Ill., 1974, Carthage HS, 1975—79, Casey-Westfield HS, Casey, 1979—2006. Mem. Far-Off Broadway Players, Casey; edn. chmn. Casey United Meth. Ch., women's cir. pres. Recipient Citizen of Yr. award, Casey, Ill., Golden Apple award, WTHI-TV.

**RICHARDS, PAUL GRANSTON,** geophysics educator, seismologist; b. Cirencester, Eng., Mar. 31, 1943; came to U.S., 1965; s. Albert George and Kathleen Margaret (Harding) R.; m. Jody Margaret Porterfield, June 1, 1968; children: Mark, Jessica, Gillian. BA, Cambridge (Eng.) U., 1965, MS, Calif. Inst. Tech., Pasadena, 1966, PhD, 1970. Prof. geol. scis. Columbia U., N.Y.C., 1971—, chmn. dept. geol. scis., 1980-83. Co-author: Quantitative Seismology, 2 vols., 1980, 2nd edit., 2002. Guggenheim Found. fellow, 1977-78, MacArthur Found. fellow, 1981-86. Fellow Royal Astron. Soc.; mem. Am. Geophys. Union (Macelwane award 1976), Coun. Fgn. Rels. Episcopalian. Office: Lamont-Doherty Earth Obs 61 Rte 9W Palisades NY 10964 E-mail: richards@ldeo.columbia.edu.

**RICHARDS, PRISCILLA ANN,** medical/surgical nurse; b. Providence, Nov. 10, 1949; d. Frank L. Thornton and Dorothy A. Maker; children: Tanya Rene, Jason Edward. Assoc. Degree Nursing, Lincoln Land C.C., Springfield, Ill., 1980. RN Ill., 1980, R.I., 1997. Cert. nursing asst. Meml. Med. Ctr., Springfield, 1971—73, lic. practical nurse, 1973—80, RN, 1980—97, South County Nursing and Subacute Ctr., North Kingstown, RI, 1997—2000, Elmhurst Extended Care, Providence, 2000—05, Maxim Health Care, Providence, 2005—. Sgt. USAF, 1968—71. Baptist. Avocations: reading, swimming, yard work. Home: 71 Wells Ave Warwick RI 02889 Personal E-mail: paramanri@aol.com.

**RICHARDS, SAMUEL J.,** secondary school educator; s. Joseph A. and Sharon Ringer Richards. BS inEdn., Ind. U. Pa., 2004. Cert. social studies edn. 7-12 Md. State Dept. Edn., 2004, basic tchg., citizenship edn. 7-12 Commonwealth of Pa., 2004. History tchr. Wicomico County Bd. Edn., Salisbury, Md., 2004—. Gr. 8 curriculum com. Wicomico County Bd. Edn., 2005, secondary adv. com., 2005—. Disaster vol. ARC, Salisbury, 2004; mem. Ea. Shore Reading Coun., Salisbury. Recipient Alumni Svc. Recognition award, Ind. U. Pa. Alumni Assn., 2003; fellow, James A. Finnegan Found., 2003. Mem.: Nat. Coun. Social Studies, Am. Hist. Assn., Phi Alpha Theta. Avocations: jogging, reading, gardening, politics, bicycling. Office: Pittsville Mid Sch 34404 Old Ocean City Rd Pittsville MD 21850

**RICHARDS, STANFORD HARVEY,** advertising agency executive, design studio executive; b. Phila., Nov. 8, 1932; s. Jack and Ruth (Stein) R.; m. Betty Jo Pugh, July 12, 1957; children— Grant Leonard, Bradford Craig Student, Pratt Inst., 1950-53. Creative dir. Bloom Advt., Dallas, 1954-55; owner Stan Richards & Assocs., Dallas, 1955-75; owner, pres. The Richards Group, Inc., Dallas, 1975—; also bd. dirs. Instr. E. Tex. State U., Commerce, 1976-77; assoc. bd. mem. Cox Sch. Bus., So. Meth. U., Dallas, 1980-84, 88—. Author: Hobo Signs, 1965 Trustee Dallas Symphony, 1978, Dallas Ballet, 1978; bd. dirs. Episcopal Sch., Dallas, 1981—, Dallas Arboretum, 1984-86, The Sci. Pl., 1987-90; mem. Dallas Citizens Council, adv. council Salvation Army Adult Rehab. Ctr., 1986—, adv. bd. Dallas County Salvation Army, 1987—; exec. com. United Way, 1990—; bd. dirs. YMCA, 1990—. Named Top Creative, AdWeek, Entrepreneur of Yr. Inc Mag.; named one of Wall Street Jours. Giants of Our Time; recipient Alumni Achievement award, Pratt Inst., Bklyn., 1985, Reddick award, U. Tex. Mem.: Aerobic Activity Ctr. Avocations: deep sea fishing, running, skiing. Office: The Richards Group 8750 N Central Expy Ste 1200 Dallas TX 75231-6436 Business E-Mail: stan_richards@richards.com.*

**RICHARDS, STEPHEN HAROLD,** engineering educator; b. Austin, Tex., July 19, 1952; s. Harold Richards Jr. and Janice Valerie (Mahone) Jackson; m. Mary Kathryn King Coleman, Aug. 15, 1974 (div. July 1981); 1 child, Adam King. BSCE, U. Tex., 1976; MCE, Tex. A&M U., 1977; PhDCE, U. Tenn., 1989. Registered profl. engr., Tenn., Tex. Rsch. asst. Tex. Transp. Inst., Tex. A&M U., 1976-77, engring. rsch. assoc., 1977-81, asst. rsch. engr., 1982-84; asst. dir. transp. ctr. U. Tenn., Knoxville, 1984-87, acting dir. transp. ctr., 1987-89, dir. transp., 1989—, assoc. prof. civil engring., 1989—; traffic engring. cons. Ctr. Transp. Rsch., 1976—. Engr., mgr. Walton & Assocs./Cons. Engrs., Inc., Houston, 1981-82; lectr. in civl engring. U. Houston, 1982, Tex. A&M U., 1978-81, 83-84; instr. Tex. Engring. Extension Svc., Tex. A&M U., 1978-84; Dwight D. Eisenhower Fellowship Rev. Com. Tenn. State U., 1993, N.C. A&T Univ., 1992, Bicentennial planning com. U. Tenn., 1993, dir. program for minority student recruitment into transp. careers, 1992—, coll. engring. awards com., 1991—, chmn. spl. events traffic planning com., 1985—. Contbr. numerous articles to profl. jours. Mem. Cumberland Gateway Com., 1993—; edn. com. Southeastern Transp. Ctr., 1992—; exec. dir. Southeastern Consortium of U. Transp. Ctrs., 1992—; chmn. Knoxville Transp. Authority, 1992-94, vice-chmn., 1990-92, commr., 1989-93; rep. Coun. of Univ. Transp. Ctrs. U. Tenn., 1987—, bd. dirs. 1992—, sec., 1994-95, v.p. 1995-96, pres., 1996—; adv. com. Ga. State u. Transp. Ctr., 1989—; traffic control device subcom. Transp. Rsch. Bd., 1989-91, traffic control devices, 1991—, many other coms. Hwy. Safety fellowship Fed. Hwy. Adminstrn., U.S. Dept. Transp., 1976-77. Mem. ASCE, Inst. of Transp. Engrs. (chmn. tech. com. Tenn. sect. 1988—, area coord. Tex. sect. 1982-84, guidelines for driveway design and location), Transp. Rsch. Bd., Soc. Profl. Engrs., Am. Road and Transp. Builders Assn. (edn. com. 1988—), Phi Kappa Phi, Chi Epsilon. Office: Ctr Transp 600 Henley St Ste 309 Knoxville TN 37996-4133 Office Phone: 865-974-5255. Personal E-mail: stephen032@comcast.net, shrichards@charter.net.

**RICHARDS, SUZANNE V.,** lawyer; b. Columbia, SC, Sept. 7, 1927; d. Raymond E. and Elise C. (Gray) R. AB, George Washington U., 1948, JD with distinction, 1957, LLM, 1959. Bar: D.C. 1958. Sole practice, Washington, 1974—. Lectr. in family and probate law; mem. D.C. Jud. Conf., 1975—2005. Bd. dirs. Coun. for Ct. Excellence. Recipient John Bell Larner award George Washington U., 1958; named Woman Lawyer of Yr., Women's Bar Assn. D.C., 1977. Mem. ABA (ho. of dels. 1988-90), Bar Assn. D.C. (pres. 1989-90, named Lawyer of Yr. 2002), Women's Bar Assn. D.C. (pres. 1977-78), Trial Lawyers Assn. of D.C. (bd. govs. 1978-82, 85-2001, treas. 1982-85), D.C. Bar. Home: 530 N St SW Washington DC 20024-4546 Office: PO Box 65466 Washington DC 20035-5466

**RICHARDS, VARGRAVE A.,** lieutenant governor; b. Santurce, PR, Sept. 15, 1950; s. Ansel, and Beulah Anduze R.; 1 child, Cherise. High School Teacher; mem. V.I. Senate, 1995—2003, pres. 1999—2000; lt. gov. Ter. of V.I., 2003—. Democrat. Office: #18 Kongens Gade St Thomas VI 00802 also: Office Lt Gov 1105 King St Christiansted VI 00820 Office Phone: 340-773-6449.

**RICHARDS, VINCENT PHILIP HASLEWOOD,** retired librarian; b. Sutton Bonington, Nottinghamshire, Eng., Aug. 1, 1933; arrived in Can., 1956, naturalized, 1961; s. Philip Haslewood and Alice Hilda (Moore) R.; m. Ann Beardshall, Apr. 3, 1961; children: Mark, Christopher, Erika. ALA, Ealing Coll., London, 1954; BLS with distinction, U. Okla., 1966. Cert. profl. libr., B.C. Joined Third Order Mt. Carmel, Roman Cath. Ch., 1976; with Brentford and Chiswick Pub. Librs., London, 1949-56; asst. librarian B.C. (Can.) Pub. Libr. Commn., Dawson Creek, 1956-57; asst. dir. Fraser Valley Regional Libr., Abbotsford, B.C., 1957-67; chief librarian Red Deer Coll., Alta., Canada, 1967-77; dir. librs. Edmonton (Alta.) Pub. Libr., Edmonton, 1977-89; libr. and book industry cons. Victoria, Canada, 1990—2006, ret. 2006. Pres. Faculty Assn. Red Deer Coll., 1971-72, bd. govs., 1972-73; pres. Libr. Assn. Alta., 1984-85. Contbr. articles to profl. jours. V.p. Jeunesses Musicales, Red Deer, 1969-70; bd. dirs. Red Deer TV Authority, 1975-76; dir. Alta. Found. Lit. Arts, 1984-86. Served with Royal Army Ed17. Corps, 1951-53. Home and office: 105 1049 Costin Ave Victoria BC Canada V9B 2T4 Office Phone: 250-391-9892. Personal E-mail: v.p.h.richards@gmail.com. *Dedication to public service, in spite of its frustrating aspects, diversity of experience, people and places, and the avoidance of overspecialization are great contributors to an enjoyable working life.*

**RICHARDS-KORTUM, REBECCA RAE,** biomedical engineering educator; b. Grand Island, Nebr., Apr. 14, 1964; d. Larry Alan and Linda Mae (Hohnstein) Richards; m. Philip Ted Kortum, May 12, 1985; children: Alexander Scott, Maxwell James, Zachary Alan. BS, U. Nebr., 1985; MS, MIT, 1987, PhD, 1990. Prof. U. Tex., Austin, 1990—, and Robert M. and Prudie Leibrock Endowed Prof., Engring., and assoc. chair, rsch., biomedical engring. dept. Prof. Howard Hughes Med. Inst., 2002—. Named Presdl. Young Investigator NSF, Washington, 1991; NSF presdl. faculty fellow, Washington, 1992; recipient Career Achievement award Assn. Advancement Med. Instrumentation, 1992, Dow Outstanding Young Faculty awd., Am. Soc. for Engring. Edn., 1992, Y.C. Fung Young Investigator award, Bioengring. Divsn., Am. Soc. of Mechanical Engrs., Howard Hughes Med. Inst. grantee in biomedical engring., 2002. Mem. AAAS, Am. Soc. Engring. Edn. (Outstanding Young Faculty award 1992), Optical Soc. Am., Am. Soc. Photobiology. Achievements include research in photochemistry, photobiology, applied optics and bioengring. Office: Dept Biomed Engring U Texas 1 U Station C0800 Austin TX 78712-0238 Office Phone: 512-471-3604. Business E-Mail: kortum@mail.utexas.edu.

**RICHARDSON, ALBERT EDWARD,** chemistry professor, researcher; b. Lovelock, Nev., Feb. 4, 1929; s. James Harold and Mary Lorraine Richardson; m. Shirley Arlene Richardson, June 10, 1959 (dec. Apr. 1997); children: Anne Ikard, John (dec.), Stephen; stepchildren: Corinne Jameson, Elisabeth Anderson, David Beckman, Margaret Chambers. BS in Chemistry, U. Nev., 1950; PhD, Iowa State U., 1956. Accredited profl. chemist Am. Inst. Chemists. Rsch. chemist Ames (Iowa) Lab. of the Atomic Energy Commn., 1950—55; asst. prof. chemistry N.Mex. State U., Las Cruces, 1955—60, radiation safety officer, 1957—75, assoc. prof. chemistry, 1960—91, assoc. prof. emeritus, 1991—. Vis. scientist N.Mex. secondary schs., 1960—91; vis. prof. chemistry Adams State Coll., Alamosa, Colo., 1963; summer rschr. Ames Lab. Atomic Energy Commn., 1964, Lawrence Livermore (Calif.) Nat. Lab., 1979; cons. White Sands (N.Mex.) Missile Range, 1965—71, contractor, 1973—74, chemist, 1981—82, 1984—92; vis. staff mem. Los Alamos (N.Mex.) Nat. Labs., 1975—80; summer faculty Sandia Nat. Lab., Albuquerque, 1983; owner, mgr. Timberline Bed and Breakfast, Cedaredge, Colo., 1992—98. Contbr. over 20 articles to profl. jours. Mem. founding cabinet The World Peace and Diplomacy Forum, 2003—; bus. mgr. Coll. Cmty. Chorus, Las Cruces, 1956—57; pres. U. Park Toastmaster's Club, Las Cruces, 1961; dir. Southwestern N.Mex. Regional Sci. Fair, Las Cruces, 1967—68; vol. reading aide to elem. schs. Las Cruces, 2000—03. Rsch. grantee NASA, 1966, Equipment grantee Atomic Energy Commn., 1968; postdoctoral rsch. fellow Atomic Energy Commn., 1968-69. Mem. Am. Chem. Soc. (chmn. so. N.Mex. sect. 1962, chmn. Rio Grande Valley sect. 1977), World Peace and Diplomacy Forum (charter), Sigma Xi, Phi Kappa Phi (pres. N.Mex. State U. chpt. 1972-73), Phi Lambda Upsilon, Sigma Pi Sigma. Democrat. Avocations: photography, collecting coins and CD's, travel, gardening, cultural activities. Home: 1185 Villita Loop Las Cruces NM 88007 Personal E-mail: aerinlc@earthlink.net.

**RICHARDSON, ALFONSO AUSTIN,** accountant, financial services executive; b. St. Nicholas, Aruba, W.I., Feb. 29, 1932; came to U.S., 1951; s. Ashley A. and Elvia H. Richardson; m. Florence C. St. Hilaire, Sept. 7, 1957 (dec. Nov. 17, 1998); children: Paula, Kathy, Peter, Steven, Edward, Vernon; m. Jennifer Harrypersad Dec., 24, 2002; stepchildren: Nicholas Binda, Devon Binda. BS, L.I. U., 1959. Cert. internat. financier. V.p., treas. Node 4 Assocs., Inc., Bklyn., 1970-71; asst. contr. Kings County Hosp. Ctr., Bklyn., 1971-74; owner Richardson Mgmt. Assoc., 1971—; contr. Kings County Hosp. Ctr., Bklyn., 1974-79; contr., CFO Harlem Hosp. Ctr., N.Y.C., 1979-95; CFO L.B.J. Health Complex, Inc., Bklyn., 1996-98; pres., CEO Accudata Sys. Svcs., Inc., N.Y.C., 1997—. Owner Empire Trading Co., 2002. Contbr. articles to profl. publs. Dir., treas. Bklyn. Local Econ. Devel. Corp., 1965-70, L.B.J. Health Complex, Inc., Bklyn., 1991-96; mem. Pub. Citizens. Sgt. U.S. Army, 1952-55. Mem. Healthcare Fin. Mgmt. Assn. (Follmer Bronze Merit award 1996), Nat. Soc. Accts., Ind. Assn. Accts. Bklyn., Caribbean Am. C. of C., Oxford Club, VFW, Disabled Am. Vets., Contrs. Orgn. (past pres.), Internat. Assn. Fin. Planning, Internat. Soc. Financiers; Am. Legion. Avocations: bowling, Scrabble, stamp collecting/philately, coin collecting/numismatics, bicycling. Home: 704 Empire Blvd Brooklyn NY 11213-5309 Office: Accudata Sys Svcs Inc Empire State Bldg Ste 4200 New York NY 10118

**RICHARDSON, ANN BISHOP,** foundation executive, lawyer; b. New Rochelle, NY, Dec. 15, 1940; d. Erwin Julius and Mary Frances (Stuart) Heilemann; children: Timothy William, Lynn Patricia, Melanie Elizabeth. BA summa cum laude, Georgetown U., 1977; JD, George Washington U., 1984; cert., Oxford U., Eng., 1986. Bar: Md. 1988, DC 1989. Student counselor Amideast, Beirut, 1967-68, program specialist, 1970-73; adminstrv. asst. UN Devel. Program, Yaounde, Cameroon, 1968-70; adminstrv. mgr. Antioch Sch. Law, Washington, 1977-79; chief adminstrv. officer for internat. ops. Peace Corps, Washington, 1980-84; dir. adminstrn. and fin. African Devel. Found., Washington, 1984-87; atty. Karr and McLain, Washington, 1987-92; v.p., gen. counsel Time Dollar, Inc., Washington, 1992-98; adj. prof. law DC Sch. Law, Washington, 1994-98; prof., acad. dean U. DC David A. Clarke Sch. Law, Washington, 1998—. Bd. dirs. Bur. Rehab., Inc. Active Neighbors, Inc., Washington, 1976—, Time Dollar, Inc. Recipient Spl. Achievement award Peace Corps, 1981, 82, African Devel. Found., 1986. Mem. ABA, ACLU, DC Bar Assn., Am. Women Univ. Grads., Soc. for Internat. Devel., Phi Beta Kappa. Office: David A Clarke Sch Law 4200 Connecticut Ave NW Washington DC 20008-1122

**RICHARDSON, BARBARA HULL,** state legislator, social worker; b. Danville, Pa., Sept. 30, 1922; d. Robert Alonzo and Clara Lucille (Woodruff) H.; widowed; children: Barbara Follansbee, Lawrence, Christine, Lovel Pratt. BA, Bryn Mawr Coll., 1944; MSW, Smith Coll. School for Social Work, 1973. Social worker child and family svcs. divsn. children and youth svcs. HHS, Keene, N.H., 1969-71, adminstr. child and family svcs. Concord, N.H., 1975-88, supr. policy writers, 1988-91; mem. N.H. Ho. Reps., Concord, 1992—. Trustee Mental Svcs. 1980—; bd. dirs. Cheshire Housing Trust, 1986-93; adv. bd. Casey Family Svcs. N.H., 1990—; vol. Hospice Monadnock Region, 1991—; mem. community coun. Luth. Social Svcs. New England, 1993—; bd. dirs. Keene Day Care Ctr. Democrat. Home: 101 Morgan Rd Richmond NH 03470-4909 Office: NH Ho of Reps State Capitol Concord NH 03301

**RICHARDSON, BETTY H.,** lawyer, former prosecutor; b. Oct. 3, 1953; BA, U. Idaho, 1976; JD, Hastings Coll. Law, 1982. Staff aide U.S. Senator Frank Church, 1976-77; tchg. asst. Hastings Coll. Law, 1980-82, 1980-82; legal rsch. asst. criminal divsn. San Francisco Superior Ct., 1982-84; jud. law clk. Chamber of Idaho Supreme Ct. Justice Robert C. Huntley Jr., 1984-86; atty. U.S. Dept. Justice, Boise, Idaho, 1993-2001, Richardson & O'Leary, Eagle, Idaho, 2001—; jud. law clk. Chamber of Chief U.S. Dist. Ct. Judge B. Lynn Winmill, Idaho, 2003—. Instr. Boise State U., 1987, 89; mem. U.S. Atty. Gen.'s Adv. Com. subcoms. on environ., civil rights and native Am. issues, others, 1993-2001; mem. hon. adv. bd. for Crime Victims Amendment in Idaho, 1994; mem. Dist. of Idaho Judges and Lawyer Reps. com., gender fairness com., Civil Justice Reform Act com. and criminal adv. com., 1993-2001; Dem. nominee Dist 1 Idaho, U.S. Ho. of Reps., 2003; adj. prof. constnl. law Boise State U., 2004; program planner Idaho State Bar and Law Found., 2004—. Mem. Idaho Indsl. Commn., 1991-93, chmn., 1993; mem. adv. bd. Family and Workplace Consortium, 1995-2001; bd. dirs. Tony Patino Fellowship. Recipient Harold E. Hughes Exceptional Svc. award Nat. Rural Inst. on Alcohol and Drug Abuse, 1999; Tony Patino fellow Hastings Coll. Law, 1982. Mem. FBA, Idaho Bar Assn. (governing coun. govt. and pub. sectors lawyers sect. 1999-01, Pro Bono Svc. award 1988), Idaho State Bar (alt. dispute resolution sect.), Idaho Women Lawyers (Kate Feltham award 2006), Idaho Legal Hist. Soc. Ptnrs. for Justice, Assistance League Boise, YMCA, City Club Boise. Office: Richardson & O'Leary 515 N 27th Boise ID 83702 Office Phone: 208-938-7900.

**RICHARDSON, BILL (WILLIAM BLAINE RICHARDSON),** governor; b. Pasadena, Calif., Nov. 15, 1947; m. Barbara Flavin, 1972. BA, Tufts U., Medford, Mass., 1970; MA, Fletcher Sch. Law and Diplomacy, 1971. Mem. staff US Ho. of Reps., 1971-72, US Dept. State, 1973-75; mem. staff fgn. relations com. US Senate, 1975-78; exec. dir. N. Mex. State Democratic Com., 1978, Bernalillo County Democratic Com., 1978; businessman Santa Fe, 1978-82; mem. 98th-103rd Congresses from 3rd N.Mex. dist., Washington, 1982-96; democratic chief dep. majority whip 103d Congress, Washington; permanent US rep. UN, NYC, 1997-98; sec. US Dept. Energy, Washington, 1998-2001; sr. mng. dir. Kissinger McLarty, Washington, 2001—02; gov. State of N. Mex., Santa Fe, 2003—. Ranking minority mem. Resources Com. on Nat. Pks., Forests and Lands; mem. Select Com. on intelligence, Helsinki Commn.; adj. prof. pub. policy Harvard U., 2001; cons. Salomon Smith Barney Author (with Michael Ruby): Between Worlds: The Making of an American Life, 2005. Vice chair Dem. Nat. Com.; active Big Bros.-Big Sisters, Santa Fe. Named one of 25 Most Influential Hispanics, Time Mag., 2005. Mem. Santa Fe Hispanic C. of C., Santa Fe C. of C., Council Fgn. Relations, NATO 2000 Bd., Congl. Hispanic Caucus, Am. G.I. Forum Democrat. Catholic. Office: Office of the Gov State Capitol Rm 400 Santa Fe NM 87501 Office Phone: 505-476-2200. Office Fax: 505-476-2226.*

**RICHARDSON, CAMPBELL,** retired lawyer; b. Woodland, Calif., June 18, 1930; s. George Arthur and Mary (Hall) R.; m. Patricia Packwood, Sept. 3, 1957 (dec. Oct. 1971); children: Catherine, Sarah, Thomas; m. Carol Tamblyn, June 1975 (div. Dec. 1977); m. Susan J. Lienhart, May 3, 1980; 1 child, Laura. AB, Dartmouth Coll., 1952; JD, NYU, 1955. Bar: Oreg. 1955, U.S. Dist. Ct. Oreg. 1957. Ptnr. Stoel Rives LLP, Portland, 1964-2000; ret., 2000—. Co-author Contemporary Trust and Will Forms for Oregon Attorneys, 2003, and for Idaho Attorneys, 2001; contbr. articles to profl. jours. Mem. Portland/Metro Govt. Boundary Commn., 1976; mem. Oreg. Adv. Com. to U.S. Commn. on Civil Rights, 1976-84; bd. dirs. Ctr. for Urban Edn., Portland, 1980-84, Dorchester Conf., Inc., 1982, Oreg. Zoo Found., 1993-2003; chmn. planned giving com. St. Vincent Med. Found., 1988-98; mem. planned giving coun. Oreg. Health Scis. Found., 1994-2003; trustee Met. Family Svc. Found., 1990-98; bd. dirs. Elders in Action, Portland, 2000-. Served with U.S. Army, 1955-57. Mem. ABA, Oreg. Bar Assn., Multnomah County Bar Assn., Estate Planning Coun. Portland (pres. 1978), Am. Coll. Trust and Estate Counsel, City Club, Multnomah Athletic Club (Portland). Republican. Home: 1500 SW 5th Ave Apt 1704 Portland OR 97201-5430 Office: Stoel Rives LLP 900 SW 5th Ave Ste 2300 Portland OR 97204-1229 Office Phone: 503-294-9337. E-mail: crichardson@stoel.com.

**RICHARDSON, CHARLES CLIFTON,** biochemist, educator; b. Wilson, NC, May 7, 1935; s. Barney Clifton and Florence Elizabeth (Barefoot) R.; m. Ute Ingrid Hanssum, July 29, 1961; children: Thomas Clifton, Matthew Wilfrid BSM., Duke U., 1959, MD, 1960; A.M. (hon.), Harvard U., 1967. Intern dept. medicine Duke U., Durham, NC, 1960-61; postdoctoral fellow dept. biochemistry Stanford U. Med. Sch., Calif., 1961-63; asst. prof. biol. chemistry Harvard Med. Sch., Boston, 1964-67, assoc. prof. 1967-69, prof. biol. chemistry, 1969—, chmn. dept. biol. chemistry, 1978-87, Edward S. Wood prof., 1979—. Physiol. chemistry study sect. NIH, 1970-74; mem. Fachbeirat of Max-Planck Inst. für Molekulare Genetik, Berlin, Fed. Republic Germany, 1980-89; sci. adv. com. U.S. Biochem. Corp., Cleve., 1983-93, Genetics Inst., Cambridge, Mass., 1986-99, NYCOMED-Amersham, U.K., 1998-2000; mem. Nat. Bd. Med. Examiners, 1973-76; nucleic acids and protein adv. com., Am. Cancer Soc. Inst., 1975-78; vis. com. Boston Biomed. Rsch. Found., 1985—; assoc. Helicon Found., San Diego, 1983-2000; sci. adv. bd. Amersham Life Sci. Inc., 1994-98. Assoc. editor: Ann. Rev. Biochemistry, 1973-82, editor, 1983-2003; mem. editl. bd. Jour. Biol. Chemistry, 1968-73, 84-88, Jour. Molecular Biology, 1976-79. Recipient Career Devel. award, NIH, 1967—76, Merit award, 1986, Herbert Tabor lectureship award, Jour. Biol. Chemistry, 2006. Fellow Am. Acad. Arts and Scis., Inst. of Medicine; mem. Nat. Acad. Scis., Am. Chem. Soc. (Eli Lilly Co. biol. chem. award 1968), Am. Soc. Biol. Chemists (mem. nominating com. 1974-75, 1983-84), Am. Cancer Soc. (coun. for rsch. and clin. investigation 1989-92), Am. Soc. Biochemistry and Molecular Biology (Merck award in biochemistry and molecular biology 1996, Herbert Tabor/Jour. Biol. Chemistry Lectureship award 2006). Business E-Mail: ccr@hms.harvard.edu.

**RICHARDSON, CINDY GUIDRY,** voice educator, music educator, religious education administrator; b. Crowley, La., Aug. 21, 1961; d. Lloyd Joseph and Pearl Hoffpauir Guidry; m. Crosby Gaar Richardson; children: Amie Victoria, Cassie Michelle, Patrick Crosby. B in Vocal Music Edn., U. La., Lafayette, 1987. Sec. Richardson Land Title Co., Lafayette, La., 1980—84; vocal music tchr. Lafayette Parish Sch. Bd., La., 1987—; dir. religious edn. St. Basil Ch., Duson, La., 2004—. Supervising tchr. Office of Tchr. Clin. Experiences-UL, Lafayette, La., 2006—. Dir. religious edn. St. Basil Ch., Duson, La., 2004—06. Recipient Tchr. of Yr., Scott Mid. Sch., 2001—02, Walmart, 2002. Mem.: APEL, Lafayette Vocal Music Tchrs. Assn. (pres. 1991—93), Lafayette Parish Vocal Music Tchrs. Assn. (sec./treas. 1988—90), La. Music Educators Assn., Music Educators Nat. Conf. Roman Catholic. Achievements include Numerous Superior Ratings for Choral Group Performances. Office: Scott Mid Sch 116 Marie St Scott LA 70583 Office Phone: 337-235-9698. Business E-Mail: cgrichardson@lpssonline.com.

**RICHARDSON, DANA ROLAND,** technology consultant; b. Mason City, Iowa, Jan. 11, 1945; s. Dana Roland Richardson and Louise Marion (Duke) Sarles; m. Sandra Anderson, June 12, 1966; children: Patricia Nan, Dana Roland, Jr. BS, UCLA, 1966, MBA, 1967. CPA, Calif., N.Y. Staff acct. Arthur Young, L.A., 1967—72, mgr., 1972—76, prin. N.Y.C., 1976—78; ptnr. Ernst & Young, N.Y.C., 1978—94; founder, ptnr. Dream Street Prodns., New Canaan, Conn., 2004—2002; pres. Richardson Media & Tech. LLC, 2003—. Author: A Manager's Guide to Computer Timesharing, 1975, Audit and Control of Information Systems, 1987. Staff sgt. Reserves USANG, 1967-73. Named one of Techology 100 Top 100 Achievers in Techn. in Am., Tech. Mag., 1982, Top 100 Influential People in Acctg., Acctg. Today mag., 2005; recipient Nat. Videographer award, Nat. Videography Assn., 1998, 1999, Telly award, 1999. Mem. AICPA (Lifetime Achievement award 2003), Calif. Soc. CPA's, Conn. Soc. CPA's. Republican. Episcopalian. Avocations: boating, fishing, music, videography, multimedia. Office: Richardson Media & Tech LLC 24 Blueberry Ln Canton CT 06019 Home: 24 Blueberry Ln Canton CT 06019-4503 Business E-Mail: rick@richardon-media-tech.com.

**RICHARDSON, DAVID L.,** lawyer; b. Washington, 1954; BA with high distinction, U. Va., Charlottesville, 1976, JD, 1978. Bar: Va. 1978. Ptnr. McGuireWoods LLP, Richmond, Va., chair firm fin. services dept., head firm pub. fin. group. Fellow: Healthcare Fin. Mgmt. Assn.; mem.: Va. Govt. Fin. Officers Assn., Va. Hosp. & Healthcare Assn., Local Govt. Attorneys of Va.,

Nat. Assn. Bond Lawyers. Office: McGuireWoods LLP One James Ctr 901 E Cary St Richmond VA 23219-4030 Office Phone: 804-775-1030. Office Fax: 804-698-2148. Business E-Mail: drichardson@mcguirewoods.com.

**RICHARDSON, DAVID WALTHALL,** cardiologist, educator, consultant; b. Nanking, China, Mar. 22, 1925; s. Donald William and Virginia (McIlwaine) R.; m. Frances Lee Wingfield, June 12, 1948; children: Donald, Sarah, David. BS, Davidson Coll., 1947; MD, Harvard U., 1951. Diplomate Am. Bd. Internal Medicine, Am. Bd. Cardiology. Intern, resident Yale New Haven Hosp., 1951-53; resident, fellow Med. Coll. Va., Richmond, 1953-56, assoc. prof. to prof. medicine, 1962-95, prof. emeritus, 1995—. Chmn. divsn. cardiology, 1972-87; interim chmn. dept. medicine, 1973-74; chief cardiology, assoc. chief staff for rsch. VA Hosp., Richmond, 1956-61, dir. cardiology tng. program, 1990-95; vis. scientist Oxford U., Eng., 1961-62; vis. prof. U. Milan, Italy, 1972-73. Contbr. articles to profl. jours. Moderator Hanover Presybery, Presbyn. Ch. U.S., Richmond, 1970; chmn. events com., NHLBI Cardiac Arrhythmia Suppression Trial, 1983-92, NHLBI Anti-Arrhythmics versus Implantable Defibrillators Trial, 1993-97. Served with USN, 1944-46. Fellow Am. Coll. Cardiology (gov. VA 1970-72), Am. Heart Assn. (coun. clin. cardiology and high blood pressure rsch.); mem. Am. Soc. Clin. Investigation, Am. Clin. and Climatol. Assn. Home: 1500 Westbrook Ct CYA 1105 Richmond VA 23227-3366 Office Phone: 804-200-1256. Personal E-mail: dwr1@wcrichmond.org.

**RICHARDSON, DEAN WHEELER,** equine surgeon, veterinary educator; b. Aug. 30, 1953; married; 1 child. Grad., Dartmouth Coll., Hanover, NH, 1974; DVM, Ohio State U., Coll. Vet. Medicine, 1975—79. Internship surgical residency training prog., U. Pa., 1979; with New Bolton Ctr., U. Pa. Sch. Vet. Medicine, Kennett Sq., Pa., 1979—, Charles W. Baker prof. equine surgery, chief of Large Animal Surgery. Mem. editl. bd. Specialty Mag. in the Sci. Biol. Chemicals, mem. adv. editl. bd. Zeitschrift für Metallkunde. Recipient Norden Disting. Teaching award, Disting. Alumni award, Coll. Vet. Medicine, Ohio State U., 2005. Mem.: Osteosynthesis Soc., Grayson-Jockey Club (mem. scientific adv. bd.). Achievements include recognized for teaching AO Veterinary in North America and Switzerland; leading authority in orthopedic surgery and long bone fractures in horses; renown for performing life saving surgery on Kentucy Derby winner Barbaro. Avocations: horseback riding, basketball, golf, birdwatching. Office: School Vet Medicine U Pa 382 W St Rd Kennett Square PA 19348 Office Phone: 610-444-5800. Office Fax: 610-925-8100.*

**RICHARDSON, DENNIS MICHAEL,** lawyer, educator; b. LA, July 30, 1949; s. Ralph Lee and Eva Catherine (McGuire) R.; 1 child from previous marriage, Scott Randol; m. Catherine Jean Coyl, July 27, 1973; children: Jennifer Eve, Valerie Jean, Rachel Catherine, Nicole Marie, Mary Rose, Marie Christina, Laura Michelle, Alyssa Rose. BA, Brigham Young U., 1976, JD, 1979. Bar: Oreg. 1979. Owner Dennis Richardson & Assocs., P.C., Central Point, Oreg., 1979—; pvt. practice law Central Point, Oreg., 1979—; state leg. Oreg. Ho. of Reps., 2003—, spkr. protem, 2005—. Chair ways and means sub com. human svcs. Oreg. Ho. of Reps., 2005—; guest lectr. in field. Contbr. articles to profl. jours. Bd. dirs. Oreg. Lung Assn., 1980, Shakespearean Festival, Ashland, 1981, Jackson County Legal Services, 1982; chmn. GOP Oreg. 2d. Congl. Dist., 1996-2000, treas. GOP Oreg. Exec. Com., 1996-2002; councilman Ctrl. Point City, 2001-2002. Served as helicopter pilot U.S. Army, 1969-71, Vietnam. Decorated Vietnamese Cross Gallantry. Republican. Office: Dennis Richardson & Assocs PC 55 S 5th St Central Point OR 97502-2474 Office Phone: 541-664-6622. Business E-Mail: dennis@justiceonline.com.

**RICHARDSON, DENNISE MARIE,** physician assistant; b. Patuxent River, Md., July 16, 1944; d. Hershel Elroy and Suzanne Marie (Ahern) R.; m. Richard Harold Browne, Aug. 10, 1970. BS, Lamar U., 1966, U. Tex., 1995; MS, Okla. State U., 1970, PhD, 1973. Cert. physician asst. Rsch. technician MD Anderson Hosp., Houston, 1967-68; fellow U. Tex., Dallas, 1974-75, rsch. assoc., 1978-93; rsch. immunologist Wadley Insts., Dallas, 1975-76; physician asst. Lakewood Med. Ctr., Dallas, 1996-97, Lewis Group, Dallas, 1997-98; pediat. physician asst. George Monroe, MD, Dallas, 1998—2002; ind. physician asst., 2002—. Fellow Am. Assn. Physician Assts.; mem. People to People Internat., Tex. Acad. Physician Assts., Alzheimer Assn. (group leader), Dallas Com. Fgn. Visitors, Dallas Camera Club (sec.), Beta Beta Beta, Phi Sigma. Republican. Avocations: photography, canoeing, writing. Home: 12045 Inwood Rd Dallas TX 75244-8016 E-mail: richb46@airmail.net.

**RICHARDSON, DON L.,** secondary school educator; s. Lloyd Anderson and Alice Joy Richardson; m. Carolyn Sue Richardson, Dec. 28, 1969; children: Sharla, Kyle. BS, Western N.Mex. U., Silver City, 1969; MS, East Tex. State U., Commerce, 1973. Master tchr. Tex. Edn. Agy. Tchr., coach Gallup H.S., N.Mex., 1969—70, Richardson Ind. Sch. Dist., Tex., 1970—73, Highland Park H.S., Dallas, 1973—2006, dept. chair social studies, 1988—92, head football coach, 1993—95, adminstr., 1996—2004. Mem. site-based com. Highland Park H.S., Dallas, 1988—92, mem. facilities com., 1992—2002, co-curricular coord., 1996—2004; spkr. football convs. and clinics, 1992—2004. Editor: U.S. History Readings, 1989. Sponsor Key Club, Dallas, 1990—92. Named Tchr. of Yr., 1998—99, All-Star Football Coach, 1980; recipient Tom Landry award, 1998, Football Dist. Coach of Yr., 1993, 1995, Football Dist. Co-Coach of Yr., 1994. Mem.: Tex. Classroom Tchrs. Assn., Tex. H.S. Coach Assn. Avocation: travel. Home: 1625 Centenary Richardson TX 75081 Office: Highland Park HS 4220 Emerson Dallas TX 75205

**RICHARDSON, DOT (DOROTHY GAY),** former Olympic softball player, physician; b. Orlando, Fla., Sept. 22, 1961; m. Bob Pinto. Student, Western Ill. U.; BS in Kinesiology, UCLA; M in Exercise, Adelphi U.; MD, U. Louisville; PhD (hon.), Western Ill. U., 2003; St. Leo Coll., 2004, Adelphi U.; LLD (hon.), Phila. Coll. Osteo. Medicine, 2005. Mem., capt. US Olympic Softball Team, 1996, 2000; resident in orthopedic surg. U. Calif. Med. Ctr.; med. dir. Nat. Tng. Ctr., Clermont, Fla., 2001—. Recipient Gold medal Pan. Am. Games, 1979, 87, 95, 99, ISF Women's World Championship, 1982, 86, 90, 94, 98, South Pacific Classic, 1994, Superball Classic, 1995, Atlanta Olympics, 1996, Sydney Olympics, 2000, Medal of Honor DAR, 2005; ERV Linda Best Defensive Player in Nation award (7 times), Flo Hyman award, 2002; named All-Am. Am. Softball Assn. (16 times), MVP Am. Softball Assn. (3 times), Major Fast Pitch Nat. Championship, Player of Decade for 80s NCAA. Office: Nat Tng Ctr 1099 Citrus Tower Blvd Clermont FL 34711 E-mail: dot.richardson@orhs.org.

**RICHARDSON, DOUGLAS J.,** career officer; b. New Britain, Conn. m. Denise Richardson; children: Erin, Megan. BS, USAF Acad., 1973; M in Pub. Adminstrn., George Washington U., 1990. Commd 2d lt. USAF, 1973, advanced through grades to col., 1994; F-4E pilot 526th Tactical Fighter Squadron, Ramstein AB, Germany, 1975-79; F-4E weapons officer 36th TFS, Osan AB, Republic of Korea, 1979-80, wing weapons, flight comdr., 1980-81; F-4 FWIC instr. pilot 414th Fighter Weapons Sch., Nellis AFB, 1981-82; exec. officer 57th Weapons Wing, Nellis AFB, Nev., 1983-84; F-16A test project mgr. Nellis AFB, 1985-86; asst. chief F-16C/LANTIRN test, 1985-86; action officer NATO divsn. Hdqr. USAF Europe, the Pentagon, Washington, 1986-87, action officer TAC divsn., 1987-89; F-16C pilot 612 Tactical Fighter Squadron, 1990-91; chief of safety 401st TFW, Torrejon AB, Spain, 1991, comdr. 613th TFS, Torrejon AB, 1991; asst. dir. of ops. 401st TFW, Torrejon AB, 1991-92; with sr. officer mgmt. divsn. Hdqs. USAFE, Ramstein Air Base, Germany, 1992-93; dep. comdr. 86th Ops. Group, Ramstein Air Base, 1993; comdr. 39th Ops. Group, Incirlik Air Base, Turkey, 1993-94; dep. chief of staff Plans and Ops., 5th ATAF, Verona, Italy, 1994-96; comdr. 48th Fighter Wing, Royal Air Force Station, Lakenheath, Eng., 1996-98, 53rd Wing, Eglin AFB, Fla., 1998—. Decorated Legion of Merit, Air medal with two oak cluster, Aerial Achievement medal, Combat Readiness medal with one oak leaf cluster, NATO medal. Office: 53 WG/CC 203 WD Ave Ste 600 Eglin Afb FL 32542-6867

**RICHARDSON, EDWARD R.,** academic administrator; b. Pensacola, Fla., Jan. 24, 1939; s. Edward H. and Doria (Parker) R.; m. Nell C.; children: Merit Lynn Richardson Smith, Laura Leigh. BS, Auburn U., 1962, MEd, 1967, EdD, 1972. Sci. tchr. Montgomery Pub. Schs., Montgomery, Ala., 1962-64, prin., 1967-70, Andalusia High Sch., Andalusia, Ala., 1972-80; asst. prof. Auburn U., Montgomery, 1980-82; supt. Auburn City Schs., Auburn, Ala., 1982-95, State of Ala., Montgomery, 2004—; interim pres. Auburn U., Montgomery, Ala., 2004—. Bd. mem. So. Regional Edn. Bd., Atlanta, 1989—; co-dir. Ala. Mgmt. Inst. Sch. Leaders, Montgomery, 1980-82. Ednl. advisor Gov. Guy Hunt, Montgomery, 1987—; active Landmarks Found., Montgomery, 1968-69. Named Supt. of Yr., State PTA, Montgomery, 1986-87, Educator of Yr., Andalusia Jaycees, 1973-74. Mem. Ala. Assn. Secondary Sch. Adminstrs. (pres. 1978-79), Ala. Assn. Sch. Adminstrs. (pres. 1986-87), Rotary (Auburn chpt. pres. 1987-88), Capitol Lions Club (pres. 1968-69), Phi Delta Kappa (Auburn U. chpt. pres. 1971-72). Republican. Methodist. Avocations: tennis, reading, gardening. Office: Off of President 107 Samford Hall Auburn University AL 36849 Office Phone: 334-844-4650. E-mail: president@auburn.edu.*

**RICHARDSON, ELIZABETH HALL,** retired ecologist; b. Waltham, Mass., June 5, 1937; d. Livingston and Elizabeth (Blodgett) Hall; m. (div.); children: Elisabeth F. Richardson, Anne K. Richardson. AB, Radcliffe Coll., 1959; MPA, U. So. Calif., 1975; MBA, U. Denver, 1986. Asst. biology tchr. Presbyn. Ladies Coll., Pymble, NSW, Australia, 1959; tchr. drama Middlesex Sch., Concord, Mass., 1961-62; adminstrv. asst. Gov. Richard D. Lamm, Denver, 1975-76; coord. govt. affairs Rocky Mountain Energy Co., Lakewood, Colo., 1977-79; exec. dir. Thorne Ecol. Inst., Boulder, Colo., 1981-82; rsch. asst. Boettcher & Co., Denver, 1988-89; land protection specialist Colo. Open Lands, Lakewood, 1991—2002. Sec. Colo. Coalition of Land Trusts, Denver, 1992-2005. Sec. Simon's Rock Coll. of Bard, 1989—; active N.Mex. Land Conservancy, 2002—. Mem. ASPA, Rocky Mountain Women's Inst. (chair 1982-97). Democrat. Home: 2400 S Jackson St Denver CO 80210-5637

**RICHARDSON, EMILIE WHITE,** manufacturing executive, investment company executive, educator; b. Chattanooga, July 08; d. Emmett and Mildred Evelyn (Harbin) White; 1 child, Julie Richardson Milunic. BA, Wheaton Coll. With Christy Mfg. Co., Inc., Fayetteville, N.C., Ft. Lauderdale, Fla., 1952—, exec. v.p., 1967-74, exec. v.p., 1975-79, pres., CEO, 1980—. V.p. E. White Investment Co., 1968-83, pres., 1983—; cons. Aerostatic Industries, 1979—; v.p. Gannon Corp., 1981—; cons. govt. contacts and offshore mfg., 1981—; lectr., spkr. in field. V.p. pub. rels. Ft. Lauderdale Symphony Soc., 1974-76, v.p. membership, 1976-77, adv. bd., 1978—; active Artistic Found., Ft. Lauderdale Mus. Art, Beaux Arts, Freedoms Found.; mem. East Broward Women's Rep. Club, 1968—, Americanism chmn., 1971-72. Mem. Internat. Platform Assn., Nat. Spkrs. Assn., Fla. Spkrs. Assn., Toastmasters, Coral Ridge Yacht Club. Methodist. Home: 1531 NE 51st St Fort Lauderdale FL 33334-5709 Office: 3311 Fort Bragg Rd Fayetteville NC 28303-4763 Personal E-mail: emilier@mindspring.com.

**RICHARDSON, EVERETT VERN,** hydraulic engineer, educator, administrator, consultant; b. Scottsbluff, Nebr., Jan. 5, 1924; s. Thomas Otis and Jean Mae (Everett) R.; m. Billie Ann Kleckner, June 23, 1948; children: Gail Lee, Thomas Everett, Jerry Ray. BS, Colo. State U., 1949, MS, 1960, PhD, 1965. Registered profl. engr., Colo. From hydraulic engr. to project chief U.S. Geol. Survey, Wyo., 1949—52, Iowa, 1952—56, rsch. hydraulic engr. Wyo., 1956—63, project chief Ft. Collins, Colo., 1963—68; adminstr. Engring. Rsch. Ctr. Colo. State U., Ft. Collins, 1968—88, dir. Egypt water use project, 1977-84, prof. in charge of hydraulic program, 1982-88, dir. hydraulic lab. Engring. Rsch. Ctr., 1982-88, prof. emeritus, 1988—, dir. Egypt irrigation improvement project, 1985-90; dir. Egypt Water Rsch. Ctr. Project, Ft. Collins, 1988-89; sr. assoc. Ayers Assocs. Inc. (formerly Resource Cons./Engr., Inc.), Ft. Collins, 1989—. Dir. Consortium for Internat. Devel., Tucson, 1972-87; developer stream stability and scour at hwy. bridges course for State Dept. Transps. for NHI, FHWA; investigator for NTSB 1987 I-90 bridge failure, NY, 1997, railroad bridge failure, Ariz., CALTRAN 1995 I-5 bridge failure; chmn. peer rev. panel Turnefairbanks Rsch. Ctr. Hydraulics Lab., 2004; cons. in field; lectr. in field. Sr. author Highways in the River Environment: Hydraulic and Environmental Considerations, FHWA, 1975, 1990, Evaluating Scour at Bridge, FHWA, 1991, 1993, 1995, 2001, FHWA Hydr. Design Series No. 6: River Engineering for Highway Encroachments, 2001, Civil Engring. Handbook, 1995; co-author: Engring. Handbook, 1995, 2003; contbr. Handbook of Fluid Dynamics and Fluid Machinery, 1996, Water Resources-Environmental Planning, Management and Development, 1996, more than 200 articles to profl. jours. Mem. Ft. Collins Water Bd., 1969-84; mem. NY State Bridge Safety Assurance Task Force, 1988-91. Decorated Bronze Star, Purple Heart, Combat Infantry Badge; named hon. diplomate Am. Acad. Water Resources Engring. 2005; U.S. Govt. fellow MIT, 1962-63. Fellow: ASCE (chair task com., bridge scour rsch. 1990—96, editor Compendium of Stream Stability and Scour Papers 1991—98, vice chair 1997—2002, J.S. Stevens award 1961, hydraulics divsn. task com. excellence award 1993, Hans Albert Einstein award 1996); mem.: Am. Acad. Water Resource Engrs. (hon. diplomate 2005), Internat. Congress for Irrigation and Drainage (bd. dirs.), Sigma Xi, Sigma Tau, Chi Epsilon. Home: 824 Gregory Rd Fort Collins CO 80524-1504 Office: Ayres Assocs PO Box 270460 Fort Collins CO 80527-0460 Office Phone: 970-223-5556. Business E-Mail: richardsone@ayresassociates.com.

**RICHARDSON, GRACE ELIZABETH,** consumer products company executive; b. Salem, Mass., Nov. 22, 1938; d. George and Julia (Sheridan) R.; m. Ralph B. Henderson, Mar. 3, 1979. BS, Simmons Coll., 1960; MS, Cornell U., 1962; MBA, NYU, 1981. Textile technologist Harris Rsch. Lab., Washington, 1962-65; instr. Simmons Coll., Boston, 1965-66; dir. consumer edn. materials J.C. Penney, N.Y.C., 1966-73; dir. residential conservation Con Edison, N.Y.C., 1974-81; dir. consumer affairs Chesebrough-Ponds, Greenwich, Conn., 1981-85; v.p. global consumer affairs Colgate Palmolive, N.Y.C., 1985—2004; chmn. of bd. YMCA of N.Y.C., 2004—. Chair Simmons Coll. Leadership Coun., 1993—97; mem. com. Juilliard Sch., 1996—; bd. dirs. SOCAP, 1996—99, Nat. Coalition Consumer Edn., 1983—93; mem. Cornell U. Coun., chair pub. rels. com., 1988—97; bd. mem. UNIFEM, 2002—. Named Nat. Bus. Home Economist of Yr., Home Economists in Bus., 1979. Mem. Women's Forum, Cornell Club N.Y.C. (bd. dirs. 1989-96). Home: 180 E 79th St New York NY 10021-0437

**RICHARDSON, HERBERT HEATH,** mechanical engineer, educator, dean; b. Lynn, Mass., Sept. 24, 1930; s. Walter Blake and Isabel Emily (Heath) R.; m. Barbara Ellsworth, Oct. 6, 1973. SB, SM with honors, MIT, 1955, ScD, 1958. Registered profl. engr., Mass., Tex. Research asst., research engr. Dynamic Analysis and Control Lab. MIT, 1953-57, instr. Dept. Mech. Engring., 1957-58, mem. faculty, 1958-84, prof. mech. engring., 1968-85, head dept., 1974-82, assoc. dean engring., 1982-84; Disting. prof. engring. Tex. A&M U., 1984—; Regents prof. Tex. A&M U. System, College Station, 1993—; dean, vice chancellor engring. Tex. A&M U. Sys., 1984-85; dep. chancellor, dean, dir. Tex. Engring. Expt. Sta. Tex. A&M U., 1991-93; chancellor Tex. A&M U. System, College Station, 1991-93, assoc. vice chancellor engring., 1994, assoc. dean engring., 1993—; dir. Tex. Trans. Inst., Tex. A&M Univ. Sys., 1993—. With Ballistics Rsch. Lab. Aberdeen Proving Ground, Md., 1958; chief scientist U.S. Dept. Transp., 1970-72; chmn. adv. com. for engring. NSF, 1987-89, adv. com. basic energy scis. U.S. Dept. Energy, 1987-91. Author: Introduction to System Dynamics, 1971; contbr. articles to profl. publs. Trustee S.W. Rsch. Inst. Officer U.S. Army, 1968. Recipient medal Am. Ordnance Assn., 1953, Gold medal Pi Tau Sigma, 1963, Meritorious Service award and medal Dept. Transp., 1972. Fellow AAAS, ASME (Moody award fluid engring. divsn. 1970, Centennial medallion 1983, Rufus Oldenberger medal 1984, Meritorious Svc. medal 1986, Disting. Svc. award 1986, hon. mem. 1987); mem. NAE (coun. 1986-92, com. on engring. edn.), Am. Soc. Engring. Edn. (Disting. Svc. medal 1993, Lamme award 1997), Inst. Transp. Engrs., Nat. Rsch. Coun. (gov. bd.

1986-92, chmn. transp. rsch. bd. 1988-89), Nat. Acads. (nat. assoc., life), Sigma Xi, Tau Beta Pi. Office: Tex A&M U Sys MS 3135 College Station TX 77843-0001 E-mail: herbert-richardson@tamu.edu.

**RICHARDSON, IAN WILLIAM,** actor; b. Edinburgh, Scotland, Apr. 7, 1934; s. John and Margaret R.; m. Maroussia Frank, Feb. 2, 1961; children: Jeremy, Miles. Diploma in Acting and Teaching, Royal Scottish Acad. Music and Drama, D in Drama, 1999; D (hon.), Stirling U., 2006. Actor Royal Shakespeare Co., Stratford on Avon and London, 1960-75, Shaw Festival Theatre, Niagara, Ont., Can., 1977. Appeared in plays including My Fair Lady, Broadway, 1976-77, The Miser, 1995, The Magistrate, 1997-98, The Seven Ages of Man, 1999, The Hollow Crown, 2002-04, The Creeper, 2005; films and TV plays include Tinker, Tailor, Soldier, Spy, Private Shulz, The Sign of Four, The Hound of the Baskervilles, Phantom of the Opera, 1990, The Gravy Train, 1990, House of Cards, 1991, The Gravy Train Goes East, 1991, To Play the King, 1993, Foreign Affairs Remember, Savage Play, 1994, The Final Cut, 1995; films include Brazil, Whoops!, Apocalypse, The Fourth Protocol, Cry Freedom, The Fifth Province, 1996, Dark City, 1998, From Hell, 2000, Remake, 2005; TV programs includes Star Quality, Porterhouse Blue, The Winslow Boy, 1989, An Ungentlemanly Act, 1992, Catherine the Great (miniseries), 1994, Gormenghast, 1999, (miniseries) Magician's House, 1999, Murder Rooms, 1999, Murder Rooms II, 2000, Strange, BBC TV, 2001, 03, (ITV) Miss Marple, 2004, Bleak House, 2005, Booze Cruise2-BBC, (films) Joyeux Noël, 2005, Greyfriars Bobby, 2005, Desaccord Parfair, 2006; author prefaces to Shakespearean works. Recipient CBE award, 1989, BAFTA award, 1991, award Royal TV Soc., 1991. Fellow Royal Scottish Acad. Music and Drama; mem. SAG, Brit. Actors Equity, Actors Equity. Office: care Diamond Mgmt 31 Percy St London W1T 2DD England E-mail: maroussia@maroussia.freeserve.co.uk.

**RICHARDSON, J. WILLIAM,** hotel executive; Acting pres. Interstate Hotels Corp., Pitts., 1999—, vice chmn., CFO, 1999—. Office: Interstate Hotels Corp Foster-Plaza Ten 680 Andersen Dr Pittsburgh PA 15220-2700 also: Interstate Hotels & Resorts 4501 Fairfax Dr Arlington VA 22203-1656

**RICHARDSON, JAMES,** computer company executive; married; 2 children. B in Mktg. and Fin., Queens U., Kingston, Ont., Can. Formerly with Unisys; with Cisco Systems, Inc., 1990—, v.p. intercontinental ops., 1992—94, v.p. N.Am. ops., 1995—96, pres., Europe, Mid. East and Africa ops., 1996—99, sr. v.p. Enterprise Line of Bus., sr. v.p., chief mktg. officer San Jose, Calif., 2001—. Avocations: hockey, skiing, sailing. Office: Cisco Systems Inc 170 W Tasman Dr San Jose CA 95134

**RICHARDSON, JAMES,** chef; Line cook Boca, sous chef, 1997; owner, head chef Atomic Café, 1998; chef Berns; line cook Bergamot Café, LA, 2001, co-exec. chef; co-owner, exec. chef Nook Bistro, LA. Named one of LA's Rising Stars, StarChefs.com, 2006. Office: Nook Bistro 11628 Santa Monica Blvd Los Angeles CA 90025 Office Phone: 310-207-5160.*

**RICHARDSON, JAMES BERNARD,** music educator; b. Smithfield, NC, Dec. 21, 1970; s. Annie Griffin Richardson and Anthoney Harris Jenkins; m. Rhonda Kay Jacobs, July 6, 1996; children: James Bernard Richardson II, Jacob Bejorn. BS Music Edn., NC Agrl. & Tech. State U., 1994. Tchr. music Corinth-Holders H.S., Zebulon, NC, 1998—2000; dir. bands Smithfield-Selma H.S., NC, 2000—03; dir. music James Kenan H.S., Warsaw, NC, 2003—04; dir. bands Pine Forest H.S., Fayetteville, NC, 2004—. Song leader Cmty. Ch. of Christ, Goldsboro, NC, 2003, Selma Ch. of Christ, NC, 1998—2003, Berkeley Ch. of Christ, Moncks Corner, SC, 1996—98. Specialist Army N.G., 1988—94. Mem.: Music Educators Nat. Conf. (assoc.; coll. chpt. pres. 1993—94), Phi Mu Alpha Sinfonia (assoc.), Kappa Kappa Psi (assoc.), Phi Beta Sigma (assoc.). Mem. Church Of Christ(Non Instrumental). Office: Pine Forest High School 525 Andrews Rd Fayetteville NC 28311 Office Fax: 910-488-0790. E-mail: jamesrichardson@ccs.k12.nc.us.

**RICHARDSON, JAMES DAVID,** surgeon; b. Morehead, Ky., 1945; MD, U. Ky., 1970. Diplomate Am. Bd. Surgeons, Am. Bd. Vascular Surgery, Am. Bd. Thoracic Surgery, Am. Bd. SCC. Intern U. Ky. Med. Ctr., Lexington, 1970, resident, 1971-72, U. Tex., San Antonio, 1972-76; surgeon Norton Hosp., Louisville, 1977—; prof. surgery U. Louisville, 1979—; pres. Am. Bd. Surgery, 1998-99. Past pres. So. Surg. Assn., Western Surg. Assn. Editor: (jour.) Am. Surgeon. Fellow ACS (bd. regents); mem. AMA, Am. Assn. Surgery of Trauma, Soc. Surgergy Alimentary Tract, Alpha Omega Alpha. Office: U Louisville Dept Surgery 550 S Jackson St Louisville KY 40202-1622 Office Phone: 502-583-8303, 502-852-5452.

**RICHARDSON, JASON ANTHONEY,** professional basketball player; b. Jan. 20, 1981; Student, U. Mich. Profl. basketball player Golden State Warriors, Oakland, Calif., 2001—. Named to NBA All-Rookie First Team, 2002; recipient Winners award, NBA All-Star Slam Dunk Contest, 2002—03. Achievements include member of NCAA championship team, 2000; won NBA Slam Dunk Contest, 2002, 2003. Office: Golden State Warriors 1011 Broadway Oakland CA 94607*

**RICHARDSON, JOHN,** retired international relations executive; b. Boston, Feb. 4, 1921; s. John and Hope (Hemenway) R.; m. Thelma Ingram, Jan. 19, 1945; children: Teren de Cossy, Hope Gravelly, Catherine Munch, Hetty L AB, Harvard U., 1943, JD, 1949. Bar: NY 1949. Assoc. Sullivan & Cromwell, NYC, 1949-55; with Paine, Webber, Jackson & Curtis, NYC, 1955-69, gen. ptnr., 1958-61, ltd. ptnr., 1961-69; pres., chief exec. officer Free Europe, Inc. (Radio Free Europe), 1961-68; asst. sec. for ednl. and cultural affairs Dept. State, 1969-77, also acting asst. sec. state for pub. affairs, 1971-73; exec. dir. for social policy Ctr. for Strategic and Internat. Studies; rsch. prof. internat. comm. Sch. Fgn. Svc., Georgetown U., Washington, 1977-78; pres., chief exec. officer Youth for Understanding, Inc., 1978-86, bd. dirs., 1986-98; counselor US Inst. of Peace, 1987-90. Spl. advisor Aspen Inst. Humanistic Studies, 1977—80. Founder Polish Med. Aid Project, 1957—61; co-founder, chmn. bd. Am. Com. to Aid Poland, 1989—95; pres. Internat. Rescue Com., 1960—61, bd. dirs., 1958—61, 1978—2004, bd. overseers, 2004—; chmn. Am. Coun. for UN U., 1977—87, Consortium for Internat. Citizens Exch., 1980—84, Delphi Internat., 1995—99, bd. dirs., 1999—2001; chmn., bd. dirs. Nat. Endowment for Democracy, 1984—88, bd. dirs., 1991—92, chmn. emeritus, 1992—; bd. dirs. Freedom House, 1963—69, pres., 1977—84; mem. Coun. Fgn. Rels., 1957—; Citizens Commn. on S.E. Asian Refugees, 1978—85; bd. dirs. Nat. Policy Assn., 1958—68, 1977—86, Japan-US Friendship Commn., 1976—77; chmn. NYC Met. Mission United Ch. of Christ, 1966—69; bd. dirs. Kennedy Ctr. for the Performing Arts, 1970—77, Inter-Am. Found., 1977—, East-West Ctr., 1975—77, Am. Forum for Global Edn., 1977—, Social Sci. Found., U. Denver, 1992—2004, World Learning, 2001—05, Meridian House Internat., 1977—83, Atlantic Coun. U.S., 1982—84, Fgn. Student Svc. Coun., 1978—82, Coun. for Advancement of Citizenship, 1991—96, Coun. Cmty. of Democracies, 1996—, chmn., 1999—2001, pres. emeritus, 2001—. With paratroops USAR, WWII. Decorated Bronze Star with v device, Japan Order of the Sacred Treasure, Gold and Silver Star; Germany Order of Merit, Commdr.'s Cross, Poland Order of Merit, Knight Cross. Home: 9707 Old Georgetown Rd Apt 1104 Bethesda MD 20814-1746

**RICHARDSON, JOHN CARROLL,** lawyer, financial consultant; b. Mobile, Ala., May 3, 1932; s. Robert Felder and Louise (Simmons) R.; m. Cicely Tomlinson, July 27, 1961; children: Nancy Louise, Robert Felder III, Leslie. BA, Tulane U., 1954; LLB cum laude, Harvard U., 1960. Bar: Colo. 1960, N.Y. 1965, D.C. 1972. Assoc. Holland & Hart, Denver, 1960-64; legal v.p. Hoover Worldwide Corp., N.Y.C., 1964-69; v.p., gen. counsel Continental Investment Corp., Boston, 1969; dep. tax legis. counsel U.S. Dept. Treasury, Washington, 1970-71, tax legis. counsel, 1972-73; ptnr. Brown, Wood, Ivey, Mitchell & Petty, N.Y.C., 1973-79, LeBoeuf, Lamb, Leiby & MacRae, N.Y.C., 1979-88, Morgan, Lewis & Bockius, N.Y.C., 1988-93; ret., 1993. Tax legis. cons., Orford, N.H., 1993—; adj. prof. Law Sch. Fordham U., 1990-94. Served to lt. comdr. USN, 1954-58. Mem. ABA (chmn. com. administrv.

practice tax sect. 1984-86), N.Y. State Bar Assn. (exec. com. tax sect. 1975-84), D.C. Bar Assn., Am. Coll. Tax Counsel, N.Y. Athletic Club, Royal Automobile Club. Office Phone: 603-353-4608.

**RICHARDSON, JOHN THOMAS,** academic administrator, clergyman; b. Dallas, Dec. 20, 1923; s. Patrick and Mary (Walsh) R. BA, St. Mary's Sem., Perryville, Mo., 1946; S.T.D., Angelicum U., Rome, Italy, 1951; MA, St. Louis U., 1954. Prof. theology, dean studies Kenrick Sem., St. Louis, 1951-54; lectr. Webster Coll., 1954; dean Grad. Sch. DePaul U., Chgo., 1954-60, exec. v.p., dean faculties, 1960-81, pres., 1981-93; prof. DePaul U. Coll. Law, Chgo., 1955; chancellor DePaul U., Chgo., 1993—. Vis. mem. theology faculty Christ the King Major Sem., Nyeri, Kenya, East Africa, 1997—. Trustee DePaul U., Chgo., 1954-93, life trustee, 1993-. Office: De Paul U 1 E Jackson Blvd Chicago IL 60604-2287

**RICHARDSON, JOHN VINSON, JR.,** library and information science professor; b. Columbus, Ohio, Dec. 27, 1949; s. John Vinson Sr. and Hope Irene (Smith) R.; m. Nancy Lee Brown, Aug. 22, 1971. BA, Ohio State U., 1971; MLS, Peabody Coll., 1972; PhD, Ind. U., 1978. Asst. prof. UCLA, 1978-83, assoc. prof., 1983-98, editor The Libr. Quar., 1994—2003, prof., 1998—, assoc. dean grad. divsn., 2002—, mem. editl. bd., The Libr. Quar., 2004—. Faculty coord. UCLA-St. Petersburg State Acad. of Culture Exch. Program, 1996—; fellow advanced rsch. Inst. U. Ill., 1991; pres. Info. Transfer, Inglewood, Calif., 1988—; vis. fellow Charles Sturt U. NSW Australia, 1990; vis. scholar ALISE Russia Project, St. Petersburg and Moscow, 1996; vis. disting. scholar OCLC Inc., Dublin, Ohio, 1996-97; presidential scholar, Libr. Sys. & Svcs., LLC, 2002—03; chmn. Calif. Pacific Ann. Conf. Com. on Archives and History, 1992-96; Henderson lectr. U. N.C., Chapel Hill, 1997; mem. UCLA Privilege and Tenure, 1999-2000, chair, 2000-02; Fulbright sr. specialist Vladivostok State U. Econ. and Svc., Russia, 2005.; cons. to U.S. Dept of State, Vladivostok, 2000, Uganda and Zambia, 2001, Eritrea, 2003, Turkmenistan, 2005. Author: Spirit of Inquiry, 1982, Gospel of Scholarship, 1992, Knowledge-based Systems for General Reference Work, 1995, Understanding Reference Transactions, 2002; mem. editl. bd. Ref. Svcs. Rev., Ann Arbor, Mich., 1991—, Jour. Govt. Info., Oxford, Eng., 1975-2005, Index to Current Urban Documents, Westport, Conn., 1987—, U. Calif. Press Catalogues and Bibliographies series, 1994-97, Jour. Edn. for Libr. and Info. Sci., 2005-07. Mem. UCLA Grad. Coun., 1992-96, chair, 1995-96; mem. U. Calif. systemwide coord. com. on grad. affairs, 1993-96; pres. Wesley Found., L.A., 1981-87; lay del. Cal-Pac Conf. United Meth. Ch., 1985, 86, 92-96, chair conf. commn. on archives and history, 1992—96. Rsch. grantee Coun. on Libr. Resources, 1985, 90, Assn. Libr. and Info. Sci. Educators rsch. grantee, 1984, 87, 98, Online Computer Libr. Ctr. Libr. and Info. Sci. grantee, 1999; Harold Lancour scholar Beta Phi Mu, 1986, 99, Kaliper Sr. scholar U. Mich., 1998-99, Presdl. scholar Libr. Systems and Svcs. LLC, 2002—03; recipient Louise Maxwell award Ind. U. Alumni Assn., 1995. Mem. ALA (Justin Winsor prize 1990, Ref. and Adult Svcs. divsn. Outstanding Paper award 1992), AAAS, Assn. Libr. and Info. Sci. Educators (rsch. paper prize 1986, 91, rsch. grants 1984, 87, 98), Am. Soc. for Info. Sci. (Best Info. Sci. book 1995), Am. Assn. Adv. Slavic Studies, Sigma Xi. Democrat. Avocations: wine tasting, reading, travel. Office: UCLA GSE&IS DIS Campus Box 951520 Los Angeles CA 90095-1520 Office Phone: 310-206-2281. Business E-mail: jrichard@ucla.edu. *By our common action, we can bend the flow of history.*

**RICHARDSON, JOSEPH HILL,** physician, medical educator; b. Rensselaer, Ind., June 16, 1928; s. William Clark and Vera (Hill) R.; m. Joan Grace Meininger, July 8, 1950; children: Lois N., Ellen M., James K. MS in Medicine, Northwestern U., 1950, MD, 1953. Diplomate Am. Bd. Internal Medicine. Intern U.S. Naval Hosp., Great Lakes, Ill., 1953-54; physician internal medicine, hematology pvt. practice, Marion, Ind., 1959-67, Ft. Wayne, Ind., 1967—. Assoc. clin. prof. medicine Ind. U. Sch. Medicine, 1993—; founding mem. The Reviewing Physician Group, 2001—. Contbr. articles to profl. jours. Fellow in medicine Cleve. Clinic, 1956-59. Fellow: AAAS, ACP; mem.: AMA, Masons. Home and Office: 8726 Fortuna Way Fort Wayne IN 46815-5725 Office Phone: 260-485-1391.

**RICHARDSON, JUDY MCEWEN,** investment banker, consultant, cartoonist; b. Appleton, Wis., June 3, 1947; d. John Mitchell and Isabel Annette (Ruble) McEwen; m. Larry Leroy Richardson, Mar. 19, 1972 (div. Oct. 1983). BA in English, Stanford U., 1968, MA in Edn., 1969; PhD in Higher Edn., U. Wash., 1975. Dir. ednl. rsch. St. Olaf Coll., Northfield, Minn., 1975-79; evaluation specialist Northwest Regional Ednl. Laboratory, Portland, 1980-82; legis. rsch. analyst Ariz. State Sen., Phoenix, 1982-87; dir. sch. fin. Ariz. Dept. Edn., Phoenix, 1987-92, assoc. supt., 1992-94; ednl. cons. Scottsdale, Ariz., 1994-96; exec. dir. Ariz. State Bd. for Sch. Capital Facilities, Phoenix, 1996-98; sch. fin. cons. Peacock, Hislop, Staley & Given, Phoenix, 1998—2002; v.p. Stone & Youngberg, Phoenix, 2002—. Cartoonist for the Ariz. Capitol Times, 1995-96. Office: Stone & Youngberg LLC 2555 E Camelback Rd Ste 280 Phoenix AZ 85016 Office Phone: 602-794-4012. Business E-Mail: jrichardson@syllc.com.

**RICHARDSON, K. SCOTT,** sales executive; b. Laurens, Iowa, Nov. 3, 1951; s. Kenneth and Lanore K.; m. Theresa Ann Fitzsimmons, Aug. 31, 1974; children: Seth Ian, Aaron Paul, Evan Scott, Claire Elizabeth, Anna Christine. BS in Radiologic Tech., Creighton U., Omaha, 1974; MS, U. Nebr., Omaha, 1976. Spl. procedures tech. Med. Coll. Va., Richmond, 1974-75; chief spl. procedure tech. St. Vincent Hosp., Sioux City, Iowa, 1975; inservice coordinator to radiology mgr. Nebr. Meth. Hosp., Omaha, 1975-78; sales rep. to sr. sales rep. Philips Med. Systems, Inc., Omaha, 1978-81; adminstrv. dir. radiology The Meth. Hosp., Houston, 1981-83, reg. mgr. P.P. Klinobiolog Co., Dallas, 1983-84, mgr. sales and svc., 1984-87, v.p. sales and svc., 1987-98, sr. v.p. sales and svc., 1998—2003; COO Perkins Electronics, Dallas, 2000—; regional sales mgr. Philip Med. Systems N.Am., 2003—04; exec. v.p. Celebrations Mgmt., 2004—, also bd. dirs., 2004—; pres. Life's a Beach Grill, SA. Bd. dirs. Strategic Med. Svcs., Inc., Strategic Med. Svcs. San Antonio, SMS Acquisition #1. Eucharistic min., svce. min., lector, tchr. continuing Cath. edn., chmn. fin. com., chmn. bldg. steering com. St. Philips Ch.; T-ball coord. Braeburn Little League, 1989—; coach YMCA Indoor Soccer League, 1987—; Highland Village Area Baseball and Softball Assn., 1998—; mgr. Lewisville Baseball Assn., 1990—, team sponsor, 1990—, bd. dirs., current, 1992—; active ARC, Glenshire Soccer Club, Braeburn Valley West Swim Team; chmn. City of Highland Village Parks and Recreation Bd.; mem. City of Highland Village Tree Bd., Highland Village Cmty. Ctr. Com.; bd. dirs. Louisville Baseball Assn. Mem. Am. Registry Radiologic Technologists, Iowa Soc. Radiologic Technologists, Assn. Univ. Radiology Technologists, Tex. Soc. Radiologic Technologists. Republican. Roman Catholic. Avocations: fishing, travel, swimming, golf, basketball, collecting wine. Home: 2415 Silverthorne Ct Highland Village TX 75077-3109 Office Phone: 972-768-6600. E-mail: ksr2531@aol.com.

**RICHARDSON, KELLY CHRISTOPHER,** literature and language educator, writer; b. Decatur, Ga., Feb. 11, 1973; s. Alan Lee and Janet Ann Richardson; m. Elizabeth Shea Turner, Dec. 29, 2001; 1 child, Jacob Christopher. BA in English, Ga. State U., 2000, MA in Edn., 2001; PhD in Ednl. Policy and Leadership, Berne U. and Internat. Grad. Sch., St. Kitts, West Indies, 2004. Cert. help desk profl. Support Techs., Ga., 1999; T5 tchr. Ga. Profl. Standards Commn., 2001. Distbn. specialist DeKalb Med. Ctr., Decatur, Ga., 1992—94; tech. support specialist DeKalb County Sch. Sys., Decatur, Ga., 1994—99; cert. help desk profl. Support Techs., Inc., Atlanta, 1999—2000; English tchr. Gwinnett County Sch. Sys., Lilburn, Ga., 2000—01, Fulton County Sch. Sys., Atlanta, 2001—; owner Richardson Inspired Interactive, Alpharetta, Ga., 2003—. Mentor DeKalb County Sch. Sys., Decatur Ga., 1994—99, coach, Atlanta, 1994—2000; mentor Gwinnett County Sch. Sys., Lilburn, Ga., 2000—01; sch. improvement plan com. Fulton County Sch. Sys., Atlanta, 2001—02, coach, mentor, nat. honor soc. selection com. 2001—04; copywriter/cons. Richardson Inspired Interactive, Alpharetta, Ga., 2003—04. Contbr. Milton H.S. Sch. Improvement Plan.

Appointed to, West Point Mil. Acad. Mem.: Ga. Coun. Tchrs. of English, Nat. Coun. Tchrs. of English, Profl. Assn. of Ga. Educators, Pi Lambda Theta. Office Phone: 678-859-2960. Personal E-mail: kellyrichardson@bellsouth.net.

**RICHARDSON, LAWRENCE, JR.,** classicist, archaeologist; b. Altoona, Pa., Dec. 2, 1920; widower. BA, Yale U., 1942, PhD in Classics, 1952. Instr. classics Yale U., New Haven, 1946-47, instr. to assoc. prof., 1955-66; prof. Duke U., Durham, NC, 1966-78, James B. Duke prof. Latin, 1978-91, prof. emeritus, 1991—. Field archeologist Am. Acad. Rome, 1952-55, Mellon prof., 1980-81; mem. Inst. Advanced Study, 1967-68. Author: Pompeii: An Architectural History, 1988, A New Topographical Dictionary of Ancient Rome, 1992, A Catalog of Identifiable Figure Painters of Ancient Pompeii, Herculaneum and Stabiae, 2000; contbr. articles to profl. jours. Guggenheim fellow, 1958-59; Am. Council Learned Socs. fellow, 1967-68, 72-73; NEH fellow, 1979-80 Mem. German Archeol. Inst. (corr.), Am. Philol. Assn., Archeol. Inst. Am.

**RICHARDSON, M. CATHERINE,** lawyer; b. Syracuse, NY, July 14, 1941; d. George Lynch and Margaret (Mansfield) R. BS, State U. Coll., Oswego, N.Y., 1963; MA, U. No. Colo., 1969; JD magna cum laude, Syracuse U., 1977; LLD (hon.), SUNY, 2005. Bar: N.Y. 1978, U.S. Dist. Ct. (no. dist.) N.Y. 1978, U.S. Ct. Appeals (2d cir.) 1982. Math. tchr. Westhill HS, NY, 1963-67, Jamesville-Dewitt (NY) HS, 1969-74; lawyer Bond, Schoeneck & King, PLLC, Syracuse, 1977—. Mem. com. on profession and the cts. and profl. edn. project Chief Judge State N.Y. With St. Camillus Health and Rehab. Ctr.; Frank H. Hiscock Legal Aid Soc. (pres. 1994-96, bd.dir.); mem. Syracuse Ksch. Corp.; mem. State of NY Univ. Hosp. Syracuse Ethics Comm. Recipient Take the Lead award Girl Scouts N.Y. Girl Scout Coun., 1988, Athena award Greater Syracuse C. of C. Small Bus. Bur., 1989, Spirit of Am. Women award Girls Inc. of Ctrl. N.Y., 1994, Syracuse Law Rev.'s Alumni Achievement award, 1995; named Outstanding Alumni SUNY Oswego, 1995; Kate Stoneman award, Albany Law Sch., 1996. Fellow ABA (bd. gov. 2003-), Am. Bar Found., N.Y. State Bar Found. (bd. dirs. 1992—), Ruth G. Shapiro award 2002); mem. N.Y. State Bar Assn. (pres. 1996-97), N.Y. State Jud. Inst., Hist. Soc. Cts. State N.Y., Onondaga County Bar Assn. (pres. 1987, Pro Bono award), Onondaga County Bar Found. (bd. dirs.), Am. Law Inst., Nat. Health Lawyers Assn., Am. Acad. Hosp. Attys., N.Y. State Assn. Sch. Attys., Lambda Sigma Tau, Kappa Delta Pi, Delta Kappa Gamma, Phi Kappa Phi, Justinian Hon. Law Soc., Ordr of Coif. Office: Bond Schoeneck & King LLP One Lincoln Ctr Syracuse NY 13202 Office Phone: 315-218-8230. Business E-Mail: crichardson@bsk.com.

**RICHARDSON, MARGARET MILNER,** retired lawyer; b. Waco, Tex., May 14, 1943; d. James W. and Margaret Wiebusch Milner; m. John L. Richardson, July 22, 1967; 1 child, Margaret Lawrence. AB in Polit. Sci., Vassar Coll., 1965; JD with honors, George Washington U., 1968. Bar: Va. 1968, D.C. 1968, U.S. Dist. Ct. D.C. 1968, U.S. Ct. Appeals (4th, 5th, D.C. and Fed. cirs.) 1968, U.S. Claims Ct. 1969, U.S. Tax Ct. 1970, U.S. Supreme Ct. 1971. Clk. U.S. Ct. Claims, Washington; with Office Chief Counsel IRS, Washington, 1969-77; with Sutherland, Asbill and Brennan, Washington, 1977-80, ptnr., 1980-93; commr. IRS, Washington, 1993-97; ptnr. Ernst & Young, Washington, 1997—2003. Mem. commr.'s adv. group IRS, 1988-90, chair, 1990; bd. advisors George Washington Law Sch.; mem. D.C. Bar Commn. on Multidisciplinary Practice, Presdl. Commn. on Holocaust Assets; bd. dirs. Legg Mason, Inc., JacksonHewitt, Eurasia Found., USA4 UNHCR. Contbr. articles to profl. jours. Assisted Clinton 1992 primary and gen. election campaign; served as team leader Justice Dept./Civil Rights Cluster during Presdl. Transition; mem. bd. Mayor's Transition Team, 1998, Women's Campaign Fund, Nat. Cathedral Sch., Hosp. for Sick Children; trustee Eurasia Found., USA for UNHCR, Woodrow Wilson Coun., U.S.-Russia Bus. Coun., 1999-03; mem. bd. dirs. Nat. Mus. Women in the Arts. Mem. ABA, D.C. Bar Assn. (tax sect.), Va. State Bar, Fed. Bar Assn. (com. taxation), Fin. Women's Assn. N.Y., Washington Women's Forum, Internat. Alliance, U.S. Russia Bus. Coun., Woodrow Wilson Ctr. Avocations: travel, antiques, needlepoint, gardening. Personal E-mail: margaretrichardson@yahoo.com.

**RICHARDSON, MARK P.,** protective services official, educator; b. St. Paul, June 27, 1962; m. Mary K Sanford, Oct. 8, 1988; children: Lara S., Sonja S. BS, St. Cloud State U., Minn., 1992; Med. St. Mary's U., Minn., 1998; JD, William Mitchell Coll. of Law, Minn., 2004. Tchr. Ind. Sch. Dist. #728, Elk River, Minn., 1993—; firefighter Elk River Fire Dept., Minn., 1997—. E-5 staff sargeant USAF, 1982—86, Ramstein Airbase, Germany. Avocations: Karate, scuba diving, horseback riding, travel. Office: Ind Sch Dist #728 900 School St Elk River MN 55330 Office Phone: 763-241-1077 2173. E-mail: mrichardson@elkriver.k12.mn.us.

**RICHARDSON, MIRANDA,** actress; b. Lancashire, Eng., Mar. 3, 1958; Studied, Drama Program Bristol. Stage performances include Moving, All My Sons, Who's Afraid of Virginia Woolf, The Life of Einstein, A Lie of the Mind, Edmond, Insignificance, Aunt Dan & Lemon, The Changeling, Mountain Language, Educating Rita, The Maids, The Designated Mourner, Ella Jenks; actor(TV appearances): The Hard Word, Sorrel and Son, A Woman of Substance, Underworld, Death of the Heart, The Scold's Bridle, 1998, Merlin, 1998, Alice, 1999,: (TV series) Black Adder II & III, Sweet as You Are; (TV miniseries) Die Kinder, The James Bond Story, 1999, (voice): The Miracle Maker, 2000,: (films) Dance with a Stranger, 1985, The Innocent, 1986, Empire of the Sun, 1987, Eat the Rich, 1987, Twisted Obsession, 1990, The Bachelor, 1991, Enchanted April, 1992 (Golden Globe award), Damage, 1992 (B.A.F.T.A. award for Best Supporting Actress), The Crying Game, 1992 (B.A.F.T.A. award for Best Supporting Actress), Fatherland, HBO, 1994 (Golden Globe award), Tom & Viv, 1994 (Acad. award nominee for best actress, 1995), La Vie en Rose, Kansas City, 1996, The Evening Star, 1996, Swann, 1996, Saint-Ex, 1997, The Apostle, 1997, The Designated Mourner, 1997, All for Love, 1998, Jacob Two Two and the Hooded Fang, 1998, Sleepy Hollow, 1999, Blackadder Back and Forth, 1999, Get Carter, 2000, Spider, 2001, The Hours, 2001, Rage on Placid Lake, 2002, The Lost Prince, 2002, Chicken Run, 2000, Snow White, 2000, The Actors, 2002, Falling Angels, 2003, The Prince and Me, 2003, Phantom of the Opera, 2003, Churchill The Hollywood Years, 2003, Wah-Wah, 2004, Harry Potter and the Goblet of Fire, 2005, Gideon's Daughter, 2005, Provoked, 2005, Morning Apprentics, 2005, Change to Save, 2005. Address: c/o Harriet Robinson 76 Oxford St London W1D 1BS England Office Phone: 0207 636 6565.

**RICHARDSON, MOZELLE GRONER,** author; b. Hereford, Tex., Jan. 26, 1914; d. Grover Cleveland and Jessie Leah (Head) Groner; m. William T. Richardson, Aug. 25, 1939; children: William T. Jr., Judith, Susan Ann, Rock Grover. Student, East Tex. Bapt. U., 1930—33, Ctrl.State U., Edmond, Okla., 1967—71, Okla. U., Norman, 1967—71; BA in Journalism, Okla. U., 2004. Speaker to writers groups, high schs., women's clubs. Author: (novels) The Curse of Kalispoint, 1971, Portrait of Fear, 1971, Masks of Thespis, 1973, Candle in the Wind, 1973, (novels) The Song of India, 1975, Daughter of the Sacred Mountain, 1977, (Non fiction Autobiographical) Dear Daddy Don't Let Mother Travel Alone- A Love Letter to Paris, 1968, (Non fiction) Six Days from Sunday - A Grand Canyon Odyessey, 1985. Recipient Writers award, Oklahoma U., 1973. Mem.: PEN, Authors Guild, Mystery Writers of Am. Democrat.

**RICHARDSON, NATASHA JANE,** actress; b. London, May 11, 1963; d. Tony Richardson and Vanessa Redgrave; m. Robert Fox, 1984 (div. 1993); m. Liam Neeson, July 3, 1994; children: Micheal Richard Antonio, Daniel Jack. Trained, Ctrl. Sch. Speech and Drama. Acting debut on stage at Leeds (Eng.) Playhouse, 1983; appearances include (plays) A Midsummer's Night Dream, Hamlet, 1985, The Seagull, 1985, High Society, 1987, Anna Christie, 1993, (Tony award nominee 1993, Drama Desk award), Cabaret, 1998 (Tony award, Drama Desk award, Outer Critics award), Closer (Broadway, 1999), A Streetcar Named Desire, 2005; (TV) In the Secret State, 1984, Sherlock Holmes, The Copper Beaches, 1984, Ghosts, 1986, Suddenly Last Summer, 1992, Hostages, 1993, Zelda, 1993, (Cable Ace nomination), Haven, 2001; (films) Gothic, 1987, A Month in the Country, 1987, Patty Hearst, 1988, Fat

Man and Little Boy, 1989, The Handmaid's Tale, 1990, The Comfort of Strangers, 1991, The Favor, The Watch and the Very Big Fish, 1992, Past Midnight, Widow's Peak, 1994, (Best Actress Karlovy Vary), Nell, 1995, The Parent Trap, 1998, Blowdry, 2001, Wakin Up in Reno, 2001, Maid in Manhattan, 2002, The White Countess, 2005; actor, exec. prodr.: (films) Asylum, 2005. Recipient Most Promising Newcomer award Plays & Players, 1986; named Best Actress by London Theatre Critics, Plays & Players, 1990, Evening Standard Best Actress, 1990; Tony Award, actress in a musical, Cabaret, 1999.*

**RICHARDSON, PATRICIA,** actress; b. Bethesda, Md., Feb. 23, 1951; d. Laurence Baxter and Elizabeth (Howard) R.; m. Raymond Baker, June 20, 1982; children: Henry, Roxanne, Joseph. BFA, So. Meth. U., 1972. Appearences include (Broadway) Gypsy, Loose Ends, The Wake of Jamie Foster; (off-Broadway) The Collected Works of Billy the Kid, The Frequency, Vanities, The Coroner's Plot, Hooters, Company, Fables for Friends, The Miss Firecracker Contest, Cruise Control; (regional theatre) King Lear, The Killing of Sister George, Relatively Speaking, The Importance of Being Earnest, Of Mice and Men, The Philadelphia Story, Room Service, Fifth of July, About Face; (nat. tours) Gypsy, Vanities; (films) Gas, 1972, You Better Watch Out, Lost Angels, 1988, In Country, 1988, Ulee's Gold, 1997; (TV) Double Trouble, 1984, Eisenhower & Lutz, 1988, FM, 1989-90, Home Improvement, 1991-99 (Lead Actress in a Comedy Series Emmy award nominee, 1994, Golden Globe award nominee, 1993, 94), Sophie and the Moonhanger, 1995, Undue Influence, 1996, Viva Las Nowhere, 2000. Office: William Morris Agy care Jonathon Howard 151 S El Camino Dr Beverly Hills CA 90212-2775

**RICHARDSON, PAUL JOSEPH,** economist; b. Pincourt, Que., Can., Oct. 26, 1965; s. Donald Herbert and Denise Marie Richardson; m. Julia Louise Adams, July 6, 1996; children: Cameron Forbes, Emily Adams. Diploma in Bus. Adminstrn., John Abbott Coll., Ste. Anne de Bellevue, Can., 1987; BA in Econs., Concordia U., Montreal, Can., 1991; M Internat. Econs. and Mgmt., Sch. Direzione Aziendale Bocconi, Milan, 1994. English tchr. Prime Acad. English, Osaka, Japan, 1991—92; mortgage banker Love Funding Corp., Washington, 1992—93; rschr. UN Econ. Commn. for Africa, Addis Ababa, Ethiopia, 1994—94; fin. analyst UN Indsl. Devel. Orgn., Milan, 1995—96, head St. Helens, England, 1996—99; dir. internat. partnership programs U.S. C. of C., Washington, 1999—2003; dir. new bus. World Vision, Washington, 2003—05; fgn. svc. officer U.S. Agy. for Internat. Devel., Washington, 2005—. Author: (research) Africa: An Overview of the Manufacturing and Agricultural Sectors and the Factors Impeding their Export Promotion. Mem.: Black Watch Assn. (life), Izaack Walton League Am. (corr.). Office: US C of C 1615 H St Washington DC 20062 Personal E-mail: pjr110@comcast.net. E-mail: prichardson@uschamber.com.

**RICHARDSON, RICHARD JUDSON,** retired political science professor; b. Poplar Bluff, Mo., Feb. 16, 1935; s. Jewell Judson and Naomi Fern (Watson) R.; m. Sammie Sue Cullum, Dec. 29, 1961; children: Jon Mark, Anna Cecile, Ellen Elizabeth, Megan Leigh. BS, Harding Coll., Searcy, Ark., 1957; cert., U. Dublin, Ireland, 1958; MA, Tulane U., New Orleans, 1961, PhD, 1967. Instr. Tulane U., 1962—65; 67asst. prof. polit. sci. Western Mich. U., Kalamazoo, 1965, assoc. prof., 1967—69; vis. assoc. prof. U. Hawaii, 1967—68; from asso. prof. to v.p. acad. affairs U. N.C., Chapel Hill, 1969—91, assoc. v.p. acad. affairs univ. gen. adminstrn., 1991—92. Adj. prof. Duke U., Durham, 1972-74; provost, vice chancellor acad. affairs U. N.C. 1995-2000; cons. in field. Author: (with Kenneth Vines) The Politics of Federal Courts, 1971, (with Darlene Walker) People and the Police, 1973, (with Marian Irish, James Prothro) The Politics of American Democracy, 1981. Del. County Dem. Conv., 1972, 83; vice chmn. Dem. Party Precinct, 1983-85; chmn. bldg. fund YMCA, 1976; chmn. Carolina Challenge for endowment U. N.C., Chapel Hill, 1979-80; chmn. U. N.C. Bicentennial Observance, 1991-94; chmn. United Way, 1983, pres., 1985; pres. PTA County Coun., 1984. Recipient Edward S. Corwin award Am. Polit. Sci. Assn., 1967, Tanner Disting. Teaching award U. N.C., 1972, Univ. award for Outstanding Teaching, 1981, Thomas Jefferson award, 1987, James Johnston Disting. Tchg. award, 1993, Alumni Faculty Disting. Svc. award, 1994, Disting. Eagle Scout award Boy Scouts Am., 1998, Laura Thomas award, 1999, C. Knox Massey award, 2000, Disting. Svc. medal U, N.C. Alumni Assn., 2001, William Richardson Davie award, 2005; named life regent Boy Scouts Am., 1998; Edgar Stern fellow, 1959-61; NEH grantee, 1970. Mem. N.C. Polit. Sci. Assn. (pres. 1978-79), Am. Polit. Sci. Assn., So. Polit. Sci. Assn., ACLU (bd. dirs. local chpt. 1985-88, state bd. dirs. 1988-89), Order of Janus, Order of the Long Leaf Pine, Order of Golden Fleece, Order of the Grail. Home: 234 Terrells Creek Ln Pittsboro NC 27312-5145

**RICHARDSON, ROBERT,** cinematographer; b. Hyannis, Mass., 1955; m. Monica Wali; 2 children. Cinematographer: (films) An Outpost of Progress, 1982, Salvador, 1986, Platoon, 1986 (Academy award nomination best cinematography 1986), Wall Street, 1987, Dudes, 1987, Eight Men Out, 1988, Talk Radio, 1988, Born on the Fourth of July, 1989 (Academy award nomination best cinematography 1989), City of Hope, 1991, The Doors, 1991, JFK, 1991 (Academy award best cinematography 1991), A Few Good Men, 1992, Heaven and Earth, 1993 (also dir. photography), Natural Born Killers, 1994, Casino, 1995, Nixon, 1995, U-Turn, 1997, Fast, Cheap & Out of Control, 1997, Wag the Dog, 1997, The Horse Whisperer, 1998, Snow Falling on Cedars, 1999, Bringing Out the Dead, 1999, The Hire: Power Keg, 2001, The Four Feathers, 2002, Kill Bill: Vol. 1, 2003, Kill Bill:Vol. 2, 2004 (also dir. photography), The Aviator, 2004 (Academy award best cinematography, 2005), (TV spl.) To the Moon, Alice, 1990 (also camera operator, visual cons.); cameraman: (films) Repo Man, 1984, Making the Grade, 1984; cinematographer, photographer Mr. Death: The Rise and Fall of Fred A. Leuchter, Jr., 1999; exec. prodr. The Wind Effect, 2003

**RICHARDSON, ROBERT ALLEN,** retired lawyer, educator; b. Cleve., Feb. 15, 1939; s. Allen B. and Margaret C. (Thomas) R.; m. Carolyn Eck Richardson, Dec. 9, 1968. BA, Ohio Wesleyan U., 1961; LLB, Harvard U., 1964. Bar: Ohio 1964, Hawaii 1990. Ptnr. Caffee, Halter & Griswold, Cleve., 1968-89; counsel Mancini, Rowland & Welch (formerly Case & Lynch), Maui, Hawaii, 1990—2001; lectr.; affirmative action officer, atty., exec. com. Maui (Hawaii) C.C., 1989—2001; ret., 2001. Chmn. gov. fin. dept., chmn. cmty. svc. com., mem. oper. com. Caffee, Halter & Griswold; past lectr. Sch. Law Cleve. State U.; counsel Maui C. of C., Kahului, 1994-98. Pres., trustee Big Bros./Big Sisters of Maui, 1990-94; v.p., trustee, pres. Ka Hole A Ke Ole Homeless Resource Ctr., 1990—; trustee Maui Acad. Performing Arts, 1990-97, Maul Counseling Svc., 1990-96, Kapalua Music Festival, Friends of Children Advocate Ctr., Legal Aid Soc. Hawaii, pres., 1998-88; trustee Hui Noeur Visual Arts Ctr., 2004—; mem. land use com. Maui Coastal Land Trust, 2004; v.p., trustee, chmn. devel. com. Cleve. Playhouse, 1984-89; trustee, mem. exec. com., program chmn. Cleve. Coun. World Affairs, 1970-89; past model UN chmn. Cleve. Com. on Fgn. Rels.; trustee, mem. exec. com., budget chmn. Neighborhood Ctrs. Assn., 1980-89; trustee Maui Symphony, 1995-98, v.p., 1999—. Recipient T.S. Shinn award Maui C. of C., 2000. Mem. Rotary Club of Maui, Maui Country Club, Rowfant Club (adv.), Cleve. Skating Club. Home: 1365 Lower Kula Rd Kula HI 96790-9724

**RICHARDSON, ROBERT COLEMAN,** physics professor, researcher; b. Washington, June 26, 1937; s. Robert Franklin and Lois (Price) R.; m. Betty Marilyn McCarthy, Sept. 2, 1962; children: Jennifer, Pamela. BS in Physics, Va. Poly. Inst. and State U., 1958, MS, 1960; PhD in Physics, Duke U., 1966; PhD (hon.), Ohio State U., 2000. Research assoc. Cornell U., Ithaca, NY, 1966-67, asst. prof., 1968-71, assoc. prof., 1972-74, prof., Low Temp. Physics, 1975—86, Floyd R. Newman prof. physics, 1987—, dir. Lab. of Atomic and Solid State Physics, 1990—97, vice provost for rsch. Ithaca, NY, 1998—. Chmn. internat. Union Pure and Applied Physics Commn. (C-5), 1981-84; mem. lab assessment Nat. Bur. Standards, 1983—; vis. scientist Bell Labs., Murray Hill, N.J., 1984; mem. adv. panel for MIT sci. rsch., 1998-; mem. NASA Life and Microgravity Sci. and Applications Adv. Panel, 1999-; mem. Internat. Space Station Mgmt. and Cost Evaluation Task Force, NASA, 2001-02; trustee Duke U., 1997—, exec. com. bd. trustees, 2001—; bd. dirs.

Brookhaven Sci. Assocs.; mem. ecec. com. of sr. rsch. officers, Am. Assn. Univs., 2002-. Author: Experimental Techniques in Condensed Matter Physics at Low Temperatures, 1988, (videotape lectr.); College Physics, 2003; mem. editorial bd. Jour. of Low Temperature Physics, 1984—. Served to 2d lt. U.S. Army, 1959-60. Guggenheim fellow 1975-76, 82-83; recipient Simon Meml. prize Brit. Phys. Soc., 1976, Disting. Grad. Sch. Alumnus Award, Va. Polytechnic Inst. and State U.; co-recipient Nobel prize in physics, 1996; commendation, Va. Gen. Assembly, 1988. Fellow AAAS (bd. dirs. 2000—), Am. Phys. Soc. (Oliver E. Buckley prize 1981), Am. Philos. Soc, Am. Acad. Arts & Scis.; mem. NAS, Nat. Sci. Bd. (exec. com. 2000—); Finnish Acad. Sci. & Letters. Achievements include research in experimental low temperature physics, especially the properties of liquids and solids at sub-millikelvin temperatures. Avocations: photography, gardening. Office: Cornell U Lab of Atomic and Solid Physics 529A Clark Hall Ithaca NY 14853-2501*

**RICHARDSON, ROBERT DALE, JR.,** language educator; b. Milw., June 14, 1934; s. Robert Dale and Lucy Baldwin (Marsh) R.; m. Elizabeth Hall, Nov. 7, 1959 (div. 1987); m. Annie Dillard, Dec. 10, 1988; children: Elisabeth, Anne, Rose. AB magna cum laude in English, Harvard U., 1956, PhD in English Lit., 1961; DHL (hon.), Meadville-Lombard Theol. Sch., 2003. Instr. English Harvard U., Cambridge, Mass., 1961-63; asst. prof. English U. Denver, 1963-68, assoc. prof., 1968-72, prof., 1972-87, Lawrence C. Phipps prof. humanities, 1979-82, chmn. dept., 1968-73, pres. Univ. senate, 1972-73, assoc. dean grad. studies, 1975-76; prof. English, U. Colo., Boulder, 1987; vis. prof. letters Wesleyan U., Middletown, Conn., 1989-94. Vis. prof. Harvard U., summer 1976, CUNY, 1978, Sichuan U., 1983, U. N.C., Chapel Hill, 2002, 05; vis. fellow Huntington Libr., 1973-74; vis. instr. Yale U., 1988; bd. dirs. David R. Godine Pub., Key West Literary Seminar. Author: Literature and Film, 1969, Henry Thoreau: A Life of the Mind, 1986 (Melcher award, 1986), Emerson: The Mind on Fire, 1995 (Parkman prize, 1995, Melcher award, 1995, Washington Irving award, 1995), Myth and Literature in the American Renaissance, 1978; author: (with Burton Feldman) The Rise of Modern Mythology 1680-1860, 1972; author: (with Allen Mandelbaum) Three Centuries of American Poetry, 1999; author: William James: In the Maelstrom of American Modernism, 2006. Trustee Meadville-Lombard Theol. Sch., 1981-87. Fellow Guggenheim Found., 1990, Nat. Humanities Ctr., 1999-2000; recipient Acad. award in lit. Am. Acad. of Arts and Letters, 1998. Mem. Soc. Am. Hist., Author's Guild, Thoreau Soc., Emerson Soc., Assn. Lit. Scholars and Critics, William James Soc. Democrat. Unitarian Universalist. Personal E-mail: rrchardson@aol.com.

**RICHARDSON, R(OSS) FRED(ERICK),** insurance company executive, consultant; b. Renfrew, Ont., Can., Feb. 4, 1928; came to U.S., 1980; s. Garfield Newton and Grace Mary (MacLean) R.; m. Betty Blanche Betts, Feb. 4, 1972; children by previous marriage— Sheri Joan, Robert John, Paul Frederick. BA in Math. and Physics with honors, Queens U., 1950. Actuarial asst. Empire Life Ins. Co., Kingston, Ont., Canada, 1950-55; sec. Maritime Life Ins. Co., Halifax, N.S., Canada, 1955-59; dir. sales, 1959-65, chief exec. officer, 1967-72; mng. dir., chief exec. officer Abbey Life Ins. Co., England, 1972-80; group gen. mgr. Hartford Europe Group, 1975-80; sr. v.p., dir. worldwide life ins. ops. Hartford Ins. Group, Conn., 1980-83, dir. worldwide life ins. ops. Conn., 1983-88; pres., COO, Hartford Life Cos., 1983-88; pvt. ins. cons., Boca Raton, Fla., 1988; pres., CEO, Crown Life Ins. Co., 1988-93; cons. INSCE, Boca Raton, 1993—. Fellow Soc. Actuaries, Can. Inst. Actuaries. Home and Office: 300 SE 5th Ave Apt 1090 Boca Raton FL 33432-6093 Office Phone: 561-417-9390. E-mail: richar_f@bellsouth.net.

**RICHARDSON, SALLY KEADLE,** academic administrator; b. Mar. 2, 1933; d. Okey P. and Viola Miriam (Graybeal) Keadle; m. Don Rule Richardson, Dec. 15, 1961; children: Miriam Paige, Ruth Evan. AB, Vassar Coll., 1954. Regional pub. info. rep. Columbia Gas Sys., Charleston, W.Va., 1958-62; dir. Children's Mus., Charleston, 1963; coord. space-related sci. project Kanawha County Schs., Charleston, 1967-68; vol. dir. Rockefeller for Gov. Campaign, Charleston, 1972, program dir., 1976, 80; dir. admissions W.Va. Wesleyan Coll., Buckhannon, 1974-75; spl. asst. Office of Gov. State of W.Va., 1977, dep. commr. dept. welfare, 1978-79, dep. dir. dept. health, 1979-83; chmn. W.Va. Health Care Cost Rev. Authority, Charleston, 1983-85. Health care cons., Charleston, 1985-89; dir. W.Va. Pub. Employees Ins. Agy., Charleston, 1989-93; vice-chmn. W.Va. Health Care Planning Task Force, 1992-93; mem. White House Health Care Reform Task Force, Washington, 1993; dir. Medicaid Bur., Health Care Financing Adminstrn., U.S. DHHS, Balt., 1993-96; acting dep. adminstr. HCFA, U.S. DHHS, Washington, 1996-97; dir. HCFA Ctr. for Medicaid and State Ops., 1997-99; mem. U.S. DHHS Governing Coun. on Children and Youth, 1993-97, co-chmn. U.S. DHHS Children's Health Initiative, 1997-99; co-chmn. U.S. DHHS Home and Cmty. Based Svcs. Task Force, 1996-99; mem. U.S. DHHS Pub. Health Coun.'s D.C. Task Force, 1994-99; mem. Nat. Adv. Com. on Rural Health, DHHS, 2000-04; bd. dir. Molina Healthcare, Inc. W.Va. rep. Task Force on So. Children, So. Growth Policies Bd., 1978-79; co-chmn. exec. com. W.Va. Internat. Yr. of Child, 1979; staff mem. Com. on Human Resources Nat. Gov. Assns., 1983-85; trustee U. Charleston, 1994-; bd. dirs. Children's Home Soc., Charleston, 1999—. Mem. Acad. Health, Nat. Rural Health Assn. Democrat. Office: WVa U Inst Health Policy Rsch 3110 Maccorkle Ave SE Rm 3015 Charleston WV 25304-1210

**RICHARDSON, SAMUEL J.,** theater educator; BS in Theatre Arts, Lees-McRae Coll., Banner Elk, N.C., 2002; MFA in Drama/Theatre for Youth, Ea. Mich. U., Ypsilanti, Mich., 2006. Acting edn. apprentice Round Ho. Theatre, Bethesda, Md., 2002—03; asst. tech. dir. Concordia U., Ann Arbor, Md., 2005—. Fellow, Ea. Mich. U., 2003—05.

**RICHARDSON, SANDRA LYNN,** mathematics professor; b. Columbus, Ga., July 15, 1980; d. Samuel and Virginia Richardson. BS in Math., Dillard U., 2000; PhD, Purdue U., 2004. Asst. prof. math. and math. edn. Lamar U., Beaumont, Tex., 2004—. Mem.: Math. Assn. Am., Am. Edn. Rsch. Assn., Psychology of Math. Edn. (N.Am. chpt.), Alpha Kappa Alpha. Office: Lamar Univ PO Box 10047 Beaumont TX 77710 Business E-Mail: richardson@math.lamar.edu.

**RICHARDSON, SCOTT,** federal official, researcher, writer; s. Stewart and Jeanne Richardson; m. Leighann Lowley, Nov. 12, 1994; 1 child, Evan Stewart. BA, Thomas Edison Coll., Trenton, NJ, 1981. Cert. in public health Bloomberg Sch. Public Health, Johns Hopkins U., Balt., 2001. Project mgr., coord. Nat. Evaluation Sys., Amherst, Mass., 1981—88; project dir. Nat. Evaluation Systems, Inc., Austin, Tex., 1988—90; mgr. bur. of labor stats. programs Tex. Workers' Compensation Commn., 1991—94, chief safety info. sys, 1994—99; dir. office of stats. Occupl. Safety and Health Adminstrn., Washington, 1999—2000; program mgr. census of fatal occupl. injuries Bur. Labor Stats., Washington, 2000—. Contbr. articles to profl. jours., chapters to books. Sr. warden, vestry Christ Our Lord Ch., Woodbridge, Va., 2004—06. Mem.: APHA. Anglican. Office: Bureau of Labor Statistics 2 Massachusetts Ave Washington DC 20212 Business E-Mail: richardson.scott@bls.gov.

**RICHARDSON, SHIRLEY MAXINE,** editor; b. Rising Sun, Ind., May 3, 1931; d. William Fenton and Mary (Phillips) Keith; m. Arthur Lee Richardson, Feb. 11, 1950; children: Mary Jane Hunt, JoDee Mayfield, Steven Lee Richardson. Pers. mgr. Mayhill Pubs., Knightstown, Ind., 1967-87, prodn. mgr., 1975-87, editor, 1967-87; info. staff, assoc. editor Ind. Farm Bur., Inc., 1987-89, dir. info. and pub. rels., 1989-94; genealogy editor AntiqueWeek, 1996-2001; exec. editor Knightstown Banner, 2001—. Avocations: travel, reading, boating, quilting. Home: 366 E Carey St Knightstown IN 46148-1208 Office: 24 N Washington St Knightstown IN 46148-1242 Office Phone: 765-345-2292.

**RICHARDSON, SHIRLEY R.,** librarian; b. Brownwood, Tex., Apr. 20, 1943; d. Raymond C. and Leta Z. Richardson. BS in Secondary Edn., Howard Payne U., 1963; MLS, Tex. Woman's U. 1970. Tchr. English Gorman (Tex.) H.S., 1964—65; tchr. art Kirby Jr. High, Converse, Tex., 1965—69; catalog libr. Pittsburg (Kans.) State U., 1971—75, U. Tex., El Paso, 1975—80; serials

project libr. U. Houston, 1980—82; catalog libr. Angelo State U., San Angelo, Tex., 1982—. Contbr. short stories and poetry to anthologies. Avocations: writing, reading, music. Home: PO Box 3060 San Angelo TX 76902 Office: Angelo State Univ Libr 2601 W Ave N San Angelo TX 76909 Personal E-mail: counselortroi2@yahoo.com.

**RICHARDSON, STEPHEN GILES,** biotechnologist, director; b. Mpls., Sept. 17, 1951; s. Richard Giles and Constance Bernice (Krieg) R. BA cum laude, Wartburg Coll., 1972; MS, U. Iowa, 1974, PhD, 1981; postdoctoral, Duke U., 1982-84. Cert. mgmt. profl. Project Mgmt. Inst. Ter. mgr. Wyeth Labs., Phila., 1974-76; rsch. asst. U. Iowa, Iowa City, 1976-82; rsch. assoc. Duke, Durham, NC, 1982-84; scientist Becton Dickinson Rsch. Ctr., Research Triangle Park, NC, 1984-86; devel. group leader Dade Diagnostics divsn. Baxter Healthcare, Miami, Fla., 1986; rsch. group leader Organon Teknika Corp divsn., Akzo Nobel N.V, Durham, NC, 1987-89, R & D sect. head, internat. R & D area mgr., 1989-90, program mgr., 1990-94, assoc. dir., head product devel., 1994-96, project mgmt. dir., microbiology bus. area R & D, 1997—2001; program dir. global mktg. and strategic devel. bioMerieux, Inc., Durham, NC, 2001—. Contbr. articles to profl. jours.; patentee in field; bd. readers IVD Technology Mag. Co-founder Libertarian Party Minn., Mpls., 1972, del. nat. conv., 1998; exec. sec. Iowa Coun. to Repeal Conscription, Waterloo, 1971. Mem. Am. Soc. for Microbiology, Am. Chem. Soc., Am. Assn. for Clin. Chemistry, Royal Soc. Chemistry (U.K.), N.Y. Acad. Scis. Electronic Frontier Found., Sigma Xi. Achievements include discovery of transient neutral heteroaryl radicals as viable organic synthetic intermediates, such as, to halopurine nucleosides; MDA-180 hemostasis analyzer system, BacT/ALERT 3D blood culture system family. Office: PO Box 17284 Chapel Hill NC 27516-7284 Office Phone: 919-619-2276. E-mail: BTA3D@aol.com.

**RICHARDSON, THADDEUS MAURICE,** funeral director; b. Amite, La., June 21, 1965; s. Samuel Richardson, Dorothy (Johnson) Richardson. FSC, Commonwealth Coll., 1985; GSC, So. U., 1986; NC, Southeaster La. U., 1997. Dir. Richardson Funeral Home, Hammond, La., 1985—. Author: How To Get the Strong Man in Marriage, 2000. Bd. dirs. La. State Bd. Funeral Dirs., New Orleans; city coun. bd. State of La., Baton Rouge, 1996—2000; v.p. L.M.A.B.C., Baton Rouge, 1998—2000; pres. L.E.T.A., Greensburg, La., 1995—96, P.D.A., Amite, 2000—; bd. dirs. Health Care, Independence, La., S.E.F.A., Covington, La., R.F.C., Amite. Mem.: Progressive Citizens (pres. 2001, Star award 2002), Mt. Nebo Grand Lodge (Master 1994). Democrat. Avocations: farming, fishing, football, hunting, racing. Office: Richardson Funeral Home 1601 W Thomas St Hammond LA 70404

**RICHARDSON, THOMAS ANDREW,** business executive, educator; b. Providence, Aug. 31, 1955; s. Edward Ferris and Olive Elizabeth (Lynaugh) R.; m. Patricia Ann Mundie, Dec. 30, 1982; children: Michael Edward, Lauren Elizabeth, Kristen Mundie. AS in Oceanography, Fla. Inst. Tech., 1977, BS in Environ. Sci., 1979, MBA, 1985; EdD, Nova Southeastern U., 2003. Asst. prof., div. head sch. marine and environ. tech. Fla. Inst. Tech., Jensen Beach, 1979-85; mng. tng. mgr. PADI Internat., Santa Ana, Calif., 1985-88, dir. tng. and edn., 1988-90, sr. v.p., 1991—2003; pres. PADI Worldwide, 2003—; v.p. Capital Investment Ventures Corp., 1991—2003; pres., COO Emergency First Response Inc., 2003—; pres. Current Publs., 2003—. Dir. lakefront City of Evanston, Ill., 1980-82; bd. dirs. CIVCO; chmn. bd. dirs. Project AWARE Found., Santa Ana; pres. DSAT Inc., Santa Ana, 1989—, DSAT Worldwide, 2003—; pres., CEO, Emergency First Responce Corp., 2003—; guest faculty Duke Med. Sch. continuing edn., Durham, N.C., 1992. Editor in chief: Open Water Diver Manual, 1988, Rescue Diver Manual, 1988, Divemaster Manual, 1990, Undersea Journal, 1987, Adventures in Diving; Open Water Diving video, Adventures in Diving video, Peak Performance video; contbr. articles to profl. jours. CPR and first aid instr. Martin County Sch. Dist., Stuart, Fla., 1982-83. Recipient Diver of Yr. award Divers Alert Network/Rolex, Inc., 1992, Craig Hoffman Meml. award for diving safety, Undersea and Hyerbaric Med. Soc., 2000; scholar Nova Southeastern U. 1998. Mem. Am. Mgmt. Assn., Am. Soc. Training and Devel., Am. Soc. Assn. Exec., Undersea and Hyperbaric Med. Soc., South Pacific Undersea Med. Soc., Sierra Club. Nat. Audubon Soc., Emergency Med. Planning Inc., Am. Acad. Underwater Scis., Nat. Assn. Search and Rescue, PADI Diving Soc. (pres. 1998—). Avocations: photography, music, woodworking, scuba diving. E-mail: drewr@padi.com.

**RICHARDSON, TOM (EDWARD THOMPSON RICHARDSON),** artist; b. Upper Darby, Pa, Aug. 12, 1948; s. Edward Thompson and Elizabeth Catherine (Fredericks) R.; m. Margaret Reed Colvin, July 1, 1972; 1 child, Edward Thompson III. BFA, U. Pa., 1974, MFA, 1975. Scenic artist San Francisco Opera Assns., 1979-84, San Francisco Ballet Assn., 1982-84; scenic designer music dept. Stanford U., Calif., 1980-84; scenic designer San Jose Opera Assn., Calif., 1985; lead scenic artist FM Prodn., Brisbane, Calif., 1984-87, artist-in-charge, 1987-93. Scenic artist: (films) James and the Giant Peach; Down Periscope; Phenomenon; A Smile Like Yours; Rainmaker; Flubber; What Dreams May Come; The Horse Whisperer; Mumford; Bicentennial Man; Invisible Circus; A Woman on Top; Boys and Girls; Bartleby; Sweet November; Forty Days and Forty Nights; High Crimes; The Matrix Reloaded; Revolutions; Twisted; The Assassination of Richard Nixon; (TV series) Nash Bridges; (films) Bee Season; Starwars; RENT: Pursuit of Happyness; Episode 3; (TV series) Partners. Mem. Internat. Alliance Theatrical Stage Employees (Bay area bus. rep. 1984-88, Bay area field rep. 2000—, pres. 1998—. Home: 87 Roosevelt Cir Palo Alto CA 94306-4219

**RICHARDSON, VERNAL EDWARD,** retired music educator; b. Bloomington, Ind., May 20, 1932; s. Edgar Lee and Olive Mae Richardson; m. Elpha Ernestine Patton, Aug. 10, 1958; children: Ernest Todd, Patricia Beth Niemann, Edward Scott. MusB, Ind. U., Bloomington, 1950—55, MusM, 1959—63; PhD in Musical Arts, Cath. U. Am., Washington, D.C., 1970—77. Cert. orch. tchr. Ga., 1989. Orch. dir. Manatee Pub. Schs., Bradenton, Fla., 1985—89, Atlanta Pub. Schs., 1989—2004. First violin sect. Atlanta Symphony Orch., 1955—56; pilot USAF, Lincoln AFB, Nebr., 1956—59; asst. prof., music David Lipscomb Coll., Nashville, 1959—63, Southeastern La. U., Hammond, 1963—65, Harding Coll., Searcy, Ark., 1965—68, Towson State U., Md., 1968—79; assoc. prof., music Lebanon Valley Coll., Annville, Pa., 1979—82, Moorhead State U., Minn., 1982—85. 1st lt. USAF, 1956—59, Lincoln, Nebr. Mem.: Am. Fedn. Musicians. Democrat. Methodist. Avocations: aviation, photography, music. Home: 5968 Brasstown Creek Estates Young Harris GA 30582 Office: Richardson String Studios 5968 Brasstown Creek Estates Young Harris GA 30582 Office Phone: 706-379-2711. E-mail: verned@alltel.net.

**RICHARDSON, VETA TERESA,** professional society administrator, lawyer; b. Phila., Aug. 4, 1962; d. William Alfred and Teresa Richardson. BS in Bus. Mgmt., U. Md., 1983, JD, 1986. Bar: Pa. 1986, N.Y. 1995, D.C. 1988. Corp. and securities counsel Sunoco, Inc., Phila., 1986-97; v.p. Am. Corp. Counsel Assn., Washington, 1997-2000, exec. dir., CEO, 2001; exec. dir. Minority Corp. Counsel Assn., Washington. Dir. publs. Diversity and the Bar mag., Washington, 2001—; mem. adv. bd. Georgetown Law Sch. Corp. Counsel Inst., Washington. Trustee Prince George's Arts Coun., 1997—; mem. steering com. Lawyers for One Am., Washington, 1999-2000. Mem. Nat. Bar Assns., Am. Corp. Counsel Assn., Am. Soc. Assn. Execs., Alpha Kappa Alpha. Avocation: african american art collector.

**RICHARDSON, WALTER JOHN,** architect; b. Long Beach, Calif., Nov. 14, 1926; s. Walter Francis and Ava Elizabeth (Brown) R.; m. Marilyn Joyce Brown, June 26, 1949 (div. 1982); children: Mark Steven, Glenn Stewart; m. Mary Sue Sutton, Dec. 4, 1982. Student, UCLA, 1944—45, Long Beach City Coll., 1946; BA, U. Calif., Berkeley, 1950. Registered arch., Ala., Ariz., Calif., Colo., Fla., Hawaii, Ill., Kans., Md., Mass., Nev., N.J., N.Y., Okla., Oreg., Tex., Utah, Vt., Va., Wash. Draftsman Skidmore, Owings & Merrill, San Francisco, 1950-51, Skidmore, Owings & Merrill, San Francisco, 1951; designer Hugh Gibbs Arch., Long Beach, 1952-58; ptnr. Thomas R & Richardson Archs., Long Beach, Costa Mesa, 1958-70; pres. Walter Richardson Assocs. Archs., Newport Beach, Calif., 1970-74; chmn. bd. Richardson, Nagy, Martin Archs. and Planners, Newport Beach, 1974—2000, RNM

Architecture-Planning, Newport Beach, 2000—. Co-author: The Architect and the Shelter Industry, 1975. Chmn. Planning Commn., City of Orange, Calif., 1967-68. With USAF, 1945. Recipient over 200 Gold Nugget Design awards Pacific Coast Builders Conf., San Francisco, 1969-96, 12 Builders Choice Design awards Builder Mag.; named Arch. of Yr. Profl. Builder mag., 1986; named to Hall of Fame Builder Mag., 2005 Fellow AIA (pres. Orange County chpt. 1970, chmn. nat. housing com. 1976, 77 design awards); mem. Nat. Assn. Home Builders, Nat. Coun. Archtl. Registration Bds., Urban Land Inst., Alpha Tau Omega. Republican. Avocations: photography, downhill skiing, travel. Office: RNM Design 4611 Teller Ave Ste 100 Newport Beach CA 92660-2104 Office Phone: 949-752-1800.

RICHARDSON, W.C., painter; Exhibitions include W.C. Richardson: New Paintings, Kiang Gallery, Atlanta, 2004, one-man shows include, Loyola U., Baltimore, 2004, Fusebox Gallery, Washington DC, 2002, 2003, Baumgartner Gallery, NYC, 2000, displayed in, Hirshhorn Twenty-five: Celebrating Modern & Contemporary Art, Hirshhorn Mus. & Sculpture Garden, 1999, two painted triptychs, reproduced in porcelanized steel, North Terminal, Ronald Reagan Nat. Airport; co-curator with Paula Crawford (exhibitions) Recent Paintings, Projectspace, Washington DC, 1998. Grantee Individual Artist Award, Md. State Arts Coun., 2002, Visual Arts Fellowship, 2002, 1998, 1987, 1981Md. State Arts Coun. Office: U Maryland 1211 Art/Sociology Bldg College Park MD 20742-1311 Office Phone: 301-405-1460. Office Fax: 301-314-9740. E-mail: wr8@umail.umd.edu.

RICHARDSON, WILLIAM CHASE, retired foundation administrator; b. Passaic, N.J., May 11, 1940; s. Henry Burtt and Frances (Chase) R.; m. Nancy Freeland, June 18, 1966; children: Elizabeth, Jennifer. BA, Trinity Coll., 1962; MBA, U. Chgo., 1964, PhD, 1971. Rsch. assoc., instr. U. Chgo., 1967-70; asst. prof. health services U. Wash., 1971-73, assoc. prof., 1973-76, prof., 1976-84, chmn. dept. health services, 1973-76, assoc. dean Sch. Pub. Health, 1976-81, acting dean, 1977, 78, dean Grad. Sch., vice provost, 1981-84; exec. v.p., provost, prof. dept. family and community medicine Pa. State U., 1984-90; pres. Johns Hopkins U., Balt., 1990-95, pres., prof. emeritus, 1995, prof. dept. health policy, mgmt., 1990-95, prof. emeritus, 1995—; pres., CEO W.K. Kellogg Found, Battle Creek, Mich., 1995—2005. Cons. in field; bd. dirs. Kellogg Co., CSX Corp., Mercantile Bankshares Corp., Mercantile-Safe Deposit & Trust Co., Coun. on Founds. Author: books, including Ambulatory Use of Physicians Services, 1971, Health Program Evaluation, 1978; contbr. articles to profl. jours. Mem. external adv. com. Fred Hutchinson Cancer Rsch. Ctr. Kellogg fellow, 1965-67 Fellow Am. Public Health Assn.; mem. Inst. Medicine, Nat. Acad. Scis.

RICHARDSON-BOWMAN, LEQUETTA DEVERA, finance company executive, consultant; d. Edward Richardson and Lonzetta Beatrice Townsend-Richardson; life ptnr. Thomas Michael Sellers; m. Michael Jerome Bowman, Mar. 24, 1987 (div. June 31, 1989); m. Ray Alexander, Dec. 27, 1963 (div. Dec. 13, 1967); children: Malik (Ray) Edward Shakur (Alexander), Briant Leonard Alexander. BA in Psychology magna cum laude, Langston U., 1995; MBA, Okla. City U., 1998. Cost risk analysis course, Dept. of Def. Logistics Mgmt. Coll., sys. acquisition funds mgmt. courses, Dept. of Def. Sys. Mgmt. Coll., Md., contractor performance measurement course, Dept. of Def. Sys. Mgmt. Coll., Md., fed. appropriation law, Grad. Sch. USDA, Okla., federal budget process, Grad. Sch. USDA, Okla., cert. acquisition profl. level I in fin. mgmt., Dept. of Air Force, Ohio, budget estimating techniques, U.S. Office of Pers. Mgmt., Tex., budget formulation, U.S. Office of Pers. Mgmt., Tex., budget execution, U.S. Office of Pers. Mgmt., Tex.; aeronautics Dept. of Transp., FAA, Okla., ISO 9000 implementation and documentation workshop Hartley Group Performance Paradigms, Inc., Okla., ISO 9000 internal quality auditor workshop Hartley Group-Performance Paradigm, Inc., Okla., Outclass the Competition PROTOCOL PLUS through Protocol Sch. of Washington, Profl. Devel. Inst. Symposium Sequoyah chpt. Am. Soc. of Mil. Comptrs., cert. acquisition profl. level I in acquisition logistics Dept. of the Air Force, Ohio, fgn. mil. sales internat. budget workshop Pentagon and Wright-Patterson AFB, appropriations law update in mgmt. field of study Learning Curve Tng. Group, Inc., Okla., cert. acquisition profl. level I in program mgmt. Dept. of the Air Force, Ohio, quality participation for employees USAF, quality leadership for mgrs. USAF, Alterations bookkeeping clk. alterations dept. Al Rosenthal's, Oklahoma City, 1966—67; sec.-receptionist ITT Continental Baking Co., Wonder Bread Regional Sales-Svc. Bus. Office, Oklahoma City, 1967—69; teller Tinker Field Credit Union, Tinker AFB, Okla., 1969; sales-svc. sec. West Coast regional sales svc. office Reynolds Metals Co., L.A., 1969—70; purchasing technician purchasing dept. Memorex Corp., Santa Clara, Calif., 1970—72; pers.-payroll clk. Unit Parts Co.-Borg Warner Corp., Oklahoma City, 1972—73; teller Tinker Field Credit Union, Tinker AFB, Okla., 1972; payroll technician acctg. divsn., C.G. Payroll Br. FAA Mike Monroney Aero. Ctr., Oklahoma City, 1974—81; payroll clk. divsn. WR Grace Petroleum, Bus. Office, payroll sect. TRG Drilling, Oklahoma City, 1981—83; payroll clk. civilian pay Dept. of Def., USAF Acctg. Br., Civilian Payroll Sect., Tinker AFB, 1973—74; mgr., supr. Cmty. Day Care Presch., Bus. Office, Pers. & Payroll, Oklahoma City, 1981; travel clk. FAA, Mike Monroney Aero. Ctr., Acctg. Divsn., Travel Br., Travel Adminstrn. Sect., Oklahoma City, 1983—83; acctg. technician FAA Mike Monroney Ctr., Acctg. Divsn., Accounts Payable Br., Oklahoma City, 1983—85; air traffic control specialist pre-developmental student flight svcs. trainee Dept. of Transp., FAA, Ea. Region, Jamaica, N.Y., Oklahoma City, 1986; mgr.-supr. family bus. Cmty. Day Care PreSch. Bus. Office, Oklahoma City, 1986—87; shipment clk. Def. Logistics Agy., Billing OS & D Sect. (Inbound), Tinker AFB, 1988—90; transp. control clk. Def. Logistics Agy., Freight Terminal Br., Tinker AFB, 1988; customer svc. rep. ATT Sales-Svc. Office, Oklahoma City, 1988; child devel. ctr. supr. HQ 72nd Air Base Wing, 72 Svcs. Divsn., Child Devel. Ctr.-West, Tinker AFB, 1990—91; budget analyst 552 Airborne Computer Squadron, Tinker AFB, 1991—93; budget anal. Okla. City Air Logistics Ctr., Commodities Mgmt. Directorate, Fin. Mgmt. Br., Tinker AFB, 1991—92; budget analyst Okla. City-Air Logistics Ctr., Tech. and Indsl. Support Directorate, Resource Mgmt. Divsn., Funds Mgmt. Br., Tinker AFB, 1992—97, Okla. City-Air Logistics Ctr., Fin. Mgmt. Directorate Workloading Sect., Tinker AFB, 1998—2001, Okla. City-Air Logistics Ctr., Fin. Mgmt. Directorate, Fin. Analysis Divsn., Tinker AFB, 2001—03. Leader participant League of Black Women, Flossmoor, Ill., 2005; treas. U.S. Green Bldg. Coun., Oklahoma City, 2005; cons. OCU Women As Servant Leaders, Oklahoma City, 2005—06. Named to Vice President's Honor Roll, Rose State Coll., 1991, President's Honor Roll, 1991, 1992; recipient Acad. Achievement award, Langston U., 1994, Spl. Act award, FAA Mike Monroney Aero. Ctr., 1979, Svc. award, 1983, Performance award, Okla. City-Air Logistics Ctr., Tech. and Indsl. Directorate, Resource Mgmt. Divsn., Funds Mgmt. Sect., 1996, Okla. Scholar-Leadership Enrichment Program' Elizabeth George Seminar fellowship, Okla. State Regents for Higher Edn. through the U. of Okla., 1995. Mem.: Union Concerned Scientists, Friends Earth, Common Cause, Nat. Wildlife Fedn., Interfaith Alliance, Price Tower Arts Ctr., Amnesty Internat. USA, Sustainable OKC, T&L Golf Club. Avocations: gardening, cooking, hiking, travel, reading. Office Phone: 405-235-2905.

RICHARDSON-LOWRY, MARY, lawyer; b. June 26, 1957; BA, U. San Francisco State, 1981; JD, Tex. So. U., 1984. Bar: U.S. Dist. Ct. (No. Dist. Ill.) 1986, Ill. Supreme Ct. 1986. Asst. corp. counsel Dept. Law City of Chgo., 1987—92, sr. supervising atty., 1992—94; asst. to Mayor Richard M. Daley City of Chgo., 1994—98, commr. dept. bldgs., 1998—2002; ptnr. Mayer, Brown, Rowe & Maw LLP, Chgo., 2002—. Commr. Devel. Commn. City of Chgo., 2004—. Office: Mayer Brown Rowe Maw Llp 230 S La Salle Ste 300 Chicago IL 60604-1407 Office Phone: 312-701-8442. Office Fax: 312-706-8427. E-mail: mbrl@mayerbrown.com.

RICHARDSON-MELECH, JOYCE SUZANNE, music educator, singer; b. Perth Amboy, N.J., Nov. 15, 1957; d. Herbert Nathaniel and Fannie Elaine (Franklin) Richardson; m. Gerald Melech, July 28, 1990. MusB, Westminster Choir Coll., 1979, MusM, 1981; postgrad. Rutgers U., 1999—. Cert. music tchr. N.J., supr. N.J. Musical play dir. Perth Amboy H.S. 1989-92, asst. band dir., 1984-94; music tchr. Perth Amboy Bd. Edn., 1981—, gifted and talented

music tchr., 1992-96; vocal soloist N.Y.C. Vocal soloist N.Y. Philharm. and Westminster Symphonic Choir, 1977, United Moravian Ch., N.Y.C., 1980-81, Ctrl. Jersey Concert Orch., Perth Amboy, 1994-96; mezzo-soprano soloist in The Messiah, John Hus Moravian Ch., Bklyn., 1998; master tchrs. collaborative with N.J. Symphony Orch., 2000-01, 2003, 2005 Contbg. author: Teacher's Resource Book, 2000, 2001, 2003, 2005, illustrator: The Peacock of Half-Way Tree: A Caribbean Fable, 2004; actor: Perth Amboy Adult Cmty. Theatre, 1983. Participant Perth Amboy Adult Cmty. Theatre, 1983. Recipient award for excellence in tchg., NJ Symphony Orch., 2000, 2001, 2003, 2005, Lois Bailey Glenn award for tchg. excellence, Nat. Music Found., 2004; grantee, Am. Music Edn. Initiative for Programmatic Ragtime, 2004. Mem. NAACP, Internat. Platform Assn., Am. Mus. Natural History (assoc.), Am. Fedn. Tchrs., Am. Fedn. Musicians (local 204-373), Music Educators Nat. Conf., Orgn. Am. Kodaly Educators, Alliance for Arts Edn. N.J., Ctrl. Jersey Music Educators, N.J. Music Educators Assn., Alpha Phi Omega. Democrat. Episcopalian. Avocations: travel, Art Deco antiques, needlecrafts, knitting, crocheting. Home: 148 Carson Ct Somerset NJ 08873-4790 Office: Samuel Shull Sch 380 Hall Ave Perth Amboy NJ 08861-3205 Office Phone: 732-376-6060 26662. Business E-Mail: joycrichardson@paps.net.

RICHARDSON-WENINEGAR, LORETTA LYNNE, biologist, educator; b. Ft. Riley, Kans., Sept. 19, 1954; d. Woodrow and Florence Myrtle Denton; children: Jennifer Lynne Weninegar-Canady, Jessica Leigh Weninegar, James Christopher Weninegar. BS in Biology and Secondary Edn./Minor Psychology, U. Mobile, 1976, MSEd in secondary edn./biology, 1993; MS in biology, Jacksonville State U., 2002. Cert. Tchr. #252735, Type B Ala., 1976, Tchr. #252735, Type A Ala., 1993. Sci. tchr. Arnold Sch. of Ala., Mobile, 1976, Berney Points Sch., Birmingham, Ala., 1977—79, Hueytown H.S., Ala., 1995—98, Jacksonville H.S., Ala., 1990—91; grad. tchg. asst., biology Jacksonville State U., Ala., 1993, adj. instr. biology, 1993—98; asst. project dir. Ala. Sci. in Motion Ala. A&M U., Huntsville, 1998—; tchr. of sci. Columbia H.S., 2006—. Field technician, botanist Natural Resource Conservation Svc., Ala., 1996; chmn., pers. com. Berney Points Sch., Birmingham, 1979—81; asst. dir. Chattooga river environ. edn. and water quality project Jacksonville State U., Ala., 1994—95, facilitator environ. edn. From Awareness to Action, 1993, staff, Little River Field Sch., 1993—97; trainer Ala. Water Watch Ala. A&M U., Huntsville, 1998—; adj. instr. Biology Calhoun C.C., Decatur/Huntsville, Ala., 2004—. Spkr. bur., hike leader The Land Trust of Huntsville and North Ala.; mem. strategic planning com. Columbia H.S., Huntsville, 2005—; outdoor amb. Ala. Bur. Tourism and Travel, 2006, amb. yr. outdoor Ala., 2006; spkr. Ala. Wildflower Soc., Huntsville. Mem.: NEA, Nat. Sci. Tchr. Assn., Nat. Assn. Biology Tchrs., Ala. Edn. Assn., The LandTrust of Huntsville and North Ala. (speaker's bur., hike leader), Beta Beta Beta, Delta Kappa Gamma (membership chmn. 2002—04). Achievements include research in water quality analysis of Cane Creek in Calhoun County, Ala; lysozyme crystal experiment; Vascular Flora of Choccolocco Creek, Calhoun, Cleburne, and Talladega Counties, Ala. Avocations: hiking, camping, gardening, birdwatching, dance. Home: 9507 Hemlock Dr SE Huntsville AL 35803 Personal E-mail: bcdh@aol.com.

RICHARDS-VITAL, CLAUDIA, small business owner, recreational facility executive; b. Banes, Oriente, Cuba, May 18, 1935; arrived in U.S., 1951; d. Vasper Zacharia Richards and Ana Louisa Coombs - Vital; m. Eugene Blackman, July 22, 1956 (div. Apr. 20, 1965); children: Emery, John, Veronica. AA in Bus. Adminstrn./English, Havana Bus. Acad., 1951; diploma in Early Childhood Devel., Miami Dade C.C., 1972. Pvt. practice nanny, Miami Beach, Fla., 1951—56; seamstress Playboy Club, Miami, Fla., 1961—65; prodn. supr. So. Bakery, 1965—69; care mother James E. Scott Cmty. Agy., 1970—75; nurse asst. North Shore Hosp., 1970—75; home health aide Total Care Home Health Agy., 1975—85; site dir. YMCA, 1985—95; sole propr. Veronica's Boutique, 1982—89, Claudia's Formal Wear, 1989—. Pres. Local #249 Am. Bakery and Confectionery Workers Internat. AFL-CIO, Fla., 1966—69. Named Parent of Yr. Metro Dade County, 1993; recipient Diamond Pendant, Queen Elizabeth II, 1965, cert. of Appreciation, YMCA of Miami, Fla., 1990. Mem.: NAFE, NAACP. Democrat. Roman Catholic. Avocations: sewing, decorating, gardening, babysitting, animals. Home: 1915 NW 49 St Miami FL 33142 Office Phone: 305-637-2090. Personal E-mail: claudia@claudiaformalwareeleganza.com.

RICHBURG, BILLY KEITH, healthcare manager, consultant, entrepreneur; b. Memphis, Tex., Dec. 16, 1946; s. Burney C. and Marjorie Mae (Draper) R.; children: Gretchen, Jeremy; m. Paula Anita Mason, July 27, 1990. BA, U. Alaska, Anchorage, 1974; MS in Health Care Administrn., Trinity U., San Antonio, 1978. Exec. dir. Med. Park Hosp. (Am. Med. Internat.), Hope, Ark., 1979-84; asst. adminstr. Columbia (Mo.) Regional Hosp. (Am. Med. Internat.), 1984-85, v.p., CFO, 1985-96; exec. dir. VNA Ctrl. Mo., Columbia, 1996-98; gen. mgr. Coram Healthcare, Earth City, Mo., 1999-2000; dir. gov't. programs and compliance IMACS, Ltd., Dallas, 2001—. Founder MPTC Svcs. With USAF, 1969-76. Fellow Healthcare Fin. Mgmt. Assn.; mem. Mensa. Episcopalian. Avocations: motorcycles, on-line computing. Office Phone: 972-692-2827, 972-755-6370.

RICHELS, JOHN, energy executive, lawyer; BA, York Univ.; LLB, Univ. Windsor, 1978. Mng. ptnr., COO, mem. exec. com. Bennett Jones; bd. dir. Northstar Energy Corp., 1993—96, exec. v.p., CFO, 1996—98; pres., CEO Devon Canada, 1998—2001; sr. v.p. Canadian div. Devon Energy Corp., Oklahoma City, 2001—04, pres., 2004—. Gen. counsel XV Olympic Winter Games, Calgary, 1986—88. Office: Devon Energy Corp 20 N Broadway Oklahoma City OK 73102-8260*

RICHELSON, PAUL WILLIAM, curator; b. Montpelier, Idaho, Sept. 27, 1939; s. Paul Newton and June (Quayle) R. BA, Yale U., 1961; MFA, Princeton U., 1967. PhD 1974 Asst. prof. Lawrence U., Appleton, Wis., 1970-77, U. Denver, 1977-84; asst. dir., curator Trisolini Gallery of Ohio U., Athens, 1984-87; chief curator Grand Rapids (Mich.) Mus., 1987-91; curator of Am. art Mobile Mus. Art, Mobile, Ala., 1991-97, asst. dir., chief curator, 1997—. Author: (book) Studies in the Personal Imagery Collection of 20th Prints Ohio University, 1985, (catalogue) The Golden Age 19th Century Prints by David Roberts, 1988, Lee Loring: A Southern Sophisticate, 1992, Modernism and American Painting of the 1930s, 1993, ThirtySomething, 1994, Alabama Impact: Contemporary Artists with Alabama Ties, 1995, Louise Lyons Heustis (1965-1951): A Retrospective, 1995, The French Connection: Jean Simon Chaudron Returns To Mobile, 1996, John Roderick Dempster MacKenzie (1865-1941): A Retrospective, 1997, Celebrating the Creative Spirit, 1998, Contemporary Southeastern Furniture, 1998, Coming Home: American Paintings, 1930-1950, from the Schoen Collection, 2003. Lt. (j.g.) USN, 1961-63. Recipient Elizabeth B. Gould Rsch. award Mobile Hist. Devel. Commn., 1997; Fulbright-Hays fellow to Italy, 1967-69; Mus. Purchase Plan grantee Nat. Endowment for the Arts, 1991; grantee Mus. Loan Network, 2002. Mem. Southeastern Museums Conf. Home: 6427 Grelot Rd Apt 405 Mobile AL 36695-2630 Office: Mobile Museum of Art 4850 Museum Dr Mobile AL 36608-1917 Fax: 251-208-5201. Office Phone: 251-208-5215. E-mail: prichelson@mobilemuseumofart.com

RICHENHAGEN, MARTIN H., manufacturing executive; b. July 1, 1952; married; 3 children. Grad., Univ. Bonn, Germany, 1975. Vice-pres. field ops. Schindler Aufzugsfabrik GmbH, Germany, 1995—98; group pres. GLAAS KgaA mbH, Germany, 1995—2003; group exec. vice-pres. Forbo Internat. SA, 2003—04; pres., CEO AGCO Corp., Duluth, Ga., 2004—06, chmn., pres., CEO, 2006—. Office: AGCO Corp 4205 River Green Pkwy Duluth GA 30096 Office Phone: 770-813-9200.*

RICHERSON, HAL BATES, internist, allergist, immunologist, educator; b. Phoenix, Feb. 16, 1929; s. George Edward and Eva Louise (Steere) R.; m. Julia Suzanne Bradley (dec. 1996), Sept. 5, 1953; children: Anne, George, Miriam, Julia, Susan. BS with distinction, U. Ariz., 1950; MD, Northwestern U., 1954. Diplomate Am. Bd. Internal Medicine, Am. Bd. Allergy and Immunology, Bd. Diagnostic Lab. Immunology; lic. physician, Iowa. Intern Kansas City (Mo.) Gen. Hosp., 1954-55; resident in pathology St. Luke's Hosp., Kansas City, 1955-56; trainee in neuropsychiatry Brooke Army Hosp.,

San Antonio, 1956; resident in medicine U. Iowa Hosps., Iowa City, 1961-64, fellow in allergy and immunology, 1964-66; fellow in immunology Mass. Gen. Hosp., Boston, 1968-69; instr. internal medicine U. Iowa Coll. Medicine, Iowa City, 1964-66, asst. prof., 1966-70, assoc. prof., 1970-74, prof., 1974-98, prof. emeritus, 1998—; acting dir. divsn. allergy/applied immunology U. Iowa Hosps. and Clinics, Iowa City, 1970-72, dir. allergy and clin. immunology sect., 1972-78, dir. divsn. allergy and immunology, 1978-91; gen. practice, asst. to Gen. Surgeon Ukiah, Calif., 1958; gen. practice medicine Holbrook, Ariz., 1958-61. Vis. lectr. medicine Harvard U. Sch. Medicine, Boston, 1968-69; vis. prof., rsch. scientist U. London and Brompton Hosp., 1984; prin. investigator Nat. Heart, Lung and Blood Inst., 1971-94, mem. pulmonary diseases adv. com., 1983-87; prin. investigator Nat. Inst. Allergy and Infectious Diseases, 1983-94; dir. Nat. Inst. Allergy and Infectious Diseases' Asthma and Allergic Diseases Ctr., U. Iowa, 1983-94; mem. VA Merit Rev. Bd. in Respiration, 1981-84; mem. NIH Gen. Clin. Rsch. Ctrs., 1989-93; mem. rev. reserve NIH, 1993-98; mem. bd. sci. advisors Merck Inst., 1990-94; presenter lectures, seminars, continuing edn. courses; mem. numerous univ., coll. and hosp. coms., 1970—; cons. Merck Manual, 1982, 87, 92, 96-97. Contbr. numerous articles and revs. to profl. jours., chpts. to books; reviewer Sci., Jour. Immunology, Jour. Allergy and Clin. Immunology, Am. Rev. Respiratory Disease, New Eng. Jour. Medicine, Ann. Internal Medicine. Served to capt. U.S. Army, 1956-58. NIH fellow 1968-69. Fellow ACP (Laureate award 1996), Am. Acad. Allergy Asthma & Immunology (Disting. Clinician award 1998); mem. AMA (mem. residency and rev. com. for allergy and immunology; mem. accreditation coun. for grad. med. edn. 1980-85, vice-chmn. 1984-85), AAAS, Iowa Med. Soc., Iowa Thoracic Soc. (chmn. program com. 1964-65, 69-71, pres. 1972-73, mem. exec. com. 1972-74), Am. Thoracic Soc. (bd. dirs. 1981-82, councilor assembly on allergy and immunology 1980-81, mem. nominating com. 1988-90), Iowa Clin. Med. Soc., Am. Fedn. Clin. Rsch., Am. Assn. Immunologists, Ctrl. Soc. Clin. Rsch. (chmn. sect. on allergy-immunology 1980-81, mem. coun. 1981-84), Alpha Omega Alpha. Avocations: reading, trombonist, swimming, scuba diving. Home: 331 Lucon Dr Iowa City IA 52246-3300 Office: U Iowa Health Care Dept Internal Medicine 200 Hawkins Dr Iowa City IA 52242-1009 Personal E-Mail: richersonh@mchsi.com. Business E-Mail: hal-richerson@uiowa.edu.

RICHERT, JOHN ROLIN, neuroimmunologist, educator; b. Boston, June 9, 1945; s. Daniel Arnold and Esther (Beamer) Richert; m. Nancy Dembeck, July 5, 1969. BA, Cornell U., 1966; MD, U. Rochester, 1970. Diplomate Am. Bd. Med. Examiners, Am. Bd. Psychiatry and Neurology. Intern, resident in medicine Strong Meml. Hosp. U. Rochester, NY, 1970-72; resident in neurology Mayo Clinic, Rochester, Minn., 1974-77; fellow Nat. Multiple Sclerosis Soc. NIH, Bethesda, Md., 1977-80; rsch. asst. prof. neurology Georgetown U. Med. Ctr., Washington, 1980-83, asst. prof. neurology, 1983-89, assoc. prof. neurology, 1989-93, prof. neurology, 1993—2005, prof., chair dept. microbiology and immunology, 1997—2005; v.p. rsch. and clin. programs Nat. Multiple Sclerosis Soc., N.Y.C., 2005—; mem. data and safety monitoring bd. Acorda Therapeutics, Hawthorne, NY, 2005—, Novartis, Basel, Switzerland, 2005—. Mem. physician adv. bd. Biogen Inc., Cambridge, Mass., 1994-2000; cons. Immunex, Inc., Seattle, 1998-2000; external adv. com. VA Multiple Sclerosis Ctr. of Excellence, U. Md. Multiple Sclerosis Ctr., Balt., 2003-2005; sci. adv. bd. TolerGenics, Inc., Rockville, Md., 2001-2005; cons. Health Sci. Ctr. for Continuing med. Edn., NY, 2003. Mem. editl. bd.: NeuroRx. Mem. immunol. scis. study sect. NIH, 1989, mem. mental health AIDS and immunology rsch. study sect., 1992, mem. neurol. disorders program project com., 2003, Brain Disorders and Clin. Neuroscience spl. emphasis panel, 2003-2004. Maj. USAF, 1972-74. Fellow Am. Acad. Neurology; mem. Internat. Soc. Neuroimmunology, Nat. Multiple Sclerosis Soc. (med. adv. bd. 1988-91, 93-96, profl. adv. com. 1988-2005, sci. peer rev. com. 1993-98), Am. Neurol. Assn., Am. Assn. Immunologists, Assn. Med. Sch. Microbiology and Immunology Chairs (pub. policy com. 2002-2005, chair 2004-2005), Am. Soc. for Biochemistry and Molecular Biology, Am. Soc. for Exptl. Neurotherapeutics, N.Y. Acad. Scis.,m Alpha Omega Alpha. Avocations: tennis, golf, skiing. Office: Nat Multiple Sclerosis Soc 733 3d Ave New York NY 10017 Office Phone: 212-476-0423. Business E-Mail: john.richertj@nmss.org

RICHERT, PAUL, law educator; b. Elwood, Ind., Aug. 31, 1948; m. Catherine George Stanton, June 24, 1972; children: John, William, AB, U. Ill.-Urbana, 1970, MS, 1971; JD, Tulane U., 1977. Bar: Ohio 1977. Asst. law librarian U. Akron, 1977-78, law librarian, asst. prof. law, 1978-83, assoc. prof., 1983-87, prof. law, 1987—. Local bd. dirs. Selective Svc. sys. Co-author: Searching the Law, 3d edit., 2005. Mem. United Chs. of Christ. With U.S. Army, 1971-74. Mem. Am. Assn. Law Librs., Akron Bar Assn., ABA. Home: 2030 Ganyard Rd Akron OH 44313-6050 Office: U Akron Sch of Law Libr 150 University Ave Akron OH 44325-2902 Office Phone: 330-972-7330. Business E-Mail: richert@uakron.edu.

RICHES, WENDY, magazine publishing executive; Dir. pub. rels. Save the Children Fund, dir. mktg. and fundraising U.K., 1985-90; exec. creative dir. Ogilvy & Mather Direct, London, 1990-92; mng. dir. Ogilvy & Mather Direct (now Ogilvy One), London, 1995-98; chmn., CEO OgilvyOne N. Am.; pres., global mktg. & e-commerce Hasbro Inc., 1998—2000; former pres. D'Arcy Mktg. Comm. Group; exec. v.p., integrated mktg. Meredith Pub. Group, NYC, now exec. v.p., 2006—. Mem., bd. dirs. Columbia House Co., Direct Marketing Association, 2000—. Office: Meredith Publishing 125 Park Ave New York NY 10017 Office Phone: 212-557-6600.*

RICHESON, JAMES GRADY, JR., dentist; m. Nancy Richeson; 1 child, Suzanne. DDS, Georgetown U. Dentist, Washington; Recipient Disting. Svc. award, Georgetown Dental Alumni, 2003. Fellow: Pierre Fauchard Acad., Am. Coll. Dentists, Acad. Gen. Dentistry (pres.-elect 2001—02, pres. 2002—03, v.p., treas., bd. trustee, budget and fin. com., regional dir., Found. bd. dirs.); mem.: ADA (alt. del. 2001—, del. 2004), DC Dental Soc. (The Sterling V. Meade award 2004), DC Acad. Gen. Dentistry (past pres.), Georgetown U. Alumni Club of Met. Washington (past pres.). Office: 4400 Jenifer St NW Ste 340 Washington DC 20015-2113 Office Phone: 202-364-5246. Business E-Mail: richeson@agd.com.

RICHESON, JENNIFER ANNE, psychology professor, researcher; b. Sept. 1972; ScB, Brown U., 1994; PhD in Social Psychology, Harvard U., 2000. Asst. prof. psychol. and brain scis. Dartmouth Coll., Hanover, NH, 2000—05; assoc. prof. Dept. Psychology Northwestern U., Evanston, 2005—, faculty fellow Inst. for Policy Rsch., 2005—. Vis. fellow Rsch. Inst. for Comparative Studies in Race and Ethnicity, Stanford U., 2004—05. Contbr. articles to profl. jours. Grantee Ford Found. Odyssey Grant, 1993, NIMH Individual Rsch. Svc. Award, 1999—2000, Walter and Constance Burke Rsch. Initiation Award, 2000—06, NIMH B/START Grant, 2002—04, NSF, 2002—05; MacArthur Fellow, John D. and Catherine T. MacArthur Found., 2006. Mem.: Soc. for Psychol. Study of Social Issues, Soc. for Personality and Social Psychology, Am. Psychol. Soc., Am. Psychol. Assn. Office: Dept Psychology Northwestern U 2029 Sheridan Rd Evanston IL 60208-2710 Office Phone: 847-467-1331. E-mail: jriches@northwestern.edu.*

RICHEY, ELLEN, credit card company executive; BA summa cum laude, Harvard U.; JD, Stanford U. Law clk. Hon. Lewis F. Powell, Jr. U.S. Supreme Ct.; law clk. Hon. Charles B. Renfrew U.S. Dist. Ct. (no. dist.); ptnr. Farella, Braun & Martel, San Francisco, 1980—94; from gen. counsel, sec. Providian Fin. Corp., San Francisco, 1995—, exec. v.p., 1997—99, vice chmn. Enterprise Risk Mgmt., 1999—. Office: Providian Financial Corp 201 Mission Street Lobby San Francisco CA 94105 Office Phone: 415-278-4634. Business E-Mail: ellen_richey@providian.com.

RICHEY, KIMBERLY KAY, singer, actress, composer; b. Zanesville, Ohio, Dec. 1, 1956; Student, Western Ky. U., Bowling Green, 1975-79; BS in Environ. Edn., Ohio U., 1980-82. With Mercury Nashville, 1994—; composer Nobody Wins, Those Words We Said, Believe Me Baby I Lied; rec. artist Kim

Richey, 1995, Bitter Sweet, 1997, Glimmer, 1999; opener, headliner various shows. Recipient Grammy nomination, 1996. Office: Mercury Records Ste 300 54 Music Sq E Nashville TN 37203-4386

**RICHEY, MARY ELLEN,** lawyer; b. Boston, Mar. 16, 1949; BA summa cum laude, Radcliffe Coll., 1970; JD, Stanford U., 1977. Bar: Calif. 1978. Law clk. to Hon. Charles B. Renfrew U.S. Dist. Ct. (no. dist.) Calif., 1977-78; law clk. to Hon. Lewis F. Powell, Jr., assoc. justice U.S. Supreme Ct., 1979-80; with Farella, Braun & Martel, San Francisco; assoc. Providian Fin. Corp., San Francisco, 1980—85, ptnr., v.p., sec., 1985—93, gen. counsel, 1985—, vice chmn., 1990-93. Symposium editor Stanford Law Rev., 1976-77. Mem. ABA (bus. law sect., real property probate and trust law sect.), State Bar Calif. (bus. law sect., real property law sect.), Bar Assn. San Francisco, Phi Beta Kappa, Order of Coif. Office: Providian Fin Corp 201 Mission St San Francisco CA 94105-1831 Office Phone: 415-543-0404. Office Fax: 415-278-6028.

**RICHIE, JEROME PAUL,** surgeon, educator; b. San Antonio, 1944; MD, U. Tex., 1969. Surg. intern UCLA, 1969—70, resident in gen. surgery, 1970—71, resident in urology, 1971—75, lectr. surg. urology, 1974—75; asst. clin. prof. U. Calif., San Diego, 1975—77; asst. prof. urology Harvard U., 1977—80, assoc. prof., 1980—86, prof., 1986—, Elliott C. Cutler prof. surgery, 1987—, chmn. program in urology, 1987—. Chief urol. Brigham and Women's Hosp., Boston, 1977—; cons. Dana Farber Cancer Ctr., Boston, 1977—. Lt. comdr. M.C. USN, 1975—77. Mem.: ACS, Am. Surg. Assn., Am. Soc. (Clin.) Oncology, Assn. Acad. Surgery, Am. Urol. Assn., Am. Assn. Gerito-Urinary Surgeons. Office: Brigham & Womens Hosp 45 Francis St # 3 Boston MA 02115-6105 E-mail: jrichie@partners.org.

**RICHIE, LIONEL B., JR.,** singer, lyricist, theater producer; b. Tuskegee, Ala., June 20, 1949; s. Lionel and Alberta Richie; m. Brenda Harvey, 1975 (div.); 1 child, Nicole; m. Diane Alexander, 1996; children: Miles, Sofia. BS in Econs., Tuskegee U., 1971, MusD (hon.), 1985, Boston Coll., 1986. Pres. Brockman Music, L.A. Mem. group The Mystics (name changed to The Commodores), 1969-81; writer, producer songs for Commodores including: Easy, Three Times a Lady (Am. Music award 1979, People's Choice award for best song 1979), Still (People's Choice award for best song 1980), Sail On, Lady (Nat. Music Pubs. award 1980, 81, People's Choice award for best composer 1981); songwriter, producer album for Kenny Rogers; albums (with The Commodores) include Midnight Magic, Machine Gun, Movin' On, Commodores, Caught in the Act, Hot on the Tracks, Natural High, Heroes, (solo albums) Lionel Richie, 1982, Can't Slow Down, 1983 (Grammy award Album of Yr. 1985), Dancing on the Ceiling, 1986, Back to Front, 1992, Louder Than Words, 1996, Truly-The Love Songs, 1997, Time, 1998, Renaissance, 2001 (Grammy nomination for Angel); prodr., composer: (songs) Truly (Grammy award 1982, 2 Am. Music awards 1983, People's Choice award Best Song 1983), All Night Long (Nat. Music Pubs. award 1984, 3 Black Gold awards 1984, Am. Music award 1984, Hello (2 Am. Music awards 1985), Say You, Say Me (ASCAP Pop award 1987, Am. Music award 1987, Oscar award Best Song 1986, Golden Globe award Best Song 1986), Dancing on the Ceiling (3 Am. Music awards 1987), (duet with Diana Ross) Endless Love (Grammy award 1982, 2 Am. Music awards 1982, Am. Movie award 1982, Rojo award Gold Status in Hong Kong 1982, People's Choice award Best Song 1982), (sung by Kenny Rogers) Lady, (with Michael Jackson) We Are The World, 1985 (Grammy awards Best Song, Record of Yr. 1986, People's Choice award Best Song 1986); actor (film) The Preacher's Wife, 1996. Recipient Best Young Artist in Film award, 1980, 2 NAACP image awards, 1983, Favorite Male Vocalist Pop/Rock award Am. Music Acad., 1987, Favorite Male Vocalist Soul/R&B award Am. Music Acad., 1987, Lifetime Achievement award San Remo Festival, Italy, 1996, Lifetime Achievement award World Music Awards; inductee Ala. Music Hall of Fame, 1997; named Man of Yr. Children's Diabetes Found., 1984, Alumnus of Yr. United Negro Coll. Fund, 1984, Favorite Male Singer People mag. Readers Poll, 1985, Entertainer of Yr. NAACP, 1987. Mem. ASCAP (Writer of Yr. 1984, 85, 86, Pub. of Yr. 1985).

**RICHIE, MARGARET BYE,** architectural historian; PhD, U. Pa., 1987. Author: Victorian Sketch Book, 1980, Stone Houses, Homes of Traditional Pennsylvania's Bucks County and Brandywine Valley, 2005. Mem. Bucks County Archtl. Rev. Bd. Fellow: Sigma Pi Kappa. Avocations: architecture, history, politics, sociology, languages. Address: Woodland Crossing T04 300 Linden Ponds Way Hingham MA 02043

**RICHIE, NICOLE,** television personality; b. Berkeley, Calif., Sept. 21, 1981; d. Lionel and Brenda Harvey Richie. Co-star: (TV series) The Simple Life, 2003; The Simple Life 2: Road Trip, 2004; The Simple Life 3: Interns, 2005; The Simple Life 4: 'Til Death Do Us Part, 2006; guest appearance Punk'd, 2003; Mad TV, 2004; Rock Me Baby, 2004; Six Feet Under, 2004; actor: (films) Kids in America, 2005; author: The Truth About Diamonds, 2005 (Publishers Weekly hardcover fiction bestseller list).*

**RICHIE, RODNEY CHARLES,** critical care and pulmonary medicine physician; b. Big Springs, Tex., Aug. 17, 1946; s. Howard Mouzon and Gloria (Hollingshead) R.; m. Sara Lee Dilley, July 13, 1968; children: Megan Kathryn, Paul Nathan. BA in Chemistry, So. Meth. U., 1968; MD cum laude, Baylor Coll., 1972. Diplomate in Internal Medicine, Pulmonary, Crit. Care and Ins. Medicine. Resident in medicine Baylor Affiliated Hosps., Houston, 1973-75, chief med. resident, 1975, fellow in pulmonary medicine, 1976-77; pres. Waco (Tex.) Lung Assocs., 1977—2004; assoc. clin. prof. cmty. medicine Heart of Tex. Cmty. Health Ctr./U. Tex. S.W. Med. Sch., 2004—. Med. dir. Tex. Life Ins., Waco, 1985—, Cmty. Hospice of Waco, 1996—, EMSI, Waco, Tex., 1997—. Chmn. med. staff Hillcrest Bapt. Med. Ctr., Waco, 1993; chmn. bd. dirs. GH Pape Found., Waco, 1993. Fellow: ACP, Am. Coll. Chest Physicians; mem.: AMA, Am. Thoracic Soc., Am. Acad. Internal Medicine (del. to AMA), Tex. Club Internists. Episcopalian. Avocations: skiing, writing, reading. Home: 3509 Lake Heights Dr Waco TX 76708-1005 Office: Waco Med Group 7125 New Sanger Ave Ste B Waco TX 76712 Office Phone: 254-761-1519. E-mail: rcrichie@earthlink.net.

**RICHIERI, KENNETH A.,** publishing executive, lawyer; b. Jersey City, 1951; married; 3 children. AB, Brown U., 1973; JD cum laude, Harvard U., 1976. Bar: 1977. Assoc. Cahill Gordon & Reindel, 1976—82; with The NY Times Co., NYC, 1983—, sr. counsel, 1989—93, asst. gen. counsel, 1993—2002, dep. gen. counsel, 2001—05, v.p., 2002—, gen. counsel, 2006—, NY Times Digital, 1999—2004. Office: The NY Times Co 229 W 43rd St New York NY 10036*

**RICHLAND, KENT LEWIS,** lawyer; b. Nov. 1946; AB, U. Calif., Berkeley, 1968; JD, UCLA, 1971. Bar: Calif. 1972, US Supreme Ct. 1975, US Ct. Appeals (9th cir.) 1972, US Dist. Ct. (ctrl. dist.) Calif. 1972. Supervising dep. atty. gen. State of Calif., 1972—76; supervising atty. for Calif. State Pub. Defender, 1976—78; sr. rsch. atty. to Presiding Justice Otto M. Kaus Calif. Ct. Appeals, 1978—79; atty. Horvitz & Greines, 1980—83; founding mem. Greines, Martin, Stein & Richard LLP, LA, 1983—. Mem. Com. on Delivery of Legal Svcs., 1977—78, Appellate Cts. Com., 1978—, Jud. Evaluation Com., 1984—85, State Appellate Jud. Evaluation Com., 1989—99, chief justice, 1992—94, Appellate Cts. Com., 1985—88, Calif. Jud. Sys. Com., 1988—90, Jud. Appointments Com., 2001—03; adj. prof. law Southwestern Sch. Law, 1986—87; guest lectr. U. So. Calif. Law Ctr., UCLA Sch. Law, U. West LA Sch. Law. Bd. editors LA Bar Jour. and LA Lawyer, 1973—78, articles editor and mng. editor, 1977—78, bd. advisors Hastings Constl. Law Quarterly, 1978—88; contbr. articles to law jours. Mem.: ABA (co-chair Nat. Inst. on Med. Malpractice 1989—90, vice-chair 1989—90, mem. Appellate Adv. Com. 2001—, mem. Torts and Insurance Practice Sect., Appellate Advocacy Com.), Calif. Judicial Coun., LA County Bar Assn. (trustee 1990—2000), Calif. Acad. Appellate Lawyers (pres. 1995—96), Calif. Supreme Ct. Hist. Soc. (pres. 1999—2004, bd. dirs.). Achievements include successfully argued Marshall versus Marshall (Anna Nicole Smith case) in the United States

Supreme Court, 2006. Office: Greines, Martin, Stein & Richard LLP Ste 375 5700 Wilshire Blvd Los Angeles CA 90036-3697 Office Phone: 310-859-7811. Office Fax: 310-276-5261. Business E-Mail: krichland@gmsr.com.

**RICHLEN, SCOTT LANE,** federal government program administrator; b. Ames, Iowa, July 23, 1949; s. Ellsworth Mark and Betty Jane (Wegner) R.; m. Deborah Lou Dick, Feb. 6, 1971; children: Mindy Lou, Gwendolyn Anne. BSME, Mont. State U., 1972; M.Engring. in Mech. Engring., U. Idaho, 1982; grad. exec. potential program, Office Pers. Mgmt., 1995. Assoc. engr. Thiokol Chem. Corp., Brigham City, Utah, 1973-75; rsch. engr. EG&G Idaho, Inc., Idaho Falls, 1975-79, sr. program specialist, 1979-84; program mgr. indsl. heat pumps U.S. Dept. Energy, Washington, 1984-87, program mgr. advanced heat exchangers, 1984-94, program mgr. continuous fiber ceramic composites, 1990-95, team leader steel industry R&D, 1995-99, integrated delivery sys. devel. team, 1998-99, dir. Office Indsl. Techs., 2000—03, team leader advanced process sys., 2003—. Lectr. profl. ext. U. Wis., Madison, 1982—83; lectr. Nat. Air & Space Mus., Smithsonian Instn., Washington, 2005—. Author: (reference text) ASM, Engineered Materials, 1992, Ceramics Information Analysis Center/American Ceramic Society Handbook on Continuous Fiber Reinforced Ceramic Matrix Composites, 1993; editor (conf. procs.) Industrial Heat Exchangers, 1985; inventor, patentee corrosive resistant heat exchanger. Vol. Martha's Table, Washington, 1986—; v.p. Aid Assn for Lutherans, Br. 2792, Annandale, Va., 1988-92. Mem. Precision Aerobatics Model Pilots Assn., No. Va. Control-line Assn. (pres. 1987-89, 91-92, 2000-04, youth com. chmn. 2005-), Mont. State Soc. Mont. State U. Alumni Assn. (life). Avocations: woodworking, martial arts, control-line model airplanes, gardening, readings in psychology, history and law. Office: US Dept Energy 1000 Independence Ave SW Washington DC 20585-0001

**RICHMAN, ALAN,** magazine editor, educator; b. Bronx, N.Y., Nov. 12, 1939; s. Louis and Sonia (Carity) R.; m. Kelli Shor, June 21, 1964; children: Lincoln Seth Shor, Matthew Mackenzie Shor. BA, Hunter Coll., 1960. Reporter Leader-Observer, N.Y.C., 1960-61; asst. editor Modern Tire Dealer, N.Y.C., 1962-64; assoc. editor ASTA Travel News, N.Y.C., 1964-65; pub. rels. rep. M.J. Jacobs, Inc., N.Y.C., 1965-66; mng. editor Modern Floor Coverings, N.Y.C., 1966-68; editor Bank Systems & Equipment, N.Y.C., 1968-79, Health Care Product News, N.Y.C., 1976; from assoc. pub. to pub. Bank Systems & Equipment, N.Y.C., 1969-79; editorial dir. Nat. Jeweler, N.Y.C., 1979-81; editor Health Foods Bus.; editorial dir. Army/Navy Store and Outdoor Merchandiser, 1981-88, The Pet Dealer, 1983-88; editor Cabinet Mfg. and Fabricating KBC Publs., 1988-94; ret., 1994. Program dir. Cabinet Mfg. Fair, 1989-94; adj. faculty NYU, 1989—, Brookdale C.C., 1992—, Bergen County C.C., 1994—. Exec. editor: Kitchen and Bath Design News, 1992-93; editor-in-chief Wood Digest, PTN Pub. Co., 1992-94; editor: Whole Foods, 1994—; author: Czechoslovakia in Pictures, 1969, A Book on the Chair, 1968. With AUS, 1961-62. Recipient Jesse H. Neal certificate merit Am. Bus. Press, 1973.

**RICHMAN, ANTHONY E.,** textile rental industry association executive; b. Dec. 13, 1941; s. Irving M. and Helen V. (Muchnic) R.; Judy Harriet Richman, Dec. 19, 1964; children: Lisa Michele, Jennifer Beth. BS, U. So. Calif., 1964. With Reliable Textile Rental Svcs., L.A., 1964—; svc. mgr., 1969; sales and svc. mgr., 1970-73; plant mgr., 1973-75; gen. mgr., bd. dirs., 1975-78; v.p., sec.-treas., 1975-82; exec. v.p., CEO, 1982-84; pres., CEO, 1984—. Bd. dirs. Guild for Children, 1979—, Valley Guild for Cystic Fibrosis, 1974—, Cystic Fibrosis Found. of L.A. and Orange Counties, 1989—; pres. Textile Rental/Svc. Assn. Am., 1993-95; exec. dir. Western Textile Svcs. Assn., Studio City, Calif., 1996—. Office: Western Textile Svcs Assn 12400 Ventura Blvd Ste 213 Studio City CA 91604-2409 Office Phone: 818-399-5408.

**RICHMAN, DAVID PAUL,** neurologist, educator, researcher; b. Boston, June 9, 1943; s. Harry S. and Anne (Goodkin) R.; m. Carol Mae von Bastian, Aug. 31, 1969; children: Sarah Ann, Jacob Charles. AB, Princeton U., 1965; MD, Johns Hopkins U., 1969. Diplomate Am. Bd. Psychiatry and Neurology. Intern, then asst. resident in medicine Albert Einstein Coll. Medicine, N.Y.C., 1969-71; resident in neurology Mass. Gen. Hosp., Boston, 1971-73, chief resident, 1973-74; instr. neurology Harvard U. Med. Sch., Boston, 1975-76; asst. prof. neurology U. Chgo., 1976-80, assoc. prof., 1981-85, prof., 1985-91, Straus prof. neurol. Scis., 1988-91; prof. neurology U. Calif., Davis, 1991—, chmn. dept., 1991-97. Mem. com. Nat. Aging, NIH, 1984-85, mem. immunological scis. study sect., 1986-90. Mem. AAAS, Am. Assn. Immunologists, Am. Acad. Neurology, Am. Neurol. Assn., Phi Beta Kappa, Sigma Xi. Office: U Calif Davis Dept Neurology 1515 Newton Ct Davis CA 95616-4859 Office Phone: 530-752-5013. Business E-Mail: dprichman@ucdavis.edu.

**RICHMAN, DOUGLAS DANIEL,** medical virologist, educator, internist; b. NYC, Feb. 15, 1943; s. Daniel Powell and Louise Kohnstamm (Woolf) R.; m. Eva Acquino, June 21, 1965; children: Sara, Matthew. AB cum laude, Dartmouth Coll., 1965; MD, Stanford U., 1970. Diplomate Am. Bd. Internal Medicine, Am. Bd. Infectious Diseases, Am. Bd. Med. Examiners. Intern Stanford Med. Sch., Calif., 1970—71, resident, 1971—72; rsch. assoc. LID/NIAID NIH, Bethesda, Md., 1972—75; fellow Beth Israel and Children's Hosps., Harvard Med. Ctr., Boston, 1975—76; asst. prof. depts. pathology and medicine U. Calif., San Diego, 1976—82, assoc. prof., 1982—88, prof., 1988—, Florence Seeley Riford chair in AIDS rsch., 2004—. Vis. prof. Hubei Med. Coll., Wuhan, People's Republic of China, 1987, Tokyo Med. and Dental U., Kumamoto U. Sch. Medicine, Inst. for Virus Rsch. at Kyoto U., St. Marianna U., Tokyo, Inst. Med. Rsch., Tokyo, Fukishima Prefecture Med. Sch., Japan, 1990; vis. fellow Clare Hall, U. Cambridge, 1984-85; mem. U. Calif. Pres.'s Cancer Rsch. Coord. Com., 1984-89, NIH AIDS Rsch. Rev. Com., 1987-90; cons. FDA Ctr. for Drugs and Biologics, 1986-89; dir. U. Calif.-San Diego Ctr. for AIDS Rsch., AIDS Rsch. Inst. Co-editor: Clin. Virology, —; mem. editl. bd.: Antimicrobial Agts. and Chemotherapy, 1987—, Jour. of AIDS, 1988—, Antiviral Agts., 1988—, AIDS, 1990—, AIDS Alert, 1990—, Antiviral Drug Resistance, 1996—, Virology, 1997—, others; contbr. more than 520 articles to profl. jours. Recipient Lowell Rantz award in infectious diseases, 1970, AMA Physicians Recgonition award, 1976, 79, 82, 85, 88, William S. Middleton award Dept. Vet. Affairs, 2002; John Simon Guggenheim fellow, 1984. Fellow: ACP, AAAS, Am. Assn. Physicians, Am. Assn. Physicians, Infectious Diseases Soc. Am.; mem.: Am. Clin. and Climatologic Assn., VA Soc. for Physicians in Infectious Diseases, Internat. AIDS Soc., Internat. Soc. Antiviral Rsch., Am. Soc. for Virology, Am. Fedn. for Clin. Rsch., Am. Soc. for Microbiology. Office: U Calif San Diego Dept Pathology & Medicine 9500 Gilman Dr La Jolla CA 92093-0679

**RICHMAN, HAROLD ALAN,** social welfare policy educator; b. Chgo., May 15, 1937; s. Leon H. and Rebecca (Klieman) R.; m. Marlene M. Forland, Apr. 25, 1965; children: Andrew, Robert. AB, Harvard U., 1959; MA, U. Chgo., 1961, PhD, 1969. Asst. prof., dir. Ctr. for Study Welfare Policy, Sch. Social Svc., U. Chgo., 1967-69, dean, prof. social welfare policy, 1969-78, Hermon Dunlap Smith prof., 1978—, dir. of ctr., 1978-81, dir. Children's Policy Rsch. Project, 1978-84, dir. Chapin Hall Ctr. for Children, 1985—2002, faculty assoc. Chapin Hall Ctr. for Children, 2002—, chmn. univ. com. on pub. policy studies, 1974-77. Chmn. Univ. Lab. Schs., 1985-88; cons. to gov. State of Ill., Edna McConnell Clark Found., 1984-95, Lilly Endowment, 1987-90, Ford Found., 1987-89; co-chair Aspen Roundtable on Cmty. Change, 1993—. Chmn. editl. bd. Social Svcs. Rev., 1970-79; contbr. articles to profl. jours. Bd. dirs. Chgo. Com. Fgn. and Domestic Policy, 1969-78, S.E. Chgo. Commn., 1970—, Jewish Fedn. Met. Chgo., 1970-75, Ill. Facilities Fund, 1989-94, Welfare Coun. Met. Chgo., 1970-72, Erikson Inst. Early Childhood Edn., 1972-79, Nat. Urban Coalition, 1975-86, Family Focus, 1980-89, Jewish Coun. Urban Affairs, 1982-87, Ctr. for Study Social Policy, 1983-92, chmn., 2003—; bd. dirs. Nat. Family Resource Coalition, 1990-93, Pub./Pvt. Ventures, 1992-98, Benton Found., 1994-2004; bd. dirs. Israel Ctr. on Childhood, chmn., 1995-2004; bd. dirs. Info. and Rsch Ctr., Amman, Jordan, 2001—, Michael Reese Health Trust, 2002—, bd. dirs. U. Capetown Childen's Inst., dep. chair, 2002—; mem. adv bd John Gardner

Ctr., Stanford U., 2003—; bd. dirs. Brookdale Inst., Jerusalem, 2004—, Interfaith Youth Core, 2005—, Bull. Atomic Scientists, 2006—. White House fellow, Washington, 1965-66; recipient Disting. Svc. citation U.S. Dept. Health, Edn. & Welfare, 1970, Quantrell award U. Chgo., 1990. Mem. White House Fellows Assn. (v.p. 1976-77), Am. Pub. Welfare Assn. (bd. dirs. 1989-92). Home: 5715 S Dorchester Ave Chicago IL 60637-1726 Office: U Chgo Chapin Hall Ctr for Children 1313 E 60th St Chicago IL 60637-2830 Office Phone: 773-256-5176. Business E-Mail: hrichman@chapinhall.org.

**RICHMAN, JOAN M.,** lawyer; b. Chicago, Dec. 15, 1965; Diploma in Internat. Bus., The Netherlands Sch. Bus.; 1989; B of Commerce with distinction, McGill U., 1988; JD, Georgetown U., 1992. Bar: Ill. 1992. Summer assoc. Baker & McKenzie, Chgo., 1991, assoc., 1992—99, ptnr., 1999—. Office: Baker and McKenzie One Prudential Plz 130 E Randolph Dr Chicago IL 60601

**RICHMAN, JOHN MARSHALL,** lawyer, food products executive; b. N.Y.C., Nov. 9, 1927; s. Arthur and Madeleine (Marshall) R.; m. Priscilla Frary, Sept. 3, 1951; children: Catherine Richman Wallace, Diana H. BA, Yale U., 1949; LLB, Harvard U., 1952. Bar: N.Y. 1953, Ill. 1973. Assoc. Leve, Hecht, Hadfield & McAlpin, N.Y.C., 1952-54; mem. law dept. Kraft, Inc., Glenview, Ill., 1954-63, gen. counsel Sealtest Foods div., 1963-67, asst. gen. counsel, 1967-70, v.p., gen. counsel, 1970-73, sr. v.p., gen. counsel, 1973-75, sr. v.p. adminstrn., gen. counsel, 1975-79, chmn. bd., chief exec. officer, 1979, Dart & Kraft, Inc. (name changed to Kraft, Inc. 1986), Glenview, 1980; chmn. Kraft Gen. Foods, Glenview, Ill., 1988-89; counsel Wachtell, Lipton, Rosen & Katz, Chgo., 1990-98. Bd. dirs. Archstone-Smith Trust; life bd. dirs. Evanston Northwestern Healthcare. Life trustee Chgo. Symphony Orch., Northwestern U.; bd. dirs. Chgo. Coun. on Fgn. Rels., Lyric Opera Chgo., Norton Mus. Art, West Palm Beach. Fla. Mem. Comml. Club, Chgo. Club, Casino Club (Chgo.), Westmoreland Country Club (Wilmette, Ill.), Old Elm Club (Highland Park, Ill.), Lost Tree Club (N. Palm Beach, Fla.), Shoreacres, Lake Bluff, Ill., Racquet Club of Chgo. Congregationalist. Office: 179 E Lake Shore Dr Chicago IL 60611-1306 E-mail: johnrichman@att.net.

**RICHMAN, JOSEPH HERBERT,** retired public health service officer; b. Balt., Aug. 13, 1941; s. Samuel and Beatrice R. BS, Howard U., 1962, MD, 1966; MPH, Johns Hopkins U., 1974. Intern Maimonides Med. Ctr., Bklyn., 1966-67; resident in pediat. Sinai Hosp. of Balt., 1967-69; chief sch. health P.G. Health Dept. of Md., Cheverly, Md., 1972-75; dir. area health svcs. Montgomery County Health Dept., Bethesda, Md., 1975-82; county chief pub. health physician State of Del., Dover, 1982-99; ret., 2000. Capt. USAF, 1969—71. Recipient Outstanding Svc. award, Delaware Health and Soc. Svc., 1999. Fellow Am. Acad. Pediatrics (emeritus), Am. Coll. Preventive Medicine; mem. AMA, Masons, Phi Beta Kappa. Democrat. Jewish. Avocations: golf, photography. Home: PO Box 880852 Boca Raton FL 33488-0852 Personal E-mail: joefortsedgwick@aol.com.

**RICHMAN, MARC HERBERT,** engineer, forensic specialist, educator; b. Boston, Oct. 14, 1936; s. Samuel and Janet (Gordon) R.; m. Ann Raeshel Yoffa, Aug. 31, 1963. BS, MIT, 1957, ScD, 1963; MA, Brown U., 1967. Registered profl. engr., Conn., Mass., R.I.; cert. forensic examiner. Cons. engr., 1957—; engr. shipbldg. div. Bethlehem Steel Corp., Quincy, Mass., 1957; instr. metallurgy MIT, Cambridge, 1957-60, research asst. dept. metallurgy, 1960-63; instr. metallurgy div. univ. extension Commonwealth of Mass., 1958-62; asst. prof. engring. Brown U., Providence, 1963-67, assoc. prof., 1967-70, prof., 1970-98, dir. central electron microscopy facility Materials Research program, 1971-86, dir. undergrad. program in engring., 1991-98; prof. emeritus, 1998—; pres. Ednl. Aids of Newton Inc., Providence, 1968-71, Marc H. Richman Inc., Providence, 1981—. Guest scientist Franklin Inst., Phila., 1959; vis. prof. U. R.I., Kingston, 1970-71; biophysicist dept. medicine Miriam Hosp., Providence, 1974-87; biogengr. dept. orthopaedics R.I. Hosp., 1979-93; prof. emeritus Brown U., Providence, 1998—. Author: Introduction to Science of Metals, 1967; also articles; editor Soviet Physics: Crystallography, 1970-94; mem. editl. adv. bd. Materials Characterization, 1970—98, Jour. Forensic Engring., 1985-88. Served to maj. Ordnance Corps, U.S. Army, 1963. Recipient Engr. of Yr. award R.I. Soc. Profl. Engrs., 1993. Fellow Nat. Acad. Forensic Engrs. (cert.), Am. Coll. Forensic Examiners (cert.), Am. Inst. Chemists, Inst. Materials (U.K.); mem. ASCE, AIME, NSPE, ASEE (Outstanding Young Faculty award 1969), NAFE (bd. cert. diplomate in forensic engring.), Am. Soc. Metals (sec.-treas. 1965-68, chmn. R.I. chpt. 1968-69, Albert Sauveur Meml. award 1968, 69), Providence Engring. Soc. (pres. 1991-92, Freeman award for engring. achievement 1989), B'nai B'rith, Sigma Xi, Tau Beta Pi. Home: 291 Cole Ave Providence RI 02906-3452 Office: One Richmond Sq Providence RI 02906 Office Phone: 401-751-9656. Personal E-mail: mhrichman@aol.com.

**RICHMAN, MARTIN FRANKLIN,** lawyer; b. Newark, Feb. 23, 1930; s. Samuel L. and Betty E. (Goldstein) R.; stepson Doris (Bloom) R.; m. Florence E. Reif, May 6, 1962; children— Judith, Andrew. BA magna cum laude, St. Lawrence U., 1950; LL.B. magna cum laude, Harvard U., 1953. Bar: N.Y. 1953. Law clk. to Judge Calvert Magruder and Chief Justice Earl Warren, 1955-57; assoc., mem. firm Lord Day & Lord, Barrett Smith (and predecessors), N.Y.C., 1957-66, 69-94; of counsel Kirkpatrick & Lockhart Nicholson Graham LLP, N.Y.C., 1994—; dep. asst. atty. gen. Office Legal Counsel, Dept. Justice, Washington, 1966-69. Public mem. Adminstrv. Conf. U.S., 1970-76; bd. dirs. Community Action for Legal Services, 1977-80 Trustee St. Lawrence U., 1979-95, trustee emeritus, 1995—, vice chmn. bd., 1988-95; bd. dirs. Friends of Law Libr. of Congress, 1992-99. Recipient Alumni citation St. Lawrence U., 1972 Fellow Am. Bar Found., N.Y. Bar Found.; mem. ABA (chmn. sect. adminstrv. law 1983-84), N.Y. State Bar Assn. (ho. of dels. 1981-84), Assn. of Bar of City of N.Y. (sec. and mem. exec. com. 1976-79, chmn. com. fed. legislation 1972-75, com. lawyer's pro bono obligations 1977-81), Am. Law Inst. Office: Kirkpatrick & Lockhart Nicholson Graham LLP 599 Lexington Ave New York NY 10022-6030 Office Phone: 212-536-3945. E-mail: mrichman@klng.com.

**RICHMAN, MURRAY,** lawyer; b. Bronx, NY, Oct. 3, 1937; children from previous marriage: Stacey Gayle, Nicole; m. Rene Arias, Sept. 22, 2002. BA, CCNY, 1959; JD, N.Y. Law Sch., 1964. Bar: U.S. Dist. Ct. (so. dist.) NY 1969, U.S. Dist. Ct. (ea. dist.) NY 1969, U.S. Ct. Internat. Trade 1982, U.S. tax Ct. 1979, U.S. Ct. Appeals (2d cir.) 1975, U.S. Supreme Ct. Sole practice, Bronx, 1964—. Recipient Humanitarian award Black Econ. Survival Assn., 1976, Honor award Borough Pres. Bronx County, 1972, Lawyer of Yr. award, United Jewish Appeal, 1985; named Man of Yr., Am. Jewish Congress, 1972. Mem. Bronx Bar Assn. (bd. dirs.), Bronx Criminal Bar Assn. (v.p., Humanitarian award 1981), NY Assn. Criminal Def. Lawyers, B'nai B'rith, Rockland. Democrat. Jewish. Office: 2027 Williamsbridge Rd Bronx NY 10461-1605 Office Phone: 718-892-8588. Personal E-mail: mrichman_mr@msn.com.

**RICHMAN, PAUL,** semiconductor industry executive, educator; b. N.Y.C., Nov. 17, 1942; s. Harry and Molly (Armel) Richman; m. Ellen Margaret Kleiman, July 3, 1966; children: Lee Stuart, Alyson Michelle, Daniel Noah. BSEE, MIT, 1963; MSEE, Columbia U., 1964. V.p.r R & D Standard Microsystems Corp., Hauppauge, NY, 1971-76, pres., 1976-81, pres., chief exec. officer, 1981-83, pres., chmn. bd., chief exec. officer, 1983-2000; co-founder Toyo Microsystems Corp., Tokyo, 1987—. Pres Consortium Technology Licensing Ltd, Nisseuogue, NY, 1994—99, chmn bd dirs, CEO, 1999—; vis prof elec eng SUNY, Stony Brook, 1976—85; mem vis comt elec eng and computer sci dept MIT, 1996—; adj. prof. elec. engring. CUNY, 1973—75. Author: (book) Characteristics and Operation of MOS Field Effect Devices, 1967, MOS Field Effect Transistors and Integrated Circuits, 1974. Named one of 30 Most Important Contributors in the World to Devel Integrated Circuit Technology, Elec Eng Times/Elec Buyer's News/VLSI Sys Design, 1988; recipient Ann Award Achievement in Electronics, Electronics

Mag, 1978. Fellow: IEEE (Award for Outstanding Technical Achievement 1980, Third Millennium Medal 2000). Achievements include invention of COPLAMOS technology. E-mail: paul.richman@smsc.com, paul_consortium@verizon.net.

**RICHMAN, PETER,** electronics executive; b. N.Y.C., Nov. 7, 1927; s. Emil H. and Janet (Seidler) R.; m. Vivian Hoffman, July 29, 1951; children: Meredith, Jeremy. BS, MIT, 1946; MS, NYU, 1953. Asst. chief engr. Reeves Instrument Corp., Garden City, NY, 1948-58; chief engr. Epsco, Inc., Cambridge, Mass., 1959-60; v.p., co-founder Rotek Instrument Corp., Watertown, Mass., 1960-64; v.p. Weston-Rotek, Lexington, Mass., 1964-67; cons. electronics engr. Lexington, 1967—. Bd. dirs. Thermo Voltek Corp, Thermo Sentron Corp.; founder, pres. KeyTek Instrument Corp., 1975-93; mem. NRC/NAS/Nat. Acad. Engring. Evaluation Panel for electricity divsn. Nat. Bur. Standards; mem. sci. adv. groups for several indsl. and sci. orgns. Patentee in precision electronic instrumentation; pioneer in precision dc and audio-frequency measurements, surge electrostatic discharge generation and electrostatic discharge measurements; author: The Insider's Guide to Growing a Small Business, 1996; contbr. articles to profl. jours. Mem. bd. overseers Boston Mus. Sci. Fellow IEEE; mem. Electromagnetics Acad., Instrument Soc. Am. (sr.), Sigma Xi, Tau Beta Pi.

**RICHMAN, PETER MARK,** actor, painter, film producer; b. Phila., Apr. 16, 1927; s. Benjamin and Yetta Dora (Peck) R.; m. Theodora Helen Landess, May 10, 1953; children: Howard Bennett, Kelly Allyn, Lucas Dion, Orien, Roger Lloyd. BS in Pharmacy, U. of the Scis., 1951; student of Lee Strasberg, N.Y.C., 1952-54; mem., Actors' Studio, N.Y.C., 1954—. Registered pharmacist, Pa., N.Y. Appeared in little theater, Phila., 1946-51, on stage radio and in live TV, Phila., N.Y.C., and Los Angeles, 1948-65, including Have I Got a Girl for You (pre-Broadway tryout), Biltmore Theater, L.A., 1963, The Deputy, Ctr. Theater Group, L.A., 1965; appeared at Grove Theater, Nuangola, Pa., 1952, Westchester Playhouse, 1953, Drury Lane, Chicago, 1957, Strand, N.J., 1957, Capri, 1959, Ogonquit (Maine) Playhouse, 1955-62, Matunuck, R.I., 1955, Falmouth, Mass., 1953-55, Westport, Conn., 1955, Harrison, Maine, 1962, Dennis, Mass., 1955-62, Phila. Playhouse in the Park, 1962-63; Broadway plays include End as a Man, 1953, Hatful of Rain,Broadway and Nat. Tour, 1956-57, Masquerade, 1959; off-Broadway plays include End as a Man, 1953, The Dybbuk, 1954, The Zoo Story (400 performances), 1960-61; Rainmaker, Private Lives, Angel Street, Arms and the Man, Rose Tattoo, Liliom, Funny Girl, Owl and the Pussycat, Hold Me, Equus, Night of the Iguana, Blithe Spirit, Twelve Angry Men, Henry Fonda Theatre, L.A., 1985, Babes in Toyland, Calif. Mus. Theater, 1988, Ray Bradbury's Next in Line, L.A., 1992, and numerous others; writer, performer (one man show) 4 Faces, L.A., 1995, NYC, 1996, The Actors Studio, NYC, 1996 and others; narrator: (composed and conducted by Lucas Richman with Spokane Symphony) 7 Circles of Life: A Subud Cantata, 1997, 7 Circles of Life: A Subud Cantata (with Tiroler Kammerorchester Instrumenti and conducted by Lucas Richman), Innsbruck, Austria, 2005, (with Knoxville Symphony conducted by Lucas Richman) A Lincoln Portrait (Aaron Copeland), 2004; motion pictures include Friendly Persuasion, 1956, The Strange One, 1956, Black Orchid, 1958, The Dark Intruder, 1965, Agent for HARM, 1965, For Singles Only, 1967, Judgement Day (formerly The Third Hand), 1988, Friday the 13th, Part 8 (Jason Takes Manhattan), 1989, Naked Gun 2 1/2 (The Smell of Fear), 1991, Pool Hall Junkies, 2003; prodr., writer, actor 4 Faces (film), 2000; appeared on TV series as Nick Cain in Cain's Hundred, 1961-62, as David in David Chapter III for CBC, 1966, as Duke Page in series Longstreet, 1971-72, as Reverend Snow in series Three's Company, 1978-79, as Andrew Laird in series Dynasty, 1981-84, as Channing Capwell in series Santa Barbara, 1984, voice of God series Heroes of the Bible, 1979, voice of the Phantom in animated series Defenders of the Earth, 1986, as Madros in Berlin series My Secret Summer (formerly Mystery of the Keys), 1991; guest star over 500 TV shows, including Hotel, Dallas, Hart to Hart, Fantasy Island, Murder She Wrote, Nothing Sacred, Three's Company, Knight Rider, Star Trek: The Next Generation, Matlock, Beverly Hills 90210, others; starred in TV movies House on Greenapple Road, 1968, McCloud, 1969, Yuma, 1970, Nightmare at 43 Hillcrest (Wide World of Entertainment), 1974, Mallory, 1975, The Islander, 1978, Greatest Heroes of the Bible, 1979, Blind Ambition, 1979, The PSI Factor, 1981, Dynasty, 1981, Dempsey, 1983, City Killer, 1984, Bonanza, The Next Generation, 1988; one-man shows (paintings) Am. Masters Gallery, L.A., 1967, Orlando Gallery, L.A., 1966, McKenzie Gallery, L.A., 1969, 73, Hopkins Gallery, L.A., 1971, Goldfield Gallery, L.A., 1979, Galerie des Stars, L.A., 1988, Crocker Mus., Sacramento, 1967, Parkhurst Gallery, Seal Beach, Calif., 1991, 1996 March thru July, inaugural exhibition of the Henley Gallery Chapman U., Orange, Calif. (a 30 yr. retrospective, A life in Art); group shows include Bednarz Gallery, L.A., 1968, Dohan Gallery, L.A., 1966, Celebrity Art Exhibits, 55-city tour, 1964-65; represented in permanent collections U.S. and abroad; playwright: Heavy, Heavy What Hangs Over?, 1971, A Medal for Murray, 1991, 4 Faces, 1995 (Communication award Prism Film Festival, 2002); dir. plays Apple of His Eye, 1954, Glass Menagerie, 1954; author: Hollander's Deal, 2000, The Rebirth of Ira Masters, 2001; featured in book Actor as Artists, 1992, Guide to Artists in Southern California, 1994; recordings: Twighlight Zone, 2005. Trustee Motion Picture and TV Fund. Served with USN, 1945-46. Recipient silver medallion Motion Picture TV Fund, 1990, Sybil Brand Humanitarian award Jeffrey Found., 1990, Spl. award, 1997, Drama-Logue critics performance award for 4 Faces, 1996, Golden Halo Eagle award, So. Calif. Motion Picture Coun., 1997, Lifetime Achievement award, 2004. Mem. SAG, AFTRA, Actors Equity Assn., Assn. Can. TV and Radio Artists, Acad. Motion Picture Arts and Scis., Acad. TV Arts and Scis. Office: 4 Faces Prodns 19528 Ventura Blvd Ste 385 Tarzana CA 91356 Office Phone: 818-623-6476. Personal E-mail: pmri@petermarkrichman.com. *I have always been grateful to be able to work in more than one medium. In a way they are all related, each solidifying and nurturing the other. I have a strong belief in God, and spiritual values. This, along with my marriage, children, and family life, has helped me enormously to express my own individuality as an artist.*

**RICHMAN, SOPHIA,** psychologist; b. Lwow, Poland, Jan. 28, 1941; arrived in US, 1951; d. Leon and Dorothy Weiss Richman; m. Spyros D. Orfanos, Nov. 25, 1976; 1 child, Lina Joanna Orfanos. BA in Psychology, CCNY, 1962, MS in Psychol. Svcs., 1965; PhD in Psychology, NYU, 1970, cert. in psychoanalysis, 1975. Lic. psychologist N.Y., 1972, N.J., 1993, diplomate in psychoanalysis Am. Bd. Profl. Psychology. Testing asst. Hunter Coll., N.Y.C., 1965—68; rsch. assoc. Harvard U., Boston, 1967—68; counselor to students NYU, N.Y.C., 1968—72; clin. psychologist SS Rockaway (N.Y.) Mental Health, 1972—74, Student Ctr. Roosevelt Hosp., N.Y.C., 1974—75; cons. psychologist Diocese of Bklyn., 1974—80; pvt. practice psychotherapy and psychoanalysis NY, 1972—, NJ, 1991—93. Adj. prof. Fordham U., Baruch Coll., N.Y.C., 1986, N.Y.C., 87; supervising analyst ICP, CCAPS, NY, 1986—, NJ, 1995—; supr. postdoctoral program NYU, NY, 2003—. One-woman shows include Cornelia St. Café, 2005; author: A Wolf in the Attic: The Legacy of a Hidden Child of the Holocaust, 2002; contbr. articles to profl. jours., chapters to books. Holocaust testimony Fortunoff Video Archive, Yale U., Conn., 1990, Survivors of the Shoah Visual History Found., L.A., 1998; pub. edn. spkr. on the holocaust various elem. and middle schs. NJ, 1994—95. Recipient scholarship, Jewish Women's Caucus of Assn. Women in Psychology, 2003; Fellowship grant, Meml. Found. for Jewish Culture, 2000—01. Fellow: Acad. Psychoanalysis; mem.: APA (divsn. 39 sect. 3 and 5 treas.), The Pen and Brush Club. Avocations: painting, writing, music. Office: Ste 5 303 Second Ave New York NY 10003 Office Phone: 212-533-3383. Personal E-mail: sophiarichman@aol.com.

**RICHMAN, STEPHEN ERIK,** lawyer, consultant; b. Austin, Tex., Mar. 10, 1945; s. Allen A. and Erika (Zimmerman) Richman; m. Frances Ellen Sharpe, Aug. 29, 1971; children: Joshua Eric, Wendy Michelle. BA magna cum laude, Amherst Coll., Mass., 1967; JD cum laude, Harvard U., Cambridge, Mass., 1970. Bar: Wis. 1972. Assoc. Webster Sheffield, N.Y.C., 1970-72, Quarles & Brady, Milw., 1972-78, ptnr. 1978—; mem. Richman Nonprofit Strategies, LLC, 2005—. Pres. Milw. Youth Symphony Orch., 1985—87; bd. dirs. Milw. Symphony Orch., 1995—2004, chmn. 2000—02; bd. dirs. Jewish Cmty. Found., Milw., 1992—; chmn. steering com. Milw. Youth Arts Ctr.,

2003—05; pres. Milw. Jewish Fedn., 1996—98. Mem.: State Bar Wis., Nat. Assn. Bond Lawyers, Phi Beta Kappa. Home and Office: 709 E Carlisle Ave Milwaukee WI 53217 Office: Quarles & Brady 411 E Wisconsin Ave Ste 2550 Milwaukee WI 53202-4497

**RICHMAN, STEPHEN I.,** lawyer; b. Washington, Pa., Mar. 26, 1933; m. Audrey May Gefsky. BS, Northwestern U., 1954; JD, U. Pa., 1957. Bar: Pa. 1958, U.S. Dist. Ct. (we. dist.) Pa. Assoc. McCune Greenlee & Richman, 1960—63, Greenlee Richman Derrico & Posa, 1963—84; ptnr. Richman, Smith Law Firm, PA, Washington, 1985—2005; of counsel Webber, Gallagher, 2005—. Lectr. U. South Fla. Sch. Medicine, Mine Safe Internat. Chamber of Mines of We. Australia, W.Va. U. Med. Ctr. Grand Rounds, Am. Coll. Chest Physicians, Pa. Thoracic Soc., Am. Thoracic Soc., The Energy Bur., Coll. Am. Pathologists, Allegheny County Health Dept., APHA, Internat. Assn. Ind. Accident Bds. and Commns., Indsl. Health Found., Nat. Coun. Self-Insurers Assn., Am. Iron and Steel Inst., Can. Thoracic Soc., I.L.O./N.I.O.S.H., Univs. Associated for Rsch. and Edn. in Pathology, Am. Ceramics Soc., Nat. Sand Assn.; mem. adv. com. U.S. Dist. ct. We. Dist. Pa., 1994—. Author: Meaning of Impairment and Disability, Chest, 1980, Legal Aspects for the Pathologist, in Pathology of Occupational and Environmental Lung Disease, 1988, A Review of the Medical and Legal Definitions of Related Impairment and Disability, Report to the Department of Labor and the Congress, 1986, Medicolegal Aspects of Asbestos for Pathologists, Arch. Pathology and Laboratory Medicine, 1983, Legal Aspects of Occupational and Environmental Disease, Human Pathology, 1993, Impairment and Disability in Pneumoconiosis, State of the Art Reviews in Occupational Medicine The Mining Industry, 1993, House Bills 2103 and 885; co-author: Act 44 and 57 amending Pa. Workmen's Compensation act. Mem. legal com. Indsl. Health Found., Pitts.; bd. dirs. Pitts. Opera Soc., Pitts. Jewish Fedn., 1994—97; dir. Jewish Family and Children's Svc., Pitts., 1995—2001. Mem.: ATLA, ABA (former vice chair workers compensation and employers liability law com, toxic and hazardous substance and environ. law com., lectr.), Pa. Chamber Bus. and Industry (worker's compensation com., chmn. subcom. on legis. drafting, lectr.), Pa. Bar Assn. (former coun. worker's compensation sect., contbr. bar assn. quar. 1992, 1993). Home: 820 E Beau St Washington PA 15301-2906 Office: Washington Trust Bldg Ste 200 Washington PA 15301 Personal E-mail: steve2633@aol.com.

**RICHMAND, ALICE ELENOR,** lawyer; b. NYC; d. Louis A. and Estelle (Muraskin) R.; m. David L. Rosenbloom, July 26, 1981; 1 child, Elizabeth Lara. BA magna cum laude, Cornell U., 1968; JD, Harvard U., 1972; grad. Owners and Pres.'s Mgmt. Program, Harvard U., Harvard Bus. Sch., 2001; DLH (hon.), North Adams State U., 1987. Bar: Mass. 1973, U.S. Dist. Ct. Mass. 1975, U.S. Ct. Appeals (1st cir.) 1982, U.S. Supreme Ct. 1985. Law clk. to justices Superior Ct., Boston, 1972-73; asst. dist. atty. Office of Dist. Atty., Boston, 1973-76; spl. asst. atty. gen. Office of Atty. Gen., Boston, 1975-77; asst. prof. New Eng. Sch. of Law, Boston, 1976-78; assoc. Lappin, Rosen, Boston, 1978-81; ptnr. Hemenway & Barnes, Boston, 1982-92, Deutsch, Williams, Boston, 1993-95, Richmond, Pauly & Ault, Boston, 1996—2002; prin. Richmond & Assocs., Boston, 2002—. Asst. team leader, faculty Trial Advocacy Course, 1978—82; examiner Mass. Bd. Bar Examiners, Boston, 1983—; trustee Mass. Continuing Legal Edn., Inc., Boston, 1985—96, Boston, 1998—2004; treas. Nat. Conf. Bar Examiners, 1995—2005, chmn., 2003—04; v.p., bd. dirs. Am. Bar Ins., Inc., 1996—; analyst CBS TV WBZ, 1991—; bd. dirs. Valora Techs., Inc. Contbr. chpts. to book; contbr. articles to profl. jours. Mem. Pres. Adv. Com on the Arts, 1995—99; bd. overseers Handel & Haydn Soc., 1985—94, bd. govs., 1994—, v.p., 1996—2002; mem. Boston 2000 Millennium Commn., 1997—98; sec., dir. Boston 2000, Inc., 1998—2001; mem., pres. Coun. of Cornell Women, Cornell U. Coun.; trustee Red Auerbach Youth Found., Fund for Justice and Edn., 1997—2002; mem. adv. bd. Ctrl. and Ea. European Law Initiative, 1998—2002; mem. Angell Meml. Hosp. Coun. of Fellows, 2001—. Named one of Outstanding Young Leaders, Boston Jaycees, 1982; Sloan Found. Urban fellow, N.Y.C., 1969. Fellow: Am. Coll. Trial Lawyers; mem.: NOW, Legal Def. and Edn. Fund (trustee 1995—2002, sec. 1998—2002), ABA (ho. of dels. 1980—, vice chmn. com. on rules and calendar 1986—88, bd. govs. 2002—05, task force on gats 2003—, standing com. on audit 2005—), Latin Am. Legal Initiatives Coun., Mass. Bar Found. (pres. 1988—91), Mass. Bar Assn. (pres. 1986—87), Am. Law Inst., Bostonian Soc. (dir.), Boston Club, Harvard Club. Office: Richmond & Assocs 39 Brimmer St Boston MA 02108 Office Phone: 617-523-8187. Business E-Mail: arichmond@rpalaw.com.

**RICHMAND, ALLEN,** conductor, educator; b. Dayton, Ohio, 1966; s. Alfred J. Richmand and Martha E. Cottle, Ted E Spetnagel (Stepfather); m. Linda Russell. MusB cum laude, Ohio U., 1990; MusM cum laude, U. of Mo., 1992. Mandolinist/vocalist PJ & The Poor Boys, Waverly, Ohio, 1974—88; asst. choral condr./organist Chillicothe Bapt. Ch., Ohio, 1984—86, orch. condr./asst. music dir., 1986—88; asst. condr. Ohio Singers/Ohio Choral Union, Athens, 1988—91; composer Scioto Pub. Ltd, Middletown, Ohio, 1988—; assoc. condr. Singing Men of Ohio, Athens, 1989—91; guest condr. Ohio Symphony Orch., Athens, 1990—90; music dir. First Bapt. Ch., Overland Park, Kans., 1991—92; interim music dir. Country Club United Meth. Ch., Kansas City, Mo., 1991—91; condr. Magnificat Singers, Kansas City, Mo., 1992—92; assoc. artistic dir./composer-in-residence Met. Musical Arts, Inc., Lee's Summit, Mo., 1995—2003; music dir. Dayton Mandolin Orch., Ohio, 2004—; mandolist/mandocellist MandolIndy, Indpls., 2004—; artistic dir. Miami Valley Mandolin Quintet, Middletown, Ohio, 2005—, DMO Concert Artist Series, Dayton, Ohio, 2005—; edn. com. mem. Classical Mandolin Soc. of Am., 2005—; mandocellist Am. Mandolin & Guitar Orch., Bristol, RI, 2005—. Mandolin orch. clinician Classical Mandolin Soc. of Am., 2006—. Composer: (symphonic composition) Symphony No. 3 for Piano & Orchestra, Symphony One: motet (instrumental instruction method) Mastering The Mandola; arranger/orchestrator (mandolin orchestra/ensemble literature) 100+ works for Mandolin Orchestra/Chamber Ensembles; musician: (performance recording) Creole Belles, March MARCH MADNESS and Other Musical Novelties, MandolIndy: Live at Eagle Creek, Singing Men of Ohio: Stand Up and Cheer; composer: (symphonic composition) Symphony II: Concert Piece for Orchestra. Edn. com. Classical Mandolin Soc. of Am., 2006—; music dir. Dayton Mandolin Orch., Ohio, 2004—06. Mem.: Chamber Music Am. (assoc.), Am. Mandolin & Guitar Summer Sch. (assoc.), Fretted Instrument Guild of Am. (assoc.), Classical Mandolin Soc. of Am. (life), Mandolin Soc. of Ctrl. Ind. (assoc.), Columbus Guitar Soc. (assoc.), U. of Mo. Alumni Assn. (corr.), Ohio U. Alumni Assn. (corr.). Avocations: travel, reading, auctions. Home: PO Box 333 Dayton OH 45475-0333 Office: Dayton Mandolin Orch PO Box 333 Dayton OH 45475-0333 Office Phone: 937-238-4323. Home Fax: 847-589-1927; Office Fax: 847-589-1927. E-mail: dmo@daytonmandolin.com.

**RICHMAND, ANTHONY HENRY,** sociologist, emeritus educator; b. Ilford, Essex, Eng., June 8, 1925; s. Henry James and Ellen Bertha R.; m. Freda Williams, Mar. 29, 1952; 1 dau., Glenys Catriona Richmond Troth. BSc in Econs., London Sch. Econs., 1949; MA, U. Liverpool, Eng., 1951; PhD, U. London, 1965. Rsch. officer U. Liverpool, 1949-51; lectr. dept. social study U. Edinburgh, Scotland, 1952-63; reader in sociology Bristol (Eng.) Coll. Sci. and Tech., 1963-65; prof. sociology York U., Toronto, Ont., Canada, 1965-89, prof. emeritus, sr. scholar, 1989—; dir. York U. (Inst. Behavioral Rsch.), 1979-82. Social rsch. cons.; vis. prof. Australian Nat. U., Canberra, 1971, 77, St. Antony's Coll., Oxford, Eng., 1984-85. Author: Colour Prejudice in Britain, 1954, 2d edit., 1971, The Colour Problem: A Study of Racial Relations in Britain, Africa and the West Indies, 1955, rev. edit., 1961, Post-War Immigrants in Canada, 1967, (with others) Immigrant Integration and Urban Renewal in Toronto, 1973, Migration and Race Relations in an English City, 1973, (with W. E. Kalbach) Factors in the Adjustment of Immigrants and Their Descendants, 1980, Immigration and Ethnic Conflict, 1988, Caribbean Immigrants: A Demoeconomic Analysis, 1989, Global Apartheid: Refugees, Racism and the New World Order, 1994; editor: Readings in Race and Ethnic Relations, 1972, (with D. Kubat) Internal Migration: The New World and the Third World, 1976; contbr. chpts. to books, articles to profl. jours. Recipient research grants and scholarships.

Fellow Royal Soc. Can.; mem. Can. Sociology and Anthropology Assn. (Outstanding Contrbn. award 2001), Can. Population Soc. Mem. Soc. Of Friends. Avocations: classical music, photography. E-mail: richmond@yorku.ca.

**RICHMOND, DAVID WALKER,** retired lawyer; b. Silver Hill, W.Va., Apr. 20, 1914; s. David Walker and Louise (Finlaw) Richmond; m. Gladys Evelyn Mallard, Dec. 19, 1936; children: David Walker, Nancy L. LLB, George Washington U., 1937. Bar: DC 1936, Ill. 1946, Md. 1950. Ptnr. Miller & Chevalier, Washington; ret. Lectr. fed. taxation. Contbr. articles to profl. jours. Served to lt. comdr. USNR, 1942—46. Decorated Bronze Star; recipient Disting. Alumni Achievement award, George Washington U., 1976. Fellow: Am. Coll. Tax Counsel, Am. Bar Found.; mem.: ABA (chmn. taxation sect. 1955—57, ho. of dels. 1958—60), Am. Law Inst., Lawyers Club Washington, Masons. Republican. Methodist. Home: 3240 Lake Pointe Blvd Apt S-359 Sarasota FL 34231 Office: 655 15th St NW Washington DC 20005-5701

**RICHMOND, DINA RAE,** retired secondary school educator; b. Shawnee, Okla., Apr. 29, 1929; d. Jack H. Williams and Bertha B. (Megehee) Williams McNair; children: Gregory, Mark, Stephanie. BA in Edn., U. Cen. Okla., 1952; MA in Edn., S.W. Tex. State U., San Marcos, 1977. Tchr. Cotton County Ind. Sch. Dist., Randlett, Okla., 1952-53, Terrell County Ind. Sch. Dist., Sanderson, Tex., 1967-71, Luling (Tex.) Ind. Sch. Dist., 1971-87, Lexington (Tex.) Ind. Sch. Dist., 1987-90, Brenham Ind. Sch. Dist., 1990—91; ret., 1991. Mem. NEA, Tex. State Tchrs. Assn., Delta Kappa Gamma. Democrat. Baptist. Home: 1613 Luza Ln Bryan TX 77802-1517 E-mail: drichmond2929@cox.net

**RICHMOND, EERO,** composer, music librarian; b. Tacoma, Wash., Jan. 5, 1938; s. Orin August and Esther Maija (Johnson) R. BA in Music, U. Wash., 1961, MLS, 1966. Music libr. N.Y.C. Pub. Libr., 1966-68, head music cataloger, 1969-80; dir. info. svcs. Am. Music Ctr., N.Y.C., 1982-93, head music cataloger, 1994-95, coord. info. svcs., 1995-99. Pianist Slavic Arts Ensemble, N.Y.C., 1985—, Inoue Chamber Ensemble, N.Y.C., 1993—. Composer musical works performed throughout U.S., Europe, South Am., Japan; contbr. articles to profl. jours. Mem. ASCAP, Internat. Soc. for Contemporary Music (v.p. 1986-90), Sibelius Soc. (v.p. 1985—), Phi Mu Alpha Sinfonia, Beta Phi Mu. Democrat. Lutheran. Avocations: travel (especially berlin), reading. Home: 152 Kent St Brooklyn NY 11222-2142 Office Phone: 718-389-6030. E-mail: kafka333@aol.com.

**RICHMOND, ERNEST LEON,** research engineer, consultant, retired engineer; b. Catskill, NY, Sept. 11, 1914; s. Leon J. and Beulah B. (Garling) R.; m. Constance R. Vroom, Oct. 9, 1943. B of Mech. Engring. cum laude, Clarkson U., Potsdam, N.Y., 1942; postgrad., N.J. Inst. Tech., Newark, 1950-60, Rutgers U., 1950-60. Registered profl. engr., N.J. Test engr. Mack Trucks, Inc., Plainfield, N.J., 1936-45; from asst chief to chief engr. Worthington Corp., Plainfield Works, 1945-58; rsch. engr. Ethicon, Inc. (div. Johnson & Johnson), Somerville, N.J., 1958-75; ret., 1975. Spkr., cons. in field. Author design papers; patentee in field. Vol. United Fund, Plainfield, 1940-50, Cancer Fund, Plainfield, 1940-50, Heart Fund, Plainfield, 1940-50; coach YMCA Ch. Basketball League, Plainfield, 1940-65, chmn. exec. com., 1964-65. Mem. ASME, NSPE, Am. Electroplaters and Surface Finishers Soc. Republican. Presbyterian. Avocations: civil war history, golf.

**RICHMOND, GAIL LEVIN,** law educator; b. Gary, Ind., Jan. 9, 1946; d. Herbert Irving and Sylvia Esther (Given) Levin; children: Henry, Amy. AB, U. Mich., 1966, MBA, 1967; JD, Duke U., 1971. Bar: Ohio 1971, U.S. Claims Ct. 1986, U.S. Ct. Mil. Appeals, 1994; CPA, Ill. Acct. Arthur Andersen & Co., Chgo., 1967-68; assoc. Jones, Day, Cleve., 1971-72; asst. prof. Capital U. Law Sch., Columbus, Ohio, 1972-73, U. N.C. Law Sch., Chapel Hill, 1973-78; vis. asst. prof. U. Tex. Law Sch., Austin, 1977-78, Nova U. Law Ctr., Ft. Lauderdale, Fla., 1979-80, assoc. prof., 1980-81, assoc. prof., assoc. dean, 1981-85, prof., assoc. dean, 1985-93, 95—, prof., acting dean, 1993-95. Author: Federal Tax Research, 6th edit., 2002; co-author: Tax Planning for Lifetime and Testamentary Dispositions, 1997, A Complete Introduction to Corporate Taxation, 2006; contbr. articles to profl. jours. Pres. Greater Ft. Lauderdale Tax Coun., 1987-88; trustee Law Sch. Admission Coun., 1994-99, chair audit com., 1991-93, chair svcs. and programs com., 1997-99. Mem. ABA (former coun. on individual income, tax sect. 2001-03, chair AMT Task Force, tax sect. 2003-2004, chair adj. com., legal edn. sect. 2002-05), Am. Assn. Atty.-CPAs (dir. Fla. chpt. 1992-98), Assn. Am. Law Schs. (mem. audit com. 1992, chair sect. adminstrn. of law sects. 1996, pres. S.E. chpt. 1993-94, sec. S.E. chpt. 1995-2002), S.E. Assn. Law Schs. (pres. 2002-03, sec. 2004—). Democrat. Jewish. Avocation: reading. Office: Nova Southeastern U Shepard Broad Law Ctr 3305 College Ave Fort Lauderdale FL 33314-7721

**RICHMOND, GERALDINE LEE,** chemist, educator; BS in Chemistry magna cum laude, Kansas State U., 1975; PhD in Phys. Chemistry, U. Calif., Berkeley, 1980. Rsch. and teaching asst. Kans. State U., 1973-76, U. Calif., Berkeley, 1976-80; asst. prof. chemistry Bryn Mawr Coll., 1980-85; assoc. prof. chemistry U. Oreg., Eugene, 1985-91, dir. rsch. experience for undergrad. program, 1987—2004, dir. chem. phys. inst., 1991-95, prof. chemistry, 1991—, Knight prof. liberal arts and sci., 1998—2001, Richard M. and Patricia H. Noyes prof. chemistry, 2001—. mem. adv. bd. Chemistry, NSF, 1986-89, Materials Sci., 1989-92; mem. adv. bd. Accounts of Chem. Rsch., 1991-94, Analytical Chemistry, 1992-95; chair, founder Com. Advancement Women Chemists (COACh), 1998-2005; mem. governor's sci. adv. bd., State of Oreg., 1986-89; mem., Basic Energy Sci. Adv. Com. Dept. Energy, 1995-2003, chair, 1998-2003; regent Oregon State Bd. Higher Edn. (Gov. Kitzhabor appointee) 1999-2003 system strategic planning com., 1999 2000, Budget and Fin. Com., 2000-03, regent, v.p. (Gov. Kulongoski appointee), 2002-, mem. exec. com., 2003-05, v.p. and interim pres., 2004, chair, chancellor's office reorganization com., 2004-05; mem. Coun. on Chem. Sciences, Dept. Energy 1996-2001; mem. bd. chem. sci. and tech. matter, NAS/NRC, 1989-92, mem.bd. on solid state sciences, 1991-94, mem. chem. sci. roundtable 2003-;chair, NAS Frontiers in Sci. Symposium, 1993-94, Women Faculty Resource Network, U. Oreg., 1992-2004;lectr. in field. Mem. editl. bd. Critical Reviews and Surface Anatomy, 1991-95, Analytical Chemistry, 1992-95, Accounts of Chemical Research, 1991-94, Vibrational Spectroscopy, 1990-94, Jour. Physical Chemistry, 1989-1994, Applied Spectroscopy, 1993-96, Langmuir, 2001-03; adv. bd. mem. Chemical and Engineering News, 2002-04; assoc. editor, Annual Review of Physical Chemistry, 2005-; contbr. articles to profl. jours. King Meml. scholar, 1973-75; Alfred P. Sloan rsch. fellow, 1985-89; recipient Rosalyn Schwartz award, 1982, NSF Presdl. Young Investigator award, 1985-90, Camile and Henry Dreyfus Tchr. award, 1986-90, Chemistry Dept. Alumni award, Kansas State U., 1986, Women Scientists and Engrs. Faculty award, NSF, 1991-96, Rsch. Creativity award, NSF, 1991, Agnes Faye Morgan Rsch. award, 1993, Coll. Arts & Sciences Alumni award, Kansas State U., 1997, Presdl. award Excellence Sci. and Engring. Mentoring White House, 1997, Women Helping Women award Soroptomist Internat., 1998, Rsch. Creativity award, NSF, 2000, Advance Leadership award, NSF, 2001, Oregon Outstanding Sci. award Oregon Acad. Sci., 2001, Spiers medal, Royal Soc. Chemistry (UK) Faraday divsn., 2004 Fellow AAAS, Am. Phys. Soc.(mem. adv. com. laser sci. topical group, 1990-95), Am. Acad. Arts & Sciences; mem. Am. Chem. Soc. (Analytical Chemistry award 1973, Francis P. Garvan medal, 1996, Women Chemist Com. Regional award Diversity, 2002, Spectrochemical Analysis award, 2005, Assn. Women in Sci., Coblentz Spectroscopy Soc. (mem. exec. com., 1988-91, award 1989), Electrochem. Soc., Soc. Applied Spectroscopy, Western Spectroscopy Assn. (exec. bd. mem. 1986-1989) Office: Dept Chemistry 1274 Univ Oregon Eugene OR 97403 Office Phone: 541-346-4635. Office Fax: 541-346-5859. Business E-Mail: richmond@uoregon.edu.

**RICHMOND, JAMES ELLIS,** retired restaurant company executive; b. Chgo., Feb. 16, 1938; s. Kenneth E. and Irene M. (Anderson) R.; m. Karen Ann Ryder, Oct. 6, 1956; children: Scott, Brian, Ann, Susan. BBA, Case Western Res. U., 1960. CPA, Ohio. Sr. auditor Ernst & Ernst, Cleve.,

1960-64; treas. Cook United, Inc., Cleve., 1964-75, Fairmont Foods Co., Houston, 1975-80, v.p. ops., 1980-82; v.p., treas. U-tote-M, Inc., 1982-84; mktg. exec. Circle K Convenience Stores, 1984-86; v.p. Consol. Products, Inc., Indpls., 1986-2000; ret. Lutheran. Home: 331 Wild Turkey Blvd Boerne TX 78006- E-mail: jkrich@gvtc.com.

**RICHMOND, JAMES GLIDDEN,** lawyer; b. Sacramento, Feb. 20, 1944; s. James Gibbs and Martha Ellen (Glidden) R.; m. Lois Marie Bennett, Oct. 22, 1988; 1 child, Mark R. BS in Mgmt., Ind. U., 1966, postgrad., 1966-69, JD, 1969. Bar: Ind. 1969, Ill. 1991, U.S. Dist. Ct. (no. dist.) Ind. 1971, U.S. Dist. Ct. (so. dist.) Ind., 1969, U.S. Ct. Appeals (7th cir.) 1975, U.S. Tax Ct. 1980. Spl. agent FBI, 1970-74; spl. agent Criminal Investigation Divsn. IRS, 1974-76; asst. U.S. atty. no. dist. U.S. Atty. Office, Ind., 1976-80; assoc. Galvin, Stalmack & Kirschner, Hammond, Ind., 1980-81; pvt. practice Highland, Ind., 1981-83; ptnr. Goodman, Ball & Van Bokkelen, Highland, Ind., 1983-85; U.S. atty. no. dist. State of Ind., Hammond, 1985-91; spl. counsel to dep. atty. gen. of the U.S. U.S. Dept. Justice, Washington, 1990-91; mng. ptnr. Ungaretti and Harris, Chgo., 1991-92, ptnr., 1995—2002; exec. v.p., gen. counsel Nat. Health Labs., 1992-95; shareholder Greenberg Traurig, Chgo., 2002—. Practitioner in residence Ind. U. Sch. Law, Bloomington, 1989. Minority counsel senate republicans October Surprise Hearings, 1992. Fellow Am. Coll. Trial Lawyers. Republican. Avocation: fly fishing. Office: Greenberg Traurig 77 W Wacker Dr Ste 2500 Chicago IL 60601 Office Phone: 312-456-5204. Business E-Mail: richmondj@gtlaw.com.

**RICHMOND, JULIUS BENJAMIN,** retired pediatrician, former Surgeon General of the United States, health policy educator; b. Chgo., Sept. 26, 1916; s. Jacob and Anna (Dayno) Richmond; m. Rhee Chidekel, June 3, 1937 (dec. Oct. 9, 1985); children: Barry J, Charles Allen; m. Jean Rabow, Jan. 11, 1987; 1 child, Dale Keith (dec.). BS, U. Ill., 1937, MS, MD, 1939; DSc (hon.), Ind. U., 1978, Rush-Presbyn.-St. Luke Med. Ctr., 1978, U. Ill., 1979, Georgetown U., 1980, SUNY, Syracuse, 1986, U. Ariz., 1991; DMS (hon.), Med. Coll. Pa., 1980; D in Pub. Svc. (hon.), Nat. Coll. Edn., Evanston, Ill., 1980; DHL (hon.), Tufts U., 1986; DMS (hon.), Yale U., 1999; DEd (hon.), Wheelock Coll., 2000; DSci, Harvard U., 2002. Intern Cook County Hosp., Chgo., 1939—41, resident, 1941—42, 1946, Mcpl. Contagious Disease Hosp., Chgo., 1941; faculty U. Ill. Med. Sch., Chgo., 1946—53, prof. pediat., 1950—53; dir. Inst. Juvenile Rsch., Chgo., 1952—53; prof., chmn. dept. pediatrics Coll. Medicine, SUNY at Syracuse, 1953—65, dean med. faculty, chmn. dept. pediatrics, 1965—70; prof. child psychiatry and human devel., prof., chmn. dept. preventive and social medicine Harvard Med. Sch., 1971—77, prof. health policy, 1981—88, dir. divsn. health policy rsch. and edn., 1983—88, prof. health policy emeritus, 1988—; asst. sec. health, surgeon gen. US Dept. Health & Human Services, Washington, 1977—81. Psychiatrist-in-chief Children's Hosp. Med. Ctr., Boston, 1971—77, adv. on child health policy, 1981—; dir. Judge Baker Children's Ctr., Boston, 1971—77; mem. Pres.'s Commn. on Mental Health, 1977. Author: Pediatric Diagnosis, 1962, Currents in American Medicine, 1969, The Health Care Mess, 2005. Nat. dir. Project Head Start; dir. Office Health Affairs, OEO, 1965—66. Flight surgeon U.S. Army Air Force, 1942—46. Recipient Agnes Bruce Greig Sch. award, 1966, Parents Mag. award, 1966, Disting. Svc. award, Office Econ. Opportunity, 1967, Family Health Mag. award, 1977, Myrdal award, Assn. for Evaluation Rsch., 1977, award for disting. sci. contbn., Soc. for Rsch. in Child Devel., 1979, Dolly Madison award, Inst. on Clin. Infants Programs, 1979, Pub. Health Disting. Svc. award, HEW, 1978, Illini Achievement award, U. Ill. Alumni Assn., 1982, Cmty. Svc. award, Health Planning Coun. Greater Boston, 1985, Lemuel Shattuck award, Mass. Pub. Health Assn., 1985, 1st Ann. Ronald McDonald Children's Charities award for Outstanding Contbns. to Child Health and Welfare, 1986, David E. Rogers award, Assn. Am. Med. Colls., 1997, A.L. Ellis award, Children's Home Soc. Fla., 1997, John Stearns award, N.Y. Acad. Medicine, 1999, Heinz Family Found. award. Fellow: Am. Psychiat. Assn. (disting.), Am. Orthopsychiat. Assn. (Ittleson award 1994); mem.: APHA (Martha May Eliot award 1970, Sedgwick medal 1992), AMA (AMA-ERF award in health edn. 1988), Am. Psychosomatic Soc., Soc. Pediatric Rsch., Am. Acad. Child Psychiatry (hon.), New Eng. Coun. Child Psychiatry (assoc.), Am. Acad. Pediat. (C. Anderson Aldrich award 1966, ann. award sect. on cmty. pediat. 1977, Outstanding Contbn. award sect. cmty. pediat. 1978, Job Lewis Smith award 2000), Am. Pediatric Soc. (John Howland award 1990), Inst. Medicine of NAS (1st ann. Gustav O. Lienhard award 1986, McDermott medal 2002), Phi Eta Sigma, Alpha Omega Alpha, Sigma Xi. Office Phone: 617-432-1410.

**RICHMOND, LYLE L.,** judge; BA, Wesleyan U., 1952; LLB, Yale U., 1955. Dep. dist. atty., San Diego, 1959—64; pvt. practice Calif., 1964—70; dist. atty. Truk/Ponape dists., 1970—73; head legal divsn. atty.'s gen. office Trust Territory of the Pacific Islands, Saipan, 1973—75; atty. gen. American Samoa, 1975—77; legal counselor to American Samoa govs. Peter T. Coleman and A. P. Lutali, 1978—89; adminstr., legal mgr. Samoa Packing Co., Pago Pago, American Samoa, 1989—91; assoc. justice High Ct., Pago Pago, American Samoa, 1991—. With USN, 1955—58, capt. JAGC USNR, 1984. Office: Courthouse PO Box 309 Pago Pago AS 96799 Office Phone: 684-633-1261. E-mail: lylerichmond72@hotmail.com.

**RICHMOND, MARILYN SUSAN,** lawyer; b. Bethesda, Md., Oct. 19, 1949; d. Carl Hutchins Jr. and Elizabeth Adeline (Saeger) R. BA with honors, U. Fla., 1971; JD, Georgetown U., 1974. Bar: Md. 1974, D.C. 1975. Atty. Office of Gen. Counsel, FTC, Washington, 1974-77, antitrust atty. Bur. of Competition, 1977-81; counsel, consumer subcom. of com. on commerce, sci. and transp. U.S. Senate, Washington, 1981-85; assoc. Heron, Burchette, Ruckert & Rothwell, Washington, 1985-87, ptnr., 1987-90; dep. asst. sec. for govtl. affairs U.S. Dept. Transp., Washington, 1990-91, acting asst. sec. for govtl. affairs, 1991-92; cons. Raffaelli, Spees, Springer & Smith, Washington, 1993-94; asst. exec. dir. govt. rels. APA Practice Orgn., 1995—. Lectr. Brookings Instn. Ctr. for Pub. Policy Edn., Washington, 1985-88. Active Lawyers for Bush-Quayle, Washington, 1988. Mem. ABA (antitrust, adminstrv. law sect., vice chair transp. industry com. antitrust sect. 1992-99). Republican. Methodist. Avocations: horseback riding, tennis. Home: Apt 601 2725 Connecticut Ave NW Washington DC 20008-5305 Office Phone: 202-336-5889.

**RICHMOND, MARVIN ELLIOT,** astronomer, educator; b. San Antonio, Sept. 6, 1942; s. Sam Doss and Koreski May Richmond; m. Marilyn Kathleen McDaniel, Jan. 15, 1967; children: Jennifer Anne Harrison, Elanor Michelle (dec.). PhD, U. Texas, Austin, 1993—2006. Adj. prof. astronomy Austin Cmty. Coll., 1993—. Editor: (encyclopedia) Macmillan Encyclopedia of Animal Science. Planter/developer Good Shepherd Christian Ch., Austin, 2004—; edn. com. chair Tex. Archeol. Soc., Austin, 2005—. Mem.: Astron. Soc. Pacific, Nat. Assn. Rsch. Tchg., Am. Ednl. Rsch. Assn., Tex. State Tchrs. Assn. (life), Tex. Archeol. Soc. Disciples Of Christ. Avocations: archaeology, astronomy, archaeoastronomy. Home: 5305 Summerset Trail Austin TX 78749-1215 Personal E-mail: mrichmond@austin.rr.com.

**RICHMOND, ROCSAN,** television executive producer, small business owner; b. Chgo., Jan. 30; d. Alphonso and Annie Lou (Combest) Richmond; 1 child from previous marriage, Tina S. Student, Wilson Jr. Coll., 1963, 2d City Theatre, Chgo., 1969, Alice Liddel Theatre, 1970; cert. fingerprint classifier, LA City Coll., 1996. Lic. 3d class radio/tel. operator FCC. Vegetarian editor Aware mag., Chgo., 1977—78; investigative reporter, film critic Chgo. Metro News, 1975—81; prodr., talk show host Sta. WSSD, Chgo., 1980—81; dir. pub. rels. IRMCO Corp., Chgo., 1981—82; pub. rels., newsletter editor Hollywood (Calif.) Reporter, 1985—86; exec. prodr. Donald Descendent's Prodns., Hollywood, 1983—, Future News, TV show, 1983—86; pres. Richmond Estates; tchr. TV prodn. Profl. Bus. Acad., Hollywood, 1998—2000; founder, pres. Richmond Acad. Fine Manners, 2000—. Invention invisible drapery tieback. Jehovah'S Witness. Achievements include invention of invisible drapery tieback. Office: PO Box 665 Los Angeles CA 90078-0665 E-mail: aaaaatoner@aol.com.

**RICHT, MARK,** college football coach; b. Feb. 18, 1960; m. Katharyn Francis; children: Jonathan, David, Zach, Anya. Graduate, Univ. Miami, 1982. Asst. coach Ea. Carolina Univ., 1989; quarterbacks coach FSU, 1985—2000, Offensive Coord., 1994—2000; head football coach Univ. Ga., 2000—. Recipient SEC Coach Yr., 2002, 2005. Office: Sanford Stadium PO Box 1472 Sanford Dr at Reed St Athens GA 30602*

**RICHTEL, MATT (THERON HEIR),** reporter, cartoonist; BA, Univ. Calif., Berkeley; M in journalism, Columbia Univ. Reporter & editor Peninsula Times Herald; reporter Oakland Tribune; telecommunications reporter New York Times, 2000—. Co-author (with Darrin Bell, under pen name Theron Heir): (syndicated comic strip) Rudy Park. Office: New York Times 201 Spear St San Francisco CA 94105 Office Phone: 415-836-6700. Business E-Mail: mattr@nytimes.com.*

**RICHTER, BURTON,** physicist, educator; b. NYC, Mar. 22, 1931; s. Abraham and Fanny (Pollack) Richter; m. Laurose Becker, July 1, 1960; children: Elizabeth, Matthew. BS, MIT, 1952, PhD, 1956; degree in physics (hon.), U. Pisa, 2001. Research assoc. Stanford U., 1956—60, asst. prof. physics, 1960—63, assoc. prof., 1963—67, prof., 1967—, Paul Pigott prof. phys. sci., 1980—2005, tech. dir. Linear Accelerator Ctr., 1982—84, dir. Linear Accelerator Ctr., 1984—99; dir. emeritus, 1999—. Loeb lectr. Harvard U., 1974; DeShalit lectr. Weizmann Inst., 1975; pres. Internat. Union of Pure and Applied Physics, 1997; cons., sec. energy adv. bd. NSF, 1999—2002; Astor vis. lectr. Oxford U., 2000; sec. Energy Adv. Bd.; bd. dirs. Varian Med. Systems, AREVA Enterprises, Inc., Litel Instruments. Contbr. over 300 articles to profl. publs. Recipient E.O. Lawrence medal, Dept. Energy, 1976, Nobel prize in Physics, 1976. Fellow: AAAS, Am. Acad. Arts and Scis., Am. Phys. Soc. (pres. 1994); mem.: NAS, Nat. Rsch. Coun. (mem. bd. physics and astronomy, chair 2003—), Internat. Coun. Sci. (mem. exec. bd. 2002—05), Regents Mercersbury Acad. (hon.), Nat. Climate Change Assessment (PCAST rev. panel), Acceleration Transmutation Nuc. Waste (chair NERAC subcom.), Am. Phil. Soc. (bd. dirs.). Achievements include research in elementary particle physics. Office: SLAC 2575 Sand Hill Rd Menlo Park CA 94025

**RICHTER, CAROLYN PETERSON,** lawyer; b. Portland, Oreg., Aug. 6, 1961; d. Ralph Edward and Elizabeth Claire Peterson; m. Werner Siegfried Richter, July 18, 1998; 1 child, Patrick Sebastian. BS, Newcomb Coll. Tulane U., 1984; JD, Tulane Law Sch., 1987. Bar: Fla. 1987, La. 1987, Ga. 1988, DC 1989. Law clk. to Hon. Judge Henry A. Mentz U.S. Dist. Ct. (ea. dist.) La., 1987—89; law clk. to Hon. Chief Judge William C. O' Kelley U.S. Dist. Ct. (no. dist.) Ga., 1989—90; assoc. Kilpatrick Stockton LLP, Atlanta, 1990—96, Troutman Sanders LLP, 1996—2001, ptnr., 2001—. Contbr. chpts. secured trans., bank deposits and collections. Mem.: ABA (vice chair creditors' rights subcom. 2003—05, chair creditors' rights subcom. 2005—), Atlanta Bar Assn. (Vol. of Yr. 1996). Avocations: travel, cooking. Office: Troutman Sanders LLP 600 Peachtree St Ste 5200 Atlanta GA 30308-2216 Office Phone: 404-885-3358. Office Fax: 404-962-6667. Business E-Mail: carolyn.richter@troutmansanders.com.

**RICHTER, DONALD PAUL,** lawyer; b. New Britain, Conn., Feb. 15, 1924; s. Paul John and Helen (Racoske) R.; m. Jane Frances Gumpright, Aug. 10, 1946; children: Christopher Dean, Cynthia Louise. AB, Bates Coll., 1947; LL.B., Yale U., 1950. Bar: NY 1951, Conn. 1953. Assoc. Winthrop, Stimson, Putnam & Roberts, N.Y.C., 1950-52; ptnr. Murtha, Cullina, Richter and Pinney, Hartford, Conn., 1954-94; counsel Murtha Cullina LLP, Hartford, Conn., 1994—. Trustee Bates Coll., 1962-94, Manchester (Conn.) Meml. Hosp., 1963-94, Hartford Sem., 1973-85; trustee Suffield Acad., 1974—, pres., 1982-89; bd. dirs. Met. YMCA Greater Hartford, 1970-94, pres., 1976-81, trustee, 1994—; mem. nat. coun. YMCA, 1978-82; bd. dirs. Church Homes, 1967-81; trustee, v.p., Silver Bay Assn., 1971-96. With USNR, 1943-46. Fellow Am. Coll. Trust and Estate Counsel; mem. ABA, Conn. Bar Assn., Univ. Club, Hartford Club, 20th Century Club, Rotary (Paul Harris fellow 1996), Phi Beta Kappa, Delta Sigma Rho. Congregationalist. Home: 140 Boulder Rd Manchester CT 06040-4508 Office: Murtha Cullina LLP City Place I 185 Asylum St Hartford CT 06103-3469

**RICHTER, FRANK M.,** geophysicist, educator; b. Dominican Republic; naturalized, US, 1974; Profl. engring. degree, Colo. Sch. Mines, 1965; MS, U. Chgo, 1971; PhD, U. Chgo., 1972. Rsch. assoc. dept. earth and planetary sci. MIT, 1972—74; asst. prof. dept. geophys. scis. U. Chgo., 1975—78, assoc. prof., 1978—81, prof., 1981—, Sewel L. Avery Disting. Svc. prof. geophys. scis., 1994—. Chmn. dept. geophys. scis. U. Chgo., 1985—94. Contbr. articles to sci. jours. Named a Fairchild Disting. Scholar, Calif. Inst. Tech., 1978, Green Scholar, Inst. Geophysics and Planetary Physics, La Jolla, Calif., 1979; recipient George Woollard award, Geol. Soc. Am., 1999, Arthur L. Day medal, 2006; grantee John Simon Guggenheim fellowship, 1974, Royal Soc. Rsch. fellowship, 1981. Fellow: Am. Geophys. Union (Norman L. Bowen award 1995), Am. Acad. Arts & Scis.; mem.: NAS (mem. dept Geophys Scis U Chgo 5734 S Ellis Ave HGS 549 Chicago IL 60637 E-mail: richter@geosci.uchicago.edu.*

**RICHTER, FRANK-JÜRGEN,** economist, consultant; b. Karlsruhe, Germany, Mar. 20, 1967; s. Ernst and Bernhilde Richter; m. Nadja Gindi. PhD, U. Stuttgart, Germany, 1995. Fin. dir. Bosch (China) Ltd, Beijing, 1996—2000; dir. World Econ. Forum, Geneva, 2001—04; pres. Horasis: The Global Visions Cmty., Geneva, 2005—. Prof. The Emirates Ctr. for Entrepreneurship, Abu Dhabi, United Arab Emirates, 2005—. Author: Global Future. Office: Horasis: The Global Visions Cmty Rue du 31-Decembre 1211 Geneva Switzerland Office Phone: 0041 79 305 3110. Office Fax: 0041 22 718 4140. E-mail: visions@horasis.org.

**RICHTER, GERHARD,** artist; b. Dresden, Germany, Feb. 9, 1932; m. Isa Genzken, 1982; 1 child, Betty. Student, Hochschule fur Bildende Kunste, Dresden, 1952-57; studied with, Karl-Otto Gotz Staatliche Kunstakademie, Dusseldorf, 1961-64. Scenery painter Stadttheatre Zittau, East Germany, 1949-50; commercial artist numerous firms Zittau, 1950-51; photolab. technician Dresden, 1957-60; painter Dusseldorf, 1963—; visual artist Staatliche Kunstakademie, Germany. Prof. Staatliche Kunstakademie, Dusseldorf, 1971; lectr. in field. One man shows include Mobelhaus Berges, Dusseldorf, 1963, Galerie Heiner Friedrich, Munich, 1964, 67, 70, 72, Galerie Rene Block, 1965, 69, 74, White Wide Space Gallery, Antwerp, 1967, Galerie Ricke, Kassel, 1968, Galleria del Naviglio, 1969, Palais des Beaux-Arts, Brussels, 1970, Galerie Konrad Fischer, Dusseldorf, 1970, 72, 75, 83, Mus. Folkwang, Essen, 1970, 80, Kunstverein, Dusseldorf, 1971, Galerie Thomas Borgmann, Cologne, 1971, 84, Galerie Rudolph Zwirner, Cologne, 1972, Galerie Seriaal, Amsterdam, 1973, Onnasch Gallery, N.Y., 1973, Galleria La Bertesca, Milan, 1973, Galerie Rolf Preisig, Basle, 1975, Nova Scotia Coll. Art, Halifax, 1978, Whitechapel Art Gallery, London, 1979, Sperone-Westwater-Fischer, N.Y., 1980, 83, Kunsthalle, Dusseldorf, 1981, Galerie Hetzler, 1982, Padiglione d'Arte Contemporanea, Milan, 1982, Galleria Lucio Amelio, Naples, 1983, Galleria Maria Pieroni, Rome, 1983, Musée d'Art et d'Industrie, St. Etienne, France, 1984, Marian Goodman Gallery, N.Y., 1985, Sperone-Westwater, N.Y., 1985, Anthony d'Offay Gallery, London, 1988, Art Gallery Ont., 1988, others; exhibited in group shows at Whitechapel Art Gallery, London, Stedelijk Mus., Amsterdam, Kunsthalle, Royal Acad. London, L.A. County Mus. Art; represented in permanent collections Kunstmuseum, Dusseldorf, Neue Gallery, Mus. Folkwang, Nationalgalerie, Berlin, Kunstmuseum, Basle, Guggenheim Mus., N.Y.; author: Bericht uber eine Demonstr., 1963, Gerhard Richter: Atlas von de fot., 1972, Gerhard Richter: Atlas der Fotos, Collgen und Skizzen, 1976. Recipient Kunstpreis Junger Westen, Recklinghausen, 1967, Arnold Bode prize, Kassel, 1972, Wolf prize in arts (painting) Wolf Found., 1994/5 Mem.: Am. Acad. Arts and Sciences (hon. fgn.). Mailing: Staatliche Kunstakademie Eiskellerstraße 1 (Altstadt) Germany*

**RICHTER, GLENN,** retail executive; BBA, George Washington U.; MBA, Duke U. Various exec. level positions with Frito-Lay Co., McKinsey and Co.; pres., CEO Specialty Foods Corp., 1994—97; sr. v.p., corp. contr. Dade

Behring, Deerfield, Ill., 1997-99, CFO, 1998—99; exec. v.p., CFO St. Paul Companies Inc., 1997—2000; v.p., controller Sears Roebuck, Hoffman Estates, Ill., 2000—02, senior v.p., CFO, 2002—05, exec. v.p., CFO, 2005—. Office: Sears Roebuck 3333 Beverly Rd Schaumburg IL 60179

**RICHTER, HARVENA,** retired literature educator, poet; b. Reading, Pa., Mar. 13, 1919; d. Conrad Michael and Harvena Maria (Achenbach) R. BA, U. N.Mex., 1938; MA, NYU, 1955, PhD, 1967. Advt. copyrighter Saks 5th Ave., N.Y.C., 1942-43, R.H. Macy, N.Y.C., 1944-46; copy chief Elizabeth Arden, N.Y.C., 1946-47; advt. dir. I. Miller, N.Y.C., 1947-48; European corr. various newspapers, 1948-49; lectr. NYU, N.Y.C., 1952-66, U. N.Mex., 1969-89. Author: The Human Shore, 1959, Virginia Woolf: The Inward Voyage, 1970, Writing to Survive: The Private Notebooks of Conrad Richter, 1988, The Yaddo Elegies and Other Poems, 1995, Green Girls, Poems Early and Late, 1996, The Innocent Island, 1999, Frozen Light, the Crystal Poems, 2002, The Golden Fountains, Sources of Energy and Life, 2002, Passage to Teheran, 2004; author numerous poems; short stories to Sat. Eve. Post, New Am., Blue Mesa Rev.; essays to Atlantic, Modern Fiction Studies, C.S. Monitor, others. AAUW fellow, 1964-65; grantee Yaddo, 1963-64, MacDowell Colony, 1965-66, Wurlitzer Found., Taos, N.Mex., 1968, 73-75, Va. Ctr. for Creative Arts, 1983, 85, Ragdale Found., 1990. Mem. Author's Guild, Virginia Woolf Soc., Kappa Kappa Gamma. Avocation: gardening. Home and Office: 1932 Candelaria Rd NW Albuquerque NM 87107

**RICHTER, JOHN CHARLES,** prosecutor; Grad., Emory U.; JD, U. Va. Law clk. to Hon. J. Owen Forrester US Dist. Ct. (no. dist.) Ga.; asst. dist. atty. Cobb County, Ga., 1998; chief of staff, criminal divsn. US Dept. Justice, 1998, acting asst. atty. gen. criminal divsn., acting US atty. (we. dist.) Okla., 2005—06, US atty., 2006—. Office: US Attys Office 210 W Park Ave Ste 400 Oklahoma City OK 73102*

**RICHTER, JUDITH ANNE,** pharmacologist, educator; b. Wilmington, Del., Mar. 4, 1942; d. Henry John and Dorothy Madelyn (Schroeder) R. BA, U. Colo., 1964; PhD, Stanford U., 1969. Postdoctoral fellow Cambridge (Eng.) U., 1969-70, U. London, 1970-71; asst. prof. pharmacology Sch. Medicine Ind. U., Indpls., 1971-78, assoc. prof. pharmacology and neurobiology, 1978-84, prof., 1984—. Vis. assoc. prof. U. Ariz. Health Sci. Ctr., Tucson, 1983; mem. biomed. rsch. rev. com. Nat. Inst. on Drug Abuse, 1983-87. Mem. editl. bd. Jour. Neurochemistry, 1982-87; contbr. numerous articles to sci. jours. Fellow, Wellcome Trust, 1969—71; scholar, Boettcher Found., 1960—64. Mem. AAAS, Am. Soc. for Pharmacology and Exptl. Therapeutics (exec. com. neuropharmacology div. 1989-91), Am. Soc. for Neurochemistry, Internat. Soc. for Neurochemistry, Soc. for Neurosci., Women in Neurosci., Assn. Women in Sci., Phi Beta Kappa, Sigma Xi. Achievements include research in neuropharmacology, especially barbiturates, neurobiology of mutant mice and dopaminergic systems, and regulation of sensory neuron glutamate release. Office: Ind U Sch Medicine 635 Barnhill Dr Indianapolis IN 46202-5126 Office Phone: 317-274-7593. Business E-Mail: jrichter@iupui.edu.

**RICHTER, MIKE (MICHAEL THOMAS RICHTER),** retired professional hockey player; b. Abington, Sept. 22, 1966; m. Veronica Richter; children: Thomas, James. Student, U. Wisconsin. With NY Rangers, NY, 1985—2003. Mem. US Olympic Hockey Team, Nagano, Japan, 1998, Salt Lake City, 2002; player NHL All-Star Game, 1992, 94, 2000. Named MVP, All-Star Game, 1994; recipient WCHA Rookie of Yr. award, 1985—86. Achievements include being a Stanley Cup Champion NY Rangers, 1994; having his number, 35, retired by NY Rangers, 2006.

**RICHTER, PETER CHRISTIAN,** lawyer; b. Opava, Czechoslovakia, June 13, 1944; came to U.S., 1951; s. Hanus and Alzbeta (Kindlarova) R.; m. Leslie Diane Rousseau, Nov. 25, 1967; children: Timothy Jason, Lindsey Berta. BS, U. Oreg., 1967, JD, 1971. Bar: Oreg. 1971, U.S. Dist. Ct. 1972, U.S. Ct. Appeals (9th cir.) 1972, U.S. Supreme Ct. 1983. Assoc. Veatch, Lovett & Stiner, Portland, Oreg., 1971-73; ptnr. Miller Nash LLP, Portland, 1978—. Adj. prof. law trial advocacy Northwestern Sch. of Law, Lewis and Clark Coll., Portland, 1986—; pro tempore judge Multnomah County Cir. Ct., Portland, 1985—1998. Oreg. State Bar Trial Advocacy Seminars, 1988—; trial advocacy coll. planner, instr. Oreg. State Bar, 1998—. Author: (handbook) Oregon State Bar, 1987, 88, 89; co-author: (chpt. in book) Oregon State Bar Damage Manual, 1985, 90; editor, program planner Sales: The Oregon Experience, 1989. Trustee, bd. dirs. Parry Ctr. for Children, Portland, 1990; former bd. dir. Boy Scouts of Am., Columbia Pacific Coun., Portland, Nat. Conf. Christians and Jews, Portland, 1983; bd. advisers Pacific Crest Outward Bound, 2000. With Oreg. Army N.G., 1967-75. Recipient Cert. of Appreciation Northwestern Sch. of Law, 1990; named one of ten Best Litigators in Oreg, Nat. Bar Jour. Fellow Am. Bar Found.; mem. ABA (trial techniques com.), Fed. Bar Assn. (Oreg. chpt.), Am. Bd. Trial Advocates (advocate), Internat. Assn. of Def. Counsel, Oreg. Bar Assn. (lectr. trial advocacy seminars 1988—, mem. jud. adminstn. com, bus. lit. sect. exec. comm.), Multnomah Bar Assn. (former bd dirs.), Oreg. Assn. Def. Counsel (cert. of appreciation 1987, 89) Inns of Ct., Multnomah Athletic Club (trustee, pres.), Arlington Club. Avocations: squash, tennis, skiing, golf, reading, motorcycling riding. Office: Miller Nash LLP 111 SW 5th Ave Ste 3500 Portland OR 97204-3699 Office Phone: 503-224-5858. E-mail: peter.richter@millernash.com.

**RICHTER, ROBERT C.,** retired automotive executive; V.p.- admin. Dana Corp., Toledo, 1997—98, v.p.- fin. and admin., 1998—99, v.p., CFO, 1999—2006; chmn. Dana Credit Corp., 2002.

**RICHTER, STUART M.,** lawyer; b. Bethlehem, Pa., July 17, 1961; BS, U. Va., 1983; JD summa cum laude, Pepperdine U., 1986. Bar: Calif. 1986, US Ct. Appeals, 9th Cir., US Dist. Ct., Dist. Ariz., US Dist. Ct., Ctrl, Ea, No. and So. Dists. Calif. Ptnr., co-head Litig. Practice Katten Muchin Zavis Rosenman, LA. Mem.: LA County Bar Assn. Office: Katten Muchin Zavis Rosenman Ste 2600 2029 Century Park E Los Angeles CA 90067 Office Phone: 310-788-4582. Office Fax: 310-712-8434. E-mail: stuart.richter@kmzr.com.

**RICHTER, W.D.,** screenwriter, director, producer; b. New Britain, Conn., Dec. 7, 1945; s. Walter Oswald and Hedwig (Duch) R.; m. Susan Booth, June 22, 1968. BA, Dartmouth Coll., 1968; postgrad., U. So. Calif., 1968-70. Freelance writer, producer, director, 1973—. Screenwriter: Slither, 1973, Peeper, 1975, Nickelodeon, 1976, Invasion of the Body Snatchers, 1978, Dracula, 1979, Brubaker, 1980 (Academy award nomination best original screenplay 1980), All Night Long, 1981, Hard Feelings, 1982, Big Trouble in Little China, 1986, Needful Things, 1993, Home for The Holidays, 1995, Stealth, 2005; prodr.: dir.: (films) Buckaroo Banzai, 1984, Late for Dinner, 1991. Mem. Writers Guild Am., Dirs. Guild Am.

**RICHTMAN, JACK,** French language educator; b. N.Y.C., Mar. 15, 1927; s. Fred and Rose (Blumenfeld) R BA, Bklyn. Coll., 1959; MA, Columbia U., 1961, PhD, 1969. Prof. French studies SUNY, Albany, 1962—95, prof. emeritus, 1995—. Assoc. dean Coll. of Humanities SUNY, Albany, 1992-94 Author: Adrienne Lecouvreur: The Actress and the Age, 1971; contbr. articles to profl. jours Fulbright fellow Fulbright Commn., 1961-62 Mem. MLA (editor Lesbian and Gay Studies Newsletter, 1999-2004), Les Amis de Jean Cocteau (Am. corr. 2002—) Home: 484 W 43d St Apt 12R New York NY 10036

**RICK, ROSELEEN P.,** lawyer; b. NYC, 1941; BA, Va. Commonwealth Univ., 1976; JD, Univ. Richmond, 1980. Bar: Va. 1980. Ptnr., practice group leader, multi-family housing Troutman Sanders LLP, Richmond, Va. Mem.: ABA, Nat. Assn. Women Bus. Owners, Va. Bar Assn., Richmond Bar Assn. Office: Troutman Sanders LLP Bank Am Ctr 1111 E Main St Richmond VA 23219 Office Phone: 804-697-1462. Office Fax: 804-698-6007. Business E-Mail: roseleen.rick@troutmansanders.com.

**RICKABAUGH, RENÉ LANE,** principal; b. Newcastle, Wyo., Sept. 1, 1957; d. James Austin and Patricia Lee (Baumgartner) Lane; m. Ronald J. Rickabaugh, Aug. 1, 1981. BA in Elem. and Spl. Edn. cum laude, U. Wyo., 1979, MA in Spl. Edn., 1989. Spl. summer program dir. Assn. for Retarded Citizens Weston County, Newcastle, 1979; spl. edn. tchr. Natrona County Sch. Dist. 1, Casper, Wyo., 1979—84, ednl. resource specialist, cons. for instrn., curriculum and materials for handicapped students, 1984—92, prin. spl. edn., 1992—94; elem. prin., Title I dir. Bar Nunn Sch., 1994—. Mem. Wyo. state com. North Ctrl. Assn. Ed. chmn. First United Meth. Ch., chair staff/parish rels. com. Mem. NEA, AAUW, Wyo. Assn. Elem. Prins. (past treas., pres.-elect 2005, pres. 2006), Nat. Assn. Elem. Prins., Coun. Exceptional Children (past membership chmn.), Assn. Direct Instrn., Assn. Retarded Citizens (past sec. N.C. chpt.), U. Wyo. Alumni Assn., PEO (past pres. chpt.), Omicron Delta Kappa, Kappa Delta Pi (past v.p.), Phi Delta Kappa (past chpt. pres.), Phi Kappa Phi. Home: 80 Magnolia St Casper WY 82604-4063 Office Phone: 307-577-4507. Personal E-mail: rener_9@msn.com.

**RICKARD, DAVID B.,** retail executive; b. Oneida, N.Y., 1946; BS, Cornell U., 1969; MBA, Harvard U., 1971. From internat. acct. to fin. control mgr. U.S. mktg. S.C. Johnson Wax, Inc., 1971-74; with Gen. Foods Corp., fin. dir. internat.; dir. investor rels. Kraft Gen. Foods; v.p. fin. and strategy Kraft USA; sr. v.p., CFO Grand Metropolitan, 1991-94, group contr. London, 1994-95; fin. dir. Internat. Distillers and Vintners, Ltd., 1995-96; exec. v.p. Internat. Distillers and Vintners-Americas, 1996-97; sr. v.p., CFO RJR Nabisco, N.Y.C., 1997-99; CFO CVS Corp., Woonsocket, RI, 1999—. Bd. dirs. Harris Corp., May Dept. Stores. Mem.: Worldwide Retail Exchange, Financial Acctg. Standards Advisory Coun. (mem. steering comt.). Office: CVS Corp 1 CVS Dr Woonsocket RI 02895*

**RICKARD, LISA ANN,** lawyer; b. Englewood, N.J., Oct. 22, 1955; d. Joseph Mitchell and Ann Marie (Samen) Moore; m. J. Scott Rickard, June 18, 1977; children: Jack Taylor, Justin Moore. BA in Govt. and French, Lafayette Coll., 1977; JD, Am. U., 1982. Legis. asst. Bank of Am., Washington, 1977-78; spl. asst. and press asst. to Sen. Richard Stone, Washington, 1978-80; legis. asst. to Sen. Frank Murkowski, Washington, 1981; assoc. and ptnr. Akin, Gump, Strauss, Hauer & Feld, Washington, 1982-93; v.p. federal affairs Ryder System, Inc., Washington, 1993-97, sr. v.p. govt. affairs, 1997; v.p. fed. & state govt. affairs Dow Chemical Co.; pres. U.S.C. of C. Inst. for Legal Reform, Washington. Bd. dirs. mem. corp. adv. coun. Women's Rsch. and Edn. Inst., Washington, 1991—. Diplome D'Etudes Francaises Cours Moyen, Deuxieme Degres, U. Strasbourg, France, 1976. Mem. ABA, D.C. Bar Assn. Episcopalian. Avocation: travel. Office: Institute for Legal Reform 1615 H St NW Washington DC 20062-2000 Office Phone: 202-463-3107. E-mail: lrickard@uschamber.com.

**RICKARD, MARGARET LYNN,** library director, consultant; b. Detroit, July 31, 1944; d. Frank Mathias and Betty Louise (Lee) Sieger; m. Cyriac Thannikary, Nov. 13, 1965 (div. Feb. 1973); 1 child, Luke Anthony Thannikary; m. Marcos T. Perez, Mar. 1973 (dec. Oct. 1973); m. Lui Gotti, Dec. 23, 1984 (dec. Aug. 1997); m. William A. Rickard, Aug. 22, 1998 (dec. Aug. 21, 2005). AB, U. Detroit, Mich., 1968; MLS, Pratt Inst., Bklyn., 1969; postgrad., NYU, 1976—77. Cert. libr. N.Y. Sr. libr. Queens Pub. Libr., Jamaica, NY, 1969-77; libr. dir. El Centro (Calif.) Pub. Libr., 1977-99; ret., 1999. Vice chmn., chmn. Serra Coop. Libr. Sys., San Diego, 1980—82, libr. cons., 1998—; county libr./cons. Imperial County Free Libr., 1993—99. Pres. Hist. Site Found., El Centro, 1988—99, 1992, sec., 1989, trustee, 1989—99, v.p., 1991—92; mem. Downtown El Centro Assn., mem. arches bus. improvement dist.; mem. comm. and arts task force Imperial County Arts Coun.; coord. arts and culture com. City of El Centro Strategic Plan; fin. sec. St. Elizabeth Luth. Ch., El Centro, 1988. Recipient Disting. Svc. award, El Dorado County ACSA, 2004, El Dorado County Disting. Employee Svc. award, ACSA, 2004; Title IIB fellow, Pratt Inst., 1968—69. Mem.: AAUW (v.p. El Centro 1988), ALA, Calif. County Librs. Assn., Calif. Libr. Assn., Toastmasters, El Centro C. of C., Women of Moose (sr. regent El Centro 1988—89, ednl. advancement chmn. 1999—2000), Soroptomist (life; v.p. El Centro 1978, corr. sec. 1990—91, 1st v.p. 1991—92, pres. 1992—93, 2d v.p. 1995—96, 1998—99, rec. sec. 1997—98). Democrat. Lutheran. Home and Office: 6169 Terrace Dr PO Box 232 Pollock Pines CA 95726 E-mail: rickmeg@worldnet.att.net.

**RICKARD, RUTH DAVID,** retired history professor, retired political science professor; b. Fed. Republic Germany, Feb. 20, 1926; came to U.S., 1940; d. Carl and Alice (Koch) David; m. Robert M. Yaffe, Oct. 1949 (dec. 1959); children: David, Steven; m. Norman G. Rickard, June 1968 (dec. 1988); 1 stepson, Douglas. BS cum laude, Northwestern U., 1947, MA, 1948. Law editor Commerce Clearing House, Chgo., 1948; instr. history U. Ill., Chgo., 1949-51, instr. extension program Waukegan, 1960-67; instr. history Waukegan Schs., 1960-69; original faculty, prof. western civilization, polit. sci. Coll. of Lake County, Grayslake, Ill., 1969-92. Mem. Inter-Univ. Seminar on Armed Forces and Soc.; mem. Hospitality Info. Svc. for Diplomatic Residents and Families affiliate Meridian Internat. Ctr.; spkr. in field. Author: History of College of Lake County, 1987 (honored by city of Waukegan 1987), (poem) I Lost My Wings, 1989, Au Revoir from Emeritusdom, 1993, Where are the Safety Zones, 1994; contbg. author: History of National Press Club: Reliable Sources, 1997; contbr. articles to profl. jours. Mem. Econ. Devel. Com., Waukegan, 1992-93; working with homeless through Samaritans of Greater Washington area, 2000—. Scholar Freedoms Found. Am. Legion, Valley Forge, Pa., 1967. Mem. AAUW (pres. Waukegan chpt. 1955-57, scholarship named for her 1985, program co-chair McLean chpt. 1997-2000), LWV (charter, v.p. Waukegan chpt.), Nat. Press Club D.C., Northwestern U. Alumni Washington (bd. dirs.). Avocations: writing, travel, lecturing, reading, theater.

**RICKEL, ANNETTE URSO,** psychology and psychiatry researcher, educator; b. Phila. d. Ralph Francis and Marguerite (Calcaterra) Urso; 1 child, John Ralph Rickel. BA, Mich. State U., 1969; PhD, MD, U. Mich., 1972. Lic. psychologist, Mich. Faculty early childhood edn. Merrill-Palmer Inst., Detroit, 1967-69; adj. faculty U. Mich., Ann Arbor, 1969-75; asst. dir. N.E. Guidance Ctr., Detroit, 1972-75; assoc. prof. psychology Wayne State U., Detroit, 1975-81; vis. assoc. prof. Columbia U., N.Y.C., 1982-83; assoc. prof. psychology Wayne State U., 1981-87, asst. provost, 1989-91, prof. psychology, 1987-95; Am. Coun. on Edn. fellow Princeton and Rutgers Univs., 1990-91; clin. prof. dept. psychiatry Georgetown U., Washington, 1995—2000; program officer Rockefeller Found., 2000—03; pres. Annette Urso Rickel Found., 2003—; prof. Weill Cornell Med. Sch., 2005—. AAAS and APA Congl. Sci. fellow on Senate Fin. Subcom. on health and Pres.'s Nat. Health Care Reform Task Force, 1992—93; prof. Weill Cornell Med. Sch., 2005. Cons. editor Jour. of Cmty. Psychology, Jour. Primary Prevention; co-author: Social and Psychological Problems of Women, 1984, Preventing Maladjustment..., 1987; author: Teenage Pregnancy and Parenting, 1989, Keeping Children From Harm's Way, 1997, High Risk Sexual Behavior, 1998, Understanding Managed Care, 2000, Attention Deficit Hyperactivity Disorder in Children and Adults, 2006; contbr. articles to profl. jours Mem. Pres.'s Task Force on Nat. Health Care Reform, 1993; bd. dirs. Children's Ctr. of Wayne County, Mich., 1989—, The Epilepsy Ctr. of Mich., 1984-92, Nat. Symphony Orch., 1997—, Reading is Fundamental, 2000—, Chamber Music Soc. of Lincoln Ctr., 2002—, Soc. Meml. Sloan Kettering Cancer Ctr., 2002—, The Kellogg Found., 1996-97, The John D. and Catherine T. MacArthur Found., 1998-99. Grantee NIMH, 1976-84. Recipient Career Devel. Chair award, 1985-86. Fellow APA (div. pres. 1984-85); mem. Internat. Women's Forum, Soc. for Rsch. in Child Devel., Soc. for Rsch. in Child and Adolescent Psychopathology, Internat. Assn. of Applied Psychologists, Sigma Xi, Psi Chi. Roman Catholic. Office Phone: 212-659-7760. Personal E-mail: rickelau@aol.com.

**RICKELS, KARL,** psychiatrist, educator; b. Wilhelmshaven, Germany, Aug. 17, 1924; came to U.S., 1954, naturalized, 1960; s. Karl E. and Stephanie (Roehrhoff) R.; m. Rosalind Wilson, June 27, 1964; children: Laurence Arthur, PhD, Stephen W., Michael R. MD, U. Muenster, 1951. Intern Dortmund (Germany) City Hosp., 1951-52; postgrad. tng. U. Erlangen, U. Frankfurt, City Hosp. Kassel, 1952-54; resident in psychiatry Mental Health Inst., Cherokee, Iowa, 1954-55. Hosp. U. Pa., Phila., 1955-57; from instr. to assoc. prof. U. Pa., Phila., 1957-69, prof. psychiatry, 1969—, prof. pharmacology, 1976-98, Stuart and Emily B.H. Mudd prof. human behavior, 1977—, chief mood and anxiety disorders program, 1964—, chmn. com. on studies involving human beings Phila., 1985-98. Chief psychiatry Phila. Gen. Hosp., 1975-77. Editor, author 9 books; contbr. over 550 articles to profl. publs. Fellow Am. Coll. Neuropsychopharmacology (life; charter), Am. Soc. Clin. Psychopharmacology, Am. Psychiat. Assn. (life), Coll. Physicians Phila., Collegium Internat. Neuro-Psychopharmacologicum; mem. Psychiat. Rsch. Soc., European Coll. Neuropsychopharmacology (corr.). Home: 1324 Youngsford Rd Gladwyne PA 19035 Office: U Pa Dept Psychiatry Ste 670 3535 Market St Philadelphia PA 19104-3515 Office Phone: 215-746-6417. Business E-mail: krickels@mail.med.upenn.edu.

**RICKERT, ANTHONY H.,** lawyer; b. Salisbury, Md., May 28, 1955; BA cum laude, Univ. Md., 1977; JD magna cum laude, Georgetown Univ., 1981. Bar: DC 1982, Md. 1982. Law clk. Judge J. Dudley Digges, Md. Ct. Appeals; ptnr., co-chmn. Private Equity practice group DLA Piper Rudnick Gray Cary, Washington. Contbr. articles to profl. jours. Office: DLA Piper Rudnick Gray Cary 1200 19th St NW Washington DC 20036-2412 Office Phone: 202-861-3894. Office Fax: 202-223-2085. Business E-Mail: anthony.rickert@dlapiper.com.

**RICKERT, JEANNE MARTIN M.,** lawyer; b. Cambridge, Mass., May 13, 1953; d. Robert Torrence and Margaret (Mutchler) Martin; m. Scott Edwin Rickert, Aug. 19, 1978. BA, Cornell U., 1975; JD, Case Western U., 1978. Bar: Ohio 1980, admitted to practice U.S Dist. Ct. (No. Dist.) Ohio 1980. Law clk. to Judge Leroy J. Contie Jr. U.S. Dist. Ct. Ohio, Akron, 1978-80; assoc. Jones, Day, Reavis & Pogue, Cleve., 1980-86; ptnr. Jones & Day, Cleve., 1987—. Author: The Limited Liability Company in Ohio: 1994 Senate Bill 74, with Commentary and Practice Pointers, 1994; co-author (with John Currivan): Ohio Limited Liability Companies, 1999. Mem.: ABA, Ohio State Bar Assn. (corp. law com. 1985—), Cleve. Bar Assn., Order of the Coif. Office: Jones Day Reavis & Pogue N Point 901 Lakeside Ave E Cleveland OH 44114-1190 Office Phone: 216-586-7220. Office Fax: 216-579-0212. Business E-Mail: jmrickert@jonesday.com.

**RICKERT, JONATHAN BRADLEY,** retired foreign service officer; b. Washington, July 23, 1937; s. Van Dusen and Margaret Eleanor (Bradley) R.; m. Ulla Gerd Margareta Granstrand, June 20, 1969; children: Ulla Margaret, Jonathan Bernt. AB cum laude, Princeton U, 1959; diploma Russian lang., U.S. Army Lang. Sch., 1962; student, Harvard U., 1976-77; MA, George Washington U., 1982. Rotational jr. officer Exec. Sec. State Dept., 1963-65; consular officer Embassy, London, 1965-66, staff aide to amb., polit. officer Moscow, 1966-68; exchanges officer Office Soviet and Eastern European Exchanges State Dept., 1969-70, with Romanian Lang. Tng. FSI, 1971; consular officer Embassy Bucharest, 1971-73, polit. officer, 1973-74; spl. asst. to U.S. Rep. U.S. Delegation MBFR, Vienna, 1974-76; polit./labor officer Embassy Port of Spain, 1977-80; desk officer Trinidad, Guyana, Suriname, acting dep. dir. Office Caribbean Affairs State Dept., 1980-82, desk officer Romania, Office Eastern European and Yugoslav Affairs, 1982-84, with Bulgarian Lang. Tng., 1984-85; dep. chief mission Embassy Sofia, 1985-88; chief European Assignments divsn. State Dept., 1988-90; legis. asst. to Sen Bob Packwood, 1990-91; dep. chief mission Embassy Bucharest, 1991-95; dir. Office of N. Cen. European Affairs State Dept., 1995-98, program officer Office of the Coord. for U.S. Assistance to Europe and Eurasia, 1998—2005; bd. dirs. Project on Ethnic Rels., Princeton, N.J., 1999. With U.S. Army, 1961-62. Mem. Am. Fgn. Svc. Assn. Episcopalian. Personal E-mail: therickets@hotmail.com.

**RICKERT, ROBERT RICHARD,** pathologist, educator; b. Harrisburg, Pa., Oct. 19, 1936; s. Alton G. and Henrietta (Gey) R.; m. Sonja Murray Hansen, Aug. 26, 1961; children: Kristin, Robin, Anne. AB, U. Mich., 1958; MD, John Hopkins U., 1962. Diplomat Am. Bd. of Pathology. Intern Yale-New Haven (Conn.) Med. Ctr., 1962-63, resident in pathology, 1963-64, 66-67; rsch. assoc. Atomic Bomb Casulty Commn., Hiroshima, Japan, 1964-66; asst. prof. pathology Yale U. Sch. Med., New Haven, 1968-70; attending pathologist Yale New Haven Med. Ctr., 1968-70; dir. surg. pathology U. Med. and Dentistry N.J.-N.J. Med. Sch., Newark, 1970-73, assoc. prof. pathology, 1970-73; clin. prof. pathology U. of Med. and Dentistry N.J.-N.J. Med. Sch., Newark, 1985—; co-chmn. dept. pathology St. Barnabas Med. Ctr., Livingston, NJ, 1973-2000, chmn. dept. pathology, 2000—. Adj. assoc. prof. pathology Columbia U. Coll. Physicians & Surgeons, N.Y.C., 1974-89. Contbr. chpts. to med. textbooks and articles to profl. jours. Chmn. med. com. Am. Cancer Soc., N.J., 1989-91, v.p. 1991-93, pres. elect 1993-94, pres. 1995-97 (Physician of Yr., N.J. Divsn., 1998), chief med. officer, bd. dirs. Ea. divsn., 1998-2000. Recipient honoree, ACS Coaches vs. Cancer Classic, 2003. Fellow Coll. Am. Pathologists (vice-chmn., internat. regional commr. commn. on lab. accreditation, Pathologist of Yr. 2001), Am. Soc. Clin. Pathologists, U.S.-Can. Acad. Pathology; mem. AMA, N.J. Soc. Pathologists (pres. 1980-82), Gastrointestinal Pathology Soc. (pres. 1988-89), Med. Soc. N.J., Acad. Medicine N.J. (trustee 1988—, treas. 1994-95, v.p. 1995-97, pres. 1998), Am. Soc. Cytopathology, Short Hills Club, Phi Beta Kappa, Alpha Omega Alpha. Republican. Congregationalist. Avocations: antiques, wine collecting, art. Office: St Barnabas Med Ctr Dept Pathology Livingston NJ 07039

**RICKETSON, MARY E.,** dean, lawyer; m. Nathan Ben Coats. JD, U. Denver, 1978. Asst. atty gen., Colo.; dep. dist. atty. Colo.; private practice specializing in employment dispute mediation; exec. dir. Colo. Lawyer's Com., dean, univ. prof. U. Denver Sturm Coll. Law, 2000. Affiliated Judicial Arbitrators and Mediators. Trustee Dian Fossey Found. Internat.; co-chair Mayor Wellington Webb's 2025 Commn., 2002. Recipient Women of Distinction award, Mill High Girl Scouts, 2004, Edwin Wolf award, Lawyers Com. Civil Rights Under Law, 2004, Mile High Coun. Girl Scouts award, 2004. Mem.: Colo. Hispanic Bar Assn. (Cmty. Svc. award 2003, award 2003), Colo. Profl. Soc. on Abuse of Children, Colo. Women's Bar Found., Colo. Women's Bar Assn. (Mary Lathrop Award 2003).

**RICKETTS, JAMES F.,** treasurer; BSBA, Ohio State U., 1969, MBA, 1973. Various treasury and controller positions Ford Motor Cor.; corp. v.p., treas. Ingram Micro Inc, Santa Ana, Calif., 1996—. Bd. dirs. Mission Aviation Fellowship, PACTEC. With U.S. Army, 1970—71. Office: Ingram Micro Inc 1600 E St Andrew Pl PO Box 25125 Santa Ana CA 92799

**RICKETTS, JOHN JOE,** securities company executive; b. Nebr. City, Nebr., July 16, 1941; s. Donovan Platte and Florence Marie (Erhart) R.; m. Marlene Margaret Volkmer, June 15, 1963; children: J. Peter, Thomas, Laura. BA, Creighton U., 1969. Counselor Father Flannagan's Boys Home, Boys Town, Nebr., 1967—68; with sales dept. Dean Witter & Co., Omaha, 1968—74; investment counselor Ricketts & Co., Omaha, 1974—75; pres. Ameritrade Inc., Omaha, 1975—82, CEO 1982—99, co-CEO 1999—. Named one of Forbes' Richest Americans, 2006. Republican. Roman Catholic. Office: Ameritrade Holding Corp 4211 S 102d St Omaha NE 68127*

**RICKETTS, SONDRA LOU,** librarian; b. McFall, Mo., Aug. 4, 1941; d. Jewell E. and Daisie Glenn (Weller) Rainey; m. Rex Errol Ricketts, June 14, 1964; children: Chad Errol, Trina Rae, Neysa Carrie. BS, U. Mo., 1963—. Cert. tchr., Mo. Libr. East Ladue Jr. High Sch., Ladue, Mo., 1963-65; administrv. asst. Jacksonville (Ill.) Pub. Libr., 1965; reference libr. Ill. Coll. Jacksonville, 1965-66; cataloger Stephens Coll., Columbia, Mo., 1966-69; libr. Clark (Mo.) Elem. Sch., 1981-95, Middle Grove Elem. Sch., 1996—2003. Sun. sch. tchr. Presbyn. Ch., Columbia, 1977-84; mem. Hallsville (Mo.) Sch. bond com., 1980; cmty. leader Hallsville 4-H, 1980-82, mem. state com., Columbia, 1985, project leader Hallsville 4-H, 1980-85, 94-2000; bd. dirs. 4-H Found., Columbia, 1991—, sec., 1997-2000; mem. Boone County 4-H Auction com., 1994-2000; mem. ways and means com., hallsville

PTA, 1980, publicity com., 1981; co-chmn. Hallsville H.S. All Night Sr. party, 1985, 90. Conf. honoree AIJCA, 1991. Mem. Am. Internat. Charolais Assn., Mo. Assn. Sch. Librs., Mid.-Mo. Regional Assn. Sch. Librs., Mo. Univ. Alumnae Assn., Boone County Alumnae Assn., Alpha Chi Omega Alumni Assn., U. Mo. Jefferson Club, Pi Lambda Theta. Avocations: crafts, swimming, reading, dance, antiques. E-mail: rex.ricketts@gte.net.

**RICKEY, HORACE B., JR.,** retired civil engineer, retired architectural engineer; b. New Orleans, July 2, 1924; s. Horace Bushnell Rickey and Marjorie Bouvier; m. Jewel Katherine Seybold, Aug. 15, 1947 (dec. Dec. 1984); chlidren: Sharon Jewel, Marjorie Anna, Priscilla Gail; m. Maude Elizabeth Dudley, Nov. 30, 1985 (div. Apr. 1995). BSCE, U. Wyo., 1947, BS in Archtl. Engring., 1948. Registered profl. engr., La.; lic. profl. surveyor, realtor, ins. agt., La. CAO Horace B. Rickey Constrn. Co., Lafayette, La., 1948—67; pvt. practice engring. Horace B. Rickey Jr. PE, Lafayette, 1948-89; pres. S.W. Materials, Lafayette, 1956-78, S.W. Homes, Lafayette, 1963-78, Buck Enterprises, Albuquerque, 1978-86; real estate agt. Lafayette, 1986-92; dir. pub. works City of Lafayette, 1992; project engr. Lafayette Consol. Govt., 1993-98; ret., 1998. V.p. Union Fed. S&L, Lafayette, 1960-85; sec., treas.. CAO Motor Lodges of Lafayette, 1966-86; operating dir. Computers for Bus. Mgmt., Lafayette, 1970-86; pres. CAO Buck Enterprises Motel, Albuquerque, 1978-86. Scoutmaster, cubmaster Boy Scouts Am., New Orleans, 1942-43; v.p. Bayou coun. Girl Scouts U.S., Lafayette, 1961-65, pres., 1965-69; bd. dirs. Hunter-Jumper Assn., La., 1971, Southwestern La. Inst. Assn., Lafayette, 1969-72, Salvation Army, Lafayette, 1960-62; chmn. constrn. divsn. United Fund, Lafayette, 1968, campaign chmn., 1969, pres., 1970, bd. dirs. Lafayette C. of C., 1960-62, 69-71, v.p., 1961; chmn. Citizen's Adv. Com. for City and Parish under Interstate Act, Lafayette, 1960-62; chmn. Rep. Parish Exec. Com., Lafayette, 1953-65; sec. Rep. State Ctrl. Com., La., 1955-65; deacon First Presbyn. Ch., Lafayette, 1958-62, ruling elder, 1962-74. Sgt. AUS, 1943-46, ETO. Recipient Thanks Badge, Bayou Coun. Girl Scouts U.S., 1969, Outstanding Svcs. to Arts award, La. Arts Coun., 1971, Expert Tapiestier award, Acadian Weavers, 1978. Avocations: flat loom weaving, Goblein tapestry weaving, genealogy. Home: 109 Falbrook Ave Lafayette LA 70506

**RICKLEFS, DALE LYNNE,** library director; b. Chgo., July 29, 1953; d. Glenn Harley and Eleanor Clara Rogers; 1 child, Reyhan. BA, Ill. Wesleyan U., 1974; MLS, U. Tex., 1977. Libr. Radian Corp., Austin, Tex., 1975—80; libr. dir. City of Round Rock, Tex., 1980—. Mem. ex officio Friends Round Rock Pub. Libr., 1983—, Round Rock Pub. Libr. Found., 1991—; bd. dirs. Round Rock Cmty. Choir, 1998—2003; pres United Way Greater Williamson Co., Round Rock, 2003—; boy scout dist. cub trainer Boy Scouts Am. Tomahawk Dist., Austin-Georgetown, Tex., 1991—92; pres. Maste St. Quilt Guild, 2002—03. Recipient Dist. Cubscouter of Yr., Boy Scouts Am. Tomahawk Dist., Texas, 1992. Mem.: ALA, Texas Mcpl. League Libr. Dir.'s Divsn. (pres. 1988—89), Tex. Libr. Assn. (chmn. dist. 3 1984—85). Avocations: machine embroidery, old house renovations, painting, quilting. Office: City Round Rock Pub Libr 216 E Main St Round Rock TX 78664 Office Phone: 512-218-7010. Business E-Mail: dale@round-rock.tx.us.

**RICKLES, DONALD JAY,** comedian, actor; b. LI, NY, May 8, 1926; s. Max S. and Etta (Feldman) R.; m. Barbara Sklar, Mar. 14, 1965; children: Mindy Beth, Lawrence Corey. Grad., Am. Acad. Dramatic Arts, N.Y.C. Appeared in TV shows The Don Rickles Show, 1971-72, C.P.O. Sharkey, 1976-77, Foul-Ups, Bleeps and Blunders, 1984, Daddy Dearest, 1993; appeared in movies Run Silent, Run Deep, 1958, The Rat Race, 1960, Kelly's Heroes, 1992, Casino, 1995, Toy Story, 1995, Quest for Camelot, 1998, Toy Story 2, 1999, The Wool Cap, 2004, others; Reno and Lake Tahoe, Nev., Stardust Hotel, Las Vegas, Resorts Atlantic City, numerous other nightclubs; numerous appearances TV variety shows; rec. albums include Don Rickles Speaks and Hello Dummy. Served with USN, 1943-45. Named Entertainer of Yr. Friars Club, 1974, Entertainer of Yr. Am. Gaming Assn., 2004, Las Vegas Comedian of Yr., Las Vegas Conv. and Visitor's Authority, 2004; awarded star on Hollywood Walk of Fame, 2000. Office: care Shefrin Co 808 S Ridgeley Dr Los Angeles CA 90036-4727

**RICKLING, IRAIDA BADILLO,** librarian; b. Aguada, P.R., Sept. 13, 1932; d. Miguel and Rosa C. (Vega) Badillo; m. John T. Rickling, Dec. 21, 1970 (div. 1977); 1 child, Mark Thomas. BA magna cum laude, U. P.R., Rio Piedras, 1952; MLS, Carnegie Inst. Tech., 1954. Cataloguer U. P.R. Library, Rio Piedras, 1954-55; post librarian Camp Losey, P.R., 1955-56; reference librarian U.S. Army War Coll. Library, Carlisle Barracks, Pa., 1956-59; cataloguer, reference librarian Martin Marietta Corp., Orlando, 1959-61; librarian Aerospace Corp./ETRO Office, Patrick AFB, Fla., 1961-68; head reference dept. U. Cen. Fla. Library, Orlando, 1968-69; circulation librarian Kennedy Space Ctr. (Fla.) Library, 1969-72; librarian Fla. Solar Energy Ctr., U. Ctrl. Fla., Cocoa, 1975—. Recipient Nina Brotherton Prize Carnegie Library Sch., 1954, Outstanding Performance award U.S. Army War Coll., 1958, award for Excellence U. Cen. Fla. Found., 1984. Mem. Spl. Libraries Assns., Fla. Library Assn., Library Assn. Brevard, Phi Kappa Phi, Beta Phi Mu. Democrat. Roman Catholic. Avocations: reading, travel, theater. Home: 347 Jack Dr Cocoa Beach FL 32931-3841 Office: Fla Solar Energy Ctr 1679 Clearlake Rd Cocoa FL 32922-5703 Office Phone: 321-638-1460. Business E-Mail: rickling@fsec.ucf.edu.

**RICKMAN, ALAN,** actor; b. Hammersmith, London, England, Feb. 21, 1946; Student, Royal Acad. of Dramatic Art. Stage appearances: The Seagull, Mephisto, Les Liaisons Dangereuses, 1985, 87 (Tony nominee Best Actor 1987), Tango at the End of Winter, 1991, Hamlet, 1992, Antony and Cleopatra, 1990, Private Lives (Tony nominee, Best Stage Actor award Variety Club Show Bus. Awards 2002); (TV movies) Romeo and Juliet, Masterpiece Theater, 1978, Therese Raquin, 1980, Barchester Chronicles, 1984, Spirit of Man, 1989, Revolutionary Witness, 1989, Victoria Wood's All Day Breakfast, 1992, Fallen Angels, 1993, Rasputin, 1996 (Golden Globe, Emmy and SAG awards for Best Actor), Victoria Wood with All the Trimmings, 2000, We Know Where You Live, 2001, Something the Lord Made, 2004; (films) Die Hard, 1988, The January Man, 1989, Robin Hood: Prince of Thieves, 1991, Quigley Down Under, 1990, Truly, Madly, Deeply, 1991, Closet Land, 1991, Close My Eyes, 1991, Bob Roberts, 1992, Mesmer, 1993, An Awfully Big Adventure, 1994, Sense and Sensibility, 1995, Michael Collins, 1996, Judas Kiss, 1998, Dogma, 1998, Dark Harbor, 1998, Galaxy Quest, 1999, Play, 2000, Blow Dry, 2001, Harry Potter and the Sorcerer's Stone, 2001, Search for John Gissin, 2001, (also exec prodr.) Willows, 2001, Harry Potter and the Chamber of Secrets, 2002, Love Actually, 2003, Harry Potter and the Prisoner of Azkaban, 2004, (voice) The Hitchhiker's Guide to the Galaxy, 2005, Harry Potter and the Goblet of Fire, 2005; writer, dir.: The Winter Guest, 1997 (Best Film award Chgo. Film Festival). Office: Oxford House 76 Oxford St London W1N 0AX England

**RICKMAN, WILLIAM THOMAS,** choral director; b. Mt. Pleasant, Tex., Oct. 31, 1977; s. Paul Wayne and Margret Etta Rickman; m. Elizabeth Leigh Foster, July 11, 1998; 1 child, Ethan Paul. B in Music Edn., Ark. Tech U., 2004; postgrad., Boston U., 2006—. Cert. svc. technician Radiant Systems, 2001, engr. Radiant Systems, 2001, hardware engr. IBM, 2000, engr. IBM, 2000, network engr. Leviton Corp., 2000, Leviton Corp., 2000; lic. tchr. Ark. Dept. Edn., 2004. Regional mgr. midwest Spartan Computer Services, Greer, 2000—01; technician Contemporary Music Services, Russellville, Ark., 2002—05; choral dir. Dardanelle HS, Ark., 2004—05, Harrison Jr. HS, Ark., 2005—. Singer Vocalis, Bentonville, Ark., 2005—. Supporter Dem. Party Boone County, Harrison, 2005. Scholar Presdl. Scholar, U. of Cen. Ark., 1996-1999. Mem.: Am. Choral Dirs. Assn., Phi Mu Alpha Sinfonia (life; pres. 2003—04). Democrat. Mem. Disciples Of Christ Ch. Achievements include research in Political Impact of Music in American and English Society; The Role of Music Education in Children's Social Development. Avocations: travel, aviation, golf. Office: Harrison Jr High School 515 S Pine Harrison AR 72601 Office Phone: 870-741-8503. Business E-Mail: trickman@gobs.k12.ar.us.

**RICKS, JOHN ADDISON, III,** history professor; b. Charlotte, NC, Aug. 18, 1939; s. John Addison Jr. and Mamye Snow (Turner) R.; m. Nancy Elaine Ricks, Apr. 23 1966; children: Elizabeth Anne, John Addison IV. BA, Davidson Coll., 1961; MA, Tulane U., 1963; PhD, U. N.C., 1974. Instr. history Montreat- Anderson Coll., NC, 1966-68; from instr. to prof. Valdosta State U., Ga., 1968-88; prof. history, chmn. social sci. edn., bus. adminstrn. div. Mid. Ga. Coll., Cochran, 1988—2003. Contbr. articles to jour., newspapers. Pres. Friends of the Libr., Cochran, 1989-90; clk. of session, elder First Presbyn. Ch., Eastman, 1990-93; 1998-2001, scoutmaster Boy Scouts Am., Valdosta, 1982-84; mem. Valdosta Bd. Edn., 1976-80. 1st lt. US Army, 1963-65. Fulbright Found. grantee, 1992, 97. Mem.: Cochran C. of C., Ga. Assn. Historians (pres. 1994—95, amb.), So. Assn. Secondary Sch. and Coll. (vis. team 1979), So. Assn. Coll. and Sch. (vis. team 1990), Rotary (pres. 1993—94, asst. gov. Dist. 6920, Rotarian of Yr. 1997, Paul Harris fellow 2001), Kiwanis (treas. 1980—82, Kiwanian of Yr. 1979). Democrat. Presbyterian. Avocations: piano, weightlifting, nordic track exercise, reading, chess. Home: 712 Beech St Cochran GA 31014 Office: Cochran Better Hometown Inc 318 Second St Cochran GA 31014 Office Phone: 478-934-0017. E-mail: jricks39@yahoo.com.

**RICKS, JOYCIA CAMILLA,** retired lawyer; b. Atlanta, Feb. 17, 1949; d. George Palmer and Johnnie Mae (Ricks) Redd. BBA, Albany State Coll., 1971; MS, Ga. State U., 1977; JD, Woodrow Wilson Coll. Law, Atlanta, 1979, LLM, 1987. Bar: Ga. 1979, US Dist. Ct. (no. dist.) Ga. 1979, US Ct. Appeals (5th cir.) 1979. Acctg. clk. Gulf Oil Corp., Atlanta, 1971; clk. EEOC, Atlanta, 1971-73, paralegal specialist, 1973-79, investigator, 1979-91, supervisory investigator, 1992-2000; complaints mgr. CDC, Atlanta, 2000—03; gen. counsel Albany State U. Alumni Assn., 1986—90, 2005—. Recipient Presdl. citation award Equal Opportunity in Higher Edn., Washington, 1981. Mem. ABA, ATLA, Atlanta Bar Assn., Albany State Coll. Alumni Assn. (pres. Atlanta chpt. 1983-85), Ga. State U. Alumni Assn., Women of the Ch. Presbyn. (hon. life), Am. Bus. Women's Assn. (Woman of Yr., Tara chpt. 1985, 91, Peach chpt. 2003), Spreading Oak Cmty. Club. Democrat. Presbyterian.

**RICKS, MARK G.,** lieutenant governor, former state senator; b. Rexburg, Idaho, July 4, 1924; s. Peter J. and Emily E. (Arnold) R.; m. Evelyn Tonks, Aug. 9, 1944; children: Michael T., Gary M., Alan D., Adele Ricks Nielsen, Glen L., Kathie Ricks Tensmeyer, Grant H., Merle K., Douglas T. AS in Agr., Ricks Coll. Mem. Idaho State Senate, 1979-94, majority leader, 1983-88, chmn. reapportionment com., 1982, chmn. senate commerce and labor commn., 1981-82, vice chmn. senate fin. com., 1989-94, state affairs com., chmn., 1989-94, chmn. revenue and projection com., 1989-94, chmn. reapportionment com., 1990-94; lt. gov., State of Idaho, 2006—; Mem. exec. and adv. bd. council Boy Scouts Am. Named to Eastern Idaho Agrl. Hall of Fame, 1989, Idaho Blue Ribbon Task Force, 2002; named One of Ten Outstanding Legislators Nat. Rep. Legislators Assn., 1987; recipient Community Svc. Prodn. and Example award Rexburg C. of C., 1976, Outstanding Svc. award Madison Sch. Dist., 1987, Distinguished Alumni award Ricks Coll., 1988. Mem. Nat. Conf. State Legis. (exec. com. 1989-94, chmn. nominating com. 1988, mem. rsch. and grants com., vice chmn. fed. taxation com., vice chmn. trade and econ. devel. com., mem. budget and rules com., co-chmn. reapportionment com. 1989, vice chmn. state fed. assembly 1988), Coun. State Govts. (exec. com., budget com. 1989-90, chmn. western legislative conf. 1988-89, ann. meeting com. 1989-90), Idaho Wheat Growers, Nat. Fedn. Ind. Bus., Rexburg C. of C. (maj. gifts com. Ricks Coll.). Republican. Mormon. Office: Office Lt Governor Rm 225 State Capitol Boise ID 83720 Office Phone: 208-334-2200. Office Fax: 208-334-3259.*

**RICKS, THOMAS MILLER,** historian, academic administrator; b. Lafayette, Ind, Oct. 15, 1938; s. Michael T. and Veronica K. (Jordan) R.; m. Janice D. Grasso, Aug. 26, 1967; children: Cynthia C., Laila M. BA, U. Notre Dame, 1961; MA, Ind. U., 1968, PhD, 1975. Tchr. history Tehran Internat. Sch., 1972-73; instr. history Macalester Coll., St. Paul, 1974-75; asst. prof. history Georgetown U., Washington, 1975-83; asst. dir. Ctr. for Arab and Islamic Studies Villanova U., Pa., 1985-92; dir. internat. studies, 1986—2002; lectr. history U. Pa., 2002—05. Adj. assoc. prof. history Ctr. for Arab and Islamic Studies, Villanova U., 1985-2002; vis. asst. prof. history Birzeit U., Palestine, 1983-85; mem. Am. Friends Svc. Com., Mid. East Panel, 1996—. Editor, compiler, author: (bibliography) Persian Studies: A Bibliography, 1970, Iran: Contemporary Persian Literature, 1974, Critical Perspectives on Persian Literature, 1976; co-author: (textbook) Middle East: Past and Present, 1986; co-founder, co-editor: (jour.) Rev. of Iranian Polit. Economy and History, 1976-80, Birzeit Rsch. Rev., 1985-90; assoc. editor: Frontiers: An Interdisciplinary Jour. of Study Abroad, 1994—. Vol. Iran III program Peace Corps, Mashhad and Mahabad, Iran, 1964-66. Scholar, Ind. U., 1966-67, Birzeit U., 1983-84, Fulbright Found., 1993, 94, 95, Guest scholar, Haverford Coll., 2003, Spencer Found., 2005—06; Nat. Def. Edn. Act grantee US Dept. Edn., 1967-70, grantee Fulbright-Hays Found., 1971-72, NEH, 1976, 91, Social Sci. Rsch. Coun., 1977, U.S. Dept. Edn., 1988-90, Pa. Dept. Edn., 1990-94, Palestinian Am. Rsch. Ctr., 2003, Spencer Found. Fellow, 2005-. Mem. Coun. for Internat. Ednl. Exch. (bd. dirs. 1997-2000), Coun. for Internat. Edn. of Scholars (bd. dirs. 1996-04), Pa. Coun. for Internat. Edn. (bd. dirs. 1994-03, pres. 1994-99), Mid. East Studies Assn. (co-editor jour. 1980-82), Ctr. for Iranian Rsch. and Analysis (bd. dirs. 1997-2000), Soc. for Iranian Studies (treas. 1974-76), Mid. East Inst., Am. Hist. Assn., Oral History Assn., Hist. Soc. Pa., Presbyn. Hist. Soc., Sons of Civil War Vets., Palestinian Am. Rsch. Ctr. Democrat. Roman Catholic. Avocations: civil war living history/reenactment, music. E-mail: tmricks@sas.upenn.edu.

**RICO-GUTIERREZ, LUIS F.,** architecture educator; BArch, ITESM, 1986; grad. degree in modular design, Rafael Leoz Found., 1988; M in Bldg. Performance, Carnegie Mellon U., 1997. Jr. designer Rafael Leoz Found., Madrid, 1988—90, projects mgr., 1990—91, mgr. arch. dept., 1991—92; prin. CAD cons. Madrid, 1992—93; prof. ITESM, Queretaro, 1993—96; asst. prof. Carnegie Mellon U. Sch. Arch., Pitts., 1996—, assoc. dean Coll. Fine Arts, 1996—, assoc. head, 1996—. Recipient Nationwide award for ednl. innovation, Borrego Dorado ITESM, Mexico, 1997, Andrew Heiskell award for tech. enhanced learning in internat. edn., Inst. for Internat. Edn., 2003. Office: Carnegie Mellon Univ Sch Arch CFA 201 201 College Fine Arts Pittsburgh PA 15213

**RICOL, RENE JEAN,** accountant; b. Lyon, France, Dec. 26, 1950; s. Benoit and Marie Antoinette (Mercier) R.; children: Raphaelle, Stephane, Matthieu, Antoine, Arthur, Victor. MBA in Econs., Lyon U., France, 1973. Ptnr. Calan Ramolino Ricol, Paris, 1978—80, mng. ptnr., 1980—86; pres. Ricol-Lasteyrie & Assocs., Paris, 1986—; hon. pres. France Defi, Paris, 1989-97, Euro Defi, 1991-94. Pres. Compagnie Regionale Des Commissaires Aux Comptes, 1982-84, Compagnie Nationale Des Commissaires Aux Comptes, 1985-89, Conseil Superieur de l'Ordre des Experts-Comptables, 1994-98; pres. Internat. Fedn. Accts., NY, 2006—. Decorated comdr. Legion of Honor, comdr. Nat. Order of Merit (France). Office: Ricol-Lasteyrie & Associes 2 Ave Hoche 75008 Paris France Business E-mail: rr@ricol-lasteyrie.fr.

**RICORDI, CAMILLO,** surgeon, medical researcher; b. N.Y.C., Apr. 1, 1957; m. Valerie A. Grace, Aug. 8, 1986; children: M. Caterina, Eliana G., Carlo A. MD, U. Milan (Italy) Sch. Medicine, 1982. Trainee in gen. surgery San Raffaele Inst., Milan, 1982-85; NIH trainee Washington U. Sch. Medicine, St. Louis, 1985-88; attending surgeon San Raffaele Inst., Milan, 1988-89; asst. prof. to assoc. prof. surgery U. Pitts., Pa., 1989-93; prof. surgery and medicine, pathology, microbiology and immunology, chief divsn. cellular transpl. Diabetes Rsch. Inst., U. Miami, Fla., 1993—, sci. dir., chief acad. officer Fla., 1996—, Stacy Joy Goodman chair in Diabetes Rsch. 1998—. Reviewer of applications for grants Can. and Am. Diabetes Assns., Juvenile Diabetes Found., NIH; chmn. First and Third Internat. Congresses of Cell Transplant Soc., Pitts., 1992, Miami, 1996, 5th Internat. Congress on Pancreas and Islet Transplantation, Miami, 1995, others; mem. editl. bd. Transplantation, Cell Transplantation, Transplantation Procs., Jour. Tissue Engring. Editor: Pancreatic Islet Cell Transplantation, 1992, Methods in Cell Transplantaion, 1995; co-editor-in-chief Cell Transplantation, Graft; assoc.

editor Am. Jour. Transplantation, 2003—; contbr. numerous chpts. to books and articles to jours. including Immunology Today, Jour. Clin. Investigation, New Eng. Jour. Medicine, Hepatology, Diabetes, Transplantation, Endocrinology, Procs. NAS, USA, Am. Jour. Physiology, Surgery, Nature, Nature Genetics, Lancet, Nature Immunology Rev. Grantee Juvenile Diabetes Found. Internat., 1988—, NIH, 1993—; recipient Nessim Habif World prize of surgery, 2001. Mem. AAAS, Cell Transplant Soc. (founder, pres. 1992-94), Am. Soc. Transplant Surgeons, Internat. Pancreas and Islet Transplant Assn. (v.p. 1979-99, pres. 1999-2001), The Transplantation Soc., Am. Diabetes Assn. (councillor, 2003-, Outstanding Sci. Achievement award 2002). Achievements include patents in cellular biotechnologies. Office: U Miami Diabetes Rsch Inst PO Box 016310 Miami FL 33101-6310 Business E-Mail: ricardi@miami.edu.

**RICOUART, JANINE,** language educator; b. Acquin, France, Jan. 27, 1955; d. André Ricouart, Anne-Marie Bernard; life ptnr. PhD, U. Calif., Davis, 1985. Vis. asst. prof. U. Miami, Oxford, Ohio, 1985—86; prof. French Mason U, Fairfax, Ohio, 1986—. Author: Ecriture féminine et violence: Une étude de Maguerite Duras, 1991; editor: Marguerite Duras Lives On, 1998, Relectures de Madeleine Monette, 1999; co-editor: Les secrets de la sphinx: relectures de L'oeuvre d'Anne-Marie Alonzo, 2004; translator: (short stories) Stephanie's Book, 1999; contbr. chapters to books, articles to profl. jours. Instr. Lit. Coun. Northern Va., Fairfax, 1988—90; mem. emergency svc. Red Cross, Carmel, 1993—94, Alexandria, 1994—2001. Recipient Grad. Student Travel award, U. Calif., Davis, 1984, Sabbatical award, George Mason U., 1993—94; fellow, U. Calif., Davis, 1984—85; grantee, 1983, Humanities Rsch. grant, 1984, Summer Rsch. grant, George Mason U., 1996, Tech. Asst. Program grant, 2001, Tchg. Across the Curriculum grant 2001—02. Mem.: Am. Coun. Quebec Studies, Conseil International d'Études Francophones, Women in French. Avocation: diving. Office: George Mason Univ MCL 3E5 4400 University Dr Fairfax VA 22030-4444 Business E-Mail: jricouar@gmu.edu.

**RIDDELL, STEPHEN W.,** lawyer; b. Quincy, Mass., 1959; BA magna cum laude, Univ. SC, 1981; JD with honors, Univ. NC, 1985. Bar: Ga. 1985, cert.: Am. Arbitration Assn. (arbitrator) 1993. Assoc. Troutman Sanders LLP, Atlanta, 1985—93, ptnr., labor, employment, 1993—, mng. ptnr., Atlanta office, and mem. exec. com. Named a Super Lawyer, Atlanta Mag., 2004—05, Legal Elite in labor/employment, Ga. Trend Mag., 2004—05; named one of Leading Lawyers for Bus., Chambers USA, 2004—05. Mem.: ABA, State Bar Ga., Phi Beta Kappa. Office: Troutman Sanders LLP Ste 5200 600 Peachtree St NE Atlanta GA 30308-2216 Office Phone: 404-885-3408. Office Fax: 404-962-6668. Business E-Mail: stephen.riddell@troutmansanders.com.

**RIDDER, LINDA GAYLE,** librarian; b. Chgo., Apr. 17, 1949; d. Gale Eugene and Yvonne Lucille (Marcotte) A.; m. George Larry Ridder, Mar. 29, 1970; 1 child, Michael Eric. BA English, St. Mary's U., 1971; MS Libr. Sci., Our Lady of the Lake U., 1977. Cert. media specialist; profl. libr.; provisional cert. secondary English and social studies, Tex. Tchr. fourth grade St. Thomas More Cath. Sch., San Antonio, Tex., 1971-72; tchr. English/dept. coord. Sam Rayburn Mid. Sch., San Antonio, 1972-77; libr. media specialist Gregorio Esparza Elem., San Antonio, 1977-85, H.B. Zachry Mid. Sch., San Antonio, 1985—. Mem. Sch. Leadership Team, 1985—, Sch. Adv. Team, 1994—, recording sec.; mem. Northside Dist. Comm. Network Com., 1996—, Zachry Tech. Task Force Com., 1996—. Author Middle School Integrated Curriculum Guide of Library Skills, 1991; dir. accreditation reports, 1979, 84. Mem. St. Luke's Cath. Ch., San Antonio, 1975—. Mem. Nat. Reading Assn., Tex. Libr. Assn., Phi Delta Kappa. Home: 4607 Lightning Ln San Antonio TX 78238-2907 Office: HB Zachry Mid Sch 9410 Timber Path San Antonio TX 78250-4921

**RIDDER, P. ANTHONY (PAUL ANTHONY RIDDER),** newspaper company executive; b. Duluth, Minn., Sept. 22, 1940; s. Bernard H. and Jane (Delano) Ridder; m. Constance Louise Meach, Nov. 6, 1960; children: Katherine Lee Pennoyer, Linda Jane, Susan Delano Cobb, Paul Anthony Jr. BA in Econs., U. Mich., 1962. With Aberdeen (S.D.) Am. News, 1962—63; With Pasadena (Calif.) Star News, 1963—64; with San Jose (Calif.) Mercury News, 1964—86, bus. mgr., 1968—75, gen. mgr., 1975—77, pub., 1977—86, pres., 1979—86, Knight-Ridder Inc., Miami, Fla., 1989—95, pres., chmn., CEO, 1995—. Bd. dirs. Seattle Times, Knight-Ridder, Inc.; adv. bd. Stanford U. Grad. Sch. Bus. Bd. trustees Santa Clara U. Named Calif. Pub. of Yr., 1983, Newspaper Exec. of Yr., Ad Week, 1991. Mem.: San Francisco Golf Club, Pine Valley Golf Club, Cypress Point Club. Office: Knight-Ridder Inc Ste 1500 50 W San Fernando St San Jose CA 95113-2413*

**RIDDICK, DANIEL HOWISON,** obstetrician, gynecologist, priest; b. Lynchburg, Va., Dec. 12, 1941; s. Joseph Henry and Nancy Eloise (Gordon) R.; m. Louisa McIntosh Spruill, June 9, 1963; children: Ellen, Daniel. BA, Duke U., 1963, MD, 1967, PhD in Physiology, 1969. Diplomate Am. Bd. Ob-Gyn, Am. Bd. Reproductive Endocrinology; ordained priest Episc. Ch., 1969. Asst. prof. physiology Duke U., Durham, NC, 1973-74; asst. prof. ob-gyn U. Conn. Sch. Medicine, Farmington, 1974-76, dir. reproductive endocrinology and infertility, 1974-85, assoc. prof. ob-gyn, 1976-81, prof. ob-gyn, 1981-85; prof., chmn. ob-gyn dept. U. Vt., Burlington, 1985-97, assoc. dean grad. med. edn., 1987-88. Editor: Reproductive Endocrinology in Clinical Practice, 1987; editor: (with others) Pathology of Infertility, 1987. Mem. ACOG, Am. Fertility Soc. (pres. 1992-93), Am. Gynecol. and Obstet. Soc. Avocation: sheep-raising. Home: 680 Mayo Rd Huntington VT 05462-9410 Office: Fletcher Allen Health Care Dept of Obstetrics & Gynecology 111 Colchester Ave Burlington VT 05401-1416 Office Phone: 802-847-1400. E-mail: dan.riddick@vtmednet.org.

**RIDDICK, FRANK ADAMS, JR.,** physician, healthcare administrator; b. Memphis, June 14, 1929; s. Frank Adams and Falba (Crawford) Riddick; m. Mary Belle Alston, June 15, 1952; children: Laura Elizabeth Dufresne, Frank Adams III, John Alston. BA cum laude, Vanderbilt U., 1951, MD, 1954. Diplomate Am. Bd. Internal Medicine. Intern Barnes Hosp., St. Louis, 1954—55, resident in medicine, 1957—60; fellow in metabolic diseases Washington U., St. Louis, 1960—61; staff Ochsner Clinic (Ochsner Found. Hosp.), New Orleans, 1961—, head sect. endocrinology and metabolic disease, 1976—83, asst. med. dir., 1968—72, assoc. med. dir., 1972—75, med. dir., 1975—92; CEO Alton Ochsner Med. Found., New Orleans, 1992—2001; CEO emeritus Ochsner Clinic Found., 2001—. Bd. govs. Am. Bd. Internal Medicine, 1973—80; clin. prof. Tulane U., New Orleans, 1977—; trustee Alton Ochsner Med. Found., 1973—, CEO, 1991—; chmn. bd. Ochsner Health Plan, 1993—92; pres. Orleans Svc. Corp., 1976—80, South La. Med. Assocs., New Orleans, 1978—; dir. Brent House Corp., New Orleans, 1980—; chmn. Accreditation Coun. on Grad. Med. Edn., 1988—90, v.p. nat. resident matching program, 1986—90, mem. accreditation coun. on med. edn., 1988—90. Bd. govs. Isidore Newman Sch., New Orleans, 1987—93; trustee St. Martin's Protestant Episc. Sch., Metairie, La., 1970—84. Recipient Tchg. award, Alton Ochsner Med. Found., 1969, Disting. Alumnus award, Castle Heights Mil. Acad., 1979, Physician Exec. award, Am. Coll. Med. Group Administrs., 1984, Disting. Alumnus award, Vanderbilt U. Sch. Medicine, 1988. Master: ACP; fellow: Am. Coll. Physician Execs. (pres. 1987—88); mem.: NAS Inst. Medicine, AMA (ho. dels. 1971—92, chmn. coun. on med. edn. 1983—85, coun. on jud. and ethical affairs 1995—2002, chair 2001—02, Disting. Service award 2003), Am. Group Practice Assn. (pres. 1992—94), Soc. Med. Adminstrs. (pres. 1995—), Am. Diabetes Assn., Endocrine Soc., Am. Soc. Internal Medicine (trustee 1970—76, Disting. Internist award), Cosmos Club, New Orleans Country Club, Boston Club. Office: Ochsner Clinic 1516 Jefferson Hwy New Orleans LA 70121-2429 Home: 150 Broadway 709 New Orleans LA 70118-7610 Office Phone: 504-842-4019. Business E-Mail: friddick@ochsner.org.

**RIDDICK, WINSTON WADE, SR.,** lawyer; b. Crowley, La., Feb. 11, 1941; s. Herbert Hobson and Elizabeth (Wade) Riddick; m. Patricia Ann Turner, Dec. 25, 1961; 1 child, Winston Wade. BA, U. Southwestern La., 1962; MA, U. N.C., 1963; PhD, Columbia U., 1965; JD, La. State U., 1973. Bar: La. 1974, U.S. Dist. Ct. Asst. prof. gov., dir. Inst. Gov. Rsch. La. State U., Baton

Rouge, 1966-67; dir. La. Higher Edn. Facilities Commn., Baton Rouge, 1967-72; exec. asst. state supt. La. Dept. Edn., Baton Rouge, 1972-73; law ptnr. Riddick & Riddick, Baton Rouge, 1973—; asst. commr., gen. counsel La. Dept. Agr., Baton Rouge, 1981-82. Cons. Riddick & Assoc., Baton Rouge, 1973—; part-time law faculty mem. Southern U. Law Ctr., Baton Rouge, 1974—95, assoc. prof., 1995—99, prof. law, 1999—; real estate investor, property mgr., 1975—; exec. asst. atty. gen. State of La., 1987—91. Spl. assst. to. Gov. John McKeithen on Nat. Tchr. Edn. Politics Fellowship, 1966—67; state campaign mgr. Gillis W. Long for Gov., Baton Rouge, 1971; mem. East Baton Rouge Parish Dem. Exec. Com., 1981—84. Mem.: La. Trial Lawyers Assn. (bd. govs. 1978—80). Presbyterian. Office: Riddick & Assocs Inc 1563 Oakley Dr Baton Rouge LA 70806-8622 Office Phone: 225-771-4900 x203. Business E-Mail: wriddick@sulc.edu.

**RIDDIFORD, LYNN MOORHEAD,** biologist, educator; b. Knoxville, Tenn., Oct. 18, 1936; d. James Eli and Virginia Amalia (Berry) Moorhead; m. Alan W. Riddiford, June 20, 1959 (div. Jan. 1966); m. James William Truman, July 28, 1970. AB magna cum laude, Radcliffe Coll., 1958; PhD, Cornell U., 1961. Rsch. fellow in biology Harvard U., Cambridge, Mass., 1961-63, 65-66, asst. prof. biology, 1966—71, assoc. prof., 1971—73; instr. biology Wellesley (Mass.) Coll., 1963—65; from assoc. prof. to prof. zoology U. Wash., Seattle, 1973—2003, prof. biology, 2003—, Virginia and Prentice Bloedel prof., 2000—05, assoc. chmn., 2003—04. Mem. study sect. tropical medicine and parasitology NIH, Bethesda, Md., 1974—78, 1997; mem. Competitive Grants panel USDA, 1979, 89, 95; mem. regulatory biology panel NSF, 1984—88, 2001, 05; mem. governing coun. Internat. Ctr. for Insect Physiology and Ecology, 1985—91, chmn. program com., 1989—91; chmn. adv. com. SeriBiotech, Bangalore, India, 1989; mem. biol. adv. com. NSF, 1992—95; mem. coun. Internat. Cong. Entomology, 1988—, pres., 2000—04; mem. coun. Internat. Fedn. Comparative Endocrine Socs., 1996—, pres., 2001—05. Mem. editl. bd. profl. jours.; contbr. articles to profl. jours. Bd. dirs. Entomol. Found., 1998—2001, chmn., 2001; bd. dirs. Whitney Lab., 2000—04, chmn., 2004. Recipient Gregor J. Mendel award, Czech Republic Acad. Scis., 1998; fellow, NSF, 1958—60, 1961—63, NIH, 1960—61, 1986—87, John S. Guggenheim Found., 1979—80, NIH, 1986—87; grantee, NSF, 1964—65, 1967—, Rockefeller Found., 1970—79, USDA, 1978—82, 1989—. Fellow: AAAS, Entomol. Soc. Am. (Recognition award in insect physiology, biochemistry and toxicology), Royal Entomol. Soc., Am. Acad. Arts and Sci.; mem.: Soc. Exptl. Biology, Soc. Devel. Biology, Am. Soc. Cell Biology, Am. Soc. Biochem. and Molecular Biology, Soc. Integrative and Comparative Biology. Methodist. Home: 16324 51st Ave SE Bothell WA 98012-6138 Office: U Wash Dept Biology PO Box 351800 Seattle WA 98195-1800 Business E-Mail: lmr@u.washington.edu.

**RIDDLE, CHARLES ADDISON, III,** district attorney, former state legislator; b. Marksville, La., June 8, 1951; s. Charles Addison Jr. and Alma Rita (Gremillion) R.; m. Margaret Susan Noone, Mar. 24, 1978; children: Charles Addison IV, John H., Michael J. BA, La. State U., 1976, JD, 1980. Bar: La. 1980, US Dist. Ct. (mid. and we. dists.) La. 1983, U.S. Ct. Appeals (5th cir.) 1988, U.S. Supreme Ct. 1991, U.S. Ct. Vets. Appeals 1994. Ptnr. Riddle & Bennett LLC, Marksville, 1980; pvt. practice Marksville, 1981—2004; mem. La. Ho. of Reps., Baton Rouge, 1992—2003; reelected La. House of Reps., Baton Rouge, 1995—99, 1999—2003; dist. atty. Avoyelles Parish 12th Jud. Dist., 2003—. Elected La. State Dem. Cen. com., Avoyelles Parish, 1983-87, Parish Exec. Demo. Com. 1987-91. Mem. Avoyelles Bar Assn. (pres. 1987-88), Bunkie Rotary (bd. dirs.), Marksville Lions, Marksville C. of C. (pres. 1988-92). Office: PO Box 608 208 E Mark St Marksville LA 71351-2416 Office Phone: 318-253-4551. Personal E-mail: criddle777@aol.com.

**RIDDLE, DOUGLAS S,** music educator; b. Vallejo, Calif., Aug. 21, 1951; m. Gabrielle Karoline Hurler, June 2, 1973. MusB, U. of the Pacific, Stockton, CA, 1973; MusM in Choral Conducting, No. Ariz. U., 1991. Teaching Credential State of Ariz., 1989, Standard Secondary Teaching Credential Calif. Choral music educator East Union H.S., Manteca, Calif., 1973—77, Lodi H.S., Lodi, Calif., 1977—89, Coconino H.S., Flagstaff, Ariz., 1989—. Vp choral activities Choral Directors of Ariz., 1996—98; nw regional gov. Ariz. Music Educator's Assn., 2002—04, sol-ensemble chair, 2004—; repertoire and standards chair (women's chorus) Ariz. Am. Choral Director's Assn., 2004—. Mem. Lodi Arts Commn., Calif., 1987—89. Scholar Paid Choir Mem., Saratoga Potsdam Chorus, 1985. D-Conservative. Office: Coconino HS 2801 N Izabel St Flagstaff AZ 86004 Office Phone: 928-773-8237. Office Fax: 928-773-8247. E-mail: driddle@apscc.org

**RIDDLE, MICHAEL LEE,** lawyer; b. Oct. 7, 1946; s. Joy Lee and Francis Irene (Brandes) R.; m. Suzan Ellen Shaw, May 25, 1969 (div.); m. Carol Jackson, Aug. 13, 1977; 1 child, Robert Andrew. BA, Tex. Tech U., 1969, JD with honors, 1972. Bar: Tex. 1972, U.S. Dist. Ct. (no. dist.) Tex. 1972, U.S. Ct. Appeals (5th cir.) Tex. 1972. Assoc. Geary Brice Barron & Stahl, Dallas, 1972-75; ptnr. Baker Glast Riddle Tuttle & Elliott, Dallas, 1975-80; ptnr., mng. ptnr. Middleburg, Riddle & Gianna, 1980—; chmn., CEO MRG Document Techs., 2000—. Bd. dirs. Dallas Opera. Bd. dirs. U.S.A. Film Festival, pres., 1984-86, North Tex. Pub. Broadcasting, 1992-97; chmn., bd. dirs. Provident Bancorp Tex., 1987-90. Mem. ABA, Tex. Bar Assn., Dallas Bar Assn., Coll. of State Bar of Tex., Lakewood Country Club, Crescent Club. Democrat. Lutheran. Office: 717 N Harwood Ste 2400 Dallas TX 75201 Office Phone: 214-220-6300. Personal E-mail: mriddle@midrid.com.

**RIDDLE, VERYL LEE,** lawyer; b. Campbell, Mo., Dec. 6, 1921; s. Elvis Lloyd and Etter Whitehead (Wood) R.; m. Mary J. Riggs, Jan. 15, 1941 (div. 1967); children— Kay, Jo, Janet, Veryl Lee, Jr.; m. Janet Lewis, Nov. 24, 1985. Student, Southeast Mo. U., 1939-41; student, U. Buffalo, 1942, 45-46; JD, Washington U., St. Louis, 1948. Bar: Mo. 1948, US Dist. Ct. (ea. and we. dists.) Mo. 1949, US Ct. Appeals (8th cir.) 1949, US Supreme Ct. 1969, US Ct. Appeals (7th cir.) 1970, US Ct. Appeals (5th cir.) 1974, US Ct. Appeals (3d cir.) 1975. Agt. US Dept. Justice, NY, Ohio, Tex., Mex., 1942-43; US atty. Eastern Dist. Mo. Dept. Justice, St. Louis, 1967-69; ptnr. Riddle, Baker & O'Herin, Malden, Mo., 1948-67; sr. ptnr. Bryan Cave, St. Louis, 1969—. Pros. atty. Dunklin County, Mo., 1950-53; chmn. merit selection panel for US Magistrate, St. Louis, 1983-84 Del., Nat. Democratic Conv., Chgo., 1956, Los Angeles, 1960. With US Army, 1943-45, European Theatre, Military Intelligence. Recipient Disting. Alumni award Washington U. Sch. Law, 1993. Fellow Am. Coll. Trial Lawyers, Internat. Acad. Trial Lawyers; mem. Acad. Mo. Squires. Clubs: Bellerive Country, Noonday, Round Table (St. Louis). Baptist. Office: Bryan Cave 211 N Broadway Saint Louis MO 63102-2733 Office Phone: 314-259-2235, vlriddle@bryancave.com.

**RIDDLE, WESLEY ALLEN,** army officer, writer; b. Houston, Apr. 19, 1961; s. Walter Abige Riddle and Gloria Texane (Longnecker) Riddle-Roe; m. Maria Aida Albesa, Dec. 21, 1985; stepchildren: Catalina Louise Oates, Danilo Albesa Calabia. BS cum laud, U.S. Mil. Acad., 1983; MPhil in Modern History with distinction, Oxford (Eng.) U., 1993. Commd. U.S. Army, 1983, advanced through grades to lt. col., 2000, platoon leader, battery exec. officer 1-62 ADA (C/V) Schofield Barracks, Hawaii, 1984-87; asst. S-3 Plans, S-4 and Battery Comdr. 2-43 ADA (Patriot) Hanau, Germany, 1988-91; battery comdr. B/2-43 ADA Gulf War SWA, 1991; asst. prof. history U.S. Mil. Acad., West Point, NY, 1993-96; Theater Missile Def. evaluation officer Air Def. Directorate Operational Test and Evaluation Command, Alexandria, Va., 1996-98; exec. officer 2-6 ADA, Ft. Bliss, Tex., 1998-99; chief AD br., requirements divsn. DCD, Ft. Bliss, 1999-2000; air def. readiness br. chief (OMC-K) USASATMO, Ft. Bragg, NC, 2000—. Chmn. Am. Civility Project, 1996-99. Mem. adv. bd. The Social Critic mag., 1996-99; U.S. corr. Fragments Mag., 1998—; contbr. chpts. to books; columnist Belton Jour., 2000—. Founder, pres. Northbrook Teenage Reps., Houston, 1975-79; youth advisor State of Tex. to Citizens for the Republic, 1978-79; pag, Rep. Nat. Conv., Kansas City, Mo., 1976. Decorated Bronze Star; Salvatori fellow Heritage Found., Washington, 1996-99; Nat. Humanities Inst. fellow, 1997—. Mem. VFW, Am. Legion, Mil. Order of Saint Barbara, Phi Kappa Phi, Phi Alpha Theta. Republican. Christian Scientist. Avocations: music, poetry, weightlifting, running, water sports.

**RIDE, SALLY KRISTEN,** physics professor, research scientist, retired astronaut; b. LA, May 26, 1951; d. Dale Burdell and Carol Joyce (Anderson) R.; m. Steven Alan Hawley, July 26, 1982 (div.). BA in English, Stanford U., 1973, BS in Physics, 1973, PhD in Physics, 1978. Tchg. asst. Stanford U., Palo Alto, Calif., rschr. Dept. Physics; astronaut candidate, trainee NASA, 1978-79, astronaut, 1979-87, on-orbit capsule communicator STS-2 mission Johnson Space Ctr. Houston, on-orbit capsule communicator STS-3 mission, mission specialist STS-7, 1983, mission specialist STS-41G, 1984; sci. fellow Stanford (Calif.) U., 1987-89; dir. Calif. Space Inst. U. Calif. San Diego, La Jolla, 1989—96, pres. space com., 1999-2000; prof. dept. physics9 U. Calif. San Diego, 1989—96; pres., CEO Imaginary Lines, Inc., 2001—. Mem. Presdl. Commn. on Space Shuttle Challenger Accident, 1986, World Resources Inst. Global Coun., 1993—, Presdl. Com. of Advisors on Sci. and Tech., 1994—, Univ. Calif. Oversight Com. for the Nat. Labs, Pacific Coun. on Internat. Policy; pres., CEO Space.com, 1999—2000; intiated NASA EarthKAM project; bd. dir. Nat. Rsch. Coun. Space Studies, Congressional Office of Tech. Assessment, Carnegie Instn. Washington; past bd. dir. NCAA Found.; bd. trustee Caltech; lectr. in field. Author: (with Susan Okie) To Space and Back, 1986, (with T.O'Shaughnessy) Voyager: An Adventure to the Edge of the Solar System, 1992, The Third Planet: Exploring the Earth From Space, 1994, (revised 2004), The Mystery of Mars, 1999, Exploring Our Solar System, 2003. Named to The Nat. Women Hall of Fame, 1988, Astronaut Hall of Fame, Kennedy Space Center, 2003; recipient Jefferson award for Pub. Svc., Nat. Spaceflight medal (twice), Von Braun award, Lindbergh Eagle award, Silver Anniversary award, NCAA, 1998, Theodore Roosevelt award, 2005. Fellow: Am. Physical Soc. Achievements include becoming the first American woman to orbit Earth when she flew aboard Space Shuttle Challenger, June, 18 1983. Avocations: tennis, running, volleyball, softball, stamp collecting. Office: U Calif San Diego Dept Physics 0426 La Jolla CA 92093-0426 Address: Sally Ride Science 9191 Towne Centre Dr San Diego CA 92122

**RIDEN, MICHAEL DAVID,** nuclear engineer; b. Maryville, Tenn., July 2, 1947; s. William Walter and Grace Ella (Elrod) R.; m. Perry Dene Thyberg, Mar. 28, 1970; children: Chad Michael, Kirk David, Eric Wesley. Cert. nuclear weapons specialist, Lowry Tng. Ctr., Denver, 1968; cert. nuclear weapons technician, Gen. Electric Co. Tng. Program, King of Prussia, Pa., 1969; BS, U. Tenn., Knoxville, 1974. Cert. regional judge, Duck Town, Tenn., 1995. Asst. engr. Duke Power Co. Oconee Nuclear Sta., Seneca, SC, 1974-78; reactor insp. Nuclear Regulatory Commn., Glen Ellyn, Ill., 1978-79; gen. mgr. Chgo. Barra Corp. Am., Inc., Wheaton, Ill., 1979-82; reg. mgr. Watpro, Inc., Orland Park, Ill., 1982-83; pres. ETs, Glen Ellyn, 1983-87; engring. assurance engr. TVA Watts Bar Nuc. Plant, Spring City, Tenn., 1987-88, Sequoyah Nuc. Plant, Soddy-Daisy, Tenn., 1988-89; supervising engr. United Energy Svcs. Corp., Palo Verde Nuc. Power Plant, Wintersburg, Ariz., 1989-90; nuc. engr. Sigma Sci. Browns Ferry Nuc. Plant, Athens, Ala., 1990-93; lead auditor SECORE Svcs. Inc., Trans-Alaska Pipeline, Anchorage, 1994; plant ops. and betterment I&C cons. engr. Raytheon Engrs. and Constructors Inc. TVA Watts Bar Nuclear, Spring City, Tenn., 1994-95; cons. nuc. engr. Sci. Applications Internat. Corp. TVA Sequoyah Nuclear Plant, Soddy-Daisy, Tenn., 1995-96; sports staff mem. Atlanta com. Olympic Games, Cherokee Nat. Forest, Tenn., 1996; cons. nuc. engring. environ. qualification Cooper Nuc. Station, Brownville, Nebr., 1996-97; sys. engring. mentor Duke Engring. & Svc. Resources, Inc., Two Rivers, Wis., 1997-98; maintenance commitment project mgr. Cook Nuc. Plant Cook Nuc. Plant, Duke Engring. & Svcs. Resources, Inc., Sun Tech. Svcs., Inc. and S&L, Bridgman, Mich., 1998-2001; agt. Ednl. Tng. Svcs., Riceville, Tenn., 2000—; elec. supt. Newberg, Perini, Stone and Webster, Braceville, Ill., 2001—02. Re-entry system evaluation team mem. minuteman III missile USAF, Minot, N.D., 1990-71. Deacon Presbyn. Ch. U.S., Seneca, 1976-77; lay spkr. United Meth. Ch. Holston Conf., 1991-2001. Sgt. USAF, 1967-71. Recipient Outstanding Achievement in Poetry During the 20th Century award Internat. Libr. of Poetry, 2000. Mem. Am. Nuclear Soc. Sovereign American.

**RIDENHOUR, MARILYN HOUSEL,** retired accountant; b. Madison, Nebr., July 12, 1931; d. Kenneth Virgil Housel and Edna Christina Reese Housel; m. Henry Clifton Ridenhour, Apr. 25, 1954 (dec.); children: Keith James, Susan Marie Ridenhour Redelfs, Jill Housel Ridenhour Cortese. Student, Nebr. Wesleyan U., 1949—50; BS in Bus. Adminstrn. with distinction, U. Nebr., 1953. CPA Mo., 1957. CPA Price Waterhouse & Co., St. Louis, 1953—54, Adolph Kahn, St. Louis, 1954—57; ptnr., CPA Adolph Kahn & Co., St. Louis, 1957—61, Kahn, Ridenhour & Co., St. Louis, 1961—65, Ridenhour Hylton & Co., St. Louis, 1965—91; cons. Baird Kurtz & Dobson, St. Louis, 1991—92, ret., 1992. Citizen leader Chesterfield, Mo. 2d Congl. Dist., 2005. Mem.: Rep. Leadership Found. (founding mem.), Am. Women's Soc. CPA, Am. Soc. Women Accts. (charter pres. 1959), Dawn Hope Soc., Soaring Eagle, Nat. Law Enforcement (founding mem. 2005), Century Soc., U. Nebr. Alumni Assn., St. Labre Indian Sch. Ednl. Assn., Chancellors Club U. Nebr., Beta Gamma Sigma, Phi Chi Theta, Alpha Lambda Delta, Delta Delta Delta. Republican. Methodist. Personal E-mail: hermhr@wchtv.net.

**RIDENOUR, AMY MORITZ,** research center administrator; b. Pitts., Nov. 9, 1959; d. Karl Berkoben and Carol Lee (Riley) M. B or Econs., U. Md., 1981. Exec. dir. Nat. Ctr. for Pub. Policy Rsch., Washington, 1982-88, trustee, 1986—; pres. The Nat. Ctr. for Pub. Policy Research, Washington, 1988—; formerly host Snoop!, Nat. Empowerment Television, Washington; nationally sundicated columnist UPI and Knight-Ridder Tribune, 1998—. Chmn. Liberty Inst., Washngton. Assoc. pub. Cath. Study Coun. Bull.; editor Nat. Policy Watch Jour., Liberation Bull.; exec. editor Liberty Letter; contbr. articles to Policy Rev. and other profl. jours. Regional coord. Reagan-Bush Nat. Campaign Volunteering, 1980, 1st v.p. Internat. Youth Yr. Commn. for U.S., 1985; chmn. Md. Fedn. Coll. Rep. Clubs, 1978-80. Mem. Accuracy in Academia (adv. bd.). Lutheran. Avocations: skiing, books, history. Office: Nat Ctr for Pub Policy Rsch 501 Capitol Court Washington DC 20002

**RIDENOUR, BRIAN KENT,** lawyer; b. Ravenna, Nebr., Nov. 2, 1947; s. Raymond Ivan and Helen May (Wilson) R.; m. Rosalie Kay Bradley, June 1, 1969; children: Jeffrey Kent, Alissabeth Kay. BS, U. Nebr., Lincoln, 1969, JD, 1974. Nebr., U.S. Dist. Ct. Nebr. 1975, U.S. Ct. Appeals (D.C. cir.) 1977, U.S. Supreme Ct. 1978. Assoc. Nelson & Harding, Lincoln, 1975-78, ptnr., 1978-89, Heron, Burchette, Ruckert & Rothwell, Lincoln, 1989-90, Kinsey, Ridenour, Becker & Kistler, Lincoln, 1990—2005; asst. gen. counsel Fiserv, Inc., Lincoln, 2005—. Dir. Info. Tech., Inc., Lincoln, 1996-93, Russian Trade & Prodn. Co. "Russkaya Bakaleya", Moscow, 1995-2001, A&Y Distbrs., Inc., Lincoln, 1992-2001. Found. pres., dir. Lincoln Sister Cities Program, Lincoln, 1989—; past pres., dir. Friendship Force of Lincoln, 1985-92; mem. Mayor's Com. Internat. Friendship, Lincoln, Nebr. Diplomats; v.p. Lincoln Coun. for Internat. Friendship. With U.S. Army, 1970-73. Named Hon. Citizen City Khujand, Tajikistan, 1992. Mem. ABA, Nebr. State Bar Assn., Lincoln Bar Assn., Order of Coif. Democrat. Office: Ste 601 121 S 13th St Lincoln NE 68508-1982 E-mail: bkridenour@hotmail.com.

**RIDENOUR, JOEY,** medical association administrator, operations research specialist; BSc in Nursing, Ariz. State U.; MN, U. Phoenix. RN Ariz. COO Maricopa Health Sys., Phoenix, 1975—95; exec. dir. Ariz. State Bd. Nursing, 1995—98; pres. Nat. Coun. State Bds. of Nursing, Chgo., 1998; exec dir Ariz State bd of nursing. Pres. Ariz. State Bd. Nursing, Phoenix, 1986—89, 1994—95; adj. faculty Ariz. State U. Recipient Disting. Achievement award, Am. Soc. Pub. Adminstrn., Ariz. State U. Coll. Nursing. U. Phoenix; fellow, Wharton. Office: Boards of Nursing Natl Coun of State 111 E Wacker Dr Ste 2900 Chicago IL 60601-4277

**RIDEOUT, JAN G.,** ship manufacturing company executive; B in acctg., Bklyn. Coll.; MBA in mgmt. info. systems, U. Dallas. Dir. integrated enterprise solutions Northrop Grumman Corp., dir. Y2K program office, various other mgmt. positions; v.p. enterprise resource planning and corp. systems Bechtel Group, Inc., San Francisco; rejoined Northrop Grumman Corp., 2001; now v.p., chief info. officer Northrop Grumman Ship Systems, Pascagoula, Miss. Named one of Premier 100 IT Leaders, Computerworld, 2005. Office: Northrop Grumman Ship Systems 1000 Access Rd Pascagoula MS 39568 Office Phone: 228-935-1122. Office Fax: 228-935-1126.*

**RIDEOUT, PATRICIA IRENE,** vocalist; b. St. John, N.B., Can., Mar. 16, 1931; d. Eric Radway and Florence May (Chase) R.; m. Rolf Edmund Dissmann, Sept. 3, 1955 (dec. 1975); m. Leonard R. Rosenberg, May 25, 1987. Student, U. Toronto Opera Sch., Royal Conservatory Music, 1952-55. Tchr. voice Queen's U., Kingston, Ont., 1980-86, Royal Conservatory Music, Toronto, 1980-91. Singer Can. Opera Co., Toronto, 1954-85; leading roles in operas, Stratford, Ont., Vancouver, B.C., Guelph, Ont., 1956-85, CBC, 1958-90. Mem.: Actors Equity Assn., Assn. Radio and TV Artists, Toronto Heliconian Club. Unitarian Universalist. Personal E-mail: prosenberg@intown.net.

**RIDER, KATHLEEN MARY,** dietician; b. Bronx, N.Y., Mar. 21, 1953; d. William Anthony and Elizabeth Catherine (Gavin) Browne; m. David York Rider, Oct. 15, 1983; children: Kathleen M., Colleen M., David Y., Elizabeth A., Erin M. AAS, Maria Coll., 1976; BS, Empire State Coll., 1978; M of Profl. Studies, SUNY, New Paltz, 1982; cert. alternative & complimentary health, Marist Coll., 1999. Cert. dietitian/nutritionist, N.Y. Food svc. dir./dietitian Lovely Hill Nursing Home, Pawling, N.Y., 1979-81; adminstrv. dietitian Hudson River Psychiat. Ctr., Poughkeepsie, N.Y., 1981-82; cmty. svc. dietitian Wassaic (N.Y.) Developmental Ctr., 1982-83; ind. cons. dietitian, 1981—. Cons. Bapt. Home, Hospice Inc., Greystone Inc., Mountainview Nursing Ctr., Victory Care Nursing Ctr., Assn. for Retarded Citizens, Ulster and Orange Counties, Home Care, Alcohol Rehab. Ctr., various other orgns.; advisor Mid Hudson Food Svc. Mgrs. Assn., Poughkeepsie. Vol. nutrition educator area parochial schs., Dutchess County, 1996; instr. religious edn. St. Peter's Ch., Poughkeepsie, 1981-84; team mem. engaged encounter Cath. Engaged Encounter, Dutchess County, 1986-89. Soroptomist scholar, Schenectady, N.Y., 1976. Fellow Am. Dietetic Assn. (del. 1999, Flora Wishart Davies Meml. award for Outstanding Caregiver 1994, Outstanding Svc. award); mem. N.Y. State Dietetic Assn. (state profl. recruitment coord. 1976—, scholar 1976), Mid Hudson Dietetic Assn. (pres. 1992-94). Democrat. Home and Office: 13 Edna Dr Hyde Park NY 12538-2939

**RIDER, LISA G,** pediatric rheumatologist, researcher; b. Newark; MD, Duke U. Sch. of Medicine, 1983—87. Pediatric Rheumatologist Am. Bd. Pediat. Med. officer and staff scientist for Biologics Evaluation and Rsch., FDA, Bethesa, Md., 1993—2001; dep. chief Environ. Autoimmunity Group, Nat. Inst. Environ. Health Scis. NIH, Bethesda, Md., 2001—. Vice chair med. adv. bd. The Myositis Assn., Washington, 1996—; spl. govt. employee FDA, Rockville, Md., 2001—03; adv. coun. Pediatric Rheumatology Collaborative Study Group, Cincinnati, Ohio, 1998—. Editor: Myositis and You; contbr. articles to profl. jours., chapters to books. Vol. Garrett Pk. Elem. Sch., Md., 2002—06. Capt. US Pub. Health Svc., 1991—, Bethesda, MD. Fellow, PhRMA, 1985—86; Eugene Stead Rsch. fellow, Duke U., 1985—86. Fellow: Am. Acad. Pediat., Am. Coll. Rheumatology (exec. coun. pediatric rheumatology sect. 2003—); mem.: Phi Beta Kappa. Achievements include research in juvenile myositis, rheumatic disease, environmental risk factors, autoantibodies, immunogenetics, outcome measures. Office: NIEHS NIH CRC 4-2332 MSC 1301 10 Center Dr Bethesda MD 20892-1301 Office Phone: 301-451-6272. Business E-Mail: riderl@mail.nih.gov.

**RIDER, RICHARD FRANCIS,** psychologist; b. Utica, N.Y., Dec. 16, 1947; s. Paul Zachary and Ruth Wind Rider; m. Julie Ann Rider, Nov. 29, 1969; children: Robyn Michelle, James Elliot. BA in Eng., San Diego State U., 1969; MA in Clin. Psychology, Forest Inst., 1999, PhD summa cum laude, 2001. V.p. SAIC, San Diego, 1977—84; bus. devel. mgr. HK Sys., Milw., W.Va., 1988—97, San Diego, 1988—97; psychologist Neurology, Learning and Behavior Ctr., Salt Lake City, 2001—. Mem. editl. bd.: J. Attention Disorders, 2005—; contbr. chapters to books. Lt. USNR, 1969—74. Mem.: APA, Psi Chi. Avocations: bicycling, golf, reading, water sports. Office: Neurology Learning and Behavior Ctr 230 S 500 E Ste 100 Salt Lake City UT 84102

**RIDGE, DAVY-JO STRIBLING,** school librarian; b. Westminster, SC, Jan. 16, 1932; d. David Waren and Thelma Josephine (Braselton) Stribling; m. George Ross Ridge, June 9, 1956 (div. Dec. 1964). BA, Queens Coll., 1954; MLN, Emory U., 1955. Catalog libr. U. Ga., Athens, 1955—56; head ref. libr. Dekalb Regional Libr., Decatur, Ga., 1956—64; ref. libr. U. S.C., Columbia, 1965—66, head ref. dept., 1967—74, asst. dir. libr., 1975—76, assoc. dir. libr., 1977—88, ret., 1988. Author: A Load of Gratitude: Audubon and South Carolina, 1985, A South Carolina Family in Wartime, 2003. Mem.: S.C. Libr. Assn. (chmn. legis. & pub.), S.C. Libr. Soc. (life), Thomas Cooper Libr. Soc. (life), S.E. Libr. Assn. (life; chmn. constrn. & bylaws 1980—84). Episcopalian. Avocations: gardening, reading, cats.

**RIDGE, TOM (THOMAS JOSEPH RIDGE),** former secretary of homeland security; b. Munhall, Pa., Aug. 26, 1945; s. Thomas Regis Ridge and Laura A. Sudimack; m. Michele Moore, 1979, children, Lesley, Tommy. BA in govt. studies, Harvard U., 1967; JD, Dickinson Sch. Law, Carlisle, Pa., 1972. Bar: Pa. 1972. Pvt. practice, Erie, Pa., 1972-82; asst. dist. atty. Erie County, Pa., 1979-82; mem. 98th-103rd Congresses from Pa. 21st dist., Washington, 1983-1995; mem. Banking, Fin., Urban Affairs com. subcoms. Econ. Growth and Credit Formation, Housing and Community mem. banking, Devel., Veteran's Affairs com.; gov. State of Pa., 1995—2001; dir. U.S. Dept. Homeland Security, Washington, 2001—02, sec., 2003—05. Bd. dirs. The Home Depot, Inc., Atlanta, 2005 , Savi Technology Inc., Sunnyvale, Calif., 2005—, Exelon Corp., Chgo., 2005—. Staff Sergeant, U.S. Army, 1968-70, Vietnam; Awarded a Bronze Star for Bravery. Republican.

**RIDGELY, HENRY DUPONT,** state supreme court justice; b. Dover, Del., May 31, 1949; s. Henry Johnson and Mary Lil (Berry) R.; m. Barbara Shepard, Mar. 17, 1973; children: Daniel, Michael. BS in Business Administration, Syracuse U., 1971; JD, Cath. U. Am. Columbus Sch. Law, 1973; LLM in Corp Law, George Washington U. Nat. Law Ctr., 1974. Atty. Ridgely and Ridgely, Dover, 1974—84, Del. State Senate, Dover, 1981—84; judge Superior Ct. Del., Dover, 1984—2004; justice Del. Supreme Ct., Wilmington, 2004—. Recipient Chief Justice's Annual award for Outstanding Judicial Service, 1997, Judicial Professionalism and Civility award, Am. Bd. Trial Advocates- Del. Chapter, 2000. Fellow: Am. Bar Found.; mem.: ABA (co-chair Ct. Technology Com. 2003—), Terry-Carey Am. Inn of Ct. (pres. 1996—98), Nat. Assn. for Ct. Mgmt., Am. Judicature Soc. (bd. dirs 2003—05). Republican. Episcopalian. Office: Del Supreme Ct 502 S State St Dover DE 19901

**RIDGEWAY, JAMES FOWLER,** journalist; b. Auburn, N.Y., Nov. 1, 1936; s. George L. and Florence (Fowler) Ridgeway; m. Patricia Carol Dodge, Nov. 1966; 1 child, David Andrew. AB, Princeton U., 1959. Assoc. editor New Republic, Washington, 1962-68, contbg. editor, 1968-70; editor Hard Times, 1968-70, Elements, 1974-78; assoc. editor Ramparts, 1970-75; assoc. fellow Inst. for Policy Studies, 1973-77; mem. Pub. Resource Center, 1977—; staff writer Village Voice, 1973—2006; corr. Washington Ulather Jones, 2006—. Author: (book) The Closed Corporation, 1969, Politics of Ecology, 1970, The Last Play, 1973, New Energy, 1975; author: (with Alexander Cockburn) Smoke, 1978; author: Political Ecology, 1979, Energy-Efficient Community Planning, 1979, Who Owns the Earth, 1980, Powering Civilization, 1983, Blood in the Face, 1991, The March to War, 1991; author: (with Jean Casella) To Cast a Cold Eye, 1991; author: The Haiti Files, 1994; author: (with Jasmika Udovicki) Yugoslavia's Ethnic Nightmare, 1995; author: (with Sylvia Plachy) Red Light, 1996; author: (with Jeffrey St. Clair) Environmental Bad Guys, 1999; author: (with Kevin Rafferty, Fran K. Kerrandren) Who Wants to Be President?; prodr., dir. (with Anne Bohlen, Kevin Rafferty): (films) Blood in the Face, 1990; prodr., dir. (with Kevin Rafferty) Feed, 1992; cons. prodr. Awful Truth, 1999; author: It's All For Sale, 2004, The 5 Unanswered Questions about 9/11, 2005, Baghdad Burning, 2005; editor (founder): Video website. With N.G. U.S. Army, 1959. Home: 3103 Macomb St NW Washington DC 20008-3325 Personal E-mail: jridgew@yahoo.com.

**RIDGLEY, FRANK NELSON,** veterinarian; b. Yankton, SD, May 25, 1975; s. Ronald Howell Ridgely and Sherilyn Kay Nelson. BS in Animal Sci., Purdue U., West Lafayette, Ind., 1997, DVM, 2001. Assoc. vet. Orchard Pk. Vet. Med. Ctr., NY, 2001—02; attending vet. Zool. Soc. Buffalo, 2002—. Animal mgmt. program adv. bd. Niagra County C.C., Sanborn, NY, 2003—; adj. faculty U. Buffalo, 2004—; part-time faculty Canisius Coll., 2003—. Bd. mem. Parkside Cmty. Assn., Buffalo, 2005—06. Mem.: NY State Vet. Med. Soc., Western NY Vet. Med. Assn., Am. Assn. Zoo Vets., Am. Vet. Med. Assn., Assn. Avian Vets., Assn. Reptile and Amphibian Vets., Am. Zoo and Aquarium Assn. Home: 32 Crescent Ave Buffalo NY 14214 Office: Buffalo Zoo 300 Parkside Ave Buffalo NY 14214 Office Phone: 716-837-3900.

**RIDGLEY, THOMAS BRENNAN,** lawyer; b. Columbus, Ohio, Apr. 29, 1940; s. Arthur G. and Elizabeth (Tracy) R.; children: Elizabeth, Jennifer, Kathryn; m. Lisa Lester, Nov. 27, 1999. BA, Princeton (N.J.) U., 1962; JD with honors, U. Mich., 1965. Bar: Ohio 1968, U.S. Dist. Ct. (so. and no. dists.) Ohio, U.S. Dist. Ct. (ea. dist.) Pa., U.S. Ct. Appeals (6th, 3d and 10th cirs.), U.S. Supreme Ct. Assoc. Dechert, Price and Rhoades, Phila., 1965-67; ptnr. Vorys, Sater, Seymour and Pease LLP, Columbus, 1967—. Author: Interstate Conflicts and Cooperation, 1986, (with others) Fending Off Corporate Raiders, 1987. Bd. dirs., mem. exec. com. United Way of Franklin County, Columbus, 1986-98; bd. dirs. Cmty. Shelter Bd., 1992-98, pres. 1997-98; bd. dirs. Columbus Bar Found., 1992-99, pres., 1998. Fellow Am. Coll. Trial Lawyers. Office: Vorys Sater Seymour and Pease LLP 52 E Gay St Columbus OH 43215-3161 Office Phone: 614-464-6229. Business E-Mail: tbridgley@vssp.com.

**RIDGWAY, DELISSA ANNE,** federal judge; b. Kirksville, Mo., June 28, 1955; d. Kenneth Driggs and Margaret Anne (Warner) R. BA with honors, U. Mo., 1975, postgrad., 1976; JD, Northeastern U., 1979. Bar: DC Ct. Appeals 1979, US Dist. Ct. DC 1980, US Ct. Appeals (DC cir.) 1980, US Supreme Ct. 1983, US Ct. Appeals (1st cir.) 1988. Law clk. to presiding justice U.S. Dist. Ct. D.C., Washington, 1979; assoc. Shaw, Pittman, Potts & Trowbridge, Washington, 1979-88, counsel, internat. practice group, 1988—94; chair, US Fgn. Claims Settlement Commn. US Dept. Justice, Washington, 1994—98; judge US Ct. Internat. Trade, NYC, 1998—. Lectr. nuclear and environ. law to various orgns. Mem. Women's Legal Def. Fund. Recipient: Hardin-Craig fellow U. Mo., Columbia, 1994, Frederick B. Abramson award, DC Bar Assn., 1996, Earl W. Kintner award, Fed. Bar Assn., 2000, Woman Lawyer of The Year, Washington, 2001. Mem. ABA, Women's Bar Assn. (sec. 1989-90), Fed. Bar Assn. (chair adminstrv. law sect. com. agy. adjudication 1985-89, chair adminstrv. law sect. com. regulatory reform 1984-85), Am. Law Inst., Fellow, Am. Bar Found. Roman Catholic. Office: US Ct Internat Trade One Federal Plz New York NY 10278-0001

**RIDGWAY, JAMES MASTIN,** retired government agency administrator; b. Sedalia, Mo., Mar. 14, 1917; s. Amelius Biddle and Maude Anna (Brandt) R.; m. Lillian Belle Shaneyfelt, May 25, 1941; children: Duressa, Richard (dec.), Cheryl. BSBA, U. Mo., 1939, MA, 1940; PhD, U. Chgo., 1953. Tchr. High Schs., Mo., Kans., 1940-44, prin. Butler, Mo., 1944-45; instr. Southwest & Ctrl. Mo. State U., Springfield, Warrensburg, Mo., 1945-47; chmn. dept. edn. Carroll Coll., Waukesha, Wis., 1949-55; instr. dept. head Nat. Civil Def. Coll., Battle Creek, Mich., 1955-62, dir. 1958-62; deputy asst. dir. tng. & edn. Office Civil Def., Def. Civil Preparedness Agy., Washington, 1963-73; adm. advisor DCPA/DOD and FEMA, Washington, 1973—80. Cons. in field. Contbr. articles to profl. jours. Mem. Am. Strategic Def. Assn., Internat. Assn. Emergency Mgrs., Am. Civil Def. Assn., Heritage Found. Avocation: stamp collecting/philately.

**RIDGWAY, MARCELLA DAVIES,** veterinarian; b. Sewickley, Pa., Dec. 24, 1957; d. Willis Eugene and Martha Ann (Davies) R. BS, Pa. State U., 1979; VMD, U. Pa., 1983; MS, U. Ill., 1997. Diplomate Am. Coll. Vet. Internal Medicine. Intern U. Ill., Urbana, 1983-84, resident in small animal internal medicine, 1984-87; small animal vet. Vet. Cons. Svcs., Savoy, Ill., 1987-97; clin. asst. prof. small animal vet. medicine U. Ill., Urbana, 1997—. Contbr. articles to profl. jours. Mem. Am. Vet. Med. Assn., Acad. Vet. Clinicians, Ea. Ill. Vet. Med. Assn. (pres. 2000-2001), Savoy Prairie Soc. (pres. 1989—), Grand Prairie Friends (bd. dirs. 1990-96), Sangamon Valley Conservancy (bd. dirs. 1995-2005 Avocations: prairie conservation activities, hiking, canine collectibles, running, dog obedience training. Office: U Ill Vet Med Teaching Hosp 1008 W Hazelwood Dr Urbana IL 61802-4714 Home: 808 Indigo Savoy IL 61874

**RIDGWAY, ROZANNE LEJEANNE,** investment company executive, retired ambassador; b. St. Paul, Aug. 22, 1935; d. H. Clay and Ethel Rozanne (Cote) R.; m. Theodore E. Deming. BA, Hamline U., 1957, LLD (hon.), 1978, George Washington U., 1986, Elizabethtown Coll., 1990, U. Helsinki, 1992; LLD in Pub. Svc. (hon.), Coll. of William and Mary, 1994; DHL (hon.), Hood Coll., 1994; LLD (hon.), Albright Coll.; DHL in Pub. Adminstrn. (hon.), The Citadel, 2003; DHL (hon.), Ill. Coll., 2003. Career diplomat U.S. Fgn. Svc., 1957-89, amb. at large for oceans and fisheries, 1975-77, US amb. to Finland Helsinki, 1977—80; counselor State Dept., 1980—81, spl. asst. to sec., 1981, amb. to German Dem. Republic, 1982-85, asst. sec. Europe and Can., 1985-89; ret.; pres. Atlantic Coun. US, 1989-92, co-chmn., 1993-96; chmn. Baltic-Am. Enterprise Fund, Washington, 1994—. Bd. dirs. 3M Corp., Emerson Electric Co., Boeing Co., Sara Lee Corp., Manpower, Inc., New Perspective Fund, Europacific Fund, New World Fund. Life trustee Hamline U., Nat. Geog. Soc., Ctr. Naval Analyses. Decorated Grand Cross Order of the Lion (Finland); recipient Profl. awards Dept. State, Presdl. Disting. Performance awards, Joseph C. Wilson Internat. Rels. Achievement award, 1982, Sharansky award Union Couns. Soviet Jewry, 1989, U.S. Presdl. Citizens medal, 1989; named Person of Yr. Nat. Fisheries Inst., 1977, Knight Comdr. Order of Merit, Germany; inducted into Nat. Women's Hall of Fame, 1998. Fellow Nat. Acad. Pub. Adminstrn.; mem. Am. Acad. Diplomacy, Army-Navy Country Club.

**RIDINGS, DOROTHY SATTES,** former association executive; b. Charleston, W.Va., Sept. 26, 1939; d. Frederick L. and Katharine E. (Backus) Sattes; m. Donald Jerome Ridings, Sept. 8, 1962 (dec. June 1997); children: Donald Jerome Jr., Matthew Lyle. Student, Randolph-Macon Woman's Coll., 1957-59; BSJ, Northwestern U., 1961; MA, U. N.C., 1968; D.Pub. Svc. (hon.), U. Louisville, 1985; LHD (hon.), Spalding U., 1986; LLD (hon.), U. Charleston, 1999. Reporter Charlotte Observer, NC, 1961-66; instr. U. N.C. Sch. Journalism, 1966-68; freelance writer Louisville, 1968-77; news editor Ky. Bus. Ledger, Louisville, 1977-80, editor, 1980-83; communications cons., editor, 1983-86; mgmt. assoc. Knight-Ridder Inc., Charlotte, NC, 1986-88; pres., pub. Bradenton Herald, Fla., 1988-96; pres., CEO Coun. on Founds., Washington, 1996—2005. Adj. prof. U. Louisville, 1982-83; v.p. Nat. Mcpl. League, 1985-86; bd. dirs. com. on Constl. Sys., Nat. Com. Against Discrimination in Housing, 1982-87, Com. for Study of Am. Electorate, 1982—; bd. dirs. Ind. Sector, 1983-88, 92-97; mem. exec. com. Leadership Conf. Civil Rights, 1982-86; mem. Accrediting Coun. on Edn. in Journalism and Mass Comm., 2000-06. Pres. LWV U.S., 1982-86, 1st v.p., 1980-82, human resources dir., 1976-80, chair edn. fund, 1982-86, 1st vice chair, 1980-82, trustee, 1976-80, pres. Louisville/Jefferson County, 1974-76, bd. dirs., 1969-76; chmn., bd. dirs. Nat. Civic League, 2000-04; trustee Louisville Presbyn. Theol. Sem., 1992—, chmn., 2000—; trustee Ford Found., 1989-96, Manatee C.C., 1992-96; bd. dirs. Benton Found., 1989-96, Fla. Press Assn., 1994-96, Leadership Ky., 1984-87, Leadership Louisville, 1983-86, Louisville YWCA, 1978-80, Jr. League Louisville, 1972-74; mem. ABA Accreditation Com., 1987-93, ABA coun. legal edn. and admissions to bar, 1997-03, Gov.'s Coun. Ednl. Reform, 1984-85; chair Prichard Com. Acad. Excellence, 1985-86; mem. Gov.'s Commn. Full Equality, 1982-83; mem. state adv. coun. U.S. Commn. Civil Rights, 1975-79; mem. steering com. Task Force for Peaceful Desegregation, 1974-75; elder 2d Presbyn. Ch., 1972-75, 78-81; mem. adv. coun. on ch. and soc. United Presbyn. Ch. in USA, 1978-84; mem.

bd. visitors U. N.C., 1993-96; mem. Nat. Commn. on Presdl. Debates, 1997—; mem. Urban Librs. Coun. Exec. Bd., 2005—; bd. dirs. Editl. Projects in Edn., 2004—. Recipient Northwestern U. award of merit, 1994, Disting. Alumna award U. N.C., 1995, Leadership award Nat. Assn. Cmty. Leadership Orgns., 1986, Alumnae Achievement award Randolph-Macon Woman's Coll., 1985, Disting. Citizen award Nat. Mcpl. League, 1983; inducted into Northwestern U. Medill Sch. Journalism Hall of Fame, 1996, U. N.C. Journalism Hall of Fame, 1997.

**RIDKER, PAUL M.,** cardiologist, medical educator; b. St. Louis, Oct. 2, 1959; BS, Brown U., 1981; MD, Harvard U., 1986, MPH, 1992. Assoc. prof. medicine Harvard U., Boston; dir. Ctr. for Cardiovascular Disease Prevention Brigham and Women's Hosp., Boston; cons. cardiologist So. Jamaica Plain Health Ctr., Boston. Simon Dack vis. prof. Mt. Sinai Med. Ctr., 2000. Recipient Doris Duke Disting. Clin. Scientist award, 2000, Linus Pauling Lecture and 2000 Prevention award, Am. Coll. for Advancement in Medicine, 2000, SmithKline Beecham Faculty Devel. award, 1997—99, Clinician Scientist award, Am. Heart Assn., 1992—97. Fellow: Am. Coll. Cardiology; mem.: Am. Soc. of Clin. Investigation, Am. Epidemiol. Soc. Office: Harvard Univ Sch Medicine Brigham & Womens Hosp 75 Francis St Boston MA 02115

**RIDLEN, SAMUEL FRANKLIN,** agriculture educator; b. Marion, Ill., Apr. 24, 1916; s. Will and Leoma Josephine (Sneed) R.; m. Helen Louise Camp, Apr. 17, 1946; children: Judith Elaine, Barbara Jo, Mark Ellis. BS, U. Ill., 1940; MS, Mich. State U., 1957. Agr. instr. Westville (Ill.) Twp. High Sch., 1940-43; gen. mgr. Honegger Breeder Hatchery, Forrest, Ill., 1953-56; assoc. prof. poultry sci. U. Conn., Storrs, 1957-58; from asst. prof. to prof. poultry extension U. Ill., Urbana-Champaign, 1946-86, prof. emeritus poultry extension, 1986—, asst. head dept. animal scis., 1978-86. Author: An Idea and An Ideal-Nabor House Fraternity 1939-1989, 1989; poultry editorial cons. Successful Farming, Wonderful World Ency., 1960; poultry editor Am. Farm Youth, 1949-53, Ill. Feed Folks, 1949-53. Founding mem., charter mem. Nabor House Frat. Recipient Superior Svc. award U.S. Dept. Agr., 1982, Paul A. Funk Recognition award Coll. Agr., U. Ill., 1983, numerous others. Fellow Poultry Sci. Assn.; mem. World's Poultry Sci. Assn., Ill. State Turkey Growers Assn., Ill. Poultry Industry Coun., Ill Egg Market Devel. Coun. (adv. mem.), Ill. Animal Industry Coun., Coun. for Agr. Sci. and Tech., Ill. Alumni Assn. (life), DAV (life), Alpha Tau Alpha, Epsilon Sigma Phi, Gamma Sigma Delta (pres. 1982-83). Home: 1901 Lakeside Dr Unit C Champaign IL 61821-5997

**RIDLEY, BETTY ANN,** theology studies educator; b. St. Louis, Oct. 19, 1926; d. Rupert Alexis and Virginia Regina (Weikel) Steber; m. Fred A. Ridley, Jr., Sept. 8, 1948; children: Drue Alexis, Clay Kent. BA, Scripps Coll., Claremont, Calif., 1948. Christian Sci. practitioner, Oklahoma City, 1973—. Tchr. Christian Sci., 1983—; mem. Christian Sci. Bd. Lectureship, 1980-85. Trustee Daystar Found., 1990-; mem. First Ch. of Christ Scientist, Boston, 1956-2005, Fifth Ch. of Christ Scientist, Oklahoma City. Mem. Jr. League Am. Home: 2933 Lansdowne Ln Oklahoma City OK 73120-4343 Office: Suite 100-G 3000 United Founders Blvd Oklahoma City OK 73112 Office Phone: 405-848-7565. Personal E-mail: baridley@aol.com.

**RIDLEY, CAROLYN FLUDD,** retired social studies educator; b. Nashville, Jan. 21, 1942; d. Quitman Daniel and Glennora Elizabeth (Cannon) F.; m. Raymond Bennett, June 23, 1962 (div. 1984); 1 child, Karen Elizabeth Bennett Moore; m. Cornelius Theodore Ridley, July 16, 1988; stepchildren: Constance Maria Ridley Smith, William Keith. BA, CUNY, 1973; MEd, Tenn. State U., 1985. Cert. tchr., prin., Tenn., N.Y. Tchr. N.Y.C. Bd. Edn., 1973-75, Dickson (Tenn.) County Bd. Edn., 1976-77, Hickman County Bd. Edn., Centerville, Tenn., 1977-86, Met. Nashville Bd. Edn., 1986—2003; ret, 2003. Dir. Hickman County Career Day, 1982-83; bd. dirs. Assn. Retarded Citizens, Centerville, 1982-86; adv. com. Hickman County Bicentennial Com., Centerville, 1984-86, initiator commemorative quilt; participant NEH lectr. Author: A Black History of Hickman County, 1985. Campaign worker Met. Nashville Bd. Edn., 1991; campaigner Met. Nashville Edn., Assn., 1992; attendant Dem. Socialization Meeting, Nashville, 1992; participant Nat. Endowment for the Humanities Summer Inst. Furman U., Greenville, Tenn., 1995; mem. Nashville Symphony Orch. League, 2005; bd. dirs. Hall of Champions/Tenn. Secondary Schs. Athletic Assn., 2005. Grantee Mid. Tenn. State U., Murfreesboro, 1990, Tenn. State U., Nashville, 1992; James R. Stokeley Inst. fellow U. Tenn., 1993; participant NEH Summer Inst. at Furman U., Greenville, Tenn., 1995; named Tchr. of Yr., 1997, 2002-03. Fellow Taft Inst. (cert. 1992, tchr. of yr. 1997, 2002-03); mem. AAUW, NEA, NASA Space Inst. (cert. 1990), Met. Nashville Edn. Assn. (campaign worker and assn. rep.), Smithsonian Instn., Internat. Platform Assn., Nat. Historic Preservation Soc., Nat. Geographic Soc., Nat. Coun. Social Studies, Internat. Platform Assn., Holocaust Meml. Mus. (charter mem.). Democrat. Mem. Ch. of Christ. Avocations: travel, reading, music, studying quilting folk art. Home: 4348 Setters Rd Nashville TN 37218-1839 Personal E-mail: CTRidley@comcast.com.

**RIDLEY, CLARENCE HAVERTY,** retail executive; b. Atlanta, June 3, 1942; s. Frank Morris Jr. and Clare (Haverty) R.; m. Eleanor Horsey, Aug. 22, 1969; children: Augusta Morgan, Clare Haverty. BA, Yale U., 1964; MBA, Harvard U., 1966; JD, U. Va., 1971. Bar: Ga. 1971. Ptnr. King & Spalding, Atlanta, 1977—2000, partner emeritus, policy com., 1995—97; chmn. bd. Haverty Furniture Cos., Inc., 2001—. Bd. dirs. Crawford & Co., Inc.; bd. trustees STI Classic Funds and Variable Trusts, 2001—. Co-author: Computer Software Agreements, 1987, 3d edit., 2003; exec. editor Va. Law Rev., 1970-71. Chmn.; bd. trustees St Joseph's Health Sys., 2003—; founding trustee Atlanta Girls Sch., 2000-2003; chmn., bd. visitors Emory U., 1999-2000; dir. Atlanta Ballet Co., 1993-2003; bd. councilors Carter Ctr., 2000-2001; mem. Atlanta bd. Am. Red Cross, 2002—. Lt. U.S. Army, 1967—68, Korea. Mem.: Atlanta Rotary Club. Roman Catholic. Home: 2982 Habersham Rd NW Atlanta GA 30305-2854 Office: Haverty Furniture Companies Inc 780 Johnson Ferry Rd Atlanta GA 30342

**RIDLEY, HARRISON, JR.,** history professor; b. Phila., Oct. 22, 1938; s. Harrison and Janet Collins Ridley; m. Jade Ridley, July 18, 1986. Cert. in Radio Tele-Type, U.S. Army, 1962. Instr. Temple U., Phila., 1975—. Host radio WRTI 90 FM Temple U., Phila., 1976—; master ceremonies African Am. Cultural Mus., Phila., 1990—2000; discographer Libr. Congress, Washington, 1992; spkr. in field; cons. in field. Specialist U.S. Army, 1961—63. Named a Day in his hon., Mayor John F. Street, Phila., Pa., 2001; nominee Excellence in Jazz Broadcasting award, Jazz Journalists Assn., 2002; recipient Master Tchr. award, Temple U., 1989, Preserving Jazz Heritage award, Vols. Am. Del. Valley, 1996, Jazz Studies citation, Commonwealth Pa. Ho. Reps., 1996, 20 Yrs. Broadcasting award, Temple U., 1996, Preservation African-Am. Music award, Nat. Assn. Negro Musicians, 1997, numerous others. Mem.: Duke Ellington Soc., Clef Club (discographer 2000, historian, rschr. 1997—2002, 25 Yrs. Radio Broacasting award 2001). Avocations: basketball, collecting recordings. Home: 243 N Wanamaker St Philadelphia PA 19139 Office: Phila School Dist 734 Schuylkill Ave Philadelphia PA 19146

**RIDLEY, JOHN A.,** lawyer; b. Jersey City, Oct. 27, 1943; AB, St. Peter's Coll., 1965; LLB, U. Va., 1968. Bar: Va. 1968, N.J. 1968, U.S. Supreme Ct. 1979. Law sec. to Hon. Lawrence A. Whipple U.S. Dist. Ct. N.J., 1968-70; mem. Gibbons, Del Deo, Dolan, Griffinger & Vecchione, Newark, 1970—2002; ptnr. co-chair, labor and employment practice group Drinker Biddle & Reath LLP, Florham Park, 2002—. Mem. ABA (labor and employment law, litigation, tort and ins. practice sects.), N.J. State Bar Assn., Essex County Bar Assn. Office: Drinker Biddle & Reath LLP 500 Campus Dr Florham Park NJ 07932-1047 Office Phone: 973-549-7030. Office Fax: 973-360-9831. Business E-mail: john.ridley@dbr.com.

**RIDLOFF, RICHARD,** real estate investment advisor, lawyer, consultant; b. NYC, July 18, 1948; s. Sol and Daisey (Metz) R.; m. Caren Sara Berger, Mar. 27, 1977; children: Michael Joshua, Daniel Joseph. BA cum laude, Queens Coll., 1969; JD, Cornell U., 1972. Bar: N.Y. 1973. Assoc. counsel MONY, N.Y.C., 1972-79; sr. v.p., gen. counsel, sec. MONY Real Estate Investors, N.Y.C., 1979-85; v.p. investments MONY Fin. Svcs., N.Y.C., 1985-87; pres. MONY Realty Ptnrs. Inc., Glen Point, N.J., 1985-91; v.p. for investment mgmt. MONY Real Estate Investment Mgmt., N.Y.C., 1991-93; exec. v.p. Tibor Pivko and Co., Clifton, N.J., 1991-94; pres., dir. Growth & Income Inc., 1993-94; spl. projects dir. Kimco Realty Corp., 1995-96; pres. The Richardson Co., 1996—. Mem. adv. commn. on real property ins. to Calif. Sen. Com. on Ins. Claims and Corps., 1986-92; adv. com. N.Y. chpt. Nat. Assn. Corp. Real Estate Execs., 1990. Author: A Practical Guide to Construction Lending, 1985; editor Real Estate Financing Newsletter, 1980-85; contbr. articles to profl. jours. Mem. secondary sch. interviewing com. Cornell U., Ithaca, NY, 1981—; treas. Lansman Housing Corp., 2000—02; chmn. fed. legis. com. Nat. Assn. Real Estate Investment Trusts; trustee Jericho Jewish Ctr., 2002—. Mem.: N.Y. Bar Assn., Alpha Epsilon Pi, Pi Sigma Alpha, Omicron Delta Epsilon. Office Phone: 516-242-1531. E-mail: ricar77@hotmail.com.

**RIDLON, KATHLEEN,** dancer, educator; b. Greenwich, Conn., May 1, 1966; d. Charles Shepard and Susan Mary Ridlon. AA in Dance, Dean Coll., Franklin, Mass., 1986; BA in Psychology, CCNY, NYC, 1996; MFA in Performance and Choreography, Smith Coll., Northampton, Mass., 1998. Lectr. dance Coll. Holy Cross, Worcester, Mass., 1999—2002; prof. dance Providence Coll., 2001—02; lectr., artist in residence Knox Coll., Galesburg, Ill., 2003—. Program coord. MJT Dance Co., Boston, 1998; dir. Movement Together, Bklyn., 1993—95, Kid's Cmty. Dance Project, 1993—95, Midwest Dance Group, Galesburg, 2005—; coord. Ctr. Cmty. Svc. Knox Coll., 2006—; guest artist U. Okla., Norman, 2004—05. Dance coord. Arts Partners Ill. Inc, Peoria, 2005—06; vol. Galesburg RR Days, 2004—06. Mem.: Ill. Arts Coun. Artists Roster. Office: Knox College PO Box K-232 2 East South Street Galesburg IL 61401 Office Phone: 309-341-7085. Business E-Mail: kridlon@knox.edu.

**RIDOLFI, DOROTHY PORTER BOULDEN,** nurse, real estate broker; b. SI, NY, Jan. 24, 1937; d. David Porter and Helen Marie (McCloskey) Boulden; m. Edward Benjamin Ridolfi, Aug. 16, 1958; children: Edward Brian, Judyann Nixon, Jacqueline Ryan. RN, St. Francis Hosp., 1957; student, Seton Hall U., 1958, Mercer CC, 1974, student, 1984, Thomas Edison Coll., 1979—84. Cert. coronary and critical care nurse; real estate cert. South Jersey Sch. Profl. Bus., 1976, lic. real estate instr. NJ, broker NJ, sales person NJ, cert. residential broker, residential specialist. Owner Stay 'N Play Day Camp, 1963—65; nurse Princeton (NJ) Med. Ctr., 1972—73; pres., broker Ridolfi Realty Inc., Trenton, NJ, 1977—91; nurse Hamilton (NJ) Hosp., 1982—85; instr. real estate Mercer County CC and Career Devel. Sch. Trustee NJ Assn. Realtors Edn. Found., No. Regional Adv. Bd. Bank Mid Jersey. Corr. sec. Hist. Soc., Hightstown, NJ, 1971—72; bd. dirs. Campfire Girls and Boys, 1984; committeewoman Burlington County Dem. Com., Willingboro, NJ, 1966—67, Mercer County Dem. Com., East Windsor, NJ, 1969—72. Mem.: TREND, Mercer County Multiple Listing, Nat. Assn. Realtors, Nat. Fedn. Ind. Bus. (RPAC chmn. 1989), NJ Assn. Realtors (bd. dirs., v.p. 5th dist. 1989, Make Am. Better award 1982), Mercer County Bd. Realtors (bd. dirs. 1981—83, treas., v.p., pres. 1988—, 1997), Soroptomist Internat. of Am. and NJ, Mercer County C. of C. Roman Catholic. Avocations: genealogy, travel, reading. Office: Gloria Nilson Realtors GMAC Real Estate 1970 Rt 33 Hamilton Square NJ 08690 Personal E-mail: dotridolfi@aol.com.

**RIDOLFI, PATRICK MURPHY,** music educator, tenor; b. San Francisco, Calif., July 29, 1954; s. Joseph Oreste Ridolfi and Lillian Ruth Scott; m. Margie Gayatin, May 22, 1993; 1 child, Justin Robert; m. Barbara Ridolfi, Sept. 20, 1980 (dec. Nov. 6, 1989); 1 child, Joseph Patrick. BA, U. of Calif. at Santa Barbara, Santa Barbara, CA, 1977; BM, Calif. State U. at Northridge, Northridge, CA, 1987. Elem. tchr. LA Unified Sch. Dist., Los Angeles, Calif., 1991—2005; free-lance operatic tenor LA Opera, LA Master Chorale, Long Beach Opera, Carnegie Hall, Roger Wagner Chorale, Los Angeles, Calif., 1981—; elem. music tchr. LA Unified Sch. Dist., Los Angeles, Calif., 1995—. Grantee ELSA Grant, Fed. Arts Grant, 1999, 2000. Mem.: UTLA, MENC. Avocations: swimming, snorkeling, travel. Office Phone: 818-620-6515.

**RIDOUT, SUSAN RAMP,** education educator; b. Peoria, Ill., Nov. 3, 1955; d. Wayne Samuel and Dorothy Bowers Ramp; m. Kyle Royce Ridout, Oct. 2, 1983; children: Patrick, Emily. MA, Murray State U., 1976; PhD, Ind. U. 1983. Tchr. S.W. Elem. Sch., Murray, Ky., 1977—81; instr. So. Ill. U., Carbondale, 1980; grad. asst. Ind. U., Bloomington, 1981—83; asst. prof. edn. Ind. U. S.E., New Albany, 1983—89, assoc. prof. edn., 1989—95, prof. edn., 1995—. Cons. Perry County Schs., Leopold, Ind., 2001—, Springs Valley Schs., French Lick, Ind., 2002—06; mem. Action Team, Success by Six, Floyd County, Ind., 2005. Contbr. articles to profl. jours. Bd. dirs. Cmty. Action (Head Start), New Albany, Ind., 1996—; parent vol. Renaissance PTO/Theatre, Floyds Knobs, Ind., 1999—2006; v.p. Philanthropic Ednl. Orgn., New Albany, Ind., 1975—. Named one of Outstanding Young Women of Am., 1988; recipient Tchg. Excellence Recognition award, Ind. U., 1998, 1999, Master Tchr. award, Ind. U. S.E., 2002, Trustees' Tchg. award, 2003, Woman of Achievement award, Bus. and Profl. Women's Club, 2003. Mem.: Ind. Profs. of Reading, Internat. Reading Assn., Phi Delta Kappa (various positions 1982—). Avocations: watching theatrical productions, reading, spending time with family.*

**RIECHMANN, DEB,** reporter; Grad., U. Kansas William Allen White Sch. Journalism & Mass Communication, 1980. Writer AP, Washington. Recipient Merriman Smith award for excellence on deadline, White House Corrs. Assn., 2006. Office: AP Washington Bur 6th Fl 2021 K St NW Washington DC 20006-1082 also: AP Headquarters 450 W 33rd St New York NY 10001 Office Phone: 212-621-1500.*

**RIECK, WILLIAM ALBERT,** education educator, academic administrator; b. Hackensack, N.J., Jan. 15, 1942; s. William Emanual and Grace Adeline (Bormann) R.; m. Judith Ann Klindt, Apr. 18, 1965; children: Melissa, William Albert Jr. BA, Jersey City State Coll., 1963; MA, Montclair (N.J.) State Coll., 1966; DEd, Loyola U., Chgo., 1976. Asst. prof. Trenton State Coll., NJ, 1966-69; area mgr. Dupont Chem., Chgo., 1969-72; chemistry tchr. Lockport H.S., 1972-74; asst. prin. Oak Forest H.S., Ill., 1974-75; prin. Evanston Twp. H.S., Ill., 1975-76, Rock Island H.S., Ill., 1975-77, Fallsburg H.S., NY, 1977-80, Hicksville H.S., NY, 1980-90, Nottingham H.S., Trenton, 1982-90; prof. edn./dir. tchr. cadet corps U. La., Lafayette, 1991—, prof., dir. grad. studies edn., 1991—. Contbr. articles to profl. jours. Mem. Hamilton (N.J.) Say No to Drugs Com., 1987—, Hamilton Citizens for Edn., 1989—; advisor DeMolay chpt., Hamilton Sq., N.J., 1987—; trustee First Presbyn. Ch., Levittown, N.Y., 1981-84. Recipient Disting. Alumni award Jersey City State Coll., 1983, Citation, N.J. Gen. Assembly, 1983, Cert. of Appreciation, N.Y. Congress Parents and Tchrs., 1982; NSF grantee, 1968, 1994-95. Mem. Nat. Assn. Secondary Sch. Prins. (Svc. award 1989), N.J. Prins. and Suprs. Assn. (exec. coun. 1985—, Svc. award 1989), Assn. for Supervision and Curriculum Devel., Mercer County Prins. and Suprs. Assn. (sec. 1988—), Masons, Shriners (youth com. chmn. 1975-80). Presbyterian. Home: 108 Shadowbrush Bnd Lafayette LA 70506-7852 Office: U La Foster Hall 221 PO Box 42051 Lafayette LA 70504-0001 Office Phone: 337-482-6413. Business E-Mail: wrieck@louisiana.edu.

**RIECKENBERG, DESIREE,** academic administrator; d. Jerry and Carolyn Rieckenberg; m. Matt Starcke. BA in Psychology, Ea. Ill. U., 2001; MS in Ednl. Adminstrn., Tex. A&M U., 2004. Program coord. Office Student Conduct U. Nev., Las Vegas, 2004—. Mem.: Am. Coll. Personnel Assn., Nat. Assn. Student Pers. Adminstrs., Assn. Student Jud. Affairs. Avocations: travel, running, hiking. Office: U Nev Box 452019 4505 Maryland Pkwy Las Vegas NV 89154

**RIEDEL, ALAN ELLIS,** manufacturing executive, lawyer; b. Bellaire, Ohio, June 28, 1930; s. Emil George and Alberta (Shafer) R.; m. Ruby P. Tignor, June 21, 1953; children: Ralph A., Amy L., John T. AB magna cum laude, Ohio U., 1952, LLD (hon.), 1994; JD, Case Western Res. U., 1955; grad., Advanced Mgmt. Program, Harvard, 1971. Bar: Ohio 1955, Tex. 1968. Assoc. Squire, Sanders & Dempsey, Cleve., 1955-60; from gen. counsel to sec. Cooper Industries Inc. (formerly Cooper Bessemer Co.), Mt. Vernon, Ohio, 1960-68; from sec. to v.p. indsl. rels. Cooper Industries Inc., Mt. Vernon, Ohio, 1963-73; from sr. v.p. adminstrn. to vice chmn. Cooper Industries, Inc., Houston, 1973-94. Dir. Factory Mut. Ins., 1999-2000; bd. dirs. Belden Inc., St. Louis, 1993-2000, Gardner Denver Inc., Quincy, Ill., 1994-2000, chmn. bd. dirs., 1994-98; of counsel Squire, Sanders & Dempsey, Houston, 1994-2000. Past chmn. bd. dirs. S.E. Tex.; trustee, past chmn. bd. trustees Ohio U. Endowment Found. Mem. Order of Coif, Phi Beta Kappa, Omicron Delta Kappa, Delta Tau Delta. Home: Bunker Hill Village 4 Heritage Ct Houston TX 77024 E-mail: aeriedel@swbell.net.

**RIEDEL, BERNARD EDWARD,** retired pharmaceutical sciences educator; b. Provost, Alta., Can., Sept. 25, 1919; s. Martin and Naomi E. (Klingaman) R.; m. Julia C. McClurg, Mar. 5, 1944 (dec. Mar. 1992); children: Gail Lynne, Dwain Edward, Barry Robert; m. Della Williams, Sept. 2, 2000. BS in Pharmacy, U. Alta., Edmonton, 1943, MS in Pharmacology, 1949, DSc (hon.), 1990; PhD in Biochemistry, U. Western Ont., 1953. Lectr., asst. prof. Faculty of Pharmacy U. Alta., Edmonton, 1946-49, asst. prof. then assoc. prof., 1953-58, prof., 1959-67, exec. asst. to v.p., 1961-67; dean, prof. Faculty Pharm. Scis. U. B.C., Vancouver, Canada, 1967-84, coord. Health Scis. Centre, 1977-84. Mem. sci. adv. com. Health Rsch. Found. of B.C., 1991-95. Contbr. numerous articles on pharmacology to profl. jours. Elder Ryerson United Ch.; mem. exec. bd. Boy Scouts Can., Edmonton Region, Alta.; mem. Cancer Control Agy. of B.C., trustee 1979-86, v.p., 1984, pres. 1985-86; bd. dirs. B.C. Lung Assn., 1988-2000, v.p., 1989, pres., 1990-91; chmn., bd. dirs. B.C. Organ Transplant Soc., 1986-89, hon. bd. dirs., 2000. Wing comdr. RCAF, 1943-46, 49-67. Decorated mem. Order of Can.; recipient Gold medal in Pharmacy, 1943; Centennial medal, 1967, 75th Anniversary medal U. B.C., 1990; Can Forces decoration, 1965; Commemorative medal for 125th Anniversary of the Confedn. of Can., 1992, Spl. Svcs. award Assn. Faculties of Pharmacy of Can., 2001, Queen Elizabeth II Golden Jubilee medal, 2002. Mem. Alta. Pharm. Assn. (hon. life), Can. Pharm. Assn. (hon. life), Assn. of Faculties of Pharmacy of Can. (hon. life, chmn. 1959, 69, Spl. Svc. award 2001), Can. Biochem. Soc., Pharmacol. Soc. Can., Can. Assn. of Univ. Tchrs., Can. Soc. Hosp. Pharmacists, B.C. Coll. Pharmacists (hon. life), U. B.C. Profs. Emeriti Divsn. Alumni Assn. (pres. 1993-95). Home: 8394 Angus Dr Vancouver BC Canada V6P 5L2 E-mail: briedel@interchange.ubc.ca.

**RIEDEL, BUNNIE,** not-for-profit organization executive; m. Daniel M. Gartland; 2 children. Formerly founder, exec. dir. Religious Coalition for Reproductive Choice of So. Calif.; formerly nat. field dir. Ams. United for Separation of Ch. and State; exec. dir. Alliance for Cmty. Media, Washington, 1998—. Spkr. in field. Author: (booklets) Faith and Freedom: Church/State Separation in Our Time, Reflections on Religious Liberty, A Matter of Conscience; contbr. articles to jour., mags., textbooks; appearances on numerous TV and radio programs. Recipient award, V.p. Al Gore, 1999, Recognition for Leadership award, Calif. State Senate. Mem.: Phi Kappa Phi. Office: Alliance for Cmty Media 666 11th St NW Washington DC 20001-4542

**RIEDEL, HOLLY,** theater director; m. Roy Burney, July 27, 2005; 1 child, John H. Matthews. BA, Eckerd Coll., St. Petersburg, 1976; MA, U. South Fla., Tampa, 1981. A.p. English, theatre dir. Ingram Tom Moore HS, Ingram, Tex., 2001—. V.p. ITM Friends and Faculty, Ingram, Tex., 2004—06. Recipient Best Supporting Actress, Hill Country Arts Found., 1998, Best Actress, 2004, Harvard Book prize, Harvard U., 2006. Mem.: Ednl. Theatre Assn., Nat. Coun. Tchr. of English, Tex. Educators in Theatre Assn. Office: Ingram Tom Moore HS 510 College St Ingram TX 78025 Office Phone: 830-367-4111. Office Fax: 830-367-7332.

**RIEDER, ERIC,** lawyer; BA, Columbia U., 1976, JD, 1985. Bar: NY 1987, US Dist. Ct. (so. and ea dists.) NY, US Ct. Appeals (2d cir.). Ptnr., leader Securities Enforcement, Compliance Litig. Group, Bryan Cave LLP, NYC. Office: Bryan Cave LLP 1290 Ave of the Americas New York NY 10104 Office Phone: 212-541-2057. E-mail: erieder@bryancave.com.

**RIEDER, SHERRY L.,** psychologist; b. Fond du Lac, Wis., July 8, 1974; d. David J. and Carol J. Rieder. BS with honors, U. Wis., 1996; MA, U. Ill., Chgo., 1999, PhD, 2003. Psychologist, owner Palmetto Health Psychology LLC, Charleston, SC, 2005—. Adj. faculty Coll. Charleston, 2004—, Walden U. online, 2005—. Contbr. articles to profl. jours. Fellow, Med. U. SC, Charleston, 2003—05. Mem.: APA, SC Psychol. Assn. Office: Palmetto Health Psychology LLC 152 Cannon St Ste A Charleston SC 29403

**RIEDESEL, LAUREEN FALK,** library director; b. Wakefield, Nebr., June 1, 1951; d. Arlyn Dale and Glaura Milly (Harry) Falk; m. Charles Paul Riedesel, May 25, 1973; children: Aprilla Florentine Lynnae, Amerilla Maye Falk. BA, Wheaton Coll., 1973; MA in Libr. Sci., U. Mo., 1974. Cert. libr. level V, Nebr. Youth svcs. libr. Dunklin County Libr., Kennett, Mo., 1974-77; dir. Beatrice (Nebr.) Pub. Libr., 1977—. Instr. Nebr. Libr. Commn., Lincoln, 1988-92; spkr. Nebr. Humanities Coun. Spkrs. Bur., 1993—. Editor: Nebraska Writers, Nebraska Readers, 1995; contbr. articles to profl. jours. Incorporator, exec. bd. Gage County Heritage Preservation, Inc., Beatrice, 1987—97, 1999—; alt. del. White House Conf. on Librs., Washington, 1991; hist. preservation rep. City Plan Coordinating Com., Beatrice, 1991—92, 1999—2001; apptd. mem. Gov.'s Task Force on Hist. Preservation, Nebr., 1992—94; co-dir. Nebr. Lit. Festival, 2000; Gov.'s appointee representing librs. to State Records Bd., 2002—; bd. dirs. Nebr. State Hist. Soc. Found., 2003—. Named Outstanding Genealogist, Nebr. State Genealogical Soc., 1992, Woman of the Yr., Beatrice Bus. and Profl. Women, 1993, Outstanding Cmty. Leader, Beatrice Jaycees, 1993, Citizen of the Yr., Beatrice C. of C., 1995, Sower award Nebr. Humanities Coun., 1998. Mem.: ALA, Nat. Libr. Assn. (pres. 1989, Excalibur Outstanding Libr. award pub. libr. sect. 1991, Meritorious Svc. award 1998), Nat. Mgmt. Assn. (charter, exec. bd. mem. 1993, 1998—99), Friends of Homestead Nat. Monument of Am. (pres. 1999—), Nebr. Lit. Heritage Assn. (bd. mem. 2001—), S.E. Nebr. Genealogical Soc. (charter, Hall of Fame 1982), S.E. Nebr. Coords. for Literacy (charter), Nebr. Ctr. for the Book (exec. bd. 1992—99, pres. 1998). Democrat. Mem. Church of the Brethren. Avocations: reading, history, genealogy, doll collecting, antiques. Home: 721 Grant St Beatrice NE 68310-2939 Office Phone: 402-223-3584.

**RIEDL, JOHN ORTH,** retired university dean; b. Milw., Dec. 9, 1937; s. John O. and Clare C. (Quirk) R.; m. Mary Lucille Priestap, Feb. 4, 1961; children: John T., Ann E., James W., Steven E., Daniel J. BS in Math. magna cum laude, Marquette U., Milw., 1958; MS in Math., U. Notre Dame, 1960, PhD in Math., 1963; postgrad., Northwestern U., 1963. Asst. prof. math. Ohio State U., Columbus, 1966-70, assoc. prof., 1970—2003, asst. dean Coll. Math. and Phys. Sci., 1969-74, assoc. dean, 1974-87, acting dean, 1984-86, spl. asst. to provost, 1987—2003, dean, dir. Mansfield (Ohio) Campus, 1988—2003, exec. dean regional campus, 1988—2003; prof. emeritus, 2003—; ret. 2003. Panelist sci. edn. NSF, 1980-91; cons. Ohio Dept. Edn., 1989, Ohio bd. regents subsidy cons., 1991, 95, 97, 99, 2001, 03; bd. dirs. Richland County Univ. and Coll. Access Network, 2001—, pres. Richland County bus. adv. coun., 2004—. Pres., v.p. exec. Univ. Cmty. Assn., Columbus, 1970-78; mem. edn. commn. St. Peter's Schs., Mansfield, 1989-95; trustee Rehab. Svc. N. Ctrl. Ohio, Mansfield, 1990-99, v.p., 1993-94, pres., 1995-97; pres. Ohio Assn. Regional Campuses, 1993-94; co-chair capital campaign St. Peter's Schs., 1998. Recipient Faculty Svc. award, Nat. U. Continuing Edn. Assn., 1988, Creative Programming award, 1988; NSF grad. fellow, 1960—62. Mem. Math. Assn. Am. (chair com. on minicourse 1981-87), Downs Am. Chestnut Found. of Ohio (bd. dirs. 2001-04), Rotary Internat. (bd. dirs., pres.-elect, pres.) C. of C. (bd. dirs.). Democrat. Roman

Catholic. Avocations: fishing, woodworking, gardening. Home: 789 Clifton Blvd Mansfield OH 44907-2284 Office: Ohio State U 1680 University Dr Mansfield OH 44906-1547 Business E-mail: riedl.1@osu.edu.

**RIEDLINGER, STEPHEN C.,** federal judge; b. 1950; BA, La. State U., 1971, JD, 1977. Bar: La. 1977, U.S. Dist. Ct. (ea. dist.) La. 1979, U.S. Dist. Ct. (mid. dist.) 1978, U.S. Ct. Appeals (5th cir.) 1983. Law clk. U.S. Dist. Ct. La., 1977-78; pvt. practice Baton Rouge, 1978-86; magistrate judge U.S. Dist. Ct. (mid. dist.) La., Baton Rouge, 1986—. With USNR, 1971-77. Office: Russell B Long Fed Bldg & Courthouse 777 Florida St Ste 260 Baton Rouge LA 70801-1717 Office Phone: 225-389-3584. Office Fax: 225-389-3585.

**RIEDMAN, MARY SUZANNE,** lawyer; b. June 1951; JD, Yale U. Bar: Wash. 1980, DC 1983, Calif. 1988. Various positions Beverly Enterprises Inc., Forth Smith, Ark.; counsel Vencor Inc., Louisville, 1995—96, assoc. gen. counsel, 1996—97, v.p.; assoc. gen. counsel, 1997—98; (In 1998 Vencor Inc. split into Vencor Inc. and Ventas Inc.); v.p., assoc. gen. counsel Vencor Inc. (renamed Kindred Healthcare Inc. in 2001), Louisville, 1998—99, sr. v.p., gen. counsel, 1999—. Office: Kindred Healthcare Inc 680 S 4th St Louisville KY 40202-2412

**RIEDY, MARK JOSEPH,** finance educator; b. Aurora, Ill., July 9, 1942; s. Paul Bernard and Kathryn Veronica R.; m. Erin Jeanne Lynch, Aug. 29, 1964; children: Jennifer Erin, John Mark. BA in Econs. maxima cum laude, Loras Coll., 1964; MBA, Washington U., St. Louis, 1966; PhD, U. Mich., 1971. Asst. prof. bus. adminstrn. U. Colo., Boulder, 1969-71; sr. staff economist Council of Econ. Advisers, Washington, 1971-72; spl. asst. to chmn. Fed. Home Loan Bank Bd., Washington, 1972; v.p., dir. research PMI Investment Corp., San Francisco, 1973; v.p., chief economist Fed. Home Loan Bank of San Francisco, 1973-77; exec. v.p., chief operating officer Mortgage Bankers Assn. of Am., Washington, 1978-84; pres., chief operating officer Fed. Nat. Mortgage Assn., Washington, 1985-86, cons., 1986-87; pres., chief operating officer J.E. Robert Cos., Alexandria, Va., 1987-88; pres., chief exec. officer Nat. Coun. Community Bankers, Washington, 1988-92, also bd. dirs.; prof. real estate fin. U. San Diego, 1993—, exec. dir. Burnham-Moores Ctr. Real Estate, 1993—. Mem. adv. coun. Credit Rsch. Ctr., Purdue U., 1981-82; bd. dirs. Fed. Nat. Mortgage Assn., Continental Savs. Bank, AccuBanc Mortgage Corp., Pan Pacific Retail Properties, Inc., Am. Mortgage Network, Inc., Bio-Med. Realty Trust, Noble Broadcast Group, Drayton Ins. Cos., Perpetual Savs. Bank, Ctr. for Fin. Studies; chmn., bd. dirs., Neighborhood Bancorp; mem. San Diego Mayor's Renaissance Commn. Bd. dirs Lambda Alpha Internat. Woodrow Wilson scholar, 1964; Nat. Def. scholar, 1964-66; U.S. Steel Found. fellow, 1966-68; Robert G. Rodkey Found. fellow, 1966-69; Earhart Found. fellow, 1968-69 Mem. Am. Econ. Assn., Am. Fin. Assn., Nat. Assn. Bus. Economists, Am. Soc. Assn. Execs., Urban Land Inst. Office: U San Diego Sch Bus Adminstrn 5998 Alcala Park San Diego CA 92110-2492 Business E-Mail: mriedy@sandiego.edu.

**RIEF, MICHELLE M.,** cultural studies educator; b. Council Bluffs, Iowa, Oct. 8, 1972; d. Thomas L. and Jeanne A. Rief; m. David F. Carpio, Aug. 16, 2003. BS, Fla. State U., 1993; MA, Temple U., 2003, PhD, 0103. Exec. dir. Thresholds in Del. County, Media, Pa., 1999—2003; asst. prof. Borough of Manhattan C.C., N.Y.C., 2003—06. Faculty fellow publs. program, CUNY, 2005. Mem.: Nat. Women's Studies Assn., Nat. Coun. Black Studies, Am. Hist. Assn., Assn. for Study of African Am. Life and History. Unitarian Universalist. Avocations: travel, films. Office Phone: 212-220-1372. Office Fax: 212-220-1508. Business E-Mail: mrief@bmcc.cuny.edu. E-mail: mreif@comcast.net.

**RIEFF, DAVID SONTAG,** editor, writer, critic; b. Boston, Sept. 28, 1952; s. Philip and Susan (Sontag) R. Student, The Lycee Francais de NY, New Lincoln Sch., B.A., Princeton U., 1978. Dir. publs. N.Y. Inst. for Humanities, 1980-85, program dir., 1984—85, now fellow; sr. editor Farrar, Straus & Giroux Inc., N.Y.C., 1979—89. vis. prof., creative writing, City Univ. NY, 1985-86; visiting faculty, Empire State Summer Writing Program, Skidmore Coll., 1990-95; freelance writer, 1989-, dep. editor, World Policy Jour., 1998-; contbg. editor, The New Republic, 1990-. Author: Texas Boots, 1979, Going to Miami: Exiles, Tourists, and Refugees in the New America, 1987, Los Angeles: Capital of the Third World, 1991, The Exile: Cuba in the Heart of Miami, 1993, Slaughterhouse: Bosnia and the Failure of the West, 1995, A Bed for the Night: Humanitarianism in Crisis, 2002, At the Point of a Gun: Democratic Dreams and Armed Intervention, 2005; contbr. numerous articles, short stories to various pubs. Club: Princeton (N.Y.C.). Office: Pentagram Design 204 5th Ave New York NY 10010-2103 Address: c/o Wylie Agy Ste 2114 250 W 57th St New York NY 10107 E-mail: davidrieff@compuserve.com.

**RIEFLER, DONALD BROWN,** financial consultant; b. Washington, Nov. 10, 1927; s. Winfield W. and Dorothy (Brown) R.; m. Patricia Hawley, Oct. 12, 1957; children: Duncan, Linda, Barbara. BA, Amherst Coll., 1949. With J.P. Morgan & Co. Inc., N.Y.C., 1952-91; v.p. Morgan Guaranty Trust Co. of N.Y., 1962-68, sr. v.p., 1968-77, chmn. sources and uses of funds com., 1977—88, comml. market risk com., 1989—91; fin. mkts. cons., 1991—. With U.S. Army, 1950-52. Mem. John's Island Club, Riomar Country Club, Quail Valley River Club, Birchwood Farms Club, Harbor Point Club. Home: 512 Bay Dr Vero Beach FL 32963-2107

**RIEGEL, BYRON WILLIAM,** ophthalmologist; b. Evanston, Ill., Jan. 19, 1938; s. Byron and Belle Mae (Huot) Riegel; m. Marilyn Hills, May 18, 1968; children: Marc William, Ryan Marie, and Elizabeth. BS, Stanford U., 1960; MD, Cornell U., 1964. Diplomate Am Bd Ophthalmology, Nat Bd Med Examiners. Intern King County Hosp., Seattle, 1964-65; asst. resident in surgery U. Wash., Seattle, 1965; resident in ophthalmology U, Fla., Fla., 1968-71; pvt. practice medicine specializing in ophthalmology Sierra Eye Med. Group, Inc., Visalia, Calif., 1972—. Mem staff Kaweah Delta Dist Hosp, chief staff, 1978—79, bd dirs, asst secy, 1983—90; asst med dir Sierra Ambulatory Surg Ctr, Visalia, Calif., 2000—. Flight surgeon USN, 1966—68. Co-recipient Fight-for-Sight Citation for rsch. in retinal dystrophy, 1970. Fellow: ACS, Am. Acad. Ophthalmology; mem.: Am. Soc. Cataract and Refractive Surgery, Calif. Acad. Ophthalmology (v.p. 3d party liaison 1994—96, dir. 1996—98), Tulare County Med Asn, Calif. Med. Assn. (del. 1978—79), Rotary (Visalia). Roman Catholic. Home: 3027 Keogh Ct Visalia CA 93291-4228 Office: 2830 W Main St Visalia CA 93291-4331 Office Phone: 559-636-1000. Personal E-mail: briegel@pacbell.net. Business E-Mail: briegel@sierraeye.com.

**RIEGEL, CAROLINE S. E.,** marketing professional; b. Flemington, NJ, Mar. 10, 1979; d. Daniel Lee and Sheila Robbins Riegel. BA, Brandeis U., Waltham, Mass., 2000; MA, Emory U., Atlanta, 2002. On-site promotions coord. Entercom Boston, 2002—03; promotions dir. Good Karma Broadcasting, Madison, Wis., 2003—05; dir. mktg. and promotions Cox Radio Group 95-5 BEAT, Atlanta, 2005—. Sunday sch. tchr. Temple Sinai, Atlanta, 2005—06. Mem.: Mensa. Liberal. Conservative Judaism. Avocations: sudoku math puzzles, science fiction literature. Office: Cox Radio Group 95-5 BEAT 1601 W Peachtree St NE Atlanta GA 30309 Office Phone: 404-962-2041. E-mail: caroline.riegel@coxradio.com.

**RIEGEL, KURT WETHERHOLD,** environmental protection executive; b. Lexington, Va., Feb. 28, 1939; s. Oscar Wetherhold and Jane Cordelia (Butterworth) R.; children: Tatiana Suzanne, Samuel Brent Oscar, Eden Sonja Jane. BA, Johns Hopkins U., 1961; PhD, U. Md., 1966; PMD, Harvard U., 1977. Asst. prof. astronomy UCLA, 1966-74; prof. astronomy U. Calif. Extension, Los Angeles, 1968-74; mgr. energy conservation program Fed. Energy Adminstrn., Washington, 1974-75; chief tech. and consumer products energy conservation Dept. Energy, Washington, 1975-78, dir. consumer products divsn., conservation and solar energy, 1978-79; assoc dir. environ. engring. and tech. EPA, 1979-82; head Astronomy Ctrs. NSF, 1982-89; dir. Environ. Protection Office USN, 1989-94, dir. environ. tech. Washington, 1994—2001. Adj. prof. George Washington U., 1995, Johns Hopkins U.,

2001—; vis. prof. Washington & Lee U., 1993; cons. Aerospace Corp., El Segundo, Calif., 1967-70, Rand Corp., Santa Monica, Calif., 1973-74; vis. fellow U. Leiden, Netherlands, 1972-73; mem. Casualty Council Underwriters Labs., Nat. Radio Astron. Observatory Users Com., 1968-74; chair gov.'s environ. edn. adv. commn. colls. and univs., Va., 2000-2003. Contbr. articles to profl. jours. Mem. AAAS, Am. Phys. Soc., Sierra Club, Audubon Soc., Internat. Radio Sci. Union, Am. Astron. Soc., Internat. Astron. Union, Assn. of Scientists and Engrs. Home: 171 Gulchleigh Ln Glasgow VA 24555-2266 E-mail: riegel.kurt@apl.jhu.edu.

**RIEGER, JAMES A.,** plastic surgeon; m. Linda M. Rieger; children: Katrina, Andrew, Claire. BS in Chem. Engring., SUNY, Buffalo; MD, St. Louis U. Cert. Am. Bd. Plastic Surgery, lic. physician Kansas, Calif. Sole practitioner Aesthetic Plastic Surgery PA, Wichita, Kans. Mem.: Am. Soc. Plastic Surgery, Am. Soc. Aesthetic Plastic Surgery. Avocations: gardening, bicycling, hiking, travel. Office: Aesthetic Plastic Surgery Ste 204 9300 E 29th St N Wichita KS 67226-2183

**RIEGER, MICHAEL IRA,** lawyer; b. N.Y.C., Oct. 19, 1952; s. Joseph and Adrienne R. BA in Sociology, SUNY, Buffalo, 1973; JD, George Mason U., 1977. Bar: Va. 1977. Pvt. practice, Fairfax, Va., 1977—. Lectr. in field. Mem. Va. State Bar Assn., Fairfax Bar Assn. co-chmn. com. law related edn. 1996-97, co-chmn. com. continuing legal edn. 1995-96, chmn. subcom. gen. dist. ct. criminal law 1993-95, com. mem. 1992—) Office: Ste 301-B 10623 Jones St Fairfax VA 22030 Office Phone: 703-352-1400. E-mail: riegerlaw@aol.com.

**RIEGER, MITCHELL SHERIDAN,** lawyer; b. Chgo., Sept. 5, 1922; s. Louis and Evelyn (Sampson) Rieger; m. Rena White Abelmann, May 17, 1949 (div. 1957); 1 child, Karen Gross Cooper; m. Nancy Homer, May 30, 1961 (div. 1972); stepchildren: Jill Levi, Linda Hanan, Susan Perlstein, James Geoffrey Felsenthal; m. Pearl Handelsman, June 10, 1973; stepchildren: Steven Newman, Mary Ann Moseley, Nancy Halbeck. AB, Northwestern U., 1944; JD, Harvard U., 1949. Bar: Ill. 1950, U.S. Dist. Ct. (no. dist.) Ill. 1950, U.S. Supreme Ct. 1953, U.S. Ct. Mil. Appeals 1953, U.S. Ct. Appeals (7th cir.) 1954. Legal asst. Rieger & Rieger, Chgo., 1949-50, assoc., 1950-54; asst. U.S. atty. No. Dist Ill., Chgo., 1954-60, 1st asst., 1958-60; assoc. gen. counsel SEC, Washington, 1960-61; ptnr. Schiff Hardin & Waite, Chgo., 1961—, sr. counsel, 1998—. Instr. John Marshall Law Sch., Chgo., 1952—54. Contbr. articles to profl. jours. Mem. Chgo. Crime Commn., 1964—, bd. dirs., 1998—; pres. Park View Home Aged, 1969—71; bd. dirs. Spertus Mus. Judaica, 1987—91, mem. vis. com., 1991—2005; Rep. precinct committeeman Highland Park, Ill., 1964—68. Served to It. (j.g.) USNR, 1943—46, PTO. Fellow: Am. Coll. Trial Lawyers; mem.: FBA (pres. Chgo. chpt. 1959—60, nat. v.p. 1960—61), ABA, 7th Cir. Bar Assn., Am. Judicature Soc., Ill. Bar Assn., Chgo. Bar Assn., Vail Racquet Club, Lawyers Club Chgo., Standard Club, Phi Beta Kappa. Jewish. Avocations: photography, skiing, sailing. Office: SchiffHardin LLP 6600 Sears Tower Chicago IL 60606 Office Phone: 312-258-5644. Personal E-mail: msheridanr@aol.com. Business E-mail: mrieger@schiffhardin.com.

**RIEGSECKER, MARVIN DEAN,** pharmacist, state senator; b. Goshen, Ind., July 5, 1937; s. Levi and Mayme (Kauffman) R.; m. Norma Jane Shrock, Aug. 3, 1958; children: Steven Scott, Michael Dean. BA in Pharmacy, U. Colo., 1967. Pharmacist Parkside Pharmacy, Goshen, Ind., 1967-73, Walgreens, Goshen, 1994-96, Meijer, Goshen, 1998—2004; pharmacist, mgr. Hooks Drugs, Inc., Goshen, 1973-94; coroner Elkhart County, Goshen, 1977-84; mem. Ind. Senate from 12th dist., Indpls., 1988—; pharmacy cons., 2003—. Bus. affairs cons. Goshen Health Sys., 1997-98. Rep. committeeman Elkhart County, 1985-88; bd. commrs. pres., 1987-88; past adv. bd. dirs. Oaklawn Hosp.; past chmn. Michiana Area Coun. of Govts. Mem. Ind. Pharm. Assn. Republican. Mennonite. Avocation: jogging. Home: 1814 Kentfield Way Goshen IN 46526-5610 Office: Ind Senate Statehouse 200 W Washington St Indianapolis IN 46204-2728

**RIEHECKY, JANET ELLEN,** writer; b. Waukegan, Ill., Mar. 5, 1953; d. Roland Wayne and Patricia Helen (Anderson) Polsgrove; m. John Jay Riehecky, Aug. 2, 1975; 1 child, Patrick William. BA summa cum laude, Ill. Wesleyan U., 1975; MA in Comm., Ill. State U., 1978; MA in English, Northwestern U., 1983. Tchr. English Blue Mound (Ill.) H.S., 1977-80, West Chicago (Ill.) H.S., 1984-86; editor Child's World Pub. Co., Elgin, Ill., 1987-90; freelance writer Elgin, 1990—. Author: Dinosaur series, 24 vols., 1988, UFOs, 1989, Saving the Forests, 1990, Irish Americans, 1995, The Mystery of the Missing Money, 1996, The Mystery of the UFO, 1996, Stegosaurus, 1998, Triceratops, 1998, Tyrannosaurus, 1998, Velociroptor, 1998, A Ticket to China, 1999, Greece, Sweden, 2000, George Lucas, 2001, The Emancipation Proclamation, 2002, The Osage Nation, 2002, The Cree Nation, 2002, Indonesia, 2002, The Plymouth Colony, 2002, The Settling of Jamestown, 2002, The Settling of St. Augustine, 2002, The Siege of the Alamo, 2002, Benjamin Franklin, 2003, Daniel Boone, 2003, The Wampanoag, 2003, Ulysses S. Grant, 2004, William McKinley, 2005, Respect, 2005, Citizenship, 2005, Cooperation, 2005, Iguanodon, 2006, Diplademos, 2006, Pteranodon, 2006, Megalodon, 2006. Nat. dir. Kids Love a Mystery, 1999-2004. Recipient Summit award for best children's nonfiction Soc. Midland Authors, 1988. Mem. Soc. Am. Magicians, Soc. Children's Book Writers and Illustrators (network rep. 2006), Mystery Writers Am. (midwest bd. dirs. 2000-04), Sisters in Crime, Phi Kappa Phi. Democrat. Baptist. Avocations: reading, hiking, dinosaur hunting. Office Phone: 847-695-9781. Personal E-mail: jr@janetriehecky.com.

**RIEHL, JANE ELLEN,** education educator; b. New Albany, Ind., Oct. 17, 1942; d. Henry Gabbart Jr. and Mary Elizabeth Willham; m. Richard Emil Riehl, June 15, 1968; 1 child, Mary Ellen. BA in Elem. Edn., U. Evansville, 1964; MS, Ind. U., Bloomington, 1966; postgrad., Spalding U., 1979, Ind. U., S.E., New Albany, 1991—2002. Cert. 1-8 and kindergarten tchr., Ind.; lic. profl. elem adminstrn., reading minor kindergarten tchr., Ind. Elem. tchr. Clarksville (Ind.) Cmty. Sch., 1964-68, 70-75, 81-82, tchr. kindergarten, 1975-81; elem. tchr. Chapelwood Sch. Wayne Twp., Indpls., 1968-70; lectr. edn. Ind. U. S.E., 1988-97, dir. tchg. and rsch. project, 1990-91, 92-93, dir. field and career placement, cert./lic. grad advisor New Albany, 1998, coord. elem./spl. edn. field and career placement, license and grad. advisor, 1998—. Cons. Riehl Assocs., Jeffersonville, Ind., 1995—. Co-author: An Integrated Language Arts Teacher Education Program, 1990, The Reading Professor, 1992, Multimedia: HyperStudio and Language Education, 1996, Technology: Hypermedia and Communications, 1997, others; author procs. Parent vol. Girl Scouts U.S.A., Jeffersonville, 1988-95; mem. adminstrtv. bd. Wall Street United Meth. Ch., Jeffersonville, 1993-95; mem. women's health adv. coun. Clark Meml. Hosp., Jeffersonville, 1995—; bd. dirs. Clark Meml. Hosp. Found., vice chair, 1999, chair 2000, sec. 2002-03; team mem. People to People Citizen Amb. Program, 1993, 95, 96; chair internat. bylaws Altrusa Internat., Inc., 2001—. Named Young Career Woman of Yr. Bus. and Profl. Women New Albany and Dist. 13 Ind., 1966; tchg. and rsch. grantee Ind. U. S.E., 1990, 94, 95, 96, 97, 2000; recipient Disting. Tchg. award Ind. U. S.E., 1997, Tchg. Excellence Recognition award, 1997. Mem. Nat. Coun. Tchrs. English, Profs. Reading Tchr. Edn., Ind. State Med. Assn. Alliance (v.p. so. area 1999-2000), Clark County Med. Soc. Alliance (pres.-elect 1997-98, pres. 1998-99), Altrusa Internat. Inc. (internat. bd. 1993-95, dist. gov. 1993-95, svc. award 1995), Phi Delta Kappa (v.p. 1991-92, pres. 1997—, svc. award 1991), Kappa Kappa Kappa (pres. Jeffersonville 1975-76, 90-91, Outstanding Mem. award 1987). Avocations: travel, reading, crafts, decorating. Home: 1610 Fox Run Trl Jeffersonville IN 47130-8204 Office: U Ind U SE 4201 Grant Line Rd New Albany IN 47150-2158

**RIEHLE, B. HUDSON,** trade association executive; b. Cin., Sept. 10, 1953; s. Robert Arthur Riehle and Lois A. Wich; m. Eileen Patricia Betit, Aug. 2, 1986; children: B. Hudson Jr., Bradley Patrick. BA, Skidmore Coll., 1975; MBA, U. Pa., 1986. Rsch. cons. Avmark, Inc., Washington, 1976-78; rsch. analyst Airline Pilots Assn., Washington, 1978-81, supr. econ. analysis, 1981-84; rsch. mgr. Nat. Restaurant Assn., Washington, 1986-91, sr. rsch. mgr., 1991-95, dir. rsch., 1995-97, sr. dir. rsch., 1997-99, v.p. rsch. & info. svcs., 1999-2000, sr. v.p. rsch. and info. svcs., 2000—; bd. dirs. Alexandria

Econ. Devel. Partnership, 2002—04. Bus. rsch. adv. coun. Bureau of Labor Stats., 2003—. Editor: Comml. Airline Fleets, 1976—78, Restaurant Industry Ops. Report, 1986—; contbr. Airline Pilot, 1978—84, Restaurants USA, 1986-2002. Mem., bd. dirs., 1st v.p. Fairlington Meadows, Arlington, 1990—92. Mem.: Alexandria Conv. and Visitors Assn. (vice chmn. bd. govs. 2001—02, chmn. bd. govs. 2002—04, treas. 2004—05). Avocations: geology, cross country skiing, photography. Home: 2431 Davis Ave Alexandria VA 22302-3209 Office: Nat Restaurant Assn 1200 17th St NW Ste 700 Washington DC 20036-3006 Office Phone: 202-331-5962. E-mail: hriehle@dineout.org.

**RIEHLE, BARRY STEVEN,** physicist, researcher; b. Cin., Jan. 8, 1952; s. James Francis and Jean Mary (Schaefer) R.; m. Kathleen Anne Giegel, May 16, 1961. BS in Physics, Xavier U., Cin., 1974, MEd in Physics, 1989; MA in Theology, Athenaeum of Ohio, Cin., 1978, MA in Bibl. Studies, 1979. Cert. tchr. 7-12 physics, math., Ohio. Tchr. physics, religion Cath. Ctrl. H.S., Springfield, Ohio, 1978-81; assoc. pastor St. Raphael's Ch., Springfield, 1978-81; tchr. religion Badin H.S., Hamilton, Ohio, 1981-82; assoc. pastor St. Peter-in-Chains Ch., Hamilton, 1981-82, St. Mary's Ch., Oxford, Ohio, 1982-84; tchr. physics Turpin H.S., Cin., 1985—, in-svc. presenter, 1993—. Bible study leader Christ Renews Luth. Ch. of Resurrection, Cin., 1996—; spiritual dir. Immaculate Heart of Mary Ch., Cin., 1991, 93, 95. Mem. Am. Assn. Physics Tchrs., Tri-State Physics Tchrs., Nat. Sci. Tchrs. Assn., Union of Concerned Scientists. Avocation: golf. Office: Turpin HS 2650 Bartels Rd Cincinnati OH 45244-4009 Office Phone: 513-232-7770. Business E-mail: briehle@foresthills.edu.

**RIEKE, FORREST NEILL,** lawyer; b. Portland, Oreg., May 26, 1942; s. Forrest Eugene and Mary Neill (Whitelaw) R.; m. Madonna Bernardi, Apr. 2, 1966; children: Mary Jane, Forrest Ermelindo. AB in Polit. Sci., Stanford U., 1968; JD, Willamette U., 1971. Bar: Oreg. 1971, U.S. Dist. Ct. Oreg. 1974, U.S. Ct. Appeals (9th cir.) 1975, U.S. Supreme Ct. 1977. Sr. dep. dist. atty. Multnomah County, Portland, 1971-76; ptnr. Rieke & Savage P.C., Portland, 1977—2003; owner Forrest Rieke and Assocs., Sandy, Oreg., 2004—. Instr. Oreg. State Police Acad., Ft. Rilea, 1979-2001 Contbr. editor Williamette U. Law Rev., 1971. Pres., bd. dirs. Council Great City Schs., Washington, 1985-93; trustee Emanuel Hosp. Found., 1987-93; bd. dirs. Portland Pub. Schs., 1978-93. Mem. ABA, Oreg. Bar Assn. (indigent accused def. com., chmn. law related edn. com. 1985, bd. dirs. criminal law sect. 1979-84, mem. pub. info. com. 1987-90, ho. dels. 1995-98), Nat. Criminal Def. Lawyers Assn., Oreg. Criminal Def. Lawyers Assn., Multnomah Athletic. Presbyterian. Avocations: skiing, reading, coaching youth sports. Home: PO Box 266 Zigzag OR 97049 Office: Forrest Rieke and Assocs 39120 SE Proctor Blvd Ste 5 Sandy OR 97055 Office Phone: 503-668-5454. Personal E-mail: jrieke@gte.net. Business E-Mail: joe.rieke@forrestrieke.com.

**RIEKE, PAUL VICTOR,** lawyer; b. Seattle, Apr. 1, 1949; s. Luvern Victor and Anna Jane (Bierstedt) R.; m. Judy Vivian Farr, Jan. 24, 1974; children: anna Katharina, Peter Johann. BA, Oberlin Coll., 1971; postgrad., U. Wash., 1971, Shoreline C.C., 1972-73; JD, Case Western Res. U., 1976. Bar: Wash. 1976, U.S. Dist. Ct. (we. dist.) Wash. 1976, U.S. Tax Ct. 1978. Assoc. Hatch & Leslie, Seattle, 1976-82, ptnr., 1982-91; Foster, Pepper & Shefelman, PLLC, 1991—. Exec. notes editor Case Western Res. U. Law Rev., 1975-76. Mem. exec. bd. coun. N. Pacific dist. Am. Luth Chs., Seattle, 1978-83, coun. pres., 1983, Am. Luth. Ch. pub. bd., 1984-87; v.p. Northwest Wash. Synod of Evangelical Luth. Ch. Am., Seattle, 1988-90, mem. Synod Coun., 1990-92, del. ELCA Nat. Assembly, 1991, ELCA Northwest Synod Regional Rep., 1992-96, region one coun. pres., 1994-96. Mem. ABA, Wash. State Bar Assn., Seattle-King County Bar Assn., Order of Coif. Lodges: Seattle Downtown Central Lions. Democrat. Home: 321 NE 161st St Shoreline WA 98155-5741 Office: Foster Pepper & Shefelman PLLC 34th Fl 1111 3rd Ave Seattle WA 98101 E-mail: RiekP@Foster.com.

**RIELLY, JOHN EDWARD,** educational association administrator; b. Rapid City, SD, Dec. 28, 1932; s. Thomas J. and Mary A. (Dowd) R.; m. Elizabeth Downs, Dec. 28, 1957 (marriage annulled 1976); children: Mary Ellen, Catherine Ann, Thomas Patrick, John Downs; m. Irene Diedrich, Aug. 1, 1987. BA, St. John's U., Collegeville, Minn., 1954; postgrad. (Fulbright scholar), London Sch. Econs. and Polit. Sci., 1955-56; PhD, Harvard U., 1961. Faculty dept. govt. Harvard U., 1958-61; with Alliance for Progress programs Dept. State, Washington, 1961-62; fgn. policy asst. to Sen. then Vice Pres. Hubert Humphrey, Washington, 1963-69; cons. office European and internat. affairs Ford Found., N.Y.C., 1969-70; sr. fellow Overseas Devel. Council, Washington, 1970-71; exec. dir. Chgo. Council on Fgn. Relations, 1971-74, pres., 1974—2001. Adj. prof. Northwestern U., 2001—; vis. prof. Grad. Sch. Internat. Rels. U. Calif., San Diego, 2003—; cons. NSC; adv. bd. Grad. Sch. Arts and Scis., Harvard U. Alumni Assoc.; bd. dirs. Am. Coun. on Germany, Nat. Com. on U.S.-China Rels., China Coun. of Asia Soc., Am. Ditchley Found., Trilateral Commn., commn. on U.S.-Brazilian Rels.; past pres. Nat. Coun. Comty. World Affairs Orgns. Contbr. articles to profl. jours.; editor: American Public Opinion and U.S. Foreign Policy, 1975, 2d edit., 1979, 83, 87, 91, 95, 99; editl. bd. Fgn. Policy Quar., 1974—. Former trustee St. John's U. Recipient Legion d'Honneur, France, Distinguished Service Cross, Germany, Commendatore of the Italian Republic, Bernardo O'Higgins Award, Chile, The Golden Decoration, Austria, European Friendship Award, European Union, Order of Leopold (Belgium), Nat. Hon. Southern Cross, Brazil. Mem.: Council on Fgn. Relations, N.Y.C. Home: 2021 Kenilworth Ave Wilmette IL 60091-1519 Office: Ctr for Info & Comparative Studies 1902 Sheridan Rd Evanston IL 60208 Office Phone: 847-491-2580.

**RIELLY, JOHN P. (J.P. RIELLY),** corporate financial executive; Ptnr. Ernst & Young; v.p., controller, chief acctg. officer Amerada Hess Corp, NYC, 2001—04, sr. v.p., CFO. Office: Amerada Hess Corp 1185 Avenue of the Americas New York NY 10036 Office Phone: 212-997-8500. Office Fax: 212-536-8390.*

**RIELY, CAROLINE ARMISTEAD,** gastroenterologist, educator; b. Washington, Feb. 1, 1944; d. John William and Jean Roy (Jones) Riely. AB, Mt. Holyoke Coll., 1966; MD, Columbia U., 1970. Diplomate Am. Bd. Internal Medicine. Med. intern Presbyn. Hosp., N.Y.C., 1970-71, resident in medicine, 1971-73; fellow in liver disease Yale U., New Haven, 1973-75, asst. prof., 1975-80, assoc. prof., 1980-88; prof. medicine U. Tenn., Memphis, 1988—. Fellow ACP, Am. Coll. Gastroenterology; mem. Am. Assn. Study Liver Disease, Internat. Assn. Study Liver, N.Am. Soc. for Pediatric Gastroenterology and Nutrition. Home: 1756 Central Ave Memphis TN 38104-5116 Office: U Tenn 951 Court Ave Rm 555D Memphis TN 38103-2813

**RIEM, MICHELLE JOHANNA,** science educator; b. Salt Lake City, Sept. 5, 1958; d. Albert Riem and Sonya Jane Beyer-Riem-Stark; m. Ricard Sterling Strauss, Nov. 9, 1990; children: Trent Sterling Strauss, Ra-shelle Brianne Strauss. AA in Natural Sci., Saddleback Coll., Mission Viejo, Calif., 1981; BA in Psychology, U. Calif., Irvine, 1984, BS in Biology, 1985; MA in Edn., U.S. Internat. U. (now Alliant Internat. U.), San Diego, 1989; ND in Naturopathy, Clayton Coll. Natural Health, Birmingham, Ala., 2003. Tchr. sci. Dana Hills H.S., Dana Point, Calif., 1986—92, San Clemente H.S., 1992—. Mem.: NEA, Nat. Tchrs. Assn., Am. Chem. Soc. Avocation: karate (brown belt). Office: San Clemente HS 700 Ave Pico San Clemente CA 92673-5682 Office Phone: 949-492-4165.

**RIEMENSCHNEIDER, PAUL ARTHUR,** retired physician, retired radiologist; b. Cleve., Apr. 17, 1920; s. Albert and Selma (Marting) R.; m. Mildred McCarty, May 12, 1945; children: Barbara Anne, Nancy Emelia, David Andrew, Paul Albert, Mary Elizabeth, Sarah Bache. BS magna cum laude, Baldwin-Wallace Coll., 1941; MD, Harvard U., 1944. Diplomate Am. Bd. Radiology (trustee 1973-85). Nat. Bd. Med. Examiners. Prof., chmn. dept. radiology SUNY, Syracuse, 1951—64; chief diagnostic radiology Santa Barbara Cottage Hosp., Calif., 1964—89, dir., 1984—90; ret., 1990. Vis. prof. in residence SUNY, Syracuse, 1983-98; vis. prof. of Radiology, U. Malaya, 1990-91. Co-editor: N.Y. State Jour. Medicine, 1960-64; mem.

editorial adv. bd. Yearbook of Cancer, 1960-64; contbr. articles to profl. jours. Mem. appropriations com. Santa Barbara Found., 1984-93; vestryman All Saints Episc. Ch., 1970-76, sr. warden, 1973; bd. dirs. ARC, Santa Barbara, 1968-72, Am. cancer Soc., Santa Barbara, 1967-70, Casa Dorinda Retirement Residence, 1975-76, 89-96, pres., 1993-96; bd. dirs. Wood Glen Hall Retirement Residence, sec., 1987, v.p. 1998, pres. 2000; bd. dirs. Cancer Found. Santa Barbara, 1966-82, 89-95, chmn. equipment com., 1973-82; bd. dirs. Direct Relief Internat., 1997-2003, sec., 1999. Lt. comdr. USNR, 1945-46, 54-56. Recipient Alumni Merit award Baldwin-Wallace Coll., 1985. Fellow Am. Coll. Radiology (cancer com. 1952-54, coun. 1956-64, bd. chancellors 1967-73, chmn. commn. stds. in radiologic practice 1968-71, v.p. 1972, pres. 1974, chmn. com. manpower 1972-86, chmn. com. manpower in armed svcs. 1975-86, Gold medal 1982); mem. AMA, Calif. Med. Assn., Santa Barbara County Med. Soc. (chmn. med. sch. com. 1967-71), Am. Roentgen Ray Soc. (publs. com. 1965-75, chmn. 1970-75, exec. coun. 1970-75, 77-82, chmn. program com. 1977-79, pres.-elect 1977-79, pres. 1979, Gold medal award 1986), South Coast Radiol. Soc. (pres. 1967), Assn. U. Radiologists (sec. 1960, pres. 1961, com. resident tng. 1984-88), Radiol. Soc. N.Am. (com. 1972-77, Gold medal award 1990), Am. Soc. Neuroradiology, Soc. Pediat. Radiology, Ea. Radiol. Soc. (pres.-elect 1987, pres. 1988-89), Calif. Radiol. Soc., So. Calif. Radiol. Soc., Detroit Roentgen Soc. (hon.), Bluegrass Radiol. Soc. (hon.), Pacific N.W. Radiol. Soc. (hon.), Birnam Wood Golf Club (bd. dirs. 1996-98), Skaneateles Country Club, Cosmopolitan Club (sec. 1996), Alpha Omega Alpha. Republican. Avocations: tennis, swimming. Home: 300 Hot Springs Rd Santa Barbara CA 93108-2038

**RIEMKE, RICHARD ALLAN,** nuclear engineer; b. Vallejo, Calif., Oct. 11, 1944; s. Allan Frederick and Frances Jewell (O'Brien) R. BA in Physiology, U. Calif., Berkeley, 1967, MA in Physiology, 1971, PhD in Engring. Sci., 1977. Postdoctoral fellow U. So. Calif., L.A., 1977-78; rsch. engr. Del Mar Avionics, Irvine, Calif., 1979; staff fellow NIH, Bethesda, Md., 1980; nuc. engr. Battelle Energy Alliance, Idaho Nat. Lab., Idaho Falls, 1980—. With USAR, 1969—75. Mem. AAAS, ANS, ASME, Biomed. Engring. Soc., Soc. Computer Simulation, Soc. Math. Biology, Soc. Engring. Sci., Order of Golden Bear, Alpha Sigma Phi. Republican. Roman Catholic. Avocations: swimming, surfing. Home: 1727 Grandview Dr # 4 Idaho Falls ID 83402-5016 Office: Battelle Energy Alliance Idaho Nat Lab Idaho Falls ID 83415-3890

**RIENDL, ROBIN WENDY,** financial planning specialist, financial advisor; b. Madison, Wis., Feb. 8, 1966; d. Jim McCaslin and Dean Naomi Brown; m. Paul Alex Riendl, Feb. 4, 1994. B in Natural Resources Mgmt., U. Alaska, Fairbanks, 1988; MBA, U. Alaska, 1991. Field investigator Harding Lawson Assocs., Anchorage, 1988-89; rsch. assist. U. Alaska, Fairbanks, 1989; planner Fairbanks N. Star Borough, 1989—90; forestry tech. Environ. Rsch. Inst., 1989—90; environ. analyst State of Alaska Dept. Transportation, Anchorage, 1992—96; fin. advisor Morgan Stanley, 1996—2002, Smith Barney, 2002—. Recipient Outstanding Young Woman of Am., 1997. Mem. Fin. Planning Assn., U. Alaska Fairbanks Alumni Assn. Avocations: martial arts, skiing, scuba diving. Office: Smith Barney 2550 Denali St 17th Fl Anchorage AK 99503

**RIEPE, JAMES SELLERS,** investment company executive; b. Bryn Mawr, Pa., June 25, 1943; s. Henry Brunt and Marjorie (Sellers) R.; m. Gail Nelms Petty, Sept. 14, 1968; children: Christina, James, Jr. BS, Wharton Sch., U. Pa., 1965, MBA, 1967. Mem. audit staff Coopers & Lybrand, C.P.A.s, Phila., 1967-69; asst. to pres. Wellington Mgmt. Co., Phila., 1969-72, 1972-75; exec. v.p. Vanguard Group, Inc., Valley Forge, Pa., 1975-82, dir., 1979-82; vice chmn., mem. mgmt. com. T. Rowe Price Group, Inc., Balt., 1982—; chmn. T. Rowe Price Investment Svcs., 1982—; exec. v.p. TRP Trust Co., 1982—, TRP Retirement Plan Svcs., 1982—. Bd. dirs. Balt. Equitable Soc., NASDAQ Stock Market, Inc. Trustee, former chmn. Balt. Mus. Art; trustee U. Pa., chmn. bd. trustees, 1999—. Mem. Investment Co. Inst. (gov.), Greenspring Valley Hunt Club, Caves Valley Golf Club. Office: T Rowe Price Group Inc 100 E Pratt St Baltimore MD 21202-1090

**RIERSON, ROBERT LEAK,** retired broadcast executive, scriptwriter; b. Walnut Cove, NC, Sept. 5, 1927; s. Sanders C. and Anna (Cox) R.; m. Barbara Eugenia McLeod, Sept. 23, 1950 (dec. Feb. 1988); children: Barbara Elaine, Richard Troy; m. Rosemary L. McCampbell, Apr. 20, 1997. Student, Duke U., 1945-46, Davidson Coll., 1946-47; BS in Speech cum laude, Northwestern U., 1948. Program dir., program ops. mgr. WBT Radio and WBTV, Charlotte, N.C., 1948-66; program mgr. WJBK-TV, Detroit, 1966-69, WTOP-TV, Washington, 1969-71; dir. broadcasting WCBS-TV, N.Y.C., 1971-73; pres. Rierson Broadcast Consultants, N.Y.C., 1973-75; program exec. Grey Advt., N.Y.C., 1975-77; v.p. dir. programming Dancer-Fitzgerald-Sample, N.Y.C., 1977-80; exec. producer Corinthian Prodns., N.Y.C., 1980-82; dir. news programming CNN TV, Atlanta, 1982-96; ret., 1996. Producer-creator TV show ABCs of Democracy, 1965; producer, writer TV show George Washington's Mt. Vernon, 1970; creator, writer TV series 24 Days of Christmas, 1978, 21 Days of America, 1979. Bd. dirs. Mich. Coun. Chs., Detroit, 1968-69, ARC, Charlotte, 1960-62; 1st v.p. Charlotte Oratorio Singers, 1960-66. Lt. USNR, 1952-54. Recipient Edn. award Charlotte Jr. Woman's Club, 1961, George Washington Honor medal Freedoms Found., 1970; named Young Man of Yr., 1960. Mem. Nat. Assn. Radio-TV Program Execs. (charter, bd. dirs.), Radio-TV News Dirs. Assn., Order Long Leaf Pine (hon. N.C. award). Republican. Mem. Moravian Episcopal Ch. Avocations: reading, travel, movies.

**RIES, CHARLES P.,** ambassador; b. 1951; BA, Johns Hopkins U., 1972, MA, 1973. Dep. asst. U.S. Trade Rep. for N.Am. Affairs Office of the U.S. Trade Rep., Washington, 1990—92; min. counselor for econ. affairs U.S. Mission to the Euorpean Union, Brussels, 1992—96, U.S. Embassy, London, 1996—2000; prin. dept. asst. sec. of state for European and Eurasian affairs Dept. of State, Washington, 2000—04, U.S. amb. to Greece, 2004—.

**RIES, EDWARD RICHARD,** petroleum geologist, consultant; b. Freeman, S.D., Sept. 18, 1918; s. August and Mary F. (Graber) R.; m. Amelia D. Capshaw, Jan. 24, 1949 (div. Oct. 1956); children: Rosemary Melinda, Victoria Elise; m. Maria Wipfler, June 12n 1964. AB magna cum laude, U. S.D., 1941; MS, U. Okla., 1943, PhD, 1951; postgrad., Harvard U., 1946-47, Harvard, 1946-47. Asst. geologist Geol. Survey S.D., White River area, 1941; geophys. interpreter Robert Ray Inc., Western Okla., Okla., 1942; jr. geologist Carter Oil Co., Mont., Wyo., 1943-44; geologist Standard Vacuum Oil Co., Mont., Wyo., Colo., India, 1944-49, sr. geologist Asam Tripura, Bangladesh, India, 1951-53; sr. regional geologist NY Standard Vacuum Petroleum, Maatschappij, NY, Indonesia, 1953-59, geol. advisor Far East and Africa White Plains, NY, 1959-62, Oceania. Mobile Petroleum Co., NYC, 1962-65; geol. advisor Europe, Far East Mobil Oil Corp., NYC, 1965-71, sr. regional explorationist Far East, Australia, New Zealand, 1971-73, sr. regional explorationist Asia-Pacific, Dallas, 1973-76, sr. geol. advisor Rsch. Geology, 1976-79; assoc. geol. advisor Geology-Geophysics, Dallas, 1979-82; sr. geol. cons., 1982-83. Ind. internat. petroleum geol. cons. Europe, Africa, Sino-Soviet and S.E. Asia, 1986—; grad. asst., teaching fellow U. Okla., 1941-43, Harvard, 1946-47. Contbr. numerous domestic and internat. proprietary and pub. hydrocarbon generation and reserve evaluations, reports and profl. papers. With AUS, 1944-46. Warden-Humble fellow, U. Okla., 1951. Mem. AAAS, Am. Inst. Econ. Rsch., Am. Assn. Petroleum Geologists (assoc. editor 1978-83, 50 Yr. Mem. Svc. award 1993, 60 Yr. Mem. Svc. award 2003), Geol. Soc. Am., Am. Geol. Inst., Nat. Wildlife Fedn., Nat. Audubon Soc., NY Acad. Sci., Soc. Exploration Geophysicists, Wilderness Soc., Am. Legion, Harvard Club (Dallas), Phi Beta Kappa, Sigma Xi, Sigma Gamma Epsilon. Republican. Mennonite. Home and office: 810 E 6th St Freeman SD 57029

**RIES, MARTIN,** artist, educator; b. Washington, Dec. 26, 1926; s. Martin Frank and Kathryn (Stretch) R.; m. Dianys d'Arcy Frobisher, June 8, 1953; children: d'Arcy, Now, Gannett, Nicole. BFA, Am. U., 1950; MA in Art History, Hunter Coll., 1968, postgrad. in mus. adminstrn., 1968. Asst. dir. pub. rels. Nat. Congl. Com., Washington, 1951; asst. to dir. Hudson River Mus., 1957-67; advisor Westchester Cultural Ctr., 1965-66; curator instnl. art

exhibits, prof. art L.I. U., Bklyn., 1967-94; juror Fulbright art scholarships Inst. Internat. Edn., UN, 1998. One-man shows include Atelier Gallery, N.Y.C., 1968, Paul Gallery, Tokyo, 1968, Atelier Terre d'Ocre, France, 1973, Unicorn Gallery, Soho, N.Y., 1976, Ganesh Gallery, Lenox, Mass., 1978, Belanthi Gallery, Bklyn., 1984, Stamford (Conn.) Mus., 1987, Raja Idris Gallery, Melbourne, Australia, 1989, Robb St. Gallery, Bairnsdale, Australia, 1989, Salena Gallery, L.I. U., 1996, 2/20 Gallery, N.Y.C., Karpeles Mus., Newburgh, N.Y., 2002, exhibited in group show at Smithsonian Inst., 1952, Mus. of Modern Art, N.Y.C., 1956, SUNY-Albany, 1967, Casa de la Cultura Ecuatoriana in Cuayaquil, Ecuador, 1979, Hammer Gallery, N.Y.C., 1980, Muestra Internacional de Obra Grafica, Spain, 1982, Aaron Berman Gallery, N.Y.C., 1983, Kenkeleba Gallery, 1985, Inst. of Contemporary Art, London, 1988, Williamsburg Art & Hist. Ctr., Bklyn., retrospective, Watkins Gallery, Am. U., Washington, 2000; U.S. editor: Irony & Rude Questions, art editor: art editor Greenwich Village News, 1974—77, contbg. editor: Arts Mag., 1974—75; contbr. articles, revs., catalog introductions, and artists' statements to publs. With Intelligence and Reconnaissance, U.S. Army, 1945-46. Mem. Artists Representing Environ. Art (bd. dirs.), Assn. Internationale des Critiques d'Art (Am. sect.), Am. Soc. Contemporary Artists, Nat. Writer's Union. Home: 36 Livingston Rd Scarsdale NY 10583-6845 E-mail: martin@MartinRies.com.

**RIES, WILLIAM CAMPBELL,** lawyer; b. Pitts., Apr. 8, 1948; s. F. William and Dorothy (Campbell) R.; m. Mallory Burns, Oct. 26, 1968; children: William Sheehan, Sean David. AB, Cath. U. Am., 1970; JD, Duquesne U., 1974; cert. Grad. Sch. Indsl. Adminstrn., Carnegie Mellon U., 1980. Bar: Pa. 1974, U.S. Dist. Ct. (we. dist.) Pa. 1974, U.S. Supreme Ct. 1979. Atty., then mng. counsel trust and investment svc. Mellon Bank, N.A., Pitts., 1974-90; ptnr. Dickie, McCamey and Chilcote, Pitts., 1990-98; mem. Sweeney, Metz, Fox, McGrann & Schermer, LLC, 1998-2001; shareholder Tucker Arensberg, 2001—. Mem. adv. com. decedents' estates and trust law Pa. Joint State Govt. Commn., 1981—; adj. prof. Duquesne U., 1984—; mem. risk mgmt. adv. group Bank Adminstrn. Inst., 2003—. Author: The Regulation of Investment Management and Fiduciary Services West, 1997. Pres. McCandless Twp. Civic Assn., Pitts., 1981—, McCandless Town Coun., chmn. pub. safety com., vice chair fin com.; sec. McCandless Indsl. Devel. Auth.; liaison McCandless zoning hearing bd. Fellow Am. Bar Found.; mem. ABA (chmn. fiduciary svcs. subcom.), Pa. Bar Assn., Allegheny County Bar Assn., Pitts. Estate Planning Coun., Am. Bankers Assn. (co-chmn. nat. conf. lawyers and corp. fiduciaries, chmn. trust counsel com.), Pa. Bankers Assn. (trust com., trust legis. com.), Rivers Club, Treesdale Golf and Country Club. Republican. Avocations: golf, sailing, cross country skiing, exercise. Home: 9602 Fawn Ln Allison Park PA 15101-1737 Office Phone: 412-594-5646. Business E-mail: wries@tuckerlaw.com.

**RIESEBERG, LOREN,** botanist, educator; BA, Southern Coll., Tenn., 1981; MS, U. of Tenn., Knoxville, 1984; PhD, Wash. State. u., 1987. Rsch. scientist Rancho Santa Ana Botanic Garden, Claremont, Calif., 1987—93; asst. prof. Claremont Grad. Sch., 1987—93; assoc. prof. biology Ind. U., Bloomington, Ind., 1993—97; dir. Plant Sci. Program, 1996—; prof. biology Ind. U., Bloomington, Ind., 1997—. Contbr. scientific papers more than 150 articles; editor (chief): (text book) Molecular Ecology, 1999. Recipient George R Cooley award in Plant Systematics, 1990, David Starr Jordan award in Evolution, Ecology, and Organismal Biology, 1998; grantee MacArthur Found. Fellowship, 2003. Fellow: Am. Acad. Arts & Sciences; mem.: Am. Genetics Assn. Office: Ind U dept of Biology 1001 E 3rd St Jordan Hall Bloomington IN 47405

**RIESENBERGER, JOHN RICHARD,** science administrator; b. NYC, Sept. 25, 1948; s. Richard Raymond and Marie Teresa (Long) R.; m. Patricia Ann Casey, Nov. 23, 1974; children: Christine, Jennifer. BS in Econs. and Bus., Hofstra U., 1970, MBA in Mgmt., 1975; cert. internat. sr. mgmt. program, Harvard U., 1989. Customer svc. supr. Chase Manhattan Bank, 1970-72; gen. sales rep. various regions Upjohn Co., Bklyn., 1972-75, sales rep., sales mgr. various locations, N.Y., 1976-81, profl. tng. and devel. officer Kalamazoo, 1981-83, dir. Chgo. sales area, 1983-87; v.p., group mgr. Upjohn Co. of Can., Toronto, Ont., 1987-89; exec. dir. worldwide med. scis. liaison Upjohn Co., Kalamazoo, 1989-92, exec. dir. worldwide strategic mktg., 1992-95; exec. dir. corp. info. tech. Pharmacia & Upjohn, Inc., Kalamazoo, 1995, v.p. bus. info., 1996-97; v.p. global bus. mgmt. Pharmacia & Upjohn Inc., Bridgewater, N.J., 1998-99; mem. pharm. cons., 1999—; exec.-in-residence Mich. State U., 2000—; pres. Consilium Ptnrs. Inc., 2000—; exec. v.p. Shaw Sci. Ptnrs., Atlanta, 2000—. Chmn. industry adv. bd. dirs. SEI Ctr. Advanced Studies in Mgmt., Wharton Sch., U. Pa.; mem. Global Adv. bd. Am. Mktg. Assn., 1999; mem. edtl. review bd. Jour. Internat. Mktg.; Ciber adv. bd. Mich. State U. Author: (with Robert T. Moran) The Global Challenge: Building the New Worldwide Enterprise, 1994, Global Business Strategies for the Year 2000, 1995. Mem. ciber adv. bd. Mich. State U. Mem. Am. Mgmt. Assn., Strategic Mgmt. Soc., Pharm. Rsch. Mfrs. Am. (chmn. mktg. practices com.), The Planning Fom, Internat. Soc. for Strategic Planning and Mgmt., Harvard Bus. Sch. Club, Pharm. Bus. Intelligence and Rsch. Group, European Pharm. Market Rsch. Assn., Harvard Bus. Sch. Health Industry Alumni Assn. Avocation: golf. Home: 42 Independence Dr Basking Ridge NJ 07920-3815

**RIESER, JOSEPH A., JR.,** tax specialist; b. Pitts., Aug. 28, 1947; s. Joseph Alexander and Ruth Margaret (Piper) R.; m. Susan Jean Irving, Feb. 28, 1976; 1 child, Alexander H.I. AB, Princeton U., 1969; JD, MPP, Harvard U., 1974. Bar: Pa. 1974, D.C. 1976, U.S. Supreme Ct. 1979. Assoc. Reed Smith LLP, Pitts. and Washington, 1974-82, ptnr. Washington, 1983—2003; mem. Arent Fox PLLC, Washington, 2003—. Mem. D.C. Office of Tax and Revenue Adv. Group, 1997-2001. Chmn. nat. alumni assn. Kennedy Sch. Govt., Cambridge, Mass., 1979-82; bd. dirs. Harvard U. Alumni Assn., 1982-84; gen. counsel 1984 Dem. Nat. Conv., Washington, 1983-84; gen. counsel Nat. Dem. Party, Washington, 1985-89; spl. counsel Clinton/Gore '92, Inc.; mem. Clinton-Gore 1992 Presdl. Transition Team. Mem. D.C. Bar (chmn. bus. related taxes com. 1989-92, tax policy steering com., chmn. D.C. Bar Nat. Fed. Tax Inst. 1991, 92, 2000, chmn. state and local taxes com. 1994-97, tax sect. steering com. 1997-2003, co-chair tax sect. 1998-2001), Ctr. for Nat. Policy Bd. Advisors, Harvard-Yale-Princeton Pitts. Club, Cosmos Club. Presbyterian. Home: 3517 Davis St NW Washington DC 20007-1426 Office: Arent Fox PLLC 1050 Connecticut Ave NW Washington DC 20036 Office Phone: 202-857-8964.

**RIESS, ADAM GUY,** astronomer, educator; b. Dec. 16, 1969; BS in Physics, MIT, 1992; AM in Astrophysics, Harvard U., 1994, PhD in Astrophysics, 1996. Undergraduate rsch. asst. MIT, 1990—92, sr. thesis student, 1991—92; rsch. assoc. Lawrence Livermore Nat. Lab., 1992; doctoral student Harvard U., 1992—96; Miller Fellow U. Calif., Berkeley, 1996—99; asst. astronomer Space Telescope Sci. Inst., Balt., 1999—2001, assoc. astronomer, 2001—; assoc. adj. prof. Johns Hopkins U., 2002—06, prof., physics and astronomy, 2006—. Tchg. fellow, physics dept., The Physics of Sports MIT, 1992; tchg. fellow, astronomy Harvard U., 1993, 94; co-taught, Hot Topics in Astrophysics, astronomy and physics dept. Harvard U., 2003; invited spkr. in field. Contbr. articles to profl. jours.; guest appearance Quirks and Quarks, CPR, 1998, News, BBC, 1998, Science Friday, NPR, 1998, 2001, Headline News, CNN, 1998, Jim Lehrer News Hour, PBS, 1998, Sound Prints, NPR, 2000, NOVA, PBS, 2002, 60 Minutes, CBS, 2003, Scientific American Frontiers, PBS, 2004. Co-recipient Shaw prize in Astronomy, Shaw Found., Hong Kong, 2006; finalist Innovator award, Discover Mag., 2003; recipient Nat. Merit Scholar, 1988, Trumpler award, Astronomical Soc. Pacific, 1999, AURA Sci. award, 2000, Innovator award, Time Mag., 2000, Bok prize, Harvard U., 2001, Helen B. Warner prize, Am. Astronomical Soc., 2003, Best and Brightest award, Esquire Mag., 2003, Raymond and Beverly Sackler prize, Tel-Aviv U., 2004; Margaret Weyerhaeuser Jewett Meml. Fellowship, 1993, Harvard GSAS Merit Fellow, 1995. Mem.: Phi Beta Kappa. Achievements include design of Space Shuttle, Leap Frog Toys, children's educational astronomy toy, 1997-98; published the first evidence that the expansion of the Universe was accelerating % filled with Dark Energy, as a result, Science Magazine called this the Breakthrough Discovery of the Year in 1998.

Avocations: bicycling, coin collecting/numismatics, home improvement. Office: Space Telescope Sci Inst 3700 San Martin Dr Baltimore MD 21218 Office Phone: 410-338-4509. Office Fax: 410-338-5090. Business E-mail: ariess@stsci.edu.*

**RIESS, GORDON SANDERSON,** management consultant; b. Thessaloniki, Greece, Feb. 25, 1928; came to U.S., 1932; s. Lewis William and Dorothy Onward Riess; m. Priscilla Rich, June 2, 1951; children: Mark C., Kimberly A., Blake G. AB with highest honors, Whitman Coll., 1949; MBA cum laude, Harvard U., 1951. Cert. mgmt. cons.; registered profl. cons.; accredited profl. cons. With Ford Internat. Div., N.Y.C., 1951-53; asst. fin. mgr. Ford Motor Co., Mid. East, Alexandria, Egypt, 1953-57; gen. sales mgr. Ford Motor Co., Rome, Italy, 1957-60; regional fin. mgr. Ford Motor Co., Scandinavia, Copenhagen, Denmark, 1960-62; gen. mgr. Ford Motor Co., European, Brussels, Belgium, 1962-67; v.p. Internat. Paper Co., Zurich, Switzerland, 1967-71; exec. v.p. Cinema Internat. Corp., London, 1971-75; chmn., pres. Stewart-Riess Labs. Inc., Tarzana, Calif., 1976-83; pres., CEO Intercontinental Enterprises Ltd., Beverly Hills, Calif., 1983—. Chmn. Vis. Nurse Found., L.A., 1985-87; bd. dirs., chmn. Vis. Nurse Assn., L.A., 1976-97; bd. dirs. Beverly Found., Pasadena, Calif., 1990-97; vice-chmn. of bd. Witman Coll., Walla Walla, Wash., 1985-96. Author: Confessions of a Corporate Centurion--Tales of International Adventures, 2000, From Communism to Capitalism, 2001, Passports to Adventure, 2005; inventor/patentee pre-fillable hypodermic syringe. Chmn. Inter-Community Sch. Zurich, 1968-71; trustee Am. Sch. London, 1972-75; vice chmn. Krafterliner Mfgs. Assn., Zurich, 1968-71; bd. dirs. Vols. in Tech. Assistance, Arlington, Va., 1986-93; bd. overseers Muhlenberg Coll., 1993—; internat. bd. Czechoslovak Mgmt. Ctr., 1992—. Sgt. U.S. Army, 1946-47. R.H. Macy scholar, Harvard Bus. Sch., 1949. Mem. Am. Assn. Profl. Cons., Am. Cons. League, Asia Acad. Mgmt., Hollywood Radio & Television Soc., Inst. Mgmt. Cons.. Lic. Execs. Soc. Avocations: skiing, scuba diving. Office: Intercontinental Enterprises Ltd 1082 Angelo Dr Beverly Hills CA 90210-2702 Personal E-mail: GSR@mindspring.com, g.riess@sbcglobal.net.

**RIESZ, PETER CHARLES,** marketing educator, consultant; b. Orange, N.J., Apr. 30, 1937; s. Kolman and Ellen (Wachs) R.; m. Elizabeth Strider Dunkman, Dec. 28, 1968; children: Sarah Kathleen BS, Rutgers U., 1958; MBA, Columbia U., 1963, PhD, 1971. From asst. prof. to assoc. prof. U. Iowa, Iowa City, 1968-80, prof. mktg., 1980—, chmn. dept. mktg., 1981-87, Williams prof. tchg., 1994-97. Vis. prof. Boston U., 1974-75, Duke U., Durham, N.C., 1984-85; guest prof. Meiji U., Japan, summer 2004; cons. in field. Contbr. articles to profl. jours. Recipient Teaching Excellence award HON Industries, 1989; named MBA Prof. of Yr., 1990; Old Gold fellow U. Iowa, 1972. Mem. Am. Chem. Soc., Am. Mktg. Assn. Democrat. Presbyterian. Avocation: photography. Home: 2411 Tudor Dr Iowa City IA 52245-3638 Office: U Iowa Dept Mktg Tippie Coll Bus Adminstrn Iowa City IA 52242 Office Phone: 319-335-0937. Business E-mail: peter-riesz@uiowa.edu.

**RIETH, ROBERT FREDRICK,** retired music educator; b. Jersey City, Feb. 22, 1933; s. Louis Robert and Viola Elvira Rieth. MusB, Manhattan Coll. Music, N.Y.C., 1956, EdM, 1957. Cert. elem. edn. tchr. N.J., vocal music K-8 N.J., instr. music K-12 N.J. Tchr. Newark Bd. Edn., 1959—72, Jersey City Bd. Edn., 1972—89; ret., 1989. Vol. Christ Hosp., Jersey City, 1992—; mem. Heights Neighborhood Liaison, Jersey City, 1998—; chmn. All Soul's Scholarship Fund St. John's Luth. Ch., Jersey City, 1997—98. Sgt. Band U.S. Army, 1954—62. Named scholarship in his honor, St. John's Luth. Ch., 2004. Mem.: AFM, Am. Legion (dir. band Union City, N.J. 1957—92). Democrat.

**RIEW, K. DANIEL,** cervical spine surgeon; b. Seoul, Republic of Korea, July 28, 1958; arrived in U.S., 1966; s. C. Keith and H. Kim Riew; m. Mary Kahng, Sept. 12, 1992. MD, Case Western Res. U., 1984. Diplomate Am. Bd. of Orthopaedic Surgery. Asst. attending physician, instr. medicine Cornell U. Med. Ctr., N.Y.C., 1987—89; resident gen. surgery Beth Israel Med. Ctr., N.Y.C., 1989—90; resident orthop. surgery George Washington U. Hosp., Washington, 1990—94; fellow spine surgery U. Hosps. Cleve./Case We. Res. U.; from asst. prof. to prof. Washington U. Sch. Medicine, St. Louis, 1995—2005, Mildred B. Simon disting. prof. orthop. surgery, prof. neurol. surgery, 2006—, chief cervical spine surgery, dir. Cervical Spine Inst. Contbr. articles to profl. jours. (Cervical Spine Rsch. Soc. Outanding Basic Sci. Rsch. award, 2000, Mayfield award for basic sci. Am. Assn. of Neurol. Surgeons, 2000, North Am. Spine Soc. Outstanding Paper award, 2000, Russell S. Hibbs Basic Sci. award Scoliosis Rsch. Soc., 2000). Recipient C. Richard Bowman award, N.Y. Hosp., Cornell Med. Ctr., 1987, Caring Spirit award, Barnes-Jewish Hosp., 2001; grantee, Orthopaedic Rsch. and Edn. Found., 2002—05. Fellow: Am. Acad. Orthopaedic Surgeons; mem.: Mo. State Orthop. Assn., Mid. Am. Orthop. Assn., Am. Orthop. Assn., Scoliosis Soc., Orthop. Rsch. Soc., N.Am. Spine Soc. (CME com. and surg. care com. 2000), Cervical Spine Rsch. Soc. (clin. outcomes com. 2001). Avocations: skiing, golf. Office: Washington U Sch of Medicine ste 11300 One Barnes-Jewish Hosp Plz Saint Louis MO 63110 Office Phone: 314-747-2565.

**RIFE, ELIZABETH,** musician, music educator; b. Zebulon, Ga., Feb. 23, 1938; d. Jack and Ouida Dorothy (Walker) Bridges; m. Robert M. Hill, June 25, 1959 (div.); child: Dorothy Hill Bremer; m. C. David Rife, Feb. 15, 1986. BS in Music Edn., Ga. State Coll. and U., 1959; postgrad., Ga. State U., 1976-81, Vanderbilt U., 1977-79. Music tchr., Marietta, Ga., 1959—; choir master, organist Holy Trinity Luth. Ch., Marietta, 1966-79. Pres., chmn. bd. Assist. Inc., Marietta, 1982-84. Guest columnist Marietta Daily Jour., 1980-84, Horizons mag., 1997. Dir. WSB-TV Call for Action, Atlanta, 1980—82; spkr. Foster Children Program, Marietta, 1980—83, United Way, 1982—83; sec. bd. dirs. Help for Hispanics, 2002; conducted seminars, workshops on hunger ch. and civic groups, Atlanta, 1981—; concert coord. Musica Sacra Atlanta, 2002—; mem. steering com. Presbyn. Answer to Hunger, 1991—; vol. Must Ministries, 2002—. Mem. Music Tchrs. Nat. Assn., Music Educators Nat. Assn., Ga. Music Educators Conf. (adjudicator piano competition 1967—), Cobb County Music Tchrs. Assn., Guild Music Sacra of Atlanta, Sigma Alpha Iota. Presbyterian. Avocations: running, reading, travel, fashion consulting, tutoring. Home: 1296 Poplar Pointe SE Smyrna GA 30082-2213

**RIFENBURGH, RICHARD PHILIP,** investment company executive; b. Syracuse, NY, Mar. 3, 1932; s. Russell D. and Edna (MacKenzie) R.; m. Doris Anita Hohn, June 24, 1950; children: David, Susan, Robert. Student, Wayne State U. With Mohawk Data Scis. Corp., Herkimer, NY, 1964-74, pres., 1970-74, chmn., CEO, 1974-74, Moval Mgmt. Corp., Herkimer, 1968—; CEO, GCA Corp., Andover, Mass., 1986-87; gen. ptnr. Hambrecht and Quist Venture Ptnrs., 1987-90; chmn. Miniscribe Corp., Longmont, Colo., 1988-91, Ironstone Group Inc., 1988-91, St. G Crystal Ltd., Jeannette, Pa., 1985—, Paradise Music and Entertainment Inc., 2000—. Chmn. Tristar Corp., 1992—2002. With USAF, 1951-55. Address: Moval Mgmt Corp PMB 133 2637 E Atlantic Blvd Pompano Beach FL 33062-4939 Office Phone: 954-941-9182. Personal E-mail: dickrif@gmail.com.

**RIFF, LAWRENCE P.,** lawyer; BA with highest honors & high distinction in History, U. Mich., 1978; JD, U. Oreg., 1982. Bar: Calif. 1982, Oreg. 1985, Washington 1987. Lawyer So. Pacific Transp. Co., San Francisco, 1982—86; mng. ptnr., toxic tort, transp. & litig. depts. Steptoe & Johnson LLP, LA, 1997—. John Williams Fellowship. Mem.: Am. Bd. Trial Advocacy, LA County Bar Assn. (Litig. Sect.), Internat. Moot Ct. Team, Jessup Competition. Office: Steptoe & Johnson LLP 633 W 5th St Ste700 Los Angeles CA 90071 Office Phone: 213-439-9494. Office Fax: 213-439-9599. Business E-mail: lriff@steptoe.com.

**RIFFE, STACY CHRISTINE,** secondary school educator; b. Beckley, W.Va., Aug. 16, 1970; d. Clinton Gilbert and Frances Loise (Martin) Forren; m. Vincent Rodger Riffe, Apr. 17, 1993. Student, So. W.Va. C.C., Pineville, BA in Edn., Glenville State Coll., 1993; M in Curriculum and Instrn., Coppin State Coll., 1991. Cert. tchr. W.Va. Waitress Pineville (W.Va.) Restaurant,

1988; teller Bank Oceana, W.Va., 1988-90; substitute tchr. Fayette County Bd. Edn., Fayetteville, W.Va., 1993; teller 1st State Bank and Trust, Rainelle, W.Va., 1993; tchr. math. Jackson County Bd. Edn., Ripley, W.Va., 1993—. Tech. specialist Jackson County Bd. Edn., Ripley, 1993—; presenter in field; freelance musician, 1995—97. Pianist West Ripley Bapt. Ch., 1993—; sponsor Young Christians Club, Ripley, 1993—. Mem.: NEA, Jackson County Tchr. Assn., W.Va. Edn. Assn., Delta Kappa Gamma. Avocations: music, arts and crafts, reading. Home: 229 Simmons Dr Ripley WV 25271-1336 Office: Ripley HS # 2 School St Ripley WV 25271 E-mail: welovejesus@charter.net.

**RIFFEL, KAREN SHEFFER,** music educator; b. Ft. Lauderdale, Fla. d. Thomas Fox and Frances McGaffick Sheffer; m. Keith Allen Riffel; children: Christopher, Kyle, Kathryne, Kirk, Carlton, Carolyn. BS in Music Edn., Bob Jones U., 1976. Tchr. elem. music Silver State Bapt. Schs., Lakewood, Colo., 1976—77, 1978—87, Schaumburg (Ill.) Christian Sch., 1987—, pvt. piano/voice tchr., 1987—. Dir. children's choir Bethel Bapt. Ch., Schaumburg. Mem.: Am. Coll. Musicians. Republican. Baptist. Avocations: stamping, crafts. Office: Schaumburg Christian Sch 200 N Roselle Rd Schaumburg IL 60194 E-mail: riffelkeith@sbcglobal.net.

**RIFFEL, LOREN DARREL,** retired entrepreneur; b. Shattuck, Okla., Mar. 3, 1936; s. Charles F. and Fern L. Riffel; m. Betty Lou Hawthorne, 1963. Gen. mgr. Best Western Inn, Woodward, Okla., 1965—84, dist. mgr., 1984—87; motel owner Motel Group, Inc., Oklahoma City, 1987—91; restaurant owner J.B. & Twin Oak Inc., Woodward, 1991—2005. Author: Country Schools, 2002, In the Shadows of the Law & Beyond, 2004. Pres. Junior Woodward C. of C., Woodward, Okla., 1971; bd. mem. Woodward C. of C., Woodward, Okla., 1975—2005, Kids Inc., Woodward, Okla., 1974—78, pres., 1978—79. Private first class U.S. Army, 1958—60, Germany. Recipient Best Restaurant award, Woodward, 1997, 1998, 1999, 2001, 2002, 2003, 2004. Mem.: Lions Club (pres. 1978—79). Republican. Avocation: history writing. Home: 4805 Cedardale Woodward OK 73801 Office: JBs Steak House 225 E Main PO Box 351 Woodward OK 73801 Office Phone: 580-256-4845.

**RIFFENBURGH, GERRYE H.,** artist, educator; d. Herman Harvey and Mary (Beryl) Harlow; m. Robert Harry Riffenburgh, Nov. 22, 1952; children: Robin, Scott, Marc, Karen, Douglas. BS, Coll. William and Mary, 1951, MS, 1955; BA summa cum laude, San Diego State U., 1979. Exhibiting artist and instr. San Diego Adult Coll., 1978—81; exhibiting artist The Hague, Netherlands, 1982—86, La Spezia, Italy, 1986—89, San Diego, 1990—. Rep. exhibitor Cosmopolitan Fine Arts Gallery, La Jolla, Calif., 2001—, Timmons Courtyard Gallery, Encinitas, Calif., 2001—. Author: (article on color choice) Jour. of Gen. Psychol.; over 45 juried exhibitions, Europe, U.S. Vol. Coastal Planning Coun., San Diego, 1971—73; leader Girl Scouts, San Diego, 1968—74, Girl Guides, Pembrokeshire, Wales, 1974—77; vol. polit. groups, San Diego, 1978—81; fund raiser vol. COTA, San Diego, 1978—82. Named hon. mention, Nat. Annual Galleon Exhibit, London, 1975, Associazione Artisti Versiliese, Italy, 1989; named to Gold Medal Exhbn., Salon d'Automne/Pasadena, Calif., 2002; recipient First pl., Pembrokeshire Artists Assn., UK, 1974, Third pl., Congressgebouw, Netherlands, 1984, Cenacolo Buttini, Italy, 1988, First pl., Maurice Braun Meml. Plein Air Exhbn., Calif., 2000, cert. merit, LaJolla Art Assn., 2001, Third pl., Offtrack Gallery, Leucadia, Calif., 2002, William Schultz award, Am. Impressionist Soc., Fla., 2002, Second pl., Municipal Art Gallery, Escondido, Calif., 2003, Spl. Merit, Internat. Mus. Contemporary Masters Fine Art, San Antonio, 2004—05, Arts Parks Excellence award, 2005, spl. merit, Coos Mus. Art, Oreg., 2003, Nat. Arts Club, N.Y.C., 2005. Mem.: Am. Soc. Marine Artists (juried artist mem.), Artists' Guild San Diego Mus. Art, Oil Painters Am., Plein Air Painters Assn. San Diego (founder), Am. Impressionists Soc. (signature mem.), San Diego Portrait Soc. (bd. dir. 1995—96), La Jolla Art Assn. (life; treas., bd. dir. 1996—2001), Calif. Art Club (juried artist mem.). Avocations: photography, piano, walking, tennis, yoga. E-mail: gerryeriff@yahoo.com.

**RIFFENBURGH, ROBERT HARRY,** biostatistician, researcher; b. Christiansburg, Va., June 19, 1931; s. Harry Buchholz and Ada Swallow Riffenburgh; m. Gerrye Harlow, Nov. 22, 1952; children: Robin, Scott, Marc, Karen, Douglas. BS, Coll. William and Mary, Richmond, Va., 1951, MS, 1953; PhD, Va. Poly. Inst., Blacksburg, 1957. Asst. prof. math. Va. Poly. Inst., Blacksburg, 1955—57, U. Hawaii, Honolulu, 1957—61; prof., head dept. stats. U. Conn., Storrs, 1962—70; prof. stats. San Diego State U., 1968—74, 1979—82, 1990—93, prof. stats, 2006—; head, biomedical program Naval Undersea Ctr., San Diego, 1970—73; scientist Naval Facility, Brawdy, Wales, 1974—77; math. statistician Naval Ocean Systems Ctr., San Diego, 1977—82; leader, naval ops. rsch. NATO SHAPE Tech. Centre, The Hague, Netherlands, 1982—86; head, ops. rsch. NATO SACLANT Undersea Rsch. Centre, La Spezia, Italy, 1986—90; chief biostats. Naval Med. Ctr. San Diego, San Diego, 1991—. Pres. and ceo Gen. Systems Analysis Co., Storrs, Conn., 1963—70. Author: Statistics in Medicine; contbr. more than 140 articles to profl. jours. Capt. USN, 1982—89. Decorated Navy Commendation Medal; Predoctoral fellow, NIH, 1954-1956. Fellow: Am. Statis. Assoc.; mem.: Internat. Biometrics Soc., Royal Statis. Soc. (life), Phi Kappa Phi, Sigma Xi. Office Phone: 619-532-9414.

**RIFKA, JUDY,** artist, educator; b. Bklyn., Sept. 25, 1945; d. Irving David Tenenbaum and Pearl Fessler; children: John Reed, Matthew Lenski. BA, SUNY, Old Westbury, 1993; MA, Adelphi U., 1994. Asst. prof. SUNY, Rochester, NY, 1974; artist-in-residence Princeton U., NJ, 1976, Tamarind Inst., N.Mex., 1983, Columbia U., NY, 1994, Md. Inst. Mt. Royal, Balt., 1985, Skowkegan Sch., Maine, 1989, Tandem Press, Madison, Wis., 1991. Grants juror NY State Coun. Arts, NYC, 1983, Mass. Coun. Arts, Boston, 1984, Nat. Found. Arts, 1988. One-woman shows include numerous others, 1974—2001, Brooke Alexander Gallery, 1982—85, Galerie de France, Paris, 1984, Anna Friebe Gallery, Cologne, Germany, 1985—86, Brooke Alexander Gallery, 1987—88, Tobias Hirschmann, Frankfurt, Germany, 1988, Pyramide Arte Contemporane, Florance, 1989, Brooke Alexander Gallery, 1991, Hofstra U., 1996, prin. works include murals Madison Sq. Garden, 1989, Union Sq. Cafe, NY, 2004; author: Opera of Worms, 1984; Exhibited in group shows at Brooke Alexander Editions, 2004, N.Y. Studio Sch., 2005, Austin Mus., Tex., 2006, Andy Warhol Mus., 2006, Berkely Art Mus., Calif., 2006, Grey Gallery NYU, 2006. Jewish. Home: 53 Market St New York NY 10002 Office Phone: 212-285-1532. Personal E-mail: jrifka@nyc.rr.com.

**RIFKIN, ARNOLD,** film company executive; b. Bklyn. m. Rita George; two children. BA, U. Cin. Founder Rifkin-David, 1974-80; merged to form Rifkin/David/Kimble/Parseghian, 1980-81, DHKPR, 1981-84; head motion picture dept. Triad Artists, Inc., 1984-92, founding ptnr.; exec. v.p., worldwide head motion picture divsn. William Morris Agy., Beverly Hills, Calif., 1992-96; pres. William Morris Talent and Lit. Agy., Beverly Hills, Calif., 1996-2000; CEO Cheyenne Enterprises, LLC, Santa Monica, Calif., 2000—. Bd. dirs. Am. Cinematheque; faculty, co-chair UCLA Sch. Theatre, Film & TV; lecturer Yale Law Sch., Harvard Sch. Bus., 2002-. Bd. councillors U. So. Calif. Office: Cheyenne Enterprises 406 Wilshire Blvd Santa Monica CA 90401-1410

**RIFKIN, BARRY R.,** dean, dental educator, researcher; b. Trenton, N.J., Mar. 30, 1940; s. Samuel H. and Ida M. Rifkin; m. Harriet Smith, Mar. 1960 (div. Sept. 1981); children: Avery, Carl; m. Linda Ruth Rosenberg, Nov. 1993; 1 child, Hannah. BS, Ohio State U., 1961; MS, U. Ill., 1964; DDS, Temple U., 1968; PhD, U. Rochester, 1974. Andrew Mellon fellow U. Rochester Med. Ctr., 1974; assoc. pathologist Strong Meml. Hosp., 1974—80; assoc. prof. NYU, NYC, 1980—84, chmn. dept. oral medicine, 1980—87, prof., 1984—91, chmn. dept. oral medicine and pathology, 1987—91, head divsn. basic scis., 1991—98, prof. emeritus, 1998—; prof. oral biology and pathology, dean SUNY Stony Brook Health Sciences Ctr. Sch. Dental Medicine, 1998—. Rschr. in field; bd. mem. Friends of the Nat. Inst. of Dental and Craniofacial Rsch., 2005—. Sr. editor Biology and Physiology of the Osteoclast, 1992; mem. editl. bd.: Jour. Dental Rsch.; contbr. articles and abstracts to profl. jours. Fellow: Am. Coll. Dentists; mem.: AAAS, Am. Soc. Bone and Mineral Rsch., Internat. Assn. Dental Rsch., Am. Soc. Cell Biology,

N.Y. Acad. Scis., Am. Assn. Oral Biologists (pres. 1992—93), Sigma Xi, Omicron Kappa Upsilon. Office: Stony Brook Univ Sch Dental Medicine 160 Rockland Hall Stony Brook NY 11794-8700 Office Phone: 631-632-8950. Office Fax: 631-632-9105. E-mail: Barry.Rifkin@stonybrook.edu.

**RIFKIN, MATTHEW D.,** radiologist; b. NYC, Mar. 26, 1949; m. Susan Greenberg, 1971; children: Adam, Jason. BA, Brandeis U., 1971; MD, Albert Einstein Coll., 1974. Intern in medicine Montefiore Hosp. and Med. Ctr., Bronx, NY, 1974—75, resident in diagnostic radiology, 1975—78; fellow in ultrasound/CT Johns Hopkins Hops. and Med. Ctr., Balt., 1978—79; instr. radiology Johns Hopkins Hosp. and Med. Sch., Balt., 1978—79; clin. asst. prof. radiology U. Miami Sch. Medicine, Fla., 1979—81, Jefferson Med. Coll., Thomas Jefferson U., Phila., 1981—83, asst. prof. radiology, 1983—85, assoc. prof. radiology, 1983—86, prof. urology, 1985—91, prof., assoc. chair dept. radiology, 1986—91; clin. prof. Coll. Allied Health Sci., Thomas Jefferson U., Phila., 1984—91, 1991; chair dept. radiology Albany Med. Coll., 1991—98, prof. radiology, 1991—98, prof. surgery, 1995—99; prof., vice chmn., chief diagnostic radiology SUNY Sch. Medicine, Stony Brook, 1999—2003, prof. urology, 1999—2003; chmn. radiology Good Samaritan Hosp., West Islip, NY, 2002—; dir. radiology St. Catherine of Siena Hosp., Smithtown, NY, 2004—, St. Charles Hosp., Port Jefferson, NY, 2005—. Cons. radiology VA, Perry Point, Md., 1978—79; staff radiologist Johns Hopkins Hosp., Balt., 1978—79, Plantation Gen. Hosp., Fla., 1979—80, St. Mary's Hosp., West Palm Beach, Fla., 1980—81; med. and ednl. dir. med. sonography St. Mary's Hosp. Sch. Diagnostic, West Palm Beach, 1980—81; staff radiology Thomas Jefferson Univ. Hosp., Phila., 1981—91; dir. radiology rsch. Jefferson Med. Coll., Thomas Jefferson U. Hosp., 1986—91, dir. divsn. magnetic resonance imaging, 1986—91; med. svc. dir. dept. radiology Albany Med. Ctr. Hosp., 1996—98, chief radiologist, 1991—98; vice chair, chief diagnostic radiology, chief clin. ops., chief abdominal radiology SUNY Health Sci. Ctr., Stony Brook, 1999—2003; presenter in field. Contbr. scientific papers and articles to profl. jours.; author: Diagnostic Imaging of the Lower Genitourinary Tract, 1985, Handbook of Normal Ultraousnd Anatomy, 1985; author: (editor) Intraoperative and Endoscopic Ultrasound, 1987; author: Ultrasound of the Prostate, 1988, 1997, Ultrasound, 1991; editor: Ultrasound of the Urinary Tract, 1991; co-editor: Interventional Radiology of the Genitourinary Tract, 1993; co-author: Pocket Atlas of Normal Ultrasound Anatomy, 2001, Diagnostic Imaging of the Scrotum and External Male Genitalia, 2002. Fellow: Phila. Coll. Physicians, Am. Coll. Radiology, Am. Inst. Ultrasound Medicine; mem.: Soc. Uroradiology. Home: 198 Field Rd East Setauket NY 11733 Office: Good Samaritan Hosp and Med Ctr Dept Radiology 1000 Montauk Hwy West Islip NY 11795 Office Phone: 631-376-4030. E-mail: matthew.rifkin@chsli.org.

**RIFKIN, NED,** museum director; b. Florence, Ala., Nov. 10, 1949; s. Arthur Robert and Ina Blanche (Steinberg) R.; children: Moses Kleinman, Amos Kleinman. BA, Syracuse U., 1972; MA in Art History, U. Mich., 1973, PhD in Art History, 1976. Asst. prof. dept. art U. Tex., Arlington, 1977-80; curator, asst. dir. New Mus. Contemporary Art, N.Y.C., 1980-84; curator contemporary art Corcoran Gallery Art, Washington, 1984-86; chief curator exhbns. Hirshhorn Mus. and Sculpture Garden, Washington, DC, 1986-90, chief curator, 1990-91, dir., 2002—05; Nancy and Holcombe T. Green Jr. dir. High Mus. Art, Atlanta, 1991—99; dir. Menil Collection and Found., Houston, 2000—01, Smithsonian Internat. Art Mus. Div., 2004—; under sect. for art Smithsonian Institution, 2004—. Address: Smithsonian Institution Bldg 1000 Jefferson Dr SW MRC 041 Washington DC 20560-0001

**RIFKIN, RON,** actor; b. NYC, Oct. 31, 1939; m. Iva Rifkin, 1966. Actor: (films) Flareup, 1969, Devil's 8, 1969, Silent Running, 1971, Rabbit Test, 1978, The Big Fix, 1978, The Chosen, 1981, The Sting II, 1983, Kidco, 1984, JFK, 1991, Husbands and Wives, 1992, Manhattan Murder Mystery, 1993, Wolf, 1994, Last Summer in the Hamptons, 1995, The Substance of Fire, 1996, I'm Not Rappaport, 1996, L.A. Confidential, 1997, The Negotiator, 1998, Sam the Man, 1999, The Boiler Room, 2000, Keeping the Faith, 2000, The Majestic, 2001, Tadpole, 2002, Dragonfly, 2002, The Sum of All Fears, 2002, Just a Kiss, 2002, Pulse, 2006; (TV films) The Sunshine Boys, 1975, The Dream Makers, 1975, The Night that Panicked America, 1975, In the Glitter Palace, 1977, A Question of Guilt, 1978, Columbo: Make Me a Perfect Murder, 1978, Mrs. R's Daughter, 1979, Day the Bubble Burst, 1981, Another Woman's Child, 1983, The Ratings Game, 1984, Concealed Enemies, 1984, Do You Remember Love, 1985, Courage, 1986, Dress Gray, 1986, Conspiracy: The Trial of the Chicago 8, 1987, Sunset Gang, 1991, W.S.H., 1994, Norma Jean and Marilyn, 1996, Flowers for Algernon, 2000, Deliberate Intent, 2000, The Warden, 2001; (TV series) Adam's Rib, 1973, When Things Were Rotten, 1975, Husbands, Wives & Lovers, 1978, One Day at a Time, 1980—81, Falcon Crest, 1983—84, Evergreen, 1985, Leaving L.A., 1997, Alias, 2001—06, Brothers & Sisters, 2006; Broadway actor Cabaret, 1998 (Tony award featured actor in a musical, 1998), The Paris Letter, 2005, TV guest appearances include The Bob Newhart Show, 1972, Mary Tyler Moore Show, 1970, The Rockford Files, 1974, Hill Street Blues, 1981, Law & Order, 1990, ER, 1994, The Outer Limits, 1995. Office: c/o SAG 1515 Broadway Fl 44 New York NY 10036-8901*

**RIFKIN, STEPHEN,** nephrologist; s. Morris and May Rifkin; children: Steven, Laura. AB, U. Rochester, 1963, MD, 1967. Diplomate in internal medicine and in nephrology Am. Bd. Internal Medicine. Pvt. practice nephrology, Tampa, Fla., 1980—; assoc. prof. medicine U. South Fla. Coll. Medicine, Tampa, 1999—. Chief of staff Tampa Gen. Hosp., 1988—90, chief nephrology sect., 2002—; pres. Fla. End Stage Renal Disease Network #7, Tampa, 1990—92, bd. dirs., 1999—. Capt. U.S. Army, 1969—71. Recipient Exemplary Practice award for nephrology, Nat. Kidney Found. of Fla., 1996. Fellow: ACP; mem.: Fla. Soc. Nephrology, Am. Soc. Internal Medicine, Am. Soc. Nephrology. Avocations: tennis, travel. Office: Stephen I Rifkin MD PA 2403 West Azeele St Tampa FL 33609-3317 Personal E-mail: sirifkin@hotmail.com.

**RIFKIND, ARLEEN B.,** pharmacologist, researcher, educator; b. NYC, June 29, 1938; d. Michael C. and Regina (Gottlieb) Brenner; m. Robert S. Rifkind, Dec. 24, 1961; children: Amy, Nina. BA, Bryn Mawr Coll., 1960; MD, NYU, 1964. Resident Bellevue Hosp., N.Y.C., 1965; clin. assoc. Endocrine br. Nat. Cancer Inst., 1965—68; rsch. assoc., asst. resident physician Rockefeller U., 1968—71; from asst. prof. to assoc. prof. Weill Med. Coll. Cornell U., N.Y.C., 1971—83, prof. pharmacology Weill Med. Coll., 1983—, chmn. Gen. Faculty Coun. Weill Med. Coll., 1984—86. Mem. Nat. Inst. Environ. Health Scis. Rev. Com., 1981-85, chmn., 1985-86; mem. toxicology study sect. NIH, 1989-91, chmn., 1991-93; bd. sci. counselors USPHS Agy. for Toxic Substances and Disease Registry, 1991-95; adv. com. FDA, Spl. Studies Relating to the Possible Long-Term Health Effects of Phenoxy Herbicides and Contaminents, 1995-99; external adv. bd. Environ. Health Scis. Ctr., Wayne State U., 1999—. Assoc. editor Drug Metabolism and Disposition, 1997-2005; mem. editl. bd. Toxicology and Applied Pharmacology, 1996-2002, Biochem. Pharmacology, 1996—2003; contbr. articles to profl. jours. Chair Friends of Libr., Jewish Theol. Sem. Am., 1984-86; trustee Dalton Sch., 1986-92; bd. govs. Am. Jewish Com., 1993—. Bd. dirs. N.Y. chpt. Am. Jewish Com. Recipient Andrew W. Mellon Tchr.-Scientist award, 1976-78, Tchg. Excellence award Weill Med. Coll. Cornell U., 2004 Mem. AAAS, Internat. Soc. Study Xenobiotics, Am. Soc. Clin. Investigation, Am. Soc. Pharmacology and Exptl. Therapeutics, Endocrine Soc., Soc. Toxicology. Office: Cornell U Med Coll Dept Pharmacology 1300 York Ave New York NY 10021-4805 Business E-Mail: arifkind@med.cornell.edu.

**RIFKIND, ROBERT S.,** lawyer; b. NYC, Aug. 31, 1936; s. Simon H. and Adele (Singer) R.; m. Arleen Brenner, Dec. 24, 1961; children: Amy, Nina. BA, Yale U., 1958; JD, Harvard U., 1961; LHD (hon.), Jewish Theol. Sem. Am., 1998. Bar: N.Y. 1961, U.S. Supreme Ct. 1965. Asst. to solicitor gen. Dept. Justice, 1965-68; assoc. firm Cravath, Swaine & Moore LLP, N.Y.C., 1962-65, 68-70, ptnr., 1971—2001, sr. counsel, 2002—. Trustee Dalton Sch., N.Y.C., 1975-83, hon. trustee, 1983—, pres., 1977-79; trustee Brandeis U., 1998—, The Loomis Inst., 1987-95; bd. dirs. Charles H. Revson Found., 1991-2005, chmn., 1997-2003; bd. dirs. Jewish Theol. Sem. Am., 1983—,

Jerusalem Found., 1998-2006, Leo Baeck Inst., 1999—, Benjamin N. Cardozo Sch. Law, 1984-89, UN Assn., 2006—; pres. Am. Jewish Com., 1994-98; chmn., adminstr. coun., Jacob Blaustein Inst. Advancement of Human Rights, 1999-. Fellow Am. Coll. Trial Lawyers, Am. Bar Found.; mem. ABA, Coun. Fgn. Rels., Am. Law Inst., Assn. of Bar of City of N.Y., UN Assn. (bd. dirs. 2006—), The Century Assn., Phi Beta Kappa. Democrat. Office: Cravath Swaine & Moore LLP Worldwide Pla 825 8th Ave Fl 40 New York NY 10019-7475 Office Phone: 212-474-1450. Business E-Mail: rrifkind@cravath.com.

**RIGALI, JUSTIN FRANCIS CARDINAL,** archbishop; b. L.A., Apr. 19, 1935; s. Henry Alphonsus and Frances Irene (White) Rigali. B in Sacred Theology, Cath. U. Am., 1961; Lic. in Canon Law, Gregorian U., Rome, 1963, D in Canon Law, 1964; LHD (hon.), St. Louis U., 1995. Ordained priest Roman Cath. Ch. 1961, ordained bishop 1985, elevated to cardinal 2003. Served at Apostolic Nunciature, Madagascar, 1966—70; named Papal Chamberlain to Pope Paul VI, 1967; titular archbishop of Bolsena, 1985—94; sec. Congregation for Bishops Holy See, Vatican City, 1989—94, sec. Coll. of Cardinals, 1990—94; archbishop Archdiocese of St. Louis, St. Louis, 1994—2003, Archdiocese of Philadelphia, Pa., 2003—; dir. English-lang. sect. Vatican Secretariat of State. Pres. Pontifical Ecclesiastical Acad., 1985—89. Office: Archdiocese of Philadelphia 222 N 17th St Philadelphia PA 19103

**RIGAN, KARWYN E.,** speech pathology/audiology services professional; b. Mpls., Nov. 3, 1918; d. Hans Peter and Minnie Martha Dahl; m. Dennis Rigan (dec.); children: Dennis Fredrick, David Allen, Paul Larry AA, Flint Jr Coll., Mich., 1938; BA, U. Mich., 1940, MA, 1942. Speech therapist Lincoln Consol. Sch., Ypsilanti, Mich., 1950—58, Ann Arbor Pub. Schs., Mich., 1960—81, home bound tchr., 1981—87. Contbr. poetry to publs., columns in newspapers. Life mem. So. Poverty Law Ctr., Montgomery, Ala.; cast mem. Comic Opera Guild, 1998—; soprano 1st Meth. Chancel Choir, 1967—. Mem.: Mich. Speech and Hearing AQssn. (life), Amnesty Internat., UN Assn. (chmn. 1997—99), U. Mich. Faculty Women's Club. Avocations: yoga, piano, reading, gardening, bicycling.

**RIGAS, JOHN NICHOLAS,** lawyer; b. Muncie, Ind., Feb. 24, 1949; s. Nicholas Peter and Edna (Krestakos) Rigas; m. Rosemary Ann Dzienis, May 19, 1979; children: Margaret Rosemary, Nicholas John. BA, Mich. State U., 1971; MA in history and polit. sci., U. Mich., 1972; JD, U. Conn., 1979. Bar: Mich. 1979, US Dist. Ct. Mich. 1979. Joined Dow Corning Corp., 1982; sr. internat. atty. Dow Corning Europe, Brussels, 1988-91; mng. counsel for bus. and comml. law Dow Corning Corp., Midland, Mich., 1992-94, sr. mng. counsel for litigation and claimant law, 1994—99; dep. gen. counsel litig. Armstrong World Industries Inc., 1999—2000, sr. v.p., gen. counsel, sec., 2001—, Armstrong Holdings Inc., Lancaster, Pa., 2000—. Dir. Armstrong Found. Bd. dirs. Lancaster C. of C. and Industry, 2000—03. Mem. ABA, State Bar Mich., Am. Corp. Counsel Assn., Internat. Bar Assn., Midland Country Club (bd. dirs.). Office: Armstrong Holdings Inc PO Box 3001 Lancaster PA 17604-3001

**RIGAUD, EDWIN JOSEPH,** museum administrator; b. New Orleans, June 25, 1943; m. Carole Rigaud; children: Simone, Edwin, Eric. BS in Chemistry, Xavier U., Louisiana, 1965; MA in BioChemistry, U. Cincinnati, Ohio, 1972; LHD (hon.), Saint Joseph Coll., N. Kentucky U. Joined Procter & Gamble, 1965, v.p., gen. mgr. food and beverage products, 1992—95, v.p. govt. relations, 1996—2001; exec. dir. Nat. Underground Railroad Freedom Ctr., Cincinnati, 1996—2001, pres., 2001—; pres., CEO Enova Tech., LLC. Trustee emeritus Nat. Conference for Community & Justice, Cincinnati; bd. mem. Amistad Rsch. Ctr., Tulane U.; bd. dirs. Hebrew Union Coll., Tofa Bus. Consulting. Bd mem. Internat. Youth Inst.; adv. coun. Ohio River Way; bd. dirs. Knowledge Funding Ohio. Recipient Annual YMCA Black Achiever award, 1980. Mem.: Queen City Club (bd. dirs.), Jr. League Cin. (mentor). Office Phone: 513-557-5311.

**RIGBY, PERRY GARDNER,** medical association administrator, internist, medical educator; b. East Liverpool, Ohio, July 1, 1932; s. Perry Lawrence and Lucille Ellen (Orin) R.; m. Joan E. Worthington, June 16, 1957; children: Martha, Peter, Thomas, Matthew. BS summa cum laude, Mt. Union Coll., 1953, D.Sc. hon., 1976; MD, Western Res. U., 1957. Diplomate: Am. Bd. Internal Medicine. Intern in medicine U. Va. Hosp., Charlottesville, 1957-58, asst. resident in medicine, 1958-60; research fellow in hematology Mass. Meml. Hosp., Boston, 1960-62; clin. asst. in medicine Boston City Hosp., 1961-62; research assoc. in medicine Mass. Meml. Hosp., Boston U. Med. Ctr., 1961-62; asst. prof. internal medicine and anatomy U. Nebr., Omaha, 1964-66, assoc. prof. internal medicine and anatomy, 1966-69, prof. internal medicine, 1969-78, prof. anatomy, 1969-74, prof. med. edn., 1973-74, head sect. hematology Eugene C. Eppley Inst. for Research in Cancer and Allied Diseases, 1964-68, dir. hematology div., 1968-74, asst. dean for curriculum Coll. Medicine, 1971-72, assoc. dean for acad. affairs, 1972-74, dir. office ednl. services, 1972-74, acting assoc. dean for allied health professions, 1973-74, vice chmn. dept. med. and ednl. adminstrn., 1974, dean, 1974-78, chmn. dept. med. and ednl. adminstrn., 1974; prof. internal medicine La. State U., Shreveport, 1978—; assoc. dean acad. affairs Sch. Medicine, 1978-81, acting dean, 1981-82, dean, 1982-85, chancellor, 1985-94, dir. Health Care Systems New Orleans, 1994—; mem. clin. bd. Univ. Hosp., 1978-94, chmn. clin. bd., 1981-85, program dir. biomed. research support grant program, 1980-81; chmn. dean's com. VA Hosp., 1978-85; mem. courtesy staff Immanuel Med. Ctr.; bd. dirs. Health Planning Council of Midlands, Omaha, 1976-78; cons. WHO, Kabul, Afghanistan, 1976. Bd. dirs. Fontenelle Forest, Omaha, 1976-78; bd. dirs. River Cities High Tech. Group, Shreveport, 1982-85. Served as capt. M.C. U.S. Army, 1962-64. Markle scholar 1965 Fellow ACP, mem. Am. Fedn. Clin. Research (councillor 1971), AMA (del.), Am. Soc. Hematology, N.Y. Acad. Scis., Am. Assn. Med. Colls. (council of deans of Midwest-Gt. Plains 1974-78, chmn. Midwest-Gt. Plains 1976), Am. Assn. Cancer Research, AAAS, Am. Heart Assn., Central Soc. Clin. Research, Internat. Soc. Hematology, Health Edn. Media Assn., Am. Assn. Physicians' Assts., So. Soc. Clin. Investigation, Shreveport C. of C. (dir. 1982-85), Sigma Xi, Alpha Omega Alpha, Phi Rho Sigma Home: 905 1/2 DALZELL Shreveport LA 71104

**RIGDON, DAVID TEDRICK,** military officer, geneticist, director; b. Laurel, Miss., Jan. 27, 1948; s. James T. and Marie T. (Taylor) R.; m. Elizabeth Sue Jones, June 1, 1973; children: Angela Denise, Michael David. BS in Biology, U. Ala., 1970; MD cum laude, U. Miss., 1975. Diplomate Am. Bd. Pediates., Am. Bd. Med. Genetics. Commd. USAF, 1975, advanced through grades to col., 1991; intern in pediatrics USAF Med. Ctr., Keesler AFB, Miss., 1975-76, resident in pediats., 1976-78; fellow in med. genetics U. Ala., Birmingham, 1978-80; med. geneticist USAF Med. Genetics Ctr., Keesler AFB, 1980-85, dir. Air Force Med. Genetics Ctr., 1985—. Cons. Surgeon Gen. USAF, Miss. State Dept. Health; clin. asst. prof. pediats. Uniformed Svcs. Univ. of Health Scis., F. Edward Herbert Sch. Medicine, Bethesda, Md. Contbr. articles to profl. jours. Recipient Physician's Recognition awards AMA. Fellow Am. Acad. Pediats.; mem. Am. Soc. Human Genetics, So. Genetics Group, Alpha Omega Alpha. Republican. Methodist. Avocations: boating, fishing. E-mail: david.rigdon@keesler.af.mil, drigdon@bellsouth.net.

**RIGDON, KEVIN LEIGH,** theater educator, lighting designer, set designer; b. Pontiac, Mich., Feb. 17, 1956; s. Donald Lee and Arlene Mae Rigdon; m. Patricia Patrick, June 21, 1998. Student, Drake U., Des Moines, Iowa, 1974—75. Resident designer Steppenwolf Theatre Co., Chgo., 1976—97; from vis. prof. to prof. U. Houston, 1997—2001, prof., 2001—. Adj. faculty The Theater Sch. De Paul U., 1991—96; assoc. dir. design The Alley Theater, Houston, 1998—. Lighting designer (plays) Steppenwolf Theatre, 1980 (The Joseph Jefferson award, 1980), Remains Theatre, 1982 (The Joseph Jefferson award, 1981, 1982), Glengarry Glen Ross, 1984, Speed the Plow, 1988, Ghetto, 1989, Our Town, 1989 (nominated Drama Desk award, 1989), The Grapes of Wrath, Broadway, 1990 (nominated Drama Desk award, 1990, Am. Theatre Wing Design award, 1990, nominated Tony award, 1990), A Streetcar

Named Desire, 1992, Steppenwolf Theatre, 1994 (The Joseph Jefferson award, 1994), The Rise and Fall of Little Voice, 1994, Buried Child, 1996, Mark Taper Forum, 1997 (Drama-Logue Critic's award, 1997), One Flew Over the Cuckoo's Nest, 2001, Lincoln Ctr. Theater (Am. Theatre Wing Design award, 1985, nominated Drama Desk award, 1985, 1985, Am. Theatre Wing Design award, 1985), A Clockwork Orange (The Joseph Jefferson award, 1997), Goodman Theatre (The Joseph Jefferson award, 1988), Remains Theatre, scenic designer, lighting designer The Caretaker, 1986, The Song of Jacob Zulu, 1993, Coast Playhouse, 1994 (The L.A. Weekly award, 1994, LA Weekly award, 1994), The Old Neighborhood, 1997, designer (over 300 other plays off-Broadway plays). Recipient Outstanding Faculty award, The Houston Alumni Orgn., 2003. Mem.: United Scenic Artists. Home: 2115 Runnels St Apt 5308 Houston TX 77003 Office: Univ Houston 133 Cynthia Woods Mitchell Houston TX 77204-4016 Office Phone: 713-743-2816. Home Fax: 713-236-0986. Personal E-mail: rigdondesign@sbcglobal.net. Business E-Mail: krigdon@uh.edu.

**RIGERMAN, RUTH UNDERHILL,** mathematics professor; b. Batavia, N.Y., Feb. 1, 1944; d. George E. and Caroline E. (Cooper) Underhill; m. David Rigerman, Nov. 17, 1967; children: Cliff, Eileen, Matthew, Glenn, Ardeen. BS, SUNY, Brockport, 1965, MS, 1967. Instr. math. Genesee C.C., Batavia, 1982—; tech. specialist Genesee Advanced Studios, Batavia, 1990—; instr. SUNY, Brockport, 1990—. Named Master Tchr., U. Tex., 1992, 96. Mem. Math. Assn. Am. Home: 4749 Batavia Elba Townline Rd Batavia NY 14020-1035 Office: Genesee C C 1 College Rd Batavia NY 14020-9703

**RIGG, CAROL MARGARET ELIZABETH RUTH,** art educator; b. Pitts., Dec. 14, 1928; d. Carl Hazlett and Ruth Standish (Massey) Rigg. BA, Fla. State U., Tallahassee, 1951; MA, Presbyn. Sch. Christian Edn., 1955; MFA, Chgo. Art Inst., Ill., 1963. Art dir. bd. publs. Fla. State U., Tallahassee, 1950-53; art editor Motive Mag., Nashville, 1954-65; artist-in-residence Fla. Presbyn. Coll., St. Petersburg, 1965-66; prof. visual arts Eckerd Coll., St. Petersburg, 1967-93, prof. emerita, 1999—. Founder Possum Press, St. Petersburg, 1969; lectr. Princeton Div. Sch., 1972; vis. art lectr. Harvard Div. Sch., 1982. Exhibitions include in more than 60 solo art shows; calligraphy featured on two CBS-TV shows, 1969, 1971; one-woman shows include calligraphy Cultural Olympics, Seoul, Republic of Korea, 1987; author: (book) Calligraphy of the Americas, 1977-95. Pres. Nashville Artists Guild, 1960—62. Fulbright grantee, 1972. Mem.: Am. Calligraphic Arts Assn., Fla. Artist Group, Fla. Gulfcoast Soc. Scribes (founder, pres. 1976—78). Mem. Religious Soc. Friends. Office Phone: 727-866-2541. Business E-Mail: riggmr@eckerd.edu.

**RIGG, CHARLES ANDREW,** pediatrician; b. Hamilton, Victoria, Australia, Oct. 18, 1926; arrived in U.S., 1963; s. Arthur Oscar and Mary Eileen (Wingrove) Rigg. B Medicine, Surgery with honors, Sydney U., 1951. Registrar, professorial unit Children's Hosp., Sydney, 1954—56; registrar pediat. unit St. Mary's Hosp. Med. Sch., London, 1956; registrar professorial unit Children's Hosp., Boston, 1957, from sr. resident to chief resident, 1957, fellow adolescent medicine, 1963—64, staff adolescent medicine, 1964—65; asst. prof. pediat. Georgetown U. Med. Sch., 1965—67; chief dept. adolescent medicine Children's Nat. Med. Ctr., Washington, 1967—80, Boston City Hosp., 1981—83; med. dir. Outer Cape Health, Provincetown, Mass., 1983—88; pediatrician, med. dir. Medicenter Five, Harwich, Mass., 1988—95, pediatrician, 1995—97; cons. pediatrician May Ctr. Child Devel., Chatham, Mass., 1990—; pediatrician Harwich Town Pub. Sch. Sys., 1997—. Cons. Nat. Naval Med. Ctr., Bethesda, Md., 1973—80, Walter Reed Army Med. Ctr., Washington, 1973—80; courtesy staff medicine Children's Hosp., Boston, 1983—2005, emeritus mem. courtesy staff, 2005—; vis. prof. Philippine Pediat. Soc., 1978, 9th Congress Brazilian Med. Assn., 1979, 16th Internat. Congress Pediat., Barcelona, 1980; from asst. prof. to assoc. prof. child health George Washington U. Med. Sch., 1967—80; assoc. prof. pediat. Boston U., 1981—83. Editor: Adolescent Medicine Present and Future Concepts, 1980; contbr. articles to profl. jours. Mem. Shakespeare Libr., Washington, Nat. Trust Hist. Preservation, Nat. Trust Australia, Tasmania, Royal Oak Soc. Maj. M.C. Royal Australian Army, 1951—60, lt. col. USAR, 1985—91. Model Typg. Program Adolescent Medicine grantee, Maternal and Child Health Svcs.-U.S. Govt., 1967—80, Comprehensive health Svcs. Adolescent Ctr. grantee, Mass. Dept. Pub. Health, 1981—83. Fellow: Royal Australasian Coll. Physicians, Am. Acad. Pediatrics (life); mem.: Soc. Adolescent Medicine (Washington, DC chpt. pres. 1974—76, New Eng. chpt. pres. 1982—84, charter, treas., chmn., legis. com.), Folger Shakespeare Libr., Royal Sydney Golf Club. Episcopalian. Avocations: historic preservation, gardening, theater, music, walking.

**RIGG, DAME DIANA,** actress; b. Doncaster, Yorkshire, Eng., July 20, 1938; d. Louis and Beryl (Helliwell) R.; m. Menahem Gueffen, July 6, 1973 (div. Sept. 1976); m. Archibald Hugh Stirling, Mar. 25, 1981 (div. Apr. 1993); 1 child, Rachael Atlanta. Grad., Fulneck Girls' Sch., Pudsey, Yorkshire; student, Royal Acad. Dramatic Art, London; D (hon.), Stirling U., Eng., 1988, Leeds U., 1992, Southbank U., 1996. Prof. of theater studies Oxford U., 1998—. Stage debut as Natella Abashwili in The Caucasian Chalk Circle, Theatre Royal, York, Eng., 1957; joined Royal Shakespeare Co., Stratford-on-Avon, 1959, debut as Andromache in Troilus and Cressida, 1960; London debut as Philippe Trincant in The Devils, London, 1961; numerous repertory appearances; joined Nat. Theatre, 1972; appeared in Jumpers, Macbeth, 1972, The Misanthrope, 1973, Pygmalion, 1974, Phaedra Britannica, 1975, Night and Day, 1978, Colette, 1982, Heartbreak House, 1983, Little Eyolf, 1985, Antony and Cleopatra, 1985, Wildlife, 1986, Follies, 1987, Love Letters, 1990, All for Love, 1991, Putting It Together, 1992, Berlin Bertie, 1992, Medea, 1992 (Tony award, Broadway prod., 1994, Eve. Standard award, Variety Club award), Mother Courage and Her Children, 1995, Who's Afraid of Virginia Wolf, 1996, Humble Boy, 2001, Honour, 2006; film appearances include A Midsummer Night's Dream, 1968, The Assassination Bureau, 1969, On Her Majesty's Secret Service, 1969, Julius Caesar, 1970, The Hospital, 1971, Theatre of Blood, 1973, A Little Night Music, 1977, The Great Muppet Caper, 1981, Evil Under the Sun, 1982, A Good Man in Africa, 1994, Parting Shots, 1998, Heidi, 2005; co-starred as Emma Peel in Brit. TV miniseries: Charles II: The Power and the Passion, 2003. TV series The Avengers, 1965-67; star TV series Diana, 1973-74; numerous TV movies including This House of Brede, 1975, Hedda Gabler, 1981, Little Eyolf, 1982, Witness for the Prosecution, 1982, King Lear, 1983, Bleak House, 1984, A Hazard of Hearts, 1987, Worst Witch, 1987, Unexplained Laughter, 1989, Mother Love (Broadcasting Guild Award, BAFTA), 1989, Genghis Cohn, 1994, Zoya, 1995, The Haunting of Helen Walker, 1995, Moll Flanders, 1996, Samson and Delilah, 1996, Rebecca, 1997 (Emmy award, 1997); host PBS series Mystery, 1989—, Mrs. Bradley Mysteries, 1999—, In the Beginning, 2000, The American, 2000, Victoria & Albert, 2001; author: No Turn Unstoned, 1982, U.S. edit., 1983, So To The Land, 1994. Decorated comdr. Brit. Empire; created dame, 1994; recipient Tony award nomination as best actress in Abelard and Heloise and The Misanthrope; Plays and Players award for Phaedra Britannica and Night and Day; Variety Club Est. Britannica award for best actress for Evil Under the Sun; Brit. Acad. Film and TV Arts award for best TV actress in Mother Love, 1989, Award for Women in TV & Film, 2001. Mem. United Brit. Artists (co-founder, dir. 1982—). Address: c/o Lionel Larner Ltd 119 W 57th St New York NY 10019-2303*

**RIGG, LYLE D.,** headmaster; m. Sharon Creech; 2 children. BA, Miami U.; MA, W.Tex. State U.; EdM, Harvard U. Former headmaster & English teacher Am. Sch. in Switzerland (TASIS) England Am. Sch.; headmaster Pennington Sch., Pennington, NJ, 1999—. Office: Pennington Sch 112 W Delaware Ave Pennington NJ 08534

**RIGGINS, WILLIAM G.,** electric power industry executive; b. 1958; BS, U. Kansas; MS, U. Mo., Kansas City; JD, U. Kansas. Bar: Mo. 1984. Atty. Great Plains Energy, Inc., Kansas City, Mo., 1991—92, staff atty., 1992—94, sr. atty., 1994—96, mng. atty., 1996, asst. gen. counsel, 1996—98, asst. chief legal officer, 1998—2000, gen. counsel, 2000—. Bd. mem. vice chmn. Swope Health Found. Office: Great Plains Energy Inc PO Box 418679 1201 Walnut St Kansas City MO 64141

**RIGGIO, LEONARD,** book store company executive; b. 1941; married; 3 children. Student, NYU; D (hon.), CUNY Baruch Coll., Bentley Coll. Mdse. mgr. NYU Bookstore, NYC, 1962—65; pres., CEO, bd. dirs. Barnes & Noble Bookstores, Inc., 1965—86; founder, CEO, pres., treas. Barnes & Noble Inc., NYC, 1986—2002, chmn. bd., 1986—; chmn. bd., prin. beneficial owner Software Etc. Stores, Inc., Mpls., MBS Textbook Exch. Inc., Columbia, Mo. Chmn. bd. Dia Art Found., 1998—2006, bd. mem., 2006—; bd. dirs. Children's Def. Fund, Black Children's Cmty. Crusade, Bklyn. Tech Found., Italian Am. Found. Named one of Top 200 Collectors, ARTnews mag., 2003—06; named to Acad. of Disting. Entrepreneurs, Babson Coll., Retailing Hall of Fame, Tex. A&M U., 2005; recipient Ellis Island Medal of Honor, Frederick Douglas Medallion, Americanism award, Anti-Defamation League, 2002. Avocation: collecting contemporary art. Office: Barnes & Noble Inc 4th Fl 122 5th Ave Fl 4 New York NY 10011-5605*

**RIGGIO, MILLA C.,** language educator, researcher; b. Ft. Smith, Ark., Nov. 15, 1940; d. Morgan William Cozort and Mildred Ella Robison; m. Thomas P. Riggio, June 21, 1970; children: Anna Riggio-Rosen, Thomas P. III 1 stepchild, Robert Brink. BA, So. Meth. U., Dallas; AM, Harvard U., Cambridge, Mass., 1968, PhD, 1973. Lectr. U. Sydney, Australia, 1968, Harvard U., Cambridge, 1971; from asst. prof. to prof. Trinity Coll., Hartford, Conn., 1973—98, James J. Goodwin prof. English, 1996—. Dramaturg, panelist, cons. Hartford Stage Co., 1995—; cons. West Indian Found., Hartford, 1998—; vis. prof. in residence U. W. Indies, St. Augustine, Trinidad and Tobago, 2000. Author, editor: Teaching Shakespeare thru Performance, 1989, Carnival: Culture in Action - The Trinidad Experience, 2004; editor: Trinidad & Tobago Carnival, 1998. Exec. bd. Hemispheric Inst. Performances and Politics, NYC; trustee E. Coast Artist, NYC; advisor Cultural Dance Troupe of West Indies, Hartford, 1996—; bd. dirs. Charter Oak Cultural Ctr., Hartford, 2001—02. Recipient award for Contbn. to West Indian Hartford Cmty.; fellow, NEH, 1998—99; vis. scholar, NYU, 2005—06; Nat. Merit scholar, Fulbright fellow, Australia, 1964. Mem.: MLA, Medieval/Renaissance Drama Soc. (sec., v.p., pres. 1988—2001), Shakespeare Assn. Am. Avocations: music, tennis, films. Home: 20 Dearborn Dr Manchester CT 06040 Office: Trinity Coll English Dept Hartford CT 06106

**RIGGIO, STEPHEN,** book store company executive; married; 3 children. BA in Anthropology, Bklyn. Coll., 1974. Buying, mktg. areas Barnes & Noble Bookstores, Inc., N.Y.C., 1974-78, gen. mdse. mgr., 1978-81, head direct mail bus., 1981-86, exec. v.p. merchandising, 1986-90, exec. v.p., chief oper. officer, 1990—97; vice-chmn. Barnes & Noble, Inc., 1997—, CEO, 2002—; vice-chmn. & acting CEO barnesandnoble.com, 2000—02. Originator Children With Special Needs collection books about and for children with learning disabilities. Bd. dirs. N.Y. chpt. Assn. Help Retarded Children. Office: Barnes & Noble, Inc 122 5th Ave New York NY 10011-5605*

**RIGGLE, BLAIR ANDREW,** educational association administrator, consultant, psychologist, educator; b. Springfield, Ohio, Apr. 16, 1942; s. Margaret Elaine and Loren Robert Riggle; m. Jennifer Sue Riggle, Aug. 16, 1986. BS in Psychology, Wright State U., Ohio, 1984, MA in Sch. Psychology, 1987; PhD in Ednl. Leadership, U. Dayton, 2001. Cert. supr., edn. of the handicapped, elem. prin., h.s. prin., sch. psychologist, asst. supt. Ohio, 1987. Sch. psychologist Del. County Bd. of Edn., Delaware, Ohio, 1987—91; dir., planning, rsch. & testing, evaluation Westerville City Schs., Ohio, 1991—95; dir., assessment intervention, sch. improvement Hilliard City Schs., Ohio, 1995—. Adj. prof. U. Dayton, 1997—. Vestry mem. St. Matthews Episcopal Ch., Westerville, 2001—02. Mem.: NASP (assoc.), Phi Delta Kappa (assoc.), Nat. Assn. of Test Dirs. (assoc.), Kappa Delta Pi (assoc.), Assn. for Suprs.and Curriculum Devel. (assoc.), Am. Ednl. Rsch. Assn. (assoc.). Achievements include design of School Improvement Template; Assessment Analysis Procedures. Home: 7558 Lynbrook Ln Westerville OH 43082 Office: Hilliard City Sch Dist 5323 Cemetery Rd Hilliard OH 43026 Office Phone: 614-771-4273. Office Fax: 614-777-2424. Personal E-mail: arigglebar@aol.com. Business E-Mail: andy_riggle@fclass.hilliard.k12.oh.us.

**RIGGLE, PATRICIA CAROL,** special education educator; b. Gallipolis, Ohio, May 28, 1965; d. Pat and Freadith Fay Price; m. Richard Allan Riggle; children: Alana, Emily. BS, U. Rio Grande, 1989. Sub. tchr. Gallia County Local Schs., Gallipolis, Ohio, 1989—92, Gallipolis City Schs., Gallipolis, Ohio, 1989—92; tchr. Wellston City Sch., Wellston, Ohio, 1992—; child care provider Rio Grande Child Devel. Ctr., Rio Grande, Ohio, 1992—93. Vol. asst. dir. drama club Wellston HS, Wellston, Ohio, 1998—; career assessment adv. com. Gallia-Jackson-Vinton Joint Vocats. Sch. Dist., Rio Grande, Ohio, 2001—03. Youth Sunday sch. tchr. Okey Chapel, Scottown, Ohio, 1985—2000. Mem.: NEA, Ohio Farm Bur., Wellston Tchrs. Assn., Ohio Edn. Assn. Avocations: camping, travel, crafts. Home: 4767 Hannan Trace Rd Patriot OH 45658 Personal E-mail: star1@aceinter.net.

**RIGGS, ARTHUR D.,** health facility administrator, research scientist; b. Modesto, Calif., Aug. 8, 1939; s. John Arlis and Nelly Laura Riggs; m. Jane Merill, June 12, 1960; children: Karen, Lynelle, Derrick. AB in Chemistry, U. Calif., Riverside, 1961; PhD in Biochemistry, Calif. Inst. Tech., Pasadena, 1966. Predoctoral fellow biology dept. Calif. Inst. Tech., 1961—66; postdoctoral fellow Salk Inst. for Biol. Studies, La Jolla, Calif., 1966—69; assoc. rsch. scientist dept. molecular biology City of Hope Nat. Med. Ctr., Duarte, Calif., 1969—74, sr. rsch. scientist, 1974—83, assoc. chmn. divsn. biology, 1979—81, chmn. divsn. biology, 1981—83, assoc. dir. rsch., 1998—99; adj. prof. U. So. Calif., Los Angeles, 1991—; assoc. dir. for lab. rsch. City of Hope Cancer Ctr., 1981—87, dir. shared resources, 1993—95; chmn. divsn. biology Beckman Rsch. Inst. City of Hope, 1983—87, 1994—2000, dir., 1999—, 2000—; founding dean City of Hope Grad. Sch., Duarte, 1994—98. Contbr. articles to profl. jours. Recipient Rsch. award, Juvenile Diabetes Found., 1979, Disting. Alumnus award, U. Calif., Riverside, 1988, Tech. Leadership award, 2004. Mem.: NAS. Achievements include first human protein produced in bacteria; first man-designed and man-made gene; discovery of new type of genetics. Avocations: hiking, kayaking, mountain biking. Office: Beckman Rsch Inst City of Hope 1450 E Duarte Rd Duarte CA 91010

**RIGGS, ARTHUR JORDY,** retired lawyer; b. Nyack, N.Y., Apr. 3, 1916; s. Oscar H. and Adele (Jordy) R.; m. Virginia Holloway, Oct. 15, 1942 (dec.); children: Arthur James (dec.), Emily Adele Riggs Freeman, Keith Holloway, George Bennett; m. Priscilla McCormack, Jan. 16, 1993. AB, Princeton U., 1937; LLB, Harvard U., 1940. Bar: Mass. 1940, Tex. 1943; cert. specialist in labor law. Assoc. Warner, Stackpole, Stetson & Bradlee, Boston, 1940-41; staff mem. Solicitors Office U.S. Dept. Labor, Washington, Dallas, 1941-42; mem. Johnson, Bromberg, Leeds & Riggs, Dallas, 1949-81; of counsel Geary & Spencer, Dallas, 1981-91. Mem. ABA, State Bar Tex., Phi Beta Kappa. Avocations: maya archeology, history, photography. Home and Office: 2110 Antibes Dr Carrollton TX 75006-4326

**RIGGS, BARBARA,** federal agency administrator; b. Albany, NY; B in Internat. Studies, Cornell U., 1974. With U.S. Secret Svc., 1975—, assigned to field office LA, NY, with presdl. protective divsn. Washington, asst. dir. office protective rsch., head tech. security divsn, head Nat. Threat Assessment Ctr., 1998, chief of staff, dep. dir., 2004—. Mem. White House Security Rev., 1995. Recipient Meritorious Exec. Presdl. Rank award, 2002. Achievements include first female supervisory agent assigned to presdl. protective divsn.; first female to serve as dep. dir. Office: US Secret Svc US Dept Homeland Security 245 Murray Dr Bldg 410 Washington DC 20223*

**RIGGS, DONALD EUGENE,** librarian, academic administrator; b. Middlebourne, W.Va., May 11, 1942; m. Jane Vasbinder, Sept. 25, 1964; children: Janna Jennifer, Krista Dyonis. BA, Glenville State Coll., 1964; MA, W.Va. U., 1966; MLS, U. Pitts., 1968; EdD, Va. Poly. Inst. and State U., 1975. Head libr., tchr. sci. Warwood HS, W.Va., 1964-65, head libr., audiovisual dir. 1965-67; sci. and econs. libr. California State Coll. of Pa., 1968-70; dir. libr. and learning ctr. Bluefield State Coll., 1970-72; dir. librs. and media svcs. Bluefield State Coll., Concord Coll., Greenbrier C.C., and So. campus W.Va. Coll. of Grad. Studies, 1972-76; dir. librs. U. Colo., Denver, Met. State Coll.,

and C.C. of Denver- Auraria Campus, 1976-79; univ. libr. Ariz. State U., 1979-88, dean univ. librs., 1988-90; prof. info. and libr. sci., dean univ. libr. U. Mich., Ann Arbor, 1991-97; prof., v.p. for info. svcs., univ. libr. Nova Southeastern U., Ft. Lauderdale, Fla., 1997—. Adj. prof. Calif. State Coll., 1968-70, W.Va. U., 1970-72, U. Colo., 1977-79, U. Ariz., 1985, Emporia State U., 1996—, U. South Fla., 1997—; fed. rels. coord. Am. and W.Va. Libr. Assns., 1970-75; chmn. bd. dirs. Ctrl. Colo. Libr. Sys., 1976-79; chmn. Colo. Coun. Acad. Librs., 1977-78; mem. exec. bd. Colo. Alliance Rsch. Librs., 1978-79; cons. to librs.; fgn. assignments in Xi'an, China, 1988, Guadalajara, Mex., 1990, Budapest, Hungary, 1991, 95, Hong Kong, 1992, 94, San Juan, PR, 1993, Melbourne, Australia, 1994, Eupatory, Republic Crimea, Ukraine, 1995, London, 1996, Prague, Czech Republic, 1996, Beijing, China, 1996, 98, Pretoria, South Africa, 1996, others; del. Users Coun. Online Computer Libr. Ctr., Dublin, Ohio, 1987-91, pres.-elect, 1990-91, chair artificial intelligence and expert systems nat. group, 1987-88; bd. govs. Rsch. Librs. Group, Inc., Mountain View, Calif., 1991-92; vice chmn. mgmt. com. William L. Clements Libr., 1991-97. Editor: W.Va. Librs., 1973-75, Libr. Hi Tech, 1993-96, Coll. & Rsch. Librs., 1996-2002; founding editor: Libr. Adminstrn. and Mgmt., 1987-89; assoc. editor: Southeastern Libr., 1973-75; contbg. editor: Libraries in the Political Process, 1980, Options for the 80's, 1982, Library and Information Technology: At the Crossroads, 1984; contbg. author, editor: Library Leadership: Visualizing the Future, 1982; author: Strategic Planning for Library Managers, 1984, (with Helen Gothberg) Time Management in Academic Libraries, 1986, (with Gordon Sabine) Libraries in the 90's: What the Leaders Expect, 1988, Creativity, Innovation and Entrepreneurship in Libraries, 1989, Library Communication: The Language of Leadership, 1991, (with Rao Aluri) Expert Systems in Libraries, 1990, Cultural Diversity in Libraries, 1994; editl. bd. Am. Librs., 1987-89, Jour. Libr. Adminstrn., 1987-97, Coll. and Rsch. Librs., 1990-96, Coll. and Rsch. Librs. News, 1996-2002. Trustee Mesa Pub. Libr., Ariz., 1980-86, chmn., 1985-86; mem. Ariz. State Libr. Adv. Coun., 1981-84; bd. dirs. Documentation Abstracts, Inc., 1986-90. Recipient Alumnus of Yr. award Glenville State Coll., 1992; named Outstanding Young Educator, Ohio County Schs., 1966; Coun. on Libr. Resources grantee, 1985; sr. fellow UCLA, 1989. Mem. ALA (councilor-at-large 1982-86, 89-93, chmn. coun.'s resolutions com. 1985-86, pub. com. 1988-92, Hugh Atkinson award 1991), Ariz. Libr. Assn. (pres. coll. and univ. divsn. 1981-82, pres. 1983-84, Spl. Svc. award 1986, Disting. Svc. award 1990), Colo. Libr. Assn. (pres. 1978-79), W.Va. Libr. Assn. (pres. 1975-76), Assn. Coll. and Rsch. Librs. (pres. Tri-State chpt. 1972-74, pres. Ariz. chpt. 1981-82), So. Libr. Assn. (chmn. coll. and univ. sect. 1982-83), Assn. Rsch. Librs. (100th meeting planning com. 1982, mgmt. of rsch. libr. resources com. 1990-93, rsch. collections com. 1993-96), AMIGOS Bibliograph Coun. (trustee 1986-90, chmn. bd. trustees 1988-89), Libr. Adminstrn. and Mgmt. Assn. (bd. dirs. 1987-89, pres.-elect 1993-94, pres. 1994-95), Libr. Info. and Tech. Assn. (bd. dirs. 1989-93), Ctr. for Rsch. Librs. (councilor 1979-97), Fla. Libr. Assn. (chair leadership devel. com. 2003-2004), Mountain Plains Libr. Assn. (bd. dirs. 1987-90, pres.-elect 1990-91), S.E. Fla. Libr. Info. Network (exec. com., bd. dirs. 1997—, pres. 1998-99), Beta Phi, Phi Beta Phi, Phi Delta Kappa, Phi Kappa Phi. Office: Nova Southeastern U Alvin Sherman Libr Rsch & Info Tech Ctr Ray Ferrero Jr Blvd Fort Lauderdale FL 33314-7721 Office Phone: 954-262-4640. Business E-Mail: driggs@nova.edu.

**RIGGS, FRED WARREN,** political science professor; b. Kuling, China, July 3, 1917; (parents Am. citizens); s. Charles H. and Grace (Frederick) R.; m. Clara-Louise Mather, June 5, 1943; children: Gwendolyn, Ronald (dec.). Student, U. Nanking, China, 1934-35; BA, U. Ill., 1938; MA, Fletcher Sch. Law and Diplomacy, 1941; PhD, Columbia U., 1948. Lectr. CUNY, 1947-48; rsch. assoc. Fgn. Policy Assn., 1948-51; asst. dir. Pub. Adminstrn. Clearing House, N.Y.C., 1951-55; Arthur F. Bentley prof. govt. Ind. U., 1956-67; dir. Social Sci. Rsch. Inst. U. Hawaii, 1970-73, prof. polit. sci., 1967-87, prof. emeritus, 1987—. Vis. assoc. prof. Yale U., 1955-56; vis. lectr. Nat. Officials Tng. Inst., Korea, 1956; vis. prof. U. Philippines, 1958-59, MIT, 1965-66, CUNY, 1974-75; vis. scholar Inst. Soc. Studies, The Hague, 1972; sr. specialist East-West Ctr. U. Hawaii, 1962-63. Author: Pressures on Congress: A Study of the Repeal of Chinese Exclusion, 1950, reprinted, 1973, Formosa under Chinese Nationalist Rule, 1952, reprinted, 1972, The Ecology of Public Administration, 1961 (pub. in Portuguese, 1964), Administration in Developing Countries: The Theory of Prismatic Society, 1964 (pub. in Korean, 1966, Portuguese, 1968); Thailand: The Modernization of a Bureaucratic Polity, 1966, Organization Theory and International Development, 1969, Administrative Reform and Political Responsiveness: A Theory of Dynamic Balancing, 1971, Prismatic Society Revisited, 1973 (pub. in Korean, 1987), Applied Prismatics, 1978, (with Daya Krishna) Development Debate, 1987; author: (with others) Contemporary Political Systems: Classifications and Typologies, 1990, Handbook of Comparative and Development Public Administration, 1991, Terminology: Application in Interdisciplinary Communication, 1993, Parliamentary vs. Presidential Government, 1993, Public Administration in the Global Village, 1994, Comparing Nations: Concepts, Strategies, Substance, 1994, Handbook of Bureaucracy, 1994, Standardizing and Harmonizing Terminology, 1995, Korea in the Era of Post-Development and Globalization, 1996, Designs for Democratic Stability, 1997, Modernity and Bureaucracy, 1997, Presidentialism vs. Parliamentarism, 1998, Public Administration in America, 1998, The Modernity of Ethnic Identity and Conflict, 1998, Beyond Area Studies, 1998, Impeachment vs. Harassment, 1999; Ethnic Diversity, Nationalism and Constitutional Democracy, 2000, The Para-Modern Context of Ethnic Nationalism, 2000, Globalization, Ethnic Diversity and Nationalism, 2002, Globalization and Faith, 2002, Electronic Nomenclators, 2002, A Comparativist's Sojourn, 2003, American Myth as Global Model, 2004, In Response to Globalization, 2004, Manifesto: The Vicious Cycle and How to Reverse It, 2005, Turbulent World, 2005, Globalization and Religion on the Web, 2005, Trends in Bureaucracy, Democracy, and Representation, 2006, Impact of Globalization on Public Administration, 2006; co-author, editor: Frontiers of Development Administration, 1971, Tower of Babel: On the Definition and Analysis of Concepts in the Social Sciences, 1975. Dir. INTERCOCTA project Internat. Social Sci. Coun., 1970-93; chair UNESCO com. INTERCONCEPT project, 1977-79; chair Comm. on Conceptual and Terminological Analysis (COCTA), Internat. Polit. Sci. Assn., Internat. Sociol. Assn. and Internat. Social Sci. Coun., 1973-79; co-chair N.AM. roundtable on cooperation Social Sci. Info. Mables., 1979; chair lexicographic terminology com. Dictionary Soc. N.Am., 1983-86; co-chair Com. on Viable Constitutionalism (COVICO), 1993—. Decorated Order of White Elephant, Kingdom of Thailand, 1986; fellow com. comparative politics Social Sci. Rsch. Coun., 1957-58, Ctr. Advanced Study in Behavioral Scis., 1966-67; recipient Disting. Ret. Faculty award U. Hawaii, 2005; honoree Eastern Regional Orgn. Pub. Adminstrn. Conf., 1983. Mem. Am. Soc. for Pub. Adminstrn. (chair comparative adminstrn. group 1960-71, Dwight Waldo award 1991), Am. Polit. Sci. Assn., Internat. Studies Assn. (chair comparative interdisciplinary studies sect. 1970-74, v.p. 1970-71, co-chair ethnicity, nationalism and migration sect. 1994-95), Internat. Polit. Sci. Assn., Internat. Sociol. Assn., Asian Studies (chair com. rsch. materials S.E. Asia 1969-73), Soc. for Comparative Rsch. (co-founder 1994—). Home: 3920 Lurline Dr Honolulu HI 96816-4006 Office: U Hawaii Political Science Dept 2424 Maile Way Honolulu HI 96822-2223 Business E-Mail: fredr@hawaii.edu.

**RIGGS, GREGORY LYNN,** lawyer; b. Columbus, Ohio, Apr. 21, 1948; s. Roy Albert and Edith Myrtle (Riggins) R.; m. Janet Kaye Adams, June 26, 1982; children: Caroline Ashley, Kristen Nicole. BA, U. NC, 1971; BA in jurisprudence, Oxford U., 1976; JD, Emory U., 1979. Bar: Ga. 1979, US Dist. Ct. No. Dist. Ga. 1979, US Ct. Appeals 7th cir. 1982, US Ct. Appeals 11th cir. 1985, US Ct. Appeals 5th cir. 1986. Atty. Delta Air Lines, Atlanta, 1979-84, sr. atty., 1984-92, asst. gen. counsel, 1992-94, assoc. gen. counsel, 1994-98, v.p.- dep. gen. counsel, asst. sec., 1998—2003, sr. v.p.- gen. counsel, 2003—04, sr. v.p.- gen. counsel, chief corp. affairs officer, 2004—05; chmn. exec. com. corp. counsel sect. State Bar Ga., 2005—. Mem.: Atlanta Vol. Lawyers Found. (bd. dirs. 2000—04), Am. Corp. Counsel Assn. (chair law dept. mgmt. com. 1995—96, bd. chs. chpt. 1998), State Bar of Ga. (justice to justice com. 1999, chair exec. com. corp. counsel sect. 2005—). Office: Delta Air Lines Inc Dept Law Hartsfield Internat Airport Atlanta GA 30320 E-mail: greg.riggs@comcast.net.

**RIGGS, HENRY EARLE,** academic administrator, engineering educator; b. Chgo., Feb. 25, 1935; s. Joseph Agnew and Gretchen (Walser) Riggs; m. Gayle Carson, May 17, 1958; children: Elizabeth, Peter, Catharine. BS, Stanford U., 1957; MBA, Harvard U., 1960. Indsl. economist SRI Internat., Menlo Park, Calif., 1960—63; v.p. Icore Industries, Sunnyvale, Calif., 1963—67, pres., 1967—70; v.p. fin. Measurex Corp., Cupertino, Calif., 1970—74; prof. engring. mgmt. Stanford U., Calif., 1974—88, Ford prof. Calif., 1986—88, Ford prof. emeritus Calif., 1990, v.p. for devel. Calif., 1983—88; pres. Harvey Mudd Coll., Claremont, Calif., 1988—97, pres. emeritus, 1997; pres. Keck Grad. Inst., Claremont, 1997—2003, pres., trustee emeritus, 2003—. Bd. dirs. Capital Rsch. Group Inst. Sys. Biology. Author: Accounting: A Survey, 1981, Managing High-Tech Companies, 1983, Financial and Economic Analysis, 1994, 2d edit., 2004; contbr. articles to profl. jours. Recipient Gores Tchg. award, Stanford U., 1980; Baker scholar, Harvard Bus. Sch., 1959. Mem.: Stanford U. Alumni Assn. (bd. dirs. 1990—94, chmn. 1993), Palo Alto Club, Sunset Club, Calif. Club, Tau Beta Pi, Phi Beta Kappa. Congregationalist. Home: 24 Peter Coutts Circle Stanford CA 94305 Personal E-mail: henryriggs@comcast.net.

**RIGGS, JACK TIMOTHY,** emergency physician, retired lieutenant governor; b. Coeur d'Alene, Idaho, Oct. 1, 1954; BS summa cum laude, U. Idaho, 1976; MD, U. Wash., 1980. Diplomate Am. Bd. Emergency Medicine. Intern Deaconess Med. Ctr., Spokane, Wash., 1980-81; mem. Idaho Senate, Dist. 4, Boise, 1996-2000; owner North Idaho Immediate Car Ctrs., 1985—; lt. gov. State of Idaho, 2001—03. Fellow Am. Coll. Emergency Physicians; mem. AMA, Am. Coll. Physician Execs., Idaho Med. Assn., Am. Coll. Occupl. and Environ. Medicine. Address: 927 E Polston Post Falls ID 83854

**RIGGS, JEANETTE TEMPLETON,** civic worker; b. Little Rock, Mar. 13, 1933; d. Donald M. and Fay (Templeton) Brewer; student Little Rock U., 1950-51, Tex. Coll. for Women, 1951-52; B.S., U. Ark., 1955; m. Byron Lawrence Riggs, June 1955; children: Byron Kent, Ann Templeton. Founder, Rochester (Minn.) Ballet Guild, 1970, pres., 1974; mem. establishing bd., exec. bd. Rochester Arts Council, 1972, producer, dir. T.S. Elliot's The Rock, 1970; founder, performer So. Minn. Ballet Co., 1974; sponsor Nat. Ballet Cos., Rochester, 1970-75; exec. bd. for restoration 1875 Pattern Book House, Rochester Heritage Assn., 1975-77; exec. bd. Savino Ballet Nat., 1975-78; founder, exec. bd. Citizens Action Com., 1977-79; asso., commentator Women, Cable TV Program for Women, Rochester, 1979; mem. Mayor's Com. on Drug Abuse, 1979-80; mem. Olmsted County Steering Com. for George Bush, 1979-80, a founder, mem. exec. bd. Olmsted County Republican Women's Orgn., 1979—, mem. Olmsted County Rep. Central Com., 1979—, exec. bd. issues com., 1979-80. Home: 1000 10TH St SW Rochester MN 55902-2090

**RIGGS, JOHN M.,** army officer; b. Mo., Dec. 2, 1946; BA in Polit. Sci., Tarkio Coll.; MA in Pers. Mgmt. and Adminstrn., Cent. Mich. U.; postgrad., Harvard U. Commd. 2d lt. U.S. Army, advanced through grades to maj. gen.; served overseas in Korea, Belgium, Vietnam, Germany; asst. divsn. comdr. Bamberg, Germany; dep. comdg. gen. U.S. Army Aviation Sch., Ft. Rucker, Ala.; asst. dep. chief staff for ops. and plans Hdqs. Dept. Army, Washington, 1997-99; comdg. gen. 1st U.S. Army, Forest Park, Ga., 1999—; dir. Objective Task Force. Decorated DSM, Legion of Merit with 3 oak leaf clusters, DFC, Bronze Star medal, others; Nat. Security fellow.

**RIGGS, LEW,** foundation executive; b. Indpls., Apr. 1, 1937; s. Frank Lloyd Riggs and Marie Loretta (Shaner) Ellis; m. Christine Marie Stiemke, Dec. 2, 2000. BS in Bus. Adminstrn., U. Ariz., 1961, EdD, 1976; MBA, George Washington U., 1968. Mktg. adminstr. TRW Systems, L.A., 1964-67; assn. exec. Electric League Ariz., Phoenix, 1967-68; pub. affairs adminstr. Ariz. Regional Med. program Coll. of Medicine, U. Ariz., Tucson, 1968-73; dir. community affairs Tucson Med. Ctr., 1973-82; dir. pub. rels. Good Samaritan Med. Ctr., Phoenix, 1982-85; pres. The Lew Riggs Co., Phoenix, 1985-88; chief exec. officer Tucson Osteo. Med. Found., Tucson, 1988—. Adj. prof. U. Ariz. Coll. Edn., Tucson, mem. internat. adv. bd., 1996-99, pres., 2000; cons. to hosps. and physicians in group practice nationally; presenter in field. Editor: Public Relations Handbook, 1982; co-author booklets; contbr. articles to profl. jours. Chmn. pub. rels. Nat. Arthritis Found., Atlanta, 1985-87; participant Ariz. Strategic Planning and Econ. Devel., 1991-92. Lt. col. USAFR, 1987. Recipient IABC gold quill award, Silver Anvil award Pub. Rels. Soc. Am., Golden Mike award Am. Legion Assn., MacEachern citation Acad. Hosp. Pub. Rels., Pres.'s citation Pub. Rels. Soc. Mem. Pub. Rels. Soc. Am. (trustee 1999—), Nat. Assn. Osteo. Founds. (pres. 1991-93), Student Osteo. Med. Assn. (found. bd. dirs. 1990—), Soc. Assn. Execs. (bd. dirs. 1995—), Rotary. Republican. Presbyterian. Home: 4566 E Camino De Oro Tucson AZ 85718-4475 E-mail: lriggs@tomf.org.

**RIGGS, LORRIN ANDREWS,** psychologist, educator; b. Harput, Turkey, June 11, 1912; parents Am. citizens; s. Ernest Wilson and Alice (Shepard) R.; m. Doris Robinson, 1937 (div.); children: Douglas Rikert, Dwight Alan; m. Caroline Cressman, 1994. AB, Dartmouth Coll., 1933; MA, Clark U., 1934, PhD, 1936; DSc, Brown U., 2001. NRC fellow biol. scis. U. Pa., 1936-37; instr. U. Vt., 1937-38, 39-41; with Brown U., 1938-39, 41—, from asst. to assoc. prof., 1938-51, prof., 1951—, L. Herbert Ballou prof., 1960-68, E.J. Marston Univ. prof., 1968-77, prof. emeritus, 1977—; Guggenheim fellow U. Cambridge, 1971-72. Author sci. articles on vision, physical psychology. Recipient Kenneth Craik award Cambridge U., 1979, Prentice medal Am. Acad. Optometry, 1973 Mem. AAAS (chmn., v.p. sect. 1 1964), APA (div. pres. 1962-63, Disting. Sci. Contn. award 1974), Eastern Psychol. Assn. (pres. 1975-76), Optical Soc. Am. (Tillyer medal 1969, Ives medal 1982), Nat. Acad. Scis., Am. Physiol. Soc., Internat. Brain Rsch. Orgn., Soc. for Neurosci., Soc. Exptl. Psychologists (Howard Crosby Warren medal 1957), Assn. Rsch. in Vision and Ophthalmology (pres. 1977, Friedenwald award 1966), Am. Acad. Arts and Scis., Am. Psychol. Soc. (William James fellow 1989), Sigma Xi (chpt. pres. 1962-64). Home: Kendal at Hanover Apt 1018 80 Lyme Rd Hanover NH 03755-1225 Personal E-mail: clriggs@valley.net.

**RIGGS, MICHAEL DAVID,** editor, writer; b. Frankfort, Ky., Apr. 30, 1951; s. Homer David and Helen Marion (Webber) R.; m. Elizabeth Susan Borman, Apr. 24, 1983; children: David B., William B. AB, Washington U., 1973. Chief trader Thomte & Co., Boston, 1975-77; tech. writer Saddlebrook Corp., Cambridge, Mass., 1977-79; assoc. editor Mini-Micro Systems Mag., Boston, 1979-80; editor High Fidelity Mag., N.Y.C., 1980-89; exec. editor Stereo Review Mag., N.Y.C., 1989-95; editor-in-chief Audio Mag., N.Y.C., 1995-2000; ind. technology writer, editor, cons. Westfield, NJ, 2000—. Author: Understanding Audio and Video, 1989; sr. contbg. editor Sound and Vision Mag., 2001—04, sr. editor; 2004—05, online editor; 2006—. Mem. Audio Engring. Soc., Boston Audio Soc. Office Phone: 212-767-6028. E-mail: michael@riggsnet.com.

**RIGGS, R. WILLIAM,** state supreme court justice; Grad., Portland State U., 1961; JD, U. Oreg., 1968. Atty. Willner Bennett & Leonard, 1968—78; judge circuit ct. 4th Jud. Dist., 1978—88; judge Oreg. Ct. of Appeals, 1988—98, presiding judge, 1995—98; judge Oreg. Supreme Ct., 1998—. Vice-chair exec. com. Oreg. Jud. Conference, 1996—98; mem. Council on Ct. Procedures, 1986—89; founder Oreg. Acad. of Family Law Practitioners. Active mem. Cmty. Law Project; founder Integra Corp. Capt. USNR. Mem.: Oreg. Trial Lawyers Assn. (pres. 1973—74), Oreg. Appellate Judges Assn. (pres. 1993—94, 2001—02), Oreg. State Bar Assn. (founding mem. chair Family Law Section 1979). Office: Supreme Ct Bldg 1163 State St Salem OR 97310-0260*

**RIGGS, RORY B.,** pharmaceutical executive; b. Orange, N.J., May 5, 1953; d. Thomas Jeffries and Virginia (Griggs) R. BA, Middlebury Coll.; MBA, Columbia U. Mng. dir. PaineWebber, Inc.; CEO RF&P Corp.; mng. dir. Pharma Ptnrs. LLC; pres. Biomatrix Inc., Ridgefield, N.J., 1995—. Bd. dirs. Biomatrix, Inc. 1990—; bd. mem. Fibrogen Corp., Spartan Corp., Pharma Ptnrs, LLC. Mem. Young Pres. Orgn. Office: Biomatrix Inc 65 Railroad Ave Ste 3 Ridgefield NJ 07657-2176

**RIGGS, TIMOTHY ALLAN,** museum curator; b. New Haven, Conn., Feb. 15, 1942; s. Douglas Shepard and Robin (Palmer) R.; divorced; 1 child, Emma; m. Carolyn P. Coolidge, June 25, 1995. BA, Swarthmore Coll., 1964; MA, Yale U., 1966, PhD, 1971. Rschr. Print Coun. Am., 1970-73; asst. curator Worcester (Mass.) Art Mus., 1973-76, curator prints and drawings, 1976-84; asst. dir. Ackland Art Mus., Chapel Hill, N.C., 1984—, acting dir., 1986, 94. Adj. prof. U. N.C., Chapel Hill, 1984-2003, curator of collections, 2003—. Contbr. catalogs. Mem. Print Coun. Am. (bd. dirs. 1981-84), Historians Netherlandish Art. Office: U NC CB # 3400 Ackland Art Mus S Columbia St near Franklin St Chapel Hill NC 27599-3400

**RIGGS, WILLIAM GERALD,** military officer, small business owner; b. Bethany, Okla., Feb. 14, 1924; s. Elvis and Merle Belle Riggs; m. Billie Jean Johnson, Aug. 22, 1946 (dec.); children: G. William Jr., Teresa Ann Riggs Carison (dec.). Grad. Polit. Sci., U. Nebr., 1971. Cert. Master Plumber Okla., 1974. Commd. lt. USAF, 1943, advanced throug grades to lt. col.; pilot air corp. U.S. Army, 1944; ret. USAF, 1973. Decorated Legion of Merit (2) USAF, Bronze Star, Army Commendation medal, Air Medal USAF, Combat Inf. Badge, Master Parachute Badge, Meritorious Svc. medal USAF. Mem.: DAV, VFW, Mil. Officers of Am., Young Men's Club of Okla. City (bd. 1974—). Avocations: bridge, fishing, reading, travel. Home: 2420 NW 111th St Oklahoma City OK 73120

**RIGGS, WILLIAM W.,** social sciences educator; b. Decatur, Ill., Apr. 26, 1945; d. William and Doris Mae Riggs; m. Karen Sue Henderson, May 19, 1998 (div.); children: Christopher. BA, The Citadel, 1967; MS, U. So. Miss., 1989; PhD, U. New Orleans, 1999. Commd. 2d lt. USMC, 1967, advanced through grades to maj., rct., 1987, tchr. Coast Episcopal High Sch., Pess Christian, Miss., 1987—89; asst. prof. polit. sci. Tex. A&M Internat. U., Larado, 2001—04, chair dept. social scis., 2004—. Vis. prof. U. West Ala., Livingston, 1989—90; external reviewer N.W. State U., Nachitoles, La., 2004; presenter in field. Contbr. chapters to books. Chair Logistics Cmty. Anchorage Sch. Dist., 2000—01; bd. dirs. Anchorage Mus., 1998—2001. Fellow, TAMU. Mem.: NEH, Am. Soc. Pub. Adminstrn. (v.p. 2004—). Avocations: golf, bridge, travel. Office: Tex A&M Internat U 5201 Univ Blvd Laredo TX 78041

**RIGGSBY, DUTCHIE SELLERS,** education educator; b. Montgomery, Ala., Oct. 26, 1940; d. Malcolm Sellers and Marcelia Sellers Dickman; m. Ernest Duward Riggsby, Aug. 25, 1962; 1 child, Lyn. BS, Troy State Coll., 1962, MS, 1965; postgrad., George Peabody Coll., 1963; EdD, Auburn U., 1972. Cert. tchr., Ala., Ga.; cert. libr., Ga. Tchr. Montgomery Pub. Schs., 1962—63, Troy City Schs., 1963—67; instr. Auburn U., Ala., 1968—69, dir. media svcs., 1972—77; asst. prof. Columbus Coll., Ga., 1972—77, assoc. prof., 1978—83, prof., 1983—. Vis. prof. U. P.R., Rio Piedras, 1972—73; leader various workshops, 1989, 1993—; software reviewer NSTA; chmn. publicity Ga. Ednl. Tech. Conf., 1997—, bd. dirs.; bridal cons. Hist. Moments, Inc., 1998—2001, v.p., 1998—2001; chair scholarship com. Ga. Ednl. Consortium, 1999—; coord. instrnl. Tech. Sch. Edn., 1996—97; coord. program Ednl. Founds., 2001—04. Contbr. more than 90 articles on state, regional, nat., and internat. programs to profl. jours., 1968—. Active Internal Aerospace Edn. CAP, Maxwell AFB, 1980-90; dir. Air and Space Camp for Kids, 1990-98; apptd. selection com. Coll. Edn. Columbus State U. Hall of Fame, 2005—. Recipient STAR Tchr. award NSTA, 1968; named to Lee H.S. Hall of Fame, Montgomery, 1997. Mem.: Ga. Assn. Instrnl. Tech. (bd. dirs. 1982—84), World Aerospace Edn. Orgn. (v.p. for Ams. 1996—98, pres. for Ams. 1998—, pres. 1999—), Nat. Congress on Aviation and Space Edn. (dir. spl. promotions 1986—90), Assn. for Ednl. Commun. and Tech. (awards com. 1994—96, non-periodical publs. com. 1994—99, chair meml. awards com. 1996—99), Phi Delta Kappa (pres. Chattahoochee Valley chpt. 1986—87, membership v.p. 2005—06, pres. Chattahoochee Valley chpt. 2006—), Svc. award 1989, Svc. Key award 1993). Baptist. Avocations: photography, mining for gemstones. Office: Columbus State U Coll Edn 4225 University Ave Columbus GA 31907-5679 Office Phone: 706-565-7802.

**RIGGSBY, ERNEST DUWARD,** science educator, educational consultant; b. Nashville, June 12, 1925; s. James Thomas and Anna Pearl (Turner) Riggsby; m. Dutchie Sellers Riggsby, Aug. 25, 1964; 1 child, Lyn-Dee. BS, Tenn. Polytech. Inst., 1948; BA, George Peabody Coll. Tchrs., 1952, BA, 1953, MA, 1956, EdS, 1961, EdD, 1964. Commd. lt. USAF, 1944, col., 1974, advanced through grades to col., 1974, ret., 1985; prof. Troy (Ala.) State U., 1956—66, Auburn (Ala.) U., 1967—69; pres. Ednl. Developers, Inc., Columbus, 1968—; prof. Columbus (Ga.) Coll., 1969—96; ret. Vis. grad. prof. George Peabody Coll., 1963—64; vis. lectr. Fla. Inst. Tech., 1967—77; vis. prof. U. P.R., Rio Piedras, PR, 1963—64. Contbr. articles to profl. jours. Named to Aerospace Edn. Hall of Fame, 1982. Fellow: AAAS; mem.: World Aerospace Edn. Assn. (v.p. for Ams., pres. for Ams. 1999—), Nat. Sci. Tchrs. Assn. Office Phone: 706-323-4154.

**RIGHINI, MARILOU MAUSTELLER,** editor, consultant; b. Savannah, Ga., June 17, 1937; d. John Ellis and Ethel Mae Mausteller; m. Massimo A. Righini, May 5, 1962; children: Giovanna, John Paolo. BA in Polit. Sci. magna cum laude, Mich. State U., East Lansing, 1958; attended, Johns Hopkins U., Bologna, Italy, 1958—60; MA in Internat. Rels., Johns Hopkins U., Washington, DC, 1963. Editor Internat. Legal Materials Am. Soc. Internat. Law, Washington, 1968—97; dir. pubs., 1992—97; editor, mem. editl. bd. Transnational Pubs., Inc., Ardsley, NY, 1994—; aquisitions editor, cons., 1998—2001. Translator IBM, Milan, 1960—61; tchr. polit. sci., internat. law, am. lit. Istituto Ugo Foscolo, Bologna, Italy, 1961—62; rschr., editl. asst. Washington Ctr. Fgn. Policy Rsch., 1963—68; program chmn. Internat. Devel. Conf., Washington, 1977; program coord. Washington Fgn. Law Soc., 1980—81, bd. govs., 1980—82; chmn. Coun. Washington Reps. UN, 1983—85; tchr. internat. law and orgn. Trinity Coll., Washington, 1965; elected com. rep. DC Dem. State Com., Ward 1, 1988—92; chmn., nominating com. Worldwide 2000, 1989, bd. dirs., 1989—91; mem. mtg. roundtable chair Am. Soc. Internat. Law, 1991, am. mtg. panel chair, 92; program developer Am. Assn. Law Librs., 1999, 2000. Mem.: Mich. State U. DC Study Devel. Coun., Am. Soc. Internat. Law, UN Assn. U.S.A., Meridian Internat. Ctr., Delta Gamma.

**RIGHTER, WALTER CAMERON,** retired bishop; b. Phila., Oct. 23, 1923; s. Richard and Dorothy Mae (Bottomley) R.; m. Nancy Ruth DeGroot, Aug. 22, 1992; children: Richard, Rebecca. BA, U. Pitts., 1948; MDiv, Berkeley Div. Sch., New Haven, 1951, DD, 1972; DCL, Iowa Wesleyan U., 1982; DD, Seabury Western Sem., 1984. Ordained priest Episcopal Ch., 1951, consecrated bishop, 1972; lay missioner St. Michael's Ch., Rector, Pa., 1947-48; priest-in-charge All Saints Ch., Aliquippa, Pa., 1951-54, St. Luke's, Georgetown, Pa., 1952-54; rector Ch. of Good Shepherd, Nashua, NH, 1954-71; bishop Diocese of Iowa, Des Moines, 1972-89; asst. bishop Dio. of Newark, 1989-91; interim rector St. Elizabeth's, Ridgewood, NJ, 1991; assisting bishop Diocese of Mass., 2003; ret. Mem. exec. coun. Protestant Episcopal Ch. U.S.A., 1979-85; spl. adv. NH Cursillo, 1994-96; interim rector Emmanuel, Rockford, Ill., 1989. Author: A Pilgrim's Way, 1998. Mem. N.H. com. White House Conf. on Youth, 1962, Regional Crime Commn., Hillsboro County, N.H., 1969-71; trustee Nashua Libr., 1968-71, Seabury Western Sem., 1986-89; founding trustee The Morris Fund, Des Moines; planning com. Town of Alstead, N.H., 1993-96. Fellow Coll. Preachers, Washington Cathedral. Episcopalian. Personal E-mail: wcrighter@alltel.com.

**RIGHTMIRE, GEORGE PHILIP,** anthropology educator; b. Boston, Sept. 15, 1942; s. Brandon Garner and Marcia (Ham) R.; m. Berit Johansson, Aug. 20, 1966; children: Anna Marcia, Eric Philip. AB, Harvard U., 1964; MS, U. Wis., 1966, PhD, 1969. Asst. prof. SUNY, Binghamton, 1969-73; assoc. prof., 1973-82, prof., 1982—2002, chmn., 1976-78, disting. prof., 2002—; rsch. assoc. Harvard U., 2006—. Vis. in archaeology U. Cape Town, South Africa, 1975-76; rsch. fellow in osteology U. Stockholm, Sweden, 1973. Author: The Evolution of Homo erectus, 1990; contbr. articles to Am Jour. Phys. Anthropology, Evolutionary Anthropology, Sci., Nature, Paleobiology, Ency. Britannica, Jour. Human Evolution. Fellow Nat. Inst. Gen. Med. Scis., 1973; rsch. grantee NSF, 1975—, Nat. Geographic Soc., 1978-79, L.S.B. Leakey

Found., 1990-91, 1992-93, 1995-96, 98-99, 2001-2003, 2006—, Am. Philos. Soc., 2003-04. Fellow AAAS; mem. Am. Assn. Phys. Anthropologists, Human Biology Assn., Paleoanthropology Soc., Sigma Xi Achievements include rsch. in skeletal biology and human paleontology, fossil evidence for hominid evolution examined in East Africa, South Africa, Europe, the Near East, the Caucasus, China and Southeast Asia. Office: Harvard Univ Dept Anthropology Peabody Mus Cambridge MA 02138 Home: 24 Whittier Dr Scituate MA 02066-2436 Office Phone: 617-495-5703. Business E-mail: gpright@binghamton.edu.

**RIGHTS, GRAHAM HENRY,** retired minister; b. Winston-Salem, N.C., Jan. 14, 1935; s. Douglas LeTell and Cecil Leona (Burton) R.; m. Sybil Critz Strupe, Sept. 7, 1963; children: Susan Elizabeth, John Graham. BA, U. N.C., 1956; BD, Yale U., 1959; postgrad., Moravian Theol. Sem., 1959-60. DHL (hon.), 1997; postgrad., U. Edinburgh, Scotland, 1965-66; DD (hon.), Wofford Coll., 1989. Ordained to ministry Moravian Ch., 1960. Pastor Union Ch., Managua, Nicaragua, 1960-63, Managua Moravian Ch., 1960-65, Mayodan (N.C.) Moravian Ch., 1966-72, Messiah Moravian Ch., Winston-Salem, 1972-81; exec. dir. Bd. World Mission Moravian Ch., Bethlehem, Pa., 1981-83, pres. exec. bd. so. province Winston-Salem, 1983-95, pres. exec. bd. world-wide, 1991-94; pastor First Moravian Ch., Greensboro, NC, 1995-2000; ret. Bd. dirs. Crisis Control Ministry, Forsyth County, 1976-, Ecumenical Inst.of the Carolinas, 1995-, Wachovia Hist. Soc., 2004-, CareNet of the Triad, 2005-. Mem. N.C. Soc. Mayflower Descendants (elder 2000—). Mem. Moravian Ch. Home: 553 Steeple View Ct Winston Salem NC 27101-5850

**RIGNEY, JAMES OLIVER, JR., (ROBERT JORDAN, CHANG LUNG, REAGAN O'NEAL, JACKSON O'REILLY),** writer; b. Charleston, S.C., Oct. 17, 1948; s. James Oliver and Eva May (Grooms) Rigney; m. Harriet Stoney Popham, Mar. 28, 1981; 1 child, William Popham McDougal. BS, The Citadel, 1974. Nuc. engr. U.S. Civil Svc., 1974—78. Author: Conan the Invincible, 1982, Conan the Defender, 1982, Conan the Triumphant, 1983, Conan the Unconquered, 1983, Conan the Destroyer, 1984, Conan the Magnificent, 1984, Conan the Victorious, 1985, The Eye of the World, 1990, The Great Hunt, 1990, The Dragon Reborn, 1991, The Shadow Rising, 1992, The Fires of Heaven, 1993, Lord of Chaos, 1994, A Crown of Swords, 1996, The Path of Daggars, 1998, Winter's Heart, 2000, Crossroads of Twighlight, 2003, New Spring, 2004, Knife of Dreams, 2005. Office: Elena Stokes Dir Publicity Tor Books 175 5th Ave New York NY 10010

**RIGOLOSI, ELAINE LA MONICA,** lawyer, educator; b. Astoria, N.Y., Oct. 12, 1944; d. Richard Anthony La Monica and Caroline La Monica; m. Robert Salvatore Rigolosi, June 15, 1997. BS, Columbia Union Coll., Takoma Park, Md., 1964; MN, U. Fla., 1967; EdD, U. Mass., 1975; JD, Benjamin N. Cardozo Sch. Law, N.Y.C., 1993. Bar: N.J. 1994, N.Y. 1994, D.C. 1995; RN, N.Y. Chair dept. nursing edn. Tchrs. Coll., Columbia U., N.Y.C., 1988-91, prof. nursing edn., 1982-96, acting chair dept. nursing edn., 1994-96, prof. dept. orgn. and leadership, 1996—; health care mgmt. cons. in pvt. practice, N.Y.C., 1974—. Bd. dirs. Hooper Holmes, Inc., Basking Ridge, N.J., 1989—; cons. Delaware Valley Transplant Program, Phila., 1998, U. Tenn. Coll. Pharmacy, Memphis, 1995-98. Author: The Nursing Process: A Humanistic Approach, 1979 (Am. Jour. Nursing Book of Yr. 1979), Management in Health Care, 1994, Management and Leadership in Nursing and Health Care, 2005. Dept. HHS grantee, 1977-80, 80-83. Fellow Am. Acad. Nursing; mem. ABA, Assn. Bar City N.Y. (com. on health law 1994-97), Am. Health Lawyers Assn., Am. Assn. Nurse Attys., Am. Coll. Legal Medicine, Sigma Theta Tau. Avocations: tennis, needlepoint, interior design. Home: 158 Summit Dr Paramus NJ 07652-1312 Office: Tchrs Coll Columbia U 525 W 120th St New York NY 10027-6625

**RIGSBY, LINDA FLORY,** lawyer; b. Topeka, Kans., Dec. 16, 1946; d. Alden E. and Lolita M. Flory; m. Michael L. Rigsby, Aug. 14, 1963; children: Michael L. Jr., Elisabeth A. MusB, Va. Commonwealth U., 1969; JD, U. Richmond, 1981. Bar: Va. 1981, D.C. 1988. Assoc. McGuire, Woods, Battle & Boothe, Richmond, Va., 1981-85; dep. gen. counsel and corp. sec. Crestar Fin. Corp., Richmond, 1985-99, gen. counsel, 1999-2000; mng. atty. Sun Trust Banks Inc., 2000—. Mem. audit com. Bon Secours Health Systems, Richmond, 1999—. Bd. dirs. Commonwealth Cath. Charities, 2004-. Recipient Disting. Svc. award U. Richmond, 1987; named Vol. of Yr. U. Richmond, 1986, Woman of Achievement. Met. Richmond Women's Bar, 1995. Mem. Va. Bar Assn. (exec. com. 1993-96), Richmond Bar Assn. (bd. dirs. 1992-95), Va. Bankers Assn. (chair legal affairs 1992-95), U. Richmond Estate Planning Coun. (chmn. 1990-92). Roman Catholic. Avocations: music, gardening. Home: 163 W Square Pl Richmond VA 23233-6157 Office: SunTrust Bank 919 E Main St Richmond VA 23219-4625 Office Phone: 804-782-7733. E-mail: liinda.rigsby@suntrust.com.

**RIGSBY, SHEILA GOREE,** accounting firm executive; b. Macon, Ga., June 13, 1955; d. David Wendell and Carolyn (Canington) Goree; children: Jason, Ryan. Student, Macon Coll., 1979. cert. tax preparer. Tax preparer Better Income Tax Svc., Macon; acct. Bass Tool and Indsl. Supply, Macon, Padgett Bus. Svc., Macon; owner Indsl. Acctg. Svcs., Macon. Mem. NAFE, Nat. Fedn. Ind. Businessmen, Nat. Soc. Tax Profls., Nat. Assn. Tax Preparers, Nat. Assn. Tax Practitioners, Ga. Assn. Pub. Accts. Office: 4000 Mercer University Dr Macon GA 31204-5702

**RIHANNA, (ROBYN RIHANNA FENTY),** singer; b. St. Michael, Barbados, Feb. 20, 1988; d. Ronald and Monica Fenty. Singer: (albums) Music of the Sun, 2005, A Girl Like Me, 2006, (songs) Pon de Replay, 2005, SOS, 2006 (Best New Video Artist, MTV Video Music Awards Japan, 2006), Unfaithful, 2006; actor: (films) Bring It On: All of Nothing, 2006. Recipient Best Internet Artist award, MuchMusic Video Awards, 2006, Female Breakout Artist award, Teen Choice Awards, 2006, Choice R&B Artist award, 2006. Office: Def Jam Entertainment Cambridge MD 21613*

**RIKARD, WILLIAM L., JR.,** lawyer; b. Canton, N.C., Apr. 7, 1945; BA, Davidson Coll., 1967; JD, Vanderbilt U., 1970. Bar: N.C. 1970, US Dist. Ct. (NC), US Ct. Appeals (4th cir.), US Supreme Ct. Ptnr., chmn litig. dept. Parker Poe Adams & Bernstein, Charlotte, NC. Bd. dir. Charlotte Merchants' Found.; mem. Charlotte Mecklenburg Bd. Assn., 1988—, vice chmn., 1990—. 1st lt. adj. gen. corps U.S. Army, 1970-72. Mem. ABA, NC Bar Assn., Mecklenburg County Bar Assn. (mem. exec. com. 1985-88), Omicron Delta Kappa. Office: Parker Poe Adams & Bernstein LLP Ste 3000 3 Wachovia Ctr 401 S Tryon St Charlotte NC 28202-1935 Office Phone: 704-335-9011. Office Fax: 704-335-9689. Business E-mail: williamrikard@parkerpoe.com.

**RIKKERS, LAYTON FREDERICK,** surgeon; b. Fond du Lac, Wis., Jan. 31, 1944; s. Judson John and Dorothy (Layton) R.; m. Diane Lynn Foster, Aug. 20, 1966; children: Steven, Kristin. BS, U. Wis., 1966; MD, Stanford U. Sch. Medicine, 1970. Diplomate Nat. Bd. Med. Examiners, Am. Bd. Surgery. Intern U. Utah Sch. Medicine, Salt Lake City, 1970-71, surgical residency, 1971-76; instr. surgery Emory U. Sch. Medicine, Atlanta, 1976-77 from asst. prof. surgery to acting chmn. div. gen. surgery U. Utah Sch. Medicine, Salt Lake City, 1977-84; prof., chmn. dept. surgery U. Nebr. Med. Ctr., Omaha, 1984-96, U. Wis., Madison, 1996—. Interim dean Coll. Medicine, U. Nebr. Coll. Medicine, 1991-93, M.M. Musselman prof. surgery, 1990—; cons. Omaha Vet. Adminstrv. Ctr., 1984-86, NIH, 1992, Gov.'s Blue Ribbon Coalition on Health Care, Nebr., 1993-94. Editor: Surgical Clinics of North America, 1990; editor-in-chief Annals of Surgery, 1996—; contbr. articles to profl. jours. Mem. Am. Surgical Assn., Am. Coll. Surgeons (com. chair 1993-95), Am. Bd. Surgery (clin. chmn. 1994-95), Soc. Clin. Surgery (pres. 1994-95), Soc. Surgery Alimentary Tract (pres. 2000), Halsted Soc. (pres. 2000). Episcopalian. Avocations: hiking, reading, skiing, travel. Office: U Wis H4/710 Clin Sci Ctr 600 Highland Ave Madison WI 53792-3284

**RIKON, MICHAEL,** lawyer; b. Bklyn., Feb. 2, 1945; s. Charles and Ruth (Shapiro) R.; m. Leslie Sharon Rein, Feb. 11, 1968; children: Carrie Rachel, Joshua Howard. BS, NY Inst. Tech., 1966; JD, Bklyn. Law Sch., 1969; LLM, NYU, 1974. Bar: NY 1970, U.S. Dist. Ct. (so. and ea. dists.) NY 1971, U.S.

Ct. Appeals (2d cir.) 1972, U.S. Supreme Ct. 1973, U.S. Ct. Appeals (5th and 11th cirs.) 1981. Asst. corp. counsel City of NY, 1969-73; law clk. NY State Ct. Claims, 1973-80; ptnr. Rudick and rikon, P.C., NYC, 1980-88; pvt. practice NYC, 1988-94; ptnr. Goldstein, Goldstein and Rikon, P.C., NYC, 1994—. Contbr. articles to profl. jours. Pres. Village Greens Residents Assn., 1978-79; chmn. bd. Arden Heights Jewish Ctr., S.I., NY, 1976-77; pres. North Shore Rep. Club., 1977; mem. cmty. bd. S.I. Borough Pres., 1977. Fellow Am. Bar Found.; mem. ABA (chair com. Condemnation) NY State Bar Assn. (spl. com. of condemnation law), Suffolk County Bar Assn., NY County lawyers Assn. (chair condemnation com.), Assn. Bar City of NY (condemnation com.), Mt. Vernon Bar Assn., Owners Counsel Am. (dir.). Republican. Jewish. Avocations: collecting stamps, photography, collecting miniature soldiers. Home: 133 Avondale Rd Ridgewood NJ 07450-1301 Office: 80 Pine St New York NY 10005-1702 Office Phone: 212-422-4000. E-mail: mrikon@ggrgpc.com.

**RIKOSKI, RICHARD ANTHONY,** electrical engineering executive; b. Kingston, Pa., Aug. 13, 1941; s. Stanley George and Nellie (Gober) R.; m. Giannina Batchelor Petrullo, Dec. 18, 1971 (div. 1979); children: Richard James, Jennifer Anne; m. Carol Westbrook. BEE, U. Detroit, 1964; MSEE. Carnegie Inst. Tech., 1965; PhD, Carnegie-Mellon U., 1968; postdoctoral fellow, Case-Western Res. U./NASA, 1971. Registered profl. engr., Ill., Mass., Pa. Engr. 1st communication satellite systems Internat. Tel. & Tel., Nutley, N.J., 1961-64; engr. Titan II ICBM program Gen. Motors, Milw., 1964; trainee NASA, 1964-67; instr. Carnegie-Mellon U., Pitts., 1966-68; asst. prof. U. Pa., Phila., 1968-74; assoc. prof., dir. hybrid microelectronics lab., chmn. ednl. TV com. IIT, Chgo., 1974-80, chmn. ednl. TV com., 1974-80; rsch. engr. nuclear effects ITT Rsch. Inst., Chgo., 1974-75; pres. Tech. Analysis Corp., Chgo., 1980—; engr. color TV colorimetry Hazeltine Rsch., Chgo., 1969; engr. Metroliner rail car/roadbed ride quality dynamics analysis U.S. Dept. Transp., ENSCO, Inc., Springfield, Va., 1970; pres. Tech. Analysis Corp., Chgo., 1978-91; contractor analysis of color TV receiver safety hazards U.S. Consumer Product Safety Commn., 1977, analysis heating effect in aluminum wire Beverly Hills Supper Club Fire, Covington, Ky., 1978; engr. GFCI patent infringement study 3M Corp., St. Paul, 1979-81; elec. systems analyst Coca-Cola Corp., Atlanta, 1983-91; fire investigator McDonald's Corp., Oak Brook, Ill., 1987-90; engring. analyst telephone switching ctrs. ATT, Chgo., 1990-91; expert witness numerous other govtl. and corp. procs.; evaluator Accreditation bd. Engring. and Tech., 2000—. Author: Hybrid Microelectronic Circuits, 1973; editor: Hybrid Microelectronic Technology, 1973; contbr. articles to profl. jours. Officer Planning Commn., Beverly Shores, Ind., 1987-93; trustee town coun., 1992—, police liason 1993-96, dir. emergency mgmt., 1998, coun. pres., 1999-2000; mem. Chgo. Coun. Fgn. Rels., USAF SAC Comdrs. Disting.is. Program; adv. coun. Nat. Park Svc. Ind. Dunes Nat. Lake Shore, 1993—. NASA fellow, 1964-67, 70. Mem. IEEE (sr. ednl. activities bd. N.Y.C. 1970-74, USAB career devel. com. 1972-74, editor Soundings 1973-75, Cassette Colloquia 1973-74, del. Popov Soc. Tech. Exch. USSR, mgr. Dial Access Tech. Edn. program 1972), Assn. for Media Based Continuing Engring. Edn. (bd. dirs.), Nat. Fire Protection Assn., Sigma Xi, Tau Beta Pi, Eta Kappa Nu. Republican. Avocations: sailing, travel. Home: One E Lakefront Dr Beverly Shores IN 46301-0444 Office: 211 E Oncand St Chicago IL 60611 Office Phone: 773-883-1333. Personal E-mail: rikoski@earthlink.net.

**RILEY, BARBARA POLK,** retired librarian; b. Roselle, N.J., Nov. 21, 1928; d. Charles Carrington and Olive Bond P.; AB, Howard U., 1950; BS, N.J. Coll. Women, 1951; MS, Columbia U., 1955; m. George Emerson Riley, Feb. 23, 1957 (dec.); children: George E., Glenn C., Karen O.; m. William I. Scott, Oct. 6, 1990 (div. 1998). Asst. librarian, Fla. A&M U., 1951-53; with Morgan State Coll., 1955; with Dept. Def., 1955-57, S.C. State Coll., 1957-59, U.Wis., 1958-59; asst. librarian Atlanta U., 1960-68; asst. dir. Union County Anti Poverty Council, 1968; librarian Union County Tech. Inst., Scotch Plains, N.J., 1968-82, Plainfield campus Union County Coll., 1982-95; ret., 1995. Contbr. articles in Past and Promise, 1990, Ency. NJ. Mem. Roselle Bd. Edn., 1976-78; bd. dirs. Union County Anti Poverty Council, 1969-72; mem. Roselle Human Relations Commn., 1971-73, Plainfield Sci. Center, 1974-76, Union County Psychiat. Clinic, 1980-83, Pinewood Sr. Citizens Council, 1981-85; bd. dirs. Project, Women of N.J, 1985-93, Pinewood Sr. Citizen Housing, 1981-85, Black Women's History Conf., 1985-92, pres., 1989-91; Mem. Heard A.M.E. Ch. Mem. N.J. Library Assn., Council Library Tech., ALA (Black caucas), N.J. Coalition of 100 Black Women, African Am. Women's Polit. Caucus, N.J. Black Librarians Network (bd. dirs.), Links, Inc. (North Jersey chpt.), Black Women's History Conf., Alpha Kappa Alpha. Club: Just-A-Mere Lit. Home: 76 Hana Rd Edison NJ 08817-2037

**RILEY, BETTY ANNE,** psychologist, educator; d. James Andrew Riley and Elizabeth Riley Deurloo; m. Ronald Robert Teed, June 14, 1997. BA in Music, Wheaton Coll., 1969, MA in Christian Edn with highest honors, 1971, MA in Counseling Psychology, 1985; PsyD in Clin. Psychology, Ill. Sch. Profl. Psychology, 1992. Lic. clin. psychologist Ill., 1993. Dir. of Christian edn. Naperville Bible Ch. (now called Grace Pointe), Ill., 1971—78; vis. instr. Wheaton Coll., Wheaton, Ill., 1980—81; writer and editor Scripture Press Pubs. Inc., Wheaton, Ill., 1971—76; pre-primary dept. mgr. Scripture Press Pubs., Inc., Wheaton, 1976—83; clin. psychologist Psychotherapy & Consultation Svcs., Wheaton, 1985—97; founder and dir. clin. psychologist Bethel Ctr. for Psychotherapy, Wheaton, 1997—. Vol. cons. Solomon Klein Orphanage, Cochabamba, Bolivia, 1988; provide respite for refugee ctr. workers The Alpenland Life Ctr., Crikvenica, Croatia, 1995—95; lectr. in field. Author: (leader's guide) Leader's Guide for Building Stronger Families; co-author (with Mary Lebar): You Can Teach 4s and 5s; editor, composer (song book) Let's Sing! for 4s and 5s; prodr.: (cassettes) Motions 'N Music 1; Motions 'N Music 2; Let's Sing! for 4s and 5s; contbr. chapters to books. Youth ministries bd. Evangel Bapt. Ch., Wheaton, Ill., 2002—03; co-founder (with husband) and co-pastor Village Ch. of Wheaton, Wheaton, Ill., 2003—. Recipient Rech award in Psychol. Studies, Wheaton Coll., 1985. Mem.: Christian Assn. for Psychol. Studies, Am. Assn. for Marriage and Family Therapy, APA, Christians for Bibl. Equality. Christian Evangelical. Avocations: attending concerts, cooking, golf. Office: Bethel Center for Psychotherapy 213 W Wesley St Ste 204 Wheaton IL 60187 Office Phone: 630-681-1900.

**RILEY, BOB (ROBERT RENFROE RILEY),** governor; b. Ashland, Ala., Oct. 3, 1944; m. Patsy (Adams) Riley; children: Rob, Jenice, Minda, Krisalyn. Degree in bus. administrn., U. Ala. Past poultry and egg bus. co-owner, Ala.; past owner automobile dealership, Ala.; owner trucking co., Ala.; past owner grocery store and local pharmacy, Ala.; mem. Ho. of Reps. from 3d Ala. dist., 1996—2002, asst. whip, mem. house armed svcs. com., mem. house banking and fin. svcs. com., mem. house agr. com., house-senate conferee on FY 1998 Def. Authorization bill, 1997, mem. ho. agrl. com.; gov. State of Ala., 2003—. Past chmn. fin. com. Clay County Hosp.; mem. First Baptist Ch., men's Sunday sch. tchr., past chmn. bd. trustees; pres., Ala. State Bd. Edn., 2003—. Named Pub. Official of Yr., Governing mag., 2003. Mem. Masons, Shriners, Jaycees (past pres. Ashland chpt.). Republican. Baptist. Office: Office of the Gov State Capitol 600 Dexter Ave Montgomery AL 36130 Office Phone: 334-242-7100. Office Fax: 334-242-0937.*

**RILEY, CARROLL LAVERN,** anthropology educator; b. Summersville, Mo., Apr. 18, 1923; s. Benjamin F. and Minnie B. (Smith) R.; m. Brent Robinson Locke, Mar. 25, 1948; children: Benjamin Locke, Victoria Smith Evans, Cynthia Winningham AB, U. N.Mex., 1948, PhD, 1952; MA, UCLA, 1950. Instr. U. Colo., Boulder, 1953-54; asst. prof. U. N.C., Chapel Hill, 1954-55, So. Ill. U., Carbondale, 1955-60, assoc. prof., 1960-67, prof., 1967-86, Disting. prof., 1986-87, Disting. prof. emeritus, 1987—, chmn. dept., 1979-82, dir. mus., 1972-74; rsch. assoc. lab. anthropology Mus. N.Mex., 1987—. Rsch. collaborator Smithsonian Instn., 1988—; adj. prof. N.Mex. Highlands U., 1989—. Author: The Origins of Civilization, 1969, The Frontier People, 1982, expanded edit., 1987, Rio del Norte, 1995, Bandelier, 1996, The Kachina and Cross, 1999, 2003, Becoming Aztlan, 2005; editor: American Historical Anthropology, 1967, Man Across the Sea, 1971, Southwestern Journals of Adolph F. Bandelier, 4 vols., 1966, 70, 75, 84, Across the

Chichimec Sea, 1978, A Zuni Life, 1998, The Casas Grandes World, 1999, others; contbr. numerous articles to profl. jours. Served in USAAF, 1942-45 Decorated 4 battle stars; grantee Social Sci. Rsch. Coun., NIH, Am. Philos. Soc., Am. Council Learned Socs., NEH, others. Home and Office: 1106 6th St Las Vegas NM 87701 E-mail: criley@newmexico.com.

**RILEY, CHERYL,** artist, educator; b. Houston, Tex., Dec. 1, 1952; d. Bennie Riley and Gladys Mae DuBois. AA in Fashion Fine Art, Columbia Coll., 1973. Advt. exec. Levi Strauss & Saatchi Saatchi, San Francisco, 1979—84; instr. mixed media Penland (N.C.) Sch. Crafts, 2004; instr. wood decorative surfaces Haystack Mountain Sch. Crafts, Deer Isle, Maine, 2003; instr. mixed media Arrowmont Sch. Arts and Crafts, Gatlinburg, Tenn., 2001; instr. visual concepts N.Y. Sch. Interior Design, N.Y.C., 2000—03; artist, furniture designer Right Angle Designs, San Francisco, 1986—99; artist, designer N.Y.C., 2000—. Designer, cons. selected site art and graphics San Francisco Redevel. Agy., 1992; designer, think tank cons. Design Revival, Rock Hill (S.C.) Art Coun., 1999, 2000; conceptualist, think tank cons. Alternative Design for Walt Disney Industries, Jersey City and Orlando, Fla., 1998; keynote spkr. ann. conf. Furniture Soc. Am., Purchase, NY, 1997; artist, comty. facilitator Mosaic Mural on Exterior of 911 Emergency Ctr., San Francisco, 1994—98; artist, civic artist Lifetime Cultural Achievement from San Francisco Bus. and Profl. Women, Inc., 1997. Included in book and panel, Women Designers in the USA, 1900-2000, 2000. Bd. dirs., chair membership com. Mus. Arts and Design, N.Y.C., 2000—; bd. dirs., chair SECA aux. San Francisco Mus. Modern Art, 1996—99; bd. dirs., exec. bd. sec. Am. Craft Coun., N.Y.C., 1992—97; bd. dirs., exec. bd. dirs.-chair Capp St. Project, San Francisco, 1990—97; fundraiser Ndebele tribe-inspired wall panels for Carver Acad. Elem. Sch. and Bayview Police Sta.'s Comty. Conf. Rm., San Francisco. Recipient visual art grant, Fleishacker Found. and Tamarack Found., 1997, design arts individual grant, NEA, 1994. Mem.: Bead Soc., Orgn. of Black Designers (panel discussion participant 1997), Furniture Soc. Avocations: reading, swimming, walking, fine dining, opera, gallery and museum visits. Office: 22 Copeces Ln East Hampton NY 11937 E-mail: mail@cherylriley.com.

**RILEY, CHERYL M.,** prosthodontist, military officer; b. Biloxi, Miss., Aug. 4, 1963; d. William Richard and Gloria Lucille Morgan; m. Kevin Gerard Riley; 1 stepchild, Jared Nolan. BS in Chemistry magna cum laude with high honors, Millsaps Coll., 1985; RDH, U. Ala., 1987, DMD, 1989; MS in Oral Scis., SUNY, Buffalo, 1993. Diplomate Am. Bd. Prosthodontics. Dental specialist Miss. Army N.G., 1983—85; dental hygienist Ala. Army N.G., 1985—87; NBC officer, phys. tng. officer, retention officer La. Army N.G., 1987—89; dental officer, NBC officer N.Y. Army N.G., 1989—90; resident in prosthodontics SUNY, Buffalo, 1990—93; NBC officer USAFR, NY, 1990—93; tng. officer, divsn. officer, chmn. children's dental health care month USN, Quantico, 1993—94, head prosthodontic dept., weapons officer Palms, 1996—97; chief prosthodontics, PROFIS officer U.S. Army, Ft. Bragg, NC, 1997—2003, chief prosthodontic mentor, 2004—05; comdr. 257th Med. Detachment, Army Commendation medal, Navy Commendation medal, NATO medal Bosnia Theater, others; Merit scholar, Millsaps Coll., 1981—82, Acad. scholar, 1982—83, 1983—84, 1984—85, Ruth Cushman scholar, 1984—85, Emma Lou Ohsburg scholar, U. Ala., 1986—87, Dorothy Perkins Campbell scholar, SUNY, Buffalo, 1991—92. Fellow: Am. Coll. Prosthodontics (diplomat); mem.: Aircraft Owners and Pilots Assn., U.S. Parachute Assn., Tri Chi, Beta Beta, Omicron Delta Kappa, Phi Eta Sigma, Eta Sigma, Alpha Epsilon Delta (pres.), Theta Nu Sigma (v.p.), Phi Mu. Personal E-mail: aeropros@aol.com. Business E-Mail: cheryl.riley@us.army.mil.

**RILEY, DAVID RICHARD,** management consultant, retired military officer; b. Spokane, Wash., Mar. 28, 1940; s. Lee James and Louise Elizabeth (Duncan) R.; m. Anna Maria Formigoni, July 6, 1963; children: David Scott, Michelle Anna. BS in Naval Sci., USN Acad., 1963; MS in Applied Math., USN Post Grad. Sch., 1972; postgrad., Armed Forces Staff Coll., 1975. Navy ops. mgmt. specialist, Navy aerospace engring. specialist, Navy material specialist, Navy weapon sys. mgmt. specialist. Ensign USN, 1963, advanced through grades to capt., 1984, antisubmarine warfare/antisubmarine rocket officer Mayport, Fla., 1963-65, pilot trainee Pensacola, Fla., 1965-67, designated naval pilot San Diego, 1967, with antisubmarine/antiair warfare, 1967-74, maintenance officer, 1976-78, officer in charge Nerra Naples, Italy, 1978-81; exec. officer Naval Aviation Depot, Alameda, Calif., 1981-84, comdg. officer Pensacola, 1987-90; aviation depot program mgr. Navairsyscom Hdqrs., Washington, 1984-87; ret., 1990; cons. bus. planning and organizational devel., internat. commerce Chula Vista, Calif., 1990-94; pres., COO Speco Corp., Springfield, Ohio, 1994-95; pres. David Riley Assocs., Inc., 1998—. Mem. Assn. Naval Aviation, Ret. Officers Assn., Am. Legion, Naval Helicopter Assn. Republican. Presbyterian. Avocation: golf. Home and Office: David Riley Assoc Inc 115 Eastwick Ct Dayton OH 45440-3647 Business E-Mail: dra-inc@earthlink.net.

**RILEY, FAITH LYNCH,** retired historian, writer; b. Lockesburg, Ark., Sept. 16, 1940; d. Lester Doss and Nina Pettigrew-Doss Shuffield; m. Bryan Riley, Mar. 12, 1962; children: Reed Lynch, Costa Lynch, Alex Lynch. BS of Edn., Henderson State Tchrs. Coll., Arkadelphia, Ark., 1962. Tchg Ark. Dept. of Edn., 1962. Dir. SW Ark. Regional Archives, Washington, Ark., 2002—; flight attendant Delta Airlines, Dallas, 1963—64; tchr. Crawfordsville H.S., Ark., 1962—63; columnist Mena Star Newspaper, Mena, Ark., 1980—92; writer, owner Riley Publications, Wickes, Ark., 1994—, ret. Author (publisher): (oral history) Legacy of Arkansas, Somewhere The Sun Is Shining: Eyewitness Accounts of the Great Depression, To Do Or Die: Ouachita Mountain Men Remember World War II; editor: (non-fiction) 25 Years at Southwest Archives: True Stories From the Collections of Southwest Arkansas Regional Archives, Washington, Arkansas. Chmn. Rich Mountain CC, Mena, Ark., 1988—89, mem. Historical Soc. Achievements include research in History of Schools Since 1836 in Twelve SW Arkansas Counties. Avocations: working on the ranch, fishing/hunting, piano playing, nature photography, four wheeling in the back woods and trails near the Cossatot River. Home: 740 Hwy 278 Wickes AR 71973 Personal E-mail: faithriley@alltel.com.

**RILEY, HAROLD JOHN, JR.,** manufacturing executive; b. Syracuse, N.Y., Nov. 13, 1940; s. Harold John and Esther Emma (Denmark) R.; m. Diane Marie Slattery, June 15, 1963; children— Beth Ann, Thomas, Patrick BS in Indsl. Engring., Syracuse U., 1961; postgrad., Harvard Bus. Sch., 1985. Mfg. tng. program Gen. Elec. Co., various locations, 1961-63; various mfg. assignments Crouse-Hinds Co., Syracuse, 1963-74; gen. mgr. Midwest Elec., Chgo., 1974-77; v.p., gen. mgr. Crouse Hinds Distbn. Equipment Div., Earlysville, VA., 1977-79; v.p. Crouse-Hinds Co. Syracuse, 1979-82; exec. v.p. Cooper Industries Inc., Houston, 1982-92, pres., chief oper. officer, 1992-95, pres., 1995—2004, CEO, 1995—, chmn., 1996—, also bd. dirs. Bd. dirs. Wyman-Gordon Co., North Grafton, Mass. Bd. dirs. Jr. Achievement Southeast Tex., Houston Ctrl., Houston Symphony, The Greater Houston Partnership, The Houston Forum, The Mus. Fine Arts, Houston, Jr. Achievement, Inc. Mem. Mfrs. Alliance for Productivity Improvement, The Bus. Roundtable, Houston Club, Lakeside Country Club, Farmington Country Club. Republican. Roman Catholic. Home: 3669 Chevy Chase Dr Houston TX 77019-3009 Office: Cooper Industries Inc PO Box 4446 Houston TX 77210-4446

**RILEY, HELENE MARIA KASTINGER,** Germanist; b. Vienna, Mar. 11, 1939; came to U.S., 1959; d. Josef and Helene (Friedl) Kastinger; m. Edward R. Riley, Nov. 6, 1957 (div. May 1970); children: India Helene, John Edward, Jesse Dale, Michael Rutledge; m. Darius G. Ornston, May 11, 1983. Grad. bus. coll., Vienna, 1955; BA in Music, North Tex. State U., 1970; MA in Germanics, Rice U., Houston, 1973, PhD in Germanics, 1975. Tchg. asst. Rice U., Houston, 1971—75; asst. prof. German Yale U., New Haven, 1975—79, head summer lang. inst., 0979—1981, assoc. prof., 1979—85; chmn. Dept. Fgn. Langs. Wash. State U., Pullman, 1981—82; head Dept. Langs. Clemson U., SC, 1985—86, prof., 1985—95, alumni Disting. prof., 1996—. Guest prof. Middlebury Coll., Vt., 1976; speaker in field. Author:

Achim von Arnim, 1979, Virginia Woolf, 1983, Clemens Brentano, 1985, Die Weibliche Muse, 1986, Max Weber, 1991, Hildegard von Bingen, 1997, John Adam Treutlen: The European Heritage of Georgia's First Governor, 1999, Clemson University, 2002; editor: Germanic Notes and Reviews, 2005—; prodr., dir. traveling exhibit Cultural Contbns. of German-speaking Settlers in SC, 1996—; others; contbr. articles to profl. jours. Recipient German-Am. Friendship award Consul Gen. of the German Fed. Republic, 1989; grantee Griswold Found., 1975-76, 78, SC Dept. Edn., 1986, NEH, 1986, Provost's award Clemson U., 1989, 96, Hilles Fund, 1976, 79, 82, SC Humanities Coun., 1996; NDEA fellow, 1972, 73, Rice fellow, 1971, 74, Morse fellow, 1977-78, Deutscher Akademischer Austausch-Dienst fellow, 1979, Yale U. sr. faculty fellow, 1981-82, Holland Fund fellow, 1982, Deutsche Forschungsgemeinschaft fellow, 1982, Mesda fellow, 1993, Davenport Coll. fellow Yale U. Mem. AAUP (v.p. 1987-88, pres. 1988-89), MLA, Am. Assn. Tchrs. German, So. Comparative Lit. Assn., others. Democrat. Avocations: reading, writing, sports, needlecrafts, painting. Office: Clemson U Dept Langs 717 Strode Twr Clemson SC 29634-0001 Office Phone: 864-656-3402. Business E-Mail: rhelene@clemson.edu.

**RILEY, HENRY CHARLES,** banker; b. Newton, Massachusetts, Mar. 23, 1932; s. Charles Matthew and Marion Anna (Armstrong) R.; m. Patricia Ann (Buchanan), Mar. 3, 1962; children: Lauren Elizabeth, Carolyn Ann, Julie Louise. BA, Yale U., 1954; MBA, Boston Coll., 1965. With BayBank Harvard Trust Co., Cambridge, Mass., 1958—89, treas., sec., 1967—70, sr. v.p., sec., 1972—82, exec. v.p., 1982—87; mng. dir. cmty. banking BayBank Systems Inc., Waltham, Mass., 1987—90; exec. v.p., dir. cmty. banking BayBank Boston, 1990—92; exec. v.p. BayBank Systems, Inc., Waltham, Mass., 1992—97. Mem. pvt. banking adv. com. Fleet Boston, Sarasota, Fla., 2000-04. Trustee, treas. Longy Sch. Music, 1970-92; bd. dir. Richard Warren Surg. Rsch. and Ednl. Fund Inc., 1984—; bd. dir., pres. Cambridge Econ. Devel. Corp., 1982-87; corporator, past asst. treas. Mt. Auburn Hosp.; mem. exec. bd. Gettysburg Coll. Parents Assn.; treas. St. John's Episcopal Ch., sr. warden, Westwood, Mass., 1982-85; mem. St. Paul's Cathedral chpt., Boston, 1990-93. Served in USNR, 1956-57. Mem. Am. Bankers Assn. (chmn. 1991-92, exec. com. br. adminstry. divsn. 1992, chmn. nat. retail banking conf. 1990), Nat. Br. Adminstr. Roundtable, Boston Coll. Sch. Mgmt. Alumni Assn. (past dir., pres.), Harvard Sq. Bus. Assn. (past dir.), Cambridge C. of C. (past dir., past treas., v.p. 1975-87), Rotary (club dir. 1976-80, pres. 1979-80), Yale Club, Yale Club of the Suncoast (bd. dir. 2001—, v.p., 2004), Harvard Club, Dennis Yacht Club (mem. bd. govs., treas. 1993-94), The Meadows Country Club, Ivy League Club, Tiger Bay Club, Kings Way Golf Club. Episcopalian. Home: 33 York Way Westwood MA 02090-2633 also: PO Box 1192 240 New Boston Rd Dennis MA 02638-2121 also: 5284 Huntingwood Ct Sarasota FL 34235-5600 Personal E-mail: Marshwind@aol.com.

**RILEY, JACK,** actor, writer; b. Cleve., Dec. 30, 1935; s. John A. and Agnes C. (Corrigan) R.; m. Ginger Lawrence, May 18, 1975; children: Jamie, Bryan. BS in English, John Carroll U., 1961. Mem. Rolling Along of 1960, Dept. Army Travelling Show; co-host: Baxter & Riley, Sta.-WERE, Cleve., 1961-65; numerous TV appearances, including: as Mr. Carlin on Bob Newhart Show, CBS-TV, 1972-78; Occasional Wife, 1966, Mary Tyler Moore, 1972, Barney Miller, 1979, Diff'rent Strokes, 1979, Hart to Hart, 1980, Love Boat, 1984, Night Court, 1985-91, St. Elsewhere, 1986, Evening Shade, 1992, Family Matters, 1993, Married with Children, 1994, Coach, 1996, The Drew Carey Show, 1996, Seinfeld, 1997, Working, 1998, Son of the Beach, 1999-2002, Lucky, 2003, Yes, Dear, 2004, That 70's Show, 2004, numerous appearances on Tonight Show with Jay Leno, 1997-99; appeared in feature films including Catch-22, 1969, McCabe and Mrs. Miller, 1970, Long Goodbye, 1972, Calif. Split, 1974, World's Greatest Lover, 1978, High Anxiety, 1978, Butch and Sundance: The Early Years, 1979, History of the World, Part I, 1981, Frances, 1983, To Be or Not To Be, 1983, Finders Keepers, 1984, Spaceballs, 1987, Rented Lips, 1987, Gleaming the Cube, 1988, The Player, 1992, T-Rex, 1995, (voice) The Rugrat's Movie, 1998, Boogie Nights, 1997, Rugrats in Paris, 2000, Rugrats Go Wild, 2003, (TV movie) McBride, 2005, (feature film) Room 6; plays West Coast premier of Small Craft Warnings, 1975, Los Angeles revival of 12 Angry Men, 1985, Zeitgeist, 1990, House of Blue Leaves, at Cleve. Playhouse and tour Ea. Europe, 1993, The Odd Couple, Beck Ctr., Cleve., 1999, Do I Hear a Waltz? at Pasadena playhouse, 2001; TV writer: Mort Sahl Show, 1967, Don Rickles Show, 1968; writer commls. for, Blore & Richman Inc., Los Angeles, 1966-84; numerous radio commls. and TV voice-overs, Rugrats (cartoon series), 1993. With U.S. Army, 1958—61. Named to, Ohio Broadcasters' Hall of Fame, 2002. Mem.: AFTRA, Acad. TV Arts and Scis., Acad. Motion Picture Arts and Scis., Writers Guild Am., Actor's Equity, Screen Actors Guild. Office: care Ho of Reps 400 S Beverly Dr Beverly Hills CA 90212-4424 Personal E-mail: jackriley2005@aol.com.

**RILEY, JACQULYN (JACQUE) DIANE,** English educator, theater educator; b. Lamesa, Tex., Mar. 4, 1953; d. John Edward and Vermell (Peggy) None Gillispie; m. Joe Ray Riley, Oct. 3, 1955; 1 child, Randi Jo. BA in English Edn., West Tex. U., Canyon, 1975. Cert. Tex. Edn. Agy., 1975. HS English, theater tchr. McLean Ind. Sch. Dist., Tex., 1975—. Author: (poetry) The Cross. Alderwoman City Coun., McLean, 2004—05. Baptist. Avocations: reading, sewing, singing. Home: 320 Gray St PO Box 41 Mclean TX 79057 Office: McLean Ind Sch Dist 4th and Rowe St Mclean TX 79057 Office Phone: 806-779-2571.

**RILEY, JAMES B., JR.,** lawyer; b. Evanston, Ill., 1954; BA magna cum laude, U. Ill., 1976; JD cum laude, George Wash. U., 1979. CPA; bar: Ill. 1979, US Dist. Ct. No. Dist. Ill. 1979, US. Ct. Fed. Claims. Ptnr. Ross & Hardies (merged with McGuireWoods LLP in 2003), Chgo., 1985—2003, McGuireWoods LLP, Chgo., 2003—, co-chair firm health care dept., 2003—. Bd. dirs. Christmas in Apr. - North Suburban Chgo., past pres.; bd. dirs., pres. Rebuilding Together North Suburban Chgo. Mem.: ABA (health law sect.), Ill. Assn. Hosp. Attorneys, Am. Health Lawyers Assn., Ill. Bar Assn. Office: McGuireWoods LLP Ste 4100 77 W Wacker Dr Chicago IL 60601-1815 Office Phone: 312-750-8665. Office Fax: 312-920-6133. Business E-Mail: jriley@mcguirewoods.com.

**RILEY, JAMES CLIFFORD,** military career officer; b. Montacello, Calif., Nov. 13, 1946; m. Linda Jean Axtater. BS, U. Nebr., 1971; MA, Webster U., 1978; grad., Command and Gen. Staff Coll., 1980, U.S. Army War Coll., 1987. Drafted U.S. Army, 1965, commd. 2d lt., 1966, advanced through grades to lt. gen., 1999, co. comdr., S4 and Battalion Maintenance Officer 1st Bn., 6th Inf., 1st Armored Divsn. Illesheim, Germany, 1972-75, dep. G3 1st Armored Divsn., exec. officer 1st Bn., 52d Inf., S3, 3d Brigade Bamberg, Germany, 1981-83, comdr. 2d Bn., 7th Cavalry, 1st Cavalry Divsn. Ft. Hood, Tex., 1983-86, G3 and chief of staff 2d Armored Divsn. (forward) Garlstedt, Germany, 1987-89, comdr. 3d Brigade, 3d Infantry Divsn. Aschaffenburg, Germany, 1989-90, with 1st Armored Divsn. Saudi Arabia, Iraq & Kuwait, 1990-91, chief European divsn., J-5, the Joint Staff, Joint Chiefs of Staff rep. for European security matters Washington, Vienna, Austria, 1992-94, asst. divsn. comdr. for support, 1st Armored Divsn. Hanau, Germany, 1994-95, chief U.S. Mil. Tng. Mission Saudi Arabia, 1995-97, comdr. 3d Inf. Divsn. (Mechanized) Ft. Stewart, Ga., 1997-99. Decorated Def. Disting. Svc. medal, Disting. Svc. medal, Def. Superior Svc. medal, Legion of Merit with oak leaf cluster, Bronze Star medal with oak leaf cluster, Meritorious Svc. medal with four oak leaf clusters, Army Commendation medal. Home and Office: 2410 W Entrada Traio #16 Saint George UT 84770

**RILEY, JOCELYN CAROL,** writer, television producer; b. Mpls., Mar. 6, 1949; d. G.D. Riley and D.J. (Berg) Riley-Jacobson; m. Jeffrey Allen Steele, Sept. 4, 1971; children: Doran Riley, Brendan Riley. BA in English, Carleton Coll., Northfield, Minn., 1971. Mng. editor Carleton Miscellany, Northfield, Minn., 1971; mkgt. asst. Beacon Press, Boston, 1971-73; freelance writer, editor, prodr., 1973—. Author: (books) Only My Mouth is Smiling, 1982, Crazy Quilt, 1984; prodr.: (TV series) Her Own Words, 1986, Belle: The Life and Writings of Belle Case La Follette, 1987, Gold Medal Internat. Film and TV Festival, 1988, Zona Gale, 1874-1938, 1988, Patchwork, 1989, Prairie Cabin, 1991, Winnebago Women Songs & Stories, 1992, Ethel Kvalheim,

Rosemaler, 1992, Her Mother Before Her, 1992, Women in Construction, 1993, America Fever, 1994, Women in Policing. 1994, Sisters & Friends, 1994, Big Sister, Little Sister, 1995, Audrey Handler, Glass Artist, 1995, Women in Dentistry, 1996, Sewing Together, 1996, Women in Nontraditional Careers, 1996, Women in Firefighting, 1996, Women in Machining, 1997, Women in Welding, 1997, Prairie Child, 1997, Math at Work, 1998, Writing on the Lakes, 1998, Women in Engineering, 2000, Work Talk, 2000, Women in Highway Construction, 2001, Women in Building Construction, 2002, The Art of Ethel Kvalheim, 2002, Writing at Work, 2003, Shifting Gears: Changing Careers, 2004, Women Entrepreneurs, 2005, Women in the Automotive Industry, 2005, Women in Electronics, 2006; columnist: Wis. State Jour., 1986—91; contbr. articles to profl. jours. Active United Way of Dane County, 1984-90, On-Site Rev. Com., Madison Area Tech. Coll., 1993, Boy Scouts Am., 1996—. Hon. fellow Women's Studies Rsch. Ctr., U. Wis., Madison, 1986-91; Film in the Cities Regional Film/Video grantee; Dane County Cultural Affairs Comm. grantee, 1986-94, 96-97, 2002, 04; Wis. Arts Bd. grantee, 1986, 88-93; Wis. Humanities Coun. grantee, 1997; Wis. Sesquicentennial grantee, 1997, Madison CitiArts grantee, 1986-87, 89-90, 92-93, 96-97, 2002; Bronze Apple award Nat. Ednl. Film & Video Festival, 1988; cert. of commendation Am. Assn. State and Local History, 1988, Gold medal Internat. Film & TV Festival, 1988, cert. of recognition Wis. Dept. Pub. Instrn. Am. Indian History & Culture Program, 1991, Write Women Back into History award Nat. Women's History Project, 1995, ALA award, 1996, Barb Landers Meml. award Assn. for Gender Equity Leadership in Edn., 2004. Mem. Women in Comm. (pres. Madison chpt. 1984-85, nat. del. 1983, Writer's Cup 1985), Coun. for Wis. Writers (1st pl. for nonfiction article 1986), Authors Guild, Madison Assn. for Multi-Image (pres. 1986-87, nat. del. 1986), Downtown Madison Rotary Club. Address: PO Box 5264 Madison WI 53705-0264

**RILEY, JOE,** real estate executive; Pres. Coldwell Banker Ira E. Berry, St. Louis.

**RILEY, JUDITH MERKLE,** writer, educator; b. Brunswick, Maine, Jan. 14, 1942; d. Theodore Charles Merkle and Helene Antonia Suarez; m. W. Parkes Riley (div.); children: Elizabeth, Marlow. BA, U. Calif., Berkeley, 1962, PhD, 1974; MA, Harvard U., 1964. Intelligence analyst Dept. of Def., Washington, 1965—66; tchg. asst., acting instr., lectr. U. Calif., Berkeley, 1967—70; vis. asst. prof., asst. prof. U. Oreg., Eugene, 1971—82; assoc. prof. Claremont (Calif.) McKenna Coll./Claremont Grad. Sch., 1982—. Author: (non-fiction) Management and Ideology, 1980, (novels) A Vision of Light, 1989, In Pursuit of the Green Lion, 1990, The Oracle Glass, 1993, The Water-Devil, 1995, The Serpent Garden, 1997, The Master of All Desires, 1999 (Libr. Jour. 100 Best of 1999). Recipient Career Achievement award, Romantic Times, 1999. Fellow: Brit. Inst. Homeopathy (Di Hom 1998); mem.: Am. Soc. Pub. Adminstrn., Am. Polit. Sci. Assn., Novelists, Inc., Pen USA West, Nat. Ctr. Homeopathy, Phi Beta Kappa. Democrat. Episcopalian. Avocations: homeopathy, painting, stained glass, choral singing. Office: Claremont McKenna Coll Dept Govt 850 Columbia Ave Claremont CA 91711 Office Phone: 909-607-2996. Business E-Mail: jmerkle@mckenna.edu.

**RILEY, LYNNE F.,** lawyer; b. Boston, Oct. 31, 1959; BA cum laude, U. Mass., 1981; JD cum laude, Suffolk U. Law Sch., 1992. Bar: Mass. 1992, U.S. Dist. Ct. Mass. 1993, U.S. Ct. Appeals First Cir. 1993. Ins. agent Fidelity Nat. Title Ins. Co., Lawyers Title Ins. Co. Title examiner Mass. Land Ct., 1994—. Author: Recent First Cir. Devel. & Persisting Problems Regarding Avoidance of Impairing Liens, 1999. Named an top Boston lawyers, Boston Mag., 2004. Mem.: U.S. Panel Bankruptcy Trustees Dist. Mass. (mem. 1995), Mass. Conveyancer's Assn., Internat. Women's Insolvency & Restructuring Confederation (network chairperson), Am. Bankruptcy Inst., Women's Bar Assn. Mass., Boston Bar Assn. (bankruptcy sect.). Office: Riley & Esher LLP 69 Thorndike St Cambridge MA 02141 Office Phone: 617-876-3755. Office Fax: 617-876-3155.

**RILEY, MARGARET FOSTER (MIMI RILEY),** law educator; b. NYC, 1959; AB in History and Polit. Sci., magna cum laude, Duke U., 1981; JD, Columbia U., 1985. Bar: NY 1986, Pa. 1988. Assoc. Rogers & Wells, NYC, 1985—88, Pepper, Hamilton & Scheetz, Phila., 1988—92; asst. prof. U. Va. Sch. Law, 1992—88, named assoc. prof., 1994, co-dir. Legal Rsch. and Writing Program, 1992—. Office: U Va Sch Law 580 Massie Rd Charlottesville VA 22903-1789 Office Phone: 434-924-4671. E-mail: mf9c@virginia.edu.

**RILEY, MARK,** radio personality, political scientist; b. New Rochelle, NY, 1951; m. Kim Riley; 1 child, Viveca Simone. BA, NYU, 1973. Writer WLIB, NYC, 1973—76, editor, 1976—79, mng. editor, 1979—82, exec. prod., 1982—92, host Urban Notebook, 1983—86, host Real Talk, 1986—, prog. dir., 1992—96, co-host The Melting Pot, 1995—97; host Politics Live!, 1999; co-host (with Marc Maron) Morning Sedition, Air Am. Radio, NYC, 2004—. Programming cons., prodr. Disco Party Mix WBLS, 1977—79; political analyst NY 1 News - Road to City Hall, CNN Reporters Roundtable, Fox New Channel. Liberal. Office: Air America Radio 641 Avenue Of The Americas Fl 4 New York NY 10011-2038

**RILEY, MARK RICHARD,** biochemical engineer, educator; b. Dearborn, Mich., Mar. 16, 1969; s. Richard A. and Mary Alice Stella (Malaski) R.; m. Jill Susan Bonita Riley, Oct. 7. 1995. BSE in Chem. Engring. cum laude, U. Mich., 1990; MS in Chem. and Biochemical Engring., Rutgers U., 1994, PhD in Chem. and Biochemical Engring., 1995; Post Doctoral in Biochemical Engring. and Analytical Chemistry, U. Iowa, 1997. Undergraduate rsch., cellular bioengineering lab., dept. chemical engring. U. Mich., 1989—90; grad. dissertation rsch., dept. chemical and biochemical engring. Rutgers U., NJ, 1992—95; postdoctoral rschr., dept. chemical and biochemical engring. and dept. chemistry U. Iowa, Iowa City, 1995-97, faculty mem. of grad. interdisciplinary program in biomedical engring. U. Ariz., Tucson, 1997, chair, activities subcommittee, 1999—, asst. prof. dept. agrl. and biosystems engring. and program in biomedical engring., 1997—2003, assoc. prof. dept. agrl. and biosystems engring., biomedical engring., 2003—, assoc. prof., chemical and environ. engring., 2004—; assoc. prof., materials sci. and engring., 2005—, assoc. prof., Bio5 Inst., 2005—. Undergraduate tchg. asst. for self-paced biochemistry class, dept. biochemistry U. Mich., 1990; tchg. asst. for grad. and undergraduate classes in transport phenomena, dept. chemical and biochemical engring. Rutgers U., 1993—94, Merck Excellence fellow, NJ, 1993—95, instructor of undergraduate class in momentum transport phenomena, dept. chemical and biochemical engring., NJ, 1994; tchg. of several workshops/seminars for small groups of students U. Ariz., 1997—2001; indsl. intern Ortho Pharma., Raritan, NJ, 1991, Exxon Rsch. and Engring., Annandale, NJ, 1993, Annandale, 94. Refereed articles for peer-reviewed jours.; contbr. chapters to books; editor for patents and lit. reviews Applied Biochemistry and Biotechnology, 1998—, biol. engring. representative to resource mag. editl. bd., 2004—06. Recipient Nat. Assn. Coll. and Teachers of Agr., Tchg. award of merit, U. Ariz, Coll. Agr. and Life Sciences, 2002; U. Ariz. Dean of Students Faculty Fellow, 2001—. Mem. Am. Chem. Soc. (membership chair for biochemical tech. divsns. 1998-2002), Biomed. Engring. Soc., AIChE, Am. Soc.Agrl. Engring. (chair, biol. engring. divsn., 1999-2000, assoc. editor, Transactions, 2005-), Am. Soc. of Engring. Soc., Inst. Biol. Engring. (councilor, 2000-02, 2003-04), Alpha Epsilon. Achievements include development of methods to predict the rates of nutrient transport and reaction in immobilized cell systems; developed near infrared spectroscopic techniques for bioreactor monitoring; invented a sticker that can tell consumers if a fruit or vegetable is ripe. Office: Dept Agrl and Biosystems Engring U Ariz Shantz Bldg Rm 403 Tucson AZ 85721-0038 Office Phone: 520-626-9120. Office Fax: 520-621-3963. Business E-Mail: riley@ag.arizona.edu.*

**RILEY, MARY JANE,** computer scientist; b. Raleigh, NC, May 26, 1946; d. Charles William and Geraldine Lucile (Adams) Hampton; m. William Walter Schubert, Dec. 30, 1967 (div. June 1979); children: Kristen, Stephen, Betsy, Kathryn; stepchildren: Lee, Scott; m. Jim Riley, Oct. 17, 1998. BA in Math., Park Coll., 1967. Cert. IBM exec. project mgr. Programmer U. Mo.

Med. Ctr., Columbia, 1968-72, City and County of Denver, 1979-80; sr. sys. programmer Citicorp Person to Person, Denver, 1980-82; sys. support rep. Software AG, NA, Denver, 1982-83; prin. info. sysm. specialist Idaho Nat. Engring. Lab., EG&G, Idaho Falls, 1983-89; adv. svcs. specialist IBM Profl. Svcs., Albuquerque, 1989-91; field mgr. IBM Svc., Boulder, Colo., 1991-93; project mgr. IBM Global Svcs., Denver, 1993-99; exec. project mgr. IBM Global Svcs. Healthcare, 1999—2002; delivery project exec. IBM Global AMS, Boulder, Colo., 2002—03, N.Y.C., 2003—06. Presenter career workshop for girls Nor. Colo. U., Greeley, 1993. Leader Girl Scout Am., Pocatello, Idaho, Columbia, Mo., 1969-79, Idaho Falls, 1986-89, cluster leader, Rigby, Idaho, 1988-89; active Albuquerque Civic Chorus, 1990-91, Luth. Ch. Coun., 1994-96; bd. dirs. LWV, Pocatello, 1977-79, 84-85, 2003—, pres., 1978-79; bd. dirs. Luth. Ch. Women, Pocatello, 1978-79; youth advisor Luth. Ch., Idaho Falls, 1984-89; tchr. Sunday sch. local ch., Albuquerque, 1990-91; youth com. chair local ch., Boulder, Colo., 1994-96; tchr. 7th and 8th grade Sunday sch., 1993-96; mem. ch. choir, 1995-96; mem. Denver Art Mus., Denver Nat. History Mus. Mem. AAUW, LWV. Episcopalian. Avocations: youth work, reading, choir, photography, swimming. Home: PO Box 2030 1172 Palmers Dr Silverthorne CO 80498-2030 E-mail: mjriley@us.ibm.com

**RILEY, MONICA,** microbiologist, educator; b. New Orleans, Oct. 4, 1926; d. Chauncey Wesley and Maude (Kemper) M.; children: Adam, Christine (dec.), Katherine. BA, Smith Coll., 1947; PhD, U. Calif.-Berkeley, 1960. Asst. prof. U. Calif., Davis, 1960-66; assoc. prof. SUNY-Stony Brook, 1966-75, prof. and provost, 1975-78, prof. biochemistry, 1975-89, acting chmn., 1984-85, emeritus prof., 1989—; sr. scientist Marine Biol. Lab., Mass., 1989-06; vis. prof. U. Paris-Sud-Orsay, 1991, 94; mem. program com. for meeting Engineered Organisms in the Environment, 1985; mem. rev. panel NSF; organizer Conf. on Orgn. Bacterial Chromosome, 1988; chair Gordon Rsch. Conf. on Population Biology of Microorganisms, 1989; mem. Recombinant DNA Adv. Com. NIH, 1988-91; lectr. Found. for Microbiology, 1987-88; co-organizer 1st Internat. Conf. on E coli Genome, 1992, organizer 3d conf., 1993-94, co-organizer Conf., 1995-2006; organizer Internat. Workshops Annotation Ecoli genome, 2003, 05. Editor: The Bacterial Chromosome, 1990; co-editor: Escherichia coli and Salmonella typhimurium, 2d edit.; contbr. articles to profl. jours., chpts. to books. Bd. dirs. Brookhaven chpt. LWV, N.Y., 1982-87, Falmouth chpt., Mass., 1990-00. Grantee NIH, 1960-00, 05, NSF, 1960-90, DOE, 1999-06. Fellow Am. Acad. Microbiologists; mem. Am. Soc. Microbiology (chmn. com. genetic and molecular microbiology of pub. and sci. affairs bd. 1984-88), Genetics Soc. Am., Am. Soc. Biol. Chemists, Phi Beta Kappa, Sigma Xi. As a graduate student at the University of California at Berkeley in the 1950s, Ms. Riley's work on how genes make protein helped forge the field of Molecular Biology. When the complete DNA sequence of the bacterium Escherichia coli was determined in the mid 1990s, she played an important role by interpreting gene functions from their sequences. As a leader in the field, she organized international workshops in 2003 and 2005 to update the annotation of this model organism, which was a major step toward learning how all the genes of a cell work. Business E-Mail: mriley@mbl.edu.

**RILEY, NANCY C.,** state legislator; b. Tulsa, Okla., June 20, 1958; m. Jerry A. Riley; children: Dan, Robin, Patrick stepchildren: Steve, Phil. Student, Okla. Christian U., 1976-79; BSE, UCT Langston, 1985. Tchr. Tulsa Pub. Schs., 1986—; mem. Okla. Senate from 37th dist., Oklahoma City, 2001—. Active PTA, Berryhill Hoover, S.W. Tulsa Chamber, Sand Springs Chamber, Bixby Chamber, Green Country Campfire Adv. Coun., Interagency Coun. Early Childhood Intervention, Okla. Fedn. Rep. Women, Okla. First Ladies, Tulsa Rep. Men's Club, After Five Rep. Women's Club, Tchr. Recruitment Com. for Minorities. Mem. Tulsa Classroom Tchrs. Assn. (del. 1986-2000), Rolling Oaks Homeowners Assn. (past pres. 1999-2000), Delta Kappa Gamma (sec. 1994-97). Republican. Mailing: State Capitol Bldg Rm 528A 2300 N Lincoln Blvd Oklahoma City OK 73105 E-mail: Rileyn@lsb.state.ok.us.

**RILEY, PATRICK JAMES,** professional basketball coach; b. Rome, N.Y., Mar. 20, 1945; s. Leon R.; m. Chris Riley; children: James Patrick, Elisabeth Marie. Grad., U. Ky., 1967. Guard San Diego Rockets, 1967-70, Phoenix Suns, 1975-76, L.A. Lakers, 1970-75, asst. coach, 1979-81, head coach, 1981-90, N.Y. Knicks, 1991-95; broadcaster L.A. Lakers games Sta. KLAC and Sta. KHJ-TV, 1977-79, NBC Sports, 1990-91; head coach Miami Heat, 1995—2003, 2005—, pres., basketball ops., 2003—05. Author: Show Time: Inside the Laker's Breakthrough Season, 1988, The Winner Within: A Life Plan for Team Players, 1993. Named NBA Coach of Yr., 1990, 93, 97 Head coach, NBA Champions, LA Lakers, 1982, 85, 87, 88, NBA Champions, Miami Heat, 2006. Achievements include setting the NBA record for most playoff wins (137). Office: Miami Heat Am Airlines Arena 601 Biscayne Blvd Miami FL 33132*

**RILEY, R. DOUGLAS,** music educator; b. Phoenixville, Pa., Mar. 1, 1952; s. Thomas M. and Maryjane Riley; children: Sean, Michael. MusB in Edn., Susquehanna U., Selinsgrove, Pa., 1974; MusM in Edn., West Chester U., Pa., 1981. Music tchr. Hazelton (Pa.) Area Schs., 1974—75, Northern York County Schs., Dillsburg, Pa., 1975—. Office: Northern York County HS 653 S Baltimore St Dillsburg PA 17019-9690

**RILEY, RAQUEL,** photographer; d. Marnita Jean Riley and James Whitney Buggs; life ptnr. Ron Thomas. BA, Hampton U., Va., 1995—98. Photojournalism Ft Ben Harrison, Ind., 1991, Photojournalism II Ft Ben Harrison, Ind., 1991. Owner/ceo PBR Studios, LLC, Atlanta, Ga., 2002—. Photographer (published work) Tranquility (Internat. Libr. of Photography, 2001). Capt. (0-3) US Army, 1998—2002, Ft. Benning, GA. Mem.: Delta Sigma Theta, Inc (hbc). Achievements include Ebony Magazine; Army Achievment Medal for Photojournalism-1992; Army Achievement Medal for Photojournalism-2000. Office: PBR Studios LLC 541 10th Street Suite #182 Atlanta GA 30318 Office Phone: 404-454-1878. E-mail: info@photographybyraquel.com

**RILEY, RAY ALLAN,** biology educator; s. Joanne Huffaker; m. Kathy A. Archer, Feb. 14, 1981; children: Kimberly Busler, Jennifer. BS, U. Tenn., Knoxville, 1979; MS, Lincoln Meml. U., Harogate, Tenn., 1992. Cert. profl. educator, highly qualified State of Tenn., 2000. Biology tchr. Karns H.S., Knoxville, Tenn., 1979—97; asst. prin. Fulton H.S., 1997—2000, Karns H.S., 2000—03; biology tchr. Farragut H.S., 2003—. Football coach Karns H.S., Knoxville, Tenn., 1979—85, track coach. Chmn. deacons Wallace Meml. Bapt. Ch., Knoxville, Tenn., 1991—92; mem. strategic planning com., 1997—98. Named KIL Track Coach of Yr., Regional Track Coach of Yr. Office: Farragut HS 11237 Kingston Pike Farragut TN 37934-2840 Office Phone: 865-966-9775.

**RILEY, RHONDA WINGATE,** music educator; d. Albert Earl Wingate and Doris Wingate Rogers; m. Michael Gerald Riley, Nov. 8, 1947; children: Jonathan Michael, Stephen Marcus, Alicia Patrice. MusB, East Carolina U., Greenville, NC, 1975; MusM, U. South Fla., Tampa, 1984. Dir. ch. music Suncoast Cathedral, St. Petersburg, Fla., 1983—85, Countryside Christian Ctr., Clearwater, 1985—87; instr. voice Pinellas County Ctr. Arts, St. Petersburg, 1989—91; instr. voice, piano pvt. studio, Greenville, NC, 1991—; tchr. music Pitt County Schs., 1993—96; instr. voice, piano Arendell Parrott Acad., Kinston, 1995—; prof. voice Barton Coll., Wilson, 1997—2000; lectr., vocal coach, accompanist dept. theatre & dance East Carolina U., Greenville, 1997—. Choral dir. Greenville Choral Soc. Chamber Chorale, 1996—2001. Singer (soprano soloist (yum - yum) gilbert & sullivan's the mikado; singer: (choral singer) Mahler's Symphony No. 8 (performed and recorded with Robert Shaw; singer: (choral member) (robert shaw's carnegie hall workshop) Stabat Mater by Francis Poulenc & K. Szymanowski & G. Verdi; singer: (soprano soloist) handel's messiah, beethoven mass in c, haydn's lord nelson mass, mendelssohn's hymn of praise; singer: (soprano soloist) Bach Magnificat, Carrissimi's Historis Di Jepthe, (soprano soloist in faculty recitals) Pinellas County Center for the Arts, (soprano soloist) appearances on nationally syndicated television, WCLF, Clearwater, Florida. Choral singer

Master Chorale, Tampa, Fla., 1977—91, Greenville Choral Soc., 1991—2000, mem., 1996—2000. Mem.: Nat. Assn. Tchrs. Singing. Office: East Carolina University Fifth Street Greenville NC 27858 Office Phone: 252-328-1199.

**RILEY, RICHARD WILSON,** lawyer, former federal official; b. Greenville, SC, Jan. 2, 1933; s. Edward Patterson and Martha Elizabeth (Dixon) Riley; m. Ann Osteen Yarborough, Aug. 23, 1957; children: Richard Wilson, Anne Y., Hubert D., Theodore D. BA, Furman U., 1954; JD, U. S.C., 1959. Bar: S.C. 1960. Ptnr. Riley & Riley, Greenville, 1959—78, Nelson, Mullins, Riley & Scarborough, Greenville and Columbia, 1987—93, Greenville, 2001—; gov. State of S.C., 1979—87; sec. U.S. Dept. Edn., Washington, 1993—2001; disting. univ. prof. U. S.C., Columbia, 2001—; disting. prof. govt., politics, and pub. policy Furman U., 2001—. Spl. asst. to subcom. U.S. Senate Jud. Com., 1960; mem. S.C. Ho. of Reps., 1963—66, S.C. Senate from Greenville-Laurens Dist., 1966—76; sr. adv. and chair Richard W. Riley Inst. Govt., Politics and Pub. Leadership, Furman U., 2001—; bd. dirs. ACT (Am. Coll. Testing Program), Pub. Broadcasting Svc. (PBS), Laureate Edn., Inc.; bd. trustees Knowledge Works Found., 2001—; trustee Carnegie Corp. N.Y., 2004—, Furman U., 2001—. Lt. (j.g.) USNR, 1954—56. Recipient Dist. Svc. award, Coun. Chief State Sch. Officers, 1994, James Bryant Conant award, Edn. Comm. of the States, 1995, T.H. Bell award for outstanding edn. advocacy, Com. for Edn. Funding, 1996, Dist. Svc. award, Am. Coun. on Edn., 1998; disting. sr. fellow, NAFSA: Assn. Internat. Educators, Wash., D.C. Mem.: Greenville Bar Assn., S.C. Bar Assn., Rotary, Phi Beta Kappa. Office: Nelson Mullins Riley & Scarborough Poinsett Plaza Ste 900 104 S Main St Greenville SC 29601 Office Phone: 864-250-2300. Business E-Mail: dick.riley@nelsonmullins.com.

**RILEY, ROBERT BARTLETT,** landscape architect; b. Chgo., Jan. 28, 1931; s. Robert James and Ruth (Collins) R.; m. Nancy Rebecca Mills, Oct. 5, 1956; children: Rebecca Hill, Kimber Bartlett. PhB, U. Chgo., 1949; BArch, MIT, 1954. Chief designer Kea, Shaw, Grimm & Crichton, Hyattsville, Md., 1959-64; prin. partner Robert B. Riley (A.I.A.), Albuquerque, 1964-70; campus planner, asso. prof. architecture, dir. Center Environ. Research and Devel., U. N.Mex., 1966-70; prof. landscape architecture and architecture U. Ill., Urbana-Champaign, 1970—, head dept. landscape architecture, 1970-85, dir. PhD program, 1999—; vis. prof. Harvard U., 1996-97; prof. emeritus, dir. joint PhD program U. Ill., 1997—. Sr. fellow landscape architecture studies Dumbarton Oaks/Harvard U., 1992—, chmn. fellows, 1996—; mem. rev. panel landscape architects Fed. Civil Service-Nat. Endowment Arts. Assoc. editor Landscape mag., 1967-70; editor Landscape Jour., 1987—. Served with USAF, 1954-58. Nell Norris fellow U. Melbourne, Australia, 1977; project fellow Nat. Endowment Arts, 1985 Fellow Am. Soc. Landscape Architects (Nat. Honor award 1979); mem. Coun. of Educators in Landscape Architecture, pres. 1984-85, chmn. bd. dirs. 1985-86, Outstanding Educator award 1992, Pres.'s award 1994, chmn. editl. adv. bd. Landscape Architecture 1996-99), AIA (Design award Md. 1962, N.Mex. 1968, Environ. Svc. award N.Mex. 1970), Environ. Design Rsch. Assn. (chmn. bd. 1990-91, Career award 2003), Phi Beta Kappa. Unitarian Universalist. Office: Univ Ill 101 Temple Buell Hall 611 E Lorado Taft Dr Champaign IL 61820-6921 Home: 407 E George Huff Dr Urbana IL 61801-6703 Business E-Mail: rbriley@uiuc.edu.

**RILEY, ROBERT SHEAN,** writer, publishing executive, retired army officer; b. West Point, Ky., Oct. 16, 1929; s. Niram Brooks and Nan Estelle (Shean) R.; m. Matsuko Uechi, Mar. 24, 1955; children: Elizabeth Mae, Robert Jr. BS in Engring., U.S. Mil. Acad., 1952; MPA, U. Okla., 1974; M in Internat. Affairs, Columbia U., 1975. Commd. 2d lt. U.S. Army, 1952, advanced through grades to col.; writer, pub. Lawton, Okla., 1978—. Author: History of Shumate Family, 1992, Our European Origins, 1992, History O'Ferrall-Shaen Family, 1994, History of Ditto Families, 1996, The Colonial Riley Families of the Tidewater Frontier, 1999, Marc Hardouin (Mark Hardin) and Descendants, 2003, History of the Woolfolk Family, 2005. Decorated Bronze Star medal with 3 oak leaf clusters, Air medal, Joint Svc. Commendation medal, Meritorious Svc. medal with 1 oak leaf clusters, Army Commendation medal. Mem. Mil. Order of World Wars, West Point Soc., TEXOMA. E-mail: rsriley29@sbcglobal.net.

**RILEY, RONALD JIM,** industrial engineer, consultant; b. Flint, Mich., Mar. 10, 1950; s. Jack Robert and Rose Alice (Millard) R.; m. Laura Jean Gill, June 23, 1979; children: Meghan Kathleen, Caitlin Rose. Student, C.S. Mott C.C., Flint, 1969-70. Asst. mgr., salesman Howat Electronics, Flint, 1968-70; proprietor Customtronics, Flint, 1970-74; engr. med. equipment Werby Labs., Flint, 1974-76; plant engr. Cara Corp., Detroit, 1976-78; indsl. controls engr. Atlas Techs., Fenton, Mich., 1978-84; engr., mgr. J.N. Fauver Co. subs. Sun Oil, Madison Heights, Mich., 1984-90; founder Riley & Assocs., Inc., Riley Cons., Inc., Riley Enterprises, Ltd., 1990—. Freelance journalist, 1980—; founder, exec. dir. InventorEd, Inc., 1996—. Contbr. articles to profl. jours.; patentee in field. Recipient MIT Invention Dimension Inventor of Week Award, UIA Website Excellence Award for 2003 & 2004, Nat. Inventor Fraud Center's "Good Guy of Year" Award, 1999, Awesome Library Editors Choice Award, Tech. Mus. Innovation Award, Hot Site Award, USA Today, Dr. Matrix Award for Sci. Excellence, Pres. Award JN Fauver. Mem. Union of Concerned Scientists, Action on Smoking and Health, Pub. Citizen, Profl. Inventors Alliance (pres. 1996—), Alliance for Am. Innovation Inc. (pres. adv. bd. 1996-2002), Intellectual Property Creators (adv. bd. 1995-2000), Student Coalition for Handling Intellectual Property. Avocations: horticulture, carpentry, solar and renewable energy, education, politics. Office: Riley Cons, Inc 1323 W Cook Rd Grand Blanc MI 48439-9364 Business E-Mail: RJR@rjriley.com.

**RILEY, RUTH ELLEN,** professional basketball player; b. Macy, Ind. d. Sharon Riley. B in psychology, U. Notre Dame, 2001. Basketball player North Miami High Sch., U. Notre Dame, Miami Sol, WNBA, 2001—03, Detroit Shock, WNBA, 2003—. Mem. USA Select Team, 1998, USA Basketball Women's Sr. Nat. Team, 2004; mem., NCAA Divsn. 1 Nat. Championship Team U. Notre Dame, 2001; mem., WNBA championship team Detroit Shock, 2003; mem. US Women's Basketball Team, Athens Olympic Games, Greece, 2004. Named Big East Female Scholar-Athlete of Yr. award, 2001, Most Outstanding Player, Final Four, 2001, Naismith and AP Coll Player of Yr., 2001, Most Valuable Player, WNBA Finals, 2003; named to Verizon Women's Basketball Academic All-American first team, 2000, 2001; recipient Silver medal, World U. Games, 1999. Achievements include No. 5 overall pick by the Miami Sol in the 2001 WNBA draft; only Norte Dame player to have reached 2,000 points and 1,000 rebounds. Office: USA Basketball 5465 Mark Dabling Blvd Colorado Springs CO 80918-3842

**RILEY, SALLY JEAN,** science educator; b. Pasadena, Calif., Feb. 24, 1941; d. Richard Dunlap Hopping and Nelle Bernice Webb-Hopping; m. Robert William Riley, Sept. 27, 1977; children: Stacie Lynn Scripter, Derrick Wayne, Stefanie Lyn Campbell. BA, Calif. State U., L.A., 1963; Tchg. Credential, U. Calif., Irvine, Calif. 1982. Social worker County of LA, Covina, Calif., 1967—71, County of Orange, Santa Ana, Calif., 1974—76; sci. tchr. Irvine Unified Sch. Dist., Irvine, Calif., 1982—. Mem. Sch. Site Coun., Irvine, Calif., 1995—. Vol. Pacific Wildlife Orgn., Laguna Niguel, Calif., 2000—04. Mem.: NEA, Calif. Tchrs. Assn., Irvine Tchrs. Assn. R-Liberal. Christian Scientist. Achievements include Dean's List - Univ. Calif., Irvine. Avocations: genealogy, gardening, reading, travel. Office: Venado Mid Sch 4 Deerfield Irvine CA 92604 Office Phone: 949-936-6856. Business E-Mail: sriley@iusd.org.

**RILEY, TERENCE,** curator, architect; Architect, ptnr. (with John Keenen) architectural practice; dir. Arthur Ross Architectural Galleries, Columbia U.; curator dept. arch. and design MoMA, NYC, 1991, chief curator, 1992—2002, Philip Johnson chief curator arch. and design, 2002—06; dir. Miami Art Mus., Fla., 2006—. Prof. Harvard U., Columbia U. Curator (exhibitions) Paul Nelson: Filter of Reason, Arthur Ross Architectural Galleries, Columbia U., 1989, Light Construction, The Un-Private House,

Mies in America, 2001, On-Site: New Architecture in Spain, 2006; contbr. articles to profl. jours. Trustee Fundació Mies van der Rohe, Barcelona; adv. bd. Parsons Grad. Sch. Design. Office: Miami Art Museum 101 West Flager St Miami FL 33130*

**RILEY, THOMAS EDWARD,** lawyer; BA, SUNY, Binghamton, 1976; JD, NYU, 1979. Bar: NY 1980, US Dist. Ct. (So. Dist.) NY 1983, US Dist. Ct. (Ea. Dist.) NY 1983, US Dist. Ct. (So. Ariz.) 1992, US Ct. Appeals (4th Cir.) 1995, US Ct. Appeals (6th Cir.) 1998, US Dist. Ct. (No. Dist.) NY 2002, US Ct. Appeals (3rd Cir.) 2004, US Dist. Ct. (2nd Cir.) 2004. Staff atty. Mfrs. Hanover Trust Co., NYC, 1979-80; law clk. to presiding justice US Dist. Ct. (We. Dist.) NY, Buffalo, 1980-82; assoc. Chadbourne & Parke LLP, NYC, 1982—, ptnr., head litig. dept., mem. mgmt. com. Staff mem. NYU Jour. Internat. Law & Politics, 1977—78, rsch. editor, 1978—79. Bd. dirs. U. Settlement Soc. of NY, 1992—2004. Mem.: ABA (product liability com., litigation sect.), Internat. Assn. Def. Counsel, NY State Bar Assn. Office: Chadbourne & Parke LLP 30 Rockefeller Plz Fl 31 New York NY 10112-0129 Office Phone: 212-554-5408. Office Fax: 212-541-5369. Business E-Mail: triley@chadbourne.com.

**RILEY, THOMAS JOSEPH,** anthropologist, educational association administrator; b. Portland, Maine, Nov. 2, 1943; s. Joseph Gerard and Virginia C. (Cunningham) R.; m. Karma Jean Ibsen, July 10, 1967 (div. 1985); children: Kirsten, Katharine, Erin; m. Carol Ann, Nov. 21, 1989; 1 child, Julia Wade. BA, Boston Coll., 1965; MA, U. Hawaii, 1970, PhD, 1973. Asst. prof. NYU, 1972—74; from asst. prof. to prof. anthropology U. Ill., Urbana, 1974—96; dean Coll. Arts, Humanities/Social Scis., prof. anthropology N.D. State U., Fargo, 1996—. Acad. adv. bd. SALT Ctr., Portland, 1988-90; assoc. dean Grad. Coll. U. Ill., 1983-86, head dept. anthropology, 1986-93, chmn. senate coun., 1995-96; dir. N.D. Inst. Regional Studies, 1996— Co-author: Prehistoric Agriculture, 1972; mem. editl. bd. Ency. World Cultures, 1993-96, Ency. Cultural Anthropology, 1994-95, Ency. World Pre-history, 1996-2001; contbr. over 100 articles to profl. jours Chmn. bd. Devel. Svcs. Ctr., Champaign, 1986—89, Human Rels. Area Files at Yale U., 1985—96, v.p., 1995, pres., 1996; sec. bd. C-U Independence, Champaign, 1987—96; bd. dirs. Disabled Citizens Found., Champaign, 1988—96, Ill. Assn. Retarded Citizens, Chgo., 1988—94, Champaign County Mental Health Bd., 1993—96, Prairie Pub. Broadcasting, 1999—2005, Plains Art Mus., Fargo, vice-chair, 2001—05, chair, 2005—06; bd. dirs. ND State Hist. Soc. Found., 2001—, Ill. State Hist. Sites Adv. Coun., 1986—89, United Way Cass-Clay, 2001—. Fellow, NSF, 1978—79; grantee, 1978—99. Mem. AAAS, Am. Assn. State and Local History, Am. Anthropology Assn., Ill. Archeol. Survey, Soc. Am. Archaeology, Soc. Archeol. Scis. (treas 1982-83), Sigma Xi (chpt. v.p. 1987-88, chpt. pres. 1988-91) Roman Catholic. Home: 1108 42nd Ave N Fargo ND 58102-5318 Office: ND State U 221 Minard Hall Fargo ND 58105 Home: 1209 18 1/2 St N Moorhead MN 56560-1828 Office Phone: 701-231-8338. E-mail: thomas.riley@ndsu.edu.

**RILEY, TOM JOSEPH,** lawyer; b. Cedar Rapids, Iowa, Jan. 9, 1929; s. Joseph Wendell and Edna (Kyle) R.; m. Nancy Evans, Jan. 21, 1952; children: Pamela Chang, Peter, Lisa Thirnbeck, Martha Brown, Sara Riley, Heather Mescher. BA, U. Iowa, 1950, JD, 1952. Bar: Iowa 1952, U.S. Dist. Ct. (no. dist.) Iowa 1952, U.S. Ct. Appeals (8th cir.) 1960, U.S. Ct. Appeals (7th cir.) 1977, U.S. Ct. Appeals (9th cir.) 1996, U.S. Supreme Ct. 1966. Assoc. Simmons, Perrine, Allbright & Ellwood, Cedar Rapids, 1952-60, ptnr., 1960-80; pres. Tom Riley Law Firm, P.C., Cedar Rapids, 1980—. Adj. prof. trial advocacy Coll. Law, U. Iowa, Iowa City, 1979. Author: Proving Punitive Damages, 1981, The Price of a Life, 1986, Trial Handbook for Iowa Lawyers (Civil), 1997, Iowa Practice: Civil Litigation Handbook, 2003, 04, 05, 06. Active Iowa Ho. of Reps., 1960-64, Iowa Senate, 1965-74. First lt. USAF, 1952-54. Named Outstanding Freshman Legislator, Des Moines Press and Radio Club, 1961. Fellow Iowa Acad. Trial Lawyers (bd. govs. 1982-91); mem. Iowa Trial Lawyers Assn. (bd. govs. 2000-2002), Cedar Rapids Country Club. Democrat. Presbyterian. Avocations: tennis, sailing. Home: 5300 Lakeside Rd Rural Route Marion IA 52302 Office: 4040 1st Ave NE Cedar Rapids IA 52402-3143 Office Phone: 319-363-4040. Business E-Mail: ellena@trlf.com.

**RILEY, WILLIAM,** wholesale distribution executive, writer, conservationist; b. Indpls., June 30, 1931; s. Leo Michael and Edna (Wilhelm) R.; m. Laura Etz, Apr. 20, 1957. AB, U. Notre Dame, 1952; LLB, Yale U., 1955. V.p., dir., chmn. Ivy Corp., Atlanta, 1960-80; CEO, chmn. Moore-Handley, Inc., Birmingham, Ala., 1981—. Bd. dirs. Fabco-Air, Inc., Gainesville, Fla. Author: (with Laura Riley) Guide to the National Wildlife Refuges, 1979 (Pulitzer prize nominee), 2d edit., 1993, Lifetime Conservation award Nat. Audubon Soc., 2000. Trustee The Raptor Trust, Basking Ridge, N.J., 1980-2000; bd. dirs. Nat. Wildlife Refuge Assn., Potomac, Md., 1985-94, Hawk Mountain Sanctuary Assn., Kempton, Pa., 1989-98, Nat. Audubon Soc., N.Y.C., 1990-94; chmn. exec. com. Everglades Fdn., 1997-2003, chmn. program com. 2003-. With U.S. Army, 1957-58. Recipient Conservationist of Yr. award Everglades Coalition, 2001. Mem.: Explorers Club of N.Y.C., Met. Club of N.Y.C. Home: 575 Madison Ave Fl 10 New York NY 10022-8511

**RILEY, WILLIAM JAY,** federal judge; b. Lincoln, Nebr., Mar. 11, 1947; s. Don Paul and Marian Frances (Munn) R.; m. Norma Jean Mason, Dec. 27, 1965; children: Brian, Kevin, Erin. BA, U. Nebr., 1969, JD with distinction, 1972. Bar: Nebr. 1972, U.S. Dist. Ct. Nebr. 1972, U.S. Ct. Appeals (8th cir.) 1974; cert. civil trial specialist Nat. Bd. Trial Advocacy, 1994-2004. Law clk. U.S. Ct. Appeals (8th cir.), Omaha, 1972-73; assoc. Fitzgerald, Schorr Law Firm, P.C., LLO, Omaha, 1973-79; shareholder Fitzgerald, Schorr Law Firm, Omaha, 1979—2001; US Circuit Judge 8th Circuit Ct. Appeals, 2001—. Adj. prof. trial practice Creighton U. Coll. Law, Omaha, 1991—, Nebr. Law Sch., Lincoln, 2006—; chmn. fed. practice com. Fed. Ct., 1992-94; mme. criminal law com. Jud. Conf. U.S., 2005—. Scoutmaster Boy Scouts Am., Omaha, 1979—89, scout membership chair Mid. Am. coun., 1995—98, trustee, 2001—. Recipient Silver Beaver award Boy Scouts Am., 1991. Fellow Am. Coll. Trial Lawyers (chair state com. 1997-99), Nebr. State Bar Found.; mem. Am. Bd. Trial Advs. (Nebr. chpt. pres. 2000), Nebr. State Bar Assn. (bd. com. ethics com. 1996-98, ho. of dels. 1998—, profl. com. 2002—), Omaha Bar Assn. (treas. 1997-98, pres. 2000-01), Robert M. Spire Inns of Ct. (master 1994—, counselor 1997-98), Order of Coif, Phi Beta Kappa. Republican. Methodist. Avocations: reading, hiking, bicycling. Office: Roman L Hruska US Courthouse 111 S 18th Plaza Ste 4303 Omaha NE 68102-1325 Office Phone: 402-661-7575.*

**RILEY, WILLIAM JOHN,** neurologist; b. Seattle, Oct. 24, 1930; s. William John and Virginia (McCarthy) R.; m. Joan Marie Weismann, 1956 (div. 1976); children: Sean, Kevan, Megan, Janeen, Michael; m. Margit Mary Winstrom, 1976; children: Britta, Shane, Timothy. MS in Anatomy, U. Chgo., 1958, MD, 1960; PhD, U. Minn., 1965. Intern Mpls. Gen. Hosp., 1961-62; resident U. Minn. Hosps., 1962-65; asst. chief neurology Mpls. Gen. Hosp., 1965-69; chief neurology St. Luke's Episcopal Hosp., Houston, 1970-85; pres., CEO Tex. Neurol. Clinic Assn., Houston, 1969—. Staff sgt. USAF, 1951-55. Recipient Disting. Tchg. award Minn. Med. Found., 1969. Fellow: ACP, Tex. Neurol. Soc. (pres. 2002—, Lifetime Achievement award 2005), Am. Acad. Neurology; mem.: Alpha Omega Alpha, AMA, Tex. Med. Assn. (pres. 9th dist. 1991), Sigma Xi. Roman Catholic. Avocation: ranching. Office: Tex Neurol Clinic Assn 4126 SW Freeway # 1210 Houston TX 77027-7306 Office Phone: 713-621-9291. Personal E-mail: wjrileymd@aol.com.

**RILL, JAMES FRANKLIN,** lawyer; b. Evanston, Ill., Mar. 4, 1933; s. John Columbus and Frances Eleanor (Hill) R.; m. Mary Elizabeth Lanes, June 14, 1957; children: James Franklin, Roderick M. AB cum laude, Dartmouth Coll., 1954; LLB, Harvard, 1959. Bar: D.C. bar 1959. Legis. asst. Congressman James P. S. Devereux, Washington, 1952; pvt. practice Washington, 1959-89; assoc. Steadman, Collier & Shannon, 1959-63; ptnr. Collier, Shannon & Rill, 1963-69, Collier, Shannon, Rill & Scott, 1969-89; asst. atty. gen., antitrust div. U.S. Dept. Justice, Washington, 1989-92; ptnr. Collier, Shannon, Rill & Scott, Washington, 1992-2000; co-chair internat. competition policy adv.

com. U.S. Dept. Justice, 1997-2000; ptnr. Howrey Simon Arnold & White LLP, Washington, 2000—. Pub. mem. Adminstrv. Conf. of U.S., 1992-94; coun. prin. Coun. for Excellence in Govt.; mem., advisor panel Office of Tech. Assessment of Multinat. Firms and U.S. Tech. Base. Contbr. articles to profl. jours. Trustee emeritus Bullis Sch., Potomac, Md. Served to 1st lt. arty. AUS, 1954-56. Fellow: Am. Bar Found.; mem.: ABA (antitrust law sect., past chmn.), DC Bar Assn., Loudoun Valley Club, Met. Club, Phi Delta Theta. Home: 7305 Masters Dr Potomac MD 20854-3850 Office: Howrey Simon Arnold & White, LLP Rm 621 1299 Pennsylvania Ave NW Washington DC 20004-2402

**RILLING, JOHN ROBERT,** history professor; b. Wausau, Wis., Apr. 28, 1932; s. John Peter and Esther Laura (Wittig) R.; m. Joanne Marilyn McCrory, Dec. 21, 1953; children: Geoffrey Alan, Andrew Peter. BA summa cum laude, U. Minn., 1953; AM, Harvard U., 1957, PhD, 1959. Asst. prof. history U. Richmond, Va., 1959-62, assoc. prof. history, 1962-68, prof. history, 1968-99, prof. English history emeritus, 1999—, chmn. dept. history, 1977-83, Westhampton Coll., 1965-71. Pres. Faculty Senate of Va., 1975—77. Contbr. articles to profl. jours. Elder, Ginter Park Presbyn. Ch., 1973-83. Served with U.S. Army, 1953-55. Recipient U. Richmond Disting. Educator award, 1975, 76, 77, 80, 87, Prof. of Yr. finalist Coun. for Advancement and Support of Edn., 1981. Woodrow Wilson fellow, 1955-59; Harvard U. travelling fellow, 1958; Coolidge fellow, 1955-56; Folger Libr. fellow, 1960. Mem.: Agecroft Assn. (bd. dir.), Am. Hist. Assn., Omicron Delta Kappa (Prof. of Yr. 1995), Phi Beta Kappa. Avocations: hiking, bicycling, enology. Home: 1507 Wilmington Ave Richmond VA 23227-4429 Office: U Richmond Dept History Richmond VA 23173 Business E-Mail: jrilling@richmond.edu.

**RIMA, INGRID HAHNE,** economics professor; b. Fed. Republic of Germany; dau. Max F. and Hertha G. (Grunsfeld) Hahne; m. Philip W. Rima; children: David, Eric. BA with honors, CUNY, 1945; MA, U. Pa., 1946, PhD, 1951. Prof. econs. Temple U., Phila., 1967—. Author: Development of Economic Analysis, 1967, 6th edit., 2000, Labor Markets Wages and Employment, 1981, The Joan Robinson Legacy, 1991, The Political Economy of Global Restructuring, Vol. I, Production and Organization, Vol. II, Trade and Finance, 1993, Measurement, Quantification and Economic Analysis, 1994, Labor Markets in a Global Economy, 1996. Fulbright Disting. Lectr., Lingnan U., China, 2000. Fellow Ea. Econ. Assn.; mem. Am. Econ. Assn., History of Econs. Soc. (pres. 1993-4), Phi Beta Kappa (pres. chpt. 2006). Office: Temple U Broad & Montgomery Ave Philadelphia PA 19122 Personal E-mail: irima@aol.com.

**RIMEL, IRA WESLEY,** writer, US Navy supply officer, real estate specialist, real estate appraiser, real estate broker; b. Wibaux, Mont., Jan. 10, 1921; s. Ira Dice and Hazel Barbara (Webber) Rimel; m. Mary Mackinlay, Dec. 13, 1943 (div.). children: Patricia, Valerie, Linda, David, Glenn. Basic sci./engring. Mont. Sch. Mines, 1943—44; BA in mgmt./acctg., U. Wash., 1943—47; Navy supply, acctg. grad., Harvard Grad. Sch. Bus., 1945—46; nat. security, econ., Indust. Coll. Armed Forces, 1965. Tech. writer Military Manuals Co., Renton, Wash., 1952—55; indsl. agent No. Pacific Railway, Seattle, 1955—58; right of way agent/supr. Mont. Hwy. Dept., Helena, 1958—65; right of way agent Lane County, Eugene, Oreg., 1965—86; columnist Fishing & Hunting News, Seattle, 1992—95; freelance writer, 1956—. Ensign, reserve, supply, disbursing, acctg. officer U.S. Navy Naval Prison, Norfolk, Va., 1946; LTJG supply officer liaison U.S. Navy, Republic of Korea, 1950—51. Author: (short stories) Dynamic Tension, 1990 (First Prize, 1990), Lucky Man, 2002 (Best of Show/Class, 2002), Winter Travel, 2002 (First Prize, 2002). Adj., publicity officer/comdr. Disabled Am. Vet., Renton, Wash., 1952—58, Wash. publicity officer Seattle, 1953—58; lifetime mem. VFW, Marcola, Oreg., 1960—2003. Lt. jr. grade USN, 1942—46, WWII, Korea, lt. jr. grade USN, 1950—51, WWII, Japan, selected for V-12 Coll. Prog. USN. Named rep. to Rep. Korea, Yokosuka, Japan, Celebration of Commissioning Frigates to Korea, U.S. Navy, 1950; recipient com., Mont. Sports Outdoors, Missoula, 1959, Author "Lady Gets Her Buck", 1959. Mem.: DAV. Avocations: hunting, fishing, boating, horseback riding, gardening.

**RIMEL, REBECCA WEBSTER,** foundation administrator; BS, U. Va., 1973; MBA, James Madison U., 1983. Head nurse, emergency dept. U. Va. Hosp., Charlottesville, 1973-74, coord. med. out-patient dept., 1974-75, nurse practitioner dept. neurosurgery, 1975-77, instr. in neurosurgery, 1975-80, asst. prof., 1981-83; program mgr. health Pew Charitable Trusts, Phila., 1983-84; asst. v.p. Glenmede Trust Co., Pew Charitable Trusts, Phila., 1984-85; v.p. for programs Pew Charitable Trusts, Phila., 1985-88, exec. dir., 1988-94, pres., 1994—. Mem. Coun. on Founds., Washington; prin. investigator dept. neurosurgery U. Va., 1981—83; adv. coun. Boxing U.S. Olympics, 1983—86; adv. coun. Nat. Inst. of Neurol. Disorders and Strokes, 1988—91. bd. dirs., Thomas Jefferson Meml. Found., Deutsche Banc Flag Investors Fund. Contbr. chpts. in books, articles and abstracts to profl. jours. Recipient Disting. Nursing Alumni award, U. Va., 1988; fellow Kellogg Nat. fellow, 1992. Mem.: APHA, ANA, Va. State Nurses Assn. (membership and credentials com. 1982—86), Emergency Dept. Nurses Assn., Am. Assn. Neurosurg. Nurses, Am. Acad. Nursing.

**RIMER, BARBARA K.,** health facility administrator, educator, dean; b. Wilkes Barre, Pa., Jan. 14, 1949; married. BA in English, U. Mich., 1970, MPH in Med. Care Adminstrn. and Health Edn., 1973; PhD in Health Edn., Johns Hopkins Sch. of Hygiene and Public Health, 1981. Instr. Wayne State U. Sch. Medicine, Detroit, 1973-75; program dir. Nat. Cancer Inst. Bethesda, Md., 1975-77; intervention coord. Johns Hopkins Oncology Ctr., Balt., 1977-79; rsch. assoc. Johns Hopkins Sch. Hygiene and Public Health, Balt., 1977-79; sr. health educator Fox Chase Cancer Ctr., Phila., 1981-87, dir. health comms. rsch., 1981-87, dir. behavioral rsch., 1987-91, dir. population sci. for behavioral rsch., 1990-91; dir. cancer prevention, detection and ctrl. rsch. Duke Comprehensive Cancer Ctr., Durham, NC, 1991-97; sr. fellow Aging Ctr. Duke U. Med. Ctr., Durham, NC, 1991-97, assoc. prof. in cmty. and family medicine, 1991-93, prof. cmty. and family medicine, 1993-97; acting dep. dir. Duke Comprehensive Cancer Ctr., Durham, NC, 1995-96; dir. cancer ctrl. and population scis. Nat. Cancer Inst., Rockville, Md., 1997—2002; dep. dir., population sciences, Lineberger Cancer Ctr. UNC, Chapel Hill, 2003—05, alumni disting. prof., Dept. Health Behavior & Health Edn., 2003—, assoc. dean Sch. Pub. Health, 2005—. Adj. assoc. dept. health behavior and health edn. U. N.C. Sch. of Public Health, Chapel Hill, NC, 1992-97; adj. mem. Fox Chase Cancer Ctr., Phila., 1992-97; preceptor, lectr. Temple U., 1983-91; guest lectr. Duke U. Med. Ctr., 1991-97, U. N.C. Sch. Public Health, 1991-97; Judith P. Schlager vis. prof. Dana-Farber Cancer Inst., 1995; disting. vis. lectr. Harvard U., 1998; mem. institutional review bd. Fox Chase Cancer Ctr., 1983-88, vice chair, 1988-91; proposal review, site visitor Nat. Cancer Inst., 1985-95; chairperson tech. advisory com. Am. Lung Assn., 1987; external advisory com. Vermont Regional Cancer Ctr., 1988-89; advisory com. Brown U., U. R.I. Cancer Prevention Rsch. unit, 1988-95; mem. Am. Assn. Retired Persons task force on smoking, 1989-91, Health Promotion adv. bd. Wesley Found., 1990-91, program com. annual mtg. Am. Soc. Preventive Oncology, 1990-93, chair, 1993 mtg., expert adv. com. AMC Cancer Rsch. Ctr./Ctrs. for Disease Ctrl. Coop. Agreement, 1991, adult edn. subcom. and tobacco materials review group Am. Cancer Soc., 1991; mem. Nat. Task Force on Breast Cancer Ctrl. Am. Cancer Soc., 1992, chair Nat. and State (NC) Task Force on Breast Cancer Ctrl., 1992; mem. Pub. Edn. subcom. on Adult Edn. Am. Cancer Soc., 1992; mem. adv. bd. Office of Cancer Comms., NCI, 1992; mem. Clin. Cancer com. Duke U. Med. Ctr., 1992-95; mem. Cancer Ctrs.' Support com. NCI, 1993-94, Recruitment and Adherence com. Office of Women's Health NIH, 1993, Report com. Internat. Workshop on Screening for breast cancer NCI, 1993, Detection and Treatment subcom. on Breast Cancer Am. Cancer Soc., 1993, 94, Nominating com. Soc. Behavioral Medicine, 1993-96, adv. com. on cancer coordination and ctrl. State of NC, 1993-97; invited participant and com. chair Frontiers of Behavioral Medicine mtg., Chantilly, Va., 1993; invited co-chair Sec. Shala-la's Mtg. to develop nat. strategic plan for breast cancer, Bethesda, Md., 1993; chair, mem. Nat. Cancer Adv. Bd. (presdl. appointment), 1994-97; bd. dirs.

Am. Family Life Assurance Corp., 1995—; fellowship selection com. Am. Assn. Cancer Rsch., 1996; mem. exec. com. Acad. Behavioral Medicine Rsch., 1998, Charles S. Mott Selection com. of Gen. Motors Cancer Rsch. Found., 1999, Inst. Medicine com. effective health comm. and behavior change strategies for diverse populations, 2000. Editor: special cancer issue Health Education Research, 1998-89; editl. bd. Health Education Quarterly, 1985-87, guest editl. bd. 1983; editl. bd. Jour. of Compliance in Health Care, 1989-90, Health Edn. Rsch., 1990-98, Cancer Prevention, Epidemiology and Biomarkers, 1990—, Patient Edn. and Counseling, 1994—, Breast Diseases, 1998—, Cancer Causes and Control, 1998—, Effective Clin. Practice, 2000—; assoc. editor: Preventive Medicine, 1990—; reviewer Am. Jour. Preventive Medicine, Am. Jour. Public Health, Annals of Internal Medicine, Health Edn. Quarterly, Health Services Research, Jour. of Am. Med. Assn., Jour. Nat. Cancer Inst., Milbank Quarterly, Women's Health, 1986—; contbr. numerous articles, papers to profl. pubs. Fellow Johns Hopkins Sch. of Hygiene and Public Health, 1979-81, Soc. of Behavioral Medicine, 1997; recipient Mayhew Derryberry award Am. Public Health Assn., 1992, Best Visual Presentation of Session award Soc. of Behavioral Medicine, San Diego, 1995, Citation award Soc. Behavioral Medicine, 1996, Disting. Achievement award Am. Soc. Preventive Oncology, 1997, Herbert J. Block Leadership award Ohio State U., 1997, John P. McGovern award in Health Promotion U. Tex. Sch. Public Health, 1999. Office: Sch Public Health Univ North Carolina 170 Rosenau Hall Campus Box 7400 Chapel Hill NC 27599-7400 Office Phone: 919-966-3215. Office Fax: 919-966-7678. E-mail: brimer@unc.edu.*

**RIMER, JOHN THOMAS,** language educator, academic administrator, writer; b. Pitts., Mar. 2, 1933; s. John T. and Naomi (Bowser) R.; m. Laurence E. Mus., Apr. 18, 1964; children: John, Mark. BA, Princeton U., 1954; MA, Columbia U., 1969, PhD, 1971. Asst. cultural officer USIA, Laos, Japan; then dir. Am. Cultural Ctr. Kobe, Japan, 1958-67; assoc. prof., then prof. Japanese lang. and lit. Washington U., St. Louis, 1973-83, chmn. dept. Chinese and Japanese, 1973-83; chief Asian div. Library of Congress, Washington, 1983-86; chmn. Hebrew and East Asian langs. and lits. U. Maryland, College Park, 1986-91; chmn. East Asian langs. and lits. U. Pitts., 1991—2005; ret., 2005. Mem. Am. adv. bd. Japan Found., 1984- Author: Toward a Modern Japanese Theatre, 1974, Traditions in Modern Japanese Fiction, 1978; translator: stories Mori Ogai, 2 vols., 1977, Mask and Sword: Two Plays for the Contemporary Japanese Theatre, 1980, On the No Drama, 1983, Pilgrimages, 1988, A Reader's Guide to Japanese Literature, 1988; editor: Multiple Meanings, 1987; editor, contbr.: Culture and Identity, Japanese Intellectuals during the Interwar Years, 1990, Shisendo, 1991, Youth and Other Stories by Mori Ogai, 1994, Kyoto Encounters, 1995, A Hidden Fire: Russian and Japanese Cultural Encounters, 1868-1929, 1995, The Blue-eyed Tarōkaja: Essays by Donald Keene, 1996, Nara Encounters, 1997, The Voyage of Japanese Theatre: Theatre Criticism of Senda Akihiko, 1997, Poems to Sing: The Wakan Rōeishū, 1997, (with Marlene J. Mayo) War, Occupation, and Creativity: Japan and East Asia 1920-1960, 2001, Collected Writings of J. Thomas Rimer, 2004, (with Van Gessel The Columbia Anthology of Japanese Literature, 2005, (with Stephen Ausiss and Gerald Broemor) Traditional Japeneses Arts and Cultures: An Illustrated Sourcebook, 2006. Served with U.S. Army, 1955-58. NEH fellow France, 1976-77; NEH grantee, 1979-81; recipient Order of the Sacred Treasure award Japanese Govt., 1997. Episcopalian. Home: 4319 Redwood #1 Marina Del Rey CA 90292-7643 Office Phone: 412-624-5568.

**RIMES, LEANN,** country music singer; b. Jackson, Miss., Aug. 28, 1982; m. Dean Sheremet, Feb. 23, 2002. Singer: (albums) Blue, 1996, Unchained Melody: The Early Years, 1997, You Light Up My Life: Inspirational Songs, 1997 (Contemporary Christian Album of Yr., 1998), Sittin' on Top of the World, 1998, LeAnn Rimes, 1999, I Need You, 2001, God Bless America, 2001, Twisted Angel, 2002, Greatest Hits, 2003, What a Wonderful World, 2004, This Woman, 2005; co-writer: (TV films) Holiday in Your Heart, 1997; guest appearance (TV films) Holiday in Your Heart, 1997, (TV series) American Dreams, 2003, (TV) Days of Our Lives, 1998, Moesha, 1999, MadTV, 2000, Tinseltown TV, 2003, and several others, (films) Coyote Ugly, 2000, host Nashville Star, 2003—; performer: (TV) LeAnn Rimes Live, 2003, LeAnn Rimes: Custom Concert, 2004; author: (children's books) Jag, 2003, Jag's New Friend, 2004; singer: (soundtrack) Can't Fight The Moonlight from Coyote Ugly (Favorite Song, Blockbuster award, 2001), Looking Through Your Eyes for Quest for Camelot, (soundtrack-TV miniseries) I Need You for Jesus, 2000. Internat. spokesperson Children's Miracle Network; established LeAnn Rimes Adventure Gym (Vanderbilt Children's Hosp.), Nashville. Nominated Best Country Singer award, Country Music Assn., 1996; recipient Best New Artist,(youngest person to win a top award) & Best Female Country Vocal Performance, Grammy award, 1997, Song of Yr. & Single Record of Yr., Blue, Top New Female Vocalist, Acad. of Country Music, 1997, Horizon award, Country Music Assn., 1997, Favorite Female Artist, Blockbuster award, 1998; named Female Rising Video Star of Yr., Country Music Television (CMT), 1997, New Country Act of Yr., Internat. Touring Talent Pub., Internat. Rising Star, British Country Music Awards, Artist of Yr., North Tex. Music Festival, Country Single Sale Artist of Yr., Female Country Artist of Yr., Contemporary Christian Artist of Yr., Billboard, 1998 and others. Office: care Curb Records 3907 W Alameda Ave 2d Fl Burbank CA 91505-4332

**RIMINGTON, JAMES EARL,** music educator, consultant; b. Canton, Ill., Jan. 6, 1950; s. Wilfred Earl and Alma Louise Rimington; m. Jill Marie Laun, June 21, 1970; children: Angela Marie Rimington Chase, James Ryan. BMusEd, Bradley U., 1972; MMusEd, U. Ill., Champaign, 1981, PhD in Curriculum and Instrn., 2000. Music educator Elmwood Pub. Schs., Ill., 1972—73, Danville Pub. Schs., 1973—77, Geneseo Pub. Schs., 1977—95; choral dir. Ea. Ill. U., Charleston, 1995—97; music educator Lincoln Way H.S., New Lenox, 1997—99; dir. music edn. Valdosta State U., Ga., 1999—2000; profl. preparation Ill. State Bd. Edn., Springfield, 2000—01; cons. music educator Pekin H.S., 2001—. Choir dir. Grace Meth. Ch., Pekin, Ill., 2004—. Contbr. articles to profl. jours. Named Outstanding Young Music Educator, Geneseo (Ill.) Jaycees, 1984; recipient Outstanding Young Religious Leader, 1982. Mem.: Ill. Edn. Assn., Ill. Music Educators Assn. (dist. svc. award 2001, pres. 1972—). Democrat. Lutheran. Avocations: singing, golf, piano, model railroads. Home: 2109 Sierra Dr Pekin IL 61554-6315 Office: Pekin Cmty HS 1903 Ct St Pekin IL 61554 Business E-Mail: jrimington@pekinhigh.net.

**RIMLAND, LISA PHILLIP,** writer, composer, lyricist; b. Stamford, Conn., Mar. 27, 1954; d. Maurice Louis and Eva (Kreiz) R. BA, U. Conn., 1978. Owner Ph Rimland Press, Storrs, Conn., 1991—. Composer numerous songs, including Your Heart or Mine, 1990, Drive Me Crazy, 1991, Send Me an Angel, 1992, Geography of Heaven, 1990, 2002, The Winds of Time (The Cloning Song), 2003; author: The Candida Manual: Candida Overgrowth and the Quest for Human Wellness, 1999, Voices From the Farm, 1999, Machronomarker Observations Conducted During the First Three Months of the Life of a Cloned Heifer Dairy Calf, 2000, An Evaluation of Machronomarker Observations, 2001, Amy and Aspen: Behavioral Observations of a Cloned Holstein Cow and Her Genetic Donor Living Together in Pasture, 2003, Betty and Cathy With Aspen In Summer, 2004, Behavioral Observations of Two Cloned Holstein Cows and Their Genetic Donor Living Together in Pasture, 2006; contbr. articles, poems, essays to profl. jours. Vol. dairy barn U. Conn., 1992—, vol. photographer Morgan horse facility, 1982-91. Recipient DAR award, 1969, Soc. Women Engrs. award, 1971, Editor's Choice award Nat. Libr. Poetry, 1995, 96; Nat. Merit scholar, 1972. Mem. ASCAP. Avocations: film and drama, art, poetry, athletics, morgan horses. Home: PO Box 408 Storrs Mansfield CT 06268-0408

**RIMLER, ANITA A.,** former state official; b. 1944; m. George W. Rimler. Campaign aide, legis. asst. former Del. Rob James, 1975; asst. to atty. gen. Mary Sue Terry State of Va., Richmond, 1985—91; fin. ops. Terry for Gov. campaign, 1993, Robb for Senate campaign, 1994, Warner's U.S. Senate campaign, 1996; sr. advisor, dir. fin. ops. Warner for Gov. campaign; sec. of state State of Va., Richmond, 2002—06. Democrat.*

**RIMOIN, DAVID LAWRENCE,** medical geneticist; b. Montreal, Nov. 9, 1936; s. Michael and Fay (Lecker) Rimoin; m. Mary Ann Singleton, 1962 (div. 1979); 1 child, Anne; m. Ann Piilani Garber, July 27, 1980; children: Michael, Lauren. BSc, McGill U., Montreal, 1957, MSc, MD, CM, 1961; PhD, Johns Hopkins U., 1967; LHD (hon.), Finch U., 1997. Asst. prof. medicine, pediat. Washington U., St. Louis, 1967—70; assoc. prof. UCLA, 1970—73, prof., 1973—; chief med. genetics, Harbor-UCLA Med. Ctr., 1970—86; chair dept. pediat., dir. Med. Genetics and Birth Defects Ctr. Cedars-Sinai Med. Ctr., L.A., 1986—2004, Steven Spielberg chair, 1989—; dir. Med. Genetics Inst., 2004—. Chmn. coun. Med. Genetics Orgn., 1993. Co-editor: Emory and Rimoin's Principles and Practice of Medical Genetics, 1983, 5th edit., 2006; contbr. articles to profl. jours., chapters to books. Recipient E. Mead Johnson award, Am. Acad. Pediat., 1976, Col. Harland Saunders award, March of Dimes, 1997, Pioneer in Medicine award, Cedars Sinai Med. Ctr., 2001, Extraordinary Merit award, UCLA Med. Alumni Assn., 2005, Legends Harbor award, UCLA Med. Ctr., 2006, Leadership award, Am. Soc. Human Genetics, 2006. Fellow: Am. Coll. Med. Genetics (pres. 1991—96, bd. dirs. 1996—2000), AAAS, ACP; mem.: Inst. of Medicine, Assn. Am. Physicians, Am. Pediat. Soc., Am. Soc. Human Genetics (pres. 1984, Leadership award 2006), Am. Bd. Med. Genetics (pres. 1979—83), Western Soc. Pediat. Rsch. (pres. 1995, Ross Outstanding Young Investigator award 1976), Western Soc. Clin. Rsch. (pres. 1978,), Am. Fedn. Clin. Rsch. (sec.-treas. 1972—75), Am. Coll. Med. Genetics Found. (pres. 1999—2002, bd. dirs. 2002—), Johns Hopkins Soc. Scholars. Office: Cedars Sinai Med Ctr 8700 Beverly Blvd Los Angeles CA 90048-1865 Office Phone: 310-423-4461. Business E-Mail: david.rimoin@cshs.org.

**RIMPEL, AUGUSTE EUGENE, JR.,** management and technical consulting executive; b. St. Thomas, V.I., Aug. 25, 1939; s. Auguste Eugene and Leah Eudora (Harris) R. B.A. magna cum laude, Inter-Am. U. P.R., 1957; M.S. in Ch.E., M.I.T., 1961; Ph.D., Carnegie Inst. Tech., 1964; M.B.A., Columbia U., 1964-65; m. Maria Czernetski, Sept. 23, 1966; children: Nicole, Christopher. Research chem. engr. Am. Cyanamid Co., Stamford, Conn., 1961-62; with Arthur D. Little, Inc., Cambridge, Mass., 1965-75, sr. staff mem., 1973-75; commr. of commerce, spl. advisor to gov. for econ. affairs Govt. U.S. V.I., St. Thomas, 1975-78; mem. corp. spl. staff Arthur D. Little, Inc., Cambridge, 1978-81, also v.p. Arthur D. Little Internat., Inc.; v.p. Booz-Allen and Hamilton, Inc., 1981-83; v.p., ptnr., Price Waterhouse, 1983-98, ptnr. Price Waterhouse Coopers, 1998—; sr. partner Boston Global Partners, 2001-; Bd. dirs. Caribbean/Lat. Am. Action, 1979-; chair, bd. dirs. U. V.I., 1997—; mem. subcoms. on internat. econ. devel. U.S.C. of C., 1980-83; bd. dirs. travel adv. bd. U.S. Dept. Commerce, 1977-78; pres. Caribbean Tourism Assn., 1977-78; bd. dirs., mem. exec. com. Caribbean Tourism Research Center, 1976-78. Mem. Am. Inst. Chem. Engrs., Am. Chem. Soc., Am. Inst. Chemists, Soc. Internat. Devel., Sigma Xi. Office: Ste 400 283 Franklin St Boston MA 02103-1195 E-mail: arimpel@aol.com.

**RIMSZA, SKIP,** former mayor; b. Chgo. m. Kim Gill; children: Brian, Jenny, Alexander, Taylor, Nicole. Mem. Phoenix City Coun., 1990-94; vice mayor City of Phoenix, 1993, mayor, 1994—2003. Former pres. Bd. Realtors. Mem. several cmty. bds.

**RINACA, JAMES M.,** lawyer; b. Harrisonburg, Va., Dec. 12, 1950; BS in Nuclear Engring. with highest distinction, Univ. Va., 1973, JD, 1976. Bar: Va. 1976. Ptnr., regulated industries, govtl. rels.; co-head, energy, telecom. team Hunton & Williams LLP, Richmond, Va. Mem.: ABA, Va. Engring. Found. (past pres., bd. dir.), Va. State Bar Assn., Richmond Bar Assn., Raven Soc., Omicron Delta Kappa, Tau Beta Pi. Office: Hunton & Williams LLP Riverfront Plz East Tower 951 Byrd St Richmond VA 23219-4074 Office Phone: 804-788-8334. Office Fax: 804-788-8218. Business E-Mail: jrinaca@hunton.com.

**RINAKER, SAMUEL MAYO, JR.,** retired utilities executive; b. Chgo., Sept. 29, 1922; s. Samuel Mayo and Marjorie (Horton) R.; m. Alice Benthey, Dec. 17, 1949 (div. 1974); children: Elizabeth Cherry, Samuel M. III, Laura Frazier, Mary Clark. Student, UCLA, 1941-42. Farmer, Nebr. and Ill., 1946-49; exec. sec. to atty. gen. Olympia, Wash., 1949-52; news dir. Sta. KTNT-TV, Tacoma, Wash., 1952-57, Sta. KIRO-TV, Seattle, 1957-60; assoc. news dir., news anchor Sta. KGTV, San Diego, 1960-75; dir. pub. policy San Diego Gas & Electric Co., 1976-84. Bd. dirs. 1st Nat. Bank, Beatrice, Neb., 1976-93. Maj. U.S. Army Air Corps, 1942-46, ETO. Mem. Rotary (bd. dirs. 1965-67), La Jolla Beach Tennis Club. Republican. Presbyterian. Avocation: golf. Home: 5935 Rutgers Rd La Jolla CA 92037-7834 E-mail: smr11@san.rr.com.

**RINALDI, ANTONIO,** engineering educator; b. Torino, Italy, Sept. 12, 1975; PhD in Mech. Engring., Ariz. State U., 2004. Cert. 6 Sigma grad. Maintenance engr. Alitalia, Rome, 2000; rsch. prof. Ariz. State U., Tempe, 2004—. Contbr. articles to profl. jours. Recipient NSF fellowship for nanotechs. study, 2003. Mem.: Ordine Ingegneri di Rome.

**RINALDI, JAMES J.,** federal agency administrator; BA in computer sci., U. North Fla. Various positions ending as sr. v.p. info. resources, ops. and services Marriott Corp., Bethesda, Md.; dir. e-Govt. program office, chief info. tech. services IRS, Washington; chief info. officer FDA, Rockville, Md., NASA Jet Propulsion Lab., Pasadena, Calif., 2005—. Named one of Premier 100 IT Leaders, Computerworld, 2005. Office: Jet Propulsion Lab 4800 Oak Grove Dr Pasadena CA 91109 Office Phone: 818-354-4321.*

**RINALDI, TINA,** travel company executive, writer; b. Newark, Nov. 13, 1966; d. Charles and Anne Marie Rinaldi. Cert. travel and tourism. Author: (book) What The Brochures Didn't Tell You. Mem.: NAFE (assoc.).

**RINALDO, PETER MERRITT,** publishing executive; b. Evanston, Ill., June 21, 1922; s. Philip Sidney and Harriet Huntington (Beach) R.; m. Dorothy Hastings Warren, July 20, 1946; children: David, Marjory, John. BA, Bowdoin Coll., 1943; BS, MIT, 1944, MS, 1947. Chem. engr. Dewey & Almy Chem. Co., Cambridge, Mass., 1947-54; v.p. overseas chem. divsn. W.R. Grace & Co., Cambridge, Mass., 1954-65, v.p. indsl. chem. group N.Y.C., 1965-77, v.p. gen. indsl. prodn. group, 1977-82; pres. Dorpete Press, Briarcliff Manor, N.Y., 1982—. Chmn. bd. Flexible Steel Lacing Co., Downers Grove, Ill., 1984-96; cons. Nat. Exec. Serv. Corps., N.Y.C., 1982-85. Author: The Five-day Week End, 1989, Unnecessary Wars?, 1993, Marrying the Natives, 1996, The Great Reindeer Caper, 1997, Nature, Nurture, and Chance, 1998, Atheists, Agnostics, and Deists in America, 2000. Pres. Briarcliff Vol. Fire Dept., Briarcliff Manor, N.Y. 1983-85; pres. bd. trustees Ossinining (N.Y.) Pub. Libr., 1990-92. Lt. USN, 1944-46. Mem. Am. Chem. Soc., Am. Inst. Chem. Engineers. Avocations: hiking, canoeing, nordic skiing. Home: 428 Savage Farm Dr Ithaca NY 14850 E-mail: prinaldo@twcny.rr.com.

**RINAMAN, JAMES CURTIS, JR.,** lawyer; b. Miami, Fla., Feb. 8, 1935; s. James Curtis and Ruth Marie (Rader) R.; m. Gloria Margaret Kaspar; children: James, Mark, Christine, Karen BA, U. Fla., 1955, JD, 1960. Bar: Fla. 1960, U.S. Dist. Ct. (so. dist.) Fla. 1960, U.S. Ct. Appeals (5th cir.) 1960, U.S. Supreme Ct. 1963, U.S. Dist. Ct. (mid. dist.) Fla. 1967, U.S. Dist. Ct. (no. dist.) Fla. 1981, U.S. Ct. Appeals (11th cir.) 1981, U.S. Ct. Claims 1991, U.S. Ct. Mil. Appeals 1994; cert. civil trial lawyer Fla. Bar. With Marks, Gray, Conroy & Gibbs, P.A., Jacksonville, Fla., 1960—. Gen. counsel Fla. Bd. Architecture, 1965-79, City of Jacksonville, 1970-71, Jacksonville C. of C., 1973-76, 90; adj. prof. Coll. Architecture, U. Fla., 1975-90; dir. gen. The Southern Acad. Letters, Arts and Scis., 1997—. Pres. Jacksonville Cmty. Coun. Inc., 1985. Leadership Jacksonville, Montreal, 1978, 1987; mem. Jacksonville Transp. Authority, 1971-80, Jacksonville Base Realignment and Closure Commn., 1993-95. Jacksonville Cecil Field Devel. Commn., 1994-96; chmn. N.E. Fla. chpt. ARC, 1996. With U.S. Army, 1955-57, Fla. NG, 1957-92 ret. brig. gen., 1992. Named to U.S. Fla. Hall of Fame. Fellow Am. Coll. Trial Lawyers, Am. Bar Found., Fla. Bar Found. (bd. dirs. 1982-87, 88, Disting. Svc. award 1983, 86, Medal of Honor 1988); mem. ABA (ho. of dels. 1982-86), Jacksonville Bar Assn. (pres. 1972-73, Lawyer of Yr. 1994), The

Fla. Bar (pres. 1982-83), Def. Rsch. Inst. (so. regional v.p. 1980-83, bd. dirs. 1976-78, 83-87), Am. Judicature Soc. (Herbert Harley award 1987), Fla. Coun. Bar Pres. (Outstanding Past Pres. award 1989), Lawyers for Civil Justice (pres. 1989-91, chmn. bd. dirs 1991-94), Vol. Lawyers Resource Ctr. of Fla., (pres. 1984-89, chmn. bd. dirs. 1989-93), So. Conf. of Bar, Nat. Conf. of Bar, Assn. Def. Trial Attys. (internat. pres. 1976-77), Internat. Assn. Def. Counsel, Jacksonville Assn. Def. Counsel, Fla. Defense Lawyers Assn. (pres. 1973), Fla. C. of C., Jacksonville C. of C. (chmn. 1994), Meninak Civic Club (pres. 1986), Jacksonville Commodores League, The Army War Coll. Alumni Assn. (life), Fla. Blue Key, San. Jose Country Club, River Club, Phi Gamma Delta (bd. trustees ednl. found. 1995—), Phi Alpha Delta. Republican. Methodist. Office: Marks Gray Conroy & Gibbs 1200 Riverplace Blvd Ste 800 Jacksonville FL 32207-1805 also: PO Box 447 Jacksonville FL 32201-0447 Office Phone: 904-398-0900. E-mail: jrinaman@marksgray.com.

**RINARD, ARTHUR CALVIN,** secondary school educator; b. Monterey Park, Calif., Oct. 2, 1955; s. Arthur Calvin Rinard and Luretta Pearl Rhoades-Rideout; m. Candy Lee Rinard, Mar. 19, 1994; children: Alexander Calvin, Nathan Shane, Noad David; m. Andrea Elizabeth Osborn, July 10, 1980 (div. May 10, 1986); children: Lawrence Tyrone Williams, Nathaniel James Williams. BA in Youth Agy. Adminstrn., Pepperdine U., Malibu, Calif., 1982. Tchr. math. Job Corps, LA, 1996—98; tchr. social sci. LA County Office Edn., Downey, 1998—2000, Whittier Union H.S. Dist., 2000—. Adult leader Boy Scouts Am., Alhambra, Calif., 1973—2006. Recipient Eagle Scout, Boy Scouts of Am., 1975; scholar, Haggi Found., 1995, Armington Found., 1980. Mem.: Whittier Secondary Edn. Assn. (chpt. pres. 2004—05), Nat. Coun. Econ. Edn., Nat. Coun. Social Studies, Calif. Coun. Social Studies. Avocation: hiking. Office: Whittier Union High Sch 12417 Philadelphia St Whittier CA 90601-3994 Office Phone: 562-698-8121.

**RINDEN, DAVID LEE,** clergyman; b. Lake Mills, Iowa, Aug. 1, 1941; s. Oscar Henry and Iva (Stensrud) R.; m. Gracia Elizabeth Carlson, Sept. 11, 1966; children: Jonathan, Elizabeth, Amy. BA, Moorhead State U., 1964; diploma, Luth. Brethren Sem., 1966; postgrad., Seattle Pacific U., 1973. Ordained to ministry Luth. Ch., 1967. Pastor Bethesda Luth. Ch., Eau Claire, Wis., 1968-72, Maple Pk. Luth. Ch., Lynnwood, Wash., 1972-79; v.p. Ch. of the Luth. Brethren of Am., Fergus Falls, Minn., 1991—; editor Faith & Fellowship, Fergus Falls, Minn., 1979-2000; exec. dir. Faith and Fellowship Press Ch. of the Luth. Brethren of Am., Fergus Falls, 1979-2000; pastor Gethsemane Lutheran Ch., Rochester, Minn., 2000—. Chmn. com. on commitment Ch. of Luth. Brethren, Fergus Falls, 1981-82, com. on role of women in ch., 1984-86, chmn. com. on 90th anniversary, chmn. bd. publs., 1968-78. Editor: Explanation of Luther's Small Catechism, 1988; author: Biblical Foundations, 1981. Founding com. JAIL, Inc., Fergus Falls, 1991; pres. bd. dirs. Fergus Falls Fed. Community Credit Union, 1987-2000. Mem. Fergus Falls Ministerial Assn. (sec. 1989-90, v.p. 1991-92, pres. 1992-93) Kiwanis (pres. 1994-95, lt. gov. 1996-97). Home: 1925 Century Valley Rd NE Rochester MN 55906-7705 Office: Gethsemane Lutheran Ch 2204 22d St NW Rochester MN 55901

**RINDER, LAWRENCE R.,** curator; Curator 20th-century art & contemporary projects Berkeley Art Museum; found. dir. Wattis Inst. Calif. Coll. of Arts, San Francisco; curator contemporary art Whitney Museum of Am. Art, NYC, 2000—04, adjunct curator, 2004—; dean grad. studies California Coll. of Arts, San Francisco, 2004—. Office: California Coll of Arts 1111 Eighth St San Francisco CA 94107-2247

**RINDFUSS, RONALD RICHARD,** social studies educator; b. Buffalo, Dec. 11, 1946; married Aug. 1968; 2 children. BA, Fordham U., 1968; PhD, Princeton U., 1974. Rsch. asst. Nat. Fertility Study, Office Population Rsch., Princeton U., 1971-73; rsch. assoc. Ctr. Demography and Ecology U. Wis., Madison, 1973-76; asst. prof. sociology U. N.C., Chapel Hill, 1976-79, assoc. prof., 1979-84, prof. sociology, 1984-2000, Robert Paul Ziff Disting. prof., 2000—; dir. Carolina Population Ctr., Chapel Hill, 1992-97; sr. fellow East-West Ctr., Honolulu, 2006—. Cons. in field Contbr. numerous articles to profl. jours.; assoc. editor Social Forces, 1976—; cons. editor Am. Jour. Sociology, 1977-80; contbg. editor Sociol Biology, 1974; referee for numerous jours. Recipient NIH traineeship, 1968—71, 1st place Erdas award for best sci. paper on remote sensing, 2000. Fellow: AAAS (mem. nominating com. sect. K 2001—03); mem.: Sociol. Rsch. Assn., Coun. on Family Rsch., So. Sociol. Soc., So. Regional Demographic Group, Nat. Coun. on Family Rels., Internat. Union for Sci. Study Population, Population Assn. Am. (bd. dirs. 1984—87, Mindel C. Sheps award com. 1990, pres. 1991), Am. Sociol. Assn. (publs. com. 1983—84, chmn. sociology of population sect. 1989—90). Office: Carolina Population Ctr CB # 8120 University Sq 123 W Franklin St Chapel Hill NC 27516-2524 Office Phone: 919-966-7779. E-mail: Ron_Rindfuss@unc.edu.

**RINDLER, ROBERT,** academic administrator; b. NYC, May 21, 1948; BArch, The Cooper Union, 1970; M in Environ. Design, Yale U., 1972; Mgmt. Devel. Program, Harvard U., 1993-95. Chair art dept. U. Vt., Burlington, 1975-79; dean of students Boston Arch. Ctr., 1980-86; assoc. provost R.I. Sch. Design, Providence, 1986-94; dean Sch. Art The Cooper Union, NYC, 1994—2004; pres. Milw. Inst. of Art & Design, 2005—. One man shows include Pace U., N.Y., 1972, U. Vt., 1980, Harvard U., 1985, R.I. Sch. Design, 1990, Richard DeMarco Gallery, Edinborough, Scotland, Boston Archtl. Ctr., Yale U. Art Gallery. mem. art steering com. R.I. State Coun. Arts, Providence, 1992-94. Grantee NEA, 1973, 74, Vt. Coun. Arts, 1977, Mass. Counc. Arts, 1980. Mem. Nat. Assn. Schs. Art and Design, Coll. Art Assn., Internat. Coun. Fine Arts Deans, Assn. Ind. Schs. Art and Design (bd. dirs. 1994—). Office: Milw Inst Art & Design 273 E Erie St Milwaukee WI 53202 E-mail: rindler@niad.edu.

**RINDSKOPF, DAVID,** statistician, educator; b. St. Louis; s. Wallace and Lorraine Rindskopf; m. Laurie Hopp. PhD, Iowa State U., Ames, 1976. Disting. prof. CUNY Grad. Ctr., NYC, 1979—. Cons. statistician Bus. Week, NY State Atty. Gen., Kaplan Ednl. Svcs. Contbr. articles to profl. jours. Grantee, US Dept. Edn., 2005. Fellow: Am. Statis. Assn. (pres. NY chpt. 1986—88, Note: Fellow status is for lifetime achievement 2002). Office: CUNY Grad Ctr 365 Fifth Ave New York NY 10016 Office Phone: 212-817-8287. E-mail: stat101@optonline.net.

**RINE, MARK BRADIGAN,** metrology specialist; b. Jacksonville, Fla., Apr. 1, 1956; s. Ronald F. and Karen Rine. BBA, The Citadel, 1978. Insp. Weber-Knapp Co., Jamestown, NY, 1978—79; chief insp. Watson Mfg. Co., Jamestown, 1979—81; gage calibration technician Cummins Engine Co., Lakewood, 1981—2000; metrology specialist Consolidated Diesel Co., Whitakers, NC, 2000—. Mem. Am. Wildlife Assn., Jamestown, 1969—73, Big Brother Assn., Charleston, SC, 1974—78, Crippled Children Assn., Charleston, 1974—78; chmn. Bd. Employees, Jamestown, 1991—95; coach Little League, Jamestown, NY, 1997—99; asst. scout master Order of the Arrow. 2d lt. USMC Res., 1974—78. Recipient Jux Weinberg award, Chautauqua County Boy Scouts Am., 1969, Eagle Scout. Mem.: Am. Soc. Quality. Republican. Baptist. Avocations: sailing, swimming. Office Phone: 252-437-9227.

**RINE, MAUREEN S.,** elementary school educator; b. Bridgeport, Conn., Oct. 4, 1946; d. Paul G. and Irene M. Duffner; m. Craig Lewis Rine; children: Brent, Todd. BS, U. Conn., Storrs, 1968; MS, U. Bridgeport, Conn., 1972. Cert. elem. tchr. Conn. Tchr. Trumbull (Conn.) Pub. Schs., 1968—77, Naugatuck (Conn.) Pub. Schs., 1995—. Recipient Celebration of Excellence award, Conn. Assn. Schs. Home: 461 Reservoir Rd Southbury CT 06488

**RINEARSON, PETER MARK,** journalist, writer, software executive; b. Seattle, Aug. 4, 1954; s. Peter Morley and Jeannette Irene (Love) R.; m. Jill Chan, Sept. 15, 1991. Student, U. Wash., 1972-78. Editor Sammamish Valley News, Redmond, Wash., 1975-76; reporter Seattle Times, 1976-78, govt. and polit. reporter, 1979-81, aerospace reporter, 1982-84, Asian corr., 1985-86; pres. Alki Software Corp., Seattle, 1990—, Raster Ranch, Ltd., 1995-99; sr.

v.p. Oxygen Media, 1999-2000; corp. pres. Microsoft Corp., 2002—. Mem. vis. com. Sch. Comm., U. Wash., 1996—; mem. nat. adv. bd. Poynter Inst. for Media Studies, 2000—. Author: Word Processing Power with Microsoft Word, 4th edit., 1991, Microsoft Word Style Sheets, 1987, Quick Reference Guide to Microsoft Word, 1988, Microsoft Word Companion Disk, 1988, Masterword, 1990, 91, 92, (with Bill Gates and Nathan Myhrvold) The Road Ahead, 1995, rev. edit., 1996, Babynamer.com, 1977-79, To The Day, 2001. Recipient Spl. Paul Myhre award-series Penney-Mo. Newspaper awards, 1983, Disting. Writing award Am. Soc. Newspaper Editors, 1984, Pulitzer prize for feature writing, 1984, Lowell Thomas Travel Writing award, 1984, John Hancock award,1985, semi-finalist NASA Journalist-in-Space Project, 1986; U.S.-Japan Leadership Program fellow Japan Soc., 1988.

**RINEBOLD, ALICE JUNE,** environmental scientist; b. Fostoria, Ohio, June 24, 1953; d. Rex Gene and Hilma Alice (Huff) Rinebold; 1 child, Nicholas Jeremy. AA, USAF C.C., 1982; BA in Psychology and Biol. Sci., U. No. Colo., 1983. Cert. Nat. Environ. Health Trainer NEHA, 2003, Administr. Profl. Excellence APEX, 2005. Vet. food insp. WAC, Ft. Carson, Colo., 1972—75; environ. health specialist Weld County Health Dept., Greeley, Colo., 1986—91; environ. specialist Environ. Health, City and County Denver, 1991—. Trainer Nat. Environ. Health Assn., Denver; environ. medicine tech. Master sgt. USAF Reserves, Colorado, ret., 1998. Recipient Outstanding Achievement Humanitarian award, USAF Caledonia, San Blas Islan. Mem.: Colo. Environ. Health Assn. (Honary award 1993), Nat. Environ. Health Assn. Achievements include being one of the first 5 women food inspectors in the US Army in 1972.

**RINEHART, JAMES FORREST,** international relations professor; b. Kansas City, Mo., Dec. 1, 1950; s. Kenneth Perry and Eleanor Louise (Lane) R.; m. Betty Keller, Feb. 3, 1973; children: Erica Christine, Andrew James. BA, U. Fla., Gainesville, 1972; M of Social Sci., Syracuse U., N.Y., 1991, PhD, 1993. Vis. prof. internat. rels. U. Tenn., Chattanooga, 1993-95; dir., prof. grad. program in internat. rels. U.S. Army John F. Kennedy Spl. Warfare Sch. Troy U., 1995—2001, lectr. regional studies program, 1996—2001; assoc. prof., chair dept. polit. sci. Troy U., 2001—. Author: Revolution and the Millennium: China, Mexico and Iran, 1997, Apocalyptic Faith and Political Violence: Prophets of Terror, 2006; contbr. articles to profl. jours. Mem. Coun. on Peace Rsch. in History, 1992-94; active Program on Analysis and Resolution of Conflict, Syracuse U., 1991-93; bd. dirs. Ulster Project Chattanooga, 1993-94. Capt. USAF, 1972-80. Recipient Cert. of Achievement U.S. Army JFK Spl. Warfare Ctr. and Sch., 1996. Mem. Am. Polit. Sci. Assn., Internat. Studies Assn. (exec. cou. South 2002-05, treas. 2005—), Internat. Soc. Polit. Psychology, Am. Radio Relay League, Fla. Blue Key Soc., Phi Gamma Delta. Democrat. Presbyterian. Home: 201 Hampton Ave Troy AL 36081-4045

**RINEHART, KENTON W.,** academic administrator; b. New Milford, Conn., Feb. 18, 1971; s. Herbert and Sally Rinehart; m. Deborah Rinehart, July 2, 1971; 1 child, Jackson Carter. BS in Bus., Marist Coll., 1994, BA in Psychology, 1994, MBA, 1999. Dir. transfer admission Marist Coll., Poughkeepsie, NY, 1994—99; product mktg. mgr. OpenText, Toronto, Ont., Canada, 1999—2001; dir. admission Bentley Coll., Waltham, Mass., 2001—. Mem. alumni exec. bd. Marist Coll., Poughkeepsie, 2005—06. Mem.: Nat. Assn. Coll. Admission Counselors (assoc.). Independent. Office: Bentley College 175 Forest St Waltham MA 02452 Office Phone: 781-891-2244. Home Fax: 781-891-3414; Office Fax: 781-891-3414. Business E-Mail: ugadmission@bentley.edu.

**RINEHART, NEIL,** financial consultant; b. Mt. Ayr, Iowa, May 9, 1951; s. Park and Joan Rinehart; m. Sheila Kay Funderburgh, Sept. 3, 1977; children: Allison Rinehart Billodeau, Matthew. MBA, U. Iowa, 1975. Fin. cons. E.F. Hutton, Dallas, 1977—90; sr. v.p. investments Smith Barney, Inc., Plano, Tex., 1990—2004; sr. v.p. investments, sr. portfolio mgr. UBS Financial Svc., Dallas, 2004—. Author: It's All The Same Game: The Sports Fan's Guide to Success in the Stock Market, 2003, Finding Your "A" Game: Golf, Investing and Life, 2005. Mem.: Assn. Authors and Pubs., U. Iowa Alumni Assn. Avocations: sports, sports psychology, travel. Office: UBS Fin Svc 5080 Spectrum Dr Ste 1000-W Addison TX 75001 Office Phone: 972-450-4367. E-mail: neil.rinehart@ubs.com.

**RINES, ROBERT HARVEY,** lawyer, educator, physicist, composer; b. Boston, Aug. 30, 1922; s. David and Lucy (Sandberg) R.; m. Carol Williamson, Dec. 29, 1972 (dec. 1993); 1 son, Justice Christopher; children by previous marriage: Robert Louis, Suzi Kay Ann; m. Joanne Hayes, June 2, 1996; 1 stepchild, Laura Ellen Hayes-Heuer. BS in Physics, MIT, 1942; JD, Georgetown U., 1947; PhD, Nat. Chiao Tung U., 1972; DJ (hon.), New Eng. Coll. Law, 1974; DSc (hon.), Notre Dame Coll., 1994; LLD (hon.), Franklin Pierce Law Ctr., 2004. Bar: Mass. 1947, D.C. 1947, N.H. 1974, Va. 1983, U.S. Supreme Ct., FCC, Tax Ct., U.S. and Can. patent offices; Registered profl. engr., Mass. Asst. examiner U.S. Patent Office, 1946; partner Rines & Rines, Boston, NH, 1947—; pres., founder, chmn. emeritus, prof. Franklin Pierce Law Ctr., 1973-97. Pres. Jura Corp., 1996-; bd. dirs. Megapulse, Inc., Nat. Inventors Hall of Fame Found., 1997-99. New Eng. Fish Farming Enterprises-D.E. Salmon Inc., 1983-99, Acad. Applied Sci.-Project Orbis Bangladesh and Singapore Opthamology Programs and Loch Ness Rsch. Program, 1972—, Seagull Tech., Inc., 1994-98, New Eng. Aquarium, 1973-75, Albavision Ltd. U.K., Promotion of Am. Chinese Tech., Knox Mt. Licensors Inc., Ctr. Broadcasting Corp. of N.H., Accelerated Genomics Inc., 2001-04, Sotti Records; Gordon McKay lectr. patent law Harvard, 1956-58; lectr. inventions and innovation MIT, 1962—; commerce tech. adv. bd. Dept. Commerce, 1963-67, nat. inventors coun., 1963-67, 81—; mem. N.H. Gov.'s Crime Study Com., 1976-78; trustee Mass. Eve and Ear Infirmary 2001 Author: A Study of Current World-Wide Sources of Electronic and Other Invention and Innovation; Computer Jurisprudence: Create or Perish--The Case for Patents and Inventions; patentee in field of radar and sonar, fish farming and plant nutrients; composer music for on and off broadway prodns. including Drums Under the Windows (S. O'Casey, P. Shyre), Different, Long Voyage Home (E. O'Neil, P. Shyre), Strindberg's Creditors, Whitman Portrait, Blasts and Bravos (H.L. Menken), Hizzoner the Mayor (Emmy winning tv prodn.), 1-800-Save Me and Friendly Acquaintances (Jack Betts), Bob's Dream Ballet, Lincoln Ctr., 1999, Life at MIT suite, (films) Search at Loch Ness, 2002, Irish Eyes, 2002-2004. Campaign chmn. United Fund, Belmont Mass., 1960; mem. adv. bd. Harvard-MIT Biomed. Engring. Ctr., 1976-80; bd. dirs. Allor Found. Capt. AUS, 1942-46, European and Pacific Theaters, WWII, Brevet Col., 1994, U.S. Army Signal Corps. Named to Nat. Inventors Hall of Fame, 1994, Wall of Fame U.S. Army Signal Corps, 1994; recipient Inventions citation Pres. Carter and U.S. Dept. Commerce, 1980, N.H. High Tech. Entrepreneur award, 1989, Beyond Peace award, 1989, Disting. Svc. award Bangladesh, 1990, 96, honors Town of Inverness, Scotland, 2003, Dinsdale award Soc. Sci. Exploration, 2004, Disting. Lifetime award Boston Patent Law Assn., 2004; Robert H. Rines Bldg. dedication at Franklin Pierce Law Ctr., 1993, Distance Learning Ctr. Bldg. dedication MIT, 1997. Fellow Internat. Soc. Cryptozoology; mem. IEEE (sr.), AAAS, ABA, Acad. Applied Sci. (pres., founder, Medal of Honor 1989), Am. Patent Law Assn. (Disting. Lifetime Achievement award Boston chpt. 2004), Sci. Rsch. Soc. Am., Aircraft Owners and Pilots Assn., Nat. Acad. Engring. (patent com. 1969-80, cons. to exec. officer 1979-80), Explorers Club, Harvard Club, Chemists Club, MIT Faculty Club, Nat. Lawyers Club, Capitol Hill Club, Highland Club, Commonwealth Club, Sigma Xi. Unitarian Universalist. Address: Harbor Towers Boston MA 02110 Home: 81 N State St Concord NH 03301-4329

**RING, ALICE RUTH BISHOP,** retired preventive medicine physician; b. Ft. Collins, Oct. 11, 1931; d. Ernest Otto and Mary Frances Bishop; m. Wallace Harold Ring, July 26, 1956 (div. 1969); children: Rebecca, Eric, Mark; m. Robert Charles Diefenbach, Sept. 10, 1977. BS, Colo. State U., 1953; MD, U. Colo., 1956; MPH, U. Calif., Berkeley, 1971. Diplomate Am. Bd. Preventive Medicine. Physician cons. Utah State Divsn. Health, Salt Lake City, 1960—65; med. dir., project head start Salt Lake City Cmty. Action Program, 1965—70; resident Utah State Divsn. Health, 1969—71; asst.

assoc. regional health dir. USPHS, San Francisco, 1971—75, med. cons. Atlanta, 1975—77, dir. primary care, 1977—84; dir. divsn. diabetes control Ctrs. Disease Control, Atlanta, 1984—88; dir. WHO Collabor Ctr., Atlanta, 1986—91; dir. preventive medicine residency Ctrs. Disease Control, Atlanta, 1988—93; exec. dir. Am. Bd. Preventive Medicine, 1993—98. Trustee Am. Bd. Preventive Medicine, 1990—92; lectr. Emory U. Sch. Pub. Health, 1988—94; bd. dirs. Redwood Coast Med. Svcs., v.p., 1994—2004; mem. adv. com. Shamli Hospice, Gualala, Calif.; mem. adv. coun. Sonoma County Area Agy. on Aging, Santa Rosa, Calif., 2001—, sec., 2004—06, vice chair, 2006—; bd. dirs. Alliance Rural Cmty. Health, Calif., 2002—04. Co-author: Clinical Diabetes, 1991; author: History of the American Board of Preventive Medicine, 2002. Bd. dirs. Diabetes Assn. Atlanta, 1985—90. Recipient Disting. Svc. award, Am. Bd. Med. Splties, 2004. Fellow: Am. Coll. Preventive Medicine (bd. dirs. 1990—94, Splt. Recognition award 1998); mem.: AMA (grad. med. edn. adv. com. 1993—97), Steering Com. Environ. Commons, Am. Bd. Med. Specialists (Disting. Svc. award 2004), Am. Acad. Pediat., Assn. Tchrs. Preventive Medicine. Office: PO Box 364 Gualala CA 95445-0364 Business E-Mail: ard@mcn.org.

**RING, ALVIN MANUEL,** pathologist, educator; s. Julius and Helen (Krolik) R.; m. Cynthia Joan Jacobson, Sept. 29, 1963; children— Jeffrey, Melinda, Heather. BS, Wayne State U., 1954; MD, U. Mich., 1958. Intern Mt. Carmel Hosp., Detroit, 1958-59; resident in pathology Michael Reese Hosp., Chgo., 1960-62; asst. pathologist Kings County Hosp., Bklyn., 1962-63; assoc. pathologist El Camino Hosp., Mountain View, Calif., 1963-65; chief pathologist, dir. labs. St. Elizabeth's Hosp., Chgo., 1965-72, Holy Cross Hosp., Chgo., 1972-87, Silver Cross Hosp., Joliet, Ill., 1990—. Instr. SUNY, 1962-63, Stanford U., 1963-65; asst. prof. pathology U. Ill., Chgo., 1966-69, assoc. prof., 1969-78, prof., 1978—; adj. clin. prof. No. Ill. U., 1981-87; adj. prof. med. edn. U. Ill. Coll. Medicine, 1988—; chmn. histotech. Nat. Accrediting Agy. for Clin. Lab Scis., 1977-81; mem. adv. com. Health Manpower, 1966-71; pres. Spear Computer Users Group, 1981-82; mem. adv. com. Mid-Am. chpt. ARC, 1979-85; pres. Pathology and Lab Cons., Inc., 1985—; adj. prof., med. dir. Med. Tech., Moraine Valley C.C., 1994—; originator, coord. pathology, med. decision-making courses Nat. Ctr. for Advanced Med. Edn., 1981—; others; co-coord. computer courses Midwest Clin. Conf., 2000—. Author: Laboratory Correlation Manual, 1968, 82, 86, Laboratory Assistant Examination Review Book, 1971, Review Book in Pathology, Anatomic, 1986, Review Book in Pathology, Clinical, 1986; mem. editorial bd. Lab. Medicine, 1975-87; contbr. articles to med. jours. Fellow Coll. Am. Pathology (insp. 1973—, ins. com. 2002—; membership com. 2005—), Am. Soc. Clin. Pathology; mem. AMA, Ill. Med. Soc., Chgo. Med. Soc. (alt. councilor 1980-85, mem. adv. com. on health care delivery), Ill. Pathol. Soc. (trustee 1997—), Chgo. Pathol. Soc. (censor 1980-88, exec. com. 1985-89, program. com. 1987—), Am. Assn. Blood Banks, Assn. Brain Tumor Rsch. (cons.), Exec. Svc. Corps (exec. com. 1988—), Phi Lambda Kappa (chpt. pres.). Home: 100 Graymoor Ln Olympia Fields IL 60461-1213 Office: Silver Cross Hosp 1200 Maple Rd Joliet IL 60432-1497

**RING, CARLYLE C.,** lawyer; b. Camen, N.Y., May 25, 1931; s. Carlyle Conwell and Mary Lois (Tooley) R.; m. Jane Norwood Lee, Oct. 16, 1954; children: Donna Lee Ring Moss, Mary Elizabeth Ring Lord, Russell Conwell John Roderick. AB, Hamilton Coll., Clinton, N.Y., 1953; JD, Duke U., 1956. Bar: U.S. Supreme Ct., D.C., U.S. Ct. (4th cir.) Appeals, Va., U.S. Ct. Appeals (D.C. cir.). Assoc. Klagsbrun, Hanes & Irwin, Washington, 1956—63; ptnr. Klagsbrun, Hanes & Irwin and successor, Washington, 1963—85; v.p., gen. counsel Atlantic Rsch. Corp., Va., 1985—99; of counsel Ober Kaler, Washington, 1985—. Mem. Nat. Conf. Commr's Uniform Laws, Chgo., 1970—, pres., 1983—85; mem. permanent editl. bd. Uniform Comml. Code, 1985—, chair Article 4A (funds transfers), chair Articles 5, 3, and 4 (letters of credit and checks); chair Uniform Computer Info. Transactions Act. Contbr. articles to profl. jours. Chair Alexandria (Va.) Sch. Bd., 1976—78; vice chair Alexandria Redevel. Housing, 2001—; mem. Alexandria (Va.) Sch. Bd., 1969—78, Alexandria City Coun., 1979—88, Alexandria Redevel. Housing, 1999—. Named one of Best Lawyers in Am. - Cyber Law, 2002; recipient Charles Murphy award, Duke U. Sch. Law, 1985, Red Cross Burke award for outstanding philanthropic and humanitarian svc., Alexandria Red Cross, 2002, George Washington Leadership award, Alexandria C. of C., 1973. Mem.: Va. Bar Assn., D.C. Bar Assn., Phi Beta Kappa. Republican. Presbyterian. Home: 308 Monticello Blvd Alexandria VA 22305 Office: Ober Kaler 1401 H St NW Washington DC 20005

**RING, GERALD J.,** real estate developer, insurance company executive; b. Madison, Wis., Oct. 6, 1928; s. John George and Mabel Sarah (Rau) R.; m. Armella Marie Dohm, Aug. 20, 1949; children: Michael J., James J., Joseph W. Student public schs., Madison. With Sub-Zero Freezer Co., Madison, 1948-70, mfr.'s rep., 1954-70; founder, pres. Parkwood Hills Corp., Madison from 1965; founder, pres. Park Towne Devel. Corp., Madison, 1969, Ring Devel. Co., 1992—. Bd. dirs. CUNA Mut. Ins. Soc., CUNA Mut. Ins. Group, CUNA Mut. Investment Corp., CUDIS Ins. Soc., all Madison, 1968-98, exec. com., 1973-83, chmn. bd., 1979-81; bd. dirs. CUMIS Ins. Soc., mem. exec. com., 1973-83, chmn. bd., 1977-79; bd. dirs. CMCI Corp., mem. exec. com., 1974-83, chmn. bd., 1981-83; treas. CUNADATA Corp., 1974-81; bd. dirs. Wis. Credit Union League, 1958-79, pres., 1965-67; mem. Wis. Credit Union Rev. Bd., 1967-83, chmn., 1973-76, 82-83; bd. dirs. CUNA Credit Union Nat. Assn., Inc., 1964-81, League Life Ins. Co., League Gen. Ins. Co., Southfield, Mich., CUNA Mut. Fin. Svcs. Corp., Century Ins. Co. Am., Waverly, Iowa. Chmn. Greater Madison C. of C., 1980, bd. dirs. 1976-89, v.p. econ. devel., 1983-85, v.p. govtl. affairs, 1985-89, mem. capital fund raising com., 1983—, chmn. 1983-86; mem. Mayor's Emergency Housing Com., 1984-85; chmn. fin. com. St. Patrick's Congregation, 1983-89; bd. dirs. Cath. Charities of Madison, 1995—, pres., 1996-99; bd. dirs. Future Madison Housing Fund, 1997—, pres. 2005—. Served with USMC, 1951-53. Mem. Aircraft Owners and Pilots Assn. Lodges: Rotary. Cath. Roman Catholic. Home: 607 Farwell Dr Madison WI 53704-6029 Office: 402 S Gammon Rd Madison WI 53719-1002

**RING, HERBERT EVERETT,** management executive; b. Norwich, Conn., Dec. 19, 1925; s. Herbert Everett and Catherine (Riordan) R.; m. Marilyn Elizabeth Dursin, May 21, 1955 (dec. Jan. 1994); children: Nancy Marie, Herbert Everett. BA, Ind. No. U., 1971, MBA, 1973; AMP, Harvard U., 1981. V.p. ops. Ogden Foods, Inc., Toledo, 1963-74; v.p. Boston, 1974-75; v.p. concessions SportSvc. Corp., Buffalo, 1976-78, sr. v.p., 1978-80, pres., 1980-83, bd. dir.; pres. Universal Mgmt. Concept Counseling, Sylvania, Ohio, 1983—2003; prin. Hysen Group II, Livonia, Mich., 1991-95. Counselor L.A. Olympic Concessions Food Svc., 1984, Phila. Meml. Stadium, 1985, Del. North Cos. Internat. London Eng., 1985-86, Chgo. Stadium Corp., 1989-92, Buffalo Sabres N.Y., 1992, Fine Host Inc. Greenwich Ct., 1993, Delaware North of Australia Ltd., 1994, Temp DNC Health Support Ltd., Wellington, New Zealand, 1995, Fanfare Enterprises, 1997, Geneva Lakes Kennel Club, Delavan, Wis., 1997, St. Francis Health Care Ctr., Greenspring, Ohio, 1998, Detroit Opera House, 2000; bd. dirs. Greenfield Restaurant Co., Inc., Letheby and Christopher Ltd., Reading, Berkshire, Eng., Air Terminal Svcs., Inc., The Aud Club, Inc., Bluegrass Turf Svc., Inc., Concession Suppliers, Inc., Cosel Drive-In Theatre, Inc., G&H Sports Concessions, Inc., Hazel Park Parking, Inc. Mem. Toledo Mus. Art., 1985-92. Sgt. Air Corps U.S. Army, 1944-46, ETO, USAF, 1950-51. Mem.: N.W. Ohio Restaurant Assn. (bd. dirs. 1990—93), Internat. Assn. Auditorium Mgrs., Am. Culinary Fedn. Inc. Roman Catholic. Home and Office: 5540 Radcliffe Rd Sylvania OH 43560-3740

**RING, JAMES WALTER,** physics professor; b. Worcester, N.Y., Feb. 24, 1929; s. Carlyle Conwell and Lois (Tooley) R.; m. Agnes Elizabeth Muir, July 18, 1959; 1 son, Andrew James. AB, Hamilton U., 1951; PhD (Root fellow), U. Rochester, 1958. Asst. prof. physics Hamilton Coll., Clinton, NY, 1957—62, assoc. prof., 1962—69, prof., 1969—75, Winslow prof. 1975—2003, chmn. dept. physics, 1968—80, 1987—88, 1991—92, radiation safety officer, 1964—84, engring. liaison officer, 1969—2002, prof. emeritus, 2003—. Attached physicist Atomic Energy Rsch. Establishment, Harwell, Eng., 1965-66; vis. physicist Phys. Chemistry Lab., Oxford (Eng.) U., 1973;

vis. fellow Ctr. for Energy and Environ. Studies, Princeton U., 1981; vis. scientist Lab. for Heating and Air Conditioning, Danish Tech. U., Copenhagen, 1987. Contbr. articles to profl. jour. and books in physics, chemistry, solar energy, environ. sci., health physics, archaeology, and engring. Recipient prize Acad. Edn./Devel., 1980, medal for outstadig achievements in physics Hamilton Coll., 2005; NSF grantee, 1959-66; NSF sci. faculty fellow, 1965-66. Mem. AAUP (chpt. pres. 1987-92), Am. Phys. Soc., Am. Assn. Physics Tchrs., Phi Beta Kappa, Sigma Xi. Achievements include solar house design and testing; indoor air studies in radon dangers and thermal comfort; study of the use of solar energy by the Romans during the Roman Empire; analysis of experimental evidence for the validity of continuous spontaneous localization theory as an alternative to standard quantum mechanics; detection of Pb210 gamma radiation to establish geochronology for sediment core samples taken in antarctic peninsula bay and straits; to study global warming. Avocations: reading, cross country skiing, landscape painting, visiting wine country, studying architecture. Office: Hamilton Coll Dept Physics Clinton NY 13323 Business E-Mail: jring@hamilton.edu.

**RING, NANCY GAIL,** artist, writer; b. Irvington, NJ, Dec. 24, 1956; d. Frank and Dorothy (Kasoff) R.; m. Eric Mark Kaplan, Aug. 1, 1993. Student, Sch. of Mus. of Fine Arts, Boston, 1975-76; BFA, Syracuse U., 1978. Food history columnist, feature food article contbr. N.J. Star Ledger, Newark, 1998—2004. Muralist pvt. commns., 2000—. Author (and illustrator): Walking on Walnuts, 1996; exhibitions include Iandor Fine Art Gallery, Newark, 2005, New Door Creative Gallery, Balt., 2005. Recipient Drawing award Barbara Chase Burke, 1978; fellow Mid-Atlantic Arts Found., 1988, N.Y. Found. for Arts, 1987, Montalvo Ctr. for Arts, 1987. Avocations: baking, cooking, exercise, travel, reading.

**RING, RENEE ETHELINE,** lawyer; b. Frankfurt, Germany, May 29, 1950; arrived in U.S., 1950; d. Vincent Martin and Etheline Bergetta (Schoolmeesters) Ring; m. Paul J. Zofnass, June 24, 1982; children: Jessica Renee, Rebecca Anne. BA magna cum laude, Catholic U. Am., 1972; JD, U. Va., 1976. Bar: NY 1977. Assoc. Whitman & Ransom, NYC, 1976-83, Carro, Spanbock, Fass, Geller, Kaster & Cuiffo, NYC, 1983-86, ptnr., 1986, Finley Kumble Wagner et. al., NYC, 1987; of counsel Kaye, Scholer, Fierman, Hays & Handler, NYC, 1988; ptnr. Kaye, Scholer, Fierman, Hays & Handler, LLP, NYC, 1989-97, Hunton & Williams, NYC, 1997—2002, McKee Nelson LLP, NYC, 2006—. Trustee The Spence Sch., 2001—02; advisor WestWind Found., 2001—; mem. exec. com. Lawyers for Clinton, Washington, 1991—92; team capt. Clinton Transition Team, Washington, 1992—93; mem. Nat. Lawyers Coun. Dem. Nat. Com., 1993—98; trustee The Clinton Legal Expense Trust, 1998—2002, Pound Ridge Land Conservancy, 2003—; v.p. Queens Bot. Garden Soc., 2005—, mem. exec. com., 2005—; mem. alumni coun. U. Va. Sch. of Law, 1997—2005, 2d v.p., 2000—01, 1st v.p., 2001—03, pres., 2003—05. Mem.: ABA. Democrat. Roman Catholic. Office Phone: 917-777-4527.

**RING, RONALD HERMAN,** lawyer; b. Flint, Mich., Nov. 30, 1938; s. Herman and Lydia (Miller) R.; m. Joan Kay Whitener, Aug. 5, 1966. AB, U. Mich., 1961, LLB, 1964. Bar: Mich. 1964. U.S. Dist. Ct. (ea. dist.) Mich. 1966. Assoc. Beagle, Benton & Hicks, Flint, 1964-69; ptnr. Beagle & Ring, Flint, 1970-80, Beagle, Ring & Beagle, Flint, 1980-85, Ring, Beagle & Busch, Flint, 1985-93, Ronald H. Ring, P.C., Flint, 1993-95; pvt. practice Flint, 1991—. Mem. meml. com. Crossroads Village, Flint, 1981; pres. Family Service Agy., Genesee County, Mich., 1986. Mem. ABA, Assn. Trial Lawyers Am., Mich. Bar Assn. (delivery of legal service com. 1986, med. malpractice panel 1986), Genesee County Bar Assn. (pres. 1980-81, bd. dirs. 1979-82, cir. ct. mediation panel 1986). Clubs: Ostego Ski (Gaylord, Mich.). Avocations: skiing, sailing. Office: 7993 Bussa Ln Rapid City MI 49676-9203 Office Phone: 616-264-5549. Business E-Mail: ronhring@cs.com.

**RING, TIMOTHY MICHAEL,** human services administrator, pharmaceutical executive; b. Buffalo, Sept. 30, 1957; s. Roger Michael and Leone Ann (Reitmeier) R.; m. Mary Lou Mauro, June 10, 1984; children: Christina and Alexandra (twins). BS in Indsl. Labor Relations, Cornell Univ., 1979. Coll. grad. in tng. GM, Detroit, 1979-80, labor relations rep., 1980, salaried personnel rep., 1980-81, sr. salaried personnel rep., 1981-82, sr. labor relations rep., 1982-83; div. personnel mgr. Abbott Labs., North Chicago, Ill., 1983-84, regional personnel mgr., 1984-86, dir. personnel Pacific, Asian and African ters., 1986-87, dir. personnel Pacific, Asian, African and European ters., 1987—92; corp. v.p., human resources CR Bard Inc., New Providence, NJ, 1992—93; group v.p.-internat., 1993—97, group pres.-coronary vascular products, 1997—99, group pres.-electrophysiology, peripheral vascular products, 1999—2003, chmn, CEO, 2003—. Advisor Midwest Personnel Forum U. Ill., Champaign. Mem. European Pharm. Mfg. Assn. Personnel, Pacific Area Personnel Assn., Human Resource Assn. Chgo. (chmn. internat. human relations com. 1986-88), Cornell U. Indsl. and Labor Relations Assn., Delta Upsilon. Republican. Roman Catholic. Avocations: real estate investments, tennis, golf, sailing. Office: CR Bard 730 Central Ave New Providence NJ 07974 Office Phone: 908-277-8000.*

**RING, YVONNE ANN,** special education educator; b. Miami, Fla., Dec. 2, 1960; d. Thomas Charles and Diane Esther Fisher (Stepmother); m. John Michael Ring, Oct. 19, 1991; children: James William Jobbitt, II, Stephanie Ann Jobbitt. BS in Spl. Edn., Piedmont Coll., Demorest, Ga., 1996, Ednl. Specialist, 2002; MS in Interrelated Spl. Edn., North Ga. Coll. and State U., Dahlonega, 2001. Cert. tchr. interrelated spl. edn. Ga., 2001, tchr. mental retardation spl. edn. Ga., 1996, tchr. middle grades math., social sci., reading, interrelated spl. edn. 2006, Wilson reading tchr. 2006. Interrelated spl. edn. tchr. Rabun County Mid. Sch., Tiger, Ga., 2000—, North Habersham Mid. Sch., Clarkesville, Ga., 1996—2000. Practicum Clayton Elem., Clayton, Ga., 1994—94. Recipient Spl. Recognition, Coun. For Exceptional Children, 2000—, Recognition of Participation, Hand-in-Hand Mentor Program, 2001—; Tony Molinaro Scholarship, Ga. Coun. of Aminstrs. of Spl. Edn., 2003. Mem.: Nat. Assn. Spl. Educators, Internat. Reading Assn., Profl. Assn. of Ga. Educators (assoc.), Coun. for Exceptional Children (assoc.), Internat. Dyslexia Found. (assoc.). Avocations: tutoring, travel, continuing education, professional conferences, museums. Home: PO Box 242 Clayton GA 30525-0007 Office: Rabun County Mid Sch 108 Wildcat Hill Drive Tiger GA 30576 E-mail: yring@rabun.k12.ga.us.

**RINGEL, DEAN,** lawyer; b. NYC, Dec. 12, 1947; m. Ronnie Sussman, Aug. 24, 1969; children: Marion, Alicia. BA, Columbia Coll., 1967; JD, Yale U., 1971. Bar: N.Y. 1972, U.S. Ct. Appeals (6th cir.) 1972, U.S. Ct. Appeals (2d and D.C. cirs.) 1974, U.S. Supreme Ct. 1976, U.S. Ct. Appeals (10th cir.) 1982, U.S. Ct. Appeals (11th cir.) 1997, U.S. Ct. Appeals (9th cir.) 2000. Law clk. to Judge Anthony J. Celebrezze U.S. Ct. Appeals (6th cir.), 1971—72; assoc. Cahill Gordon & Reindel, N.Y.C., 1972—79; ptnr. Cahill, Gordon & Reindel LLP, N.Y.C., 1979—. Sec. def. coun. sect. Media Law Resource Ctr., 2006—. Mem.: ABA (vice chmn. com. on freedom of speech and press 1978—79), Pub. Edn. Assn. (trustee, sec. 1997—2000, trustee CEI-PEA 2000—), Assn. Bar City NY (commn. comm., fed. litigation, antitrust and trade regulation), NY State Bar (chmn. antitrust litigation com., sect. comml. and fed. litigation 1994—96, co-chmn. fed. judiciary com. 1997—2001, co-chair newsgathering com. Media Law Resource Ctr. 2001—05, sec. media law resource ctr. def. counsel sect. 2005—, media law com., mem. exec. com.). Office: Cahill Gordon & Reindel LLP 80 Pine St 17th Fl New York NY 10005-1790 Office Phone: 212-701-3521.

**RINGEL, JUDY G.,** writer; b. Cleve., Aug. 31, 1940; d. Leo and Ernestine F. Greenberger; m. Neil E. Ringel, June 30, 1960; children: Elizabeth Ringel Saslawsky, James M., Jonathan L. Student, Goucher Coll., 1958—60; BA magna cum laude, Cast Western Res. U., 1962. Assoc. editor Memphis Mag., 1982—86, sr. editor, 1986—91, assoc. pub., 1991—92; freelance writer Memphis, 1992—. Author: Children of Israel, 2004 (cert. of commendation Am. Assn. State and Local History, 2005); contbr. numerous articles to mags. Chmn. bd. dirs. Memphis Planned Parenthood, Memphis, 1995—97; pres.

Jewish Fedn. Women's Divsn., Memphis, 1976—77. Mem.: Memphis Jewish Hist. Soc., West Tenn. Hist. Soc., Am. Assn. for State and Local History, Phi Beta Kappa. Avocations: golf, gardening, jogging, reading.

**RINGEL, ROBERT LEWIS,** academic administrator; b. N.Y.C., Jan. 27, 1937; s. Benjamin Seymour and Beatrice (Salb) R.; m. Estelle Neuman, Jan. 18, 1959; children— Stuart Alan, Mark Joseph. BA, Bklyn. Coll., 1959; MS, Purdue U., 1960, PhD, 1962. cert. speech pathologist. Rsch. scientist, laryngeal rsch. lab. Ctr. Health Scis., UCLA, 1962-64; asst. prof. communication disorders U. Wis., 1964-66; from mem. faculty to provost Purdue U., 1966—91, provost, 1991—2001, prof. speech, lang. & hearing scis., Donald S. Powers disting. univ. adminstr., 2001—. Vis. prof. Inst. Neurology and Nat. Hosps. Coll. Speech Scis., U. London, 1985; cons. NIH, NEH, Bur. Edn. Handicapped of U.S. Office Edn.; bd. dirs. Indpls. Ctr. for Advanced Rsch., 1988-92; hon. prof. Coll. of Computer Scis. and Mgmt., Rzeszów, Poland, 2000—; bd. dir., faculty adv. Hillel Found. Purdue U., 2000—. Author sci. articles; contbr. to monographs and textbooks; cons. editor Chapman & Hall, London. Bd. dirs. Lafayette Home Hosp., 1978-87, Lafayette Symphony Orch., 1983-85. Recipient Rsch. Career Devel. award Nat. Inst. Dental Rsch., 1967-70, Award for highest merit for sci. article Jour. Speech and Hearing Rsch., 1979, Disting. Alumnus award Bklyn. Coll., 1985; Para-Rabbi fellow Hebrew Union Coll., 2001—; Robert L. Ringel Art Gallery at Purdue U. named in his honor. Fellow Am. Speech and Hearing Assn. (v.p. Found. 1990—, honors 1998); mem. Nat. Assn. State Univs. and Land Grant Colls. (exec. com. 1988-91, rsch. policy and grad. edn., exec. com. on acad. affairs 1991-2001, com. on instnl. coop., exec. com. provosts instn. coop. com. 1991-2001), Sigma Xi (v.p. 1986-90). Office: Purdue U Speech Lang & Hearing Scis 1353 Heavilon Hall G-12B West Lafayette IN 47907-1353 Home: 208 Rosebank Ln West Lafayette IN 47906-8613 Business E-Mail: rringel@purdue.edu.

**RINGENBERG, DONNA LOU,** music educator, conductor; b. Mt. Joy, Pa., Jan. 22, 1954; d. Robert George Landvater and June Kathleen Wenger; m. Paul David Ringenberg, July 2, 1977; children: Rebekah, Ruth, Rachel, Paul Jr., Rose, Rosalyn, Peter, Priscilla. BS in Music Edn., Bob Jones U., 1976, student in Elem. Edn.; student, Converse Coll., 1998—99, Furman U., summer sessions. Cert. tchr. S.C. Tchr. music, dir. chorus Goldsboro (N.C.) Christian Sch., 1976—77; tchr. Southgate Christian Sch., Augusta, Ga., 1977—78; tchr. music, dir. orch. Acad. Arts, Taylors, SC, 1991—93; pvt. music instr. Greenville, SC, 1991—; tchr. music Hampton Park Christian Sch., Greenville, 1997—99. Music dir. Camp of Nations, South Gibson, Pa., 1976; dir. home schooling string orch. Pecknel Music, Greenville, SC, 1997—; judge various competitions. Musician: Greenville (S.C.) Cmty. Chamber Orch., 2001. Organist Tabernacle Bapt. Ch., Clayton, Ga., 1977—81; pianist, dir. children's choir Colonial Hills Bapt. Ch., Taylors, SC, 1991—93; dir. children's choir Hampton Pk. Bapt. Ch., Greenville, 1998—99; musician Greenville (S.C.) Rescue Mission, 1995—. Recipient Musicianship award, Park Hills Elem. Sch., 1966, Bus. award, Southwestern H.S., 1972. Mem.: Nat. Guild Piano Tchrs., Suzuki Assn. Am. Republican. Bapt. Avocations: sewing, crafts. Home: 16 Brookview Cir Greenville SC 29605

**RINGER, PAULA DENISE HOLLENSHEAD,** elementary school educator; b. Urania, La., Sept. 15, 1961; d. Feldor Herold and Betty Jane Hollenshead; m. William Craig Ringer, June 14, 1986; 1 child, William Chase. BA in Tchg., Sam Houston State U., Huntsville, Tex., 1984. Cert. tchr. in math. and computer info. sys. Tex., 1984. Tchr. Hull-Daisetta Ind. Sch. Dist., Tex., 1994—2000, Hardin Ind. Sch. Dist., Tex., 2000—. Participant Conf. for the Advancement of Math. Tchg., Tex., 1988—; tchr. Brazos-Sabine Connection, Daisetta, Tex., 1996—2000; math. textbook panel mem. Tex. Edn. Agy., Austin, 2006. Mem. Hardin United Meth. Ch., 1988. Mem.: Assn. of Tex. Profl. Educators (assoc.). Home: PO Box 383 Hardin TX 77561 Office: Hardin Ind Sch Dist PO Box 330 Hardin TX 77561 Office Phone: 936-298-2112. Personal E-mail: pringer@esc5.net.

**RINGGOLD, FAITH,** artist; b. NYC, Oct. 8, 1930; BS, CCNY, 1955, MA, 1959; DFA (hon.), Moore Coll. Art, Phila., 1986, Coll. Wooster, Ohio, 1987, Mass. Coll. Art, Boston, 1991, CCNY of CUNY, 1991, RI Sch. Design, 1994, Russell Sage Coll., NY, 1996, Parsons Sch. Design, 1996, Marymount Coll., 1999, Mary Grove Coll., 2000, William Patterson U., 2001, Chgo. Art Inst., 2001, Bloomfield Coll., 2005; DSc (hon.), Brockport State U., NY, 1992, Calif. Coll. Arts and Crafts, Oakland, 1993; DHL (hon.), Malloy Coll., 1997, Bank St. Coll., 1999, William Patterson U., 2001, St. Joseph Coll., 2004; DEd (hon.), Wheelock Coll., 1997. Art tchr. N.Y. Pub. Schs., 1955-73; lectr. Bank St. Coll. Grad. Sch., N.Y.C., 1970-80; prof. art U. Calif., San Diego, 1984—2002, prof. emeritus, 2002—, ret., 2002. Solo exhbns. include Bernice Steinbaum Gallery, 1991, ACA, 2000, Spectrum Gallery, N.Y.C., 1967, 70 10 year retrospective, Studio Mus. in Harlem, N.Y.C., 1984, Bernice Steinbaum Gallerym N.Y.C., 1987-88, Balt. Mus., Deland (Fla.) Mus., Faith Ringgold 25 Yr. Survey Fine Arts Mus. L.I., Hempstead, 1990-93, Textile Mus., Washington, 1993, Children's Mus. of Manhattan, N.Y.C., 1993-95, Hewlett-Woodmere Pub. Libr., Hewlett, N.Y., 1993-94, St. Louis Art Mus., 1994, Athenaeum, La Jolla, Calif., 1995, A.C.A. Gallery, N.Y.C., 1995, 98, Ind. U. of Pa., 1995, Bowling Green State U. Ind., 1996, New Mus. Contemporary Art, N.Y.C., 1998; exhibited in group shows at Harlem Cultural Coun., N.Y.C., 1966, Meml. Exhibit for MLK, Mus. Modern Art N.Y.C., 1968, Chase Manhattan Bank Collection, Martha Jackson Gallery, N.Y.C., 1970, Am. Women Artists, Gedok, Kunstalle, Hamburg, Ger., 1972, Jubilee, Boston Mus. Fine Arts, 1975, Major Contemporary Women Artists, Suzanne Gross Gallery, Phila., 1984, Committed to Print Mus. Modern Art, N.Y.C., 1988, The Art of Black Am. in Japan, Terada Warehouse, Tokyo, Made in the USA, Art in the 50s and 60s U. Calif. Berkeley Art Mus., Craft Today Poetry of the Physical, Am. Craft Mus., N.Y.C., Portraits and Homage to Mothers Hecksher Mus. Huntington, 1987, N.J. State Mus., Trenton, 1992-94, Fukui Fine Art Mus., Fuki, Japan, 1992, Takushima Modern Art Mus., Japan, 1993, Otani Meml. Art Mus., Japan, 1993, Salina Art Ctr., Kans., 1993, Bruce Watkins Ctr. Kansas City, Mo., 1993, Barton County C.C., Great Bend, Kans., 1993, Del. State Coll. Arts Ctr. Gallery, Dover, 1993-94, Roswell Mus. and Art Ctr., N.Mex., 1994, Aknaton Gallery, Cairo, Alexandria, Egypt, Exit Art, N.Y.C., 1994, New Mus. Contemporary Art, N.Y.C., 1996, Spellman Coll. Mus., Atlanta, 1996, Whitney Mus., N.Y.C., 1996, Centre Georges Pompidou, Paris, 1997, Mus. Art, Ft. Lauderdale, Fla., 1997, N.J. Ctr. Arts, Summit, N.J., 1997, Trout Gallery Dickenson Coll., Carlisle, Pa., numerous others; represented in collections at Chase Manhattan Bank, N.Y.C., Philip Morris Collection, N.Y.C., Children's Mus., Bklyn., Newark Mus., The Women's House of Detention, Rikers Island, N.Y., The Studio Mus., N.Y.C., High Mus., Atlanta, Guggenheim Mus., Met. Mus. Art, Boston Mus. Fine Arts, MOMA, AARP, Washington, Am. Craft Mus., N.Y.C., Clark Mus. Williamstown, Mass., ARCO Chem., Phila., Coca-Cola, Atlanta, Ft. Wayne Mus. Fine Art, Ind., Harold Washington Libr. Ctr., Chgo., Lang Comm. Corp., Coll., Phila. Mus. Art, Pub. Art Pub. Schs., P.S. 22, Bklyn., Spenser Mus. Lawr., Kans., St. Louis Mus. Art, Balt. Mus., Nat. Mus., Washington, Woman's Mus. Washington, Eugenio Maria de Hostos C.C., N.Y.C., MTA 125th St. IRT subway sta. installation, N.Y.C., numerous others; author: Tar Beach, 1991, Aunt Harriet's Underground Railroad in the Sky, 1992 (Picture Book award 1993, Best Children's Book of Yr. 1993), Dinner at Aunt Connie's House, 1993 (Reading Magic award 1993), We Flew Over the Bridge: Memoirs of Faith Ringgold, 1995, Talking to Faith Ringgold, 1995, Bonjour Lonnie, 1996, My Dream of Martin Luther King, Jr., 1996, The Invisible Princess, 1999, If a Bus Could Talk: The Story of Rosa Parks, 1999, Counting to Tar Beach, 1999, Cassie's Colorful Day with Daddy, 1999, Cassie's Word Quilt, 2000, O Holy Night, 2004, Three Witches, 2006; author: (video prodn.) Goodnight Moon: and Other Sleepy Time Tales, Tar Beach, 2000; contbr. articles to profl. jours. Recipient AAUW travel award to Africa, 1976; John Simon Guggenheim Meml. Found. Fellowship (painting), 1987, N.Y. Found. for Arts award (painting), 1988, Nat. Endowment Arts award (sculpture), 1978, (painting) 1989, La Napoule Found. award (painting in So. of France), 1990, Video and Software award Calif. children's book, 1991, Parent's Choice Gold award, 1991, Artist award Studio Mus., Harlem, 1991, Artist of Yr. award Sch. Art League N.Y., 1991, Coretta Scott King award for illustration, 1992, Dist. Artist award Nat. Coun. Art Adminstrs., 1992, award, 1993, Arts Internat. award (travel to Morocco), 1992, Honors award for outstanding achievement in the visual arts Woman's Caucus Arts, N.Y., 1994, Towsend Harris medal City Coll. Alumni Assn., 1995, N.J. Artist of Yr. award N.J. Ctr. Visual Arts, 1997, 31st NAACP Image award, 1999, Visionary Woman award, Moore Coll. Art & Design, 2005. Home: PO Box 429 Englewood NJ 07631-0429 Office: ACA Galleries 529 W 20th St Fl 5 New York NY 10011-2800 Office Phone: 858-576-0397. Personal E-mail: ringgoldfaith@aol.com.

**RINGLE, BRETT ADELBERT**, lawyer; oil industry executive, gas industry executive; b. Berkeley, Calif., Mar. 17, 1951; s. Forrest A. and Elizabeth V. (Darnall) R.; m. Sue Kinslow, May 26, 1973. BA, U. Tex., 1973, JD, 1976. Bar: Tex. 1976, U.S. Dist. Ct. (no. dist.) Tex. 1976, U.S. Supreme Ct. 1980, U.S. Ct. Appeals (5th cir.) 1984. Ptnr. Shank, Irwin & Conant, Dallas, 1976-86, Jones, Day, Reavis & Pogue, Dallas, 1986-96; v.p. Hunt Petroleum Corp., Dallas, 1996—. Adj. prof. law So. Meth. U., Dallas, 1983. Author: (with J.W. Moore and H.I. Bendix) Moore's Federal Practice, 2d edit., Vol. 12, 1980, Vol. 13, 1981, (with J.W. Moore) Vol. 1A, 1982, Vol. 1A Part 2, 1989. Mem. Dallas Bar Assn. Home: 3514 Gillon Ave Dallas TX 75205-3220 Office: Hunt Petroleum Corp 5000 Thanksgiving Tower 1601 Elm St Dallas TX 75201 Office Phone: 215-338-3658. Business E-Mail: bar@huntpetroleum.com.

**RINGLEE, ROBERT JAMES**, consulting engineering executive; b. Sacramento, Apr. 23, 1926; s. Francis and Marie N. R.; m. Helen Laura Carleton, Aug. 27, 1949; children— Sarah N., Jane C., Robert K. BSEE, U. Wash. 1946, MSEE, 1948; PhD in Mechanics, Rensselaer Poly. Inst., 1964. Registered profl. engr., N.Y. With advanced engring. program Gen. Electric Co., 1948-51, advanced devel. engr., power transformer dept., 1951-55, supr. power transformer design, 1955-60, sr. analytical engr., 1960-65, mgr. system and equipment reliability, 1965-69; prin. engr. dir. Power Technologies, Inc., Schenectady, 1969-86, prin cons., 1986-93; TAG assoc. Power Techs., Inc., 1993-94, assoc. cons., 1994-98. Contbr. articles to profl. publs.; patentee in field. Mem. Schalmont Bd. Edn., 1966-70, pres., 1968-69; mem. environ. adv. coun. mem. NYISO, 2004-. Served with USNR, 1944-46. Recipient Managerial award Gen. Electric Co., 1953 Fellow IEEE (3 prize paper awards), AAAS; mem. Internat. Conf. on High Voltage Power Systems (expert advisor, Attwood Assoc.), Adirondack Mountain Club (pres. 1990-93, acting exec. dir. 1994). Democrat. Unitarian Universalist. Home and Office: 315 Juniper Dr Schenectady NY 12306-1705 E-mail: robert.ringlee1@verizon.net.

**RINGLER, JAMES M. (JAMES M. RINGLER)**, computer services company executive; b. 1945; BS, U. Buffalo, 1967, MBA, 1968. Mgr., cons. Arthur Andersen & Co., 1968-76; v.p. appliance group Tappan Co., Mansfield, Ohio, 1976-78, gen. v.p., mgr. appliance div., 1978-87, pres., COO, 1987-90, also bd. dirs., 1987-90; exec. v.p. Premark Internat., Inc., Deerfield, Ill., 1990-92, pres., COO, 1992-96, pres., CEO, 1996—99, chmn., 1997—99; vice chmn. Ill. Tool Works, Inc., Glenview, 1999—2004; interim CEO NCR Corp., Dayton, Ohio, 2005, chmn., 2005—. Bd. dir. Union Carbide Corp., 1996—2001, Dow Chemical Co., 2001—, Corn Products Internat., 2001—, FMC Tech., 2001—, Autoliv Lic., 2002—, NCR Corp., 2003—. Bd. mem. Lyric Opera Chgo.; trustee Boys & Girls Club of No. Am., Midwest region. Office: NCR Corp 1700 S Patterson Blvd Dayton OH 45479*

**RINGLER, KENNETH J., JR.**, state agency administrator; b. May 29, 1948; m. Marty DeLaney; 3 children. Grad., Siena Coll. Chmn. planning bd. Town of Bethlehem, Albany County, NY, 1988—89, supr. NY, 1990—93; first dep. sec. state State of NY, 1996—99, commr. gen. svcs., 2001—04; exec. dep. commr. NY State Dept. Motor Vehicles, 1999—2001; exec. dir. Port Authority of NY and NJ, NYC, 2004—. Former chmn. Emergency Fin. Control Bd., City of Yonkers; bd. mem. Capitalize Albany Transp. Com., Com. on Open Govt., Coun. of Contracting Agencies, Gov. Nelson A. Rockefeller Empire State Plaza - Performing Arts Ctr. Corp., Gov.'s Seventh Regiment Armory Adv. Coun., Nat. Emergency Repatriation, Police Officers Meml. Adv. Coun., NY State Procurement Coun., Purchase Coun. for State and Local Govt. Procurement Officers, State Civil Defense Commn., State Commn. on Restoration of Capital, State Interagency Coun. on mental Hygiene Property Utilization. Mem.: Nat. Assn. State Purchasing Officers, Nat. Assn. of State Chief Adminstr., NY State Heritage Commn., Am. Commodity Distribution Assn., Exec. Mansion Preservation Soc. Office: Port Authority of NY & NJ 225 Park Ave S New York NY 10003 Office Phone: 212-435-7000.*

**RINGLESBACH, DOROTHY LOUISE**, retired nurse, writer; b. Ft. Wayne, Ind., Aug. 14, 1925; d. Paul Frederick and Elizabeth Barbara Sauerteig; m. John Clyde Ringlesbach, July 5, 1980; m. Robert Salisbury (div.); children: David, Claudia Ann, Evelyn, Claude, Jane. RN, Wishard Meml. Hosp., 1947. RN Ind., Ky., Va. RN staff Mary Chiles Hosp., Mt. Sterling, Ky., 1958—60; interperter Colonial Williamsburg, Williamsburg, Va., 1968—73; house supr. Williamsburg Cmty. Hosp., Williamsburg, Va., 1973—80, 1985—93; ret. Author: OSS Stories that can Now Be Told, 2005; contbr. articles publ. to profl. jour. Mem. US Cadet Nurse Corps., 1944—47; state pres. Aux. to Kymedical Assn., Louisville, 1965—66, rec. sec., 1962—65. Cadet nurse corps, 1944—47. Mem.: OSS Com. Vets, OSS Soc. Luth. Association. Avocations: reading, raise orchids, travel, writing. Home: 303 Farmville Ln Williamsburg VA 23188 Office Phone: 757-564-8299. Personal E-mail: esp22693@widomaker.com.

**RINGO, JEROME**, conservationist; Founder Progressive Resources Inc. Bd. mem. Nat. Wildlife Fedn., 1996—, chmn., 2005—. Mem. Coalition to Restore Coastal La, North Lake Charles Econ. Devel. Distr., Calcasieu Estuary Environ. Task Force. Named Vol. of Yr., Dupont Corp., 1985; named one of best cmty. activists, Times mag. of La., 1998, Most Influential Black Americans, Ebony mag., 2006. Office: Nat Wildlife Fedn 11100 Wildlife Ctr Dr Reston VA 20190-5362 Office Phone: 800-822-9919.*

**RINGWALD, MOLLY**, actress; b. Sacramento, Feb. 18, 1968; d. Bob and Adele Ringwald; m. Valery Lameignère, July 28, 1999 (div. Nov. 2002); life ptnr. Panio Gianopoulos; 1 child, Mathilda Ereni. Grad. high sch., Los Angeles. Actress: (stage prodns.) The Glass Harp, 1973, Annie, 1977, Cabaret, 2001, Enchanted April, 2004, When Harry Met Sally, 2004, Sweet Charity, 2006;(feature films) Tempest, 1982, Spacehunter: Adventures in the Forbidden Zone, 1983, Sixteen Candles, 1984, The Breakfast Club, 1985, Pretty in Pink, 1986, The Pick-Up Artist, 1987, For Keeps, 1988, Betsy's Wedding, 1990, Seven Sunday, 1994, Office Killer, 1996, Kimberly, 1999, Requiem For Murder, 1999, Teaching Mrs. Tingle, 1999, Cut, 2000, In the Weeds, 2000, Ring of Fire, 2000, Not Another Teen Movie, 2001, The Tulse Luper Suitcases: The Moab Story, 2003; (TV movies) Packin' It In, 1983, P.K. and the Kid, Something to Live For: The Alison Gertz Story, 1992, Twice Upon a Time, 1998, Since You've Been Gone, 1998, The Big Time, 2002; (TV mini-series) The Stand, 1994; regular (TV series) The Facts of Life, 1979-80, Townies, 1996; guest-star (TV shows) Diff'rent Strokes, The Merv Griffin Show; (Album) Molly Sings, 1974. Office: William Morris Agy 151 S El Camino Dr Beverly Hills CA 90212-2775*

**RINI, JOEL**, language educator, linguist; b. Cleve., Dec. 4, 1957; s. Joseph Charles and Virginia Ann Rini; m. Pamela Jean De Vries; children: Christopher Michael, Marcus Joel. BS in Edn., Kent State U., 1981; PhD, U. Mich., 1987. Asst. prof. Spanish linguistics U. Va., Charlottesville, 1987—93, assoc. prof. Spanish linguistics, 1993—2000, prof. Spanish linguistics, 2000—, chmn. Spanish, Italian and Portuguese, 1998—2004. Author: (books) Motives for Linguistic Change in the Formation of the Spanish Object Pronouns, 1992, Exploring the Role of Morphology in the Evolution of Spanish, 1999; contbr. articles to profl. jours. Home: 1039 Hayrake Ln Charlottesville VA 22903 Office: Univ Virginia 115 Wilson Hall Charlottesville VA 22904 Office Phone: 434-924-4657. Personal E-mail: jrini@adelphia.net. E-mail: jr6b@virginia.edu.

**RINI, JOSEPHINE NANCY**, nuclear medicine physician; b. Astoria, N.Y., Apr. 29, 1964; d. Joseph Anthony and Nancy Rini; m. Gary Limoncelli, Sept. 7, 1996; 1 child, Grace Ann Limoncelli. MD, Mayo Med. Sch., Rochester, MN, 1989. Diplomate Am. Bd. Nuc. Medicine, 1998, Am. Bd. Internal Medicine, 1996. Staff physician divsn. of nuc. medicine L.I. Jewish Med. Ctr., New Hyde Park, NY, 1999—. Mem.: SNM, Acad. of Molecular Imaging, RSNA. Achievements include research in PET and lymphoma, PET of FDG labeled WBC. Office: LI Jewish Med Ctr 270-05 76th Ave New Hyde Park NY 11040 Office Phone: 718-470-7080. Personal E-mail: rinlim2@aol.com. E-mail: rini@lij.edu.

**RINK, LAWRENCE DONALD**, cardiologist; b. Indpls., Oct. 14, 1940; s. Joe Donald and Mary Ellen (Rand) R.; m. Eleanor Jane Zimmerly, Aug. 10, 1963; children: Scott, Virginia. BS, DePauw U., 1962; MD, Ind. U., 1966. Diplomate Am. Bd. Internal Medicine, Am. Bd. Cardiology, Critical Care Medicine. Clin. asst. prof. U. Med. Sch., Indpls., 1973-79, clin. assoc. prof., 1979-85, clin. prof. medicine, 1985—; cardiologist IMA, Inc., Bloomington, Ind., 1974—; med. dir. Ind. U. Human Performance Lab., 1994—; dir. cardiac rehab. Bloomington Hosp., 1976—, dir. cardiology, 1983—; CEO, chmn. bd. dirs. IMA Inc., 1995—. Physician Ind. U. Basketball Team, 1979—; dir. med. edn. Bloomington Hosp., 1976—; med. dir. Track and Field Pan Am. Games, 1987; U.S. Olympic Physician Olympic Sports Festival, 1989, World Univ. Games, 1990, Olympic Games, Barcelona, 1992, World Univ. Games, Daegu, Korea, 1993, Fukuoka, Japan, 1995, Korea, 1997, Majorca, Spain, 1999, Beijing, 2001, Korea, 2003, Innsbruck, 2005; N.Am. continent rep. Fed. Internat. Student Univ. Sports, pres., 2004—, pres. med. commn. bd. dirs. J.O. Ritchie Soc., Ind. U. Med. Sch. Bd. dirs., dean's coun. Ind. U. Med. Sch., 1992—. Recipient Quality of Life award Major Bloomington, 1978; named Most Outstanding Flight Surgeon, USN, 1968, Most Outstanding Alumnus, Ind. U. Med. Sch., 1998. Fellow Am. Coll. Cardiology, Am. Heart Assn. (Corvitae award 2003), Am. Soc. Critical Care, Am. Coll. Sports Medicine; mem. AMA, Ind. U. Med. Alumnae Assn. (pres. 1986-87, exec. alumna coun.). Avocations: reading, writing, golf, tennis. Office: IMA Inc 550 Landmark Ave Bloomington IN 47403 E-mail: lrink@ima-md.com

**RINK, ROBERT P.**, secondary school educator; m. Stacia Margaret Stockwell, June 17, 1988; children: Kyle, Andrew, Mikaela. MusB, U. Puget Sound, Tacoma, 1986; MA in Music Edn., Pacific Luth. U., Tacoma, 1992. Band dir. Ballou Jr. HS, Puyallup, Wash., 1986—94, Ferrucci Jr. HS, Puyallup, 1995—. Office: Ferrucci Jr High Sch 3213 Wildwood Park Dr Puyallup WA 98374-1399

**RINK, WESLEY WINFRED**, retired bank executive; b. Hickory, N.C., June 14, 1922; s. Dewey Lee and Mabel E. (Yount) R.; m. Patricia A. Jones, Aug. 19, 2000; children from previous marriage: Rebecca S., Christopher L BS in Accountancy, U. Ill., 1947, MS, 1948. Acct., Glidden Co., Chgo., 1948-58; adminstrv. mgr. Central Soya Co., Chgo., 1958-65; v.p. comptroller State Nat. Bank, Evanston, Ill., 1965-71; exec. v.p., dir. Pioneer Trust & Savs. Bank, Chgo., 1971-76; corp. v.p. Exchange Bancorp., Inc., Tampa, 1977-82; sr. v.p. NCNB Nat. Bank Fla., Tampa, 1982-86; fin cons. Temple Terrace, Fla., 1986-2001; ret., 2001. Served to capt. USAAF, 1942—46. Home: 11402 Robles Del Rio Pl Temple Terrace FL 33617-2627

**RINKENBERGER, RICHARD KRUG**, physical scientist, geologist, consultant; b. Gridley, Ill., May 15, 1933; s. Burl E. and Olive J. (Krug) R.; m. Marilyn Ruth Ratliff, Feb. 19, 1960; children: Janice L., Ginger R., Rebekah P. BA in Geology, U. Colo., Boulder, 1959. Dir. prospecting Grubstake Assn., Sask., Can., 1958-59; engr. Martin-Marietta Aerospace Co., Denver, 1960-75; geologist U.S. Geol. Survey, Denver, 1975; geologist remote sensing U.S. Mine Safety and Health Adminstrn., Denver, 1975-79; pres., exploration geologist Banner Set, Ltd., Denver, 1980-84; pres., cons. geologist R.K. Rinkenberger & Assocs., Aurora, Colo., 1979-87; phys. scientist U.S. Dept. Energy, Germantown, Md., 1987-97; cons. geologist, rsch. geologist Denver, Rockville, Md., 1988—. Educator prospecting Denver Sch. Prospecting, 1968-71, U. Colo., Denver, Boulder, 1970-75; rsch. geochemist Heritage Chem. Co., Englewood, 1984-86; prospecting researcher, gold and silver prospector R.K. Rinkenberger & Assocs., 1965—. Contbr. articles to profl. jours. Mem. parent adv. bd, supt. of schs. Westminster, Colo., 1982-83. Grantee Sask. Dept. Mineral Resources, 1958, 59; remote sensing grantee U.S. Geol. Survey, 1978. Mem. Denver Mining Club, Sigma Gamma Epsilon, Mem. Ch. of the Nazarene. Achievements include geological theory and experimentation, research on animal and plant killing mechanisms responsible for dinosaur extinction and other mass plant and animal extinctions. Office: 12183 Monaco Dr Brighton CO 80602-9603

**RINKER, RUBY STEWART**, foundation administrator; b. Dayton, Ohio, June 11, 1936; d. Encle Stewart and Addie (Hamilton) Stewart-Smith; children: William Bertram Klawonn, Elizabeth Lynn Dennis, William Stewart-Bradley Klawonn. Human relations counselor Palm Beach County Sch. System, West Palm Beach, Fla., 1974-84; adminstrv. asst. Bohmfalk Estate, Palm Beach, Fla., N.Y.C, Newport, R.I., 1984—; pres., CEO Ruby S. Rinker Co., Inc., Palm Beach. Hon. counselor U.S. Naval Acad., U.S. Air Force Acad.; mem. exec. bd. Intercoastal Health Care Sys. Trustee Bohmfalk Charitable Found., Crystal Cathedral Ministries; bd. dirs. Crystal Cathedral Ministries Internat. Bd. Vatican Mus.; mem. adv. bd. Drug Free Am. Mem. Phi Delta Kappa. Office: 225 Peruvian Ave Palm Beach FL 33480-4672 Home: 1840 S Ocean Blvd Palm Beach FL 33480-5104

**RINNE, AUSTIN DEAN**, retired insurance company executive; b. Aug. 14, 1919; s. Hermann Henry and Marie (Knudsen) R.; m. Martha Jo Runyan, Dec. 29, 1941; children: Erik Knudsen, Barbara Jane Rivera. Student, Ind. U., 1938—40; grad. in Mktg., Purdue U., 1947. Spl. agt. Northwestern Mut. Life, Indpls., 1946-56, dist. agt. 1956-58 gen agt. Dallas, 1958-84, gen. agt. emeritus, 1984—. Bd. dirs., v.p. English Speaking Union, Dallas, 1972, Dallas Opera, 1984—; Indianapolis Philarmonic Orch., 2001— (hon.), Taca Bd., Dallas Cultural Arts Assn. Capt. USAF, 1941-45, ETO. Decorated Purple Heart, Air Medal with cluster, POW medal, Presdl. unit citation Happy Warriors WWII Combat pilots, 8th Air Force assn., 1995; recipient Trail Boss award S.W. Gen. Agts. and Mgrs. Assn., 1993. Mem. Dallas Estate Planning Coun. (pres. 1965-66), Dallas Assn. Life Underwriters (bd. dirs. 1960-63, Hall of Fame 1989), Million Dollar Roundtable (life), Dallas Knife and Fork (pres., bd. dirs. 1986—), Mil. Order World Wars, English-Speaking Union (dir., v.p. Dallas chpt. 1972—), Dallas Coun. on World Affairs, Dallas Sales and Mktg. Execs. (bd. dirs. 1970-73), Am. Legion Dallas (comdr. met. post 1967), VFW, Sertoma (pres. Dallas chpt. 1967-68, mem. found. bd. 1975—, Sertoman of Yr. 1990), Phi Kappa Psi Alumni Assn. (pres. 1951-52), Ind. U. Alumni Assn. (pres. Dallas/Ft. Worth 1968-69), Phi Kappa Psi (exec. coun. 1972-76, endowment bd. 1989—, Dallas sales and mktg. chpt. bd. 1969-72), Park City Club, Dallas Country Club, Northshore Club. Republican. Methodist. Home: 4311 Bordeaux Ave Dallas TX 75205-3719 Office: 3102 Oak Lawn Ave Ste 650 Dallas TX 75219-6400 Fax: (214) 521-4760.

**RINO, BARBARA ELIZABETH**, music educator, musician; b. Lincoln, Nebr., Jan. 14, 1945; d. Howard Gillette and Elizabeth Lucille Cook; m. Louis Stanislaus Rino, Dec. 22, 1974 (dec. Aug. 31, 2004); 1 child, John Gaspare. MusB (with distinction), Nebr. Wesleyan U., Lincoln, 1966; violin study, Harold Wippler, Denver, Colo., 1974—77. Lic. tchr. Colo., 1967. Violinist Lincoln Symphony Orch., Lincoln, Nebr., 1962—66; music educator Denver Pub. Sch., Denver, 1966—68; orch. dir. Adams County Sch. Dist. 50, Westminster, Colo., 1969—78, Adams County Sch. Dist. 12 Five Star Schs., Thornton, Colo., 1988—2001; pvt. studio tchr. self employed, Westminster, Colo., 1971—; concertmaster Brico Symphony Orch., Denver, 1972—74; dir. orch. Denver Youth Musicians Inc., 1973—77, 1984—89; free lance violinist Denver Musicians Assn., Denver, 1973—95; orch. clinician, adj. Solo and Group Competitions Youth Orch. Chair Auditions, Colo., 1973—; concertmaster Rocky Mountain Chamber Orch., 1985—87. Conductor: Colo. Music Educators State Conf., 1972, 1975; musician: Disneyland and Universal Studios, Kennedy Arts Ctr., 1976, Expo '86; author (curriculum): Dist. Orch. grades 6-12, 1990. Music activities Westminister United Meth. Ch., Colo., 1980—. Recipient Outstanding Alumni award, Nebr. Wesleyan U. Dept.

Music, 2006. Mem.: Music Tchrs'. Nat. Assn., Am. String Tchrs. Assn. (Colo. Outstanding Tchr. of the Yr. 2003), Music Educators Nat. Conf., Phi Kappa Phi, Kappa Delta Pi. Meth. Achievements include pvt. violin and viola students consistently chosen to participate in Colo. All State HS Orch., Western States Honor Orch., Denver Young Artist Orch., MTNA divsn., Nat. solo competitions.

**RINSCH, MARYANN ELIZABETH**, occupational therapist; b. L.A., Aug. 8, 1939; d. Harry William and Thora Analine (Langlie) Hitchcock; m. Charles Emil Rinsch, June 18, 1964; children: Christopher, Daniel, Carl. BS, U. Minn., 1961. Registered occupational therapist Calif., lic. Calif., 2003. Staff occupational therapist Hastings (Minn.) State Hosp., 1961-62, Neuropsychiat. Inst., L.A., 1962-64; staff and sr. occupational therapist Calif. Children's Svcs., L.A., 1964-66, head occupational therapist, 1966-68; researcher A. Jean Ayres, U. So. Calif., L.A., 1968-69; pvt. practice neurodevel. and sensory integraton Tarzana, Calif., 1969-74; pediat. occupational therapist neurodevel. & sensory integration St. Johns Hosp., Santa Monica, Calif., 1991-95; pvt. practice, cons. Santa Monica-Malibu Unified Sch. Dist., 1994-2001; pvt. practice, 2001—. Mem. alliance bd. Natural History Mus., L.A. County, 1983—, pres., 1998-99; cub scouts den mother Boy Souts Am., Sherman Oaks, Calif., 1986-88, advancement chair Boy Scout Troop 474, 1989-92; mem. Vol. League San Fernando Valley, Van Nuys, Calif., 1985-93; trustee Viewpoint Sch., Calabasas, Calif., 1987-90; bd. dirs. Valley Women's Ctr., 1990-91. Mem. Am. Occupational Therapy Assn., Calif. Occupational Therapy Assn. Home: 19849 Greenbriar Dr Tarzana CA 91356-5428 Personal E-mail: merinsch@sbcglobal.net.

**RINSKY, ARTHUR C.**, lawyer; b. Cin., July 10, 1944; AB with honors. U. Cin., 1966; JD cum laude, U. Mich., 1969; LLM in Taxation, NYU, 1974. Bar: Fla. 1969, Calif. 1975, U.S. Tax Ct. 1974; cert. tax specialist. Ptr. DLA Piper Rudnick Gray Cary US LLP, Palo Alto, Calif., 1975—. Mem. ABA, State Bar Calif., Phi Beta Kappa, Phi Eta Sigma. Office: DLA Piper Rudnick Gray Cary US LLP 2000 University Ave East Palo Alto CA 94303

**RINSKY, JOEL CHARLES**, lawyer; b. Bklyn., Jan. 29, 1938; s. Irving C. and Elsie (Millman) R.; m. Judith L. Lynn, Jan. 26, 1963; children: Heidi M., Heather S., Jason W. BS, Rutgers U., 1961, LLB, 1962, JD, 1968. Bar: NJ 1963, U.S. Dist. Ct. NJ 1963, U.S. Supreme Ct. 1967, U.S. Ct. Appeals (3d cir.) 1986. Sole practice, Livingston, NJ, 1964—97; sr. ptnr. Rinsky & Marley L.L.C., Livingston, 1997—98; of counsel Poles, Tublin, Stratakis, Gonzalez and Weichert LLP, Livingston, 1999—. Committeeman Millburn-Short Hills (N.J.) Dem. Com., 1982-87, vice chmn., 1983-87; trustee Student Loan Fund, Millburn, 1983-91. Fellow Am. Acad. Matrimonial Lawyers; mem. N.J. Bar Assn., Essex County Bar Assn. (exec. com. sect. family law). Jewish. Avocations: tennis, chess, golf, piano. Home: 87 Sullivan Dr West Orange NJ 07052-2262 Office: 127 E Mount Pleasant Ave Livingston NJ 07039-3005 Office Phone: 973-992-3555. Personal E-mail: rinsky3@aol.com. Business E-Mail: rinsky2@comcast.org. E-mail: jrinsky@polestublin.com.

**RINSKY, JUDITH SUE LYNN**, foundation administrator, educator consultant; b. Sept. 12, 1941; d. Allan A. and Sophie (Schwartz) Lynn; m. Joel C. Rinsky, Jan. 29, 1963; children: Heidi Mae Schnapp, Heather Star Maxon, Jason Wayne. BA in Home Econs., Montclair State U., 1963. Tchr. home econs. Florence Ave. Sch.. Irvington, NJ, 1963—66; substitute tchr. Millburn-Short Hills Sch. Sys., Millburn Twp., NJ, 1978—82, Millburn-Short Hills Sch. Sys., Millburn Twp., 1990—98; sr. citizen coord. Millburn-Short Hills Sch. Sys., Millburn Twp., 1982—87; coord. respite care Essex County Divsn. on Aging, East Orange, NJ, 1988—90; pvt. practice educator Short Hills, NJ, 1990—98; tchr. basic skills Millburn H.S., 1998—. Bd. mem. adv. com. gerontology Seton Hall U., 1984—90; coord. Mayor's Adv. Bd. Sr. Citizens, Millburn-Short Hills, 1982—87; home instrn. Millburn-Short Hills Sch. Sys., 1997—98; tchr. adv. Millburn H.S. Interart Club, 2000—. Pres. Deerfield Sch. PTA, 1979-80, Millburn H.S. PTA, 1983-85; co-chmn. dinner dance Charles T. King Student Loan Fund, 1981; active Handicapped Access Study Com., 1983-85; bd. dirs. Coun. on Health and Human Svcs., 1985-90, 94-97; acting dir. B'nai Israel Nursery Sch., 1994. Mem. Lake Naomi Assn. (chmn. sailing com. 1981), N.J. Home Econs. Assn., Am. Home Econs. Assn., Rotary (hon., pres. Millburn-Short Hills club 1992-93, bd. dirs. 1992-2000, advisor Millburn interact club 1987-98, 2000-04, chmn. internat. interact dist. 7470 1993-95, advisor 1995-98). Home and Office: 87 Sullivan Dr West Orange NJ 07052-2262 Office Phone: 973-376-3600. Personal E-mail: jsr_07041@yahoo.com. Business E-Mail: rinsky@millburn.org.

**RINZEL, DENNIS JOSEPH**, media specialist, director; b. Port Washington, Wis., Mar. 18, 1946; s. Benedict Steven and Leona Olga (Ebert) R.; m. Kathleen Agnes Bodilly, Aug. 12, 1978; children: Micah, Jonah, Uriah, Eliah Jesse, Tirzah, Justina. BA, Marquette U., 1968; MA, U. Wis., 1975. Cameraman, set design builder Marquette U. Sch. Nursing, Milw., 1967-68, S.C. Ednl. TV Network, Columbia, 1968-69; dir. video resource ctr. U. Wis. Madison, 1972—. Co-chmn. Com. on Use of Media in Social Work Edn., Phoenix, 1979-83. Producer, dir. record album: Works of God, 1980, also numerous ednl. video programs. Co-leader marriage ministry team St. James Cath. Ch., 1986-92. With U.S. Army, 1968-70, Vietnam. Decorated Bronze Star. Avocations: singing, bicycling, gardening, swimming, photography. Home: 941 E Dayton St Madison WI 53703-2319 Office: U Wis Video Resource Ctr 279 Van Hise Hall 1220 Linden Dr Madison WI 53706-1525 Office Phone: 608-263-3828. Business E-Mail: dennis@lss.wisc.edu.

**RION, JOHN HAYES**, lawyer; b. Dayton, Ohio, Aug. 4, 1943; s. Paul West and Vera E. (Spitler) R.; m. Barbara Smith, July 31, 1965; children: Stacey, Jennifer, Jon Paul. BA, Ohio State U., 1965, JD, U. Toledo, 1969. Bar: Ohio 1970, U.S. Dist. Ct. (so. dist.) Ohio 1970, U.S. Ct. Appeals (6th cir.) 1983, U.S. Supreme Ct. 1977; cert. Criminal Trial Advocate, Nat. Bd. Trial Advocacy. Ptnr., Rion, Rion & Rion, Dayton, Ohio, 1969-78; v.p. Rion, Rion & Rion, L.P.A., 1978-88; pres. John H. Rion & Assocts., 1988-97; ptnr., chmn. Rion, Rion & Rion, L.P.A., Inc., Dayton, 1997—; lectr. in field. Contbr. articles to profl. jours. Mem. jud. selection com. Republican Com., 1974. Mem. NACDL (life), ABA, Ohio State Bar Assn. (faculty 1983, chmn. criminal justice com. 1989-91, setting standards for bd. cert. com. 1999), Dayton Bar Assn. (Outstanding Service award 1977, 80, chmn. bar briefs 1975), Ohio Assn. Criminal Def. Lawyers (life, pres. 1989, chmn. 1990), Montgomery County Trial Lawyers (v.p. 1989-90, mem. bd. trustees 1990), Calif. Def. Lawyers Assn., Ohio Trial Lawyers Assn. Republican. Methodist (pres. Grace United Ch. Ushers Club 1982-84). Clubs: Dayton Racquet, Comos (pres. 1982-84), Briarwood Sportsman. Lodges: Masons (32 degree), Shriners. Avocations: fly fishing, tennis. Office: Rion Rion and Rion PO Box 1262 Dayton OH 45402-9762 E-mail: info@rionlaw.com.

**RIOPELLE, ARTHUR JEAN**, psychologist; b. Thorp, Wis., Apr. 22, 1920; s. Wilfred Gaspar and Anne Marie (Schroeder) R.; m. Mary Jane Astell, May 2, 1942; children— Mary Ann, James Michael, Jean Elizabeth. BS, U. Wis., 1941, MS, 1948, PhD, 1950. Asst. prof., then assoc. prof. Emory U., 1950-57; dir. psychology div. U.S. Army Med. Research Lab., Ft. Knox, Ky., 1957-59; dir. Yerkes Labs. Primate Biology, Orange Park, Fla., 1959-62, Delta Regional Primate Research Ctr., Covington, La., 1962-71; prof. psychology La. State U., Baton Rouge, 1971—, Boyd prof., 1977-89, Boyd prof. emeritus, 1989—. Mem. NRC panel on manganese, Com. on Med. and Biol. Effects of Environ. Pollutants Editor Jour. Gen. Psychology, 1978-95; asst. editor Animal Behavior, 1962-65; cons. editor Jour. Genetic Psychology and Genetic Psychology Monograph, 1973-95; contbr. chpts. to books. La. Bd. Examiners of Psychologists, 1972-75; mem. panel on Air Force tng. Nat. Acad. Sci.-NRC, 1955-56; primate research study sect. Am. Inst. Biol. Scis.-NASA, 1959-63; mem. on man Lunar Receiving Lab. Study, 1970-71; chmn. U.S.-Japan Conf. Primate Research, 1963-64; chmn. subcom. primate standards Inst. Lab. Animal Resources, NRC, 1964-69. Served with USAAF, 1942-46, ETO. Mem. Am Psychol. Assn., Am. Physiol. Soc., So. Soc. Philosophy and Psychology, Internat. Primatological Soc., AAAS, Psychonomic Soc., Southeastern Psychol. Assn., Sigma Xi, Phi Kappa Phi,

Sigma Chi. Home: 9710 Highland Rd Baton Rouge LA 70810-4031 Office: La State U Dept Psychology Baton Rouge LA 70803-0001 Personal E-mail: ariope@bellsouth.net. Business E-Mail: ariope@lsu.edu.

**RIOPKA, TARAS P.,** computer engineer; s. John and Stefanie Riopka. BSc in Mech. Engring., U. Toronto, 1986, MSc in Mech. Engring., 1989; MSc in Computer Sci., U. Rochester, N.Y., 1995; Phd in Computer Sci., The George Wash. U., Washington, D.C., 2001. Adminstr. Image Analysis Lab. U. Toronto, 1987—89; rsch. engr. Perceptive Sci. Instruments, Inc., League City, Tex., 1990—94; post-doctoral rschr. Lehigh U., Bethlehem, Pa., 2002—04; sr. imaging scientist Aware, Inc., Bedford, Mass., 2004—. Course instr. The George Wash. U., Washington, 1997—2001; cons. in field. Author: The Collective Learning Genetic Algorithm; contbr. chapters to books. Mem.: IEEE (assoc.). Achievements include invention of collective learning genetic algorithm; patents pending for classification system improvement via prediction and perturbations. Avocations: astronomy, skiing, travel. Office: Aware Inc 40 Middlesex Turnpike Bedford MA 01730 Office Phone: 781-687-0473. Personal E-mail: riopka@kantbelievemyeyes.com. Business E-Mail: triopka@aware.com.

**RIORDAN, GEORGE NICKERSON,** investment banker; b. Patchogue, NY, May 16, 1933; s. E. Arthur and Constance E. (Whelden) R.; m. Ann Wiggins, Jan. 4, 1958; children— Susan M., Peter G. BS, Cornell U., 1955; MBA, Harvard U., 1960. Vice-pres. Lehman Bros., N.Y.C., 1960-71; mng. dir. Blyth Eastman Paine Webber, Los Angeles and N.Y.C., 1971-81; Prudential-Bache Securities, Los Angeles, 1981-88, Bear Stearns & Co., Inc., L.A., 1988-89, Dean Witter Reynolds Inc., 1989-91. Chmn. bd. MSC Software, Inc., 1997-99; bd. dirs. MSC Software, Inc., L.A. Served to capt. USAF, 1955-57 Mem. Calif. Club, Quoque Field Club (L.I., N.Y.), Athenaeum Club, Valley Hunt Club (Pasadena, Calif.). Office: 815 Colorado Blvd Ste 104 Los Angeles CA 90041-1720 Business E-Mail: george.riordan@mscsoftware.com.

**RIORDAN, JAMES QUENTIN,** retired oil industry executive, lawyer; b. Bklyn., June 17, 1927; s. James A. and Ruth M. (Boomer) R.; m. Gloria H. Carlson, June 23, 1951; children: Harris, Susan, James, Ruth. BA, Bklyn. Coll., 1945; LLB, Columbia U., 1949. Bar: N.Y. 1951, U.S. Supreme Ct. 1954. Atty. Winthrop, Stimson, Putnam & Roberts, N.Y.C., 1949-51; mem. staff Ways and Means sub-com., Washington, 1951-52; atty. tax div. Justice Dept., Washington, 1952-55; atty. Chadbourne, Parke, Whiteside & Wolff, N.Y.C., 1955-57; various positions to vice chmn., chief fin. officer Mobil Corp., 1957-89; pres. Bekaert Corp., 1989-92; chmn. Quentin Ptnrs. Co., 1996—. Bd. dirs. Com. Econ. Devel., Tax Found., Inc.; trustee Bklyn. Mus. Mem. Rembrandt Club (N.Y.C.), Blind Brook Club, Sailfish Point (Fla.), Stockbridge Club. Office: 851 Johnson Ave Stuart FL 34994 Office Phone: 772-220-4127.

**RIORDAN, JOHN THOMAS,** trade association executive, consultant; b. Newark, June 5, 1937; s. Daniel Francis and Kathleen May (Hanan) R.; m. Mary Theresa Fleming, Sept. 10, 1966; children: Sheila, Patrick, Aidan, Meghan, Brendan, Caitlin. BA, Montclair St. Coll., 1959; MA, Laval U., Que., Can., 1963; postgrad., Harvard U., 1980. Tchr. Princeton (N.J.) Pub. Schs., 1959-64; instr. SUNY, Cortland, 1965; editor McGraw-Hill Book Co., St. Louis, 1966; assoc. examiner Ednl. Testing Svc., Princeton, 1967-68; mgr. Houghton Mifflin Co., Boston, 1968-73, editl. dir., 1973-74; v.p. Hougton Mifflin Co., Boston, 1974-75, dir., 1975, sr. v.p., 1975-81; dir. programs Internat. Coun. Shopping Ctrs., N.Y.C., 1982-83, gen. mgr., 1983-85, exec. v.p., 1986-96, pres., CEO, 1997—2001, vice chmn., 2001—03, lifetime trustee, 2003. Cons., leader Experiment in Internat. Living, Brattleboro, Vt., 1961-64; mem. adv. bd. Sch. Internat. Tng., Brattleboro, 1971-79, Real Estate Ctr. U. Pa., 1991—, Ctr. for Real Estate MIT, 1992—; mem. fin. adv. bd. City of Georgetown, Mass., 1972-75, chmn. 2001-03; trustee The Pike Sch., Andover, Mass., 1973-76; bd. trustees Travel Bus. Roundtable; mem. adv. bd. Baruch Coll., adv. bd. MIT ctr. for real estate, adv. bd. U Pa. real estate ctr.; bd. dirs. Gen. Growth Properties, 2003—. Mem.: Am. Soc. Assn. Execs. (bd. dirs. Ivanhoe/Cambridge 2005—). E-mail: jtriordan@aol.com.

**RIORDAN, MICHAEL C.,** hospital administrator; b. N.J., 1959; BA in liberal arts and English, Columbia U., 1980, MA in edn. and psychology, 1981; M in health sys., Ga. Inst. Tech., 1986. Various positions Crawford Long Hosp., Atlanta; COO Emory U. Hosp. Sys., 1995—2000; exec. v.p. and COO U. Chgo. Hospitals, 2000—01, pres. and CEO, 2001—. With USMC, 1981—85. Office: U Chgo Hosps and Health Sys 5841 S Maryland Ave Chicago IL 60637*

**RIORDAN, RICHARD J.,** former state official, former mayor; b. Flushing, NY, 1930; m. Eugenia Riordan; 6 children (2 dec.); m. Jill Riordan; m. Nancy Daly Riordan; 3 children. Attended, U. Calif., Santa Clara; grad., Princeton U., 1952; JD, U. Mich., 1956. With O'Melveny & Myers, LA; owner, operator Original Pantry Cafe; founder Total Pharmaceutical Care, Tetra Tech; atty. Riordan & McKinzie, 1970—2003; mayor LA, 1993—2001; sec. of edn. State of Calif., Sacramento, 2003—05. Co-founder LEARN, 1991; sponsor Writing to Read computer labs Riordan Found.; active Eastside Boys and Girls Club. Lt. U.S. Army, Korea.

**RIORDAN, RICK,** writer; b. San Antonio, Tex. married; 2 children. Graduate, Univ. Tex., Austin. Former English, history tchr., Calif. and Tex. Author: (novels) Big Red Tequila, 1997 (Anthony award for best original paperback novel, Shamus award for best first private eye novel), Widower's Two-Step, 1998 (Edgar Allen Poe award for best original paperback novel, 1999), Last King of Texas, 2000, Devil Went Down to Texas, 2001, Cold Springs, 2003 (One of top 10 suspense novels, Am.Libr. Assn., 2003), South Town, 2004 (Edgar award, 2004), Mission Road, 2005, (childrens books) Percy Jackson & the Olympians: The Lightning Thief, 2005. Inducted into Tex. Inst. Letters, 2003. Mailing: c/o Nancy Gallt Lit Agcy 273 Charlton Ave South Orange NJ 07079 Address: c/o Gina Maccoby Lit Agy PO Box 60 Chappaqua NY 10514 E-mail: rick@rickriordan.com.

**RIORDAN, ROBERT P.,** lawyer; b. Milw., Feb. 6, 1958; AB, Duke Univ., 1980, JD, 1984. Bar: Ga. 1984. Ptnr., head, labor and employment group Alston & Bird LLP, Atlanta. Mem.: ABA, Henry L. Lumpkin Am. Inn of Ct., Atlanta Bar Assn., Ga. Bar Assn. Office: Alston & Bird LLP One Atlantic Ctr 1201 W Peachtree St NW Atlanta GA 30309-3424 Office Phone: 404-881-7682. Office Fax: 404-881-7777. Business E-Mail: briordan@alston.com.

**RIOS, ELENA,** health association administrator; BA, Stanford U., 1977; M in Health Policy and Planning Analysis, UCLA, 1980, MD, 1987. With State of Calif. Office of Statewide Health Planning and Devel.; mem. Nat. Health Care Reform Task Force; coord. outreach groups for White House; advisor regional and minority women's health U.S. Dept. Health and Human Svcs., 1994—98; pres., CEO Nat. Hispanic Med. Assn. Primary care health svcs. rsch. fellow UCLA, 1990; CEO Hispanic-Serving Health Professions Schools, Inc.; bd. dirs. Nat. Hispanic Leadership Agenda, Women's Policy Inc., Partnerships for Prevention; co-chair Hispanic Health Coalition; mem. advisory panel Medicare Edn.; lectr. in field. Named one of Top 10 Latinos in Healthcare, LatinoLeaders mag., 2004. Office: Nat Hispanic Med Assn 1411 K St NW Ste 1100 Washington DC 20005*

**RIOS, EVELYN DEERWESTER,** columnist, musician, artist, writer; b. Payne, Ohio, June 25, 1916; d. Jay Russell and Flossie Edith (Fell) Deerwester; m. Edwin Tietjen Rios, Sept. 19, 1942 (dec. Feb. 1987); children: Jane Evelyn, Linda Sue Rios Stahlman. BA with honors, San Jose State U., 1964, MA, 1968. Cert. elem., secondary tchr. Calif. Lectr. in music San Jose (Calif.) State U., 1969-75; from bilingual cons. to assoc. editor Ednl. Factors, Inc., San Jose, 1969-76, mgr. field rsch., 1977-78; writer, editor Calif. MediCorps Program, 1978-83; contbg. editor, illustrator Cmty. Family Mag., Wimberly, Tex., 1983-85; columnist The Springer, Dripping Springs, Tex., 1985-90. Author, illustrator, health instr. textbooks elem. schs., 1980—82. Author: The Best of It Seems To Me, 2002. Chmn. Dripping Springs Planning

and Zoning Commn., 1991—93; music dir. Cambrian Park (Calif.) Meth. Ch., 1961—64; choir dir. Bethel Luth. Ch., Cupertino, Calif., 1965—66, 1968—83; dir. music St. Aban's Ch., Bogota, Colombia; organist Holy Spirit Episcopal Ch., Dripping Springs, 1987—94. Mem.: Am. Guild Organists (dean 1963—64), Phi Kappa Phi (pres. San Jose chpt. 1973—74). Avocations: weaving, stitching, painting. Home: PO Box 3175 Atascadero CA 93423-3175

**RIOUX, PIERRE AUGUST,** psychiatrist; b. Hartford, Conn., Sept. 2, 1953; s. Berchmans and Mary (Sauter) R. BA, Concordia Coll., 1975; MD U. N.D. 1981. Diplomate Am. Bd. Psychiatry and Neurology. Intern U. Mich. 1981-82, resident, 1982-85; asst. prof. dept. psychiatry Emory U., Atlanta, 1985-86; attending physician VA Med. Ctr., Atlanta, 1985-86; staff physician UniMed Med. Ctr., Minot, ND, 1986-87, med. dir. adult partial hospitalization program, 1988-98, dir. behavioral health svcs., 1990—2001; med. dir. North Ctrl. Human Svc. Ctr., Minot, 1987-98; med. dir. stress unit Austin Med. Ctr., 2001—; med. dir. behavioral health Mayo Health Sys., Austin, 2003—06, med. dir. dept. psychiatry and psychology, 2006—; instr. Mayo Med. Sch., 2003—. Cons. North Ctrl. Human Svc. Ctr., 1986—2001; mem. chem. dependency unit UniMed Med. Ctr., 1986—; mem. adv. bd. UniMed Med. Ctr., 1998—2001; clin. prof. neurosci. U. ND Sch. Medicine, 1986—96; mem. family practice residence adv. bd. com. U. N.D., 1987—95; physician advisor N.D. Health Care Rev., Inc., 1987—2001; dir. psychiat. svcs. Dakota Boys Ranch, Minot, 1990—94; med. dir. Rural Mental Health Consortium, 1999—2001; instr. Mayo Med. Sch., 2003—. Bd. Am. Coll. of Heraldry, 2003; comsumer rsch. coun. America's Top Psychiatrists, 2002—. Recipient Nat. Alliance for the Mentally Ill Exemplary Psychiatrist award, 1993, Top Psychiatrists in Am. award Consumers Rsch. Coun. Am., 2003. Fellow Am. Coll. Forensic Examiners (life); mem. AMA, Am. Psychiat. Assn. (pres. N.D. dist. br. 1993-96, dep. rep. area IV coun. 1993-98, mem. psychiat. svcs. achievement awards bd. 1996-97, chmn. 1998, fellowship award 1996, disting. fellowship award 2003), Assn. Am. Physicians and Surgeons, Am. Soc. Clin. Psychopharmacology, N.D. Psychiat. Assn. (dist. br. exec. coun. 1997-2001), N.D. Med. Assn. (mem. commn. on socio-econ. affairs 1997-2001), Internat. Soc. for Philos. Enquiry (pres.2002-05) Avocation: art. Office: PO Box 188 Austin MN 55912-0188

**RIPA, KELLY MARIA,** television personality, actress; b. Stratford, N.J., Oct. 2, 1970; d. Joseph and Esther Ripa; m. Mark Consuelos, 1996; children: Michael Joseph, Lola Grace, Joaquin Antonio. Student, Camden CC, NJ. Co-host Live with Regis and Kelly, NY, 2001—. Dancer (TV series) Dance Party USA, 1990; actor: (TV series) All My Children, 1990—2002 (Soap Opera Digest award, 1996, 1998, 2000, 3 Daytime Emmy nominations); (films) Marvin's Room, 1996, The Stand-In, 1999 (Best Actress award N.Y. Internat. Ind. Film and Video Festival, 1999), It's a Very Merry Muppet Christmas Movie, 2002, Cheaper by the Dozen, 2003; (TV films) Someone to Love, 2001; voice: (film) Kim Possible: A Stitch in Time, 2003; Batman: Mystery of the Batwoman, 2003; actor: (TV series) Hope & Faith, 2003—. Nominee Outstanding Talkshow Host award, Daytime Emmy; named one of 25 Most Intriguing People, People Mag., 2001, Top 20 Entertainers of Yr., E! Entertainment. Office: Live with Regis and Kelly 7 Lincoln Sq New York NY 10023*

**RIPERT, ERIC,** food service executive; b. Antibes, France, Mar. 2, 1965; married. Grad., Culinary Sch., Perpignan, France, 1982. Apprentice La Tour D'Argent, Paris; with Jamin; sous chef Watergate Hotel, Washington; with Bouley, N.Y.C.; exec. chef Le Bernardin, N.Y.C., 1991—94, chef, 1994—, co-owner. Active French Mil. Recipient Top Chef in N.Y.C. award James Beard Found., 2003. Avocations: eating, travel, skiing.*

**RIPKEN, CALVIN EDWIN, JR., (CAL RIPKEN)** retired professional baseball player; b. Havre de Grace, Md., Aug. 24, 1960; Player minor league teams, Bluefield, Miami, Charlotte, Rochester, 1978—81; player Balt. Orioles, 1978—2001. Named Am. League MVP, 1983, 1991, MLB All-Star Game MVP, 1983, 2001, Male Athlete of Yr., AP, 1995; named to All-Star Team, Am. League, 1983—2001, MLB All-Century Team, 1999; recipient Rookie of Yr. award, 1982, Golden Glove award, 1991—92. Achievements include being a holder of the major league record for consecutive games played; breaking Lou Gehrig's record of 2131 consecutive games played, 1995; maj. league record home runs by shortstop; highest single season fielding percentage (.996), 1990; most consecutive errorless games at shortstop (95); led Am. League in Runs (121), Hits (211), 1983.

**RIPLEY, CHARLENE A.,** lawyer; BA, U. Alberta; JD, Dalhousie U., Nova Scotia. Counsel Amoco Can. Petroleum Co. Limited, 1990—97; sr. counsel Norcen Energy Resources Limited (predecessor to Anadarko Can. Corp.), 1997—98, v.p., gen. counsel, corp. sec., 1998—2003; v.p., gen. counsel Anadarko Petroleum Corp., 2003—, corp. sec., 2004—. Mem.: Alberta Arbitration & Mediation Soc., Tex. State Bar, API Gen. Com. on Law, Tex. Gen. Counsel Group, Assn. Corp. Counsel, Law Soc. Alberta, Can. Bar Assn. Office: Anadarko Petroleum Corp 1201 Lake Robbins Dr The Woodlands TX 77380-1046 Office Fax: 832-636-8220, 832-636-1000.

**RIPLEY, RANDALL BUTLER,** political scientist, educator; b. Des Moines, Jan. 24, 1938; s. Henry Dayton and Aletha (Butler) R.; m. Grace A. Franklin, Oct. 15, 1974; children: Frederick Joseph, Vanessa Gail. BA, DePauw U., 1959; MA, Harvard U., 1961, PhD, 1963. Tchg. fellow Harvard, 1960-62; mem. staff Brookings Inst., Washington, 1963-67, rsch. asst., 1963-64, rsch. assoc., 1964-67; intern Office Dem. Whip, US Ho. of Reps., Washington, 1963; assoc. prof. dept. polit. sci. Ohio State U., Columbus, 1967-69, prof., 1969—2005, prof. emeritus, 2005, chmn., 1969-91, dean Coll. Social and Behavioral Scis., 1992—2004. Lectr. Cath. U., Washington, 1963-64; professorial lectr. Am. U., Washington, 1964-67; vis. prof. U. Okla., 1969-91. Author: Public Policies and Their Politics, 1966, Party Leaders in the House of Representatives, 1967, Majority Party Leadership in Congress, 1969, Power in the Senate, 1969, The Politics of Economic and Human Resource Development, 1972, Legislative Politics U.S.A, 1973, American National Government and Public Policy, 1974, Congress: Process and Policy, 1975, 4th edit., 1988, Policy-making in the Federal Executive Branch, 1975, Congress, the Bureaucracy, and Public Policy, 1976, 5th edit., 1991, National Government and Policy in the United States, 1977, A More Perfect Union, 1979, 4th edit., 1989, Policy Implementation and Bureaucracy, 1982, 2d edit., 1986, CETA: Politics and Policy, 1973-82, 1984, Policy Analysis in Political Science, 1985, Readings in American Government and Politics, 1989, 2d edit. 1993, 3d edit., 1999, Congress Resurgent, 1993, U.S. Foreign Policy After the Cold War, 1997, American Labor Unions in the Electoral Arena, 2001; contbr. articles to profl. jours. Bd. govs. Stratford Festival, Ont., Can., 1994-98. Woodrow Wilson fellow, 1959-60; Danforth fellow, 1959-63; recipient Sumner prize Harvard, 1963 Mem. Am. Polit. Sci. Assn. (sec. 1978), Phi Beta Kappa. Democrat. Home: 11465 Cable Rd SW Pataskala OH 43062-8809 Office Phone: 614-292-4392. Personal E-mail: ripley.1@osu.edu.

**RIPMA, MARY,** librarian; b. St. Johns, Mich., Aug. 7, 1952; d. Charles William and Vera Elizabeth Austin; m. Mark Gale Ripma, Apr. 29, 1978; children: Lee, Tye, Clay. BA, Mich. State U., 1974; MLS, San Jose State U., Calif., 1977; cert. in bus. mgmt., Cañada Coll., Redwood City, Calif., 2000. Dir. editl. Info. Access Corp., Redwood City, 1977—83; info. advisor Mothers with Babies, Menlo Park, Calif., 1983—88; reference libr. Menlo Park Pub. Libr., 1988—92; bus. specialist Dialog Inc., Mountain View, Calif., 1992—98; mgr. Menlo Park Rsch. Inc., 1998—2001; mgr., owner www.yourgetawayhouse.com, Santa Cruz, Calif., 2001—. Vol. libr. Kristin Sch., Albany, New Zealand, 2004—; music program organizer, rm. mother PTA, Menlo Park, 1987—2004. Seeburg scholar, San Jose State U., 1977. Mem.: AAUW, Forest & Bird, Warkworth Quilting Club, Collie Club of Am. Democrat. Unitarian. Avocations: quilting, swimming. Home: 217 Goatley Rd Warkworth 1241 New Zealand Mailing: 849 Almar Ave Ste C 190 Santa Cruz CA 95060 E-mail: ripma@hotmail.com.

**RIPOLL, SHAKIRA ISABEL MEBARAK See SHAKIRA**

**RIPP, JOSEPH ALLEN,** information technology executive; b. N.Y.C., Nov. 29, 1951; m. Virginia Nolan. BA, Manhattan Coll.; MBA, Bernard M. Baruch Coll. CUNY, 1980. Mgr. Ernst & Whinney, N.Y.C., 1973-82; asst. contr. Time Inc., N.Y.C., 1982-85, v.p. fin., 1985-90, v.p., CFO, 1990-92, sr. v.p., CFO, 1992-94, exec. v.p., CFO, 1994-99, Time Warner Inc., N.Y.C., 1999-01; CFO America On-Line, Inc., 2001—03, vice chmn., 2002—04; sr. v.p. media & comm. group Time Warner Inc., 2004—05; pres., COO Dendrite Internat. Inc., Bedminster, NJ, 2005—. Bd. dirs. Greenfield Online Inc. Trustee Manhattan Coll.; bd. dir. Advt. Edn. Found.; bd. dir. mem. exec. com., chmn. fin. com. Ad Council Office: Dendrite Internat Inc 1405-1425 Rt 206 S Bedminster NJ 07921*

**RIPP, KENNETH LEON,** secondary school educator; b. Waunakee, Wis., Jan. 12, 1953; s. Jerome Jacob and Dolores Mary Ripp; m. Sue Ellen Ripp, June 2, 1973; children: Brian, Christopher Steven. BA, Milton Coll., Wis., 1975; MA, U. Colo., Boulder, 1982; postgrad., U. Minn., Mpls., 2001. Econs. and psychology tchr. Eau Claire Meml. HS, Wis., 1975—. Presenter in field. Named Tchr. of Yr., Wis. Coun. Econ. Edn., Milw., 1980, 1983, 1993, 1999; recipient Nat. Tchr. of Yr. in Econs., Found. Tchg. Econs., Davis, 1997. Mem.: Wis. Coun. Social Studies, Nat. Coun. Social Studies. Home: 127 E MacArthur Ave Eau Claire WI 54701 Office: Eau Claire Meml HS 2225 Keith St Eau Claire WI 54701

**RIPPE, LYNN E.,** portfolio manager; b. Superior, Nebr., Dec. 27, 1947; children: Douglas E., Christopher C. BA in Econs., Kansas State U., 1969; MBA, So. Ill. U., Edwardsville, 1977. Contract specialist, contracting officer Naval Constrn. Bn. Ctr., Port Hueneme, Calif., 1989-93; sr. contract adminstr. U. Calif. Lawrence Livermore (Calif.) Nat. Lab., 1993-98; computing scis. subcontracts mgr. U. Calif. Lawrence Berkeley Nat. Lab., 1998—. Mem. Nat. Contract Mgmt. Assn. (v.p. Tri Valley chpt. 1995-96, pres. 1996-97, nat. dir. 1997-98, 2000-01, nat. v.p. 2001-03). Republican. Roman Catholic. Home: 3478 FM 1670 Belton TX 76513 Office: U Calif Lawrence Berkeley Nat Lab M-50B One Cyclotron Rd Berkeley CA 94720 Office Phone: 254-939-5514. E-mail: lerippe@nersc.gov.

**RIPPERT, ERIC THEODORE,** oral and maxillofacial surgeon, healthcare consultant; b. Ft. Devens, Mass., Feb. 22, 1942; s. Jacob Kopf and Kathleen (Faughnan) R.; m. Mary Ellen Dormer, Nov. 25, 1965; children: Thomas, Kathleen. AB, Holy Cross Coll., 1964; DMD, U. Pa., 1968. Diplomate Am. Bd. Oral and Maxillofacial Surgery. Intern Phila. Gen. Hosp., 1968-69, resident, 1973-76; dental officer U.S. Navy, 1965-95; asst. prof. oral and maxillofacial surgery U. Nebr., Lincoln, 1996-99; asst. prof. U. Pitts. 1999-2000; assoc. prof. Med. Coll. Va., Richmond, 2000—02; assoc. prof., dir. residency tng., oral and maxillofacial surgery Med. Coll. Ga., Augusta, Ga., 2002—05; cons. in health care, 2005—. Clin. asst. prof. Med. Coll. Va., Richmond, 1979-81; adj. assoc. prof. Temple U., Phila., 1984-87; asst. prof. U. Calif., San Francisco, 1991-93. Fellow Am. Assn. Oral and Maxillofacial Surgeons, Am. Coll. Dentists, Internat. Coll. Dentists; mem. Varsity Club Coll. Holy Cross, Delta Sigma Delta. Republican. Roman Catholic. Avocations: tennis, skiing, speech and dialogue, writing. Office Phone: 706-836-0781. Personal E-mail: etrippert@yahoo.com.

**RIPPETEAU, DARREL DOWNING,** retired architect; b. Clay Center, Nebr., Jan. 14, 1917; s. Claude LaVerne and Eva (Downing) R.; m. Donna Doris Hiatt, Jan. 8, 1939 (dec. 1988); children: Bruce Estes, Darrel Downing, Jane Upson Heffron; m. Joyce Spencer, May 18, 1991. BA in Architecture, U. Nebr., 1941. Staff architect FHA, Omaha, 1941-42; project mgr., mng. ptnr. Sargent-Webster-Crenshaw & Folley, Archs. and Engrs., Watertown, Buffalo, Syracuse, N.Y., Burlington, Vt, Bangor, Maine, 1946-81; treas., dir. Empire Forest System, Albany, N.Y., 1984-89; ret., 1990. Bd. dirs. Archtl. Corp. Atlanta, Key Bank No. N.Y., Watertown Assn. Island Recreational Corp.; commr. N.Y. State Coun. Architecture, 1975-85; mem. N.Y. State Forest Practice Bd., 1980-2000, chmn., 1994-98; bd. adv. bd. mem. Remington Art Mus., Ogdensburg, N.Y., 1983-95. Prin. works include Justice Bldg, Albany, N.Y. State Office Bldg Watertown, Toomey Abbott Towers Syracuse, State U. N.Y. Cortland, U.S. P.O. Facility Syracuse. Mem. nat. fin. com. Rep. Party, 1971-73; bd. trustees The Antique Boat Mus., Clayton, N.Y., 1973-99, Glenn Curtiss Mus., Hammondsport, N.Y. Maj. U.S. Army, 1942-46; lt. col. Corps of Engrs. retired, 1977. Recipient North Country citation St. Lawrence U., Canton, N.Y., 1971; Sears-Roebuck scholar, 1936-37; U. Nebr. Dept. Architecture grantee, 1940-41; Nebr. master U. Nebr., 1971; Disting. Alumni award Coll. of Architecture Alumni Assn., U. Nebr., 1996. Fellow AIA (nat. dir. 1969-73, trustee AIA Found. 1970-73); mem. Greater Watertown C. of C. (past pres.), N.Y. State Assn. Indsl. Devel. Agys. (past v.p.), N.Y. State Assn. Architects (pres. 1968-69, polit. action com. 1980-98, James Kideney award 1987), Bldg. Rsch. Inst., Res. Officers Assn. (past pres.), Am. Tree Farm Assn., Jefferson County Hist. Soc. (dir. 1974-78), OX-5 Aviation Pioneers (chpt. pres.), Assn. U.S. Army (chpt. pres. 1985-86). Republican. Presbyterian. Home: 1011 NW 3rd Ave Delray Beach FL 33444-2938

**RIPPL, FRANK GEORGE,** retired music educator, retired organist; b. Neenah, Wis., Aug. 8, 1947; s. Paul Frank and Marilla Terrien Rippl; m. Carol Ann Jegen. MusB, Lawrence U., 1965—69; MA, U. of Denver, 1977—80. Orff-Schulwerk U. of Toronto, 1973. Elem. vocal music tchr. Appleton Area Sch. Dist., Wis., 1969—2002; organist/choirmaster All Saints' Episcopal Ch., Appleton, Wis., 1971—; co-founder, dir. Appleton Boychoir, INC, Wis., 1979—2001. Dean Northeastern Wis. Chpt. of the Am. Guild of Organists, Appleton, Wis., 1974—76, bd. of directors, 2001—04. Author: (monograph) An Architectural and Historical Walking Tour of The Columbus Elementary School Neighborhood, A Brief History of Pipe Organs in Lawrence University's Memorial Chapel, A History of Lincoln Elementary School, Appleton, A Brief History of Pipe Organs in the Appleton Area. Founder/coord. Lunchtime Organ Recital Series, Wis., 1995—. Recipient First Ann. Appreciation award, Appleton Heritage Soc., 1999. Mem.: Packerland Theatre Organ Soc., Organ Hist. Soc., Am. Guild of Organists (dean 1974—76). Home: 503 East Pacific St Appleton WI 54911 Office: All Saints' Episcopal Ch 100 North Drew St Appleton WI 54911 Office Phone: 920-734-3656.

**RIPPLE, KENNETH FRANCIS,** federal judge; b. Pitts., May 19, 1943; s. Raymond John and Rita (Holden) Ripple; m. Mary Andrea DeWeese, July 27, 1968; children: Gregory, Raymond, Christopher. AB, Fordham U., 1965; JD, U. Va., 1968; LLM, George Washington U., 1972, LLD (hon.), 1992. Bar: Va. 1968, N.Y. 1969, U.S. Supreme Ct. 1972, U.S. Supreme Ct. 1972, D.C. 1976, Ind. 1984, U.S. Ct. Appeals (7th cir.), U.S. Ct. Mil. Appeals, U.S. Dist. Ct. (no. dist.) Ind. Atty. IBM Corp., Armonk, NY, 1968; legal officer U.S. Supreme Ct., Washington, 1972—73, spl. asst. to chief justice Warren E. Burger, 1973—77; prof. law U. Notre Dame, 1977—; judge U.S. Ct. Appeals (7th cir.), South Bend, 1985—. Reporter Appellate Rules Com., Washington, 1978—85; commn. on mil. justice U.S. Dept. Def., Washington, 1984—85; cons. Supreme Ct. Ala., 1983, Calif. Bd. Bar Examiners, 1981, Anglo-Am. Jud. Exch., 1977; adv. com. Bill of Rights to Bicentennial Constn. Commn., 1989; adv. com. on appellate rules Jud. Conf. U.S., 1985—90, chmn., 1990—93; chmn. adv. com. on appellate judge edn. Fed. Jud. Ctr., 1996—2003; mem. jud. conf. administrv. office U.S. Cts. Com., 2003—; mem. faculty Law Clerkship Inst., Pepperdine U., 2001—04; mem. vis. com. U. Chgo. Sch. Divinity, 2005—, U. Chgo. Sch. Law, 2005—. Author: Constitutional Litigation, 1984. With JAGC USN, 1968—72. Mem.: ABA, Am. Law Inst., Phi Beta Kappa. Office: US Ct of Appeals 208 US Courthouse 204 S Main St South Bend IN 46601-2122 also: Fed Bldg 219 S Dearborn St Ste 2660 Chicago IL 60604-1803*

**RIPPLINGER, GEORGE RAYMOND, JR.,** lawyer; b. East St. Louis, Ill., Apr. 19, 1945; s. George Raymond and Virginia Lee (Toupnot) R. AB, U. Ill., 1967, JD, 1970. Bar: Ill. 1970, U.S. Dist. Ct. (so. dist.) Ill. 1970, U.S. Ct. Appeals (7th cir.) 1970, U.S. Dist. Ct. (ctrl. dist.) Ill. 1972, U.S. Tax Ct. 1971, U.S. Ct. Internat. Trade 1973, U.S. Dist. Ct. (ea. dist.) Mo. 1977, U.S. Ct. Appeals (8th cir.) 1977. Assoc. Meyer & Meyer, Belleville and Greenville, Ill., 1970-72; assoc. Meyer & Kaucher, 1972—73; sole practice Belleville, 1974; ptnr. Ripplinger & Walsh, Clayton, Mo., 1974-76, Ripplinger, Dixon &

Johnston, Belleville, Ill., St. Louis, Scott AFB, and Bellvue, Neb., 1976-94; prin. George Ripplinger & Assocs., Belleville, 1994—2005; mng. mem. Ripplinger & Zimmer LLC, Belleville, 2006—. Mem. com. minimum continuing legal edn. Ill. Supreme Ct., 2005—. Bd. visitors Coll. Law U. Ill., 1979-86, pres., 1983-84; pres., bd. dirs. Ill. Legal Aid on Line, 2006—, bd. dirs. 2005—. Col. USAR, 1970-2001. Recipient Disting. Alumnus award, U. Ill., Coll. Law, 2006. Fellow Am. Bar Found., Ill. Bar Found. (bd. dirs. 1988-2004, treas. 1998-2004); mem. ABA (ho. of dels. 1989-93, 95-99, chmn. workers compensation com. 1985-88, divsn. dir. 1988-89, 95-99, mem. coun. 1989-93, 99-2003, sec. 1999-2000, vice-chmn. 2000-2001, chmn. 2001-02, gen. practice/solo and small firm sect.), ATLA, Lawyers Trust Fund Ill. (bd. dirs. 1988-94), Ill. Bar Assn. (bd. govs. 1981-83, 87-93, sec. 1991-92), St. Clair County Bar Assn., Bar Assn. Met. St. Louis, Mo. Bar Assn., Ill. Trial Lawyers Assn. (bd. advs. 1993—), Land of Lincoln Legal Assistance Found. (bd. dirs. 1982-88, vice-chmn. 1987-88), Res. Officers Assn. Democrat. Office: Ripplinger and Zimmer LLC 2215 W Main St Belleville IL 62226-6668 Office Phone: 800-753-8333. Business E-Mail: george@ripplingerlaw.com

**RIPS, LANCE JEFFREY**, psychology professor; b. Omaha, Dec. 19, 1947; s. Norman Julian and Barbara (Taxman) R.; m. Julie West Johnson; 1 child, Eve Clare Johnson. BA, Swarthmore (Pa.) Coll., 1970; PhD, Stanford U., 1974. Asst. prof. U. Chgo., 1974-80, assoc. prof., 1980-91, prof., 1991-93, Northwestern U., Evanston, Ill., 1993—. Author: Psychology of Proof, 1994, Psychology of Survey Response, 2000; mem. editl. bd. Cognition; contbr. articles to profl. jours. James McKeen Cattell fellow, 1989-90, Fulbright fellow, 2004-2005. Fellow APA, Am. Psychol. Soc.; mem. Psychonomic Soc., Cognitive Sci. Soc., Phi Beta Kappa.

**RISBERG, ERICA LYNN**, archivist, film producer; b. New Milford, Conn., Feb. 17, 1969; d. Roland Eric and Linda Ann Risberg. BA, Western Conn. State U., 1991, MA, 1996; postgrad., U. Maine, 2000—. Underwriter Gt. Western Mortgage Corp., Southport, Conn., 1994—96; adminstrv. asst. Duke Engring. and Svcs., Inc., Portland, Maine, 1997—2000; sound archivist Maine Folklife Ctr., Orono, Maine, 2001—03; asst. prodr. Edge Pictures, Bangor, Maine, 2002—; rsch. asst. Maine Atlas Project, 2003—04; radio announcer Maine Pub. Radio, 2003—; prodr. 3leggedog Productions, 2003—04. Cons. Old Town (Maine) Hist. Soc., 2002—03, Bangor Mus. and Ctr. for History, 2001—02. Prodr., writer, narrator (audio documentary) Community in Maine: Life During the Great Depression. Reader Maine Audio Info. and Reading Svcs., Brewer, 2000—02; candidate for state senate Maine Rep. Party, Portland, 1998; sec. Cumberland County Rep. Party, Portland, 1998—99. Recipient Gold award, Girl Scouts of Am., 1987. Mem.: Maine Hist. Soc., Orgn. Am. Historians, Oral History Assn., Am. Hist. Assn., Phi Alpha Theta. Avocations: swimming, hiking, writing, filmmaking, music. Office: Maine Folklife Ctr/U Maine 5773 S Stevens Hall Orono ME 04469-5773 also: Maine Pub Radio 65 Texas Ave Bangor ME 04401 E-mail: erica_risberg@umit.maine.edu, elrisberg@suscom-maine.net.

**RISCH, JAMES E.**, governor, former lieutenant governor, former state legislator; b. Milw., May 3, 1943; s. Elroy A. and Helen B. (Levi) R.; m. Vicki L. Choborda, June 8, 1968; children: James E., Jason S., Jordan D. BS in Forestry, U. Idaho, 1965, JD, 1968. Dep. pros. atty. Ada County, Idaho, 1968-69, chief dep. pros. atty. Idaho, 1969-70, pros. atty. Idaho, 1971-75; mem. Idaho Senate, Dist. 18, Boise, 1974—88, 1995—2002, majority leader, 1977—82, 1997—2002, pres. pro tem, 1983-88; ind. counsel to Gov. State of Idaho, Boise, 1996; ptnr. Risch Goss & Insinger, Boise, 1975—; lt. gov. State of Idaho, Boise, 2003—06, gov., 2006—. Prof. law Boise State U., 1972-75. Bd. dirs. Nat. Dist. Attys. Assn., 1973, Idaho Co., 1992-94, State Legis. Leaders Found., 2002; chmn. bd. dirs. Am. Trailer Mfg. Co., 1995—; pres. Idaho Pros. Attys., 1970-74; chmn. George Bush Presdl. Campaign, Idaho, 1988; gen. counsel Idaho Rep. Party, 1991-2002. Mem. ABA, Idaho Bar Assn., Boise Bar Assn., Ducks Unlimited, Nat. Rifle Assn., Nat. Cattlemans Assn., Idaho Cattlemans Assn., Am. Angus Assn., Idaho Angus Assn., Am. Legis. Exch. Coun., Boise Valley Angus Assn., Phi Delta Theta, Xi Sigma Pi Republican. Roman Catholic. Avocations: hunting, fishing, skiing. Office: Office of Gov PO Box 83720 Boise ID 83720 Office Phone: 208-334-2100. Office Fax: 208-334-2175.

**RISDON, MICHAEL PAUL**, manufacturing executive; b. Hamburg, Iowa, Feb. 24, 1946; s. Paul A. and Vesta Mae (Melton) R.; m. Ann Lorraine Grandowski, June 4, 1966; children: Anita Ann, Carter Paul. BS, Iowa State U., Ames, 1967, U. Ky., Lexington, 1968; MBA, U. Pitts., 1971. Sr. acct. Ernst & Young, Indpls., 1971-75; audit supr. Ashland Oil, Inc., Ky., 1975—77; v.p. fin. and sys. Diesel ReCon Co., Memphis, 1982-86; budget analyst Cummins Engine Co., Columbus, Ind., 1969-70, mgr. corp. audit, 1977-78, dir. corp. and EDP audit, 1978-82, dir. fin. and planning power sys. group, 1987-88; v.p. Cummins Power Generation, Columbus, 1989; v.p. fin., CFO Metal Powder Products Co., Inc., Indpls., 1989-99; pres. MPM LLC, Carmel, Ind., 1998-99; pres., CEO The Cumbernauld Group, 1999—; exec. v.p., chief adminstrv. officer PiezoTech, LLC, Indpls., 1999—2003. V.p. Columbus Child Care Ctr., 1981-82; vol. Big Sisters Ctr. Ind., 1994-98. Mem. AICPA, Ind. CPA Soc., Metal Powder Industry Fedn. (fin. com. 1991-98, chmn. 1994-98), APMI Internat., Fin. Execs. Internat. (sec. 1997-98, v.p. 1998, pres. 1999), Inst. Mgmt. Accts. (nat. bd. dirs. 1981-87, v.p. 1985), Kiwanis (v.p. Columbus 1981). Roman Catholic. Avocations: bicycling, hiking, sports.

**RISEBROUGH, DOUG**, professional sports team executive; b. 1954; m. Marilyn Risenbrough; children: Allison, Lindsay. Former player Montreal Canadiens, for 8 years, Calgary Flames, for 5 years, former asst. coach, 1987-89, asst. gen. mgr. 1989-90 to 1991-92, gen. mgr. 1990-91, team pres. 1991-92, 1993-? v.p. hockey ops. Edmonton Oilers, 1996—99; gen. mgr. Minn. Wild, 1999—; pres. Minn. Sports & Entertainment (MSE), 2003—. Office: Minn Wild 317 Washington St Saint Paul MN 55102*

**RISEN, JAMES E.**, journalist; b. Cinn., Apr. 27, 1955; married; 3 children. BA in history, Brown U., 1977; MS in journalism, Northwestern U., 1978. Reporter Detroit Free Press, 1981—84; bur. chief LA Times, Detroit, 1984—90, chief econ. corr. Washington, 1990—95, nat. sec. & intelligence corr., 1995—98; investigative corr. NY Times, Washington, 1998—. Recipient Pulitzer Prize for nat. reporting, 2006. Office: NY Times Washington Bur 7th Fl 1627 I St NW Washington DC 20006 Office Phone: 202-862-0300. Office Fax: 202-862-0340. E-mail: risenj@nytimes.com.*

**RISHEL, JAMES BURTON**, manufacturing executive, director; b. Omaha, Apr. 27, 1920; s. James Blaine and Elizabeth Helen (Kerr) R.; m. Alice Jane Snyder, June 30, 1945; children: James Richard, Sara Jane Rishel Fields. BSME, U. Nebr., 1946. Profl. engr., Ohio. Pres. Corp. Equipment Co., Cin., 1962-82; chmn. bd. Systecon Inc., Cin., 1982-2000; cons. Pumping Solutions LLC, 2000—. Author: The Water Management Manual, 1994, HVAC Pump Handbook, 1996, 2d edit., 2006, Water Pumps and Pumping Systems, 2002; patentee hydraulic systems; contbr. numerous articles to profl. jours. Capt. USAF, 1942-46, 51-52. Fellow ASHRAE. Avocations: philanthropy, walking. Home: 6470 Post Rd Apt 305 Dublin OH 43016-5200

**RISHEL, RICHARD CLINTON**, retired bank executive; b. Oreland, Pa., June 7, 1943; S. Herbert Beale and Evelyn (Lauer) R.; m. Carol Staub, Apr. 3, 1965; children: Christian Daniel, Peter James. BA, Pa. State U., 1965; postgrad., Drexel Inst. Tech., 1965-66. Credit analyst 1st Pa. Banking & Trust Co., Phila., 1965-69; comml. lending officer Nat. Bank of Chester County, West Chester, Pa., 1969; asst. v.p. Continental Bank of Norristown, Pa., 1969-70, sec., 1970-71, v.p. 1971-73, sr. v.p., chief fin. officer, 1973-75, exec. v.p., chief fin. officer, 1975-81, vice chmn., 1981-83, pres., chief adminstrv. officer, 1984-89, also dir.; pres., chief exec. officer Continental Bank, Continental Bancorp, 1990-92; vice chmn. bd. Continental Bank, 1981-89; pres. parent co. Continental Bancorp., 1981-92; dir. Barnett Inst. U. North Fla., 1993-94; sec. of banking Commonwealth of Pa., 1995-99; ret., 1999.

**RISHER, JAMES A.**, electronics executive; b. 1943; MS in Econs. and Stats., U. Tex., 1943. With IBM Corps., 1969-80; v.p. Wang Labs., 1980-84; sr. v.p. Motorola Computer Systems, Inc., 1984-86; pres., CEO Exide Electronics Group, Inc., Raleigh, NC, 1986—98, chmn., 1997—98; mng. ptnr. Lumina Group LLC, 1998—; chmn., CEO Blue Star Battery Systems Internat., 2001—02; CEO Del Global Technologies, Valhalla, NY, 2006—. Bd. dir. SL Industries Inc, New Century Equity Holdings Corp. Office: Exide Electronics Corp 8609 Six Forks Rd Raleigh NC 27615-2966*

**RISHER, WILLIAM HENRY**, cardiothoracic surgeon, educator; b. New Orleans, Oct. 3, 1958; m. Michele Helene Van Kuren, July 11, 1981; children: Amelia Alexandra, Jordan Prescott, Olivia Leigh. Student, U. New Orleans, 1981; BS in Biomed. Engring., Tulane U., 1981; MD, La. State U., 1985. Diplomate Am. Bd. Surgery, Am. Bd. Thoracic Surgery; lic. surgeon, N.Y.; cert. ACLS, advanced trauma life support, pediatric advanced life support provider, basic life support provider. Resident in gen. surgery Alton Ochsner Med. Found., New Orleans, 1985-90, chief resident, 1989-90, resident and fellow in cardiovascular surgery, 1990-92, chief resident, 1991-92; flight care physician Ochsner Flight Care, 1986-92; assoc. prof. cardiothoracic surgery Med. Ctr. U. Rochester, NY, 1992—2002; chief St. Luke's Regional Heart Program, Bethlehem, Pa., 2002—. Presenter in field. Contbr. over 20 articles to med. and sci. jours. T.H. Harris scholar Tulane U, 1977-79, full scholar, 1979-81. Fellow ACS, Am. Coll. Cardiology (assoc.); mem. AMA, Am. Coll. Chest Physicians, Soc. Thoracic Surgeons, Internat. Soc. Heart and Lung Transplantation, S.E. Surg. Congress, So. Med. Assn., Med. Soc. County Monroe, Rochester Acad. Medicine, Rochester Cardiovascular Soc., Upstate Soc. Thoracic Surgeons, Rochester Surg Soc, Assn. for Advancement of Med. Instrumentation, Alton Ochsner Med. Soc., Tau Beta Pi, Alpha Omega Alpha. Home: 1875 Augusta Dr Center Valley PA 18034-8924 Office Phone: 610-954-3990. Personal E-mail: mbaj05@aol.com.

**RISHWAIN, JAMES MICHAEL, JR.**, lawyer; b. Stockton, Calif., Apr. 28, 1959; BA with honors, UCLA, 1981; JD cum laude, Pepperdine U., 1984. Bar: Calif. Co-mng. ptnr. Pillsbury Winthrop Shaw Pittman LLP, Century City, Calif., 2001—04, LA, 2004—, former co-head Real Estate Group, chair-elect, former mem., vice chmn., ptnr. compensation com. Mem., vice-chmn. Partner Compensation Com. Pillsbury Winthrop Shaw Pittman. Editor (Note & Comment): Pepperdine Law Rev. Mem. adv. bd. LA City Coun. for Holmby Pk., Calif. Coalition for Adequate Sch. Housing, Jonathan Club; bd. mem. Bldg. Owners and Mgrs. Assn.; bd. experts Internat. Real Estate Trade Orgn., mem. pres.'s cir. Named Best Lawyer Am., 2005—06; named one of Calif. Super Lawyers, 2004, 2005, 2006; recipient Calif. Lawyer of Yr. award, 2004, 2005. Mem.: ABA, State Calif. Bar Assn., LA County Bar Assn., Urban Land Inst. Office: Pillsbury Winthrop Shaw Pittman LLP 725 S Figueroa St 28th Fl Los Angeles CA 90017 Office Phone: 213-488-1111. Office Fax: 213-488-3737. Business E-Mail: jrishwain@pillsburylaw.com.

**RISHWORTH, SUSAN KNOKE**, archivist, researcher; b. Appleton, Wis., Aug. 25, 1945; d. Leland Leonard and Gertrude Helen Martha Posselt Knoke; m. Clarence Douglas Rishworth, Apr. 7, 1971; children: Corey Adam, Benjamin Tobey, Amelia Marzieh. BA, U. Wis., Madison, 1967; MLS, Ind. U., Bloomington, 1968; MA, U. Md., College Park, 1998. Cert. archivist Modern Archives Inst., 1994. Libr. African studies Mich. State U., East Lansing, 1968—70; Africana bibliographer Libr. Congress, 1970—74; libr. to libr. dir. Southeastern U., 1983—90; interim dir. libr. svcs. U. Md. U., College Park, 1985; history libr., archivist Am. Coll. Ob/Gyns, 1990—2001; archivist ACS, Chgo., 2002—. Founder Chgo. Area Med. Archivists, 2002—; co-initiator Lone Arrangers Roundtable SAA, Birmingham, Ala., 2002—; presenter in field. Co-founder Ann. Martin Luther King Tribute, College Park, 1991—2001; facilitator Human Rels. Com. Race Study Circles, Prince George's County, Md., 1996—2000; Baha'i travel tchr. Nat. Spiritual Assembly of Baha'is of US, Wilmette, Ill., 1972—73; Baha'i pioneer Nat. Spiritual Assembly of Leeward Islands, Antigua and Barbuda, 1981—83; Baha'i travel tchr. Nat. Spiritual Assembly of Baha'is of Cameroon, Yaounde, 1998; sec. Spiritual Assembly of Baha'i, College Park, 1973—2001; facilitator study circles Baha'i, Chgo., 2002—. Recipient 10 Yr. Svc. on MLK tribute award, City of Coll. Pk., 1991—2001, Murray Gottlieb prize, Med. Libr. Assn., 1994; fellow Wood Found. History of Women in Medicine award, Coll. Physicians Phila., 2005—06. Mem.: Midwest Archives Conf., Soc. Am. Archivists, Am. Assn. for History Medicine (shryock award com. 2005—), Archivists and Librs. in History of Health Sci. (sec., steering com. 1994—95, 2004—06), Assn. Bahai Studies. Baha'I. Office: Am Coll Surgeons 633 N St Clair St Chicago IL 60611

**RISI, LOUIS JAMES, JR.**, manufacturing executive; b. Highland Park, Ill., July 2, 1937; s. Louis J. and Ann E. Risi; m. Mary Jean Anson, Jan. 15, 1958; children: Steven, Janet, Andrew. BS, Bradley U.; MBA, U. Chgo. Pres. and CEO, bd. dirs., mem. exec. com. Norin Corp., Miami, Fla., 1969-81; exec. com. dir. Maple Leaf Mills Ltd., Toronto, Can., 1970-81, Corp. Foods, Inc., 1970-81; chmn. bd. dirs. Louis Sherry, Inc., 1976-81; chmn. bd., chief exec. officer Nat. Investors Fire & Casualty Co., 1975-77; exec. com. dir. Investors Equity Life Ins. Co. of Hawaii, 1970-75; pres., dir. The Abbey, Lake Geneva, 1970-75; exec. com., dir. Upper Lakes Shipping, Ltd., Toronto, Can., 1970-76; pres., dir. The Pioneer, Lake Oshkosh, 1971-76; exec. com. dir. Port Weller and St. Lawrence Dry Dock, Ltd., St. Catharines, Can., 1971-76; pres., dir. Homosassa Springs, Fla., 1971-78, Ivan Tors Films Inc., Culver City, Calif., 1971-78, Ivan Tors Studios Inc., Miami, Fla., 1976-80; exec. com. dir. Midland Nat. Bank, 1976-80; pres., dir. Norris Grain Co., 1980-82; chmn. bd., CEO CTC Corp., 1981-83. Exec. com. dir. Nat. Investors Life Ins. Co., 1970-77; chmn. bd., pres. Victory Industries, Inc.; chmn. bd. dirs. Red Wing Co., Ottawaha Farms, Inc.; Assured Security Co.; dir. Breckinridge Group; exec. v.p. Ft. Worth Red Wings Hockey Club, Inc., 1975-78, Detroit Red Wings Hockey Club, Inc., 1976-82, Adirondack Red Wings Hockey Club, Inc., 1976-82; bd. govs. Nat. Hockey League, 1976-82; bd. dirs. Chgo. Rock Island and Pacific R.R.; exec. com. AfriAir Corp., 1972-79, Southeastern Airlines, Inc., 1972-78; exec. com., bd. dirs. Peter Bowden Drilling Ltd., Bankmgrs. Corp.; U.S. rep. Grain negotiations with USSR; U.S. rep. Feedstuffs negotiations with China; adv. coun. Am. Stock Exch.; mem. Agrl. Processors Liaison com. FTC; adv. bd. Nat. Millers Assn.; bd. govs. Internat. Hockey League, 1978-82, Am. Hockey League, 1975-79; pres., chmn. bd. dirs. Kinnard Body Works, Inc., 1970-73. Trustee Fairchild Tropical Garden, Miami, Fla. Lt. comdr. USN, 1959—67. Mem. Ocean Reef Yacht Club (Key Largo, Fla.), Santa Rosa (Calif.) Country Club, Riviera Country Club (Coral Gables, Fla.), Lake Toxaway Country Club (Lake Toxaway, NC), Coral Reef Yacht Club (Miami, Fla.), Anabelle's Club (London), St. James Club (London). Home: 10915 Lakeside Dr Coral Gables FL 33156-4209 Office: 9200 S Dadeland Blvd Miami FL 33156-2715

**RISIN, JACK** See BUTCHER, JACK

**RISIN, SEMYON AARON**, pathologist, educator; b. Belarus; m. Diana Risin; 1 child, Michael. MD, PhD, Minsk State Med. Inst., Belarus, 1964. Diplomate Am. Bd. of Pathology, 2003. Physician, physician-in-chief Village Hosp., Khominka, Belarus, 1964—66; rschr. Minsk State Med. Inst., 1971—79, prof., 1979—89; rschr. prof. U. Tex. M. D. Anderson Cancer Ctr., Houston, 1990—97; resident physician dept. pathology & lab. medicine U. Tex.-Houston Med. Sch., 1997—2001, prof. dept. pathology & lab. medicine, 2001—. Med. cons. Am. Biomed. Houston, 1990—91; med. interpretor and cons. Johnson Space Ctr., NASA, Houston, 1996—97. Avocation: travel. Office: UT-Houston Medical School 6431 Fannin Street MSB 2290 Houston TX 77030 Office Phone: 713-500-5320. Office Fax: 713-500-0730.

**RISING, KEVIN D.**, lawyer; BA in Criminology, Law and Society, U. Calif., Irvine, 1997; JD, U. Calif., Los Angeles, 2000. Bar: Calif., US Ct. of Appeals, 9th Circuit, US Dist. Ct. (So., Ea., Central & No. dist.), DC. Assoc., litigation dept. Akin Gump Strauss Hauer & Feld LLP, Los Angeles, Calif., 2001—. Recipient Award for Excellence in Preparation for Trial Practice of the Law,

Am. Bd. of Trial Advocates. Office: Akin Gump Strauss Hauer & Feld LLP 2029 Century Park E Ste 2400 Los Angeles CA 90067 Office Phone: 310-229-1000. Office Fax: 310-229-1001. Business E-Mail: krising@akingump.com.

**RISINGER, BETH N.**, elementary school educator; b. New Orleans, June 24, 1959; d. Merrill J. and Betty S. Nunez; m. Kurt S. Risinger, May 21, 1983; children: Kristofer, Kevin. BA in Elem. Edn., Nicholls State U., 1982. Sci. tchr. St. Bernard Parish Schs., Chalmette, La., 1982—83; 4th and 5th grade tchr. West Ascension Elem., Donaldsonville, La., 1986—92; 3rd and 4th grade tchr. G.W. Carver Primary, Gonzales, La., 1992—. Named Tchr. of Yr., Carver Primary, 1996—97. Mem.: La. Fedn. Tchrs., Internat. Reading Assn. Home: 13668 Parwood Ave Baton Rouge LA 70816-1473

**RISINGER, C. FREDERICK**, social studies educator; b. Paducah, Ky., July 15, 1939; s. Charles Morris and Mary Neal (Barfield) R.; m. Margaret M. Marker, July 4, 1994; children: Donna Lyne, Alyson, Laura, John. BS in Edn., So. Ill. U., 1961; MA in History, No. Ill. U., 1968. Newscaster, disc jockey WMOK Radio, Metropolis, Ill., 1955-61; tchr., adminstr., coach Lake Park H.S., Roselle, Ill., 1962-73; coord. sch. social studies Ind. U., Bloomington, 1973-86, assoc. dir. social studies devel. ctr., 1986-90, dir. nat. clearinghouse for U.S.-Japan studies, 1990—, assoc. dir. tchr. edn., 1995-97, dir. profl. devel., sch. svcs. and summer sessions, 1997—. Mem. adv. bd. Learning Mag., Boston, 1988—; pres. Nat. Coun. for the Social Studies, 1990-91. Co-author: America! America!, 1974, America's Past and Promise, 1997, Surfing Social Studies: The Internet Book, 1999, Creating America, 2000, Scott Foresman Social Studies K-6 Series, 2004; editor jour. News and Notes on the Social Sciences, 1973-86. Pres. Social Studies Suprs. Assn., Washington, 1985-86; exec. dir. Ind. Coun. for Social Studies, Bloomington, 1975-87. Recipient numerous pub. and pvt. ednl. grants; named Tchr. of Yr. DuPage County Edn. Assn., 1973. Mem. ASCD, Nat. Coun. for Social Studies, Ind. Assn. Historians, Phi Delta Kappa. Democrat. Home: 7039 E State Rd 45 Bloomington IN 47408-9580 E-mail: risinger@indiana.edu.

**RISKE, WILLIAM KENNETH**, producer, cultural services consultant; b. Lamont, Alta., Can., May 9, 1949; s. Norman Elmer and Clara Jeanette (Krause) R.; m. Barbara Elizabeth Malcolm, Apr. 28, 1973; children: Elizabeth Nicola, William Norman Malcolm. BFA, U. Alta., 1969. Stage mgr. Royal Winnipeg Ballet, Man., Can., 1971-73, prodn. stage mgr., 1973-76, prodn. mgr., 1976-77, assoc. gen. mgr., 1978-79, gen. mgr., 1979-92, cultural svcs. cons., 1992—; assoc. prodr., gen. mgr. Cirque Du Soleil-Mystère, 1994-96; gen. mgr. Cirque du Soleil U.S., Inc., 1996—2003. Mem. Assn. Cultural Execs. Home: 227 Deer Crossing Way Henderson NV 89012-2289

**RISKIN, VICTORIA**, former trade association administrator; d. Robert Riskin and Fay Wray; m. David Rintels. Pres. Writers Guild Am., West, 2001—04. Author: (TV films) My Antonia, 1995; prodr.: (TV films) The Last Best Year, 1990, A Town Torn Apart, 1992, World War II: When Lions Roared, 1994, The Member of the Wedding, 1997.

**RISKO, VICTORIA J.**, language educator; BS, U. Pitts., 1966; MS, W.Va. U., 1969, EdD, 1971; postgrad., U. London, 1975. Fellow Learning Disabilities Inst. W.Va. U., 1969—70; tchr. Johnstown (Pa.) Pub. Sch. Sys., 1967—68; tchr. remedial reading Johnstown (Pa.) Pub. Sch. Dist., 1967; instr. home econs. W.Va. U., 1968—69, instr., supr. reading clinic, 1969; rschr.-tchr. Robert F. Kennedy Youth Ctr., Morgantown, W.Va., 1969—70; tchr.-cons. inservice edn. of tchrs. Belair-Manchester Schs. of Mandeville, Jamaica, 1974—75; instr., asst. prof., assoc. prof., dir. reading clinic programs, mem. grad. faculty SUNY, Fredonia, 1970—75; rsch. scientist Learning Tech. Ctr., mem. faculty interdisciplinary team Child Study Ctr., Kennedy Ctr. Peabody Coll., Vanderbilt U., Nashville, 1978—89, assoc. prof., 1975—94, prof. lang. and learning, 1994—. Vis. prof. reading W.Va. U., 1971. Recipient Disting. Svc. and Leadership award, Coll. Reading Assn., 1995, Disting. Rsch. in Tchr.'s Edn. award, Assn. Tchr. Educators Conf., 1992. Office: Vanderbilt U Peabody Coll 367 Wyatt Ctr Box 330 Nashville TN 37203

**RISKOWSKI, GERALD LEE**, engineering educator; b. Loup City, Nebr., Feb. 26, 1952; s. Stanley George and Rose Marie (Eurek) R.; m. Janet Ann Riskowski, June 19, 1976; 1 child, Ryan Lee. BS in Agrl. Engring., U. Nebr., 1974, MS in Agrl. Engring., 1976; PhD in Agrl. Engring., Iowa State U., 1986. Registered profl. engr., Ill., Iowa, Wis. Design engr. Lesters Bldgs., Lester Prairie, Minn., 1976-77; product engr. Wick Bldg. Systems, Mazomanie, Wis., 1977-80; instr. Iowa State U., Ames, 1980-86; prof. dept. agrl. engring. U. Ill., Urbana, 1986—2001; prof., head biol. and agrl. engring. dept. Tex. A&M U., College Station, 2002—. Swine facilities cons. Am. Tech. Products, Savoy, Ill., 1997-2002; pres. Internat. Air Technologies, Savoy, 1994-2003. Author: Designing Facilities for Pesticide and Fertilizer Containment, 1991 (Am. Soc. Agrl. Engrs. Blue Ribbon 1992); editor: Swine Housing and Equipment Handbook, 1983 (Am. Soc. Agrl. Engrs. Blue Ribbon 1984), Livestock Waste Facilities, 1985, Farm Buildings Wiring Handbook, 1986 (Am. Soc. Agrl. Engrs. Blue Ribbon 1987). Named to Rural Builders Hall of Fame, 1998. Mem. ASHRAE (TC.2 Handbook chair 1993-2000), Am. Soc. Agrl. Engrs. (S&E program chair, stds. chair, Henry Giese award 2001). Office: Tex A&M U 2117 TAMU College Station TX 77843-2117 E-mail: riskowski@tamu.edu.

**RISLEY, DAVID MILO**, controller; b. Davenport, Iowa, Dec. 3, 1944; s. Ernest and Emma (Remke) R.; m. Karen Ann McConkey, Aug. 26, 1967; children: Kristen Anne, Christopher. BBA in Acctg., U. Iowa, 1966; MBA in Fin., Loyola U., Chgo., 1970. CPA, Ill. Staff auditor Authur Young & Co., Chgo., 1970-76; dir. internal audit Trans. Union Corp., Lincolnshire, Ill., 1976-79, group controller, 1979-81, v.p., controller Hultor Corp., Chgo., 1981-84; corp. controller Trinova Corp., Maumee, Ohio, 1984—. Trustee Knox Presbyn. Ch., Naperville, Ill., 1976-84, Toledo Hearing and speech ctr., Ohio, 1988—; bd. dirs. Toledo Opera, 1989—; instr. Jr. Achievement, Toledo, 1985—. Served as 1st lt. U.S. Army, 1966-69, Vietnam. Mem. AICPA, Ohio Soc. of CPAs, Fin. Exec. Inst., Nat. Assn. Accts. Clubs: Inverness Golf (Toledo). Republican. Methodist. Home: 2710 Derby Rd Toledo OH 43615-2144 Office: Trinova Corp 1705 Indian Wood Cir Maumee OH 43537-4097

**RISLEY, ROD ALAN**, educational association administrator; b. Hutchinson, Kans., Oct. 17, 1954; s. Ralph Edward and Patricia Ann (Gaulding) R. AA, San Jacinto Coll., 1975; BBA, Sam Houston State U., 1982; AA (hon.), Austin Community Coll., 1991; MBA, Millsap Coll., 1995; PhD (hon.), Highpoint U., 1996, Mt. Ida Coll., 1996, Landmark Coll., 2003; postgrad., Miss. State U., 2003. Dir. alumni affairs Phi Theta Kappa, 1976-82; assoc. dir. Phi Theta Kappa Internat. Hdqrs., Jackson, Miss., 1982-85, exec. dir., 1985—. Bd. dirs. Miss. Humanities Coun., Jack Kent Cooke Found., CC Transfer Initiative Bd.; bd. mem. Miss. Ctr. Non-Profit Orgns.; grant reviewer NSF, CC Humanities Assn., NEH; mem. adv. bd. Horne CPA Group. Judge Truman Scholarship Found., 1993, 94, Coca-Cola Scholars Found., 2001-04, USA Today's All-USA Acad. Team HS, 2003-04, Jack Kent Cooke Found., 2004-06, Nat. Assn. C.C. Tchr. Edn. Program, 2004-06. Named one of Outstanding Young Men of Am., 1982, 83, 84, 85, 86, 87, 88, 89, Top Bus. Leaders Miss., 1994, Disting. Alumnus, San Jacinto Coll., 1997; Mid South Found. C.C. fellow, 2001. Mem. Am. Assn. of Cmty. Colls. (commr. coun. for acad., student and cmty. devel., grant reviewer, Disting. Alumnus award 1996), Phi Theta Kappa (sec., pub. jour.), Phi Kappa Phi. Episcopalian. Office: Phi Theta Kappa Soc PO Box 13729 Jackson MS 39236-3729 Office Phone: 601-984-3518. E-Mail: rod.risley@ptk.org.

**RISLEY, TODD ROBERT**, psychologist, educator; b. Palmer, Alaska, Sept. 8, 1937; s. Robert and Eva Lou (Todd) R.; 1 child, Todd Michael; m. Cheryl Thomas, Mar. 30, 1996. AB with distinction in Psychology, San Diego State Coll., 1960; MS, U. Wash., 1963, PhD, 1966. Asst. prof. psychology Fla. State U., Tallahassee, 1964-65; rsch. assoc. Bur. Child Rsch., U. Kans., Lawrence, 1965-77, sr. scientist, 1977—2003, emeritus, 2003—, asst. prof. human devel., 1967-69, assoc. prof., 1969-73, prof., 1973-84; prof. psychology U. Alaska, Anchorage, 1982—2003, prof. emeritus, 2003—. Pres. Ctr. for

Applied Behavior Analysis, 1970-82; dir. Johnny Cake Child Study Ctr., Mansfield, Ark., 1973-74; vis. prof. U. Auckland (N.Z.), 1978; acting dir. Western Carolina Ctr., Morgantown, N.C., 1981; dir. Alaska Div. Mental Health and Devel. Disabilities, 1988-91; cons. in field to numerous orgns. and instns. Co-author: The Infant Center, 1977, Shopping with Children: Advice for parents, 1978, The Toddler Center, 1979, Meaningful Differences, 1995, The Social World of Children, 1999; editor: Jour. Applied Behavior Analysis, 1971-74; mng. editor: Behavior Therapy, The Behavior Therapist, Behavioral Asessment, 1977-80; assoc. editor: Jour. Positive Behavior Support, 1998—; mem. editl. bds. of numerous profl. jours.; contbr. revs. and numerous articles. Co-chmn. Fla. task force on use of behavioral procedures in state programs for retarded, 1974—; mem. resident abuse investigating com. div. retardation Fla. Dept. Health and Rehab. Services, 1972—; mem. adv. com. Social Research Inst., U. Utah, 1977—; mem. Alaska Gov.'s Council on Handicapped and Gifted, 1983-88, NIH Mental Retardation Research Com., 1987-88, Alaska Mental Health Bd., 1988. Grantee NIMH, 1971-72, 72-73; rsch. grantee Nat. Ctr. Health Services, 1976-79; grantee Nat. Inst. Edn., 1973, NIH, 1967-86; grantee U.S. Dept. Edn., 1997-2002. Fellow APA (coun. of reps. 1982-85, pres. div 25, 1989, Edgar Doll award 2000), Am. Psychol. Soc.; mem. AAAS, Am. Assn. Mental Deficiency (Rsch. award 2000), Assn. Advancement of Behavior Therapy (dir. 1975-80, pres. 1976-77, chmn. profl. rev. com. 1977—, series editor Readings in Behavior Therapy 1977—), Soc. Behavioral Medicine, Assn. Behavior Analysis, Sigma Xi. Office Phone: 907-745-4360. Business E-Mail: risley@alaska.net.

**RISMAN, MICHAEL,** lawyer, real estate developer, broker; b. Everett, Mass., Apr. 2, 1938; s. Morris Charles and Doris (Rosenbaum) R.; m. Rebecca R. Fuchs, Mar. 23, 1974; 1 stepchild, Ian Carlton Murray; children: Matthew Craig, Deborah Risman Kyle, Jared Evan. BA, U. Mich., 1960; LLB, Georgetown U., 1964. Bar: D.C. 1964. Staff mem. Democratic Nat. Com., Washington, 1964; atty. U.S. Fgn. Claims Settlement Commn., Washington, 1964-66, SEC, Washington, 1966-67; counsel Seaboard Planning Corp., Beverly Hills, Calif., 1967-72, pres., 1970-72; v.p. Seaboard Corp., Beverly Hills, 1970-72; sec. B.C. Morton Realty Trust, 1967-71; with Arlington Investments Corp., Santa Monica, Calif., 1979-86; founder The Quincey Group, 1986; owner, pres. Armstrong Kitchens, San Francisco, 1988-90; sr. v.p. AFC Am. Housing Corp., L.A., Calif., 1991-97; mng. dir. Hollingsworth & Lord, L.A., 1997—; ptnr. Dorama, L.L.C., 2002—. Bd. dir. Competitive Capital Fund, Income Fund Boston, Inc., Admiralty Fund. Home: 1133 Centinela Ave Santa Monica CA 90403-2316 Office Phone: 310-392-9681 x 29. Personal E-mail: mrisman02@aol.com.

**RISNER, DOUG S.,** performing arts educator, researcher; b. Bellefontaine, Ohio, May 14, 1959; life ptnr. Jon D. Anderson, Apr. 30, 1976; 1 child, Hannah K. BFA summa cum laude, U. N.C. Greensboro, 1988, MFA, 1990, PhD, 2001. Assoc. prof. Luther Coll., Decorah, Iowa, 1988—98; assoc. dir. rsch. & sponsored program U. North Tex., Denton, 2002—03; chmn., assoc. prof. Maggie Allesee dept. dance Wayne State U., Detroit, 2003—. Editor: Jour. Dance Edn.; contbr. articles to profl. jours., chapters to books. Recipient Ethel Martus Lawther Alumni award, U. N.C. Greensboro, 2006; grantee Nat. Coll. Choreography Initiative, DanceUSA & Nat. Endowment for the Arts, 2005—06; Hester Doctoral fellow, U. N.C. Greensboro, 1998—2001, George Hayes Doctoral fellow, 1999, Luther Selfe Dissertation fellow, 2001. Mem.: Congress on Rsch. in Dance, Nat. Assn. of Schools of Dance, Dance Edn. Orgn. (sec. 2005), Am. Coll. Dance Festival. Office: Wayne State Univ 4841 Cass Ave Detroit MI 48202 Office Phone: 313-577-9879. Office Fax: 313-577-5691. Business E-Mail: drisner@wayne.edu.

**RISOM, JENS,** furniture designer, consultant, manufacturing executive; b. Copenhagen, May 8, 1916; came to U.S., 1939; naturalized, 1944; s. Sven J. and Inger Risom; m. Iben Haderup, Dec. 12, 1939 (dec. Jan. 1977); children: Helen Ann, Peggy Ann, Thomas Christian, Sven Christian; m. Henny Panduro, May 12, 1979. Student, Krebs, Denmark, 1922-27, St. Annae, 1927-32, Niels Brock Bus. Coll., 1932-34, Sch. for Arts and Indust., Denmark, 1935—37; DFA (hon.), R.I. Sch. Design, 2003. With design and decorating divsn. Nordiska Kompanet, Stockholm, Inge Westin, Stockholm, 1934-35, Ernst Kühn, Arch., Copenhagen and N.Y.C., 1937-38; with Dan Cooper, Inc., N.Y., 1939-41; freelance furniture designer, 1941-46; founder, pres. Jens Risom Design Inc., 1946-71; pres. Jens Risom Design, Inc. (became subs. Dictaphone Corp. 1971); v.p. Dictaphone Corp., 1971-73; pres. Design Control, New Canaan, Conn., 1973—. Cons. design, mktg., space planning. Trustee RISD, New Canaan Libr., Indsl. Design Soc. Am. With U.S. Army, 1943-45, ETO. Decorated Danish Knight's Cross (Denmark); recipient awards Archtl. League, Am. Inst. Internat. Design, Lifetime Achievement award Bklyn. Mus. Art, 1996, numerous Danish and Am. design awards. Home and Office: 24 Parade Hill Ln New Canaan CT 06840-4119 also: PO Box 596 Block Island RI 02807-0596 Home Fax: 203-966-6144.

**RISS, ERIC,** psychologist; m. Miriam Barbara Schoen; children: Arthur, Suzanne, Wendy. BA, Bklyn. Coll., 1950; PhD, NYU, 1958. Diplomate Am. Bd. Psychotherapy. Pvt. practice psychotherapy, family therapy and marriage counseling, N.Y.C., 1952; sr. psychologist N.Y.C. Diagnostic Ctr., 1954-57; with Marriage and Family Life Inst., N.Y.C., 1956-62, cons., 1956-58, dir. pub. edn., 1960-73, chmn. bd. dirs., 1961-73, dir., 1973-92; mem. attending staff, supr. psychotherapy and family therapy Payne Whitney Psychiat. Clinic, N.Y. Hosp., N.Y.C., 1971-78; clin. instr. psychology and psychiatry Cornell U. Med. Coll., 1971-72, clin. asst. prof., 1973-78; dir. Inst. for Exploration of Marriage, 1976-84; chief psychologist Artists, Writers and Performers Psychotherapy Ctr., 1978-92. Sr. psychologist N.Y.C. Diagnostic Center, 1954-57; with Marriage and Family Life Inst., N.Y.C., 1956-92; cons., 1956-58, dir. pub. edn., 1960-73, chmn. bd. dirs., 1961-73, dir., 1973-92; mem. attending staff, supr. psychotherapy and family therapy Payne Whitney Psychiat. Clinic, N.Y. Hosp., N.Y.C., 1971-78; clin. instr. psychology and psychiatry Cornell U. Med. Coll., 1971-72, clin. asst. prof., 1973-78; dir. Inst. for Exploration of Marriage, 1976-84; chief psychologist Artists, Writers and Performers Psychotherapy Center, 1978-92; lectr. Bklyn. Coll., 1955-62; cons. Fordham Hosp., 1956-68; psychotherapist N.Y. Neuropsychiat. Center, 1958-60; psychotherapist Community Guidance Service, N.Y.C., 1958-61; founder, head Natural Psychotherapy Internat., 1999—; webmaster www.naturalpsychotherapy.com. Contbr. numerous articles to profl. jours. Mem. APA, N.Y. State Psychol. Assn., Am. Acad. Psychotherapy, N.Y. State Marriage, Family and Child Counseling Assn. (pres. 1971-72), Acad. Family Psychology. Office: 174 E 73rd St New York NY 10021-4352 Office Phone: 212-988-4700. E-mail: eriss@naturalpsychotherapy.com, eriss@npsy.com.

**RISS, MURRAY,** photographer, educator; b. Stryj, Poland, Feb. 6, 1940; arrived in U.S., 1951, naturalized, 1958; s. Elias and Dora (Feit) Riss; m. Karen Mason; children: Shanna, Adya 1 stepchild, Jarrod Mason. Student, CCNY, 1958-63; BA, Cooper Union, 1966; M.F.A., R.I. Sch. Design, 1968. Prof., chmn. dept photography Memphis Acad. Arts, 1969-84; lectr. film and photography Southwestern U., Memphis, 1972-82; artist-in-residence U. Syracuse, N.Y., 1980, U. Haifa, Israel, 1976 One-man shows include Art Inst. Chgo., 1971, Mpls. Inst. Fine Arts, 1971, U. Rochester, NY, 1975, Photographers Gallery, London, 1977, Afterimage Gallery, Dallas, 1979, Visual Studies Workshop, Rochester, 1980, Hampshire (Mass.) Coll., 1981, Loomis Inst., Conn., 1984, exhibited in group shows at Mus. Modern Art, NYC, 1970, 1971, New Orleans Mus. Art, 1975, Nexus Gallery, Atlanta, 1981, Askew Nixon Gallery, touring show, So. Arts Fedn., 1985—86; conceived, organizer, dir. Southern Eye, Southern Mind, A Photographic Inquiry, Memphis, 1981; illustrator: History of Memphis Architecture until 1900, 1983, Guide to Mud Island, 1989, Elmwood-In the Shadow of the Elms, 2002; curator, dir. Emerging So. Photographers, Memphis Coll. Art Gallery, 1992, Memphis Brooks Mus. Art, 1994. Nat. Endowment for Arts fellow, 1979. Mem.: Soc. Photographic Edn. Home: 1306 Harbert Ave Memphis TN 38104-4514 Office: Murray Riss Photography 516 S Main St Memphis TN 38103-4443 Personal E-mail: mur3435ris@aol.com. *Had I designed the events and outcomes of my life I would not have done as well as my fate has done for me.*

**RISSE, GUENTER BERNHARD,** physician, historian, educator; b. Buenos Aires, Apr. 28, 1932; s. Francisco B. and Kaete A. R.; m. Alexandra G. Paradzinski, Oct. 14, 1961; children— Heidi, Monica, Alisa. MD, U. Buenos Aires, 1958; PhD, U. Chgo., 1971. Intern Mercy Hosp., Buffalo, 1958-59; resident in medicine Henry Ford Hosp., Detroit, 1960-61, Mt. Carmel Hosp., Columbus, Ohio, 1962-63; asst. dept. medicine U. Chgo., 1963-67; asst. prof. dept. history of medicine U. Minn., 1969-71; asso. prof. dept. history of medicine and dept. history of sci. U. Wis., Madison, 1971-76, prof., 1976-85, chmn. dept. history of medicine, 1971-77; prof. dept. history health scis. U. Calif., San Francisco, 1985-99, prof. dept. anthropology, history and social medicine, 1999-2001, prof. emeritus, 2001—, dept. chair, 1985—99; affiliate prof. dept med. history and ethics Univ. Wash. Sch. of Medicine, Seattle, 2002—. Mem. project com. Ctr. for Photog. Images in Medicine and Health Care. Author: Paleopathology of Ancient Egypt, 1964, Hospital Life in Enlightenment Scotland, 1986, Mending Bodies-Saving Souls: A History of Hospitals, 1999, New Medical Challenges During the Scottish Enlightenment, 2005; editor: Modern China and Traditional Chinese Medicine, 1973, History of Physiology, 1973, Medicine Without Doctors, 1977, AIDS and the Historian, 1991, Culture, Knowledge and Healing, Historical Perspectives of Homeopathic Medicine in Europe and North America, 1998; mem. editl. bd. Jour. History of Medicine, 1971-74, 90-93, Clio Medica, 1973-88, Bull. History of Medicine, 1980-94, Medizinhistorisches Jour., 1981—, Med. History, 1989-95, NTM Internat. Jour. of History, Ethics, Medicine, 1992—, History of Philos. Life Scis., 1993—, Asclepio, 1995—, Health and History, 1998—. With Argentine Armed Forces, 1955. Recipient NIH grants, 1971-73, 82-84, WHO grant, 1979, named Logan Campbell Disting. Lectr., New Zealand, 1994, Karl Sudhoff Meml. Lectr., Germany, 2000. Mem. Am. Assn. History of Medicine (pres. 1988-90, William H. Welch medal 1988, Lifetime Achievement award 2005), History Sci. Soc., Deutsche Gesellschaft fur Geschichte der Medizin, European Assn. History of Medicine and Health, Internat. Network for History of Pub. Health, Mex. Soc. History and Philosophy of Medicine, Peruvian Assn. Med. Ethnology and History, Brit. Soc. for Social History of Medicine, Argentine Ateneo de Historia de la Medicina, AIDS History Group (co-chair 1988-94), Internat. Network for History of Hosps. (convenor 1995—), Bay Area Med. Hist. Club (pres. 1994-96). Home: 2612 SW 167th St Burien WA 98166-3228 Business E-Mail: risseg@u.washington.edu.

**RISSER, JAMES VAULX, JR.,** journalist, educator; b. Lincoln, Nebr., May 8, 1938; s. James Vaulx and Ella Caroline (Schacht) R.; m. Sandra Elizabeth Laaker, June 10, 1961; children: David James, John Daniel. BA, U. Nebr., 1959, cert. in journalism, 1964; JD, U. San Francisco, 1962. Bar: Nebr. 1962. Pvt. practice law, Lincoln, 1962-64; reporter Des Moines Register and Tribune, 1964-85, Washington corr., 1969-85, bur. chief, 1976-85; dir. John S. Knight fellowships for profl. journalists, prof. communication Stanford U., 1985-2000. Lectr. Wells Coll., 1981; mem. com. on agrl. edn. in secondary schs. Nat. Acad. Scis., 1985-88. Trustee Reuter Found., 1989-00, Am. Conservatory Theater, 2000-03, Oreg. Shakespear Fest., 2003—, Jefferson Pub. Radio, 2003-; mem. Pulitzer Prize Bd., 1990-99; mem. journalism adv. com. Knight Found., 2000-06. Profl. Journalism fellow Stanford U., 1973-74; recipient award for disting. reporting public affairs Am. Polit. Sci. Assn., 1969; Thomas L. Stokes award for environ. reporting Washington Journalism Center, 1971, 79; Pulitzer prize for nat. reporting, 1976, 79; Worth Bingham Found. prize for investigative reporting, 1976; Raymond Clapper Meml. Assn. award for Washington reporting, 1976, 78; Edward J. Meeman award for Conservation Reporting, 1985. Mem. Soc. Environ. Journalists, Soc. Profl. Journalists (Disting. Svc. award 1976), Investigative Reporters and Editors Assn., Com. Concerned Journalists, Gridiron Club. Clubs: Gridiron. Home: 71 Water St 206 Ashland OR 97520 E-mail: jimrisser@earthlink.net.

**RISSER, PAUL GILLAN,** academic administrator, botanist; b. Blackwell, Okla., Sept. 14, 1939; s. Paul Crane and Jean (McCluskey) R.; children: David, Mark, Stephen, Scott. BA, Grinnell Coll., 1961; MS in Botany, U. Wis., 1965, PhD in Botany and Soils, 1967. From asst. prof. to prof. botany U. Okla., 1967-81, also asst. dir. biol. sta., chmn. dept. botany and microbiology, 1977-81; dir. Okla. Biol. Survey, 1971-77; chief Ill. Natural History Survey, 1981-86; program dir., ecosystem studies NSF; provost and v.p. acad. affairs U. N.Mex., 1989-92; former pres. Miami U., Oxford, Ohio; pres. Oreg. State U., 1996—2002; chancellor Okla. Sys. Higher Edn., 2003—. Author: (with Kathy Cornelison) Man and the Biosphere, 1979, (with others) The True Prairie Ecosystem, 1981; research, numerous publs. in field. Trustee Pioneer Multi-County Library Bd. Mem. Am. Acad. Arts and Scis., Ecol. Soc. Am. (pres.), Brit. Ecol. Soc., Soc. Range Mgmt., Southwestern Assn. Naturalists (pres.), Am. Inst. Biol. Sci. (pres.), Torrey Bot. Club. Presbyterian. Address: OK State Regents Higher Edn Off Chancellor 655 Rsch Pky Ste 200 Oklahoma City OK 73104

**RISSETTO, HARRY A.,** lawyer; b. Dec. 1, 1943; AB, Fairfield U., 1965; JD, Georgetown U., 1968. Bar: N.Y. 1969, D.C. 1970, U.S. Supreme Ct. Law clk. to Hon. John J. Sirica U.S. Dist. Ct. D.C., 1968-69; law clk. to Chief Justice Warren E. Burger U.S. Supreme Ct., 1969-70; ptnr. Morgan, Lewis & Bockius, Washington, dep. leader labor & employment law practice group. Adj. prof. Law Ctr., Georgetown U., 1986-89. Mem. ABA (co-chmn. railway labor act com. sect. of labor and employment law 1987-89), Coll. Labor & Employment Lawyers. Office: Morgan Lewis & Bockius 1111 Pennsylvania Ave NW Washington DC 20004 Office Phone: 202-739-5130. Business E-Mail: hrissetto@morganlewis.com.

**RISSMAN, BURTON RICHARD,** lawyer; b. Chgo., Nov. 13, 1927; s. Louis and Eva (Lyons) R.; m. Francine Greenberg, June 15, 1952; children: Lawrence E., Thomas W., Michael P. BS, U. Ill., 1947, JD, 1951; LLM, NYU, 1952. Bar: Ill. 1951, U.S. Dist. Ct. (no. dist.) Ill. 1954, U.S. Ct. Appeals (7th cir.) 1978, U.S. Supreme Ct. 1982. Assoc. Schiff, Hardin & Waite, Chgo., 1953-59, ptnr., 1959—2003, mem. mgmt. com., 1984-92, chmn. mgmt. com., 1986-90; ret., 2003. Mem. faculty Practicing Law Inst. Bd. editor U. Ill. Law Forum, 1949-51; contbr. articles to profl. jours. 1st lt. JAGC USAF, 1952—53. Food Law fellow, 1951. Mem. ABA, Ill. Bar Assn., Chgo. Bar Assn., Chgo. Coun. Lawyers, Carlton Club.

**RISSMANN, WILLIAM JOHN,** medical products executive; b. Evanston, Ill., July 23, 1949; s. Charles R. and Elise M. Rissmann; m. Mary Beth A. Anglin, Nov. 3, 1984; children: Bridget K., Mark C. BSEE, U. Ill., Urbana, 1972; MSEE, U. Ill., 1975; MBA, U. Minn., Mpls., 1982—87. V.p. R&D Angeion Corp., Plymouth, 1994—99; v.p. product devel. Data Sciences, Inc., St. Paul, 1999—2000; pres., founder Cameron Health, Inc., San Clemente, Calif., 2001—02. v.p. R&D, 2002—04; COO Bioelectric Med. Solutions, Inc., San Diego, 2004—05; v.p. product devel. and mfg. HeartWare, Inc., Miramar, Fla., 2005—. Cubmaster Boy Scouts Am., Coto de Caza, Calif., 2002—04; gen. festival chmn. Mpls. Aquatennial, Mpls., 1988—89, pres., 1995—97. Mem.: IEEE (sr.). Achievements include patents in field; patents pending in field. Home: 7631 Hyannis Ln Parkland FL 33067 Office: HeartWare Inc 3351 Executive Way Miramar FL 33025 Personal E-mail: brissmann@aol.com.

**RISTAU, JACOB ROBERT,** art educator, graphics designer; b. Lawrence, Kans., Jan. 3, 1978; s. Mel H. and Jacque A. Ristau; m. Melissa Dawn Sheldon, July 15, 2000. BFA, Abilene Christian U., Tex., 2000; MFA in Visual Comm., Sch. Art Inst. Chgo., 2005. Asst. artist Mel Ristau Design/Media Garden, Inc., Ft. Collins, Colo., 1998—; designer Richards, Brock, Miller, Mitchell and Assoc., Dallas, 2002—03; freelance artist and designer, 2003—; instr. Sch. Art Inst. Chgo., 2005; asst. prof. dept. art and art history U. Redlands, Calif., 2005—. Exhibited in group shows at Virginia Shore Gallery Abilene Christian U., Tex., 2001, exhibitions include Grad. Thesis Exhbn. at Gallery 2, Sch. Art Inst. Chgo., 2005, 45th Ann. Dallas Show, 2003, Faculty Exhbn. Peppers Art Ctr., Redlands, Calif., 2005, illustrations, The Business of Holidays, edited by Maud Lavin, 2004, appearing in collections and trade publs. Recipient Graphic Designer of Yr.,

Abilene Christian U., 1998, awards of excellence (4), Houston Art Dirs. Club, 2002. Mem.: Coll. Arts Assn. Avocations: linguistics, word games, board games, card games. Office: Univ Redlands Dept Art and Art History 1200 E Colton Ave Redlands CA 92373

**RISTER, GENE ARNOLD,** humanities educator; b. Merkel, Tex., Apr. 18, 1943; s. Jettie William and Mary Evelyn (Scott) R.; m. Janet Kathleen Ledermann, Jan. 21, 1967. BA summa cum laude, McMurry U., 1965; MA, Tex. Christian U., 1966; PhD, U. Wis., 1972; postgrad., U. Ariz., 1990, No. Ariz. U., 1990. Prof. divsn. chmn. McMurry U., Abilene, Tex., 1970-81, East Ctrl. U., Ada, Okla., 1981-83, Paradise Valley Coll., Maricopa C.C., Phoenix, 1983—. Adj. prof. No. Ariz. U., Phoenix, 1994—; del. Nat. Inst. Higher Edn. for Mex.-Ams., Albuquerque, 1975. Author: (poems) Canticles I, 2002, Canticles II, 2003, Canticles III, 2004, Rumors of Unruh, 2006; book reviewer Tex. Rev., 1985; illustrator Tex. Rev. and Tex. Anthology, 1979-82; contbr. articles to profl. jours.; contbr. numerous poems to jours., anthologies. Regional cons. Human Rels. Coun., Midland; moderator, dir. West Tex. Coun. Govts.; mem. Tex. Com. for Humanities and Pub. Policy, 1975-81; ECU rep. Intertribal Coun., Five Nations, Sulphur, Okla., 1981; co-sponsor Tex. Reading Ctr. Consortium of Univs., 1977-79. Recipient Faculty Recognition award Consortium for C.C. Devel., 1996; named Innovator of the Yr. Maricopa CCD/League for Innovation, 1988, Outstanding Faculty Employee award Maricopa C.C. Dist., 1985, 89, 92; NDEA Title VI fellow, 1965-67, Am. Grad. Sch. Internat. Mgmt. fellow, 1995, East-West Ctr. fellow, 1994, Japan Found. fellow, 1995; U.S. Dept. Edn. Title VIA grantee, 1996-98. Mem. C.C. Humanities Assn. (Ariz. state rep. to nat. bd. 1992). Democrat. Baptist. Avocations: archaeology, art, movies, music, travel. Home: 14407 N 60th St Scottsdale AZ 85254-5540 Office: Paradise Valley Cmty Coll 18401 N 32nd St Phoenix AZ 85032-1210 Office Phone: 602-787-6575. E-mail: gene.rister@pvmail.maricopa.edu.

**RISTICH, MIODRAG,** psychiatrist; b. Belgrade, Yugoslavia, July 19, 1938; arrived in US, 1967; s. Teodosije and Gordana (Isailovic) Ristich; m. Yvonne Muriel Cunliffe, May 6, 1967; children: Katharine Alexandra, Elizabeth Victoria. MD, U. Belgrade, 1962. Resident psychiatry Manhattan Psychiat. Ctr., NYU, 1980-83; med. dir. Cambridge (Minn.) State Hosp., 1967-72; dir. Willowbrook State Sch., Staten Island, NY, 1972-74; med. dir. DeWitt Rehab. Nursing Ctr., NYC, 1976—; clin. asst. prof. psychiatry NYU Med. Sch., 1996—. Pvt. practice psychiatry, NYC, 1973—. Mem.: AMA, Royal Coll. Psychiatrists, Am. Assn. Geriatric Psychiatry, Am. Psychiat. Assn. Republican. Avocation: tennis. Home: 37 Sunrise Ln Upper Saddle River NJ 07458-1631 Office: 201 E 79th St Apt 7J New York NY 10021-0833 Office Phone: 212-737-6990. E-mail: mristich@yahoo.com.

**RISTOW, BRUNNO,** plastic surgeon; b. Brusque, Brazil, Oct. 18, 1940; s. Arno and Ally Odette (von Bruettner) Ristow; m. Urannia Carrasquilla Gutierrez, Nov. 10, 1979; children from previous marriage: Christian Kilian, Trevor Roland. Student, Coll. Sinodal, Brazil, 1956—57; MD magna cum laude, U. Brazil, 1966. Diplomate Am. Bd. Plastic and Reconstructive Surgery. Intern in surgery Hosp. dos Estrangeiros, Rio de Janeiro, 1965, Hosp. Estuadual Miguel Couto, Brazil, 1965—66, Instituto Aposentadoria Pensao Comerciarios Hosp. for Gen. Surgery, 1966; resident in plastic and reconstructive surgery Dr. Ivo Pitanguy Hosp. Santa Casa de Misericordia, Rio de Janeiro, 1967; fellow Inst. Reconstructive Plastic Surgery NYU Med. Ctr., N.Y.C., 1967—68, jr. resident, 1971—72, sr. and chief resident, 1972—73; practice medicine specializing in plastic surgery Rio de Janeiro, 1967, NYC, 1968—73, San Francisco, 1973—; asst. surgeon NY Hosp., Cornell Med. Ctr., NYC, 1968—71. Clin. instr. surgery NYU Sch. Medicine, 1972—73; chmn. plastic and reconstructive surgery divsn. Presbyn. Hosp., Pacific Med. Ctr., San Francisco, 1974—92, chmn. emeritus, 1992—. Contbg. author: Cancer of the Hand, 1975, Current Therapy in Plastic and Reconstructive Surgery, 1988, Male Aesthetic Surgery, 1989, How They Do It: Procedures in Plastic and Reconstructive Surgery, 1990, Middle Crus: The Missing Link in Alar Cratilage Anatomy, 1991, Surgical Technology International, 1992, Aesthetic Plastic Surgery, 1993, Mastery of Surgery: Plastic and Reconstructive Surgery, 1993, Reoperative Aesthetic Plastic Surgery of the Face and Breast, 1994; contbr. articles to profl. jours. With M.C. Brazilian Army Res., 1959—70. Decorated knight Venerable Order of St. Hubertus, Knight Order St. John of Jerusalem; fellow in surgery, Cornell Med. Sch., 1968—71. Fellow: ACS, Internat.Coll. Surgeons; mem.: AMA (Physician's Recognition award 1971—83), San Francisco Med. Assn., Calif. Med. Assn., Calif. Soc. Plastic Surgeons, Internat. Soc. Aesthetic Plastic Surgeons, Am. Soc. Plastic and Reconstructive Surgeons, Am. Soc. Aesthetic Plastic Surgery (chmn. edn.), San Francisco Olympic Club. Republican. Evangelical. Office: Calif Pacific Med Ctr 2100 Webster St Ste 501 San Francisco CA 94115-2373 Office Phone: 415-202-1507. Personal E-mail: info@brunnoristow.com.

**RISTOW, GEORGE EDWARD,** neurologist, educator; b. Albion, Mich., Dec. 15, 1943; s. George Julius and Margaret (Beattie) R.; 1 child, George Andrew Martin. BA, Albion Coll., 1965; DO, Coll. Osteo. Medicine/Surgery, Des Moines, 1969. Diplomate Am. Bd. Psychiatry and Neurology. Intern Garden City Hosp., 1969-70; resident Wayne State U., 1970-74; fellow U. Newcastle Upon Tyne, 1974-75; asst. prof. dept. neurology Wayne State U., Detroit, 1975-77; assoc. prof. Mich. State U., East Lansing, 1977-83, prof., 1983-84, 95—, prof., chmn., 1984-95, prof. emeritus, 2001—. Fellow Am. Acad. Neurology, Royal Soc. Medicine; mem. AMA, Am. Osteo. Assn., Pan Am. Med. Assn., World Fedn. Neurology, Am. Coll. Neuropsychiatrists (sr.). Home: 6149 Bridgewater Cir East Lansing MI 48823 Office Phone: 517-374-7600. Personal E-mail: gristow@cimamed.com.

**RISTOW, THELMA FRANCES,** retired elementary school educator; b. Plymouth, Wis., Sept. 9, 1938; d. Ambrose J. and Marie A. (Lauby) Enders; m. William A. Ristow, Nov. 7, 1964; children: James, Lora, Kim Marie, Robert, Donald. BS, U. Wis., Oshkosh, 1960, MS in Edn., 1995. Cert. elem. tchr. Peer coach Oshkosh Area Sch. Dist., 2000—, ret., 2003. Contbr. chapters to books; co-author (with Dr. Ava McCall): Teaching State History: A Guide to Developing a Multicultural Curriculum. Mem. ASCD, Internat. Reading Assn. (state coord.), Wis. State Reading Assn., Ctrl. Wis. Reading Coun., Mid-East Reading Coun., Wolf River Reading Coun., Fox Valley Reading Coun., Headwaters Reading Coun., Phi Delta Kappa, Kappa Delta Pi. Home: 1600 Northpoint St Oshkosh WI 54901-3119 Office: Oshkosh Area Sch Dist Adminstrn 215 S Eagle St Oshkosh WI 54903 Personal E-mail: tfristow@sbcglobal.net.

**RISUKHIN, VLADIMIR NIKOLAYEVICH,** aeronautical engineer, educator; b. Verkhnyaya Pokrovka, Ukraine, Dec. 26, 1946; arrived in U.S., 2001; s. Nikolay Ostapovich Risukhin and Nina Josephovna (Linevich) Risukhina; m. Tatyana Vasilyevna Chernysh, July 12, 1969; children: Dmitry, Ekaterina. BS in Radio Comm., Coll. Elec. Comm., 1965; BS in Flight Ops., Coll. Civil Aviation, 1968; MS in Aeronautical Engring., Acad. Civil Aviation, 1974, PhD in Aeronautical Engring., 1988. Radio tech. Airport, Lugansk, Ukraine, 1964—65; pilot Regoinal Adminstrn. Civil Aviation, Yakutsk, 1968—77; flight ops. mgr. Ctrl. Adminstrn. Internat. Airline, Moscow, 1977—83; flight tng. mgr. Min. Aviation Industry, 1983—90; sr. instr. pilot Aepoflot-Russian Airlines, 1990—2002; assoc. prof. Coll. Aviation, Western Mich. U., Battle Creek, 2002—. Cons. Internat. Air Transp. Assn., Montreal, 2000—. Author: Controlling Pilot Error: Automation, 2001. Mem.: AIAA, Univ. Aviation Assn. Avocations: photography, tennis. Office: Coll Aviation Western Mich U 237 N Helmer Rd Battle Creek MI 49015 E-mail: vladimir.risukhin@wmich.edu.

**RITACCO, PATSY RICHARD,** sales executive; b. Newark, Aug. 27, 1956; s. Michael Patsy and Adelaide (Caruso) Ritacco; m. Linda La Falce, Nov. 5, 1978; children: Michael A., Patsy Richard Jr. B in History, William Paterson Coll., 1978. Notary pub. N.J. Tchr. Belleville (N.J.) HS, 1978-82; bd. pneumatics Robert Tool, Saddle Brook, NJ, 1983-94; dist. sales mgr. Std. Abrasives, Simi Valley, Calif., 1994—. Concert promotion dir. edn. groups 50s and 60s Bklyn. Bridge, Coasters, 1980—; scholar bd. Unico Nat., Nutley, NJ, 1995—, treas., 1998—99, v.p., 2000—; chpt. pres., 2005—; guest lectr. in field. Contbr. poetry to anthologies; contbg. writer: Italian Tribune. Fellow bdlgs. and grounds pub. rels. Christ Ch. Sch. Bd., 1985—88; chmn. com. Nutley Hall of Fame, 2002—; chmn. Ferraro Found., 2004; mem. planning bd. Township of Nutley, 2005; mem. Nutley Planning Bd., 2005—; coun. mem. NIAF; assoc. mem. Mus. Natural History. Named in Greatest Poets and Poems of the 20th Century, 1999; recipient Editor's Choice award "Riddle of the Rose", Internat. Libr. of Poetry, Color of Heart, 2000, Poetry's Elite: The Best Poets, 2000, Unican of the Yr. award, Nutley chpt. Unico Nat., 2002, Poetry's Elite: The Best Poet, 2001, 2002, 2003, 2004, Outstanding Achievement award, Ferraro Found., 2003, Cmty. Svc. award, 2003, Parable of Time Editor's Choice award, 2003, Civic award, Nutley Jaycees, 2006. Mem.: Internat. Soc. Poets, Platers Assn. (contbg.), Soc. Engrs. (contbg.), Am. Softball Assn. (assoc.). Roman Catholic. Avocations: reading, cooking, music, sports. Office: Standard Abrasives 4201 Guardian St Simi Valley CA 93063-3372 Office Phone: 800-423-5444. Personal E-mail: BaBiBard@aol.com. Business E-mail: pritacco@standardabrasives.com.

**RITCH, KATHLEEN,** diversified financial services company executive; b. Harbor Beach, Mich., Jan. 23, 1943; d. Eunice (Spry) R. BA, Mich. State U., 1965; student, Katharine Gibbs Sch., 1965—66. Exec. sec., adminstrv. asst. to pres. Katy Industries, Inc., N.Y.C., 1969-70; exec. sec., adminstrv. asst. to chmn. Kobrand Corp., N.Y.C., 1970-72; adminstrv. asst. to chmn. and pres. Ogden Corp., N.Y.C., 1972-74, asst. sec., adminstr. office svcs., asst. to chmn., 1974-81, corp. sec., adminsr. office svcs., 1981-84, v.p., corp. sec., adminstr. office svcs., 1984-92, v.p. corp. sec., 1992-2000; freelance executive NYC, 2000—. Co-owner Unell Mfg. Co., Port Hope, Mich., 1966-87. Bd. dir. Young Concert Artists, Inc. Home: 500 E 77th St New York NY 10162-0025

**RITCH, ROBERT HARRY,** ophthalmologist, educator; b. New Haven, May 14, 1942; s. Edward Lewis and Minerva (Grosberg) R. BA cum laude, Harvard U., 1965, MA, 1967; postgrad., Rice U., 1967—68; MD, Albert Einstein Coll. Medicine, 1972. Diplomate Am. Bd. Ophthalmology, Am. Bd. Laser Surgery. Intern St. Vincent's Med. Ctr., NYC, 1972-73; resident in ophthalmology Mt. Sinai Sch. Medicine, NYC, 1973-75, chief resident, 1975-76, Heed Ophthalmic Found. fellow, 1976-77, NIH-Nat. Rsch. Svc. fellow, 1976-78, asst. clin. ophthalmologist, 1976-77, instr., 1977-78, asst. prof., 1978-80, assoc. prof., 1980-82; attending ophthalmologist Beth Israel Med. Ctr., NYC, 1978—. Cons. ophthalmologist VA Hosp., Bronx, 1978—82, Manhattan Eye, Ear & Throat Hosp., 1989—; dir. glaucoma svc. Elmhurst Hosp., 1978—82, acting dir. dept. ophthalmology, 1979—82; chief glaucoma svc. N.Y. Eye and Ear Infirmary, N.Y.C., 1983—, surgeon dir., 1991—; prof. clin. ophthalmology N.Y. Med. Coll., Valhalla, 1983—; Arthur Bedell Meml. lectr. Wills Eye Hosp., Phila., 1995; John Edwin Brown Meml. lectr. Ohio State U., Columbus, 1996; Schoenburg Meml. lectr. Ill. Eye and Ear Infirmary, Chgo., 1996; Schlaegel lectr. U. Ind., Indpls., 1996; Gerasimos Frenimopoulos Meml. lectr. Duke U., 1997, Joseph M. Bryan Meml. lectr. 97; Roger P. Mason Meml. lectr. Howard U., 1997; Abraham S. Ticho lectr., Jerusalem, 98; Anagnostakis-Trantus lectr., Athens, 98; Sanford Gifford Meml. lectr., Chgo., 98; Annie Wong lectr. Chinese U., Hong Kong, 1999; Arthur Lim lectr., Hong Kong, 2001; Am. Glaucoma Soc. Subspecialty Day lectr. Am. Acad. Ophthalmology, New Orleans, 2001; King Khaled Meml. lectr., Riyadh, 03; Chew Sek-Jin Meml. lectr., Hong Kong, 03; Irving Leopold Meml. lectr., Irvine, Calif., 04; Francis Proctor Meml. lectr., San Francisco, 05; program chmn. East Coast Glaucoma Symposium, NY, 2000; cons. Sukhumvit Hosp., Bangkok, 1994—; pres. Internat. Eye Cons., Ltd., 1995—, N.Y. Glaucoma Rsch. Inst., 1996; adj. sr. scientist Singapore Eye Rsch. Inst., 1997; mem. adv. bd. Dr. to Dr., Berkeley, Calif., 1995—; sec., treas., chmn. sci. adv. bd. Glaucoma Found., 1984—; med. dir., chmn., grant rev. com.; med. dir. Children's Right to Sight, prin. investigator Collaborative Initial Glaucoma Treatment Study, 1993—2000; mem. adv. bd. Sturge-Weber Found., 1996; mem. glaucoma adv. com. Nat. Soc. to Prevent Blindness, 1986—; organizing chmn. Bangkok Ophthal. Congress, 1985—93, Optic Nerve Rescue & Restoration Think Tank, NY, 1994—2003, First Internat. Think Tank on Exfoliation Syndrome, NY, 1999, Myanmar Internat. Ophthal. Congress, 1997, 99, 2003; internat. sci. com. Internat. Congress of Ophthalmology, Sydney, Australia, 2002; sci. organizing com. mem. 4th Internat. Glaucoma Congress, Barcelona, 2003; external assessor U. Malaya, 1988—96; cons. Tun Hussein Onn Nat. Eye Hosp., Kuala Lumpur, Malaysia, 1996—; internat. adv. bd. 4th Internat. Symposium of Ophthalmology, Shantou, China, 2002; mem. steering com. Assn. Internat. Glaucoma Soc., 2002—; internat. advisor Tianjin Med. Ctr., China, 2002—; hon. pres. Chinese Internat. Glaucoma Congress, Beijing, 2004; adj. prof. Mt. Sinai Sch. Medicine, N.Y.C., 2005—; mem. sci. organizing com. 5th Internat. Glaucoma Congress, Capetown, South Africa, 2005; chmn. sci. organizing com. glaucoma sect. World Congress Ophthalmology, Sao Paulo, Brazil, 2006; bd. dirs. Helen Keller Internat. Author (with M.B. Shields): The Secondary Glaucomas, 1982, The Glaucomas, 1988, 1996; author: (with R. Caronia) Classic Papers in Glaucoma, 2000; spl. sect. editor: Jour. Glaucoma, 1991—98, mem. editl. bd.: Sightsaving, 1981—86, Opthalmic Laser Therapy, 1984—88, Ophthalmic Resident, 1992—95, Ophthalmic Surgery and Lasers, 1995—, Microsurgery, 1994—2004, Ophthalmology Times, 1996—2001, Jour. Glaucoma, 1998—, Internat. Glaucoma Rev., 1999—, Archives Ophthalmology, 2004—, BMC Ophthalmology, 2005—, Expert Rev. Ophthalmology, 2005—, contbg. editor: Ophthalmic Practice, 1993—; contbr. to films on laser therapy, over 900 articles and abstracts in field. Bd. dirs. Dooley Found./Intermed. U.S.A., 1991—, UN, Southeastern Nigeria Eye Care Outreach Coll. Med. Scis. U. Calabar, Nigeria, 1996—; vol. Devel. Coun., 1991-93; chmn. bd. dirs. I-Med. Devel Corp., 1991-94; sci. adv. bd. Singapore Eye Rsch. Inst.; bd. govs. Internat. Soc. for Imaging of the Eye, 2002—; adv. com. Internat. Coun. Ophthalmology, 2002—. Decorated comdr. Grace Cross badge Order of Orthodox Knights Hospitalier of St. John of Jerusalem; named spl. honoree, Helen Keller Found., 2000, Glaucoma Found., 2000; recipient Acad. Investigator award, NIH, 1978—81, Disting. Svc. award, Internat. Ctr. N.Y., 1981, Exec. Dirs. award, 1985, Founders award, Nat. Exhibits by Blind Artists, 1985, Gold medal of Merit and Honor, Greek Glaucoma Soc., 1998, Ophthalmology Times Achievement in Ophthalmology award, 1998, Louis Rudin award for rsch. in glaucoma, 1999, Jesse H. Neal award for editl. achievement, 2000, John Kearny Rodgers Physician of Yr. award, N.Y. Eye and Ear Infirmary, 2005; Hon. scholar, Harvard U., 1965, NSF fellow, 1966—67, Harvard Traveling fellow, Rice U., 1967—68. Fellow Am. Acad. Ophthalmology (edn. distbn. subcom. 1994-97, book/jour. link subcom. 1994-97, distbn. adv. subcom. 1997-2000, chmn. subcom., 2001—, Honor award, 1985, sr. honor award 1995), Heed Ophthalmic Found. (ophthalmologist of Yr. 1996), Am. Ophthalmol. Soc. (program com. 2002—), NY Acad. Medicine, Royal Coll. Ophthalmologists (U.K.), ACS, Internat. Coll. Surgeons, Am. Soc. Laser Surgery Medicine (chmn. ophthalmology sect. 1991-92, moderator and program chmn. joint sci. symposium on glaucoma 1991), NY Acad. Medicine (sec. sect. on ophthalmology 1991-92, chmn. 1993-94, Charles May Meml. Lectr. 1991, bd. trustees 2003—); mem. AMA, AAAS, NY State Med. Soc., NY County Med. Soc., Assn. Rsch. in Vision and Ophthalmology (program com., glaucoma sect. 1991-93, program chmn. 1993-94, internat. com. 2003—, bd. trustees 2003—), Am. Assn. Ophthalmology, Ophthal. Soc. U.K., Internat. Assn. Ocular surgeons, Internat. Congress Ophthalmology (glaucoma com. 1994—), NY Intra-Ocular Lens Implant Soc., Manhattan Ophthal. Soc., Assn. Internat. Glaucoma Soc., European Eye Rsch., Soc. Clin. Trials, Pan-Pacific Anterior Segment Soc. (v.p. 1985-88), Internat. Coun. Ophthalmology (adv. com.), NY Acad. Sci., Ophthalmic Laser Surgery Soc. (sec.-treas. 1982-98, 2000-, pres. 1998-2000), NY Soc. Clin. Ophthalmology (rec. sec. 1988-90, program chmn. 1990-91, pres. 1991-92), NY Glaucoma Rsch. Inst. (pres. 1996—), Am. Soc. Cell Biology, Am. Telemed Assn., Internat. Soc. On-Line Ophthalmology (mem. orgn. com., chmn. glaucoma sect. 1995—), Internat. Fedn. Cell Biologists, Philippine Soc. Ophthalmology (hon.), Thailand Ophthal. Soc. (hon.), Italian Assn. for Study of Glaucoma (hon.), La.-Miss. Ophthal. and Otolargyol. Soc. (hon.), Can. Implant Soc. (hon). Home: 455 E 57th St # 14D New York NY 10022-3065 Office: NY Eye and Ear Infirmary 310 E 14th St New York NY 10003-4201 Office Phone: 212-477-7540. Personal E-mail: ritchmd@earthlink.net.

**RITCHEY, BRENT DYLAN,** lawyer; b. Sycamore, Ill., Apr. 27, 1970; s. Ronald G. and Carla Edris Ritchey; m. Crystal Anne Ritchey, Aug. 14, 1993. BA with honors, U. Wis., 2000; JD, U. Tex., 2003. Bar: Tex. 2003. Intern Tex.

Atty. Gen., Austin, 2002; assoc. Jorge G. Pineda and Assocs., Austin, 2003—04; hearing officer Tex. Workforce Commn., Austin, 2004; ptnr., trial atty. Ritchey & Marbut, LLP, Austin, 2004—. Editor: (law jour.) Rev. of Litigation, 2002—03. Mem.: ATLA, ABA, Coll. of State Bar of Tex., Phi Beta Kappa. Avocations: playing drums, astronomy, painting. Office: Ritchey & Marbut LLP Ste C 3823 Airport Blvd Austin TX 78722

**RITCHEY, KENNETH WILLIAM,** educational association administrator; b. Washington, June 7, 1947; s. Conrad Monroe and Katherine Costance (Sheris) (dec. 2004) R.; m. Nancy Jayne Kirk, Aug. 22, 1970; children: Kirk Damon, Erin Kathryn (dec. Apr. 1988). BS in Edn., Shippensburg U., 1969; MEd in Spl. Edn., U. Va., 1972; MS in Ednl. Adminstrn., U. Dayton, 1980; grad. sr. execs. in state & local govt. program, Harvard U., 1992. Spl. edn. tchr. Shippensburg (Pa.) Area Sch. Dist., 1969-71; head cross country and track coach Shippensburg U., 1970-74; master tchr., coord. work experience program Lincoln Intermediate Unit, New Oxford, Pa., 1971-76; adult edn. tchr. Franklin County Prison, Chambersburg, Pa., 1972-76; asst. supt. mgmt. svcs. Montgomery County Bd. Mental Retardation & Devel. Disabilities, Dayton, Ohio, 1977-83, supt. bd., 1983-99; dir. Ohio Dept. Mental Retardation and Devel. Disabilities, Columbus, 1999—; mem. Gov.'s Cabinet. Mem. part-time faculty edn. dept. U. Dayton, 1983-97; mem., vice-chair cmty. and mil. adv. com. ARC, 1986-95, needs and priorities com. Human Svcs. Levy Coun., 1982-84, 87-99; trustee Ohio Polit. Action Com., Brighter Tomorrow Found., 1990-2000, County Corp., 1992-98, Leadership Dayton, 1991. Former editor statewide newsletter for tchrs. and profls. in Work Experience. Vol. mem. cmty. and agys. resources coun. United Way, 1986—98; v.p. HelpLink Bd., pres.; mem. Gov.'s Vision Com., Ill., 1997—2000; bd. dirs. Ohio Pub. Images, Inc., past pres. Recipient Harold Hilty Humanitarian award, United Cerebral Palsy Rehab. Svcs., 1994, Robert Weaver Disting. Svc. award, Montgomery County Bd. Mental Retardation and Devel. Disabilities, 1999, Svc. award, Profl. Assn. on Retardation, 2002, Chair's Recognition award, Wright State U. Dept. Psychiatry, 2005; honored by, Ohio Assn. County Bds., 2005. Mem.: Ohio Self Determination Assn. (Catalyst award 2003), Nat. Assn. State Dirs. Developmental Disabilities Svcs. (chair nat. policy work group 2002, bd. trustees 2004, sec.-treas. 2005), Supts. Assn. (exec. com.), Ohio Supts. County Bds. Mental Retardation (v.p., pres.), Am. Assn. Mental Retardation, Phi Beta Kappa. Democrat. Methodist. Home: 7660 Turtle Creek Dr Dayton OH 45414-1756 Office: 1810 Sullivant Ave Columbus OH 43222-1055 Office Phone: 614-466-0129. E-mail: k1ritchey@aol.com.

**RITCHEY, LAURETTA MARIE,** secondary school educator; b. Chgo., Oct. 17, 1947; d. Thomas Joseph and Marien LaFond Fay; m. Richard Wayne Ritchey, July 17, 1971; children: Richard Thomas, Christopher Milo, Timothy James. BA, Dominican U., River Forest, Ill., 1969; MA in Tchg. in Biology, Northeastern U., Chgo., 1975; CAS Early Childhood, Nat. Lewis U., Evanston, Ill., 1982. Cert. secondary tchr. Ill. Sci. tchr. Proviso West HS, Hillside, Ill., 1969—78, ValleyView Sch. Dist., Romeoville and Bolingbrook, Ill., 1986—91, Carl Sandburg HS, Ill., 1991—. Tchr. rep. Pk. Dist., Orland Park, 2005—06. Recipient Connections award (2), State of Ill. Mem.: NIABT. Home: 15W770 82nd St Burr Ridge IL 60527 Office: Carl Sandburg HS 131st and LaGrange Road Orland Park IL 60462 Office Phone: 708067103100. Business E-mail: lritchey@d230.org.

**RITCHEY, SAMUEL DONLEY, JR.,** retired retail executive; b. Derry Twp., Pa., July 16, 1933; s. Samuel Donley and Florence Catherine (Litsch) R.; m. Sharon Marie Anderson, Apr. 6, 1956; children: Michael Donley, Tamara Louise, Shawn Christopher. BS, San Diego State U., 1955, MS, 1963; postgrad., Stanford U., 1964. With Lucky Stores Inc., 1951-61, 64-86, pres., chief operating officer, 1978-80, pres., chief exec. officer, 1980-81, chmn., chief exec. officer, 1981-85, chmn. bd., 1981-86. Bd. dirs AT&T, Inc., The McClatchy Co., De La Salle Inst., John Muir Health; grad. mgr. San Diego State U., 1961-63; lectr. in field; past chmn. Calif. Power Exch., mem. adv. coun. Grad. Sch. Bus., Stanford U. Sloan Found. fellow. Mem. Mex. Am. Legal Def. and Edn. Fund, Western Assn. Food Chains (bd. dirs., pres.), Food Mktg. Inst. (bd. dirs., vice chmn.), Sloan Alumni Assn. (adv. bd., pres.).

**RITCHIE, ALBERT,** lawyer; b. Charlottesville, Va., Sept. 29, 1939; s. John and Sarah Dunlop (Wallace) R.; m. Jennie Wayland, Apr. 29, 1967; children: John, Mary. BA, Yale U., 1961; LLB, U. Va., 1964. Bar: Ill. 1964, Tenn. 2000. Assoc. Sidley & Austin, Chgo., 1964-71, ptnr., 1972-99, ret., 1999. Bd. dirs. Erie Neighborhood House, Chgo., 1978-88; bd. dirs. United Charities of Chgo., 1979-90; trustee U. Va. Law Sch. Found., 1997-99. Capt. U.S. Army, 1965-67. Mem. ABA, Am. Coll. Real Estate Lawyers, Chgo. Legal Aid Soc., Legal Club Chgo. (pres. 1986-87), U. Va. Law Sch. Alumni Assn. (v.p. 1989-93, pres. 1993-95), Cherokee Country Club, Hillsboro Club. Episcopalian. Home: 436 Boxwood Sq Knoxville TN 37919-6627 Personal E-mail: ritchiea@bellsouth.net.

**RITCHIE, ALEXANDER BUCHAN,** lawyer; b. Detroit, Apr. 19, 1923; s. Alexander Stevenson and Margaret (May) R.; m. Sheila Spellacy, June 1998; 1 child, Barbara Ritchie Drolshagen. BA, Wayne State U., 1947, JD, 1949. Bar: Mich. 1949. Pvt. practice, Detroit, 1949-52, 84—; asst. gen. counsel, asst. v.p. Maccabees Mutual Life Ins. Co., Detroit, 1952-65, v.p., sec., gen. counsel Southfield, Mich., 1977-84; sec., house counsel Wayne Nat. Life Ins. Co., Detroit, 1966-67; ptnr. Fenton, Nederlander, Dodge & Ritchie, Detroit, 1967-77. Spl. asst. atty. gen. State Mich., 1974-77. Bd. mem. Detroit Bd. Edn., 1971-77, Montgomery Bd. Edn., 1971-73; bd. Police Commrs., Detroit, 1974-77; bd. dirs. Doctor's Hosp., Detroit, 1974-89. With U.S. Army, 1943-46. Recipient Key to the City of Detroit, Mayor Coleman Young, 1977. Mem. Mich. State Bar Assn. Avocations: reading, golf, theater, gourmet. Home: 29255 Laurel Woods Dr Apt 201 Southfield MI 48034-1017

**RITCHIE, ALLEN W.,** insurance company executive; Degree, U. Ala. Ptnr. Arthur Andersen & Co., Atlanta; from CFO to pres. Fin. and Adminstrv. Group AGCO Corp., 1991—96, pres. Fin. and Adminstrv. Group, 1996—97; exec. v.p., CFO, COO Per-Se Technologies, 1998, pres., CEO, 1998—2000; exec. v.p. Protective Life Corp., Birmingham, Ala., 2001—, CFO, 2001—. Office: Protective Life Corp 2801 Hwy 280 S Birmingham AL 35223

**RITCHIE, DANIEL LEE,** former academic administrator; b. Springfield, Ill., Sept. 19, 1931; s. Daniel Felix and Jessie Dee (Binney) R. BA, Harvard U., 1954, MBA, 1956. Exec. v.p., CFO MCA Inc., LA, 1962—70; pres. Archon Pure Products Co., LA, 1970-73; exec. v.p. Westinghouse Electric Corp., Pitts., 1975-78; pres. corp. staff and strategic planning Westinghouse Broadcasting Co., 1978-79, pres., CEO, 1979-81; chmn., CEO Westinghouse Broadcasting & Cable, Inc., 1981-87; owner Rancho Cielo, Montecito, Colo., 1977—; chancellor U. Denver, Colo., 1989—2005, chancellor emeritus, 2005—, chmn. bd. trustees, 1999—. Mem. bd. dirs. Nat. Assn. Ind. Coll. & Univ., Internat. Assn of Univ. Pres.; pres. Ind. Higher Edn. of Colo. Trustee, vice chmn., chmn. of bd., U. Denver, 1983-89; pres., Temple Hoyne Buell Found., Denver; chmn. Ctrl. City Opera; mem., adv. bd. Nat. Park Sys. With U.S. Army, 1956-58. Office: Chmn Bd U Denver 270 Saint Paul St, Ste 300 Denver CO 80206 Office Phone: 303-871-2122. Office Fax: 303-871-3770. E-mail: dritchie@du.edu.*

**RITCHIE, GISELA FUHRMANN,** foreign language educator; b. Germany; came to U.S., 1953; d. Ernst and Martha (Mahraun) Fuhrmann; m. R. Bowland Ritchie, Nov. 27, 1958 (dec. 1971); children: Irene, George. MA, Free Univ., Berlin, 1952, PhD, U. Mich, 1965. Instr. Bob Jones U., Greenville, S.C., 1953-54, Wayne State U., Detroit, 1954-56; teaching fellow U. Mich., Ann Arbor, 1956-59; asst. prof. Wichita (Kans.) State U., 1965-68, assoc. prof., 1968—. Vis. prof. Vanderbilt U., Nashville, 1991. Author: (books) Caroline Schlegel-Schelling in Wahrheit und Dichtung, 1968, Der Dichter und die Frau, 1989; contbr. articles to profl. jours. Mem. Internat. Soc. for Study of European Ideas, Modern Lang. Assn., Am. Assn. Tchrs. of German, Lessing Soc., Internat. Brecht Soc., Phi Beta Kappa. Avocations: reading, writing, swimming, walking.

**RITCHIE, J. MURDOCH,** pharmacologist, educator; b. Aberdeen, Scotland, June 10, 1925; came to U.S. 1956; s. Alexander Farquharson and Agnes Jane (Bremner) R.; m. Brenda Rachel Bigland; children: Alasdair J., A. Jocelyn. BSc, Aberdeen (Scotland) U., 1944, U. Coll. London, 1949, PhD, 1952, DSc, 1960, MA, Yale U., 1968; DSc, Aberdeen U., 1987. Lectr. physiology U. Coll. London, 1949-51; sci. staff Nat. Inst. Med. Rsch., London, 1951-55; asst. prof. to prof. Albert Einstein Coll. Medicine, N.Y.C., 1954-63, prof. pharmacology, 1963-68; prof. and chmn. pharmacology Yale U., New Haven, 1968-74, dir. biol. scis., 1975-78, prof. pharmacology, 1968—. Contbr. articles to profl. jours.; editor sci. books and jours. Fellow Royal Soc., Univ. Coll. London. Home: 200 Leeder Hill Dr Apt 400A Hamden CT 06517-2729 E-mail: murdoch.ritchie@yale.edu.

**RITCHIE, KEVIN,** semiconductor company executive; BS in elec. engring., U. Dayton, 1978. Product engr. def. bus. Tex. Instruments Inc., 1978—80, with semiconductor group, 1980—90, wafer fab mgr., 1990—96, mgr. worldwide application-specific products mfg. ops., 1996—2000, v.p. worldwide mfg. ops., tech. and mfg. group Dallas, 2000—. Office: Tex Instruments Inc 12500 TI Blvd Dallas TX 75243 Office Phone: 972-995-2011. Office Fax: 972-995-4360.

**RITCHIE, P. SCOTT,** lawyer; BS, Purdue U., 1983; JD, DePaul U., 1989. Bar: Ill. 1989, U.S. Dist. Ct. (no. dist.) Ill. 1989. Acct. exec. Hallmark Mktg., Kansas City, Mo., 1983-86; assoc. atty. Clausen Miller P.C., Chgo., 1989-96, ptnr., 1997—. Rep. precinct capt., Mt. Prospect, Ill., 1992-94. Named Ill. Super Lawyer, Law and Politics. Mem. Chgo. Bar Assn., Ill. Assn. Def. Trial Counsel, Brain Injury Assn., Specialized Carriers and Rigging Assn., Order of Barristers, Am. Alpine Club, Glacier Mountaineering Soc., Glacier Natural History Assn. Avocations: mountain climbing, golf. Office: Clausen Miller PC 10 S La Salle St Ste 1600 Chicago IL 60603-1098 Office Phone: 312-855-1010. Business E-mail: pritchie@clausen.com.

**RITCHIE, RICHARD LEE,** media company executive; b. Grand Rapids, Mich., Nov. 16, 1969; children: Gabrielle Gay, Steven Barton. BA, Mich. State U., 1968, MBA, 1972; P.MD, Harvard U., 1982. C.P.A., Mich. Sr. acct. Peat, Marwick, Mitchell & Co., Detroit, 1968-69, 72-74; mgr. corp. acctg. Grand Trunk Western R.R., Detroit, 1974-76, treas., 1976-79, asst. v.p., treas., 1980-83; v.p., treas. James River Corp., Richmond, Va., 1984-86; v.p.-fin., chief fin. officer Harte Hanks Communications, San Antonio, 1987-96; exec. v.p., CFO Big Flower Holdings, Inc., N.Y.C., 1997-2000. Prof. Oakland Community Coll., Farmington, Mich. Served with AUS, 1969-71. Mem. AICPA, Mich. Assn. CPAs, Am. Acctg. Assn., Beta Alpha Psi, Beta Gamma Sigma. Jewish. Office: Bice Mercato 551 Madison Ave #1601 New York NY 10022-3261

**RITCHIE, ROBERT JAMES See KID ROCK**

**RITCHIE, ROBERT OLIVER,** materials science educator, director; b. Plymouth, Devon, Jan. 2, 1948; arrived in US, 1974; s. Kenneth Ian and Kathleen Joy (Sims) Ritchie; m. Connie Olesen (div. 1978); 1 child, James Oliver; m. HaiYing Soong, 1991; 1 child, Duncan Soong. BA with honors, U. Cambridge, Eng., 1969, MA, PhD, 1973, ScD, 1990. Cert. engr., UK. Goldsmith's rsch. fellow Churchill Coll. U. Cambridge, 1972-74; Miller fellow in basic rsch. sci. U. Calif., Berkeley, 1974-76, prof., 1981—, chair Materials Sci. and Engring. Dept., 2005—; assoc. prof. mech. engring. MIT, Cambridge, 1977-81; dep. dir. Materials Scis. Divsn. Lawrence Berkeley Nat. Lab., Cambridge, 1990-94, dir. Ctr. for Advanced Materials, 1987-95, head structural Materials Dept., Materials Scis. Divsn., 1995—. Cons. Alcan, Allison, Applied Materials, Boeing, Chevron, Cordis, Exxon, GE, GM, Grumman, Guidant, Instron, Northrop, Rockwell, Westinghouse, Baxter, Carbomedics, Med. Inc., Shiley, St. Jude Med.; Van Horn Disting. lectr. Case Western U., 1997. Editor: 17 books; contbr. articles to profl. jours. Named one of Top 100 Scientists, Sci. Digest mag., 1984; recipient G. R. Irwin medal, ASTM, 1985, Mathewson gold medal, TMS-AME, 1985, Curtis W. McGraw Rsch. award, Am. Soc. Engring. Educators, 1987, Rosenhain medal, Inst. Materials London, 1992, Wohler medal, European Structural Integrity Soc., 2006, Van Horn Disting. Lectr. award, Case Western U., 1997. Fellow: Royal Acad. Engring. (London), Minerals, Materials and Metals Soc. (Mathewson Gold medal 1985, Disting. Structural Materials Scientist/Engr. award 1996), Internat. Congress on Fracture (pres. 1997—2001), Am. Soc. Metals Internat., Inst. Materials (London); mem.: NAE, ASME (NADAI medal 2004), Am. Ceramic Soc., Materials Rsch. Soc. Avocations: skiing, hiking, antiques, orchids. Home: 590 Grizzly Peak Blvd Berkeley CA 94708-1238 Office: U Calif Dept Materials Sci and Engring Berkeley CA 94720-1760 Office Phone: 510-486-5798. Business E-mail: roritchie@lbl.gov.

**RITCHIE, RONALD THOMAS,** history educator; b. Waterloo, Iowa, Apr. 22, 1946; s. Philip Gordon and Zelpha Leota Ritchie; m. Barbara Jean Hocken, Aug. 11, 1968; children: Andrew David, Sarah Kristine Schmidt. BA, U. No. Iowa, 1968, MA, 1974, U. Iowa, 2001. Lic. permanent prof. tchr. State of Iowa Bd. Edn. Tchr. LeMars Comty. Schs., LeMars, Iowa, 1972—82; dept. chair Linn-Mar Comty. Schs., Marion, Iowa, 1982—2004, facilitator for gifted and advanced placement programs, 2004—. Reader Advanced Placement European History Exams. Candidate for Iowa Gen. Assembly Dem. Party, 1978; pres. tchrs. union LeMars Edn. Assn., 1979—81. With U.S. Army, 1969—71. Sr. fellow, James Madison Meml. Fellowship Found., 1993. Mem.: ASCD, NEA, Soc. for History Edn., Orgn. Am. Historians, Am. Hist. Assn. Democrat. Evangelical Lutheran. Avocations: travel, book collecting, reading, numismatics. Home: 180 Landau St Robins IA 52328 Office: Linn-Mar H S 3111 N 10th St Marion IA 52302 Office Phone: 319-447-3125

**RITCHIE, WALLACE PARKS, JR.,** retired surgeon, educator; b. St. Paul, Nov. 4, 1935; s. Wallace Parks and Alice Ransome (Otis) R.; m. Barbara Carey Jewell, Aug. 10, 1960; children: Stephanie, David, Jessica. BA, Yale U., 1957; MD, Johns Hopkins U., 1961; PhD, U. Minn., 1971. Diplomate Am. Bd. Surgery. Intern, resident in surgery Yale U., New Haven, 1961-63; resident in surgery U. Minn. Hosps., Mpls., 1963-69, instr. in surgery, 1969-70; from asst. prof. to prof. surgery U. Va. Sch. Medicine, Charlottesville, 1973-83; prof., chmn. dept. surgery Temple U. Sch. Medicine, Phila., 1983-93; exec. dir. Am. Bd. Surgery, Phila., 1994—2002; ret. Editor textbook: Essentials of Surgery, 1994; contbr. over 160 sci. articles to profl. jours. Lt. col. M.C., U.S. Army, 1970-73. USPHS grantee, 1974-85. Office: Am Bd Surgery Inc 1617 John F Kennedy Blvd Philadelphia PA 19103-1821 Office Phone: 215-568-4000. E-mail: wallace.ritchie@verizon.net.

**RITCHIE, WILLIAM PAUL,** lawyer; b. Columbus, Ohio, June 3, 1946; s. Austin Everett and Helen (Drake) R.; m. Diane Smith, Aug. 2, 1969; 1 child, Elizabeth Drake. BS in Bus. Adminstrn., Ohio State U., 1968, JD, U. Va., 1971. Bar: Ohio 1971, Calif. 1973, Ill. 1987. Assoc. Jones, Day, Reavis & Pogue, Cleve., 1971-77, ptnr., 1977—, ptnr.-in-charge, Chgo., 1987—. Served to lt. USAR, 1972. Mem. ABA, Ohio Bar Assn., Calif. Bar Assn., Chgo. Bar Assn., Mayfield Country Club (Cleve.), Chgo. Club. Republican. Office: Jones Day 77 W Wacker Dr Fl 35 Chicago IL 60601-1662 Office Phone: 312-782-3939. Office Fax: 312-782-8585. Business E-mail: wpritchie@jonesday.com.

**RITER, ROBERT C., JR.,** lawyer; b. Pierre, SD, July 8, 1948; BS, U. SD, 1970, JD, 1973. Bar: SD 1973. Asst. city atty., 1973—; with Riter, Rogers, Wattier & Brown, LLP, Pierre, SD, 1973—, ptnr. Lectr. in field. Contbr. articles to profl. jours. Fellow: Am. Bar Found., Am. Bd. Trial Advocates, Am. Coll. Trial Lawyers; mem.: ABA, Def. Rsch. Inst. (state rep. 1994—99, bd. dirs. 1999—2003), Am. Counsel Assn., SD Def. Lawyers Assn. (pres. 1994—95), State Bar SD (chmn. adminstrv. law com. 1979—81, continuing legal edn. com. 1983—86, ethics com. 1986—89, commr. 2002—05, pres. 2005—06), Phi Delta Phi. Office: Riter Rogers Wattier & Brown LLP Profl and Exec Bldg 319 S Coteau St PO Box 280 Pierre SD 57501 Office Phone: 605-224-5825. Office Fax: 605-224-7102. E-mail: r.riter@riterlaw.com.

**RITER, STEPHEN,** academic administrator, electrical engineer; b. Providence, Mar. 7, 1940; s. Max and Jeannette (Finn) R.; m. Eve R. Hirsch, Aug. 11, 1963; children—Heidi L., Theodore H. BA, Rice U., Houston, 1961, BS in Elec. Engring. 1962; MS, U. Houston, 1967, PhD, 1968. Registered profl. engr., Tex. Dir. Center Urban Programs, Tex. A&M U., 1974-76, mem. univ. faculty, 1968-80, prof. elec. engring., 1976-80; dir. Tex. Energy Extension Service, 1976-79; prof. elec. engring., chmn. dept. elec. engring. and computer sci. U. Tex., El Paso 1980-89, dean engring., 1989-95, dir. Ctr. for Environ. Resource Mgmt., 1989-95, interim v.p. acad. affairs, 1995-96, provost, v.p., 1996—2005, v.p. info. rsch. and planning, 2005—. Active El Paso Pub. Svc. Bd., El Paso Utility Regulatory Bd., 1982-89; cons. in field. Author papers in field.; Editor: Trans. Geosci. Electronics, 1972-76. Mem. policy adv. com. Tex. Dept. Community Affairs, 1979-81; Tex. Border Health and Environ. Issues Task Force, 1990—. Served with U.S. Army, 1962-64. Mem. IEEE, Am. Soc. Engring. Edn. Home: 836 Cherry Hill Ln El Paso TX 79912-3325 Office: U Tex Info Rsch and Planning El Paso TX 79968-0001 Office Phone: 915-747-5216. Business E-Mail: sriter@utep.edu.

**RITSCH, FREDERICK FIELD,** academic administrator, historian; b. Covington, Va., Nov. 25, 1935; s. Frederick Field and Harriet Curtis (Miller) R.; m. Jeannette McClung, June 14, 1957 (dec.); children: Frederick Field III, Lise Catherina; m. Debra Ronning, Dec. 21, 1991; 1 child, Anne Ronning. BA, U. Va., 1956, MA, 1959, PhD, 1962; student, Univ. de Strasbourg, France, 1957-58. Instr. Randolph-Macon Women's Coll., Lynchburg, Va., 1959; vis. lectr. Sweet Briar (Va.) Coll., 1959-60; from asst. prof. to prof. Dana history and humanities Converse Coll., Spartanburg, SC, 1960-83, dir. ctr. for humanities, head div. humanities; dean of faculty Elizabethtown (Pa.) Coll., 1984-85, provost, 1986-96, prof., 1997—2003, prof. and provost emeritus, 2004—. Cons. Ednl. Services, Inc., Washington, 1975-77; vice chmn. Communication Services, Inc., Spartanburg, 1978-82; dir. Ctr. for Study Contemporary Humanities, Spartanburg, 1972-81. Author: French Left and European Idea, 1967; author, editor: Issues and Commitment, 1976; editor: (with M. Goldberg) Probes and Projections, 1974; contbr. articles to profl. jours. and collections. Elder Donegal Presbyn. Ch., Mt. Joy, Pa. Fulbright fellow, 1957-58; NEH grantee, 1969; recipient Cert. Merit, Inst. Internat. Edn. 1978. Mem. Am. Hist. Assn., Pa. Acad. Deans Conf. (program chmn. 1984), So. Humanities Conf. (editor jour. Humanities in the South 1971-83, chmn. 1984), Phi Beta Kappa. Home: 102 Meadowbrook Ln Elizabethtown PA 17022-2239 Business E-mail: ritschf@etown.edu.

**RITT, ROGER MERRILL,** lawyer; b. N.Y.C., Mar. 26, 1950; m. Mimi Santini, Aug. 25, 1974; children: Evan Samuel, David Martin. BA, U. Pa., 1972; JD, Boston U., 1975, LLM, 1976. Bar: Mass. 1977, Pa. 1975, U.S. Tax Ct. Sr. ptnr. Wilmer Cutler Pickering Hale and Dorr LLP, Boston, 1984—. Adj. prof. grad. tax program Boston U., 1979-92; panelist Am. Law Inst., Mass. Continuing Legal Edn.; mem. World Trade Inst., NYU Inst. on Fed. Taxation; mem. exec. com. Fed. Tax Inst. New Eng. Treas. Found. for Tax Edn. Mem. ABA (tax sect.), Boston Bar Assn. Office: Wilmer Cutler Pickering Hale and Dorr 60 State St Boston MA 02109-1816 Office Phone: 617-526-6475. Business E-mail: roger.ritt@wilmerhale.com.

**RITTENHOUSE, NANCY CAROL,** elementary school educator; b. Humeston, Iowa, May 26, 1941; d. Myrl Matthews and Opal L. (McCartney) Hixson; m. J. Kent Rittenhouse, Dec. 18, 1960 (div. Mar. 1984); children: Brenda L. Carroll, J. Aaron, Timothy K. Grad., Kirksville State Tchrs. Coll., 1960; student, St. Mary of the Plains Coll., 1984-87; degree in elem. edn., Ft. Hays State Coll., 1989. Cert. tchr., Kans. Reading instr. Sacred Heart Sch., Dodge City, Kans., 1984; elem. tchr. Miller Sch., Dodge City, Kans., 1985-86, Washington Sch., Hays, 1987; city-county recreation dir. Sherman County, Goodland, 1988; elem. tchr. Northside Sch., Larned, 1989-90; with Great Bend (Kans.) Tribune. Artist numerous paintings; author poetry. Mem. Menninger Found., Topeka, 1984—; hon. mem. Boy Scouts Am., 1978; camp instr. Spl. Olympics Blind Found., Junction City, Kans., 1985-90, Dodge City, 1984; leader Girl Scouts USA, 1975-77. Recipient Hon. award Spl. Olympics, 1984, 1st pl. leader award, 1990, watercolor award, 1990, oils award, 1988, pen and ink award, 1984. Mem. AAAS, Nat. Trust for Hist. Preservation, Nat. Geog. Soc., Planetary Soc., Smithsonian Assn., MIT. Republican. Avocations: painting, drawing, walking, swimming, writing prose. Home: PO Box 1872 Great Bend KS 67530-1872 Office: Great Bend Tribune 2012 Forest Ave Great Bend KS 67530-4014

**RITTER, ANN L.,** lawyer; b. N.Y.C., May 20, 1933; d. Joseph and Grace (Goodman) R. BA, Hunter Coll., 1954; JD, N.Y. Law Sch., 1970; postgrad. Law Sch., NYU, 1971-72. Bar: N.Y. 1971, U.S. Ct. Appeals (2d cir.) 1975, U.S. Supreme Ct. 1975. Writer, 1954-70; editor, 1955-66; tchr., 1966-70; atty. Am. Soc. Composers, Authors and Pubs., N.Y.C., 1971-72, Greater N.Y. Ins. Co., N.Y.C., 1973-74; sr. ptnr. Brenhouse & Ritter, N.Y.C., 1974-78; sole practice N.Y.C., 1978—. Editor N.Y. Immigration News, 1975-76. Mem. ABA, Am. Immigration Lawyers Assn. (treas. 1983-84, sec. 1984-85, vice-chair 1985-86, chair 1986-87, chair program com. 1989-90, chair spkrs. bur. 1989-90, chair media liaison 1989-90), N.Y. State Bar Assn., N.Y. County Lawyers Assn., Assn. Trial Lawyers Am., N.Y. State Trial Lawyers Assn., N.Y.C. Bar Assn., Watergate East Assn. (v.p., asst. treas. 1990—). Democrat. Jewish. Home: 47 E 87th St New York NY 10128-1005 Office: 420 Madison Ave Rm 1200 New York NY 10017-1171 Personal E-mail: annlritter@aol.com.

**RITTER, C. DOWD,** diversified financial services company executive; b. Birmingham; m. Susan; 2 children. BA, Birmingham-Southern Coll., 1969; grad., Sch. Banking of South, L.S.U. With AmSouth Bancorporation and AmSouth Bank, Birmingham, Ala., 1969—, exec. v.p., 1980-88, sr. exec. v.p., 1988-93, vice chmn. bd., 1993-94, pres., COO, 1994-96, chmn., pres., CEO, 1996—. Bd. dirs. Ala. Power Co., Protective Life Corp. Bd. trustees Tuskegee Inst., Bus. Council Ala., Ala. Econ. Develop. Partnership, Region 2020 Inc., Birmingham Mus. Art, Burmingham-Southern Coll., Leadership Birmingham, adv. bd. Birmingham Crime Commn., Juvenile Diabetes Found., bd. visitors U. ala. Coll. Commerce and Bus. Adminstrn., campaign co-chmn. Am. Cancer Soc. Five Points South Ctr. and Hope Lodge, campaign steering com. YWCA Birmingham, pres's. coun. U. Ala., campaign chmn. United Way Central Ala., 1993. Named Ala. Outstanding Young Banker 1984. Mem. Ala. Young Bankers (past pres.), Birmingham Festival Arts (past pres.). Office: Amsouth Bancorporation 1900 6th Ave N Birmingham AL 35203-2610

**RITTER, DANIEL BENJAMIN,** lawyer; b. Wilmington, Del., Apr. 6, 1937; s. David Moore and Bernice Elizabeth (Carlson) R.; m. Shirley F. Sether, Jan. 29, 1971 (dec. Jan. 1998); 1 child, Roxane Elise. AB with honors, U. Chgo., 1957; LLB, U. Wash., 1963. Bar: Wash. 1963, U.S. Dist. Ct. (we. dist.) Wash. 1963, U.S. Tax Ct. 1965, U.S. Ct. Appeals (9th cir.) 1963. Assoc. Davis, Wright Tremaine LLP (formerly Davis, Wright and Jones), 1963-69, ptnr., 1969—. Lectr. Bar Rev. Assocs. Wash., Seattle, 1964—86; chmn. internat. dept. Davis, Wright and Jones, Seattle, 1984—85, chmn. banking dept., 1986—89. Casenote editor U. Wash. Law Rev., 1962-63; editor-in-chief, contbg. author Washington Revised Article 9 Deskbook, 2003; contbg. author: Washington Commercial Law Desk Book, 1982, rev. edit., 1987, Washington Community Property Desk Book, 1977. Trustee Cathedral Assoc., Seattle, 1980-86; legal counsel Wash. State Reps., Bellevue, 1983-92; bd. dirs. U. Chgo. Club Puget Sound, Seattle, 1982-95, pres., 1984-86; bd. dirs. Am. Lung Assn. Wash., Seattle, 1983-92; mem. vis. com. U. Wash. Law Sch., 1984-88; trustee U. Wash. Law Sch. Found. 1989-92; chmn. alumni rels. coun. U. Chgo., 1986-88; mem. statute law com. State of Wash. 1978-87; bd. dirs. Seattle Camerata, 1991-93; bd. dirs. Early Music Guild, Seattle, 1993-96. Mem. ABA (bus. law sect.), Wash. State Bar Assn. (chmn. bus. law sect. 1988-89, uniform comml. code com. 1980—, chmn. 1980-86, chmn. internat. law com. 1979-81, jud. recommendations com. 1991-93), Seattle-King County Bar Assn. (chmn. internat. and comparative law sect. 1980-82), Rainier Club, Order of Coif. Republican. Lutheran. Avocations: reading, theater, early music. Home: 907 Warren Ave N Apt 202 Seattle WA 98109-5635 Office: Davis Wright Tremaine 2600 Century Sq 1501 4th Ave Seattle WA 98101-1688 Business E-Mail: danritter@dwt.com.

**RITTER, ELISE DAWN,** therapist, clinical social worker, writer, artist, photographer; b. Balt., Aug. 14, 1952; d. Nelson Fred and Marjorie Jean (Corke) Ritter; m. Philip Anthony Gibson, Apr. 7, 1979 (div. Feb. 1990); 1 child, Christopher Ritter Gibson; m. Victor Wayne Clough, Jr., Mar. 3, 1990; stepchildren: Wesley T., Lindsay, Sharon. Student, Austro-Am. Inst., Vienna, Austria, 1973; BS, U. Kans., 1974; M Psychiatric Social Work, Va. Commonwealth U., 1998. LCSW. Rschr. impeachment inquiry staff U.S. Ho. of Reps., Washington, 1974; rschr. APA, Washington, 1975; editor prodn. The New Republic Mag., Washington, 1976-77; copy editor Time-Life Books, Alexandria, Va., 1977-79, assoc. editor, 1979-83, adminstrv. editor, 1983-87, asst. dir. editl. resources, 1988-90; dir. editl. resources Time Warner, Time-Life Books, Alexandria, 1990-94; pvt. psychotherapy, 2000—04. Juried show, Summer Memories, Yates House Gallery, 2000 (1st and 2d prize), exhbn. juried show, Peace, Yates House, 2004 (honorable mention), dirs. show, Rappahannock Art League Studio Gallery, Va., 2005, Mathews Art Group, 2005—. With Arlingtonians Ministering to Emergency Needs-AMEN, 1995; vol. Mental Health Program, Visiting Nurse Assn., 1996, Women's Ctr., Vienna, Va., 1997-99, PsychologyNetwork.com, 2000-02, DiscoveryHealth.com, 2002-03.

**RITTER, ELZA K.,** music educator; b. Moscow, Apr. 27, 1964; arrived in U.S., 1999, permanent resident, 2003; d. Radic Kmassanou and Olija Kmassanoua; m. Steven A. Ritter, Mar. 31, 1999; 1 child, Tim. MusB, Music Coll., Moscow, Russia, 1982—99; MusM, The Russian Acad., Moscow, Russia, 1983—89. Opera coach Nat. Inst. of Theatrical Art, Moscow, 1982—99; pvt. practice Va., 1982—; piano inst. No. Va. Cmty. Coll., Sterling, Va., 1999—2003; pres. The Russian Music Acad. of Am., Reston, Va., 2003—. Concert master Bolshio Theater, 1999—. Mem.: Music Tchr. Nat. Assn. (assoc.). Buddhist. Home: 11407 Fieldstone Ln Reston VA 20191 Office: The Russian Music Acad of America PO Box 710083 Oak Hill VA 20171 Office Phone: 703-758-1915.

**RITTER, HAL,** newspaper editor; Mng. editor money sect. USA Today, Arlington, Va., 1985-95, mng. editor news, 1995—2004. Office: USA Today 7950 Jones Branch Dr Mc Lean VA 22108-0001

**RITTER, JACK CHARLES,** mathematician, computer graphics designer; b. Hokkaido, Japan, Apr. 4, 1948; arrived in U.S., 1949; s. James William Ritter and Maureen Ruth Gutenkunst; m. Barbie Jane Jacobs, Sept. 5, 1973. Student, Princeton U., 1966—68; BA in Philosophy, U. Wis., 1970, MS in Computer Sci., 1973. Software engr. Nat. Cash Register, San Diego, 1974—78; video game designer Atari Games, Sunnyvale, Calif., 1983—85; 2D graphics engr. Versatec-Xerox, Santa Clara, Calif., 1987—90; 3D programmer-artist Sho Graphics, Mountain View, Calif., 1990—93; 3D hardware mktg. nVidia, Sunnyvale, 1995—96; PC video game programmer Accolade Games, San Jose, Calif., 1997—2000. Author: Graphics Gems, Vol. 1 & 2, 1990. Mem. Homicide Rsch. Working Group, Chgo., 2000—; vol. City of Racchi, Sacred Valley, Peru, 2000—. Mem.: The Manly Club (Hartland, Wis.). Achievements include design of prototype for computer controlled electronic dog trainer; Infogramme's Ecstacy Graphics Engine used in PC game Slave Zero; design and programming of a software image synthesizer Rat Racer. Avocations: teaching, wearable audio response gear, artificial intelligence, stereoscopic video, large-format ink-jet fine art. Office Phone: 214-520-0933. E-mail: jack@the-empty-set.com.

**RITTER, JASON,** actor; b. LA, Calif., Feb. 17, 1980; s. John Ritter and Nancy Morgan. Attended, NYU. Actor: (TV series) Joan of Arcadia, 2003—05, The Class, 2006—; (TV films) The Dreamer of Oz, 1990, Who's Your Momma?, 2004; (films) Mumford, 1999, PG, 2002, Swimfan, 2002, Smash the Kitty, 2003, Freddy vs. Jason, 2003, Raise Your Voice, 2004, Perceptions, 2005, Happy Endings, 2005, Our Very Own, 2005, Placebo, 2005, The Wicker Man, 2006, (off-Broadway) The Beginning of August; (plays) The Distance from Here, Third, 2005 (Clarence Derwent award, Actors' Equity Found., 2006). Mailing: c/o The Burstein Co Ste 208 15304 Sunset Blvd Pacific Palisades CA 90272*

**RITTER, JODI GOTTESFELD,** lawyer; b. Bklyn., May 1966; BA cum laude, SUNY, Albany, 1988; JD, NY Law Sch., 1992. Bar: NY 1993, Conn. 1993, US Dist. Ct. So. Dist. NY, US Dist. Ct. Ea. Dist. NY, US Supreme Ct. Asst. dist. atty. Kings County Dist. Atty.'s Office, NY, Spl. Narcotics Prosecutor's Office; ptnr. Wilson, Elser, Moskowitz, Edelman & Dicker LLP, NYC. Mem.: NY State Bar Assn. Office: Wilson Elser Moskowitz Edelman & Dicker LLP 23rd Fl 150 E 42nd St New York NY 10017-5639 Office Phone: 212-490-3000 ext. 2245. Office Fax: 212-490-3038. Business E-mail: ritterj@wemed.com.

**RITTER, RENÉE,** artist, educator; b. Bronx, N.Y. d. Marvin and Helen Gaylinn; m. Seymour David Ritter; children: Edward, Steven, Jennifer. BA, Queens Coll.; MFA, L.I. U. Adj. prof. art CW Post Coll., L.I. U., Greenvale, N.Y., 1982—. Juror scholastic art and writing awards Alliance for Young Artists and Writers, Inc., 1999—2000; adj. prof. art history Nassau C.C., 2000—. One-woman shows include Elaine Benson Gallery, Bridgehampton, N.Y., 1988, 91, 97, Islip (N.Y.) Mus., 1992, 2004, Viridian Gallery, N.Y.C., 1981, 82, 84, 86, 91, 92, Nassau County Mus. of Art, Roslyn, N.Y., 1988, Smithtown Arts Coun., Mills Pond House, Smithtown, N.Y., 1988, Danville Mus. of Art, 1987, others.; group exhibits include Guild Hall, East Hampton, N.Y., 1998, Heckscher Mus., Huntington, N.Y., 1990, 92, 94, 96, Silvermine Guild, New Canaan, Conn., 1992, 94, Bergen County Mus. of Art, Paramus, N.J., 1983, 91, Ft. Hays Kansas State U., 1991, Lubbock Fine Arts Ctr., Tex., 1992, Reece Gallery, N.Y.C., 1995, Francine Ellman Gallery, L.A., 1991, NAWA Traveling Centenary Exhibit, 1987, Parrish Art Mus., Southampton, 1984, Muscarelle Mus., Va., 1994, 96, Smithtown Twp. Arts Coun.-Mills Pond House, St. James, N.Y., 1994, Md. Fedn. Art, 1994, 95, 96, Valdosta (Ga.) State U., 1996, Eleftherias Park Art Ctr., Athens, Greece, 1996, others; represented in permanent collections Muscarelle Mus. of Art-Coll. of William and Mary, Williamsburg, Va., Jane Voorhis Zimmerli Mus. Art-Rutgers U., New Brunswick, N.J., Hillwood Mus.-L.I. U., Greenvale, Islip Mus. Art, FAMLI Mus., Hempstead, N.Y., Danville (Va.) Mus. Arts Docent Nassau County Mus. Art, Roslyn, N.Y., 1979-92. Recipient awards Nassau County Mus. Art, Roslyn, 1986, Islip (N.Y.) Mus. Art, 1987, Heckscher Mus. Art, Huntington, N.Y., 1996, Muscarelel Mus. Art, Williamsburg, 1996. Mem. Nat. Assn. Women Artists, Nat. Drawing Assn. (exec. bd. 1991-98). E-mail: Reneegritter@yahoo.com.

**RITTER, RENEE O.,** theater educator; b. Knoxville, Tenn., May 10, 1975; d. Kenneth, Jr. Frost and Paula Hinton; m. Wesley E. Ritter (div.); children: Cole W., Savannah R. BS in theater, Middle Tenn. State U., Murfreesboro, 1998. Theater tchr. Hendersonville HS, Tenn., 1999—2002, Station Camp. HS, Gallatin, Tenn., 2002—. Dir. Portland Arts Council, Tenn., 1994; tchr. Hendersonville Arts Council, Tenn., 2001—03; dir. Theatre of Summer County, Gallatin, Tenn., 2001. Grantee, Hendersonville C. of C., 2001, 2002. Republican. Baptist. Avocations: theater, dance, music, art. Home: 152 Putter Point Dr Gallatin TN 37066 Office: Station Camp HS 1040 Bison Trail Gallatin TN 37066 Personal E-mail: ritterr@k12tn.net.

**RITTER, ROBERT T.,** diversified financial services company executive; BBA in Acctg., Coll. William and Mary, 1973. Various fin. positions Am. Cyanamid Co.; CFP WLR Foods, Inc.; v.p., CFO The Pittston Co., Glen Allen, Va., 1998—. Mem. AICPAs. Office: The Pittston Co 1801 Bayberry Ct PO Box 18100 Richmond VA 23226

**RITTER, STACEY JILL,** music educator; b. Lincoln, Nebr., Nov. 23, 1979; d. Arlan Dale and Jennifer Jill Stohre; m. Michael Joseph Ritter, Dec. 20, 2002. B in Music Edn., Greenville Coll., Ill., 2002; M in Music Edn., So. Ill. U., Edwardsville, 2006. Elem. music tchr. Francis Howell Sch. Dist., St. Charles, Mo., 2003—04; mid. sch. choir dir. Hazelwood Sch. Dist., Mo., 2006—. Mem.: Music Educator's Nat. Conf., Am. Choral Dirs. Assn., Pi Kappa Lambda.

**RITTER, WILLIAM FREDERICK,** civil and agricultural engineering educator, consultant; b. Stratford, Ont., Can., Mar. 25, 1942; came to U.S., 1966. s. John Louis and Norma Willehmine (Foerster) R.; m. Carol-Anne Gertrude Turner, June 25, 1966; children: John WIlliam, Amy Lynn. BSA, U. Guelph, Ont., 1965; BAS, U. Toronto, 1966; MS, Iowa State U., 1968, PhD, 1971. Rsch. assoc. Iowa State U., Ames, 1966-71; asst. prof. U. Del., Newark, 1971-77, assoc. prof., 1977-82, prof., 1982—, dept. chair, 1992—98, 2003—; owner Ritter Engring., Elkton, Md., 1990—. Sr. engr. Environ. Cons. Internat., Rehoboth Beach, Del., 1991-94. Editor: Irrigation and Drainage Conf. Procs., 1991, Jour. Irrigation and Drainage Engrs., 2001—; contbr. more than 290 articles to profl. jours. and tech. reports. Pres. Newark Day Nursery, 1984-86. Recipient Superior Achievement award U.S. EPA, Phila., 1979; Salzberg fellow U. Del., 1987. Fellow ASCE (editor Jour. Irrigation and Drainage Engring. 2001—, News Corr. award 1997, Outstanding Svc. award 1993, Svc. to Divsn. award 1997, Civil Engr. of Yr. award 1999, Royce J. Tipton award, 2004), Am. Soc. Agrl. Engrs. (Young Engr. of Yr. 1981, Country Side Engring. award 1988, Disting. SVc. award, 2003); mem. (life)Am. Water Works Assn., Water Environment Fedn., Am. Acad. Environ. Engrs. (diplomate). Lutheran. Home: 63 Papermill Rd Elkton MD 21921-3518 Office: U Del Newark DE 19717 Office Phone: 302-831-2468. Business E-Mail: w.ritter@udel.edu.

**RITTERSKAMP, DOUGLAS DOLVIN,** lawyer; b. St. Louis, July 7, 1948; s. James Johnstone Jr. and Linn M. (Dolvin) R.; m. Linda S. Vansant, Mar. 23, 1974; 1 child, Tammy. AB, Washington U., 1970, JD, 1973; LLM in Taxation, NYU, 1978. Bar: N.Y. 1974, Mo. 1979. Assoc. Patterson, Belknap, Webb & Tyler, N.Y.C., 1974-78; jr. ptnr. Bryan Cave LLP (and predecessors), St. Louis, 1978-82; ptnr. Bryan Cave LLP, St. Louis, 1983—2004, of counsel, 2005—. Trustee Scottish Rite Clinic for Childhood Lang. Disorders of St. Louis, Inc., 1987-97, St. Louis Mission and Ch. Ext. Soc., United Meth. Ch., 1987-97, Mo. United Meth. Found., 1994—2003, pres., 2000—03; trustee The Coll. Sch., 1995-2001. Served to capt. USAR, 1970—79. Mem. ABA (employee benefits com. sect. taxation 1987-91, 96—), Bar Assn. Met. St. Louis (steering com. employee benefits 1989—), Masons (32d degree, knight comdr. ct. of honor), Shriner. Methodist. Home: 5223 Sutherland Ave Saint Louis MO 63109-2338

**RITVO, HARRIET,** historian; b. Cambridge, Mass., Sept. 19, 1946; d. Martin and Zelma R. AB, Harvard U., 1968, PhD, 1975; attended, U. Cambridge, Eng., 1968-69. Staff assoc. AAAS, Boston, 1976-79; from asst. to full prof. MIT, Cambridge, 1979—, assoc. dean humanities & social scis., 1992-95, Arthur J. Conner prof. of history, 1995—, head history faculty, 1999—2006. Author: The Animal Estate, 1987, The Platypus and the Mermaid, 1997; co-editor: Macropolitics of 19th Century Literature, 1991. Rsch. fellow Stanford Humanities Ctr., 1985-86, fellow NEH, 1989, Guggenheim fellow, 1990, sr. fellow Nat. Humanities Ctr., 1990, 2002-03; recipient Whiting Writer's award Whiting Found., 1990. Fellow: Am. Acad. Arts and Scis. Office: MIT E51-285 Cambridge MA 02139 Office Phone: 617-253-6960. Business E-Mail: ritvo@mit.edu.

**RITZ, DAVID M.,** photographic retail company executive; Various positions Ritz Camera, Beltsville, Md., 1969-74, mmgt. positions to pres., 1974—, former pres., now CEO; also chmn. Ritz Interactive, Irvine, Calif. Past pres. PMA Internat. Recipient PMA Hall of Fame award. Office: Ritz Camera 6711 Ritz Way Beltsville MD 20705-1318 also: Ritz Interactive 2010 Main St Ste 400 Irvine CA 92614*

**RITZ, GEORGE F.,** forester, consultant; s. George Augustus and Ethel Maria Ritz; m. Sylvia J. Brackett, Aug. 26; children: Jeremy, Andrea. BS, U. Maine, 1971, MS, 1972. Lic. forester Maine. Forester Peace Corps, Chile, 1968—71; cons. forester self, Bradford, Maine, 1971—82, 1987—90; assoc. dir. U.S. Peace Corp. Asuncion, Paraguay, 1982—87; forester Maine Dept. Conservation, Old Town, Maine, 1990—; coord. Andrea Ritz Clinics, Paraguay, 1997—. Co-author: Los Arboles Comunes del Paraguay. Selectman Town of Bradford (Maine), 1987—93. Recipient Spl. Achievement award, Peace Corps, 1982, 1985, Outstanding Achievement award, Paraguaym Soc. Foresters, 1985. Mem.: Internat. Soc. Tropical Foresters, Soc. Am. Foresters (Outstanding Field Forester award for New Eng. Area 2006). Home: 572 Main Rd Bradford ME 04410 Office: Maine Dept Conservation PO Box 415 Airport Rd Old Town ME 04468

**RITZ, THORSTEN,** biophysics professor; b. Hanau, Germany, Apr. 17, 1971; s. Dietmar and Seol-Ok Ritz; m. Brooke Ritz. Diploma, JW Goethe U., Frankfurt, Germany, 1996; PhD, U. Ulm, Germany, 2001. Rsch. assoc. Va. Tech, Blacksburg, 2001—03; asst. prof. U. Calif., Irvine, 2003—. Author: The Quantum Physics of the Bacterial Photosynthetic System. Fellow in molecular biology, Alfred P Sloan Found., 2005; Cottrell scholar, Rsch. Cooperation, 2006. Fellow: Inst. of Physics (UK), German Nat. Merit Found.; mem.: Am. Phys. Soc. Mem. Lab. Os Office: Dept Physics and Astronomy U Calif Irvine 4129 Frederick Reines Hall Irvine CA 92697-4575 Office Phone: 949-824-4345. Office Fax: 949-824-2174. E-mail: tritz@uci.edu.

**RITZEL, BRENT PAUL,** publishing executive, consultant; b. Carbondale, Ill., Feb. 5, 1968; s. Dale Owen and Janet Elvera Ritzel. BA in Philosophy, Northwestern U., 1990. Prin., owner Happy Tails Records/Crank Records, Chgo., 1990—96; pub., editor, journalist Zine Guide & Tail Spins Mag., Evanston, Ill., 1992—2004, supr. pers. and interns, 2000—04; grad. rschr., tchg. asst. Loyola U., Chgo., 1992—93; asst. exec. dir., coord. showcase Ind. Label Festival, Chgo., 1993; intern assoc. prodr. Mother Jones Mag., San Francisco, 1994—95; adminstrv. asst. Evanston (Ill.) Cultural Arts Divsn. Noyes Cultural Arts Ctr., 2004; product specialist ednl. tech. McDougal Littell, Evanston, 2004—05; mortgage broker, wealth advisor, pres., CEO, Source Fin. LLC, Denver, 2006—. Event organizer, promoter ind. media cmty. Self-Publishers Event Coun. Chgo., Chgo., 2000—05; extended faculties faculty Naropa U., Boulder, Colo., 2006—. Musician (singer, songwriter): (albums) Multiple Cartoon Dogs (Coll. Music Jour. Jackpot! selection, 1991), Hong Kong Supermarket, Algorithm, Satan Superman. Mem. coun., chmn-talk arts com. Evanston (Ill.) Arts Coun., 2005. Progressive. Buddhist. Avocations: writing, reading, researching. Office: Source Fin LLC POB 1949 Boulder CO 80306 E-mail: SourceFinancialLLC@yahoo.com.

**RITZEL, TRACEY L.,** special education educator; b. Centralia, Ill., Nov. 7, 1971; d. William A. and Linda B. Brasket; m. Matthew A. Ritzel, Mar. 15, 1997; children: Nealey J., Camden M. BS, So. Ill. U., 2000; M, Lindenwood U., 2004. Tchr. O'Fallon Twp. H.S., Ill., 2000—. Intramural dir. O'Fallon Twp. H.S., 2001—04. Sponsor Bleachermaniac Pep Club, 2005—. Mem. United Church Christ. Home: 615 ABC Dr Okawville IL 62271 Office: O'Fallon Twp High Sch 600 South Smiley O'Fallon IL 62269 Office Phone: 618-632-3507. Business E-Mail: ritzelt@oths.k12.il.us.

**RITZENTHALER, BEATRIZ AUGUSTA,** musician, educator; arrived in U.S., 2001; d. Adilson Ferreira and Beatriz Pereira Da Silva; m. Robert Joseph Ritzenthaler, Aug. 10, 2003. BA in Piano Performance with honors, Brazilian Conservatory Music, 1998; MusM with honors, Andrews U., 2004. Piano instr. Villa Lobos Conservatory Music, Aracatuba, Brazil, 1991—2000; piano instr., adj. prof. Andrews U., Berrien Springs, Mich., 2001—. Concert pianist Brazil, Europe and Brazil. Performer: (recordings) Sacred Concerts for Piano, 1998. Pianist Seventh Day Adventist Ch., Berrien Springs, Mich., 2001—04. Named winner young artists competition, Andrews U., 2004; recipient 1st pl. Internat. Piano Competition, France, 1992, 2d pl. nat. piano competition, Heitor Villa Lobos, 1986; grantee, Fundação Manoel de Barros, Brazil, 2001—04; scholar, Music Dept. Andrews U., 2001—04. Mem.: Phi Kappa Phi. Home: 2472 Honeysuckle Ln Berrien Springs MI 49103 Office Phone: 269-591-2904. Business E-Mail: bas@andrews.edu.

**RIVARA, FREDERICK PETER,** pediatrician, educator; b. Far Rockaway, NY, May 17, 1949; s. Frederick P. and Mary Lillian (Caparelli) R.; m. J'May Bertrand, May 17, 1975; children: Matthew, Maggie. BA, Holy Cross Coll.,

1970; MD, U. Pa., 1974; MPH, U. Wash., 1980. Diplomate Am. Bd. Pediatrics. Intern Children's Hosp. and Med. Ctr., Boston, 1974-75, resident, 1975-76, Seattle, 1978-80; RWJ clin. scholar U. Wash., Seattle, 1978-80, assoc. prof. pediatrics, 1984-89, prof. pediatrics, head divsn. gen. pediatrics, 1990—; mem. staff Nat. Health Svc. Corps, Hazard, Ky., 1976-78; asst. prof. pediatrics U. Tenn., Memphis, 1981-84. Editor Archives of Pedatrics and Adolescent Medicine. Fellow Am. Acad. Pediatrics; mem. Ambulatory Pediatrics Assn., Internat. Assn. Child, Adolescent and Injury Prevention (pres. 1993-2000), Inst. of Medicine. Office: Harborview Med Ctr 325 9th Ave PO Box 359960 Seattle WA 98195-9960 Business E-mail: fpr@uwashington.edu.

**RIVARD, ROBERT,** newspaper executive; b. Nov. 17, 1952; m. Monika Maeckle, Sept. 19, 1981; children: Nicolas, Alex. BA in Polit. Sci., U. Tex., San Antonio, 1996; postgrad., Northwestern U., 1996. Sportswriter Brownsville Herald, 1977-78; news reporter Corpus Christi (Tex.) Caller, 1978-79; reporter Dallas Times Herald, 1979-81, Ctrl. Am. bur. chief, 1981-83, Newsweek, 1983-85, sr. editor, chief corr. N.Y.C., 1985-90; dep. mng. editor San Antonio Light, 1990-93; mng. editor Express News, San Antonio, 1993-97, editor, sr. v.p., 1997—. Author: (non-fiction) Trail of Feathers: Searching for Philip True, 2005. Named Editor's and Pub.'s Editor of Yr., 2000. Mem.: Soc. Profl. Journalists (Disting. Svc. award 1982).

**RIVAS, ARIEL L.,** biomedical researcher, educator; b. Montevideo, Uruguay, July 20, 1949; s. Washington G. Rivas-Mela and Mirta E. Lopez; life ptnr. Almira L. Hoogesteyn. Diploma, Royal Vet. Coll., Uppsala, Sweden, 1980; DVM, U. Republic, Montevideo, Uruguay, 1976; MS, Cornell U. Ithaca, NY, 1986, PhD, 1992, PhD, 1996. Vis. fellow Cornell U., 2004—; prof. epidemiology Autonomous U. Yucatan, Merida, Mexico, 2006—. Contbr. articles to profl. jours. Grantee, NY Dept. Agrimarkets, 2003. Mem., Assn. Vet. Epidemiology and Preventive Medicine, Am. Assn. Vet. Immunologists, Conf. Rsch. Workers Animal Diseases. Achievements include patents for A method for diagnosis of, and determination of susceptibility to bovine mastitis; patents pending for A geo-statistical method to identify geographically continuous and discontinuous clusters. Home: 119 First St Ithaca NY 14850 Personal E-mail: alr4@cornell.edu.

**RIVERA, BAVI EDNA (NEDI RIVERA),** bishop; b. 1946; d. Bishop Victor Manuel Rivera; m. Rev. Bob Moore, 1979. AB in Physics, Wheaton Coll. Norton, Mass., 1968; MDiv, Ch. Div. Sch. of the Pacific, Berkeley, Calif., 1976; cert. in Parish Revitalization, Vancouver Sch. Theology. Ordained priest, 1979; served at churches in Diocese of Calif., Diocese of El Camino Real; rector St. George's Episcopal Ch., Salinas, Calif., 1984—93, St. Aidan's Episcopal Ch., San Francisco; then canon to ordinary, canon for global mission Diocese of Calif., 1997-2004; ordained & consecrated bishop suffragen Diocese of Olympia, 2005—. Achievements include Ordained as first Hispanic woman bishop, Meydenbauer Ctr., Bellevue, Wash, Jan. 22, 2005. Office: Diocese of Olympia PO Box 12126 1551 10th Ave E Seattle WA 98102 Office Phone: 206-325-4200 ext. 312. Business E-mail: nrivera@ecww.org.

**RIVERA, CHITA (CONCHITA DEL RIVERO),** actress, singer, dancer; b. Wash., Jan. 23, 1933; d. Pedro Julio Figuerva del Rivero; m. Anthony Mordente. Student, Am. Sch. Ballet, N.Y.C. Broadway debut: Call Me Madam, 1952; appeared on stage in: Guys and Dolls, Can-Can, Seventh Heaven, Mister Wonderful, West Side Story, Father's Day, Bye Bye Birdie, Three Penny Opera, Flower Drum Song, Zorba, Sweet Charity, Born Yesterday, Jacques Brel is Alive and Well and Living in Paris, Sondheim-A Musical Tribute, Kiss Me Kate, Ivanhoe, Chicago, Bring Back Birdie, Merlin, Jerry's Girls, 1985, The Rink, 1984 (Tony award 1984), Can-Can, 1988, Kiss of the Spider Woman (Tony award, Best Actress in a musical), 1993, The Dancer's Life, 2005; performs in cabarets and nightclubs around world; starred in: film Sweet Charity, 1969; numerous TV appearances include Kojak and the Marcus Nelson Murders, 1973, The New Dick Van Dyke Show, 1973-74, Kennedy Ctr. Tonight-Broadway to Washington!, Pippin, 1982, The Mayflower Madam, 1987, Sammy Davis Jr.'s 60th Birthday Celebration, 1990, Ira Gershwin at 100: A Celebration at Carnegie Hall, 1997, Venecia, 2001, Anything Goes, 2000, The Visit, 2001. Recipient Best Actress, Outer Critics Circle award, 1993, Drama League award, Spider Woman, 1993, Best Leading Actress in a Musical, Tony award, Ellis Island Medal of Honor, 2000, Kennedy Center Honor, 2002—02. Mem. AFTRA, SAG, Actors Equity Assn. Office: William Morris Agy c/o Samuel Liff 1325 Ave of the Ams New York NY 10019

**RIVERA, GEORGE,** museum director; b. Japan, Nov. 5, 1955; arrived in U.S., 1956; s. Manuel and Shizuko Rivera; m. Kristin Ann Lindseth-Rivera, June 28, 2003 (div.); children: Karinna, Marisa, Rachael. AA, Monterey Peninsula Coll., 1976; BA, San Jose State U., 1979, MA, 1982. Exec. dir. San Jose Art League, Calif., 1982—86; assoc. dir. Allegra Gallery, San Jose, 1985; assoc. faculty Mission Coll., Santa Clara, 1986—; chief curator, curator art Triton Mus. Art, 1986—97, acting dir., asst. dir., 1994—97, exec. dir. 1997—; assoc. faculty De Anza Coll., Cupertino, 2005. Instr. art Pacific Art League, Palo Alto, Calif., 1998—, Triton Mus. Art, 1993—94, 2003—, U. Calif., Berkeley, 1996—2000. Mem. Leadership City of Santa Clara, 1997—. Recipient Asian Heritage Coun. award, 1992, Jean Bock Spirit Art award, Avart Festival, Santa Clara, 2000; grantee, Smithsonian Inst., Washington, 1988. Democrat. Avocations: music, motorcycling, golf, travel. Office: Triton Mus Art 1505 Warburton Ave Santa Clara CA 95050 Office Phone: 408-247-0742. E-mail: tritongeorge@aol.com.

**RIVERA, GERALDO,** television personality, journalist; b NYC July 4 1943, s. Cruz Allen and Lillian (Friedman) R.; m. Sheri Rivera (div. 1984); m. C.C. Dyer, 1987 (div. 2002); children: Gabriel, Cruz, Isabella, Simone, m. Erica Levy, 1 child, Solita Liliana. BS, U. Ariz., 1965; JD, Bklyn. Law Sch., 1969; postgrad., U. Pa., 1969, Sch. Journalism, Columbia U., 1970. Bar: NY 1970. Mem. anti-poverty neighborhood law firms Harlem Assertion of Rights and Community Action for Legal Svcs., NYC, 1968-70; with Eyewitness News, WABC-TV, NYC, 1970-75; reporter Good Morning America program ABC-TV, 1973-76, corr. host Good Night America program, 1975-77, corr., sr. producer 20/20 Newsmag., 1978-85; host syndicated talk show The Geraldo Rivera show, NYC, 1987-98; host investigative show on cable CNBC Rivera Live, NYC, 1994—2001; host nightly news show on cable CNBC Upfront Tonight, NJ, 1998—2000; spl. corr. Fox News Channel, 2001—; host weekend show on cable At Large with Geraldo Rivera; contbr. Fox newsmag. The Pulse. Author: Willowbrook, 1972, Island of Contrasts, 1974, Miguel, 1972, A Special Kind of Courage, 1976, Exposing Myself, 1991; host numerous syndicated TV spls.; film appearances: The Bonfire of the Vanities, 1990; television movie: Perry Mason: The Case of the Reckless Romeo. Recipient 7 Emmy awards, Peabody award, Kennedy Journalism award, 1973, 75, numerous others; named Broadcaster of Yr. N.Y. State AP, 1971, 72, 74; Smith fellow U. Pa., 1969. Jewish. Office: Fox News Channel 1211 Ave of Ams New York NY 10036

**RIVERA, JOSE DE JESUS,** lawyer; b. Zacatecas, Mex., 1950; m. Nina Rivera; 5 children. BA, No. Ariz. U.; JD, Ariz. State U. Atty. civil rights divsn. Dept. of Justice, 1976—77; asst. U.S. atty. Dist. Ariz., 1977—81; with Langerman, Begam, Lewis and Marks, 1981—84; ptnr. Rivera, Scales and Kizer, 1984—98; atty. City of El Mirage, U.S. Atty., Dist. of Ariz., 1998—2001; with Haralson, Miller, Pitt & McAnally PLC, Phoenix, 2001—. Vice-chair adv. com. civil rights Atty. Gen. Ariz. dist., 1998-2001, adv. com. Native Am. issues, domestic terrorism subcom., 1998-2001, chair subcom. no Mem. com. Los Abogados; bd. dirs. Inst. for County Initiatives, 1996-98; with N.G. Ariz. Ariz. State Bar. (bd. govs. 1995-98, bd. officer, sec. treas. 1996, 2d v.p. 1997-98, exec. dir. search com. 1996-97, chair appointments com. 1997-98), Hispanic Bar Assn., Los Abogados Bar Assn. (pres. 1982-83). Democrat. Avocation: reading. Office: Haralson Miller Pitt Feldman & McAnally PLC 2800 N Ctrl Ste 840 Phoenix AZ 85004 Office Phone: 602-266-5557. Business E-Mail: jrivera@hpmplaw.com.

**RIVERA, LIONEL,** mayor; b. El Paso, Tex. B in Microbiology, Tex. Tech. U.; MBA, Jacksonville State U., 1986. V.p. investments UBS. Mem. Colorado Springs (Colo.) City Coun., 1997—2001; vice mayor City of Colorado Springs, 2001—03, mayor, 2003—; founder, past pres. Colorado Springs Hispanic C. of C.; trustee United Way; mem. exec. com., co-chair The Springs Cmty. Action Plan; mentor Big Bros.-Big Sisters. Capt. U.S. Army, 1979—87. Office: PO Box 1575 Colorado Springs CO 80901 Office Phone: 719-385-5986. Office Fax: 719-385-5495. E-mail: lrivera@ci.colospgs.co.us.

**RIVERA, MARIANO,** professional baseball player; b. Panama City, Panama, Nov. 29, 1969; Baseball player N.Y. Yankees, 1995—. Named World Series MVP, 1999, ALCS MVP, 2003; named to Am. League All-Star Team, 1997, 1999—2002, 2004; recipient Am. League Rolaids Relief Award, 1999, 2001. Achievements include mem. of World Series Champions New York Yankees, 1996, 1998, 1999, 2000; led Am. League in saves (45), 1999, (50), 2001, (53), 2004. Office: New York Yankees Yankee Stadium East 161St and River Ave Bronx NY 10451

**RIVERA, MAXIMIANO MARQUEZ,** academic administrator, educator, researcher, writer; b. Mindoro, Philippines, Aug. 24, 1946; arrived in U.S., 1991; s. Maximiano Corea Rivera, Sr. and Rosita Marquez Rivera; m. Roela Victoria Rivera, Oct. 5, 1974; children: Paul Christian, Paul John, Norman Vincent Paul. BS, U. East, Manila, 1967, BS Biosci., 1969, BS Edn., 1970, MEd, 1974; diploma aquaculture, U. Philippines, 1985, M Aquaculture, 1985; profl. diploma, Centro Escolar U., Manila, 1979, DEd, 1980. Cert. sci./technol. specialist. Supervising tchr. Secondary Sch. U. East, Manila, 1969—70, prof., 1971—81; rschr., sta. head S.E. Asian Fisheries, Iloilo, Philippines, 1982—85; gen. mgr., rschr. Seahorse Aquaculture, Mindoro, 1986—87; exec. asst. Dept. Edn., Pasig, Philippines, 1988—92; v.p., prof. Makati U., Philippines, 1993—96; coord. NSE program Tenn. State U. Nashville, 1997—, asst. dir. honors program, 2004—. Cons. Seoul Art Theol. Sch., Korea and the Philippines, 1994—95; adj. faculty Vol. State C.C., Gallatin, Tenn., 1997—98; faculty honors program Tenn. State U. Nashville, 1998—; pres. Tenn. Collegiate Honors Coun., 2005—06. Author: (book) Thesis/Dissertation Writing, 1999; co-author: Practical Guide to Thesis and Dissertation, 1996; contbr. articles to profl. jours. Election coord., supr. Election Commn. Makati U., 1993—95. Named Outstanding Father, Devel. of Filipino Youth Inc., 1998; recipient Man of Yr. award, New Life Family Devel. Coun., 1994, Golden medal of honor, Philippine Exptl. Ednl. Rsch. Soc. Inc., 1995, Profl. Achievement award, Media for Devel. and Progress Inc., 1995, Golden Record Achievement award in field of edn., Asian Inst. Humanitarian Devel., 1995, Dr. Jose Rizal Immortal award, Philippine Exptl. Ednl. Rsch. Soc. Inc., 1994, Golden Leadership award for outstanding educator, Social Action and Civic Movement Inc., 1994, Golden Scroll of Honor award, New Life on Family Devel. and Youth Coun. Inc., 1997, Recognition Outstanding Svc. and Leadership cert., City of Nashville, 2004, Noble Svc. Disting. Univ. Svc. cert., Tenn. State U., 2004, Recognition Outstanding Svc. to Nat. Student Exch. Program cert., Tenn. State U. Honors Program, 2005, scholarships, Japan Internat. Coop. Agy., SEAFDEC, AQD, State of Israel, Fund for Assistance to Pvt. Edn., U. East, Coun. Internat. Ednl. Exch., travel grant, Tenn. State U.; fellow, Exxon Mobil. Mem.: So. Regional Honors Coun., Am. Soc. for Pub. Adminstrn., Philippine Geog. Soc. (life), Philippine Soc. for Microbiology (life; bus. mgr. 1980—), Philippine Assn. for Advancement of Sci. (life), Biology Tchrs. Assn., Inc. (life; bd. dirs.-Outstanding Svc. award 1991), Phi Kappa Phi (scholarship chair 1999—, chpt. pres.-elect). Achievements include patents for anti-pimples formula; massaging device. Avocations: reading, sitar, gardening. Office: Tenn State U Honors Program 3500 John A Merritt Blvd Nashville TN 37209 Office Phone: 615-963-5612. Business E-Mail: mrivera@tnstate.edu.

**RIVERA, MILUKA,** actress, journalist, poet; b. San Juan, P.R., Mar. 24, 1953; d. Francisco and Fidelina (Rabell) R.; m. Paul Navarre Matlovsky, Sept. 28, 1981; children: Élan Lixander, Miluette Nalin Matlovsky. Student, Inter-Am. U., Hato Rey, P.R., 1971-74; diploma in pub. rels., U. P.R., Rio Piedras, 1974; student in writing and journalism, UCLA, 1986. Lic. in real estate, Calif. Model Polianna/Barbizon, San Juan, 1968-74; instr. modeling, advisor, co-founder Barbizon Sch. of Modeling, San Juan, 1971-74; freelance dir., 1994—; hostess Buena Vista Cable TV, L.A., 1997—; instr. acting, modeling and etiquette Creative Arts Ctr., Burbank, Calif., 1998—2004; co-founder, artistic dir., instr. Kumaras Ctr. Arts and Etiquette, 2004—. Appeared in T.V. shows including Kojak, Nurse and General Hospital; films include Taxi Driver, All That Jazz, Fort Apache: The Bronx; prodr. documentaries; author (poems), "Unequaled Raul Julia", Hollywood Latinos Offspring, 1998; contbr. articles to profl. publs. Founder, pres. Alliance of Latin Artists, N.Y.C., 1982-84. Recipient Governor Mario Cuomo's Citation award for service, N.Y.C., 1984, Excellent Svc. award Assn. Cronistas Espectaculo, N.Y.C., 1996. Mem. AFTRA, SAG (nat. bd. dirs. 1992-93, chair com., 1998—), Actors Equity Assn. Avocations: poetry, drawing, ballroom dancing, horseback riding, skiing. Office: Kumaras Ctr Arts & Etiquette 1616 W Magnolia Blvd Burbank CA 91506 Office Phone: 818-848-9333. Business E-Mail: kumarascenter@aol.com.

**RIVERA, MIRIAM,** information technology executive, lawyer; AB, Stanford U., AM in Spanish, JD, MBA, Stanford U. Assoc. bus. and tech. Brobeck, Phleger & Harrison; strategy cons. Andersen Consulting (now Accenture); co-founder On Your Mind; in-house counsel Ariba Inc., Sunnyvale, Calif.; v.p., dep. gen. counsel Google Inc., Mountain View, Calif. Bd. sec. Google Found. Vol. A Better Chance, La Casa de las Madres, First Congregational Ch. of Palo Alto. Office: Google Inc 1600 Amphitheatre Pky Mountain View CA 94043 Office Phone: 650-253-0000. Office Fax: 650-253-0001.*

**RIVERA, RICHARD EDWIN,** former restaurant chain executive; b. Jan. 6, 1947; m. Leslie Suzanne Pliner, Nov. 18, 1984. BA, Washington & Lee U., 1968. Credit analyst Nat. Bank Commerce, Dallas, 1970-71; from mgmt. trainee to exec. v.p., dir. Steak and Ale Restaurants of Am., Dallas, 1971-80; pres. restaurant div. El Chico Corp., 1980-82; exec. v.p., chief operating officer T.J. Applebee's and Taco Villa Mexican Restaurant, Dallas, 1982-87; exec. v.p. ops. TGI Friday's Inc., Dallas, 1987-88, pres., CEO, 1988-94, RARE Hosp. Internat., Inc., Atlanta, 1994-97, Chart House Restaurants, Inc., 1997; pres. Red Lobster Restaurants, Orlando, Fla., 1997—2002, 2003—04; vice-chmn. Darden Restaurants, Inc., Orlando, Fla., 2002; interim pres. Bahama Breeze Restaurants, 2002—03; pres., COO Darden Restaurants, Inc., 2003—04.

**RIVERA, SALVADOR, JR.,** history and sociology educator, researcher; b. Glendale, Calif., Aug. 14, 1957; s. Salvador Joseph Rivera and Mary Rodriguez; m. Rosina A. Pezzati, Apr. 8, 1995. PhD, SUNY, Albany, 2003. Prof. history and sociology SUNY, 1992—. Mem. coun. Zion Luth. Ch., Cobleskill, 1996—99. Grad. fellow, SUNY at Albany, 1996. Mem.: Soc. Historians for Am. Fgn. Rels. Baptist. Achievements include research in concerning US efforts to promote European and Latin American economic integration; efforts of former New York Senator Jacob K. Javits to promote Latin American economic integration. Avocations: sailing, swimming, ice hockey, lacrosse. Home: 203 Elm St # 5 Cobleskill NY 12043 Office: SUNY Rt 7 Cobleskill NY 12043 Office Phone: 518-255-6238. Office Fax: 518-255-5113. Business E-Mail: riveras@cobleskill.edu.

**RIVERA-DOMINGUEZ, ALBERTO,** mathematician, educator, mechanical engineer; b. Vega Baja, P.R., June 17, 1958; s. Angel Rivera-Delgado and Concepcion Dominguez-Suarez; m. Elli Reyes-Grote, Jan. 6, 1985; 1 child, Albert Vincent Rivera-Reyes. BSME magna cum laude, U. P.R., 1981; MSME, La. Tech. U., 1990. Engr. Boeing Comml. A/P Co., Seattle, 1981-82; lectr. U. P.R., Mayaguez, P.R., 1983-84, asst. to the assoc. dean of engring., 1984; tchg. asst. La. Tech. U., Ruston, 1985-86; mech. engr. U.S. Army, Fort Buchanan/San Juan, P.R., 1987-90, USN/AFWTF, Ceiba, P.R., 1990-91; gen. engr. USN - NUWC, Newport, R.I., 1991-95; engr. Breeze-Eastern, Union, NJ, 1995—2001; tchr. h.s. math NJ 2001—. Lectr. U. P.R., 1983-84. Contbr. articles to profl. jours. Recipient tuition award MIT, Cambridge, Mass., 1982-84, Panam. Surety Assn. scholarship La. Tech. U., Ruston, 1986.

Mem. ASME, NSPE, Am. Soc. for Composites, Colegio de Ingenieros Y Agrimensores de P.R. Achievements include research on viscoelastic characterization of composite materials; theoretical rsch. findings include: co-established the prin. of virtual equillibrium state of viscoelasticity; devel. a generalized predictive creep response formulation suitable for composite materials; developed algorithm and techniques for performance and reliability prediction of assembled products. Home: PO Box 868 Matawan NJ 07747-1370

**RIVERA PEREZ, EFRAIN E.,** judge; b. Mayaguez, PR, July 15, 1951; s. Efrain Rivera Padilla and Irene Perez Camacho; m. Border Mariluz; 1 child, Mariela Mariluz. B in Adminstrn. of Cos., U. P.R., 1971; JD, Pontifica Caht. U., 1975. Dist. judge Judicial Region Mayaguez, 1982—84, superior judge, 1984—85; pvt. practice law Maguayez, 1985—92; chmn. U. Enclosure Mayaguez U. P.R., 1986—92; dir. office of commn. Judicial Reformation; judge Ct. Cir. Appeals, 1995—2000; assoc. justice PR Supreme Ct., 2000—. Office: PO Box 902 2392 San Juan PR 00902-2392*

**RIVERA-SOTO, ROBERTO A.,** state supreme court justice; b. NYC, 1954; m. Mary Catherine Mullaney; 3 children. Grad., Colegio Nuesra Senora Del Pilar, Rio Piedras, P.R., 1970, Haverford Coll., 1974; JD, Cornell U. Sch. of Law, 1977. Asst. US atty. criminal divsn. US Atty. Office, Pa., 1978—80; litigation assoc. Fox Rothschild, O'Brien & Frankel, 1980—83; v.p., gen. counsel, corp. sec. Sands Hotel Casino, Atlantic City, 1984—94, Caesars World, Las Vegas, 1994—99; prtnr. Fox Rothschild, Princeton, NJ, 1999—2004; justice NJ Supreme Ct., 2004—. Former instructor trial advocacy Rutgers Sch. of Law; certified mediator U.S. Dist. Ct. for Dist. of N.J.; mem., chair N.J. Supreme Ct. Dist. VII Ethics Com. Former mem. bd. dirs. Please Touch Museum, N.J. Devel. Authority for Small Bus., Minorities and Women's Enterprises. Recipient Director's award for superior performance as asst. U.S. atty., U.S. Dept. Justice, 1980. Office: NJ Supreme Ct PO Box 970 Trenton NJ 08625*

**RIVERA-VELAZQUEZ, MARIA,** marketing professional; BA in Econs. cum laude, U. P.R., San Juan, 1993; MA in Econs., U. Wis., Milw., 1995. Statistician Blue Shield P.R., San Juan, 1996—97; rsch. analyst Info. Resources, Inc., Chgo., 1998—2001; sr. rsch. analyst Northwestern Mut., Milw., 2001—04; mgr. corp. and market rsch., 2004—. Spkr. Wis. SAS Users Group Conf., Milw., 2003. Vol. Vecinos Unidos Pro Macun, Toa Baja, PR, 1996—97; vol. United Way campaign Northwestern Mut. Friends, Milw., 2001—; pres. Young Dems. Macun, Toa Baja, PR, 1990—94. Scholar, NEA-P.R. chpt., 1994—95. Mem.: Am. Mktg. Assn. Office: Northwestern Mutual 720 E Wisconsin Ave Milwaukee WI 53202

**RIVERO, DENNIS P.,** orthopedist; b. Albuquerque, Mar. 11, 1952; MD, Ctrl. U. Venezuela, Caracas, 1981. Chief sect. adult reconstrn. U. N.Mex., Albuquerque, 1992—. Author: (with others) Surgical Infections, 1995. Mem. Am. Acad. Orthopaedic Surgeons, Am. Assn. Hip and Knee Surgeons. Office: U NMex Sch Med Dept Orthopaedics Albuquerque NM 87131-5296 Office Phone: 505-272-4107. Business E-Mail: drivero@salud.unm.edu.

**RIVERO, MARILYN ELAINE KEITH,** state legislator; b. Burlington, Vt., Aug. 22, 1942; d. Kenneth Charles and Irene (Haskell) Keith; m. Victor Paul Rivero, Sr., 1966; children: Lina, Mita, Victor Jr., Amy, Nicholas. BS, U. Vt., 1964, MS, 1988; postgrad., Middlebury Coll., 1973, St. Michaels Coll., 1986. Vol. Peace Corps., 1964-66; mem. Vt. Ho. of Reps., 1991—; mem. health and welfare com., 1991—. Recipient Beyond War award. Mem. ANA, Vt. Nurses Assn., Returned Peace Corps. Vol., Am. Assn. Retired People. Roman Catholic. Home: PO Box 37 Milton VT 05468-0037 E-mail: m149rivero@aol.com.

**RIVERS, ALMA FAYE,** secondary school educator; b. Marion, N.C., Oct. 13, 1949; d. Arthur Henry and Lena (Deyton) Letterman; m. Charles Edwin Rivers, June 29, 1980. BA, Mars Hill Coll., 1971; MEd, W. Ga. Coll., 1978. Tchr., choral dir. W. Fannin H.S., Blue Ridge, Ga., 1971-76, W. Fannin Jr. H.S., Blue Ridge, 1976-80; tchr. Truett-McConnell Coll., Young Harris, Ga., 1975-76, 78-80, Sprayberry H.S., Marietta, Ga., 1980—. Student tchr. supr. State of Ga., 1988—, tchr. mentoring program, 1990—; tchr., cons. Kennesaw (Ga.) State U., 1995—; presenter workshops, confs., and confs. on 19th century women's lit. and multiculture lit. Mem. Standing Presbyterian Ch. Atlanta, 1994—; vol. PGA Tournament. NEH fellow, 1995. Mem. Nat. Coun. Tchrs. English, Ga. Coun. Tchrs. English, Thomas Wolfe Soc., Cooking Club of Am., Alpha Delta Kappa. Methodist. Avocations: golf, piano, literature, travel, book collecting. Office: Sprayberry High Sch 2525 Sandy Plains Rd Marietta GA 30066-5799

**RIVERS, BEVERLY D.,** former district secretary; b. 1965; JD U. Ala. Sch. Law; BS in bus. mgmt., Oakwood Coll., Huntsville, Ala. Sec. D.C.; spl. asst. CFO; chief legis. asst. State Senator Henry L. Marsh, Richmond, Va.; atty. Hill Tucker Firm, Marsh Firm; acting sec. of dist. D.C. Govt., 1999, sec. of dist., 1999—2003. Mem.: Nat. Forum Black Pub. Adminstr., Wash. Bar Assn., Ala. Bar Assn., D.C. Bar Assn.

**RIVERS, BOBBY,** television personality, host, actor, writer; b. LA; Studied Film Journalism and Comm. Marquette U., Milw. Entertainment reporter WPIX-TV, WB11, 1985—87; reporter Weekend Today in NY, News 4, WNBC, 1992—95, Good Day NY, FOX 5, WNYW, 1995—99. Veejay (TV series) Sunday Brunch, VH1, 1987—90, regular appearances The Pat Sajak Show, CBS Late Night, 1989, game show host Bedroom Buddies, WB Syndication, 1992, host, writer Metro Movies, Metro Channel, 1999—2000, entertainment editor Lifetime Live, Lifetime Network, 2000, host Top 5, Food Network 2002—04, guest appearances The Equalizer, 1988, The Sopranos, 1999, 2001, reader, writer (plays) Happiness is Just a Thing Called José, Dixon Place Theatre, NYC, The Chelsea Diaries, writer, performer We Can't All Be Matt Lauer: Misadventures in Broadcasting, NYC, I Look Thinner on TV.*

**RIVERS, EMANUEL P.,** emergency physician, medical educator; b. Detroit; m. Kandis Rivers; 2 children. BS, MD, MPH, U. Mich., Ann Arbor. Cert. Emergency Medicine, Internal Medicine, Critical Care Medicine. Dir. rsch., dept. emergency medicine & surg. critical care Henry Ford Hosp., Detroit, asst. prof. internal medicine & surgery, sr. staff attending physician. Assoc. prof. emergency medicine Case Western Reserve U., Cleveland. Internat. lectr.; contbr. articles, scientific papers. Recipient Outstanding Contbn. in Rsch. award, Am. Coll. Emergency Physicians (ACEP), 2005, Teacher of Yr. award, Emergency Medicine Resident's assn. (Mich. chpt.), Clin. Sci. Faculty award, Soc. Academic Emergency Medicine. Fellow: Am. Acad. Emergency Medicine, Am. Coll. Chest Physicians; mem.: AMA, Soc. Critical Care, Am. Coll. Emergency Physicians, Soc. Academic Emergency Medicine, Inst. Medicine. Achievements include patents for Selective Aortic Arch Perfusion & Oxygenation; development of Early Goal Directed Therapy (EGDT). Office: Henry Ford Hosp 2799 W Grand Blvd Detroit MI 48202 Office Phone: 313-916-1801, 313-916-7437. E-mail: erivers1@hfhs.org.*

**RIVERS, GLENN ANTON (DOC RIVERS),** professional basketball coach; b. Maywood, Ill., Oct. 13, 1961; m. Kris Rivers, 1987. Student, Marquette U., 1980-83. Player Atlanta Hawks, 1983-91, Los Angeles Clippers, 1991-92, New York Knicks, 1992-94, San Antonio Spurs, 1994-96; sports analyst Turner Sports, 1996-1999; head coach Orlando Magic, 1999—2003, Boston Celtics, 2004—. Mem. NBA All-Star Team, 1988; recipient Coach of Yr. award, 1999-2000. Office: c/o Boston Celtics 151 Merrimac St Boston MA 02114*

**RIVERS, JOAN,** entertainer; b. NYC, June 8, 1937; d. Meyer C. Molinsky; m. Edgar Rosenberg, July 15, 1965 (dec.); 1 child, Melissa. BA, Barnard Coll., 1958. Formerly fashion coordinator Bond Clothing Stores. Debut entertaining; mem. From Second City, 1961-62; TV debut Tonight Show, 1965; Las Vegas debut, 1969; nat. syndicated columnist Chgo. Tribune, 1973-76; creator: CBS TV series Husbands and Wives, 1976-77; host: Emmy

Awards, 1983; guest hostess: Tonight Show, 1983-86; hostess The Late Show Starring Joan Rivers, 1987, Hollywood Squares, 1987, (morning talk show) Joan Rivers (Daytime Emmy award 1990), 1989-93, Can We Shop? Home Shopping Network, 1994, (radio) The Joan Rivers Show, 1997—, E! Pre-awards Show, 1995-2004; originator, screenwriter TV movie The Girl Most Likely To, ABC, 1973; other TV movies include: How to Murder a Millionaire, 1990, Jackie Collins' Lady Boss, 1992, Tears and Laughter: The Joan and Melissa Rivers Story, 1994; cable TV spl. Joan Rivers and Friends Salute Heidi Abromowitz, 1985; film appearances include The Swimmer, 1968, Uncle Sam, The Muppets Take Manhattan, 1984; co-author, in: (films) Rabbit Test, 1978 (also acted), Spaceballs, 1987, Serial Mom, 1994; actress: theatre prodn. Broadway Bound, 1988, Sally Marr...and her escorts, 1994; recs. include: comedy album What Becomes a Semi-Legend Most, 1983; author: Having a Baby Can be a Scream, 1974, The Life and Hard Times of Heidi Abromowitz, 1984, (autobiography with Richard Meryman) Enter Talking, 1986, (with Richard Meryman), Still Talking, 1991, From Mother to Daughter: Thoughts and Advice on Life, Love and Marriage, 1998, Don't Count the Candle, Just Keep the Fire Lit, 1999; debuted on Broadway (play) Broadway Bound, 1988, creator Seminar You Deserve To Be happy, 1995. Nat. chmn. Cystic Fibrosis, 1982—, benefit performer for AIDS, 1984. Recipient Cleo awards for commls., 1976, 82, Jimmy award for best comedian, 1981; named Hadassah Woman of Yr., 1983, Harvard Hasty Pudding Soc. Woman of Yr., 1984. Mem. Phi Beta Kappa. Office: William Morris Agy 151 S El Camino Dr Beverly Hills CA 90212-2775 also: JR Worldwide 150 E 58th St New York NY 10155-0002

**RIVERS, NANCY LEE,** retired elementary school educator; b. Bridgeport, Conn., Aug. 20, 1943; d. Ralph Warren and Hazel (Barnhart) R. BA, Olivet (Mich.) Coll., 1965; MS, U. Bridgeport, 1974. Cert. tchr., Conn. Tchr. Fairfield (Conn.) Woods Sch., 1965-67, Jennings, 1967-76, Mill Hill, 1976-81, Riverfield Sch., Fairfield, Conn., 1981—2000; ret., 2000. Mem. AAUW, Eastern Star, White Shrine, Delta Kappa Gamma. Congregationalist. Avocations: needlepoint, reading, golf.

**RIVERS, ROBERT ALFRED,** microwave company executive; b. Phillipston, Mass., Sept. 5, 1923; s. Frank Allen and Marie Ange (Pelchat) R.; m. Priscilla Bradford, Oct. 8, 1944; children: Lucy Marie, Rosalind Dolley, Robert Bradford. BSEE, MIT, 1953. Registered profl. engr., NH. Flight radio officer Pan Am. Airways, various locations, 1942-50; design engr. Gen. Electronic Labs., Boston, 1953-54; pres. Aircom, Inc., various cities, 1954—. Editor Tech. Employment and Engring. Manpower Newsletter, 1989-2002; contbr. articles to profl. jours. Inventor wideband cavity resonator; designer over 1300 microwave components, portable and desktop microcomputer systems. Fellow IEEE (life, bd. dirs. 1975-76, mem. numerous coms. and bds., ethics rev. panel 1982-88, Centennial medal 1984, US Activities Bd. citation of hon., Profl. Achievement award 1992, Haradan Pratt award 1997); mem. IEEE Microwave Theory and Techs. Soc. (pres. 1974, mem. numerous coms., chmn. Boston chpt. 1958-59, digest editor 1967, MTT Disting. Svc. award 1978), Eta Kappa Nu, Tau Beta Pi. Republican. Avocations: gardening, travel, reading. Office: Aircom Inc 334 E Main St Orange MA 01364

**RIVES, JACK L.,** judge, career military officer; BA in Polit. Sci., U. Ga., 1974, JD, 1976; postgrad., Squadron Officer Sch., 1982, Air Command and Staff Coll., 1983, Nat. Security Mgmt., 1985, Naval War Coll., 1993. Advanced through ranks to maj. gen. USAF, 2002; asst. staff judge advocate Griffiss AFB, NY, 1977; area def. counsel, 1977—78; dep. staff judge advocate Kunsan AB, Republic of Korea, 1978—79; asst. staff judge advocate Hellenikon AB, Greece, 1979—81; cir. def. counsel Pacific Cir., Clark AB, Philippines, 1981—83; judge advocate air staff tng. officer The Pentagon, Washington, 1983—84; staff judge advocate Plattsburgh AFB, NY, 1984—86; chief officer br., judge advocate profl. devel. divsn. Office of Judge Advocate Gen., Washington, 1986—90; appellate judge USAF Ct. Mil. Rev., Bolling AFB, DC, 1990—92; dep. legal counsel Chmn. Joint Chiefs of Staff, Washington, 1993—95; commandant Air Force JAG Sch., Maxwell AFB, Ala., 1995—98; chief AF Exec. Issues Team Office of Sec. of Air Force, Washington, 1998—2000; staff judge advocate Hdqrs. Air Combat Command, Langley AFB, Va., 2000—02; dep. JAG USAF, Washington, 2002—. Decorated Legion of Merit with oak leaf cluster, Superior Svc. Medal, Meritorious Svc. Medal with six oak leaf clusters, Air Force Commendation Medal. Office: JAG 1420 Air Force Pentagon Washington DC 20330

**RIVES, STANLEY GENE,** retired academic administrator; b. Decatur, Ill., Sept. 27, 1930; s. James A. and Frances (Bunker) R.; m. Sandra Lou Belt, Dec. 28, 1957; children: Jacqueline Ann, Joseph Alan. BS, Ill. State U., 1952, MS, 1955; PhD, Northwestern U., 1963; EdD (hon.), Lincoln Coll., 1998. Instr. W.Va. U., 1955-56, Northwestern U., 1956-58; prof. Ill. State U., Normal, 1958-80, Am. Coun. on Edn. Fellows Program, 1969-70, assoc. dean faculties, 1970-72, dean undergrad. instrn., 1972-80, assoc. provost, 1976-80, acting provost, 1979-80; provost, v.p. acad. affairs, prof. Eastern Ill. U., Charleston, 1981-83, pres., 1983-92, pres. emeritus, 1992—. Vis. prof. U. Hawaii, 1963—64. Author: (with Donald Klopf) Individual Speaking Contests: Preparation for Participation, 1967, (with Gene Budig) Academic Quicksand: Trends and Issues in Higher Education, 1973, (with others) Academic Innovation: Faculty and Instructional Development at Illinois State University, 1979, The Fundamentals of Oral Interpretation, 1981; contbr. articles to profl. jours. Bd. dirs. Ill. State Univs. Ret. Sys., 1992-2005, treas., 1995-2001, pres., 2001-05; bd. dirs. Ea. Ill. Univ. Found., 1993-98, also pres., 1996-98, East Ctrl. Ill. Devel. Corp., 1983-92, Charleston Area Econ. Devel. Found., 1986-92, Coles Together, 1988-92; mem. pres. commn. NCAA, 1986-91; trustee Nat. Debate Tournament, 1967-75. With U.S. Army, 1952-54. Named to Co. of Edn. Hall of Fame; recipient Alumni Achievement award, Ill. State U., 1998. Mem. Am. Assn. State Colls. and Univs., Ill. State C. of C. (bd. dirs. 1990-92), Charleston C. of C. (bd. dirs. 1985-88), Theta Alpha Phi, Phi Kappa Delta, Pi Gamma Mu, Alpha Phi Omega, Alpha Zeta, Sigma Phi Epsilon (hon.). Home: 2231 Andover Pl Charleston IL 61920-3807 Personal E-mail: srives@consolidated.net.

**RIVES, TERRY EDWARD,** public health service officer, researcher, epidemiologist; b. Cleburne, Tex., Jan. 31, 1947; s. T. E. and Lora Earline Rives; m. Najiba Sayeed Rives, May 6, 2001; children: Lori, Justin. BS, LeTourneau U., Longview, Tex., 1992, MPH, 1994; DPH, U. Tex. Health Svcs. Ctr., Houston, 1996. Cert. Am. Coll. of Epidemiology. Epidemiologist Tex. Children's Hosp., Houston, 1993—97; rsch. scientist M.D. Anderson Cancer Ctr., Houston, 1997; chief epidemiologist City of Ft. Worth, 1998—99; dir. inst. rsch. U. Tex., Brownsville, 1999—2000; dir. assessment and biostatistical svcs. U. Tex. Health Svcs. Ctr., Houston, 2000—. Health assessor UN High Command Refugees, Peshawar, Pakistan, 2001, Peshawar, 02. With USAF, 1966—69, Vietnam. Mem.: Am. Pub. Health Assn., Am. Coll. Epidemiology. Office: Univ of Texas Health Svcs Ctr 7000 Fannin M60 Houston TX 77030 Business E-mail: terry.e.rives@uth.tmc.edu.

**RIVEST, RONALD L.,** engineer; BS, Yale Univ., 1969; PhD, Stanford Univ., 1974. Andrew and Erna Viterbi prof. elec. engring. and computer sci. Mass. Inst. Tech., 1974—; mem. MIT Computer Sci. and Artificial Intelligence Lab (CSAIL). Dir., founding inventor Peppercorn Corp.; founder RSA Data Security, Inc. Recipient ACM Turing award, 2002, Secure Computing Lifetime Achievement award, 2004 Paris Kanallakis award, 1996. Fellow World Tech. Network; mem. NAS, IEEE (Koji Kobayashi Computers and Comm. award 2000), Nat. Acad. Engr., Assn. Computer Mach., Internat. Assn. Cryptographic Rsch., Am. Acad. Arts and Scis. Office: CSAIL 32 Vassar St Rm 32-G692 Cambridge MA 02139 E-mail: rivest@mit.edu.*

**RIVET, JEANNINE M.,** insurance company executive; BS in Nursing, Boston Coll.; MPH, Boston U. Sch. Public Health. V.p. grp. ops. Prudential Ins. Co. Am.; v.p. health svc. ops. to CEO United HealthCare, Minnetonka, Minn., 1990-98, CEO, 1998—2000, Ingenix; exec. v.p. UnitedHealth Grp., 2000—. Office: UnitedHealth Group 9900 Bren Rd E Minnetonka MN 55343-9664

**RIVETTE, FRANCIS ROBERT,** lawyer; b. Syracuse, N.Y., May 1, 1952; s. Francis Patrick and Barbara Parker (Smith) R.; m. Judith A. La Manna, 1993. BA, Allegheny Coll., 1974; JD, Syracuse U., 1977. Bar: N.Y. 1978, D.C. 1980. U.S. Dist. Ct. (no. dist.) N.Y. 1978, U.S. Supreme Ct. 1993. Ptnr. Rivette & Rivette P.C., Syracuse, 1978—; corp. counsel Nicom Techs., Inc., 1995—, Group 52, Inc., 2002—. Corp. counsel Fangand Enterprises Ltd., 1978—; co-founder Apex Racing. Mem. ATLA, N.Y. State Trial Lawyers Assn., N.Y. State Acad. Trial Lawyers, Syracuse Corvette Club (pres. 1985-86), Sportscar Vintage Racing Assn., Nat. Corvette Restorers Soc. (nat. judge, 1985, 88, 95, 97), Historic Sportscar Racing Ltd., Phi Delta Phi, Phi Gamma Mu. Republican. Home: 200 Old Liverpool Rd Liverpool NY 13088-6354 Office: Rivette & Rivette PC 224 Harrison St Ste 306 Syracuse NY 13202-3067 Office Phone: 315-478-1122. Business E-mail: frr-rr@accucom.net.

**RIVIERE, JIM EDMOND, JR.,** pharmacologist, educator, toxicologist; b. New Bedford, Mass., Mar. 3, 1953; s. Raymond R. Riviere and Gertrude E. Pelletier-Riviere; m. Nancy Ann Monteiro-Riviere, May 31, 1976; children: Christopher, Brian, Jessica. BS, MS, Boston Coll., 1976; DVM, PhD, Purdue U., 1980. Lic. vet. medicine; diplomate Am. Bd. Forensic Medicine, Acad. Toxicological Sci. From asst. prof. to assoc. prof. NC State U., Raleigh, 1981-88, prof., 1988-92, Burroughs-Wellcome disting. prof. pharmacology, 1992—, dir. Ctr. Chem. Toxicology Rsch. and Pharmacokinetics, 1989—, dir. Biomath. Program, 2005—. Cons. for govt. and pharm. cos.; mem. com. on revision U.S. Pharmacopeia; mem. sci. bd. FDA. Author, editor 10 books, author over 410 rsch. manuscripts. Recipient Ebert prize Am. Pharm. Assn., 1991, Outstanding Rsch. award N.C. State U. Alumni Assn., 1993, Disting. Alumni award Purdue U., 1991, Harvey Wiley medal, 1997, FDA Commrs. Spl. citation, 1997, O. Max Gardner award U. N.C. Sys., 1999, numerous rsch. grants. Fellow Am. Acad. Vet. Pharmacology and Therapeutics (editor 1989-92, 99—, First Rsch. award 1998), Inst. Medicine Nat. Acad.; mem. Am. Assn. Pharm. Scientist, Soc. Toxicology, Am. Vet. Med. Assn., Am. Coll. Forensic Examiners. Achievements include 5 patents in field. Avocations: baseball, boating, beachcombing. Office: NC State U 4700 Hillsborough St Raleigh NC 27606-1428 Business E-mail: Jim_Riviere@ncsu.edu.

**RIVIN, EVGENY IZRAILEVICH,** mechanical engineer, consultant; b. Moscow, June 11, 1932; came to U.S., 1979; s. Izrail Borisovich and Frida Mikhailovna Rivin; m. Irina Rivin, Dec. 30, 1958; children: Igor, Natasha. Machine Tool Engr., Moscow Machine Tool Inst., 1954, PhD in Engring., 1962; DSc in Engring., USSR State Attestation Bd., 1972. Registered profl. engr., Ont., Can. Sr. engr. Profl. Movie Cameras Plant, Moscow, 1954-57; sr. rschr. Exptl. Rsch. Inst. for Machine Tools, Moscow, 1957-68; lab. head Rsch. Inst. for Standardization, Moscow, 1968-75; cons. Burroughs Co., Winnipeg, Man., Can., 1976; prin. staff engr. Ford Sci. Rsch. Lab., Dearborn, Mich., 1976-81; prof. mech. engring. Wayne State U., Detroit, 1981—, dir. machine tool rsch. lab., 1988—. Co-prin. The TRIZ Group, West Bloomfield, Mich., 1995—, cons., 1981—. Author: Dynamics of Machine Drives, 1966, Mechanical Design of Robots, 1988, The Science of Innovation, 1997, Stiffness and Damping in Mechanical Design, 1999, Passive Vibration Isolation, 2003, Innovation on Demand, 2005; author 13 books/monographs; editor 10 books; contbr. some 150 articles to profl. jours.; holder more than 60 patents. Recipient Shingo prize for excellence in mfg. Shingo Found., 1992, DeVlieg Rsch. awards Wayne State U., 1987-89; Eminent Scholar Invitation, Loughborough Univ. Tech., 1995. Fellow ASME, Soc. Mfg. Engrs., Internat. Acad. for Prodn. Engring. (membership com. 1990). Achievements include installation/isolation system for industrial machinery; noise abatement methodology for manufacturing plants developed at Ford; advanced metal cutting tooling systems; research in TRIZ methodology. Office: Wayne State U 5050 Anthony Wayne Dr Detroit MI 48202-3902 Office Phone: 313-577-3898. Fax: 313-577-8789. Business E-Mail: rivin@eng.wayne.edu.

**RIVKIN, DAVID WOLFE,** lawyer; b. NYC, Oct. 17, 1955; s. Donald H. and Lois (Herman) R.; m. Marilyn Aloi, Sept. 13, 1981; children: Jessica, Catherine. BA, Yale U., 1977, JD, 1980. Bar: NY 1981. Law clk. to Hon. Luther M. Swygert US Ct. Appeals (7th cir.), Chgo., 1980-81; assoc. Debevoise & Plimpton, NYC, 1982-88, ptnr., 1988—. Author: (with others) Stockbroker Supervision: Managing Stockbrokers and Surviving Sanctions, 1990, Commercial Arbitration for the 1990's, 1991, Competition and Arbitration Law, 1993; contbr. articles to profl. publs. Mem. ABA (co-chmn. internat. litigation com. litigation sect. 1990—, task force on liaison with internat. profl. assns. 1989—, task force on broker-dealer supervision and compliance 1987-89), Inter-Am. Bar Assn., Am. Arbitration Assn. (panel comml. arbitrators 1986—, internat. arbitration, arbitration practice and corp. counsel coms. 1988—), Assn. Bar City NY (com. on US in global economy 1991—, com. on internat. trade 1984-89), London Ct. Internat. Arbitration, N.Am. Users' Coun. (sec. 1992—), Inst. for Transnat. Arbitration (adv. bd. dirs. 1988—), Internat. Bar Assn. (internat. litigation com., com. on procedures for settling disputes, sect. on bus. law), Internat. Law Assn. (chmn. com. on internat. arbitration am. br. 1989—). Home: 62 Park Rd Scarsdale NY 10583-2140 Office: Debevoise & Plimpton LLP 919 Third Ave New York NY 10022 Office Phone: 212-909-6671, 212-909-6836. E-mail: dwrivkin@debevoise.com.

**RIVLIN, ALICE MITCHELL,** economics professor, former federal official; b. Phila., Mar. 4, 1931; d. Allan C. G. and Georgianna (Fales) Mitchell; m. Lewis Allen Rivlin, 1955 (div. 1977); children: Catherine Amy, Allan Mitchell, Douglas Gray; m. Sidney Graham Winter, 1989. AB, Bryn Mawr Coll., 1952; MA, Radcliffe Coll., 1955, PhD, 1958; LLD (hon.), U. Mich., 1975, U. Md., 1975; DSc (hon.), U. Ind., 1976; LLD (hon.), Yale U., 1984; DSc (hon.), N.J. Inst. Tech., 1998; LLD (hon.), U. Dist. of Columbia, 1999, Harvard U., 2001. Mem. staff Brookings Instn., Washington, 1957-66, 69-75, 83-93; dir. econ. studies Brookings Inst., 1983-87; dir. Congl. Budget Office, 1975-83; prof. pub. policy George Mason U., 1992—93; dep. dir. Office Mgmt. and Budget Exec. Office of the Pres., Washington, 1993-94, dir., 1994-96; vice chmn. Fed. Res. Sys., Washington, 1996-99; chair Fin. Assistance and Mgmt. Authority, 1998—2001; sr. fellow, econ. studies program Brookings Instn., Washington, 1999—; Henry J. Cohen prof. New Sch. U., 2001—; co-dir. Greater Wash. Rsch. Program, Brookings Instn., 2001—. Dep. asst. sec. program coordination HEW, Washington, 1966-68, asst. sec. planning and evaluation, 1968-69; mem. Staff Adv. Commn. on Intergovtl. Rels., 1961-62; bd. dirs. NY Stock Exch., 2005-06, NYSE Group, Inc., 2006—, BearingPoint, Inc., Washington Post Co. Author: The Role of the Federal Governemnt in Financing Higher Education, 1961, (with others) Microanalysis of Socioeconomic Systems, 1961, Systematic Thinking for Social Action, 1971, (with others) Economic Choices 1987, 1986, (with others The Swedish Economy, 1987, (with others) Caring for the Disabled Elderly: Who Will Pay?, 1988, Reviving the American Dream, 1992, The Economic Payoff from the Internet Revolution (co-edited with Robert E. Litan), 2001, Beyond the Dot.Coms: The Economic Promise of the Internet (with Robert E. Litan), 2001. MacArthur fellow, 1983-87, Elliot J. Richardson prize for excellence in pub. svc., 2002, Barnard medal of distinction, Barnard Coll., 2002. Mem. Am. Econ. Assn. (nat. pres. 1986), Nat. Acad. Pub. Administrn., Nat. Acad. of Social Insurance, Coun. on Fgn. Rels., Women's Econ. Roundtable Office: Brookings Instn 1755 Massachusetts Ave Washington DC 20036 also: NYSE Group Inc 11 Wall St New York NY 10005

**RIVLIN, BENJAMIN,** political science professor; b. Bklyn., July 10, 1921; s. Moses and Esther (Ribnick) R.; m. Leanne Green, Aug. 9, 1957; 1 child, Marc Alexander. BA, Bklyn. Coll., 1942; MA, Harvard U., 1947, PhD, 1949. With OSS, 1943-45; teaching fellow Harvard U., 1948; mem. trusteeship dept. UN Secretariat, 1948, 50, 52; research assoc. Hoover Commn., 1948; mem. faculty Bklyn. Coll., 1949-75, Grad. Sch. faculty CUNY, 1949-75, prof. polit. sci. Ph.D. program, 1970-75, dean research and univ. programs Grad. Sch. and Univ. Center, 1975-78, prof. emeritus, 1985—, dir. Ralph Bunche Inst. on UN, 1984—91, dir. emeritus, 1991—. Vis. lectr. Johns Hopkins Sch. Advanced Internat. Studies, 1965; vis. prof. African and Middle East Insts., Columbia U., 1963-68; co-chair RalphBunche Centenary Commemoration com., 2001—. Author: The United Nations and The Italian Colonies, 1950,

Self-Determination and Dependent Areas, 1955, (with J.S. Szyliowicz) The Contemporary Middle East: Tradition and Innovation, 1965, Ralph Bunche: The Man and His Times, 1990, (with Leon Gordenker) The Challenging Role of the UN Secretary-General, 1993; also articles. Served with AUS, 1942-45. Grantee Social Sci. Research Council, 1951, 54, 64; Fulbright scholar France and N. Africa, 1956-57 Fellow Middle East Studies Assn.; mem. Internat. Studies Assn. (pres. Middle Atlantic region 1978-80), Am. Polit. Sci. Assn., Acad. Coun. on UN System (vice chair 1990-91). Office: CUNY Grad Ctr 365 5th Ave New York NY 10016-4334 Office Phone: 212-817-2100. E-mail: brivlin@gc.cuny.edu.

**RIVLIN, GARY,** writer, reporter; b. NYC, June 20, 1958; s. Kenneth and Naomi Rivlin. Staff writer Chgo. Reader, 1985—89; reporter Conta Costa Times, 1990—91; editor East Bay Express, 1999; sr. writer & editor Industry Standard, 2000—01; contbg. editor Wired mag., 2001—04; tech. reporter NYTimes, 2004—. Author: Fire on the Prairie, 1992 (Nonfiction Book of the Yr., Chgo. Tribune, 1992, Carl Sandburg award, 1992), Drive-By, 1995 (one of NY Times' notable books of the yr., 1995, non-fiction book of yr. finalist, San Francisco Bay Area Book Reviewers Assn., 1995, non-fiction finalist for Pen-WEST Best of West, 1995), The Plot to Get Bill Gates, 1999, The Godfather of Silicon Valley, 2001; contbr. to magazines such as NY Times Magazine Newsweek, Fortune, The New Republic, Parada and GQ. Named best writer non-daily newspaper, Calif. Newspaper Pub. Assn., 1993; recipient print journalism prize, San Francisco Bay Area Media Alliance, 1993, Best Enterprise reporting award, Soc. Profl. Journalists, 1993, Gold Medallion award, Calif. Bar Assn., 1996, Gerald Loeb award for disting. bus. & fin. journalism in the mag. category, 2001, Gerald Loeb award, 2005. Office: New York Times 201 Spear St San Francisco CA 94105 Office Phone: 415-836-6700. Business E-Mail: rivlin@nytimes.com.*

**RIVLIN, RACHEL,** lawyer; b. Bangor, Maine, Sept. 1, 1945; d. Lawrence and A. Sara (Rich) Lait. BA, U. Maine, 1965; MA, U. Louisville, 1968; JD, Boston Coll., 1977. Bar: Mass. 1977, U.S. Dist. 1978, U.S. Ct. Appeals (1st cir.) 1983, U.S. Supreme Ct. 1985. Audiologist Boston City Hosp., 1969-72; dir. audiology Beth Israel Hosp., Boston, 1972-74; atty. Legal Sys. Devel., Boston, 1977-78, Liberty Mut. Ins., Boston, 1978-82; counsel, sec. Lexington Ins. Co., Boston, 1982-85, v.p., assoc. gen. counsel, sec., 1985—. Mem. task force fin. literacy students U.S. Bankruptcy Ct. and Boston Bar Assn., 2004—05. Mem. civil rights com. Anti-Defamation League, Boston, 1982—2005; bd. dirs. Dance Art, Inc., Boston, 1985—92. Mem.: ABA (mem. ins. regulation sect. 1980, vice chair internat. ins. law com 1983—84, chair internat. ins. law com. 1985—86, sr. vice chair nat. inst. insurer insolvency 1987—88, sr. vice chair pub. regulation of ins. 1987—90, nat. inst. reins. collections and insolvency 1988, chair excess surplus lines and resins. com. 1988—89, nat. inst. insurer insolvency 1989, vice chair internat. ins. law com. 1997—2005, task force ins. and corp. counsel interests and involvement 1999—2003, vice chair corp. counsel com. 2003—05), Boston Bar Assn. (mem. coun. 1983—86, chmn. corp. counsel 1987, steering com. corp. bus. law and fin. sect. 1987—89, chmn. ins. law com. 1987—90, nominating com. 1988, edn. com. 1989, 1990—91, chmn. ins. com. 1990—93, ethics com. 1993—2005, edn. com. 1994, multi-disciplinary practice task force 2000—02, comprehensive revision Mass. corp. law 2000—02, mem. coun. 2002—05, edn. com. 2003, mem. task force fin. literacy students 2004—05), Boston Coll. Law Sch. Alumni Assn. (ann. fund com. 1981—89, chmn. telethon com. 1989—94, nominating com. 1990, search com. for dean 1993, search com. for sch. fund dir. 1993, leadership gifts exec. com. 1994—98, search com. for dir. instl. advancement 1995, reunion com. 2002, Father James Malley award 1996). Home: 122 Lincoln St Newton MA 02461-1528 Office Phone: 617-244-0092. Business E-Mail: rachelrivlin@mac.com.

**RIVLIN, RICHARD SAUL,** internist; b. Forest Hills, NY, May 15, 1934; s. Harry Nathaniel and Eugenie (Graciany) R.; m. Barbara Melinda Pogul, Aug. 28, 1960 (div.); children: Kenneth Stewart, Claire Phyllis; m. Rita Klausner, Feb. 29, 1976; children: Michelle Elizabeth, Daniel Elliott. AB cum laude in Biochem. Scis., Harvard U., 1955, MD cum laude, 1959. Diplomate Am. Bd. Internal Medicine. Intern Bellevue Hosp., NYC, 1959-60; asst. resident in medicine Johns Hopkins U. Hosp., Balt., 1960-61, asst. resident, 1963-64; fellow dept. physiol. chemistry, medicine Johns Hopkins U. Sch. Medicine, 1964-66, lectr. clin. medicine, 1965-66; clin. assoc. endocrinology br. Nat. Cancer Inst., NIH, Bethesda, Md., 1961-63; attending physician med. service Balt. City Hosps., 1964-66; assoc. in medicine Columbia U. Coll. Physicians and Surgeons, NYC, 1966-67, asst. prof. medicine, 1967-71, assoc. prof. medicine, 1971-79; mem. Inst. Human Nutrition, 1972-79; chief endocrinology, asst. physician Francis Delafield Hosp., NYC, 1966-75; asst. physician Presbyterian Hosp., NYC, 1966-73, assoc. attending physician, 1973-79; chief nutrition service Meml. Sloan-Kettering Cancer Ctr., NYC, 1979-90; prof. medicine Cornell U. Med. Coll., 1979—; chief div. nutrition dept. medicine NY Hosp. -Cornell Med. Ctr., 1979—2001; NIH Nutrition Study Sec., 2000—02; vis. prof. Creighton U., 1974, U. Guadalajara (Mexico), 1974, N.J. Coll. Medicine and East Orange VA Hosp., Newark Med. Sch., NJ, 1974, 1976, 1983; Upjohn vis. prof. in nutrition Med. Coll. Ga., 1976; vis. prof. Syracuse U., 1980; Nat. Dairy Coun. vis. prof. in nutrition U. Mich., Ann Arbor, 1982; vis. prof. Washington U.-Jewish Hosp., St. Louis, 1983; external examiner in physiology Calcutta U., India; prin. investigator clin. nutrition rsch. unit Strang Cancer Rsch. Lab., NYC, 1980—, dir. Anne Fisher Nutrition Ctr., 2004—; sr. v.p. med. affairs, Naylor-Dana chair in nutrition Inst. Cancer Prevention, NYC, 2001—04; vis. prof. UCLA, 2000, Emory U., 2002, Purdue U., 2002. Rsch. program oversight com. Am. Inst. Cancer Rsch., 1995—; Sydenstricker lectr. Med. Coll. Ga., 1989. Editor: Riboflavin, 1975; referee numerous profl. jours.; contbr. articles to profl. jours. Served with USPHS, 1961-63. Recipient Grace A. Goldsmith Lectre award Am. Coll. Nutrition, 1981, Lifetime Achievement award, 2001. Fellow ACP, AAAS; mem. Am. Soc. Clin. Nutrition (v.p. 1992-93, pres. 1993-94), Am. Fedn. Clin. Rsch., Endocrine Soc., Am. Thyroid Assn., Am. Physiol. Soc., Am. Soc. Clin. Investigation, Am. Inst. Nutrition, Soc. Exptl. Biology and Medicine. Home: 30 Farragut Rd Scarsdale NY 10583-7206 Office: Strang Cancer Rsch Lab Rockefeller Univ 1230 York Avenue Box 231 New York NY 10021 Office Phone: 212-734-1436. Office Fax: 212-794-5129. Business E-Mail: rrivlin@mail.rockefeller.edu.

**RIZER, MAGGIE,** model; b. Watertown, NY, Jan. 9, 1978; Model Elite Modeling Agy.; appeared in ads for Calvin Klein, Versace, the Gap. Actor(guest appearances): (TV series) Sex and the City, The Victoria's Secret Fashion Show, 2001, America's Top Model, 2003. Office: Elite Premier 111 E 22nd St New York NY 10010

**RIZKALLAH, MORRIS Z.,** translator; b. Cairo, Nov. 24, 1945; arrived in U.S., 1975; s. Zachari Rizkallah and Hanem Morcos Ghabbour; m. Nadia Elkes Girgis, Aug. 20, 1947; children: Matta, Mouhab, Christine. BS in Mech. Engring., Helwan U., Cairo, 1967; MS in Engring. Mgmt., Fla. Inst. Tech., 1981. Mech. engr. U.S. Army Armament R&D Command, Dover, NJ, 1979—85; translator Dept. Justice, N.Y.C., 1999—. With U.S. Army, 1975—78.

**RIZKIN, IOSIF,** systems, circuits, and computer scientist, writer; b. Leningrad, Russia, Apr. 10, 1931; came to U.S., 1988; s. Chaim Aronovitch Rizkin and Sosja Eljevna Itsikson; m. Lyudmila Chudnovskaya, Oct. 28, 1930; 1 child, Yelena. PhD Moscow Telecomm. Inst., 1962, DSc in Engring., 1972. Assoc. prof. Moscow Telecomm. Inst., 1969-82; programmer-analyst Chem. Bank, N.Y.C., 1989-94; programmer Amarex Tech., Inc., N.Y.C., 1994-95, Metropolitan Transp. Authority (MTA), N.Y.C., 1997—2001; freelance cons. N.Y.C., 2001—. Author: Frequency Multipliers and Dividers, 1966, 2d edit., 1976, Computer Aided Analysis and Design in Engineering, 1985, Night Skies, 1999, Scenes from the Previous Life, Pseudo-Poetry, 2002 (in Russian, in English); contbr. articles to profl. jours. in Russia, Europe and U.S. Mem. sci. adv. bd. N.Y. Assn. for New Americans, 1990-94. Mem. IEEE (sr., former section chmn. Popov Soc.). Jewish. Avocations: poetry, stories and plays. Home and Office: 186 Pinehurst Ave Apt 2B New York NY 10033-1731 Office Phone: 212-795-2478. E-mail: iyr@mindspring.com.

**RIZOWY, CARLOS GUILLERMO,** lawyer, educator, political analyst; b. Sarandi Grande, Uruguay, Mar. 5, 1949; arrived in U.S., 1973, naturalized, 1981; s. Gerszon and Eva (Visnia) R.; m. Charlotte Gordon, Mar. 14, 1976; children: Brian Isaac, Yael Deborah, Michal Evie. BA, Hebrew U., Jerusalem, 1971; MA, U. Chgo., 1975, PhD, 1981; JD, Chgo. Kent Coll. Law, Ill. Inst. Tech., 1983. Bar: Ill. 1983, U.S. Dist. Ct. (no. dist.) Ill. 1983, U.S. Ct. Appeals (7th cir.) 1983. Asst. prof. polit. sci. Roosevelt U., Chgo., 1982-89, chmn. dept. polit. sci., 1983-86, dir. internat. studies program, 1986-89; mng. ptnr. Ray, Rizowy & Fleischer, Chgo., 1983-90; ptnr. corp. law dept. Gottlieb and Schwartz, 1990-92; ptnr. Levenfeld, Eisenberg, Janger, Glassberg, Samotny & Halper, 1993-94; of counsel Sonnenschein, Nath & Rosenthal, 1994—2004; internat. bus. cons., 2004—. Hon. consul of Uruguay, Chgo., 1994—; adj. assoc. prof. Spertus Coll. Judaica, Chgo., 1984—; weekly polit. analyst on Mid. East, internat. law and fgn. policy, resource specialist Sta. WBEZ Pub. Radio and BBC L.Am.; mem. panel of arbitrators of Mediation and Arbitration Ctr., Internat. Arbitration Ct. for Mercosur Bolsa de Comercio, Uruguay, 1999—; gen. counsel Assn. Iberoamerican Consuls, 2003-; internat. bus. cons., 2004-; spkr. and presenter to CEOs on Am. fgn. policy. Author: Avoiding Premises Liability Suits by Improving Security, 1991, Middle East Security: Five Areas to Watch, 1997, May 17, Elections in Isreal, National Stragey Forum, 1999, Guidelines for US Mideast Policy, National Strategy Forum, 2001; co-editor: Latin American Business Cultures-Crossing Cultural Barriers, Prentice Hall, 2005; contbr. articles to profl. jours. V.p., resource specialist to exec. com. Orgn. Children of Holocaust Survivors, Chgo., 1982; pres. Am. Children Holocaust Survivors, 1986-91; pres. bd. dirs. Soviet Jewry Legal Advocacy Ctr., 1986-88; rsch. com. Nat. Strategy Forum, bd. dirs. UN Assn. U.S., 1985-89; mem. cmty. rels. com. Jewish Fedn. Met. Chgo., 1983-84; mem. adv. bd., chmn. internat. affairs commn. Am. Jewish Congress, Chgo., 1983-85, chmn. subcom. for Israel, 1986-88; mem. Nat. Spkrs. Bur. United Jewish Appeal, Nat. Spkrs. Bur. Devel. Coun. for Israel; spkr. to CEOs The Exec. Com., 1980-; mem. adv. bd. Chgo. Action for Soviet Jewry, 1983-85; bd. dirs. Am. Friends of Hebrew U., Chgo., 1984-86, Florence Heller Jewish Cmty. Ctr., 1986-88; mem. human rights com. Anti-Defamation League, 1986, bd. dirs., 1989—; bd. dirs. Bd. Jewish Edn., 1989-91, Hispanic Coalition for Jobs, 1991-94; chmn. univ. educators divsn. Jewish United Fund, 1988-90; mem. consular corp. adv. bd. Internat. Vis. Ctr. Chgo., 1995—, com. fgn. affairs Chgo. Coun. Fgn. Rels., 1994—. Scholar Hebrew U., 1967-72, U. Chgo., 1972-78, Hillman Found., 1978, Peter Volid Found., 1980; recipient Globalist award Heritage Internat. Trade Assn., 1997. Mem. ATLA, ABA (chmn. bus. com. 1993-95), Assn. Ibero-Am. Consuls of Chgo., Ill. State Bar Assn., Chgo. Bar Assn. (internat. trade com.), Latin Am. Bar Assn., Nat. Hispanic Bar Assn., Am. Immigration Lawyers Assn., Am. Polit. Sci. Assn., Am. Judicature Soc., Exec. Club Chgo., Internat. Platform Assn., Wexner Heritage Found., Am. Forum, Latin Am. C. of C. (bd. dirs. 1991—, gen. counsel 1992—), Anshe Emet Congregation, Masons. Mailing: 143 Reade St New York NY 10013 E-mail: crizowy49@hotmail.com.

**RIZZA, FRANK ALFONSO,** retired surgeon, educator; b. Savannah, Ga., Sept. 28, 1928; s. Alfonso Joseph and Georgia Hall Rizza. BS, Med. Coll. Ga., 1950, MD, 1954. Gen. surgeon New Orleans, 1960—96; chief surgery West Jefferson Gen. Hosp., Marrero, La., 1980—84. Assoc. prof. La. State Med. Sch., New Orleans. Archives rschr. Savannah (Ga.) Cath. Diocese, 2001—06. Capt. Med. Corps U.S. Army, 1956—58. Fellow: AMA, ACS, Royal Soc. Medicine; mem.: Parish Med. Soc., La. State Med. Soc., AMA of Vienna.

**RIZZI, JOSEPH VITO,** banker; b. Berwyn, Ill., Dec. 5, 1949; s. Joseph and Mary Catherine (Mancini) R.; m. Candace Kunz, June 24, 1972; children: Jennifer, Joseph, Sammantha. BS in Commerce summa cum laude, DePaul U., 1971; MBA, U. Chgo., 1973; JD magna cum laude, U. Notre Dame, 1976. Bar: Ill. 1976. Law clk. to judge U.S. Dist. Ct. (no. dist.) Ill., 1976—77; exec. v.p. T.B.R. Enterprises, Inc., Downers Grove, Ill., 1977—83; mng. dir., exec. v.p. ABN AMRO, N.Y.C., 1983—. Mem. Delta Epsilon Sigma. Roman Catholic. Home: 287 Bartram Rd Riverside IL 60546-1886 Office: Gustav Mahlerlaan 10 HQ 2040 ABN AMRO Bank 1082 PP Amsterdam Netherlands Office Phone: 31-20-628-0396. E-mail: joe.rizzi@nl.abnamro.com.

**RIZZI, ROBERT A.,** lawyer; b. Madison, WI, 1949; Attended, Dartmouth Coll., 1968—72; AB, Princeton U., 1972; MLitt, Oxford U., Oxford, Eng., 1975; JD cum laude, Harvard U., 1978. Bar: Calif. 1978, DC 1997. Mem., Office of Gen. Counsel CIA, 1981—82; joined O'Melveny & Myers LLP, Newport Beach, Calif., 1994, one of group of ptnrs. to open in Silicon Valley firm, ptnr. litig. Washington, 1995—, chair tax dept. Adj. faculty Golden Gate U. Law Sch., 1991—94, Catholic U. Law Sch., 1997—98; lectr. in field. Bd. contrbg. editors Jour. Corp. Taxation, 1987—, Mergers & Acquisitions: The Monthly Tax Jour., 1999—; contbr. articles to profl. jours. Mem. bd. student advisors Harvard U.; bd. trustee Am. Friends of New Coll. Marshall Scholar, New Coll., Oxford, Wilson Sch. Scholar, Princeton U. Mem.: ABA (Tax Sect., Corp. Tax Subsection), Phi Beta Kappa. Office: O'Melveny & Myers LLP 1625 Eye St NW Washington DC 20006-4001 Address: O'Melveny & Myers LLP 2765 Sand Hill Rd Menlo Park CA 94025-7019 Office Phone: 202-383-5322. Office Fax: 202-383-5414. Business E-Mail: rrizzi@omm.com.

**RIZZLE, DAN,** artist; b. Poughkeepsie, NY, 1951; BFA, Hendrix Coll., Conway, Ark., 1973; MFA, So. Meth. U., Dallas, 1975. One-man shows include Lizan Tops Gallery, East Hampton, NY, 1999, 2002, Allene Lapides Gallery, Santa Fe, N.Mex., 1999, McKinney Ave. Contemporary, Dallas, 2000, Pillsbury Peters Fine Art, 2000, Harmon Meeks Gallery, Naples, Fla., 2003, Gerald Peters Gallery, Dallas, 2004, Hendrix Coll., 2004, Hampton Rd. Gallery, Southampton, NY, 2005, Armory Art Gallery, Palm Beach, Fla., 2005, Gallery Aurora, San Miguel, Mex., 2005, numerous others, exhibited in group shows at Flatbed Gallery, Austin, Tex., 1999, Austin, 2000, Amarillo (Tex.) Mus. Art, 1999, ACA Gallery, Austin, 1999, Represented in permanent collections Flatbed Press, exhibited in group shows, 2002, Wilson Stephens Fine Art, London, 1999, Guild Hall Mus., East Hampton, 2001, Horowitz Gallery 2003, Wilson Stephens Fine Art, London, 2003, Arthur Roger Gallery, New Orleans, 2004, exhibited in group shows at Amagansett (NY) Arts, 2004, Royal Acad. Art, London, 2005, Remy Toledo Gallery, NYC, 2005, numerous others, Represented in permanent collections Am. Airlines, Am. Embassy, Riyadh, Saudi Arabia, ARCO, AT&T Corp. Ctr., Chgo., Cadillac Fairview, Cigna Investment, Inc., Dallas, City of Phoenix, Cleve. Browns Football Club, Crescent Hotel, Dallas, Dallas Mus. Art, Delta Airlines, El Paso Mus. Art, Enron Corp., Houston, Fidelity Investments, MBNA Am., Hyatt Hotels, Mobil Oil, Mus. Modern Art, NYC, Mus. Fine Art, Houston, numerous others. Recipient Disting. Alumnus award, Hendrix Coll., 2005. Address: PO Box 1672 Sag Harbor NY 11963-0060

**RIZZO, RONALD STEPHEN,** lawyer; b. Kenosha, Wis., July 15, 1941; s. Frank Emmanuel and Rosalie (Lo Cicero); m. Mary Rizzo; children: Ronald Stephen Jr., Michael Robert. BA, St. Norbert Coll., 1963; JD, Georgetown U., 1965, LLM in Taxation, 1966. Bar: Wis. 1965, Calif. 1967, Ill. 1999. Assoc. Kindel & Anderson, L.A., 1966-71, ptnr., 1971-86, Jones & Day, L.A., 1986—93, Chgo., 1993—2004, of counsel, 2005—. Bd. dirs. Guy LoCicero & Son Inc., Kenosha, Bristol Oaks Country Club Enterprises, Bristol, Wis. Contbg. editor ERISA Litigation Reporter, 1994-99; mem. internat. adv. editl. bd. Jour. Pensions Mgmt. and Mktg. Schulte zur Hausen fellow Inst. Internat. and Fgn. Trade Law, Georgetown U., 1966. Fellow Am. Coll. Tax Counsel, Am. Coll. Employee Benefits Counsel (charter); mem. ABA (chmn. com. on employee benefits sect. on taxation 1988-89, vice chair com. on govt. submissions 1995-99), Los Angeles County Bar Assn. (chmn. com. on employee benefits sect. on taxation 1977-79, exec. com. 1977-78, 90-92), State Bar Calif. (co-chmn. com. on employee benefits sect. on taxation 1980), West Pension Conf. (steering com. L.A. chpt. 1980-83). Avocations: reading, golf, travel. Home: 1040 N Lake Shore Dr #19C Chicago IL 60611-6164 Office: Jones Day 77 W Wacker Ste 3500 Chicago IL 60601-1692 Office Phone: 312-269-1568. Business E-Mail: rsrizzo@jonesday.com.

**RIZZO, STEPHEN WAYNE BURTON,** secondary school educator, music minister; s. Fredrick Stephen and Betty Burton Rizzo; m. Kristi Lynn Longsworth; children: Olivia Lynnea, Nicholas Stephen Martin. BA in Music, Jacksonville State U., Ala., 1987; MA in Edn. in English, U. Ala., 1987; ham, 1989; MusM, Samford U., Birmingham, 1997. Instr., devel. studies dept. chair Bevill State C.C., Sumiton, Ala., 1995—. Mem. ministerial staff Living Water Cmty. Ch. of God, Fultondale, Ala., 2005—. Editor: (newsletter) Music in Ministry; contbr. articles to profl. jours. and presentations. Vol. Am. Cancer Soc., Sumiton, Ala., 2002—05; mem. state music com. Ch. of God, Birmingham, 1986—95. Recipient Svc. award, Warrior River Chpt., SAR, 2002. Mem.: SAR (Wiregrass chpt., past chpt. pres. Warrior chpt. 2001—05), NEA, Ala. Edn. Assn., Internat. Trumpet Guild, Music Tchrs. Nat. Assn., Music Educators Nat. Conf., Nat. Assn. Devel. Edn., Contessa Entellina Heritage Assn. (New Orleans), Order Sons of Italy in Am., Italian-Am. Progressive Lodge. Conservative. Mem. Church Of God. Achievements include research in the relationship between types/learning styles and developmental placement of rural two-year college students. Avocation: genealogy. Home: PO Box 1408 Sumiton AL 35148 Office: Bevill State CC PO Box 800 101 State St Sumiton AL 35148

**RIZZUTO, RICHARD PETER,** entrepreneur; s. Richard S. and Theresa A. Rizzuto; m. Alexis C. Koch, Apr. 30, 2004. BS, Rider U., Lawrenceville, NJ, 1996. Owner, CEO R.P. Rizzuto Enterprises, New Vernon, NJ, 1997—2000; sr. ptnr. RPR Mktg. Solutions, NYC, 2001—. Hon. co-chmn. Nat. Rep. Congress Com., 2003. Recipient Nat. Leadership award, Nat. Rep. Com. 2003. Mem.: Advt. Club NY, Exec. Assn. NJ. Avocations: skiing, skydiving, wine tasting. Office: RPR Mktg Solutions 22 W 21st Ste 801 New York NY 10010 Office Phone: 212-352-9090. Fax: 212-352-9099. E-mail: rick@RPRmarketingsolutions.com.

**ROACH, BRADLEY CHARLES,** music educator; b. Kettering, Ohio, Sept. 25, 1972; s. Michael and Patsy Jayne Roach; m. Shelba Jean Stebelton, Feb. 14, 1998; children: Micah Wayne Riggenbach, Sarah Kristen Riggenbach. MusB, Bowling Green State U., 1994; MS in Edn. and Allied Professions, U. Dayton, 2002. Cert. K-12 music tchr. Ohio. Dir. bands Bloom Carroll Local Schs., Carroll, Ohio, 1994—97, Elida Local Schs., Elida, Ohio, 1997—. Recipient Elida Employee Excellence award, Elida Bd. Edn., 2004. Mem.: Nat. Band Assn., Am. Sch. Band Dirs. Assn., Music Educators Nat. Conf., Elida Edn. Assn. (pres. 2005—), Ohio Edn. Assn., Ohio Music Edn. Assn. (pres. elect 2005—06), Kappa Kappa Psi. Office: Elida HS 101 East North St Elida OH 45807 Office Phone: 419-339-6325. Personal E-mail: b_roach_hoosier@yahoo.com. Business E-mail: broach@elida.k12.oh.us.

**ROACH, CAROLE HYDE,** music educator; d. Clyde Eugene Hyde and Mary Evelyn Springer; m. Samuel Frederick Roach, Nov. 14, 1970. BMus, Ga. State U., 1962; MusM, Fla. State U., 1963; postgrad., U. Ga., 1974. Nat. cert. voice and piano Tchrs. Nat. Assn., 1974, cert. piano & voice Music Tchrs. Nat. Assn., 1985. Voice & piano tchr. Mary Hardin-Baylor Coll., Belton, Tex., 1964—65, Kennesaw State U., Ga., 1967—70, Perimeter Coll., Decatur, Ga., 1970—71; choral dir. Jerusalem Ave. Jr. HS, North Bellmore, NY, 1965—67; choir dir. Ch. of Ascension, Cartersville, Ga., 1993—96, St. Teresa's Episcopal Ch., Acworth, Ga., 2000—; mezzo-soprano soloist Peachtree Presbyterian, Atlanta, 1967—84, Peachtree Meth., Atlanta, 1984—86. Soloist Fletcher Wolfe Chorale, Atlanta, 1968—71, state vocal auditions chmn., 2003, Atlanta, 04; soloist Atlanta Chamber Opera, 1968—71; musical dir. Canton Theatre, Canton, Ga., 2004. Actress: Gooch (Best Supporting Actress, 1991); Bloody Mary (Best Supporting Actress, 1995); dir.: Fantasticks (Best Dir., 1998), Lend Me a Tenor (Best Dir., 1999), I Hate Hamlet (Best Dir., 2000). Pres., treas. Pumphouse Players, Cartersville, Ga., 1990—2003. Mem.: Music Tchrs. Nat. Assn., Ga. Music Tchrs. Assn., Greater Marietta Music Tchrs. Assn. (pres. 2003—), Cobb County Music Tchrs. Assn. (pres. 1975—76, state chair for vocal auditions). Democrat. Episcopal. Avocations: theater, travel, dog breeding, dog showing, dog rescue. Office: Music Acad So Keyboards 1898-B Leland Dr Marietta GA 30067 Home: 22 Glory Ln Cartersville GA 30120 Personal E-mail: roachs@msn.com.

**ROACH, DANIEL T., JR., (TAD ROACH)** headmaster; BA, Williams Coll.; MA, Middlebury Coll. English teacher, dorm parent, and coach in 1979 St. Andrew's Sch., Middletown, Del., 1979—84, various positions including dean of students, asst. headmaster for student life, academic dean, and asst. headmaster for academic affairs, 1984—97, headmaster, 1997—. Mem. bd. trustees St. Andrew's Sch. Office: St Andrew's Sch 350 Noxontown Rd Middletown DE 19709-1605

**ROACH, JAMES CLARK,** federal agency administrator; b. Charleston, W. Va., Sept. 29, 1943; m. Susan Roelke Roach, June 27, 1970; children: Edward J., Andrew A. BA in Social Studies and History, W. Va. Wesleyan Coll., 1965; MA in Am. History, W. Va. U. Historian Harpers Ferry (W. Va.) Nat. Hist. Pk., 1967-68, 70-72; chief interpretation resource mgmt. Ft. Frederica Nat. Monument, St. Simons Island, Ga., 1972-74; asst. chief interpretation visitor svcs. Colonial Nat. Hist. Pk., Yorktown, Va., asst. chief interpretation visitor svc. Jamestown, Va.; chief interpretation visitor svcs. Gettysburg (Pa.) Nat. Mil. Pk., Eisenhower Nat. Hist. Site, 1981-94; site mgr. Eisenhower Nat. Hist. Site, 1995—2001; sch.-to-work coord. Adams County Bus. Edn. Partnership, Gettysburg, Pa., 2001—. Sec. Gettysburg Peace Celebration Commn. Inc. (former bd. dirs.); sec. Tri-County Econ. Edn. Found.; vice chair Blue and Grey dist. coms. York Admas coun. Boy Scouts Am. With U.S. Army, 1968-70, Vietnam. Recipient Freeman Tilden award Mid-Atlantic Region Interpreter of Yr., 1984, Ea. Superior Performance award Nat. Park and Monument Assn., 1985, Spl. Events award GETT Travel Coun. award, 1986, 87. Mem. Nat. Rec. Park Rangers, Lincoln Fellowship Pa. (sec., past pres.), Adams County Torch Club (past pres.), Rotary (bd. dirs. Gettysburg club). Lutheran. Avocations: gardening, reading, fishing, stamp collecting/philately. Home: 84 Knoxlyn Orrtanna Rd Gettysburg PA 17325 7215 Office: Adams County Bus Edu Partnership 18 Carlisle St Ste 203 Gettysburg PA 17325 Office Phone: 717-338-0861. E-mail: acbep@blazenet.net.

**ROACH, JAMES ROBERT,** retired political science professor; b. Rock Rapids, Iowa, Aug. 25, 1922; s. Paul Ramsey and Doris (Kline) R. BA, U. Iowa, 1943; AM, Harvard U., 1948, PhD, 1950. Mem. faculty, adminstrn. U. Tex., Austin, 1949—, prof. govt., 1965-95, prof. emeritus, 1995—, dir. spl. programs, 1965-69, vice provost, dean interdisciplinary programs, 1971-72, dean divsn. gen. and comparative studies, 1972-74; counselor for cultural affairs Am. embassy, New Delhi, 1974-78. Fulbright vis. lectr. polit. sci. Rajasthan U., India, 1961-62; mem. Bd. Fgn. Scholarships, 1965-74, chmn., 1969-71; mem. U.S. Commn. for UNESCO, 1966-69. With USNR, 1943-46. Fulbright rsch. grantee, Australia, 1951-52, Ford Found. fgn. fellow, India, 1956-57. Mem. Phi Beta Kappa, Kappa Tau Alpha, Phi Kappa Psi. Democrat. Congregationalist. Home: 8604 Dorotha Ct Austin TX 78759-8113 Office: U Tex Dept Govt Austin TX 78712-1087

**ROACH, JANET ANN,** music educator; b. Knoxville, Tenn., May 16, 1963; d. Vernon Thomas and Carolyn Ann Hamilton; m. Steve Lane Roach, Nov. 20, 1962; children: Andrew Steven, Katie Ann, Emily Marie. BS in Music Edn., U. Tenn., 1985. Elementary Educators TN, 1988. Choral dir. Powell Mid. Sch., Powell, Tenn., 1995—. Youth choir dir. First Bapt. Ch., Powell, Tenn., 1995. Curriculum devel. Joy of Music, Powell, Tenn., 2000—04; active Tenn. Music Educators, Knoxville, 1995—. Mem.: Tenn. Music Educators (festival chair 2003—04). Home: 7532 Berkshire Blvd Powell TN 37849 Office: Powell Mid Sch 3329 W Emory Rd Powell TN 37849 Office Phone: 865-938-2846. Personal E-mail: janetroach@frontiernet.net.

**ROACH, JOHN C.,** state supreme court justice; b. Frankfort, Ky., 1967; m. Maria Roach; 3 children. BA, Washington & Lee Univ.; JD with high distinction, Univ. Ky. Bar: 1992. Law clk. to Hon. Pierce Lively, sr. judge US Ct. Appeals (6th cir.); atty. Akin Gump Strauss Hauer & Feld LLP, Washington; ptnr. Ransdell Roach & Wier PLLC, Lexington, Ky., 1996—2001; gen. counsel to gov. State of Ky., 2001—05; assoc. justice Ky. Supreme Ct., 2005—. Office: Ky Supreme Ct Ste 200 155 E Main St Lexington KY 40507-1332 Office Phone: 859-246-2220.*

**ROACH, JOHN D.,** building products company executive; b. West Palm Beach, Fla., Dec. 3, 1943; s. Benjamin Browning and Margaret (York) R.; m. Pam Flebbe, Dec. 29, 1967 (div. Aug. 1981); children: Vanessa, Alexandra; m. Betty Lou (Elizabeth Louise) Phillips, Aug. 28, 1982; children: Bruce Phillips, Bryce Phillips, Brian Phillips. BS in Indsl. Mgmt., MIT, 1965; MBA, Stanford U., 1967. Dir. mgmt. acctg. and info. sys. Ventura divsn. Northrop Corp., Thousand Oaks, Calif., 1967—70; co-founder, mgr. Northrop Venture Capital, Century City, Calif., 1970—71; v.p. dir. Boston Consulting Group, Boston and Menlo Park, Calif., 1971—80; v.p., world-wide strategic mgmt. practice mng. officer Booz, Allen, Hamilton, San Francisco, 1980—82, Houston, 1982—83; vice chmn., mng. dir. Braxton Assocs., Houston, 1983—87; sr. v.p., CFO Manville Corp., Denver, 1987—88, exec. v.p. ops., 1988-91; pres. Manville Bldg. Products Group, Denver, 1988-90, Manville Mining and Minerals Group, Denver, 1990-91, Celite Corp., Denver, 1990-91; chmn., pres., CEO Fibreboard Corp., Walnut Creek, Calif., 1991—97, Stonegate Resources, Dallas, 1997—2001; founder, chmn., pres., CEO Builders FirstSource, Inc., Dallas, 1998—2001; chmn., CEO Stonegate Internat., Dallas, 2001—; chmn. Unidare U.S., Muskogee, Okla., 2002—. Bd. dirs. PMI Group, Kaiser Aluminum, URS Corp., Mat. Scis., NCI Bldg. Systems, Wash. Internat., Am. Stock Exch., Thompson PBE, Magma Power, Fibreboard Corp., Builders First Source. Author: Strategic Management Handbook, 1983. Bd. dirs. Opera Colo., Denver, 1987-91, Bay Area Coun., San Francisco, 1991-96, Dallas Symphony, 1996-03, mem. exec. com., 1996-03; bd. trustees Alta Bates Med. Ctr.; mem. exec. com. San Francisco Opera Assn. Mem.: MIT Alumni Club, Stanford Grad. Sch. Bus. Club, Dallas Country Club, Cordillera Country Club (Colo.), Beaver Creek (Colo.) Country Club, Red Sky Golf Club (Wolcott, Colo.), Preston Trail Golf Club (Dallas), Cherry Hills Country Club (Englewood, Colo.). Avocations: golf, skiing, hunting. Home: 4278 Bordeaux Ave Dallas TX 75205-3718 Office: Stonegate Internat 100 Crescent Ct 7th Fl Dallas TX 75201 Office Phone: 214-459-3460. Personal E-mail: johndcroach@aol.com.

**ROACH, JOHN HENDEE, JR.,** bank executive, investment banker, financial services executive; b. NYC, Oct. 24, 1941; s. John Hendee and Julia (Casey) R.; m. Joan Hayden Muchmore, Sept. 23, 1972; children: Hayden, Cameron, John, Lauriston, Schuyler. BA, Washington and Jefferson Coll., 1964; postgrad., Aspen Inst., 1987, Harvard U., 1989. With Chem. Bank, N.Y.C., 1968-71, sr. v.p. corp. bank, 1972-87, mng. dir. corp. fin., 1987-92, ret., 1992; sr. mng. dir., vice chmn. The Geneva Cos., N.Y.C., 1992-94; sr. mng. dir., client mgmt. and mktg. Am. Internat. Group, N.Y.C., 1994-97; sr. mng. dir. Reliance Nat., N.Y.C., 1998-99, JP Morgan Pvt. Bank, Greenwich, Conn., 2000—01, Jamison Prince Asset Mgmt., 2003—. Bd. dirs. Strategic Capital Resources Inc., Boca Raton, Fla., PrivaTechnologies, Arlington, Va., MBAs 4 N.Y.C. Capt. U.S. Army, 1964-66. Mem. Round Hill Club. Republican. Roman Catholic. Home: 16 Oakwood Ln Greenwich CT 06830-3909 Office: 530 Fifth Ave New York NY 10036 Office Phone: 212-944-7153. Personal E-mail: jhr.jr@att.net.

**ROACH, JOHN VINSON, II,** retail company executive; b. Stamford, Tex., Nov. 22, 1938; s. John V. and Agnes M. (Hanson) R.; m. Barbara Jean Wiggin, Mar. 31, 1960; children: Amy, Lori. BA in Physics and Math., Tex. Christian U., 1961, MBA, 1965. V.p. Radio Shack, 1972-75, Radio Shack Mfg., 1975-78; exec. v.p. Radio Shack, 1978-80; gen. mgr. data processing Tandy Corp., Ft. Worth, 1973-75, pres., from 1980, CEO, from 1981, chmn., 1982—99, Roach Enterprises, 1999—. Chmn. bd. Justin Ind., 1999—2001. Bd. dirs. Van Cliburn Found.; former chmn. bd. Tex. Christian U. Mem. Ft. Worth Club, City Club, Colonial Country Club. Office: 777 Taylor St PII-J Fort Worth TX 76102

**ROACH, LONNIE CALVIN,** social studies educator; b. Brewster, Wash., Aug. 3, 1951; s. Nolen Calvin and Berta Ellen (Lackey) Roach; m. Vickie Lynn Johnson, 1976 (div. Jan. 1994); children: Megan Bridget, Cameron Holt. BS in Edn., U. Ark., Fayetteville, 1972, MEd, 1978, EdS, 1987, EdD, 1995. Cert. global studies tchr., K-12 ESL tchr., K-12 curriculum specialist, 6-12 social studies tchr., tchr. trainer, K-12 gifted and talented tchr. Tchr. math. Huntsville Mid. Sch., Ark., 1973; photo collector Shiloh History Mus., Springdale, Ark., 1983—85; tchr. observer Ark. Dept. Edn.; job counselor U.S. Dept. Labor, Ark., 1990—95, Ark., 1997—98; gifted & talented/advanced placement tchr./facilitator Huntsville HS, 1987—2006, tchr. social studies, 1973—. Adj. prof. N. Ark. Coll., Harrison, 2004—06; mem. approval team U. Ark. Ark. Dept. Edn., 1998. Co-author: No Smoke, No Soot, No Clinkers, 1974; author: Arkansas in a Changing World: A Global Studies Historical Approach, 1986. Coord. Huntsville Centennial, 1977; chmn. Madison County Ark. Reps., Huntsville, 1984—86; commr. Madison County Ark. Election Commn., 1984—85; co-founder AEA Dist. 10 Fed. Credit Union, Ark., 1977; pres. Hunstville Jaycees, 1980; chmn. scholarship com. Madison County Med. Mentors. Named Ark. HS Tchr. of Yr., VFW, 2000—01, Outstanding Young Man of Am., Am. Mensa, Ltd.; recipient Svc. award, Am. Legion, 1998. Mem.: Global Assn. Tchrs. Econs., Ark. Geog. Alliance. Republican. Mem. Lds Ch. Avocations: history, genealogy, writing, sci. fiction, reading. Home: PO Box 134 635 Hwy 412B Huntsville AR 72740 Office: Huntsville Mid Sch 133 School Dr PO Box G Huntsville AR 72740 Office Phone: 479-738-6520.

**ROACH, MARGARET,** editor-in-chief; Editor, mgr. NY Times; garden columnist Newsday Newspapers; creative developer Martha Stewart Living Omnimedia, 1995; gardening editor Martha Stewart Living; mgr. devel. and execution marthastewart.com; editor-in-chief Martha Stewart Living, NYC, 2001—. Author: A Way to Garden, 1998 (Garden Writers Assn. Am. Best Book, 1998). Mailing: Martha Stewart Living 11 West 42nd St 25th Floor New York NY 10036*

**ROACH, MARGOT RUTH,** retired biophysicist, educator; b. Moncton, N.B., Can., Dec. 24, 1934; d. Robert Dickson and Katherine Roach; m. Franklyn St. Aubyn House, Dec. 30, 1994 (wid. Feb. 2000). B.Sc. in Math. and Physics with honors, U. N.B., Fredericton, Can., 1955; MD, CM. cum laude, McGill U., Montreal, Can., 1959; PhD in Biophysics, U. Western Ont., Can., 1963; D.Sc. (hon.), U. N.B., St. John, Can., 1981. Jr. intern Victoria Hosp., London, Ont., Can., 1959-60, fellow in cardiology, 1962-63, asst. resident in medicine, 1963-64, Toronto Gen. Hosp., 1964-65; mem. faculty, dept. biophysics U. Western Ont., London, 1965—98, head dept. biophysics, 1970-78, prof., 1971-98, asst. prof. medicine, 1965-72, assoc. prof., 1972-78, prof., 1978-98, prof. emeritus Biophysics & Med., 1998. Mem. staff dept. medicine Victoria Hosp., 1967-72. U. Hosp., London, 1972-98; Commonwealth vis. sci., dept. applied math. theoretical physics Cambridge U., 1975; vis. sci. Bioengring. Inst., Chonqing U., People's Republic of China, 1991; mem. bioengring. grants com. Med. Rsch. Coun. Can., 1993-96; cons. and lectr. in field. Mem. editl. bd.: Imprints, 2003—06. Active civic orgns. and coms. including Univ. Rsch. Com., 1976-79; mem. interview bd. London Conf. of United Ch., 1967-90; steward United Ch. of Can., 1967-73, elder, 1973-82, mem. com. on ministry vocations, 2004-, chair unified bd. Tatama-gouche Pastoral Charge, 2001-; chmn. stewardship devel. com. Colborne St. United Ch., 1990-93. Recipient A. Wilmer Duff prize in physics U. N.B., 1955, Cushing prize in pediatrics, 1959, Clup Found. award for research in aging, 1959, Teaching award Faculty of Medicine U. Western Ont., 1990, Dean's award, 1997, Women of Distinction award YWCA, 1997; Med. Research Council fellow U. Western Ont., 1960-62, Arthur Guyton award Internat. Soc. Cardiovascular Medicine and Sci., 1997; numerous other fellowships and grants in medicine. Fellow Royal Coll. Physicians (Can.), Am. Coll. Cardiology (Young Investigator's award 1963); mem. Can. Physiol. Soc., Can. Cardiovascular Soc. (of council), Can. Clin. Investigation Soc. (council 1980-84), Can. Soc. Internal Medicine. Address: RR #1 104 Sea Shore Dr Tatamagouche NS Canada B0K 1V0 Personal E-mail: mroach@pchg.net.

**ROACH, MAUREEN S.,** primary school educator; Bachelors Degree, Boston U.; Masters Degree, U. Mass. Primary sch. educator Lyndon Pilot Sch., West Roxbury, Mass. Presenter Nat. Bd. Insts.; mem. adv. bd. Nat. Bd.

Profl. Tchg. Standards, 2005. Mem.: Nat. Bd. for Profl. Tchg. Stds. (bd. mem.). Avocations: cross country skiing, reading. Office: Patrick Lydon School 20 Mount Vernon St West Roxbury MA 02132-2809*

**ROACH, PAM,** state legislator; m. Jim Roach; 5 children. BA in History, Brigham Young U., 1970. Mem. Wash. Legislature, Olympia, 1991—, mem. govtl. ops. and election com., mem. internat. trade and econ. devel. com., mem. ways and means com., mem. sentencing guidelines commn. Past mem. Gov.'s Juvenile Issues Task Force; mem. local coun. Boy Scouts Am.; past mem. adv. com.; founder, dir. Escuela de Esperanza; mem. Joint Com. Vets. and Mil. Affairs; mem. Sentencing Guidelines Commn. Mem. Wash. Policy Coun., Rotary. Republican. Office: 202 Irving Newhouse Bldg Olympia WA 98504-0001 also: PO Box 40431 Olympia WA 98504 Office Phone: 360-786-7660. Business E-Mail: roach-pam@leg.wa.gov.

**ROACH, ROBERT MICHAEL, JR., (RANDY ROACH),** lawyer; b. Bronxville, N.Y., May 27, 1955; s. Robert M. and Mary Dee R.; m. Elizabeth Preston Roach, Sept. 22, 2000. BA, Georgetown U., 1977; JD, U. Tex., 1981. Bar: Tex. 1981, U.S. Dist. Ct. (so. dist.) Tex. 1982, U.S. Ct. Appeals (5th cir.) 1982, U.S. Dist. Ct. (we. dist.) Tex. 1984, U.S. Supreme Ct. 1986, U.S. Dist. Ct. (ea. dist.) 1986, U.S. Dist. Ct. (no. dist.) Tex. 1988. Assoc. Vinson & Elkins, Houston, 1981-83, Ryan & Marshall, Houston, 1983, Mayor, Day & Caldwell, Houston, 1983-88; ptnr. Mayor, Day, Caldwell & Keeton, Houston, 1989-93; founding ptnr. Cook & Roach LLP, Houston, 1993—; dir. appellate advocacy U. Houston Law Ctr., 1994—; adj. prof. U. Tex., 2000—; ptnr. RBS Napa Winery, 2000—. Adj. prof. law U. Houston, 1990-; lectr. continuing legal edn. U. Houston Law Ctr., 1989—; lectr. continuing legal edn. State Bar Tex., U. Tex., U. Houston, South Tex. Coll. Law. So. Meth. U., ABA; rschr., editor U.S. Senate Com. on Nutrition, 1975, 76, 77; rschr. U.S Supreme Ct., Washington, 1977; mem. Tex. Law Rev., 1979-81. Editor Def. Counsel Jour., 1990-93. Mem. Product Liability Adv. Coun., Internat. Assn. Def. Counsel, Fedn. Defense and Corp. Counsel, Def. Rsch. Inst., Tex. Assn. Def. Counsel, State Bar Tex. (appellate sect. chmn., grievance com., insurance section judicial liaison), Houston Bar Assn. (former chmn., appellate sect.), Meadowood of NAPA Valley, Coronado Club, Spanish Oaks Golf Club, Houston Racquet Club. Avocations: oenology, music, travel, tennis. Office: Cook & Roach LLP Heritage Plaza Ste 2650 1111 Bagby St Houston TX 77002-2543 Office Phone: 713-652-2032. Business E-Mail: rroach@cookroach.com.

**ROACH, WESLEY LINVILLE,** lawyer, insurance executive; b. Norlina, N.C., Oct. 8, 1931; s. Joseph Franklin and Florence G. (Sink) R.; m. Mary Jon Gerald, Aug. 13, 1955; children: Gerald, Mary Virginia. BS, Wake Forest U., 1953, JD, 1955. Bar: N.C. 1955. With Pilot Life Ins. Co., Greensboro, NC, 1958-86, also bd. dirs.; sr. v.p., gen. counsel Jefferson-Pilot Life Ins. Co., Greensboro, 1986-88; sec. Great Ea. Lif. Ins. Co., 1975-85; of counsel Smith, Anderson, Blount, Dorsett, Mitchell & Jernigan, Attys. at Law, Raleigh, NC, 1988—. Former chmn. bd. dirs. N.C. Life and Accident and Health Ins. Guaranty Assn., Va. Life, Accident and Health Guaranty Assn., S.C. Life, Accident and Health Guaranty Assn.; sec. JP Investment Mgmt. Co., Jefferson-Pilot Equity Sales, Inc., Spl. Services Agy., Inc., 1974-84; mem. exec. com., bd. dirs. N.C. Ins. Edn. Found., 1978—; trustee In-Home Care, Inc., 1999—, chmn., 2001. Mem. fin. com. Greensboro United Fund, 1964-65; mem. fin. com. Greensboro 1st Bapt. Ch., 1963-66, 83-86, chmn., 1983-85, chmn. bd. deacons, 1974-76, 80-81; nat. chmn. alumni coun. coll. fund Wake Forest U., 1971-76, pres. nat. alumni coun., 1975-76, trustee univ., 1978-82, emeritus trustee, 1999—; trustee So. Bapt. Theol. Sem., Louisville, 1973-84; trustee Bapt. Retirement Homes N.C., Inc., 1992-2000, chmn., 1993-94, emeritus trustee, 2001-; trustee In Home Care, Inc., 1997—, chmn., 2001; trustee Bapt. Retirement Homes Found. 2001-. With USNR, 1955-58. Mem. ABA, N.C. Bar Assn., Raleigh Bar Assn., Assn. Life Ins. Counsel (bd. govs. 1984-88), Greensboro C. of C. (chmn. nat. legis. com. 1973—), Nat. Orgn. Life Guaranty Assn. (bd. dirs. 1982-87). Democrat. Home: PO Box 1690 601 Selma Rd Wendell NC 27591-8648 Office: 2500 First Union Capitol Ctr PO Box 2611 Raleigh NC 27602-2611 Office Phone: 919-821-6630.

**ROACHE, PATRICK MICHAEL, JR.,** management consultant; b. Elizabeth, N.J., Oct. 8, 1946; s. Patrick Michael and Rose Marie (Remite) R. BS, St. Peter's Coll., 1969. Adminstrv. aide to a state assemblyman N.J. Assembly, NJ, 1969-71; supr. acctg. Dept. Pub. Works Newark, Newark, 1971-78, asst. to dir. pub. works, 1978-79, mgr. div. motors, 1979-84; mgmt. specialist Dept. Gen. Svcs., Newark, 1985-86, 2002; pvt. practice as mgmt. and fin. cons. Brick, NJ, 1986—. Mem. Lions (treas. 1983-86, pres. 1988-89). Republican. Roman Catholic. Home and Office: 170 Binnacle Rd Brick NJ 08723-6704 Office Phone: 732-477-9162. E-mail: proache@haywardnet.com.

**ROADARMEL, STANLEY BRUCE,** civilian military employee; b. Albion, N.Y., May 5, 1937; s. Kenneth A. and Catherine Louise (Bobel) R.; m. Carole Ann Hayes, Nov. 26, 1959; children: Karen Marie, Oscar Pacific, Ann Catherine, William Hayes. Student, Purdue U., 1956—58; BA, Syracuse U., 1962; grad., Squadron Officer Sch., 1965, Air Command Staff Coll., 1976, Indsl. Coll. Armed Forces, 1976; postgrad., Golden Gate U., 1976—78. Commd. 2d lt. USAF, 1962, advanced through grades to maj.; adminstrv., security and recruiting ops. officer Air Tng. Command, Tex. and W.Va., 1962—69; chief field maintenance Titan II ICBM Strategic Air Command, Davis Monthan AFB, Ariz., 1969—71, chief Hq SAC's 3901st Titan II maintenance evaluation team Vandenberg AFB, Calif., 1971—74, logistics staff officer, 1974—77, contract specialist, 1977—82, U.S. Air Forces Europe, Adana, Turkey, 1980—81; ret. USAF, 1982; launch complex constrn. contract negotiator, adminstr. NASA/USAF Space Shuttle Program, Lompoc, Calif., 1983—89, USAF Titan IV Space Booster, Vandenberg AFB, 1991—92; constrn. and maj. svcs. contract negotiator, adminstr. 30th Contracting Squadron USAF Space Command, Vandenberg AFB, 1992—2001; ret. active fed. svc., 2001. With Civil Coast Profls., Mut. Profl. Counseling/Placement, Santa Maria, Calif., 1990-91. Author manual: Man Lifting Crane Operations, 1976 (Air Force Commendation award 1977); revision officer Air Force Manual 66-1 Maintenance Management, 1976 (Air Force Commendation award 1977); contbr. Strategic Air Command Manual 66-12 ICBM Maintenance Mgmt. Spkr. World Orgn. Ovulation Method, Calif., 1987—; pro life advocate, activist Am. Life League, Nat. Right to Life, 1980—; mem. and vol. Rep. Party, 1992—; marriage preparation instr. Cath. Archdiocese of LA, Santa Maria, 1995—; life mem. Holy Family Inst., Soc. St. Paul. Mem. NRA, Air Force Assn. (life), Mil. Officers Assn. Am. (life), Disabled Am. Vets. (life), Assn. Air Force Missileers (life), Am. Legion, Couple to Couple League, The Heritage Found., Exptl. Aircraft Assn. Avocations: aviation, music, marksmanship, travel, literature. Home and Office: 4532 Glines Ave Santa Maria CA 93455-4313 Personal E-mail: csroadarmel@earthlink.net.

**ROADEN, ARLISS LLOYD,** retired academic administrator; b. Bark Camp, Ky., Sept. 27, 1930; s. Johnie Samuel and Ethel Nora (Killian) R.; m. Mary Etta Mitchell, Sept. 1, 1951; children: Janice Arletta Roaden Skelton, Sharon Kay Roaden Vogt. Grad., Cumberland Coll., 1949; AB, Carson Newman Coll., 1951; MS, U. Tenn., 1958, EdD, 1961; PhD (hon.), Cumberland Coll., 1986; DLitt (hon.), Tusculum Coll., 1992. With Oak Ridge Inst. Nuclear Studies, 1957-59, Auburn U., 1961-62; mem. faculty Ohio State U., 1962-74, prof. edn., 1967-74, acting dean Coll. Edn., 1968-70, vice provost for research, dean Grad. Sch., 1970-74; pres. Tenn. Tech. U., 1974-85, pres. emeritus, 1985—; dir. Tenn. Higher Edn. Commn., Nashville, 1985-95, exec. dir. emeritus, 1995—. Summer vis. prof. Marshall U., 1961, U. So. Calif., 1964, Ind. U., 1967; cons. edni. instns., 1961—; pres. Tenn. Coll. Assn., 1978; chmn. sci. and tech. com. Am. Assn. State Colls. and Univs., 1980; chmn. task force on program and instl. assessment State Higher Edn. Exec. Officers', 1987, pres. 1993-94, chmn. coun. postsecondary accreditation liaison com., 1986-88, exec. com., 1988-95, pres. elect 1992-93; mem. exec. bd. trustees Southern Assn. Colls. and Schs., 1986—, chair communications com., 1990—, mem. task force, 1990—; mem. Southern Regional Edn. Bd., 1985—, chmn. procedures com. for reviewing bylaw changes and revisions, 1988-89; mem. exec. com., state rep., treas., chair Internal Audit Com. 1990-91, Edn. Commn. States, 1987-90; mem. Tenn. Econ. Cabinet Coun. 1988—, chmn.n 1988-91, bd. dirs. 1988—, Fgn. Lang. Inst.; treas., chair

Internal Audit Com., 1990-91; mem. Performance Standards in Vocat.-Tech. Edn. Working Group, U.S. Dept. Edn., 1990. Co-author: The Research Assistantship: Recommendations for Colleges and Universities, 1975, Cultures of the States: A Handbook on the Effectiveness of State Governments, 2003; editor: Problems of School Men in Depressed Urban Areas, 1967; contbr. articles to profl. jours. State chmn. Tenn. Cancer Soc. Crusade, 1986-88, bd. dirs., 1987—; mem. exec. bd., commr. Mid. Tenn. coun. Boy Scouts Am., 1987-88, mem. nat. coun., 1988—, chmn. scouts membership rels. com.; mem. Phi Delta Kappa Found., 1965—, past chmn. bd. govs., mem. futures and diamond jubilee coms., 1989—; chmn. Blue Ribbon Com. To Respond to Edn. Goals, 1990; bd. dirs. Nat. Project 714, 1986—, pres.-elect, 1987-88, chmn., 1988-89; pres. alumni assn. bd. Cumberland Coll., 1987-88, chmn. devel. bd., 1994—; adult Sunday sch. tchr. Woodmont Bapt. Ch., chmn. pers. com., 1989—, chmn. deacons, ch. moderator, 1998-99. With U.S. Army, 1951-53. Rsch.grantee Phi Delta Kappa Internat., 1968; named Disting. Alumnus Cumberland Coll., 1970; recipient Disting. Alumni and Faculty Centennial medallion Coll. Edn., 1970, Disting. Service award Coun. Grad. Students, 1974, both Ohio State U.; recipient Silver Beaver award Boy Scouts Am.; named Rotarian of Yr., 1984; Eagle Scout honoree Middle Tenn. Coun. Boy Scouts Am., 1989, others. Fellow Oxford Soc. Scholars; mem. AAAS, Am. Assn. Higher Edn., Acad. Polit. and Social Scis., Am. Edni. Rsch. Assn. (chmn. publs. com. 1979-80), Nat. Soc. Study Edn., Nat. Assn. State Colls. and Land Grant Univs., Lions (bd. dirs. Nashville 1988-90, pres. 1991-92, zone chmn. 1992-93, dist. gov. 1996), Rotary (bd. dirs.), Order of Lion and Eagle, Phi Kappa Phi, Phi Delta Kappa (Disting. Svc. award Ohio State U. chpt. 1974), Kappa Phi Kappa, Kappa Delta Pi. Baptist.

**ROAF, ANDREE LAYTON,** judge; b. Mar. 31, 1941; m. Clifton G. Roaf; 4 children. BS in Zoology, Mich. State U., 1962; JD with high honors, U. Ark., 1978; LLD (hon.), Mich. State U., 1996. Bar: Ark. 1978. Bacteriologist Mich. Dept. Health, Lansing, 1963—65; rsch. biologist FDA, Washington, 1965—69; staff asst. Pine Bluff (Ark.) Urban Renewal Agy., 1971—75; biologist Nat. Ctr. for Toxicological Rsch., Jefferson, Ark., 1978—79; assoc. Walker, Roaf, Campbell, Ivory & Dunklin, Little Rock, 1979—86, ptnr., 1986—95; assoc. justice Ark. Supreme Ct., Little Rock, 1995—96; appellate judge Ark. Ct. Appeals, 1997—. Editor: Ark. Law Rev. Mem. PTA bd. Forest Park Elem. Sch., 1972—74, 34th Ave. Sch., 1974—76, 1980—83, Southeast Jr. High, 1976—77; mem. ad hoc com. for voter registration Jefferson County, 1972—73; bd. trustees Southeast Ark. Arts and Scis. Ctr., 1972—75, sec., 1974—75, Pine Bluff OIC Bd., 1972—78, Pine Bluff Police-Cmty. Rels Task Force, 1973; mem. Jefferson County Com. on Black Adoptions, 1973—75, chmn., 1974—75; mem. Ark. Code of Ethics Commn., 1987, Friends of Sta. KRLE-FM, 1982—88, 1990—94, pres., 1985—86; trustee Winthrop Rockefeller Found., 1990—94; mem. Jefferson County Dem. Com., 1980—82; mem. vestry Grace Episcopal Ch., 1995—; bd. dirs. Ark. Coun. on Human Rels., 1972—73, Ark. for Arts, 1983, Ark. Student Loan Authority, 1977—81, Vocals, 1989—. Named Gayle Pettus Pontz outstanding Ark. woman lawyer, 1996; named to Ark. Black Hall of Fame, 1996; recipient disting. alumni award, Mich. State U., 1996. Mem.: ABA, W. Harold Flowers Law Soc., Jefferson County Bar Assn., Pulaski County Bar Assn. (chmn. hist. com. 1986—87), Ark. Bar Assn. (chmn. youth edn. com. 1979—80). Office: Justice Bldg 625 Marshall St Ste 1230 Little Rock AR 72201-1052

**ROALOFS, LINDA A.,** language educator; b. Cin., Sept. 4, 1943; d. Stanley Randolph and Inis Frances (Prater) Brown; m. Roger Leonard Roalfs, Sept. 19, 1964; children: Scott, Christine, Karen, Eric, Katherine. BS in Edn., Ohio U., 1964; MS in Edn., U. Louisville, 1980. Tchr. English Parma City Schs., Ohio, 1964—65, St. Augustine Acad., Lakewood, 1967—71, St. Jerome, Fairdale, Ky., 1977—78, St. Martha, Louisville, 1978—83, Mercy Acad., 1983—99, Ky. Country Day, 2000—02. Chair fundraising com. Highview United Ministries, Louisville, 1999—2003; sec. RLS Enterprises (dba Papa John's Pizza), 1987—2003. Contbr. articles to newspapers. Grantee, Ky. Shakespeare Festival, 1994—95. Avocations: scrapbooks, reading, travel, gardening. E-mail: lindar0904@aol.com.

**ROAN, FORREST CALVIN, JR.,** lawyer; b. Waco, Tex., Dec. 18, 1944; s. Forrest Calvin and Lucille Elizabeth (McKinney) R.; m. Vickie Joan Howard, Feb. 15, 1969 (div. Dec. 1983); children: Amy Katherine, Jennifer Louise; m. Leslie D. Hampton Roan, Jan. 2, 1999. BBA, U. Tex., Austin, 1973, JD, 1976. Bar: Tex. 1976, U.S. Dist. Ct. (we. dist.) Tex. 1977, U.S. Dist. Ct. (so. dist.) Tex. 1998, U.S. Ct. Appeals (5th cir.) 1977, U.S. Supreme Ct. 1979, U.S. Ct. Appeals (11th cir.) 1981, U.S. Ct. Appeals (fed. cir.) 1998, U.S. Ct. Internat. Trade, 1998. Prin. Roan & Assocs., Austin, 1977-81; counsel, com. dir. Tex. Ho. of Reps., 1972-75; assoc. Heath, Davis & McCalla, Austin, 1975-78; prin. Roan & Gullahorn, P.C., Austin, 1978-85, Roan & Autrey (formerly Roan & Simpson), P.C., 1986-99; sr. ptnr. Cantey, Hanger, Roan & Autrey, 1999—2003; shareholder Winstead, Sechrest & Minick, P.C., Austin, 2003—. Bd. dirs. Lawyers Credit Union, chmn., 1982-83; bd. dirs. pub. law sect. State Bar Tex., 1980-84; trustee, Safeplace Found.; mem. Chancellor's Coun., U. Tex.; life mem. Mensa. With Tex. Army N.G., 1966-74. Fellow Tex. Bar Found., Travis County Bar Found. (founding fellow); mem. ABA, Tex. Assn. Def. Counsel, Tex. Assn. Bank Counsel, Def. Rsch. Inst., Travis County Bar Assn., Tex.-Mex. Bar Assn., Knights of the Symphony (Lord Chancellor 2003-04), Tex. Lyceum Assn. (v.p. bd. dirs. 1980-87), Austin C. of C., Austin Club, Headliners Club, Masons, Shriners (Parsons Masonic master 1976-77). Methodist. Office: Winstead Sechrest & Minick PC 401 Congress Ste 2100 Austin TX 78701 Office Phone: 512-370-2999. E-mail: froan@winstead.com.

**ROAN, WILLIAM C.,** mathematics professor; b. Stonewall, Okla., Mar. 15, 1941; s. Jass Nunn Roan and Violet Pauline Ellis; m. Waverly Christine Stroope; children: Tristin, Lindsey, Ash, Josh. BS in Edn., East Ctrl. Okla. U., Ada, 1963; MA, La. State U., Baton Rouge, 1968. Math. tchr. Amarillo (Tex.) Pub. Schs., 1963—69; math. instr. Howard Coll., Big Spring, Tex., 1969—74; prof. math. N.Mex. Jr. Coll., Hobbs, 1974—2000; assoc. prof. math. Coll. of the SW, Hobbs, 2000—. Statistician Coll. of the SW Baseball, 2000—; prof. emeritus N.Mex. Jr. Coll., 2000. Mem.: Math. Assn. Am. Republican. Roman Catholic. Avocations: baseball, reading, movies. Home: 1200 Roan Way Hobbs NM 88242 Office: Coll of the SW 6610 Lovington Hwy Hobbs NM 88240 Office Phone: 505-392-6561. E-mail: wroan@csw.edu.

**ROANE, DAVID JAMES, JR.,** information technology auditor; b. Petersburg, Va., Nov. 11, 1960; s. David James Roane, Sr. and Anne (Vest) Savage; m. Bonnie L. Dear, Dec. 3, 1983; two children. BS, Va. Commonwealth U., 1984. CPA, Va.; cert. info. systems auditor. Audit intern Continental Fin. Services Co., Richmond, Va., 1983-84, staff auditor, 1984-85; EDP auditor Life Ins. Co. of Va., Richmond, 1985-86, Fort James Corp., Richmond, Va., 1986-88, sr. EDP auditor, 1990-2000; technologies group specialist Mgmt. Info. Systems, 1989-90; info. tech. audit cons. Ft. James Corp./Ga. Pacific, 2000-01; info. tech. audit supr. The Brink's Co., Richmond, Va., 2001—06, info. tech. audit mgr., 2006—. Treas. Civic Assn., Chester, Va., 1985-91; chmn. fin. com. Matoaca United Meth. Ch., 1990-92, 1997-98, chmn. adminstrv. bd., 1993-95. Methodist. Avocation: micro computers. Home: 3148 Talleywood Ln Chester VA 23831-7036 Office Phone: 804-289-9649. E-mail: droane@brinkscompany.com.

**ROARK, BARBARA ANN,** librarian; b. Evanston, Ill., July 24, 1958; d. Edward B. and Ann H. Rowe; m. Paul E. Roark, Sept. 18, 1982; children: Sarah, John. BA in History. U. Ky., 1981, MLS, 1982. Dir. Hopkins County Madisonville (Ky.) Pub. Libr., 1983-85; ops. mgr. Wurzburg Inc., Nashville, 1985-91; dir. Spies Pub. Libr., Menominee, Mich., 1991-98, Franklin (Wis.) Pub. Libr., 1998—. V.p. adv. coun. Mid-Peninsula Libr. Coop., Mich., 1993-95, sec. adv. coun., 1991-93; chair tech. adv. com. Milwaukee County Federated Libr. Sys., 2001—. Grant writer Title II, 1994, Title I, 1995. Treas. Franklin Area Jr. Woman's Club. Recipient Cert. of Excellence Libr. of Mich., 1995, Cert. of Appreciation Menominee Area C. of C., 1998. Mem. ALA, Wis. Libr. Assn. (pers. and profl. concerns com. 1999—, Muriel Fuller award 2002), Spies Pub. Libr. Found., PEO, Order Ea. Star, U. Ky. Alumni Assn.,

Franklin Area Jr. Women's Club (treas. 1999—), Kiwanis (pres. Milw. suburban S.W. chpt. 2002—), Zeta Tau Alpha. Methodist. Avocations: golf, reading, cross stitching, travel. Office Phone: 414-425-8214. E-mail: barbara.roark@mcfls.org.

**ROARK, IAN R.,** school system administrator; b. Laramie, Wyo., Nov. 11, 1977; s. Ben T. and Eileen R. Roark; m. Landi D. Orr, July 4, 1998; 1 child, Ireland Malone. MusB in Edn. magna cum laude, Angelo State U., San Angelo, Tex., 1999; MA in Edn. and Ednl. Leadership, U. of Tex. of the Permian Basin, Odessa, 2004. Cert. prin. Tex., tchr.- all level music Tex., tchr.- social studies composite Tex., tchr.- English as second lang. Tex. Music tchr. choir San Angelo Ind. Sch. Dist., 2000—01; asst. prin. Midland (Tex.) Ind. Sch. Dist., 2004—05; social studies tchr., dept. chair Ector County Ind. Sch. Dist., Odessa, 2001—04, social studies coord., 2005—. Cmty. outreach Kelview Heights Bapt. Ch., Midland. Named Oustanding Tchr. of the Yr., Ector County Ind. Sch. Dist., 2004, Outstanding New Vocalist, Angelo State U. Concert Choir, 1996; recipient IMPACT Edn. grant, U. of Tex. of the Permian Basin, USDE, 2002—04, Carr Acad. scholarship, Angelo State U., 1995—99, Choir scholarship, 1996—99, FAME scholarship, Angelo State Friends of Art and Music, 1999, Randy Bell Meml. scholarship, Angelo State U., 1997—98, Charles Van Pelt Music scholarship, 1996—97, Choir Dir.'s award, Angelo State U. Concert Choir, 1999. Mem.: Nat. Coun. for Social Studies, Tex. Coun. for Social Studies, Tex. Social Studies Supr., West Tex. Regional Coun. for Social Studies (bd. dirs. 2005—06), Pi Kappa Lambda, Alpha Chi. Avocations: musician, hiking, fishing, reading. Office Phone: 432-332-9151.

**ROARK, ROBERT CAMERON,** insurance agent; b. San Diego, Jan. 11, 1931; s. Alfred T. and Virginia J. Roark; m. Lois J. Maynard, July 19, 1952; children: Cynthia, Susan, Kellie, Robert. BA, San Diego State U., 1954. Life underwriter Mass. Mut. Life, San Diego, 1955-57; supr. John Hancock Mut., San Diego, 1957-59; gen. agt., mgr. Am. Mut. Life Ins., San Diego, 1959-65; regional v.p. Northwestern Life Ins., Seattle, 1965-68; broker, owner Roark Ins., Menifee, Calif., 1968—. Author: Good News Letter, 1991—. Divsn. capt. USCG Aux., 1990, flotilla comdr., 1987, vice capt., 1989, publs. officer, 1997. Mem. Mission Hills Homeowners Assn. (pres. 1970-73, bd. mem. 1991-92), Lions Internat. (zone chmn. 1972, club pres. 1971). Office: Roark Ins 28032 Whittington Rd Menifee CA 92584

**ROARK, TERRY PAUL,** astronomer, educator; b. Okeene, Okla., June 11, 1938; s. Paul J. and Erma K. (Morrison) R.; m. Beverly Brown, Sept. 7, 1963; 1 child, David. C. BA in Physics, Oklahoma City U., 1960; MS in Astronomy, Rensselaer Poly. Inst., 1962, PhD in Astronomy, 1966. Asst. provost for curricula Ohio State U., Columbus, 1977-79, assoc. provost for instrn., 1979-83; prof. physics Kent (Ohio) State U., 1983-87, v.p. acad. and student affairs, 1983-87, provost, 1985-87; pres. U. Wyo., Laramie, 1987-97, prof. physics and astronomy, 1987-2001; interim pres. Mont. State U., Bozeman, 2000. Bd. dirs. Rocky Mountain Fed. Savs. Bank, chmn. audit com., 1989-93; commr. Western Interstate Commn. for Higher Edn., 1987-97, chmn., 1991; bd. dirs. Associated Western Univs., 1987-94, chmn., 1991, bd. trustees, 1994-97, chmn. 1996; adv. bd. Wyo. Geol. Survey, 1987-97; mem. Warren AFB Civilian Adv. Coun., 1987-97; bd. dirs. First Interstate Bank of Wyo.; bd. dirs. Albany County Hosp. Dist., chmn. 2006. Mem., treas. Ctr. for Pub. Edn., Columbus 1980-83; mem. fin. adv. coun. LWV, Kent, 1986; mem. long range planning com. Cleve. Urban League, 1985-86; mem. adv. com. Battelle youth sci. program Columbus and Ohio Pub. Schs., 1982; bd. dirs. Ivinson Hosp. Found., 1987-97, 2005—. Mem. Am. Astron. Soc., Internat. Astron. Union, Nat. Assn. State Univs. and Land Grant Colls. (bd. dirs. 1994-96, chair commn. on intenat. affairs 1995), Astron. Soc. Pacific, Sigma Xi, Phi Kappa Phi, Omicron Delta Kappa. Avocations: photography, music, hiking. Office: U Wyo Dept Physics & Astronomy Dept No 3905 1000 E University Ave Laramie WY 82071-3905

**ROARKE, MICHAEL CHARLES,** medical educator, nuclear medicine physician; b. Albany, N.Y., May 8, 1959; s. Charles Augustus and Joan Ann Roarke; m. Maria Giuliani, June 25, 1988; 1 child, Michael Andrew. BS, SUNY, Albany, 1981, MS, 1982; MD, U. Rochester Sch. Medicine, N.Y., 1990. Cert. Am. Bd. Radiology, 1995, Am. Bd. Nuc. Medicine, 1996. Chemistry tchr. Albany Acad. Boys, NY, 1982—86; intern internal medicine St. Mary's Hosp., Rochester, 1990—91; resident diagnostic radiology Mallinckrodt Inst. Radiology, St. Louis, 1991—95, fellow nuc. medicine, 1995—96; asst. prof. radiology U. Tex. Med. Ctr., Houston, 1996—97, Mayo Med. Sch., Scottdale, 1997—. Sect. head nuc. radiology Mayo Clinic Ariz., Scottsdale, Ariz., 1997—; med. dir. nuc. radiology, 1997—. Named one of Best Doctors in Am., 2003—06, America's Top Physicians, Consumer's Rsch. Coun., 2005; recipient Best Intern award, St. Mary's Hosp. Internal Medicine Program, 1991; Klingenstein Summer Tchg. fellow, Columbia U., 1983. Mem.: Acad. Molecular Imaging (assoc.), Soc. Nuc. Medicine (assoc.), Radiol. Soc. N.Am. (assoc.), Am. Coll. Radiology (assoc.), Beta Beta Beta, Alpha Omega Alpha (life). Avocations: musician, composer. Office: Mayo Clinic Ariz 13400 East Shea Blvd Scottsdale AZ 85259 Office Phone: 480-301-8016. E-mail: mroarke@aol.com.

**ROB, MOHAMMAD ABDUR,** education educator, researcher; s. Moslem Uddin Howlader and Hamidunnessa Khatun; m. Mahbuba Sultana, Oct. 1, 1957; children: Farhana, Washik Abdur. MS in Physics, Marquette U., Milw., 1982; PhD in Physics, U. Ala., Tuscaloosa, 1989. MS in Computer Info. Systems, U. Houston-Clear Lake, 2000. Rsch. asst. U. Ala., 1983—87; asst. prof. Talladega Coll., Ala., 1987; asst. prof. electro-optics U. Houston-Clear Lake, 1990—95; summer faculty fellow NASA Johnson Space Ctr., Houston, 1994—95; scientist/ops. specialist Lockheed Martin/NASA Johnson Space Ctr., Houston, 1996—97; programmer/analyst Zebec Data Systems, Houston, 1998—99; curricular coord. Dar-ul-Arqam Schs., Houston, 2005—06; asst. prof. U. Houston-Clear Lake, 2000—. Summer faculty fellow NASA GISS Lab. at Columbia U., N.Y.C., 2002. Author: numerous rsch. articles and grant proposals. Dir. Bangladesh-American Soc. Greater Houston, 2001—05; sci. fair judge Crlear Creek Sch. Dist., Houston, Friendswood, League City, Tex.; councilor Islamic Soc. Greater Houston, 2004—06; dir. Bangladesh-America Lit., Art & Cultural Assn., 1992—2000. Recipient Best Student Paper, Labama Acad. of Sci., 1985. Office Phone: 281-283-3191. Office Fax: 281-283-3951. Business E-Mail: rob@uhcl.edu.

**ROBAK, KIM M.,** lawyer; b. Columbus, Nebr., Oct. 4, 1955; m. William J. Mueller; children: Katherine, Claire. BS with distinction, U. Nebr., 1977, JD with highest distinction, 1985. Tchr. Lincoln Pub. Schs., Nebr., 1978—82; clerk Cline Williams Wright Johnson & Oldfather, 1983; summer assoc. Cooley Godward Castro Huddleson & Tatum, San Francisco, 1984, Steptoe & Johnson, Washington, 1985; ptnr. Rembolt Ludtke Parker & Berger, Lincoln, 1985—91; legal counsel Gov. E. Benjamin Nelson/State of Nebr., 1991—92, chief of staff, 1992—93; lt. gov. State of Nebr., 1993—98; v.p. external affairs, corp. sec. U. Nebr., 1999—2004; with Ruth Mueller Robak, LLC, Lincoln, Nebr., 2004—. Chair Prairie Fire Internat. Symposium on Edn., 1986; bd. dirs. Fiserv, Inc., First Ameritas Life Ins. Corp. NY, Union Bank & Trust Co. Program com. Leadership Lincoln, 1987—90; chair program com. Leadership Lincoln Alumni Assn., 1987, selection com., 1990; mem. Toll Fellowship Program, 1995; chair Nat. Conf. Lt. Govs., 1996; hon. chair Daffodil Day Campaign An, Cancer Soc.; hon chair Walktoberfest Am. Diabetes Assn.; hon. chair Prevent Blindness Campaign, Nebr.; hon. mem. Red Ribbon Campaign Mothers Against Drunk Driving, 1994—95; active Groundwater Found., 1997, Medicaid Managed Care Commn., 1993—98; bd. dirs. Nebr. Health Sys., 1997—2004, Nat. Found. Women Legislators Found., 1997—98; chair Nebr. Info. Tech. Commn., 1997—98; hon. Christmas chair Salvation Army, 1997; cert. program chair Nat. Order Women Legislators, 1997; mem. Martin Luther Home Soc., 1999—2001, Dem. Gen. Counsel, Nebr., 1985—92; bd. dirs. women's ministries First Congl. Ch., 1993—97, trustee, 1991—99, asst. moderator, 1999—; trustee Plymouth Congl. Ch., 1998—; bd. dirs. Doane Coll., 1997—, Lincoln Pub. Sch. Found., 1998—2004, Lincoln Partnership for Econ. Devel. Bd., 2000—, Nebr. Found. for the Humanities, 2003—, Lincoln Cmty. Found., 2004—, United Way of Lincoln and Lancaster County, 2000—, Strategic Air and Space Mus.,

2006—, Exec. Women's Golf Assn., 2005—. Named Notable Woman, First Plymouth Congl. Ch.'s Bd. Women's Ministries, 1996; fellow, Leadership Lincoln, 1986—87. Mem.: ABA (steering com. 1997—), Lincoln Bar Assn., Nebr. State Bar Assn. (ethics com. 1987—92, chair com. yellow pages advt. 1988, vice chair com. pub. rels. 1988—92, ho. of dels. 1988—95), Nat. Inst. Trial Advocacy, Alzheimers Assn. (hon. chair Lincoln-Greater Nebr. chpt. 1996—98), Updowntowners, Exec. Women's Golf Assn. (trustee 2005—), Order of Coif, U. Nebr. Coll. Alumni Assn. (bd. dirs. 1986—89). Office: Ruth Mueller Robak LLC 530 S 13th St Ste 110 Lincoln NE 68508 Business E-Mail: robak@ruthmueller.com.

**ROBARDS, THOMAS FREDERICK,** banker; b. Sewickley, Pa., June 10, 1946; s. Woodford Lee and Elizabeth Jane (Linscheid) R.; m. Karen Ann Puskarz, June 19, 1976; children: David Woodford, Christopher Joseph, Katherine Elizabeth. BA, Brown U., 1968; MBA, Harvard Bus. Sch., 1976. Asst. treas. Republic N.Y. Corp., N.Y.C., 1976-82, 1st v.p., treas., 1983-85, sr. v.p., treas., 1985-87, exec. v.p., treas., 1987—; asst. v.p. J. Aron div. Goldman Sachs, N.Y.C., 1982-83; CFO Republic New York Corp., N.Y.C., 1995—, Datek Online Holding Corp., Iselin, N.J., 2000—. Bd. dirs. Nat. Down Syndrome Soc., N.Y.C., 1986-87. Served to 1st lt. U.S. Army, 1968-72. Mem.: Harvard (N.Y.C.). Avocations: cross-country skiing, reading, racquet sports.

**ROBART, JAMES LOUIS,** federal judge, lawyer; AB, Whitman Coll., 1969; JD, Georgetown U., 1973. Bar: Wash. 1973, U.S. Dist. Ct. (we. dist.) Wash. 1973, U.S. Supreme Ct. 1977, U.S. Ct. Appeals (9th cir.) 1978, U.S. Dist. Ct. (ea. dist.) Wash. 1981, Alaska 1985, U.S. Dist. Ct. Alaska 1985, U.S. Ct. Appeals (fed. cir.) 1985. Assoc. Lane Powell Moss Miller LLP, Seattle, 1973—79, ptnr. 1980—90, Lane Powell Spears Lubersky LLP, 1990—98; co-mng. ptnr. Lane Powel Spears Lubersky, 1998—2002, mng. ptnr., 2003—04; judge US Dist. Ct. (we. dist.) Wash., 2004—. Trustee Children's Home Soc., 1991-92, Seattle Children's Home, pres., 1984, Whitman Coll., bd trustees, 2000-, bd. overseers, 1988-2000. Mem. Fed. Cir. Bar Assn. (trustee 1985-88). Office Phone: 206-370-8920.

**ROBB, CAMERON,** wireless communications company executive; Founder, dir. PetsMobility, Inc., Scottsdale, Ariz. Achievements include inventor of PetsCell, which is shaped like a bone attached to the dog's collar. It will allow pet owners to talk to their pets as well as allowing owners to request assistance if help is required. Office: PetsMobility Networks Inc 10575 114th St Ste 2 Scottsdale AZ 85259 Address: PetsMobility Networks Inc Unit 135 11300 No 5 Road Richmond BC Canada V7A5J7 Office Phone: 480-344-7724.

**ROBB, CHUCK (CHARLES SPITTAL ROBB),** law educator, former senator; b. Phoenix, Ariz., June 26, 1939; s. James Spittal and Francis Howard (Wooley) R.; m. Lynda Bird Johnson, Dec. 9, 1967; children: Lucinda Desha, Catherine Lewis, Jennifer Wickliffe. BBA, U. Wis., 1961; JD, U. Va., 1973. Bar: Va. 1973, U.S. Supreme Ct. 1976. Law clk. to Hon. John D. Butzner 4th U.S. Ct. Appeals, 1973—74; atty. Williams & Connolly, 1974-77; lt. gov. State of Va., 1978—82, gov., 1982—86; ptnr. Hunton & Williams, 1986—88; U.S. Senator from Va., 1989—2001; disting. prof. law and pub. policy George Mason U., 2001—. Former mem. armed svcs. com., intelligence.com., senate Dem. policy com., senate Dem. tech. and comm. com., subcom. on readiness, subcom. on seapower, subcom. on strategic forces Com. on Fin., subcom. on internat. trade, subcom. on social security and family policy, subcom. on taxation and IRS oversight Select Com. on Intelligence, Joint Econ. Com., Dem. Policy Com.; former Nat. Conf. Lt. Govs., 1979-80, Am. Coun. Young Polit. Leaders Dels. to Peoples Republic of China, 1979, dir. Commn. of the States, 1985; vis. prof. pub. affairs George Mason U., spring 1987; co-chmn. Commn. on the Intelligence Capabilities of the US Regarding Weapons of Mass Destruction, 2004 Chmn. Jobs for Am.'s Grads. Inc., 1985-90, Dem. Leadership Coun., 1986-88; gov. Atlantic Inst. for Internat. Affairs, 1987. With USMC, 1961—70. Decorated Bronze Star, Vietnam Service medal with 4 Stars; Vietnamese Cross of Gallantry with Silver Star; recipient Raven award, 1973, Seven Soc. award U. Va. Mem. ABA, Va. Bar Assn., So. Govs. Assn. (chmn.), Dem. Govs. Assn. (chmn.), Coalition for Dem. Majority, Res. Officers Assn., USMC Res. Officers Assn., U.Fa. La. Alumni Assn. (bd. dirs. 1974-85), Am. Legion, Raven Soc., Navy League U.S., Coun. on Fgn. Rels., Omicron Delta Kappa. Democrat. Episcopalian. Office: George Mason U Sch Law 3301 N Fairfax Dr Rm 409 Arlington VA 22201-4498

**ROBB, CURTIS,** air transportation executive; B in Physics, Emporia State U. With Citicorp Credit Svcs., IBM; sr. v.p., chief tech. officer Delta Tech., Inc., 2000—02, pres., CEO, 2002—; sr. v.p., chief info. officer Delta Air Lines, Inc., Atlanta, 2002—. With USAF. Office: Delta Air Lines Inc Hartsfield Atlanta Internat Airport 1030 Delta Blvd Atlanta GA 30320-6001

**ROBB, GARY CHARLES,** lawyer; b. Kansas City, Mo., May 17, 1955; m. Anita Candace Porte, Apr. 30, 1983. BA with distinction, U. Mo., Kansas City, 1977, MA in Econs., 1978; JD cum laude, U. Mich., 1981. Bar: Ill. 1981, U.S. Dist. Ct. (no. dist.) Ill. 1981, Mo. 1982, U.S. Dist. Ct. (we. dist.) Mo. 1982, U.S. Ct. Appeals (8th cir.) 1982. Assoc. Mayer, Brown & Platt, Chgo., 1981—82, Shughart, Thomson & Kilroy, Kansas City, Mo., 1982—84; ptnr. Robb & Robb LLC, Kansas City, Mo., 1984—. Adj. prof. law U. Mo., Kansas City; lectr., program chmn. Nat. Conf. on Products Liability Law, Chgo., 1983, lectr., 84. Contbg. author: Tort Law, Missouri Bar Handbook, 1982, Products Liability, 1984; editor: U. Mich. Jour. Law Reform, 1980—81; contbg. editor: Products Liability, 1983; mem. bd. editors: Products Liability Newsletter, 1982—, mem. bd. experts: Lawyers Alert Newsmag.; contbr. articles. Mem.: ATLA (tort and aviation sects.), ABA (tort and ins. practice 1981— trial evidence com. 1981—, sect. litigation, chmn. future programs and projects subcom., products, liability and consumer law com., co-chmn.Aviation Litig. Com. Jour. of Litig. 2004-2005), Lawyers Assn. Kansas City, Mo. Bar Assn. (fed. practice com.), Kansas City Bar Assn., Mo. Assn. Trial Attys. (bd. govs. 1993—, pres. elect), Univ. Mo.-Kansas City Alumni Assn. (chmn. career planning com.), Pi Sigma Alpha (pres. 1977—78), Omicron Delta Epsilon, Phi Kappa Phi. Republican. Office: Robb & Robb LLC One Kans City Pl Ste 3900 1200 Main St Kansas City MO 64105-2100

**ROBB, GEOFFREY LAWRENCE,** plastic surgeon; b. El Paso, Tex., May 28, 1947; s. Giles Anthony and Mary Jo (Lawrence) R.; m. Cathy Jean Cross, May 31, 1974; children: Tiffany, Kimberly, Courtney, Carly, Melaney, Mary. BS, U. Miami, 1969, MD, 1974. Diplomate Am. Bd. Otolaryngology. Commd. ensign USNR, 1970-92; advanced through grades to capt., 1989; resident in otalaryngology, mem. staff US Naval Hosp., San Diego, 1974-79, otolaryngologist Orlando, Fla., 1979-83; plastic surgeon USN Sponsorship at U. Pitts., 1983-85, microvascular surgeon, 1985; plastic surgeon U.S. Naval Hosp., Portsmouth, Va., 1985-88; ret., 1992; chief plastic surgery U.S. Naval Hosp., Portsmouth, Va., 1988-92; vice chmn. plastic surgery M.D. Anderson Cancer Ctr., Houston, 1992-97, chmn., 1997—, dep. chmn. divsn. surgery, 1994—, dir. postgrad. med. edn., 1992—, med. dir. plastic surgery clinic, 1994—, assoc. med. dir. skin cancer etc., 1994-97. Contbg. author: Reconstructive Plastic Surgery for Cancer, 1995, Endoscopic Plastic Surgery, 1995, Advanced Skin Cancer of Head and Neck, 1995; contbr. articles to profl. jours. Fellow ACS, Am. Soc. Plastic Reconstructive Surgeons, Am. Soc. Reconstructive Microsurgeons, Am. Assn. Plastic Surgeons; mem. Internat. Soc. Reconstructive Microsurgery, Tex. Soc. Plastic Surgeons, Houston Soc. Plastic Surgeons, KC. Avocations: physical fitness, weightlifting, tennis, running. Office: MD Anderson Cancer Ctr 1515 Holcombe Blvd # 443 Houston TX 77030-4009 E-mail: grobb@mdanderson.org.

**ROBB, JAMES ALEXANDER,** lawyer; b. Huntingdon, Que., Can., May 3, 1930; s. Alexander George and Irma Mary (Martin) R.; m. Katherine Ann Teare, June 26, 1960; children: Laura, John, Andrew. BA, McGill U., 1951, B.C.L., 1954; postgrad., U. Montreal, 1961-63. Bar: Que. 1955, queen's counsel 1970. Lectr. comml. law and taxation Sir George Williams U., 1958-60; ptnr. Stikeman Elliott LLP and predecessor firm Stikeman, Elliott, Tamaki, Mercier & Robb, Montreal, 1967—2002, ret., 2003. Pres. Que-Japan Bus. Forum, 1993—95; bd. dirs. Itochu Can. Ltd., YKK Can. Inc., NGK Spark Plugs Can. Ltd., Western Life Assurance Co., Bank West. Mem. Protestant Sch. Bd. Greater Montreal, 1971-75; chmn. bd. trustees Martlet Found., 1967-69; v.p. Que. Liberal Party, 1976-79; mem. adv. com. McGill Ctr. for Study of Regulated Industries; bd. dirs. Montreal Mus. Fine Arts, 1987-90; bd. govs. McGill U., 1991-95. Mem.: Consumers Assn. Can. (past chmn. regulated industries program), Bar Que. (chmn. multidisciplinary com. 1998—2001), Can. C. of C. (internat. arbitration com.), McGill Alumni Assn. (pres. 1996—98), Hillside Tennis Club, Royal Montreal Curling Club (pres. 1999—2000), Kanawaki Golf Club (Que.), Univ. Club (pres. 1988—89), Can. Club Montreal (pres. 1990—91). Home: 9 Renfrew Ave Westmount PQ Canada H3Y 2X3 Office: 1155 Renè Lèvesque Blvd W 40th Fl Montreal PQ Canada H3B 3V2 Office Phone: 514-397-3086. Personal E-mail: jrobb@stikeman.com.

**ROBB, JAMES WILLIS,** romance languages educator; b. Jamaica, N.Y., June 27, 1918; s. Stewart Everts and Clara Johanna (Mohrmann) R.; m. Cecilia Uribe-Noguera, 1972. Student, Inst. de Touraine, Sorbonne, 1937-38; BA cum laude, Colgate U., 1939; postgrad., U. Nacional de Mex., 1948; MA, Middlebury Coll., 1950; PhD, Cath. U. Am., 1958. Instr. romance langs. Norwich U., 1946-50; from asst. prof. to prof. romance langs. George Washington U., Washington, 1950-88, prof. emeritus, 1988—. Corr. mem. Academia Mexicana de la Lengua, 1998. Author: El Estilo de Alfonso Reyes, 1965, 78, Repertorio Bibliográfico de Alfonso Reyes, 1974, Prosa y Poesía de Alfonso Reyes, 1975, 84, Estudios sobre Alfonso Reyes, 1976, Por Los Caminos de Alfonso Reyes, 1981, Imágenes de América en Alfonso Reyes y en Germán Arciniegas, 1990, Más Páginas Sobre Alfonso Reyes, 1996-97; contbr. articles to profl. jours. With USNR, 1942—44, Brazil, with USNR, 1944—46, PTO. Recipient Alfonso Reyes Internat. Lit. prize, 1978; Lit. Diploma of Merit, State of Nuevo León and City of Monterrey, Mex., 1979; OAS grantee, 1964; Am. Philos. Soc. grantee, 1977 Mem. MLA, Internat. Assn. Ibero-Am. Lit., Am. Assn. Tchrs. Spanish and Portuguese, Assn. Colombianistas, Phi Beta Kappa. Office: George Washington U Romance Langs Dept Washington DC 20052-0001

**ROBB, JOHN WESLEY,** religion educator; b. L.A., Dec. 1, 1919; s. Edgar Milton and Alta (Boger) R.; m. Ethel Edna Tosh, June 13, 1942; children: Lydia Joan Robb Durbin, Judith Nadine Robb Eggerman. AB, Greenville Coll., 1941; Th.M., U. So. Calif., 1945, PhD, 1952; L.H.D., Hebrew Union Coll.-Jewish Inst. Religion, 1977. Asst. prof. philosophy and religion Dickinson Coll., Pa., 1948-51; fellow Fund for Advancement in Edn., 1951-52; asso. prof. U. So. Calif., L.A., 1954-62, chmn. dept. religion, 1954-67, assoc. dean humanities Coll. Letters, Arts and Scis., 1963-68, Leonard K. Firestone prof., 1974-75, prof., 1962-87, prof. emeritus, 1987—, prof. Sch. Medicine, 1981-87; coun. mem. Inst. of Lab. Animal Resources Nat. Acad. Scis. Nat. Rsch. Coun., 1986-93. Vis. disting. prof. USAF Med. Ctr., Wilford Hall, Tex., 1985; mem. rev. com. NIH Guide for the Care and Use of Lab. Animals, NRC, NAS, 1993-96; advisor/tutor Med. Quality Assurance Commn., Dept. Health, State of Wash., 1994-2001; mem. ethics com. Swedish Med. Ctr., N.W. Hosp., Seattle, 1992-2002; adj. prof. bioethics Sch. Medicine, U. So. Calif., 1989-91, adj. prof. emeritus, 1991—. Author: Inquiry Into Faith, 1960; co-editor: Readings in Religious Philosophy; The Reverent Skeptic, 1979. Served as lt. (j.g.) USNR, 1945—47, o lt., 1952—54. Recipient award for excellence in tchg. U. So. Calif., 1960, 74, Dart award for acad. innovation, 1970, Raubenheimer Disting. Faculty award divsn. humanities, 1980, Robert Fenton Craig award Blue Key, 1980, Outstanding Faculty award Student Senate, 1981, Disting. Emeritus award, 1995, Educator of Yr. award Swedish Med. Ctr., Providence, Seattle, 2002. Fellow Soc. for Values in Higher Edn.; mem. Am. Acad. Religion (v.p. 1966, pres. 1967), Am. Philos. Assn., AAUP (v.p. Calif. Conf. 1977, pres. 1978-79), Phi Beta Kappa (hon.), Phi Kappa Phi, Phi Chi Phi. United Methodist. Home: 12507 Green Wood Ave N A-405 Seattle WA 98133

**ROBB, KATHY MCCLESKEY,** lawyer; b. Bklyn., Nov. 14, 1954; BA cum laude, spl. honors, Plan II, Univ. Tex., 1976; JD, Univ. Va., 1980. Bar: Va. 1982, NY 1989, US Dist. Ct. (ea. and so. dists.) NY, US Supreme Ct. Law clk. to Hon. Glen M. Williams US Dist. Ct. (we. dist.) Va., 1980—81; ptnr. resources, regulatory and environ. law Hunton & Williams LLP, NYC, 1988—. Adv. bd. BNA's Environ. Due Diligence Guide. Fellow: ABA; mem.: Assn. of City Bar of NY. Office: Hunton & Williams LLP 200 Park Ave New York NY 10166 Office Phone: 202-995-1128, 212-309-1128. Office Fax: 202-309-1100. Business E-Mail: krobb@hunton.com.

**ROBB, LYNDA JOHNSON,** writer; b. Washington, Mar. 19, 1944; d. Lyndon Baines and Claudia Alta (Taylor) Johnson; m. Charles Spittal Robb, Dec. 9, 1967; children: Lucinda Desha, Catherine Lewis, Jennifer Wickliffe. BA with honors, U. Tex., 1966. Writer McCall's Mag., 1966-68; contbg. editor Ladies Home Jour., 1968-80; lectr., bd. dirs. Reading Is Fundamental, 1968—, Lyndon B. Johnson Family Found., 1969-95. Past mem. Va. State Coun. on Infant Mortality, Va. Maternal & Child Health Coun.; mem. Nat. Commn. to Prevent Infant Mortality, 1987-93; chmn. Pres.'s Adv. Com. for Women, 1979-81; pres. bd. dirs. Nat. Home Libr. Found.; chmn. Va. Women's Cultural History Project, 1982-85; chmn. Reading is Fundamental, 1996-2001. Mem.: Zeta Tau Alpha. Office: Reading is Fundamental Ste 400 1825 Connecticut Ave NW Washington DC 20009-5708

**ROBBINS, ALICE ELIZABETH,** musician; b. N.Y.C., Aug. 29, 1950; d. Jacob and Jean Robbins; m. Gregory Hayes (div.); m. Walter Denny. AB in Renaissance Music Performance, Ind. U., 1973; grad. degree, Schola Cantorum Basiliensis, Switzerland, 1977. Adj. faculty Boston U., 1990—2002, Five Coll. Early Music Program Northampton, Mass., 1979 Musician (violin, viola da gamba): Concerto Castello, 1980—85, Smithsonian Chamber Players, 1979—82, 1986—91, 2005; musician: (cello, basse de violon) Boston Early Music Festival Orch., 1997—; musician: (viola da gamba) Oberlin Consort of Viols, 1979—; musician: (prin. cello, viola da gamba) Wash. Bach Consort, 1996—; musician: (cello) Handel and Haydn Soc., 1987—; musician: (prin. cello, viola da gamba) Arcadia Players, 1988—; musician: (CD) Electrola, 1975, Arabesque, 1990, Centaur, 2000. Mem.: Early Music Am., Viola da Gamba Soc. of Am., Boston Musicians Assn. E-mail: arobbins@smith.edu.

**ROBBINS, ALLEN BISHOP,** physics professor; b. New Brunswick, N.J., Mar. 31, 1930; s. William Rei and Helen Grace (Bishop) R.; m. Shirley Mae Gernert, June 14, 1952 (div. 1978); children: Catherine Jean, Marilyn Elizabeth, Carol Ann, Melanie Barbara; m. Alice Harriet Ayars, Jan. 1, 1979. Student, Oberlin Coll., 1948—49; BS, Rutgers U., 1952; MS, Yale U., 1953, PhD, 1956. Rsch. fellow U. Birmingham (Eng.), 1957-58, lectr., 1960-61; instr. physics Rutgers U., New Brunswick, 1956-57, asst. prof. physics, 1957-60, assoc. prof., 1960-68, prof., 1968-97, prof. emeritus, 1997—, chmn. dept. physics and astronomy, 1979-95. Contbr. articles on nuc. physics to profl. jours. Recipient Lindbach Christian and Mary F. Lindbach Found., Rutgers U., 1975. Fellow Am. Phys. Soc.; mem. Am. Assn. Physics Tchrs., AAAS, Phi Beta Kappa, Sigma Xi. Office: Rutgers U Dept Physics and Astronomy 136 Frelinghuysen Rd Piscataway NJ 08854-8019 Personal E-mail: allenbrobbins@aol.com.

**ROBBINS, ANNE FRANCIS See REAGAN, NANCY**

**ROBBINS, AUDREY,** county official; b. Chgo., Mar. 1, 1932; d. Philip I. and Manya Lehr; children: Dana Merfeld, Cindy Buss. BA, DePaul U., Chgo., 1993. Mfrs. rep. Museum Reprodns. - Marwall Industries, N.Y.C., 1969—79; asst. to chief counsel Arthur Andersen & Co., Chgo., 1979—98; mem. staff Office of Chief Judge, Cook County Cir. Ct., Chgo., 1999—. Author: Goldblatt's Galloping Gourmets, 1974 (Tribune award, 74). Vol. intensive care infants Northwestern Meml. Hosp., Chgo., 1970—80; vol. Art Inst. Chgo., 1984—86; touring docent Terra Mus. Am. Art, Chgo., 1999—2004, Clarke/Glessner House, 2005—, Loyola U. Mus. Art, 2005—; bd. dirs., sec.,

pres. Nathan & Francis Goldblatt Soc. for Cancer Rsch., 1955—83. Mem.: Golden Key (life). Avocations: art history, watercolors, cooking. Home: 910 N Lake Shore Dr # 718 Chicago IL 60611 Office: Cir Ct Cook County 50 W Washington Chicago IL 60602

**ROBBINS, CORNELIUS (CORNELIUS VAN VORSE),** educational administration educator; b. Wilmington, Del., Nov. 2, 1931; s. Cornelius V. and Irene (Tatman) R.; m. Janet Porter, Aug. 1953; children: Eva Robbins Burke, Laurel Robbins, Susan Robbins, Melissa Robbins Beegle. BA in Polit. Sci, U. Del., 1953, MEd in Social Scis, 1961; EdD in Ednl. Adminstrn, U. Pa., 1964. Asst. mgr. Robbins & Clark Hardware, 1953-57; asst. provost U. Del., 1957-58, 1964—65; tchr. Marshallton (Del.) Sch. Dist., 1958-60, Mt. Pleasant (Del.) Sch. Dist., 1960-62; asst. to dir. sch. study councils U. Del., 1962-64; dir. mgmt. sys. U. Del., 1964—65; dean instrn. Ocean County Coll., 1965-67; dean of coll. C/C. of Delaware County, Pa., 1967-69; sr. assoc., coll. div. dir. McManis Assocs., Washington, 1969-70; pres. Genesee C.C., 1970-75; assoc. chancellor for community colls. SUNY, 1975-85; acting pres. Potsdam State Coll. (N.Y.), 1982-83; pres. Cobleskill (N.Y.) Coll. Agr. & Tech., 1985-92; prof. edn. adminstrn. SUNY, Albany, NY, 1992—. Cons. Middle States Assn. Colls.; area liaison officer U.S. Mil. Acad., 1971-75; chmn. SUNY West Pres.'s Council and mem. Chancellor's Council, 1973-91. Contbr. articles to profl. publs. Served with U.S. Army, 1954-56; maj. USAR ret. Recipient Outstanding Educator's award N.Y. State Assn. Jr. Colls., 1975, Disting. Svc. award Faculty Coun. Community Colls., 1988. Mem. Am. Assn. Higher Edn., State Dirs. of Community Colls. Assn., Phi Delta Kappa. Office: SUNY Albany Ed 332 Albany NY 12222-0001 Office Phone: 518-442-5085. Business E-Mail: crobbins@uamail.albany.edu.

**ROBBINS, DAN S.,** theater educator, theater director; b. Ft. Worth, Tex., Dec. 11, 1957; s. Winfred L. Robbins and Julia Ann Phillips; m. Karen Sue Stigura, June 20, 1998. PhD in Theatre, U. Tex., Austin, 1992. Dir. theatre Jacksonville U., Fla., 1998—2000, Gordon Coll., Barnesville, Ga., 2000—. Mem.: Southeastern Theatre Conf. (assoc.; chmn. small theatre programs 2005—), Ga. Theatre Conf. (assoc.; chmn. colls. and univs. 2005—), Phi Kappa Phi (assoc.). Office: Gordon College 419 College Drive Barnesville GA 30204 Office Phone: 770-358-5040. Office Fax: 770-358-5140. Business E-Mail: drobbins@gdn.edu.

**ROBBINS, DOREN GURSTEIN,** poet, educator, artist; b. LA, Aug. 20, 1949; s. Ralph and Florence R.; m. Linda Drand Mazak Janakos; 1 child, Samantha. MFA, U. Iowa, 1993. Instr. English Umpqua C.C., Roseburg, Oreg., 1993-95, Linfield Coll., McMinnville, Oreg., 1994-95; instr. creative writing U. Iowa, Iowa City, 1991-93; English instr. East Los Angels Coll., Monterey Park, Calif., 1997—2000; instr. creative writing, poetry L. Calif., L.A., 1996-99; English instr. Santa Monica (Calif.) Coll., 1998—2000. Author: (poetry) Driving Face Down, 2001 (Blue Lynx prize 2001), The Donkey's Tale, 1998 (The Villon prize 1998), Sympathetic Manifesto, 1988 (Emma Goldman award 1988), Seducation of the Groom, 1982, Dignity in Naples and North Hollywood, 1996, My Piece of the Puzzle, 2005; (fiction) Parking Lot Mood Swing, 2004. Poet, artist Salvadoran Med. Relief Fund, Salinas, Calif., 1984-85; poet-activist Ctrl. Am. Refugee Com. L.A. 1984-86; poetry organizer Amnesty Internat., L.A. 1980. Recipient Anna Davidson Roseberg award Judah Magnes Mus., Commendation prize Chester H. Jones Found., 1993, 96, 97; poetry fellowship Oreg. Literary Arts, L.A. County Mus. of Art, 1999, The Loft Found., 1985. Jewish. Avocations: travel, walking, meditation. Office: Foothill Coll care Lang Arts 12345 El Monte Rd Los Altos Hills CA 94022-4599 Home: 152 Montclair Dr Santa Cruz CA 95060-1025 Office Phone: 650-949-7678. Personal E-mail: pantagruli@aol.com. Business E-Mail: robbinsdoren@foothill.edu.

**ROBBINS, ELLEN SUE,** lawyer, educator; b. Chgo., Mar. 15, 1967; d. Sheldon Neal and Barbara Lynn (Corenman) R. BS in Bus. Adminstrn. summa cum laude, U. Ill., 1988; JD magna cum laude, Harvard U., 1991. Bar: Ill. 1991. Jud. clk. to Judge Charles Kocoras U.S. Dist. Ct., Chgo., 1991-92; ptnr. Sidley & Austin, Chgo., 1992—. Adj. prof. law DePaul Coll. Law, Chgo., 1997—. Mem. ABA. Chgo. Bar Assn. Avocations: jogging, golf, sports. Office: Sidley & Austin One First Nat Plz Chicago IL 60603-2003 E-mail: erobbins@sidley.com.

**ROBBINS, EMMALEE ELIZABETH,** theater director, speech professional; b. Kingstree, SC, Mar. 29, 1941; d. Thomas Earl and Elizabeth Eloise (Payne) Gaddy; children: Alicia Rhett Howard, Christopher Michael. BA in speech and drama, Columbia Coll., 1963; MFA in theatre, U. N.C., Greensboro, N.C., 1977. Cert. teaching 1965. Dance instr. Columbia Coll., 1961—63; dir. Christian youth activities Kingstree Meth. Ch., 1962; dir. Christian edn. Main St. Meth. Ch., Columbia, SC, 1963—64; dir., prod., choreographer Charleston County Playhouse, Summer Playhouse and St. Andrew's Parish H.S., 1969—72; tchg. asst. U. N.C., Greensboro, 1972—74; hostess Today's Woman CBS, 1972—74; dir., prod., choreographer Charleston County Playhouse, Summer Playhouse and St. Andrew's Parish H.S., 1974—79; tchr. Charleston Southern U., 1969—70; guest, choreographer ABC, 1977; theatre dir. Town Theatre, Columbia, SC, 1979—97; instr. Newberry Coll., Newberry, SC, 1979—80; dir. Young Town Players and Young People's Theatre, 1985—97; tchr. Buckley Sch. of Pub. Speaking, Camden, SC, 1998—. Vol., tchg. character edn. Lugoff Elem. Sch., Camden, SC, 2002—03; vol. tchg. character edn. Carolina Care Plan, 2003. Author: (9 story books on character edn.) The Lighthouse Learning Express. Recipient Career Achievement award, Columbia Coll., 1990. Mem.: SC Theater's Assn., Daughters of Am. Colonists. Republican. Presbyterian. Avocations: ballroom dancing, travel, reading, writing, pilates. Home: 30 Royal Gate Columbia SC 29223 Office Phone: 803-736-1555. E-mail: eer_productions@msn.com.

**ROBBINS, ETTA JO,** music educator; b. Fayetteville, Ark., Dec. 29, 1951; d. Memo Conrad and Dena Neva Robbins; children: Timothy Morris, Jessica Mitchell, Benjamin Morris. BA, Ark. Tech. U., Russellville, 1974, MEd. 1979. Instr. choir and band Yellville- Summit H.S., Yellville, Ark., 1974—75. Mountain Burg H.S., 1991—93; instr. band Westside H.S., Coal Hill, 1993—96; instr. choir and band Augusta H.S., 1996—98, Concord H.S., 1999—2001, West Side H.S., Greers Ferry, 2001—. Mem.: Ark. Sch. Band and Orch. Assn., Ark. Choral Dirs. Assn., Ark. Women Band Dirs. Assn. Baptist. Avocations: church choir, handbells, community theater. Office: West Side HS 7295 Greers Ferry Rd Greers Ferry AR 72067-9416

**ROBBINS, HENRY ZANE,** public relations and marketing executive; b. Winston-Salem, N.C., Jan. 17, 1930; s. Romulus Mayfield and Vera Ethel (Daniel) R.; m. Barbara Anne Brown, Jan. 19, 1955; children: Zane Scott, Jill Stewart, Gail Ruth. AB, U. N.C., 1952; student, Emory U., 1952. Reporter Atlanta Constn., 1952; exhibit specialist Gen. Electric Co., Schenectady, 1952, employee relations specialist Cin., 1955, editor Schenectady, 1955, account supr. Winston-Salem, 1956-58, group supr. Schenectady, 1958-60; v.p., gen. mgr. Burson-Marsteller, Pitts. and Chgo., 1960-70, sr. v.p., 1970; pres., chief exec. officer SL&H-Robbins Inc., Chgo., 1970-72; also dir. pres., chief exec. officer Beveridge and Robbins Inc., Chgo., 1975-77; pres., chief exec. officer Financial Advt. of Ill., Inc., Chgo.; mng. dir. Sports Mgmt. Group, Chgo., 1975-77; dir. communications Arthur Andersen & Co., Chgo. and Geneva, Switzerland, 1977-81, dir. mktg. support services, 1981-89, dir. mktg. and comms., 1989-91; mem. Worldwide Alpha Group, 1991-96, exec. dir. global markets program, 1995—2000; prin. Arthur Andersen & Co., 1980—2000; cons. Exec. Svc. Corps, 2004—. Mem. journalism adv. com. Harper Coll., Palatine, Ill., exec. svc. corp.; dir. Evanston Environ. Assn.; mem. Ladd Arboretum Commn., Evanston, Ill.; pub. rels. com. Mobil, Inc. Mem. Nat. Task Force on Environment; cons. sec. Dept. Health, Edn. and Welfare, 1970; chmn. pub. rels. com. Honor Am. Day Com., 1970. Author: Vision of Grandeur, 1988, Globalizing the Enterprise, 2000, Tradition of Excellence, 2001; contbr. articles to profl. jours. Counselor Council of Mojave, 1972-74; gen. chmn. Chgo. Children's Classic Golf Tournament, 1974-77; chmn. Chgo. fin. com. Am.'s Freedom Train, 1976; chmn. fund devel. com. Presbytery of Chgo.

1977-83, maj. mission fund, 1977-79; dist. commr. Boy Scouts Am., 1976-79, chmn. Wildcat dist., 1980-83; mem. exec. bd. N.E. Ill. council, 1980-85; mem. Republican Citizens Com. Ill., 1960-61, Allegheny County (Pa.) Rep. Com., 1962-65; Trustee Roycemore Sch., Evanston, 1971-74; trustee, v.p. devel. Child and Family Services Chgo.; bd. dirs. Fellowship of Christian Athletes, U. N.C. Alumni Ill., Stockbrokers Assn. Chgo.; chmn. devel. com. Potawotamie Dist., 2000, chmn. fin. com., 2001; bd. dirs. Evanston Environ. Ctr., Ladd Arboretum, North Shore Nature Ctr., 2001-; mem. Ctr. for the Rehab. of Wildlife; bd. visitors U. N.C., 2004-. Served to 1st lt. AUS, 1952-54. Elected to N.C. Pub. Rels. Hall of Fame, 1994. Mem.: Chgo. Assn. Commerce and Industry, Environ. Writers Assn. Am., Am. Mgmt. Assn., Pub. Rels. Counselors Roundtable, Chgo. Ednl. TV Assn., Midwest Travel Writers Assn., Nat. Investor Rels. Inst., Pub. Rels. Soc. Am., Art Inst. Chgo., Sunset Ridge Country Club, OptimistClub of Wilmette (pres. 2005—07), Univ. Club, Chi Psi. Republican. Presbyterian. Home: 2759 Broadway Ave Evanston IL 60201-1556 Personal E-mail: hzrobbins@sbcglobal.net.

**ROBBINS, HULDA DORNBLATT,** artist, printmaker; b. Atlanta, Oct. 19, 1910; d. Adolph Benno and Lina (Rosenthal) Domblatt. Student, Phila. Mus's. Sch. Indsl. Art, 1928-29, Prussian Acad., Berlin, 1929-31, Barnes Found., Merion, Pa., 1939. Poster designer and maker ITE Circuit Breaker Co. Inc., Phila., 1944; instr. serigraphy Nat. Serigraph Soc. Sch., N.Y.C., 1953-60; instr. creative painting Atlantic County Jewish Cmty. Ctrs., Margate, Atlantic City, NJ, 1960-67. Represented by William P. Carl, Fine Prints, Boston, Picture Store, Boston. One-woman shows include Lehigh U. Art Galleries, 1933, ACA Galleries, Phila., 1939, 8th St. Gallery, N.Y.C., 1941, Serigraph Gallery, 1947, Atlantic City Art Ctr., 1961, 1971, exhibited in group shows at 2d Nat. Print Ann. Bklyn. Mus., Carnegie Inst., Libr. of Congress, LaNapoule Art Found., Am. Graphic Contemporary Art, Represented in permanent collections Met. Mus. Art, N.Y.C., Mus. Modern Art, Biblioteque Nationale, Smithsonian Instn., Art Mus. Ont., Can., Victoria and Albert Mus., London, U.S. embassies abroad, Lehigh U., Princeton Print Club, 6 prints, Phila. Mus. Art. Recipient Purchase prize, Prints for Children, Mus. Modern Art, N.Y.C., 1941, prize, 2d Portrait Am. Competition, 1945, 2d prize, Paintings by Printmakers, 1948. Mem.: Serigraph Soc. (mem. founding group, charter sec., Ninth Ann. prize 1948, 1949), Graphics Soc., Print Club, Am. Color Print Soc. Home and Office: 16 S Buffalo Ave Ventnor City NJ 08406-2635 Office Phone: 609-823-7314. *To cherish and express living through devotion to art.*

**ROBBINS, JAMES O.,** former communications executive; BS in Am. studies, Univ. Pa.; MBA, Harvard Univ. Mng. editor WBZ-TV News, Boston, 1969-72; mgmt. position Continental Cablevision, 1972-79, Montachusett Cable Television, 1972-79, v.p., gen. mgr. Viacom Cablevision, Long Island, N.Y., 1979-83; pres., CEO Cox Communications, Inc., 1983—2005. Bd. dirs. NCR Corp., Teleport Communications, Inc., TeleWest. Treas., bd. dirs. Nat. Cable Television Assn., exec. com. Cable Satellite Pub. Affairs Network; v.p. Cable in Classroom; trustee Westminster Sch., Atlanta.

**ROBBINS, JEFFREY HOWARD,** media consultant, research writer, educator; b. N.Y.C., Mar. 29, 1941; s. Stanley Samuel and Miriam (Cooper) R.; m. Marsha Sue Rimler, Nov. 3, 1984 (div. Dec. 1996); 1 child, Nina Camille. BSME, Carnegie Mellon U., 1962; MS in Physics, U. N.Mex., 1966, ABD in Physics, 1967; postgrad., U. Calif., Berkeley and L.A., 1963-64. Summer rsch. assoc. Linde Co., Tonawanda, NY, 1961; rsch. engr. N.Am. Aviation (Rockwell), Downey, Calif., 1962—64; summer rsch. assoc. Los Alamos Nat. Lab., N.Mex., 1965; sr. engr. Radio Engring. Labs., L.I., NY, 1968—70; engring. cons. PRD Electronics, Syosset, NY, 1972—73; sr. cons. Bendix Corp., Teterboro, NJ, 1974—76; sr. engr. Giordano Assocs., Franklin Lakes, NJ, 1977—81; sr. applications engr. Racal-Redak, Mahwah, NJ, 1981—83; tech. media cons. Allied Signal Corp., Teterboro, 1983—92, U.S. Army, Picatinny Arsenal, NJ, 1992; tech. cons. Ford Motor Co., Lansdale, Pa., 1992—98, Visteon Automotive Electronics, Markham, Ont., Canada, 1998; adj. prof. Rutgers U., New Brunswick, NJ, 2002—. Cons. Tyco Internat., Clark, N.J., 1998-2002; tech. cons., rsch. writer media literacy programs Packer Collegiate Inst., Bklyn., N.Y.C., 1992-93, On TV, Inc., N.Y.C., 1992; initiator, moderator Media Literacy Forum, 1995; evening sch. instr. New Sch. for Social Rsch., N.Y.C., 1979-85; presenter in field. Author: On Balance and Higher Education, 1970; contbr. articles to profl. jours. Organizer, co-moderator Future Impact of Artificial Intelligence, Robotics Forum, 1984. Recipient 1st prize for essay The World and I Mag., 1990; nominee Grawemeyer award in Edn., 1988; NDEA fellow, 1966-67, others; feature essay premier issue Plain mag., 1994; contbr. essays to publs. Mem. IEEE (presenter Internat. Symposium and Soc. and Soc., 1993, 96, 98, 2006, Internat. Soc. Sys. Scis. Conf. 1993, 95, 97, 99, 2000, 02, initiator, moderator, media literacy forum Packer Collegiate Inst. 1995, presenter World Order Conf., Toronto 1999, 2001, 02, 04, judge sci. engring. fair 2003-06, spkr.), N.Y. Acad. Scis., Sigma Xi, Phi Kappa Phi, Pi Tau Sigma. Home and Office: PO Box 335 Long Beach NY 11561-0335 E-mail: jhrobbins@erols.com.

**ROBBINS, JERRY HAL,** educational administration educator; b. DeQueen, Ark., Feb. 28, 1939; s. James Hal and Barbara I. (Rogers) R. BA in Math, Hendrix Coll., 1960; M.Ed., U. Ark., 1963, Ed.D., 1966. Tchr. math. and music Clinton (Ark.) pub. schs., 1960-61; prin. Adrian (Mo.) High Sch., 1961-63; exec. sec. Ark. Sch. Study Council, Fayetteville, 1963-64; mem. faculty U. Miss., University, 1965-74, prof. ednl. adminstrn., 1970-74, chmn. dept. ednl. adminstrn., 1970-74; dean Coll. Edn., U. Ark., Little Rock, 1974-79; asso. v.p. for acad. affairs Ga. State U., Atlanta, 1979-84, dean Coll. Edn., 1984-90, prof. ednl. adminstrn., 1990-91; dean. Coll. Edn. Ea. Mich U., Ypsilanti, 1991—2004, prof. ednl. leadership, 2004—05. Co-author: (with S. B. Williams Jr.) Student Activities in the Innovative School, 1969, School Custodian's Handbook, 1970, Administrator's Manual of School Plant Administration, 1970. Mem. NEA, Am. Assn. Sch. Adminstrs., Am. Assn. Colls. Tchr. Edn. (dir. 1979-82, 2000-04), Nat. Assn. Secondary Sch. Prins., So. Regional Council Ednl. Adminstrn. (pres. 1970-71), Tchr. Edn. Coun. State Colls. and Univs. (pres. 1998-99), Phi Delta Kappa, Kappa Delta Pi (v.p. chpt. devel. 1978-80, pres. elect 1980-82, pres. 1982-84, past pres. 1984-86) Mem. United Meth. Ch. Home and Office: 3384 Bent Trail Dr Ann Arbor MI 48108-9310 Office: Ea Mich U 310 Porter Bldg Ypsilanti MI 48197 E-mail: jerry.robbins@emich.edu.

**ROBBINS, JOHN BENNETT,** medical researcher; b. Bklyn., Dec. 1, 1932; BA, NYU, 1956; MD (hon.), U. Goteborg, Sweden, 1959. Intern, resident Children's Med. Svc. Mass. Gen. Hosp., Boston, 1959—60; rsch. fellow dept. pediat. U. Fla., 1961—64; guest scientist dept. chem. immunology Weizmann Inst. Sci., Rehovot, Israel, 1965—66; asst. prof. pediat. and microbiology U. Fla., Gainesville, 1964—67; from asst. prof. to assoc. prof. pediat. Albert Einstein Coll. Medicine, 1967—70; clin. dir. Nat. Inst. Child Health and Human Devel. NIH, 1970—72; chief devel. immunology br. NIH, 1971—74; dir. divsn. bacterial products FDA, 1974—83; chief lab. devel. and molecular immunity Nat. Inst. Child Health and Human Devel. NIH, 1983—. Henry Bale Meml. lectr. Nat. Inst. Biol. Stds. and Control, 1979; Erwin Neter Meml. lectr. U. Buffalo, 1984; Henry L. Barnett lectr. Albert Einstein Coll. Medicine, 1985; Maxwell Finland lectr. Infectious Disease Soc. Am., 1989; Louis Weinstein lectr. Tufts U., 1989. Recipient E. Mead Johnson award, Am. Acad. Pediat., 1975, Albert Lasker Clin. Med. Rsch. award, Albert and Mary Lasker Found., 1996. Fellow: Am. Acad. Microbiology; mem.: NAS, Am. Philos. Soc., Nat. Inst. Medicine, Am. Assn. Immunologists, Assn. Am. Physicians, Am. Soc. Clin. Investigation, Soc. Infectious Disease, Soc. Pediatric Rsch. Achievements include development of first effective typhoid fever vaccine for children. Office: Nat Inst Child Health & Human Devel 9000 Rockville Pike Rm 424 Bethesda MD 20892-0001*

**ROBBINS, JOHN CLAPP,** management consultant; b. Cleveland, Jan. 22, 1921; s. John Clapp and Esther Turner (Holland) R.; m. Louise Severance Nash, Jan. 10, 1951 (div. Oct. 1974); children: Anne Millikin, Julia Severance, John Nash; m. Beatrice Blair, Aug. 2, 1975 (dec. July 1994); m. Sylvia Hordosch, Dec. 20, 2000. AB, Harvard U., 1942. Copy boy, reporter, writer, promotion editor Cleve. Press, 1946-57; exec. internat. div. Mobil Oil Corp., N.Y.C., Istanbul, 1957-70; chief exec. officer Planned Parenthood/World

Population, N.Y.C., 1970-75; prin. mgmt. cons. Stanford Research Inst., 1976-83; v.p. GPA Inc., N.Y.C., 1983—; pres. John Robbins Assocs. Spl. fin. cons. Internat. Helsinki Fedn., Vienna, Parkinson Disease Found., N.Y.C., Alan Guttmacher Inst. U. Mich., Ann Arbor, 2001—03; substitute tchr. Okemos (Mich.) Pub. Schs., 2003; tchg. asst. Johns Hopkins U., Eastern, Pa., 2003, Bristol, RI, 2004, Brown U., Providence, 2004—. Vol. Hemophilia Found. Mich., Ann Arbor, 2000—01. Fellow, Brown U., 2003. Mem.: Am. Hist. Assn., Phi Alpha Theta. Avocations: fishing, trumpet, sports, cross country skiing. Office: Brown U Dept History Box N Providence RI 02912

**ROBBINS, MARK WALTER,** historian; b. Lansing, Mich., Aug. 31, 1981; s. Lawrence Harry and Martha Edwards Robbins. BA in History magna cum laude, U. Mich., 2003; AM in History, Brown U., 2004. Reference asst. Bently Hist. Libr. U. Mich., Ann Arbor, 2001—03; substitute tchr. Okemos (Mich.) Pub. Schs., 2003; tchg. asst. Johns Hopkins U., Eastern, Pa., 2003, Bristol, RI, 2004, Brown U., Providence, 2004—. Vol. Hemophilia Found. Mich., Ann Arbor, 2000—01. Fellow, Brown U., 2003. Mem.: Am. Hist. Assn., Phi Alpha Theta. Avocations: fishing, trumpet, sports, cross country skiing. Office: Brown U Dept History Box N Providence RI 02912

**ROBBINS, N. CLAY,** foundation administrator; b. Indpls., May 30, 1957; m. Amy Robbins; 3 children. BA, Wabash Coll., Crawfordsville, Ind., 1979; JD, Vanderbilt U., 1982; LLD (hon.), Ind. State U., 2004; LHD (hon.), Rose-Hulman Inst. Tech., 2006. Exch. assoc. European Econ. Cmty. law dept. Rycken Burlion Bolle & Houben, Brussels, 1985-86; assoc. Baker & Daniels, 1982-85, ptnr., 1988—92; v.p. cmty. devel. Lilly Endowment Inc., Indpls., 1993-94, pres., 1994—. Mem. drafting com. Ind. Nonprofit Corp. Act 1991. Past dir., pres. Indpls. Chamber Orch.; past dir. Damar Homes, Inc.; bd. dirs., exec. com. Ind. Corp. Partnership; bd. dirs. United Way Ctrl. Ind. Mem. Ind. State Bar Assn., Indpls. C. of C. Methodist. Office: Lilly Endowment Inc 2801 N Meridian St PO Box 88068 Indianapolis IN 46208-0068

**ROBBINS, NANCY LOUISE See MANN, NANCY**

**ROBBINS, NANCY SLINKER,** volunteer; b. New Kensington, Pa., Jan. 28, 1923; d. Charles Morris and Nancy Grace (Moore) Slinker; m. James Bingham Murray, Aug. 1, 1946 (div. 1959); m. Daniel Harvey Robbins, Nov. 21, 1964; children: Nancy Caroline, Christina Chapman. BA, Westminster Coll., 1945; grad., U. Pitts., 1946. Cert. tchr., Pa. Tchr. Lower Burrell Sch., New Kensington, 1945-48; asst. buyer Gimbel's, Pitts., 1951-53, buyer, 1953-57, La Salle's, Toledo, 1957-61, Sibley's, Rochester, N.Y., 1961-66. Editor: Fan Fare, 1980-81. Pres. bd. Woman's Edn. and Indsl. Union, Rochester, 1973-76, Women's Coalition for Downtown, Rochester, 1982-84; pres. bd. Ronald McDonald House, Rochester, 1986-90, adminstr. grants program, 1996—2004; chmn. Pub. TV Auction, Rochester, 1980. Recipient Jefferson award Am. Inst. Pub. Svc., 1988, Forman Flair award for outstanding volunteerism, 1990, DeWitt Clinton award for pub. svc. Masons, 1989, Miracle Maker award Golisano Children's Hosp., 2005. Avocations: antiques, travel, cooking. Home: 35 Schoolhouse Ln Rochester NY 14618-3231 E-mail: nandan0035@aol.com.

**ROBBINS, NORMAN NELSON,** lawyer; b. Detroit, Sept. 27, 1919; s. Charles and Eva (Gold) R.; m. Pamela Anne Eldred, April 22, 1946; children: Susan, Aimee. LLB, JD, Wayne State U., 1943. Bar: Mich. 1943. Pvt. practice, Birmingham, Mich., 1943—. Chmn. Mich. Bd. for Marriage Counselors, 1971-75; lectr. Inst. Continuing Legal Edn. Editor Mich. Family Law Jour., 1974—; mem. editorial bd. Am. Jour. Family Law; co-editor: Michigan Family Law, 2 vols., 1988; contbr. 600 articles to legal publs. Chmn. Wayne County unit Am. Cancer Soc., Detroit, 1971-76, Mich. Dept. Vets. Trust Fund, 1977-78. Capt. USMCR, 1943-46, PTO. Recipient Gov.'s award State of Mich., Cert. of Appreciation, Gov. of Mich., Cert. of Recognition, Detroit Common Coun. award Mich. Assn. Marriage Counselors, Lifetime Achievement award Mich. Family Law Sect. Mem. ABA (mem. family law coun. 1993-95, sr. editor ABA Family Adv. 1991—), Mich. Bar Assn. (chmn. family law sect. 1974-75), Oakland County Bar Assn., Am. Acad. Matrimonial Lawyers (pres. Mich. chpt. 1982), Am. Legion (judge adv. Mich. dept. 1968-69, comdr. Detroit chpt. 1970-71).

**ROBBINS, OREM OLFORD,** insurance company executive; b. Mpls., Feb. 5, 1915; s. Douglas Ford and Grace (Rorem) R.; m. Annette Strand Scherer, May 17, 1992; children: Ford M., Ross S., Gail R. Tomei, Cynthia R. Rothbard. BBA with distinction, U. Minn., 1936; BS in Law, William Mitchell Coll. Law, 1946, JD, 1949. Comml. rep. NW Bell Telephone Co., Mpls., 1936-48; dep dir. U.S. Treas. Dept., Mpls., 1948-49; sales rep. Conn. Gen. Life Ins. Co., Mpls., 1949-56; founder, chmn. Security Life Ins. Co. Am., Mpls., 1956—. Bd. dirs., past pres. Family and Children's Svcs., Mpls., 1968—; bd. govs., past chmn. Meth. Hosp., 1960-90; past treas., bd. dirs. Goodwill/Easter Seals, St. Paul, 1958-68, 75-88; life trustee Hamline U., St. Paul, 1979—, chmn. bd. trustees, 1990-91. Col. U.S. Army, 1941-46. Decorated Legion of Merit; recipient Outstanding Achievement award U. Minn., 2001. Fellow Life Mgmt. Assn.; mem. Am. Soc. CLU (pres. Mpls. chpt. 1959), Health Underwriters Assn., Chartered Fin. Cons., Am. Legion, Skylight Club (Mpls.), Naples Yacht Club, Mpls. Club, Officer's Club, Masons. Republican. Methodist. Office: Security Life Ins Co Am 10901 Red Circle Dr Minnetonka MN 55343-9304 E-mail: oorobbins@securitylife.com

**ROBBINS, RAY C.,** retired manufacturing executive; b. Syracuse, NY, Sept. 15, 1920; s. Frederick and Mary Elizabeth (Field) R.; children: Sandra Robbins Jannetta, Ray Charles Jr., Eric L. With Lennox Internat. Inc. (formerly Lennox Co.), 1940-48; asst sales mgr. Lennox Industries Inc., Syracuse, 1948-52, gen. mgr. new factory and sales office, Toronto, Ont., Canada, 1952-67; dir. Lennox Can. and Timeplan Fin. Co. Ltd., 1953-65; pres. Lennox Can., 1965-69, chmn. bd., 1976-92; exec. v.p. Lennox Internat. Inc., 1969-70, pres., CEO, 1970-77, chmn. bd., chief exec. officer, 1977-80, chmn. bd., 1980-91, chmn. emeritus, 1991—. Bd. dirs. Lennox Internat., First Interstate of Iowa, Inc., Hawkeye Security Ins. Co., Des Moines, Fin. Security Group, Inc., Des Moines, Q-Dot, Garland, Tex.; pres., founder, bd. dirs. Exec. Inst., Inc., Dallas, 1983—; cons. Internat. Exec. Svc. Corp., 1992—; bd. adv., 1993-. Bd. dirs. Metro Toronto Big Bros., 1964-69, Queensway Gen. Hosp., 1957-69, Texx Found., 1979-81, Bus. Industry Polit. Action Com.; bd. govs., mem. exec. com Iowa Coll. Found., 1975-78; v.p., mem. exec. bd Mid-Iowa County Boy Scouts Am., 1972-78; mem. Pres.' Phys. Fitness Council, from 1979; exec. bd. Circle 10 council Boy Scouts Am. from 1979; mem. Dallas Citizens Council; bd. of govs. Nat. Women's Econ. Alliance Found.; bd. dirs. North Tex. Commn.; fellow Legacy for Pub. Opinion, 2001—. Served with AUS, 1942-45, PTO. Mem. ASHRAE (life), Am. Refrigeration Inst. (bd. dirs. 1973-74, 78, life from 1979, v.p. 1975-76, chmn. 1977), NAM (bd. dirs 1974-75, dir. at large 1976, dir. State of Iowa 1977-78, dir. State of Tex. 1979-92), Nat. Mgmt. Assn. (exec. adv. com. 1979-92), Gas Appliance Mfrs. Assn. (past bd. dirs.), Can. Gas Assn. (pres.), Can. Mfg. Assn. (chmn. Toronto dist.), U.S.C. of C. (Can.-U.S. sect.), Bus.-Industry Polit. Action Com. (bd. dirs. 1991). Clubs: Park Cen., Landmark Athletic, Cooper Fitness Ctr. (Dallas); Canyon Creek Country (Richardson, Tex.).

**ROBBINS, ROBERT B.,** lawyer; b. Canton, Ohio, Aug. 31, 1951; s. Nathan H. and Evelyn (Cohen) R.; m. Melinda Abbot Street, Oct. 18, 1981; children: Julia Bates, Katherine Melinda, Caroline Rachel, Eli Street. AB magna cum laude, Cornell U., 1972; JD cum laude, Harvard U., 1975. Bar: D.C. 1975. Ptnr. Shaw Pittman LLP, Washington, 1976—, also chmn. corp. securities group; (Shaw Pittman LLP merged with Pillsbury Winthrop LLP, 2005); ptnr., chmn., REITs & real estate capital markets group & co-head, corp. & securities practice Pillsbury Winthrop Shaw Pittman LLP, Washington,

2005—. Chmn. D.C. Bar Commn. on Broker-Dealer Regulation, 1985-90; co-chmn. Ann. Course Study on Pvt. Placements and Regulation D, Am. Law Inst.-ABA, 1992—. Mem. ABA, Nat. Assn. Corp. Dir., Nat. Assn. Real Estate Investment Trusts, D.C. Bar (steering com., sect. corp., fin. and securities law 1991-94, chmn. 1993-94), Phi Beta Kappa. Office: Pillsbury Winthrop Shaw Pittman LLP 2300 N St NW Washington DC 20037-1172 Office Phone: 202-663-8136. Office Fax: 202-663-8137. Business E-mail: robert.robbins@pillsburylaw.com.

**ROBBINS, ROBERT CLAYTON,** surgeon; b. Laurel, Miss., Nov. 20, 1957; MD, U. Miss., 1983. Cert. cardiothoracic surgery Am. Bd. Thoracic Surgery, gen. surgery Am. Bd. Surgery. Intern U. Miss. Med. Ctr., 1983—84, resident, 1984—88; fellow Stanford U., 1989—91, asst. prof. then assoc. prof., 1993—; dir. Inst. Cardiovasc. Medicine, 2004—. Mem.: Western Thoracic Surgical Assn., Am. Assn. Thoracic Surgery, Cardiothoracic Surgery Network. Office: Falk Cardiovasc Rsch Ctr 300 Pasteur Dr CVRB MC 5407 Stanford CA 94305 Office Phone: 650-725-3828.

**ROBBINS, ROBERT MARVIN,** accountant; b. Warren, Ohio, Aug. 2, 1924; s. Edward and May (Rubenson) R.; m. Phyllis Ann Dillon, Sept. 29, 1951; children: Michael C., Pat D., Robert J., Susan Jo Burkey. BSBA, Ohio State U., 1948; postgrad., NYU, 1972, 76, 79. CPA, Ohio. Sr. acct. Albert F. Turrell & Assocs. CPAs, Warren, Ohio, 1948-52; comptroller Harts Jewelry Stores, Ohio, 1952-54; pvt. practice Warren, 1954-59; mng. ptnr. Griffith & Robbins, CPAs, Warren, 1959-65; owner R.M. Robbins & Assocs., CPAs, Warren, 1966-82; pres., mgr. R.M. Robbins & Assocs., Inc., Warren, 1982-98; retired. Sec. and acctg. cons. Ohio-Ont. Clean Fuels, Inc., Warren, 1986-90; area owner, franchisee Red Barn Restaurants, Omaha, 1968-72. Treas. Planned Parenthood, Youngstown, Ohio, 1970s; asst. Sisters of Humility of Mary, Villa Maria, Pa., 1978-83. Sgt. U.S. Army armored div., 1943-45, ETO. Mem. Am. Inst. CPAs, (mem. tax div. subcoms.), ACUTE, Ohio Soc. CPAs, Rotary, Exchange Club (treas. Warren chpt. 1968-73), Squaw Creek Country Club (past bd. dirs.), Elks, Buckeye Club (Warren), Ohio State U. Pres. Club. Avocations: flying, golf, history of american revolution and civil war. Home: 376 Wainwood Dr SE Warren OH 44484-4650 E-mail: roberobbi3@aol.com.

**ROBBINS, STEPHEN J. M.,** lawyer; b. Seattle, Apr. 13, 1942; s. Robert Mads and Aneita Elberta (West) R.; m. Nina Winifred Tanner, Aug. 11, 1967; children: Sarah E.T., Alicia S.T. AB, UCLA, 1964; JD, Yale U., 1971. Bar: D.C. 1973, U.S. Dist. Ct. 1973, U.S. Ct. Appeals (D.C. cir.) 1973, U.S. Ct. Appeals (3d cir.) 1973, U.S. Dist. Ct. (ea. and no. dists.) Calif. 1982, U.S. Dist. Ct. (cen. dist.) Calif. 1983, Supreme Ct. of Republic of Palau, 1994. Pres. U.S. Nat. Student Assn., Washington, 1964-65; dir. scheduling McGovern for Pres., Washington, 1971-72; assoc. Steptoe & Johnson, Washington, 1972-75; chief counsel spl. inquiry on food prices, com. on nutrition and human needs U.S. Senate, Washington, 1975; v.p., gen. counsel Straight Arrow Pubs., San Francisco, 1975-77; dep. dist. atty. City and County of San Francisco, 1977-78; regional counsel U.S. SBA, San Francisco, 1978-80; spl. counsel Warner-Amex Cable Communications, Sacramento, 1981-82; ptnr. McDonough, Holland and Allen, Sacramento, 1982-84; v.p. Straight Arrow Pubs., N.Y.C., 1984-86; gen. legal counsel Govt. State of Koror, Rep. of Palau, Western Caroline Islands, 1994-95; pvt. practice law, 1986—. Adj. prof. govt. Calif. State U., Sacramento, 1999—. Staff sgt. U.S. Army, 1966-68. Mem. ABA (sect. urban, state and local govt. sect. real property, probate and trust law, sect. natural resources energy, environ. law, forum com. on affordable housing and cmty. devel.), D.C. Bar, State Bar of Calif., Urban Land Inst., Am. Hist. Assn., Supreme Ct. Hist. Soc., Acad. Polit. Sci., Chamber Music Soc. of Sacramento, Oreg. Shakespeare Festival, Shaw Island Hist. Soc. Democrat. Unitarian. Avocations: theater, art, hiking. Office: 2150 3rd Ave Sacramento CA 95818-3102

**ROBBINS, SUSAN PAULA,** social work educator; b. Bklyn., Aug. 15, 1948; d. Harold Jess and Rose (Bernstein) R. AA, Manhattan C.C., 1972; BA summa cum laude, Hamline U., 1974; MSW, U. Minn., 1976; PhD, Tulane U., 1979. Adj. instr. dept. sociology and social work Augsburg Coll., Mpls., 1975-76; part-time instr. women's studies program U. Minn., Mpls., 1976; rsch. and grant cons. Seminole Tribe of Fla., Hollywood, 1978-79, child and adolescent caseworker, program planning cons., 1979-80; coord. criminal justice/corrections program St. Mary's Dominican Coll., New Orleans, 1979-80; asst. prof. social work New Orleans Consortium, 1978-80, U. Houston, 1980-86, assoc. prof., 1986—, assoc. dean acad. affairs, 1998-2000. Cons. ABA Multi Door Program, Houston, Cmty. Svc. Option Program, Houston; mediator Dispute Resolution Ctrs., Houston, 1982—; trainer Tex. Dept. Protective Svcs. Tng. Inst., 1995—. Author (with others): Encyclopedia of Social Work, Social Workers' Desk Reference; contbr. articles and book chpts. to profl. jours. Women's Club of Mpls. fellow, 1975, Nat. Inst. of Mental Health fellow, 1976-78; recipient Nat. Faculty Excellence award Univ. Continuing Edn. Assn., 1998. Mem. NASW, Coun. on Social Work Edn., Social Welfare Action Alliance, Assn. for Cmty. Orgn. and Social Adminstrn., So. Sociol. Soc., Phi Kappa Phi (sec. Houston chpt. 1984—). Democrat. Jewish. Office: Univ Houston 4800 Calhoun Rd Houston TX 77204-4013 Office Phone: 713-743-8103. Business E-mail: srobbins@uh.edu.

**ROBBINS, THOMAS EUGENE,** writer; b. Blowing Rock, NC, 1936; m. Terrie Hemingway (div.); m. Alexa d'Avalon, 1995; 1 child, Fleetwood Starr. Student, Washington and Lee U., 1954-56, U. Wash., 1963; degree in social sci., Va. Commonwealth U., 1959. Former copy editor Richmond (Va.) Times-Dispatch, 1959—62, Seattle Post-Intelligencer, 1967—69; art critic Seattle Times, 1962—65. Author: Guy Anderson, 1965, Another Roadside Attraction, 1971, Even Cowgirls Get the Blues, 1976 (Best Am. Short Story 1977), Still Life with Woodpecker, 1980, Jitterbug Perfume, 1984, Skinny Legs and All, 1990, Half Asleep in Frog Pajamas, 1994, Fierce Invalids Home from Hot Climates, 2000, Villa Incognito, 2003, Wild Ducks Flying Backward, 2005. With USAF. Named one of 100 Best Writers of 20th Century, Writer's Digest. Office: PO Box 338 La Conner WA 98257-0338

**ROBBINS, THOMAS LANDAU,** researcher, editor; b. N.Y.C., Oct. 13, 1943; s. Manuel Lee and Elly (Landau) R. AB, Harvard U., 1965; MA, U. N.C., 1968, PhD in Sociology, 1973. Instr., asst. prof. Queens Coll., 1971-78; instr. Cen. Mich. U., 1982-83; NIMH postdoctoral trainee in sociology Yale U., New Haven, 1979-81; sr. rsch. assoc. Santa Barbara (Calif.) Ctr. for Humanistic Studies, 1990—. Author: Cults, Converts and Charisma, 1988; co-editor: In Gods We Trust, 1981, 2d edit., 1990, Cults, Culture and the Law, 1985, Church-State Relations, 1987, Millennium, Messiahs and Mayhem, 1997, Misunderstanding Cults, 2000, New Religious Movements in the 21st Century, 2000; assoc. editor Sociol. Analysis, 1984-90; editl. cons. Nova Religio, 1997—; contbr. articles to various publs. Mem. Soc. for the Sci. Study of Religion (exec. coun. 1988-91), Assn. for the Sociology Religion, (exec. coun. 1985-87), Am. Sociol. Assn., Soc. for the Study of Social Problems. Meher Baba. Home and Office: 427 4th St SW Apt F-1 Rochester MN 55902-3226 Personal E-mail: tomrobbins427@aol.com. *I am becoming concerned these days about threats to freedom of religion in the United States and Europe.*

**ROBBINS, TIM (TIMOTHY FRANCIS ROBBINS),** actor, film director; b. West Covina, Calif., Oct. 16, 1958; s. Gil Robbins; life ptnr. Susan Sarandon; children: John Henry, Miles 1 stepchild, Eva Maria. BA with honors, UCLA, 1981. Founder, artistic dir. The Actor's Gang, 1981—. Actor: (films) No Small Affair, 1984, Toy Soldiers, 1984, Fraternity Vacation, 1985, The Sure Thing, 1985, Howard the Duck, 1986, Top Gun, 1986, Five Corners, 1987, Bill Durham, 1988, Tapeheads, 1989, Eric The Viking, 1989, Miss Firecracker, 1989, Cadillac Man, 1990, Twister, 1990, Jacob's Ladder, 1990, Jungle Fever, 1991, The Player, 1992 (Best Actor award Cannes Film Festival 1992), Short Cuts, 1993, The Hudsucker Proxy, 1994, The Shawshank Redemption, 1994, Ready to Wear (Prêt-à-Porter), 1994, I.Q., 1994, Nothing to Lose, 1997, Arlington Road, 1999, Austin Powers: The Spy Who Shagged Me, 1999, Mission to Mars, 2000, High Fidelity, 2000, Antitrust, 2001, Human Nature, 2001, The Truth About Charlie, 2002, The Day My God Died (voice), 2003, Mystic River, 2003 (Golden Globe for best supporting actor in a drama, 2004, Screen Actors Guild Award for best supporting actor, 2004,

Acad. Award for best supporting actor in a drama, 2004), Code 46, 2004, Anchorman: The Legend of Ron Burgundy, 2004, War of the Worlds, 2005, The Secret Life of Words, 2005, Zathura, 2005; (TV movies) Quarterback Princess, 1983, Alice in Wonderland, 1985; (TV appearances) St. Elsewhere, 1982, Legmen, 1984, Hardcastle and McCormick, 1984, Hill Street Blues, 1984, Moonlighting, 1985, Amazing Stories, 1986, (voice) The Simpsons, 1999, Jack & Bobby, 2005; actor, dir., writer, composer: Bob Roberts, 1992; dir., writer, prodr.: Dead Man Walking, 1995 (Golden Globe nomination for best dir. of film 1996, Acad. Award nomination for best dir. 1996), The Cradle Will Rock, 1999; exec. prodr., The Typewriter, the Rifle, and the Movie Camera, 1994, The Spectre of Hope, 2000; dir. (plays) Ubu Roi (L.A. Weekly Dir. award), A Midsummer's Night Dream, Methusalem, the Eternal Bourgeois, The Good Woman of Setzuan (L.A. Drama Critics Circle nominee), and others, (TV series) Queen's Supreme, 2003; co-writer: (plays) Alagazam...After the Dog Wars, Violence: The Misadventures of Spike Spangle, Farmer, Carnage, a Comedy, Embedded, and others. Recipient Tribute to Ind. Vision Award, Sundance Film Festival, 1997. Office: ICM c/o Elaine Goldsmith Thomas 40 W 57th St New York NY 10019*

**ROBBINS, TONY (ANTHONY ROBBINS),** writer; b. Glendora, Calif., Feb. 29, 1960; m. Becky Robbins, 1985 (div. 2001); 3 children; m. Sage Bonnie Humphrey, Oct. 14, 2001; 1 child. Founder The Anthony Robbins Found. Author: (book) Awaken the Giant Within: How to Take Immediate Control of Your Mental, Emotional, Physical, and Financial Destiny, 1992, Giant Steps: Small Changes to Make a Big Difference, 1994, Unlimited Power: The New Science of Personal Achievement, 1997, (audio programs) Lessons in Mastery, 2002, Personal Power II, Get the Edge; actor: (films) Shallow Hal, 2001, (guest appearances): (TV series) Roseanne, 1997, The Sopranos, 2004. Achievements include invention of the neuro-linguistic programming based motivational technique "neuroassociative conditioning". Office: Anthony Robbins Companies 9888 Carroll Centre Rd San Diego CA 92126

**ROBBINS-WILF, MARCIA,** educational consultant; b. Newark, Mar. 22, 1949; d. Saul and Ruth (Fern) Robbins; 1 child, Orin. Student, Emerson Coll., 1967-69, Seton Hall U., 1969, Fairleigh Dickinson U., 1970; BA, George Washington U., 1971; MA, NYU, 1975; postgrad., St. Peter's Coll., Jersey City, 1979, Fordham U., 1980; MS, Yeshiva U., 1981, EdD, 1986; postgrad., Monmouth Coll., 1986. Cert. elem. tchr., N.Y., N.J., reading specialist, N.J., prin., supr., N.J., adminstr., supr., N.Y. Tchr. Sleepy Hollow Elem. Sch., Falls Church, Va., 1971-72, Yeshiva Konvitz, N.Y.C., 1972-73; intern Wee Folk Nursery Sch., Short Hills, NJ, 1978-81, dir. day camp, 1980-81, tchr., dir., owner, 1980-81; adj. prof. reading Seton Hall U., South Orange, NJ, 1987, Middlesex County Coll., Edison, NJ, 1987-88; asst. adj. prof. L.I. U., Bklyn., 1988, Pace U., N.Y.C., 1988—. Ednl. cons. Cranford High Sch., 1988; presenter numerous workshops; founding bd. dirs. Stern Coll. Women Yeshiva U., N.Y.C., 1987; adj. vis. lectr. Rutgers U., New Brunswick, N.J., 1988. Chairperson Jewish Book Festival, YM-YWHA, West Orange, N.J., 1986-87, mem. early childhood com., 1986—, bd. dirs., 1986—; vice chairperson dinner com. Nat. Leadership Conf. Christians and Jews, 1986; mem. Hadassah, Valerie Children's Fund, Women's League Conservative Judaism, City of Hope; assoc. bd. bus. and women's profl. divsn. United Jewish Appeal, 1979; vol. reader Goddard Riverside Day Care Ctr., N.Y.C., 1973; friend N.Y.C. Pub. Libr., 1980—; life friend Millburn (N.J.) Pub. Libr.; pres. Seton-Essex Reading Coun., 1991-94. Co-recipient Am. Heritage award, Essex County, 1985; recipient Award Appreciation City of Hope, 1984, Profl. Improvement awards Seton-Essex Reading Council, 1984-86, Cert. Attendance award Seton-Essex Reading Counci, 1987. Mem. N.Y. Acad. Scis. (life), N.J. Council Tchrs. English, Nat. Council Tchrs. English, Am. Ednl. Research Assn., Coll. Reading Assn. (life), Assn. Supervision and Curriculum Devel., N.Y. State Reading Assn. (council Manhattan), N.J. Reading Assn. (council Seton-Essex), Internat. Reading Assn., Nat. Assn. for Edn. of Young Children (life N.J. chpt., Kenyon group), Nat. Council Jewish Women (vice chairperson membership com. evening br. N.Y. sect. 1974-75), George Washington U. Alumni Club, Emerson Coll. Alumni Club, NYU Alumni Club, Phi Delta Kappa (life), Kappa Gamma Chi (historian). Clubs: Greenbrook Country (Caldwell, N.J.); George Washington Univ. Avocations: reading, theater. Home: 242 Hartshorn Dr Short Hills NJ 07078-1914 E-mail: dr.mrw349@aol.com.

**ROBBOY, STANLEY J.,** pathologist, educator; s. John and Sarah (Shapiro) R.; m. Anita Wyzanski, July 21, 1968 (div. 1981); children: Elizabeth, Caroline; m. Marion Meyer, June 14, 1990. Student, U. Mich., 1958-61, MD, 1965. Diplomate Am. Bd. Pathology, Am. Bd. Med. Mgmt. Intern Mt. Sinai Hosp, Cleve., 1965-66; resident to chief in pathology Mass. Gen. Hosp., 1966-70, asst. in pathology, 1972-73, asst. pathologist, 1973-76, assoc. pathologist, 1976-84; resident in pathology Boston Hosp. for Women, 1970; instr. Tufts Med. Sch., 1968-69; asst. prof. pathology Harvard Med. Sch., Boston, 1972-76, assoc. prof., 1976-84; prof. pathology U. Medicine and Dentistry N.J.-N.J. Med. Sch., Newark, 1984—92, chmn. dept., 1984-89, prof. ob-gyn, 1990—92, pathologist-in-chief, 1984-89, dir. faculty practice service, 1985-89; prof., vice chmn. dept. pathology Duke U., 1992—. Cons. pathologist St. Joseph Hosp., Paterson, N.J., 1985—92, St. Barnabas Hosp., Livingston, N.J., 1985—92, Beth Israel Hosp., Newark, 1985—92, VA Med. Ctr., Durham, 1992-, Durham Reg. Hosp., 2003-, Raleigh Com. Hosp., 2003-; pathologist (DES) Registry Rsch. Transplacental Hormonal Carcinogenesis (formerly Clear-Cell Adenocarcinoma Registry), 1972-83; pathologist, prin. investigator Nat. Collaborative Diethylstilbestrol project, 1974-82; vis. scientist New Eng. Primate Ctr., 1973-84; vis. prof. U. Shiraz Med. Sch., Iran, 1976; commr. N.J. Commn. on Cancer Research, 1987-92; sr. advisor East Asia Cons. Group, Boston, Los Angeles and Tokyo, 1984-85; reference panel for diagnostic and therapeutic tech. AMA, 1992-99; mem. nat. med. com. Planned Parenthood Fedn. Am., 1990-93, vice chmn. com. on oncology, 1993; mem. DES steering com. Nat. Cancer Inst., 1995—; mem. exec. editl. bd. ArchPathhab Med, 2005-; bd. dir. Pamet Sys. Inc. Mem. editorial bd. Human Pathology, 1980-90, Cervix and the Low Female Genital Tract, 1983-94, Internat. Jour. Gynecologic Pathology, 1985-; editor: Informatics in Pathology, 1985-88, Pathology Rsch. and Practice, 1990-, Gynecologic Oncology, 1997-2004, InsSight, 1998-; sect. editor Functional Biomarkers in Disease, 2005-; contbr. articles to profl. jours. Trustee Am. Pathology Found., 1984—86; NJ commn. Cancer Rsch., 1987—92; co-pres. Chapel Hill Kehillah, 2005—. Maj. U.S. Army, 1970—72. Recipient Jr. Faculty award Am. Cancer Soc., 1972-75, Found. prize Am. Coll. Ob-Gyn, 1975; Pardee fellow U. Mich., 1961, Lederle Lab. fellow, 1962, Eliza Howell fellow, 1964, Ford Found. fellow, 1964-65; clin. fellow Am. Cancer Soc., 1967-68. Fellow Am. Soc. Clin. Pathologists (chmn. pathology telecommunications network com. 1983, task force on computers 1980-83, council on med. informatics 1983-84, planning and scope com. 1983-84, co-chmn. pathology communication network 1983-87, coun. anatomic pathology, 1995-2001, future directions, 1995-98), Coll. Am. Pathologists (alt. Mass. del. to house dels. 1981-84, co-chmn. pathology communication network 1983-85, alt. N.J. del. to house dels. 1985-92, exec. com. and advisor nomenclature and classification of disease 1975-80, editorial bd. Systematized Nomenclature Medicine 1976-80, gov. 1999-2005, mem. reimbursement com., 1992-94, profl. and econ. affairs com., 1995-97, outcomes com., 1999-2000, vice chmn. coun. on pub. affairs 2000-2004, coun. of govt. prof. affairs, 2000-2004, credentials com., 2000-2004, spokesperson, 2001—), performance measurement com., 2000, nat. meeting planning com. 2003—, vice chmn. oversight com., 2006-); Soc. Gynecologic Oncologists Assocs.; mem. Arthur Purdy Stout Soc. Surg. Pathology (membership com. 1980-86, treas. 1993-2001, pres.-elect 2001-03, pres. 2003-2005), Internat. Acad. Cytology, Internat. Acad. Pathology (mem. com. 1979-83), Internat. Soc. Gynecologic Pathologists (chmn. membership com. 1982-84), Mass. Soc. Pathology (3d party relations 1978-84, chmn. computer com. 1981-84), N.C. Med. Soc., N.C. Soc. Pathology, N.J. Med. Soc., N.J. Soc. Pathology (edn. and profl. relations Coms. 1984-92, exec. com. 1985-92), Chapel Hill Kehillah (co-pres. 2004—). Jewish. Office: Duke U Med Ctr PO Box 3712 Durham NC 27710-0001 Office Phone: 919-684-3656. Business E-mail: stanley.robboy@duke.edu.

**ROBE, THURLOW RICHARD,** engineering educator, dean; b. Petersburg, Ohio, Jan. 25, 1934; s. Thrulow Scott and Mary Alice (McKibben) R.; m. Eleanora C. Komyati, Aug. 27, 1955; children: Julia, Kevin, Stephen, Edward. BSC.E., Ohio U., 1955, MS in Mech. Engring., 1962; PhD in Applied Mechanics, Stanford U., 1966. Engr. Gen. Electric Co., Niles, Ohio. Cleve., Erie, Pa., Evendale,Ohio, 1954-60; instr. Ohio U., Athens, 1960-63; asst. prof to prof., assoc. dean U. Ky., Lexington, 1965-80; dean Ohio U., Athens, 1980-96, Cruse W. Moss prof. Engring. Edn., 1992-96, dir. Innovation Ctr. Authority, 1983-96; dean emeritus, Moss prof. emeritus Russ Coll. Engring. and Tech., Ohio U., Athens, 1996—; pres., chmn. bd. Q.E.D. Assocs., Inc., Lexington, 1975-83. Trustee Engring. Found. Ohio, 1988-94; bd. govs. Edison Materials Tech. Ctr., 1987-96; dir. T. Richard and Eleanora K. Robe Leadership Inst., Ohio U., 1997-2005; mem. adv. bd. Robe Leadership Inst., 2005—; liaison engring. accreditation commn. Accreditation Bd. Engring. and Tech., 1989-91; mem. Russ Prize Selection Com., NAE, 2000—. Contbr. articles to profl. jours.; patentee trailer hitch. Bd. dirs. Athens County Cmty. Redevel. Corp., 1980-86; treas. South Lexington Little League, 1976-80; vice chmn. Thoroughbred dist., Boy Scouts Am., 1975-77; pres. Tates Creek H.S. PTA, Lexington, 1975-76; bd. dirs. U. Ky. Athletics Assn., 1975-80; trustee Ohio U. Found., 1998—. Maj. USAF Res., 1955-85. Recipient Alumni medal of merit Ohio U., 1993; named Am. Coun. on Edn. Adminstrn. fellow, 1970-71, Ohio U. Alumnus of Yr., 1996, inductee Acad. Disting. Grads., Russ Coll. Engring. & Tech., 2001. Mem. ASME, NSPE (profl. engring. in edn. exec. bd., ctrl. region vice-chmn. 1987-89), Am. Soc. Engring. Edn. (Outstanding Contbn. in Rsch. award 1966), Athens Reading Club, Athens Symposiarchs, Rotary, Sigma Xi, Tau Beta Pi, Omicron Delta Kappa, Alpha Lambda Delta Office: Russ Coll Engring & Tech Ohio U Athens OH 45701 Business E-mail: robe@ohio.edu.

**ROBECK, MILDRED COEN,** education educator, writer; b. Walum, N.D., July 29, 1915; d. Archie Blain and Mary Henrietta (Hoffman) Coen; m. Martin Julius Robeck, Jr., June 2, 1936; children: Martin Jay Robeck, Donna Jayne Robeck Thompson, Bruce Wayne Robeck. BS, U. Wash., 1950, MEd, 1954, PhD, 1958. Ordnance foreman Sherman Williams, U.S. Navy, Bremerton, Wash., 1942-45; demonstration tchr. Seattle Pub. Schs., 1946-57; reading clinic dir. U. Calif., Santa Barbara, 1957-64; rsch. cons. State Dept. Edn., Sacramento, Calif., 1964-67; prof., head early childhood edn. U. Oreg., Eugene, Oreg., 1967-86; vis. scholar West Australia Inst. Tech., Perth, 1985; v.p. acad. affairs U. Santa Barbara, Calif., 1987-95. Vis. prof. Victoria Coll., B.C. Can., summer 1958, Dalhousie U., Halifax, 1964; trainer evaluator U.S. Office of Edn. Head Start, Follow Thru, 1967-72; cons., evaluator Native Am. Edn. Programs, Sioux, Navajo, Umatilla, 1967-86; cons. on gifted Oreg. Task Force on Talented and Gifted, Salem, 1974-76; evaluator Early Childhood Edn., Bi-Ling. program, Petroleum and Minerology, Dhahran, Saudi Arabia, 1985. Author: Materials KELP: Kgn. Evaluation Learning Pot, 1967, Infants and Children, 1978, Psychology of Reading, 1990, Oscar: His Story, 1997, 2d edit., 2000; contbr. articles to profl. jours. Evaluation cons. Rosenburg Found. Project, Santa Barbara, 1966-67; faculty advisor Pi Lambda Theta, Eugene, Oreg, 1969-74; guest columnist Oreg. Assn. Gifted and Talented, Salem, Oreg., 1979-81; editorial review bd. ERQ, U.S. Calif., L.A., 1981-91. Recipient Nat. Dairy award 4-H Clubs, Wis., 1934, NYA and U. Wis. scholar, Madison, 1934-35, Faculty Rsch. grant U. Calif., Santa Barbara, 1958-64, NDEA fellow Retraining U.S. Office Edn., U. Oreg., 1967-70. Mem. APA, Am. Ednl. Rsch. Assn., Internat. Reading Assn., Phi Beta Kappa, Pi Lambda Theta. Democrat. Avocations: dyslexia research, historical research, writing. Home: 95999 Highway 101 S Yachats OR 97498-9714 E-mail: mrobeck@casco.net.

**ROBEK, MARY FRANCES,** business education educator; b. Superior, Wis., Jan. 30, 1927; d. Stephen and Mary (Hervert) R. BE, U. Wis., 1948; MA, Northwestern U., 1951; MBA, U. Mich., 1962, PhD, 1967. Tchr. Bergland (Mich.) High Sch., 1948, Tony (Wis.) High Sch., 1948-50, Sch. Vocat. and Adult Edn., Superior, 1950-58; prof. bus. and office tech. Ea. Mich. U., Ypsilanti, 1958-93; instr. Jazyckova Gymnasium, Banská, Stiavnica, Slovakia, 1994. Author: Information and Records Management, 1995. Assn. of Records Mgrs. and Adminstrs. fellow, 1992. Mem. Assn. Records Mgrs. and Adminstrs. (life), Inst. Cert. Mgrs. (pres. 1980-81, Emmett Leahy award 2000), Cath. Daus. Am., Delta Pi Epsilon, Delta Kappa Gamma, Pi Lambda Theta. Republican. Roman Catholic. Home: 515 Clough Ave Superior WI 54880 Office Phone: 715-394-5400. Personal E-mail: RobekMary@aol.com. *Opportunity to do creative and innovative things without infringing on the rights of others is limited only by priorities set considering people and technology.*

**ROBEL, LAUREN,** dean, law educator; b. Dec. 1953; BA, Auburn U., 1978; JD, Ind. U., 1983, postgrad., 1985. Bar: US Supreme Ct., Ind., Ill. Law clk. to Hon. Jesse Eschbach, U.S. Ct. Appeals (7th cir.), 1983—85; dean, Val Nolan prof. law Ind. U. Sch. Law, Bloomington, Vis. faculty U. Pantheion-Assas, Paris; reporter rules com. U.S. Dist. Ct. (so. dist.) Ind.; mem. rules com. Ind. Supreme Ct. Author: Les États des Noirs: Federalisme et question raciale aux États-unis, 2000, Federal Courts: Cases and Materials on Judicial Federalism and The Lawyering Process, 2005; contbr. articles to profl. jours. Mem.: Ind. State Bar Women (Law Recognition award), Ind. Bar Found. (Pro Bono Publico award), Order of Coif. Office: Ind Univ Sch Law 211 S Indiana Ave Bloomington IN 47405 Office Phone: 812-855-8885. Business E-mail: lrobel@indiana.edu.

**ROBELOT, JANE,** anchor; b. Greenville, S.C., Oct. 9, 1960; married; 1 child. BA in Econs., Clemson U. News and sports dir., reporter WCCP-AM Radio, Clemson, SC; anchor, reporter WSPA-TV, CBS affiliate, Spartanburg, SC, 1983—90; gen. assignment reporter WCAU-TV, Phila., 1990—92, co-anchor 6:00 PM news, 1991—92, co-anchor 11:00 PM news, 1992—95; co-anchor CBS Morning News, N.Y.C., 1995; news reader This Morning CBS News, N.Y.C., 1995-96, co-anchor This Morning, 1996—99, co-anchor CBS Atlanta News, 1999—. Office: WGCL TV 46 Meredith Corp 425 14th St NW Atlanta GA 30318-7965

**ROBENALT, JOHN ALTON,** lawyer; b. Ottawa, Ohio, May 2, 1922; s. Alton Ray and Kathryn (Straman) R.; m. Margaret Morgan Durbin, Aug. 25, 1951 (dec. July 1990); children: John F., William A., James D., Robert M., Mary K., Margaret E., Thomas D.; m. Nancy Leech Kidder, Sept. 21, 1991. BA, Miami U., 1943; LL.B., JD, Ohio State U., 1948. Bar: Ohio 1948. Asst. atty. gen., Ohio, 1949-51; practice in Lima, Ohio, 1951-59; acting municipal judge Lima Municipal Ct., 1955-59; partner Robenalt, Daley, Balyeat & Balyeat, 1959-82; ptnr. Robenalt, Kendall & Robenalt, 1983-85, Robenalt, Kendall, Rodabaugh & Staley, 1985-92, Robenalt & Robenalt, 1993—. Chmn. Lima March of Dimes, 1957-58; Bd. dirs. Lima Civic Center, pres., 1971-72; bd. dirs. Lima Rotating Fund; trustee Allen County Regional Transit Authority, Lima, pres., 1975—. Served with AUS, 1943-45. Mem. ABA, Ohio Bar Assn., Allen County Bar Assn. (pres. 1969-70), Am. Legion, Lima Automobile Club (bd. dirs., pres. 1975-82), Shawnee Country Club (pres. 1968-70), Ohio Automobile Club (trustee 1982-2002, 1995-97), Elks (bd. trustees 1991-97), Rotary, Delta Tau Delta, Phi Delta Phi. Home: 1755 Shawnee Rd Apt 700 Lima OH 45805-3857 Office Phone: 419-229-0054. Personal E-mail: jarobenalt@wcoil.com.

**ROBERDS, WYATT KAYNE,** music educator; b. West Plains, Mo., Mar. 17, 1971; s. William Keith and Cheryl Diane Roberds; m. Theresa Suzanne Corona, Apr. 19, 1996; 1 child, Samson Kayne. AA in Music Edn., Lewis and Clark C.C., 1992; BA in Music Edn., So. Ill. U., 1994. Dir. band and music Brussels (Ill.) Ctrl. Unified Sch. Dist., 1994—95; dir. mid. sch. band Granite City Ctrl. Unified Sch. Dist., 1995—2002, dir. high sch. band, 2002—. Mem.: Madison County Band Dirs. Assn., Music Educators Nat. Conf., Ill. Music Educators Assn. Avocations: saxophone, piano, guitar. Office: Granite City High Sch 3101 Madison Ave Granite City IL 62040 E-mail: wyatt.roberds@gcsd9.net.

**ROBERSON, BRUCE HEERDT,** lawyer; b. Wilmington, Del., Mar. 7, 1941; s. A. L. and Virginia Amelia (Heerdt) R.; m. Mary E. Abrams; children: Cheryl Anne, David B., Douglas M. BS cum laude, Washington and Lee U.,

1963; JD, U. Va., 1966. Bar: Del. 1966, Fla. 1969. Assoc. Morris, Nichols, Arsht & Tunnell, Wilmington, 1966-67; assoc. Holland & Knight, Tampa, Fla., 1969-74; ptnr. Holland & Knight LLP, Tampa, Fla., 1975—. Contbg. editor Pratt's Banking and Lending Institution Forms, 1992—. Capt. U.S. Army, 1967-69 Decorated Bronze Star. Fellow Am. Bar Found. (life), Fla. Bar Found.(life), Am. Coll. Consumer Fin. Svcs. Lawyers; mem. ABA (bus. law sect. com. on consumer fin. svcs. 1976—, banking law com. 1980—, savs. instns. com. 1989-96), Am. Judicature Soc., Fla. Bar Assn. (corp. banking and bus. law sect. exec. coun. 1978-86, chmn. banking law com. 1982-84), Del. Bar Assn., Hillsborough County Bar Assn., Univ. Club, Tampa Yacht and Country Club, Lambda Chi Alpha. Republican. Methodist. Office: Holland & Knight LLP PO Box 1288 Tampa FL 33601-1288 Office Phone: 813-227-8500. Business E-mail: bruce.roberson@hklaw.com.

**ROBERSON, DORIS JEAN HEROLD,** retired social worker; b. N.Y.C., Oct. 15, 1924; d. Albert and Rosalind (Lowenstein) Herold; m. Lloyd Willis Roberson, Aug. 31, 1949; children: Lynn, Patricia, Katherine, Irene. BA cum laude, Mount Holyoke Coll., 1945; MSW, Fordham U., 1947. lic. master social worker, N.Y. Social worker Children's Aid Soc., N.Y.C., 1947-52, Yonkers (N.Y.) Pub. Schs., 1969-89; ret., 1989. Mem. NASW, Acad. Cert. Social Workers, N.Y. State Sch. Social Workers Assn., Phi Beta Kappa. Home: 145 Hoover Rd Yonkers NY 10710-3408

**ROBERSON, JAMES O.,** foundation executive; m. Rita Quinn; children: Melanie Merrill, Sharyl Shatz, James Jr., Trisha, Joel. AB in Journalism, Baylor U., 1956; student Indsl. Devel. Inst., U. Okla.; student Inst. Orgnl. Mgmt., U. Houston. Cert. econ. developer. Dir. econ. devel. West Tex. C. of C., Abilene, 1956-59; area devel. mgr. Mo.-Kans.-Tex. R.R., 1959-63; exec. dir. Albuquerque Indsl. Devel. Svc., 1963-65; dir. N.Mex. Dept. Devel., Santa Fe, 1965-69; mgr. Forward Metro Denver, 1969-72; dir. R.I. Dept. Econ. Devel., Providence, 1972-77; v.p., dir. new bus. devel. Howard Rsch. and Devel. Corp. subs. Rouse Co., Columbia, Md., 1977-79; sec. Md. Dept. Econ. and Community Devel., Annapolis, 1979-83; pres. Louisville C. of C., 1983-88; pres., CEO Rsch. Triangle Found. N.C., 1988—. Chmn. bd. dirs. Charlotte br. Fed. Res. Bank Richmond; cons., speaker in field. Editor West Tex. Today mag., 1956-59. Trustee, vice chmn. Wake Tech. C.C.; bd. dirs. N.C. Biotech. Ctr. Fellow Am. Econ. Devel. Coun. (past chmn.); mem. Indsl. Devel. Rsch. Coun., Nat. Assn. State Devel. Agys. (past pres.), Assn. Univ. Related Rsch. Parks (pres.).

**ROBERSON, ROBERT S.,** investment company executive; b. Mt. Kisco, NY, 1942; m. Barbara Drane, 1967; children: Elizabeth de V., Merritt B., Barbara D. BS, NYU, 1964; MBA, Coll. William and Mary, 1973. Various positions in fin. and bldg. industries, 1964—67; mem. N.Y. Produce Exchange, 1965—66; with Weaver Bros., Inc., Newport News, Va., 1967—, now pres., dir. Former dir. Peninsula unit Am. Cancer Soc., Newport News; former dir. Heritage Coun. Girl Scouts U.S.A., Hampton; former trustee Newport News Pub. Libr., former trustee Va. Living Mus., Newport News; former trustee, chmn. com. on devel. Hampton Roads Acad., Newport News; former mem. bd. visitors to George Washington's Mt. Vernon Nat. Shrine; hon. dep. chief NYC Fire Dept.; trustee, pres., chief curator Golf Mus., Newport News; mem., chmn. Newport News Arts Commn.; trustee, pres. Va. War Mus. Found., Newport News; former mem. bd. visitors, mem. exec. com., chmn. com. on devel. and alumni affairs Coll. William and Mary, Williamsburg, Va.; trustee, vice chmn. N.Y. Geneal. and Biog. Soc., NYC; former mem. bd. visitors, mem. exec. com. Richard Bland Coll., Petersburg, Va. Decorated officer Order of St. John (England). Mem. Newcomen Soc. U.S., Hon. Fire Officers Assn., U.S. Golf Assn. (former nat. com. mem. mus. and libr.), Gen. Soc. Colonial Wars, St. Nicholas Soc. City N.Y., Colonial Order Acorn, Sovereign Mil. Order Temple of Jerusalem (knight comdr.), Squadron A, Pilgrims U.S./U.K., Union Club, The Brook, Church Club (N.Y.C.), Southampton Club (N.Y.), Farmville Country Club (Charlottesville, Va.), Cypher Soc. of William and Mary (exec. mem.), James River Country Club, Hampton Roads German Club (past pres.), Hampton Roads Assembly, The Hundred Club (Newport News, Va.), N.Y. Yacht Club, Fishers Island Yacht Club (N.Y.), Rotary Internat. (Paul Harris fellow), Blue Key, Delta Sigma Pi. Republican. Episcopalian. Home: PO Box 3 Williamsburg VA 23187-0003

**ROBERT, KALB GORDON,** neuroscientist, educator, neurologist; b. Bronx, N.Y., Nov. 4, 1956; s. Philip and Alma Kalb; m. Marianne Bernstein, June 17, 1984; children: Jacob Aaron Kalb, Benjamin Gordon Kalb. BA, Wesleyan U., Middletown, Conn., 1978; MD, Cornell U., N.Y.C. 1982. Diplomate Am. Bd. Psychiatry and Neurology, 1988. Chief resident Yale U. Sch. Medicine, New Haven, 1986, asst. prof. neurology, 1990—95, assoc. prof. of neurology, 1995—2003; assoc. prof. U. Pa., Phila., 2003—06. rsch. scientist, 2003—, assoc. prof., 2006—. Contbr. scientific papers. Named Attending of Yr. for Tchng. Dedication, Yale U. Sch. Medicine, 1992, 1997, 2000; recipient Upjohn Achievement award for Acad. Excellance, Cornell U. Sch. Medicine, 1982, Achievement award, NASA, 2001; David Barr Rsch. fellow, Cornell U. Sch. Medicine, 1980. Home: 401 S 3rd St Philadelphia PA 19147 Office: Chop/Arc #814 3615 Civic Center Blvd Philadelphia PA 19104 Office Phone: 215-590-0691. Office Fax: 267-426-5134. Business E-mail: kalb@email.chop.edu.

**ROBERT, STEPHEN,** academic administrator; b. Haverhill, Mass., June 13, 1940; s. Samuel R.; m. Catherine Price; children: Tracey Alexandra, Elisabeth Amory. AB with honors, Brown U., 1962; postgrad., London Sch. Econs., 1962-63, Columbia Bus. Sch., 1963-65. Co-chmn., CEO Faulkner Dawkins and Sullivan, 1965-67; v.p. Oppenheimer Funds, N.Y.C., 1968-76, chief portfolio mgr., 1969-76; gen. ptnr. Oppenheimer & Co., Inc., N.Y.C., 1970-83, dir. research, 1976 78, pres., 1979-83, chmn., 1983-97; chancellor Brown U., Providence. Dir. NacRe Corp. Bd. dirs., chmn. fin. com. Wiltwyck Sch., 1968-78; bd. dirs. Joffrey Ballet, 1981—; trustee The Dalton Sch., 1984—, Brown U., 1984—. Mem.: Harmonie (N.Y.C.). Office: Brown Univ Presidents Office Box 1860 Providence RI 02912-1860 Office Phone: 401-863-2234.*

**ROBERTS, ALAN SILVERMAN,** orthopedic surgeon; b. Apr. 20, 1939; s. Joseph William and Fannie (Margolies) S.; children: Michael Eric, Daniel Ian. BA, Conn. Wesleyan U., 1960; MD, Jefferson Med. Coll., 1966. Rotating intern Lankenau Hosp., Phila., 1966—67; resident in orthop. Tulane U. Med. Coll., 1967—71; pvt. practice specializing in orthop. and hand surgery L.A., 1971—. Mem. clin. faculty UCLA Med. Coll., 1971-76. Contbr. articles to profl. jours. With AUS, 1961. Riordan Hand fellow, 1969, Boyes Hand fellow, 1971. Mem. AMA, ACS, Am. Acad. Orthop. Surgeons, Calif. Med. Assn., L.A. County Med. Assn., We. Orthop. Assn., Riordan Hand Soc. Republican. Jewish. Office Phone: 310-276-7748. Personal E-mail: arobertsmd@earthlink.net.

**ROBERTS, ALBERT DEE,** internist; b. Ft. Worth, Mar. 7, 1930; s. Albert D. and Irene Burnett (Lewis) R.; m. Diane Truett, Dec. 22, 1952; children: Truett, Hillary. BS, So. Meth. U., 1951; MD, U. Tex. Southwestern, Dallas, 1954. Diplomate Am. Bd. Internal Medicine, Am. Bd. Nephrology. Pvt. practice, Dallas, 1960-75, 88-91; assoc. dean, prof. medicine U. Tex. Southwestern, 1975-88, prof. medicine, 1991—, Hartman prof. medicine, 1995—2004, clin. prof. medicine, 2005—. Mem. ACP (master, gov. 1977-81, regent 1981-87, vice chair 1986-87), AMA, Am. Soc. Nephrology, Internat. Soc. Nephrology, Tex. Med Assn., Dallas County Med. Assn. Avocations: reading, music, tennis, travel. Office Phone: 214-648-7868.

**ROBERTS, ANNE MARIE GABRIELLE,** chemistry educator; b. Kingston, Pa., Apr. 2, 1951; d. Samuel Louis and Jennie Ida (Lunetta) Luzier; m. Curtis Wesley Roberts, July 8, 1978 (dec. Jan. 25, 2005). BA in Chemistry, summa cum laude, Wilkes Coll., Wilkes-Barre, Pa., 1972, MS in Chemistry Edn., 1975. Cert. tchr. Chemistry tchr. Pittston Area Sr. HS, Yatesville, Pa., 1972—. Head sci. dept., coord. greenhouse tomato genetics project Pittston Area Sr. HS, 1997—; coach Sci. Olympiad, 1998—, tchr. mentor, 2002—; Sunday sch. tchr. Christian Missionary Alliance Ch. and Grace Bible Ch.,

West Pittston and Wilkes-Barre, Pa., 1978—96, daily vacation bible sch. tchr., 1988—96. Recipient State Senatorial citation for tchg. excellence, award, Am. Chem. Soc., 1995, Outstanding Sci. Tchr. award, U. of Scis. in Phila., 1999, Gerard Musto Tchr. of Yr. award, Nat. Honor Soc., 2002. Mem.: Am. Fedn. Tchrs. Avocations: interior design, reading, gardening, theater. Office: Pittston Area Sch Dist 5 Stout St Yatesville PA 18640 Office Phone: 570-654-3541. E-mail: amroberts@adelphia.net.

**ROBERTS, BARRY LESTER,** biologist, educator; b. Bexley, Kent, England, May 2, 1942; s. William Percival and Mary Martha Roberts; m. Gloria Evelyn Meredith, Sept. 17, 1993; children: Bryn Daniel Meredith, Christopher Colin Meredith; m. Elizabeth Mavis Stock, July 16, 1969 (div. Nov. 27, 1992); 1 child, Nicola. BA, U. Cambridge, England, 1964, MA, PhD, U. Cambridge, England, 1967. Rsch. scientist Marine Biol. Assn., Plymouth, England, 1967—84; prof. gen. zoology U. Amsterdam, 1984—93; prof. zoology and comparative anatomy Trinity Coll., Dublin, 1993—2003; rsch. prof. Chgo. Med. Sch., Rosalind Franklin U. Medicine and Sci., North Chicago, Ill., 2003—. Vis. prof. U. Groningen, Netherlands, 1981. Co-author (with W.J.A.J. Smeets and R. Nieuwenhuys): (research textbook) The Central Nervous System of Cartilaginous Fishes; co-editor (with A. Roberts): Neural Origin of Rhythmic Movements; contbr. articles to profl. jours. Mem. coun. Dublin Zoo. Fellow, Trinity Coll., Dublin, Ireland, 1996—; scholar, U. Cambridge, 1961—67. Mem.: Soc. Exptl. Biology (mem. coun. 1980—83), Physiol. Soc., Soc. Neurosci. Avocation: gardening. Home: 153 Washington Road Lake Forest IL 60045 Office: Chicago Medical School 3333 Green Bay Road North Chicago IL 60064 Office Phone: 847-578-8664. Office Fax: 847-578-3268. E-mail: barry.roberts@rosalindfranklin.edu.

**ROBERTS, BILL GLEN,** retired protective services official; b. Deport, Tex., June 2, 1938; s. Samuel Westbrook and Ann Lee (Rhodes) R.; m. Ramona Ryall, June 1, 1963 (dec. Nov. 1988); 1 child, Renee Ann; m. Johana R. Caines, Oct. 14, 2000. Student, So. Meth. U., 1968, North Tex. State U., 1974; grad. paramedic course, U. Tex. Southwestern Med. Sch., 1974; grad. Exec. Program for Fire Service, Tex. A&M U., 1978; AAS, El Centro Jr. Coll., Dallas, 1980; grad. exec. fire officer program, Nat. Fire Acad., 1989. With Dallas Fire Dept., 1958-82, lt., 1964-67, capt., 1967-71, div. fire chief, 1971-79, asst. fire chief, 1979-83; fire chief Austin (Tex.) Fire Dept., 1983-94. Tech. bd. dirs. Found. Fire Safety, Washington, 1982-85; adj. faculty Nat. Fire Acad., 1981-86; aft. State Life of Indpls., Dallas, 1962; owner Personnel Testing Lab., Dallas, 1963; real estate salesman Dale Copus Realtor, Dallas, 1963-66; salesman intercommunications equipment Chandler Sound, Dallas, 1966-67; field engr. IBM Corp., Dallas, 1968; cons. U. Tenn., 1974, Ga. Inst. Tech., 1974, Tex. Dept. Health Resources, 1973-78, Rand Corp., Washington, Mission Rsch., Santa Barbara, Calif., Macro Author: EMS Dallas, 1978; (with others) Anesthesia for Surgery Trauma, 1976, EMS Measures to Improve Care, 1980; contbr. articles to periodicals. Com. chmn. Dallas Jaycees, 1962-65; mem. task force Am. Heart Assn., Austin, 1973-83; bd. dirs. Brackenridge Hosp., 1989, Rehab. Hosp. Austin, 1992-94, Austin Police Pensions Bd., 1989, Capital Area coun. Boy Scouts Am., 1989-92. Recipient John Stemmons Service award Dallas Fire Dept., 1979; Internat. Assn. Fire Chiefs scholar, 1967. Mem. Internat. Assn. Fire Chiefs, Am. Heart Assn., North Tex. Coun. of Govts. (regional emergency svc. adv. coun. 1973-79), Found. Fire Safety (tech. bd. dirs. 1982-85), Tex. Assn. Realtors, Rotary. Methodist. Home: 192 Hunter's Ridge Rd Canton NC 28716 Office Phone: 828-648-4345. E-mail: bglenrob@aol.com.

**ROBERTS, BRIAN,** professional baseball player; b. Durham, NC, Oct. 9, 1977; Attended, Univ. S.C. Second baseman Baltimore Orioles, 2001—. Named to MLB All-Star Game, 2005.

**ROBERTS, BRIAN L.,** communications executive; b. Phila., June 28, 1959; s. Ralph J. and Suzanne F. Roberts; m. Aileen Kennedy, Dec. 28, 1985; children: Sarah, Tucker, Amanda. BS, U. Pa., 1981. V.p. ops. Comcast Cable Communications, Inc., Phila., 1985-86; exec. v.p. Comcast Corp., 1986-92, pres., 1990—97, CEO, 1997—; bd. dir. Comcast Holdings, 2000. Bd. dirs. The Bank of NY; bd. trustees Simon Wiesenthal Ctr.; founding co-chair Phila. 2000; dir., exec. com. CableLabs, 1999, now chmn. bd. dir. Vice chmn. The Walter Katz Found. Recipient Humanitarian Award, Simon Wiesenthal Ctr., 2004. Mem.: Nat. Cable & Telecommunications Assn. (chmn. 1995—96, treas., bd. dirs., exec. com., now chmn.). Avocation: squash (All-American, silver medal with U.S. team 1981, 85 and 97). Office: Comcast Corp Fl 35 East Twr 1500 Market St Fl 33 Philadelphia PA 19102-2100*

**ROBERTS, BRIAN WAYNE,** middle school educator, minister; b. Owensboro, Ky., Dec. 2, 1974; s. Clyde Wayne and Donna Lynn Roberts; m. Jenny Rebecca Westerfield. ThM, Luther Rice Sem., Lithonia, Ga., 2001. Ordained minister Green Brier Baptist, Utica, Ky., 1997; cert. tchr. Pastor New Life Bapt. Ch., Hawesville, Ky., 1997—2002, Sorgho (Ky.) Bapt. Ch., 2002—. Faculty sponsor Christian Student Fellowship, Owensboro, 1998—. Author: (study guide) God's Apocalypse: According to John, 1996. Student counselor Daviess/McLean Bapt. Assn., 1993—98, Ky. Wesleyan Meth. Workers, 1993—98. Recipient Elizabeth Munday Cmty. Svc. award, Ky. Wesleyan Coll., 1997. Mem.: Christian Educators Assn. Internat. R-Consevative. Avocation: University of Kentucky basketball. Home: 7030 Jack Hinton Rd Philpot KY 42366 Office: Daviess County Mid Sch 1415 E Fourth St Owensboro KY 42303

**ROBERTS, BURTON BENNETT,** lawyer, retired judge; b. N.Y.C., July 25, 1922; s. Alfred S. and Cecelia (Schanfein) R.; m. Gerhild Ukryn. BA, NYU, 1943, LL.M., 1953; LL.B., Cornell U., 1949. Bar: N.Y. 1949. Asst. dist. atty., New York County, 1949-66; chief asst. dist. atty. Bronx County, Bronx, NY, 1966-68, acting dist. atty., 1968-69, dist. atty., 1969-72; justice Supreme Ct. State N.Y., 1973-98, adminstrv. judge criminal br. Bronx County 12th Jud. Dist., 1984-98, adminstrv. judge civil br. Bronx County 12th Dist., 1988-98; ret., 1998; counsel Fischbein, Badillo, Wagner & Harding, 1999—2005, Dreier LLP, 2005—. Pres. Bronx div. Hebrew Home for Aged, 1967-72. With U.S. Army, 1943-45. Decorated Purple Heart, Bronze Star with oak leaf cluster, Combat Infantry badge Mem. Assn. Bar City N.Y., Am. Bar Assn., N.Y. Bar Assn., Bronx County Bar Assn., N.Y. State Dist. Attys. Assn. (pres. 1971-72) Jewish (exec. bd. temple). Home: 215 E 68th St Apt 19A New York NY 10021-5727 Office: Dreier LLP 499 Park Ave New York NY 10022 Office Phone: 212-328-6103. Business E-Mail: broberts@dreierllp.com.

**ROBERTS, CARL GEOFFREY,** lawyer; b. Boston, June 17, 1948; s. Simon Matthew and Ruth (Gorfinkle) Roberts; m. Sharon Ash, Mar. 24, 1979 (div. June 19, 2002); 1 child, Dennis; m. Susan Busch, Dec. 28, 2002. BA, Harvard U., 1970; JD, U. Pa., 1974. Bar: Pa. 1974, U.S. Dist. Ct. (ea. dist.) Pa. 1974, U.S. Ct. Appeals (3d cir.) 1978, U.S. Supreme Ct. 1980, U.S. Ct. Claims 1980, U.S. Dist. Ct. (mid. dist.) Pa. 1986. Law clk. U.S. Dist. Ct. (ea. dist.) Pa., Phila., 1974-76; assoc Dilworth, Paxson, Kalish & Kauffman, Phila., 1978-82, ptnr., 1982-92, Ballard, Spahr, Andrews & Ingersoll, Phila., 1992—. Bd. dirs. Phila. Chamber Ensemble, sec., 1977-92, pres., 1992-95; mem. Hillel com. U. Pa., 1999—, chair 2001-05; bd. dirs. Hillel of Greater Phila., 2000—. Mem.: ABA (law practice mgmt. sect. sec. 2002—03, vice chmn. 2003—04, SCOTIS 2004—, chmn.-elect 2004—05, chmn. 2005—). Office: Ballard Spahr Andrews & Ingersoll 1735 Market St Fl 51 Philadelphia PA 19103-7599 Office Phone: 215-864-8120. Business E-Mail: cgroberts@ballardspahr.com.

**ROBERTS, CAROLYN C.,** former hospital administrator; b. Parkersburg, W.Va., Dec. 4, 1938; married. M, Northeastern U., 1981. Various positions, 1962-75; dir. clin. adminstrn. svcs. Sidney Farber Cancer Inst., Boston, 1975-82; pres., CEO Copley Health Sys., Morrisville, Vt., 1982—. Author books; contbr. articles to profl. jours. Recipient cmty. svc. awards. Fellow Am. Acad. Med. Administrs.; mem. Am. Hosp. Assn. (bd. dirs., chmn., del., trustee), Am. Soc. Healthcare Risk Mgmt. (coms.), Vt. Hosp. Assn. (coms., trustee). Home: RR 1 Box 3290 Hyde Park VT 05655-9759

**ROBERTS, CARTER S.,** environmental services administrator; married; 3 children. AB, Princeton U., 1982; MBA, Harvard U., 1988. Led mktg. and mgmt. teams at Procter & Gamble and Gillette; Mass. state dir. Nature Conservancy, 1990—96, dir., strategic planning, divsn. v.p., C.Am., v.p., dir., strategic planning and global priorities; chief conservation officer, COO World Wildlife Fund, Washington, 2004—05, pres., CEO, 2005—. Office: World Wildlife Fund 1250 Twenty Fourth St NW Washington DC 20003-1132

**ROBERTS, CATHERINE C.,** radiologist, educator; MD, U. Ariz. Diplomate diagnostic radiology Am. Bd. Radiology. Staff cons. radiologist Mayo Clinic, Scottsdale, Ariz. Assoc. dean Mayo Sch. Health Scis.; chmn., edn. com. Assn. U. Radiologists; editl. bd. mem. Am. Jour. Roentgenology, Integrative Imaging, Radiology Case Reports Jour. Author: Musculoskeletal Imaging: A Teaching File. Mem.: Soc. Skeletal Radiology (chmn. electronic comm. com.). Office: Mayo Clinic 13400 E Shea Blvd Scottsdale AZ 85259 Office Phone: 480-301-4850.

**ROBERTS, CECIL EDWARD, JR.,** labor union administrator; b. Oct. 31, 1946; s. Cecil Edward and Evelyn Roberts; m. Carolyn Sue Stewart; children: Kyle Edward, Melissa Dawn. Student, Beckley Jr. Coll.; grad., W.Va. Technical Coll., 1987; HHD (hon.), W.Va. U. Tech. Gen. inside laborer, shuttle car operator, unitrack operator, greaser, beltman & mechanic Carbon Fuels Mine, Winifred, W.Va., 1971-77; v.p. dist. 17 United Mine Workers of Am., 1977-82, v.p., 1982-95, pres., 1995—. Mem. Com. Employer Support Vet. Employment, 1985, v.p.; pres. Nat. Coun. Holmes Safety Assn., 1985; mem. W. Va. Employment Opportunities and Econ. Devel. Commn. Gen. v.p. Nat. Coun. Sr. Citizens; adv. bd., Inst. Labor Studies and Rsch. W.Va. U., 1996; bd. dir. Blue Cross and Blue Shield So. W.Va., Cabin Creek Clinic, W.Va.; mem. adv. com. Black Lung Program. With U.S. Army, 1966—67, Vietnam. Recipient Martin Luther King award, Rainbow Coalition. Mem.: Vietnam Vets. of Am., Am. Legion, VFW (life). Office: United Mine Workers of Am Internat Union 8315 Lee Hwy Fairfax VA 22031-2215*

**ROBERTS, CELIA ANN,** librarian; b. Bangor, Maine, Feb. 6, 1935; d. William Lewis and Ruey Pearl (Logan) Roberts. AA, U. Hartford, 1957, BA, 1961; postgrad., So. Conn. State Coll., 1963—. With catalog, acquisition and circulation depts. U. Hartford Libr., 1956-65; libr. Simsbury Free Libr., Simsbury, Conn., 1965-69; reference libr. Simsbury Pub. Libr., 1969—. Tchr. ballet, 1965—66; tchr. genealogy, 1977—; ballet mistress Ballet Soc. Conn., Inc., 1968—70; with corps de ballet Conn. Opera Assn., 1963—64; active in prodns. Simsbury Light Opera Assn., 1964—69. Contbr. articles to profl. jours. Vol. Family History Ctr., 1970—. Mem.: DAR (Abigail Phelps chpt.), AAUW (past pres. Greater Hartford br.), ALA, Simsbury Hist. Soc., Conn. Libr. Assn., Denison Soc., Inc., Daus. of Scotia, Simsbury Geneal. and Hist. Rsch. Libr., Chateauguay Valley Hist. Soc., New Brunswick Geneal. Soc., Conn. Hist. Soc., Dance Masters Am. (Conn. Dance Tchrs. Club chpt.), Soc. Mayflower Descs. Conn., Conn. Soc. Genealogists (registrar Hartford 1983), Pro Dance, New Eng. Historic Geneal. Soc., Ont. Geneal. Soc. Unitarian Universalist. Office: Simsbury Public Libr 725 Hopmeadow St Simsbury CT 06070-2243 Business E-Mail: croberts@simsburylibrary.info.

**ROBERTS, CHARLES MURRAY,** retired publishing executive, writer; b. New Haven, Conn., Mar. 30, 1937; s. Samuel S. and Bertha L. Roberts; m. Sally Miller, June 19, 1960; children: Susan Hilary, Julie Handel. BA, U. Pa., 1958. V.p. field sales dir. western region Simon & Schuster, N.Y.C., 1960—2002; pres. Author Escort & Media Svcs., Houston, 2002—. PBR Mag. Bd. trustees Congregation Beth Israel, Houston, 1972—74. With Air N.G., 1961—64. Mem.: Houston Forum. Avocations: tennis, travel, walking. Home: 49 Briar Hollow Ln #1002 Houston TX 77027 Home Fax: 713-572-5785. Personal E-Mail: charles@authortours.net.

**ROBERTS, CHARLES PATRICK (PAT ROBERTS),** senator; b. Topeka, Kans., Apr. 20, 1936; m. Frankie Fann, 1969; children: David, Ashleigh, Anne-Wesley. BA in Journalism, Kans. State U., 1958. Pub. Litchfield Park, Ariz., 1962-67; adminstrv. asst. to U.S. Senator Frank Carlson, U.S. Senate, Washington, 1967-68; adminstrv. asst. to U.S. Congressman Keith Sebelius U.S. Ho. of Reps., Washington, 1968-80; mem. 97th to 104th Congresses from Kans. 1st Dist., Washington, 1980-96; US Senator from Kansas, 1997—. Com. agr. US Senate, com. armed services, com. health, edn., labor and pensions, select com. ethics, chmn. select com. intelligence. Served with USMC, 1958—62. Recipient Am. Farmer award, Future Farmers of Am., 1986, Disting. Leadership award, Prodn. Credit Assn., Disting. Svc. award, Kans. Farm Bur., Wheat Man of Yr., Assn. Wheat Growers, 1993, Public Svc. award, Am. Chem. Soc., 2001, John H. Chafee award public svc., Rep. Main Street Partnership, 2003. Republican. Methodist. Office: US Senate 109 Hart Senate Off Bldg Washington DC 20510-1605 also: District Office Ste 203 100 Military Plz Dodge City KS 67801 Office Phone: 202-224-4774, 620-227-2244. Office Fax: 202-224-3514, 620-227-2264.*

**ROBERTS, CHRIS,** strategy and finance educator, researcher; b. New Castle, Pa., July 16, 1954; s. Samuel Bruce and Jan Roberts, Della V. Roberts (Stepmother), Sheldon S. Smith (Stepfather). BS in Mgmt., U. Utah, 1975, BS in Fin., 1981; MBA, U. Phoenix, Salt Lake City, 1986; PhD in Mgmt., U. Mass., 1995. Supr. Holiday Inns Reservation Ctr., Memphis, Utah, 1972—78; product mgr. Mountain Bell/Qwest Comms., Salt Lake City, 1978—89; prof. Isenberg Sch. Mgmt. U. Mass., Amherst, 1993—; assoc. dept. head Isenberg Sch. Mgmt., 2001—. Contbr. articles to profl. jours.; editor: Jour. Hospitality and Tourism Edn. Mem.: Acad. Mgmt., Strategic Mgmt. Soc., Coun. Hotel, Restaurant & Instnl. Edn. (chair symposium com. 1998—2002, Outstanding Peer Reviewer 1999), Beta Gamma Sigma. Avocations: contract bridge, international travel. Home: PO Box 4 Millers Falls MA 01376 Office: U Mass Flint 206 90 Campus Center Way Amherst MA 01003-9247 Office Phone: 413-545-4411. Personal E-Mail: q@qutah.edu. Business E-Mail: q@ht.umass.edu.

**ROBERTS, CHRISTOPHER WAYNE,** psychologist, educational consultant; b. Richmond, Va., June 5, 1971; s. Eddie Donald and Patricia Walker Roberts; m. Robin Lee Reinert, Aug. 14, 2005; 1 child, Tatum Grace. BS in Psychology cum laude, Va. Poly. Inst. and State U., 1996; MS in Psychology, Radford U., Va., 1998, EdS in Sch. Psychology, 1999; postgrad., Ariz. State U., 2002—. Nat. cert. sch. psychologist, cert. sch. psychologist Ariz. Dept. Edn., Calif. Dept. Edn., NC Dept. Edn., Va. Dept. Edn. Tchr. The Children's Ho., Chesterfield, Va., 1991—96; svc. provider New River Valley Cmty. Svcs., Radford, 1996—98; psychologist Cumberland County Pub. Schs., Fayetteville, NC, 1998—2000; psychologist, diagnostician Piedmont Psychol. Svcs., Farmville, Va., 2000—01; sch. psychologist Dept. Correctional Edn., Richmond, 2001—02; contract sch. psychologist Phoenix 1 Elem. Sch. Dist., 2002—, Whittier Area Coop. Sch. Dist. Program, Calif., 2002—, Balsz Elem. Sch. Dist., Phoenix, 2004—05, Ariz. Dept. Juvenile Corrections, Phoenix, 2004—; pres. Valley Ednl. Specialists, Phoenix, 2004—. Camp counselor, svc. provider Camp Baker, Chesterfield, Va., 1995—96; substitute tchr. Montgomery County Pub. Schs., Christiansburg, Va., 1996—97, Chesterfield County Pub. Schs., 2000; intern Montgomery County Pub. Schs., 1997—98; mem. local arrangements com. 19th Internat. Conf. on Learning Disabilities, Washington, 1997; grad. counselor Disability Resource Office, Radford U., 1997—98; adj. prof. edn. psychology, developmental psychology and behavior modification Fayetteville Tech. CC, 1998—2000; evaluator Maricopa County Juvenile Probation/Vocat. Rehab. Program, Ariz. State U., Phoenix, 2002, 03; mem. conf. com. 26th Ann. Conf. on Severe Behavior Disorders of Children and Youth, Tempe, Ariz., 2002; rsch. asst. Ctr. on Edn., Disability and Juvenile Justice, Ariz. State U., Tempe, 2002—03; intern, co-instr. Ariz. State U., 2003, instr., 2003—05; presenter in field. Recipient Tara Reilly Meml. Scholarship award, Behavioral Inst. for Children and Adolescents, 2004. Mem.: Tchr. Educators for Children with Behavior Disorders, Nat. Assn. Sch. Psychologists (nat. cert.), Coun. Exceptional Children (divsn. learning disabilities, coun. for children with behavioral

disorders), Pi Lambda Phi. Avocations: racing, exercise, movies, football. Home and Office: Valley Ednl Specialists Inc 418 E Beth Dr Phoenix AZ 85042 Office Phone: 602-690-1502. Fax: 602-304-9332. E-mail: skoolpsyco@aol.com.

**ROBERTS, CHUCK,** cable news anchor; B in Journalism, U. Mo. Various newscaster positions, 1970-75; anchor, writer, prodr. Sta. KMTV-TV, Omaha; from newscaster to anchor CNN Headline News, Atlanta, 1981—. Office: CNN Cable News Network 1 CNN Ctr NW Atlanta GA 30303-2762

**ROBERTS, COKIE (CORINNE BOGGS ROBERTS),** newscaster; b. New Orleans, Dec. 27, 1943; d. Thomas Hale and Corinne Morrison (Claiborne) Boggs; m. Steven V. Roberts, Sept. 10, 1966; children: Lee Harriss, Rebecca Boggs. BA in Polit. Sci., Wellesley Coll., 1964; degree (hon.), Amherst Coll., Columbia Coll., Loyola U. of the South, Manhattanville Coll., Gonzaga U., Bradeson Coll., Hood Coll., Chestnut Hill Coll., Miss. Women's U., Notre Dame U., Duke U. Assoc. prodr., host Altman Prodns., Washington, 1964—66, prodr. L.A., 1969—72; reporter, editor Cowles Comm., N.Y.C., 1967; prodr. Sta. WNEW-TV, N.Y.C., 1968, Sta. KNBC-TV, L.A., 1972—74; reporter CBS News, Athens, Greece, 1974—77; sr. news analyst. Nat. Pub. Radio, Washington, 1977—; corr. MacNeil/Lehrer Newshour, Washington, 1984—88; spl. Washington corr. ABC News, Washington, 1988—92; interviewer, commentator This Week With David Brinkley, Washington, 1992—96; co-anchor This Week with Sam Donaldson & Cokie Roberts, 1996—2002; chief congrl. analyst ABC News, 1998—; polit. commentator, analyst ABC News, World News Tonight and other ABC News broadcasts. Lectr. in field. Co-host weekly pub. TV program on Congress The Lawmakers, 1981—84, prodr., host pub. affairs program Sta. WRC-TV, Washington; prodr.: Sta. KNBC-TV Serendipity (award for excellence in local programming, Emmy nomination for children's programming); author: We Are Our Mother's Daughters, 1998, Founding Mothers: The Women Who Raised Our Nation, 2004; contbr. articles to newspapers, mags.; writer of a weekly column along with husband for newspapers around the country by United Media; contbg. editor (with husband): USA Magazine; co-author: From this Day Forward. Bd. dir. Presidential Commn. on Service and Civic Participation, Dirksen Ctr., Pekin, Ill., 1988—95, Fgn. Students Svc. Ctr., Washington, 1990—, Manhattanville Coll., Purchase, NY, 1991—99, Children's Inn at NIH, Bethesda, Md., 1992—. Named one of 50 Greatest Women in the History of Broadcasting, Am. Women in Radio and Television; named to Broadcasting Hall of Fame, Cable Hall of Fame; recipient Broadcast award, Nat. Orgn. Working Women, 1984, Distinguished Alumnae Achievement awards, Wellesley Coll., 1985, Everett McKinley Dirksen disting. reporting of Congress, 1987, Weintal award, Georgetown U., 1987, Corp. Pub. Broadcasting award, 1988, Edward R. Murrow award, Corp. Pub. Broadcasting, 1990, Broadcast award, Nat. Women's Polit. Caucus, 1990, David Brinkley Comm. award, 1991, Mother of Yr. award, Nat. Mother's Day Com., 1992, Emmy award news and documentary, 1991. Mem.: Radio-TV Corrs. Assn. (pres. 1981—82, bd. dirs. 1980—94), U.S. Capitol Hist. Soc. Roman Catholic. Mailing: 1717 DeSales St NW Washington DC 20036

**ROBERTS, CURTIS CREED,** minister, writer; b. Lenox, Ga., Nov. 20, 1920; s. Walter C. Roberts and LeeAnn Goodwin; m. Pauline Powell Roberts (dec.); children: Don Wayne, Marcus Carroll, Randy Curtis. BA, Valdosta State Coll., Ga., 1967. Co-owner Roberts Furniture Co., Lenox, Ga., 1947—58, Bradenton, Fla., 1958—60; pastor United Meth. Ch., Ga., 1963—2001; bookkeeper Roberts Reliant Property Mgmt., Tifton, Ga., 1988—. Co-author: (book) The Leesburg Methodist Story, 1974; author: More Precious Than Gold, 2002, Korn on the Kob, 2006. Ordained elder United Meth. Ch., 1970. Sgt. U.S. Army, 1942—45. Decorated EAMET Svc. medal U.S. Army, Am. Theatre Ribbon, World War II Victory medal. Methodist. Avocations: art, woodworking. Home: 88 Richards Dr Apt A-5 Tifton GA 31793 Office: Roberts Reliant Property Mgmt 1015 E 12th St Tifton GA

**ROBERTS, CYNTHIA JEANNE,** history educator; d. Rae Winford and Christine Shanks Klepper; m. Alan Richard Roberts, July 3, 1980; children: Nikina Dawn, Sabrina Kay stepchildren: Cory Lenn, Cody Alan. AA in Edn., Western Tex. Coll., Snyder, 1975; BS in Edn., Angelo State U., San Angelo, Tex., 1977. Tchr. history and math. coach Sabinal Sch. Dist., Tex., 1977—78; tchr. history, coach Snyder Jr. H.S., Tex., 1978—80; tchr. history Clyde Jr. H.S., Tex., 1982—. Sponsor Jr. Beta Clyde Jr. H.S., Tex., 1995—2006. Recipient Tchr. of Yr. award, Clyde C. of C., 1998—99, Tchr. Tribute award, Tchr. Tribute, 2000. Mem.: Tex. Classroom Tchr.'s Assn. Southern Baptist. Avocations: music, reading, collecting antique books, historical travel throughout U.S. Office: Clyde Jr HS 211 S Third W Clyde TX 79510 Office Phone: 325-893-5788. E-mail: croberts@valornet.com.

**ROBERTS, DALE (TY),** digital music and media company executive; Sr. engr. Pixar; founder, sr. mgr. LightSource; founder ION, 1993; joined (after acquiring ION) Gracenote, Emeryville, Calif., 1998—, now chief technology officer. Rep. for Gracenote Secure Digital Music Initiative. Widely recognized as one of the inventors of enhanced CD technology and is accredited with producing the industry's first enhanced CD. Office: Gracenote 2000 Powell St Ste 1380 Emeryville CA 94608 Office Phone: 510-547-9680. Office Fax: 510-547-9681.

**ROBERTS, DAVID E., JR.,** oil industry executive; BS in Min. Engring., Univ. Alabama, Tuscaloosa, Ala. Engr., oil and gas ops. Texaco No. Am., 1983—96, regional mgr., 1997, dir. strategic mgmt., worldwide ops., 1999—2001; adv. to vice-chmn. Chevron Texaco Corp., 2001—03; exec. v.p., mng. dir. BG Group, 2003—06; sr. v.p. bus. devel. Marathon Oil Corp. Office: Marathon Oil Co 5555 San Felipe St Houston TX 77056*

**ROBERTS, DAVID GLEN,** prospector, investor; b. Plainview, Tex., Feb. 8, 1952; s. Doris Glen and Anna Grace (Mathis) R. Student, Tex. A&M U., 1970-71, Dallas Bapt. Coll. 1971-75; BA in Comm., U. Tex. Permian Basin, 1987. Lic. minister Bapt. Ch.; cert. profl. landman. Profl. stuntman, actor, 1972-76; mgr. Channel 100, Midland, Tex., 1976-78; pub., owner Basin Voice newspaper, 1987—; owner Diamond Developers Fire and Enviro-Safety Co., Midland, 1989—; regional mktg. dir. Nochar Inc.-Region 11, Midland, Tex., 1990-96; owner D.G. Roberts Land Mgmt., Midland, Tex., 1978—2004; CEO Permian Basin Diamond Developers, Inc., Skelly Oil Co., Inc., Heart of Tex. Quik Internet, Inc., 2004—. Cons. EPA, Indpls., 1991—. Appeared in film Giovanni & Ben, 1974, Drive In, 1976; theatre appearance at Globe Theatre, Odessa, Tex., 1975, Shakespeare in the Park, Dallas, 1976. Past chair Midland County Libertarian Party; past mem. exec. com. Dist. 31 Tex. Libertarian Party; organizer Sons of Liberty, Midland, 1990—; candidate US Congress Dist. 21, Tex., 2002. Mem. Am. Assn. Petroleum-Landmen, Five Aces, NRA, Tex. State Rifle Assn., Permian Basin Landman's Assn., N.O.R.M.L., Rep. Nat. Com. (libertarian). Avocations: golf, motorcycling, hiking, shooting, photography. Office. Office Phone: 432-520-0012. Business E-Mail: droberts@quik.com.

**ROBERTS, DAVID LOWELL,** journalist, educator; b. Lusk, Wyo., Jan. 12, 1954; s. Leslie James and LaVerne Elizabeth (Johns) R. BA, U. Ariz., 1979; MA, U. Nebr., 1997. Founder, editor, publisher Medicine Bow (Wyo.) Post, 1977-88; journalism instr. U. Wyo., Laramie, 1987-92; adviser U. Wyo. Student Publs., Laramie, 1987-92; gen. mgr. Student Media Corp U No. Colo., Greeley, 1995-98; founder, publisher Hanna Herald, Wyo., 1979-80; asst. prof. mass comm. Missouri Valley Coll., Marshall, Mo., 2001—. Exch. reporter The Washington Post, 1982; freelance reporter Casper (Wyo.) Star-Tribune, 1978-83, various publs.; freelancer, 1977—. Co-author: (book) The Wyoming Almanac, 1988, 90, 94, 96, 2001; author: (book) Sage Street, 1991; columnist Sage Street, 1989-92. Chmn. Medicine Bow Film Commn., 1984; treas. Friends of the Medicine Bow Mus., 1984-88; pres. Medicine Bow Area C. of C., 1984; dir. Habitat for Humanity of Albany County, Laramie, 1991-92. Recipient Nat. Newspaper Assn. awards, over 40 Wyo. Press Assn. awards, Five Editorial awards U. Wyo., Citizen of Yr. award People of Medicine Bow, 1986, Student Publs. awards U. Wyo., 1990, 92. Mem.

Friends of Medicine Bow Mus. Mem. Green Party. Methodist. Avocations: writing, golf, visiting museums, photography. Office Phone: 660-831-4211. Business E-Mail: robertsd@moval.edu.

**ROBERTS, DEBORAH MARIE,** historian, consultant; b. Riverside, Calif., Oct. 5, 1956; d. Edward Nelson Morgan, Sr. and Margaret Mary Morgan; m. James Howard Roberts, Jr., Sept. 27, 1981; children: Michael James, Anastacio Edward, Misty Dawn, Monique Sincere. MA in History, Calif. State U., Sacramento, 1989—96. Grants officer Yavapai-Prescott Indian Tribe, Prescott, Ariz., 1996—2002; historian, Yavapai Coll., Prescott, Ariz., 1997—. Regional dir. Yavapai County Nat. History Day. Mem.: Am. Hist. Assn. (assoc.). Democrat. Avocations: reading, travel. Home: 120 S Rocky Dells Dr Prescott AZ 86303 Office: Yavapai Coll 1100 E Sheldon St Prescott AZ 86301 Office Phone: 928-776-2342. E-mail: debbie_roberts@yc.edu.

**ROBERTS, DELMAR LEE,** editor; b. Raleigh, NC, Apr. 9, 1933; s. James Delmer and Nellie Brockelbank (Tyson) R. BS in Textile Mgmt., NC State U., 1956; postgrad., Inst. Polit. Studies, U. Paris, 1963; MA in Journalism, U. SC, 1974. Product devel. engr. U.S. Rubber Co. (Uniroyal), Winnsboro, SC, 1959—63; process improvement engr. Allied Chem. Co., Irmo, SC, 1965-67; assoc. editor S.C. History Illustrated Mag., Columbia, 1970; editor-in-chief, editl. v.p. Sandlapper-The Mag. of S.C., Columbia, 1968-74; mng. editor, art dir. Legal Econs. mag. of the ABA, Chgo., 1975-89, Law Practice Mgmt. mag. of the ABA, Chgo., 1990-2000, editor emeritus, 2000—. Editor: The Best of Legal Economics, 1979; freelance editor and/or designer of over 35 books. Active World Affairs Coun. Columbia, 1997-; 1st v.p. English-Speaking Union, 1996-97, pres. 1997-2003, bd. dirs. 2003-. With U.S. Army, 1956-58. Hon. fellow Coll. of Law Practice Mgmt., Golden, Colo., 1995—. Mem. Soc. Profl. Journalists, Capital City Club (Columbia), Phi Kappa Tau, Kappa Tau Alpha. Avocations: travel, turkish carpet/kilim collecting, antiques.

**ROBERTS, DENISE (DENISE ROBERTS HURLIN),** dancer; Studied dance with Ilene Danek; BFA in dance, SUNY, Purchase. Dancer Paul Taylor Dance Co., N.Y.C., 1989—95. Dancer with Hannah Kahn, Kevin Wynn, Douglas Wright; founding mem., toured with David Parsons Co.; faculty mem. SUNY, The Juilliard Sch., SUNY, 99; co-founder (with Hernando Cortez), Dancers Responding to AIDS, 1991-; panelist, Arts Alive Grants Com. of Westchester, NY, Broadway Cares/Equity Fights AIDS Nat. Grants prog. Named Outstanding performer by Joan Acocella, 1994. Office: Dancers Responding to AIDS 165 W 46th St 1300 New York NY 10036

**ROBERTS, DENNIS WILLIAM,** construction executive; b. Chgo., Jan. 7, 1943; s. William Owen and Florence Harriet (Denman) R. BA in Journalism, U. N.Mex., 1968; MA in Legal Studies, Antioch U., 1982; MA, St. John's Coll., 1984. Gen. assignment reporter Albuquerque Pub. Co., 1964, sports writer, 1960-64, advt. and display salesman, 1967-68; dir. info. N.Mex. bldg. br. Assoc. Gen. Contractors Am., Albuquerque, 1968-79, asst. exec. dir., 1979-82, dir., 1982—. Adj. prof. civil engring. U. N.Mex., 2004—06. Active United Way, Albuquerque, 1969-78; chmn. Albuquerque Crime Prevention Coun., 1982; bd. dirs. Rio Grande chpt. ARC, 1992-95, Albuquerque Lit. Coun., 1998-2004, Luth. Campus Ministry, U. N.Mex., 2003—; mem. cmty. adv. coun. Albuquerque Jobs Corps. Recipient Pub. Rels. Achievement award Assoc. Gen. Contractors Am., 1975, 78. Mem. N.Mex. Pub. Rels. Conf. (chmn. 1975, 82-83), Pub. Rels. Soc. Am. (accredited, pres. N.Mex. chpt. 1981, chmn. S.W. dist. 1984, chmn. sect. 1988), Constrn. Specifications Inst. (Outstanding Industry Mem. 1974, Outstanding Com. Chmn. 1978), Am. Soc. Safety Engrs., Toastmasters Club (dist. gov. 1977-78, Disting. Dist. award 1978, Toastmaster of Yr. 1979-80), Masons, Shriners, Sigma Delta Chi (pres. N.Mex. chpt. 1969). Republican. Lutheran. Home: Apt 21 1410 Girard NE Albuquerque NM 87106 Office: Assn Gen Contractors 1615 University Blvd NE Albuquerque NM 87102-1717 Office Phone: 505-842-1462. Business E-Mail: dennisr@agc-nm.org. *Personal philosophy: Set your priorities in life, then your goals. In pursuing your goals, visualize their accomplishment. Be persistent, and you will accomplish what you set out to accomplish. Learn to be fair to others and empathetic.*

**ROBERTS, DONALD FRANK, JR.,** communications educator; b. Seattle, Mar. 30, 1939; s. Donald Frank Sr. and Ruth Amalia (Geiger) R.; m. Karlene Hahn, 1963 (div. 1981): 1 child, Donald Brett; m. Wendy G. Roberts, Aug. 26, 1983; stepchildren: Richard L., David L., Katherine M. AB, Columbia U., 1961; MA, U. Calif., Berkeley, 1963; PhD, Stanford U., 1968. Instr., dept. English U. Hawaii, Honolulu, 1963-64; asst. dir. ednl. svc. bur. The Wall Street Jour., Princeton, NJ, 1964-65; asst. prof., rsch. assoc. dept. Comm., Inst. Comm. Rsch. Stanford (Calif.) U., 1970-76, assoc. prof., 1976-84, prof. Comm., 1984—, dir. Inst. Comm. Rsch., 1985-90, chmn. dept. Comm., 1990-96, Thomas More Storke Prof., 1991—. Cons. WHO, 1974, Rand Corp., 1972—74, Sta. KQED-TV, 1975—77, Far West Lab. Ednl. Rsch. and Devel., 1978—79, FTC, 1978—80, Westinghouse Broadcasting, 1983—86, Soc. Nutrition Edn., 1984—86, The Disney Channel, 1986—87, WHO, 1988—89, SRI Internat., 1988—89, Carnegie Coun. Adolescence, 1989—90, NBC, 1992, Ctr. Disease Control, 1992, Children Now, 1992—2004, Software Pubs. Assn., 1994, Nickelodeon, 1994, JP Kids, 1995—97, MGM Animation, 1996—98, DIC Entertainment, 1997—, Planet Lingo, 1997—2001, Sunbow Entertainment, 1999—2000, ABC/Disney TV Animation, 2000—02, Disney Online, 2000—02, Nelvana, Ltd., 2000—01; bd. advisors Media Scope, 1992—94; proposal reviewer NIMH, NSF, U.S. Agy. Internat. Devel., Can. Coun., John and Mary R. Markle Found., W.T. Grant Found.; spkr. numerous seminars, confs., symposia. Co-author: Process and Effects of Mass Communication, 1971, Television and Human Behavior, 1978, It's not ONLY Rock and Roll, 1998, Kids and Media at the New Millennium, 1999, Kids and Media in America, 2004, Generation M: Media in the Lives of 8-18 Year-olds 2005; mem. editl. bd. Jour. Broadcasting, 1900—88, Pub. Opinion Quarterly, 1981—86, Communicare, 1986—2004, editl. reviewer Commn. Rsch.—, Comm. Monograph, Comm. Yearbook, Human Comm. Rsch., Jour. Comm., Jour. Quarterly, Child Devel., Jour. Applied Psychology, Jour. Ednl. Psychology, Psychology Bull., Jour. Adolescent Health; contbr. articles, chapters to books. Fellow Human Scis. Rsch. Coun., Pretoria, South Africa, 1985, 1987, Fullbright Teaching fellow Inst. for Unterrichtstechnologie Und Medienpadagogic, Austria, 1987. Mem. APA, Internat. Comm. Assn., Assn. Edn. in Journalism and Mass Comm., Soc. Rsch. Child Devel., Soc. Personality and Soc. Psychology. Office: Stanford U Dept Comm McClatchy Hall Stanford CA 94305-2050 Office Phone: 650-723-0780. Business E-Mail: droberts@stanford.edu.

**ROBERTS, DONALD JOHN,** economics professor, business professor, consultant; b. Winnipeg, Man., Can., Feb. 11, 1945; came to U.S., 1967; s. Donald Victor and Margaret Mabel R.; m. Kathleen Eleanor Taylor, Aug. 26, 1967 (dec. 2006). BA with honors, U. Man., 1967; PhD, U. Minn., 1972. Instr. dept. managerial econs. and decision scis. J.L. Kellogg Grad. Sch. Mgmt., Northwestern U., Evanston, Ill., 1971—72, asst. prof., 1972—74; assoc. prof. J. L. Kellogg Grad. Sch. Mgmt., Northwestern U., Evanston, Ill., 1974—77; prof. J.L. Kellogg Grad. Sch. Mgmt., Northwestern U., Evanston, Ill., 1977—80, Grad. Sch. Bus., Stanford (Calif.) U., 1980, Jonathan B. Lovelace prof., 1980—2001, assoc. dean, dir. rsch., 1987—90, dir. exec. program in strategy and orgn., 1992—, dir. global mgmt. program, 1994—, sr. assoc. dean, 2000—, John H. Scully prof., 2001—; co-dir. Ctr. for Global Bus. and the Economy, 2003. Prof. (by courtesy) dept. econs. Stanford U., 1986—; vis. rsch. faculty U. Catholique de Louvain, Belgium, 1974-75; inaugural Clarendon lectr. mgmt. studies Oxford U., 1997; cons. bus., econs. and antitrust, 1976—; vis. fellow All Souls Coll., Oxford U., 1995, Nuffield Coll., Oxford U., 1999-00; vis. acad. fellow in leadership and orgn. McKinsey & Co., London, 1999-00. Author The Modern Firm: Organizational Design for Performance and Growth, 2004; co-author: Economics, Organization and Management, 1992; assoc. editor Jour. Econ. Theory, 1977-92, Econometrica, 1985-87, Games and Economic Behavior, 1988-; mem. editl. bd. Am. Econ. Rev., 1991-95, Jour. Econs. and Mgmt. Strategy, 1991-98, Orgns. and Markets Abstracts, 1996-; contbr. articles to profl. jours. NSF grantee, 1973-93; rsch. fellow Ctr. Ops. Research, Heverlee, Belgium, 1973-93.

1974, fellow Ctr. for Advanced Study in the Behavioral Scis., 1991-92. Fellow Am. Acad. Arts and Scis., Econometric Soc. (coun. 1994-96); mem. Am. Econ. Assn., Beta Gamma Sigma. Home: 835 Santa Fe Ave Stanford CA 94305-1022 E-mail: roberts_john@gsb.stanford.edu.

**ROBERTS, DONALD MUNIER,** retired banker, trust company executive; b. Paterson, N.J., Aug. 3, 1935; s. Edward and Dorothy (Munier) R.; m. Sally D. Ingram, Sept. 6, 1958 (dec. Feb. 1978); 1 dau., Sarah M.; m. Mary Ayer Gordon, June 23, 1978; children: Edward (dec.), John, Martha. BS, Yale U., 1957; MBA, NYU, 1961. Exec. v.p., 1979-90; vice chmn., treas. U.S. Trust Co. N.Y., N.Y.C., 1990-95; retired, 1995. Bd. dirs. Burlington Resources, Inc. Mem. N.Y. Road Runners Club Inc. (bd. dirs., past chmn.), Tau Beta Pi. Clubs: Links (N.Y.C.). Republican. Office: 18th Fl 645 Fifth Ave New York NY 10022-5910

**ROBERTS, DONALD WILSON,** pathologist, consultant; b. Phoenix, Jan. 20, 1933; s. Alpha Wilson and Rubye Clotilde R.; m. Mae Astrid Strand, June 17, 1959; children: Marc Donald, Sara Judith Roberts Roundy. BS, Brigham Young U., 1957; MS, Iowa State U., 1959; PhD, U. Calif., Berkeley, 1964. Postdoctoral Swiss Fed. Inst. Tech., Zurich, 1964—65; insect pathologist Boyce Thompson Inst. for Plant Rsch., Ithaca, NY, 1965—96; insect pathologist, rsch. prof. dept. biology Utah State U., Logan, 1997—. Cons. WHO, Kaduna, Nigeria, 1974, 76, Empresa Brasileira de Pesquisa Agropecuraria, Brasilia, Brazil, 1978, 79, 80, 94, 96; mem. sci. adv. bd. EcoSci. Corp., Worcester, Mass., 1990-95; project reviewer UN Devel. Program, Africa and South Am., 1993-96, USAID Africa, 1991-96; adj. prof. dept. entomology Cornell U., Ithaca, N.Y., 1993-2000, adj. prof. dept. plant pathology, 1994-99. Editor: (3 books) Diseases of Medically Important Arthropods, 1977, 80, 83, Invasion Processes of Fungi, 1983, Biotechnology in Pest Control, 1989; contbr. over 250 articles to profl. jours. Recipient Fulbright Sr. Rsch. scholarship Fulbright Found., Australia, 1985; named Family of Yr., Utah State U. Internat. Students, 1999. Mem. Soc. for Invertebrate Pathology (hon. 1998, founding mem., pres. 1988-90, Founder's Lectr. 1996, Svc. to Brazilian Insect Pathology award 2002), Entomol. Soc. Am. (Ea: br., Ciba-Geigy Recognition award 1985, 86, L.O. Howard Disting. Achievement award 1989), Am. Soc. Microbiology, Mycol. Soc. Am., Brazilian Entomol. Soc. (hon., recognition award 1996). Avocation: ballroom and swing dance. Office: Utah State U Dept Biology Logan UT 84322-5305 Office Phone: 435-797-0049. Business E-Mail: dwroberts@biology.usu.edu.

**ROBERTS, DORIS,** actress; b. St. Louis, Nov. 4, 1930; d. Larry and Ann (Meltzer) R.; m. Michael E. Cannata, June 21, 1950; 1 child, Michael R.; m. William Goyen, Nov. 10, 1963 (dec.). Student, NYU, 1950-51; studies with, Sanford Meisner, Neighborhood Playhouse, N.Y.C., 1952-53, Lee Strasberg, Actors' Studio, 1956. Ind. stage, screen and TV actress, 1953—. Profl. stage debut, Ann Arbor, Mich., 1953; appeared in summer stock Chatham, Mass., 1955; Broadway debut in The Time of Your Life, 1955; other Broadway and off-Broadway appearances include The Desk Set, 1955, The American Dream, 1961, The Death of Bessie Smith, 1961, The Office, 1965, The Color of Darkness, 1963, Marathon 33, 1963, Secret Affair of Mildred Wilde, 1972, Last of the Red Hot Lovers, 1969-71, Bad Habits, 1973 (Outer Circle Critics award 1974), Cheaters, 1976, Fairie Tale Theatre, 1985, The Fig Tree, 1987, It's Only a Play, 1992, Bye Bye Birdie, 2004; movie debut Something Wild, 1961, film appearances include: Barefoot in the Park, 1968, No Way to Treat a Lady, 1973, A Lovely Way to Die, 1969, Honeymoon Killers, 1969, A New Leaf, 1970, Such Good Friends, 1971, Little Murders, 1971, Heartbreak Kid, 1972, Hester Street, 1975, The Taking of Pelham, One, Two, Three, 1974, The Rose, 1979, Good Luck, Miss Wyckoff, 1979, Rabbit Test, 1979, Ordinary Hero, 1986, #1 with a Bullet, 1987, For Better or for Worse-Street Law, 1988, National Lampoon's Xmas Vacation, 1989, Used People, 1992, The Night We Never Met, Momma Mia, 1994, Walking to Waldheim, 1995, The Grass Harp, 1995, A Fish in the Bathtub, 1997, My Giant, 1998, All Over the Guy, 2001, Dickie Roberts-Child Star, 2003, Lucky 13, I Can See You.Com, Grandma's Boy, 2005; TV debut on Studio One, 1958, Mary Hartman, Mary Hartman, 1975, Mary Tyler Moore Hour, 1976, Soap, 1978-79, Angie, 1979-80, Remington Steele, 1984-88, Lily Tomlin Comedy Hour, Barney Miller, Alice, Full House, Perfect Strangers, Sunday Dinner, A Family Man, The Fig Tree (PBS), 1987, (TV films) The Story Teller, 1979, Ruby and Oswald, 1978, It Happened One Christmas, 1978, Jennifer: A Woman's Story, 1979, The Diary of Anne Frank, 1982, A Letter to Three Wives, Blind Faith, 1989, A Mom For Christmas, 1990, The Sunset Gang, 1990, Crossroads, 1993, Dream On, 1993, The Boys, 1993, A Time To Heal, 1994, A Thousand Men and a Baby, 1997, One True Love, 2000, Sons of Miseltoe, 2001, A Time to Remember (Hallmark channel) 2003, Raising Waylon, (CBS) 2003, Lucky 13, 2004, (Hallmark channel) Our House, 2005, Grandma's Boy, 2005, Keeping Up With The Sterns, 2006; (TV series) include St. Elsewhere, 1982 (Emmy award best sup. actress drama) Murder She Wrote, 1990, Step By Step, 1994, Burk's Law, 1994, Walker Texas Ranger, 1995, High Society, 1996, Everybody Loves Raymond, 1996-05 (Amer. Comedy award, 1999, Emmy award outstanding supporting actress in a comedy series, 2001, 02, 03, 2005, Gracie Allen award, 2004). Recipient People's Choice award, 2006. Mem. SAG (Ensemble award 2002), AFTRA, Actors Equity Assn., Dirs. Guild Am.

**ROBERTS, DOROTHY E.,** law educator; BA magna cum laude, Yale U., 1977; JD, Harvard U., 1980. Bar: NY 1981. Law clk. to Hon. Constance Baker Motley US Dist. Ct. (so. dist.) NY, 1980—81; assoc. Paul, Weiss, Rifkind, Wharton & Garrison, NYC, 1981—88; assoc. prof. Rutgers U. Sch. Law, Newark, 1988—94, prof., 1994—98; vis. prof. Northwestern U. Sch. Law, Chgo., 1997, prof., 1998—2001, Kirkland and Ellis prof., 2001—, faculty fellow Inst. for Policy Rsch., faculty affiliate Joint Ctr. for Poverty Rsch., 1998—. Vis. assoc. prof. U. Pa. Law Sch., 1994; fellow Program in Ethics and the Professions Harvard U., 1994—95; vis. prof. Stanford Law Sch., 1998; fulbright fellow Ctr. for Gender and Devel. Studies U. West Indies, Trinidad and Tobago, 2002—03. Author: A First Amendment Anthology, 1994, Constitutional Law Anthology, 1996, Killing the Black Body: Race, Reproduction, and The Meaning of Liberty, 1997, Shattered Bonds: The Color of Child Welfare, 2002; co-author: Frug's Women and The Law, 1998, Constitutional Law: Cases, History and Dialogues, 2000, First Amendment Law: Cases, Comparative Perspectives, and Dialogues, 2003; contbr. articles to profl. jours. Office: Northwestern U Sch Law 357 E Chicago Ave Chicago IL 60611 Office Phone: 312-503-0397. E-mail: d-roberts@law.northwestern.edu.

**ROBERTS, DWIGHT LOREN,** engineering consultant, writer; b. San Diego, June 3, 1949; s. James Albert and Cleva Lorraine (Conn) R.; B.A., U. San Diego, 1976, M.A., 1979; m. Phyllis Ann Adair, Mar. 29, 1969; children: Aimee Renee, Michael Loren, Daniel Alexandr. Engring. aide Benton Engring. Inc., San Diego, 1968-73; pres. Robert's Tech. Research Co., also subs. Marine Technique Ltd., San Diego, 1973-76; pres. Research Technique Internat., 1978—; freelance writer, 1979—; owner Agrl. Analysis, 1985-88; constrn. mgr. Homestead Land Devel. Corp., 1988-92; sr. engr. cons. Morrison Knudson, 1992-95; sr. soils analyst Geotechnics, Inc., 1995-98; offsite field supt. coastal divsn. Kaufman and Broad, 1998—. Served with U.S. Army, 1969-71. Mem. ASTM, AAAS, Nat. Inst. Scis., N.Y. Acad. Scis., Nat. Inst. Cert. in Engring. Techs., Soil and Found. Engr. Assn., Phi Alpha Theta. Baptist. Author: Geological Exploration of Alaska, 1898-1924, Alfred Hulse Brooks, Alaskan Trailblazer, Papaveraceae of the World, Demarchism, Arid Regions Gardening, Visions of Dame Kind: Dreams, Imagination and Reality, Antal's Theory of the Solar System, Science Fair-A Teacher's Manual, Common Ground: Similarities of the World Religions, Black Sheep-Scientific Discoveries From the Fringe, After Manhattan, The Christofilos Effect; and others; contbr. articles to profl. jours. Office: 3111 E Victoria Dr Alpine CA 91901-3679 *Personal philosophy: Honesty and ethical behavior at all times. Trueness of being throughout my life. Love of my wife and children makes my life worth living and is always a light when there is darkness. God watches over my shoulder.*

**ROBERTS, E. F.,** law educator; b. 1930; m. Alice A. Dunn, July 4, 1955; children: Martha, Ernest III, Michael, Marianne. BA, Northeastern U., Boston, 1952; LL.B., Boston Coll., 1954. Bar: Mass. 1954. Asst. prof. law

Villanova U., Pa., 1957-59, assoc. prof. law Pa., 1959-60, prof. law Pa., 1960-64, Cornell U., Ithaca, NY, 1964-96, Edwin H. Woodruff prof. law, emeritus/prof., 1996. Vis. prof. Nottingham U., Eng., 1962-63, Harvard U., 1983. Author: Public Regulation of Title Insurance, 1960, Land Use Planning, 2d edit., 1975, Law and the Preservation of Agricultural Land, 1982, (with Broun et al) McCormick on Evidence, 6th edit., 2006. Mem. Am. Law Inst. (life). Office: Cornell U Sch Law Ithaca NY 14853 Office Phone: 607-255-2356. Business E-Mail: e-f-roberts@postoffice.law.cornell.edu.

**ROBERTS, EDWARD BAER,** technology management educator; b. Chelsea, Mass., Nov. 18, 1935; s. Nathan and Edna (Podrachik) Roberts; m. Nancy Helen Rosenthal, July 14, 1959; children: Valerie Jo Friedman, Mitchell Jonathan, Andrea Lynne. BSEE, MSEE, MIT, 1958, MS in Mgmt., 1960, PhD in Econs., 1962. Founding mem. system dynamics program MIT, 1958-84, instr., 1959-61, asst. prof., 1961-65, assoc. prof., 1965-70, prof., 1970—, David Sarnoff prof. mgmt. of tech., 1974—, assoc. dir. research program on mgmt. of sci. and tech., 1963-73, chmn. tech. and health mgmt. group, 1973-88, chmn. mgmt. of tech. and innovation, 1988-99, founder, chmn. ctr. for entrepreneurship, 1992—94, 1997—, co-dir. internat. ctr. rsch. mgmt. tech., 1993-2000, dir. mgmt. of tech. program, 1980-89, co-chmn., 1989-99, chmn. mgmt. tech. innovation and entrepreneurship, 1999—2003. Co-founder, dir. Med. Info. Tech., Inc., Westwood, Mass., 1969—; co-founder, gen. ptnr. Zero Stage Capital Group, 1981—99; co-founder, dir. SOHU.com, Inc., Beijing, 1996—; bd. dirs. Advanced Magnetics, Inc., Cambridge, PR Restaurants, LLC, Andover, Mass., Interactive Supercomputers Inc., Visible Measures, Inc. Author: (book) The Dynamics of Research and Development, 1964, Systems Simulation for Regional Analysis, 1969, The Persistent Poppy, 1975, The Dynamics of Human Service Delivery, 1976, Entrepreneurs in High Technology, 1991; prin. author, editor: book Managerial Applications of System Dynamics, 1978; editor (with others): Biomedical Innovation, 1981; editor: Generating Technological Innovation, 1987, Innovation, 2002; mem. editl. bd. IEEE Trans. on Engring. Mgmt., Jour. Engring. and Tech. Mgmt., Jour. Product Innovation Mgmt., Sloan Mgmt. Rev., Tech. Forecasting and Social Change, Internat. Jour. Entrepreneurship and Innovation, Internat. Jour. Product Devel., Internat. Jour. Tech. Mgmt. Mem.: IEEE, Tau Kappa Alpha, Eta Kappa Nu, Tau Beta Pi, Sigma Xi. Office: MIT E52-535 50 Memorial Dr Cambridge MA 02142-1347 Office Phone: 617-253-4934. Business E-Mail: eroberts@mit.edu.

**ROBERTS, EDWARD GRAHAM,** librarian; s. Samuel Noble and Frances Johnson (Boykin) R.; m. Anna Jean Walker, Nov. 12, 1949; children: Galer Walker, Edward Graham, John Boykin. BA, U. South, 1943; BA in Library Sci., Emory U., 1948, U. Va., 1950. Curator manuscripts Duke U., Durham, NC, 1948-52; dir. libraries (Drake U.), Des Moines, 1952-56; dir. Southeastern Interlibrary Research Facility, Atlanta, 1956-59; asst. prof. info. sci. Ga. Inst. Tech., Atlanta, 1963-66, assoc. prof., 1966-69, prof., 1969-73, assoc. dir. libraries, 1966-71, dir. libraries, 1971-84, dir. emeritus, 1984—. Chmn. info. bank com. Ga. Tech. Service Program, Atlanta, 1965-67; mem. exec. bd. Southeastern Library Network, Atlanta, 1973-74; library cons. So. Regional Edn. Bd., Atlanta, 1958-59 Compiler, editor: Southeastern Supplement to the Union List of Serials, 1959; author: Literature of Science and Engineering, 1966, 2d edit.,1969. Served with U.S. Army, 1942-43. Mem. ALA, Southeastern Library Assn., Ga. Library Assn. Democrat. Episcopalian. Home: 1639 Adelia Pl NE Atlanta GA 30329-3807

**ROBERTS, EDWIN ALBERT, JR.,** editor, journalist; b. Weehawken, N.J., Nov. 14, 1932; s. Edwin Albert and Agnes Rita (Seuferling) R.; m. Barbara Anne Collins, June 14, 1958; children: Elizabeth Adams, Leslie Carol, Amy Barbara, Jacqueline Harding. Student, Coll. William and Mary, 1952-53, NYU, evenings 1955-58; AA in Coll. & Cmty. Svc., St. Petersburg Jr. Coll., 1994. Reporter N.J. Courier, Toms River, 1953-54, Asbury Park (N.J.) Press, 1954-57; reporter Wall Street Jour., N.Y.C., 1957, editorial writer, 1957-63; news editor Nat. Observer, Silver Spring, Md., 1963-68, columnist, 1968-77; editorial writer, columnist Detroit News, 1977-78, editorial page editor, 1978-83; editor editorial page Tampa Tribune, 1983—2003, ret., 2003. Author: Elections, 1964, 1964, Latin America, 1965, The Smut Rakers, 1966, Russia Today, 1967; Editor anthology: America Outdoors, 1965. Recipient Disting. Reporting Bus. award U. Mo., 1969; Pulitzer prize for distinguished commentary, 1974 Business E-Mail: ededitor@tampabay.rr.com.

**ROBERTS, ELIZABETH ANNE STEPHENS,** educational consultant; b. Bklyn., N.Y., Oct. 23, 1942; d. Edward Joseph and Mary Agnes (Donlon) Stephens; m. James Patrick Roberts, July 31, 1976; children: Sean Michael, Kerri Elizabeth Stephens. BA in Latin, Seat of Wisdom Coll., Litchfield, Conn., 1967; MA in English, CUNY, 1972; PhD in Adminstrn. and Supervision, L.I. U., 1976. Cert. tchr. Latin N.Y., tchr. English N.Y., sch. adminstrn. and supervision N.Y.; sch. dist. adminstrn. N.Y. Tchr. Christ the King HS, Middle Village, NY, 1964—73, asst. prin., 1973—74; asst. prin., tchr. English Elwood (N.Y.) Sch. Dist., 1974—78; ednl. cons. Huntington, NY, 1978—87, 2002—; instr. English, adminstr. Touro Coll, Huntington, 1987—91; tchr. Latin South Huntington (N.Y.) Sch. Dist., 1990—2002, chairperson world langs. dept. grades 6-12, 1997—2002. Coord. student internat. travels South Huntington Schs., 1990—2002. Coord. parish-wide renew program Our Lady Queen Martyrs Ch., Centerport, 1987—90. Mem.: Fgn. Lang. Assn. Chairpersons and Suprs. (pres. 1997—2002), Classical Assn. N.Y. State, N.Y. State Assn. Fgn. Lang. Tchrs., Am. Classical League, Phi Delta Kappa (treas. 1990—). Avocations: travel, reading, crossword puzzles. Home: 24 Platt Pl Huntington NY 11743-3528 Personal E-mail: JSEKR@aol.com.

**ROBERTS, ERNST EDWARD,** marketing consultant; b. Wheeling, W.Va., Dec. 19, 1926; s. Charles Ernest and Virginia Mae (Stephenson) R.; m. Donna Clare Davis, Dec. 27, 1949; children: Ernst Edward II, Carol Lee Roberts Gayda. BS, U.S. Mil. Acad., 1949; MBA, Xavier U., Cin., 1954; MS in Mech. Engring., U. So. Calif., 1957; grad. with distinction, Air War Coll., 1970. Commd. 2nd lt. U.S. Army, 1949, advanced through grades to brig. gen., 1971, served as officer in combat Korea, 1950-52; prof. mil. sci. Xavier U., 1952-54; mgmt. assist. to asst. comdt. U.S. Army Air Def. Sch., Fort Bliss, Tex., 1957-60; admissions officer U.S. Mil. Acad., West Point, NY, 1961-62, asst. to supt. (pres.), 1962-64, dir. admissions, 1964-65; comdg. officer 3d Missile Bn., 71st Arty., Fed. Republic of Germany, 1965-67; staff officer Gen. Staff U.S. Army, Washington, 1968-70; comdg. officer NATO Air Def. Arty. Group, Germany, 1970-71; commdg. gen. 38th Air Def. Arty. Brigade, Korea, 1971-72; dep. commanding gen. U.S. Army Air Def. Sch. and Ctr., Fort Bliss, 1972-74; ret. U.S. Army, 1974; v.p. bldg. and property mgr. El Paso (Tex.) Nat. Bank and Corp., 1974-79, sr. v.p., dir. pers. and tng., 1979-83, exec. v.p., dir. mktg., 1983-92; mktg. cons., 1992—. Mem. exec. mgmt. com. Tex. Commerce Bank, El Paso, 1983-92; vis. lectr. mktg. Webster U. Mem. bd. advisors SBA; mem. mayor's Citizens Com. on Police Dept. Matters, El Paso; mem. Task Force to Evaluate Mgmt. of Sheriff's Dept.; head bond-issue campaign, El Paso; adv. dir. Armed Svcs. YMCA, past pres.; adv. dir. nat. bd. dirs. Armed Svcs. YMCA, El Paso Cmty. Found.; past pres. U. Tex.-El Paso Eldorados; past mem. bd. dirs., trustee Found. Lighthouse for Blind; chmn. adv. bd. dirs. El Paso Bus. Com. for Arts; chmn. capital fund drive com. Rio Grande Girl Scouts Am., Plz. Theatre-Plz. Park Restoration bd.; past mem. campaign cabinet United Way El Paso County; chmn. Capital Fund Drive, Air Def. Arty. Mus., Ft. Bliss; bd. dirs. City of El Paso, mem. steering com. Safe 2000; bd. dirs. Crimestoppers of El Paso. Decorated D.S.M., Legion of Merit, Silver Star, Meritorious Svc. medal; recipient Pro Eclesio Et Pontifice, Vatican, 1971; Conquistador award City of El Paso, Liberty Bell award Legal Cmty. El Paso, 1988. Mem. Am. Inst. Banking, Assn. U.S. Army (Gen. Army Omar N. Bradley chpt.), El Paso C. of C. (mem. armed forces com., chmn. spl. task force to evaluate chamber mgmt.), Mil. Order Worldwar I chpt. chmn. citizen of yr. award 1996-2001), U.S. Army Air Def. Arty. Assn. (past pres., named Disting. Korean War Vet. 2004), El Paso Club (past pres., bd. dirs.), Rotary (past pres.). Republican. Roman Catholic. Home: 8212 Antero Pl El Paso TX 79904-2401

**ROBERTS, FLETCHER,** editor; Arts & Leisure sect. writer, editor NY Times, 1987—. Office: NY Times 229 W 43rd St New York NY 10036 Office Phone: 212-556-4260.*

**ROBERTS, FRANCIS STONE,** advertising executive; b. Scranton, Pa., Aug. 15, 1944; s. Gordon Link and Eleanor Swartz (Stone) R.; m. Julie Ann Dolan; children: Francis Stone, Link McGregor. BA, Grove City Coll., Pa., 1966; A.M.P., U. Chgo., 1984. With media dept., then account exec. Compton Advt. Inc., N.Y.C., 1966-69; account exec. Tatham-Laird & Kudner Advt., N.Y.C., 1969-70; account supr., v.p. SSC&B Advt. Inc., N.Y.C., 1970-78, sr. v.p., mgmt. supr., 1994; group exec. v.p. SSC&B: Lintas Advt. Worldwide, 1987-89; COO, pres. Lintas, NY, 1990-94; mem. policy and ops. coms., chmn. strategy rev. bd. Lintas N.Y.; also dir. Lintas N.Y. and U.S.A.; CEO, chmn. The CEO-Gotham Grp., N.Y.C., 1994-95; chmn., CEO Gotham Inc., N.Y.C., 1995—2004; mng. dir. Gotham Ltd., London, 1996—2004; CEO, pres. Carlson & Ptnrs., N.Y.C., 2004—05, Roberts & Tarlow, N.Y.C., 2005. Mem. bd. dirs. Am. Assn. Advertising Agencies, Am. Advertising Fedn., The Ad Coun.; bd. trustees Pro Ad PAC. Alumni coun. Grove City Coll., 1999—. Mem. William Penn Charter Alumni Assn. (pres. N.Y. chpt. 1984-88), Ad Club N.Y., The Union League N.Y. Clubs: New Canaan Field, New Canaan Winter, New Canaan Country, Congl. Country. Republican. Presbyterian. Home: 28 Landing Dr Dobbs Ferry NY 10522 Office: Roberts and Tarlow 437 Madison New York NY 10022 Office Phone: 646-289-7301. Business E-Mail: stone@robertsntarlow.com.

**ROBERTS, FRANK ALAN,** periodontist, researcher, dental educator; b. Ill. s. Glynn W. and Joanna B. Roberts; m. Laura J. Theobald; children: Hannah L., Elizabeth G. BS, Davidson Coll., NC, 1986; DDS, U. Tenn., 1990; PhD, U. Ala., Birmingham, 1996; cert. in Periodontics, U. Ala., 1996. Diplomate Am. Bd. Periodontology, 2002. Assoc. prof. U. Wash., Seattle, 1996—; staff periodontist Vets. Healthcare Sys., Seattle, 1997—. Infection control cons. Dental Quality Assurance Bd. State of Wash. and Wash. State Medicaid Program, Olympia, Wash., 2002—; infection control cons. Dept. of Labor and Industries State of Wash. and Wash. Indsl. Safety and Health Act, Olympia, 2002—; reviewer Jour. Periodontology, Chgo., 1998—. Jour. Periodontal Rsch., Oxford, 1998—. Jour. Dental Rsch., Washington, 2005—. Contbr. articles to profl. jours. Grantee, Nat. Ctr. Minority and Minority Health Disparities, 2002—, NIH, 1999—. Fellow: Am. Acad. Periodontology (Tarrson fellowship 2000—03); mem.: ADA (accreditation site visitor 2002—). Internat. Assn. Dental Rsch. Office: Univ Wash HSB D580C Box 357444 Seattle WA 98195-7444 Office Phone: 206-685-9046.

**ROBERTS, GARY RAYMOND,** lawyer, educator; b. Owatonna, Minn., Apr. 24, 1948; s. Ronald Raymond and Evelyn Mary (Halverson) R.; m. Nancy Louise Crnkovich, Sept. 30, 1983; 1 child, Andrew August. BA, Bradley U., 1970; JD, Stanford U., 1975. Tchr. Limestone High Sch., Bartonville, Ill., 1970-72; instr. Bradley U., Peoria, Ill., 1971-72; law clk. to judge U.S. Ct. Appeals (9th cir.) Calif., San Francisco, 1975-76; assoc. Covington and Burling, Washington, 1976-83; prof. law Tulane U. Law Sch., New Orleans, 1983—, vice dean, 1990—95, dep. dean, 2001—. Sports law cons. to athletes, leagues and univs.; faculty rep. NCAA; mem. pres.'s adv. com., ad-hoc com. on men's basketball, univ. senate Tulane U.; chmn. athlete career counseling and agt. screening com. Tulane U. Author: Cases and Materials on Sports and the Law, 1993; editor-in-chief The Sports Lawyer; contbr. articles to numerous univ. law revs. Recipient Felix Frankfuter Tchg. Award, 2001. Mem. ABA (com. antitrust sect., litigation sect., forum com. on sports and entertainment), Am. Assn. Law Schs. (past chmn. law and sports sect.), Sports Lawyers Assn. (v.p., bd. dirs., pres. 1995-97). Democrat. Office: Tulane Law Sch 6801 Freret St Ste 2 New Orleans LA 70118-5697

**ROBERTS, GEORGE BERNARD, JR.,** management and government relations consultant, former state legislator; b. Andover, Mass., June 13, 1939; s. George Bernard and Helene F. (Eversen) R.; m. Margaret Fay Edmunds, Aug. 26, 1967; children: Abigail Emerson, Jessica Swift. BS, U. N.H., 1964, M.P.A., 1967. Ptnr. Roberts Real Estate Assocs., Gilmanton, N.H. 1966—; mem. N.H. Ho. of Reps., 1967-80, majority leader, 1971-74, speaker, 1975-76, 77-78, 79-80; pres. Policy Mgmt. Assocs., Concord, NH, 1980—. Pres. and treas. Concord, Concord Coach Soc. Del. Nat. Rep. Conv., 1972-76; mem. N.H. Constl. Conv., 1974, 84, N.H. Rep. Party Fin. Com.; pres. Nat. Conf. State Legislatures, 1979-80; chmn. exec. com. 1st Congl. Soc. Gilmanton. Mem. Nat. Rep. Legislators Assn. (founding, past pres.), Masons, Shriners, Scottish Rite, Historic Dist. Commn. Gilmanton, Sigma Alpha Epsilon. Republican. Office: Concord Policy Mgmt Assocs 4 Park St Ste 100 Concord NH 03301-6313

**ROBERTS, GEORGE R.,** investment banking company executive; b. Houston, Tex., 1945; married; 3 children. Grad., Claremont McKenna Coll.; JD, U. Calif. Hastings Law Sch., San Francisco, 1969. Joined corp. fin. dept. to partner Bear Stearns & Co., New York, 1969—79; founding sr. ptnr. Kohlberg, Kravis, Roberts, San Francisco, 1976—. Dir. Kodel-KKR, Safeway, Inc., DPL, Inc., KinderCare Learning Centers, Inc., Owens-Illinois, Inc. and PRIMEDIA Inc. Bd. San Francisco Symphony, San Francisco Ballet, Fine Arts Mus., San Francisco, Claremont McKenna Coll. Named one of Forbes' Richest Americans, 2006; recipient Man of Yr. award, Culver Ednl. Found., 2006. Achievements include historic billion dollar buyout of Wometco Companies in 1984; $25 billion RJR Nabisco buyout in 1989. Office: Kohlberg Kravis Roberts & Co 2800 Sand Hill Rd Ste 200 Menlo Park CA 94025-7055*

**ROBERTS, HARRY MORRIS, JR.,** lawyer; b. Dallas, June 10, 1938; s. Harry Morris and La Frances (Reilly) R.; m. Nancy Beth Johnson, Mar. 7, 1964; children: Richard Whitfield, Elizabeth Lee. BBA, So. Meth. U., 1960; LLB, Harvard U., 1963. Bar: Tex. 1963, U.S. Dist. Ct. (no. dist.) Tex. 1964, U.S. Ct. Appeals (5th cir.) 1972, U.S. Supreme Ct. 1971. Assoc. Thompson & Knight, Dallas, 1963-69, ptnr., 1970-75, sr. ptnr., 1975—. Lawyer; chmn. real estate, probate and trust law sect. State Bar Tex., 1984-85; vis. scholar U. Tex. Law Sch., 1986. Contbr. articles to profl. jours. Trustee Shelter Ministries of Dallas, 1982—, chmn. bd. trustees, 1992-95, 2004-05. Mem. ABA, Dallas Bar Assn. (chmn. real estate sect. 1981), Am. Bar Found., Tex. Bar Found., Dallas Bar Found. (dir.), Am. Coll. Real Estate Lawyers, Tex. Coll. Real Estate Attys., Salesmanship Club (Dallas), Dallas Country Club. Episcopalian. Office: Thompson & Knight 1700 Pacific Ave Ste 3300 Dallas TX 75201-4693 Office Phone: 214-969-1616. Business E-Mail: harry.roberts@tklaw.com.

**ROBERTS, JAMES ALLEN,** retired urologist, educator; b. Beach, N.D., May 31, 1934; s. Earl Fernando and Maria Ellen Roberts; m. Hilda Peachy Roberts, Nov. 29, 1896; children from previous marriage: Jennifer Lou Roberts Walsh, Mary Ellen Roberts Wargo, Thomas Jay. MD, U. Chgo., 1959. Diplomate: Am. Bd. Urology. Intern U. Chgo. Sch. Medicine, 1959-60, resident in urology, 1961-65; from mem. faculty to prof. Tulane U. Med. Sch., New Orleans, 1971-99, prof. urology, 1986—, assoc. chmn., 1986—99; sr. research scientist, head dept. urology Tulane Regional Primate Research Center, Covington, 1972-99; prof. emeritus, 1999—; fellow Tougaby Sch. Internat. NIH, 1941; ret., 2005. Mem. editorial bd. Am. Jour. Kidney Diseases and Urol. Rsch.; contbr. articles to profl. jours. Bd. dirs. Highland Park Hosp., 1985-87. With USN, 1965—67. Recipient grants NIH, Original Rsch. award Southern Med. Assn., 1990, Cert. Achievement Am. Urological Assn., 1997 Fulbright Sr. scholar, 1999-2000. Fellow ACS; mem.: AUA (pub. Biology and Medicine, Nat. Inst. Health (SAT study sect. 1995-99), Sigma Xi. Office: 83 Towne Place Dr Hendersonville NC 28792 Personal E-Mail: jrhr285@mchsi.com.

**ROBERTS, JAMES HAROLD, III,** lawyer; b. Omaha, Aug. 11, 1949; s. James Harold Jr. and Evelyn Doris (Young) R.; m. Marilyn Novak, June 29, 1974; children: Jessica Noël, Meredith Caitlin. BA, U. Notre Dame, 1971; JD, St. Louis U., 1974. Bar: Iowa 1974, U.S. Ct. Mil. Appeals 1974, U.S. Supreme Ct. 1979, D.C. 1981. Govt. contract atty. U.S. Gen. Acctg. Office, Washington, 1978-83, US Dept. Treasury, Washington, 1983-88; pvt. practice Van Scoyoc Kelly PLLC, Washington, 1988—. Editor St. Louis U. law rev., 1973-74. Lt. col. JAGC, U.S. Army, 1974-78, USAR/NG, 1978-99. Mem. ABA (pub. contract law sect.), D.C. Bar Assn., Fed. Bar Assn. Roman

---

Catholic. Home: 308 N Monroe St Arlington VA 22201-1736 Office: Van Scoyoc Kelly PLLC Ste 665E 101 Constitution Ave NW Washington DC 20001-1737 Office Phone: 202-898-1898. Business E-Mail: jroberts@vsklaw.com.

**ROBERTS, JAMES MCGREGOR,** retired trade association administrator; b. Moncton, N.B., Can., Nov. 24, 1923; came to U.S., 1949, naturalized, 1956; s. Roland M. and Edith M. (Shields) R.; m. Thelma E. Williams, May 6, 1944; 1 dau., Jana M. B.Commerce, U. Toronto, Ont., Can., 1949. Auditor Citizens Bank, Los Angeles, 1949-54; auditor Acad. Motion Picture Arts and Scis., Hollywood, Calif., 1954—, controller, 1956-71, exec. dir., 1971-89, exec. sec. acad. found., 1971-89, exec. cons. Hollywood, Calif., 1989-92, 1990-93; ret., 1994. Served as pilot Royal Can. Air Force, World War II. Home: 4968 Lerkas Way Oceanside CA 92056-7428 E-mail: jmrter@cox.net.

**ROBERTS, JEANNE ADDISON,** retired literature educator; b. Washington; d. John West and Sue Fisher (Nichols) Addison; m. Markley Roberts, Feb. 19, 1966; children: Addison Cary Steed Masengill, Ellen Carraway Masengill Coster. AB, Agnes Scott Coll., 1946; MA, U. Pa., 1947; PhD, U. Va., 1964. Instr. Mary Washington Coll., 1947-48; instr., chmn. English Fairfax Hall Jr. Coll., 1950-51; tchr. Am. U. Assn. Lang. Center, Bangkok, Thailand, 1952-56; instr. Beirut (Lebanon) Coll. for Women, 1956-57, asst. prof., 1957-60, chmn. English dept., 1957-60; instr. lit. Am. U., Washington, 1960-62, asst. prof., 1962-65, asso. prof., 1965-68, prof., 1968-93. Dean faculties Am. U., 1974; lectr. Howard U., 1971-72; seminar prof. Folger Shakespeare Libr. Inst. for Renaissance and 18th Century Studies, 1974; dir. NEH Summer Inst. for HS Tchrs. on Teaching Shakespeare, Folger Shakespeare Libr., 1984-86; dir. NEH summer inst. Va. Commonwealth U. 1995-96 Writings By and About Women in The English Renaissance; study group leader Inst. Learning in Retirement, Am. U., 1999-, mem. study groups. Author: Shakespeare's English Comedy: The Merry Wives of Windsor in Context, 1979, The Shakespearean Wild: Geography, Genus and Gender, 1991; editor: (with James G. McManaway) A Selective Bibliography of Shakespeare: Editions, Textual Studies, Commentary, 1975; (with Peggy O'Brien) Shakespeare Set Free, vol. 1, 1993, vol. 2, 1994, vol. 3, 1995, (with Georgianna Ziegler) Shakespeare's Unruly Women, 1997; contbr. articles to profl. jours. and scholarly collections. Danforth Tchr. grantee, 1962—63, Folger Sr. fellow, 1969—70, 1988. Mem. MLA (chmn. Shakespeare div. 1981-82), Renaissance Soc. Am., Milton Soc., Shakespeare Assn. Am. (trustee 1978-81, 87-89, pres. 1986-87), AAUP (pres. Am. U. chpt. 1966-67), Southeastern Renaissance Conf. (pres. 1981-82), English Speaking Union (bd. dirs. 2005-06). Phi Beta Kappa, Mortar Board, Phi Kappa Phi. Episcopalian. Home: 4931 Albemarle St NW Washington DC 20016-4359 Personal E-mail: jeannerobe@aol.com.

**ROBERTS, JILL CAROLYNE,** researcher, educator; b. South Bend, Ind., Oct. 2, 1972; d. Carolyne Sue Roberts. BS in Microbiology, Ind. U., Bloomington, 1996; MPH in Infectious Disease, U. South Fla., Tampa, 1998; PhD in Infectious Disease, U. South Fla., 2006; MS in Microbiology, U. Tex. Houston, 2003. Adj. faculty Hillsborough C.C., Tampa, 2005—; postdoctoral rschr., adj. faculty U. South Fla., 2006—. Contbr. articles to profl. jours. Rsch. grantee, Sam Bell Found., Jacksonville, Fla., 2005, tchg. grantee, Dept. Global Health, U. South Fla., 2006. Mem.: Am. Soc. Microbiology, Am. Pub. Health Assn. Avocations: marathon running, bicycling, swimming, rollerblading. Office: Ctr for Biol Def 3602 Spectrum Blvd MDC 56 Tampa FL 33672 Office Phone: 813-974-3429. Office Fax: 813-974-1479. E-mail: jroberts@hsc.usf.edu.

**ROBERTS, JIM,** editor; m. Debby Krenek, Feb. 1987; 2 children. Grad, Univ. N.C., 1977. Reporter Richmond Times Dispatch; copy editor Baltimore News American; news editor Dallas Times Herald; copy editor, dep. metro. editor, nat. policital editor New York Times, 1987—2001, dep. nat. editor, 2001—02, nat. editor, 2002—05, sr. editor, nat. desk, 2005—06, editor, digital news, 2006—. Office: New York Times 229 W 43d St New York NY 10036*

**ROBERTS, JOHN,** news anchor; b. Toronto, Ont., Nov. 15, 1956; Student, U. Toronto. Anchor, corr. several broadcasts City TV, Toronto, 1979—89; anchor, corr. WCIX TV (now WFOR-TV), Miami, Fla., 1989—90; co-anchor Can. A.M., 1990—92, CBS Morning News, 1992, WCBS-TV, NYC, 1994—95; anchor CBS Evening News Sunday, NYC, 1995—2006; chief White House corr. CBS News, NYC, 1999—2006; sr. nat. corr. CNN, Washington, 2006—. Recipient Emmy award for best newscast (live coverage of the 1994 elections), New York Press Club award. Office: CNN Bldg 820 First St NE Washington DC 20002*

**ROBERTS, JOHN CHARLES,** law educator; b. Aberdeen, S.D., Feb. 29, 1940; s. Jacob John Schmitt and Leona (Blethen) Blake; m. Nathleen Kelly (div. 1985); children: Katherine, John Charles Jr.; m. Lynn Dale Friedman, Dec. 22, 1985; 1 child, Emily Sara. BS, Northwestern U., 1961; LL.B., Yale U., 1968. Bar: U.S. Dist. Ct. D.C. 1969, Mich. 1981. Assoc. Covington & Burling, Washington, 1968-71; assoc. dean, lectr. Yale U. Law Sch., New Haven, 1971-77; gen. counsel US Senate Com. on Armed Services, 1977-80; adj. prof. law Washington Coll. Law, Am. U., 1978-80; dean, prof. law Wayne State U. Law Sch., Detroit, 1980-86; prof., dean Law Sch. DePaul U., Chgo., 1986-96, v.p. for univ. advancement, 1996-97, prof. law, 1997—. Mem. exec. com. Inst. for Continuing Legal Edn., Chgo., 1988-91. Mem. adv. com. Mich. Psychiat. Soc., 1980-86; bd. dirs. Constl. Rights Found., 1992-96. Lt. USN, 1961-65. Mem. ABA, Assn. Am. Law Schs. (mem. exec. com., chmn. sect. instn. advancement 1987-88, chmn., sec. adminstrn. law schs. 1993-94), Order of Coif. Democrat. Avocation: collecting modern first editions. Office: DePaul U Coll Law 25 E Jackson Blvd Chicago IL 60604-2289 Office Phone: 312-362-8776. Business E-Mail: jroberts@depaul.edu.

**ROBERTS, JOHN D.,** chemist, educator; b. LA, June 8, 1918; s. Allen Andrew and Flora (Dombrowski) Roberts; m. Edith Mary Johnson, July 11, 1942; children: Anne Christine, Donald William, John Paul, Allen Walter. AB, UCLA, 1941, PhD, 1944; D in Natural Scis. (hon.), U. Munich, 1962; DSc (hon.), Temple U., 1964, Notre Dame U., 1993, U. Wales, 1993, Scripps Rsch. Inst., 1996. Instr. chemistry UCLA, 1944—45; NRC fellow chemistry Harvard U., 1945—46, instr. chemistry, 1946, MIT, 1946, asst. prof., 1947—50, assoc. prof., 1950—52; vis. prof. Ohio State U., 1952, Stanford U., 1973—74; prof. organic chemistry Calif. Inst. Tech., 1953—72, inst. prof. chemistry, 1972—88, inst. prof. chemistry emeritus, lectr., 1988—, dean of faculty, v.p., provost, 1980—83, lectr., 1988—, chmn. divsn. chemistry and chem. engring., 1963—68, acting chmn., 1972—73. Bd. dirs. Huntington Med. Rsch. Insts., 1984—99, Organic Syntheses Inc.; Robert Noyce vis. prof. sci. Grinnell Coll., 2001. Author: Basic Organic Chemistry Part I, 1955, Nuclear Magnetic Resonance, 1959, Spin-Spin Splitting in High-Resolution Nuclear Magnetic Resonance Spectra, 1961, Molecular Orbital Calculations, 1961; author: (with M.C. Caserio) Basic Principles of Organic Chemistry, 1964, 2d edit., 1977, Modern Organic Chemistry, 1967; author: (with R. Stewart and M.C. Caserio) Organic Chemistry-Methane To Macromolecules, 1971; author: At The Right Place at the Right Time, 1990, ABCs of FT-NMR, 2000; contbg. editor: McGraw-Hill Series in Advanced Chemistry, 1957—60; editor: Organic Syntheses, Vol. 41, 1961; Spectroscopy, mem. editl. bd.: Organic Magnetic Resonance in Chemistry. Trustee L.S.B. Leakey Found., 1983—92; bd. dirs. Coleman Chamber Music Assn.; adv. com. Calif. Competitive Tech., 1989—92. Co-recipient Robert A. Welch award, 1990; named Hon. Alumnus, Calif. Inst. Tech., 1990, SURF dedicatee, 1992; named one of Most Influential Chemists of Last 75 yrs., Chem. and Engring. News, 1998; recipient Alumni Profl. Achievement award, UCLA, 1967, Nichols medal, 1972, Tolman medal, 1975, Michelson-Morley award, 1976, Norris award, 1978, Pauling award, 1980, Theodore Wm. Richards medal, 1982, Willard Gibbs Gold medal, 1983, Golden Plate award, Am. Acad. Achievement, 1983, Priestley medal, 1987, Madison Marshall award, 1989, Nat. Medal Sci., NSF, 1990, Glenn T. Seaborg medal, 1991, Award in nuclear magnetic resource, 1991, Svec to Chemistry award, 1991, History Maker award, Pasadena Hist. Soc., 1994, Panting Legacy award, 2006, Pauling

---

Legacy award, 2006;, Guggenheim fellow, 1952—53, 1955—56. Mem.: AAAS (councillor 1992—95), NAS (councillor 1980—83, com. on sci. and engring. pub. policy 1983—87, Chem. Scis. award 1999), Am. Acad. Arts and Scis., Am. Philos. Soc. (coun. mem. 1983—86), Am. Chem. Soc. (chmn. organic chemistry divsn. 1956—57, award pure chemistry 1954, Harrison Howe award 1957, Roger Adams award in organic chemistry 1967, Arthur C. Cope award, Chem. Pioneer award 1994, Nakanishi prize 2001, Auburn Kosolapoff award 2003), Phi Lambda Upsilon, Sigma Xi. Office: Calif Inst Tech Crellin Lab Pasadena CA 91125-0001

**ROBERTS, JOHN DERHAM,** lawyer; 1 child. Cert., Richmond (Va.) Bus. Coll., 1960; BS, Hampden-Sydney (Va.) Coll., 1964; LLB, Washington & Lee U., 1968. Bar: Va. 1968, Fla. 1969, U.S. Supreme Ct. 1969, U.S. Ct. Customs and Patent Appeals 1970, U.S. Tax Ct. 1970, U.S. Ct. Appeals (5th cir.) 1970, U.S. Ct. Appeals (9th cir.) 1974, U.S. Supreme Ct. 1969. Law clk. U.S. Dist. Ct., Jacksonville, Fla., 1968-69; assoc. Phillips, Kendrick, Gearhart & Aylor, Arlington, Va., 1969-70; asst. U.S. Atty. mid. dist. Fla. U.S. Dept. Justice, Jacksonville, 1970-74. Dist. of Alaska, Anchorage, 1974-77, U.S. magistrate judge, 1977—. Bd. dirs. Teen Challenge Alaska, Anchorage, 1984-93; chmn. Eagle Scout Rev. Bd., 1993—; bd. dirs. Alaska Youth for Christ, 1993-96; govs.'s Prayer Breakfast Com., 1994—, vice-chair, 1998—. Recipient Citizenship award DAR, Anchorage, 1984, plaque, U.S. Navy, Citizen Day, Adak, Alaska, 1980, Silver Beaver award, 2004. Mem. ABA, Nat. Conf. Spl. Ct. Judges (exec. bd. 1985-92), 9th Cir. Conf. Magistrate Judges (exec. bd. 1982-85, chmn. 1984-85, 2005—), Alaska Bar Assn., Anchorage Bar Assn., Chi Phi, Psi Chi, Phi Alpha Delta. Republican. Office: US Magistrate Judge 222 W 7th Ave Unit 46 Anchorage AK 99513-7504 Office Phone: 907-677-6255.

**ROBERTS, JOHN GLOVER, JR.,** United States Supreme Court Chief Justice; b. Buffalo, Jan. 27, 1955; s. John Glover and Rosemary (Podrasky) R.; m. Jane Marie Sullivan Roberts, July 27, 1996; children Jack, Josie. AB summa cum laude, Harvard U., 1976, JD magna cum laude, 1979. Bar: DC 1981, US Ct. Appeals (Fed. Cir.) 1982, US Ct. Appeals (DC, 5th, 9th Cirs.) 1988, US Ct. Appeals (3rd, 7th, and 10th Cirs.) 1996, US Ct. Claims 1982, US Supreme Ct. 1987. Law clk. to Hon. Henry Friendly US Ct. Appeals (2nd Cir.), NYC, 1979-80; law clk. to Assoc. Justice William H. Rehnquist US Supreme Ct., Washington, 1980-81; spl. asst. to US Atty. Gen. William French Smith US Dept. Justice, Washington, 1981-82; assoc. counsel to Pres. Ronald Reagan The White House, Washington, 1982-86; assoc. Hogan & Hartson, Washington, 1986-87, ptnr., 1988—89, 1993—2003; prin. dep. solicitor gen. US Dept. Justice, Washington, 1989-93; judge US Ct. Appeals (DC Cir.), Washington, 2003—05; initially nominee for assoc. justice US Supreme Ct., 2005, chief justice, 2005—. Editor: Harvard Law Rev., 1977-79 Named one of 100 Most Influential People, Time Mag., 2006. Mem. Am. Law Inst., Am. Acad. Appellate Lawyers, Edward Coke Appellate Inn of Ct., Supreme Ct. Hist. Soc., Lawyers Club, Met. Club, Robert Trent Jones Golf Club, Phi Beta Kappa; fellow Am. Acad. Arts & Sciences Republican. Argued 39 cases before the US Supreme Court. Office: US Supreme Ct One First St SE Washington DC 20543*

**ROBERTS, JOHN W.,** historian, federal agency official; b. NJ, 1954; s. Walter I. and Lucile K. Roberts. BA, Coll. of N.J., Trenton, 1976; MA, U. Md., 1979, PhD, 1992. Instr. rschr. U. of Md., College Park, 1976—82; archives technician Nat. Archives, Washington, 1978—82; dir. devel. svcs. Trinity Coll., Washington, 1982—85; archivist Nat. Archives, Washington, 1985—87; chief of archives Fed. Bur. of Prisons, Washington, 1987—98; sr. historian, archivist History Assocs. Inc., Rockville, Md., 1998—2002; chief mus. mgmt. Nat. Pk. Svc., Washington, 2002—05, chief Nat. Register of Hist. Places and Nat. Hist. Landmarks program, 2005—. Author: (book) Escaping Prison Myths: Selected Topics on the History of Federal Corrections, Putting Foreign Policy to Work: The Role of Organized Labor in American Foreign Relations, 1932-1941, Reform and Retribution: An Illustrated History of American Prisons; co-author (with Richard Phillips): Quick Reference to Correctional Administration; contbr. articles to profl. jours. and encys. Mem.: Am. Assn. of Mus., Soc. of Am. Archivists, Soc. for History in the Fed. Govt. (exec. coun. 2002—04, v.p. 2005—06, pres. 2006—). Office: Nat Park Svc 1201 I St NW Washington DC 20005 Business E-Mail: john_w_roberts@nps.gov.

**ROBERTS, JUDITH ANN,** secondary school educator; b. Hammond, Ind., July 8, 1958; d. Edmund Carl and Norma Jean (Holmes) Huke; m. Ashton Lindsey Roberts, July 10, 1981; children: Stephanie Louise, Matthew Ashton. BS, Manchester Coll., 1980; MS, Purdue U., Hammond, Ind., 1987. Cert. tchr., Ind. Tchr. math. Kankakee Valley Sch. Corp., Wheatfield, Ind., 1980—, head dept., 1985-89. Mem. Cedar Creek Twp. Adv. Bd., Lowell, Ind., 1991-94. Named Tchr. of Month, Kankakee Valley Sch. Corp., 1990. Mem. Kankakee Valley Tchrs. Assn. (negotiations com. 1990-98, high sch. bldg. rep., treas.).

**ROBERTS, JUDITH MARIE,** librarian, educator; b. Bluefield, W.Va., Aug. 5, 1939; d. Charles Bowen Lowder and Frances Marie (Bourne) Lowder Alberts; m. Craig Currence Johnson, July 1, 1957 (div. 1962); 1 child, Craig Jr.; m. Milton Rinehart Roberts, Aug. 13, 1966 (div. 1987). BS, Concord State Tchrs. Coll., 1965. Libr. Cape Henlopen Sch. Dist., Lewes, Del., 1965—91; with Lily's Gift Shop, St. Petersburg, Fla., 1991—. Pres. Friends of Lewes Pub. Libr., 1986—90; chmn. exhibits Govs. Conf. Librs. and Info. Svcs., Dover, Del., 1978; mem. Gov.'s State Libr. Adv. Coun., 1977—91. Mem.: NEA, ALA, Del. Learning Resources Assn. (pres. 1976—77), Del. Library Assn. (pres. 1982—83), Sussex Help Orgn. for Resources Exch. (pres. 1984—85), Del. State Edn. Assn. Methodist. Office Phone: 727-867-7974. Business E-Mail: judyoffice2003@yahoo.com.

**ROBERTS, JULIA FIONA,** actress; b. Smyrna, Ga., Oct. 28, 1967; d. Betty and Walter Roberts; m. Lyle Lovett, Jun. 25, 1993 (div. March 22, 1995); m. Daniel Moder, July 4, 2002; children Hazel Patricia, Phinnaeus Walter. Actress (films) Blood Red, 1986, Satisfaction, 1987, Mystic Pizza, 1988, Steel Magnolias, 1989 (Acad. Award nominee, Golden Globe award), Pretty Woman, 1990 (Acad. Award nominee, Golden Globe Award), Flatliners, 1990, Sleeping With the Enemy, 1991, Hook, 1991, Dying Young, 1991, The Player, 1992, The Pelican Brief, 1993, I Love Trouble, 1994, Ready to Wear (Prêt-à-Porter), 1994, Something To Talk About, 1995, Mary Reilly, 1996, Everybody Says I Love You, 1996, Michael Collins, 1996, My Best Friend's Wedding, 1997, Conspiracy Theory, 1997, Stepmom, 1998 (also exec. prodr.), Notting Hill, 1999, Runaway Bride, 1999, Erin Brockovich, 2000 (Acad. award for Best Actress, Golden Globe for Best Performance by an Actress), The Mexican, 2001, America's Sweethearts, 2001, Ocean's Eleven, 2001, Full Frontal, 2002, Confessions of a Dangerous Mind, 2002, Mona Lisa Smile, 2003, Closer, 2004, Ocean's Twelve, 2004, (voice) The Ant Bully, 2006; (TV movies) Baja Oklahoma, 1988, Before Your Eyes: Angelie's Secret (voice only), 1995; (TV appearances) Crime Story, 1987, Miami Vice, 1988, Friends, 1996, Murphy Brown, 1998, Sesame Street, 1998, AFI's 100 Years...100 Movies, 1998, In the Wild, 1998, Law & Order, 1999; Broadway plays include Three Days of Rain, 2006. Involved with UNICEF; lent celebrity name to help raise money for research to develop a cure for Rett Syndrome. Named Female Star of the Yr., Nat. Assn. Theatre Owners, 1991; recipient People's Choice awards Favorite Motion Picture Actress, 1991, 98, Favorite Comedy/Dramatic Motion Picture Actress, 1992, Favorite Dramatic Motion Picture Actres, 1994; recipient Woman of Yr. award Hasty Pudding Theatricals, 1997, Spc. award Internat. Star of Yr., ShoWest Conv., 1998; named one of '50 Most Beautiful People in the World, People Mag., 1990, 1991, '50 Most Beautiful List', People Mag.(USA), 2000, 2002, '25 Most Intriguing People, People Mag., 2001, Top Entertainers, E!, 2001.; named one of 50 Most Powerful People in Hollywood Premiere mag., 2002-06. One of the most popular and sought-after talents in Hollywood; highest paid actress in film history. Office: c/o Kevin Huvane Creative Artists Agency 9830 Wilshire Blvd Beverly Hills CA 90212-1825*

**ROBERTS, KATHARINE ADAIR,** retired bookkeeper; b. Columbus, Ga., June 4, 1930; d. William Lynn and Ella Miller (Adair) R. BA, U. Redlands, 1955; postgrad., San Bernardino Valley Coll., 1971—74, Calif. State U., San Bernardino, 1975—78. Bookkeeper Rettig Machine Shop, Inc., Redlands, Calif., 1970-97, ret., 1997. Pres. Dem. Study Club, San Bernardino, 1967-68, Redlands Dem. Club, 1976, Wilsonian Club, San Bernardino, 1986; chair Redlands/San Bernardino chpt. Citizens for Global Solutions, 1987—, San Bernardino leader ptnrs. for global change program; active San Bernardino County Dem. Cent. Com., treas. 1977-80. Named one of 63 Women of Distinction, 63rd Assembly Dist., Calif., Assemblyman Bill Emmerson, 2005; recipient Citizen Achievement award, LWV, 1989. Mem. Dem. Luncheon Club (George E. Brown Amb. of Peace award 2000), Humane Soc. of San Bernardino Valley, Redlands Humane Soc., Redlands Dem. Club (treas.), LWV, Inland Empire Debating Soc. (treas.). Democrat. Home: 798 W 18th St San Bernardino CA 92405-4235

**ROBERTS, KATHLEEN JOY DOTY,** secondary school educator; b. Jamaica, NY, Apr. 19, 1951; d. Alfred Arthur and Helen Caroline (Sohl) Doty; m. Robert Louis Roberts, Nov. 24, 1974; children: Robert Louis, Michael Sean, Kathleen Meagan. BA in Edn., CUNY, 1972, MS in Spl. Edn., 1974; cert. advanced study in ednl. adminstrn., Hofstra U., 1982; Ednl. Specialist, Nova Southeastern U., 2003, PhD Computing Tech. in Edn., 2004. Cert. sch. adminstrn., tchr. math., N.Y.; cert. N.Y. Dept. Mental Hygiene; lic. spl. edn. supr., ednl. adminstr., N.Y. Tchr. health conservation Woodside (N.Y.) Jr. H.S., 1973-77; coord. spl. edn. dept. Ridgewood (N.Y.) Jr. H.S., 1977-81; adminstrv. asst., health, compliance and mainstream coord., grant writer Grover Cleveland H.S., Ridgewood, 1981—2004, also coord. transition linkage, resource tchr. mentor, 1981—2004; tech. staff developer Region 4, N.Y.C. Dept. Edn., 2004—06; collaborative team tchr. Queens H.S. for Tchg., 2006—. Instr. Grad. Sch. U. Phoenix. Author: Closed Circuit TV and Other Devices for the Partially Sighted, 1971, Nat. Soc. Colonial Daughters of the Seventeenth Century Lineage Book (Centennial Remembrance edit.), 1999; contbr. articles to profl. jours. Legis. chmn. Fairfield Jr. and Sr. H.S. PTA and Massapequa coun., 1987-92. Mem.: ACM, DAR, NEA, Internat. Soc. Tech. in Edn., N.Y. State Tchrs. Assn., Colonial Dames of the XVII Century, Colonial Daus. of the XVII Century (pres. 1985—91, nat. chmn. hist. activities com. 1988—91, registrar, historian Founders chpt. 1991—94, nat. councillor, publicity chmn. 1991—94, centennial com. 1994—96, registrar gen. nat. soc. 1997—2000, pres. 2000—), Republican. Roman Catholic. Home: 52 Hicksville Rd Massapequa NY 11758-5843 Office: NYC Dept Edn Region 4 Queens Plaza N Long Island City NY 11101 Business E-Mail: drkathleenroberts@yahoo.com.

**ROBERTS, KATHLEEN MARY,** retired school system administrator; b. Syracuse, NY, Apr. 15, 1947; d. Casimer and Lorrayne Arletta (Molloy) Piegdon; m. James C. Roberts, June 29, 1968 (div. Sept. 1988). BA, Cen. State U., Edmond, Okla., 1968, MEd, 1971; PhD, U. Okla., 1977. Cert. tchr., prin., supt., Okla.; cert. supt., N.Y. Tchr. Putnam City Schs., Oklahoma City, 1960-72; reading specialist Moore (Okla.) Pub. Schs., 1973-74, Crooked Oak Pub. Schs., 1977-80; supt. Okla. Dept. Corrections, Oklahoma City, 1980-86, Healdton (Okla.) Pub. Schs., 1986-90; supr. Crooked Oak Schs., Oklahoma City, 1990—95; supt. Piedmont (Okla.) Pub. Schs., 1995-98, ret., 1998; registered fin. advisor McDonald & Assocs., 1998—. Contbr. articles to profl. publs. Bd. dirs. United Meth. Prism Ministry, Oklahoma City, 1986—, Children's Shelter, Ardmore, Okla., 1989-90; mem. State Vocat. Edn. Coun., Oklahoma City, 1980-85. Recipient citation Okla. State Senate, 1986. Mem. ASCD, Internat. Reading Assn., Am. Assn. Sch. Adminstrs., Okla. Assn. Sch. Adminstrs., Piedmont C. of C. (v.p. 1997—), Phi Delta Kappa, Alpha Chi, Kappa Delta Phi. Democrat. Roman Catholic. Avocations: furniture refinishing, reading, gardening.

**ROBERTS, KATY,** editor; married. BA politics, U. Calif., Santa Cuz, 1974; MA journalism & Russian studies, Ind. U., 1977. With Hayward Daily Rev., Calif., 1977—79, Minneapolis Star, 1979—82; op-ed editor NY Times, 1995—2000, nat. editor, 2000—02, editor, The Week in Review, 2002—. Recipient Alumni Achievement award, U. Calif., Santa Cruz, 2001. Office: NY Times 229 W 43rd St New York NY 10036 Office Phone: 212-556-1748. Office Fax: 212-556-3738. E-mail: krobe@nytimes.com.*

**ROBERTS, KENNETH LEWIS,** investor, lawyer, foundation administrator; b. Dungannon, Va., Dec. 12, 1932; s. Clarence Eugene and Katherine (Osborne) R.; m. Anne Foster Cook, Sept. 10, 1955 (dec. Dec. 5, 1999); children— Kenneth L., Patrick Hagan Foster; m. Delphine Oman Sloan, July 20, 2002. BA, Vanderbilt U., 1954, LLB, 1959. Bar: Tenn. Assoc. prof. law Vanderbilt U., 1959-60; assoc. Waller, Lansden & Dortch, Nashville, 1960-66; exec. v.p Commerce Union Bank, Nashville, 1966-71; pres., CEO, dir. Cen. Nat. Bank, Richmond, Va., 1971-76; pres., CEO First Am. Nat. Bank, Nashville, 1976-90; dir. First Am. Corp., Nashville, 1976-90, vice-chmn., 1976-77, pres., CEO, 1977-79, chmn., CEO, 1979-90; pres., exec. dir. FRIST Found., Nashville, 1991—2002, pres. emeritus, 2002—. Past pres. Cen. Nat. Corp. Trustee Vanderbilt U.; bd. dirs. Leadership Nashville, Country Music Found. Lt. Chem. Corps, AUS, 1955-57. Mem. ABA, Tenn. Bar Assn., Nashville Bar Assn., Nashville C. of C., Belle Meade Country Club, Univ. Club, Ponte Vedra (Fla.) Inn & Club. Office: FRIST Found 3100 W End Ave Ste 1200 Nashville TN 37203-6827

**ROBERTS, KEVIN,** advertising executive; b. Lancaster, Eng. m. Rowena Roberts; children: Ben, Rebecca, Dan. D (hon.), Waikato U., Hamilton, New Zealand, 1998. With Mary Quant, London, Gillette, Procter & Gamble; CEO Pepsi-Cola Middle East, 1987—89; COO Lion Breweries, New Zealand, 1989—96; CEO Worldwide Saatchi & Saatchi, NYC, 1997—. Prof. sustainable enterprise U. Waikato Mgmt. Sch., New Zealand, 2003, U. Limerick, Ireland, 2003; CEO in residence Judge Inst. Mgmt., Cambridge U.; mem. Global Bus. Policy Coun. A.T. Kearney; mem. judging panel Fast Co.'s "Fast 50" Competition. Bd. mem. New Zealand Rugby Football Union; coach, mentor Turn Your Life Around Trust, Auckland, New Zealand. Office: Saatchi & Saatchi 375 Hudson St New York NY 10014-3520*

**ROBERTS, LARRY SPURGEON,** biological science educator, zoologist; b. Texon, Tex., June 30, 1935; s. E. Fowler and Frances Wray (Huggins) R.; m. Maria Elek, Feb. 7, 1962; children: Gregory Lorinc, Bruce Tibor, Teresa Margit, Eric Miklos. BS, So. Meth. U., Dallas, 1956; MS (NSF fellow), U. Ill., 1958; DSc, Johns Hopkins U., Balt., 1961. Cert. scuba instr. Nat. Assn. Underwater Instrs. From asst. prof. to prof. zoology U. Mass., Amherst, 1963-79; prof. biol. scis. Tex. Tech U., Lubbock, 1979-90, chmn. dept., 1979-84. Adj. prof. biol. scis. U. Miami, 1990-99, Fla. Internat. U., 1990-93, 99—. Author (with others): Foundations of Parasitology, 1977, 7th edit., 2005; author: Integrated Principles of Zoology, 1979, 13th edit., 2006, Biology of Animals, 1982, 7th edit., 1998, The Underwater World of Sport Diving, 1991, Animal Diversity, 3d edit., 2003. Mem. Amherst Town Com., 1968-79, vice chmn., 1972-76; mem. Amherst Town Meeting, 1966-76; mem. Amherst Zoning Bd. Appeals, 1972-75, vice chmn., 1972-75; recorder West Tex. Dems., 1985-86; mem. Dade County Dem. Exec. Com., 1991—. NIH postdoctoral trainee, 1961-63; NIH fellow, 1969-70; recipient Disting. Service cert. Mass. Tchrs. Assn., 1979 Mem. AAAS, ACLU (vice chmn. Hampshire County chpt. 1966-68, bd. dirs. Lubbock chpt. 1985-89, vice chmn. 1988-89, bd. dirs. Miami, Fla. chpt. 1991—, 1st v.p. 1998-2000, treas. 2000—, Fla. State bd. dirs., treas. 2006-), Am. Soc. Parasitologists (Henry Baldwin Ward medal 1971, council mem. at large 1980-83, v.p. 1984-85, 96-97, pres. 1998-99), Am. Micros. Soc. (v.p. 1974-75, exec. com. 1978-81), Mass. Soc. Profs. (pres. 1977-78), Soc. Protozoologists, Am. Soc. Tropical Medicine and Hygiene, Southwestern Assn. Parasitologists (v.p. 1982, pres. 1983), Southeastern Soc. Parasitologists (pres. elect 1993, pres. 1994), Internat. Soc. Reef Studies, Crustacean Soc., Am. Acad. Underwater Scis., Sigma Xi. Home: 27700 SW 164th Ave Homestead FL 33031-2846 E-mail: Lroberts1@compuserve.com

**ROBERTS, LAWRENCE GILMAN,** telecommunications industry executive; b. Conn., Dec. 21, 1937; s. Elliott John and Elizabeth (Gilman) R.; m. June Ellen Stuller, 1959 (div. 1973); children: Paul, Kenny. BSEE, MIT, 1959, MSEE, 1960, PhD, 1963. Dir. info. proc. Advanced Rsch. Projects Agy. U.S. Dept. Def., Arlington, Va., 1969-73; pres., CEO, GTE Telenet Corp., Vienna, Va., 1973-82; pres. DHL, Redwood City, Calif., 1982-83; chmn., CEO, NetExpress, Inc., Foster City, Calif., 1983-93; pres. ATM Systems, Santa Clara, Calif., 1993-98; founder, chief tech. officer Caspian Networks, San Jose, Calif., 1998—2004; founder, CEO Anagran Inc., Woodside, Calif., 2004—. Recipient L.M. Ericsson award for comms., 1981, Prince of Asturias award, 2002, NEC Computer Comms award, 2005. Mem.: AAAS, IEEE (W. Wallace McDowell award 1992, Internet award 2000), NAE (Draper award 2001), Assn. Computing Machinery (SIGCOM award 1998), Am. Fedn. Info. Processing, IEEE Computer Soc., Sigma Xi. E-mail: lroberts@packet.cc.

**ROBERTS, LEIGH MILTON,** psychiatrist; b. Jacksonville, Ill., June 9, 1925; s. Victor Harold and Ruby Harriet (Kelsey) R.; m. Marilyn Edith Kadow, 1946 (dec. 1995); m. Ellen Rabenhorst, 2003; children: David, Carol Troxell, Paul, Nancy Mills. BS, U. Ill., 1945, MD, 1947. Diplomate Am. Bd. Psychiatry and Neurology. Intern St. Francis Hosp., Peoria, Ill., 1947-48; gen. practice medicine Macomb, Ill., 1948-50; resident in psychiatry U. Wis. Hosps., Madison, 1953-56; staff psychiatrist Mendota (Wis.) State Hosp., 1956-58; mem. faculty U. Wis. Med. Sch., Madison, 1959-89, prof. psychiatry, 1971-89, acting chmn. dept., 1972-75. Cons. in psychiatry, 1989-; mem. spl. rev. bd. Wis. Parole Bd. Sex Crimes Law, 1962-88, forensic cons., 1988—; mem. Dane County Devel. Disabilities Bd., 1962-66, Wis. Planning Com. Mental Health, 1963-65, Wis. Planning Com. Health, 1969-71, Wis. Planning Com. Vocat. Rehab., 1966-68, Wis. Planning Com. Health Centers, 1967-71, Wis. Mental Health Adv. Com., 1973-78; bd. dirs. Methodist Hosp., Madison, Dane County Rehab. House, Dane County Assn. Mental Health; cons. in field. Editor: Community Psychiatry, 1966, Comprehensive Mental Health, 1968; contbr. articles profl. jours. Pres. Wis. Coun. Chs., 1976-78; bd. dirs. Madison Campus Ministry, St. Benedict Center; trustee North Central Coll., Naperville, Ill. Served with USNR, 1943-45, 50-53. Decorated Bronze Stars, Purple Heart. Fellow Am. Psychiat. Assn. (trustee 1981-84), Wis. Psychiat. Assn. (pres. 1967) Methodist. Home and Office: 33 S Midvale Blvd Madison WI 53705 *Life is a precious gift whose journey is molded and shaped by cumulative experiences and relationships. Religious belief and practice which provides future-oriented hope, disciplined accountability and living service are balanced by professional psychiatric vistas on the uniqueness and worth of each human person.*

**ROBERTS, LIA,** investor, political organization worker; b. Bucharest, Romania, 1949; arrived in U.S., 1979, naturalized, 1982; married; 1 child. Degree in Geology and Geotechnical Engring., U. Bucharest. Prin., owner, Las Vegas, 1979—93; pvt. investor, 1993—; chmn. Nev. Rep. Party, Las Vegas, 2003—. Mailing: Nevada Republican Party Chmn 8625 W Sahara Ave Las Vegas NV 89117

**ROBERTS, LINDA M.,** science educator; b. Kenosha, Wis. Aug. 24, 1948; d. David L. and Joyce M. Schmelling; m. John A. Roberts, June 13, 1970; children: Jennifer, Karin. BS, U. Wis., 1971; MEd, Cardinal Stritch U., 2002. Cert. tchg. Univ. Wis. Parkside, 1988. Bacteriologist FDA, Chgo., 1971—72, investigator, 1972—79; tchr. sci. Armitage Acad., Kenosha, Wis., 1988—. Co-dir. Sci. Acad. U. Wis. Parkside, Kenosha, 1998—2003; co-dir. summer sch. Armitage Acad., Kenosha, Wis., 2000—02; workshop presenter Sci. Kit & Boreal Labs, Tonawanda, NY, 2002—. Sci. advisor Girl Scouts, Kenosha; planning com. Chiwaukee Acad., Sci. on Sat.; co-chairperson Wis. Independ. Sch. Educators, 1998—2001, sec., 1996—2001. Recipient Honor Pin, Girl Scouts, 1995, Disting. Tchg. award, Wis. Elem. Sci. Tchrs., 2001, Presdl. Award Excellence in Math and Sci. Tchg., Nat. Sci. Found., 2002, Disting. Alumni Achievement award, U. Wis., 2003. Mem.: NSTA, Wis. Elem. Sci. Tchrs. Avocations: stained glass, sewing, silversmithing.

**ROBERTS, LORIN WATSON,** botanist, educator; b. Clarksdale, Mo., June 28, 1923; s. Lorin Cornelius and Irene (Watson) Roberts; m. Florence Ruth Greathouse, July 10, 1967; children: Michael Hamlin, Daniel Hamlin, Margaret Susan. BA, U. Mo., 1948, MA, 1950; PhD in Botany, U. Mo.-Columbia, 1952. Asst. prof., then assoc. prof. botany Agnes Scott Coll. Decaur, Ga., 1952-57; vis. asst. prof. Emory U., 1952-55; mem. faculty U. Idaho, 1957—, prof. botany, 1967-91, prof. botany emeritus, 1991—; Fulbright research prof. Kyoto (Japan) U., 1967-68; research fellow U. Bari, Italy, 1968; Cabot fellow Harvard, 1974; Fulbright teaching fellow Northeastern Hill U., Shillong, Meghalaya, India, 1977; Fulbright sr. scholar and fellow Australian Nat. U., Canberra, 1980; sr. researcher U. London; 1984; pres. botany sect. 1st Internat. Congress Histochemistry and Cytochemistry, Paris, 1960; Alexander von Humboldt vis. fellow Australian Nat. U., 1992. Author: Cytodifferentiation in Plants, 1976; author: (with J. H. Dodds) Experiments in Plant Tissue Culture, 1982, 3d edit., 1995; author: (with P. B. Gahan and R. Aloni) Vascular Differentiation and Plant Growth Regulators, 1988; contbr. articles to profl. jours. Fellow AAAS; mem.: Idaho Acad. Scis., Am. Inst. Biol. Scis., Internat. Assn. Plant Tissue Culture, Am. Soc. Plant Physiologists, Bot. Soc. Am., N.W. Sci. Assn. (pres. 1970—71), Sigma Xi, Phi Sigma, Phi Kappa Phi. Home (Winter): 920 Mabelle St Moscow ID 83843-3834

**ROBERTS, MADELYN ALPERT,** publishing executive; V.p., assoc. pub. McCall's Magazine, 1993—99; pub. McCall's Gruner & Jahr USA Pub., N.Y.C., 1999—2001; pub. Mode Magazine, 2001; v.p., pub. 360 Youth, N.Y.C., NY, 2003—. Office: Alloy Inc 151 W 26th St New York NY 10001

**ROBERTS, MARGARET A,** elementary school educator; children: Jennifer, Jesse. BA in Elem. Edn., State U. Coll., Cortland, NY, 1969; MS in Spl. Edn., U. No. Colo., Greeley, 1972; MS in Math. Leadership, Bank St. Coll. Edn., NYC, 2005. Tchr. spl. edn. Tuba City Boarding Sch., Ariz., 1972—74; head start trainer Ctrl. Ariz. Coll., Coolidge, 1974—76; tchr. elem., mid. sch. Kodiak Island Borough Sch. Dist., Chiniak, Alaska, 1976—78; tchr. elem., spl. edn., 1983—97, tchr. elem., 1997—2004; tchr. mentor U. Alaska, Fairbanks, 2004—06; tchr. elem., mid. sch. Kodiak Island Borough Sch. Dist., 2006—. Mem.: AAUW, ASCD, Nat. Coun. Tchrs. Math., Alaska State Literacy Assn., Internat. Reading Assn., Kodiak Reading Coun. (pres. membership chair). Personal E-mail: mroberts3@gci.net.

**ROBERTS, MARGARET HAROLD,** editor, publisher; b. Aug. 18, 1928; AB, U. Chattanooga, 1950. Editor, pres Award Winning Art, 1960-70, New Woman mag., Palm Beach, Fla., 1971-84; editor, pub. BONKERS mag., 1992—2001. Author: juvenile book series Daddy is a Doctor, 1965.

**ROBERTS, MARK SCOTT,** lawyer; b. Fullerton, Calif. s. Emil Seidel and Theda (Wymer) R. BA in Theater, Pepperdine U., 1975; JD, Western State U., 1978; cert. civil trial advocacy program, U. Calif., San Francisco, 1985; cert. program of instrn. for lawyers, Harvard U., 1990. Bar: Calif. 1980, U.S. Dist. Ct. (cen. dist.) Calif. 1980, U.S. Supreme Ct. 1989, U.S. Ct. Mil. Appeals 1989, U.S. Tax Ct. 1990. Prin. Law Offices of Mark S. Roberts, APLC, Fullerton, Calif., 1980—. Instr. bus. law Biola U., La Mirada, Calif., 1980-82; judge pro tem Orange County Superior Ct., Santa Ana, 1989—; adj. prof. wills and trusts Trinity Law Sch., Santa Ana, 2000—. Co-author: Legacy-Plan, Protect and Preserve Your Estate, 1996, Generations Planning Your Legacy, 1999. Mem. Calif. State Bar Assn., Orange County Bar Assn. (charter), Nat. Network Estate Planning Attys., Soc. Cert. Sr. Advisors. Office: 1440 N Harbor Blvd Ste 900 Fullerton CA 92835-4122 Office Phone: 714-449-3353. Personal E-mail: mroberts@marksroberts.com.

**ROBERTS, MARKLEY,** economist, educator; b. Shanghai, Sept. 3, 1930; s. Donald and Frances Charlotte (Markley) R.; m. Jeanne Addison, Feb. 19, 1966; children: Addison, Ellen. AB, Princeton U., 1951; MA, Am. U., 1960, PhD, 1970. Reporter Washington Star newspaper, 1952-57; legis. asst. Office of Senator Hubert Humphrey of Minn., Washington, 1957-62; legis. asst.,

economist AFL-CIO, Washington, 1962-96, asst. dir. econ. rsch. dept., 1989-96. Bd. dirs., vice-chmn. Econ. Edn. Found. for Clergy, 1972-80; chmn. labor rsch. adv. coun. Bur. Labor Stats.-Dept. Labor, 1972-96; adj. prof. econs. U. Md., 1966—, George Washington U., 1972-96; bd. dirs., chair Inst. Learning in Retirement, 2002—. Contbr. numerous articles on labor and econ. affairs, tech., productivity to various publs.; author monographs in field. Mem. D.C. Dem. Ctrl. Com., 1964-68; ward III coord. Washington Mayor Walter Washington, 1974-78; bd. dirs. Laymen's Nat. Bible Com. Inc., N.Y.C., 1972-82. Mem. UN Assn. (bd. dirs., labor chair nat. capitol area chpt. 1995—), Am. Econ. Assn., Indsl. Rels. Rsch. Assn. (exec. bd. 1975-77), Am. Polit. Sci. Assn., Nat. Acad. Social Ins., Assn. Evolutionary Econs., Am. Statis. Assn., Nat. Consumers League (bd. dirs. 1991-99), Newspaper Guild, Ams. Dem. Action (exec. bd. 1992—), Social Dems. USA, Cosmos Club. Democrat. Episcopalian. Home: 4931 Albemarle St NW Washington DC 20016-4359

**ROBERTS, MELVILLE PARKER,** retired neurosurgeon; b. Phila., Oct. 15, 1931; s. Melville Parker and Marguerite Louise (Reimann) R.; m. Sigrid Marianne Magnusson, Mar. 27, 1954; children: Melville Parker III, Julia Perl, Erik Emerson. BS, Washington and Lee U., 1953; MD, Yale U., 1957. Diplomate: Am. Bd. Neurol. Surgery. Intern Yale Med. Ctr., 1957, neurosurgical resident, 1958-60, 62-64, Am. Cancer Soc. fellow in neurosurgery, 1962-64, instr., 1964; asst. prof. surgery Sch. Medicine U. Va., Charlottesville, 1965-69; practice medicine specializing in neurol. surgery Hartford, Conn., 1970-1998; mem. staff Hartford Hosp.; asst. prof. surgery Sch. Medicine U. Conn., Farmington, 1970-71, assoc. prof., 1972-75, assoc. prof. neurology, 1974-77, chmn. divsn. neurosurgery, 1971-84, prof. surgery, 1975—, acting chmn. dept. neurology, 1973-77, acting chmn. dept. surgery, 1974-77, William Beecher Scoville prof. neurosurgery, 1976-98, prof. emeritus, 1998—. James Hudson Brown rsch. fellow Yale U., 1957. Author: Atlas of the Human Brain in Section, 1970, 2d edit., 1987, The Brain Atlas, 1998; mem. editl. bd. Conn. Medicine, 1973-98; contbr. articles to profl. jours. Capt. MC, US Army, 1960-61. Fellow Royal Soc. Medicine London (life); mem. Am. Assn. Neurol. Surgeons, Soc. Neurol. Surgeons, Congress Neurol. Surgeons (bd. dirs. joint spinal sect. with Am. Assn. Neurol. Surgeons, chmn. ann. meeting 1987, sci. program chmn. ann. meeting 1988), Assn. for Rsch. in Nervous and Mental Diseases, New Eng. Neurosurg. Soc. (bd. dirs. 1976-79, pres. 1989-91), Soc. Brit. Neurol. Surgeons, Rsch. Soc. Neurol. Surgeons, Soc. Rsch. into Hydrocephalus and Spina Bifida, Conn. Acad. Arts and Sci., Vereingung Schweizer Neurochirugen, Mory's Assn., Beaumont Med. Club (pres. 1988, New Haven), Yale Club NY, Sloane Club (London).

**ROBERTS, MICHAEL G.,** lawyer; b. 1956; BA with high honors, Mich. State Univ., 1977; jd cum laude, Am. Univ. 1982. Bar: DC 1983, Fla. 1984. Law clerk DC Superior Ct., 1983; maritime atty. Washington; from corp. counsel to v.p., govt. rels. Crowley Maritime Corp., 1991—2000; with Thompson Coburn LLP, Washington, 2000—04; ptnr., transp. law Venable LLP, Washington, 2004—. Adj. prof., bus. law Am. Univ. Mem. Navy League US; bd. gov. Propeller Club US, 1994—2003; founding chmn. CoastWise Coalition. Mem.: Maritime Adminstrv. Bar Assn. (pres. 1999—2000), Nat. Def. Transp. Assn. (life). Office: Venable LLP 575 Seventh St NW Washington DC 20004 Office Phone: 202-344-4350. Office Fax: 202-344-8300. Business E-Mail: mgroberts@venable.com.

**ROBERTS, MICHAEL J.,** former food products executive; b. Chgo., Oct. 20, 1950; m. Maureen Long; children: Lauren, Lindsey, Michelle. BA in Sociology, Loyola U. V.p., supply chain mgmt. McDonald's Corp, 1990—95; asst. v.p., district mgr., McDonald's LA region McDonald's Corp., 1989—90, regional v.p., Chgo. north region, 1995—96, v.p., field ops.; pres. West div. McDonald's USA, pres., 2001—04, CEO, 2004; pres., COO McDonald's Corp., 2004—06. Adv. dir. McDonald's Corp., bd. dirs., 2004—06.*

**ROBERTS, MICHAEL T.,** law educator, lawyer; Attended, Drake Univ., Des Moines; BS, Univ. Utah, 1986, JD, 1989; LLM, Univ. Ark. Sch. Law, 2001. Bar: Utah. Atty. Van Cott Bagley Cornwall & McCarthy, Ogden, Utah; rsch. assoc. prof. Univ. Ark. Sch. Law, 2001—; dir. Law Ctr., Univ. Ark., 2003—. Past chmn., Agribusiness Practice Group Lex Mundi. Mem.: Am. Agrl. Law Assn. Officer: National AgLaw Ctr University of Arkansas Law School 1 University of Arkansas Fayetteville AR 72701

**ROBERTS, MICHELE A.,** lawyer; b. NYC, Sept. 14, 1956; BA, Wesleyan U., 1977; JD, Boalt Hall Sch. Law, U. Calif., Berkeley, 1980. Bar: Wash. DC 1980. Atty. Pub. Defender Svc., Washington, 1986—92; ptnr. Rochon & Roberts, 1992—2001, Shea & Gardner, 2001—04; ptnr., civil/white collar litig. Akin Gump Strauss Hauer & Feld LLP, Washington, 2004—. Former mem. adj. faculty George Wash. U. Sch. Law; former lectr. Pub. Defender Svc. Tng. Program; past instr. Nat. Inst. Trial Advocacy; mem. adj. faculty Harvard Law Sch.; serves on DC Adv. Commn. on Sentencing. Named First Among Washington's Top 75 Lawyers, Washingtonian mag. survey, 2002; named one of 75 Best Lawyers in Washington, 2004, Am. Top Black Lawyers, Black Enterprise Mag., 2003. Fellow: Am. Coll. Trial Lawyers; mem.: Nat. Assn. Criminal Def. Lawyers, Nat. Bar Assn., ABA, DC Bar. Office: Akin Gump Strauss Hauer & Feld LLP Robert S Strauss Bldg 1333 New Hampshire Ave NW Washington DC 20036-1564 Office Phone: 202-887-4306. Business E-Mail: mroberts@akingump.com.

**ROBERTS, MONTY,** horse trainer, writer; b. Calif., 1935; m. Pat, 3 children, 47 foster children. D (hon.), Univ. Zurich. Stuntman, Hollywood; owner, operator, thoroughbred breeding, training facility Flag Is Up Farms, Solvang, Calif.; owner, operator Monty Roberts Equestrian Acad., Join Up Internat. Inc., Solvang, Calif. Creator Join Up method for non-violent equine training. Author: The Man Who Listens to Horses, 1997 (NY Times Bestseller list), Shy Boy: The Horse that Came in from the Wild, 1999 (NY Times Bestseller list), Horse Sense for People, 2001, From My Hands to Yours, 2002, The Horses in My Life, 2005; subject, with Shy Boy, the mustang (PBS/BBC documentary) Monty Roberts: The Real Horse Whisperer. Achievements include being invited by Queen Elizabeth II to teach Join Up method to her equestrian team, London. Home and Office: Flag Is Up Farms 901 E Hwy 246 PO Box 1700 Solvang CA 93464 Office Phone: 805-688-6288. Office Fax: 805-688-2242. Business E-Mail: admin@montyroberts.com

**ROBERTS, NANCY,** computer scientist, educator; b. Boston, Jan. 25, 1938; d. Harold and Annette (Zion) Rosenthal; m. Edward B. Roberts, June 14, 1959; children: Valerie Friedman, Mitchell, Andrea. AB, Boston U., 1959, MEd, 1961, EdD, 1975. Elem. tchr. Sharon (Mass.) Pub. Schs., 1959-63; asst. prof. Lesley U., Cambridge, Mass., 1975-79, assoc. prof., 1980-83, prof., 1983—, dir. grad. programs in tech. in edn., 1980—99, dir. Project Bridge, 1987-92, dir. divsn. tchg., learning and leadership, 2001—04; dir. Ctr. for Math., Sci. and Tech. in Edn., Cambridge, Mass., 1990-91. Rsch. assoc. MIT, Cambridge, 1976-79;mem. nat. steering com. Nat. Edn. Computing Conf., Eugene, Oreg., 1976-96; co-chmn. nat. conf., 1989, vice chmn. steering com., 1991-95. Author: Dynamics of Human Service Delivery, 1976, Practical Guide to Computers in Education, 1982, Computers in Teaching Mathematics, 1983, Introduction to Computer Simulation, 1983 (J.W. Forrester award 1983), Integrating Computers into the Elementary and Middle School, 1987, Computers and the Social Studies, 1988, Integrating Telecommunications into Education, 1990, Computer Modeling and Simulation in Science and Mathematics Education, 1999; mem. editl. bd. Jour. Ednl. Computing, 1983—, Jour. Rsch. in Sci. Teaching; editor Computers in Edn. book series, 1984-89. Mem. Computer Policy Com., Boston, 1982-84, mem. adv. bd. Electronic Learning, 1989-91; bd. dirs. Computers for Kids, Cambridge, 1983-85; mem. State Ednl. Tech. Adv. Coun., 1990-93; bd. dirs. Boston Ctr. Adult Edn. 2000—, Citizens Charter Schs. 1997-05; pres. bd. Littleton Mus. Fine Arts, 2003—. Grantee, NSF, 1985—96, DOE, 1994—2003. Mem. System Dynamics Soc. (bd. dirs. policy com. 1987-89). Republican. Jewish. Home: 300 Boylston St Apt 1102 Boston MA 02116-3940 Office: Lesley Coll 29 Everett St Cambridge MA 02138-2702 Office Phone: 617-349-8419. Business E-Mail: nroberts@lesley.edu.

**ROBERTS, NORA,** writer; b. Silver Spring, Md., Oct. 10, 1950; m. Ronald Aufdem-Brinke, 1970 (div. 1983); children: Dan, Jason; m. Bruce Wilder, 1985. Former legal secy. Author: Promise Me Tomorrow, 1984, Hot Ice, 1987, Sacred Sins, 1987, Brazen Virtue, 1988, Sweet Revenge, 1989, Public Secrets, 1990, Genuine Lies, 1991, Carnal Innocence, 1992, Divine Evil, 1992, Honest Illusions, 1992, reprint, 1993, Private Scandals, 1993, Hidden Riches, 1994, Born in Fire, 1994, Born in Ice, 1995, True Betrayals, 1995, reprint, 1996, Born in Shame, 1996, Daring to Dream, 1996, Montana Sky, 1996, reprint, 1997, Holding the Dream, 1997, Finding the Dream, 1997, Sanctuary, 1997, Rising Tides, 1998, Once Upon a Castle, 1998, Homeport, 1998, Sea Swept, 1998, The Reef, 1998, Inner Harbor, 1999, Jewels of the Sun, 1999, River's End, 1999, Heart of the Sea, 2000, Tears of the Moon, 2000, Carolina Moon, 2001, Heaven and Earth, 2001, The Villa, 2002, Three Fates, 2002, Chesapeake Blue, 2002, Key of Knowledge, 2003, Key of Light, 2003, Once Upon a Midnight, 2003, Birthright, 2003, Blue Dahlia, 2004, Once Upon a Moon, 2004, Northern Lights, 2004, A Little Fate, 2004, Key of Valor, 2004, Black Rose, 2005, Blue Smoke, 2005; (under pseudonym J.D. Robb) Naked in Death, 1995, Glory in Death, 1995, Immortal in Death, 1996, Rapture in Death, 1996, Ceremony in Death, 1997, Vengeance in Death, 1997, Holiday in Death, 1998, Loyalty in Death, 1999, Conspiracy in Death, 1999, Judgment in Death, 2000, Witness in Death, 2000, Betrayal in Death, 2001, Seduction in Death, 2001, Interlude in Death, 2001, Purity in Death, 2002, Reunion in Death, 2002, Imitation in Death, 2003, Portrait in Death, 2003, Visions in Death, 2004, Survivor in Death, 2005, Origin in Death, 2005, Memory in Death, 2006; author numerous category romances for Silhouette. Recipient Lifetime Achievement award Waldenbooks. Mem. Romance Writers Am. (charter, mem. Washington chpt., inductee Hall of Fame, Centennial award, Lifetime Achievement award 1997), Mystery Writers Am., Sisters in Crime, The Crime League of Am., Novelists, Inc. Office: GP Putnams Sons 375 Hudson St New York NY 10014-3658*

**ROBERTS, ORAL (GRANVILLE ORAL ROBERTS),** clergyman; b. nr. Ada, Okla., Jan. 24, 1918; s. Ellis Melvin and Claudius Priscilla (Irwin) R.; m. Evelyn Lutman (dec. 2005), Dec. 25, 1938; children: Rebecca Ann (dec.), Ronald (dec.), Richard Lee, Roberta Jean. Student, Okla. Bapt. U., 1942-44, Phillips U., 1945-47; LLD (hon.), Centenary Coll., 1975; MDiv, Oral Roberts U., 1981; DD, Internat. Ch. Foursquare, 1988. Ordained to ministry Pentecostal Holiness Ch., 1936, United Meth. Ch., 1968. Evangelist, 1936-41; pastor Fuquay Springs, N.C., 1941, Shawnee, Okla., 1942-45, Toccoa, Ga., 1944, Enid, Okla., 1947; began worldwide evangelistic ministry thru crusades, radio, TV, printed page, 1947; founder Oral Roberts Evangelistic Assn., Inc., Tulsa, 1948, Univ. Village Retirement Center, 1970, City of Faith Med./Research Ctr., 1981, Healing Outreach Ctr., 1986; founder, pub. Miracles Now mag., Your Daily Guide; founder, pres. Oral Roberts U., Tulsa, 1963-93, chancellor, 1993—. Founding chmn. Internat. Charismatic Bible Ministries, 1986. Author over 122 books including: If You Need Healing, Do These Things, 1947, God is a Good God, 1960, If I Were You, 1967, Miracle of Seed-Faith, 1970, The Miracle Book, 1972, A Daily Guide to Miracles, 1975, 3 Most Important Steps to Your Better Health and Miracle Living, 1976, How to Get Through Your Struggles, 1977, Don't Give Up, 1980, Your Road to Recovery, 1986, Attack Your Lack, 1985, How to Resist the Devil and His Demons, 1989, Fear Not!, 1989, A Prayer Cover Over Your Life, 1990, Is God Your Source?, 1992, Unleashing the Power of Praying in the Spirit, 1993, (autobiography) Expect a Miracle, My Life and Ministry, 1995, A Thousand Times More!, 1997, Don't Park Here!, 1997, Keys to Success, 1998, Seed-Faith 2000, 1999, Still Doing the Impossible, 2002; also numerous tracts, brochures, Bible commentaries. Recipient Outstanding Am. Indian of Yr. award Am. Indian Expo., 1963; inducted into Okla. Hall of Fame, 1972; named Oklahoman of Yr., Am. Broadcasters Assn., 197, One of 50 Most Influential Oklahomans, Okla. Today mag., 2000. Mem.: Rotary. Methodist. Office: Oral Roberts U 7777 S Lewis Ave Tulsa OK 74171-0001

**ROBERTS, OWEN A,** school system administrator, researcher; s. Arnold Joseph and Irene Maud Roberts; m. Sheila M. Crawford, Aug. 3, 1980; children: Jeremy Andre, Jevawn Sebastian, Joann Simone. BSc, WI Coll., Mandeville, Jamaica, 1979; MA, Andrews U., 1984; MSc, Nova Southeastern U., 1991; PhD, U. Miami, 1998. Cert. tchr. Fla. Tchr. math. and sci. WI Coll., 1980; tchr. of math. and sci. Bahamas Acad., Nassau, Bahamas, 1981—83; tchr. math. and computer sci. Bermuda Inst., Southampton, 1984—89; head dept., tchr. math. and sci. Sandys Secondary Sch., Sandys, Bermuda, 1989—96; rsch. asst. U. Miami, Coral Gables, Fla., 1996—98; exec. dir. accountability and assessment Monroe County Sch. Bd., Key West, Fla., 1998—2004; asst. supt. curriculum, accountability and assessment St. Lucie County Sch. Bd., Fort Pierce, Fla., 2004—. Tech. advisor assessment Fla. Dept. Edn., Tallahassee, 1998—; pres. Fla. Rsch. Coun., Tampa, 2003—04. Researcher (exploration) JASON Project: Volcanism and the Formation of New Land Mass on Earth; contbr. articles to profl. publs. Leader Seventh-Day Adventist Ch., Fort Lauderdale, 1996. Recipient meritorious svc. award, Assn. Sci. Tchrs. Jamaica, special recognition award, Nat. Sci. Tchrs. Assn.; Goal 2000 grantee, Fla. Dept. Edn., 1999. Mem.: ASCD, Fla. Assn. Test Adminstrs. (sec./treas. 2005—), Fla. Ednl. Rsch. Assn. (mem. exec. bd. 2003—), Fla. Assn. Sch. Administrs. (assoc.), Fla. Orgn. Instrnl. Leaders (assoc.), Am. Ednl. Rsch. Assn. (assoc.). Office: St Lucie County Sch Bd 4204 Okeechobee Rd Fort Pierce FL 34947 Office Phone: 772-429-5546. Business E-Mail: robertso@stlucie.k12.fl.us.

**ROBERTS, PAMELA RANGER,** secondary school educator; b. Royal Oak, Mich., May 19, 1960; d. Richard Lee and Carol Bruce (Roland) Ranger; m. John Jack Roberts, Sept. 23, 1989. BA Anthropology, U. Colo., 1983. Retail sales book buyer Neptune Mountaineering, Boulder, Colo., 1985—92; tchr. coach, advisor Phillips Acad., Andover, Mass., 1989; tchr. Spanish Broomfield (Colo.) H.S., 1992—97; retail sales, floor mgr. Neptune Mountaineering, 1997—99; tchr. Spanish Broomfield H.S., 1999—. Dept. chair world lang. Broomfield High Sch., 2001—, mem. emergency first response team, 1999—. Mem.: Am. Assn. Tchrs. Spanish and Portugese, Sigma Delta Pi. Avocations: rock climbing, skiing, surfing, swimming, travel. Home: 130 S 33d St Boulder CO 80305 E-mail: pam.roberts@bvsd.org.

**ROBERTS, PATRICIA LEE,** education educator; b. Coffeyville, Kans. d. Philip Lee Brighton and Lois Ethel Wortham; m. James E. Roberts, Oct. 5, 1953; children: James Michael, Jill Frances. BA, Calif. State U., Fresno, 1953, MA, 1964; EdD, U. Pacific, 1975. Lifetime tchg. diploma; sch. adminstrn. cert. Prof. edn. Calif. State U., Sacramento, 1969—. Cons. in field. Author (textbooks): Alphabet: A Handbook of ABC Books and Book Extensions for the Elementary Classroom, 2d edit., 1994, Integrating Language Arts and Social Studies for Kindergarten and Primary Children, 1996, Literature-Based History Activities for Children, Grades 4-8, 1997, Taking Humor Seriously in Children's Literature, 1997, Multicultural Friendship Stories and Activities for Children Ages 5-14, 1997, Language Arts and Environmental Awareness, 1998, Literature-Based History Activities for Children, Grades 1-3, 1998, Family Values Through Children's Literature, Grades K-3, 1999, Family Values Through Children's Literature, Grades 4-6, 2005, A Guide for Developing an Interdisciplinary Thematic Unit, 2006, A Resource Guide for Elementary School Teaching. 6th edit., 2005. Named Disting. Alumnae of Yr., U. Pacific, 1975-76. Mem. Internat. Reading Assn., Nat. Coun. Rsch. on English.

**ROBERTS, PATRICIA LEE,** small business owner, consultant; b. Tuscaloosa, Ala., Feb. 13, 1942; d. Felton H. and Floy Robin Lee; m. Tom David, July 27, 1993; m. Ralph Myron Roberts (div.); children: Sharon DeeAnne Aizer, Frances Lee Revere. BA in Elem. Edn., U. Ala., Tuscaloosa, 1968; BA in Social Work, U. Western Fla., Pensacola, 1975; MA, Troy State, Mobile, Ala., 1977. Loan officer First Am. Bank, Pensacola, 1970—74; social worker CETA, Pensacola, 1974—78; owner constrn. cleaning co., Pensacola, 1978—2005; ct. appt. receiver Ct. Sys., Pensacola, 1985—91; owner, mgr. golf course, Pensacola, 1989—91; tchr. Returning Women U. West Fla., Pensacola, 1989—91; cons., counselor. Adv. bd. Coun. on Aging, Pensacola, Am. Red Cross, Pensacola, United Way, Pensacola. Com. chmn. Am. Red Cross; com. mem. Jaycess, Lions Club. Recipient Outstanding Svcs., Jaycees, Cancer Soc., numerous awards to contrb. to cmty. and social svc. activities.

Mem.: Home Bldg. Assn. NW Fla., Pensacola Beach Yacht Club. Achievements include patents pending in field. Avocations: boating, skiing, golf, walking, beach. Office Phone: 850-932-0087.

**ROBERTS, PAUL,** chef; Master sommelier Cafe Annie, Houston. Recipient Krug Cup. Achievements include being the only Master Sommelier in the State of Tex. and 1 of only 50 in country; becoming the first person in six years to pass the very intense Master Sommelier's test. Office: 1728 Post Oak Blvd Houston TX 77001

**ROBERTS, PAUL C,** paper company executive; CFO, treas. Schweitzer Mauduit Internat. Inc., Alpharetta, Ga., 1995—. Office: Schweitzer Mauduit Internat Inc 100 N Point Ctr E Ste 600 Alpharetta GA 30022-8263

**ROBERTS, PAUL CRAIG, III,** economics professor, writer, columnist; b. Atlanta, Apr. 3, 1939; s. Paul Craig and Ellen Lamar (Dryman) R.; m. Becky B. Bickerstaff, 1959 (div. 1968); m. Linda Jane Fisher, July 3, 1969 (div. 1994); children: Becky Ellen, Stephanie Bradford, Pendaran Struan Sherman. BS, Ga. Inst. Tech., 1961; postgrad., U. Calif., Berkeley, 1962—63, Merton Coll., Oxford U., Eng., 1964—65; PhD, U. Va., 1967. Asst. prof. econs. Va. Poly. Inst., 1965-69; assoc. prof. U. N.Mex., 1969-71; rsch. fellow Hoover Instn., Stanford U., 1971-77, sr. rsch. fellow, 1978—2004; mem. U.S. Congl. Staff, 1975-78; asst. sec. of treasury for econ. policy Dept. Treasury, Washington, 1981-82; William E. Simon prof. polit. economy Georgetown U. Ctr. for Strategic and Internat. Studies, Washington, 1982-93; chmn. Inst. for Polit. Economy, 1985—; John M. Olin fellow, 1994—2004; rsch. fellow Ind. Inst., 1990—. Disting. adj. scholar Ctr. Strategic and Internat. Studies, Washington, 1993-96; adj. scholar Cato Inst., 1987-93, disting. fellow, 1993-96; assoc. editor, columnist Wall St. Jour., N.Y.C., 1978-80; columnist Bus. Week, 1983-98, Fin. Post, Can., 1988-89, Liberation, Paris, 1988-89, Erfolg, Fed. Rep. of Germany, 1988, Washington Times, 1988—, San Diego Union, 1988-92, Le Figaro, Paris, 1992-96, Investors Bus. Daily, 1998-2005; nationally syndicated columnist Scripps Howard News Svc., 1989-97, Creators Syndicate, 1997—; contbr. editor: Nat. Rev., 1993-2003, Reason Mag., 1993-95, World Trade mag., 1997-98; mem. Pres.-elect Reagan's Task Force on Tax Policy, 1980; dir. Value Line Investment Funds, N.Y.C., A. Schulman, Akron, Ohio; cons. Morgan Guaranty Trust Co., Lazard Freres Asset Mgmt., 1983-97; pres. Econ. & Communication Svcs. Inc.; cons. Dept. Commerce, 1983, Dept. Def., 1983-84; mem. adv. bd. Marvin and Palmer, 1986-96, Am. studies program Harding U.; mem. ad. com. Ctr. for the Am. Founding; mem. Wright Investors' Svc. Internat. Bd. Econ. and Invesment Advisors; bd. dirs. Com. on Present Danger; trustee Intercollegiate Studies Inst., Com. on Developing Am. Capitalism; mem. selection com. Frank E. Seidman disting. award in Polit. Economy; pres. Inlet Beach Water Co., 2000—. Author: Alienation and the Soviet Economy, 1971, new edit., 1990, Marx's Theory of Exchange, 1973, new edit., 1983, The Supply-Side Revolution: An Insider's Account of Policymaking in Washington, 1984, The Cost of Corporate Capital in the U.S. and Japan, 1985, Meltdown: Inside the Soviet Economy, 1990, The New Color Line: How Quotas and Privilege Destroy Democracy, 1995; The Capitalist Revolution in Latin America, Oxford U. Press, 1997, The Tyranny of Good Intentions, 2000, Chile: Dos Visiones-la Era Allende-Pinochet, 2000; mem. editl. bd. Modern Age, Intercollegiate Rev.; contbg. editor Harper's. Mag. Drafted original Kemp-Roth Bill, 1976. Recipient Meritorious Svc. award Dept. Treasury, 1982, Pub. Svc. award GSA, 1991, Warren Brookes award for Excellence in Journalism, 1992; Am. Philos. Soc. grantee, 1968; named to Chevalier de la Légion d'Honneur, 1987, Gridiron Secret Soc., U.S. Ga.; Earhart fellow U. Va., 1966-67, Nat. Chamber Found. fellow, 1984-85. Mem. Mont Pelerin Soc., Beethoven Soc., Am. Soc. French Legion of Honor, U.S. C. of C. (taxation com.), Polanyi Soc. Home and Office: 169 Pompano St Panama City FL 32413-7245

**ROBERTS, PAUL DALE,** state agency administrator, writer; b. Fresno, Calif., Jan. 17, 1955; s. Paul Marceau and Rosemarie Roberts; divorced; 1 child, Jason Randall Porter. AA, Sacramento City Coll., 1977; diploma in pvt. investigations, Ctrl. Investigation & Security, 1984. Office asst. I, Dept. Benefit Payments, Sacramento, Calif., 1976-77; firefighter Calif. Divsn. Forestry, Colfax, 1977; key data operator Dept. Justice, Sacramento, 1977-78; intelligence analyst, spl. forces instr. U.S. Army Mil. Intelligence, Seoul, Korea, 1979-84; office asst. 1 Calif. State Lottery Commn., 1987-89; law libr. Employment Devel. Dept., Sacramento, 1989-92; office asst. II, Calif. Dept. Health Svcs., Sacramento, 1992-98, chief cert. support, 1992-93; supervising program technician II Dept. Cmty. Svcs. and Devel., State Calif., Sacramento, 1998-2000; divsn. supr. polit. reform Sec. of State, Sacramento, 2000—. Office asst I, Calif. Lottery Commn., 1987-89; disaster courier dept. social svcs. Gov.'s Office of Emergency Svcs., L.A., 1994. Author: Organization of D.E.A.T.H. (Destroy Evildoers and Teach Harmony), 1984, The Cosmic Bleeder, 1991, Madam Zara, Vampiress, 1993, People's Comic Book Newsletter, 1996, The Legendary Dark Silhouette, 1997, Vacationing in Dublin, Ireland and Newry, Northern Ireland, 1997, (comic book) The Legendary Dark Silhouette, 1997, Jazma Universe Online!, 1998, Jazma League of Justice, 1999, Jazma Man/Jazma Girl, 2000, My Adventures in Brazil, 2001, My Adventures in Thailand/Burma, 2003, My Adventures in Moscow, Russia, 2004, Nicole Mila Phengaroune Growing Up Years, 2005, My 50th Birthday on Catalina Island, 2005, My Crazy Adventure to Spain, Gibralter, Portugal and Tangiers/Morocco- North Africa, 2005 Sgt. U.S. Army Mil. Police, 1973-76. Republican. Roman Catholic. Avocations: flying, tennis, photography, ballooning, skydiving. Home: 5606 Moonlight Way Elk Grove CA 95758-6837 Office: 1500 11th St Rm 495 Sacramento CA 95814 Office Phone: 916-653-8504. Personal E-mail: jazmapika@cs.com.

**ROBERTS, PAUL HARRY,** mathematics professor; b. Aberystwyth, Wales, Eng., Sept. 13, 1929; s. Percy Harry and Ethel Frances (Mann) R.; m. Maureen Frances Tabbett, Dec. 16, 1989. BA, Cambridge U., Eng., 1951, MA, PhD, 1954, ScD, 1966. Rsch. assoc. U. Chgo., 1954-55, assoc. prof., 1961-63; scientific officer Atomic Weapons Rsch. Establishment, Aldermaston, U.K. 1955-56; rsch. fellow U. Durham, Newcastle, U.K., 1956-59, lectr., 1959-61; prof. math. U. Newcastle upon Tyne, Eng., 1963-86; prof. math. and geophysical scis. U. Calif., L.A., 1986—. Author: (book) An Introduction to Magnetohydrodynamics, 1967; co-editor: (book) Rotating Fluids in Geophysics, 1979; editor: Geophysical and Astrophysical Fluid Dynamics, 1976—. Mem. Royal Astronomical Soc., Royal Soc. London, Am. Geophysical Union (John Adam Fleming medal, 1999. Office: UCLA Inst of Geophysics & Planetary Physics Los Angeles CA 90095-1567

**ROBERTS, PHILIP JOHN,** history professor, editor; b. Lusk, Wyo., July 8, 1948; s. Leslie J. and LaVerne Elizabeth (Johns) R. BA, U. Wyo., 1973, JD, 1977; PhD, U. Wash., 1990. Bar: Wyo. 1977. Editor Lake Powell Chronicle, Page, Ariz., 1972-73; pvt. practice in law Carbon and Laramie County, Wyo., 1977-84; historian Wyo. State Hist. Dept., Cheyenne, 1979-84; owner, pub. Capitol Times, Cheyenne, 1982-84; co-editor Wyo. History Jour., 1995-96; editor Annals of Wyo., Cheyenne, 1980—84, 1995—2004; owner, pub. Skyline West Press, Seattle, 1985-90; prof. history U. Wyo., Laramie, 1990—; law liaison ABA-Ctrl. European and Eurasian Law Initiative, Baku, Azerbaijan, 2004—05. Indexer Osborne-McGraw-Hill, Berkeley, 1988-95; guest lectr. media law, Dubai, United Arab Emirates, 1996, Cairo, 2001; mem. editl. bd. Annals of Wyo., 1990-95, 2005—. Author: Wyoming Almanac, 1989 (pub. annually), Buffalo Bones: Stories from Wyoming's Past, 1979, 3d edit., 1984, Readings in Wyoming History, 1994, 4th edit., 2004, Penny for the Governor, A Dollar for Uncle Sam: The Politics of Taxation in Washington, 2002; contbr. articles to profl. jours. Cand. for gov. of Wyo., 1998; chmn. Albany County Dem. Party, 1999-2001, 2003-04; pres. Albany County Hist. Soc., 2000-02; mem. Albany County Hist. Preservation Commn., 2000—; bd. mem. Laramie Plains Mus., 2000-2004; apptd. mem. Wyo. Coin Adv. Commn, 2005. With USMC, 1970-72. Mem. Wyo. State Hist. Soc. (life), Wyo. State Bar, Am. Bar Assn., Pacific N.W. Historians' Guild, 9th Judicial Cir. Hist. Soc., Western History Assn., Am. Hist. Assn., Orgn. of Am. Historians, Albany County Hist. Soc. (pres. 2000-02). Office Phone: 307-766-5311. Personal E-mail: philwyo@yahoo.com. Business E-Mail: philr@uwyo.edu.

**ROBERTS, R. MICHAEL,** animal scientist, biochemist, educator; b. U.K., 1941; BA in Botany, Oxford U., PhD in Plant Physiology and Biochemistry; doctorate (hon.), U. Liege, Belgium, 1998. Prof. animal scis. and biochemistry U. Mo., Columbia, 1985—, curators' prof., 1996—, dir. Life Scis. Ctr., 2004—. Vice-chmn. Gordon Conf. on Mammalian Genital Tract Plymouth State Coll., 1986; chmn. Gordon Conf. on Reproductive Tract Biology Brewster Acad., 1988; fgn. specialist Nat. Inst. Animal Industry, Japan, 1998; chief scientist Nat. Rsch. Initiative Competitive Grants Program/Coop. State Rsch., Edn., Extension Svc./USDA, 1998—2000. Contbr. articles to profl. jours. Named Disting. Scientist, USDA, 1992; recipient Rsch. award, Soc. for Study of Reproduction, 1990, Merit award, NIH, 1990—2000, Milstein award, Internat. Soc. Interferon and Cytokine Rsch., 1995, Alexander von Humboldt award for agr., 1996, Wolf prize in agr., Wolf Found., Israel, 2003. Mem.: NAS. Office: U Mo Columbia Life Scis Ctr Columbia MO 65211*

**ROBERTS, RALPH JOEL,** telecommunications industry executive, cable broadcast executive; b. NYC, Mar. 13, 1920; s. Robert and Sara (Wahl) Roberts; m. Suzanne Fleisher, Aug. 23, 1942; children: Catherine, Lisa, Ralph Jr., Brian, Douglas. BS in Econs., U. Pa., 1941; LHD (hon.), Holy Family Coll., 1994; HHD (hon.), Arcadia U., 2004; LLD (hon.), U. Pa., 2005. Account exec. Aitken Kynett Advt., Phila., 1946-48; v.p. Muzak Corp., NYC, 1948-50; pres., chief exec. officer Pioneer Industries, Inc., Darby, Pa., 1950-61; pres. Internat. Equity Corp., Bala Cynwyd, Pa., 1961-83; chmn. bd., Comcast Corp., Phila., 1969—; chmn., chief exec. officer Sural Corp. (merger with Internat. Equity Corp. 1983); chmn. Comcast Corp., Phila. Trustee, chmn. conflict interest com. Albert Einstein Med. Ctr.; bd. dirs. Phila. Electric Co., Phila. Nat. Bank, Corestates, Penn Medicine; bd. trustees U. Pa. Health Sys., 2002. Bd. dirs. regional NCCJ; trustee Brandywine Mus. and Conservancy, charter mem. World Bus. Coun.; past mem. mentor program and Benjamin Franklin assocs. U. Pa.; bd. dirs. Phila. Orch., 1993; past v.p. Family Svc. Phila.; past bd. dirs., mem. budget and fees com. State Coll. and Univ. Dirs.; mem. re-regulation and legis. affairs coms. Nat. Cable TV Assn.; past mem. Gov.'s Rev. of Govt. Mgmt., Inc. Lt. USNR, 1942-45. Reipient Americanism award Anti-Defamation League of B'nai B'rith, Brotherhood award NCCJ, 1989, award for outstanding svc. to cable TV industry Walter Kaitz Found., 1990, Acres of Diamonds Entrepreneurial Excellence award Entrepreneurial Inst. Temple U., 1991, Disting. Vanguard award for leadership Nat. Cable TV Assn., 1993, Golden Plate award Am. Acad. Achievement, 1994, PAL award Police Athletic League Phila., 1995, Edward Powell award for cmty. svc. City of Phila., 1995, Joseph P. Wharton award U. Pa., 1995, Whitney M. Young Jr. Leadership award Urban League Phila., 1997, Disting. Cmty. Leadership award Operation Understanding, 1997, Cable TV Hall of Fame award, 2000, Mensa Achievement award, 2000, Heroes of Liberty award Liberty Mus., 2000, William Penn award Greater Phila. C. of C., 2002, Am. Horizon award for Visionary Leadership, Media Inst., Washington, 2002, Humanitarian award United Jewish Appeal Fedn. of NY, 2003, Trustee Leader award NATAS, 2003, Excellence in Leadership award Temple U., 2005, Partnership for Drug Free Am. hon., 2005; named to Broadcasting and Cable Hall of Fame, 1993. Avocations: tennis, travel. Home: Sural Farm 505 Fairview Rd East Fallowfield Township PA 19320-4451 Office: Comcast Corp 1500 Market St Philadelphia PA 19102-2148 Office Fax: 215-981-7790. Business E-Mail: rroberts@comcast.net.

**ROBERTS, RICHARD CHARLTON, III,** lawyer; b. Jackson, Miss., Mar. 18, 1951; BA, U. Miss., 1973, JD with distinction, 1976. Bar: Miss. 1976, U.S. Dist. Ct. (no. and so. dists.) Miss. 1976, U.S. Ct. Appeals (5th cir.) 1976, U.S. Ct. Appeals (11th cir.) 1981, U.S. Supreme Ct. 1989. Pvt. practice, Jackson, Miss. Assoc. editor Miss. Law Jour., 1976. Named one of Best Lawyers in Am., Outstanding Lawyers Am. Fellow: Nat. Conf. Bar Pres., Miss. Bar Found.; mem.: ABA (sect. on family law, gen. practice, solo and small firm practice), Nat. Lawyer's Assn., Bar Assn. 5th Fed. Cir., Miss. Bar (chmn. solo and small firm practitioner's task force 1993—94, exec. com. family law sect. 1994—95, chmn. 1996, bd. bar commrs. 1996—99, nominating com. 1999—99, bench-bar liaison standing com. 2001—, bd. bar commrs. 2002—05, pres. 2003—04), Hinds County Bar Assn. (bd. dirs. 1990—96, sec.-treas. 1992—93, pres. 1994—95, chmn. long range planning com. 1995—97), Fed. Bar Assn. (pres. Miss. chpt. 1987—88, nat. coun. 1988, jud. liaison for U.S. Dist. Cts.-So. Dist. Miss. 1989), Am. Inss of Ct., Phi Kappa Phi. Office: PO Box 55882 Jackson MS 39296-5882

**ROBERTS, RICHARD JOHN,** molecular biologist, consultant, research director; b. Derby, Eng., Sept. 6, 1943; came to U.S., 1969; s. John Walter and Edna Wilhelmina (Allsop) R.; m. Elizabeth Dyson, Aug. 21, 1965 (dec.); children: Alison, Andrew; m. Jean E. Tagliabue, Feb. 14, 1986; children: Christopher, Amanda. BS, Sheffield (Eng.) U., 1965, PhD, 1968. Rsch. fellow Harvard U., Cambridge, Mass., 1969-70, rsch. assoc., 1971-72; sr. staff investigator Cold Spring Harbor Lab., N.Y., 1972-87, asst. dir., 1987-92; cons. New Eng. Biolabs, Ipswich, Mass., 1974-92, rsch. dir., 1992—; sci. adv. bd. Genex, Rockville, Md., 1977-85; chief scientific officer Molecular Tool, Balt., 1994—. Contbr. articles to profl. jours. Recipient Nobel prize in physiology or medicine, Nobel Found. 1993. John Simon Guggenheim Found. fellow, 1979. Fellow Royal Soc.; mem. Am. Soc. Microbiology. Office: New Eng Biolabs 240 County Rd Ipswich MA 01938-2723 Office Phone: 978-380-7405. E-mail: roberts@neb.com.

**ROBERTS, ROBERT WINSTON,** social worker, educator, dean; b. Balt., July 23, 1932; s. Kelmer Swan Roberts and Lettie Mae (Collins) Johnston; m. Helen Elizabeth Perpich, Mar. 4, 1964 (div. Aug. 1997); life ptnr. Paul Edwards. BA with high honors, San Francisco State U., 1957; MSW, U. Calif., Berkeley, 1959; D in Social Welfare, Columbia U., 1970. Caseworker Edgewood Protestant Orphanage, San Francisco, 1959-62, Jewish Family Service, San Francisco, 1962-63; research assoc. U. Calif., Berkeley, 1963-65; research analyst Family Service Assn. Am., N.Y.C., 1965-69; asst. prof. U. Chgo., 1967-70; prof. U. So. Calif., Los Angeles, 1970-90, dean sch. social work, 1980-88, dean emeritus, prof. emeritus, 1990—. Vis. prof. Western Australia Inst. Tech. (now Curtin U.), Perth, 1976-77, Chinese U. Hong Kong and U. Hong Kong, 1980; cons. Crittenton Services, Los Angeles, 1970-72, James Weldon Johnson Community Ctr., N.Y., 1966-67; bd. dirs. El Centro, Los Angeles. Editor: The Unwed Mother, 1966; co-editor: Theories of Social Casework, 1970, Child Caring: Social Policy and the Institution, 1973, Theories of Social Work with Groups, 1976, Theory and Practice of Community Social Work, 1980; editorial bd. Social Work Jour.; contbr. articles to profl. jours. Staff sgt. USAF, 1950-54; sgt. 1st class USAR, 1956-59. Fellow NIMH, 1957-58, 65-67, Crown Zellerbach Found., 1958-59; recipient Outstanding Educator award Los Amigos de la Humanidad, 1979; named Disting. Assoc., Nat. Acad. Practice in Social Work, 1985; decorated Commendation ribbon USAF, Korean Svc. ribbon USAF, Svc. medal UN, Good Conduct medal USAF, Nat. Def. Svc. medal, Ribbon medal, USAF. Mem. ACLU, NASW (chmn. social action com. 1960-61), Coun. on Social Work Edn. (bd. dirs. 1970-73, del. to assembly 1971-72, commn. minority groups 1972-73). Avocations: cooking, reading, travel, photography. Office: U So Calif Montgomery Ross Fisher Rm 21 Los Angeles CA 90089-0001

**ROBERTS, RONALD JOHN,** education educator, director; b. Liverpool, England, Mar. 28, 1941; s. Ronald George Roberts and Marjorie Kneale; m. Helen Macgregor; children: Gavin, Calum. DVM, U. Glasgow, 1966, PhD, 1968. Lectr. U. Glasgow, 1966—71; dir. Inst. of Aquaculture, Scotland, 1971—96; adj. disting. prof. U. Idaho, 1996—. Dir. Landcatch, Ltd., 1996— Bradan, Ltd., 2002—. Editor: Jour. of Fish Diseases, 1978—; author: (book) Fish Pathology, 3d edit., 1999. Vice chmn. vet. bd. European Food Stds. Authority, Belgium, 2002—06. Named to Royal Order Commander of Crown Thailand, His Royal Highness King Bumibol Ayaludej, 1994; recipient Gold medal, Buckland prize, 1983. Fellow: Royal Soc. Edinburgh, Royal Coll. Vet. Surgeons. Avocations: golf, gardening. Home: 9 Alexander Dr Bridge of Allan FK96QR Scotland Office: Hagerman Lab U Idaho Hagerman ID 83332 Office Phone: 208-837-9096. E-mail: heronpisces@btinternet.com.

**ROBERTS, ROSALINDA CUSIDO,** medical researcher, educator; b. LA, Oct. 26, 1957; d. Frederic Cusido and Orpha Linda Roberts. BS, U. Calif., Irvine, 1979, PhD, 1986. Postdoctoral fellow Mass. Gen. Hosp., Harvard

Med. Sch., Boston, 1986—89, instr., 1989—90; asst. prof. psychiatry U. Md., Balt., 1990—96, assoc. prof., 1996—2000, prof. psychiatry, anatomy and neurobiology, 2000—. Dir. Md. brain collection Md. Psychiat. Rsch. Ctr., Balt., 1996—. Grantee, NIH, 1996—. Mem.: Soc. Neurosci. Achievements include patents for disease related genes. Avocations: animals, nature lover, gourmet food and wine, exercise. Office: MPRC Univ Md Sch Medicine PO Box 21247 Baltimore MD 21228 Office Phone: 410-402-7608. E-mail: rroberts@mprc.umaryland.edu.

**ROBERTS, ROXANN MAE,** secondary school educator; b. Dansville, N.Y., Oct. 28, 1941; d. James Vincent and Victoria Marie (Ashley) Argennia; m. James L. Roberts, Feb. 1, 1964; children: Donald James, Ronald Ashley, William Carl. BS in Edn., SUNY, Geneseo, 1969, MS in Edn., 1978; cert. in vol. adminstrn., St. John Fisher Coll., 1996. Cert. tchr., N.Y. Sub. tchr. Perry (N.Y.) Cen. Sch. Dist., 1965-71, reading aide, 1971-74, elem. tchr., 1974, 1975-86; tchr. remedial reading Keshequa Cen. Sch. Dist., Nunda, N.Y., 1975-86; prin. Wyoming (N.Y.) Cen. Sch. Dist., 1986-88; pupil personnel Pavilion (N.Y.) Cen., 1988-89; bridge coord. Genesee Community Coll., Batavia, N.Y., 1990-91; asst. dir. edn. Rochester (N.Y.) Mental Health Ctr., 1992; prin. St. Michael's, Warsaw, N.Y., 1993-94; vol. adminstr. liv. Wyo. Arc., Mt. Morris, N.Y., 1995-97. Part-time faculty State Univ. Coll. at Geneseo, 1997—; Genesee Community Coll. in Batavia; charter mem. N.Y.State Staff Devel. Coun. Sec. Genesee-Wyoming Prins. Assn., N.Y., 1986-89. Mem. Sch. Adminstrs. Assn. N.Y. State, Internat. Reading Assn., Children's Book Coun., Assn. for Supervison and Curriculum Devel., NEA of N.Y., N.Y. State Tchrs. Retirement System, N.Y. Coll. Learning Skills Assn., United Univ. Profs., Phi Delta Kappa. Avocations: duplicate bridge, collecting cookbooks.

**ROBERTS, SAMUEL SMITH,** television news executive; b. Port Chester, N.Y., Feb. 8, 1936; s. Robert M. and Lillian (Smith) R.; m. Harriet Rubin, July 27, 1975; children: Rachel, David; children by previous marriage: Nancy, Pamela. BS, Northwestern U., 1957. With UPI, N.Y.C., 1961, Capital Cities Broadcasting, Providence, 1962, CBS News, 1962-95; sr. prodr. CBS Evening News, N.Y.C., 1978-81, nat. editor, 1982-84, fgn. editor, 1984-87; exec. prodr. CBS News Prodns., 1992-95, 20th Century, 1994-95; pres. Roberts Media Internat., N.Y.C., 1995-96; v.p., gen. mgr. TV programming Electronic Media Co., N.Y. Times, 1996-99; Frances L. Wolfson chair U. Miami, Coral Gables, Fla., 1999—. Served to It. USN, 1957-61. Office: U Miami Sch Comm PO Box 248127 Coral Gables FL 33124-8127

**ROBERTS, SANDRA BROWN,** real estate company executive; b. Boston, May 26, 1939; d. Frederick Thomas and Christine (Peyton) Brown; m. Joseph Peter Roberts Aug. 26, 1962 (div. May 1984); children: Christine, Joseph, Paul. BA, Boston Coll., 1981. Lic. real estate broker, Mass. Owner, mgr. real estate, Wellesley, Mass., 1963—; pres. Riverview Realty, Wellesley, 1970—; comml. realtor Boston, 1974—. Cons. Berkshire Hathaway, New Bedford, Mass., 1983-87; asst. to pres. BHR, Inc., New Bedford, 1988-2000. Founder, pres., bd. dirs. Friends of Ft. Washington, Inc., 1985-95; active Friends of Boston Ballet, 1983—. Mem. DAR (Boston Tea Party chpt. regent 1983-84, 84-85), Navy League of U.S., New Eng. Hist. Geneal. Soc., Boston Coll. Club (bd. dirs.), Order of Crown of Charlemagne (life), Order of Lafayette). Republican. Roman Catholic. Home and Office: 52 Kenilworth Rd Wellesley MA 02482-7428

**ROBERTS, SIDNEY,** biological chemist; b. Boston, Mar. 11, 1918; s. Samuel Richard and Elizabeth (Gilbert) R.; m. Clara Marian Szego, Sept. 14, 1943. BS, MIT, 1939; postgrad., Harvard U., 1939-41; MS, U. Minn., 1942, PhD, 1943. Instr. physiology U. Minn. Med. Sch., 1943-44, George Washington U. Med. Sch., 1944-45; rsch. assoc. Worcester Found. Exptl. Biology, Shrewsbury, Mass., 1945-47; asst. prof. physiol. chemistry Yale U. Med. Sch., 1947-48; mem. faculty U. Calif. Med. Sch., Los Angeles, 1948—, prof. biol. chemistry, 1957—; chmn. acad. senate UCLA, 1989-90; mem. adv. panel regulatory biology NSF, 1955-57, adv. panel metabolic biology, 1957-59; mem. metabolism study sect. NIH, 1960-63; basic sci. study sect. Los Angeles County Heart Assn., 1958-63. Cons. VA Hosp., Long Beach, Calif., 1951-55, Los Angeles, 1958-62, Pew Fin. Biomed. Scholar Program, 1992-; air conservation tech. adv. com. Los Angeles County Lung Assn., 1972-76 Author articles, revs.; editor med. jours. Served to 2d lt. AUS, 1944-48. MIT Nat. Entrance scholar, 1935; Guggenheim fellow, 1957-58. Fellow AAAS; mem. Am. Physiol. Soc., Endocrine Soc. (v.p. 1968-69, Ciba award 1953), Brit. Biochem. Soc., Soc. Neurosci., Am. Chem. Soc. (exec. com. div. biol. chemistry 1956-59), Am. Soc. Biol. Chemists, Am. Soc. Neurochemistry, Internat. Soc. Neurochemistry, Phi Beta Kappa, Sigma Xi (pres. UCLA chpt. 1959-60). Home: 1371 Marinette Rd Pacific Palisades CA 90272-2627 Office: UCLA Sch Med Dept Biol Chemistry Los Angeles CA 90095-1737 Office Phone: 310-825-6997. Business E-Mail: sr@ucla.edu.

**ROBERTS, STANLEY DWAYNE,** physician, educator, academic administrator; b. Edmonton, Alta., Can., Sept. 17, 1959; came to U.S., 1994; s. Stan and Margaret Rosslyn (Rye) R.; m. Debra Elizabeth Bell, Aug. 20, 1981; children: Matthew, Brent, Michelle, Jared, Bradley. BSc with honors, U. Alta., Edmonton, 1980, BSc in Psychology with distinction, 1981, MD, 1985; grad., IHC Inst., 1990. Diplomate in family practice and sports medicine Am. Bd. Family Practice; cert. Family Medicine and Emergency Medicine, Coll. Family Physicians of Can. Resident in family medicine U. Alta., 1985-87; resident in physical rehab. and sports medicine McMaster U., Hamilton, Ont., Can., 1987-88; resident in emergency medicine, 1988-89, asst. prof. family and emergency medicine, 1989-94; med. dir., internat. med. cons. Med. Emergency, Inc., Toronto, Ont., Can., 1990-94; chief emergency svcs. Queensway Gen. Hosp., Toronto, Ont., Can., 1992-94; employee health physician, family physician Norman (Okla.) Regional Hosp., 1994-95; family physician Bigstone Cree Indian Reserve, Alberta, 1995—96; pvt. practice Provo, Utah, 1996-97; faculty physician Utah Valley Family Practice Residency, Provo, 1997—2003; emergency physician Utah Valley Regional Med. Ctr., Provo, 1997—; assoc. team physician Brigham Young U., 1999—2002. Med. dir. Redcliff Ascent Wilderness Behavioral Reclamation Program Youth, 2000—; moderator, panelee Telemedicine Can./USA Broadcasts, 1990—98; team doctor World Cup Speed Skating, 1999; dir. Utah Valley Sports Medicine Fellowship, 1999—2003; site physician 2002 Winter Olympics and Paralympics/Ice Hockey, Sledge Hockey; developer internat. tng. program for physicians, Nepal, 2000, Western Samoa, 01, Fiji, 01; cons. Global Emergency Medicine Support; cons. devel. plan emergency svcs., Malaysia, 1990—92, Thailand, 1990—92; mem. spkrs. burs. Abbott Labs., Glaxo-Smith-Kline, Burroughs-Wellcoje, Pfizer, 1999—; lectr. in field. Contbr. articles to profl. jours.; guest radio talk shows; developer internat. tng. program in emergency medicine: Art in EM = Advanced Resuscitation Training in Emergency Medicine. Chmn. coms. life support Heart and Stroke Found. (Can.) Ont., 1991-93; scoutmaster Boy Scouts Am., Kaysville, Utah, 1995, Orem, Utah, 1998-99. Recipient Achievement award for internat. distinction in music Govt. Alberta, 1976, Disting. Lectr. award Thailand and Asia Coll. Surgeons, 1993. Mem. AMA, Am. Acad. Family Physicians, Utah Med. Assn., Coll. Family Physicians (Can.), Am. Coll. Sports Medicine, Spkrs. Bureau. Mem. Lds Ch. Avocations: mountain biking, photography. E-mail: sdwayne.roberts@ihc.com.

**ROBERTS, STEPHEN M.,** library director; Asst. v.p. univ. libbns. SUNY, Buffalo, acting assoc. v.p. univ. librs. Office: U at Buffalo Librs 433 Capen Hall, N Campus Buffalo NY 14260-1625 Office Phone: 716-645-2966. Office Fax: 716-645-3844. E-mail: sroberts@buffalo.edu.*

**ROBERTS, SUSAN STURGEON,** art educator, writer; b. Aurora, Colo., Aug. 15, 1953; d. Thomas James Sturgeon, Lela Selby Nagle; m. Eugene Arden Roberts. BS, Calif. State Poly. U., 1978. Tchr. Redlands Unified Sch. Dist., Calif., 1978—80; needle arts tchr. Grants Pass, Oreg., 1974—. Double knits designer Western Textile MIll., Ontario, Calif., 1978. Author: (book) The Complete Needlepoint Guide 400+ Needlepoint Stitches, 2000; sculpture, Stitchin Suzi and Three Ply, 1998. Mem.: Embroiderer's Guild Am. Inc. (asst. editor 1973—76, program dir. 2001—03), Am. Needlepoint Guild Inc. Fax: 541-471-0917. Office Phone: 541-471-0917. Business E-Mail: susanroberts15@hotmail.com.

**ROBERTS, SUZANNE CATHERINE,** artist; b. San Antonio, Oct. 27, 1953; d. Thomas Simons and Marceline Margaret (Conrady) Garrett; m. Ted Blake Roberts, May 22, 1976; 1 child, Elizabeth. BS Radio-TV-Film, U. Tex., 1975, B Journalism, 1977; MA Interdisciplinary Studies, Corpus Christi State U., Tex., 1982; MS Gen. Counseling, Corpus Christi State U., 1989; MA Polit. Sci., S.W. Tex. State U., 1995. News announcer Sta. KIXL Radio, Austin, Tex., 1976, Sta. KSIX Radio, Corpus Christi, 1977—78; news anchor Sta. KZTV-TV, Corpus Christi, 1979, news reporter, 1977—80; news announcer, reporter Sta. KRYS-AM-FM, Corpus Christi, 1983—87; freelance reporter UPI, Austin, 1989—94, Tex. State Network, Austin, 1995—97, Des Moines, 1997—2000; artist, 1998—.

**ROBERTS, TERI ALANE,** finance educator, volunteer; b. Mission Hills, Calif., Oct. 25, 1963; d. Alan Lewis and Barbara Ann (Taylor) R. BA in Speech Comm., Calif. State U., Northridge, 1990, BA in Polit. Sci. with honors, 1993, MA in Polit. Sci., 1997, MA in History Progress. Peer educator on rape Discovering Alternatives to Today's Encounters, Northridge, 1996-97; dir. Save the Animals Fund, Pasadena, Calif., 1997. Vol. Ga. Mercer for City Coun., Encino, Calif., 1997; mem. planning com., presenter at workshop Ending Violence Against Women Conf., Northridge, 1997; mem. planning com. Rainbow Sisters Project, L.A., 1999. Recipient Commendation for Rainbow Sisters Project, L.A. County, 1999. Mem. Polit. Sci. Club Calif. State U. (dir. fundraising 1992-93, dir. graduation com. 1992-93), Student Speech Comm. Assn. Calif. State U. (dir. social activities 1987-88), Delta Sigma (life). Democrat. Avocations: reading, dance, church activities. Home: 8545 Balboa Blvd Apt 250 Northridge CA 91325-3531 E-mail: teriroberts@socal.rr.com.

**ROBERTS, THEODORE HARRIS,** banker; b. Gillett, Ark., May 14, 1929; s. Edward and Gertrude (Harris) R.; m. Elizabeth Law, July 17, 1953; children: Susan, William(dec.), Julia, John. BA in Govt., Northwestern State U., 1949; MA in Polit. Sci., Okla. State U., 1950; postgrad., U. Chgo. Grad. Sch. Bus., 1956. With Harris Trust and Savs. Bank, Chgo., 1953-82; exec. v.p., sec., treas. Harris Bank and Harris Bankcorp Inc., 1971-82, dir., exec. com., 1975-82; pres. Fed. Res. Bank St. Louis, 1983-85; chmn. bd., chief exec. officer Talman Home Fed. Savs. & Loan, Chgo., 1985-92; pres. LaSalle Nat. Corp., 1992-95, retired. Sr. cons. ABN AMRO, 1995—. Mem. Chgo. Club, Comml. Club Chgo., Econ. Club Chgo., Exmoor Country Club (Highland Park, Ill.). Office: 135 S La Salle St Ste 260 Chicago IL 60603-4500 E-mail: ted.roberts@abnamro.com.

**ROBERTS, THOMAS ALBA,** lawyer; b. Ft. Wayne, Ind., Sept. 7, 1946; s. Jack and Elizabeth (Wallace) R.; m. Mary Alice Buckley, Aug. 11, 1973; children: Kaitrin M., John A., Kara B. BA, Georgetown U., 1969, JD, 1972. Bar: NY 1973, US Dist. Ct. (So. Dist.) NY 1973, US Ct. Appeals (2nd cir. 1973, Tex. 1976, US Supreme Ct. 1977, US Dist. Ct. (So. Dist.) Tex. 1978, US Ct. Appeals (5th and 11th cirs.) 1982. Assoc. Winthrop, Stimson, Putnam & Roberts, NYC, 1972-76; ptnr. Moore & Peterson, Dallas, 1976-89, mng. ptnr., 1980-88; ptnr. Johnson & Gibbs, Dallas, 1989-92; sr. ptnr., head corp. dept. Weil, Gotshal & Manges, LLP, NYC, 1992—. Chmn. Internat. Corp. Practice Group, 1997—2001, chmn. corp. dept., 2001—, mem. mgmt. com., 1997—; adj. prof. law Sw. Meth. U., Dallas, 1977—78; lectr. in field. Mem. Georgetown Law Jour. 1971-72; contbr. to pubs. Mem. lawyers com. N.Y. Pub. Libr., 2006—; mem. fin. com. St. Rita Ch., Dallas 1983—88; mem. Ch. of the Resurrection; mem. fin. com. Our Lady of the Lake, Rockwall, Tex., 1995—98; mem. exec. com., bd. dir. Make-A-Wish Found. Met. N.Y., 1998—; mem. exec. com., bd. dir. chmn. fin. com. Make-A-Wish of Am., 2002—, chmn. elect bd. dirs., 2006—; bd. dir. Memorial Sloan Kettering Cancer Ctr. Prostrate Cancer Rsch. Fund; mem. bd. visitors Georgetown Law Ctr., 2004—. Recipient Dealmakers for the Yr., Am. Lawyer, 2001. Mem. ABA, State Bar Tex., Dallas Bar Assn., Assn. of Bar of NY Roman Catholic. Avocations: skiing, golf, literature. Home: 133 Grandview Ave Rye NY 10580-2030 Office: Weil Gotshal & Manges LLP 767 Fifth Ave New York NY 10153 Office Phone: 212-310-8479. Office Fax: 212-310-6717. E-mail: thomas.roberts@weil.com.

**ROBERTS, THOMAS GEORGE,** retired physicist; b. Ft. Smith, Ark., Apr. 27, 1929; s. Thomas Lawrence and Emma Lee (Stanley) R.; m. Alice Anne Harbin, Nov. 14, 1958 (dec. 1994); children: Lawrence Dewey, Regina Anne; foster child, Marcia Roberts Dale; m. Betty Howard McElyea, July 28, 1995. AA, Armstrong Coll., 1953; BS, U. Ga., 1956, MS, 1957; PhD, N.C. State U., 1967. Rsch. physicist U.S. Army Missile Command, Huntsville, Ala., 1958-85; cons. industry and govt. agys., 1970—, SAIC, Huntsville, Ala., 1997-2001; owner Technoco, Huntsville, 1985-96. Contbr. articles to profl. jours.; patentee in field. Sgt. USAF, 1948-52. Fellow Am. Optical Soc.; mem. Am. Phys. Soc., IEEE, Huntsville Optical Soc. Am. (pres. 1980, 92), Toastmaster Internat. (pres. 1963). Episcopalian. Achievements include research in laser physics, optics, particle beams and instrumentation; diagnostic devices and techniques development. Personal E-mail: robertsbetty@bellsouth.net.

**ROBERTS, THOMASENE BLOUNT,** entrepreneur; b. Americus, Ga., Sept. 5, 1943; d. Thomas Watson and Mary Elizabeth (Smith) Blount; m. Henry Lee Roberts, Apr. 24, 1970 (div. 1991); 1 child, Asha Maia. Student, Fisk U., 1960-63; BA, Morris Brown Coll., 1965; MA, Atlanta U., 1970, postgrad., 1979-82, Clark Atlanta U. Social worker Gate City Day Nursery Assn., Atlanta, 1965-66; ticket agt. Delta Air Lines, Inc., Atlanta, 1966-68; clk. accounts payable Kraft Foods, Inc., Decatur, Ga., 1968; cons. family svcs. Atlanta Housing Authority, 1970-72, supr. family svcs., 1972-73, mgr. family relocation, 1974-79; grad. rsch. asst. Sch. Edn. Atlanta U., 1979-82; city coun. asst. City of Atlanta, 1984-88, rsch. assoc. Dept. Pub. Safety 1988; dir. govt'l rels., Morris Brown Coll., Atlanta, 1988-93, owner TBR Ent., Atlanta, 1993—2002; adminstrv. analyst human svcs. City of Atlanta, 1995-97, adminstrv. analyst, prin. dept. adminstrv. svcs., 1997; owner Dream Catcher Events, Inc., 1997—; psychol. svcs. specialist City of Atlanta, 1998—2002. Researcher/intern Project Focus Teen Mother Program, Atlanta, 1981-82; moderator Nat. Black Women's Health Project, Atlanta, 1985; workshop leader Assn. Human Resources Mgrs., Atlanta, 1989; pres.'s rep U. Ctr. Devel. Corp., Inc., 1989-93; cons. entrepreneur devel. workshop Morris Brown Coll. Chairperson Ida Prather YWCA Cmty. Bd., Atlanta, 1985-90; bd. dirs. YWCA Met. Atlanta, 1986-90, Met. Atlanta Coalition 100 Black Women, 1988-90, 92-2001, sec., mem. bd. dirs. 1994-96, 1st v.p., 1997-2000; trustee Hammonds House Mus., 1995-2001; active fund dr. com. Jomandi Prodn., 1988-89; v.p. maj. gifts com. Camp Best Friends, City of Atlanta, 1989; mem. Multi-Cultural Leadership Group, Gov.'s Coun. on Developmental Disabilities, 2000; bd. dirs. Atlanta Black/Jewish Coalition, 1997-2000; apptd. mem. Atlanta Sister Cities Comm.; presenter, cons. Youth Motivation Task Force, 1998-2001; co-chmn. Atlanta AIDS Partnership Fund, 2000-04. Mem. Atlanta-Trinidad/Tobago Exch. (sec., treas. 1983-89, Pt. of Spain cert. 1986), Nat. Polit. Congress Black Women (corr. sec. 1989-90), Nat. Assn. for Equal Opportunity Higher Edn. (coll. liaison 1988-93), Coun. for Advancement-Support of Edn., Info. Forum, Atlanta Urban League, Inc., Nat. Assn. for Equal Opportunity in Higher Edn. (Disting. Alumni award 1991), Nat. Soc. Fund-Raising Execs. (cert. 1992), Nat. Soc. Fund-Raising Execs. Leadership Inst., Friends of Morehouse Sch. Medicine, Assn. Bridal Execs. Internat. Spl. Events Soc. (v.p. programs 2001-02), Atlanta Bus. League, Delta Sigma Theta (pub. rels. asst. 1986-89). Avocations: theater, music, films, art, fine dining. Home and Office: 1817 King Charles Rd SW Atlanta GA 30331-4909 Office Phone: 404-344-5052. Home Fax: 404-344-0378. E-mail: dreamcatcherevents2000@yahoo.com.

**ROBERTS, TIFFANY MARIE,** former soccer player; b. Petaluma, Calif., May 5, 1977; BA in Comm. Studies, U. N.C., 1998. Mem. U.S. Women's Nat. Soccer Team, 1994—; including CONCAFAF Qualifying Championship Montreal, 1994; 3d place FIFA Women's World Cup Sweden, 1995; gold medal U.S. Olympic Team, 1996; mem. Under-20 Nat. Team 1997 Nordic Cup, Denmark; mem. Tri Valley Team, San Ramon, Calif.; profl. soccer player Carolina Courage, 2001—03. Named 1994 Calif. H.S. Player of Yr.,

Most Valuable Player, Far Western Regional, 1993, World Cup Champion, 1999. Achievements include member U. N.C. NCAA national championship teams, 1996, 97. Office: US Soccer Fedn 1801-1811 S Prairie Ave Chicago IL 60616

**ROBERTS, TONY (DAVID ANTHONY ROBERTS),** actor; b. NYC, Oct. 22, 1939; s. Kenneth and Norma R.; 1 child, Nicole. BS, Northwestern U., 1961. Movie debut in The Million Dollar Duck, 1971; other film appearances include Star Spangled Girl, 1971, Play It Again, Sam, 1972, Serpico, 1974, The Taking of Pelham, One Two Three, 1974, Annie Hall, 1977, Lovers Like Us, 1977, Just Tell Me What You Want, Stardust Memories, 1980, A Midsummer Nights Sex Comedy, 1982, Question of Honor, 1982, Packin' It In, 1983, Amityville IIID, 1983, Hannah and her Sisters, 1986, 18 Again!, 1988, Popcorn, 1990, Switch, 1991; TV movies The Lindbergh Kidnapping Case, 1976, Girls in the Office, 1979, If Things Were Different, 1980, A Question of Honor, 1982, Our Sons, 1992, Not in My Family, 1993, The American Clock, 1993, Perry Mason: The Case of the Jealous Jokester, 1995; regular on TV series The Edge of Night, 1963-65, Rosetti and Ryan, 1977, The Four Seasons, 1986, The Lucy Arnaz Show, 1987, The Thorns, 1989; other TV appearances include The Way They Were, 1980; Broadway debut in Something about a Soldier, 1962; toured with nat. co. of Come Blow Your Horn, 1962; other Broadway stage appearances Take Her, She's Mine, 1964, Never Too Late, Barefoot in the Park, The Last Analysis, 1964, Don't Drink the Water, 1966, How Now, Dow Jones, 1967 (nominated for Tony award), Play It Again, Sam, 1969 (nominated for Tony award), Promises, Promises, 1971, Sugar, 1972, Absurd Person Singular, 1974, Murder at the Howard Johnson's, 1979, They're Playing Our Song, 1981, Doubles, 1985, Arsenic and Old Lace, 1986, Jerome Robbins Broadway, 1990, The Seagull, 1992, Tale of the Allergist's Wife, 2002, Sleuth, 2005; London debut in Promises, Promises, 1969 (London Critics Poll award as Best Actor in Musical); 1974; appeared in: Darkroom, Yale Repertory Theatre, New Haven, Hamlet, Otterbein Coll. (Ohio) Winter Drama Festival, 1975, Taming of the Shrew, Atlanta, 1978, Let 'Em Eat Cake, Berkshire Theatre Festival, Serenading Louis, Acad. Festival Theatre; The Seagull, Saratoga Performance Arts Festival, 1985, Who's Afraid of Virginia Woolf, 1986, (voice) audio books The Short Forever, 2002, Leadership, 2002. Served in U.S. Army. Mem. SAG (bd. dirs. 1990—, v.p. of NY div.,2001-), Actors Equity Assn. (governing coun. 1968-74) Office: Innovative Artists 1505 10th Ave Santa Monica CA 90401

**ROBERTS, VICTORIA LYNN P.,** antique expert; b. N.Y.C., Sept. 15, 1953; d. Edgar Alan Parmer and Nina Joyce (Ash) Gross; m. George E. Roberts, Dec. 1, 1978 (div 1985); 1 child, Joshua Henry. BA in Polit. Sci., Am. govt., const. law, Yale U., 1998; MBA, Fairfield U., 1999. Lic. real estate broker N.C., 2005, Conn., 2005. Pres. High Gear Creative Svcs., Savannah, Ga., 1979-81; v.p. Rossignol Modeling Agy., N.Y.C., 1981-82; mgr., dir. Parc Monceau Antiques, Westport, Conn., 1982-85; pres., owner, CEO Victoria & Cie LLC, Custom Furniture Mfg., Norwalk, Conn., 1985—; pres., owner L.L.C. Custom Furniture Mfg.; with Prudential Conn. Real Estate, 2005. Antiques tchr. Sacred Heart U., Fairfield, Conn., 1988, 89, Norwalk Community Coll., 1989; antique lectr. various hist. socs., Conn., 1989-90; speaker in antiques field; antique expert seminars to interior designers, Norwalk, 1989; creator, sole contbr. spls. on antiques CNBC TV, 1989, 90. Antiques editor Brooks Community Newspaper, Westport, 1989-91; contbr. Antiques Mag., 1991—. Mem. Appraisers Assn. Am. (sr.), Coll. Arts Assn., Norwalk Rotary, Yale Club (N.Y.C. admissions com. mem.), Alpha Sigma Lambda. Avocations: scenic photography, bicycling, history, rose gardening.

**ROBERTS, WALTER RONALD,** retired diplomat; b. Waltendorf, Austria, Aug. 26, 1916; arrived in U.S., 1939, naturalized, 1944; s. Ignatius and Elizabeth (Diamant) R.; m. Gisela K. Schmarak, Aug. 22, 1939; children: William M., Charles E., Lawrence H. MLitt, Cambridge U., Eng., 1940, PhD, 1980. Rsch. asst. Harvard U. Law Sch., 1940-42; writer, editor Voice of Am., 1942-49; press officer U.S. del. to Austrian Treaty talks, 1949, 55; fgn. affairs officer Dept. State, 1950-53; dep. asst. dir. USIA, 1954-60; counselor of embassy for pub. affairs Am. Embassy, Belgrade, Yugoslavia, 1960-66; diplomat-in-residence Brown U., Providence, 1966-67; counselor U.S. Mission to Internat. Orgns., Geneva, 1967-69; dep. assoc. dir. USIA, Washington, 1969-71, assoc. dir., 1971-74; dir. diplomatic studies Ctr. Strategic and Internat. Studies Georgetown U., Washington, 1974-75; exec. dir. Bd. Internat. Broadcasting, Washington, 1975-85; diplomat-in-residence George Washington U., Washington, 1986-96. Author: Tito, Mihailovic and the Allies, 1941-45, 73, paperback, 1987, (with Terry L. Deibel) Culture and Information: Two Foreign Policy Functions, 1976; contbr. articles to profl. pubs. Apptd. mem. U.S. Adv. Commn. on Pub. Diplomacy, 1991-97, sr. advisor, 1998-2003; bd. dirs. Salzburg Seminar, 1993-97, Coun. Sr. Fellows, 1998—, Oxford and Cambridge com., 1975-, Pub. Diplomacy Coun., 1996—; mem. emeritus bd. dirs. 2005—; bd. dirs. Pub. Diplomacy Inst., George Washington U., 2001-2004, sr. advisor 2006—. Recipient Disting. Honor award USIA, 1974. Mem. Washington Inst. Fgn. Affairs, Coun. Fgn. Rels., Oxford-Cambridge Com., USA Alumni Assn. (bd. dirs. 1995-98), Met. Club. Home: 4449 Sedgwick St NW Washington DC 20016-2713

**ROBERTS, WILLIAM B.,** lawyer; b. Detroit, Aug. 23, 1939; s. Edwin Stuart and Marjorie Jean (Wardle) R.; m. Cathleen Anne Thompson, Sept. 1, 1962; children: Bradford William, Brent William, Katrina Marjorie. BA, Mich. State U., 1961; JD with distinction, U. Mich., 1963; China law diploma, U. East Asia, Macau, 1989. Bar: Mo. 1964, Fla. 1983, U.S. Dist. Ct. (ea. dist.) Mo. 1964, U.S. Dist. Ct. (mid. dist.) Fla. 1993. Mem. firm Thompson & Mitchell, St. Louis, 1963-67; atty. Monsanto Co., 1967-70; sr. exec. v.p. adminstrn., sec., gen. counsel Chromalloy Am. Corp. (successor Segua Corp. N.Y.), St. Louis, 1970-78, exec. v.p. adminstrn., gen. counsel sec Clayton, Mo., 1978-80; pvt. practice law, 1980-87, mng. ptnr. Roberts and Nordahl, St. Louis and Naples, Fla., 1988-89, Law Offices of William B. Roberts, St. Louis and Naples, 1989-90, Darrow & Roberts, P.A., Naples, 1992-93; pres., mng. dir. Law Offices of William B. Roberts, Naples, 1994—, Kansas City, Mo., 1999—. Pres., mng. dir. The Fairborne Group, Ltd., St. Louis and Naples, 1988-91, William B. Roberts & Assocs. Co., Merger and Acquisitions Specialists, 1982—; mem. exam. com. of policyowners Northwestern Mut. Life Ins. Co., Milw., 1978; del. to U.S.-China Joint Session on Trade Investment and Econ. Law, Beijing, 1987; sports rep. Steve Carlton, St. Louis Cardinals, Phila. Phillies baseball clubs, 1985-89; pres., CEO Tropical Tracks, Inc., Naples, 1994—. Mem. ABA, Fed. Bar Assn. (Mid. Dist. Fla.), Mo. Bar Assn., St. Louis Bar Assn. (chmn. antitrust sect. 1973), Fla. Bar Assn., Collier County Bar Assn., Delta Theta Phi. Methodist. Home: 133 Crestview Terr Lake Placid FL 33852 Also: 321 NE Landings Dr Lees Summit MO 64064-1586 Personal E-mail: billkcmo@swbell.net.

**ROBERTS, WILLIAM CLIFFORD,** medical association administrator; b. Atlanta, Sept. 11, 1932; s. Stewart Ralph and Ruby (Holbrook) R.; m. Frances Carey Cansler, Aug. 20, 1955 (div. Apr. 1993); children: William Clifford, Charles Stewart, Frances Carey, John David. AB, So. Meth. U., 1954; MD, Emory U., 1958. Chief pathology br. Nat. Heart, Lung & Blood Inst., NIH, Bethesda, Md., 1959-93; dir. Baylor Heart and Vascular Inst., Baylor U. Med. Ctr., Dallas, 1993—. Editor-in-chief: The Am. Jour. Cardiology, 1994, Baylor U. Med. Ctr. Procs., 1994—; contbr. articles to profl. jours. With USPHS, 1959-93. Fellow Am. Coll. Cardiology (bd. trustees, Gifted Tchr. award 1978, Coll. Medalist award 1983), Am. Heart Assn. (Richard and Linda Rosenthal Found. award Coun. Cardiology 1984); mem. North Tex. Cardiovascular Soc. (pres. 1993—), Assn. U. Cardiologists (elected mem.), Halsted Soc. (elected mem.). Avocations: reading, tennis. Home: 3415 Harvard Ave Dallas TX 75205-3242 Office: Baylor Univ Med Ctr 3500 Gaston Ave Dallas TX 75246-2096 Office Phone: 214-820-7911. E-mail: wc.roberts@baylorhealth.edu.

**ROBERTS, WILLIAM EVERETT,** lawyer; b. Pierre, SD, May 12, 1926; s. Everett David and Bonnie (Martin) R.; m. Cynthia Cline, July 18, 1953; children: Catherine C. Roberts-Martin, Laura M., Nancy F., David H. BS, U. Minn., 1947; LLB, Yale U., 1950. Bar: Ind. 1950, U.S. Supreme Ct. 1964. Employee, ptnr. Duck and Neighbours, Indpls., 1950-58; ptnr. Cadick, Burns,

Duck & Neighbours, Indpls., 1958-60, Roberts, Ryder, Rogers & Scism, Indpls., 1960-85, Barnes & Thornburg, Indpls., 1986-93, of counsel, 1994—. Pres., bd. dirs. Park-Tudor Sch., Indpls., 1982-83; elder Second Presbyn. Ch., Indpls., 1962—; trustee Indpls. Mus. Art, 1978—; pres. New Hope of Ind., Indpls., 1986-87. Fellow Am. Bar Found.; mem. ABA, Ind. Bar Assn., Indpls. Bar Assn., Rotary, Meridian Hills Country Club (pres. 1983-84). Republican. Home: 10466 Spring Highland Dr Indianapolis IN 46290-1101 Office: Barnes & Thornburg 11 S Meridian St Ste 1313 Indianapolis IN 46204-3535 Office Phone: 317-231-7520.

**ROBERTS, WILLIAM H.,** lawyer; b. Buffalo, June 14, 1945; s. Esther C. Roberts and William H. Roberts, Jr. JD, U. Pa., Phila., 1970; AB, Harvard Coll., Cambridge, MA, 1967. Bar: Pa. 1970, U.S. Ct. Appeals (3d cir.) 1972, U.S. Supreme Ct. 1974, U.S. Ct. Appeals (11th cir.) 1982, U.S. Claims Ct. 1986, U.S. Ct. Appeals (4th cir.) 1987, U.S. Ct. Appeals (9th cir.) 2000. Ptnr. Blank Rome LLP, Phila., 1977—. Co-author: (book) Com. Free Speech, 1985. Trustee The Curtis Inst. of Music, Phila., 1997—; trustee, pres. Chamber Orch. of Phila., Phila., 1988—; trustee Harvard Rev. of Philosophy, Cambridge, Mass., 1993—, Marlboro Music Sch., 2004—. Named Disting. Honoree, Nat. Assn. of Fundraising Execs., 2002. Mem.: Phila. Bot. Club, Harvard Club NYC. Avocations: violin, botany, salmon fishing.

**ROBERTS, WILLIAM J.,** mathematics professor; s. William F. and Alice B. Roberts; m. Barbara A. Abbott, June 26, 1976 (dec. Feb. 15, 2000); m. Elaine M. Maron, June 15, 2003; children: William R., Beth L. BS, U. Mass., 1964, D Math. Edn., 1970; MEd, U. Hartford, 1966; CAS, Wesleyan U., Middletown, Conn., 1968. Math. tchr. Windsor Locks (Conn.) Sch. Sys., Windsor Locks, Conn., 1963—67; asst. prof. Westfield (Mass.) State Coll., 1968—71; assoc. prof. math. Plymouth (NH) State Coll., 1971—82; prof. of math. Plymouth State U., 1982—. Cons. New Hampton (NH) Village Precinct, 1977—2000, treas., 2000—05; mem. troop com. Boy Scouts Am., Bridgewater, NH, 1993—2000. Mem.: NH Tchrs. Math. (bus. mgr. 1978—), Nat. Coun. Tchrs. Math., Math. Assn. Am. Office: Plymouth State U 17 High St - Hyde Hall MSC #29 Plymouth NH 03264 Office Phone: 603-535-2433. Business E-Mail: wjr@plymouth.edu.

**ROBERTS, WILLIAM O.,** sports medicine physician; b. Napoleon, N.D., Mar. 17, 1952; s. Robert O. and Myrtle Margaret Roberts; m. Debra Ann Wood, Aug. 21, 1976; children: Jessie Marie, Kelly Lynne, Dana Margaret. BS in Biology, Rennselaer Poly. Inst., 1974; MD, U. Minn. Med. Sch., 1978; MSc in Family Practice and Cmty. Health, U. Minn., 1981. Diplomate Am. Bd. Family Medicine, 1981, Sports Medicine Am. Bd. Family Medicine, 1993. Physician MinnHealth Family Physicians, White Bear Lake, 1986—2003; assoc. prof. family medicine U. Minn. Med. Sch., Mpls., 2003—. Editor in chief Your Patient and Fitness, Mpls., 1991—95, McGraw Hill HealthCare Info. Products, Mpls., 1995—2005; med. dir. Twin Cities Marathon, Mpls., 1985—; mem. editl. bd. Physician and Sportsmedicine, Mpls., 1992—2005, Medicine and Sci. in Sports and Exercise, Balt., 2000—, Brit. Jour. Sports Medicine, London, 2001—, Clin. Jour. Sports Medicine, Balt. Editor: (handbook) Bull's Handbook of Sports Injuries, 2d edit., 2004. Sports medicine adv. com. Minn. State HS League, Bklyn. Center, Minn., 1986—2006, Schwan's USA Soccer Cup, Blaine, Minn.; sch. bd. mem. and clk. Mahtomedi Dist. 832 Schs., Minn., 1996—2006. Named to Minnesota's Best Doctors List for Family Practice, Best Doctors Inc., Minn. Monthly, 2003, Twin Cities Top Doc's List for Sports Medicine, Mpls.-St. Paul Mag., 2004—05; recipient Merit award for Sports Medicine, Minn. State HS League, 1993, Larry "Stosh" Neumann award, Minn. Athletic Trainers' Assn., 2002. Fellow: Am. Coll. Sports Medicine (pres. 2004—05); mem.: Internat. Marathon Med. Dirs. Assn. (pres. 1996—98), Am. Rd. Race Med. Soc. (pres. 2004—06). Home: 59 Birchwood Rd Mahtomedi MN 55115 Office: Univ MInn Medical School 1414 Maryland Ave E Saint Paul MN 55106 Office Phone: 651-793-5603. Office Fax: 651-772-2605. Business E-Mail: rober037@umn.edu.

**ROBERTS, WILLIAM S.,** lawyer; b. Riverside, Calif., June 26, 1946; BA, U. Colo., 1969; MS, U. So. Calif., 1979; JD, U. San Diego, 1989. Bar: Calif. 1989, US Dist. Ct. Ctrl. Dist. Calif. 1989, US Dist. Ct. So. Dist. Calif. 1989, Nev. 2000, US Dist. Ct. Dist. Nev. 2000. Regional mng. ptnr. San Diego office Wilson, Elser, Moskowitz, Edelman & Dicker LLP. Mem.: Am. Soc. Naval Engineers, San Diego Bar Assn. Office: Wilson Elser Moskowitz Edelman & Dicker LLP Emerald Tower Plz Ste 1500 402 W Broadway San Diego CA 92101 Office Phone: 619-595-3181 ext. 3166. Office Fax: 619-595-3183. Business E-Mail: robertsw@wememd.com.

**ROBERTS-MAMONE, LISA A.,** lawyer; BA magna cum laude, Grove City Coll., 1985; JD magna cum laude, Case Western Res. U., 1988. Bar: Ohio 1988. With Jones Day, Cleve., 1988—, ptnr., 2000—. Mem. Estate Planning Coun. of Cleve.; trustee The Laub Found.; mem. Estate Planning Discussion Group, Cleve.; mem. diamond adv. group U. Hosps. Cleve.; mem. Case Western Reserve U. Estate Planning Adv. Coun., Hathaway Brown Sch. Profl. Advisors Com. Mem.: Cleve. Bar Assn. (estate planning, probate and trust law sect.), Ohio State Bar Assn. (estate planning, trust and probate sect.). Office: Jones Day North Point 901 Lakeside Ave Cleveland OH 44114-1190 Office Phone: 216-586-7172.

**ROBERTSON, A. HAEWORTH,** actuary, foundation executive, benefits consultant; b. Oklahoma City, Mar. 10, 1930; s. Albert Haeworth and Bonnie Tennessee (Duckett) R.; m. Mary Adeline Kissee, Feb. 3, 1952 (div. July 1979); children— Valerie Lynn, Alan Haeworth, Mary Kathryn. BA in Math., U. Okla., 1951; MA in Actuarial Sci., U. Mich., 1953. Actuary Wyatt Co., Washington and Dallas, 1955-58; actuary Bowles, Andrews & Towne, Dallas, 1958-60; v.p., actuary W. Alfred Hayes & Co., St. Louis, 1960-63; pres. First Am. Security Life Ins. Co. Mo., St. Louis, 1964-68; pvt. practice internat. cons. actuary Barbados and Ghana, 1969-72; sr. actuary ILO, Geneva, Switzerland, 1973-75; chief actuary U.S. Social Security Adminstrn., Balt., 1975-78; mng. dir. William M. Mercer, Inc., Washington, 1978-88; pvt. practice, internat. cons., actuary Washington, Kuwait, Turkey, Guyana, Zimbabwe, China, The Philippines, 1988—. Chmn. Retirement Bd. Actuaries, Dept. Def., 1984-95; mem. Benefits Bd. Actuaries, 1985-95; pres., founder Retirement Policy Inst. Inc., 1986—. Author: The Coming Revolution in Social Security, 1981, Social Security: What Every Taxpayer Should Know, 1992, The Big Lie: What Every Baby Boomer Should Know About Social Security and Medicare, 1997. Served to 1st lt. USAF, 1953-55 Recipient Commrs. citation, Social Security Adminstrn., Washington, 1976, Arthur J. Altmeyer award, HEW, Washington, 1978, Disting. Alumni award, Ctrl. H.S., Oklahoma City, 1997. Fellow Soc. Actuaries (bd. govs. 1979-81, v.p. 1985-87), Conf. Cons. Actuaries; mem. Am. Acad. Actuaries (Robert J. Myers Pub. Svc. award 2004), Internat. Actuarial Assn., Internat. Assn. Cons. Actuaries, U.K. Inst. Actuaries (assoc.), Cosmos Club, Phi Beta Kappa, Phi Eta Sigma, Phi Kappa Sigma. Republican. Methodist. E-mail: haeworth@aol.com.

**ROBERTSON, ABEL L., JR.,** pathologist; b. St. Andrews, Argentina, July 21, 1926; came to U.S., 1952, naturalized, 1957; s. Abel Alfred Lazzarini and Margaret Theresa G. (Anderson) R.; m. Irene Kirmayr Mauch, Dec. 26, 1958; children: Margaret Anne, Abel Martin, Andrew Duncan, Malcolm Alexander. BS, Coll. D.F. Sarmiento, Buenos Aires, Argentina, 1946; MD suma cum laude, U. Buenos Aires, 1951; PhD, Cornell U., 1959. Fellow tissue culture div. Inst. Histology and Embryology, Sch. Medicine Inst. Histology and Embryology, 1947-49; surg. intern Hosp. Ramos Mejia, Buenos Aires, 1948-50; fellow in tissue culture research Ministry of Health, Buenos Aires, 1950-51; resident Hosp. Nacional de Clinicas, Buenos Aires, 1950-51; head blood vessel bank and organ transplants Research Ctr. Ministry of Health, Buenos Aires, 1951-53; fellow dept. surgery and pathology Sch. Medicine Cornell U., N.Y.C., 1953-55; asst. vis. surgery U. Hosp. N.Y., N.Y.C., 1955-60; asst. prof. research surgery Postgrad. Med. Sch. NYU, N.Y.C., 1955-56; asst. vis. surgeon Bellevue Hosp., N.Y.C., 1955-60; assoc. prof. research surgery NYU, 1956-60, assoc. prof. pathology Sch. Medicine and Postgrad Med. Sch., 1960-63; staff mem. div. research Cleve. Clinic Found., 1963-73, prof. research, 1972-73; assoc. clin. prof. pathology Case Western

Res. U. Sch. Medicine, Cleve., 1968-72, prof. pathology, 1973-82, dir. interdisciplinary cardiovascular research, 1975-82; exec. head dept. pathology Coll. Medicine, U. Ill., Chgo., 1982-88; prof. pathology Coll. Medicine U. Ill., 1982-93, prof. emeritus, 1993—; vis. prof. emeritus cardiovascular med. Core Analysis Lab., Stanford U. Coll. Medicine, 1995—, cardiac pathologist, 2000—. Rsch. fellow N.Y. Soc. Cardiovasc. Surgery, 1957-58; mem. rsch. study subcom. of heart com. N.E. Ohio Regional Med. Program, 1969—. Mem. internat. editorial bd.: Atherosclerosis, Jour. Exptl. and Molecular Pathology, 1964—, Lab. Investigation, 1989—, Acta Pathologica Japonica, 1991—; contbr. articles to profl. jours. Recipient Rsch. Devel. award NIH, 1961-63; recipient Disting. Alumnus award, Grad. Sch. Med. Sci., Cornell U., 2003. Fellow AAAS, Am. Coll. Cardiology, Am. Coll. Clin. Pharmacology, Am. Heart Assn. (established investigator 1956-61, nominating com. coun. on arteriosclerosis 1972), Royal Microscopical Soc., Royal Soc. Promotion Health (Gt. Britain), Am. Geriat. Soc., N.Y. Acad. Scis., Cleve. Med. Library Assn.; mem. AMA, AAUP, Am. Soc. for Investigative Pathology, Am. Inst. Biol. Scis., Am. Judicature Soc., Am. Soc. Cell Biology, Am. Soc. Pathologists, Am. Soc. Nephrology, Assn. Am. Physicians and Surgeons, Assn. Computing Machinery, Electron Microscopy Soc. Am., Assn. Pathology Chmn., Internat. Acad. Pathology, Soc. Cardiovasc. Pathology, Internat. Cardiovasc. Soc., Internat. Soc. Cardiology (sci. council on arteriosclerosis and ischemic heart disease), Internat. Fed. on Genetic Engring. and Biotechnology, Internat. Soc. for Heart Rsch., Internat. Soc. Nephrology, Internat. Soc. Stereology, Pan Am. Med. Assn. (life, councillor in angiology 1966), Ill. Registry Anatomical Pathology (treas. 1985-87), Chgo. Pathology Soc., Reticuloendothelial Soc. Leucocyte Biology, Soc. Cryobiology, Tissue Culture Assn., Ohio Soc. Pathologists, Electron Microscopy Soc. Northeastern Ohio (pres., trustee 11966-68), Heart Assn. Northeastern Ohio, N.Y. Soc. Cardiovasc. Surgery, N.Y. Soc. Electron Microscopists, Cuyahoga County Med. Soc., Cleve. Soc. Pathologists, The Oxygen Soc., Sigma Xi. Home: PO Box 3125 340 5th Ave Half Moon Bay CA 94019-3125 Office Phone: 650-712-0357. Office Fax: 650-712-0357. Personal E-mail: abelrobertsonmd@yahoo.com.

**ROBERTSON, ANDREW,** advertising executive; b. Zimbabwe; Degree in econ., London U. Joined as media planner Ogilvy & Mather, London, 1982, account mgr., bd. dirs., 1986—89, mgmt. supr., new bus. dir., 1989; group account dir. J. Walter Thompson, London, 1989—90; CEO WCRS, London, 1990—95; mng. dir. Abbott Mead Vickers BBDO, London, 1995—99; CEO, pres. BBDO N. Am., NYC, 2001—04; pres. BBDO Worldwide, NYC, 2002—04, CEO, pres., 2004—. Office: BBDO Worldwide Inc 1285 Ave of the Americas New York NY 10019-6028*

**ROBERTSON, ARMAND JAMES, II,** judge; b. San Diego, Sept. 23, 1937; s. Armand James and Muriel H. R.; m. Marion Sperry, Aug. 11, 1962; children: Armand James, Laura Marie. A.M. in Econs., Stanford U., 1960; LL.B., Harvard U., 1965. Bar: Calif. 1966. Law clk. to Charles M. Merrill, U.S. Ct. Appeals (9th cir.), 1965-66; assoc. firm Howard, Prim, Rice, Nemerovski, Canady & Pollak, San Francisco, 1966-71, ptnr., 1971-77; dir. Howard, Rice, Nemerovski, Canady, Robertson & Falk (P.C.), San Francisco, 1977-95; judge of the Superior Ct. City and County of San Francisco, 1995—. Bd. dirs. St. Francis Found., 1996—, chmn., 1999—. Lt. (j.g.) USN, 1960-62. Mem. Am. Law Inst., ABA (antitrust sect.), CPR Inst. for Dispute Resolution, Phi Beta Kappa. Office: San Francisco Superior Ct 400 Mcallister St Rm 210 San Francisco CA 94102-4512

**ROBERTSON, BEVERLY CARRUTH,** retired steel company executive; b. Texarkana, Ark., May 16, 1922; s. Glenn C. Robertson (dec.); m. Ruth Mulcare, Oct. 31, 1945 (dec. Oct. 1993); children: Glenn J., Beverly R. Dodds, Rebecca A. Robertson Deans; m. Charlotte Doty Lawler, June 2, 1995. In sales Nat. Supply Co., Laurel, Miss., 1941-51; purchasing agt. Kirby Petroleum Co., Houston, 1951-54; exec. v.p. mktg. Lone Star Steel Co., Dallas, 1954-85, exec. v.p., 1985-86; pres., dir., chief exec. officer LSSCO Trading Corp., 1985-86; owner BSEER Enterprises, Dallas, 1986—; ptnr. Clayton Equipment Co., Dallas, 1992-97, retired, 1997—. Chmn. Sir Alec Inc., 1985-94; cons. Pipeco, Inc., Houston, 1986-88; exec. v.p. mktg. and procurement Nat. Pipe and Tube Co., Houston, 1988-89; pres., CEO Tex. Am. Pipe & Supply Co., Inc., Dallas, 1989—; cons. Ipsco Steel, Inc., Camanche, Iowa, 1991-92. Served to capt. USAF, 1943-46, ETO. Named Supplier of Yr. Petroleum Industry Buyers group Nat. Assn. Purchasing Mgmt., 1982 Mem. Dallas Country Club, Dallas Petroleum Club. Republican. Episcopalian. Home: PO Box 12688 Dallas TX 75225-0688 E-mail: tapsco@airmail.net, tapsco@earthlink.net.

**ROBERTSON, CHARLES JAMES,** museum director emeritus; b. Houston, Sept. 12, 1934; s. Charles James and Felide Corinne (O'Brien) R. BA, U. Va., Charlottesville, 1956; MA, Harvard U., 1958; student, U. London Courtauld Inst., 1960; JD, George Washington U., 1964. Atty. Dow, Lohnes & Albertson, Washington, 1964-69; adminstr. Richard H. Chamberlain, M.D. & Assoc., Phila., 1969-75; assoc. dir. N.C. Mus. Art, Raleigh, 1975-77; deputy dir. Smithsonian Am. Art Mus., Washington, 1977—2001. Treas., exec. com. Am. Assn. Mus., Washington, 1982-84; mem. adv. com. Octagon House Mus., Washington, 1989-97, chmn. 1993-96; bd. dirs. Victorian Soc. in Am., Phila., 1990—, v.p., 1994-2000, 2006—; mem. Hist. Preservation Rev. Bd. of the Dist. of Columbia, 1992-2004; bd. regents Am. Archtl. Found., Washington, 1993-96; trustee Cosmos Club Historic Preservation Found., Washington, 1993—, treas., 1999—2003. Author: Temple of Invention: History of a National Landmark, 2006; contbr. articles to profl. jours. Pres. Dupont Circle Conservancy, Washington, 1978-92; v.p., bd. mem., Dupont Circle Citizens Assn. Washington, 1980-83, 86; mem. com. 100 Fed. City Washington, 2005—, trustee, 2006—. Recipient Rumrill fellowship Harvard U., Cambridge, Mass., 1956-57. Mem. Cosmos Club, Phi Beta Kappa, Phi Pi Theta, Delta Theta Phi.

**ROBERTSON, DAVID,** neurologist, educator; b. Sylvia, Tenn., May 23, 1947; s. David Herlie and Lucille Luther (Bowen) R.; m. Rose Marie Stevens, Oct. 30, 1976; 1 child, Rose. BA, Vanderbilt U., 1969, MD, 1973. Diplomate Am. Bd. Internal. Medicine, Am. Bd. Clin. Pharmacology. Intern Johns Hopkins U., Balt., 1973-74, asst. resident, 1974-75, asst. chief svc. in medicine, 1977-78; fellow in clin. pharmacology Vanderbilt U., Nashville, 1975-77, asst. prof. medicine and pharmacology, 1978-82, assoc. prof., 1982-86, prof., 1986—, prof. neurology 1991—, Elton Yates prof. autonomic disorders, 1998—, dir. clin. rsch. ctr., 1987—; dir. Ctr. Space Physiology and Medicine, 1989—, Med. Sci. Tng. Program, 1993—2003; mem. staff Vanderbilt Hosp., Burroughs Wellcome scholar in clin. pharmacology, 1985-91. Author: (with B.M. Greene and G.J. Taylor) Problems in Internal Medicine, 1980, (with C.R. Smith) Manual of Clinical Pharmacology, 1981, (with Italo Biaggioni) Disorders of the Autonomic Nervous System, 1995, (with Italo Biaggioni, Geoffrey Burnstock and Phillip A. Low) Primer on the Autonomic Nervous System, 1996, 2d edit., 2004; editor-in-chief: Drug Therapy, 1991-94; assoc. editor, Jour. Pharmacol. Exptl. Therapy, 1998—; mem. editl. bd. Am. Jour. Medicine, Autonomic Neuroscience, Clin. Pharm. and Therapeutics, Clin. Autonomic Rsch., Am. Jour. Med. Sci., Current Topics in Pharmacology, Logan Clendening fellow, Reykjavik, Iceland, 1969; Adolph-Morsbach grantee Bonn, Germany, 1968; recipient Rsch. Career Devel. award NIH, 1981, Grant W. Liddle award for leadership in rsch., 1991, Tchg. award Nat. Program Dir.'s Assn., 2003, Rschr. of Yr. award Nat. Dysautomia Rsch. Found., 2001. Fellow Am. Heart Assn. Coun. Hypertension and Circulation, ACP (tchg. and rsch. scholar 1978-81), Am. Autonomic Soc. (pres. 1992-94); mem. Am. Acad. Neurology, Soc. Neurosci., Am. Inst. Aeronautics and Astronautics, U.S Pharmacological Conv., Nat. Bd. Med. Examiners, Aerospace Med. Assn. (space sta. sci. and applications com.), NASA (microgravity human rsch. com.), FDA Consortium Rare Disorders, Rare Disorder Network, Am. Fedn. Med. Rsch., Am. Soc. Clin. Investigation, Am. Physicians. Assn. Patient-Oriented Rsch. (bd. dirs., pres.), So. Soc. Clin. Investigation, Am. Soc. Clin. Pharmacology and Therapeutics, Phi Beta Kappa, Alpha Omega Alpha (hon., bd. dirs. 1995—. William Danfroy award 2000). Baptist. Home: 4003 Newman Pl Nashville TN 37204-4308 Office: Vanderbilt U Clin Rsch Ctr 21st Ave S Nashville TN 37232-2195 Office Phone: 615-343-6499. Business E-Mail: david.robertson@vanderbilt.edu.

**ROBERTSON, DAVID,** conductor, music director; b. Santa Monica, Calif. m. Orli Shaham; 2 children. Student in French horn and composition, Royal Acad. Music. Resident condr. Jerusalem Symphony Orch., 1985—87; music dir. Ensemble Intercontemporain, Paris, 1992—2000; musical dir. Orchestre Nat. de Lyon, France, 2000—; artistic dir. Lyon Auditorium, 2000; music dir. St. Louis Symphony Orch., 2005—. Guest condr. Minn. Orch., 2001, Phila. Orch., 2001, Chgo. Symphony, 2001, Boston Symphony, 2001, San Francisco Symphony, 2001, NDR Symphony Orch. Hamburg, Germany, 2001, Royal Concertgebouw Orch., 2001, Orch. del Maggio Musicale Fiorentino, 2001, London Symphony Orch., Halle Orch., Bayerisches Staatorchester, Munich, Berlin Staatskapelle, La Scala Philharm., Boston Symphony, Chgo. Orch., NY Philharm., L.A. Philharm., many others; prin. guest condr. BBC Symphony, 2005—. Active outreach programs Ensemble Intercontemporain, Orchestre Nat. de Lyon, Paris Conservatory, Juilliard Sch., Tanglewood, Aspen Music Festival. Named Condr. of Yr., Musical Am., 2000; recipient Seaver/Nat. Endowment for Arts Condr. award, 1997, Ditson Conductor's award, Columbia U., 2006, ASCAP Morton Gould award, Am. Symphony Orch. League, 2006. Office: 82 rue de Bonnel 69431 Lyon France Office Fax: 33 4 78 60 13 08.*

**ROBERTSON, DAVID ALAN,** museum director, educator; b. Jefferson City, Mo., Oct. 10, 1950; s. Roy Victor and Mary Jane (Threlkeld) R. BA in English, U. Mo., 1973, MA in Art History, 1976; PhD in Art History, U. Pa., 1983. Museum asst. U. Mo. Museum, Columbia, 1975-76; rsch. asst. Victoria and Albert Museum, London, 1976; curatorial asst. Yale Ctr. for British Art, New Haven, 1977-78; teaching fellow U. Pa., Phila., 1978-81; staff supr. Rosenbach Museum and Library, Phila., 1980-82; dir. Dickinson Coll., Carlisle, Pa., 1982—2002; dir. Mary and Leigh Block Mus Art Northwestern U., Evanston, Ill., 2002—, lectr. Art Hist. Dept., 2003—. Fulbright prof. U. Munich, Germany, 1989-90; mem. selection com. Fulbright Commn., Bonn, Germany, 1989; grant reviewer Inst. Mus. Svcs., Washington, 1989-91. Penfield fellow U. Pa., Vienna, Austria, 1981-82, Kress fellow Kress Found., London, 1976, Vienna, 1980. Mem. Am. Assn. Mus., Coll. Art Assn., Assn. Coll. and U. Mus. and Galleries. Office: Mary and Leigh Block Mus Art Northwestern U 40 Arts Circle Dr Evanston IL 60208 Office Phone: 847-491-2562. Business E-Mail: d-robertson@northwestern.edu.

**ROBERTSON, DONNA VIRGINIA,** architect, educator, dean; b. Richmond, Va., Feb. 26, 1952; d. Charles Henry and Florence (Givens) R.; m. Robert M. McAnulty, May 24, 1986; 1 child, Robertson. Cert. theater arts studies, Webster Coll., St. Louis, 1972; BA, Stanford U., 1974; MArch, U. Va., 1978. Registered arch., N.Y. Asst. prof. Harvard U., Cambridge, Mass., 1983-84; asst. prof. Barnard Coll. Columbia U., N.Y.C., 1984-92; dean Sch. Arch. Tulane U., New Orleans, 1992-96; dean Coll. Arch. Ill. Inst. Tech., Chgo., 1996—; ptnr. Robertson McAnulty Archs., Chgo., 1986—; owner Donna V. Robertson Archs., N.Y.C., 1982-86; sr. designer Kohn Pedersen Fox Archs., N.Y.C., 1980-82, Mitchell Giurgola Archs., N.Y.C., 1979-80. Adj. asst. prof. Barnard Coll., Columbia U., N.Y., 1982-83, dir. arch. program, fall 1985-92; vis. critic in design Harvard U., Cambridge, fall 1990, U. Va., Charlottesville, fall 1991; organizer, panelist Arch. and Lit. Symposium, N.Y.C., 1985; jury chair Am. Collegiate Schs. Arch., Boston, 1996; mem. bd. dirs. Nat. Archtl. Accrediting Bd., 2000-03; profl. advisor Ford Calumet Environ. Ctr. Competition, City of Chgo., 2004. Prin. arch. Fishback residence, New Orleans, Sunkel residence, New Orleans, Pisar residence, N.Y.C., Dachs residence, N.Y.C.; pres. Nat. Archtl. Accrediting Bd., 2002-03; profiled in Archtl. Record May 2004. Jur invitational competition Seoul Performing Arts Ctr., Republic of Korea, 2006. Named one of Most Influential Women in Chgo., Crain's Chgo. Bus., 2004; recipient Honor award, Chgo. Landmarks Commn., 2005. Mem. AIA (juror national design hons. awards 1996, Educators and Practitioners Network, co-chair tchrs. seminar 2006, mem. Chgo. bd.), Coll. Fellows of AIA, Am. Coll. Student Assn. (co-chair 2006), Chgo. Network-Internat. Women's Forum, Raven Soc. (U. Va.), Arts Club (Chgo.), Phi Beta Kappa. Office: Ill Inst Tech Coll Architecture 3360 S State St Chicago IL 60616 Office Phone: 312-567-3263. E-mail: robertson@iit.edu.

**ROBERTSON, EDWARD NEIL,** dentist; b. Rumford, Maine, Mar. 3, 1950; s. Edward Norris and Edith Louise (Kirk) Robertson; m. Susan Elizabeth Valentine, July 24, 2004; 1 child, Olivia; children: Christie Portia, Juliet Melissa(dec.), Jenni Celia, Edward Noah, Jessica Edith. BS in Biology, Antioch Coll., Yellow Springs, Ohio, 1973; MS in Epidemiology, Ohio State U., 1977, DDS, Case Western Res. U., 1983, DMD, 2004. Faculty adv. to med. students Ohio State U., Columbus, 1975-77; rsch. cons. Ohio Dept. Health, Columbus, 1976-77; rsch. assoc. UCLA, 1977; epidemiologic/statis. cons. L.A., 1977; medic J & L Steel Corp., Cleve., 1979-84; pvt. practice Cleveland Heights, Ohio, 1983-94, Lyndhurst, Ohio, 1995-2000. Mem. adj. faculty Cuyahoga C.C., Cleve., 1986-88; assoc. prof. Sch. Dentistry Case Western Res. U., 1991-96; asst. prof. Case Western Res. U. Sch. Dentistry, Cleve., 1997—; pvt. contractor Indian Health Svc. Dental Clinic, Pine Ridge, S.D., 1999-2000; clin. instr. U. Md. Dental Sch., 1999-00. Pres. Robertson Family Assn. of N.Am., 1986-88. Recipient numerous rsch. grants. Mem.: ADA, Internat. Congress Oral Implantologists, Am. Acad. Craniofacial Pain, Internat. Assn. for Study of Pain, Greater Cleve. Dental Soc., Ohio Dental Assn., Acad. Gen. Dentistry, Midwest Pain Soc., Acad. Laser Surgery, U.S. Dental Inst., Am. Chronic Pain Assn., Ohio Acad. Gen. Dentistry, Am. Pain Soc., Am. Acad. Pain Mgmt. Avocations: scuba diving, cross country skiing, camping, canoeing, bicycling. Office: 24755 Chagrin Blvd Ste 145 Beachwood OH 44122-5692 Office Phone: 216-468-0041. Business E-Mail: dentalned@aol.com.

**ROBERTSON, EDWIN DAVID,** lawyer; b. Roanoke, Va., July 5, 1946; s. Edwin Traylor and Norma Burns (Bowles) R.; m. Anne Littelle Ferratt, Sept. 7, 1968, 1 child, Thomas Therit. BA with honors, U. Va., 1968, LLB, 1971. Bar: N.Y. 1972, U.S. Ct. Appeals (2d cir.) 1972, U.S. Dist. Ct. (ea. and so. dists.) N.Y. 1973, U.S. Supreme Ct. 1975, U.S. Dist. Ct. (ea. dist.) Mich. 1986. Assoc. Cadwalader, Wickersham & Taft, N.Y.C., 1972-80, ptnr., 1980—, Bd. dirs. Early Music Found. N.Y.C., 1983-99, chmn., 1993-99; bd. dirs. Oratorio Soc. of N.Y.C., 1988—2004, sec., 1990—2004; judge Ct. of Rev., Episcopal Ch., 2001-03. 1st lt. USAF, 1971-72. Echols scholar. Mem. ABA (ho. of dels. 2004—), Nat. Conf. Bar Presidents, Fed. Bar Coun., N.Y. County Lawyers Assn. (chmn. bankruptcy com. 1983-87, chmn. fin. com., bd. dirs. 1985-88, 95-99, 2000—, investment com. 1992—, exec. com. 1996—, treas. 2001-02, v.p. 2002-04, pres. 2006—), N.Y. State Bar Assn. (ho. of dels. 2001-04, 05—, nominatng com. 2002-), Assn. Bar City N.Y., Soc. Colonial Wars, Jefferson Soc., Sons of Revolution, Order of Coif, Phi Beta Kappa, Phi Kappa Psi. Republican. Episcopalian. Home: 315 E 72nd St New York NY 10021-4625 Office: Cadwalader Wickersham & Taft OneWorld Fin Ctr New York NY 10281 Office Phone: 212-504-6000. E-mail: darob@cwt.com.

**ROBERTSON, EVERETT B.,** performing arts educator, consultant; b. Calhoun, Ky., Feb. 8, 1945; s. Everette Gerald Robertson and Marjorie Bohanon; m. Barbara Joy Boone, June 14, 1975; 1 child, Brian Everett-Boone. BA, Baylor U., Waco, Tex., 1969; MA, U. Mont., Missoula, 1972. Actor, co. mgr. Utah Shakespeare Festival, Cedar City; actor, dir. Victoria Fair Repertory Theater Co., B.C., Canada, 1969—72; prof. Wayland Bapt. U., Plainview, Tex., 1972—74; sr. theatre specialist Bapt. S.S. Bd., Nashville, 1974—94; cons. Tenn. Bapt. Commn., Nashville, 1995—98; dir. theatre Carson-Newman Coll., Jefferson City, 1998—. Bd. trustees Face to Face Theatre Co., Birmingham, Ala., 1997—2000; founder Nat. Creative Arts Festival, State Dramatic Arts Festival. Author: The Dramatic Arts in Ministry, 1989, Drama in Worship, 1999, Ministries with Puppets, 1993. Chmn. Tenn. Appointments to Naval Acad., Nashville, 1998—2006. Recipient Career of Excellence award, Bapt. S.S. Bd., 1987. Mem.: S.W. Theatre Conf., Christian Creative Arts Assn. (chmn. bd. 2004). Avocations: lic. pilot, ordained minister, sports, travel. Office: Carson Newman Coll CN Box 71999 Jefferson City TN 37760 Office Phone: 865-471-3293. Office Fax: 865-471-3416. E-mail: erobertson@cn.edu.

**ROBERTSON, GREGORY B.,** lawyer; b. Sandusky, Ohio, Apr. 2, 1951; BA, Washington & Lee Univ., 1973; JD, Univ. Richmond, 1976. Bar: Va. 1976. Ptnr., co-chmn. labor, employment practice group Hunton & Williams LLP, Richmond, Va. Mem.: ABA, Va. Bar Assn., Energy and Mineral Law Found. (past pres.), Va. CofC (bd. dir., counsel), Phi Delta Phi, Pi Sigma Alpha. Office: Hunton & Williams LLP Riverfront Plz East Tower 951 E Byrd St Richmond VA 23219-4074 Office Phone: 804-788-8526. Office Fax: 804-788-8218. Business E-Mail: grobertson@hunton.com.

**ROBERTSON, HORACE BASCOMB, JR.,** retired law educator; b. Charlotte, N.C., Nov. 13, 1923; s. Horace Bascomb and Ruth (Montgomery) R.; m. Patricia Lavell, Aug. 11, 1947; children— Mark L., James D. BS, U.S. Naval Acad., 1945; JD, Georgetown U., 1953; MS, George Washington U., 1968. Commd. ensign U.S. Navy, 1945, advanced through grades to rear adm., 1972; line officer, 1945-55; law specialist, 1955-68; spl. counsel to sec. Navy, Washington, 1964-67, judge adv., 1968-76; spl. counsel to chief naval ops. Washington, 1970-72; dep. judge adv. gen. Navy Dept., Washington, 1972-75, judge adv. gen., 1975-76; prof. law Duke U., 1976-89, sr. assoc. dean, 1986-89, ret., 1990; Chas H. Stockton chair of internat. law Naval War Coll., Newport, R.I., 1991-92. Decorated D.S.M. Mem. ABA, Am. Soc. Internat. Law. Home: 9 Silver Maple Ct Durham NC 27705-5642 Office: Duke U Sch Law Durham NC 27708 Office Phone: 919-613-7038. Business E-Mail: hbr@law.duke.edu.

**ROBERTSON, HUGH (ELIHU F. ROBERTSON),** lawyer; b. Annapolis, Md., 1953; BA, Yale Univ., 1976; JD, Univ. Va., 1979. Bar: N.Y. 1980. Atty. Milbank Tweed Hadley & McCloy, London, Hong Kong, ptnr. Global Fin. Dept. N.Y.C., 1987—. Mem.: ABA, N.Y. State Bar Assn. Office: Milbank Tweed Hadley & McCloy 1 Chase Manhattan Plz New York NY 10005-1413 Office Phone: 212-530-5187. Office Fax: 212-530-5219. Business E-Mail: erobertson@milbank.com.

**ROBERTSON, JACK CLARK,** finance educator; b. Marlin, Tex., Apr. 27, 1943; s. Rupert Cook and Lois Lucille (Rose) R.; m. Caroline Susan Hughes, Oct. 23, 1965; children: Sara Ellen, Elizabeth Hughes. Student, Rice U., 1961-63; BBA with honors, U. Tex., Austin, 1965, M in Profl. Acctg., 1967; PhD, U. N.C., 1970. CPA, Tex. Tax acct. Humble Oil and Refining Co., Houston, 1964-65; auditor Peat, Marwick, Mitchell & Co., Houston, 1965-66; acct. Wade, Barton, Marsh CPAs, Austin, Tex., 1966-67; from asst. prof. to prof. emeritus U. Tex., Austin, 1970—2003, C.T. Zlatkovich Centennial prof. emeritus, 2003—. Acad. assoc. Coopers & Lybrand, N.Y.C., 1975-76; acad. fellow U.S. Securities and Exchange Commn. Office of the Chief Acct., Washington, 1982-83; Erskine fellow U. Canterbury, Christchurch, New Zealand, 1988; tng. the trainers instr. Vilnius, Lithuania, 1993; lectr. in field. Contbr. articles to profl. jours. Lay reader St. Matthews Episcopal Ch., Austin, 1972-75, mem. vestry, 1973-75, 77-79, 84-86, treas., 1974-75, 77-96, chmn. bldg. fund, 1976-87, chmn. everymen. canvass, 1980, sr. warden, 1986; del. Diocese of Tex. Coun., 1993-95; Trompetista El Grupo Valor Latino, 2000-, lector laico, 2000-03, Miembro comité del obispo Iglesia San Francisco de Asis, 2000-03, treas., 2002-03; trustee, treas. Austin Chamber Music Ctr., 2003-; official U.S.A Track and Field, 1996-. Mem. AICPA, Am. Acctg. Assn. (sec.-treas. auditing sect. 1976-77, v.p. auditing sect. 1977-78, pres. auditing sect. 1978-79, chmn. auditing stds. com. 1980-81, chmn. SEC liaison com. 1983-84, historian auditing sect. 1999-2001), Tex. Soc. CPAs (vice-chmn., profl. ethics com. 1986-94, 95-97, Presdl. citation 1994), Assn. Cert. Fraud Examiners (regent emeritus, cert.), Phi Kappa Phi, Beta Gamma Sigma, Beta Alpha Psi.

**ROBERTSON, JAMES,** federal judge; b. Cleve., May 18, 1938; s. Frederick Irving and Doris Mary (Byars) R.; m. Berit Selma Persson, Sept. 19, 1959; children: Stephen Irving, Catherine Anne, Peter Arvid. AB, Princeton U., 1959; LLB, George Washington U., 1965. Bar: D.C. 1966, U.S. Supreme Ct. 1969. Assoc. Wilmer, Cutler & Pickering, Washington, 1965-69, ptnr., 1973-94; judge US Dist. Ct. (D.C. dist.), 1994—, Fgn. Intelligence Adv. Ct., 2002—06. Chief counsel, Lawyers Com. for Civil Rights Under Law, 1969-70, dir., 1970-72, co-chmn., 1982-84; mem. com. on grievances U.S. Dist. Ct., 1988-92, vice chmn., 1989-92; bd. dirs. South Africa Legal Svcs. and Edn. Project, Inc., 1987-01, pres., 1989-94; bd. dirs. D.C. Prisoners Legal Svcs., Inc., 1992-94. Editor in chief George Washington Law Rev., 1964-65. Lt. USN, 1959-64. Fellow Am. Coll. Trial Lawyers, Am. Bar Found.; mem. ABA, D.C. Bar (bd. govs. 1986-93, pres.-elect 1990-92, pres. 1991-92), Am. Law Inst. Home: 3318 N St NW Washington DC 20007-2807 Office: US Courthouse Rm 6315 333 Constitution Ave NW Washington DC 20001-2854*

**ROBERTSON, JAMES MUELLER,** civil engineer, educator; b. Champaign, Ill., Apr. 18, 1916; s. William Spence and Gertrude (Mueller) R.; m. Margaret Dillinger, Oct. 23, 1943; children: Bruce D., Alan S. BSCE, U. Ill., 1938; MS, U. Iowa, 1940, PhD, 1941. Asst. physicist U.S. Navy Dept., Taylor Model Basin, 1941-42; mem. engring. faculty, dir. Water Tunnel Pa. State U., 1942-54; rsch. engr. Douglas Aircraft, Santa Monica, Calif., 1944-45; prof. theoretical and applied mechanics U. Ill., Urbana, 1954-82, acting head dept., 1982, prof. emeritus, 1982—. Cons. U.S. Army, various indsl. orgns., 1957-73; vis. lectr. hydraulic engring. Kans. State U., 1967; course instr. TAPPI, 1969; lectr. U. Tenn. Space Inst., 1973; vis. prof. civil engring. Colo. State U., 1974; adj. prof. mech. engring. Naval Postgrad. Sch., 1984; bd. dirs. Internat. Mgmt. and Engring. Ltd., Colo., Terabyte, Inc., Boulder, Colo. Author: Hydrodynamics in Theory and Application, 1965; contbr. numerous articles to profl. pubs. Sec., v.p., pres. Summit County Sr. Citizens, Frisco, Colo., 1983-97; sec. Skylin Six Area Agy. on Aging Coun., Frisco, 1986-95, chair, 1995-96; bd. dirs. Breckenridge (Colo.) Music Inst., 1984-95, sec., 1989-93, mem. adv. coun., 1995-2002. Recipient Alumni Honor award, Coll. Engring., 1989. Fellow ASCE (life, Hilgard prize 1955), ASME (life); mem. Sigma Xi, Phi Eta Sigma, Chi Epsilon, Tau Beta Pi, Phi Kappa Phi. Achievements include co-design of hydrodynamics wind water tunnel at Pennsylvania State University. Home: 14091 E Marina Dr Apt 202 Aurora CO 80014-3712

**ROBERTSON, JAMES THOMAS,** neurosurgeon; b. McComb, Miss., Apr. 5, 1931; s. Clyde Aubrey and Catherine Roberta (Darville) R.; m. Valeria Ann Brower, Nov. 26, 1952; children: James T. Jr., Elizabeth, Catherine Clay, Roberta, Daniel. BS, Southwestern U., 1951; MD, U. Tenn., 1954. Diplomat Am. Bd. Neurol. Surgeons, 1962. Intern Bapt. Meml. Hosp., Memphis, 1955; resident U. Tenn., Memphis, 1956-59, Peter Bent Brigham & Children's Hosp., Boston, 1959-60; chief neurosurgery Travis AFB, Fairfield, Calif., 1960-63; asst. chief nuerosurgery Lackland AFB, San Antonio, 1963-64; assoc. physician Semmes Murphey Clinic, Memphis, 1964-65; asst. prof. neurosurgery U. Tenn., 1964-69, assoc. prof., 1969-73, prof., chmn. dept. neurosurgery, 1973—98, prof., 1998—. Physician dept. neurosurgery U. Tenn., Memphis, 1973—97; med. dir. Medtronic Sofamarc Dansk, Memphis, 2003. Editor: Subarachnoid Hemorrhage and Cerebrovascular Vasopasm, 1975; contbr. articles to mags. Vice chair Rep. Party, Shelby County, Memphis, 1980, treas., DeSoto County, Miss., 1993; pres. Shelby County chpt. Am. Heart Assn., 1996, chmn. stroke coun., 1992-94. Capt. USNR, 1982-98. Recipient Disting. Alumni award U. Tenn., 1990, Rhodes Coll., 1994. Fellow Am. Coll. Surgeons (bd. govs. 1987-92); mem. Am. Assn. Neurol. Surgeons (pres. 1990-91), Congress Neurol. Surgeons (pres. 1975), Am. Acad. Neurol. Surgery (pres. 1988), Soc. Univ. Neurosurgeons (pres. 1965). Presbyterian. Avocations: gardening, fly fishing. Home: 8570 Jones Rd Olive Branch MS 38654-9001 Office: U Tenn 847 Monroe Ave # 427 Memphis TN 38103-4901 Office Phone: 901-448-6375. Business E-Mail: jrober52@aol.com.

**ROBERTSON, JAMES WOOLSEY,** lawyer; b. Ft. Sam Houston, Tex., Aug. 6, 1942; s. Robert Charles Lee and Marjorie Evelyn (Woolsey) R.; 1 child, William Angus; m. Laura Ann Koons, Apr. 24, 1993. BBA, U. Tex., 1966, JD, 1967. Bar: Tex.; cert. real estate law specialist. Ptnr. Locke Liddell & Sapp L.L.P., Houston, 1971—, chmn. fin. com., 1985-90, chmn. banking and real estate sect., 1992-98. Bd. dirs., sec., chmn. Lighthouse for the Blind, Houston, 1998—; chancellor Episcopal Ch. Holy Spirit, Houston, 1964—92,

trustee, 1984—87. Lt. comdr. USCGR, 1968—71. Mem. State Bar Tex., Houston Bar Assn., Houston Real Estate Lawyers Coun. Republican. Avocations: fly fishing, skiing, hunting. Office: 600 Travis St Ste 3400 Houston TX 77002-3095

**ROBERTSON, JOEL THOMAS,** railroad executive; b. Milo, Maine, Aug. 30, 1947; s. Paul Russell Robertson and Denice Luella Stevens; m. Bonita Louise Hosford, July 29, 1966 (div. Nov. 1968); m. Patricia Rae Willinski, Mar. 14, 1970 (div. May 1990); children: Jason Thomas, April Dawn Robertson Bishop; m. Marie Paulette Melvin, Dec. 31, 1994; 1 child, Stuart Spencer Stratton. BS, W.Va. State U., 1982; MS, Marshall U., 1986. Cert. safety mgr. World Safety Orgn., 85. Agt. Bangor (Maine) & Aroosook R.R., 1966—70, Can. Pacific Rwy., St. John, NB, 1970—80; hazardous materials inspector Fed. RR Adminstrn., Washington, 1980—2001, hazardous materials specialist, 2001—02; ptnr. Robertson & Assocs., LLC, 2002—; regulatory specialist Am. Honda Co. Inc., 2004—. Transp. cons. Union Carbide Corp., Danbury, Conn., 1989—90; expert witness/accident investigator Collins, Collins & Dinardo, Buffalo, 1989—; bus. devel. cons. Brothers Coal Cons., Charleston, W.Va., 1989—90, TransMar Inc., Spokane, Wash., 1994, Coal Tech. Corp., Bristol, Va., 1989—97; appearance on nat. news program ABC Wide World News Tonight, 1985; interviewed by Tass Soviet News Agy., 89; owner Guest Nat. Soc. of Profl. Engrs., Nat. Press Club, Washington, 1989; founder, devel. dir. Stuart Spencer Stratton Meml. Found., unit of Nat. Heritage Found., 2002—; regional sci. fair judge and scholarship founder for environ. scis. INTEL N.W., 2000—; adj. tech. faculty Marshall U., Transp. Safety Inst., 1987—; adv. U.S. Senate Murray U.S. Dept. State, Volpentest Hammer Tng. Inst., Transportation Safety Security, Richland, Wash.; leader, organizer Multi-Agy Internat. Transp. Safety-Security Strike Force, 2000; internat. trade and devel. cons. Govt. Cameroon, West Africa; loaned exec. Combined Fed. Campaign, 2001—02; assoc. Oreg. Fed. Bd., 2001—02; mem. exec. potential program USDA Grad. Sch. Leadership, 2002; internat. lectr. and citizen amb. China Assn. of Sci. and Tech., 1989; acting regional adminstr., acting staff dir. U.S. Hazardous Materials, 1994—2002. Contbr. articles to profl. pubs. Organizer, master of ceremonies First Joint Chem. Industry/Rwy. Safety Symposium, W.Va., 1985, Celebration of Engring. Career Day, Huntington, W.Va., 1989; sci. advisor Bush White House Space Coun., Washington, 1989. Recipient Commendation, Gov. of W.Va., 1985, Superior Achievement award, U.S. DOT-FRA. Mem.: Am. Soc. Metals, Am. Inst. Hygiene Assn., Soc. Mechanical Engrs., AIChE, Am. Soc. Quality Control, Am. Soc. Safety Engrs., Am. Soc. Profl. Engrs. (exec. affiliate 1983—89), Engrs. Club of Huntington (pres. 1987—88), Kiwanis (pres. West Huntington chpt. 1989—90). Republican. Mem. Lds Ch. Avocations: fundraising activities, event organizing, photography, travel, writing. Address: 16505 A SE 1st St Ste 285 Vancouver WA 98684 Home: 32154 E Punkin Center Rd Hermiston OR 97838-7510 Office Phone: 360-873-2329. E-mail: joel@safety.specialist.com, cameroon313@aol.com.

**ROBERTSON, JOHN,** principal; MEd, Delta State U., Cleveland, Miss. Athletic trainer Decatur (Tex.) Ind. Sch. Dist., 1997—2002, Azle (Tex.) Ind. Sch. Dist., 1992—97; prin., asst. supt. Megargel (Tex.) Ind. Sch. Dist., 2002—. Office: Megargel Ind Sch Dist PO Box 39 Megargel TX 76370

**ROBERTSON, JOHN ARCHIBALD LAW,** nuclear scientist; b. Dundee, Scotland, July 4, 1925; arrived in Can., 1957, naturalized, 1963; s. John Carr and Ellen (Law) R.; m. Betty-Jean Moffatt, June 26, 1954; children: Ean Stuart, Clare Deborah, Fiona Heather. BA, Cambridge U., Eng., 1950, MA, 1953. Sci. officer UK Atomic Energy Authority, Harwell, England, 1950-57; rsch. officer Atomic Energy Can. Ltd., Chalk River, Ont., Canada, 1957-63, head reactor materials br., 1963-70, dir. fuels and materials div., 1970-75, asst. to v.p., 1975-82; dir. program planning Atomic Energy Can. Ltd. (Rsch. Co. Head Office), 1982-85; cons., 1985—. Mem. Atomic Energy Control Bd.'s Adv. Com. on Nuc. Safety, 1988-97. Author: Irradiation Effects in Nuclear Fuels, 1969, Decide the Nuclear Issues for Yourself: Nuclear Need Not Be Unclear, 2000; editor: Jour. Nuclear Materials, 1967-71. Capt. Royal Engrs. Brit. and Indian Armies, 1943—47. Recipient W.B. Lewis medal Can. Nuc. Assn., 1987, W.J. Kroll Zirconium medal W.J. Kroll Inst. for Extractive Metallurgy, 1993, Queen's Golden Jubilee medal, 2004, Edn. and Comm. award Can. Nuc. Assn., 2005. Fellow Royal Soc. Can. Office Phone: 613-584-2765. E-mail: jalrober@magma.ca.

**ROBERTSON, JOSEPH E., JR.,** ophthalmologist, educator, dean; b. Jackson County, Ind., July 24, 1952; s. Joseph E. and Virginia Faye (Baxter) R.; children: Kathryn Faye, Charles Joseph. BS in Neuroscience, cum laude, Yale U., 1974; MD, Ind. U., 1978; MBA, U. Oreg., 1997. Diplomate Am. Bd. Ophthalmology. Intern Bapt. Med. Ctr., Birmingham, Ala., 1978-79; resident Oreg. Health Sci. U., Portland, 1979-82; pvt. practice Vancouver, Wash., 1982-83; fellow Oreg. Health Sci. U./Devers Hosp./Good Samaritan Hosp., Portland, 1983-84; vitreous surgery fellow Steve Charles, M.D., Memphis, 1984-85; asst. prof. Oreg. Health Sci. U., Portland, 1985-92, assoc. prof., 1992-97, prof., chmn. dept. ophthalmology, 1997—, interim dean, 2001—02, dean Sch. Medicine, 2003—. Contbr. articles to profl. jours., chpts. to books; editor videotapes. Apptd. mem. Oreg. Commn. for the Blind, 1988-94. Mem. Am. Acad. Ophthalmology (Oreg. rep. to coun. 1992-95, COVE com 1988-93, skills transfer adv. com 1994-98, nat. chair and state coord. Diabetes 2000), Oreg. Acad. Ophthalmology (pres. 1990-91), Univ. Med. Group (exec. com. 1997—, v.p. 1997—), Oreg. Med. Assn. Democrat. Presbyterian. Avocations: skiing, windsurfing, snowboarding, hiking, jogging. Office: Casey Eye Inst OHSU 3375 SW Terwilliger Blvd Portland OR 97239

**ROBERTSON, JOSEPH EDMOND,** grain processing company executive; b. Brownstown, Ind., Feb. 16, 1918; s. Roscoe Melvin and Edith Penina (Shields) R.; m. Virginia Faye Baxter, Nov. 23, 1941; 1 son, Joseph Edmond, Jr. BS, postgrad. Kans. State U., 1940. Cereal chemist Ewing Mill Co., 1940—43, engr. flour milling, 1946—50, feed nutritionist, 1951—59; v.p., sec. Robertson Corp., Brownstown, Ind., 1960—80, pres., 1980—97, chmn., 1997—. Author: On Kilroy's Trail, 1998. Mem. Kans. State U. Varsity Basketball Team, 1937-40; pres. Jackson County (Ind.) Welfare Bd., 1948-52; mem. Ind. Port Commn., 1986-91; mem. Ind. Gov.'s Coun. of Sagamores of the Wabash. Served with USAAF, 1943-45. Named to Hon. Order Ky. Cols.; recipient Brownstown (Ind.) First Lifetime Achievement award, 1999. Mem. Hardwood Plywood Mfrs. Assn. (v.p. affiliate div. 1971-73, 87-88, internat. lectr. forest products industry 1973-97), Am. Assn. Cereal Chemists, Assn. Operative Millers, Am. Legion, Brownstown C. of C. (dir. All Am. city program 1955), Kans. State U. Alumni Assn. (life), Blue Key, Phi Delta Theta, Phi Kappa Phi, Alpha Mu. Clubs: Internat. Travelers Century (L.A.), Circumnavigators Club (N.Y.C.), Elks. Presbyterian. Home: Lake and Forest Club 1268 E Lake Shore Dr PO Box A Brownstown IN 47220 Office: 200 N Front St Brownstown IN 47220-1040 E-mail: robmark@glux.com.

**ROBERTSON, KENNETH CARL,** music educator; b. Bethany, Mo., Oct. 14, 1963; s. Hal Dean and IRetha Robertson. MusB Edn., Drake U., 1986, MusB Performance, 1986; MusM, Conservatory of Music, Kansas City, Mo., 1988. Cert. Orff- Schulwerk Music Specialist 1999. Organist 1st Christian Ch., Pattonsburg, Mo., 1976—82, Glen Echo Christian Ch., Des Moines, 1982—86, Congl. United Ch. Of Christ, Prairie Village, Kans., 1986—89; organist/choirmaster St. Charles Ch., Gladstone, Mo., 1989—91; organist Pk. Christian Ch., Kansas City, Mo., 1991—99; music tchr. North Kans. City Schs., Kansas City, 1993—. Soloist Drake U. Choir, Des Moines, 1982—86; dance accompanist Alvin Ailey Dance Co., Kansas City, Mo., 1987—87. Singer: (recording) Handel's Messiah, 1983, (radio live recording) Three French Songs - Bernstein, 1986. Recipient Ctrl. Iowa 1st Pl. Music, Yamah Corp. Competition, 1979, 5 #1 music ratings, State of Mo., 1978—82. Mem.: Am. Orff-Schulwerk Assn. Office: Gracemor Elem Sch 5125 N Sycamore Kansas City MO 64119 Office Phone: 816-413-6445. Business E-Mail: krobert1@nkcsd.k12.mo.us.

**ROBERTSON, LAVERNE,** minister; MS, Nova Southeastern U., 1995. Pastor Mansion Ave. Triumphant Bapt. Ch., Richmond, Va., 2001—04. Singer: (songs) Freedom Day Has Come. Gospel music writer and performer,

Richmond, 1980—99. Named 3rd runner up, Miss Black Richmond Pageant. Office: Mansion Ave Triumphant Baptist Ch PO Box 24245 1801 Mansion Ave Richmond VA 23224 Office Phone: 804-232-6046. Personal E-mail: laverroberts@aol.com.

**ROBERTSON, LAWRENCE MARSHALL, JR.,** neurosurgeon; b. Denver, Feb. 4, 1932; s. Lawrence M. and Mildred Eleanor (Blackwood) R.; m. Joan T. White, May 13, 1958 (div. Oct. 1973); children: Colette M., Michele E., Laurienne J., Lawrence M. III; m. Lee Ann Crawford, Sept. 24, 1982; one child, William M. BA, U. Colo., 1954; MD, U. Colo., Denver, 1957; postgrad., U. Denver, 1981-85. Diplomate Am. Bd. Med.-Legal Analysis in Medicine and Surgery, Am. Bd. Clin. Neurol. Surgery, Am. Bd. Forensic Medicine. Intern Kings County Hosp., Bklyn., 1957-58; resident in gen. surgery St. Joseph Hosp., Denver, 1958-59; resident in neurology U. Colo., Denver, 1959-60; resident in neurosurgery Boston City Hosp., 1960-64; fellow in neurosurgery Lahey Clinic, Boston, 1963; practice medicine specializing in neurosurgery Denver, 1964—. Contbr. articles on malpractice to legal jours. Capt. USNR, 1979-83, 85. Recipient Continuing Edn. Cert., Am. Assn. Neurol. Surgeons and Cong. Neurol. Surgeons, 1976, 1980-83, Physicians Recognition award AMA 1976-79, 80-83, 84-87. Fellow Internat. Coll. Surgeons, Royal Coll. Surgeons; mem. AAAS, ACS, AMA, Colo. Neurosurg. Soc., N.Y. Acad. Scis., Naval Res. Assn., U.S. Naval Inst., Interurban Neurosurg. Soc., Rocky Mountain Traumatologic Soc., Phi Alpha Delta. Office: Colo Neurosurgery PC 1635 Gilpin St Denver CO 80218-1632

**ROBERTSON, LEON H.,** management consultant, educator; b. Atlanta; s. Grady Jospeh and Pearline (Chandler) R. BS in Indsl. Mgmt., Ga. Inst Tech., 1957, MS, 1959, postgrad., U. Okla.-Norman, 1958, U. Mich., 1961; PhD in Bus. Adminstrn., Ga. State U., 1968. Mgr. mgmt. cons. divsn. Arthur Andersen & Co., Atlanta, 1960-65; prof. bus. adminstrn. Ga. State U., 1965-75; corp. v.p. Tex. Gas Corp., Owensboro, Ky., 1975-78, sr. v.p., 1982-83; chmn., CEO Am. Carriers, Inc., Overland Park, Kans., 1978-88; chmn. bd. dirs. Midwest Coast Transport, Overland Park, 1988-89; prof. mgmt., dir. divsn. bus. adminstrn. U. Mo., Kansas City, 1990-96, prof. Internat. Acad. Programs, 1996-98, dir. Ctr. for Internat. Bus., 1999—. Office: Univ of Mo-Kansas City Henry W Bloch Sch Bus & Pub Admn 5110 Cherry St Kansas City MO 64110-2426 Business E-Mail: robertsonl@umkc.edu.

**ROBERTSON, LINDA F.,** educational administrator; b. Powell, Wyo., July 15, 1946; d. Lee and Dorothy W. (Schweighart) Brunk; m. Darrell G. Robertson II, July 2, 1965; 1 child, Michelle. BA in elem. edn., U. Wyo., 1968; MA in edn. adminstrn., U. Akron, 1978; PhD in higher edn. adminstrn., Kent State U., 2005. Cert. supt., elem. prin., secondary prin., Ohio. Elem. prin. Aurora (Ohio) City Schs., asst. supt., high sch. prin.; dir. Ctr. for Internat. and Intercultural Edn., Kent State U. Named Ohio Prin. of Yr., 1992. Mem.: Kappa Delta Pi, Phi Delta Kappa. Home: 8220 Timber Trl Chagrin Falls OH 44023-5071 Business E-Mail: lfrobert@kent.edu.

**ROBERTSON, MICHAEL,** Internet company executive; B in Cognitive Sci., U. Calif. San Diego. Founder MR Mac Software, 1994—95, Media Minds, Inc., 1995—96; founder, pres. The Z Co., 1996; founder, CEO, chmn. MP3.com, San Diego, 1998—2001; founder, CEO Linspire, Inc., San Diego, 2001—; CEO SIPphone, 2003—. Cons. San Diego Super Computer Ctr.; cons. in field. Founder Robertson Educational Empowerment Found. (REEF) San Diego, 2002—. Named one of 100 most influential individuals in the music industry BAM Mag. Achievements include established Filez and Websitez. Office: Linspire 9333 Genesee Ave 3rd Fl San Diego CA 92121

**ROBERTSON, MICHAEL SWING,** minister; b. Boston, July 20, 1935; s. Charles Stuart and Elizabeth (Swing) R.; m. Margaret Filoon, Sept. 17, 1960 (dec. Oct. 1996); children: Michael Swing, Ashlee Whipple, Christopher Filoon, Andrew Stuart; m. Emily Erickson, Feb. 22, 1998. AB, Harvard U., 1957, grad. Advanced Mgmt. Program, 1979. With Robertson Factories, Inc., 1957-80, exec. v.p., 1968-73, pres., 1973-79, chmn. bd., 1979-80; dir. Robertson-Swing Co., 1980—; pres. The Berkley Co. Inc., 1981-90, Reactions Inc., 1985-90; treas. Falmouth Marine Inc., 1981-88; pres., treas. Orchard Computer Inc., 1984-91, chmn., treas., 1991-93; exec. sec. Nat. Assn. Congl. Christian Chs., Oak Creek, Wis., 1991-97; minister Pilgrim Congl. Ch., Taunton, Mass., 2000—02; ch. coord. Cmty. Faith Alliance, Milw., 1997-2000; exec. dir. Cmty. Village, Ltd., 1998-2000, 2003—; pastor Pilgrim Congrl. Ch., Taunton, 2001—02, Urban Ministry Cmty. Bapt. Ch., Milw., 2003, Union Congl. Ch., Braintree, Mass., 2004—. V.p. adv. coun. Coll. of Bus. and Industry, Southeastern Mass. U., North Dartmouth, Mass., 1979-91; selectman, Town of Berkley, Mass., 1974-80, chmn. 1979-80; mem. Pres.'s Adv. Com. for Trade Negotiations, 1983-86; bd. dirs. Mass. Easter Seal Soc., 1977-91, pres. 1982-83; bd. dirs. Nat. Easter Seal Soc., 1985-91, Wis. Easter Seal Soc., 1994-95, Trips for Kids, New Bedford, 2005-; chmn. Berkley Rep. Town com., 1977-91; Rep. nominee U.S. Senate Mass., 1976, nominee for Mass. state auditor, 1982; co-chmn. Mass Reagan for Pres. Com., 1980; Bristol County coord. Reagan/Bush campaign; co-chmn. Mass. Dole for Pres. Commn., 1987; chmn. Southeastern Mass. campaign Harvard Coll., 1981; chmn. Friends of Harvard Track, 1986-91; trustee Barnstable County Hosp., 1985-90, chmn., 1988. Mem. Harvard Varsity Club, Falmouth Yacht Club, Harvard Club of Boston. Congregationalist. Home: 7 Swing Lane Falmouth MA 02540 Office: 74 Commercial St Braintree MA 02184 Office Phone: 781-843-1333. Personal e-mail: emmyandmike@verizon.net. Accept responsibility with enthusiasm and gratitude. Our individual freedom is unmatched in history, compelling us to remain true to our heritage and our God.

**ROBERTSON, OSCAR PALMER (BIG O ROBERTSON),** chemical company executive, former professional basketball player; b. Charlotte, Tenn., Nov. 24, 1938; BBA, U. Cin., 1960. Player U.S. Olympic Basketball Team, 1960; basketball player Cin. Royals, 1960-70, Milw. Bucks, 1970-74; founder, pres., CEO, Orchem, Inc., Cin., 1981-1996, Orpack-Stone Corp., Herrin, Ill., 1990—, Orflex Ltd., Cin., 1995—, ORDMS, Marlton, N.J., 1997—. Player NBA Championship Team, 1971. Named Sporting News Coll. Player of Yr., 1958, 59, 60, Sporting News All-Star Fitrst Team, 1958, 59, 60, NBA Rookie of Yr., 1961, All NBA First Team, 1961-69; player NBA All Star Games, 1961-72; named MVP, NBA, 1964, M VP in NBA All-Star Games, 1961, 64, 69; named to NBA 35th Anniversary All-Star Team, 1980; elected to Naismith Meml. Basketball Hall of Fame, 1979 Office: Orchem Corp 4293 Mulhauser Rd Fairfield OH 45014-5450

**ROBERTSON, PAT (MARION GORDON ROBERTSON),** religious broadcasting executive, university president and chancellor; b. Lexington, Va., Mar. 22, 1930; s. A. Willis and Gladys (Churchill) R.; m. Adelia Elmer; children: Timothy, Elizabeth, Gordon, Ann. BA, Washington and Lee U., 1950; JD, Yale U., 1955; MDiv, N.Y. Theol. Sem., 1959; ThD (hon.), Oral Roberts U., 1983. Ordained minister So. Bapt. Conv., 1961-87. Founder, CEO, chmn. Christian Broadcasting Network, Virginia Beach, Va., 1960—; host 700 Club, 1968—; founder, chancellor, pres. Regent Univ. (formerly CBN Univ.), 1977—; founder, chmn. Operation Blessing Internat. Relief and Devel. Inc., 1978—. Internat. Family Entertainment, Inc., 1990-97, Asia Pacific Media Corp., 1993—; chmn. Starguide Digital Networks, Inc., 1995—, Porchlight Entertainment, Inc., 1995—; founder, pres. The Christian Coalition, 1989—, The Am. Ctr. for Law and Justice, 1990—, also chmn. Bd. dirs. United Va. Bank, Norfolk; mem. Pres. Task Force on Victims of Crime, Washington, 1984. Author: (with Jamie Buckingham) Shout It From the Housetops: The Story of the Founder of the Christian Broadcasting Network, 1972, My Prayer for You, 1977, The Secret Kingdom, 1982, Answers to 200 of Life's Most Probing Questions, 1984, (with William Proctor) Beyond Reason: How Miracles Can Change Your Life, 1984, America's Dates with Destiny, 1986, The Plan, 1989, The New Millennium: 10 Trends that Will Impact Your Family by the Year 2000, 1990, The New World Order, 1991, The Turning Tide: The Fall of Liberalism and the Rise of Common Sense, 1993, The End of the Age, 1995, Six Steps to Spiritual Revival: God's Awesome Power in Your Life, 2002, Bring It On: Tough Questions. Candid Answers, 2002, The Ten Offenses: Reclaim the Blessings of God's Eternal Truth, 2003, Courting Disaster: How the Supreme Court Is Usurping the

Power of Congress and the People, 2004, Miracles Can Be Yours Today, 2005 Candidate for Rep. nomination for Pres. U.S., 1988. Served in USMC, 1950—52. Recipient Disting. Merit citation NCCJ, Knesset medallion Israel Pilgrimage Com., Faith and Freedom award Religious Heritage Am., Bronze Halo award So. Calif. Motion Picture Council, Humanitarian award Food for the Hungry, 1982, George Washington Honor medal Freedoms Found. at Valley Forge, 1983, Defender of Israel award Christians Israel Pub. Action Campaign, 1994, John Connor Humanitarian Svc. award Operation Smile Internat., 1994, Cross of Nails award, 2000, The State of Israel Friendship award, Zionist Org. of Am., 2002; named Internat. Clergyman of Yr. Religion in Media, 1981, Man of Yr. Internat. Com. for Goodwill, 1981. Mem. Nat. Religious Broadcasters (bd. dirs. 1973—2006), Kentucky Colonels. Office: The Christian Broadcasting Network 977 Centerville Tpke Virginia Beach VA 23463-7701 also: Regent U 1000 Regent U Dr Virginia Beach VA 23464

**ROBERTSON, PAUL FRANCIS,** mathematician, educator; b. Galveston, Tex., Aug. 23, 1953; s. Gilfred and Wilda Robertson; m. Ana Cecilia Moreno, May 17, 1988 (div. Nov. 1993); m. Cynthia Arnet Gilford, June 3, 1978 (div. Dec. 1980); children: Chiquita Monique, Paul Alexander, Andrea Celeste. BA in Math., Tex. So. U., 1975. Cert. tchr. Tex., 1997. Data processing instr. Houston C.C. Sys., 1981; math./ computer literacy tchr. Galveston Ind. Sch. Dist., Tex., 1997—99; adj. prof. math. Galveston Coll., Tex., 1999; math./ instrnl. tech. tchr. Galveston Cath. Sch., Tex., 1999—2004; adj. prof. math. Galveston Coll., 2004; sub. tchr. Tex. City Ind. Sch. Dist., 2004—. Instrnl. tech. chairperson Galveston Cath. Sch., Tex., 2001—. Author (chairperson): (technical writing) Galveston Cath. Sch. Instrnl. Tech. Plan. Recipient Unsung Hero award, Galveston County - The Daily News, 2002, Cert. of Appreciation, Communities in Schs. Galveston, Inc., 2002, Cert. for Outstanding Support, Big Bros. Big Sisters of Gulf Coast, 2002; Four Yr. Acad. Scholarship award, The Moody Found., 1971. Mem.: Sheriffs Assn. of Tex., Tex. Libr. Assn., Tex. Computer Edn. Assn. (corr.), Tex. Coun. Tchrs. of Math. (corr.). D-Conservative. Catholic. Avocations: reading, tutoring, volunteering, poetry. Office: 8801 Palmer Hwy 2205 Texas City TX 77591 E-mail: pfr0853@earthlink.net.

**ROBERTSON, PAULINE DURRETT,** publishing executive; b. Amarillo, Tex., Apr. 17, 1922; d. Walter Lucius and Mary Eddie (Jones) Durrett; m. Roy Lewis Robertson, Dec. 18, 1940; children: Kay Linda Robertson Savage, Kent Lewis, Robyn M. Robertson Turner, Paula Jo Robertson Pierce, Roy Durrett, Laurel Annette Robertson Gibson, Virginia Lee Robertson-Baker, Ellen Robertson Green, Neil Thomas, Carrie Beth. AA, Amarillo Coll., 1969; BA in English Writing, St. Edward's U., Austin, Tex., 1992. Editor project history U.S. Reclamation Bur., Amarillo, 1942-43; editor post newsletter U.S. Army Air Force, Amarillo, 1943-44; freelance writer, 1944-73; writer books of history Staked Plains Press, Canyon, Tex., 1973-77; writer books of history and poetry Paramount Pub. Co., Amarillo, 1977—; pub. house pres., editor, 1977—; tchr. poetry writing and history Amarillo Coll., 1971—2002. Tchr. poetry writing Elderhostel, U. Tex., Austin, 1988-89; writer book revs. Amarillo Globe News, 1968—; editor books, articles, newspapers, 1985-; spkr. in field. Author: (with R.L. Robertson) Panhandle Pilgrimage: Illustrated Tales Tracing History in the Texas Panhandle, 1976, 77, 81, 85, 90, Tascosa: Historic Site in the Texas Panhandle, 1978, 2d edit., 1995, Mystery Woman of Old Tascosa: The Legend of Frenchy McCormick, 1979, 2d edit., 1995, Cowman's Country: Fifty Frontier Ranches in the Texas Panhandle 1876-1887, 1981, 2d edit., 1995, (poetry) Fringe Benefits: Light Verse From Living, 1985, Borrowed Moccasins: Poems From Other Viewpoints, 1986, Field Notes: Poems on Late Light, 1987; editor and designer: Austin Originals: Chats With Colorful Characters by Robyn Turner, 1982, Long Shadows: Indian Leaders Standing in the Path of Manifest Destiny 1600-1900 (by Jack Jackson), 1985; designer, editor: (poetry) Bootsteps: Poems of the West-Then and Now (by Mildred C. Speer), 1978, 83, coauthor, editor: Eve's Version: 150 Women of the Bible, 1983; featured in documentary Story Of A Family on NBC-TV, 1960; mem. writing team Ch. Women United U.S.A., 2001—. Co-founder, sec. Cerebral Palsy Treatment Ctr., Amarillo, 1948-60, Opportunity House, Amarillo, 1970-87; founder, pres. Children's Cottage, Amarillo, 1964-84, Women's Coalition for Change: Focus on Poverty, Amarillo, 1989-95; founder, bd. for underprivileged children Camp Friendship, Ceta Glen, Tex., 1971-74; vol. tutor neighborhood pub. schs., 1992-; chair of elders First Christian Ch., 1979-81; host family Internat. Christian Youth Exch., 1963-64, sending family, 1968, 78; active Potter County Hist. Commn., Tex., 1988-96; pres.-elect Ch. Women United of Tex., 1996-98, pres., 1998-2000; chair Amarillo Mayor's Commn. on Early Childhood Nurture/Neglect, 1997—; nat. del. Christian Ch. Named Amarillo's Family of the Yr., Amarillo Globe-News, 1957, Tex. Merit Mother, Am. Mothers Assn., Boston, 1991, 1995 Woman of the Yr. in Amarillo, Beta Sigma Phi, Amarillo, 1995, Yellow Rose Tex., Gov. Anne Richards, 1991, Mayor's Friend of Young Children, 1999, Tex. Mother of Yr., Am. Mothers Assn., Boston, 2003; named to Amarillo HS Hall Fame, 1998; recipient Tex. Panhandle Disting. Svc. award West Tex. A&M U., Canyon, 1977, Lifetime Career Achievement award Amarillo Women's Network, 1996, Woman of Distinction award Girl Scouts Tex. Plains Coun., 2002. Mem. AAUW, LWV (v.p., Amarillo program chair), Western Writers Am., Acad. Am. Poets, Amarillo Photog. Soc. (publicity com., Salon award 1961—), Panhandle Prof. Writers (pres. 1966—, bd. mem.), Poetry Soc. Tex. (founder. area chpt. 1972, pres. area chpt. 1979-81, Tex. state councilor 1973—), Tex. Tchrs. of Creative Writing, Common Cause (area rep. 1971—). Democrat. Avocations: photography, travel, reading, walking. Home: 124 Wayside Dr Amarillo TX 79106-6425 Office: Paramount Pub Co PO Box 3730 Amarillo TX 79116-3730 E-mail: pdr-rlr@cox.net.

**ROBERTSON, PENETHA BROWNING,** secondary school educator; b. Welch, W.Va., Oct. 23, 1963; d. Danny Wayne and Martha Nester Browning; m. Mark David Robertson, Aug. 17, 1985; 1 child, Hope Alexa. BS in Edn., Concord U., 1986; MS in Edn., Longwood U., 2003. Postgrad. profl. lic. Va. Dept. Edn., 2004. Tchr. Franklin County Schs., Louisburg, NC, 1987—90, Durham Pub. Schs., NC, 1990—94, Archdiocese of Louisville, 1995—97, Powhatan County Pub. Schs., Va., 1999—. V.p. Sigma Sigma Sigma, Woodstock, Va., 1998—2004. Recipient Tchr. of Yr., Powhatan HS, 2004. Home: 1310 Pine Creek Bluff Drive Powhatan VA 23139 Office: Powhatan HS 1800 Judes Ferry Rd Powhatan VA 23139 Office Phone: 804-598-5710. Personal E-mail: dukefans63@msn.com. Business E-mail: penny.robertson@powhatan.k12.va.us.

**ROBERTSON, PETER JAMES,** oil company executive; b. Edinburgh, Scotland, Jan. 31, 1947; came to U.S., 1969; s. James Donald and Evelyn Patricia (McNaughton) R.; m. Candace Povey, Dec. 29, 1971; children: James Darrell, Nicole Povey, Emily Jemma. BS in Mech. Engring., Edinburgh U., 1969; MBA, U. Pa., 1971. Refinery engr. Union Oil Co. of Calif., Chgo., 1971-72; mcht. banker Noble Grossart Ltd., Edinburgh, 1972-73; fin. analyst Standard Oil Co. of Calif. (Chevron), San Francisco, 1973-78, audit mgr. Europe London, 1978-80; comptr. Chevron Oil Europe, London, 1980-83; asst. comptr. Chevron U.S.A., Inc., San Francisco, 1983-86, comptr., 1987-89, v.p. fin., 1989-91; asst. comptr. Chevron Corp., San Francisco, 1986-87; pres. Warren Petroleum Co., Tulsa, 1991—94; exec. V.P. Chevron U.S.A., 1996—97, pres., 1997—2000; VP Chevron Corp., 1997—2000; pres. Chevron Overseas Petroleum Co., San Ramon, Calif., 2000—02; vice chmn. bd. dir. Chevron/Texaco Corp., 2002—. Bd. dirs. Okla. chpt. The Nature Conservancy, Tulsa area United Way, Indian Nations coun. Boy Scouts Am., Tulsa. Recipient Thouron award Thouron Scholarship Found., U. Pa., 1969-71. Mem. Met. Tulsa C. of C., U.S. Hispanic C. of C. (sr. exec. adv com. 1990-92), Midcontinent Oil and Gas Assn. Avocations: travel, collecting antique maps, skiing. Office: Chevron/Texaco 6001 Bollinger Canyon Rd San Ramon CA 94583-2324*

**ROBERTSON, RALPH S.,** secondary school principal; Prin. Richmond Sr. High Sch., Rockingham, N.C. Recipient Blue Ribbon Sch. award U.S. Dept. Edn., 1990-91, Nat. award Dale Parnell Tech. Prep Program of Excellence, 1991; named Prin. of Yr., N.C. Burger King/Nat. Assn. of Secondary Sch. Prins., 1987. Office: US Hwy 1 North PO Box 1748 Rockingham NC 28380-1748 Office Phone: 910-997-9812. E-mail: ralphrobertson@richmond.k12.nc.us.

**ROBERTSON, RICHARD EARL,** physical chemist, educator; b. Long Beach, Calif., Nov. 12, 1933; s. Earl Austin and A. Isobel (Roberts) R.; m. Joyce W. Conger, Sept. 4, 1955 (div. 1972); children: Christopher, Jill; m. Patricia L. Richmond, Apr. 20, 1974. BA, Occidental Coll., L.A., 1955; student, UCLA, 1955-56; PhD, Calif. Inst. Tech., 1960. Phys. chemist rsch. lab. GE, Schenectady, NY, 1960-70; staff scientist Ford Motor Co., Dearborn, Mich., 1970-86; prof. materials sci. and engring. U. Mich., Ann Arbor, 1986—; dir. Macromolecular Sci. and Engring. Ctr., 1995—2000. Contbr. articles to profl. jours. Postdoctoral fellow Washington U., St. Louis, 1959-60. Fellow Am. Phys. Soc.; mem. Am. Chem. Soc., Sigma Xi. Office: U Mich Dept Materials Sci Eng Ann Arbor MI 48109-2136 E-mail: rer@umich.edu.

**ROBERTSON, ROBERT GRAHAM HAMISH,** physicist; b. Ottawa, Ont., Can., Oct. 3, 1943; arrived in US, 1971, naturalized, 1993; s. Hugh Douglas and Alice Madeleine (Bell) R.; m. Peggy Lynn Dyer, July 4, 1980; 1 child, Ian. BA, Oxford U., Eng., 1965, MA, 1969; PhD, McMaster U., Can. 1971. Rsch. assoc. Mich. State U., East Lansing, 1971-72, asst. rsch. prof., 1972-73, asst. prof., 1973-78, assoc. prof., 1978-81, prof., 1981-82; mem. staff Los Alamos (N.Mex.) Nat. Lab., 1981—, fellow, 1988—; prof. U. Washington, Seattle, 1994—; sci. dir. Ctr. for Exptl. Nuc. Physics and Astrophysics, 2000—. Rsch. assoc. Princeton U., NJ, 1975—76; vis. scientist Argonne Nat. Lab, Ill., 1979, Chalk River Nuc. Labs., Ont., Canada, 1980; dir. Sudbur Neutrino Obs., 2003. Contbr. over 60 articles to profl. jours. Alfred P. Sloan Found. fellow Mich. State U., 1976; Trevelyan scholar Eng., 1962-65, NRC scholar McMaster U., 1965-69, Oriel Coll. scholar, 1962-65. Fellow Am. Phys. Soc. (chair divsn. nuclear physics 2000, Tom W. Bonner prize 1997), Inst. Physics of Eng., Am. Acad. Arts and Scis.; mem. NAS, Can. Assn. Physicists. Achievements include first observation of nuclear isobaric quintet; development of technique for precise measurement of neutrino mass; determination of Lithium-6 synthesis in early universe; demonstration of neutrino mass, oscillations with Sudbury Neutrino Obs. E-mail: rghr@u.washington.eu.

**ROBERTSON, ROBIN ALAYNE,** headmaster, anthropologist; b. Tex. B. U. Penn.: M in Anthropology, PhD in Anthropology, Harvard U. Former asst. prof. So. Methodist U., former assoc. dean for gen. ed., 1984—90; head of sch. Emma Willard Sch., Troy, NY, 1990—99, Milton Acad., Milton, Mass., 1999—. Trustee-at-large CASE; bd. v.p. Nat. Coalition of Girls' Schools, 1994—; mem. pres. council Sage Colleges, Troy, NY. Mem. Troy Redevelopment Found., 1994—, pres., 1995—96. Office: Milton Acad 170 Centre St Milton MA 02186

**ROBERTSON, ROSE MARIE,** cardiologist, educator; b. Detroit, May 15, 1945; d. Joseph Michael and Rose Marie (Pink) Stevens; m. David Robertson, Oct. 31, 1978; 1 child, Rose Marie. BA, Manhattanville Coll., 1966; MD, Harvard Med. Sch., 1970. Diplomate Nat. Bd. Medicine, 1971, Am. Bd. Internal Medicine, 1974, Cardiovascular Medicine, 1975. Intern in medicine Mass. Gen. Hosp., Boston, 1970-71, resident in medicine, 1970-72; fellow in cardiovasc. medicine Johns Hopkins Med. Sch., Balt., 1973-75, asst. prof. medicine, 1976—77, Vanderbilt U. Med. Ctr., Nashville, 1975-82, assoc. prof. medicine, 1982-89, dir. cardiovasc. tng. program, 1990—2000, assoc. dir. cardiology, 1987—2000, prof. medicine, 1989—. Mem. adv. bd. Robert Wood Johnson Found., 1990-, chair, 2003-; mem. adv. bd. Assn. for Patient-Oriented Rsch.; mem. cardiovasc. study sect. NIH, Bethesda, Md., 1993-97; invited spkr., lectr. Contbr. articles to profl. jours., chpts. to books. Fellow Am. Coll. Cardiology, Am. Heart Assn. (pres. 2000-01, chief sci. officer 2003-), European Soc. Cardiology; mem. Am. Autonomic Soc., Am. Fedn. for Clin. Rsch., Am. Soc. Clin. Investigation, Am. Clin. and Climatol. Assn., Assn. Univ. Cardiologists. Home: 4003 Newman Pl Nashville TN 37204-4308 Office: 7272 Greenville Ave Dallas TX 75240 Office Phone: 214-706-1295. E-mail: rosemarie.robertson@heart.org.

**ROBERTSON, SAMUEL LUTHER, JR.,** psychotherapist, educator; b. Houston, Apr. 28, 1940; s. Sam L. and Portia Louise (Burns) R.; children: Samuel Luther IV, Sean Lee (dec.). Ryan William, Susan Elizabeth (dec.), Henry Philmore. BS, McMurry U., 1969; MA, Hardin-Simmons U., 1973; PhD, U. Tex., 1993. Cert. tchr. adminstr., counselor, Tex.; lic. chem. dependency counselor, Tex., lic. clin. mental health counselor, N. Mex. Instr., coach, athletic dir. Tex. and La. schs., 1969-94; social worker, supr. Children's Protective Svcs., Abilene, Tex., 1978-79; instr. adminstr. Harlandale Sch. Dist., San Antonio, 1980-84, 87-90; adminstr. night sch. Harlandale Ind. Sch. Dist., San Antonio, 1988-89; instr. Edgewood Ind. Sch. Dist., San Antonio, 1985-87; developer, instr., integrated unit program San Antonio, 1990—; CEO The Educative Inst., San Antonio, 1992—. CEO Educative Therapeutic Processes, 1972—; co-founder, dir. Inst. Organizational Personal Devel.; lectr. U. Tex. at San Antonio, 2000-, founder, dir. Recovery Ctr., U. Tex., San Antonio, 2004-05. Author: (play) The Challenged, 1965, Dream Poems, 1998; (poem) Trains in the Night, 1969; (screenplay) Tom & Jane, 2000; dir. (film) Tom & Jane, 2003. State co-chmn. Youth for Kennedy-Johnson, Tex., 1960; mem. W. Tex. Dem. Steering Com., Abilene, 1962-63; founding dir. Way Off Broadway Cmty. Theater, Eagle Pass, Tex., 1971-72; founding bd. dirs. Battered Women's Shelter, Abilene, 1978-79; v.p. bd. dirs. Mental Health Assn., San Antonio, 1980-83, bd. dirs Palmer Drug Abuse Program, San Antonio, 1985-87; pres., bd. dir. Alcoholic Rehab. Ctr., 1985-86, 1987-92, Woman at the Well, 2006-; vice-chmn. Civilian and Mil. Addictive Programs, San Antonio, 1991-92; author, implementer Cmty. Vitalization Program, 1994—; mem. vestry St. George Episcopal Ch., mem. sch. bd., St. George Sch.1999—02; mem. standards chair Tex. Certification Bd. of Addiction Profls.; chmn. 1999—01. Named Tchr. of Yr. Southside Ind. Sch. Dist., San Antonio, 1970-71, Harlandale Alternative Ctr., San Antonio, 1987-88; Vol. of Yr., Mental Health Assn., San Antonio, 1982, Alcoholic Rehab. Ctr., San Antonio, 1992-93; Businessman of Yr., 2003. Mem. ACA, NEA, Am. Mental Health Counseling Assn., Tex. State Tchrs. Assn., Am. Ednl. Rsch. Assn., Am. Assn. Sch. Adminstrs. (mem. exec. com.), Internat. Consortium Reciprocity Commn. Nat. Alcoholism and Drug Abuse Counselors, N.Mex. Mental Health Counselors Assn., N.Mex. Profl. Counselors Assn., Phi Kappa Phi, Kappa Delta Pi. Episcopalian. Avocations: reading, writing, travel, theater, sports. Office: Educative Therapeutic Processes 339 E Hildebrand Ave San Antonio TX 78212-2412 Office Phone: 210-828-9919. Personal E-mail: slr.junior@netscape.net. *I have participated in my life, my family's life, and my community's life in a responsible fashion through the Grace of God.*

**ROBERTSON, STEPHEN WILLIAM,** corporate compliance officer, government relations executive; b. Nebr., U. Nebr., 1976. Gen. counsel Nebr. Dept. Ins., Lincoln, 1977—80; v.p., fed. and state govt. rels. officer Health Ins. Assn. Am., Chgo., 1980—94; chief compliance and regulatory affairs officer, fed. and state govt. rels. officer Conseco, Inc., Carmel, Ind., 1994—. Mem. adv. bd. Lexis Nexis. Recipient Founders award, Health Ins. Assn. Am., 2002. Mem.: ABA, The Heroes Club Inc. (bd. dirs.), Nebr. State Bar Assn., Ins. Inst. Ind. (bd. dirs., exec. and legis. com. 1998—2005), Am. Coun. Life Insurers (state policy oversight com., corr. officer 2001—05), Ams. Health Ins. Plans (state govt. rels. com. 1995—2005, fed. govt. rels. com. 1995—2005). Office: Conseco Inc 11825 N Pennsylvania St Carmel IN 46032 Office Phone: 317-817-3539.

**ROBERTSON, STERLING CLIFTON,** music educator, musician; b. Tientsin, Tiangjin, China, Jan. 22, 1928; arrived in U.S., 1932; s. Sterling Clifton and Mary Letitia (Grimes) Robertson. Student, Tex. Christian U., 1945—47, U. Tex., 1948—50, Julliard Sch. Music, N.Y.C., 1952—53, Columbia U., 1952—53, Royaumont-12th Century Monastery-Libr. and Found. Artists; grad., Ft. Worth Conservatory Music, 1945. Tchr. piano, N.Y.C., 1950—70, San Antonio, 1970—. Staff pianist Four Seasons Hotels, San Antonio, Hyatt Regency, San Antonio, Wyndham-St. Anthony, San Antonio; concert pianist Carnegie Hall, 1961, 63, Royal Danish Ballet, Royal Danish Ballet, Columbia Artist, 1961, Boston Music Ctr. (Music Circus), Ted Shawn's Jacob's Pillow. Grantee for piano study with George Copeland, Fairfield Found. and William Hale Harkness/Rebekah Harkness, 1952—53. Democrat. Avocations: theater, films, art. Mailing: 314 Bryn Mawr Dr San Antonio TX 78209 Office Phone: 210-826-3376.

**ROBERTSON, STEWART,** conductor; b. Glasgow, Scotland; m. Meryl Owen; children: Keren, Niel. Attended, Royal Scottish Acad. of Music; studied with, Hans Swarowsky & Otmar Sultner. Past music dir., prin. condr. Santa Fe (N.Mex.) Symphony; music dir. Glimmerglass Summer Opera Festival, 1988—, Inland Empire Symphony Orchestra, San Bernardino, Calif.; music dir., prin. condr. San Bernardino Symphony Orchestra, 1989—2001; music dir. Fla. Grand Opera, Miami, 2005—. Guest condr. BBC Scottish Symphony, Ukraine State Philharm., Buenos Aires Philharm., Lille Festival, Fla. Philharm., Louisville Orch., Cluj. Lyric, N.Y.C. Opera, Cologne, Zurich, Scottish Opera, Sicily Symphony Orch., North German Philharm., Mecklenburg Staatskapelle; recs. Chandos, New World, Verdi-EMI.

**ROBERTSON, THOMAS SINCLAIR,** academic administrator; b. Scotland, Nov. 16, 1942; s. Thomas C. and Ann Gorman (Mundie) R.; m. Diana S. Conway, June 18, 1966; children: Brian, Ashley, Alexandra BA, Wayne State U., Detroit, 1963; MA, PhD, Northwestern U., 1966. Asst. prof. mktg. UCLA, 1966-68, Harvard U., 1968-77; prof. mktg. Wharton Sch., U. Pa., 1971, chmn. mktg. dept., 1978-84, assoc. dean, 1984—88, London Bus. Sch., 1994-98; dean Goizueta Bus. Sch., Emory U., Atlanta, 1998—2004; spl. asst. to pres. for internat. strategy Emory U., 2005—. Bd. dirs. Profit Recovery Group. Author: Innovative Behavior and Communication, 1971, Televised Medicine Advertising and Children, 1979, Consumer Behavior, 1984, Handbook of Consumer Behavior, 1991. Grantee NSF NIH. Mem. Am. Mktg. Assn., Assn. Consumer Rsch., Cherokee Town Club, Commerce Club. Republican.

**ROBERTSON, TIMOTHY JOEL,** statistician, educator; b. Denver, Oct. 4, 1937; s. Flavel P. and Helen C. (Oliver) Girdner; m. Joan K. Slater, Aug. 18, 1959; children— Kelly, Jana, Doug, Mike BA in Math., U. Mo., 1959, MS in Math., 1961, PhD in Stats., 1966. Asst. prof. Cornell Coll., Mt. Vernon, Iowa, 1961-63; prof. stats. U. Iowa, Iowa City, 1965—2004, prof. emeritus, 2004—. Vis. prof. U. N.C., Chapel Hill, 1974-75, U. Calif.-Davis, 1983-84; Eugene Lukacs Disting. vis. prof. Bowling Green State U., 1991-92; vis. lectr. Com. Pres. Statis. Soc., 1971-74. Author: (with F.T. Wright and R.L. Dykstra) Order Restricted Statistical Inference; assoc. editor Am. Math. Monthly, 1977-81; mem. editl. bd. Comms. in Stats., 1981-92; assoc. editor Jour. Am. Statis. Assn., 1990-96; contbr. numerous articles to profl. jours. Recipient Collegiate Teaching award U. Iowa, 1990. Fellow Am. Statis. Assn. (council 1974-75), Inst. Math. Stats., Internat. Statis. Inst.; mem. Math. Assn. Am., Sigma Xi, Sierra Club Democrat. Avocations: canoeing, camping, bicycling, walking. Home: 673 Garfield Rd West Branch IA 52358-8574 Office: Univ Iowa Dept Stats/Actuarial Sci Iowa City IA 52242 Office Phone: 319-335-2019. Personal E-mail: rtticity@aol.com.

**ROBERTSON, WANDA SUE,** secondary school educator; b. Martin, Tenn., Jan. 24, 1949; d. Charles Eugene and Ruby Velma (Edwards) Bailey; m. Gene Revelle Robertson, June 13, 1970 (div. Jan. 1984); 1 child, Alecia Revelle. BS in Edn., U. Tenn., Martin, 1970, MS in Math. Edn., 1974. Cert. secondary math. tchr., Tenn. Computer operator U. Tenn., 1969-72, instr. math., 1981-88; tchr. math. Milan H.S. 1972—81, Dyersburg H.S., 1988—. Adj. math faculty Dyersburg State C.C., Tenn., 1990—. Newsletter editor Parents without Ptnrs., 1988—. Named Outstanding H.S. Tchr., U. Tenn., Martin. Mem. Nat. Coun. Tchrs. Math., Tenn. Edn. Assn., Delta Kappa Gamma. Democrat. Baptist. Avocations: travel, reading, bicycling. Home: 2502 Stoneville St Dyersburg TN 38024-5230 Office: Dyersburg High Sch Hwy 51 By-Pass Dyersburg TN 38024 Office Phone: 731-286-3630.

**ROBERTSON, WILLIAM OSBORNE,** physician; b. NYC, Nov. 24, 1925; s. William Osborne and Barbara Konvalinka (Bennett) R.; m. Barbara Foster Simpson, Feb. 23, 1952; children: Kathy, Lynn, Kerry, Douglas, Andrew. BA, U. Rochester, 1946, MD, 1949. Intern Strong Meml. Hosp., Rochester, NY, 1949-51, resident, 1951-52, Grace New Haven Hosp., 1954-56; acting med. dir. Ross Labs., Columbus, Ohio, 1956-59; mem. faculty Ohio State Coll. Medicine, 1956-63, assoc. prof. pediatrics, 1961-63; mem. faculty dept. pediatrics U. Wash., Seattle, 1963—, prof., 1972—, assoc. dean, 1967-72, med. dir., 1963-67, acting chmn. dept. pediatrics, 1972-73, 80-84, head div. ambulatory pediatrics, 1975-77, 78-79; dir. med. edn. div. Children's Orthopedic Hosp., 1971-90, med. dir., poison control ctr., 1971—. Mem. staffs Children's, Harborview, Univ. hosps.; mem. advisory com., chmn. Wash. Alaska Regional Med. Program; bd. dirs. Wash. Med. Edn. and Research Found., 1968-73 Contbr. articles to profl. pubs. Served with USNR, 1943-45, 52-54. Mem. Am. Acad. Pediatrics (chmn. edn. com. 1971-73, med. liability com. 1985-90, chmn. task force on quality assurance 1988-92), Am. Clin. Acad. Toxicology, King County Med. Soc. (pres. 1971-72), Wash. State Med. Assn. (pres. 1975-76), Am. Assn. Poison Control Ctrs. (pres. 1988-90), Phi Beta Kappa, Alpha Omega Alpha, Am. Coll. Med. Toxicology. Home: 18724 40th Pl NE Seattle WA 98155-2806 Office: Wash Poison Ctr 155 NE 100th St Seattle WA 98125 Office Phone: 206-517-2356. E-mail: mryuk@wapc.org.

**ROBERTSON, WILLIAM WITHERS,** lawyer; b. Morristown, N.J., Nov. 3, 1941; s. Thomas Withers and Jessie (Swain) R.; m. Elizabeth Jeanne Robertson; children: Barbara Ellen Richmond, William Withers, Jr., Jessie Swain Wilt. BA, Rutgers U., 1964, LL.B., 1967. Bar: N.J. 1968. Law sec. to judge Superior Ct. N.J., 1967-68; asst. U.S. atty., 1972-76; 1st asst. U.S. atty., 1978-80; U.S. atty. N.J., 1980-81; chief Newark Organized Crime Strike Force, 1976-78; ptnr. Hannoch Weisman, Roseland, NJ, 1981-99, Robertson, Freilich, Bruno & Cohen, LLC, Newark, 1999—. Mng. editor: Rutgers Law Rev., 1966—67. Trustee Rutgers U., 1984-88. Served to capt. JAGC USAR, 1968-72. Mem. Nat. Assn. Former U.S. Attys. (pres. 1990-93, 2005-, pres. 2002-2003), Rutgers U. Law Sch. Alumni Assn. (pres. 1990-91), Rutgers U. Alumni Fedn. (pres. 1981-83). Office: Robertson Freilich et al 1 Riverfront Plz Newark NJ 07102-5401 Office Phone: 973-848-2100. Business E-Mail: wrobertson@rfbclaw.com.

**ROBERTSON, WILLIAM WRIGHT, JR.,** orthopedist, educator; b. Mayfield, Ky., Dec. 26, 1946; m. Karel Virginia Dierks, Jan. 26, 1974. BA, Rhodes Coll., 1968; MD, Vanderbilt U., 1972; MBA, Geo Washington U., 2000. Intern U. Calif., San Diego, 1972-73, resident in orthop. surgery, 1975-76, Vanderbilt U., Nashville, 1976-79; asst. prof. orthop. Tex. Tech U., Lubbock, 1979-86; assoc. prof. U. Pa., Phila., 1986-90; prof. orthop. surgery George Washington U., Washington, 1990-2000; chmn. pediat. orthop. Children's Nat. Med. Ctr., Washington, 1990-99. Field rep. accreditation coun. grad. med. edn. Fellow Am. Acad. Orthop. Surgeons, Am. Orthop. Assn., Pediat. Orthop. Soc. (bd. dirs. 1993-96—). Avocations: gardening, music. Office: Accreditation Coun Grad Med Edn 515 N State St Chicago IL 60610 Business E-Mail: wrobertson@acgme.org.

**ROBERTSON, WYNDHAM GAY,** university official, journalist; b. Salisbury, N.C., Sept. 25, 1937; d. Julian Hart and Blanche Williamson (Spencer) R. AB in Econs., Hollins Coll., Roanoke, Va., 1958. Rsch. asst. Standard Oil Co., N.Y.C., 1958-61; rschr. Fortune Mag., N.Y.C., 1961-67, assoc. editor, 1968-74, bd. of editors, 1974-81, 1984-86; bus. editor Time Mag., N.Y.C., 1982-83; v.p. comm. U. N.C., Chapel Hill, 1986-96. Contbr. numerous articles to Fortune Mag. Trustee Thomas S. Kenan Inst. for the Arts, Hollins U. Recipient Gerald M. Loeb Achievement award, U. of Conn., 1972. Mem. Phi Beta Kappa. Episcopalian.

**ROBERTS-RAMSBOTHAM, HAZEL RUTH,** piano educator; b. Graham, Tex., Apr. 1, 1930; d. John Charles and Daisy Mae (Glosup) Roby; m. Quentin Cyrus Roberts, Sept. 4, 1949 (div. June 1977); children: Roma Ruth, Randall Ray, Ronda Renee, Ronald Roy, Ronelda Ree; m. Elwyn Clare Ramsbotham, Sept. 30, 1990. BA, U. Wyo., 1959; MusM, U. Idaho, 1967. Cert. Music Tchrs. Nat. Assn. Tchr. Las Vegas Pub. Schs., 1955-56, Butler (Wyo.) Pub. Sch., 1956-57, 58-59, Cowdrey (Colo.) Pub. Sch., 1957-58, Lander (Wyo.) Pub. Sch., 1959-60; prvt. practice piano instr. Roberts Studio, Lander, 1959-80, Aurora, Colo., 1980-90, Roberts Ramsbotham Studio, Aurora, Colo., 1990—. Recipient Cmty. Svc. award Lander Seventh Day Adventist Ch., 1978, Colo. Music Tchr. Yr., Colo. Music Tchrs. Assn., 2006.

Mem. Nat. Piano Guild (organizer Lander Ctr., 1962-80, Aurora Ctr., 1981—), Am. Coll. Musicians, Wyo. Music Tchrs. Assn. (from treas. to pres. 1974-80), Lander Music Tchrs. Assn. (pres., others 1967-79), Aurora Music Tchrs. Assn. (pres., others 1980—). Republican. Mem. Ch. of Christ. Avocations: gardening, travel, crocheting, quilting. Home: 377 S Wheeling Way Aurora CO 80012-2448

**ROBEY, MARK DOUGLAS,** lawyer; b. Denver, Apr. 23, 1965; s. Kenneth and Theresa Stone; m. Katherine Robert, Apr. 2, 1993; children: Michele Elizabeth, David Christopher. BS in Acctg., Met. State Coll. Denver, 1989; JD, U. Denver, 2004. Dir. of info. and rsch. Colo. Credit Union League, Arvada, 1997—2005; gen. counsel Colo. Credit Union League (now named Credit Union Assn. of Colo.), 2005—. Mem.: ABA. Republican. Lutheran. Avocations: golf, private pilot. Office: Colo Credit Union League 4905 W 60th Ave Arvada CO 80003 Office Phone: 303-427-4222. E-mail: mrobey@colocu.com.

**ROBFOGEL, SUSAN SALITAN,** lawyer; b. Rochester, NY, Apr. 4, 1943; d. Victor and Janet (Rosenthal) Salitan; m. Nathan Joshua Robfogel, July 12, 1965; children: Jacob Morris, Samuel Salitan. BA cum laude, Smith Coll., 1964; JD, Cornell U., 1967. Bar: N.Y.1967, U.S. Dist. Ct. (we. dist.) 1968, U.S. Ct. Appeals (2d cir.) 1971, U.S. Supreme Ct. 1971, U.S. Dist. Ct. (no. dist.) 1974, D.C. 1982. From asst. corp. counsel to sr. asst. corp. counsel City of Rochester, NY, 1967-70; assoc. Harris, Beach & Wilcox, Rochester, 1970-75; ptnr. Harris, Beach, Wilcox, Rubin & Levey, Rochester, 1975-85, Nixon, Peabody, LLP, Rochester and N.Y.C., 1985—; chair bd. Office of Compliance, Washington, 1999—. Panel mem., Fed. Svc. Impasses Panel, Washington, 1983-94; mem., past chair Data Protection Rev. Bd., Albany, N.Y., 1984—. Recipient Brockport Coll. Found. Community award, 1989. Fellow Am. Bar Found., N.Y State Bar Found., Coll. Labor and Employment Lawyers; mem. ABA, N.Y. State Bar Assn., Washington D.C. Bar Assn., Monroe County Bar Assn. (Rodenbeck award 1988). Home: 1090 Park Ave Rochester NY 14610-1728 also: 437 Madison Ave New York NY 10022-7001 Office Phone: 212-940-3116. Business E-Mail: srobfogel@nixonpeabody.com.

**ROBILA, STEFAN ALEXANDRU,** education educator; s. Ioan Robila; m. Mihaela Robila. PhD, Syracuse U., 2002. Asst. prof. U. New Orleans, 2002—03, Montclair (N.J.) State U., 2003—. Dir. ctr. for imaging and optics Montclair (N.J.) State U., 2004—. Grantee Tech. Initiative, HP Found., 2006; Wilbur LePage Scholarship, Syracuse U., 2002, SPIE Ednl. Grant, The Internat. Soc. for Optical Engrng., 2004, 2005, 2006, Academic Excellence Grant, Sun Microsystems inc., 2005. Office: Montclair State Univ RI 301 Computer Sci Montclair NJ 07043 Office Phone: 973-655-4230. Office Fax: 973-655-4164. Business E-Mail: robilas@mail.montclair.edu.

**ROBILLARD, JEAN EUGENE,** dean, educator; b. Montreal, 1943; m. Renee Robillard. BA, U. Montreal, 1964, MD, 1968. Pediat. residency Saint Justine Hosp., Montreal, 1969—72; pediat. nephrology fellowship UCLA Med. Ctr., Los Angeles, 1972—73, U. Iowa Med. Ctr., Iowa City, 1973—74; asst. prof., dept. pediat. U. Montreal Coll. Med., 1975—76; asst. prof. Dept. Pediat., Coll. Med., U. Iowa, 1974—75, 1976—78, assoc. prof., 1978—82, dir. nephrology div., 1976—96, prof., 1982—96, vice chmn.; chief pediat. U. Mich., Ann Arbor, 1996—2003; physician-in-chief C.S. Mott Children's Hosp., 1996—2003; dean Roy J. and Lucille A. Carver Coll Medicine, U. Iowa, 2003—. Editl. bd. Jour. Pediat., 2001—; bd. dirs. Am. Bd. Pediat., 2001—, chmn. bd. dirs., 2006—. Author of over 220 sci. papers. Recipient Disting. Alumni Award for Achievement, U. Iowa, 2002. Fellow: Coun. for High Blood Pressure Rsch., Am. Heart Assn., Royal Coll. Physicians & Surgeons; mem.: Assn. Med. Sch. Pediat. Dept. Chairs, Inc., Am. Soc. Transplant Physicians, The Perinatal Rsch. Soc., Soc. for Gynecologic Investigation, Am. Physiol. Soc., Am. Assn. for Advancement Sci. (fellow 1999), Am. Soc. Pediat. Nephrology (pres. 1994—95), Soc. Pediat. Rsch., Am. Heart Assn., Soc. Nephrology, Internat. Soc. Nephrology, Internat. Pediat. Nephrology Assn., Midwest Soc. Pediat. Rsch. (Founder's Award 2002), Am. Acad. Pediat., Am Pediat. Soc. Office: Roy J & Lucille A Carver Coll Med 200 CMAB Iowa City IA 52242

**ROBIN, ALAN JAY,** lawyer; b. Norwich, Conn., Oct. 8, 1950; s. Louis and Rose (Rutchik) R.; m. Jean D. Wizig, July 15, 1973; children: Jeffrey Scott, Ross Michael. BBA, U. Tex., 1972, JD, 1975. Bar: Tex. 1975, U.S. Dist. Ct. (so. dist.) Tex., U.S. Tax Ct., U.S. Ct. Appeals (5th cir.), U.S. Ct. Claims. Assoc. Vinson & Elkins LLP, Houston, 1975-82, ptnr., 1983—, head Employee Benefits and Exec. Compensation Sect. Mem. Houston Bar Assn., Tex. Soc. CPAs, Order of Coif, Beta Alpha Psi, Beta Gamma Sigma, Phi Kappa Phi. Home: 11635 Arrowwood Cir Houston TX 77063-1401 Office: Vinson & Elkins First City Tower 1001 Fannin St Ste 2300 Houston TX 77002-6706 E-mail: arobin@velaw.com.

**ROBIN, CLARA NELL (CLAIRE ROBIN),** English language educator; b. Harrisonburg, Va., Feb. 19, 1945; d. Robert Franklin and Marguerite Ausherman (Long) Wampler; m. Phil Camden Branner, June 10, 1967 (div. May 1984); m. John Charles Robin, Nov. 22, 1984 (div. Dec. 1990) BA English, Mary Washington Coll., 1967; MA English, James Madison U., 1974; postgrad., Jesus Coll., Cambridge, Eng., 1982, Princeton U., 1985—86, Auburn U., 1988, U. No. Tex., 1990—91. Cert. tchr. English, French, master cert., Tex. Tchr. 7th grade John C. Myers Intermediate Sch., Broadway, Va., 1967—68; tchr. 10th grade Waynesville H.S., Mo., 1968—70; tchr. 6th, 7th, 8th grades Mary Mount Jr. H.S., Santa Barbara, Calif., 1970—72; tchr. 9th grade Forest Meadow Jr. H.S. Richardson Ind. Sch. Dist., Tex., 1972—78, tchr. 10th grade Lake Highlands H.S., 1972—84; tchr. 11th, 12th grades Burleson H.S. Burleson Ind. Sch. Dist., Tex., 1986—2003; tchr. 9th and 10th grade English Ft. Worth Country Day Sch., 2003—. Instr. composition Hill Coll., 1989-90 Contbg. author (book revs.) English lit., 1989-91, (lit. criticism) Eric, 1993 Vol. Dallas Theater Crit., 1990—96; active Kimbell Art Mus., Ft. Worth, 1990—, Modern Art Mus., Ft. Worth, 1992—, KERA Pub. TV, Dallas, 1990—; Amon Carter Mus., Ft. Worth, 2001—. Fellow NEH, 1988, 89, 92, 95, Fulbright-Hays Summer Seminar Abroad, 1991; ind. study grantee Coun. Basic Ednl., 1990; recipient Chpt. Achievement award Epsilon Nu Delta Kappa Gamma, 1993, Hon. Mention Tex. Outstanding Tchg. of Humanities award, 1995, Burleson Ind. Sch. Dist., Campus Ednl. Improvement Com., 1997-2000, Dist. Ednl. Improvement Com., 1998-2001 Mem.: Tex. State Reading Assn., Nat. Coun. Tchrs. English (spring conf. presenter 2000, 2002), Epsilon Nu of Delta Kappa Gamma (1st v.p. 1988—94, v.p. 1992—94, profl. affairs com. 1996—98, comms. chair 1994—). Avocations: bicycling, travel, reading, writing, landscaping. Home: 4009 W 6th St Fort Worth TX 76107-1619 Office: Ft Worth Country Day Sch 4200 Country Day Ln Fort Worth TX 76109-4299 Office Phone: 817-302-3203 ext. 102. Personal E-mail: crbkrd@aol.com. Business E-Mail: crobin@fwcds.org.

**ROBINETT, BETTY WALLACE,** linguist, educator; b. Detroit, June 23, 1919; d. Henry Guy and Beulah (Reid) Wallace; m. Ralph F. Robinett, Apr. 10, 1952 (div. 1960); 1 child, Richard Wallace. BA, Wayne State U., 1940; MA, U. Mich., 1941, PhD, 1951. Instr., adminstrv. asst. English Lang. Inst., U. Mich., Ann Arbor, 1945-50; cons. Dept. Edn., San Juan, P.R., 1950-51, 52-57; lectr. English, U. Mich., 1951-52, 55-56; asso. prof. English InterAm. U., San German, P.R., 1957-59; asst. prof. English and linguistics Ball State U., Muncie, Ind., 1959-63, assoc. prof. English and linguistics, 1963-67, prof., 1967-68; prof. dept. linguistics U. Minn., Mpls., 1968-88, dir. program in English as a second lang., 1968-80, acting asst. v.p. acad. affairs, 1979-80, asst. v.p. acad. affairs, 1980-84, assoc. v.p. acad. affairs, 1984-88, prof. emerita, 1988, Morse alumni disting. tchg. prof. emerita, 1996; chmn. Univ. Senate Consultative Com., 1977-78. Vis. prof. Pa. State U., 1994-95; chmn. adv. panel on English tchg. USIA, 1988-93. Author: (with C.H. Prator) Manual of American English Pronunciation, 1972, 4th edit., 1985, Teaching English to Speakers of Other Languages, Substance and Technique, 1978, (with J. Schachter) Second Language Learning: Contrastive Analysis, Error Analysis and Related Aspects, 1983, (with Virginia F. Allen) Easy Latin Crossword Puzzles: Quid Pro Quo, 1999, Easy French Crossword Puzzles: Le mot Juste, 2002; editor Tesol Quar., 1967-72. Internat. Programs travel

grantee, 1972, 77; recipient Morse-Amoco award for Excellence in Teaching, 1977 Mem. Tchrs. English to Speakers of Other Langs. (pres. 1974, James Alatis Svc. award 1990), Assn. Tchrs. ESL (chmn. 1976-77), Am. Assn. Applied Linguistics (v.p., pres. 1980-82), Linguistic Soc. Am. (life). Home: 1936 Park Forest Ave State College PA 16803-1329 E-mail: brobin4049@aol.com.

**ROBINOV, JEFF,** film company executive; Literary agent Internat. Creative Mgmt., 1992—97; with Warner Bros. Pictures, 1997—, exec. v.p. prodn., pres. prodn., 2002—. Exec. prodr.: (films) On Deadly Ground, 1994. Office: Warner Bros Entertainment Inc 4000 Warner Blvd Burbank CA 91522 Office Phone: 818-954-6000.*

**ROBINS, DAVID,** chef; Chef Stars restaurant, San Francisco; mng. ptnr., corp. chef Wolfgang Puck Fine Dining Grp., Las Vegas. Avocations: travel, softball, tennis. Office: Spago Las Vegas 3500 Las Vegas Blvd S Las Vegas NV 89109*

**ROBINS, JOEL,** import/export company executive; Pres. Robbins Trading Co., Chgo., 1983—. Office: Robbins Trading Co 8700 W Bryn Mawr Ave Ste 760 Chicago IL 60631-3512

**ROBINS, LEE NELKEN,** medical educator; b. New Orleans, Aug. 29, 1922; d. Abe and Leona (Reiman) Nelken; m. Eli Robins, Feb. 22, 1946 (dec. Dec. 1994); children: Paul, James, Thomas, Nicholas; m. Hugh Chaplin, Aug. 5, 1998. Student, Newcomb Coll., 1938-40; BA, Radcliffe Coll., 1942, MA, 1943; PhD, Harvard U., 1951. Mem. faculty Washington U., St. Louis, 1954—, prof. sociology in psychiatry, 1968-91, prof. sociology, 1969-91, prof. social sci. and social sci. in psychiatry, 1991-2000, prof. emeritus, 2001—. Past mem. Nat. Adv. Coun. on Drug Abuse; past mem. task panels Pres.'s Commn. on Mental Health; mem. expert adv. panel on mental health WHO; Salmon lectr. NY Acad. Medicine, 1983; Cutter lectr. Harvard U., 1997. Author: Deviant Children Grown Up, 1966; editor 11 books; mem. editl. bd. Psychol. Medicine, Jour. Studies on Alcohol, Social Psychiatry and Psychiatric Epidemiology, Epidemiol. e Psichiat. Sociale; contbr. articles to profl. jours. Recipient Rsch. Scientist award USPHS, 1970-90, Pacesetter Rsch. award Nat. Inst. Drug Abuse, 1978, Radcliffe Coll. Grad. Soc. medal, 1979, Sutherland award Am. Soc. Criminology, 1991, Nathan B. Eddy award Com. on Problems of Drug Dependence, 1993, Spl. Presdl. Commendation Am. Psychiat. Assn., 1999, Am. Acad. Arts and Scis., 1999, Commendation and Appreciation award Harvard Inst. Psychiat. Epidemiology and Genetics, 2000, Disting. Sci. Devel. award Soc. Rsch. in Child Devel., 2003, Peter Raven Lifetime award Acad. Sci. St. Louis, 2006; rsch. grantee NIMH, Nat. Inst. on Drug Abuse, Nat. Inst. on Alcohol Abuse and Alcoholism. Fellow Am. Coll. Epidemiology, Royal Coll. Psychiatrists (hon.), Am. Soc. Psychiatrists (hon.), Soc. Study of Addiction (hon.); mem. APHA (Rema Lapouse award 1979, Lifetime Achievement award sect. on alcohol and drug abuse 1994), Internat. Fedn. Psychiat. Epidemiology (com.1992-2002), World Psychiat. Assn. (sect. com. on epidemiology and cmty. psychiatry, 1985-2002, co-chmn. sect. on rsch. instruments in psychiatry), Soc. Life History Rsch. in Psychopathology, Am. Coll. Neuropsychopharmacology, Inst. Medicine, Am. Psychopath. Assn. (pres. 1987-88, Paul Hoch award 1978), World Innovation Found. (hon. mem. 2004). Office: Washington U Med Sch Dept Psychiatry Saint Louis MO 63110 Business E-Mail: robinsl@psychiatry.wustl.edu.

**ROBINS, MITCHELL JAMES,** management consultant; b. Detroit, May 23, 1956; s. Melvin M. Robins and Judith (Bell) Martin; m. Amy Elizabeth Green, July 2, 1978; children: Alexander Philip, Sean Lewis, Emily Dinah. BBA, U. Mich., 1977; postgrad., U. Detroit, Oakland U. CPA, Mich., Fla., Ind., Nev., Calif. Exec. mgr. GM; founder, mng. ptnr., CEO Robins-Assocs., CPAs and Cons., Southfield, Mich., 1981—, founder, mng. ptnr. La Jolla, Calif., 1980—; founder, mgr., ptnr. Lumedics, Ltd., La Jolla, Calif., Paris. Bd. dirs. Campus Distbn., Inc., Ann Arbor, Mich., Internat. Med.-Dental Hypnotherapy Assn., LumeDics Ltd., San Diego; mem. Restaurant Bus. Research Adv. Panel, N.Y.C. Mem. steering com. Rep. 300 Com. of Mich., Oakland County, zoning bd. appeals City of Farmington Hills, Rep. Senatorial Inner Circle; mem. Carmel Valley Planning Bd., 1997. Named Nat. Rep. Congl. Com. Businessman of the Yr., 1999. Mem. AICPA, ABA, Mich. Assn. CPA's, Mich. Soc. Planning Ofcls., Assn. MBA Execs., U. Mich. Alumni Assn., Internat. Platform Assn. Clubs: Economic (Detroit), Detroit Athletic, Heritage Hills Country, Skyline. Republican. Avocations: golf, tennis, history, politics, travel. Home: 12885 Ralston Cir San Diego CA 92130-2447 Fax: 858-551-1215. E-mail: mrobinsooo@usa.net.

**ROBINS, NORMAN ALAN,** management consultant, retired metal products executive; b. Chgo., Nov. 19, 1934; s. Irving and Sylvia (Robbin) Robins; m. Sandra Ross, June 10, 1956; children: Lawrence Richard, Sherry Lynn. BSChemE, MIT, 1955, MSChemE, 1956; PhD in Math., Ill. Inst. Tech., 1972. Asst. mgr. process sys. and controls Inland Steel Co., East Chicago, Ind., 1962—67, assoc. mgr. process sys. and controls 1967—72, dir. process rsch., 1972—77, v.p. rsch., 1977—84, v.p. technol. assessment, 1984—86, v.p. strategic planning, 1986—91; ret., 1991; ind. cons. in strategic planning, 1991—. Mem. bd. edn. Homewood-Flossmoor HS, Ill., 1974—77. Mem.: AIChE, Assn. Iron and Steel Tech. (Nat. Open Hearth Conf. award 1972).

**ROBINS, ROBERT SIDWAR,** political science professor, department chairman; b. Spangler, Pa., Apr. 20, 1938; s. Sydney and Katherine (Sidwar) R.; m. Marjorie McGann, Nov. 25, 1959; children: Anthony P., Nicholas A. BA, U. Pitts., 1959; MA, Duke U., 1961, PhD, 1963. Prof. polit. sci. Tulane U., New Orleans, 1965—, comm. dept. polit. sci., 1979-90, dep. provost, 1991-98. Acad. visitor Inst. Commonwealth Studies, U. London, 1969-70, 78-79, mem. 1987-88; sr. assoc. mem. St, Antony's Coll. Oxford, Eng., 1977-78, vis. scholar Hastings Ctr., 1982; vis. scientist Tavistock Clinic, London, 1987-88. Author: Political Institutionalization and the Integration of Elites, 1976 (Carnegie Commn. report) Legislative Attitudes Toward Higher Education in Louisiana, 1968, Psychopathology and Political Leadership, 1977, Disease and Political Leadership, 1990; co-author: When Illness Strikes the Leader, Political Paranoia; contbr. articles to profl. publs. Vice chmn. Elections Integrity Commn., State of La., 1981-82; mem. Stamford (Conn.) Rep. Town Com. Recipient Excellence in Tchg. award Tulane U., 1978; Fulbright scholar, 1961-62. Mem. Am. Polit. Sci. Assn., Internat. Soc. Polit. Psychology. Avocations: carpentry, gardening. Home: 64 Pond Rd Stamford CT 06902 Office Phone: 203-323-2935. E-mail: robins_06902@yahoo.com.

**ROBINSON, ALEXANDER JACOB,** retired psychologist; b. St. John, Kans., Nov. 7, 1920; s. Oscar Frank and Lydia May (Beitler) R.; m. Elsie Louise Riggs, July 29, 1942; children: Madelyn K., Alicia A., David J., Charles A., Paul S., Marietta J., Stephen N. BA in Psychology, Ft. Hays State U., Kans., 1942, MS in Clin. Psychology, 1942; postgrad., U. Ill., 1942-44. Cert. psychologist, sch. psychologist. Chief psychologist Larned (Kans.) State Hosp., 1948-53, with employee selection, outpatient services, 1953-55; sch. psychologist County Schs., Modesto, Calif., 1955-61, Pratt (Kans.) Jr. Coll., 1961-66; fed. grantee, writer assoc. dir. Exemplary Federally Funded Program for Spl. Edn., Pratt, 1966-70; dir. spl. edn., researcher Stafford County Schs., St. John, 1970-81, ret., 1981. Supr. testing and data Incidence of Exceptional Children in Kansas, Kans. State U., Ft. Hays, 1946; writer, asst. dir. Best Exemplary Federally Funded Program on Spl. Edn., Pratt, 1966-70; fed. grantee, researcher, writer, study dir. Edn. for the High-Performance Child, St. John, 1970—, Psychogenesis of the Sociopathic Personality, a longitudinal study. Minister, The Ch. of Jesus Christ. Served to 2d lt. U.S. Army, 1944-46, PTO. Mem. N.Y. Acad. Scis., Libr. of Congress. Lodges: Lions (program chmn. St. John 1974-76). Achievements include research in normal children with a learning disability and their specific developmental requirement. Avocations: history, ethnology, anthropology, music, literature. Home and Office: 402 E 1st Saint John KS 67576 Office Phone: 620-549-3373.

**ROBINSON, AMINAH BRENDA LYNN,** artist, illustrator; b. Columbus, Ohio, Feb. 18, 1940; d. Leroy Edward William and Helen Elizabeth (Zimmerman) R.; m. Clarence Adrian Robinson (div. 1981); 1 child, Sydney

Edward (dec. July 17, 1994). Student, Columbus Coll. of Art & Design, 1956-60, Ohio State U., 1960-61, Franklin U., 1961-62, Bliss Coll., 1963. Asst. libr., illustrator, artist Ohio Pub. Libr., Columbus, 1958-64; draftsman Mountain State Telephone Co., Boise, Idaho, 1964-66; illustrator TV Oper. Br. TV, Miss., 1966-67; sr. illustrator N.Am. Rockwell Corp., Columbus, 1971; with City Recreation and Pks. Dept., Columbus, 1972—. Lectr. to numerous orgns., 1971—; spkr. numerous workshops, 1970—. One woman shows include Otterbein Coll., Worthington, Ohio, 1982, 89, 91, Columbus Mus. Art, 1983, 90, 2003, Esther Saks Gallery, Chgo., 1984, Akron Art Mus., 1987, 88, So. Ohio Mus., Portsmouth, 1990, U. Wis., Greenbay, 1990, Museo Nacional de Bellas Artes, Santiago, 2004; exhibited in group shows at Wexner Art Ctr., Columbus, 1992, Nat. Mus. Women in the Arts, Washington, 1990, 91, Memphis Brooks Mus. Art, 1991; represented in permanent collections Cin. Art Mus., Newark Art Mus., Otterbein Coll., Nat. Underground R.R. Freedom Ctr.; numerous others; seried artist: Pages in History, 1981-, Afrikan Pilgrimage: the Extended Family, Sapelo Series, New York Stories, People of the Book, Chilean Suite; author: A Street Called Home; illustrator: Elijah's Angel, 1992, Sophie, 1994, A School for Pompey Walker, 1995, To Be A Drum, 1998. Ohio Arts Coun. fellow 1979-80, 86-87, 88-89, 991-92, Travel-Study fellow Am. Forum for Internat. Study, 1979, PSI Residency fellow, 1989; resident Israel, 1998, Santiago, Chile, 2004; recipient Gov.'s award for the visual arts in Ohio, 1984, Columbus Star of 1980 Achievement award, 1980; named Outstanding Citizen in the Community, Nat. Epicureans, 1974, named a MacArthur Fellow, 2004.

**ROBINSON, AMORIE ALEXIA,** psychologist, educator; b. Detroit, Oct. 19, 1956, d. David Everett Robinson, II and Jane Marian Robinson; m. Hattie Corine Francis, Oct. 17, 2001. BA in Psychology, Oberlin Coll., Ohio, 1978; MA in Ednl. Psychology, U. Mich., 1979, PhD in Clin. Psychology, 1996. Dir. counseling svcs. Lewis Coll. Bus., Detroit, 1981—84; admissions counselor U. Detroit, 1984—89; forensic psychologist Recorders Ct. Psychiat. Clinic, Detroit, 1996—2002; psychotherapist Counseling Assocs., Farmington Hills, Mich., 1996—; guest lectr. U. Mich., Ann Arbor, 2002—. Adv. bd. Gay Lesbian Straight Edn. Network, Detroit, 2004—; co-founder Com. for Study of Culture, Class and Mental Health, U. Mich., 1990—96; condr. workshops in field; lectr. in field; designer Kofi Kards. Illustrator, cartoonist children's coloring books, 1975—2004; author: There's A Stranger in This House: African American Lesbians and Domestic Violence in Battered Black and Blue: Violence in the Lives of Black Women, 2000, Misunderstood, Misled, & Misfit: The Marginalization Experiences of African American Lesbian Youth, 2000. Co-founder, v.p. bd. dirs. Ruth Ellis Ctr., Detroit, 1999—; co-founder, pres., bd. dirs. Karibu House, Detroit, 1997—; co-founder, bd. dirs. African-Am. Lesbians Organized to Renew Dignity and Empowerment, Detroit, 1994—, Unity Fellowship Ch., Detroit, 1989—. Recipient Catalyst Activist award, Triangle Found., Detroit, 2001, Lorraine Hansberry award, Affirmations Gay and Lesbian Cmty. Ctr., 1997, Coretta Scott-King Black Achievement award, Alpha Phi Alpha, 1989; fellow half-term fellow, U. Mich., 1994—95, Rackham Minority Merit fellow, 1989—95. Mem.: APA (Sci. Directorate award 1993), Detroit Metro Assn. Black Psychologists (sec. 1997—, Outstanding Svc. award 2002), Assn. for Women in Psychology (suite coord. 1993—95). Avocations: violin, tennis, African drumming. Office: Counseling Associates 33045 Hamilton Ct #W-300 Farmington Hills MI 48334 Business E-Mail: kofi@umich.edu.

**ROBINSON, ANDREA J.,** lawyer; b. 1960; AB magna cum laude, Harvard Univ., 1981; JD, Univ. Va., 1984. Bar: NY 1985, DC 1988, Mass. 1990. Atty. Debevoise & Plimpton, NYC, Washington; ptnr., Litigation dept. Wilmer Cutler Pickering Hale & Dorr, Boston, 1990—, co-vice chmn., Securities dept. Spl. asst. dist. atty. Middlesex County, Mass., 1994. Named a Mass. Super Lawyer, Boston Mag., 2004, Top 50 Female Mass. Super Lawyer, 2004. Mem.: ABA, Boston Bar Assn., Phi Beta Kappa, Order of the Coif. Office: Wilmer Cutler Pickering Hale & Dorr 60 State St Boston MA 02109 Office Phone: 617-526-6360. Office Fax: 617-526-5000. Business E-Mail: andrea.robinson@wilmerhale.com.

**ROBINSON, ANTHONY CHRISTOPHER,** novelist, educator; b. Biskupitz, Germany, Mar. 10, 1931; came to U.S., 1931; s. Henry Morton and Gertrude (Ludwig) R.; m. Mary Chika, Nov. 16, 1957 (dec. Mar. 1976); children: Jennifer Eve, Henry David; m. Tatiana Padwa, Feb. 14, 1998. BA, Columbia Coll., N.Y.C., 1953; MA cum laude, Columbia U., 1960; grad., Phillips Acad., Andover, Mass., 1949. Prof. English, dir. creative writing SUNY, New Paltz, 1964-2000, prof. English emeritus, 2000—. Vis. prof. U. Paris, 1971-72. Author: A Departure From the Rules, 1960 (Bread Loaf fellow 1960), The Easy Way, 1963, Home Again, Home Again, 1969, The Whole Truth, 1990, The Member-Guest, 1991. Lt. USNR, 1953-56. Democrat. Roman Catholic. Avocations: golf, fly fishing, golf club making, hiking. Home: 153 Huguenot St New Paltz NY 12561 E-mail: robinsoa@newpaltz.edu.

**ROBINSON, ARCHIE STIRLING,** lawyer; b. Long Beach, Calif., May 28, 1939; s. Wendell Stirling and Bonnie Mae (Noble) R.; m. Joy Young; children— Jennifer, Christopher, Matthew, Benjamin. A.B., Columbia U., 1960; J.D., Stanford U., 1963. Bar: Calif. 1964, U.S. Dist. Ct. (no. dist.) Calif. 1964, U.S. Ct. Appeals (9th cir.) 1964; Mng. ptnr. Robinson & Wood, Inc. and predecessors, San Jose, Calif., 1964—; pres. Def. Rsch. Inst. Chmn., bd. dirs. City Team Ministries; bd. dirs. Good Samaritan Hosp., bd. dirs. Advent Group Ministries; trustee Saratoga Federated Ch. Mem. ABA, Calif. State Bar Assn., Santa Clara County Bar Assn., Assn. Def. Counsel (past pres.), Am. Coll. Trial Lawyers, Calif. Def. Counsel (pres.), Assn. Ins. Attys., Am. Bd. Trial Advs., Internat. Assn. Ins. Counsel, Fedn. Ins. Counsel, San Jose C. of C., Assn. Calif. Tort Reform (bd. dirs.), Democrat Club: Stanford Golf (past pres.), Saint Claire (San Jose), San Jose Athletic. Contbr. numerous articles to profl. jours. Office: 227 N 1st St Ste 300 San Jose CA 95113-1003 Office Phone: 408-298-7120. E-mail: asr@robinsonwood.com

**ROBINSON, BARBARA PAUL,** lawyer; b. Oct. 19, 1941; d. Leo and Pauline G. Paul; m. Charles Raskob Robinson, June 11, 1965; children: Charles Paul, Torrance Webster. AB magna cum laude, Bryn Mawr Coll., 1962; LLB, Yale U., 1965, Order of the Coif. Bar: N.Y. 1966, U.S. Dist. Ct. (so. and ea. dists.) N.Y. 1975, U.S. Tax Ct. 1972, U.S. Ct. Appeals (2d cir.) 1974. Assoc. Debevoise & Plimpton LLP, NYC, 1966-75, ptnr., 1976—, with Trusts and Estates Dept.; commr. Mayor's Commn. on Women's Issues, 2002—. Mem. adv. bd. Practicing Law Inst.; bd. dirs. Am. Arbitration Assn., 1997—2003. Mem. bd. editors: Chase Jour., 1997—2001; contbr. articles to profl. jours. Mem. adv. coun., bd. vis. CUNY Law Sch., Queens, 1984—90; active Coun. on Fgn. Rels.; trustee Trinity Sch., 1982—88, pres., 1986—88; bd. dirs. Found. for Child Devel., 1988—2000, 2001—, chmn., 1991—2000; bd. dirs. Catalyst, 1993—, treas., 1993—; bd. dirs. Fund for Modern Cts., 1994—2003, Wave Hill, 1994—, Garden Conservancy, 1996—2002, Lawyers Com. for Civil Rights Under Law, 1997—2003, William Nelson Cromwell Found., 1993—, Irish Legal Rsch. Found. Inc., 1996—, Citizens Union Found. Inc., 1996—2004, Am. Friends Brit. Mus., 2003—, The Ocean Conservancy, 2004—, Teagle Found., 2005—, The Grumwald Found., 2006—, The John A. Found., 2006—; trustee Bryn Mawr Coll., 2000—. Recipient Laura Parsons Pratt award, 1996. Fellow Am. Coll. Trust and Estate Counsel, Am. Bar Found., N.Y. Bar Found.; mem. ABA (commn. on women in profession 1999-2002), N.Y. State Bar Assn. (vice chmn. com. on trust adminstrn., trusts and estates law sect. 1977-81, ho. of dels. 1984-87, 90-92, com. ann. award 1993-94), Assn. of Bar of City of N.Y. (chmn. com. on trusts, estates and surrogates ct. 1981-84, judiciary com. 1981-84, coun. on jud. adminstrn. 1982-84, chair nominating com. 1984-85, 99-2000, exec. com. 1986-91, chair 1989-90, v.p. 1990-91, Found. com. on honors 1993-94, com. on long-range planning 1991-94, co-chair coun. on childen 1997-98, pres. 1994-96), Assn. of Bar of City of N.Y. Fund Inc. (bd. dirs. 2000-03, pres. 1994-96), Women's Forum, Yale Coun., Yale Law Sch. Assn. N.Y. (devel. bd., exec. com. 1981-85, 93—, pres. 1988-93), The Century Assn., Yale Club, Washington Club. Office: Debevoise & Plimpton LLP 919 Third Ave New York NY 10022 Office Phone: 212-909-6325. Business E-Mail: bprobinson@debevoise.com.

**ROBINSON, BARRY R.,** lawyer; b. Dover, Ohio, Dec. 8, 1946; AB, Princeton U., 1969; JD cum laude, Ohio State U., 1972. Bar: Ohio 1972. Ptnr. Baker & Hostetler, Columbus, Ohio. Fellow Am. Coll. Trust and Estate Counsel; mem. ABA, Ohio State Bar Assn., Columbus Bar Assn. Office: Baker & Hostetler Capital Sq 65 E State St Ste 2100 Columbus OH 43215-4260

**ROBINSON, BERNARD PAHL,** retired thoracic surgeon, educator; b. NYC, Apr. 12, 1919; s. Nathaniel and Augusta (Strauss) R.; m. Gloria Joyce Rehfuss, Oct. 3, 1943; children: Lawrence, Andrew. BS, NYU, 1938; MD, L.I. Coll. Medicine, 1942. Diplomate Am. Bd. Surgery, Am. Bd. Thoracic Surgery. Intern Mount Sinai Hosp., N.Y.C., 1942-43, resident in surgery, 1946-47, Beth Israel Hosp., Boston, 1948-49; resident in thoracic surgery VA Hosp, Castle Point, N.Y., 1949-50; assoc. attending surgeon Mt. Sinai Hosp., N.Y.C., 1956—; asst. clin. prof. surgery Mt. Sinai Sch. Medicine, N.Y.C., 1968—. Capt. U.S. Army, 1943-46. Fellow Am. Coll. Surgeons, Am. Coll. Chest Physicians; mem. N.Y. Soc. for Thoracic Surgery. Jewish. Avocations: sailing, golf, photography, travel.

**ROBINSON, BROOKS CALBERT, JR.,** former professional baseball player, sports commentator, business consultant; b. Little Rock, May 18, 1937; s. Brooks Calbert and Ethel (Denker) R.; m. Constance Louise Butcher, Oct. 8, 1960; children— Brooks David, Christopher Leslie, Michael Patrick, Diana Agnes. Student, U. Little Rock, 1956-57. Profl. baseball player Balt. Orioles, 1955-77; sports commentator for Baltimore Oriole Games Sta. WMAR-TV, Balt., 1978-90; spl. asst. mktg. dept. Crown Central Petroleum Corp., 1979—; v.p. Personal Mgmt. Assocs., 1979—; spl. asst. Crown Ctrl. Petroleum Co. Selected Most Valuable Oriole, 1960, 62, 64, 71; named Am. League's Most Valuable Player, 1964, Most Valuable Player in Major League All-Star game at St. Louis, 1966; Most Valuable Player, 1970 World Series; recipient Hickock Athlete of Yr. award, 1970; Balt. Decade award, 1970; mem. World Series Championship Team, 1965, 70; named to Baseball Hall of Fame, Cooperstown, N.Y. Office: Crown Ctrl PO Box 1168 Petroleum Corp/Dept Mktg 1 N Charles St Ste 1168 Baltimore MD 21201-3740*

**ROBINSON, CATHY D.,** science educator; m. Chuck Robinson; children: Catherine, Tommy, Richie. BS in Med. Tech., U. So. Miss., Hattiesburg, 1974; MS in Adminstrn., Ctrl. Mich. U., Mt. Pleasant, 2004. Lab. dir. Dynacare Labs., Alexandria, La., 1999—2001; dir. phlebotomy program La. State U., 2001—. Mem. Jr. League Alexandria, La., 1990—2006, First United Meth. Ch., Alexandria, 1974—2006; sec. Ctrl. LA Soc. Med. Technologists, 1995—2006; editor state newsletter La. Soc. Clin. Lab. Sci., Monroe, 2005—06. Recipient Presdl. Svc. award, La. Soc. Clin. Lab. Sci., 2006. Mem.: ASCP (assoc.). Office: Louisiana State University at Alexandria 8100 Hwy 71 South Alexandria LA 71302 Office Phone: 318-427-4474. Business E-Mail: crobinson@lsua.edu

**ROBINSON, CHARLES PAUL,** nuclear energy industry executive, diplomat; b. Detroit, Oct. 9, 1941; s. Edward Leonard and Mary Opal (Edmondson) R.; m. Barbara Thomas Woodard; children by previous marriage: Paula S., Colin C. BS in Physics, Christian Bros. U., 1963; PhD in Physics, Fla. State U., 1967; doctorate (hon.), Christian Brothers U. Mem. nuclear test staff Los Alamos (N.Mex.) Nat. Lab., 1967-69, chief test operator, 1969-70, mem. advanced concepts staff, 1971-72, assoc. div. leader, lasers, 1972-76, div. leader, 1976-79, assoc. dir., 1980-85; v.p., p., bd. dirs. Ebasco Services Inc. subs. Enserch Corp., N.Y.C., 1985-88; ambass. to nuclear testing talks U.S. Dept. State, Geneva, 1988-90; v.p. Sandia Nat. Labs., Albuquerque, 1990-95, pres., 1995—2005; capture exec. Lockheed Martin Corp., 2005—. Instr. U. N.Mex., Los Alamos, 1974-76; mem. sci. adv. group Def. Nuclear Agy., Washington, 1981-86; mem. nat. security bd. Los Alamos Nat. Lab., 1985-88; chmn. Presdl. Tech. Adv. Bd., 1991; mem. U.S. Strategic Command Adv. Bd.; bd. dirs. Wells Fargo Bank, Tech. Ventures Corp., Fla. State U. Rsch. Found.; trustee Kazakhstan Nonproliferation Inst. Mem. strategic adv. group for comdr. U.S. Strategic Command; chmn. policy panel, tech. adv. group Verification of Warhead Dismantlement and Spl. Nuc. Materials Controls; mem. threat reduction adv. com. Dept. Def., exec. bd. Boy Scouts of N.Mex. Recipient Outstanding Pub. Svc. medal Joint Chiefs of Staff, 1996. Mem. Am. Phys. Soc. (Pake Prize 2003), Am. Nuclear Soc., NAE. Achievements include testifing before Congress more than 80 times. Avocation: choral singing. Office: Lockheed Martin 1155 Univ Blvd SE Albuquerque NM 87106 Office Phone: 505-843-4153. Business E-Mail: c.p.robinson@lmco.com, c.probinson@lmco.com

**ROBINSON, CHARLOTTE HILL,** artist; b. San Antonio, Nov. 28, 1924; d. Lucius Davis and Charlotte (Moore) Hill; m. Floyd I. Robinson, Mar. 1943; children: Floyd I. Jr., Lawrence H., Elizabeth H. Student, Incarnate Word Coll., 1942—45, NYU, 1947-48, Corcoran Sch. Art, 1951-52. Painting instr. Art League No. Va., Alexandria, 1967-75. Condr. Art World Seminar Washington Women's Art Ctr., 1975-80, drawing workshop Smithsonian Instn. Resident Assocs. Program, Washington, 1977; program dir. Nat. Women's Caucus for Art, 1979; project coord.; exhbn. curator The Artist and the Quilt, nat. mus. traveling exhbn., 1983-86; vis. artist S.W. Craft Ctr., San Antonio, 1983-85; lectr. WFUV 90 FM, Fordham U., NYC, 1990, San Antonio Art Inst., 1991, Nat. Mus. for Women in Arts, Washington, 1991, Iowa State U., Ames, 1991; panelist Nat. Mus. Women in Arts, 1997, Woman and the Arts, Douglass Coll./ Rutgers U., 1998, Washington Women's Caucus for Art at the Millenium Art Ctr., 2001. Editor: The Artist & The Quilt, 1983; one-person shows include Thames Sic. Ctr., New London, Conn., 1991, Brunner Gallery & Mus., Iowa State U., 1991, 92, San Antonio Art. Inst., 1991, Fordham U., 1991, de Andino Fine Arts, Washington, 1992, Masur Mus. Art, Monroe, La., 1993, 96, 2001, Lee Hansley Art Gallery, Raleigh, NC, 1993, 97, 2001, Sol Del Rio, San Antonio, 1995, 97-98, 1812 Artic Gallery, Virginia Beach, Va., 1995, Savannah Coll. Art and Design, 1997, Duke U. Sch. Law, 1998, No. Va. CC, 1999, McLean Project for the Arts, 2002, Southwest Sch. Art & Craft, San Antonio, 2003; exhibited in group shows at Franklin Square and Watkins Gallery, Washington, 1992, Rutgers U., New Brunswick, NJ, 1992, 96, 98, Brody's Gallery, Washington, 1992, Lee Hansley Art Gallery, Raleigh, 1993, 96, 98-2001, 02, 03, 05, 06, Emerson Gallery, McLean, 1993, 95, 99, No. Va. CC, 1994, 99, Harvard U., 1996, Ceres Gallery, NYC, 1999-2000, Millennium Art Ctr., Washington, 2001, Am. Ctr. Physics, 2003. Trustee Bronx Mus., NY, 1977; bd. dirs. Washington Women's Art Ctr., 1977, New Art Examiner, 1985-86; nat. bd. dirs. Women's Caucus for Art, 1983-84. Recipient Concourse award Corcoran Sch. Art, 1952; Telfair Acad. Art scholar, Savannah, Ga., 1959; Nat. Endowment for Arts grantee, 1977-81; fellow Va. Ctr. for Creative Arts, Sweet Briar, Va., 1985. Address: Lee Hansley Gallery 225 Glenwood Ave Raleigh NC 27603 Office Phone: 703-941-3865. E-mail: bjohnb@mchs1.com, chardyrob@cox.net.

**ROBINSON, CHRIS (CHRIS MARK ROBINSON),** musician; b. Atlanta, Dec. 20, 1966; m. Kate Hudson, Dec. 31, 2000 (separated Aug. 2006); 1 child, Ryder. Co-founder & lead singer Mr. Crowe's Garden (name changed to Black Crowes), 1985—. Singer (albums) Shake Your Money Maker, 1990 (Album of Yr. Internat. Rock Awards 1991, double platinum record 1991), The Southern Harmony and Musical Companion, 1992, Amorica, 1994, Three Snakes and One Charm, 1996, Souled Out Live, 1998, By Your Side, 1999, Lions, 2001, Live, 2002, The Lost Crows, 2006, Freak N Roll...into the Fog, 2006; solo albums New Earth Mud, 2002, This Magnificent Distance, 2004; guest appearances include Saturday Night Live, 1991, 1992, Kids in the Hall, 1995; actor (films) Medicine Chest, 2004. Recipient (with Black Crowes) Grammy award nomination for Best New artist, 1991; voted Best New Am. band Rolling Stone readers and critics polls; named Artist of Yr., 1991.*

**ROBINSON, CHRISTINA ANNE,** secondary school educator; d. John Filmore and Catherine Lavona Neese; m. James Howard Jr. Robinson, July 31, 1971; 1 child, James Howard III. BS, Ind. State U., Terre Haute, 1971. Tchr. Ctr. Grove Jr. High, Greenwood, Ind., 1973—75; mgr. Emma Parrish

Theatre, Titusville, Fla., 1983—85; tchr. Cocoa HS, Fla., 1992—97, Astronaut HS, Titusville, 1997—. Named Tchr. of Yr., Cocoa HS, 1994, Wal-Mart, Titusville, 2005. Office: Astronaut High Sch 800 War Eagle Blvd Titusville FL 32796

**ROBINSON, CHRISTINE MARIE,** mathematics professor; b. Savannah, Ga. d. Aaron Sr. and Lucille (Jones) Williams; m. Amos Robinson, Aug. 2, 1953; children: Michael Anthony, Pamela Michele. BS in Math. magna cum laude, Savannah State U., 1951; MA, U. Mich., 1965. Instr. in math. Chatham County Bd. of Instruction, Savannah, 1951-64, Duval County Bd. of Instruction, Jacksonville, Fla., 1964-71, master and resource tchr., 1971-76; prof. math. Fla. C.C., Jacksonville, 1976-99, ret., 1999. Mem. faculty task force Fla. Dept. Edn./Fla. Assn. C.C., Tallahassee, 1979-81; on-site coord. Fla. Devel. Edn. Assn. Conv., Jacksonville, 1986; chmn. Fla. C.C. EA/EO Com., Jacksonville, 1988, 89. Mem. YWCA, Jacksonville, 1989—; vol. driver Wheels for Cancer-AKA Sorority, Jacksonville, 1986; chmn. United Way, Jacksonville, 1987. Recipient Outstanding Faculty Mem. award, Fla. C.C., 1987, Tchg. Excellence award, U. Tex., 1988; grantee, NSF; scholar, U. Mich., U. Ill. Mem. Am. Math. Assn. Two-Yr. Colls., Fla. Devel. Edn. Assn. (bd. dirs. Jacksonville chpt. 1983-86), Fla. Assn. C.C., Math. Assn. Am., So. Assn. Colls. and Schs. (Fla. com.), LWV, Alpha Kappa Alpha. Democrat. Roman Catholic. Avocations: reading, piano, dance, bicycling. Home: 7426 Simms Dr Jacksonville FL 32209-1023

**ROBINSON, CLEO PARKER,** artistic director; Degree in Dance Edn. Psychology, Denver U., DFA (hon.), 1991. Founder, exec. artistic dir., choreographer Cleo Parker Robinson Dance, Denver. Mem. dance, expansion arts and inter-arts panels NEA; bd. dirs. Denver Ctr. Performing Arts; tchr. in workshops. Co-creator (documentary) African-Americans at Festae, Run Sister Run, (film) Black Women in the Arts, (music video) Borderline. Apptd. Nat. Coun. on Arts, 1999. Recipient Thelma Hill Ctr. for the Performing Arts award, 1986; Choreography fellow NEA; named one of Colo. 100, 1992, Colo. Governor's award for Excellence in the Arts; named to Blacks in Colo. Hall of Fame, 1994. Mem. Internat. Assn. Blacks in Dance (2nd v.p.). Office: 119 Park Ave W Denver CO 80205 Office Phone: 303-295-1759. Business E-Mail: cleodance@aol.com

**ROBINSON, CLIFFORD,** professional basketball player; b. Buffalo, N.Y., Dec. 16, 1966; Student, Conn., 1989. Basketball player Portland Trail Blazers, 1989—97, Phoenix Suns, 1997—99, Det. Pistons, 2001—03, Golden State Warriors, 2003—05, New Jersey Nets, 2005—. Office: c/oi New Jersey Nets 390 Murray Hill Pkwy East Rutherford NJ 07073

**ROBINSON, CRYSTAL,** professional basketball player; b. Atoka, Okla., Jan. 22, 1974; d. Billy and Nancy Robinson. Grad., S.E. Okla. State, 1996. Forward, WNBA New York Liberty, N.Y.C., 1999—. Named MVP, U.S. Sports Festival, 1993; named to Nat. Assoc. of Intercollegiate Athletics Hall of Fame, 2003; recipient ABL Rookie of the Yr. award, 1996—97.

**ROBINSON, DAVID BRADFORD,** writer, poet; b. Richmond, Va., Apr. 14, 1937; s. Albert Lewis and Martha Ellen (Lovern) R. BS, U. Miami, 1959, MS, 1961; JD, Calif. Ctrl. U., 1961, MA, 1994; AA, Miami-Dade C.C., 1970; DSc, Northwestern Coll., 1978, PhD, 1979, MA, 1994. Author: Characteristics of Cesium, 1978, Collected Poems, 1987. Founder Ronald Reagan Rep. Ctr., Washington; exhibitor Statue of Liberty, Port of NY, 1986; mem. Heritage Found., 1989; sustaining sponsor Ronald Reagan Presdl. Found.; 1987; charter mem. Ronald Reagan Trust; charter mem. Honor Roll Rep. Presdl. Task Force, 1990, life mem., 1989, Commemorative Honor Roll, 1991; mem. Nat. Rep. Senatorial Com. with Presdl. Commn., 1992; founding sponsor, founding mem. Space Life Sta., 1989; spkrs. citizen task force Inaugural Mem. Cert. of Honor; life mem. Rep. Nat. Com.; expert solver US Chess Fedn., 2005. Recipient 2d pl. Amateur Trophy, Capablanca Chess Club, 1964, Presdl. Sports award bicycling, 1976, Presdl. Achievement award Rep. Nat. Com., 1982, Cert. Good Standing Rep. Presdl. Task Force, 1982-85, Presdl. Merit medal, 1982, Appreciation cert. Sen. Paula Hawkins, 1986, Golden Poet Trophy award World of Poetry, 1987, Silver Anniversary Album, Nat. Geog. Soc., 1990, Pres. Ronald Reagan Appreciation cert., 1988, Pres. Bush Congl. Victory Squadron Recognition cert., 1989, Affidavit of Life Membership, Cert. from Rep. Nat. Com., Bush Inaugural/ Freedom medal, 1989, World Time-Capsule cert., 1990, Am. in Space medal, 1990, Cert. of Appreciation, Nat. Rep. Congl. Com., 1990, Pegasus Time Capsule plaque, 1991, Congl. Merit cert. Nat. Rep. Congl. Com., 1992, Battle of Normandy Found. Appreciation award, 1993, Presdl. Legion of Merit medal, 1993, Congl. Order of Liberty award, 1993, Appreciation cert. Sen. Kay Bailey Hutchinson, 1993, Rep. Presdl. award, 1994, Albert Einstein medal Brit. Bar. Degree Promotion, 1994, Cert. of Appreciation, The Golden Heart Club, Mil. Order of Purple Heart Svc. Found.; Congl. Order of Freedom, 1995, Cert. of Meritorious Svc. Rep. Party Planning Com., 1996, Cert. Appreciation World War II Meml. 1997, Chmn.'s Honor Roll cert., Rep. Nat. Com., 1997, Eisenhower Commn., 1997, Caesar medal Trinity Broadcasting Network, 1998, Cert. Recognition Rep. Nat. Com., 1999, Jubilee Yr. Blessing Cert. His Holiness John Paul II/Missionary Assn. Mary Immaculate, 1999, US Congl. Medal of His Holiness Pope John Paul II, 2005, Cert. of Appreciation Concerns of Police Survivors, 2000, Cert. of Appreciation Rep. Nat. Com., 2000, 2004, 2005, Cert. Appreciation, Planetary Soc., 2001, Reagan Ranch Mem. cert. recognition Young Am.'s Found., 2005; rated expert solver U.S. Chess Fedn., 2005. Mem. Am. Air Mus. (Brit., founder 1991), Battle of Normandy Meml. Mus. (charter 1988), Sigma Xi, Russian Club, Phi Theta Kappa. Avocation: chess.

**ROBINSON, DAVID BROOKS,** retired naval officer; b. Alexandria, La., Oct. 26, 1939; s. Donald and Marion (Holloman) R.; m. Gene Kirkpatrick, Aug. 1, 1964; children: Kirk, David. Student, Tex. A&M U., 1958—59; BS, U.S. Naval Acad., 1963; MS in Physics, Naval Postgrad. Sch., Monterey, Calif., 1969. Commd. ensign USN, 1963, advanced through grades to vice adm., 1993; commdg. officer USS Canon and USS Ready, Guam, 1969-71; adminstrv. aide to Chmn. Joint Chiefs Staff, Washington, 1971-74; commdg. officer USS Luce, Mayport, Fla., 1976-78; surface comdr. assignment officer. and dir. fiscal mgmt. and procedural control divsn. Naval Mil. Pers. Command, 1979-81; mem. Fgn. Svc. Inst. Exec. Seminar, Washington, 1982; commdg. officer USS Richmond K. Turner, Charleston, SC, 1983-84; chief of staff, comdr. Naval Surface Force, Atlantic Fleet, Norfolk, Va., 1984; exec. asst. and sr. aide to vice chief Naval Ops., Washington, 1985; dir. Manpower and Tng. divsn., 1986, dir. Surface Warfare divsn., 1987-88; comdr. cruiser destroyer group 8, 1988-89; vice dir. and subsequently dir. operational plans and inter-operability directorate Joint Staff, Washington, 1989-91; dep., chief of staff to comdr. U.S. Pacific Fleet, 1991-93, comdr. naval surface force, 1993-96; ret. USN, 1996. Decorated Navy Cross, Def. D.S.M., D.S.M., Legion of Merit with 4 gold stars, Bronze Star, Purple Heart. Mem. Optimists (pres. Oakton, Va. 1986-87). Methodist. Avocations: golf, bicycling, stamp collecting/philately, reading. Office Phone: 703-902-5001.

**ROBINSON, DAVID LOWELL,** biology professor; b. Charleston, W.Va., Sept. 10, 1955; s. Barbara Munson and Lytle Webb Robinson; m. Snake C. Jones, Mar. 22, 1956. BS, U. Ariz., Tucson, 1978, MS, 1986; PhD, U. Minn., St. Paul, 1993. Contract scientist U.S. AID, Sanaa, Yemen, 1978—80; staff scientist U. Ariz., Tucson, 1980—89; grad. rsch. asst. U. Minn., St. Paul, 1989—93, rsch. assoc., 1993—95; assoc. prof. of biology Bellarmine U., Louisville, 1995—. Chair dept. biology Bellarmine U., Louisville, 2004—. Mem. Friends of Louisville Free Pub. Libr., 1997—99. Ky. Biomedical Rsch. Infrastructure Network grant, NIH, 2001-2004. Mem.: Ky. Acad. of Sci. (chair botany and microbiology divsn. 1999—2000), Weed Sci. Soc. of Japan, Am. Soc. of Plant Biologists. Independent. Avocation: hiking. Office: Bellarmine Univ Dept Biology 2001 Newburg Rd Louisville KY 40205 Office Phone: 502-452-8197. Business E-Mail: drobinson@bellarmine.edu.

**ROBINSON, DAVID MAURICE,** professional basketball player; b. Key West, Fla., Aug. 6, 1965; Grad., U.S. Naval Acad., 1987. Commd. ensign USN, 1987; with San Antonio Spurs, 1989—. Mem. US Olympic Basketball Team, 1988, 92, 96, NBA Champions, 1999. Named Coll. Player of Yr.,

Sporting News, 1987, NBA Rookie of Yr., 1990, NBA Defensive Player of Yr., 1992, Most Valuable Player, 1994—95, Season Most Valuable Player, 1995; named to All-Am. 1st team, Sporting News, 1986, 1987, All-NBA 1st team, 1991; recipient Naismith award, 1987, Wooden award, 1987, IBM award, 1990, 1991, 1994, Schick Pivotal Player award, 1990, 1991, All-NBA 1st team, 1992, All-Star team, 1990—94. Achievements include being a holder of NCAA divsn. 1 single season record most block shots per game (5.91), 1986; being holder of NCAA divsn. 1 single record most blocked shots in 1 game (14), 1986; holding NBA career record most blocked shots per game (3.65). Office: care San Antonio Spurs 100 Montana St San Antonio TX 78203-1033

**ROBINSON, DAVID ZAV,** not-for-profit consultant; b. Montreal, Que., Can., Sept. 29, 1927; s. Benjamin and Antonia (Seiden) R.; m. Nan Senior, Sept. 6, 1954; children: Marc, Eric. AB, Harvard U., 1946, AM, 1947, PhD, 1950. Assoc. dir. rsch. Baird-Atomic Inc., Cambridge, Mass., 1949-59, 60-61; sci. liaison officer Office Naval Rsch., London, 1959-60; sci. advisor staff Office of Pres., Washington, 1961-67; v.p. acad. affairs NYU, 1967-70; v.p. Carnegie Corp. NY, NYC, 1970-80, exec. v.p., 1981-85, exec. v.p., treas., 1986-88; exec. dir. Carnegie Commn. on Sci Tech. and Govt., 1988-97; cons., 1997—. Dir. Urban Research Corp., Chgo., 1965-75; cons. Congressional Office of Tech. Assessment, 1975-78; mem. com. women in sci. NRC, 1975-82, chair com. on tchr. testing, 1999-2000; mem. vis. com. dept. chemistry Harvard U., 1977-83; physics dept. Princeton U., 1970-76 Mem. NY Energy Rsch. and Devel. Authority, 1971-77; trustee CUNY, 1976-81, Amideast, 1983-88, Citizen Union Found., 1985-, Insts. Schs. of the Future, 1986-, NC Sch. Sci. and Math., 1989-97, Santa Fe Inst., 1987-2004, Prep for Prep, 1989-98. Mem. AAAS, Optical Soc. Am., Coun. on Fgn. Rels., Am. Contract Bridge League, Fedn. Am. Scientists Coun., Bar assoc. of City of NY (commn. on future of CUNY 1999-2000), Harvard Club (NYC).

**ROBINSON, DAVIS ROWLAND,** lawyer, international arbitrator; b. NYC, July 11, 1940; s. Thomas Porter and Cynthia (Davis) R.; m. Suzanne Walker, June 11, 1966; children: Christopher Champlin II, Gracyn Walker. BA magna cum laude, Yale U., 1961; LLB cum laude, Harvard U., 1967. Bar: N.Y. 1968, D.C. 1971, U.S. Supreme Ct. 1972. Fgn. svc. officer U.S. Dept. State, Washington, 1961-69; assoc. Sullivan & Cromwell, N.Y.C., 1969—71; assoc., then ptnr. Leva, Hawes, Symington, Martin and Oppenheimer, Washington, 1971-81; the legal adviser U.S. Dept. State, Washington, 1981-85; ptnr. Pillsbury, Madison & Sutro, Washington, 1985-88, Le Boeuf, Lamb, Greene & MacRae LLP, Washington, 1988—2002, ret., 2002—; mng. dir. Richard C. Breeden & Co., LLC, 2003—. Dir. Mid. East Policy Coun., Washington, 1999—. Pres. Harvard Legal Aid Bur., 1966-67. Mem. Am. Law Inst. (adviser fgn. rels. law of U.S.), Am. Soc. Internat. Law, Internat. Centre for Settlement of Investment Disputes (U.S. panel, 2002-), Coun. on Fgn. Rels., Phi Beta Kappa. Business E-Mail: drrobins@breedenco.com

**ROBINSON, DOUGLAS,** computer company executive; BBA, St. Michael's Coll.; M in Fin., Babson Coll. Acct. exec. Fred S. James & Co.; comml. underwriter Liberty Mutual Ins. Co.; CFO Cullinet Software; from v.p. fin. to sr. v.p. fin. Computer Assoc. Internat., Islandia, NY, 1989—2003, sr. v.p. fin., interim CFO, 2003—04, sr. v.p., corp. controller, 2004—. Office: Computer Assoc Internat One Computer Assoc Plz Islandia NY 11749

**ROBINSON, E. GLENN,** lawyer; b. Charleston, W.Va., Jan. 1, 1924; s. Elmer George and Eva Elena (Rexrode) Robinson; m. Emma Lou Legg, Dec. 23, 1947; children: Richard G., Martha L., William E., Ann K. BSc, Ohio State U., 1948; JD, W.Va. U., 1950. Bar: W.Va. 1950, U.S. Ct. Appeals (4th cir.) 1953, U.S. Ct. Appeals (3d cir.) 1980, U.S. Supreme Ct. 1982. Ptnr. Shannon & Robinson, Charleston, 1950—52, James, Wise, Robinson, & Magnuson, Charleston, 1952—76, Love, Wise, Robinson & Woodroe, Charleston, 1976—83, Robinson & McElwee, Charleston, 1983—91, of counsel, 1991—. With AUS, 1942—45. Fellow: W.Va. Bar Found., Am. Coll. Trial Lawyers, Am. Bar Found.; mem.: Am. Bd. Trial Advocates, Kanawha County Bar Assn. (pres. 1968—69), W.Va. Bar Assn. (pres. 1982—83), W.Va. State Bar (pres. 1972—73), Rotary. Republican. Home: 507 Superior Ave South Charleston WV 25303-2024 Office: 400 Fifth Third Ctr 700 Virginia St E Charleston WV 25301 Office Phone: 304-347-8334. Business E-Mail: egr@ramlaw.com.

**ROBINSON, EARL, JR.,** marketing executive, transportation executive, educator, retired air force officer; b. St. George, Bermuda, Nov. 5, 1954; s. Willie Earl and Jeanette (Wilson) Robinson; m. Indera Rodgers, Dec. 11, 1999; children: Aiyana Spring, Jasmine Summer, Earl III. BA in Radio, TV, U. Detroit, 1976; MS in Mgmt., Troy State U., 1986; postgrad., Old Dominion U., 1986—95; MS in Computer Info. Sys., U. Detroit, 1998; PhD in Legal Letters, Sunbelt Paralegal Inst., 1999. Commd. lt. USAF, 1976, advanced through grades to lt. col., 1992, gen. officer aide, adminstrv. staff officer Sembach, Germany, 1982-85, with tactical air command Hampton, Va., 1986-88, mem. faculty Air Command and Staff Coll. Montgomery, Ala., 1989-92, commdr. recruiting squadron Clinton Twp., Mich., 1992-94, ret., 1994; pres. Power-Base USA, 1994—; chief advisor solar energy co., 1994—; exec. dir. Detroit Transit Authority, 1994-95, 1995—. Maj. prof. Spring Arbor (Mich.) Coll., 1992—; adj. prof. Faulkner U., Montgomery, 1991—; pres. CEO ERJ Corp. Ltd., Hampton, Va., 1986-88; pres. Paddle King Corp., Zaragoza, Spain, 1980-82; cons. Inst. Def. Analysis. Inventor info. resource mgmt. system. Mem. Nat. Tech. Assn. (publicity chmn. 1984-85), Urban Youth Action (case worker 1984-85), Housing Opportunity, Inc., Hampton Host Lions Club, Tuskegee Airmen (past chpt. pres.). Avocations: computers, reading, table-trennis, team sports, fishing, golf. Home: 1035 Roslyn St Mount Clemens MI 48043-2934 Office Phone: 313-492-0845. E-mail: erobinson@powerbaseusa.us.

**ROBINSON, EDDIE GAY,** college football coach; m. Doris Robinson; children: Lillian Rose, Eddie Jr. BA, Leland Coll., 1940; MS, U. Iowa; LLD (hon.), La. Tech. Coach football Grambling U., La., 1941—97, v.p. athletics La., asst. v.p. univ. rels. La., sr. advisor to pres. for instnl. advancement La., 1998—. Head coach East-West Shrine Game, 1977. Recipient Horatio Alger award, Nat. Football Found. award, NAACP award, VFW award, Bear Bryant award, Liberty Bowl award, others, Spl. Commendations from Pres. Ronald Reagan, Nat. Collegiate Athletic Assn., U.S. Congress, State of La., B'nai B'rith; holds record of most college football victories. Mem. Nat. Assn. Sports & Phys. Edn., Nat. Assn. Intercollegiate Athletics, Southwestern Athletic Conf., La. Sports Hall of Fame, Pop Warner, Sugar Bowl, Black Coll. Achievements include winning 10 nat. Black coll. football championships. Office: Grambling State Univ Pres's Office PO Box 607 Grambling LA 71245-0607

**ROBINSON, EDWARD LEE,** retired physics professor, consultant; b. Clanton, Ala., Nov. 6, 1933; s. Alonzo Lee and Ollie Sarah (Mims) R.; m. Shirley Anne Burnett (div. Sept. 1972); children: Edward Lee Jr., James Allan, Paul David; m. Linda G. Moon, 1990. AB with honors, Samford U., 1954; MS, Purdue U., 1958, PhD, 1962. Dir. Cyclotron Lab. Samford U., Birmingham, Ala., 1961-67, asst. prof. physics, chmn. dept., 1961-62, assoc. prof., chmn. dept., 1962-66, prof., chmn. dept., 1966-67; assoc. prof. U. Ala., Birmingham, 1967-77, co-radiation safety officer, 1967-85, dir. Van de Graaff Accelerator Lab., 1970-91, acting chmn. dept., 1973-74, prof. physics, 1977-91, adj. prof. forensic sci., 1983-91, cons. in applied physics and accident reconstrn., 1991—; prin., owner Robinson & Assocs., LLC, 1998—. Cons. Hayes Internat. Corp., Birmingham, 1963-68, So. Rsch. Inst., Birmingham, 1968-69; rschr. Oak Ridge (Tenn.) Nat. Lab., 1968, 74-75, 82, U. Md., College Park, 1966, 67; bd. overseers Samford U., 1999—; adv. com. to dean Howard Coll. of Arts and Scis. of Samford U., 2002—. Active Birmingham YMCA; mem. at large nat. coun., chmn. sci. adv. com. for explorer scouting Boy Scouts Am., 1999—2002. Mem. Am. Phys. Soc., Soc. Automotive Engrs., AAAS, Ala. Acad. Sci. (life, v.p. 1964-65), Tex. Assn. Accident Reconstrn. Specialists (bd. dirs. 1999-2003), numerous other nat. and internat. profl. assns. Baptist. Achievements include discovery, co-discover of six radioisotopes. Home: 233 Oakmont Rd Birmingham AL 35244-3264 Office Phone: 205-995-8330. Personal E-mail: elrobinson@charter.net.

**ROBINSON, ENDERS ANTHONY,** geophysicist, educator, writer; b. Boston, Mar. 18, 1930; s. Edward Arthur and Doris Gertrude (Goodale) Robinson; m. Eva Arborelius, Sept. 9, 1962 (div. 1973); children: Anna, Erik Arthur, Karin; m. Joyce McPeake, Aug. 8, 1992. BS in Math., MIT, 1950, MS in Econs., 1952, PhD in Geophysics, 1954. Dir. geophys. analysis group MIT, Cambridge, Mass., 1952-54, instr. math. 1955-56; geophysicist Gulf Oil Corp., Pitts., 1954-55; petroleum economist Standard Oil Co. NJ, NYC, 1956-57; asst. prof. stats. Mich. State U., East Lansing, 1958; asst. prof. math. U. Wis., Madison, 1958-61, assoc. prof. math. (with tenure), 1961-62; dep. prof. stats. Uppsala (Sweden) U., 1960-64; v.p., dir. Digicon Inc., Houston, 1965-70; pres. Robinson Rsch. Inc., Houston, 1970-82; vis. prof. theoretical and applied mechanics Cornell U., Ithaca, NY, 1981-82; McMan prof. geophysics U. Tulsa, 1983-93; Maurice Ewing and J.L. Worzel prof. geophysics Columbia U., NYC, 1993—2000, prof. emeritus, 2000—. Author: (book) Seismic Inversion and Deconvolution, Dual Sensor Technology, 1999, 31 other books on sci., tech. and history; editor: Internat. Jour. Imaging Sys. & Tech., 1988—; mem. editl. bd.: Multidimensional Sys. and Signal Processing, An Internat. Jour., 1990—. 2d lt. U.S. Army, 1950—51. Recipient Donald G. Fink Prize award, IEEE, 1984, Achievement award, Thayer Acad. Alumni, 1997, Alexander von Humboldt Rsch. award for sr. U.S. scientists, 1999, Medal award in recognition of outstanding contribr. to the digital processing of seismic data, Soc. Exploration Geophysicists, Conrad Schlumberger award, European Assn. Exploration Geophysicists, Blaise Pascal medal Earth Scis., European Acad. Scis., 2003. Fellow: European Acad. Scis.; mem.: Nat. Rsch. Coun. (com. undiscovered oil and gas resources), Nat. Acad. Engring. (petroleum and mining sect.), Soc. Exploration Geophysicists (hon. Classic Paper award 1953, 1957, Best Paper award 1964, Reginald Fessenden medal 1969, father of deconvolution 1983, Best Paper award 2001, Maurice Ewing Gold medal 2001), European Assn. Geoscientists and Engrs. (Conrad Schlumberger award 1969), Renaissance Inst. Washington, NY Athletic Club, MIT Club NY. Known as the "Father of Digital Geophysics". Office: 8 Dorothy E Lucey dr Newburyport MA 01950-1781 Office Phone: 978-465-2053. E-mail: endersrobinson@comcast.net.

**ROBINSON, EVELYN EDNA,** secondary school educator; b. St. John, Maine, Feb. 23, 1911; d. Registe Jalbert and Olive Michaud; m. Carl Robinson, July 19, 1939; children: Robert, James. BA in Math., U. Maine, 1934; MS, U. N.H., 1963; MEd, Hillyer Coll. U., 1960. Tchr. English and math. Ft. Kent (Maine) H.S., 1934; tchr. English and math., coach girls basketball Madewaska (Maine) H.S., 1935-55; tchr. math. Stamford (Conn.) H.S., 1955-56; tchr. math and English, Bristol (Conn.) H.S., 1956-63; prof. math. Worcester (Mass.) State Coll., 1963-77, chmn. dept., 1970-77. Coord. cmty. bus. Worcester State Coll., 1970-77, class advisor, 1968-72, salary equity bd., 1971-73. Vol. libr. Madawaska Pub. Libr., 1936-55; lector Christ the King, Worcester, 1974-2000. Mem. Delta Kappa Gamma. Republican. Roman Catholic. Avocations: decorating, flower arrangements, ceramics, tailoring. Home: 167 N Spencer Rd Spencer MA 01562-1232

**ROBINSON, EVELYN ETTA,** principal; b. Pocatello, Idaho, Nov. 5, 1946; d. Luther Nelson Robinson and Marian Rose Smith. Tchr. diploma, Bapt. Bible Coll., 1968; BA, U. Ill. Springfield, 1978, MA, 1979; edn. specialist, Idaho State U., Boise, 1988. Cert. elementary tchr., sch. prin., superintendent. 1st grade tchr. Villa Christian Sch., Broadview, Ill., 1968—74, North Jacksonville Elem., Jacksonville, Ill., 1978—79, Bonneville Elem., Pocatello, Idaho, 1979—88; edn. supr. Grace Acad., Springfield, Ill., 1977—78; prin. Westfair Acad., Jacksonville, 1977—84, Lewis & Clark Elem., Pocatello, Idaho, 1988—. Instr. Idaho Sate U. Coll. Edn., Pocatello, 1987—; District #25 Tech. Portfolio, 1997—; curriculum instr. Integration of Tech. into Idaho history, 1999—; inservice instr. District #25, Pocatello, 1988—; mentor District #25 Tech. Mentor Program, 1996—; mem. District #25 Curriculum Com., 1996—2000, Leadership for the 21st Century Com., 1997—, Home Page Devel. Com., 1999—, Tchr. Evaluation Com., 2000—01, Sch. Improvement Criteria Com., 2000—01, Enhancement Learning Project Com., 2000—; commr. Idaho State Bd. Edn. Accountability Commn., 2003—; presenter in field. Author: Lewis & Clark School Improvement Profile, 1988—2005. Tchr. children's program Idaho State Mus. Natural History, Pocatello, 1984; mem. Salvation Army Canned Food Drive Com., Pocatello, 1994—, Neighborhood Watch Program, Pocatello, 1994—, Neighborhood Support Group for the Elderly, Pocatello, 1996—, Ross Park Zoological Soc., Pocatello, 2003—; tchr. Sunday Sch. Workshop Nazarene Ch., Pocatello, 1985—; bd. dirs. Pocatello Zoo, 2003—. Nominee Idaho Tchr. of Yr., 1982—83, Outstanding Adminstr., Pocatello Edn. Assn., 1994; named Tchr. of Yr., Bonneville Elem. Parent-Tchr. Assn., 1982—83, Bonneville Elem., 1988—89; recipient Outstanding Svc. award, Messiah Baptist Ch., 1972, Outstanding Leadership award, Am. Assn. Sunday Schools, 1977, Sunday Sch. Leadership award, Westfair Baptist Ch., 1979, Dedication to Youth award, Ctr. for Leadership, Edn., and Devel., 1989, 8 Who Make a Difference award, Idaho Channel 8, Pocatello, 1997, Woman of Achievement award, ZONTA Internat., 2005, Excellence in Edn. award, Northwest Region, 2006, Idaho's Excellence in Edn. award, Alpha Delta Kappa, 2006. Mem.: SE Idaho Reading Assn. (bldg. rep. 1983—88, chair newspspaper in edn. week 1984—88), Internat. Reading Assn. (chair newspaper in edn. 1986—87, chair Idaho Honors coun. 1987—88), Assn. Supervision and Curriculum Devel., District #25 Assn. Elem. Sch. Principals (v.p. 1989—90, pres. 1990—91), Region V Assn. Elem. Sch. Principals, Idaho Assn. Sch. Administrators, Idaho Assn. Elem. Sch. Principals (Idaho Gem award 1990—91, Idaho's Nat. Disting. Prin. award 2005), Nat. Assn. Elem. Sch. Principals, Internat. and Portneuf Valley Audubon Assn., Phi Delta Kappa (chair program com. 1987—88, v.p. program com. 1988—89, v.p. membership 1989—90, pres. 1990—91), Alpha Delta Kappa (sgt. at arms 1982—84, chair altruistic com. 1986—88, chair courtesy com. 1990—92, historian 1992—94, Idaho Excellence in Edn. award 2006). Avocations: gardening, hunting, fishing, birdwatching, hiking. Office: Lewis & Clark Elem 800 Grace Dr Pocatello ID 83201 Business E-Mail: robinsev@d25.k12.id.us.

**ROBINSON, FRANK,** professional baseball manager, retired professional baseball player; b. Beaumont, Tex., Aug. 31, 1935; s. Frank and Ruth (Shaw) R.; m. Barbara Ann Cole, Oct. 28, 1961; children: Frank Kevin, Nichelle. Student, Xavier U., Cin. Baseball player Cin. Reds, 1956-65, Balt. Orioles, 1966-71, L.A., 1972, Calif. Angels, 1973-74, Cleve. Indians, 1974-76, mgr., 1975-77; coach Calif. Angels, 1977, Balt. Orioles, 1978-80, 85-87, mgr., 1988-91, asst. to gen. mgr., 1991-95; mgr. San Francisco Giants, 1981-84; batting coach Milw. Brewers, 1984; dir. baseball ops. Arizona Fall League Major League Baseball, 1997—99, v.p. on-field operations, 1999—2002; mgr. Wash. Nationals (formerly Montreal Expos), 2002—. Author: (with Al Silverman) My Life is Baseball, 1967, (with Barry Steinbach) Extra Innings, 1989, Frank the First Year, 1976. Named Rookie of Yr. Nat. League, 1956, Most Valuable Player, 1961, Am. League, 1966, Am. League Mgr. of Yr., 1982, 89; mem. World Series Championship Team, 1966, 70, Nat. League All-Star Team, 1956-57, 59, 61.62, 65, Am. League All-Star Team, 1966-67, 69-71, 74; inducted into Baseball Hall of Fame, 1982; recipient Presdl. Medal of Freedom, The White House, 2005. Office: RFK Stadium 2400 E Capitol St SE Washington DC 20003*

**ROBINSON, FRED COLSON,** language educator; b. Birmingham, Ala., Sept. 23, 1930; s. Emmett Colson and Morwenna Hope (Bennett) R.; m. Helen Caroline Wild, June 21, 1959; children: Lisa Karen, Eric Wild. BA, Birmingham So. Coll., 1953; MA, U. N.C., 1954, PhD, 1961; DLitt (hon.), Williams Coll., 1985; MA (hon.), Yale U., 1989. Instr. Stanford (Calif.) U., 1960-61, asst. prof., 1961-65, assoc. prof., 1967-71, prof. English philology, 1971-72; asst. prof. Cornell U., Ithaca, NY, 1965-66, assoc. prof., 1966-67; prof. Yale U., New Haven, 1972-83, Douglas Tracy Smith prof., 1983—2000, prof. emeritus, 2000—, chmn. medieval studies, 1975-78, 80. Vis. prof. Harvard U., Cambridge, Mass., 1983; pub. com. Medieval Acad. Monographs, Cambridge, 1987-90. Author: Old English Literature: Select Bibliography, 1970, Beowulf and the Appositive Style, 1985, The Tomb of Beowulf, 1993, The Editing of Old English, 1994; co-author: A Bibliography...ed Old English Literature, 1980, Old English Verse Texts from Many Sources: A Comprehensive Collection, 1991, A Guide to Old English, 6th edit., 2001, Beowulf: An Edition with Relevant Shorter Texts, 1998; editor Old English

Newsletter, 1966-73, Early English MSS in Facsimile, 1971-2002. Jour. English Linguistics, 1971—, Anglo-Saxon England, 1972—, Anglistica, 1981—; contbr. over 100 articles to profl. jours. Trustee Yale Univ. Libr. Assocs., New Haven, 1986-89, 91-95, 97-2000, 03—. With U.S. Army, 1954-56. Recipient Disting. Vis. Scholar award U. Ala., 1999, William Clyde DeVane medal, fellow Guggenheim Found., 1974-75, Am. Coun. Learned Socs., 1968-69, Inst. Social and Econ. Rsch., Rhodes U., 1978, Japan Soc. Promotion of Sci., 1989; grantee NEH, 1976, 79, 81, 85, Am. Philos. Soc., 1973, 85; named Professore solo per ricerca Univ. di Roma "La Sapienza", 2000 Fellow AAAS, Medieval Acad. Am. (pres. 1983-84, Haskins medal 1984), Brit. Acad. (corr., Sir Israel Gollancz prize 1997), Meddeleeuevereniging van Suidelike Afrika (corr.); mem. Finnish Acad. of Sci. and Letters (fgn. mem.), New Eng. Medieval Conf. (pres. 1982-83), Conn. Acad. Arts and Scis. (pres. 1980-85), Internat. Soc. Anglo-Saxonists (elected hon.), Elizabethan Club (bd. govs. 1986-88, v.p. 1989-90, pres. 1990-92), Manuscript Club (v.p. New Haven chpt. 1990-92), Phi Beta Kappa. Episcopalian. Office: Yale Univ Dept English New Haven CT 06520 Business E-Mail: fred.robinson@yale.edu.

**ROBINSON, GAIL PATRICIA,** retired mental health counselor; b. Medford, Oreg., Dec. 31, 1936; d. Ivan T. and Evelyn H. (Hamilton) Skyrman; m. Douglas L. Smith; children: Shauna J. BS in Edn., Oreg. State U., 1958, PhD in Counseling, 1978; MS in Counseling, Western Oreg. State Coll., 1974. Tchr. Monterey (Calif.) Pub. Schs., 1958-59, Corvallis (Oreg.) Pub. Schs., 1959-62, 69-75, counselor, 1977-81; pvt. practice Corvallis, 1977-95. Vol. therapist Children's Svcs. divsn., Linn and Benton Counties, 1982-83; asst. prof. Western Oreg. State coll., 1977, counselor, 1982-83; mem. grad. faculty Oreg. State U., Corvallis, 1978-95; presenter workshops, lectr. in field. Contbr. articles to profl. jours. Mem. Benton County Mental Helath Citizens Adv. Bd., 1979-85, chair, 1982-83; trustee WCTU Children's Farm Home, 1978-84, chair child welfare com., 1983-85, pres., 1984; mem. Old Mill Sch. Adv. Bd., 1979-85, chair, 1979-81; bd. dirs. Cmty. Outreach, 1979-83; mem. Benton Com. for Prevention of Child Abuse, 1978-85, v.p., 1982; mem. Oreg. Bd. Lic. Profl. Counselors and Therapists, 1989-95, chair, 1989-90, Aurora Colony Historical Soc., vol., 2000-, bd. mem. 2005-. Mem. ACA (govt. rels. com. 1988-91, professionalization com. 1988-92, pres. 1996-97), Am. Mental Health Counselors Assn. (chair consumer and pub. rels. com. 1988-91, bd. dirs. Western region 1989-91, chair strategic planning com. 1994-95, pres. 1992-93), Oreg. Counseling Assn. (chair licensure liaison com. 1985-91, exec. bd. 1985-88, steering com. 1986-87, register editorial com. 1985-86, Disting. Svc. award 1985, 87, Leona Tyler award 1989), Oreg. Mental Health Counselors Assn. Personal E-Mail: robinsgp@comcast.net.

**ROBINSON, GARRY LEWIN,** television news executive; b. Kansas City, Mo., Oct. 26, 1951; s. Calvin Luin and Reba Kathleen (Owen) R.; m. Linda Sue Payton, Oct. 21, 1973 (div. 1982); children: Penny Lynn, Larry Calvin II, Jeff Noel BS, Ark. State U., 1981. Cert. tech. Dynatech Newstar and AP Newscenter Computer Sys. Various positions Sta. KAWW-AM-FM, Heber Springs, Ark., 1969—76, dir. news, ops., 1978; asst. news dir. Sta. KARV-AM, Russellville, Ark., 1976—78; ops. mgr., news dir. Sta. KCON-AM, Conway, Ark., 1978—79; asst. news dir. Sta. KTVE-TV, El Dorado, Ark., 1979—81; mng. prodr. Sta. KAIT-TV, Jonesboro, Ark., 1981—84; newscast prodr. Sta. KOLD-TV, Tucson, 1984—85; newscast prodr., now news ops. mgr. Sta. KSLA-TV, Shreveport, La., 1984—, exec. prodr., 10 PM prodr., newsroom computer sys. mgr., 1985—2005, exec. prodr., computer sys. mgr., news ops. mgr., 1985—2005, info. sys. engr., 2005—. Bd. dirs. North Ark. Fire Dist., Russellville, 1977; bd. advisors City Cable TV Commn., Conway, 1978; chmn. drama divsn. Conway Regional Arts Commn., 1977-78; advisor Explorer Scouts, Shreveport, 1987 Recipient numerous reporter awards Ark. AP, Little Rock, 1984, Radio Documentary award Ark. AP, 1984, Women in Radio and TV, Little Rock, 1978, various TV news awards La., Tex., Ark., AP Broadcasters Assn., 1985-90 Mem. Radio TV News Dirs. Assn. (Edward R. Murrow award 1987), Sigma Delta Chi (North La. chpt., bd. dirs. 1987), Phi Eta Sigma (pres. 1970-71) Democrat. Baptist. Avocations: reading, writing, guitar, computers, outdoor sports. Home: 5063 Town North Dr Shreveport LA 71107-2843 Office: Sta KSLA-TV 1812 Fairfield Ave Shreveport LA 71101-4431 Office Phone: 318-677-6720. E-mail: garry@garryrobinson.com.

**ROBINSON, GENE EZIA,** biologist, educator; b. Buffalo, Jan. 9, 1955; s. Jack and Sonja (Rubin) R.; m. Julia O. Robinson, Aug. 29, 1982; children: Aaron, Daniel, Sol. BS in Life Sciences, Cornell U., 1977, MS, 1982, PhD, 1986. Postdoctoral assoc. Ohio State U., Columbus, 1986-89; asst. prof. biology U. Ill., Urbana, 1989-93, assoc. prof. biology, 1993-98, prof. biology, 1998—2003, dir. neuroscience prog., 2001—, G. William Arends prof. of integrative biology, 2003—; team leader Inst. for Genomic Biology, 2004—. Cons. Songbird Genomic Initiative, 2003—. Assoc. editor Ann. Rev. Entomology, 1998—, editl. bd. Jour. Insect Physiology, 1992—, Genes, Brain, and Behavior, 2002—, Jour. Insect Biology, 2002—. Recipient Fulbright Sr. Rsch. Fellowship, Hebrew U., 1995-96, Guggenheim Fellowship, 2003. Fellow AAAS, Am. Acad. Arts & Sciences; mem. Am. Assn. Behavioral Neuroendocrinology, Animal Behavior Soc., Entomol. Soc. Am. (Founders Meml. award, 2003, Recognition award in insect physiology, 2004), Internat. Bee Rsch. Assn., Internat. Soc. Neuroethology, Soc. Neurosci., Internat. Union Study of Social Insects, Internat. Behavioural and Neural Genetics Soc., NAS, Sigma Xi. Achievements include discovery of hormone, neural and genetic factors that regulate behavioral plasticity and division of labor in honeybee colonies. Office: The Robinson Lab--Univ Ill 320 Morrill Hall 505 S Goodwin Ave Urbana IL 61801-3707 E-Mail: generobi@uiuc.edu.*

**ROBINSON, GLENN,** professional basketball player; b. Gary, Ind., Jan. 10, 1973; Student, Purdue U. Basketball player Milw. Bucks, 1994—2002; small forward Atlanta Hawks, 2002, Phila. 76ers, 2003, San Antonio Spurs, 2004—05. Named mem., Ea. Conf. All-Star Team, 2000, 2001. Achievements include member NBA National Championship Team, 2005. Office: San Antonio Spurs One SBC Ctr San Antonio TX 78219

**ROBINSON, HARLOW LOOMIS,** language educator, historian, writer; b. Bristol, Conn., Sept. 20, 1950; s. Raymond Loomis and Katherine Chaffee Robinson; life ptnr. Robert Frank Holley. BA magna cum laude, Yale U., 1972; MA, PhD, U. Calif., Berkeley, 1980. Prof. Russian SUNY, Albany, 1980—96; prof. modern langs. and history Northeastern U., Boston, 1996—. Presenter in field. Author: (biography) Sergei Prokofiev: A Biography, 1987, 1988, 2002, The Last Impresario: The Life, Times and Legacy of Sol Hurok, 1994 (Albany, NY, Pub. Libr. Author of the Yr., 1994); translator (editor): (translation) Selected Letters of Sergei Prokofiev, 1998; contbr. articles to profl. jours. Editl. bd. Northeastern U. Press, Boston, 2002—03; bd. mem. Citizen Exch. Coun., N.Y.C., 1988—94, Troy (N.Y.) Savs. Bank Music Hall, 1992—95. Fellow Grad. Student Rsch. in Eng. and France, Fulbright-Hayes, 1978—79, Grad. Student rsch. in USSR, IREX/Fulbright, 1979—80; Nat. Def. Fgn. Lang. fellow, 1973—75, Faculty Rsch. fellow, Am. Coun. Learned Socs., 1985, Sr. Scholar Rsch. fellow, Fulbright-Hayes/IREX in USSR, 1991—92, travel fellow for Czech Republic, Whiting Found., 2002, Sr. Rsch. grantee, NEH, 1988, Soviet Scholars Travel grantee, Soros Found., 1991, Short-Term Rsch. grantee, Kennan Inst., 1993. Mem.: MLA, Am. Assn. for the Advancement Slavic Studies, Authors Guild, Am. Assn. Tchrs. Slavic and East European Langs. (assoc.; v.p. 2001—03), Phi Beta Kappa. Avocations: travel, swimming, singing, piano. E-Mail: h.robinson@neu.edu.

**ROBINSON, HENRY WARD,** meteorologist; b. Schoharie, NY, June 30, 1940; s. Frank Locklyn and Esther (Lawyer) R.; m. Muriel Scott, Aug. 15, 1964; children: Katherine, Heather, David. BS, SUNY, Oneonta, 1964; MS, Pa. State U., 1970. Tchg. asst. Pa. State U. State College, 1968-72; instr. Upsala Coll., East Orange, NJ, 1973-75; analyst Computer Sci. Corp., Silver Spring, Md., 1975-78; meteorologist Nat. Westher Svc. NOAA, Silver Spring, 1978—2005; faculty Embry-Riddle Aeronautical U., 2006—. Adj. prof. Montgomery Coll., Germantown, Md., 1983-2005; mentor NASA Goddard Space Flight Ctr. Ea. Region Remote Sensing Applications Ctr.; vis. instr. NSF program Notre Dame U., South Bend, Ind.; data stream instr., adv. Am. Meteorol. Data Stream Project Contbr. numerous articles to profl. jours.; writer, coord., dir., editor tng. videos. Mem. Am. Meteorol. Soc. (bd. sch. and

popular meteorol. and oceanograph edn., contbg. editor operational terms Glossary of Meteorology, bd. women and minorities), Am. Geophys. Union. Home: 19622 Enterprise Way Montgomery Village MD 20886 Business E-Mail: henry.robinson@eras.edu.

**ROBINSON, HERBERT HENRY, III,** psychotherapist, educator; b. Leavenworth, Wash., Mar. 31, 1933; s. Herbert Henry II and Alberta (Sperber) R.; m. Georgia Murial Jones, Nov. 24, 1954 (div. 1974); children: Cheri Dean Asbury, David Keith, Peri Elizabeth Layton, Tanda Rene Graff, Gaila Daire. Grad. of Theology, Bapt. Bible Coll., 1959; BA in Philosophy/Greek, Whitworth Coll., 1968; MA in Coll. Teaching, Ea. Wash. U., 1976; PhD, Gonzaga U., 2002. Cert. psychotherapist, perpetrator treatment program supervision; nat. bd. cert. counselor. Choir dir. Twin City Bapt. Temple, Mishawaka, Ind., 1959-61; min. Inland Empire Bapt. Ch., Spokane, Wash., 1961-73; tchr. philosophy Spokane C.C., 1969-72; dir. Alternatives to Violence, Women in Crisis, Fairbanks, Alaska, 1985-87; tchr. pub. rels. U. Alaska, Fairbanks, 1986-87; dir. Alternatives to Violence Men Inc., Juneau, 1988-89; tchr. leadership mgmt. U. Alaska S.E., Juneau, 1988-89; min. Sci. of Mind Ctr., Sandpoint, Idaho, 1989-92; dir., therapist Tapio Counseling Ctr., Spokane, 1991—; cert. psychotherapist, supr. perpetrator treatment program Wash. Cons. Lilac Blind/Alpha Inc./Marshall Coll., Spokane, 1975-85, Alaska Placer Mining Co., Fairbanks, 1987; tchr. Spokane Falls C.C., Spokane, 1979-85; seminar, presenter Human Resource Devel., Spokane and Seattle, Wash., Pa., 1980; guest trainer United Way/Kellogg Found. Inst. for Volunteerism, Spokane, 1983. 1st trombone San Diego Marine Band, 1953-56, Spokane Symphony, 1961; bd. dirs. Tanani Learning Ctr., Fairbanks, 1987; mem. consensus bldg. team Sci. of Mind Ctr., Sandpoint, 1989-92. Cpl. USMC, 1953-56. Mem. ACA, Assn. for Humanistic Edn. and Devel., Assn. for Religious Values in Counseling, Internat. Assn. Addictions and Offender Counselors, Internat. Assn. Marriage and Family Counselors, Am. Assn. Profl. Hypnotherapists, American Assn. Christian Counselors. Office: Tapio Counseling 5325 E Sprague Ave Spokane WA 99212-0820 Office Phone: 509-534-5028. E-mail: peace@herb-robinson.com.

**ROBINSON, HOBART KRUM,** management consulting company executive; b. Quincy, Mass., Oct. 8, 1937; s. Hobart Krum and Charlotte Elizabeth (Hall) R.; m. Gerd Ingela Janhede, Oct. 17, 1964; children: Steven Whitney, Karina Jill, Peter Danforth. BA, Williams Coll., 1959; MBA, Columbia U., 1964. Market analyst Mobil Chem. Co., Richmond, Va., 1964-67; mgr. program analysis and control Polaroid Corp., Cambridge, Mass., 1967-69; exec. v.p., dir. Simplex Wire and Cable, Inc., North Berwick, Maine, 1969-73; sr. engagement mgr. McKinsey and Co., Inc., N.Y.C., 1973-76, prin. Copenhagen, 1977-81, N.Y.C., 1985-89, Stockholm, 1989-95, dir. adminstrn. Eastern Europe, 1993-95, dir. adminstrn. N.Y.C., 1995-98; pres. CEO Brink's Inc., Darien, Conn., 1981-84; ret., 1998. Dir. Burlington No. Air Freight, Inc., Newport Beach, Calif., 1982-84. Pres. Am. Club in Copenhagen, 1980-81; dir. Fulbright Commn., Copenhagen, 1980-81; vice chair Williams Coll. Alumni Fund, 1999—2004. Lt. USNR, 1959-62. Mem. Tournament Players Club (Ponte Vedra, Fla.), Taconic Golf Club (Williamstown, Mass.), Marsh Landing Country Club (Ponte Vedra, Fla.), Sawgrass Country Club (Ponte Vedra), Ponte Vedra Golf and Country Club. Republican. Episcopalian. Home: 94 Ide Rd Williamstown MA 01267-2815 E-mail: bartrobin@aol.com.

**ROBINSON, HOWARD ARTHUR, JR.,** minister; s. Howard Arthur Sr. and Mary Hairston Robinson; children: Dionne Carol, Angela Marie, Howard Arthur III. MDiv, Morehouse Sch. of Religion / Interdenominational Theol. Ctr., 1976. Cert. advanced marriage and family therapy Puget Sound Counseling Ctr., 1979, consecrated as Bishop Full Gospel Bapt. Ch. Fellowship Internat., 2000. Pres. Berean Kingdom Ctr., Renton, Wash., 1995—2002; adj. prof. N.W. Coll. Assemblies God, Kirkland, 1999—2001; provost Sunday sch. curriculum Full Gospel Bapt. Ch. Fellowship, Seattle, 1999—2003, aux. bishop New Orleans, 2000—03, bishop for Wash. and Oreg. states Seattle, 2000—03; pres. Berean Acad. Christian Devel., Renton, 1995—; presiding bishop and chief apostle Agape Christian Fellowship Internat., Seattle, 2002—; pres. Howard A. Robinson, Jr. Ministries, Kent, Wash., 2002—. Pres. Black United Clergy for Action Pacific N.W., Seattle, 1995—2000; moderator Macedonia Dist. Bapt. Assn.; pres. pastors conf. Nat. Bapt. Conv. Am., Inc., v.p. congress of christian workers, Shreveport, La., 1998—99; sec. Gen. Bapt. Conv. N.W. Reg. Author: Changing the 21st Century Ch., 2003. Adv. bd. mem. Wells Fargo Bank, Seattle, 1995—96, First Interstate Bank, Seattle. Maj. USAFR, 1967—90. Decorated Am. Spirit Honor Medal U. S. Army, Trainee of the Cycle; M. L. King scholar, Coun. Chs. Seattle Wash. 1974—76. Avocations: swimming, travel, photography. Office: Agape Christian Fellowship International P O Box # 58009 Tukwila WA 98138 Office Phone: 425-255-4562.

**ROBINSON, HUGH GRANVILLE,** consulting management company executive; b. Washington, Aug. 4, 1932; s. James Hill and Wilhelmina (Thomas) R.; 1 stepchild, Mia; children by previous marriage: Hugh Granville, Susan K. Student, Williams Coll., 1949-50; BS, U.S. Mil. Acad. 1954; MS, MIT, 1959; LLD, Williams Coll., 1983. Commd. 2d lt. U.S. Army, 1954, advanced through grades to maj. gen.; 1983; platoon leader, co. comdr. Co. B, 185th Engrs. Bn., Korea, 1955; platoon leader, ops. officer 74th Engr. Co., Korea, 1955-56; br. chief Engr. Supply Control Office, St. Louis, 1956-58; chief Catalog and Authorization div. Engr. Supply Control Agy., Orleans, France, 1960-62; co. comdr. 553d Engr. Bn., Orleans, 1962-63; chief combat br. War Plans divsn. Engr. Strategic Studies Group, Washington, 1963-65; Army asst. to armed forces aide to Pres. Washington, 1965-69; comdr. 39th Engr. Bn., Vietnam, 1969-70; br. chief war plans divsn. Office Dep. Chief Staff for Ops., Washington, 1970-71; assigned Nat. War Coll., 1972; comdr. 3rd regt. U.S. Corps Cadets, West Point, NY, 1973-74, U.S. Army Engr. Sch. Brigade, Fort Belvoir, Va., 1974-76; dist. engr. U.S. Army Engr. Dist., L.A., 1976-78, dir. div. civil works office Chief of Engrs., Washington, 1978-80; comdr. Southwestern Divsn., U.S. Army C.E., 1980-83; ret., 1983; v.p. Southland Corp., Dallas, 1983-88; pres. Cityplace Devel. Corp.; sr. v.p. Grigsby Brandford Powell, Inc., 1988-94; chmn., CEO The Tetra Group, Inc., Dallas, 1989—2002; chmn. Granville Cons. and Devel. Co., Inc., 2001—03, Global Bldg. Sys., Dallas, 2004—. Mem. Mississippi River Commn., 1980-83, bd. engrs. for rivers and harbors, 1980-83, Coastal Engring. Rsch. Bd., 1980-83; bd. dirs. Carmax, Inc., Guaranty Bank, Aleris Internat., New Market Tech.; chmn. Dallas Fed. Res. Bd., 1991; adv. bd. TXU; with Tex. Pub. Broadcasting, LBJ Found., 1989—. Mem. nat. bd. dirs. Keep Am. Beautiful, 1981-85; bd. dirs. Dallas Symphony, 1981-85, Dallas United Way, 1984-92, Baylor U. Med. Ctr. Found., 1983-91, Dallas Opera, 1983-90, Dallas Citizens Coun., 1987-91, Greater Dallas C. of C., 1986-91, Vietnam Vets Meml. Fund Tex.; chmn. African Am. Mus., Dallas Youth Svcs. Corp.; trustee Dallas Mus. Fine Arts, 1988-93; mem. adv. coun. U.S. Tex. Engring. Fedn., 1991—. Mem. Am. Soc. Mil. Engrs. (past sec. Orleans chpt., regional v.p. Tex., pres. Dallas chpt.), Assn. U.S. Army, Dallas Black C. of C., ASCE Methodist. Office Phone: 214-415-4200. Personal E-mail: general2star@aol.com.

**ROBINSON, HUGH R.,** retired marketing executive; b. Syracuse, NY, Sept. 18, 1922; s. Frank J. and Gladys (Hunt) R.; m. Evelyn De Mattia, Nov. 24, 1949; children: Susan, Hugh R., Patrice. BS, Syracuse U., 1949. Dist. mgr. Syracuse China, 1949-59; with Royal Worcester Porcelain Co., N.Y.C. 1959-77, v.p. sales, 1971-75, pres., 1975-76, Royal Worcester Spode, Inc., 1977, Lance Internat., N.Y.C., 1977-84; v.p., dir. Christians Glass Inc., N.Y.C., 1980-84; v.p. sales and mktg. Weil Ceramics & Glass Inc., 1985-86, CEO, exec. v.p., 1986-88; CEO LLadro U.S.A. Inc., 1988-91; v.p. Lladro Realty, Inc., 1988-94, Lladro Galleries, Inc., 1988-94; retired, 1994. Advisor Lladro Group, Valencia, Spain, 1991-97; cons. in giftware industry. Served with USAAF, 1942-46. Mem. Alumni Assn. Syracuse U. Home: 3433 57th Ave DRW Bradenton FL 34210

**ROBINSON, IRWIN JAY,** lawyer; b. Bay City, Mich., Oct. 8, 1928; s. Robert R. and Anne (Kaplan) R.; m. Janet Binder, July 7, 1957; children: Elizabeth Binder Schubiner, Jonathan Meyer, Eve Kimberly Wiener. AB, U. Mich., 1950; JD, Columbia U., 1953. Bar: N.Y. 1956. Assoc. Breed Abbott & Morgan, N.Y.C., 1955-58; asst. to ptnrs. Dreyfus & Co., N.Y.C., 1958-59;

assoc. Greenbaum Wolff & Ernst, N.Y.C., 1959-65, ptnr., 1966-76; sr. ptnr. Rosenman & Colin, N.Y.C., 1976-90; of counsel Pryor, Cashman, Sherman & Flynn, 1990-92; sr. ptnr. Phillips, Nizer, Benjamin, Krim & Ballon, N.Y.C., 1992-99; pvt. practice N.Y.C., 1999—. Asst. treas. Saarsteel, Inc., Whitestone, N.Y., 1970—. Bd. dirs. Henry St. Settlement, N.Y.C., 1960-85, Jewish Cmty. Ctr. Assn. N.Am., N.Y.C., 1986-94, mem. adv. bd., 1998—; bd. dirs. Heart Rsch. Found., 1989-94, pres., 1991-93. Mem. ABA, N.Y. State Bar Assn., Assn. Bar City of N.Y., Internat. Bar Assn., Thai-Am. C. of C. (founder, bd. dirs. 1992-95, pres. 1992-95), Vietnam-Am. C. of C. (founder, bd. dirs. 1992-95, pres. 1992-95), Philippine-Am. C. of C. (bd. dirs. 1960-98), Sunningdale Country Club, The Desert Mountain Club. Jewish. Home: 290 West End Ave New York NY 10023 Office: care Kramer Levin Naftalis & Frankel 1177 Avenue of The Americas New York NY 10036 Office Phone: 212-715-7656. Personal E-mail: ijrjbr@aol.com.

**ROBINSON, J. MACK,** communications executive; Chmn. Gulf Capital Corp; owner, chmn. Atlantic Am. Corp., Atlanta, 1974—. Office: Gray Communications Systems Inc 126 N Washington St Albany GA 31701

**ROBINSON, J. MICHAEL,** chemistry professor, researcher; m. Mary Robinson; children: Jim, Will, Chris, John, Jenny. BS in Chemistry, La. Tech. U., 1967—67, MS in Chemistry, 1969; PhD in Organic Chemistry, La. State U., 1973. Bench scale pilot plant chemist DOW Chem. Co., Plaquemine, La., 1968; analytical environ. chemist Continental Can Co., Hodge, La., 1969; nih postdoctoral rsch. assoc. Purdue U., West Lafayette, Ind., 1973—75; postdoctoral rsch. assoc. Tulane U., New Orleans, 1975—76; asst. prof. of chemistry U. of Tex. of the Permian Basin, Odessa, Tex., 1976—80, assoc. prof. of chemistry, 1981—92; enhanced oil recovery rsch. Gulf Oil & Exploration, Monahans, Tex., 1984—85; prof. of chemistry U. of Tex. of the Permian Basin, Odessa, Tex., 1993—94, ashbel smith prof., 1994—96, Ellen and Bill Noël disting. prof. for energy rsch., 1996—. Chair, acs permian basin sect. Am. Chem. Soc., Odessa, Tex., 1999—2002. Sec. North Ector County Little League Baseball, Odessa, Tex., 1994—96; asst. coach Burnett Elem. JV Football, Odessa, Tex., 1993; baseball coach & asst. coach North Ector County Little League, Odessa, Tex., 1996—99; asst. baseball coach Eastside Sr. Baseball League, Odessa, Tex., 2000–01. Fellow Postdoctoral fellow, NIH, 1974-1975; grantee Petroleum Rsch. Fund, Type G, Am. Chem. Soc., 1977-1980, Chemistry Dept. Rsch. grant, The Robert A. Welch Found., 1987-2008, Biomass Derived Transp. Fuels, Nat. Renewable Energy Lab., 1994-1995, Advanced Rsch. Project, Dept of Energy, Basic Energy Scis., 1995-1998, Advanced Tech. Program, Tex. Higher Edn. Coordinating Bd., 2002-2004, Wastewater Rsch. grant, Spectrum Labs, 2004, Energy Related Lab. Equipment grants, Dept of Energy, 1993 - 1997; grant, UTPB Ctr. for Energy & Econ. Diversification, 1980, 1985, 2000-2003. Mem.: Coun. on Undergraduate Rsch., Am. Chem. Soc., Gamma Sigma Epsilon Chemistry Honor Soc. (hon.). Methodist. Achievements include patents for Process for Producing Hydrocarbon Fuels (from biomass) 1996; development of Catalyst Enhanced Solvent Refining of Waste Motor Oil 2003; patents pending for Lactones as Oxygenate Fuels Additives 2005; development of Continuous Removal of Phenols from Oil Refinery Wastewater 2004; Accurate Fire Assay Method for Platium Ores in the US 1992; Enhanced Crude Oil Recovery from Salt Water Disposals 1986. Avocations: mineral exploration, mountain climbing, hunting, fishing, tennis, racquetball. Office: Univ Tex Permian Basin 4901 East University Blvd Odessa TX 79762 Office Phone: 432-552-2237. Office Fax: 432-552-2236. E-mail: robinson_m@utpb.edu.

**ROBINSON, JACK ALBERT,** retail executive; b. Detroit, Feb. 26, 1930; s. Julius and Fannie (Aizkowitz) Robinson; m. Aviva Freedman, Dec. 21, 1952; children: Shelby, Beth, Abigail. B in Pharmacy, Wayne State U., 1952. Founder, chief exec. officer, chmn. bd. Perry Drug Stores, Inc., Pontiac, Mich., 1957-95; founder, chmn., pres. JAR Group LLC, Bloomfield Hills, Mich., 1996—. Chmn. Wayne State U. Fund, Detroit, 1986, Concerned Citizens for Arts Mich., 1990, 1991—; chmn. ann. fund Detroit Symphony Orch.; bd. dirs. United Way Pontiac, Mich., 1986, United Found. Detroit, 1986, Pontiac Area Urban League, Cmty. Found., S.E. Mich., Detroit Svc. Group, Save Orch. Hall, Inc., Cranbrook Inst. Sci., Jewish Fedn. Apts., Wetzman Inst. Sci., Holocaust Meml. Ctr., Harper-Grace Hosp., Detroit; past dir. Pontiac Symphony, Boys Club, Detroit Osteo. Hosp.; pres. United Jewish Found. Met. Detroit, 1992—94; co-chmn. Greater Detroit Interfaith Round Table NCCJ, 1986—92, v.p., 1994—95; pres. Jewish Fedn. Met. Detroit, 1992—94. Named Entrepreneur of the Yr., Harvard Bus. Sch., Detroit, 1982; recipient Disting. Alumni award, Wayne State U. Coll. Pharmacy, 1975, Eleanor Roosevelt Humanities award, State of Israel, 1978, Youth Svcs. Am. Tradition award, B'nai B'rith, 1982, Gt. Am. Traditions award, 1991, Disting. Alumni award, Wayne State U., 1985, Corp. Leadership award, 1985, Tree of Life award, Jewish Nat. Fund, 1985, Disting. Citizen award, Pontiac Boy Scouts Am., 1985, Brotherhood award, Booker T. Washington Bus. Assn., 1986, Humanitarian award, March of Dimes, 1987, Variety Club, 1988, award, Weizmann Rsch. Inst., 1987, Fred M. Butzel award, Jewish Fedn. Met. Detroit, 1991, Cmty. Svc. award, Am. Arabic and Jewish Friends, 1995, Outstanding Philanthropic award, Nat. Soc. Fundraising Execs., 1999, Mich. Hall of Fame award in Real Estate and Retailing, Internat. Coun. Shopping Ctrs., 2001, Gov.'s Arts award Spl. Recognition, 2003. Mem.: Econ. Club (bd. dirs. Detroit chpt.), Am. Found. for Pharm. Edn. (bd. dirs.), Am. Pharm. Assn., Nat. Assn. Chain Drug Stores (chmn. 1987, Lifetime Achievement award 1995, Robert B. Begley award 1995). Avocations: skiing, jogging, photography, classical music, glass collecting. Office: JAR Group LLC Ste 3100 4190 Telegraph Rd Bloomfield Hills MI 48302-2082

**ROBINSON, JAMES ALFRED,** middle school educator; b. Phila., May 13, 1939; s. James Alfred Sr. and Evelyn (Perry) R.; children: James, John, Marce Balais; m. Gladys Acaba, Mar. 9, 1996. BS, Cheyney (Pa.) U., 1961; postgrad., U. Pa., 1962, Temple U., 1966—68, Goddard Coll., 1989—90, C.C. Phila., 1989. Mid. sch. tchr. Phila. Pub. Schs., 1962-95. Mem. reading program grades 4-6, TV lang. arts Project Climb, Sch. Dist. Phila., 1974; mem. panel, asst. prodr. video prodn. Skills for New Teachers, Sch. Dist. Phila., 1975; social sci. specialist Samson L. Freedman Sch. Humanities Alternative Middle sch., Dist. Phila., 1977; chmn. J.A. Robinson Assocs. Video Prodn. Cons., Phila., 1988—; instr. ednl. media Temple U., 1988-90; video prodn. cons. In Search of History: The Underground Railroad, History channel, 1999; video documentaries include Linda Creed Concert, Mayoral Race: Phila., 1985, Duality, Bicentennial Celebration. Media arts fellow Mid-Atlantic region Pitts. Filmmakers NEA, Pa. Coun. for Arts, 1993. Mem. HTML Writers Guild. Baptist. Avocations: photography, music, tennis.

**ROBINSON, JAMES ARTHUR,** political scientist; b. Blackwell, Okla., June 9, 1932; s. William L. and Ethel Bell (Hicks) R.; children: Adelaide, Luke; m. Andrea C. Hatcher, Jan. 20, 2006 AB, George Washington U., 1954, DPS (hon.), 1977; MA, U. Okla., 1955; PhD, Northwestern U., 1957. Congl. fellow Am. Polit. Sci. Assn., 1957-58; Instr. polit. sci. Northwestern U., 1958-59, asst. prof., 1959-62, assoc. prof., 1962-64; prof. polit. sci. Ohio State U., Columbus, 1964-71; dir. Mershon Center, 1967-70, v.p. acad. affairs, provost, 1969-71; pres., prof. polit. sci. Macalester Coll., St. Paul, 1971-74; pres. U. West Fla., Pensacola, 1974-88, pres. emeritus, 1988—, Regents prof., 1988—2002. Author: (with R. C. Snyder) National and International Decision Making, 1961, Congress and Foreign Policy Making, rev. edit, 1967, House Rules Committee, 1963, (with J. Baum) Party Primaries in Taiwan, 1999, (with D. Brown and E. Moon) Appraising Steps in Democratization: Elections in Taiwan, 1986-2000, 2000. Mem.: Cosmos (Washington).

**ROBINSON, JAMES D., III,** venture capitalist; b. Atlanta, Nov. 19, 1935; m. Bettye Bradley (div.), 2 children; m. Linda Gosden, 1984; 2 children. BS, Ga. Inst. Tech., 1957; MBA, Harvard U., 1961. Officer various depts. Morgan Guaranty Trust Co. of N.Y., N.Y.C., 1961-66, asst. v.p.; staff asst. to chmn. bd. and pres., 1967-68; gen. ptnr. White, Weld & Co., 1968-70; exec. v.p. Am. Express Co. N.Y.C., 1970-75, pres., dir., 1975-77, chmn. bd. dirs. CEO, 1977-93. Pres., CEO Am. Express Internat. Banking Corp., 1970-73; chair Am. Express Credit Corp., 1973-75; co-founder, gen. ptnr. RRE Ventures, 1994—; chmn., CEO RRE Investors LLC; bd. dirs. Coca Cola Co., Novell, Inc., First Data Corp.; former co-chair Bus. Roundtable; non-exec. chmn.

Bristol-Myers Squibb Co., 2005—. Author: Inflation Overkill, 1994, Full Steam Ahead, 2000. Active Bus. Coun., Coun. on Fgn. Rels., U.S. Japan Bus. Coun., Dean's Adv. Coun. Roberto C. Goizueta Sch. Bus. Emory U., Exec. Adv. Bd., Van Allen Coll.; hon. chmn. bd. Meml. Sloan-Kettering Cancer Ctr.; hon. mem. The Brookings Instn.; mem. bd. dirs. Nat. Acad. Found.; mem. Pres.' Cir. The Asia Soc.; bd. dirs., chair emeritus Partnership of N.Y.C.; chair emeritus World Travel & Tourism Coun.; former chair Internat. Trade and Investment Task Force of the Bus. Roundtable, former chair svcs. policy adv. com.; former chmn. adv. com. on trade and policy negotiations United Way of Am.; former mem. Coun. on Competitiveness; former trustee Alfred P. Sloan Found., Coun. on Econ. Devel.; former mem Dewitt Wallace Found. Lt. USNR, 1957-59. Mem. Econ. Club (N.Y.C.). Office: RRE Ventures 126 E 56th St Fl 22 New York NY 10022-3613 Office Phone: 212-418-5100.

**ROBINSON, JAMES W.,** fire captain; b. Calif. m. Erika Robinson. MPA, Kennedy Sch. of Govt., Harvard U., Cambridge, MA, 2000—01; Fire Protection Adminstrn./ Pub. Adminstrn., Calif. State U. LA, Los Angeles, 1996—99. Exec. projects LA County Fire Dept., Los Angeles, Calif., 2001—, engr., 1998—2004, firefighter, 1992—98. Mem. Inst. of Supply Mgmt., Los Angeles, Calif., 2002—; treas. LA County Fire Fighters Assoc., Los Angeles, Calif., 2001—. Interviewer and evaluator Harvard U. Schools Com., Los Angeles, Calif., 2002—. Recipient Alumni Achievement Award, Calif. State U. LA, 2000, Commendation, LA County Bd. of Supervisors, 2000, Magna Cum Laude, Calif. State U. LA, 1999; fellow Robert Wilmers State and Local Govt. Pub. Svc. Fellow, Kennedy Sch. of Govt., Harvard U., 2000-2001. Mem.: Harvard-Radcliffe Club of So. Calif. Avocations: reading, golf, travel. Office: LA County Fire Dept 1320 N Eastern Ave Los Angeles CA 90063 E-mail: jrobinso@lacofd.org.

**ROBINSON, JAMES WILLIAM,** chemistry professor; b. Kidderminster, England, July 12, 1923; arrived in U.S., 1955, naturalized, 1958; s. James William and Eva Robinson; m. Winifred Gladys Nixon, Jan. 8, 1940; children: James William, Linda Juanita, Sandra Jacqueline. BSc with hons., U. Birmingham, England, 1949, PhD, 1952, DSc, 1978. Sr. sci. officer Brit. Civil Svc., Birmingham, England, 1952—55; from rsch. assoc. to prof. emeritus La. State U., Baton Rouge, 1955—93, prof. emeritus, 1993—; sr. chemist Esso Rsch. Labs., Baton Rouge, 1956—63; tech. advisor Ethyl Corp., Baton Rouge, 1963—64. Mem. rsch. grants adv. com. EPA, 1969—73; vis. prof. U. Sydney, Australia, 1983; lectr. in field. Author: Atomic Absorption Spectroscopy, 1966, 2d edit., 1975, Undergraduate Instrumental Analysis, 1970, 6th edit., 2005, Atomic Spectroscopy, 1990, 2d edit., 1996; editor: Analytica Chemica Acta, 1956—80, Spectroscopy Letters, 1966—98, Environl. Sci. and Health, 1971—97, Monograph Series Analysis Environ. Control, 1977—85, Applied Spectroscopy Revs., 1977—90, Jour. Applied Spectroscopy, 2003, Handbook of Spectroscopy, Vol. I, 1974, Handbook of Spectroscopy, Vol. II, 1974, Handbook of Spectroscopy, Vol. III, 1981, Practical Handbook of Spectroscopy, 1991; contbr. chapters to books, over 200 articles to profl. jours. Recipient Gold medal, N.Y. Soc. Applied Spectroscopy, 2000; fellow, Guggenheim Found., 1975. Fellow: Royal Chem. Soc. Avocations: gardening, travel, snorkeling. Office: Dept Chemistry La Sate Univ Baton Rouge LA 70803

**ROBINSON, JANET L.,** publishing executive; BA in English cum laude, Salve Regina Coll., Newport, R.I., 1972; diploma in Exec. Edn., Dartmouth U., 1996; DBA (hon.), Salve Regina U., Newport, R.I., 1998. Tchr., reading specialist, 1972—83; account exec., Tennis Mag. The N.Y. Times Co., 1983—85, nat. resort and travel mgr., Golf Digest/Tennis, 1985—87, advt. dir., Tennis Mag., 1987—90, v.p. advt. sales and mktg., The Women's Mag. Group, 1990—92, group sr. v.p., advt. sales and mktg., The Women's Mag. Group, 1992—93, v.p., dir. advt., 1994, sr. v.p. advt., 1995, pres., gen. mgr., N.Y. Times newspaper, 1996—, sr. v.p. newspaper ops., 2001—04, exec. v.p., COO, 2004—, dir., 2004—, pres., CEO, 2005—. Coun. Dept. Edn., Mass., 1977—83; chair. Advertising Council, 2004—. Mem. Literacy Vols. N.Y.; mem. adv. bd. Salve Regina Coll.; trustee Carnegie Corp., 2004—. Named Outstanding Newspaper Exec.; Frohlinger's Mktg. Report, 1994; named one of 100 Most Powerful Women in World, Forbes Mag., 2005—06. Mem.: Women in Comm., Advt. Women N.Y., Advt. Club N.Y. Office: NY Times 229 W 43rd St New York NY 10036-3959*

**ROBINSON, JAY (JAY THURSTON ROBINSON),** artist; b. Detroit, Aug. 1, 1915; s. Carter Boston and Marie Rose (Steger) R.; m. Dorothy June Whipple, Sept. 15, 1937 (dec. 1968); children: Theodore Carter, Thomas Whipple, James Jay; m. Anne Frances Helen Posch, Nov. 5, 1970 (dec. 1999). BA, Yale U., 1937; MFA, Cranbrook Acad. Art, 1943. One-man shows include, Guggenheim Mus. Non-Objective Painting, N.Y.C., 1947, Milch Galleries, N.Y.C., 1948, 51, 53, 54, 55, 56, J.B. Speed Art Mus., Louisville, 1953, Dayton Art Inst., 1953, Phila. Art Alliance, 1957, Monede Gallery, N.Y.C., 1961, 62, Raymond Burr Galleries, Beverly Hills, Calif., 1963, xxth Century West Gallery, N.Y.C., 1968, E. Kuhlik Gallery, N.Y.C., 1971, New Canaan Soc. for Arts, 1983, Broome St. Gallery, N.Y.C., 1994, group shows include, Guggenheim Mus., 1947, 49, Carnegie Inst., Pitts., 1949, Des Moines Art Center, 1950, Butler Inst., Youngstown, Ohio, 1953, also Audubon Artists, N.Y.C., Corcoran Gallery, Washington, Mich. Artists, Detroit, NAD, N.Y., Pa. Acad., Phila., Provincetown (Mass.) Annual, Va. Biennial, Richmond; represented in permanent collections, including, Detroit Inst. Art, Houston Mus. Fine Art, Witte Meml. Mus., San Antonio, Philbrook Art Center, Tulsa; Berea Coll., Goucher Coll., Fisk U.; represented also in corp. collections, including, IBM; Republic Steel Co., Bristol-Myers Squibb, portrait painter, designer china and textiles; illustrator: Seventeenth Summer (Maureen Daly), 1948, The New York Guide Book, 1964; contbr. illustrations to other books. Served with OSS, 1943; Served with USN, 1943-46. Louis Comfort Tiffany Found. award, 1950; various purchase awards Am. Acad. Arts and Letters, 1951-64; Outstanding Alumnus award Detroit Country Day Sch., 1966 Home: 305 E Landing Williamsburg VA 23185-8254 *I have always been drawn to the theme of Man in His Environment. By extension to our own, I love jazz music, many of whose players I have painted; classic cars; Japanese gardens; good company and active social life. Travel enables me to see what others have done and are doing.*

**ROBINSON, JEFFREY P.,** lawyer; b. Memphis, Aug. 30, 1956; BA cum laude, Marquette U., 1978; JD, Harvard U., 1981. Bar: Wash. 1981, US Dist. Ct., We. Dist. Wash. 1981, US Ct. Appeals, Ninth Circuit 1986. Public defender state, fed. courts, 1981—88; atty., criminal def. Schroeter, Goldmark & Bender, PS, Seattle. Instr. trial advocacy program U. Wash. Sch. Law, 1988—; faculty Nat. Criminal Def. Coll., Macon Ga.; mem. trial advocacy workshop Harvard Law Sch., 1990—. Contbr. articles to law jour. Named Lawyer of Yr., Kings County Bar Assn., 2003; named one of Am. Top Black Lawyers, Black Enterprise Mag., 2003. Fellow: Am. Coll. Trial Lawyers; mem.: Nat. Inst. Trial Advocacy, Nat. Assn. Criminal Def. Lawyers (bd. dirs.), Wash. Assn. Criminal Def. Lawyers (past pres.), Wash. State Trial Lawyers Assn., Wash. State Bar Assn. (mem. criminal law com. 1989). Office: Schroeter Goldmark & Bender PS 810 Third Ave Ste 500 Seattle WA 98104 Office Phone: 206-622-8000.

**ROBINSON, JENNIFER JANKE,** voice educator, singer; d. Charles Janke and Barbara Jean Dressel; m. Bradley Craig Robinson, Jan. 26, 1985; children: Zachary Lewis, Jacob Taylor. B of Music Edn. and Vocal Performance, Western Mich. U., Kalamazoo, 1981; MusM, Fla. State U., Tallahassee, 1984. Grad. tchg. asst. Fla. State U., Tallahassee, 1981—83; instr. of voice Meredith Coll., Raleigh, NC, 1988—95; grad. asst. U. Ill., Urbana, 1995—97; instr. of voice U. Miss., Oxford, 1997—.

**ROBINSON, JENNIFER META,** academic administrator, consultant; b. Boston, 1962; d. Samuel Sachs and Catherine Greenacre Robinson; m. J. A. Hartenfeld, 1946; 1 child. Sarah Meghan Hartenfeld. PhD, Ind. U., 2001. Dir. campus instrnl. cons. and scholarship of tchg. and learning Ind. U., Bloomington, 2002—. Author: "Kate Douglas Wiggin." Bibliography of American Fiction, 1866 to 1918. Ed. James Nagel and Gwen L. Nagel., of poems; contbr. chapters to books, articles to profl. jours. Treas. People and Animal Learning Svcs., Bloomington, Ind., 2000—05. Recipient Hesburgh award for

a faculty devel. program, TIAA-CREF, 2003. Mem.: Internat. Soc. Scholarship of Tchg. and Learning (founding mem., v.p. 2005—06). Office: Indiana Univ 601 East Kirwood Ave Bloomington IN 47405 Office Phone: 812-855-9023. E-mail: jenmetar@indiana.edu.

**ROBINSON, JOE SAM,** neurosurgeon, educator; b. Atlanta, Ga., July 21, 1945; s. Joe Sam and Nell (Mixon) R.; m. Elizabeth Ann Moate, Apr. 3, 1982; children: Joe Sam III, Edward Richard, Thomas McRae. AB cum laude, Harvard Coll., 1967; MD, U. Va., 1971; MS, Northwestern U., 1975. Surg. intern Emory U., 1971-72, resident in surgery, 1972-73; resident in neurosurgery Northwestern U., 1973-78; instr. U. Ill., 1978-79, Yale U., 1979-81; pres. Ga. Neurosurg. Inst. P.A., Macon, 1981—. Prof., chief neurosurgery Mercer U. Sch. Medicine, Macon, 1986; chief surgery Med. Ctr. Ctrl. Ga., Macon, 1989—, vice chmn. surgery, 1991-97, chmn. dept. surgery, 1996—; vis. neurosurgeon China, 1992, Konaus Acad. Neurosurgery Inst., Lithuania, 1992; clin. prof. Med. Coll. Ga., 2002. Lt. col. USANG, 1972-95. Fellow Internat. Coll. Surgeons (vice regent 1983-93); mem. Am. Assn. Neurol. Surgeons, Congress Neurol. Surgeons, AAAS, Ga. Neurosurg. Soc., Alpha Omega Alpha. Republican. Methodist. Office: Ga Neurosurg Inst PA 840 Pine St Ste 880 Macon GA 31201-7525 E-mail: teriwyn@hotmail.com.

**ROBINSON, JOEL D.,** manufacturing executive; 3 children. Dir. Body-in-White assemble Chrysler; dir. vehicle assembly Am. Motors; Ford personnel devel. program Ford Motor Co.; dir. mfg. planning Am. Axle & Mfg., Detroit, 1994, dir. GMT800 program, exec. dir. mfg., v.p. mfg., exec. v.p., COO, 1998—2001, pres., COO, 2001—. Office: Am Axle and Mfg 1840 Holbrook Detroit MI 48212-3488

**ROBINSON, JOHN ALAN,** information scientist, educator; b. Halifax, Eng., Mar. 9, 1930; came to U.S., 1952; naturalized citizen, 1990. s. Harry and Clara (Pilkington) R.; m. Gwen Groves, Dec. 18, 1954; children: Alan Groves, Hugh Parke Custis, Gwen Owen. BA in Classics with honours, Corpus Christi Coll., Cambridge U., Eng., 1952; MA, 1955; MA in Philosophy, U. Ore., 1953; MA, Princeton U., 1955, PhD, 1956; D in Applied Sci. honoris causa, U. Leuven, 1988; D in Philosophy honoris causa, U. Uppsala, 1994; D in Informatics honoris causa, U. Politechnica, Madrid, 2003. Operations research analyst E.I. du Pont de Nemours & Co., Inc., 1956-60; post-doctoral research fellow U. Pitts., 1960-61; mem. faculty Rice U., 1961-67, prof. philosophy, 1964-65, prof. computer sci. and philosophy, 1965-66, prof. computer sci., 1966-67; disting. prof. logic and computer sci. Syracuse U., 1967-84, Univ. prof., 1984-92, univ. prof. emeritus, 1993—. Cons. in applied math. divsn. Argonne Nat. Lab., 1961-67, Stanford Linear Acceleration Ctr., 1966-68; vis. rsch. fellow Australian Nat. U., 1989; Fujitsu vis. prof. U. Tokyo, 1991-92. Author: Logic: Form and Function, 1979; founder, editor-in-chief Jour. Logic Programming, 1984-86; contbr. articles to profl. jours. Served with RAF, 1948-49. Recipient Sr. U.S. Scientists prize Humboldt Found., 1995, Herbrand award, 1996; Guggenheim Found. fellow, 1967-68; hon. rsch. fellow U. Edinburgh, 1967—. Fellow Am. Assn. for Artificial Intelligence; mem. Kokusai Bunka Kaikan (Tokyo). Home and Office: PO Box 988 Northampton MA 01601-0988

**ROBINSON, JOHN BECKWITH,** development management consultant; b. Portland, Oreg., May 23, 1922; s. Jewell King and Arvilla Agnes (Beckwith) R.; m. Dilys Walters, Sept. 8, 1945; children— John Gwilym, David Gwyn. BA, U. Oreg., 1944; postgrad., U. Shrivenham, Eng., 1945, U. Oxford, 1946, Am. U., 1947. Staff U.S. Bur. Budget, 1947—48; sr. program and budget officer UNESCO, 1948—51; mem. staff U.S. Bur. Budget, 1951—52; chief personnel policy Mut. Security Agy., Washington, 1952-54, program officer Guatemala, 1954-59, planning officer, Latin Am. region asst. dep. dir. for program and planning AID Washington, 1959-61; dep. U.S. rep. devel. assistance com. OECD, 1961-64, asst. dir. devel. policy Pakistan, 1964-68; dep. dir. North Coast Affairs, AID, State Dept., Washington, 1969-71; dep. mission dir. U.S. Econ. Aid Program, Colombia, 1971-73, mission dir. Dominican Republic, 1973-76, mission dir. Honduras, 1976—79; privatization adviser Gov. of Costa Rica, 1986-88; prin. assoc. J.B. Robinson & Assocs. (devel. mgmt. cons.), 1979—. Mem. faculty, fellow Harvard U., 1968-69; cons. NATO, 1951, UN, 1951. Served to 1st lt., inf. AUS. 1943-46, ETO. Mem. Oriental Club (London), DACOR BACON House (Washington), Minchinhampton Probus Club (pres. 1983-84). Episcopalian. Address: Anglezarke The Hithe Rodborough Common Stroud GL5 5BN Gloucestershire England also: 2323 SW Park Pl Portland OR 97205 Office Phone: 44-1453-873346. Business E-Mail: jbrdil@ukonline.co.uk. *Summary: always do more than what is asked for the task at hand. The extra effort always leads to unexpected opportunities for career advancement. Helping others to realize their potential has its own rewards and their success helps to realize your own hopes and aspirations, and improve your own quality of life and satisfaction in a life well-spent. Never underestimate the contribution of your wife and family.*

**ROBINSON, JOHN CHRISTOPHER,** music educator; s. Marlyn Eugene and Marion Robinson; m. Kristina Parker. MusB in Edn., Shorter Coll., Rome, Ga., 1996; MEd, Valdosta (Ga.) State U., 2005. Cert. tchr. Ga. Profl. Standards Commn., 1996, pub. sch. leadership Ga. Profl. Standards Commn., 2005. Asst. music dir. First Bapt. Ch., Rome, Ga., 1993—96; dir. choral 8th St. Mid. Sch., Tifton, Ga., 1996—. Singer: Tallahassee Symphony, Carnegie Hall. Interim music min. Northside Bapt. Ch., TIfton, 2003—04. Marion Wallace Music scholarship, Shorter Coll., 1992—96. Mem.: Pa. of Ga. Educators, Am. Choral Dirs. Assn., Music Educators Nat. Conf., Ga. Music Educators Assn. Republican. Southern Bapt. Avocations: hunting, golf, outdoors activities. Home: 608 46th Street East Tifton GA 31794 Office: 8th Street Middle School 700 West 8th Street Tifton GA 31794 Office Phone: 229-387-2445.

**ROBINSON, J(OHN) E(RIC),** history professor, travel company executive; b. Alton, Ill., Oct. 8, 1965; s. Ralph Preston and Joyce Lauretta Robinson. BA, Howard U., 1987; MA, U. Mo., 1989. Lectr. history various colls., St. Louis, 1989—94; instr. history Lewis and Clark C.C., Godfrey, Ill., 1994—; proprietor J.E. Robinson Tours, Alton, 1995—. Prodr., host Eavesdropping WBGZ-AM, Alton, 1993—2004. Author: Five Verses: Poems, 2000, Skip Macalester, 2005. Sec. Alton Mus. History and Art, 1994—99; pres. Elijah P. Lovejoy Meml., Alton, 1995—2003; mem., vice-chmn. Alton Hist. Commn., 1996—98; vol. Big Bros. Big Sisters, 2004—; mem. African Meth. Episcopal Ch. Nominee Puschart prize, 2004; recipient Lit. award in prose, Ill. Arts Coun., 2005; grantee, NEH, 1985, Ill. Arts Coun., 2000—02. Mem.: Ill. Underground R.R. Assn. Avocations: genealogy, antiques. Office Phone: 618-462-5590.

**ROBINSON, JOHN HAYES,** law educator; b. Providence, Apr. 4, 1943; s. William Philip and Dorothy Frances (Hayes) R.; m. Deborah Ann Deery, Aug. 15, 1981; children: Gena, John. BA, Boston Coll., 1967; MA, Notre Dame U., 1972, PhD, 1975; JD, U. Calif.-Berkeley, 1979. Bar: R.I. 1980. Asst. prof. U. San Francisco, 1973-76; instr. law U. Miami, Coral Gables, Fla., 1979-80; jud. clk. U.S. Dist. Ct., Hartford, Conn., 1980-81; asst. prof. law and philosophy U. Notre Dame (Ind.), 1981-96, assoc. prof. law, 1996—, assoc. dean acad. affairs, 2002—04, exec. assoc. dean, 2005—. Office: U Notre Dame Law Sch Box 780 Notre Dame IN 46556 Office Phone: 574-631-6980. Business E-Mail: robinson.1@nd.edu.

**ROBINSON, JOHN WILLIAM, IV,** lawyer; b. Atlanta, Apr. 29, 1950; s. J. William III and Elizabeth (Smith) R.; m. Ellen Showalter, Dec. 28, 1976; children: William, Anna. BA with honors, Washington & Lee U., 1972; JD, U. Ga., 1975. Bar: Fla., Ga., U.S. Dist. Ct. (no., so. and mid. dists.) Fla., U.S. Ct. Mil. Appeals, U.S. Ct. Appeals (5th and 11th circs.), U.S. Supreme Ct.; cert. labor & employment law, civil trial and bus. litigation lawyer, Fla., Nat. Bd. Trial Advocacy. Trial atty. Nat. Labor Rels. Bd., New Orleans, 1975—76; trial def. counsel 8th infantry U.S. Army, Mainz, Germany, 1977—78; trial counsel 8th infantry, 1979; law clk., commr. Ct. Mil. Rev., Washington, 1980; atty. Fowler, White, Boggs & Banker, PA, Tampa, Fla., 1980—, head labor and employment law dept., 1993—, dir., 1998—, sec./treas., 2001—. Mem. faculty U. Md., 1977-79; arbitrator U.S. Dist. Ct. (mid. dist.) Fla.; mem.

Leadership Fla., 2004— Editor-in-chief: Employment & Labor Relations Law, 1991-95; editor: Developing Labor Law, 1982—, Model Jury Instructions for Employment Litigation, 1994—; editor: Employment Litigation Handbook, 1998. Chmn. Tampa Bay Internat. Trade Coun., 1990-91, Rough Riders Dist. Boy Scouts Am., 1990; legal counsel, chair Drug Free Workplace Task Force, 1999-00; legal counsel, chair, gen. counsel, bd. dirs., 1996, 04-, Greater Tampa C. of C., 1996, 05-; bd. fellows, chair bus. symposia U. Tampa, 2006—. Capt. U.S. Army, 1976-80. Named one of Best Lawyers in Am. for labor and employment law, Top Ten Super Lawyers in Fla., Fla. Legal Elite. Fellow: Coll. Labor and Employment Lawyers (Founding fellow); mem.: ABA (chmn. employment and labor rels. com. 1993—96, divsn. dir. 1996—2000, mem. coun. 2000—03, chmn. com. on multijurisdictional practice 2000—, task force on electronic discovery 2003—04, litigation sect.), Acad. Fla. Mgmt. Attys. (chair-elect 2006—, charter mem.), Leadership Tampa (chmn. 2006), Hillsborough County Bar Assn. Trial Lawyers (bd. dirs. 1996—, chmn. 2003—), Am. Inn of Ct. (pres., dir. and master barrister, trustee Am. Inns of Ct. Found., exec. com. Am. Inns of Ct. Found.), Washington & Lee U. Bd. (pres. nat. alumni bd. 1990—91, trustee 1995—2005), Fla. Bar Assn. (chmn. labor and employment law sect. 1992—93), Rotary (bd. fellows 2004—, exec. com. 2004—, pres. Tampa Bay chpt.). Avocations: tennis, history. Office: Fowler White Boggs Banker PA 501 E Kennedy Blvd Tampa FL 33602-5237

**ROBINSON, JOYCE MCPEAKE,** academic administrator; b. Newark, July 28, 1941; d. Salvatore and Wilhelmina (Cervetto) Guinta; m. John David McPeake, June 15, 1963 (div. Aug. 1974); children: John Paul, David Samuel; m. Enders Anthony Robinson, Aug. 8, 1992. BA in English, Tufts U., 1962; MA in English, Boston U., 1965, EdD, 1979, Asst. to dean women & dept. administrn. Boston U., 1962—63, 1965—67; reading specialist Hingham Pub. Schs., Mass., 1963—64; reading and learning specialist Manter Hall Sch., Cambridge, Mass., 1964—67; reporter Patriot Ledger, Quincy, Mass., 1967—69; dir. Christ Luth. Sch., Scituate, Mass., 1971—74; prin. and reading specialist Scituate Pub. Schs., 1974—80; chair English, dir. reading programs St. Andrew's Sch., Boca Raton, Fla., 1980—85; chair English, learning specialist Broadwater Acad., Exmore, Va., 1988—89; dir. learning resources, English Fountain Valley Sch., Colorado Springs, Colo., 1989—91; asst. prin. Islamic Saudi Acad., Alexandria, Va., 1991—93; chair English Masters Sch., Dobbs Ferry, NY, 1993—94; head QUEST program Dwight Sch., N.Y.C., 1994—96, head of sch., 1996—. Adj. prof. Nova U., Ft. Lauderdale, Fla., 1984-88, St. Thomas U., Miami, Fla., 1987-88; sch. evaluator Fla. Coun. Ind. Schs., 1985-88; cons. in field. Author: Teaching Study Skills, 1987, Wordworks, 1990; contbr. (poetry) Rhyme and Reason, 1987; editor: How to Double Your Child's Grades in School, 1997; contbr.: Fostering Creativity in Children, K-8, 2000. Coord. Am. Inst. Fgn. Study, Boston, 1987; parent agt. Hamilton Coll. Parents Fund, Clinton, N.Y., 1986—; mem. town adv. com. Scituate Town Com., 1975-80. Mem. Nat. Coun. Tchrs. English, Am. Acad. Poets, Nat. Assn. Ind. Schs., Fla. Coun. Librs., Ea. Ednl. Rsch. Assn. (membership chair 1993-95), Internat. Reading Assn., Coun. Exceptional Children, Modern Lang. Assn., Hemingway Soc., Am. Assn. Ednl. Rsch. (pres.), Nat. Acad. Ednl. Rsch. Home: 8 Dorothy Lucey Dr Newburyport MA 01950 Business E-Mail: jrobinson@dwight.edu.

**ROBINSON, JULIE ANN,** judge; b. 1957; BS, U. Kans., 1978, JD, 1981. Bar: Kans. 1981. Asst. U.S. atty. for dist. Kans. U.S. Dept. Justice, Kansas City, Kans., 1983—94, sr. litigation counsel, 1991—94; law clk. to hon. Benjamin E. Franklin, U.S. Bankruptcy Ct. for Dist. Kans., Kansas City, Kans., 1981—83, bankruptcy judge, 1994—2001; judge bankruptcy appellate panel U.S. Ct. Appeals (10th cir.), Topeka, 1996—2001; U.S. dist. judge State of Kans., 2001—. Instr. trial practice U. Kans. Sch. Law, 1989—90. Fellow: Am. Bar Found.; mem.: ABA, Kans. Bar Assn. Office: US Dist Ct 405 US Courthouse 444 SE Quincy Topeka KS 66683

**ROBINSON, JUNE KERSWELL,** dermatologist, educator; b. Phila., Jan. 26, 1950; d. George and Helen S. (Kerswell) R.; m. William T. Barker, Jan. 31, 1981. BA cum laude, U. Pa., 1970; MD, U. Md., 1974. Diplomate Am. Bd. Dermatology, Nat. Bd. Med. Examiners, Am. Bd. Mohs Micrographic Surgery and Cutaneous Oncology. Intern Greater Balt. Med. Ctr., Hanover, NH, 1974, resident in medicine, 1974—75; resident in dermatology Dartmouth-Hitchcock Med. Ctr., Hanover, 1975—78, chief resident, clin. instr., 1977—78, instr. in dermatology, 1978; fellow Mohs; chemosurgery and dermatologic surgery NYU Skin and Cancer Clinic, N.Y.C., 1978—79; instr. in dermatology NYU, N.Y.C., 1979; asst. prof. dermatology Northwestern U. Med. Sch., Chgo., 1979, asst. prof. surgery, 1980—85, assoc. prof. dermatology and surgery, 1985—91, prof. dermatology and surgery, 1991—98; prof. medicine and pathology, dir. divsn. dermatology Cardinal Bernardin Cancer Ctr., Loyola U. Med. Ctr., 1998—2004, program leader skin cancer clin. program, 1998—2004; prof. medicine Med. Sch. Dartmouth U., 2004—05, chief Dermatology Sect. Hitchcock Med. Ctr., 2004—05; prof. clin. dermatology Feinberg Sch. Medicine, Northwestern U., Chgo., 2004—. Mem. consensus devel. conf. NIH, 1992; mem. panel on use of sunscreens Internat. Agy. for Rsch. on Cancer, WHO, 2000; lectr. in field. Author: Fundamentals of Skin Biopsy, 1985, also audiovisual materials; editor: (textbooks) Atlas of Cutaneous Surgery, 1996, Cutaneous Medicine and Surgery: An Integrated Program in Dermatology, 1996, Surgery of the Skin, 2005; mem. editl. bd. Archives of Dermatology, 1988-97; sect. editor The Cutting Edge: Challenges in Med. and Surg. Therapeutics, 1989-97. editor, 2004—; contbg. editor Jour. Dermatol. Surgery and Oncology, 1985-88; mem. editl. com. 18th World Congress of Dermatology, 1982; contbr. numerous articles, abstracts to profl. publs., chpts. to books. Bd. dirs. Northwestern Med. Faculty Found., 1982-84, chmn. com. on benefits and leaves, 1984, nominating com. 1988. Grantee Nat. Cancer Inst. 1985-91, 2004—. Am. Cancer Soc., 1986-89. Skin Cancer Found., 1981 85. Dermatology Found., 1981-83, Northwestern U. Biomed. Rsch., 1981, Syntex, 1984. Fellow: Am. Coll. Chemosurgery (chmn. sci. program ann. meeting 1983, chmn. publs. com. 1986—87, chmn. task force on ednl. needs 1989—90, co-editor bull. 1984—87); mem.: Chgo. Dermatol. Soc., Women's Dermatol. Soc. (pres. 1990—92, Wilma Bergeld, MD Visionary and Leadership award 2002), Soc. Investigative Dermatology, Am. Soc. Dermatol. Surgery (pres. 1994—95), Dermatology Found. (trustee 1995—98), Am. Acad. Dermatology (asst. sec.-treas. 1995—98, sec.-treas. 1998—2001, bd. dirs. 1993—95, Stephen Rothman Lectr. award 1992, Presdl. citation 1992, 2000), Am. Dermatol. Assn., Am. Cancer Soc. (pres. Ill. divsn. 1996—98, St. George Disting. Svc. medal 2004). Office: Northwestern U Feinberg Sch Med Dept Dermatology 132 E Delaware Pl #5806 Chicago IL 60611

**ROBINSON, KAREN VAJDA,** dietician; BS in Home Econs., Montclair State Coll., 1980; MS in Health Scis./Dietetics, James Madison U., 1992. Cert. food svc. sanitation mgr., N.J. 1984. Dietician Roosevelt Hosp., Edison, NJ, 1980-85; asst. mgr. UVA (U. Va.) Dining Svcs., Charlottesville, 1985-86; temp. sales sec., mem. banquet prep. staff Boar's Head Inn, Charlottesville, 1986-88; head diet counselor Diet Ctr., Charlottesville, 1986-90; dietetic intern VA Med. Ctr., Hampton, Va., 1991; pub. health nutritionist Cen. Shenandoah Health Dist., Waynesboro (Va.) Health Dept., 1993-97. Grad. dietetic intern mentor, 1993—97; cons. dietetate Hebrew Hosp. Home, Bronx, NY, 1998; food svc. mgr. Sodexho Marriott Svcs., Morningside House Nursing Home, Bronx, 1998—99; clin. dietitian Yonkers (NY) Gen. Hosp., 1999—2001; cmty. svcs. instr. Westchester C.C., Valhalla, NY, 2001; inpatient/out patient dietitian Park Care Pavilion (formerly Yonkers Gen. Hosp.), 2001—; clin. dietitian St. John's Riverside Hosp., Yonkers, 2002—; outpatient dietitian St. John's Riverside, Valentine Lane Family Practice, Yonkers, 2005. Contbr. articles to local newspapers. Mem. Charlottesville Health Promotion Coalition, 1993-97. Mem.: Westchester Rockland Dietetic Assn. (health fairs chair 1998—2001, scholarship com. 2000, pub. rels. co-chair 2000—01, sec. 2001—06, chmn. nominating com. 2003—04, health fairs com. 2005—06, grantee 2000), Va. Dietetic Assn. (exec. bd. 1996—97), Blue Ridge Dietetics Assn. (nat. nutrition month coord. 1993—95, editor newsletter 1993—96, mem. exec. bd. 1993—97, pres.-elect 1995—96, scholarship com. 1996, pres. 1996—97), Va. Pub. Health Assn. (sec. 1995,

awards chair 1996—97), Dietitians in Nutrition Support, Gerontol. Nutritionists Practice Group, Cons. Dietitians in Health Care Facilities, Am. Dietetic Assn. (registered). Home: 10-02 Hunter Ln Ossining NY 10562 Personal E-mail: kvrobinson@aol.com.

**ROBINSON, KAYNE B.,** lobbyist, former political organization officer; m. Donna R. Robinson, B, Drake U. With Des Moines Police Dept., 1968—99; dep. Iowa chmn. Dole Presdl. campaign, 1988; Iowa chmn. Gramm Presdl. campaign, 1996; chmn. Iowa Rep. Party, 1999—2001; 1st v.p. NRA, Fairfax, Va., 1997—2003, pres., 2003—. With USMC. Named Police Officer of the Yr. Iowa Assn. Women Police. Office: NRA 11250 Waples Mill Rd Fairfax VA 22030

**ROBINSON, KENNETH CHARLES,** management educator; b. Macon, Ga. s. Charles William Robinson and Joyce R. Sorrow. BBA, U. Ga., 1984, MBA, 1991, PhD, 1995. Gen. mgr., CFO Shoe Shack, Inc., Macon, 1984-90, controller, buyer, 1990-91, mgmt. advisor, 1991-94; grad. tchg. asst. U. Ga., Athens, 1991-95; lectr. U. Wollongong, NSW, Australia, 1995-96; assoc. prof. strategy & entrepreneurship Kennesaw (Ga.) State U., 1996—. Mem. rels. com. Greater Macon C. of C., 1988—90, vice chmn. small bus. coun., 1989—90. Recipient Heizer Best Doctoral Dissertation award, Entrepreneurship Divsn., Acad. Mgmt., 1996, Mescon/Coles Best Empirical Paper award, Acad. Mgmt., 1999, Best Paper award, Entrepreneurship/Ethics Track, So. Mgmt. Assn., 2001; fellow Kauffman Ctr. Entrepreneurial Leadership, 1994, Comer fellow, U. Ga., 1994. Mem.: Strategic Mgmt. Soc., U.S. Assn. Small Bus. and Entrepreneurship (Runner-Up award 1999), Acad. Mgmt. (mem. exec. com. entrepreneurship divsn. 1996—, chair awards com. 1998—), Presbyterian. Avocations: travel, skiing, scuba diving, hiking. Office: Kennesaw State U Coles Coll Bus 1000 Chastain Rd NW #0404 Kennesaw GA 30144-5591 Home: 2941 Lookout Pl Ne Atlanta GA 30305-3217 Office Phone: 770-423-6446. Office Fax: 770-423-6606. Personal E-mail: kcrobinson@bellsouth.net.

**ROBINSON, KIM STANLEY,** science fiction author; b. Waukegan, Ill., Mar. 23, 1952; m. Lisa Howell; 2 children. BS, U. Calif., San Diego, PhD in English and Am. Lit., 1982; MS, Boston U. Author: (book series) Mars (Red Mars 1992, Green Mars 1993, Blue Mars 1995), Orange County (The Wild Shore 1984, The Gold Coast 1988, Pacific Edge 1990), (novels) Icehenge, 1984, The Memory of Whiteness, 1985, Escape from Kathmandu, 1989, A Short, Sharp Shock, 1990, Antarctica, 1998, The Years of Rice & Salt, 2002, Forty Signs of Rain, 2004, (collections) The Planet on the Table, 1986, Escape From Kathmandu, 1990, Remaking History, 1991, The Martians, 1999, (anthologies) Future Primitive: The New Ecotopias, 1994, (non-fiction series) Studies in Speculative Fiction, 1984; author numerous short fiction, essays and articles. Recipient World Fantasy award, 1984, John W. Campbell Meml. award, 1991, Nebula award, 1987, 93, Locus Poll award, 1985, 91, 94, 97, Hugo award, 1994, 97, SF Chronicle award, 1984, 92, Brit. Sci. Fiction award, 1993. Avocations: mountain trekking, swimming. Office: c/o Random House Inc Bantam Books 1540 Broadway New York NY 10036-4039

**ROBINSON, LARRY CLARK,** former professional hockey coach; b. Winchester, Ont., Can., June 2, 1951; m. Jeannette; children: Jeffery, Rachelle. Player Montreal Canadiens, 1971—89, LA Kings, 1989—92; asst. coach NJ Devils, 1993—95, 1999—2000; head coach L.A. Kings, 1995—99, NJ Devils, 2000—02, 2005, spl. assignment coach, 2002—05. Player Team Canada, 1976, 81, 84. Recipient, Norris trophy (NHL best defenseman) 1977, 1980, Conne Smythe trophy (playoff MVP) 1978, named to NHL All-Star game, 1974, 1976-1978, 1980, 1982, 1986, 1988, 1989, 1992. Achievements include being a member of 9 Stanley Cup Championship teams; being inducted into the Hockey Hall of Fame, 1995. Avocations: polo, boating.

**ROBINSON, LAURIE OVERBY,** former assistant attorney general; b. Washington, July 7, 1946; d. Kermit and Ethel Esther (Schlasinger) Overby; m. Craig Baab, Oct. 22, 1977 (div. 1991); 1 child, Teddy Baab; m. Sheldon Krantz, Dec. 8, 1991. BA in Polit. Sci. magna cum laude, Brown U., 1968. Desk editor Cmty. News Svc., N.Y.C., 1968-71; asst. staff dir. sect. criminal justice ABA, Washington, 1972-74; dir. sect. criminal justice, 1979-93; assoc. dep. atty. gen. U.S. Dept. Justice, Washington, 1993-94, asst. atty. gen. Office Justice Programs, 1994-2000; sr. fellow program on crime policy U. Pa. Jerry Lee Ctr. Criminology, 2000—, exec. dir. Forum Crime & Justice; dir. Master of Sci. in Criminology program U. Pa., 2004—. Mem. ex-officio, bd. regents Nat. Coll. Dist. Attys., Houston, 1979—93; adv. bd. Fed. Sentencing Reporter, N.Y.C., 1990—; chair Nat. Forum Criminal Justice, Washington, 1991—93; bd. dirs. Nat. Ctr. Victims of Crime. Adv. bd. George Mason U. Adminstrn. of Justice Adv. Program.; Clinton transition com. Dept. Justice, 1992; trustee Vera Inst. Justice, 2001—; bd. dirs. Police Found. Mem.: ABA, Phi Beta Kappa. Democrat. Office Phone: 215-573-9109. Business E-Mail: robinsol@sas.upenn.edu. E-mail: laurieorob@aol.com.

**ROBINSON, LAWRENCE DEWITT,** lawyer; b. Saginaw, Mich., Sept. 15, 1943; m. Lynne Howe; children: Tiffany, Julia. BS, Cen. Mich. U., 1965; JD, U. Mich., 1968. Bar: Mo. 1968, Tex. 1983. Ptnr. Stinson, Mag & Fizzell, Kansas City, Mo., 1968-89, Bracewell & Patterson, Dallas, 1991-1996; exec. v.p., gen. counsel, sec. FelCor Lodging Trust, Irving, Tex., 1996—. Tchr. navigational class. Mem. ABA. Office: FelCor Lodging Trust 545 E John Carpenter Freeway, Ste 130 Irving TX 75062 E-mail: lrobinson@felcor.com.

**ROBINSON, LINDA GOSDEN,** communications executive; b. LA, Jan. 10, 1953; d. Freeman Fisher and Jane Elizabeth (Stoneham) Gosden; m. Stephen M. Dart (div. June 1977); m. James Dixon Robinson III, July 1984. Student, UCLA, 1970-72; BA summa cum laude in Psychology, U. So. Calif., 1978. Dep. press sec. Reagan Presdl. Campaign, LA, 1979; press sec. dir. pub. relations Rep. Nat. Com., Washington, 1979-80; dir. pub. affairs US Dept. Transp., Washington, 1981-83; sr. v.p. corp. affairs Warner Amex Cable Communications, NYC, 1983-86; chmn. Robinson Lerer & Montgomery, LLC, NYC, 1986—, CEO, 1986—2002. Bd. dirs. Revlon, Inc., NYC; dir. BlackRock, Inc., NYC. Del. Rep. Nat. Conv., 1985; trustee NYU Sch. Medicine Found. Bd., vice chair; trustee NYU Hosp. Ctr.; bd. dirs. Lustgarten Found. Pancreatic Rsch. Mem.: Phi Beta Kappa. Avocations: tennis, horseback riding.

**ROBINSON, LOGAN GILMORE,** lawyer; b. Cin., Dec. 26, 1949; s. Landon Graves and Alis (Rule) R.; m. Edrie Baker Sowell, Sept. 22, 1983; children: Leyland G., Landon G., Linden G., Lane G. BA in Econ. and History magna cum laude, Cornell U., 1972; JD, Harvard U., 1976; Cert. Competence in German, Goethe Inst., Freiburg, Germany, 1978. Bar: Ohio 1977, N.Y. 1979, Mich. 1989, U.S. Ct. Internat. Trade 1983. Rsch. faculty Leningrad State U., Russia, 1976-77; rsch. officer U. Leiden, Netherlands, 1977-78; assoc. Wender, Murase & White, NYC, 1978-81, Coudert Bros., NYC, 1981-83; sr. counsel TRW Inc., Cleve., 1983-87; asst. gen. counsel Chrysler Corp., Highland Park, 1987—96; sec., v.p., gen. counsel ITT Automotive, Auburn Hills, Mich., 1996—98; v.p., gen. counsel Delphi Corp., Troy, Mich., 1998—2006; exec. v.p., gen. counsel, govt. rels. Metaldyne Corp., Plymouth, Mich., 2006—. Author: An American in Leningrad, 1982, paperback, 1984, Evil Star, 1986, paperback, 1987. Mem. Assoc. Gen. Counsels. Internat. Bar Assn. (co-chair corp. counsel forum), Mich. State Bar (former chmn. internat. sect., Outstanding Contbn. award), German Am. C. of C. Mich. (bd. dirs.), Coun. US and Italy, Phi Beta Kappa. Office: Metaldyne Corp 47603 Halyard Dr Plymouth MI 48170-2429

**ROBINSON, MARGUERITE STERN,** anthropologist, educator, consultant; b. NYC, Oct. 11, 1935; d. Philip Van Doren and Lillian (Diamond) Stern; m. Allan Richard Robinson, June 12, 1965; children: Sarah Penelope, Perrine, Laura Ondine. BA, Radcliffe Coll., 1956; PhD, Harvard U., 1965. Assoc. scholar Radcliffe Inst. for Advanced Studies, Cambridge, Mass., 1964-65; asst. prof. anthropology Brandeis U., 1965-72, assoc. prof., 1972-78, prof., 1978-85, dean Coll. Arts and Scis., 1973-75; assoc. fellow Inst. Internat. Devel. Harvard U., Cambridge, 1978-80, fellow Inst. Internat. Devel., 1980-85, inst. fellow Internat. Devel., 1985-2000, inst. fellow emeritus

Inst. Internat. Devel., 2000—; dir. Cultural Survival Inc., 1981-99, Am. Inst. Indian Studies, Chgo., 1977—, chmn., 1983-84; faculty mem. Microfinance Tng. Program, Boulder, Colo. and Turin, Italy, 1995—2006. Cons. in field. Author: Political Structure in a Changing Sinhalese Village, 1975, Local Politics: The Law of the Fishes, 1988, Pembiayaan Pertanian Pedesaan, 1993, The Microfinance Revolution, Vol. 1: Sustainable Finance for the Poor, 2001, Vol. 2: Lessons from Indonesia, 2002, Mobilizing Savings from the Public: Basic Principles and Practices, 2005, The Future of the Commercial Microfinance Industry in Asia, 2005, Commercial Microfinance and Employment in Developing Countries, 2005; contbg. author: Cambridge Papers in Social Anthropology 3, 1962, Cambridge Papers in Social Anthropology 5, 1968, Enterprises for the Recycling and Composting of Municipal Solid Waste, 1993, The New World of Microenterprise Finance, 1994, New Perspectives on Financing Small Business in Developing Countries, 1995, Assisting Development in a Changing World, 1997, New World of Microfinance, 1997, Agricultural Development in the Third World, 1998, Strategic Issues in Microfinance, 1998, Microfinance: Conversations with the Experts, 1999, Microbanking: Creating Opportunities for the Poor Through Innovation, 2005; contbr. articles to profl. jours. Mem. internat. coun. advisors Calmeadow Found., 1996-2000; pres. The Greatest Gift Corp. Fellow NIH, 1964-65; grantee NSF, 1966-70, Ford Found., 1972-74, 79, Calmeadow Found., 1994; fellow Indo-Am. Fellowship Program-Indo-U.S. Subcomm. on Edn. and Culture, 1976-77, Am. Inst. Indian Studies, 1976-77; grantee Calmeadow Found., 1994. Fellow Am. Anthrop. Assn., Soc. Bunting Inst. Fellows; mem. Assn. Asian Studies, India Internat. Centre. Personal E-mail: MRobinso1@aol.com.

**ROBINSON, MARIE HADLEY,** voice educator; b. Thomas County, Ga., Dec. 2, 1940; d. King Dennis Hadley and Rosetta James; m. Emmett Robinson; children: Emmett Jr., Carl Dennis, Gregory Lloyd, Angelyn Rosetta, Tobie Norwood Robinson. BS in Music Edn., Fla. A&M U., 1968; MusM, Fla. State U., 1972, MusD, 1973. Gen. music tchr. Detroit Pub. Schs., 1968—70; pvt. tchr. Mannheim, Germany, 1979—83; assoc. prof. voice U. Del., Newark, 1988. Bd. dirs. Opera Del., Delaware Valley Chorale. Singer: (Operas) Bayerishe Staatsoper, Deutsche Oper an Rhein, 1975, 1976, 1978, 1979, 1986, Deutsche Staatsoper unter den Linden, 1977, 1982, 1983, 1984, Deutsche Oper Berlin, 1980—83, Vereinigte Buhen, 1978—81, Mich. Opera Theater, 1979, L.A. Opera Repertory Theater, 1981, Landestheater Linz, 1982, many others. Recipient award, Thomasville (Ga.) Entertainment Found., 1969, First Pl. award, Civic Opera Palm Beaches Auditions, 1973; grantee, Ford Found., 1969; scholar, Fla. A&M U., 1962—68; Presdl. scholar, 1968, grad. fellow, Fla. State U., 1970, Duiguid fellow, So. Fellowship Found., 1973. Mem.: OperaDelaware, W. Russell Johnson Music Guild, Nat. Assn. Negro Musicians, Opera Am. (bd. dirs., artist planning com., opera selection and audition com., mem. adv. com.), Nat. Assn. Tchrs. Singing, Nat. Opera Assn. (bd. dirs. 1999—, coord. opera auditions, chairperson Legacy Fund), Delta Sigma Theta, Phi Kappa Phi. Roman Catholic. Avocation: sewing. Home: 298 Pickett Ln Newark DE 19711 Office: Univ Del Amy du Pont Music Bldg Newark DE

**ROBINSON, MARIETTA S.,** lawyer; b. Platteville, Wis., Dec. 26, 1951; BA, U. Mich., 1973; JD, UCLA, 1978. Bar: Calif. 1978, Mich. 1979, U.S. Dist. Ct. (ea. dist.) Mich. 1979, U.S. Ct. Appeals (6th cir.) 1983, U.S. Supreme Ct. 1989. Data processing mktg. rep. IBM Corp., Flint, Mich., 1973-75; assoc. The Bank of Bermuda Legal Dept., Hamilton, 1978-79; from assoc. to ptnr. Dickinson, Wright, Moon, VanDusen & Freeman, Detroit, 1979-94; ptnr. Sommers, Schwartz, Silver & Schwartz, P.C., Southfield, Mich., 1985-89; pvt. practice Detroit, 1989—. Adj. prof. U. Detroit Sch. of Law, 1982-83, Wayne State U., Detroit, 1983-84; mem. Rep. of State Bar Rep. Assembly, 1984-85; Dem. nominee for Mich. Supreme Ct., 2000; lectr. in field. Contbg. author: Evidence in America, The Federal Rules in the States, 1987, Introducing Evidence, A Practical Guide for Michigan Lawyers, 1988; contbr. articles to profl. jours. Trustee Dalkon Shield Claimants Trust, 1989-97; appointee Gov. James Blanchard, State of Mich. Bldg. Authority, 1985-89, State Bar Mich./Mich. State Med. Soc. Coalition, 1993—; appointee Transition Team of Wayne County Exec. Robert Ficano, 2002; bd. dirs. Mich. Women's Found., 2003—. Named one of ten Mich. Lawyers of Yr., Lawyers Weekly, 2000. Fellow ABA, Internat. Soc. Barristers (bd. govs.), Am. Bar Found., Mich. State Bar Found.; mem. State Bar Mich., State Bar Calif., ATLA, Mich. Trial Lawyers Assn., Women Lawyers Mich., Am. Bd. of Trial Advocates, Detroit Bar Assn., Oakland Bar Assn., U.S. Ct. Appeals (6th cir.) Jud. Conf. (life). Democrat. Avocations: running, biking, tennis, boating, skiing, reading, horseback riding. Office: 436 S Broadway St Ste C Lake Orion MI 48362 Office Phone: 248-693-6245. E-mail: msebreerobinson@aol.com.

**ROBINSON, MARILYNNE,** writer; b. Sandpoint, Idaho, Nov. 26, 1943; d. John J. and Ellen (Harris) Summers; children: James, Joseph. BA, Brown U., 1966; PhD in English lit., U. Wash., 1977. Mem. faculty Writer's Workshop U. Iowa, 1991—. Spkr. in field. Author: (novels) Housekeeping, 1981 (PEN/Hemingway Award, 1981, Richard and Hinda Rosenthal Award, AAAL), Gilead, 2004 (Nat. Book Critics Cir. prize for fiction, 2004, Pulitzer Prize for fiction, 2005, Publishers Weekly Hardcover Bestseller list, 2005), (non-fiction) Mother Country: Britain, the Welfare State and Nuclear Pollution, 1989, (essay collection) The Death of Adam: Essays on Modern Thought, 1998; Has contbd. to Harper's, Paris Rev., The NY Times Book Rev., others. Recipient Mildred and Howard Strauss Living Award, AAAL, 1998; Lila Acheson Wallace Reader's Digest Grant, 1991. Office: Farrar Straus & Giroux 19 Union Sq W New York NY 10003*

**ROBINSON, MARK LEIGHTON,** gas industry executive, petroleum engineer, farmer; b. San Bernardino, Calif., Aug. 4, 1927; s. Ernest Guy and Florence Inla(l(unun) R.; m. Jean Marie Ries, Feb. 8, 1954; children: Francis Willis, Mark Ries, Paul Leighton. AB cum laude in Geology, Princeton U., 1950; postgrad., Stanford U., 1950-51. Geologist Shell Oil Co., Billings, Mont., Rapid City, S.D., Denver, Midland, Tex., dist. geologist Roswell, N.Mex., 1957-60. divsn. mgr., 1961-63, Jackson, Miss., 1964-65, Bakersfield, Calif., 1967-68, mgr. exploration econs. N.Y.C. 1969; cntrl. office staff BIPM (Royal Dutch Shell Oil Co.), The Hague, The Netherlands, 1969; pres., chmn. bd. dirs. Robinson Resource Devel. Co., Inc., Roswell, 1970—. Chmn., pres. Como Petroleum Corp., Roswell, 1994—. Campaign chmn. Chaves County Rep. Com., Roswell, 1962; mem. alumni schs. com. Princeton U., 1980—; vestry St. Andrew's Episcopal Ch., Roswell, N.Mex., 1999-2002. With USNR, 1945-46. Mem. Assn. Petroleum Geologists, Stanford U. Earth Scientists Assn., Yellowstone Bighorn Rsch. Assn., Am. Horse Show Assn., SAR, Sigma Xi. Episcopalian. Achievements include discovery of Lake Como oil field, Miss., 1971, McNeal oil field, Miss., 1973, North Deer Creek gas field, Mont., 1983, Bloomfield East oil field, Mont., 1986, West Cat Claw Draw gas field, N.Mex., 1997, Southeast Cemetary Gas Field, N.Mex., 2000. Office: Robinson Resource Devel Co Inc PO Box 1227 Roswell NM 88202-1227 Office Phone: 505-623-5275.

**ROBINSON, MARLA HOLBROOK,** community care nurse; b. Grass Valley, Calif., Sept. 15, 1934; d. Hilmer Harrison and Mable Lucille (Kline) Holbrook; m. Donald Wilson Robinson Jr., June 25, 1961; children: Jeffrey Brian, Jennifer Lee. BSN, PHN, U. Calif. Chico, 1956. RN; cert. audiometer. Nurse U. Calif. San Francisco Hosp., 1956-59; supr. clinic St. Luke's Hosp., San Francisco, 1959-60; sch. nurse, pub. health nurse San Francisco City and County, 1960-62; sch. nurse All Saints Sch., Carmel, Calif., 1969-79; cmty. care nurse, founder Care & Choice Home Health Care, 1994. Mem. Carmel Found., 2003. Mem. AAUW, Quata Internat. Monterey Peninsula (pres. 1993), Jacettes (pres. 1967), Long Term Dir. of Nursing Salinas, Calif., Ea. Star Monterey (50 Yr. mem.). Episcopalian. Avocations: growing orchids, crafts, reading, travel. Office: Community Care 80 Garden Ct Ste 105 Monterey CA 93940 Office Phone: 831-657-1994, 831-657-1998. Personal E-mail: marlarob@yahoo.com.

**ROBINSON, MARTIN (MARTY ROBINSON),** television and radio broadcaster, media consultant; b. Chgo., Sept. 7, 1932; s. Edward Emmanuel Robinson and Florence Ruth (Cohen) Mayer; m. Mary Alice Wellingham,

May 31, 1959; children: Paul Edward, Jill Marie. Broadcaster, host Stas. WAAF, WGN and WNIB, Chgo., 1956-58, Sta. WFMT, Chgo., 1958-63. Sta. WTTW-TV, Chgo., 1971-99. Speaker, concert narrator; lectr. Lyric Opera Chgo.; media cons. J. Walter Thompson, Hill & Knowlton, Burson Marsteller, Newell & Matthews, 1973—. Host, narrator programs (Peabody award, 15 Emmy awards, 8 Ohio State awards, Chgo. and San Francisco Film Festival Gold medals); prodr., host nationally syndicated opera program The First Fifty Years, 1967-93. Served with USN, 1950-53. Recipient Emmy awards, 1977, 78. Avocations: biking, weight training, the internet. Office: 5 Lynnbrook Dr Prospect Heights IL 60070-1022 E-mail: martyrob@comcast.net.

**ROBINSON, MARY,** former United Nations official; b. Ballina, County Mayo, Ireland, May 21, 1944; d. Aubrey Bourke and Tessa O'Donnell; m. Nicholas Robinson; children: Tessa, William, Aubrey. MA, Dublin U., Trinity Coll., Ireland, 1967; Barrister, King's Inns, Ireland, 1967, Mid. Temple, 1973; LLM, Harvard U., 1968; DCL, Oxford U.; LLD (hon.), Basle U., Cambridge U., Columbia U., Coventry U., Dublin U., Fordham U., Harvard U., Kyung-Hee U., Seoul, Katholieke U., Leuven, Liverpool U., London U., Melbourne U., U. Montpellier U., Nat. U. Ireland, Nat. U. Mongolia, Nat. U. Wales, U. Poznan, Queen's U., Belfast, St. Andrews U., Toronto U., Uppsala U., Yale U.; D Internat. Law (hon.), U. Costa Rica; Dr., Essex U.; PhD (hon.), Dublin City U.; DPS (hon.), Northeastern U.; DSc (hon.), Humaines U. Kennes, A Schweitzer U. Berne. Reid prof. constitutional and criminal law Trinity Coll., Dublin, 1969-75; lectr. in European Cmty. law Trinity Coll., Dublin, 1975-90; senator Irish Parliament, 1969-89; pres. Ireland, 1990-97; high commr. for human rights UN, 1997—2002; hon. pres. Oxfam Internat., 2002—. Mem. Dublin City Coun., 1979-83; chancellor Dublin U., 1998—. Mem. Editorial Bd. Irish Current Law Statutes Annotated, 1984-90; adv. bd. Common Market Law Rev., 1976-90. Pres. Cherish, 1973-90; mem. Internatl. Commn. Jurists, 1987-90. Recipient Marisa Bellisario prize, Italy, CARE Humanitarian award, 1993, Internat. Human Rights award Internat. League of Human Rights, N.Y., Liberal Internat. prize for freedom, New Zealand Suffrage Centennial medal, Berkeley medal U. Calif., Medal of Honour, U. Coimbra, Portugal, Ordem dos Advogados, Portugal, Gold Medal of Honour, U. Salamanca, Spain, U. Chile, Global Leadership award UN Assn., Freedom prize Max Schmidheiny Found., Switzerland, UNIFEM award Noel Found., U.S., Collar of Hussein Bin Ali, Hashemite Kingdom of Jordan, North South prize Coun. of Europe, 1997, F.D. Roosevelt Four Freedoms medal, 1998, Dag Hammarskjold Medal, 1998, Erasmus prize, Govt. The Netherlands, 1999, Fulbright prize, 1999, Indira Gandhi Peace prize, 2000, Sydney Peace Prize, 2002; named to Internat. Hall of Fame, Internat. Women's Forum, USA; named one of 100 Most Influential People, Time Mag., 2005. Fellow Instn. Engrs. of Ireland (hon.), Royal Coll. Physicians Ireland (hon.), Royal Coll. Psychiatrists London (hon.), Royal Coll. Surgeons, Ireland (hon.), Royal Coll. Obstetricians and Gynecologists London; mem. Royal Irish Acad., Am. Philos. Soc. Office: Oxfam International Ste 20 266 Banbury Rd OX2 7DL Oxford England E-mail: secrt.hchr@unog.ch.

**ROBINSON, MARY ELIZABETH GOFF,** retired historian, researcher; b. East Providence, R.I., Jan. 3, 1925; d. Newell Darius and Eva Agnes (Crane) Goff; m. Charles Albert Robinson, July 30, 1954; 1 child, Thomas Goff (dec.). BA, Wheaton Coll., Norton, Mass., 1947. Cataloger, fine arts Chester County Hist. Soc., Pa., 1973-80, trustee Pa., 1974-80. Cataloger artifacts Chadds Ford (Pa.) Hist. Soc., 1992-95. Co-author: (monograph) Ada Clendenin Williamson, 1983, (history) The Ingalls and the Hoyts, The Crane Sawmill, The Ingalls-Crane House, 1995; author: (monograph) The Life of a Young Entrepreneur at the Turn of the Twentieth Century, 1992; editor: A Quiet Man from West Chester, 1974. Mem. Jr. League, Providence, 1957-62, Providence Athenaeum, 1955-63, Providence Preservation Soc., 1959-63, Brandywine Conservancy, Del. Symphony Orch., Winterthur Mus.; donor Newell D. Goff Fund Chester County Cmty. Found.; founder Chester County Artists Register, Chester County Art Assn., acting libr., 1994-2000. Donor T. Morris Longstreth Libr. endowment West Chester U., Greater Lewes (DE) Found., Friends of Lewes Pub. Mem. AAUW, R.I. Hist. Soc. (trustee 1994-99, founder Newell D. Goff Edn. Ctr.), Danville (Vt.) Hist. Soc., Hershey's Mill Country Club, Hope Club (Providence), Chester County Cmty. Fdn. Avocations: writing, reading, hiking, travel.

**ROBINSON, MARY LOU,** federal judge; b. Dodge City, Kans., Aug. 25, 1926; d. Gerald J. and Frances Strueber; m. A.J. Robinson, Aug. 28, 1949; 3 children. BA, U. Tex., 1948, LL.B., 1950. Bar: Tex. 1949. Ptnr. Robinson & Robinson, Amarillo, 1950-55; judge County Ct. at Law, Potter County, Tex., 1955-59, (108th Dist. Ct.), Amarillo, 1961-73; assoc. justice Ct. of Civil Appeals for 7th Supreme Jud. Dist. of Tex., Amarillo, 1973-77, chief justice, 1977-79; U.S. dist. judge No. Dist. Tex., Amarillo, 1979—. Named Woman of Year Tex. Fedn. Bus. and Profl. Women, 1973; recipient Sandra Day O'Connor award profl. excellence, 2005. Mem. Nat. Assn. Women Lawyers, ABA, Tex. Bar Assn. (Outstanding 50-Yr. Lawyer award 2002), Tex. Bar Found. (Samuel Pessara Outstanding Judge award) Amarillo Bar Assn., Delta Kappa Gamma. Presbyterian. Office: US Dist Ct Rm 226 205 E 5th Ave # F13248 Amarillo TX 79101-1559

**ROBINSON, MAUREEN LORETTA,** retired secondary school educator; b. NYC, May 17, 1945; d. Arthur Vincent and Paula (Dillon) R.; m. Derish Michael Wolff, Feb. 13, 1992. BA in English, Wagner Coll., 1967; MS, CUNY, 1970; LHD (hon.), Wagner Coll., 2003. Cert. tchr. secondary sch. English, K-12 reading, N.Y. Tchr. English Curtis H.S., S.I., NY, 1968-95, coord. student activities, 1985-94. Vis. lectr. Coll. of S.I., 1982; guest lectr. NYU, 1991, Pace U., N.Y.C., 1993; dir. Soc. de Management de Projets Internat., Paris, 1996—. Class agt. Wagner Coll., 1995—; mem. nat. alumni bd.; trustee Wagner Coll., 1998—, vice chair bd. trustees, 2001—03; pub chair Bernardsville Garden Club, 1995—97, pres., 1997—99, sec., 1999—2001, pub chair, 2001—03, nominations chair, 2004—, bd. dirs., yearbook chair, 2005—; trustee Somerset Hills Edn. Found., 1996—97; pub. chair Friends of the Bernardsville Libr., 1996—2002, bd. dirs., nominations chair, 2004—; elected mem. Somerset Hills Bd. Edn., Bernardsville, NJ, 1997—2003; v.p Somerset County Ednl. Svcs. Commn., Raritan, 2002—03, pres., 2002—03; bd. dirs Clarence Dillon Pub. Libr., 2002—03; sec. Friends for a Greener Bernardsville Inc., 2003—04, pres., 2005, co-pres., 2006—. Staff sgt. USAR, 1979—85. Recipient Human Rels. award Greater N.Y. Region of NCCJ, 1994, Army Achievement medal Dept. of Army, 1983, Bernardsville Vol. of Yr. award, 2003, Outstanding Comty. vol. award Borough Coun. and Mayor Bernardsville, 2003. Mem. AAUW, Wagner Coll. Nat. Alumni Assn. (1st v.p. 1999-2001), Friends of the Shelter. Avocations: reading, gardening, skiing, cooking, travel. Home: 160 Jockey Hollow Rd Bernardsville NJ 07924-1312

**ROBINSON, MICHAEL HILL,** retired zoological park director, biologist; b. Preston, Eng., Jan. 7, 1929; came to U.S. 1984; s. Samuel and Ethel (Hill) R.; m. Barbara Cragg Robinson, May 19, 1955 (divorced). BS, U. Wales, U.K., 1963; DPhil, U. Oxford, Eng., 1966; DSc (hon.), U. Westminster, Eng., 2000. Tchr. sci. U.K. Secondary Schs., 1953-60; sr. sci. master Camborne Grammar Sch., 1958-60; biologist Smith. Tropical Research Inst., Panama, 1966-71; vis. lectr. U. Pa., Phila., 1969; reader in biology New U. Ulster, No. Ireland, 1971; biologist Smithsonian Tropical Research Inst., Panama, 1971-84, asst. dir., 1980, acting dir., 1980-81, dep. dir., 1981-84; dir. Nat. Zool. Park, Washington, 1984—2000; sr. scientist emeritus Smithsonian Tropical Rsch. Inst., 1999—. Contbr. articles to profl. jours. Mem.: Soc. for Study of Animal Behavior. Address: 8291 SW Bent Oak Ct Stuart FL 34997 Personal E-mail: michael-robinson@usa.net.

**ROBINSON, MICHAEL KEVIN,** lawyer; s. Russell Eugene and Betty Jane R.; 1 child, Nicholas Grant. AB, U. Calif., Berkeley, 1976; JD, Golden Gate U., 1980. Bar: Calif. 1980, U.S. Ct. Appeals (9th cir.) 1980, U.S. Dist. Ct. (no. dist.) Calif. 1980. Dep. dist. atty. Riverside (Calif.) County Dist. Attys. Office, 1980-84; dept. dist. atty. Humboldt County Dist. Attys. Office, Eureka, Calif., 1984-86, chief asst. dist. atty., 1986-93; ptnr. Scott, Scott, Robinson & Pavlich, Eureka, Calif., 1993—. Instr. Coll. of the Redwoods Police Acad., Eureka, 1985—. Author: (with others) The Berkeley Guide to Employment of New College Graduates, 1984. Founding dir. Ct. Apptd. Spl. Advocate,

Eureka, 1991. Recipient Outstanding Achievement in Environ. Protection award Pres. of U.S., 1972. Mem. State Bar of Calif. (criminal law sect. 1993—), Consumer Attys. Calif. Office: Scott Scott Robinson & Pavlich 1118 6th St Eureka CA 95501-1174

**ROBINSON, MICHAEL LEE,** biologist; b. Dayton, Ohio, July 9, 1965; s. Ronald Mac Robinson and Priscilla Elaine Lang; m. Julia Eileen Gerringer, July 15, 1989; children: Emily Megan Sahm, Eric Stephen Douglass, Jessica Rosemary Dare, Ian Matthew Conner. BS, Purdue U., West Lafayette, Ind., 1987; PhD, U. S.C., Columbia, 1992. Postdoctoral rsch. fellow Baylor Coll. of Medicine, Houston, 1992—96; prin. investigator Columbus Children's Rsch. Inst., Columbus, Ohio, 1996—2005; asst. prof. Ohio State U., Columbus, Ohio, 1996—2004, assoc. prof., 2004—05, Miami U., Oxford, Ohio, 2005—. Dir. transgenic and embryonic stem cell core lab. Children's Rsch. Inst., Columbus, Ohio, 1997—2005. Editor: Development of the Ocular Lens. Grantee NIH, Nat. Eye Inst., 2000-2005, Postional cloning of an autosomal recessive gene for congenital hydrocephalus, Mar. of Dimes, 2000-2003. Mem.: Internat. Soc. for Eye Rsch. (meeting organizer 2006), Assn. for Rsch. in Vision and Ophthalmology (program com. 2006—). Conservative-R. Roman Catholic. Achievements include discovery of Discovered and cloned the Hydin gene; research in role of fibroblast growth factors in lens devel; Transgenic mice and eye devel; role of cilia in hydrocephalus; role of FGF in lens devel; Transgenic mice and mammalian genetics. Avocations: genealogy, swimming, singing, theater. Home: 1854 S Stone Rd Liberty IN 47353 Office: Zoology Dept Miami U 256 Pearson Hall Oxford OH 45056 Office Phone: 513-529-2353. Office Fax: 513-529-6900. E-mail: robinsm5@muohio.edu.

**ROBINSON, MICHELLE A.,** elementary school educator; b. Yale, Mich., Nov. 15, 1971; d. Mitch and Laura Robinson. AA, St. Clair County C.C., Pt. Huron, Mich., 1992; BS in Edn., Cen. Mich. U., 1995; MA in Tchg., Saginaw Valley State U., 2003. Profl. tchg. cert. Mich. Elem. tchr. Holy Cross Cath. Sch., Marine City, Mich., 1999—. Office: Holy Cross Cath Sch 618 S Water St Marine City MI 48039 Office Phone: 810-765-3591. Personal E-mail: shellshell22@yahoo.com.

**ROBINSON, MILDRED WIGFALL,** law educator; b. Charleston, SC, Dec. 1, 1944; d. Switzon Samuel and Mildred Gwendolyn (Mance) Wigfall; m. William Hudson Ravenell, Aug. 29, 1969 (div. Apr. 1986); children: William Samuel, Teressa Emlynne; m. Armstead Louis Robinson, June 27, 1987; 1 child, Allison Louise Wigfall. BA, Fisk U., 1965; JD, Howard U., 1968; LLM, Harvard U., 1971. Bar: Mass. 1971. Dir. admissions, asst. dean Boston U., 1971-72; asst. prof. law Fla. State U., Tallahassee, 1972-76, assoc. prof., 1976-84, assoc. dean, 1983-84; vis. assoc. prof. U. Va., Charlottesville, 1984-85, assoc. prof., 1985-88, prof., 1988—, currently Henry L. & Grace Doherty Charitable Found. prof. law. Currently trustee Martha Jefferson Hosp.; bd. dir. Law Access, Inc., 1993—96; mem. exec. com. Assoc. Am. Law Sch., 2000—03; commr. Nat. Conf. of Commn. on Uniform State Laws, 1990—94; bd. visitors J. Reuben Clark Law Sch. Brigham Young U., Provo, Utah, 1993—96. Mem.: ALI, Phi Beta Kappa. Democrat. Episcopalian. Avocations: aerobics, needlecrafts, reading. Office: U Va Sch Law 580 Massie Rd Charlottesville VA 22901 E-mail: mwr@virginia.edu.

**ROBINSON, MITCHELL,** music educator; s. Kenneth Charles and Barbara Mary Robinson; m. Catherine Ann Fox; children: Jacob Fox, Andrew Mitchell. PhD, Eastman Sch. Music, 1999. Cert. Music Tchr. (Kindergarten through twelfth grade) NY State, 1980. Tchr. Fulton City Sch. Dist., NY, 1983—93; asst. prof. Eastman Sch. Music, Rochester, NY, 1998—2000, U. Conn., Storrs, 2000—03; assoc. prof. Mich. State U., East Lansing, 2003—. Ednl. cons., Okemos, Mich. Co-author: (book) Great Beginnings for Music Teachers (Reston prize, 1999). Office: Michigan State Univ Sch Music East Lansing MI 48824

**ROBINSON, MURIEL COX,** psychiatrist; d. Henry Willard and Veola Garry Cox; m. Julius Ceasar Robinson (div.); children: Julius W., Rosalyn P. Student, Ohio State U., 1948; MD, Meharry Med. Coll., 1952. Psychiatry resident Homer Phillips Hosp./Washington U., St. Louis, 1953—56; staff psychiatrist St. Louis Child Guidance Ctr., St. Louis, 1956—57, Napa (Calif.) St. Hosp., 1958, Cmty. Mental Health Centers Richmond, Calif., 1958—75; pvt. practice psychiatry Calif., 1960—79; staff psychiatrist East Oakland Mental Health Ctr., Calif., 1976—79, Calif. Youth Authority, Sacramento, 1979—92; with Locum Tenens Physicians Group, 1992—94. Mem. mental health adv. bd. Contra Costa County, Martinez, Calif., 1960—64. Bd. dirs. North Richmond Neighborhood Ho., Calif., 1961—63. Mem.: AAAS, AMA, NAACP, Am. Psychiat. Assn. (life). Avocations: block flute, keyboards. Home: PO Box 292148 Sacramento CA 95829-2148 Office Phone: 916-427-8070.

**ROBINSON, NANCY NOWAKOWSKI,** academic administrator; b. Pitts., Nov. 2, 1945; d. Theodore Joseph Nowakowski and Martha Radick; 1 child, David A. BA cum laude, U. Pitts., 1983, MA, 2000. Founding mem. bd. dirs., treas. Extrasolar Planetary Found., Pitts., 1980—97; mem. adv. com. Nazareth Housing Svcs., 1991—; assoc. Sisters of the Holy Family of Nazareth, Pitts., 1998—; pres. City of God Found., Pitts., 2000—02, bd. dir., 2000—, treas., 2004—. Author: Institutional Anti-Judaism: Pope Pius VI and the Edict Concerning the Jews, 2000; editor: Pittsburgh Lubber's Line, 2003—05. Chaplain and diversity advisor divsn. 7, 8th eastern region U.S. Coast Guard Aux., 2003—, publs. officer, 2003—05; treas. City of God Found. Recipient Sister Noel Kernan award, Seton Hill Coll., 1999, Weiner Israel Heritage Nationality Rms. award, U. Pitts., 1999, Dorot Found. grantee for study in Israel, 1999, Pax Christi grantee, Pax Christi, 1999. Mem.: Soc. Bibl. Lit., Am. Acad. Religion, Golden Key. Roman Catholic. Avocations: Jewish/Catholic relations, history, music, travel, outdoors. E-mail: nancy1@pitt.edu.

**ROBINSON, NATHANIEL DAVID, JR.,** physician, consultant; b. Kansas City, Mar. 6, 1941; s. Nathaniel David Robinson and Dorothy Mae McLaughlin; m. Joanne Marie Kaleida, July 7, 1979; children: Donelle, Nathaniel David Robinson III. BSEE, U. RI, 1963; MD, U. Bologna, 1975. Cert. bd. cert. ins. medicine. Intern Roger Williams Gen. Hosp. Brown U., Providence, 1975—76; resident St. Francis Hosp. and Med. Ctr. U. Conn., Hartford, 1976—77; resident Hamot Med. Ctr., Erie, Pa., 1977—79, Mt. Sinai Med. Ctr., Miami Beach, Fla., 1981—82; med. officer USPHS Hosp., Seattle, 1979—81, VA, Nashville, 1982—85; med. dir. CNA, Nashville, 1985—95, v.p., med. dir., 1997—2004; asst. med. dir. Am. United Life, Indpls., 1995—97; med. cons. AIG Am. Gen., Nashville, 2005—. Cons. in field. Contbr. articles to profl. jours. Mem.: IEEE, AMA, Fla. Med. Assn., Midwest Med. Dirs. Assn., So. Med. Assn., Providence Engring. Soc., Nashville Acad. Medicine, Tenn. Med. Assn., Am. Acad. Ins. Medicine, Am. Radio Relay League. Avocation: amateur radio. Personal E-mail: djdrobinson@comcast.net. E-mail: klant@ieee.org.

**ROBINSON, NEIL CIBLEY, JR.,** lawyer; b. Columbia, SC, Oct. 25, 1942; s. Neil C. and Ernestine (Carns) R.; m. Judith Ann Hunter, Sept. 4, 1971 (div. Nov. 1979); 1 child, Hunter Leigh; m. Vicki Elizabeth Kornahrens, Mar. 2, 1985; children: Neil C. III, Taylor Elizabeth. BS in Indsl. Mgmt., Clemson U., 1966; JD, U. S.C., 1973. Bar: S.C. 1974, U.S. Ct. Appeals (4th cir.) 1974, U.S. Dist. Ct. S.C. 1976. Asst. to dean U.S. Law Sch., Columbia, 1973-74; law clk. to Hon. Charles E. Jr. Simons Jr. U.S. Dist. Ct. S.C., Aiken, 1974-76; assoc. Grimball & Cabaniss, Charleston, SC, 1976-78; ptnr. Grimball, Cabaniss, Vaughan & Robinson, Charleston, 1978-84; ptnr., pres. Robinson, Wall & Hastie, P.A., Charleston, 1984-91; ptnr., exec. mem. Nexsen, Pruet, Jacobs, Pollard & Robinson, Charleston, 1991—2003; mem. exec. com. Nexsen Pruet, LLC, 2004—. Permanent mem. 4th Cir. Jud. Conf., 1982—; pres. Coastal Properties Inst., Charleston, 1981—. Co-founder, chmn. Charleston Planning Project Pub. Edn., 1996; pres. Clemson Advancement Found., 2003—; mem. S.C. Edn. Oversight Com., 2005—; mem. devel. coun. S.C. Homebuilders Assn.; mem. Gov. Sanford's Quality of Life Task Force, 2003; bd. dirs Charleston Edn. Found., Clemson U. Humanities Found., 2000—03 Charleston Edn. Network, chmn. bd. dirs 2000—03; edn. adv. bd.

Coll. of Charleston; bd. dirs. Clemson U. Found., 2003—; pres. Southeastern Wildlife Expn., 1994—99, Southeastern Wildlife Expn. Found., 2003—, bd. dirs., 1987—, Charleston Maritime Festival, 1993—99, pres., 1994—98; bd. dirs. Parklands Found. of Charleston Counrty, pres.; bd. dirs. S.C. Tourism Coun., Columbia, 1991—2000. Cpl. USMCR, 1960—66. Recipient Order of Palmetto, Gov. David Beasley, S.C., 1996. Mem. ABA, Urban Land Inst. (recreational devel. coun.), S.C. Bar Assn., Fed. Bar Assn., S.C. Def. Trial Lawyers Assn. (pres.), Hibernian Soc. (mgmt. com. 1984—98, sec. 1998-2000, chmn. 2000-02, v.p. 2002-04, pres. 2004-06), Kiawah Club, Haig Point Club, Country Club of Charleston, Carolina Yacht Club, Phi Delta Phi. Presbyn. Avocations: golf, boating. Home: PO Box 121 Charleston SC 29402-0121 Office: Nexsen Pruet LLC 205 King St Ste 400 Charleston SC 29401 Office Phone: 843-577-9440. Personal E-mail: nrobinson@nexsenprenet.com. Business E-mail: nrobinson@njp.com.

**ROBINSON, NICHOLAS ADAMS,** law educator; b. NYC, Jan. 20, 1945; s. Albert Lewis and Agnes Claflin (Adams) R.; m. Shelley Miner, Jan. 5, 1969; children: Cynthia M., Laura V. BA cum laude, Brown U., 1967; JD cum laude, Columbia U., 1970. Bar: N.Y. 1971, U.S. Dist. Ct. (so. and ea. dists.) N.Y. 1972, U.S. Supreme Ct. 1974, U.S. Ct. Appeals (2d and 7th cirs.) 1972. Law clk. to U.S. dist. judge So. Dist. Ct., NY, 1970-72; assoc. Marshall, Bratter, Greene, Allison & Tucker, NYC, 1972-78, counsel, 1978-82; assoc. prof. Pace U. Sch. Law, White Plains, NY, 1978-81, prof., 1981-99, Gilbert and Sarah Kerlin Disting. prof. environ. law, 1999—; counsel Winer, Neuburger & Sive, NYC, 1982-83; dep. commr., gen. counsel NY State Dept. Environ. Conservation, Albany, 1983-85; counsel Sive, Paget & Reisel, 1985-92, Sidley & Austin, N.Y., London, 1992-96; legal advisor Internat. Union Conservation of Nature and Natural Resources, 1996—2004; counsel to Internat. Union Conservation of Nature and Natural Resources Observer Mission to UN, 2002—05, counsel to Asian African Consultative Orgn., 2005—; chmn. Internat. Union Conservation of Nature and Natural Resources Acad. Environ. Law, 2003—. Co-dir. Ctr. for Environ. Legal Studies, Pace U., 1982—; mem. environ. adv. coun. European Bank for Reconstron. and Devel., 2005—; del. U.S.A. environ. law meetings with USSR, 1974-92; chmn. Environ. Adv. Bd. to Gov. Mario Cuomo, 1995-94. Contbr. articles to profl. jours. Nat. bd. dirs. UN Assn. U.S.A., 1966-76, 79-84, U.S. Com. for UNICEF, 1970-80, World Environment Ctr., 1981—, chmn., 1993-96; bd. dirs. Westchester County Soil and Water Conservation Dist., 1976-83; chmn. N.Y. State Freshwater Wetlands Appeals Bd., 1976-83; chmn. planning bd. Village of Sleepy Hollow, N.Y., 1999—; bd. edn. Union Free Sch. Dist., Tarrytown, 1981-83, 85. Recipient N.Y. State Gov.'s Citation for Hist. Preservation, 1983, Eliz Haub prize in environ. law Frasses, 1992, Nat. Environ. Quality award Natural Resources Coun. Am., 2002. Fellow Am. Bar Found.; mem. Internat. Coun. Environ. Law (gov. 1993—), Commn. Environ. Law (chmn. 1996-2004), Am. Soc. Internat. Law, ABA, ALI, N.Y. State Bar Assn. (chmn. environ. law sect. 1979-80, Environ. Law award 1981), Assn. Am. Law Schs. (chair sect. on postgrad. legal edn. 1999-2000, chair sect. environ. law 1987-88), Assn. Bar City N.Y. (chmn. environ. law com. 1977-78, internat. law com. 1985-88, internat. environ. law com. 1990-92, Russian law com. 1992-95), Westchester County Bar Assn., Sierra Club (nat. bd. dirs. 1979-83), Phi Beta Kappa. Democrat. Unitarian Universalist. Home: 258 Kelbourne Ave Sleepy Hollow NY 10591-1322 Office: Pace U Sch Law 78 N Broadway White Plains NY 10603-3710 Office Phone: 914-422-4244. Business E-mail: nrobinson@law.pace.edu.

**ROBINSON, PAUL ARNOLD,** historian, educator, writer; b. San Diego, Oct. 1, 1940; s. Joseph Cook and Beryl Marie (Lippincott) R.; m. Ute Brosche, Aug. 3, 1964 (div. Aug. 1967); 1 child, Susan Marie; life ptnr. Stephen Dunatov. BA, Yale U., 1962; postgrad., Free U. Berlin, 1962-63; PhD, Harvard U., 1968. Asst. prof. history Stanford U. (Calif.), 1967-73, assoc. prof., 1973-80, prof. history, 1980—, Richard W. Lyman prof. in the humanities, 1994—. Author: The Freudian Left, 1969, The Modernization of Sex, 1976, Opera and Ideas: From Mozart to Strauss, 1985, Freud and His Critics, 1993, Ludwig van Beethoven: Fidelio, 1996, Gay Lives: Homosexual Autobiography from John Addington Symonds to Paul Monette, 1999, Opera, Sex and Other Vital Matters, 2002, Queer Wars: The New Gay Right and Its Critics, 2005; editor: Social Thought in America and Europe, 1970; contbg. editor The New Republic, 1979—85. Guggenheim fellow, 1970-71, Stanford Humanities Ctr. fellow, 1984-85, 96-97, Inst. for Advanced Study fellow, 1990-91, Ctr. for Advanced Study in the Behavioral Scis. fellow, 2002-03. Mem. Am. Acad. Arts and Scis., Am. Hist. Assn. Home: 671 Santa Ynez St Stanford CA 94305-8542 Office: Stanford Univ Dept History Stanford CA 94305 Business E-mail: paulr@stanford.edu.

**ROBINSON, PAUL HARPER,** lawyer, educator; b. Waterbury, Conn., Nov. 12, 1948; s. Edward Raymond and Ann (Harper) R.; m. Jane Grall, June 23, 1984; children by previous marriage— Samuel, Amanda. B.S., Rensselaer Poly. Inst., 1970; JD, UCLA, 1973; LL.M., Harvard U., 1974; diploma in legal studies Cambridge U., Eng., 1976. Bar: Mass. 1974. Faculty fellow Nat. Ctr. for State Courts, Washington, 1973; fed. prosecutor US Atty.'s Office, Alexandria, Va., 1976; legis. counsel U.S. Senate Jud. Com., Washington, 1977; asst. prof. law Rutgers U. Sch. Law, Camden, NJ, 1977—80, disting. prof., 1985-93, acting dean, 1989-90; commnr. US Sentencing Commn., Washington, 1985—; adj. prof. law, Georgetown U. Law Ctr., Washington, 1986-88; vis. prof. Northwestern U., 1992-93, prof. law, 1993-98, Edna & Ednyfed Williams prof., 1998-2002; Colin S. Diver disting. prof. law U. Pa. Law Sch., 2003-; dir. RI Criminal Code Revision Project. Author: Criminal Law Defenses, 1984. Contbr. numerous articles to profl. jours. Mem. ABA (chmn. criminal justice sect. com. on state legislation). Home: 230 S Cooper River Dr Collingswood NJ 08108-1100 Office: U Pa Law Sch 3400 Chestnut St Philadelphia PA 19104 Office Phone: 215-898-1017. E-mail: phr@law.upenn.edu.

**ROBINSON, PETER J.,** dean, periodontal educator, pathologist; b. St. Louis, May 31, 1941; s. Hamilton Burrows-Greaves and Katherine (Long) R.; m. Letticia Schumacher, July 18, 1964; children: Elizabeth Haskins Vance, Emily Hamilton. BA, Drake U., Des Moines, 1963; DDS, U. Mo., Kansas City, 1966; PhD, U. Pa., Phila., 1972. Dental intern U.S. Army, Washington, 1966-67; asst. prof. U. Pa., Phila., 1973-75; prof., chmn. periodontics Northwestern U., Chgo., 1975-88, chmn. stomatology, 1988-97; dean, prof. periodontology U. Conn. Sch. Dental Medicine, 1997—. Co-author: Transplantation for Dental Specialties, 1980. Pres. Dist. 38 Sch. Bd., Kenilworth, Ill., 1985-87. Capt. U.S. Army, 1966-69. Recipient Procter & Gamble Guest Scientist award Am. Dental Assn. Rsch. Inst., Chgo., 1983, Fogarty award NIH, Washington, 1984. Mem. ADA (sci. rsch. instt.), Internat. Assn. Dental Rsch. (pres. periodontal rsch. group 1990-92), Midwest Soc. Periodontology (pres. 1986-87), Ill. Soc. Periodontology (pres. 1985-86). Achievements include patent on Northwestern periodontal probe. Office: U Conn Sch Dental Medicine 263 Farmington Ave Farmington CT 06030*

**ROBINSON, PETER M.,** business association executive; BA, U. Del., 1977; MA in Internat. Affairs, Columbia U., 1979. Dir. Inbound Div. Am. Inst. Fgn. Study, 1986—89; mng. Trade and Transport Policy US Coun. for Internat. Bus., v.p. memberships, sr. v.p., COO, pres., 2005—. Bd. dirs. Am. Field Svc.-USA; mem. internat. bd. trustees Am. Field Svc. Intercultural Programs, 1997—2004; bd. dirs. WAND, Inc. Fellow: Fgn. Policy Assn.; mem.: Econ. Club of NY. Office: US Coun for Internat Bus 1212 Ave of Americas New York NY 10036 Office Phone: 212-354-4480. Office Fax: 212-575-0327. E-mail: probinson@uscib.org.*

**ROBINSON, PREZELL RUSSELL,** academic administrator; b. Batesburg, SC, Aug. 25, 1922; s. Clarence and Annie (Folks) R.; m. Lulu Harris, Apr. 9, 1950; 1 dau. AB in Econs. Social Sci., St. Augustine's Coll., 1946; MA in Sociology, Econs., Cornell U., 1951, EdD in Sociology-Ednl. Adminstrn., 1956; degree (hon.), St. Augustine's Coll.; DCL (hon.), U. South, 1970; LHD, degree, Cuttington Coll., Monrovia, Liberia; LHD (hon.), Voorhees Coll., 1981, degree (hon.); LHD (hon.), Episcopal Theol. Sem., 1982; LLD (hon.), Bishop Coll., 1979; DCL (hon.), Columbia U., 1980, degree (hon.); DHL (hon.), Kenyon Coll., 1988; degree (hon.), Va. Theology Sem., Alexandria, Barton Coll., Campbell U., NC State U., Shaw U. Tchr. social sci., French

Bettis Jr. Coll., Trenton, SC, 1946-48; sucessively registrar, tchr., acting prin. high sch., acting dean jr. coll., instr., dir. adult edn. Voorhees Jr. Coll., Denmark, SC, 1948-56; prof. sociology, dean coll. St. Augustine's Coll., Raleigh, NC, 1956-64, exec. dean, 1964-66, acting pres., 1966-67, pres., 1967-95, pres. emeritus, 1995—. Pres. United Negro Coll. Fund, Inc., 1978-81, Nat. Assn. Equal Opportunity Higher Edn., 1981-84, N.C. Assn. Coll. & U., Cooperating Raleigh Colls., 1981, 86—; bd. dirs. Learning Inst. N.C.; scholar-in-residence Nairobi (Kenya) U., 1973; vis. lectr. Dept. State del. to African nations, 1971, 73, 78; dir. Wachovia Bank & Trust Co.; vice chmn. N.C. State Bd. Edn., mem., 1973-99, vice-chmn., 1994-99. Contbr. articles to profl. publs. Exec. com. N.C. Edn. Com. on Tchr. Edn.; active N.C. Bd. Edn.; chmn. bd. Assn. Episcopal Colls.; mem. Mayor's Community Relations Com.; vice-chmn. Wake County divsn. Occoneechee coun. Boy Scouts Am., 1959-67; chmn. Wake Occoneechee coun., 1963-66, exec. com., 1965—; vice-chmn. Wake County chpt. ARC; chmn. edn. divsn. United Fund of Raleigh, budget com., 1965—; exec. com. Wake County Libraries.; trustee Voorhees Coll. Fulbright fellow to India, 1965; appointed US alt. rep. or public mem. amb. Gen. Assembly UN, by Pres. George Bush, 1992, by Pres. Clinton, 1996. Served with AUS, 1942. Recipient Distinguished Alumni award Voorhees Coll., 1967, Silver Anniversary award N.C. Community System, 1989; decorated Star of Africia Liberia; recipient numerous service awards and citations; named one of the most effective coll. pres.s in U.S. Coun. for Advancement and Support of Edn., Washington, 1986; Univ. fellow Cornell U., 1954, rsch. fellow, 1955-56; Fulbright fellow, 1965. Mem. AAAS, Nat. Assn. Collegiate Deans and Registrars, Am. Acad. Polit. and Social Sci., Am. Sociol. Soc., N.C. Sociol. Soc. (exec. com.), Ctrl. Intercollegiate Athletic Assn. (exec. com.), N.C. Assn. Ind. Colls. and Univs. (dir.), Raleigh C. of C. (A.E. Finley Disting. Svc. award 1989), So. Sociol. Assn., Am. Acad. Polit. Sci., N.C. Lit. and Hist. Soc., N.C. Hist. Soc., Delta Mu Delta, Phi Delta Kappa, Phi Kappa Phi, Alpha Kappa Mu, Phi Beta Lambda. Protestant Episcopalian (lay reader). Home: 821 Glascock St Raleigh NC 27604-2317 Office: St Augustine's Coll 1315 Oakwood Ave Raleigh NC 27610-2247

**ROBINSON, RALPH W.,** lawyer; b. San Francisco, Mar. 26, 1947; BA, U. Calif., Berkeley, 1968; JD, Golden Gate U., 1971. Bar: Calif. 1972, US Supreme Ct., Supreme Ct. Calif. Mng ptnr. San Francisco office Wilson, Elser, Moskowitz, Edelman & Dicker LLP, head San Francisco trial practice area. Mem.: ABA, Alameda County Bar Assn., Bar Assn. San Francisco. Office: Wilson Elser Moskowitz Edelman & Dicker 14th Fl 650 California St San Francisco CA 94108 Office Phone: 415-433-0990 ext. 3001. Office Fax: 415-434-1370. Business E-Mail: robinsonr@wemed.com.

**ROBINSON, RAYMOND EDWIN,** conductor, music educator, writer; b. San Jose, Calif., Dec. 26, 1932; s. Elam Edwin and Zula Mai (Hatley) R.; m. Ruth Aleen Chamberlain, Mar. 12, 1954; children: Cynthia Rae, Greg Edwin, David L., Brent Steven, Jeffrey Vernon. BA, San Jose State U., 1956; MMus, Ind. U., 1958, D in Mus. Edn., 1969; LHD, Westminster Choir Coll. 1987; postdoctoral study, Jagiellonian U., Poland, 1995, Cambridge U., 1987—89, postdoctoral study, 2002—03. Instr. music Ind. U., Bloomington, 1958-59; music critic Portland Reporter, 1962-63, Balt. Evening Sun, 1964-68, Palm Beach (Fla.) Post, 1991—, Palm Beach Daily News, 2003—04; founder, tchr. seminar for music adminstrs., 1972—; chmn. divsn. fine arts Cascade Coll., Portland, Oreg., 1959-63; dean Peabody Inst., Balt., 1963-69; pres. Westminster Choir Coll., Princeton, NJ, 1969-87; vis. fellow Wolfson Coll. U. Cambridge, England, 1987—88, 2002—03; disting. prof. choral studies, choral condr. Palm Beach Atlantic U., West Palm Beach, Fla., 1989—; pres. Prestige Publs., Inc., 1978—; prof. Sch. Ch. Music Knox Theol. Sem., Ft. Lauderdale, Fla., 1989—; vis. prof. U. Miami, 2001—. Choral condr. Palm Beach C.C., Lake Worth, Fla., 1992-93; condr.-in-residence, dir. music First Presbyn. Ch., West Palm Beach, 1989-97; dir. music Coral Ridge Presbyn. Ch., Ft. Lauderdale, Fla., 1997, music dir. Palm Beach Symphony Orch., 2004—; spl. guest choral condr. Palm Beach Opera, 1990—; interim condr. Choral Soc. Palm Beaches, 1992; condr. Ray Robinson Chorale, 1994—, Cambridge (Eng.) U., Cambridge, Eng., 1987-89, 2002-03, Kiev, Ukraine, 1997, Budapest, 1997, Cracow, 2002, Coral Ridge Presbyn. Ch., 1997; vis. prof. U. Miami, Fla., 2001-2002. Author: The Choral Experience, 1976, Choral Music, 1978; Krzysztof Penderecki, A Guide to His Works, 1983, A Study of the Penderecki St. Luke Passion, 1983, John Finley Williamson: A Centennial Appreciation, 1987; co-author: German Diction for the Choral Singer, 1992, A Bach Tribute: Bach Essays in Honor of William H. Scheide, 1993; co-author, editor: Studies in Penderecki, 1998, 2003; editor: Labyrinth of Time: Postcards from Cambridge, 2005, Five Addresses for the End of the Millenium, 1998; The Choral Tradition Series, Hinshaw Music Inc., 1978—. Bd. dirs. Balt. Symphony Orch., 1967-69, Am. Boy Choir Sch., 1970-73, N.Y. Choral Soc., 1972—, Palm Beach Atlantic U. choral series Hinshaw Music Inc., 1990—; bd. dirs. Palm Beach County Coun. Arts, chmn. profl. artists com., mem. task force for master plan, 1990-92; mem. cultural plan com. Palm Beach County Cultural Coun., 1992; mem. task force for edn. Fla. Philharm. Orch., 1994-95; mem. art in pub. places com. West Palm Beach, Fla. 2004—. Recipient Disting. Alumni Merit award Ind. U., 1975, Disting. Alumni award Sch. Music Ind. U., 1973, Disting. Alumni award San Jose State U., 1990. Mem. Coll. Music Soc. (life), Am. Choral Dirs. Assn. (life, chmn. rsch. and publs. com. 1986—), Internat. Heinrich Schütz Soc. (chmn. Am. sect. 1984-87), Univ. Club N.Y., Nassau Club Princeton, Govs. Club West Palm Beach. Presbyterian. Home: 2413 Medina Way West Palm Beach FL 33401-8019 Office Phone: 561-803-2416. Business E-Mail: Ray_Robinson@pba.edu.

**ROBINSON, REBECCA LYNNE,** medical researcher; b. Evansville, Ind., Dec. 9, 1967; d. Sherman Joseph and Joyce Jeane Black; m. Robert Wayne Robinson, Aug. 8, 1992; children: Calder Luke, Mary Helen Ellie. BA, U. So. Ind., 1990; MS, Purdue U., 1995. Tchg. asst. Ind. U.-Purdue U., 1990—92; rsch. asst. Osgood Lab. for Cross-Cultural Rsch., Indpls., 1990—93; rsch. analyst Regenstrief Inst./Bowen Rsch. at Ind. U. Sch. Medicine, Indpls., 1993—98; rsch. scientist St. Vincent Hosp., Indpls., 1996—98; health outcomes rsch. cons. U.S. Med. Divsn., Eli Lilly and Co., Indpls., 1998—. Cons. Osgood Lab. for Cross-Cultural Rsch., 1993—98, Ind. Hand Ctr., Indpls., 1996—98, Ind. State Dept. Health, Indpls., 1998—; presenter in field. Contbr. articles to profl. jours. Facilitator, team leader, participant Ministry of Moms, Nativity Ch., Indpls., 2001—05. Recipient Outstanding Grad. Student award, Purdue U., 1992, Best Author Presentation award, 17th World Congress on Psychosomatic Medicine, 2003, Marketscan Rsch. award, 2005; grantee Agy. for Health Care Policy and Rsch., 1990—95. Office: Eli Lilly and Co Lilly Corp Ctr Indianapolis IN 46285 Office Phone: 317-433-1323. Office Fax: 317-277-7444. E-mail: rlrobinson@lilly.com.

**ROBINSON, REGINALD R.,** musician; b. Chgo., Oct. 19, 1972; Pianist and composer of classical ragtime music; signed by Delmark Records, 1992. Composer: (albums) The Strongman, 1993, Sounds in Silhouette, 1994, Euphonic Sounds, 1998, Man Out of Time, 2003. Named MacArthur Fellow, John D. and Catherine T. MacArthur Found., 2004. Office: c/o Delmark Records 4121 N Rockwell Chicago IL 60618

**ROBINSON, RETIANA CECELIA,** secondary school educator; b. Balt. m. Allen and Rosa Lee (Jones) Branch; m. Larry James Robinson, July 15, 1978. BS, Coppin State Coll., 1973; postgrad., Morgan U., 1974, Towson U. Cert. advanced profl. tchr. Md. Math. instr. Balt. City Pub. Schs., 1973—, head dept. math., 1996-98. Mem. Regional Adv. Coun. High Schs., 1977-80; evaluator Mid. States Evaluation Com., Balt., 1983, 85; math instr. summer program Upward Bound Program, Balt., 1993-95, Tech Bridge Engring. Program, Balt., 1996; advisor Student Mentoring Program, 1996—. Active Task Force for Mid. Schs., Balt., 1977-78; treas. Harlem Park Cmty. Assn., Balt., 1990-91; asst. planner ASCD, Balt., 1994-95. Recipient Champion of Courage award Sta. WNUV-TV, Balt., 1989. Mem. Nat. Coun. Tchrs. Math., Coppin State Coll. Avocations: flower arranging, collecting African-American artwork, collecting old photo albums, collecting African-American figurines. Home: 6700 Queens Ferry Rd Baltimore MD 21239-1428 Office: Upton Sch 811 W Lanvale St Baltimore MD 21217 Office Phone: 410-396-0775. Personal E-Mail: retiana#1@aol.com.

**ROBINSON, RICH,** musician; b. Atlanta, May 24, 1969; s. Stan and Nancy Robinson. Co-founder & band mem. Mr. Crowe's Garden (name changed to Black Crowes), 1985—; founder Hookah Brown, 2003. Musician (albums): Shake Your Money Maker, 1990 (Album of Yr. Internat. Rock Awards 1991, double platinum record 1991), The Southern Harmony and Musical Companion, 1992, America, 1994, Three Snakes and One Charm, 1996, Souled Out Live, 1998, By Your Side, 1999, Armorica, 2000, Lions, 2001, Live, 2002, Freak 'n' Roll...Into the Fog, 2006, (solo albums) Paper, 2004. Recipient (with Black Crowes) Grammy award nomination for Best New Artist; voted Best New Am. Band, Rolling Stone readers and critics polls; named Artist of Yr., 1991.*

**ROBINSON, RICHARD,** publishing executive; b. Pitts., May 15, 1937; s. Maurice Richard and Florence (Liddell) Robinson; children: John Benham, Maurice. BA in English magna cum laude, Harvard U., 1959; postgrad., St. Catharines Coll., Cambridge U., 1959-60, Columbia U., 1959-61. Tchr. English, Evanston Twp. (Ill.) H.S., 1960-62; asst. editor Lit. Cavalcade, Scholastic Inc., N.Y.C., 1962-63; editor Scholastic lit. units Scholastic Inc., 1963-64; founder, editor Scope mag., 1964, editorial dir. English, 1967-71, pub. sch. divsn., 1971-74; pres. Scholastic Corp., 1974—, CEO, 1975—, chmn. bd., 1982—. Named Corp. Citizen of Yr., Robin Hood Found., 1999, The Creative Coalition, 2000. Publisher of Yr., UJA Fedn., N.Y., 2000; recipient EdPress Hall of Fame award, Assn. Ednl. Publrs., Cleveland E. Dodge medal, Tchrs. Coll. Columbia U., Best Friend award, LA's BEST After Sch. Enrichment Program, For the Love of Reading award, UJA-Fedn., Spotlight award, Creative Coalition, British Am. Bus. award Save the Children, Partners for Children award, 2003. Mem. Nat. Coun. Tchrs. English, Nat. Assn. Bilingual Edn. (Corp. Citizen of Yr. 1996), Assn. Am. Pubs. (bd. dirs. 1989—, exec. com., chmn. 1996-98, LMP Publ. of Yr. 1998), Century Assn., Pubs. Lunch Club, University Club (N.Y.C.), Phi Beta Kappa Office: Scholastic Inc 557 Broadway New York NY 10012-3919 E-mail: drobinson@scholastic.com.

**ROBINSON, RICHARD ALLEN, II,** security firm executive, director; s. Richard Allen, Sr. Robinson and Barbara Ortt Haege; m. Patty Ruth Crawford, July 27, 1990; children: Rebecca, Christie, Richard III, Jessica, Jacklyn. AS, South Fla. C.C., 1979; BS, Rollins Coll., Fla., 1982; M in bus. adminstrn., Warner So. Coll., Fla., 2004. Patrolman Sebrins (Fla.) Police Dept., 1976—80, sgt., 1980—84, lt., 1984—88, capt., 1988—90; chief of security Werner Southern Coll., Lake Wales, Fla., 1992—95, physical plant dir., chief security, 1995—. Pres. Mallard Point Home Owners Assn., Winter Haven, Fla., 2005—06. Mem.: Nat. Fire Prevention Assn., Internat. Assn. Campus Law Enforcement, Fla. Assn. Campus Safety and Security (pres. 1996, v.p. 1994). Office: Warner Southern Coll 13895 US Hwy 27 Lake Wales FL 33884

**ROBINSON, RICHARD M.,** communications executive; b. Bklyn., Nov. 28, 1934; s. Allen and Syd (Bell) R.; m. Rochelle Wolf, Dec. 25, 1967; children: Michelle P., Steven E. BS in Physics, Rensselaer Poly. Inst., 1956, MS in Tech. Comm., 1959. Assoc. engr. Convair-Astronautics, San Diego, 1956—57; tech. writer Raytheon, Andover, Mass., 1957—58; pubs. engr. Hazeltine Electronics, Little Neck, NY, 1959—61; sr. pubs. engr. Sperry Gyroscope, Great Neck, NY, 1961—68; mgr. editl. svcs. Grumman Corp., Bethpage, NY, 1968—94; tech. comm. specialist/cons. Setauket, NY, 1995—. Adj. faculty Suffolk County C.C. Contbr. articles to profl. jours. Mem. IEEE (life sr., conf. chmn. 1989, tech. activities bd. 1992-93, Profl. Com. Soc. adminstrv. com. 1977-97, Profl. Com. Soc. pres. 1992-93, referee papers Trans. on Profl. Comm., Alfred N. Goldsmith award 1983, 3d Millennium medal 2000), Soc. Tech. Comms. (sr. mem.), Miramar Ski Club (pres. 1966-67), Amateur Ski Instrs. Assn. (cert. instr.). Home and Office: 10 Penelope Dr Setauket NY 11733-2010 Personal E-mail: r.robinson@ieee.org.

**ROBINSON, ROBERT BLACQUE,** foundation administrator; b. Long Beach, Calif., Apr. 24, 1927; s. Joseph LeRoi and Frances Hansel R.; m. Susan Amelia Thomas, Jan. 21, 1960; children: Victoria, Shelly, Blake, Sarah. Student, Oreg. State Coll., 1946; BA, UCLA, 1950; student, U. Hawaii. Partner, Pritchard Assocs. (Mgmt. Cons.), Honolulu, 1956-58; asst. dir. Econ. Planning and Coordination Authority, Hawaii, 1959; dep. dir. dept. econ. devel. State of Hawaii, 1960-63; asst. mgr. Pacific Concrete and Rock Co., Ltd., Honolulu, 1963-66, exec. v.p. and gen. mgr., 1966-68, pres. and gen. mgr., 1968-75, chmn., 1976-77; pres. C. of C. of Hawaii, Honolulu, 1977—. Bd. govs. Hawaii Employers Coun., 1969-74, mem. exec. com., 1969-74, vice chmn., 1973-74; bd. dirs. Pacific Aerospace Mus., 1982-86; mem. Hawaii Tourism Conf., 1977, chmn., 1981-82; bd. dirs. Aloha United Fund, 1970-76, sec., 1972, v.p., 1973-76; bd. dirs. Oahu Devel. Conf., 1970-75; treas., bd. dirs. Crime Stoppers Hawaii, 1981—; mem. Hawaii Joint Coun. on Econ. Edn., 1985—; bd. dirs. Jr. Achievement Hawaii, 1967-73, pres., 1969; bd. dirs. Hawaii Ednl. Coun., 1974-75, Health and Community Services Coun. Hawaii, 1982-84; mem. exec. com. Hawaii Conv. Ctr. Coun., 1984—, Interagency Energy Conservation Coun., State of Hawaii, 1978—; trustee Cen. Union Ch., 1983-86; bd. dirs. Waikiki Improvement Assn. Inc., 1986—; mem. Ctr. for Tropical and Subtropical Aquaculture Industry Adv. Coun., 1987—; chmn. Mayor's Adv. Com. on Pacific Nations Ctr., 1988-89. Lt. comdr. USNR, 1945-46, ret. Mem. Japan-Am. Conf. of Mayors and C. of C. Pres. (mem. Am. exec. com. 1974—), Am. Soc. Assn. Execs. (past dir. Hawaii chpt.), Hawaii Execs. Coun. (found., Young Pres. Assn. (past mem.), Aloha Soc. Assn. Execs., C. of C. Hawaii (dir. 1972-75, chmn. 1975), Coun. of Profit Sharing Industries (past dir. Hawaii sect.), Cement and Concrete Products Industry of Hawaii (pres. 1968), Hawaii Mfrs. Assn. (past dir.), Navy League of U.S. (Hawaii council), Engring. Assn. Hawaii, Pacific Club, Rotary, Sigma Chi. Home: 1437 Kalaepohaku St Honolulu HI 96816-1804 Office: C of C Hawaii 735 Bishop St Ste 220 Honolulu HI 96813-4816

**ROBINSON, ROBERT L.,** retired diversified financial services company executive, lawyer; b. Ridgeway, Va., Feb. 22, 1936; s. Gerald L. and Annie (McBride) R.; m. Audrey M. Allen, July 30, 1960; children: Robert, Diane, Kelly. BA, Va. State Coll., 1957; LL.B., Harvard U., 1960; MBA, U. Conn. 1976. Bar: N.Y. 1961, Pa. 1978. Atty. N.Y. Central Ry. Co., N.Y.C., 1960-63; asst. gen. counsel Crane Co., N.Y.C., 1963-71; counsel Xerox Corp. Stamford, Conn., 1971-77; v.p., asst. gen. counsel and sec. INA Corp., Phila. 1977-82; sr. v.p., gen. counsel investment group CIGNA Corp., Bloomfield, Conn., 1982-84, sr. v.p., asst. gen. counsel, corp. sec., 1984-87; sr. v.p., gen. counsel property & casualty group Phila., 1987-88, sr. v.p., chief counsel litigation and ins., 1988-2000; ret., 2000. Dir. Phila. Reinsurance Corp., Am. Arbitration Assn., CPR Inst. for Dispute Resolution. Served to lt. U.S. Army, 1957. Mem. ABA, Pa. Bar Assn., Westchester-Fairfield Corp. Counsel Assn. (founder, bd. dirs. pres. 1976-77), Great Oak Yacht Club, Harvard Club (N.Y.C.), Merion Cricket Club, Phila. Club., Phila. Cricket Club. Republican. Office: 451 Moreno Rd Wynnewood PA 19096 Office Phone: 610-896-0758. Personal E-mail: rlrobinson@verizon.net.

**ROBINSON, ROBIN,** newscaster; b. Chgo. m. Terrence Brantley, 1986 (div. 1989). B, San Diego State U., 1980. Reporter KGTV, San Diego, 1979—81; consumer reporter CBS affiliate, Denver, 1981—84; reporter WBBM-TV, Chgo., 1984—87; co-anchor Fox News at 9 WFLD-TV, Chgo., 1987—. Co-recipient Emmy awards. Office: WFLD-TV 205 N Mich Ave Chicago IL 60601

**ROBINSON, RONALD ALAN,** manufacturing executive; b. Louisville, Mar. 23, 1952; s. J. Kenneth and Juanita M. (Crosier) R.; m. Joan Parker, 1986; children: Rex, Jay. BS, GA Inst. Tech., 1974; MBA, Harvard U., 1978 Staff engr., asst. to exec. v.p. ops. Dual Drilling Co., Wichita Falls, Tex., 1978-80; v.p. Dreco, Inc., Houston, 1980-84, pres., dir. subs. Triflo Industries Internat., Inc.; pres., COO Ramteck Sys., Inc., 1984-87; chmn., CEO Denver Techs. Inc., 1988-95; pres. Svedala Industries, Inc., 1996-99; pres., CEO Alamo Group Inc., Seguin, Tex., 1999—. Recipient Optimist Internat. Citizenship award, 1970; Gardiner Symonds fellow, 1978. Mem. Harvard Alumni Assn. Home: 18 Pourtales Colorado Springs CO 80906 Office: Alamo Group Inc 1502 E Walnut St Seguin TX 78155-5202 Office Phone: 830-372-9615.

**ROBINSON, RONALD GENE,** military officer, political science professor; b. Detroit, June 13, 1952; s. John Henry and Linnie (Mattingly) R.; m. Cheryl Lee Robinson, Aug. 27, 1982 (div. July 2000); children: Ronald Jr., Lindee Marie, Ryan John; m. Dee Robinson, May 6, 2001. AA, Schoolcraft Coll., 1972; B in Gen. Studies, U. Mich., 1974; MA, Western Mich. U., 1977. Cert. govt. contracting level III. Prof. polit. sci. Schoolcraft Coll., Livonia, Mich., 1976—; contract negotiator U.S. Army, Warren, Mich., 1981—. Pres. R&B Advt. Agy., Warren, 1996-98. Author: Judicial Character, 1977; columnist The County Line, Warren, 1990-97, The Warren Examiner, 1996-97. Candidate Warren City Coun., 1991, nominee, 1995, 2003; chmn. Hartsig Pk. Homeowners Assn., Warren, 1990-97; precinct del. Livonia Rep. Party, 1974-81; mem. Oakland County Young Reps., 2000—; bd. dirs. Warren-Centerline Right to Life, 1991—. Mem. So. Polit. Sci. Assn. Avocations: swimming, travel, dance, playing stratego, playing pool. Personal E-mail: rgr11897@aol.com.

**ROBINSON, RONALD MICHAEL,** financial executive, financial consultant; b. N.Y.C., May 1, 1942; s. Arthur John and Matilda (Siegel) R.; m. Mary Jane Reemelin, Feb. 25, 1972; children: Scott Edward, Elizabeth Drew. BS, Ohio State U., Ohio State U. Pa., 1966. CPA, Pa. Fin. mgr. Am. Airlines, Inc., N.Y.C., 1969-72; mgmt. cons. Coopers & Lybrand, Phila., 1973-75; pres. Robinson Assocs., Inc., Paoli, Pa., 1975-81; dir. fin. and adminstrn., chief fin. officer Presbyn. Homes, Inc., Camp Hill, Pa., 1982-99. Bd. dirs. Healthamerica, Healthassurance, Mems. First Fed. Credit Union, Continuing Care Rx, Geneva House. Mem. Carlisle (Pa.) Borough Coun., 1988-92. Home: 1214 Georgetown Circle Carlisle PA 17013-3548 Office: PO Box 908 Carlisle PA 11701 Fax: 717-379-3275. Office Phone: 717-379-3275. E-mail: ronaldmrobinson@comcast.net.

**ROBINSON, ROXANA BARRY,** writer, art historian; b. Pine Mountain, Ky., Nov. 30, 1946; Student, Bennington Coll., 1964—66; BA, U. Mich., 1969. Art cataloguer Sotheby's, N.Y.C., 1970-74; exhbn. dir. Terry Dintenfass Gallery, N.Y.C., 1974-76; freelance writer, 1976—. Author: (novels) Summer Light, 1988 (Washington Irving award Westchester Libr. Assn.), This is My Daughter, 1998 (Notable Book of the Yr. award N.Y. Times, 1998, Washington Irving award Westchester Libr. Assn.), Sweetwater, 2003 (named Notable Book, N.Y. Times), (biography) Georgia O'Keeffe: A Life, 1989 (Notable Book of the Yr. award N.Y. Times, 1989, Washington Irving award Westchester Libr. Assn.), (short stories) A Glimpse of Scarlet, 1991 (Notable Book of the Yr. award N.Y. Times, 1991), Asking for Love, 1995 (Washington Irving award Westchester Libr. Assn., Notable Book of the Yr. Nat. Libr. Assn.), A Perfect Stranger, 2005. Trustee Eugene Lang Coll., NY, Nat. Humanities Ctr., NC, 1995—, PEN Am. Ctr., NY, 1998—. Recipient Lit. Lion award, N.Y. Pub. Libr., 1991; fellow, Nat. Endowment Arts, 1987, MacDowell Colony, 1999; John S. Guggenheim Found. fellow, 2000. Office: c/o Lynn Nesbit Janklow-Nesbit 445 Park Ave New York NY 10022

**ROBINSON, SALLY WINSTON,** artist; b. Detroit, Nov. 2, 1924; d. Harry Lewis and Lydia (Kahn) Winston; m. Eliot F. Robinson, June 28, 1949; children: Peter Eliot, Lydia Winston, Sarah Mitchell, Suzanne Finley. BA, Bennington Coll., 1947; postgrad., Cranbrook Acad. Art, 1949; grad., Sch. Social Work, Wayne U., 1948, MA, 1972; MFA, Wayne State U., 1973. Psychol. tester Detroit Bd. Edn., 1944; psychol. counselor and tester YMCA, N.Y.C., 1946; social caseworker Family Svc., Pontiac, Mich., 1947; instr. printmaking Wayne State U., Detroit, 1973—. Tchr. children's art Detroit Inst. Art, 1949-50, now artistic advisor, bd. dirs. drawing and pring orgn. One-woman shows include: U. Mich., 1973, Wayne State U., 1974, Klein-Vogel Gallery, 1974, Rina Gallery, 1976, Park McCullough House, Vt., 1976, Williams Coll., 1976, Arnold Klein Gallery, 1977, exhibited in group shows, Bennington Coll., Cranbrook Mus., Detroit Inst. Art, Detroit Artists Market, Soc. Women Painters, Soc. Arts and Crafts, Bloomfield Art Assn., Flint Left Bank Gallery, Balough Gallery, Detroit Soc. Women Painters, U. Mich., U. Ind., U. Wis., U. Pitts., Toledo Mus., Krannert Mus., Represented in permanent collections, Detroit, N.Y.C., Birmingham, Bloomfield Hills. Bd. dirs. Planned Parenthood, 1951—, mem. exec. bd., 1963—; bd. dirs. PTA, 1956-60, Roeper City and Country Sch., U. Mich. Mus. Art, 1978; trustee Putnam Hosp. Med. Rsch. Inst., 1978; mem. Gov.'s Commn. Art in State Bldgs., 1978-79; mem. art and devel. coms. So. Vt. Art Ctr., 1987-88; mem. vol. com. Marie Selby Gardens; patron Graphic Art Studio, U. So. Fla., Tampa; patron, benefactor Clark Mus., Williamstown, Mass. Fellow: Williams Coll. Mus. Art (mem. visiting com.); mem.: Bloomfield Art Assn. (program co-chmn. 1956), Birmingham Soc. Women Painters (pres. 1974—76), Detroit Soc. Women Painters, Detroit Artists Market (dir. 1956—, hon. bd. mem.), Founders Soc. Detroit Inst. Art, Bennington Coll. Alumnae Assn. (regional co-chmn. 1954), Cosmopolitan Club (N.Y.C.), Founders Garden Club (Sarasota, Fla.), Garden Club Am. (bd. dirs.), Oaks Club (Fla.), Women's City Club (coord. art shows Detroit 1950), Village Women's Club (Birmingham, Mich.), Unitarian Universalist. Home: 209 Hills Point Rd Charlotte VT 05445-9698 also: 639 Eagle Watch Rd Osprey FL 34229 Personal E-mail: sallyrobinsonflorida@msn.com.

**ROBINSON, SHARON BETH,** health science association administrator; b. Balt., Sept. 28, 1959; BS, Towson State U., 1981; MS, Johns Hopkins U., 1986. Exec. asst. Congress of Neurol. Surgeons, Balt., 1983-86; office adminstr. Md. Inst. Emergency Med. Svcs., Balt., 1986-87; coord. spl. projects U. Md. Med. Systems, Balt., 1986-88; adminstr. Am. Bd. Med. Genetics, Bethesda, Md., 1988—. Am. Coll. Med. Genetics, Bethesda, 1992-98, Am. Bd. Genetic Counseling, Bethesda, 1993—. Mem. Catonsville Community Coll. Alumni Assn. (bd. dirs. 1984-89, sec. 1986, v.p. 1987, pres. 1988). Office: ABMG/ABGC 9650 Rockville Pike Bethesda MD 20814-3998 E-mail: srobinson@genetics.faseb.org.

**ROBINSON, SMOKEY (WILLIAM ROBINSON),** singer, composer; b. Detroit; m. Claudette Rogers, 1959 (div. 1986); children: Berry William, Tamla Claudette; m. Frances (Gladney) Robinson, 2002. V.p. Motown Record Corp., 1961-1988; bd. dirs. Smokey Robinson Foods. Formed group, Smokey Robinson and the Miracles, with Miracles, 1957-72, performed Detroit nightclubs, co-founder, Tamla record label, 1959; numerous singles and album recs. including: Sweet Harmony, 1973, Virgin Man, 1974, Agony and the Ecstasy, 1975, Quiet Storm, 1976, Open, 1976, There will Come a Day (I'm Gonna Happen to You), 1977; appearances at clubs, colls., also network TV shows including Shindig; star own TV spl., 1971; solo albums include Smokey, 1973, A Quiet Storm, 1975, Smokey's Family Robinson, 1976, Deep in My Soul, 1977 Smokin', 1978, Warm Thoughts, 1980, Being with You, 1981, Touch the Sky, 1983, Smoke Signals, 1986, One Heartbeat, 1987, Love Smokey, 1990, Blame It on Love & All the Great Hits, 1990, Double Good Everything, 1992, Motown Legends, 1995, Intimate, 1999, Food for the Spirit, 2004; appeared on Broadway in An Evening with Smokey Robinson, 1985, Chicago, 2006; author: (autobiography with David Ritz) Smokey: Inside My Life, 1989. Inducted Rock 'n Roll Hall of Fame, 1986, Songwriters Hall of Fame, 1986; recipient Grammy award for best male rhythm & blues vocal perfomance, 1987, Founders award ASCAP, 1988, Lifetime Achievement award, Motor City Music Awards, 1992, Kennedy Ctr. Honor, John F. Kennedy Center for Performing Arts, 2006. Office: SFGL Foods Inc #200 100 N Brand Ave Glendale CA 91203 also: SBK Records 1290 Ave of the Americas New York NY 10104*

**ROBINSON, STEPHEN MICHAEL,** mathematician, educator; b. Columbus, Ohio, Apr. 12, 1942; s. Arthur Howard and Mary Elizabeth (Coffin) R.; m. Chong-Suk Han, May 10, 1968; children: Diana Marie Oestreich, James Andrew. BA, U. Wis., 1962, PhD, 1971; MS, NYU, 1963; Diploma, U.S. Army War Coll., 1986; Dr. honoris causa, Univ. Zürich, 1996. Adminstr. U. Wis., Madison, 1969-72, asst. prof., 1972-75, assoc. prof., 1975-79, prof. indsl. and sys. engring. and computer scis., 1979—, chmn. dept. indsl. engring., 1981-84. Cons. to various agys. Dept. Def., 1971—. Author: (with Jagdish Chandra) An Uneasy Alliance: The Mathematics Research Center at the University of Wisconsin, 1956-1987, 2005; editor: Math. of Ops. Rsch., 1981-86, assoc. editor, 1975-80, Jour. Ops. Rsch., 1974-86, Math. Programming, 1986-91; mem. bd. editors Annals Ops. Rsch., 1984-99, Set-Valued Analysis, 1992-99, Jour. Convex Analysis, 1994—2002; adv. editor Math. of

Ops. Rsch., 1987—, Ops. Rsch. Letters, 2002-; mem. editl. bd. Springer Series in Ops. Rsch. and Fin. Engring., 1996—; contbr. numerous articles to profl. jours. Trustee Village of Shorewood Hills, Wis., 1974-76, mem. fin. com., 1973-87; bd. on math. scis. and their applications NRC, 2001—, bd. overseers Simon's Rock Coll., Great Barrington, Mass., 1991-02. Served to capt. U.S. Army, 1963—69, Korea, Vietnam, col. AUS, ret. Decorated Legion of Merit, Bronze star, Air medal, Army Commendation medal with 2 oak leaf clusters; recipient John K. Walker Jr. award, Mil. Ops. Rsch. Soc., 2001. Fellow Inst. Ops. Rsch. and Mgmt. Scis. (mem. Ops. Rsch. Soc. Am. coun. 1991-94, sec. 2000-03); mem. Inst. Indsl. Engrs., Soc. Indsl. and Applied Math., Math. Programming Soc. (mem.-at-large of coun. 1991-94, George B. Dantzig prize 1997). Madison Club. Home: 1014 University Bay Dr Madison WI 53705-2251 Office: U Wis Dept Indsl and Sys Engring 1513 University Ave Madison WI 53706-1572 Office Phone: 608-263-6862. Business E-Mail: smrobins@wisc.edu.

**ROBINSON, SUE L(EWIS),** federal judge; b. 1952; BA with highest honors, U. Del., 1974; JD, U. Pa., 1978. Assoc. Potter, Anderson & Corron, Wilmington, Del., 1978-83; asst. U.S. atty. U.S. Attys. Office, 1983-88; U.S. magistrate judge U.S. Dist. Ct. (Del. dist.), 1988-91, dist. judge, 1991—, chief judge. Named to U. Del. Wall of Fame, 1994. Mem.: Del. State Bar Assn. (sec. 1986—87). Office: US Dist Ct J Caleb Boggs Fed Bldg 844 N King St Lockbox 31 Wilmington DE 19801-3519

**ROBINSON, SUSAN ESTES,** pharmacology educator; b. Radford, Va., Apr. 26, 1950; d. Cecil Bennett and Helen Elizabeth (Buckner) Estes; m. Robert McMurdo Gillespie, Nov. 7, 1981; children: William Bennett, James Campbell. BA in Chemistry, Vanderbilt U., 1972, PhD in Pharmacology, 1976. Staff fellow Lab. Preclin. Pharmacology St. Elizabeth's Hosp., NIMH, Washington, 1976-79; asst. prof. dept. med. pharmacology and toxicology Coll. Medicine, Tex. A&M U., College Station, 1979-81; asst. prof. dept. pharmacology and toxicology Med. Coll. Va., Va. Commonwealth U., Richmond, 1981-87, assoc. prof., 1987-95, prof., 1995—, Med. Coll. Va., Va. Commonwealth U., Richmond, 1995—. Mem. study sect. Internat. and Coop. Projects Div. Rsch. Grants, NIH, Bethesda, Md., 1990-93, mem. Devel. brain Disroders Study Sect., 1999-2004. Contbr. articles to profl. jours. Recipient Lyndon Baines Johnson Rsch. award Am. Heart Assn., Tex. affiliate, 1980; rsch. grantee Nat. Inst. Drug Abuse. 1989, 90, 95, NIH, 1989. Mem. Am. Soc. Neurochemistry, Am. Soc. Pharmacology and Exptl. Therapeutics (exec. com. divsn. for neuropharmacology 1992-96), Soc. Neurosci. (councillor Ctrl. Va. chpt. 1989-90, pres. 1991-92, 98-99, sec.-treas. 2005—), Coll. on Problems of Drug Dependence Neurobehavioral Teratology Soc. Office: Med Coll Va Va Commonwealth U Dept Pharmacology Toxicology PO Box 980613 Richmond VA 23298-0613 Office Phone: 804-828-8396.

**ROBINSON, THOMAS CHRISTOPHER,** health science educator; b. Buffalo, Oct. 16, 1944; s. Christopher Sidney and Eleanor Florence (Martin) R.; m. Helen Dare Tew, June 21, 1986; children: Diane Dunn, Kristen O'Melia, Molly Lindsay, Norman Ashley. BA, SUNY, Buffalo, 1966, EdM, 1968, PhD, 1971; grad. mgmt. devel. program, Harvard U., 1989. Admissions officer, office of admissions and records SUNY, Buffalo, 1966-72, assoc. dean Sch. Health Related Professions, 1975-78; asst. dir. Erie County Lab., Buffalo, 1972-75; assoc. dean Coll. Allied Health Professions, U. Ky., Lexington, 1978-84, dean Coll. Health Scis., 1984—2004, prof., 1984—, dean emeritus, 2005—. Cons. MDS Labs., Hamilton, Ont., Can., 1973-73, Joint U.S.-Arabian Commn. on Econ. Cooperation, 1986-87, West Sussex Inst. Higher Edn., Bogner Regis, U.K., 1987, U. Wis. Sys. Ctrs. of Excellence Program, 1988, Pub. Health Svc. Health Resources Adminstrn., 1983, 90-91; mem. exec. com. Nat. Practitioner Data Bank, 1992-94, cons. 1994-95; hon. mem. faculty Khabarovsk (Russia) Med. Inst., 1996; bd. dirs. Health Ky. Contbr. articles to profl. jours. Mem. Health Sys. Agy. Coun., Buffalo, 1977-78, Western N.Y. Hemophilia Soc. Bd. Buffalo, 1977-78, Lexington-Fayette County Bd. Health, Lexington, 1987-91, program excellence project Ohio Bd. Regents, United Way of Bluegrass Healthcare Devel. Bd., 1991; cons. La. Bd. Regents, 1995, 98, 2001, 04, Univ. Wolverhampton fellow, U.K., 1991. Sgt. N.Y. Army N.G., 1968-74. Recipient Svc. award, Jour. Allied Health, 1986; Internat fellow, Hatfield Coll., Un. Durham, Eng., 2005. Mem. Assn. Schs. Allied Health Professions (bd. dirs. 1985-87, Svc. award 1987, Fellow award 1988, pres. 1991-94, past pres. 1994-95, Outstanding Member award 1995), Ky. Allied Health Consortium (bd. dirs. 1985-93, chair 1995-96), So. Assn. Allied Health Deans (sec. 1986-88, chmn. 1988-90), Assn. Schs. Allied Health Professions (pres. 1991-94), Ky. Hosp. Assn., Ky. Assn. Healthcare Facilities, Lexington C. of C., Sigma Phi Epsilon. Avocations: golf, travel, genealogy, gardening. Home: 620 Centennial Ln Lexington KY 40502-2770 Office: U Ky Coll Health Scis CTW Bldg 900 S Limestone Rm 209H Lexington KY 40536-0200 Office Phone: 859-323-1100 x 80559. Business E-Mail: tcrobi@uky.edu.

**ROBINSON, V. GENE (THE RIGHT REVEREND V. GENE ROBINSON),** bishop; life ptnr. Mark Andrew; children: Jamee, Ella. BA in Am. Studies and History. U. South, 1969; MDiv, Gen. Theol. Sem., 1973. Curate Christ Ch., Ridgewood, NJ, 1973—75, youth ministries coord. Province 1, 1978—85; exec. sec. Episc. Province New England, 1983—2003; canon to the ordinary Episc. Diocese N.H., 1988—2003, bishop coadjutor, 2003—04, Bishop Diocesan, 2004—. Bd. trustees Gen. Theol. Sem., 2001—; co-owner, dir. Girl's Summer Camp and Horse Farm, 1975—78; founding dir. Sign of the Dove Retreat Ctr., Temple, NH; mem. Nat. Youth Ministries Devel. Team. Founder Concord Outright. Avocations: cooking, gardening, music, running. Office: Episcopal Diocese of NH 63 Green St Concord NH 03301-4243 Office Phone: 603-224-1914.

**ROBINSON, VERNA COTTEN,** retired librarian, real estate manager; b. Enfield, N.C., Oct. 6, 1927; d. Ernest and Ida (Faulcon) Cotten; m. Elbert Crutcher Robinson, Aug. 14, 1953 (dec. Feb. 1992); children: Angela, Elbert Cotten. BS, N.C. Cen. U., 1948; MS in Libr. Sci., Carnegie Mellon U., 1950. Br. libr. Blyden br. Norfolk (Va.) Pub. Libr., 1950-51; serials libr. Howard U., Washington, 1951-52; sch. libr. Spingarn H.S., Washington, 1952-53, Cardozo H.S., Washington, 1955-60, Roosevelt H.S., Washington, 1960-67, 70-85; ret. D.C. Pub. Schs., 1985. Pres. Robinson Property Mgmt. Inc., Washington, 1993—; bd. dirs. New Birth Corp., Miami. V.p. D.C. Assn. Sch. Librs., Washington, 1972-74; vice-chair Diaconate Lincoln Congrl. Temple/United Ch. of Christ, 1999—, chair 2000-02. Recipient Elder Wise Woman award, Ctrl. Atlantic Conf. of United Ch. Christ, 2002, Pioneer's Achiever's award United Ch. Christ, 1995; Daisy Scarborough scholar N.C. Cen. U., 1946-48, Carnegie Libr. Alumni scholar Carnegie Libr. Sch. Alumni Assn., 1948-50. Mem. African Am. Women's Assn. (internat. com. 1992-95), Delta Sigma Theta (tuition scholar Grand chpt. 1948-50), Delta Sigma Theta Alumnae Assn. (Wash. D.C. Chpt., 1970-). Avocations: reading, walking. Office Phone: 202-882-1737.

**ROBINSON, W. LEE,** lawyer; b. Rome, Ga., Sept. 24, 1943; m. Irene Scales, 1966; children: Christine, Jacquelyn. BS, Ga. Inst. Tech.; MBA, JD, Mercer U., 1985. With Robinson Hardware Store, Macon, Ga., 1954-86; mem. Ga. Senate, Atlanta, 1975-83; mayor City of Macon, Macon, 1988-92; pvt. practice Macon, 1985—2004; circuit pub. defender Macon Jud. Circuit, 2005—. Judge mcpl. ct. (part time), Macon. Bd. dirs. Cherry Blossom Festival, 2006—. 2d lt. U.S. Army, col. USAR. Decorated Bronze Star with two oak leaf clusters, Legion of Merit with oak leaf cluster. Named to U.S. Army Officer Candidate Sch. Hall of Fame. Mem. Ga. Assn. Criminal Def. Lawyers, Macon C. of C. (former bd. dirs.), Macon Bar Assn. Alzheimer's Assn. (chmn., bd. govs. Ga. chpt. 2005-) Address: 3824 Overlook Ave Macon GA 31204-1325 Office: 201 2nd St Ste 550 Macon GA 31201-8282 also: PO Box 4852 Macon GA 31208-4852 E-mail: wlrmcnlaw@aol.com.

**ROBINSON, WALTER J., III,** lawyer; b. Seattle, Apr. 24, 1941; BA magna cum laude, Univ. Wash., 1963; JD magna cum laude, Univ. Chgo., 1966. Bar: Calif. 1967, Wash. 1967. Ptnr., chmn. Securities Litigation group Pillsbury Winthrop Shaw Pittman, Palo Alto, Calif. Contbr. articles to profl. jours.

Mem.: ABA, San Francisco Bar Assn. Office: Pillsbury Winthrop Shaw Pittman 2475 Hanover St Palo Alto CA 94304-1114 Office Phone: 650-233-4792. Office Fax: 650-233-4545. Business E-Mail: walter.robinson@pillsburylaw.com.

**ROBINSON, WARREN LOWE,** utilities executive; b. Logan, Utah, Apr. 11, 1950; s. Floyd Comish and Grace (Lowe) R.; m. Ann Decker, May 21, 1977 (div. Dec. 1981); 1 child, Stephanie; m. Joan Cunningham, June 17, 1983; children: Jennifer, John. BBA, Brigham Young U., 1974; MBA, Boise State U., 1976; cert., Stanford U., 1985, Harvard U., 1991. Fin. analyst Intermountain Gas Co., Boise, 1976-77, dir. budgets and fin. planning, 1977-79, mgr. planning services, 1979-80, asst. to pres., 1980-81; v.p., treas., chief fin. officer Great Falls (Mont.) Gas Co., 1981-87, sr. v.p., chief fin. officer, 1987-88. Pres., co-founder, bd. dirs. Mont. Overthrust Energy Found., Great Falls, 1983-87; v.p., treas., co-founder Great Falls Capital Corp., 1984-87; mgr. corp. devel. MDU Resources Group, Inc., 1988-89, treas., asst. sec., 1988-92, v.p., treas., CFO, 1992—. Commr. Garden City, Idaho, 1981. Served with N.G., 1968-75. Mem. Nat. Assn. Corp. Treas., Nat. Investor Rels. Inst., Leadership Bismarck Alumni Assn. (pres., co-founder), Fin. Execs. Inst. Lodges: Rotary (pres. Great Falls chpt. 1985-86, bd. dirs. 1985-87). Republican. Mem. Lds Ch. Office: MDU Resources Group Inc 400 N 4th St Bismarck ND 58501-4092 Home: 1533 Galleon Pl Bismarck ND 58504-8984

**ROBINSON, WENDY Y.,** school system administrator; Under grad., DePauw U., Ind. U.-Purdue U., Ball State U. Tchr. Ward Elem., 1973—86; asst. prin. Meml. Pk. Mid. Sch., 1986—87, Weisser Pk. Elem., 1987—89; prin. Price Elem., 1989—91; area admin., asst. supt. Wayne HS, 1991—95; dep. supt. Fort Wayne Comm. Schs., 1995—2003, supt. Fort Wayne, Ind., 2003—. Office: Fort Wayne Comm Sch 1200 S Clinton St Fort Wayne IN 46802

**ROBINSON, WILKES COLEMAN,** retired federal judge; b. Anniston, Ala., Sept. 30, 1923; s. Walter Wade and Catherine Elizabeth (Coleman) R.; m. Julia Von Poellnitz Rowan, June 24, 1955 (dec.); children: Randolph C., Peyton H., Thomas Wilkes Coleman; m. Dorothy Anne LaVictoire, Jan. 17, 2004. BA with honors, U. Ala., 1948; JD, U. Va., 1951. Bar: Ala. 1951, Va. 1962, Mo. 1966, Kans. 1983; cert. mediator, Fla., Ala. Assoc. Bibb & Hemphill, Anniston, 1951-54; city recorder City of Anniston, 1953-55; judge Juvenile and Domestic Rels. Ct. of Calhoun County, Ala., 1954-56; atty. legal dept. GM&O R.R., Mobile, Ala., 1956-58; commerce counsel, asst. gen. atty. Seaboard Air Line R.R., Richmond, Va., 1958-66; chief commerce counsel Monsanto Co. St. Louis, 1966-70; gen. counsel, v.p. Marion Labs., Inc., Kansas City, Mo., 1970-79; pres. Gulf and Gt. Plains Legal Found., Kansas City, Mo. 1980-85, also bd. dirs.; atty. Howard, Needles, Tammen & Bergendoff, Kansas City, 1985-86, also bd. dirs.; v.p. S.R. Fin. Group, Inc., Overland Park, Kans., 1986-87; judge U.S. Ct. Fed. Claims, Washington, 1987-97, sr. judge, 1997—2003; ret., 2003—; of counsel Morris, Cary, Andrews, Talmadge, Jones & Driggers, Dothan, Ala., 2006—. Bd. govs. Kansas City Philharm. Orch., 1975-77. Served with USNR, 1943-44. Mem. Indian Bayou Golf Club, Destin Athletic Club, Scottish Rite, Phi Beta Kappa (past treas. Kansas City, Mo. chpt.), Phi Eta Sigma, Phi Alpha Theta, Kappa Alpha. Episcopalian. Home: 12 Weekewachee Cir Destin FL 32541-4426 Office Phone: 850-654-9137. E-mail: wilkescrob@cox.net.

### ROBINSON, WILLIAM See ROBINSON, SMOKEY

**ROBINSON, WILLIAM I.,** sociologist; b. NYC, Mar. 28, 1959; s. Howard Sydney and Jo-Ann Phyllis Robinson; m. Gloconda Lucia Robinson, May 10, 1985 (div. Oct. 9, 2000); children: Amaru Alejandro, Tamara Yoconda; m. Marielle Mayorga, Sept. 27, 2003. BA, Friends World Coll., N.Y.C., 1982; M, U. N.Mex., 1992, PhD, 1994. Editor, reporter Agencia Nueva Nicaragua, Managua, 1982-87; Washington bur. chief Agencia Nueva Nicaragua Internat. News Agy., Washington, 1987-90; news analyst, cons. Latin Am. Data Base, Albuquerque, 1990-94; prof. sociology U. N.Mex., Albuquerque, 1994-96, U. Tenn., Knoxville, 1996-98, N.Mex. State U., Las Cruces, 1998-2001; prof. sociology and global studies U. Calif., Santa Barbara, 2001—. Author: David & Goliath, 1987, A Faustian Bargain, 1992, Promoting Polyarchy, 1996, Transnational Conflicts: Central America, Globalization and Social Change, 2003, A Theory of Global Capitalism, 2004, Critical Globalization Studies, 2005. Mem.: Internat. Studies Assn., Latin Am. Studies Assn., Am. Sociol. Assn., Global Studies Assn., Phi Kappa Phi. Avocation: Latin dance. Office Phone: 805-893-5607. Business E-Mail: wirobins@soc.ucsb.edu.

**ROBINSON, WILLIAM PHILIP, III,** state supreme court justice; b. Providence, Jan. 30, 1940; s. William Philip and Dorothy Frances (Hayes) R. BA, U. de Louvain, Belgium, 1962; MA, U. R.I., 1966; PhD, U. Conn., 1971; JD, Boston Coll., 1975. Bar: R.I. 1975, Mass. 1985, U.S. Ct. Appeals (1st cir.) 1977, U.S. Supreme Ct. 1989. Instr. U. Conn., Storrs, 1967-71; law clk. U.S. Ct. Appeals, Boston, 1975-77; assoc. Edwards & Angell, Providence, 1977-81, ptnr., 1981—2003; justice R.I Supreme Ct., 2004—. Bd. trustees Providence Country Day Sch., East Providence, 1991-97. Mem. East Greenwich Sch. Com., 1988-96, vice chmn., 1990-94; mem. exec. com. R.I. Assn. of Sch. Coms., 1990-96; mem. East Greenwich Dem. Town Com., 1988-2004; mem. Fed. Bd. Bar Examiners, R.I., 1994-2004; mem. R.I. Jud. Performance Evaluation Com., 1993-2004, R.I. Bd. Govs. for Higher Edn., 2000-03. Mem. Boston Coll. Law Sch. Alumni Assn. (v.p. R.I. chpt. 1990-93, pres. 1993-97, nat. del. 1997—), Order of Coif, Phi Beta Kappa. Avocations: reading, skiing, literary translation. Office: RI Supreme Ct Frank Licht Jud Complex 250 Benefit St Providence RI 02903 E-mail: wrobinson@courts.ri.gov.*

**ROBINSON, WILLIAM RICHARD,** lawyer; b. Paterson, NJ, Dec. 27, 1946; s. Raymond Pellington and Jessie Fremont Robinson; m. Elaine Carol Puchalsky, Oct. 6, 1991; children: Corinne, Jessica, Gregg, Julie, Lauren. BS in Chem. Engring., Rutgers U., 1969; JD, U. Md., 1972. Bar: NY, U.S. Patent Office, NJ. Assoc. Brumbagh, Graves, Donohue and Raymond, N.Y.C., 1972—74; patent atty. Stauffer Chem. Co., Dobbs Ferry, NY, 1974—78; sr. patent atty., corp. counsel CPC Internat. Inc., Englewood Cliffs, NJ, 1978—89; ptnr., mng. ptnr. Brooks, Haidt, Haffner and Delchanty, N.Y.C., 1998—; sr. ptnr., chair IP dept. Norris, McLaughlin and Marcus, Somerville, NJ, 1998—. Dir. Peterson Puritan Inc., Danville, Ill., 1984—88. Mem.: ABA, NY State Bar Assn., Assn. Bar City NY. Republican. Avocations: golf, skiing, boating, woodworking. Office: Norris McLaughlin and Marcus PO Box 1018 721 Rt 202 206 Somerville NJ 08876 Office Phone: 908-722-0700.

**ROBINSON, WILLIAM T.(BILL), III,** lawyer; b. Covington, Ky., Jan. 6, 1945; s. William T. Jr. and Hilda C. (Tatermann) R.; m. Joan Mary Wernersbach, Aug. 2, 1969; children: William Taylor IV, Todd Arthur. AB, Thomas More Coll., 1967; JD, U. Ky., 1971. Bar: Ohio 1971, Ky. 1972, Tenn. 1999, U.S. Dist. Ct. (ea. dist.) Ky. 1972, U.S. Dist. Ct. (so. dist.) Ohio 1971, U.S. Dist. Ct. (we. dist.) Ky. 1993, U.S. Dist. Ct. (so. dist.) Ind. 1996, U.S. Ct. Appeals (6th cir.) 1972, U.S. Supreme Ct. 1978. Ptnr. Robinson, Arnzen, Parry & Wentz, P.S.C., Covington, Ky., 1971—; mem. in charge, Greater Cincinnati & No. Ky., exec. comm. Greenebaum Doll & McDonald, Covington, Ky. Found. bd. mem. Appellate Judges Edn. Inst., 2003; adj. prof. No. Ky. U., 1977—; lectr. numerous seminars. Bd. of trustees Redwood Sch. and Rehabilitation Ctr., 1971-81, 83—, sec., 1972-73, 1st v.p., 1973-75, pres., 1975-78, bd. of overseers, 1981-83; bd. of trustees, chmn. Dorothy Wood Found., 1980—, bd. mem. emeritus 2003-; bd. dirs. Cin. chpt. ARC, 1979-85; sust. atty. mem. Product Liability Adv. Council 1997-; Coll. Law Univ. Ky. Lafferty Soc. 1981-, mem. visiting comm. 1988- (chmn. 1995 & 1998), commencement speaker 1988, Hall of Fame 2004; bd. mem. Boy Scouts Am. Powder Horn dist. 1994-; bd. mem. Cincinnati Inst. Fine Arts 1999-2004; bd. dir. Cincinnati/No. Ky. Internat. Airport 1998-, vice chmn. 2004-; bd. trustees Cincinnati Symphony 1998-2004; found. bd. mem. Cincy-Tech USA, 2002-; found. bd. mem. Forward Quest 1997-; policy bd. mem. Partnership for Greater Cincinnati 1999-, chmn. 1999-2003; bd. mem. Greater Cincinnati C. of C. 1994-, exec. comm. 1999-2003; bd. mem. Greater Cincinnati Scholrship Assn. 1994-; bd. mem. Kentuckians for Better Transp. 1996-2004; bd. mem. Ky. C. of C. 1987-93, chmn. 1992-92, Dunlevy frontiersman Comm. Svc.

award 1991; mem. Legatus Cincinnati chptr. 1996-2004; bd. trustees Mt. St. Joseph Coll. 1997-; bd. mem. Nat. Conf. Community & Justice 1986-97, treas. 1990-97, co-chmn. 1995-97, emeritus bd. 1997-, Disting. Svc. Citation 2004; adv. trustee Nat. Underground Railroad Freedom Ctr. 2001-; found. bd. mem. & sec./treas. Tri-County Econ. Dev. Corp. 1987-; co-found. & charter bd. mem. Tri-County Econ. Devel. Found. 1996-, charter sec./treas. 1996-2000, treas. 2000-; life mem. Univ. Ky. Alum. Assn., fellow 1981-. Recipient Covington award, Friends of Covington, 1998, Judge Learned Hand Human Rels. award, Am. Jewish Comm., 1998, Governor's Econ. Devel. Leadership award, Ky., 1997, Knight of Malta, 1992. Fellow Am. Acad. Appellate Lawyers 1998, Internat. Soc. Barristers 1988; Mem. ABA (bd. govs. 2000-, exec. comm. 2002-03, treas.-elect 2004-, chmn. fin. comm. 2002-03), Ohio Bar Assn., Fed. Bar Assn. (mem. steering comm. 2002-), Ky. Bar Assn. (Outstanding Lawyer award, 1989), Am. Bar Found. (life fellow, fellows chmn Ky. 2000-04), Am. Law Inst., Sixth Cir. Jud. Conf. (life mem.), Ky. Bar Found. (pres. 1988-89, charter life fellow 1986-), No. Ky. Bar Assn., Louisville bar Assn., Cincinnati Bar Assn. (Themis award 2003), Kenton County Bar Assn. (mem. exec. com. 1972-73, chmn. legal-med. com. 1978-83, Ann. Merit award 1973), Ky. Def. Counsel Assn., Internat. Assn. Ins. Counsel, Internat. Assn. Def. Counsel, Salmon P. Chase Am. Inn Ct. (co-founder & pres. 1993-94, master 1993-),Acad. Trial Lawyers Am., So. Conf. Bar Pres., Nat. Conf. Bar Pres.s', U. Ky. Alumni Assn. (bd. dirs. 1981—), No. Ky. C. of C. (vice chmn. 1985-86, bd. dirs. 1980—, Profl. of Yr. 1980), Thomas More Coll. Alumni Assn. (bd. dirs. 1972—, pres. 1974-75, chmn. alumni fund drive 1974-75, Disting. Alum. award 1982), Phi Alpha Theta, Alpha Delta Gamma, Phi Delta Phi. Office: Greenebaum Doll & McDonald PO Box 122673 Covington KY 41012-2673

**ROBINSON, ZELIG,** lawyer; b. Balt., July 7, 1934; s. Morton Matthew and Mary (Ackerman) R.; m. Karen Ann Bergstrom (div. Oct. 1987); children: John, Christopher, Kristin; m. Linda Portner Strangmann, Dec. 23, 1987. BA, Johns Hopkins U., 1954; LLB, Harvard U., 1957. Bar: Md. 1958. Legis. analyst Md. Ho. of Dels., Annapolis, 1958; tech. asst. IRS, Washington, 1958-60; pvt. practice Balt., 1960-62; assoc. gen. counsel commerce com. U.S. Ho. of Reps., Washington, 1962-64; assoc. Weinberg & Green, Balt., 1964-66; spl. legal cons. commerce com. U.S. Ho. of Reps., Washington, 1966-68; pvt. practice Balt., 1966—70; mem. Gordon, Feinblatt, Rothman, Hoffberger & Hollander, LLC, 1971—. Chmn. Balt. City Minimum Wage Commn., 1974-82, Md. Pub. Broadcasting Commn., 1991-95; mem. Gov's. Commn. to revise Md. Code, Annapolis, 1968-90. Contbr. articles to profl. jour. Bd. dirs., v.p., sec. Gov.'s Mansion Found., Annapolis, Md.; v.p. bd. dirs. Md. Cmty. and Citizens Fund, Chestertown, Md.; sec. bd. dirs. William Donald Schaefer Civic Fund, 1980-88; bd. dirs. Md. Arts Pl., Balt., Balt. Coalition of Homeowners, 1989—; v.p., bd. dirs. Everyman Theatre, 2002—03, pres., 2004—; mem. Found. for Md. Pub. Broadcasting; sec., trustee Balt. City Hist. Soc.; bd. dirs., pres. Celebration 2000, Inc., 1998—; founder, bd. dirs. Balt. Efficiency and Econ. Found., 1999—; chmn., Balt. City Coun. Transition Commn., 2003. With U.S. Army. 1958. Mem. ABA, Md. State Bar Assn. (laws com., internat. law com.). Democrat. Office: Gordon Feinblatt Rothman Hoffberger & Hollander LLC 233 E Redwood St Baltimore MD 21202-3332 Business E-Mail: zrobinson@gfrlaw.com.

**ROBISON, BRUCE H.,** marine biologist; BS in Biol. Scis., Purdue U., 1965; MA in Marine Sci., Coll. William & Mary, Va. Inst. Marine Sci., 1968; PhD in Biol. Oceanography, Stanford U., Hopkins Marine Sta., 1973. Cert. sci. rsch. pilot for ADS submersibles 1982, 2000. Postdoctoral fellow Woods Hole Oceanog. Instn., Mass., 1973, postdoctoral investigator, 1974; asst. rsch. oceanographer U. Calif. Santa Barbara Marine Sci. Inst., 1974—82, assoc. rsch. oceanographer, 1982—88; sr. scientist Monterey Bay Aquarium Rsch. Inst., 1987—. Chair sci. dept. Monterey Bay Aquarium Rsch. Inst., 1991—96; Morris scholar in residence U. Md. Horn Point, 1996. Contbr. articles to profl. jours.; mem. editl. bd.: Marine Tech. Soc. Jour., 1997—2004. Recipient Sci./Rsch. award, Monterey Bay Nat. Marine Sanctuary, 1997, Lockheed-Martin award, Ocean Sci. and Engring., Marine Tech. Soc., 2002. Fellow: Calif. Acad. Scis., AAAS. Office: Monterey Bay Aquarium Rsch Inst 7700 Sandholdt Rd Moss Landing CA 95039 E-mail: robr@mbari.org.*

**ROBISON, CAROLYN LOVE,** retired librarian; b. Orlinda, Tenn., Aug. 9, 1940; d. Fount Love and Martha Desha (Jones) R. BA, Denison U., 1962; MLS, Emory U., 1965; PhD, Ga. State U., 1982. Tchr. Dag Hammarsjhjold Jr. H.S., Wallingford, Conn., 1962-64; asst. libr., lectr. Architecture Libr., Ga. Inst. Tech., Atlanta, 1965-67; head circulation Ga. State U., Atlanta, 1967-71, asst. prof., then assoc. prof., asst. libr., 1971-75, prof., assoc. libr., 1975-98, prof. emeritus, 1998. Active Friends of Atlanta-Fulton County Pub. Libr., 1981—98. Recipient Woman of Achievement award YWCA, 1989. Mem. ALA, AAUP, Ga. Libr. Assn., Delta Kappa Gamma, Phi Kappa Phi, Kappa Delta Pi. Republican. Presbyterian. Home: 1057 Capital Club Cir NE Atlanta GA 30319-2662 Personal E-mail: clrobison@mindspring.com.

**ROBISON, EMILY BURNS,** musician; b. Pittsfield, Mass., Aug. 16, 1972; d. Paul and Barbara Burns; m. Charlie Robison, May 1, 1999; children: Charles Augustus, Julianna Tex, Henry Benjamin. Performer Blue Night Express, 1984—89; banjo player, guitarist, vocalist Dixie Chicks, 1989—. Musician: (albums) Thank Heavens for Dale Evans, 1990, LIttle Ol' Cowgirl, 1992, Shouldn't a Told You That, 1993, Wide Open Spaces, 1998 (Maximum Vision Clip of Yr., Billboard, 1998, Best New Country Artist Clip of Yr., Billboard, 1998, Best Country Album, Grammy Awards, 1998, Album of Yr., Acad. Country Music, 1998, Best Selling Album, Can. Country Music Awards, 1999, Song of Yr., WB Radio Music Award, 1999, Album of Yr., ACM, 1999), Fly, 1999 (Best Country Album, Grammy Awards, 1999, Best Selling Album, Can. Country Musc Awards, 2000, Internat. Album, British Country Music Award, 2000, Country Album of Yr., Billboard Awards, 2000, Album of Yr., ACM, 2000, Album of Yr., CMA, 2000), Home, 2002 (Favorite Country Album, Am. Music Awards, 2002, Best Recording Package, Grammy Awards, 2002, Best Country Album, Grammy Awards, 2002), Top of the World Tour: Live, 2003 (Grammy award for Best Country Group Vocal Performance, 2005), Taking the Long Way, 2006. Named Most Significant New Country Act, Country Monitor, 1998, Top New Country Artist, Billboard, 1998, Top Vocal Group, Acad. Country Music, 1998, Country Artist of Yr., Rolling Stone, 1999, Top Country Artist, Billboard, 1999, Internat. Rising Star, British Country Music Awards, 1999, Artist of Yr. (Country), WB Radio Music Award, 1999, Favorite New Artist (Country), AMA, 1999, Vocal Group of Yr., CMA, 1999, Country Artist of Yr., Billboard, 1999, 2000, Entertainer of Yr., CMA, 2000, ACM, 2000, Vocal Group of Yr., 2001, Entertainer of Yr., 2001, Favorite Musical Group or Band, People's Choice Award, 2002, Vocal Group of Yr., Country Music Assn., 2002, others; named one of 100 Most Influential People, Time Mag., 2006; recipient Horizon award, CMA, 1998. Office: Monument Sony Nashville 34 Music Sq East Nashville TN 37203*

**ROBISON, KENT RICHARD,** lawyer; b. Reno, Nev., May 22, 1947; s. Burle and Helen Jean (Martin-Szymanski) R.; m. Tonya Robison, 2 children. BA, U. Nev.-Reno, 1969; JD, U. San Francisco, 1972. Bar: Nev. 1972, U.S. Dist. Ct. Nev. 1973, U.S. Ct. Claims 1973, U.S. Ct. Appeals (9th cir.) 1976, U.S. Supreme Ct. 1977, U.S. Tax Ct. 1982. Law clk. Carson City Dist. Atty.'s Office, 1971; dep. pub. defender Washoe County, Reno, 1972-75; pvt. practice Johnson Belaustegui & Robison, Reno, 1975-79, Johnson, Belaustegui, Robison & Adams, Reno, 1979-81, Robison, Lyle, Belaustegui & Robb, Reno, 1981-88, Robison, Belaustegui, Robb & Sharp, Reno, 1988-99, Robison, Belaustegui, Sharp & Low, Reno, 1999—. Lectr. West Nev. Community Coll., Reno Police Acad., Calif. Legal Secs., U. Nev., Reno Bus. Coll., assns., socs., others; mem. com. on costs and speedy trials Nev. Supreme Ct.; mem. Nev. State Commn. on Sentencing Felony Offenders, Exec. Com. to Establish Appellate Ct., Commn. to Implement Cameras in the Courtroom, Com. on Rules of Civil Procedure, Ad Hoc Com. for Improved Tech. in Nev. Fed. Courtroom; mem. No. Nev. Legal-Med. Screening Panel, 1981-85; Washoe County Juvenile Master pro tem, 1975-77; ex-officio mem. ethics com., jury instrn. com. Nev. State Bar. Contbr. articles to law jours. Mem. ABA, ATLA, Am. Bd. trial Advocacy (pres. 1991), Nat. Bd. Trial Advocacy (diplomat civil and criminal), Nev. State Bar Assn. (bd. dirs., bd. govs.), Washoe County Bar Assn., Nev. Trial Lawyers Assn. (past pres., bd.

govs.), Nat. Assn. Criminal Def. Lawyers, Am. Bd. Criminal Lawyers, Am. Inns of Ct. (charter, master), Am. Coll. Barristers, Roscoe Pound Found. Republican. Office: Robison Belaustegui Sharp & Low 71 Washington St Reno NV 89503 Office Phone: 775-329-3151. Business E-Mail: krobison@rbslattys.com.

**ROBISON, PAULA JUDITH,** flutist; b. Nashville, June 8, 1941; d. David Victor and Naomi Florence R.; m. Scott Nickrenz; Dec. 29, 1971; 1 child, Elizabeth Hadley Amadea Nickrenz. Student, U. So. Calif., 1958-60; BS, Juilliard Sch. Music, 1963. Founding artist, player Chamber Music Soc., N.Y.C., 1970-90, N.Y. ChôroBand, 1994; co-dir. chamber music Spoleto Festival, Charleston, SC, 1978-88; Filene artist-in-residence Skidmore Coll., Saratoga Springs, NY, 1988-89; mem. faculty New Eng. Conservatory Music, 1991—, mem. faculty, Donna Heiken flut chair 1st occupant, 2005—; co-dir. Gardner Chamber Orch., Boston, 1995—; artist-in-residence Gardner Mus., 2005. Faculty Juilliard Sch., N.Y.C., 1978-82; annual concert series, Met. Mus. Art, N.Y., 1990—, With Art series, P.S. 1 Art Gallery, N.Y., 2000, Mass. Mus. Contemporary Art, 2001; dir. Vivaldi in the Courtyard, Gardner Mus., Boston, 2002—, faculty NE Conservatory, 2005—; founder, Pergola Recordings, 2006; collaboration with Sol LeWitt, Variations on a Theme, Gardner Mus., 2005. Soloist with various major orchs., including N.Y. Philharm., London Symphony Orch.; player, presenter Concerti di Mezzogiorno, Spoleto (Italy) Festival, 1970-2003; commd. flute concertos by Leon Kirchner, Toru Takemitsu, Oliver Knussen, Robert Beaser, Kenneth Frazelle; premiered works by Pierre Boulez, Elliott Carter, William Schuman, Thea Musgrave, Carla Bley, John Tavener, Michael Tilson Thomas; premiered Rio Days Rio Nights, Music Theatre Group prodn. in N.Y.C., 1998; participant Marlboro Music Festival, 1999-2005; author: The Paula Robison Flute Warmups Book, 1989, The Andersen Collection, 1994, Paula Robison Masterclass: Paul Hindemith, 1995, The Sidney Lanier Collection, 1997, Frank Martin: Ballade, 2002, To a Wild Rose, 2003, MasterClass Series, Diller-Quaile Sch of Music, 2004-; co-author: Places of the Spirit, 2003; recs. on CBS Masterworks, Music Masters, Vanguard Classics, New World Records, Omega, Arabesque, Sony Classical, King Recs., Mode Recs., Artemis Recs.; two person show Gardner Mus., Boston, 2005; featured in PBS documentary and book: Juilliard. Recipient First prize Geneva Internat. Competition, 1966, Adelaide Ristori prize, 1987, Lifetime Achievement award Nat. Flute Assn., 2004; named Musician of Month, Musical Am., 1979, House Musician for Isamu Noguchi Garden Mus., N.Y.C., 1988; Martha Baird Rockefeller grantee, 1966; Nat. Endowment for Arts grantee, 1978, 86; Fromm Found. grantee, 1980; Housewright Eminent scholar Fla. State U., 1990-91. Recipient Disting. Svc. award, Music Tchrs. Nat. Assn., 1989, Laurence Lesser Presdl. award, 1999, Lifetime Achievement award, Usdan Ctr. for Creative and Performing Arts, 2000, Hon. Citizen for Life award, City of Charleston, S.C., 2002, Lifetime Achievement award, Nat. Flute Assn., 2004. Mem. Sigma Alpha Iota (hon.). Office: Kirshbaum Demler & Assoc 711 W End Ave #5KN New York NY 10025

**ROBISON, SHANE V.,** computer company executive; BS in Computer Sci., MS in Computer Sci., U. Utah. With Apple Computer Co., 1988, v.p., gen. mgr., 1994—95; exec. v.p. rsch. & developt., pres. design productivity grp. Cadence Design Systems; exec. v.p. AT&T, 1995—99, pres. internet tech. and devel., 1999—2000; sr. v.p., chief tech. officer strategy and tech. Compaq Computer Corpn., 2000—02; exec. v.p., chief strategy and tech. officer Hewlett-Packard Co., Palo Alto, Calif., 2002—. Cons. database systems architecture U. Utah. Office: Hewlett-Packard Co 3000 Hanover St Palo Alto CA 94304*

**ROBISON, VICTOR JAMES, JR.,** retired military officer; b. Youngstown, Ohio, Apr. 29, 1920; s. Victor James Robison and Babe Albert. BS, Case We. Res. U., 1942, MA, 1948; Qualified Comms. Officer, U.S. Naval Acad. Grad. Sch., 1943; student, Sorbonne U., Paris, 1949—50, Columbia U., 1950—51. Commd. ensign USN, 1943, advanced through grades to comdr., comm. officer USS Taylor Pacific PTO, 1943—45, tng. officer U.S. Naval Res. Tng. Ctr. Balt., 1952—55, asst. ops. officer USS Worcester Mediterranean and Pacific, 1955—56; U.S. Naval attaché and U.S. Naval attaché for air U.S. Embassy, Warsaw, 1957—58, Brussels, 1962—65; officer in charge Navy Liaison Group and Chief Plant Engring and Maintenance Divsn. Joint Commns. Ctr., Ft. Ritchie, Md., 1958—61; asst. curator for Navy Dept., Office Chief of Naval Ops. USN, Washington, 1966—69, ret., 1969; tchr. English Corcoran Coll. Art, Washington, 1969—70; pvt. practice appraiser Navy artifacts and memorabilia Washington and Annapolis, Md., 1970—84. Decorated Order of Leopold II, 1966, Navy Unit Commendation, 13 Battle Stars, USN, Asiatic Pacific Campaign medal, others. Mem. VFW, Am. Legion, Fleet Res. Assn., Smithsonian Instn., Beta Theta Pi. Avocations: stamp collecting/philately, jogging, poetry, learning. Home: 423 7th St SE Washington DC 20003-2756

**ROBITAILLE, CAROLYN ANN,** music educator; b. Ft. Wayne, Ind., Nov. 25, 1930; d. Edgar Herman and Della Katharina Neuenschwander; m. Anthony McLeon Robitaille, June 29, 1957; children: Beth Ann Smyth, Robert Scott; children: Melody Joy Berryhill, Douglas Eric. Student, St. Louis Inst. Music, 1948—50, Washington U., 1948—49. Pvt. piano tchr. Compton, Calif., 1946—48, Brea, Calif., 1968—2005; piano tchr. Del Burg's Music Store, South Gate, Calif., 1946—48; exec. sec. Sears, Roebuck and Co., LA, 1953—68; pianist Faith Bapt. Ch., Yorba Linda, Calif., 1969—83, Crossroad Ch., Fullerton, Calif., 1983—. Piano tchr. Nat. Piano Guild, Austin, Tex., 1984—2004, evaluator, 2004—; adjudicator Assn. Christian Schs. Internat. Piano Festivals, La Habra, Calif., 1999—; pianist Gideon State Convs., 2000—05, Rep. State Convs., 2000—05. Pianist North Intermediate Sch., Saginaw, Mich., 1942—45, Christian and Missionary Alliance Ch., Saginaw, 1942—45, Huntington Park (Calif.) H.S., Calif., 1945—48; pianist, Sunday sch. tchr. Lynton Village Chapel, Lynwood, Calif., 1947—48, 1950—68; chaplain Gideon Internat Aux., 2005—; Piano scholar ft. Louis Inst. Music, 1948—50. Mem.: Music Tchrs. Assn. Calif. (treas. Orange County br. 2004—06), Gideons Internat. Aux. (sec.-treas. 2001—05). Republican. Baptist. Avocations: tennis, croquet, swimming, badminton, board games.

**ROBITAILLE, LUC,** retired professional hockey player; b. Montreal, Que., Can., Feb. 17, 1966; mem. Hull Olympiques Major Jr. Hockey League, Que., 1983—84, LA Kings, 1984—94, 1997—2001, 2003—06, Pitts. Penguins, 1994—95, NY Rangers, 1995—97, Detroit Red Wings, 2001—03. Named NHL Rookie of Yr., 1986—87; named to NHL All-Star Team, 1987, 1988, 1990—91, 1992—93; recipient Guy LaFleur Trophy, 1985—86, Can. Hockey Player of Yr. award, 1985—86, Calder Meml. Trophy. Achievements include scoring the winning goal for the national team of Canada at the 1994 World Hockey Championship; being a member of the Stanley Cup Champion Detroit Red Wings team in 2002. Office: c/o LA Kings Suite 3100 1111 S Figueroa St Los Angeles CA 90015*

**ROBLE, CAROLE MARCIA,** accountant; b. Bklyn., Aug. 22, 1938; d. Carl and Edith (Brown) Dusowitz; m. Richard F. Roble, Nov. 30, 1969. MBA with distinction, N.Y. Inst. Tech., 1984. CPA, Calif., N.Y. Compt. various orgns. various orgns., 1956-66; staff acct. ZTBG CPA'S, L.A., 1966-67; sr. acct. J.H. Cohn & Co., Newark, 1967-71; prin. Carole M. Roble, CPA, South Hempstead, NY, 1971-90; ptnr. Roble & Libman, CPAs, Baldwin, NY, 1990-93; prin. Carole M. Roble, CPA, Baldwin, NY, 1993—. Speaker, moderator Found. for Acctg. Edn., N.Y., 1971—; lectr. acctg. various schs. including New Sch., Queens Coll., Empire State Coll., Touro Coll., N.Y. Inst. Tech., N.Y.C., (Parsons Sch., 1971—. Guest various N.Y. radio and TV stas., 2 noted various newspapers. Treas. Builders Devel. Corp. of L.I., Westbury, N.Y., 1985; dir. Women Econ. Devels. of L.I., 1985-87. Recipient Sisterhood citation Nat. Orgn. Women, 1984, 85, cert. of Appreciation Women Life Underwriters, 1988, Women in Sales, 1982, 84; named top Tax Practitioner Money Mag., 1987, one of Top 100 Most Influential People, Acctg. Today, 1999. Mem. AICPA (mem. small firm advocacy com. 1996—), Am. Acct. Assn. (auditing sect.), Am. Soc. Women Accts. (pres. N.Y. chpt. 1980-81), Am. Woman's Soc. CPAs, Nat. Conf. CPA Practitioners (trustee L.I. chpt. 1981-82, sec. 1982-83, treas. 1983-84, v.p. 1984-85, 1st v.p. 1985-86, pres.

1986-87, nat. nominating com. 1983-84, 88-89, nat. continuing profl. edn. chmn. 1988-90, nat. treas. 1991-94, nat. v.p. 1994-96, exec. v.p. 1996-98, first woman nat. pres. 1998-99), Calif. Soc. CPAs, N.Y. State Soc. CPAs (bd. dirs. Nassau chpt. 1981-86, 91-93, bd. dirs. profl. devel., 1982-86, sec., mem. fin. acctg. standards com. 1990-95), Kiwanis (program chmn. County Seat chpt. 1989-90, sec. 1990-91, pres. 1991-92), Baldwin C. of C. (treas. 1990-93). Avocations: golf, gourmet cuisine, water-skiing, music. Home: 626 Willis St Hempstead NY 11550-8000

**ROBLE, RAYMOND GERALD,** science administrator; b. Mar. 14, 1935; BS in Engring. Physics, U. Mich., 1957, BS in Engring. Math., 1957, MSME, 1961, PhD in Aeronomy. 1969. Engr. Bendix Rsch. Labs., Southfield, Mich., 1961-64; rsch. sci. Space Physics Rsch. Lab., U. Mich., 1964-69; postdoctoral fellow advanced study program Nat. Ctr. Atmospheric Rsch., 1969-70, scientist lab. for atmospheric scis., 1970-73, scientist atmospheric quality and modification div., 1973-77, project leader thermospheric dynamics and aeronomy project atmosphericchem. and aeronomy div., 1977-81, sr. scientist atmospheric chem. and aeronomy div., 1978-84, sr. scientist high altitude obs., 1984—, head, terrestrial impact of solar output sect. high altitude obs., 1986—2001, dep. dir. high altitude obs., 1993-95, acting dir. high altitude obs., 1995—. Commn. URSI III Working Group 8 Incoherent Scatter, 1975-77; guest investigator OSO-8 Satellite Team Occultation Studes, 1975-79, NASA Atmospheric Explorer Satelite Team, 1975-80; panel mem. USRA Sci. Definition for Atmosphere, Magnetosphere and Plasmas in Space Payload, 1976-78, Upper Atmoshpere Geophysics, Geophysics Study com., Geophysical Rsch. bd., NAS, 1976-77, USRA Computer Simulation in Space Physics, 1977-79, NASA Sci. Definition Panel UARS Satellite Program, 1977-78, Sun, Weather and Climate Geophysics Study com., Geophysical Rsch. bd., NAS, 1977-82, Survey on Solar-Terrestrial Rsch. in the 1980's, com. on Solar-Terrstrial Rsch. Geophysical Rsch. bd., NAS program, 1979-81, Mid. Atmosphere Program Panel, NAS, 1981-86; theoretician NASA Dynamics Explorer Satellite Team, 1977—; mem. AGU com. for Pub., 1977-84, Atmospheric and Space Physics Mgmt. Ops. Working Group, NASA Solar-Terrestrial Physics Program, 1978-81, Space Power Sys. Overviewcom Inst. Telecomms., 1978-82; lecturer Dept. Astrophysical, Planetary and Atmospheric Scis. U. Colo., 1978—; com. Solar and Space Physics, Space Sci. bd. NAS, 1980-83, Geophysics Study com. Geophysical Rsch. bd. NAS, 1980-84, IUGG on Atmospheric Electricity, 1981—, AGU for Pub. Affairs, 1982-84, IUGG com. Solar-Terrestrial film Planet earth, 1984-86; sec. Aeronomy Div. Solar-Planetary Relationships Sect. AGU, 1982-84; mem. Earth Scis. Task Group Study Major Dirs. for Space Scis.: 1995-, Space Sci. bd., 1984-88; chmn. Am. Geophysical Union com. on Atmospheric and Space Electricity, 1984-88; co-investigator, prin. investigator, NASA; mem. Arecibo Observatory vis. com. Cornell U., 1997-2001; mem. rev. bd. Geophys. Inst. U. Alaska, 1984-. Contbr. over 250 articles to profl. jours. With USN, 1957-60. Recipient CEDAR Prize Lecture, 1994; grantee NASA, USAF. Fellow Am. Geophys. Union (atmos. space physics and aeronomy fellows com. 1996-98); mem. NAS (Arctowski medal, 1996), Am. Inst. Aeronautics and Astronautics. Office: Nat Ctr Atmospheric Rsch High Altitude Obs PO Box 3000 Boulder CO 80307-3000 Business E-Mail: roble@ncar.ucar.edu.

**ROBLES, DARLINE P.,** school system administrator; AA in History, East L.A. Coll., 1968; B in History, Calif. State U. L.A., 1972; MEd, Claremont Grad. Sch., 1976; D in Edn. Policy and Adminstrn., U. So. Calif. Cert. tchr., adminstr. Tchr. Montebello Intermediate Sch., Calif., 1973—79; dir. bilingual program Montebellow Unified Sch. Dist., Calif., 1979—81; prin. Washington Elem., Montebello, Calif., 1981—85, Montebello Intermediate, Montebello, Calif., 1985—88; asst. supt. Montebello Unified Sch. Dist., Montebello, Calif., 1988—91, acting supt., 1991—92, supt., 1992—95, Salt Lake City Sch. Dist., 1995—2002; county supt. schs. L.A. County Office of Edn.. 2002—. Office: LA County Office of Edn 9300 Imperial Hwy Rm EC109 Downey CA 90242-2890

**ROBLES, JOSUE, JR.,** insurance company executive; b. Rio Piedras, Puerto Rico, Jan. 24, 1946; B in Acctg., Kent State U, 1972; M in Bus. Adminstrn., Ind. State U. CFO, sr. v.p., treas. USAA, San Antonio, 1994—. Mem. Def. Base Closure and Realignment Comm., 1995. Joined U.S. Army, 1966, ret., maj. gen. U.S. Army, 1994. Office: USAA 9800 Fredericksburg Rd San Antonio TX 78288-0002*

**ROBLES, ROSALIE MIRANDA,** elementary school educator; b. L.A., Oct. 30, 1942; d. Richard and Carmen (Garcia) Miranda; m. Ralph Rex Robles, July 12, 1986; children: Gregory, Eric, Karen Cassandra. BA, Calif. State Coll., L.A., 1964; postgrad., Northridge State Coll. Playground supr. L.A. City Schs., 1961-64; elem. tchr. Montebello Unified Schs., Calif., 1964—; sch. site rep., faculty club chair, PTA La Merced Elem., 2006—. Rep. Montebello Credit Union, 1973-75, Bilingual Com., 1983-88; mem. Sch. Site Coun., 1989-92, chmn. 1980-83; union rep. Montebello Unified Schs. Chmn. Monterey Park Christmas Food Baskets, 1973-91; boys coord. Am. Youth Soccer, 1993-94, girls coord.; chmn. Boy Scouts Am., 1980-85; exec. bd. PTA, 1978, 80, 85, 87, 92—, pres. 1990-92; sec. St. Paul Parent Group, 1992-93, Palimentarian, 1993—; rep. Cost Containment Com., 1994-96; Eucharistic minister Roman Cath. Ch.; team mother Boys and Girls Club, 2005-06. Recipient Hon. Svc. award PTA, 1979, Hon. Svc. Continuing award, 1982, Golden Oak award, 1995. Mem. AAUW (pres. 2001-2003, v.p. program 2003—, cultural chair); Montebello Tchrs. Assn. (facult club chair), Delta Kappa Gamma (sec., recording sec., pres., 2004—). Roman Catholic.

**ROBLETO, DARIO,** artist; b. 1972; Attended, U. Tex., San Antonio, 1991—93, U. Tex., El Paso, 1993—96, Yale Summer Sch. Music & Art, 1996; BFA, U. Tex., San Antonio, 1996—97. Visiting lectr. Corcoran Coll. Art & Design, Washington, 2001, U. New Orleans, 2001, Calif. Inst. Arts, Valencia, Calif., 2002, Calif. Coll Arts & Crafts, San Francisco, 2002. Lngola Marymount, LA, 2002, Otis Art Inst., LA, 2002. One-man shows include Goldie love's Bjork, DiverseWorks, Houston, 1998, I Love Everything Rock n' Roll (Except the Music), Mint Mus. Art, Charlotte, NC, 1999, Your Cheeks Have Lost Their Luster, Inman Gallery, Houston, 1999, Factory Girl, ACME, LA, 2000, Polar Soul, ArtPace, San Antonio, Tex., 2000, I Thought I Knew Negation Until You Said Goodbye, Contemporary Arts Mus., Houston, 2001, Deep Down I Don't Believe in Hymns, ACME, LA, 2002, A Surgeon, A Scalpel & A Soul, Mus. Contemporary Art, San Diego, 2003, Roses in the Hosp., Inman Gallery, Houston, 2003, Say Goodbye to Substance, Whitney Mus. Am. Art, 2003, Eunuch Euthanasia, Ulrich Mus. Art, Wichita State U., Kans., 2004, Southern Bacteria, ACME, LA, 2004, exhibited in group shows at Close To The Border VI, U. Art Gallery, NM State U., 1996, Inside the Loop, Blue Star Art Space, San Antonio, 1998, Paradise 8, Exit Art, NY, 1999, Meat Market Art Fair, Inman Gallery, NY, 2000, Fresh: Altoids Curiously Strong Collection, New Mus. Contemporary Art, NY, 2001, Rapper's Delight, Yerba Buena Ctr. Arts, San Francisco, 2001, One Planet Under a Groove, Bronx Mus., NY, 2001, Rock My World, CCAC Inst. Gallery, San Francisco, 2002, Gene(sis): Contemporary Art Explores Human Genomics, Henry Art Gallery, U. Washington, Seattle, 2002, Pill & Psaches, Cleve. Mus. Art, 2003, Dust Memories, Swiss Inst., NY, 2003, Harlem Postcards, Studio Mus., Harlem, NY, 2003, Whitney Biennial, Whitney Mus. Am. Art, 2004, Treble, Sculpture Ctr., Long Island City, NY, 2004. Mailing: c/o ACME 6150 Wlishire Blvd #1 Los Angeles CA 90048

**ROBOCK, ALAN,** meteorology professor; b. Boston, Sept. 7, 1949; s. Stefan Hyman and Shirley Robock; m. Sherri Robock, May 12, 1990; children: Brian, Daniel. BA, U. Wis., 1970; SM, MIT, 1974, PhD, 1977. Vol. Peace Corps, The Philippines, 1970-72; rsch. scientist Lawrence Livermore (Calif.) Lab., 1973; asst. prof. dept. meteorology U. Md., College Park, 1977-82, assoc. prof., 1982-86, prof., 1996-97; prof. dept. environ. scis. Rutgers U., New Brunswick, NJ, 1998—2003, prof. II, 2003—. Dir. Ctr. Environ. Prediction Rutgers U., 2003-05; snow forecaster Montgomery County (Md.) Pub. Schs., 1980-81; state climatologist State of Md., 1991-97; vis. rsch. scientist Princeton U., NOAA/Geophys. Fluid Dynamics Lab., 1994-95 Editor Jour. Climate and Applied Meteorology, 1985—87, Jour. Geophys. Rsch-Atmospheres, 2000—05, assoc. editor, 1998—2000; assoc. editor: Jour. Geophys. Rsch-Atmospheres, 2006—; assoc. editor Revs.

Geophysics, 1994—2000, 2006—; contbr. articles to profl. jours., chapters to books. Fellow Am. Meteorol. Soc.; mem. AAAS (Congressional sci. fellow 1986-87), Am. Geophys. Union. Avocations: tennis, Bob Dylan music, travel, politics. Office: Rutgers U Dept Environ Scis 14 College Farm Rd New Brunswick NJ 08901-8551 E-mail: robock@envsci.rutgers.edu.

**ROBOCK, STEFAN HYMAN,** retired economics professor: b. Redgranite, Wis., July 31, 1915; s. Samuel and Elizabeth (Kushner) R.; m. Shirley Bernstein, June 17, 1946 (div. Mar. 1980); children: Alan David, Jerry, Lisa (Mrs. Stephen Shaffer); m. Hanne Miree, June 13, 1998. BA, U. Wis., 1938; MA (Adminstrn. fellow), Harvard U., 1941, PhD, 1948; Prof. Honoris Causa. U. Recife, Brazil, 1956; M. Honoris Causa, E.S.T.E., San Sebastian. Spain. 1974. Economist Nat. Resources Planning Bd., Washington, 1940-41; antitrust div. U.S. Dept. Justice, Washington, 1941-42, Boston, 1948-49; chief economist TVA, Knoxville, 1949-54; devel. adviser UN, Brazil, 1954-56, tech. asst. missions India, 1959, Bolivia, 1963; with Midwest Rsch. Inst., 1956-58, Com. Econ. Devel., 1958-60; prof. internat. bus. Ind. U., Bloomington, 1960-67; with World Bank, Philippines, 1961, Ford Found., Pakistan, 1964; R.D. Calkins prof. internat. bus. Columbia U., N.Y.C., 1967-84, prof. emeritus, 1984—. Internat. economist Dept. Commerce, 1975-76; trustee Inst. Current World Affairs, 1981-86; cons. fgn. countries, 1959—; bd. dirs. Econs. Inst., Boulder, Colo., 1984-89; adv. bd. World Trade Inst., 1974-95; mem. bd. sci. and tech. NAS, 1969-72; vis. prof. Beijing Mgmt. Inst., 1985, U. Internat. Bus. and Econ., Beijing, 1989, Internat. Mgmt. Ctr., Budapest, Hungary, 1992. Author: Brazil's Developing Northeast, 1963, Brazil: A Study in Development Progress, 1975, International Business and Multinational Enterprises, 4th edit., 1989; Editorial bd.: Columbia Jour. World Bus, 1975-85. Served with USNR, 1942-46. Mem. Soc. Internat. Devel. (mem. council 1966-69), Am. Econ. Assn., Acad. Internat. Bus. (v.p. 1983-85), Harvard Club NYC, Phi Kappa Phi, Beta Gamma Sigma, Phi Eta Sigma. Clubs: Columbia Tennis. Home: 560 Riverside Dr Apt 21J New York NY 10027-3237

**ROBOL, RICHARD THOMAS,** lawyer; b. Norfolk, Va., Feb. 8, 1952; s. Harry James and Lucy Henley (Johnson) R. BA, U. Va., 1974; JD, Harvard U., 1978. Bar: Va. 1979, Ohio 1996, U.S. Dist. Ct. (ea. dist.) Va. 1979, U.S. Ct. Appeals (4th cir.) 1979, U.S. Dist. Ct. (we. dist.) Va. 1981, U.S. Supreme Ct. 1982, D.C. 1991, U.S. Ct. Appeals (4th, 6th and 9th cirs.) 1995. Law clk. to presiding justice U.S. Dist. Ct. (ea. dist.) Va., 1978-79; ptnr. Seawell, Dalton, Hughes & Timms, Norfolk, 1979-87, Hunton and Williams, Norfolk, 1987-92; exec. v.p., gen. counsel Columbus Am. Discovery Group, Inc., 1992—. Adj. prof. U. Dayton Law Sch.; asst. prof. mil. sci Capital U.; pro bono counsel Nat. Commn. for Prevention Child Abuse, Norfolk, 1983, Tidewater Profl. Assn. on Child Abuse, 1983, Parents United Va., 1981-82, Sexual Abuse Help Line, 1983-86; mem. Boyd-Graves Conf. on Civil Procedure in Va., 1981-87. Contbr. articles to law revs.; contbg. editor: International Law for General Practitioners, 1981. Bd. dirs. Va. Opera Assn. Guild, Norfolk, 1983-87, Tidewater br. NCCJ, 1991-92; deacon Ctrl. Bapt. Ch., Norfolk, 1980-83. Maj. USAR, 1992—. Fulbright scholar, 1974. Mem. Va. State Bar Assn. (bd. dirs. internat. law sect. 1984-87, chmn 1982-83), Va. Young Lawyers Assn. (cir. rep. 1984-88), Va. Assn. Def. Attys., Maritime Law Assn., Norfolk-Portsmouth Bar assn. (chmn. speakers bur. 1987-88), Assn. Def. Trial Attys. (chmn. Va. 1987), Def. Rsch. Inst., 1982-88. Avocations: camping, rowing, scuba diving. Home: 60 Kenyon Brook Dr Worthington OH 43085-3629 Office: Robol Law Office LPA 555 City Park Ave Columbus OH 43215 Office Phone: 614-737-3739. Business E-Mail: rrobol@robolllaw.com.

**ROBRENO, EDUARDO C.,** federal judge; b. 1945; BA, Westfield State Coll., 1967; MA, U. Mass., 1969; JD, Rutgers U., 1978. With antitrust divsn. U.S. Dept Justice, Phila., 1978-81; ptnr. Meltzer & Schiffrin, Phila., 1981-86, Fox, Rothschild, O'Brien & Frankel, Phila., 1987-92; judge U.S. Dist. Ct. for Ea. Dist. Pa., Phila., 1992—. Mem. Jud. Conf. Com. on Bankruptcy Rules. Fellow Am. Law Inst. Office: US Courthouse Rm 3810 Philadelphia PA 19106

**ROBSON, CAROL ANN SHAFFNER,** retired secondary school educator; b. Jacksonville, Ill, July 19, 1936; d. Carl Merle and Patricia Beatrice (Brown) Shaffner; children: David, Glen, Anne, Patricia, Susan. BA, Ill. Coll., 1958; MS, So. Conn. State U., 1978, diploma in Advanced Studies, 1991, Cert. tchr., Ill., Conn., Mass. Tchr. New Berlin Bd. Edn., Ill., 1958-59, Arenzville Bd. Edn., Ill., 1960, Weston Bd. Edn., Mass., 1960-63, Hamden Bd. Edn., Conn., 1975-79, Elkhart Grade Sch., Ill., 1979-80, Hartford Bd. Edn., Conn., 1984—2002, ret., 2002. Tchr. Hamden Adult Edn., 1984—. Mem. Hamden Orgn. Women Educators, Hartford Fedn. Tchr., Conn. Coun. Adult Educators, Weston Tchrs. Assn. (pres. 1962-63), New Haven County Ret. Tchrs. Assn., Conn. Coun. English Tchr., Alpha Delta Kappa, Phi Delta Kappa, Delta Kappa Gamma. Republican. Avocation: cooking. Home: 331 Broadway Hamden CT 06518-2617

**ROBSON, DONALD,** physics professor; b. Leeds, Eng., Mar. 19, 1937; came to U.S., 1963; s. Albert and Rose Hannah (Parbutt) Robson; m. Joy Olivia Burkitt Findlay, Aug. 1960 (div. May 1971); children: Donald Peter, David Ian, Karen Joy; m. Martha Breitenlohner, Aug. 26, 1971 (div. Sept. 1999); m. Kimberly G. Kitchen, Dec. 18, 1999; 1 child. Nadirah Berge. BSc, U. Melbourne, Australia, 1959, MSc, 1961, PhD, 1963. Rsch. assoc. Fla. State U., Tallahassee, 1963-64, asst. prof. physics, 1964-65, assoc. prof., 1965-67, prof., 1967—, chmn. dept. physics, 1985-91, Disting. prof., 1990—2003, emeritus prof., 2003—. Editor: (with J.D. Fox) Isobaric Spin in Nuclear Physics, 1966, Nuclear Analogue States, 1976; assoc. editor Nuclear Physics A., 1972-96; contbr. more than 100 articles to profl. jours. Chmn. bd. trustees Southeastern Univ Rsch Assn., 1996-98. Fulbright scholar, 1963-64; A.P. Sloan fellow, 1966-67; Alexander Von Humboldt sr. scientist. 1976-77. Fellow Am. Phys. Soc. (co-recipient Tom W. Bonner prize 1972). Avocations: chess, golf, running. Office: Fla State U Dept Physics Tallahassee FL 32306 Office Phone: 850-644-1767. Business E-Mail: robson@csit.fsu.edu.

**ROBSON, GLENN R.,** engineering and design company executive; BS in Econs., U. Pa.; MBA, Harvard U. Various positions to mng. dir. investment banking divsn. Morgan Stanley, 1990—2002; sr. v.p., CFO Aecom Tech., LA, 2002—. Office: Aecom Tech 555 S Flower St Los Angeles CA 90071 Office Phone: 213-593-8000. Office Fax: 213-593-8730. Business E-Mail: info@aecom.com

**ROBSON, MARTIN CECIL,** surgery educator, plastic surgeon: b. Lancaster, Ohio, Mar. 8, 1939; children: Karen Iredell, Douglas Spears, Martin Cecil Robson III. Student, Northwestern U., 1957—59; BA, Johns Hopkins U., 1961, MD, 1964. Diplomate Am. Bd. Surgery, Am. Bd. Plastic Surgery. Intern U. Chgo. Hosps. and Clinics, 1964—65; resident in surgery Balt. City Hosp., 1965—67, Brooke Gen. Hosp., Ft. Sam Houston, Tex., 1967—69; resident in plastic surgery Yale-New Haven Hosp., 1971—73; instr. dept. surgery Yale U. Sch. Medicine, New Haven, 1973—74, instr. prof. plastic surgery, 1973—74, assoc. prof., 1974, assoc. prof., chief plastic surgery U. Chgo., 1974—77, prof. and chief plastic surgery, 1977—83; dir. U. Chgo. Burn Ctr., 1976—83; prof., chmn. divsn. plastic and reconstructive surgery Wayne State U., Detroit, 1983—88; dir. Detroit Med. Ctr. Burn Ctr. 1983—88; Truman Blocker Disting. prof., chief divsn. plastic surgery U. Tex. Med. Br., 1988—93; dir. surg. svcs. Shriners' Burn Inst., Galveston, Tex., 1988—93; prof. surgery U. South Fla., Tampa, 1993—2001, prof. surgery emeritus, 2001—, chair divsn. surgery rsch., 1993—97; chmn. surg. svc. Bay Pines (Fla.) VA Med. Ctr., 1993—97. Chmn., mem. Am. Bd. Plastic Surgery, 1996—97. Mem. editl. bd.: Jour. Trauma. Maj. M.C. U.S. Army, 1967—71, col. M.C. USAR, 1991—97. Recipient Lifetime Achievement award, Assn. Advanced Wound Care, 2003. Fellow: ACS, Royal Coll. Surgeons of Eng. (hon.), Royal Australasian Coll. Surgeons (hon.); mem.: Am. Bd. Med. Specialties, Am. Assn. Plastic Surgery, Wound Healing Soc. (pres. 1995—96, Lifetime Sci. Achievement award 1998), Am. Surg. Assn., Am. Burn Assn. (pres. 1985—86, Disting. Svc. award), Plastic Surgery Rsch. Coun. (chmn. 1983—84), Alpha Omega Alpha, Phi Delta Theta, Nu Sigma Nu.

**ROBY, BRIAN L.**, bank executive; b. Kansas City, Mo., Apr. 16, 1960; s. F. Alan Roby and Mimi Jean (Halliburton) King; m. M. Elizabeth Santander, June 6, 1987. BSBA, U. Mo., 1982, MBA, 1983. V.p. Commerce Bank of Kansas City, 1983-90; sr. v.p. First Nat. Bank of Olathe, Kans., 1990—98, exec. v.p., 1998—2001, pres., CEO, 2001—. Mem. U. Mo. Bus. and Pub. Adminstrn. Alumni Assn. (v.p. 1989-92), Overland Park C. of C. (dir. 1993—). Republican. Roman Catholic. Avocations: tennis, bicycling. Office: First Nat Bank Olathe PO Box 1500 Olathe KS 66051-1500

**ROBY, JASPER**, bishop; Sr. bishop, exec. head Apostolic Overcoming Holy Ch. of God, Inc., Birmingham, Ala. Office: Apostolic Overcoming Church of God PO Box 6238 Mobile AL 36660-0238

**ROBY, JOE LINDELL**, investment banker; b. Metropolis, Ill., May 22, 1939; s. Gerald C. and Inez (DeLaine) R.; m. Elizabeth Shute, June 17, 1967 (dec. Oct. 1980); m. Hilppa Pirila, June 15, 1984 BA cum laude, Vanderbilt U., 1961; MBA with distinction, Harvard U., 1967. Asst. v.p. Kidder, Peabody & Co., N.Y.C., 1967-72; v.p. Donaldson, Lufkin & Jenrette, N.Y.C., 1972-75, sr. v.p., 1976-83, mng. dir. investment banking, 1984-89, chair. banking grp., 1989-95, COO, 1995-99, pres., 1996-99; CEO, pres. Donaldson, Lufkin & Jenrette (merged with Credit Suisse First Boston in 2000), N.Y.C., 1999-2000; chmn. Credit Suisse First Boston, N.Y.C., 2000—01, chmn. emeritus and sr. advisor, 2002. Bd. dirs. Maersk Lines Ltd., Ctrl. Pk. Conservancy, Vanderbilt U., Harvard Bus. Sch., Sybron, Inc., Musicland Group, Inc. Served to lt. USN, 1961-65 Mem.: Southampton Bath & Tennis Club, Bathing Corp. of Southampton, Meadow Club of Southampton, Stanwich Club, Links Club, Lyford Cay Club.

**ROBY, MARY LORRAINE**, special education educator; b. Balt., Nov. 17, 1952; d. Robert Edelen and Lorraine Teresa Roby. BA in Edn., Loyola Coll., Balt., 1974, MEd, 1977; postgrad., NYU, 2003—. Spl. edn. educator St. Francis Sch. for Spl. Edn., Balt., 1975—77, Balt. County Pub. Schs., Balt., 1977—. Adj. prof. spl. edn. Loyola Coll., Balt., 2000—; dir., choreographer Balt. Area Schs., Essex C.C., Balt. area cmty. theaters, 1977—; ednl. rsch. cons. Johns Hopkins U., Balt., 2001—03; mem. tchg. staff Carver Ctr. for Arts and Tech. magnet sch., Balt., 1993—97. Recipient Excellence in Edn. award, Balt. (Md.) C. of C. Avocations: teaching dance, choreography, musical theater. Office: Loyola Coll 4501 N Charles St Baltimore MD 21210-2699

**ROBY, PAMELA ANN**, sociologist, educator; b. Milw., Nov. 17, 1942; d. Clark Dearborn and Marianna (Gillman) Roby; m. James Peter Mulherin, July 15, 1977 (div. 1987). BA, U. Denver, 1963; MA, Syracuse U., N.Y., 1966; PhD, NYU, 1971. Instr. ednl. sociology NYU, N.Y.C., 1966; asst. prof. George Washington U., Washington, 1970—71; asst. prof. sociology and social welfare Brandeis U., Waltham, Mass., 1971—73; assoc. prof. U. Calif., Santa Cruz, 1973—77, prof. sociology and women's studies, 1977—, chair cmty. studies bd., 1974-76, 79, dir. sociology doctoral program, 1988—91, chair sociology dept., 1998—2001. Mem. social sci. rsch. rev. com. NIMH, Washington, 1976—80; vice chair Nat. Commn. Working Women, Washington, 1977—80; cons. James Irvine Found., San Francisco, 1986; mem. sociology program rev. com. Northeastern U., Boston, 1990; mem. anthropology, linguistics and sociology panel NSF, Washington, 1993; assessor Social Scis. and Humanities Rsch. Coun. Can., Toronto, 1993; mem. U. Calif San Francisco Sociology Grad. Dept. External Review Panel, 2005, Ford Found. Post-Doctoral and Dissertation Fellowship Evaluation Panel, 2005, 06. Co-author: The Future of Inequality, 1970; editor: Child Care: Who Cares? Foreign and Domestic Infant and Early Childhood Development Policies, 1973—75, The Poverty Establishment, 1974; author: Women in the Workplace, 1981; adv. editor: Social Quar., 1990—93, Gender and Society, 1986—89. Vis. scholar, Indian Coun. Social Sci. Rsch., 1979, U. Wash., Seattle, 1991—92; Andrew W. Mellon Sr. scholar, Wellesley Coll., 1978—79. Mem.: Alpha Kappa Delta, Re-Evaluation Counseling (coll. and univ. faculty reference person 1980—), Eastern Sociol. Assn. (exec. coun. mem.-at-large 1973—74), Pacific Sociol. Assn. (v.p. 1996—97), Internat. Sociol. Assn. (rsch. coun. mem.-at-large 1978—82), Am. Sociol. Assn. (chair sect. sex and gender 1974—78, exec. coun. mem.-at-large 1975—78), Sociologists Women in Soc. (pres. 1978—80), Soc. Study Social Problems (pres. 1996—97), Phi Beta Kappa. Avocations: camping, hiking, painting, swimming, pen and ink drawing. Office: U Calif Dept Sociology C8 Santa Cruz CA 95064

**ROBY, THOMAS CARTER**, conservator; b. Phila., Nov. 12, 1957; s. Rochester Ross Roby and Juliet Carter Dulany; m. Rachel Anne Burch; 1 child, Elena Juliet. BA in Classical Archaeology, Haverford Coll., 1979; MA in Archtl. History, U. Va., 1985; MA in Conservation studies, U. York, 1987. Pvt. conservator, Rome, 1987—2001; sr. project specialist Getty Conservation Inst., L.A., 2001—. Contbr. articles to profl. jours. Coord. Mid. East peace edn. program Am. Friends Svc. Com., Balt., 1980—82. Fellow: Am. Acad. Rome; mem.: Internat. Inst. Conservation, Am. Inst. Conservation (assoc.). Mem. Soc. Of Friends. Avocations: tennis, walking, choral singing. Office: Getty Conservation Inst 1200 Getty Center Dr Los Angeles CA 90049 Business E-Mail: troby@getty.edu.

**ROCCA, CHRISTINA B.**, ambassador, former federal agency administrator; b. Washington, 1957; m. Gordon L. Rocca; 2 children. BA in History, King's Coll., London, 1980. Staff ops. officer, Directorate of Ops. CIA, Washington, 1982—97; fgn. affairs advisor to Senator Sam Brownback US Senate, Washington; asst. sec for South Asian Affairs US Dept. State, Washington, 2001—06, US rep. to Conf. on Disarmament, 2006—.*

**ROCCO, ANGELO GREGORY**, anesthesiologist; b. Lawrence, Mass., July 17, 1925; s. Angelo Gregory Rocco and Antoinetta Iacobo Roccoo; m. Celia Caprio Caprio, Apr. 20, 1953; children: Angelo Gregory, JulieAnn Jamies, Alfred Paul, Arthur Todd, Anthony Stephen, Andrew Marvin. AB, Boston U., 1945; MS in Chemistry, U. Mich., Ann Arbor, 1946; MD, Tufts U., Boston, 1950. Diplomate Am. Bd. Anesthesiologists, 1958, Nat. Bd. Med. Examiners, 1951. NIH fellow Peter Bent Brigham Hosp., Harvard Med. Sch., Boston, 1955—56; chief anesthesiology West Roxbury Va. Hosp.; chief anesthesia Exeter Hosp., 1959—79; anethesiologist Peter Bent Brigham Hosp., Brigham & Women's Hosp., Boston, 1979—84; dir. pain treatment svc. Brigham & Women's Hosp., Boston, 1984—92; vis. scientist Johns Hopkins Med. Instns., Balt., 1989—90; anesthesiologist Harvard Vanguard Med. Ctr., Boston, 1994—. Asst. prof. anesthesia Harvard Med. Sch., Boston, 1982—91, assoc. prof., 0091—1996. Contbr. articles to profl. jours. Dir. Am. Lung Assn., Concord, NH, 1968—79. Capt. U.S. Army, 1951—53, Korea. Fellow: Am. Coll. Anesthesiologists. Avocation: hiking. Office: Harvard Vanguard Medical Associates 133 Brookline Ave Boston MA 02215

**ROCCO, NIKKI**, film company executive; m. Joseph Rocco. Sales dept. Universal Pictures, 1967, asst. to gen. sales mgr., 1981—84, v.p. distbn., 1984—90, sr. v.p. distbn and mktg., 1990—95, exec. v.p., distbn., 1995—96, pres., distbn., 1996—. Bd. dirs. Will Rogers Motion Picture Pioneers Found. Named one of 100 Most Powerful Women in Entertainment, Hollywood Reporter, 2004, 2005; recipient Crystal award, Women in Film, 2000. Office: Universal Pictures 100 Universal City Plaza Universal City CA 91608*

**ROCCO, RON**, artist; b. Ft. Hood, Tex., Nov. 21, 1953; s. Raymond and Dorothy Ann (D'Angelo) R. Student, Fordham U., 1972; BFA, SUNY, Purchase, 1976; MS in Visual Studies, MIT Ctr. for Advanced Visual Studies, 1983. Artist-in-residence Exptl. TV Ctr., Owego, NY, 1982—; guest lectr., artist-in-residence The Banff (Alta., Can.) Ctr., 1987; artist-in-residence Kunstlerhaus Bethanian, Berlin, 1991; artist-in-residence inter. studio program Kunst and Complex, Rotterdam, Netherlands, 1993. Guest lectr. various univs., 1977-90; mem. UN Internat. Conf. on Communication Tech. and Traditional Cultures, N.Y.C., 1983; bd. dirs. Art & Sci. Collaborations, Inc. Performance at The Solomon R. Guggenheim Mus., N.Y.C. (1983) works exhibited: Arnot Art Mus., Elmira, N.Y., 1976, The Showing Room, N.Y.C., 1979, IV Biennale Internazionale Dantesca, Ravenna, Italy, 1979, The Ithaca Festival, N.Y., 1979, Gallery Danielli, Toronto, Can., 1981, Pratt Inst., Brooklyn, 1981, The Fifth Floor Studio, N.Y.C., 1981, Herbert F. Johnson Mus., Ithaca, 1981, The Asia Soc., N.Y.C., 1985, Video Image Invitational, Found. Georgio Ronchi, Capri, Italy; Bronx Mus. Art, N.Y., 1985; Internat. Exhibit of Computer Art Forms, Kortijk, Belgium, 1986, P.S.1 Mus./MOMA Inc., N.Y.C., 1987, Found. Artgarden, Amsterdam, The Netherlands, 1989, The Katonah (N.Y.) Mus. Art, 1990, The Bklyn. Mus., 1990, Fundacao Rocha, Fortalesca, Brazil, 1991, Kunstlerhaus Bethanien, Berlin, 1991, Amerika Haus, Berlin, 1992, Rotunda Gallery, N.Y.C., 1996, Neuberger Mus. Art, Purchase, N.Y., 1996, Warehouse Galerie, Amsterdam, 1993, ISEA95/Internat. Exhbn. Electronic Art, Montreal, 1995, Sylvia White Gallery, N.Y.C., 1996, The Brooklyn Mus., 1997, List Ctr. MIT, Cambridge, 1997, Snug Harbor Cultural Ctr., N.Y.C., 1998, U. Mass., Lowell, 1999, Campo and Campo, Antwerp, Belgium, 1999, Galerie Volcker and Freunde, Berlin, Germany, 2000, Islip Art Mus., N.Y., 2000, Collaborative Concepts, Beacon, N.Y., 2001, ABC NO RIO and Hudson Guild, N.Y.C., 2001, Galerie Volcker & Freunde, Berlin, 2002, Scope Art, N.Y., 2004, Hudson Guild, N.Y.C., 2004, Brklyn. Pub. Libr., 2004; artistic dir. Laser Sculpture/Dance, 1981; producer, dir. Zaroff's Tale, 1983 (N.Y. State Coun. on Arts grantee); co-dir., collaborator Buddah Meets Einstein at the Great Wall, 1985 (Nat. Endowment Arts award); collaborator, sculptor Light and Sound Sphere Study, 1986 (N.Y. State Coun. on Arts grantee); collaborator Communicating Vessels, 1998 (sponsors: CBK/Centrum Bildende Kunst, Rotterdam and Netherlands Consul to N. Am.). Founder, dir. Ithaca Artists Coop., 1977-80; pub. commns. N.J. Light Rail Project, West Ave. Station, 1997. Creative and Performing Arts Coun. grantee Cornell U., Ithaca, N.Y., 1977, expansion arts program grantee Nat. Endowment Arts, 1977-79; recipient Netherland-Am. Found. award, 1989, Art Matters award, 1989, N.Y. Found. for the Arts award, 1989, The Found. for Contemporary Performance Arts award, 1989, Sculpture award, Ithaca Art Assn., 1976, Printmaking award, NY Found. for Arts, 2003; nominated Joan Mitchell Found. award, 2002. Mem. ACLU, Film/Video Arts, Am. Assn. Mus. Buddhist. Studio: 285 N 6th St 5th Fl Brooklyn NY 11211-8115 E-mail: rr192@columbia.edu.

**ROCEK, JAN**, chemist, educator; b. Prague, Czech Republic, Mar. 24, 1924; came to U.S., 1960, naturalized, 1966; s. Hugo and Frida (Loebl) Robitschek; m. Eva Trojan, June 26, 1947; children: Martin, Thomas. MS, Tech. U., Prague, 1949, PhD, 1953. Scientist Czechoslovak Acad. Sci., Prague, 1953-57, sr. scientist, 1957-60; vis. scientist U. Coll., London, 1958; research fellow Harvard U., 1960-62; asso. prof., then prof. Cath. U. Am., 1962-66; prof. chemistry U. Ill., Chgo., 1966-95, acting head dept., 1980-81, head dept., 1981-93, vice chancellor rsch., dean grad. coll. Chgo., 1993-95, acting dean Grad. Coll., 1990-70, dean Grad. Coll., 1970-79, asso. mem. Ctr. for Advanced Studies, 1968-69; ret., 1995. Vis. scholar Stanford U., 1979-80, Cambridge U., 1980 Contbr. articles to profl. jours. Mem. Am. Chem. Soc., AAAS, Czechoslovak Soc. Arts and Scis. in Am., AAUP, Sigma Xi (pres. chpt. 1976-77, 85-86), Phi Kappa Phi. Home: 2636 Laurel Ln Wilmette IL 60091-2202 Personal E-mail: rocek@uic.edu.

**ROCH, LEWIS MARSHALL, II**, ophthalmic surgeon, medical entrepreneur; b. Mineola, Tex., Aug. 13, 1934; s. Lewis Marshall Roch III, Katrina Ann Seitz. BA, U. Tex., Austin, 1955; MD, U. Tex. Southwestern, Dallas, 1959. Diplomate Am. Bd. Ophthalmology. Intern USPHS Hosp., Boston, 1959-60, resident in ophthalmology New Orleans, 1960-63, dep. chief ophthalmology, 1963-64, chief opthalmology Seattle, 1964-67; attending ophthalmic surgeon Ball Meml. Hosp., Muncie, Ind., 1967—, chmn. dept. surgery, chmn. clin. staff, 1975, chmn. exec. com., 1984—87, bd. dirs., 1984—90, mem. fin. com., 1984—87, founder, CEO, med. dir. The Eye Ctr. Group, Muncie, 1985—, The Surgi Ctr. Group, Muncie, 1985—. Mem. exec. com. Ind. Acad. Ophthalmology, 1978-82; bd. dirs. Cardinal Health Ventures, Paragent, LLC, Cardinal Ethanol LLC, Cardinal Health Found., Inc., 1999-, Ball Meml. Found., 1998-; clin. asst. prof. Ind. U. Sch. Medicine, 1978—. Chmn. Muncie-Delaware Devel., 2000-03; active Ball State U. Bus. Forecasting Roundtable, 2000—; exec. v.p. Muncie-Delaware Econ. Devel., 2000-02; trustee Minnetrista Cultural Ctr., 2002—; bd. dirs. United Way Delaware County, 2003-06. Fellow ACS, Am. Acad. Ophthalmology; mem. AMA, Ind. State Med. Assn., Muncie Acad. Medicine (pres. 1981-82), Am. Soc. Cataract and Refractive Surgeons, Am. Coll. Physician Execs., Muncie-Delaware C. of C. (bd. dirs. 1999-2003), Rotary. Republican. Achievements include first to work in outpatient ambulatory surgery; innovation in intraocular lens implantation in cataract surgery; integration of physician's practices with hospital health care delivery systems. Home: 2006 E Robinwood Dr Muncie IN 47304-2857 Office: The Eye Ctr Group LLC 200 N Tillotson Ave Muncie IN 47304-3988 Office Phone: 765-289-7073. E-mail: lmroch@comcast.net.

**ROCHA, BRENDA DUVALL**, theater educator; b. Ft. Knox, Ky., Feb. 15, 1952; d. Lowell Edgar and Mary Lois Duvall; m. Lear Anthony Rocha, Dec. 24, 1997; children: Randal Craig, Scott Leandro. AA, Altus Jr. Coll., Okla., 1972; BA, Okla. Coll. Liberal Arts, Chickasha, Okla., 1973; MEd, Ctrl. State U., Edmond, Okla., 1977. Tchr. Homerville Elem. Sch., Ga., 1976—80; reading specialist South Houston Elem. Sch., Pasadena, Tex., 1981—85; tchr. speech and drama Pk. View Intermediate Sch., 1985—89; dir. theatre Sam Rayburn H.S., 1989—. Ednl. standing com. Pasadena Local Emergency Planning Com., Pasadena, 1993—2003; shelter-in-place team coord. SE Regioanal Local Emergency Planning Com., Houston, 2003. Mem.: NEA (assoc.), Tex. State Tchrs. Assn. (assoc.), Delta Kappa Gamma (assoc.). Office: Sam Rayburn High School 2121 Cherrybrook Lane Pasadena TX 77502 Office Phone: 713-477-3601 15051503. Personal E-mail: brendarocha@aol.com. E-mail: brocha@pasadenaisd.org.

**ROCHA, GUY LOUIS**, archivist, consultant, historian; b. Long Beach, Calif., Sept. 23, 1951; s. Ernest Louis and Charlotte (Sobus) R. BA in Social Studies and Edn., Syracuse U., 1973; MA in Am. Studies, San Diego State U., 1975; postgrad., U. Nev., 1975—. Cert. archivist Am. Acad. Cert. Archivists. Tchr. Washoe County Sch. Dist., Reno, Nev., 1975-76; history instr. Western Nev. C.C., Carson City, 1976; curator manuscripts Nev. Hist. Soc., Reno, 1976-81, interim asst. dir., 1980, interim dir., 1980-81; state adminstr. archives and records Nev. State Libr. and Archives, Carson City, 1981—. Hist. cons. Janus Assocs., Tempe, Ariz., 1980, Rainshadow Assocs., Carson City, 1983— Co-author: The Ignoble Conspiracy: Radicalism on Trial in Nevada, 1986, The Earp's Last Frontier: Wyatt and Virgil Earp in Nevada 1902-1905, 1988; contbr. to books and govt. study; host weekly radio talk show Sta. KPTL, Carson City, 1988-2000, KUNR/NPR, Reno, 2001-; hist. cons. to documentary Las Vegas, A&E Network, 1996, documentary Truckee and Carson Rivers, PBS Network, 1997, documentary Hoover Dam, PBS Network, 1999, documentary Lake Tahoe, PBS Network, 2001; dir. documentary Comstock Miners Union, 2003, Goldfield, 2004, They Died to Make the Desert Bloom, 2005, Whose Right to Work?, 2006, Nev. AFL-CIO; mem. editl. bd. Nev. Hist. Soc., 1983-2003. Mem. Washoe Heritage Coun., Reno, 1983—85; ex-officio mem. Nev. Commn. Bicentennial U.S. Constn., 1986—91; mem. Washoe County Dem. Ctrl. Com., Reno, 1984—87. Mem. Conf. Intermountain Archivists (coun. mem. 1979-87, v.p. 1984-85, pres. 1985-86), No. Nev. Pub. Adminstrs. Group (pres. 1986-87), S.W. Labor Studies Assn., State Hist. Records Adv. Bd. (dep. coord. 1984-86, coord. 1986—), Westerners Internat. Nev. Corral (dep. sheriff 1980-81, sheriff 1984-85, mem. state coords. steering com. 1985-87, vice chmn. 1986-87), Soc. Am. Archivists, Western History Assn., Nat. Assn. Govt. Archives and Records Adminstrs., Orgn. Am. Historians. Home: 1824 Pyrenees St Carson City NV 89703-2331 Office: Nev State Libr & Archives 100 N Stewart St Carson City NV 89701-4285 Office Phone: 775-684-3317.

**ROCHA, V. MANUEL**, former diplomat, international trade consultant; Grad. cum laude, Yale U., 1973; MPA, Harvard U., 1976; M. Internat. Relations, Georgetown U., 1978. Desk officer Dept. State, Honduras, 1981-83, polit. officer U.S. Embassy Santo Domingo, Dominican Republic, 1983, watch officer Ops. Ctr., consul for polit. and econ. affairs Florence, Italy, politico-mil. officer U.S. Embassy Tegucigalpa, Honduras, 1987, dep. polit. counselor Mexico City, dep. chief of mission Santo Domingo, 1991-94; dir. Inter-Am. Affairs Nat. Security Coun., Washington; dep. prin. officer U.S.

Interests Section Dept. State, Havana, Cuba, dep. chief of mission Buenos Aires, 1997, charge d'affaires, 1997—2000, U.S. amb. to Bolivia, 2000—02; sr. counselor internat. trade and govt. affairs Steel Hector & Davis LLP, Miami, Fla., 2002—.

**ROCHE, GAIL CONNOR**, editor; b. Phila., Aug. 14, 1953; d. Donald Russell Connor; m. Richard Roche, Nov. 21, 1981; children: Alex James, Clare Evelyn. AB cum laude, Franklin & Marshall Coll., Lancaster, Pa., 1975; MA with distinction, Rider U., 1988. Cert. tchr., Pa. Tchr. Pennsbury Schs., Fallsington, Pa., 1975-76, Cen. Bucks Sch., Doylestown, Pa., 1977-79; reporter Trenton Times, NJ, 1979-82; editor Dow Jones & Co., Princeton, NJ, 1982-95; mem. adv. bd. Dow Jones Women's Network, Princeton, 1990-95; tech. editor Bloomberg News, Princeton, 1995-2000; sr. editor, letters editor Bloomberg Markets, 2000—. Contbr. articles to mags. Mem. Phi Beta Kappa. Home: 23 Jericho Run Washington Crossing PA 18977-1027 Office Phone: 609-394-0738. Personal E-mail: groche@bloomberg.net.

**ROCHE, GEORGE AUGUSTINE**, investment management executive; b. Rochester, N.Y., July 6, 1941; s. John David and Elizabeth Ann (Switzer) R.; m. Nancy Keen, July 30, 1966; children: Kathryn Elizabeth, Anne Patricia. Student, U. Fribourg, Switzerland, 1961-62; AB, Georgetown U., 1963; MBA, Harvard U., 1966. Brand asst. Procter & Gamble Co., Cin., 1966-68; with T. Rowe Price, Balt., 1968—, rsch. analyst, 1968-72, v.p., 1972—, CFO, 1984—97, also bd. dirs., mng. dir., 1989, chmn., CEO, 1997—. Pres. Rowe Price New Era Fund, Balt., 1979—; bd. dir. B.R.P. Inc. Contbr. articles to profl. jours. Mem. Urban Coalition, Balt., 1976; bd. dirs. Roland Park Country Sch., 1982-89, French Pratt Free Libr., 1985—. With U.S. Army, 1963-64. Mem. AIME, Ctr. Club, L'Hirondelle Club, Harvard Bus. Club, Md. Club. Republican. Roman Catholic. Office: T Rowe Price Assocs Inc 100 E Pratt St Fl 4 Baltimore MD 21202-1090

**ROCHE, GERARD RAYMOND**, management consultant; b. Scranton, Pa., July 27, 1931; s. Joseph Arthur and Amelia Jane (Garcia) R.; m. Marie Terotta, Apr. 27, 1957; children: Mary Margaret, Anne Elizabeth, Paul Joseph. BS in Acctg., U. Scranton, 1953; MBA, NYU, 1958. Mgmt. trainee AT&T, Phila., 1955-56; account exec. ABC-TV, N.Y.C., 1956-58; sales and mktg. positions Kordite Corp. subs. Mobil Oil Co., Macedon, NY, 1959-63; assoc. Heidrick & Struggles, Inc., N.Y.C., 1964-68, ptnr., 1968—, mgr. N.Y., 1968-73, mgr. East, 1973-77, pres., chief exec. officer, 1978—81, chmn., 1981-2000, sr. chmn., 2000—. Former trustee Cath. U. Am.; U. Scranton; mentor Nat. Mentoring Partnership. Served to lt. USN, 1953-55. Mem.: Cmty. Anti-Drug Coalitions of am. (bd. dirs.), Knights of Malta, Loblolly Pines Country Club, Blind Brook Club, Sleepy Hollow Country Club, Univ. Club, Yale Club, Alpha Sigma Nu (past pres.). Roman Catholic. Office: Heidrick & Struggles Inc 245 Park Ave Fl 43 New York NY 10167-0152 Office Phone: 212-551-0505.

**ROCHE, JAMES GERARD**, former civilian military employee; m. Diane Lee. BS in Language, Lit. & Philosophy, Illinois Inst. Tech., Chicago, 1960; MS, U.S. Naval Postgrad. Sch., Monterey, Calif., 1966; PhD in Bus. Adminstrn., Harvard U., Cambridge, Mass., 1972; PhD (hon.), Illinois Inst. of Tech., 2002, St. Thomas Aquinas Coll., 2003. Advanced through ranks to capt. USN, 1960-83; with Office Sec. Def., 1975-79; sr. profl. staff mem. Senate Select Com. Intelligence, 1979-81; princ. dep. dir. policy planning staff US Dept. State, 1981-83; Dem. staff dir. U.S. Senate Com. on Armed Svcs., 1983—84; v.p., dir. analysis ctr. Northrop Grumman Corp., Washington, 1984-89, v.p., special asst. to chmn., pres., CEO L.A., 1989-91, v.p., adv. devel. planning, 1991—92, chief advanced develop., planning, pub. affairs, 1992—96, corp. v.p., pres. elec. sensors, systems sector Balt., 1996—2001; sec. USAF, Washington, 2001—05. Mem. The Coun. Fgn. Relations, Internat. Institute of Strategic Studies, Fleet Reserve Assn., Mil. Order of the Carabao, Conquistadores Del Cielo. Decorated Def. Superior Svc. medal, Legion of Merit, Navy Commendation medal, Navy Expeditionary medal, Nat. Def. Svc. medal, Vietnam Svc. medal, USN Disting. Pub. Svc. medal; recipient Disting. Civilian Svc. medal, Dept. Army, 2003, Ill. Inst. Tech. Profl. Achievement award, 2003, Air Force Order of the Sword, 2003, Exceptional Civilian Svc. award, 2005.

**ROCHE, JEFF**, history professor; s. Steve Roche and Sheila Nelson; m. Cathy Gensler Roche, Dec. 15, 9199; 1 child, Christopher Matthew. BA, Ga. State U., 1992, MA, 1995; PhD, U. N.Mex., 2001. Asst. prof. College of Wooster, Ohio, 2001—06, assoc. prof., 2006—, dean Class 2010, 2006—. Vis. asst. prof. Trinity Coll., Hartford, Conn., 2000—01. Author: Restructured Resistence, 1996; co-editor: The Conservative Sixties, 2001. Trustee Montesorri Schs. Wooster, 2005—. Mem.: Western History Assn., Orgn. Am. Historians. Democrat. Avocations: golf, snowboarding, poker.

**ROCHE, JOHN EDWARD**, college administrator, human resources specialist, educator; b. St. Albans, NY, Nov. 11, 1946; s. John F. and Carolyn C. (Miller) R.; m. Valerie Vastola; children: Christopher B., Danielle, Ryan J., Jennifer M. BA, Marist Coll., 1968, MBA, 1975; MS in Edn., SUNY, New Paltz, 1974; EdD, Nova Southeastern U., 1998. Tchr. Kingston City Schs., NY, 1968-76; employment supr. ACLI Internat. Inc., NYC, 1976-78; dir. pers. Balfour MacLaine Internat., NYC, 1978-80; mgr. employee rels. Harcourt Brace Jovanovich, NYC, 1980-82; nat. dir. pers. Hayt, Hayt & Landau, Great Neck, NY, 1982-86; pres. Pers. Mgmt. Svcs., Great Neck, NY, 1983-86, Martin-Roche Assocs., Inc., Levittown, NY, 1986-94, Human Resources Dept. Inc., Syosset, NY, 1994—2002, LI Bus. Network, Inc., 1994-2000, Martin-Roche Internat. Ltd., Plainview, NY, 1992—94; prof. instrnl. tech. NY Inst. Tech., Old Westbury, 1989-2000, chair Sch. Edn. Manhattan Campus, 1997-2000, acting dir. Ctr. Labor & Indsl. Rels., 2000; dean Sch. Continuing Studies LI U., Bklyn., 2000—04; dean Sch. Profl. Devel. Berkeley Coll., NYC, 2004—, v.p. career svcs., 2006—. Mem. Pres.'s Coun. Berkeley Coll., 2004—, mem. academic affairs com., 2005, mem. exec. com. NY Exec. dir. Jr. Achievement, Kingston, 1972-76, coach Syosset Baseball Assn., 1993-97, CYO Basketball Assn., CYO Girls Softball Assn., 2004-; mem. Syosset Youth Athletic Commn., 2000-04; human resource com. mem. Adults and Children with Learning and Devel. Disabilities, 1990-2000; mem. LI U. Coun. Deans, 2000-04, Middle States Com., 2001-03. Mem. ASTD, Assn. Continuing Higher Edn. (exec. com. region III), WorldatWork (cert. compensation profl.), Soc. for Human Resource Mgmt. (cert. sr. profl. in human resources), KC (grand knight 1967-68). Republican. Roman Catholic. Avocations: astronomy, photography, painting. Home: 17 Meadow Ln Syosset NY 11791-4126 Office: Berkeley Coll Career Services New York NY 10038 Office Phone: 212-986-4343. Personal E-mail: jeroche@juno.com. Business E-Mail: jer@berkeleycollege.edu.

**ROCHE, JOYCE M.**, marketing executive; Sales exec. Avon Inc., 1976-91, sr. v.p. mktg., 1991-93, v.p. global mktg., 1993-94; exec. v.p. global mktg. Carson Prods. Co., Savannah, Ga., 1995-96, pres., COO, 1996—98; pres., CEO Girls Inc. Office: Girls Inc 120 Wall St New York NY 10005-3902

**ROCHE, (EAMONN) KEVIN**, architect; b. Dublin, June 14, 1922; came to U.S., 1948, naturalized, 1964; s. Eamon and Alice (Harding) R.; m. Jane Tuohy, June 10, 1963; children: Eamon, Paud, Denis, Anne, Alice. B.Arch., Nat. U. Ireland, 1945; D.Sci. (hon.), Nat. U. Ireland, 1977; postgrad., Ill. Inst. Tech., 1948; D.F.A. (hon.), Wesleyan U., 1981, Yale U., 1995. With Eero Saarinen and Assocs., Bloomfield Hills, Mich., 1950—61; prin. Kevin Roche John Dinkeloo and Assocs., Hamden, 1966—. Prin. works include Ford Found. Hdqs., 1967, Oakland (Calif.) Mus, 1968, Met. Mus. Art, NYC, Creative Arts Ctr., Wesleyan U., Middletown, Conn., 1971, Fine Arts Ctr., U. Mass., 1971, Union Carbide Corp. World Hdqs., Conn., Gen. Foods Corp. Hdqs., Rye, N.Y., 1977, 1978, Conoco Inc. Hdqs., Houston, 1979, Central Pk. Zoo, N.Y.C., 1980, DeWitt Wallace Mus. Fine Arts, Williamsburg, Va., 1980, Bouygues World Hdqrs., Paris, 1983, J.P. Morgan and Co. Hdqrs., N.Y.C., 1983, UNICEF Hdqs., N.Y.C., 1984, Leo Burnett Co. Hdqrs., Chgo., 1985, Cummins Engine Co. Corp. Hdqrs., Columbus, Ind., 1985, Corning (N.Y.) Inc. Hdqs. 1986, Merck & Co. Hdqs., N.J., 1987, Dai Ichi Hdqs./Norinchukin Bank Hdqrs., Tokyo, 1989, Nations Bank Hdqs., Atlanta,

1989, Pontiac Marina Pvt. Ltd., Singapore, 1990, Metropolitano, Madrid, 1990, Borland Internat. Headquarters, Scotts Valley, Calif., 1990, Tanjong & Binariang/Ampang Tower, Kuala Lumpur, Malaysia, 1993, Mus. Jewish Heritage Holocaust Meml., N.Y.C., 1993, Tata Cummins Pvt. Ltd., Jamshedpur, India, 1994, Vis. Ctr., Columbus, Ind., 1994, Cummins Engine Co. APEX Mfg. Facility, 1994, Lucent Techs. Hdqs., Murray Hill, N.J., 1996, Wuxi Newage Cummins, Wuxi, China, 1996, Total Sys. Svcs. Corp. Hdqrs., Columbus, Ga., 1997, Zesiger Sports and Fitness Ctr., MIT, Cambridge, 2000, Lucent Tech. R&D Facilities, various locations including The Netherlands and Germany, 2001, Shiodome City Ctr., Tokyo, 2003, Hdqrs. Santander Ctrl. Hispano, Madrid, 2005, SEC, Washington, 2005, Bouygues SA Holding Co. Hdqrs., Paris, 2005, Nat. Conf. Ctr., Dublin, 2005. Mem. Fine Arts Commn., Washington; trustee Am. Acad. in Rome, 1968-71, Woodrow Wilson Center for Scholars in Smithsonian Instn. Recipient Creative Arts award Brandeis U., 1967; A.S. Bard award City Club N.Y., 1968, 77, 79; award Gov. of Calif., 1968; N.Y. State award Citizens Union N.Y., 1968; total design award Am. Soc. Interior Design; Pritzker Archtl. prize, 1982; Albert S. Bard award, 1990. Fellow AIA (medal of honor N.Y. chpt. 1968, Gold Medal award 1993, 25-yr. award 1995), AAAS; mem. NAD (academician), AAAL (pres. 1994-97), Am. Acad. Arts and Letters (Brunner award 1965, Gold medal 1990), Académie d'Architecture (Grand Gold medal 1977), Mcpl. Art Soc. N.Y. (Brendan Gill prize 1989), Acad. di San Luca. Office: Kevin Roche John Dinkeloo & Assoc PO Box 6127 20 Davis St Hamden CT 06517-0127 Office Phone: 203-777-7251. Business E-mail: info@krjda.com.

**ROCHE, MARK A.,** consumer products company executive, lawyer; b. 1954; m. Barbara Roche. BA, U. Va.; JD, Cornell U. Bar: N.Y. 1980. From assoc. to counsel Chadbourne & Park LLP, N.Y.C., 1981-88; group gen. counsel Fortune Brands Inc., Deerfield, Ill., 1988-91, Lincolnshire, Ill., 1991-96, v.p., assoc. gen. counsel, 1996-98, v.p., gen. counsel, 1998-99, sr. v.p., gen. counsel, 1999—. Office: Fortune Brands Inc 300 Tower Pky Lincolnshire IL 60069-3640

**ROCHE, PAULINE JENNIFER,** artist; b. London, Sept. 22, 1961; arrived in U.S., 1995; d. Walter Daniel and Doreen Molly Roche; m. Hany Massarany, Feb. 27, 1986; children: Thomas Daniel, Natalie Jane. BS, Monash U., Melbourne, Australia, 1982. Rsch. physiology dept. physiology Monash U., Melbourne, 1983—86; rsch., policy and planning officer Victorian State Govt. Dept. Edn./Pub. Svc. Bd., Melbourne, 1986—92; artist, 1989—. Exhibitions include Sherbrooke Art Award exhbns., 1991—97, Victorian Artists Soc. Ann. Exhbns., 1992—2001, Alice Bale Art Nat. Exhbns., 1993—98, Camberwell Rotary Ann. Juried Art Exhbn., 1992—98, 1993, 2000, Kew Gallery Invitational Exhbn., 1994, Victorian Artists Soc. Artist of Yr. Invitational Exhbn., 1997, Salmagundi Club 20st Ann. Open Exhbn., Salmagundi Club, 1997—98, Catherine Lorillard Wolfe Art Club 101st Art Exhbn., 1997, Am. Artists Profl. League 69th Grand Nat. Exhbn., 1997, Newbury Fine Arts, Boston, 1998, Newbury Fine Arts Figurative Art Group Exhbn., 2000, Celebrate! Exhbn., Tucson, 2002, Catherine Lorillard Wolfe Art Club 109st Art Exhbn., 2004, El Presidio Gallery, Tucson, 2005—06, one-woman shows include Cato Gallery, Victorian Artists Soc. Galleries, Melbourne, 1994, Ventana Med. Sys. Nat. Hdqs., Tucson, 2003. Recipient Gold Medal of Honor, Audubon Artists 55th Ann. Exhn., 1997, Hans Heysen award, Sherbrooke Art Soc., 1992, Award for Oil Painting, Alice Bale Nat. Art Awards, 1994, Mavis Hill Acquisitive Award, Sherbrooke Spring Exhbn., 1995, Gordon Moffat award, Victorian Artists Soc., 1997, Highly Commended, Victorian Artists Soc. Dep. Lord Mayor's Exhbn., 1999, N.J. Chpt. award for artistic excellence, Am. Artists Profl. League, 1997, Pres. award, Salmagundi Club, 1997, Artist Showcase award, Manhattan Arts Internat., 1997, 1998, Leonard J. Meiselman Meml. award, Catherine Lorillard Wolfe Art Club, 1997, Sharon and Danielle Ortlip Meml. award, Salmagundi Club, 1998, Highly Commended award, Australian Guild Realist Artists, 2006. Mem.: Australian Guild Realist Artists, Portrait Soc. Am., Victorian Artists Soc. (signatory mem., Gordon Moffat award 1997). Office Phone: 520-219-2902. E-mail: paulineroche@comcast.net.

**ROCHÉ, ROBERT RICHARD,** artist; m. Bettie Fistere, Dec. 6, 1945. Apprenticeship, Studio of Sebastian Cruset, N.Y.C., 1931—32; at, Nat. Acad. Design, N.Y.C., 1933—36, Art Students League, 1936—40, Columbia U., 1941. Artist Roché Studio, N.Y., Conn., N.H. and Maine, 1941—2004; instr. Roché Tchg. Studio, N.Y., Conn. and N.H., 1942—79. Curator Mus. Fine Arts, Richmond, Va., 1947—48; art commentator Nat. Antiques Rev., Portland, Maine, 1969—71; critic and art judge; lectr. in field. Represented in permanent collections N.Y. Racing Assn., Aqueduct and Belmont, Wilmington Race Track, Del., prin. works include portraiture, including Pres. Harry S. Truman, Eleanor Roosevelt, Dr. Ralph Bunche, James Farley, Old Saratoga Race Track, 1960, FB-111 Before Take-Off, 1982, Amish Children, 1984, Cat Portfolio, 1984, prin. works and pvt. collections in publs., Sunny Jim: The life of America's Most Beloved Horseman, 1962, American Racetracks and Contemporary Art, 1966, Birds and Beasts of Mark Twain, 1966, Thoroughbred Record, 1973, 1974, one-man shows include Frank K.M. Gallery, 1949, 1952, Retrospectives, U.S. Air Force Acad., 1988, Nat. Mus. Racing, Saratoga Springs, N.Y., 2000—01. Instr. diagnostic rsch. Northampton State Hosp., Mass., 1946—47; dir. art auction Cerebral Palsy, Conn., 1950. Mem.: Royal Soc. Arts, Am. Watercolor Soc. Avocations: writing, music, antiques, farming and animal husbandry, literature. Home: Windswept Farm PO Box 467 York ME 03909-0467

**ROCHELLE, DUDLEY CECILE,** lawyer; b. Franklinton, La., Sept. 10, 1950; s. James Cecil and Mildred Grace (Stennis) R. BA in Polit. Sci., La. State U., 1972; JD, Yale U., 1975. Bar: Ga. 1976, US Dist. Ct. (no. dist.) Ga. 1976, US Ct. Appeals (5th cir.) 1976, US Ct. Appeals (11th cir.) 1997. Vista atty. Atlanta Legal Aid Soc., 1975-76; law clk. to Hon. Joel J. Fryer Fulton County Superior Ct., Atlanta, 1976-77; trial atty. U.S. Dept. Labor, Atlanta, 1977-82; assoc. Hansell Sponns & Phillips PC, Atlanta, 1984-88, shareholder (ptnr.), 1988-94, Spanos & Rochelle, P.C., Atlanta, 1994-97; shareholder Littler Mendelson, P.C., Atlanta, 1997—. Mem. adv. bd. Coverdell Leadership Inst., Atlanta, 1996—; mem. Ga. Commn. on Equal Opportunity; bd. dirs. Ga. Pub. Policy Found., 1996—; So. Inst. Bus. and Profl. Ethics, 2001—, Midtown Alliance, Atlanta, 1982—92. Mem. State Bar Ga. (mem. labor sect.), Atlanta Bar Assn. (mem. labor/employment sect., chairperson alt. dispute resolution com. 1986-92, mem. bench and bar com. 1986-87), Christian Legal Soc., Federalist Soc., Yale Club Ga. (bd. dirs. 1982-86), So. Inst. Bus. and Profl. Ethics (bd. dirs.). Republican. Avocations: outdoor activity, scuba diving, music. Home: 2769 Brook Grove Ln Atlanta GA 30339-5331 Office: Littler Mendelson PC 3348 Peachtree Rd NE Ste 1100 Atlanta GA 30326-1447 Office Phone: 404-233-0330. E-mail: DRochelle@littler.com.

**ROCHELLE, LUGENIA,** academic administrator; b. Maple Hill, N.C., July 14, 1943; d. John Edward and Ruby Lee (Holmes) R. BA, St. Augustine's Coll., 1965; MS, N.C. A & T State U., 1969; D of Pedagogy, Barbar-Scotia Coll., 1993. Cert. tchr., N.C. Tchr. French, English Butler High Sch., Barnwell, SC, 1965-67; instr. English N.C. A & T State U., Greensboro, 1970-77, St. Augustine's Coll., Raleigh, NC, 1977-86, dir. freshman studies program, 1986-91, dean lower coll., 1991-95, asst. to v.p. acad. affairs, 1991-92; dir. gen. studies, asst. prof. English Voorhees Coll., Denmark, SC, 1996-98, spl. asst. to pres. external affairs, 1999—2002, dir. Hons. Coll., 1999—, dean, Coll. of General Studies, 2002—. Dir. Mellon program St. Augustine's Coll., Raleigh, 1980-83; adv. bd. cooperating Raleigh Colls., 1986—, Off to Coll., Montgomery, Ala., 1993—; mem. profl. practices commn. N.C. Dept. Pub. Instrn., 1994-96; coord. Title III, 1999-00, coord. Bd. Trustees Rels., 1999-02; dir. Ctr. Excellence in Humanities, Voorhees Coll., April 2000-02; Hostess for Radio Talk Show, Views and News from Voorhees Coll., Sept. 2001-03. Author: English Manual of Writing, 1980, (with others) Off to College, 1997, 98, reprinted, 1999, 2000, 01; editor: Can't Nobody Do You Like Jesus, 1998. Judge oratorical contests, Optimist Club, Raleigh, 1985-93; chair pro tem Raleigh Bicentennial Hist. Com., Raleigh, 1991-92; initiated, effected chartering of Phi Eta Sigma St. Augustine's Coll., 1995; bd. dirs. Garner Rd. YMCA, Raleigh, 1994-1996; coord. Honda Campus All-Star Challenge, 1996—; lay min., sec. vestry St. Philip's

---

Episcopal Ch., 1997—; instnl. rep. S.C. Women in Higher Edn., Voorhees Coll., 1998—. Nat. teaching fellow N.C. A & T State U., Greensboro, 1968-70. NCTE Fellow Nat. Coun. Tchrs. English; mem. ASCD (assoc.), Am. Assn. U. Women (pres. Denmark Br.), Cardinal Club. Avocations: reading, collecting antique birds, travel. E-mail: rochelle@voorhees.edu.

**ROCHELSON, BURTON L.,** obstetrician; MD, U. Mich., 1978. Cert. Maternal Fetal Medicine Am. Coll. Ob-Gyn, 1988. Dir. obstetrics and maternal fetal medicine North Shore U. Hosp., Manhasset, NY, 1999—. Contbr. numerous articles to profl. jours. Office: North Shore Univ Hosp 300 Community Dr Manhasset NY 11030 Office Phone: 516-562-2892. E-mail: brochels@nshs.edu.

**ROCHESTER, MICHAEL GRANT,** geophysics educator; b. Toronto, Ont., Can., 1932; s. Reginald Rochester and Ruth Rochester Konrad; m. Elizabeth Manser, 1958; children: Susan, Fiona, John. BA with honors, U. Toronto, 1954, MA, 1956; PhD, U. Utah, 1959. Aerodynamicist A. V. Roe Can. Ltd., Malton, Ont., 1954-55; lectr. geophysics U. Toronto, 1959-60, asst. prof., 1960-61, U. Waterloo, Ont., 1961-65, assoc. prof., 1965-67, Meml. U. Nfld. St. John's, Canada, 1967-70, prof., 1970-98, univ. research prof., 1986—, prof. emeritus, 1998—. Officer Nat. Spiritual Assembly of Baha'is of Can., 1963—92. Grantee, NRC, Natural Scis. and Engring. Rsch. Coun. Can., 1961—2002. Fellow Royal Soc. Can.; mem. Internat. Union Geodesy and Geophysics (Can. nat. com. 1971-75, 84-88), AAAS, Am. Geophys. Union, Can. Assn. Physicists, Can. Geophys. Union (Tuzo Wilson medal, 1986), Internat. Astron. Union (commn. rotation of the Earth 1973—), Royal Astron. Soc. London, Sigma Xi Avocations: hiking, swimming, history. Office: Meml Univ Nfld Dept Earth Scis Saint John's NL Canada A1B 3X5 Office Phone: 709-737-7565. E-mail: mrochest@mun.ca.

**ROCHETTE, ALEXANDRE C.,** computer scientist; b. Saint Martin d'Heres, France, Sept. 5, 1973; s. Philippe and Nicole Suzanne Rochette. BA in econ., Pierre Mendes France U., France, 1998; BS, MS in computer sci., applied math., network telecom. engring., INP-ENSEEIHT, Toulouse, France, 1998. EIT European Engineer, FEANI, 1998. Bus. analyst Total Fina Elf, Paris La Def., France, 1998—98; cons. Accenture, Paris, 1998—2000; program mgr. MicroStrategy, McLean, Va., 2000—02; engagement mgr. Premiere Intelligence, Fairfax, Va., 2002—. Author: Time Zone. Mem.: Enseeiht Internat. Network, PMI, Rotary. Achievements include patents for voice applications. Avocations: mountain climbing, sailing, travel. Personal E-mail: alexrochette@yahoo.com.

**ROCHETTE, LOUIS,** water transportation executive; b. Quebec City, Que., Can., Feb. 19, 1923; s. Evariste and Blanche (Gaudry) R.; m. Nicole Barbeau, Oct. 12, 1968; children: Louise (dec.), Anne, Guy. M. Commerce, Laval U., Que., 1948. Chartered acct., Que. Chief auditor Sales Tax Govt. Que., Quebec City, 1952—55; treas. Davie Ltd., Lauzon, Que., 1955—65; chmn., CEO Davie Ltd., Lauzon, Que., 1976—81; exec. v.p. Marine Industries, Ltd., Montreal, 1965—76; pres., CEO Soconav Inc., Quebec, 1976—86; pres. Gesconav Inc., 1986—. Past chmn. Lloyd's Com. for Can. Author: Le Reve Separatiste, 1969. Bd. dirs. Gov. Coun. for Can. Unity; gov. Laval U. Found., Quebec Opera Found. Pilot RCAF, 1943-45, ETO. Fellow Inst. Chartered Accts. Can., Can. Inst. Mgmt. Accts. Home and Office: 2500 Pierre Dupuy 508 Montreal PQ Canada H3C 4L1 *Whatever success I have met with throughout my career was mainly achieved through perseverance in the face of what often looked like insurmountable obstacles.*

**ROCHINSKI, STEPHEN JAMES,** musician, educator; b. Washington, Jan. 20, 1954; s. Stanley James Rochinski, Jr. and Lorraine Agnes Rochinski, Carol Rochinski (Stepmother); m. Laurie Fox, May 24, 1986; children: Anna F., Alex F. Diploma, Berklee Coll. Music, 1980. Freelance guitarist, Washington, 1972—77; freelance guitarist, arranger Boston, 1977—80; guitarist, arranger, music dir. Anthony Tillman Show with The East Coast Brass, 1980—84; prof. Berklee Coll. Music, 1984—. Writer Hal Leonard Corp., Milw., 1995—; jazz clinician numerous nat. and internat. locations, 1996—. Musician: (recording) Until Further Notice, 1993, A Bird In The Hand, 1999, Otherwise, 2001; author: The Jazz Style of Tal Farlow, 1994, The Motivic Basis for Jazz Guitar Improvisation, 1998, composer numerous jazz compositions and arrangements; Jardis Records, Spiesen-Elversberg, Germany, 1999—; contbg. editor (and author): Berklee Press and Advance Music, 1991—; performances with Tal Farlow, Tim Hagans, Jimmy Raney, Attila Zoller, Pete and Conte Candoli, Chuck Redd and Brad Goode. Jazz artist-in-residence Nat. and Internat. locations. Recipient Paul Revere award Graphic Excellence, Music Pubs. Assn., 1995; grantee, NEA, 1992, Berklee Coll. Music, 1989, 1994, 1998, 2001. Mem.: Broadcast Music Inc. (writer, pub. affiliate 1991—2003), Rec. Acad. (voting mem. 2001—03). Roman Catholic. Avocations: reading, political affairs, history. Home: 2 Wellington Terr Brookline MA 02445 Office: Berklee Coll Music Faculty Box #273 1140 Boylston St Boston MA 02215 Office Phone: 617-747-8335. Business E-Mail: srochinski@berklee.edu.

**ROCHKIND, LOUIS PHILIPP,** lawyer; b. Miami, Fla., June 25, 1948; s. Reuben and Sarah R.; m. Rosalind H. Rochkind, July 4, 1971. BA in Psychology cum laude, U. Mich., 1970, JD cum laude, 1974. Bar: Mich. 1974, U.S. Dist. Ct. (ea. dist.) Mich. 1974. Ptnr. Jaffe, Raitt, Heuer & Weiss, Detroit, 1974—; adj. prof. law Wayne St. U. Law Sch.; lectr. various profl. assns. and orgns. Assoc. editor U. Mich. Law Rev.; contbr. articles to profl. jours. publs. Mem. Am. Coll. Bankruptcy Lawyers, Detroit Bar Assn. (local rules in bankruptcy subcom. creditor-debtor law sect. 1980—), Phi Kappa Phi. Office: Jaffe Raitt Heuer Weiss 27777 Franklin Rd Ste 2500 Southfield MI 48034-8222 E-mail: larrol@jafferaitt.com

**ROCHLIN, PAUL R.,** lawyer; b. Balt., Dec. 14, 1934; s. Jack and Sara (Levin) Rochlin; m. Lois David, Oct. 25, 1962 (div. 1969); children: Greg, Jennifer; m. Joyce Tretick, July 12, 1973; children: Keith Sopher, Maura Sopher. JD, U. Balt., 1958. Bar: Md. 59, U.S. Dist. Ct. Md. 59. Assoc. Milton Talkin, Balt., 1959—61, Rochlin & Settleman, Balt., 1961—63, ptnr., 1963—78; pres., sr. ptnr. Rochlin Settleman & Dobres, P.A., Balt., 1978—2001, of counsel, 2001—. Bd. dirs. Balt. Jewish Coun., 1979. Mem.: Balt. City Bar Assn., Md. Trial Lawyers Assn. (bd. dirs. 1988—92), Md. State Bar Assn., Suburban Club (pres. 2003—05). Jewish. Office Phone: 410-733-6660.

**ROCHON, MARK,** lawyer; b. Detroit, Mich. BS, Western Mich. U., 1980, JD, Stanford U., 1983. Bar: DC 1983, Md. 1990. Former chief, trial divsn. Pub. Defender Svc., Washington; ptnr. Rochon & Roberts, Miller & Chevalier Chartered, Washington. Lectr. on trial practice to students and practitioners. USN, 1977—. Named one of 75 Best Lawyers in Washington, Washingtonian Mag., 2002. Office: Miller & Chevalier Chartered 655 Fifteenth St NW Ste 900 Washington DC 20005-5701 Office Phone: 202-626-5819. Office Fax: 202-628-0858. Business E-Mail: mrochon@milchev.com.

**ROCHON, THOMAS RICHARD,** academic administrator; b. Wash., DC, July 29, 1952; s. Lawrence Charles and Elizabeth Rochon. BA, U. Mich., 1973, MA, 1976, PhD, 1980. Asst. prof. Princeton (NJ) U., 1980—87; assoc. prof. Claremont (Calif.) Grad. U., 1987—96, prof., dean, 1996—2000, interim provost, 1997—98; fulbright scholar Kobe (Japan) U., 1992—93; exec. dir., grad. record examination Ednl. Testing Svc., Princeton, 2000—03; exec. v.p. U. St. Thomas, St. Paul, 2003—. Author: Mobilizing For Peace, 1988 (Choice award, 1988), Culture Moves, 1998 (Sociology award, 2000), The Netherlands, 1999. Roman Cath. Avocation: tennis.

**ROCHOWICZ, JOHN ANTHONY, JR.,** mathematician, mathematics educator, physics educator; b. Reading, Pa., Mar. 20, 1950; s. John Anthony and Sara Jane (Binckley) R. BS in Math., Albright Coll., Reading, Pa., 1972, secondary edn. cert. math., 1975; MS in Math., Lehigh U., Bethlehem, Pa., 1974, EdD in Ednl. Tech., 1993. Cert. secondary tchr., Pa. Tchr. math. Bethlehem Cath. H.S., Pa., 1980—81; instr. math. Pa. State U.-Berks, Reading, 1982—84, Kutztown U., Pa., 1983—84, Lehigh County C.C.,

---

Schnecksville, Pa., 1984, Alvernia Coll., Reading, 1984, prof. math., 1984—; instr. math. Reading Area C.C., 1984—86. Contbr. articles to profl. jours. Recipient Alumni Educator award Albright Coll., Reading, 1987. Mem. Math. Assn. Am., Assn. for Advancement Computing in Edn., Assn. for Ednl. Comm. and Tech., Nat. Coun. Tchrs. Math., Beta Kappa Chi. Democrat. Roman Catholic. Avocations: music, computers, calculators, billiards, swimming. Home: 825 Brighton Ave Reading PA 19606-1316 Office: Alvernia College 400 Saint Bernardine St Reading PA 19607-1799 Office Phone: 610-796-8257. Business E-Mail: john.rochowicz@alvernia.edu.

**ROCK, ALLAN MICHAEL,** ambassador, former Canadian government official; b. Ottawa, Ont., Can., Aug. 30, 1947; s. James Thomas and Anne (Torley) R.; m. Deborah Kathleen, June 24, 1983; children: Jason, Lauren, Andrew, Stephen. BA, U. Ottawa, 1968, LLB, 1971. Certified specialist in civil litigation. Sr. ptnr. Fasken Campbell & Godfrey, Toronto, Ont.; min. of justice, atty. gen. Govt. of Can., 1993-97, min. of health, 1997—2002, min. of industry, 2002—03; permanent Can. rep. UN, New York, 2004—. Treas. Law Soc. Upper Can., 1992-93; bencher Law Soc., 1983, 87, 91; former chmn. discipline and legal edn. coms.; past chmn. litigation dept. Fasken Campbell Godfrey. Fellow Am. Coll. Trial Lawyers. Office: UN One Dag Hamarskjold Plz 885 Second Ave 14th Fl New York NY 10017

**ROCK, ARTHUR,** venture capitalist; b. Rochester, NY, Aug. 19, 1926; s. Hyman A. and Reva (Cohen) Rock; m. Toni Rembe, July 19, 1975. BA, Syracuse U., 1948; MBA, Harvard U., 1951. Gen. ptnr. Davis & Rock, San Francisco, 1961-68, Arthur Rock & Assocs., San Francisco, 1969-80. Mem. exec. com. Teledyne, Inc., L.A., 1961-94; dir. emeritus, founder, past chmn. chmn. exec. com., lead dir. Intel Corp., Santa Clara, Calif.; bd. dirs. Echelon Corp., San Jose, Calif.; bd. govs. Nasdaq Stock Market, Inc. Trustee Calif. Inst. Tech.; pres. Basic Fund; bd. dirs. San Francisco Opera Assn., 1970-92, San Francisco Mus. Modern Art; mem. vis. com. Harvard U. Bus. Sch., 1982-88. Recipient Medal of Achievement Am. Electronics Assn., 1987, Am. Acad. Achievement, 1989, Lifetime Achievement in Entrepreneurship and Innovation award U. Calif., 1999; named to Jr. Achievement Hall of Fame, 1990, Calif. Bus. Hall of Fame, 1990, Bay Area Bus. Coun. Hall of Fame, 1995, Arents Pioneer medal Syracuse U., 1997, Outstanding Dir., Corp. Am., 1999, SDForum Visionary award, 2001, Bus. Leader of Yr. award Harvard Bus. Sch. Assn. No. Calif., 2002. Office: 1 Maritime Plz Ste 1220 San Francisco CA 94111-3502

**ROCK, CHRIS,** actor, comedian; b. Bklyn., Feb. 7, 1965; s. Julius and Rose Rock; m. Malaak Compton, 1996; 1 child, Lola. Actor (films) Beverly Hills Cop II, 1987, I'm Gonna Git You Sucka, 1988, New Jack City, 1991, Boomerang, 1992, Panther, 1995, The Immortals, 1995, Sgt. Bilko, 1996, Beverly Hills Ninja, 1997, (voice) Doctor Dolittle, 1998, Lethal Weapon 4, 1998, Dogma, 1999, Torrance Rises, 1999, Spin Doctor, 1999, Nurse Betty, 2000, (voice) Artificial Intelligence, 2001, Pootie Tang, 2001, (voice) Osmosis Jones, 2001, Jay and Silent Bob Strike Back, 2001, Bad Company, 2002, Paparazzi, 2004, (voice) Madagascar, 2005, The Longest Yard, 2005; (TV series) Saturday Night Live, 1990-93, Def Comedy Jam, 1992, In Living Color, 1993-94, (voice) Happily Ever After: Fairy Tales for Every Child, 1995, Politically Incorrect, 1996, The Remarkable Journey, 2000; actor, writer (films) Comedy's Dirtiest Dozen, 1988, actor, writer, exec. prodr. Down to Earth, 2001; actor, dir., prodr. Head of State, 2003; actor, writer, prodr. (with Nelson George) CB4, 1993; actor, writer, exec. prodr. (TV series) The Chris Rock Show, 1997-2000 (Emmy for Outstanding Writing for a Variety or Music Program, 1998); exec. prodr. The Hughleys, 1998; writer (TV special) Chris Rock: Big Ass Jokes, 1993, Saturday Night Live: The Best of Chris Rock, 1999; writer, exec. prodr. Chris Rock: Bring the Pain, 1996 (Emmy for Outstanding Variety, Music or Comedy Special), Chris Rock: Bigger and Blacker, 1999 (American Comedy award for Funniest Male Performer in a TV Special, 2000), Chris Rock: Never Scared, 2004 (Grammy award, Best Comedy Album, 2006), Everybody Hates Chris, 2005-; writer, prodr. Best of Chris Rock, 1999; (voice) Whatever Happened to Michael Ray?, 2000; TV appearances include Miami Vice, 1987, The Fresh Prince of Bel-Air, 1995, Martin, 1996, Homicide: Life on the Street, 1996, (voice) King of the Hill, 1998, Chappelle's Show, 2003; albums: Born Suspect, 1991, Roll with the New, 1997 (Grammy award for Best Spoken Comedy Album, 1997), Bigger & Blacker, 1999 (Grammy award for Best Spoken Comedy Album, 1999), Never Scared, 2004; Author Rock This!, 1998. Recipient Star, Hollywood Walk of Fame, 2003.*

**ROCK, DOUGLAS LAWRENCE,** manufacturing executive; b. Glen Cove, N.Y., Jan. 25, 1947; s. Herb and Beatrice (Vyse) R.; m. Cindy Pegoraro, May 11, 1967 (div. Apr. 1973); 1 child, Jason; m. Mary Sue Bell, Mar. 23, 1991 (div. Jan. 1996). BS in Psychology and Chemistry, Pa. State U., 1968; postgrad., U. Chgo., 1971-73. Rsch. chemist FMC Corp., Princeton, NJ, 1968-69; mfg. system project leader A.O. Smith Corp., Erie, Pa., 1969-71; dir. materials and info. systems Joy Mfg., Michigan City, Ind., 1971-74; dir. info. systems Smith Tool div. Smith Internat. Inc., Irvine, Calif., 1974-75, dir. materials, 1975-77, v.p. mfg., 1977-80, sr. v.p. ops., 1980-82, pres., 1985-87, Drilco div. Smith Internat. Inc., Houston, 1982-85; pres., chief exec. officer Smith Internat. Inc., Houston, 1987—, chmn. bd., 1991—. Bd. dirs. Viad Corp. Named Golden Knight, Nat. Mgmt. Assn., 1983. Mem. Internat. Assn. Drilling Contractors, Am. Petroleum Inst., Petroleum Equipment Suppliers Assn. (bd. dirs. Houston chpt. 1987—, 1st v.p. 1996), Nat. Offshore Industries Assn. (fin. com. 1988, audit com. 1989), Greenspoint Club. Avocations: golf, racquetball, reading. Office: Smith Internat PO Box 60068 16740 Hardy Rd Houston TX 77205*

**ROCK, EDWARD BARON,** law educator; b. Phila. June 16, 1956; s. Eli and Florence (Baron) R.; m. Andrea White, Jan. 9, 1983; children: Aaron Faith, BA cum laude, Yale U., 1977; DA first class honors, Oxford U., Eng., 1980; JD magna cum laude, U. Pa., 1983. Bar: Pa. 1983, U.S. Dist. Ct. (ea. dist.) Pa. 1983, U.S. Ct. Appeals (3rd cir.) 1988. Assoc. Fine, Kaplan & Black, Phila., 1983-87, ptnr., 1988; asst. prof. Univ. Pa. Law Sch., Phila., 1989—93, prof., 1993—2001, Saul A. Fox disting. prof., 2001—; co-dir. Inst. Law & Econ., Univ. Pa., 1998—. Vis. prof. Goethe Universität, Frankfurt am Main, Germany, 1994; vis. prof. & Fulbright scholar Hebrew Univ., Jerusalem, 1995—97; vis. prof. Columbia Univ. Law Sch., N.Y., 2000. Contbr. articles to profl. jour.; co-author (with Reinier Kraakman, et al.): The Anatomy of Corporate Law: A Comparative and Functional Approach, 2004. Home: 620 W Upsal St Philadelphia PA 19119-3626 Office: U Pa Law Sch 3400 Chestnut St Philadelphia PA 19104-6204*

**ROCK, HAROLD L.,** lawyer; b. Sioux City, Iowa, Mar. 13, 1932; s. Harold L. and Helen J. (Gormally) R.; m. Marilyn Beth Clark Rock, Dec. 28, 1954; children: Michael, Susan, John, Patrick, Michele, Thomas. BS, Creighton U., 1954, JD, 1959. Bar: Nebr., N.Y., Wyo. Law clk. to judge Woodrough U.S. Ct. Appeals 8th Circuit, Omaha, 1959-60; law clk. Fitzgerald Hamer Brown & Leahy, Omaha, 1960-65; of counsel Kutak Rock, Omaha, 1965—. Chmn. Nebr. Bd. Bar Examiners, 1989-96; bd. dirs. Mid City Bank, Omaha. Bd. dirs. Douglas County Hist. Soc., 1992-99, Nat. Equal Justice Libr., 1995—; Nebr. Humanities Coun., 1996-2002. Served to 1st Lt. U.S. Army, 1954-56. Recipient Alumni Achievement award Creighton U., 1995. Mem. ABA (ho. of dels. 1970-96, bd. govs. 1992-95), Nebr. Bar Assn. (ho. of dels., bd. dirs. 1985—, pres. 1988, Nebr. Bar found. bd. dirs., 1982-2003), Omaha Bar Assn. (pres. 1972-73), Omaha Legal Aid Soc. (pres. 1969-72), Nebr. State Bd. Pub. Accts. (bd. dirs. 1981-85). Roman Catholic. Office: Kutak Rock The Omaha Bldg 1650 Farnam St Omaha NE 68102-2186

**ROCK, JANICE C.,** electronics engineer; b. Birmingham, Ala., Nov. 7, 1967; d. Howard Fred and Elizabeth Irene Craven. AS, Wallace State Coll. Hanceville, Ala., 2000; BS, U. of Ala., Huntsville, 2002. Rsch. engr. U.S. Army Aviation and Missile RDEC, Redstone Arsenal, Ala., 2002—. Mem. UAH Indsl. Adv. Bd., Huntsville, 2003—. Named Engring. Student of the Yr., 2002; named to Order of the Engr., U. of Ala., 2002. Mem.: IEEE, Tau Beta Pi. Achievements include patents for Passive Radar Detector; patents pending for Design Concept for a Hybrid Array; invention of Design Concept for a Reconfigurable Phased Array; Novel Guidance Technique Using Multiple

Aperture Derived Delta Signal. Avocations: figure skating, pottery, kayaking. Home: 391 Deaton Rd Laceys Spring AL 35754 Office Phone: 256-876-1426. Business E-Mail: janice.rock@us.army.mil

**ROCK, JOHN AUBREY,** gynecologist, obstetrician, educator, healthcare administrator, retired chancellor; b. Corpus Christi, Tex., Oct. 21, 1946; s. William A. and Burta (Wheeler) R.; children: John Aubrey Jr., Deborah Ellen, Daniel Authur; m. Martha Miller. BS in Zoology, La. State U., Baton Rouge, 1968; MD, La. State U., New Orleans, 1972; MS in Healthcare Mgmt., Harvard U., 2003. From asst. prof. to prof. ob-gyn. Sch. Medicine Johns Hopkins U., Balt., 1978-80, prof. pediatrics Sch. Medicine, 1988-92, dir. reproductive endocrinology Sch. Medicine, 1979-91, dep. dir. Sch. Medicine, 1985-88; chmn. Union Meml. Hosp., Balt., 1991-92; James Robert McCord prof., chmn. dept. ob-gyn. Emory U. Sch. Medicine, Atlanta, 1992—2002; chancellor La. State U. Health Scis. Ctr., New Orleans, 2002—06, chancellor emeritus, prof. ob-gyn., pediat. and pub. health, 2002—. Cons. Dept. Army, Washington, 1982-93, NASA, Houston, 1988—; chmn. ad hoc com. on in vitro fertilization State of Md., 1985. Author: Reparative and Constructive Surgery of the Female Generative Tract, 1983, Endometriosis, 1988, TeLinde's Operative Gynecology, 1991, 9th edit., 2003, Reproductive Endocrinology, Surgery and Technology, 1995; mem. editl. bd. Fertility and Sterility jour., 1986-94, Gynecology Surgery, 1989—. Fellow ACOG; mem. Am. Gynecol. and Obstet. Soc., Soc. Gynecol. Surgeons (pres. 1998-99), Am. Soc. for Reproductive Medicine (pres. 1996-97), Soc. Gynecologic Investigation, Soc. Reproductive Surgeons (pres. 1986), World Endometriosis Soc. (pres. 2000-02), Rotary, Phi Kappa Phi, Alpha Omega Alpha. Methodist. Office: La State U Health Scis Ctr 433 Bolivar St New Orleans LA 70112 Office Phone: 504-568-4800.

**ROCK, MARY ANN,** artist, educator; b. St. Louis, Mar. 2, 1931; d. Clobert Bernard and Mary Henrietta (Jones) Broussard; m. William Ralph Rock, Mar. 18, 1960 (div. Sept. 1967); 1 child, John Henry C. BS, Bennett Coll., 1952; postgrad., Chgo. Art Inst., 1953—54, So. Ill. U., Carbondale, 1955. Instr. arts and crafts Presidio Hill Sch., San Francisco, 1966; dir. gallery Cannery House Gallery, Friday Harbor, Wash., 1974—76; co-founder Island Artisans, Friday Harbor, 1980—85; gallery asst. Waterworks Gallery, Friday Harbor, 1986—95; with European study tour, 1996; patron sponsored painting sabbatical, 2001—03; prin. owner Dream Keeper Art Card Co., 2002—. Guest instr. Spring St Sch., Friday Harbor, 2001, Friday Harbor, 02; presenter art workshops Friday Harbor Elem. Sch., 1976, 87, Portland CC, 1989, 90. Author, illustrator: DreamKeeper, 1995; brochures, one-woman shows include Trofes Gallery, Seattle, 2006, exhibitions include 13th Saloon Internat. del Alpha, Lyon, France, Waterworks Gallery, Friday Harbor, 1986—, 7th Whatcomb County Mus., Bellingham, 1988, Portland CC, 1990, Chetwynn Stapleton Gallery, Portland, 1989—98. Curator African art exhibit NAACP, San Francisco, 1961. Vt. Studio Ctr. fellow, Johnson, 1999. Democrat. Avocations: collecting ethnic artifacts, skiing, rock climbing, travel, reading.

**ROCKABOVE, MAGDALENE M.,** special education educator; d. Walter M. Stewart Sr. and Meto M. Stewart; married; 3 children. AA, Mont. State U., 1996, BS in Elem. Edn., 1997, M in Spl. Edn., 2001. Clk. Indian Health Sci., Billings, Mont., 1999—2000, stats. asst., 2000—01; spl. edn. tchr. Lodge Grass (Mont.) H.S., 2001—05. Mentor Mont. Youth Leadership, Dillon, 2004—; mem. World Vision, 2000—. Recipient Partnerships for Diversity award, U. Mont., 2004—05. Democrat. Avocations: jogging, reading, singing. Home: PO Box 176 Pryor MT 59066 Office: Lodge Grass High Sch PO Box 810 Lodge Grass MT 59050

**ROCKAS, ANASTASIA T.,** lawyer; b. Rochester, N.Y., 1963; BA, Smith-Coll., 1985; JD with hons., U. Conn., 1990. Bar: Conn. 1990, N.Y. 1993. Atty. Skadden, Arps, Slate, Meagher & Flom LLP, N.Y., 1992, ptnr. Office: Skadden Arps Slate Meagher & Flom LLP Four Times Sq New York NY 10036

**ROCKBURNE, DOROTHEA GRACE,** artist; b. Montreal; naturalized; Student, Black Mountain Coll.; PhD (hon.), Coll. of Creative Studies, Detroit, 2002. Milton and Sally Avery Disting. prof. Bard Coll., 1986. Trustee Ind. Curators Inc., N.Y., Art in Gen.; artist in residence Am. Acad. in Rome, 1991; vis. artist Skowhegan Sch. Painting and Sculpture, 1984; Rockefeller Found. resident Bellagio (Italy) Conf. and Study Ctr., 1997. One-woman shows at Sonnabend Gallery, Paris, 1971, New Gallery, Cleve., 1972, Bykert Gallery, NYC, 1970, 72-73, Galleria Toselli, Milan, Italy, 1972-74, Galleria D'Arte, Bari, Italy, 1972, Lisson Gallery, London, 1973, Daniel Weinberg Gallery, San Francisco, 1973, Galerie Charles Kriwin, Brussels, 1975, Galleria Schema, Florence, Italy, 1973, 75, 92, John Weber Gallery, NYC, 1976, 78, Galleria la Polena, Geona, Italy, 1977, Tex. Gallery, Houston, 1979-81, Xavier Fourcade Gallery, NYC, 1981-83, 85-86, David Bellman, Toronto, 1980-81, Margo Leavin, Calif., 1982, Arts Club Chgo., 1987, André Emmerich Gallery, NYC, 1988-89, 91-92, 94-95, Rose Art Mus., 1989, P. Fong & Spratt Galleries, San Jose, Calif., 1991, Sony Music Hdqs., NYC, 1993, Frederick Spratt Gallery, San Jose, 1994, Guild Hall Mus., Easthampton, N.Y., 1995, Portland Mus. Art, Maine, 1996, Ingrid Raab Gall., Berlin, 1997, Art in Gen., NY, 1999, Greenberg, Van Doren, NYC, 2000, Dieu Donne Papermill, NYC, 2003, Jan Abrams Fine Art, NY, 2003; group exhbns. at Leo Castelli Gallery, NYC, 1966, Whitney Mus. Am. Art, 1970, 73, 77, 79, 82, 05, Mus. Modern Art, NYC, 71, 73, 81, 84, 86, 91, 93-94, 05, Buenos Aires, 1971, Kolner Kunst Market, Cologne, Germany, 1971, Stedelijk Mus., Holland, 1971, Spoleto (Italy) Festival, 1972, Palazzo Taverna, Rome, 1973, Nat. Gallery Victoria, Melbourne, Australia, 1973, Art Gallery NSW, Sydney, 1973, Auckland (New Zealand) City Art Gallery, 1973, Inst. Contemporary Art, London, 1974, Mus. d'Arte de la Ville, Paris, 1975, Galerie Aronowitsch, Stockholm, 1975, Stadtiches Mus., Manchengladbach, Germany, 1975, Galleria D'Arte Moderna, Bologna, Italy, 1975, Art Gallery Ont., Toronto, Can., 1975, Mus. Fine Art, Houston, 1975, Contemporary Arts Ctr., Cin., 1973, 75, 81, Mus. Contemporary Art, Chgo., 1971, 77, 86, Corcoran Gallery of Art, Washington, 1975, 87, Städtisches Mus., Leverkusen, Germany, 1975, Cannaviella Studio d'Arte Rome, 1976, Phila. Coll. Art, 1976, 83, New Mus., NYC, 1977, 80, 84, 83, Renaissance Soc. of U. Chgo., 1976, Lowe Art Mus., U. Miami, Fla., 1976, Inst. Contemporary Art, Boston, 1976, Seibu Mus. Art, Tokyo, 1976, NY State Mus., Albany, 1977, Drawing Ctr., 1977, Kansas City (Mo.) Art Inst., 1977, Smithsonian Inst., Washington, 1977, Kassel, Fed. Republic Germany, 1972, 77, Ackland Art Ctr., Chapel Hill, NC, 1979, 84, Milw. Art Ctr., 1978, 81, Biblioteca Nacional, Madrid, 1980, Gulbenkian Mus., Lisbon, Portugal, 1980, Bklyn. Mus., 1981, 89, Guggenheim Mus., 1982, 88-89, 2004, Albright Knox Art Gallery, Buffalo, 1979-80, 88-89, Kuustforeningen Mus., Copenhagen, 1980, Venice Biennale, 1980, Cranbrook (Mich.) Acad. Art, 1981, Mus. Fine Arts, Boston, 1983, Contemporary Arts Mus., Houston, 1983, Norman Mackenzie Art Gallery, U. Regina, Sask., Can., 1983, Galleriet, Sweden, 1983-84, Seattle Art Mus., 1979-84, Nat. Mus. Art., Osaka, Japan, 1984, Fogg Art Mus., Cambridge, Mass., 1984, Am. Acad. and Inst. Arts and Letters, NYC, 1984, 87, LA County Mus. Art, 1984, 86, Wadsworth Atheneum, Hartford, Conn., 1981, 84, Everhart Mus., Pa., 1984, Grey Art Gallery, NYU, 1977, 84, 87, Avery Ctr. Arts, Bard Coll., N.Y., 1985, 87-88, Stamford (Conn.) Mus., 1985, Aldrich Mus., Conn., 1979, 82, 95, Bronx Mus. Arts, N.Y.C., 1985, High Mus., Atlanta, 1975, 81, Phila. Mus. Art, 1986, Nat. Gallery Art, Washington, 1984, 94, 97, Mus. Art, Ft. Lauderdale, Fla., 1986, Nat. Mus. Women in Art, Washington, 1987, Xavier Fourcade Gallery, 1982, 83, 86-87, LA County Mus. Modern Art, 1986-87, The Hague, The Netherlands, 1986, Carnegie-Mellon Art Gallery, Pitts., 1979, 87, Balt. Mus. Art, 1975-76, 88, Ctr. for Fine Arts, Miami, 1989, Milw. Art Mus., 1989, Cin. Art Mus., 1989, New Orleans Mus., 1989, Denver Art Mus., 1989, Parrish Art Mus., South Hampton, NY, 1990-91, 99, Margo Leavin Gallery, LA. 1991, Guild Hall Mus., East Hampton, NY, 1991, Am. Acad., Rome, 1991, Mus. Contemporary Art, LA, 1991, 99, Hunter Coll., NY, 1991, CentroCultural/Arte Contemporanea, MexicoCity, 1991, Hilton, San Jose. Calif.,1992, Hillwood Art Mus., L.I., NY, 1992, Am. Acad. and Inst. Arts and Letters, 1992, Neuberger Mus., 1992, 00, Kohn-Abrams Gallerie, LA, 1993, Gallery at Bristol Myers Squibb, NJ, 1993-94, Friends of Art and Preservation in Embassies, NYC, 1993, Andre Emmerich Gallery, NYC, 1993, Fred Spratt Gallery, San Jose, Calif., 1994, Raab Galarie, Berlin, 1994,

NY Studio Sch., NYC, 1995, 02, Rose Art Mus., Brandeis U., 1996, Addison Gallery Am. Art, Andover, Mass., 1997, 04, Fine Arts Mus. San Francisco, 1997, Wexner Ctr., Columbus, 1997, Dieu Donne Papermill, Inc., NYC, 1998, Pub. Sch. 1, Long Island City, NYC, 1999, Gemini G.E.L., 1998, Am. Acad. Arts and Letters, 1999, 01, Parsons Sch. Design, NYC, 1999, David Dorsky Gallery, NY, 2000, Greenberg, Van Doren Fine Art, NYC, 2000, 02, 04, NAD, NYC, 2002, Armory Show, NYC, 2002, Nat. Gallery of Art, 2001, Krannert Art Mus., 2002, Selby Gallery, Fla., 2002, Geffen Contemporary, LA, 2002, Marcus Ritter, NYC, 2002, Bowdoin Coll. Mus. Art, 2002, Reina Sophia Mus., Madrid, 2003, Cleve. Mus. Art, 2003, New Britain (Conn.) Mus. Am. Art, 2003, Mus. New Zealand, 2003, Guggenheim Mus., NYC, 2004, ACA Galleries, NYC, 2004, Bruce Mus., Greenwich, Conn., 2004, MOCA at Calif. Plz., LA, 2004, Boca Raton Mus. Art, 2005, Betty Cunningham Gallery, 2005, Spanierman Gallery, East Hampton, NY, 2005, Black Mtn. Coll. Mus., Asheville, NC, 2005, Mus. Modern Art, NYC, 2006, Nat. Acad. Design, NYC, 2006, Yellow Bird Gallery, Newburgh, NY, 2005, Pa. Acad. Fine Arts, Phila., 2006, Cleve. Mus. Art, 2006, Weatherspoon Mus., Greensboro, NC, 2006, others; print exhbns. at Nat. Gallery, Washington, 1994, 97, 2001, Kate Ganz, Ltd., NYC, 2000, David Adamson Gallery, Washington, 2000, Fine Arts Mus. San Francisco, 1997, Bklyn. Mus., 1989, Mt. Holyoke Coll. Art Mus., 1987, Harcus Gallery, Boston, 1985, Xavier Fourcade Gallery, NYC, 1982, Mus. Modern Art, NYC, 1981, 91, Yale U. Art Gallery, New Haven, 1981, New Gallery Contemporary Art, Cleve., 1978, Art Gallery Ont., Toronto, 1978, Stadtiches Mus., Monchengladbach, Germany, 1971, Mus. New Zealand Te Papa Tongarewa, Wellington, 2003, Ralls Collection, Washington, 2004, Addison Gallery Am. Art, Mass., 2004, Mus. Fine Arts, Boston, 2003, 04, 05; represented in permanent collections Milw. Art Ctr., Mus. Modern Art NYC, Fogg Mus., Cambridge, Mass., Phila. Mus. Art, High Mus. Art, Atlanta, Houston Mus. Fine Arts, Corcoran Gallery, Washington, Mpls. Art Inst., Mpls. Art Mus., Met. Mus. Art, NYC, Guggenheim Mus., NYC, Nat. Acad. Design, NYC, J. Paul Getty Trust, LA, Ludwig Mus., Aachen, Fed. Republic Germany, Holladay, Washington, Saatchi, London, Bard, Albright-Knox Art Gallery, Buffalo, Whitney Mus. Am. Art, NYC, U. Mich., Ann Arbor, Ohio State U., Columbus, Gilman Paper Co., NY, Auckland (New Zealand) City Art Mus., Portland (Oreg.) Art Mus., Aaken Art Mus., Oberlin, Ohio, Highhold Internat., South Africa, U. Ohio Art Gallery, Columbus, HHK Charitable Found., Milw., Art Gallery Ont., Nat. Mus. Women in Art, Washington, Chase Manhattan Bank, NYC; installations: Hilton Hotel, San Jose, Calif., Sony Music Hdqrs., Aldridge Mus., Conn., Edward T. Gignoux Courthouse, Portland, Maine. Recipient Witowsky prize, Art Inst., Chgo., 1976, Creative Arts award, Brandeis U., 1985, Bard Coll. 1986, Alliance for Young Artists and Writers Inc. award, 1997, Jimmy Ernst Lifetime Achievement award in art, Am. Acad. Arts and Letters, 1999, Pike award, Nat. Acad. of Art and Design, 2002, Adolph and Clara Obrig prize, Nat. Acad. Design, 2002, Pollock Krasner award, 2002, 2004, Omi Internat. Francis J. Greenberger award, 2003; fellow, Guggenheim fellow, 1972; grantee, Nat. Endowment Arts, 1974, Am. Acad. Rome, 1991. Mem.: AAAL. Personal E-mail: drockburne@gmail.com.

**ROCKEFELLER, DAVID,** banker; b. NYC, June 12, 1915; s. John Davison Jr. and Abby Greene (Aldrich) R.; m. Margaret McGrath, Sept. 7, 1940 (dec. Mar. 1996); children: David, Abby A., Neva, Margaret D., Richard G., Eileen M. BS, Harvard Coll., 1936; student, London Sch. Econs.: PhD, U. Chgo., 1940; LLD (hon.), Columbia U., 1954, Bowdoin Coll., 1958, Jewish Theol. Sem., 1958, Williams Coll., 1966, Wagner Coll., 1967, Harvard U., 1969, Pace Coll., 1970. St. John's U., 1971, Middlebury, 1974, U. Liberia, 1979, Rockefeller U., 1980, Am. U., 1987, U. Miami, 1988; DEng (hon.), Colo. Sch. Mines, 1974, U. Notre Dame, 1987. Sec. to Mayor Fiorello H. La Guardia, 1940-41; asst. regional dir. Office Def., Health and Welfare Services, 1941-42; asst. mgr. for. dept. Chase Nat. Bank, N.Y.C., 1946-47, asst. cashier, 1947-48, 2d v.p., 1948-49, v.p., 1949-51, sr. v.p., 1951-55; exec. v.p. Chase Manhattan Bank (Chase Nat. Bank merged with Bank of Manhattan), 1955-57; vice chmn. bd. Chase Manhattan Bank, 1957-61, pres., chmn. exec. com., 1961-69, chmn., 1969-81, CEO, 1969-80. Chmn. Chase Internat. Adv. Com., 1981-99, Rockefeller Group, Inc., 1981-95, N.Y. Clearing House, 1971-78, Ctr. for Intern-Am. Rels., 1966-70, Overseas Devel. Coun., U.S.-USSR Trade and Econ. Coun. Inc.; chmn. Internat. Exec. Svc. Corps., 1964-68; chmn. Rockefeller Ctr. Properties Trust, Inc., 1996-2000 Author: Unused Resources and Economic Waste, 1940, Creative Management in Banking, 1964. Active Urban Devel. Corp., N.Y. State Bus. Adv. Coun., 1968-72, U.S. Adv. Com. on Reform on Internat. Monetary System, 1973-77, U.S. exec. com. Dartmouth Conf. Bd. Inst. Internat. Econs., Am. Friends of LSE, U.S. Hon. Fellows LSE, Bus. Com. for Arts; founding mem. Commn. on White House Fellows, hon. mem., 1964-65; exec. com., chmn. Downtown Lower Manhattan Assn., 1958-75; trustee Rockefeller U., 1940-95, Carnegie Endowment Internat. Peace, Hist. Hudson Valley, 1981-95; chmn. Rockefeller Bros. Fund, 1981-87, vice-chmn., 1968-80; hon. trustee Rockefeller Family Fund; life trustee U. Chgo.; trustee, chmn. emeritus, Mus. Modern Art, N.Y.C.; bd. overseers Harvard Coll., 1954-60, 62-68; co-founder Trilateral Commn., 1973-91, N.Am. chmn. 1981-92, hon. chmn., 1992; hon. chmn. Internat. House, 1940—, dir., 1940-63; pres. Morningside Heights, Inc., 1947-57, chmn., 1957-65; chmn. Am. Soc., 1981-92, hon. chmn., 1992—; N.Y.C. Partnership, 1979-88. Capt. AUS, 1942-45, NATOUSA, ETO. Decorated Legion of Honor France, Order of Arts and Letters; Order of the Liberator San Martin, Argentina, Order of Valor, Rep. of Cameroun, Order of Boyaca, Colombia, Order of Christopher Columbus, Dominican Republica, Nat. Order of Merit, Ecuador, Knight Comdr.'s Cross of the Order of Merit, Germany, Order of the Republic, Guinea, Gwengha Medal of the Rep. of Korea, Order of the Aztec Eagle, Mexico, Order of the Throne, Morocco, Hilal-i'Quaid-e-Azam, Pakistan, Order of Vasco Nunez de Balboa, Panama, Order of Manuel Amador Guerrero, Panama, Nat. Order of Merit/Grand Cross, Paraguay, Order of Merit, Italy, Order of Southern Cross, Brazil, Order of the White Elephant and Order of Crown, Thailand, Order of the Cedars, Lebanon, Order of the Sun, Peru, Nicholas Copernicus award, Porland, Order of Prince Henry the Navigator, Portugal, Nat. Order of the Lion, Rep. of Senegal, Order of Francisco de Miranda, Venezuela, Order of the Humane African Redemption, Liberia, Order of the Crown, Belgium, Nat. Order of Ivory Coast, Grand Cordon Order of Sacred Treasure, Japan, Order Bernardo O'Higgins, Chile, others; recipient Merit award N.Y. chpt. AIA, 1965, Gold medal Nat. Inst. Social Scis., 1967, AIA medal of Honor for City Planning N.Y.C., 1968, Charles Evans Hughes award NCCJ, 1974, World Brotherhood award Jewish Theol. Sem, 1953, C. Walter Nichols award NYU, 1970, Regional Planning Assn. award, 1971; Hadrian award, World Monuments Fund, 1994, U.S. Presdl. Medal of Freedom, 1998; named one of Top 200 Collectors, ARTnews Mag., 2004, Forbes' Richest Americans, 2006. Mem. Council Fgn. Relations (dir. 1949-51, v.p. 1951-70, chmn. 1970-85), Japan Soc. (hon. chmn.), Internat. House (hon. chmn.), Bilderberg Conf., Harvard Club, Univ. Club, Century Club, The Links, The Knickerbocker. Avocations: sailing, collecting 19th-century Am. art, impressionism and American art, porcelain. Address: 30 Rockefeller Plz Rm 5600 New York NY 10112-0002

**ROCKEFELLER, EDWIN SHAFFER,** lawyer; b. Sept. 10, 1927; s. Edwin and Nancy Rhea (McCullough) R.; m. Marilie Gould Wallace, Dec. 22, 1952; children: Ben Wallace, Edwin Palmer. AB, Yale U., 1948, LLB, 1951; M in Internat. Pub. Policy, Johns Hopkins U., 1989. Bar: Conn. 1951, D.C. 1956, U.S. Supreme Ct. 1957. Atty. FTC, 1956—61, asst. to gen. counsel, 1958—59, exec. asst. to chmn., 1960—61; pvt. practice Washington, 1961; chmn. adv. bd. bna.antitrust rept., 1961—. Mem. USIA Inspection Team, Pakistan, 1971; adj. prof. Georgetown U. Law Ctr., Washington, 1987. Author: Antitrust Questions & Answers, 1974, Desk Book of FTC Practice & Procedure, 3d edit., 1979, Antitrust Counseling for the 1980s, 1983. Mem.: ABA (chmn. sect. antitrust law 1976—77, bd. of dels. 1979—82), Met. Club, Chevy Chase Club. Office: Ste 1024 2801 New Mexico Ave NW Washington DC 20007-3940

**ROCKEFELLER, JOHN DAVISON, IV, (JAY ROCKEFELLER),** senator, retired governor; b. NYC, June 18, 1937; s. John Davison III and Blanchette Ferry (Hooker) R.; m. Sharon Percy, Apr. 1, 1967; children: John, Valerie, Charles, Justin. Student, Japanese lang. Internat. Christian U., Tokyo, 1957-60; BA in Far Eastern Languages and History, Harvard U., 1961, MA,

1954—57; postgrad. in Chinese, Yale U. Inst. Far Eastern Langs., 1961-62. Apptd. mem. nat. adv. council Peace Corps, 1961, spl. asst. to dir. corps, 1962, ops. officer in charge work in Philippines, until 1963; desk officer for Indonesian affairs Bur. Far Eastern Affairs, U.S. State Dept., 1963; later asst. to asst. sec. state for Far Eastern affairs; cons. Pres.'s Commn. on Juvenile Delinquency and Youth Crime, 1964; field worker Action for Appalachian Youth program, from 1964; mem. W.Va. Ho. of Dels., 1966-68; sec. of state W.Va., 1968-72; pres. W.Va. Wesleyan Coll., Buckhannon, 1973-75; gov. State of W.Va., 1977—85; U.S. senator from W.Va., 1985—. Mem. com. commerce, sci. and transp. US Senate, com. fin., com. veterans affairs, joint com. taxation, vice chmn., select com. intelligence. Contbr. articles to mags. including N.Y. Times Sunday mag. Trustee U. Chgo., 1967—; chmn. White House Conf. Balanced Nat. Growth and Econ. Devel., 1978, Pres.'s Commn. on Coal, 1978-80, White House Adv. Com. on Coal, 1980 Named one of Top 200 Collectors, ARTnews Mag., 2004, 2005, 2006; recipient Excellence in Public Svc. award, Am. Acad. Pediatrics, 1990, Congressional Adv. of Yr. award, Child Welfare League of Am., 1997, Langer Chip award, Sci. Coalition, 1999, Award Excellence in Public Svc., Consortium Sch. Networking, 2002, Wellstone award, United Steelworkers of Am., 2003. Mem.: Nat. Gov. Assn. Democrat. Presbyn. Avocation: collecting 19th-century Am. art and Am. impressionism. Office: US Senate 531 Hart Senate Bldg Washington DC 20510-0001 also: District Office Ste 308 405 Capitol St Charleston WV 25301-1786 Office Phone: 202-224-6472, 304-347-5372. Office Fax: 202-224-7665, 202-228-4656, 304-347-5371. Business E-Mail: senator@rockefeller.senate.gov.*

**ROCKEFELLER, RICHARD GILDER,** medical association administrator; b. N.Y.C., Jan. 20, 1949; MD, Harvard U., 1979, EdM. Diplomate Am. Bd. Family Practice. Intern Highland Hosp.-U. Rochester, 1979—80, resident family practice, 1980—82; founder, pres. Health Commons Inst., Portland, Maine, 1992—; clin. instr. family medicine Maine Med. Ctr.-Mercy Hosp. Family Practice Residency Program. Chmn. adv. bd. Doctors Without Borders. Bd. dirs. Rockefeller U.; bd. trustees Rockefeller Family Fund, Rockefeller Bros. Fund; bd. dirs. Maine Summer Dramatic Inst. Office: Health Commons Inst PO Box 9715 135 Marginal Way #375 Portland ME 04104-5015

**ROCKEFELLER, SHARON PERCY,** broadcast executive; b. Oakland, Calif., Dec. 10, 1944; d. Charles H. and Jeanne (Dickerson) Percy; m. John D. (Jay) Rockefeller IV; children: John, Valerie, Charles, Justin. BA cum laude, Stanford U.; LLD (hon.), U. Charleston, 1977, Beloit Coll., 1978; LHD (hon.), West Liberty State Coll., 1980, Hamilton Coll., 1982, Wheeling Coll., 1984. Founder, chmn. Mountain Artisans, 1968—78; teacher's asst., Head Start Head Start program, Coal Branch Heights, W.Va.; chmn. Corp. Pub. Broadcasting, Washington, 1981—84; bd. dirs. Stas. WETA-TV-FM, Washington, 1987—89, pres., CEO, 1989—. Bd. dirs. Pub. Broadcasting Svc., W.Va. Edn. Broadcasting Authority, PepsiCo, Smithsonian Instn., Nat. Gallery of Art, Nat. Cathedral, Stanford Univ., Chgo. Univ., George Washington Univ., Phillips Collection, Colonial Williamsburg Found.; trustees coun. Nat. Gallery of Art. Mem.-at-large Dem. Nat. Conv., del., 1976, 1980, 1984; trustee Fed. City Coun.; bd. dirs. Rockefeller Bros. Fund; former mem. bd. dir. Sunrise Mus., W.Va.; bd. mem. Sotheby's, NYC, Mus. Modern Art, NYC, Colonial Williamsburg Found; former chmn. Va. Assn. Pub. TV Stas. Named Washingtonian of Yr., Washingtonian Mag., 1994; named one of Top 200 Collectors, ARTnews Mag., 2004, 2005, 2006; recipient Charles Frankel Prize, Nat. Endowment for the Humanities, 1994, Distinguished Broadcaster Award, 1994, Woman of Vision Award, Women in Film & Video, CINE Lifetime Achievement Award. Fellow: Am. Acad. Arts & Sciences, Smithsonian Am. Art Commn. (bd. mem.); mem.: Stanford-in-Washington Coun. (former chmn.). Avocation: collecting 19th-century Am. art and Am. impressionism. Office: Sta WETA-FM 2775 S Quincy St Arlington VA 22206-2236*

**ROCKENSIES, JOHN WILLIAM,** mechanical engineer; b. N.Y.C., May 30, 1932; s. John William and Wilma (Mercz) R.; m. Marion Pauline Peachman, Sept. 16, 1956; children: Kenneth John, Karen Martha Rockensies Steinbeck. B of Mech. Engring., CCNY, 1954, M of Mech. Engring., 1960; postgrad., Bklyn. Poly. Inst., 1955, Columbia U., 1956. Registered profl. engr., N.Y. Jet engine performance and compressor devel. Curtiss Wright Corp., Woodridge, NJ, 1954—56; product devel. engr. Sperry Gyroscope Corp., Lake Success, NY, 1956—60; sr. exptl. test engr. Pratt & Whitney Corp., East Hartford, Conn., 1960—62; project engr. Stratos Corp., Bayshore, NY, 1962; prin. propulsion engr. Republic Aviation Corp., Farmingdale, NY, 1963—64; power plant design engr., group and project leader, project engr. engr. specialist and mgr. Grumman Aerospace Corp., Bethpage, NY, 1964—95; ret., 1995; contract staff engr. Northrop-Grumman Corp., Bethpage, 1996—98. Mem. SAE E-32 Engine Condition Monitoring com., 1983; lt. comdr. Smithtown Bay Power Squadron, instr. navigation. Author tech. papers in field; co-author chpt. in book. Deacon, trustee, elder First Presbyn Ch. Smithtown; docent Cradle of Aviation Mus., Garden City, N.Y., 2002-. Recipient Apollo Achievement award NASA, Washington, 1970. Assoc. fellow AIAA (mem. air breathing propulsion tech. com. 1996—, mem. coun. L.I. sect. 2002—, Chmn.'s award 2003); mem. NSPE, ASME, U.S. Power Squadrons (sr. navigator). Avocations: sailing, boating, jogging, camping, travel, model aircraft. Home: 65 Parnell Dr Smithtown NY 11787-2428 Personal E-mail: jrock8@optonline.net.

**ROCKENSTEIN, WALTER HARRISON, II,** lawyer; s. Walter Harrison and Martha Lee (Morris) R.; m. Jodell Lynn Steinke, July 29, 1972; children: Martha Liv, Andrew Harrison. BA cum laude, Coll. of Wooster, 1965; LLB, Yale U., 1968. Bar: Minn. 1968, U.S. Dist. Ct. Minn. 1968, U.S. Ct. Appeals (8th crct.) 1977. Spl. asst. atty. gen., chief antitrust divsn. Office of Minn. Atty. Gen., 1970-72; assoc. Head & Truhn, 1972-73; alderman 11th ward Mpls. City Coun., 1974-83; assoc. Faegre & Benson, Mpls., 1984-85, ptnr., 1986—. Mem. Capital Long-Range Improvements Com., 1974-82, Gov.'s Econ. Roundtable, 1980-82, Hennepin County Waste Disposal & Energy Recovery Adv. Com., 1976-77; chmn. devel. strategies com. League of Minn. Cities, 1979-80, bd. dirs., 1980-83; Mpls. del. Metro. Aircraft Sound Abatement Coun., 1977-90, chmn., 1982-90; mem. aviation subcom. of transp. tech. adv. com. Metro. Coun., 1977-83; mem. airport noise adv. bd. Minn. Pollution Control Agy., bd. dirs. noise com., 1982-85, mem. tech. adv. com., 1990; adv. com. Nat. League of Cities, steering com. Environmental Quality, 1975-79, vice chmn., 1976, chmn., 1978, steering com. Energy, Environment and Natural Resources, 1980-83, Energy Task Force, 1977-79, Nat. Urban Policy Com., 1978; mem. Noise Task Force, Nat. League of Cities/Nat. Assn. of Counties, 1977-80; regional dir. Nat. Org. to Insure a Sound-Controlled Environment, 1976-90, v.p. legal affairs, 1983-90; cons. group nuclear waste mgt., U.S. Dept. Energy, 1978. Elder Westminster Presbyn. Ch., 1975-80, 95-2001, trustee, 1982-87, chair stewardship com., 1989, chair pastor nominating com., 1992-94, co-chair bldg. centennial com.; bd. dirs. Loring Nicollet-Bethlehem Cmty. Ctrs., Inc., 1984—, pres., 1988-92; bd. dirs. U. Minn. Underground Space Ctr. Adv. Bd., 1985-95, chair, 1988-95; bd. dirs. Minn. Ctr. for Book Arts, 1988-93; com. mem. Cub Scout pack 196, Diamond Lake Luth Ch., 1988-91, com. chair, 1990-91; alumni trustee, alumni bd. dirs. The Coll. of Wooster, 1990-96; com. mem. Boy Scout Troop 187, 1994-97; bd. dirs. Minn. Safety Coun., 1997-2002, v.p., 2001-2002, chair, 2003—. Recipient Cert. of Appreciation, Upper Midwest chpt. Acoustical Soc. Am., 1977, Resolution of Appreciation, City of Mpls., 1983, Citation of Honor, Hennepin County, 1983, Cert. of Recognition, League of Minn. Cities, 1983, Hope of Rotary award City of Lakes Rotary Club, 1989, WCCO Good Neighbor award, 1992. Mem. Minn. State Bar Assn. (coun. mem. environ. and natural resources law sect. 1997-98, 2000-2001), Hennepin County Bar Assn., Delta Sigma Rho-Tau Kappa Alpha, Phi Sigma Alpha. Republican. Presbyterian. Avocations: reading, backpacking, cross country skiing, woodworking. Office: Faegre & Benson LLP 2200 Wells Fargo Ctr 90 S 7th St Minneapolis MN 55402-3901 E-mail: wrockenstein@faegre.com.

**ROCKETT, D. JOE,** lawyer, director; b. Drumright, Okla., May 3, 1942; s. Gordon Richard and Hazel Peggy (Rigsby) R.; m. Mary Montgomery, Aug. 31, 1963; children: David Montgomery, Ann Morley. BA, U. Okla., 1964, JD, 1967. Bar: Okla. 1967, U.S. Dist. Ct. (we. dist.) Okla. 1968. Assoc. Kerr,

Davis, Irvine & Burbage, Oklahoma City, 1967-69, Andrews Davis Legg Bixler Milsten & Price, Oklahoma City, 1969—, mem., 1973—, also bd. dirs., pres., 1986-90, 96-00. Securities law advisor Oil Investment Inst., Washington, 1984-87. Bd. dirs. Myriad Gardens Found., Oklahoma City, 1987—, chmn., 1991-92. Mem. ABA (fed. regulation of securities and partnership coms. of bus. law sect. 1984), Okla. Bar Assn. (securities liaison com. 1983, chmn. bus. assocs. sect. 1985, securities adminstr.'s select com. 1986—). Avocations: sailing, fishing, skiing. Office: Andrews Davis 100 N Broadway Ste 3300 Oklahoma City OK 73102-8812 Office Phone: 405-272-9241. Business E-Mail: djrockett@andrewsdavis.com.

**ROCKHOLD, FRANK W.**, statistician, pharmaceutical executive; b. Chgo., Dec. 1, 1952; s. Wesley F. and Elizabeth A. Rockhold; m. Julie C. Callahan, Aug. 1, 1976; 1 child, Katherine. BA, U. Conn., Storrs Conn., 1974; MSc in Pub. Health, Johns Hopkins U., Balt., 1976; PhD, Va. Commonwealth U., Richmond, Va., 1978. Rsch. fellow Lilly Rsch. Labs, Indpls., 1979—87; sr. v.p. GlaxoSmithKline R&D, King of Prussia, Pa., 1987—; exec. dir. Merck Rsch. Labs., Blue Bell, Pa., 1994—97. Pres. bd. trustees St John's Presbyn. Ch., Devon, Pa., 2001—04. Fellow: Am. Statis. Assn. (life); mem.: WHO (mem. sci. adv. bd. 2005—), Soc. Clin. Trials (pres. 1986—87). Office: GlaxoSmithKline R&D 2301 Renaissance Blvd King Of Prussia PA 19087 Office Phone: 610-787-3890. Business E-Mail: frank.w.rockhold@gsk.com.

**ROCKLAND, LAWRENCE HOWARD**, psychiatrist, educator; b. N.Y.C., Apr. 13, 1932; s. Milton and Bess Sherry Rockland; m. Charlotte Francis Roberts, June 29, 1957; children: Nancy, Thomas, Peter. BS, Union Coll., 1952; MD, Albany Med. Ctr., 1956. Diplomate Am. Bd. Psychiatry and Neurology. Rsch. psychiatrist NIMH, Bethesda, Md., 1959—61; pvt. practice Scarsdale, Larchmont, NY, 1961—; instr. psychiatry Georgetown Med. Coll., Washington, 1961—63; asst. prof. psychiatry Albert Einstein Coll. Medicine, N.Y.C., 1967—76; assoc. prof. clin. psychiatry Cornell U. Med. Coll., N.Y.C., 1982—99; assoc. prof. psychiatry emeritus Weill/Cornell Med. Coll., N.Y.C., 1999—; assoc. prof. clin. psychiatry U. Mass. Med. Coll., Worcester, 1999—2002. Cons. Montgomery County Child Clinic, Rockville, Md., 1962—66, US Peace Corps, Washington, 1963—66, Carson Adult Family Clinic, Westfield, Mass., 1999—2002. Contbr. articles to profl. jours., chapters to books; author: Supportive Therapy, 1989, Supportive Therapy for Borderlines, 1992, La Terapia di Sostegno, 1994. Surgeon USPHS, 1959—2005. Fellow: Am. Psychoanalytic Assn. (exec. coun. 1976—79, 1985—2005), Am. Psychiat. Assn. (disting. life fellow); mem.: Group for Advancement Psychiatry, Sigma Xi, Phi Beta Kappa, Alpha Omega Alpha. Avocations: music, hiking, physical exercise, reading. Home and Office: 7 East Drive Larchmont NY 10538 Office Phone: 914-834-7601.

**ROCKLEN, KATHY HELLENBRAND**, lawyer; b. NYC, June 30, 1951; BA, Barnard Coll., N.Y.C., 1973; JD magna cum laude, New England Sch. Law, 1977. Bar: NY 1978, US Dist. Ct. (so. and ea. dists.) NY 1982, US Dist. Ct. (no. dist.) Calif. 1985. Interpretive counsel NY Stock Exchange, NYC; 1st v.p. E.F. Hutton & Co. Inc., NYC; v.p., gen. counsel, sec. S.G Warburg (USA) Inc., NYC; mem. Proskauer Rose LLP, NYC. Adj. prof. Fordham Sch. Law. Vice-chair, mem. exec. com. NY lawyers Pub. Interest; mem. exec. com. lawyers divsn Am. Friends Hebrew U.; mem. lawyers' divsn. exec. com. ADL; mem. adv. bd. NY Women's Bar Found. Mem. NY State Bar Assn., NY Women's Bar Assn., Assn. Bar City NY (v.p., chmn. exec. com., chmn. drugs law com., chmn. fed. legis. com., chmn. libr. com., securities law com., sec. 2d century com., sex law com., young lawyers' com., corp. law com.). Office: Proskauer Rose LLP 1585 Broadway New York NY 10036 Office Phone: 212-969-3755. E-mail: krocklen@proskauer.com.

**ROCKMORE, DANIEL NAHUM**, mathematician; b. Boston, Dec. 5, 1961; s. Ronald Marshall and Miriam (Miller) R. AB in Math. cum laude, Princeton U., 1984; MA in Math., Harvard U., 1986, PhD in Math., 1989. Rsch. scientist Thinking Machines Corp., 1986; asst. prof. math. Columbia U., N.Y.C., 1989—91; asst. prof., dept. math and computer sci. Dartmouth Coll., Hanover, NH, 1991—96, assoc. prof., dept. math and computer sci., 1996—2000, prof., dept. math., 1999—, vice chmn., dept. math., 1999—; also mem. faculty, Ctr. for Cognitive Neuroscience. Vis. scientist IBM, 1989, mem. Inst. for Advanced Study, 1995-96, 2002; external faculty, Santa Fe Inst., 2000-; bd. mem., Defense Sci. Study Group, Inst. Defense Analyses, 2000-2002; sci. adv. bd., Poindexter Sys.; adv. bd. InSite One; co-dir. fMRI Data Ctr., Dartmouth Coll., 1999-; sr. search chair, dept. math., 2003, search chair, dept. math., 2004, 2005; search chair, Bioinformatics, 2004; vis. positions: dept. math., Harvard U., 1992, dept. computer sci., U. Chgo., 1992, 1993, Nat. Ctr. for Atmospheric Rsch., 1997, 1998, 1999, NYU Courant Inst., 2000, 2001-02; spkr. in field. Author: Stalking the Reimann Hypothesis, 2005; editl. bd. mem. SIAM Review; editor: Spl. Issue on Computer Algebra and Signal Processing, Journal of Symbolic Computation; contbr. articles to profl. jours., documentaries. Fellow Fulbright, 1984, NSF, 1985-87, 1991-93, 1995-2000, IBM, 1988, Phi Beta Kappa; named Sigma XI, Disting. Lectr., 2005-07 Mem. Am. Math. Soc. Office: Math Dept Dartmouth Coll Hanover NH 03755 Office Phone: 603-646-3260. Office Fax: 603-646-1672. Business E-Mail: rockmore@cs.dartmouth.edu.

**ROCKOFF, HUGH TOUFF**, economist, educator; b. Dayton, Ohio, Feb. 8, 1945; s. Joseph Rockoff and Mildred Touff; m. Hope Cormani; children: Jessica, Steven. BA, Earlham Coll., 1967; PhD, U. of Chgo., 1971. Prof. of economics Rutgers U., New Brunswick, NJ, 1971—. Author: The Free Banking Era, 1975, Drastic Measures: A History of Wage and Price Controls, 1984, History of the American Economy, 2002. Mem.: Econ. History Assn. (v.p. 2002—03). Office: Rutgers University 75 Hamilton Street New Brunswick NJ 08901 Office Phone: 732-932-7857.

**ROCKOFF, MARK ALAN**, pediatric anesthesiologist; b. Jersey City, Apr. 11, 1948; s. Aaron and Rose Rockoff; m. Elizabeth Sceery, Aug. 6, 1978; children: Benjamin, Jillian, Michael. BS, MIT, 1969; MD, Johns Hopkins U., 1973. Diplomate Am. Bd. Pediatrics, Am. Bd. Anesthesiology. Pediatric intern and resident Mass. Gen. Hosp., Boston, 1973-75, anesthesia resident, 1975-77, assoc. dir. pediatric ICU, 1979-81; neuroanesthesia fellow U. Calif., San Diego, 1978-79; assoc. dir. ICU Children's Hosp., Boston, 1981-89, assoc. anesthesiologist-in-chief, 1988—; med. dir. operating rm., 1992-99; prof. anaesthesia Harvard Med. Sch., Boston, 1999—. Editor jours. Survey of Anesthesiology, 1984-94, Jour. Neurosurg. Anesthesiology, 1994-98. Fellow: Soc. Critical Care Medicine, Am. Acad. Pediats., Am. Soc. Anesthesiologists; mem.: Soc. Pediat. Anesthesia (pres. 1996—98), Am. Bd. Anesthesiology (dir. 2000—). Office: Children's Hosp 300 Longwood Ave Boston MA 02115-5737

**ROCKOFF, S. DAVID**, radiologist, physician, educator; b. Utica, N.Y., July 21, 1931; s. Samuel and Sarah (Rattinger) R.; m. Jacqueline Garsh; children— Lisa E., Todd E., Kevin D. AB, Syracuse U., 1951; MD, Albany Med. Coll., 1955; M.Sc. in Medicine, U. Pa., 1961. Diplomate: Am. Bd. Radiology. Intern U.S. Naval Hosp., Bethesda, Md., 1955-56; resident and fellow in radiology, USPHS trainee dept. radiology p. of U. Pa., Phila., 1958-61; staff radiologist NIH, Bethesda, Md., 1961-65; asst. prof. radiology Yale U. Sch. Medicine, New Haven, 1965-68, assoc. prof.; 1968; asst. attending radiologist Yale-New Haven Med. Center, 1965-68; assoc. prof. radiology Washington U. Sch. Medicine, St. Louis, 1968-71; asst. radiologist Barnes and Allied Hosps., St. Louis, 1969-71; cons. radiologist VA Hosp., St. Louis, 1969-71, Homer G. Phillips Hosp., St. Louis, 1968-71; prof. radiology George Washington U. Sch. Medicine, Washington, 1971—, chmn. dept. radiology, 1971-77, head pulmonary radiology, 1978—, interim chmn. dept. radiology, 1989-90, prof. emeritus radiology 1993—. Cons. NIH, 1972—; vis. prof. Hadassah U., Beersheba U., Rambam Hosp., Israel, 1977; cons. in radiology VA Hosp., Washington, 1972-77, U.S. Naval Med. Center, Bethesda, 1973-77; mem. diagnostic radiology adv. com. NIH, 1973-76; mem. Cancer Research Manpower Rev. Com., NIH, 1978 Editor-in-chief: Investigative Radiology, 1965-76; editor-in-chief emeritus, 1976—; editor Jour. Thoracic Imaging, 1985; reviewer Jour. Computed Tomography, 1997—; contbr. numerous articles to med. jours. Served with USN, 1955-58; Served with USPHS, 1961-63. Recipient numerous USPHS grants. Fellow Am. Coll.

Radiology (pres.-elect D.C. chpt. 1976), Am. Coll. Chest Physicians; mem. Am. Fedn. Clin. Research, D.C. Med. Soc. (mem. med.-legal com. 1975-78), AMA, Radiol. Soc. N.Am. (mem. roster of disting. sci. advisors Rsch. and Edn. Found. 1999), Assn. Univ. Radiologists, Soc. Thoracic Radiology (pres. 1983-84, exec. dir. 1984-87). Home: PO Box 675650 Rancho Santa Fe CA 92067-5650 E-mail: drockoff@cox.net.

**ROCKWELL, DAVID**, architectural firm executive; b. Chgo., 1956; Founder, CEO Rockwell Architecture, Planning & Design, P.C., N.Y., 1984—. Book about firm Pleasure: The Architecture Design of Rockwell Group, 2002. Chmn. bd. Design Industries Found. Fighting AIDS (DIFFA); bd. dir. The Public Theater, City Meals on Wheels. Named one of Magnificent Seven Gurus of Innovation, BusinessWeek, 2005; named to Hall of Fame, Interior Design Mag.; recipient Lifetime Achievement award, Interiors Mag., Presidential Design award for Grand Central Terminal Renovation. Projects include the new theatre for the Academy of Motion Picture Arts and Sciences in LA, renovation of Radio City Music Hall, interiors on the Disney Cruise ships, the Mohegan Sun Casino, the Cirque du Soleil theatre in Orlando, and the Loew's Theatre at E-Walk in Manhattan. Office: Rockwell Architecture Planning & Design PC 5 Union Sq W New York NY 10003 Office Phone: 212-463-0334. Office Fax: 212-463-0335.

**ROCKWELL, DON ARTHUR**, retired psychiatrist; b. Wheatland, Wyo, Apr. 24, 1938; s. Orson Arthur and Kathleen Emily Rockwell; m. Frances Pepitone-Arreola, Dec. 23, 1965; children: Grant, Chad. BA, Wash. U., 1959; MD, U. Okla., 1963; MA in Sociology, U. Calif., Berkeley, 1967. Diplomate Am. Bd. Psychiatry and Neurology. Intern in surgery San Francisco Gen. Hosp., 1963-64; resident in psychiatry Langley-Porter Neuropsychiatric Inst. U. Calif. Med. Ctr., San Francisco, 1964-67; instr. dept. psychiatry U. Calif. Sch. Medicine, Davis, 1969-70, asst. prof., 1970-74, assoc. prof., 1974-80, acting. assoc., dean curricular affairs, 1979-80, acting assoc. dean student affairs, 1980, assoc. dean student affairs, 1980-82, prof., 1980-84; career tchr. NIMH, 1970-72; assoc. psychiatrist Sacramento Med. Ctr.; med. dir. U. Calif. Med. Ctr., Davis, 1982-84; prof., vice chmn. dept. psychiatry and biobehavioral sci. UCLA, 1984-96; dir. UCLA Neuropsychiat. Hosp., 1984-95; chief profl. staff Neuropsychiat. Inst., UCLA, 1984-85, also dir. outpatient svc. Chmn. U. Calif. Hosp. Dir. Council, 1988-89; cons. Nat. Commn. on Marijuana, Washington, 1971-73; mem. Santa Barbara County Civil Grand Jury, 2001-02. Co-author: Psychiatric Disorders, 1982; contbr. chpts. to books; articles to profl. jour. Mem. bd. visitors U. Okla. Sch. Medicine; chmn. hosp. dirs. coun. U. Calif. Hosp.; mem. governing coun. AHA Psychiat. Hosp.; mem. County of Santa Barbara Civil Grand Jury, 2001—02; bd. dir. Bereavement Outreach, Sacramento, 1974—84, Suicide Prevention, Yolo County, 1969—84. Fellow APA (disting. life), Am. Coll. Psychiatrists, Am. Coll. Mental Health Adminstr.; mem. AMA (gov. coun. psych. hosp.), Am. Sociologic Assn., Calif. Med. Assn. (med. staff survey com.), Cen. Calif. Psychiat. Assn. (sec.-pres. 1977-78), U. Okla. Alumni Assn. (trustee 1981-86), Alpha Omega Alpha. Home: 2293 Ginger Hill Loop Lincoln CA 95648

**ROCKWELL, ELIZABETH GOODE**, dance company director, consultant, educator; b. Portland, Oreg., Sept. 10, 1920; d. Henry Walton and Elizabeth (Harmon) Goode; m. William Hearne Rockwell, Feb. 3, 1948; children: Enid, Karen, William. Ba, Mills Coll., 1941; MA, NYU, 1946. Instr. dance Monticello Jr. Coll., Alton, Ill., 1941-42; dir. masters program in dance Smith Coll., Northampton, Mass., 1946-48; 1st dir. dance dept. High Sch. of Performing Arts, N.Y.C., 1948-51, 53-54; dir. Elizabeth Rockwell Sch. Dance, Bedford, N.Y., 1956-86, Rondo Dance Theater Internat. Dance Touring Co., Bedford, 1971-93; tchr. continuing dance classes CCAE, 1994—; with Martha Graham, 1944-46; with Hanya Holm, 1946-48; with José Limon, 1949-52. Mem. adv. ednl. com. Calif. Ctr. for Arts, Escondido, Calif., 1993-95, dir. dance classes, 1994—; tchr. master class, choreographer Waitukubuli Dance Theater, Dominica, 1999; dir. prime dance performance Artists Coming of Age, U. San Diego, 1999. Choreographer (suite of dances) Jazz Suite, 1966, (50-minute dances) Catch the Wind, 1969, Genesis, 1972, (narrative modern ballet) The Executioner, 1974, Decathalon, 1982; dir. (subscription series) Dance-Art-Poetry-Jazz, 1978-79, (dance/music 1600-1900) Stages in Ages, 1981, (Am. dance revivals) Masterpieces of American Dance, 1982-84, Dances of the Decades, 1985-90, (revival & new choreography) Dances of Our Times, 1991; dir. dance workshops for Calif. Ctr. Arts, 1994, 95, 96; creator, founder performing group of older dancers Golden Connections Dance Ensemble of Women, CCAE, (touring San Diego area), 1996—. Bd. dirs. Coun. for Arts in Westchester, White Plains, N.Y., 1978-79, affiliate, 1978— Recipient Medal for Performance, Israeli Army, 1966, Award for Excellence in Arts Edn. Alumnae of High Sch. of Performing Arts, 1990, Tommy Dance award of distinction San Diego Area Dance Alliance, 1999; various grants N.Y. State Coun. on Arts, 1971-93, Coun. Arts in Westchester, 1973-92, dance touring program grant Nat. Endowment for Arts, 1975-79. Mem. Am. Dance Guild, Westchester Dance Coun. (program dir. 1965-69), Assn. Am. Dance Cos., San Diego Area Dance Alliance (bd. dirs. 1995—). Avocations: writing, swimming, touring, reading. Home: 205 Tampico Gln Escondido CA 92025-7359

**ROCKWELL, JOHN SARGENT**, dance critic, writer, former arts administrator; b. Washington, Sept. 16, 1940; s. Alvin John and Anna Sargent (Hayward) Rockwell; m. Linda Mevorach; 1 child, Sasha Eve. BA, Harvard U., 1962; postgrad., U. Munich, 1962-63; MA, U. Calif., Berkeley, 1964, PhD, 1972. Music and dance critic Oakland Tribune, Calif., 1969; asst. music and dance critic LA Times, 1970-72; freelance music critic NY Times, 1972-74, staff music critic, 1974-91, European cultural corr. and prin. classical recordings critic Paris, 1992-94, editor Arts & Leisure sect., 1998—2002, sr. cultural corr., 2002—05, chief dance critic, 2003—; dir. Lincoln Ctr. Festival Lincoln Ctr. Festival, NYC, 1994—98. Lectr. in field. Author: All American Music: Composition in the Late 20th Century, 1983, Sinatra: An American Classic, 1984, The Idiots, 2003, Outsider: John Rockwell on the Arts 1967-2006, 2006. Harvard-German Govt. fellow, 1962—63, Woodrow Wilson fellow, 1963—64. Mem.: Dance Critics Assn., Century Assn., Music Critics Assn., Phi Beta Kappa. Office: NY Times Dance Critic 229 W 43rd St New York NY 10036 Office Phone: 212-556-1418. Office Fax: 212-334-5073. Business E-Mail: rockwell@nytimes.com.

**ROCKWELL, THEODORE**, nuclear engineer; b. Chgo., June 26, 1922; s. Theodore G. and Paisley (Shane) R.; m. Mary Juanita Compton, Jan. 25, 1947; children: Robert C. (dec.), W. Teed, Lawrence E., Juanita C. BS in Engring, Princeton U., 1943, Chem.E. (MS), 1945; grad. courses, Oak Ridge, 1944-49; D.Sc. (hon.), Tri-State U., 1960. Registered profl. engr., D.C. 1964-1990. Process improvement engr. Manhattan Project, Oak Ridge, 1944-45; head shield engring. group Oak Ridge Nat. Lab., 1945-49; nuclear engr., naval reactors br. AEC, also nuclear propulsion divs. Navy Bur. Ships, 1949-55, tech. dir., 1955-64; founding officer, dir. MPR Assos., Inc., Washington, 1964—; research assos. Johns Hopkins U. Center Fgn. Policy Research, 1965-66. Chmn. Atomic Indsl. Forum Reactor Safety Task Force, 1966-72; mem. adv. group artificial heart program NIH, 1966; cons. to joint Congl. Com. on Atomic Energy, 1967; founding officer, dir. Radiation, Sci. & Health, Inc., 1996—. Author: The Rickover Effect; How One Man Made a Difference, 1992, Creating the New World, 2003 (First Place award nonfiction JADA Pub. Ann. Book Competition, 2005, Ind. Publishers award, 2005); co-author: Shippingport Pressurized Water Reactor, 1958, Arms Control Agreements/Designs Verification, 1968; co-founder Princeton Engr.; editor: Reactor Shield Design Manual, 1956; contbg. editor: New Realities, 1988—92; contbr. sci. articles to profl. pubs., non-tech. articles to nat. mags. Mem. adv. council dept. chem. engring. Princeton, 1966-72. Recipient Disting. Civilian Svc. medal USN, 1960, Disting. Svc. medal AEC, 1960, Lifetime Contbn. award Am. Nuclear Soc. (1st, now known as Rockwell award), 1986. Fellow Am. Nuclear Soc., Am. Soc. Psychical Rsch. (life); mem. AAAS (rep. of Parapsychol. Assn. to AAAS 1975-87), N.Y. Acad. Scis., Soc. for Sci. Exploration, U.S. Psychotronic Assn. (dir. 1988-91), Nat. Inst. for Discovery Sci. (sci. adv. bd. 1995—), Nat. Acad. Engring. (Sigma XI disting. lectr. 2003—), Authors Guild, Writers Ctr., Washington Ind. Writers,

Cosmos Club (Washington), Nat. Press Club. Presbyterian (elder). Achievements include patent applications for neutron-absorbing cermets and plastics; patents in field. Address: 3403 Woolsey Dr Chevy Chase MD 20815-3924 E-mail: tedrock@starpower.net.

**ROCKWELL, WINTHROP ADAMS**, lawyer; b. Pittsfield, Mass., May 7, 1948; s. Landon Gale Rockwell and Ruth (Adams) Lonsdale; m. Barbara Washburn Wood, June 20, 1970; children: Samuel Adams, Madeleine McCord. AB, Dartmouth Coll., 1970; JD, NYU, 1975. Bar: N.Y. 1975, US Dist. Ct. Minn. 1975. Asst. newsman fgn. desk N.Y. Times, N.Y.C., 1970-71; asst. to pres. Dartmouth Coll., Hanover, NH, 1971-72; assoc. Faegre & Benson, Mpls., 1975-79; assoc. chief counsel Pres.'s Commn. on Accident at Three Mile Island, Washington, 1979; assoc. Faegre & Benson, Mpls., 1979-82, ptnr., 1983—. Chmn. diversity com. Faegre & Benson, 1990—95, head gen. litig. group, 1995—2004, mem. mgmt. com., 2004—, head internat. ops., 2004—. Bd. dirs. v.p. Children's Theatre, Mpls., 1982-83; bd. dirs. Actors Theatre St. Paul, 1975-79, Trinity Films, Mpls., 1978-82, Minn. Ctr. for Book Arts, 1996-2003; adv. bd. U. Minn. Joint Degree Program in Law, Health and the Life Scis. Brit.-Am. Project fellow, 1987. Mem. ABA, Minn. Bar Assn., Hennepin County Bar Assn., Am. Agrl. Law Assn., Adirondack 46ers, Adirondack Mountain Club. Avocations: writing, tennis, mountain climbing, gardening. Home: 1901 Knox Ave S Minneapolis MN 55403-2840 Office: Faegre & Benson 2200 Wells Fargo Ctr 90 S 7th St Ste 2200 Minneapolis MN 55402-3901 Office Phone: 612-766-6901. E-mail: wrockwell@faegre.com.

**ROCKWOOD, FREDERICK WHITNEY**, insurance company executive; b. Salt Lake City, Dec. 18, 1947; s. Lewis Frederick and Muriel (Whitney) R.; m. Alyce Jolene Edmunds, Aug. 26, 1970; children: Justin, Melissa, Jennifer, Katherine, Elizabeth, David. Student, U. Utah, 1966-67, Columbia U., N.Y.C., 1970; AB in Anthropology, Stanford U., 1972; JD, Harvard U., 1975. Bar: Mass. Corp. strategy cons. Boston Cons., 1975-77; corp. strategy cons. Bain & Co., Boston, 1977; dir. corp. strategy Hillenbrand Industries, Inc., Batesville, Ind., 1977-78, sr. v.p., 1978-85; pres. The Forethought Group. Batesville, 1985—. Mem. adj. faculty U. Mich. Grad. Sch. Bus., 1980; pres., bd. dirs. Rockwood Furniture, Inc., Salt Lake City, 1985—; chmn. curriculum adv. coun. Ind. State Bd. Edn., 1987-92. Rep. Ch. of Jesus Christ of Latter-day Saints, Hong Kong, 1967-69; unit scouting coord. Dan Beard coun. Boy Scouts Am., Cin., 1982-91; bishop Ch. of Jesus Christ, Batesville, 1986-90. Mem. ABA, Fellow Life Mgmt. Inst. (chartered life underwriter 1990, chartered fin. cons. 1992), Am. Mgmt. Assn., Phi Beta Kappa. Republican. Avocations: philately, genealogy.

**ROCKWOOD, IRVING E., JR.**, publisher; b. Norwood, Mass., Dec. 13, 1944; s. Irving E. and Cassie A. (Richardson) R.; m. Nancy E. Wilcox, June 14, 1969; children: Catherine Anne, Margaret Elaine. BA in Polit. Sci., No. Ill. U., 1967, MA in Polit. Sci., 1969. Sales rep. Coll. Divsn. Houghton Mifflin Co., Geneva, Ill., 1970-72, maths. editor Coll. Divsn. Boston, 1972-74; editor, math. and econs. Coll. Divsn. D.C. Heath, Lexington, Mass., 1974-76; gen. editor U. Wis. Press, Madison, 1976-79; exec. editor Longman, Inc., N.Y.C., 1979-85; pres. Irving Rockwood & Assocs., Inc., Chappaqua, N.Y. 1985-89; pub. Dushkin Pub. Group, Guilford, Conn., 1989-95; editor and pub. Choice, Middletown, Conn., 1995—. Mem. rsch. libr. delegation Citizen Amb. Program People to People, S. Africa, 1997; chair N.Am. chpt. Assn. Learned and Profl. Soc. Pubs. Mem. Soc. for Scholarly Pub., ALA, Assn. Coll. and Rsch. Librs. Mem. Ch. of Christ. Avocations: reading, hiking, do-it-yourself projects, choral singing. Office: Choice 100 Riverview Ctr Ste 298 Middletown CT 06457-3401 Office Phone: 860-347-6933. Business E-Mail: irockwood@ala-choice.org.

**ROCKWOOD, MARCIA**, magazine editor; Exec. editor Reader's Digest, Pleasantville, N.Y. Office: Reader's Digest Reader's Digest Rd Pleasantville NY 10570-7000

**ROCQUE, VINCENT JOSEPH**, lawyer; b. Franklin, N.H., Nov. 27, 1945; s. Francis Albert and Mary Helen (O'Grady) R.; m. Emily Adams Arnold, May 31, 1969; children: Amanda Adams, Peter O'Connor, Caroline Quin. BA magna cum laude, Georgetown U., 1967; JD, Columbia U., N.Y.C., 1970. Bar: D.C. 1971, U.S. Supreme Ct., 1973. Assoc. Hogan & Hartson, Washington, 1970-73; counsel, spl. asst. to Commr. Barbara Franklin, U. S. Consumer Product Safety Commn., Washington, 1973-77; asst. dir. bur. trade regulation U.S. Dept. Commerce, Washington, 1977-80; ptnr. Sullivan & Worcester, Washington, 1980-90; pvt. practice law Washington, 1990—. V.p., co-pres. Janney Pub. Elem. Sch. PTA, Washington, 1982-84; vol. coord. homeless shelters Cath. Charities, Washington and Silver Spring, Md., 1984-90. Staff sgt. USAR, 1969-75. Mem. ABA (adminstrv. law and regulatory practice sect. and internat. law and practice sect.), D.C. Bar (internat. law sect. and adminstrv. law and agy. sect.), Mid-Atlantic Literary Edification Soc., Nat. Capital YMCA, Phi Beta Kappa. Catholic. Avocations: reading, travel, American Civil War history. Office: Ste 1000 1155 Connecticut Ave NW Washington DC 20036-4306

**RODAK, SHARON LORRAINE**, elementary school educator, researcher; b. San Francisco, July 20, 1962; d. James Langdon Rodak and Florence Nerona Hunt; 1 child, Samuel Joseph Oakes. AA, MiraCosta C.C., Oceanside, Calif., 1984; BA, San Diego State U., 1988; postgrad., Ind. U., 2002. Tchg. credential Calif., 1990, Ind., 1994, cert. ESL instr. Calif. Cmty. Colleges, MiraCosta C.C., 1989. ESL educator Mira Costa C.C., Oceanside, 1989—92; elem. educator Murrieta (Calif.) Valley Unified Sch. Dist., 1990—93, mid. sch. educator, 1993—95, Carlsbad (Calif.) Unified Sch. Dist., 1991—; ESL educator Vista (Calif.) Unified Sch. Dist., 1993—94; gifted and talented educator Met. Sch. Dist. Martinsville, Ind., 1997—99; tchr. educator assoc. instr. Ind. U. Sch. Edn., Bloomington, 1999—2001. Gifted and talented site coord. E. Hale Curran Elem. Sch., Murrieta, 1991—92; doctoral dissertation participant Ind. U. Sch. Edn., Bloomington, 2000—01; site coun. mem. Aviara Oaks Mid. Sch., Carlsbad, Calif., 2001—; presenter in field. MiraCosta Spartan scholar, MiraCosta C.C., 1980, Mildred R. Lowel scholar, Ind. U. Sch. Edn., 1999, 2000, 2001. Mem.: NEA, Calif. Tchrs.' Union, Nat. Art Edn. Assn., Am. Ednl. Rsch. Assn., Pi Lambda Theta. Democrat. Roman Catholic. Achievements include development of Vocational English As A Second Language Curriculum and Instruction; research in arts integration curriculum and instruction. Avocations: reading, exercise, art. Home: 1351 Enchante Way Oceanside CA 92056 Office: Carlsbad Unified Sch Dist 6225 El Camino Real Carlsbad CA 92008

**RODALE, ARDATH HARTER**, publishing executive; 5 children. B in art edn., Kutztown U., LLD (hon.), 1995. Chmn. Prevention Mag., Rodale Press, Inc., 1990—; owner, CEO Rodale Press Inc., Emmaus, Pa., 1990—2002. Chmn. emeritus on the bd. Rodale Inst. Author: Climbing Toward the Light, 1989, Gifts of the Spirit, 1997, Reflections: Finding, Love, Hope and Joy in Everyday Life, 2002. Office: Rodale Press Inc 33 E Minor St Emmaus PA 18098-0099

**RODAMAKER, MARTI TOMSON**, bank executive; m. Bill Rodamaker; children: Mackenzie, Meeghan. BA in Econs., U. No. Iowa; MBA in Fin., U. St. Thomas. Credit analyst Marquette Bank, Mpls., 1984—87; field examiner Norwest Bank, 1987—93; from mem. staff to pres. First Citizens Nat. Bank, Mason City, Iowa, 1993—2000, pres., 2000—. Mem. adv. coun. Fed. Res. Iowa. Chmn. Hosp. Found.; treas. campaign YMCA; bd. regents Luther Coll., 2003—. Named One of 25 Women to Watch, U.S. Banker Mag., 2003; mem. Iowa Ind. Bankers Assn. (pres. 2001), Mason City C. of C. (bd. dir.). Office: First Citizens National Bank 2601 Fourth St SW Mason City IA 50401-1708

**RODBELL, CLYDE ARMAND**, retired distribution executive; b. Atlanta, Aug. 16, 1927; s. Joseph Hirsch and Fannie (Turetzky) R.; m. Cecile Rosenson, Mar. 27, 1949 (div.); children: Marsha, Jeffrey, Keith, Kim; m. Robin Graham McKenzie Rodbell, Dec. 15, 1974; 1 child, Lindsey. BBA, Emory U., 1949. Chmn. Apex Supply Co. Inc., Atlanta, 1949—2002. Co-chmn. George Bush Presdl. Fund Raising, Ga., 1988-89; mem. State of

Ga. Electoral Coll., 1989, exec. commr. Am. Bicentenial Pres. Inaugural Bus. Adv., 1989, Pres' Commn. on White House Fellowships, 1989-92. With U.S. Army, 1945. Mem. Wholesale Assn. Ga., Southern Wholesalers Assn., Am. Supply Assn., Standard Club, Rotary Club. Republican. Jewish. Avocations: reading, gardening, antiques, politics. Personal E-mail: rrodbell@aol.com.

**RODDE, JAMES F.,** music educator; s. Frederick O. and Shirley Rodde; m. Kathleen M. Dooley, Nov. 10, 1960. DMA, U. Iowa, 1983. Dir. choral studies U. N.D., Grand Forks, 1985—2000; dir. choral activities Iowa State U., Ames. Artistic dir. Des Moines Choral Soc., 2003—. Musician: (conductor) ACDA Conv. (Performances, 2005). Mem.: ACDA (assoc.; divisional male choirs r&s chair 1996—2006). Office: Iowa State Univ Music Hall Ames IA 50011 Office Phone: 515-294-0395.

**RODDEY, CYNTHIA PLAIR,** education educator; b. Rock Hill, SC, Apr. 6, 1940; d. Isaiah Burris and Ruth Jordan Plair; m. James Eddie Roddey Sr., Dec. 23, 1961; children: James Eddie Jr., Thomas Grier, Oresa Denise. BA, Johnson C. Smith U., Charlotte, N.C., 1960; MA Tchg., Winthrop Coll., Rock Hill, S.C., 1967; DMin, Mid-Atlantic Theol. Sems., Richmond, Va., 2000. Libr. asst. Johnson C. Smith U., Charlotte, NC, 1960—61; tchr. York County Sch. Dist., Rock Hill, SC, 1961—62, tchr., asst. libr., 1963—64; dir. Carolina Cmty. Action, Rock Hill, 1968; media coord. Charl-Meck Bd. of Edn., Charlotte, NC, 1964—93; dir. info. Clinton Jr. Coll., Rock Hill, SC, 1994—; site coord. 21st Century Communities Sch., Chester, SC, 2004—05. Chmn. of bd. 1st Steps, Chester County, SC, 2004—06; cons. owner Christian Edn. Cons., Catawba, SC; owner Rock Hill House of Beauty, Inc., Rock Hill, SC, 1968—. Author: This Far For Faith, Teaching Dewey System Through Poetry. Musician OES, Edgemoor, SC; guardian ad litem State of SC, Chester County, SC. Recipient Edn. award, NAACP. Mem.: ILC Nat. Alumni Assn., Delta Sigma Theta Sorority (chpt. pres. 2004—06). Achievements include first Afro-Am. enrollee and graduate of Winthrop Coll. Avocations: music, creative writing, reading, travel, volunteerism. Home: 5079 Theodore Rd Catawba SC 29704-7724 Office: Clinton Jr Coll 1029 Crawford Rd Rock Hill SC 29703 Office Phone: 803-327-7402 X 228. Office Fax: 803-328-2086. Business E-Mail: fisherlibrary@clintonjuriorcollege.edu.

**RODDICK, ANDY,** professional tennis player; b. Omaha, Aug. 30, 1982; s. Jerry and Blanche Roddick. Turned pro, 2000—; winner jr. Grand Slam titles Australian Open and U.S. Open, 2000; quarter-finalist Roland Garros, 2000; singles titles, Atlanta, Houston, Washington U.S. Clay Court Championships, 2001, singles titles, Memphis, Houston, 2002; runner up U.S. Open, 2002; quarterfinalist Indian Wells TMS, 2003; semifinalist Paris TMS, Basel, Tennis Masters Cup, Wimbledon, Australian Open, Washington, 2003; finalist Houston, Memphis, 2003; winner Raiffeisen Internat. Grand Prix, 2003, Stella Artois Championships, 2003, RCA Championships, 2003, Montreal Masters, 2003, Cin. Masters, 2003, 2006; winner Grand Slam title U.S. Open, 2003. Mem. U.S. Olympic Tennis Team, Athens, 2004. Host: Saturday Night Live, 2003. Founder The Andy Roddick Found. Recipient Espy Award for Best Male Tennis Player, 2004. Achievements include finishing the year as the youngest player at 18 years, 3 months in the top 200 and as the No. 1 junior in the world, 2000. Avocations: movies, music, skydiving.*

**RODDICK, HAWLEY,** writer, editor, personal historian; d. Harrison Arnold and Mary Elizabeth (Henrici) R.; m. Karl W. Haffenreffer, Mar. 11, 1961 (div. 1965); m. Walter W. Meade, Nov. 2, 1967 (div. 1993); 1 child, Luke Harrison. BA, Wellesley Coll., 1958. Exec. dir. Boehm Biography Group, Inc., Santa Barbara, Calif., 2002—06. Cons., trainer, editor, writer, personal historian, Santa Barbara, 1968—. Author: (fiction) Together, 1979, Holding Pattern, 1981; (nonfiction) Young Filmmakers, 1969 (N.Y. Pub. Library prize 1969), Writing That Means Business, 1984, Everyone Can Write: Thinking Skills for Writing (Activities Kit for grades 4-8), 1987; contbr. articles to mags., profl. jours; design and presentation of writing workshops. Vol. various pro-environ. and anti-nuclear activities; founding mem. Seal Watch, New Mex. Green Party, People for Peace, PEN N.Mex. br.; mem. Santa Barbara chpt. Progressive Dems. Mem.: Progressive Democrats of Am. (founding mem., Santa Barbara chpt.), Authors Guild, PEN Internat. (founding mem. N.Mex. chpt. 1996—97), Wellesley Club. Office: Hawley Roddick PO Box 3794 Santa Barbara CA 93130 Office Phone: 877-377-8912. Personal E-mail: hroddick@hawleyroddick.com.

**RODECKER, STEPHEN BAILEY,** science specialist, secondary school educator; b. San Bernardino, Calif., July 10, 1953; s. Charles and Merilyn Rodecker; m. Jelen Gonzales, July 24, 1993. BA in German, San Diego State U., 1975, BA in Biology, 1977, MA in German, 1977, MS in Biology, 1987. Cert. tchr. Calif., 1978. Tchr. San Diego (Calif.) Office Edn., 1983—84; instr. Upward Bound San Diego (Calif.) State U., 1990; tchr. Sweetwater Union H.S. dist., Chula Vista, Calif., 1985—, specialist sci. curriculum, 1999—. Prin., owner Spectrum Pubs., Bonita, Calif., 1990—; bd. dirs. Greater San Diego (Calif.) Sci. and Engring. Fair; cons. in field. Author: Laboratory Experiments and Activity in Physical Science, 1995, Biological Experiments and Activities Integrating Math, 1999. Named Tchr. of Yr., Tandy Tech., 1995, Nat. Sci. Tchr. of Yr., Disney, 1995; grantee, Tapestry, 1995, Gen. Telephone and Electronics, 1996, Dept. of Def., 1996, Calif. Tchr. Appreciation and Advancement Program, 1996, 2000. Master: San Diego (Calif.) Sci. Educators Assn. (pres. 2005—); mem.: Calif. Sci. Tchrs. Assn. (bd. dirs. 1990—91). Avocations: tennis, gardening, collecting porcelain.

**RODEMEYER, MICHAEL LEONARD, JR.,** lawyer; b. Balt., May 25, 1950; s. Michael Leonard and Claire Isabel (Gunther) R.; m. Dorrit Carolyn Green, June 7, 1975; children: Justin, Christoffer. AB, Princeton U., 1972; JD, Harvard U., 1975. Bar: Md. 1977, D.C. 1980, U.S. Ct. Appeals (10th cir.) 1980. Atty. Fed. Trade Commn., Washington, 1976-78, atty. advisor, 1981-84; counsel Subcom. on Natural Resources, Agr. Rsch. & Environ., Washington, 1984-88; staff dir., counsel U.S. Ho. of Reps., Washington, 1988-90, house com. on sci., chief dem. counsel, 1990-98; asst. for environment White House Office of Sci. and Tech. Policy, Washington, 1998-99, dem. legis. dir., 1999-2000; exec. dir. Pew Initiative on Food and Biotech., Washington, 2000—. Democrat. Avocations: computing, bicycling. Home: 6000 Harvard Ave Glen Echo MD 20812-1114 Office: Pew Initiative on Food and Biotech 1331 H SI NW Ste 900 Washington DC 20005 Office Phone: 202-347-9044. Business E-Mail: mrodemeyer@pewagbiotech.org.

**RODEN, JON-PAUL,** retired educator, labor union organizer, educational consultant; b. Vernon, Conn., July 15, 1943; s. Paul James and Evelyn Mary Roden. BS, SUNY, Oswego, 1965; MS, Ctrl. Conn. State U., 1970. Cert. pioneer in professionalism Nat. Bd. Profl. Tchg. Stds., registered lobbyist Conn. Gen. Assembly, notary public Conn. Tchr. elem. sch. Vernon Pub. Schs., 1965—68, tchr. anatomy and physiology, 1969—79, tchr. computer sci., 1980—82, dist. chmn. computer sci., 1982—2000, presenter staff devel., 1986—; union organizer Conn. Edn. Assn., Hartford, 2000—02, state treas. ret. tchrs., 2002—. Tech. advisor Capitol Region Edn. Coun., 1981-85; presenter Inst. for Tchrs. and Learning, Conn. Dept. Edn., 1990-91, N.E. Holmes Group, Boston, 1994; mem. adv. com. Affiliate Newsletter Svc., 1992-2000; provider mgr. Conn. Dept. Edn., 1994-98; mem. Legis. Task Force on ednl. tech., 1995-97; mem. Legis. Task Force on tchrs. retirement health ins. sys., 2000-2001; mem. Conn. stakeholders com. Nat. Bd. Profl. Tchg. Stds, 1995, 2000; mem. educator preparation program rev. com. Conn. State Bd. Edn., 1996-99; mem. nat. parent-tchr. adv. coun. Am. Online; presenter Nat. Sch. Bd. Assn. Tech. Conf., 1995, 96, 97, 98; keynote spkr. Minn. High Success Consortium, 1997; mem. bd. examiners Nat. Coun. Accreditation Tchr. Edn.; mem. tech. adv. commn. Nat. Coun. State Edn. Affiliates, 1999-2001; presenter NEA, Chgo., 2000, L.A., 2001; mem. task force on Conn. low performing schs. Assoc. editor: Logo Activities, 1985; writer, editor numerous teaching guides. Pres. U. Conn. Friends of Soccer, 1987—89; corporator Newington (Conn.) Children's Hosp., 1978—98; celebrant Celebration of Excellence Conn. State Dept. Edn., 1991, 1995, 1999; mem. Vernon Rep. Town Com., 1978—98, Vernon Recreation Com., 1978—84, chmn., 1982—84; mem. Vernon Traffic Authority, 1988—94, vice chair, 1996—; spl. dep. sheriff Tolland County, Conn., 1977—82; bd. gov. Conn. Children's Hosp., 1995—; mem. adv. bd. Vernon

Law Enforcement Block Grant, 1997—2000; bd. dirs. Hockanum Valley Cmty. Coun., 2003—, exec. bd, 2004—, pres. bd. dirs., 2005—, Lakeview Condo Assn., Inc., 2005—. Recipient Ofcl. Citation of Recognition Conn. Gen. Assembly, 1991, 95, 96, Celebration of Excellence Emeritus award Conn. State Dept. Edn., 1999; nominated Disney Tchr. awards, 2000. Mem.: NEA (design com. 1995, conv. del. 1995, presenter 1995, tchr./cons. Washington 1995—, conv. del. 1996, panelist N.E. regional leaders conf. Phila. 1997, panelist N.E. regional leaders conf. Rochester 1999, presenter 2000), ASCD, Conn. Computer Educators, Conn. Edn. Assn. (editl. bd. 1991—), Nat. Coun. State Edn. Affiliates (tech. com. 1999), Shriners, Elks (exalted ruler 1969—70, dist. dep. grand exalted ruler 1973—74, named Elk of the Yr. 2003), Masons, Phi Delta Kappa (exec. bd. 1991—2005, chpt. pres. 1994—96, selection com. 1995, internat. doctoral dissertation com.). Roman Catholic. Avocations: racquetball, bicycling, skiing. Home: 105 Maple Ave Vernon Rockville CT 06066-5450

**RODENBERG, JOHANNA KRISTINE,** education educator, consultant; d. Edward Ellis and Francess Irene Rodenberg; m. Andrew Thomas Myers, Sept. 3, 1994; children: Justin Grant, Jeffrey Richard Myers, Jakob Edward Myers. AA in Fine Art, Mesa C.C., 1980; BA in Linguistics, San Diego State U., 1982; MA in Ednl. Psychology, U.S. Internat. U., San Diego, 1987; postgrad., U. San Diego/San Diego State U., 2000—. Cert. Nat. Bd. Profl. Tchg. Stds. English lang. tchr. EF Internat. Sch., San Diego, 1983—90; reading specialist San Diego Unified Sch. Dist., 1996—99, peer coach/staff developer 1999—2002, peer assistance and support consulting tchr., 2002—. Ednl. cons. Nat. Ctr. on Edn. and the Economy, Washington, 1999—2002; ind. ednl. cons., faculty devel., 2003—; faculty San Diego State U., 2000—; spkr., presenter in field. Rm. mom Holmes Elem. Sch., San Diego, 2003. Mem.: ASCD, Internat. TESOL, Nat. Coun. Tchrs. of English, Internat. Reading Assn. Avocations: cooking, reading, gardening. Office: San Diego Unified Schs/SDSU San Diego CA Office Phone: 858-496-1883. Personal E-mail: jkr1007@earthlink.net.

**RODENBERGER, CHARLES ALVARD,** aerospace engineer, consultant; b. Muskogee, Okla., Sept. 11, 1926; s. Darcy Owen and Kathryn Martha (Percival) R.; m. Molcie Lou Halsell, Sept. 3, 1949; children: Kathryn Sue Wilcox, Charles Mark. Student, U. Ark., 1944-45; BS in Gen. Engring., Okla. State U., 1948; MSM.E., So. Meth. U., 1959; PhD in Aero. Engring., U. Tex.-Austin, 1968. Registered profl. engr., Tex. Petroleum engr. Amoco Oil Co., Levelland, Tex., 1948-51; chief engr. McGregor Bros., Odessa, Tex., 1953; petroleum engr. Gen. Crude Oil Co., Hamlin, Tex., 1954; sr. design engr. Gen. Dynamics, Ft. Worth, 1954-60; aerospace engr. NASA, Houston, summer 1962; prof. aerospace engring. Tex. A&M U., College Station, 1960-82, prof. emeritus, 1982—; chmn. bd. Meiller Research, Inc., College Station, 1967-82; pres. JETS, Inc., N.Y.C., 1977-79; cons. Southwest Research Inst., Gen. Motors Corp., Gen. Dynamics. Patentee hypervelocity gun and orthotic device; newspaper columnist: Livestock Weekly, 1986—; mag. columnist, Santa Gertrudis, Tex., 2002. Served with USAAF, 1945; served with USAF, 1951-53. NSF fellow, 1964-65; recipient Distng. Teaching award Tex. A&M U., 1962 Fellow AIAA (assoc.); mem. ASME, NSPE (v.p. 1980-81), Tex. Soc. Profl. Engrs., Am. Soc. for Engring. Edn., Sigma Xi, Kiwanis Club (pres. Cross Plains chpt. 2002-03). Methodist. Home: 8377 FM 2228 Baird TX 79504-4813 Office Phone: 254-725-6816. E-mail: crodenberg@aol.com, car926@aol.com.

**RODENBURG, CLIFTON GLENN,** lawyer; b. Jamestown, ND, Apr. 5, 1949; s. Clarence and Dorothy Irene (Peterman) R.; m. Donna Michele Stockman, Mar. 1, 1980. BS, N.D. State U., 1971; JD, U. N.D., 1974; M.L.I.R., Mich. State U., 1976. Bar: N.D. 1974, U.S. Dist. Ct. N.D. 1974, U.S. Ct. Appeals (8th cir.) 1974, Minn. 1980, U.S. Supreme Ct. 1980. S.D. 1983, Nebr. 1984, U.S. Dist. Ct. Minn. 1984, U.S. Dist. Ct. Nebr. 1984, Wis. 1985, U.S. Dist. Ct. Wis. 1985, Mont. 1986, U.S. Dist. Ct. Mont. 1986, bd. cert. Creditors' Rights Law, Am. Bd. Cert. Four. Johnson, Rodenburg & Lauinger, Fargo, ND, 1976—; pres., gen. counsel Rodenburg Group, Inc., Fargo, 1980—. Contbg. editor: The Developing Labor Law, 1976-80; drafter N.D. garnishment statutes, 1982. Mem. Acad. Comml. and Bankruptcy Law Specialists.

**RODER, HANS MARTIN,** retired physicist, consultant; b. Schenectady, N.Y., June 30, 1930; s. Johann Nikolaus and Elsa Margarethe (von Kujawa) R.; m. Mary Margaret Ball, Aug. 4, 1951; children: Jenny Brooks, Nicholas, Renate Pearson. BA in Chemistry, U. Colo., 1955, postgrad. in chemistry and physics, 1955-60. Physicist divsn. cryogenics Nat. Inst. Stds. and Tech. (formerly Nat. Bur. Stds.), Boulder, Colo., 1955-66, leader data compilation group, 1966-73, physicist divsn. thermophysics, 1973-87. V.p., sec. Doggie Biscuits, Inc., Breckenridge, Colo., 1989—. Contbr. to books: Technology and Uses of Liquid Hydrogen, 1964, Transport Properties of Fluids, 1990; editor: The Nat. Ski Patrol Ski Mountaineering Man., 1980; contbr. over 75 articles to profl. jours. Patrol leader Nat. Ski Patrol, Loveland Basin, Colo., 1962-87, ski mountaineering advisor, Denver, 1978-85. 1st lt. AUS, 1952-54. Recipient Gold Medal award U.S. Dept. Commerce, 1966, Tech. and Utilization award NASA, 1967, 68, 70, 71; R.B. Scott Meml. award Cryogenic Engring. Conf., 1969. Avocations: skiing, hiking, mountain climbing. Home: PO Box 684 340 W Buffalo Dillon CO 80435

**RODERER, JOSHUA A.,** music educator; b. Dayton, Ohio, Mar. 25, 1975; s. Thomas A. and Patricia A. Roderer. MusB in Music Edn., Wright State U., 1998, MusM in Music Edn., 2005. Lic. music K-12 Ohio, 1999. Asst. band dir. Miami East (Ohio) H.S., 1994—96, Centerville (Ohio) H.S., 1996—99; dir. bands Colerain H.S., Cin., 1999—2002; grad. tchg. asst. Wright State U., Dayton, Ohio, 2003—05; music dir. Clifton Sch., Cin., 2005—. Adj. faculty instr. clarinet Stivers Sch. Arts, Dayton, Ohio, 2002—04; jazz ensemble dir. Cin. Youth Jazz Ensemble, 2002—05. Exec. dir. Tri State Youth Performing Arts Assn., Cin., 2002—05. Recipient Stouffer Leadership award, 1996; scholar, Wright State U., 2003—05. Mem.: Internat. Jazz Educators Assn., Internat. Clarinet Soc., Music Educators Nat., Ohio Music Edn. Assn. Home: 35 Bishopsgate Dr Apt 1111 Cincinnati OH 45246 Personal E-mail: joshroderer@aol.com.

**RODGERS, BERNARD FRANCIS, JR.,** literature and language professor; b. Hazleton, Pa., Mar. 21, 1947; s. Bernard F. and Mary W. (Gulla) R.; m. Patricia Hick, Dec. 9, 1969 (div. 1982); m. Jane Powell, Oct. 27, 1984 (dec. Sept. 2002). BS in English and Edn., Mt. St. Mary's Coll., 1969; MA in English, U. Bridgeport, 1972; PhD in English with honors, U. Chgo., 1975. Tchr. Eng., dir. drama Somers Ctrl. High Sch., Lincolndale, NY, 1969-72; instr., asst. prof. lit. and humanities City Colls. Chgo., 1975-82, spl. asst. to chancellor, 1984—85; faculty Eng. Simon's Rock Coll. of Bard, Great Barrington, Mass., 1985—, dean acad. affairs, 1985—87, v.p. and dean, 1987—2004, Emily H. Fisher prof. lit., 2004—. Chair lit. and humanities sect. coll. accreditaiton program Chgo. City-Wide Coll., 1977—78, chair coll. acceleration program, 1977—78, mem. adminstrv. coun., 1980—81; bd. overseers Simon's Rock Coll. of Bard, 1987—2004; mem. planning com. humanists Write On, Chgo., 1982—83; mem. nom. com. Eisenhower Fellowship Am. Embassy, Warsaw, 1980; mem. writing panel artists-in-residence program Chgo. Coun. Fine Arts, 1978; spkr. in field. Author: Philip Roth: A Bibliography, 1974, 2nd edit., 1984, Philip Roth, 1978, Contemporary American Fiction 1944-79: A Chronology, 1980, Voices and Visions: Selected Essays, 2001; essayist, reviewer in field; contbr. articles; assoc. prodr. TV talk show U. Chgo., 1975—76; prodr.: TV talk show U. Chgo., 1975—76; prodr., host interview program City Colls. Chgo., 1981—82. Bd. dirs. Fairview Hosp., Great Barrington, 1988-94, Mass. Found. for Humanities, chair, 1992-94, vice chair, 1991-92, chair program com., 1990-92, pres., 1992-94, Friends of Chgo. Pub. Libr., 1982; mem. South County cluster Berkshires United Way, 1988, mem. planning com. humanists Read Ill., 1984-85, ad hoc com. excellence Ill. C.C. Trustees Assn., 1984-85. U. Chgo. fellow, 1973, Ford Found. fellow, 1974-75, Fulbright-Hays sr. lectr. to Poland, 1979-80, Chgo. Pub. Libr. assoc. scholar, 1976-78. Mem. So. Berkshire C. of C. (bd. dirs. 1987-90), New Eng. Assn. Schs. and Colls. (evaluation team chair commn. instns. higher edn. 1986—), North Ctrl. Assn. Colls. and Schs. (asst. dir. commn. instns. higher edn 1982-84), Soc. Midland Authors (chair fiction

award com. 1985). Home: PO Box 778 Great Barrington MA 01230-0778 Office: Simon's Rock Coll of Bard 84 Alford Rd Great Barrington MA 01230-1559 Office Phone: 413-528-7496. Business E-Mail: brodgers@simons-rock.edu.

**RODGERS, BRUCE ALAN,** government agency administrator, psychologist; s. Bernice Junior and Louise Andreason Rodgers; m. Angela Lei Lani Wiseman; children: Diana Louise, Sarah Brooke, Daniel Alan, Hartley Elizabeth, Alexus Lei Lani Maldonado. BS, Tex. State U., 1969; PhD, U. Denver, 2000. Undersheriff Park County Sheriff's Office, Fairplay, Colo., 1996—98; dir. Ea. Colo. Plains Drug Task Force, Yuma, 1998—2000; immigration adjudication officer US Dept. Homeland Security, Dallas, 2000—. Author: The Psychological Aspects of Police Work: An Officer's Guide to Street Psychology. Mem.: APA, Soc. Police and Criminal Psychology, Soc. for Theoretical and Philos. Psychology, Sovereign Mil Order of Temple of Jerusalem. Personal E-mail: rodgersbruce@sbcglobal.net.

**RODGERS, CLIFTON EUGENE, JR.,** trade association administrator, lobbyist; b. Harrisburg, Pa., Sept. 15, 1954; s. Clifton Eugene and Jean Rodgers; m. Shelley Church Rodgers; children: Henry A. children: John S. BA in History and Lit., Hampshire Coll., 1978. Corp. sales rep. Mellon Bank, NA, Pitts., 1979—81; spl. asst. to exec. v.p.s Fannie Mae, Washington, 1981—83; mgr. secondary mktg. The First Boston Corp., N.Y.C., 1983—85; v.p. Phillips Realty Capital, Bethesda, Md., 1985—91; dir. Office of Bus. Liaison U.S. Dept. Treasury, Washington, 1991—93; asset mgr. Archon Group L.P., Alexandria, Va., 1993—94; v.p. Legg Mason, Bethesda, 1994—96; sr. v.p. The Real Estate Roundtable, Washington, 1996—; founding dir. The Bank of Georgetown, Washington, 2004—. Mid-Atlantic pres. Starlight Children's Found., Washington, 1998—, bd. dirs., 1999; vestry Christ Ch., Georgetown, Washington, 1998—; dir. Starlight Children's Found. Internat., L.A., 1999—. Mem. Urban Land Inst., Mortgage Bankers Assn. of Am. (vice chmn. capital mkts. com. 1999—). Republican. Episcopalian. Avocations: skiing, shooting, fly fishing, mountain biking. Office: The Real Estate Roundtable Ste 1100 1420 New York Ave NW Washington DC 20005 Office Phone: 202-639-8400. Business E-Mail: crodgers@rer.org.

**RODGERS, DANIEL TRACY,** historian, educator; b. Darby, Pa., Sept. 29, 1942; s. Oliver Eliot and Dorothy (Welch) R.; m. Irene Wylie, 1971; children: Peter Samuel, Dwight Oliver. AB, BS in Engring., Brown U., 1965; PhD in History, Yale U., 1973. Instr. history U. Wis., Madison, 1971-73, asst. prof., 1973-78, assoc. prof., 1978-80; assoc. prof. history Princeton (N.J.) U., 1980-86, prof., 1986-98; Henry Charles Lea prof. history, 1998—, chair, 1988-95, 97-98. Fulbright lectr., Frankfurt, Fed. Republic Germany, 1983-84; Pitt prof., Cambridge Univ., 2003-04. Author: The Work Ethic in Industrial America, 1860-1920 (Frederick Jackson Turner award 1978), 1978, Contested Truths: Keywords in American Politics since Independence, 1987, Atlantic Crossings: Social Politics in a Progressive Age, 1998 (Ellis W. Hawley award 1979, George Louis Beer prize 1979). Recipient Chancellor's award U. Wis., Madison, 1978, Am. Coun. Learned Socs. fellow, 1976, NEH fellow, 1987-88, Ctr. for Advanced Study in Behavioral Scis. fellow, 1991-92; Woodrow Wilson Ctr. fellow, 1999-2000. Office: Princeton U Dept History Princeton NJ 08544-0001 E-mail: drodgers@princeton.edu.

**RODGERS, FRANK,** librarian; b. Darlington, Eng., July 28, 1927; came to U.S., 1956; s. Charles Bede and Frances (Page) R.; m. Sarah Louise Edelson, Dec. 18, 1971; children: Hilda Marie, Norah Frances. BA with honors, King's Coll., U. Durham, 1947; diploma librarianship, London U., 1952. Libr. Poplar Tech. Coll., London, 1951-53, St. Martin's Sch. Art, 1953-56; sr. libr. adult svcs. divsn. Akron (Ohio) Pub. Libr., 1956-59; asst. reference libr. U. Ill., 1959-64; chief reference libr., then asst. dir. pub. svcs. Pa. State U. Librs., 1965-69; dir. Portland (Oreg.) State U. Libr., 1969-79; dir. librs. U. Miami, Fla., 1979-97. Mem. Oreg. adv. coun. librs., 1973-74; bd. dirs. Pacific N.W. Bibliog. Ctr., 1973-77; tech. adv. com. librs. Columbia Regional Assn. Govts., 1976-79; vis. fellow U. Southampton Eng., 1975-76; pres. Oreg. Libr. Assn., 1974-75; mem. nominating com. Southeastern Libr. Network, 1984-85; bd. dirs. S.E. Fla. Libr. Info. Network, 1984-97, pres. 1991-92; mem. exec. coun. Assn. Caribbean U. Rsch. and Instl. Librs., 1985-88; chmn. local organizing com. for 1981 and 1987 confs. in Miami; mem. Fla. Libr. Network Coun., 1985-91; NEH challenge grant rev. panel, 1987, Howard U. ann. inspection team, 1989, Reaffirmation com., Tex. Christian U., 1993. Author, editor various libr. publs., guides. Sr. fellow Grad. Sch. Libr. and Info. Sci. UCLA, 1983; grantee Coun. Libr. Resources, 1975-76. Fellow Libr. Assn. ALA; mem. ALA, Assn. Rsch. Librs. (office mgmt. studies adv. com. 1981-83, stats. and measurements com. 1993-96), Assn. Specialized and Coop. Libr. Agys. (membership promotion com. 1994-96, chair 1990 program com.), Assn. Southeastern Rsch. Librs. (chmn. membership com. 1982-97). Address: 7a Avenida Norte #25 Antigua Guatemala E-mail: frodgers@conexion.com.gt.

**RODGERS, FREDERIC BARKER,** judge; b. Albany, NY, Sept. 29, 1940; s. Prentice Johnson and Jane (Weed) R.; m. Valerie McNaughton, Oct. 8, 1988; 1 child: Gabriel Moore. AB, Amherst Coll., 1963; JD, Union U., 1966. Bar: N.Y. 1966, U.S. Ct. Mil. Appeals 1968, Colo. 1972, U.S. Supreme Ct. 1974, U.S. Ct. Appeals (10th cir.) 1981, U.S. Ct. Appeals (fed. cir.) 2001. Chief dep. dist. atty., Denver, 1972-73; commr. Denver Juvenile Ct., 1973-79; mem. Mulligan Reeves Teasley & Joyce, P.C., Denver, 1979-80; mem. Frederic B. Rodgers, P.C., Breckenridge, Colo., 1980-89; ptnr. McNaughton & Rodgers, Central City, Colo., 1989-91; county ct. judge Gilpin County Combined Cts., Colo., 1987—; probate judge Jefferson County Dist. Ct., 2005—. Presiding mcpl. judge cities of Breckenridge, Blue River, Black Hawk, Central City, Edgewater, Empire, Idaho Springs, Silver Plume and Westminster, Colo., 1978-96; chmn. com. on mcpl. ct. rules of procedure Colo. Supreme Ct., 1984-96; mem. gen faculty Nat. Jud. Coll. U. Nev., Reno, 1990—, elected to faculty coun., 1993-99, chair 1999, bd. trustees 2004-. Author (with Dilweg, Fretz, Murphy and Wicker): Modern Judicial Ethics, 1992; contbr. articles to profl. jours., chapters to books; author: The Improvement of The Administration of Justice 7th edit., 2001. Mem. Colo. Commn. on Children, 1982-85, Colo. Youth Devel. Coun., 1989-98, Colo. Family Peace Task Force, 1994-96. Served with JAGC, U.S. Army, 1967-72; to maj. USAR, 1972-88. Decorated Bronze Star with oak leaf cluster, Air medal. Recipient Outstanding County Judge award Colo. 17th Judicial Dist. Victim Adv. Coalition, 1991; Spl. Community Svc. award Colo. Am. Legion, 1979, Lifetime Achievement award Denver Law Club, 2003; USAID grant, 2002-2003. Fellow Am. Bar Found. (Colo. state chair 2005—), Colo. Bar Found. (life); mem. ABA (jud. div. exec. coun. 1989-2000, vice-chair 1996-97, chair-elect 1997, chair 1998-99, mem. Ho. of Dels. 1993-2004, jud. divsn. del. to ABA nominating com. 2000-01, bd. govrs. Dist. 11 2001-04, chair traffic ct. program com. 2005—), Colo. Bar Assn. (bd. govs. 1986-88, 90-92, 93-99, 2002—, sr. v.p. 2004-05), Continental Divide Bar Assn., Denver Bar Assn. (trustee 1979-82), First Jud. Dist. Bar Assn. (trustee 2000-02), Nat. Conf. Spl. Ct. Judges (chmn 1989-90), Colo. County Judges Assn. (pres. 1995-96), Colo. Mcpl. Judges Assn. (pres. 1986-87), Colo. Trial Judges Coun. (v.p. 1994-95, sec. 1996-97), Denver Law Club (pres. 1981-82), Colo. Women's Bar Assn., Am. Judicature Soc. (bd. dirs. 2003—), Nat. Coun. Juvenile and Family Ct. Judges, Federalist Soc. for Law and Pub. Policy Studies, Judge Advs. Assn., Univ. Club (Denver), Arlberg Club (Winter Park), Marines Meml. Club (San Francisco), Rotary (charter pres. Peak to Peak 2000-2001, Paul Harris fellow 1996). Episcopalian. Office: Gilpin County Combined Trial Cts 2960 Dory Hill Rd Golden CO 80403-8827 Office Phone: 303-582-5323 x16. Business E-Mail: frederic.rodgers@judicial.state.co.us. E-mail: rodgers@abanet.org.

**RODGERS, JAMES FOSTER,** insurance research executive, economist; b. Columbus, Ga., Jan. 15, 1951; s. Laban Jackson and Martha (Jackson) R.; m. Cynthia Lynne Bathurst, Aug. 20, 1975. BA, U. Ala., Tuscaloosa, 1973; PhD, U. Iowa, 1980. Fed. intern Office Rsch. and Stats., Social Security Adminstrn., Washington, 1976-77; rsch. assoc. Ctr. Health Policy Rsch., AMA, Chgo., 1979-80, rsch. dir., 1980-82, asst. to dep. exec. vp AMA, 1982-85; dir. AMA Ctr. Health Policy Rsch., Chgo., 1985-96, v.p. health policy, 1996—2003; sr. rsch. exec. Blue Cross Blue Shield Assn., Chgo., 2003—. Contbr. articles on health econs. to profl. jours. Pharm. Mfrs. Assn. grantee,

1978; NSF grantee, 1978; Hohenberg fellow, 1969-70 Mem. Am. Econ. Assn., Am. Statis. Assn. Home: 2233 N Orchard St Chicago IL 60614-3713 Office: Blue Cross Blue Shield Assn 225 N Michigan Ave Chicago IL 60601 Office Phone: 312-297-6535.

**RODGERS, JOHN HUNTER,** lawyer; b. Lubbock, Tex., Jan. 18, 1944; s. James O'Donnell Rodgers and Dorothy (Ulin) Carpenter; m. Anne C. Smith, Nov. 29, 1969; children: Anne Elizabeth, Catherine Hunter. BA, Tex. A&M, 1966; JD, U. Tex., 1969. Bar: Tex. 1969, U.S. Supreme Ct. 1973. Atty. The Southland Corp., Dallas, 1973-79, gen. counsel, 1979-91, sec., 1987-95, sr. v.p., chief adminstrv. officer, 1991-93, exec. v.p., chief adminstrv. officer, 1993-95; pres. Clairemead Corp., Dallas, 1996-2000; sr. v.p., gen. counsel, sec. Am. Pad & Paper Co., Dallas, 1998-2000, pres., 2000—04; prin. J. Hunter & Assocs., Dallas, 2003—. Mem. visual arts com. Tex. A&M U., 1985-94, bd. dirs. student fund enrichment bd., 1986-94; mem. exec. com. Jr. Achievement Dallas, 1988-93; mem. Dallas Citizens Coun., 1992-95; bd. dirs. Boys and Girls Clubs of Greater Dallas, 1998—, vice chmn., 2003-04, chmn., 2005—; nat. chair Tulane U. Parents Coun., 1997-98; trustee Goals for Dallas, 1991-92; bd. trustees The Sci. Place Mus., 2004—; nat. bd. dirs. Boys and Girls Clubs Am., 1993-98; bd. dirs. The Sci. Play Mus., Dallas, 2004—; mem. mktg. com. Dallas Mus. Art, 1994-97. Capt. JAGC, US Army, 1969-73, Vietnam. Mem. ABA, Tex. Bar Assn. (coun. mem. corp. counsel sect. 1988), Dallas Bar Assn., Southwestern Legal Found. (adv. bd. Internat. and Comparative Law Ctr., rsch. fellow 1986-94), Nat. Assn. Convenience Stores (bd. dirs. 1993-95). Roman Catholic. Office: 4655 Insurance Ln Ste 100 Dallas TX 75205 E-mail: Jhunterlp@sbcglobal.net.

**RODGERS, JOHN JOSEPH, III,** educational administration consultant, educator; b. Jamaica, N.Y., Oct. 13, 1941; s. John Joseph Rodgers, Edith (McInerney) Rodgers; m. Iris Rodgers; children: Janet, John Joseph IV, Yvette. BS, Fordham U., 1962; Profl. diploma, St. Johns U., 1970, EdD, 1979; postgrad., CUNY, Flushing. Asst. prin. N.Y.C. Bd. Edn., 1972-82; prin. Howard T. Herber Sch., Malverne, N.Y., 1982-85, Norman Thomas H.S., N.Y.C., 1988-96, Matawan Regional H.S., Aberdeen, N.J., 1996-97; cons. on ednl. adminstrn. Valley Stream, NY, 1999—; prof. math. Farleigh Dickinson U., Madison, N.J., 1999-2001; prof. ednl. adminstrn. Coll. New Rochelle, N.Y., 2000-01; dean acad. affairs Five Towns Coll., Dix Hills, NY, 2001—02; acad. dean Bus. Informatics Ctr., The Coll. for Bus., Valley Stream, NY, 2002—05. Mem. ASCD, Am. Assn. Sch. Adminstrs., Math. Assn. Am., Nat. Assn. Secondary Sch. Prins. Home: 350-34 N Corona Ave Valley Stream NY 11580-3403 E-mail: drjohnrodgers@hotmail.com.

**RODGERS, JOHNATHAN,** broadcast executive; b. San Antonio, Jan. 18, 1946; s. Marion Alford and Barbara (Merriwether) Rodgers; m. Royal Graves Kennedy, Sept. 27, 1976; children: David, Jamie. BA, U. Calif., Berkeley, 1967; MA, Stanford U., 1972; PhD (hon.), Columbia Coll., Chgo., 1991. Writer-reporter Sports Illustrated, NYC, 1966—68; assoc. editor Newsweek, NYC, 1968—72; prodr. WNBC-TV, NYC, 1972—73; reporter WKYC-TV (NBC), Cleve., 1973—74; sta. mgr., news dir. KCBS-TV, LA, 1978—83; exec. prodr. CBS News, NYC, 1983—86; v.p., gen. mgr. WBBM-TV (CBS), Chgo., 1986—90; former pres. CBS TV Stas., Chgo.; pres. Discovery Networks, US, Bethesda, Md., 1996—2003; pres., CEO TV One, LLC, Silver Spring, Md., 2003—. Bd. dirs. Procter & Gamble. Trustee U. Calif., Berkeley, 2000—. With U.S. Army, 1969—71, Korea. Mem.: Nat. Assn. Black Journalists. Home: 3120 Newark St NW Washington DC 20008-3343 Office: TV One, LLC 1010 Wayne Ave Silver Spring MD 20910

**RODGERS, LAWRENCE RODNEY,** internist, educator; b. Clovis, N.Mex., Mar. 9, 1920; s. Samuel Frank and Lillian (O'Connor) R.; m. Ivy Lorna Piper, Aug. 6, 1943; children: Lawrence Rodney (dec.), Ivy Elizabeth, George Piper. BS, West Tex. State U., 1940; MD, U. Tex., 1943. Diplomate Am. Bd. Internal Medicine. Intern Phila. Gen. Hosp., 1943-44, resident in medicine, 1946-49; assoc. internist Tumor Inst., U. Tex. M.D. Anderson Hosp., Houston, 1949—; chmn. dept. medicine Hermann Hosp., Houston, 1966-71; assoc. prof. clin. medicine Baylor U., 1949—; prof. clin. medicine U. Tex., 1972—. Editor: Harris County Physician, 1976-80. Bd. dirs. Tex. Med. Found.; trustee Houston Mus. Med. Sci., 1981. Served to maj. M.C. AUS, 1944-46. Decorated Bronze Star with two oak leaf clusters; recipient Ashbel Smith Disting. Alumnus award U. Tex. Med. Br.-Galveston, 1993, Mastership award Am. Coll. Physicians, 1996. Fellow ACP (gov. for Tex. 1979-83, Laureate Internist Tex. award 1994); mem. AMA (del. 1975-94), Tex. Med. Assn. (elected emeritus), Harris County Med. Soc. (exec. bd. 1978-82, v.p. 1984), Am. Heart Assn., Houston Soc. Internal Medicine (pres. 1974), Houston Acad. Medicine (pres. 1981), Houston Philos. Soc. (pres. 1993-94), Doctor's Club Houston (bd. govs. 1984-88, pres. 1986). Personal E-mail: rod3920@aol.com.

**RODGERS, LOIS EVE,** secondary school educator; BA, U. So. Miss.; MEd, William Carey Coll.; student, Bread Loaf Sch. English. Tchr. Hattiesburg (Miss.) High Sch. Named Miss. State English Tchr. of Yr., 1993.

**RODGERS, MARY COLUMBRO,** literature educator, writer, academic administrator; b. Aurora, Ohio, Apr. 17, 1925; d. Nicola and Nancy (DeNicola) Columbro; m. Daniel Richard Rodgers, July 24, 1965; children: Robert, Patricia, Kristine. AB, Notre Dame Coll., 1957; MA, Western Res. U., 1962; PhD, Ohio State U., 1964; postgrad., U. Rome, 1964-65; EdD, Calif. Nat. Open U., 1975, DLitt, 1978. Tchr. English Cleve. elem. schs., 1945-52, Cleve. secondary schs., 1952-62; supr. English student tchrs. Ohio State U., 1962-64; asst. prof. English U. Md., 1965-66; assoc. prof. Trinity Coll., 1967-68; prof. English D.C. Tchrs. Coll., U. D.C., 1968—2006; pres. Md. Nat. U., 1972—2006; founder, chancellor Open U. Am., 1965—; dean Am. Open U. Acad.; ret., 2000; ind. rschr., writer, 2000—. Author: A Short Course in English Composition, 1976, Chapbook of Children's Literature, 1977, Comprehensive Catalogue The Open University of America System, 1978-80, Open University of America System Source Book, V, VII, VII, 1978, Essays and Poems on Life and Literature, 1979, Modes and Models: Four Lessons for Young Writers, 1981, Open University Structures and Adult Learning, 1982, Papers in Applied English Linguistics, 1982, Twelve Lectures on the American Open University, 1982, English Pedagogy in the American Open University, 1983, Design for Personalized English Graduate Degrees in the Urban University, 1984, Open University English Teaching, 1945-85: Conceptual History and Rationale, 1985, Claims and Counterclaims Regarding Instruction Given in Personalized Degree Residency Programs Completed by Graduates of California National Open University, 1986, The American Open University, 1965 to 1985: History and Sourcebook, 1986, New Design II: English Pedagogy in the American Open University, 1987, The American Open University, 1965 to 1985: A Research Report, 1987, The American Open University and Other Universities: A Comparative Study Report, 1988, Poet and Pedagogue in Moscow and Leningrad: A Travel Report, 1989, Foundations of English Scholarship in the American Open University, 1989, Twelve Lectures in Literary Analysis, 1990, Ten Lectures in Literary Production, 1990, Analyzing Fact and Fiction, 1991, Analyzing Poetry and Drama, 1991, Some Successful Literary Research Papers: An Inventory of Titles and Theses, 1991, Catalogue for the Mary Columbro Rodgers Literary Trust, 1992, A Chapbook of Poetry and Drama Analysis, 1992, Convent Poems, 1943-1961, 1992, Catholic Marriage Poems 1962, 1979, 1993, Catholic Widow with Children Poems 1979-1993, 1994, First Access List to the Mary Columbro Rodgers Trust by Year, 1994, Nicola Columbro: A Brief Biography, 3d edit., 1994, Biographical Sourcebook I: Mary Columbro Rodgers 1969-1995, 1995, Catholic Teacher Poems 1945-1995, 1995, Fables and Farm Stories for Fiction Analysis, 1995, Second Access List to the Mary Columbro Rodgers Literary Trust by Alphabet, 1995, Third Access List to the Mary Columbro Rodgers Literary Trust by Subject, 1996, Fourth Access List to the Mary Columbro Rodgers Literary Trust for K-PhD Open Learning-Open University Methods with Data Batches Delineated, 2002, Journals: Reflections and Resolves 1992-2002, 03, 04, 16 vols., 2002, Fifth and Final Access List to the Mary Columbro Rodgers Literary Trust with Annotations, 2004, Journals: Reflections and Resolves, 2005, Catholic Open University of America System Poems, 1962-2005, 2005; contrb. articles to profl. jours. Fulbright scholar U. Rome, 1964-65. Fellow Cath. Scholars; mem. U.S.

Distance Learning Assn., Poetry Soc. Am., Nat. Coun. Tchrs. English, Am. Ednl. Rsch. Assn., Am. Acad. Poets, Pi Lambda Theta. Home and Office: Coll Heights Estates 3916 Commander Dr Hyattsville MD 20782-1027 Office Phone: 301-779-0220. Personal E-mail: openuniv@aol.com.

**RODGERS, STEPHEN JOHN,** lawyer, physician, consultant; b. Phila., July 10, 1943; s. Harry Edward Rodgers and Antoinette Julia Muckenfuss; m. Roberta Elaine Rhine, Sept. 21, 1974; children: Abigail Elizabeth, Rebecca Elizabeth. MD, Hahnemann U., 1969; JD, Widener U., 1989. Bar: Pa. 1990, N.J. 1990; med. lic., Pa., Del., N.J. Pvt. practice in family practice and emergency medicine Del. Pain Clinic, Wilmington, 1975-89, asst. dir., 1989-92; pvt. practice as medicolegal cons. Wilmington, 1992—. Mem. Med. Assistance and Health Svcs. Adv. Bd., NJ, 1996-98; chair Task Force on Ind. Med. Exam., Dept. Labor and Industry, Commonwealth of Pa., 1996-98. Comdr. USN, 1968-75; capt. USNR, 1975—; surgeon gen. N.J. Naval Militia Joint Command. Fellow Am. Acad. Family Physicians, Am. Acad. Disability Evaluating Physicians, Am. Acad. Emergency Medicine, Am. Coll. Legal Medicine; mem. Aerospace Med. Assn., Pa. Bar Assn. (health care com. 1991—), Del. Acad. Medicine, NJ Acad. Family Physicians (ho. of dels. 1989-91), Vietnam Vets. Am. Republican. Roman Catholic. Avocations: equestrian, pro bono veterans and disability advocate. Home: PO Box 54 Alloway NJ 08001-0054 Office: Ste 14 1701 Augustine Wilmington DE 19803

**RODGERS, STEVEN EDWARD,** tax practitioner, educator; b. Pierre, S.D., Feb. 8, 1947; s. Thomas Edward and Dorothy Zoe (Barker) R.; m. Donna Lynn Joyner, June 10, 1984; 1 child, Michelle Ann. Student, State U. S.D., 1964-65, U. Calif., Berkeley, 1968-72; cert., Coll. for Fin. Planning, 1986-87, fellow, Nat. Tax Practice Inst., 1988-89. CFP, Enrolled Agent. Collection mgr. Cenval Leasing-Ctrl. Bank, Long Beach, Calif., 1972-77; tax preparer Rodgers Tax Svc., Las Vegas, 1977-78; CEO Rainbow Tax Svc. Inc., Las Vegas, 1978—. Pres. Rainbow Tax Svc., Inc., Las Vegas, 1978-90. Author: Marketing To Build Your Tax Practice, 1994. Active Amnesty Internat., Mensa; chmn. Best in the West Edn. Found., Las Vegas, 1994—, Nat. Assn. Enrolled Agents Edn. Found., 1995-96. With U.S. Army, 1965-68, Vietnam. Mem. Nat. Assn. Enrolled Agts. (nat. sec. 1989-90, nat. treas. 1991-92, nat. edn. chair 1994-95, named Tax Educator of the Yr., 1995), Nat. Assn. Enrolled Agents Edn. Found. (chair 1995-96), Nev. Soc. Enrolled Agts. (charter pres. 1985-86, fellow edn. found.), So. Nev. Assn. Tax Cons. (pres. 1981-82), Nat. Soc. Pub. Accts., Vietnam Vets. Am. Home: 1101 Cahill Ave Las Vegas NV 89128-3335 also: 777 N Rainbow Blvd Ste 245 Las Vegas NV 89107-1192

**RODGERS, SUZANNE HOOKER,** physiologist, consultant; b. Rochester, N.Y., Dec. 26, 1939; d. John Ashmead and Priscilla May (Bodman) Rodgers AB, Vassar Coll., 1961; PhD, U. Rochester Med. Ctr., 1967. Postdoctoral fellow USPHS Middlesex Hosp., London, 1966—68; ergonomist Eastman Kodak Co., Rochester, 1968—82; cons. Rochester, 1982—. Author: Working With Backache, 1985; tech. editor, co-author Ergonomic Design for People at Work, 1983, 86, co-editor, contr. Kodak's Ergonomic Design for People at Work 2d edit., 2003 Bd. dirs., chmn. com., v.p. Rochester Philharm. Orch. Inc., 1969-75; bd. dirs. Opera Theatre Rochester, 1969-75; bd. dirs., chmn com., pres. Monroe County Bd. Health, Rochester, 1979-88 Mem. Human Factors and Ergonomics Soc., (pres. We. N.Y. chpt. 1971-72), Am. Coll. Sports Medicine Avocations: photography, gardening, reading, silent films. Home and Office: 169 Huntington Hls Rochester NY 14622-1121 Office Phone: 585-544-3587. Personal E-mail: shrodgers@aol.com.

**RODGMAN, ALAN,** chemist, consultant; b. Aberdare, Wales, Feb. 7, 1924; came to U.S. from Canada, 1954, naturalized, 1961; s. Arch and Margaret (Llewellyn) R.; m. Doris Curley, June 7, 1947; children: Eric, Paul, Mark. BA in Chemistry, U. Toronto, 1949, MA in Organic Chemistry, 1951, PhD in Organic Chemistry, 1953, Rsch. asst. med. rsch. dept. U. Toronto, 1947-51, rsch. assoc., 1951-54; tchr., courses in organic chemistry, phys. chemistry, math. Chem. Inst. Can., 1951-54; sr. rsch. chemist R.J. Reynolds Tobacco Co., Winston-Salem, N.C., 1954-65, head smoke rsch. sect., 1965-75, mgr. analytical rsch., 1975-76, dir. rsch., 1976-80, dir. fundamental rsch. and devel., 1980-87; cons. in field, 1987—. Mem. editl. bd. Tobacco Sci., 1963-67 (Vol. 31 Tobacco Sci. dedicated in his name 1987), Beitrage zur Tabakforschung Internat., 1978-87. Mem. Tobacco Working Group, Nat. Cancer Inst., 1976-77, Tech. Study Group on Cigarette and Little Cigar Fire Safety, 1984-87, Sci. Commn. Cooperation Ctr. for Sci. Rsch. Relative to Tobacco, 1982-84. With Royal Can. Navy, 1942-45. Mem. Coun. for Tobacco Rsch. (industry tech. com. 1956-62, Tobacco Sci. Rsch. Conf. Inaugural Lifetime Achievement award 2005), Chem. Inst. Can., Can. Chem. Soc., Am. Chem. Soc., N.Y. Acad. Scis. Episcopalian. Home: 2828 Birchwood Dr Winston Salem NC 27103-3410

**RODIN, EUGENE,** aerospace scientist, researcher, engineering educator; b. Moscow, Feb. 20, 1937; arrived in U.S., 1993; s. Ivan Fedotovich Rodin and Maria Ivanovna Rodina; m. Bella Medvedeva, Jan. 15, 1981; children: Oleg Medvedev, Karmela Medvedeva. MS, Bauman State Tech. U., Moscow, 1960, PhD, 1969. Instr. Bauman State Tech. U., Moscow, 1960—64, asst. prof., 1964—70, assoc. prof., 1970—93; head sci. lab. Suffolk U., Boston, 1995—2005, asst. prof., 2005—. Sci. rschr. Inst. Spl. Mech. Engring., Moscow, 1970—93, Heat Engring. Rsch. inst., Moscow, 1972—93. Author: Heat Exchanges in Cryogenic Engineering, 1988, Heat Calculation of Cryogenic System, 1990; contbr. articles to profl. publs. Recipient Gold medal, Ministry Spl. Engring., Moscow, 1985, Jubilee Gagarin's medal, NASA, Russia, 2001, Jubilee Tereshkova's medal, 2002. Avocations: travel, reading, sailing, skiing.

**RODIN, JUDITH SEITZ,** foundation administrator, former academic administrator, psychologist, educator; b. Phila., Sept. 9, 1944; d. Morris and Sally R. (Winson) Seitz. m. Paul Verkuil. AB, U. Pa., 1966; PhD, U. Columbia, 1970. Asst. prof. psychology NYU, 1970—72; assoc. prof. Yale U., 1975—79, prof., dir. grad. studies, 1982—89, Philip R. Allen prof. psychology, medicine and psychiatry, 1984—94, chmn. dept. psychology, 1989—91, dean Grad. Sch., 1991—92, provost, 1992—94; pres. U. Pa., Phila., 1994—2004, prof. psychology, medicine and psychiatry, 1994—2004; pres. Rockefeller Found., NYC, 2005—. Chmn. John D. and Catherine T. MacArthur Found. Rsch. Network on Determinants and Consequences of Health-Promoting and Health-Damaging Behavior, 1983-93; vice chair coun. press. U. Rsch. Assn., 1994-95, chair, 1995-96; mem. Ind. Panel to Review Safety Procedures at The White House, 1994-95; chair adv. com. Robert Wood Johnson Found., 1994—; mem. Pres. Clinton's Com. Advisors Sci. and Tech., 1994—; mem. Coun. Competitiveness, 1997—; mem. nominating com. N.Y. Stock Exch., 1998—; bd. dirs. Aetna, Electronic Data Sys., AMR, Citigroup Inc., 2004-. Author: (with S. Schachter) Obese Humans and Rats, 1978, Exploding the Weight Myths, 1982, Body Traps, 1992; chief editor Appetite Jour., 1979-92; contbr. articles to profl. jours. Mem. Pa. Task Force on Higher Edn. Funding, 1994; bd. dirs. Catalyst, N.Y.C., 1994—; trustee Brookings Inst., 1995—; pres. steering com. Am. Reads, 1997—. Recipient Phila. award, 2004, William Penn award; grantee NSF, 1973—82, NIH, 1981—. Fellow AAAS, APA (bd. sci. affairs 1979-82, pres. divsn. 38 health psychology 1982-83, Outstanding Contbn. award 1980, Disting. Sci. award 1977, Lifetime Achievement award 2005), Am. Acad. Arts and Scis., Soc. Behavioral Medicicine; mem. AAU (mem. exec. com. 1996—), Am. Philosophical Soc., Inst. Medicine of NAS, Acad. Behavioral Medicine Rsch., Ea. Psychol. Assn. (exec. bd. 1980-82), Phi Beta Kappa, Sigma Xi (pres. Yale chpt. 1986-87). Office: Rockefeller Found 420 Fifth Ave New York NY 10018 Business E-mail: president@rockfound.org

**RODIN, RITA ANGELA,** lawyer; b. NYC, 1968; BS magna cum laude, Boston Coll., 1990; JD, St. John's U., 1990. Bar: N.J. 1994, N.Y. 1994. Law clk. Hon. Thomas C. Platt U.S. Dist. Ct. (ea. dist.) NY, 1993—94; atty. Skadden, Arps, Slate, Meagher & Flom LLP, NYC, 1994—2001, ptnr. Intellectual Property and Tech. Group, 2001—. Office: Skadden Arps Slate Meagher & Flom LLP Four Times Sq New York NY 10036 Office Phone: 212-735-3774. Business E-mail: rrodin@skadden.com.

**RODINO, VINCENT LOUIS,** insurance company executive; b. N.Y.C., June 25, 1929; s. Vincenzo and Sofia (De Toro) R.; m. Marie Green; children: Peter Vincent, Vincent Douglas. BA, NYU, 1957. CLU. With Equitable Fin. Cos., N.Y.C., 1946—, chief mktg. svcs. sector, 1983—84, chief traditional products sector, 1984—86, chmn., CEO Traebco subs. 1984—86, chief sales support sector, 1986—89; dep. pres. northeastern region Equitable Ins. Cos., N.Y.C., 1989—92; bd. dirs. Traebco subs. Equitable. Trustee Life Underwriter Tng. Coun., Washington, 1987. Served as sgt. U.S. Army, 1951-53. Mem. Assn. Advanced Life Underwriting, Nat. Assn. Life Underwriters, N.Y.C. Chpt. CLUs. Business E-Mail: vlrodino@aol.com.

**RODITE, ROBERT R.R.,** research scientist, finance and computer consultant, educator; b. Easton, Pa., Oct. 17, 1942; s. Victor James and Alice Cecilia (Zatovich) R.; m. Patricia Ann Sule, Apr. 8, 1967; children: Colleen P., Robert J. BSEE, Lafayette Coll., 1964; MSEE, Caif. Inst. Tech., 1965. Rsch. engr. mgr. mfg. rsch. lab. IBM, Endicott, N.Y., 1965-70, mfg. engring. mgr. electronic packaging mfg., 1970-72, devel. engring. mgr. electronic packaging engring., 1972-77, program dir. corp. engring., programming & tech. staff Armonk, N.Y., 1977-79, product engring. mgr., sr. engr. multichip module devel. East Fishkill, N.Y., 1979-81, system mgr., sr. tech. staff mem. fin. industry devel. Charlotte, N.C., 1981-92, sr. tech. staff mem. corp. tech. strategy devel. staff Armonk, 1992-93; pres. Rodite Assocs., Inc., Charlotte, 1993—; lectr. math. and bus. Belmont Abbey Coll., 2001—04. Workgroup mem. Am. Nat. Standards Inst. Com. X9B Stds. Com., 1991-97; chmn. IBM Image Processing and Visualization Interdivisional Tech. Liaison Com., 1992-93. Contbr. articles to profl. jours.; patentee in field. Asst. scoutmaster Boy Scouts Am., Charlotte, 1991, 92; mid. sch. basketball asst. coach, Charlotte, 1991-92, 93-94, coun. mem. Town County Consolidation Com., Endicott, 1970s; mem. Cath. sch. bd. Diocese of Charlotte, 1988-90; pres. Homeowners Assn., Charlotte, 2001-03. Tau Beta Pi fellow, Calif. Inst. Tech., 1964. Mem. IEEE (sr.), Assn. for Info. and Image Mgmt. Internat. (designated Master Info. Tech. 1997, cert. document Image Architech, Laureate of Info. Technologies 1998), Phi Beta Kappa, Eta Kappa Nu, Eta Kappa Nu. Avocations: personal computers, travel. Home: 9664 Chaumont Ln Charlotte NC 28277-2140

**RODITTI, ESTHER C(LAIRE),** lawyer, writer; b. LA, Feb. 7, 1933; d. David and Lucy Roditti; m. Oscar H. Schachter, Aug. 8, 1957 (div. Oct. 1992); children: Charles David, Susan Dayana. BA, UCLA, 1954; JD, Harvard U., 1957. Bar: N.Y. 1959. Assoc. Stickles, Hayden and Kennedy, N.Y.C., 1957-62; asst. dir. Legis. Drafting Fund Columbia U., N.Y.C., 1962-65, cons., 1965-67; U.N.Y.C. Air Pollution Control Dept., 1965-67; instr. and cons. New Sch. for Social Rsch., N.Y.C., 1968-70; cons. Internat. League for Rights of Man, N.Y.C., 1969, Rand Inst., N.Y.C., 1969, U.S. Soviet Environ. Studies Program, UN Assn., N.Y.C., 1969; sr. rsch. assoc. Ctr. for Policy Rsch. Columbia U., 1970-73; sr. program officer Ford Found., N.Y.C., 1972-78; pres. Esther Roditti Schachter, P.C., N.Y.C., 1978-83; ptnr. Schachter & Froling, N.Y.C., 1983-85, Schachter, Courter, Purcell & Kobert, N.Y.C., 1985-92; pres. Esther C. Roditti, P.C., 1992—. Spkr., lectr., panelist profl. assn. confs., forums, workshops, U.S., Can., Tokyo, London. Author: N.Y.C. Air Pollution Control Code Annotated, 1965, Enforcing Air Pollution Controls, 1979, Financial Support of Women's Programs in the 1970's, 1979, Computer Contracts Reference Directory, 1979-83, Hiring and Firing Knowledge Workers, 1995, Tax and Business Handbook for Consultants and Clients, 1998; co-author: Charities and Charitable Foundations, 1974; author, co-author articles in field; legal editor: Computer Economics, 1983-89; editor Computer Law & Tax Report, 1984-86, pub., editor, 1986-2000; author, editor Computer Contracts-Negotiating Drafting Treatise, 1992—. Nat. governing bd. Common Cause, 1979-82, mem. state governing bd., N.Y., 1982-84; mem. com. on urban environ. Citizens Union, N.Y.C., 1969-73; mem. West Side Dem. Club, 1958-63. Recipient Outstanding Svc. award Brandeis U., Nat. Women's Com., 1973; grantee Ford Found., 1970, NSF, 1971. Mem. ABA (lectr. 1987), Assn. Bar City NY (founder, chmn. com. on computer law 1980—), NY State Bar Assn., Computer Law Assn. (lectr. 1985, bulletin editor 1998-, bd. dirs. 2000-), Am. Arbitration Assn. (chair com. for computer disputes 1985-), Phi Beta Kappa. Office Phone: 212-879-3322.

**RODKIN, GARY M.,** food products executive; B.A., Rutgers U.; M.B.A., Harvard Business School. Pres., served other mktg. and gen. mgmt. positions Gen. Mills (Yoplait-Colombo yogurt unit); pres. Tropicana N.Am., 1995—98, pres., CEO, 1998—99, PepsiCola N.Am., 1999—2002; pres. PepsiCo, Beverages and Foods, 2002—03, CEO, 2002—05, chmn., 2003—05; pres. CEO ConAgra Foods Inc., Omaha, 2005—. Office: ConAgra Foods Inc 1 ConAgra Dr Omaha NE 68102-5001*

**RODLEY, CAROL A.,** federal agency administrator; b. Mass. married; 3 children. Grad., Smith Coll. Dep. chief of mission Am. Embassy, Phnom Pehn, Cambodia, 1997—2000; dep. exec. sec. US Dept. State, Washington, 2001—03, prin. dep. asst. sec. Bur. Internat. Orgn. Affairs, 2003—, acting asst. sec. Bur. Intelligence and Rsch., 2005—. Recipient Christian A. Herter award, Am. Fgn. Svc. Assn., 2000, Sr. Performance award, US Dept. State, Human Rights & Democracy award, James Clement Dunn award for Leadership, Dir. Ctrl. Intelligence Exceptional Humint Collector award, Intelligence Community Seal Medalion. Office: Bur Intelligence and Rsch US Dept State 2201 C St NW Washington DC 20520

**RODMAN, ALPINE C.,** arts and crafts company executive, photographer; b. Roswell, N.Mex., June 23, 1952; s. Robert Elsworth and Verna Mae (Means) R.; m. Sue Arlene Lawson, Dec. 13, 1970; 1 child, Connie Lynn. Student, Colo. State U., 1970—71, U. No. Colo. Ptnr. Pinel Silver Shop, Loveland, Colo., 1965-68, salesman, 1968-71; real estate salesman Loveland, 1971-73; mgr. Traveling Traders, Loveland, 1974-75; co-owner Deer Track Traders, Loveland, 1975-85, pres. Deer Track Traders, Ltd., Loveland, 1985—. Spkr., lectrs. at seminars in field, 2004—. Author: The Vanishing Indian: Fact or Fiction?, 1985. Mem. Civil Air Patrol, 1965-72, 87-92, dep. comdr. for cadets Greeley, Colo., 1988-90; cadet comdr. Ft. Collins, Colo., 1968, 70, Colo. rep. to youth tng. program, 1969, U.S. youth rep. to Japan, 1970. Mem. We. and English Salesmen's Assn. (bd. dirs. 1996), Internat. Platform Assn., Indian Arts and Crafts Assn. (bd. dirs. 1988-94, exec. com. 1989-92, v.p. 1990, pres. 1991, market chmn. 1992), Crazy Horse Grass Roots Club. Office: Deer Track Traders Ltd PO Box 448 Loveland CO 80539-0448 *Personal philosophy: I believe that most good and bad in the world comes out of respect or lack of respect for one's self, fellow man, environment and creator.*

**RODMAN, LEIBA,** mathematician; b. Riga, Latvia, June 9, 1949; arrived in U.S., 1985; s. Zalman and Haya Rodman; m. Ella Levitan, Feb. 2, 1983; children: Daniel, Ruth, Benjamin, Naomi. Diploma in maths., Latvian State U., 1971; MA in Statis., Tel Aviv (Israel) U., 1976, PhD in Maths., 1978. Instr. Tel Aviv U., 1976-78, sr. lectr., 1981-83, assoc. prof., 1983-85; postdoctoral fellow U. Calgary, Can., 1978-80; from assoc. to full prof. Ariz. State U., Tempe, 1985-87; prof. math. Coll. William and Mary, Williamsburg, Va., 1987—. Author: Introduction to Operator Polynomials, 1989, (with others) Matrix Polynomials, 1982, Matrices and Indefinite Scalar Products, 1983, Invariant Subspaces of Matrices with Applications, 1986, Interpolation of Rational Matrix Functions, 1990, Algebraic Riccati Equations, 1995, Indefinite Linear Algebra and Applications, 2005; co-editor: Contributions to Operator Theory and Its Applications, 1988, Current Trends in Operator Theory and its Applications, 2004. Mem. Am. Math. Soc., Internat. Linear-Algebra Soc., Soc. Indsl. and Applied Math. Office: Coll of William & Mary Dept Math PO Box 8795 Williamsburg VA 23187-8795 Office Phone: 757-221-2027. E-mail: lxrodm@math.wm.edu.

**RODMAN, LEONARD C.,** engineering and construction executive; BS in Civil Engring., Iowa State U., 1971; MS in Environ. Engring., U. Mo., 1978. Joined Black & Veatch, Kansas City, Mo., 1971, various project mgmt. positions environ. divsn., named head N.Am. divsn. infrastructure bus., 1992, CEO, pres., 1998—, also chmn., 2000—. Bd. trustees, cmty./legis. affairs com. U. Mo., Kansas City; bd. advisors U. Kans. - Edward Campus; mem. Iowa State Engring Coll. Indsl. Adv. Consul. Recipient Profl. Achievement Citation in Engring., U. Iowa Coll. Engring., 2003. Mem.: Am. Acad.

Environ. Engineers, Water Environment Fedn., Nat. Soc. Profl. Engineers, Mo. Soc. Profl. Engineers, Am. Water Works Assn., Am. Soc. Civil Engineers. Office: Black & Veatch 11401 Lamar Ave Overland Park KS 66211*

**RODMAN, LEROY ELI,** lawyer; b. NYC, Feb. 22, 1914; s. Morris and Sadie (Specter) R.; m. Toby Chertcoff, Mar. 14, 1943; children: John Stephen, Lawrence Bernard. AB, CCNY, 1933; JD (James Kent scholar), Columbia, 1936. Bar: NY 1937. Pvt. practice, NYC, 1937—43, 1946—; law sec. to US dist. judge Bklyn., 1936; law asst. Am. Law Inst., NYC, 1937; chief food enforcement unit NY Regional Office, OPA, 1942—43; mem. firm Lawrence R. Condon, NYC, 1937—42; ptnr. Joseph & Rodman, NYC, 1946—53; sr. ptnr. Rodman, Maurer & Dansker, NYC, 1964—73, Carro, Spanbock, Londin, Rodman & Fass, NYC, 1973—78, Rodman & Rodman, NYC, 1978—89, Teitelbaum, Hiller, Rodman, Paden & Hibsher, P.C., NYC, 1990—96; of counsel Morrison, Cohen, Singer & Weinstein LLP, NYC, 1996—2004. Edtl. bd.: Columbia Law Rev., 1934-36; Contbr. articles to legal jours. V.p. Ctrl. Synagogue, pres. brotherhood, 1958—60, hon. trustee; bd. dirs. Manhattan coun. Boy Scouts Am., v.p., 1961—68, pres., 1972—75, exec. bd. Greater NY coun. Capt. JAGD U.S. Army, 1943—46. Recipient Certs. Svc., Silver Beaver award Boy Scouts Am., 1962, Eagle Scout, Ten Mile River Camps Hallop Fame award, 2005. Fellow: Am. Coll. Trust Estate Counsel; mem.: ABA, Judge Adv. Assn., Assn. Bar City NY, NY County Lawyers Assn., Metropolis Country Club (White Plains, NY) (sec. 1976—77, 1980—82, v.p. 1977—78, bd. govs. 1976—82), Univ. Club (NYC), Phi Beta Kappa. Home and Office: 535 E 86th St New York NY 10028-7533 Office Phone: 212-737-8559.

**RODMAN, PETER WARREN,** federal agency administrator; b. Boston, Nov. 24, 1943; s. Sumner and Helen Rhoda (Morris) R.; m. F. Veronique Boulad, Apr. 13, 1980; children: Theodora, Nicholas. BA summa cum laude, Harvard U., 1964, JD, 1969; BA, MA, Oxford U., Eng., 1966. Staff mem. NSC, Washington, 1969-77; fellow in diplomatic studies Ctr. for Strategic and Internat. Studies, Washington, 1977-83; dir. rsch. Kissinger Assocs., Washington, 1982-83; mem. policy planning council US Dept. State, Washington, 1983-84, dir. policy planning staff, 1984-86; dep. asst. to pres. for nat. security affairs (fgn. policy) NSC, Washington, 1986-87, NSC counselor, spl. asst. to pres. for nat. security affairs, 1987-90; fellow Johns Hopkins Fgn. Policy Inst., Washington, 1990-93; dir. Middle East and Eurasian studies Ctr. for Strategic and Internat. Studies, Washington, 1994-95; dir. nat. security programs Nixon Ctr., Washington, 1995-2001; asst. sec. for internat. security affairs US Dept. Def., Washington, 2001—. Author: More Precious Than Peace: The Cold War and the Struggle for the Third World, 1994; sr. editor Nat. Rev., 1991-99; contbr. articles to profl. jours. V.p. World Affairs Coun., Washington, 1996-2001; trustee Freedom House, 1997-2001. Mem. Coun. on Fgn. Rels., Internat. Inst. for Strategic Studies, Atlantic Coun. U.S., Cosmos Club. Office: 2400 Defense Pentagon Washington DC 20301-2400 Office Phone: 703-695-4351. E-mail: peter.rodman@osd.mil.

**RODMAN, SARAH,** music critic; b. 1969; Popular music critic, staff columnist Boston Herald, 2000—06; popular music critic Boston Globe, 2006—. Office: Boston Globe 135 Morrissey Blvd Boston MA 02125 Mailing: Boston Globe PO Box 55819 Boston MA 02205-5819*

**RODMAN, SUE A.,** wholesale company executive, artist, writer; b. Ft. Collins, Colo., Oct. 1, 1951; d. Marvin F. Lawson and Barbara I. (Miller) Lawson Shue; m. Alpine C. Rodman, Dec. 13, 1970; 1 child, Connie L. Rodman; m. Graham L. Jackson. Student, Woodbury Bus./Arts Coll., Calif., 1969, Colo. State U., 1970—73. Silversmith Pinel Silver Shop, Loveland, Colo., 1970-71; asst. mgr. Traveling Traders, Phoenix, 1974-75; co-owner, co-mgr. Deer Track Traders, Loveland, 1975-85; v.p. Deer Track Traders, Ltd., Loveland, 1985—. Author: The Book of Contemporary Indian Arts and Crafts, 1985, short stories; contbr. articles to popular mags. Mem. U.S. Senatorial Club, 1982-87, Rep. Presdl. Task Force, 1983-90; mem. Civil Air Patrol, 1969-73, 87-90, pers. officer, 1988-90. Mem.: Internat. Platform Assn., Indian Arts and Crafts Assn., Western and English Sales Assn., Crazy Horse Grass Roots Club. Mem. Am. Baptist Ch. Avocations: museums, piano, recreation research, fashion design. Office: Deer Track Traders Ltd PO Box 448 Loveland CO 80539-0448

**RODMAN, SUMNER,** insurance company executive; b. Malden, Mass., Aug. 5, 1915; s. Nathan Markel and Sara Ruth (Slater) Rodman; m. Helen Rhoda Morris, July 2, 1942; children: Peter Warren, John Slater. AB cum laude, Harvard U., 1935. CLU. Ins. broker, employee benefits specialist Aetna Life Ins. and Annuity Co., Boston, 1935-98; with Rodman Ins. Agy., Inc., Needham, Mass.; life ins. adviser, 1953—. Pres. Boston Life Ins. and Trust Coun., 1958—59. Bd. dirs. Boston Estate Planning Coun., 1960—85, pres., 1958; mem. Anti-Defamation League B'nai Brith, World Affairs Coun. Boston; chmn. class com. Harvard, 1935; bd. dirs. Jewish Family and Children's Svc., Boston, 1953—85; active Am. Jewish Com.; hon. trustee Temple Israel, Boston; bd. dirs. Youth Tennis Found. New Eng., 1963—85, Simons-Gutman Found., 1965—, Alzheimers Assn. Ea. Mass., 1990—97; hon. trustee Combined Jewish Philanthropies of Greater Boston, 1967—. Served to capt. AUS, 1941-45, ETO. Fellow CLU Inst., 1952, 1961. Mem.: New Eng. Tennis Assn. (bd. dirs. 1966—68, Hall of Fame 1992), Am. Soc. CLUs (pres. 1972—73), Boston Life Underwriters Assn. (pres. 1965—66), Am. Coll. (trustee 1971—74), Million Dollar Round Table (life), Wightman Tennis Ctr. Club (Weston, Mass.), Harvard Varsity Club (Boston), Harvard Club (Boston), Newton Club (Mass.), Squash and Tennis Club, Masons, Golden Key Soc. Jewish. Office: Rodman Ins Agy Inc 145 Rosemary St Needham MA 02494-3238 Office Phone: 781-247-7835. Business E-Mail: srodman@rodmanins.com.

**RODNING, CHARLES BERNARD,** surgeon; b. Pipestone, Minn., Aug. 4, 1943; s. Selmer Bernard and Ida Amanda (Selness) R.; m. Mary Elizabeth Lipke, June 15, 1968; children: Christopher Bernard, Soren Piers, Kai Johannes. BS, Gustavus Adolphus Coll., St. Peter, Minn., 1965; MD, U. Rochester, 1970; PhD, U. Minn., 1979. Diplomate Am. Bd. Med. Examiners, Am. Bd. Surgery. Intern, asst. resident dept. surgery U. Rochester Sch. Medicine and Dentistry, 1970-72; assoc. resident to chief resident, med. fellow dept. surgery U. Minn. Health Scis. Ctr., Mpls., 1972-79; prof. dept cell biology and neurosci. U. South Ala., Mobile, 1981—, prof. dept. surgery, 1981—, vice chmn. dept. surgery, 1981—2006, chmn. dept. surgery, 2006—, dir. gen. surgery, 1996—. Field liaison physician Commn. on Cancer-ACS, Chgo., 1984—; mem. med. adv. bd. Ala. Organ & Tissue Ctr., Birmingham, 1988—. Author: Elan Vital, 1988, Wode and Ston, 1988, Sorrowful Wheel, 1989, Ponderings, 1990, The Sea Rises in the West, 1991, Stepping Stones, 1991, Snowbound Below the Fire Line, 1991, Love Knot, 1994, Papering Dreams, 1994, Carry Onward, 1996, Swaying Grass, 1998, Tradition of Excellence: Pictorial History of Surgical Education at the Mobile General Hospital and University of South Alabama College of Medicine and Medical Center, 1999; reviewer: Jour. Histochem. Cytochem., 1988—; contbr. (articles) Clin. Anatomy, Surg. Endoscopy, Pharos, Jours. Thoracic Cardiovasc. Surgery, So. Med. Jour., others. Bd. dirs. Mobile Mental Health Ctr., Mental Health Found. of South Ala., Mobile Med. Mus.; mem. Bd. of Health, Couty of Mobile Comdr. USN, 1974-81. Recipient Physicians Recognition award AMA, 1980, 85, 88, 91, 95, 99, 02, Bacaner Rsch. award Minn. Med. Found., 1979, Humanism in Medicine award Arnold P. Gold Found., Healthcare Found. N.J., 2002, Howard L. Holley award Med. Assn. State Ala., 2002. Fellow ACS, Internat. Coll. Surgeons (vice regent Ala. chpt. 1989—); mem. Iota Delta Gamma, Alpha Omega Alpha, Phi Kappa Phi. Office: U South Ala Coll Med Allied Health Professions Mobile AL 36617-2293 Office Phone: 251-471-7034. Business E-Mail: crodning@usouthal.edu.

**RODNUNSKY, SIDNEY,** lawyer, educator; b. Edmonton, Alta., Can., Feb. 3, 1946; s. B. and I. Rodnunsky; m. Teresita Asuncion; children: Naomi, Shawna, Rachel, Tevie, Claire, Donna, Sidney Jr. BEd, U. Alberta, 1966, LLB, 1973; MEd, U. Calgary, 1969, grad. diploma, 1990; BS, U. of State of N.Y., 1988; MBA, Greenwich U., 1990. Served as regional counsel to Her Majesty the Queen in Right of the Dominion of Can.; former gov. Grande Prairie Regional Coll.; now prin. legal counsel Can. Nat. exec., Alta. coord.

for gifted children, ombudsman, SIG coord. Mensa Can.; past pres. Grande Prairie and Dist. Bar Assn., Alta Tchrs. Assn., Aspenview. Author: Breathalyzer Casebook; editor: The Children Speak. Decorated knight Grand Cross Sovereign and Royal Order of Piast, knight Grand Cross Order of St. John the Baptist; knight Hospitaller Order St. John of Jerusalem; Prince of Kiev, Prince of Trabzon, Prince and Duke of Rodari, Duke of Chernigov, Count of Riga, Count of St. John of Alexandria; named to Honorable Order of Ky. Colonels; named adm. State of Tex.; recipient Presdl. Legion of Merit. Mem. Law Soc. Alta., Law Soc. Sask., Can. Bar Assn., Inst. Can. Mgmt., Phi Delta Kappa. Address: Box 213 Kugaaruk NU Canada X0B 1K0 Office Phone: 867-769-6211. E-mail: wonderfulschool@hotmail.com.

**RODOLPH, GRANT,** lawyer; b. Aberdeen, Scotland, Nov. 21, 1974; s. Larry Don and Averil Irene Rodolph; m. Jennifer Elise van Dyk, Mar. 14, 2003. BS in Chem. Engring., U. Okla., 1998; JD, So. Meth. U., 2003. Bar: Tex. 2003, U.S. Patent & Trademark Office 2001. Quality engr. The Pro-Quip Corp., A Divsn. of Linde AG, Tulsa, Okla., 1998—99; assoc., patent agt., tech. writer Siegesmund & Assocs., Dallas, 2001—04; assoc. Conley Rose, P.C., Plano, Tex., 2004—. Mem.: Lawyer-Pilots Bar Assn., Intellectual Property Sect., Tex. Bar Assn., Am. Intellectual Property Law Assn. Avocation: flying. Office: Conley Rose PC 5700 Granite Parkway Suite 330 Plano TX 75024 Office Phone: 972-731-2272. Office Fax: 972-731-2289. Business E-Mail: grodolph@dfw.conleyrose.com.

**RODOWSKY, LAWRENCE FRANCIS,** retired state judge; b. Balt., Nov. 10, 1930; s. Lawrence Anthony and Frances (Gardner) R.; m. Colby Fossett, Aug. 7, 1954; children: Laura Rodowsky Ramos, Alice Rodowsky-Seegers, Emily Rodowsky Savopoulos, Sarah Jones Rodowsky, Gregory, Katherine Rodowsky O'Connor. AB, Loyola Coll., Balt., 1952; LLB, U. Md., 1956. Bar: Md. 1956. Cr. crier, law clk. U.S. Dist. Ct. Md., 1954-56; asst. atty. gen. Md., 1960-61; assoc., ptnr. firm Frank, Bernstein, Conaway & Goldman, Balt., 1956-79; judge Ct. Appeals Md., Annapolis, 1980-2000, mem. rules com., 1969-80; sr. status judge Ct. of Spl. Appeals Md., Annapolis, 2001—. Lectr., asst. instr. U. Md. Law Sch., 1958-68, 87-91; reporter jud. dept. Md. Constl. Conv. Commn., 1966-67. Chmn. Gov. Md. Commn. Racing Reform, 1979. Fellow Am. Coll. Trial Lawyers; mem. Md. Bar Assn., Balt. Bar Assn. Roman Catholic. Home: 6614 Linwood Cir Baltimore MD 21212-1213 Office: 620 CM Mitchell Jr Courthse 100 N Calvert St Baltimore MD 21202 Office Phone: 410-333-4374. Business E-Mail: Lawrence.Rodowsky@courts.state.md.us.

**RODRICKS, DANIEL JOHN,** columnist, television commentator; b. Brockton, Mass., Mar. 8, 1954; s. Joseph Allen and Rose Mary (Popolo) Rodricks; m. Lillian M. Donnard, Sept. 6, 1980. BA, U. Bridgeport, 1976. Reporter Patriot Ledger, Quincy, Mass., 1973-75; wire editor Middletown Times Record, NY, 1975; reporter Balt. Evening Sun, 1976-79; columnist Balt. Sun, 1979—; reporter, commentator Sta. WBAL-TV, Balt., 1980-93; host The Dan Rodricks Show Sta. WBAL Radio, 1989-93; host Rodricks For Breakfast Sta. WMAR-TV, Balt., 1995-99. Author: Mencken Doesn't Live Here Anymore, 1989, Balt., Charm City, 1998. Recipient Heywood Broun award Newspaper Guild, 1983, Front Page award, 1983, numerous regional journalism awards, 1990-2000; awards from Sigma Delta Chi, Md.-Del.-D.C. Press Assn., AP, Firefighters Internat., and others. Mem. Sigma Delta Chi Democrat. Roman Catholic. Avocations: cooking, fishing, theater, operetta. Office: Balt Sun 501 N Calvert St PO Box 1377 Baltimore MD 21278 E-mail: TJIDAN@aol.com.

**RODRIGUE, GEORGE P.,** newpaper executive; Grad, Univ. Va., 1978. City hall reporter to city editor, European bur. chief, Washington corr. Dallas Morning News (Belo Corp.), Dallas, 1982—98, v.p., mng. editor, 2004—; exec. editor, v.p. news The Press Enterprise (Belo Corp.), Riverside, Calif., 1998; v.p. Capital Bur. Belo Corp., Washington. Co-recipient Two Pulitzer Prizes.

**RODRIGUES, AZAEL MAGALHAES, JR.,** musician; s. Azael Magalhaes Rodrigues and Maria Olga Soares Cunha. Student, U. Sao Paulo, 1975—79. Drummer, composer Pau Brasil, Divina Increnca, Preme, Sao Paulo, 1978—82, Pau Brasil, Preme, Prisma, 1982—87; drummer, composer, arranger, prodr. Band Z/Gremio Recreativo, 1988—94; mgr., musical prodr. Bourbon St. Music Club, 1995—96; prodr., musician Free lancer/Corda Toda, 1997—2000; mgr., musician Haveli Inc./Free Lancer, Miami. Lectr., tchr. U. Miami, 2002—03. Author: The Rhythm Within: a Brazilian passport to the groove, (music critic) Folha De Sao Paulo; musician (arranger): (c.d.) 23 (Engenho de Dentro, Princesa) (# 1 Hit Parade, 1993); prodr.(composer+arranger): (c.d.) Universal 18 _ Questing for Virtual Transportation. Achievements include One of the three best drummers of the year, Readers pool, Jornal da Tarde. Avocations: tennis, jogging, swimming, travel.

**RODRIGUES, STANLEY JOHN,** materials engineer, researcher; arrived in US, 1985; s. John Germano and Caraciola Rodrigues; m. Mary Rodrigues, Dec. 11, 1993; 3 children. BS, Bombay U., 1984; MS, U. Bonaventure U., 1987, U. Dayton, 1993, PhD, 2000. Grad. tchg. asst. St. Bonaventure U., Olean, NY, 1985—87; from grad. rsch. asst. to assoc. rsch. engr. U. Dayton (Ohio) Rsch. Inst., 1989—2002; rsch. scientist USAF Rsch. Labs, Dayton, 2002—03, rsch. engr., 2003—. Faculty Sinclair CC, Dayton, 1992—; moderator GM, Vandalia, Ohio, 1998—2000. Contbr. articles to profl. jours. Vol. Livingston Care Ctr., Dayton, 1992—; mentor TeenWorks, Dayton, 1994—96; vestry mem. Christ the King Reformed Episcopal Ch., Dayton, 2005—. Recipient Outstanding Physics award, St. Bonaventure U., 1987. Mem.: AIAA, Electro Chem. Soc. Achievements include patents for colloidal electrolyte. Avocations: music, walking, travel, reading. Office: Air Force Rsch Lab Propulsion Directorate 1950 Fifth St Bldg 18 Wright Patterson Afb OH 45433-7251

**RODRIGUEZ, ALEX (ALEXANDER EMMANUEL RODRIGUEZ),** professional baseball player; b. NYC, July 27, 1975; s. Victor Rodriguez and Lourdes Navarro; m. Cynthia Scurtis, Nov. 2, 2002; 1 child, Natasha Alexander. Grad. Westminster Christian Sch., Miami. Baseball player Seattle Mariners, 1995—2001, Tex. Rangers, 2001—03, NY Yankees, 2004—. Mem. Team USA World Baseball Classic, 2006. Co-author: (children's book) Hit a Grand Slam, 1998. Founder Grand Slam for Kids, 1996, Alex Rodriguez Found., 1998. Named Am. League Batting Champion, 1996, Am. League MVP, 2003, 2005; named to MLB All-Star Game, 1996—98, 2000—06; recipient Gold Glove award, 2002, 2003, Silver Slugger award, MLB, 2005. Achievements include being the third player in major league history with 40 home runs and 40 stolen bases in one season; leading the Am. League in home runs, 2001-03; leading the Am. League in runs scored, 2001, 2003; leading the Am. League in RBI's, 2002; youngest player in MLB history to hit 400 home runs, June 8, 2005; most home runs in a season by right-handed hitter in Yankee History, 2005. Office: c/o NY Yankees E 161st St and River Ave Bronx NY 10452*

**RODRIGUEZ, ANNABELLE,** judge, former attorney general; b. Santurce, PR; m. Francisco de Jesus-Schuck; children: Ricardo Enrique Candle, Fernando Manuel Vela. BA in history magna cum laude, U. PR, JD, 1985. From asst. solicitor gen. to solicitor gen. PR Dept. Justice, 1986—93; ptnr. Martino, Odell & Calabria, Hato Rey, PR, 1993—96; judge US Dist Ct. (PR dist.), 1996; sec. justice PR, 2001—04; assoc. judge PR Supreme Ct., 2004—. Democrat. Office: Tribunal Supremo de PR PO Box 2392 San Juan PR 00902*

**RODRIGUEZ, ANNE O'MEARA,** medical educator; MD, Northwestern U., Chgo. Diplomate Am. Bd. Obstetrics & Gynecology. Asst. prof. U. So. Calif., LA, 1999—2004, U. Calif. Davis Med. Ctr., Sacramento, 2004—. Editor: Current Opinion in Obstetrics and Gynecology; contbr. articles to profl. pubs. Physician educator Physicians for Social Responsibility, L.A., 2002—04. Mem.: Alpha Omega Alpha.

**RODRIGUEZ, ANTONIO JOSE,** lawyer; b. New Orleans, Dec. 7, 1944; s. Anthony Joseph and Josephine Olga (Cox) R.; m. Virginia Anne Soignet, Aug. 23, 1969; children: Henry Jacob, Stephen Anthony. BS, US Naval Acad., 1966; JD cum laude, Loyola U. of the South, New Orleans, 1973. Bar: La. 1973, U.S. Dist. Ct. (ea. dist.) La. 1973, U.S. Ct. Appeals (5th cir.) 1973, U.S. Dist. Ct. (mid. dist.) La. 1975, U.S. Dist. Ct. (we. dist.) La. 1977, U.S. Ct. Appeals (11th cir.) 1981, U.S. Supreme Ct. 1987, U.S. Dist. Ct. (so. dist.) Miss. 1991, U.S. Ct. Appeals (4th cir.) 1991, U.S. Ct. Appeals (1st cir.) 1997, U.S. Ct. Internat. Trade, 1991. Assoc. Phelps, Dunbar, Marks, Claverie & Sims, New Orleans, 1973-77; ptnr. Phelps Dunbar, New Orleans, 1977-92, Fowler Rodriguez & Chalos, New Orleans, 1992—. Prof. Law Tulane U., New Orleans, 1981—; mem. nat. rules of the road adv. coun. U.S. Dept. Transp., Washington, 1987-90, chmn. nat. navigation safety adv. coun., 1990-94, mem., 2000—; spkr. on admiralty and environ. Co-author: Admiralty-Limitation of Liability, 1981—, Admiralty-Law of Collision, 1990—; author: (chpt.) Benedict on Admiralty, 1995—; assoc. editor Loyola Law Rev., 1971-73; contbr. articles to profl. maritime and environ. jours. Bd. dirs. Greater New Orleans Coun. Navy League, 1988—, Propeller Club of New Orleans, 1997—. Lt. USN, 1966-70; capt. USNR, 1970-95. Decorated Navy Commendation medal; recipient Disting. Pub. Svc. award U.S. Dept. Transp., 1993. Fellow La. Bar Found.; mem. ABA, La. State Bar Assn., La. State Law Inst., Maritime Law Assn. U.S. (proctor 1975—), New Orleans Bar Assn., Southeastern Admiralty Law Inst., Assn. Average Adjusters U.S., Assn. Average Adjusters U.K., Naval Res. Assn. (chpt. pres. 1982-84), U.S. Naval Acad. Alumni Assn. (chpt. pres. 1981-83), Bienville Club, Phi Alpha Delta, Alpha Sigma Nu. Republican. Roman Catholic. Home: 4029 Mouton St Metairie LA 70002-1303 Office: Fowler Rodriguez & Chalos Texaco Ctr 400 Poydras St 30th Fl New Orleans LA 70130-1000 Office Phone: 504-523-2600. Business E-Mail: ajr@frc-law.com.

**RODRIGUEZ, CARLOS A.,** lawyer; b. 1960; AB, Harvard Coll., 1982; JD, Columbia Law Sch., 1985. Bar: NY 1986. Ptnr., securitization and structured fin. Sidley Austin Brown & Wood LLP, NYC, mem. exec. com. Mem.: Assn. of Bar City of NY (com. to enhance diversity in the profession). Office: Sidley Austin Brown & Wood LLP 878 Seventh Ave New York NY 10019 Office Phone: 212-839-5857. Office Fax: 212-839-5599. Business E-Mail: crodriguez@sidley.com.

**RODRIGUEZ, CARLOS AUGUSTO,** lawyer; b. Havana, Cuba, Sept. 1, 1954; came to U.S., 1960; s. Urbano and Estela (Cardenas) R.; m. Valerie Carr, May 27, 1989. BA magna cum laude, Furman U., 1977; JD, U. Fla., 1980. Bar: Fla. 1980, U.S. Ct. Appeals (5th cir.) 1981, U.S. Dist. Ct. (so. dist. and trial bar) Fla. 1984, U.S. Ct. Appeals (11th cir.) 1995; bd. cert. civil trial atty. Asst. pub. defender Broward County Pub. Defender's Office, Ft. Lauderdale, Fla., 1980-83, chief asst. pub. defender, 1983-85; assoc. Fazio, Dawson & DiSalvo, Ft. Lauderdale, Fla., 1985-87; sole practice Ft. Lauderdale, Fla., 1987—. Assoc. prof. U. Miami Sch. Law, Miami, 1983-85; lectr. criminal procedure Nova Law Cen., Ft. Lauderdale, 1983-85, lectr. on law Broward Community Coll., Ft. Lauderdale, 1983-87; mem. Nuisance Abatement Bd., 1989—, chmn., 1996—; vice chmn. Marine ADv. Bd., 1990. Mem. Marine Adv. Bd., Broward, Fla., 1986-96; rep. Primary Rep. Port Everglades Commn., Broward, 1984. Mem. ABA, ATLA, Am. Bd. Trial Advocacy, Acad. Fla. Trial Lawyers, Broward County Bar Assn., Phi Beta Kappa. Republican. Roman Catholic. Avocations: scuba diving, fishing, water and snow skiing. Home: 2448 SE 12th St Pompano Beach FL 33062-7040 Office: 633 S Andrews Ave Ste 402 Fort Lauderdale FL 33301-2857 Fax: 954-463-9492.

**RODRIGUEZ, CAROLYN,** lawyer; b. N.Y.C., Sept. 26, 1961; d. Emilio and Emma (Vasquez) R.; m. Warren Dondero, Jan. 4, 1991; children: Michelle Alicia, Nikki Taylor, Alexis Nicole. BA, Fordham U., 1982; JD, Pace U., 1987. Bar: Conn. 1987, N.Y. 1988, U.S. Dist. Ct. (so. and ea. dists.) N.Y. 1990. Asst. corp. counsel N.Y.C. Law Dept., 1987-89; assoc. David M. Lee, Esquire, N.Y.C., 1989-95; pvt. practice Suffolk, N.Y., 1995—. Mem. N.Y. State Trial Lawyers Assn., P.R. Bar Assn., Assn. Trial Lawyers of Am., N.Y. State Bar Assn.

**RODRIGUEZ, CHI CHI (JUAN RODRIGUEZ),** professional golfer; b. Bayamon, P.R., Oct. 23, 1935; m. Donnette Iwalani, Apr. 6, 1962. Profl. golfer PGA, 1960—; joined Sr. PGA, 1985—. Contbg. columnist golf. mags. Winner Denver Open Invitational, 1963, Lucky Internat. Open, 1964, Western Open, 1964, Tex. Open Invitational, 1967, Sahara Invitational, 1968, Byron Nelson Golf Classic, 1972, Greater Greensboro Open, 1973, Tallahassee Open, 1979, Sr. Tournament Players Championship, 1986, Digital Srs. Classic, 1986-88, United Va. Bank Srs., 1986, Gen. Foods PGA Srs.' Championship, 1987, Vantage at The Dominion, 1987, United Hosps. Sr. Golf Championship, 1987, Silver Pages Classic, 1987, Sr. Players Reunion Pro-Am., 1987, GTE Northwest Classic, 1987, Doug Sanders Kingwood Celebrity Classic, 1988, Crestar Classic, 1989, Las Vegas Sr. Classic, 1990, 91, Vintage Arco Invitational, 1990, 91, Ameritech Sr. Open, 1990, Sunwest/Charley Pride Classic, 1990, GTE West Classic, 1991, Murata Reunion Pro-Am., 1991, KO Olina Sr. Invitational, 1992, Burnet Sr. Classic, 1993; winner with JoAnn Washam Pepsi Mixed Team Championship, 1976, Bahamas Open, 1979, Sr. Skins Games, 1988-89, Vantage Championship Mastercard Charity Team, 1999; named to Ryder Cup Team, 1973; inducted into the World Sports Humanitarian Hall of Fame, 1994; Best Sr. PGA Tour Finish T5 Comfort Classic, 1998. Achievements include being the leading money winner on sr. tour, 1987; representing P.R. in 12 world cups; ranked # 5 on PGA sr. tour, 1987 & 4 among scoring leaders PGA sr. tour, 1992. Office: PGAAmerica PO Box 109601 112 Tpc Blvd Ponte Vedra Beach FL 32082-3077 Address: The Chi Chi Rodriguez Foun 3030 N Mcmullen Booth Rd Clearwater FL 33761-3331 also: care Eddie Elias Enterprises LLC 1720 Merriman Rd 3916 Clock Pointe Trl Ste 101 Stow OH 44224-2932

**RODRIGUEZ, CIRO DAVIS,** former congressman; b. Dec. 9, 1946; m. Carolina Pena; 1 child. BA, St. Mary's U., 1973; MSW, Our Lady of the Lake U., 1978. Mem. Harlandale Ind. Sch. Dist. Bd., 1975-87; faculty assoc., Worden Sch. Social Work Our Lady of the Lake U., 1987-96; mem. Tex. Ho. of Reps., 1987-97, 105th-108th Congress from 28th Tex. dist., 1997—2005. Mem. Mil. Readiness subcom. House Nat. Security Com., Health subcom. House Vets. Affairs Com.; 2d vice chair and health care task force chair Congrl. Hispanic Caucus, 2004-2005. Democrat. Roman Catholic.

**RODRIGUEZ, DANIEL,** tenor, former protective services official; Police officer NYC Police Dept., 1995—2004, singer ceremonial unit, ret., 2004—; tenor, 2004—; known as "the singing policeman." Performances include: 2002 Winter Olympics, PBS Meml. Day concert, Tournament of Roses Parade, Rep. Nat. Convention, 2004, Celebration of Freedom Inauguration concert; singer: (albums) God Bless America, 2001, The Spirit of America, 2002, Be My Love, 2003, From My Heart, 2003, In The Presence, 2005. Office: c/o POW Inc 5657 Wilshire Blvd Ste 280 Los Angeles CA 90036*

**RODRIGUEZ, DANIEL B.,** dean, law educator; b. 1962; BA, Calif. State U., Long Beach, 1984; JD, Harvard U., 1987. Law clk. to Hon. Alex Kozinski U.S. Ct. Appeals (9th cir.), Pasadena, Calif., 1987-88; acting prof. U. Calif., Boalt Hall Sch. Law, Berkeley, 1988—94, prof., 1994—98; dean U. San Diego Sch. Law, 1998—. Vis. scholar Hoover Inst., Stanford U.; vis. prof. McGeorge Sch. Law-Govt. Affairs Prog.; John M. Olin Fellow in Law and Econs. Office: U San Diego Sch Law 5998 Alcalá Park San Diego CA 92110

**RODRIGUEZ, DANIELA M.,** plastic surgeon; b. Detroit; BA, U. Mich., Ann Arbor, 1993; MD, U. Health Scis./Chgo. Med. Sch., 1997, M in Clin. Physiology, 1997. Cert. Am. Bd. Plastic Surgery. Resident plastic surgery Montefiore Med. Ctr., N.Y.C., 1997—2002; solo practitioner Daniela Rodriguez, M.D., St. Clair Shores, Mich., 2002—. Staff Bon Secours Cottage Hosp., St. John Hosp. and Med. Ctr., St. John Macomb Hosp., St. Joseph's Hosp. Clinton Twp., Troy Beaumont Hosp. Contbr. articles to profl. jours. Named one of Outstanding Women Surgeons, Assn. Women Surgeons, 2002;

grantee, Brown U., 1999, N.Y. Acad. Medicine, 2000. Mem.: AMA, Am. Bd. Plastic Surgeons, Am. Soc. Plastic Surgeons, Alpha Omega Alpha. Office: Daniela Rodriguez MD 21727 Greater Mack Ave Saint Clair Shores MI 48080 Office Phone: 586-777-7260.

**RODRIGUEZ, DONNA JEANNE ANGLIN,** dietician, writer; b. Albuquerque, July 21, 1953; d. Randolph Sterling and Audrey Miriam (Kubach) Anglin; m. Ralph A. Rodriguez, Feb. 19, 1977. BS, N.Mex. State U., 1975; MS, U. N.Mex., 1996. Cert. nutrition support dietitian; registered dietitian. Clin. dietitian N.Mex. Hosp., Albuquerque, 1977-91, nutrition support coord., 1991-95, rsch. coord., 1995-96, vis. prof./lectr., 1996-97; proff. healthcare writer Lovelace Healthcare Innovations, Albuquerque, 1997-98; clin. dietitian West Albuquerque Dialysis Ctr., 1999—; instr. TVI C.C., Albuquerque, 2005—. Assoc. editor: (jour.) Support Line, 1996-99; contbr. articles to profl. jours., chpts. to books. Mem. Am. Dietetic Assn., N.Mex. Dietetic Assn., Am. Burn Assn. (chmn. nutrition spl. interest group 1994-96). Avocations: camping, needlecrafts.

**RODRIGUEZ, ELENA GARCIA,** retired pension fund administrator; b. Havana, Cuba, Mar. 21, 1944; came to U.S., 1959; d. Eliseo and Elena (Suarez) Garcia; divorced; children: Victor, Yvonne, Daniel. B in Profl. Studies, Barry U., 1983; MS in Mgmt., St. Thomas U., 1985; postgrad., U. Phila., 1989, UCLA, 1990. With City of Miami, Fla., 1969-95, pension adminstr. Fla., 1978-95, ret. Fla., 1995. Bd. dirs. Mediation Ethics Adv. Bd. Author: General and Sanitation Pension Benefit Booklet, 1982, Fire and Police Pension Benefit Booklet, 1982, Retirement Planning Booklet, 1985 Mem. Leadership Miami, 1985—; mediator Cir. Ct., family, County Ct.; vol. Reading Blind and Dyslexic. Mem.: Better Bus. Bur. (former arbitrator, mediator), Assn. South Fla. Mediators (mediator), Fed. Emergency Mgmt. Agency, N.Y. Stock Exch. (arbitrator), Nat. Ctr. Dispute Resolution (arbitrator). Democrat. Roman Catholic. Avocations: growing orchids, stained glass, tile mosaics, painting.

**RODRIGUEZ, ERNESTO A.,** artist, researcher; b. NYC; s. Pedro and Hazel Valencia Rodriguez. BFA, Parsons Sch. Design, 1979. Art specialist Camp Oakhurst, NJ, 1982—86; art instr. St. Francis of the Assisi, NYC, 1984—93; sr. crafts instr. Jewish Guild for the Blind, NYC, 1987—88; supr. trainer Saks Fifth Ave, 1990—94; commn. artist/owner E. A. Rodriguez, NYC, 1990—2005; tchr. Bd. Edn., Bronx, 2001—02. Tchr. Trinity Luth. Sch., Bronx, 1983—86. One-man shows include St. Francis Assisi Ch., 1984, Represented in permanent collections N.Y.C., represented in pvt. collections. Counselor Covenant House, NYC, 1988; rehabilitation specialist Project Reachout, NYC, 1988. Max Beckmann fellow, 1968. Mem.: NY Soc. Sci., Internat. Soc. Poets. Avocations: acting, canoeing, horseback riding, travel, art.

**RODRÍGUEZ, FERDINAND,** chemical engineer, educator; b. Cleve., July 8, 1928; s. José and Concha (Luís) R.; m. Ethel V. Koster, July 28, 1951; children: Holly Edith, Lida Concha. BS, Case Western Res. U., 1950, MS, 1954; PhD, Cornell U., 1958. Devel. engr. Ferro Corp., Bedford, Ohio, 1950-54; asst. prof. chem. engring. Cornell U., 1958-61, asso. prof., 1961-71, prof., 1971—. On sabbatic leave at Union Carbide Corp., 1964-65, Imperial Chem. Industries Ltd., 1971, Eastman Kodak Co., 1978-79; cons. to industry. Author: Principles of Polymer Systems, 5th edit., 2003; contbr. articles; songwriter: Served with U.S. Army, 1954-56. Recipient Excellence in Teaching award Cornell Soc. Engrs., 1966, Edn. Achievement award Hispanic Engr. Mag., 1991. Fellow Am. Inst. Chem. Engrs.; mem. Am. Chem. Soc., Soc. Hispanic Profl. Engrs., Soc. Plastics Engrs. Lutheran. Office: Cornell U 267 Olin Hall Ithaca NY 14853 Business E-Mail: FR13@cornell.edu.

**RODRIGUEZ, FREDDY,** actor; b. Chgo., Jan. 17, 1975; m. Elsie Rodriguez; 3 children. Actor: (TV series) Oh Grow Up, 1999, Six Feet Under, 2001—05; (films) The Force, 1994, A Walk in the Clouds, 1995, Dead Presidents, 1995, The Pest, 1997, Can't Hardly Wait, 1998, Shock Television, 1998, Joseph's Gift, 1998, Payback, 1999, Beyond City Limits, 2001, Chasing Papi, 2003, Dallas 362, 2003, Harsh Times, 2005, Dreamer: Inspired by a True Story, 2005; actor, actor: (films) Pledge of Allegiance, 2005, Poseidon, 2006, Lady in the Water, 2006; (TV films) Seduced by Madness: The Diane Borchardt Story, 1996, For Love or Country: The Arturo Sandoval Story, 2000. Office: c/o Innovative Artist Talent Agy 7th Fl 235 Park Ave South New York NY 10003*

**RODRIGUEZ, IRMINA BESTARD,** science educator; b. Havana, Cuba, Apr. 29, 1945; came to U.S., 1961; d. Gaspar and Ester Antonia (Bas) Bestard; m. Luis Felipe Rodriguez, June 8, 1968; children: Damien Brandon, Leslie Christina. BA in Chemistry, Coll. of New Rochelle, 1967; postgrad., U. Bridgeport, 1969-71, Barry U., Fla. Internat. U. Ctr. Fla. Rsch. technician in pharmacology N.Y. Med. Coll., N.Y.C., 1967-70; rsch. chemist Clairol, Inc., Stamford, Conn., 1970-74; pre-sch. instr. Happi-tymes, Miami, 1981-84; educator St. John Neumann Sch., Miami, 1984-92; sci. educator Carrollton Sch., Miami, 1992—. Coord. sci. dept. Carrollton Sch., 2004—. Contbr. articles to profl. jours. Mem. ways/means chmn. Stamford Women's Rep. Club, 1975-79, v.p. 1979. Mem. AAUW, Nat. Sci. Tchrs. Assn., Fla. Sci. Tchrs. Assn., Dade County Sci. Tchrs. Assn. Republican. Roman Catholic. Avocations: swimming, biking, reading, art collecting, ecology club advisor. Office: Carrollton Sch of the Sacred Heart 3747 Main Hwy Miami FL 33133-5907 Office Phone: 305-446-5673. Business E-Mail: irodriguez@carrollton.org.

**RODRIGUEZ, IVAN TORRES,** professional baseball player; b. Vega Baja, P.R., Nov. 30, 1971; Catcher Tex. Rangers, 1991—2002, Florida Marlins, 2003, Detroit Tigers, 2004—. Mem. Am. League All-Star Team, 1992-2001, 2004, Am. League Silver Slugger Team The Sporting News, 1994-99, American League MVP, 1999, NLCS MVP, 2003, mem. of World Series Championship Team, 2003. Recipient Gold Glove award, 1992-2001, 2004. Office: c/o Detroit Tigers 2100 Woodward Ave Detroit MI 48201

**RODRIGUEZ, JAI,** television personality; b. Brentwood, NY, June 22, 1977; Actor: (films) The New Guy, 2002; (Broadway plays) Rent, Spinning into Butter, (off broadway plays) Zanna, Don't!, 2003; co-author: (books) Queer Eye for the Straight Guy: The Fab 5's Guide to Looking Better, Cooking Better, Dressing Better, Behaving Better, and Living Better, 2004; culture specialist (TV series) Queer Eye for the Straight Guy, 2003—; actor, actor: (Broadway plays) The Producers, 2005.*

**RODRIGUEZ, JOSEFA NIEVES,** special education educator, language educator; b. Mantanzaz, Cuba, Nov. 7, 1942; d. Basilio Gonzalez Santana and Edelmira Margarita Escalona; m. Manuel B. Rodriguez, June 17, 1972; children: Josie, Aimee, Manuel Jr. B in Secretarial Sci., Barry U., Miami Shores, Fla., 1965, BS, 1980, MS, 1992. Profl. educator's cert. Fla., cert. ESOL, Spanish, specific learning disabilities, mentally handicapped. Sales agt. Eastern Airlines, Inc., Miami, Fla., 1965—90; pre-sch. tchr. Archdiocese Miami, 1990—96; ESOL tchr. adult edn. Dade County Pub. Schs., Miami, 1996—, spl. edn. tchr., 2000—, tchr. of students with phys. impairments, 2005—06. Substitute tchr. Dade County Pub. Schs., Miami, 1992—2000; adj. prof. Miami Dade CC, Miami, 1997, ESOL instr., 2000; facilitator U. Miami Reading Inst.; ESOL tutor adult edn. Dade County Pub. Schs., Miami, 2005—06. Mem.: AFT, NEA, Dade Art Educators Assn., Coun. for Exceptional Student Edn., Fla. Edn. Assn., United Tchrs. Dade, Barry U. Alumnae Assn. Republican. Roman Catholic. Avocations: opera, piano, painting, tennis, languages. Office: Dade County Pub Schs 1500 Biscayne Blvd Miami FL 33132 Office Phone: 305-995-1000.

**RODRIGUEZ, JUAN ALFONSO,** information technology executive; b. Santiago, Cuba, Feb. 10, 1941; came to U.S., 1953; s. Alfonso and Marie Madeleine (Hourcadette) R. BEE, CCNY, 1962; MEE, NYU, 1963. Engr. IBM, Poughkeepsie, NY, 1963-68, Boulder, Colo., 1963—68, engring. mgr., 1968-69; dir. tech. Storage Tech. Corp., Louisville, Colo., 1969-74, v.p. engring., 1974-77, v.p., gen. mgr. disk, 1977-79, v.p., gen. mgr. optical disk

Longmont, Colo., 1979-85; pres., CEO Exabyte Corp., Boulder, 1985-87, CEO, 1987-90, chmn., 1987-92; pres. Sweetwater Corp., 1992-93, chmn., 1992-95, also bd. dirs.; prof. elec. and computer engring. and engring. mgmt. U. Colo., 1992—, co-exec. dir. Ctr. for Entrepreneurship, 1994-2000; chmn. Datasonix, 1992-96, Vixel, 1995-99; chmn., CEO Ecrix Corp., 1996—2001; chief technologist, bd. dirs. Exabyte Corp., 2001—03, interim CEO, pres., 2003, chmn., 2003—. Mem. devel. coun. Coll. Engring. U. Colo., 1990-92; Decisionism Corp.; mem. engring. adv. bd. CCNY, bd. dirs. Colo. Advanced Tech. Enterprise, 1994-98; Robert J. Appel Disting. lectr. law and tech. Law Sch. U. Denver, 1990. Patentee in field. Bd. dir. Boulder YMCA, 1982-87, U. Colo. Artist Series, 1988-92; mem. bd. govs. Boulder County United Way, 1989-93, chairperson campaign, 1992; commr. Colo. Advance Tech. Inst., 1988-92. Finalist Entrepreneur of Yr., Arthur Young & Inc Mag., 1989; named Boulder Spirit Entrepreneur of Yr., 1989, Entrepreneur of the Decade, Boulder C. of C., 1994; named one of Top 50 Tech. Innovators, VAR Bus., 2004; recipient Ind. Quality award, Am. Soc. Quality Control (Rocky Mountain sect.), 1990, Gen. Palmer award Outstanding Engr. in Industry, Am. Cons. Engrs. Coun. Colo., 1995, Career Achievement award, Engring. Sch. Alumni CCNY, 2002, Townsend Harris medal, Alumni Assn. CCNY, 2003, Hispanic Engr. of Yr., Entrepreneur Hispanic Engr. Nat. Achievement Awards Coun., 1995. Fellow IEEE; mem. Computer Soc. of IEEE (mem. steering com. on mass storage 1981-93), Soc. Photo-Optical Instrumentation Engrs., Boulder C. of C. (chmn. entrepreneurs support program 1989), Greater Denver C. of C. (bd. dirs. 1990-91); mem. Beta Gamma Sigma (medallion of Entrepreneurship 2003). Office: Exabyte Corp 2108 55th St Boulder CO 80301 Personal E-mail: jar@ieee.org.

**RODRIGUEZ, LUIS J.,** writer; b. El Paso, Tex., July 9, 1954; s. Alfonso and Maria Estela (Jimenez) R.; m. Camila Barros, Aug. 10, 1974 (div. Nov. 1979); children: Ramiro Daniel, Andrea Victoria; m. María Trinidad Cárdenas, Mar. 31, 1988; children: Ruben Joaquin, Luis Jacinto. Cert., U. Calif., Berkeley, 1980. Freelance poet, journalist, critic, 1980—; reporter San Bernardino (Calif.) Sun and other newspapers, 1980-88; newswriter, reporter WMAQ-AM All News Radio, Chgo., 1988-92; typesetter Liturgy Tng. Publs., Chgo., 1988-92; dir. poetry press Tía Chucha Press, Chgo., 1989—. Bd. dirs. Guild Complex Lit. Arts, Chgo., 1991—. Author: (poetry) Poems Across the Pavement, 1989 (Poetry Ctr. Book award), The Concrete River, 1991 (Pen West/Josephine Miles award 1991), Trochemoche, 2002, (memoir) Always Running, Gang Days in L.A., 1993 (Chgo. Sun Times Book award 1994, Carl Sandburg Literary award, designated NY Times Notable Book), The Republic of East LA, 2002, Music of the Mill, 2005, (children's) America is Her Name, 1997. Facilitator Youth Struggling for Survival, Chgo., 1994—; elder, tchr. Mosaic Multicultural Found., Washon, Wash., 1993—; participant Increase the Peace, Chgo., 1995—. Recipient PEN Josephine Miles Literary award, 1991, Dorothea Lang/Paul Taylor prize Ctr. for Documentary Studies, Duke U., 1993, Lila Wallace-Reader's Digest Writers award, 1996, Nat. Assn. Poetry Therapy Pub.Svc. award 1997, Hispanic Heritage award for Lit., 1998, Poetry Center Book award, 1999, Silver Book award, Foreword Mag., 1999, Patterson Young Adult Book award, 1999, Skipping Stones Honor award, 1999, 2000, Parent's Choice Book award, 1999, Ill. Author of Yr. award, 2000, Premio Fronterizo, 2001, Unsung Heroes of Compassion award from His Holiness the Dalai Lama., 2001; Lannan fellow in poetry, 1993, Sundance Inst. Art Writers Fellowship, 2002, Calif. Arts Coun. Fellowship, 2002. Mem. Poetry Soc. Am., Acad. Am. Poets, Nat. Writers Union, Assn. Am. Cultures. Mailing: c/o Kathryn Barcos Steven Barclay Agy 12 Western Ave Petaluma CA 94952 E-mail: luis@luisjrodriguez.com.

**RODRIGUEZ, MICHELLE (MAYTE MICHELLE RODRIGUEZ),** actress; b. Bexar County, Tx, July 12, 1978; Actor: (films) Girlfight, 2000, 3 A.M., 2001, The Fast and the Furious, 2001, Resident Evil, 2002, Blue Crush, 2003, S.W.A.T., 2003, Control, 2004, Sian Ka'an (voice), 2005, BloodRayne, 2005; (TV series) Lost, 2005— (Outstanding Performance by an Ensemble in a Drama Series, Screen Actors Guild award, 2006, Outstanding Supporting Actress in a TV Series, Nat. Coun. La Raza ALMA award (Am. Latin Media Arts), 2006); voice over: (video game) True Crime: Streets of L.A., 2003; Driv3r, 2004; Halo 2, 2004.

**RODRIGUEZ, NARCISO,** fashion designer; b. NJ, 1961; Studied, Parsons Sch. Design, NY. With Anne Klein, Calvin Klein; design dir. TSE, 1995, Cerruti, Paris, Loewe leather, Madrid, 1997—2001; owner Narciso Rodriguez, NYC, 1997—. Released signature fragrance Musc for Her. Women's ready-to-wear signature collection debuted in 1998 in Milan. Named one of 25 Most Influential Hispanics, Time Mag., 2005; recipient Best New Designer, VH1 Fashion Awards, 1997, Perry Ellis award, Coun. of Fashion Designers Am., 1998, Womenswear Designer of Yr., 2002, 2003, Hispanic Designer of Yr., 1997. Achievements include becoming a household name after designing Carolyn Bessette's wedding dress for her marriage to John F. Kennedy, Jr. Office: PR Consulting 50 Bond St New York NY 10012 also: 9th fl 30 Irving Pl New York NY 10003 Office Phone: 212-677-2989.

**RODRIGUEZ, RICH,** college football coach; b. Grant Town, W.Va. m. Rita Rodriguez; children: Raquel, Rhett. BS in Phys. Edn., W. Va. Univ., 1986. Secondary coach, spl. teams coord. Salem Coll., 1986, asst. head coach, defensive coord., 1987, head coach, 1988; asst. coach WVU, 1989; head football coach Glenville State Coll., 1990—96; offensive coord. Tulane, 1997—98; head coach WVU, 2000—. Named to Glenville Sports Hall of Fame, 2003; recipient Coach Yr., WVIAC, 1993—94, Nat. Coach Yr., NAIA, 1993, Coll. Coach Yr., W.Va. Sports Writer's Assn., 1993, Big East Coach Yr., 2002, Dist. I Coach Yr., Am. Football Coaches Assn., 2003. Office: WVU Athletics PO Box 0877 Morgantown WV 26507-0877*

**RODRIGUEZ, RITA MARIA,** economist; b. La Havana, Cuba, Sept. 6, 1944; came to U.S., 1960; Tomas and Adela (Medero) R.; m. E. Eugene Carter, Jan. 7, 1972, 1 child, Adela-Marie R. Carter. BBA, U. PR, 1964; MBA, NYU, 1968, PhD, 1969. Bus. adminstrn. asst. prof., then assoc. prof. Harvard Bus. Sch., Cambridge, Mass., 1969-74, 74-78; fin. prof. U. Ill., Chgo., 1978-82; dir. Export-Import Bank of U.S., Washington, 1982-99. Cons. Polaroid Corp. and Indsl. Devel. Bank in Ecuador (Corporacion Financiera Nacional), 1978-82, U.S. IRS, 1982; bd. dirs. Acad. Ednl. Devel., Washington, 1989-93, 2000—; bd. advisors Pew Econ. Freedom Fellows, Washington, 1991-94, World Bank, MIGA, Washington, 2000; bd. dirs. Affiliated Mgrs. Group, Boston, 2000-, Pvt. Export Funding Corp., N.Y., 2001—; sr. fellow Woodstock Theol. Ctr., Georgetown U., Washington, 2002—; bd. dirs. ENSCO, Dallas, 2003—. Author: (with E. Eugene Carter) International Financial Management, 1976, 2d edit., 1979, 3rd edit., 1984, (with Heinz Riehl) Foreign Exchange Markets: A Guide to Foreign Currency Operations, 1977, Foreign Exchange Management in U.S. Multinationals, 1980 (with Heinz Riehl) Foreign Exchange and Money Markets, 1983, Japanese, Spanish, Portuguese translations, The Export-Import Bank at Fifty, 1987; co-editor (with G.C. Hufbauer) Ex-Im Bank: Overview, Challenges, and Policy Options in the Ex-Im Bank in the 21st Century, 2001; editor (with Gary Hufbauer) The Ex-Im Bank in the 21st Century; contbr. numerous fin. articles to profl. publs. Bd. dirs. Am. Friends of Turkey, 2001. Recipient Outstanding Achievement award Nat. Coun. of Hispanic Women, 1986; Outstanding Hispanic Achievement award Hispanic Corp. Achievers, 1988; Nat. Leadership award Government The Nat. Network of Hispanic Women, 1989. Mem.: Coun. Fgn. Rels. Roman Catholic. Avocations: gardening, music. Office: 3075 Ordway St NW Washington DC 20008-3255

**RODRIGUEZ, ROBERT,** filmmaker; b. San Antonio, June 20, 1968; s. Cecilio and Rebecca Rodriguez; m. Elizabeth Avellan, 1990 (separated), 5 children. Student, U. Tex. Dir. (films) Bedhead, 1991 El Mariachi, 1992, Desperado, 1995, Four Rooms (segment The Misbehaviors), 1995, From Dusk Till Dawn, 1995, The Faculty, 1998, Spy Kids, 2001, Spy Kids II: Island of Lost Dreams, 2002, Spy Kids 3-D: Game Over, Once Upon A Time in Mexico, 2003; Sin City (co-directed with Frank Miller & Quentin Tarantino), 2005; The Adventures of Shark Boy & Lava Girl in 3-D, 2005; TV movies: Roadracers (also wrote), 1994; wrote and prod.(films), From Dusk Til Dawn 3: The Hangman's Daughter, 2000, Once Upon A Time in Mexico, 2003; prod. only (films), From Dusk Til Dawn II: Texas Blood Money, 1999; TV

appearances: Nash Bridges, 1997, Deadline, 2000. Named one of 25 Most Influential Hispanics, Time Mag., 2005, 50 Most Powerful People in Hollywood, Premiere mag., 2005. Office: care Internat Creative Mgmt 8942 Wilshire Blvd Beverly Hills CA 90211-1934

**RODRÍGUEZ, ROCÍO,** artist; b. Caibarién, Las Villas, Cuba, 1952; BFA, MFA, U. Ga. One-woman shows include Carl Solway Gallery, Cin., 1982, 1985, Young Harris Coll., Ga., 1986, The Arts Exch., Atlanta, 1989, McIntosh Gallery, 1989, Sandler Hudson Gallery, 1991, 1993, 1995, Studio Exhbn., 1992, Brenau Coll., Gainesville,Ga., 1995, Nexus Contemporary Art Ctr., Atlanta, 1996, Fay Gold Gallery, 1998, Hemphill Fine Arts, Washington, 1999, exhibited in group shows at Birmingham (Ala.) Art Mus., 1989, High Mus. Art, Atlanta, 1990, Nexus Contemporary Arts Ctr., 1991, Galerie Simonne Stern, New Orleans, 1992, Montgomery (Ala.) Mus. Fine Arts, 1994, Michael Solway Gallery, Cin., 1996, Spelman Mus., Atlanta, 1997, New Orleans Mus., 1998, numerous others, Represented in permanent collections; contbr. articles to profl. jours. Recipient So. Regioanl Vis. Artists award, Am. Acad. Rome, 1997; fellow, Ford Found., 1978, Oscar B. Cintas fellow, 1980, Mayor's fellowship in arts, 1990, regional fellow, So. Arts Fedn./NEA, 1990. Office: Fay Gold Gallery 764 Miami Cir Ne Ste 210 Atlanta GA 30324-3026

**RODRIGUEZ, SERGIO RAUL,** music educator, conductor; b. San Pedro Sula, Cortes, Honduras, Aug. 29, 1961; s. Maria Alicia Mejia and Juan Pablo Rodriguez; m. Silvia Maria Montoya, Dec. 19, 1995; children: Yasmin Elizabeth, Arianna Rocio. MusB, Victoriano Lopez Music Sch., San Pedro Sula, Honduras, 1980, U. Ky., 1993; MusM, Southeastern La. U., 1999. Cert. tchr. Ga. Profl. Standards Com., 1998. Carl Orff music tchr. Exptl. Sch. for Children, Tegucigalpa, Francisco Morazan, Honduras, 1981—95; condr. violin and viola tchr. Nat. Sch. Music, Tegucigalpa, 1994—95, Conservatory of Music Fco. Zelaya, Tegucigalpa, 1994—95; music theory, violin and viola tchr. Honduras Nat. U., Tegucigalpa, 1994—95; violin and viola tchr. String Acad. of Southeastern La. U., Hammond, 1995—96; orch. dir., violin and viola tchr. Acadiana Conservatory of Music, Lafayette, La., 1996—97; orch. tchr. Dougherty County Sch. Sys., Albany, Ga., 1997—; orch. condr. Dougherty County Youth Symphony Orch., Albany, Ga., 1997—. Violinist Vermont Symphony Orch., Ga., 1986—89, Dartmouth Symphony Orch., Hanover, NH, 1987—89, Harvard-Radcliffe Symphony Orch., Cambridge, Mass., 1988—88, Lexington Philharm., Ky., 1989—93, Baton Rouge Symphony Orch., 1995—97, Albany Symphony Orch., Ga., 1997—, Macon Symphony Orch., Ga., 1998—, Valdosta Symphony Orch., Ga., 1998—; educator Radium Springs Magnet Mid. Sch. for the Arts; educator, dir. orchs. North Cobb HS. Composer: (string orchestra) A Silvia, Flint River Dusk to Dawn for chamber orch. Founder Nat. Youth Orch., Honduras; founder, conductor Dougherty County Youth Symphony Orch. Recipient 2d pl., Music in the Parks, 2003, 1st pl., 2005; scholar, Longy Sch. of Music, 1987—89; Academic Excellence scholar, U. Ky., 1989, Fellowship Condr., S.C.'s Conducting Inst., 1998. Mem.: Nat. Assn. Music Edn., Music Educators Nat. Conf., Nat. Assn. Music Educators. Office: Dougherty County Youth Symphony Orchestr 1615 Newton Rd Albany GA 31701 Home: 1750 Shiloh Rd #1020 Kennesaw GA 30144 Office Phone: 229-431-1262, 229-431-1261. Personal E-mail: sergio.rodriguez@gmail.com.

**RODRIGUEZ, TIMOTHY ALLEN,** language educator; b. Fond Du Lac, Wis., July 11, 1958; s. Donald William and Margaret Ann Rodriguez; m. Kathryn Marie Hébert, July 9, 1988; children: William Joseph, Kathryn Ann, Bryan Allen. BS, Western Ill. U., 1982, MS, 1984; PhD, U. Iowa, 1995. Tchr. bilingual edn. Danville (Ill.) Sch. Dist. 118, 1982-83, Houston Ind. Sch. Dist., 1984-86; ESL tchr. Palm Beach (Fla.) County Sch. Dist., 1986-88, 95-97, Martin County Sch. Dist., Stuart, Fla., 1988-91, 98-99; asst. prof. Western Ill. U., Macomb, 1993-95; adj. prof. Nova Southeastern U., Ft. Lauderdale, Fla., 1996-2000; asst. prof. U Findlay, Ohio, 2001—03; lectr. Ohio State U. Lima, 2003—. Vis. prof. Fla. Atlantic U., 2000-01, Port St. Lucie; validator Nat. Bd. for Profl. Tchg. Stds. Contbr. articles to profl. jours.; presenter Internat. TESOL Conf., 1996. Named Ellecllence in Edn., Ohio mag., 2005; recipient Outstanding Tchg. award, Ohio State U., 2005. Mem. Internat. TESOL, Internat. Reading Assn., Nat. Assn. Bilingual Edn., Sunshine State TESOL (bd. dirs. 1998-2001). Office Phone: 419-495-8250. Business E-Mail: rodriguez.238@osu.edu.

**RODRIGUEZ, VINCENT ANGEL,** lawyer, director; b. Cayey, P.R., 1921; s. Vicente and Maria (Antongiorgi) R. BS, Harvard U., 1941; LLB, Yale U., 1944. Bar: N.Y. 1947. Assoc. Sullivan & Cromwell, N.Y.C., 1944-56, ptnr., 1956—. Mem. Council Fgn. Relations, ABA, Assn. Bar City N.Y., Am. Soc. Internat. Law Clubs: River (N.Y.C.). Home: 3400 Southwest 27th Ave Apt 902 Coconut Grove FL 33133 Office: Sullivan & Cromwell 125 Broad St Fl 28 New York NY 10004-2489

**RODRIGUEZ, WILLIAM JULIO,** physician; b. Ponce, P.R., June 18, 1941; BS, MD, Georgetown U., Washington, 1967; PhD, Georgetown U., 1976. Intern Univ. Hosp., San Juan, PR, 1967—68, resident in pediat., 1970—72; fellow Children's Hosp., Washington, 1972-75; attending in infectious disease Children's Hosp. Nat. Med. Ctr., Washington, 1975—; pediat. sci. dir. Office of Counterterrorism and Pediatric Drug Devel. Ctr. for Drug Evaluation and Rsch./FDA, 2000—; med. officer USN, 1968—70. Assoc. chief infectious disease and microbiology rsch. Children's Hosp. Med. Ctr., 1979—80, chmn. infectious disease dept., microbiology rsch., 1983—2000; cons. staff Hosp. for Sick Children, Washington, 1985—2000, Shady Grove Adventist Hosp., Rockville, Md., 1988—2001, Holy Cross Hosp., Silver Spring, Md., 1988—2001, Columbia Hosp. for Women, 1990—2000; prof. emeritus pediat. George Washington Med. Sch., 2000—. Contbr. articles to profl. jours. MARC fellow, XIII, 1973-76. Fellow Infectious Disease Soc.; mem. AAAS, AIM, Am. Acad. Pediat., Soc. Pediat. Rsch., Am. Fedn. Clin. Rsch., Am. Soc. Microbiology, Ctr. Drug Evaluation and Rsch.

**RODRIGUEZ-CAMILLONI, HUMBERTO LEONARDO,** architect, historian, educator; b. Lima, Peru, May 30, 1945; came to U.S., 1963; s. Alfonso and Elda (Camilloni) R.; m. Mary Ann Alexanderson, July 1, 1972; children: Elizabeth Marie, William Howard. BA magna cum laude, Yale U., 1967, MArch, 1971, MPhil, 1973, PhD, 1981. Rsch. asst. Sch. Architecture Yale U., 1964-70, teaching fellow dept. history art, 1971-72, 74-75; chmn. research dept. Centro de Investigacion y Restauracion de Bienes Monumentales Instituto Nacional de Cultura, Lima, 1973; restoration architect OAS, Washington, 1976—; prof. Sch. Architecture Tulane U., New Orleans, 1975-82; prof., dir. Henry H. Wiss Ctr. Theory and History of Art and Architecture, Coll. Architecture and Urban Studies Va. Poly. Inst. and State U., Blacksburg, 1983—, dir. Ctr. for Preservation and Rehab. Tech., Coll. Architecture, 1986—. Vis. prof. U. Ill., Chgo., 1982-83; reviewer, cons. Choice, 1975—; interim bd. dirs. Ctr. Planning Handbook Latin-Am. Art, 1978-87; cons., adviser Internat. Exhbn. and Symposium Latin-Am. Baroque Art and Architecture, 1980; adv. bd. Mountain Lake Symposium on Art and Architecture Criticism, 1985—, Internat. Symposium Luis Barragan, 1990; coord., advisor exhbn. Tradition and Innovation: Painting, Architecture and Music in Brazil, Mex. and Venezuela between 1950-80, 1991, Internat. Art History Colloquium, 1993, 48th Internat. Congress of Americanists, 1994, Congress Internat. Union Architects, 1997, Internat. Congress Americanists, 1997, European Assn. for Archtl. Edn./Archtl. Rsch. Ctrs. Consortium Conf., 2000; coord., adv. exhbn. Frank Lloyd Wright: An Architect in America, 1995, The Jesuits, Conf. II: Cultures, Scis. and the Arts, 1540-1773, 2002, Internat. Congress on Constrn. History, 2003, 06, 52d Internat. Congress of Americanists, 2006. Author: (with Walter D. Harris) The Growth of Latin American Cities, 1971; (with Charles Seymour, Jr.) Italian Primitives, The Case History of a Collection and its Conservation, 1972, Religious Architecture in Lima of the Seventeenth and Eighteenth Centuries: The Monastic Complex of San Francisco el Grande, 1984; contbg. editor Handbook of Latin American Studies, 1987—, The Retablo Facade as Transparency: A Study of the Frontispiece of Saint San Francisco, Lima, 1991, Tradición e Innovación en la Arquitectura del Virreinato del Perú, Constantino de Vasconcelos y la Invención de la Arquitectura de Quincha en Lima Durante el Siglo XVII,

1994, (with Graziano Gasparini) Arquitectura Iberoamericana, 1997, Manuel de Amat y Junyent y la Navona de Lima: un ejemplo de diseño urbano barroco del siglo XVIII en el virreinato del Perú, 1999, (with Mehdi Setareh) Monticello's Dome: Development of an Integrated Resource for the Study of Thomas Jefferson's Architecture, 2000, Quincha Architecture: The Development of an Antiseismic Structural System in Seventeenth Century Lima, 2003, The Rural Churches of the Jesuit Haciendas in the Southern Peruvian Coast, 2004, The Survival of Gothic Rib Vaulting in the Viceroyalty of Peru, 2006; contbg. editor: The Dictionary of Art, 1991-96, Encyclopedia of Twentieth Century Architecture, 1999. Named Ellen Battell Eldridge fellow, 1970-72, Robert C. Bates Jr. fellow Jonathan Edwards Coll., Yale U., 1970-71. Social Sci. Rsch. Coun. fellow, 1972-74, Yale Concilium Internat. Studies fellow, 1972-73, Giles Whiting fellow, 1974-75, NEH fellow Columbia U., 1983, Hobart and William Smith Colls. fellow, 1987, U. Ill. fellow, 1990, Edilia De Montequin fellow, 1991, NEH fellow U. N.Mex., 1992. Mem.: KC, Preservation Resource Ctr. (past bd. dirs.), Inter-Am. Inst. Advanced Studies in Cultural History (bd. dirs. 1998—), Blacksburg Regional Art Assn., Assn. for Preservation Tech., Save Our Cemeteries (past bd.dirs.), Nat. Trust Hist. Preservation, New River Valley Preservation League (bd. dirs. 1987—), Assn. Preservation Va. Antiquities, Coll. Art Assn. Am., S.E. section Soc. Archtl. Historians, Soc. Archtl. Historians (bd. dirs. 1977—80, past pres., past sec. South Gulf chpt.), Internat.Archive of Women in Architecture (treas. 1999—2002), Assn. Latin Am. Art, S.E. Coll. Art Conf., Latin Am. Studies Assn., Phi Beta Delta, Sigma Delta Pi, Tau Sigma Delta. Roman Catholic. Office: Va Poly Inst and State U Coll Architecture & Urban Studies Blacksburg VA 24061-0205 Office Phone: 540-231-5324. E-mail: hcami@vt.edu. *As an educator across the years, I have come to realize that the true art of teaching consists of reaching both the human mind and the human heart.*

**RODRIGUEZ-CRUZ, SANDRA ENID,** chemist, researcher; d. Nicolas Rodriguez and Maria Cristina Cruz; m. Seth Mason Cohen, July 7, 2001; 1 child, Sabrina Maricia Cohen. BS in Chemistry, U. P.R., Rio Piedras, P.R., 1993; PhD in Chemistry, U. Calif., Berkeley, Calif., 1999. Postdoctoral fellow Rowland Inst. Harvard U., Cambridge, Mass., 1999—2001; analyst mass spectrometry U. Calif., La Jolla, Calif., 2001—02; forensic chemist Drug Enforcement Adminstrn., Vista, Calif., 2002—. Contbr. articles to profl. jours. Recipient Exceptional Performance award, Drug Enforcement Adminstrn., 2004, 2005. Mem.: Am. Soc. Mass Spectrometry, Am. Chem. Soc., Am. Acad. Forensic Scis. (assoc.). Avocations: travel, reading, piano. Office: Drug Enforcement Administration 2815 Scott Street Vista CA 92078 Office Phone: 760-597-7900. Office Fax: 760-597-7884. Business E-Mail: sandra.e.rodriguez-cruz@usdoj.gov.

**RODRIGUEZ-DIAZ, JUAN E.,** lawyer; b. Ponce, P.R., Dec. 27, 1941; s. Juan and Auristela (Diaz-Alvarado) Rodriguez de Jesus; m. Sonia de Hostos-Anca, Aug. 10, 1966; children: Juan Eugenio, Jorge Eduardo, Ingrid Marie Rodriguez. BA, Yale U., 1963; LLB, Harvard U., 1966; LLM in Taxation, NYU, 1969. Bar: N.Y. 1968, P.R. 1970. Assoc. Baker & McKenzie, N.Y.C., 1966-68, McConnell, Valdes, San Juan, P.R.; undersec. Dept. Treasury P.R., 1971-73; mem. Sweeting, Pons, Gonzalez & Rodriguez, 1973-81; pvt. practice San Juan, 1981-94, Totti & Rodriguez-Diaz, 1994—. Bd. dirs. Ochoa Indsl. Sales Corp., Ensco Caribe, Inc., Industrias Vassallo, Inc., Luis Ayala Colon Sucres., Inc., Triangle Cargo Sucres., Inc., Triple S, Inc., Triple S Mgmt., Inc Bd. govs. Aqueduct and Sewer Authority P.R., 1979-84; mem. adv. com. collective bargaining negotiation of P.R. elec. Power Authority to Gov. P.R. 1977-78; bd. govs. P.R. coun. Boy Scouts Am., mem. transition com., 1984-85; mem. adminstrv. coun. Ballajá, 1993-2000. Mem. N.Y. State Bar Assn., P.R. Bar Assn., AFDA Club, Berwind Country Club, Palmas de Mar Country Club. Office: Suite 1200 416 Ave Ponce De Leon Hato Rey San Juan PR 00918-3418 Office Phone: 787-753-7910. Business E-Mail: JERD@TRDLAW.com.

**RODRIGUEZ-VELEZ, ROSA,** prosecutor; Bar: PR 1977. US Atty., PR US Dept. Justice, 2006—. Office: US Attys Office Torre Chardon Ste 1201 350 Carlos Chardon Ave San Juan 00918 United States*

**RODRIGUEZ-WALLING, MATILDE BARCELO,** special education educator; b. Santiago, Cuba, Aug. 15, 1950; d. Humberto Jacinto and Matilde Amelia (Cuervo) Barcelo; m. Luis Alfredo Rodriguez-Walling, June 29, 1973; 1 child, Alfredo Luis. BA, U. Miami, Fla., 1972; MS in Diagnostic Tchg., Fla. Internat. U., 1981; EdS, Barry U., 1988. Cert. edln. specialist computer edn., Fla. Tchr., chair fgn. lang. dept. Notre Dame Acad., Miami, Fla., 1972-80; tchr., coord. English as 2d lang. adult edn. program Dade County Pub. Schs., Miami, elem. sch. tchr., tchr. middle sch. spl. edn. Homestead, Fla., elem. spl. edn. tchr. Miami, 1986—, behavior mgmt. specialist, exceptional edn. dept. chair; tchr. on spl. assignment Fla. Dept. of Edn., 1994—. Mem. spkrs. bur. Nat. Clearinghouse for Professions in Spl. Edn.; sch. adv. chairperson Blueprint 2000; presenter and spkr. at state and nat. profl. confs.; coord. Fla. Spkrs. Bur.; mem. Fla. Edn. Stds. Commn. Commr. Fla. Edn. Stds. Commn.; mem. State Adv. Com.; mem. Commrs. Blue Ribbon Panel Edn. Governance; co-chair Nat Commn. Improve Spl. Edn. Teaching & Learning. Recipient Gran Orden Martiana, Cuban Lyceum, Miami, 1976. Mem. Coun. Exceptional Children (sec. 1989, v.p. 1990, pres. 1991-92, multicultural chair 1992-93, Mainstreaming Tchr. of Yr. 1983, region finalist Dade County Tchr. of Yr. 1991, Fla. Tchr. of Yr.), Fla. Fedn. Coun. for Exceptional Children (pres. 1997-98, past pres. 1998-99), Coun. Children with Behavior Disorders, Nat. Bd. for Profl. Tchg. Stds. (exceptional needs com.), Internat. Coun. for Exceptional Children (Tchr. of Yr. 1994), Delta Kappa Gamma (Epsilon chpt.). Roman Catholic. Avocations: travel, guitar. Office: Miami-Dade County Pub Schs 1500 Biscayne Blvd Ste 409G Miami FL 33132-1400 Home: 12501 SW 78th St Miami FL 33183-3516 E-mail: mrodriguez-walling@dadeschools.net.

**RODRIK, DANI,** economics and international affairs educator; b. Istanbul, Turkey, Aug. 14, 1957; AB in Govt. and Econs. summa cum laude, Harvard U., 1979; MPA with distinction, Princeton U., 1981, PhD in Econs., 1985. Asst. econ. affairs officer UN Conf. on Trade and Devel., Geneva, 1980, 81-82; asst. prof. pub. policy Kennedy Sch. Govt. Harvard U., Cambridge, Mass., 1985-89, assoc. prof. pub. policy, 1989-92; prof. econs. and internat. affairs Columbia U., N.Y.C., 1992-96; Rafiq Hariri prof. internat. polit. econs. Kennedy Sch. Govt., Harvard U., 1996—, chmn. MPA/ID prog., 2005—. Mem. adv. bd. METU Studies in Devel., New Perspectives on Turkey; Wei Lun vis. prof. Chinese U. of Hong Kong, 1992-93; vis. scholar fiscal affairs dept. Internat. Monetary Fund, 1990, Internat. Fin. div. Bd. Govs. Fed. Reserve System, 1987; advisor Ministry of Fgn. Econ. Rels., Govt. of Poland, 1990; rsch. assoc. Nat. Bur. Econ. Rsch.; rsch. fellow Ctr. Econ. Policy Rsch.; cons. in field. Author: Has Globalization Gone Too Far?, 1997; co-author: Eastern Europe and the Soviet Union in the World Economy, 1991, External Debt, Adjustment and Burden Sharing: A Unified Framework, 1992; co-editor: The Political Economy of Turkey: Debt, Adjustment and Sustainability, 1990, The Economics of Middle-East Peace, 1993; assoc. editor Jour. Internat. Econs., Jour. Devel. Econs., Econs. & Politics; contbr. articles to profl. publs., chpts. to books. Sr. rsch. fellow Inst. for Policy Reform, vis. fellow inst. for internat. Econs., NBER Olin fellow, 1990-91, Robert S. McNamara fellow, 1987-88, Hoover Instn. Nat. fellow, 1991-92, Harbison fellow, 1980-81; recipient Raymond Vernon prize Assn. for Pub. Policy Analysis and Mgmt., 1988. Office: Harvard U Kennedy Sch Govt 79 Jfk St Cambridge MA 02138-5801

**ROE, BENSON BERTHEAU,** surgeon, educator; b. LA, July 7, 1918; s. Hall and Helene Louise (Bertheau) R.; m. Jane Faulkner St. John, Jan. 20, 1945; children: David B., Virginia St. John. AB, U. Calif., Berkeley, 1939; MD cum laude, Harvard U., 1943. Diplomate Am. Bd. Surgery, Am. Bd. Thoracic Surgery (dir. 1971-83, chmn. bd. 1981-83, chmn. exam. com. 1978, long-range planning com. 1980, chmn. program com. 1977). Intern Mass. Gen. Hosp., Boston, 1943-44, resident, 1946-50; nat. rsch. fellow dept. physiology Med. Sch., Harvard U., Boston, Mass., 1947, instr. surgery 1950; Moseley Traveling fellow Harvard. U. at U. Edinburgh, Scotland, 1951; asst. clin. prof. surgery U. Calif., San Francisco, 1951-58, chief cardiothoracic

surgery, 1958-76, prof. surgery, 1966-89, emeritus prof., 1989—; pvt. practice medicine specializing in cardiothoracic surgery San Francisco, 1952-85. Sr. scientist Cardiovascular Rsch. Inst., 1956-89; cons. thoracic surgery VA Hosp., San Francisco Gen. Hosp., Letterman Army Hosp., St. Lukes Hosp., Blue Shield of Calif., Baxter Labs., Ethicon, Inc.; bd. dirs. Control Laser Corp.; vis. prof. U. Utah, U. Ky., U. Gdansk, Poland, Nat. Heart Hosp., London, U. Ibadan, Nigeria, Sanger Clinic, Charlotte, Rush-Presbyn. Hosp., Chgo., Penrose Hosp., Colorado Springs. Author: Maverick Among the Moguls, 2002; mem. editl. bd. Annals of Thoracic Surgery, 1969-82, Pharos, E-Medicine; editor 2 med. texts; author 21 textbook chpts.; contbr. more than 175 articles to profl. jours. Bd. dirs. United Bay Area Crusade, 1958-70, exec. com., 1964-65; bd. dirs. chmn. exec. com. San Francisco chpt. Am. Cancer Soc., 1955-57; bd. dirs. San Francisco Heart Assn., 1964-72, pres., 1964-65, chmn. rsch. com., 1966-71; com. mem. Am. Heart Assn., 1967-70; pres. Miranda Lux Found., 1982-94; trustee Avery-Fuller-Welch Found.; bd. dirs. Internat. Bioethics Inst., Point Reyes Bird Obs. With M.C., USNR, 1944-46. Named to Rowing Hall of Fame, 1979, Athletic Hall of Fame, U. Calif., 1995. Fellow Am. Coll. Cardiology, ACS (chmn. adv. coun. thoracic surgery, program chmn. thoracic surgery, cardiovascular com.), Polish Surg. Assn. (hon.); mem. Am. Assn. Thoracic Surgery (chmn. membership com. 1974-75), AMA (residency rev. com. for thoracic surgery), Am. Surg. Assn., Pacific Coast Surg. Assn., Calif. Acad. Medicine (pres. 1974), Calif. Med. Assn., Soc. Univ. Surgeons, Soc. Thoracic Surgeons (pres. 1972, chmn. standards and ethics com.), Soc. Vascular Surgery (v.p.). Clubs: Cruising of Am, Pacific Union, St. Francis Yacht, Calif. Tennis. Office: U Calif Div Cardiothoracic Surgery 350 Parnassus Ave # 101 San Francisco CA 94143-0118 Personal E-mail: ghotieg@earthlink.net.

**ROE, BYRON PAUL,** physics professor; b. St. Louis, Apr. 4, 1934; s. Sam S. and Gertrude Harriet (Claris) R.; m. Alice Susan Krauss, Aug. 27, 1961; children: Kenneth David, Diana Carol. BA, Washington U., St. Louis, 1954; PhD, Cornell U., 1959. Instr: physics U. Mich., Ann Arbor, 1959-61, asst. prof., 1961-64, assoc. prof., 1964-69, prof., 1969—. Guest physicist SSC Lab., 1991. Author: Probability and Statistics in Experimental Physics, 1992, 2d edit., 2001, Particle Physics at the New Millennium, 1996 (Libr. Sci. Book Club selection). CERN vis. scientist Geneva, 1967, 89; Brit. Sci. Rsch. Coun. fellow, Oxford, 1979; recipient inventor's prize CDC Worldtech, Edina, Minn., 1982, 83. Fellow Am. Phys. Soc. Home: 3610 Charter Pl Ann Arbor MI 48105-2825 Office: U Mich Physics Dept 500 E University Ave Ann Arbor MI 48109-1040 E-mail: byronroe@umich.edu.

**ROE, CHARLES BARNETT,** lawyer; b. Tacoma, June 25, 1932; s. Charles Brown and Gladys Luvena (Harding) Roe; m. Marilyn Marie Quam, July 31, 1954; children: Sharon Lynn Roe De Groot, Jeannine Carole Roe Deilwo. AB, U. Puget Sound, 1953; postgrad. Boalt Hall, U. Calif. Law Sch., Berkeley, 1957—58; JD, U. Wash., 1960. Bar: Wash. 1960, U.S. Dist. Ct. (ea. and we. dists.) Wash. 1960, U.S. Ct. Appeals (9th cir. 1963, U.S. Supreme Ct. 1963, U.S. Ct. Appeals (D.C. cir.) 1964. Asst. atty. gen. depts. natural resources, conservation, water resources and pollution control commn. State of Wash., Olympia, 1960—70, asst. dir. dept. water resources, 1967—69, sr. asst. atty. gen., 1970—90; of counsel Perkins Coie, Olympia, 1991—. Chief counsel Dept. Ecology, 1970—85, Nuclear Waste Bd., 1983—90; counsel natural resources com. Wash. Ho. of Reps., Olympia, 1970; supr. sea grant trainees U. Wash. Law Sch., 1970—72; adj. prof. Gonzaga U. Sch. Law, Spokane, 1973—76, U. Puget Sound Law Sch., 1985—90; contr. Nat. Water Commn., Washington, 1970—71; environ. aide Gov. Daniel J. Evans, 1969—77. Spl. asst. atty gen. State of Mont, Helena, 1983; rep. Western States Water Coun., Salt Lake City, 1970—90; sec. Olympia Audubon Soc., 1962—63; chmn. bd. mgrs. United Chs., 1967—68. 1st lt. USAF, 1954—57. Mem.: SAR, ABA (chmn. water resources com. natural resources sect. 1981—83), Wash. Cts. Hist. Soc. (bd. dirs. 1998—), Wash. State Bar Assn. (chmn. environ. law sect. 1971—72), Rotary, Am. Legion, Masons, Phi Delta Phi, Kappa Sigma. United Ch. Of Christ. Home: 2400 Wedgewood Dr SE Olympia WA 98501-3841 Office: 111 Market St NE Olympia WA 98501-6965 Office Phone: 360-956-3300. Business E-Mail: croe@perkinscoie.com.

**ROE, FRED DAVIS, JR.,** electronics engineer, director; b. Fayetteville, Tenn., Dec. 18, 1943; s. Fred Davis Roe and Leatha Kathrine Hudson; m. Nancy Carol Currey, June 25, 1967; children: William Davis, Kevin Lee. BSEE, Vanderbilt U., 1966. Avionics group mgr. NASA Marshall Space Ctr., Huntsville, Ala., 1990—2005, avionics divsn. mgr., 2005; v.p., prin. engr. Advanced Optical Sys., 2005—. Pres. North South Gun Club, Huntsville, 2003—05, range officer, 1990—2003. Recipient Exceptional Svc. medal, NASA, 1999, Exceptional Achievement medal, 2004. Baptist. Achievements include patents for computer desk/work station; video guidance sensor with integrated range finding. Avocations: shooting, travel, crafts. Home: 4005 Granada Drive SE Huntsville AL 35802 Office: Advanced Optical Sys 6767 Old Madison Pike Ste 410 Huntsville AL 35806 Office Phone: 256-971-0036. Personal E-mail: roe@aos-inc.com.

**ROE, GERALD BRUCE,** director, writer; b. Cushing, Wis., June 16, 1940; s. Fred Walter and Maybell Meranda (Swenson) R.; m. Laurel A. Nagel, Sept. 12, 1964 (dec. Feb. 1990); children: Stephen, David. BA, U. Minn., 1964, postgrad., 1969-71; MA, Coll. St. Thomas, 1967. Tchr. St. Anthony Padua H.S., Mpls., 1965-68, Cath. H.S., St. Paul, 1968-69; asst. to dir. bur. recommendations U. Minn., Mpls., 1973 assoc. dir. ednl. placement U. Iowa, Iowa City, 1974—. Co-author: (with Rebecca Anthony) Over 40 and Looking for Work, 1991, The Curriculum Vitae Handbook, 1994, 3d edit., 2003, 101 Grade A Resumés for Teachers, 1994, 3d edit., 2003; contbr. articles to profl. jours. Bd. dirs. Iowa City Cmty. Theatre, 1994-98. Mem. Phi Delta Kappa (chpt. 0005, v.p. 1990-94, pres. 1994-97). Avocation: theater. Office: Univ Iowa Ednl Placement 302 Lindquist Ctr N Iowa City IA 52242-1529 Business E-Mail: gerald-roe@uiowa.edu.

**ROE, JOHN H.,** manufacturing executive; b. 1939; BA, Williams Coll., 1962; MBA, Harvard U., 1964. With Bemis Co. Inc., Mpls., 1964—, plant supt., 1964-67, sales rep., 1967-68, sales mgr., 1968-70, plant mgr., 1970-73, gen. mgr. film div., 1973-76, exec. v.p. ops., 1976-87, pres., chief oper. officer, from 1987, chief exec. officer, 1990—, also bd. dirs., chmn. Office: Bemis Co Inc 222 S 9th St Ste 2300 Minneapolis MN 55402-4099

**ROE, LESA B.,** federal agency administrator; b. 1963; m. Ralph Roe. B. in elec. engring., U. Fla., Gainesville; M. in elec. engring., U. Ctrl. Fla., Orlando. Satellite comm. analyst Hughes Space & Comm., El Segundo, Calif.; with NASA, 1987—, comm. engr. Space Shuttle Engring. Directorate Kennedy Space Ctr., Fla., 1987, payloads office mgr. Internat. Space Sta. (ISS) Program Office. Johnson Space Ctr. Houston; assoc. dir. bus. mgmt. Langley Rsch. Ctr., NASA, Hampton, Va., 2003—04, dep. dir., 2004—05, dir., 2005—. Office: Bldg 1219 100 NASA Rd Mail Stop 106 Hampton VA 23681-2199 also: Langley Rsch Ctr 100 NASA Rd Hampton VA 23681 Office Phone: 757-864-4111. E-mail: lesa.b.roe@nasa.gov.*

**ROE, MARK J.,** law educator; b. NYC, Aug. 8, 1951; m. Helen Hsu, Aug. 12, 1974; children: Andrea Hsu, Jessica Hsu. BA, Columbia U., 1972; JD, Harvard U., 1975. Bar: N.Y. 1976. Atty. Fed. Res. Bank, N.Y.C., 1975-77; assoc. Cahill Gordon & Reindel, N.Y.C., 1977-80; prof. Rutgers U. Law Sch., Newark, 1980-86, U. Pa. Law Sch., 1986-88, Columbia U. Law Sch., N.Y.C., 1988-2001, Harvard Law Sch., Cambridge, Mass., 2001—. Author: (book) Strong Managers, Weak Owners: The Political Roots of Amercian Corporate Finance, 1994, Corporate Reorganization and Bankruptcy, 2000, Political Determinants of Corporate Governance, 2003. Business E-Mail: mroe@law.harvard.edu.

**ROE, MARY ANN,** postmaster; b. Greenwich, Conn., Jan. 10, 1945; d. Frederick Johnston and Doris Irene Capp; m. Robert Andrew Roe, June 17, 1966; children: Jeffrey Brian, Jennifer Yvonne. Student, S.W. Mo. State U., 1969, N.E. Mo. State U., 1970. US Postal Svc., Brookfield, Mo., 1977-82, supt. postal ops., 1983-93, postmaster, 1993—. Author: Roe's Reference, 1987; contbr. articles to mags. Sec.-treas. Busy Women's Club,

Brookfield, 1990—; asst. leader Girl Scouts U.S.A., Brookfield, 1990-99. Recipient Best Column award Show Me Postmaster, 1997. Mem. Nat. Assn. Postmasters U.S. (instr. conv. 1996, 97, 2001,& 2002. Mo. Career Devel. com. 1996-98, state editor 1999-2002). Methodist. Avocations: reading, sewing, travel. Office: US Postal Svc 104 N Grant St Wheeling MO 64688-9998

**ROE, ROGER ROLLAND, JR.,** lawyer; b. Mpls., Dec. 31, 1947; s. Roger Rolland Roe Jr.; m. Paula Speltz, 1974; children: Elena, Madeline. BA, Grinnell Coll., 1970; JD, U. Minn., 1973. Bar: Minn. 1973, U.S. Dist. Ct. Minn. 1974, U.S. Ct. Appeals (8th cir.) 1977, U.S. Supreme Ct. 1978, Wis. 1988, U.S. Dist. Ct. Nebr. 1995, U.S. Dist. Ct. (ea. and we. dists.) Wis. Law clk. to Hon. Judge Amdahl Hennepin County Dist. Ct., Mpls., 1973-74; from assoc. to ptnr. Rider, Bennett, Egan & Arundel, Mpls., 1974-91; mng. ptnr. Yaeger, Jungbauer, Barczak, Roe & Vucinovich, PLC, Mpls., 1992-2000; ptnr. Best & Flanagan LLP, Mpls., 2000—. Mem. nat. panel arbitrators Am. Arbitration Assn.; judge trial practice class and moot ct. competitions law sch. U. Minn.; guest lectr. Minn. Continuing Legal Edn. courses. Fellow Internat. Soc. Barristers; mem. ATLA (guest lectr.), Am. Bd. Trial Advs. (diplomat., Minn. chpt. pres. 1996-97), Million Dollar Round Table. Avocations: golf, skiing. Office: Best & Flanagan LLP 225 S 6th St # 4000 Minneapolis MN 55402 Office Phone: 612-349-5683. Business E-Mail: rroe@bestlaw.com.

**ROE, SANDY C.,** gifted and talented educator; d. Garvin and Peggy Catherine Bennett; m. James David Roe, Oct. 19, 1990; children: Kathryn, Preston. AA, Ark. State U., Beebe, 1994; BS, Harding U., 1998, MEd, 2001, U. Ark., Little Rock, 2005. Cert. gifted and talented edn. K-12 Ark., tchr. art K-12 Ark., curriculum K-12 Ark., ESL K-12 Ark., advanced placement art Ark. Layout artist Bennett Stained Glass, Searcy, Ark., 1987—2000; gifted and talented coord., tchr. Pangburn (Ark.) Pub. Sch., 1999—2000, ESL coord., 2002—04, gifted and talented coord., 2004—; art tchr. Pangburn (Ark.) H.S., 2000—05, coord. advanced placement, 2004—. Webmaster Pangburn Pub. Schs., 2002—; adj. instr. Ark. State U., Beebe, Ark., 2002—. Sunday sch. tchr. Foster's Chapel Missionary Bapt., 1994, 1998. Grantee, Ark. Dept. Securities, 2004—. Mem.: ASCD, Ark. Gifted and Talented Edn., Ark. TESOL, Gamma Beta Pi. Avocations: drawing, painting, gardening. Office: Pangburn Pub Schs 1100 Short St Pangburn AR 72121 Office Phone: 501-728-3513.

**ROE, THOMAS COOMBE,** former utility company executive; b. Dover, Del., Sept. 22, 1914; s. John Moore and Elizabeth Lindale (Cooper) R.; m. Emma Lillian Scotton, Oct. 16, 1937 (dec.); children: Thomas C., Margaret Ruth (dec.); m. Carolyn Scotton, May 4, 2002. BS in Elec. Engring. U. Del., Newark, 1935; DHL (hon.), Wesley Coll., Dover, Del., 1987. With Eastern Shore Public Service, 1936-43; with Delmarva Power & Light Co., 1943—; pres. subs. Delmara Power & Light Co., 1971-76, chmn. bd., 1976-79, dir., 1971-80, ret., 1980. Hon. trustee Peninsula Regional Med. Ctr., Salisbury, Md.; hon. trustee, former chmn. Wesley Coll., Dover, Del.; former trustee Wesley Theol. Sem., Washington. Served with AUS, 1941-45. Mem.: Rotary (past pres.). Republican. Methodist.

**ROE, THOMAS LEROY WILLIS,** retired pediatrician; b. Bend, Oreg., Sept. 1, 1936; MD, U. Oregon Health Scis. U., Portland, 1961. Diplomate Am. Bd. Pediatrics. Intern U. Calif., San Francisco, 1961-62, resident, 1962-64; physician Sacred Heart Med. Ctr., Eugene, Oreg.; pvt. practice Peace Health Med. Group, Eugene, 1969—2006; clin prof. pediatrics U. Oreg., Portland, 1985—2006; ret., 2006. Fellow Am. Acad. Pediatricians; mem. AMA, North Pacific Pediatrics Soc. Office: Peace Health Med Clinic 1162 Willamette St Eugene OR 97401-3568 Business E-Mail: troe@peacehealth.org.

**ROE, W. BARTON,** engineering executive; b. N.Y.C., Aug. 29, 1955; s. Kenneth Andrew R.; m. Lynne Roe, 1983; 4 children. BS in Mech. Engring., U. Pa., 1978; MSEE, Stevens Inst. Tech., 1987. Engr. analyst Sargent & Lundy Engrs., Chgo., 1978-80; engr. Stone & Webster Engring. Co., N.Y.C., 1980-85; supr. mech. thermal group Am. Rocket Co., Camarillo, Calif., 1987; project engr. Burns & Roe Group Inc., Oradell, NJ, 1988-92, v.p. bus. devel., 1992-96, v.p. infrastructure, 1996—2002, v.p. svcs., 2002—05, sr. v.p. fed. svcs., also bd. dirs., 2005—. Bd. dirs. Polar Molecular Corp., 1991-92. Mem. ASME (sect. dir. 1998-2001), IEEE, NSPE, Greenwich Country Club, Psi Upsilon of Phila. (trustee 2000—). Avocations: golf, skiing. Office: Burns and Roe Group Inc 800 Kinderkamack Rd Oradell NJ 07649

**ROEBUCK, DEBORAH MAE BRITT,** management consultant, educator; b. San Antonio, Tex., Apr. 11, 1952; d. Aubrey Clarence and Marian Lavita Britt; m. Robert Leroy Roebuck; 1 child, Hillary Grace. BSE, Truman State U., Kirksville, 1972—74, MA, 1975; PhD, Ga. State U., Atlanta, 1986—90. Cert. tchr. Mo., Iowa, 1974. Prof. mgmt. Kennesaw State U., Ga., 1992—2001, chair leadership and profl. devel., 2001—05; exec. dir., prof. mgmt. Inst. Leadership, Ethics and Character, 2006—. Author: (textbook) Improving Business Communication Skills; contbr. articles to profl. jours. Mem.: Orgnl. Behavior Tchg. Soc., Acad. Mgmt. Baptist. Avocations: travel, reading. Office: Kennesaw State Univ 1000 Chastain Rd Kennesaw GA 30144 Office Phone: 770-423-6364. Personal E-mail: droebuck@kennesaw.edu.

**ROEBUCK, JAMES RANDOLPH, JR.,** state legislator; b. Phila., Feb. 12, 1945; m. Cheryl Arrington. BA cum laude, Va. Union U., 1966; MA, U. Va., 1969, PhD, 1977. Lectr. Drexel U., 1970—77, asst. prof., 1977—84; legis. asst. Office of Mayor, Phila., 1984—85; mem. Pa. Ho. of Reps., Harrisburg, 1985—. Chmn. Pa. Legis. Black Caucus, 1998-2000; Democratic chmn. Ho. Edn. Com., 2003—; mem. Pa. History and Mus. Commn., 1990-95; bd. dirs. Pa. Higher Ednl. Assistance Agy., 1995-. Author: The Shaping of William Howard Tafts View of East Asia 1900-1908; co-editor: Biographical Dictionary of Internationalists, 1983. Recipient Young Leadership award Hamilton Watch Co., 1966, Outstanding Svc. award Va. Union U. Alumni Assn., 1973, Legion of Honor award Chapel Four Chaplains, 1980. Mem. Nat. Black Caucus State Legislators, Alpha Phi Alpha. Address: 4800 Baltimore Ave Philadelphia PA 19143-3419 Office Phone: 215-724-2227. E-mail: jroebuck@pahouse.net.

**ROEDDER, WILLIAM CHAPMAN, JR.,** lawyer; b. St. Louis, June 21, 1946; s. William Chapman and Dorothy (Reifeiss) R.; m. Gwendolyn Arnold, Sept. 13, 1968; children: William Chapman, Barcley Shane. BS, U. Ala., 1968; JD cum laude, Cumberland U., 1972. Bar: Ala. Law clk. to chief justice Ala. Supreme Ct., Montgomery, 1972; ptnr. McDowell Knight Roedder & Sledge, L.L.C., Mobile, Ala., 1997—. Comments editor Cumberland-Samford Law Rev.; contbr. articles to legal publs. Bd. dirs. Def. Rsch. Inst. 1999—2002; mem. Bd. Lawyers for Civil Justice. Named to Best Lawyers in Am. Mem.: ABA (vice chair com. trial tactics, torts and ins. practice 1995—96), Lawyers for Civil Justice (bd. dirs, pres.-elect 2005), Def. Rsch. Inst. (bd. dirs. 1999—2002), Ala. Def. Lawyers Assn., Fedn. Def. and Corp. Counsel (chmn. products liability sect. 1990—93, bd. dirs. 1993—2000, regional v.p. 1994—96, exec. com. 1997—, sec.-treas. 1999—2000, pres.-elect 2000—01, pres. 2001—02, chmn. bd. dirs. 2002—03), Mobile County Bar Assn. (sec., chmn. ethics com. 1988—90, grievance com. 1994—96), Ala. State Bar Assn., Order of Barristers, Curia Honoris, Phi Alpha Delta (pres. 1971—72). Home: 211 Levert Ave Mobile AL 36607-3219 Office: McDowell Knight Roedder & Sledge LLC PO Box 350 Mobile AL 36601-0350 E-mail: broedder@mcdowellknight.com.

**ROEDER, RICHARD KENNETH,** business owner, lawyer; b. Phila., Oct. 11, 1948; s. Walter August and Gloria (Miller) R.; 1 child, William Frederick; m. Allison Nunn Roeder, June 12, 1999. AB, Amherst Coll., 1970; JD, U. Calif., Berkeley, 1973, Cambridge U., 1973-74. Assoc. Paul, Hastings, Janofky & Walker, L.A., 1974-81, ptnr., 1981-90; founding ptnr. Aurora Capital Group, L.A., 1990—. Office: Aurora Capital Group Ste 2100 10877 Wilshire Blvd Los Angeles CA 90024-4341

**ROEDER, ROBERT GAYLE,** biochemist, molecular biologist, educator; b. Boonville, Ind., June 3, 1942; s. Frederick John and Helene (Bredenkamp) Roeder; m. Suzanne Himsel, July 11, 1964 (div. 1981); children: Kimberly, Michael; m. Cun Jing Hong, June 2, 1990; 1 child, Maxine. BA summa cum laude (Gilbert scholar), Wabash Coll., 1964, DSc (hon.), 1990; MS, U. Ill., 1965; PhD (USPHS fellow), U. Wash., 1969; DSc (hon.), Washington U., 2005. Am. Cancer Soc. fellow dept. embryology Carnegie Instn. Washington, Balt., 1969-71; asst. prof. biol. chemistry Washington U., St. Louis, 1971-75, assoc. prof., 1975-76, prof., 1976-82, prof. genetics, 1978-82, James S. McDonnell prof. biochem. genetics, 1979-82; prof. lab. biochemistry and molecular biology Rockefeller U., N.Y.C., 1982—, Arnold O. and Mabel S. Beckmann prof. molecular biology and biochemistry, 1985—. Cons. USPHS, 1975-79, Am. Cancer Soc., 1983-86. Recipient Dreyfus Tchr.-Scholar award Dreyfus Found., 1976, molecular biology award NAS-U.S. Steel Found., 1986, outstanding investigator award Nat. Cancer Inst., 1986-2002, Dickson prize in medicine, 2001, Albert Lasker Basic Med. Rsch. award 2003; co-recipient Lewis S. Rosensteil award for disting. work in basic med. scis. Brandeis U., 1995, Passano award Passano Found., Inc., 1995, Alfred P. Sloan prize GM Cancer Rsch. Found., 1999, Louisa Gross Horowitz award Columbia U., 1999, Gairdner Found. Internat. award, 2000, ASBMB-Merck Award, 2002; grantee NIH, 1972-, NSF, 1975-79, Am. Cancer Soc., 1979-85. Fellow AAAS, Am. Acad. Arts and Scis., Am. Acad. Microbiology, NY Acad. Scis.; mem. NAS, Am. Chem. Soc. (Eli Lilly award 1977), Am. Soc. Biol. Chemists, Am. Soc. Microbiologists, Am. Soc. Immunologists, Am. Diabetes Assn., European Molecular Biology Orgn. (assoc.), Harvey Soc. (pres. 1994), Phi Beta Kappa. Office: Rockefeller U 1230 York Ave New York NY 10021-6399 Office Phone: 212-327-7600. Business E-Mail: roeder@rockefeller.edu.

**ROEDER, THOMAS M., JR.,** electrical engineer, consultant, education educator; s. Thomas M., Sr. and Alice L. Roeder; m. Karen E. Walsh, Dec. 28, 1991; children: Joseph T., Jessica Anne. BS, Purdue U., 1991. Registered profl. engr., Ohio, 2004, cert. energy mgr., Assn. Energy Engrs., 1995. Elec. engr. Design-Aire Engring., Inc., Indpls., 2001—; assoc. prof. ind. U. Purdue U. at Indpls., 2002—, Ivy Tech State Coll., Indpls., 2005—. Office Phone: 317-464-9090.

**ROEDERER, JUAN GUALTERIO,** retired physics professor; b. Trieste, Italy, Sept. 2, 1929; came to U.S., 1967, naturalized, 1972; s. Ludwig Alexander and Anna Rafaela (Lohr) R.; m. Beatriz Susana Cougnet, Dec. 20, 1952; children: Ernesto, Irene, Silvia, Mario. PhD, U. Buenos Aires, 1952. Research scientist Max Planck Inst., Gottingen, W.Ger., 1952-55; group leader Argentine Atomic Energy Commn., Buenos Aires, 1953-59; prof. physics U. Buenos Aires, 1959-66, U. Denver, 1967-77, U. Alaska, Fairbanks, 1977-93, prof. emeritus, 1993—, dir. Geophys. Inst., 1977-86, dean Coll. Environ. Scis., 1978-82. Vis. staff Los Alamos Nat. Lab., 1969-81; chmn. U.S. Arctic Research Com., 1987-91; sr. adviser Internat. Ctr. Theoretical Physics, Trieste, Italy, 1998—2002. Author: Dynamics of Geomagnetically Trapped Radiation, 1970, Physics and Psychophysics of Music, 1973, 3d edit., 1995, Mecanica Elemental, 2002, Information and Its Role in Nature, 2005; contbr. articles to profl. jours Nat. Acad. Sci. NASA sr. rsch. fellow, 1964—66. Fellow AAAS, Am. Geophys. Union (Edward A. Flinn III award, 2000); mem. Assn. Argentina de Geodestas y Geofisicos (hon.), Nat. Acad. Sci. Argentina (corr.), Nat. Acad. Sci. Austria (corr.), Third World Acad. Scis. (assoc.), Internat. Assn. Geomagnetism and Aeronomy (hon.), Sci. Com. on Solar-Terrestrial Physics (hon.). Lutheran. Achievements include research in plasma and energetic particles in earth's and Jupiter's magnetosphere, policy issues for Arctic, perception of music, information theory. Home: 105 Concordia Dr Fairbanks AK 99709-3029 Office: U Alaska Geophys Inst Fairbanks AK 99775-7320 Business E-Mail: jgr@gi.alaska.edu.

**ROEG, NICOLAS JACK,** film director; b. London, Aug. 15, 1928; s. Jack Nicolas and Mabel Getrude (Silk) R.; m. Susan Rennie Stephen, May 12, 1957; children: Joscelin Nicolas, Nicolas Jack, Lucien John, Sholto Jules; m. Theresa Russell, 1985; children: Maximilian Nicolas Sextus, Statten Jack. Student Brit. schs.; LittD honoris causa, Hull U., Eng., 1995; DFA (hon.), CUNY, 2004. Cinematographer films The Caretaker, 1963, Masque of Red Death, 1964, Fahrenheit 451, 1966, A Funny Thing Happened on the Way to the Forum, 1966, Far from the Madding Crowd, 1967, Petulia, 1968; co-dir. film Performance, 1970; dir. films Walkabout, 1970, Don't Look Now, 1973, Glastonbury Fayre, 1973, The Man Who Fell to Earth, 1976, Bad Timing, 1980, Eureka, 1982, Insignificance, 1985, Castaway, 1986, 89, Track 29, 1987, Aria, 1987, The Witches, 1988-89, Cold Heaven, 1990, Heart of Darkness, 1994, Two Deaths, 1994, Hotel Paradise, 1995, Full Body Massage, 1995, Samson & Delilah, 1996, Puffball, 2006; dir. TV films: Sweet Bird of Youth, 1989, Heart of Darkness, 1994; exec. prodr. Without You I'm Nothing, 1989, Young Indy, 1991, The Sound of Claudia Schiffer, 1999-; co-prodr. Rock Concert, 2002; writer (screenplays) Night Train, 2000, Ivanhoe, 2000, History Play, 2004. Decorated comdr. Brit. Empire. Fellow Brit. Film Inst.; mem. Dirs. Guild Am., Dir. Guild Gt. Britain, Acad. Motion Picture Arts and Scis., Assn. Cinematograph, TV and Allied Technicians. Office Phone: 02072578723. Business E-Mail: nicolas@roegmovies.com.

**ROEHL, JERRALD J.,** lawyer; b. Austin, Tex., Dec. 6, 1945; s. Joseph E. and Jeanne Foster (Scott) R.; m. Nancy J. Meyers, Jan. 15, 1977; children: Daniel J., Katherine C., J. Ryan, J. Taylor. BA, U. N.Mex., 1968; JD, Washington and Lee U., 1971. Bar: N.Mex. 1972, U.S. Ct. Appeals (10th cir.) 1972, U.S. Supreme Ct. 1977. Practice of law, Albuquerque, 1972—; pres. Roehl Law Firm P.C. and predecessors, Albuquerque, 1976—; cons. to profl. groups; real estate developer, Albuquerque. Bd. advs. ABA Jour. 1981-83; bd. editors Washington and Lee Law Rev., 1970-71. Bd. dirs. Rehab. Ctr. of Albuquerque, 1974-78; mem. assocs. Presbyn. Hosp. Ctr., Albuquerque, 1974-82; incorporator, then treas. exec. com. Ctr. City Coun., 1991-98, law coun. Washington & Lee U. Law, 1973-77. Mem. ABA (award of achievement Young Lawyers divsn. 1975, coun. econs. of law practice sect. 1978-80, exec. coun. Young Lawyers divsn. 1979-81, fellow divsn. 1984—, coun. tort and ins. practice sect. 1981-83), N.Mex. Bar Assn. (pres. young lawyers sect. 1975-76), Albuquerque Bar Assn. (bd. dirs. 1976-79), N.Mex. Def. Lawyers Assn. (pres. 1983-84), Albuquerque Country Club, Albuquerque Petroleum Club, Sigma Alpha Epsilon, Sigma Delta Chi, Phi Delta Phi. Roman Catholic. Office: 300 Central Ave SW Ste 2500e Albuquerque NM 87102-2320 Office Phone: 505-242-6900. Business E-Mail: jjr@roehl.com.

**ROEHMHOLDT, JOHN MICHAEL,** urologist, educator; b. Buffalo, Jan. 3, 1960; s. Robert Louis and Mary Elizabeth Roehmholdt; m. Sheliah Joan Jung, Aug. 25, 1990; children: Peter, Max, Julie. BA in Biology summa cum laude, Canisius Coll., Buffalo, 1981; MD cum laude, Albany Med. Coll., 1985. Diplomate Am. Bd. Urology; lic. capt. USCG. Pvt. practice; resident surgery U. Wis. Hosp. and Clinics, Madison, 1985-87, resident in urology, 1987-90; pvt. practice, Amherst, N.Y., 1990—. Clin. instr. urology SUNY, Buffalo, 1996—; mem. staff DeGraff Meml. Hosp., North Tonawanda, N.Y., pres. med. staff, 1995, dir., 1996-97; mem. trustee coun. Kaleida Health Sys., Buffalo, 1998—2002. Bd. dirs. West Seneca Davol Ctr. chpt. N.Y. State ARC, 1994—; chmn. stewardship and devel. com. parish coun. Sts. Peter and Paul Ch., Williamsville, N.Y., 1999—, pres. parish coun., 2001-02. Recipient physician's recognition award AMA, 2000. Fellow ACS; mem. AMA (Physicians Recognition award 2000), Am. Urol. Assn., Buffalo Urol. Soc. (pres.-elect 2001-02, pres. 2002-2003), Olcott Yacht Club (N.Y.) (sr. mem., fleet surgeon 1999—), Alpha Omega Alpha. Office: Northtown Urology Assocs PC 3580 Sheridan Dr Amherst NY 14226

**ROEHRIG, C(HARLES) BURNS,** internist, consultant; b. Brookline, Mass., Jan. 21, 1923; s. Gilbert Haven and Helen (Burns) R.; m. Patricia Joan Orme, July 22, 1952 (dec. 2002); children: Joan Russell Roehrig Vater, Jennifer Orme Roehrig Munn, Charles Burns, Jr. Student, Amherst Coll., 1941-43, Vanderbilt U., 1943-44; MD, U. Md., 1949; cert. in internal medicine, U. Pa., Phila., 1953. Diplomate Am. Bd. Internal Medicine. Intern Boston City Hosp., 1949-50; resident in internal medicine and diabetes Joslin Clinic, New Eng. Deaconess Hosp., Boston, 1952-54; practice medicine specializing in internal medicine and diabetes Boston, 1954-91; chief of staff, pres. med. adminstrv. bd. New Eng. Deaconess Hosp., Boston, 1972-75; dir., mem. exec. com. Blue Shield of Mass., Inc., Boston, 1977-88; exec. com. Met. Boston Hosp. Coun., 1982-86; physician adv. coun. Mass. Hosp. Assn., Burlington, 1982-86. Editor: Today's Internist, Washington, 1987-99; contbr. articles to profl. jours. Bd. dirs. Camping Svcs. Bd., Greater Boston YMCA, 1966—; mem. physician adv. group Health Care Financing Adminstrn., Washington, 1983-88; mem. adv. panel on physician payment and med. tech. Office of Tech. Assessment, U.S. Congress, Washington, 1984-85; chmn. Federated Coun. for Internal Medicine, Washington, 1985-86; trustee New Eng. Deaconess Hosp. Capt. (flight surgeon) USAF, 1949-52. Master ACP (pres. emeritus); mem. AMA (chmn. coun. on long range planning and devel., Chgo.), New Eng. Diabetes Assn. (pres. 1963-64), Mass. Soc. Internal Medicine (pres. 1971-72), Am. Soc. Internal Medicine (pres. 1984-85), Country Club of Hilton Head, Wellesley (Mass.) Country Club. Republican. Episcopalian. Office: 5 Summer Breeze Ct Hilton Head Island SC 29926-2536 Personal E-mail: burnsroehrigmd@aol.com.

**ROEHRMAN, TODD FREDERICK,** costume designer, educator; s. Kenneth Earl and Judith Roehrman. BFA, U. Ariz., Tucson, 1987; MFA, Calif. Inst. Arts, Valencia, Calif., 1990. Resident costume designer Pepperdine U., Malibu, Calif., 1992—96; prof. costume design and tech. San Francisco State U., 1996—. Resident costume design asst. Mark Taper Forum, LA, 1990—92; costume designer San Francisco Shakespeare Festival, 2001—. Costume designer Cisco Systems Global Sales Mtg. Recipient Critics Circle award for Best Costume Design, San Francisco Bay Area, 2001. Mem.: United Scenic Artists local 829 (assoc.; trustee No. Calif. chpt. 2000—06), Bay Area Costumers' Alliance (assoc.; pres. 2003—05). Office: San Francisco State University 1600 Holloway Avenue San Francisco CA 94132 Office Phone: 415-338-7781. Office Fax: 415-338-0575. Personal E-mail: todd947@comcast.net.

**ROEHRS, CHRISTOPHER SCOTT,** lawyer; b. King of Prussia, Pa., Oct. 20, 1963; s. Anthony Gair and Janet Affleck Asch. BA, U. BC, 1991, LLB, 1994. Bar: BC 1995, NY 1999. Collections field auditor Revenue Can. Taxation, Vancouver, BC, Canada, 1982—86; assoc. atty. Baker and McKenzie, NYC, 1999—2004; asst. gen. counsel Am. Internat. Group, Inc., NYC. Mem.: Travelers Century Club. Avocation: photography. Office: Am Internat Group Inc 175 Water St 23d Flr New York NY 10038 Office Phone: 212-458-2426.

**ROELANDTS, WILLEM P.,** data processing executive; b. Jan. 4, 1945; came to U.S., 1982; BEE, Rijks Hogere Technische Sch., Belgium, 1965. Various position including sr. v.p. Hewlett-Packard, 1966—96; CEO, pres. Xilinx Inc., San Jose, 1996—, chmn., 2003—. Spkr. in field. Mem.: Fabless Semiconductor Assn. (pres.), Tech. Network (bd. dirs.), Semiconductor Industry Assn. (bd. dirs.). Office: Xilinx Inc 2100 Logic Dr San Jose CA 95124-3400*

**ROELL, STEPHEN A.,** manufacturing executive; CFO Johnson Controls, Inc., Milw., 1991—2004, exec. v.p., vice-chmn., 2004—, also bd. dir., 2004—. Bd. dir. Covenant Healthcare Sys., Inc., Interstate Battery Svc. of Am., Inc. Office: Johnson Controls Inc 5757 W Green Bay Ave Milwaukee WI 53201

**ROELLER, HERBERT ALFRED,** biology professor; b. Magdeburg, Germany, Aug. 2, 1927; came to U.S., 1962; s. Alfred H. and Elfriede (Wartner) R.; m. Manuela R. Buresch, Dec. 20, 1957. Abiturium, Christian Thomasius Schule, Halle/Saale, 1946; PhD, Georg August U., Goettingen, 1962; MD, U. Muenster, 1955. Project assoc. zoology U. Wis., Madison, 1962-65, asst. prof. pharmacology, 1965-66, rsch. assoc. zoology, 1966-67, assoc. prof. zoology, 1967-68; prof. biology Tex. A&M U., 1968-83, prof. biochemistry and biophysics, 1974-83, dir. Inst. Devel. Biology, 1973-83, Disting. prof., 1977—, Alumni prof., 1980-85. V.p. rsch. Zoecon Corp., Palo Alto, Calif., 1968-72, sci. adv., 1972-85, chief scientist, Zoecon Rsch. Inst., Palo Alto, 1985-88; sci. advisor Syntex Rsch., Palo Alto, 1966-68, European Cmty., 1988—; Affymax Rsch. Inst., Palo Alto, 1989-96; corp. advisor Symyx Techs., Sunnyvale, Calif., 1996—; mem. adv. panel regulatory biology, divsn. biol. and med. scis. NSF, 1969-72; mem. Internat. Centre Insect Physiology and Ecology, Nairobi, Kenya, 1970—, dir. rsch., 1970-75. Mem. editl. bd. Jour. Chem. Ecology, 1974—; Contbr. articles to profl. jours. Recipient Disting. Achievement award for research Tex. A&M U., 1976. Fellow Tex. Acad. Sci.; mem. German Acad. Naturforscher Leopoldina, AAAS, Am. Soc. Zoologists, Entomol. Soc. Am., Am. Soc. Devel. Biology, Sigma Xi.

**ROELLIG, LEONARD OSCAR,** physics professor; b. Detroit, May 17, 1927; s. Oscar Otto and Laura K. (Rutz) R.; m. B. Pauline Owen, June 20, 1952; children: Thomas Leonard, Mark Douglas, Paul David. AB, U. Mich., 1950, MS, 1956, PhD, 1959. From asst. prof. to prof. physics Wayne State U., Detroit, 1958-78, dean, 1971-72, asso. provost, 1972-76; pres. Central Solar Energy Research Corp., Detroit, 1977; prof. physics CCNY, 1978-96, prof. emeritus, 1996—; vice chancellor acad. affairs CUNY, 1978-83. Vis. prof. Univ. Coll., London, 1968-69, Tata Inst. Fundamental Rsch., Bombay, India, 1973, Paul Scherrer Inst., Villigen, Switzerland, 1991-92; chmn. bd. advisers Midwest Regional Solar Energy Planning Venture, 1977. Co-author: Positron Annihilation, 1967; contbr. articles to profl. jours. Bd. dirs. Luth. Publicity Bur., 1981-91, v.p., 1984-85, pres., 1985-89; v.p. Grosse Pointe (Mich.) Human Rels. Coun., 1969-70. With USN, 1945-46, U.S. Army, 1950-52. Recipient Wayne State U. Fund Research Recognition award, 1963, Probus Club award for acad. achievement, 1968, Probus Club award for acad. leadership, 1977 Mem. Am. Phys. Soc. Home: 4520 Sioux Dr Boulder CO 80303-3733 Office: U Colo Dept Physics Boulder CO 80302 Office Phone: 303-492-8707; Personal E-mail: lnroellig@aol.com.

**ROELLIG, MARK D.,** lawyer; BS in Applied Maths. with highest distinction, U. Mich., 1976; JD, George Washington U., 1979; MBA, U. Washington, 1988. Assoc. Perry & Smity, Seattle, Reed, McClure, Moceri & Thonn, Seattle; litigation and regulator atty. law dept. Pacific Northwest Bell Telephone Co., Seattle, 1983-92, v.p. law and litigation sect. Denver, 1992-95, v.p. law and human resources, asst. sec. corp. sect., 1995, exec. v.p. pub. policy and regulatory law, 1996-97, exec. v.p. pub. policy, human resources, law, gen. counsel, 1997—2000; dir., sec., consultant Bulletin News Network, Inc., 2000—02; v.p., gen. counsel, sec. StorageTek, 2002—. Mem. Beta Gamma Sigma. Office: StorageTek 1 StorageTek Dr Louisville CO 80028

**ROELOFS, LYLE DEAN,** physicist, researcher; b. Grand Rapids, Mich., Dec. 19, 1953; s. Harlan Ray and Cynthia Clara (Van Dyke) R.; m. Lauren Beth Mulder, June 14, 1975; children: Christopher Dean, Brian Alexander. BS, Calvin Coll., 1975; MS, U. Md., 1978, PhD, 1980. Instr. Calvin Coll., Grand Rapids, 1977; rsch. asst., instr. U. Md., College Park, 1977-80; rsch. assoc. Brown U., Providence, 1980-82; asst. prof. physics Haverford (Pa.) Coll., 1982-87, assoc. prof. physics, 1987-93, prof. physics, 1993—. Author: Electricity and Magnetism Simulations, 1995, Handbook of Surface Science, Vol. 1, 1996; contbr. articles to profl. jours. Democrat. Office: Haverford Coll Dept Physics 370 Lancaster Ave Haverford PA 19041-1336

**ROELOFS, WENDELL LEE,** biochemistry professor, consultant; b. Orange City, Iowa, July 26, 1938; s. Edward and Edith (Beyers) Roelofs; m. Joanna Roelofs, Jan. 13, 2005; children: Brenda Jo, Caryn Jean, Jeffrey Lee, Kevin Jon. BS, Central Coll., Pella, Iowa, 1960; PhD, Ind. U., 1964; DSc (hon.) (hon.), Central Coll., Pella, Iowa, 1985, Ind. U., 1986, Hobart and William Smith Colls., 1988; DSc (hon.), U. of Lund, Sweden, 1989, Free U. Brussels, 1989. Predoctoral fellow NIH, 1962—64; NIH postdoctoral fellow MIT, 1964; asst. prof. Dept. Entomology Cornell U., Geneva, NY, 1965—69, assoc. prof. Dept. Entomology, 1969—76, prof., 1976—, Liberty Hyde Bailey prof. insect biochemistry, 1978—, chmn. dept., 1991—. Contbr. articles to sci. jours. Recipient Alexander von Humboldt award in agr., 1977, Outstanding Alumni award, Central Coll., 1978, Wolf prize for agr., Wolf Found.,

Israel, 1982, Disting. Alumnus award, Ind. U., 1983, Nat. Medal of Sci., 1983, Disting. Svc. award, USDA, 1986, Silver medal, Internat. Soc. Chem. Ecology, 1990. Fellow: Entomol. Soc. Am. (J. Everett Bussart Meml. award 1973, Founder's Meml. award 1980, Disting. Achievement award Ea. br. 1983), AAAS; mem.: Am. Acad. Arts and Sci., Am. Chem. Soc. (Sterling B. Hendricks award 1994, Spencer award 2001), NAS, Sigma Xi. Republican. Presbyterian. Achievements include patents in field. Home: 4 Crescence Dr Geneva NY 14456-1302 Office: Cornell Univ Dept Entomology Barton Lab Geneva NY 14456*

**ROEMER, CAROL KALUGA,** art educator; b. Cleve., Sept. 24, 1941; d. Joseph and Helen (Belavich) Kaluga; m. William Daniel Roemer, Dec. 21, 1974 (dec. Mar. 1998). BA, Calif. State U., Long Beach, 1970, MA, 1972; PhD, Claremont (Calif.) Grad. Sch., 1992. Cert. c.c. tchr., Calif. Classroom tchr. Holy Spirit Sch., L.A., 1966-67; adj. instr. Cerritos C.C., Norwalk, Calif., 1972-81, Calif. State U., Long Beach, 1973-79. Golden West Coll., Huntington Beach, Calif., 1980-81; replacement instr. (full-time) Pasadena City Coll., 1977-80; prof. art Long Beach City Coll., 1981—2004, prof. emeritus, 2004—. Author: The Bread of Angels: Charles Eliot Norton's Art History, 1992; multi-media author/developer: Looking at Art, 1997-98. Recipient Tchg. Excellence award Nat. Inst. for Staff and Organizational Devel., U. Tex., 1995. Mem. Coll. Art Assn., Mus. Latin Am. Art, Long Beach Mus. Art (guest lectr. 1990-93), L.A. County Mus. Art (guest lectr. 1997), Cairn Terrier Club of So. Calif. (bd. dirs., newsletter editor). Avocations: cairn terrior exhibitor, breeder.

**ROEMER, ELIZABETH,** retired astronomer, retired educator; b. Calif., Sept. 4, 1929; d. Richard Quirin and Elsie Roemer. BA with honors, U. Calif., Berkeley, 1950, PhD (Lick Obs. fellow), 1955. Tchr. adult class Oakland pub. schs., 1950-52; lab technician U. Calif. at Mt. Hamilton, 1954-55; grad. research astronomer U. Calif. at Berkeley, 1955-56; research asso. Yerkes Obs. U. Chgo., 1956; astronomer U.S. Naval Obs., Flagstaff, Ariz., 1957-66; asso. prof. dept. astronomy, also in lunar and planetary lab. U. Ariz., Tucson, 1966-69, prof., 1969-97; prof. emerita, 1997—; astronomer Steward Obs., 1980-97, astronomer emerita, 1997—. Chmn. working group on orbits and ephemerides of comets commn. 20 Internat. Astron. Union, 1964-79, 85-88, v.p. commn. 20, 1979-82, pres., 1982-85, v.p. commn. 6, 1973-76, 85-88, pres., 1976-79, 88-91; mem. adv. panels Office Naval Research, Nat. Acad. Scis.-NRC, NASA; researcher and author numerous publs. on astrometry and astrophysics of comets and minor planets including 79 recoveries of returning periodic comets, visual and spectroscopic binary stars, computation of orbits of comets and minor planets. Recipient Dorothea Klumpke Roberts prize U. Calif. at Berkeley, 1950, Mademoiselle Merit award, 1959; asteroid (1657) named Roemera, 1965; Benjamin Apthorp Gould prize Nat. Acad. Scis., 1971; NASA Spl. award, 1986. Fellow AAAS (council 1966-69, 72-73), Royal Astron. Soc. (London); mem. Am. Astron. Soc. (program vis. profs. astronomy 1960-75, council 1967-70, chmn. div. dynamical astronomy 1974), Astron. Soc. Pacific (publs. com. 1962-73, Comet medal com. 1968-74, Donohoe lectr. 1962), Internat. Astron. Union, Am. Geophys. Union, Brit. Astron. Assn., Phi Beta Kappa, Sigma Xi. Office: U Ariz PO Box 210092 Lunar & Planetary Lab Tucson AZ 85721-0092

**ROEMER, JAMES PAUL,** data processing executive, writer; b. Cin., June 6, 1947; s. Charles William and Lillian (Vollman) R.; m. Patricia Pipenger; children: Kimberly, Michelle. Student, U. Cin., 1965-68; A.M.P., U. Va., 1978. Systems analyst Union Central Life Ins. Co., Cin., 1965-70; program and systems mgr. Computer Systems, Inc., Florence, Ky., 1970-72; mgr. data processing Mead Products, Dayton, Ohio, 1972-77; dir. ops. Mead Data Central, Dayton, 1977-78, v.p. ops., 1978-80, acting pres., 1980-81, v.p. product devel., 1981-82, sr. v.p. legal, govt., acctg., sr. v.p. with responsibility for lexis, 1982-89; pres. Michie Group, Charlottesville, Va., 1989-91; pres., COO Bell and Howell Publs. Systems Co., 1991-93; pres., CEO Univ. Microfilms Internat., Ann Arbor, 1994-95; chmn., pres., CEO Bell & Howell, Skokie, Ill., 1995—. Active Harvard, 1989. Mem. Info. Industry Assn., Assn. for info. and Image Mgmt. Republican. Roman Catholic. Home: 6271 Canterbury Dr Hudson OH 44236-3558

**ROEMER, JOHN E.,** economics educator; b. Washington, Feb. 1, 1945; s. Milton I. and Ruth J. (Rosenbaum) R.; m. Carla N. Muldavin, 1968. BA in Math., summa cum laude, Harvard U., 1966; PhD in Economics, U. Calif., Berkeley, 1974. Math. tchr. Lowell HS, San Francisco, 1969—74, Pelton Jr. HS, San Francisco, 1969—74; Ford Found. grad. fellow U. Calif., Berkeley, 1966—68, Nat. Sci. Found. grad. fellow, 1966—68; Social Sci. Rsch. Coun. postdoctoral rsch. fellow Stanford U., 1977; asst. prof. economics U. Calif., Davis, 1974—78, assoc. prof., 1978—81, prof., 1981—2000, acting chair Dept. Economics, 1987—88, dir. Program on Economy, Justice and Society, 1988—2000; Elizabeth S. and A. Varick Stout prof. polit. sci. and economics Yale U., 2000—. Editor Marxian economics Ency. of Economics, 1984—; Fundamentals of Pure and Applied Economics, 1984—; editl. bd. Economics and Philosophy, 1983—, Ethics, 1989—, Social Choice and Welfare, 1990—, Mathematical Social Sciences, 1993—, Jour. Economic Inequality, 2001—; assoc. editor Jour. Economic Perspectives, 1988—96, Economics and Politics, 1988—90, Jour. Economic Literature, 1988—97, Rev. Economic Design, 1992—, Jour. Ethics, 1997—, Jour. Economics, 2004—; vis. prof. Dept. Economics and Dept. Polit. Sci. UCLA, 1987; vis. prof. Université de Cergy-Pontoise, 1995, Ecole Polytechnique, Paris, Université de Paris I 2006. Author: Analytical Foundations of Marxian Economic Theory, 1981, A General Theory of Exploitation and Class, 1982, Value, Exploitation and Class, 1986, Free To Lose: An Introduction to Marxist Economic Philosophy, 1988, Egalitarian Perspectives: Essays in Philosophical Economics, 1994, A Future for Socialism, 1994, Theories of Distinctive Justice, 1996, Equality of Opportunity, 1998, Political Competition: Theory and Applications, 2001, Democracy, education and equality, 2006, coauthor: Sustainable Democracy, 1995. Fellow John Simon Guggenheim Meml., 1980—81, Russell Sage Found., 1998—99. Fellow: Econometric Soc., Am. Acad. Arts and Sciences; mem.: Am. Polit. Sci. Assn., Soc. for Social Choice and Welfare (exec. bd. mem. 1991—), Am. Economic Assn. (exec. bd. mem. 1995—97), The Brit. Acad. (corr. fellow 2005—). Office: Dept Politcal Science Yale Univ PO Box 208302 New Haven CT 06520 Office Phone: 203-432-5249. Office Fax: 203-432-6196. E-mail: john.roemer@yale.edu.*

**ROEMER, TIMOTHY JOHN,** think-tank executive, former congressman; b. South Bend, Ind., Oct. 30, 1956; m. Sarah Lee Johnson, 1989. BA in pol. sci, U. Calif., San Diego, 1979; MA, PhD in internat. rels., U. Notre Dame, 1986. Staff asst. to congressman John Brademas U.S. Congress, def., trade and fgn. policy advisor to senator Dennis DeConcini; mem. U.S. Congress from 3rd Ind. dist., 1991—2003, mem. economic and ednl. opportunity com., mem. sci. com., mem. edn. and the workforce com., mem. permanent select committee on intelligence; ptnr. Johnston & Assocs., Washington, 2003; pres. Ctr. for Nat. Policy, Washington, 2003—. Adj. prof. Am. U.; commr. The Nat. Commn. on Terrorist Attacks Upon the U.S. (The 9-11 Commn.), 2002—04. Mem.: Nat. Commn. Terrorists Attacks U.S. Democrat. Office: Ctr for Nat Policy One Massachusetts Ave NW Ste 333 Washington DC 20001

**ROEN, SHELDON R.,** publishing executive, psychologist; b. N.Y.C. Morris Rosenthal and Gussie (Weininger) R.; children: Randa M., Marjorie A., Harris L. BS, City U. N.Y., 1950, MA, 1951; PhD, Columbia U., 1955; postgrad., New Sch. Social Research, 1951-53, Harvard Sch. Pub. Health, 1961-62. Diplomate: Am. Bd. Examiners in Profl. Psychology. Tchr. pub. schs., N.Y.C., 1950-53; chief Clin. Psychology Svc., Ft. Sill, Okla., 1955-58; instr. Cameron Coll., Okla. A. and M. U., 1956-58; asst. prof. U. N.H., 1958-60; asst. chief psychol. services Mass. Mental Health Center, Boston, 1960-63; instr. Harvard, 1961-63; rsch. assoc. Med. Sch., 1960-63; dir. rsch. S. Shore Mental Health Center, Quincy, Mass., 1962-66; assoc. prof. dept. psychology Tchrs. Coll., Columbia, N.Y.C., 1966-72; dir. Psychol. Consultation Center, 1966-72; chmn. bd., pres. human scis. Human Scis. Press, N.Y.C., 1972—90. Lectr. L.I. U., summer 1968, Tufts U., 1961-62; mem. N.H. Gov.'s Com. on Spl. Edn., also Study Com. on Mental Health Reorgn., 1962; cons. VISTA program OEO, 1966-67; mem. juvenile problems research rev. com. NIMH, 1968-69; mem. research rev. com. Title III Elementary and

Secondary Edn. Act project application Ohio Dept. Edn., 1969-72; mem. mental health coordinating com. local sch. dist. 5, N.Y.C., 1969-72; mem., research dir. work incentive program for welfare recipients Wharton Sch. Pa., U.S. Dept. Labor, 1969-72; mem. mental health and community control com. N.Y. Psychologists for Social Action, 1969-72 Authors, editor books.; Editor: Mass. Psychol. Assn. Newsletter, 1963-65, Community Mental Health Jour; contbr. articles to profl. jours. and chpts. to books. Chmn. bd. trustees Bristol Acres Sch., Taunton, Mass., 1965-67. Fellow Am. Psychol. Assn. (mem. com. pre-coll. behavioral scis. 1968-71, founder div. 27 community psychology div. 1969, chmn. subcom. pre-high sch. behavioral sci. 1969-72), Am. Pub. Health Assn., Am. Orthopsychiat. Assn. (com. on research edn. 1965-67), Am. Sociol. Assn.; mem. New Eng. Psychol. Assn. (steering com. 1965-68), N.H. Psychol. Assn. (legis. chmn. 1961-62) Office: 3205 Beacon St Pompano Beach FL 33062-1207

**ROENICK, JEREMY,** professional hockey player; b. Boston, Jan. 17, 1970; m. Tracy Roenick; children: Brandi, Brett. Center Chgo. Blackhawks, 1988—96, Phoenix Coyotes, 1996—2001, Pheonix Coyotes, 2006—, Phila. Flyers, 2001—05, LA Kings, 2005—06. Mem. US Olympic Hockey Team, Nagano, Japan, 1998, Salt Lake City, 2002; player NHL All-Star Game, 1991—94, 1999, 2000, 2002—04. Named NHL Rookie of Yr., The Sporting News, 1989—90. Office: Pheonix Coyotes Hockey Club 5800 W Glenn Dr, Ste 350 Glendale AZ 85301*

**ROENICKE, NORMA JEAN,** music educator, pianist, organist, small business owner; b. Saginaw, Mich., Oct. 28, 1942; d. Walter William and Evelyn Hulda (Riethmeier) Moderow; m. W. Ruppal (div. 1966); m. Walter Allen Roenicke, Oct. 25, 1967; children: Scott Walter, Charisse Leigh Roenicke Taylor. Student, Delta Coll., U. Mich. Music tchr., performer Grinnell Bros., Saginaw, Mich., 1960-69; organist, choir accompanist Resurrection Luth Ch., Saginaw, Mich., 1974-97; organist, choir dir. Messiah Luth. Ch., Bay City, Mich., 1998—; accompanist Germania Club, Saginaw, Mich., 1997—; sub. organist St. Lorenz Luth. Ch., Frankenmuth, Mich., 1975—. Bd. dirs. Saginaw Symphony, 1985-94. Mem. Am. Guild Organists, Mich. Music Tchrs. Assn., Nat. Music Tchrs. Assn., PEO (pres. 1995-97, 2004), Rotary (internat. svc. dir. Frankenmuth chpt. 1997-99, Paul Harris fellow). Republican. Lutheran. Avocations: travel, reading, skiing, walking. Office Phone: 989-777-7000. E-mail: njrpiano@hotmail.com.

**ROENIGK, MARTIN ALLEN,** insurance company executive; b. Cleve., Sept. 19, 1942; s. Henry Herman and Irene Lena (Rini) Roenigk; m. Elise Feutz, July 5, 1965. BA, Antioch Coll., 1965; MBA, U. Chgo., 1967. CPA Conn. Staff auditor Arthur Andersen & Co., Cleve., 1968; with Travelers Ins. Co., Hartford, Conn., 1970—80, v.p., 1980—. Editor (pub.): MBS News Bull, 1976—. Pres. Greater Middletown Preservation Trust, Conn., 1981, trustee Conn., 1978—; mem. Rep. Town Com., 1981—. With U.S. Army, 1968-70. Mem.: Am. Inst. CPAs, Musical Box Soc. (trustee). Home: 26 Barton Hl E Hampton CT 06247

**ROENS, STEVEN THOMAS,** music educator, associate dean; b. Phila., Mar. 1, 1949; s. Burt Beaudry and Jacqueline Roens; m. Cheryl Anne Clarke, Aug. 18, 1994; stepchildren: David Hart, Sarah Hart, Edward Alexander Hart, Isaac Hart. BA, Swarthmore Coll., Pa., 1971; MFA, Brandeis U., Mass., 1977; DMA, Columbia U., N.Y.C., 1986. Vis. asst. prof. music Wellesley Coll., Mass., 1986—90; assoc. prof. music U. of UT, Salt Lake City, 1990—, assoc. dean, 1998—. Composer: (musical compositions) Time and Again, 1991 (Commn. from Stony Brook Contemporary Chamber Players), (musical composition) Delicate Arch, 1992, In the Night Fields, 1977, Invocation, (piano solo) starry skies, 1978, quartet for clarinet, violin, cello and piano. Mem. League of Composers Internat. Soc. for Contemporary Music, N.Y.C., 1983—86. Fellow, MacDowell Colony, 1987. Mem.: Soc. of Composers. Democrat. Avocations: astronomy, photography, hiking. Office: U of UT Sch of Music 1375 E Presidents Cir Salt Lake City UT 84112 Personal E-mail: steve.roens@music.utah.edu.

**ROEPER, RICHARD,** columnist; b. Chgo., Oct. 17, 1959; s. Robert and Margaret R. BA, Ill. State U., 1982. Freelance writer, 1982-87; syndicated columnist Chgo.-Sun Times, 1987—, NY Times; regular contbr., film crtic WBBM-CBS 2, Chgo., 2002—; and co-host Ebert & Roeper, 2000—. Talk show host Sta. WLS-FM, Chgo.; commentator Fox Thing in the Morning, Sta. WFLD-TV, Fox TV, Chgo.; contbr., film critic WLS-Channel 7. Author: Ten Sure Signs a Movie Character is Doomed and Other Surprising Movie Lists, 2002, Schlock Value: Hollywood at Its Worst, 2005; contbr. monthly essays on film in Esquire. Recipient Outstanding Columnist Ill. Press Assn., 1992, Nat. Headliner award for top columnist Atlantic City Press Club, 1992, Emmy award, 1994. Mem. Am. Fedn. TV & Radio Artists, Chgo. Newspaper Guild. Office: Chicago Sun Times 350 N Orleans St Ste 1270 Chicago IL 60654-2148*

**ROEPER, THOMAS WALTER,** linguist, educator; b. Bennington, Vt., Aug. 23, 1943; s. George Alexander Roeper and Annemarie Bondy ROeper; m. Laura Jane Holland, Sept. 22, 1973; children: Maria Ann, Timothy Abraham. PhD, Harvard U., Cambridge, Mass., 1971. Prof. U Mass., Amherst, Mass., 1973, U. Chgo., 1971—. Cons. Laureate Learning Co., Burlington, Vt.; editor lang. acquisition Erlbaum Pub. Co., Mahwah, NJ, 1990—2004; mng. editor studies in theoretical psycholinguistics Springer Pub. Co., Germany, 1980—. Author: The Prism of Grammar, Understanding and Producing Speech with Ed Matthei, (school test) Diagnostic Evaluation of Language Variation; author: (with E. Williams) (acad. book) Parametersetting; author: Theoretical Approaches to Language Acquisition. Civil rights worker SNCC, Jackson, Miss., 1965; founding mem. Faculty and Staff for Peace in C.Am., Amherst, Mass., 1984—89; mem. SAGE, 2000. Recipient Pub. Svc. award, U. Mass., 2005; grantee Contract: Develop Dialect Neutral Assessment grant, NIH, 1993—2004, Acquisition grant, NSF, 1987—90; Conti fellow, U. Mass., 1998, Theory of Mind grant, NIH, 1991—94, Evidentials in English, Navajo, and Tibetan grant, 2006—. Mem.: Linguistic Soc. Am. Achievements include research in applied principles of linguistic theory to the domain of language acquisition; applied principles of syntax below the word level; developed assessment tecniques for children based on linguistic theory. Avocations: bicycling, tennis, squash, travel. Home: 149 High St Amherst MA 01002 Office: U Mass Amherst Mass Amherst MA 01003 Office Phone: 413-545-0889.

**ROER, RICKI E.,** lawyer; b. NYC, May 22, 1956; BA, U. Pa., 1978; JD, Am. U., 1981; LLM in internat. law, Oxford U., 1982. Bar: NY 1982, US Dist. Ct. Ea. Dist. NY, US Dist. So. Dist. NY, US Ct. Appeals 2nd Cir. Ptnr. Wilson, Elser, Moskowitz, Edelman & Dicker LLP, NYC, head nat. employment litig. team. Mem.: ABA, NY State Women's Bar Assn., Assn. of the Bar of the City of NY. Office: Wilson Elser Moskowitz Edelman & Dicker LLP 23rd Fl 150 E 42nd St New York NY 10017-5639 Office Phone: 212-490-3000 ext. 2375. Office Fax: 212-490-3038. Business E-Mail: roerr@wemed.com.

**ROES, NICHOLAS A.,** communications consultant, writer; b. Jersey City, Dec. 26, 1952; s. Nicholas R. and Mimi (Maresca) R.; m. Nancy Bennett. BS in Edn., U. Bridgeport, 1974, MA in Bus. and Pub. Mgmt., 1983; PhD in Addictions Treatment, Westbrook U., 1997. Credentialed substance abuse counselor NY, credentialed alcohol and substance abuse counselor, credentialed justice counselor, registered addiction specialist. Chmn. bd. Tchr. Update, Inc., Saddle River, NJ, 1976—; pres., cons., author Nicholas A. Roes & Assocs., Saddle River, 1979—; mng. ptnr. Barryville (N.Y.) Investors, 1985—; exec. dir. New Hope Manor, residential substance abuse treatment ctr. for women, Barryville, NY, 1992—. Dir. NAR Prodns., 1987, Idea Group, Inc., 1986—; instr. Marist Coll., Poughkeepsie, N.Y., 1989—. Author: Helping Children Watch TV, 1978, rev., 1992, America's Lowest College, 1977, 10th edit., 1997, Gambling for Fun, 1988, Pick Your Own, 1989, Solutions for The Treatment Resistant Addicted Client, 2002; editor (newsletter) Tchr. Update, 1977; columnist The Investment Column, 1980—, Addiction Profl. Mag., 2003—. Exec. dir. New Hope Manor, Barryville,

1992—; chair alcohol and substance abuse subcom. Sullivan County Cmty. Svcs. Bd. Recipient Cert. of Recognition, N.Y. State Office Alcohol and Substance Abuse Svcs., 2002. Mem. Internat. Assn. Fin. Planners, Direct Mail Club of N.Y., EDPRESS, C. of C., Mensa, Internat. Platform Assn. Avocation: music. Office: Nicholas A Roes & Assocs PO Box 205 Saddle River NJ 07458-0205 Office Phone: 845-557-8713. Personal E-mail: nickaroes@aol.com.

**ROESCH, CLARENCE HENRY,** banker; b. Egg Harbor City, N.J., Aug. 22, 1925; s. Joseph Aloysius and Bertha (Heumann) R.; m. Helen Regina Owens, Sept. 25, 1954; children: Kathleen Marie, Helena Patricia, Maryanne Cornelia. BBA, Rutgers U., 1949, postgrad., 1961; certificate, Am. Inst. Banking, 1961; grad., Trust Sch., Bucknell U., 1971. Cert. internal auditor, data processing auditor. Bookkeeper, teller, head teller, asst. sec., trust officer, auditor Egg Harbor Bank & Trust Co., 1949-61; bank examiner Phila. Fed. Res. Bank, 1962-65; chief auditor Am. Bank & Trust Co. of Pa. (name changed to Meridian Bancorp Inc. 1985), Reading, 1966-88, v.p. audit dept., 1968-88, ret. officer, 1988; parish sec. St. Benedict Ch., Plowville, 1989-99; sr. staff auditor Nat. Penn Bank, Boyertown, 1990-97. Census enumerator, 2000; mem. faculty Berks County chpt. Am. Inst. Banking, 1966-68; instr. bank auditing Bank Adminstrn. Inst., U. Richmond, 1968; pres., past mems. chpt. Am. Banking Inst., Atlantic County, N.J., 1958-59. Budget com. Berks County chpt. United Way, 1967-73; bd. dirs. Berks Reading Coun. Camp Fire, 1966-93, chmn. fin. coun., 1973, 75, treas., 1974-84; instr. 55 Alive Program AARP, 1989-93. Recipient John Johnston award as outstanding banker N.J., 1955; award U.S. Savs. Bond Com., 1961; Luther Halsey Gulick award for vol. services Camp Fire, 1975; John C. Collier award for outstanding bus. and fin. services, 1981, Blue Ribbon award for vol. services Camp Fire, 1984, award for corp. vol. of yr. Meridian Bancorp Inc., 1984, 85, Outstanding Svc. in Fin. Mgmt. award Camp Fire, 1988. Mem. Inst. Internal Auditors (dir. ctrl. Pa. chpt.), Berks County Bankers Assn., Travelers Protective Assn., Berks Reading C. of C., Bank Administration Inst. (past pres., dir. Penn-Jersey chpt.), Spring Lawn Optimist Club (bd. dirs. 1992, Key Mem. award 1992, chmn. fin. and budget com. 1992-94), St. BEnedict Ch. Prime Timers Srs. Home: 6-E Doral Dr Reading PA 19607-3379

**ROESCH, ROBERT EUGENE,** dentist; b. July 10, 1951; s. Wilber H. and Vivian (Reese) R.; m. Susan M. Tuttle, Aug. 25, 1973. BA, Midland Luth. Coll., 1973; DDS, U. Nebr., 1976. Pvt. practice, Fremont, Nebr., 1979—; mem. bd. Three Rivers Pub. Health Dept., 2002—, pres., 2006—. Dental cons. Dodge County Am. Cancer Soc., Fremont, 1984—98. Campaign chmn. Fremont United Way, 1987, v.p., 1988; mem. orgn. com. Main St. Fremont 1995—, chmn. orgn. com., 1998—2000, 2nd v.p., 1998, 1st v.p., 1999, pres., 2000, bd. dirs., 1997—2001; pres. Sinai Luth. Ch. Coun., Fremont, 1983—84, bd. dirs., 1987—90; mem. endowment com. Sinai Luth. Ch., 1990—94. Master: Acad. Gen. Dentistry (v.p. region 10 1990—91, dir. 1991—93, trustee 1993—94, chmn. budget and fin. com., spkr. of house 1999—2005); fellow: Pierre Fauchard Acad., Am. Coll. Dentristry, Internat. Acad. Dentristry, Internat. Coll. Dentristry (pres. Nebr. chpt. 2006—); mem.: ADA (del. 2002, 2005—06), Acad. Gen. Dentistry Found. (bd. dirs. 2005—), Fremont Indsl. Found., Fremont C. of C. (diplomate 1985—94, vice-chmn. memberships and membership svcs. 1989—90, bd. dirs. 1991—94, vice-chmn. pub. affairs 1992—94), Fremont Wellness Coun. (bd. dirs. 1996—98), Omaha Dist. Dental Soc. (bd. dirs.), Am. Equilibration Soc., Am. Assn. Functional Orthodontists, Am. Orthodontic Soc., Nebr. Dental Assn. (v.p. 2000—02, pres. 2002), Nebr. Acad. Gen. Dentistry (pub. info. officer 1983—85, sec., treas. 1985—88, pres. 1990—92, exec. dir. 1992—94, legis. chmn. 1997—), Acad. Operative Dentistry, Midland Coll. Alumni (bd. dirs. 1981—97, pres. 1983—84), Dodge County Hist. Soc., Salmon Soc., Fremont Tennis Assn., Fremont Cmty. Players, R.V. Tucker Nebr. Study Club (treas. 2005), Tri Valley Dental Study Club (sec.-treas. 1983, v.p. 1984, pres. 1985, v.p. 1989), Midland Luth. Coll. Boosters Club (bd. dirs. 1988—94), Main St. Ambs. (co-chmn. 1997—98, chmn. 1998—2000, pres. 2000), Optimists (bd. dirs. 1981—83, 1984—88, pres. 1987, bd. dirs. Fremont club 1991—93), Am. Legion. Avocations: tennis, travel. Home: 2137 Nye Dr Fremont NE 68025-2210 Office: 553 N Broad St Fremont NE 68025-4930 E-mail: broesch@agd.org.

**ROESE, NEAL J.,** psychology professor, consultant; b. Vancouver, Canada, Feb. 13, 1965; s. Joseph and Geraldine Roese; m. Karen Grabowski, June 4, 1994; children: Emma, Anna. PhD, U. Western Ont., London, Can., 1993. Asst. prof. Northwestern U., Evanston, Ill., 1994—2000; assoc. prof., rsch. chair social psychology Simon Fraser U., Vancouver, Canada, 2000—02; prof. U. Ill., Champaign, 2002—. Cons. FORESIGHT Reconstruction, Inc, Northbrook, Ill., 2006—. Author: If Only, 2005. Grantee Nat. Inst. Mental Health, 1997—2002, 2004—. Avocation: skiing. Office: U Ill 603 East Daniel St Champaign IL 61820 Office Phone: 217-244-0751.

**ROESLER, JOHN BRUCE,** lawyer; b. Portland, Oreg., Oct. 9, 1943; s. Bruce Emil and Charlotte Amanda (Naess) R.; m. Kathryne Elise Nilsen, Aug. 14, 1965; children: Paul, Mark, Nico. BA, U. Kans., 1966, JD, 1971. Bar: Mo. 1971, N.Mex. 1979, Colo. 1998, U.S. Dist. Ct. (we. dist.) Mo. 1971, U.S. Dist. Ct. N.Mex. 1979, U.S. Dist. Ct. Colo. 1998. U.S. Ct. Appeals (10th cir.) 1979, U.S. Ct. Appeals (5th cir.) 1988, U.S. Ct. Appeals (4th cir.) 1992, U.S. Supreme Ct. 1987. Assoc. The Gage Firm, Kansas City, Mo., 1971—74; civil rights advocate State of N.Mex. Human Rights, Santa Fe, 1977—78; law clk. Hon. Edwin L. Felter N.Mex. Supreme Ct., Santa Fe, 1978—79; asst. dist. atty. Taos Dist. Atty.'s Office, N.Mex., 1979—80; asst. dist. pros. Santa Fe Dist. Atty.'s Office, 1980—82; pvt. practice Santa Fe, 1982—97; of counsel Roth, Van Amberg, Gross, Rogers & Ortiz, 1991—94; spl. asst. atty. gen. Colo. Atty. Gen.'s Office, 1997—99; assoc. Jones & Keller, Denver, 1999—2000; pvt. practice Denver, 2000—. Instr. John Marshall Law Sch., Chgo., 1974; spkr. edn. law and civil rights issues U. Miami Law Sch., 2000, Nat. Com. for Prevention of Child Abuse, Chgo., 1989, Little Rock, 90, Lorman Educators Svcs., 2004. Author: (books) How To Find the Best Lawyers; In Harm's Way: Is Your Child Safe in School, Beyond Special Education and the IDEA; mem. law rev. U. Kans. Sch. Law, 1970-71; contbr. articles to profl. jours. and Am. Jur. treatise. Mem. Colo. Bar Assn., Denver Bar Assn. Democrat. Roman Catholic. Avocations: skiing, hiking, gardening. Home: 2571 S Sherman St Denver CO 80210-5725 Office: 303 E 17th Ave Ste 200 Denver CO 80203 Office Phone: 303-832-1282. E-mail: jroesler@lawyer.com.

**ROESLER, ROBERT HARRY,** media consultant; b. Hammond, La., Oct. 5, 1927; s. Albert N. and Hilda (Schwartz) R.; m. Cloe Alferez, May 7, 1955; children: Kim, Bob, Toby. Student, Tulane U. Mem. sports staff Times Picayune, New Orleans, 1949-94, sports editor, 1964-80; exec. sports editor Times Picayune and States-Item, 1980-94; sports coord. New Orleans Met. Conv. and Visitors Bur., 1994—; CEO Roesler Media Cons. Chmn. faculty coun., Student Publs. Bd., U. New Orleans, 1998-2001. Author: Fair Grounds: Big Shots and Long Shots, 1998. Vice-chmn. Navy Recruiting Dist.; mem. assistance coun., New Orleans, 1992-96. With USN, WWII, Korean conflict. Mem. Profl. Football Writers Assn. Am. (pres. 1976-77, PFWA McCAnn Meml. award NFL Hall of Fame, 1997), Nat. Turf Writers Assn., Football Writers Am., Am. Legion, Navy League U.S., New Orleans Press Club (pres. 1959-60, sports writing awards). Office: 6458 Colbert St New Orleans LA 70124-2334 Home: 1700 Bailey Hill Rd #9 Eugene OR 97402 Office Phone: 541-338-3066. E-mail: bobroesler@gmail.com.

**ROESNER, LARRY AUGUST,** civil engineer; b. Denver, Mar. 14, 1941; s. Walter George and Sarah Jane (Merrick) R.; m. Kathleen Ann Fahrenbruch, Dec. 13, 1964; children: David John, Kevin Walter, Nathan August, Melissa Jane. BS in Civil Engring., Valparaiso U., Ind., 1959—63; MS in Civil Engring, Hydrology, Colo. State U., 1963—65; PhD, U. Wash., Seattle, 1969. Registered profl. engr., Calif., Colo., hydrologist. From assoc. engr. to prin. engr. Water Resources Engrs., Inc., Walnut Creek, Calif., 1968-77; from assoc. to v.p Camp Dresser & McKee Inc., Annandale, Va., 1977-85, sr. v.p., dir. water resources Maitland, Fla., 1985-92, chief tech. officer, 1992-98; dean Camp Dresser & McKee Corp. U., 1998-99; Harold H. Short prof. urban water infrastructure systems Colo. State U., Ft. Collins, 1999—, interim head

dept. civil engring., 2000. Guest lectr., cons. urban hydrology and surface water quality; NRC exec. com. Wastewater Mgmt. in Urban Coastal Areas, 1992; chair Engring. Found. Conf. Stormwater Mgmt.-Sustainable Urban Water Resources in the 21st Century, 1997, NRC study panel Oil in the Sea, 2001; urban wet weather adv. Water Environ. Rsch. Found. Contbr. articles to profl. jours. Recipient Water Resource Planning and Mgmt. Divsn. Svc. to the Profession award 1999. Fellow ASCE (life, chmn. 1995 water resources planning and mgmt. divsn. splty. conf., Walter L. Huber civil engring. rsch. prize 1975); mem. NAE (elected mem. 1990), Am. Water Resources Assn., Water Environ. Fedn. (chmn. urban quality runoff task force, 2005—), Tau Beta Pi (eminent engr.). Democrat. Lutheran. Achievements include development of mathematical models for U.S. government agencies including QUAL-II stream quality model for the EPA; an urban stormwater management model, the dynamic hydraulics model SWMMEXTRAN for storm drainage and sewer systems. Home: 5926 Huntington Hills Dr Fort Collins CO 80525-7118 Office: Colo State U Dept Civil Engring Fort Collins CO 80523-1372 Business E-Mail: larry.roesner@colostate.edu. *An environmental engineer is a caretaker in God's garden, the earth. The challenge for the environmental engineer is to maintain a balance between the needs of people and those of nature so that we may both use and enjoy the garden. It is the responsibility of the environmental engineer to leave the garden a little nicer than he found it.*

**ROESNER, PETER LOWELL,** manufacturing executive; b. Winchester, Ind., July 3, 1937; s. Lowell LeClair and Martha Christine (Overmyer) R.; children: Peter Lowell II, David Brandon, John Franklin. Student, Durham U., Eng., 1957-58; BA, DePauw U., 1959; JD, U. Mich., 1962; MBA, Harvard U., 1964. Bar: Ind. 1962, N.J. 1992. Asst. to pres. Overmyer Corp., Muncie, Ind., 1964-65, corp. sec., 1965-69, pres., 1969-84, also dir.; pres. Clinitemp Inc., Indpls., 1985-89, pres., owner Middletown (N.J.) Interiors Inc., 1993—. Dir. Mchts. Nat. Bank, 1974-84 Trustee Purdue U., 1978. Mem. Ind. Mfrs. Assn. (dir. 1970-82, pres. 1975, chmn. Phoenix Award com. 1974), Glass Packaging Inst. (trustee 1981-84), ABA Episcopalian.

**ROESSER, JEAN WOLBERG,** state official; b. Washington, May 8, 1930; d. Solomon Harry Wolberg and Mary Frances Brown; m. Eugene Francis Roesser, Aug. 3, 1957 (dec.); children: Eugene Francis, Jr., Mary Roesser Calderon, Anne. BA, Trinity Coll., Washington, 1951; postgrad. in econs., Cath. U. of Am., 1951-53. Congl. relations asst. U.S. Info. Agy., Washington, 1954-58; news reporter for Montgomery County Coun., Suburban Record, 1983-86; mem. Md. Ho. of Dels., Annapolis, 1986-94, Md. Senate, Annapolis, 1994—2002; mem. fin. coms., ethics com. State Senate, Md. Gen. Assembly, Annapolis, 1994—2002, joint com. welfare reform, 1996, joint com. healthcare delivery & financing, 1996—2002, joint budget & audit com., 1997—2002, chair joint com. on welfare reform, 2002; sec. Md. Dept. Aging, 2003—. Former mem. Md. Gov.'s Task Force on Energy; former pres. Montgomery County Fedn. Rep. Women, Potomac Women's Rep. Club; former 3d v.p. Md. Fedn. Rep. Women; founding mem. Montgomery County Arts Coun.; alt. del. Rep. Nat. Conv., 1992, del., 1996. Named one of Md.'s Top 100 Women, Daily Record, 2002; recipient Cmty. Achievement award, Washington Psychiat. Soc., 1994, 1998, Trinity Coll. Leadership award, 1994, Common Cause Md. award, 1993, Md. Underage Drinking Preventio Coalition award, 1994, Legislator of the Yr. award, Montgomery County Med. Soc., 1996, 2000, Best in Class award, Md. C. of C., 1997, Cmty. Svc. award, Washington Psychiatric Soc., 1998, Legislator of Yr. award, Md. State's Atty.'s Assn., 2000. Republican. Roman Catholic. Home: 10830 Fox Hunt Ln Potomac MD 20854-1553 E-mail: jeanroesser@aol.com.

**ROESSLER, CAROL ANN,** state legislator; b. Madison, Wis., Jan. 16, 1948; m. Paul Roessler. BS, U. Wis., Oshkosh, 1972. Dir. nutrition program for older adults County of Winnebago, Wis., 1973-82; elected to assembly, 1982—86; mem. Wis. Assembly, Madison, 1983-87; elected to senate in spl. election, 1987; mem. Wis. Senate from 18th dist., Madison, 1987—. Instr. pre-retirement planning Fox Valley Tech. Inst., 1978-81. Home: 1506 Jackson St Oshkosh WI 54901-2942 Office: PO Box 7882 Madison WI 53707-7882 E-mail: Sen.Roessler@legis.state.wi.us.

**ROETHE, JAMES NORTON,** lawyer; b. Milw., Jan. 27, 1942; s. Arthur Frantz and Bess Irma (Norton) R.; m. Nita May Dorris, July 15, 1967; children: Melissa Dorris, Sarah Rebacca. BBA, U. Wis., Madison, 1964, JD, 1967. Bar: Wis. 1967, Calif. 1968, U.S. Dist. Ct. (we. dist.) Wis. 1967, U.S. Dist. Ct. (no. dist.) Calif. 1972, U.S. Ct. Claims 1975, U.S. Ct. Appeals (9th cir.) 1980, U.S. Dist. Ct. (ea. dist.) Calif. 1982, U.S. Dist. Ct. (ctrl. dist.) Calif. 1986). U.S. Ct. Appeals (4th cir.) 1988, U.S. Ct. Appeals (2d cir.) 1989. Assoc. Pillsbury, Madison & Sutro, San Francisco, 1971-77, ptnr., 1978-92; sr. v.p., dir. litigation Bank of Am., San Francisco, 1992-96, exec. v.p., gen. counsel, 1996-98, dep. gen. counsel, 1998-99; ptnr. Litigation, Corp. & Securities practices Pillsbury Winthrop LLP (now Pillsbury Winthrop Shaw Pittman), San Francisco, 2000—. Staff atty. Commn. on CIA Activities within U.S., Washington, 1975. Editor: Africa, 1967; editor-in-chief Wis. Law Rev., 1966-67. Bd. dirs. Orinda (Calif.) Assn., 1984-85, pres., 1986; active City of Orinda Planning Commn., 1988-94, chmn., 1990, 93; bd. dirs. Calif. Shakespeare Festival, 1993—, pres., 2001-06; bd. vis. U. Wis. Law Sch., 1994-99. Lt. USNR, 1967-71 Fellow Am. Bar Found.; mem. ABA, Wis. Bar Assn., Calif. Bar Assn., Bar Assn. San Francisco, Wis. Law Alumni Assn. (bd. dirs. 2000—), Legal Aid Soc. (bd. dirs.), Orinda Country Club (pres. 2003-04), Order of Coif, Phi Kappa Phi Office: Pillsbury Winthrop Shaw Pittman 50 Fremont St San Francisco CA 94105 Office Phone: 415-983-1414. Office Fax: 415-983-1200. Business E-Mail: james.roethe@pillsburylaw.com.

**ROETHENMUND, OTTO EMIL,** finance company executive, bank executive; b. Thun, Switzerland, Sept. 1, 1928; came to U.S., 1951, naturalized, 1957; s. Franz and Berta (Dallenbach) R.; m. Ermina Grassi, May 7, 1955; children—Robert, Denise. MA, U. Neuchatel, 1948. Mgmt. trainee Kantonalbank, Bern, 1948-51; exec. trainee J. Henry Schroeder Banking and Trust Corp., N.Y.C., 1951-56; with Deak-Perera Group, N.Y.C., 1956—, vice chmn., group partner, 1962—; v.p., then sr. v.p. Deak & Co. (holding co.), 1962-74, exec. v.p., 1974-80, pres., chief exec. officer, 1980-86; pres., dir. Inter-Nation Capital Mgmt. Corp., 1986—. Lectr. internat. monetary and investment seminars. Served to lt. Swiss Army, 1948-51. Decorated knight Mil. Order Sts. Salvador and Brigitta (Sweden). Mem. Explorers Club, Met. Club (N.Y.C.), Westchester Country Club. Home: 2 Shore Rd Rye NY 10580-1031 Office: Inter-Nation Capital Mgmt Corp 230 Park Ave Rm 1536 New York NY 10169-0699 E-mail: oeraticnm@aol.com.

**ROETHLISBERGER, BEN,** professional football player; b. Findlay, OH, Mar. 2, 1982; s. Ken and Brenda Roethlisberger (Stepmother). BA, Miami U. of Ohio, 2004. Quarterback Pitts. Steelers, 2004—. Named Offensive Rookie of the Yr., AP, 2004. Achievements include setting NFL record for wins by a rookie quarterback (15); holding the highest competelion percentage by a rookie quarterback (66.1%), 2004; being a member of Super Bowl XL Champion Pittsburgh Steelers, 2006; being the youngest starting QB in NFL history to win a Super Bowl, 2006. Office: c/o Pittsburgh Steelers 3400 S Water St Pittsburgh PA 15203*

**ROEWE, ROBIN HUGHES,** music educator, artist, musician; s. August George and Rosemarie Roewe; m. Suzanne Schrade, Oct. 12, 1991; children: Adam Hughes, Lauren Kay. MusM, MusB, Baylor U. Lectr. in music Simpson Coll., Indianola, Iowa, 1997—2000; asst. prof. music, voice and opera Houston Bapt. U., 2000—06; music assoc. Kingsland Bapt. Ch., Katy, Tex., 2003—06. Fellow, Aspen Music Festival, 1996; apprenticeship, Des Moines Metro Opera, 1997. Mem.: Nat. Assn. Teachers of Singing, Pi Kappa Lambda (life), Phi Mu Alpha Sinfonia. Office: Houston Baptist Univ 7502 Fondren Rd Houston TX 77074-3298 Office Phone: 281-649-3000. Office Fax: 281-649-3313. Business E-Mail: rroewe@hbu.edu.

**ROFF, J(OHN) HUGH, JR.,** energy executive; b. Wewoka, Okla., Oct. 27, 1931; s. Hugh and Louise Roff; m. Ann Green, Dec. 23, 1956; children—John, Charles, Andrew, Elizabeth, Jennifer AB, U. Okla., 1954, LL.B., 1955. Bar: Okla., 1955. N.Y. Law clk. to presiding justice U.S. Ct. Appeals (10th cir.), 1958; atty. Southwestern Bell Telephone Co., St. Louis, 1959-63, AT&T, N.Y.C., 1964-68; v.p., gen. atty. Long Lines, N.Y.C., 1969-73, gen. atty., 1973-74; chmn., pres., chief exec. officer United Energy Resources, Houston, 1974-86; chmn. PetroUnited Terminals Inc., Houston, 1986-98, Roff Resources LLC, Houston, 1998—. Past chmn. Cen. Houston Inc.; mem. adv. bd. Ctr. for Strategic and Internat. Studies, Washington; mem. coun. overseers Jones Sch. Bus. Adminstrn., Rice U.; trustee Baylor Coll. Medicine; past chmn. adv. bd. The Salvation Army, Houston. 1st lt. U.S. Army, 1955-58. Mem. Order of Coif, Phi Beta Kappa, Beta Theta Pi. Clubs: Houston Country, Coronado, Houstonian. Office: 333 Clay St Ste 4300 Houston TX 77002-4103 E-mail: hughroff@roffresources.com

**ROFF, SANDRA,** library and information scientist, educator, archivist; b. Bronx, N.Y., Dec. 17, 1945; d. Charles and Clara Shoiock; m. Kenneth Roff, June 27, 1971; 1 child, Felicia. AB, CUNY, N.Y., N.Y., 1967; MA, SUNY, Oneonta, N.Y., 1969, U. Pa., Phila., 1972; MLS, Pratt Inst., Bklyn., 1981. Rsch. asst. L.I. Hist. Soc., Bklyn., 1968—70; sr. reference libr. N.Y. Hist. Soc., N.Y., 1981—84; libr. U.S. History, Genealogy and Local History Sect. N.Y. Pub. Libr., N.Y., 1984—87; prof. Baruch Coll. CUNY, N.Y., 1987—, archivist Baruch Coll., 1987—. Contbr. numerous articles to profl. jours. Mem.: ALA, Am. Assn. Mus., Beta Phi Mu, Phi Alpha Theta. Office: Baruch Coll CUNY 151 East 25th St New York NY 10010

**ROFF, WILLIAM ROBERT,** historian, educator, writer; b. Glasgow, Scotland, May 2, 1929; arrived in U.S., 1969; s. Robert Henry William and Isabella (Anderson) R.; m. Susanne Rabbitt, Aug. 2, 1978; children: Sarah, Emily. BA, U. New Zealand, 1957, MA, 1959; PhD, Australian Nat. U., 1965. Lectr. history Monash U., Australia, 1963-66; lectr., sr. lectr. U. Malaya, Malaysia, 1966-69; assoc. prof. Columbia U., N.Y.C., 1969-73, prof., 1973-90, prof. emeritus, 1990—. Vis. prof. Yale U., 1971, L'Ecole des Hautes Etudes en Scis. Sociales, Paris, 1985; vis. fellow Australian Nat. U., 1974; hon. fellow Edinburgh U., Scotland, 1992—. Author: The Origins of Malay Nationalism, 1967, Bibliography of Malay and Arabic Periodicals, 1972, (with others) The Emergence of Modern Southeast Asia, 2004; author, editor: Kelantan: Religion, Society and Politics, 1973; editor: Islam and the Political Economy of Meaning, 1987. Guggenheim Found. fellow 1973; Rockefeller Found. fellow, 1982. Mem. Royal Asiatic Soc. (life), Assn. for Asian Studies, Asian Studies Assn. Australia, Brit. Soc. for Mid. East Studies, Mid. East Studies Assn. Avocation: parenting. Home: 29 Shore St Cellardyke Fife KY10 3BD Scotland Personal E-mail: william.roff@btinternet.com

**ROG, JOSEPH W.,** engineering company executive; BS, Kent State U. Pres. Corrpro Cos., inc., Medina, Ohio, 1984—93, chmn., 1993—2004, CEO, 1984—2004, bd. dirs., 2004—. Office: Corrpro Cos Inc 1090 Enterprise Dr Medina OH 44256-1328 Office Phone: 330-723-5082.

**ROGACZEWSKI, SHERRIE REECE,** small business owner, singer; b. Greenwood, S.C., Nov. 23, 1966; d. George Washington and Hazel Irene Reece; m. Wayne Robert Rogaczewski, Nov. 29, 1986; 1 child, Brett. Grad. high sch., Greenwood, S.C. Singer, songwriter Sherreece, New Orleans, 1990—; co-owner World Gym, 2001—. Singer, songwriter: recs. Wild Life, 1997, New Age Dawning, 2000, Holy of Holies, 2004. Mem.: Gospel Music Assn. Avocations: history, archaeology. Office Phone: 504-813-8486. E-mail: sherreece@hotmail.com.

**ROGAL, ANDREW L.,** insurance company executive; b. Pitts., Dec. 13, 1948; s. Alvin and Ann (Lawrence) R.; m. Vicki Loveness, Dec. 30, 1971; children: Erin, Lisa, Samuel. BS in Journalism, Northwestern U., Chgo., 1970; JD, U. Pitts., 1975. Law clk. Hon. Hubert I. Teitelbaum, Fed. Dist. Ct. of We. Dist. Pa., Pitts., 1975-77; jr. ptnr. Titus, Marcus & Shapira, Pitts., 1977-80; pres., chief exec. officer Hilb, Rogal and Hamilton Co. of Pitts., Inc., 1987-91, Hilb, Rogal and Hamilton Internat. Ltd., 1991—; exec. v.p. Hilb, Rogal & Hamilton Co., Glen Allen, Va., 1990—. Mem. bd. trustees Children's Hosp., Pitts.; mem. investment com.; bd. dirs. Pitts. Ballet Theatre, Jewish Community Ctr., Pitts., United Jewish Feds., Pitts., Jewish Healthcare Found., Pitts., mem. investment com., mem. distbn. com.; mem. budget and allocations com. United Jewish Fedn. of Pitts. Avocation: skiing. Office: Hilb Rogal & Hamilton Co 4951 Lake Brook Dr Ste 400 Glen Allen VA 23060-9273

**ROGAL, GARY JEFFREY,** cardiologist; b. Newark, Nov. 20, 1952; s. David and Bert Shane Rogal; m. Camille Elizabeth Rogal, Oct. 18, 1981; children: David, Jennifer, Sarah. BA, George Washington U., 1974, MD, 1978. Diplomate Am. Bd. Internal Medicine, Am. Bd. Cardiovasc. Disease. Resident in internal medicine I.I. Jewish-Hillside Med. Ctr., 1978-81; resident in cardiology U. Rochester-Strong Meml. Hosp., 1981-84; asst. prof. medicine Albany Med. Coll., NY, 1984-86; chief cardiology St. Barnabas Med. Ctr., Livingston, NJ, 1998—, dir. cardiac rehab.; pvt. practice gen. and invasive cardiology, spl. interest complementary medicine and cardiology, 1986—. Fellow Am. Coll. Cardiology; mem. Am. Heart Assn. (bd. dirs.), Hertiage Affiliation (bd. dirs.), Phi Beta Kappa Avocations: photography, skiing, resistance/aerobic training. Office: Diagnostic and Clin Cardiology PA 769 Northfield Ave West Orange NJ 07052-1198 Office Phone: 973-731-9442. E-mail: grogal@sbhcs.com.

**ROGAN, ELEANOR GROENIGER,** oncologist, educator; b. Nov. 25, 1942; d. Louis Martin and Esther (Levinson) G.; m. William John Robert Rogan June 12, 1965 (div.) 1 child, Elizabeth Rebecca. AB, Mt Holyoke Coll., 1963; PhD, Johns Hopkins U., 1968. Lectr. Goucher Coll., Towson, Md., 1968-69; rsch. assoc. U. Tenn., Knoxville, 1969-73, U. Nebr. Med. Ctr., Omaha, 1973-76, asst. prof., 1976-80; assoc. prof. Eppley Inst., dept. pharm. scis. U. Nebr., Omaha, 1980-90, prof. dept. pharm. scis. and dept. biochem. & molecular biol, 1990—. Contbr. articles to profl. jours. Predoctoral fellow USPHS, Johns Hopkins U., 1965-68; recipient Linus Pauling Functional Medicine award, 2006. Mem. AAAS, Am. Assn. Cancer Rsch., Soc. Toxicology. Democrat. Roman Catholic. Home: 8210 Bowie Dr Omaha NE 68114-1526 Office: U Nebr Med Ctr Eppley Inst 986805 Nebr Med Ctr Omaha NE 68198-6805 Office Phone: 402-559-4095. Business E-Mail: egrogan@unmc.edu.

**ROGAN, JAMES EDWARD,** former federal agency administrator, former congressman; b. San Francisco, Aug. 21, 1957; s. John and Alice (Kleupfer) Rogan; m. Christine Apffel; children: Dana, Claire. BA in Polit. Sci., U. Calif., Berkeley, 1979; JD, UCLA, 1983. Past atty. Lillick McHose and Charles (now Pillsbury, Madison and Sutro), L.A.; past dep. dist. atty. L.A. County; judge Glendale (Calif.) Mcpl. Ct., 1990—93, presiding judge, 1993—94; past mem. Calif. Assembly, 1994—96, assembly majority leader, 1996; mem. U.S. Congress from 27th Calif. dist., 1996—2001; mem. house jud. com., mem. commerce com., asst. minority whip; ptnr. Venable, Baetjer, Howard & Civiletti, Washington, 2001; under sec. for intellectual property US Dept. Commerce, Washington, 2001—04; dir. US Patent & Trademark Office, Washington, 2001—04; of counsel Preston Gates Ellis LLP, Irvine, Calif., 2006—. Adj. prof. trial advocacy Sch. Law Southwestern U.; adj. prof. criminal law Coll. Law Glendale U.; past adj. prof. criminal law Glendale C.C.; mem. Selective Svc. Sys. U.S. Govt., 1981—; adj. prof. trial practice Chapman U. Law Sch. Republican. Office: Preston Gates Ellis LLP 1900 Main Ste Ste 600 Irvine CA 92614-7319

**ROGAN, MICHAEL P.,** lawyer; BA, Oberlin Coll., 1970; JD, U. Conn., 1974. Joined Skadden, Arps, Slate, Meagher & Flom LLP, Washington, 1980—, ptnr., 1984—, head, corp. mergers and acquisitions, 1994—, leader, 1998—. Office: Skadden Arps Slate Meagher & Flom LLP 1440 New York Ave NW Washington DC 20005 Office Phone: 202-371-7550. Office Fax: 202-661-8200. Business E-Mail: mrogan@skadden.com.

**ROGAN, MICHAEL T.,** neuroscientist; s. James F and Marie G Rogan. PhD, NYU, N.Y.C., 1998. Rsch. scientist Columbia U., NY State Psychiat. Inst., N.Y.C., 1998—. Office Phone: 212-543-5594.

**ROGAN, RICHARD A.,** lawyer; b. LA, Sept. 6, 1950; AB with honors, Hamilton Coll., 1972; JD, U. Calif., 1975. Bar: Calif. 1975. Ptnr. Broad, Schulz, Larson & Wineberg, 1978-94, chmn., 1991-93; ptnr. Jeffer, Mangels, Butler & Marmaro, San Francisco, 1994—, mng. ptnr., San Francisco office, 2002—. Editorial assoc. Hastings Law Jour., 1974-75. Trustee Bentley Sch. 1989-92. Mem. ABA (mem. corp., banking, and bus. sect.), Bar Assn. of San Francisco (mem. comml. law and bankruptcy sect.), Calif. Receivers Forum (bd. dirs. Bay Area chpt.), Delta Sigma Rho. Office: Jeffer Mangels Butler Marmaro-JMBM 2 Embarcadero Ctr 5th Fl San Francisco CA 94111-3823 Office Phone: 415-398-8080. E-mail: rrogan@jmbm.com.

**ROGAN, ROBERT WILLIAM,** management educator, consultant, osteopath, psychiatrist; BA, MBA, SUNY, Buffalo; cert. in data processing, Cornell U.; DO, W.Va. Sch. Osteo. Medicine, 1983; postgrad., Virginia Beach, 1986-88; JD, Regent U., 1990. Bar: Pa. 1992; diplomate Nat. Bd Examiners for Osteo. Medicine and Surgery, Am. Bd. Psychiatry; cert. data processor, data educator. Assoc. prof. bus. West Liberty (W.Va.) State Coll., 1976-79; chief intern Metro Health Ctr., Erie, Pa., 1983-84; asst. prof. computer sci. Gannon U., Erie, Pa., 1984-85; asst. prof. mgmt. Slippery Rock (Pa.) U., 1985-86; practice medicine specializing in osteopathy Harborcreek Family Practice, Erie, Pa., 1985; resident physician Univ. Med. Ctr.-East Carolina U., Greenville, N.C., 1992-96; med. officer M/V Anastasis, 1988—89, M/V Logos II, 2006. Temp. physician Oceana (W.Va.) Med. Ctr., 1992-95; rschr., tchr. law Inst. Fine Mechanics and Optics, St. Petersburg, Russia, 1993, Poland, 1994; part-time radio announcer Sta. WGHB, Farmville, N.C., 1993-96; psychiat. and mgmt. cons., critical incident stress debriefer, 1996—; asst. prof. W.Va. U. Sch. Medicine, 1999—; chmn. ethics com. William R. Sharpe Hosp., 2000— Counselor Contact Crisis Care, Lewisburg, W.Va., 1980—81; constrn. vol. various locations internationally, 1991; mem. Hist. Preservation Commn., City of Greenville, 1995—96, disaster vol., 2001—; med. vol. various orgns., Jamaica, 1988—; candidate for U.S. Congress Ho. of Rep., 2004. Scholar U. Buffalo, N.Y. State Bd. Regents; grantee NSF, Cornell U.; Group for Advancement of Psychiatry fellow, 1995-96. Mem. Am. Osteo. Assn., N.C. Psychiat. Assn. (psychiatry and law rep. 1994-96, mem. econ. affairs com 1995-96, mem. exec. coun. 1994-96, candidate Raleigh city coun., 2003). Avocations: travel, sports, volunteering. Personal E-mail: nagor36@hotmail.com. Business E-Mail: doulos@di-ve.com.

**ROGATZ, PETER,** retired physician; b. N.Y.C., Aug. 5, 1926; s. Julian and Sally (Levy) Rogatz; m. Marjorie Plaut, June 10, 1949; children: Peggy Joy, William Peter. BA, Columbia Coll., 1945; MD, Cornell U., 1949; M.P.H., Columbia U., 1956. Cert. Am. Bd. Preventive Medicine 1958. Intern Lenox Hill Hosp., N.Y.C., 1949-50, resident, 1950-51, VA Hosp., Bronx, NY, 1951-52, N.Y. Hosp., N.Y.C., 1952-53; dep. dir. Montefiore Hosp., N.Y.C., 1960-63; dir. L.I. Jewish Med. Center, 1964-68, Univ. Hosp., SUNY, Stony Brook, 1968-71; sr. v.p. Blue Cross/Blue Shield of Greater N.Y., 1971-76; prin., founding ptnr. RMR Health and Hosp. Mgmt. Cons., Inc., Roslyn Heights, NY, 1984-98; v.p. med. affairs Vis. Nurse Service, NY, 1984-91; med. dir. Staff Builders, Inc., 1992-98. Prof. cmty. medicine SUNY, Stony Brook, 1968—94; mem. N.Y.C. Mayor's Commn. on Delivery of Health Svcs., 1967; v.p. Health and Welfare Coun. of Nassau County, 1968—72; bd. dirs. Cmty. Coun. Greater N.Y., 1974—77; mem. Task Force on N.Y.C. Crisis, 1976—81; chmn. bd. dirs. Cmty. Health Program affiliated with L.I. Jewish Med. Ctr., 1989—94; chmn. bd. dirs. Managed Health Inc., 1990—94. Author: Organized Home Medical Care in New York City, 1956; co-author (with Eli Ginzberg): Planning for Better Hospital Care, 1961; mem. editl. bd. Preventive Medicine, 1975—81; contbr. articles to profl. jours. Bd. dirs. Choice in Dying, 1994—2000, Compassion and Choices of N.Y., 1998—. Recipient Dean Conley award, Am. Coll. Hosp. Adminstrs., 1975; fellow, Commonwealth Fund, 1955. Fellow: ACP, Am. Coll. Preventive Medicine, N.Y. Acad. Medicine, APHA; mem.: N.Y. County Med. Soc., N.Y. State Med. Soc., N.Y. Pub. Health Assn., Am. Hosp. Assn., AMA. Home and Office: 76 Oakdale Ln Roslyn Heights NY 11577-1535 Personal E-mail: rogatz2@aol.com.

**ROGEL, EDWARD P.,** corporate human resources executive; BA in Psychology, Ctrl. Wash. U., 1969. Employee rels. supr. Pulp and Wood Products Weyerhaeuser Co., Everett, Wash., 1969—, area pers. supr. for No. Wash. Region, regional pers. mgr. for S.W. Oreg., pers. mgr. ops., corp. pers., 1970—78, exec. devel. and succession planning mgr. for corp. pers., 1978—86, dir. human resources for Forest Products Co., 1986—88, v.p. human resources Forest Products Co. Timberlands, 1988—94, v.p. human resources and total quality, 1994—2000, v.p. human resources ops., 2000—03, sr. v.p. human resources, 2003—. Mem. MacMillan Bloedel Transition Team for Timberlands and Wood Products, Willamette and Trus Joist Integration Teams, Culture Change Project Weyerhaeuser Co. Co-chmn. facilities fundraiser campaign for Pierce County Jr. Achievement New Experience; bd. chmn. Pierce County Jr. Achievement; mem. conf. bd. Performance Improvement Coun. Recipient Leadership award, Jr. Achievement, 1998. Mem.: Human Resource Planning Soc. (treas., exec. com., past co-chair corp. sponsors), Performance Mfrs. Alliance. Office: Weyerhaeuser Co 33553 Weyerhaeuser Way S Federal Way WA 98063-9777

**ROGEL, STEVEN R.,** forest products company executive; BS in Chem. Engring., U. Wash., 1965. With St. Regis Paper Co., 1965—70; asst. mgr. St. Anne-Nackawic Pulp and Paper, Nackawic, N.B., Canada, 1970—72; tech. dir. Willamette Industries, Inc., Albany, Oreg., 1972—95, pres., CEO, 1995, 07 Weyerhaeuser Co., Tacoma, 1997—, chmn., 1999—. Bd. dirs. Kroger Co. Trustee Pacific U.; bd. dirs. Pacific Harbors coun. Boy Scouts Am. Mem.: Am. Forest and Paper Assn. (bd. dirs.). Office: 33663 Weyerhaeuser Way S Federal Way WA 98003-9620*

**ROGENESS, MARY SPEER,** state legislator; b. Kansas City, Kans., May 18, 1941; d. Frederic A. and Jeannette (Hybskmann) Speer; m. Dean Rogeness, Aug. 31, 1964; children: Emily, James, Paul. BA, Carleton Coll., 1963. Computer analyst Dept. Def., Ft. Meade, Md., 1963-66; freelance writer, editor Longmeadow, Mass., 1982-91; mem. Mass. Ho. of Reps., Boston, 1991—, asst. minority leader, 2003—. Editor: Reflections of Longmeadow, 1983. Mem. Longmeadow Rep. Town Com., 1983—; bd. dirs. Goodwill Industries Hartford-Springfield, 1996—2004; mem. Longmeadow Sch. Com., 1982-88. Mem. Am. Legis. Exch. Coun., World Affairs Coun. of Western Mass. Office: Mass House of Reps State House Rm 124 Boston MA 02133 Office Phone: 617-722-2100.

**ROGER, EDWIN MCLENDON,** education educator; s. Vivian W. and Harold Edwin Mclendon; m. Patti Swain; children: Patrick Edwin Mclendon, Erin Elizabeth Mclendon, Ryan Hodges Mclendon. MD, Med. Coll. of Ga., 1983. Diplomate Am. Bd. Pathology, 1987. Prof. Duke Sch. of Medicine, Durham, NC, 1992—; asst clin. prof. pathology Mercer U. Sch. of Medicine, Macon, Ga., 1988—2006. Dir. anatomic pathology, chief of neuropathology Duke Sch. of Medicine, Durham, NC, 2003—. Editor (author): (multiple chpts. ref. book) Russell And Rubinstein's Pathology of Tumors of The Nervous System; author: (textbook) Pathology of Tumors of the Central Nervous System. Scoutmaster Boy Scouts Of Am., Durham, NC, 2000—06. Fellow: Am. U. Pathologists (bd. councilors 2004—06); mem.: Am. Assn. Neuropathology (bd. councilors 2004—06), Am. Bd. Pathology (neuropathology com. mem. 1997—2006). Avocations: coaching youth baseball, reading. Office: Duke Univ Med Ctr M216 Davison Bldg Erwin Rd Durham NC 27710 Office Phone: 919-684-6940.

**ROGER, JANICE LOWENSTEIN,** cantor; b. Chgo., July 6, 1951; d. Herbert and Gertrude Tauf Lowenstein; m. Brandon Anthony Roger, Nov. 30, 1980; children: Edwin Sidney, Miles Lawrence. B of sacred music, Hebrew Union Coll.Jewish Inst. of Religion, 1975—79; MusB, Roosevelt U.,

1969—73; MusD (hon.), Hebrew Union Coll.-Jewish Inst. of Religion, 2004—04. Cantor Am. Conf. of Cantors, 1979. Cantor Indpls. Hebrew Congregation, 1979—. Cantorial chmn., nat. commn. on cantorial/congl. rels. Union for Reform Judaism, NY, 1995—; chmn., conv. adminstrn. com. Am. Conf. of Cantors, NY, 2004—, v.p., 1991—95, conv. co-chairman 1987, 1993; mem., artist evaluation com. Young Audiences, Indpls., 1991—92; bd. mem. Indpls. Chamber Orch., 1997—99; com. mem. Arts Coun., 2002. Singer: (concert) Hymns and Anthems, Ronen Chamber Ensemble; collaborating producer (dance performance) Avodah Dance Ensemble. Allocations com. United Way, 1990—91. Creative Renewal, Arts Coun. of Indpls., 1999. Mem.: Coalition on Advancements in Jewish Edn., Music Educators' Nat. Conf., Am. Conf. of Cantors. Avocations: reading, knitting, playing scrabble. Office: Indpls Hebrew Congregation 6501 North Meridian St Indianapolis IN 46260 Office Phone: 317-255-6647. Personal E-mail: janicer@ihcindy.org.

**ROGER, JERRY LEE,** academic administrator; b. Chase, Kans., Mar. 11, 1945; s. LeRoy J. and Lottie E. (Maphet) R.; m. Tucky Saint Roger, 1995. BS, U. Tulsa, 1966, MA, 1969, EdD, 1975. Cert. tchr., supt., Okla. Math. tchr. Kansas City (Mo.) Pub. Schs., 1966-67, Shawnee Mission (Kans.) Pub. Schs., 1967-71; rsch. asst. Tulsa Pub. Schs., 1972-73, rsch. coord., 1973-81, adminstrv. asst., 1981-90, rsch. dir., 1990-95, dir. planning and assessment, 1995-2000; chmn. U. Phoenix Sch. Gen. Studies, Tulsa, 2000; dir. acad. affairs U. Phoenix, Tulsa, 2001—05, doctoral faculty, 2005—. Adj. instr. U. Phoenix, Tulsa, 2001—05, doctoral faculty, 2005—. Adj. instr. U. Phoenix, Tulsa campus, 1998-2000. Contbr. book revs. to Tulsa Sunday World, 1990-92. Paul Harris fellow; Rotary benefactor. Mem. NEA, Am. Ednl. Res. Assn., Nat. Book Critics Cir., Nature Conservancy, Nat. Conf. for Cmty. and Justice, Phi Delta Kappa. Home: 3504 N Narcissus Ave Broken Arrow OK 74012 Office: U Phoenix 10810 E 45th St Tulsa OK 74146-3818 E-mail: jerryroger@yahoo.com.

**ROGER, KENT M.,** lawyer; b. San Francisco, May 8, 1955; s. Alberto Vasquez del Mercado and LaVerne Annette (Stadler) Newcombe; m. Margaret Ann Murphy, Aug. 10, 1985; children: Nicole, Lauren. AB, U. Calif., Berkeley, 1977; JD, U. Calif., San Francisco, 1980. Bar: Calif. 1980. Assoc. Brobeck, Phleger & Harrison, San Francisco, 1980-87, ptnr., 1987—2003; ptnr., leader litig. practice group Morgan, Lewis & Bockius LLP, San Francisco. Mem. ABA, Bar Assn. San Francisco, San Francisco Bank Atty. Assn Roman Catholic. Office: Morgan Lewis & Bockius LLP Spear St Tower 1 Market Plz San Francisco CA 94105-1420

**ROGERS, ALAN VICTOR,** former career officer; b. Hannibal, Mo., Nov. 13, 1942; s. Julian Alan and Gladys Cuneo R.; m. Linda Rae Peterson, May 8, 1966; children: Kimberly Rae, Krista Anne, Peter Alan. BS in Mil. Sci., USAF Acad., 1964; MBA with distinction, Harvard Bus. Sch., 1972; grad. with distinction, Air War Coll., 1980. Commd. 2d lt. USAF, 1964, advanced through grades to maj. gen., 1989, ret., 1993; combat fighter pilot 355th Tactical Fighter Wing, Takhli, Thailand, 1966-67; jet pilot instr. Flying Tng. Wing, Williams AFB, Ariz., 1967-69; student Harvard Bus. Sch., Cambridge, Mass., 1970-72; pers. officer Cols. Group USAF Pentagon, Washington, 1972-75; student Air War Coll., Maxwell AFB, Ariz., 1980; wing comdr. 5th Bomb Wing, Minot AFB, ND, 1982-84, 96th Bomb Wing (1st B-1 Wing), Dyess AFB, Tex., 1984-86; dir. ops. SAC, Offutt AFB, Nebr., 1986-89; asst. chief of staff ops. Supreme HQ Allied Powers Europe NATO, Mons, Belgium, 1989-91; dir. J-7 Joint Staff, Pentagon, Washington, 1991-93; assoc. Burdeshaw Assocs., Ltd., Bethesda, Md., 1993-94; prin. Gemini Consulting, Morristown, NJ, 1994-97; sr. v.p., gen. mgr. Fed. Defense Group, Am. Mgmt. Sys., Inc., Fairfax, Va., 1997—2002; exec. v.p. CACI Internat., 2003—. Mem. Active Angel Investors, Vienna, 2003—; mem. adv. bd. Infodata, Inc., 2003—06; bd. dirs. RGS & Assocs., Inc. Mem., mil. adviser C. of C., Minot, N.D., 1982-84, Abilene, Tex. 1984-86; trustee The Falcon Found., Colorado Springs, 2003—; mem. bd. advisors Our Mil. Kids, 2006—. Decorated Defense Disting. Svc. Medal, Legion of Merit, D.F.C. with two oak leaf clusters, Purple Heart, Def. Superior Svc. medal, Disting. Svc. medal, Def. Disting. Svc. medal; recipient Am. U. Leadership award, 2000. Mem.: Nat. Assn. Corp. Dirs., Nat. Def. Industry Assn. (bd. dirs.), Potomac Officers Club, Daedalians (chpt. pres. 1986), Nat. Eagle Scout Assn., Red River Valley Fighter Pilots Assn., Sabre Soc., USAF Acad. Assn. Grads. (bd. dirs. 1999—), Air Force Assn. Republican. Lutheran. Avocations: skiing, travel, antiques. Home: 4600 32nd Rd N Arlington VA 22207-4406 Office Phone: 703-679-3566. E-mail: alanvrogers@aol.com.

**ROGERS, ALICE LOUISE,** retired bank executive, writer, researcher; b. McLoud, Okla., Feb. 18, 1929; d. John Edmond and Katy McNora (Williams) Stanka; m. Jesse Ray Rogers, Apr. 18, 1948; children: Jimmy Allen Rogers, Bonnie Kay (Rogers) Calhoun. Student, Am. Inst. Banking, 1967-69. Clk. typist loan dept. Security Pacific Nat. Bank, L.A., 1960-64; office mgr., adminstrv. asst. to v.p. loan adminstrn. divsn. City Nat. Bank, Beverly Hills, 1964-75, credit mgr. Pershing Square branch, 1975-77. Author, editor: Dance Bands and Big Bands Reference Book and Price Guide, 1986, Dance Bands, Big Bands and Swing Reference Book and Price Guide, 1993; contbr. articles to DISCoveries mag., Internat. Assn. of Jazz Record Collectors Jour., Joslin's Jazz Jour., Dancing USA mag., Am.'s Registry of Outstanding Profls. Mem.: Big Band Acad. Am. Republican. Avocations: phonograph record collection, researching jazz and dance information, postcard collection. Home: 700 Clark St Apt 108 Deming NM 88030-4589

**ROGERS, ARTHUR HAMILTON, III,** lawyer; b. Florence, S.C., Apr. 19, 1945; s. Arthur Hamilton Jr. and Suzanne (Wilson) R.; m. Karen Lyn Hess, June 22, 1968; children: Sarah Elizabeth, Thomas Hess. BA, Rice U., 1967; JD, Harvard U., 1970. Bar: Tex. 1970. Assoc. Fulbright & Jaworski LLP, Houston, 1970-74; participating assoc. Fulbright & Jaworski LLP, Houston, 1974-77; ptnr. Fulbright & Jaworski, L.L.P., Houston, 1977—; gen. counsel Lifemark Corp., Houston, 1981-82. Sec. Mosher, Inc., Houston, 1984-97. Bd. dirs. Alley Theatre, Houston, 1990—, v.p. fin., 2001—, mem. exec. com., 2001—; bd. dirs. Autry House, 1994-97; mem. exec. com. Rice U. Fund Coun., Houston, 1993-99, vice chmn., 1996-97, chmn., 1997-98. Mem. ABA, State Bar Tex., Assn. of Rice Alumni (treas. 1995-97), Petroleum Club of Houston, The Forest Club. Episcopalian. Home: 5309 Bordley Dr Houston TX 77056-2323 Office: Fulbright & Jaworski LLP 1301 Mckinney St Fl 51 Houston TX 77010-3031 E-mail: arogers@fulbright.com.

**ROGERS, BARBARA RADCLIFFE,** writer; b. Bedford, Ind., Apr. 23, 1939; d. George Charles and Liddie (Bacom) Radcliffe; m. Stillman David Rogers, Aug. 12, 1967; children: Juliette Radcliffe, Lura Jeanne. AB, Boston U., 1961. Author: Encyclopedia of Everlastings, 1988, Fresh Herbs, 1989, Giant Pandas, 1989, The Portugal Traveler, 1989, Big Cats, 1990, Galapagos, 1990, Safari, 1990, Country Gardens, 1992, New Hampshire Off the Beaten Path, 1992. Mem. Commn. on the Status of Women, NH, 1971—73. Episcopalian. Office: 686 Old Homestead Hwy Richmond NH 03470-5012

**ROGERS, BENJAMIN FRANKLIN,** retired history professor; b. St. Paul, Minn., Dec. 10, 1917; s. Benjamin Franklin and Ruth De Coster Rogers; m. Peggy Louise Brodrick, Sept. 9, 1972; children: Ruth, Benjamin, Karl, David, Susan, Sara, Clay. AB, Harvard U., 1940, MA, 1941; PhD, U. Minn., 1951. Prof. history Fla. State U., Tallahassee, 1950—61; v.p. Jacksonville U., Fla., 1960—64; dean Coll. Humanities Fla. Atlantic U., Boca Raton, Fla., 1964—66; head Dept. History Parsons Coll., Fairfield, Iowa, 1966—73; prof. history Ohumwa Heights Coll., Iowa, 1973—80, ret., 1980. Lt. USNR, 1942—45. Mem.: Fla. Hist. Soc. (bd. dirs.), Am. editl. bd.), Am. Hist. Assn. Democrat. Episcopalian. Home: PO Box 877 Fairfield IA 52556

**ROGERS, BENJAMIN TALBOT,** mechanical engineer, consultant; b. Cleve., Oct. 4, 1920; s. Benjamin Talbot and Marie Aline (Miller) Rogers; m. Dale Hays Rogers, Sept. 11, 1961 (dec. Nov. 1975); children: Leslie, Phyllis. BSME, U. Wis., 1944. Registered profl. engr., N.Mex, Colo., Ariz., Tex. Mech. engr. Black & Veatch, Kansas City, Mo., 1946-49; staff mem. U. Calif., Los Alamos, N.Mex., 1949-76; cons. engring. Los Alamos, N.Mex., 1949-76, Embudo, N.Mex, 1976-80, 81-2000; ret., 2000. Vis. prof. Ariz. State U.,

1980—81, 1984; v.p. Barkmann & Rogers Cons. Engrs., Santa Fe, 1964—70. One-man shows include Millicent Rogers Mus., Taos, N.Mex., 1994, Roller Mill Mus., Cleveland, N.Mex, 1995, Ariz. State U. Coll. Architecture, Tempe, 1996, First State Bank Taos, 1997 (Artist of the Month, 1997), Johnson Gallery, Madrid, N.Mex, 1998—99; contbr. articles to tech. and profl. jours. Commr. Rinconada Cmty. Acequia, Embudo, 1961—70; v.p. adv. bd. Embudo Presbyn. Hosp., 1972; pres. Embudo Valley Health Found., 1974. 1st lt. C.E. U.S. Army, 1942—46. Recipient Solar Design award, HUD, Dept. Energy, Solar Energy Rsch. Inst., 1978, Peter van Dresser award, N.Mex Solar Energy Assn., 1983, Maharishi award, Maharishi Found., 1984; grantee, Graham Found. Advanced Studies Fine Arts, 1992, 1995. Fellow: ASHRAE; mem.: NSPE (life), ASME (life), Nat. Assn. Scholars, Am. Soc. Materials (life), Celtic Confederation (founding sec. 2000—03). Republican. Achievements include patents in field. Home: PO Box 2 Embudo NM 87531

**ROGERS, BERNARD WILLIAM,** military officer; b. Fairview, Kans., July 16, 1921; s. William Henry and Lora (Haynes) R.; m. Ann Ellen Jones, Dec. 28, 1944; children: Michael W., Diane E., Susan A. Student, Kans. State Coll., 1939-40; BS, U.S. Mil. Acad., 1943; BA (Rhodes scholar), Oxford U., Eng., 1950, MA, 1954, DCL (hon.), 1983; grad., Command and Gen. Staff Coll., 1954-55, Army War Coll., 1959-60; LLD, Akron U., 1978, Boston U., 1981. Commd. lt. U.S. Army, 1943, advanced through grades to gen., 1974; aide to supt. U.S. Mil. Acad., 1945-46, comdr. cadets, 1967-69; aide to high commr. Austria Gen. Mark W. Clark, 1946-47; bn. comdr. Republic of Korea, 1952; exec. to comdr.-in-chief Far East Command, 1953-54; mil. asst. to Chief of Staff, U.S. Army, 1956-59; exec. to chmn. Joint Chiefs of Staff, 1962-66; asst. divsn. comdr. 1st Inf. Divsn., Vietnam, 1966-67; comdg. gen. 5th Inf. Divsn., Ft. Carson, Colo., 1969-70; chief legis. liaison Dept. Army, 1971-72, dep. chief of staff for personnel, 1972-74; comdg. gen. U.S. Army Forces Command, 1974-76; chief of staff U.S. Army, 1976-79; NATO supreme allied comdr., comdr. in chief U.S. European Command, 1979-87; ret. U.S. Army, 1987. Former bd. dirs. Atlantic Coun. U.S., George C. Marshall Found., Gen. Dynamics Co., Kemper Nat. Ins. Co., Thomas Industries; former sr. couns. The Coca-Cola Co.; vol. chmn. USO World Bd. of Govs., 1988-94. Decorated DSC, DSM with oak leaf cluster, DSM of Army, Navy and Air Force, Silver Star, Legion of Merit with 3 oak leaf clusters, D.F.C. with 2 oak leaf clusters, Bronze Star medal with V device; hon. fellow Univ. Coll., Oxford U.; recipient Disting. Svc. Citation U. Kans., 1984, Disting. Grad. award U.S. Mil. Acad., 1995, Assn. U.S. Army George C. Marshall medal, 1999. Mem.: VFW, Mil. Order of World Wars, Ret. Officers Assn., Assn. Am. Rhodes Scholars, Assn. U.S. Army (bd. dirs.), Soc. 1st Inf. Divsn., Am. Soc. French Legion of Honor, Alibi, Alfalfa, Army and Navy Club, The Pilgrims, Army-Navy Country Club, Phi Delta Theta. Personal E-mail: rogers1467@aol.com.

**ROGERS, BRENDA GAYLE,** educational administrator, educator, consultant; b. Atlanta, July 27, 1949; d. Claude Thomas and Louise (Williams) Todd; m. Emanuel Julius Jones Jr., Dec. 17, 1978; children: Lavelle, Brandon, Albre Jede, Briana Adanne. BA, Spelman Coll., Atlanta, 1970; MA, Atlanta U., 1971, EdS, 1972; PhD, Georgia State U., 1975; postgrad., Howard U., Washington, D.C., 1980, Emory U., Atlanta, 1986. Program devel. specialist HEW, Atlanta, 1972; rsch. assoc. Ohio State U., Columbus, 1973-75; asst. prof. spl. edn. Atlanta U., 1975-78, program administr., 1978—, CIT project dir., 1977-91, exec. dir. Impact project, 1992—. Tech. cons. Dept. Edn., Washington, 1978-93, 96, 97-98, cons. Head Start, 1990-91; cons. Princeton Testing Svcs., 1996—; due process regional hearing officer Ga. State Dept. Edn., Atlanta, 1978-84, adv. bd., 1980-84; regional cons. Access project, 1995—; mem. parent adv. coun. APS, 1988—; cons. program devel. Ga. Respite Care, Inc., 1988-89; mem. test verification panel Edn. Testing Svcs., Princeton, N.J., 1995-96; cons. So. Assn. Colls. & Univs., 1988. Mem. Ga. Assessment Project com. Atlanta Pub. Schs. Adv. Coun., 1986—; bd. dirs. Mountain Pines Civic Assn., 1988—; mem. Grady Meml. Hosp. Cmty. Action Network, Atlanta, 1982-83; exec. bd. PTA Shadow Rock Elem. Sch., 1992-94. Recipient disting. svc. award Atlanta Bur. Pub. Safety, 1982, Mountain Sch. PTA, 1995, award Atlanta Pub. Sch. Sys., 1980, 82, 83, 89-90, Disting. Svc. award CAU, 1998; bd. Ohio State U., 1972-74, Howard U., 1980. Mem. NAFE, Assn. for Retarded Citizens, Coun. for Exceptional Children, So. Assn. Colls. and Univs. (cons. com. 1998—), Nat. Assn. Learning Disabilities, Phi Delta Kappa, Phi Lambda Theta. Democrat. Roman Catholic. Avocation: gourmet cooking. Office: Clark Atlanta U James P Brawley Atlanta GA 30314-3913 Personal E-mail: drbrendarogers@comcast.net.

**ROGERS, BRIAN CHARLES,** portfolio manager, investment company executive; b. Beverly, Mass., June 27, 1955; s. Charles E. and Margaret A. (Sweeney) R.; m. Mary Jo Skayhan, Oct. 7, 1979; children: Hilary, Peter, Sydney. AB, Harvard U., 1977, MBA, 1982. Chartered fin. analyst, investment counselor. Asst. treas. Bankers Trust Co., NYC, 1977-80; mng. dir. T. Rowe Price Assocs., Balt., 1982—, chief investment officer, 2004—; portfolio mgr. T. Rowe Price Equity Income Fund, Balt., 1985—. Bd. dirs. Balt. County Econ. Devel. Commn., 1988—, Fund for Ednl. Excellence, Balt. 1988-92. Home: 1708 Ruxton Rd Baltimore MD 21204-3505 Office: T Rowe Price Group, Inc 100 E Pratt St Fl 4 Baltimore MD 21202-1090 Office Phone: 410-547-5758. Office Fax: 410-752-3477.*

**ROGERS, BRIAN DEANE,** librarian; b. New London, Conn., June 26, 1937; s. Albert Nash and Janette (Loofboro) R.; m. Carol Mallett, May 18, 1962; children: Alison, Paul. Amy. BA, Alfred U., N.Y., 1959; MLS, Rutgers U., 1967. Asst. registrar Salem Coll., W.Va., 1964-66; libr. staff Wesleyan U., Middletown, Conn., 1967-75; librarian Conn. Coll., New London, 1975-93, spl. collections libr., 1993-99. Mem. State Adv. Coun. on Librs., Hartford, 1976, chair 1977; mem. libr. bd. Mystic Seaport Maritime Mus., Conn., 1987-01. Contbr. edit. The Battery Park City Broadsheet, NYC, 1998—. Mem. accreditation teams New England Assn. Sch. & Colls., 1985-90. Mem. Eugene O'Neill Soc. (bd. dirs. 2001-05), Columbiad Club(Meriden, Conn.), Acorn Club (Hartford, Conn.). Home: 114 Library St Mystic CT 06355-2420 E-mail: bdrog@conncoll.edu.

**ROGERS, BRYAN L.,** dean; Chmn. Sch. Art Carnegie Mellon U., 1988—99; Dean Sch. Art & Design U. Mich., 1999—. Office: Office of the Dean U Mich Sch Art & Design 2055 Art & Arch Bldg Ann Arbor MI 48109 Office Phone: 734-763-4093. E-mail: blrogers@umich.edu.

**ROGERS, BRYAN LEIGH,** artist, art educator; b. Amarillo, Tex., Jan. 7, 1941: s. Bryan Austin and Virginia Leigh (Bull) R.; m. Cynthia Louise Rice; 1 child, Kyle Austin Rogers. BE, Yale U., 1963; MS, U. Calif., Berkeley, 1966, MA, 1969, PhD, 1971. Design engr. Monsanto Co., Texas City, Tex., 1962; research engr. Rocketdyne, Canoga Park, Calif., 1963-64; research scientist Lawrence Livermore (Calif.) Lab., 1966; lectr. U. Calif., Berkeley, 1972-73; fellow Akademie der Bildenden Künste, Munich, 1974-75; prof. art San Francisco State U., 1975-88; head, prof. sch. art Carnegie Mellon U., Pitts., 1988-99, dir. Studio for Creative Inquiry, 1989-99; dean, prof. Sch. of Art and Design U. Mich., Ann Arbor, 2000—. Fellow Ctr. Advanced Visual Studies MIT, Cambridge, Mass., 1981. Editor Leonardo Jour., San Francisco, 1982-85. One-man shows include: Laguna Beach (Calif.) Mus. Art, 1974, DeSaisset Art Gallery U. Santa Clara, Calif., 1974, San Francisco Mus. Modern Art, 1974, Baxter Art Gallery Calif. Inst. Tech., Pasadena, 1979, Contemporary Crafts gallery, Portland, Oreg., 1987; group exhbns. include: Berkeley (Calif.) Art Ctr., 1969, Hansen-Fuller Gallery, San Francisco, 1970, San Francisco Arts Commn. Gallery, 1984, Clocktower Gallery, N.Y.C., 1984, Otis-Parsons Gallery, L.A., 1985, P.P.O.W. Gallery, N.Y.C., 1985, 18th Internat. Bienal, São Paulo, Brazil, 1985, MIT, Cambridge, 1990, Objects Gallery, Chgo., 1992, ARTEC 93 Internat Biennale, Nagoya, Japan, 1993, Chgo. Cultural Ctr., 1993, Am. Iron and Steel Expo., Pitts., 1993, Pitts. Ctr. for Arts, 1994, Allegheny Coll. Gallery, Meadville, Pa., 1997, Aichi Art Ctr., Nagoya, Japan, 1997. Fellow NEA, Washington, 1981, 82, Deutscher Akademischer Austauschdienst, Fed. Republic of Germany, 1974, NSF, Washington, 1965-69; recipient SECA award San Francisco Mus. Modern Art, 1974. Office: Sch Art & Design Univ Michigan Ann Arbor MI 48109 Office Phone: 734-763-4093. Business E-Mail: blrogers@umich.edu.

**ROGERS, CARLETON CARSON, JR.,** trade show and convention executive; b. Chgo., Nov. 5, 1935; s. Carleton Carson and Eleanor (Lowell) Rogers; m. Loretta Zirkel; children: Kirsten Ann, Mark, Brett. BS in Bus. Adminstrn., Am. U., 1957; postgrad., Northwestern U., 1957, Chgo.-Kent Coll. Law, 1957—58. Mgmt. trainee Ill. Bell Telephone Co., Chgo., 1959-61; sales mgr. Programs Internat., Chgo., 1961-64, pres., 1964-71; show mgr. Indsl. & Sci. Conf. Mgmt., Chgo., 1975-78; pres. Expo Mgmt., Inc., Chgo., 1978-82, Trade Expositions and Assoc. Mgmt. Ltd., Chgo., 1982-92, Expn. Mmgt., Inc., Elgin, 1992-99, National Show Mgmt., Inc., Elgin, 1999—. Adj. prof. Roosevelt U., Chgo. Pres. Kane County, Ill., Young Republican Club, 1962-64; trustee Gail Borden Pub. Libr., Elgin; bd. dirs. Area C Coun. on Aging for Ill., Upper Kane County chpt. Am. Heart Assn., Chgo. Conv. and Tourism Bur.; mem. adminstrv. bd., pres. bd. trustees First United Meth. Ch., Elgin.; sec.-treas. found. pres. Ctr. for Exhbn. Industry Rsch. Mem. Internat. Assn. Exhibit Mgmt. (chmn. bd., recipient Disting. Svc. award), Masons, Shriners, Omicron Delta Kappa, Alpha Tau Omega. Home: 11n937 Almora Ter Elgin IL 60124-4705 Office: Nat Show Mgmt Inc PO Box 6282 Elgin IL 60121-6282 Office Phone: 847-695-5330. Personal E-mail: expomgmt@juno.com.

**ROGERS, CARTON (H. CARTON ROGERS III),** school librarian, academic administrator; BA in History, Marietta Coll., Ohio, 1970; MLS, Drexel U., 1973. Joined libraries staff U. Pa., Phila., 1975; head reference & tech. services Biomedical Libr., 1975—79; sr. bus. officer U. Pa. Libr., 1979—85; Patricia and Bernard Goldstein Dir. Info. Processing U. Pa. Libraries, 1985—2003, acting dir. collections devel. & mgmt., 2003; interim vice provost & dir. libraries U. Pa., 2003—04, vice provost & dir. libraries, 2004—. Office: Van Pelt-Dietrich Libr Ctr 3420 Walnut St Philadelphia PA 19104-6206 Office Phone: 215-898-7091. Office Fax: 215-898-0559. Business E-Mail: rogers@pobox.upenn.edu.*

**ROGERS, CHARLES EDWIN,** physical chemistry professor; b. Rochester, N.Y., Dec. 29, 1929; s. Charles Harold and Maybelle (Johnson) R.; m. Barbara June Depuy, June 12, 1954; children: Gregory Newton, Linda Frances, Diana Suzanne. BS in Chemistry, Syracuse U., 1954; PhD in Phys. Chemistry, SUNY at Syracuse U., 1957. Rsch. assoc. dept. chemistry Princeton U., 1957-59, Goodyear fellow, 1957-59; mem. tech. staff Bell Telephone Labs., Murray Hill, NJ, 1959-65; assoc. prof. macromolecular sci. Case Western Res. U., Cleve., 1965-74, prof., 1974-98, prof. emeritus, 1998—. Sr. vis. fellow Imperial Coll., U. London, 1971; assoc. dir. Ctr. for Adhesives Sealants Coatings, Case Western Res. U., 1984-88, dir., 1988-91; co-dir. Edison Polymer Innovation Corp., Ctr. for Adhesives, Sealants and Coatings, 1991-97; cons. to polymer and chem. industries; devel. overseas ednl. instns. Editor: Permselective Membranes, 1971, Structure and Properties of Block Copolymers, 1977; contbr. numerous articles to profl. jours.; patentee in field. Mem.: Adhesion Soc., N.Am. Membrane Soc., Am. Phys. Soc., Am. Chem. Soc. Home: 8400 Rockspring Dr Chagrin Falls OH 44023-4645 Office: Case Western Reserve U Dept Macromolecular Sci Cleveland OH 44106-7202 Office Phone: 216-368-6376. Business E-Mail: cer@case.edu.

**ROGERS, CHARLES RAY,** minister, religious organization administrator; b. Grapevine, Tex., Nov. 26, 1935; s. Arlin Avery and Bessie Lorene (Deaton) R.; m. Oma Fay Hines, Aug. 21, 1954; children: Sheree Gay Rogers, Charles Denne Ray, Robin Celeste Rogers Eddins. MS in Christian Edn., Faith Bible Coll., 1980, DD in Humanities (hon.), 1981; B of Theology, M of Theology, Ctrl. Am. Theol. Sem., Escuintla, Guatemala, 2000; D of Ministry in Humanities (hon.), Sem. of Theol. Missions, Escuintla, Guatemala, 1992. Pastor various Bapt. chs., Athens, Dallas, Ft. Worth, 1960-64, various interdenominational chs., Houston, Longview, 1965-69; pres. Evangelism in Action, Ft. Worth, 1969—. Bd. dirs. World Ministry Fellowship, Plano, Tex., dir. world missions, 1970—; leader Over 100 Mission, humanitarian trips Evangelism in Action, Ft. Worth, 1976—. Author: Joy, 1979, Handbook for Victorious Living, 1980, How to Develop Christian Love, 1981; vocalist (rec.) Charlie, 1981. Recreation: golf, tennis, swimming, running, computers. Home: 6417 Rogers Dr Fort Worth TX 76180-4817 Office: Evangelism in Action PO Box 820724 Fort Worth TX 76182-0724 Office Phone: 817-498-3589. E-mail: chasrog@swbell.net.

**ROGERS, CHERYL LYNN,** music and dance educator; b. Tyler, Tex., Sept. 14, 1949; d. Lewis Barton and Edna Elaine (Hunt) Whisenant; m. Carl Michael Rogers, May 23, 1971; children: Jennifer Leigh, Christopher Lewis. AA, Tyler Jr. Coll., 1969; B Music Edn., North Tex. State U., 1971; MA, Stephen F. Austin State U., 1972; EdD, Texas A&M U., 1997. Instr. math Kilgore Ind. Sch. Dist., Tex., 1972—73, dir. jr. high choral, 1973—75; instr. music Tyler Jr. Coll., 1975—88, dir. fine and performing arts, 1988—. Dir. Concert Chorus, Chamber Singers, Harmony and Understanding, Tyler, 1980—; adjudicator All-Region, All-Area Vocal Auditions, Tyler, 1975—. Mem. Tyler Friends of Gifted, 1990—; mem. social com. Hollytree Country Club, Tyler, 1989-90; v.p. edn. Women's Symphony League, Tyler, 2001—; mem. adminstrv. bd. Marvin United Meth. Ch.; Tyler, 1988—; chmn. yearbook commn. Kilgore Music Club, 1974-75. Grad. Teaching fellow Stephen F. Austin State U., 1971-72. Mem. Am. Choral Dirs. Assn., Tex. Music Educators Conf., Tex. Assn. Music Schs. (past pres.), Tex. Jr. Coll. Tchr. Assn., Nat. Assn. Tchrs. Singing, Tex. Choral Dirs. Assn., Young Audiences N.E. Tex. (past pres.), Mortar Bd., Alpha Chi, Pi Kappa Lambda, Phi Theta Kappa, Kappa Delta Pi Edn. Honor Soc. Republican. Avocations: needlepoint, reading. Office: Tyler Jr Coll PO Box 9020 Tyler TX 75711-9020 Business E-Mail: crog@tjc.edu.

**ROGERS, CHRIS ELLEN,** judge; b. Tulsa, Okla., Apr. 26, 1953; d. Dan A. and Eloise B. Rogers; children: Carolyn, Zachary, Jeffrey, Julie. BA, Oral Roberts U., 1988; JD, U. Tulsa, 1990. Prof. family law Tulsa (Okla.) U. Sch. Paralegal, 1995—97; judge municipal Spavinaw, Okla., 2002—, Disney, Okla., 2005—; city atty. Langley, Okla.—2004—05, Kans., Okla., 2005—. Bd. mem. Okla. Reserve Law Officers, Langley, 2002—04. Mem.: ABA, Okla. Bar Assn., Rotary Club. Avocations: horseback riding, gardening, boating. Office: PO Box 68 Langley OK 74350

**ROGERS, DAVID,** playwright, actor; b. NYC; s. George and Deborah (Samuels) Rosenberg; m. June Lois Walker, Oct. 14, 1962; children: Dulcy Dru, Amanda Brooke. Student, Am. Theatre Wing Sch., 1948, 49. Author (N.Y.C. prodns.): Ziegfeld Follies, 1957, Vintage '60, 1960, New Faces of 1962, Fun City, 1967, Charlie and Algernon, 1980 (Tony award nomination); author: (London prodns.) Jubilee Girl, 1956, Young at Heart, 1961, Flowers for Algernon, 1979, Killing Jessica, 1986; pub. plays Tom Jones, 1964, Flowers for Algernon, 1969, Brave New World, 1970, F.L.I.P.P.E.D., 1971, Here and Now, 1973, Soft Soap, 1982, Rehearsal for Murder, 1983, pub. musical Best of Broadway, 1961, Cheaper by the Dozen, 1969, The Hobbit, 1972, The Truth About Cinderella, 1974, The Dream on Royal Street, 1981; author: (TV series) The Hero, 1966, Opera, 1966 (winner Prix d'Italia Concorso Internat. Per Opera Radiofoniche e Televisive), The Carol Burnett Show, 1970, (novels) Oh Eden, 1974, The Bedroom Set, 1976, Somewhere There's Music, 1977, The Great American Alimony Escape, 1979, The In-Laws, 1979; actor: (Broadway plays) Doubles, 1985, George Abbott's Broadway, 1987, A Funny Thing Happened On the Way to the Forum, 1997, (Off Broadway Play) Down the Garden Paths, 2000, Jewtopia, 2006, internat. tour Grand Hotel, 1991, (regional theatre appearances): Players Theatre, 1992,: Birmingham Theatre, 1993, Jupiter Theatre, 1993, Great Lakes Theatre Festival, 1994, Phoenix Theatre, 1995, Denver Ctr. Theatre Co., 1996, Repertory Theatre of St. Louis, 1998, Cin. Playhouse in the Park, 1998, Westport Playhouse, 1998, San Jose Repertory Theatre, 1999 (Dean Goodman Choice award), Va. Stage Co., 2000, Fla. Studio Theatre, 2002, Two Rivers Theatre Co., 2002, Merrimack Repertory Theatre, 2003—04, Rich Forum, 2004, 2005, Conn. Repertory, 2005, (TV guest appearances): Law and Order, 2000, Law and Order: Criminal Intent, 2001, 2005, Law and Order: Special Victims Unit, 2003; writer, performer: (one-man show) Naked on Broadway, 2004. With U.S. Army, 1951—52, Korea. Mem.: AFTRA, SAG, Actors Equity, Broadcast Music Inc., Writers Guild Am. East, Dramatists Guild, Theatre Artists Workshop Westport (bd. dirs. 1985).

**ROGERS, DAVID BOOTH,** lawyer; BA with honors and distinction, Stanford Univ., 1980, JD, 1983. Bar: Calif. 1983, DC 2002. With Latham & Watkins, 1983—, chair, fin. dept., 1997—2001, ptnr. LA, 2001—. Exec. com. Latham & Watkins, 2001—. Named one of Top 20 Lawyers in Calif. under age 40, Calif. Law Bus. mag., 1997. Mem.: ABA. Office: Latham & Watkins Ste 4000 633 W Fifth St Los Angeles CA 90071-2007

**ROGERS, DAVID FREEMAN,** aerospace engineering educator; b. Theresa, NY, Sept. 3, 1937; s. Lewis Freeman and Gladys Marion Zoller; m. Nancy Ann Nuttall, Sept. 5, 1959; children: Stephen David, Karen Nanci, Ransom Robert. B in Aero. Engring., Rensselaer Poly. Inst., 1959, MS in Aero. Engring., 1960, PhD, 1967. From asst. prof. to prof. U.S. Naval Acad., Annapolis, Md., 1964—2003, dir. aeronautics, 1999—2003, prof. emeritus, 2004—. Fujitsu Rsch. prof. Royal Melbourne Inst. Tech.; hon. rsch. scholar U. Coll. London, 1977-78. Author: Mathematical Elements for Computer Graphics, 1976, 2d edit. 1990; Procedural Elements for Computer Graphics, 1985, 2d edit., 1997, Laminar Flow Analysis, 1992, Flying Adventures, Vols. 1-2, 1999, An Introduction to NURBS: with Historical Perspective, 2001; editor Meml. edit. for P. Bezier, CAD Jour.; mem. editl. bd. Visual Computer, CAD, the Computer Aided Design Jour.; contbg. editor World Beechcraft Soc. Mag., 1995—; contbr. articles to profl. jours. David F. Rogers Chair in Aerospace Engineering named in his honor, 2000. Avocations: flying, photography, sailing. Office: US Naval Acad Aerospace Engring Dept Annapolis MD 21402

**ROGERS, DAVID HUGHES,** banking and financial service professor, dean, real estate company executive; b. Chgo., May 21, 1947; s. Joseph Gordon and Viola Winifred (Hughes) R.; Bonnie Hope Sinai, 1997; children: Kirsten Morgan, Loren Avery, Daniel Jay. BA, U. Mich., 1968; PhD, Columbia U., 1975. Economist Fed. Res. Bank of Chicago, 1975-77; asst. treas. B.F. Goodrich Co., Akron, Ohio, 1975-82; exec. v.p., chief fin. officer First Tex. Savs. Assn., Dallas, 1982-83; sr. exec. v.p., chief operating officer PriMerit Bank, Las Vegas, 1984-87, pres., dir., 1987-91, vice chmn., 1991-92; COO, The Baird Cos., Las Vegas, 1992-99; v.p., chief fin. officer Norall Labs., Las Vegas, 1999—2001; v.p., relationship mgr. Wells Fargo Bank, Las Vegas, Nev., 2001—04; CFO Lloyd Cos., Sioux Falls, SD, 2004—06; prof. banking and fin. svcs., asst. dean external programs No. State U., 2006—. Adj. prof. econs. C.C. So. Nev., 1998-2004. Author: Consumer Banking in New York, 1975; also articles. Bd. dirs. Boulder Dam Area coun. Boy Scouts Am., 1986—2004; bd. dirs. Nev. Sch. Arts, 1988-98; chmn. Las Vegas Bus. Bank, 1995-99. Office: No State U 2205 Career Ave Rm 268 D Sioux Falls SD 57107 Office Phone: 605-782-3236. Personal E-mail: dhrogers14@aol.com. Business E-mail: dhrogers@northern.edu.

**ROGERS, DEWITT RALPH,** lawyer; b. Durham, N.C., Sept. 26, 1952; s. Ralph P. and Elizabeth (Stutts) R.; m. Claire Hamby, Sept. 25, 1982; children: DeWitt Ralph Jr., Elizabeth Lee, Laura Alice. BA, Emory U., 1974, JD with distinction, 1986; MS in Journalism, Columbia U., 1975. Bar: Ga. 1986. Staff writer The Atlanta Constn., 1975-77, bus. editor, 1977-79, city editor, 1979-82; asst. mng. editor The Atlanta Jour. & Constn., 1982-83; assoc. Troutman Sanders LLP, Atlanta, 1986-93, ptnr., regulatory group, 1994—. Bd. dirs. So. Inst. for Bus. and Profl. Ethics, 1998-. Editor-in-chief Emory Law Jour. Mem.: Order of Coif. Office: Troutman Sanders LLP 600 Peachtree St NE Ste 5200 Atlanta GA 30308-2216 Office Phone: 404-885-3412. Office Fax: 404-962-6671. Business E-Mail: dewitt.rogers@troutmansanders.com.

**ROGERS, DONALD L.,** music educator, department chairman, animal breeder; b. Bayshore, NY, Jan. 22, 1945; s. Donald Hampton and Laura Rogers; m. Bonnie L. Nieman, June 25, 1967; 1 child, Rebecca L. B.S, SUNY, Fredonia, 1966. Tchg. cert. Bd. of Regents State of NY, 1966. H.s. band dir. Attica (NY) Ctrl. Sch. Dist., 1966—. Music dept. chmn. Attica Ctrl. Sch., 1980—. Dir.: (band performance) Tournament of Roses Parade, 2003. Pres. Western NY Pheasant & Waterfowl Assn., NY, 1985—. Sgt. U.S. Army, 1969—72. Decorated Army Commendation U.S. Army; named Tchr. of Yr., U. Rochester, 1993, Educator of Yr., Phi Delta Kappa, 2001; recipient Service award, Wyoming County Youth Bd., 2001, Lifetime Achievement award, Wyo. County Arts Coun. Mem.: Music Educators Nat. Conf., NY State Sch. Music Assn., Am. Pheasant & Waterfowl Assn., Western NY Pheasant and Waterfowl Assn. (life; pres. 1985—). Home: 2338 Chick Rd Darien Center NY 14040 Office: Attica Senior High Sch 3338 East Main St Attica NY 14011 Office Phone: 585-591-0400 Ext.1433. Personal E-mail: wildwingedhaven2@aol.com.

**ROGERS, DOROTHEA MAY,** education educator; b. Detroit, Dec. 14, 1951; d. Lawrence Edward Peter Dietrich and Thelma Louise St. Clair; m. Paul Douglas, Sr. Rogers, Apr. 12, 1971; children: Paul Douglas Jr., Matthew Lawrence. AA in Gen. Bus., Schoolcraft Coll., Mich., 1991; BA in Religious Edn., Christian Bible Coll. and Seminary, Independance, Mo., 1996; BA in Family Life Edn. magna cum laude, Spring Arbor U., Mich., 1998; MA in Family and Consumer Sci., Western Mich. U., 2001; D in Ministry Family Studies, Am. Christian Coll. and Seminary, Oklahoma City, 2005. Cert. family life educator, presch. tchr., gerontology, child devel. assoc. Asst. preschool tchr. Children's Care Ctr., Howell, Mich., 1993—95; head preschool tchr. A Helping Hand Preschool, Linden, Mich., 1996—97; sub. tchr. Howell (Mich.) Pub. Schs., 1998—2001; prof. health & human svcs. Baker Coll., Flint, Mich., 1999—2003; social work prevention Kids in New Directions, Lapeer, Mich., 2001—03; prof. Spring Arbor U., 2005—. Adv. bd. Making A Difference For Children Conf., Flint, Mich., 1999—2002; advisor curriculum Baker Coll., Flint, Mich., 1999—2003, sys. meeting cons., 1999—2003. Author: (book) First-Line Supervision, 1990, The Postparental Life Stage in Middle Age Women, 2005; composer, presenter (seminar) Preventing and Treating Job Burnout for Childcare Workers, 2002. Quiz bowl moderator Hartland (Mich.) HS, 1992—96; geriatric advocate Stephen Ministry, Fenton, Mich., 1997—2006; tutor, mentor Family Literacy Ctr., Lapeer, Mich., 2003—06. Mem.: Nat. Assn. Edn. of Young Children, Am. Assn. Christian Counselors, Nat. Counsel on Family Rels., Phi Kappa Phi. Democrat. Presbyterian. Avocations: gardening, hiking, flower arranging, photography. Office Phone: 810-245-0255.

**ROGERS, EARL LESLIE,** artist, educator; b. Oakland, Calif., July 8, 1918; s. Robert Ray and Addie Myrtle (Dice) R.; m. Eileen Estelle MacKenzie, Apr. 9, 1945; children: Leslie Eileen, Brian Donald (dec.). Student, L.A. Valley Coll., 1949-52, Northridge State U., 1958-59, UCLA Extension, 1967, Sergei Bongart Sch. Art, 1967-68; AA, Pierce Coll., 1958; MA equivalency, Merced Coll., 1996. Cert. tchr., Calif. Various positions City of L.A., Van Nuys, Calif., 1948-55, Reseda, Calif., 1955-68; pvt. practice Canoga Park, Calif., 1948-68; art tchr. Mariposa (Calif.) County High Sch., 1969-70; art instr. Merced (Calif.) County Coll., 1970—. Instr. Earl Rogers Studio Workshop, Mariposa, Calif., 1969—; art dir. Yosemite Nat. Park, Calif., 1973; instr. at Asilomar Conf. Grounds, Pacific Grove, Calif., 1980; juror various art orgns., 1971-2004; demonstrator Clovis (Calif.) Art Guild, 1971, 89, Sierra Artists, Mariposa, 1972, 81, 82, 84, 91, 2000, Merced Art League, 1976, Yosemite Western Artists, Oakhurst, Calif., 1973, Madera (Calif.) Art Assn., 1978, Chowchilla (Calif.) Art Guild, 1983, 86, 87, 89, 91, Soc. Western Artists, 1981, 89, 93, 97. One-man shows include L.A. City Hall, 1968, Merced Coll., 1969, 1995, Mariposa Title Co. Bldg., 1969, Coffee's Gallery, 1970, Bear Valley Hist. Bon-Ton, Calif., 1999, others, exhibited in group shows at West Valley Artists Assn., 1966—68, L.A. City Hall, 1967, Yosemite Nat. Park, 1973, Soc. Western Artists, 1977—78, Cannon Bldg. Rotunda, Washington, 1982, Mother Lode Gallery, Columbia, Calif., 1977—78, Arbor Gallery, Merced, 1988, 1998, 2001, Gold Country Gallery 1990—91, Merced Coll., 1969—92, 1996, Mariposa County Arts Coun., 1999, at others, Represented in permanent collections John C. Fremont Hosp., Mariposa, Mariposa County Arts Coun., Mariposa Mus. and History Ctr., Capitol Hill Br. Pub. Libr., Seattle, Merced Coll. Asst. scout master Boy Scouts of Am., Canoga Park, Calif., 1956-58; art instr. L.A. Recreation Corps, L.A. Parks and Recreation Dept. 1967. Mem. Soc. Western Artists (Neva Rall Meml. award 1978), Mariposa Mus. and Hist. Ctr. (life). Avocations: piano, reading. Home and Office: 5323 State Hwy 49 N Mariposa CA 95338-9503

**ROGERS, EDWARD SAMUEL,** communications company executive; b. Toronto, May 27, 1933; s. Edward Samuel and Velma Melissa (Taylor) R.; m. Loretta Anne Robinson, Sept. 25, 1963; children: Lisa Anne, Edward Samuel, Melinda Mary, Martha Loretta. BA, Trinity Coll., U. Toronto, 1956; LLB, Osgoode Hall Law Sch., 1961; DSc (hon.), Clarkson U., 1989; LLD (hon.), U. Victoria, 1990; LLD, York U., 1994; LittD, U. of New Brunswick, 2001; LLD, U. of Toronto, 2002, D of sacred letters, 1997. Bar: Ont., 1962. Founder, prin. Rogers Telecomm. Ltd., Toronto, 1960—; pres., CEO Rogers Comm. Inc., Toronto, 1978—, Rogers Cablesystems, Toronto, 1990—96; vice chmn. Rogers Media Inc., Toronto, 1994, Rogers Cable Inc., Toronto, 1997—; chmn. Rogers Wrieless Comms. Inc., 1991. Bd. dirs. Toronto Blue Jays Baseball Club. Bd. dirs. Jr. Achievement Can. Mem. Royal Can. Yacht Club, Albany Club, Granite Club, York Club, Muskoka Golf & Country Club, Rideau Club Ottawa, Lyford Cay Club (gov.), Balboa Bay Club, Sigma Chi (Beta Omega chpt.). Progressive Conservative. Mem. Anglican Ch. Office: Rogers Comm Inc 333 Bloor St E Toronto ON Canada M4W 1G9 Business E-Mail: ted.rogers@rci.rogers.com.

**ROGERS, ELIZABETH (BETTY) CARLISLE,** education educator, consultant; d. Charles Bunyan and Maggie Era (Little) Carlisle; children: Kellie Elizabeth, Sean Lewis. BS, U. Miss., 1972, MS, 1974; PhD, U. Ga., 1997. Chair divsn. sci. and math. Truett-McConnell Coll., Cleveland, Ga., 1974—84; chair dept. math. Lakeview Acad., Gainesville, Ga., 1984—89; prof. math. and edn. Piedmont Coll., Demorest, Ga., 1989—; prin. R&H Analytics, 2004—. Pres. BCR Inc., Gainesville, Ga., 1990—; ptnr. The Ednl. Solutions Task Force, Washington, 2000—. Author: (profl. book) A Study of Curriculum and Pedagogy, 1997; editor (contbg. author): Cooperative Learning In Undergraduate Mathematics, 2001; author: (textbook) Mathematics for Agriculture, 2000. Chair, ceremonies and events Spl. Olympics of Ga., 2001—04. Grantee Faculty Devel. in Ga., State of Ga., 1992—95; scholar Carrier Scholarship, Carrier Found.; Tchg. Fellow, U. of Miss., 1971—73. Mem.: Women in Math., Math. Assn. of Am., Alpha Delta Pi (Dorothy Shaw Leadership award), Alpha Lambda Delta (pres.), Kappa Delta Phi (pres.), Phi Kappa Phi. Achievements include research in advantages of coop. learning for undergraduate math. students; history of math. in Ctrl. and South Am. Home: 4733 Highland Rd Gainesville GA 30506 Office: Piedmont Coll Ctrl Ave Demorest GA 30535 Office Phone: 770-287-4634. Personal E-mail: b.rogers@prodigy.net. E-mail: brogers@piedmont.edu.

**ROGERS, ELIZABETH LONDON,** retired geriatrics services professional; MD, Jefferson Med. Sch., 1971. Lic. internal medicine, gastroenterology, and geriatrics Am. Bd. of Internal Medicine. Chief of staff Balt. VA Med. Ctr., 1982—93; prof. dept. of medicine U. of Md. Med. Sch., Baltimore, 1990—93; assoc. dean for clin. medicine Duke U. Med. Sch., Durham, NC, 1993—96; acting chief of staff VA Healthcare Sys., New Haven, 1996—2002; ret., 2002. Pres. Bradmer Biotech, Miami, 2002—05; dir. Cardiome Pharma, Vancouver, B.C., Canada, 2003—04. Recipient Geriat. scholarship, Hartford Found., 1984—85. Fellow: ACP.

**ROGERS, ELIZABETH PARKER,** retired chemistry professor; b. Plymouth, Mass., Aug. 27, 1919; d. Edward R. and Helen L. (Barnes) Belcher; m. Warren H. Yudkin, Dec. 23, 1951 (dec. June 1954); children: Michael Yudkin, David Yudkin; m. Robert W. Rogers, Nov. 23, 1956; children: Susan, Sarah, John. BA, Mount Holyoke Coll., 1940, MA, 1942; PhD, Northwestern U., 1951. Rsch. chemist Armstrong Cork Co., Lancaster, Pa., 1942-45, Evanston (Ill.) Health Dept., 1951-54; asst. prof. U. Ill., Urbana, 1963-87; ret., 1987. Author: Fundamentals of Chemistry, 1987; author: (with W. H. Brown) General, Organic and Biochemistry, 1980, 1987. Staff asst. ARC, France, 1945—46; dir. sec. E. Ctrl. Ill. Alzheimer's, Champaign, 1989—91, pres., 1991—95; dir. Friends U. Ill. Libr., Champaign, 1989—92; sec. LWV, Champaign, 1987—89. Recipient Achievement award, Sid Granet Aging Network, Ill. Area Agys. Aging, 1992, cert. of Lifetime Achievement, Ill. Dept. Aging, 1995. Mem.: Am. Chem. Soc. Avocations: golf, reading.

**ROGERS, ELYSE MACFADYEN,** communications and foundation executive; b. Kearny, N.J., Sept. 28, 1932; d. Frank H. and Silvia (Simms) MacFadyen; m. Edward W. Rogers, July 18, 1952; children: Pamela, Cynthia, Jenifer. RN, Mountainside, 1953; BS, Ind. U., 1957; MA, Purdue U., 1973. Pres. Sci. Syntax Services, Midland, Mich., 1976-81; exec. v.p. OAK Assoc. KK, Tokyo, 1981-84; pres. MAC Internat. Ltd., Tokyo, 1984-87, MAC Internat. Ltd.-USA, Midland, 1987—; asst. v.p. Herbert H. and Grace A. Dow Found., 1990—. Vice chmn. Asian Pacific Council Am. C. of C., Japan, 1985-87; bd. govs. Am. C. of C., Japan, 1985-87. Author: Staying Healthy in Japan, 1983, Cross Cultural Dialogues, 1985, Home Nursing Care, 1978; columnist: Japan Times, Yomiuri Shimbun, and Tokyo Weekender, 1980—; contbr. articles to profl. jours. Bd. dirs. Midland Symphony Orch., 1995-2002, chair, 1998-2000; bd. dirs. MidMich. Health, 1995—, MidMich. Med. Ctr., 1998—, Little Forks Conservancy, 2003—; bd. dirs. MidMich. Vis. Nurse Assn., 1990-96, chair, 1995-96; bd. fellows Saginaw Valley State U., 1997—; bd. govs. Northwood U., 2000-04; chair exec. women's bd. Northwood U., 2002—. Recipient Disting. Woman award Mitten Bay Girl Scouts U.S., 1997, Athena award Athena Found., 1998. Fellow: Am. Med. Writers Assn.; mem.: Fgn. Corrs. Club of Japan, Mich. Non Profit Assn. (bd. dirs. 1999—), Detroit Working Writers, Am. Soc. Journalists and Authors, Fgn. Exec. Women (founder, pres. 1981—84), Rotary, Midland Country Club. Republican. Episcopalian.

**ROGERS, ERNEST MABRY,** lawyer; b. Demopolis, Ala., Sept. 22, 1947; s. James B. and Ernestine B. (Brewer) R.; m. Jeanne Edwards, Dec. 15, 1979; children: Gilbert B., Katherine B., Mary C. BA, Yale U., 1969; JD, Harvard U., 1974. Bar: Ala. 1974, U.S. Dist. Ct. (no. dist.) Ala. 1975, U.S. Ct. Appeals (5th cir.) 1976, U.S. Ct. Appeals (11th cir.) 1981, U.S. Supreme Ct. 1981, U.S. Ct. Claims 1983, U.S. Ct. Appeals (6th cir.) 1987. Law clk. to judge U.S. Dist. Ct. (no. dist.) Ala. 1974—75; ptnr Bradley Arant Rose & White LLP, Birmingham, Ala., 1981—. Contbr. articles to profl. jours. Mem. Jefferson County (Ala.) Bd. of Code Appeals, 2001—. Fellow: Am. Coll. Constrn. Lawyers; mem.: Am. Arbitration Assn. (bd. dirs. 2001—05), Kiwanis. Episcopalian. Office: One Federal Pl 1819 5th Ave N Birmingham AL 35203-2104 Office Phone: 205-521-8225. Business E-Mail: mrogers@bradleyarant.com.

**ROGERS, EUGENE JACK,** retired medical educator; b. Vienna, June 13, 1921; came to U.S., 1937; s. Louis and Malvina (Haller) R.; m. Joyce M. Lighter, Feb. 9, 1952; children: Jay A., Robert J. BS, CCNY; M.B., Chgo. Med. Sch., 1946, MD, 1947. Diplomate Am. Bd. Phys. Medicine and Rehab. Intern Our Lady of Mercy Med. Ctr. and Cabrini Meml. Hosps., N.Y.C., 1946-48; resident Madigan Hosp., Tacoma, 1951, Mayo Clinic, Rochester, Minn., 1951, N.Y. Med. Coll. Met. Med. Ctr., 1953-55; USPHS fellow, 1955-56; ship's surgeon U.S. Lines, Grace Lines, N.Y.C., 1948-49; indsl. physician Abraham & Strauss Stores, Bklyn., 1949-51; practice medicine specializing in phys. medicine and rehab. Bklyn., 1956-73; dir. rehab. service, attending physician N.Y. City Hosp. Dept., 1955-73; prof., chmn. dept. rehab. medicine Chgo. Med. Sch., North Chicago, Ill., 1973—2005, prof. emeritus dept. rehab. medicine, 2005—, Rosalind Franklin U. Medicine & Sci., 2005. Cons. N.Y.C. Mayor's Adv. Com. for Aged, 1957; asst. prof. SUNY Downstate Med. Sch., Bklyn., 1958-73; med. dir. Schwab Rehab. Hosp., Chgo., 1973-75; acting chief rehab. service VA Center, North Chicgo, 1975-77; chmn. Ill. Phys. Therapy Exam. Com., 1977-78; examiner Am. Bd. Phys. Medicine and Rehab., 1983; sec., dir. Microtherapeutics, Inc., 1972 Editor: Total Cancer Care, 1975; contbr. articles to med. jours.; contbg. editor Ill. Med. Jour., 1983-89 Served to capt. U.S. Army, 1951—53. Recipient Bronze medal Am. Congress Rehab. Medicine, 1974 Fellow: ACP, Am. Acad. Phys. Medicine and Rehab.; mem.: Chgo. Med. Sch. Alumni Assn. (asst. treas. 1983—93, treas. 1993—95, sec. 1995—97, 1st v.p. 1999, pres. 2001—03, exec. com., Disting. Alumnus award 1980, Pencil plaque Greater N.Y. chpt.), Chgo. Med. Sch. Faculty Assembly (spkr. 1978—80), Ill. Soc. Phys. Medicine and Rehab. (pres. 1983—84), Ill. Med. Soc. (chmn. workmen's compensation com. 1980—83), Odd Fellows (pres. 1961—62), Phi Lambda Kappa (trustee 1980), Alpha Omega Alpha. Home: 1110 N Lake Shore Dr Chicago IL 60611-5248 Personal E-mail:

---

eugenerogers@att.com. To render good medical care: Prevent disease, evaluate the patient, treat the condition, educate patient and family, restore function, support group referral, on-line medical knowledge maintenance, never neglect or lie to or for patients, never divulging patient med. info. without consent.

**ROGERS, FRED BAKER,** medical educator; b. Trenton, N.J., Aug. 25, 1926; s. Lawrence H. and Eliza C. (Thropp) R. AA, Princeton U., 1947; MD, Temple U., 1948; MS in Medicine, U. Pa., 1951; MPH, Columbia U., 1957; spl. student, Johns Hopkins U., 1962. Diplomate: Am. Bd. Preventive Medicine. Intern Temple U. Hosp., Phila., 1948-49, chief resident physician 1953-54; USPHS fellow Temple U. Sch. Medicine, 1954-55, asst. prof. preventive medicine, 1956-58, assoc. prof., 1958-60, prof., 1960-90, prof. emeritus, 1991—, chmn. dept., 1970-77. Lectr. epidemiology Columbia U. Sch. Pub. Health, 1957-68, Sch. Nursing, U. Pa., 1964-67; cons. USN Hosp., Phila., 1964-73 Author: A Syllabus of Medical History, 1958, Help-Bringers: Versatile Physicians of N.J, 1960, Epidemiology and Communicable Disease Control, 1963, Studies in Epidemiology, 1965, (with A.R. Sayre) The Healing Art, 1966, (with M.E. Cashel) Your Body is Wonderfully Made, 1974; mem. editorial bd. Am. Jour. Pub. Health, 1967-73; contbr. articles to profl. jours. With M.C. USNR, 1950-53, Korea, capt. (ret.) USNR. Recipient Chapel of Four Chaplains award, 1982. Fellow ACP; mem. AMA (past chmn. sect. preventive medicine, Am. Pub. Health Assn., Royal Soc. Medicine of London (hon.), Sigma Xi, Alpha Omega Alpha, Phi Rho Sigma. Clubs: Campus (Princeton); Franklin Inn (Phila.); Charaka (N.Y.C.); Osler (London). Home: 333 W State St Apt 6K Trenton NJ 08618-5722 Office: Temple U Sch Med Philadelphia PA 19140

**ROGERS, GARDNER SPENCER,** railroad company executive; b. Bryn Mawr, Pa., Sept. 16, 1926; s. Gardner Spencer and Frances (Lloyd) R.; m. Margaret Elizabeth Windsor, July 18, 1954; children: Ann Rogers Wilbanks, Barbara Rogers Coombs. Student, Episc. Acad., 1940-44, MIT, 1944-45; BS, U. Colo., 1951. Registered ret. profl. engr., Calif. With We. Pacific R R. Co., San Francisco, 1947-70, engr. costs, valuation and stats., 1964-69, asst. to gen. mgr. planning and control, 1969, asst. gen. mgr., 1970; gen. mgr. Civil & Mech. Maintenance Pty. Ltd., Perth, Australia, 1970-77; mgr. We. Australian ops. Fluor Australia Pty. Ltd., 1971-73, gen. mgr. ry. divsn., 1973-77; gen. mgr. Pilbara Industries, 1971-73; dir. budgets and control Consol. Rail Corp., 1978-79, sr. dir. budgets, planning and control, 1980, dir. corp. planning, 1981-87; cons., 1987—2001. Adv. com. on R.R. property ICC, 1966-70; mem. spl. adv. team R.R. Ofcls. to U.S. Govt., 1962. Mng. trustee Daniel B. Gardner Trust, Chgo.; alt. trustee Cathedral Sq. Found., Perth; vestryman Ch. of Eng., 1971-77, mem. synod and provincial synod, 1973-77, mem. diocesan coun., 1974-77, bd. dirs. sch.'s trust, 1975-77; vestryman, chmn. fin. com., sr. warden St. Mary's-by-the-Sea Episc. Ch., Pacific Grove, Calif., 1989-91; vestryman, chmn. stewardship com., jr. warden St. Mark's Epis. Ch., Medford, Oreg., 1996-98. Mem. Instn. Engrs. Australia, Am. C. of C. in Australia (bd. dirs., v.p.-chmn. We. Australian exec. com. 1976-77), Swanleigh (chmn. exec. com. 1974-77, coun.), Am. Mgmt. Assn., Am. Ry. Engr. Assn. (sec. com. 11 1983-87), Epis. Diocese of El Camino Real (bd. dirs. 1991-93, lay Eucharistic Min. 1991-94), Diocese of Oreg. (lay Eucaristic Min. 1995—, lic. lay reader 1996—), Ry. and Locomotive Hist. Soc., Soc. of Cal. R.R. Ofcls., Mil. Order Loyal Legion (vice comdr.), Colo. Alumni Assn. No. Calif. (pres. 1951-52), Rogue Valley Manor (pres. residents coun. 1999-2000), Berkeley Tennis Club, Pacific Ry. Club, Commonwealth Club, Australian-Am. Club, Alpha Tau Omega (high coun. 1964-68, 82-90). Home: Apt 1020 1200 Mira Mar Ave Medford OR 97504 E-mail: grogersRVM@charter.net.

**ROGERS, GARTH WINFIELD,** lawyer; b. Fort Collins, Colo., Nov. 4, 1938; s. Harlan Winfield and Helen Marie (Orr) R.; m. Joanne Kathleen Rapp, June 16, 1962; children: Todd Winfield, Christopher Jay, Gregory Lynn, Clay Charles. BS, U. Colo., 1958, LLB, 1962. Bar: Colo. 1962; U.S. Dist. Ct. Colo. 1962. Law clk. to presiding justice U.S. Dist. Ct., Denver, 1962-63; assoc. Allen, Stover & Mitchell, Ft. Collins, 1963-68; ptnr. Allen, Rogers & Vahrenwald, Ft. Collins, 1968-97; ret., 1997. Articles editor Rocky Mountain Law Rev., 1961-62. Past bd. dirs. Salvation Army, Ft. Collins, Ft. Collins of C., United Way of Ft. Collins, Trinity Luth. Ch., Ft. Collins, Poudre Sch. Dist. Bd. Edn., others. Mem. ABA, Colo. Bar Assn., Larimer County Bar Assn. Avocations: nicaragua projects, participative sports, amateur writing, reading. Office: 215 W Oak St Ste 777 Fort Collins CO 80521-2734

**ROGERS, GINA INSCO,** medical association administrator; AD in Nursing, We. Ky. U., 1987, BSN, 1994. RN, cert. legal nurse cons., 1999, nat. managed care, 2000, CPR instr., 1989, pediatric advanced life support instr., 1989, lic. advanced cardiac life support, 1989, Ky. With CCU Med. Ctr. at Bowling Green, 1988—89, with cardiac cath lab., 1989—90, with CCU, ICU emergency dept., 1990—93, ho. dir., 1993—94, utilization mgmt., 1994—2000; CEO Med. Review Cons., LLC, Russellville, Ky., 1999—. Faculty Med. Legal Cons. Inst., Inc., Houston, 2002—05; spkr. in field. Mem. consolidated planning com. Logan County Sch. Sys., 1998—2000, mem. safety assessment com., 1999, mem. consolidated planning com., 2002—02. Mem.: Ky. Acad. Trial Attys., Am. Assn. Legal Nurse Cons. (pres.-elect 2002—03, pres. Ky. chpt. 2003—04), Sigma Theta Tau. Office: Medical Review Cons LLC 560 Stonewall Dr Russellville KY 42276 Office Phone: 270-726-3211. Personal E-mail: girogers@hotmail.com.

**ROGERS, HAROLD DALLAS (HAL ROGERS),** congressman; b. Barrier, KY, Dec. 31, 1937; BA, U. Ky., 1962, LLB, 1964. Bar: La. 1964. Assoc. Smith & Blackburn, 1964—67; pvt. practice Somerset, Ky., 1967-69; Commonwealth atty. Pulaski and Rockcastle counties, Ky., 1969-80; mem. US Congress from 5th Ky. dist., 1981—, mem. appropriations com., subcom. homeland security, transp., commerce, justice and state. Mem. Congressional House Caucus, Tenn. Valley Authority Caucus. Founder So. Ky. Economic Council. With KY and NC Nat. Guard, 1957—64. Mem.: Ky. Commonwealth Atty. Assn. (past pres.). Republican. Office: US Ho Reps 2406 Rayburn Ho Office Bldg Washington DC 20515-1705

**ROGERS, HELEN LYNCH,** physical therapist, educator; d. Bernard Walden and Mari Louise Lynch; m. Randall Lee Rogers, Nov. 10, 1984; children: Ian Michael, Eric Randall. BS, U. Tex., Galveston, 1983; MA in Behavioral Psychology, U. Houston, Clear Lake, 1990. Cert. phys. therapy Tex. State Bd. Phys. Therapy Examiners, 1983. Phys. therapist U. Tex. Med. Br., Galveston, 1983—87, supr. adult rehab., 1987—90; assoc. dir. for edn. and rsch. U. Tex. Med. Br. Physical Therapy, 1990—95; asst. prof. U. Tex. Med. Br. Sch. Allied Health Sci., 1995—2005. Cons. for Galveston ind. sch. dist. U. Tex. Med. Br., Galveston, 1985—86, cons. for project launch early childhood intervention, 1989—90. Named Grand Marshall for Commencement, U. Tex. Med. Br. Sch. Allied Health Scis., 2004; recipient Outstanding Faculty Mem. award, 1998, 2001, 2004, Outstanding New Faculty Mem. award, 1998, Edn. award, Tex. Phys. Therapy Found., 2003. Mem.: Tex. Phys. Therapy Assn. (publs. chair for southeastern dist. 1991—95, mem. nominating com. 2000—03), Am. Phys. Therapy Assn. (elected del. from Tex. 1999—2003), Psi Chi, Phi Beta Kappa. Democrat-Npl. Avocations: running, reading, needlecrafts. Office: Univ Tex Med Br 301 University Blvd Rte 1144 Galveston TX 77555-1144 Office Phone: 409-772-3068.

**ROGERS, HON PAULLETTO,** researcher, writer; b. Washington, Mich., Aug. 22, 1961; s. Paulleto Rogers I and Dorothy L.R. Rogers; children: Alexis R. Roycia July, Ambre L. Magissa, Ericka J. Student, Wayne County C.C.; cert. computer ops., Mother Waddles Sch. Cert. paralegal; notary pub. Pres. C.C.O.A, L.A., 1983; gen. operator CBOU, 1983—; regent agent Security MGN, 1984; collector Nat. Cert. Credit Corp., L.A., 1985; craftman Vinyl Indsl. Products, Chgo., 1986; field insp. Mortgage Svcs. Assoc., Inc., 1995; sales cons. Swepo, 1996; legal tech. Probone Legal Svcs., 1997; directorate Prousa Internat. Projects 2001, 1998. Sustaining member Rep. Platform Commn., 1986; substaining sponsor Ronald Reagan Presdl. Found., Libr., and Ctr. Pub. Affairs, Ventura County, Calif., 1988; sponsor Statue of Liberty Ellis Island Centennial Commn., 1985, Ronald Reagan Congressional-Vicotry Fund, 1987; advisorate Senate Adv. Coun., 1997; co-founder Justice Inst.; vol.

---

Mother Waddles-Petr. Mission Support; del. at large Del. Adv. Coun.; legal adv. Alexis, Ambre, Dorthy-Lewis, Paul, Paulleto, Rogers, Sutton, Proff. Corp., 2001. Creator, founder The Collectionals Survey. At-large-del. Rep. Presdl. Task Force, 1992—, lobbyist, 1994—; activist U.S. Def. Com., 1985; lobbyist Prousa Legal Corpsusa, 1999; del. Wayne County Clk. Office; Mich. state advisor Rep. Senatorial Com.; mem. Jaycees, 1981, GOPAC, congl. VIP, 1984; GOP Victory Fund sponsor NRCC, 1984; supporter KIDSFIRST YESMI, 2000; assoc. mem. Ch. Tae Adv., 2000—. Decorated Rogers Coat of Arms, Medieval Knight, Chevron, 2000; recipient Cert. Recognition, NRCC, 1990, Cert. Appreciation, Presdl. Commn. A.A., 1990, Presdl. award Rep. Presdl. Legion of Merit, 1994. Mem. Oahspe (assoc.), World Peace Tonite/Freedom Inst. (assoc.), 2nd Ch. of Tae. Avocations: copyrights, activism, lobbying, community reinvesting. Home: PO Box 27473 Detroit MI 48227-0473 Personal E-mail: rogerspaulleto@yahoo.com.

**ROGERS, HOWARD H.,** retired chemist; b. NYC, Dec. 26, 1926; s. Julian Herbert and Minnie (Jaffa) R.; m. Barbara Kniaz, Mar. 27, 1954 (div. 1978); children: Lynne, Mark David, Susan; m. Maureen Dohn, Dec. 28, 1978. BS in Chemistry, U. Ill., 1949; PhD in Inorganic Chemistry, MIT, 1953. Research group leader Allis-Chalmers Mfg. Co., West Allis, Wis., 1952-61; sr. tech. specialist Rocketdyne div., Rockwell, Canoga Park, Calif., 1961-70; chief research scientist Martek Instruments, Newport Beach, Calif., 1970-73; scientist Boeing Satellite Systems, Torrance, Calif., 1973—2002; ret., 2002. Contbr. sci. papers to profl. publs. in field. Vol. LA County Disaster Comm. Svc., 1998—. With USN, 1944—46. Recipient Lawrence A. Hyland Patent award Hughes Aircraft Co., 1987. Mem. Electrochem. Soc. (chmn. So. Calif./Nev. sect. 1976-78), Am. Chem. Soc. Achievements include development of nickel-hydrogen battery; 27 US patents. Avocation: amateur radio. Home: 18361 Van Ness Ave Torrance CA 90504-5309 Personal E-mail: howard.rogers@alum.mit.edu. In my 75 plus years of living experience I have found that these two items are vital: focus on what you intend to do, not what you have already done; complete honesty to yourself and to others in interpreting and reporting results is mandatory.

**ROGERS, JACK DAVID,** plant pathologist, educator; b. Point Pleasant, W.Va., Sept. 3, 1937; s. Jack and Thelma Grace R.; m. Belle C. Spencer, June 7, 1958. BS in Biology, Davis and Elkins Coll., 1960; MF, Duke U., 1960; PhD, U. Wis., 1963. From asst. prof. to prof. Wash. State U., Pullman, 1963-72, chmn. dept. plant pathology, 1986-99. Contbr. articles to profl. jours. Recipient Eminent Faculty award, Wash. State U., 2006. Mem. Mycol. Soc. Am. (pres. 1977-78, William H. Weston Tchg. Excellence award 1992, Disting. Mycologist award 2004), Am. Phytopathol. Soc., Bot. Soc. Am., Brit. Mycol. Soc.

**ROGERS, JAMES BEELAND, JR., (JIM ROGERS),** retired investment company executive; b. Balt., Oct. 19, 1942; s. James Beeland and Ernestine Barbera (Brewer) Rogers; m. Paige Parker; 1 child, Hilton Augusta. BA cum laude, Yale U., 1964; BA with honors, Balliol Coll., Oxford U., Eng., 1966, MA in Politics, Philosophy, Econs. Investment analyst Bache & Co., NYC, 1968-69, R. Gilder & Co., NYC, 1969-70; asst. to chmn. Neuberger & Berman, NYC, 1970-71; with Arnhold and S. Belichroeder, Inc., 1971-73; exec. v.p. Soros Fund Mgmt., NYC, 1973-80; chmn. bd. dirs Rogers Holdings, 1980—. Adj. prof. Columbia U. Sch. Bus., 1983—85, prof. fin., 1986—90, vis. prof., 1994—96. Host (TV series) The Profit Motive with Jim Rogers, 1989—90, Guinness Record Motorcycle Trip Around World, 1990—92, co-host, commentator various TV shows, 1992—; author: Investment Biker: On the Road with Jim Rogers, 1994, Guiness Record Drive Around the World on Millennium Adventure, 1999—2001, Adventure Capitalist: The Ultimate Road Trip, 2003, Hot Commodities: How Anyone Can Invest Profitably in the World's Best Market, 2004. With U.S. Army, 1966—68. Achievements include being listed 3 timess in Guinness Book of World Records for Henley Regatta Race, for 100,000 mile motorcycle trip across six continents in 1990-92, for automobile trip around world, 1999-2001. Home: 352 Riverside Dr New York NY 10025-2731 E-mail: jim@jimrogers.com.

**ROGERS, JAMES DEVITT,** judge; b. Mpls., May 5, 1929; s. Harold Neil and Dorothy (Devitt) R.; m. Leanna Morrison, Oct. 19, 1968. AB, Dartmouth Coll., 1951; JD, U. Minn., 1954. Bar: Minn. 1954, U.S. Supreme Ct. 1983. Assoc. Johnson & Sands, Mpls., 1956-60; sole practice Mpls., 1960-62; judge Mpls. Municipal and Dist. Ct., 1959-91. Mem. faculty Nat. Judicial Coll. Bd. dirs. Mpls. chpt. Am. Red Cross, chmn. service to mil. families and vets. com.; bd. dirs. Minn. Safety Coun., St. Paul, 1988-91; founding dir., sec. Forest Landowners Tax Coun. Served sgt. U.S. Army, 1954-56. Mem. ABA (chmn. nat. conf. spl. ct. judge, spl. com. housing and urban devel. law, traffic ct. program com., chmn. criminal justice sect., jud. adminstrn. div.), Nat. Jud. Coll. (bd. dirs.), Nat. Christmas Tree Grower's Assn. (pres. 1976-78), Mpls. Athletic Club. Congregationalist. Office: 14110 Prince Pl Minnetonka MN 55345-3027

**ROGERS, JAMES EUGENE,** electric and gas utility executive; b. Birmingham, Ala., Sept. 20, 1947; s. James E. and Margaret (Whatley) R.; m. Robyn McGill (div.); children: Chrissi, Kara, Ben; m. Mary Anne Boldrick, Oct. 28, 1977. BBA, U. Ky., 1970, JD, 1974; LLD (hon.), Ind. State U. Reporter Lexington (Ky.) Herald Leader, 1967—70; asst. atty. gen. Commonwealth Ky., Louisville; asst. chief trial atty. Fed. Energy Regulation Commn., Washington, dep. gen. counsel litigation and enforcement; law clk. to presiding justice Supreme Ct Ky., Louisville; ptnr. Akin, Gump, Strauss, Hauer & Feld LLP, Dallas, Akin Gump Strauss Hauer & Feld LLP, Houston, 1985-86; exec. v.p. Enron Gas Pipeline Group, 1986-88; pres., CEO, chmn. PSI Resources, Inc, 1988—94, Cinergy Corp. (formerly PSI Resources, Inc.), Cin., 1994—2006; pres., CEO Duke Energy Corp., Charlotte, NC, 2006—, 2nd vice chmn. Cinergy Electric Inst., 2004—05, vice chmn., 2005—06, chmn., 2006—; bd. dirs. Chesapeake Corp., 1999—2004, Duke Energy Corp., 2006—, Fifth Third Bancorp, Fifth Third Bank, Am. Gas Assn., US C. of C., Bus. Roundtable, Nat. Coal Coun. Trustee Nat. Symphony Orch.; bd. dirs. Cin. Mus. Assn., The Nature Conservancy-Ind. chpt., U. Ky. Bus. Partnership Found. Recipient Disting. Svc. Citation, NCCJ, 2004, Keystone Ctr. in Leadership in Industry award, 2005, Ronald McDonald House Lifetime Achievement award, 2005, Human Rels. award, Am. Jewish Com., 2006. Mem. Ky. Bar Assn., D.C. Bar Assn., Meridian Hills Country Club, Crooked Stick Golf Club, Queen City Club, Met. Club. Baptist. Avocations: tennis, bicycling, skiing, golf. Office: Duke Energy Corp 526 S Church St Charlotte NC 28202 also: Edison Electric Inst 701 Pennsylvania Ave NW Washington DC 20004*

**ROGERS, JAMES FREDERICK,** banker, management consultant; b. Centerville, Iowa, June 27, 1935; s. John W. and Mildred Holly (Morris) R.; m. Janet L. Marsden, July 27, 1957; children: Jennifer Burke, John William. AB, U. Mo., 1957; postgrad., Rutgers U. Grad. Sch. Banking, 1970-72. With Am. Security and Trust Co., Washington, 1959-85, exec. v.p., 1980-83. Bd. dirs., mem. Am. Security Corp., 1983-85; cons. B.E.I.-Golembe Assoc., 1985-93; chmn. Nat. Bank of No. Va., 1988-89. Commr. Arlington County Planning Commn., 1979-80; asst. treas. Kennedy Ctr. Performing Arts; pres., trustee Leonard Wood Found.; trustee Friends of Nat. Zoo, Greater Washington Rsch. Ctr., Washington Dulles Task Force, Arena Stage, Sch. Commerce U. Va. Officer AUS, 1958-59. Mem. D.C. Bankers Assn. (pres. 1984-85), Davenport Soc., U. Mo. Club (Washington), Chevy Chase Club. Presbyterian. Home: 4201 38th Rd N Arlington VA 22207-4554

**ROGERS, JAMES GORDON, JR.,** art educator; b. Dec. 16, 1944; AB in English, U. Mo., 1967, MA in Art History and Archaeology, 1983, PhD, 1989. Asst. prof. art history William Woods Coll., Fulton, Mo., 1989-90; prof. art history Savannah (Ga.) Coll. Art & Design, 1990-92, Florida So. Coll., Lakeland, Fla., 1992—. Adj. prof. Sch. Arch. and Comty. Design, U. South Fla., 1995-2002; cons. The Design Ctr., 1977—, chair, Dept. of Art and Art History, dir. Melvin Art Gallery, Art & Art History Study Abroad Program, 1999—; lectr. in field. Contbr. articles to profl. jours. Past mem. peer rev. com. Fla. Arts Coun.; past bd. dirs. Mid-Mo. chpt. Am. Heart Assn., Sta KBIA Pub. Radio, Columbia, Mo., Columbia Art League, also co-chmn. finance com.;

bd. dirs. Hist. Lakeland, Inc.; active Nat. Holocaust Meml. Mus Mem. AAUP, Am. Soc. Hispanic Art Hist. Studies, Soc. Archtl. Historians, Coll. Art Assn., Hist. Lakeland Inc. (bd. dirs.) Office: Fla So Coll Lake Hollingsworth Dr Lakeland FL 33803 Office Phone: 863-680-4223. E-mail: jrogers@flsouthern.edu.

**ROGERS, JEFFERY PAUL**, music educator; b. Bloomington, Ill., Jan. 18, 1959; s. Paul Marshall and Ruthannis Hastings Rogers; m. Karen Ann Coolegde, Dec. 19, 1981; children: Keith, Renee, Katie. BA, West Va. U., 1981; MS, Western Md. Coll., 1992. Music tchr. K-12 Roane Co. Public Sch., Spencer, W.Va., 1981—82; band dir. FS Key HS, Carroll Co. Public Sch., Westminster, Md., 1982—88; band dir. Westminster HS, 1988—92; asst. prin. North Carroll HS, 1992—99, fine arts supr., 1999—. Recipient Asst. Prin. of Yr., Nat. Assn. Secondary Sch. Prin., Md., 1998. Mem.: Assn. Supervision & Curriculum Devel., Nat. Assn. Music Educators. Office: Carroll Co Public Schs 125 N Ct St Westminster MD 21157-5192 Office Phone: 410-751-3055.

**ROGERS, JENNY**, artist, interior designer, consultant; d. Byron Wayne Fallesen and Susan Carol Rogers; life ptnr. Clove Galilee, Feb. 16, 2004. BA in Art and Semiotics magna cum laude, Brown U., 1993; MFA, Pa. State U., 2003. Recreation dir. City and County of San Francisco Recreation and Parks Dept., San Francisco, 1996—2001; videographer, video editor Video Studio 55, NYC, 2003; interior design cons. Uncommon Abode, NYC, 2005—. Video work, Herzliya Mus. Contemporary Art (Mus. located in Tel Aviv, Israel), 2006), Walker Arts Ctr., Mpls. Recipient 1st Pl. for poem, St. Mary's Coll. Nat. Lit. Competition, 1996, Exptl. Grand Festival award, Berkeley Video and Film Festival, 2004; Individual Artist grantee, Jerome Found., 2003, Dance and Performance Art grantee, Greenwall Found., 2004—06, Artist and Fiscal Sponsorship Program grantee, NY Found. for Arts, 2004, Individual Artist grantee, NY State Coun. on the Arts, 2006. Mem.: Coll. Art Assn. Home: 55 East 9th Street TE New York NY 10003 Office: Video Studio 55 55 East 9th Street TE New York NY 10003 Office Phone: 917-414-2234. Personal E-mail: jenny@jenrogers.com. Business E-Mail: jenny@videostudio55.com.

**ROGERS, JOE**, former lieutenant governor; b. Omaha, Nebraska, July 8, 1964; m. Juanita (Kay); children: Trent, Jordan, Haley. Degree in bus., Colo. State U., 1986; JD, Ariz. State U., 1989. Past law clk. to Hon. Robert Broomfield U.S. Dist. Ct.; assoc. Davis, Graham, and Stubbs, Colo., 1989-93; staff counsel to Senator Hank Brown U.S. Congress, Washington, 1993-95; lt. gov. State of Colo., 1998—2002; pvt. practice lawyer, 2002—. Past atty. Lend A Lawyer Program, Colo. Mem. Denver Bar Assn. (bd. dir. credit union 1990-93), Colo. Bar Assn., Sam Carey Bar Assn. Republican.

**ROGERS, JOHN JAMES WILLIAM**, geology educator; b. Chgo., June 27, 1930; s. Edward James and Josephine (Dickey) R.; m. Barbara Bongard, Nov. 30, 1956; children: Peter, Timothy. BS, Calif. Inst. Tech., 1952, PhD, 1955; MS, U. Minn., 1952. Lic. geologist, N.C. From instr. to prof. Rice U., Houston, 1954-75, master Brown Coll., 1966-71, chmn. dept. geol., 1971-74; W.R. Kenan Jr. prof. geology U. N.C., Chapel Hill, 1975-97, W.R. Kenan Jr. prof. geology emeritus, 1997—. Author: A History of the Earth, 1993, History and Environment of North Carolina's Piedmont, 1999; co-author: Fundamentals of Geology, 1966, Precambrian Geology of India, 1987, Continents and Supercontinents, 2004; co-editor: Holocene Geology of Galveston Bay, 1969, Precambrian of South India, 1983, Basalts, 1984, African Rifting, 1989, People and the Earth, 1998; regional editor Jour. African Earth Scis., 1982-93; contbr. articles to profl. jours. Fellow Geol. Soc. Am., Geol. Soc. India, Geol. Soc. Africa (hon.); mem. Am. Assn. Petroleum Geologists. Home: 114 Woodbridge Ln Chapel Hill NC 27514 Office: U NC Dept Geology CB 3315 Chapel Hill NC 27599-0001 E-mail: jjwr@mac.com.

**ROGERS, JOHN MARSHALL**, judge, law educator; b. Rochester, NY, June 26, 1948; s. Harry Lovejoy III and Virginia Kathryn (Meyers) R.; m. Ying Juan Xiong, 1990. BA, Stanford U., 1970; JD, U. Mich., 1974. Bar: D.C. 1975, Ky. 1980, U.S. Ct. Appeals, U.S. Supreme Ct. Commd. USAR, 1970; appellate atty. civil div. U.S. Dept. Justice, Washington, 1974-78; asst. prof. U. Ky., Lexington, 1978-81, assoc. prof., 1981-86, prof., 1986—2002, prof. emeritus, 2002—; cir. judge U.S. Ct. Appeals for Sixth Cir., 2002—. Vis. prof. Civil Divsn. U.S. Dept. Justice, Washington, 1983-85; Fulbright lectr. Fgn. Affairs Coll., Beijing, 1987-88, Zhongshan U., Guangzhou, People's Republic of China, 1994-95; spl. counsel impeachment com. Ky. Ho. of Reps., 1991. Author: Internat. Law and U.S. Law, 1999; contbr. articles to profl. jours. Mem. Coun. on Fgn. Rels., Am. Law Inst., Order of Coif, Phi Beta Kappa. Office: 532 Potter Stewart US Courthouse 100 E 5th St Cincinnati OH 45202-3988 also: US Courthouse Community Trust Bank Bldg Ste 400 100 E Vine St Lexington KY 40507*

**ROGERS, JOHN W., JR.**, investment company executive; s. John W. Sr. and Jewel (Mankarious) R.; m. Sharon Fairley. AB in Econs., Princeton U., 1980. Broker William Blair & Co.; founder, chmn., CEO Ariel Capital Mgmt., LLC, Chgo., 1982—. Bd. dirs. Aon Corp., Bally Total Fitness Holding Corp., Exelon Corp., McDonald's Corp., Ariel Investment Trust. Columnist: Forbes mag. Trustee U. Chgo.; dir. Chgo. Urban League; with alumnus Leadership Greater Chgo. Named one of 50 for the Future, Time mag., 1994; recipient Disting. Fellow award, Leadership Greater Chgo., 1988, Most Influential Black Americans, Ebony mag., 2006. Office: Ariel Capital Mgmt # 2900 200 E Randolph St Chicago IL 60601-6436

**ROGERS, JOSEPH A.**, mental health association administrator; With Mental Health Assn Southeastern Pa, Phila., 1984—, exec. dir., 1997—; founder Self-Help & Advocacy Resource Exch. (Project SHARE), 1984. Mem. Congl. Task Force on the Rights & Empowerment of Americans with Disabilities; former chmn. Pa Protection & Advocacy Inc. Recipient Heinz award for the Human Condition, 2005. Office: Mental Health Assn Southeastern Pa 1211 Chestnut St Philadelphia PA 19107

**ROGERS, JUDITH ANN WILSON**, federal judge; b. NYC. 1939; AB cum laude, Radcliffe Coll., 1961; LLB, Harvard U., 1964; LLM, U. Va., 1988; LLD (hon.), D.C. Sch. Law, 1992. Bar: D.C. 1965. Law clk. Juvenile Ct. D.C., 1964-65; asst. U.S. atty. D.C., 1965-68; trial atty. San Francisco Neighborhood Legal Assistance Found., 1968-69; atty. assoc. atty.'s office U.S. Dept. Justice, 1969-71, atty. criminal divsn., 1969-71; gen. counsel Congl. Commn. on Organization of D.C. Govt., 1971-72; coordinator legis. program Office of Dep. Mayor D.C., 1972-74, spl. assist. to mayor for legis., 1974-79, corp. counsel, 1979-83; assoc. judge D.C. Ct. Appeals, 1983-88, chief judge, 1988-94; judge U.S. Ct. Appeals (D.C. cir.), 1994—. Mem. D.C. Law Revision Commn., 1979-83; mem. grievance com. U.S. Dist. Ct. D.C., 1982-83; mem. exec. com. Conf. Chief Justices, 1993-94. Bd. dirs. Wider Opportunities for Women, 1972-74; mem. vis. com. Harvard U. Sch. Law, 1984-90; trustee Radcliffe Coll., 1982-88. Recipient citation for work on D.C. Self-Govt. Act, 1973, Disting. Pub. Svc. award D.C. Govt., 1983, award Nat. Bar Assn., 1989; named Woman Lawyer of Yr., Women's Bar Assn. D.C., 1990. Fellow ABA; mem. D.C. Bar, Nat. Assn. Women Judges, Conf. Chief Justices (bd. dirs. 1988-94), Am. Law Inst., Phi Beta Kappa. Office: US Ct Appeals Fed Cir 717 Madison Pl NW Washington DC 20001-2866 also: US Courthouse 333 Constitution Ave NW STE 5800 Washington DC 20001*

**ROGERS, JUSTIN TOWNER, JR.**, retired utility company executive; b. Sandusky, Ohio, Aug. 4, 1929; s. Justin Towner and Barbara Eloise (Larkin) R. AB cum laude, Princeton U., 1951; JD, U. Mich., 1954. Bar: Ohio 1954. Assoc. Wright, Harlor, Purpus, Morris & Arnold, Columbus, 1956-58; with Ohio Edison Co., Akron, 1958-93, v.p., then exec. v.p., 1970-79, pres., 1980-91, chmn. bd., 1991-93; ret., 1993. Past mem. coal adv. bd. Internat. Energy Agy. Past pres., trustee Akron Cmty. Trusts, Akron Child Guidance Ctr.; past chmn. Akron Assoc. Health Agys., U. Akron Assocs., Ohio Electric Utility Inst.; past chmn., trustee, Akron Gen. Health Sys.; trustee Sisler McFawn Found.; former trustee Stan Hywet Hall & Gardens, VNS-Hospice Found.; past dir. Edison Elec. Inst., Elec. Power Rsch. Inst., Assn. of Edison

---

Illuminating Co.'s. Mem. Portage Country Club, Mayflower Club, Rockwell Springs Trout Club (Castalia, Ohio), Princeton Club (NYC), Columbus Beach Club, Phi Delta Phi, Beta Gamma Sigma.

**ROGERS, KATHARINE MUNZER**, retired English language educator, writer; b. NYC, June 6, 1932; d. Martin and Jean (Thompson) Munzer; B.A. summa cum laude, Barnard Coll., 1952; Fulbright scholar, Newnham Coll., Cambridge U., 1952-53; Ph.D., Columbia U., 1957; m. Kenneth C. Rogers, Aug. 4, 1956; children: Margaret, Christopher, Thomas. Instr. English, Skidmore Coll., Saratoga Springs, N.Y., 1954-55, Cornell U., 1955-57; lectr. to prof. English, Bklyn. Coll., 1958-88; mem. doctoral faculty CUNY, 1972-88. Author: The Troublesome Helpmate: A History of Misogyny in Literature, 1966; William Wycherley, 1972; Feminism in Eighteenth Century England, 1982; Frances Burney: The World of "Female Difficulties", 1990, The Cat and the Human Imagination, 1998, L. Frank Baum: Creator of Oz: A Biography, 2002, First Friend: A History of Dogs and Humans, 2005. Editor anthologies: The Signet Classic Book of 18th and 19th Century British Drama; Selected Writings of Samuel Johnson, 1981, The Meridian Anthology of Early American Women Writers, 1991, The Meridian Anthology of Restoration & Eighteenth Century Plays by Women, 1994; co-editor: (with William McCarthy) The Meridian Anthology of Early Women Writers: British Literary Women from Aphra Behn to Maria Edgeworth, 1987. Contbr. articles to profl. jours.

**ROGERS, KENNETH DONALD**, entertainer, recording artist; b. Houston, Aug. 21, 1938; s. Edward Floyd and Lucille (Hester) R.; m. Janice Gordon, 1958 (div. 1960), 1 child: Carole; m. Jean Rogers, 1960 (div. 1963); m. Margo Anderson, 1964 (div. 1976), 1 child: Kenneth; m. Marianne Gordon, 1977 (div. 1993), 1 child: Christopher Cody; m. Wanda Miller, June 1, 1997; children: Justin Charles, Jordan Edward. Student, U. Houston. Founder Kenny Roger's Roasters. Recording artist, Liberty Records, 1976-82, RCA Records, 1983-88, Warner Records, 1988-93, Atlantic Records, 1993-94, Magnatone Records, 1996-97, co-founder and rec. artist, Dreamcatcher Entertainment, 1998-2000. Appeared on American Bandstand, 1958; mem. Bobby Doyle Trio, 1959-66, Christy Minstrels, 1966-67, The First Edition, 1967-69, Kenny Rogers and The First Edition, 1969-75, pursued solo career, 1975—; hosted TV spls. Kenny Rogers Classic Weekend, 1988-90, Kenny, Dolly & Willie, 1989, Kenny Rogers in Concert, 1989, Goodwill Games, 1990; starred in TV series Rollin' with The First Edition, 1972; appeared in movies Six Pack, 1982; TV appearances include The Muppet Show, 1979, Evening Shade, 1991, A&E The Real West, 1993, MacShayne, 1994, Touched by an Angel, 2000, Reno 911, 2004; appeared in TV movies: Kenny Rogers as the Gambler, 1980, Coward of the County, 1981, Gambler, Part II, 1983, Gambler III: The Adventure Continues, 1987, Christmas in America, 1989, The Gambler Returns, Gamvler IV: The Luck of the Draw, 1991, Rio Diablo, 1993, Gambler V: Playing for Keeps, 1994, Big Dreams & Broken Hearts: The Dottie West Story, 1995; recordings include: That Crazy Feeling (Gold single), I Don't Need You (Brit. Country Music Assn. award, Acad. Country Music award), Love is What We Make It, 1985, The Heart of the Matter, 1985, They Don't Make Them Like They Used To, What About Me, I Prefer the Moonlight, 1987, When You Put Your Heart in It, 1988 (ofcl. theme song U.S. Gymnastics Fedn.), Christmas in America, 1989, Love Is Strange, 1990, Greatest Country Hits, 1990, If Only My Heart Had a Voice, 1993, Greatest Hits, 1994; albums include Kenny Rogers-Lucille, 1976, Love or Something Like It, 1978, The Gambler, 1978, Kenny, 1979, Gideon, 1980, Share Your Love, 1981, Eyes That See in the Dark, 1983, Something Inside So Strong, 1989, Timepiece, 1994, The Gift, 1996, Across My Heart, 1997, Christmas From the Heart, 1998, She Rides Wild Horses, 1999, Christmas Greetings, 2000, There You Go Again, 2000, The Way It Used to Be, 2001, Calico Silver, 2002, Heart of the Matter, 2003, Christmas with Kenny, 2004, Water & Bridges, 2006, After Dark, 2006; author: Kenny Roger's America, 1986, Your Friends and Mine, 1987. Hon. capt. 1988 U.S. Gymnastics Team. Named Cross-Over Artist of Year Billboard mag., 1977, named Top Male vocalist People mag., 1979, 80; recipient Country Music Assn. award, 1978, 79, Am. Music award, Best Male Vocalist, Best Album, 1984, Am. Music award, Best Male Country Vocalist, Best Album, 1985, Country Music Found. Roy Acuff award, 1985, UN Peace award, 1984, Rec. Industry Assn. Am. Most Awarded Artist award, 1984 (11 platinum, 18 gold albums), Grammy award for best male country vocal, 1977, 79, co-recipient (with Ronnie Milsap) for best country vocal duet, 1987, 1st Harry Chapin award for humanitarianism ASCAP, 1988, Horatio Alger award, 1990, Awd. for sales in excess of ten million copies for "Greatest Hits", Lifetime Achievement Awd., Songwriters Hall of Fame, N.A.R.M. Chmns. Awd. for Sustained Achievement, 1999; numerous other music awards.*

**ROGERS, KENNY (KENNETH SCOTT ROGERS)**, professional baseball player; b. Savannah, Ga., Nov. 10, 1964; Student, Plant City, Fla. Pitcher Texas Rangers, 1989-95, 2000—02, 2004—, NY Yankees, 1996—97, Oakland A's, 1998—99, New York Mets, 1999, Toronto Blue Jays, 1999, Minnesota Twins, 2003. Named to Am. League All-Star Team, 1995, 2004, 2005; pitched perfect game against Calif. Angels, 1994, recipient Am. League Gold Glove Award, 2000, 2004, 2005; 200 career wins, 2006. Office: Texas Rangers 1000 Ballpark Way #400 Arlington TX 76011*

**ROGERS, LEE FRANK**, radiologist; b. Colchester, Vt., Sept. 24, 1934; s. Watson Frank and Marguerite Mortimer (Cole) R.; m. Donna Mae Brinker, June 20, 1956; children: Michelle, Cynthia, Christopher, Matthew. BS, Northwestern U., 1956, MD, 1959. Commd. 2d lt. U.S. Army, 1959, advanced through grades to maj., 1967; rotating intern Walter Reed Gen. Hosp., 1959-60; resident radiology Fitzsimons Gen. Hosp., 1960-63; ret., 1967; radiologist Bapt. Meml. Hosp., San Antonio, 1967-68, U. Tex. Med. Sch., San Antonio, 1968-71, dir. residency tng., radiologist Houston, 1972-74; prof., chmn. dept. radiology Northwestern U. Med. Sch., Chgo., 1974-95; editor-in-chief Am. Jour. Roentgenology, Winston-Salem, NC, 1995—2003; prof. radiology U. Ariz. Health Scis. Ctr., 2003—. Fellow Am. Coll. Radiology (past pres.), Am. Roentgen Ray Soc. (past pres.); mem. Assn. Univ. Radiologists (past pres.), Radiol. Soc. N.Am., Am. Bd. Radiology (past pres.), Alpha Omega Alpha. Episcopalian. Home: 8235 N Fairway View Dr Tucson AZ 85742 Office Phone: 520-626-6794. Personal E-mail: lfrogers@comcast.net. *The source of most problems is previous solutions.*

**ROGERS, MALCOLM AUSTIN**, museum director, art historian; b. Scarborough, Yorkshire, Eng., Oct. 3, 1948; s. James Eric and Frances Anne (Elsey) R. BA in English Language & Literature, Oxford U.; MA, Magdalen Coll., U. Oxford, Eng., 1976; DPhil, Oxford U., 1976. Asst. keeper Nat. Portrait Gallery, London, 1974-83, dep. dir., 1983—85, dep. keeper, 1985—94; Ann and Graham Gund dir. Mus. Fine Arts, Boston, 1994—. Noted authority on 16th, 17th & early 18th century portraits. Author: Blue Guide: Museums and Galleries of London, 1983; contbr. articles to profl. publs. Mem. Harvard overseers' com. Visit the Art Mus.; trustee Found. for the Arts, Nagoya, Japan, Wednesday Evening Club of 1777, Club of Odd Volumes. Comdr. British Empire, 2004. Fellow Soc. Antiquaries; mem. Thursday Evening Club of 1846, Comml. Club Boston. Avocations: wine and food, travel, opera. Home: 540 Chestnut Hill Ave Brookline MA 02445-4155 Office: Mus Fine Arts 465 Huntington Ave Boston MA 02115-5597 E-Mail: mrogers@mfa.org.

**ROGERS, MARK CHARLES**, physician, entrepreneur, anesthesiologist, pediatrician, educator; b. NYC, Oct. 25, 1942; s. Gerald and Inez Rogers; m. Elizabeth; children: Bradley, Meredith. BA, Columbia U., 1964; MD, SUNY, Syracuse, 1969; MBA, U. Pa., 1991; PhD (hon.), U. Ljubljana Slovenia, 1995. Diplomate Am. Bd. Anesthesiology (examiner 1982-96), Am. Bd. Pediatrics. Intern Mass. Gen. Hosp., Boston, 1969-70, resident, 1973-75, Boston Children's Hosp., 1970-71; fellow Duke U. Med. Ctr., Durham, NC, 1971-73; asst. prof. dept. anesthesiology and critical care medicine Johns Hopkins U., Balt., 1977-79, assoc. prof., 1979-80, prof., chmn. dept., 1980-93, assoc. dean Sch. Medicine, 1990-93, dir. pediatric ICU, 1977-93; CEO Duke Hosp. and Health Network, 1993-96; sr. v.p. Perkin Elmer, Wilton, Conn., 1996-98; pres. Paramount Capital, N.Y.C., 1998—2002; chmn. Cardiome Pharma, 2002—, Adherex Pharma, 2002—04, Aptamera,

---

2004—05, Bradmer Ventures, LLC, 2004—, Bradmer Pharm., 2005—. Pres. Critical Care Found., Balt., 1981-96; cons. WHO, Bangkok, 1982-83. Editor in chief: Yearbook of Critical Care, 1983-96, Textbook of Pediatric Intensive Care, 1987, 91, 96, Principles and Practices of Anesthesiology, 1990; editor: Perioperative Management, 1989, dep. editor in chief Critical Care Medicine Jour., 1990-96. Maj. U.S. Army, 1975-77. Recipient Club of Mainz award, Mainz, Fed. Republic of Germany, 1981, award Assn. Univ. Anesthetists, 1980; Fulbright scholar, Ljubljana, Yugoslavia, 1990. Mem. NAS, Inst. Medicine. Home: 7772 Fisher Island Dr Miami Beach FL 33109 E-mail: mrogers@bradmer.com.

**ROGERS, MICHAEL ALAN**, writer; b. Santa Monica, Calif., Nov. 29, 1950; s. Don Easterday and Mary Othilda (Gilbertson) R.; m. Donna Rini, Oct. 9, 2000. BA in Creative Writing, Stanford U., 1972. Assoc. editor Rolling Stone Mag., San Francisco, 1972-76; editor-at-large Outside mag., San Francisco, 1976-78; vis. lectr. fiction U. Calif., Davis, 1980; sr. writer Newsweek mag., San Francisco, 1983—; mng. editor Newsweek InterActive, San Francisco, 1993-97; exec. prodr. broadband divsn. The Washington Post Co., 1995-96; v.p. Washingtonpost.Newsweek Interactive, 1996—2004. Editor, gen. mgr. Newsweek.MSNBC.com, NYC, 1998-2004, columnist, 2005—; prin. Practical Futurist, 2005-; futurist-in-residence NY Times, 2006-. Author: Mindfogger, 1973, Biohazard, 1977, Do Not Worry About The Bear, 1979, Silicon Valley, 1982, Forbidden Sequence, 1988; contbr. articles to mags., newspapers. Recipient Disting. Sci. Writing award AAAS, 1976, Best Feature Articles award Computer Press Assn., 1987. Mem. Author Guild, Sierra Club. Achievements include patents for for multimedia storytelling technology. Avocations: travel, hiking. Address: 535 Dean St # 704 Brooklyn NY 11217 E-mail: mr@practicalfuturist.com.

**ROGERS, MICHAEL BRUCE**, orthodontist; b. Augusta, Ga., Aug. 25, 1945; s. Bruce Latimer and Dorothy (Baird) R.; m. Elizabeth Bennett, Dec. 21, 1968; children: Bruce, Kay, Alison, Lisa. Student, Emory U., 1963-65, DDS, 1969; cert. in orthodontics, Med. Coll. Ga., 1973. Diplomate Am. Bd. Orthodontists. Pvt. practice orthodontia, Augusta, 1973—. Part-time asst. clin. prof. Sch. Dentistry, Med. Coll. Ga., Augusta, 1973—. Capt. Dental Corps U.S. Army, 1971-73. Decorated Army Commendation medal. Fellow: Ga. Acad. Dental Practice, The Internat. Acad. Dentists, Pierre Fauchard Acad., Ga. Dental Assn. (hon.; spkr. ho. of dels. 1999—2004, v.p. 2004—05, pres.-elect 2005—06, pres. 2006), Internat. Acad. Dental Studies, Am. Coll. Dentists; mem.: Ea. Dist. Dental Soc. (pres. 1982—83), Med. Coll. Ga. Orthodontic Alumni Assn. (pres. 1981—83), Ga. Assn. Orthodontists (v.p. 1983—84, pres. 1984—85, exemplary svc. award), So. Assn. Orthodontists (spokesperson, sec.-treas. 1993—95, dir. 1995, pres. 2000, Disting. Svc. award 2001—), Am. Assn. Orthodontists (Ga. del., chmn. mem., ethics and jud. conderns, spkr. of house 1995—97, trustee 2002—), ADA (del.), Omicron Kappa Upsilon, Psi Omega (pres. 1967—68). Roman Catholic. Home: 3214 Candace Dr Augusta GA 30909-3259 Office: 3545 Wheeler Rd Augusta GA 30909-6517

**ROGERS, MICHAEL E.**, exercise physiology educator, researcher; b. Seneca Falls, N.Y. s. Philip W. and Martha A. Rogers; m. Nicole L. Dassinger. BS in Sports Medicine, Mt. Union Coll., Alliance, Ohio, 1991; PhD, Kent State U., 1996. Cert. strength and conditioning specialist Nat. Strength and Conditioning Assoc., 2000. Rsch. assoc. Brooks AFB, San Antonio, 1996—98; assoc. prof. Wichita (Kans.) State U., 1998—. Rsch. dir. Ctr. for Phys. Activity and Aging Wichita State U., 1999—. Contbr. articles to profl. jours. Mem.: Am. Coll. Sports Medicine (pres. regional chpt. 2002—02). Achievements include development of low cost, safe, and effective physical activity programs to improve strength and balance in older adults. Office: Wichita State Univ 110 Heskett Ctr Wichita KS 67260-0016 Business E-Mail: michael.rogers@wichita.edu.

**ROGERS, MIKE (MICHAEL J. ROGERS)**, congressman; b. Livonia, Mich., June 2, 1963; m. Diane Rogers; 1 child. BA in Sociology and Criminal Justice, Adrian Coll., 1985. Spl. agt. FBI, 1989—94; small bus. owner; mem. Mich. Senate from 26th dist., 1995-2000; vice chmn. judiciary com. Mich. Senate. mem. fin. svc., human resources, labor and vet affairs coms., mem. reappropriations com., mem. tech. and energy commn., mem. banking and fin. com.; mem. US Congress from Mich. 8th dist., Washington, 2001—; mem. fin. svcs. and transp. coms.; mem. Com. on Energy and Commerce. Bd. trustees Cleary Coll., Mich. Served as 2nd Lt. rapid deployment U.S. Army, 1985—88. Recipient Nextel Prepared award, Nextel Comm. Inc., 2004, ITS Congl. Champion awrad, Intelligent Transp. Systems Am., 2005, Joseph M. Magliochetti Industry Champion award, Motor and Equipment Manufacturers Assn., 2005. Mem.: Soc. Former Spl. Agents for FBI, Home Builders Assn., Livingston County, Mich., Am. Heart Assn. Republican. Meth. Office: US Congress 133 Cannon HOB Washington DC 20515-2208 also: District Office 1327 E Michigan Ave Lansing MI 48912 Office Phone: 202-225-4872, 517-702-8000. Office Fax: 202-225-5820, 517-702-8642.*

**ROGERS, MIKE**, congressman; b. Hammond, Ind., July 16, 1958; m. Beth Rogers; children: Emily, Evan, Elliot. BA in Polit. Sci., Jacksonville State U., 1981, MPA, 1983; JD, U. Birmingham, 1991. Dir., dislocated worker's project United Way of Etowah County; community rep., psychiatric counselor Northeast Ala. Regional Med. Ctr.; atty. Bolt, Isom, Jackson and Bailey; assoc. then ptnr. Rogers, Young, Wollstein and Hughes; mem. Ala. Ho. Reps., 1994—2002; congressman 3rd Dist. Ala. U.S. Ho. Reps., 2003—. Mem. Calhoun County Commn., 1987—91; active State Rep. Exec. Com., 1990—. Republican. Baptist. Office: US Ho of Reps 514 Cannon Ho Office Bldg Washington DC 20515-0103

**ROGERS, MIMI**, actress; b. Coral Gables, Fla., Jan. 27, 1956; m. Jim Rogers, 1977 (div. 1980); m. Tom Cruise, May 9, 1987 (div. 1990); m. Chris Ciaffa, Mar. 20, 2003; children: Lucy Julia, Charlie. Appeared in films Blue Skies Again, 1983, Gung Ho, 1985, Someone to Watch over Me, 1987, Street Smart, 1987, Hider in the House, 1989, The Mighty Quinn, 1989, Desperate Hours, 1990, The Palermo Connections, 1990, The Doors, 1991, The Rapture, 1991, Dark Horse, 1992, The Player, 1992, Monkey Trouble, 1994. Far From Home: The Adventures of Yellow Dog, 1995, Lost in Space, 1998, Austin Powers: International Man of Mystery, 1997, Seven Girlfriends, 1999, Ginger Snaps, 2000, The Upgrade, 2000, Dumb and Dumberer: When Harry Met Lloyd, 2003, Seeing Other People, 2004, The Gunman, 2004, The Door in the Floor, 2004, Dancing in Twilight, 2005, others; appeared on TV series The Rousters, 1983-84, Paper Dolls, 1984, The Geena Davis Show, 2000, The Loop, 2006-; appeared on TV spls. and pilots; TV movies include Divorce Wars, 1982, Deadlock, 1991, Fourth Story, 1991, Ladykiller, 1992, A Kiss to Die For, 1993, Tricks, 1997, The Christmas List, 1997, Weapons of Mass Distraction, 1997, Virtual Obsession, 1998, Host, 1998, Devil's Arithmetic, 1999, Manchester Prep, 1999, Common Ground, 2000, My Horrible Year!, 2001, Reel Comedy: Austin Powers in Goldmember, 2002, Charms for the Easy Life, 2002, Cave In, 2003, Stone Cold, 2005, Selling Innocence, 2005. Office: Creative Artists Agy c/o Jane Berliner 9830 Wilshire Blvd Beverly Hills CA 90212-1825*

**ROGERS, NANCY HARDIN**, dean, law educator; b. Lansing, Mich., Sept. 18, 1948; d. Clifford Morris and Martha (Wood) Hardin; m. Douglas Langston Rogers, Jan. 30, 1970; children: Lynne, Jill, Kim. BA with highest distinction, U. Kans., 1969; JD, Yale U., 1972. Bar: D.C. 1975, Ohio 1972, U.S. Ct. Appeals (6th cir.) 1973, U.S. Dist. Ct. (no. dist.) Ohio 1974, U.S. Dist. Ct. (so. dist.) Ohio 1975. Law clk. U.S. Dist. Judge Thomas D. Lambros, Cleve., 1972-74; staff atty. Cleve. Legal Aid Soc., 1974-75; vis. assoc. prof. Coll. of Law Ohio State U., Columbus, 1975-76, asst. prof., 1976-78, 83-89, assoc. prof., 1989-92, prof., assoc. dean acad. affairs, 1992-97, prof., 1992—; Joseph S. Platt, Porter, Wright, Morris & Arthur prof. law Columbus, 1995—2001, vice provost acad. adminstrn., 1999—2001, dean, Michael E. Moritz chair in alternative dispute resolution Michael E. Moritz Coll. Law, 2001—. Adj. prof. Ohio State Coll., 1981-83; vis. prof. law Harvard Law Sch., 2000. Author (with Frank E.A. Sander, Sarah R. Cole, Stephen B. Goldberg): (Book) Dispute Resolution: Negotiation, Mediation and Other Processes), 2003; author: (book with Craig A. McEwen and Sarah R. Cole)

Mediation: Law, Policy, Practice, 2nd edit., 1994; mem. (adv. bd.) World Arbitration and Mediation Report, 1991—, Alternatives, 1992—, co-chair (editl. bd. with Frank E.A. Sander) Dispute Resolution mag., 1994—2002; contbr. chapters to books, articles to profl. jours. Bd. dirs. Assn. for Developmentally Disabled, Columbus, 1980-85; Legal Svcs. Corp. 1995-2003. Named Outstanding Prof., Ohio State U. Coll. Law Alumni Assn., 1996; recipient Book prize, Ctr. Pub. Resources for A Student's Guide to Mediation and the Law, 1987, Ctr. Pub. Resources for Mediation: Law, Policy, Practice, 1989, Peacemaker of Yr. award, Comty. Mediation Svcs. Ctrl. Ohio, 1990, Disting. Svc. Recognition, Soc. Profls. in Dispute Resolution, 1990, Whitney North Seymour sr. medal, Am. Arbitration Assn., 1990, Svc. Recognition award, Legal Aid Soc. Columbus, 1996, Ritter award, Ohio State Bar Found for outstanding contbns. to adminstrn. of justice, 1998; grantee Exxon Edn. Found., 1986, William and Flora Hewlett Found., 1990, Ohio State U. Interdisciplinary Seed, 1990, Ohio State U. Symposium, 1992, William and Flora Hewlett Found., 1992—96, Nat. Sci. Found., 1993—95, State Justice Instn., 1994, Fund for Improvement Post-Secondary Edn., U. Mo., 1996—97, William and Flora Hewlett Found., 1997—2003. Mem. ABA (chair, standing com. dispute resolution 1988-91, D'Alemberte-Raven award sect. on dispute resolution 2002), Assn. Am. Law Schs. (pres.-elect 2006—), Phi Beta Kappa. Office: Ohio State U Coll Law 55 W 12th Ave Columbus OH 43210-1306 Office Phone: 614-292-0574. Business E-Mail: rogers.23@osu.edu.

**ROGERS, PATRICIA LOUISE,** education educator, consultant; b. St. Paul, 1956; life ptnr. W. S. Larson. BS, U. Minn., Twin Cities, 1979, MA, 1982, PhD, 1997. Lic. tchr. art and theatre Minn., 1979. Tchr. St. Paul Schs. 1979—82; cancer rschr. U. Minn. Sch. Pub. Health, Mpls., 1984—95; prof. Bemidji State U., Minn., 1996—2006; dean Sch. Edn. and Grad. Studies Valley City State U., ND, 2006—. Cons. and trainer for online tchg. Minn. State Colls. and Univs., Twin Cities, cons., 1998—; spkr. in field. Editor: (book) Designing Instruction for Technology-Enhanced Learning, Ency. of Distance Learning, Teaching, Technologies and Applications; contbr. articles to profl. jours. Vice chair Minn. Online Coun., 2003—04, chair, 2004—. Grantee, Minn. State Colls. and Univs. under a FIPSE Grant, 2001—02; scholar, Fulbright, Coun. for Internat. Exch. Scholars, 2000—01; Dissertation fellow, Getty Ctr. for Arts in Edn., 1996. Mem.: Nat. Art Edn. Assn., Assn. for Ednl. Comm. and Tech., Rotary Internat. (assoc.). Dfl. Office: Valley City State Univ Sch Edn and Grad Studies 101 College St SW Valley City ND 58072 Office Phone: 701-845-7300. Business E-Mail: patricia.rogers@vcsu.edu.

**ROGERS, PAUL A'COURT,** management consulting executive; b. Detroit, Oct. 12, 1939; s. Noel and Jessie (Adams) Rogers; 1 child, Ashley. BSBA, U. Md., 1982. Field engr. Gen. Dynamics, Pomona, Calif., 1962—65, project mgr., 1968—72; field engr. Hughes Aircraft Co., L.A., 1965—68; sys. engr. Sci. Mgmt. Assocs., Riverdale, Md., 1972—73, program mgr., 1975—82, corp. planner, 1982—; pres. R & M Assocs., 1989—; pres./CEO Parinc Corp. Project mgr. Sys. Cons., Washington, 1973—75; bd. dirs. Applied Sys. Planning, Mut. Human Concerns. With USNR, 1959—62. Mem.: Am. Soc. Naval Engrs., Project Mgmt. Inst., Am. Mktg. Assn., Am. Mgmt. Assn., Naval Inst. Democrat. Presbyterian. Home: 7524 Republic Ct Alexandria VA 22306 E-mail: paul_acourt@msn.com.

**ROGERS, PAULA MCGIVERN,** secondary school educator; d. Thomas and Lois Gregory McGivern; m. Paula McGivern, Aug. 4, 1990; children: Matthew John, Christina Marie. M in Reading, Cen. Conn. State U., 1989. Profl. tchg. cert. Conn. Tchr. grades 5-8 Indian Mountain Sch., Lakeville, Conn., 1979—88; tchr. grades 6-8 lang. arts Kingswood Oxford Sch., West Hartford, Conn., 1988—89; tchr. grades 6-8 English Lee H. Kellogg Sch., Falls Village, Conn., 1989—. Lang. arts coord. Lee H. Kellogg Sch., Falls Village, 2000—. Avocations: reading, scrapbooks, knitting. Office Phone: 860-824-7791.

**ROGERS, PETER PHILLIPS,** environmental engineer, educator, urban planner; b. Liverpool., England, Apr. 30, 1937; arrived in U.S., 1960, naturalized, 1970; s. Edward Joseph and Ellen (Duggan) R.; m. Suzanne Ogden, Oct. 24, 1998; children: Christopher, Justin. B in Engring., Liverpool U., 1958; MS, Northwestern U., 1961; PhD, Harvard U., 1966. Asst. engr. Sir Alfred McAlpine & Sons Ltd., Cheshire, Eng., 1958-60; mem. faculty Harvard U., 1966—, Gordon McKay prof. environ. engring., 1974—, prof. city planning, 1974—. Mem. Ctr. for Environment Harvard U., 2002—; cons. World Bank, UN, U.S. Agy. for Internat. Devel., Govt. India, Govt. Pakistan, Govt. Bangladesh, Govt. Nepal, Govt. Italy, Govt. Costa Rica, Commonwealth P.R. Co-author: Urbanization and Change, 1970, Land Use and The Pipe: Planning for Sewerage, 1975, Resource Inventory and Baseline Study Methods for Developing Countries, 1983, Systems Analysis for River Basin Management, 1985, Evaluacion de Projectos de Desarrollo, 1990, America's Waters, 1993, Water in the Arab World, 1994, Measuring Environmental Quality in Asia, 1997, Science with a Human Face, 1997, Water Crisis: Myth or Reality, 2006, Introduction to Sustainable Development, 2006. Mem. World Commn. for Water in 21st Century. Gordon McKay tchg. fellow 1961; Radley rsch. student, 1962-64; doctoral dissertation fellow Resources for Future 1964-65; recipient Clemens Herschel prize Harvard U., 1964; Guggenheim fellow, 1973, 20th Century Found. fellowship, 1989, Maass-White fellow U.S. Army C.E., 2003. Mem.: ASCE, Third World Acad. Scis. (corr.), Indian Inst. Agrl. Engring. (life), Cambridge Univ. Club, Cosmos Club (Washington). Home: 20 Berkeley St Cambridge MA 02138 Office: Harvard U 116 Pierce Hall Cambridge MA 02138 Office Phone: 617-495-2025. Business E-Mail: rogers@deas.harvard.edu.

**ROGERS, RAYMOND JESSE,** retired federal railroad associate administrator; b. Eugene, Oreg., Mar. 1, 1941; s. Raymond Everett and Virginia Elaine (Simpkins) R.; m. Joan Katherine Peterson, June 6, 1964 (div. 1974); 1 child, Virginia Arlene; m. Kim Lien Nguyen, Dec. 26, 1974; children: Kim Lan, Vincent Minh. Student, Santa Rosa (Calif.) Jr. Coll., 1960-61, U.S. Army Non-commd. Officer Acad., Anchorage, Alaska, 1963, U. Md., 1967-74, Fed. Exec. Inst., Charlottsville, Va., 1981. Lic. real estate agt., Va. Sr. asst. mgr. Household Fin. Corp., Md., 1964-67; contract specialist Dept. Navy, Washington, 1967-71; contract svcs. officer AID, Saigon, Vietnam, 1971-76; contracting officer Dept. Transp., Fed. R.R. Adminstrn., Washington, 1976-80, dir. fin. svcs., 1980-84, assoc. adminstr. for adminstrn., 1984—2002, CFO, CIO, 1994—2002, ret., 2002. Leader local group Boy Scouts Am., Vienna, Va., 1987-92, Izaac Walton League of Am., Am. Legion, Am. Assn. of Retired Persons. Sgt. U.S. Army, 1961-64. Decorated Vietnam Civilian Svc. medal. Mem. U.S. Sr. Exec. Svc., Fed. Exec. Inst. Alumni Assn. Avocations: fishing, hiking, camping, waterskiing. Home: 102 Yeonas Dr SW Vienna VA 22180-6557 Personal E-mail: Rayvin78@aol.com.

**ROGERS, RICHARD DEAN,** federal judge; b. Oberlin, Kans., Dec. 29, 1921; s. William Clark and Evelyn May (Christian) R.; m. Helen Elizabeth Stewart, June 6, 1947; children— Letitia Ann, Cappi Christian, Richard Kurt. BS, Kans. State U., 1943; JD, Kans. U., 1947. Bar: Kans. 1947. Ptnr. firm Springer and Rogers (Attys.), Manhattan, Kans., 1947-58; instr. bus. law Kans. State U., 1948-52; partner firm Rogers, Stites & Hill, Manhattan, 1959-75; gen. counsel Kans. Farm Bur. & Service Cos., Manhattan, 1960-75; judge U.S. Dist. Ct., Topeka, Kans., 1975—. City commr., Manhattan, 1950-52, 60-64, mayor, 1952, 64, county atty., Riley County, Kans., 1954-58, state rep., 1964-68, state senator, 1968—. Kans. Senate, 1975. Served with USAAF, 1943-46. Decorated Air medal, Dfc. Mem. Kans., Am. bar assns., Beta Theta Pi. Clubs: Masons. Republican. Presbyterian. Office: US Dist Ct 444 SE Quincy St Topeka KS 66683 Office Phone: 785-295-2735.

**ROGERS, RICHARD HILTON,** hotel executive; b. Florence, SC, May 26, 1935; s. Leslie Vaughan and Bessie (Holloway) R.; m. Evelyn Pasciuto; children: Richard Shannon, Leslie Anne. Student, U. N.C., 1953-55; BA in Bus. Adminstrn. cum laude, Bryant U., 1961; postgrad., Memphis State U., 1964; DHL (hon.), Schiller Internat. U. Innkeeper Helmsley Spear, N.Y.C., 1961-62; v.p. Holiday Inns of Am., Memphis, 1962-73; exec. v.p. First Hospitality Corp., Hackensack, NJ, 1974-77; v.p., chief oper. officer Cindy's

Inc., Atlanta, 1978-82; v.p. 1982 World's Fair, Knoxville, Tenn.; pres., chief exec. officer Hospitality Internat., Atlanta, 1982-92; dir. franchise devel. Baymont Inns, Milw., 1992, 2000. Developer, operator The Warehouse Restaurant, Oxford, Miss., 1973-75, Beauregard's Restaurant, Hattiesburg, Miss., 1975-78. Contbr. to profl. jours. Mem. adv. bd. U. South Fla. With USN, 1954-58, Korea. Mem. Am. Hotel/Motel Assn. (mktg. com. 1986-92, adv. coun. 1987-92, industry adv. bd., chmn.), Economy Lodging Coun. Avocations: sailing, photography. Home and Office: 8525 Hope Vine Roswell GA 30076 Personal E-mail: innkeeper@charter.net.

**ROGERS, RICHARD HUNTER,** lawyer; b. Flushing, N.Y., Sept. 11, 1939; s. Royden Harrison and Frances Wilma (Hunter) R.; children: Gregory P., Lynne A., Reade H. BS in Bus. Adminstrn, Miami U., 1961; JD, Duke, 1964. Bar: Ill. 1964, Ohio 1973. Atty. Continental Ill. Nat. Bank, Chgo., 1964-65; sr. atty. Brunswick Corp., Chgo., 1965-70; corporate counsel The A. Epstein Cos., Inc. (real estate developers), Chgo., 1970-73; v.p., gen. counsel, sec. Price Bros. Co., Dayton, Ohio, 1973-82; v.p., divsn. mgr. Water Systems Tech. div. Price Bros. Co., Dayton, Ohio, 1982-85; pres. Internat. divsn. Price Bros. Co., Dayton, Ohio, 1986—88; pvt. practice law Dayton, 1988—; pres. Richard H. Rogers & Assocs. LPA. Pres. adv. coun. Miami U. Bus. Sch.; bd. dirs. Red and White Club, Miami U.; mem. Washington Twp. Task Force on Future Govt.; trustee Woodhaven, Inc.; mem. Washington Twp. Zoning Commn., 1990—, chmn., 1999—. Mem. ABA (forum com. on constrn.), Ill. Bar Assn., Ohio Bar Assn., Dayton Bar Assn. (chmn. corp. law dept. com. 1983-84, exec. com. 1986-87, editor Bar Briefs 1990-91), Miami U. Alumni Assn. (pres.), Miami U. Pres.'s Club. Office: 7333 Paragon Rd Ste 200 Dayton OH 45459-4157 Address: PO Box 751144 Dayton OH 45475-1144 Office Phone: 937-438-0555. Personal E-mail: rhrlawoffice@aol.com.

**ROGERS, RICHARD RAYMOND,** cosmetics company executive; b. Houston, Apr. 15, 1943; s. J. Ben and Mary Kay (Ash) Rogers; children: Terri, Rick, Ryan. BA, North Tex. State U. Co-founder Mary Kay Cosmetics, Inc., Dallas, 1963, gen. mgr., 1963—65, v.p., 1965—68, pres., 1968—87, chmn. bd., dir., 1987—. With USMCR. Named Man of Yr., North Tex. Mktg. Assn., 1968. Republican. Baptist. Office: Mary Kay Cosmetics Inc 16251 Dallas Pkwy Addison TX 75001-6801*

**ROGERS, RITA DORIS LUCK,** family nurse practitioner; b. Lincoln County, Kans., Feb. 6, 1948; d. Ernest F. and Rea N. (Nelson) Luck; m. Eugene W. Rogers, Mar. 15, 1969; children: R. Michelle, Sara J (dec.), Brandon G. Diploma, Wesley Sch. Nursing, 1969; BSN cum laude, Ft. Hays State U., 1992, MSN, 1996. RN, ARNP, Kans., Mo., Nebr.; cert. family nurse practitioner ANCC, AANP. Float, relief charge nurse Wesley Med. Ctr., Wichita, 1969-71; charge nurse Mitchell County Hosp., Beloit, Kans., 1971-72; dir. PHN III Jewell County Health Dept., Mankato, Kans., 1973-74; office nurse Dr. A.T. Llana, Superior, Nebr., 1975-76; head nurse, evening supr. Jewell County Hosp., 1977-97; family nurse practitioner Dr. Judith Butler, Superior, 1997-99; interim dir. nursing Sterling (Kans.) Presbyn. Manor, 1998-99, Kansas City Presbyn. Manor, 1999, Wichita Presbyn. Manor, 2004; nurse cons. Presbyn. Manors Mid-Am., Wichita, Kans., 1999—2003; interim nurse practitioner Statcare Minor Emergency Ctr., Salina, Kans., 2000; edn. spec. Hospice Care of Kans., Wichita, 2004; clin. edn. spec. Presbyn. Manors Mid-Am, Wichita, Kans., 2003—05; dir. health svcs. Asbury Park, Inc., Newton, 2005—. Allied health adj. faculty Cloud C.C., Concordia, Kans., 1988-2000, Perkins grant coord. North Ctrl. Kans. Area Vo-Tech., Beloit, 1988; county chair Am. Cancer Soc., Mankato, 1972-74; sec. Jewell County Mental Health Assn., 1973-75; parliamentarian Dist. XII Kans. State Nurses Assn., Topeka, 1975-79; infection control com. Brodstone Meml. Hosp., Superior, Nebr., med. staff mem., 1997-98; mem. nursing standards com. and products specifications com. Presyn. Manors of Mid-Am., 1998-2005, ind. contractor, Nation's Care Link, 2003-; cert. leader for Arthritis Found. Aquatics Program, 2004-. Columnist Rap with Rita, 1973-74. County and club leader 4-H, Jewell County, 1977-91, Mitchell County, 2000—; tchr. Sunday sch. Luth. Ch., Mankato, 1979-82. Scholar Kans. Health Found., 1993, Midwest Organ Bank, 1994, Ft. Hays State U., 1994, Dane G. Hansen Found., 1994, Kans. Nurses' Found Wesley Alumni, 1995. Mem. Am. Acad. Nurse Practitioners, Sigma Theta Tau. Avocations: gardening, crocheting, computing. Home: Rte 2 Box 252 309 N Columbus St Jewell KS 66949-9582 Office: PO Box 648 200 SW 14th St Newton KS 67114-0648 Home Fax: 785-428-7929. Business E-mail: ritar@asbury-park.org.

**ROGERS, ROBERT D.,** steel company executive; b. 1936; Grad., Yale U., 1958; MBA, Harvard U., 1962. With Tex. Industries, Inc., Dallas, 1963—, v.p. ops., 1968-70, pres., chief adminstrv. officer, 1970-74, pres., CEO, 1974—, also bd. dirs., chmn. bd. dirs., Chaparral Steel Co., Midlothian, Tex. Served with USN, 1958-60. Office: Chaparral Steel Co 300 Ward Rd Midlothian TX 76065-9646 also: Texas Industries 1341 W Mockingbird Ln Dallas TX 75247

**ROGERS, ROBERT ERNEST,** medical educator; s. Jessie H. and Willie L. (Bahr) Rogers; m. Barbara Ann Hill, May 16, 1950; children: Robert E., Jr., Stephanie Ann Thompson, Cheri Lee Heck. BS in Biology, John B. Stetson U., 1949; MD, U. Miami, 1957. Diplomate Am. Bd. Ob-Gyn. Commd. 1st lt. M.C., U.S. Army, 1952, advanced through grades to col., 1971—74; ret. U.S. Army, 1974; intern Brooke Gen. Hosp., San Antonio, 1957-58, chief resident ob-gyn, 1960-61; resident in ob-gyn Jackson Meml. Hosp., Miami, Fla., 1958-60; fellow gynecology M.D. Anderson Hosp., Houston, 1965-66; asst. chief ob-gyn Tripler Army Med. Ctr., Honolulu, 1966-69; chmn. ob-gyn Walter Reed Med. Ctr., Washington, 1969-70, Madigan Army Med. Ctr., Tacoma, 1970-74; prof. ind. U. Sch. Medicine Indpls. 1974—, also chief gynecol. div., 1974—, chief ob-gyn svd. Wishard Meml. Hosp., Indpls., 1983-87. Contbr. articles to profl. jours.; editl. bd. Jour. Am. Coll. Surgeons, 2003—. Bd. dirs. Lake Stonebridge Homeowner's Assn., 2000—03, sec., 2000—03. Recipient Army Commendation medal, 1969, Army Meritorious Service Medal, 1971, Army Legion of Merit, 1974, Army Surgeon General's "A" Prefix for Profl. Excellence, 1974. Mem.: ACS, ACOG (chmn. gynecol. practice com., commr. practice, Sci. Exhibit award Armed Forces dist. 1971, Zimmerman Cons. award Armed Forces dist.), AMA (Certificate Merit for Sci. Exhibit 1971), Felix Rutledge Soc. (pres. 1981, historian), Internat. Soc. Advancement Humanistic Studies Medicine (pres. 1997—98), Soc. Gynecol. Oncologists, Soc. Gynecol. Surgeons (pres. 1983—84). Avocations: gardening, photography. Office: Ind U Sch Medicine 550 University Blvd Indianapolis IN 46202-5149 Office Phone: 317-849-4026. Personal E-mail: Bobberogers@hotmail.com. Business E-Mail: reroger@iupui.edu.

**ROGERS, ROBERT MARK,** physician; b. Upper Darby, Pa., June 9, 1933; s. John Francis and Clara (Baumann) R.; m. Sandra Betz, Feb. 14, 1968; children: Janet Marie, Robert Mark, Linda, William Bradford, David Philip. BA cum laude, LaSalle Coll., Phila., 1956; MD, U. Pa., 1960. Intern Hosp. of U. Pa., 1960-61, chief emergency svcs., 1968-69, founder, dir. respiratory ICU, 1968-72, dir. pulmonary disease sect. tng. program, 1970-72; resident Case Western Res. U. Hosps., Cleve., 1961-63; fellow in pulmonary disease VA Hosp., Cleve., 1963-64, U. Pa., 1964-65; postdoctoral trainee in physiology, 1966-68, asst. prof. medicine and assoc. in physiology, 1968-72; prof.medicine, assoc. prof. physiology Okla. Health Scis. Ctr. Coll. Medicine, 1972-80, also chief pulmonary disease sect., dept. medicine, dir. clin. pulmonary physiology lab. hosp. and clinics; dir. Comprehensive Lung Ctr. U. Pitts. Med. Sch., 1990-97, chief pulmonary, allergy and critical care medicine, 1980-96, prof. medicine, 1980—. Editor: Respiratory Intensive Care, 1977; mem. editl. bd. Current Opinion in Pulmonary Medicine and Critical Care; contbr. rsch. articles to profl. publs. Mem. ACP (U.S. rep. to Chinese Med. Assn. 1979, founding editor-in-chief audio cassettes program 1978-80), Am. Thoracic Soc. (founding dir. Learning Resources Ctr. 1971-77, Presdl. commendation 1977, Outstanding Achievement award 2002), Am. Fedn. Clin. Rsch., Am. Coll. Chest Physicians (Presdl. citation 1998), Am. Physiol. Soc., Soc. Critical Care Medicine, Am. Heart Assn., Ctrl. Soc. Clin. Rsch., So. Soc. Clin. Rsch., Pa. Thoracic Soc. (pres. 1985-88), Coll.

Physicians Phila. Home: 4116 Bigelow Blvd Pittsburgh PA 15213-1408 Office: U Pitts Sch Medicine 628 NW Montefiore Hosp 3459 Fifth Ave Pittsburgh PA 15213 E-mail: rogersrm@msx.upmc.edu.

**ROGERS, ROBERT REED,** manufacturing executive; b. Oak Park, Ill., Feb. 22, 1929; s. Glen Charles and Lucile (Reed) R.; m. Barbara June Fain, Feb. 22, 1951 (div.); children: Robin, Janeen, Kevin; m. Celeste Sim, Sept. 29, 1993. BS in Chemistry, Berea Coll., 1951; MBA, Ill. Inst. Tech., 1958, postgrad., 1959-62. Asst. mgr. metallurgy rsch. dept. Armour Rsch. Found., Ill. Inst. Tech., Chgo. 1955-56, faculty econs. dept. 1956—62; cons. McKinsey & Co., Inc., 1962-64; mgr. devel. planning, profl. group Litton Industries, Inc., 1964-67; pres. N.Am. subs. Muirhead & Co., Ltd., 1967-68; group v.p. Am. Electric Inc. subs., City Investing Co., 1968-70; pres. Cleartight Corp., 1971-73, Newport Internat. Metals Corp., 1973-76, Kensington Assocs., Inc., Newport Beach, Calif., 1976-83; pres., chmn. bd. Proteus Group, Inc., Newport Beach, 1981-83; pres., chmn. bd. dirs. Comparator Sys. Corp., Newport Beach, 1983-96; chmn. bd. UltraCard, Inc., Newport Beach, 1997-98, Vantage Assocs. Inc., Newport Beach, 1998—. Officer USN, 1951-55. Decorated Knight of Grace Sovereign Order St. John; Machinery and Allied Products Inst. fellow, 1956-62; Berea Coll. grantee. Mem. Navy League, Mensa, Intertel. Democrat. Mem. Ch. Of Religious Science. Office: MagnaCarda Inc 5001 Birch St Newport Beach CA 92660-2116 Business E-Mail: rrr@magnacardainc.com. E-mail: rogersrr@compuserve.com.

**ROGERS, ROY STEELE, III,** dermatologist, educator, dean; b. Hillsboro, Ohio, Mar. 3, 1940; s. Roy S. Jr. and Anna Mary (Murray) R.; m. Susan Camille Hudson, Aug. 22, 1964; children: Roy Steele IV, Katherine Hudson. BA, Denison U., 1962; MD, Ohio State U., 1966; MS, U. Minn., 1974. Cert. dermatologist, dermatopathologist and immunodermatologist. Intern Strong Meml. Hosp., Rochester, NY, 1966—67; resident Duke U. Med. Ctr., Durham, NC, 1969—71, Mayo Clinic, Rochester, Minn., 1972—73, cons., 1973—, prof. dermatology, 1983—, dean Sch. Health Related Scis., 1991—99. Adv. coun. Rochester Community Coll., 1991-2000. Contbr. over 250 sci. articles to publs. Capt. USAF, 1967-69. Recipient Alumni Achievement award Ohio State U. Coll. Medicine, 1991, Alumni citation Denison U., 1993, Faculty Svc. award Mayo Med. Sch., 1993, Gold medal 2d Med. Sch., Charles U., Prague, 2002; named Disting. Educator, Mayo Clinic, 2004, Thomas G. Pearson Meml. Edn. award, 2004, Everett J. Fox Lectureship, 2005, Paul A. O'Leary Lectureship, 2005. Mem. Am. Acad. Dermatology (bd. dirs. 1987-91, v.p. 1999, Everett C. Fox lectureship 2005, Gold Triangle award 2004, Thomas G. Pearson Meml. Edn. award 2005), Am. Soc. Dermatologic Allergy and Immunology (sec.-treas. 1988-2000), Am. Dermatologic Assn. (v.p. 2002-03). Soc. Investigative Dermatology, Assn. Schs. Allied Health Professions, Dermatology Found. (Annenberg Circle 2002). Avocations: travel, reading, walking. Office: Mayo Clinic 200 1st St SW Rochester MN 55905-0002 Home: 1924 Greenfield Lane SW # 204 Rochester MN 55902-1083 Office Phone: 507-284-2555. Business E-Mail: rogers.roy@mayo.edu.

**ROGERS, RUTH FRANCES,** retired microbiologist; b. Chgo., Nov. 5, 1925; d. Frank Joseph and Ruth Elizabeth (Abbott) Kucera; m. James Alvin Rogers, June 17, 1950; children: Kenneth James, David Wayne. BS, U. Ill., 1948. Microbiologist No. Rsch. Ctr., Nat. Ctr. for Agrl. Utilization Rsch. Peoria, Ill., 1963—85; ret., 1985. Contbr. articles to profl. jours. Recipient Sustained Superior Performance award USDA, 1984. Methodist.

**ROGERS, RUTHERFORD DAVID,** librarian; b. Jesup, Iowa, June 22, 1915; s. David Earl and Carrie Zoe (Beckel) R.; m. E. Margaret Stoddard, June 4, 1937; 1 child, Jane Shelley; m. Bernette W. Barton, Feb. 28, 2002. BA, U. No. Iowa, 1936, Litt.D., 1977; MA, Columbia, 1937, BS (Lydia Roberts fellow), 1938; D.Library Adminstrn. (hon.), U. Dayton, 1971. Asst. N.Y. Pub. Library, 1937-38; reference librarian Columbia Coll. Library, Columbia U., 1938- 41, acting librarian 1941-42, librarian 1942-45; research analyst Smith, Barney & Co., N.Y.C., 1946-48; dir. Grosvenor Library, Buffalo, 1948-52, Rochester Pub. Library, 1952-54; chief pers. office N.Y. Pub. Libr., 1954-55; chief reference dept., 1955-57; chief asst. librarian of Congress, Washington, 1957-62, dep. librarian of, 1962-64; dir. univ. libraries Stanford U., 1964-69; univ. librarian Yale U., 1969-85; univ. librarian emeritus, 1985—. Founder, chmn. bd. dirs. Rsch. Librs. Group, Inc.; mem. Exam. Com. for Pub. Librarians' Certs., N.Y. State, 1951-54; mem. U.S. Adv. Coun. Coll. Libr. Resources; bd. govs. Yale U. Press; bd. dirs., v.p. H.W. Wilson Found., 1969-98; chmn. program mgmt. com. Internat. Fedn. Libr. Assns. Author: Columbia Coll. Library Handbook, 1941, (with David C. Weber) University Library Administration, 1971; also articles in profl. jours. Served from pvt. to 1st sgt. Air Transp. Command USAAF, 1942-43; from 2d lt. to capt., planning officer, chief, spl. Planning Div., Office Asst. Chief Staff, Plans, Air Transport Command 1943-46. Decorated officier de L'Ordre de la Couronne Belge; recipient U. No. Iowa Alumni Achievement award, 1958, Disting. Alumni award Columbia U. Sch. Libr. Svc., 1992, medal Internat. Fedn. of Libr. Assns., 1977. Fellow Am. Acad. Arts and Scis.; mem. A.L.A. (chmn. com. Intellectual Freedom 1950-51), (1950-60), (2d v.p. 1965-66), (mem. exec. bd. 1961-66), (trustee endowment fund), Assn. Research Libraries (pres. 1967-68), N.Y. Library Assn., AAUP, Bibliog. Soc. Am., Assn. Coll. and Reference Libraries, Blue Key, Kappa Delta Pi, Sigma Tau Delta, Theta Alpha Phi. Clubs: Grolier; N.Y. Library (N.Y.C.), Columbia U. (N.Y.C.), Yale (N.Y.C.); Cosmos (Washington), Kenwood Country (Washington); Roxburghe (San Francisco); Book of Calif. Home (Winter): 1081 Lakemont Ct Winter Park FL 32792-5025

**ROGERS, SAMUEL SHEPARD See SHEPARD, SAM**

**ROGERS, SHARON J.,** education consultant; b. Grantsburg, Wis., Sept. 24, 1941; d. Clifford M and Dorothy L (Beckman) Dickau; m. Evan D Rogers, June 15, 1962 (div. Dec. 1980); m. Joseph Y. Ruth, Dec. 22, 2003. BA summa cum laude, Bethel Coll., St. Paul, 1963; MA in Libr. Sci., U. Minn., 1967; PhD in Sociology, Wash. State U., Pullman, 1976. Lectr., instr. Alfred (N.Y.) U., 1972-76; assoc. prof. U. Toledo, 1977-80; assoc. dean Bowling Green (Ohio) State U. Librs., 1980-84; univ. libr. George Washington U., Washington, 1984-92, asst. v.p. acad. affairs, 1989-92, assoc. v.p. acad. affairs, 1992-97, co-dir. Univ. Teaching Ctr., 1990-97; cons. in higher edn. and librs., 1997—. Mem Online Computer Library Ctr Users Coun, 1985—92; pres. Online Computer Library Ctr Users Coun., 1989—90, rsch. advt. com., 1990—92; trustee Online Computer Library Ctr., 1992—2002; exec dir Assn Libr. and Info. Sci. Edn., 1997—2000. Contbr. articles to profl jours. Bd dirs CapAccess, 1993—97, treas, 1993—95; bd dirs ACLU, Toledo, 1978—84. Fellow Jackson, Univ Minn, 1964—65; grantee NSF, Wash State Univ, 1969—72. Mem.: ALA (exec coun 1987—91, pub comt 1989—93, chair 1990—93), Universal Serials and Book Exchange (bd dirs, treas 1987), Washington Research Library Consortium (bd dirs 1987—90), Am Sociological Asn, Asn Col and Research Libraries (pres 1984—85). Home: 2922 24th St N Arlington VA 22207 E-mail: sjdrr@verizon.net.

**ROGERS, SHERRY ANNE,** physician; b. Syracuse, NY, Apr. 15, 1943; d. Rodney Wellington and Jayne Hammond; m. Robert Hamilton Rogers, June 30, 1970. BA, Syracuse U., 1969; MD, SUNY, 1969-70. Diplomate Am. Bd. Family Practice, 1973, Am. Bd. Environ. Medicine, 1985. Intern Health Scis. Ctr. Syracuse, 1969-70; pvt. practice pediat., Auburn, NY, 1970-71; emergency physician Cmty. Gen. Hosp., Syracuse, NY, 1971-72; pvt. practice family medicine, Syracuse, 1972-85; pvt. practice environ. medicine, 1978—. Lectr. in field. Author: (books) Total Health, 1989, Tired or Toxic?, 1990, Wellness Against All Odds, 1994, Chemical Sensitivity, 1995, You Are What You Ate, The E.I. Syndrome, 1997, Depression Cured At Last, 1997, Alternative and Complementary Veterinary Medicine, 1998, No More Heartburn, 2000, The Cure is in the Kitchen, The Scientific Basis of Environmental Medicine Techniques, 2000, Pain Free in 6 Weeks, 2001, Detoxify or Die, 2003, The High Blood Pressure Hoax, 2005, Total Wellness, 2006; editor: Internal Medical World Report, 1992—93; contbr. articles to profl. jours., chapters to books Molds & Mycotoxins, Arch. Environ. Health, others.

Fellow: Am. Coll. Nutrition, Am. Coll. Asthma, Allergy and Immunology. Office: Northeast Center Environmental Medicine PO Box 2716 Syracuse NY 13220-2716 Office Phone: 800-846-6687, 315-488-2856.

**ROGERS, STEFFEN H.,** retired academic administrator; m. Athena Rogers. B in Biology, Ga. So. Coll., 1964; PhD in Biology, Vanderbilt U., 1968. Postdoctoral rschr. Johns Hopkins U. Sch. Pub. Health, Balt., 1968—70; asst. prof. biology, acting dean Coll. Arts and Scis. Tulsa (Okla.) U., 1970—91; prof. zoology, dean Coll. Arts and Scis. U. R.I., 1991—96; prof. biology, acting pres., v.p. acad. affairs, provost Clemson (S.C.) U., 1996—2001; pres. Bucknell U., Lewisburg, Pa., 2001—04. Past dir. Okla. Ctr. of Excellence in Molecular Medicine, Tulsa, Mervin Bovaird Ctr. for Studies in Molecular Biology and Biotech., Tulsa; presenter in field.

**ROGERS, STEPHEN HITCHCOCK,** retired ambassador; b. Flushing, NY, June 21, 1930; s. Francis Walker and Julia (Wheeler) R.; m. Kent Brian, June 23, 1956; children: Kryston R. Fischer, F. Halsey, Julia L., John H. BA, Princeton U., 1952; MA, Columbia U., 1956; MPA, Harvard U., 1962. Fgn. svc. officer Dept. of State, 1956-93; econ. counselor Am. Embassy, London, 1970-72; counselor U.S. Mission to OECD, Paris, 1972-75; office dir. Pan Inter.-Am. Affairs Dept. of State, Washington, 1975-78; econ. counselor Am. Embassy, Mexico City, 1978-82; prof. Nat. Def. U., Washington, 1982-85; econ. counselor Am. Embassy, Pretoria, South Africa, 1986-90, amb. Mbabane, Swaziland, 1990-93; ret., 1993. Bd. dirs. Cen. Atlantic Conf., United Ch. of Christ, 2000-03; v.p. Princeton U. Class 1952, 2002—. Lt. (jg) USN, 1952-55. Recipient Outstanding Civilian Svc. award Dept. of Army, 1985. Mem. Am. Fgn. Svc. Assn., Diplomatic and Consular Officers Ret., Nassau Club (Princeton, N.J.). Mem. United Ch. Of Christ. Home: 3803 Ivydale Dr Annandale VA 22003-2006

**ROGERS, SUZANNE C.,** actress; d. Grant Christian Crumpler and Edna Mary Allen. Diploma, Christine Parks Sch. Dance, Petersburg, Va., 1957, Marion Mease Sch. Dance, Richmond, 1961, Stella Adler Drama Sch., N.Y.C., 1963. Rockette Radio City Music Hall, 1961—63. Performer: (Broadway plays) CoCo, Music Man, 110 In The Shade, Funny Girl, Halleliah Baby & Follies; actor: (TV series) Days of Our Lives, 1973—. Recipient Best Actress, Daytime TV Mag. Annual Readers Poll, 1977, Best Supporting Actress Emmy, Days of Our Lives, 1979, Women in Film Living Legacy Humanitarian award, 2002. Home: 11266 Canton Dr Studio City CA 91604-4154

**ROGERS, THEODORE COURTNEY,** investment company executive; b. Lorain, Ohio, Aug. 25, 1934; s. William Theodore and Leona Ruth (Gerhart) Rogers; m. Elizabeth B. Barlow, June 28, 1984; children from previous marriage: Pamela Anne Rogers Harmon, Theodore Courtney Jr. BS in Social Sci., Miami U., Oxford, Ohio, 1956, LHD (hon.), 2001; postgrad., Johns Hopkins U., 1957; MBA summa cum laude, Marquette U., 1968; MALA, St. John's Coll., Annapolis, Md., 2004. With Armco Inc., 1958-80; pres. Olympic Fastening Sys., 1970-74; exec. v.p. Nat. Supply Co. subs., Houston, 1974-76, pres., 1976-80, v.p. parent co., 1976-79, group v.p. parent co., 1979-80; pres., COO NL Industries, Inc., N.Y.C., 1980-82, pres., CEO, 1982-83, chmn., pres., CEO, 1983-87; chmn. Am. Indsl. Ptnrs., N.Y.C., 1987—. Chmn. Bucyrus Internat., Consoltex Inc., Gt. Lakes Carbon Corp., JHT Holdings Inc.; bd. trustees St. John's Coll. Nat. coun. Theatre Comm. Group; bd. dirs. Lincoln Ctr. Peforming Arts, City Ctr. Music and Drama; chmn. bd. dirs. Theatre for New Audience; former chmn. Ctr. Cmty. Interests; emeritus chmn. N.Y.C. Ballet; bd. dirs., trustee Ballet Rev. Qur. Lt. USN, 1956—58. Mem.: Poets and Writers (bd. dirs.), Bus. Roundtable, N.Y. Soc. Libr. (trustee), Grolier Club, Univ. Club (Milw.), Met. Club (Washington), Sky Club, Achilles Track Club (founder, bd. dirs.), Century Assn. (N.Y.), Links Club, Econs. Club (N.Y.), Union Club (Cleve.), Kappa Phi Kappa, Sigma Chi (Significant Sig, Sigma Chi Hall of Fame 2005), Beta Gamma Sigma (bd. dirs.). Office: Am Indsl Ptnr 551 5th Ave Ste 3800 New York NY 10176-0001 Office Phone: 212-983-1399.

**ROGERS, THOMAS FRANCIS,** foundation administrator; b. Providence, Aug. 11, 1923; s. Thomas Francis and H. Ann (Flaherty) R.; m. Estelle E. Hunt, July 6, 1946; children: Clare Hibschman, Judith Reynolds, Hope Grove. BS cum laude, Providence Coll., 1945; MA, Boston U., 1949. Rsch. assoc. Radio Rsch. Lab. Harvard U., Cambridge, Mass., 1944-45; TV engr. Bell and Howell Co., Chgo., 1945-46; electronics scientist AF Cambridge Rsch. Ctr., Cambridge, Mass., 1946-54; assoc. group leader MIT Lincoln Lab., Cambridge, 1951-53; lab. head AF Cambridge Rsch. Ctr., Bedford, Mass., 1954-59; div. head and steering com. mem. MIT Lincoln Lab., Bedford, 1959-64; asst. dir. def. rsch. and engring. Office of Sec. Def., Washington, 1964-65, dep. dir. def. rsch. and engring., 1965-67; dir. rsch. and tech. Office of Sec. HUD, Washington, 1967-69; v.p. The Mitre Corp., Washington, Bedford, 1969-72; chmn. The Sophron Found., McLean, Va., 1980—; dir. U.S. Congress Office of Tech. Assessment Study on Civilian Space Stas. and U.S. Future in Space, Washington, 1982-84; from pres. to chief scientist The Space Transp. Assn., Arlington, Va., 1992—2005. Founding chmn. bd. dirs. External Tanks Corp., Boulder, Colo.; bd. dirs. Internat. Radio Satellite Corp., Washington, Space Destinations Svcs., Inc., 1992-94; chmn. bd. dirs. Luna Corp., Great Falls, Va., 1991-95; dir. Share Space Found., 2000; chmn. POLARIS Command-Comm. Co., USN, 1960-64; mem. Satellite Comm. Panel, Pres.'s Sci. Adv. Com., 1961-63; mem. Dept. Def. NASA Satellite Comm. Com., 1961-64; U.S.A. del. UN Conf. on Applications of Sci. and Tech. by Lesser Developed Nations, Geneva, 1963; mem. Fed. Aeronautics and Astronautics Coordinating Bd., 1965-67; Fed. Coun. on Sci. and Tech., 1967-69; mem. Space Program Adv. Coun., NASA, 1971-73, chmn. applications com., 1972-73; mem. NAS com. on regional emergency med. comm. systems, 1976-78; mem. space applications bd. com. on NASA space comms. 1986-87; mem. com. on antenna, satellite broadcasting and emergency preparedness for Voice of Am., 1986-88; mem. adv. com. study space transp. U.S. Congrl. Office Tech. Assessment, 1994-95. Contbr. articles to jours., chpts. to books. Trustee X-Prize Found., 1995-2000. Recipient Outstanding Performance award CSC, 1957, cert. commendation Sec. Navy, 1961, Meritorious Civilian Svc. award and medal, Sec. Def., Constrn.'s Man of Yr. award Engring. News Record, 1969, Space Pioneer award Nat. Space Soc., 1988, Best Vision of the Future award Space Frontier Found., 1997, NASA Disting. Pub. Svc. award, 1999, Pioneer award Visionary Lifetime Achievement award Space Tourism Soc. Fellow IEEE (mem. transp. and aerospace policy com., chmn. 1991-95, Profl. Achievement award 1995, Citation of Honor 2005); mem. Internat. Acad. Astronautics, Cosmos Club (Washington). Home and Office: 5400 Vantage Point Rd # 210 Columbia MD 21044 Office Phone: 410-992-1210.

**ROGERS, THOMAS SYDNEY,** communications company executive; b. New Rochelle, NY, Aug. 19, 1954; s. Sydney Michael Rogers Jr. and Alice Steinhardt; m. Sylvia Texon, Oct. 9, 1983; children: Robert, Jessica, Jason. BA, Wesleyan U., 1975; JD, Columbia U., 1979. Bar: N.Y. 1980, U.S. Dist. Ct. (so. and ea. dists.) N.Y. 1980, U.S. Ct. Appeals (D.C. cir.) 1981. Legis. aide to Congressman Richard Ottinger U.S. Ho. Reps., Washington, 1975-76, sr. counsel subcom. telecommunications, 1981-86; assoc. Lord, Day & Lord, N.Y.C., 1979-81; v.p. policy planning and bus. devel. Nat. Broadcasting Co., Inc., N.Y.C., 1987-88; pres. NBC Cable, 1988-89, NBC Cable & Bus. Devel., 1989-99; exec. v.p. NBC, N.Y.C., 1992-99; pres., CEO internat. coun. NATAS, 1994—97, chmn., 1998—99; vice chmn. NBC Internet, N.Y.C., 1999; chmn., CEO Primedia, Inc., N.Y.C., 1999—2003; chmn. TRget Media, N.Y.C., 2003—; vice chmn. Tivo, Inc., Alviso, Calif., 2003—05, pres., CEO, 2005—; chmn. Teleglobe, Inc., 2004—. Named one of Outstanding Young Men in Am., 1985. Mem. N.Y. State Bar Assn., Internat. Radio and TV Soc. Office: TiVo Inc 2160 Gold St PO Box 2160 Alviso CA 95002*

**ROGERS, THOMASINA VENESE,** federal commissioner; Student, Northwestern U.; JD, Columbia U. Chmn. Administrv. Conf. U.S., Washington, 1994-95; presdl. pers. staff The White House, Washington; dep. legal counsel, then legal counsel EEOC, Washington; mem. Occupl. Safety and Health Rev.

Commn., Washington, 1998—, chmn., 1999—2002. Bd. dirs. Children's Nat. Med. Ctr. Mem. Am. Arbitration Assn. (bd. dirs.) Office: Occupl Safety and Health Review Commn One Lafayette Ctr 1120 20th St NW Washington DC 20036-3457

**ROGERS, WANDA FAYE,** vocalist; b. Oct. 24, 1929; d. John Riley and Bessie Louise Narmore; m. Weldon Nelson Rogers Sr., Feb. 27, 1959 (div. 1967); 1 child, Weldon Nelson. Student, Modesto Jr. Coll. Lic. radio broadcast. Author: (song book) Wanda Faye Song Book, 2004; singer: (CD) UFO, recorded with Jewel Records, 1958-64, Germanys Bear Import Records, 1998, Columbia Records, 1965, The Sunset Westerners, Sta. KGFL, 1946—53, Sta. WBAP, Ft. Worth, Tex., 1954—57. Named to, Cowgirl Mus. Hall of Fame, 2002, Hall of Fame, Western Swing Soc., Sacramento, 2003. Avocations: music, writing songs. Office: PO Box 383372 Modesto CA 95350

**ROGERS, WARD JUNIOR,** retired industrial designer; b. Savanna, Ill., May 8, 1924; s. Charles Clarence Rogers and Lucille Mae Woods; m. Marilyn Ruth Edwards, May 30, 1945; children: Douglas, Renee, Toni, Ward J. Grad., Mpls. Sch. Fine Arts, 1947. Chef Old Elm Club, Highland Park, Ill., 1947—49; engr. Clinton Engine, Manquota, Iowa, 1950—51; engr., indsl. designer GE, Morrison, Ill., 1951—71; art dir. Color Arts Inc., Racine, Wis. 1971—74; owner Dairy Bar, Mt. Carroll, 1976—86; custodian US Post Office, Mt. Carroll, 1973—91. Freelance designer Savanna Fabricators, Sterling (Ill.) Ambulance; drafting tchr. local coll.; mem. round table U. Iowa. Author: (column) Remember When, 1980. Pres. Art Guild, Morrison, Ill.; chmn. Mt. Carroll Hist. Soc., 1998—; pres. Hist. Soc.; precinct com. Dem. Party, Morrison, Ill. S/sgt. USMC, 1941—45, PTO, 2d lt. reserves U.S. Army, 1949. Mem.: VFW (life), Indsl. Design Inst., Am. Legion. Avocations: antiques, records, collecting cars, painting. Home: 207 E Rapp St Mount Carroll IL 61053

**ROGERS, WAYNE M.,** actor, investor, investment strategist, consultant; b. Birmingham, Ala., Apr. 7, 1933; m. Mitzi, 1960-79; children Laura, Billy; m. Amy Hirsh, 1988. BA, Princeton U., 1954; student acting, Sanford Meisners Neighborhood Playhouse, Martha Graham. Founder Wayne Rogers & Co. Bd. dirs. Vishay Intertechnology Inc., 2006—. Stage appearances in Misalliance, Bus Stop, Under the Yum-Yum Tree; TV series Housecalls, 1979 (also writer, dir.), Stagecoach West, 1960, M*A*S*H, 1972-75, City of Angels, 1976, High Risk, 1988; film debut Odds Against Tomorrow, 1959; other films include The Glory Guys, 1965, Chamber of Horrors, 1966, Cool Hand Luke, 1967, WUSA, 1970, Pocket Money, 1972, The Hot Touch, 1982, The Gig, 1985, The Goodbye Bird, 1993, Ghost of Mississippi, 1996, Love Lies Bleeding, 1999, Frozen with Fear, 2000, Coo Coo Cafe, 2000, 3 Days of Rain, 2000, Miracle Dogs, 2003, Nobody Knows Anything!, 2003 (also prodr.); TV appearances The Top of the Hill, 1980, The Edge of Night, Attack on Terror: The F.B.I. vs Ku Klux Klan, 1975, The November Plan, 1976, Having Babies II, 1977, It Happened One Christmas, 1977, Thou Shalt Not Commit Adultry, 1978, Once in Paris, 1978, (mini series) Chiefs, 1983, He's Fired, She's Hired, 1984, The Lady from Yesterday, 1985, I Dream of Jeannie: 15 Years Later, 1985, One Terrific Guy, 1986, The Girl Who Spelled Freedom, 1986, American Harvest, 1987, The Killing Time, 1987, Drop-Out Mother, 1988, Bluegrass, 1988, Passion and Paradise, 1989, Miracle Landing, 1990; guest appearances include Gunsmoke, 1959, 1962, 1965, Gomer Pyle, U.S.M.C., 1964, The F.B.I. (6 episodes), 1966-73, Barnaby Jones, 1973, Murder, Memories of M*A*S*H, 1991, She Wrote, 1993, 1994, & 1997, Diagnosis Murder, 1997, M*A*S*H: TV Tales, 2002, M*A*S*H 30th Anniversary Reunion, 2002, TV Land Confidential, 2005, The O'Reilly Factor, 2005 and several others; exec. prodr., writer Dr. Sex, 1964, The Astro-Zombies, 1969; exec. prodr. (TV) Perfect Witness, 1989, Night of the Twisters, 1996, Money Plays, 1997; regular contbr., finances and stocks, Fox News Channel. With USN. Named to Hollywood Walk of Fame, 2005. Avocations: basketball, tennis, reading. Office: Wayne M Rogers & Co 11828 La Grange Ave Los Angeles CA 90025*

**ROGERS, WILLIAM DILL,** lawyer; b. Wilmington, Del., May 12, 1927; m. Suzanne Rochford, Sept. 7, 1926; children: William Rogers, Daniel. BA, Princeton U., 1948; LL.B., Yale U., 1951. Bar: DC 1952, U.S. Supreme Ct. 1954. Ptnr. Arnold & Porter, Washington, intermittently 1953—; dep. U.S. coordinator Alliance for Progress, AID, 1962-65; pres. N.Y. Ctr. Inter.-Am. Relations, 1965-72; asst. sec. of state inter.-Am. relations Dept. State, 1974-76, undersec. of state for econ. affairs, 1976-77; mem. law faculty Cambridge U., Eng., 1982-83. Sr. counselor Bipartisan Commn. on Central Am., 1983-84; vice chmn. Kissinger Assocs. Inc. Author: The Twilight Struggle: The Alliance for Progress and U.S.-Latin-American Relations, 1967. Co-chmn. U.S.-Mexico Binat. Commn.; bd. dirs. Coun. Fgn. Rels., 1981-90. Mem. Am. Soc. Internat. Law (pres. 1971-73). ABA. Office: Arnold & Porter 555 12th St NW Washington DC 20004-1206 Office Phone: 202-942-5915. E-mail: william_rogers@apnter.com.

**ROGERS, WILLIAM RAYMOND,** retired academic administrator, psychologist, educator; b. Oswego, N.Y., June 20, 1932; s. William Raymond and A. Elizabeth (Hollis) R.; m. Beverley Claire Partington, Aug. 14, 1954; children: John Partington, Susan Elizabeth Apple, Nancy Claire Glassman. BA magna cum laude, Kalamazoo Coll., 1954; BD, U. Chgo. and Chgo. Theol. Sem., 1958; PhD, U. Chgo., 1965; MA (hon.), Harvard U., 1970. Cons., staff counselor Counseling and Psychotherapy Rsch. Ctr., U. Chgo. 1960-62; tchg. fellow, counselor to students Chgo. Theol. Sem., 1961-62; asst. prof. psychology and religion. dir. student counseling Earlham Coll., Richmond, Ind., 1962-68, assoc. prof. psychology and religion, assoc. dean of Coll., 1968-70; vis. lectr. pastoral counseling Harvard U. Div. Sch., Cambridge, Mass., 1969-70, prof. religion and psychology Div. and Edn. Schs., 1970-80, faculty chmn. clin. psychology and pub. practice, 1970-72, chmn. counseling and cons. psychology, 1979-80; prof. psychology and religious studies Guilford Coll., Greensboro, NC, 1980—, pres., 1980-96, pres. emeritus, 1996—. Bd. dirs. Moses Cone Health Sys., 1984-96, Moses Cone-Wesley Long Cmty. Health Found., 1996-2002, chmn. 1996-2002; bd. dirs. BB&T, Kendal Corp., chmn. 2005—. Author: The Alienated Student, 1969, Project Listening, 1974, Nourishing the Humanistic in Medicine, 1979; Contbr. articles to profl. jours. Bd. dirs. Greensboro Symphony Soc.; mem. Cemala Found. Danforth Found. fellow, Blatchford Traveling fellow U. Chgo. and Chgo. Theol. Sem. mem.: Islesboro Hist. Soc. (pres. 1999—2002), So. Assn. Colls. and Schs., Nat. Assn. Ind. Colls. and Univs., Friends Com. on Nat. Legislation (mem. policy com.), Friends Assn. Higher Edn., Soc. Values in Higher Edn., Tarratine Club of Dark Harbor (bd. govs.), Rotary (past pres.). Mem. Soc. Of Friends. Home: 661 Main Rd Islesboro ME 04848-4201

**ROGERS, WILLIAM WARREN,** historian, educator, publishing executive, writer; b. Sandy Ridge, Ala., Aug. 18, 1929; s. Harry Ernest Rogers and Mittie Pate Loftin; m. Miriam Arnold Rogers, June 6, 1951; children: Warren, Arnold, Kate, Amy. BS, MS, Auburn U., Ala., 1951; PhD, U. N.C., Chapel Hill, 1959. With U.S. Army Counter Intelligence Corps, Stuttgart, Germany, 1954—56; instr. U. Md., Stuttgart, Germany, 1955—56; dir. Moody AFB program Fla. State U., Valdosta, Ga., 1958—59, prof. history Tallahassee, 1959—96; vis. prof. Fla. A&M, 1990, Auburn U., Ala., 1993, 1996; dir. Sentry Press, Inc., Tallahassee, 1996—. Bd. editors Fla. Historical Quarterly, 1970—2000; bd, dir Southern Studies, Nachitaches, La.; spkr. on politics and history to groups and orgns. Author: Ante-Bellum Thomas County, 1825-1861, 1963, Thomas County During the Civil War, 1964, The One-Gallused Rebellion, 1970 (Am. Assn. State and Local History award of Merit, 1972), Thomas County 1865-1900, 1973, Transition to the Twentieth Century Thomas County, Ga., 1900-1920, 2002, A Historic Sampler of Tallahassee and Leon County, 2005; co-author: Montgomery as the Confederate Capital: A View of a New Nation, 1964, Labor Revolt In Ala.: The Great Strike of 1894, 1965, Stephen S. Renfroe Ala.'s Outlaw Sheriff, 1972, Favored Land: A History of Tallahassee and Leon County, 1972 (Tallahassee/Leon County Historic Preservation Bd. award, 1972), August Reckoning Jack Turner and Racism in Post Civil War Ala., 1973, Convict's, Coal and the Banner Mine Tragedy, 1987, Ala.: The History of a Deep South State, 1994 (James F. Sulzby award, 1995), Fla.'s Clerks of the Circuit Ct. Their History and

Experiences, 1996, Fla. Sheriffs: A History 1821-1945, 2001 (James J. Horgan award, 2002), The Croom Faily and Goodwood Plantation, 2001 (Nat. Assn. State and Local History Commendation of Merit, 2002), Ala.'s Response to the Penitentiary Movement, 1829-1865, 2003; editor: Am. Siberia by J.C. Powell, 1976; co-editor: Fla.'s Heritage of Diversity Essays in Honor of Samuel Proctor, 1997; contbr. scholarly articles to profl. jours. Finalist Prof. of Yr., Am. Hist. Assn.; named Outstanding Alumnus, Auburn U.; recipient Coyle Moore award Outstanding Tchg., Fla. State U. Faculty and Student Com., 1972, Lifetime Commitment commendation, Am. Assn. for State and Local History, 1994, Outstanding Tchr. award, Phi Alpha Theta (Fla. State chpt.), 1996; fellow, NEH, 1980; grantee, Am. Philosophical Soc., 1970. Democrat. Avocations: reading, walking, tennis, birdwatching, antique books. Office: Sentry Press Inc 424 E Call St Tallahassee FL 32301 Office Phone: 850-224-7423. Business E-Mail: www.wrogers@fsu.edu.

**ROGERS-BEARD, DONNA JANE,** history educator; d. Carmen Winifred and Robert Madison Hornbeak; m. Derex Beard, May 28, 1994; 1 child, Robert Coleman Rogers. MAT, Webster U., Mo., 1973. Cert. social studies tchr. Mo., 1969. Tchr. history U. City Sch. Dist., University City, Mo., 1969—91, Clayton H.S., Mo., 1991—. Advance placement cons. Coll. Bd., N.Y.C., 2000—. Pres. Historyonics, St. Louis, 1998—2005. Named Mo. Social Studies Tchr. of Yr., Mo. Coun. Social Studies, 2006; Woodrow Wilson fellow, Princeton U., 1992. Mem.: NEA, World History Assn., Nat. Coun. Social Studies. Avocations: travel, reading, yoga. Office: Clayton High School 1 Mark Twain Cir Clayton MO 63105 Office Phone: 314-726-2575. Home Fax: 314-854-6793; Office Fax: 314-854-6793. Business E-Mail: donna_rogers-beard@clayton.k12.mo.us.

**ROGERSON, CRAIG ALLAN,** manufacturing executive; b. Detroit, July 4, 1956; s. William Durie and Eunice Clara (Richert) R.; m. Carina Joy Ballato, Sept. 11, 1982; children: Scott Allan, Kristen Joy, Colin William. BS in Chem. Engring., Mich. State U., 1979. Tech. rep. Water Mgmt. Chemicals div. Hercules Inc., Charlotte and Wilmington, N.C., 1979-82, sales rep. Fibers div. Atlanta, 1982-85, market devel. supr., 1985-87, product mgr., 1987-88, nat. sales mgr., 1989-90, dir. ops. Oxford, Ga., 1991-92, bus. dir. Wilmington, Del., 1992-94, sales dir. paper tech. divsn., 1995-96, v.p., gen. mgr. fibers divsn., 1996—97; pres., CEO Wacker Silicones Corp., 1997—2000; v.p., Betz Dearborn Div. Hercules Inc., 2000, pres., Betz Dearborn Div., 2000—02, pres., FiberVisions, 2002—03, pres., Pinova, 2002—03, v.p., Global Procurement, 2002—03, acting pres., COO, 2003, pres., CEO, 2003—. Bd. dirs. PRL Corp., First State Innovation. Mem. Del. Bus. Roundtable (bd. dirs.), Am. Chemistry Coun. (bd. dirs.). Republican. Lutheran. Avocations: racquetball, golf, travel. Home: PO Box 702 Gwynedd Valley PA 19437-0702 Office: Hercules Inc Hercules Plz Wilmington DE 19801-6101 Office Phone: 302-594-6601.

**ROGGENSACK, PATIENCE DRAKE,** state supreme court justice; b. Joliet, Ill., 1941; BA, Drake U., 1962; JD, U. Wis. Law Sch., 1980. Atty. Dewitt Ross and Stevens, 1980—96; judge Wis. Ct. of Appeals, 1996—2003; justice Wis. Supreme Ct., 2003—. Mem.: ABA, Wis. Bar Assn. Office: Wis Supreme Ct PO Box 1688 Madison WI 53701-1688

**ROGIN, GILBERT LESLIE,** editor, author; b. N.Y.C., Nov. 14, 1929; s. Robert I. and Lillian Carol (Ruderman) R. Student, State U. Iowa, 1947-49; AB, Columbia, 1951. Editor-at-large Miller Pub., L.A., 1955—. Author: The Fencing Master, 1965, What Happens Next?, 1971, Preparations for the Ascent, 1980. Served with AUS, 1952-54. Recipient award for creative work in lit. Am. Acad. Inst. Arts and Letters 1972 Home: 21 W 10th St New York NY 10011

**ROGNESS, MICHAEL,** religious studies educator, minister; b. Duluth, Minn., Mar. 23, 1935; s. Alvin Nathaniel and Nora Margaret Rogness; m. Eva Maria Kirchner, June 2, 1958; children: Maria, Paul John, Jonathan Peter. BA, Augustana Coll., Sioux Falls, SD, 1956; MDiv, Luther Sem., St. Paul, 1960; ThD, Erlangen-Nürnberg (Germany) U., 1963. Ordained Am. Luth. Ch., 1964. Assoc. prof. Ecumenical Inst., Luth. World Fedn., Strasbourg, France, 1967—70; pastor 1st Luth. Ch., Duluth, 1970—85; prof. Luther Sem., St. Paul, 1985—. Faculty dept. chmn. Luther Sem., 1995—2001. Author: Philip Melanchthon, Reformer, 1965, The Church Nobody Knows, 1971, The Hand That Holds Me, 1980, Preaching to a TV Generation, 1987. Nat. ch. coun. mem. Am. Luth. Ch., Mpls., 1980—85. Avocations: skiing, swimming. Home: 1340 Keston Saint Paul MN 55108 Office: Luther Sem 2481 Como Saint Paul MN 55108 Office Phone: 651-641-3456. E-mail: mrogness@luthersem.edu.

**ROGNSTAD, RICHARD L.,** music educator, cellist; b. Casper, Wyo., Aug. 29, 1950; s. Louis C. and Lucy b. Rognstad; m. Lynn B. Bartholow; 1 child, Matthew. BA in Music, New Coll. Sarasota, Fla., 1973; M.Music Performance, U. Colo., Boulder, 1979; PhD in Mus. Arts, U. Colo., 1986. Pvt. music instr., Boulder, Colo., 1973—86; prof. music U. SD, Vermillion, 1986—; cellist Rawlins Piano Trio, Vermillion, 1987—2004. Musician (cellist): (CDs) Three American Piano Trios, 1993, A World Premier Recording, 1998, American Romance, 2003; musician: (cellone player) Homage to Stelzner, 2005. Mem.: Am. String Tchrs. Assn. Cap. Soc. Am. Music. Avocation: tennis. Home: 415 Canby St Vermillion SD 57069 Office: University of South Dakota Dept Music 414 E Clark St Vermillion SD 57069

**ROGOFF, JEROME HOWARD,** psychiatrist, psychoanalyst, forensic expert; b. Detroit, Dec. 21, 1938; s. Abraham Solomon and Sarah Riva (Epstein) R.; (div. 1983); m. Erika Kathleen Keller, Sept. 25, 1983. BA cum laude, Harvard Coll., Cambridge, Mass., 1960; MD, Case Western Res. U., Cleve., 1965. Diplomate Am. Bd. Psychiatry and Neurology. Physician Peace Corps USPHS, Kathmandu, Nepal, 1966-68; clin. fellow psychiatry Harvard Med. Sch., Boston, 1975-79; staff psychiatrist Westwood (Mass.) Lodge Hosp., 1972-74; assoc. clin. prof. psychiatry Tufts Med. Sch., Boston, 1977-86; assoc. chief, psychiatry and dir. inpatient Psychiatry, day hosp. Faulkner Hosp., Boston, 1975-94; pvt. practice psychiatry, psychoanalysis and forensic psychiatry, 1994—. Cons. psychiatrist Mass. Parole Bd. Probate Ct. Plymouth County, Mass., LEEA, Washington, 1971-78; psychiat. dir. ct. diversion program Boston TASC-A, 1974-75; treas. Guild for Continuing Edn., Boston, 1981-95; founding dir. Law and Psychiatry Resource Ctr., Boston, 1983-2005; adj. prof. Simmons Sch. Social Work, Boston, 1981-85; lectr. psychiatry Harvard Med. Sch., Boston, 1986-94, 2001-. Chmn. psychiatry team Combined Jewish Philanthropies, Boston, 1978-83, assoc. chmn. med. team, 1984-87, social planning and allocations com., 1991-98, cmty. svcs. com., 1998—, chmn. chronic mental illness com., 1999-2000, disabilities com., 2000-04; bd. dirs. Jewish Vocat. Svc., Boston, 1987-91. Fellow Am. Psychiat. Assn. (life, Disting., pub. affairs rep. 1988-94, budget com. 1996-2002, assembly rep. 2004—, chmn. corr. com. on confidentiality 2003—); mem. AMA, Mass. Psychiat. Soc. (councillor 1988-94, chair pub. affairs com. 1988-92, 93-94, chair nominating com. 1990, 2000, pres.-elect 1998-99, pres. 1999-2000, Mass. rep. to Assembly, 2000—), Am. Acad. Psychiatry and Law, Am. Assn. Pvt. Practice Psychiatrists, APA. Democrat. Avocations: cabinetry, carpentry, cooking, classical music, languages. Home and Office: 659 Chestnut St Waban MA 02468-2035 *Two guiding principles, both from my father: "When in doubt, do the right thing." Sounds trite and naive, but turns out in the event to be profound; one almost always knows deep down what the right thing is. "When you are born, you cry, and everyone around you laughs. So live your life that when you come to leave it, you laugh, and everyone around you cries." On my profession of psychiatry and psychoanalysis: psychotherapy adds insight to injury.*

**ROGOFF, KENNETH SAUL,** economics professor; b. Rochester, N.Y., Mar. 22, 1953; s. Stanley Miron and June Beatrice (Goldman) R.; m. Evelyn Jane Brody, Aug. 18, 1979 (div. 1989); m. Natasha Lance, June 25, 1995; children: Gabriel, Juliana. BA/MA in Econs., Yale U., 1975; PhD in Econs., MIT, 1980. Economist Internat. Monetary Fund, Washington, 1983; economist, sect. chief Internat. Fin. divsn., Bd. Govs. of the Fed. Res. Sys., Washington, 1979-84; assoc. prof. econs. U. Wis., Madison, 1985-89; prof.

econs. U. Calif., Berkeley, 1989-92; prof. econs. and internat. affairs Princeton U., 1992—, Charles and Marie Robertson prof. of internat. affairs, 1995-98; prof. econs. Harvard U., 1999—, Thomas D. Cabot prof. pub. policy, 2004—, dir. Ctr. Internat. Devel., 2003—04; econ. counselor, dir. rsch. IMF, 2001—03. Vis. scholar San Francisco Fed. Res., 1990-92, World Bank, Washington, 1989, IMF, Washington, 1988-94. Author books and contbr. articles to profl. jours. Alfred P. Sloan Rsch. fellow, 1986-87, Hoover Instn. Nat. fellow, 1986-87, NSF fellow, 1985—, John Simon Guggenheim fellow, 1998. Fellow World Econ. Forum, Econometric Soc., Am. Acad. Arts and Scis., World Econ. Forum; mem. Am. Econ. Assn.(mem. trilateral commn.), Coun. on Fgn. Rels., Internat. Grandmaster Chess. Office: Harvard U Econs Dept Littauer Ctr Cambridge MA 02138-3001 Office Phone: 617-495-4022. Business E-Mail: krogoff@harvard.edu.

**ROGOFF, PAULA DRIMMER,** English and foreign language educator; b. N.Y.C. d. George and Florence (Levine) Drimmer; m. Arnold Stevan Rogoff; children: Jeffrey Scott, Eric Todd, Brian Craig. BA cum laude, Hunter Coll., 1961; MEd summa cum laude, William Paterson Coll., 1979. Cert. elem. tchr., ESL tchr., supr., N.J. Tchr. handicapped Herricks Bd. Edn., Williston Park, NJ, 1965—68; tchr. reading compensatory edn. Oakland Bd. Edn., Oakland, NJ, 1981—84; tchr., coord. gifted-talented program North Haldeon Bd. Edn., NJ, 1984—85; ESL adult tchr., h.s. students Passaic County Tech. Inst., Wayne, NJ, 1989—2004. Presenter Children's Libr. programs. Named Tchr. of Yr., Passaic County Tech. Inst., 1999-2000. Mem. ASCD, NEA, TESOL, Internat. Platform Assn., N.J. Edn. Assn., Phi Beta Kappa, Phi Lambda Theta, Kappa Delta Pi. Home: 11 Furman Dr Wayne NJ 07470-5304 Office: Passaic County Tech Inst 45 Reinhardt Rd Wayne NJ 07470

**ROGOSKI, PATRICIA DIANA,** corporate financial executive; b. Chgo., Dec. 29, 1939; d. Raymond Michael and Bernice Rose (Konkol) R. BS in Acctg. and Econs., Marquette U., 1961, postgrad., 1965-66, NYU, 1966-68, St. John's U., N.Y.C., 1975-76; cert. mgmt. acct., 1979. Sr. fin. analyst Blackhawk Mfg. Co., Milw., 1961-66; mgr., sr. analyst Shell Oil Co., N.Y.C., 1966-71; mgr. data processing Bradford Nat./Penn Bradford, Pitts., 1971-75; asst. mgr. fin. controls ITT, N.Y.C., 1975-79; v.p., comptr. ITT Consumer Fin. Corp., Mpls., 1979-80; sr. v.p. fin. ITT Fin. Corp., St. Louis 1980-84; v.p., exec. asst., group exec. ITT Coins, Secaucus, NJ, 1984-85; pres. Patron S. Ltd., Wilmington, Del., 1986—; CFO, sr. v.p. Guardsmark, Inc., Memphis, 1989-94; sr. v.p. Peoplemark, Inc., Memphis, 1989-94. Bd. dirs. St. Louis Repertory Theater, 1983-84. Named to Acad. Women Achievers, YWCA, N.Y.C., 1980. Mem. Fin. Execs. Internat., Inst. Mgmt. Acctg., Econ. Club, Memphis Symphony Chorus. Avocation: duplicate bridge. Office: Patron S Ltd 2711 Centerville Rd Ste 400 Wilmington DE 19808-

**ROGOVIN, JOHN A.,** lawyer; b. Washington, July 10, 1961; s. Mitchell and Sheila Ann (Ender) R. AB, Columbia U., 1983; JD, U. Va., 1987. Bar: NY 1989, DC 1990. Law clk. Hon. Laurence Silberman U.S. Ct. Appeals (DC Cir.), Washington, 1987—88; assoc. Kramer, Levin et al, N.Y.C., 1988—89, O'Melveny & Myers, Washington, 1990—92, spl. counsel, 1996—97, ptnr., 1997—2001; dep. transition counsel Presdl. Transition, Little Rock, 1992—93; asst. to atty. gen. U.S. Dept. Justice, Washington, 1993, dep. asst. atty. gen. Civil Divsn., 1993—96; dep. gen. counsel FCC, Washington, 2001—02, gen. counsel, 2003—05; ptnr., Comm., E-Commerce and Litig. Dept. Wilmer Culter Pickering Hale & Dorr LLP, Washington, 2005—. Mem. ABA, DC Bar Assn. Office: Wilmer Culter Pickering Hale & Dorr LLP 1875 Pensylvania Ave NW Washington DC 20006 Office Phone: 202-663-6270. Office Fax: 202-663-6363. Business E-Mail: john.rogovin@wilmerhale.com.

**ROGOVIN, LAWRENCE H.,** lawyer; b. NYC, June 10, 1932; s. Abraham and Laura R.; m. Saundra Schwartz, Aug. 11, 1957; children: Jayne Lina, Wendy Renee, Evan Lewis. BS in Econ., U. Pa., 1953; LLB cum laude, NYU Law Sch., 1956. Bar: NY 1956, Fla. 1971. Dep. asst. atty. gen. State of N.Y., 1956-57, asst. atty. gen., 1960-61; assoc. Squadron, Gartenberg, Ellenoff & Plesent and predecessors, N.Y.C., 1962-67, ptnr., 1967-72; pvt. practice Miami, Fla., 1972—74, Lawrence H. Rogovin, P.A., Fla., 1983—98, Miami, 2002—; ptnr. Squadron, Ellenoff, Plesent & Lehrer, N.Y.C., 1974-75, Cohen, Angel & Rogovin, North Miami, Fla., 1978-82, Cohen, Rogovin, Reed & Ivans, Miami, 1982-83; v.p., gen. counsel Rare, Inc., Miami, 1998—2002. 1st lt. JAGC, USAFR, 1957-60. Recipient NYU Founders Day award, 1956. Mem.: FBA, ABA, Fla. Bar Assn. Office: Ste 265 South 4000 Hollywood Blvd Hollywood FL 33021 Office Phone: 954-367-0666. Office Fax: 954-272-0225. Business E-Mail: lrogovin@bellsouth.net.

**ROGOWSKI, CHERYL,** farmer; AS, Orange County CC, 1981; BS, Mount St. Mary Coll., 1984. Farm mgr., 1977—. Founder Warwick Valley Farmer's Market, 1993; mentor New Farmer Devel. Project. Named MacArthur fellow, John D. and Catherine T. MacArthur Found., 2004. Achievements include establishment of the first low-income Cmty. Supported Agrl. program (CSA) in NY; creation of literary programs for migrant farm workers. Mailing: 327-329 Glenwood Rd Pine Island NY 10969 Office Phone: 845-258-4574.

**ROGOWSKY, ROBERT ARTHUR,** federal official, educator; b. Vancouver, B.C., Can., Mar. 12, 1951; s. Michael Randall and Ruth Ann (Wellman) R.; m. Linda Sue George, June 17, 1972; children: Vanessa, Heather, Tara, Nichole, Alexis. BA in Econs., Boston U., 1973; MA in Econs., U. Va., 1975, PhD in Econs., 1982. Asst. prof. dept. econs. George Mason U., Fairfax, Va., 1977-78; rsch. economist Bur. Econs. FTC, Washington, 1979-83; econ. advisor to commrs. Consumer Product Safety Commn., Washington, 1983-84, acting exec. dir., asst. to dir., 1984; pres. Econ. Edn. for Clergy, Inc., Bethesda, Md., 1985-86; exec. assist. to chmn. Internat. Trade Commn., Washington, 1986-87; dir. office of industries U.S. Internat. Commn., Washington, 1989-92, dir. ops., 1992—; adj. prof. George Mason U. Instr. U. Va., 1976-77; econ. rschr. Am. Enterprise Inst., 1976; econ. rsch. analyst Econ. Policy Office, U.S. Dept. Justice, 1974-75; adj. prof. George Mason U., 1997—; presenter in field. Contbr. articles to profl. jours. Mem. Am. Econ. Assn. Lutheran. Home: 9542 Locust Hill Dr Great Falls VA 22066 Office: US International Trade Comm Operations 500 E St NW Washington DC 20436-0003

**ROHATYN, FELIX GEORGE,** diversified financial services company executive, former ambassador; b. Vienna, May 29, 1928; came to U.S., 1942, naturalized, 1950; s. Alexander and Edith (Knoll) R.; m. Jeannette Streit, June 9, 1956; children: Pierre, Nicolas, Michael; m. Elizabeth Fly, May 31, 1979. BS, Middlebury Coll., Vt., 1948; LLD (hon.), Adelphi U., Bard Coll., Hofstra U., 1981, L.I. U., 1981, Middlebury Coll., 1982, Fordham U., 1983; LLB (hon.), NYU, 1979, Brandeis U., 1987. With Lazard Freres & Co., LLC, NYC, 1948—97, mng. dir., 1960—97; US amb. to France US Dept. State, Paris, 1997—2001; pres. Rohatyn Assocs., NYC, 2002—05; sr. adv. to chmn. Lehman Brothers Inc., NYC, 2006—. Bd. dirs. Publicis Group, Rothschild, Lagardere Group, LVMH, Inc.; mem. bd. govs. N.Y. Stock Exch., 1968—72. Served with AUS, 1951—53, Korea. Office: Lehman Brothers Inc 745 7th Ave 30th Fl New York NY 10019

**ROHDE, BRUCE C.,** food company executive, lawyer; b. Sidney, Nebr., Dec. 17, 1948; BS, BA, Creighton U., 1971, JD cum laude, 1973. Bar: Nebr. 1974, U.S. Dist. Ct. Nebr. 1974, U.S. Ct. Appeals 1975, U.S. Ct. Appeals (8th cir.) 1976, U.S. Ct. Appeals (5th cir.) 1979, U.S. Supreme Ct. 1980, U.S. Claims Ct. 1981, U.S. Ct. Appeals (D.C. cir.) 1982. Lawyer, pres. McGrath, North, Mullin & Kratz, Omaha, 1984—96; gen. counsel ConAgra Inc., Omaha, 1984—96, vice chmn., pres., 1996—97, CEO, 1997—2005, chmn., 1998—2005. Bd. dirs. Valmont Industries Inc., Grocery Mfr. Am. Vice chmn. bd. dirs. Creighton U.; chmn. bd. dirs. Strategic Air and Space Mus.; bd. dirs. Preventive Medicine Rsch. Inst. Mem.: ATLA, ABA (corp., banking and bus. law sect., taxation sect., antitrust law sect., litigation sect.), Omaha Bar Assn., Nebr. Soc. CPA, Nebr. State Bar Assn., Nebr. Assn. Trial Lawyers, Beta Alpha Psi, Beta Gamma Sigma.

**ROHDE, JAMES VINCENT,** software systems company executive; b. O'Neill, Nebr., Jan. 25, 1939; s. Ambrose Vincent and Loretta Cecillia Rohde; children: Maria, Sonja, Daniele, Olga. B of Comml. Sci., Seattle U., 1962. Chmn. bd. dirs., pres. Applied Telephone Tech., Oakland, Calif., 1974; v.p. sales and mktg. Automation Electronics Corp., Oakland, 1975-82; founder, pres., CEO, chmn. Am. Telecorp, Inc., Redwood City, Calif., 1982-99; founder, vice-chmn., bd. dirs. Ceon Corp., Redwood City, 1999—. Chmn. exec. com., chmn. emeritus Pres.'s Coun. Heritage Coll., Toppenish, Wash., 1985—; chmn. bd. dirs. Calif. chpt. Coun. Growing Cos., 1990—93; bd. dirs. Ind. Colls. No. Calif., 1991—93. Mem. USCG Aux., 2005—; bd. dirs. Ind. Colls. No. Calif., 1991—93. With USCG Aux., 2005—. Named Export Exec. of the Yr. No. Calif., US Dept. Commerce, 1993. Mem.: Am. Electronics Assn. (bd. dirs. 1992—94, vice-chmn. No. Calif. coun. 1992—93, chmn. 1993—94). Republican. Roman Catholic. Office: Ceon Corp 1600 Seaport Blvd Redwood City CA 94063 Personal E-mail: jvrohde@aol.com.

**ROHDE, JOE (JOSEPH MARTIN ROHDE),** theme park executive, designer; b. Sacramento, Calif., Sept. 10, 1955; m. Melody Malmberg; children: Kellan, Brandt. BA in Fine Arts, Occidental Coll., LA. With Walt Disney Imagineering, Walt Disney Co., Lake Buena Vista, Fla., 1980—, exec. designer and v.p. creative; lead designer Disney's Animal Kingdom, Lake Buena Vista. Featured (documentaries) Expedition Everest: Journey to Sacred Lands, Travel Channel, 2006. Achievements include principal creative force behind Disney's Animal Kingdom Expedition Everest thrill ride; model designer, scenic painter Epcot's Mexico pavilion; designer on refurbishment of Fantasyland at Disneyland, Captain EO 3-D film attraction, Epcot's Norway pavilion, and Adventurers Club. Avocations: painting, travel, reading non-fiction.

**ROHLF, F. JAMES,** biologist, educator; b. Blythe, Calif., Oct. 24, 1936; BS, San Diego State Coll., 1958; PhD in Entomology, U. Kans., 1962. Asst. prof. biology U. Calif., Santa Barbara, 1962-65; assoc. prof. statis. biology U. Kans., 1965-69; assoc. prof. biology SUNY, Stony Brook, 1969-72, prof., 1972—2004, chmn. dept. ecology and evolution, 1975—80, 1990—91, disting. prof., 2004—; grad. program dir., 2005—06. Statis. cons. N.Y. Pub. Svc. Commn., 1975-78, IBM, 1977-81, U.S. EPA, 1978-80; vis. scientist IBM, Yorktown Heights, N.Y., 1976-77, 80-81; vis. prof. U. Rome, 1997, 99; guest prof. U. Vienna, 2004. Fellow: Am. Acad. Arts and Scis.; mem.: Internat. Fedn. Classification Socs. (pres. 1975—78), Classification Soc. N.Am. (pres. 1975—78, editl. bd. 1984—, bd. dirs. 1994—97, rep. to coun. 2004—, fin. com. 2004—06, election com. 2006—, bd. dirs. 2006—), Soc. Systematic Biologists, Biometric Soc. Achievements include research and development of statistical methods and software for geometric morphometrics and applications of multivariate analysis to systematics and population biology. Office: Stony Brook U Dept Ecology And Evolution Stony Brook NY 11794-5245

**ROHLFING, FREDERICK WILLIAM,** lawyer, retired judge, political scientist; b. Honolulu, Nov. 2, 1928; s. Romayne Raymond and Kathryn (Coe) R.; m. Joan Halford, July 15, 1952 (div. Sept. 1982); children: Frederick W., Karl A., Brad (dec.); m. Patricia Ann Santos, Aug. 23, 1983. BA, Yale U., 1950; JD, George Washington U., 1955. Bar: Hawaii 1955, Am. Samoa 1978. Assoc. Moore, Torkildson & Rice, Honolulu, 1955-60; ptnr. Rohlfing, Nakamura & Low, Honolulu, 1963-68, Hughes, Steiner & Rohlfing, Honolulu, 1968-71, Rohlfing, Smith & Coates, Honolulu, 1981-84; pvt. practice Honolulu, 1960-63, 71-81. Maui County, Hawaii, 1988—; dep. corp. counsel County of Maui, Wailuku, Hawaii, 1984-87, corp. counsel, 1987-88; land and legal counsel Maui Open Space Trust, 1992-97, also bd. dirs. Polit. cons., 1996, 98, 2002; magistrate judge U.S. Dist. Ct. Hawaii, 1991-96. Active Hawaii Ho. Reps., 1959-65, 80-84, Hawaii State Senate, 1966-75; US alt. rep. So. Pacific Commn., Noumea, New Caledonia, 1975-77, 1982-84; mem. adv. coun. State Reapportionment Commn., Maui, Hawaii, 2001, mem. salary commn. Maui (Hawaii) County, 2005—; chmn. Maui coms. George W. Bush for Pres., 2000. Mem. Hawaii Bar Assn., Maui Country Club, Naval Intelligence Profls. Avocations: golf, skiing. Home: 2807 Kekaulike Ave Kula HI 96790

**ROHM, ROBERT HERMANN,** sculptor, educator; b. Cin., Feb. 6, 1934; s. Hermann George and Anna Katherine (Sager) R.; m. Patricia Jean Cutlip, Dec. 6, 1959 (div. 1978); children: Hans Tobin, Kyle Curtis. B in Indsl. Design, Pratt Inst., 1956; MFA in Sculpture, Cranbrook Acad. Art, 1960. Instr. Columbus (Ohio) Coll. Art and Design, 1956-59, Pratt Inst., Bklyn., 1960-65; prof. art U. R.I., Kingston, 1965-95, pres. emeritus, 1996—. One-man shows include O.K. Harris Gallery, N.Y.C., 1970, 72, 73, 75, 77, 80, 83, 84, 86, 89, 92, 94, 97, 99, 2002, 05, Parker St. 470 Gallery, Boston, 1970, 72, Univ. Rochester, N.Y., 1971, N.S. Coll. Art, Halifax, 1970, Worcester Art Mus. (Mass.), 1978, Univ. R.I., 1981, 88, 94, Nielsen Gallery, Boston, 1985, 86, 92, 93, 2001, Wheaton Coll., Norton, Mass., 2002, La Jolla Mus. Contemporary Art, Calif., 1985, Lenore Gray Gallery, Providence, 1990, 93, 95, Wheeler Gallery, Providence, 1996, R.I. Coll., Providence, 1998, Salve Regina U., Newport, R.I., 2003; group shows include Boston Mus., 1974, Whitney Mus., N.Y.C., 1962, 64, 69, 70, 73, 83, Va. Mus., Richmond, 1970, Fogg Mus., Cambridge, Mass., 1971, Seattle Art Mus., 1969, Vancouver Art Mus., B.C., Can., 1970, N.J. State Mus., Trenton, 1969, R.I. State Coun. on Arts, 1973, 82, Vassar Coll., 1971, Inst. Contemporary Art, Boston, 1975, Miss. Mus. Art, Jackson, 1979-80. Grey Art Gallery, NYU, 1980, Montclair (N.J.) Art Mus., 1978, Aldrich Mus. Contemporary Art, Ridgefield, Conn.,1981, 82, SUNY-Plattsburgh, 1981, Zone Gallery, Springfield, Mass., 1982, Cumberland Gallery, Nashville, 1986, 93, Allan Frumkin Gallery, N.Y.C., 1989, Beitzel Fine Arts Inc., N.Y.C., Addison Gallery Am. Art, Andover, Mass., 1989, Nielsen Gallery, Boston, 1990-91, 99, 2004, Soma Gallery, San Diego, 1993, Palo Alto (Calif.) Cultural Ctr., Centre Coll., Danville, Ky., Harn Mus., U. Fla., Gainesville, 2004, Brevard Mus. Art & Sci. Melbourne, Fla., 2004; represented in permanent collections Columbus Gallery Fine Art, Finch Coll., N.Y.C., Pa. State U., Kunsthalle, Zurich, Va. Mus. Fine Arts, Mus. Modern Art, N.Y.C., U. N.Mex., Albuquerque, Albright-Knox Gallery, Buffalo, Whitney Mus. Am. Art, N.Y.C., Met. Mus. Art, N.Y.C., Rose Art Mus., Brandeis U., Waltham Mass., Mus. Fine Art, Boston, Mus. of Contemporary Art, Chgo., Newport (R.I.) Art Mus., Tucson Mus. of Art, Ariz., Flint Inst. Arts, Mich., Butler Inst. Am. Art, Youngstown, Ohio, Munson-Williams Proctor Arts Inst. Mus. Art, Utica, N.Y., Harn Mus., U. Fla., Gainesville, Amarillo Mus. Art, Tex. Grantee Guggenheim Found., 1964, R.I. State Council on Arts, 1973, 82, 93, NEA, 1974, 86; recipient Cassandra Found. award, 1967, award Boston 200 Bicentennial Commn., 1975. Achievements include subject of numerous articles in jours. and catalogues. Home: PO Box 1679 Charlestown RI 02813-0909 Personal E-mail: robertrohm@netsense.net.

**ROHMAN, THOMAS P.,** lawyer; b. Portsmouth, Va., 1955; BBA in acctg., Notre Dame U., 1977; JD summa cum laude, Wash. State U., 1982; LLM in Taxation, NYU, 1983. CPA Va. 1980; bar: Va. 1983, US Tax Ct. 1986. With KPMG Peat Marwick, 1977—80; ptnr. McGuireWoods LLP, Richmond, Va., 1991—, chmn. firm taxation & employee benefits dept., 1991—2005. Adj. prof. corp. reorganizatiosn Va. Commonwealth U. Grad. Tax Program, 1986—92; adj. prof. partnership taxation & corp. taxation TC Williams Sch. Law, U. Richmond, 1989—; mem. adv. coun. William and Mary Tax Conf., 1994—. Co-author of S Corporations: Federal Taxation, 1989. Mem. adv. bd. Meml. Found. for Children, 1987—. Fellow: Am. Coll. Tax Counsel; mem.: ABA (mem. com. on S corporations, com. on corp. tax, com. on partnerships), Va. Soc. Cert. Pub. Accountants, Am. Inst. Cert. Pub. Accountants. Office: McGuireWoods LLP One James Ctr 901 E Cary St Richmond VA 23219-4030 Office Phone: 804-775-1032. Office Fax: 804-698-2154. Business E-Mail: trohman@mcguirewoods.com.

**ROHN, REUBEN DAVID,** medical educator, director; b. Israel, Apr. 12, 1945; came to U.S., 1954; s. Aryeh and Rachel (Brenner) R.; m. Judith Semel, Sept. 6, 1971; 1 child, Karen. BA cum laude, Bklyn. Coll., 1967; MD, N.Y. Med. Coll., 1971. Diplomate Am. Bd. Pediat., Am. Bd. Pediatric Endocrinology, Am. Bd. Pediatrics-Adolescent Medicine. Intern in pediat. Montefiore Hosp., Bronx, N.Y., 1971-72, resident in pediat., 1972-74; fellow in adoles-

cent medicine U. Md. Hosp., Balt., 1974-76; preceptor in pediat. Johns Hopkins U. Sch. Health Svcs., Balt., 1975-76; asst. prof. dept. pediat. Ea. Va. Med. Sch., Norfolk, 1976-82; coord. pediat. clerkship Ea. Va. Med. Sch., Children's Hosp. of King's Daus., Norfolk, 1977-90; prof. dept. pediat. Ea. Va. Med. Sch., Norfolk, 1989—; adj. prof. chemistry Old Dominion U., Norfolk, 1984—; dir. adolescent medicine/endocrinology Children's Hosp. of King's Daus., Norfolk, 1976—. Mem. curriculum com. Ea. Va. Med. Sch., 1977-79, clerkship coords. com. 1977-90, genetics com., 1978-80, evaluation com. 1979-91, chmn. selectives com., 1981-82, ad hoc com. on consultation, 1982-83, student progress com., 1983-85, student health com., 1985-87, LCME com. on curriculum, 1990-92; mem. child abuse com. Children's Hosp. of King's Daus., 1976-80, chmn. adolescent adv. com., 1976-80, patient care com. 1980-94, nutrition com. 1980-94, utilization rev. com., 1980-82, med. records com., 1987-89, gen. med./surg. task force com., 1987-88, chmn. dept. promotions com., 1990—; bd. dirs. Pediat. Faculty Assocs., 1994-98, mgmt. com. Children's Specialty Group, 1998-2000; spkr. in field. Reviewer Jour. Adolescent Health Care, 1986—, mem. editl. bd.; 1989-92; contbr. articles to profl. jours. Mem. Norfolk Sch. Health Coun., 1977—93, mem. ad hoc com. infant screening program for hypothroidism Commonwealth of Va., 1977-79, cons., 1979—; mem. cmty. adv. bd. Norfolk Adolescent Pregnancy Prevention Svc. Project, 1981-83; bd. dirs. Elizabeth River chpt. Am. Diabetes Assn., 1982-85, South Hampton Roads chpt. 1985-93; mem. adv. com. Norfolk-Virginia Beach Jr. League, 1987-88; judge ann. Health Edn. Fair, Norfolk Pub. schs., 1980-94; pres. VA/Carolines chpt. Soc. Adolescent Medicine, 1998-2000. Recipient grant Bressler Rsch. Fund, 1975-76, Biomed. Rsch. Devel. grant Ea. Va. Med. Sch., 1978, 78-79, 79-80. 81-82, 83-84, Children's Health Found. grant, 1988-89. Fellow. Am. Acad. Pediat. (youth and adolescence com. nat. chpt. 1978—2000); mem.: Lawson Wilkins Pediat. Endocrine Soc., Soc. Adolescent Medicine (abstract reviewer 1984—91), Sigma Xi. Avocations: photography, folk dancing. Home: 4653 Larkwood Dr Virginia Beach VA 23464-5815 Office: Childrens Hosp Kings Daus 601 Childrens Ln Norfolk VA 23507-1910 Office Phone: 757-668-7237. Business E-Mail: reuben.rohn@chkd.org.

**ROHN, WILLIAM R.,** biotechnology company executive; BA, Mich. U. Mktg. and sales mgmt. positions Abbott Labs., Warren-Teed Pharms., Miles Labs., Mead Johnson Labs.; sr. v.p. sales and mktg. Adria Labs. (Pharmacia Corp.), 1984—93; sr. v.p. comml. and corp. devel. IDEC Pharms., Inc., San Diego, 1993—96, sr. v.p. comml. ops., 1996—98, COO, 1998—2003, pres., 2002—03; COO Biogen Idec, 2003—. Bd. dirs. Pharmacyclics, Cerus Corp., 2002—. Office: Biogen Idec 5200 Research Pl San Diego CA 92122-4616

**ROHNER, BONNIE-JEAN,** small business owner, computer scientist, consultant; b. Waltham, Mass., Aug. 2, 1946; d. Gerrit John and Marjorie Lorraine (Hollis) Rohner; children: David Harrison Sackett, Amanda Marjorie Sackett. BFA in Fashion, Pratt Inst., Bklyn., 1967; BA in Biology, Adelphi U., 1983; MS, CIS, U. New Haven, 1993. Freelance fashion designer, Garden City, NY, 1971-76; owner, mgr. Printing Workshop, Massapequa, NY, 1976-78; personnel mgr. Doron Ltd., Norwich, Conn., 1978-79; computer related trainer Gen. Dynamics, Groton, Conn., 1979-89; acad. computing coord. Three Rivers Com./Tech. Coll., Norwich, 1989-94; owner, mgr. bytestream, Norwichtown, Conn., 1993—. Tech. advisor Countywide Network Com., 1989—90; computer cons. U. New Haven, Groton, 1990—92; sec. Connbug, Rocky Hill, Conn., 1992—93; tech. cons. Am. Online, 1996—. Mem.: ACM, AAUP, AAUW, NAFE, Women's Network S.E. Conn. Avocations: creative writing, Web surfing. Office Phone: 860-886-7977. Business E-Mail: bonnie-jean@bytestream.org.

**ROHNER, RALPH JOHN,** lawyer, educator, dean; b. East Orange, N.J., Aug. 10, 1938; AB, Cath. U. Am., 1960, JD, 1963. Bar: Md. 1964. Teaching fellow Stanford (Calif.) U., 1963-64; atty. pub. health div. HEW, 1964-65; prof. law Cath. U. Am. Sch. Law, Washington, 1965—, acting dean, 1968-69, assoc. dean, 1969-71, dean, 1987-95; staff counsel consumer affairs subcom. U.S. Senate Banking Com., 1975-76; cons. Fed. Res. Bd., 1976-83, chmn. consumer adv. council, 1981; cons. FDIC, 1978-80; spl. counsel Consumer Bankers Assn., 1984—. Cons. U.S. Regulatory Coun., 1978-80. Co-author: Consumer Law: Cases and Materials, 1979, 2d edit., 1991; co-author, editor The Law of Truth in Lending, 1984, republished, 2000. Bd. dirs. Migrant Legal Action Program, Inc., Washington, Automobile Owners Action Coun., Washington, Credit Rsch. Ctr., Georgetown U., Am. Fin. Svcs. Assn. Edn. Found. Conf. on Consumer Fin. Law. Mem. ABA, Am. Law Inst., Coll. of Consumer Fin. Svcs. Lawyers. Home: 10909 Forestgate Pl Glenn Dale MD 20769-2047 Office: Cath U Sch Law 620 Michigan Ave NE Washington DC 20064-0001 E-mail: rohner@law.edu. *We learn from those we teach, we are inspired to write by those who read, and we should serve as examples to those who aspire.*

**ROHR, CAROL ANN,** composer, music educator; d. Herbert Samuel and Cecil Leotta Neale; m. Stephen P. Rohr, May 30, 1968. MusM, U. S.D., 1967—71. Composer: (piano composition) Dorian Grey for Piano (Cedar Rapids, Iowa Beethoven Club, 2004), (piano, violin and cello composition) Stream of Consciousness (Iowa Composer's Concert, 1994), (piano composition) Sonata and Postlude (Iowa Composers Forum Ann. Concert at Coe Coll., Cedar Rapids, Iowa, 1980). Chair, orgn. support Cedar Rapids City Music Contest, 1975—2004. Scholar Swensrud scholarship award, Northwood Pub. Sch., 1955—58. Mem.: Nat. Music Tchrs. Assn. (assoc.), Iowa Music Tchrs. Assn. (assoc.; student performance auditions and festivals 1980—), Iowa Composers Forum (assoc.), Beethoven Club of Cedar Rapids, Iowa (assoc.; libr./historian 1995—2005). Home: 4008 Glen Elm Drive NE Cedar Rapids IA 52400-2667 Office: Carol A Rohr Private Piano Instruction 4008 Glen Elm Dr NE Cedar Rapids IA 52402-2667

**ROHR, DAVIS CHARLES,** aerospace consultant, retired military officer; b. Burlington, Wis., Oct. 29, 1929; s. Charles Davis Rohr and Dorothy Elizabeth (Hahn) Rohr Larson; m. Gayle Lynn White, Aug. 22, 1959; children— Ellen Louise, Jean Elizabeth Student, Northwestern U., 1947-48; B.Sc., U.S. Mil. Acad., 1952; MA, U. Wash., 1960. Commd. 2d lt. USAF, 1952, advanced through grades to maj. gen. 1980, fighter pilot Ohio, Korea, Japan, 1954-58; asst. prof. history USAF Acad., Colo., 1960-64; fighter pilot, squadron ops. officer Idaho and, Fed. Republic Germany, 1965-69; fighter squadron comdr. Vietnam, 1969-70; country dir. S.Am. Office of Sec. of Def., Washington, 1970-73; exec. officer, dep. dir. maintenance Hdqrs. Tactical Air Command, 1973-75; tactical fighter wing comdr. Tex., Utah, 1976-79; chief Office of Mil. Coop., Cairo, 1979—81; dir. plans and policy U.S. European Command, Stuttgart, Fed. Republic Germany, 1981-84; dep. comdr. in chief U.S. Cen. Command, MacDill AFB, Fla., 1984-87, ret.; aerospace cons., 1988—. Adj. prof. history Paradise Valley C.C., 1991-94; real estate broker, 1991—. Decorated Def. D.S.M., 2 Def. Superior Service medals, Legion of Merit with cluster, D.F.C., Meritorious Service medal, Air medal with 14 clusters, Air Force Commendation medal, Purple Heart

**ROHR, DONALD GERARD,** history professor; b. Toledo, Oct. 10, 1920; s. Lewis Walter and Marie (Pilliod) R.; m. Joan Willis Michener, Sept. 14, 1948; children: Karen, Kristin. BA, U. Toronto, Can., 1943, MA, 1949; PhD, Harvard U., 1958. Instr., then asst. prof. Williams Coll., 1953—59; mem. faculty Brown U., 1959—, prof. history, 1963—86, prof. history emeritus, 1986—, chmn. dept., 1960—65, 1966—69, 1972—74, sec. faculty, 1969—72, assoc. dean faculty and acad. affairs, 1976—81; adminstrv. dir. Howard Rel., 1989—92. Author: The Origins of Social Liberalism in Germany, 1963, (with Robert Ergang) Europe Since Waterloo, 1967; editor: The Young John Carter Brown in Europe, 2005. Served with AUS, 1943-46, ETO. Mem. Am. Hist. Assn., Conf. Group Ctrl. European History, Providence Com. Fgn. Rels. (sec. 1968-81, chmn. 1981-92), Thomas Becket Fedn. (v.p. 1983-84, pres. 1984-86), English Speaking Union (pres. Providence br. 1986-88), U. Club, Faculty Club (Providence, pres. 1981-83). Roman Catholic. Home: 71 Grotto Ave Providence RI 02906 Office Phone: 401-863-2131.

**ROHR, JAMES EDWARD,** diversified financial services company executive; b. Cleve., Oct. 18, 1948; s. Charles E. and Loretta (Kramer) R.; m. Sharon Lynn Chambers, Dec. 29, 1970; children: Julie, James, Kristen. BA, Notre Dame U., 1970; MBA, Ohio State U., 1972. From comml. banking officer to pres. Pitts. Nat. Bank, 1974-89, chmn., CEO, 1989-93, pres., CEO, 1993—; vice-chmn. PNC Bank Corp., 1989-92, pres., 1992—2000, COO, 1998—2000; CEO, pres. PNC Fin. Svcs. Group, Inc., Pitts., 2000—, chmn., 2001—. Bd. dirs. Allegheny Techs. Corp., Equitable Resources, Inc., Rand Corp., Black Rock, Inc., PFPC Worldwide, Inc. Bd. dirs. Greater Pitts. coun. Boy Scouts Am., Carnegie-Mellon U.; chair Cultural Trust. Mem. Am. Bankers Assn., Internat. Monetary Conf., Fin. Svcs. Roundtable, Allegheny Conf., Orgn., Pa. Bus. Roundtable. Roman Catholic. Office: PNC Financial Services Group Inc 249 5th Ave Pittsburgh PA 15222-2709

**ROHR, MARK C.,** chemicals executive; Sr. v.p. Occidental Chem. Corp.; exec v.p. ops. Albemarle Corp., Richmond, Va., 1999, pres., COO, 2000—02, pres., CEO, 2002—. Office: Albemarle Corp 330 S 4th St Richmond VA 23219*

**ROHRABACHER, DANA,** congressman; b. Coronado, Calif., June 21, 1947; s. Donald and Doris Rohrabacher; m. Rhonda Carmont, Aug. 1997. Student, L.A. Harbor Coll., 1965-67; BA in History, Long Beach State Coll., 1969; MA in Am. Studies, U. So. Calif., 1976. Reporter City News Svc./Radio West, L.A.; editorial writer Orange County Register, 1979-80; asst. press. sec. Reagan for Pres. Campaign, 1976, 80; speechwriter, spl. asst. to Pres. Reagan White House, Washington, 1981-88; mem. U.S. Congress from 46th Calif. dist., Washington, 1989—. U.S. del. Young Polit. Leaders Conf., USSR; disting. lectr. Internat. Terrorism Conf., Paris, 1985; mem. Internat. Rels. com.; chmn. Sci. Subcom. on Space and Aeronautics. Recipient Disting. Alumnus award L.A. Harbor Coll., 1987. Republican. Avocations: surfing, white water rafting. Office: US Ho Reps 2338 Rayburn HOB Washington DC 20515-0546

**ROHRABACHER, JANET HAMMOND,** genealogist, archivist; b. Williamston, Mich., Apr. 24, 1913; d. Herbert Moore and Anna Eugenia (Lane) Hammond; m. Albert Hazen Rohrabacher (dec.); children: Ardenne Anna Brigham, Jeffrey. Tchg. cert., We. Mich. U., Kalamazoo, 1936; degree in practical nursing, McPherson Nursing Sch., Howell, Mich., 1965; student, Mich. State U., East Lansing, 1940. Cert. Geneologist, LPN. Nurse Mich. State Sanatorium, Howell, 1939-41, Ingham County Chest Hosp., Lansing, 1940, Ea. Mich. Sanatorium, Ypsilanty, 1941, McPherson Hosp., Howell, 1942-66; archivist Howell Carnegie Libr., Howell, 1977-2001. Author: Livingston County Courthouse, 2006; writer Bicentennial History of Howell. Chmn. Livingston County Civil War Obs. Com., 1963; active Bicentennial Com. Howell, 1973-77, Mich. State Sesquicentennial Com., 1985-89, The Livingston County Courthouse: An Historic Site, 2005; sec. Howell Archives Bd., 1977—. Recipient award, Mich. Geneal. Coun., 1997. Mem. DAR (award 1976), Livingston County Historical Soc. (charter, founder), Livingston County Genealogical Soc. (founder, 1982), Ancient and Honorable Artillery Soc. Mass, Descendents of Early Quakers, Palatines Am., Detroit Soc. Geneol. Rsch., Descendents of the Latin Kingdom of Jersulam (crusader). Methodist. Avocations: antiques, dance, genealogy. Home: 1320 Ashebury Ln # 356 Howell MI 48843

**ROHRBACH, HEIDI A.,** lawyer; b. Buffalo, Jan. 25, 1953; d. William R. and A.T. R.; m. Leonard Lance, Aug. 9, 1996; 1 child, Peter R. Frank. BA, Northwestern U., 1974; JD, Vanderbilt U., 1977. Bar: NY, 1978. V.p., asst. gen. counsel J.P. Morgan Chase & Co., NYC, 1985—2004.

**ROHRBACH, PETER ALPAUGH,** lawyer; b. Hartford, Conn., Apr. 11, 1953; s. John Grandin and Caroline (Hanson) R.; m. Linda Alperin, Sept. 1, 1976; children: James, Andrew. BA, Yale U., 1975; JD, Stanford U., 1979. Bar: D.C. 1979. Ptnr. Hogan & Hartson, Washington, 1979—, mem. exec. com., dir. comm. practice group. Sr. notes editor: Stanford U. Law Rev., 1978-79. Mem. Fed. Communications Bar Assn. Office: Hogan & Hartson 555 13th St NW Ste 800E Washington DC 20004-1161 Office Phone: 202-637-8631. Office Fax: 202-637-5910. Business E-mail: parohrbach@hhlaw.com.

**ROHRBAUGH, LISA ANNE,** librarian; b. Girard, Ohio, Sept. 17, 1956; d. John Michael and Josephine Antoinette (Oliva) Sultan; m. Paul Hugh Rohrbaugh Jr., July 28, 1979. BA, Youngstown State U., 1978; MLS, Kent State U., 1979. Libr. readers assistance dept. Youngstown (Ohio) Pub. Libr., 1979-86; libr., researcher Ajax Magnethermic Corp., Warren, Ohio, 1986-90; asst. reference libr. Youngstown State U., 1990-93; dir. East Palestine (Ohio) Meml. Pub. Libr., 1993—. Translator articles dealing with electronics and induction heating/melting tech. from Spanish, German and French into English; mem. Ohio Regional Libr. Sys. Reviewer for Libr. Jour. Recipient Quest '91 Creative Scholarship award Youngstown State U., 1991. Named one of. America. 500 Notable Women; recipient People Who Made a Difference award, Vindicator Pub. Co., 2003. Mem. Ohio Libr. Coun., Rotary (pres. East Palestine, Ohio, 1999-2000, 2003-2004), Oxford Round Table Avocations: reading, cooking, baseball. Office: East Palestine Meml Pub Libr 309 N Market St East Palestine OH 44413-2153

**ROHRBAUGH, NOVA R.,** retired music educator; b. Brodbecks, Pa., Jan. 28, 1915; d. Adam Kaltreider and Florence Viola Grote; m. Norman S. Rohrbaugh, Oct. 13, 1934; children: Machree M Baumgardner, Marlet R, Laura J Summers. BM, U. Ext. Conservatory, Chicago, IL, 1961. Music tchr. Conewago Twp., Hanover, Pa., 1956—59; elem. tchr. Southwestern Sch. Dist., Hanover, Pa., 1959—69; music tchr. Conewago Valley Sch. Dist., Hanover, Pa., 1970—74, Spring Grove Sch. Dist., Spring Grove, Pa., 1970—78. Pvt. music tchr., Pa., 1941—2000; church organist. Composer: (choral anthem) I Want to Live for the Master, The Lord is My Light, author several books of poetry including Words from the Heart: Heartstrings More Heartstrings, (childrens book) Chester the Nosy Pig, Daisy the Little Gosling, Benny the Little Goat, Mousey's Ride, Peppy and His Friends and Sonny the Bunny, Curious Molly, (autobiography) Life Line, 2004. Vol. Hanover Hall Nursing Home, Homewood Retirement Ctr, Hanover, Pa., 1982—2001; organist Salem United Methodist Ch., Gettysburg, Pa. Recipient Editors Choice Award, Nat. Libr. of Poetry, 1994, 1995. Mem.: AARP (sec. 1986—2000, outstanding svc. to cmty. 1992). Democrat-Npl. United Church Of Christ. Avocations: sewing, writing poetry and childrens stories, quilting. Home: 120 Amy Ln New Oxford PA 17350

**ROHRER, GREGORY SCOTT,** materials engineer, educator; b. Oct. 2, 1962; s. Clarence Eugene and Patricia Ann Rohrer; m. Cathy Ann Lane, Sept. 8, 1990; children: Scott, Molly, Eric. BA, Franklin and Marshall Coll., Lancaster, Pa., 1984; PhD, U. Pa., 1989. Registered profl. engr., Pa. Asst. prof. Carnegie Mellon U., Pitts., 1990—95, assoc. prof., 1995—99, prof., 1999—, head dept., 2005—. Dir. Materials Rsch. Sci. and Engring. Ctr. Carnegie Mellon U., 1999—. Recipient Superior Achievement New or Unique Materials award, Electro-Sci. Lab, U. Pa., 1989; grantee, NSF, 1994; Kirschner scholar, Franklin and Marshall Coll., 1984. Fellow: Am. Ceramic Soc. (chmn. basic sci. divsn., 2005—06, Ross Coffin Purdy award 2002, Roland B. Snow award 1998). Home: 5620 Aylesboro Avenue Pittsburgh PA 15217 Office: Carnegie Mellon University/Mse Dept 5000 Forbes Avenue Pittsburgh PA 15236 Office Phone: 412-268-2696. Office Fax: 412-268-7596. Business E-Mail: gr20@andrew.cmu.edu.

**ROHRER, JAMES RUSSELL,** history professor; b. Canton, Ohio, May 13, 1960; s. William Howard and Doris Jeanne Rohrer; children: Caleb Matthew, Aaron Andrew. BA witn honors, Kent State U., 1982; MA, Ohio State U., 1985, PhD, 1991; MDiv, Dubuque Theol. Sem., 1995. Tchg. asst. history Ohio State U., Columbus, 1982—89, instr. history Newark, 1989—91; adj. prof. history U. Dubuque, Iowa, 1991—93; prof. ch. history Hushan Coll. and Sem., Hualien, Taiwan, 1995—98; from asst. prof. to profl. history and religion Northwestern Coll., Orange City, Iowa, 1998—2005; vis. assoc. prof. history Western Wash. U., Bellingham, 2004—05; asst. prof. history U. Nebr.,

---

Kearney, 2005—. Vis. prof. history Western Wash. U., Bellingham; hist. cons. Postmodern Prodns., Toronto, Ont., Canada, 2005. Author: Keepers of the Covenant, 1995; contbr. articles to profl. jours., poems to lit. publs. Recipient Teaching Excellence award, Northwestern Coll., 2001. Mem.: Soc. for Historians of Early Republic, Am. Soc. Ch. History, Am. Hist. Assn., Ohio Poetry Assn., Haiku Soc. Canada, Am. Tanka Soc., Haiku Soc. Am. Mem. United Ch. Of Christ. Office: U Nebr Kearney Kearney NE 68849 Business E-Mail: rohrerjr@unk.edu.

**ROHRER, RICHARD JEFFREY,** surgeon, educator; b. Columbus, Mar. 14, 1950; s. James William and Nancy Lenore (Acheson) R.; m. Jill Ellen Stein, Nov. 29, 1981; children: Benjamin, Noah. BS, Yale U., 1973; MD, Columbia U., 1977. Surgeon New Eng. Deaconess and Harvard Med. Sch., Boston, 1984—87; surgeon, chief transplantation New Eng. Med. Ctr., Boston, 1988—; vice chmn. dept. surgery Tufts-New Eng. Med. Ctr., Boston, 2004—; prof. surgery Tufts U. Sch. Medicine, Boston, 2004—. Trustee New Eng. Organ Bank, Boston, 1988—, chmn. bd. dirs., 1999—2002; councillor United Network for Organ Sharing, 1966—2000, sec. 2000—02. Fellow ACS; mem. Am. Soc. Transplant Surgeons, Transplantation Soc., Physicians for Social Responsibility, Assn. for Acad. Surgery, Assn. for Surg. Edn., Soc. Critical Care Medicine. Office: New England Med Ctr Box 40 750 Washington St Boston MA 02111-1526 Office Phone: 617-636-5592.

**ROHRER, SUSAN EARLEY,** film producer, film director, scriptwriter; b. Richmond, Va., Mar. 24; d. Charles Marion Jr. and Gloria Jean (Ripley) Earley; m. Mark Brooks Rohrer. BA in Art cum laude, James Madison U. Prodr., dir., co-story writer (tv shows) Never Say Goodbye, 1988 (Emmy award, Humanitas Prize finalist), Terrible Things My Mother Told Me, 1988 (Emmy nomination, Gold award Nat. Film Festival); prodr., dir. (TV movies) For Jenny With Love (TV Movie award), Mother's Day, 1989 (3 Image award nominations), prodr., dir., writer (TV show) The Emancipation of Lizzie Stern, 1991 (Angel award, Bronze award Nat. Ednl. Film Festival, Emmy nomination, Monitor award finalist, TV Movie award), If I Die Before I Wake, 1993 (Emmy nomination, Humanitas Prize finalist, Cine Golden Eagle, TV Movie award); dir. (TV show) Sweet Valley High, 1996; dir. TV pilot Dojo Kids, 1996; prodr., dir., co-writer About Sarah, TV movie, 1998 (award of excellence Film Adv. Bd., Best of Festival award Breckenridge Film Festival, The Christopher award, Angel award, N.Y. Festivals finalist); writer (TV movies) Another Pretty Face, 2002, Book of Days, 2003. Recipient Resolution of Recognition Virginia Beach City Coun., 1988. Mem. ATAS, SAG, Writers Guild Am., Dirs. Guild Am. Office: Josh Schechter IPG 9200 Sunset Blvd Ste 820 Los Angeles CA 90069

**ROHRICH, RODNEY JAMES (ROD),** plastic surgeon, educator; b. Eureka, SD, Aug. 5, 1953; s. Claude and Katie (Schumacher) R.; m. Diane Louise Gibby, July 3, 1990; children: Taylor Rodney, Rachel Nicole. BA summa cum laude, ND State U., 1975; MD with honors, Baylor Coll., 1979; LittD (hon.), U. ND, 2006. Diplomate Am. Bd. Plastic Surgery, Nat. Bd. Med. Examiners. Instr. surgery Harvard Med. Sch. Mass. Gen. Hosp., Boston, 1985-86; asst. prof. U. Tex. Southwestern Med. Ctr., Dallas, 1986-89, assoc. prof., 1989-91, prof., chmn. dept. plastic surgery, 1991—, Betty and Warren Woodward chair in plastic surgery, 1999; chief plastic surgery Parkland/Zale Univ. Med. Ctr., Dallas, 1989-99. Pres., faculty senate U. Tex., crystal charity ball disting. chair in plastic surgery. Mem. editl. bd. Selected Readings in Plastic Surgery, The Cleft Palate and Craniofacial Jour.; editor Plastic and Reconstructive Surgery, 2005—; contbr. articles to med. jours. Bd. dirs. Save-the-Children Found., Dallas, March of Dimes, Dallas, Dallas for Children; class mem. Leadership Dallas, 1989-90; mem. Adopt-A-Sch., Dallas Summer Mus. Guild, Dallas Mus. Art, Dallas Symphony Assn., Tex. Health Found., Youth Leadership Dallas. Grantee Urban Rsch. Fund, 1982, United Kingdom Ltd. Ednl. Rsch. Fund, 1983, Oxford Cleft Palate Found., 1983, Am. Assn. Plastic Surgeons, 1985, Plastic Surgery Ednl. Found., 1985, 89, 90, U. Tex. Health Sci. Ctr. Dept. Surgery, 1986, Howmedica, 1989, ConvaTec-Squibb, 1989, 91, ConvaTec, 1991; recipient Disting. Svc. award Plastic Surg. Ednl. Found., 1997, Alumni Achievement award, N.D. State U., 1997. Mem. AAAS, AMA (Thomas Cronin award 1988, 90, Clifford C. Snyder award 1990), fellow, ACS, Am. Assn. Hand Surgery, Am. Burn Assn., Am. Cleft Palate Assn., Am. Soc. Law and Medicine, Am. Soc. Maxillofacial Surgeons, Am. Soc. for Surgery the Hand, Am. Soc. Plastic and Reconstructive Surgeons, Am. Trauma Soc., British Med. Assn., Nat. Vascular Malformations Found. Inc. (med. and sci. adv. bd.) Tex. Med. Assn., Tex. Soc. Plastic Surgeons, Mass. Gen. Hosp. Hand Club, Dallas County Med. Soc., Assn. Acad. Chmn. Plastic Surgery, Dallas Soc. Plastic Surgeons, Harvard Med. Sch. Alumni Assn., Inst. for Study of Profl. Risk, Plastic Surgery Rsch. Coun., Reed O. Dingman Soc. Plastic Surgeons, So. Med. Assn., Am. Soc. Plastic Surgeons (pres. 2004). Republican. Roman Catholic. Office: U Tex Southwestern Med Ctr Dept Plastic Surgery 5323 Harry Hines Blvd Dallas TX 75390-9132 Office Phone: 214-821-9114. Business E-Mail: Rod.Rohrich@UTSouthwestern.edu.

**ROHR-KIRCHGRABER, THERESA M.B.,** adolescent medicine; BA, Cornell U., 1984, MD, 1988. Cert. Internal Medicine, Adolescent Medicine. Intern U. Hosp. Cleveland, 1988—89, resident, 1989—91; hosp. appointment Meridia Huron Hosp., Cleve., 1991—94, Crouse-Irving Meml. Hosp., Syracuse, 1994—2003, Grady Hosp., Atlanta, 2004, SUNY Health Sci. Ctr., Syracuse, 1994—2003, academic appointment, 1994—2003, Case Western U., Cleve., 1991—94, Morehouse Sch. Medicine, Atlanta, 2004; asst. prof. Emory U. Sch. Medicine, Atlanta, 2005—. Fellow: Am. Coll. Physicians-Am. Soc. Internal Medicine; mem.: Soc. for Adolescent Medicine. Office: Emory U Sch Medicine 1440 Clifton Rd NE Atlanta GA 30322*

**ROHSENOW, WARREN MAX,** retired mechanical engineer, educator; b. Chgo., Feb. 12, 1921; s. Fred and Selma (Gorss) R.; m. Katharine Towneley Smith, Sept. 20, 1946; children: John, Brian, Damaris, Sandra, Anne. BS, Northwestern U., 1941; M.Eng., Yale, 1943, D.Eng., 1944. Teaching asst., instr. mech. engring. Yale, 1941-44; mem. faculty Mass. Inst. Tech., 1946-85, prof. mech. engring., 1955-85, dir. heat transfer lab., 1954-85, prof. emeritus, 1985. Co-founder, chmn. bd. dirs. Dynatech Corp., Thermal Process System. Author: (with Choi) Heat Mass and Momentum Transfer, 1961; Editor: Developments in Heat Transfer, 1964, (with Hartnett) Handbook of Heat Transfer, 1973, 3d edit., 1998. Served as lt. (j.g.) USNR, 1944-46; lt. comdr. USNR, ret. 1956. Recipient Pi Tau Sigma gold medal ASME, 1951; award for advancement sci. Yale Engring. Assn., 1952; merit award Northwestern Alumni, 1955; named hon. alumnus MIT, 2004. Fellow Am. Acad. Arts and Scis., Nat. Acad. Engring., ASME (hon. mem., Heat Transfer Meml. award 1967, Max Jakob Meml. award 1970, ASME medal 2001, Classic Paper award 2003); mem. Sigma Xi, Tau Beta Pi, Pi Tau Sigma. Home: 32 Carroll St Falmouth ME 04105-1908

**ROI, ALICE (ALICE ROY BLUMENTHAL),** apparel designer; b. 1976; m. Marc Beckman, 2005. BA in Fine Arts, NYU; grad., Parson's Sch. of Design. Former fashion consultant Elle mag., Fashion Group Internat.; designer Alice Roi Collection, 1999—. Recipient Perry Ellis award nomination, Council of Fashion Designers of Am., 2001. Office: c/o Designer Mgmt Agy 446 Broadway New York NY 10013*

**ROIG-ALVARADO, PEDRO J.,** archivist; s. Pedro J. Roig and Maria Esther Alvarado. BA in Edn., Inter-Am. U. of P.R., Bayamon, 1993; M of Archivist, U. of Seville, Spain, 1999. Cert. history tchr. Edn. Dept. of P.R. Archivist II Gen. Archives of P.R., San Juan, PR, 1995—. Recipient Luis Pales Matos medal, 0987. Mem.: Soc. of Am. Archivists. Roman Catholic. Avocations: genealogy, bowling. Office: Gen Archives of P R # 500 Ave Constitucion San Juan PR 00902-4184 Personal E-mail: pjroal@yahoo.es. E-mail: proig@icp.gobierno.pr.

**ROIN, JULIE,** law educator; b. 1955; BA in Social Studies, magna cum laude, Radcliffe Coll., 1977; JD, Yale U., 1980. Bar: DC 1981. Law clk. to Hon. Patricia M. Wald US Ct. Appeals DC Cir., 1980—81; assoc. Caplin & Drysdale, Chartered, Washington, 1981—84; asst. prof. law U. Va. Sch. Law,

---

1985—90, prof., 1990—98, Class of 1963 rsch. prof. law, 1992—95, Henry L. and Grace Doherty Charitable Found. prof. law, 1996—98; prof. law U. Chgo. Law Sch., 1998—, Seymour Logan prof. law, 2002—. Vis. asst. prof. law Yale Law Sch., 1986—87, U. Va. Sch. Law, 1984—85; vis. prof. law Harvard Law Sch., 1990—91, U. Chgo. Law Sch., 1993, U. Mich. Law Sch., 1997; Jack N. Pritzker disting. vis. prof. law Northwestern U. Law Sch., 1998. Co-author (with P. Stephan & D. Wallace): International Business and Economics: Law and Policy, 1993. Office: U Chgo Law Sch 1111 E 60th St Chicago IL 60637 Office Phone: 773-702-5314. E-mail: julie_roin@law.uchicago.edu.

**ROISMAN, LILA,** retired advertising writer; d. Jack and Rose Stoll; children: Roger, Richard. BA, Hunter Coll., NYC, 1943; MA, U. Pa., 1968. Asst. prof. Temple U., Phila., 1969—72; assoc. prof. U. Pa., 1969—72; proprietor Lila Roisman Enterprises, Phila., 1973—75; promotion writer, mktg. Phila. Inquirer, Daily News, 1975—95; ret. 1995. V.p. Newspaper Guild Phila., 1978—95; book reviewer Phila. Inquirer, 50 Plus Mag.; docent Pa. Acad. Fine Arts, 1995—98, mem. women's com., 1998—2001. Program chair Women in Comm., Phila., 1980—90; bd. mem. Mayor's Commn. Svcs. to Aging, Phila., 1985—90; vol. Phila. Mus. Art, 2000—, Jewish Cmty. Ctr. Film Festival, Phila., Manna. Mem.: Cosmopolitan Club (Phila.). Avocations: writing, travel, bridge. Home: 1901 John F Kennedy Blvd Apt 1221 Philadelphia PA 19103 E-mail: lilagol@aol.com.

**ROITMAN, JUDITH,** mathematician, educator; b. N.Y.C., Nov. 12, 1945; d. Leo and Ethel (Gottesman) R.; m. Stanley Lombardo, Sept. 26, 1978; 1 child, Ben Lombardo. BA in English, Sarah Lawrence Coll., 1966; MA in Math., U. Calif., Berkeley, 1971, PhD in Math., 1974. Asst. prof. math. Wellesley (Mass.) Coll., 1974-77; from asst. prof. to prof. math. U. Kans., Lawrence, 1977—. Author: Introduction to Modern Set Theory, 1990; contbr. articles to profl. jours. Grantee, NSF, 1975—87, 1992—95. Mem. Assn. Symbolic Logic, Am. Math. Soc., Assn. Women in Math. (pres. 1979-81, Louise Hay award 1996), Kans. Assn. Tchrs. Math., Nat. Assn. Tchrs. Math. Avocation: poetry. Business E-Mail: roitman@math.ku.edu.

**ROIZEN, MICHAEL F.,** anesthesiologist, medical educator; b. N.Y., Jan. 7, 1946; m. Nancy J. Roizen; children: Jeffery, Jennifer. AB in Chemistry with honors, Williams Coll., Williamstown, Mass., 1967; MD, U. Calif., San Francisco, 1971. Intern Beth Israel Hosp., Boston, 1972, resident in medicine, 1973; rsch. assoc. in pharmacology NIH, Bethesda, Md., 1973-75; resident in anesthesia U. Calif., San Francisco, 1977, asst. prof., 1977-81, assoc. prof., 1981-85; prof. internal medicine U. Chgo., 1985—, prof. and chair dept. anesthesia and critical care, 1985; prof., anesthesiology SUNY Upstate Med. Ctr. and Univ., Syracuse, NY. Panel mem. FDA. Author: Essence of Anesthesia Practice, 1997, RealAge: Are You as Young as You Can Be?, 1999, (with Mehmet C Oz) You: The Owners Manual, 2005 (#1 Publishers Weekly Hardcover Bestseller list); reviewer numerous anesthesia and med. jours. Mem. Am. Bd. Anesthesiology (assoc.), Am. Bd. Internal Medicine (assoc.), Am. Soc. Anesthesiologists, Soc. of Cardiovascular Anesthesiologists (pres. 1995-97), U.S. Squash Racquets Assn., Alpha Omega Alpha, Phi Beta Kappa. Avocation: squash.

**ROIZEN, NANCY J.,** physician, educator; b. Hartford, Conn. m. Michael F. Roizen; children: Jeffrey, Jennifer. BS, Tufts U., 1968, MD, 1972. Diplomate Am. Bd. Pediats. Staff physician Oakland (Calif.) Children's Hosp., 1976-84; asst. prof. clin. pediats. Johns Hopkins Hosp., Balt., 1984-85; assoc. prof. pediat. and psychiatry U. Chgo., 1985—. Fellow Am. Acad. Pediats.; mem. Soc. for Devel. Pediats. (pres. 1996-98). Office: U Chgo Hosps MC 900 5841 S Maryland Ave Chicago IL 60637-1463

**ROIZMAN, BERNARD,** virologist, educator; b. Chisinau, Rumania, Apr. 17, 1929; arrived in U.S., 1947, naturalized, 1954; s. Abram and Liudmilla (Seinberg) Roizman; m. Betty Cohen, Aug. 26, 1950; children: Arthur, Niels. BA, Temple U., 1952, MS, 1954; ScD in Microbiology, Johns Hopkins, 1956; DHL (hon.), Gov.'s State U., 1984; MD (hon.), U. Ferrara, Italy, 1991; DSc (hon.), U. Paris, 1997, U. Valladolid, Spain, 2001. From instr. microbiology to asst. prof. Johns Hopkins Med. Sch., 1956—65; from mem. faculty Divsn. Biol. Scis. to prof. U. Chgo., 1965—69, prof., 1969—, chmn. dept. molecular genetics and cell biology, 1985—88, Joseph Regoustein Disting. Svc. prof., 1984—. Co-founder Aviron, Inc., 1992; convener herpes virus workshop, Cold Spring Harbor, NY, 72; lectr. Am. Found. for Microbiology, 1974—75; mem. spl. virus cancer program devel. rsch. working group Nat. Cancer Inst., 1967—71; mem. steering com. human cell biology program NSF, 1971—74; mem. adv. com. cell biology and virology Am. Cancer Soc., 1970—74; chmn. herpes virus study group Internat. Commn. Taxonomy of Viruses, 1971—73; mem. Internat. Microbiol. Genetics Commn. Internat. Assn. Microbiol. Scis., 1974—81; mem. sci. adv. coun. N.Y. Cancer Inst., 1971—88; mem. adv. bd. Leukemia Rsch. Found., 1972—77; mem. herpes-virus working team WHO/FDA, 1978—81; mem. bd. sci. cons. Sloan Kettering Inst., N.Y.C., 1975—81; mem. study sect. exptl. virology NIH, 1976—80; mem. task force on virology Nat. Inst. Allergy and Infectious Disease, 1976—77; mem. com. to establish vaccine priorities Nat. Inst. Medicine, 1983—85; chmn. sci. adv. bd. Tampa Bay Rsch. Inst., 1983—, chmn. bd. trustees, 1991—97; cons. in field. Editor: (book) Herpes Viruses, Vol. 1, 1982, Herpes Viruses, Vol. 2, 1983, Herpes Viruses, Vols. 3 and 4, 1985, The Human Herpesviruses, 1993, Infectious Diseases in an Age of Change, 1995; editor-in-chief: Jour. Infectious Agts. and Disease, 1992—96, mem. editl. bd.: Infectious Diseases, 1965—69, Jour. Virology, 1970—, Jour. Intervirology, 1972—85, Archives of Virology, 1975—81, Virology, 1976—78, Microbiologica, 1978—, Cell, 1979—80, Virology, 1983—, Jour. Hygiene, 1985—91, Gene Therapy, 1994, Wiley Encyclopedia of Molecular Medicine, 2002; contbr. scientific papers, chapters to books. Trustee Goodwin Inst. Cancer Rsch., 1977—. Named hon. prof., Shandong Acad. Med. Scis., China, 1985; recipient Lederle Med. Faculty award, 1960—61, Career Devel. award, USPHS, 1963—65, Pasteur award, Ill. Soc. Microbiology, 1972, Esther Langer award for Achievement in Cancer Rsch., 1974, Outstanding Alumnus in Pub. Health award, Johns Hopkins U., 1984, ICN Internat. prize in Virology, 1988, J. Allyn Taylor Internat. prize in Medicine, 1997, Bristol-Myers Squibb award for Disting. Infectious Disease Rsch., 1998; fellow Travelling, Internat. Agy. Rsch. Against Cancer, Karolinska Inst., Stockholm, 1970; grantee Facutly Rsch. Assoc., Am. Cancer Soc., 1966—71, USPHS/NIH, 1958—, Am. Cancer Soc., 1962—90, NSF, 1962—79; scholar Am. Cancer Soc., Pasteur Inst. Paris, 1961—62. Fellow: AAAS, Japanese Soc. for Promotion of Sci., Am. Acad. Arts and Scis.; mem.: NAS, Johns Hopkins U. Soc. Scholars, Chinese Acad. Engring. (fgn.), Hungarian Acad. Scis. (fgn.), Brit. Soc. Gen. Microbiology, Am. Soc. Molecular Biology and Biochemistry, Am. Soc. Virology, Am. Soc. Microbiology, Am. Assn. Immunologists, Am. Acad. Microbiology, Inst. Medicine, Quadrangle Club (hon.). Home: 5555 S Everett Ave Chicago IL 60637-1968 Office: U Chgo MB Kovler Viral Oncology Labs 910 E 58th St Chicago IL 60637-1432 Office Phone: 773-702-1898. Business E-Mail: bernard.roizman@bsd.uchicago.edu.

**ROJANY, LISA ADRIENNE,** publishing company executive, writer; b. L.A., Feb. 14, 1964; d. Aviezer Rojany and Mary Marks; m. Kristian Buccieri. B of Comms. magna cum laude, UCLA; cert. in translation, Sorbonne U., Paris; M English and Am. Lit., Brown U. Newspaper journalist UCLA Daily Bruin, Together Newsmag., L.A., 1985-86; English tutor Paris, 1986-87; writer, reviewer TV Guide, L.A., 1987-88; sr. editor Intervisual Books, Santa Monica, Calif., 1991-93; editl. dir. Price Stern Sloan divsn. Penguin Putnam Pub., L.A., 1993-97, Gateway Learning Corp., 1997; west coast publ. dir. Golden Books Family Entertainment, L.A., 1998-2000; editl. dir. bus. devel. MyPotential.com, 2000-01; editor/writer, pres. Editl. Svcs. of LA, 1988—; v.p., pub. Americhip Books, 2002—. Proofreader MIT U. Press, Cambridge, Mass., 1990, Fidelity, Inc., Boston, 1990, Heinle & Heinle Pubs., Inc., Boston, 1990; copyeditor, proofreader Houghton Mifflin Co., Boston, 1990; v.p. and pub. Americhip Books, 2002—; spkr. in field. Author: (childrens books) The Hands-on Book of Big Machines, 1992, Exploring the Human Body, 1992 (10 Best New Parenting Books, Child Mag., 1993), King Arthur's Camelot, 1993 (Book of the Month Club selection, 1993), The Story of Hanukkah, 1993, Where's That Pig?, 1993, Santa's New Suit, 1993, Jake and

Jenny on the Town, 1993, 1996, Andrews & McMeel Mini Pop-Up Quote Books, 1993, Alice in Wonderland, 1994, Token of Love and Spring Gardens, 1994, Mickey Mouse: Where's the Picnic, 1994, Winnie the Pooh: The Suprise Party, 1994, Make Your Own Valentines, 1994, Make Your Own Valentines, 3d edit., 1996 (Pub.'s Weekly Bestseller list, 1994, 1995), Melvin Martian, Dumbo's Circus Train, 1995, Cinderella's Coach, 1995, The Magic Feather, 1995 (Parents Choice Silver Honor award, 1995), Pandora's Box (CD ROM), 1995, Over in the Meadow (CD ROM), 1995, Tell Me About When I Was a Baby, 1996, Gold Diggers: The Novelization, 1996, Hanukkah Candles, 1995, Dragonheart: The Jr. Novelization, 1996, Giant Animal Fold-Outs: Big Trucks & Bigger Diggers, 1996, Giant Giants & Magic Mermaids, 1996, Hippo & Pals, 1996 (Am. Booksellers Pick of the List, 1995), Kangaroo & Company, 1996 (Am. Booksellers Pick of the List, 1995), Dena Dinosaur, Morty Monster, Wanda Witch, 1996, Code Blue: In the Emergency Room, 1996, Code Blue: Making the Grade, 1996, Leave It to Beaver: The Novelization, 1997, Love You Because...Love, Barbie, 1999, Make Your Own Valentine Cards, 2000, (children's books) At the Airport, 2006, At the Ballpark, 2006, Around the House, 2006; co-author: (books) Fund Your Future, 2001 (NY Times Bus. Hardcover Bestseller list #10, 2002, NY Times hardcover bus. bestseller, 2001), Writing Children's Books for Dummies, 2005, Let's Make Noise series, 2005; ghostwriter: childrens books Dinotopia Pop-Up Book, 1993, Sliding Surprise Books, 1993—97, The Facts of Life, 1994, All Mixed Up, 1994, Little Merlin's Book of Magic Pets, 1994, Claverie Fairytale Theater, 1994. Spkr. UCLA Extension, 1993-98, SCBWI Ventura, 2005; mem. comms. bd., fin. com. UCLA, 2002-04. Recipient one of 10 Best New Parenting Books award Child Mag., 1993. Mem. PEN Ctr. U.S.A. West (editor-in-chief 1992-95), Soc. Children's Book Writers and Illustrators (manuscript reviewer 1995-2003), Internat. Women's Writing Guild, Author's Guild, Brown Alumni Assn. (interviewer 1993-98), UCLA Alumni Assn. (bd. dirs., comms., fin. com. 2002-2004), Phi Beta Kappa Avocations: reading, moderating writing workshops, rollerblading. E-mail: esola@adelphia.net.

**ROJAS, CARLOS,** literature and language educator; b. Barcelona, Aug. 12, 1928; s. Carlos and Luisa (Vila) R.; m. Eunice Anne Mitcham, Mar. 19, 1966; children: Carlos, Eunice Anne. MA, U. Barcelona, 1951; PhD, U. Cen., Madrid, 1955; PhD (hon.), U. Simón Bólivar, Barranquilla, Colombia, 1985. Teaching asst. U. Barcelona, 1951-52; fgn. asst. U. Glasgow, Scotland, 1952-54; asst. prof. Rollins Coll., Winter Park, Fla., 1957-60, Emory U., Atlanta, 1960-63, assoc. prof., 1963-68, prof., 1968-80, Charles Howard Candler prof. Spanish lit., 1980-96, Charles Howard Candler prof. emeritus, 1996. Author: Auto de fe, 1968 (Premio Nacional de Literatura 1968), Azana, 1973 (Planeta award 1973), El Igenioso Hidalgo y Poeta F.G. asciende a los infiernos, 1980 (Nadal award 1980), El Sueno de Sarajevo, 1982, El Jardin de las Hespèrides, 1988, El Jardin de Atocha, 1990, Yo, Goya, 1990, Proceso A Godoy, 1992, Salvador Dali, or the Art of Spitting on Your Mother's Portrait, 1993, Alfonso de Borbón Habla Con El Demonio, 1995, !Muera La Inteligencia! !Viva La Muerte! Salamanca, 1995, The Garden of Janus, 1996, Crónica de la Guerra Civil Española, 1996; co-author, contbg. editor Spanish Civil War documents, Momentos estelares de la guerra de España, 1996, La Vida y la Época de Carlos IV, 1997, Los Borbones Destronados, 1997, El bastardo del Rey, 1999, The Garden of the Hesperides, 1999, Puneta La Espaneta, 2000, Despiada Memoria: Memorias, 2002, Diez Crisis del Franquismo, 2003. Recipient Premio Espejo de España award, Madrid, 1984, Encomienda al Mérito Civil, King of Spain, 1986, Univ. Scholar/Tchr. award Emory U., 1987, Arts and Scis. award of Distinction, Emory U., 2001; honoree of yr. Philol. Assn. of Carolinas, 1987, Llave de Barcelona, 2003. Mem. MLA, Am. Assn. Tchrs. Spanish and Portuguese (Premio a la Lealtad Republicana Madrid 2004), Assn. Doctores y Licenciados Españoles en los Estados Unidos (bd. dirs.), South Atlantic MLA (hon.). Avocation: painting. Home: 1378 Harvard Rd NE Atlanta GA 30306-2413 E-mail: crojas@emory.edu.

**ROJAS, EDDY M.,** engineering educator; b. San Jose, Costa Rica, Feb. 26, 1969; came to U.S., 1993; s. Jorge L. Rojas and Hannia Molina; m. Denise Murillo, Aug. 10, 1991. MSCE, U. Colo., 1995, MA in Econs., 1997, PhD in Civil Engring., 1997. Registered civil engr., Costa Rica. Rschr. Earthquake Engring. Lab. U. Costa Rica, San Jose, 1991, instr., 1991-93; asst. prof. U. Buffalo, 1997—2001, U. Wash., 2001—04, assoc. prof., 2004—. Contbr. papers to profl. jours. Recipient Making Virtual Teams Work award, Constrn. Industry Inst., 2000, Tech. Transfer for Mex. Electrical Contracting Firms award, Electrical Contracting Found., 2000, Automating N.Y. State Dept. Transp. Data Collection, 1998, Millennium Generation award, Electrical Contracting Found., 2001. Mem. ASCE (mem. constrn. rsch. coun. 1997—, computing in constrn. com. 1997—). Roman Catholic. Office: U Washington 116 Architecture Box 351610 Seattle WA 98195-1610 Office Phone: 206-616-1917. E-mail: er@u.washington.edu.

**ROJAS, JESUS JON,** health products executive, researcher; b. Havana, Cuba, Oct. 29, 1970; s. Bienvenido Amado Rojas and Edelmira Nena Caballero; 1 child, Jonathan Richard-Alexander. Clin. rsch. coord. SFBC Internat., Miami, Fla., 1996—97, dir. pharmacy, 1997—99, assoc. dir. clin. ops., 1999—2004, dir. clin. ops., 2004—06; v.p. project mgmt. OmniComm Sys., Inc., Ft. Lauderdale, Fla., 2006—. Clin. rsch. cons., Miami, 1998—. Dir. activities abused children Cath. Ch., Miami, 1994—2006. Named Best New Artist, 1994. Mem.: Project Mgr. Inst. (licentiate; mem. 1996), Assn. Clin. Rsch. Profls. (assoc. cert. clin. rsch. assoc.). Avocations: martial arts, surfing, reading, running. Home: 17096 Collins Ave # 200 Sunny Isles Beach FL 33160 Office: OmniComm Sys Inc 2101 W Commercial Blvd Fort Lauderdale FL 33309 Office Phone: 954-473-1254. Home Fax: 954-473-1254; Office Fax: 954-473-1256. Personal E-mail: rojasjonn@aol.com. Business E-mail: jrojas@omnicomm.com.

**ROJAS, ROBERTO G.,** electrical engineer; PhD, Ohio State U., Columbus, 1985. Prof. Ohio State U., 2002—. Fellow: IEEE (Browder J. Thompson Meml. Prize award 1990). Office: Ohio State U 1320 Kinnear Rd Columbus OH 43212 Office Phone: 614-292-2530. E-mail: rojas-teran.1@osu.edu.

**ROJAS, VICTOR HUGO MACEDO,** retired vocational education educator; b. Mollendo, Peru, Jan. 11, 1923; came to U.S., 1944; s. Mariano A. and Maria Santos (Macedo) R.; m. Mary Emily Bush, Apr. 28, 1945 (dec. 1984). AA, Miami-Dade C.C., 1982; BS in Vocat. Edn., Fla. Internat. U., 1986. Cert. tchr., Fla. Engine tech. Nat. Sch., 1943; automotive mechanic various Ford dealerships, Miami, Fla., 1945-60; automotive technician East Tenn. Motors, Knoxville, 1960-63; car and truck salesman Ford Mktg. Inst., 1963; automotive technician Tally-Embry Ford, Inc., Miami, 1964-66, shop foreman, then mgr., 1966-75, master technician, automotive instr., 1973-75; instr. automotive tech. Dade County Pub. Schs., Miami, 1975-91; bus. exec. Internat. Correspondence, 1976; ret., 1991. Adviser, sponsor Vocat.-Indsl. Clubs Am., Miami, 1988-91. Contbr. articles to newspapers. With Armada Peruana, 1940-44, USN, 1945. Recipient Cert. of Achievement Motor Age mag., 1961, 62, St. Mary's Cathedral, Miami, 1988, Automotive Svc. Excellence award Nat. Inst. Automotive Svc., 1975, Hon. award Prefect of Arequipa, Peru, 2005. Mem. Am. Legion (historian 1989), Elks. Democrat. Roman Catholic. Avocations: music, ballroom dancing, reading, writing, photography. Personal E-mail: vicbullfighter@aol.com.

**ROJESKI, HALLIE E.,** elementary school educator; b. Denver, May 28, 1944; d. Richard Leonard and Elizabeth R. Roscoe; m. Donn Kent Rojeski, June 18, 1972; children: Paul Andrew, Diane Michelle. BA in Edn., Nebr. Wesleyan U., Lincoln, 1966. Tchr. h.s. Wilber-Clatonia Schs., Nebr., 1966—69; tchr. jr. high sch. Racine Unified Sch. Dist., Wis., 1969—71; tchr. jr. high sch., team leader Cherry Creek Schs., Englewood, Colo., 1971—72, Lincoln Pub. Schs., Nebr., 1972—75; tchr. jr. high sch. Wheatland Schs., Madrid, 1975—77, Fresno Christian Schs., Calif., 1989—. Advisor Calif. Jr. Scholarship Fedn., 1990—. Author: (textbook) Grammar Rules Notebook. Sch. coord. Odyssey Mind/Destination Imagination, Fresno, Calif., 1989—2006; coach NE Spartans Baseball League, 1985—87; chair New Life Fellowship-North Fresno MB Ch., 1985—99, treas., 2000—06; dir. North Fresno MB Ch., 1984—89, libr., 1982—89. Named Local Tchr. Yr., Wal-

Mart, 2003. Conservative. Avocation: reading. Home: 1515 E Mesa Fresno CA 93710 Office: Fresno Christian Schools 7280 N Cedar Fresno CA 93720 Office Phone: 559-299-1695. Business E-Mail: hrojeski@fresnochristian.com.

**ROJO, RUTH M.,** nutritionist, consultant, director; b. San Antonio, Tex., Oct. 23, 1938; d. Fernando Sosa and Margie Macias Rojo; 1 child, Amina Ruth. Dr. Naturopathy, Clayton Coll. Natural Health, Birmingham, Ala., 1996, U.S. Sch. Naturopathy, Atlanta, 1999; PhD in Nutrition, Am. Holistic Coll. Nutrition, Birmingham, 1996; Dr. Naturopathic Medicine, Colo. U. Naturopathic Medicine, Denver, 1999. Board Certified Naturopath Am. Naturopathic Med. Certification and Accreditation Bd. Pres. / founder Tex. State Naturopathic Med. Assn., San Antonio, 1998—; Tex. rep. Am. Naturopathic Med. Assn., Las Vegas, Nev., 1998—, bd. dirs., 2000—; founder Tex. Complimentary and Alternative Medicine Assn., 2003; cons. in complimentary and alternative medicine. Founder togetwell.com, 2004. Author: Priority 1--A Guide to Natural Health. Legis. chair N.E. Bexar County Rep. Women's Club, San Antonio, 2001—02. Recipient Hall of Fame award, Tex. State Naturopathic Assn., 2000. Avocations: painting, walking, reading, sports. Office: PO Box 1583 Helotes TX 78023 Office Phone: 210-979-0802. Personal E-mail: rrojo@drrojo.com. Business E-Mail: durojo@togetwell.com.

**ROJO DE SANTOS, ANITA,** shop owner, writer; b. Bacamopa Mocorito, Sinaloa, Mexico, Feb. 5, 1941; arrived in US, 1985; d. Rafael Rojo and Mercedes Beltran; m. Raul Santos, June 3, 1972; children: Raul Santos Rojo, Adrian Santos Rojo, Paul Santos Rojo. Owner Rojo Bros. Market, Gua muchil, Sinaloa, Mexico, 1955—84, Santa Anita Pharmacy, Guamuchil, Sinaloa, Mexico, 1960—84, Sombrereria Panama (hat store), Los Mochis, Sinaloa, Mexico, 1972—84, Santa Anita Flowers, L.A., Calif., 1992—. Mem. Commerce Adv. Com., Guamuchil/Los Mochis, Mexico, 1956—84. Author: (book) Amor del Bueno y Mas, 1991, The Grandest Love in the World, 2003. Finalist Hispanic Family of the Yr., Hispanic Am. Family of the Yr. Found., 1990; named hon. vol., Leukemia Soc. of Am., 1988. Avocations: reading, painting. Office: PO Box 2021 La Puente CA 91746 Office Phone: 626-806-7285. Personal E-mail: anitarojob@yahoo.com.

**ROKER, AL,** newscaster; b. Queens, NY, Aug. 20, 1954; m. Alice Bell, Dec. 22, 1984 (div. 1994); m. Deborah Roberts, Sept. 16, 1995; 3 children. Grad., SUNY, Oswego. Weathercaster, graphic artist WTVH-TV, Syracuse, N.Y., 1974-76; weathercaster WTTG-TV, Washington, 1976-78, WKYC-TV, Cleve., 1978-83, WNBC-TV, N.Y.C., 1983—; weatherman NBC News Today Show, N.Y.C., 1995—; founder Al Roker Productions, 1994—. Exec. prodr.: (TV series) Roker on the Road, 2003; actor: (TV films) Broadway on Broadway, 2000, (voice): (films) Wholey Moses, 2003, Robots, 2005; author (non-fiction): Don't Make Me Stop this Car: Adventures in Fatherhood, 2000, Big Shoes: In Celebration of Dads and Fatherhood, 2005; author: (cook-books) Al Roker's Big Bad Book of Barbecue: 100 Easy Recipes for Backyard Barbecue, 2002, Al Roker's Hassle-Free Holiday Cookbook, 2003. Named Best Weatherman, N.Y. mag., 1985. Mem. Am. Meteorol. Soc. (recipient Seal of Approval). Office: NBC News 30 Rockefeller Plz Rm 1420 New York NY 10112-0002

**ROKER, CHRISTOPHER A.,** microbiologist, photographer; arrived in US, 1986; s. John A. T. and LueElla Roker; m. Elizabeth M. Roker, Apr. 14, 1984; children: Krislar, Kwame, Kofi. BS in Med. Tech., LI U., 1996, post graduate, 2003—; student, NY Inst. Photography, 1975—78, Germain Sch. Photography, 1982. Cert. clin. lab. scientist Nat. Certify Agy. Lab. Profls. Profl. photographer, studio owner Esquire Photography Studio, Nassau, 1983—88; retoucher Color Wheel, NYC, 1986—95; microbiologist Shield Med. Lab., Bklyn., 1995—99, Sherman-Abrams Med. Lab, Bklyn., 1999—, Analytical Diagnostic Lab., Bklyn., 1999—. Photographer (exhibitions), NYC, Nassau, Bahamas, Down by the Sea, Body Works, New York After Dark. Mem.: Am. Soc. Clin. Lab. Sci., Am. Soc. Microbiology (mem. sub-com. 2002—). Avocations: sports, poetry, writing, jazz. Home: 118 Ave D Apt 8H New York NY 10009 Office: Analytical Diagnostic Lab 2115 Ave X Brooklyn NY 11235 Office Phone: 718-646-6000. Office Fax: 718-646-0820. Business E-Mail: CARokers@msn.com.

**ROKHLENKO, ALEXANDER,** research scientist, educator; b. Kiev, Ukraine, June 13, 1935; s. Victor Nathan Rokhlenko and Rosa Sakhnovskaya; m. Tatyana Kukavskaya, Aug. 13, 1964; 1 child, Vadim. Physicist, tchr. (hon.), Kiev State U., 1958; PhD in Physics, Inst. Physics, Kiev, 1966. Electronic engr. mil. radio plant, Kiev, 1958—60; engr.-rschr. Inst. of Hydromechanics, Kiev, 1960—63; rsch. scientist Inst. of Material Sci., Kiev, 1963—89; rsch. assoc. Rutgers U., Piscataway, NJ, 1990—. Adj. prof. Drexel U., Phila., 1990—92; cons. Am. Inst. of Physics, Melville, NY, 1991—. Achievements include research in Spectral properties of Schroedinger operator; Plasma in external fields; first to Beams of charged particles; Atomic ionization in external fields; research in Mathematical modelling of corrosion protection; first to Recombination of atoms on solids. Avocations: electronic construction, mechanical devices, swimming, social study, world literature. Home: 26 Greenbriar Row Princeton NJ 08540 Office: Rutgers Univ 110 Frelinghuysen Rd Piscataway NJ 08854 Office Phone: 732-445-3989. E-mail: rokhlenk@math.rutgers.edu.

**ROKICKI, LORI ANN,** psychologist; d. Frank and Joan Rokicki. PhD, Ohio U., Athens, 1993. Asst. prof. Miss. State U., Starkville, 1994—97, Ill. Inst. Tech., Chgo., 1997—2003; dir. med. psychology Ctr. Behavioral Medicine, 1999—2003; dir. River Centre Clinic, Sylvania, Ohio, 2003—05; ind. pvt. practice Lori Rokicki PhD, Toledo, 2005—. Ind. contractor Med. U. Ohio, Toledo, 2005—, clin. dir. pain ctr. St. Francis Healthcare Centre, Greensprings, 2005—. Contbr. scientific papers to profl. jours. Named Disting. Faculty Mem., Miss. State U., 1995; recipient Goekerman/Erlbaum award, U. Toledo, 1988; grantee, Miss. State U., 1995, Ill. Inst. Tech., 1998; Trisolini fellow, Ohio U., 1992—93. Mem.: Midwest Pain Soc. (bd. dir. 2000—06). Office: Lori Rokicki PhD Ste 210 5151 Monroe St Toledo OH 43623 Office Phone: 419-842-0804. Office Fax: 419-841-8985.

**ROKITA, TODD,** state official; m. Kathy Rokita. BA in Political Sci., Wabash Coll.; JD, Ind. Univ. Sch. of Law. Atty.; gen. counsel sec. state State of Ind., 1997, dep. sec. of state, sec. of state, 2003—. Mem.: Indiana Coun. for Economic Edn. (Director's Circle), St. Thomas More Parish, Indiana State Bar Association's Aviation Law Com. (past chair). Republican. Office: Office Sec of State 201 State House Indianapolis IN 46204 Office Phone: 317-232-6531, 317-232-6536. Office Fax: 317-233-3283. Business E-Mail: aa@sos.state.in.us.*

**ROKKE, ERVIN JEROME,** military officer, academic administrator; b. Warren, Minn., Dec. 12, 1939; s. Edwin K. and Joan (Ivery) R.; m. Pamela Mae Patterson, June 6, 1962; children: Lisa Mae, Eric Scott. Student, St. Olaf Coll., 1957-58; BS, USAF Acad., 1962; MPA, Harvard U., 1964, PhD in Polit. Sci., 1970. Commd. 2d lt. USAF, 1962, advanced through grades to lt. gen., 1994; intelligence officer Pacific Air Forces, Hawaii, Japan, 1965-68; assoc. prof. dept. polit. sci. USAF Acad., Colorado Springs, Colo., 1968-73, permanent prof., 1976-80, dean of faculty, 1982-86; plans officer NATO Hdqrs., Brussels, 1973-76; air attache Am. Embassy, London, 1980-82, def. attache Moscow, 1987-89; sr. staff Nat. Security Agy., Ft. Meade, Md., 1989-91; dir. intelligence Hdqrs. European Command, Stuttgart, Fed. Republic Germany, 1991-93; assigned to Hdqrs. USAF, Washington, 1993-94; pres. Nat. Def. U., Ft. Lesley J. McNair, DC, 1994-97, Moravian Coll. and Moravian Theol. Sem., 1997—. Cons. Dept. State, 1969. Editor: American Defense Policy, 1973. Decorated Def. Disting. Svc. medal, Disting. Svc. medal, Def. Superior Svc. medal, Legion of Merit. Mem. Coun. on Fgn. Rels., Falcon Found. Lutheran. Avocations: reading, skiing, squash. Home: 79 W Church St Bethlehem PA 18018-5821 Office: Moravian Coll 1200 Main St Bethlehem PA 18018-6614 Office Phone: 610-861-1364. Personal E-mail: chaos01@aol.com.

**ROKNALDIN, FARZAM,** mechanical engineer, educator; b. Tehran, Iran, Jan. 17, 1965; s. Hassan Roknaldin and Alye Tohidi; m. Maria S. Valera; 1 child, Aleyeh. PhD, Stanford (Calif.) U., 2001. Sr. thermal cons. Applied Thermal Technologies, Santa Clara, Calif., 2000—. Adj. instr. San Jose (Calif.) State U., 2002—, master's degree advisor, 2004—. Mem.: ASME (assoc. Recognition award 2001), Planetary Soc. (assoc.), Pars FC Soccer Club (founder). Democrat. Achievements include discovery of commom system level cooling design flaw in telecommunucation chassis; design of tapered base heat sink; development of simplified computational fluid dynamic model for radia blower; design of cooling solutions for telecmmu-nication equipments and small hand held laptops. Avocations: soccer, snowboarding, guitar, cars. Office: Applied Thermal Technologies 3255 Kifer Road Santa Clara CA 95051 Office Phone: 408-522-8730. Home Fax: 408-522-8729; Office Fax: 408-522-8729. Business E-Mail: roknaldi@athermal.com.

**ROLAND, ANNE,** registrar Supreme Court of Canada; m. Alphonse Morisette; 1 child, Julien BA Philosophy, Caen, France, 1965; diploma, Inst. Supérieur d'interprétation et de traduction, 1969; lic. in law, Paris, 1969; LLB, U. Ottawa, 1979. Bar: Quebec 1980. Legal trans., revisor, Can., 1971-75; chief trans. svcs. customs and excise Sec. of State, Can., 1975-76; spl. asst. to chief justice Can., 1976-81; chief law editor Supreme Ct. Can., 1981-88, dep. registrar, 1988-90, registrar, 1990. Mem. Can. Bar Assn., Assn. Can. Ct. Adminstrs., Assn. Francophone Jurists, Can. Inst. Adminstrn. Justice, Assn. Reporters Jud. Decisions. Office: Supreme Ct Can Office Reg 301 Wellington St Ottawa ON Canada K1A 0J1 Office Phone: 613-996-9277. E-mail: rolanda@scc-csc.gc.ca.

**ROLAND, BILLY RAY,** electronics company executive; b. Grandview, Tex., June 12, 1926; s. Marvin Wesley and Minnie Mae (Martin) R.; m. Ruth Ranell Sheets, Mar. 9, 1950 (div. 1982); children: Carl Ray and Darla Kay (twins); m. Linda Sue Leslie, Feb. 21, 1986 (div. Nov. 1991); m. Martha Kay Redford, May 17, 1993. BS, Tex. Christian U., 1954. Ticket and baggage agt. Southwestern Greyhound Co., Ft. Worth, 1943-44, 46-51; supr. acctg. dept. Tandy Leather Co., 1954-60; controller, asst. sec., treas. Tandy Corp., 1960-75; v.p., 1978-85; ret.; controller, asst. sec., treas. Tandy Crafts, Inc., 1975-78. V.p., treas. David L. Tandy Found., 1966-2003, dir. administs., 2004—; mng. trustee James L. and Eunice West Charitable Trust, 1980-91; treas. Benjamin F. Johnston Found., 1984—. Served with U.S. Army, 1944-46. Mem. AICPA, Tex. Soc. CPAs, Colonial Country Club, Petroleum Club. Republican. Methodist. Home: 8937 Random Rd Fort Worth TX 76179-2739

**ROLAND, CHARLES GORDON,** physician, medical educator, historian; b. Winnipeg, Man., Can., Jan. 25, 1933; s. John Sanford and Leona (McLaughlin) R.; m. Marjorie Ethel Kyles, 1953 (div. 1973); children: John Kenneth, Christopher Franklin, David Charles, Kathleen Siobhan; m. Connie Rankin, 1979; step-children: Gregory Irvine, Christopher Irvine, Randi Irvine. Student, U. Toronto, Ont., Can., 1952—54; MD, BSc, U. Man., 1958, DSc (hon.), 1997. Intern St. Boniface Hosp., Man., 1958—59; pvt. practice medicine specializing in family medicine Tillsonburg, Ont., 1959—60, Grimsby, Ont., 1960—64; sr. editor Jour. Am. Med. Assn., Chgo., 1964—69; head sect. publs. Mayo Clinic, 1969—70, chmn. dept. biomed. communications, 1970—77; prof. history medicine, prof. biomed. comm., coord. family practice track, chmn. adminstrv. com. dept. family medicine Mayo Med. Sch., 1971—77; mem. admissions, edn. and curriculum coordinators coms., hon. mem. med. staff West Lincoln Meml. Hosp., Grimsby; mem. grants com. Hannah Inst. History of Medicine, Toronto, 1974—77, 1987—91, mem. publs. com., 1991—95; Jason A. Hannah prof. history of medicine McMaster U., Hamilton, Ont., Canada, 1977—99, Hannah prof. emeritus, 1999—, assoc. mem. dept. history, 1978—96, chmn. archives com. Faculty of Health Scis., 1983—98; chmn. spl. grants com. Hannah Inst. for History of Medicine, 1981—85; Sid W. Richardson vis. prof. Inst. Med. Humanities U. Tex. Med. Br., Galveston, 1984. Mem. devel. adv. com. Assoc. Med. Svcs., 1999-2003; inaugural Osler-McGovern lectr. Green Coll., Oxford U., Eng., 2001. Author: (with L.S. King) Scientific Writing, 1968, (with J.P. McGovern) William Osler, The Continuing Education, 1969, Good Scientific Writing, 1971, William Osler's The Master Word in Medicine: A Study in Rhetoric, 1972, (with L.S. Baker) You and Leukemia: A Day at a Time, 1976, (with P. Potter) An Annotated Bibliography of Canadian Medical Periodicals, 1826-1975, 1979, Clarence Meredith Hincks 1885-1964: Mental Health Crusader, 1990, Courage Under Siege: Starvation, Disease and Death in the Warsaw Ghetto, 1992, (with Henry Friedlander, Benno Muller-Hill) Medicine Wihout Compassion, Past and Present: Fall Meeting, Colonge, September 28-30, 1988, Harold Nathan Segall: Pioneer Canadian Cardiologist, 1995, Long Night's Journey Into Day: Prisoners of War in the Far East, 1941-45, 2001; editor: (E.P. Scarlett) In Sickness and In Health, 1972; co-editor: An Annotated Checklist of Osleriana, 1976, vol. 2, 2000, Sir William Osler 1849-1919: A Selection for Medical Students, 1982, Health Disease and Medicine: Essays in Canadian History, 1984, Sir William Osler 1849-1919: petite anthologie à l'intention des étudiants en médecine, 1987, Bibliography of Secondary Sources in Canadian Medical History, 1985, 2nd edition, 2000, (with J. Bernier) The Collected Essays of Sir William Osler (3 vols.), 1985; editor, author introduction: Medical Topography of Upper Canada, 1985; (with Richard Golden) Sir William Osler: An Annotated Bibiography with Illustrations, 1987; co-editor: The Persisting Osler, 1984, The Persisting Osler II, 1994, The Persisting Osler III, 2001, Biography of Archibald Malloch, 2006; editor-in-chief Can. Bulletin of Med. History, 1987-90; mem. editl. adv. bd. Can. Family Physician, 1964-72, Chest, 1966-95, Med. Comm., 1971-75, Postgrad. Med. Jour., London, 1967-72, Mayo Clinic Procs., 1969-77, Bioscis. Comm., 1975-80, Ont. Med. Rev., 1979-84, HSTC Jour., 1980-87, Can. Bull. Med. History, 1982-90, Med. History (London), 1984-87, Jour. History of Medicine and Allied Scis., 1991-94, 96—. Mem. bd. curators Osler Libr., McGill U., Montreal, 1981—. Recipient Jason A. Hannah medal Royal Soc. Can., 1994. Fellow AAAS (coun. 1969-74), Am. Med. Writers Assn. (pres. 1969-70); mem. Can. Med. Assn., Am. Assn. History Medicine (sec.-treas. 1976-80, publs. com. 1979-85, mem. Garrison lectr. com. 2005—), Acad. Medicine Toronto (Grogan lecture com. 1978-83), Am. Mil. Inst., Internat. Inst. Prisoners of War, Soc. Internat. d'Histoire de la Medicine (internat. del. for Can. 1983-86), Can. Soc. for History of Medicine (v.p. 1982-87, pres. 1993-95), Can. Med. History Chgo. (sec.-treas. 1966-69), Can. Ctr. for Studies in Hist. Horticulture (exec. com. 1982-89), Coun. Biology Editors, Med. Hist. Club Toronto (pres. 1977-78), Ont. Hist. Soc., Can. Hist. Assn., Bibliog. Soc. Can., Am. Osler Soc. (sec.-treas. 1975-85, v.p. 1985-86, pres. 1986-87, historian, 1999-), Japan Osler Soc. (hon.), Royal Soc. Medicine (London), Royal Can. Mil. Inst., Champlain Soc. (Toronto), History of Second World War (Can. com.), Soc. Army Hist. Rsch., Univ. Club (Rochester); Osler Club (London), Alpine Club Can., Lit. Club (Chgo.), Sigma Xi. Office: McMaster U 3N10-HSC Med Ctr 1200 Main St W Hamilton ON Canada L8N 3Z5 Business E-Mail: croland@cogeco.ca.

**ROLAND, DAVID LEONARD,** retired broadcast production educator; b. Port Jefferson, NY, Oct. 2, 1947; s. Leonard Ernest and Dorothy (Stewart) R.; m. Susan Mary Becht, July 10, 1971 (div. Nov. 1979); m. Theresa Regina Ryan, Dec. 27, 1980. BS, Empire State Coll., 1976; MA, L.I. U., 1981. Tchr. photography Bd. Coop. Ednl. Svcs., Patchoque, NY, 1975—85, tchr. TV prodns., graphic arts module leader, 1985—2003; ret., 2003. Video arts prof. Five Towns Coll., Dix Hills, NY. Dir. CBS TV Worth Teaching Video (cert. merit), Camp Pa-gua-tuck Video (Outstanding Svc. award); audio engr. Children of the Cradle. Named Disting. Occupational Tchr. of Yr. State of N.Y., 1988. 020. Vocat. Indsl. Clubs Am. (advisor 1976-2003, chair), Internat. TV Assn., L.I. Media Arts Com., Assn. of BTC Educators. Home: 523 Washington Ave Riverhead NY 11901-2742

**ROLAND, DONALD EDWARD,** advertising executive; b. Dalhart, Tex., Nov. 14, 1942; s. Vernon O. Roland and Doris M. (Cox) Roland Hutson; m. Kathleen Marie Bennett, Feb. 1, 1964; children: Aileen, Donald E., Jenny. BS, Calif. State U., 1964; MA, Calif., Riverside, 1967; cert. scite. mgmt., UCLA. Dir. computer graphics Times Mirror Press, L.A., 1966-78, plant mgr., 1978-81, v.p. prodn., 1981-83; group v.p. ops. Treasure Chest Advt., Glendora, Calif., 1983-84, sr. v.p. ops., 1984-93, exec. v.p., 1993-94, pres., CEO, 1995-2000, Vertis Inc., Balt., 2000—, chmn., 2001—. Republican. E-mail: droland@vertisinc.com.

**ROLAND, RAYMOND WILLIAM,** lawyer, mediator; b. Ocala, Fla., Jan. 3, 1947; s. Raymond W. and Hazel (Dunn) R.; m. Jane Allen, Dec. 28, 1968; children: John Allen, Jason William. BA, Fla. State U., 1969, JD, 1972. Bar: Fla. 1972, U.S. Dist. Ct. (no. dist.) Fla. 1973, U.S. Dist. Ct. (mid. dist.) Fla. 1985, U.S. Ct. Appeals (5th cir.) 1974, U.S. Ct. Appeals (11th cir.) 1983, U.S. Supreme Ct. 1985; cert. cir. ct. mediator. Assoc. Keen, O'Kelley & Spitz, Tallahassee, 1972-74, ptnr., 1974-77; ptnr., v.p. McConnaughhay, Roland, Maida & Cherr, P.A., Tallahassee, 1978-97; owner Roland Mediation Svcs., Tallahassee, 1997—2002; cir. mediator U.S. Ct. Appeals 11th Cir., 2002—. Adj. prof. Bapt. Coll. Fla.; diplomate mem. Fla. Acad. of Profl. Mediators, Inc. Bd. visitors Bapt. Coll. Fla.; bd. dirs. So. Scholarship Found., Tallahassee, 1985—89, 1998—99, v.p., 1989. Mem.: Fla. Kiwanis Found. (life fellow), Capital City Kiwanis Club (pres. 1979, Kiwanian of Yr. 1978), Kiwanis (life; lt. gov. 1984—85). Baptist. Avocations: reading, hiking, camping, golf. Home: 800 Freedom Ln Roswell GA 30075 Office Phone: 404-335-6272. Personal E-mail: BRoland487@aol.com.

**ROLEN, SCOTT BRUCE,** professional baseball player; b. Jasper, Ind., Apr. 4, 1975; m. Niki Warner, Feb. 2, 2002. 3d base Phila. Phillies, 1993—2002, St. Louis Cardinals, 2002—. Named Nat. League Rookie Player of Yr., The Sporting News, 1997, Baseball Writers Assn. of Am., 1997; named to Nat. League All-Star Team, 2002—04; recipient Nat. League Gold Glove Award, 1997—2004. Office: c/o St Louis Cardinals 250 Stadium Plaza Saint Louis MO 63102*

**ROLETT, ELLIS LAWRENCE,** cardiologist, educator; b. NYC, July 10, 1930; s. Daniel Meyer and Mary Elaine (Warshaw) R.; m. Virginia Ann Vladimir, Mar. 25, 1956; children: Roderic Lawrence, Barry Vladimir, Daniel Alfred. BS, Yale U., 1952; MD cum laude, Harvard U., 1955. Diplomate: Am. Bd. Internal Medicine, Am. Bd. Cardiovas. Disease. Intern, resident in medicine Mass. Gen. Hosp., Boston, 1955-56, 59-61; asst. resident N.Y. Hosp.-Cornell U. Med. Ctr., N.Y.C., 1956-57; Am. Heart Assn. research fellow Peter Bent Brigham Hosp., Boston, 1961-63; mem. faculty U. N.C., Chapel Hill, 1963-74, then prof., 1971-74; prof. UCLA, 1974-77; chief cardiology VA Wadsworth Hosp., L.A., 1974-77, Dartmouth-Hitchcock Med. Ctr., Hanover, NH, 1977—87; prof. Dartmouth Med. Sch., Hanover, 1977-97, prof. medicine active emeritus, 1997—. Vis. scientist August Krogh Inst., Copenhagen, 1984; mem. merit rev. bd. Cardiovasc. studies VA, 1976-79, chmn., 1978-79; mem. regional rsch. rev. com. New Eng. Am. Heart Assn., 1978-83; mem. sci. bd. Stanley J. Sarnoff Endowment for Cardiovasc. Sci., 1992-97, chmn., 1994-95, bd. dirs., 1997-2000; mem. lit. sect. rev. com. Nat. Libr. Medicine, 1995-99, chmn., 1998-99; dir. Vt.-Karelia (Russia) Med. Project, St. Petersburg Univ. Global Fund. Bd. dirs. N.H. affiliate Am. Heart Assn., 1978-85; pres. N.H. affiliate Am. Heart Assn., 1983-85. Served to capt. M.C. USAF, 1957-59. Recipient Lederle Med. Faculty award, 1965-68, USPHS Career Devel. award, 1967-72; grantee USPHS/NIH, 1964-76, VA Merit Rev. Rsch. Program, 1975-77, Mathers Found., 1984-86, 93-96, Am. Heart Assn., 1989-91. Mem. AAAS, Am. Physiol. Soc., Internat. Soc. Heart Rsch., Phi Beta Kappa, Alpha Omega Alpha Home: 4 Balch Hill Ln Hanover NH 03755-1622 Office: Dartmouth Med Sch Hanover NH 03755 Business E-Mail: ellis.rolett@dartmouth.edu.

**ROLEY, V. VANCE,** dean, finance educator; b. Nov. 26, 1951; m. Sharon Roley; children: Susie, Vance. BA in economics and statistics with honors, U. Calif., Berkeley, 1973; MA in economics, Harvard U., 1976, PhD in economics, 1977. Tchg. fellow Harvard U., 1975—76; fin. economist Fed. Res. Bank, Kansas City, 1977—79, asst. v.p., economist, 1981—83; sr. staff economist Pres.'s Coun. Econ. Advisors, 1979—80; assoc. prof. fin. U. Wash. Bus. Sch., 1983—86, dir. Ctr. Study Banking and Fin. Markets, 1983—86, prof. fin., 1986—2005, Rainier Nat. Bank prof. banking and fin., 1987—88, Security Pacific Bank Wash. prof. banking and fin., 1988—92, dir. Pacific Rim Fin. Ctr., 1995—96, Seafirst Faculty Scholar banking and fin., 1992—95, Hughes M. Blake prof. bus. adminstrn., 1995—2005, assoc. dean acad. and faculty affairs, 2000—04, interim dean, 2004—05; dean Coll. Bus. Adminstrn., U. Hawaii Manoa, Honolulu, 2005—, First Hawaiian Bank disting. prof. leadership and mgmt., 2005—. Vis. asst. prof. economics U. Wash. Bus. Sch., 1979; vis. scholar Fed. Res. Bank, Kansas City, 1993—2000; rsch. affiliate then rsch. assoc. Nat. Bur. Econ. Rsch., 1980—92. Recipient Merton Miller prize, Jour. Bus., 1998. Office: U Hawaii Manoa Coll Bus Adminstrn 2404 Maile Way Honolulu HI 96822 Office Phone: 808-956-8377. E-mail: vroley@hawaii.edu.*

**ROLFE, ROBERT MARTIN,** lawyer; b. Richmond, Va., May 16, 1951; s. Norman and Bertha (Cohen) R.; m. Catherine Dennis Stone, July 14, 1973; children: P. Alexander, Asher B., Joel A., Zachary A. BA, U. Va., 1973, JD, 1976. Bar: Va. 1976, U.S. Dist. Ct. (ea. and we. dists.) Va. 1976, U.S. Ct. Appeals (4th cir.) 1976, U.S. Ct. Appeals (2d cir.) 1979, U.S. Dist. Ct. (ea. dist.) Mich. 1985, U.S. Ct. Appeals (D.C. cir.) 1985, U.S. Dist. Ct. (so. and ea. dists.) N.Y. 1985, U.S. Ct. Appeals (7th cir.) 1995, U.S. Ct. Fed. Claims, 1997, U.S. Supreme Ct. 1979. Assoc. Hunton & Williams, Richmond, 1976-83, ptnr., 1983—, gen. counsel, co-head litig., intellectual property and antitrust team, exec. com., 1998—2004. Editorial bd. Va. Law Rev., 1976; contbr. articles to profl. jours. Trustee, pres. bd. trustees Jewish Family Supporting Found., chmn. of bd. trustees, 2005—; bd. dirs. Jewish Family Svcs., Richmond, pres., 1993-95; bd. mgrs., 2d v.p. Congregation Beth Ahabah, 1995-97, 1st v.p., 1997-99. Fellow Am. Bar Found.; mem. ABA (litig. sect.), Va. Bar Assn., Va. State Bar, Richmond Bar Assn., Order of Coif (Alumni award for acad. excellence U. Va. 1976). Home: 18 Greenway Ln Richmond VA 23226-1630 Office: Hunton & Williams Riverfront Plz East Tower PO Box 1535 Richmond VA 23218-1535 also: 200 Park Ave New York NY 10166-0005 Office Phone: 804-788-8466, 804-343-4568. Business E-Mail: rrolfe@hunton.com.

**ROLFE, RONALD STUART,** lawyer; b. NYC, Sept. 5, 1945; s. Nat and Florence I. (Roth) R.; m. Yvonne S. Quinn, Sept. 1, 1979 (div. Apr. 2002); m. Sara Darehshori; children: Andrew, Dare. AB, Harvard U., 1966; JD, Columbia U., 1969. Bar: N.Y. 1969, U.S. Ct. Appeals (2d cir.) 1970, U.S. Dist. Ct. (so. and ea. dists.) N.Y. 1971, U.S. Supreme Ct. 1973, U.S. Dist. Ct. (no. dist.) Calif. 1982, U.S. Ct. Appeals (6th and 5th cirs.) 1982, U.S. Ct. Appeals (9th cir.) 1983, U.S. Dist. Ct. (ea. dist.) Ky. 1984, U.S. Ct. Appeals (7th and 10th cirs.) 1989, U.S. Ct. Appeals (fed. cir.) 1991, U.S. Ct. Appeals (3d cir.) 1992, U.S. Ct. Appeals (4th cir.) 1991. Law clk. to judge U.S. Dist. Ct. (so. dist.) N.Y., 1969-70; assoc. Cravath, Swaine & Moore, 1970-77, ptnr., litig., 1977—. Trustee Allen-Stevenson Sch., 1980—91, pres., 1992—; trustee Lawrenceville Sch., 1987—, v.p., 2001—05; bd. visitors Law Sch. Columbia U., emeritus bd. adv. Ctr. Corp. Governance, dean's coun. Law Sch. Trustee DeLaSalle Acad., 2002—. Fellow Am. Bar Found.; mem.: ABA, Am. Law Inst., Fed. Bar Coun. (trustee 1989—94), Assn. Bar City NY, NY State Bar Assn., Century Assn., Stanwich Club (Greenwich, Conn.), Univ. Club, Union Club. Office: Cravath Swaine & Moore LLP Worldwide Plz 825 8th Ave 40th Fl New York NY 10019-7475 Office Phone: 212-474-1714. Office Fax: 212-474-3700. Business E-Mail: rrolfe@cravath.com.

**ROLL, DAVID LEE,** lawyer; b. Pontiac, Mich., May 1, 1940; s. Everett Edgar and Garnette (Houts) R.; m. Nancy E. Spindle, Aug. 17, 1963; children: Richard, Molly. BA cum laude, Amherst Coll., 1962; JD, U. Mich., 1965. Bar: Mich. 1965, U.S. Dist. Ct. (ea. dist.) Mich. 1965, U.S. Ct. Appeals (6th cir.) 1969, D.C. 1974, U.S. Dist. Ct. D.C. 1975, U.S. Supreme Ct. 1975, U.S. Ct. Appeals (4th cir.) 1976, U.S. Ct. Appeals (D.C. cir.) 1983, U.S. Ct. Appeals (3rd and 11th cirs.) 1985, U.S. Ct. Appeals (9th cir.) 1992, U.S. Ct. Appeals (fed. cir.) 1993. Assoc. Hill, Lewis, Detroit, 1965-70, ptnr., 1970-72; asst. dir. gen. litigation Bur. of Competition Fed. Trade Commn., Washington, 1972-75; ptnr. Steptoe & Johnson, Washington, 1975—1993—98. V.p. bus. devel., bd. dirs. eLawForum, 2000-04; mng. dir. Lex Mund Pro Bono Found., 2005—. Co-author: Louis Johnson and the Arming of America: The

Roosevelt and Truman Years, 2005. Mem. ABA (chair Robinson Patman Act com., antitrust sect. 1984-86, Clayton Act com., antitrust sect. 1986-88, Energy Litigation com., litigation sect. 1992-93, mem. task force on indsl. competitiveness 1987, coun., antitrust sect. 1988-91, author, editor antitrust sect.), Lex Mundi (bd. dirs., chair competition com., chair pro bono steering com.). Office: 1330 Connecticut Ave NW Washington DC 20036-1704 E-mail: droll@steptoe.com.

**ROLL, JOHN MCCARTHY,** judge; s. Paul Herbert and Esther Marie (McCarthy) Roll; m. Maureen O'Connor; 3 children. BA, U. Ariz., 1969, JD, 1972; LLM, U. Va., 1990. Bar: Ariz. 1972, U.S. Dist. Ct. Ariz. 1974, U.S. Ct. Appeals (9th cir.) 1980, U.S. Supreme Ct. 1977. Asst. pros. atty. City of Tucson, 1973; dep. county atty. Pima County (Ariz.), 1973-80; asst. U.S. Atty. U.S. Attys. Office, Tucson, 1980-87; judge Ariz. Ct. Appeals, 1987-91, U.S. Dist. Ct. Ariz., 1991—. Mem. criminal justice mental health standards project ABA, 1980—83, mem. com. model jury instrns. 9th circ., 1994—2001, chair com. model jury instrns. 9th circ., 1998—2001; mem. panel workshop criminal law CEELI Program, Moscow, 1997; mem. U.S. Jud. Conf. Adv. Com. Criminal Rules, 1997—2003. Contbr. Merit Selection: the Arizona Experience, Ariz. State Law Jour., 1991, The Rules Have Changed: Amendments to the Rules of Civil procedure, Defense Law Jour., 1994, Ninth Cir. Judges' Benchbook on Pretrial Proceedings, 1998, 00, 02. Recipient Disting. Faculty award Nat. Coll. Dist. Attys., U. Houston, 1979, Outstanding Alumnus award U. Ariz. Coll. Law, 1992. Mem. Fed. Judges Assn., KC (adv. coun. 1991). Republican. Office: US Dist Ct 405 W Congress Tucson AZ 85701

**ROLL, RENÉE F.,** retired psychologist; d. Leo and Helen Feldman; children: Stewart Daniel, Jeri Ann. BA, U. Calif., 1965, MS, 1967. Lic. psychologist Bd. Med. Examiners, Calif., 1973, marriage and family therapist Bd. Behavioral Scis. Calif., 1968, cert. diplomate psychologist Am. Psychotherapy Assn., 1998, therapist Nat. Bd. Cognitive Behavioral Therapists, 1999. Tchr. Manesquan Sch. Dist., NJ, 1959—60, Montebello Unified Sch. Dist., Calif., 1961—70, psychologist, 1961—70; pvt. practice counselor Glendale, Calif., 1970—73; pvt. practice psychologist Chico, Calif., 1974; ret., 1974; cons. Dr. J.P. Haddock, Chico, 1975—82. Author: The Seeds of Growth, A History for the Future, 2002 (appears in the Libr. of Congress, DC), A Crooked Christmas Tree, 2004, A Tale of Two Boys and Wolf Pups, 2006. Vol. fireman Calif. Dept. Forestry, Butte Meadows, Calif., 1983. Recipient Outstanding Achievement award, Internat. Soc. Poets, 2003, Poet of Merit award, 2003. Mem.: AAUW, Natural Wildlife Assn., Writing Group Stockton, Purse Club. Avocations: piano, poetry, flowers, writing. Home: 4089 Five Mile Dr Stockton CA 95219 Office Phone: 209-481-0273. Personal E-mail: reneeroll@comcast.net.

**ROLLAND, CLARA,** pianist, educator; b. Budapest, Hungary, Apr. 20, 1916; arrived in U.S., 1939; d. Alexander and Katalin (Stein) Szekely; m. Paul Rolland, Dec. 24, 1940 (dec. Nov. 9, 1978); children: Peter Thomas, John Paul. Grad., Royal Franz Liszt Acad. Music, 1939, Cleve. Inst. Music, 1941; diploma (hon.), Franz Liszt Acad. Music, 1990. Founder, instr. prep. dept. piano, theory and ear tng. Simpson Coll., Indianola, Iowa, 1941—45; pvt. studio Urbana, Ill., 1946—73; founder, tchr. fun with music class Fine Arts Ctr., Clinton, Ill., 1966—70; co-dir. Music Divsn. Nat. Acad. Arts, 1973—79. Judge Three Rivers Piano Competition, St. Louis, 1978; lectr. in field. Performer, WILL-FM, 1950—55. Mem.: Music Tchr. Nat. Assn. (Baldwin Jr. Achievement award 1972, 1973, 1974, 1975, 1977, Mason & Hamlin Tchr. Achievement award 1974, H.S. Auditions winner 1974), Am. String Tchr. Assn. (life), Mu Phi Epsilon (pres. Mu Alpha chpt. 1961).

**ROLLAND, KATHY ANN,** elementary school educator; b. Pottsville, Pa., May 10, 1963; d. Kenneth Warren Rolland, Sr. and Lilla Catherine Telepchak. BS in Early Childhood Edn., Pa. State U., 1985; MEd in Sch. Leadership and Instrn., Wilmington Coll., 1998. Cert. generalist, early childhood Nat. Bd. Profl. Tchg. Stds. Tchr. Colonial Sch. Dist., New Castle, Del., 1990—. Mem. Investigations Math. Adv. Bd., New Castle, 2002—, Bridges Learning Sys. Dist., New Castle, 2002—. Vol. Freedom Outreach, Wilmington, 1999—. Excellence in Edn. grantee, MBNA Found., 2002. Mem.: NEA, Del. Coun. Tchrs. Math., Del. State Edn. Assn. Avocations: travel, guitar, volunteering. Office: So Elem Sch 795 Cox Neck Rd New Castle DE 19720 Office Phone: 302-832-2828.

**ROLLAND, LUCIEN GILBERT,** paper company executive, director; b. St. Jerome, Que., Can., Dec. 21, 1916; s. Olivier and Aline (Dorion) R.; m. Marie de Lorimier, May 30, 1942; children: Nicolas, Natalie, Stanislas, Dominique, Christine, Etienne, David. Student, Coll. Jean de Brebeuf, Montreal, U. Montreal, BA, BASc., C.E., also D.C.Sc. (hon.), 1960. Registered profl. engr. With Rolland Paper Co. Ltd. (name changed to Rolland inc. 1979), 1942—, v.p., gen. mgr, 1952, pres., gen. mgr., 1952-78, pres., CEO, 1978—, chmn., pres., CEO, 1984, chmn., CEO, 1985, chmn., 1991. Cons. in field, 1995; chmn. bd. Tarascon, Inc. Bd. dirs. Notre-Dame Hosp., Montreal Children's Hosp., Montreal Gen. Hosp., Hôpital Marie Enfant. Decorated Knight Comdr. Order St. Gregory, officer Order of Can. Mem. Can. Pulp and Paper Assn. (hon.), Corp. Profl. Engrs., Montreal Bd. Trade, Province of Que., C of C, Montreal C. of C., Engring. Inst. Can. Home: Apt B-60 1321 Sherbrooke St W Montreal PQ Canada H3G 1J4 Office: Tarascon Inc 1200 McGill College #1100 Montreal PQ Canada H3B 4G7

**ROLLAND, PETER GEORGE,** landscape architect; b. Frankfurt, Germany, July 2, 1930; came to U.S., 1936; s. Curt Henry and Lise (Kahn) R.; m. Wendy Diana Altschul, Dec. 26, 1955; children: David, Seth, Janna. B.Sc., Delaware Valley Coll., 1952; M.L.A., Harvard U., 1955. Registered landscape architect, N.Y., Conn., Coun. Landscape Archtl. Rev. Bds. Chief site planner Perkins & Will Architects, White Plains, NY, 1955-60; project landscape architect Lawrence Halprin & Assocs., San Francisco, 1960-63; prin. Peter G. Rolland & Assocs., Rye, NY, 1963—81, Canberra, Australia, 1963—81; ptnr. Rolland/Towers, Rye, New Haven, 1981—97. Andrew Mellon vis. prof. Yale U. Sch. Forestry, 1979; faculty Sch. Architecture, Yale U., 1973-94; vis. prof. Harvard Grad. Sch. Design, 1990; mem. Office Bldg. Ops., architecture adv. bd., US Dept. State, 2000-05; disting. prof. landscape architecture, Sch. Architecture, CCNY, 2004. Prin. landscape architect, New Parliament House, Canberra, Australia, 1980, SUNY, Coll. at Purchase, 1964-75. Mem., chmn. N.Y. State Bd. Landscape Architects, 1972-82; mem. N.Y. State Coun. on Arts, 1979-82, Rye Archtl. Bd. Rev., 1973-78; trustee Delaware Valley Coll., 1991-2003; mem. grad. coun. Grad. Sch. Design, Harvard U., Cambridge, Mass., 1978-88; trustee Am. Acad. in Rome, 1992-96, pres. Soc. Fellows, 1992-96. Served with U.S. Army, 1956-58. Recipient Arthur Brown award Del. Valley Coll., 1978, Pres.'s award, 2003; Design award AIA, 1975, 78, 85, 90, 92, 94, Inst. Honors award, 1990; Tucker award for IBM Conf. Ctr., 1982; Sir Zelman Cowens award Royal Australian Inst. Archs., 1989; Tucker award for New Parliament Ho., Canberra, Australia, 1990; Rome Prize fellow Am. Acad. in Rome, 1978, Pierson Coll. fellow Yale U., 1982-92. Fellow Am. Soc. Landscape Architects (ann. design awards 1972-85, 92, award of Excellence, 1991); mem. NAD (Academician), Australian Inst. Landscape Architects (Landmarks award for New Parliament House, Canberra, 1988). Office: 731 Milton Rd Rye NY 10580

**ROLLANS, JAMES O.,** service company executive; b. Glendale, Calif., July 7, 1942; s. Henry Leo and Geraldine Ada (Berg) R.; children: Jodie Helene, Thomas James, Daniel Joseph. BS, Calif. State U., Northridge, 1967. Vice pres., dir. Chase Manhattan Bank, 1976-78; v.p. corp. communications Dart Industries, Los Angeles, 1978-80; v.p. bus. analysis and investor relations Dart & Kraft, Chgo., 1980-82; sr. v.p., CFO Fluor Corp., Irvine, Calif., 1982-99, also bd. dirs., 1998—; pres., group exec. Bus. Svcs., Aliso Viejo, Calif., 1999. Bd. dirs. Cupertino Elec.; mem. Flowserve Corp. Bd. dirs. Irvine Med. Ctr. Episcopalian. Avocations: boating, skiing, fishing, hunting. Home: 14 Saint Remy Ct Newport Coast CA 92657-1626

**ROLLE, ANDREW,** historian, writer; b. Providence, Apr. 12, 1922; m. Frances Squires, Dec. 1945 (div.); children: John Warren, Alexander Frederick, Julia Elisabeth; m. Myra Moss, Nov. 1983. BA, Occidental Coll., 1943; MA, UCLA, 1949, PhD, 1953; grad., So. Calif. Psychoanalytic Inst., 1976. Am. vice consul, Genoa, Italy, 1945-48; editorial asso. Pacific Hist. Rev., 1952-53; from asst. prof. to Cleland prof. history Occidental Coll., 1953-88; rsch. scholar Huntington Libr., San Marino, Calif., 1988—. Author: Riviera Path, 1946, An American in California, 1956, reprinted, 1982, The Road to Virginia City, 1960, reprinted, 1989, Lincoln: A Contemporary Portrait, 1961, (with Allan Nevins, Irving Stone) California: A History, 1963, rev. edits., 1963, 69, 78, 87, 98, 2002, Occidental College: The First Seventy-Five Years, 1963, The Lost Cause: Confederate Exiles in Mexico, 1965, 1992, The Golden State, 1967, rev. edit., 1978, 1989, 2000, California, A Student Guide, 1965, Los Angeles, A Student Guide, 1965; Editor: A Century of Dishonor (Helen Hunt Jackson), 1964, Life in California (Alfred Robinson), 1971, Voyage to California (Jour. of Lucy Herrick), 1998; The Immigrant Upraised, 1968, The American Italians: Their History and Culture, 1972, Gli Emigrati Vittoriosi, 1973, reprinted, 2003; (with George Knoles others) Essays and Assays, 1973, (with others) Studies in Italian American Social History, 1975, (with others) Los Angeles: The Biography of a City, 1976, 2d edit., 1981; (with Allan Weinstein and others) Crisis in America, 1977, The Italian Americans: Troubled Roots, 1980, 2d edit. 1985, Los Angeles: From Pueblo to Tomorrow's City, 1981, 2nd edit., 1995, Occidental College: A Centennial History, 1986, John Charles Frémont: Character as Destiny, 1991, Henry Mayo Newhall and His Times, 1992, Westward the Immigrants, 1999, The Victorious Immigrants, 2005. Served to 1st lt. M.I. AUS, 1943-45, 51-52. Decorated Cavaliere Ordine Merito Italy; recipient silver medal Italian Ministry Fgn. Affairs; Commonwealth award for non-fiction; Huntington Libr.-Rockefeller Found. fellow; resident scholar Rockefeller Found. Ctr., Bellagio, Italy. Fellow Calif. Hist. Soc.; mem. Phi Beta Kappa. Office: Huntington Libr Rsch Div San Marino CA 91108 Office Phone: 626-405-2100 ext 2321.

**ROLLE, MARTHA COLLINS (MARTHA TRAUDT COLLINS),** lawyer; b. Colorado Springs, Colo., July 23, 1952; d. Verne O.M. and Helen Louise Traudt; m. Alexander F. Rolle; children: Joseph T. Collins, Alexander S. Rolle. BS in Math., U. Nebr., 1974; JD, U. Colo., 1977. Bar: Colo. 1977, N.Y. 1997. Assoc. Holme Roberts & Owen LLC, Denver, 1977-82, ptnr., 1983—, mng. ptnr. London, 2002—; English solicitor, 2004. Contbg. author: Rocky Mountain Mineral Law Foundation's Law of Federal Oil and Gas Leases, 1988; author: Hedging Transactions for Oil and Gas Producers: Rocky Mountain Mineral Law Foundation Special Institute, 1995; contbr. articles to profl. jours. Mem. ABA, Colo. Bar Assn., N.Y. Bar Assn., Order of Coif, Phi Beta Kappa. Office: Five Chancery Ln Clifford's Inn London EC4A 1BU England Office Phone: +44 (0)20 7320 6464. Office Fax: +44 (0)20 7320 6463. E-mail: marty.rolle@hro.com.

**ROLLE, MYRA MOSS See MOSS, MYRA**

**ROLLER, MARION,** sculptor; b. Boston; Student, Vesper George Sch. Art, Art Students League; BA in Art, Queens Coll., 1980. Sculptor in residence, 1999-2000. Instr. Fashion Inst. Tech., N.Y.C., Sculpture Ctr.; head design dept. Traphagen Sch. of Fashion. Exhbns. include The Newark Mus., 1995-96, Nat. Acad. Design, N.Y., 1994, Nat. Sculpture Soc., N.Y., 1996-97, Scottsdale, Ariz., Serravezza, Italy, 1994, Transco Mus., Phila., U.S. Mint, San Francisco, Denver, Albany, NY, Inst. History and Art, Pittsfield, Mass., Mus., Fedn. Internat. de la Medaille, Helsinki, Finland, Budapest, Hungary, 1993, Price Waterhouse Galleries, NYC, 1997, Janus Gallery, Santa Fe, Chesterwood, Stockbridge, Mass., 1997, Hillsdale, Mich., Coll., 1997, Nat. Sculpture Soc., 2000, 2001, UN, NYC, 1995, Cannon House Rotunda, Washington, Butler Inst. of Am. Art, 2001, Nat. Acad. Annual, 2001, others; first sculptor in residence, designer Plantation Life medal, The Wall, Brookgreen Gardens; commns. include Nassau Ctr. for Emotionally Disturbed Children, St. Mary's Children and Families Found., Traphagen Sch. Fashion, Rosemary Harris Meml., Brookgreen Gardens, medal Nat. Acad. Design, Butler Mus., others; contbr. articles, book reviews to Sculpture Review. Recipient Helen Gapen Oehler Meml. award Allied Artists, 1991, Samuel Cashwan Meml. award Audubon Artists, 1992, Audubon Artists award, 1994, Pen & Brush award for Watercolor, 1997, Nat. Sulpture Soc. Annual Exhibit award, 1998, Lou Magnani award Salmagundi Club, 1998, Gold medal of Honor 56th Annual Audubon Artists Exhibit, 1998, medal Internat. Exhibit of Medallic Art Museum Beelden aan Vee, 1998, award for Medallic Sculpture Pen & Brush, 1999, medal of Ethel Traphagen Medallic Art Co., 2001. Fellow Nat. Sculpture Soc. (sec., Kalos Kagathos Found. prize, C. Percival Dietsch Sculpture prize, Tallix Foundry prize, Edith H. & Richman Proskauer prize, Joel Meisner Foundry award); mem. Nat. Acad. Design (academician), Audubon Artists (treas., past pres., Gold medal of honor, Art Students League award, 1999), The Pen & Brush (chmn. sculpture sect., Pen and Brush award for watercolor, 1997, Bronze medal for sculpture, Chaim Gross Found. award, 1996, Samuel Cashwan meml. award, 1992, Margaret Sussman award 2000, Charlotte Dunwiddie award for medallic art 2000), Allied Artists Am. (past pres., Silver medal honor, Sybil and Bob Porton award, Helen Gapen Oehler Meml. award, 1991), Am. Medallic Sculpture Assn., Fine Arts Fedn. (bd. mem.).

**ROLLER, PAMELA JO,** elementary school educator; b. Logansport, Ind., Mar. 22, 1952; d. Glen B. Roller and Clara Evelyn Sizemore. BS, Ind. U., Kokomo, 1974; MS, Ind. U/Purdue U. Indpls., 1976. Cert. CFG Coach for Nat. Sch. Reform Faculty 2006. Tchr. 5th and 6th grade Southeastern Sch. Corp., Logansport, 1974—76, tchr. 1st grade, 1976—79, tchr. 2d grade, 1979—82, tchr. 1st grade, 1982—88, readiness tchr. 1st grade, 1988—94, tchr. 2d grade, 1994—2006. Founder/coord., mentoring program K-12 Tender Loving Care, 1989—; coord. Young Astronauts, 1988—; founder/coord. Sch. on Sat., Galveston, Ind., 1994—2006; third grade tchr., Bolivia, 2004. Flight dir. Mission Possible, Galveston, 1996—; dist. lay spkr. United Meth., Logansport, Ind., 1992—. Recipient Disney's Am. Tchr. Awards Honoree, Calif., 2003, Make a Difference award, USA Weekend Mag., 2006; scholar, Japan Fulbright Meml. Fund, 2005. Mem.: NSTA, Profl. Assn. in Edn., Hoosier Assn. Sci. Tchrs., Ind. State Tchrs. Assn., Pi Lambda Theta. Democrat. Methodist. Avocations include classroom business called chocolate lollipops, Inc. has earned over 5,000 dollars, and given to numerous charities. Office Phone: 574-699-6687. Personal E-mail: proller1@msn.com.

**ROLLER, ROBERT H.,** academic administrator, finance educator; b. Columbus, Ohio, May 13, 1957; s. Robert F and Emmalou Nunamaker Roller; m. Wanda C Hammack, May 12, 1979; children: Laura Elizabeth, Rachel Marie. BS, Oral Roberts U., Tulsa, 1979; MBA, Oral Roberts U., 1986; PhD, Okla. State U., 1995. Bus. mgr. Cone-Lewis Printing Co., Tulsa, 1979—80; youth pastor Carbondale Assembly of God, Tulsa, 1979—81; assoc. pastor First Assembly of God, Warren, Ohio, 1981—85; asst. prof. bus. Oral Roberts U., Tulsa, 1986—92; asst. prof. mgmt. Kennesaw State U. Ga., 1992—96; chair, divsn. bus. & mgmt. Roberts Wesleyan Coll., Rochester, NY, 1996—98; dean sch. bus. LeTourneau U., Longview, Tex., 1998—2006; pres. Internat. Assembly for Collegiate Bus. Edn., Ill., 2006—. Commr. Internat. Assembly for Collegiate Bus. Edn., Overland Park, Kans., 1999—; review Christian Bus. Acad. Review. Editl. bd. (acad. jours.) Jour. of Ministry Mktg. and Mgmt., Jour. of Biblical Integration in Bus.; editl. bd.: Christian Bus. Rev.; author: (accreditation manual) IACBE Accreditation Manual; contbr. articles to profl. jours. Mem. class of 2000 Leadership Longview, Tex., 1999—2000; nat. adv. bd. mem. Assembly of God Bible Quiz, Springfield, Mo., 1981—90; league coord. N.E. Tex. Jr. Bible Quiz League, Longview, 2002—05; elder First Assembly of God, Longview, 1998—2004; state coord. Ga. Dist. Bible Quiz, Ga., 1995—96. Named Outstanding Young Man of Am., 1996; fellow Disting. Grad. fellow, Robert Glenn Rapp Found., 1988. Mem.: Internat. Assembly for Collegiate Bus. Edn. (chair bd. of commrs. 2001—02, 2004—05), Okla. Small Bus. Inst. Dirs. Assn. (2nd v.p. 1991—92), Christian Bus. Faculty Assn. (bd. dirs., Richard C.

Chewning award 2004), Acad. of Mgmt. Assemblies Of God. Avocations: travel, swimming. Office: International Assembly Collegiate Business Education PO Box 3960 Olathe KS 66063 Office Phone: 913-631-3009. Business E-Mail: bobroller@iacbe.org.

**ROLLERSON, MARNIE LOREEN,** secondary school educator, art educator; b. Biddeford, Maine, Jan. 6, 1969; d. Darrell D. and Carol A. Rollerson. BS in Art Edn., U. So. Maine, 1992. Art tchr. Spaulding H.S., Rochester, NH, 1992—95, Kennebunk (Maine) H.S., 1995—. Class advisor Kennebunk H.S., 1997—2000, 2001—05. Mem.: Maine Art Edn. Assn., Nat. Wildlife Fedn., Humane Soc. U.S. Avocations: painting, drawing, hiking, reading. Office: Kennebunk HS 89 Fletcher St Kennebunk ME 04043-6867

**ROLLIN, BETTY,** writer, television journalist; b. NYC, Jan. 3, 1936; d. Leon and Ida R.; m. Harold M. Edwards, Jan. 21, 1979. BA, Sarah Lawrence Coll., 1957. Assoc. features editor Vogue mag., 1964; sr. editor Look mag., 1965-71; network corr. NBC News, N.Y.C., 1971-80, contbg. corr., 1985—2003; network corr. ABC News Nightline, 1982-84. Contbr. corr. Religion and Ethics Newsweekly PBS; lectr. in field. Profl. actress: on stage and TV, 1958—64; author: I Thee Wed, 1962, Mothers Are Funnier Than Children, 1964, The Non-Drinkers' Drink Book, 1966, First, You Cry, 1976, reissue, 2000, Am I Getting Paid for This?, 1982, Last Wish, 1985, reissue, 1998; columnist: Here, N.Y. Times; contbr. articles to popular mags. Bd. mem. Death With Dignity Nat. Ctr., 1997—. Office: Care NS Bienstock Inc 1740 Broadway New York NY 10019-4315 Office Phone: 212-664-7171.

**ROLLIN, MICHAEL FREDRICK,** history professor; b. Laredo, Tex., Apr. 25, 1975; s. Michael William and Maria Farias Rollin. BA in Polit. Sci., St Mary's U., San Antonio, 1996; MA, U. Tex., San Antonio, 2000—02. Adj. instr., history St. Philip's Coll., San Antonio, 2003—05; lectr. U. Tex., San Antonio, 2004—. Mem.: Am. Hist. Assn., The Sons of the Republic of Tex. Republican. Roman Catholic. Home: 13122 Brook Garden Ln San Antonio TX 78232-5155 Office: Univ Texas 6900 N Loop 1604 W San Antonio TX 78249-0652 Home Fax: 210-402-5413. E-mail: michael.rollin@utsa.edu.

**ROLLINS, ALBERT WILLIAMSON,** civil engineer, consultant; b. Dallas, July 31, 1930; s. Andrew Peach and Mary (Williamson) R.; m. Martha Ann James, Dec. 28, 1954; children: Elizabeth Ann, Mark Martin. BS in Civil Engring., Tex. A&M U., 1951, MS in Civil Engring., 1956, disting. grad. in Civil Engring., 2005. Registered profl. engr., Tex., La., Okla. Engring. asst. Tex. Hwy. Dept., Dallas, 1953-55; dir. pub. works City of Arlington, Tex., 1956-63, city mgr., 1963-67; ptnr. Schrickel, Rollins & Assocs., Land Planners-Engrs., Arlington, 1967—. Contbr. articles to profl. jours. Mem. Gov.'s Energy Adv. Coun.; chmn Tex. Mass Transp. Commn.; bd. dirs. Tex. Turnpike Authority. Served as 1st lt. AUS, 1951-53. Mem. ASCE (Award of Honor Tex. sect. 2002), NSPE, Internat. City Mgmt. Assn., Am. Water Works Assn., Water Pollution Control Fedn., Sigma Xi, Phi Eta Sigma, Tau Beta Pi, Phi Kappa Phi, Chi Epsilon. Home: 3004 Yellowstone Dr Arlington TX 76013-1166 Office: Suite 200 1161 Corporate Dr W Ste 200 Arlington TX 76006-6819

**ROLLINS, ALDEN MILTON,** archivist; b. Billerica, Mass., July 31, 1946; s. Alden Milton and Agnes Morgan (Simpson) R. BA, Am. U., 1968; MLS, U. R.I., 1973. Cert. geneal. record specialist, Bd. for Certification of Genealogists., Vt.; N.H. Documents libr. U. Alaska Libr., Anchorage, 1973—. Author: The Fall of Rome: A Reference Guide, 1983, Rome in the Fourth Century A.D., 1991, Vermont Warnings Out, 1995, Vermont Religious Certificates, 2003. With U.S. Army, 1969-71. Mem. Nat. Geneal. Soc., Geneal. Soc. U.S.A., N.H. Geneal. Soc., New Eng. Hist. Geneal. Soc., N.H. Hist. Soc., Vt. Hist. Soc. (life), Piscataqua Pioneers (life), Am. Congl. Assn. (life). Avocation: genealogy. Home: 221 E 7th Ave Apt 114 Anchorage AK 99501-3639 Office: U Alaska Libr Govt Documents 3211 Providence Dr Anchorage AK 99508-4614

**ROLLINS, ALFRED BROOKS, JR.,** historian, educator; b. Presque Isle, Maine, May 28, 1921; s. Alfred Brooks and Clarissa (Jack) R.; m. Ernestine Emma McMullin, Nov. 6, 1942 (dec. Aug. 28, 1972); children: John Douglas, Nancy Jane, James Scott; m. Faith Kenyon, June 16, 1973 (dec. Mar. 8, 1979); m. Helen Anrod Jones, Feb. 28, 1981. BA, Wesleyan U., Middletown, Conn., 1942, MA, Harvard U., 1953. From instr. to prof. history State U. N.Y. at New Paltz, 1948-63; prof., chmn. dept. history State U. N.Y. at Binghamton, 1964-67; dean U. Vt., Burlington, 1967-70, v.p. acad. affairs, 1970-76; pres. Old Dominion U., Norfolk, Va., 1976-85, prof. history, 1976-91, pres. emeritus, prof. emeritus, 1991—. Cons. oral history project John F. Kennedy Library, 1965 Author: Roosevelt and Howe, 1962; Editor narrative: Franklin D. Roosevelt and the Age of Action, 1960, Woodrow Wilson and the New America, 1965; Contbr. articles to profl. jours. Served to 1st lt. USAAF, 1943-46. Decorated D.F.C., Air medal with four clusters. Mem. Am. Hist. Assn., Orgn. Am. Historians, Phi Beta Kappa, Chi Psi.

**ROLLINS, DIANN ELIZABETH,** occupational health nurse, primary school educator; b. Newark, Dec. 13, 1943; d. Lewis Paul and Letitia Lavinia Rollins. RN, Meth. Hosp. Sch. Nursing, Phila., 1964; postgrad., Howard U., 1966, Milton Coll., 1969—72, West Chester State Coll., 1972—79; cert. bldg. maintenance, John F. Kennedy Vocat. Tech., 1992; BSN, Thomas Jefferson U., 2000. RN Pa., N.J.; lic. religious sci. practioner United Ch. Religious Sci., 2003. Nurse Meth. Hosp., Phila., 1964—66, 1967—69, Mercy Hosp., Janesville, Wis., 1969—72, Chester County Hosp., West Chester, Pa., 1972—74, Cheyney U., Pa., 1974—75, Embreeville State Hosp., coatesville, 1976—78; agy. nurse Norristown, Phila., 1978—86, Medox, Olsten, Kimberly, Phila., 1985-86; RN supr. New Ralston House, Phila., 1986-87, 88-89; agy. nurse Kimberly, Quality Care, Olsten, Medox, others, Phila., 1987-89; info. and referral specialist Nat. Mental Health Consumer Self Help Clearing House, Phila., 1990-93; intern ACT NOW Southeastern Mental Health Program, Phila., 1993-94; nursery sch. tchr. Bambino Gesu Child Devel. Ctr., Phila., 1994-99; primary instr. nursing assts. ARC, 2000—01, Clin. Pathways Educators Ins., 2001—02; supplemental staff nurse Breslin Learning Ctr., 2002—, LPN instr., 2003—; staff nurse Bayada Nurses, 2002—; postal nurse (occupl. health nurse) U.S. Post Office, 2003—. Spkr. in field. Vol. instr. program Franklin Inst., Phila., 1973-74; vol. multimedia first aide instr. ARC, Wilmington, Del., 1975-83; vol. plan II nurse blood mobiles ARC, S.E. Pa., 1982-85. Recipient Stella M. Mummert maternal/child care award, Meth. Hosp., 1964. Mem. Alumnae Meth. Hosp. Sch. Nursing, Four Chaplains Legion of Honor. Avocations: reading, writing, walking. Office Phone: 215-829-1609. Personal E-mail: dynamyte19107@yahoo.com.

**ROLLINS, DORIS CALLELA,** music educator, pianist, performing accompanist; arrived in U.S., 1925; d. Samuel Ezekiel and Ismay Henrietta Jones; m. Valdemar W. Rollins, Sept. 9, 1951; 1 child, Gabrielle Valerie. MusB, Oberlin Conservatory, Ohio, 1945; M in Music Lit., Eastman Sch. Music, 1950; postgrad., NYU, Columbia U., N.Y.C., Manhattan Sch. Music, Julliard Sch. Music. Cert. music tchr. N.Y. Music tchr.-piano Fisk U., Nashville, 1945—52; music tchr.-gen. Yorkville H.S., N.Y., 1952—53; tchr. music-choral and gen., choral music dir. James Monroe H.S., Bronx, NY, 1955—65; tchr. music choral-gen., choral music dir. Isaac E. Young Jr. H.S., Bronx, 1970—86; tchr. music history Coll. New Rochelle, 1990—93. Choir dir. St. Lukes Episcopal Ch., St. Catherine AME Zion Ch., New Rochelle; piano music tchr. Rye Country Day Sch., NY; piano music tchr., accompanist Greenwich Acad., Conn. Pres. Womens Aux. to Nat. Med. Assn.; pres., v.p., treas. The Group. Mem.: Southwestern Ret. Tchrs. Assn. (v.p.), NY State Music Tchrs. Assn., Music Educators Nat. Conf., Alpha Kappa Alpha (choral dir.). Democrat. Episcopalian.

**ROLLINS, EDWARD TYLER, JR.,** retired newspaper executive; b. Durham, N.C., May 23, 1922; s. Edward Tyler and Bessie (Steed) R.; m. Frances Louise Page, Oct. 5, 1963; children: Edward Tyler III, William Lawson. AB, U. N.C., 1947. V.p., asst. sec. Durham (N.C.) Herald Co. 1949-69, v.p., sec.-treas., 1969-81, pres., pub., 1982-88, chmn., bd. dirs., 1985—2004; ret., 2004. Pres. Durham Radio Corp. Stas. WDNC-AM,

WDCG-FM, 1982-88. Bd. dirs. Chowan Coll. Graphic Arts Found., 1986-95; bd. dirs. Sch. of Journalism Found. of N.C., 1982-88; mem. Friends of Duke Art Mus., mem. adv. bd. N.C. Nat. Bank, 1979-89; mem. Gov.'s Bus. Coun. on Arts and Humanities, 1989-90; mem. Duke Pres.'s Art Mus. com., 1994-2001; trustee Meredith Coll., Raleigh, N.C., 1966-69, Durham Pub. Libr., 1961-81; former bd. dirs. Durham Salvation Army; pres. Durham YMCA, 1952; former bd. dirs. Family Svc. Assn. With U.S. Army, 1943-46. Mem. The English Speaking Union, Durham C. of C. (bd. dirs. 1969), Brummer Soc. (Nasher) Art Mus., Kiwanis, Hope Valley Country Club, Univ. Club, Carolina Club. Presbyterian.

**ROLLINS, JAMES (JIM CZAJKOWSKI, JAMES CLEMENS),** writer, veterinarian; b. Chgo., 1961; DVM, Univ. Mo., 1985. Author: (novels) Subterranean, 1999, Excavation, 2000, Deep Fathom, 2001, Amazonia, 2002, Ice Hunt, 2003, Sandstorm, 2004 (named one of best Mystery/Thrillers by Readers Read, 2004, Publishers Weekly paperback bestseller, 2005), Map of Bones, 2005; author: (as James Clemens) (fantasy) Wit'ch Fire, 1999, Wit'ch Storm, 2000, Wit'ch War, 2000, Wit'ch Gate, 2001, Wit'ch Star, 2001—02, Shadowfall, 2005. Avocations: scuba diving, spelunking. Mailing: c/o Author Mail William Morrow/HarperCollins 10 E 53d St New York NY 10022 E-mail: jpcdvm@aol.com.

**ROLLINS, JAMES CALVIN (JIMMY ROLLINS),** professional baseball player; b. Oakland, Calif., Nov. 27, 1978; Grad., Encinal HS, 1996. Profl. baseball player Phila. Phillies, 2000—. Co-recipient NL Cool Papa Bell award, Negro League Hall of Fame; named 5th Best Rookie in Major Leagues, Baseball Am., 3d Best in Nat. League; named to Topps Major League Rookie All-Star team, MLB mgrs., NL All-Star Team, 2001—02, 2005. Achievements include eighth longest hitting-streak in MLB history (38 games), 2005-2006. Avocation: recreational activities. Office: Citizens Bank Park 1 Citizens Bank Way Philadelphia PA 19148*

**ROLLINS, JOHN MAXWELL,** mathematics professor, disc jockey; b. Blakely, Ga., Jan. 2, 1959; s. Hursteen West and Miriam Christine Rollins; m. Donna Jean McDaniel, Apr. 20, 1991; children: Rebecca, Robert. BS in Math., Coll. Charleston, 1988; MA in Edn. Math., Citadel, 1990; MBA, Charleston So. U., 1995. Owner, disc jockey Jay Maxwell's Music by Request, Summerville, SC, 1982—; disc jockey Sta. WXLY, Charleston, SC, 1990—93; math. prof. Charleston So. U., 1993—. Weddiing cons. Jay Maxwell's Music by Request, Summerville, 1983—; chair admissions com. Charleston So. U., 2004—, chair faculty senate, 1999—2000; mem. edn. com. Low Country Wedding Profls., Charleston, 1997—2000, pres., 2000—02, mem., 2002—04. Author: (book) Play Something We Can Dance To, 1997; contbr. articles to Mobile Beat mag. Sunday sch. tchr. 1st grade Old Fort Bapt. Ch., Summerville. With USN, 1977—83. Recipient Excellence in Tchg. award, Charleston So. U., 1999, Faculty of Yr. award, 1998. Mem.: Math. Assn. Am. Republican. Baptist. Avocation: music. Home: 422 Eastover Cir Summerville SC 29483 Office: Charleston So U 9200 University Blvd Charleston SC 29423 E-mail: jay@jaymaxwell.com.

**ROLLINS, KEVIN B.,** computer company executive; m. Debra Rollins; children: Marisa, Stephanie, Lauren. Alex. BS, Brigham Young U., MBA, 1984. Ptnr. Bain & Co., 1984—96; cons. Dell Computer Corp., 1993—96, sr. v.p., corp. strategy, 1996—97, pres. Dell Americas, 1997—2001, vice-chmn., 1997—2001, pres., COO, 2001—04, pres., CEO 2004—. Mem. Am. Enterprise Inst.; pres. leadership council Brigham Young U., Marriot Sch. Nat. Advisory Council, founder, Rollins Ctr. E-commerce; mem. Presdl. Adv. Com. Trade Policy and Negotiation. High tech chmn. Juvenile Diabetes Rsch. Found.; trustee Arts Center Stage; bd. dir. Austin Symphony, KLRU. Office: Dell Computer Corp Hdqs One Dell Way Round Rock TX 78682*

**ROLLINS, SONNY (THEODORE ROLLINS),** composer, musician; b. NYC, Sept. 7, 1930; s. Walter and Valborg (Solomon) R.; m. Dawn Finney, 1956 (div.); m. Lucille Pearson, Sept. 7, 1959. ArtsD, Bard Coll., 1992, Long Island U., 1998, Wesleyan U., 1998, Duke U., 1999; D of Music, New Eng. Conservatory of Music, 2002; MusD (hon.), Berklee Coll. Music, 2003. Ann.concert tours in Europe and Asia; more than 100 original compositions recorded including Freedom Suite, Oleo, Alegria, Sonnymoon for Two, Way Out West; composer, musician: (film) Alfie, 1966 (Grammy nomination 1966), (albums) This is What I Do, 2001 (Grammy award 2001), Without a Song: The 9/11 Concert, 2005 (Grammy award for Best Jazz Instrumental Solo, 2006). Recipient Lifetime Achievement award, Nat. Acad. Recording Arts and Scis., 2004, numerous others; Guggenheim fellow, 1972. Home: RR 9 # G Germantown NY 12526

**ROLLO, F. DAVID,** healthcare company executive, cardiologist; b. Endicott, NY, Apr. 15, 1939; s. Frank C. and Augustine L. (Dumont) R.; m. Linda Wood, June 1, 1991; children: Mindee, Alex. BA, Harpur Coll., 1959; MS, U. Miami, 1965; PhD, Johns Hopkins U., 1968; MD, Upstate Med. Ctr., Syracuse, N.Y., 1972. Diplomate Am. Bd. Nuc. Medicine. Asst. chief nuc. medicine svcs. VA Hosp., San Francisco, 1974-77, chief nuc. medicine Nashville, 1977-79; sr. v.p. med. affairs Humana Inc., Louisville, 1980-92; dir. nuc. medicine div. Vanderbilt U. Med. Ctr., Nashville, 1977-81; prof. radiology Vanderbilt U., Nashville, 1979—; pres., CEO Metricor Inc., Louisville, 1992-95; sr. v.p. med. affairs HCIA, Louisville, 1995-96; sr. v.p. med. affairs, med. dir. Raytel Med. Corp., San Mateo, Calif., 1996-99; chief med. officer ADAC Labs., Milpitas, Calif., 1999—2002; internat. chief med. officer Philips Med. Sys., 2003—. Mem. med. adv. com. IBT, Washington, 1984—; mem. pvt. sector liaison panel Inst. of Medicine, Washington, 1983—; bd. dirs. ADAC Labs. Editor: Nuclear Medicine Physics, Instruments and Agents, 1977 (rendition Physical Basis of Medical Imaging, 1980, Digital Radiology: Focus on Clinical Utility, 1982, Nuclear Medicine Resonance Imaging, 1983; mem. editorial adv. bd. ECRI, 1981—. Pres. bd. dirs. Youth Performing Arts Coun., Louisville, 1984-85; bd. dirs. Louisville-Jefferson County Youth Orch., 1983-85; sr. v.p., exec. com. USA Internat. Harp Competition, 1992-, chmn., 1994-. Fellow Am. Coll. Cardiology, Am. Coll. Nuc. Physicians (profl. Am. Coll. Radiology com. 1982-84, chmn. 1984); mem. AMA, Soc. Nuc. Medicine (trustee 1979-83, Am.—, Cassen Meml. lectr. western region 1980, 84), Radiol. Soc. N.Am., NEMA (chmn. nuc. medicine sect., 2002-, bd. mem., 2002-, testimony medicine expert, 2003-), Am. Coll. Radiology, Ky. Sci. Tech. Coun. (exec. bd. 1987—), Advancement Med. Instrumentation (bd. dirs. 1986—), Louisville C. of C. (chmn. MIC com. 1987—). Avocations: racquetball, squash, golf. Home: 15735 Peach Hill Rd Saratoga CA 95070-6447

**ROLLO, RICHARD JAMES,** music educator; b. Warren, Ohio, May 29, 1957; s. Matteo and Josephine Antoinette Rollo. B Music Edn., Youngstown State U., Ohio, 1983; M Music Edn., VanderCook Coll. Music, Chgo., 1997. Cert. tchr. Ohio. Band dir. Youngstown Diocese Schs., 1983—84, Warren City Schs., 1984—, Hubbard (Ohio) Exempted Village Schs., 1987—88, Brookfield (Ohio) Schs., 1989—90; jazz ensemble instr. Youngstown State U., 1993. Freelance musician, 1979—; alto saxophone player Packard Band, Warren, 1999—. Musician: (jazz CD) Cruise Control, 2000. Mem.: NEA, Internat. Assn. Jazz Educators, Music Educators Nat. Conf., Am. Fedn. Musicians. Avocations: woodworking, gardening, computers, cooking. Home: 2252 Wilson Ave NE Warren OH 44483-2922 Office: Warren G Harding HS 860 Elm Rd NE Warren OH 44483

**ROLLO, SHERRY LEE,** lawyer; b. Baytown, Tex., Nov. 1, 1977; d. Larry Richard and Gwen Lee Rollo. BS in Physics, U. Tex., 2001; JD, John Marshall Law Sch., 2004. Atty. Welsh & Katz, Ltd., Chgo., 2004—. Contbr. articles to profl. jours. Presentor-mentor Chgo. Metro History Edn. Ctr., 2005. Mem.: Nat. Assn. Women Bus. Owners (chair Chgo. chpt. 2005—06), North Suburban Bar Assn. bd. mem. 2005—06), ABA, Chgo. Bar Assn., Intellectual Property Assn. Chgo. Office: Welsh & Katz Ltd 120 S Riverside Plaza Chicago IL 60606 Office Phone: 312-655-1500. Office Fax: 312-655-1501. Business E-Mail: srollo@welshkatz.com.

**ROLSTEN, KATHY,** music educator, choir director; b. Van Wert, Ohio, June 8, 1950; BS in Music Edn., Bowling Green State U., Ohio, 1972; MEd in Principalship, Curriculum, Wright State U., 1982; cert., Silver Lake Coll. 1988; MusM, Bowling Green State U., Ohio, 2003; postgrad. in Music Edn., U. South Fla., 2005—. Cert. tchr. kodaly, supr., elem. music, adminstrn. Supr. educator, New Knoxville, Ohio, 1974-80; tchr. music Oklahoma City Schs., 1982-85; adminstr. arts in edn. Toledo Pub. Schs., 1989-91, elem. music specialist, 1985—2003, HS choir dir., 1992—2003; grad. asst. Bowling Green State U., 2003—05; voice instr., 2005—; grad. asst. U. South Fla., 2005—. Mem. elem. music curriculum com. Oklahoma City Schs., 1983—84; organizer Three Tchr. Workshops, Toledo, 1984, 85, 86; demonstrator tchr. workshops Toledo Pub. Schs., 1987, 88, 89, 91; vol. music specialist cons., Toledo, 1989—92. Writer: dir. student Christmas prodn. Southside Bapt. Grace Gospel Mission, Toledo, 1992; fellowship coord. Christian Rsch. and Fellowship. Mem.: Am. Choral Dirs. Assn., Orgn. Am. Kodaly Educators, Music Educators Nat. Conf. Avocations: reading, gardening.

**ROLSTON, HOLMES, III,** theology studies educator, philosopher; b. Staunton, Va., Nov. 19, 1932; s. Holmes and Mary Winifred (Long) R.; m. Jane Irving Wilson, June 1, 1956; children: Shonny Hunter, Giles Campbell. BS, Davidson Coll., 1953; BD, Union Theol. Sem., Richmond, Va., 1956; MA in Philosophy of Sci., U. Pitts., 1968; PhD in Theology, U. Edinburgh, Scotland, 1958. Ordained ministry Presbyn. Ch. (USA), 1956. Asst. prof. philosophy Colo. State U., Ft. Collins, 1968-71, assoc. prof., 1971-76, prof., 1976—. Vis. scholar Ctr. Study World Religions, Harvard U., 1974-75; ofcl. observer UN Conf. on Environ. and Devel., Rio de Janiero, 1992; vis. prof. bioethics Yale U., 2005-06. Author: Religious Inquiry. Participation and Detachment, 1985, Philosophy Gone Wild, 1986, Science and Religion: A Critical Survey, 1987, Environmental Ethics, 1988, Conserving Natural Value, 1994, Genes, Genesis and God, 1999; assoc. editor Environ. Ethics, 1979—; mem. editl. bd. Zygon: Jour. of Religion and Sci.; contbr. chpts. to books, articles to profl. jours. Recipient Univ. Disting. Prof., 1992; Disting. Russell fellow Grad. Theol. Union, 1991, Disting. Lectr., Chinese Acad. of Social Scis., 1991, Disting. Lectr., Nobel Conf. XXVII, Gifford Lectr., U. Edinburgh, 1997; featured in Fifty Key Thinkers on the Environment, 2001, Templeton Prize in Religion, 2003, Gregor Mendel medal, Villanova Univ., 2005 Mem. AAAS, Am. Acad. Religion, Soc. Bibl. Lit. (pres. Rocky Mountain-Gt. Plains region), Am. Philos. Assn., Internat. Soc. Environ. Ethics (pres. 1989-94), Phi Beta Kappa. Avocation: bryology. Home: 1712 Concord Dr Fort Collins CO 80526-1602 Office: Colo State U Dept Philosophy Fort Collins CO 80523-0001 Office Phone: 970-491-6315. Business E-Mail: rolston@lamar.colostate.edu.

**ROMA, AIDA CLARA,** artist; b. Phila., July 17, 1924; d. Carlo and Giustina S. R.; widowed; 4 children. Student, Camden County Coll., 1990-99. Dental Dr. Martin Apother, Runnemede, N.J., 1956-66; owner Rogers Auto Sales, Runnemede, N.J., 1966-90; tchr. St. Joseph's Sch., Camden, N.J., 1956-66. Author of poems, Jealousy, 1999, My 2 Best Friends, 2001, "Pal" My Pal, 2004. Art tutor, Haddenfield, N.J.; v.p. Girl Scouts Am., Runnemede, 1964; sec. Boy Scouts Am., 1960; mem. St. Teresa's Choir, 1993—, Atlantic City Choirs. Recipient Internat. Poet award, Artistic Artistry award, England, 2004. Mem. Sons of Italy. Republican. Achievements include invention of Rack on the Back auto addition. Avocation: singing. Home: PO Box 2076 Laurel Springs NJ 08021

**ROMAINE, HENRY SIMMONS,** retired investment company executive, consultant; b. NYC, May 30, 1933; s. Theodore Cole and Cornelia (Simmons) R.; m. Susan Donaldson; children: Henry, Hilary, Kathryn. BA, Harvard U., 1954. Asst. security analyst Mutual Life Ins. Co., N.Y.C., 1958-60, investment analyst, 1960-61, investment specialist, 1961-64, asst. dir. investments, 1964, dir. investments, 1964-66, asst. v.p. for securities investment, 1966-68, 2d v.p. for securities investment, 1969-71, v.p. for securities investment, 1971-72, sr. v.p., 1972-78, sr. v.p., chief investment officer, 1976-78, exec. v.p., 1978-81, pres., 1981-86; vice chmn., chief investment officer Am. Gen. Corp., Houston, 1986-93. Dir. MONY Life Ins. Co. of Can.; chmn. bd. MONY Real Estate Investors, 1978-86; mem. adv. bd. Chem. Bank, 1974-93. Served with USN, 1954-57. Mem.: Harvard Club. Home: 7 Conquest Ave Sullivans Island SC 29482-9779

**ROMAN, ALFRED VICTOR,** science education educator; b. Yonkers, NY, Feb. 26, 1940; s. Alfred Ignatius and Helen Marie (Danin) R.; m. Patricia Jeanne Gardinier, Oct. 25, 1946; 1 child, Caroline Elizabeth. BA, Montclair State Coll., N.J., 1961; MA, NYU, 1963, D Edn, 1967. Speed reading specialist N.Y. Speed Reading Inst., N.Y.C., 1965-67; teaching fellow NYU, N.Y.C., 1965-67, instr., 1967; asst. prof. N.Y.C. Community Coll., Bklyn., 1965-67; dir. rsch. and devel. and ednl. adminstrn. Universal Edn. and Visual Arts, div. Universal City Studios, Calif., 1967-71; dir. div. media arts and tech. Potsdam Coll. SUNY, 1971-87, asst. prof. ednl. communications, 1988—, prof. ednl. edn., 1987—. Film cons., N.Y.C., 1967—. Contbr. articles to profl. jours. Bd. mem. Ch. of the Nazarene, Potsdam, 1988-89; v.p. Potsdam Interfaith Community Svc. Coun., 1989, Nixa Area Arts Coun., 2002-06; supr. info. svcs. Olympic Village XIII Olympic Winter Games, Lake Placid, N.Y., 1980; adv. bd. Nixa Cmty. Found., 2004-06; Life Group leader The Bridge Ch., 2004-06. Recipient Pres. award Potsdam Coll., 1981; award NEH, 1980. Mem. Alexandria Bay Flotilla, U.S. Coast Guard Aux., Rotary, Masons, Shriners, Sigma Xi, Sigma Pi Sigma, Tau Epsilon Pi, Phi Delta Kappa, Kappa Delta Pi. Republican. Nazarene. Avocations: music, decorating, films. Home: 1220 S Becky St Nixa MO 65714-7958 Personal E-mail: alpatroman@earthlink.net.

**ROMAN, NANCY GRACE,** astronomer, consultant; b. Nashville, May 16, 1925; d. Irwin and Georgia Frances (Smith) R. BA (Joshua Lippincott Meml. fellow), Swarthmore Coll., 1946; PhD, U. Chgo., 1949; D.Sc., Russell Sage Coll., 1966, Hood Coll., 1969, Bates Coll., 1971, Swarthmore Coll., 1976. Asst. Sproul Obs., Swarthmore Coll., 1943-46; asst. Yerkes Obs., U. Chgo., at Williams Bay, Wis., 1946-48, research asso., 1949-52, instr. stellar astronomy, 1952-55, asst. prof., 1955; research asso. Warner and Swasey Obs., Case Inst. Tech., Cleve., summer 1949; physicist radio astronomy br. U.S. Naval Research Lab., Washington, 1955-56, astronomer, head microwave spectroscopy sect., 1956-58, astronomer cons., 1958-59; head observational astronomy program Office Space Flight Devel., NASA, Washington, 1959-60, chief astronomy and solar physics, geophysics and astronomy programs, 1960—79, chief astronomy and relativity programs, 1965—80, program scientist for space telescope, 1979-80; astronomy cons., 1980-89; prin. scientist Astronomical Data Ctr., NASA, 1981—97. With McDonnell Douglas Space Systems, 1988-94. Contbr. articles to sci. periodicals. Trustee Russell Sage Coll., 1973-78; bd. mgrs. Swarthmore Coll., 1979-83. Recipient Fed. Woman's award., 1962; citation for pub. service Colo. Woman's Coll., 1966; 90th Anniversary award Women's Ednl. and Indsl. Union, 1967; NASA Exceptional Sci. Achievement award, 1969; NASA Outstanding Leadership medal, 1978 Fellow AAAS, Am. Astronautical Soc. (William Randolph Lovelace II award 1980); mem. AAUW, Am. Astron. Soc., Internat. Astron. Union (editor symposia 1956-58), Astron. Soc. Pacific. Achievements include rsch. on stellar clusters, high velocity stars, radio astronomy; 1st noted correlation of metallic lines in stars with their space velocity; asteroid named Roman, 1989. Personal E-mail: nancy.roman6@verizon.net. *This guiding principle sounds old fashioned but I have found it useful: "Forget that you are a woman but never forget that you are a lady.".*

**ROMAN, RAY,** communications executive; BS finance, U. of Ill., Chicago; MBA finance and marketing, U. of Chicago. Gen. mgr., sales and service Ameritech Small Business Services; corp. controller, v.p. of financial planning and analysis Alliant Foodservice, pres. N.E. div.; v.p. sales AT&T Wireless, 2001—03; corp v.p., gen. mgr. of No. Am., mobile devices Motorola Inc., 2003—03, sr. v.p. worldwide sales, mobile devices, 2005—. Named one of the best 40 under 40 in business, Crain's Chicago Business, 2005. Office: c/o Motorola Inc 1303 E Algonquin Rd Schaumburg IL 60196*

**ROMAN, STANFORD AUGUSTUS, JR.,** medical educator, dean; b. N.Y.C. s. Stanford Augustas and Ivy L. (White) D.; m. Norma Dabney Roman; children: Mawiyah Lythcott, Jane E. Roman-Brown. AB, Dartmouth Coll., 1964, MA (hon.), 1992; MD, Columbia U., 1968; MPH, U. Mich., 1975. Diplomate Nat. Bd. of Med. Examiners. Intern Columbia U.-Harlem Hosp. Ctr., N.Y.C., 1966—69, resident in medicine, 1969—71, chief resident in medicine, 1971—73; 1972assoc. dir. ambulatory care Columbia U. Harlem Hosp., 1972—73; instr. medicine Columbia U., N.Y.C., 1972—73; asst. physician Presbyn. Hosp., 1972—73; clin. dir. Healthco, Inc., Soul City, NC, 1973—74; dir. ambulatory care, asst. prof. medicine/sociomed. scis. Boston City Hosp., Boston 1974—78; asst. prof. medicine U. N.C., Chapel Hill, 1973—74; asst. dean Boston U. Sch. Medicine, 1974—78; med. dir. D.C. Gen. Hosp., Washington, 1978—81; from assoc. dean acad. affairs to dep. dean Dartmouth Med. Sch., Hanover, NH, 1981—87, assoc. prof., 1981—87, dep. dean, 1986—87; dean, v.p., prof. medicine Morehouse Sch. Med., Atlanta, 1987—89; sr. v.p., med. and profl. affairs Health and Hosps. Corp., N.Y.C., 1989—90; dean med. sch., prof. cmty. health and social medicine Sophie Davis Sch. Biomed. Edn., 1990—; interim pres. CCNY, 1999—2001. Dir. Boston Comprehensive Sickle Cell Ctr., 1975—78; bd. dirs. Winifred Masterson Burke Rehab. Hosp., White Plains, NY, 1993—94; mem. Dartmouth Hitchcock Med. Ctr. Bd. of Medicine, NY, 1993—2002; mem. bd. trustees Dartmouth Coll., Hanover, NH, 1992—2002. Contbr. to book chpts. and profl. jours. and editls. Fellow N.Y. Acad. Medicine; mem. AMA, APHA, Nat. Med. Assn., N.Y. State Coun. Grad. Med. Edn., N.Y. State Dept. Edn. Bd. Medicine. Democrat. Episcopalian. Avocations: photography, travel, music.

**ROMANCE, MARY C.,** library director; b. Rabat, Morocco, June 20, 1957; d. Francis Joseph and Ann (Pickert) Romance. BA in Orgnl. Comms. and Mgmt., U. Mich., 1979; MLS, Rutgers U., 1992. Libr. coord. Bernardsville (N.J.) Pub. Libr., 1991-93; libr. dir. Rockaway (N.J.) Borough Pub. Libr., 1993-94, Lincoln Park (N.J.) Pub. Libr., 1994-97, Roxbury Twp. Pub. Libr., Succasunna, N.J., 1997—. Pres. Morris Automated Info. Network Inc. Mem.: Roxbury Area C. of C. (bd. dirs.). Office: Roxbury Public Library 103 Main St Succasunna NJ 07876-1417

**ROMANI, JOHN HENRY,** health science association administrator, educator; b. Milan, Mar. 6, 1925; s. Henry Arthur and Hazel (Pettengill) R.; m. Barbara A. Anderson; children: David John, Paul Nichols, Theresa A. Anderson. BA, MA, U. N.H., 1949; PhD, U. Mich., 1955. Instr. U. N.H., 1950-51; instr. U. Mich., Ann Arbor, 1954-55, assoc. prof., asst. to assoc. dean Sch. Pub. Health, 1961-69, assoc. v.p., 1971-75, chmn. health planning and adminstrn., 1975-80, prof., 1971-93, prof. emeritus pub. health adminstrn., 1993—, faculty assoc. program on the environment, 2004—; interim chair Pub. Health Policy and Adminstrn., 1991-92. Asst. prof. W. Mich. U., 1956-57; assoc. dir. Cleve. Met. Svcs. Commn., 1957-59; assoc. prof. U. Pitts., 1959-61; vice chancellor, prof. U. Wis.-Milw., 1969-71; rsch. fellow Brookings Instn., 1955-56; mem. task force Nat. Commn. on Orgn. Cmty. Health Svcs., 1963-66; dir. staff Sec.'s Com. on Orgn. Health Activities, HEW, 1965-66; dir. Govtl. Affairs Inst., 1969-75, chmn., 1970-72; trustee Pub. Adminstrn. Svc., 1969-75, chmn., 1973-75; mem. Delta Dental Plan Mich., 1972-78, bd. dirs 1972-78, chmn. consumers' adv. coun., 1975-77; bd. dirs. Ctr. for Population Activities, 1975-81, chmn., 1975-81; lifetime vis. prof. Capital U. Economics and Bus., Beijing, 1996—; vis. rschr. Human Scis. Rsch. Coun., Pretoria, South Africa, 1999—. Author: The Philippine Presidency, 1956; editor: Changing Dimensions in Public Administration, 1962; contbr. articles to profl. jours. Mem. Citizens League, Cleve., 1957-59; mem. Ann Arbor Citizens Coun., 1965-69; bd. dirs. Southeastern Mich. Family Planning Project, 1975-77; trustee Geographical Summer Assembly, 1982-85; commr. Accrediting Commn. on Edn. for Health Svcs. Adminstrn., 1989-95. Served with AUS, 1943-46, ETO. Fellow Am. Pub. Health Assn. (chmn. program devel. bd. 1975-77, exec. bd. 1975-80, governing coun. 1975—, pres. 1979, chmn. publs. bd. 1984-88), Royal Soc. Health (hon.), Am. Polit. Sci. Assn. (life); mem. ASPA (past mem. coun.), Population Assn. Am., Phi Kappa Phi, Pi Sigma Alpha, Pi Gamma Mu, Delta Omega. Home and Office: 2125 Nature Cove Apt 108 Ann Arbor MI 48104

**ROMANO, CARMEN J.,** lawyer; b. Phila., 1955; BS, U. Pa., 1977; JD, Columbia U., 1980. Note editor Columbia U. Law Review, 1979—80; law clk. to Hon. Dolores K. Sloviter US Ct. Appeals (3rd cir.), 1980—81; ptnr. Dechert LLP, Phila., chmn. bus. dept. Office: Dechert LLP Cira Ctr 2929 Arch St Philadelphia PA 19104 Office Phone: 215-994-2971. E-mail: carmen.romano@dechert.com.

**ROMANO, CLARE,** artist; b. Palisade, NJ, 1922; m. John Ross; 2 children. BFA, Cooper Union, NY; student, Inst. d'Arte, Florence, Ecole des Beaux Arts, Fontainebleau. Faculty New Sch., NYC, Univ. Wash., Seattle, Vt. Studio Sch., Okla. Arts Inst., Pratt Inst., NYC, 1964—; prof. emeritus Pace Univ. Co-author (with John Ross): Complete Printmaker, 1972, (rev. ed. with Tim Ross), 1990, John Ross and Clare Romano: Artists and the Book, 2001; one-woman shows include AAA Gallery, NYC, Galleria Segno Grafica, Venice, Jane Haslem Gallery, Washington, NJ State Mus., Represented in permanent collections MoMA, Whitney Mus., Met. Mus. Art, Bklyn. Mus., Tokyo Art Ctr., Queensland Mus., Moderna Galloria, Ljubljana, Slovenia, British Mus. Grantee Fulbright Fellow, Louis Comfort Tiffany Grant, NJ States Coun. Arts grant, five fellowships to MacDowell Colony. Mem.: NAD (Academician 1979—). Mailing: PO Box 1122 New York NY 10159-1122

**ROMANO, GAETANO,** research scientist, educator; b. Milan, Italy, May 11, 1959; s. Antonio Romano and Gemma Matilde Santangelo. PhD, State U. Milan, 1985. Asst. prof. dept. neurosurgery Thomas Jefferson U., Phila., 2000—; adj. asst. prof. cell. sci. Temple U., Phila., 2003—, assoc. prof. biology and medicine, 2006—. Editor, co-author Cell Cycle Control and Dysregulation Protocols: Cyclins, Cyclin-dependent Kinases and Other Factors, 2004, review editor Jour. Exptl. & Clin. Cancer Rsch., 2004—; contbr. articles to profl. jours. Grantee Pilot Rsch. award, Thomas Jefferson U., 2004. Mem.: Internat. Soc. Stem Cell Rsch. (assoc.). Achievements include research in engineering of an inducible system based on a retroviral-encoded Drosophila HSP70 promoter to deliver a proapoptotic factor into cancer cells; characterization of the biology of the receptor of the insulin-like growth factor 1 (IGF-1R) in cancer research; retroviral-mediated gene transfer of the retinoblastoma-related gene Rb2/p130 to suppress lung tumor growth; characterization of the tissue-specific gene expression of the human tyrosine hydroxylase promoter; development of retroviral and lentiviral vector systems. Office Phone: 215-204-9521. Personal E-mail: gromano@temple.edu.

**ROMANO, JAMES JOHN,** plastic surgeon; b. Roanoke, Va., Nov. 14, 1952; BS, Coll. William and Mary, 1976; MD, Ea. Va. Med. Sch., 1980. Diplomate Am. Bd. Surgery, Am. Bd. Plastic Surgery. Asst. chief of plastic surgery svc. Johns Hopkins Hosp., Balt., 1987—88; asst. prof. plastic surgery U. So. Calif., L.A., 1988—91; pvt. practice cosmetic surgery of the face and body San Francisco, 1991—. Contbr. articles to profl. publs. Vol. plastic surgeon San Francisco Free Clinic, 1996—2006. Fellow: Am. Bd. Plastic Surgery; mem.: Am. Soc. Maxillofacial Surgeons, Am. Soc. Aesthetic Plastic Surgery. Office: 126 Post St Suite 618 San Francisco CA 94108 Office Phone: 415-981-3911.

**ROMANO, JOHN FRANCIS,** dermatologist; b. S.I., N.Y., July 4, 1948; BS, St. Peter's Coll., 1969; MD, Cornell U., 1973. Diplomate Am. Bd. Dermatology. Intern Einstein Hosps., N.Y.C., 1973—74; resident in medicine St. Vincent's Hosp., N.Y.C., 1974—76; resident in dermatology N.Y. Hosp., N.Y.C., 1976—78; pvt. practice dermatology N.Y.C., 1979—; attending physician St. Vincent's Hosp., N.Y.C., 1979—; clin. assist. clin. prof. dermatology Weill Hosp. Cornell U., 1979—; also asst. attending dermatologist N.Y. Presbyterian Hosp. Mem.: N.Y. State Dermatologic Soc., Am. Soc. for Laser Medicine and Surgery, Am. Soc. for Dermatologic Surgery, Am. Acad. Dermatology. Avocation: sailing. Office: 36 7th Ave New York NY 10011-6609 Office Phone: 212-242-5815. Business E-mail: info@romanodermatology.com.

**ROMANO, JOSEPH ANTHONY,** healthcare education and marketing consultant; b. Bklyn., Sept. 5, 1946; s. Anthony Wilbur and Anne R.; m. Linda Rose Giacalone, Sept. 23, 1972; children: Nicholas Joseph, Christine Dianne. Student, Villanova U., 1964-66; BS Pharm. Sci., Columbia U., 1970, D Pharmacy, 1972. Clin. resident Lenox Hill Hosp., N.Y.C., 1970-72; asst. dean, asst. prof. Columbia U., N.Y.C., 1972-76, SUNY, Buffalo, 1976-78; assoc. dean, assoc. prof. U. Wash., Seattle, 1978-83; assoc. dir. external affairs Sandoz (Novartis), N.Y.C., 1983-85; product mgr., 1985, assoc. to pres., 1985-87; sr. v.p., group dir. Hill & Knowlton, Inc., N.Y.C., 1987-88; exec. dir. external affairs Sandoz (Novartis), N.Y.C., 1988-89; pres., COO, Visual Med. Mktg., N.Y.C., 1989-92; vice chair Nelson Communications, Inc. Worldwide (divsn. Publicis), N.Y.C., 1992-2001; chmn., CEO, SCIENS Worldwide Healthcare Comms., 1996-2001; co-chmn. Nelson Profl. Sales, 1998-2000. Mem. U.S. Nat. Adv. Com. Health Profls., Washington, 1980-86. Co-author: Clinical Pharmacology, 1980, Pharmacy State Board Reviews, 1976, 78, 85, The Vitamin Book, 1985, 2000; contbr. articles to profl. jours. Fellow Royal Soc. Health London; mem. Am. Pharm. Assn., Am. Soc. Healthcare Pharmacists, Am. Assoc. Study Headaches, U.S. Golf Assn., Rho Chi. Avocations: photography, stamp collecting/philately, golf, music, cooking. Personal E-mail: josepharomano@earthlink.net.

**ROMANO, MICHAEL,** publishing executive, consultant; b. IndianTown Gap, Pa., Nov. 23, 1952; s. Frank and Patricia Romano; m. Elaine A. Ambrose, July 22, 2000; children: Daniel Martin, Emily Brooke Nielson, Adam Jeffery Nielson. BS in Environ. Health, Colo. State U., 1979. Cert. EMT Colo.; LPN, Wash., Colo. Environ. specialist Hewlett Packard Co., Boise, Idaho, 1979—99; pub. Mill Pk. Pub., McCall, Idaho, 2003—. Fin. cons. E & M Group, McCall, 1999—2003. Mem. capital campaign U. Idaho, Moscow, 2000—03. With U.S. Army, 1971—75. Recipient Best New Children's Book, 2003, Statewide Literacy award. Mem.: Small Publishers Assn. Am. (assoc.). Independent. Home and Office: PO Box 1932 1510 McCall Ave Mccall ID 83638 Office Phone: 208-634-1358. E-mail: millparkpublish@aol.com.

**ROMANO, RAY,** actor, comedian; b. Forest Hills, N.Y., Dec. 21, 1957; m. Anna Scarpula; 4 children. Stand-up comedian; sitcom actor. Actor: (TV series) Everybody Loves Raymond, 1996—2005 (Best Actor, Quality Comedy, Viewers for Quality TV, 1998, TV Critics Assn. award for outstanding ind. achievement in comedy, 1999, nominee Emmy award outstanding lead actor in comedy series, 1999, nominee Golden Globe award best performance by actor in comedy, People's Choice award favorite male TV performer, 2002, nominee Screen Actors Guild award outstanding performance by a male actor in comedy series, 2002, TV Guide award Favorite Actor in a Comedy, Funniest Male Lead in a TV Series at 14th Ann. Am. Comedy Awards), (voice): (films) Ice Age, 2002, Welcome to Mooseport, 2004, Eulogy, 2004, Grilled, 2005, (voice) Ice Age: The Meltdown, 2006; TV guest appearances in Dr. Katz Professional Therapist, 1995, The King of Queens, 1998, Hollywood Squares, 1998—2004, Becker, 1998, Who Wants to Be a Millionaire, 1999; author: Everything and a Kite, 1999; co-author (with Richard & Robert Romano): (children's book) Raymie, Dickie & the Bean: Why I Love and Hate My Brothers, 2005; performer: (CD) Ray Ramono: Live at Carnegie Hall, 1999; (appeared in (TV films) Ray Romano & Kevin James: Making the Cut (HBO), 2005; prodr.: 95 Miles to Go, 2004. Recipient People's Choice award, favorite male TV star, 2006.*

**ROMANO, SHEILA JUNE,** telecommunications industry professional, writer, artist; b. Elko, Nev., June 11, 1951; d. John Lewis and June Florene (Lani) C. BA, U. Nev., 1974. Various svc. positions Citizens Comm. (formerly Alltel-Nevada Inc.), Elko, 1974-78, svc. rep., 1978-84, bus. office supr., 1984-87, bus. supr. Nev. office, 1987-94, bus. supr., state pub. rels. coord., 1994-97, results coord., project mgmt. support person Elk Grove, Calif., 1997, supr. customer ops. escalations and exec. complaints, 1998-2000, specialist state gov. affairs, 2001—02; sr. regulatory analyst Frontier Comm., 2002—. Active Citizens Amb. program People to People Internat., 1995—98; writer, artist, 1974—. Contbg. author: Fence Post to Fiber, 1998. Officer, organizer Freedom Com., Elko, 1984; mem., treas. Elk Grove Cmty. Action Team, 1997-98. Mem. NOW, AAUW (editor newsletter Elko 1980-82, v.p. programs 1991-93, sec. 1995-96), Soroptimists Internat. (treas. 1992-93, sec. 1993-94, v.p. 1995-96, pres. 1996-97). Office: Frontier PO Box 340 Elk Grove CA 95759-0340

**ROMANOFF, MARJORIE REINWALD,** retired education educator; b. Chgo., Sept. 29, 1923; d. David Edward and Gertrude (Rosenfield) Reinwald; m. Milford M. Romanoff, Nov. 6, 1945; children: Bennett Sanford, Lawrence Michael, Janet Beth (dec.). Student, Northwestern U., 1941-42, 43-45, Chgo. Coll. Jewish Studies, 1942-43; BEd, U. Toledo, 1947, MEd, 1968, EdD, 1976. Tchr. Old Orchard Elem. Sch., Toledo, 1946-47, McKinley Sch., Toledo 1964-65; substitute tchr. Toledo, 1964-68; instr. Mary Manse Coll., Toledo, 1974; instr. children's lit. Sylvania (Ohio) Bd. Edn., 1977; supr. student tchrs. U. Toledo, 1968—73, 1985—2001, instr. advanced comms., 1977, rschr., 1973-74; instr. Am. Lang. Inst., 1978—2002. Asst. prof. elem. edn. Bowling Green (Ohio) State U., 1978—88; chair rsch. com. Am. Lang. Inst., U. Toledo, 1985—94, asst. prof. elem. edn. in lang. arts, 1985—87, asst. prof. elem. edn., ESL specialist, 1978—2002; condr. workshop Internat. Conf./Teaching Langs., U. Cin., 1996; presenter in field. Author: Language and Study Skills: For Learners of English, Prentice Hall Regents, 1991. Trustee Children's Svcs. Bd., 1974-76; pres. bd. Cummings Treatment Ctr. for Adolescents, 1978-80; mem. Crosby Gardens Adv. Bd., 1976-82, Cmty. Planning Coun., 1980-84, Citizens Rev. Bd. of Juv. Ct., 1979—; allocations com. Mental Health and Retardation Bd., 1980-81; active Bd. Jewish Edn., 1976—, pres., 1982-84; active Jewish Family Svc., 1978-85, v.p., 1980-85; allocations com. Jewish Welfare Fedn., 1980, 89-91; bd. dirs. Family Life Edn. Coun., 1984-90, sec., 1988-90; budget and allocations com. Jewish Fedn., 1989-93; bd. dirs. Friends Toledo-Lucas County Libs., 1991—, bd. pres., 1991-93; program chair U. Toledo Women's Commn., 1991-93; bd. dirs. Ohio Friends of Pub. Librs. 1992-94. Named One of Ten Women of Yr., St. Vincent's Hosp., Guild, 1984, Outstanding Instructional Staff Woman, U. Toledo, 1990, Excellence award Citizen's Rev. Bd., 2003. Mem. Tchrs. English to Speakers Other Langs., Toledo Libr. Legacy Found., Orgn. Rehab. and Tng. (named Outstanding Woman in Cmty. Svc. 1987), Hadassah (chpt. pres. regional bd. 1961-64), Northwestern U. Alumni Assn., Phi Kappa Phi, Phi Delta Kappa, Kappa Delta Pi (pres., faculty adv. 1971-75, Point of Excellence award 1992), Pi Lambda Theta (chpt. pres. 1978-80, nat. com. 1979-84). Home: Stratford in the Hills 4343 W Bancroft St Apt 4B Toledo OH 43615

**ROMANOFF, MILFORD MARTIN,** retired building contractor; b. Cleve., Aug. 21, 1921; s. Barney Sanford and Edythe Stolpher (Bort) R.; m. Marjorie Reinwald, Nov. 6, 1945; children: Bennett S., Lawrence M., Janet Beth (dec.). Student, U. Mich. Coll. Arch., 1939-42; BBA, U. Toledo, 1943. Pres. Glass City Constrn. Co., Toledo, 1951-55, Milford Romanoff, Inc., Toledo, 1956—2003. Co-founder Neighborhood Improvement Found. Toledo, 1960; active Lucas County Econ. Devel. Com., 1979—, Childrens Svcs. Bd. Lucas County, 1981—97, Arthritis Bd. Dirs., Crosby Gardens Bd. Advisors, 1983—96, Toledo Met. Area Govt. Exec. Com., 1996—; citizens adv. bd. Recreation Commn. Toledo, 1973—86; campus adv. com. Med. Coll. Ohio, 1980—; trustee Cummings Treatment Ctr. for Adolescents, 1981—; pres. bd. dirs. Anti-Defamation League, 1955—60, Ohio Hillel Orgns., Lucas County Dept. Human Svcs., Arthritis Assn., 1995—, Comprehensive Addiction Svc. Sys., 1998, Kidney Found. Northwestern Ohio, 1986—, sec., 1989; chmn. Comprehensive Addiction Svc. Sys., 1999, Toledo Amateur Baseball and Softball Com., 1979—81; cons. U.S. Care Corp., 1985—; bd. govs. Toledo Housing for Elderly, 1982—84, sec., 1989, pres. bd. govs., 1990—, pres., 1991—; bd. adv. Ret. Sr. Vol. Program, 1987—89, chmn., 1988—90, 1993—, sec., adv. bd., 1993—, adv. bd., 2000—; vice chmn. adv. bd. Salvation Army, 1986—87, chmn. adv. bd., 1988—90, ct. apptd. spl. advocate adv. bd. treas., 1989—; chmn. Mental Health Adv. Bd., 1983—84, sec., 1989; bd. dirs. Toledo Urban Forestry Commn., 1991—, pres., 1993, 1995, Lucas County Dept. Human Svcs. Bd.; adv. coun. Renaissance Sr. Apts., 1997,

chmn. adv. coun., 1999; adv. bd. Lucas Co. Correctional Facility, 1999—; chmn. Compass Bd., 2002—; bd. dirs. Area Office on Aging of Northwest Ohio, 2001, Lucas County Mental Health, 2001; chair Compass Corp. for Recovery Svcs., 2002—; mem. Lucas County Mental Health Bd., 2002, Juvenile Correction Bd. Lucas County, 2004—; bd. dirs. Mental Health Lucas Co.; mem. Juvenile Correction Bd. Lucas County, 2003—; mem. adv. bd. ACLU, 2005—, 2005—; active Dem. Precinct Com., 1975—78; trustee Temple Brotherhood, 1956—58, bd. dirs., 1981—; pres. Ohio B'nai Brith, 1959—60; bd. mem. ACLU, 2005—. Mem.: Friends Libr. Bd., Mental Health Bd. of Lucas County, U. Mich. Alumni Assn., Juvenile Justice (adv. bd.), Toledo Zool. Soc., Econ. Opportunity Planning Assn. Greater Toledo (adv. bd.), Nat. Coun. on Alcoholism & Drug Dependence, Toledo Mus. Art (assoc.), U. Toledo Alumni Assn., Am. Legion, Hadassah (assoc. Toledo chpt.), Masons (Outstanding Cmty. Svc. award of Lucas County 2001), Zeta Beta Tau. Home: Stratford in the Hills 4343 W Bancroft St Apt 4B Toledo OH 43615-3956 Office Phone: 419-536-5090.

**ROMANOS, JOHN, JR., (JACK ROMANOS),** publisher; b. Stamford, Conn., Nov. 1, 1942; s. John and Grace (Frano) R.; m. Mary Jane Veach, Jan. 29, 1972; 1 child, Cary Lynne. BS, U. Conn., 1965. Sales mgr. Fawcett Publs., Inc., Greenwich, Conn., 1966-73, Bantam Books, Inc., N.Y.C., 1973-76, dep. to pres., 1976-78, v.p., dir. sales planning, 1978-79, dir. mktg., 1979-81, pub., 1981-85; pres. Simon and Schuster Trade Pub. Group, 1985-87, pres. Mass Market Pub., 1987-91; pres., chief exec. officer Simon & Schuster Consumer Pub. Group, N.Y.C., 1991-93; pres., COO Simon & Schuster, N.Y.C.; pres., CEO Simon & Schuster (Viacom Entertainment Group), N.Y.C., 2002—; pres., chief exec. officer Paramount Pub. Consumer Group, N.Y.C., 1993—. Bd. dirs. Periodicals Inst., N.Y.C., 1980-81 With Army N.G., 1967. Mem. Assn. Am. Pubs. (mem. heads of houses com.), Internat. Periodical Distbrs. Assn. (bd. dirs.), Country Club of Darien (Conn.), exec. com. The Quills. Republican. Greek Orthodox. Office: Simon and Schuster Inc Ste 383 1230 Avenue Of The Americas Fl Conc1 New York NY 10020-1586 Office Phone: 212-698-7000. Office Fax: 212-698-7099.*

**ROMANOSKY, LUANN,** elementary school educator; d. Thomas Forese and Minnie Ann Bianchini Forese; m. David Charles Romanosky, May 20, 1978; children: David C. Jr., Maria. BS in Elem. Edn., West Chester State Coll., 1976; MS in Elem. Edn., West Chester U., 1983. Cert. middle sch. math. Pa. Dept. Edn., elem. instrnl. II Pa. Dept. Edn. Remedial math. tchr. Chester County Intermediate Unit, Downingtown, Pa., 1996—, chairperson math. program, 1996—. Workshop presenter Chester County Intermediate Unit, Downingtown, 1976—. Mem.: Math. Assn. Am., Nat. Coun. Tchrs. Math., ASCD. Avocations: reading, exercise. Office: Chester County Intermediate Unit 455 Boot Rd Downingtown PA 19335 Office Phone: 610-269-8675.

**ROMANOVSKI, MIKHAIL REM,** mathematician; b. Samara, Russia, June 22, 1952; s. Rem Vladimir and Lubov Mikhail (Volgina) R.; m. Elena Vladimir Kurtashina, Aug. 27, 1983 (div.); children: Victoria, Valeria. MS, Moscow Tech. U., 1975; PhD, Heat and Mass Transfer Inst., Kiev, Ukraine, 1982. Engr. Ctrl. Constrn. Bur., Moscow, 1975-78; head dept. math. Kriogenmash, Balashikha, Russia, 1978-93; head dept. CAD/CAE Point Ltd., Moscow, 1992—. Tcrh. math. modeling Chem. Industry Inst., Moscow, 1982-93. Contbr. articles to profl. jours. Mem. N.Y. Acad. Sci. Avocations: sports, skiing. Home: Schelkovskoe Ave 79-1-334 107497 Moscow Russia Office: Point Ltd Lomonosovskiy pr 43/2 Moscow Russia

**ROMANOW, JOSH,** lawyer; b. 1964; BA, Brandeis Univ.; JD, Tulane Univ., 1991. Bar: Pa. 1992, DC 1993. Ptnr. Aviation practice, chmn. Travel Leisure & Hospitality practice Pillsbury Winthrop Shaw Pittman, Washington. Contbr. articles to profl. jours & newspapers; commentator (NPR, CNBC), mem. editl. bd. Gaming Law Rev. Office: Pillsbury Winthrop Shaw Pittman 1133 Connecticut Ave NW Washington DC 20036 Office Phone: 202-775-9864. Office Fax: 202-833-8491. Business E-Mail: romanow@pillsburylaw.com.

**ROMANOWITZ, BYRON FOSTER,** architect, engineer; b. Covington, Ky., Nov. 14, 1929; s. Harry Alex and Mildred (Foster) R.; m. Mildred Elaine Gize, June 15, 1957; children: Laura Ann, Mark Walter, Cynthia Ellen. BS in Civil Engring. U. Ky., 1951; M.F.A. in Architecture, Princeton, 1953. Instr. sch. architecture Princeton U., 1954; architect Brock & Johnson, Lexington, 1958-59, Johnson & Romanowitz, Architects, Lexington and Louisville, 1960-2000; ret., 2000. Pres. Ky. Bd. examiners and Registration of Archs., 1975-91; instr. U. Ky. Sch. Architecture, 1996, 2000. Prin. works include U. Ky. campus bldgs., 1959-96, Ea. Ky. U. campus bldgs., 1959-77, Centre Coll., Danville, Ky., campus bldgs., 1967-89, Georgetown (Ky.) Coll. campus bldgs., 1964-84, Asbury Coll., Wilmore, Ky., 1972-78, Asbury Theol. Sem., 1978-93, Berea Coll. bldgs., 1978-91, Transylvania U. bldgs., 1974-98, U. Louisville, 1990-98, 11 downtown Lexington office bldgs.; leader Men of Note Orch., 1986—, Jazzberry Jam Combo, 1993—. Mem. Lexington Urban Renewal Commn., 1963-69; chmn. adv. bd. Salvation Army, 1971-72; trustee Midway (Ky.) Coll., 1986-95; appt. architect svcs. sel. com. Commonwealth Ky., 20050172. With USNR, 1955-58; lt. comdr. Res. Recipient award of merit nat. archtl. competition AIA/Ednl. Facilities Lab., 1966 Fellow AIA (1st honor awards Ky. archtl. competition 1959, 61, 68, 70, 73, 78, 80, 81, pres. East Ky. chpt. 1965); mem. Ky. Soc. Architects (pres. 1966), Masons, Rotary, Lexington Club, Navy League, Tau Beta Pi, Phi Mu Alpha, Phi Sigma Kappa. Home: 2057 Lakeside Dr Lexington KY 40502-3016

**ROMANOWSKI, AUTUMN DAWN,** health facility administrator; b. Clarion, Pa., Mar. 17, 1974; d. Dennis Mark Powell and Mary Ann Trigilio; m. Matthew Romanowski, Sept. 18, 2004. BS, Slippery Rock U., Pa., 1996; MA, U. Md., College Park, 1999. Cert. exercise specialist, ACLS, BLS. Wellness mgr. Peninsula Regional Med. Ctr., Salisbury, Md., 1999—; fitness instr. Merritt Athletic Club, Salisbury, 1999—; faculty mem. Warwic C.C., Salisbury, 2006—. Co-chair relay for life ACS, 2003—04. Named Woman of Achievement, County Coun., Salisbury, 2004. Mem.: ACSM, Ea. Shine Running Club (pres. 2006—). Avocations: running, golf, walking. Home: 1709 S Kaywood Dr Salisbury MD 21804-8652

**ROMANOWSKI, THOMAS ANDREW,** physicist, educator; b. Warsaw, Apr. 17, 1925; came to U.S., 1946, naturalized, 1949; s. Bohdan and Alina (Sumowski) R.; m. Carmen des Rochers, Nov. 15, 1952; children: Alina, Dominique. BS, MIT, Boston, 1952; MS, Case Inst. Tech., 1956, PhD, 1957. Rsch. assoc. physics Carnegie Inst. Tech., 1956-60; asst. physicist high energy physics Argonne Nat. Lab., Ill., 1960-63, assoc. physicist, 1963-72, physicist, 1972-78; prof. physics Ohio State U., Columbus, 1964-92, prof. emeritus, 1992-98; sr. scientist Argonne Nat. Lab., 1992; physicist U.S. Dept. Energy, Washington, 1992-98; cons. in pvt. practice, 1998—. Contbr. articles to profl. jours. With high energy program U.S. Dept. Energy, 1993-98. Served with C.E. AUS, 1946-47. Fellow Am. Phys. Soc., AAAS; mem. Lambda Chi Alpha. Achievements include research in nuclear and high energy physics. Personal E-mail: romanowski@santafe-newmexico.com.

**ROMANS, DONALD BISHOP,** manufacturing executive; b. Louisville, Apr. 22, 1931; s. Albert D. and Moneta (Bishop) R.; m. Marilyn Yvonne Neff, June 13, 1953 (dec. Aug. 2000); children: Rebecca Ann, Jennifer. BS, U. Louisville, 1953; MBA, Harvard U., 1958. Mgr. internal auditing and data processing, mem. corp. staff Container Corp. Am., Chgo., 1958-62; successively asst. to pres., asst. treas., treas., v.p. fin., sr. v.p. fin. mem. bd. Trans Union Corp., Chgo. 1962-81; exec. v.p., chief fin. officer Sunbeam Corp., Chgo., 1981-82; Bally Mfg. Corp., Chgo. 1982-87; fin. cons. Chgo., 1987; pres. Romans and Co, Chgo. 1987-93. Bd. dirs. Burnham Investment Trust, N.Y.C.; trustee PhoenixFunds, Hartford, Conn.; life trustee St. Mary of Nazareth Hosp. Capt. USMCR, 1953-56. Republican. Avocations: tennis, boating. Home: 39 S Sheridan Rd Lake Forest IL 60045-3269 Office Phone: 847-615-2537. Personal E-mail: dbromans@yahoo.com.

**ROMANS, JOHN NIEBRUGGE,** lawyer; b. Bklyn., May 23, 1942; s. John McDowell and Helen Pond (Niebrugge) R.; m. Caroline Ward; children: John A., Andrew C. BA, Williams Coll., 1964; LLB, Columbia U., 1967. Bar: N.Y. 1967, U.S. Dist. Ct. (so. and ea. dists.) N.Y. 1971, U.S. Ct. Appeals (2d cir.) 1971, U.S. Supreme Ct. 1971, U.S. Ct. Appeals (3rd cir.) 1976, U.S. Ct. Appeals (4th and 7th cirs.) 1987, U.S. Ct. Appeals (9th cir.) 1992, U.S. Ct. Appeals (11th cir.) 1996, U.S. Ct. Appeals (D.C. cir.), 2004. Ptnr. Curtis, Mallet-Prevost, Colt & Mosle, N.Y.C., 1980—; Katten Muchin & Zavis, N.Y.C., 1990—98, Rosen Weinhaus, LLP, N.Y.C., 1998—. Lectr. on air law topics at various seminars. Contbr. articles to profl. jours. Trustee Summit (N.J.) Unitarian-Universalist Ch., 1978, Mamaroneck Pub. Libr. Dist., 1990-99; mem. budget com. Village of Mamaroneck, 2001-05, chmn., 2002-2005; dir. The Univ. Glee Club NYC, 1993-. Lt. USNR, 1968-71. Mem. Assn. Bar City N.Y. (aero. com. 1983-85, 2004-, chmn. 1986-89, 92-94, 2000, products liability com. 1989-91), Larchmont (N.Y.) Yacht Club. Avocation: sailing. Office: Rosen Weinhaus LLP 40 Wall St 32d Fl New York NY 10005-1304 Office Phone: 212-530-4827.

**ROMANUCCI-ROSS, LOLA,** anthropologist, educator; b. Hershey, Pa., June 13, 1928; d. Ignazio and Josephine (Giovannozzi) R.; m. John Ross Jr., Aug. 26, 1972; children: Deborah Lee, Adan Anthony. BA, Ohio U., 1948; MA, U. Minn., 1953; postgrad., Ecole des Hautes Etudes, Paris, 1961-63; PhD in Anthropology, Ind. U., 1963. Rsch. assoc. Am. Mus. Natural History, N.Y.C., 1963-67; assoc. prof. U. Hawaii, Honolulu, 1967-68; from asst. prof. to prof. family and preventive medicine and anthropology Sch. Medicine U. Calif., San Diego, 1969—. Mem. study sect. HEW Maternal and Child Health, Bethesda, Md., 1973-75; cons. NSF, 1988—. Author: Conflict, Violence and Morality in a Mexican Village, 1973, 2d edit., 1986, Mead's Other Manus: Phenomenology of the Encounter, 1985, One Hundred Towers; an Italian Odyssey of Cultural Survival, 1991; editor: Ethnic Identity, 1975, 4th edit., 2006, The Anthropology of Medicine, 1982, 3d edit., 1997, When Law and Medicine Meet: A Cultural View, 2004; mem. editl. bd.: Anthropology and Humanism Quarterly, Interdisciplinary Jour. Study of Health, Illness and Medicine, 1997—, contbr. articles to profl. jours., book chpts. Grantee Wenner-Gren Found. for Anthropol. Rsch., 1974-75. Fellow Am. Anthropol. Soc.; mem. Soc. Med. Anthropology, Soc. Psychol. Anthropology, Soc. Anthropology of Europe, Soc. Cultural Anthropology, Soc. Health and Human Values. Achievements include research in New Guinea, South Pacific, Italy and Mexico. Avocations: music, hiking, literature, writing.

**ROMANZI, KENNETH,** toy manufacturing executive; Grad., Babson Coll. With Frito-Lay, Inc.; v.p.-mktg./strategic planning Cadbury Schweppes, 1992—93; pres. and gen. mgr., Fleishmann's divsn. Nabisco, 1993—96, sr. v.p.-sales and customer svc., 1996—2000; pres. and CEO Balducci's Direct, 2000—01, Ultimate Juice Co., 2002—03; pres.-US Toys Hasbro, Inc., 2003—. Office: Hasbro Inc 1027 Newport Ave Pawtucket RI 02862

**ROMARY, THOMAS GERALD,** mathematician, educator, writer; b. Ft. Wayne, Ind., July 8, 1943; m. Becky M. Spycyalski, Aug. 16, 1969; children: Tammy M., Tyler T. BS in Math. and Edn., Purdue U., 1966; MS in Math and Edn., St. Francis Coll., 1969; MS in Secondary Adminstrn., Ind. U., 1985. Lic. tchr. Ind., Math. tchr. various schs., Ind., 1965—78; prof. math. Ind. Inst. Tech., Ft. Wayne, 1978—. Author: (8 book series) Toms Tips, 1996—. Mem.: Nat. Coun. Tchrs. Math. Office: IIT 1600 E Washington Fort Wayne IN 46803 Office Phone: 260-422-5561 x 2286. Business E-Mail: romary@indtech.edu.

**ROMAS, NICHOLAS ACHILLES,** urologist, educator; b. Endicott, N.Y., Jan. 17, 1936; s. Peter Angelo and Stavroula Romas; m. Serene Karikas, June 19, 1968; children: Stavra Nicole, Eva Maria, Pamela Stephanie. AB, Colgate U., 1958; MD, Columbia U., 1962. Bd. cert. urologist, 1974. Asst. prof. clin. urology Columbia U. Coll. Physicians and Surgeons, N.Y.C., 1970-78, assoc. prof. clin. urology, 1978-89, prof. clin. urology, 1989—; dir. urology St. Luke's-Roosevelt Hosp. Ctr., N.Y.C., 1984—. Editor: Prostate Acid Phosphatase Measurement, 1982; contbr. articles to profl. jours. Maj. USAF, 1968-70. Mem. Am. Urol. Assn. (rsch. com. 1990—, fin. com. 1991—, pub. com. 1998—, pres NY sect. 2003), N.Y. Acad. Medicine (adv. com. 1986—, sec. urology sect. 1987-88, chmn. 1988-89). Greek Orthodox. Achievements include research in the role of prostate acid phosphates in different stages of prostate cancer. Office: St Lukes-Roosevelt Hosp Ctr 425 W 59th St New York NY 10019 Office Phone: 212-523-7788. E-mail: nromas@chpnet.org.

**ROMASCO, ROBERT G.,** insurance company executive; BA, Brandeis U., 1969; MBA, Harvard U., 1978. Various mgmt. positions Epsilon Data Mgmt.; prin. Corp. Decisions, Inc.; head corp. mktg. Am. Century Investments; pres., CEO JC Penny Direct Mktg. Svcs.; exec. v.p., chief mktg. officer Cigna Corp., Phila., 2002—.

**ROME, ELLEN S.,** physician; d. Leonard P. and Nancy Rome; m. Frederick S. Asbeck, Jr., July 29, 1995; children: Andrew Asbeck, Katherine Asbeck. BA, Yale U., 1984; MD, Case We. Res. U., 1988; MPH, Harvard Sch. Pub. Health, 1994. Cert. Am. Bd. Pediat., 1991, in adolescent medicine 1994. Head, sect. adolescent medicine Cleve. Clinic, 1994—; resident pediat. Johns Hopkins Hosp., 1988—91; fellowship adolescent medicine Children's Hosp., Boston, 1991—94. Faculty mem. Ctr. for Adolescent Health, Case We. Res. U., Cleve., 1994—; mem. sci. com. U.S. Tennis Assn., Cleve., 2004—; assoc. prof. Cleve. Clinic Lerner Coll. Medicine Case We. Res. U., 2005—. Contbr. articles to profl. jours. Fellow: Am. Acad. Pediat. (coon adolescence 1996—2002, chair, planning com. 2005—); mem.: N.Am. Soc. for Pediatric and Adolescent Gynecology (chair, planning com. for ann. meeting 2005 and 2006), Acad. of Eating Disorders (com. pub. affairs 2003—, chmn. media com. 2004—), Soc. for Adolescent Medicine (chair, membership com. 1996—2002, nominations com. 2002—04). Avocation: skiing. Office: The Childrens Hosp at Cleve Clinic 9500 Euclid Ave A120 Cleveland OH 44195 Office Phone: 216-444-3566.

**ROMEO, JOANNE JOSEFA MARINO,** mathematics educator; b. Youngstown, Ohio, Nov. 21, 1943; d. Joseph James and Ann Marie (Bonamase) Marino; m. John Homer Romeo, Aug. 14, 1965; children: Christopher, Chrisanne, Jonathan; m. Harwood D. Schaffer, Apr. 25, 2003. BS, Ohio State U., 1965; postgrad., Youngstown State U., 1969-70; MS, Purdue U., 1974; postgrad. in computer sci., U. Tenn., Knoxville, 1982-91. Substitute tchr. Columbus, Ohio, 1964-65; tchr. geometry, math. and French Hamilton Sch. Dist., Columbus, Ohio, 1965-66; tchr. gifted children Bluegrass Elem. Sch., Knoxville, Tenn., 1976-77; tchr. math. and sci. Webb Sch., Knoxville, 1977-85, also developer computer sci. program, 1977-85; headmistress Greenbrier Acad., Sevierville, Tenn., 1985-86; instr. math. Pellissippi State Tech. Community Coll., Knoxville, Tenn., 1986—; dir. religious edn. Sacred Heart Parish, Knoxville, Tenn., 1987—2001; tchr. advanced math. Knox County Sch., Knoxville, Tenn., 2000—02; math. dept. chair, Washburn H.S. Grainger County Schs., Washburn, Tenn., 2004—. Delegate to go to Russia and Lithuania Ministries of Edn., NCEA. Vol dir. religious edn. Sacred Heart Parish, Knoxville, 1979-87, lay pastoral minister, 1988-2004. Mem. Nat. Council Tchrs. Math., Nat. Cath. Edn. Assn., Nat. Council Parish and Religious Coordinators and Dirs., Nat. Sci. Tchrs. Assn., Nat. Assn. Exec. Females, Ohio State U. Alumni Assn., Tenn. Assn. Dirs. Religious Edn., Purdue U. Alumni Assn., Alpha Gamma Delta. Independent. Home: 1708 Capistrano Dr Knoxville TN 37922-6302 Personal E-mail: joannejmr@yahoo.com.

**ROMEO, PETER JOHN,** lawyer; b. Darby, Pa., Aug. 1, 1942; s. Joseph Paul and Rose Marie (Beckett) R.; m. Nancy Virginia Schmidt, July 15, 1972; children: Christopher, Jeffrey, Michael. BSBA, Georgetown U., 1964; JD, George Washington U., 1967, LLM, 1969. Bar: N.Y. 1968, U.S. Dist. Ct. D.C. 1969, U.S. Supreme Ct. 1972; CPA, D.C. Acct. Schumaker & Yates, Washington, 1964-69; atty. U.S. Securities and Exch. Com., Washington, 1969-72, spl. counsel, 1972-79, chief counsel divsn. corp. fin., 1980-84; ptnr. Hogan & Hartson LLP, Washington, 1984—. Author: The Registration Process (updated biannually), 1985; co-author: Section 16 Reporting Guide,

1989, Section 16 Forms and Filing Handbook, 1991, 8th edit., 2005, Section 16 Treatise and Reporting Guide, 1994, 2d edit., Section 16 Deskbook (updated annally), 2006; contbr. articles to profl. jours. Mem. ABA (mem. fed. regulation securities com.), D.C. Bar, Va. State Bar. Roman Catholic. Office: Hogan & Hartson LLP 555 13th St NW Washington DC 20004-1161 Office Phone: 202-637-5805. Business E-Mail: pjromeo@hhlaw.com.

**ROMER, CHRISTINA DUCKWORTH,** economist, educator; b. Alton, Ill., Dec. 25, 1958; d. Clifford Lee and Carol (Greer) Duckworth; m. David Hibbard Romer, Aug. 20, 1983; children: Katherine, Paul, Matthew. BA, Coll. William & Mary, Williamsburg, Va., 1981; PhD, MIT, Cambridge, Mass., 1985. Asst. prof. Princeton (N.J.) U., 1985—88; acting assoc. prof. U. Calif., Berkeley, 1988—90, assoc. prof., 1990—93, prof., 1993—97, Class of 1957 prof., 1997—; co-dir. Monetary Econs. Program Nat. Bur. Econ. Rsch., Cambridge, Mass., 2003—. Rsch. assoc. Nat. Bur. Econ. Rcsch., Cambridge, Mass., 1990—; mem. rsch. adv. bd. Com. for Econ. Devel., Washington, 1994—98; mem. editl. bd. Jour. Econ. History, 1994—97, Rev. Economics & Statistics. Editor: (book) Reducing Inflation, 1997; contbr. articles to profl. jours. Recipient Presdl. Young Investigator award, NSF, 1989—94; fellow, John Simon Guggenheim Meml. Found., 1998—99. Fellow: Am. Acad. Arts & Sci.; mem.: Econ. History Assn. (nominating com. 2001—02), Am. Econs. Assn. (exec. com. 2000—03, com. honors & awards 2004—, adv. com. editl. appointments 2002—04, chair, adv. com. editl. appointments 2003). Democrat. United Church Of Christ. Achievements include research in new statistical evidence of the effects of monetary policy on output, inflation and interest. Showed that historical macroeconomic indicators overstate the size of business cycles before World War II. Office: Univ Calif Dept Econs Berkeley CA 94720-3880

**ROMER, DANIEL,** university official, psychologist, educator; b. Caracas, Venezuela, Apr. 19, 1947; arrived in U.S., 1948; s. Adolf and Eleanor (Rittermann) R.; m. Lauren B. Alloy, Jan. 4, 1985; 1 child, Adrienne. AB, Dartmouth Coll., 1969; PhD, U. Ill., Chgo., 1974. Rsch. fellow Dept Mental Health, Chgo., 1976-79; vis. asst. prof. Northwestern U., Evanston, Ill., 1979-81; adj. assoc. prof. U. Ill., 1981-89; assoc. rsch. dir. Leo Burnett Co., Chgo., 1982-89; sr. rschr. Annenberg Sch. for Comm., U. Pa., Phila., 1990—2000, sr. fellow Ctr. for Cmty. Partnerships, 1996—, rsch. dir. Inst. for Adolescent Risk Comm., 2001—. Mem. nat. expert panel on adolescent STD prevention Ctr. for Disease Control and Prevention, Atlanta, 2000-01; mem. rev. panels NIH, Washington, 1994-97, 98—. Mem. editl. bd. Jour. Exptl. Social Psychology, 1988-91, Youth and Society, 2001—; contbr. over 60 articles to psychol. and pub. health jours., chpts. to books. Grantee NIMH, 1992—, Ford Found., 1994. Mem. APA, APHA. Office: Annenberg Pub Policy Ctr 3535 Market St Ste 550 Philadelphia PA 19104 E-mail: dromer@asc.upenn.edu.

**ROMER, DAVID,** economics professor; AB, Princeton U., 1980; PhD, MIT, 1985. Jr. staff economist Coun. Economic Advisors, 1980—81; asst. prof. Princeton U., 1985—88; acting assoc. prof. U. Calif., Berkeley, 1988—90, assoc. prof., 1990—93, prof., 1993—2000, Herman Royer prof. polit. economy, 2000—. Vis. assoc. prof. MIT, 1988; vis. assoc. prof. Stanford U., 1993, vis. prof., 95; vis. scholar Nat. Bur. Economic Rsch., 1987—88, faculty rsch. fellow, 1986—93, rsch. assoc., 1993—, mem. bus. cycle dating com., 2003—, co-dir. Monetary Economics program, 2003—; co-editor B.E. Journals in Macroeconomics, 2000—; adv. editor Economic Letters, 1992—2003; assoc. editor Jour. Money, Credit, and Banking, 1992—, Quarterly Jour. Economics, 1990—98; bd. editors Am. Economic Rev., 1996—2002. Author: Advanced Macroeconomics, 1996; co-editor (with N. Gregory Mankiw): New Keynesian Economics, 1991; co-editor: (with Christina D. Romer) Reducing Inflation, 1997; contbr. articles to profl. journals. Fellow: Am. Acad. Arts and Sciences. Office: Dept Economics Univ Calif Berkeley 549 Evans Hall #3880 Berkeley CA 94720-3880 Office Phone: 510-642-1785. E-mail: dromer@econ.berkeley.edu.*

**ROMER, DENISE PATRICE,** lawyer; b. Tulsa, Jan. 11, 1975; d. Franz Karl and Trudy Maria Romer. BS in Sociology, Okla. State U., 1997; M in Alternative Dispute Resolution, Pepperdine U., 2000, JD, 2000. Bar: Calif. 2001, Wis. 2002, Okla. 2004. Clk. Tulsa Early Settlement - Divsn. Tulsa County Cir. Sys., 1999—99, Tulsa County Office Dist. Atty., 1998—98; asst. to counsel Nat. Assn. Securities Dealers, L.A., 1999—99; legal clk. Calif. Lawyers for Arts, Santa Monica, 2000—00; assoc. atty. Korenberg, Abramowitz & Feldun, Sherman Oaks, Calif., 2001—02; criminal def. atty. Boyle, Boyle & Paulus, S.C., Milw., 2002—03; litig. and employment support GE Med. Sys., Waukesha, Wis., 2003—; assoc. atty. Gibbs, Armstrong, Borochoff, Hillican & Hart, 2003—. Apprentice KFAQ Talk Radio, Tulsa, Okla., 2004. Author poetry. Rep. internet team leader Rep. Nat. Com., Tulsa, Okla., 2003—; supporter/ mem. So. Poverty Law Ctr.- Nat. Campaign for Tolerance, L.A., 2001—. Mem.: ABA (assoc.), State Bar Okla. (assoc.), State Bar Calif. (assoc.), State Bar Wis. (assoc.), L.A. County Bar Assn. (assoc.), The Smithsonian Instn. (assoc.), Pepperdine U. Alumni Assn. (life). Conservative. Roman Catholic. Avocations: writing, yoga, travel. Home: 6904 White Walnut Way Braselton GA 30517 Personal E-mail: romer33@hotmail.com.

**ROMERO, ANTHONY D.,** legal association administrator; b. NYC; s. Demetrio and Coralie Romero. Grad., Princeton U., 1987; JD, Stanford U., 1990. With Rockefeller Found., 1990—92; program officer for civil rights and racial justice Ford Found., 1992—96, program dir. for human rights and internat. cooperation, 1996—2001; exec. dir. ACLU, NYC, 2001—. Named Stanford Pub. Interest Lawyer of Yr., Stanford U., 2003; named one of 25 Most Influential Hispanics, Time mag., 2005; Cane scholar, Princeton U., Nat. Hispanic scholar, Dinkelspiel scholar, Stanford U., Nat. Hispanic scholar. Mem.: Coun. Fgn. Rels. NY State Bar Assn. Office: ACLU 100 Fl 125 Broad St New York NY 10004

**ROMERO, GEORGE A.,** film director; b. NYC, Feb. 4, 1940; m. Nancy Romero, 1971 (div. 1978); m. Christine Forrest, 1981. Grad., Carnegie-Mellon Inst. Dir.: (films) There's Always Vanilla, 1971, O.J. Simpson: Juice on the Loose, 1974, Creepshow, 1982, (TV series) The Winners, 1973; writer: (films) Creepshow 2, 1987, Tales from the Darkside: The Movie, 1990; dir., writer: (films) Night of the Living Dead, 1968, The Crazies, 1973, Hungry Wives, 1973, Knightriders, 1981, Monkey Shines, 1988, Two Evil Eyes, 1990, Bruiser, 2000, Land of the Dead, 2005; actor, writer, dir.: (films) Martin, 1977, Dawn of the Dead, 1978, Day of the Dead, 1985; writer, exec. prodr.: (films) Night of the Living Dead, 1990, (TV series) Tales from the Darkside, 1984; writer, dir., exec. prodr.: (films) The Dark Half, 1993, actor: (films) Flight of the Spruce Goose, 1987, The Silence of the Lambs, 1991. Office: care The Gersh Agy 232 N Canon Dr Beverly Hills CA 90210-5302

**ROMERO, JAVIER ANTONIO,** surgeon; b. Guayaquil, Ecuador, Jan. 16, 1965; arrived in U.S., 1968; d. Miguel A. and Cecilia V. Romero; m. Leah Kory, June 17, 2004; children: Sienna, Sophia, Eva. AA, AS, Mt. Sac, Walnut, Calif., 1990; BS, U. Calif., Irvine, 1991; MD, U. Calif., Davis, 1996. Diplomate Am. Bd. Surgeons. Trauma fellow U. So. Calif. County Hosp., L.A., 2001—02; attending surgeon Ventura (Calif.) County Hosp., 2002—, chief surgery, 2005—06. Office Phone: 805-641-4431. Office Fax: 805-641-4916.

**ROMERO, JESSE CHARLES,** political consultant; b. Corpus Christi, Tex., Nov. 4, 1960; s. Juan Leos and Amelia Ramirez Romero; m. Anna Alicia Arteaga, June 2, 1991; children: Emiliano Sandino, Antonio Cesar, Victor Aetius Emmanuel. BA, S.W. Tex. State U., 1987. Field organizer S.W. Voter Registration Edn. Project, San Antonio, 1987—90; exec. dir. Mexican Am. Legis. Caucus, Austin, Tex., 1991—93; spl. asst. State Senator Rodney Ellis, Austin, Tex., 1994—95; policy analyst Mexican Am. Legal Def. Ednl. Fund, San Antonio, 1995—97; spl. projects dir. Congressman Ciro Rodriguez, San Antonio, 1997—2000; S.W. dir. Ctr. Policy Alternatives, Washington, 2000—03; ptnr. Haley, Romero & Winick, Austin, 2004—. Dir. Adelante Con Clinton, Austin, Tex., 1992; dir. latino vote Dem. Congl. Campaign Com.,

Washington, 2002. Recipient Aguila Activism award, Mexican Am. Dems., 1992, Chmn.'s Advocacy award, Tex. Assn. Mexican Am. C. of C., 1997. Mem.: YMCA, San Antonio Hispanic C. of C. (legis. adv. bd. 1995—). Roman Catholic. Avocations: basketball, football, softball, weightlifting. Office: Haley Romero & Winick Ste 200 815 Brazos St Austin TX 78701 Personal E-mail: romero.jesse@sbcglobal.net.

**ROMERO, JOSEFINO TABERNILLA,** nurse anesthetist; b. Tayabas, Quezon, The Philippines; came to U.S., 1963; s. Melanio Merca and Teodorica (Tabernilla) R. Diploma, Quezon Meml. Hosp., 1961; cert. nurse anesthetist, Mt. Carmel Hosp., Detroit, 1968; D in Art, U. Found., Malta, 1986. RN, Mich. Psychiat. nurse Nat. Mental Hosp., Manila, 1961-63; operating room nurse St. Vincent Hosp., Worcester, Mass., 1963-64, Michael Reese Hosp., Chgo., 1964-65, Sarnia (Canada) Gen. Hosp., 1965-66; operating room nurse, nurse anesthetist Quezon Meml. Hosp., 1971-72; nurse anesthetist Mt. Carmel Hosp., 1973-74, Brent Hosp., Detroit, 1974-86, Smith Hosp., Southfield, Mich., 1986—. Exhibited paintings in numerous one-man shows including Beijing Internat. Conv. Ctr., 1991, Pontiac Art Ctr., 1989, Troy Libr. and Gallery, 1989, Scarab Club Detroit, 1989, Lawrence St. Gallery, Pontiac, Mich., 1989, Acad. Art Gallery, Paris, 1988, Gallert in the Grove, Canada, 1987, Southfield Civic Ctr., 1986, Electric Fantasy Gallery, 1986, Philippine Orgn. and Filipino Artists, Chgo., 1978, others; exhibited in several group shows including Detroit Press Club, 1989, Mich. Design Ctr., 1988, Philippine Cultural Ctr., Ayala Mus., Casa de Communidad de Tayabas, 1997, Seattle Asian Art Mus., 1997, Gov.'s Mansion-The Philippine, 1998, Galleria Romero, The Philippines, 1998. Named one of Outstanding Men. Mich., City of Detroit, 1976, Outstanding Alumnus quezon Meml. Hosp. Sch. Nursing, 1994; recipient Albert Einstein award Internat. Acad. Found., 1991, Merit award Mich. Ann. Art Festival, 1975, Cert. of Appreciation Gov. of Mich., 1986, Quezon medal honor (The Philippines), 1997. Mem. Am. Assn. Nurse Anesthetists, Mich. Assn. Nurse Anesthetists, Filipino Nurse Assn., Beijing Watercolor Soc., Scarab Club Detroit (bd. dirs. 1988—), Knights of Rizal, Internat. Assn. Educators for World Peace. Roman Catholic. Avocations: photography, travel, tennis. Home: 2230 S Shore Ct Rochester Hills MI 48307

**ROMERO, PEDRO RAFAEL,** information scientist, researcher; b. Caracas, Venezuela, May 22, 1959; s. Luis Octavio Romero and María Candelaria Muñoz; m. María Angélica Hernández, June 4, 1988. Chem. Engr., Universidad Simon Bolívar, Caracas, Venezuela, 1981; MSE in Chem. and Biochem. Engring., U. of Pa., Phila., 1984; PhD in Computer Sci., Wash. State U., 1999. Informatics coord. and rschr. Desarrollo Empresarial, Caracas, Miranda, Venezuela, 1985—93; post doctoral rschr. SRI Internat., Menlo Park, Calif., 1999—2003; vis. asst. scientist Ind. U. - Purdue U. Indpls., 2003—04, asst. prof. of bioinformatics, 2004—. Sci. cons. Molecular Kinetics, Indpls., 2003—. Mem.: Biophysical Soc., Internat. Soc. for Computational Biology. Achievements include first to first computational predictors of protein disorder. First to show the incidence of intrinsic disorder in nature. Helped establish intrinsic disorder as a new field in molecular biology. Office Phone: 317-278-9236.

**ROMERO, TONY,** information technology executive; Mgr. tech. svc. Western Airlines; tech. support specialist Mitsubishi Motors No. Am., Cypress, Calif., 1982, chief info. officer, 2001—, and sr. v.p. info. tech., 2003—. Named one of the Premier 100 IT Leaders, Computerworld mag., 2004. Office: SVP & CIO Mitsubishi Motors No Am 6400 Katella Ave Cypress CA 90630-0064

**ROMERO-RAINEY, REBECA,** bank executive; d. Martin and Cheryl Romero; m. John Rainey. Degree, Wellesley Coll. Pres., CEO Centinal Bank Taos, N.Mex., 1999—, bd. dir., 1999—. Bd. admissions Wellesley Coll. V.p. Taos Chpt. Habitat for Humanity; sec., treas. Bridges Project Edn. Taos; mem. Leadership N.Mex.; treas. N.Mex. Cmty. Found.; bd. dir. Taos (N.Mex.) Feeds Taos; treas. bd. dirs. Rocky Mountain Youth Corps. Named One of 25 Women to Watch, U.S. Banker Mag., 2003. Mem.: Ind. Cmty. Bankers Assn. N.Mex. (bd. dir. 2003—).

**ROMETTY, GINNY (VIRGINIA M. ROMETTY),** information technology executive; b. 1957; BS in Computer Sci., Elec. Engring. with high hon., Northwestern U. Applications, sys. devel. GM Corp.; bus., IT cons. IBM, 1985—91, supr. ops. ins. rsch., gen. mgr. strategy mktg., sales ops., gen. mgr. global services Am., mng. ptnr. bus. cons. services, 2002—05, sr. v.p., global bus. services, 2005—. Mem. bd. IBM Worldwide Mgmt. Coun., Sr. Leadership Team; bd. dirs. Am. Internat. Group (AIG), 2006—. Named a Global Bus. Influential, Time Mag., 2002. Office: IBM Corp 1133 Westchester Ave White Plains NY 10604

**ROMEY, WILLIAM DOWDEN,** geologist, educator; b. Richmond, Ind., Oct. 26, 1930; s. William Minter and Grace Warring (Dowden) R.; m. Lucretia Alice Leonard, July 16, 1955; children: Catherine Louise Keener, Gretchen Elizabeth Tanzer, William Leonard. AB with highest honors, Ind. U., 1952; student, U. Paris, 1950—51, student, 1952—53; PhD, U. Calif., Berkeley, 1962. Asst. prof. geology and sci. edn. Syracuse (NY) U., 1962-66, assoc. prof., 1966-69; exec. dir. earth sci. ednl. program Am. Geol. Inst., 1969-72; prof.-chmn. dept. geology and geography St. Lawrence U., Canton, NY, 1971-76, prof., 1976—93, prof.-chmn. dept. geography 1983-93, prof. emeritus, 1993—. Ednl. cons., 1962—; NAS visitor USSR Acad. Sci., 1967; vis. geoscientist Am. Geol. Inst., 1964-66, 71; earth sci. cons. Compton's Ency., 1970-71; adj. prof. Union Grad. Sch., 1974-2000; bd. rsch. advisors and readers Walden U., 1981-2000; prof. Grad. Sch. Am., 1993-99; travel writer and cruise ship lectr., 1990—. Author: (with others) Investigating the Earth, 1967, (with I. Kramer, F. Muller, J. Lewin) Investigation in Geology, 1967, Inquiry Techniques for Teaching Science, 1968, Risk-Trust-Love, 1972, Consciousness and Creativity, 1975, Confluent Education in Science, 1976, Plus Ça Change..., 1996, Illustrated Guide to the Geology of commonly visited sites on the Antarctic Peninsula, South Georgia, and the Falkland Islands, 2004, Norway Through a Geologist's Eyes, 2006; co-editor: Geochemical Prospecting for Petroleum, 1959; assoc. editor: Jour. Coll. Sci. Tchg., 1972-74, Geol. Soc. Am. Bull., 1979-84, Jour. Geol. Edn., 1980—2003; editor-in-chief: Ash Lad Press, 1975—; contbr. articles to profl. jours. Bd. dirs. Onondaga Nature Ctrs., Inc., 1966—69. Served to lt. j.g. USNR, 1953—57, lt. comdr. res., 1957—66. Woodrow Wilson Found. fellow, 1959-60, 61-62; NSF sci. faculty fellow U. Oslo, 1967-68. Fellow AAAS, Geol. Soc. Am., Explorers Club; mem. Nat. Assn. Geology Tchrs. (v.p. 1971-72), NY Acad. Scis., Nat. Assn. Geology Tchrs. (pres. 1972-73), Assn. Am. Geographers, Am. Geophys. Union, Geol. Soc. Norway, Can. Assn. Geographers, Assn. Can. Studies in US, Internat. Assn. Volcanology and Chemistry Earth's Interior, Phi Beta Kappa, Sigma Xi, Phi Delta Kappa. Home and office: PO Box 294 East Orleans MA 02643-0294 Office Phone: 508-255-2301. Personal E-mail: ashladpress@earthlink.net.

**ROMEYN, PRESCOTT C.,** venture capitalist; BA, Dartmouth Coll.; MBA, Amos Tuck Sch. Bus. Adminstrn. With merchant banking group Shearson Lehman Hutton, Inc.; various positions including mng. dir. AEA Investors, Inc., 1988—99; mng. dir. Perry Ptnrs., 2000—01; prin. Kohlberg & Co., 2001—. Office: Kohlberg & Co 111 Radio Cir Mount Kisco NY 10549 Office Phone: 914-241-7430. Office Fax: 914-241-7476.

**ROMICK, JOYCE TRUDEAU,** elementary school educator; b. Plattsburgh, N.Y., Jan. 23, 1939; d. Norman Samuel and Lurena (Flemming) Trudeau; m. Ronald Virgil Romick, Jan. 3, 1959; children: Cynthia Lynne, Norman Charles. BS in Early Childhood Edn., SUNY, Plattsburgh, 1959, MS in Elem. Edn., 1965; EdS in Reading Edn., Ariz. State U., Tempe, 1970. Cert. tchr., elem. prin., elem. supr., Ariz., Wash. 1st grade tchr. Heartwood Elem. Sch., Tacoma, 1960-62, Tolleson (Ariz.) Grammar Sch., 1963; tchr. 2nd grade Cartwright Elem. Sch., Phoenix, 1963-72, tchr. 6th grade, 1973-92. Intermediate rep. for lang. arts curriculum Consortium Sch. Dists., Phoenix, 1974-77; mem. cadre corps Ariz. Dept. Edn., 1977-79. Contbr. articles to Boston Bull., 1982-83. Mem. fin. com. Shepherd of the Valley United Meth. Ch., Phoenix,

1985-90, mem. choir, 1963-93, mem. adminstrv. bd., 1965-68, mem. stewardship com., 1990-98; assoc. mem. worship com. Calvary United Meth. Ch., Lake Worth, Fla., 2001—; adult Sunday sch. tchr., 2002—. Mem.: NEA (life), Bus. and Profl. Women, Ladies Oriental Shrine (page to High Priestess), Daus. of Nile, Nefertiti Club (v.p. Ariz. chpt. 1999—2000), Phi Delta Kappa, Alpha Delta Kappa (life; state historian 1984—86, Ariz. state treas. 1988—90, Nu chpt. historian 1990—92, Ariz. state treas. 1990—92, Ariz. state ways and means chmn. 1992—94, ctrl. dist. co-chmn. 1997—98, v.p. Fla. Beta Phi chpt. 2004—06, silver sister). Republican. Avocations: travel, theater, music, reading. Home (Winter): 121 Harbor Lake Cir Greenacres FL 33413

ROMIG, THOMAS J., judge, career military officer; b. Manhattan, Kans., Dec. 27, 1948; married; 2 children. Grad., Nat. War Coll., Armed Forces Staff Coll.; BS, Kans. State U., 1970; JD with honors, Santa Clara U., 1980. Commd. U.S. Army, 1971, advanced through grades to maj. gen., mil. intelligence officer Ft. Bragg, NC, Ft. Huachuca, Ariz.; trial counsel, sr. trial counsel, chief of legal assistance and chief criminal law 2d Armored Divsn., Ft. Hood, Tex., 1980—83; instr. internat. and operational law Judge Advocate Gen.'s Sch., Charlottesville, Va., 1984—87, plans officer, pers., plans and tng. office, 1989—90; staff judge advocate 32d Army Air Def. Command, Darmstadt, Germany, 1990—93, chief pers./asst. chief pers., plans and tng. office, 1993—95; staff judge advocate V Corps, Heidelberg, Germany and Taszar, Hungary, 1996—98; asst. JAG for mil. law and ops. Office of the JAG, Rosslyn, Va., 1999—2001, JAG Washington, 2001—. Decorated Legion of Merit, Meritorious Svc. medal with 4 oak leaf clusters, Army Commendation medal, Army Achievement medal, Nat. Def. Svc. medal with 1 bronze service star, Armed Forces Svc. medal, NATO medal, Army Svc. Ribbon, Army Overseas Svc. Ribbonn (2d award), Parachutist Badge, Army Staff Identification Badge. Office: Office of the JAG US Army Pentagon Washington DC 20310-1500

ROMIJN, REBECCA, actress, model; b. Berkeley, Calif., Nov. 6, 1972; m. John Stamos, Sept. 19, 1998 (div. Mar. 1, 2005); children: Jaap Romihn Stamos, Elizabeth Kuizenga Stamos. Attended, U. Calif., Santa Cruz. Model Sports Illustrated, Christian Dior, Victoria's Secret, Biotherm, Clarins, Dillards, Escada, Furla, Got Milk?, J.Crew, La Senza, Liz Claiborne, Matrix Essentials, Maybelline, Pantene Pro V, Tommy Hilfiger, various others. Actor: (films) Dirty Work, 1998, X-Men, 2000, Rollerball, 2002, Femme Fatale, 2002, X2, 2003, The Punisher, 2004, Godsend, 2004, The Alibi, 2006, Man About Town, 2006, X-Men: The Last Stand, 2006; (TV films) Hefner: Unauthorized, 1999; (TV series) Just Shoot Me, 1999—2000, Pepper Dennis, 2006—, (TV appearances) Friends, 1997, Jack & Jill, 2000. Office: Bragman Nyman Cafarelli 8687 Melrose Ave West Hollywood CA 90069-5701*

ROMITA, MAURO CHARLES, plastic surgeon; b. N.Y.C., Jan. 16, 1947; MD, U. Miami, 1973. Diplomate Am. Bd. Surgery, Am. Bd. Plastic Surgery. Resident, fellow NYU Med. Ctr., 1974—81; pvt. practice plastic surgery N.Y.C., 1999—. Attending physician St. Vincent Hosp. Med. Ctr., N.Y.C.; asst. clin. prof. surgery N.Y. Med. Coll. Contbr. articles to numerous profl. jours. Mem. Boys Town of Italy; bd. govs. Sound Shore Med. Ctr. Mem.: Am. Bd. Plastic Surgery (diplomate), Am. Soc. Plastic Surgeons. Office: 853 5th Ave New York NY 10021-5802*

ROMJUE, JOHN LAWSON, historian, writer; b. Washington, D.C., Oct. 4, 1936; s. Lawson Rodney Romjue, Joanne Romjue; m. Ingeborg Gertrud Schaefer, Mar. 25, 1961; children: Martin John, Kristin Elisabeth. BA in History and Polit. Sci., U. Mo., 1962, MA in Modern European History and German Lit., 1963. Staff historian USN Facilities Engring. Command, Port Hueneme, Calif., 1966—69; command historian US Army Combat Devel. Experimentation, Fort Ord, Calif., 1969—74; staff historian, dep. staff historian field programs Mil. Hist. Office US Army Tng. and Doctrine Command, Fort Monroe, Va., 1974—85, chief hist. studies and publs. Mil. Hist. Office, 1985—98. Author: From Active Defense to Airland Battle, 1984, The Army of Excellence, 1993, American Army Doctrine for the Post-Cold War, 1996, Out of the Riven Century, 2001, Merry Town, Missouri, 1945-1948, A Novel, 2005; co-author: Prepare the Army for War, 1993. Specialist 5 U.S. Army, 1957—61. Grantee Fulbright Commn., 1963—64. Mem.: Va. Writers Club (1st v.p. 1995—96, bd. govs. 1997—2001). Republican. Lutheran. Home: 105 Lochmere Ct Yorktown VA 23693 E-mail: johnlromjue@verizon.net.

ROMM, DANIEL F., writer, retired computer technician; b. LA, Dec. 2, 1940; s. Abe and Katherine Romm; children: Gary, Janelle. BS, Calif. Inst. Tech., 1962; MA, UCLA, 1967; JD, U. Ill., 1997. Computer programmer Blue Cross, LA, 1978—80; info. sys. mgr. ARCO (formerly Atlantic Richfield Co.), 1981—94; ret., 1994. Author: (books) A Grain of Salt: Why You Must Make Your Own Decisions, 2004, Things Your Bridge Teacher Won't Tell You, 2006. Mem.: Am. Math. Assn. Avocations: duplicate bridge, physics, philosophy, travel. Home: 1221 1st Ave #25F Seattle WA 98101

ROMMEL, A. ROSS, JR., lawyer; b. Houston, Tex., 1947; BA, U. Va., 1969; JD, U. Houston, 1973. Bar: Tex. 1973, admitted to practice: US Dist. Ct. (No. Dist.) Tex., US Dist. Ct. (So. Dist.) Tex., US Dist. Ct. (Ea. Dist.) Tex., US Dist. Ct. (We. Dist.) Tex., US Ct. Appeals (5th Cir.), US Ct. Appeals (11th Cir.). Asst. dist. atty. Harris County, Tex., 1973-81; mcpl. judge West Univ. Place, Tex., 1984-87; gen. counsel Andrews & Kurth LLP, Houston. Lectr. - investigation of fraud in fin. inst. FBI Nat. Acad.; instr. U. Houston Law Ctr. (Trial Advocacy Inst.). Commr. Harris County Civil Svc. Commn., 1990—98; pres. bd. dir. AA White Dispute Resolution Inst., 1996—97; bd. arbitrators Nat. Assn. Securities Dealers. USMC. Mem.: Houston Bar Assn., State Bar Tex., ABA, Order of Barons, Phi Delta Phi. Office: Andrews Kurth LLP 600 Travis St Ste 4200 Houston TX 77002-3090 Office Phone: 713-238-3830. Office Fax: 713-238-7227. Business E-mail: rrommel@andrewskurth.com.

ROMMEL, JAMES JOSEPH, elementary school educator; b. Adrian, Mich., Jan. 9, 1976; s. James Howard and Elizabeth Marie Rommel; m. Becky Ann Jore, June 14, 2003; 1 child, Grace Elizabeth. BA, Hillsdale Coll., 1998; MA, Western Mich. U., 2002. Co-tchr. Blissfield (Mich.) Migrant Program, 1994—98; tchr. Will Carleton Acad., Hillsdale, Mich., 1998—99, St. Joseph (Mich.) Sch., 1999—2000, edn. tech. cons., 2004—, tchr., 2004—. Grade level rep. St. Joseph (Mich.) Sch., 2004—, vertical steering com., 2004—, profl. devel. com., 2005—. Mem.: Mich. Assn. Computer Using in Learning, Phi Lambda Theta. Home: 1208 Main St Saint Joseph MI 49085 Office Phone: 269-925-3500. Business E-mail: jrommel@sjschools.org.

ROMNEY, CARL F., seismologist; b. Salt Lake City, June 5, 1924; m. Barbara Doughty; children: Carolyn Ann, Kim. BS in Meteorology, Calif. Inst. Tech. 1945; PhD, U. Calif., Berkeley, 1956. Seismologist U.S. Dept. Air Force, 1955-58; asst. tech. dir. Air Force Tech. Applications Center, 1958-73; dep. dir. Nuclear Monitoring Research Office, Def. Advanced Research Projects Agy., 1973-75, dir., 1975-79; dep. dir. Def. Advanced Research Projects Agy., 1979-83; dir. VELA Seismic Studies, 1983-91; v.p. Sci. Applications Internat. Corp., 1987—2001. Tech. adviser U.S. reps. in negotiations Test Ban Treaty; mem. U.S. del. Geneva Conf. Experts, 1958, Conf. on Discontinuance Nuclear Weapons Tests, 1959, 60; negotiations on threshold Test Ban Treaty, Moscow, 1974; mem. U.S. del. Peaceful Nuclear Explosions Treaty, Moscow, 1974-75. Contbr. articles to tech. jours. Recipient Exceptional Civilian Service awards Air Force, 1959, Exceptional Civilian Service awards Dept. Def., 1964, 79; Pres.'s award for Distinguished Fed. Civilian Service, for outstanding contbns. to devel. of control system for underground nuclear tests, 1967; Presdl. Rank of Meritorious Exec., 1980; inducted in Hall of Honor, Air Intelligence Agy., 1996. Achievements include research on earthquake mechanism, seismic noise; generation, propagation, detection seismic waves from underground explosions. Home: 4105 Sulgrave Dr Alexandria VA 22309-2629 E-mail: cromney@earthlink.net.

ROMNEY, MITT (WILLARD MITT ROMNEY), governor; b. Detroit, Mar. 12, 1947; s. George W. and Lenore (Lafount) R.; m. Ann D., Mar. 21, 1969; children: Taggart, Matthew, Joshua, Benjamin, Craig. BA, Brigham Young U., 1971; JD, MBA, Harvard U., 1975. Cons. Boston Consuting Group, 1975-77, Bain & Co., Boston, 1977-78, v.p., 1978-84, chmn., CEO, 1991—2001; mng. ptnr., CEO Bain Capital, Inc., Boston, 1984—2001; pres., CEO Salt Lake Organizing Com. (Winter Olympics), Utah, 1999—2002; gov. State of Mass., 2003—. Bd. dirs. Marriott Corp., Bethesda, Md., Staples Inc., Framingham, Mass., Babbages Inc., Dallas, Tex., Damon Corp., Needham, Mass. Pres. Boston Stake LDS Ch., 1986-1994; adv. bd. Brigham Young U. Sch. Bus., Provo, Utah, 1990—; vis. com. Harvard Bus. Sch., Cambridge, Mass; mem. nat. exec. bd. Boy Scouts Am.; trustee Belmont (Mass.) Hill Sch., 1989—. Baker scholar Harvard Bus. Sch., Cambridge, Mass., 1975. Mem. Belmont Hill Club. Republican. Latter Day Saints. Office: Gov Office State House Rm 360 Boston MA 02133 also: Bain Capital 111 Huntington Ave Ste 3500 Boston MA 02199-7615 Office Phone: 617-727-4000. Office Fax: 617-727-9725.*

ROMNEY, RICHARD BRUCE, lawyer; b. Kingston, Jamaica, Dec. 29, 1942; arrived in U.S., 1945, naturalized, 1956; s. Frank Oswald and Mary Ellen (Burton) Romney; m. Beverly Cochran, Sept. 11, 1965 (dec. 1984); children: Richard Bruce Jr., Stephanie Cochran; m. Lynthia H. Walker, Aug. 14, 1988; children: Alisa Dawn, Kristen Elizabeth. BA, U. Pa., 1964; JD, U. Va., 1972. Bar: N.Y. 1973, U.S. Ct. Appeals (2d cir.) 1975. Assoc. Dewey, Ballantine, Bushby, Palmer & Wood, N.Y.C., 1972—80, ptnr., 1981—2004, of counsel, 2004—05. Mem. editl. bd. U. Va. Law Rev., 1970—72. Lt. USN, 1964—68. Mem.: ABA, Assn. Bar City of N.Y., N.Y. State Bar Assn., Order of Coif. Home and Office: 35 Deerfield Rd Chappaqua NY 10514-1604 Office Phone: 914-238-3222. Personal E-mail: rromney@aol.com.

ROMNEY, SEYMOUR LEONARD, obstetrician, educator; b. NYC, June 8, 1917; s. Benjamin and Anne (Senter) Romney; m. Shirley Gordon, Nov. 4, 1945; children: Benjamin, Tim, Anne. AB, Johns Hopkins, 1938; MD, N.Y. U., 1942. Intern Beth Israel Hosp., Boston, 1942-43; resident Boston Lying-in Hosp., Free Hosp. for Women, Boston, 1946-51; fellow, instr. Harvard Med. Sch., 1947-51, asst. prof. obstetrics and gynecology, 1951-57; prof., chmn. dept. gynecology and obstetrics Albert Einstein Coll. Medicine, N.Y.C., 1957-72, prof., 1972-89, prof. emeritus, 1989—; dir. research gynecol. oncology, 1972—. Dir. obstetrics and gynecology Bronx Mcpl. Hosp. Ctr., N.Y.C., 1957-72; cons. WHO, Geneva, 1969-70. Founding chair Soc. of Physicians for Reproductive Choice and Health; bd. dirs. NARAL, N.Y.; mem. Nat. Abortion and Reproductive Rights Action League, N.Y. Abortion and Reproductive Rights Action League. Served to it. M.C. USNR, 1943-45. Mem. ACOG, AAAS, Am. Assn. Med. Colls. (life), Am. Gynecol. and Obstet. Soc., Soc. Gynecologic Investigation, Am. Assn. Cancer Rsch., Population Assn. Am., N.Y. Obstet. Soc., N.Y. Acad. Medicine, N.Y. Acad. Sci. Home: Glenbrooke Dr White Plains NY 10605-5008 Office: Einstein Coll Morris Park Ave Bronx NY 10461-2534

ROMNEY-MANOOKIN, ELAINE CLIVE, retired music educator, composer; b. Salt Lake City, July 11, 1922; d. Joseph Campbell Clive and Katie Winifred Gilroy; m. Eldon Brigham Romney, May 5, 1941 (dec. May 1998); children: Ruth Romney Powell, Frederic Clive Romney, Clive Jay Romney, Stanley Clive Romney, Eldon Clive Romney, Roslyn Kay Romney Reynolds, Rae Lynne Romney Johnson, Vincent Clive Romney; m. Stuart Midgley Manookin. Studied piano, violin and cello, Clive Music Studios, Salt Lake City, 1938; cert., U. Utah, 1941; studied organ, U. S.C., 1954; studied piano with Frederic Dixon, McCune Sch., 1938—42; studied piano with Alton O'Steen, Juilliard, 1936. Musician: Assembly Hall with McCune Symphony, 1941, author organ book for beginning organists; composer: (sch. song) South H.S., 1939, Skyline H.S., 1962, Wasatch Jr. H.S., 1964; organist Grandview Second Ward, 2001—; organist: Columbia (S.C.) Stake Ctr., 1953—54, East Millcreek Stake, 1956—, Monument Pk. Stake, 1955—56. Bd. dirs. Utah Hemophilia Found., Salt Lake City, 1965—99; vol. specialist Welfare Employment; vice chmn. dist. Rep. Party, Salt Lake City, 1970—90. Recipient Dedicated Svc. award, Hemophilia Found., 1991. Mem.: Alpha Dorian Fine Arts Soc. (past pres.), AXO Luncheon Club (pres.), Agalia Mu (past pres.). Avocations: travel, writing, volunteering. Address: 2987 Hartford St Salt Lake City UT 84106-3468

ROMOFF, JEFFREY ALAN, healthcare executive; b. NYC, Nov. 30, 1945; s. Richard Warren and Evelyn (Alter) Romoff; m. Vivian Irene Goodman, Aug. 25, 1966 (dec. June 1983); children: Jennifer Ann, Rebecca Lynn; m. Stefania Ferrarese, Dec. 2002. BS magna cum laude in Social Scis., CCNY, 1967; M.Phil. in Polit. Scis., Yale U., 1971; Doctor Pub. Svc. (hon.), Chatham Coll., 2005. Teaching fellow Yale U., 1969-70, teaching assoc., 1970-71; exec. dir. Central Naugatuck Valley Mental Health Council, Waterbury, Conn., 1971-73; regional programing dir. Western Psychiat. Inst. and Clinic (U. Pitts.), 1973-74, assoc. dir. div. edn. and research, 1974-75; assoc. dir. Western Psychiat. Inst. and Clinic, 1975—86; adj. asst. prof. pub. health U. Pitts., 1981—, instr. psychiatry, 1982—, assoc. v.p. health svcs., 1984-86, vice chancellor health scis., 1986-92, sr. vice chancellor for Health Adminstrn., 1992—96; exec. v.p. U. Pitts. Med. Ctr., 1986-92, pres., 1992—. N.Y.C. Regents scholar CCNY, 1963-67 Mem. Am. Hosp. Assn. (governing coun. sect. for mental health and psychiat. svcs. 1986-89), Am. Psychiat. Assn. (chmn. joint com. with Am. Hosp. Assn. 1983-84), Hosp. Assn. Pa., Coun. Psychiat. Svc. Providers (exec. com. 1981-84) Jewish. Home: 3208 Fox Run Rd Allison Park PA 15101-1506 Office: U Pitts Med Ctr Forbes Tower 200 Lothrop St Ste 11045 Pittsburgh PA 15213-2546*

ROMOSER, GEORGE KENNETH, political and social science educator; b. Kingston, NY, Sept. 14, 1929; s. Carl August and Alva (Becker) R.; m. Mechthild von Tresckow, Apr. 30, 1967; children: Alexandra Ada, Valerie Anna. AB, Rutgers U., 1951; A.M., U. Chgo., 1954, PhD, 1958. Research asst. Nat. Opinion Research Center, 1953; fellow Social Sci. Rsch. Coun., 1953-54; lectr. Indiana Univ., 1954—55; asst. Freiburg (Germany) U., 1955-56; instr. Ohio State U., 1957-61; from asst. prof. to assoc. prof. Conn. Coll., 1963-67; assoc. prof., prof. polit. sci. U. N.H., Durham, 1961-62, 67-96, chmn. dept., 1968-71, prof. internat. affairs, 1986-93, course dir. Internat. Perspective Ctr., 1986-88, dir. program on tech., society and values, 1996-2000. Fulbright prof. Faculty of Law, Mainz U., Fed. Republic Germany, 1962-63; dir. Émigré Meml. German Internship Programs, 1965-2005; vis. prof. Free U., Berlin, 1964, Mannheim U., 1968, 82-83, Johns Hopkins, Bologna, Italy, 1969, Munich U., 1973-74, U. Pa., 1986, Kobe U., Japan, 1988-89, Bowdoin Coll., 1990, Freiburg U., Germany, 1993-94, Fulbright Sr. Prof.; adj. prof. Mannheim U., Fed. Republic Germany, 1983—; Fulbright sr. rsch. fellow Munich U., 1974; Rockefeller fellow Aspen Inst. for Humanistic Studies, 1978-79; rsch. fellow Inst. on Far Ea. Studies, Kyungnam U., Republic of Korea, 1997; cons. Com. on Internat. Exchange of Persons, 1965-66; NEH fellow Yale U., 1993; co-founder Working Group on German Politics, 1968—, chmn., 1968-84, regional dir., 1984-87; founder, dir. New Eng. Workshops on German Affairs, 1980—; co-founder Pacific Coast Workshops on German Affairs, 1983-93; commuting fellow Ctr. European Studies Harvard U., 1983—; founder The Japanese Circle, 1989-2000; coord. German programs in rsch. and pub. affairs, 2004-. Co-author: West German Politics in the Mid-Eighties, 1985, Germany's New Politics, 1995; contbr. articles to profl. jours., books. Chmn. com. on govtl. reorgn. Democratic party N.H., 1962; chair Eliot (Maine) Planning Bd., 1969—72; chmn. Eliot Conservation Commn., 1984—88; vice chair Eliot Bd. Appeals, Eliot, Maine, 1977—82. Decorated Civilian Knight's Cross Fed. Republic of Germany, 1972. Mem. Am. Coun. on Germany, Internat. Polit. Sci. Assn., Am. Polit. Sci. Assn., New England Circle, Phi Delta Theta, Pi Sigma Alpha, Delta Phi Alpha, Phi Alpha Theta. Home: Shipmast Farm 86 Worster Rd Eliot ME 03903-1113 Office: PO Box 345 Durham NH 03824 Business E-mail: gkr@unh.edu.

ROMOSER, W. DAVID, lawyer; b. Oak Park, Ill., July 12, 1943; BA, U. Ill., 1965; JD, Ill. Inst. Tech., 1970. Bar: Ill. 1970. Mem. Witwer, Moran and Burlage, Chgo., 1970—75; v.p., gen. counsel, sec. Amsted Industries, Inc., Chgo., 1975—92, A.O. Smith Corp., Milw., 1992—. Bd. dirs., dir. emeritus

Siebert Lutheran Found.; bd. dirs. Wis. Equal Justice Fund, Inc.; mem. pres. coun. U. Ill.; sec. Next Door Found. Mem.: Am. Corp. Counsel Assn., Ill. State Bar Assn., Chgo. Bar Assn. Office: AO Smith Corp 11270 West Park Pl PO Box 245008 Milwaukee WI 53224-9508 Office Phone: 414-359-4137. Office Fax: 414-359-4198.

ROMPALA, RICHARD M., chemical company executive; B in Liberal Arts and Chem. Engring., Columbia U.; MBA, Harvard U. Bus. mgr. Olin Corp.; sr. v.p. ops. Mueller Brass Co.; joined PPG Industries, 1985, v.p. corp. devel., group v.p. chems., group v.p. coatings and resins; pres. Valspar Corp., Mpls., 1994, CEO, 1995—, chmn., 1998. Office: The Valspar Corp 1101 Third St S Minneapolis MN 55415

RONALD, PAMELA C., plant pathologist, educator; Diploma in French Lang. Studies, U. Strasbourg, France, 1981; BA in Biology, Reed Coll., Portland, Oreg., 1982; MA in Biology, Stanford U., Calif., 1984; MS in Plant Physiology, U. Uppsala, Sweden, 1985; PhD in Molecular and Physiol. Plant Biology, U. Calif., Berkeley, 1990. Rsch. asst. dept. biology Stanford U., Calif., 1983—84; Fulbright fellow Inst. Botany U. Uppsala, Sweden, 1984—85; postdoctoral fellow dept. plant breeding Cornell U., 1990—92; asst. prof. dept. plant pathology U. Calif., Davis, 1992—97, assoc. prof., 1997—2002, prof., 2002—. Founder, CEO Tellus Genetics, Davis, Calif., 1998—2000; Guggenheim fellow Lab. Molecular Biology of Plant-Microorganism Interactions Nat. Ctr. Sci. Rsch., Nat. Inst. Agronomic Rsch., Castanet-Tolosan, France, 2000; hon. scientist Nat. Inst. Agrl. Biotechnology, Republic of Korea, 2002—; chair plant genomics prog. U. Calif., Davis, 2004—05; external adv. Zhejiang U. Agrl. Inst., 2005—. Contbr. articles to sci. jours.; mem. editl. bd.: Planta, 1997—2002, Molecular Plant Pathology, 2002—, assoc. editor: Transgenic Rsch., 2003—, sr. editor: Molecular Plant Microbe Interactions, 2003—. Mem.: AAAS, Internat. Soc. Molecular Plant-Microbe Interactions, Am. Soc. Plant Biologists, Am. Phytopathological Soc. Office: Genome and Biomedical Scis Facility U Calif Davis 451 E Health Scis Dr Davis CA 95616-8816 E-mail: pcronald@ucdavis.edu.*

RONALD, PETER, utilities executive; b. Duluth, Minn., Aug. 26, 1926; s. George W. and Florence (Jones) R.; m. Mary Locke Boyd, Nov. 25, 1950 (div. 2003); children: Peter Webb, Pauline Morton, Samuel Herschel; m. Anne H. Moore, Dec. 28, 2005. BA, U. Va., 1950. With Louisville Gas & Electric Co., 1950-88, treas., 1962—, v.p., 1969-82, sr. v.p., 1982-88, dir., 1979-89. Bd. dirs., mem. exec. com. Bus. Devel. Corp. Ky., 1967-75, pres., 1971-72; bd. dirs. Louisville Community Chest, 1967-72, v.p., 1969-72; bd. dirs., v.p. Louisville Rehab. Ctr., 1964-82, pres., 1970-71; bd. overseers Louisville Country Day Sch., 1967-70; trustee Children's Hosp. Found., 1978-81, sec.-treas., 1978-81; bd. govs. Captiva (Fla.) Civic Assn., 1990-94, v.p., 1992; commr. Captiva, Fla. Erosion Prevention Dist., 1996-98. With USNR, 1945-46. Mem. Louisville Country Club, Captiva Yacht Club, Zeta Psi. Home: 4710 Indian Hills Green Louisville KY 40207-1366 also: PO Box 877 Captiva FL 33924

RONALDINHO, (RONALDO DE ASSIS MOREIRA), professional soccer player; b. Porto Alegre, Brazil, Mar. 21, 1980; Player Gremio FC, Brazil, 1998—2001, Paris Saint Germain, France, 2001—03, FC Barcelona, Spain, 2003—. Mem. Brazil Nat. Team, 1999—, World Cup Champion, Brazil, 2002; mem. & capt. Confederations Cup Champion, Brazil, 2005. Named FIFA World Player of the Yr., 2004, FIFPro World Player of the Year, 2005; named to FIFA 100, 2004, FIFPro World XI, 2005; recipient Best Soccer Player, ESPY award, 2006. Mailing: FC Barcelona Av Arístedes Maillol 08028 Barcelona Spain

RONALTER, CHELSEA MARIA, artist, graphic designer; b. Manchester, N.H., Jan. 30, 1974; d. Donald Edward and Lynn Elise Ronalter. AA summa cum laude in Comml. Design and Illustration, Manchester Cmty. Tech. Coll., N.H., 1997; AA in Interior Design, Hesser Coll., Manchester, N.H., 2001; postgrad., Notre Dame Coll., Manchester, N.H., 2001, Rivier Coll., Nashua, 2006. Graphic designer Notre Dame Coll., Manchester, NH, 1998—2002; instl. advancement So. NH U., Manchester, 2002. Event planner Notre Dame Coll., Manchester, NH, 1999—2000. Mem.: Phi Theta Kappa. Roman Catholic. Avocations: art, literature, history.

RONAN, CLIFFORD JOHN, literature and language professor; b. Boston, July 22, 1935; s. J(ohn) Clifford and Frances Goodwin Ronan; m. Denise Shual, Dec. 2, 1960; children: David Goodwin, Michelle Ronan Noteboom. AB, Amherst Coll., Mass., 1957; PhD in English Lit., U. Calif., Berkeley, 1971. Asst. prof. English U. Tex., Austin, 1965—72; prof. English Tex. State U., San Marcos, 1972—. Reader in Advanced Placement in English Ednl. Testing Svc., 1976—79; exec. sec.-treas. South-Central Renaissance Conf., 1978—80; core faculty Nat. Endowment for Humanities, 1987—93; sr. Fulbright lectr. in Am. Lit. U. Silesia, Poland, 1995—96; cons., presenter, lectr. in field. Author: Antike Roman: Power Symbology and the Roman Play in Early Modern England 1585-1635, 1995; contbr. articles to profl. jours., chapters to books. Mem. Voluntary Action Ctr., Caldwell County, Lockhart, Tex., 1973—75, sec., 1973—75; adv. bd. mem. Catholic Student Ctrs., U Tex., Austin, 1973—75, Catholic Student Ctrs., Tex. State U., 1989—. Sgt. U.S. Army, 1957—58. Recipient Presdl. Seminar award, SW Tex. State U., 1997. Democrat. Roman Catholic. Home: 211 Harvard St San Marcos TX 78666 Office: Tex State Univ Dept English San Marcos TX 78666 Office Phone: 512-245-2163. Office Fax: 512-245-8546. Business E-mail: cr06@txstate.edu.

RONAN, WILLIAM JOHN, management consultant; b. Buffalo, Nov. 8, 1912; s. William and Charlotte (Ramp) R.; m. Elena Vinadé, May 29, 1939; children: Monica, Diana Quasha. AB, Syracuse U., 1934; PhD, NYU, 1940, LLD, 1969; certificate, Geneva Sch. Internat. Studies, 1933. Mus. asst. Buffalo Mus. Sci., 1928-30; with Niagara-Hudson Power Co., 1931; transfer dept. NYC R.R., 1932; Penfield fellow internat. law, diplomacy and belles lettres, 1935; Univ. fellow, 1936; editor Fed. Bank Service, Prentice-Hall, Inc., 1937; instr. govt. NYU, 1938, exec. sec. grad. div. for tng. in pub. services, 1938, asst. dir., 1940, asst. prof. govt., dir. grad. div. for tng. pub. service, 1940, assoc. prof. govt., 1946-47, prof., 1947, dean, grad. sch. pub. adminstrn. and social service, 1953-58; Cons. NYC Civil Service Commn., 1938; prin. rev. officer, negotiations officer US Civil Service Commn.; 1942; prin. div. asst. US Dept. State, 1943; cons. Dept. State, 1948, Dept. Def., 1954; dir. studies NY State Coordination Commn., 1951-58; project mgr. NYU-U. Ankara project, 1954-59; cons. ICA, 1955, NY State Welfare Conf., adminstrv. co-dir. Albany Grad. Program in Pub. Adminstrn.; 1st dep. city adminstr. NYC, 1956-57; exec. dir. NY State Temporary Commn. Constl. Conv., 1956-58; sec. to Gov. NY, 1959-66; chmn. interdept. com. traffic safety, commr. Port Authority NY and NJ, 1967-90, vice chmn., 1972-74, chmn., 1974-77; with UTDC Corp., West Palm Beach, Fla. Trustee Crosslands Savs. Bank; chmn. bd. LI R.R., 1966-74; chmn. Tri-State Transp. Com., NY, NJ, Conn., 1961-67; chmn. interstate com. New Haven R.R., 1960-63; chmn. NY Com. on LI R.R., 1964-65; mem. NY State Comm. Interstate Coop., 1961, NY State Com. Fgn. Ofcl. Visitors, 1961, NY State Coordination Commn., 1960; mem. NY Civil Svc. Commn., Temporary State Commn. on Constl. Conv., 1966-67; chmn. NY State Met. Commuter Transp. Authority, 1965-68, Met. Transp. Authority, 1968-74, Tri-Borough Bridge and Tunnel Authority, 1968-74, NYC Transit Authority, 1968-74, Manhattan and Bronx Surface Transit Operating Authority, 1968-74; chmn. bd., pres. 3d Century Corp., 1974-94; mem. Commn. Critical Choices for Am., 1973—, acting chmn., 1975—; mem. urban transp. adv. com. US Dept. Transp.; sr. adviser Rockefeller family, 1974-80; pres. Nelson Rockefeller Collection, Inc., 1977-80; trustee Power Authority of State of NY, 1974-77; cons. to trustees Penn Ctrl. Transp. Co.; vice chmn. bd. OCX, Inc.; sec.-treas. Sarabam Corp. N.V.; chmn., dir. UTDC (USA) Inc., 1987-88; chmn. UTDC Corp., 1989-94, Transit Svcs. Corp., 1989-94; cons. Herzog Transit Svcs., 1995-99, Dime Savs. Bank, Metal Powder Products Inc., Flomet Inc., 1997—, Teckna Seal, LLC, 2002—; Internat. Mining and Metals Inc., Quadrant Mgmt. Inc., 1990—, Ohio Highspeed Rail Authority 1991-93; chmn. NY and NJ Inland Rail Rate Com.; dir. Nat. Mgmt. Coun., 1951. Author: Money Power of States in International Law, 1940, The Board of Regents and the Commissioner,

1948, Our War Economy, 1943, (with others); articles in profl. jours.; adviser: Jour. Inst. Socio-Econ. Studies. Mem. US FOA, Am. Public Health Assn.; staff relations officer NYC Bd. Edn.; Mem. Nat. Conf. Social Work, Nat. Conf. on Met. Areas, Citizens Com. on Corrections, Council on Social Work Edn.; bd. dirs. World Trade Club; adv. bd. World Trade Inst.; mem. 42d St. Redevel. Corp. (chmn., 1980-94; mem. Assn. for a Better NY; bd. advisers Inst. for Socioecon. Studies, 1977—; dir. Nat. Health Council, 1980-86; dep. dir. policy Nelson Rockefeller campaign for Republican presdl. nomination, 1964; mem. NY State Gov.'s Com. on Shoreham Nuclear Plant, 1983-85, Nassau County Indsl. Devel. Authority, 1982-90, US Dept. Transp. Com. on Washington and Capital Dist. Airports, 1985-86; bd. dirs. Ctr. Study Presidency, 1986-90, Alcoholism Council of NY, 1986—; trustee NY Coll. Osteopathic Medicine, 1986-91; v.p. Am. Cancer Soc., Palm Beach. Served as lt. USNR, 1943-46. Mem. ASPA, NEA, Am. Polit. Sci. Assn., Am. Acad. Pub. Adminstrn., Civil Svc. Assembly of US and Can., Internat. Assn. Met. Rsch. and Devel., Nat. Mcpl. League, Mcpl. Pers. Soc., Citizens Union of NY, Nat. Civil Svc. League, Am. Acad. Polit. and Social Sci., LI Assn. Commerce and Industry (dir.); Internat. Inst. Adminstrv. Scis., Am. Fgn. Law Assn., Internat. Union Pub. Transport (mgmt. com., v.p.), Am. Pub. Transit Assn. (chmn. 1974-76), Nat. Def. Transp. Assn. (v.p. for Mass transit), English Speaking Union (bd. dirs. Palm Beach), Met. Opera Club, Maidstone Club, Devon Yacht Club, Knickerbocker Club, Hemisphere Club, Harvard Club, Creek Club, Wings Club, Traffic Club, Univ. Club, Am. Club Riviera, Beach Club (Palm Beach), Everglades Club. Home: 525 S Flagler Dr West Palm Beach FL 33401-5922 Address: Villa La Pointe Du Cap 29 Ave de La Corniche 06230 Saint Jean Cap Ferrat France Personal E-mail: w.j.ramp@aol.com.

**RONAY, MATTHEW,** sculptor; b. Louisville, 1976; Grad., Md. Inst. Coll. Art, 1998; MFA, Yale U., 2000. One-man shows include Gallery Luhmann, Nils Staerk, Copenhagen, 2002, Galerie Grimm/Rosenfeld, Munich, 2003, Vedanta Gallery, Chgo., 2003, exhibited in group shows at Richard Telles Gallery, L.A., 1999, Andrew Kreps Gallery, N.Y.C., 2000, Exit Art, 2001, Marc Foxx, L.A., 2001, 2002, Dorsky Gallery, L.I., N.Y., 2002, Wattis Inst. for Contemporary Arts, San Francisco, 2002, Logan Gallery, 2002, Gallery Luhmann, Nils Staerk, Copenhagen, 2002, Inst. Contemporary Art, Boston, 2002, Gallery 2 Andrea Rosen, N.Y.C., 2002, Whitney Biennial, Whitney Mus. Am. Art, NY, 2004, The Stars Are So Big, The Earth Is So Small...Say As You Are, Esther Schipper, Berlin, 2004. Named Invited Exhibitor, 2004 Biennial Exhbn., Whitney Mus. Am. Art, N.Y., 2004; recipient award for set design, N.Y. Internat. Fringe Festival, 2001.

**RONAYNE, MICHAEL RICHARD, JR.,** academic dean; b. Boston, Apr. 29, 1937; s. Michael Richard and Margaret (Fahey) R.; m. Joanne Maria, Aug. 7, 1971; 1 child, Michelle Eileen. BS, Boston Coll., 1958; PhD, U. Notre Dame, 1962. Instr. chemistry Providence Coll., 1962-63, asst. prof. chemistry, 1963-64; rsch. chemist Panametrics, Inc., Waltham, Mass., 1964-66; asst. prof. chemistry Suffolk U., Boston, 1966-67, assoc. prof., 1967-70, prof., chmn. dept. chemistry, 1970-72, dean Coll. Arts and Sci., 1972—. Reaccreditation vis. team mem. New Eng. Assn. Schs. and Colls., Winchester, Mass., 1974-80, Mass. Dept. Edn., Boston, 1975; mem. acad. adv. com. Mass. Bd. Higher Edn., Boston, 1977. Contbr. articles to sci. jours., profl. publs. Mem. Winchester Sch. Com., 1983-92, chmn., 1984-85, 86-87; mem. Winchester Town Meeting, 1983-98, mem. town capital planning com., 1983-84, town coun. on youth, 1987-88, 89-90; mem. exec. com., bd. dirs. Mass. Bay Marine Studies Consortium, 1985-87; project dir. U.S. Dept. of Edn. Title III Grants. Shell Oil Corp. fellow, 1958-59, AEC fellow 1959-62; recipient Contbns. in Sci. and Edn. citation New Eng. Sch. Art and Design, Boston, 1991; named to Matignon High Sch. Alumni Achievement Hall of Fame, 1997. Mem. AAAS, Am. Chem. Soc., Am. Conf. Acad. Deans, Coun. for Liberal Learning, Am. Assn. for Higher Edn., Sigma Xi, Phi Alpha Theta, Phi Gamma Mu, Sigma Tau Delta, Omicron Delta Epsilon, Sigma Zeta, Pi Sigma Alpha. Office: Suffolk U Beacon Hill Boston MA 02114 E-mail: mronayne@suffolk.edu.

**RONCAL, ROGELIO,** psychiatrist; b. Bataan, Philippines, 1939; MD magna cum laude, Manila Ctrl. U., 1962. Diplomate Am. Bd. Psychiatry and Neurology, Am. Bd. Forensic Medicine, Am. Acad. Integrative Medicine. Intern French Hosp., NYC, 1963; resident in psychiatry Middletown PC-NY Psychiat. Inst., NYC, 1965-67; physician Horton Meml. Hosp., Middletown, NY; founding dir. Middletown Alcohol Treatment Ctr. (now R. Ward Addictions Treatment Ctr.), 1974—; pvt. practice., 1974-89; clin. dir. Middletown Psychiat. Ctr., NY; attending psychiatrist Mid Hudson Psychiat. Ctr., New Hampton, NY, 1984-95; med. dir. chemical dependency program Pius XII Youth and Family Svcs., 1995—. Instr. clin. psychiat. Columbia U.; psychiatrist N.Am. Province Order Carmelites, 1975-95; med. cons. NY State Divsn. Alcoholism and Alcohol Abuse, 1981-84; psychiat. cons. McQuade Found. for Children, 1974-81; attending psychiatrist NY State Dept. Corrections, 1992-95. Maj. MC, USAR, 1983. Recipient Life Achievement award Alcoholism and Drug Abuse Coun. Orange County, N.Y., 2001, medal of honor MCU Coll. Medicine, 2000, MCU Alumni in Am. Eagle award, 2004, MCU Centennial Medallion, 2004; donor M. Roncal achievement award for acad. excellence given to delinquent youth in group homes served by Pius XII Youth and Family Svcs., 1990-95; named to First Alumni Hall of Fame, Manila Ctrl. U., 2001. Fellow: APA (disting. life), Am. Assn. Integrative Medicine (life; cert.), Am. Psychiat. Assn. (life); mem.: Caloocan H.S. Alumni Assn., Acad. Internat. Med. Study, Manila Ctrl U. Med. Alumni Assn. (pres. N.E. chpt. 1998, pres. found. in Am. 1999, pres. 2000—), West Hudson Psychiat. Soc. (sec. 1979, pres. 1981), NY State Med. Soc. (task force on smoking cessation 1997—), Am. Soc. Addiction Medicine, Am. Acad. Psychiat. Adminstrn., Am. Coll. Forensic Examiners, Orange County Med. Soc., Am. Coll. Physician Execs., Am. Med. Dirs. Assn., Med. Staff Orgn. Middletown Psychiat. Ctr., Med. Staff Orgn. Mid-Hudson Forensic Psychiat. Ctr. (pres. 1995), Filipino Psychiatrists in Am. (life). Fax: 914-294-1402.

**RONDE, JOHN HERMAN,** writer, translator; b. Lonneker, Overyssel, The Netherlands, July 12, 1929; arrived in US, 1961; s. Johannes Maria Ronde and Lamberdina Hulsschreuder. BA in Econs., Columbia U., 1973, MA in Social Studies, 1974, MPhil in Geography, 1983. With Irving Trust Co., NYC, Loeb, Rhoades & Co., NYC, Bache & Co., NYC, Import-Export Industries, NYC, Winter-Wolff Internat. Corp., NYC; substitute tchr. NYC HS, 1985-86, 92-93; asst. geographer US Census Bur., NYC, 1988-91. Author: Migration, Social Infrastructure and Urban Devel. in Selected German Cities, and Housing Policy and Supply in the Fed. German Republic (1970-85), 1996, Urban Devel. and Migration in Kiel with Reference to City Ctr. and Fringe Area Devel. Initiatives, 1971-84, Philosophical Interpretations of Modern Science, The Developing New World View of Man and His Activities for The Fulfillment of His Needs, An Introd. To and A Discussion of A Model of The Location of Man and His Activities, or: Geography as a Theory of Man. Aide, advisor to Sen. George McGovern, 1972; advisor Dem. Party. Mem.: AAAS, Baron Johannes Hermanus Ronde Inst. Urban Geography and Locational Studies (founder), Am. Geog. Soc. (nat. affil.), NY Acad. Sci. Democrat. Avocations: bibliophile in history, philosophy of science, music, Bandonion player. Home: 75 East 3rd St C-3 New York NY 10003-9015

**RONDEAU, CLEMENT ROBERT,** petroleum geologist; b. Ironwood, Mich., July 6, 1928; BS, Tulane U., 1955. Geol. supr. Texaco, Inc., New Orleans, 1955-63; area mgr. Pubco Petroleum Corp., New Orleans, 1963-69; cons. petroleum geologist Harahan, La., 1969—; owner Natural Gas Exploration Co., Harahan, 1977—. Mem. AAAS, Am. Assn. Petroleum Geologists, Soc. Exploration Geophysicists, New Orleans Geol. Soc., N.Y. Acad. Sci., The Explorers Club, Phi Beta Kappa, Sigma Gamma Epsilon. Democrat. Roman Catholic. Home and Office: 119 W Southland Ave Ironwood MI 49938 Personal E-mail: gasfinder@aol.com.

**RONDEAU, DORIS JEAN,** entrepreneur, consultant; b. Winston-Salem, N.C., Nov. 25, 1941; d. John Delbert and Eldora Virginia (Klutz) Robinson; m. Robert Breen Corrente, Sept. 4, 1965 (div. 1970); m. Wilfrid Dolor Rondeau, June 3, 1972. Student Syracuse U., 1959-62, Fullerton Jr. Coll., 1974-75; BA in Philosophy, Calif. State U.-Fullerton, 1976, postgrad., 1976-80. Ordained to ministry The Spirit of Divine Love, 1974. Trust real estate clk. Security First Nat. Bank, Riverside, Calif., 1965-68; entertainer Talent, Inc., Hollywood, Calif., 1969-72; co-founder, dir. Spirit of Divine Love, Huntington Beach, Calif., 1974—; pub., co-founder Passing Through, Inc., Huntington Beach, 1983—; instr. Learning Activity, Anaheim, Calif., 1984—; chmn. bd., prin. D.J. Rondeau, Entrepreneur, Inc., Huntington Beach, 1984—; co-founder, dir. Spiritual Positive Attitude, Inc., Moon In Pisces, Inc., Vibrations By Rondeau, Inc., Divine Consciousness, Expressed, Inc., Huntington Beach, Doris Wilfrid Rondeau, Inc., Huntington Beach, Calif. Author, editor: A Short Introduction To The Spirit of Divine Love, 1984; writer, producer, dir. performer spiritual vignettes for NBS Radio Network, KWVE-FM, 1982-84; author: Spiritual Meditations to Uplift the Soul, 1988. Served with USAF, 1963-65. Recipient Pop Vocalist First Place award USAF Talent Show, 1964, Sigma chpt. Epsilon Delta Chi, 1985, others. Mem. Hamel Bus. Grads., Smithsonian Assocs., Am. Mgmt. Assn., Nat. Assn. Female Execs. Fax: (714) 841-3286. Avocations: long-distance running, body fitness, arts and crafts, snorkeling, musical composition.

**RONDEAU, GEORGE CHARLES, JR.,** lawyer; b. Phila., May 2, 1946; BSEE, Drexel U., Phila., 1969; MBA, U. So. Calif., LA, 1972; JD, UCLA, 1976. Assoc. atty. Fulwider, Patton, Lee & Utecht, LA, 1976—82; ptnr., atty. Seed Intellectual Property Law Group PLLC, Seattle, 1983—2002, Davis Wright Tremaine, LLP, Seattle, 2002—. Mem.: ABA, Licensing Execs. Soc. (chmn. seattle chpt. 1995—99), Wash. State Patent Law Assn., Wash. State Bar Assn. (chmn. 1990—91, intellectual property sect.). Office: Davis Wright Tremaine LLP 2600 Century Sq 1501 Fourth Ave Seattle WA 98101-1688 Office Phone: 206-628-7739. Office Fax: 206-903-3739. Business E-Mail: georgerondeau@dwt.com.

**RONDEAU, PATRICK JOHN,** lawyer; b. South Hadley, Mass., July 13, 1959; s. John Patrick and Norine Patricia (Shevlin) R.; m. Valerie Anne Cameron, May 4, 1991. BA summa cum laude, Williams Coll., 1981; JD cum laude, Harvard U., 1984. Bar: Mass. 1985. Assoc. Hale and Dorr, Boston, 1984-89, jr. ptnr., 1989—92, sr. ptnr., 1994—2004; ptnr., vice chmn. Corp dept., co-chmn. Venture Capital group Wilmer Cutler Pickering Hale & Dorr, Boston, 2004—. Lectr. MIT Sloan Sch. Mgmt. Named a Mass. Super Lawyer, Boston Mag., 2004. Mem. ABA, Mass. Bar Assn., Boston Bar Assn. (past co-chmn. securities law com.), Phi Beta Kappa. Roman Catholic. Avocation: sports. Office: Wilmer Cutler Pickering Hale & Dorr 60 State St Boston MA 02109-1816 Office Phone: 617-526-6670. Office Fax: 617-526-5000. Business E-Mail: patrick.rondeau@wilmerhale.com.

**RONDINELLI, DENNIS A(UGUST),** business administration educator, researcher; b. Trenton, N.J., Mar. 30, 1943; s. August P. and Vincentia Rondinelli; m. Soonyoung Chang, Dec. 19, 1976; children: Linda, Lisa. BA, Rutgers U., 1965; PhD, Cornell U., 1969. Asst. prof. urban affairs U. Wis., Milw., 1971-73; assoc. prof. grad. sch. of mgmt. Vanderbilt U., Nashville, 1973-76; assoc. prof. planning Maxwell Sch. of Citizenship and Pub. Affairs Syracuse U., NY, 1976-79; prof. social scis. NY, 1979-86; prin. scientist and sr. policy analyst Office for Internat. Programs, Research Triangle Inst., Research Triangle Park, NC, 1986-90; Glaxo Disting. Internat. Prof. Mgmt. emeritus Kenan-Flagler Bus. Sch., 2005—, emeritus, 2005—; sr. rsch. scholar Duke Ctr. Internat. Devel., 2005—; dir. Pacific Basin Rsch. Ctr., Soka U. Am., 2005—. Cons. World Bank, U.S. Dept. State, UN Devel. Program, Govts. of Colombia, South Korea, Can., Indonesia, Philippines, China, India, mem. com. of experts on pub. adminstrn. UN Econ. and Social Coun., 2002—. Author: Decentralization and Development: Policy Implementation in Developing Countries, 1983, Applied Methods of Regional Analysis: The Spatial Dimensions of Development Policy, 1985, Development Administration and U.S. Foreign Aid Policy, 1987, Urban Services in Developing Countries: Public and Private Roles in Urban Development, 1988, Planning Education Reforms in Developing Countries, 1990, Development Projects as Policy Experiments, 1993, Privatization and Economic Reform in Central Europe, 1994, Expanding Sino-American Business and Trade: China's Economic Transition, 1994, Great Policies: Strategic Innovations in Asia and the Pacific, 1995, Policies and Institutions for Managing Privatization, 1996, Market Reform in Vietnam, 1999, Reinventing Government for the 21st Century, 2003, Beyond Reconstruction in Afghanistan, 2004, Globalizataion and Change in Asia, 2006; mem. editl. adv. bd. Leadership Rev., Jour. Internat. Bus. Edn., Jour. Internat. Devel. Planning; contbr. articles to jours. Mem. expert com. pub. admin. econ. and social coun. UN, 2002—. Capt. U.S. Army, 1965—72. Decorated Julio Lieras Order of Merit (Colombia). 1988; recipient Rural Devel. medal Republic of Vietnam, 1971, Ethnic Minorities Devel. medal, 1971, W. Bloomberg award for excellence in futures studies, 1997, Weatherspoon Disting. Rsch. award, 1997; East-West Ctr. sr. fellow, 1975-76, Pacific Basin Rsch. Ctr./Soka U. of Am./Harvard U. rsch. fellow, 1991-92. Avocations: gardening, writing nonfiction. Office: Duke Univ Duke Ctr Internat Devel Box 90237 Durham NC 27708 E-mail: rondined@duke.edu.

**RONDUM, KAI DAMIEN,** marketing executive; b. Phila., Oct. 7, 1956; s. Steen Eigel Rondum and Rita Marie Bernadette Rondum; m. Nancy Janet Brinkmann; 1 child, Nicole Amber. BS, Rutgers U., New Brunswick, NJ, 1982. Insp. Dept. Environ. Protection Solid Waste Adminstrn. Enforcement Divsn. State NJ, Trenton, 1976—78; draftsman Squibb, New Brunswick, 1978—82; tech. sales rep. Hercules, Wilmington, Del., 1982—85; product specialist to sr. product specialist to product suprv. to product mgr. Drew Industl. Divsn. Ashland Speciality Chem., Boonton, NJ, 1985—. Conf. presenter in field, 1985—. Contbr. articles to profl. jours. Mem.: VASA, Nat. Assn. Corrosion Engrs. (chmn. 1990, conv. presenter) Achievements include patents for process for dispersing iron oxide in steam generated boilers; method for inhibiting foulant formation in organic streams using erythorbic acid or oximes; a non-aqueous process stream; patents pending for a process for removing iron oxide deposit from a metal surface in contact with an aqueous system. Avocations: sailing, tennis. Business E-Mail: kdrondum@ashland.com.

**RONEL, DANIEL NOEL,** plastic surgeon; b. Princeton, NJ; AB, Princeton U., NJ, 1986; MD, Columbia U., NYC, 1991. Instr. Hurricane Island Outward Bound Sch., Rockport/Bethel, Maine, 1986—87; pediatric intern Children's Hosp. Phila., 1991—92; pediatric resident Children's Hosp., Boston, 1992—94; chief resident Boston City Hosp., 1994—95; chief pediatric services Columbus AFB Hosp., Columbus, Miss., 1995—97, chief med. staff, 1997—98; intern gen. surgery Mt. Sinai Med. Ctr., NYC, 1999—2000; resident gen. surgery Columbia Presbyn. Med. Ctr., 2000—02; plastic surgeon N.Mex Plastic Surgery, Albuquerque, 2004—. Clin. asst. prof. dept. surgery U. N.Mex Med. Sch., Albuquerque, 2005—, clin. asst. prof. dept. pediat., 2004—. Contbr. scientific papers. Maj. USAF, 1995—99. Fellow, NY Presbyn. Hosp., NYC, 2002—04. Fellow: ACS, Am. Acad. Pediat.; mem.: Greater Albuquerque Med. Assn., Am. Soc. Aesthetic Plastic Surgery, Am. Soc. Plastic Surgery. Office: New Mexico Plastic Surgery 1020 Tijeras NE Suite 16 Albuquerque NM 87106 Office Phone: 505-842-6868. Office Fax: 505-842-9325. E-mail: drronel@nmplasticsurgery.com.

**RONEY, CARLEY,** wedding company executive, writer; m. David Liu; 2 children. BFA, NYU Tisch Sch. Arts, Inst. Film & TV; MA Cultural Studies, NYU. Creative dir., editor Nat. Mus. Am. History, McGraw-Hill Co., Simon & Schuster, 1988—94; cofounder RunTime Inc., 1994, pres., 1994—96; cofounder The Knot, 1996, v.p. creative devel., 1996—99, editor in chief, 1996—; syndicated columnist Scripps Howard News Svc., 2003—. Author: The Knot's Complete Guide to Weddings, 1998, The Knot Ultimate Wedding Planner, 1999, The Knot Book of Wedding Vows & Traditions, 2000, The Knot Book of Wedding Gowns, 2001, The Knot Book of Wedding Flowers, 2002, The Knot Complete Guide to Weddings in the Real World, 2003, The Knot Guide for the Groom, 2005, The Knot Guide for the Mother of the Bride, 2005; author: (foreword) Forever & a Day, 1999; author: (syndicated column) Ask Carley, 2003—; contbr.: NY Times, Wall St. Jour, USA Today, Glamour, Vogue, Elle, Self, Naples Daily News; appearances on Oprah, The View, ABC, Today Show, NBC, The Early Show, CBS. Achievements include The Knot named Best Wedding Hub 4 years in a row by Yahoo! Internet Life. Office: The Knot 6th Fl 462 Broadway New York NY 10013 Office Phone: 212-219-0724. Office Fax: 212-219-1929.*

**RONEY, GLEN E.,** finance company executive; Chmn., pres., CEO Tex. Regional Bancshares, Inc., McAllen, Tex., 1978—. Office: Texas Regional Bancshares Inc 3900 N 10th Fl Mcallen TX 78501

**RONEY, JOHN M.,** lawyer; b. Sept. 21, 1939; m. Barbara Kennedy; children: Christopher, Carley, Kristina. BA, Providence Coll.; JD, Cath. U. Am.; degree (hon.), Katherine Gibbs Sch., 2002. Senator R.I. State Senate, 1994—2002; sr. staff atty. R.I. Legal Svcs., 1970—75; assoc. Winograd Shine & Zacks, PC, 1975—78; ptnr. Mann & Roney, 1978—83, Roney & Labinger LLP, Providence, 1983—. Dep. majority leader, vice chair fin., health, edn. welfare R.I. State Senate. Mem. Leadership R.I., R.I. Coun. on Alcoholism, Narragansett Bay Commn., 1996—2003; bd. dirs. Sophia Acad., 2003—, Katherine Gibbs Sch., 2002—, R.I. Philharmonic, 1996—2001, Family Svc., Inc., 1973—90, pres., 1987—89; mem. neighborhood coun. Mayor, 2003—; mem. R.I. Commn. Women, 2000—03, R.I. Retirement Bd., 1998—2003. Recipient Dorothy Lohmann Cmty. Svc. award, 1995, Unsung Hero award, R.I. Assn. Developmentally Disabled Children, 1999, Bronze Key award, Nat. Coun. Alcoholism, 1999, Disting. Alumni award, Cath. U. Am., 2004. Mem.: R.I. Bar Assn. (pres.-elect 2002—03, exec. com., pres. 2003—04, pres. 1999—2002, sec. 2000—01), Fox Point Citizens Assn. (bd. dirs. 2002—). Democrat. Office: Roney & Labinger LLP 344 Wickenden St Providence RI 02903 Office Phone: 401-421-9794.

**RONEY, PAUL HITCH,** federal judge; b. Olney, Ill., Sept. 5, 1921; m. Sarah E. Eustis; children: Susan M., Paul Hitch Jr., Timothy Eustis. Student, St. Petersburg Jr. Coll., 1938—40; BS in Econs., U. Pa., 1942; LLB, Harvard U., 1948; LLD, Stetson U., 1977; I I M U. Va., 1949. Bar: N.Y. 1949, Fla. 1950. Assoc. Root, Ballantine, Harlan, Bushby & Palmer, N.Y.C., 1948—50; ptnr. Mann, Harrison, Roney, Mann & Masterson (and predecessors), St. Petersburg, Fla., 1950—57; pvt. practice, 1957—63; ptnr. Roney & Beach, St. Petersburg, 1963—69, Roney, Ulmer, Woodworth & Jacobs, St. Petersburg, 1969—70; judge U.S. Ct. Appeals (5th cir.), St. Petersburg, 1970—81, U.S. Ct. Appeals (11th cir.), St. Petersburg, 1981—86, chief judge, 1986—89, sr. cir. judge, 1989—. Adv. com. on adminstrv. law judges U.S. CSC, 1976—77; pres. judge U.S. Fgn. Intelligence Surveillance Ct. of Rev., 1994—2001; lectr. Stetson U. Coll. of Law. With U.S. Army, 1942—46. Fellow: Am. Bar Found.; mem.: ABA (chmn. legal adv. com. Fair Trial-Free Press 1973—76, task force on cts. and public 1973—76, jud. adminstrn. divsn., chmn. appellate judges conf. 1978—79, Gavel Awards com. 1980—83), Jud. Conf. U.S. (subcom. on jud. improvements 1978—84, exec. com. 1986—89, com. to review circuit coun. conduct and disability orders 1991—93), Nat. Jud. Coll. (faculty 1974—75), St. Peturbug Bar Assn. (pres. 1964—65), Fla. Bar Assn., Am. Law Inst., Am. Judicature Soc. (bd. dirs. 1972—76); Office: US Ct Appeals Bank of Am One Progress Plz 200 Central Ave Saint Petersburg FL 33701-3326*

**RONEY, ROBERT KENNETH,** retired aerospace transportation executive; b. Newton, Iowa, Aug. 5, 1922; s. Louie Earl and Hazel Iona (Cure) R.; m. Alice Lorraine Mann, Oct. 6, 1951; children: Stephen P., Karen Margaret Dahl. BSEE, U. Mo., 1944; MSEE, Calif. Inst. Tech., 1947, PhD, 1950. Engr. rsch. Jet Propulsion Lab. Calif. Inst. Tech., Pasadena, 1948-50, Hughes Aircraft Co., Culver City, Calif., 1950-54, mgr. sys. analysis, 1955-59, dir. tech. R&D, 1960, assoc. mgr. space sys. divsn., 1961-68, mgr. space sys. divsn., 1968-70, v.p. asst. group exec., 1970-83, sr. v.p. corp. tech., 1986-88, ret., 1988. Mem. adv. bd. Dept. Aerospace Sci. Space Transp., 1984-87, Engring. Sch. U. Kans., 1988-91. Lt. (j.g.) USNR, 1944-46, PTO. Recipient Honor award for Disting. Svc. in Engring. U. Mo.-Columbia, 1979. Fellow IEEE; mem. NAE, Caltech Assocs. Home: 1105 Georgina Ave Santa Monica CA 90402-2027

**RONG, HAISHENG,** research scientist; s. Chengzhen Rong and Yaqin Guan; m. Qi Tian; children: Robert, Clara. BS (hon.), Nankai U., Tianjin, China, 1983, MS, 1986; PhD, U. Heidelberg, Germany, 1992. Rschr. U. oHeidelberg, Germany, 1992—96, MIT, Cambridge, 1996—98, Calif. Inst. of Tech., Pasadena, 1998—2000, Intel Corp., Santa Clara, Calif., 2000—. Contbr. articles to profl. jours. Recipient Achievement award, Intel Corp., 2004, Rsch. Leader, Sci. Am., 2005. Mem.: IEEE, Materials Rsch. Soc., Internat. Soc. for Optical Engring., Optical Soc. of Am. Achievements include development of the world's first continuous-wave Raman silicon laser. Office: Intel Corp 2200 Mission College Blvd Santa Clara CA 95054 Office Phone: 408-765-0331.

**RONG, SHU,** materials scientist, researcher; b. QingDao, ShanDong, China, Oct. 15, 1972; arrived in U.S., 1998; s. Yuexin Shu and Yong Li; m. Hua G Shu. PhD (hon.), China Acad.Sci U. Sci.Tech.China, Hefei, 1993—98; M in Materials Sci., U. Houston - Clearlake, 2002. Rsch. engr. U. Science and Tech. China, Hefei, Anhui, China, 1994—98; cons RHIC, Houston, 2001; sr. rsch. engr. Rock Solid Images, Houston, 2001—. Author: (Journal) several papers; contbr. articles to profl. jours. Mem.: AAAS, Am. Phys. Soc. Home: 14915 Sugar Cup Ct Sugar Land TX 77478 Office: Rock Solid Images 2600 S Gessner Ste 650 Houston TX 77099

**RONGEN, THOMAS,** professional soccer coach; b. Netherlands, Oct. 31, 1956; arrived in US, 1979; m. Gail Megaloudis, Apr. 13, 1996. AA in Lang., Snellius Lyceum, Netherlands; MA in Phys. Edn. and Recreation, Central Inst. for Training of Sportsleaders, Netherlands. "A" coaching lic. U.S. Soccer Fedn., Dutch coaching lic.; cert. in sports massage Netherlands Sports Fedn. Midfielder/defender LA Aztecs, 1979, Wash. Diplomats, 1980, Strikers, Ft. Lauderdal, 1980-84, 86, Chgo., 1984-86; asst. coach Nova Southeastern U., 1986-92, head coach, 1992-96; coach New England Revolution, 1996-98; head coach DC United, 1999—2001, US Nat. Men's Under-20 Team, 2001—. Dir. coaching and player devel. Plantation (Fla.) Eagles Soccer Club, coach Am. Soccer League All-Star team, 1991. Named MLS Coach of the Yr., 1996, Am. Soccer League Coach of the Yr., 1991.

**RONSTADT, LINDA MARIE,** singer; b. Tucson, July 15, 1946; d. Gilbert and Ruthmary (Copeman) R. Rec. artist numerous albums including Evergreen 1967, Evergreen Vol. 2, 1967, Linda Ronstadt, The Stone Poneys and Friends, Vol. 3, 1968, Hand Sown, Home Grown, 1969, Silk Purse, 1970, Linda Ronstadt, 1972, Don't Cry Now, 1973, Heart Like a Wheel, 1974, Different Drum, 1974, Prisoner In Disguise, 1975, Hasten Down the Wind, 1976, Greatest Hits, 1976, Simple Dreams, Blue Bayou, 1977, Living in the U.S.A., 1978, Mad Love, Greatest Hits Vol. II, 1980, Get Closer, 1982, What's New, 1983, Lush Life, 1984, For Sentimental Reasons, 1986, Trio (with Dolly Parton, Emmylou Harris), 1986, 'Round Midnight, 1987, Canciones de Mi Padre, 1987, Cry Like a Rainstorm-Howl Like the Wind, 1989, Mas Canciones, 1991, Frenesi, 1992, Winter Light, 1993, Feels Like Home, 1995, Dedicated to the One I Love, 1996, We Ran, 1998, Trio 2, 1999 (with Emmylou Harris & Dolly Parton), Western Wall: The Tucson Sessions (with Emmylou Harris), A Merry Little Christmas, 2000, Hummin' to Myself, 2004, Adieu False Heart, 2006; starred in Broadway prodn. of Pirates of Penzance, 1981, also in film, 1983, off Broadway as Mimi in La Boheme, 1984. Recipient Am. Music awards, 1978, 1979, Grammy awards, 1975, 1976, 1987 (with Emmylou Harris and Dolly Parton), 1988, 1989 (with Aaron Neville), 1990, 1991, (with Aaron Neville), 1992 (2), 1996, 2000, Acad. Country Music award, 1987, 1988; named one of 100 Greatest Women of Rock 'n' Roll, VH1, 1999. Office: Electra Records 75 Rockefeller Plz New York NY 10019-6908

**ROOBOL, NORMAN RICHARD,** chemistry professor, consultant; b. Grand Rapids, Mich., Aug. 19, 1934; s. Pleune and Henrietta (Sietsema) Roobol; m. Joan Lois Ezinga, Aug. 15, 1957; children: Kerri Linda, Michael Eric, Victoria May, Sara Elizabeth Angelique. BS, Calvin Coll., 1958; PhD in Organic Chemistry, Mich. State U., 1962. Rsch. chemist Shell Oil Co., Emeryville, Calif., 1962-65; asst. prof. chemistry GMI Engring. Inst., Flint, Mich., 1965-68, assoc. prof., asst. head dept. math., sci., 1968-72, prof., 1972-89; pres. NR Painting Cons. Co., Peachtree City, Ga., 1989—. Rhodes prof., Russelsheim, Germany, 1980—81; tchr. short courses paint; cons. coatings application processes; spkr. indsl. painting methods; painting advisor, instr. Outboard Marine Corp., 1986—2001, Bombardier Can., 1988—, Compaq-Asia, Singapore, 1991—, Harley-Davidson, 1992—, Metagal Commercie e Industri, San Paulo, Brazil, 1996—, Decometal S.A., Panama City, Panama, 1997—2001, J. R. McDermott Corp., Jebel Ali, 2000—; adj. prof. Kent (Ohio) State U., 1986—94, Okla. State U., 1994—98, U. Wis., 1992—2001; chmn. Peruvian Decorative & Protective Finishes Coun., 2005—. Author: (book) Painting Problems Solved, 1987, Industrial Paint and Powder Coating Principles and Practices, 3d edit., 2003; monthly columnist, tech. editor: Indsl. Paint and Powder Jour.; contbr. articles to profl. jours. Treas. Fayette (Ga.) Cmty. Hosp.; bd. dirs. With Signal Corps U.S. Army, 1954—56. Fellow Johnson, 1957—58, NSF, 1960—62, Dow, 1961—62. Fellow: Am. Inst. Chemists; mem.: AAUP, Assn. Finishings Proc. (v.p. profl. devel. coun.), Soc. Mfg. Engrs. (bd. dirs.), Am. Sci. Affiliation, Atlanta Oenophilic Soc., Pi Tau Sigma (chpt. sr. adviser 1979—86), Alpha Tau Omega, Sigma Xi. Achievements include patents in field. Home and Office: Powder Coating & Painting Cons 507 Haddington Ln Peachtree City GA 30269-3340 Personal E-mail: drpaint@consultant.com.

**ROOD, DAVID S.,** linguistics educator; b. Albany, NY, Sept. 14, 1940; s. J. Henry and Pearl B. (Stanley) R.; m. Juliette A. Victor; 1 child, Jennifer. AB, Cornell U., 1963; MA, U. Calif., Berkeley, 1965; PhD, U. Calif., 1969. Instr. U. Colo., Boulder, 1967-69, asst. prof., 1969-77, assoc. prof., 1977-82, prof., 1982—; vis. prof. U. Köln, Germany, 1998-99. Author: Wichita Grammar, 1975, Siouan Languages Archive, 1982; (with others) Beginning Lakhota, 1976; editor Internat. Jour. of Am. Linguistics, 1981-2002, (with others) Linguistic Diversity and Language Theories, 2005; contbr. articles to profl. jours. Grantee NSF, 1972-96, 06-, NEH, 1972-96, Volkswagen Stiftung, 2000-05. Mem.: Tchrs. English to Speakers Other Langs., Soc. for Study Indigenous Langs. Am. (pres. 2004), Linguistic Soc. Am. Office: U Colo Dept Linguistics 295 UCB Boulder CO 80309-0295 Office Phone: 303-492-2747. Business E-Mail: rood@colorado.edu.

**ROODMAN, DAVID A.,** lawyer; b. St. Louis, Apr. 17, 1962; BSME, U. Mo., 1984, JD, 1990. Bar: Mo., Ill., U.s. Dist. Ct. (ea. dist.) Mo., U.S. Patent and Trademark Office, U.s. Ct. Appeals (fed. cir.), U.S. Dist. Ct. (so. dist.) Ill. Mech. design engr. Unidynamics Corp., St. Louis, 1985; sales engr. Reliance Elec. Co., Kansas City, Mo., 1985-87; assoc. Bryan Cave LLP, St. Louis, 1990, ptnr., group co-leader Intellectual Property. Assoc. editor-in-chief Mo. Law Rev. Mem. ABA (intellectual property law sect., patent legislation com., litigation sect.), Mo. Bar Assn. (civil practice and procedure com., tech. and computer law com., patent, trademark and copyright law com.), Order of Coif, Order of Barristers. Office: Bryan Cave One Metropolitan Sq 211 N Broadway Saint Louis MO 63102-2733 Office Phone: 314-259-2614. E-mail: daroodman@bryancave.com.

**ROOF, ROBERT L.,** broadcast executive, sales executive; b. Circleville, Ohio, Apr. 15, 1946; s. Roger D. and Doris (Kraft) R.; m. Linda Anderson, Nov. 28, 1969; children: Jennifer, Leslie. BA, Franklin U. Sales, disc jockey Sta. WPKO Radio, Waverly, Ohio, 1969-72, Sta. WSCR Radio, Scranton, Pa., 1972-75; sales Sta. WSPD Radio, Toledo, Ohio, 1975-78, Sta. WTVN Radio, Columbus, Ohio, 1978-81, local sales mgr., 1981-83, gen. sales mgr., 1984-87; v.p., gen. mgr. Sta. WDVE Radio, Pitts., 1987-93, pres., gen. mgr., 1993—. Bd. dirs. Southwest PA Jr. Achievement, Pitts., 1994—. Recipient Bronze Leadership award Jr. Achievement, Pitts., 1994. Mem. Columbus Sales Club (pres. 1982), Pitts. Sales Club (pres. 1989), Pitts. Radio Orgn. (pres. 1994). Methodist. Avocations: golf, hunting, history. Office: Sta WDVE-FM 200 Fleet St Pittsburgh PA 15220-2908

**ROOF, SALLY JEAN-MARIE,** library and information scientist, educator; b. Cleve., Dec. 29, 1947; d. James William and Marie Monreal Roof; m. Christian John Hoffmann III, Sept. 22, 1973; children: Christian Graham Hoffmann, Joscelyn Nicole Hoffmann, Gavin Leigh Hoffmann. BA in English Lit., Dunbarton Coll. of Holy Cross, Washington, D. C., 1969; MS in Libr. and Info. Sci., Cath. U. of Am., 1972; degree in Profl. Mgmt. (hon.), Miami U., 1976; MA in Elem. Edn., No. Ariz. U., 2001. Cert. tchr. in libr. media ctr. adminstrn. Nat. Bd. of Cert. Tchrs., 2004. Asst. libr. U.S. Postal Svc. Libr., Washington, 1971—72; head of acquisitions George Wash. U. Libr., Washington, 1972—74; libr. adminstr. and mgr. Calgon Corp. Libr. Merck Inc., Pitts., 1974—77; libr. info. specialist U. of Phoenix, 1979—81; reference libr. Grand Canyon U., Phoenix, 1990—91; reference libr. West Campus Libr. Ariz. State U., Phoenix, 1994—95; libr. tchr. info. specialist Madison Meadows Sch., Phoenix, 1998—. Libr. cons. U. of Phoenix, 1981—82; presenter Ariz. Libr. Assn., Scottsdale, 2003; mem., presenter People to People Amb. Program Children's Lit. Del., Spokane, Wash., 2004; participant rep., 04; cons. in field. Editor: Serial Titles in the Washington, D. C. University Consortium Libraries, No School Left Behind at Your Library. Librarians Meet Arizona Legislators, 2004; author: (pamphlet) Madison Meadows Library Media Center; designer (school website) Madison Meadows Sch. website. Chmn. grade level patroness Nat. Charity League, Phoenix, 1994—99; pres. Phoenix (Ariz.) Mus. of History, 1991—94. Mem.: ALA (assoc.), Ariz. Libr. Assn. (assoc.), Phi Kappa Phi, Beta Phi Mu, Jr. League of Phoenix. Democrat-Npl. Roman Catholic. Avocations: yoga, fast walking, reading, bicycling. Office: Madison Meadows School 225 W Ocotillo Rd Phoenix AZ 85013 Office Phone: 602-664-7640. Personal E-mail: sroofhoff@cox.net. E-mail: sroof@msd38.org.

**ROOK, JUDITH RAWIE,** television producer, writer; d. Wilmer Ernest and Margaret Jane (Towle) Rawie; m. Dr. John Holland, 1964 (div. 1978); children: Daryn Simons, Dawn Reinard; m. Tim Rook, 1993. BA, Loyola-Marymount Univ., 1964; postgrad., U. Calif., San Diego, 1978. Syndicated columnist Environ. Forum, 1971-74; dir. video IABC, San Francisco, 1982; dir. programming Westinghouse Cable, 1983-85; dir. devel. Embassy/Nelson Home Entertainment, 1990-91; ptnr. Real Magic, 1987-89; prodr., writer, ptnr. BrantHol Prodns., 1990-93; co-sponsorship Beetle Juice, The Last Emperor, 1987—89; founder, pres. R2 Group, 1990—. Assoc. dir.: (off-broadway play) Arms and the Man, 1967; The Man Who Came to Dinner, 1981; exec. prodr.: Neighborhood Without Bars (Emmy award, 1986); prodr., writer: PBS series Focus, 1980; Achieving, 1982 (Emmy award, ACE nominee, PBS nominee); NBC pilot Christmas Comes to Silverton, 1990—93; CNN pilot Clever Encounters, 1991; prodr.: One Creative Moment, 1992, Close up: The 60s, 1995—97; assoc. prodr.: Fox Latin Am. Billboard Music Awards, 1998—2000; (TV pilot) Fempresario, 2005; assoc. prodr. (documentaries) Rising From the Plains Revisited, 2005, (films) Somewhere in Between, 2005; playwright: Theatre 40 Writer's Workshop Anniversary for Three, 2003; assoc. prodr.: (films) Highway 101, 2005—. Mem. adv. bd. U. Calif. Irvine Screenwriting/Film Prodn., 1996-2000; mem. adv. bd. Univ. Art Mus., 1996-97, co-pres. contemporary coun., 1996-97; mem. exec. bd. Long Beach Mus. Art, 1995-96; bd. dirs. Counseling 4 Kids, 1998-2005, bd. sec., 2001-2005; editor: bd. LWV, Santa Monica, 2004-05, Getty Mus., 2005-. Mem. Am. Film Inst., Women in Film (dir. seminars on women in film), IFP West. Democrat. Episcopalian. Office Phone: 310-633-3292. Personal E-mail: tirook@earthlink.net.

**ROOK, VICKI LYNN,** safety specialist; b. Denton, Tex., Oct. 14, 1954; d. Lonzo Lester and Myrtle Jodelle Roberts; m. Rickey Hugh Rook, Jan. 27, 1979; children: Brandon Nicholas, Katy Lynn Student, Richland Jr. Coll., Dallas, 1974-75. Safety supr. United Parcel Svc., Dallas, 1975-81; safety administr. Boeing Airport Equipment, Carrollton, Tex., 1981-83; safety rep. Loral Vought Sys., Grand Prairie, Tex., 1983-95; sr. safety specialist Fed. Express Corp., Dallas, 1995—. Mem. workers comp claims mgmt. various cos., Dallas, 1975—; mgr. union contract negotiation Boeing Airport Equipment, Dallas, 1983; com. mem. mgmt. safety program Fed. Express, Memphis, 1997-2001 Tchr. Sunday sch. Walnut Ridge Bapt. Ch., Mansfield, Tex., 1978; 1st Bapt. Ch., Grand Prairie, 1980-82, counselor ch. camp, 1980-82; vol. ednl. TV Loral Vought Sys., Dallas, 1993. Named Safety Specialist of Yr. Fed. Express, 1997. Mem. Am. Soc. Safety Engineers, Nat. Safety Coun. Republican. Office: Fed Express 4500 W Mockingbird Ln Dallas TX 75247-4929 Office Phone: 469-524-4623. Business E-Mail: vlrook@fedex.com.

**ROOKE, ALLEN DRISCOLL, JR.,** civil engineer, consultant; b. San Antonio, Oct. 5, 1924; s. Allen Driscoll and Jean Edna (Lackner) R.; m. Betty Ruth Whitson, Oct. 17, 1949; children: Victoria Lynn Lewis, Cornelia Ruth. BSCE, Tex. A&M U., 1957; MSCE, Miss. State U., 1980. Registered prof. engr., Miss. Enlisted U.S. Army, 1942, advanced through grades to brig. gen., ret., 1984; rsch. civil engr. U.S. Army Corps Engrs., Vicksburg, Miss., 1958-83; ptnr. F.B. Rooke & Sons, Woodsboro, Tex., 1964—; sr. engr. Sci & Tech. Corp., Vicksburg, Miss., 1984-95. Bd. dirs. First Nat. Bank, Woodsboro, 1985—. Contbr. articles to profl. jours. Mem. Res. Officers Assn. U.S. (dept. pres. 1980-82, svc. award 1980, 84), Assn. of U.S. Army, Ret. Officer's Assn. (chpt. v.p. 1985-86), Soc. Am. Mil. Engrs. (post v.p. 1979). Clubs: Army and Navy Vicksburg (pres. 1980, 82). Episcopalian. Avocation: chess.

**ROOKE, BEN G.,** finance company executive, lawyer; b. Charleston, W.Va., Apr. 22, 1949; Student, Cedarville Coll.; BA cum laude, Wheaton Coll., 1973; JD, Ohio State U., 1976. Bar: Pa. 1977, U.S. Dist. Ct. (we. dist.) Pa. 1978, U.S. Supreme Ct. 1989. Asst. counsel Pennbancorp, Titusville, Pa., 1978-81; vice chmn., gen. coun., sec. Keystone Fin., Harrisburg, Pa. With U.S. Army, 1969-70. Mem. ABA, Am. Bankers Assn. (mem. legal affairs com. 1992—), Pa. Bar Assn., Pa. Bankers Assn. (mem. legal adv. com. 1988-93, vice chmn., gen. counsel, sec.). Office: 3607 Derry St Harrisburg PA 17111-1920

**ROOKE, DAVID LEE,** retired chemical company executive; b. San Antonio, Tex., May 2, 1923; s. Henry Levi, Jr. and Annie (Davidson) R.; m. Esthermae Litherland, June 2, 1945; children— Eugene, Mark, Paul, Bruce. BS in Chem. Engring, Rice Inst., Houston, 1944; postgrad., U. Houston. With Dow Chem., Midland, Mich., 1946-88, v.p. ops., 1977-78; pres. Dow U.S.A., 1978-82; v.p. Dow Chem. Corp., 1978-82, exec. v.p., 1982-83, sr. v.p., 1983-86, sr. cons., 1986-88, ret., 1988. Bd. dirs. Dow Corning Corp., James Avery Craftsman, Inc. Nat. exec. bd. Boy Scouts Am., 1979-86; bd. dirs. Meth. Mission Home, San Antonio. Served with USNR, 1944-46. Mem. AICE, United Meth. Reporter Found. (Dallas). Methodist.

**ROOKE, WILLIAM WEBSTER,** retired music educator; b. Glens Falls, N.Y., Jan. 1, 1939; s. George Harris and Mildred Webster Rooke; m. Katherine Jean Cooley, July 3, 1967; 1 child, Fawn Jeanette. AS in Math., Clinton C.C., Plattsburgh, N.Y.; BS, SUNY, Potsdam, 1961; MusM, Kans. State Tchr.'s Coll., Emporia, 1968. Permanent tchg. cert. music K-12 N.Y., 1968, permanent tchg. cert. math. 7-12 N.Y. Tchr. music Plattsburgh City Sch., NY, 1961—69; tchr. music grades K-12 Dannemora Union Free Sch., NY, 1969—89; tchr. music grades 4-8 Saranac Ctrl. Sch., NY, 1989—96. Musician: Plattsburgh Coll. Cmty. Orch., 1970—2000. Mem.: Music Educator's Nat. Conf., N.Y. State Sch. Music Assn. (past zone rep., on site coord. winter conf. 1998—, chair various sch. music festivals), Nat. Model Railroader Assn. Methodist. Avocation: model railroading.

**ROOKLIDGE, WILLIAM CHARLES,** lawyer; b. Portland, Oreg., Aug. 10, 1957; s. Chester Herbert and Barbara Kathryn (Dodson) R.; m. Kathryn Elaine Roosa, Aug. 20, 1983; children: Elizabeth Jill, Matthew Joseph. BS, U. Portland, 1979; JD, Lewis & Clark, 1984; LLM, George Washington U., 1985. Bar: Oreg. 1985, U.S. Patent Office 1985, U.S. Ct. Appeals (fed. cir.) 1985, Calif. 1988, U.S. Ct. Appeals (9th cir.) 1988, U.S. Supreme Ct. 1993. Engr. Tube Forgings Am., Inc., Portland, 1978-82; jud. clk. U.S. Ct. Appeals (fed. cir.), Washington, 1985-87; assoc. Knobbe, Martens, Olson & Bear, Newport Beach, Calif., 1987-89; ptnr., 1990-94; dir. Howard, Rice, Nemerovski, Canady, Falk & Rabkin, Newport Beach, Calif., 1995—2000. Contbr. articles to profl. jours. Recipient Joseph Rossman Meml. award Patent & Trademark Office Soc., 1988, Gerald Rose Meml. award John Marshall Law Sch., 1993. Mem. ABA (sect. intellectual property law, com. chair 1992-96), Am. Intellectual Property Law Assn. (com. chair 1988-93, dir. 1995-98, pres. 2005, Robert C. Watson award 1987), Orange County Patent Law Assn. (bd. dirs. 1990-93, pres. 1994). Republican. Presbyterian. Office: Howrey LLP 2020 Main St Ste 1000 Irvine CA 92614-8224 Office Phone: 949-759-3904. Office Fax: 949-721-6910. Business E-Mail: rooklidgew@howrey.com.

**ROOKS, CHARLES S.,** foundation administrator; b. Whiteville, NC, June 29, 1937; BA in English, Wake Forest Coll., 1959; Rockefeller Brothers fellow, Harvard U., 1959-60; MA in Polit. Sci., Duke U., 1964, PhD in Polit. Sci., 1968. Rsch. assoc. Voter Edn. Project, Atlanta, 1969-70, dir. tech. assistance programs, 1970-71, dep. dir., 1971-72; exec. dir. Southeastern Coun. of Founds., Atlanta, 1972-78; dir. mem. svcs. Coun. on Founds., Washington, 1979-80, v.p., 1981-82, acting CEO, 1987-88; exec. dir. Meyer Meml. Trust, Portland, Oreg., 1982—. Instr. polit. sci. Duke U., Durham, N.C., 1963, 65-67; asst. prof. of govt. Lake Forest Coll., Ill., 1967-69; asst. prof. polit. sci. Clark Coll., Atlanta, 1969-71; bd. dirs. Pacific Northwest Grantmakers Forum, Forum of Regional Assns. of Grantmakers; mem. adv. bd. Neighborhood Partnership Fund (Oreg. Cmty. Found.); mem., adv. bd. Giving in Oreg. Coun.; co-chair Northwest Giving Project. Contbr. articles to profl. jours. Home: 2706 SW English Ct Portland OR 97201-1622

**ROOKS, LINDA,** writer; d. Harold John and Marianna Wieck; m. Marvin Edward Rooks, Dec. 19, 1967; children: Juliana Wolf, Laura Katherine. BA, San Francisco State U., 1965. Tchr. Seminole Jr. H.S., Fla., 1970—72; pro-life liaison for Paula Hawkins senatorial campaign Nat. Right to Life, Winter Park, Fla., 1986; asst. editor Ctr. Stage Mag., Maitland, Fla., 1987—89; office coord., newsletter editor Adoption by Shepherd Care, Orlando, Fla., 1994—2000; freelance writer Maitland, 2000—. Author: Broken Heart on Hold, 2006, (devotional) Tapestry; scriptwriter: radio and tv Testimony of An Unborn Child (Cammeo Award for Best of Show, 1987); contbr. articles to profl. jours. Pres. Ctrl. Fla. Right to Life, 1984—85, 1990—96; staff position state coord. for families Bob Dole Presdl. Campaign, Fla., 1995—96; pub. rels. co-chmn. Nat. Right to Life Conv., Orlando, 1983. Mem.: Word Weavers Writers Group (sec. steering com. 2002—). Republican. Avocation: travel. Office: PO Box 241 Winter Park FL 32790-0241 Personal E-mail: linda@brokenheartonhold.com.

**ROONEY, ANDREW AITKEN,** writer, journalist; b. Albany, N.Y., Jan. 14, 1919; s. Walter S. and Ellinor (Reynolds) R.; m. Marguerite Howard, Mar. 21, 1942; children: Ellen, Martha, Emily, Brian. Student, Colgate U., 1942. Writer-producer CBS-TV News, 1959—; newspaper columnist Tribune Co. Syndicate, 1979—. Author: (with O.C. Hutton) Air Gunner, 1944, The Story of Stars and Stripes, 1946, Conquerors' Peace, 1947, The Fortunes of War, 1962, A Few Minutes with Andy Rooney, 1981, And More By Andy Rooney, 1982, Pieces of My Mind, 1984, Word for Word, 1986, Not That You Asked, 1989, Sweet and Sour, 1992, My War, 1995, Sincerely, Andy Rooney, 1999, Common Nonsense, 2002, Years of Minutes, 2003; TV programs include An Essay on War, Mr. Rooney Goes to Washington, Mr. Rooney Goes to Dinner; regular commentator-essayist: 60 Minutes, 1978—. Served with AUS, 1941-45. Decorated Air Medal, Bronze Star; recipient awards for best written TV documentary Writers Guild Am., 1966, 68, 71, 75, 76, Emmy awards, 1968, 78, 81, 82

**ROONEY, DANIEL M.,** professional football team executive; b. Pitts., July 20, 1932; s. Arthur Joseph and Kathleen (McNulty) Rooney; m. Patricia Rooney; 9 children. BA in Acctg., Dusquene Univ., 1955. Former salesman advt., editor, other positions Pitts. Steelers Program, 1955—75; pres. Pitts. Steelers, 1975—; mem. exec. coms. NFL. Bd. dir. United Way of Am., Am. Ireland Fund, Am. Diabetes Assn., Presbyn. Univ. Hosp., Pitts. History and Landmarks Found., Dusquesne Univ. Recipient Reds Bagnell award for Outstanding Contributions to the Game of Football, Maxwell Football Club, 1999. Achievements include presented with Vince Lombardi Trophy for the winning team, Pittsburgh Steelers at Super Bowl XL in 2006. Office: Three Rivers Stadium 3400 S Water St Pittsburgh PA 15203-2349

**ROONEY, FRANCIS,** ambassador; married; 3 children. AB, Georgetown U., 1975, JD, 1978. Bar: DC, Tex.; 100-Ton Master's Lic. U.S. Coast Guard. CEO Rooney Holdings, Inc., Naples, Fla.; US amb. to Holy See US Dept. State, Vatican City, 2005—. Vice-chmn. Okla. Turnpike Authority; dir. Okla.

Capital Investment Bd.; dir. 20/20 com., Wash. adv. coun. Ctr. Strategic and Internat. Studies, Washington; officer Tex. Bus. Hall of Fame, Houston; dir. Inst. Nautical Archaeology, College Station, Tex., Young President's Orgn., 1992—98, internat. pres., 1997—98. Bd. dirs., chmn. strategic planning com. St. Francis Health Sys., Okla.; chmn. bd. Cascia Hall Preparatory Sch., Tulsa; mem. sch. of architecture coun. U. Notre Dame; mem. Fla. Coun. 100. Mem.: Sovereign Mil. Order of Malta. Office: Am Embassy 5660 Vatican City Pl Washington DC 20521*

**ROONEY, JOE DON,** country musician; b. Baxter Springs, Kans., Sept. 13, 1975; s. Windell and Jo Rooney. Student, A&M Jr. Coll. (Northwestern Okla. A&M). Performer Printers Alley, Nashville, Chely Wright Band; guitarist Rascal Flatts, 2000—. Music: (albums) East to West, 1993, Rascal Flatts, 2000, Melt, 2002, Feels Like Today, 2004 (Group/Duo Video of Yr., Country Music Television Music awards, 2005), Me and My Gang, 2006; performer: (songs) "Walk the Llama Llama", Emperor's New Grove (Original Soundtrack), 2000. Recipient Vocal Group Yr., Country Music Assn., 2002, 2004, 2005, Song Yr. for "I'm Movin On", Acad. Country Music Awards, 2002, Top Vocal Group, 2003, 2005, 2006, Country Song Yr. for Bless the Broken Road, Radio Music Awards, 2005, Best Country Song, Grammy Awards, 2006, Group/Duo Video of Yr. for Skin (Sarabeth), CMT Awards (Country Music TV), 2006. Office: Lyric Street Records 1100 Demonbreun St Nashville TN 37203-3108 Office Phone: 615-963-4848.*

**ROONEY, JOHN EDWARD,** communications company executive; b. Evergreen Park, Ill., Apr. 24, 1942; s. John Edward and Margaret Wilma (Stolte) R.; m. Germaine Rose Dettloff, June 26, 1965; children: Kathleen, John, Colleen. BS, John Carroll U., 1964; MBA, Loyola U., 1969. Credit analyst Fed. Res. Bank, Chgo., 1964-69, adminstrv. asst., 1969-70; asst. treas. Pullman Inc., 1970-73, asst. contr., 1973-78; v.p. fin. Pullman Standard, 1978-79; sr. v.p. fin. Trailmobile, Chgo., 1979-81; treas. Firestone Tire & Rubber Co., Akron, Ohio, 1981-87, v.p. retail fin. services, 1987-88, sr. v.p. MasterCare Svc. Ctrs., 1988-90; v.p., treas. Ameritech, Chgo., 1990-92; pres. Ameritech Cellular Svcs., Chgo., 1992—. Instr. fin. Ill. Benedictine Coll., 1975-80 Mem. Ohio Mfrs. Assn. (trustee 1983-87), Ohio Pub. Expenditure Coun. (trustee 1986-87), Glen Oak Country Club (Glen Ellyn, Ill.), Boulders Club (Carefree, Ariz.), The Tavern Club (Chgo.). Home: 2S 311 Davis Ct Wheaton IL 60187 Office: Ameritech # 3H 70 2000 W Ameritech Center Dr Hoffman Estates IL 60196-1025

**ROONEY, KEVIN DAVITT,** lawyer; b. Springfield, Mass., June 23, 1944; s. Davitt Michael and Elizabeth Isabel (Wlodyka) R.; m. Annette Eloise Benevento, Nov. 11, 1972; children: Kathryn Denise, Mary Elizabeth. BA, St. Marys Coll., 1966; JD, George Washington U., 1975. Bar: Va. 1975, D.C. 1977. Computer systems analyst VA, Washington, 1967-68, 70-73; chief legal programs and budget Dept. Justice, Washington, 1973-77, exec. asst. to assoc. atty. gen., 1977, asst. atty. gen. for adminstrn., 1977-84; prin. Rooney & Assocs, Washington, 1984-87, 90-94, Rooney & Barry, Washington, 1987-89; assoc. dir. Exec. Office for Immigration Rev. Dept. Justice, Falls Church, Va., 1995-97, asst. dir. Fed. Bur. Prisons Washington, 1997-99, dir. Exec. Office for Immigration Falls Church, Va., 1999—, acting commr. Immigration and Naturalization Svc., 2001. Bd. dirs., v.p. Joint Action in Cmty. Svcs., Inc., Washington, 1988-94. With U.S. Army, 1968-70. Mem. ASPA, Fed. Bar Assn., Va. Bar Assn., D.C. Bar Assn. Office: Executive Office for Immigration Review 5107 Leesburg Pike Falls Church VA 22041

**ROONEY, LAURENCE FRANCIS, III,** ambassador to the Vatican, construction executive; b. Mar. 4, 1953; m. Kathleen Rooney; 3 children. AB, Georgetown U., 1975, JD, 1978. CEO Rooney Bros., Tulsa, Okla.; CEO, chmn. Rooney Holdings, Naples, Fla.; US ambassador to The Holy See, 2005—. Bd. dirs. BOL Fin. Corp., NASDAQ, Helmerich and Payne, Inc., NY Stock Exch., Cimarex Energy Co.; vice chmn. Okla. Turnpike Authority; dir. Okla. Capital Investment Bd., 20/20 com., Wash. Advisory Coun. Ctr. for Strategic and Internat. Studies; transition team for gov. elect Brad Henry State of Okla.; bd. advisors Panama Canal Authority Republic of Panama. Mem. Sch. of Architecture Coun. U. of Notre Dame; mem. Sovereign Military Order of Malta (Fed. Assn.). Mem.: Young President's Org. (dir. 1992—98, internat. pres. 1997—98). Republican. Roman Catholic. Office: Rooney Bros 111 W 5th St Ste 1000 Tulsa OK 74103-4264 also: Am Embassy to the Holy See via delle Terme Deciane 26 00153 Rome Italy Office Phone: (39) 06-4674-3428. Office Fax: (39) 06-575-8346.*

**ROONEY, MARIA DEWING,** photographer; b. N.Y.C., July 25; d. Madeleine L'Engle Franklin; m. John Bryan Rooney, Jan. 21, 1984; children: Bryson, Alexander. BFA, Phila. Coll. Art. Tchr. photography Bishop Bright Grammar Sch., Leamington Spa, Eng., Mid-Warwickshire Sch. of Further Edn., Leamington Spa, 1976-80; photographer, owner The Studios, Shipston-on-Stour, Eng., 1977-80; photographer Gary Studios & Comini Studios, Dallas, 1980-83; pvt. practice Mystic, Conn., 1990—. One-woman shows include Emporium Gallery, 2004, exhibitions include Warwick (Eng.) Gallery, Derby (Eng.) Coll. Art Gallery, Bath (Eng.) Pt. Cmty. Gallery, Midland Group Galley, Nottingham, Eng., Wimbledon Sch. Art, London, Warwich U. Arts Ctr., Birmingham, Eng., Essex Art Assn., 1998, R. J. Julia, Madison, Conn., 1998, State Capitol Hartford, Conn., 1999, Emporium Gallery, 2003, Brick Gallery, Essex, Conn., 2003, 2004, Emporium Gallery, 2004, Mystic Art Ctr., 2005; contbr. photographs Anytime Prayers, 1994, Mothers and Daughters, 1997, Mothers and Sons, 1999, photographs published in Co-Optic Publs., London, 1976—80; prodr.: series greeting cards with personal photography. Mem. Child and Family Svcs. Mem.: AAUW, Mystic Art Assn., Essex Art Assn. (photography award 1997, 2002, 2003). Avocations: sailing, writing. Home and Office: 77 High St Mystic CT 06355 Office Phone: 860-884-7582. E-mail: vlad0121@aol.com.

**ROONEY, MATTHEW A.,** lawyer; b. Jersey City, May 19, 1949; s. Charles John and Eileen (Dunphy) R.; m. Jean M. Alletag, June 20, 1973 (div. Dec. 1979); 1 child, Jessica Margaret; m. Diane S. Kaplan, July 6, 1981; children: Kathryn Olivia, S. Benjamin. AB magna cum laude, Georgetown U., 1971; JD with honors, U. Chgo., 1974. Bar: Ill. 1975, U.S. Dist. Ct. (no. dist.) Ill. 1975, U.S. Ct. Appeals (7th cir.) 1990. Law clk. to cir. judge US Ct. Appeals (7th cir.), Chgo., 1974-75; assoc. Mayer, Brown, Rowe & Maw LLP, Chgo., 1975-80, ptnr., 1981—. Assoc. editor U. Chgo. Law Rev., 1973. Fellow Am. Coll. Trial Lawyers; mem. ABA, 7th Cir. Bar Assn., Order of Coif, Phi Beta Kappa. Democrat. Roman Catholic. Avocations: jogging, golf. Home: 2718 Sheridan Rd Evanston IL 60201-1754 Office: Mayer Brown Rowe & Maw LLP 71 S Wacker Dr Chicago IL 60606-4637 Office Phone: 312-702-7279. Business E-Mail: mrooney@mayerbrownrowe.com.

**ROONEY, MICKEY (JOE YULE JR.),** actor; b. Bklyn., Sept. 23, 1920; s. Joe and Nell (Carter) Yule; m. Ava Gardner, Jan. 10, 1942 (div. May 1943); m. Betty Jane Rase, Sept. 30, 1944 (div. 1949); children: Mickey Jr., Timothy; m. Martha Vickers, June 3, 1949 (div.); m. Elaine Mahnken (div. 1958); m. Barbara Thomason, Dec. 1958; children: Kerry, Kyle, Kelly Ann, Kimmy Sue; m. Margie Lang, Sept. 1966 (div. 1967); m. Carolyn Hockett, (div.); 1 adopted child, Jimmy, 1 child, Jonell; m. Jan Chamberlin, July 28, 1978; stepchildren: Chris Aber, Mark Aber. Student, Pacific Mil. Acad. First appeared in vaudeville with parents; then appeared with Sid Gould, numerous TV programs; appeared in motion pictures Judge Hardy's Children, Hold That Kiss, Lord Jeff, Love Finds Andy Hardy, Boys Town, Stablemates, Out West With the Hardys, Huckleberry Finn, Andy Hardy Gets Spring Fever, Babes in Arms, Young Tom Edison, Judge Hardy and Son, Andy Hardy Meets Debutante, Strike Up the Band, Andy Hardy's Private Secretary, Men of Boystown, Life Begins for Andy Hardy, Babes on Broadway, A Yank at Eton, The Human Comedy, Andy Hardy's Blonde Trouble, Girl Crazy, Thousands Cheer, National Velvet, Ziegfeld Follies, The Strip, Sound Off, Off Limits, All Ashore, Light Case of Larceny, Drive A Crooked Road, Bridges at Toko-Ri, The Bold and Brave, Eddie, Private Lives of Adam and Eve, Comedian, The Grabbers, St. Joseph Plays the Horses, Breakfast at Tiffany's, Somebody's Waiting, Requiem For A Heavyweight, Richard, Pulp, It's a Mad, Mad, Mad, Mad World, Everything's Ducky, The Secret Invasion, The Extraordinary Seaman, The Comic, The Cockeyed Cowboys of Calico County, Skidoo, B.J.

Presents, That's Entertainment, The Domino Principle, Pete's Dragon, The Magic of Lassie, Black Stallion, Arabian Adventure, Erik the Viking, My Heroes Have Always Been Cowboys, 1991, (voice) Little Nimo: Adventures in Slumberland, 1992, Long Road Home, 1996, Kings of the Court, 1997, Animals, 1997, Babe: Pig in the City, 1998, Internet Love, 1998, The First of May, 1999, (voice) Lady and the Tramp II: Scamps Adventure, 2001, Topa Topa Bluffs, 2002; starred in TV prodns. Pinocchio, 1957, Leave 'Em Laughing, 1981, Bill, 1981 (Emmy, Golden Globe), Senior Trip!, 1981, Bill on His Own, 1983, Little Spies (Acad. Hon. award 1982), It Came upon the Midnight Clear, 1984, Bluegrass, 1988, Legend of Wolf Mountain, 1992, That's Entertainment! III, 1994, Revente of the Red Baron, 1994, Radio Star-die AFN-Story, 1994, The Legend of O.B. Taggart, 1995; appeared on stage in Sugar Babies, 1979, The Will Rogers Follies, 1993; appeared in TV series A Year at the Top, The Mickey Rooney Show; author: I.E. An Autobiography, 1965, Life Is Too Short, 1991, Search for Sonny Skies, 1994, Brother's Destiny (T.V.), 1995, Michael Kael in Katango, 1997, Boys Will be Boys, 1997, Sinbad: The Battle of the Dark Knights, 1998, The First of May, 1998, The Face on the Barroom Floor, 1998, Babe: Pig in the City, 1998; fgn. films: Midsummer Nights Dream, 1937, Words and Music, 1946, Rachels, 1973, To Hong Kong with Love, 1975, Oddessy of the Pacific, 1979. With AUS, WWII. Recipient Spl. Acad. Award, 1940, Tony award for best mus. actor, 1980; named One of Top 10 Money-Making Stars, Herald-Fame Poll, 1938-43 Office: PO Box 3186 Thousand Oaks CA 91359-0186

**ROONEY, PAUL C., JR.,** retired lawyer; b. Winnetka, Ill., Oct. 23, 1943; s. Paul C. and Mary K. (Brennan) R.; m. Maria Elena Del Canto, Sept. 6, 1980. BA, Harvard U., 1963, LLB, 1966. Bar: Mass. 1968, N.Y. 1972, Fla. 1980, U.S. Dist. Ct. (ea. and so. dists.) N.Y., U.S. Ct. Appeals (2d cir.). Ptnr. White & Case, N.Y.C., 1983-98, ret., 1998. Served to lt. USNR, 1966-69. Mem. N.Y. State Bar Assn., Univ. Club (N.Y.C.), Mashomack Preserve (N.Y.), Sharon Country Club (Conn.). Home: 11 Lilac Ln PO Box 271 Sharon CT 06069-0271 Office: White & Case 1155 Avenue Of The Americas New York NY 10036-2787 Office Phone: 212-819-8200.

**ROONEY, PAUL GEORGE,** mathematics professor; b. N.Y.C., July 14, 1925; s. Geoffrey Daniel and Doris Elizabeth (Babcock) R.; m. Mary Elizabeth Carlisle, June 20, 1950; children: Francis Timothy, Elizabeth Anne, Kathleen Doris, John Edward, James Carlisle. B.Sc., U. Alta., 1949; PhD, Calif. Inst. Tech., 1952. Asst. prof. math. U. Alta., 1952-55; asst. prof. U. Toronto, 1955-60, assoc. prof., 1960-62, prof., 1962-91, prof. emeritus, 1991—. Dir. Commonwealth Petroleum Co., Calgary, 1946-59 Editor in chief Can. Jour. Math. 1971-75; contbr. articles to profl. jours. Bd. dirs. Francis F. Reeve Found., 1954-85. Served with Can. Army, 1943-45. Fellow Royal Soc. Can.; Mem. Can. Math. Soc. (councillor 1960-64, 60-70, 76-78, v.p. 1979-81, pres. 1981-83), Am. Math. Soc., Math. Assn. Am. Office: U Toronto Dept Math 40 St George St Toronto ON Canada M5S 2E4 Business E-Mail: rooney@math.toronto.edu.

**ROONEY, PHILLIP BERNARD,** service company executive; b. Chgo., July 8, 1944; BA magna cum laude, St. Bernard Coll., 1966. With Waste Mgmt., 1969-97, Service Master Co., Downers Grove, Ill., 1997—2003; chmn. Claddaugh Investments LLC, 2004—. Trustee U. Notre Dame. Capt. USMC, 1966—69. Decorated Bronze Star USMC, 1966-69; recipient Semper Fidelis award Marine Corps Scholarship Found., El Valor's Corp. Visionary award, Man of Yr. award Ill. Viet Nam Vets. Mem.: Econ. Club Chgo. (past chmn.). Roman Catholic. Office: 1301 W 35th St Chicago IL 60609 Office Phone: 773-579-2474. E-mail: pbrooney78@aol.com.

**ROOP, JAMES JOHN,** public relations executive; b. Parkersburg, W.Va., Oct. 29, 1949; s. J. Vaun and Mary Louise (McGinnis) R.; m. Margaret Mary Kuneck (div. 1982); m. Susan Lynn Hoell (div. 1989); m. Daisy P. Billue, 1990 (div. 1999); m. Constance E. West, 2005. BS in Journalism, W.Va. U., 1971. Various account mgmt. postions Ketchum Pub. Rels., Pitts., 1972-77, v.p., 1977-79, Burson-Marsteller, Chgo., 1979-81; sr. v.p. Hesselbart & Mitten/Watt, Cleve., 1981-84, exec. v.p., 1984-86, pres., 1986-87, Watt, Roop & Co. (formerly Hesselbart & Mitten/Watt), Cleve., 1987-96; chmn., pres., CEO Roop & Co., Cleve., 1996—. Contbr. articles to profl. jours. Mem. Leadership Clevel.; former bd. dirs. Ctr. for Families and Children, Boys Hope, Girls Hope, Kidney Found., Police Athletic League, Econs. Am. Fellow Pub. Rels. Soc. Am. (chmn. investor rels. sect. 1984-85, chmn. honors and awards com. 1995); mem. Nat. Investor Rels. Inst. (pres. Cleve./Akron/Pitts. chpt., sr. investor rels. roundtable), Cleve. Skating Club, Mayfield Country Club, Hermit Club Republican. Home: 2697 Scarborough Rd Cleveland Heights OH 44106-3241 Office: Roop & Co 650 Huntington Bldg 925 Euclid Ave Cleveland OH 44115-1408

**ROOP, JOSEPH MCLEOD,** economist; b. Montgomery, Ala., Sept. 29, 1941; s. Joseph Ezra and Mae Elizabeth (McLeod) R.; m. Betty Jane Reed, Sept. 4, 1965; 1 dau., Elizabeth Rachael. BS, Ctrl. Mo. State U., Warrensburg, 1963; PhD, Wash. State U., Pullman, 1973. Economist Econ. Rsch. Svc., USDA, Washington, 1975-79; sr. economist Evans Econs., Inc., Washington, 1979-81; staff scientist Battelle Pacific N.W. Nat. Lab., Richland, Wash., 1981—. Adj. prof. dept. econs. Wash. State U., 1999—; with Internat. Energy Agy., Paris, 1990-91. Contbr. articles to profl. jours. With U.S. Army, 1966—68. Grantee Rsch. grant, Dept. Agr. Coop. State Rsch. Svc., 1971—73. Mem. Am. Econ. Assn., Econometric Soc., Internat. Assn. Energy Econs., Am. Statis. Assn. Home: 715 S Taft St Kennewick WA 99336-9587 Office: PO Box 999 MSIN K6-05 Richland WA 99352-0999 Business E-Mail: joe.roop@pnl.gov.

**ROOP, MITCHELL A.,** information scientist; b. Ocala, Fla., Feb. 12, 1955; s. James Q. and Bobbie P. Roop; m. Elizabeth S Roop, Feb. 14, 1992, RA, U. Fla., 1989, M.Liberal Arts, U. South Fla., 1992. Programmer/tech. writer Rare Comms. Inc., Oldsman, Fla., 1990—94; writer Kronus Inc., Tampa, 1994—97; tech. dir. Sites on Demand, Inc., Tampa, 1997—98, chief tech. officer, CIO, 1998—99; CEO MTG Internat., Inc., Tampa, 1999—2002; pres. Mitch Roop, Inc., Tampa, 2002—. Mem. Leadership Tampa, 2002—03; exec. com., bd. dirs. Faces of Courage Found., Inc., Tampa, 2002—; mem. pres.'s coun. U. Fla., Tampa, 2001—. With U.S. Army, 1973—85. Republican. Methodist. Avocations: weight training, martial arts. Office: Mitch Roop Inc 12601 Wood Ibis Way Tampa FL 33624-5717

**ROORBACH, BILL FORSYTH,** English language educator, writer; b. Chgo., Aug. 18, 1953; s. John E. and Reba (Burkhardt) R.; m. Juliet Karelsen, June 15, 1962. BA in Gen. Studies cum laude, Ithaca Coll., 1976; MFA in Creative Writing, Columbia U., 1990. Instr. in logic and rhetoric dept. English Columbia U., NYC, 1988-90; asst. prof. U. Maine, Farmington, 1991—95; faculty Ohio State Univ., Columbus, 1995—2001; Jenks Chair in Contemporary. Am. Letters Coll. of Holy Cross, Worcester, Mass., 2004—. Author: Summers with Juliet, 1992, Turning Toward Home: Reflections on the Family from Harper's Magazine, 1993, The Quotable Moose, 1994, The Smallest Color, 2001, Big Bend, 2001 (Flannery O'Connor award for short fiction, 2001, Silver Rose Award for Excellence in the short story, 2001, O. Henry award, 2002), Temple Stream: A Rural Odyssey, 2005, (essays) Into Woods, 2002, A Place on Water, 2004, (instructional) Writing Life Stories, 1998. Editor: Contemporary Creative Nonfiction: The Art of Truth, 2001. Grantee NEA fellowship, 2002. Office: Jenks Chair Arts & Letters Coll of Holy Cross 1 College St Worcester MA 01610 Business E-Mail: broorbac@holycross.edu.

**ROORDA, JOHN FRANCIS, JR.,** manufacturing executive, consultant; b. Evanston, Ill., Jan. 16, 1923; s. John Francis and Sadie M. (Daley) R.; m. Elizabeth Mulcahy, July 2, 1949; children: Elizabeth Roorda Barker, John F., Ann Roorda Hollis. BSChemE, Purdue U., 1943, PhD, 1949. With Shell Oil Co., 1949-83; gen. mgr. combined oil products/chem. econs. dept., 1973-74; v.p. planning and econs., 1974-77; v.p. Shell Devel. Co., Houston, 1977-78; v.p. corp. planning Shell Oil Co., 1978-83; pres. John Roorda, 1983—; Coordinator Exec. Service Corps, Houston, 1985— Served to lt. (j.g.) USNR

1943-46. Recipient Disting. Engring. Alumnus award Purdue U., 1976, Outstanding Chem. Engr. award Purdue U., 1993. Mem. Sigma Xi. Roman Catholic. Personal E-mail: graycell@houston.rr.com, tyro@houston.rr.com.

**ROOS, CASPER,** actor; b. N.Y.C., Mar. 21, 1925; s. Jacob and Sabina (Uhlenbusch) R.; m. Shirley Anne Nicholson, June 27, 1953; 1 child, Pieter Nicholson. Student, N.Y. Coll. Music. Treas. Actors Equity Found., N.Y.C., 1982-88; co-chmn. research subcom. Nat. Theater Com., N.Y.C., 1983—; chair supv. com. Actors Fed. Credit Union, 1990-2001, 2003—. Prin. actor Shenandoah, N.Y.C., 1975-78, Brigadoon, N.Y.C., 1979-80, My One and Only, N.Y.C., 1982-85, Into the Light, 1986, Man of La Mancha, Zurich, 1988, (Broadway prodn.) Shenandoah Revival, 1989; numerous regional theater prodns. Served with U.S. Mcht. Marines, 1943-46. Mem. Actors Equity (treas. 1982-88, councilor 1964-79, 88-93). Home: 3 Cozzens Ct Newport RI 02840 Office Phone: 800-484-1081 x4081. *Don Quixote wanted to 'add a little grace to the world.' I, too, would like to add a 'little' to this world, whether it be grace or laughter or tears to an audience or service to my colleagues. If, like Don Quixote, I look a little foolish, so be it. I prefer a life of striving for the ultimate to the easier smug acceptance of the status quo.*

**ROOS, CHARLES EDWIN,** physicist; b. Chgo., Apr. 23, 1927; s. Charles Frederick and Mary Barkuloo Roos; m. Anne Friedrich, Aug. 30, 1952; children: Margit Josephine, Alice Marie, Carlton Friedrich, Charles David. BA in Zoology, U. Tex., Austin, 1948; PhD in Physics, Johns Hopkins U., 1953. Faculty assoc. in physics Johns Hopkins U., Balt., 1953-54; asst. prof. physics U. Calif., Riverside, 1954-59; rsch. fellow Calif. Inst. Tech., Pasadena, 1955-67; assoc. prof. physics Vanderbilt U., Nashville, 1959-65, prof. physics, 1965-89, prof. emeritus, 1989—; chmn. Nat. Recovery Tech., Nashville, 1982—. Regular visitor, Be. Labs., Holmdale, N.J., 1973-76, scientific assoc. CERN, Geneva, Switzerland, 1969-80, founder, dir. Am. Magnetics, Oak Ridge, Tenn., 1966-85, mng. ptnr. Seofon Assocs., Baytown, Tex., 1960—; prin. investigator, NSF, 1955-89, U.S. Dept. Energy, 1970—. Contbr. over 140 articles to profl. jours.; U.S. and fgn. patentee in field. Mem. Condominium bdl, 817 5th Ave. Condominium, N.Y.C., 1975—, pres. bd., 1999—. With USN, 1945-46. Recipient Tibbets award, SBA, 1996, Nat. Conservation medal, DAR, 1992; guest Nobel awards, Royal Acad. Physics, Stockholm, 1989; sr. NATO fellow, NSF, Max Planck Inst., 1968. Fellow Am. Physics Soc.; mem. Cosmos Club. Avocations: cross country skiing, scuba diving. Office: 566 Mainstream Dr Ste 300 Nashville TN 37228-1234 E-mail: ceroos@comcast.net.

**ROOS, DANIEL,** engineering educator; b. Bklyn., Apr. 12, 1939; s. Sigmund and Anita (Sperling) R.; m. Eva Bonis, June 1, 1969; children— Richard Joseph, Linda Suzanne. BS in Civil Engring. M.I.T., 1961, MS, 1963, PhD, 1966. Mem. faculty MIT, Cambridge, 1963—, assoc. prof. civil engring., 1970-76, prof., 1976—, head transp. systems div., 1977-78, dir. Ctr. for Transp. Studies, 1978-85, dir. Ctr. Tech., Policy and Indsl. Devel., 1985-97, Japan Steel Industry prof., 1985—, mem. Commn. on Indsl. Productivity, 1987-89, assoc. dean engring. systems, 1997—, spl. asst. provost and chancellor, 1996—2003, co-dir. Ford Indsl. Ptnrships, dir. engring. sys. divsn., 1998—2004. Founder, dir. Multisystems Inc., Cambridge, 1965—85; chmn. com. to assess advanced vehicle and hwy techs. NRC, 1990—91, mem. com. on fuel economy, 1991—92; dir. Internat. Motor Vehicle Program, 1980—99; co-dir. Lean Aircraft Initiative, 1992—97; mem. coun. indsl. relationships MIT, 1996—97. Author: ICES System Design, 1964; The Future of the Automobile, 1984, Auto Futures, 1990; co-author: Made in America, 1989, The Machine That Changed the World, 1990; contbr. articles to profl. jours. Mem. U.S. Task Force on Transp., 1969. Recipient Shingo Prize for Excellence in Mfg. Rsch., 1994. Mem. ASCE (Frank M. Masters Transp. Engring. award 1989), Assn. Computing Machinery, Ops. Research Soc. (treas. transp. sci. sect. 1970-71), Transp. Research Bd. (chmn. para-transit com. 1974-80, group coun. 1980-84), Coun. Univ. Transp. Ctrs. (pres. 1983). Achievements include developing Dial-A-Ride transp. concept, 1965; dir. Internat. Motor Vehicle. Home: 28 Baskin Rd Lexington MA 02421-6929 Office: MIT Engring Sys Divsn 77 Massachusetts Ave Cambridge MA 02139-4307 Office Phone: 617-253-1661. E-mail: roos@mit.edu.

**ROOS, JOHN VICTOR,** lawyer; b. San Francisco, Feb. 14, 1955; AB, Stanford U., 1977, JD, 1980. Ptnr. Wilson, Sonsini Goodrich & Rosati, San Francisco, 1988—, mng. dir. profl. services, CEO, 2005—, mem. exec. mgmt. com. & policy com. Mem.: Order of the Coif. Office: Wilson Sonsini Goodrich & Rosati 650 Page Mill Rd Palo Alto CA 94304 Office Phone: 650-493-9300. Office Fax: 650-493-6811. E-mail: jroos@wsgr.com.*

**ROOSA, JAN BERTOROTTA,** psychologist, writer; b. Champaign, Ill., Apr. 19, 1927; s. Walter Laidlaw and Giannina (Bertorotta) Roosa; m. Joan Herr. BS, U. Ill., 1950; MA, U. Denver, 1951, PhD, 1957. Coord., clin. psychologist Child Rsch. Coun., Kansas City, Mo., 1954-57, dir. neighborhood rsch. project, 1957; supr., psychologist State Hosp., Fulton, Mo., 1957-59; chief of psychotherapy VA Hosp., Kansas City, 1959-63; pvt. practice clin. psychologist Kansas City, 1963—. Dir., co-founder Learning Resource Ctr., Kansas City, 1969—79; dir. Gestalt, Social Competence Inst., Kansas City, 1969—89, Competence and Coop. Group, 1992—. Author: Situation-Options-Consequences-Simulation: A Technique for Teaching Social Skills, 1973, Psychological and Social Competence Model and Skills, 1975, 1992, Pet Peeves of a Psychologist and Other Flights into Reality, 2005, Brainspire.com: Psychological Tools for a New Way of Life, 2006; creator SOCCSS and SOCCSS: A Decision Making Process, 1973, 1996, The Competence and Cooperation Based Program, 1995. With USN, 1945—47, with USN, 1951—52. Mem.: APA, Nat. Register Health Providers Psychology, Mental Health Profls., Kans. Assn. Profl. Psychologists, Mo. Psychol. Assn., Greater Kansas City Psychol. Assn. Office: 9229 Ward Pkwy Ste 365 Kansas City MO 64114 3334 Office Phone: 816-444-3366. E-mail: jbroosa@planetkc.com.

**ROOSEVELT, JAMES, JR.,** insurance company executive, lawyer; b. LA, Nov. 9, 1945; s. James and Romelle (Schneider) R.; m. Ann M. Conlon, June 15, 1968; children: Kathy, Tracy, Maura. AB, Harvard U., 1968, JD, 1971. Bar: Mass. 1971, DC 1973, US Ct. Appeals (DC cir.) 1973, US Ct. Appeals (1st cir.) 1976, US Supreme Ct. 1975. Assoc. Winthrop, Stimson, Putnam & Roberts, NYC, 1971, Herrick & Smith, Boston, 1975-80, ptnr., 1981-86, Nutter, McClennen & Fish, Boston, 1986-88, Choate, Hall & Stewart, Boston, 1988-98; assoc. commr. for retirement policy Social Security Adminstrn., Washington, 1998-99; sr. v.p., gen. counsel Tufts Health Plan, Waltham, Mass., 1999—2005, pres., 2005—, CEO, 2005—. Mem. Dem. Nat. Com., Washington, 1980—, Dem. State Com., Boston, 1980—; trustee Emmanuel Coll., Boston, 1982-92, 95—; trustee Care Group, Inc., Boston, 1990-00. Mt. Auburn Hosp., Cambridge, Mass., 1984-2000, chmn., 1988-92, chmn. bd. overseers, 2000—06. Lt. JAGC, USN, 1972-75. Mem. ABA, Boston Bar Assn., Mass. Bar Assn., Am. Health Lawyers Assn. (pres. 2002-03), Mass. Hosp. Assn. (trustee 1987-99, chmn. 1996-97), Harvard Club. Roman Catholic. Avocation: public policy. Office: Tufts Health Plan 333 Wyman St Waltham MA 02451-1282 Office Phone: 781-466-8564. Business E-Mail: james_roosevelt@tufts-health.com.

**ROOSEVELT, KERMIT,** law educator; b. Washington, July 14, 1971; s. Kermit and Priscilla Reynolds Roosevelt. AB, Harvard U., 1993; JD, Yale U., 1997. Bar: U.S. Ct. Appeals (7th cir.) 2001. Law clk. D.C. Cir. Ct. Appeals, Washington, 1997—98, U.S. Supreme Ct., Washington, 1999—2000; assoc. Mayer, Brown, Rowe & Maw, Chgo., 2000—02; asst. prof. U. Pa. Law Sch., Phila., 2002—. Author: (novels) In the Shadow of the Law, 2005; contbr. articles to profl. jours. Mem.: Phi Beta Kappa. Office: Univ Pa Law Sch 3400 Chestnut St Philadelphia PA 19104 Office Phone: 215-746-8775. Business E-Mail: krooseve@law.upenn.edu.

**ROOSEVELT, MARY WINSKILL,** elementary school educator; b. Birkenhead, Cheshire, Eng., June 5, 1939; came to U.S., 1968, 72; d. Joseph Hesford and Irene Myrtle (Mansfield) Winskill; m. James Roosevelt, Oct. 3, 1969; 1 child, Rebecca Mary. Grad., U. London, 1960; cert., U. Calif., Irvine, 1974.

Cert. multiple subject elem. tchr., Eng. Tchr. elem. London County Coun., 1960-62, The Queens Sch., Chester, Eng., 1962-63, The Internat Sch. of Geneva, 1963-68; prin U.N. Internat. Sch., 1968-70; dept. edn., supr. multiple subject credential U. Calif., Irvine, 1975—2002. Mem. faculty U. Calif., Irvine, 1975-99; pres. rsch. assocs., Calif. Coll. Medicine, Irvine, 1985-96. Bd. dirs. Sage Hill Sch., 2002—; friend Griffith U., Queensland, Australia, 2003—. Lawrence scholar Montefiore Found., London, 1960, Lauds and Laurels Univ. Svc., 1984, U. Calif.-Irvine medal, 1990. Democrat. Methodist.

**ROOSEVELT, PHIL,** periodical editor; BA, Tufts U., 1979; MBA, Columbia U., 1985. Editor Am. Banker, Inc., N.Y.C., 1999—.

**ROOSEVELT, THEODORE, IV,** investment banker; b. Jacksonville, Fla., Nov. 27, 1942; s. Theodore III and Anne Mason (Babcock) Roosevelt; m. Constance Lane Rogers, Aug. 1, 1970; 1 child, Theodore V. AB, Harvard U., 1965, MBA, 1972. Fgn. svc. officer U.S. Dept. of State, 1967—70; assoc. Lehman Bros., N.Y.C., 1972-76; corp. v.p. Lehman Bros. Kuhn Loeb, N.Y.C., 1976-82; sr. v.p. Lehman Comml. Paper Inc., N.Y.C., 1982-85; mng. dir. Lehman Brothers (formerly Shearson Lehman Bros., Inc.), N.Y.C., 1985—. Chmn., bd. dirs. Lehman Bros. Fin. Products, Inc.; dir. Inst. Environ. and Natural Resources U. Wyo. Mem. N.Y. State Pk. Recreation and Hist. Preservation Commn. City of N.Y.; commr. Hudson River Pk. Conservancy; mem., governing coun. Cultural Inst. Retirement Sys.; chmn. Pew Ctr. Global Change; co-chmn. Allicance for Climate Protection; trustee World Resources Inst. With underwater demolition team USN, 1965—67. Mem.: Fgn. Policy Assn. (gov.), Coun. Fgn. Rels., Trout Unlimited, Wilderness Soc. (vice chmn.), Clove Valley Rod and Gun Club, Econ. Club N.Y., Harvard Club (N.Y.C.), Explorers Club, Heights Casino Club (Bklyn.), Edgartown Yacht Club, Links (N.Y.C.). Republican. Home: 1 Pierrepont St Brooklyn NY 11201-3302 Office: Lehman Bros 745 7th Ave 20th Fl New York NY 10019 Office Phone: 212-526-8363. E-mail: troosere@lehman.com.

**ROOT, ALAN CHARLES,** diversified manufacturing company executive; b. Essex, Eng., Apr. 11, 1921; arrived in U.S., 1951, naturalized, 1959; s. Charles Stanley and Lillian (Collins) Root. BA, Oxford U., 1943; MA, Cambridge U., 1951; MBA, Stanford U., 1953. Rsch. analyst Dow Chem. Co., Midland, Mich., 1954—55; mgr. mktg. rsch. GE Co., 1955—61; v.p. bus. planning Mosler Safe Co., Hamilton, Ohio, 1961—70; v.p. corp. planning Am. Standard Inc., N.Y.C., 1970—76, sr. v.p. ops. svcs., 1976—86, sr. v.p., 1986—88, sr. advisor, 1989. Trustee 1995 Trust Fund; sr. advisor Unit Ice, 1995—; bd. dirs. Am.-Standard Energy Inc., Amstan Trucking Inc., 1976-86. Trustee, treas. N.J. Chamber Music Soc., 1988—95; mem. Sheriff's Jury, N.Y. Cty., 1971—79; bd. dirs., chmn. Brit. Schs. and Univs. Found., 1970—2002, hon. dir., 2002—. Capt. Brit. Army, 1944—48. Admission to Order of St. John of Jerusalem sanctioned by Her Majesty Queen Elizabeth II, 1986, comdr., 1994. Mem. AIChE (assoc. producer TV series Midland sect. 1955), Pilgrims U.S., Newcomen Soc. N.Am., Univ. Club (N.Y.C.). Home: 4934 Mount Pleasant Ln Las Vegas NV 89113-0114 Fax: 702-227-8885. *Good luck meant that my industrial career drew on the education I enjoyed as a young man. Professional advancement came by building on prior experience at each step and through long-term, managerial continuity.*

**ROOT, ALLEN WILLIAM,** pediatrician, educator; b. Phila., Sept. 24, 1933; s. Morris Jacob and Priscilla R.; m. Janet Greenberg, June 15, 1958; children: Jonathan, Jennifer, Michael. AB, Dartmouth Coll., 1955, postgrad. Med. Sch., 1954-56; MD, Harvard U., 1958. Diplomate Am. Bd. Pediatrics (mem. bd. 1985—), Am. Bd. Pediatric Endocrinology (mem. bd. 1985-90, chmn. 1990). Intern Strong Meml. Hosp., Rochester, NY, 1958-60; resident in pediatrics Hosp. U. Pa., Phila., 1960-63; fellow in pediatric endocrinology Children's Hosp. of Phila., 1962-65; assoc. physician in pediatrics U. Pa. Sch. Medicine, 1964-66, asst. prof. pediatrics, 1966-69; assoc. prof. pediatrics Temple U. Sch. Medicine, Phila., 1969-73, prof., 1973; asst. physician in endocrinology Children's Hosp. Phila., 1965-69; chmn. divsn. pediatrics Albert Einstein Med. Center, Phila., 1969-73; prof. pediatrics U. South Fla. Coll. Medicine, Tampa, 1973—, prof. biochemistry, 1987—, assoc. chmn. dept. pediatrics, 1974-99, dir. sect. pediatric endocrinology, 1973-96. Dir. univ. tchg. svcs. All Children's Hosp., St. Petersburg, 1973-89; mem. Fla. Infant Screening Adv. Coun., 1979-06, chmn., 1994-06; mem. Hillsborough County Thyroid Adv. Com., 1980; mem. med. adv. com. Nat. Pituitary Agy., 1974-78, mem. growth hormone subcom., 1972-79, 81-85; chmn. Fla. Legis. Infant Screening Task Force, 2002. Author: Human Pituitary Growth Hormone, 1972; editor Endocrinology and Metabolism Current Opinion in Pediats., 1993—; co-editor: (with C. La Cauza) Problems in Pediatric Endocrinology, 1980; mem. editl. bd. Jour. Pediats., 1973-81, Jour. Adolescent Health Care, 1979-95, Jour. Pediat. Endocrinology and Metabolism, 1985—, Jour. Clin. Endocrinology and Metabolism, 1993-96, 2001-04, Growth, Genetics and Hormones, 1993—, Pediat. in Rev., 1995-2001; assoc. editor Adolescent and Pediat. Gynecology, 1992-95, Current Opinion in Pediats., 2006-. USPHS grantee; Birth Defects Found. grantee. Mem. AAAS, Am. Pediatric Soc., Soc. Pediatric Rsch., Lawson Wilkins Pediatric Endocrine Soc. (treas. 1979-88, pres. 1988-89), Endocrine Soc., Am. Acad. Pediatrics, Am. Fedn. Clin. Rsch., Soc. Exptl. Biology and Medicine, Soc. Nuclear Medicine, N.Y. Acad. Sci., Phila. Coll. Physicians, Phila. Endocrine Soc. (bd. dirs. 1971-72, treas. 1973), Dartmouth Coll. Alumni Coun., Dartmouth Club. Office: 801 6th St S Saint Petersburg FL 33701-4816 Business E-Mail: roota@allkids.org.

**ROOT, BRIAN K.,** journalist; b. Sharon, Pa., Sept. 25, 1981; s. Clyde O., Jr. (Stepfather) and Diane M. Heckman. BA in English Writing, U. Pitts., Greensburg, 2004; postgrad., Ind. (Pa.) U., 2004—. Journalist Record-Argus, Inc., Greenville, Pa., 2004—; mem.: Assocs. Student Devel (v.p. pub, relp. 2004—05), Pa. Coll. Pers. Assn., U. Pitts. Greensburg Alumni Assn. (pres. student senate 2003—04). Home: 90 Shenango Park Rd Lot 8 Transfer PA 16154 Office: Record Argus Inc 10 Penn Ave Greenville PA 16125

**ROOT, EDWARD LAKIN,** education educator, academic administrator; b. Cumberland, Md., Dec. 5, 1940; s. Lakin and Edna Grace (Adams) Root. BS, Frostburg (Md.) State Coll., 1962, MEd, 1966; EdD, U. Md., 1970. Cert. tchr. Md. Tchr. Allegany County Bd. of Edn., Cumberland, 1962-66; grad. fellow U. Md., College Park, 1966-67, fellow, 1967-69; with Frostburg (Md.) State U., 1969-99, prof., head edn. dept., 1980-87, dean, 1987-95, prof., head MEd adminstrn., 1995-99; gubernatorial appointee Md. State Bd. Edn., 1999—, pres., 2000—. mem. Profl. Stds. Bd. Md., Balt., 1980—87, Balt., 1995—99, Cert. Rev. Bd. Md., Balt., 1987—90, Md. Task Force Adminstrn., Balt., 1985—88, Md. Task Force: Prisoners Time and Response, task force vice chmn., 1995—97, Md. Task Force Tchr. Quality, 2002—03, Md. Task Force Disadvantaged but Capable Students, 2000—02; chmn. Md. Tchr. Quality Task Group, 2002—03. Mem. Allegany County (Md.) Planning and Zoning Bd. Appeals, 1995—96. Named Md. Ednl. Leader of Yr., 2003. Mem.: ASCD, Nat. Soc. Study Edn., Nat. Assn. Secondary Sch. Prins., Mensa, Masons, Shriners, Phi Delta Kappa. Democrat. Methodist. Avocations: photography, travel. Home: 100 Pennsylvania Ave Cumberland MD 21502-4236 Office: Frostburg State U College Ave Frostburg MD 21532-1724

**ROOT, GEORGE LINCOLN, JR.,** lawyer; b. 1947; BA, Syracuse U.; JD cum laude, U. San Diego. Ptnr. Foley & Lardner LLP, San Diego, mem. mgmt. com., chmn. regulated ind. dept. Guest lectr. U. Calif., San Diego; adj. prof. San Diego State U. Mem. San Diego County Bar Assn. (chmn. mental health com. 1983, task force on children at risk 1995), Calif. Soc. Healthcare Attys., Healthcare Fin. Mgmt. Assn., Nat. Health Lawyers Assn. Office: Foley & Lardner LLP 402 W Broadway Fl 23 San Diego CA 92101-3542 Office Phone: 619-234-6655. Business E-Mail: groot@foley.com.

**ROOT, JAMES BENJAMIN,** landscape architect; b. Detroit, Jan. 26, 1934; s. William Jehial and Helen Elizabeth (English) R. BBA, Memphis State U., 1960; B Landscape Architecture, U. Ga., 1966. Registered landscape architect; lic. real estate agt., Va. Asst. prof. W.Va. U., Morgantown, 1973-75, 93;

pvt. practice Charlottesville, Va., 1976-85, 91—; site planner LBA, PH&R, Charles P. Johnson & Assocs., Fairfax, Va., 1986-90. Pvt. practice as golf course architect, Charlottesville, 1976—; instr. Parkersburg C.C., 1975, Piedmont Va. C.C., 1981. Author: Fundamentals of Landscaping and Site Planning, 1985; contbr. articles to profl. jours., also poetry. Mem. Planning Commn., Marietta, Ohio, 1972. Mem. Nat. Golf Found., Golf Course Builders Assn. Am. (assoc.), Elks, Va. Writers Club. Avocations: piano, drums. Office: PO Box 7017 Charlottesville VA 22906-7017 Office phone: 434-971-4000. E-mail: jamesbroot@aol.com.

ROOT, NINA J., librarian, writer; b. 1934; d. Jacob J. and Fannie (Slivinsky) R. BA, Hunter Coll.; MSLS, Pratt Inst.; postgrad., USDA Grad. Sch., 1964-65, CUNY, 1970-75. Reference and serials libr. Albert Einstein Coll. Medicine Libr., Bronx, NY, 1958-59; asst. chief libr. Am. Cancer Soc., N.Y.C., 1959-62; chief libr. Am. Inst. Aeros. and Astronautics, N.Y.C., 1962-64; head ref. and libr. svcs. sci. and tech. divsn. Libr. Congress, Washington, 1964-66; mgmt. cons. Nelson Assocs., Inc., N.Y.C., 1966-70; dir. libr. svcs. Am. Mus. Natural History, N.Y.C., 1970-97; freelance mgmt. cons. and libr. planning, 1970-99. Trustee Barnard Found., 1984-91; mem. libr. adv. coun. N.Y. State Bd. Regents, 1984-89, trustee Metro, 1987-92; bd. dirs. Hampden/Booth Libr. Players, 1990-97, Sutton Area Cmty., 1997-2001; trustee Mercantile Libr. N.Y., 1993-95; dir. emerita Libr. AMNH, 1998—. Recipient Meritorious Svc. award Libr. of Congress, 1965, Founders medal SHNH, 1997. Mem. ALA (preservation com. 1977-79, chmn. libr./binders com. 1978-80, chmn. preservation sect. 1980-81, mem. coun. 1983-86), Spl. Librs. Assn. (sec. documentation group N.Y. chpt. 1972-73, 2d v.p. N.Y. 1975-76, treas. sci. and tech. group N.Y. 1975-76, mus. arts and humanities divsn. program planning chairperson-conf. 1977), Archons of Colophon (convener 1978-79), Soc. for Hist. of Natural History (N.Am. rep. 1977-85), N.Y. Acad. Scis. (mem. publs. com. 1975-80, 89-91, archives com. 1976-78, search. com. 1976), Explorers Club. Home: 400 E 59th St New York NY 10022-2342

ROOT, STUART DOWLING, lawyer, retired government agency administrator, retired banker; b. Chagrin Falls, Ohio, Oct. 14, 1932; s. Elton Albert and Virginia Saxton (Dowling) R.; m. Jean D. Youse, Dec. 28, 1957 (div. Jan. 1972); children: Bryan, Kathleen, Timothy, Todd; m. Patricia Stoneman Graff, Apr. 24, 1976. BA, Ohio Wesleyan U., 1955; JD, Columbia U., 1960. Bar: N.Y. 1960. Assoc. Cadwalader Wickersham and Taft, N.Y.C., 1960-68, ptnr., 1969-81, 84-87; pres. Bowery Savs. Bank, N.Y.C., 1981-82, vice chmn., 1982-83; exec. dir. Office Fed Savs. and Loan Ins. Corp., Washington, 1988-89; chmn. bd. Fin. Instn. Svcs. Corp., Washington, 1989. Lectr. ABA, Practicing Law Inst., Infocast, Am. Law Inst.; bd. dirs Bowest Corp., 1969-81. Contbr. articles to profl. jours. Chmn. bd. dirs. Harlem Sch. Arts, N.Y.C., 1974-83, trustee emeritus, 1984—; bd. dirs. Open Space Inst., 1976-80, 84-87, 89—, Nat. Choral Soc. N.Y.C., 1981-86, Canterbury Choral Soc., N.Y.C.; trustee N.Y. Geneal. and Biographical Soc., 1981-85; pub. interest dir. Fed. Home Loan Bank N.Y., N.Y.C., 1985-87. With U.S. Army, 1955-57. Mem. Century Assn. (N.Y.C.). Republican. Episcopalian. Avocations: liturgical music, fly fishing, golf. Home and Office: Beaverkill/Campsite Rd PO Box 417 Livingston Manor NY 12758-0417 Office Phone: 845-439-4255. E-mail: rootlaw32@aol.com.

ROOT, WILLIAM LUCAS, electrical engineering educator; b. Des Moines, Oct. 6, 1919; s. Frank Stephenson and Helen (Lucas) R.; m. Harriett Jean Johnson, Dec. 10, 1918; children: William Lucas Jr., Wendy Elizabeth Root Cate. BEE, Iowa State U., 1940; MEE, MIT, 1943, PhD in Math., 1952. Staff mem. MIT Lincoln Lab., Lexington, Mass., 1952-61, group leader, 1959-61; lectr. Harvard U., Cambridge, Mass., 1958-59; visitor U. Wis., Madison, 1963-64; vis. prof. Mich. State U., East Lansing, 1966, 68, U. Calif., Berkeley, 1966-67; prof. aerospace engring. U. Mich., Ann Arbor, 1961-87, prof. emeritus, 1988—. Visitor U. Cambridge (Eng.) 1970; mem. U.S. Army Sci. Bd., 1979-82. Co-author: Random Signals and Noise, 1958 (Russian and Japanese transls.); assoc. editor: (IEEE) Information Theory Transactions, 1977-79; Soc. Indsl. and Applied Math. Jour. Applied Mathematics, 1962-72; contbr. 65 articles to profl. jours., book chpts. and conf. procs. Served to lt. USMCR, 1943—45. NSF Sr. postdoctoral fellow, 1970, vis. fellow Cambridge Clare Hall, 1970; recipient Claude E. Shannon award IEEE Info. Theory Soc., 1986, Career Achievement award ComCon Conf. Bd., 1987. Life fellow IEEE (vice chmn. adminstrv. com. info. theory group 1965-66); mem. Am. Math. Soc. Home: PO Box 3785 Ann Arbor MI 48106-3785 Office: Univ Mich Dept Aerospace Engring Ann Arbor MI 48109 Office Phone: 734-763-9300.

ROOT, WILLIAM PITT, poet, educator; b. Austin, Minn., Dec. 28, 1941; s. William Pitt and Bonita Joy (Hilbert) R.; m. Judith Carol Bechtold, 1965 (div. 1970); 1 dau., Jennifer Lorca; m. Pamela Uschuk, 1987. BA, U. Wash., 1964; MFA, U. N.C. at Greensboro, 1967; postgrad., Stanford, 1968-69. Asst. prof. Mich. State U., 1967-68; tchr. writing Mid-peninsula Free U., 1969; writer-in-residence Amherst Coll., U. Southwestern La., 1976, U. Mont., 1978, 80, 83-84; with poet-in-schs. program state art councils Oreg., Miss., Idaho, Ariz., Vt., Mont., Wyo., Wash., Tex., 1971—; Distinguished writer-in-residence Wichita State U., 1976; vis. writer in residence U. Mont., 1978, 80, 83-86, Hunter Coll., N.Y.C., 1986—; vis. writer NYU, 1986. Vis. writer Westside Young Men's Hebrew Assn., N.Y.C., 1988; disting. writer-in-residence Pacific Luth. U., 1990. Author: The Storm and Other Poems, 1969, Striking the Dark Air for Music, 1973, The Port of Galveston, 1974, Coot and Other Characters, 1977, 7 Mendocino Songs, 1977, A Journey South, 1977, Fireclock, 1981, Reasons for Going It on Foot, 1981, In the World's Common Grasses, 1981, The Unbroken Diamond: Nightletter to the Mujahideen, 1983, Invisible Guests, 1984, Faultdancing, 1986, Trace Elements from a Recurring Kingdom, 1994; collaborated (with filmmaker Ray Rice) on poetry films Song of the Woman and the Butterflyman (Orpheus award 1st Internat. Poetry Film Festival 1975), 7 for a Magician, 1976, Faces, 1981. Rockefeller Found. grantee, 1969-70; Guggenheim Found. grantee, 1970-71; Nat. Endowment for Arts grantee, 1973-74; US/U.K. Bicentennial Exchange Artist, 1978-79; Wallace Stegner creative writing fellow Stanford U., 1968-69; recipient 1st prize univ. poetry contest Acad. Am. Poets, 1966, Atlantic Young Poet award, 1967, Stanley Kunitz Poetry award, 1981, Guy Owen Poetry Prize, 1982, Pushcart Prize (Poetry), 1977, 1980, 1985; named Poet Laureate of Tucson, 1997-2002. Address: CUNY Hunter Coll Dept Eng 695 Park Ave New York NY 10021-5024 *With Rilke I believe the measure of one's life consists in a growing capacity to engage ever more fully in that dance between what we call will and what we call fate until the result is a contagion of vitality powerful enough to dissipate the spell of habits and to recreate in oneself that first spirit which is intuitive, sympathetic, and clear. Poems simply record the complex effort.*

ROOT-BERNSTEIN, ROBERT SCOTT, biologist, educator; b. Washington, Aug. 7, 1953; s. Morton Ira and Maurine (Berkstresser) Bernstein; m. Michèle Marie Root-Bernstein, Sept. 2, 1978; children: Meredith Marie, Brian Robert. AB, Princeton U., 1975, PhD, 1980. Postdoctoral fellow Salk Inst. for Biol. Studies, La Jolla, Calif., 1981-82, rsch. assoc., 1983-84; from asst. to assoc. prof. Mich. State U., East Lansing, 1987-96, prof., 1996—. Cons. Parke-Davis Pharm. Rsch. Divsn., Ann Arbor, 1990-96, Chiron Corp., 1992-96; mem. adv. bd. Soc. for Advancement Gifted Edn., Chgo., 1987-92; Sigma Xi nat. lectr., 1994-96. Author: Discovering, 1989, Rethinking AIDS, 1993, Honey, Mud, Maggots and Other Medical Marvels, 1997, Sparks of Genius, 1999; columnist The Scis. mag., 1989-92, The Leonardo mag., 2004—; contbr. numerous articles to profl. jours. MacArthur Found. fellow, 1981-86; recipient D.J. Ingle Meml. Writing prize, 1988. Mem. Phi Beta Kappa (hon.), Sigma Xi. Avocations: drawing, painting, photography, cello. Office: Mich State U Dept Physiology Biomed & Phys Scis Bldg East Lansing MI 48824 Office Phone: 517-355-6475 x 1101. Business E-Mail: rootbern@msu.edu.

ROOTH, SIGNE ALICE, editor, consultant; b. NYC, Aug. 14, 1924; d. Gerhard Teodor and Florence Elizabeth (Miner) Rooth. BA summa cum laude, U. Miami, 1944; MA, U. So. Calif., 1945; PhD, U. Chgo., 1953. Translator IMF, Washington, 1954—56, UN Secretariat, NYC, 1956—58,

editor Official Records Editing sect., 1958—69; translator/interpreter UN Mission to Congo, Leopoldville, 1962—63; editor/sr. editor divsn. Gen. Assembly Affairs UN Secretariat, NYC, 1969—84, cons. editor UN Devel. Programme, 1985—92, cons. editor Trusteeship Dept., Gen. Assembly and Conf. Mgmt., Dept. Pub. Info., 1993—2006. Editor Econ. and Social Commn. for Asia and the Pacific, Bangkok, 1999; bd. mem. Assn. Culturelle Francophone, UN Secretariat. Author: Seeress of the Northland: Fredrika Bremer's American Journey, 1849-1851, 1955; editor: Procs. of UN Congress on Pub. Internat. Law: International Law as a Language for International Relations, 1995; contbr. articles and essays to jours. Recipient Am. Swedish Woman of Yr., Woman's Auxiliary of Am. Swedish Hist. Mus., Phila., 1984. Mem.: French Inst./Alliance Francaise, Swedish Women's Ednl. Assn., Am. Scandinavian Soc., Am.-Scandinavian Found., Am. Swedish Hist. Found. (life), Southampton Hist. Mus., Rogers Meml. Libr., Parrish Art Mus., Paris Am. Club. Avocations: reading, travel, art, music, collecting F. Bremer autographs.

ROOTHAAN, JOHN, music educator, jazz pianist; s. Clemens and Judith Roothaan; m. Lynn Payer, 1982; 1 child, Steven. MusB, Chgo. Musical Coll., 1992, MusM, 1995; ArtsD in Music, Ball State U., 1999. Spl. lectr. in jazz piano Chgo. Musical Coll., 1990—93; instr. music theory and composition Ball State U., Muncie, Ind., 1997—. Freelance pianist, band leader, Chgo., 1980—. Pianist, prodr. Star Eyes, 2002, It Might as Well Be Spring, 2004. Doctoral fellow, Ball State U., 1995—97. Mem.: ASCAP. Office: Ball State U Muncie IN 47306 Office Phone: 312-515-0483. Personal E-mail: jproothaan@sbcglobal.net.

ROPER, BERYL CAIN, writer, retired library director, publishing executive; b. Long Beach, Calif., Mar. 1, 1931; d. Albert Verne and Ollie Fern (Collins) Cain; m. Max H. Young, Aug. 22, 1947 (div. 1958); children: Howard, Wade, Debra, Kevin, John R., Christopher; m. George Albert Roper, Mar. 24, 1962 (dec. July 1978); children: Ellen, Georgianne; m. Jack T. Hughes, Sept. 21, 1993 (dec. May 2001). BA, West Tex. State U., 1986; MA, Tex. Womans U., 1989. Libr. clk. Cornette Libr., West Tex. State U., Canyon, 1981-87; dir. Clarendon (Tex.) Coll. Libr., 1988-96. Lectr. in history and archaeology; owner Aquamarine Publs. Editor, pub.: In the Light of Past Experience, 1989, Transactions of the Southwest Federation of Archaeological Societies, 1993, Greenbelt Site, 1996, Presbyterian Mission Work in New Mexico: Memoirs of Alice Blake, 1997; author, pub.: Trementina, 1990, Trementina Revisited, 1994, Seekers After Truth, 1998, The Queen of Sciences: Personal Ramblings in Anthropologia, 2006; author articles on women and history. Mem.: Biblical Archaeology Soc., Internat. Soc. for Archeology and the Bible, Panhandle Archaeol. Soc., (newsletter editor) Archeology Conservancy, Phi Alpha Theta, Alpha Chi, Beta Phi Mu, Pi Gamma Mu. Republican. Mem. Lds Ch. Avocations: music, gardening, decorating, remodeling old houses, genealogy. Office: Aquamarine Publs 8001 Cattle Dr Canyon TX 79015 E-mail: beryl0I@sprynet.com.

ROPER, HARRY JOSEPH, lawyer; b. Bridgeport, Conn., Apr. 15, 1940; BEE, Rensselaer Poly. Inst., 1962; LLB, NYU, 1966. Assoc. Neuman, Williams, Anderson & Olson, 1966-70, ptnr., 1970-90, Roper & Quigg, 1990—2004, Jenner & Block, 2004—. Home: 611 W Fullerton Pky Chicago IL 60614-2613 Office: Jenner & Block 1 IBM Plz 330 N Wabash Ave Chicago IL 60611-7603 Office Phone: 312-923-8303. Business E-Mail: hroper@jenner.com.

ROPER, JOHN MARLIN, SR., federal magistrate judge; b. Greenville, Ala., Dec. 11, 1942; s. Marlin Ross and Ruby Lois (Martin) R.; m. Virginia Gene Kerth, Apr. 2, 1966; 1 son, John Marlin. BS, Auburn U., 1964; JD, Tulane U., 1968. Bar: Ala. 1968, Miss. 1974. Counselor, program dir. Juvenile Delinquency Instn., New Orleans, 1966-69; sr. law clk. to judge U.S. Dist. Ct. (so. dist.) Miss., 1969-75, magistrate judge, 1975—. Mem. Fed. Magistrate Judges Assn. (dir. 5th cir. 1976-82, nat. officer 1982-86, nat. pres. 1986-87, security com. jud. conf. 1987-89, budget com., jud. conf. 1989-97, judge rep. 5th cir. jud. coun. 2004—, mag. judge rep. jud. conf. 2004—). Methodist.

ROPER, NICOLE ELIZABETH, history educator; b. Norristown, Pa., Mar. 11, 1978; d. Richard Kenneth and Faye Elizabeth Roper. BA in History, DeSales U., 2000; Masters in Ednl. Leadership, Immaculata U., 2005. Secondary Certificate to teach Social Studies Pa., 2005, Supervisor Certificate in Social Studies Pa., 2006. World history tchr. West Phila. Cath. H.S., Pa., 2002—, algebra tchr., 2000—02; mythology tchr. Gwynedd-Mercy Coll. Upward Bound Program, Phila., study skills tchr., 2005, edgar allen poe tchr., 2001, drama tchr., 2000—00. Mem. social studies curriculum com. Archdiocese of Phila., 2003—; title i coord. Phila. Pub. Sch. Sys., 2004—, title i tutor, 2003—; world affairs club moderator West Phila. Cath. H.S., 2000—, nat. history day club moderator, 2005—, set designer, lighting dir., sound dir., stage mgr., 2004—, bowling moderator, 2000—02; mem. World Affairs Coun. of Phila., 2000—; counselors-in-training supr. Malvern Prep. H.S. Summer Camp, Pa., 2004—05, asst. adminstr., 2003—05, computer tchr., 2001—02, art tchr., 1999—2000, camp counselor, 1994—98. Mem.: ASCD, Nat. Constn. Ctr., U. Pa. Mus. of Archeology and Anthropology, Nat. Coun. for History Edn., Pa. Coun. for the Social Studies, Orgn. of Am. Historians, Mid-Atlantic Region Assn. for Asian Studies, World Affairs Coun. of Phila., History Channel Club (life). Avocations: reading, bowling, softball, volleyball. Office: West Phila Catholic High Sch 4501 Chestnut St Philadelphia PA 19139 Office Phone: 215-386-2244 325. Personal E-mail: wchsroper@yahoo.com.

ROPER, PAUL KIRK, elementary school educator; b. Fort Smith, Ark., Dec. 29, 1972; s. Sheila Yvonne and Lyman Lincoln Roper; m. Davina Rose Lewis, July 11, 2000; children: Samuel Lewis, Alex Clayton. BS in Edn., U. Ctrl. Ark., Conway, 1996. Social studies tchr. Mountainburg Sch. Dist., Ark., 1996—. Office: Mountainburg Sch Dist 129 Hwy 71 SW Mountainburg AR 72946 Office Phone: 479-369-2146.

ROPER, RICHARD B., III, prosecutor; BA, U. Tex., Arlington; JD, Tex. Tech. U. Asst. dist. atty. Tarrant County, Tex., 1982—87; asst. U.S. atty. (no. dist.) Tex. US Dept. Justice, Dallas, 1987—2004, interim US atty. (no. dist.) Tex., 2004, US atty. (no. dist.) Tex., 2004—. Office: US Attys Office Third Fl 1100 Commerce St Dallas TX 75242-1699 Office Phone: 214-659-8600.*

ROPER, SCOTT CHRISTOPHER, geographer, researcher, research scientist; b. Quincy, Mass., Oct. 24, 1969; s. James Henry and Lynne Patricia (Dunlop) Roper; m. Stephanie Abbot, Aug. 3, 1991. BA, Clark U., Mass., 1991; MA, U. ND, 1993; PhD, U. Kans., 1997. Grad. tchg. asst. U. of ND, Grand Forks, ND, 1991—93, U. of Kans., Lawrence, 1993—96; adj. prof. Rivier Coll., Nashua, NH, 1999—2002; asst. prof. of geography West Tex. A&M U., Canyon, Tex., 2002—05, Castleton (Vt.) State Coll., 2005—. Co-president Lyndeborough Hist. Soc., NH, 1998—2001; book rev. editor Material Culture, Springfield, Ohio, 2003—; rsch. cons., Lyndeborough, NH, 1997—2002. Co-author (nonfiction book) Citizen Soldiers: New Hampshire's Lafayette Artillery Company, 1804-2004; author: (nonfiction book) The Peterborough Savings Bank, 1847-1997, (monograph) Citizens' Hall: A History of Lyndeborough's 'Other' Town Hall, 1888-2000; co-editor (monograph) A Soldier's Life: Reminiscences of the Civil War; contbr. articles to profl. jours. Selectman, Lyndeborough, NH, 1999—2002. Recipient Govs. Citation, Gov. of the State of NH., 2000, Award for Excellence in Geography, Assn. of Am. Geographers and Nat. Coun. for Geog. Edn., 1991, Ellen Churchill Semple Geography award, Clark U., 1991, Paul P. Vouras Social Scis. award, 1991; Summer scholar, ND State Bd. of Higher Edn., 1992. Mem.: Soc. for Am. Baseball Rsch., Nat. Coun. for Geog. Edn., Assn. Am. Geographers, Pioneer Am. Soc. (life; editor Pioneer Am. Soc. Transactions 2006—), Phi Kappa Phi, Phi Beta Kappa, Gamma Theta Upsilon (chpt. pres. pro tem 1991). Home: 157 Pettingill Hill Rd Lyndeborough NH 03082 Office: Castleton State Coll Dept History, Geography, Econs and Polit Castleton VT 05735

ROPER, WILLIAM LEE, dean, preventive medicine physician, health facility administrator; b. Birmingham, Ala., July 6, 1948; s. Richard Barnard and Jean (Fyfe) R.; m. Maryann Roper, Jan. 14, 1978 AA, Fla. Coll., 1968; BS, U. Ala, 1970, MD, 1974, M.P.H., 1981. Diplomate Am. Bd. Pediatrics, Am. Bd. Preventive Medicine. Intern, resident in pediatrics U. Colo. Med. Ctr., Denver, 1974-77; health officer Jefferson County Dept. Health, Birmingham, 1977-82, 83; White House fellow Washington, 1982-83; spl. asst. to Pres. for health policy, 1983-86; adminstr., Health Care Finance Adminstrn. HHS, Washington, 1986-89; dep. asst. to pres. for domestic policy The White House, Washington, 1989-90; adminstr. Agy. for Toxic Substances and Disease Registry and dir. Ctrs. for Disease Control and Prevention, Atlanta, 1990-93; sr. v.p. Prudential Health Care, Roseland, NJ, 1994-97; pres. Prudential Ctr. for Health Care Rsch., Atlanta, 1993-95; dean, sch. pub. health, prof. medicine and health policy U. NC, Chapel Hill, 1997—2004, dean sch. medicine, 2004—, vice chancellor med. affairs, 2004—, CEO U. NC Health Care, 2004—. Mem. Inst. Medicine, Phi Beta Kappa, Alpha Omega Alpha Republican. Office: Office of Dean U NC Med School 125 MacNider Bldg CB #7000 Chapel Hill NC 27599 Office Phone: 919-966-4161.*

ROPP, MICHAEL E., engineering educator; m. Susan L. Spilker, June 29, 1991. PhD in Elec. Engring., Ga. Inst. of Tech., Atlanta, 1998. Registered profl. engr., NCEES. Asst. prof. of elec engring. S.D. State U., Brookings, 1999—2004, assoc. prof. of elec. engring., 2004—. Author: (book chpt.) Handbook of Power Electronics; contbr. articles to profl. jours. Dir. S.D. Energy Infrastructure Authority, Pierre, 2005—; dir. engring. advisor Trans-Am. Grid Inst., Memphis, 2002—06. Grantee NSF Early Faculty CAREER award, 2003—08. Mem.: IEEE (advisor of student br. 1999—2006, Tech. Prize Paper award 2003). Achievements include patents for method for preventing islanding of distributed generators connected to utility grids; research in determining relative effectiveness of islanding detection methods using phase criteria and nondetection zones. Office: SD State U EECS Dept Harding Hall 205 Brookings SD 57007-2220 Office Phone: 605-688-4664. E-mail: michael.ropp@sdstate.edu.

ROPPEL, MARK, lawyer; b. Calgary, Can., Aug. 29, 1963; arrived in U.S., 1989; s. Howard Ross and Karen Elaine Roppel. Student, U. Alberta, Edmonton, Can., 1981—84; LLB, BCL, McGill U., Montreal, 1988; LLM, Columbia U., NYC, 1990. Assoc. LeBoeuf, Lamb, Greene & MacRae, NYC, 1990—94, Shearman & Sterling, NYC, 1994—2000, ptnr., 2000—05, Cadwalader, Wickersham & Taft, NYC, 2005—. Author: Practical Law Handbook, 2005—06; contbr. articles to profl. jours. Mem.: ABA, Bar of City of NY, NY Bar Assn. Office: Cadwalader Wickersham & Taft One World Financial Ctr New York NY 10281 Office Phone: 212-504-5674. Office Fax: 212-504-6666. Business E-Mail: mark.roppel@cwt.com.

ROPPLE, LISA M., lawyer; b. June 25, 1962; BA summa cum laude, Holy Cross Coll., 1984; JD magna cum laude, Boston Coll., 1989. Bar: Mass. 1989, US Ct. Appeals (1st cir.). Ptnr., co-chair litigation dept. Ropes & Gray, Boston, 1989—. Editor (articles): Boston Coll. Law Rev. Office: Ropes & Gray 1 International Pl Boston MA 02110-2624 Office Phone: 617-951-7554. Office Fax: 617-951-7050. Business E-Mail: lisa.ropple@ropesgray.com.

ROPSKI, GARY MELCHIOR, lawyer; b. Erie, Pa., Apr. 19, 1952; s. Joseph Albert and Irene Stefania (Mszanowski) R.; m. Barbara Mary Schleck, May 15, 1982. BS in Physics, Carnegie-Mellon U., 1972; JD cum laude, Northwestern U. Sch. Law, 1976. Bar: Ill. 1976, U.S. Patent and Trademark Office 1976, U.S. Dist. Ct. (no. dist.) Ill. 1976, U.S. Ct. Appeals (7th cir.) 1977, U.S. Dist. Ct. (ea. dist.) Wis. 1977, U.S. Ct. Appeals (3d cir.) 1981, Pa. 1982, U.S. Ct. Claims 1982, U.S. Ct. Appeals (fed. cir.) 1982, U.S. Supreme Ct. 1982, U.S. Dist. Ct. (ea. dist.) Mich. 1984, U.S. Dist. Ct. (no. dist.) Calif. 1986. Assoc. Brinks Hofer Gilson & Lione, Chgo., 1976-81, shareholder, 1981—, pres., 2006—. Adj. prof. patents and copyrights Northwestern U. Sch. Law, Chgo., 1982-97. Contbr. numerous articles to profl. jours. Mem. ABA, Internat. Bar Assn., Internat. Trademark Assn., Am. Intellectual Property Law Assn., Ill. Bar Assn., Intellectual Property Law Assn. Chgo., Chgo. Bar Assn., Univ. Club, Chgo. Yacht Club. Roman Catholic. Office: Brinks Hofer Gilson & Lione Ste 3600 455 N Cityfront Plaza Dr Chicago IL 60611-5599 Office Phone: 312-321-4216. E-mail: gropski@brinkshofer.com.

ROQUE-MALHERBE, ROLANDO MARCOS ANTONIO, research scientist, institute director; b. Guines, Cuba; s. Rolando Roque and Silvia Malherbe; m. Teresa Fernandez, Dec. 7, 1992; children: Edelin Roque, Rolando Roque, Ruben Perez. Lic. in physics, Havana U., Cuba, 1970; MSc, Nat. Ctr. Sci. Rsch.-Tech. U. of Dresden, Havana, 1972; PhD, Moscow Inst. Steel and Alloys, 1978. Rsch. scientist Nat. Ctr. Sci. Rsch., Havana, 1971—92; rsch. assoc. ITQ-Poly. U. of Valencia, Spain, 1993—96; rsch. prof. CTSPS-Clark Atlanta U., 1997—98; dean sch. of sci. U. del Turabo, Gurabo, PR, 1999—2004, dir. inst. chem. and biol. tech., 2004—. Author 3 books; contbr. articles to profl. jours., chapters to books; patentee in field. Mem. Cuban Civic Movement, Havana, 1992; chmn. Cuban Valencian Assn. for Democracy, Valencia, 1994—96; del. in Valencia, mem. internat. bd. Cuban Liberal Union and Cuban Dem. Platform, 1993—96; bd. dirs. Statehood for Cuba, San Juan, PR, 2004. Mem.: Internat. Zeolite Assn. (assoc.), Am. Phys. Soc. (assoc.), Am. Chem. Soc. (assoc.). Roman Catholic. Achievements include discovery of new carbon oxides; heading research group that is one of the world's leaders in natural zeolite activities. Avocation: opera. Office Phone: 787-743-7979. E-mail: rroque@suagm.edu.

ROREM, NED, composer, writer; b. Richmond, Ind., Oct. 23, 1923; s. Clarence Rufus and Gladys (Miller) R. Student, Northwestern U., 1940-42, Curtis Inst., Phila., 1943; BA, Juilliard Sch. Music, 1946, MA, 1948; D.F.A. (hon.), Northwestern U., 1977, Curtis Inst., 1982. Slee prof., composer-in-residence Buffalo U., 1959-61; prof. composition U. Utah, 1965-67, Curtis Inst., 1980—2004, Yale U., New Haven, 1998—, Manhattan Sch. of Music, 1995—2000. Guest composer New Music New Haven Series Sch. Music Yale U., 1998, vis. prof., 1998-99; composer-in-residence Great Lakes Chamber Music Festival, 1999. Composer: symphonies No. 1, premiere Vienna, Austria, 1951, No. 2, premiere La Jolla, Calif., 1956, No. 3, premiere with Leonard Bernstein and N.Y. Philharmonic, 1959, Three Piano Sonatas, 1949, 50, 54, Lento for Strings, 1950, Design for Orch., 1954, The Robbers, 1956, Pilgrims for Strings, 1958, Eagles for Orch., 1958, Last Day, 1959, Lions, 1964, Ideas for Easy Orch., 1961, Piano Concerto No. 2, 1951, 3d Piano Concerto, 1970, Eleven Studies for Eleven Players, 1959, Water Music, 1966, Sun; for voice and orch., commd. by N.Y. Philharmonic, 1966, Air Music for Orch, 1974 (Pulitzer prize 1976), Assembly and Fall, 1975, Sunday Morning for Orch., 1977, Remembering Tommy, 1981; numerous chorus works, latest being Letters from Paris, 1965; for chorus and orch., commd. by Koussevitzky Found. in Library of Congress, Little Prayers, 1972, Whitman Cantata, 1982, An American Oratorio, 1983, Homer, 1986, Seven Motets, 1986, Te Deum, 1986, What is Pink?, 1987, The Death of Moses, 1987, Goodbye My Fancy, 1988; operas A Childhood Miracle, 1952, Three Sisters Who Are Not Sisters, 1969, Fables, 1970, Bertha, 1968, Miss Julie, 1964 (Ford Found. grantee), Hearing, 1976, Cycles: War Scenes, 1969, Six Songs for High Voice and Orchestra, 1954, Six Irish Poems, 1951, Poems of Love and the Rain, 1964, Ariel for Voice, clarinet and piano, 1971, Last Poems of Wallace Stevens for voice, cello and piano, 1971, Serenade for voice, violin, viola and piano, Women's Voices, 1975, The Nantucket Songs, 1979, Three Calamus Poems, 1982, The Schuyler Songs, 1987, Day Music and Night Music for Violin, 1972-73, Etudes for Piano, 1975, Book of Hours for flute and harp, A Quaker Reader for Organ, 1976, The Santa Fe Songs, 1980, Remembering Tommy, 1980, Views From the Oldest House for organ, 1981, Winter Pages, 1981, Picnic on the Marne for saxophone and piano, 1982, Dances for Cello, 1983, Violin Concerto, 1984, Organ Concerto, 1985, String Symphony, 1985, Septet: Scenes from Childhood, 1985, Trio: End of Summer, 1985, Quintet: Bright Music, 1988, Diversions for Brass Quintet, 1989, Trio (Spring Music), 1990, Three Organbooks; The Auden Poems, Trio for Violin, Cello, Piano, 1990, Swords and Plowshares (for 4 solo voices and orch.), 1991, Third Quartet, 1991, Fourth Concerto for Piano (left hand) and Orch., 1991, Present Laughter for mixed chorus, piano and brass, 1993, Fourth Quartet, 1994,

Songs of Sadness for quartet of baritone, guitar, clarinet and cello, 1994, More Than a Day for countertenor and orch., 1995, Six Variations for Two Pianos, 1995. Evidence of Things Not Seen, 1997; Autumn Music for Violin and Piano, 1997, Six Organ Pieces, 1998, Double Concerto for Violin, Cello and Orchestra, 1998, An Oboe Book, 1999, Another Sleep, Cello Concerto, 2001 Aftermath, 2002, Pas de Trois (oboe, violin, piano), 2002, Fifth String Quartet, 2002, Flute Concerto, 2002, Mallet Concerto, 2003, Our Town, an opera, 2005; commns. for U.S. Bicentennial include compositions for, Cin. Symphony, N.C. Symphony, Nat. Endowment of the Arts, Am. Harp Soc.; author: The Paris Diary of Ned Rorem, 1966, Music from Inside Out, 1967, The New York Diary, 1967, Music and People, 1968, Critical Affairs, 1970, Pure Contraption, 1973, The Later Diaries, 1974, An Absolute Gift, 1978, Setting the Tone, 1983, Paul's Blues, 1985, The Nantucket Diary, 1987, Settling the Score, 1988, Knowing When To Stop, 1994, Other Entertainment, 1996, Dear Paul, Dear Ned, 1997 (letters between Paul Bowles and Ned Rorem), Lies: A Diary (1986-1999), 2000 A Ned Rorem Reader, 2002, Wings of Friendship, 2005, Facing the Night, 2006; also articles newspapers, mags., Recs. for, Columbia, Decca, Odyssey, Desto, Phillips, Premier, C.R.I., Westminster, Orion, New World Records. Recipient Music Libraries Assn. award for song Lordly Hudson 1948, Gershwin Meml. award 1949, Lili Boulanger award 1950, Nat. Inst. Arts and Letters award 1968, Pulitzer prize in music 1976, Grammy award for Best Orchestral Rec., 1989; Fulbright fellow Paris, 1951-52; Guggenheim fellow, 1957-58, 77-78 Mem.: AAAL (pres. 2000—), ASCAP, PEN, Am. Acad. Arts & Letters (pres. 2000—03), Soc. Friends. Mem. Soc. Of Friends. Address: PO Box 764 Nantucket MA 02554-0764

**RORER, JOHN WHITELEY,** publisher, consultant; b. Phila., Aug. 4, 1930; s. Ronald Erle and Hazel (Whiteley) R.; m. Beverly Case, June 6, 1953. BS, U. Pa., 1952; MBA, Drexel U., 1956. Credit analyst Phila. Nat. Bank, 1954-56; with Curtis Pub. Co., Phila., 1956-68; dir. purchasing Chilton Pub. Co., Phila., 1968-70; founding pres. Focus Bus. Weekly, Bus. News, Inc., Phila., 1968—, pres., pub., 1974—; owner Pubs. Systems Assocs., Upper Darby, Pa., 1979—. Mem. Phila. World Affairs Council, 1979—. Served to capt. U.S. Army, 1952-54. Mem. Nat. Assn. Bus. Publs. (co-founder, bd. dirs. 1978-81), Nat. Assn. Indsl. Advt., Mktg. and Communications Execs. Assn., Union League Club (Phila.), Downtown Club. Republican. Episcopalian. Avocation: economics research. Office: 1015 Chestnut St Philadelphia PA 19107-4316

**RORICK, WILLIAM CALVIN,** librarian, educator, portrait artist; b. Elyria, Ohio, June 23, 1941; s. Harold R. and Edythe E. (Harris) R.; m. Anne L. Sherbondy, Aug. 21, 1971. BA in Econs. and Bus. Adminstrn., Ohio Wesleyan U., 1963; MusB in Music History and Lit., U. Utah, 1968; MusM in Music History and Lit., Northwestern U., 1970; MLS, Pratt Inst., 1974; MA in Musicology, NYU, 1982; studied portraiture, various art schs., workshops. Curator orchestral-choral libr., reference asst., office mgr. Manhattan Sch. Music Libr., NYC, 1970-74; music reference libr. CUNY Queens Coll. Music Libr., Flushing, 1974-96, instr., 1974-79, asst. prof., 1979-96, asst. prof. emeritus, 1996—, mem. senate nominating com., del.-at-large arts divsn., 1984-86. Portrait painting demonstrator various art orgns. Corp., instnl., pub. and pvt. portrait commns.; contbr. articles and revs. to profl. jours. Bd. deacons South Britain (Conn.) Congl. Ch., 1998—2001, historian, 2002. With U.S. Army, 1964—66. Grantee Rsch. Found. CUNY, 1981-84; recipient regional and nat. art awards including Best in Show Conn. Classic Arts Assn. Mem.: Kent Art Assn. (elected artist, bd. dirs. 2003—, mem. exhbn. com.), Acad. Artists Assn. (artist mem.), N.Y. Soc. Portrait Artists (mem. leadership team 2001—02), Conn. Soc. Portrait Artists, Portrait Soc. Atlanta, Portrait Soc. of Am., Inc., Soc. Creative Artists of Newtown (corr. sec. 1999—2002), Conn. Classic Arts, Inc. (publicity chmn. 1996—99), Sonneck Soc., Am. Soc. Portrait Artists, Music Libr. Assn. (program chmn. Greater N.Y. chpt. 1977—79, mem. nat. subcom. on basic music collection 1977—79, sec.-treas. 1979—81, chmn. nat. membership com. 1979—82, chpt. chmn. 1983—85, mem. Music Pub. Assn. joint com. 1986—88), Libr. Assn. CUNY (chmn. grants com. 1978—80, mem. publ. com. 1979—81, editor Directory 1980—81, del. 1983—85), Internat. Assn. Music Libr., Assn. for Recorded Sound Collections, Am. Printing History Assn., Am. Musicological Soc., Portrait Clubs Am. (cert. leader-instr. 2003—), Greater Southbury chpt.), Beta Phi Mu. Home: 63 Beacon Hill Dr Southbury CT 06488-1914 Office Phone: 203-264-4380.

**RORIE, CONRAD JONATHAN,** research scientist, retired military officer; b. Henning, Tenn., Oct. 28, 1930; s. Elvy and Lena (Jenkins) R.; m. Patricia Paris Cunliffe, Feb. 7, 1952; children: Michael Stephen, Catherine Jean, Patrick Jonathan. BS, Union U., 1952; MSEE, U.S. Naval Postgrad. Sch., 1961; PhD in Elect. Engring., Vanderbilt U., 1970. Enlisted USN, 1952, advanced through grades to adm., 1971; comdg. officer various ships, 1957—72; comdr. U.S. Naval Surface Weapons Ctr., Dahlgren, Va., 1974—77; dep. comdr. for surface combatants and weapons sys. engr. Naval Sea Sys. Command, Washington, 1977—81; comdr. Naval Surface Forces Mid. Pacific & Naval Base Pearl Harbor, Hawaii, 1981—84. Planning dir. Johns Hopkins U., Applied Physics Lab., 1984—; mem. numerous naval bd. for officer career devel., chmn. Weapons Systems Mgr./Ordnance Adv. Bd. to Naval Postgrad. Sch. President Hawaii Navy Relief Soc. and Red Cross, 1980; chmn. Combined Fed. Campaign Charity Dr., 1981; bd. dirs. Govs. for Navy Charity Retail Store, 1981; commissioning chmn. USS Antietam, 1987, USS Arleigh Burke, 1991; mem. Navy/Civilian U. Lab., 1988; mem. curricula rev. com. Naval Postgrad. Sch., 1977-81; bd. dirs. Historic USS Constellation, 1996; mem. warfare sys. adv. panel for 21st century aircraft carriers. Decorated Legion of Merit (4), Meritorious Svc. medal with gold star; recipient Ann. Disting. Alumnus award Union U., 1975, Am. Spirit of Honor medal, APL Disting. Svc. award Johns Hopkins U., 1998; named Tenn. Number One State Future Farmer 1948; C.J. Rorie annual award for Excellence established in his honor, 1987, Navy Surface Warfare Ctr. established in his honor. Mem. Naval Inst., Am. Soc. Naval Engrs., Nat. Security Indsl. Assn., AIAA, Am. Astronaut. Soc., U.S. Navy League, Armed Forces Communications and Electronics Assn., Mil. Order of Carabao, Masons, Bapt. Club, Sigma Xi, Eta Kappa Nu, Alpha Tau Omega. Conservative. Baptist. Office: Johns Hopkins U Applied Physics Lab Johns Hopkins Rd Laurel MD 20707 Home: 2124 McDonough Lane San Diego CA 92106 Personal E-mail: conradrorie@aol.com.

**RORIG, KURT JOACHIM,** chemist, science association director, educator; b. Bremerhaven, Germany, Dec. 1, 1920; came to U.S., 1924, naturalized 1929; s. Robert Herman and Martha (Grundke) R.; m. Helen Yonan, Mar. 20, 1949; children: James, Elizabeth, Miriam. BS, U. Chgo., 1942; MA, Carleton Coll., 1944; PhD, U. Wis., 1947. Lectr. Loyola U. Chgo., 1950-62; chemist to dir. Chem. Research G.D. Searle & Co., Chgo., 1947-87; pres. Chemo-Delphic Cons. Ltd., Chgo., 1987—. Adj. prof. chemistry U. Ill., Chgo., 1989—. Patentee in field. Mem. Sch. Bd., Wilmette, Ill., 1969-71. Mem. Am. Chem. Soc. (dir. Chgo. sect.), Am. Soc. Pharm. and Exptl. Therapeutics, N.Y. Acad. Scis., AAAS, Chgo. Chemists Club (past pres.). Presbyterian. Home and Office: 337 Hager Ln Glenview IL 60025-3329 Office Phone: 847-724-2808.

**RORISSA, ABEBE,** information scientist, educator; s. Rorissa Abdulie and Keneni Tolla; m. Mekdes Mulugeta, Dec. 14, 1995; 1 child, Amehe Abebe. BS in Math. Addis Ababa U., Ethiopia, 1988, MS in Info. Sci., 1993; PhD, U. North Tex., Denton, 2005. Grad. asst., supr. and head, computer sect. Addis Ababa U. Librs., Ethiopia, 1988—96; automation libr. Nat. U. of Lesotho, Roma, 1996—98; systems libr. and head, systems divsn. U. Namibia, Windhoek, 1998—2001, lectr., 2001; tchg./rsch. asst., instr. U. North Tex., 2001—05; asst. prof. SUNY, Albany, 2005—. Cons. UN Econ. Commn. for Africa, Addis Ababa, 1995—99, The World Conservation Union Regional Office for So. Africa, Harare, Zimbabwe, 2000, Ministry of Higher Edn., Sci., and Tech., Maputo, Mozambique, 2001. Fellow Inst. Mus. and Libr. Svcs., 2001—02. Mem.: ALA, Am. Soc. Info. Sci. and Tech. (adv. bd. bull. 2006). Office Phone: 518-442-5123. Fax: 518-442-5367. E-mail: arorissa@albany.edu.

**RORKE-ADAMS, LUCY BALIAN,** pathologist, educator; b. St. Paul, June 22, 1929; d. Aram Haji and Karzouhy (Ousdigian) Balian; m. Robert Radcliffe Rorke, June 4, 1960 (dec. Mar. 31, 2002); m. Boyce M. Adams, Apr. 16, 2004 (dec. June 21, 2006). AB, U. Minn., 1951, MA, 1952, BS, 1955, MD, 1957. Diplomate Am. Bd. Pathology. Intern Phila. Gen. Hosp., 1957-58, resident anat. pathology and neuropathology, 1958-62, asst. neuropathologist, 1963-67, chief pediat. pathologist, 1967-68, chief neuropathologist, 1968-69, chmn. dept. anat. pathology and chief neuropathologist, 1969-73, chmn. dept. pathology, 1973-77, pres. med. staff, 1973-75; neuropathologist Children's Hosp., Phila., 1965—, pres. med. staff, 1986-88, acting pathologist-in-chief, 1995-2000. Cons. neuropathologist Wyeth Rsch. Labs., Radnor, Pa., 1961—87, Wistar Inst. Anatomy and Biology, Phila., 1967—93; assoc. prof. pathology U. Pa. Sch. Medicine, Phila., 1970—, prof. pathology, 1973—, clin. prof. neurology, 1979—, clin. prof. pediat., 1997—; forensic neuropathologist Office Med. Examiner, Phila., 1977—2004. Author: Myelinization of the Brain in the Newborn, 1969, Pathology of Perinatal Brain Injury, 1982; mem. editl. bd. Jours. Neuropathology Exptl. Neurology, 1980—85, 1993—98, Pediat. Neurosurgery, 1984—2002, Child's Nervous Sys., 1984—88, Brain Pathology, 1990—95; contbr. articles to profl. jours. NIH fellow, 1961—62, NIH grantee, 1963—68. Fellow: Coll. Am. Pathologists; mem.: AMA, Phila. Coll. Physicians (trustee 2002—04, treas. 2004—), Burlington County Med. Soc., Am. Neurol. Soc., Am. Soc. Neuroradiology (hon.), Am. Assn. Neuropathologists (exec. coun. 1976—85, v.p. 1979—80, pres. 1981—82, Meritorious Svc. award 1999), Phila. Neurol. Soc. (v.p. 1971—72, editor transactions 1973, pres. 1975—76). Office: Childrens Hosp Phila 324 S 34th St Philadelphia PA 19104-4399 Home: 316 E Maple Ave Moorestown NJ 08057-2014 Business E-Mail: Rorke@email.chop.edu.

**RORSCHACH, KIMBERLY,** museum director; m. John Hart; 2 children. BA, Brandeis U.; PhD in art hist., Yale U. Curator Phila. Mus. Art, Rosenbach Mus. & Libr., Phila.; Dana Feitler dir. Smart Mus. Art, U. Chgo., 1994—2004; dir. Nasher Mus. Art, Duke U. (scheduled to open Oct. 2005), Durham, NC, 2004—. Mem.: Assn. Art Mus. Dirs. (trustee). Office: Nasher Mus Art PO Box 90732 Durham NC 27708 Office Phone: 919-684-8420.

**RORSCHACH, RICHARD GORDON,** lawyer; b. Tulsa, Aug. 9, 1928; s. Harold Emil and Margaret (Hermes) R.; m. Martha Kay King, Dec. 23, 1979; children by previous marriage: Richard Helm, Reagan Cartwright, Andrew Maxwell. BS, MIT, 1950; MS, U. Okla., 1952; JD, U. Houston, 1961. Bar: Tex. 1961; lic. prof. engr., Tex. Cons. civil engr. Freese & Nichols, Ft. Worth, 1955; cons. engr. Freese, Nichols & Turner, Houston, 1955-56; petroleum engr. Marathon Oil Co., Bay City, Tex., 1956-57, Houston, 1957-61, atty., 1961-64; ptnr. Broady, Kells & Rorschsch, Houston, 1964-68, Ragan, Russell & Rorschach, Houston, 1968-80, R.G. Rorschach & Assocs., Kilgore, Tex., 1980—. Mem. exec. com. Colonial Royalties Co., Tulsa, 1970-77; officer Little River Oil & Gas Co., 1980-88; mng. ptnr. Pentagon Oil Co., 1988—; pres. Nat. Assn. Royalty Owners-Tex., 1993-96, trustee, 2004-05; chmn. Nat. Assn. Royalty Owners, Inc., 1996-99, bd. dirs., 1999-2000, adv. bd. dirs., 2004-05; mem. exec. com. Nat. Assn. Royalty Owners, Inc.; owner, breeder, exhibitor Arabian Horses Shadowbrook Farm, Kilgore, Tex., 1980—. Author: How to Protect Your Royalty Interests: Texas Perspectives, Vols. 1 & 2, 2002. Served to 1st It. C.E., AUS, 1952-54, Korea. Mem. ASME, ASCE, Tex. Bar Assn., Rotary Club (pres. Kilgore chpt. 1984-85), Sigma Xi, Sigma Alpha Epsilon. Republican. Presbyterian. Home: 1893 CR 186 East Kilgore TX 75662-9023 Office: 1100 Stone Rd PO Box 1934 Kilgore TX 75663-1934

**ROSA, JOHN WILLIAM,** academic administrator, career military officer; m. Donna Kangeter; children: Jonathan, Brad. BA in Bus. Adminstrn., The Citadel, 1973; M in Pub. Adminstrn., Golden Gate U., 1985. Commd. 2d. lt. USAF, 1973, advanced through grades to lt. gen., 2003; A-7D pilot, scheduler, weapons officer 353rd Tactical Fighter Fighter Squadron, Myrtle Beach AFB, SC, 1975-77; A-10 pilot 356th Tactical Fighter Squadron, Myrtle Beach AFB, 1977—78; weapons officer 353rd Tactical Figher Squadron, Myrtle Beach AFB, 1979—80; pilot Hunter and Jaguar Aircraft, RAF Lossiemouth, Scotland, 1980-81; weapons instr. RAF Lossiemouth, 1981-83; instr. pilot, weapons officer, flight comdr. 61st Tactical Fighter Tng. Squadron, MacDill AFB, Fla., 1983-86; programmer, dir. of programs and resources Hdqrs. USAF, Washington, 1987-90; comdr. 35th Tactical Fighter Squadron, Kunsan AB, Korea, 1991-92, 366th Ops. Support Squadron, Mountain Home AFB, Idaho, 1992, dep. comdr., 1992-93; dep. comdr. to comdr. 49th Ops. Group, Holloman AFB, N.Mex., 1994-95; comdr. 20th Fighter Wing, Shaw AFB, SC, 1995-97; inspector gen. Hdqrs. Pacific Air Forces, Hickman AFB, Hawaii, 1997-98; comdt. Air Command and State Coll.. Air U.. Maxwell AFB, Ala., 1998—2000; comdr. 347th Wing, Moody AFB, Ga., 2000—01, 347th Rescue Wing, Moody AFB, 2001; dep. dir. ops. Ops. Directorate, the Joint Staff, Washington, DC, 2001—03; supt. USAF Acad., Colorado Springs, 2003—05; pres. The Citadel, Charleston, SC, 2005—. Decorated Def. Superior Svc. award, Meritorious Svc. medal with four oak leaf clusters, Air Force Commendation medal, Legion of Merit with oak leaf cluster, Combat Readiness medal with two oak leaf clusters. Office: The Citadel Office of Pres 171 Moultrie St Charleston SC 29409 Office Phone: 843-225-3294.*

**ROSA, RAYMOND ULRIC,** retired banker; b. New Britain, Conn., Jan. 30, 1927; s. Kenneth E. and Regina (Chenette) R.; m. Irene M. Asselin, Feb. 5, 1949; children: R. James, David M., Cathryn P., Michael F., Nancy A., Kenneth E. AS, Hillyer Coll., 1949. CPA, Conn. Pvt. practice pub. accounting, Manchester, Conn., 1949-52; auditor Auditors of Pub. Accounts, State of Conn., Hartford, 1952-65; dir. Fed.-State Relations Dept. Finance and Control, Conn., 1965-69; dep. commr. Finance and Control, Conn., 1969-71; sr. v.p., auditor Svgs. Savings, Hartford, 1971-90, ret., 1990. Mem. Windsor Locks (Conn.) Bd. Fin., 1973—81; pres. Savs. Bank Forum, 1981—82; trustee, sec.-treas. Mease Manor, Inc., Dunedin, Fla., 1995—2001, vice chmn., 2001—03, chmn., 2003—05. Treas. Mental Health Assn. Conn., 1974-77, pres., 1977-80, pron., 1980-83; bd. dirs. Nat. Assn. Mental Health, 1977-85, v.p. region 1, 1982-83; bd. dirs. Combined Health Appeal of Greater Hartford, 1982-90. Served with USNR, 1944-46. Mem. AICPA, Conn. Soc. CPAs, Conn. Soc. Govtl. Accts., KC, Dunedin Country Club (bd. dirs. 1997-2000, v.p. 1998-99, pres. 1999-00), Suffield Country Club (bd. govs. 1984-91). Home: 2060 Golf View Dr Dunedin FL 34698-2330 E-mail: rrosa1@tampabay.rr.com.

**ROSALDO, RENATO IGNACIO, JR.,** cultural anthropology educator; b. Champaign, Ill., Apr. 15, 1941; s. Renato Ignacio and Mary Louise Pratt (Potter) R.; m. Michelle Sharon Zimbalist, June 12, 1966 (dec. Oct. 1981); children: Samuel Mario, Manuel Zimbalist; m. Mary Louise Pratt, Nov. 26, 1983; 1 child, Olivia Emilia Rosaldo-Pratt. AB, Harvard U., 1963, PhD, 1971. Asst. prof. cultural anthropology Stanford (Calif.) U., 1970-76, assoc. prof., 1976-85, prof., 1985—2003, Mellon prof. interdisciplinary studies, 1987-90, dir. Ctr. for Chicano Rsch. 1985-90. chair anthropology, 1994-96, Lucie Stern prof. social scis., 1993—. Author: Ilongot Headhunting 1883-1974, 1980, Culture and Truth, 1989, Prayer to Spider Woman/Rezo a la mujer araña, 2003. Recipient Harry Benda prize Assn. for Asian Studies, 1983 Am. Book award, 2004; Guggenheim fellow, 1993. Fellow Am. Acad. Arts and Scis. Avocations: poetry, swimming, drawing, dance. Home: 12 W 15th St Apt 7H New York NY 10011-6792 Office: NYU Dept Anthropology 25 Waverly Pl New York NY 10003-6790 Business E-Mail: renato.rosaldo@nyu.edu.

**ROSALES, JENNIFER,** professional golfer; b. Manila, Philippines, Sept. 17, 1978; Attened, U. So. Calif. Winner Philippine Ladies Amateur Open, 1994—98, Chick Fil-A Charity Championship, 2004. NCCC individual champion, 1998; winner Golf World Invitational, 1998. Achievements include being tied for lead after three rounds of the 2004 US Open. Avocations: shopping, movies, pets. Office: c/o LPGA 100 International Golf Dr Daytona Beach FL 32124-1092*

**ROSALES, MONICA D.,** social studies educator; b. Hialeah, Fla., Oct. 24, 1974; d. Roberto F. and Maria A. Valdes; m. Ivan J. Rosales, Aug. 29, 1992; children: Ivan R., Marilyn I. AA in Secondary Edn., Miami Dade Coll., 1999; B Social Studies Edn., Fla. Internat. U., 2003, M L.Am. History, 2006. Cert.

grades 6-12 social studies tchr. Fla. Social studies tchr. Doral Mid. Sch., Miami, Fla., 2003—. Screenwriter Revolution. Mem.: AFLCIO, NEA, Oral History Assn., Am. Hist. Assn., Fla. Edn. Assn., Am. Fedn. Teachers, United Teachers Dade (Doral Mid. Sch. Rookie Tchr. of Yr. 2004), Nat. Coun. Social Studies, Nat. Assn. Latino Ind. Producers (writers group coord. 2003—06). Office Phone: 305-592-2822.

**ROSALES, SUZANNE MARIE,** hospital coordinator; b. Merced, Calif., July 23, 1946; d. Walter Marshall and Ethel Marie (Earl) Potter; children: Anita Carol, Michelle Suzanne. AA, City Coll., San Francisco, 1966. Diplomate Am. Coll. Utilization Review Physicians. Utilization review coord. San Francisco Gen. Hosp., 1967-74; mgr. utilization review/discharge planning UCLA Hosp. and Clinics, 1974-79; nurse III Hawaii State Hosp., Kaneohe, 1979-80; review coord. Pacific Profl. Std. Review Orgn., Honolulu, 1980-81; coord. admission and utilization reviewq The Rehab. Hosp. of the Pacific, Honolulu, 1981-85; coord. Pacific Med. Referral Project, Honolulu, 1985-87; dir. profl. svcs. The Queen's Healthcare Plan, Honolulu, 1987-88; utilization mgmt. coord. Vista Psychiat. Physician Assocs., San Diego, 1989; admission coord. utilization review San Francisco Gen. Hosp., 1989-91, quality improvement coordinator, 1991—. Cons. Am. Med. Records Assn. Contbr. articles to profl. jours. Mem. Nat. Assn. Utilization Review Profls. Home: 138 Alta Vista Way Daly City CA 94014-1402 Office: San Francisco Gen Hosp 1001 Potrero Ave San Francisco CA 94110-3594

**ROSALES HERRERA, RAÚL JOAQUIN,** language educator; b. N.Y.C., NY, June 29, 1978; s. Jose Joaquin and Paula Rosales. BA, Drew U., 1999; MA, Columbia U., 2000, MPhil, 2001, PhD, 2006. Tchg. fellow Spanish Columbia U., N.Y.C., 2000—03; asst. prof. Spanish Drew U., Madison, NJ, 2004—. Adj. instr. Spanish New Sch. U., N.Y.C., 2003—05; mem. Columbia U., Lang. Program Com., Dept. Spanish, 2003—. Summer Rsch. fellowship, Columbia U., 2002—05. Mem.: Am. Assn. Tchrs. Spanish and Portugese, Rocky Mt. Modern Lang. Assn., Modern Lang. Assn. Office: Drew U Dept Spanish 36 Madison Ave Madison NJ 07940 Home: 42 F Loantaka Way Madison NJ 07940 Office Phone: 973-408-3751. Personal E-mail: raulrh29@gmail.com.

**ROSALSKY, BARBARA ELLEN,** artist, community health nurse; b. N.Y.C., Nov. 16, 1948; d. Ellis M. Rosalsky and Claire (Schwartz) Rosalsky Shapiro; m. Dennis Robinson. BA, SUNY, Plattsburgh, 1970. Sales girl Cambridge Artist mag., Mass., 1970—71; artist Pillar of Fire mag., Zarephath, NJ, 1977; home health aide CMR, Bound Brook, NJ, 1978—; designer New Brunswick Tomorrow, NJ, 1980; art therapist Middlesex Hosp., New Brunswick, 1981—83; vol. office Robert Wood Johnson Hosp., 1995—. One-woman shows include The Bird and Me, 1980, Highland Pk. Libr., N.J., 2003, The City, 2003, exhibited in group shows at Other Artists Other Art, Robeson Newark Gallery, N.J., 1983. Mem. Cultural Arts Commn., Piscataway, N.J., 1993—. SUNY Plattsburgh scholar, 1970. Mem.: Women's Caucus Art, Quality Inn Swim Club. Democrat. Avocations: piano, swimming, dance, print making. Home: 114 Woodland Rd Piscataway NJ 08854-4222

**ROSAND, DAVID,** art historian, educator; b. Bklyn., Sept. 6, 1938; s. Johan Herbert and Frieda (Grotenstein) R.; m. Ellen Fineman, June 18, 1961; children: Jonathan, Eric. AB, Columbia Coll., 1959; MA, Columbia U., 1962, PhD, 1965. Instr. art history Columbia U., NYC, 1964-67, asst. prof., 1967-69, assoc. prof., 1969-73, prof., 1973-95, chmn. Soc. of Fellows in the Humanities, 1979-83, Meyer Schapiro prof. art history, 1995—. Co-author (with Michelangelo Muraro): Titian and the Venetian Woodcut, 1976, Titian, 1978; author: Painting in Cinquecento Venice: Titian, Veronese Tintoretto, 1982. rev. edit., 1997; author: (with others) Places of Delight: The Pastoral Landscape, 1988; author: The Meaning of the Mark: Leonardo and Titian, 1988, Painting in Sixteenth-Century Venice, rev. edit., 1997, Robert Motherwell on Paper, 1997, Myths of Venice: The Figuration of a State, 2001, Drawing Acts: Studies in Graphic Expression and Representation, 2002, The Invention of Painting in America, 2004; editor: Titian: His World and His Legacy, 1982; editor: (with Robert W. Hanning) Castiglione: The Ideal and the Real in Renaissance Culture, 1983; editor: Interpretazioni Veneziane, 1984. Mem. bd. advisors CASVA Nat. Gallery Art., 1990-94. Fulbright Commn. fellow, 1962-63; NEH fellow, 1971-72, 85-86, 91-92; John S. Guggenheim Meml. Found. fellow, 1974-75. Mem. Coll. Art Assn. Am., Renaissance Soc. Am. (mem. exec. bd. 1981—), Save Venice, Inc. (bd. dirs.), Ateneo Veneto (fgn.), Am. Acad. Arts and Scis. Home: 560 Riverside Dr New York NY 10027-3212 Office: Columbia U Dept Art History & Archaeology 826 Schermerhorn Hall Mail Code 5517 New York NY 10027 Office Phone: 212-854-4502. Business E-Mail: dr17@columbia.edu.

**ROSARIO-OLMEDO, CARMEN GLORIA,** principal; b. Mayaguez, P.R., Jan. 4, 1940; d. Rafael and Emilia (Derieux) Rosario; m. William Galindo, Apr. 19, 1968 (div. 1974); m. Ruben Eduardo Olmedo, Dec. 25, 1976. BA, CCNY, 1963; MA, NYU, 1982; profl. diploma, L.I. U., 1987. Cert. elem. prin., asst. prin., sch. dist. adminstr., sch. adminstr. and supr., permanent tchg. cert., N.Y.C. Tchr. N.Y.C. Bd. Edn., 1963-89, asst. prin., 1989-95, prin. I.A., 1995-97, prin.—1997—2001. Curriculum designer Cmty. Sch. Dist. 17, Bklyn., 1965-66, tchr. trainer, 1967-70; exch. tchr. trainer San Juan, P.R., 1970-71; founder, artistic dir. Children in the Arts, Bklyn., 1979-86; coord. sch. vol. program Pub. Sch. 316, Bklyn., 1988-95. Contbr.: The Mexican Family, 1979, The Chilean Family Structure, 1982. Mem. Puerto Rican Educator's Assn., NYC, 1979—, Atlas, NYC, 1972—93; mem. internat. com. YMCA, NYC, 2002—05; mem. global teens com., 2003—05; mem. Nat. Conf. Puerto Rican Women, 1998—. Recipient Women's Hist. Month award, Borough Pres. Office, 1986, McDonald cert. of appreciation, Anonymous Heroes of our Cmty., 1989, cert. of recognition, NYC Adminstrv. Women in Edn., 1989. NYC Coun. Proclamation annual, 2002, Bklyn. Borough Pres. Citation, 2002, NY State Senate 20th Dist. award, 2002, NY State Exec. Chamber Cert. of Merit, 2002, Cmty. Sch. Dist. 17 Dedicated Svc. award, 2001, Admin. of Yr. award, Fordham U. chpt., Phi Delta Kappa, 2001; Fulbright scholar, 1972, 1982, NDEA grantee, 1965. US Office Edn. Inst. for Tchg. Disadvantaged Children, 1965—66, Operation Understanding rsch. program grantee, NYC Bd. Edn., 1970—71. Mem. ASCD, Counsel of Supervisors and Adminstrs., Nat. Assn. P.R. Women, Hispanic Orgn. Latino Actors, Fulbright Assn. (life). Avocations: acting, adminstr., travel, writer, archaeology. Home: 176 Prospect Park W Brooklyn NY 11215-5285 Office: CGO Prop Corp Brooklyn NY Office Phone: 917-815-8424. E-mail: cgopropcorp@aol.com.

**ROSASCHI, JIM,** librarian; b. Alma, Mich., Apr. 4, 1949; s. Mary Henry and True Rosaschi; m. Gaylene Reynolds, Aug. 22, 1975; children: Nicole, Daniel, Michelle, Emma. MLS, Brigham Young U., 1979. Cert. K-12 tchrg. Calif., 1982. Dir. Nampa (Idaho) Pub. Libr., 1979—82; mgr. Petaluma br. libr. Sonoma County Libr., Sana Rosa, Calif., 1982—95, mgr. tech. svcs. Santa Rosa, 1985—89, mgr. tech. svcs. 1989—. Pres. Customers of Dynix, Inc., Salt Lake City, 2003; libr. tech. presentations, Melbourne, Australia, 03. Edinburgh, Scotland, 04. Adult sunday sch. tchr. Ch. of Jesus Christ of Latter-Day Saints, Santa Rosa, 1998—2003. With US Army, 1969-73. Mem.: Calif. Libr. Assn., ALA, Mormon History Assn. Home: 925 Hyland Dr Santa Rosa CA 95407 Office: Sonoma County Libr 3rd and E St Santa Rosa CA 95404 Office Phone: 707-545-0831.

**ROSATI, DIANE CLAIRE,** epidemiologist, educator, artist; d. Samual J. Castonguay and Edna Tomasulo; m. Vincent Rosati; children: Elissa, Alexander. Diplioma, Bklyn. Hosp. Sch. Nursing, 1962; BS cum laude, Wagner Coll., 1976; MPH, Columbia U., 1980. One-woman shows include Mooruing Gallery, Mahone Bay, 1995, Open Ho. Gallery, Anapolis, 1995, McKay List., 1996, Herman Hines Mus. Photography & Art Gallery, 1998, Shelburne County Mus., 1999, others, exhibitions include Nat. Art Club, 1997, Art Lab, Snug Harbor, 1997, St. Francis Xavier U., 1997, Krasedale Art Gallery, 1998, Pastel Soc. Can., 2000, Acadia U. Art Gallery, 2001, 2003, others, Represented in permanent collections Housatonic Mus. Art. Recipient Solo Show awards, Pen & Brush, 15 various awards for pastel, graphics, mixed media, 1992—2000, Philip Isenburg award for graphics, Salmagundi Club, Dorothy

Koatz Meyer award for innovative work, Augie Napoli Mem. award, Gerald Mennin award for graphics, Nat. Art Club, silver medal award, Audubon Artist Show, 56th Annual. Mem.: Nat. League Am. Pen Women, Pastel Soc. Can., Visual Arts Nova Scotia, Soc. Am. Graphic Artists, Nat. Assn. Women Artists, Pastel Soc. Am., Nova Scotia Print Makers Assn., Pen & Brush Soc. (bd.dirs., pastel chair), Print Club Albany, Nat. Art Club. Avocations: beekeeping, sailing.

**ROSATO, ANTHONY DOMINICK,** mechanical engineer, educator; b. Bklyn., Aug. 28, 1953; s. Michael Joseph and Betty (Rispoli) R. BME, Pratt Inst., 1975; MS in Theoretical and Applied Mechanics, Northwestern U., 1979; MS in Applied Maths., Carnegie Mellon U., 1981, PhD in Mech. Engring., 1985. Devel. engr. Green Fan Co., Beacon, NY, 1975—77; rsch. asst. dept. civil engring. Northwestern U., Evanston, Ill., 1977—79; tchg. asst. mech. engring. and maths. Carnegie Mellon U., Pitts., 1979—82, rsch. asst., 1981—84, rsch. assoc. dept. mech. engring., 1985—86; adj. faculty dept. exact scis. Carlow Coll., Pitts., 1986; asst. prof. mech. engring. N.J. Inst. Tech., Newark, 1987—93, assoc. prof. mech. engring., 1993—2002, prof. mech. engring., 2002—, dir. Particle Tech. Ctr., 1995—99, dir. Granular Sci. Lab., 2000—, coord. undergrad. rsch. in mech. engring., 2000—02. Faculty Gov.'s Sch. in Scis., Drew U., Madison, N.J., 1988; vis. faculty fellow, physicist dept. earth scis. Lawrence Livermore (Calif.) Nat. Lab., 1989, 90; Joliot professorship Ecole Superieure de Physique et de Chimie Industrielles, Laboratoire H.M.P., Paris, 1994; mem. nat. materials adv. bd. NRC, 1995; vis. scientist The Lovelace Insts., Albuquerque, 1995-96; vis. assoc. prof. mech. engring. Worcester Poly. Inst., 1995; assoc. chmn. mech. engring. grad. studies, N.J. Inst. Tech., 2001-2003; vis. scholar Stanford U., 2003 Co-editor-in-chief Mechanics Rsch. Comms.; mem. editl. bd. Internat. Jour. Nonlinear Sci. and Numerical Simulation. Chair sci. com. IUTAM Symposium, Cape May, N.J., 1999. Vis. scholar mech. engring. Stanford U., 2003. Fellow ASME; mem. Am. Soc. Engring. Edn. (program chair elect grad. studies divsn. 1995), Am. Acad. Mechanics, N.J. Inst. Tech. Ctr. for Applied Maths., Sigma Xi, Tau Beta Pi, Pi Tau Sigma. Roman Catholic. Office: NJ Inst Tech Mech Engring Dept University Heights Newark NJ 07102 Office Phone: 973-596-5829. E-mail: rosato@adm.njit.edu.

**ROSATO, JENNIFER L.,** dean, law educator; BS, Cornell U., 1983; JD, U. Pa., 1987. Law clk. to Hon. Thomas N. O'Neill, Jr. Fed. Dist. Ct., Ea. Dist. Pa.; assoc. Hangley Connolly Epstein Chicco Foxman and Ewing, Phila.; prof. Villanova Law Sch.; assoc. dean student affairs, co-dir. Ctr. for Health, Sci. and Pub. Policy Brooklyn Law Sch.; assoc. dean students, sr. prof. Coll. Law, Drexel U., Phila., 2006—, acting dean, 2006—. Vis. prof. U. Pa. Law Sch. Contbr. articles to profl. jours. Office: Drexel U Coll Law 3141 Chestnut St Philadelphia PA 19104 E-mail: jennifer.l.rosato@drexel.edu.*

**ROSBOTTOM, RONALD CARLISLE,** language educator, humanities educator; b. New Orleans, July 5, 1942; s. Albert Carlisle and Marjorie Catherine (Chavez) R.; m. Betty Elane Griffin, Sept. 5, 1964; 1 child, Michael K. BA, Tulane U., 1964; MA, Princeton U., 1966, PhD, 1969; MA (hon.), Amherst Coll., 1990. Instr. U. Pa., Phila., 1967-69, asst. prof., 1969-73; assoc. prof. Ohio State U., Columbus, 1973-78, prof. French lit., 1978-89, chmn. Romance langs., 1982-88; dean of faculty Amherst (Mass.) Coll., 1989-95, prof. French lit. and European studies, 1989—, Winifred L. Arms prof. arts and humanities, 1996—, chair European studies program, 1996—2005, acting chmn. dept. Spanish, 2004—06. Author: Marivaux's Novels, 1974, Choderlos de Laclos, 1979 (Havens prize 1980); editor: Studies in 18th Century Culture, 1975, 76, Essays in the French Enlightenment, 1991 Decorated Ordre des Palmes Académiques; Woodrow Wilson Found. fellow, 1964-65, 66-67; Am. Council Learned Socs. summer fellow, 1970 Mem. Am. Soc. 18th Century Studies (exec. sec. 1978-83, 2d v.p 1992-93, 1st v.p 1993-94, pres. 1994-95), Am. Assn. Tchrs. French, Phi Beta Kappa Democrat. Home: 326 Shays St Amherst MA 01002-2943 Office: Amherst Coll PO Box 2255 Amherst MA 01002-2255 Business E-Mail: rcrosbottom@amherst.edu.

**ROSCH, JOHN THOMAS (TOM ROSCH),** commissioner, lawyer; b. Council Bluffs, Iowa, Oct. 4, 1939; s. H.P. and Phebe Florence (Jamison) Rosch; m. Carolyn Lee, Aug. 18, 1961; children: Thomas Lee, Laura Lee. BA, Harvard U., 1961, LLB, 1965. Bar: Calif. 1966, US Dist. Ct. No. Dist. Calif. 1966, US Dist. Ct. Ea. Dist. Calif. 1967, US Ct. Appeals 9th cir. 1966. Assoc. McCutchen, Doyle, Brown & Enersen, San Francisco, 1965-72, ptnr., 1972-73, 75-93; dir. Bur. Consumer Protection FTC, Washington, 1973—75; ptnr. Latham & Watkins, San Francisco, 1994—2006, office mng. ptnr., 1994—99; commr. FTC, Washington, 2006—. Adv. bd. Antitrust and Trade Regulation Report, Bur. Nat. Affairs, 1976—2006, Practising Law Inst., NYC; bd. dirs. Eisenhower Inst., Washington, 2003—06. Contbr. articles to profl. jours. Knox Fellow, Cambridge U., 1962. Fellow Am. Bar Found., Am. Coll. Trial Lawyers; mem. ABA (chmn. antitrust sect. 1990), Calif. State Bar Assn. (past chair Antitrust and Unfair Competition Sect., Antitrust Lawyer of Yr. 2003) San Francisco Bar Assn. Republican. Episcopalian. Office: FTC 600 Pennsylvania Ave NW Rm 540 Washington DC 20580 Business E-Mail: trosch@ftc.gov.

**ROSCH, PAUL JOHN,** internist, educator; b. Yonkers, N.Y., June 30, 1927; s. Samuel Joseph and Mary (Gang) R.; m. Lorraine Marie Hunt, June 27, 1951; children: David Carl, Jonathan Hunt, Jane Ellen, Michael Edward, Richard Joseph, Donna Marie; m. Marguerite Delamater, Sept. 12, 1972. AB, Brown U., NYU, 1948, MA, 1950; MD, Albany Med. Coll., 1954. Diplomate Am. Bd. Internal Medicine. Fellow Inst. Exptl. Medicine and Surgery, U. Montreal, Que., Canada, 1951-52; intern, asst. resident in medicine Johns Hopkins Hosp., 1954-56; resident in medicine, then chief dept. metabolism Walter Reed Med. Ctr., 1956-58; physician-in-charge nuclear medicine St. John's Riverside Hosp., Yonkers, 1959-67, dir. endocrine clinic, sr. attending physician, 1959-96, vice chief of staff, 1977; chief endocrine clinic St. Joseph's Hosp., 1959, sr. cons. in medicine, 1980—; pres. Am. Inst. Stress, Yonkers, 1978—, sr. cons. in medicine, 1980—; clin. prof. medicine and psychiatry N.Y. Med. Coll., 1980—. Asst. clin. prof. medicine Mt. Sinai Hosp. Sch. Medicine, 1963-67; former adj. prof. medicine in psychiatry U. Md. Sch. Medicine. From asst. to assoc. editor Health Comm. and Informatics; editor-in-chief Stress Medicine, 1990—; mem. institutional bd. AMA Archives Internal Medicine, Folia Clinica Internat. Jour. Human Stress, Internat. Jour. Psychosomatics, Am. Jour. Health Promotion, Cardiovascular Revs. & Reports, Internat. Jour. Stress Mgmt., Comprehensive Therapy, Jour. Human Behavior; contbg. editor Creative Living; contbr. articles to profl. jours. Bd. govs. Jewish Community Ctr.; bd. dirs. Family Svc. Soc., Mensana Clinic, 1980—; chmn. bd. Internat. Found. Biosocial Devel. and Human Health, 1980—; mem. adv. bd. Image Inst., 1980—. Capt. AUS, 1956-58. Fellow ACP, Internat. Stress Mgmt. Assn. (hon. v.p. 1991—), Am. Coll. Cardiology, Internat. Acad. Medicine, Am. Coll. Angiology, N.Y. Diabetes Assn.; mem. Westchester Diabetes Assn. (pres. 1968), Internat. Law Enforcement Stress Assn. (adv. bd. 1980—), Yonkers Acad. Medicine (bd. govs., pres. 1971), N.Y. Cardiology Soc., Acad. Psychosomatic Medicine, Soc. Behavioral Medicine, N.Y. Acad. Scis., Endocrine Soc., Am. Diabetes Assn., Westchester Soc. Internat. Medicine (past pres.), Stress Mgmt. Assn. (hon. v.p.), N.Y. State Soc. Internal Medicine (pres. 1974), Soc. Nuclear Medicine (bd. dirs.), Am. Fedn. Clin. Rsch., Am. Soc. Internal Medicine, Am. Geriatrics Soc., Elmwood Country Club, Atlantis Golf Club, Breakers Golf Club, St. Andrews Golf Club, La Coquille Club (Palm Beach, Fla.). Home: 10 Old Jackson Ave Hastings On Hudson NY 10706-3203 Office Phone: 914-963-1200. Personal E-mail: stress124@optonline.net.

**ROSCOE, STANLEY NELSON,** psychologist, aeronautical engineer; b. Eureka, Calif., Nov. 4, 1920; s. Stanley Boughton and Martha Emma (Beer) R.; m. Margaret Hazel Brookins, Dec. 21, 1948 (dec.); children: Lee Marin Roscoe Bragg, Jack; m. Elizabeth Frances Lage, Mar. 12, 1977 (dec.); 1 child, Catherine Marie; m. Gayle Buchanan Karshner, Mar. 15, 1990. AB in Speech and English, Humboldt State U., 1943; postgrad., U. Calif., Berkeley, 1942, 46; MA in Psychology, U. Ill., 1947, PhD in Psychology, 1950. Cert. psychologist, Calif. Research inst. U. Ill., Urbana-Champaign, 1946-50, research assoc., 1950-51, asst. prof., 1951-52; assoc. dir. Inst. Aviation, head aviation rsch. lab., Savoy, 1969—75, prof. aviation, psychology, aero. and

astronautical engring., 1969—79, prof. emeritus, 1979—; prof. psychology N.Mex. State U., Las Cruces, 1979-86, prof. emeritus, 1986—; with Hughes Aircraft Co., Culver City, Calif., 1952-69, 75-77, dept. mgr., 1962-69, sr. scientist, 1975-77; tech. adviser, cons. in field. Pres. Illiana Aviation Scis. Ltd., Las Cruces, N.Mex., 1976—; v.p. Aero Innovation, Inc., Montreal. Author: Aviation Psychology, 1980, Flightdeck Performance: The Human Factor, 1990, Heydays in Mattole, 1996, Predicting Human Performance, 1997, Keeping the Picture: The Measurement of Flow Control, 1999; editor: Aviation Research Monographs, 1971-72, Heydays in Humboldt, 1991, From Humboldt to Kodiak, 1992; assoc. cons. editor Human Factors Jour., 1982—, Internat. Jour. Aviation Psychology, 1991—; contbr. more than 200 articles to profl. jours.; patentee, inventor in field. 1st lt. AC, U.S. Army, 1943-46. Fellow APA (divsn. of applied and engring. psychology, Franklin V. Taylor award 1976), Human Factors and Ergonomics Soc. (pres. 1960-61, Jerome H. Ely award 1968, 73, 89, 91, Alexander C. Williams award 1973, Paul M. Fitts award 1974, Pres.'s award 1990), Royal Aero Soc. (Eng.); mem. IEEE, AIAA, Inst. Navigation, Assn. Aviation Psychologists (ann. career award 1978), Aerospace Human Factors Assn. (Paul T. Hansen award 1994), Sigma Xi, Phi Kappa Phi, Phi Sigma, Chi Sigma Epsilon. Home: 2750 Sunnygrove Ave Mckinleyville CA 95519-7912 Office: PO Box 4498 Las Cruces NM 88003-4498

**ROSCOPF, CHARLES BUFORD,** lawyer; b. Marvell, Ark., Apr. 21, 1928; s. Emmett Lee and Sally Virginia (King) R.; m. Mary Anne Maddox, Aug. 22, 1954; children— Charles David; Ann Karen. Student, Hendrix Coll., 1948-50; JD, U. Ark., 1954. Bar: Ark. bar 1954, U.S. Dist. Cts 1955, 64, U.S. Supreme Ct. bar 1965. Pvt. practice, Helena, Ark., 1954—; assoc. firm Burke, Moore & Burke, 1954-58; ptnr. firm Burke & Roscopf, 1958-64; sr. ptnr. Roscopf and Roscopf, P.A., 1964—. Mem. Ark. Ho. of Reps., 1953-58; del. Ark. Constl. Conv., 1968; mem. Ark. Probate Drafting Com.; mem. Ark. State Bd. Law Examiners, 1973-79; spl. justice Ark. Supreme Ct. Served with USN, 1946-48; served with USAFR, 1962-68. Fellow Am. Bar Found., Ark. Bar Found. (pres. 1995-96); mem. ABA, Ark. Bar Assn. (pres. 1990-91), Am. Law Inst., Rotary (Paul Harris fellow), Masons, Shriners, Kappa Sigma. Methodist. Home: 117 Avalon Pl Helena AR 72342-1715 Office: Helena Nat Bank Bldg PO Box 610 Helena AR 72342-0610 Office Phone: 870-338-3438.

**ROSDEUTSCHER, JOHN DAVID,** plastic surgeon; b. Lexington, Ky., Jan. 7, 1965; BA, Vanderbilt U., 1987; MD, Vanderbilt Sch. Medicine, 1991. Diplomate Am. Bd. Plastic Surgery, Am. Bd. Otolaryngolgy. Plastic surgeon Mid South Plastic Surgery, PA, Hermitage, Tenn., 1998—2000; asst. prof. surgery Meharry Med. Coll., 2000—03; asst. clin. prof. Vanderbilt Sch. Medicine, Nashville, 2000—; plastic surgeon Cumberland Plastic Surgery, Hermitage, Tenn., 2003—. Mem.: Southeastern Soc. Plastic Surgeons, Am. Acad. Otolaryngology, Am. Soc. Plastic Surgeons. Presbyn. Office: Cumberland Plastic Surgery PC 5651 Frist Blvd Ste 708 Hermitage TN 37076

**ROSE, ALAN F.,** human factors engineer; b. Plattsburgh, Ny, June 26, 1971; m. Janet Liu, 2006. BS in Tech. Comm., Clarkson U., 1993; MS in Human Factors & Info. Design, Bentley Coll., 2005. Software usability engr. IBM Corp., Boca Raton, Fla., 1993—96; sr. usability engr. Open Market, Inc., Burlington, Mass., 1997—98; art dir. Lycos, Inc., Waltham, 1999—2001; user experience lead Partners HealthCare Sys., Inc., Wellesley, 2002—. Della Whitaker Scholarship, Soc. Tech. Communication, 1992. Mem.: Usability Professionals Assn., Acm Sigchi, Beta Gamma Sigma (life). Personal E-mail: alan@uexperience.com.

**ROSE, ALBERT SCHOENBURG,** lawyer, educator; b. Nov. 9, 1945; s. Albert Schoenberg Sr. and Karleen (Klein) Rose; m. Nancy K. Rose; children: Claudia, Micah Daniel. BSBA, U. Ala., 1967; JD, Washington U., St. Louis, 1970; LLM in Taxation, George Washington U., 1974. Bar: Mo. 1970, U.S. Dist. Ct. (ea. dist.) Mo. 1970, U.S. Tax Ct. 1970, U.S. Ct. Mil. Appeals 1970, U.S. Supreme Ct. 1970. Ptnr. Lewis Rice & Fingersh, St. Louis, 2001—. Adj. prof. law Washington U., 1979-98, Fontbonne Coll., 1993-96. Co-author: Missouri Taxation Law and Practice, 1986, supplement, 1989. Capt. U.S. Army, 1970-74, Korea. Mem.: Civic Entrepreneurs Orgn. (Bd. dirs., sec.), Tax Lawyers Club, Mid.Am. Tax Conf. (chmn.). Office: Lewis Rice & Fingersh 500 North Broadway Ste 2000 Saint Louis MO 63102 Office Phone: 314-444-1300. E-mail: arose@lewisrice.com.

**ROSE, ALFRED O.,** lawyer; b. Townshend, Vt., Dec. 9, 1957; married. BA summa cum laude, Dartmouth Coll., 1979; JD, Yale U., 1982. Bar: Mass. 1984. Law clk. U.S. Dist. Ct. NY (so. dist.), 1982—83; ptnr. Ropes & Gray, Boston, 1991—. Mem.: Phi Beta Kappa. Avocation: skiing. Office: Ropes & Gray One Internat Plz Boston MA 02110-2624 Office Phone: 617-951-7372. Office Fax: 617-951-7050. E-mail: alfred.rose@ropesgray.com.

**ROSE, ARON D.,** ophthalmologist, educator; b. Norwalk, Conn., Sept. 23, 1958; s. Gilbert and Anne Rose; m. Stacey L. Miller; children: Jenna, Lauren, Hannah. BA (hon.), Brown U., Providence, 1980; MD, NY Med. Coll., Valhalla, 1985; degree in ophthalmology, Mt. Sinai Sch. of Medicine, NYC, 1989. Fellow Am. Bd. Ophthalmology, 1989. Assoc. clin. prof. Yale U. Sch. Medicine, New Haven, 1989—, Yale U. Sch. Nursing, New Haven, 1996—. Dir., residency tng. Yale U. Dept. Ophthalmology and Visual Scis., New Haven, 1992—94; cons. Advanced Med. Optics, Santa Ana, Calif., 2003—; sect. editor Techniques in Ophthalmology, 2004—. Composer: Quartet for Clarinet & Strings, 1980; contbr. articles various profl. jours. Advisor JusticeWorks Med. Humanitarian Assn., Newtown, Pa., 1994—99; bd. mem. New Haven Med. Assn., 1995—2004; strategic oversight New Haven Hunger & Relief, 1997—2006; invited faculty Project Orbis Internat., NYC, 1992—2006; advisor Yale China Health Adv. Com. Recipient Brand Music Premium for Excellence in Musical Composition, Brown U., 1980, Departmental Honors, 1980. Fellow: Am. Acad. Ophthalmology (life); mem.: European Soc. Cataract and Refractive Surgeons, Conn. Soc. Eye Physicians, Conn. Glaucoma Soc., New Eng. Ophthal. Soc., Conn. State Med. Soc., Am. Soc. Cataract and Refractive Surgeons. Office: Eye Care Group PC 40 Temple St 5B New Haven CT 06405 Office Phone: 203-789-2020.

**ROSE, ARTHUR LOUIS,** neurologist, educator; b. Cracow, Poland, July 21, 1932; arrived in U.S., 1960; s. Jan and Irena Rose; m. Anne Maguire, Aug. 1963 (div.); children: Simon, Julia; m. Victoria Azara, Mar. 19, 1989. MBChB, Bristol U., Eng., 1957; Diploma of Child Health, U. London, 1958; MD, SUNY, 1979. Diplomate Am. Bd. Pediat., Am. Bd. Psychiatry & Neurology, Am. Bd. Psychiatry & Neurology-Child Neurology. Instr Harvard Med. Sch., Boston, 1961—63; registrar Regional Neurol. Ctr., Newcastle, 1964—65; acad. registrar Nat. Hosp. Queen Sq., London, 1965—66; instr. Columbia U., N.Y.C., 1966—67; from asst. to assoc. prof. Albert Einstein Sch. Medicine, N.Y.C., 1967—75; dir. divsn. pediat. neurology SUNY Downstate Med. Ctr., Bklyn., 1975—97, assoc. prof. neurology, 1975—80, prof. neurology and pediat., 1980—. Vis. scientist N.Y. Inst. for Basic Rsch., Staten Island, NY, 1997—98; examiner child neurology Am. Bd. Psychiatry & Neurology, 1985—. Contbr. articles to profl. jours. Founding pres. Tristate Child Neurol. Soc., N.Y.C., 1978. Fellow: Am. Acad. Neurology; mem.: Soc. Pediat. Rsch., Assn. Rsch. Nervous and Mental Diseases, Profs. Child Neurology (bd. dirs., com. mem. 1975—), Child Neurology Soc. Office: SUNY Downstate Med Ctr PO Box 118 Brooklyn NY 11203

**ROSE, ARTHUR ROYAL,** financial planner, tax consultant; b. Red Bank, NJ, July 22, 1955; s. Melvin S. and Margaret L. R. BS in Bus. summa cum laude, Monmouth U., 1986, BA in Psychology summa cum laude, 1986, MBA, 1990. CFP; Accredited tax preparer; registered investment advisor N.J.; enrolled agt. IRS. CFO, Interphase Industries Inc., Red Bank, 1986-91; pres. World-View Inc, Red Bank, 1991—. Office: World-View Inc 114B Monmouth St Red Bank NJ 07701-1109

**ROSE, BEATRICE SCHROEDER (MRS. WILLIAM H. ROSE),** harpist, educator; b. Ridgewood, NJ, Nov. 15, 1922; d. Henry William and Ida (LeHovey) Schroeder; m. William Harrison Rose, Apr. 10, 1954; 1 child, Daniel. Student, Inst. Musical Art, 1940—41, Mannes Coll. Music,

1942—44; studies with, Lucile Lawrence and Carlos Salzedo. Concert and radio debut NY World's Fair, NYC, 1939; soloist Damrosch Music Appreciation Hour broadcast, 1940, Duke of Windsor's Save the Children Fund, Nassau, The Bahamas, 1941; assoc. harpist Radio City Music Hall Orch., NYC, 1944-50; various radio and solo performances NY area, 1944-51; concert artist Italy, US and Can., 1952; prin. harpist Houston Symphony, 1953-84; prof. harp Moores Sch. Music, U. Houston, 1953—98. Soloist Contemporary Music Soc., 1959, 60, Houston Chamber Orch., 1969; dir. Christmas Festival of Harps, Houston Harp Ensemble, PBS, 1978, Harps of Gold, 1983; staff harpist Heritage Club, 1987-95, High Tea Ritz Carlton, 1996-97, St. Regis, 1998-2003. Author: The Harp in the Orchestra: A Reference Book for Harpists, Teachers, Composers and Conductors, 2003; composer works include Enchanted Harp, rev. edit., 1995; recs. for Houston Symphony, Stokowski, Everest, Capitol, Comissiona, Vanguard Records. Recipient 1st prize Federated Music Clubs Contest, 1936; NY Hour of Music award, 1945. Mem. Am. Harp Soc., Tex. Music Educators Assn. (adjudicator All-State competitions), Nat. Fedn. Music Clubs (harp adviser 1991), Phi Beta. Home: 1315 Friarcreek Ln Houston TX 77055-6714 Office: U Houston Sch Music Houston TX 77004

**ROSE, CAROL ANN,** retired air transportation executive; b. Toledo, Ohio; d. Donald Lucien and Dorothy Josephine (Maus) Edmunds; m. Saul Rose, Feb. 3, 1971 (div. 1976). BA, Kent State U., 1963. Entertainer, restaurant supr. S.S. Aquarama Cruiseship, Cleve., 1961-63; airline reservation agt. United Airlines, Cleve., 1963-68, internat. passenger svc. rep. Miami, Fla., 1969-70, V.I.P. customer svc. receptionist-expediter Phila., 1971-79, account exec., 1980-84, spl. events mgr. Chgo., 1984-87, red carpet club coord., 1987-88, corp. meeting planner, 1988-90, comml. aircraft weight and balance planner Seattle, 1991-96, comms. coord., 1996-98, mktg. and promotion coord., 1998-99, coord. workers compensation-comm./return to work Chgo., 1999—2001; ret., 2001; vol. editor Spiceline cmty. newsletter. Speaker Am. Mktg. Assn., Chgo., 1989. Author: Red Carpet Club Procedure Manual-O'Hare, 1987, Corporate Meeting Planners Manual, 1989, United Airlines Foundation Community Connection Report; Editor: Sky Lines Seattle Station Newsletter, 1992, United Airlines Workers' Compensation Newsletter, 1999 Vol. Relay for Life Am. Cancer Soc. Recipient Oustanding Svc. award Airline Passengers Assn., Phila., 1981, Outstanding Contbn. award Muscular Dystrophy Assn.-Jerry Lewis Telethon, Las Vegas, 1985, 86, 89, Leadership award United Way Campaign, Chgo., 1988. Mem. Meeting Planners Assn. Mgmt. Club (v.p. 1983, pres. 1984), Women United (exec. bd. 1982-83), Spicer Estates Homeowners Assn. (pres.), Delta Zeta. Avocations: reading, walking, writing, dance. Home: 468 Woodruff Trl Mullica Hill NJ 08062-2026

**ROSE, CAROL MARGUERITE,** law educator; b. Washington, Apr. 12, 1940; d. J. Hugh and Marie (Meenehan) R. BA, Antioch Coll., 1962; MA, U. Chgo., 1963, JD, 1977; PhD, Cornell U., 1970. Bar: Ill. 1977, Calif. 1978, D.C. 1978. Instr. history Ohio St. U., Columbus, 1969-73; assoc. dir. So. Govtl. Monitor Project, Atlanta, 1975-76; law clk. to judge U.S. Ct. Appeals (5th cir.), Austin, Tex., 1977-78; asst. prof. law Stanford U., 1978-80; acting prof. law U. Calif., Berkeley, 1980-82; prof. law Northwestern U., Chgo., 1982-88, Yale U., 1989—90, Fred A. Johnston prof. New Haven, 1990—94, Gordon Bradford Tweedy prof. of law and orgn., 1994—2005; emerita, 2005—. Bd. editors Found. Press, Mineola, N.Y., 1986—. Mem. Am. Assn. Law Schs., Am. Acad. Arts and Scis., Order of Coif. Office: U Ariz Coll of Law PO Box 210176 Tucson AZ 85721-0176 E-mail: carol.rose@yale.edu.

**ROSE, CHARLES ALEXANDER,** lawyer; b. Louisville, June 14, 1932; s. Hector Edward and Mary (Shepard) R.; m. Moncie Watson; children: Marc, Craig, Lorna, Gordon, Alex, Sara. BA, U. Louisville, 1954, JD, 1960. Bar: Ky. 1960, U.S. Ct. Appeals (6th cir.) 1970, Ind. 1978, U.S. Supreme Ct. 1978. Pvt. practice, Louisville, 1960-63; assoc. Jones, Ewen & McKenzie, Louisville, 1963-65; ptnr. Curtis & Rose, Louisville, 1965-81, Weber & Rose, Louisville, 1981—. Organist Scottish Rite Temple, Louisville. Lt. USAF, 1954-56. Mem. ABA, Ky. Bar Assn., Ind. Bar Assn., Louisville Bar Assn., Am. Soc. Hosp. Attys., Am. Bd. Trial Advocates, Brandeis Soc., Fedn. Ins. Counsel, River Road Country Club, Pendennis Club (Louisville), Jefferson Club. Republican. Episcopalian. Office: 400 W Market St Ste 2700 Louisville KY 40202-3358

**ROSE, CHARLIE (CHARLES PEETE ROSE JR.),** television journalist; b. Henderson, NC, Jan. 5, 1942; s. Charles Rose Sr. and Margaret Rose; m. Mary King (div. 1980). B in History, Duke U., JD; Ph.D (hon.), C.W. Post Coll., UNC-Pembroke. Interviewer Sta. WPIX-TV, N.Y.C., 1972; mng. editor Bill Moyers Internat. Report, 1974—75; exec. producer Bill Moyers Jour., 1975—76; corr. USA.E.: A People in Politics, PBS, 1976; polit. corr. NBC News, 1976-77; co-host A.M. Chgo., 1978; host The Charlie Rose Show Sta. KXAS-TV, Dallas, Ft. Worth, 1979-81, Sta. WRC-TV, Washington, 1981-83; host, interviewer CBS News Nightwatch, Washington, 1984—90; exec. prodr., exec. editor and host The Charlies Rose Show, 1991—; corr. Sixty Minutes II, 1999—. Producer: (TV program) A Conversation with Jimmy Carter (George Peabody Broadcasting award). Recipient News and Documentary Emmy award for Conversation with Roger Payne, 1992, Cable ACE award, 1992, Futrell award, 2005. Office: 499 Park Ave New York NY 10022-1240

**ROSE, DALE A.J.,** performing arts educator; b. Detroit, Sept. 5, 1946; s. Ora Henry Rose and Vida Blanche Birkett. BA, Mich. State U., 1966, MA, 1968. Performing arts coord. Mich. State Arts Coun. for the Arts, 1968—69; asst. prof. U. South Fla., Tampa, 1973—77; asst. prof. divsn. theatre So. Meth. U., Dallas, 1977—81, adj. prof. 1984—85, assoc. prof., 1985—88, Mo. Repertory Theatre/U. Mo., Kansas City, 1988—97, prof., 1997—2004; dir. Sch. Theatre and Dance U. South Fla., Tampa, 2004—05; dir. performance studies U. Conn., Storrs, 2005—; master tchr. acting The Actors Ctr., N.Y.C., 2005—; assoc. artistic dir. Conn. Repertory Theatre, Storrs, 2005—. Artistic dir. Shakespeare Festival of Dallas, 1986—90, The Plaza Theatre, Dallas, 1983—84; acting tchr. George Morrison Studio and Warren Robertson Theatre Workshop, N.Y.C., 1981—83; co-founder, dir. Stage #1, Dallas, 1979—85; artistic dir., founder The Alice People Theatre Co., Tampa, 1974—77; host, commentator The Bergman Films-WUSF-TV, 1975; co-host, theatre/film critic Variety, WTOG-TV, St. Petersburg, Fla., 1973—76; actor, N.Y.C., 1970—73. Dir.: (plays) The Boys Next Door, 1991, Hydrophobia, 1993, The First Family of Africa, 1993, The Very First Family, 1994, The Belle of Amherst, 1996, Babes in Arms, 1996, Les Liaisons Dangereuses, 1998, Charley's Aunt, 2000; author: (plays) The Pearl, 1994; screenwriter Eye for Eye, 1996—98; dir.: (plays) numerous plays, as You Like It, 2006. Office: University of Connecticut 802 Bolton Rd Unit 1127 Storrs Mansfield CT 06269

**ROSE, DANIEL,** real estate company executive, consultant; b. NYC, Oct. 31, 1929; s. Samuel B. and Belle (Bernstein) R.; m. Joanna Semel, Sept. 16, 1956; children: David Semel, Joseph Benedict, Emily, Gideon Gregory. Student, Yale U., 1947-50; cert. of proficiency in Russian lang., U.S. Air Force Program, 1951; BA, Syracuse U., 1952; postgrad., U. Paris. With Dwelling Mgrs., Inc., N.Y.C., 1954—; pres., 1960—, vice-chmn., sec.-treas. Baltic-Am. Enterprise Fund, 1994—; dir. Dreyfus Tax Exempt Bond Fund Inc., 1976-82, Dreyfus Money Market Fund, Inc., 1980-82; pres., CEO Rose Assocs., Inc., N.Y.C., 1980-99, chmn., 1999—, 22 Dreyfus Funds, 1992—. Assoc. fellow Pierson Coll. Yale U., 1974—; bd. govs., hon. life mem. Technion-Israel Inst. Tech.; bd. dirs., grants com. Realty Found. N.Y.; vice-chmn. Lionel Trilling seminars Columbia U., 1977—; bd. dirs. Ventures in Edn.; trustee, mem. exec. and compensation and benefits coms. U.S. Trust Co. of N.Y., 1982-92; trustee, vice-chmn. mixed use devel. coun. Urban Land Inst., 1986-93; exec. com. Urban Land Found., 1989—, gov., 1993—; designated Cert. Property Mgr. Inst. for Real Estate Mgmt. Expert adv. to sec. HUD, 1972; expert/cons. to commr. edn. HEW, 1977; cons. HUD panel on urban devel., 1984-86; dir. N.Y. Coun. Humanities, 1980-86, N.Y. Conv. Ctr. Devel. Corp., 1980-90, Get Ahead Found., 1989-98, Fifth Ave. Assn. 1989-98; mem. Governor's Task Force on Housing, 1975, Task Force on Taxation, Mcpl. Assistance Corp., 1976-77, Planning Commn. Theatre Adv.

Group, coun. of fellows, vis. com. to grad. faculty, bd. overseers Ctr. for Study of N.Y.C. affairs New Sch. for Social Rsch.; overseers com. to visit Ctr. Internat. Affairs Harvard U., 1992-98; Mcpl. Broadcasting System, 1977-78, MIT Ctr. for Real Estate Devel.; donor Daniel Rose chair urban econs., trustee NYU N.Y. Inst. for Humanistic Studies, Mus. of City of N.Y., 1984-90; chmn. bd. trustees, Horace Mann-Barnard Sch., 1971-74, trustee, 1962-89, hon. trustee, 1989—; v.p., assoc. treas., bd. dirs. Police Athletic League of N.Y., vice chmn. Cen. Harlem Facility; founder and pres. Harlem Ednl. Activities Fund Inc., YM & YWHA of the Bronx, 1963-67; v.p. N.Y. Landmarks Conservancy, bd. dirs. 1977-90; bd. dirs. Jewish Cmty. Ctrs. Assn., 1970—; pres. 1974-78, hon. pres. 1978—; v.p. World Confedn. of Jewish Cmty. Ctrs., 1977-83; former trustee and exec. com. mem. Fedn. of Jewish Philanthropies of N.Y., chmn. standing functional com. on cmty. ctrs., 1969-73; ptnr. N.Y.C. Partnership, 1990—; treas., bd. dirs. Citizens Housing and Planning Coun. of N.Y., 1972—; chmn. Dem. platform adv. com., 1984 Nat. Conv.; bd. advisors Dem. Leadership Coun., 1992—; Progressive Policy Inst.; trustee Dem. Nat. Com., 1988; chmn. Del. Svcs. Host Com., N.Y.C.; bd. trustees MBA of N.Y. Scholarship Found., Inc., 1996—. Served with USAF, 1951-54. Mem. Internat. Inst. Strategic Studies (dir. am. com. for IISS 1987—), Coun. on Fgn. Rels., Econ. Policy Inst. (pub. policy com. 1971—, chmn. fgn. policy assocs. 1972-75), East-West Inst. (bd. dirs. 1982—, treas. 1988—, co-chmn. fin. com. 1990—, chmn. exec. com. 2000—), Am. Soc. Real Estate Counselors (mem. publs.-rsch. com.), Real Estate Bd. of N.Y. Inc. (chmn. housing com. 1975—, mem. bd. govs. 1977-80, 90—, mem. REBNY Found.), Assn. of Yale Alumni (del.-at-large 1978-81, class of 1951 del. 1986-89), Century Assn. (N.Y.C.), Coffee House, Yale, Union League Club, Cosmos (Washington), Quaker Ridge Country Club, Noyac Country Club, Econ. Club N.Y. Office: Rose Associates Inc 200 Madison Ave Fl 5 New York NY 10016-3912 E-mail: drose@rosenyc.com.

**ROSE, DEBRA FIELDS See FIELDS, DEBBI**

**ROSE, DEEDIE POTTER,** arts patron; BA in French, Tex. Christian U. Mem. Nat. Coun. on Arts Nat. Endowment for Arts, 2002—; past pres. bd., bd. trustee Dallas Mus. Art; bd. dir. Dallas Ctr. for Performing Arts, Dallas Theater Ctr., Dallas Inst. for Humanities and Culture, Dallas Architectural Forum, Pub. Radio Internat., Channel 13/KERA 90.1, Tex. Internat. Theatrical Arts Soc., Dallas Found., Tex. Christian U.; adv. bd. U. Tex. Sch. Architecture; coun. mem. Dallas Women's Found. Recipient Neiman Marcus Silver Cup award, TACA, 1997. Mailing: Nat Endowment for Arts 1100 Pennsylvania Ave NW Washington DC 20505*

**ROSE, DONALD JOSEPH,** orthopedist, surgeon; b. Oakland, Calif., Feb. 7, 1953; s. David and Audrey Rose; m. Victoria Lasdou Rose, June 25, 1994; children: Dylan, Alexandra. BA, Cornell U., 1975; MD, U. Medicine and Dentistry N.J., 1980. Diplomate Am. Bd. Orthop. Surgery. Intern Beth Israel Med. Ctr., NYC; resident in orthop. surgery Hosp. Joint Diseases; fellow in sports medicine Temple U. Hosp., Phila.; assoc. clin. prof. NYU Med. Sch., N.Y.C.; dir. ambulatory surgery NYU-Hosp. for Joint Diseases, N.Y.C., dir. Harkness Ctr. for Sports Injuries. Recipient Documents of Dance award, Dance Libr. Israel, 1997, Disting. Alumnus award, U. Medicine and Dentistry N.J., 2002. Fellow: Am. Acad. Orthop. Surgeons, Am. Coll. Surgeons; mem.: Anthroscopy Assn. N.Am. Achievements include U.S. Nat. Champion in rowing; gold medalist in rowing World Maccabiah Games 1977. Avocations: tennis, skiing, sailing. Office: JMR Sports Medicine PC 1095 Park ave New York NY 10128 Office Phone: 212-427-7750. Business E-mail: jhrsports@aol.com.

**ROSE, DONALD MCGREGOR,** retired lawyer; b. Cin., Feb. 6, 1933; s. John Kreimer and Helen (Morris) R.; m. Constance Ruth Lanner, Nov. 29, 1958; children: Barbara Rose Burgess, Ann Rose Weston. AB in Econs., U. Cin., 1955; JD, Harvard U., 1958. Bar: Ohio 1958, U.S. Supreme Ct. 1962. Asst. legal officer USNR, Subic Bay, The Philippines, 1959-62, with Office of JAG The Pentagon, Va.; 1963-63; assoc. Frost & Jacobs, LLP, Cin., 1963-70, ptnr., 1970-93, sr. ptnr., 1993-97, ret. ptnr., 1997. Co-chmn. 6th Cir. Appellate Practice Inst., Cin., 1983, 90, 6th Cir. adv. com., 1990-98, chmn. subcom. on rules, 1990-94, chmn., 1994-96. Trustee Friends of Cin. Pks., Inc., 1980-89, 93-98, pres. 1980-86; trustee Am. Music Scholarship Assn., Cin., 1985-88; pres. Social Health Assn. Greater Cin. Area Inc., 1969-72; co-chmn. Harvard Law Sch. Fund for So. Ohio, Cin., 1985-87; pres. Meth. Union, Cin., 1983-85; chmn. trustees Hyde Pk. Cmty. United Meth. Ch., Cin., 1974-76, chmn. coun. on ministries, 1979-81, chmn. administrv. bd., 1982-84, chmn. missions, 1993-95; trustee Meth. Theol. Sch. Ohio, vice chmn. devel. com., 1990-94, sec. 1992-94, chmn. devel. com., 1994-98, vice chmn., 1998, chmn., 1999—2004; loaned exec. United Way, Cin., 1999. Lt. USNR, 1959-63. Mem.: 6th Cir. Judicial Conf. (sr.), Boothbay Harbor Yacht Club (bd. dirs. 2005—), Cin. Country Club. Republican. Avocations: sailing, golf. Home: 8 Walsh Ln Cincinnati OH 45208-3435 also: 11 Blackstone Rd Boothbay Harbor ME 04538-1943 Business E-mail: dmrose@fbtlaw.com.

**ROSE, DONNA MARIE,** secondary school educator, farmer; b. Rochester, N.Y., May 11, 1951; d. Robert James and Dorothy Lorraine (Shortsleeve) Weagley; m. Francis Ernest Rose, Aug. 18, 1973; children: Daniel Richard, William Michael. Student, SUNY, Albany, 1969-70; BS in Math./Edn., Nazareth Coll., Pittsford, N.Y., 1973-76; MA in Edn./Spl. Edn., U. Rochester, 1991, postgrad., 1991—94. Tchr. math. and bus. East Irondequoit Schs., Irondequoit, N.Y., 1973-78; tchr. math. Greece (N.Y.) Arcadia H.S., 1978, Rush Henrietta (N.Y.) Schs., 1978-79; tchr. math./computers East Rochester (N.Y.) Schs., 1979-82, Palmyra-Macedon H.S., NY, 1982—2006, K-12 math. curriculum coord., 1996—2002. Pres., sec., county math coord. Monroe County Math. League, Rochester, 1973—2000, state meet coord.; math. team coach, advisor Pal-Mac Math. Team. Palmyra 1982—. Cantor, flutist St. Louis Ch. folk Group-Choir, Pittsford, N.Y., 1980—2001, mem. choir 2001—; mgr. Farmer (N.Y) Farmer's Market, 1976—. Mem. Nat. Coun. Tchrs. Math. (life), Assn. Math. Tchrs. N.Y. State, Nat. Arbor Day Found., N.Y. State Assn. Math. Suprs., Women's Internat. Bowling Congress, Ontario County Farm Bur. Roman Catholic. Avocations: sewing, baking, gardening, stamp collecting/philately, doll collecting. Home: 7335 Valentown Rd Victor NY 14564-9714 Office: Palmyra-Macedon HS 151 Hyde Pky Palmyra NY 14522-1235 Office Phone: 315-597-3420 1115. Business E-mail: drose1@rochester.rr.com.

**ROSE, DWIGHT DEAN,** music educator; b. Omaha, Nebr., Apr. 6, 1970; s. Marvin Alan Rose (Deceased) and Betty Jane Rose. BA, Midland Luth. Coll., Fremont, NE, 1993; MA Music Ed., Univ. Nebr., Omaha, NE, 2002. Music educator Laurel-Concord Schools, Laurel, Nebr., 1993—97, Lyons-Decatur Schools, Lyons, 1997—2003. Recipient Snider Young Band Dir., Nebr. State Bandmasters Assn., 1998. Mem.: Music Educators Nat. Conf., Nebr. Music Educators Assn., Nebr. State Bandmasters Assn. Office: Lyons-Decatur Public Schools PO Box 526 Lyons NE 68038 Office Phone: 402-687-2363.

**ROSE, ELIHU,** real estate executive; b. NYC, Mar. 30, 1933; s. Samuel B. and Belle (Bernstein) R.; m. Susan Wechsler, Feb. 6, 1965; children: Amy, Isabel, Abigail. BS, Yale U., 1954; MA, NYU, 1969, PhD, 1978. Vice chmn. Rose Assocs., N.Y.C., 1956—. Contbr. articles to profl. mil. jours. Former chmn. bd. dirs. Internat. Ctr. Photography; bd. dirs. Sta. WNET (PBS), Lincoln Ctr. Theater, 1992—, Nat. Mus. Am. History, Smithsonian Instn. Fellow Am. Acad. Arts and Scis.; mem. Internat. Inst. Strategic Studies, Coun. Fgn. Rels., Literary Assn., Union League Club, Yale Club of N.Y., Army and Navy Club (Washington). Office: Rose Assocs 200 Madison Ave New York NY 10016-3903

**ROSE, ERIC,** physician, consultant; s. Israel and Susan Rose; m. Eleni Ledesma, 1997. BSc, Brown U., 1988; MD, Albert Einstein Coll. Medicine, 1993. Diplomate Am. Bd. Family Medicine. Physician U. Wash. Physicians, Seattle, 1997—2004; physician cons. IDX Sys. Corp., Seattle, 2004—05; product mgr. Practice Ptnr., Inc., Seattle, 2005—. Work group on functionality Cert. Commn. for Health Info. Tech., 2004—. Bd. dirs. Queen Anne Helpline,

Seattle, 2005—. Fellow: Am. Acad. Family Physicians; mem.: Am. Med. Informatics Assn. (pub. policy com. 2004—). Avocations: homebrewing, cycling. Office: Practice Ptnr Inc 2401 4th Ave Ste 700 Seattle WA 98121

**ROSE, GEORGE ANDREW,** application developer, information systems specialist; b. Mt. Clemens, Mich., Dec. 17, 1950; s. George Hubert and Geraldine Marie (Benoit) R. BA, BSW in Psychology and Biology, Ea. Mich. U., 1975; MBA in Internat. Fin., George Washington U., 1987. Inpatient substance abuse therapist St. Joseph's Hosp., Mt. Clemens, 1974—77; dep. twp. clk. Twp. of Clinton, Mich., 1977—79; social worker Bur. Rehab, Washington, 1979—84; sr. social worker Comprehensive Alcohol and Drug Abuse Ctr., Washington, 1984—88; contract mgmt. UMWA Health and Retirement Funds, Washington, 1988—91; dir. software devel., info. svcs. United Seniors Health Coop., Washington, 1993—98; pres., CEO Portsmouth Group, Inc., Washington, 1997—. Home: 2929 Connecticut Ave NW Ste 306 Washington DC 20008-1435 Office: The Portsmouth Group Inc Ste 605 1522 K St Washington DC 20005 Business E-Mail: georgerose@portsmouthgroup.net.

**ROSE, HERMAN,** artist; b. Bklyn., Nov. 6, 1909; s. Charles and Bella (Washelevsky) Rappaport; m. Tilly Lomsky, Mar. 15, 1934 (div.); children: George, Andrew; m. Elia Braca, Oct. 18, 1955. Student, N.A.D., 1927-29. Mem. staff art project Works Progress Adminstrn., 1934-39; tchr. Hofstra Coll., 1959-60, Bklyn. Coll., 1949-51, 58-61; instr. New Sch. Social Research, 1954-55, 63—; artist-in-residence U. Va., 1966, U. N.Mex., 1970-71, Queens Coll., 1974. One man shows include Egan Gallery, 1946-47, 48, A.C.A. Gallery, 1952-55, Forum Gallery, 1962, U. Va., Charlottesville, 1966, Bard Coll., Annandale-on-Hudson, N.Y., 1967, Nova Scotia Coll. Art, 1969, Zabriskie Gallery, 1967-69, 71-74, Fishbach Gallery, 1983, 86, 89, Coll. William and Mary, Williamsburg, Va., 1984; group shows include Mus. Modern Art, 1952, Barcelona, 1955, Paris, 1955, Tate Mus., London, 1956, Pa. Acad., 1953, Whitney Mus., 1948, 49, 53, 55, 56, Nat. Inst. Arts and Letters, 1956, 70, 72, Parrish Mus., Southhampton, N.Y., 1975, San Francsico Mus. Modern Art, 1985, Mus. at Stony Brook, L.I., N.Y., 1990, Macon Coll., Fredericksburg, Va., 1990; works in permanent collection Mus. Modern Art, Whitney Mus., U. Tex., U. Calif., Smithsonian Instn. Print Collection, Washington, Commerce Bancshares, Kans. City, Cigna Corp., Hallmark Coll., Reader's Digest, N.Y., Allied Bank of Tex., Sheldon Meml. Art Gallery, U. Nebr., Lincoln, Hirshhorn Mus. and Sculpture Garden, Washington, Weatherspoon Art Gallery, N.Y., Munson-Williams-Proctor Inst., Utica, N.Y., Parrish Art Mus., Southampton, Vassar Coll., Poughkeepsie, N.Y., NAD, N.Y.C., Palm Desert Mus., Palm Springs, Calif. Recipient Longview award, 1959, 60, 61, award Inst. Arts and Letters, 1972, Childe Hassam award, 1970, 73, Adolph and Esther Gottlieb Found. award, 1989, Oscar Williams and Gene Derwood award N.Y. Community Trust, 1984; Yaddo Scholar, 1955; Nat. Endowment for Arts grantee, 1976, 80; Pollack Krasner Found. grantee, 1989-90. Mem. NAD (Benjamin Altman 1st prize landscape 1976, 83, Henry Ward Ranger Fund purchase 1977, 85, Grumbacher gold medal, 1982, 85, Emil and Dines Carlsen award 1989). Office: care Fishbach Gallery 24 W 57th St New York NY 10019-3918

**ROSE, HUGH,** management consultant; b. Evanston, Ill., Sept. 10, 1926; s. Howard Gray and Catherine (Wilcox) R.; m. Mary Moore Austin, Oct. 25, 1952; children: Susan, Nancy, Gregory, Matthew, Mary. BS in Physics, U. Mich., 1951, MS in Geology, 1952; MBA with highest distinction, Pepperdine U., 1982. Mgr. Caterpillar, Inc., Peoria, Ill., 1952-66; v.p. mktg. mgr. Cummins Engine Co., Columbus, Ind., 1966-69; pres., CEO Cummins Northeastern, Inc., Boston, 1969-77; pres. Power Systems Assocs., L.A., 1980-83, CD High Tech., Inc., Austin, Tex., 1984-87; mgmt. cons. Rose and Assocs., Tucson, 1984, 87—; molecular cell biology rschr. U. Ariz. Cardio-Thoracic Lab., 2004—. Polit. activist. Contbr. articles to profl. jours. Bd. dirs. Raymond Alf Mus., Claremont, Calif., 1975—, Comstock Found., Tucson, 1988, Environ. Edn. Found., 1991, Heart Ctr. U. Ariz., Tucson, 1992. With USAAF, WWII. Fellow AAAS; mem. Acacia, Soc. Vertebrate Paleontology, Beacon Soc. Boston (pres. 1979-80), Algonquin Club Boston (v.p., bd. dirs. 1974-80), Duxbury Yacht Club, Longwood Cricket Club, Skyline Country Club, Phi Beta Kappa, Delta Mu Delta, Sigma Gamma Epsilon, Sigma Pi Sigma, Beta Beta Beta, Sigma Xi, Beta Gamma Sigma. Republican. Presbyterian. Office: Rose & Assocs 5320 N Camino Sumo Tucson AZ 85718-5132

**ROSE, I. NELSON,** lawyer, educator; b. LA, May 23, 1950; s. Bernard and Helen Mae (Nelson) Rose. BA, UCLA, 1973; JD, Harvard U., 1979. Bar: Hawaii 79, U.S. Dist. Ct. Hawaii 79, Calif. 80, U.S. Supreme Ct. 91. Pvt. practice, Honolulu, 1979-82; asst. prof. law Whittier Coll., LA, 1982—85, assoc. prof., 1985—89, tenured prof. law, 1989—. Cons. legal gaming; vis. scholar Inst. for Study of Gambling and Comml. Gaming, U. Nev., Reno. Author: Gambling and the Law, 1986; author: (with Robert A. Loeb) Blackjack and the Law, 1998; co-author (with Robert M. Jarvis, J. Wesley Cochran. Ronald J. Rychlak): Gaming Law: Cases and Materials, 2003; co-author: (with Martin D. Owens) Internet Gaming Law, 2005; contbr. articles profl. jour. and books. Founder, counsel Hawaii Lions Eye Bank, Honolulu; founder, v.p., counsel Calif. Coun. on Compulsive Gambling; mem. Calif. Gambling Policy Adv. Com., 2002—04. Mem.: ABA, Internat. Assn. Gaming Attys., Hawaii Bar Assn., Calif. State Bar Assn. Democrat. Jewish. Home: 17031 Encino Hills Dr Encino CA 91436-4009 Office: Whittier Law Sch 3333 Harbor Blvd Costa Mesa CA 92626-1501 Office Phone: 818-788-8509. Personal E-mail: rose@sprintmail.com.

**ROSE, IRWIN A. (ERNIE ROSE),** biochemist, educator; b. NYC, July 16, 1926; BS, U. Chgo., 1948, PhD in biochemistry, 1952. Specialist, Dept. Physiology and Biophysics, Sch. Med. U. Calif., Irvine, Calif. Contbr. articles to profl. jour. Co-recipient Nobel Prize in Chemistry, 2004. Mem.: NAS. Achievements include discovery of ubiquitin-mediated protein degradation. Office: U Calif Dept Physiology and Biophysics Coll Medicine Irvine CA 92697*

**ROSE, ISRAEL HAROLD,** mathematics professor; b. New Britain, Conn., May 17, 1917; s. Abraham and Dora (Dubrow) R.; m. Pearl Nitzberg, Jan. 24, 1942 (div. Feb. 1956); 1 son, Steven Philip; m. Susan Ann Lazarus, Mar. 26, 1961; children: Dora, Eric. Student, CCNY, 1934-36; AB, Bklyn. Coll., 1938, A.M., 1941; PhD, Harvard, 1951. Tutor, instr. Bklyn. Coll., 1938-41; instr. Pa. State Coll., 1942-46; asst. prof. U. Mass., 1948-54, assoc. prof., 1954-60; faculty Hunter Coll., 1960-68, prof. math., 1965-68, chmn. dept., 1966-68; prof. math. Lehman Coll., CUNY, 1968-82, prof. emeritus 1983—, chmn. dept., 1968-72, 80-82, resident prof., 1983—; vis. assoc. prof. Mt. Holyoke Coll., 1951-52, vis. assoc. prof., 1954-55, 58-59; sci. cons. AID, India, summer 1965 Author: A Modern Introduction to College Mathematics, 1959, Algebra: An Introduction to Finite Mathematics, 1963, Vectors and Analytic Geometry, 1968, Elementary Functions: A Precalculus Primer, 1973, (with Esther R. Phillips) Elementary Functions, 1978. NRC predoctoral fellow Harvard, 1946-48; fellow Fund Advancement Edn., 1952-53 Mem. Am. Math. Soc., Math. Assn. Am. (chmn. Met. N.Y. sect. 1973-75), Nat. Council Tchrs. Math., Assn. Math. Tchrs. Math. New Eng. (pres. Conn. Valley sect. 1956-57), Sigma Xi (pres. Hunter Coll. chpt. 1966-67) Home: 18 Floral Dr Hastings On Hudson NY 10706-1202 Office: Lehman Coll Bedford Park Blvd W Bronx NY 10468

**ROSE, JALEN,** professional basketball player; b. Detroit, Jan. 30, 1973; s. Jeanne R. Student, U. Mich. Guard Denver Nuggets, 1994-96, Ind. Pacers, 1996—2002, Chicago Bulls, 2002—04, Toronto Raptors, 2004—06, NY Knicks, 2006—. Named Honorable Mention All-Am. AP, 1991; set Michigan freshman scoring record, 1991; selected as All-Am., Parade Magazine, Third-Team All-Am., USA Today; set Nuggets' rookie record for assists, 1994-95 season; named to All-Rookie Second Team, NBA, 1995 Office: New York Knicks MSG 4 Penn Plz New York NY 10001*

**ROSE, JAMES TURNER,** aerospace engineer, consultant; b. Louisburg, NC, Sept. 21, 1935; s. Frank Rogers and Mary Burt (Turner) R.; m. Sandie Raymond, Sept. 15, 1984. BS with high honors, N.C. State U., 1957. Aero. rsch. engr. NASA, Langley Field, Va., 1957-59; project engr. NASA (Mercury and Gemini), Langley Field, Va. and Houston, 1959-64; program sys. mgr. McDonnell Douglas Astronautics Co (MDAC), St. Louis, 1964-69; mgr. shuttle ops. and implementation MDAC McDonnell Douglas Astronautics Co., St. Louis, 1969-72, mgr. shuttle support (MDAC), 1972-74, mgr. space processing programs, 1976-83; dir. electrophoresis ops. in space McDonnell Douglas Astronautics Co (MDAC), St. Louis 1983-86; dir. space shuttle engrng. NASA, Washington, 1974-76, asst. adminstr. comml. programs, 1987-91; aerospace cons., 1992—. Chmn. Fla. Space Bus. Roundtable, 1995-98. Recipient Silver award for mgmt. leadership AIAA, 1983, Presdl. Meritorious Rank award, 1989, NASA Exceptional Svc. medal, 1990, Laurels award Aviation Week, 1990, Aerospace Contribution to Soc. award AIAA, 1993. Mem. Phi Kappa Phi. Epsicopalian. Personal E-mail: jrose935@aol.com.

**ROSE, JANE A.,** financial planner; b. Phila., Sept. 30, 1940; d. Maurice and Miriam (Blank) Auritt; divorced; children: Lynne C., Wendy J., Debora J. Rose-Stewart. Student, Pa. State U., 1958; BA, Rutgers U., 1975; MBA, Temple U., 1978, postgrad., 1978-80. CPA, N.J.; CFP; cert. mgmt. acct., personal fin. specialist. Asst. v.p. Data Control Ctr., Cherry Hill, N.J., 1966-70; statistician, sr. staff asst. I.U. Internat. Corp., Phila., 1970-72; ops. mgr. Bus. Data Ctr., Cherry Hill, N.J., 1972-75; instr. acctg. and mgmt. Rutgers U., Camden, N.J., 1975-80; cost acctg. supr., acctg. mgr. Phila. Nat. Bank, 1980-82; asst. dir. fiscal planning N.J. Dept. Higher Edn., Trenton, 1982-85; contr., CFO Essex County Coll., Newark, 1985-87; v.p. fin. Horizon House, Inc., Phila., 1987-89; v.p. RTD Fin. Advisors Inc., Phila., 1989—. Instr., advisor Cen. Mich. U., McGuire AFB, N.J., 1978-80; instr. MBA Program, Widener U., Chester, Pa., 1980-82; rsch. asst. Temple U. Sch. Bus., Phila., 1975-76. Trustee Contact Cmty. Helpline, Cherry Hill, N.J., 1987-97, v.p., 1988-89, pres., 1989-94, mem. fin. com., 1995—; chair planned giving com. Women's Way, 2001—. Fellow Temple U. Sch. Bus., Phila., 1976-78. Fellow N.J. Soc. CPAs (chair subcom. 1985-89); mem. AICPA (grader CPA exam. 1987), Am. Woman's Soc. CPAs, Inst. Mgmt. Accts. (sec. South Jersey chpt. 1971-73, v.p. 1982-84, bd. dirs. 1971-75, 84-85, 91-93; grader, cons. CMA exam. 1986-99), Fin. Planning Assn., Am. Soc. Women Accts. (sec. Phila. chpt. 1972-74, bd. dirs. 1970-75), Choral Arts Soc. Phila. (singer, 2003—). Office: RTD Fin Advisors Inc 30 S 17th St Ste 1720 Philadelphia PA 19103-1752 Office Phone: 215-557-3800. E-mail: jrose@rtdfinancial.com.

**ROSE, JEFFREY RAYMOND,** economist, educator, public servant, trade unionist; b. Toronto, Ont., Can., 1946; s. Albert and Thelma R.; m. Sandra Black; 1 child, Adam. BA with honors, U. Toronto, 1968, M.Indsl. Relations, 1983; postgrad., London Sch. Econs., 1968-69. Planner planning dept. City of Toronto, 1976-80; pres. local 79 Can. Union Pub. Employees, Toronto, 1980-83, nat. pres. Ottawa, Ont., 1983—91, nat. pres. emeritus, 1991—; dep. min. intergovtl. affairs Govt. of Ont., Toronto, 1991-95; sr. fellow Harrowston program in conflict mgmt.-negotiation U. Toronto, 1995—2002. Gen. v.p. Can. Labour Congress, 1983—91. Exec. mem. Ont. New Dem. Party, 1982-91; bd. dirs. Inst. for Rsch. on Pub. Policy, 1988-91; mem. fed. coun. New Dem. Party, 1988-91; co-chmn. Ont.-Que. Commn. for Cooperation, 1991-95. Home: 55 Sunnydene Crescent Toronto ON Canada M4N 3J5

**ROSE, JOANNA SEMEL,** volunteer; b. Orange, NJ, Nov. 22, 1930; d. Philip Ephraim and Lillian (Mindlin) Semel; m. Daniel Rose, Sept. 16, 1956; children: David S., Joseph B., Emily, Gideon G. Cert., Shakespeare Inst., U.K., 1951; BA summa cum laude, Bryn Mawr Coll., 1952; postgrad., St. Hilda's Coll., Oxford U., 1953; grad., CUNY Ctr. for Humanities. Mem. exec. com. Am. Friends St. Hilda's Coll., former chmn.; bd. dir., former pres. Paper Bag Players, N.Y.C.; former bd. dir., current mem. adv. coun. Poets and Writers, Inc., N.Y.C.; former chmn. adv. bd. Partisan Rev., N.Y.C.; mem. adv. coun. Nat. Dance Inst., N.Y.C.; bd. mem. NY Coun. for Humanities. Bd. dir. Bay St. Theatre, Sag Harbor; former bd. dir. Am. Friends Jewish Mus. Greece; assoc. fellow Berkeley Coll. Yale U.; mem. N.Y. Inst. for Humanities; bd. dirs. N.Y. Gate Coun. for Humanities; bd. dirs. Ctr. Humanities CUNY. Former bd. dirs. Eldridge St. Project, N.Y.C. Named an Hon. fellow, St. Hilda's Coll. Oxford. Mem. Cosmopolitan Club, Bryn Mawr Club of NY, LVIS East Hampton. Home: 895 Park Ave New York NY 10021-0327 also: 1 Lily Pond Ln East Hampton NY 11937

**ROSE, JOANNE W.,** rating service executive; BA in Polit. Sci. and History magna cum laude, U. Rochester; JD, Columbia U. Assoc. White & Case, NYC; sr. mng. dir., gen. counsel Standard & Poor's Rating Svcs. divsn. McGraw Hill, NYC, 1989—99, chair rating policy bd.; exec. mng. dir., structured fin. ratings Standard & Poor's, NYC, 1999—. Office: Standard & Poors 55 Water St New York NY 10041-0003

**ROSE, JOEL ALAN,** legal consultant; b. Bklyn., Dec. 26, 1936; s. Edward Isadore and Adele R. Rose; m. Isadora Fenig, Apr. 12, 1964; children: Susan, Terri Angstriech. BS in Econs., NYU, 1958; MBA, Wharton Grad. Sch., U. Pa., 1960. Asst. purchasing agt. McDonnell Inc., N.Y.C., 1960-62; personnel dir. E.J. Korvette Inc., N.Y.C., 1962-66; mgmt. cons. Daniel J. Cantor & Co. Inc., Phila., 1966—, sr. v.p., 1987—; mgmt. cons. to legal profession. Coord. Ann. Conf. on Law Firm Mgmt. and Econs. Author: Managing the Law Office; mem. adv. bd. Law Office Economics and Management, 1987; contbg. columnist N.Y. Law Jour., 1984—, Nat. Law Jour. Extra, 1996—, Phila. Legal Intelligencer, 1995—, L.A. Daily Times, 1999—, Legal Times of Washington, 1998—, N.J. Law Jour., 2000-, The Barrister, 1995-. contbr. articles to profl. jours.; bd. editors Acctg. for Law Firms, Law Firm Partnership and Benefits Report, 2001—; editl. adv. bd. Corp. Counsel's Guide to Law Dept. Mgmt. With U.S. Army 1960, Res., 1960-66. Fellow Coll. of Law Practice Mgmt.; mem. ABA (chmn. acquisition and mergers com., practice mgmt. sect., large law firm interest group), Inst. Mgmt. Cons., Am Arbitration Assn. (nat. panel), Adminstrv. Mgmt. Soc. (past chpt. pres.), Am. Mgmt. Assn., Assn. Legal Adminstrs. Office: Joel A Rose & Assoc Inc PO Box 162 Cherry Hill NJ 08003-0162 Office Phone: 856-427-0050. E-mail: jrose63827@aol.com.

**ROSE, JOHN CHARLES,** internist, educator; b. N.Y.C., Dec. 13, 1924; s. Hugh Stanley and Marie-Louise (Delury) R.; m. Dorothy Anne Donnelly, June 26, 1948; children: Nancy, Ellen, John Charles, Richard, Christopher. BS, Fordham U., 1946; MD magna cum laude, Georgetown U., 1950, D.Sc. (hon.), 1973; D.C.L. (hon.). Diplomate: Am. Bd. Internal Medicine, Am. Bd. Family Practice. Intern Walter Reed Army Hosp., 1950-51; resident, research fellow Georgetown U., VA hosps., Washington, 1950-54; established investigator Am. Heart Assn., 1954-57; instr., asst. prof. medicine Georgetown U., 1954-57, coord. med. edn., 1957-58, assoc. prof. physiology and biophysics, 1958-60, prof., 1960-91, chmn. dept. physiology and biophysics, 1958-63, dean Sch. Medicine, 1963-73, 78-79, prof. medicine, 1973-91, prof. emeritus, 1991—, vice chancellor Med. Ctr., 1984-87. Assoc. editor Am. Family Physician, 1955-62, chief med. editor, 1962-88; assoc. editor Acad. Medicine, 1992-95; contbr. articles to sci. publs. Trustee Charles E. Culpeper Found., 1986-96. Served to 2d lt. USAAF, 1943-45. Decorated Air medal. Master ACP; mem. Am. Physiol. Soc., Soc. Exptl. Biology and Medicine (nat. councillor 1962-63), Am. Heart Assn. (fellow sect. circulation). Clubs: Cosmos (Washington). Home: 5710 Surrey St Chevy Chase MD 20815-5520 E-mail: jrosemd@earthlink.net.

**ROSE, JOHN THOMAS,** finance educator; b. Ft. Worth, Aug. 20, 1943; s. Paul Pittman and Francis Nan (White) R.; m. Sandra Kaye Rolen, Sept. 5, 1969; children: Melanie Ann, Leah Nan, Lynnelle Renee. BA with honors, Tex. A&M U., 1965; MA, Washington U., St. Louis, 1968, PhD, 1976. Economist Bd. Govs. of FRS, Washington, 1972-82, sr. economist, 1982-84; prof. fin., Harriette L. & Walter G. Lacy, Jr. chair banking Baylor U., Waco, Tex., 1984—, acting chmn. dept. fin. ins. and real estate, 1996-97, chmn. dept., 1997—2006. Contbr. articles to profl. jours. Bd. visitors Abilene (Tex.) Christian U., 1989-92. Capt. U.S. Army, 1969-71. Decorated Bronze Star; recipient Disting. Bus. Prof. award, 1988, Alpha Kappa Psi Favorite Prof. award Hankamer Sch. Bus. Baylor U., 2004; Econ. Devel. Adminstrn. U.S.

Dept. Commerce fellow, 1968-69; Ernst & Young Found. Rsch. grantee, 1991. Mem. Am. Fin. Assn., So. Fin. Assn., Southwestern Fin. Assn., Fin. Mgmt. Assn., Omicron Delta Epsilon, Beta Gamma Sigma. Mem. Ch. of Christ. Office: Baylor U Hankamer Sch of Bus Dept Fin Ins and Real Estate One Bear Pl # 98004 Waco TX 76798-8004 Business E-Mail: jt_rose@baylor.edu.

ROSE, JONATHAN CHAPMAN, lawyer; b. Cleve., June 8, 1941; s. Horace Chapman and Katherine Virginia (Cast) R.; m. Susan Anne Porter, Jan. 26, 1980; 1 son, Benjamin Chapman. AB, Yale U., 1963; LL.B. cum laude, Harvard U., 1967. Bar: Mass. 1968, D.C. 1972, U.S. Supreme Ct. 1976, Circuit Ct. Appeals 1977, Ohio 1978. Law clk. Justice R. Ammi Cutter, Mass. Supreme Jud. Ct., 1967-68; spl. asst. to U.S. pres., 1971-73; gen. counsel Coun. on Internat. Econ. Policy, 1973-74, The White House; assoc. dept. atty. gen. U.S. Dept. Justice, 1974-75; dept. asst. atty. gen. U.S. Dept. Justice (Antitrust Div.), 1975-77, asst. atty. gen. Office of Legal Policy, 1981-84; ptnr. firm Jones Day, Washington, 1977-81, 84—. Prin. Ctr. for Excellence in Govt.; pres. Yale Daily News Found.; bd. govs. Yale Alumni Assn., 1996-99. 1st lt. U.S. Army, 1969-71. Mem. ABA, D.C. Bar Assn., Mass. Bar Assn., Ohio Bar Assn., Fed. Bar Assn., Am. Law Inst. Clubs: Met, Chevy Chase, Union, Yale, Harvard. Republican. Episcopalian. Office: Jones Day 51 Louisiana Ave NW Washington DC 20001-2113 Office Phone: 202-879-3888. Business E-Mail: jcrose@jonesday.com.

ROSE, L. STEVEN See JASHEL, LARRY

ROSE, MARIAN HENRIETTA, physics researcher; b. Brussels; (parents Am. citizens); m. Simon Rose, Oct. 20, 1948 (dec. Jan. 1981); children: Ann, James, David, Simon. BA, Barnard Coll., 1942; MA, Columbia U., 1944; PhD, Harvard U., 1947. Teaching fellow Harvard U., Cambridge, Mass., 1945-46; adj. asst. prof. Courant Inst., N.Y.C., 1947-48; rsch. assoc., 1951-65, sr. rsch. scientist, 1965-75; vis. fellow Yale U., New Haven, Conn., 1981-93. Bd. dirs. Minna-James-Heineman Stiftung, Essen, Fed. Republic of Germany. Contbr. articles to profl. jours. Bd. dirs. Jay Heritage Ctr., Rye, N.Y.; mem. Wetlands Control Commn., Bedford, N.Y., 1992-99, Conservation Bd., Bedford, 1989-93; pres. Croton Watershed Clean Water Coalition, 1997—. Mem.: Sierra Club (conservation chair Atlantic chpt. 1992—95, del. at large to Westchester County Environ. Mgmt. Coun. 1994—, chair N.E. regional conservation com. 1995—98, conservation chair Atlantic chpt. 1998—2000, steering com. Atlantic chpt. 2000—02, del. at large N.E. regional conservation com., del. at large Atlantic chpt., exec. com. Atlantic chpt.), Sigma Xi, Phi Beta Kappa. Avocations: skiing, hiking. Personal E-mail: marianr451@aol.com.

ROSE, MARK ALLEN, humanities educator; b. NYC, Aug. 4, 1939; s. Sydney Aaron and Rose (Shapiro) R.; m. Ann (Bermingham); 1 son, Edward Gordon. AB (hon.), Princeton, 1961; LittB, Merton Coll., Oxford, Eng., 1963; PhD, Harvard Univ., 1967. Instr. to assoc. prof. in English Yale U., 1967-74; prof. English U. Ill., 1974-77; prof. U. Calif., Santa Barbara, 1977—, chmn. dept. English, 1987-89; dir. U. Calif., Humanities Rsch. Inst., Santa Barbara, 1989-94, chmn. dept. English, 1997—2001, assoc. vice chancellor, 2002—. Author: Heroic Love, 1968; (fiction) Golding's Tale, 1972; Shakespearean Design, 1972; Spenser's Art, 1975; Alien Encounters, 1981; Authors and Owners, 1993; editor: Twentieth Century Views of Science Fiction, 1976; Twentieth Century Interpretations of Antony and Cleopatra, 1977, (with Slusser and Guffey); Bridges to Science Fiction, 1980; Shakespeare's Early Tragedies, 1994; (CD-ROM) Norton Shakespeare Workshops. Woodrow Wilson Fellow, 1961; Henry Fellow, 1961-62; Dexter Fellow, 1966; Morse Fellow, 1970-71; NEH Fellow, 1979-80, 90-91. Mem. MLA, Renaissance Soc. Am., Shakespeare Soc. Am., Phi Beta Kappa. Office: U Calif English Dept Santa Barbara CA 93106 Business E-Mail: mrose@english.ucsb.edu.

ROSE, MARY MABEL, retired elementary school educator; b. Monticello, Iowa, Dec. 16, 1940; d. Ralph Richard and Flora Birdena (Hawkins) Ganfield; m. Paul Roger Rose, Dec. 30, 1961 (dec. Oct. 1999); children: Lynn Marie, Carol Ann. BA, Upper Iowa U., Fayette, 1962; postgrad., U. No. Iowa, Cedar Falls, 1990—93. Cert. profl. tchr., Iowa. Elem. tchr. North Fayette County Cmty. Schs., West Union, Iowa, 1962-67, Marion Ind. Schs., Iowa, 1963—64; instr. adult edn. West Central Sch. Dist., Iowa, 1967; substitute tchr. Bremer County Schs., Waverly, Iowa, 1974-84; tchr. Waverly-Shell Rock Schs., Iowa, 1984—2006, early childhood adv. bd., 1990—91; ret., 2006. Mem. edn. com. Waverly Trinity Meth. Ch., 1979-84, trustee, 1984-86, mem. fin. com., 1989-92, staff parish relationship com., 1999-2001, mem. mission commn., 2005—; vol. Waverly Hosp. Aux., 1984-86 Mem. ASCD, Nat. Assn. for Edn. Young Children, Shell Rock Music Assn. (bd. dirs. 1995-98). Home: 107 S Ridge Dr Waverly IA 50677-3908

ROSE, MARY MCNALLY, federal official; b. Apr. 10, 1946; d. Hugh B. and Margaret (Brady) McNally; m. Philip David Rose, Sept. 12, 1970; children: Sarina Josephine, Aimee Elizabeth, Michael Roddy, Maureen Erin. RN, Bon Secours Sch. Nursing, 1967. Spl. asst. to dir. Fed. Exec. Inst. - Washington; asst. dir. office exec. personnel The White House, Washington, 1983-85, asst. office personnel mgmt., 1985, dir. personnel, 1985-86; dep. under sec. for mgmt. U.S. Dept. Edn., Washington; vice chmn. Fed. Salary Coun.; mem. US Merit Systems Protection Bd, Washington, 2005—. Office: US Merit Systems Protection Bd 1615 M St NW Rm 680 Washington DC 20419*

ROSE, MARYA MERNITZ, lawyer; b. Sept. 1962; m. Anthony J Rose. BA, Williams College, Williamstown, Mass.; JD, Ind. U. Corp. counsel Cummins Inc, 1997—98, corp. counsel & dir. public relations, 1998—99, corp. counsel & dir. public relations & comm. strategy, 1999—2000, v.p., gen. counsel, 2001—. Office: Cummins Inc 500 Jackson St Columbus IN 47202

ROSE, MATTHEW K., rail transportation executive; BS in Mktg., U. Missouri. With Missouri Pacific Railroad; various positions Schneider Nat., Internat. Utilities; former v.p., transportation Triple Crown Services (Norfolk So. Railroad subsidiary); various v.p. positions Burlington No. Santa Fe Corp., 1993—96, sr. v.p., merchandise bus. unit, 1996—97, sr. v.p., COO, 1997—99, COO, 1999—2000, pres., CEO, 2000—, chmn., 2002—. Bd. dirs. AMR Corp., Ctr. for Energy & Economic Develop., Centex Corp., Dallas, 2006—; mem. exec. bd. Boy Scouts of Am. Mem.: Assn. of Am. Railroads (bd. dirs.). Office: Burlington No Santa Fe Corp PO Box 961052 Fort Worth TX 76161-0052*

ROSE, MICHAEL DEAN, retired lawyer, educator; b. Johnstown, Pa., Oct. 22, 1937; BA, Ohio Wesleyan U., 1959; JD, Case Western Res. U., 1963; LLM, Columbia U., 1967. Bar: Ohio 1963. Assoc. firm Porter, Stanley, Treffinger & Platt, Columbus, Ohio, 1963-66; asst. prof. law Ohio State U., Columbus, 1967-69, assoc. prof., 1969-72, prof., 1972-99, Lawrence D. Stanley prof. law, 1987-99, prof. emeritus, 1999—. Staff asst. to chief counsel IRS, Washington, 1970-71. Author: (with Leo J. Raskind) Advanced Federal Income Taxation: Corporate Transactions, 1978, (with Joseph S. Platt) A Federal Taxation Primer, 1973, Hornbook on Federal Income Taxation, 3d edit., 1988; editor Selected Federal Taxation Statutes and Regulations, 1973-99, Ohio Will Manual, 1986-2002. Mem.: Am. Law Inst. Home: 1327 Friar Ln Columbus OH 43221-1527 Office: Ohio State U 55 W 12th Ave Columbus OH 43210-1338 Business E-Mail: rose.4@osu.edu.

ROSE, MICHAEL ELVIN, oil and gas exploration company executive; b. Beaumont, Tex., Mar. 8, 1947; s. Harold Elvin and Onita (Buckelew) R.; m. Patricia Jan Howell, Aug. 21, 1971; children: Jaime Erin, Dana Lyn. BBA, Lamar U., 1970. CPA, Tex. Various positions Atlantic Richfield Co., Dallas, Midland, Tex., L.A., 1971-77; chief acct. Anadarko Prodn. Co., Houston, 1978-79, asst. contr., 1979-80, contr., 1981-85, Ana-darko Petroleum Corp., Houston, 1985-86, exec. v.p. fin., chief fin. officer, 1986—2003. Mem. Fin. Execs. Inst., AICPA, Tex. Soc. CPAs. Avocations: golf, hunting, sailing. Home: Po Box 611194 Rosemary Beach FL 32461-1001

ROSE, MICHAEL LEONARD, film, television and video producer; b. St. Paul, Aug. 9, 1952; s. Robert L. and Beverly Bain (McKee) R.; m. Carol L. King, 1991. BA, UCLA, 1978, MFA, 1990. Media dir. Com. to Bridge the Gap, L.A., 1980-82; producer KPFK Pacifica, L.A., 1982-83, GM, Detroit, 1983-92, Network USA, Inc., Rockville, Md., 1993-96; producer 30-part documentary series Automobiles, 1995—; prodr., writer, dir. Michael Rose Prodns., Santa Monica, Calif., 1996—. Prodr. (film) Character, 1984 (Cine award 1984, 96), (videotape) A New Me, 1985 (U.S. Industry award 1985), Safety Belts for Dummies and People, 1986 (ITVA award, U.S. Industry award, Nat. Com. Films for Safety award), (TV series) Wheels of Survival, History Channel, Dream Machines, Ultimate Autos, History Channel, Great Cars, Wealth TV and PBS, Great Drives, Pvt. Jets, (video) ZZ Top; prodr. (for Travel Channel), Private Jets Revealed, Hot Rod TV; prodr., writer (video-tape) I Need the Earth and the Earth Needs Me, 1990 (Cine Golden Eagle award, Nat. Edn. Film and Video award 1991), (film) A Tale of Two Cities, 1990 (Expo of Short Film and Video Award, Outstanding Student Documen-taty Bklyn. Arts Coun. 1991); dir. pub. svc. announcement Eye Exam, 1988 (ITVA award 1988); prodr. The Game of Your Life, 1989 (Am. Film and Video award, ITVA award), Precious Cargo, (TV series) Wheels of Survival, Dream Machines, Ultimate Autos Active, prodr. Mahaffey for Coun. campaign, Detroit, 1989; prodr. radio comml. Friends of the Nuclear Freeze, L.A., 1982. Recipient E.P. Ingersoll award Soc. Automotive Historians, 1998, Nat. Ednl. Media Network award, 1998; scriptwriting grantee Calif. Coun. for Humanities, 1999. Mem.: Nat. Acad. Television Arts & Scis., Writers Guild Am., Dirs. Guild Am., Internat. Documentary Assn. (bd. dirs.). Office Phone: 310-821-0800.

ROSE, MICHAEL ROBERTSON, evolutionary biology educator, consultant; b. Iserlohn, Germany; s. James Barry and Charlotte Julia Rose; children: Darius, Caitlin, Liam, Muireann. BS, Queen's U., Kingston, Ont., Can., 1975, MS, 1976; PhD, U. Sussex, Eng., 1979. NATO sci. fellow U. Wis., Madison, 1979-81; asst. prof. Dalhousie U., Halifax, N.S., Canada, 1981-85, assoc. prof., 1985-87; assoc. prof. evolutionary biology U. Calif., Irvine, 1987-90, prof., 1990—, dir. Intercampus Rsch. Program Exptl. Evolution, 2004—05, dir. Network Exptl. Rsch. Evolution, 2006—. Author: Evolutionary Biology of Aging, 1991, Adaptation, 1996, Darwin's Spectre, 1998, Methuselah Flies, 2004, The Long Tomorrow, 2005, Evolution and Ecology of the Organism, 2006. Recipient President's prize Am. Soc. Naturalists, 1992, Busse award World Congress Gerontology, Adelaide, Australia, 1997. Mem. Soc. for Study Evolution. Avocation: music. Office Phone: 949-824-8121. E-mail: mrrose@uci.edu.

ROSE, NOEL RICHARD, immunologist, microbiologist, educator; b. Stamford, Conn., Dec. 3, 1927; s. Samuel Allison and Helen (Richard) R.; m. Deborah S. Harber, June 14, 1951; children: Alison, David, Bethany, Jonathan. BS, Yale U., 1948; MA, U. Pa., 1949, PhD, 1951; MD, SUNY, Buffalo, 1964; MD (hon.), U. Cagliari, Italy, 1990; ScD (hon.), U. Sassari, Italy, 1992; Order of the First Class (hon.), Ctrl. U. Venezuela, 1997. From instr. to prof. microbiology SUNY Sch. Medicine, Buffalo, 1951-73, dir. Center for Immunology, 1970-73, dir. Erie County Labs., 1964-70; dir. WHO Collaborating Center for Autoimmune Disorders, 1968—; prof. immunology and microbiology, chmn. dept. immunology and microbiology Wayne State U. Sch. Medicine, 1973— 82; prof., chmn. dept. immunology and infectious diseases Johns Hopkins U. Sch. Hygiene and Pub. Health, Balt., 1982-93, prof. medicine and environ. health sci.s., 1982—, prof. molecular microbiol-ogy and immunology, 1993—; prof. pathology Johns Hopkins U. Sch. Medicine, 1994—; dir. Johns Hopkins Autoimmune Disease Rsch. Ctr., 1998. Cons. in field. Editor: (with others) International Convocation on Immunol-ogy, 1969, Methods in Immunodiagnosis, 1973, 3d rev. edit., 1986, The Autoimmune Diseases, 1986, 2d edit., 1992, 3d edit., 1998, Microbiology, Basic Principles and Clinical Applications, 1983 Principles of Immunology, 1973, 2d rev. edit., 1979, Specific Receptors of Antibodies, Antigens and Cells, 1973, Manual of Clinical Laboratory Immunology, 1976, 6th edit., 2002, Genetic Control of Autoimmune Disease, 1978, Recent Advances in Clinical Immunology, 1983, Clinical Immunotoxicology, 1992, Manual of Human Immunology, 1997; editor in chief Clin. Immunology and Immuno-pathology, 1988-98; contbr. articles to profl. jours. Recipient award Sigma Xi, 1952, award Alpha Omega Alpha, 1976, Lamp award, 1975, Faculty Recognition award Wayne State U. Bd. Govs., 1979, Pres.'s award for excellence in teaching, Disting. Service award Wayne State U. Sch. Medicine, 1982, U. Pisa medal, 1986, U. Venezuela medal, 1998; named to Acad. Scholars Wayne State U., 1981; Josiah Macy fellow, 1979 Fellow AAAS (coun. 2004—), APHA, Am. Acad. Allergy and Immunology, Am. Acad. Microbiology, Assn. Med. Lab Immunologists; mem. Acad. Clin. Lab. Physicians and Scientists, Am. Assn. Immunologists, Am. Soc. Investigative Pathology, Am. Soc. Clin. Pathologists, Am. Soc. Microbiology (hon.; Abbott Lab. Clin. and Diagnostic Immunology award 1993, Profl. Achievement award 2003), Brit. Soc. Immunology, Coll. Am. Pathologists, Sociète Française d'Immunologie, Can. Soc. Immunology, Soc. Exptl. Biology and Medicine Coun., Clin. Immunology Soc. (sec., treas., pres. 1993), Austrian Immunology Soc. (hon. mem.), Sigma Xi (pres. Johns Hopkins U. chpt. 1988), Alpha Omega Alpha, Delta Omega. Office: Johns Hopkins U 615 N Wolfe St Baltimore MD 21205-2103

ROSE, PATRICIA, artist, educator; 1 child, Nicholas Flores. BA, U. Calif., Berkeley, 1968; MA, Roosevelt U., 2002. Cert. elem. secondary tchr. Ill. Tchr. Cook and Lake Counties, Ill., 1991—95; dir. Ravenswood Gallery and Studios, Chgo., 1995—96; founder, dir. Art Odyssey, Wilmette, Ill., 1997—; tchr. Muslim Cmty. Ctr. Full Time Sch., Morton Grove, Ill., 1999—2000; instr. gifted edn. and arts Sch. of Art Inst., Chgo., 2001. One-woman shows include Union League Club, Chgo., 1999, Rush Presbyn. St. Lukes Med. Ctr., Core Gallery, 2005—06, exhibited in group shows at Montserrat Gallery, N.Y.C., 2000, Chgo. Art Open, 2000, Art Odyssey, Willmette, 2002—04, Represented in permanent collections Chgo. Bd. Edn. Office Langs. and Culture. Mem.: Am. for the Arts, Nat. Mus. Women in Arts, Art Alumni Group U. Calif. Berkeley, Ill. Assn. Gifted Children, Nat. Assn. Gifted Children. Avocations: theater, social science. Office Phone: 312-286-7422. Personal E-mail: artodyssey@sbcglobal.net. E-mail: patrose253@comcast.net.

ROSE, PAUL EDWARD, systems administrator, educator; b. Denver, Oct. 14, 1978; s. Robert Ferguson and Kathleen Marie Rose; life ptnr. Shontience Nicole Morris; 1 child, Imani Brianna-Lee. Cert. A+ CompTia, Network+ CompTia, CompTia, CompTia, Server+ CompTia, i-Net+ CompTia, CIW cert. instr. ProSoft, cert. master CIW adminstr. ProSoft, CIW assoc. ProSoft, CIW profl. ProSoft, master CIW site designer ProSoft, CIW security analyst ProSoft, ITCAP designated instr. MCP Microsoft, MCSA Windows 2000 Microsoft, MCDST Windows XP Microsoft, MCSA Windows 2003 Mi-crosoft, MCSE Microsoft, Security Microsoft, Microsoft cert. trainer Mi-crosoft. Migration cons. Oxford Global Resources, Mountain View, Calif., 2000; owner RoseNet Solutions, Oakland, Calif., 2000—; sr. instr. TechSkills, San Francisco 2003—; chief tech. officer Computer Svcs. Group, San Jose, Calif., 2004—. Cons. Young Cmty. Developers, San Francisco, 2005—. Bd. dirs. African-American.com, San Jose, 2003—06. With USMC, 1996—99. Decorated Good Conduct medal USMC, Meritorious Mast. Master: Masons (3d degree). Democrat. Avocations: travel, baseball, football, softball. Office Phone: 415-842-0150. Personal E-mail: paul@paulrose.net. Business E-Mail: prose@techskills.com.

ROSE, PETER HENRY, nuclear physicist; b. Lincoln, England, Jan. 16, 1925; arrived in U.S., 1951; PhD in Nuc. Physics, U. London, 1955. Lectr. physics, rschr. U. Birmingham, England, 1953—56; scientist High Voltage Engring. Corp., Mass., 1956—67, chief scientist Mass., 1967—71; founder, pres. Extrion Corp. (later Varian Assocs.), 1971—77; founder Nova Assocs., 1978—81; pres. Eaton Semiconductor Equipment Divsn. (formerly Nova Assocs.), 1981—93; founder Krytek Corp., 1993—, Orion Equipment Inc, Beverly, Mass.—1996—. Recipient nat. medal of tech., U.S. Dept. Commerce, 1996. Office: Orion Equipment Corp 66 Cherry Hill Dr Ste 5 Beverly MA 01915-1055 Home: 89 Phillips Ave Rockport MA 01966-1036

ROSE, PETER ISAAC, sociologist, writer; b. Rochester, N.Y., Sept. 5, 1933; s. Aaron E. and Lillian (Feld) R.; m. Hedwig Hella Cohen, Mar. 25, 1956; children: Elisabeth Anne, Daniel Eric. AB, Syracuse U., 1954; MA, Cornell U., 1957, PhD, 1959. Mem. faculty Smith Coll., Northampton, Mass., 1960—2003, sr. fellow Kahn Inst., 2000—, Sophia Smith prof. emeritus, 2003—; mem. grad. faculty U. Mass., 1961—. Fulbright prof. U. Leicester, Eng., 1964-65, Kyoto (Japan) Am. Studies Inst., Flinders U., Australia, 1970, U. Vienna, 2004; vis. prof. Wesleyan U., Middletown, Conn., 1966-67, U. Colo., 1968, Yale U., 1970, Clark U., 1970-71, Doshisha U., Kyoto, Japan, fall 1999; vis. scholar Harvard U., 1983, 84-85, vis. prof., spring 1984; vis. scholar Chinese Acad. Social Sci., Beijing, 1986; resident scholar Rockefeller Study Ctr., Bellagio, Italy, summer 1987; vis. fellow St. Catherine's Coll., Oxford, spring, 1995, Stanford U., 1996, 2005, Liguria Study Ctr., Bogliasco, Italy, spring 1998, fall 2001. Author: They and We, 1964, 6th edit., 2006, The Subject is Race, 1968, Strangers in Their Midst, 1977, Mainstream and Margins, 1983, Tempest-Tost, 1997, Guest Appearances and Other Travels in Time and Space, 2003; co-author: Sociology, 1977, 2d edit., 1982, Under-standing Society, 1978, 3d edit.; 1986; editor: The Study of Society, 1967, 4th edit., 1977, The Ghetto and Beyond, 1969, Americans From Africa, 1970, Nation of Nations, 1972, reissued, 1981, Seeing Ourselves, 1972, rev. edit., 1975, Socialization and the Life Cycle, 1979, Working With Refugees, 1986, Interminority Relations in the U.S., 1993, Professorial Passions, 1998, The Dispossessed, 2005; co-editor: Through Different Eyes, 1973. Mem. Am. Sociol. Assn. (mem. coun. 1974-77), Mass. Sociol. Assn. (pres. 1967-68), Soc. Study of Social Problems (v.p. 1968-69), Ea. Sociol. Soc. (v.p. 1970-71, pres. 1991-92). Home: 96 Round Hill Rd Northampton MA 01060-2907 Office Phone: 413-585-3515. Business E-Mail: prose@smith.edu.

ROSE, PETER J., delivery service executive; V.p. air divsn. The Harper Group, San Francisco, 1969-81; exec. v.p. Expeditors Internat. Wash. Inc., Seattle, 1981-88, pres., CEO, 1988—, chmn., 1996—. Office: Expeditors Internat Wash Inc 1015 3rd Ave Seattle WA 98104

ROSE, RICHARD, secondary school educator; BA, Cornell U., 1990; MA, U. Pa., 1993. Lic. tchr. N.Y., 1995. Tchr. Elwood Schs., East Northport, NY, 1995—. Office: Elwood John Glenn High Sch 478 Elwood Rd East Northport NY 11731

ROSE, RICHARD LOOMIS, lawyer; b. Long Branch, NJ, Oct. 21, 1936; s. Charles Frederick Perrott and Jane Mary (Crotta) R.; m. Marian Frances Irons, Apr. 1, 1960; children: Linda, Cynthia, Bonnie. BA, Cornell U., 1958; JD, Washington and Lee U., 1963. Bar: N.Y. 1963, Conn. 1966, U.S. Dist. Ct. (so. dist.) N.Y. 1964, U.S. Dist. Ct. Conn. 1966, U.S. Ct. Appeals (2d cir.) 1965, U.S. Supreme Ct. 1970. Ptnr. Cummings & Lockwood, Stamford, Conn., 1965-71, 1971-91, Kleban & Samor, P.C., Southport, 1991-93; of counsel Whitman Breed Abbott & Morgan, Greenwich, Conn., 1993-95; prin. Roberts, Rose & Bates, P.C., Stamford, Conn., 1995—2005, Murtha Cullina LLP, 2005—. Mem. adv. com. Conn. Banking Commr. on Conn. Securities Laws, 1982—; bd. dirs. Conn. World Trade Assn. Editor: Washington and Lee Law Rev. Chmn. Fgn. Trade Zone Com. to Mayor of City of Bridgeport, Conn., 1988-90; mem. fgn. trade awareness com. S.W. Area Industry and Commerce Assn., Task Force, 1987-88; bd. dirs. German Sch. of Conn., Inc., 1992—; commr. New Canaan (Conn.) Hist. Dist. Commn., 1995—. 1st lt. U.S. Army, 1958-60, Korea. Mem. ABA, Conn. Bar Assn. (exec. com. corp. sect.), Internat. Bar Assn., New Canaan Country Club, Gridiron Club New Canaan, Phi Delta Phi, Omicron Delta Kappa, Phi Delta Theta. Republican. Office: Murtha Cullina 177 Broad st Stamford CT 06901

ROSE, ROBERT CHARLES, virologist, researcher; s. Robert Charles and Mary Jean Rose; children: Jennifer Lynn, Michael Robert, Christine Marie. PhD, U. Rochester Sch. of Medicine and Dentistry, Rochester, NY, 1994. Assoc. prof. of medicine U. of Rochester, Rochester, NY, 2005—. Recipient Melville Hare Award for Excellence in Rsch., U. Rochester, 1995, Davey Award for Excellence in Cancer Rsch., 2005, Disting. Inventor of the Yr., Rochester Intellectual Property Law Assn., 2006. Achievements include invention of Human papillomavirus vaccine for prevention of cervical cancer; patents for Human papillomavirus virus-like particle vaccine; Oral immuni-zation against human papillomavirus diseases; Human papillomavirus cap-somer subunit vaccine. Office: U Rochester Med Ctr 601 Elmwood Ave Rochester NY 14642 Office Phone: 585-275-0263. Office Fax: 585-442-9328. E-mail: robert_rose@urmc.rochester.edu.

ROSE, ROBERT DIDIER, neurophysiologist; b. Washington, Oct. 10, 1954; s. Richard Contee and Mary Estill (Martin) R. AB, Transylvania U., 1976; MS, Emory U., 1981; PhD, SUNY, Stony Brook, 1986. Tchg. asst. Emory U., 1977-81, SUNY, Stony Brook, 1981-82, NIMH predoctoral rsch. fellow, 1982-84, rsch. asst., 1984-86; rsch. assoc. prof. dept. pharmacology U. Pitts. Med. Sch., 1987-88; clin. neurophysiologist dept. neurosurgery U. Pitts. Med. Ctr., 1992; clin. fellow Ctr. Clin. Neurophysiology U. Pitts. Sch. Medicine, 1992-97; asst. prof. dept. biol. sci. Duquesne U., Pitts., 1988-90; asst. prof. dept. biology Slippery Rock U., Pa., 1991-92; vis. prof. dept. anatomy and histology U. Pitts. Dental Sch., 1998—; COO Neurex, Inc., 1999—. Pres., CEO Neuro-Resource, 1998—; cons. Computational Diagnos-tics, Inc., Pitts., 1992—; cons. dept. otolaryngology Children's Hosp. of Pitts., 1994—, NuVasive, Inc., 2000—; adj. faculty C.C. Allegheny County, Pitts., 1988—; trainee activities com. Ctr. for Neurosci., U. Pitts., 1988—; naturalist-cons. Queens Coll. Ctr. for Environ. Edn., 1982-84; grant reviewer US-Israel Binational Sci. Found., Tel Aviv, 1990—; mem. panel NSF, Wash-ington, 1990, 92; exec. dir. Childrens Rights Inst., 1999—; bd. dir. Child & Family Advocates; clin. dir. PRAG Group, 2000—; bd. dir. PT Works, 2003—; Neurophysiology Program Dir. Integrative Med. Ctr., Atlantic City, 2003—; lectr., reviewer in field. Contbr. articles, chpts., abstracts to profl. publs. Fellow Marine Biol. Lab., Woods Hole, Mass., 1978, Luft-Brückendank fellow Inst. Tierphysiologie und Angewandte Zoologie, Arbeitsgruppe Neu-robiologie, Freie U. Berlin, 1979, Deutscher Akademischer Austauschdienst fellow, 1979, NIMH/NRSA fellow SUNY-Stony Brook, 1982-84; grantee Emory U., 1978-81, Freie U., 1979, Hunkele Devel. Fund, 1988, State of Pa., 1989, NSF, 1989-91, Copeland Found., 1992-94, Children's Hosp. of Pitts., 1994, 94-95. Mem. AAAS, Am. Soc. Neurophysiol. Monitoring, Soc. Neurosci. Avocations: white water kayaking, fishing, skiing, rugby. Office: 440 Broadway Pitcairn PA 15140-1447

ROSE, ROBERT EDGAR, state supreme court justice; b. Orange, NJ, Oct. 7, 1939; BA, Juniata Coll., Huntington, Pa., 1961; LL.B., NYU, 1964. Bar: Nev. 1965. Dist. atty. Washoe County, 1971-75; lt. gov. State of Nev., 1975-79; judge Nev. Dist. Ct., 8th Jud. Dist., Las Vegas, 1983-88; justice Nev. Supreme Ct., Carson City, 1989—, chief justice, 1993-94, 1999—2000. Office: Nev Supreme Ct Capitol Complex 201 S Carson St Carson City NV 89701-4702

ROSE, ROBERT GORDON, lawyer; b. Newark, June 25, 1943; s. Harry and Ann Shirley (Gordon) R.; m. Ellen Nadley Berkowitz, July 2, 1966; children: Lisa Pauline, Michael Allan. BA, SUNY, Buffalo, 1965; MA, Columbia U., 1969; JD, Seton Hall U., 1974. Bar: NJ 1974, US Dist. Ct. NJ 1974, US Ct. Appeals (3rd cir.) 1974, US Ct. Appeals (2nd cir.) 1975. Law clk. to Hon. John J. Gibbons US Ct. Appeals (3rd cir.), Newark, 1974-75; assoc. Pitney Hardin LLP, Morristown, NJ, 1975-80, ptnr., 1980—. Mem. com. on unauthorized practice of law NJ Supreme Ct., 1989-2001, apptd. com. chair, 2000-2001; apptd. lawyers adv. com. US Dist. Ct., Dist. NJ, 2002—; trustee Legal Svcs. NJ, 2001—. Contbr. articles to profl. jours. Recipient Disting. Grad. award Seton Hall U. Law Sch., 2000. Mem. ABA, NJ Bar Assn., Morris County Bar Assn. (trustee 1989-90). Avocation: travel, stamp collecting/philately. Office: Pitney Hardin LLP Park Ave at Morris County PO Box 1945 Morristown NJ 07962-1945 Office Phone: 973-966-8070. Business E-Mail: rrose@pitneyhardin.com.

ROSE, ROBERT MICHAEL, materials engineering educator; b. N.Y.C., Apr. 15, 1937; s. Lawrence Lapidus and Lillian (Rosen) R.; m. Martha Gibbs, Oct. 15, 1961; children: Cynthia J., James L., Joshua S. BS, MIT, 1958, DSc,

1961. Registered profl. engr., Mass. Asst. prof. materials sci. and engring MIT, Cambridge, 1961-66, assoc. prof., 1966-72, prof., 1972—2003, prof. emeritus, 2003—; dir. MIT Concourse program, 1988—; prof. health scis. and tech. Harvard Med. Sch.- MIT, 1978-90; dir. Cryoelectro Assocs., Wenham, Mass., 1978-90. Author: Structure and Properties of Materials, 1964, Practical Biomechanics for the Orthopedic Surgeon, 1979, 92, The Chicken From Minsk, 1995. Recipient Kappa Delta prize Am. Acad. Orthop. Surgeons, 1973. Mem. Am. Soc. Metals (vice chmn. 1971-72, Bradley Stoughton prize, chmn. 1972-73), Metal Soc. AIME, Boston Yacht Club. Jewish. Home: 18 Morgan St Wenham MA 01984-1114 Office: Room 4-132 MIT 77 Massachusetts Ave Cambridge MA 02139-4301 Business E-Mail: rose@mit.edu. *I would share my thoughts with you if I were satisfied with what I am. But I submit to you that anyone who is truly satisfied with his personal success doesn't understand the nature of his own achievement.*

**ROSE, ROBERT NEAL,** investment banker; b. Chgo., Feb. 27, 1951; s. James Allan Rose and Hazel (Gordon) Kaufman; m. Anna Yvette Trujillo, Aug. 23, 1981; children: David James, Michelle Elizabeth, Daniel Jonathan. BS, Georgetown U., 1973; MPA, Harvard U., 1995. Trader Salomon Bros., N.Y.C., 1974-75; regional coord. Latin Am. Merrill Lynch Govt. Securities, N.Y.C., 1975-76; dir. fed. govt. affairs Pub. Svc. of N.Mex., Albuquerque, 1977-78; exec. dir. Gov. Jerry Apodaca, Washington, 1979-80; expert cons. U.S. Dept. Commerce, Washington, 1980-81; asst. treas. Am. Express Internat. Bank, N.Y.C., 1981-82; sr. v.p. Refco, Inc., N.Y.C., 1982-84; v.p. mgr. Thomson McKinnon Securities, N.Y.C., 1984-88; sr. v.p. Lehman Bros., N.Y.C., 1988-92; mng. dir. Credit Agricole Futures inc., N.Y.C., 1992-95; sr. mng. dir. Bear Stearns, N.Y.C., 1995—. Cons. BDM Corp., McLean, Va., 1981-88; Presdl. appointee J. William Fulbright Fgn. Scholarship Bd., 1993-97; bd. adv. Shenandoah U. Sch. Bus., 2001—. Exec. com. Conn. Yankee Coun. Boy Scouts Am., 2000—, v.p. exec. com., 2003—; mem. arrangements com. Dem. Nat. Conv., San Francisco, 1984, mem. site selection com., 1989—90, alt. del. Boston, 2004, mem.rules com. L.A., 2000; chmn. nat. fin. coun. Dem. Nat. Com., 1998—2005; fin. chmn. Conn. Dem. State Ctrl. Com., 1993, 2003—05; trustee Conservative Synagogue of Westport, 2000—02. Wexner Heritage Found. fellow, 1992-94; recipient Disting. Citizen award Conn. Yankee Coun. Boy Scouts Am., 2004. Jewish. Avocation: skiing. Home: 326 Bayberry Ln Westport CT 06880-1315 Office: 383 Madison Ave New York NY 10179 Office Phone: 212-272-2822. E-mail: robrose@att.net.

**ROSE, SARAH ELIZABETH,** genealogist, writer, counselor, web site designer; d. H. S. Agsanian & B. M. Phillips; children: Julie, Tory, Mary, Alesandra, Vinnie, Sasha, Zachary. Grad. with honors, U.S. Army Signal Sch., 1975; grad. with distinction, Non-Commd. Officer's Leadership Acad. U.S. Army, 1976; BA in Social Sci., San Jose State U., 1980; MA in History with honors, Hawking Inst., 2004. Prof. genealogist Hearldry. Author: Many Branches, One Tree, 1997, World Wide Roots, 2001, Poetry: A Tribute to Life, 2003, (novel) Extraordinary Journey: Daughter of Destiny, 2005, numerous poems. Army specialist U.S. Army, 1974-77. Decorated Good Conduct medal, Nat. Def. Svc. medal, weapons medal M-16 U.S. Army; recipient Cold War Recognition Cert., U.S. Dept. Def. Mem.: Nat. Fedn. Poetry Socs., Iowa Pioneers, Oreg. Poetry Soc., Women in Mil. Svc. for Am. (charter), Pioneer Families Nebr., Nat. Soc. Colonial Dames XVII Century, Nat. Soc. Daus. of the Am. Colonists, The Winthrop Soc. (assoc.), Nat. Soc. DAR, Am. First Families, Ill. Prairie Pioneers, Pioneers of Kans., Internat. Soc. Daus. Utah Pioneers, Am. Legion. Avocation: collecting Egyptian, African, Native American objects. Address: PO Box 945 Sutherlin OR 97479 Personal E-mail: genealogical2002@yahoo.com.

**ROSE, SCOTT A.,** lawyer; b. Flint, Mich., Feb. 10, 1953; BS with distinction, Ariz. State U., 1975, JD cum laude, 1979. Bar: Ariz. 1979. Chmn. bd. The Cavanagh Law Firm, Phoenix, Ariz. Articles editor Ariz. State Law Jour., 1978-79. Ariz. Govt. Affairs chmn. Internat. Coun. Shopping Ctrs. Mem. ABA, State Bar Ariz., Maricopa County Bar Assn., Downtown Phoenix Rotary Club 100 (bd. dirs.). Office: The Cavanagh Law Firm 1850 N Central Ave Ste 2400 Phoenix AZ 85004

**ROSE, SELWYN H.,** chemicals executive; b. N.Y.C., May 1, 1933; s. Rubin and Ruth Rosenthall; m. Helen Diana De Mov, July 25, 1957; children: Michelle, Wendy, Suzanne. BS, CCNY, 1954; MS, Ohio State U., 1958, PhD, 1961; MBA with honors, U. Chgo., 1979; CFP, Coll. Fin. Planning, 1994. Sr. rsch. chemist Pennwalk Corp., King of Prussia, Pa., 1961-65; dept. mgr. Horizons Inc., Beachwood, Ohio, 1965-72, dir. rsch., 1972-74; mgr. long range rsch. De Soto Inc., Des Plaines, Ill., 1974-79; dir. rsch., cen. rsch. lab. Borg-Warner Chem., Des Plaines 1979-85; v.p. tech. Parker Chem. Co., Madison Heights, Mich., 1985-88; gen. mgr. rsch. and devel. Himont Inc., Wilmington, Del., 1988-91, v.p. product devel., 1991-93; pres. SHR Fin. Advisors, Wilmington, 1993—. Coritbr. articles to profl. jours.; patentee in field. 1st lt. U.S. Army, 1954-56. Recipient IR 100 award Indsl. Rsch. mag., 1971, award Roon Found., 1979. Mem. Am. Chem. soc., Nat. Assn. Personal Fin. Advisors, Fin. Planners Assn. Achievements include development of polyphosphazene polymers. Home: 1503 Evergreen Ln Wilmington DE 19810-4431

**ROSE, STEPHEN F.,** columnist; b. Kansas City, Mo., Nov. 5, 1947; s. Stanley J. and Shirley Rose; m. Carol S. Brady, May 31, 1970; children: Joshua Scott, Melissa Rose Faulkner, Rebecca Kathryn. BJ, U. Mo., Columbia, 1966—70. Chmn. Sun Publs., Overland Park, Kans., 1977—. Vice-chmn. Greater Kans. City C. of C., Kansas City, 1995—2003; chmn. U. Kans. Sch. Nursing, Kansas City, 1997—99, UMB Scout Mut. Funds, 1990—2005, dir., 1990—2005; pres. Suburban Newspapers Am., Chgo., 1998—99; dir. Metcalf Bank, Overland Park, Kans., 1986—99; roundtable panelist Sta. KCPT-TV, Kansas City, 1995—2003, weekly Sta. PBS-TV program host. Specialist 4th class/corr. U.S. Army, 1968—69 Vietnam. Recipient Johnson Countian of Yr., Johnson County CC Found., 1999. Achievements include co-chairing the first bi-state cultural initiative in America. Home: 2110 Stratford Rd Mission Hills KS 66208 Home Fax: 913-722-5353. Personal E-mail: srose@kc.rr.com.

**ROSE, SUSAN PORTER,** management and governmental affairs consultant; b. Cin., Sept. 20, 1941; d. Elmer Johnson and Dorothy (Wurst) Porter; m. Jonathan Chapman Rose, Jan. 26, 1980; 1 child, Benjamin Chapman. BA, Earlham Coll., 1963; MS, Ind. State U., 1970; HDL (hon.), Rose-Hulman Inst. Tech., 2002. Staff asst. Congressman Richard L. Roudebush, Washington, 1963-64; asst. dean George Sch., Bucks County, Pa., 1964-66; asst. dir. admissions Mt. Holyoke Coll., South Hadley, Mass., 1966-71; asst. dir. correspondence First Lady Pat Nixon The White House, 1971-72, dir. of scheduling to First Lady Pat Nixon, 1972-74, to First Lady Betty Ford, 1974-77; spl. asst. to asst. atty. gen. Office Improvements in Adminstrn. Justice, Washington, 1977-79; spl. asst. to dep. asst. atty. gen. Justice Mgmt. divsn. U.S. Dept. Justice, Washington, 1978-81; chief of staff to Barbara Bush, asst. to U.S. v.p. Washington, 1981—89; chief of staff to First Lady Barbara Bush, dept. asst. pres. of U.S. The White House, 1989—93; commr. U.S. Commn. Fine Arts, 1993-98. Bd. dirs. Barbara Bush Found. for Family Literacy, 1993—2002; trustee Bush Presdl. Libr.; mem. alumni coun. Earlham Coll., 1977—78, pres. alumni assn., 1978—81. Recipient Disting. Alumni award, Earlham Coll., 1992, Ind. State U., 1991. Mem.: Ind. Acad. Home: 5955 Ranleigh Manor Dr Mc Lean VA 22101-2428

**ROSE, THOMAS ALBERT,** artist, educator; b. Washington, Oct. 15, 1942; s. Francis John and Ann Elizabeth (Voelkel) R.; m. Mary Melinda Moyer, Aug. 21, 1965; children: Sarah, Jessica. BFA, U. Ill., 1965; MA, U. Calif., Berkeley, 1967; postgrad., Lund U., Sweden, 1967-68. Instr. U. Calif., Berkeley, 1968-69, N.Mex. State U., Las Cruces, 1969-72; faculty mem. U. Minn., Mpls., 1972—, prof. art, 1983—, Fesler-Lampert chair in humanities, 2001—. Author: Winter Book, 1995, Where Do We Start?, 2003, 1018 W. Scott St., 2005; one-man shows include Clock Tower, N.Y.C., 1977, Truman Gallery, N.Y.C., 1978, Rosa Esman Gallery, N.Y.C., 1979, 81, 82, Marianne Deson Gallery, Chgo., 1984-86, Robert Thomson Gallery, Mpls., 1986, 91, 92, 95, Deson Saunders Gallery, Chgo., 1989, Mpls. Inst. Art, 1992,

Weisman Art Mus., Mpls., 1994, Tweed Mus., Duluth, Minn., 1995, Steinbaum/Krauss Gallery, N.Y.C., 1996, 99, Brevard Mus. Art, Melbourne, Fla., 1997, Gensler Arch., Washington, 1999, 2004, Flanders Gallery, Mpls., 2000, 05, Bernice Steinbaum Gallery, Miami, Fla., 2001, 03, 05, Intermedia Arts, Mpls. Bernice Steinbaum Gallery, 2003, Kent Mueller Gallery, Milw., 2005, Bernice Steinbaum Gallery, 2005; exhibited in group shows at Walker Art Ctr., Mpls., 1974, 76, 77, Whitney Mus. Downtown, N.Y.C., P.S. #1, N.Y.C., 1978, Wave Hill, Bronx, N.Y., 1981, Hirshhorne Mus., Washington, 1981, Am. Ctr. in Paris, 1982, Harvard U. Sch. Architecture, 1983, Cultural Ctr., Chgo., 1983, Hal Bromm Gallery, N.Y.C., Sheldon Mus., Lincoln, Nebr., 1989, Tampa (Fla.) Mus., 1988, MCAD, Mpls., 1996, Minn. Mus. Art, 1996, Socrates Sculpture Park, N.Y.C., Fla. Internat. U., Miami, 1997, Gallerie Lipanjepuntin, Trieste, Italy, 2004; represented in permanent collections Whitney Mus., N.Y.C., N.Y., Getty Inst. L.A., Walker Art Ctr., Joslyn Mus., Omaha, Park St. Lofts, Springfield, Mass., U. Minn., Mpls., Am. Lung Assn. Target Ctr., Mpls., St. Lukes Episcopal Ch., Mpls., Wonkwang U., Republic of Korea, 2005, Luxun Acad. Art, Shenyang, China, 2006, Mpls. Inst. Art, Weisman Mus. Art, Mpls., Stanford U. Libr., Sch. of the ARt Inst., Chgo., Milw. Pub. Libr.; set designer: Fool for Love, Cricket Theater, Mpls., 1985, Circus, Theater de Jeune Lune, 1986; project dir. Works of Art in Pub. Places for Humphrey Inst. Pub. Affairs, Mpls., 1988; prin. works include Minn. Zoo, Marine Edn. Ctr., Sacred Heart U., Fairfield, Conn., Berniece Steinbaum Gallery, Miami, 1999, Steinbaum residence, 2002, Bennett Meml., Mpls., 2002. Named Rockefeller resident, Bellagio, Italy, 1993; recipient McKnight Artist fellow, 1995, travel fellow, Dayton-Hudson/Jerome, 1990, 1995, Jerome Found. Arts, 1993—94, Mellon Found., 1993, Fesler-Lampert Chair in Humanities, 2002; fellow, Nat. Endowment for Arts, 1977, 1981, Bush Found., 1979, Minn. State Arts Bd., 1979, 1984, McKnight Found., 1981, McKnight Found. Rsch., 1993—96, McKnight Photography, 2002; grantee, Arts Bd. Opportunities, 1993. Home: 91 Nicollet St Minneapolis MN 55401-1513 Office: Univ Minn 208 Studio Arts 23D S Avenue Minneapolis MN 55425 Office Phone: 612-889-9871. Personal E-mail: rosex00l@umn.edu.

**ROSE, VICTORIA LASDON,** publishing executive; Pub. YM/Young & Modern mag., NYC, Mademoiselle mag., style365.com, US Weekly mag., NYC, 2000—. Named Pub. the Yr., Delaney Report, 2004. Office: US Weekly 1290 Avenue of the Americas New York NY 10104-0298*

**ROSE, WALTER DEANE,** retired engineering educator; b. Liberty, Ind., Jan. 10, 1920; s. Joseph Sims Rose.. Sr and Dorothy Gray Rose; m. Edith Magdalena Dora Schroeder, May 11, 1959; m. Dorris Evelyn Dailey, Mar. 20, 1939 (dec. Feb. 2, 1945); m. Zoe Fern Wilcox, July 14, 1945 (div. Oct. 31, 1952); children: Dixie Rachel Rose-Phillips, Walter Deane Jr., John Gregory, Bonnie Zoe, Deane Michael, Edith Elisabeth. BS, U. of Chgo., 1944. Registered profl. engr., Colo. Rsch. chemist Affils. of Std. Oil of N.J., N.Y.C., 1944—48; rsch. physicist Gulf R&D Co., Physics Divsn., Pitts. and Harmarville, Pa., 1948—50; lectr. in petroleum engring., asst. dir. Tex. petroleum rsch. com. U. Tex. and State of Tex. RR Commn., Austin, 1950—52; editor Gulf Coast dist. Oil and Gas Jour., Houston, 1952—53; group leader oil recovery processes Continental Oil Co. Rsch. Ctr., Ponca City, Okla., 1954—56; fossil energy recovery specialist Petroleum Rsch. Corp., Denver, 1954—55; prof. of petroleum engring. U. of Ill., Champaign, 1955—68; scholar French Petroleum Inst., Rueil Malmaison, France, 1962—63; Albert Albermann vis. prof. of civil engring. TECHNION, Israel Inst. of Tech., Haifa, 1968—69; vis. prof. of freshman engring. Purdue U., West Lafayette, Ind., 1970—71; dean of sci. and prof. of engring. Abadan (Iran) Inst. of Tech., 1971—72; editor, ghost writer Authors and Spkrs. Svc., Chicago and Champaign, Ill., 1975—2001. Vis. prof. developing grad. student programs Mid. East Tech. U., Ankara, Turkey, 1969—70; rsch. lab. innovator Amdel Spl. Core Labs., Adelaide and Brisbane, Australia, 1991—92; tech. cons. Petronas Rsch. Inst., Kuala Lumpur, Malaysia, 1992—94; cons. in petroleum reservoir engring. matters Mex. Petroleum Inst., Mexico City, 2000—06; reservoir engring. cons. Woodside Peroleum, Perth, Australia, 2000; cons. Mex. Inst. of Petroleum, Mexico City, 2004—05, U. of NSW, Sydney, Australia, 1991, Chevron, Brisbane, Australia, 1991, Santos, Adelaide, Australia, 1991; vis. scientist Brit. Nat. Oil Co., London, 1976; vis. prof. U. Ibadan, Nigeria, 1971—74; dir. rsch. and v.p. EG&G Continental Labs., Denver, 1984—86; vis. prof. UNESCO, Dacca, East Pakistan, 1970—71; vis. prof., head of dept. N.Mex. Inst. of Mining and Tech., Socorro, 1974—76; vis. prof., departmental head U. of Wyo., Laramie, 1976—77; vis. specialist on prodn. of coal bed methane Sci. Applications Internat. Assigned to DOE Funded Natural Gas Recovery Rsch. Projects, Morgantown, W.Va., 1978—79; assoc. dir. U.S. Dept. Fossil Energy Rsch. Projects Inst. of Gas Tech., Chgo., 1980—82; vis. sci. rsch. instigator Commonwealth Sci. Indsl. Rsch. Orgn., Canberra, Australia, 1987—89; vis. scientist Chinese Inst. of Porous Flow, Lang Feng, China, 1988. Contbr. articles to profl. jours. and books (travel and rsch. grants various insts. and univs.). Advocate 'natural law party concept. Recipient Cert. of Appreciation award, CEO of the Alta. Rsch. Coun. in Edmonton, 1998. Mem.: Soc. Petroleum Engring. (sr. Legion of Honor), Chgo. Press Club, Houston Press Club. Achievements include patents for Research Lab and Field Equipment Designs; Developing Mathematical Modeling Ideas; patents for dealing with design and utilization of laboratory and field equipment facilities, also mathematical modeling schemes; research in so-called APTPA applications (Additional Prospective Transport Process Algorithms). Home: POBox 2424 409 E Springfield Ave Champaign IL 61820 Office Phone: 217-352-0474. Business E-Mail: wdrose@uiuc.edu.

**ROSE-ACKERMAN, SUSAN,** law and political economy educator; b. Mineola, NY, Apr. 23, 1942; d. William and Rosalie Rose; m. Bruce A. Ackerman, May 29, 1967; children: Sybil, John. BA, Wellesley Coll., 1964; PhD, Yale U., 1970. Asst. prof. U. Pa., Phila., 1970-74; lectr. Yale U., New Haven, 1974-75, asst. prof., 1975-78, assoc. prof. 1978-82; prof. law and polit. economy Columbia U., N.Y.C., 1982-87; Ely prof. of law and polit. econ. Yale U., New Haven, 1987-92, co-dir. Ctr. Law, Econ. and Pub. Policy, 1988—, Henry R. Luce prof. jurisprudence law and polit. sci., 1992—. Vis. rsch. fellow World Bank, 1995-96. Author: (with Ackerman, Sawyer and Henderson) Uncertain Search for Environmental Quality, 1974 (Henderson prize 1982); Corruption: A Study in Political Economy, 1978, (with E. James) The Nonprofit Enterprise in Market Economies, 1986; editor: The Economics of Nonprofit Institutions, 1986, (with J. Coffee and L. Lowenstein) Knights, Raiders, and Targets: The Impact of the Hostile Takeover, 1988, Rethinking the Progressive Agenda: The Reform of the American Regulatory State, 1992, Controlling Environmental Policy: The Limits of Public Law in Germany and the United States, 1995, Corruption and Government: Causes, Consequences and Reform, 1999 (Levine Prize 2000), (with János Kornai) Building a Trustworthy State in Post-Socialist Transition, 2004, (with Kornai and B. Rothstein) Creating Social Trust in Post-Socialist Transition, 2004, From Elections to Democracy: Building Accountable Government in Hungary and Poland, 2005, International Handbook on the Economics of Corruption, 2006+; contbr. articles to profl. jours.; mem. editl. bd. Jour. Law, Econs. and Orgn., 1984—, Internat. Rev. Law and Econs., 1986—, Jour. Policy Analysis and Mgmt., 1989—, Polit. Sci. Quar., 1988—. Guggenheim fellow 1991-92, Fulbright fellow, Free U. Berlin, 1991-92; fellow Ctr. for Advanced Study in the Behavioral Scis., Stanford, Calif., 2002, Collegium Budapest, 2002. Mem. Am. Law and Econs. Assn. (bd. dirs. 1993-96, 2002-), Am. Econ. Assn. (mem. exec. com. 1990-93), Am. Polit. Sci. Assn., Assn. Am. Law Schs., Assn. Pub. Policy and Mgmt. (policy coun. 1984-88, treas. 1998-2000). Democrat. Office: Yale U Law Sch PO Box 208215 New Haven CT 06520-8215 Office Phone: 203-432-4891. Business E-Mail: susan.rose-ackerman@yale.edu.

**ROSEANNE, (ROSEANNE BARR),** actress, comedienne, television producer, writer; b. Salt Lake City, Nov. 3, 1952; d. Jerry and Helen Barr; m. Bill Pentland, 1974 (div. 1989); children: Jessica, Jennifer, Brandi, Buck, Jake; m. Tom Arnold, 1990 (div. 1994); m. Ben Thomas, 1994. Former window dresser, cocktail waitress; prin. Full Moon & High Tide Prodns., Inc. As comic, worked in bars, chntr. coffeehouse, Denver; produced showcase for women performers Take Back the Mike, U. Boulder (Colo.); performer The Comedy Store, L.A.; showcased on TV special Funny, 1986, also The Tonight

Show; featured in HBO-TV spl. On Location: The Roseanne Barr Show, 1987 (Am. comedy award Funniest Female Performer in TV spl., 1987, Ace award Funniest Female in Comedy, 1987, Ace award Best Comedy Spl. 1987); writer, dir., star of TV series Roseanne ABC, 1988-97 (U.S. Mag. 2nd Ann. Readers Poll Best Actress in Comedy Series, 1989, Golden Globe nomination Outstanding Lead Actress in Comedy Series 1988, Emmy award Outstanding Lead Actress in Comedy Series, 1993), The Real Roseanne Show, 2003; actress: (motion pictures) She-Devil, 1989, Look Who's Talking Too (voice), 1990, Freddy's Dead, 1991, Even Cowgirls Get the Blues, 1994, Blue in the Face, 1995, Unzipped, 1995, Meet Wally Sparks, 1997, Home on the Range (voice), 2004; TV movies: Backfield in Motion, The Woman Who Loved Elvis, 1993; appeared in TV spl. Sinatra: 80 Years My Way, 1995; exec. prodr. Saturday Night Spl., Fox-TV; author: Roseanne: My Life as a Woman, 1989, My Lives, 1994; (host) Roseanne Show, 1998-2000, I am Your Child, 1997 (TV), Get Bruce, 1999. Active various child advocate orgns. Recipient Peabody award, People's Choice award (4), Golden Globe award (2), Am. Comedy award, Humanitas award, Nickelodeon Kids Choice award, 1990, Eleanor Roosevelt award for Outstanding Am. Women, Emmy award, 1993.

**ROSEBERRY, EDWIN SOUTHALL,** retired state agency administrator; b. Roanoke, Va., July 4, 1925; s. Edwin Alexander and Gladys Edmonia (Southall) R.; m. Mary Louise Sprengel, Sept. 2, 1949 (dec. 1978); children: Edwin Jr., David, Kevin; m. Alice Proffit Boger, Dec. 27, 1980; 1 stepdaughter, Elizabeth Leigh Boger. BS in Commerce, U. Va., 1949. Registered sanitarian, Hawaii, Va. Store mgr. Allied Arts, Charlottesville, Va., 1949-51; retail credit sales mgr. B.F. Goodrich Co., Charlottesville, 1951-53; environ. health specialist Dept. of Health, Charlottesville, 1953-84, Dept. of Labor, Honolulu, 1987-2000; ret., 1999. Freelance photographer, Charlottesville, 1949-85, Honolulu, 1985—. Contbr. photographs: The Inward Eye, 1986. Election ofcl. State of Hawaii, Honolulu, 1988—. With USN, 1944-46. Recipient Nat. awards Eastman Kodak Co., nat. newspapers, and photography mags., 1951-69. Mem. VFW (life), Am. Indsl. Hygiene Assn., Austrian Hawaiian Club (v.p., bd. dirs. 1985), Antique Auto Assn. (pres. Piedmont region 1964), Hawaii Photo Soc. (v.p. 1989), Elks (tiler and inner guard 1985, officer Honolulu chpt. 1985-2001); Am. Legion (dept. historian, VFW jr. vice commdr.), Mason (32 degree), Shriners (sojourners, heroes of '76, eastern star), Pi Delta Epsilon. Episcopalian. Avocations: photography, stamp collecting/philately, antique automobiles, figure skating. Home: Carriage Hill Apts #302 820 Beverly Dr Charlottesville VA 22911 Personal E-mail: uvaflashed@adelphia.net.

**ROSEBOROUGH, TERESA WYNN,** lawyer; b. Iowa City, Nov. 28, 1958; d. Robert Larry Wynn Jr. and Ethel (Crawford) Wynn; m. Joseph Anthony Roseborough, May 24, 1980. BA, U. Va., 1980; MEd, Boston U., 1983; JD with high honors, U. N.C., 1986. Bar: Ga. 1987, U.S. Ct. Appeals (4th cir.) 1987, U.S. Dist. Ct. (no. dist.) Ga. 1989, U.S. Ct. Appeals (11th cir.) 1989, U.S. Ct Appeals (5th, 6th and 7th cir.), U.S. Supreme Ct. Counselor U.S. Dept. of Army, Giebelstadt, Fed. Republic of Germany, 1980-83; law clk. to hon. Judge J. Dickson Phillips U.S. Ct. Appeals (4th cir.), 1986-87; law clk. to hon. Justice John Paul Stevens U.S. Supreme Ct.. Washington, 1987-88; assoc. Sutherland, Asbill & Brennan, Atlanta, 1988-93; dep. asst. atty. gen. office legal counsel U.S. Dept. Justice, Washington, 1994—96; ptnr. Sutherland Asbill & Brennan LLP, Atlanta. Adj. prof. litig. Emory U. Sch. Law, 1996—98. Editor in chief U. N.C. Law Rev., 1985-86. Bd. dirs. Howard Schs., Atlanta, 1990—, Neighborhood Justice Ctr., 1993—, Nat. Assn. for Pub. Interest Law, The Children's Sch.; chair pro bono com. Atlanta Coun. Younger Lawyers, 1990-92, bd. dirs., 1990-93. Named to Am.'s Top Black Lawyers, Black Enterprise mag., 2004. Mem. ABA (vice chair young lawyers sect. pro bono com. 1990-92, vice chair water quality com. sect. on natural resources energy and environment 1992—), Am. Constn. Soc. (chair, 2004-), State Bar Ga., Gate City Bar Assn., Ga. Assn. Black Women Attys., Order of Coif. Avocations: skiing, golf. Office: Sutherland Asbill & Brennan LLP 999 Peachtree St NE Atlanta GA 30309-3996 Office Phone: 404-853-8100. E-mail: teresa.roseborough@sablaw.com.

**ROSEBROUGH, CAROL BELVILLE,** cable television company executive; b. Ironton, Ohio, June 5, 1940; d. Lindsey and Bessie (Reed) Belville; m. John R. Rosebrough, Mar. 4, 1960 (dec. Nov. 1974); children: G. Suzanne, John R., Rebecca J. Student, Columbia (Mo.) Coll., 1958-59; BSBA, Franklin U., 1985. Cons. CBR and Assocs., Columbus, 1978-82; dir. adminstrn. United Cerebral Palsy Columbus and Franklin County, 1972-82; bus. mgr. Times Mirror, Newark, Ohio, 1982-83; opns. mgr., 1983-85, gen. mgr. Logan/Waverly/Greenfield, Ohio, 1985-86, Times Mirror doing bus. as Dimension Cable Svcs., Marion, Ohio, 1986-88; v.p., gen. mgr. Cable TV div. Comcast of S.E. Pa. (formerly Susquehanna Comms., Times Mirror and Cox Comms.), Williamsport, Pa., 1988—. Bd. dirs United Way, Marion County, 1987-88, Lycoming County, 1989-2000, 2001-, Williamsport/Lycoming C. of C.; personal and bus. coach Coach U., 2002. Named one of Pa.'s Best 50 Women in Bus., 1997, One of Top 100 Bus. Persons in the State of Pa., 1997-99; fellow Betsy Magness Leadership Inst. 1999-2000, Pa. Economy League 2003—. Mem. Ohio Cable TV Assn. (bd. dirs. 1986-88), Pa. Cable TV Assn. (bd. dirs. 1990-96), Pa. Edn. Comms. Sys. (bd. dirs.), Pa. Rural Devel. Coun. (exec. com. telecomms. task force 1992-95), Mid-Ohio Regional Planning Commn. (transp. com. 1980-82), Internat. Women's Writers Guild, Internat. Assn. Counselors and Therapists. Avocations: writing, reading, music, arts/therapies. Office: Susquehana Comms 330 Basin St Williamsport PA 17701-5216 Personal E-mail: carolrosebrough@suscom.net. Business E-Mail: carol_rosebrough@cable.comcast.com.

**ROSEBUSH, JAMES SCOTT,** management consulting executive, former government official; b. Flint, Mich., June 1, 1949; s. Kenneth F. and Jacqueline (Porter) R.; m. Nancy Paull, May 18, 1974; children: Claire Haisley, Lauren Culver. BA, The Principia, Elsah, Ill., 1971; MA, Boston U., 1973. Cons., Boston, 1972-76; v.p. Nat. Chamber Found., Washington, 1976-79; assoc. dir. corp. contbn. Std. Oil Co., Cleve., 1979-81; dir. Office Bus. Liaison, U.S. Dept. Commerce, Washington, 1981, spl. asst. to Pres. for pvt. sector initiatives, Washington, 1981-82; dept. asst. to Pres., chief staff for First Lady The White House, Washington, 1982-86; pres. James Rosebush & Co., 1986—; CEO Growth Strategy, Inc., OurfamilyManager.com. Lectr. Georgetown U., Washington, 1977-79, George Washington U., Washington, 1977-79; presdl. appointee Nat. Mus. Svcs. Bd. Author: First Lady, Public Wife, 1987; contbr. articles to profl. jours. Mem. rev. com. United Way, Cleve., 1979; mem. cmty. rels. com. Cleve. Orch., 1979; bd. dirs. Phillips Collection Mus., SDC, Inc.; art adv. panel Fed. Res. Bd.; mem. adv. bd. Boston U. Recipient Internat. award Rotary Internat., 1970 Republican. Avocations: tennis, skiing, reading, travel. Office: 1250 24th St NW Ste 350 Washington DC 20037-1124 Office Phone: 202-835-1695. Personal E-mail: jsrosebush@aol.com.

**ROSEDALE, PHILIP,** computer software company executive; BS, Univ. Calif., San Diego. V.p., chief tech. officer RealNetworks; entrepreneur-in-residence Accel Partners, San Francisco, 1999; founder, CEO Linden Lab, San Francisco 1999—. Recipient Rave award (Business), Wired mag., 2006. Achievements include development of Second Life computer game software. Office: Linden Lab 1100 Sansome St San Francisco CA 94111*

**ROSEFSKY, JONATHAN BENENSOHN,** pediatrician; b. Johnson City, N.Y., June 28, 1939; s. I. J. and Elsie S. Rosefsky; m. Sue Perel, 1964 (div. 2005); children: Katherine, Douglas, Matthew. AB, Cornell U., 1960; B in Med. Sci., Dartmouth U., 1962; MD, Harvard U., 1964. Diplomate Am. Bd. Pediat., iic. Pa., Va. Intern in surgery Vanderbilt Univ. Hosp., Nashville, 1964-65; resident in pediatrics Children's Hosp. Med. Ctr., Boston, 1965-67; pediatrician USAF Med. Corps, Langley AFB, Va., 1967-69; dir. neonatal ICU United Health Svcs. Hosp., Johnson City, NY, 1969-74; pvt. practice Binghamton, NY, 1969-86; pres. Notation Systems, Inc., Binghamton, 1981-89; asst. clin. devel. McNeil Consumer Products Co., Ft. Washington, Pa., 1986-89; dir. med. svcs., sr. dir. med. affairs Wyeth-Ayerst Labs., St. David's, Pa., 1989—99; pres. Fluidmotive, Inc., Haverford, Pa., 2000—, Simulatrix, Inc., Wynnewood, Pa., 2004—, HydroCoil Power, Inc., Wynnewood, Pa., 2006—. Cons. pediat. N.Y. State Dept. Social Svcs., Albany, 1976—86; FDA adv. com. Gen. Hosp. and Personal Use Devices, Rockville, Md., 1986; industry rep. FDA Adv. Com. on Immunology Devices, Rockville, 1987—93; asst. prof. Pediat. Jefferson Med. Sch., Phila., 1987—; chmn. com. on ethics in clin. trials, pharm. sponsored conf., 1998; cons. Pharm. Device Mfrs. 2004—. Contbr. articles to profl. jours. Chmn. Citizen's Adv. Com. to Mayor of Binghamton, NY, 1971. Capt. USAF, 1967—69. Recipient Physician's Recognition award, AMA, 2004. Fellow: Am. Coll. Nutrition, Am. Acad. Pediat.; mem.: Mainline YMCA (bd. dirs. 2005—), Harvard Club NYC. Achievements include invention of back wedge, mole marker, ribbon drive, DecTRR electronic camouflage; propulsion, pump, low head hydroelectric turbine. Avocations: skiing, swimming, photography, languages, travel. Home: 1359 Arbordale Rd Wynnewood PA 19096 Office Phone: 877-790-7972. Business E-Mail: fluidmotive.inc@att.net.

**ROSEGARTEN, RORY**, personal manager, television producer, theater producer, film producer; b. N.Y.C., Feb. 12, 1962; s. Robert Joel and Rita Honey (Mandel) Rosegarten; m. Wendy Jill Korn, May 4, 1991; children: Danielle Sydney, Ryan Harris. Student, Ariz. State U., 1980-81. Pres. The Conversation Co., Ltd., Great Neck, NY, 1983—. Prodr.: (Broadway plays) Late Nite Comic, 1987; exec. prodr.: (albums) Robert Klein: Let's Not Make Love, 1990, Brian Regan: Live, 1997; exec. prodr.: (DVD) Brian Regan: I Walked on the Moon, 2004; exec. prodr.: (albums) Ray Romano: Live at Carnegie Hall, 2002, (TV spl.) A Pair of Jokers: Brian Regan and Dennis Regan, 1991, Something's Wrong with the Regan Boy, 1992, Robert Klein: It All Started Here, 1996, Sketch Pad, 2001, Sketch Pad 2, 2003; exec. prodr.: (TV spl.) Making The Cut, 2005; exec. prodr.: (TV series) Everybody Loves Raymond, 1996—2005, New Joke City, 2000—01, The John Henson Project, 2004; exec. prodr.: (TV series) The Lance Krall Show, 2005, (TV spl.) Robert Klein: Child in His 50's, 2000; exec. prodr.: (TV spl., DVD) Clint Holmes: A Night to Remember, 2001, (TV spl.) Robert Klein: The Amorous Busboy of Decature Ave, 2005; exec. prodr.: (films) Welcome to Mooseport, 2004; prodr.: Grilled, 2004; exec. prodr.: Eulogy, 2004. Assoc. trustee North Shore L.I. Jewish Health Sys. Found., 2004—; assoc. bd. dir. Parker Jewish Geriat. Inst., New Hyde Park, NY, 1995—98; bd. gov. Comic Relief, 1999—2002. Recipient Primetime Emmy award for Outstanding Comedy Series: Everybody Loves Raymond, 2002—03, 2004—05. Mem.: SAG, NATAS, Friars Club. Avocation: autograph and memorabilia collecting. Office: The Conversation Co Ltd 1044 No Blvd Ste 304 Roslyn NY 11576

**ROSEIG, ESTHER MARIAN See FOGEL, ESTHER**

**ROSELIEB, CRAIG ALAN**, band director; b. Dekalb, Ill., Sept. 3, 1961; s. Alan David and Beverly Joan Roselieb; m. Joy Belt Belt, July 4, 2004; children: Jousha Elijah Belt, Abigail Margaret. MusB, No. Ill. U., 1984; MusM, Northwestern U., Evanston, Ill., 1988. Cert. tchr. Ill., 1984. Band dir. Glenbrook North H.S., Northbrook, Ill., 1984—87, Wheaton Ctrl. H.S., Wheaton, Ill., 1988—90, Downers Grove South H.S., Downers Grove, Ill., 1990—. Recipient Citation of Excellence, Nat. Band Assn., 1997. Mem.: Ill. Music Educators Assn. (Dist. I pres. 1999—), Am. Sch. Band Directors Assn. D-Liberal. Methodist. Avocations: running, bicycling. Office: Downers Grove South High School 1436 Norfolk Downers Grove IL 60516 Office Phone: 630-795-8693. Office Fax: 630-795-8599. E-mail: croselieb@csd99.org.

**ROSELL, KURT F.**, lawyer; b. Ithaca, NY, May 12, 1960; BS magna cum laude, Wake Forest U., NC, 1982; JD, Columbia Law Sch., 1985; LLM in Taxation, 1992, 1993. Bar: NY 1986. Atty. Cravath, Swaine & Moore, NYC; hiring ptnr., recruiting coon. Schulte Roth & Zapel LLP, NYC. Spkr. in field, sr. editor Columbia Law Rev., 1983—85; contbr. articles to profl. jour. Harlan Fiske Stone Scholar. Mem.: Assn. Bar City NY, Phi Beta Kappa. Office: Schulte Roth & Zapel LLP 919 Third Ave New York NY 10022 Office Phone: 212-756-2099. Office Fax: 212-593-5955. Business E-Mail: kurt.rosell@srz.com.

**ROSELLA, JOHN DANIEL**, clinical psychologist, educator; b. Phila., Sept. 12, 1938; s. Orazio and Angela Theresa (Caramado Rosella; m. Rose Mary Theresa Malloy, Nov. 14, 1964; children: Anne-Marie, John Daniel Jr. BS in Psychology, Villanova U., 1961; MEd Temple U., 1966, postgrad. Temple U., 1969—72, PhD Walden U., 1981. Diplomate Am. Bd. Forensic Examiners, Am. Bd. Psychol. Spltys., Profl. Acad. Custody Evaluators, cert. hypnotherapist, lic. psychologist, Pa.; cert. in edn. St. Joseph's U., 1963. Tchr., counselor Father Judge H.S., Phila., 1962—67; counselor Bristol Twp. Sch. Dist., Bucks County, Pa., 1967—69; prof. dept. social and behavioral scis. Bucks County C.C., 1994—2005, prof. emeritus, 2005—, subject area coord., 2004, Newtown, Pa., 1968—, adj. prof., 2005, founder coll. reading and study skills program Newtown, Pa., 1968—70, founding chmn. dept. basic studies, 1970—76; dir. psychol. svcs. Fairless Hills (Pa.) Med. Ctr., 1978—89, dir. clin. svcs., 1989—96; asst. clin. prof. Widener U., 1990—. Cons. Office of Vocat. Rehab., 1977—; psychol. cons. Eugenia Hosp.19890, 1980—, Bur. Disability Determination, 1982—, Human Growth Ctr., Inc. 1982—2003, Crestview North Nursing Home and Rehab. Ctr., 1990—2003; cons. staff psychologist Attleboro Nursing Home and Rehab. Ctr., 1993—2001, Pickering Manor Nursing Home, 1997—2001; clin. assoc. mem., Dept. Mental Health Scis. Hahnemann U., 1982—94; cons. Bucks County (Pa.) Family Ct., 1985—2004; grad. clin. supr. Coll. of N.J., 1985—86; grad. counseling intern supr. Rider Coll., 1988—95; participant 1st Internat. Colloquium on Family Health, Sri Lanka, 1983, Australia, 88; ednl. profl. travel Italy and Switzerland; 1991; clin. supr. doctor of psychology program, 2005—06; lectr. in field. Author: Reading and Study Skills: A Counseling Approach, 1970, Effects of the Basic Studies Program on the Academic Achievement of High Risk Students, 1973—74, The Professor and the Law, 1975, Research in Hypnosis for Students, 1976, Marriage and Family Therapy: Its Evolution from Revolution, 1980, others; author: (audiotapes) Developing Successful Study Skills, Guided Imagery Exercises; author: articles. Active Right to Read Task Force, 1972—73; project dir. Fairless Hills Psychiat. Hosp. bldg. program, 1982—83; pres. bd. trustees Friends of the Libr. Found., Bucks County C.C., 1984—; co-founder Newtown Twp. Dem. Party, 1978, 1st vice chmn., 1979—80, Dem. committeeman, 1989—92; mem. 8th Congressional Dist. Adv. Coun. on Health Care, 1981—83; bd. dirs. Valley Day Sch., 1978—81; Bucks County Cmty. Ctrs., 1980—85. Recipient Man of Yr. award, Assn. to Advance Ethical Hypnosis, 1976, Disting. Tchg. recognition, Phi Theta Kappa, 1981, 1983, Faculty Svc. award, 1989, Profl. AChievement award, Bucks County C.C. Alumni Assn., 1991. Fellow: Pa. Psychol. Assn., Internat. Coun. for Sex Edn. and Parenthood of Am. U.; mem.: APA, Profl. Acad. Custody Evaluators, Pa. Assn. Marriage and Family Therapy, Am. Assn. Marriage and Family Therapy, Am. Coll. Forensic Examiners, Sons of Italy, KC, Am. Legion. Office: Offices at Oxford Crossing Ste 202 333 N Oxford Valley Rd Fairless Hills PA 19030-2626 E-mail: fairrlesspsychassoc@comcast.net.

**ROSELLE, DAVID PAUL**, academic administrator, mathematician, educator; b. Vandergrift, Pa., May 30, 1939; s. William John and Esther Suzanne (Clever) R.; m. Louise Helen Dowling, June 19, 1967; children—Arthur Charles, Cynthia Dowling BS, West Chester State Coll., 1961; PhD, Duke U., 1965; LLD (hon.), West Chester U., 1994; degree (hon.), Westchester U., Soka U. Japan. Asst. prof. math. U. Md., College Park, 1965-68; assoc. prof. math. La. State U., Baton Rouge, 1968-73; prof., 1973-74, Va. Poly. Inst. and State U., Blacksburg, 1974-87, dean grad. sch., 1979-81, dean research and grad. studies, 1981-83, provost, 1983-87, chmn. Commn. on Rsch., 1981-83, chmn. Commn. on Grad. Studies, 1983-87; prof. U. Ky., 1987-90, pres., 1987-90; pres., prof. math. U. Del., 1990—. Pres. COMAP, Inc., Lexington, Mass., 1986-95; bd. dirs. Wilmington Trust Corp., VTLS, Inc. Editor: Proc. of the First Louisiana Conf. on Combinatorics, Graph Theory and Computing, 1970, Proc. of the Second Louisiana Conf. on Combinatorics, Graph Theory and Computing, 1971; mem. editorial bd. The Bicentennial Tribute to American Mathematics, 1977; contbr. numerous research articles to profl. jours. Mem. Del. Roundtable, 1990—, Bus.and Pub. Edn. Coun., 1990—; trustee Winterthur Mus., 1991—; bd. dirs. Del. Acad. Medicine, 1991—, Med. Ctr. Del., 1991—, OCLC, Inc., 2004—; mem. USAID adv. com. vol. fgn: aid, 2000-04. Named Outstanding Alumnus West Chester State Coll., 1979; Westinghouse Coop. scholar, 1957; NSF grantee, 1965-75; Teaching

Excellence Cert., 1978; Digital Equipment grant, 1984; Nat. Coun. Tchrs. Math. Cert. of Appreciation, 1984; founding fellow of Inst. for Combinatorics and Its Applications, 1990; numerous invited addresses at univs. and profl. soc. meetings. Mem. Am. Math. Soc., Math. Assn. Am. (sec., fin. com., exec. com., com. on publs. 1975-84; com. on spl. funds 1985—; chmn. com. on accreditation 1985; numerous other coms.). Home: 47 Kent Way Newark DE 19711-5201 Office: U Del Hullihen Hall Rm 104 Newark DE 19716-0101 Business E-Mail: roselle@udel.edu.

**ROSELLE, WILLIAM CHARLES**, librarian; b. Vandergrift, Pa., June 30, 1936; s. William John and Suzanne Esther (Clever) R.; m. Marsha Louise Lucas, Aug. 2, 1959; 1 child, Paul Lucas. BA, Thiel Coll., 1958; MLS, U. Pitts., 1963. Lic. profl. guide State of Mont., 1978. Mem. media Temple Hershey (Pa.) Sch., 1960-62; trainee Pa. State Library, 1962-63; asst. catalog librarian Pa. State U., 1963-65; engring., math. librarian U. Iowa, 1965-66, library adminstrv. asst., 1966-69, asst. dir. libraries, 1969-71; prof., dir. library U. Wis.-Milw., 1971-89; dir. univ. library system U. Pitts., 1989-90; pvt. cons. Thiensville, Wis., 1991—. Chmn. Morris Fromkin Meml. Lectr. Com., 1972-89; chmn. planning task force on computing U. Wis. System, 1973-74, mem. library planning study com., 1978-79, co-chmn. library automation task force, 1983-85; chmn. computing mgmt. rev. team U. Wis.-Stout, 1976; chmn. Council for U. Wis. Libraries, 1981-82; library cons. Grambling (La.) State U., Viterbo Coll., LaCrosse, Wis., N.C. A&T U., Greensboro, Mt. Mary Coll., Milw., U. Ill. at Chgo., Milw. Sch. Engring., Bklyn. Coll., U. South Ala., Concordia Coll., Milw., Metrics Rsch. Corp., Cardinal Stritch Coll., Milw., N.Y. Inst. Tech., Indiana U. of Pa., Med. Coll. Wis., Wis. Luth. Coll., Milw.; participant Library Adminstrs. Devel. Program, U. Md., 1973, micrographics seminar Nat. Microfilm Assn., 1973, Mgmt. Skills Inst., Assn. Rsch. Libraries, Kansas City, Mo., 1977, Meadowbrook Symposium Midwest Library Network, 1976; mem. sect. geography and map libraries Internat. Fedn. Library Assns. and Instns., 1978-83; mem. bldg. com. Ctr. for Rsch. Libraries, 1980-82. Editorial cons. The Quest for Social Justice, 1983, Current Geographical Publications, 1978-89; contbr. articles to profl. jours. Pres. Thiensville (Wis.) Village Bd., 1987; bd. dirs. Charles Allis Art Mus., 1979-84. Served with AUS, 1958-60. Named Disting. Alumnus, Thiel Coll., 1985 Hon. fellow Am. Geog. Soc.; mem. Spl. Libraries Assn. (spl. citation 1979), ALA (life), Iowa Library Assn. (chmn. audit com. 1968-70, chmn. intellectual freedom com. 1969-70), Wis. Library Assn., Midwest Acad. Librarians Conf. (chmn. 1969-71), AAUP (treas. U. Iowa chpt. 1969-70), Coun. Wis. Libraries (chmn. 1973-74), Soc. Tympanuchus Cupido Pinnatus, Internat. CBX Owners Assn., Milw. Civil War Round Table, Ozaukee Corvette Club, Beta Beta Beta, Beta Phi Mu, Phi Alpha Theta, Phi Kappa Phi, Phi Delta Kappa. Lutheran. Home: 324 Sunny Ln Thiensville WI 53092-1334

**ROSELLI, RICHARD JOSEPH**, lawyer; b. Chgo., Mar. 2, 1954; s. H. Joseph and Dolores Roselli; m. Lisa McNelis; children: Nicholas Joseph, Christiana Elise, Alexandra Grace, Michaela Luciana, Anthony Santino. BA, Tulane U., 1976, JD, 1980. Bar: Fla. 1981, U.S. Dist. Ct. (so. dist.) Fla. 1981, U.S. Ct. Appeals (5th and 11th cirs.); bd. cert. civil trial lawyer. Ptnr. Krupnick, Campbell, Malone, Roselli et al, Ft. Lauderdale, 1981—2002, Roselli & Campbell Trial Lawyers, Boca Raton, Fla., 2002—06, Roselli & McNelis, PA, Boca Raton, Fla., 2006—. Adj. asst. prof., mem. bd. advisors physician asst. program Nova Southeastern U. Trustee Fla. Dem. Party, 1992-95. Mem. ATLA (pres.' coun. 1996-97), Am. Bd. Trial Advocates, Am. Soc. Law and Medicine, So. Trial Lawyers Assn. (founder), Acad. Fla. Trial Lawyers (bd. dirs. 1987—, exec. com. 1990-97, sec. 1993, treas. 1994, pres. elect. 1995, pres. 1996, chmn. Fla. lawyers action group-PAC 1996, Golden Eagle award, 1989, 1996, 98, Silver Eagle award, 1990, Crystal Eagle award 1995), Broward County Trial Lawyers (bd. dirs.), Trial Lawyers for Pub. Justice, Lawyer Pilots Bar Assn., St. Jude Catholic Ch. Office: 4800 N Federal Hwy Ste 202E Boca Raton FL 33431 Office Phone: 954-568-0700. Business E-Mail: rroselli@rosellimcnelis.com.

**ROSEMAN, CHARLES SANFORD**, lawyer; b. Jersey City, Feb. 26, 1945; s. Leon and Edith (Neidorf) R.; children: Rochelle Lynn, Loren Scott. BA, Calif. State U., Northridge, 1968; JD, U. San Diego, 1971. Bar: Calif. 1972, U.S. Dist. Ct. (so. dist.) Calif. 1972, U.S. Dist. Ct. (cen. dist.) Calif. 1975, U.S. Supreme Ct. 1980, U.S. Claim Ct. 1990. Assoc. Greer, Popko, Nickoloff & Miller, San Diego, 1972-73; ptnr. Roseman & Roseman, San Diego, 1973-78, Roseman & Small, San Diego, 1978-82, Frank, Roseman, Freedus & Mann, San Diego, 1982-86, Roseman and Mann, 1986-92; pvt. practice San Diego, 1992—; judge pro tem San Diego County Superior Ct., 1975—; also arbitrator, mediator, 1977—; founding ptnr. i2i Resolutions, 2001. Bd. dirs. Glenn Aire Cmty. Devel. Assn., San Diego, 1972-73, Big Bros. San Diego County, 1973-81,; bd. dirs. San Diego County Anti-Defamation League, 1985—; chmn. exec. com. 1984-85, assoc. nat. commr., 1995—; bd. dirs. San Diego County Legal Aid Soc., 1988-89, Tifereth Israel Synagogue, pres. 1982-84, Homeys Youth Found., 2002—. Mem. ABA, ATLA, Fed. Bar. Assn., Consumer Attys. of Calif. (Recognition of Experience award 1985), Calif. Bar Assn., Am. Arbitration Assn. (arbitrator, panel 1985-86), San Diego Bar Assn., Consumer Attys. of San Diego (bd. dirs. 1982-84), U. San Diego Sch. Law Alumni assn. (bd. dirs. 1972-73), B'nai B'rith (pres. 1978). Democrat. Office: Law Offices Charles S Roseman & Assocs 1761 Hotel Cir S Ste 250 San Diego CA 92108 Office Phone: 619-544-1500. E-mail: csroseman@rosemanlaw.com.

**ROSEMAN, JACK**, computer services company executive; b. Lynn, Mass., June 13, 1931; s. Abraham and Bessie (Guz) Roseman; m. Judith Ann Rosenthal, Feb. 21, 1960; children: Laura, Alan, Shari. BA, Boston U., 1954; MS, U. Mass., 1955. Instr. U. Mass., 1958—60; dir. info. processing CEIR, Inc., Washington, 1960—66; v.p. KMS Tech. Ctr., Washington, 1966—70; pres., bd. dirs. On-Line Systems, Inc., Pitts., 1970—79; pres., chmn. United Computing Internat. subs. of SPRINT, 1979—80; pres., bd. dirs., later chmn. Actronics, 1981—85; pvt. investor, ptnr. J.R Assocs., Pitts., 1988—92; chmn. of bd. dirs. Omega Systems, 1994—96; CEO/dir. Roseman Inst., 2001—. Disting. adj. prof. Donald H. Jones Ctr. Entrepreneurship, 1992—2000, assoc. dir., 1992—2001; John Thorne prof. entrepreneurship Carnegie Mellon U., 2000—01; dir. emeritus Pitts. High Tech. Coun.; chmn. Cerebellum, Inc., 1997—2000; bd. dirs. Roseman Inst., Collaborate, Inc., 2001—05, MIT Forum; advisor Donald H. Jones Ctr. for Entrepreneurship, Carnegie Mellon U., Akustica, Inc., Echo Internat.; bd. dirs. RHS Industries, ChemDAQ, VoCollect. Co-author: Outrageous Optimism: Wisdom for the Entrepreneurial Journey. Adv. Kobold Found.; mem. Nat. Found. Tchg. Entrepreneurships. Recipient Judges' award, Ernst & Young, and Merrill Lynch Inc. mags., 1991. Office Phone: 412-369-5306. Business E-Mail: rosemanj@rosemaninstitute.com.

**ROSEMAN, SAUL**, biochemist, educator; b. Bklyn., Mar. 9, 1921; s. Emil and Rose (Markowitz) R.; m. Martha Ozrowitz, Sept. 9, 1941; children: Mark Alan, Dorinda Ann, Cynthia Bernice. BS, CCNY, 1941; MS, U. Wis., 1944, PhD, 1947; MD (hon.), U. Lund, Sweden, 1984. From instr. to asst. prof. U. Chgo., 1948-53; from asst. prof. to prof. biol. chemistry, also Rackham Arthritis Research Unit, U. Mich., 1953-65; S. O'Connor prof. biology Johns Hopkins U., Balt., 1965—, chmn. dept., 1969-73; dir. McCollum-Pratt Inst., 1969-73, chmn. dept. biology, dir., 1988-90. Cons. NIH, NSF, Am. Cancer Soc., Hosp. for Sick Children, Toronto; sci. counselor Nat. Cancer Inst.; Lynch lectr. U. Notre Dame, 1989; Van Niel lectr. Stanford U., 1992. Author articles on metabolism of complex molecules containing carbohydrates and on solute transport.; former mem. editorial bd.: Biochemistry, Jour. Biol. Chemistry. Served with AUS, 1944-46. Recipient Sesquicentennial award U. Mich., 1967, T. Duckett Jones Meml. award Helen Hay Whitney Found., 1973, Rosensteihl award Brandeis U., 1974, Internat. award Gairdner Found. award, 1981, Townsend Harris award CUNY, 1987, Spl. award 11th Internat. Symposium on Glycoconjugates, 1991, Karl Meyer award Soc. Glycobiology, 1993. Fellow Am. Acad. Microbiology; mem. Am. Soc. Biol. Chemists, Am. Soc. Cell Biology, Am. Acad. Arts and Scis., Nat. Acad. Scis., Am. Chem. Soc., Am. Soc. Microbiologists, Biochem. Soc. Japan (hon.). Office: Johns Hopkins U 34th Charles St Baltimore MD 21218 Office Phone: 410-516-7333.

**ROSEMAN, STEVEN A.**, insurance company executive, lawyer; BA in Econs., Brandeis U.; JD, U. Pa. Assoc., ptnr. Ervin Cohen & Jessup, Beverly Hills, Calif.; v.p. bus. affairs Worldwide Pay TV Paramount Pictures Corp.; sr. v.p., gen. counsel, sec. Am. Health Properties Inc., Englewood, Colo., 1997—2000; counsel LeBoeus Lamb Green & MacRae LLP, Denver, 2001—02; exec. v.p., gen. counsel, sec. Sun Healthcare Group, Albuquerque, 2002—. Office: Sun Healthcare Group 101 Sun Ave NE Albuquerque NM 87109

**ROSEMARIN, CAREY STEPHEN**, lawyer; b. Englewood, NJ, Aug. 19, 1950; s. Jack L. and Muriel Ruth (Gordon) R.; m. Joan Maxine Lafer, June 17, 1973; children: Benjamin Joseph, Meryl Ruth. BS, U. Mich., 1972; MS, Pa. State U., 1974; JD, U. Tenn., 1978. Bar: Tenn. 1978, Ill. 1982, U.S. Dist. Ct. (ea. dist.) Tenn. 1978, U.S. Dist. Ct. (no. dist.) Ill. 1982. Rsch. assoc. Union Carbide Corp., Oak Ridge Nat. Lab., 1974-80; asst. regional counsel U.S. EPA, Chgo., 1980-86; ptnr. Katten, Muchin, & Zavis, Chgo., 1986-90, Jenner & Block, Chgo., 1990-99; prin. Law Offices of Carey S. Rosemarin, P.C., Northbrook, Ill., 1999—. Participant Israel Environ. Bike Ride, 2004, Alyn Pediat. Hosp. Charity Bike Ride, 2005; v.p. facilities Congregation Beth Judea, Long Grove, Ill. Mem. ABA, Tenn. Bar Assn., Chgo. Bar Assn. (chmn. environ. law com. 1985-86), Environ. Law Inst. (assoc.), North Suburban Bar Assn. (v.p.). Jewish. Avocations: licensed glider pilot, bicycling. Office: Law Offices of Carey S Rosemarin PC 500 Skokie Blvd Ste 510 Northbrook IL 60062-2893 Fax: 312-896-5786. Office Phone: 847-897-8000. Business E-Mail: csr@rosemarinlaw.com.

**ROSEN, ABY J.**, real estate developer; Cofounder RFR Holding LLC, NYC; works with Ian Schrafer. Helped develop properties at 390 Park Ave., NYC, 400 Park Ave., NYC, 516 Fifth Ave., NYC, 521 Fifth Ave., NYC, 275 Madison Ave., NYC, 636 Madison Ave., NYC, many other commercial and residential properties. Named one of Top 200 Collectors, ARTnews mag., 2006; recipient Man of Yr. award, Spring Ahead Gala, Jeffrey Modell Found., 2000. Avocation: collecting modern and contemporary art and contemporary photography. Office: c/o RFR Holding LLC 400 Park Ave New York NY 10022*

**ROSEN, ADAM B.**, lawyer; b. Queens, NY, May 4, 1967; BA in History, LI U., 1989; JD cum laude, Touro Coll., 1993. Bar: NJ 1993, US Dist. Ct. Dist. NJ 1993, NY 1994, US Dist. Ct. Ea. Dist. NY 1995, US Dist. Ct. So. Dist. NY 1995. Ptnr. Wilson, Elser, Moskowitz, Edelman & Dicker LLP, NYC. Mem.: NY State Bar Assn., Nassau County Bar Assn., Assn. of the Bar of the City of NY. Office: Wilson Elser Moskowitz Edelman & Dicker LLP 23rd Fl 150 E 42nd St New York NY 10017-5639 Office Phone: 212-490-3000 ext. 2693. Office Fax: 212-490-3038. Business E-Mail: rosena@wemed.com.

**ROSEN, ALLEN DAVID**, plastic surgeon; b. Bklyn., Mar. 5, 1957; MD, SUNY-Buffalo, 1983. Diplomate Am. Bd. Plastic Surgery with subspecialty in hand surgery. Intern Columbia-Presbyn. Med. Ctr., N.Y.C., 1983—84, resident in surgery, 1984—86, resident in plastic surgery, 1986—88, fellow in hand surgery, 1987; pvt. practice plastic surgery, 1987—; founding ptnr., med. dir. The Plastic Surgery Group, Montclair, NJ, 1995—. Attending plastic surgeon Passaic Gen. Hosp., NJ, Mountainside Hosp., NJ, St. Barnabas Med. Ctr.; clin. asst. prof. U. Medicine and Dentistry N.J.; spokesperson Am. Soc. Plastic and Reconstructive Surgery, 1990—. Fellow: ACS; mem.: N.J. Soc. Plastic and Reconstructive Surgery, Am. Cancer Soc. (past pres.). Office: 37 N Fullerton Ave Montclair NJ 07042*

**ROSEN, ARTHUR MARVIN**, advertising executive; b. N.Y.C., Dec. 28, 1930; s. Joseph and Cornelia (Grob) R.; m. Maureen Elizabeth Reilly; children: Ellen Jessica, Deborah Lynn, Daniel Joshua. BA, CUNY, 1952; MA, Yale U., 1953; postgrad., Columbia U., 1955-57. Analyst research Dancer-Fitzgerald-Sample, N.Y.C., 1955-56; supr. research Benton and Bowles, N.Y.C., 1956-61; account exec. Young and Rubicam, N.Y.C., 1961-66; v.p. account supr. Grey Advt., N.Y.C., 1966-69; pres. Met. Diagnostic, N.Y.C., 1969-73; v.p. group mgmt. Grey Advt., N.Y.C., 1973-81; exec. v.p. Sudler and Hennessey, N.Y.C., 1981-94; mktg. cons. Himmel Nutrition, Inc., 1994-95, Martin Himmel, Inc., 1994-95. Spkr. in field. Contbr. articles to profl. jours. Pres. Temple Beth Or, Washington Twp., N.J., 1973-74; chmn. Soc. Families, Colgate U., 1983-84; chmn. curriculum com., mem. exec. coun., study leader ILEAD, 2004-05; Dartmouth Coll.; trustee, study leader Adventures in Learning, Colby-Sawyer Coll.; mem. bd. dirs. Lake Sunapee Protective Assn.; mem. Jewish-Christian Interfaith Partnership. Capt. U.S. Army, 1953-55. Republican. Jewish. E-mail: ponderosen@tds.net.

**ROSEN, ARYE**, microwave, optoelectronics and medical researcher; b. June 26, 1937; BSEE cum laude, Howard U., 1963; MScE, Johns Hopkins U., 1965; MSc in Physiology, Thomas Jefferson U., 1975; PhD in Elec. Engring., Drexel U., 1993. Registered profl. engr., B.C., Can. Assoc. in medicine Jefferson Med. Coll., Phila., 1977—; rsch. prof. Sch. of Biomed. Engring. Sci. and Health Sys. Drexel U., Phila., adj. prof. elec. and computer engring., 1981—2003, acad. prof. biomed. engring. and elec. engring., 2003—. Mem. com. on sci. and the arts The Franklin Inst., 2003—. Co-editor: High-Power Optically Activated Solid-State Switches, 1993, New Frontiers in Medical Device Technology, 1995; co-author: RF/microwave Interaction with Biological Tissues, 2000; contbr. more than 150 articles to profl. jours. Mem. adv. com. John Scott award Phila. Bd. Dirs. City Trusts, 2004—. Recipient Microwave prize 16th European Microwave Conf., 1986, Disting. Alumni award Drexel U. Coll. Engring., Elec. and Computer Engring. Dept., 1997, IEEE MTT-S Microwave Application award, 2000, IEEE Third Millennium medal, 2000, IEEE Reg. I award, 1989. Mem.: NAE, IEEE (mem. MMT-S tech. com. for light-wave tech. 1979—, mem. MTT-S tech. program com., chmn. MTT-S tech. com. on biol. effects and med. applications, mem. editl. bd., assoc. editor IEEE Jour. Light-Wave Tech., editl. bd. Transactions on Microwave Theory and Techniques, editl. bd. Microwave and Optical Tech. Letters, mem. tech. com. IEEE Internat. Conf. Microwaves in Medicine 1991, ednl. activities bd., mem.-at-large health care engring. policy com., Disting. Microwave lectr. 1997—2001). Achievements include 55 patents in the fields of engineering and medicine, including Percutaneous Transluminal Microwave Catheter Angioplasty, Method and Apparatus for High Frequency Catheter Ablation, Catheter with Distally Located Integrated Circuit Radiation Generator, Electrical Phase Shifter Controlled by Light, Direct DC to RF Conversion by Impulse Excitation, Light Controlled Antennas, High Power Optical Switch, Radiation Protection Circuit for Protection Against Gamma Ray and Neutron Radiation. Office: Drexel Univ Sch Biomed Engring Sci and Health Sys 3141 Chestnut St Philadelphia PA 19104-2875 Office Phone: 215-895-1913.

**ROSEN, BARRY S.**, lawyer; BS magna cum laude, U. Ill., 1974; JD, Harvard U., 1977. Bar: Mass. 1977, Ill. 1978. Asst. atty. gen. Antitrust Divsn., Mass., 1977—79; ptnr. Sachnoff & Weaver, Chgo., 1979—. Recipient Bronze Tablet, Univ. Ill., Charles Merriam Scholar. Mem.: Phi Beta Kappa. Office: Sachnoff & Weaver Ltd 40th Fl 10 S Wacker Dr Chicago IL 60606 Office Phone: 312-207-6483. Business E-Mail: brosen@sachnoff.com.

**ROSEN, BENSON**, business administration educator; b. Detroit, Oct. 9, 1942; s. David and Laura R.; m. Brenda M. Lisbroder, Dec. 17, 1966; children: Gregory Scott, David Loren. BS, Wayne State U., 1964, MA, 1968, PhD, 1969. Asst. prof. U. N.C., Chapel Hill, 1969-74, assoc. prof., 1974-80, prof. bus. adminstrn., 1980—, Hanes prof. mgmt., 1992—, sr. assoc. dean acad. affairs, 1995-98. Vis. prof. U. Minn., 1981; cons. to bus., industry, govt.; cons. EEOC. Author: Becoming Aware, 1980, Older Employees: New Roles for Valued Resources, 1985; mem. editorial rev. bd. Acad. Mgmt. Jour., 1978-84; contbr. articles to profl. jours. Bd. dirs. SHRM Found., 1994-2001. Recipient Young Scholars award Spencer Found., 1976, 78, Disting. Rsch. award, 1993, PhD Teaching award, 1994; NSF grantee, 1973-75; Adminstrn. on Aging grantee, 1978-80. Fellow APA; mem. Acad. Mgmt., Soc. Human Resource Mgmt. Office: U NC CB 3490 Kenan Flagler Bus Sch Chapel Hill NC 27599-3490 Office Phone: 919-962-3166. E-mail: Ben_Rosen@unc.edu.

**ROSEN, CAROL MENDES,** artist; b. N.Y.C., Jan. 15, 1933; d. Bram de Sola and Mildred (Bertuch) Mendes; m. Elliot A. Rosen, June 30, 1957. BA, Hunter Coll., 1954; MA, CUNY, 1962. Tchr. art West Orange (N.J.) Pub. Schs., 1959—85. Co-curator exhibit Printmaking Coun. N.J., Somerville, 1981; exhibit curator 14 Sculptors Gallery, N.Y.C., 1988; collection: Nat. Collection of Fine Arts, Smithsonian Instn., Newark Mus., N.J. State Mus., Bristol-Myers Squibb, AT&T, Noyes Mus., N.Y. Pub. Libr., Zimmerli Art Mus., Mus. of Modern Art, Whitney Mus., Libr. Collection Bklyn. Mus., Victoria & Albert Mus., Nat. Art Gallery, London, Mus. of Tolerance, L.A., Hunterdon Mus. Art, Nat. Mus. Women in Arts, Tel Aviv U. and The Jewish Nat. & U. Libr., Jerusalem, Houghton Libr., Harvard U., Yale U., Clark Art Inst., Skidmore, Williams Coll. Mus. Art, Oberlin Coll., William Paterson U., Stanford U., Smith Coll., Wellesley Coll., Tate Britain, Kreitman Rsch. Ctr. Contbr. articles to arts mags. Recipient Hudson River Mus. award, Yonkers, 1983; fellow, N.J. State Coun. Arts, 1980, 1983. Jewish. Avocations: gardening, reading. Home: 10 Beavers Rd Califon NJ 07830-3433 Personal E-mail: earosen@earthlink.net.

**ROSEN, CHARLES, II,** retired lawyer; b. New Orleans, Jan. 29, 1925; s. Louis Leucht and Nita (Silverstein) R.; m. Mary Alice Waldauer (div. 1976); children: Charles III, Virginia, Jane, James Louis; m. Sandra Reed (div. 1995); m. Emily Hart, 1995. BA, Tulane U., 1948, LLB, 1951. Bar: La. 1951. Assoc. Rosen, Kammer, Wolff, Hopkins & Burke, New Orleans, 1951-55, Jones, Walker, Waechter, Poitevent, Carrere & Denegre, New Orleans, 1955-58, ptnr., 1958-90; spl. counsel Locke, Purnell, Rain, Harrell (now Locke Liddell & Sapp), New Orleans, 1990-97; of counsel Sullivan Stolier & Resor, New Orleans, 1997—2005; ret. Past chmn. and mem. exec. com. Golf & Sports Attractions, Inc., ret. mem. fore kids Found. Past trustee Touro Synagogue; hon. trustee Touro Infirmary; chmn. lawyers div. Jewish Fedn. Greater New Orleans, 1969; past chmn. lawyers div. United Fund. 1st lt. U.S. Army, 1944-46, PTO. Mem. ABA, La. Bar Assn., New Orleans Bar Assn., Am. Coll. Real Estate Attys., Anglo Am. Real Property Inst., So. Golf Assn. (past bd. dirs.), New Orleans Golf Assn. (past pres., past bd. dirs.), Tulane Green Wave Club (past bd. dirs.), Lakewood Country Club (past pres., bd. dirs.). Republican. Avocation: golf. Home: 126 Brokenbraugh Ct Metairie LA 70005 also: 126 Brockenbraugh Ct Metairie LA 70005 Office Phone: 504-561-1044. Business E-mail: atty@ssrlawfirm.com.

**ROSEN, CLIFFORD JAMES,** internist; b. Utica, N.Y., Feb. 18, 1950; s. Harry N. and Harriett P. (Rubin) R.; m. Donna Peckham, June 17, 1973; (div Dec. 1983); 1 child, Aaron; m. Rebecca Harless, Aug. 7, 1986; 1 child, Isaac. BS, U. Maine, 1971; MD, SUNY, Syracuse, 1975. Diplomate Nat. Bd. Med. Examiners, Am. Bd. Internal Medicine. Chief resident in medicine U. Mass./Berkshire Med. Ctr., Pittsfield, 1978-79, instr. medicine, 1978-79; fellow in endocrinology Dartmouth Hitchcock Med. Ctr., Hanover, N.H., 1982-84; cooperating prof. nutrition U. Maine, Orono, 1986-88, rsch. asst. prof., 1988-91, rsch. assoc. prof., 1991-94; clin. assoc. prof. Tufts U. Sch. Medicine, Boston, 1991-94, Boston U. Sch. Medicine, 1993—; rsch. prof. U Maine, 1995—, prof. nutrition, 1999—. Adv. bd. Inst. Cellular Rsch., Bangor, 1991-93; exec. dir. Maine Ctr. for Osteoporosis Rsch.; chief medicine St. Joseph Hosp., Bangor, 1989-99; sr. staff scientist Jackson Lab., Ben Harbor, Maine Editor-in-chief Jour. Clin. Densitometry, 1998—; editor Osteoporosis in Clin. Medicine, 1995—; contbr. chpts. to books, articles to profl. jours. Founder Physicians for Nat. Health Plan, Maine, 1991; com. person Am. Health Reform Com., Washington, 1993. Recipient Katherine Musgrave award Maine Nutrition Coun., Augusta, 1994, Excellence in Aging Rsch. award Glenn Found., 1996. Mem. Am. Fedn. Clin. Rsch., Soc. of Insulin Growth Factor Rschrs., Endocrine Soc., Am. Soc. Bone Mineral Rsch. (bd. dirs. adult bone and mineral working group 1993—, pub. affairs com. 1994-, pres., 2002-03), Soc. Clin. Densitometry (founding mem.). Democrat. Jewish. Avocations: running, gardening. Home: 16 Mckinley St Bangor ME 04401-3830 Office: St Joseph Hosp Maine Ctr Osteoporosis Rsch Bangor ME 04402 Personal E-mail: rofe@aol.com.

**ROSEN, ERIC S.,** state supreme court justice; b. Topeka, Kansas, May 25, 1953; BA, MA, U. Kansas; JD, Washburn U., 1984. Former social worker Topeka Public Sch.; former ptnr. Hein, Ebert and Rosen; former asst. dist. atty. & asst. public defender Shawnee County; judge domestic div. U.S. Dist. Ct., Third Dist., Shawnee County, Kans., 1993—95, judge Kans., 1993—2005; justice Kansas Supreme Ct., 2005—. Former assoc. gen. counsel Kans. Securities Commn.; former adjunct prof. Washburn U. Sch. of Law; mem. Koch Crime Commn., 1994; lecturer Menninger Sch. of Law and Psychiatry; mem. Kans. Sentencing Commn., 2004—. Recipient Atty. General's Victim's Svc. award, 2000, Martin Luther King Living the Dream Humanitarian award, 2002. Mem.: ABA, Kans. Bar Assn., Kans. Dist. Judges Assn., Am. Judicature Soc., Am. Judges Assn. Office: Kans Supreme Ct 301 W 10th Topeka KS 66612*

**ROSEN, FRED,** travel company executive; b. Windsor, Ont., Can., May 19, 1926; arrived in U.S., 1946; s. Harry and Dora Rosen; m. Gertrude Rush, May 13, 1952; 1 child, Robert Martin. Cert. Elec. Tech., Washington U., St. Louis, 1964; AA in Tourism, Forest Park C.C., St. Louis, 1993; Cert. Microcomputers, Meramec C.C., St. Louis, 2000. X-ray maint. staff Keleket X-Ray, Covington, Ky., 1953—54; whse. mgr. Western Shoe Jobbers, St. Louis, 1954—64, prodn. supr., 1977—92; owner Vanity Shoes, Kirkwood, Mo., 1964—77; travel cons. Hausler Travel, St. Louis, 1995—97; owner Accessible Travel, St. Louis, 1997—. Contbg. editor the Independence, 1997—98; author: (guidebook) How to Travel - A Guidebook for Persons with a Disability, 1997, How to Travel in Canada - A Guidebook for a Visitor with a Disability, 2000, Hot to Travel To and In Britain and Northern Ireland - A Guidebook for a Visitor with a Disability. Pres. Kirkwood Noonday Optimist Club, 1971—72; commr. Kirkwood Disabled Commn., 1984—91, Kirkwood Housing Authority, 1977—83, Kirkwood Human Rights, 1974—77; bd. dirs. Mo. Assn. Retarded Citizens, Jefferson City, 1962—65, St. Louis Assn. Retarded Citizens, 1962—89, mem. recreation com., 1962—89. Sgt. 1st class U.S. Army, 1946—53, ETO. Mem.: Masons (worshipful master 1990—91, Achievement award 1991). Jewish. Avocations: dance, cruising. Home: 144 Oakside Ln Saint Louis MO 63122-1211

**ROSEN, GEORGE,** economist, educator; b. St. Petersburg, Russia, Feb. 7, 1920; s. Leon and Rebecca (Rosenoer) R.; m. Sylvia Vatuk; 1 son, Mark. BA, Bklyn. Coll., 1940; MA, Princeton U., 1942, PhD, 1949. Prof. econs. Bard Coll., Annandale-on-Hudson, NY, 1946-50; economist Dept. State, Washington, 1951-54, Council Econ. Indsl. Research, Washington, 1954-55, MIT, CENIS, Cambridge, 1956-59, UN, N.Y.C., 1959-60, Ford Found., N.Y.C., Nepal and India, 1960-62, Rand Corp., Santa Monica, Calif., 1962-67; chief economist Asian Devel. Bank, Manila, Philippines, 1967-71; prof. econs. U. Ill.-Chgo., 1972-85, prof. econs. emeritus, 1985—, head dept., 1972-77; fellow Woodrow Wilson Internat. Ctr., Washington, 1989-90. Adj. prof. Johns Hopkins U.-Nanjing U. Ctr. Chinese-Am. Studies, 1986-87; cons. USAID, Egypt, 1990, book rev. editor Econ. Devel. and Cultural Change, 1980-2000; treas. Am. Com. for Asian Econ. Studies, 1990-2000; Golden Jubilee spkr. Dept. Commerce Osmania U., Hyderabad, India, 1999; disting. spkr. Ctr. for Advanced Study of Internat. Devel., Mich. State U., East Lansing, 1999. Author: Industrial Change in India, 1958, Some Aspects of Industrial Finance in India, 1962, Democracy and Economic Change in India, 1966, 67, Peasant Society in a Changing Economy, 1975, Decision-Making Chicago-Style, 1980, Western Economists and Eastern Societies, 1985, Industrial Change in India 1970-2000, 1988, Contrasting Styles of Industrial Reform: China and India in the 1980s, 1992, Economic Development in Asia, 1996; contbr. The India Handbook, 1997, Globalization and Some of its Contents: The Autobiography of a Russian Immigrant, 2005. Ford Found. fellow NYU, 1971-72; grantee U. Ill., 1977-78, Social Sci. Research Council and Am. Inst. Indian Studies, 1980-81, Am. Inst. Indian Studies, 1983-84, 87-88, Rockefeller Found. Bellagio Study Ctr., 1984. Office: U Ill Dept Econs M/C 144 601 S Morgan St Chicago IL 60607-7121 Home: 5830 S Stony Island Ave Apt 11a Chicago IL 60637-2024

**ROSEN, GERALD ELLIS,** federal judge; b. Chandler, Ariz., Oct. 26, 1951; s. Stanley Rosen and Marjorie (Sherman) Cahn; m. Laurie DeMond; 1 child, Jacob DeMond. BA, Kalamazoo Coll., 1973; JD, George Washington U., 1979. Researchist Swedish Inst., Stockholm, 1973; legis. asst. U.S. Senator Robert P. Griffin, Washington, 1974-79; law clk. Seyfarth, Shaw, Fairweather & Gerardson, Wash., 1979; from assoc. to sr. ptnr. Miller, Canfield, Paddock and Stone, Detroit, 1979-90; judge U.S. Dist. Ct. (ea. dist.) Mich., Detroit, 1990—. Mem. Jud. Evaluation Com., Detroit, co-chmn. 1983-88; adj. prof. law Wayne State U., 1992—, U. Detroit Law Sch., 1994-98, Cooley Law Sch., 2005-; mem. U.S. Jud. Conf. Com. on Criminal Law; lectr. CLE confs., 1996-05, others. Co-author: Federal Civil Trials and Evidence, 1999, Michigan Civil Trials and Evidence, 2001; contbr. articles to profl. jours. Rep. candidate for U.S. Congress, Mich., 1982; chmn. 17th Congl. Dist. Rep. Com., 1983-85; mem. Mich. Criminal Justice Commn., 1985-87; mem. Birmingham Athletic Club; bd. visitors George Washington U. Law Sch., 2000—; bd. dirs. Focus Hope, 2000—. Fellow Kalamazoo Coll. (sr. 1972); recipient Career Achievement award Rolex/Intercollegiate Tennis Assn. Mem. Fed. Judges Assn. (bd. dirs.). Jewish. Office: US Courthouse 231 W Lafayette Blvd Rm 730 Detroit MI 48226-2707 Office Phone: 313-234-5135.

**ROSEN, GERALD HARRIS,** physicist, consultant, educator; b. Mount Vernon, NY, Aug. 10, 1933; s. David A. and Shirley (Schapiro) R.; m. Sarah Louise Sweet, June 8, 1963; children: Lawrence A., Karlyn Rosen Aires. BSE, Princeton U., 1955, MA, 1956, PhD, 1958. Rsch. assoc. dept. aero. engring. Princeton U., 1958-59, NSF predoctoral fellow, 1956, Inst. Theoretical Physics, Utrecht, Netherlands, 1957-58, NSF postdoctoral fellow Stockholm, 1959-60; tech. cons. weapon sys. evaluation divsn. The Pentagon, 1960; prin. scientist Martin-Marietta Aerospace divsn., Balt., 1960-63; cons. to a tech. v.p. Southwest Rsch. Inst., 1963-66; prof. physics Drexel U., Phila., 1966-73, M.R. Wehr prof. physics, 1973-98, prof. emeritus, 1998—. Cons. fin., indsl. and govt. agys., 1966—. Author: Formulations of Classical and Quantum Dynamical Theory, 1969, A New Science of Stock Market Investing, 1990; assoc. editor Bull. Math. Biology, 1982-98; contbr. over 300 articles to profl. jours.; patentee in field. Sponsor San Antonio Chamber Music Soc., 1963-66; mem. Franklin Inst., 1967—; mem. publ. bd. Soc. Math. Biol., 1983—. Guggenheim Jet Propulsion scholar, Princeton U., 1955, Whiton Engring.-Physics scholar, 1955. Fellow Am. Phys. Soc., AAAS; mem. Am. Math. Soc. Home and Office: 415 Charles Ln Wynnewood PA 19096-1604     Office    Phone:    610-896-8727.     Personal    E-mail: gerald@geraldrosen.com. *The meaning of life has transcended human understanding up to the present time, but there are reasons to believe that future discoveries in science will illuminate the significance of life in nature. We must break completely free of non-rational dogma and illusion, and attempt to solve this mystery with factual clues revealed by scientific progress.*

**ROSEN, GERALD ROBERT,** editor; b. NYC, Nov. 17, 1930; s. Sol and Essie (Shapiro) R.; m. Lois Lehrman, May 9, 1958; 1 son, Evan Mark. BS, Ind. U., 1951, MA, 1953. Intelligence analyst Dept. Def., N.Y.C., 1955-58; assoc. editor Challenge: The Mag. of Econ. Affairs, N.Y.C., 1959-61, mng. editor, 1961-64, 65-66; sr. editor Dun's Rev., N.Y.C., 1964-65, nat. affairs editor, 1967—; exec. editor Dun's Rev. (now Bus. Month), 1978-90; editor IMF survey Washington, 1990-93; mng. dir. Global Insights Svcs., Washington, 1993—. Fin. corr. Westinghouse Broadcasting Co. Served with CIC U.S. Army, 1953-55. Mem. Soc. Am. Bus. and Econ. Writers, N.Y. Fin. Writers Assn., White House Corrs. Assn. Clubs: Nat. Press. Home: 1625 31st St NW Washington DC 20007-3628 Office Phone: 202-337-7748. Personal E-mail: gerry308@aol.com.

**ROSEN, HARVEY SHELDON,** economics professor, former federal official; b. Chgo., Mar. 29, 1949; s. Edward and Eleanor (Altman) R.; m. Marsha E. Novick, June 20, 1976; children: Lynne, Jonathan. AB, U. Mich., 1970; AM, Harvard U., 1972, PhD, 1974. Dep. asst. sec., tax analysis US Dept. Treasury, Washington, 1989-91; asst. prof. econs. Princeton (N.J.) U., 1974-80, assoc. prof., 1980-84, prof., 1984—, chmn. dept. econs., 1993—96, John L. Weinberg prof. economics & bus. policy, 1995—, co-dir. Ctr. for Econ. Policy Studies, 1991—; mem. Coun. Econ. Advisers The White House, Washington, 2003—05, chmn., 2005. Vis. fellow Inst. Advanced Studies, Hebrew U., Jerusalem, 1978; vis. scholar Hoover Intsn., Stanford, Calif., 1981. Author: Public Finance, 1985; co-author (with (Michael Katz): Microeconomics, 1991; editor: Studies in State and Local Public Finance, 1986, Fiscal Federalism: Quantitative Studies, 1988. Recipient Pres. award for Disting. Teaching, Princeton U., 2003. Fellow Econometric Soc.; mem. Phi Beta Kappa Office: Princeton U Dept Econs Princeton NJ 08544-0001

**ROSEN, JACQUELINE I.,** musician, educator; b. Los Angeles, Sept. 28, 1952; d. Samuel Morris and Blanche (Seigel) R.; m. James Andrew Meckel, July 14, 1979; children: Sean Aaron, Eric Rosen. Student, Music Acad. of the West, Santa Barbara, Calif., 1973-74; BS in Music, UCLA, 1974; studies with Julius Baker, James Galway, Jean-Pierre Rampal, 1974-80. Freelance musician, Los Angeles, San Francisco and Monterey, Calif., 1974—; mem. Laurel Wind Quintet, 1977-80, Allegra Trio, 1980—, Farrell/Rosen Duo, Carmel, Calif., 1978-87, Terrence Farrell Consort, Carmel, 1980—. Instr. flute pvt. studio, Monterey, 1976—, Monterey Peninsula Coll., 1981-85; instr. Hidden Valley music seminars, Cazadero Music Camp; prin. flutist Hidden Valley Opera, Carmel Valley, Calif., 1976—; condr. master classes numerous Calif. colls., 1982—; music specialist Salinas City Sch. Dist. Premiere performance (flute-guitar duo) Sonatine for Flute and Guitar, 1981; rec. artist (with Terrence Farrell) Alla Romanza, Merry Christmas; appearances with San Francisco Spring Opera, 1979, Cabrillo Music Festival, 1978-84, Carmel Bach Festival, 1996, 98, 99, Camerata Singers; flutist Michael Culver Trio; editor CTB/Macmillan-McGraw-Hill; radio broadcasts, 1977—. Recipient Southwestern Music Conf. award, 1972; Leonard Bernstein fellow, Tanglewood, 1977. Mem.: Calif. Music Educators Assn., Music Educators Nat. Conf. Avocations: playing jazz, gourmet cooking. Home: 15 Paseo Primero Salinas CA 93908-9110 Personal E-mail: jjmeckel@pacbell.net.

**ROSEN, JAY SAMUEL,** urologist, surgeon; b. Paterson, NJ, Dec. 16, 1950; s. Sidney and Fern Rosen; m. Sue DeGregorio; children: Jessica, Jordan. BS, Fairleigh Dickinson U., 1972; MD, U. Autonoma de Guadalajara, Mexico, 1978. Diplomate Am. Bd. Urology. Resident in urology Mayo Clinic Grad. Sch. Medicine, Rochester, Minn., 1980—84; attending urologist Hackensack (NJ) U. Med. Ctr., 1984—, Valley Hosp., Ridgewood, NJ, 1984—; asst. clin. prof. urology U. Medicine and Dentistry of NJ, Newark, 1986—. Mem. USCG Auxiliary. Named Top Minimally Invasive Urologic Surgeon, NY Mag., 2002; named to Best Doctors of NY Metro Area, Castle-Connolley, 2002—05. Jewish. Achievements include first to urologist in Northeast to perform a robotic prostatectomy for treatment of prostate cancer. Avocation: flying. Home: 10 Berwick Cir Highland Mills NY 10930-8309 Office: Urology Specialty Care 555 Kinderkamack Rd Oradell NJ 07649 Office Phone: 201-225-1644.

**ROSEN, JEFFREY ADAM,** lawyer, federal agency administrator; b. Boston, Apr. 2, 1958; m. Kathleen Nichols, May 29, 1982. BA in Econ., Northwestern U., 1979; JD magna cum laude, Harvard U., 1982. Bar: D.C. 1982, U.S. Ct. Appeals (fed. cir.) 1983, U.D. Dist. Ct. D.C. 1983, U.S. Supreme Ct. 1986, U.S. Ct. Appeals (11th cir.) 1988, U.S. Ct. Appeals (6th cir.) 1990, U.S. Ct. Appeals (3rd cir.) 1996, U.S. Ct. Appeals (4th cir.) 1995, U.S. Dist. Ct. (ea. dist.) Mich., U.S. Dist. Ct. (no. dist.) Ill. Assoc. Kirkland & Ellis, Washington, 1982-88, ptnr., 1988—2003; gen. counsel U.S. Dept. Transp., Washington, 2003—. Adj. prof. Georgetown U. Law Ctr., 1996—2003; mem. Arlington County Hist. Affairs and Landmark Rev. Bd., 1991—93. Mem.: Va. Hist. Soc., U.S. Supreme Ct. Hist. Soc., Am. Law Inst. Office: US Dept Transp 400 Seventh St SW Rm 10428 Washington DC 20590-0001 Office Phone: 202-366-4702. Office Fax: 202-366-3388.

**ROSEN, JEFFREY J.,** lawyer; b. NYC, May 13, 1949; s. Fred and Jane (Krieger) R. BA, Harvard U., 1971, JD, 1978. Bar: D.C. 1980. Reporter, columnist Rocky Mountain News, Denver, 1971-75; law clk. to presiding justice U.S. Ct. Appeals, Washington, 1978-79; law clk. to justice William J. Brennan U.S. Supreme Ct., Washington, 1979-80; spl. asst. to sec. U.S.

**ROSEN, CAROL MENDES,** _(continued from prior column)_

Treasury, Washington, 1980-81; assoc. Paul, Weiss et al, Washington, 1981-85, O'Melveny & Myers, Washington, 1985-87, ptnr., 1987—2001, Debevoise & Plimpton, 2001—. Supreme Ct. editor Harvard Law Rev. Named one of 12 "Dealmakers of the Yr.", The American Lawyer, 2004. Mem. ABA (tax sect., com. on govt. submissions), D.C. Bar Assn. Home: PO Box 273 Clinton Corners NY 12514-0273 Office: Devevoise & Plimpton 919 3rd Ave New York NY 10022

**ROSEN, JON HOWARD,** lawyer; b. Bklyn., May 20, 1943; s. Eli and Vera Horowitz Rosen; m. Patricia R. Marshall; children: Jason Marc, Hope Terry. BA, Hobart Coll., 1965; JD, St. John's U., 1968; postgrad. in bus., CCNY, 1969—71. Bar: N.Y. 1969, Calif. 1975, Wash. 1977. Atty. FAA, N.Y.C., 1968-71; regional atty., contract adminstr. Air Line Pilots Assn., N.Y.C., Chgo., L.A., San Francisco, 1971-77; pvt. practice Seattle, 1977-80; ptnr. Frank and Rosen, Seattle, 1981-98, Frank Rosen Freed Roberts LLP, Seattle, 1999—2002, The Rosen Law Firm, 2002—. Instr. labor studies Shoreline C.C., 1978-90; bd. dirs. Music of Remembrance. Chair Ward Springs Pk. Steering Com.; active African-Am./Jewish Coalition for Justice, Interfaith Alliance; trustee Temple DeHirsch Sinai, 1991—98, v.p., 1998—2000, pres.-elect, 2000—01, pres., 2001—03; active Union for Reform Judaism Commn. on Outreach and Synagogue Cmty. Fellow: Am. Bar Found., Coll. Labor and Employment Lawyers; mem.: ABA (union co-chmn. com. on employee rights and responsibilities 1992—96, union co-chmn. regional programs subcom. 1998—2000, union co-chmn. nat. programs. subcom. 2000—02, union co-chmn. ADR in labor and employment law com. 2002—05, co-regional EEOC liaison), Wash. State Trial Lawyers Assn. (past chair employment law com.), Nat. Employment Lawyers Assn. (state steering com. 1990—95, founding state chair); King County Bar Assn. (past chmn. aviation and space law sect., past chmn. Pacific Coast Labor and Employment Law Conf., past chmn. labor law sect.). Office: Rosen Law Firm 705 2nd Ave Ste 1200 Seattle WA 98104-1729 Office Phone: 206-652-1464. Business E-Mail: jhr@jonrosenlaw.com.

**ROSEN, JOSHUA NATHAN,** lawyer; b. Chicago Heights, Ill., Aug. 9, 1966; s. Stanley and Margit (Kir-Stimon) R.; m. Wen-Ying Rosen. BA, U. Ill., 1988; JD, So. Ill. U., 1993. Bar: Ill. 1993, Calif. 1999, U.S. Dist. Ct. (so. dist.) Ill. 1994, U.S. Dist. Ct. (no. dist.) Calif. 1999, U.S. Ct. Appeals (9th cir.) 1999. Assoc. Craig & Craig, Mt. Vernon, Ill., 1994—98, Hayes & Assocs., 1999—2001; trial atty. Law Offices of Larry Kloenhamer, 2001—04, Law Offices of Dennis Issac, 2004—. Mem. State Bar Calif., Bar Assn. San Francisco (Outstanding Barrister award, 2004), Barristers Club (litigation sec. 1999—, vice chmn. judges reception com. 2002-04), So. Ill. Am. Inn of Ct. (barrister). Office: Law Offices of Dennis Issac 2 Rincon Ctr 121 Spear St Ste 410 San Francisco CA 94105

**ROSEN, J(OSHUA) PHILIP,** lawyer; b. NYC, Aug. 24, 1956; s. Irving and Tauba (Krieger) Rosen. BA, Yeshiva U., 1978; JD, Georgetown U., 1981. Bar: NY 1982. Law clk. to Hon. David N. Edelstein U.S. Dist. Ct. (So. Dist.) NY, NYC, 1981-82; corp. ptnr., co-head real estate transactions and fin. dept. Weil, Gotshal & Manges LLP, NYC, co-head, Middle East practice. Appt. to Lower Manhattan Develop. Corp. Profl. Firms Adv. Coun., 2002; spkr. in field; spkr. and chaired at seminars on doing bus. in Israel and the Middle East; assoc. mem. Real Estate Bd. NY, 1990—; mem. Nat. Assn. Real Estate Investment Trusts, Urban Land Inst.; bd. advisors NY Real Estate Law Reporter, NYC, 1987. Editor: Jour. Law and Policy Internat. Bus., Georgetown Internat. Law Review, author numerous articles and books on opportunity fund representation, real estate mergers & acquisitions, real estate investment trusts, fin., loan restructuring, workouts and turnarounds, leasing, developing and securitization. Vice-chmn. bd. dirs. Yeshiva Coll. of Yeshiva U., NY; mem. Conf. of Presidents of Major Jewish Am. Orgns., Internat. Council of Shopping Ctrs.; vice-chmn. Republican Jewish Coalition; legal counsel, spkr. on real estate topics NY Holocaust Meml. Commn., NYC, 1983. Named "40 Under 40 People to Watch in the 1990's", Crain's NY Bus., 1990; named one of Leading Power Brokers in NY Real Estate, GRID Mag. Fellow: Wexner Heritage Found. (Wexner Heritage Scholar); mem.: Am. Coll. Real Estate Lawyers. Jewish. Avocation: tennis. Home: 431 Mistletoe Way Lawrence NY 11559-2716 Office: Weil Gotshal & Manges LLP 767 Fifth Ave New York NY 10153 Office Phone: 212-310-8604. Office Fax: 212-735-4857.

**ROSEN, JUDAH BEN,** computer scientist; b. Phila., May 5, 1922; s. Benjamin and Susan (Hurwich) R.; children— Susan Beth, Lynn Ruth. BSEE, Johns Hopkins U., 1943; PhD in Applied Math., Columbia U., 1952. Rschr. Manhattan (N.Y.) Project, 1944—46, Brookhaven (N.Y.) Nat. Lab., 1946—48; rsch. assoc. Princeton (N.J.) U., 1952-54; head applied math. dept. Shell Devel. Co., 1954-62; vis. prof. computer sci. dept. Stanford (Calif.) U., 1962-64; prof. dept. computer sci. and math. rsch. ctr. U. Wis., Madison, 1964-71; prof., head dept. computer sci. U. Minn., Mpls., 1971-92, fellow Supercomputer Inst., 1985—; sr. fellow Supercomputer Ctr., San Diego, 1993—; adj. rsch. prof. dept. computer sci. and engrin. U. Calif. San Diego, La Jolla, 1992—, bioinformatics grad. program faculty, 2001—. Fulbright prof. Technion, Israel, 1968-69, Davis vis. prof. 1980; invited lectr. Chinese Acad. Sci., Peking, 1980, Guilin, 1996, Samos, Greece, 2000; lectr., cons. Argonne (Ill.) Nat. Lab.; mem. Nat. Computer Sci. Bd. Author: Topics in Parallel Computing, 1992; editor: Nonlinear Programming, 1970, Supercomputers and Large-Scale Optimization, 1988; assoc. editor Global Optimization, 1990—, Annals of Ops. Rsch., 1984—; contbr. articles to profl. jours. and procs. Grantee, NSF, 1995—, ARPA/NIST, 1994—97. Mem. Assn. Computing Machinery, Soc. Indsl. and Applied Math., Math. Programming Soc., European Acad. Scis. Achievements include research in supercomputers and parallel algorithms for optimization, computation of molecular structure and drug design by energy minimization and homology models, algorithms for structured approximation in signal processing. Office: U Calif San Diego Dept Computer Sci Engring 9500 Gilman Dr La Jolla CA 92093-0114 Business E-Mail: jbrosen@cs.ucsd.edu.

**ROSEN, KEVIN S.,** lawyer; b. 1962; AB magna cum laude with honors, Dartmouth Coll., 1984; JD, Columbia Univ., 1987. Bar: Calif. 1988. Law clk. Hon. William D. Keller US Dist. Ct. (ctrl. dist.) Calif., 1987—88; assoc. Gibson Dunn & Crutcher LLP, LA, 1988—95, ptnr. litig. dept. and head, legal malpractice def. group, 1995—. Chmn. legal malpractice def. practice group and mem. exec. com. Gibson Dunn & Crutcher. Named one of California's Top 20 Lawyers Under 40, Daily Journal. Office: Gibson Dunn & Crutcher LLP 333 S Grand Ave Los Angeles CA 90071-3197 Office Phone: 213-229-7635.    Office    Fax:    213-229-6635.    Business    E-Mail: Krosen@gibsondunn.com.

**ROSEN, LAWRENCE,** anthropologist, educator; b. Cin., Dec. 9, 1941; s. George and Hannah (Persky) Rosen. BA, Brandeis U., 1963; MA, U. Chgo., 1965, PhD, 1968, JD, 1974. Bar: N.C. 1975, U.S. Supreme Ct. 1979. Asst. prof. anthropology U. Ill., Urbana, 1968-70; mem. Inst. Advanced Study, Princeton, NJ, 1970-71; assoc. prof. Duke U., Durham, NC, 1974-77; prof. Princeton (N.J.) U., 1977—, William Nelson Cromwell Prof., 2002. Adj. prof. Columbia U. Law Sch., 1979—; vis. prof. Northwestern U. Law Sch., Chgo., 1985—87, U. Pa. Law Sch., Phila., 1985—86, Georgetown Law Ctr., 1994; Lewis H. Morgan lectr. U. Rochester, 1985; mem. commons Wolfson Coll. Oxford U., Corpus Christi Coll. Cambridge U., 1998—99. Editor: The American Indian and the Law, 1974, Other Intentions, 1995, The Culture of Islam, 2002; co-author: Meaning and Order in Morrocan Society, 1978; author: Bargaining for Reality, 1984, The Anthropology of Justice, 1989, The Justice of Islam, 2000, The Culture of Islam, 2004. Legal asst. Native Am. Rights Fund, Boulder, Colo., 1973. Recipient John and Catherine MacArthur Found. award, 1981; scholar, Carnegie Corp., 2005—; vis. scholar, Phi Beta Kappa, 1997; Woodrow Wilson fellow, 1964, Guggenheim fellow, 1989, Fulbright fellow, 1991. Fellow: Am. Anthrop. Assn.

**ROSEN, LEON,** lawyer; b. N.Y.C., May 21, 1924; s. Irving and Kate (Woronoff) R. BA, Coll. of William and Mary, 1949; JD, NYU, 1953. Bar: N.Y. 1954, U.S. Supreme Ct. 1960, U.S. Ct. Appeals (2d, 3d and 9th cirs.). Investigator, atty. U.S. Immigration and Naturalization Svc., Dept. Justice,

N.Y.C., 1951-55; pvt. practice N.Y.C., 1955-87; spl. counsel Clifton, Budd & DeMaria, N.Y.C., 1987—; with Garcia-Mendoza & Snavely, Las Vegas, Nev. With USAAC, 1943-46. Decorated Air medal, 2 oak leaf clusters; recipient Presdl. Citation award. Mem. Am. Immigration Lawyers Assn. (past. nat. pres.). Democrat. Jewish. Avocation: golf. Home: 10701 Dover Creek Ave Las Vegas NV 89134 Office: Garcia-Mendoza & Shavely 501 S 7th St Las Vegas NV 89101 Office Phone: 702-870-1444. E-mail: lombardierlawyer@aol.com.

**ROSEN, LOUIS,** physicist; b. NYC, June 10, 1918; s. Jacob and Rose (Lipionski) R.; m. Mary Terry, Sept. 4, 1941; 1 son, Terry Leon. BA, U. Ala., 1939, MS, 1941; PhD, Pa. State U., 1944; DSc (hon.), U. N.Mex., 1979, U. Colo., 1987. Instr. physics U. Ala., 1940-41, Pa. State U., 1943-44; mem. staff Los Alamos Sci. Lab., 1944-90, group leader nuclear plate lab., 1949-65, alt. div. leader exptl. physics div., 1962-65, dir. meson physics facility, 1965-85, div. leader medium energy physics div., 1965-86, sr. lab. fellow, 1985-90, sr. fellow emeritus, 1990—; Sesquicentennial hon. prof. U. Ala., 1981. Panel on future of nuclear sci., chmn. subpanel on accelerators NRC of NAS, 1976, panel on instnl. arrangements for orbiting space telescope, 1976; mem. U.S.A.-USSR Coordinating Com. on Fundamental Properties of Matter, 1971-90 Mem. editl. bd. Applications of Nuclear Physics; co-editor Climate Change and Energy Policy, 1992; contbr. articles to profl. jours. Mem. Los Alamos Town Planning Bd., 1962-64; mem. Gov.'s Com. on Tech. Excellence in N.Mex.; mem. N.Mex. Cancer Control Bd., 1976-80, v.p., 1979-81; co-chmn. Los Alamos Vols. for Stevenson, 1956; Dem. candidate for county commr., 1962; bd. dirs. Los Alamos Med. Ctr., 1977-83, chmn., 1983; bd. govs. Tel Aviv U., 1986; bd. dirs. Sombillo Nursing and Rehab. Facility, 2004. Recipient E.O. Lawrence award AEC, 1963, Golden Plate award Am. Acad. Achievement, 1964, N.Mex. Disting. Pub. Svc. award, 1978; named Citizen of Yr., N.Mex. Realtors Assn., 1973; Guggenheim fellow, 1959-60; alumni fellow Pa. State U., 1978; Louis Rosen prize established in his honor by bd. dirs. Meson Facility Users Group, 1984; Louis Rosen Auditorium dedicated, 1995; recipient Los Alamos Nat. Lab. medal, 2002. Fellow AAAS (coun. 1989), Am. Phys. Soc. (coun. 1975-78, chmn. panel on pub. affairs 1980, div. nuclear physics 1985, mem. subcom. on internat. sci. affairs 1988). Achievements include research in nuc. sci. and applications of particle accelerators. Home: 1170 41st St Los Alamos NM 87544-1913 Office: Los Alamos Sci Lab PO Box 1663 Los Alamos NM 87544-0600 Office Phone: 505-667-4361. *I have come to believe that only after one has learned to manage and set worthy goals for himself should he attempt to do so for others.*

**ROSEN, MARVIN SHELBY,** lawyer; b. Detroit, Aug. 8, 1947; s. Joseph P. and Rachel K. (Kaplan) R.; m. Sandra Mira Levy, Nov. 22, 1970; children: Joseph H., Bradley J. BA, Columbia U., 1970, JD, MBA, 1973; BHL in Philosophy, Jewish Theol. Sem., N.Y.C., 1970. Bar: Mich. 1974, Fla. 1984. Assoc. Honigman Miller Schwartz and Cohn, Detroit, 1974-78, ptnr., 1978-84, mng. ptnr. West Palm Beach, Fla., 1984-97; shareholder Ruden, McClosky, Smith, Schuster & Russell, P.A., West Palm Beach, 1997—. Contbr. articles to profl. jours. V.p. Pres. Country Club, 1995-99, Jewish Fedn. Palm Beach County, 1992-99; pres. Jewish Cmty. Day Sch., 1987-88; founding chmn. Commn. for Jewish Edn., 1990-93; pres. Temple Emanu-El, Palm Beach, 2000-2004. Named one of Best Lawyers in Am., 1989—. Mem. Mich. State Bar (chmn. com. on mortgages, land contracts and related security devices real property sect. 1982-84), Detroit Bar Assn. (chmn. real property sect. 1982-83). Office: Ruden McClosky Smith Schuster & Russell PA 222 Lakeview Ave Ste 800 West Palm Beach FL 33401-6148 Office Fax: 561-514-3401. Business E-Mail: marvin.rosen@ruden.com.

**ROSEN, MATTHEW A.,** lawyer; b. Phila., 1952; BA, Swarthmore Coll., 1973; JD cum laude, Boston U., 1976; LLM, NYU, 1979. Bar: Pa. 1976, N.Y. 1979. Sr. ptnr. Skadden, Arps, Slate, Meagher & Flom LLP, NYC, co-head, tax law group. Spkr. in the field. Contbr. articles to profl. publs. Named one of 45 Lawyers in the Country under the age of 45 who "are making their mark now and will lead the profession tomorrow", Am. Lawyer Mag. Mem.: NY State Bar Assn. (co-chair, subcommittee on net operating losses 1985—87, co-chair, subcommittee on bankruptcy 1988—89, exec. com. mem., tax sect. 1985—89). Office: Skadden Arps Slate Meagher & Flom LLP 4 Times Sq New York NY 10036 Office Phone: 212-735-2230. Office Fax: 917-777-2230. Business E-Mail: mrosen@skadden.com.

**ROSEN, MATTHEW STEPHEN,** botanist, consultant; b. NYC, Oct. 7, 1943; s. Norman and Lucille (Cass) R.; m. Deborah Louise Mackay, June 16, 1974 (div. Feb. 1983); children: Gabriel Mackay, Rebecca Mackay; m. Kay Eloise Williams, July 11, 1987. MFSc, Yale U., 1972; BS, Cornell U., 1967. Instr. ornamental horticulture SUNY-Farmingdale, 1968-69; landscape designer Manhattan Gardener, N.Y.C., 1969-70; instr. ornamental horticulture McHenry County Coll., Crystal Lake, Ill., 1972-74; coord. agrl. studies, asst. prof. biology, chemistry Mercer County Community Coll., West Windsor, NJ, 1974-79; adminstr. Des Moines Botanical Ctr., 1979-96, horticulture divsn. mgr., 1996—. Cons. dir. West Mich. Hort. Soc., 1993; nat. judge Communities in Bloom, 2001-05, Winter Lights, 2002-04, Am. in Bloom, 2002, sr. nat. judge, 2005; cons. in field. Contbr. articles to profl. jours. Com. chmn. United Way Cen. Iowa, 1982, divsn. chmn. 1983-86, 88-89, 91, 2000, group chmn. 1987, chmn. arts adv. com. 1985-86, pres. 1986, bd. dirs. Arts and Recreation Coun., 1985-86, com. chmn., 1992; career vocat. com. Des Moines Indsl. Sch. Dist., 1986, co-chmn., 1987, ptnrs. for progress com., 1988-90, sci. monitoring program, 1991-92; chmn. Two Rivers Festival, 1987-88; active Des Moines Sister City Program, Kofu, Japan, 1984, delegation, 1989, Naucalpan, Mexico, 1986, 87, Shijiazhuang, China, 1986, 90, 92, 95, 97; vice-chmn. Greater Des Moines Sister City Commn., 2004-05, chmn., 2005—; mem. edn. com. Am. Assn. Bot. Gardens and Arboretum, membership com., conservation com., bd. dirs., 1997—. Mem. Am. Assn. Bot. Gardens and Arboreta (edn. com.), Greater Des Moines C. of C. (team leader 1984—, chmn. new mem. sales, chmn. 8 O'clock new, Pres. Cabinet award 1983-85, bd. dirs., exec. com. 1995—, Achievement award C. of C. Fedn. 1986, exec. com. 1995-97), East Des Moines C. of C. (bd. dirs. 1992—, v.p., sec. 1993—, pres.-elect 1994, pres. 1995-96, sister cities commn. 1994, china chair 1995—, treas. 1995—, vice chair 2003, 04, chair 2005—), Greater Des Moines Conv. and Visitors Bur. (mem. new mem. sales com. 1988-89), Iowa Advt. Rev. Coun., Affiliate Pres.'s Coun. of Chambers (chair 1995, 97), bd. dirs. DM Gen. Hosp., 1994-97, Bd. Coun. Internat. Trade, Latinos Unidos (bd. dirs. 1996-97), Rotary, Phi Kappa Phi, Pi Alpha Xi. Democrat. Jewish. Avocations: photography, reading, model trains, collecting old books, writing. Home: 1042 22nd St West Des Moines IA 50265-2219 Office: Park and Recreation Dept 3226 University Ave Des Moines IA 50317 Office Phone: 515-323-8901. Business E-Mail: msrosen@dmgov.org.

**ROSEN, MEYER ROBERT,** chemical engineer; b. Bklyn., Mar. 9, 1943; s. Philip and Jeanne (Rosenzweig) R.; children: Carrie, David; m. Selma Schwartz Mirman. BS, Poly. Inst. Bklyn., 1964, MS, 1966. Diplomate, Am. Bd. Forensic Engring. and Tech., cert. forensic examiner, profl. chemist, profl. chem. engr.; fire and explosion investigator Nat. Cert. Bd., Nat. Assn. Fire Investigators. Rsch. engr. Union Carbide Corp., Tonawanda, NY, 1966-73, project scientist, 1973-79, devel. scientist Tarrytown and Boundbrook, NJ, 1979-92; dir. chemistry and fire investigation Inter-City Testing and Cons. Corp., Mineola, NY, 1993—2003; pres. Interactive Cons. Inc., 1993—. Cons. Brookfield Engring. Labs., Stoughton, Mass., 1979-81; cons. to chem. industry; course dir. Ctr. for Profl. Advancement, East Brunswick, N.J., 1994; adj. prof. chemistry Westchester C.C., 1970-84; exec. advisor Am. Bd. Forensic Engring. and Tech.; spkr. in field; forensic litigation expert in field, Vaaler Awards Judge Chemical Processing Mag., 2003. Co-author: Rheology Modifier Handbook: Practical Use & Application, 2000; editor: Delivery System Handbook for Personal Care and Cosmetic Products Technology, Applications, Formulations, 2005; series editor Breakthroughs in Personal Care and Cosmetic Technology; contbr. articles to profl. jours. Fellow Am. Coll. Forensic Examiners, Royal Soc. Chemistry London (chartered chemist); Am. Inst. Chemists (dir., exec. bd. dirs.), Am. Coll. Forensic Examiners; mem. ASTM (mem. various subcoms.), Am. Inst. of Chem. Engrs., Am. Chem. Soc. (divsn. colloid and surface chemistry, mem. noise com., organizer, session leader nat. mtgs. 2002-, chmn. and organizer first HBA

regulatory summit 2006), Am. Indsl. Hygiene Assn. (cons. spl. interest group), Am. Soc. Safety Engrs. (v.p.), Assn. Cons. Chemists and Chem. Engrs., Am. Assn. Colorists and Textile Chemists, Am. Med. Writers Assn., Nat. Assn. Sci. Writers, Soc. de Chimie Industrielle (Am. sect.), Nat. Fire Protection Assn., Soc. Indsl. Chemistry (Am. sect.). Am. Acupuncture and Oriental Medicine, Acupuncture Soc. Pa., Nat. Dental Acupuncture Soc. (exec. bd.), Nat. Alliance of Acupuncture and Oriental Medicine (bd. cert. in pain mgmt.), Nat. Hearing Conservation Assn. Achievements include 21 patents for process for fire fighting foams, antifoams; flocculation of phosphatic slimes, high molecular weight water soluble polymers and flocculating method, process for producing polymer water-in-oil emulsion, process for agglomerating ore concentrate utilizing clay and dispersions of polymer binders or dry powder binders, removal of residual ethylene oxide from poly(ethylene oxide); development of treatment of previously incurable ear disorder, seminar leader in Reflex-Correspondence Training. Publications include Polyox R Water Soluble Resin Worldwide Technical Literature; Rheology of Non-Newtonian Fluids; Energy Medicine; Auriculotherapy; Korean Hand Therapy. Office: Interactive Cons Inc PO Box 66 East Norwich NY 11732-0066 Office Phone: 516-922-2167. Office Fax: 516-922-3830. Business E-Mail: meyer.rosen@chemicalconsult.com.

**ROSEN, MICHAEL N.,** lawyer; AB, Princeton U., 1962; LLB, Harvard U., 1965. Bar: NY 1966, US Dist. Ct., So. Dist NY 1974. Ptnr., mem. exec. com. Bryan Cave LLP, NYC. Office: Bryan Cave LLP 1290 Ave of the Americas New York NY 10104 Office Phone: 212-541-2200. E-mail: mnrosen@bryancave.com.

**ROSEN, MOISHE,** religious organization founder; b. Kansas City, Mo., Apr. 12, 1932; s. Ben and Rose (Baker) R.; m. Ceil Starr, Aug. 18, 1950; children: Lyn Rosen Bond, Ruth. Diploma, Northeastern Bible Coll., 1957; DD, Western Conservative Bapt. Sem., 1986. Ordained to ministry Bapt. Ch., 1957. Missionary Am. Bd. Missions to the Jews, N.Y.C., 1956, minister in charge Beth Sar Shalom Los Angeles, 1957-67, dir. recruiting and tng. N.Y.C., 1967-70; leader Jews for Jesus Movement, San Francisco, 1970-73, exec. dir., 1973-96, founder, 1973—. Speaker in field. Author: Sayings of Chairman Moishe, 1972, Jews for Jesus, 1974, Share the New Life with a Jew, 1976, Christ in the Passover, 1977, Y'shua, The Jewish Way to Say Jesus, 1982, Overture to Armageddon, 1991, The Universe is Broken: Who on Earth Can Fix It?, 1991, Demystifying Personal Evangelism, 1992, Witnessing to Jews, 1998. Trustee Western Conservative Bapt. Sem., Portland, Oreg., 1979-85, 89-91, Bibl. Internat. Coun. on Bibl. Inerrancy, Oakland, Calif., 1979-89; bd. dirs. Christian Advs. Serving Evangelism, 1987-91. Named Hero of the Faith, Conservative Bapt. Assn. Am., 1997. Office: Jews for Jesus 90 Miraloma Dr San Francisco CA 94127-1641 Office Phone: 415-661-2263. Personal E-Mail: MityMo@aol.com.

**ROSEN, MYOR,** harpist, educator; b. N.Y.C., May 28, 1917; s. Caesar and Rose (Seidenberg) R.; m. Esther Rosen, May 25, 1941; children: Linda, David. Diploma, Juilliard Sch. Music, 1940. Faculty Juilliard Sch. Music, 1947-69. Prin. harpist, Mexico Symphony Orch., 1941-42, Indpls. Symphony Orch., 1941-42, Mpls. Symphony Orch., 1943-44, staff harpist, CBS, Columbia Records and free lanced, 1945-60, prin. harpist, N.Y. Philharm., 1960-87; Composer incidental music for; NBC series Arts and the Gods, 1946, CBS Camera Three, 1947, Solomon, The King, 1948. Served with U.S. Army, 1945. Mem. Am. Fedn. Musicians, Bohemians. Office: Phone: 561-624-5531. Personal E-Mail: roymnesor@adelphia.net. *Having been the fortunate recipient of a 7-year scholarship through the New York Philharmonic Symphony Society and the Juilliard School of Music when I began my career as a harpist, I can think of no greater honor than my privilege in having been accepted as principal harpist with the same organization which trained me. I now bend my efforts to train future harpists to excel in like manner. In my opinion, the most important function of a teacher is to teach his students how to teach themselves; self-development.*

**ROSEN, NATHANIEL KENT,** cellist; b. Altadena, Calif., June 9, 1948; s. David Leon and Frances Jean (Kaufman) R.; m. Jennifer Langham, Aug. 27, 1976 (div. 1986); m. Margo Shohl, May 21, 1989 (div. 2001); children: Samuel Gregory, Stella Rosalie. Student, Pasadena City Coll., Calif., 1965-67; MusB, U. So. Calif., 1971. Teaching asst. U. So. Calif., 1974-75, mem. faculty 7th ann. Gregor Piatigorsky Seminar Sch. Music, 1984; asst. prof. Calif. State U. at Northridge, 1970-74; mem. faculty Manhattan Sch. Music, N.Y.C., 1981—, U. Ill., Urbana, 1988-94; artist-in-residence So. Meth. U., Dallas, 2002—05. Prin. cellist, Los Angeles Chamber Orch., 1970-76, Pitts. Symphony, 1977-79, concert cellist worldwide; recordings include Orientale: Romantic Music for the Cello. Recipient 1st prize Naumburg Competition, 1977, 1st prize Moscow Tchaikovsky Competition, 1978; Ford Found. grantee, 1970-71; Rockefeller Found. grantee, 1973-74 Mem. Violoncello Soc. N.Y., Century Assn. N.Y. Office: John Gingrich Mgmt Inc PO Box 1515 New York NY 10023-9462 Office Phone: 212-799-5080. E-mail: NRosen8794@aol.com.

**ROSEN, NORMA,** writer; b. N.Y.C., Aug. 11, 1925; d. Louis and Rose (Miller) Gangel; m. Robert S. Rosen, Aug. 23, 1960; children: Anna, Jonathan. BA, Mt. Holyoke Coll., 1946; MA, Columbia U., 1953. Tchr. New Sch., U. Pa., Yale U., Harvard U., Columbia U., Hofstra U., NYU, others. Author: Joy to Levine!, 1962, Green, 1967, Touching Evil, 1969, At The Center, 1982, reissued, 1996, The Story of Sarah's Late Pregnancy, 1996, John and Anzia: An American Romance, 1989, reissued, 1997, Accidents of Influence: Writing as a Woman and a Jew in America, 1992, Biblical Women Unbound, 1996, The Lovemaking of I.B. Singer, 1996, The Collaborators Quarrel, 1999, Elixir, 1999, Writer's Gift, Writer's Grudge, 2001, Orphan Lovers, 2001, The Lovemaking of I.B. Singer, 2004, Deconstructing Jacques (Derrida), 2005, The WRiters Among Us, 2006; contbr. articles to profl. jours. Eugene Saxton grantee, 1960; fellow Radcliffe Inst., 1971-73; recipient CAPS award N.Y. State. Mem. PEN Am. Ctr., Authors Guild, Phi Beta Kappa.

**ROSEN, RAYMOND,** health facility executive; b. Louisville, Feb. 5, 1950; s. Sam and Olga Rosen; m. Deborah Joy Rubinow, June 25, 1972; children: Lisa, Jessica. BS, Pa. State U., 1972; MA, George Washington U., 1974. Adminstrv. resident York (Pa.) Hosp., 1973-74; asst. to pres., 1974-75, asst. adminstr.-adminstrn., 1975-77, asst. adminstr.-med. affairs, 1977-79, adminstr.-med. affairs, 1979-87, v.p.-opers., 1987—. Pres. Young Adminstrs. Group Ctrl. Pa., 1980-82, Rabbit Transit, Inc., 1992—, vice chmn., 1989-92, chmn., 1992—; bd. dirs. Fedn. South Ctrl. Pa. Emergency Health Svcs., 1978-92, mem. adv. com., 1992-93, York Emergency Health Svcs. Coun., 1978-92, Jewish Cmty. Ctr., 1986-91; divsn. chmn. United Way York County, 1988, York County Transp. Auth., 1995—; bd. mem. York County Econ. Devel. Corp., 2005—. Fellow: Am. Coll. Healthcare Execs. (regent south ctrl. Pa. 1991—95); mem. Am. Hosp. Assn. Pa. (planning com. 1992—), Am. Hosp. Assn. Office: York Hosp 1001 S George St York PA 17403-3676 Office Phone: 717-851-2122.

**ROSEN, RICHARD S.,** lawyer; b. Charleston, S.C., Aug. 15, 1949; BA, Tulane U., 1971; JD, U. S.C., 1975. Bar: S.C. 1975, U.S. Dist. Ct. S.C. 1975, U.S. Ct. Appeals (4th cir.) 1993, U.S. Supreme Ct. 1993. Mem.: ABA, Am. Bd. Trial Advs., Assn. Trial Lawyers Am., S.C. Trial Lawyers Assn., S.C. Bar (bd. govs. 1991—94, Ho. of Dels. 1984, chmn. 1996, nominating com. 1986—89, continuing legal edn. com. 1995, law practice mgmt. com. 1995, sec. 1999, treas. 2000, pres.-elect 2001, pres. 2002), Charleston County Bar Assn. (exec. com. 1982—83), Soc. Wig and Robe, Charleston Lawyer's Club (pres. 1982). Office: Rosen Rosen & Hagood LLC PO Box 893 134 Meeting St Ste 200 Charleston SC 29402

**ROSEN, ROBERT ARNOLD,** management consultant, real estate owner, manager, developer, investor, farmer; b. NYC, June 19, 1936; s. Louis and Helen (Weiss) R.; m. Florence Cohen, Oct. 23, 1960; children: David S., Kenneth A., Mark A., Emily B. BBA, CUNY, 1957, MBA, 1960; postgrad. (Ford Found. scholar), NYU, 1961; grad., Indsl. Coll. Armed Forces, Air War Coll., 1960, U.S. Air Force U.; various courses, Naval Edn. and Tng.

Command. Sales promotion mgr. Leipzig & Lippe, Inc., 1956-58; advt. and sales promotion mgr. Zenith Radio, 1957-62; chmn., pres., founder Am. Bus. Resources Corp., 1963-64; v.p., dir. Royal Bus. Funds Corp., 1964-68; chmn., CEO Rosen Assocs. Mgmt. Corp., Jericho, NY, 1983—. V.p. corp. finance div., dir. Brand Grumet & Siegel, Inc., 1969-70; pres. Brand Grumet & Siegel Equities, Inc., 1970; former pres., chief oper. officer Bell TV, Inc., N.Y.C.; pres., former chmn. bd. Holmes Protection, Inc.; former chmn. bd., pres. Union Small Bus. Investment Co., 1968-77, Skyway-Laguardia Corp.; dir. past chmn. bd. Okuraya Davos Internat., Inc.; chmn. bd., pres., chief exec. officer, treas. Suburban Broadcasting Corp., 1970-80; chmn., pres. Affiliated Comms. Corp.; vice chmn., pres. Comm. Svcs. Corp.; pres. Wescom Corp.; pres. Androse Corp., 1983—; cons. Asian Devel. Bank, Albert Einstein Coll. Medicine, Nat. Housing Bank of Brazil, 1972-76; mem. U.S. Senatorial Bus. Adv. Bd.; lectr. Baruch Coll. Grad. Sch. Bus., CUNY, 1960-63; adj. prof. Fairleigh Dickinson U. Grad. Sch. Bus., 1968-75; ret. pres., ret. dean Internat. Inst. Real Estate Studies; dir. Ctr. for Real Estate Studies, Adelphi U.; adj. prof. mgmt. NYU; mem. faculty New Sch. for Social Rsch.; guest lectr., mem. bd. advs. Fordham U.; prin. owner, developer shopping ctrs., comml. real estate throughout, U.S.; chmn. UN Trade and Tech. Adv. Mission to Israel, 1972, Econ. Devel. Corp./UJA Fedn.; active Nat. Builder Mktg. Bd.; owner, investor seat on N.Y. Stock Exch. Chmn. Borough Pres.'s of Manhattan Com. on Narcotics Addiction Control, 1970—75; N.Y. mem. adv. coun. USAF Acad.; mem. editl. policy com. Internat. Property Investment Jour. of Hofstra U. Law Sch.; mem. Navy Recruiting Dist., N.Y. Assistance Coun.; chmn. Navy Task Force to Study Navy Budgeting, Acquisition and Procurement; former mem. Pres.'s Pvt. Sector Survey on Cost Control (Grace Commn.); mem. N.Y. State Gov.'s Bus. Adv. Coun.; former trustee Zachary and Elizabeth M. Fisher Found.; trustee Fisher House Found., Inc., North Shore L.I.J. Health Sys., Florence and Robert A. Rosen Family Found.; chmn. econ. devel. com., former bd. dirs. United Jewish Appeal/Fedn.; former mem. corp. adv. bd. Queens Coll.; mem. adv. bd. Roundabout Theatre; advisor Disaster Preparedness Commn.; chmn. sys. emergency preparedness com. North Shore-L.I. (N.Y.) Jewish Health Sys., Inc., chmn.Florence and Robert A. Rosen Family Wellness Ctr. Law Enforcement and Mil.; chmn. sys. emeregency preparedness com. of bd. trustees North Shore-L.I. Jewish Health Sys., chmn. Florence and Robert A. Rosen Family Wellness Ctr. for Law Enforcement and the Mil.; bd. dirs. The Film Forum, 1979—86, N.Y.C. Housing Partnership, Housing Partnership Devel. Corp.; bd. dirs., trustee Intrepid, Sea Air Space Mus.; bd. dirs. Fed. Law Enforcement Found.; trustee Florence and Robert A. Rosen Family Found. With USAFR and USNR, 1959—90, ret. as capt. USNR, 1990, rear adm. upper half N.Y. Naval Militia, comdr. Divsn. Mil. and Naval Affairs, naval aide to the Gov. Mem. Soc. Internat. Devel., Internat. Inst. Valuers (SCV designation), NRA, Nat. Def. Exec. Res., Chief Execs. Orgn., Nat. IPres.'s Orgn., Young Pres.'s Orgn. (past chmn. Met. chpt.), Real Estate Bd. N.Y., Assn. for Better N.Y., Internat. Coun. Shopping Ctrs., Property Cons. Soc., Nat. Assn. Rev. Appraisers (cert. rev. appraiser), Air Force Assn., Res. Officers Assn., Nat. Guard Assn. (life), Naval Res. Assn. (life), U.S. Naval Inst., Navy League U.S., Naval War Coll. Found. (assoc.), Am. Legion, Naval Militia Assn. (chmn.), Jewish War Vets. U.S., Wine Inst. Group Stony Brook State U. N.Y., Militia Assn. N.Y., U.S. Navy Pub. Affairs Assn., Alpha Delta Sigma, Pi Sigma Delta, Sigma Alpha. Home: 60 Apple Lake Ln PO Box 8 Rhinebeck NY 12572 Office: Rosen Associates Mgmnt Corp 33 South Service Rd Jericho NY 11753-1006 Office Phone: 516-333-2000. Business E-Mail: rar@rosenmgmt.com.

**ROSEN, SANFORD JAY,** lawyer; b. N.Y.C., Dec. 19, 1937; s. Alexander Charles and Viola S. (Grad) R.; m. Catherine Picard, June 22, 1958; children: Caren E. Andrews, R. Durelle Schacter, Ian D., Melissa S. AB, Cornell U., 1959; LLB, Yale U., 1962. Bar: Conn. 1962, Calif. 1974, U.S. Supreme Ct. 1966. Law clk. to Hon. Simon E. Sobeloff U.S. Ct. Appeals, Balt., 1962-63; prof. sch. law U. Md., Balt., 1963-71; assoc. dir. Coun. on Legal Edn. Opportunity, Atlanta, 1969-70; vis. prof. law U. Tex., Austin, 1970-71; asst. legal dir. Nat. ACLU, N.Y.C., 1971-73; legal dir. Mex.-Am. Legal Def. Fund, San Francisco, 1973-75; ptnr. Rosen, Remcho & Henderson, San Francisco, 1976-80, Rosen & Remcho, San Francisco, 1980-82; prin. Law Offices of Sanford Jay Rosen, San Francisco, 1982-86; sr. ptnr. Rosen & Phillips, San Francisco, 1986-89; prin. Rosen & Assocs., San Francisco, 1990; sr. ptnr. Rosen, Bien & Asaro, San Francisco, 1991—2006, Rosen, Bien & Galvan LLP, San Francisco, 2006—. Mem. Calif. Cmty. Rels. Commn., 1966-69; mem. com. Patuxent Instn., Md., 1967-69; ad hoc adminstrv. law judge Calif. Agrl. Labor Rels. Bd., San Francisco, 1975-80; interim monitor U.S. Dist. Ct. for no. dist. Calif., San Francisco, 1989, early reversal evaluator, 1987—; mediator, 1993—; mediator Calif. Ct. Appeal 1st dist., 2004—; permanent atty. del. Jud. Conf. U.S. Ct. Appeal for 4th Cir.; atty. del. Jud. Conf. U.S. Ct. Appeals 9th cir., 1996-98. Contbr. articles to profl. jours. Mem. Com. on Adminstrn. of Criminal Justice, Balt., 1968; mem. adv. com. HEW, Washington, 1974-75. Mem. ABA, Assn. Trial Lawyers Am. (chair civil rights sect. 1993-94), Calif. Bar Assn., Bar Assn. San Francisco. Avocations: reading, travel, movies. Office: Rosen Bien & Asaro 155 Montgomery St Fl 8 San Francisco CA 94104-4113 Office Phone: 415-433-6830. Business E-Mail: srosen@rbalaw.com.

**ROSEN, SAUL WOOLF,** research scientist, health facility administrator; b. Boston, July 29, 1928; s. David Tsvi and Ida (Hannah) Sadwin; m. Mary Jean Westfall, June 14, 1959 (div. 1986); children: Craig, Laura, David; m. Deborah Susan Kieffer, Nov. 3, 1989. BA cum laude, Harvard U., 1947, MD, 1956; PhD, Northwestern U., 1955. Intern U. Calif. Med. Ctr., San Francisco, 1956-57, resident, 1957-58, sr. res., 1960-61; clin. assoc. Nat. Inst. Arthritis and Metabolic Diseases, Bethesda, Md., 1958-60, sr. investigator NIH, 1961-84; dep. dir. Clin. Ctr. NIH, Bethesda, Md., 1984-90, acting dir. clin. ctr., 1990-94. Vis. scientist Nat. Inst. Med. Rsch., London, 1975-76. Contbr. articles to profl. jours. U.S. Rubber Co. fellow, Northwestern U., 1950. Fellow ACP; mem. Assn. Am. Physicians, Endocrine Soc. Avocations: opera, lexicography, weightlifting. Home: 11801 Rockville Pike Apt 1204 Rockville MD 20852-2728 E-mail: saulrosen@earthlink.net.

**ROSEN, STANLEY HOWARD,** humanities educator; b. Warren, Ohio, July 29, 1929; s. Nathan A. and Celia (Narotsky) R.; m. Francoise Harlepp, Sept. 5, 1955; children: Nicholas David, Paul Mark, Valerie. BA, U. Chgo., 1949, PhD, 1955; postgrad., Am. Sch. Classical Studies, Athens, Greece, 1955-56; D honoris causa, New U. Lisbon, 1997. Mem. faculty Pa. State U., 1956-94, prof. philosophy, 1966-94; Fulbright research prof. U. Paris, 1960-61; research fellow Humanities Research Inst., U. Wis., 1963-64; Inst. Arts and Humanities research sr. fellow Pa. State U., 1972—, Evan Pugh prof. philosophy, 1985-94; Bowne prof. philosophy Boston U., 1994—, univ. prof., 2000—. Vis. prof. U. Calif., San Diego, 1978, U. Nice, 1981, Scuola Superiore Pisa, 1989; vis. lectr. U. Barcelona, Spain, 1992; Priestly lectr. U. Toronto, 1997; Cardinal Mercier lectr. Louvain U., 1998; Gilson lectr. Institut Catholique, Paris, 2003. Author: Plato's Symposium, 1968, Nihilism, 1969, G.W.F. Hegel, 1974, The Limits of Analysis, 1980, Plato's Sophist: The Drama of Original and Image, 1983, Hermeneutics as Politics, 1987, The Quarrel Between Philosophy and Poetry, 1988, The Ancients and the Moderns, 1989, The Question of Being, 1993, Plato's Statesman: The Web of Politics, 1995, The Mask of Enlightenment, 1995, Metaphysics in Ordinary Language, 1999; editor: The Examined Life: A Treasury of Western Philosophy, 2000, The Elusiveness of the Ordinary, 2002, La Production Platonicienne, 2005, Plato's Republic, 2005 Research grantee Am. Philos. Soc., 1961; Research grantee Earhart Found., 1971, 73, 81, 2000. Mem. Metaphys. Soc. Am (pres. 1990-91). Home: 117 Brook St Wellesley MA 02482-6632 Office: 745 Commonwealth Ave Boston MA 02215-1401 E-mail: srosen@bu.edu.

**ROSEN, STEVEN O.,** lawyer; b. NYC, Jan. 11, 1949; s. Albert I. and Yvette (Sterbuch) R. BS Aerospace Engring., SUNY, 1970; MS System and Control Engring., Case Western Reserve, 1973; JD, Lewis & Clark Coll., 1977. Bar: Ill. 1977, Oreg. 1978, Wash. 2004. Assoc. Lord, Bissell & Brook, Chgo., 1977-79, Miller, Nash, Wiener, Hager & Carlsen, Portland, Oreg., 1979-84, ptnr., 1984-97; pvt. practice Rosen Law Firm, Portland and Salem, Oreg., 1997—. Disting. adj. prof. Lewis & Clark Law Sch., 1986. Mem. ABA (dir. divsns. sect. of litigation 1996-97, chmn. aviation litigation com. 1990-93), Am. Bd. Trial Advocates, Oreg. State Bar Assn. (exec. com.

aviation sect. 1984-2001, chmn. 1994-95), Washington State Bar Assn. Avocations: skiing, bicycling. Address: The Rosen Law Firm 620 SW Main St Ste 702 Portland OR 97205-3030 Office Phone: 503-525-2525. Business E-Mail: rosen@rosenlawfirm.com.

**ROSEN, STEVEN TERRY,** oncologist, hematologist; b. Bklyn., Feb. 18, 1952; married, 1976; 4 children. MB, Northwestern U., Evanston, Ill., 1972, MD, 1976. Genevieve Teuton prof., med. sch. Northwestern U., 1989—, dir. Robert H. Lurie Comprehensive Cancer Ctr., 1989—. Dir. clin. programs Northwestern Meml. Hosp., 1989—. Editor-in-chief Jour. Northwestern U. Cancer Center, 1989—, Contemporary Oncology, 1990-95, Cancer Treatment and Rsch., 1995—, In Touch, 1998-02. Mem. AAAS, ACP, AMA, Am. Soc. Hematology, Am. Soc. Clin. Oncology, Ctrl. Soc. Clin. Rsch. Achievements include research in hematologic malignancies, lung cancer, breast cancer, biologic and hormonal therapies. Office: Northwestern U Olson Pavilion Rm 8250 303 E Chicago Ave Chicago IL 60611-3093 Office Phone: 312-908-5250. Business E-Mail: s-rosen@northwestern.edu.

**ROSEN, WILLIAM WARREN,** lawyer; b. New Orleans, July 22, 1936; s. Warren Leucht and Erma (Stich) R.; m. Eddy Kahn, Nov. 26, 1965; children: Elizabeth K., Victoria A. BA, Tulane U., 1958, JD, 1964. Bar: La. 1964, U.S. Dist. Ct. (ea. dist.) La. 1965, U.S. Ct. Appeals (5th cir.) 1965, U.S. Supreme Ct. 1984, U.S. Dist. Ct. (mid. dist.) La. 1985, Colo. 1989. Assoc. Dodge & Friend, New Orleans, 1965-68, Law Office of J.R. Martzell, New Orleans, 1968-70; pvt. practice New Orleans, 1970-79, 89-90; ptnr. Lucas & Rosen (and predecessor firm), New Orleans, 1979-87, Herman, Herman, Katz & Cotlar, New Orleans, 1987-88, Rosen and Samuel, New Orleans, 1990-95; of counsel Rittenberg & Samuel, New Orleans, 1996-99; founder & dir. Litigation Consultation Svcs., New Orleans, 1996—; ptnr. Rosen & Lundeen, L.L.P., New Orleans, 1999—2002; pvt. practice New Orleans, 2002—. Adj. prof. trial advocacy Law Sch. Tulane U., 1988-2006, mem. adv. com. paralegal studies program, 1977-86, instr. bus. orgns., 1978, instr. legal interviewing, 1980-81; mem. adv. com. Paralegal Inst. U. New Orleans, 1990—, instr. legal interviewing and investigations, 1986-87; lectr. legal and paralegal fields; lectr. real and demonstrative evidence Nat. Edn. Network, 1993; lectr. new judges seminar La. Jud. Coll., 2000, 01, 02, 03. Author: (with others) Trial Techniques publ. La. Trial Lawyers Assn., 1981; columnist Briefly Speaking publ. New Orleans Bar Assn., 1993-2000. Mem. budget and planning com. Jewish Welfare Fedn., 1970-73; mem. adv. coun. on drug edn. La. Dept. Edn., 1973; mem. profl. adv. com. Jewish Endowment Found., 1982—; mem. exec. com. U.S. Olympic Com., La., 1982-84; bd. dirs. Planned Parenthood La., 1994-2001, Hillel Found. New Orleans, 2003-05, Dad's Club, Isidore Newman Sch., 1984-85, Uptown Flood Assn., 1982-85; bd. dirs. Jewish Children's Home Svc., 1973-76, Met. Crime Commn. New Orleans, 1976-82; spl. agt. Office Spl. Investigations USAF, 1958-61. Fellow, Inst. of Politics. Loyola U. Mem. ABA, ATLA (keyperson com. 1986-89, vice chmn. paralegal com. 1986-89, mem. family law adv. com. 1989-90, sec. family law sect. 1990-91, lectr. legal edn. 1979, 81, 83, 86, 88); mem. La. Bar Assn. (vice chmn. pub. rels. com. 1970-73, 88-89, past chmn. state youth drug abuse edn. program, vol. lawyers for arts 1986-96, chmn. sr. counsel com. 1995-96), Am. Arbitration Assn., Nat. Fedn. Paralegal Assn. (adv. coun. 1989-1998), Assn. Atty. Mediators (sec. La. chpt. 1995), Nat. Choice in Dying (legal adv. com. 1992-96), Nat. Edn. Network (lectr. legal edn. 1993), New Orleans Bar Assn. (CLE com. 1990-91, chmn. 1991-92, mem. alternative dispute resolution com. 1996-2000, panel moderator 1997), Inn of Ct. (master 1992-2004), Rotary Club New Orleans (bd. dirs. 1996-98, 2003-05, chmn. legal com. 1996—2005), Audubon Park Tennis Club (pres. 2004-06). Avocation: photography. Office: 210 Baronne St 18th Flr New Orleans LA 70112-4132 Office Phone: 504-473-2200. E-mail: lcsno@aol.com.

**ROSENAU, JAMES NATHAN,** political scientist, educator, writer; b. Phila., Nov. 25, 1924; s. Walter Nathan and Fanny Fox (Baum) R.; m. Norah McCarthy, Aug. 5, 1955 (dec. July 1974); 1 child, Heidi Margaret; m. Pauline Vaillancourt, June 14, 1987 (div. 1993); m. Hongying Wang, Dec. 11, 1993; children: Fan Elizabeth, Patrick Rosenau (adopted). AB, Bard Coll., 1948; AM, Johns Hopkins U., 1949; PhD, Princeton U., 1957. From instr. to prof. Rutgers U., New Brunswick, NJ, 1949-70; prof. Ohio State U., Columbus, 1970-73; prof. polit. sci. U. So. Calif., L.A., 1973-92; prof. internat. affairs George Washington U., 1992—. Rsch. asst. Inst. Advanced Study, Princeton, N.J., 1953-54; rsch. assoc. Princeton U., N.J., 1960-70; dir. Sch. Internat. Rels. U. So. Calif., L.A., 1976-79; dir. Inst. for Transnat. Studies. U. Southern Calif., L.A., 1973-92. Author: Public Opinion and Foreign Policy, 1961, National Leadership and Foreign Policy, 1963, The Dramas of Politics, 1973, Citizenship between Elections, 1974, The Scientific Study of Foreign Policy, 1980, Turbulence in World Politics, 1990, The United Nations in a Turbulent World, 1992, Along the Domestic-Foreign Frontier, 1997, Distant Proximities, 2003, The Study of World Politics: Vol. 1, Theoretical and Methodological Challenges, Vol. 2, Globalization and Governance, 2005; (play) Kwangju: An Escalatory Spree, 1991; co-author: American Leadership in World Affairs, 1984, Global Voices, 1993, Thinking Theory Thoroughly, 1995, 2nd edit., 2000, International Political Economy, 1995, Understanding Globalization, 1998, On the Cutting Edge of Globalization, 2005; co-editor: Journeys through World Politics, 1989, Global Changes and Theoretical Challenges, 1989, Governance without Government, 1992, Strange Power, 2000, Information Technologies and Global Politics, 2002, Globalization, Security and the Nation State, 2005, Governance and Sustainability, 2005. Trustee Bard Coll., Annandale-on-Hudson, 1968-70, Odyssey Theater Ensemble, L.A., 1987-88. With U.S. Army, 1942-46. Ford Found. fellow, 1958-59, Guggenheim fellow, 1987-88; Rsch. grantee NSF, 1970, 73, 78-79, 83, 88, 92, 96, NEH grantee, 1976. Fellow World Acad. Art and Sci.; mem. Internat. Studies Assn. (pres. 1984 85), Am. Polit. Sci. Assn. (cons. coun. 1975-77) Democrat. Office: 2130 H St NW Washington DC 20052-2521 Business E-Mail: jnr@gwu.edu.

**ROSENBACH, LEOPOLD,** engineer, consultant; b. Walbrzych, Poland, Jan. 10, 1947; came to the U.S., 1969; s. Samuel and Halina (Kormicz) R.; m. Pola Knott, Dec. 23, 1969; 1 child, Coleene Rosenbach. MSEE, Polytechnic, Wroclaw, Poland, 1968. Cert. mfg. engr. Mfg. Mgr. Leviton Mfg. Co., Bklyn., 1973-77; mfg. engr. Eagle Electric, Long Island City, N.Y., 1977-78; electric mfg. engr. Standard Motor Products, Long Island City, 1979-83, product devel. mgr., 1984-87, design mgr., 1988-90, engring. mgr., 1991-93, dir. materials, 1994-96, dir. ops., 1996—. Contbr. numerous articles to sci. jours. Mem. IEEE, Am. Soc. Metals, Am. Purchasing Soc., Internat. Soc. for Hybrid Microelectronics (met. chpt. treas. 1988-89, sec. 89-90, pres. 90-91), Soc. Mfg. Engrs. Avocations: music, astronomy. Office: Standard Motor Electronics 170 Sunport Ln Orlando FL 32809-7892 also: 7709 Windbreak Rd Orlando FL 32819-5163 E-mail: leor@smpe.net.

**ROSENBAUM, BELLE SARA,** religious studies educator, religious organization administrator; b. N.Y.C., Apr. 1, 1922; d. Harry and Hinda (Sits) Heimowitz; m. Jacob H. Rosenbaum, Mar. 12, 1939; children: Linda Zelinger, Simmi Brodie, Martin, Arlene Levene. Cert., N.Y. Sch. Interior Design, 1945; MA in Judaic Art, U.B.C., 1997, PhD, 1997. Sr. mem. Am. Soc. Appraisers, Washington, 1979—; tchr. Judaica Yeshiva U., 1984—; dir. Mus. Contemporary Judaica; pres. Jarvis Designs, Inc., Union City, NJ, 1955-75, Design Assocs., BLS, Monsey, NY, 1970-78; v.p. Lord & Lady Inc., Union City, 1955-70, Cardio-Bionic Scanning, Inc., Spring Valley, NY, 1975-78; v.p., treas. Rapitech Sys., Inc., 1985; exec. bd. State of Israel Bonds Orgn., 1992—. Author short stories, 1947-48, Chronicle of Jewish Traditions, 1992, Upon Thy Doorposts, 1996; contbr. articles on interior design to profl. jours. Chmn. bd. artifacts Rockland Holocaust Ctr., 1991—; trustee Rockland Ct. Holocaust Studies, 1994; pres. Ednl. Ctr. Jewish Values Jerusalem St. Synagogue, Israel, 1998—; co-chair Nat. Jewish Art Week, 2000; curator arts Holocaust Mus. Rockland County, 2000; Bd. dirs. Midgal Ohr Schs., 1971—, Shaare Zedek Hosp., Jerusalem, 1998—, Jewish Fedn. Rockland County, 1999—, Riverdale (N.Y.) Jewish Mus., 1999—, Am. Guild Judaic Art, 1999—, Judaica Mus. Riverdale, 2001—.

**ROSENBAUM, DAVID MARK,** engineering executive, consultant, educator; b. Boston, Feb. 11, 1935; s. Frederick and Elizabeth (Gelman) R.; m. Karen Jeanne Smith, Dec. 27, 1964; children: Benjamin Micah, Shoshana Elizabeth. BSc, Brown U., 1956; MS, Renessaler Poly. Inst., 1958; PhD, Brandeis U., 1964. Asst. rsch. prof. Boston U., 1964-65; assoc. prof. Poly. U., Bklyn., 1969-70; pres. Network Analysis Corp., Glen Cove, NY, 1970-72; asst. dir. Office of Nat. Narcotics Intelligence, Washington, 1973-74; cons. to comptr. gen. GAO, Washington, 1975-78; dir. Office of Radiation Programs EPA, Washington, 1978-81; pres. Tech. Analysis Corp., McLean, Va., 1981—. Cons. Dir. of Licensing, AEC, Washington, 1972-73. Author: Super Hilbert Space and the Quantum Time Operator, 1969, Liquefied Energy Gases Safety, 1978, A Statistical Procedure for Testing Pacemakers, 1978, Health Effects of Low-Level Radiation, 1981, A Statistical Procedure for Cluster Recognition with Application to Atlanta Leukemia Data, 1983. Mem. IEEE, Am. Phys. Soc. Office: Tech Analysts Corp # 202 6723 Whittier Ave Mc Lean VA 22101-4533 Personal E-mail: dmrose@radix.net.

**ROSENBAUM, GREG ALAN,** merchant banker, consultant; b. Toledo, Aug. 7, 1952; s. Marvin and Ida Edith (Millman) R.; m. Martha Jane Radlo, Sept. 3, 1978; children: Eli Samuel, Eve Hannah, Elliott Jacob. AB, Harvard U., 1974, M in Pub. Policy, 1978, JD, 1978. Bar: Ohio 1978, Ill. 1980. Summer assoc. Jones, Day, Reavis & Pogue, Cleve., 1977; tchg. fellow in govt. and social scis. Harvard U., Cambridge, Mass., 1976-78; cons. Boston Consulting Group, Boston and Chgo., 1978-82; v.p. Dyson-Kissner-Moran Corp., N.Y.C., 1982-87; mng. dir. Carlyle Group, Washington, 1987-88; pres. Palisades Assocs., Inc., Bethesda, Md., 1988—. Debating coach Harvard U., 1976-79; dir. Varlen Corp., Naperville, Ill., 1985-99, Richey Electronics, Inc., Garden Grove, Calif., 1993-99, McLaren/Hart Inc., Rancho Cordova, Calif., 1995-2000, Expressions Furniture, Inc., Anaheim, Calif., 1992-97, AMCO Corp., Chgo., 1993-97, The Whaler on Kaanapali Beach, 1999—, PlayCore Holdings, Inc., 2000—. Co-author: The Crime of Poverty, 1973, Beyond Politics, 1974, World Without Plenty, 1975. Dir. Lifeline, A Mental Retardation Partnership, Washington, 1993-98; baseball coach Potomac (Md.) Boys' Club, 1992-96; co-chair Harvard Debate Centennial, 1991—; mem. Harvard Law Sch. 20th Reunion gift com., 1997-98, 25th Reunion gift com., 1998-99. Winner Ames Moot Ct. competition Harvard Law Sch., 1976. Mem. ABA, Am. Forensic Assn. (nat. intercollegiate debate champion 1974, coach nat. intercollegiate debate champion 1979), Am. Acad. Polit. and Social Scis., Ctr. for Study of Presidency, Toledo Bar Assn., Chgo. Bar Assn., Phi Beta Kappa. Democrat. Jewish. Avocations: major league baseball, golf, computers, sports memorabilia. Office: Palisades Assocs Inc 9140 Vendome Dr Bethesda MD 20817-4021

**ROSENBAUM, HERBERT EDWIN,** neurology educator; b. Los Angeles, Dec. 11, 1924; s. Samuel P. and Rebecca (Goldberg) R.; m. Dorothy Goldner, Nov. 2, 1944 (div. Aug. 1972); children: Robert, Barbara, Nancy; m. Velma Rosenbaum, Nov. 5, 1988. BS, U. Oreg., 1947, MD, 1949. Prof. neurology Washington U. Sch. Medicine, St. Louis, 1978—. Served to 1st lt. USAF, 1952-53. Fellow Am. Acad. Neurology (counselor 1970-74); mem. Am. Psychiat. Assn. (life mem., pres. Mo. chpt. 1964-65), Soc. Clin. Neurologists (pres. 1974-75). Avocation: golf. Office: Wash U Sch Medicine Campus Box 8111 660 S Euclid Ave Saint Louis MO 63110-1010 Home: 13 Sackston Woods Ln Creve Coeur MO 63141-8228 Office Phone: 314-747-5355.

**ROSENBAUM, JACOB I.,** retired lawyer; b. Cleve., Oct. 4, 1927; s. Lionel C. and Dora (Heldman) R.; m. Marjorie Jean Arnold, Apr. 20, 1952; children: Laura Rosenbaum, Alexander, Judith Bartell. JD, U. N.Mex., 1951. Bar: N.Mex. 1951, Ohio 1952. Pres. Ohio Savs. Bank., Cleve., 1955—60, sr. v.p., 1960—92, also dir., 1995—; ptnr. Burke, Haber & Berick, 1955-79, Arter & Hadden, 1979-94, of counsel, 1994—2003, Tucker Ellis & West, 2003—05; ret., 2005. Active Judson Retirement Cmty., Cleveland Heights, Ohio, 1990—, trustee, 1994—2003, 2006—, pres., 1992; trustee Cleve. Zool. Soc., 1983—; Cleve. Nat. Air Show, 1981—, pres., 1987—90, 1994—, pres. Found., 1995—2003; trustee Golden Age Ctrs. of Cleve., 1996—; pres. Temple Emanu El, University Heights, Ohio, 1965—67, 1995—. Mem. Cleve. Execs. Assn. (pres. 1989, chmn. 1990, pres. 2003), Greater Cleve. Bar Assn., Ohio Bar Assn. (chmn. aviation law com. 1981—84), Lawyer-Pilots Bar Assn. (pres. 1981—82, editor jour. 1982—97), Kiwanis Club of Cleve. (pres. 1970—71, pres. found. 1999—). Democrat. Jewish. Home: 28050 N Woodland Rd Cleveland OH 44124-4521 Office: Tucker Ellis & West 1150 Huntington Bldg 925 Euclid Ave Cleveland OH 44115-1475 Office Phone: 216-696-2480. Business E-Mail: jrosenbaum@tuckerellis.com.

**ROSENBAUM, JAMES MICHAEL,** federal judge; b. Ft. Snelling, Minn., Oct. 12, 1944; s. Sam H. and Ilene D. (Bernstein) Rosenbaum; m. Marilyn Brown, July 30, 1972. BA, U. Minn., 1966, JD, 1969. Bar: (Minn) 1969, (Ill.) 1970, (U.S. Supreme Ct.) 1979. Atty. AmeriCorps, 1969—70; VISTA staff atty. Leadership Coun. for Met. Open Cmtys., Chgo., 1970—72; assoc. Katz, Taube, Lange & Frommelt, Mpls., 1972-77; ptnr. Rosenbaum & Rosenbaum, Mpls., 1977-79, Gainsley, Squier & Korsh, Mpls., 1979-81; US dist. atty. US Dept. Justice, Mpls., 1981-85; judge US Dist. Ct., Minn., 1985—, chief judge Minn., 2001—. 8th cir. rep. Jud. Conf. U.S., 1997—, mem. exec. com., 1999—2001. Author: (booklet) Guide to Practice Civil Rights Housing, 1972; co-author: U.S. Courts Design Guide, 1991—96; contbr. U.S. Courts Design Guide, In Defense of the Hard Drive. Campaign chmn. People for Boschwitz, Minn., 1978; bd. vis. U. Minn. Law Sch. (pres. 1996-97). Mem.: FBA (bd. dirs.). Jewish. Office: US Courthouse 300 S 4th St Minneapolis MN 55415-1320

**ROSENBAUM, JOAN HANNAH,** museum director; b. Hartford, Conn. d. Charles Leon and Lillian (Sharasheff) Grossman; m. Peter S. Rosenbaum, July 1962 (div. 1970). AA, Hartford Coll. for Women, 1962; BA, Boston U., 1964; student, Hunter Coll. Grad Sch., 1970-73; cert., Columbia U. Bus. Sch. Inst. Non Profit Mgmt., 1976 (hon.), Jewish Theol. Sem., 1993. Curatorial asst. Mus. Modern Art, N.Y.C., 1966-72; dir. mus. program N.Y. Council on Arts, N.Y.C., 1972-79; cons. Michal Washburn & Assocs., N.Y.C., 1979-80; dir. Jewish Mus., N.Y.C., 1980—. Mem. adv. bd. Pub. Ctr., N.Y.C.; bd. dirs. Creative Time. Bd. dirs. Artists Space, 1988-93; mem. coun. Am. Jewish Mus., 1981-90; mem. policy panel Nat. Endowment Arts, 1982-83. Created knight (Denmark); recipient Disting. Alumni award Boston U. Coll. Libera Arts, 1994, Woman of Distinction award Hadassah, 1997, diploma Chevalier of Order of Arts and Letters (France), 1999; European travel grantee Internat. Coun. Mus., 1972. Mem. Am. Assn. Mus. (cons. 1979—), Assn. Art Mus. Dirs. (com. chair), N.Y. State Assn. Mus. (mem. coun. 1981-90), Art Table. Office: Jewish Mus 1109 5th Ave New York NY 10128-0118

**ROSENBAUM, RICHARD A.,** lawyer; b. Bklyn., Sept. 21, 1954; BA, SUNY, Stony Brook, 1975; JD, St. John's Univ., 1982. Bar: NY 1983, Fla. 1985. Joined Greenberg Traurig, 1985, now nat. operating shareholder, shareholder-in-charge No. Ea. Region, mem. exec. com. NYC. Mem.: Fla. Bar Assn., NY State Bar Assn. Office: Greenberg Traurig LLP MetLife Bldg 200 Park Ave New York NY 10166 Office Phone: 212-801-9320. Office Fax: 212-801-6400. Business E-Mail: rosenbaumr@gtlaw.com.

**ROSENBERG, ALAN,** actors guild executive; b. Passaic, NJ, Oct. 4, 1950; m. Robin Bartlett (div.); m. Marg Helgenberger, Sept. 9, 1989; 1 child. Actor: (Broadway plays) Lost in Yonkers; (films) The Wanderers, 1979, Happy Birthday, Gemini, 1980, Not for Publication, 1984, Stewardess School, 1986, White of the Eye, 1987, The Last Temptation of Christ, 1988, Miracle Mile, 1988, After Midnight, 1989, Impulse, 1990, The Bum, 2002, (voice) Robots, 2005.; (TV films) Kojak: The Belarus File, 1985, Promise, 1986, The King of Love, 1987, The Revenge of Al Capone, 1989, The Preppie Murder, 1989, Parker Kane, 1990, The Boys, 1991, Partners, 1993, On Hope, 1994, Witch Hunt, 1994, Freaky Friday, 1995, On Seventh Avenue, 1996, Undue Influence, 1996, Breaking Through, 1996, Cloned, 1997, Bronx County, 1998, Giving Up the Ghost, 1998, The Temptations, 1998, A Touch of Hope, 1999, A Mother's Fight for Justice, 2001, On the Edge, 2001; (TV series) Civil Wars, 1991—93, L.A. Law, 1993—94, Cybill, 1995—98, The Guardian, 2001—04, (guest appearances) Barnaby Jones, 1978, The Days and Nights of

Molly Dodd, 1987, Coach, 1989, Empty Nest, 1989, ER, 1994, Murphy Brown, 1998, Touched by an Angel, 1999, Chicago Hope, 1999, 2000, NYPD Blue, 2005, CSI, 2005, Numb3rs, 2005. Mem.: SAG (pres. 2005—). Office: SAG 5757 Wilshire Blvd Los Angeles CA 90036

**ROSENBERG, ALAN DAVID,** accountant; b. Mt. Vernon, N.Y., Apr. 11, 1946; s. Benjamin Bernard and Miriam (Nierenberg) R.; m. Wendy Patricia Cutler, May 25, 1975; children: Kerri L., Joshua Z., Brian S. BS in Acctg., NYU, 1967; MBA in Taxation, Baruch Coll., 1970. CPA, N.Y. Sr. acct. Ernst & Ernst, N.Y.C., 1967-70; dir. acctg., CFO various firms, N.Y.C., 1970-75; pres. Alan D. Rosenberg, CPA, P.C., N.Y.C., New Rochelle, N.Y., 1975—. Mem. AICPA (mem. tax practice mgmt. com. 1992—), N.Y. State Soc. CPAs, Inst. Mgmt. Accts., Nat. Conf. CPA Practitioners, Alliance of Practicing CPAs, Estate Planning Coun. Westchester County, Tax Soc. NYU. Jewish. Avocations: sports, reading, family activities. Office: 2 W 45th St Ste 1208 New York NY 10036-4212

**ROSENBERG, ALAN GENE,** editor; b. Chgo., Sept. 14, 1957; s. Earl David and Lorraine Faith (Blum) R.; m. Avis Beth Gunther-Rosenberg, Apr. 8, 1984; children: Ethan Elijah, Rebecca Greer, Jacob Sigmund. BS in Journalism, Northwestern U., 1978. From state staff reporter to asst. features editor Providence Jour., 1978—. Mem. Am. Assn. Sunday and Feature Editors. Office: Providence Jour 75 Fountain St Providence RI 02902-0050 Office Phone: 401-277-7253. E-mail: alan_rosenberg@projo.com.

**ROSENBERG, ALAN STEWART,** lawyer; b. NYC, Mar. 29, 1930; s. Louis and Sadye (Knobler) R.; m. Ilse Rosenberg/Klein, Aug. 15, 1963; children: Gary, Robert. BA, Stanford U., 1949; LLB, Columbia U., 1952; LLM, NYU, 1960. Bar: N.Y. 1955. Assoc. Wolf Haldenstein Adler & Freeman, NYC, 1955-56; ptnr., chmn. tax dept. Proskauer Rose LLP, NYC, 1957—92. Contbr. articles to profl. jours. Mem. exec. com., bd. visitors Stanford (Calif.) U. Law Sch., 1982-85, Jewish studies program, 1986—; chmn. bd. N.Y. Alliance for the Pub. Sch., 1988-91; mem. adv. com. on pub. issues Advt. Coun., 1991-94; bd. dirs., sec. Univ.-Urban Schs. Nat. Task Force Inc., 1981-96; mem. bd. visitors Columbia U. Law Sch., 1991-96; trustee Ctr. Ednl. Innovation Pub. Edn. Assn., 2000—; mem. bd advisors Spl. Music Sch Am., 1999—; bd. dirs., treas. Justice Resource Ctr., 1994-97; bd. dirs., mem. exec. com. The Abraham Fund; chmn. bd. dirs. Richalan Found., 1996-2003. Lt. (j.g.) USN, 1952-55. Lt (jr. grade) USNR, 1952—55. Jewish. Avocations: singing, tennis. Home: 115 Central Park W New York NY 10023-4153 E-mail: aandi98@aol.com.

**ROSENBERG, ALEX JACOB,** art appraiser, art dealer; b. N.Y.C., May 25, 1919; s. Israel and Lena (Zar) R. Student, Albright Coll., 1935-37, Sch. Phila. Mus. Art, 1937-40; BS, Phila. U., 1948; DHL (hon.), Hofstra U., 1989; DSc in Art, Inst. Superior Art, Havana, Cuba, 2003. completed Personal Property courses, levels I, II, III and IV, Am. Soc. of Appraisers, Uniform Standards of Profl. Appraisal Practice, 1994, 2000. Pres. Ansenphore, 1959-66; sec., dir. Gen. Cablevision Tex., 1968-72; v.p., dir. Communicable, Inc., Fla., 1967-71, Gen. Cablevision Palatka, Fla., 1967-71, Rosenberg Cable Corp., 1966-71; pres., dir. Modern Cable Corp., 1966-71, B.F.C.-C.A.T.V. Corp., 1966-71; v.p., dir. Starfax Corp. Real Estate, 1968-70; gen. ptnr. Lakewood Plaza Assocs., NJ, 1973-92, Rostin Assocs., Austin, Tex., 1970-83; pres. Transworld Art Inc., Alex Rosenberg Gallery and Alba Edits., N.Y.C., 1968-89, Rostin Mgmt. Corp., 1986-89, The Abbot Group, 1987-89, Ardmore Affiliates Ltd., Alex Rosenberg Fine Art, 1985—, Neikrug-Rosenberg Associates, 1989-97. Lectr. Parsons Sch. Design, N.Y.C., 1979—88; instr. appraising modern art NYU, 1992—95, adj. asst. prof. appraising, 1995—; vis. prof. fine art Inst. Superior Art, Havana, Cuba, 1993—; organizer Henry Moore exhbn. Mus. Budapest, Bratislava and Prague, Hungary, 1993; co-curator Leonoid Sokov, Albright Coll., Reading, Pa., 2002; guest lectr. CUNY, N.Y.C., 2000—03; organizer Henry Moore Exhbn., Havana, 1998; chmn. Salvadore Dali Rsch. Ctr., 2006. Curator An American Portrait, 1976—78, Mus. Fine Art, Havana, 1992—93, co-curator Romare Bearden as Printmaker, 1992—97, Henry Moore Mother and Child Exhbn., 1987—88, assoc. editor exhbn. catalogue. Trustee Alice Baber Art Fund, 1991-93, Phila. Coll. Textiles and Sci., 1992-95; mem. internat. bd. dirs. Tel Aviv Mus. Art, 1999—, bd. dirs., 2000—; bd. dirs. Artists' Rights Today, 1974-80; mus. adv. bd. Hofstra Mus., Hempstead, N.Y., 1987-92; mem. collection and exhbn. com. Parrish Art Mus., Southhampton, N.Y., 1989-95; mem. adv. com. Pollock-Krasner House and Study Ctr., 2000—; trustee Guttman Inst., 1979-92; mem. exec. bd. Nat. Emergency Civil Liberties Com., 1970-98, treas., 1981-98; trustee Nat. Emergency Civil Liberties Found., 1964-98, chmn., 1992-98; nat. bd. dirs. and bd. dirs. local coun. SANE, 1974-83, bd. dirs. Ctr. for Constitutional Rights, 1998—, v.p. 2003—; trustee, treas. New Lincoln Sch., 1968-71; trustee Givat Haviva Ednl. Found., N.Y.C., 1969—, chmn. exec. com., 1992-99, v.p., 1998—; trustee Stephen Wise Free synagogue, 1967-70, 73-76, 99-2000, Mus. Borough Bklyn., 1986-89; del. World Zionist Congress, Jerusalem, 1972; mem. Cmty. Planning Bd. # 7, 1965-67, 70-72; mem. Lower West Side Anti-Poverty Bd., 1965-66, Lincoln Ctr. Cmty. Coun., 1968-74, Com. for Ind. Civilian Police Rev. Bd., 1967; mem. steering com. Com. Pub. Edn. and Religious Liberty; chmn. Am. Israel Civil Liberties Coalition, 1988-89; Dem. dist. leader, 1964-74, state committeeman, 1970-73, mem. county exec. com., 1964-74; del. Dem. Nat. Convs., 1968, 72; bd. dirs. Raoul Wallenberg Commn. of U.S., 1986-90, chmn., 1990-92; mem. print and drawing coun. Israel Mus., 1980-85; assoc. dir. Snug Harbor Cultural Ctr., S.I., 1982-88; mem. AAA del. to Pres. Coun. of Appraisal Orgns., 1995-96; bd. mem. Ludwig Found. of Cuba, 1995—; Am. Friends Ludwig Found. Cuba, 2000—; mem. Assn. Governing Bds. of Univs. and Colls., 1994-96, Nat. Registry of Forensic Examiners, 1994-96; hon. fellow Tel. Aviv Mus. Art, 2002. Recipient Spl. prize Grenschen Triennial, Switzerland, 1976, Cuban Order of Culture, 1995, Cert. of Commendation, Am. Soc. Appraisers, 1994. Disting Svc. Appraisers Assn of Am, 1997, Graham J. Littlewood III award for profl. excellence Phila. Coll. of Textiles and Sci., 1996, Alex and Carole Rosenberg Collection, Savannah Coll. of Art and Design, 1999. Alex Rosenberg Gallery Hofstra U., 1996—, Alex and Carole Rosenberg Collection Albright Coll., Reading, Pa.; named to Bronze Ctr., Pres.'s Coun. Albright Coll., 2002, Diploma for Service, Nat. Mus. of Fine Art, Havana, Cuba, 2003. Mem. Am. Soc. Appraisers (sr., bd. examiners 1987-95, personal property com. 1987-89), Appraisers Assn. Am. (cert. mem., bd. dirs. 1990-96, v.p. 1992-94, 1st v.p. 1994, pres. award 2005), Fine Art Pubs. Assn. (v.p., bd. dirs. 1981-83, pres. 1983-86, treas. 1986-89), Nat. Arts Club (Lifetime Achievement Gold medal 2004). Home and Office: 3 E 69th St New York NY 10021-4943 Fax: 212-628-4969. Office Phone: 212-628-0606.

**ROSENBERG, ALISON P.,** public information officer; b. Miami, Fla., Sept. 5, 1945; d. Mortimer I. and Gail (Sklar) Podell; m. Jeffrey Alan Rosenberg, May 4, 1969; 1 child, Robert Aaron. BS in Econs., Smith Coll., 1967. Mng. officer Citibank, N.Y.C., 1967-69; legis. aide Senator Charles Percy, Washington, 1969-80; profl. staff mem. Senate Fgn. Rels. Com., Washington, 1981-85; assoc. asst. administr. Agy. for Internat. Devel., Washington, 1985-87; dir. African affairs Nat. Security Coun., Washington, 1987-88; dep. asst. sec. for Africa State Dept., Washington, 1988-92; asst. administr. for Africa Agy. for Internat. Devel., Washington, 1992-93; lead partnerships specialist (Africa) The World Bank, Washington, 1993—. E-mail: arosenberg@worldbank.org.

**ROSENBERG, AURIA ELEANOR,** secondary school educator; b. Detroit, Mar. 27, 1935; d. Paulino and Emelia (Phillip) Aromin; m. Jonah Rosenberg, Jan. 23, 1967 (div. June 1974); children: Pamela Reynée, Jonathan David, Deena Robyn. BA in French, Univ. Wash., 1961; MA in edn., Nat.-Louis Univ., 1992. Cert. tchr. Ill., Wash. Tchr. Tyee Jr H.S., Bellevue, Wash., 1961-62, Bais-Yaakov Parochial Sch., Chgo., 1979-84, Audy Home Cook County Detention Ctr., Chgo., 1984-89, Pleasant Ridge Elem. Sch., Glenview, Ill., 1988-90, Lyon Elem. Sch., Glenview, Ill., 1989-91; chair world lang. dept. Phillips Acad., Chgo., 1991—. Rep. committeewoman of 49th ward, Chgo., 1970-82, mem. Cook County Rep. Committeewomens Orgn. Chgo., 1970-82, sec. 1970-74. Recipient Merit award Excellence for Outstanding Tchr. of Yr., Ill. State Bd. Edn. Mem. Alumni assn. Univ. Wash. Nat. Coun. Tchg. Fgn. Lang., Ill. Coun. Tchg. Fgn. Lang. (adv. coun., ctrl. states), Ctr.

States Coun. Tchrs. Fgn. Langs. (mem. adv. coun.), Internat. Reading Assn., Ill. Reading Assn., Pi Lambda Theta (v.p. 1996-98, sec. 1992), Delta Kappa Gamma (historian 1994—), Phi Delta Kappa. Republican. Avocations: watercoloring, illustration. Home: One Ct of Harborside Northbrook IL 60062 Office Phone: 312-773-1503. Personal E-mail: laprof61@yahoo.com.

**ROSENBERG, BETSY,** radio personality, environmentalist; Reporter, anchor KCBS, San Francisco, host Trash Talk, 1997; host EcoTalk, Air Am. Radio, 2004—; nat. anchor CBS Radio, NYC. Recipient awards, EPA, Nat. Recycling Assn., Calif. Resource Recovery Assn., Peninsula Cmty. Conservation Fund, Keep Calif. Beautiful. Office: KCBS 865 Battery St San Francisco CA 94111

**ROSENBERG, BRIAN C,** academic administrator; BA in English, Cornell U.; MA in English, PhD in English, Columbia U. Tchg. asst. Columbia U., NYC, 1979—80; English instr. Queens Coll., NY, 1980—82; asst. prof. The Cooper Union, NYC, 1982—83; asst. prof. to assoc. prof. to prof. to chmn. dept. of English Allegheny Coll., Meadville, Pa., 1983—98; chief acad. officer to dean of faculty and prof. English Lawrence U., Appleton, Wis., 1998—2003; pres. Macalester Coll., 2003—. Pres. fellowship Columbia U., 1977—78, 1980—81; bd. trustees The Dickens Soc., 2000—. Author: (book) Mary Lee Settle's Beulah Quintet: The Price of Freedom, 1991, Little Dorrit's Shadow's: Character and Contradiction in Dickens, 1996. Mem.: Phi Beta Kappa. Office: Office of the Pres. Macalester Coll 208 Weyerhaeuser Hall 62 Macalester St Saint Paul MN 55105 Office Phone: 651-696-6207.

**ROSENBERG, CHARLES ERNEST,** historian, educator; b. NYC, Nov. 11, 1936; s. Bernard and Marion (Roberts) R.; m. Carroll Ann Smith, June 22, 1961 (div. 1977); 1 child, Leah; m. Drew Gilpin Faust, June 7, 1980; 1 child, Jessica. BA, U. Wis., 1956; MA, Columbia U., 1957, PhD, 1961; DHL, U. Wis., 1997. Fellow Johns Hopkins U., Balt., 1960-61; asst. prof. U. Wis., 1961-63; assoc. prof. U. Pa., Phila., 1965-68; prof. history, 1968—, chmn. dept., 1974—75, 1979—83, 1991—95; prof. history of sci. Harvard U., 2001—, chmn. dept. history of sci., 2003—04. Author: The Cholera Years: The United States in 1832, 1849 and 1866, 1962, The Trial of the Assassin Guiteau: Psychiatry and Law in the Gilded Age, 1968, No Other Gods: On Science and Social Thought in America, 1976, The Care of Strangers: The Rise of America's Hospital System, 1987, Explaining Epidemics and Other Studies in the History of Medicine, 1992; editor Isis, 1986-89. Bd. dirs. Mental Health Assn. Southea. Pa., 1973—76, Libr. Co. of Phila., 1980—, Ctr. Advanced Study Behavioral Scis., 1999—2005. Nat. Inst. Health Research grantee, 1964-70; Guggenheim Found. fellow, 1965-66, 89-90; Nat. Endowment Humanities fellow, 1972-73; Rockefeller Found. humanities fellow, 1975-76; fellow Inst. Advanced Study, 1979-80, Ctr. Advanced Study in Behavioral Scis., 1982-83. Fellow: Am. Philos. Soc. (coun. 2006—), Am. Acad. Arts and Scis.; mem.: Orgn. Am. Historians (exec. bd. 1985—88), Soc. Social History of Medicine (pres. 1981), History of Sci. Soc. (coun. 1972—75, George Sarton medal 1995), Am. Assn. History of Medicine (coun. 1974—76, pres. 1992—94, William H. Welch medal 1969), Inst. Medicine of NAS. Home: 76 Brattle Cambridge MA 02138 Office: Harvard U Dept History of Sci Cambridge MA 02138 Office Phone: 617-495-9953. Business E-Mail: rosenb3@fas.harvard.edu.

**ROSENBERG, CHUCK (CHARLES P. ROSENBERG),** prosecutor; b. 1960; BA, Tufts U., 1982; MA in Pub. Policy, Harvard U.; JD, U. Va. Atty. Hunton & Williams LLP, McLean, Va., 2000—02; legal analyst NBC TV; asst. US atty. (ea. dist.) Va. 2002-2003; counsel, chief of staff to dep. atty. gen. Washington, counselor to atty. gen. John Ashcroft, counselor to FBI Dir. Robert S. Mueller III, interim US atty. (so. dist.) Tex. Houston, 2005—06, interim US atty (ea. dist.) Va. Alexandria, 2006, US atty. (ea. dist.) Va., 2006—. Office: US Atty's Office 2100 Jamieson Ave Alexandria VA 22314*

**ROSENBERG, DAN YALE,** retired plant pathologist; b. Stockton, Calif., Jan. 8, 1922; s. Meyer and Bertha (Naliboff) R.; m. Marilyn Kohn, Dec. 5, 1954; 1 son, Morton Karl. AA, Stockton Jr. Coll., 1942; AB, Coll. of the Pacific, 1949; MS, U. Calif., Davis, 1952. Jr. plant pathologist State of Calif. Dept. Agr., Riverside, 1952-55, asst. plant pathologist Sacramento, 1955-59, assoc. plant pathologist, 1959-60, pathologist IV, 1960—63, program supr. Riverside, 1963-71, chief exclusion and detectin, divsn. plant industry, 1971-76, chief nursery and seed svcs. divsn. plant industry, 1976-82, spl. asst. divsn. plant industry, 1982-87; pres. Health Inc., 1972-73. Agrl. cons., 1988—; mem. Citrus Rsch. Adm. Com., U. Calif., Riverside, 1992—; mem. Gov.'s Interagy. Task Force on Biotech., 1986—; agrl. cons. Calif. Avocado Commn., 1994—. Contbr. articles to profl. jours. Served with AUS, 1942-46, ETO. Mem. Am. Phytopath. Soc. (fgn. and regulatory com. 1975—, chmn. 1978, grape diseases and pests 1977-98), Calif. State Employees Assn. (pres. 1967-69), Sacto. Met. C. of C. (internat. trade com. 1993-97), N.Am. Plant Protection Orgn. (industry adv. group), Plant Patents Fruit Trees and Ornamental Trees, Olive Trees and Grapevines Achievements include research in grape genetics; new olive varieties. Home and Office: 2328 Swarthmore Dr Sacramento CA 95825-6867 Office Phone: 916-929-4620.

**ROSENBERG, DAVID ALAN,** military historian, educator; b. NYC, Aug. 30, 1948; s. Sidney and Fay (Breitman) R.; m. Deborah Lee Haines, July 1, 1973; 1 child, Rebecca Haines. BA in History, Am. U., 1970; MA in History, U. Chgo., 1971, PhD in History, 1983. Asst. historian, cons. Lulejian & Assocs., Inc., Falls Church, Va., 1974-75; instr. history U. Wis., Milw., 1976-78; pvt. practice cons., rschr. Chgo., Washington, 1978-82; asst. prof. history U. Houston, University Park, 1982-83; sr. fellow Strategic Concepts Devel. Ctr., Nat. Def. U., Washington, 1983-85; prof. strategy and ops. U.S. Naval War Coll., Newport, RI, 1985-90; assoc. prof. history Temple U., Phila., 1990-2000, professorial lectr., 2001—; Adm. Harry W. Hill prof. maritime strategy Nat. War Coll., Washington, 1996—2003; sr. prof. U.S. Naval War Coll., 1998—2006, asst. to vice chief naval ops., 1996—2004; dir. Task Force History for chief naval ops. Operation Iraqi Freedom, Global War on Terror, 2003—04; rsch. staff mem. intelligence studies Inst. for Defence Analyses, 2006—. USA econ. coun. Found four Nation Nuc. History Program, project dir. Berlin Crisis, 1989-95; cons. Office of Sec. Def., 1991-93, Office Chief of Naval Ops., 1991-2005, Office Sec. of Navy, 1992-2003; chair Sec. Navy's Adv. Subcom. Naval History, 1995-2005 Co-author: The Admiral's Advantage U.S. Navy Operational Intelligence in World War II and the Cold War, 2005; co-editor: (15 vol.) U.S. Plans for War, 1945-1950, 1990; contbr. articles to profl. jours., chpts. to books. With USNR, 1982—. Recipient Meritorious Pub. Svc. award Dept. of Navy, 1995, Superior Civilian Svc. medal, 2000; Advanced rsch. scholar U.S. Naval War Coll., 1974-79; Ford Found grantee, 1985-86, MacArthur rsch. grantee 1987-88; MacArthur fellow 1988-93. Mem. Orgn. Am. Historians (Binkley-Stephenson article prize), Soc. for Historians of Am. Fgn. Rels. (Bernath article prize), Soc. for Mil. History, U.S. Naval Inst., Internat. Inst. for Strategic Studies. Jewish.

**ROSENBERG, DEBORAH A.,** special education educator; d. Samuel and Ethelle Wells Luque; married, June 6, 1970; children: Aimee, Corey. BSc in Bus. Adminstrn. Pers. Mgmt., SUNY, Albany, 1971; MSc in Spl. Edn., LI U., 1987; profl. diploma in Adminstrn. and Supervision, St. Johns U., 2003. Cert. Sch. Dist. Adminstr. U. of State of NY Edn. Dept., Provisional Cert. in Sch. Adminstrn. and Supervision. Prodn., sales office mgr. Electronic Essentials, Inc., Woodside, NY, 1974—85; reading, English tchr. NYC Bd. Edn. Bushwick, NY, 1985—88, tchr Rikers Island, NY, 1988—89, spl. edn. tchr. Jamaica, NY, 1989—92, edn. evaluator Hollis, NY, 1992—2003; spl. edn. math. tchr. NYC Dept. Edn., Flushing, NY, 2003—. Pvt. tutor, NYC, 1985—; adult edn. tchr. Phoenix House, LI, NY, 1987—93; reading tchr. Jamaica Learning Ctr., NYC, 1993—2002. Mem.: Assn. of Tchrs. of Math. NYC, Phi Delta Kappa (UFT chpt. leader JHS189 2006—). Democrat. Avocations: reading, crossword puzzles, role playing games. Office: JHS189Q Dist 25 Region 3 144 80 Barclay Ave Flushing NY 11355 Office Phone: 718-359-6676. Personal E-mail: debrose49@aol.com.

**ROSENBERG, EDWIN HAROLD,** systems analyst; b. Balt., June 17, 1949; s. Mervin and Helen Rosenberg. BS, Towson U., 1976, MS, 1984. Rsch. psychologist Gerontology Rsch. Ctr., Nat. Inst. on Aging NIH, Balt., 1983—92; programmer analyst Johns Hopkins Health Sys., Balt., 1993—. Contbr. articles to profl. jours. Avocations: writing, computers, bridge, crossword puzzles. Home: 4501-A Dunton Terr Perry Hall MD 21128 Office: Johns Hopkins Health System 5300 Alpha Commons Suite 200 Baltimore MD 21224 Personal E-mail: erosenb@comcast.net.

**ROSENBERG, ELI IRA,** physicist, educator; b. Bklyn., Feb. 19, 1943; s. Milton and Beatrice Rosenberg; m. Wendy Jean Harrod, July 23, 1990; m. Eileen Ewig, Aug. 29, 1965 (div. Dec. 1, 1987); children: Elliot Michael, Evan Robert. BS, CCNY, 1964; MS, U. Ill., 1966, PhD, 1971. Enrico Fermi postdoctoral fellow U. Chgo., 1971—72, instr. 1972—74, asst. prof. 1974—79; assoc. physicist Ames (Iowa) Lab., U.S. Dept. Energy, 1979—81, program dir., 1988—93, physicist, 1981, sr. physicist, 1993—93; asst. prof. Iowa State U., Ames, 1979—81, assoc. prof., 1981—87, prof., 1987—, chmn. dept. physics and astronomy, 2002—. Contbr. more than 400 articles to profl. jours. Grantee, U.S. Dept. of Energy, 1979—. Mem.: Am. Phys. Soc. (life), Sigma Xi, Phi Beta Kappa.

**ROSENBERG, ERIC,** mathematician; s. Sidney Rosenberg and Vita Himber; children: David, Alexa. BA, Oberlin Coll., Ohio, 1975; PhD, Stanford U., Calif., 1979. Sr. tech. specialist AT&T Labs, Middletown, NJ, 1979—; instr. Princeton U., 1994. Adj. prof. NJ Inst. Tech., Newark, 1992—97. Mem. editl. adv. bd.: Jour. Recent Patents Engring., 2006—; contbr. articles to profl. jours. Mentor women and minority engring. and math. students MentorNet, 2000—06. Liberal. Achievements include patents for hierarchical topological network designing system and method. Office: AT&T Labs 200 S Laurel Ave Rm C2-3D24 Middletown NJ 07748 Office Phone: 732-420-1955. Business E-Mail: ericr@att.com.

**ROSENBERG, FRANK BLAUSTEIN,** petroleum company executive; b. Balt., Sept. 24, 1958; s. Henry A. Jr. and Eleanor (Kantor) R.; m. Ann Lockwood, Feb. 1, 1986. BS in Chem. Engring., Bucknell U., 1980; MBA, Emory U., 1982. Mktg. and project mgr. Gen. Electric Credit Corp., Chgo., 1982-86; feedstock trader Crown Cen. Petroleum Corp., Houston, 1986—; exec. v.p. Rosemore, Balt., 2003—. Mem. jr. bd. Chgo. Symphony Orch., 1983-86. Mem. Am. Inst. Chem. Engrs. Clubs: Union League of Chgo., Royal Automobile. Avocations: theater, golf. Office: Rosemore Calvert Inc 1 N Charles St Ste 2200 Baltimore MD 21201-3759

**ROSENBERG, GARY A.,** neurologist; b. Oct. 27, 1942; BS, Georgetown U., 1964; MD, Albert Einstein Coll. Medicine, Bronx, 1968. Intern Genesee Hosp., Rochester, N.Y., 1968-69; resident Albert Einstein Coll Medicine, Bronx, N.Y., 1973-76; chief neurology svcs. U. N.Mex. Hosp., Albuquerque, 1986—; from asst. to assoc. prof. neurology U. N.Mex., Albuquerque, 1976-86, prof. and chair dept. neurology, 1986—, prof. neurosci., cell biology and physiology, 1998—. Contbr. articles to profl. jours. Office: Univ NMex Sch Medicine 915 Camino De Salud NE Albuquerque NM 87131-0001

**ROSENBERG, HAROLD NMI,** preventive medicine physician, consultant; b. N.Y.C., Nov. 23, 1921; s. Jacob and Rose Rosenberg; m. Sharon Rosenberg, June 6, 1962; children: Marla Holben, Victor. BA, Drake U.; DO, Phila. Coll. of Osteo. Medicine, 1951; MS, Columbia Coll. Physicians and Surgeons, 1999. Physician Health Awareness/lifesustainer, N.Y.C., 1999—; cons./advisor LIFESUSTAINER, N.Y.C., 1999—. Pres. Internat. Acad. Of Preventive Medicine, Houston. Author: (sr. editor): Book Of Vitamin Therapy/web Site:lifesustainer. With U.S. Army, 1944—46, ETO. Decorated Purple Heart, Bronze Star medal. Mem.: Internat. Acad. Preventive Medicine (pres. 1970—75), Mil. Order Of The Purple Heart (life; sr. vice comdr./N.Y. Dept. 2002—04). Independent-Republican. Hebrew. Avocations: swimming, hiking, painting landscape, portrates. Home: Po Box 678 New York NY 10023 Office: Lifesustainer 37 West 72nd St New York NY 10023 E-mail: hr89@columbia.edu.

**ROSENBERG, HENRY A., JR.,** petroleum executive; b. Pitts., Nov. 7, 1929; s. Henry A. and Ruth (Blaustein) R.; children: Henry A. III, Edward Lee, Frank Blaustein; m. Dorothy Lucibello, June 30, 1984. BA in Econs., Hobart Coll., 1952. With Crown Cen. Petroleum Corp., Balt., 1952—, pres., 1966-75, chmn. exec. com., 1966—, chmn. bd., 1975—, also CEO. Dir. Am. Trading & Prodn. Corp., USF&G Corp., Signet Banking Corp. Bd. dirs. Johns Hopkins Hosp., Goucher Coll., McDonogh Sch., Nat. Flag Day Found., YMCA Greater Balt., United Way Ctrl. Med., Crohn's and Colitis Found. Md., Nat. Aquarium Balt.; mem. nat. exec. bd., mem. N.E. regional bd., v.p. program group nat. coun., past pres., exec. bd., adv. coun. Balt. Area coun. Boy Scouts Am.; past chmn., mem. adv. bd William Donald Schaefer Ctr. for Pub. Policy; past chmn. bd. dirs. Balt. Area Conv. and Visitors Assn.; trustee Hobart and William Smith Colls. and Loyola Coll. Med. Mem. Nat. Petroleum Refiners Assn. (chmn., bd. dirs., exec. com.), Nat. Petroleum Coun., 25 Yr. Club Petroleum Industry, Nat. Assn. Mfrs. (bd. dirs.). Office: Crown Cen Petroleum Corp 1 N Charles St PO Box 1168 Baltimore MD 21203-1168*

**ROSENBERG, HOWELL K.,** lawyer; b. Phila., June 3, 1950; s. Martin and Thelma Rosenberg; m. Sondra Kramer, Dec. 25, 1971; children: Sydney, Carrie, Jake. BA in Polit. Sci., Pa. State U., 1971; JD cum laude, Villanova U., 1974. Bar: Pa. 1974, U.S. Dist. Ct. (ea. dist.) Pa. 1976, U.S. Ct. Appeals (4th cir.) 1993, U.S. Ct. Appeals (3d cir.) 1994, U.S. Surpeme Ct. 1997. Asst. dist. atty. Phila. Dist. Attys. Office, 1974—80, asst. dist. atty. chief spl. investigations, 1980—82; assoc. Shein & Brookman, 1982—84; founding ptnr. Brookman, Rosenberg, Brown & Sandler, 1984—. Clin. prof. law Widener Law Sch., Del., 1985—91. Assoc. editor: Villanova U. Law Rev., 1973—74. Bd. dirs. Libr. Co. of Phila. Named Pa. Super Lawyer, Pa. Mag. Law and Politics, 2004, 2005, 2006. Mem.: ATLA, Phila. Trial Lawyers Assn. (bd. dirs. 2001—), Order of Coif. Office: Brookman Rosenberg Brown & Sandler 305 15th St 17th Fl Philadelphia PA 19102 Office Phone: 215-569-4000. Business E-Mail: hrosenberg@brbs.com.

**ROSENBERG, JEROME DAVID,** physicist; s. Hyman D. and Hilda (Cantor) R.; m. Shirley Sirota, 1947; children: Jonathan, Hindy. BS in Physics, CCNY, 1948; postgrad., Nat. Bur. Standards Grad. Sch., 1949-52, George Washington U., 1952, U. Md., 1951-53, Cath. U. Am., 1953-54. Engr. officer USCG Acad., 1942, APA-34, 1943-45; dir. microphonics Nat. Bur. Stds.; project mgr., mgr. Triga test nuclear reactor Harry Diamond Labs., Washington, 1952-62; ops. mgr. tech. utilization NASA, Washington, 1962-64, program and project mgr. Nat. Geodetic Satellite Program, Satellites Pageos, GEOS 1 and 2, 1964—72, dep. dir. comm. divsn., 1972-74, dir. tech. applications divsn., 1974-77, dir. office energy programs divsn. bus. mgmt., 1977-78; spl. assignment to solar applications & conservation, barriers and incentive dir. Dept. Energy, 1978-79; leader solar energy group Mitre Corp., McLean, Va., 1979-80; prin. cons. energy and environ. divsn. Booz, Allen & Hamilton, Washington, 1980-82; sr. staff officer Bd. Telecom. and Computer Applications, NRC-NAS, Washington, 1982-85. Exec. dir. NASA Alumni League, Washington, 1986—; mem. Outlook for Space Study Group, NASA planning group to develop U.S. space programs, 1975. Lt. (j.g.) USCG, 1943—45. Recipient NASA Exceptional Svc. medal, 1973. Mem.: Fed. Exec. Inst., Sigma Pi Sigma. Office: NASA Alumni League 750 1st St NE Washington DC 20002-4241 Office Phone: 202-336-6136. Personal E-mail: jerry@ssrinc.com.

**ROSENBERG, JEROME IRA,** lawyer; b. Passaic, N.J., June 9, 1931; s. Emanuel and Sylvia S. (Schwartz) R.; m. Dorothy Elaine Teninbaum, Aug. 21, 1955; children: Peter, Michael BA, NYU, 1953; LLB, Harvard U., 1956. Bar: N.Y. 1966, D.C. 1957, U.S. Supreme Ct. 1961. Tax law specialist IRS, Washington, 1960-63; ptnr. Hughes Hubbard & Reed LLP, N.Y.C., 1968—2000, counsel, 2000—. Lectr. NYU Tax Inst.; pres. Close Encounters with Music; trustee The Austen Riggs Hosp. Ctr. Contbr. articles to Jour. of

Taxation. Served as lt. USAF, 1957-60. Mem. Phi Beta Kappa. Office: Hughes Hubbard & Reed LLP One Battery Park Plz New York NY 10004-1466 Office Phone: 212-837-6788. E-mail: rosenber@hugheshubbard.com.

**ROSENBERG, JEROME LAIB,** chemist, educator; b. Harrisburg, Pa., June 20, 1921; s. Robert and Mary (Katzman) R.; m. Shoshana Gabriel, Sept. 15, 1946; children— Jonathan, Judith. AB, Columbia U., 1941; MA, Columbia U., 1944, PhD, 1948. Rsch. chemist S.A.M. Labs., 1944-46; Instr. chemistry Columbia U., 1944-48; rsch. assoc. (asst. prof.) inst. Radiobiology and Biophysics, U. Chgo., 1950-53; mem. faculty U. Pitts., 1953-91, chmn. dept. biophysics and microbiology, 1969-71, prof. biol. scis., 1976-91, dean faculty arts and scis., 1970-86, vice provost, 1978-89, chmn. biol. scis., 1989-90, interim chmn. communication, 1991, assoc. dean faculty arts and scis., 1991-92, rsch. integrity officer, 1992—, instr. Washington U., 1977—, dir. Jewish studies program, 1991-99. Author: Photosynthesis, 1965; editor, reviser: Outline Theory and Problems of College Chemistry (Schaum), 1949, 58, 66, 80, 90, 97; contbr. articles to profl. jours. NSF sr. fellow Technion Israel Inst. Tech., 1962-63, AEC fellow U. Chgo., 1948-50; recipient Pitts. award Am. Chem. Soc., 1987. Mem. AAUP (nat. coun. 1968-69, pres. Pa. div. 1968-69). Home: 1029 S Negley Ave Pittsburgh PA 15217-1045 Office Phone: 412-624-3007. Business E-Mail: jrosenb@pitt.edu.

**ROSENBERG, JERRY C.,** lab administrator, surgeon; s. Abraham and Harriet Francis Rosenberg; m. Corliss Ethel Bestland, July 3, 1955; children: David Rolf, Andrew Leon. BS, Wagner Coll., 1950; MD, Chgo. Med. Sch., 1954; PhD, U. Minn., 1963, MBA, Mich. State U., 1983. Intern U. Minn., 1954—55, resident surgery, 1956—61; fellow U. Vienna, 1955—56; lab. dir. Gift Life Mich., Ann Arbor, 1985—2005. Office: Gift Life Mich 2203 Platt Rd Ann Arbor MI 48104 Office Phone: 734-973-1294. Office Fax: 734-973-0332. Personal E-mail: jcrosenbergmd@comcast.net. Business E-Mail: jcrosenbergmd@giftoflifemichigan.org.

**ROSENBERG, JOEL BARRY,** government economist; b. Bronx, Aug. 14, 1942; s. Benjamin and Miriam Dorothy (Yellin) Rosenberg; m. Judith Lynne Jackler, Aug. 26, 1965; children: Jeffrey Alan, Marc David. BA, Queens Coll., 1964, MA, 1966; PhD, Brown U., 1972. Accredited valuation appraiser 2002. Cons. Commonwealth Svcs., Washington, 1970—71; asst. prof. econs. SUNY, Geneseo, 1971—75, Case Western Res. U., Cleve., 1975—76; mgr. industry economist IRS, Washington, 1976—; NDEA fellow Brown U., 1966—69. Contbr. articles to profl. jours. Mem.: Am. Statis. Assn., Nat. Assn. Bus. Economists, Am. Econ. Assn. Home: 16 Flameleaf Ct Gaithersburg MD 20878-5216 Office: IRS 500 N Capitol St NW Washington DC 20221-0003

**ROSENBERG, JOHN DAVID,** language educator, critic; b. NYC, Apr. 17, 1929; s. David and Dorothy Lilian (Shatz) R.; m. Barbara E. Hatch, 1952 (div. 1969); m. Maurine Ann Hellner, June 11, 1972; 1 child, Matthew John. BA, Columbia U., 1950, MA, 1951, PhD, 1958; BA, Clare Coll., Cambridge U., 1953, MA, 1958. Editor-in-chief Columbia Rev., 1949-50; lectr. English Columbia U. N.Y.C., 1953-54, asst. prof., 1962-65, assoc. prof., 1966-67, prof. English, 1967—, William Peterfield Trent prof., 1994—; instr. CCNY, 1954-62; chmn. Columbia Coll. humanities program, 1970-73, dir. grad. studies in English, 1986-89. Vis. prof. English Harvard U., 1968, U. B.C., 1970, Princeton U., 1978; vis. fellow Clare Hall Cambridge U., England, 1969; guest lectr. U.S. Mil. Acad., Cambridge U., Lancaster U. Author: The Darkening Glass: A Portrait of Ruskin's Genius, 1961, The Fall of Camelot: A Study of Tennyson's Idylls of the King, 1973, Carlyle and the Burden of History, 1985, Elegy for an Age: The Presence of the Past in Victorian Literature, 2005; editor: The Genius of John Ruskin, 1963, 2nd edit., 98, Mayhew, 1968, Swinburne: Selected Poetry and Prose, 1968, The Poems of Alfred, Lord Tennyson, 1975; contbr. essays and reviews on English lit. to N.Y. Times Book Rev., N.Y. Rev. Books, Harper's mag., Hudson Rev. and profl. jours. Recipient Clarke F. Ansley award Columbia U., 1960, Disting. Svc. award Columbian Coll. Core Curriculum, 1997; Coun. for Rsch. in Humanities grant-in-aid, 1965; Euretta J. Kellett fellow Cambridge U., 1951-53, Edward Coe fellow, 1956-57, Samuel S. Fels fellow, 1959-60, Am. Coun. Learned Soc. fellow, 1965-66, 70, Lawrence H. Chamberlain fellow, 1965-66, Guggenheim fellow, 1968-69, NEH fellow, 1982-83. Mem. MLA (life), Tennyson Soc., Ruskin Assn., Camp Rising Sun Alumni Assn., Columbia Coll. Alumni Assn. (dir. 1980-82, Alexander Hamilton medal 1994), Phi Beta Kappa. Office: Columbia U Dept English 1150 Amsterdam Ave New York NY 10027-7051 Office Phone: 212-854-6407. Business E-Mail: jdr6@columbia.edu.

**ROSENBERG, JONATHAN,** information technology executive; BA in econ. with honors, Claremont McKenna Coll.; MBA, U. Chgo. Former mgr. eWorld product line Apple Computer Inc.; former dir. product mktg. Knight-Ridder Info. Svcs., Palo Alto, Calif.; former sr. v.p. online products and svcs. Excite@Home, Redwood City, Calif.; founder @Home Product Group, Redwood City; v.p. product mgmt. Google Inc., Mountain View, Calif., 2002—. Office: Google Inc 1600 Amphitheatre Pky Mountain View CA 94043 Office Phone: 650-623-4000. Office Fax: 650-618-1499.*

**ROSENBERG, LAWRENCE,** lawyer; b. NYC; BBA with spl. honors & distinction, George Washington U., 1974, JD with honors, 1978; LLM Taxation, NYU Sch. Law, 1980. Bar: Pa. 1978, NY 1982, US Tax Ct. Law clk. to Judge Sheldon V. Ekman US Tax Ct., 1980—81, law clk. to Judge Theofore Tannenwald, 1981—82; ptnr. taxation Chadbourne & Parke LLP, NYC, mem. mgmt. com. Contbr. articles to profl. jour. Mem.: ABA (Taxation Sect.), NY State Bar Assn. (Tax Sect.). Office: Chadbourne & Parke LLLP 30 Rockefeller Plaza New York NY 10112 Office Phone: 212-408-5274. Office Fax: 212-541-5369. Business E-Mail: lrosenberg@chadbourne.com.

**ROSENBERG, LEE EVAN,** financial planner; b. Bklyn., Nov. 6, 1952; s. Daniel and Rita (Blanket) R.; m. Saralee Hymen, Aug. 27, 1977; children: Zachary Martin, Alexandra Lynn, Taryn Jessica. BA, Bklyn. Coll., 1974. Cert. fin. planner. Underwriter Fin. Life Ins. Co., N.Y.C., 1974-75, Mony, N.Y.C., 1975-80; pres. Lee Rosenberg Assoc., N.Y.C., 1980-83; co-founder, sr. ptnr. ARS Fin. Svcs. Inc., Valley Stream, NY, 1983—2003, Jericho, NY, 2003—. Co-host radio show Moneytalk WBAB, L.I., 1991; guest Nat. CNBC TV show Money Club, 1995, 96; cons. fin. sections New Choices Mag., 1995-2002; mem. adv. bd. Forum for Investor Advice, 2000-02. Author (with Saralee Rosenberg): Destination Fla.: Guide to a Successful Relocation, 1989, 50 Fabulous Places to Retire in Am., 1991, 50 Fabulous Places to Raise Your Family, 1993, Retirement Ready or Not! How to Get Financially Prepared in a Hurry, 1993; guest CNBC Power Lunch, 1997—2005, contbr. CNBC.com, 2000—06; contbr. chapters to books, articles to profl. jours. Named one of Best 200 Fin. Advisors in USA, Worth Mag., 1996, 97, 98. Mem. Internat. Assn. Fin. Planners, Internat. Assn. Registered Fin. Planners, Internat. Soc. Preretirement Planners, L.I. Inst. Cert. Fin. Planners (bd. dirs., pres. 1988-90), Nat. Speakers Assn. (bd. dirs. N.Y. chpt.). Home: 5 Cobblers Ln Dix Hills NY 11746-5001 also: 500 N Broadway Jericho NY 11753-2127 Office: Boca Corp Plaza 1801 Clint Moore Rd Ste 109 Boca Raton FL 33487 Office Phone: 561-932-5130. Business E-Mail: leerosb@yahoo.com.

**ROSENBERG, LEON JOSEPH,** marketing educator; b. Atlanta, Oct. 9, 1918; s. Harry Manville and Gertrude Dora (Hassenbusch) R.; m. Phylis Jane Israel, Feb. 6, 1943 (dec. Mar. 1976); children: Joanne Rosenberg Larson, Paul Harvey; m. Louise Nachman Mayer, Oct. 15, 1977. BS in Indsl. Mgmt. Ga. Inst. Tech., 1939; MS, Columbia U., 1940; PhD, NYU, 1967. Mem. staff Nat. Retail Mchts. Assn., N.Y.C., 1947-49; rsch. analyst Federated Dept. Stores, Inc., Cin., 1949-52; rsch. dir. Sanger Harris Dept. Store, Dallas, 1952-56, gen. supt., 1956-67; assoc. prof. Coll. Bus. Adminstrn., U. Ark, Fayetteville, 1967-74; prof. mktg. and transp. Sam M. Walton Coll. Bus. Adminstrn., U. Ark., 1975-89; dept. head mktg. and transp. U. Ark., 1986-88, prof. emeritus, 1989—; mktg. cons., sales analyst Lindsey & Assocs. Inc., Fayetteville, 1990—. Disting. vis. prof. Calif. State U., San Bernardino, 1990. Contbr. articles to profl. jours. Pres. Jewish Family Svc., Dallas, 1960-62, Temple Shalom, Fayetteville, 1992-96; mem. exec. com. Dallas Jewish Fedn., 1963-67; bd. dirs. New Orleans Jewish Children's Regional Svc., 1962-73,

75-2003, Jewish Fedn. Ark., 1992-96; pres. N.W. Ark. unit B'nai B'rith, 1992-2001; bd. dirs. Washington County (Ark.) chpt. Am. Cancer Soc., 1979-86, pres., 1982-83. Capt. USAAF, 1940-46. Mem. Am. Mktg. Assn., So. Mktg. Assn., Nat. Bd. Realtors, Ark. Bd. Realtors, Econs. and Bus. History Soc. (trustee 1986-89), Alpha Phi Omega (Svc. award 1971), Beta Gamma Sigma, Delta Nu Alpha. Home: 1923 E Joyce Blvd # 168 Fayetteville AR 72703 Office: Lindsey & Assocs Inc 3900 Front St Fayetteville AR 72703

**ROSENBERG, MARILYN ROSENTHAL,** artist, poet; b. Phila., Oct. 11, 1934; m. Robert Rosenberg, June 12, 1955; 2 children. B in Profl. Studies in Studio Arts, SUNY, Empire State Coll., 1978; MA in Liberal Studies, NYU, 1993. Represented in permanent collections Avant Writing Collection, The Ohio State U. Librs., Whitney Mus. Libr., N.Y.C., Tate Gallery Libr., London, Mus. Modern Art Libr., NYC, Bklyn. Mus. Lib., Bibliotheque Nat., Paris, Fogg Arts Lib., Harvard U., one-woman shows include Westchester CC, Valhalla, N.Y., 2002, exhibited in group shows at Fla. Atlantic U., Boca Raton, Fla., 2000, U. Ctrl. Ark., Conway, 2000, Ocean Grove Libr., Victoria, Australia, 2000, City Gallery, Szekesfehervar, Hungary, 2000, The Temple Judea, Elkins Park, Pa., 2001, Art Acad. Cin., 2002, Ohio State U. Librs., Columbus, 2002, Cuesta Coll. Art Gallery, San Luis Obispo, Calif., 2002, Pensacola (Fla.) Mus. Art, 2002, U. Indpls. (Ind.) Gallery, 2002, Lowenstein Gallery, Miami, Fla., 2003, Starr Gallery, Newton Ctr., Mass., 2003, Wexford (Ireland) Arts Centre, 2003, The Buddy Holly Ctr., Lubbock, Tex., 2003, Peck Arts Ctr. Gallery, Ctrl. Wyo. Coll., Riverton, 2003, Purdue U. Galleries, Lafayette, Ind., 2003, Ellipse Art Ctr., Arlington, Va., 2003, The Ctr. for Book Arts, NYC, 2003, 2005, Durango Art Ctr., Colo., 2004, Neopolis Gallery, Cleve., 2004, Ceres Gallery, N.Y.C., 2004, 2005, Westchester Gallery/Westchester Art Workshop, 2004, Futernic Gallery, Alper Jewish Cmty. Ctr., Miami, Fla., 2005, Art Ctr. Hasselt Belgium, 2005, Gallery Durban Segnini, Miami, Fla., 2005, Rutgers U., Camden, N.J., 2005, Gallery 308, Mpls., 2005, Pelham (N.Y.) Art Ctr., 2006, works in exhib. catalogs, reviews, ref. books, anthologies and websites. Home: 67 Lakeview Ave W Cortlandt Manor NY 10567-6415

**ROSENBERG, MARK FLETCHER,** lawyer; b. Perth Amboy, NJ, Dec. 3, 1954; s. Leonard and Rita Frances (Jaffe) R.; m. Sandra Rosenberg, Aug. 30, 1980; 1 child, Melissa. BA, Mich. State U., 1977; JD, George Washington U., 1980. Bar: NJ. Ptnr. litig. Sullivan & Cromwell, NYC, 1993—. Coord., Sullivan & Cromwell Environ. Group, NYC; dep. coord. Ins. Group. Editor: Attorney-Client Privileges Under Siege, 1989. Mem. ABA (chmn. toxic and hazardous substances and environ. law com. of tort and ins. practice sect., chmn. subcom. on revisions to CGL policy), NY State Bar Assn. (chmn. environ. law com. internat. law sect.). Avocations: theater, tennis, music. Office: Sullivan & Cromwell 125 Broad St Fl 28 New York NY 10004-2489 Office Phone: 212-558-4000. Office Fax: 212-558-3588. Business E-Mail: rosenbergm@sullcrom.com.

**ROSENBERG, MARK L.,** health facility administrator; b. Newark, July 30, 1945; m. Jill Alison Dimond; children: Julie, Ben. BA in Biology magna cum laude, Harvard Coll., 1967, MD cum laude, 1972, M of Pub. Policy, 1972. Diplomate Am. Bd. Internal Medicine, Am. Bd. Psychiatry and Neurology. Intern Mass. Gen. Hosp., Boston, 1972—73, resident in medicine, 1973—74; resident in preventive medicine Ctrs. for Disease Control, Atlanta, 1975—76; resident in psychiatry Beth Israel Hosp., Boston, 1980—83; clin. prof. dept. cmty. medicine and family practice Morehouse Sch. Medicine, Atlanta, 1984—93; clin. prof. psychiatry Emory U. Sch. Medicine, Atlanta, 1994—99; exec. dir. Task Force for Child Survival and Devel., 1999—; dir. sci. devel., dir. programs Ctr. for Child Well-being, 1999—. Dir. Nat. Ctr. for Injury Prevention and Control, Atlanta, 1994—99, acting assoc. dir. for pub. health practice, 1992—93; dir. divsn. injury control Ctr. for Environ. Health and Injury Control, 1989—92; spl. asst. for behavioral sci., office of dep. dir. CDC, Atlanta, 1989, advisor to dep. dir., 88, asst. dir. for sci. divsn. injury epidemiology and control, 1986—88, liaison officer office program planning and evaluation, 1979—80; assoc. dir. office extramural health programs Harvard Sch. Pub. Health, Boston, 1979—80; clin. fellow in psychiatry Harvard Med. Sch., Boston, 1980—83; vis. prof. dept. cmty. health Emory U. Sch. Medicine, Atlanta, 1984—91, clin. asst. prof. psychiatry, 1985—87, clin. assoc. prof., 1988—93; adj. prof. Emory U. Sch. Pub. Health, Atlanta, 1991—; clin. prof. dept. cmty. health and preventive medicine Morehouse Sch. Medicine, Atlanta, 1993—; staff physician Women's Med. Clinic, Atlanta, 1974—76, Harvard St. Neighborhood Health Ctr., Boston, 1976—77, Winchester (Mass.) Hosp., 1978—83; emergency rm. physician Burbank Hosp., Fitchburg, Mass., 1976—77, Harrington Hosp., Southbridge, Mass., 1976—77; vis. physician dept. psychiatry Grady Meml. Hosp., Atlanta, 1985—; lectr. and cons. in field. Author: Patients: The Experience of Illness, 1980, Violence in America: A Public Health Approach, 1990; mem. editl. bd. Violence and Victims, 1985—88, Violence, Aggression and Terrorism, 1986—; contbr. articles to profl. jours. Active Calif. Wellness Found., 1993—; bd. dirs. southeastern divsn., sci. adv. coun. Am. Suicide Found., 1990—. Recipient Coulter Lecture award, Am. congress Rehab. Medicine, 1991, William S. one award, Am. Trauma Soc., 1991, Outstanding Achievement award, 1994, World Health Day award, Am. Assn. for World Health, 1993, Disting. Svc. award, Ga. Assn. Family and Marital Therapists, 1994, Disting. Achievement award, Disability Wellness Assn., 1998, Outstanding Svc. medal, USPHS, 2000, Meritorious Svc. medal, 2000, Disting. Svc. medal, 2000; fellow, Mass. Gen. Hosp., 1977—78, Mead-Johnson, 1982; scholar, John Harvard, 1964. Mem.: Alpha Omega Alpha, Inst. of Medicine of NAS, Phi Beta Kappa. Avocation: photography. Home: 972 Oakdale Rd NE Atlanta GA 30307-1272 Office: 750 Commerce Dr Ste 400 Decatur GA 30030

**ROSENBERG, MARK LOUIS,** lawyer; b. Lexington, Ky., Sept. 21, 1947; s. Edward George and Shirley Lee (Berkin) R.; m. Betty Adler, May 16, 1982; stepchildren: Aaron, Sarah Clayton; children: Eli, Daniel. BA, U. Mich., 1969; JD, harvard U., 1973; LLM in Taxation, Georgetown U., 1985. Bar: D.C. 1973, Md. 1991, U.S. Dist. Ct. D.C. 1973, U.S. Ct. Appeals (D.C. cir.) 1973. Asst. to v.p. George Washington U., 1973-75; counsel U.S. Ho. of Reps., Washington, 1975-77; sr. atty. FTC, Washington, 1977-85; ptnr. Gordon, Feinblatt et al, Washington, 1989-91; prin. Law Offices of Mark L. Rosenberg, 1991—; of counsel The Jacobovitz Law Firm, 1994-97, Spirer & Goldberg, PC, Bethesda, Md. Mem. Fed. Bar Assn. (dep. sect. coord., Disting. Svc. award 1982, 83, 87). Democrat. Jewish. Home: 6101 Shady Oak Ln Bethesda MD 20817-6027 Office: Spirer & Goldberg PC 7101 Wisconsin Ave Ste 1201 Bethesda MD 20814 Office Phone: 301-913-0077. Personal E-mail: marklro@aol.com.

**ROSENBERG, MICHAEL,** lawyer; b. NYC, Oct. 13, 1937; s. Walter and Eva (Bernstein) Rosenberg; m. Jacqueline Raymonde Combe, Apr. 29, 1966; children: Andrew James, Suzanne Jennifer. AB in Econs. with honors, Ind. U., 1959; LLB, Columbia U., 1962. Bar: NY 1963, US Ct Appeals (2d cir) 1975, US Dist Ct (ea dist so div) Mich 1989. From dep. asst. atty. gen. to asst. atty. gen. N.Y. State Dept. Law, N.Y.C., 1963-66; assoc. Hellerstein, Rosier & Rembar, N.Y.C., 1966-73; assoc. gen. counsel Gen. Instrument Corp., N.Y.C., 1973-78; from assoc. gen. counsel to dep. gen. counsel U.S. Filter Corp., N.Y.C., 1978-82; v.p., gen. counsel, sec. Alfa-Laval Inc., Ft. Lee, NJ, 1982-88; counsel Becker Ross Stone De Stefano & Klein, N.Y.C., 1988-89; ptnr. Rosenberg & Rich, White Plains, NY, 1989-95, Quinn, Marantis & Rosenberg, LLP, White Plains, NY, 1995-97, Marantis, Rosenberg & van Nes, LLP, 1997-2001; atty. Law Offices of Michael Rosenberg, Armonk, 2001—. Mem Zoning Bd. Appeals Town of North Castle, NY, 1995—2006. Mem.: ABA, Westchester County Bar Assn., NY State Bar Assn. Office: Law Offices of Michael Rosenberg 20 Maryland Ave Armonk NY 10504

**ROSENBERG, NORMAN JACK,** agricultural meteorologist, educator; b. Bklyn., Feb. 22, 1930; s. Jacob and Rae (Dombrowitz) R.; m. Sarah Zacher, Dec. 30, 1950; children: Daniel Jonathon, Alyssa Yael. BS, Mich. State U., 1951; MS, Okla. State U., 1958; PhD, Rutgers U., 1961. Soil scientist Israel Soil Conservation Service, Haifa, 1953-55, Israel Water Authority, Haifa, 1955-57; asst. prof. agrl. meteorology U. Nebr., Lincoln, 1961-64, assoc. prof., 1964-67, prof. agrl. meteorology, 1967—, prof. agrl. engring., 1975—,

prof. agronomy, 1976—, George Holmes prof. agrl. meteorology, 1981-87, prof. emeritus, 1987—, leader sect. agrl. meteorology, 1975-79, acting asst. vice chancellor for research, 1983-85; sr. fellow, dir. climate resources program Resources for the Future, Washington, 1987-92; chief scientist integrated earth studies energy sci. divsn. Battelle Pacific N.W. Nat. Lab., Washington, 1992—2003, lab. fellow emeritus, 2003—; scientist Joint Global Change Rsch. Inst., Pacific N.W. Nat. Lab., U. Md. 2001—; affiliate mem. Washington Adv. Group, 2003—. Cons. Dept. State AID, NOAA Oak Ridge Assoc. Univs., 1986—87; cons. Elec. Power Rsch. Inst., 1989—92, Sandia Nat. Labs., 1990; mem. numerous ad hoc coms. and mem. standing com. on atmsopheric sci. NAS/NRC, 1975—78, mem. bd. atmospheric sci. and climate, 1982—85; mem. U.S. com. Internat. Geosphere-Biosphere Program, 1984—86; mem. panel on policy implications of climate change, 1990—91; mem. bd. coun. Agrl. Sci. and Tech.; vis. prof. agrl. meteorology Israel Inst. Tech., Haifa, 1968; trustee Nat. Inst. Global Environ. Change, 1992, vice-chmn., 1992—95, chmn., 1996—2000; adj. prof. dept. geography U. Md., College Park, adj. prof. Sch. Natural Resources Sci., 2003; bd. dirs. Ctr. for Rsch. on the Changing Earth Sys., Columbia, Md., 2002. Author: Microclimate: The Biological Environment, 1974, 2d edit., 1983, Chinese transl., 1983, Malay transl., 1987; editor: North American Droughts, 1978, Drought in the Great Plains: Research on Impacts and Strategies, 1980, Greenhouse Warming: Abatement and Adaptation, 1989, Toward an Integrated Impact Assessment of Climate Change: The MINK Study, 1993, Carbon Sequestration in Soils: New Science, Monitoring and Beyond, 1999; editor: (with V.C. Cole and K. Paustian) Mitigation of Greenhouse Gas Emissions by the Agricultural Sector, Spl. issue of Climate Change, 1998; editor: (with R.C. Izaurralde) Storing Carbon in Agricultural Soils: A multipurpose environmental strategy, Spl. issue of Climatic Change, 2001; tech. editor: Agronomy Jour., 1974—79, cons. editor: Agrl. and Forest Meteorology, Climatic Change; contbr. articles to profl. jours.; editor (with J.A. Edmonds): Climate Change Impacts for the Conterminous USA: An Integrated Assessment, 2005. Mem. Intergovernmental Panel on Climate Change, 1993—. Recipient Centennial medal Nat. Weather Svc., 1970; sr. fellow in sci., NATO, 1968, rsch. fellow U. Nebr., 1968, Lady Davis fellow Hebrew U., Jerusalem, 1977, nat. resources fellow Resources for Future, 1986; grantee State of Nebr., 1970-73, NSF, 1971-87, 96, U.S. Dept. Commerce, 1972-74, 80-82, 83-85, 88-89, NASA, 1972-73, 85-86, U.S. Dept. Interior, 1974-75, 77-79, 88—, USDA, 1979-82, 88-89, U. Nebr. Found., 1982, Nat. Ctr. Atmospheric Rsch., 1984-85, U.S. Dept. Energy, 1989-92, G. Gunnar Vetleson Found., 1987-92, UN Environ. Program, 1989, EPA, 1988-89, 98, NASA, 1995-97, 98, NOAA, 1996. Fellow AAAS (com. climate 1984-89, com. global change 1992-96, adv. panel Earth Explorer ency. 1992-95), Am. Soc. Agronomy, Am. Meteorol. Soc. (Outstanding Achievement in Bioclimatology award 1978, councillor 1981-84), Am. Water Resources Assn. (Boggess award, 2004); mem. Am. Assn. State Climatologists (Nebr. rep. 1979-81), Arid Zone Soc. India, Sigma Xi, Alpha Eta, Gamma Sigma Rho. Clubs: Cosmos (Washington). Jewish. Office: Joint Global Change Rsch Inst 8400 Baltimore Ave College Park MD 20740-2496 Office Phone: 301-314-6753. E-mail: nj.rosenberg@pnl.gov.

**ROSENBERG, PAMELA,** opera director, conductor; b. LA, 1945; m. Wolf Rosenberg (dec. 1996); 2 children. Diploma, London Opera Ctr.; B, U. Calif. at Berkely, 1966; M in Russian hist., Ohio State U. Various positions Frankfurt Opera, 1974—87; dir. of ops. Deutscher Schauspielhaus, Hamburg, Germany, 1987—88; mgr., artistic affairs Netherlands Opera, 1988—90; co-gen. dir. Stuggart Opera, 1990—2000; gen. dir. San Francisco Opera, 2001—06, exec. adv., 2006. Office: San Francisco Opera 301 VanNess Ave San Francisco CA 94102*

**ROSENBERG, PETER N.,** lawyer; b. Aug. 29, 1958; BA, Dartmouth Coll., 1980; JD, Boston Univ., 1984. Bar: Mass. 1985. Assoc. to ptnr. Ropes & Gray, Boston, 1984—, head employee benefits practice group. Editor: Boston Univ. Law Rev. Office: Ropes & Gray 1 International Pl Boston MA 02110-2624 Office Phone: 617-951-7273. Office Fax: 617-951-7050. Business E-Mail: peter.rosenberg@ropesgray.com.

**ROSENBERG, RAYMOND DAVID,** special education educator, consultant; b. Jersey City, Apr. 25, 1951; s. Fabulous Sam and Arlene (White) R.; m. JoAnn Gabriella Simchera, June 10, 1984; 1 child, Anna Teresa. BA, Boston U., 1974; MEd in Spl. Edn., William Paterson Coll., 1978, MEd in Ednl. Adminstrn. and Supervision, 1994. Cert. tchr., N.J.; profl. recognized spl. educator in ednl. diagnosis, PRSE, 2005. Tchr. reading Passaic County Tech. Vocat. High Sch., Wayne, NJ, 1980-82; specialist learning disabilities North Jersey Devel. Ctr., Totowa, 1983-84; ednl. specialist Div. Devel. Disabilities, Totowa, NJ, 1984-85, North Jersey Devel. Ctr., Totowa, NJ, 1986—93; learning disabilities tchr., cons. Office of Edn., N.J. 1993-96; learning cons. child study team North Bergen (N.J.) H.S., 1996-98; supr. child study team, tchr.-cons. learning disabilities Morris Plains Elem. Sch. Dist., 2005—. Learning disabilities tchr., cons., 1997—2002; pres. Ednl. Assessment Svcs., Inc.; mem. child study team West N.Y. Early Childhood Sch., 2002—03. With ABA discrete trial learning with PDD autistic students, 2002—; staff Office of the Child Study Team, Garfield, NJ, 2003—03. Mem. Nat. Eagle Scout Assn., Pi Lambda Theta (Beta Chi chpt.). Episcopal. Lodge: Order of Arrow. Office Phone:   973-538-1650   x   134.   Business   E-Mail: raymond.rosenberg@mps.morris.k12.nj.us. E-mail: advocate@nj.rr.com.

**ROSENBERG, RICHARD F.,** physician, radiologist; b. NYC, June 13, 1942; s. Henry J. and Sylvia (Harris) R.; m. Judith Wolf, May 5, 1985; 1 child, Glen. BA, Colgate U., 1964; MD, N.Y. Med. Coll., 1968. Diplomate Am. Bd. Radiology. Intern Met. Hosp., N.Y.C., 1968-69; resident Montefiore Hosp. and Med. Ctr., Bronx, NY, 1969-70, 72-74, chief resident, 1974; radiologist Lipsay & Rosenberg, Great Neck, NY, 1974-78; dir. gastrointestinal radiology North Shore U. Hosp., Manhasset, NY, 1978-82; radiologist, owner Great Neck Radiologists, 1982—; Mem. adv. bd. Bank of Great Neck, 1990-94. Contbr. articles to profl. jours. Lt. comdr. USN, 1970-72. Fellow Am. Coll. Gastroenterology; mem. Am. Coll. Radiology, Alpha Omega Alpha. Republican. Office: Great Neck Radiologists 935 Northern Blvd Great Neck NY 11021-5309 Office Phone: 516-829-4414.

**ROSENBERG, ROBERT BRINKMANN,** information technology executive; b. Chgo., Mar. 19, 1937; s. Sidney and Gertrude (Brinkmann) Rosenberg; m. Patricia Margaret Kane, Aug. 1, 1959 (dec. Feb. 1988); children: John Richard, Debra Ann; m. Maryann Bartoli Manrot, June 25, 1989. BSChemE with distinction, Ill. Inst. Tech., 1958, MS in Gas Tech, 1961, PhD in Gas Tech, 1964. Registered profl. engr., Ill. Adj. asst. prof. Ill. Inst. Tech., 1965-69; mem. staff Inst. Gas Tech., Chgo., 1962-77, v.p. engring. rsch., 1973-77; v.p. R & D Gas Rsch. Inst., Chgo., 1977-78, exec. v.p., sr. v.p., 1978-84, v.p., 1984-96; pres. RBR Vision, Burr Ridge, Ill., 1996—; bd. dirs. IEA Internat. Ctr. Gas Tech. Info. Tech. program dir. World Energy Congress, 1996—98. Pres. Triangle Frat. Edn. Found., 1974—96, bd. dirs., 1996—2001, dir. emeritus; bd. dirs. Hinsdale Arts Coun., 1977—85, dir. emeritus, 1985—95; mem. adv. coun. U. Tex. Coll. Natural Scis. Found., 1990—95; mem. giving com. Morton Arboretum, 2004—; mem. Hinsdale (Ill.) Home Rule Ad Hoc Com., 1975—77; mem. vis. com. dept. chemistry U. Tex.; bd. advisors Chgo. (Ill.) 502, 2004—; pres. Lake Ridge Club Homeowners Assn., 2001—. Recipient Gas Industry Rsch. award, 1985, Energy Exec. of the Yr. award, 1987, Profl. Achievement award, Ill. Inst. Tech. Alumni Assn., 1991. Mem.: AIChE, Triangle (Svc. Key and Outstanding Alumnus award 1987), Air Pollution Control Assn. (past sect. com. residential pollution sources), Gas Appliance Engrs. Soc. (past trustee), Internat. Gas Union, Atlantic Gas Rsch. Exch., Combustion Inst. (past treas. bd. dirs. ctrl. states sect.), Inst. Gas Engrs., Am. Gas Assn. (oper. sect. award of merit 1989). Achievements include patents for 13 patents in field. Office: Lake Ridge Club Dr Burr Ridge IL 60527-7937 Office: RBR @ Vision 28 Lake Ridge Club Dr Burr Ridge IL 60527-7937 Home Phone: 630-654-3213. Personal E-Mail: RBR3@comcast.net.

**ROSENBERG, ROBERT CHARLES,** housing corporation executive; b. Bronx, N.Y., Oct. 21, 1934; s. Bernard L. and Flora (Popiel) R.; m. Diane Stricof, Jan. 29, 1962 (dec.); children: Andrew, Scott; m. Frances Kaufman,

Sept. 11, 1976; stepchildren: Michael Kaufman, Benjamin Kaufman. BS, NYU, 1955, JD (hon.), 1995; LLB, Columbia U., 1958. Bar: N.Y. 1959. Adminstrv. asst. N.Y. State Dept. Law, N.Y.C., 1957-58; assoc. firm Barron Rice & Rochmore, N.Y.C., 1959-62; Carro Spanbock & Londin, N.Y.C., 1962-68; 1st dep. commr. for devel. dept. N.Y.C. Housing and Devel. Adminstrn., 1968-73; 1st sr. v.p., dir. Starrett Corp., N.Y.c., 1973-97; gen. mgr. Starrett City; pres., chmn. bd. Grenadier Realty Corp., 1976-97; pres. Rosenberg Housing Group, 1997—. Lectr. Practicing Law Inst., Real Estate Bd. N.Y.C., Harvard U. Kennedy Sch. of Govt., Beijing Inst. of Design, U. Nancy (France), Columbia U., NYU, others; fed. receiver Chester (Pa.) Housing Authority, 1994—; adj. prof. dept. urban affairs Hunter Coll., N.Y.C. 1998—. Author N.Y. acts for residential constrn., rent. Candidate for N.Y. State Assembly, 1958, 65; sec. N.Y. State Assn. Young Rep. Clubs, 1959-61; bd. dirs., chmn. emeritus Bklyn. Philharm.; bd. dirs. Bklyn. Acad. Music, 1978-99; v.p. Citizens Housing and Planning Coun.; dir. Nat. Housing Conf. Served with USAF, 1958. Mem. ABA, N.Y. State Bar Assn., N.Y. County Lawyers Assn., Nat. Assn. Housing and Renewal Ofcls., Urban Land Inst., N.Y.C. Assn. Builders and Owners (v.p.). Home: 201 E 79th St New York NY 10021-0830 Office: 419 Park Ave S New York NY 10016-8410 E-mail: bob@rhgcommunities.com.

**ROSENBERG, ROBERT MICHAEL,** retired restaurant franchise company executive; b. Boston, Mar. 4, 1938; s. William and Bertha (Greenberg) R.; children: James Lee, John Matthew, Jennifer Beth. BS in Hotel and Restaurant Adminstrn., Cornell U., 1959; MBA, Harvard U., 1963; DBA (hon.), Nathaniel Hawthorne Coll., Antrim, N.H., 1980; LLD (hon.), N.H. Coll., 1982; D in Food Svc. Mgmt. (hon.), Johnson and Wales U., 1990. Pres. Dunkin' Donuts Inc., Randolph, Mass., from 1963; now chmn.; CEO Allied Domecq Retailing, 1993—99. Bd. dirs. Sonic Industries, Buffets, Inc., Domino's Pizza, 1998-. Co-author: Profits from Franchising, 1969. Bd. dirs., trustee Dana Farber Cancer Found.; mem. bd. overseers Mus. Fine Arts. Boston; past dir. Am. Bus. Dir. Recipient Outstanding Man of Yr. award Jr. C. of Co., Boston, 1968, Bus. award Bryant and Stratton Coll., Boston, 1968, award of excellence Am. Acad. Achievement, 1968, Leadership award Restaurant Bus. Mag., 1987, Gold Plate Winner as Foodsvc. Op. of Yr. 1983 Internat. Food Svc. Mfrs. Assn. Mem. Nat. Restaurant Assn. (bd. dirs., Silver Plate award 1984, 86, 87), Internat. Franchise Assn. (past pres., bd. dirs.), Am. Bus. Conf., Harvard Bus. Sch. Assn.*

**ROSENBERG, ROGER NEWMAN,** neurologist, educator, department chair; b. Milw., Mar. 3, 1939; s. Sol J. and Cora D. (Newman) R.; m. Adrienne Turick, June 24, 1962; children— Jennifer, Lara Student, Tufts U., 1957-60; BS, Northwestern U., 1961, MD with distinction, 1964. Diplomate Am. Bd. Psychiatry and Neurology. Intern Harvard Med. Service, Beth Israel Hosp., Boston, 1964-65; resident in neurology Neurol. Inst., Columbia U., N.Y.C., 1965-67, instr. neurology, 1967-68; research assoc. Lab. of Biochem. Genetics, NIH, Bethesda, Md., 1968-70; clin. instr. Howard U. Med. Sch., Washington, 1969-70; asst. prof. neuroscis. Sch. Medicine, U. Calif.-San Diego, 1970-71; assoc. prof. neuroscis. and pediatrics, attending neurologist Univ. Hosp., U. Calif.-La Jolla, 1971-74; prof., chmn. dept. neurology U. Tex. Southwestern Med. Ctr., Dallas, 1973-91, prof. physiology, 1976—; Zale Disting. chair, prof. neurology, 1990—, dir. Alzheimer's Disease Rsch. Ctr., 1989—. Attending neurologist Parkland Meml. Hosp. and Children's Med. Ctr., Dallas, 1974—, Zale Lipshy Univ. Hosp., 1990—; mem. staff Presbyn. Hosp., Dallas, 1974—, St. Paul's Hosp., Dallas, 1974—; cons. staff VA Hosp., Dallas, 1971—; mem. nat. med. adv. bd. Nat. Ataxia Found., Mpls., 1971—, Myasthenia Gravis Found., 1973; chmn. med. adv. bd. dir. med. sci. research Internat. Joseph Diseases Found., Livermore, Calif., 1977—; lectr. Japanese Soc. Neurology, 1987, 94, Chinese Neurol. Soc., 1987, Spanish Neurol. Soc., 1992; chmn. bd. sci. councilors NINDS/NIH, 1984-86; pres. (hon.), Intl. Neurosci. Soc. of Neurology Charcot Centenary Symposium, 1993. Editor Jour. Neurogenetics; mem. editl. bd. Neurology, 1977-82, 91-97, Trends in Neurosci., 1980-86, Current Opinion in Neurology & Neurosurgery, 1990—, Jour. of AMA, 1997—; chief editor Archives of Neurology, 1997—; contbr. articles to med. jours. Bd. dirs. Winston Sch., Dallas, 1974-80; trustee World Fedn. Neurology. 2005. 1st Woody Guthrie scholar, 1971; USPHS grantee; recipient Disting. Alumnus award Neurol. Inst., N.Y., 1994, Nancy R. McCune Alzheimer's Rsch. award Alzheimer's Ass., 2005, Lifetime Achievement award Tex. Neurol. Soc., 2005. Fellow AAAS; mem. Am. Acad. Neurology (chmn. sci. program com. nat. meetings 1979-84, elected councillor exec. bd. 1984-89, pres. 1991-93), Am. Neurochem. Soc., Tissue Culture Soc., Soc. Neurosci., Am. Fedn. Clin. Rsch., Soc. Pediat. Rsch., Internat. Child Neurology Assn., Am. Neurol. Assn. (1st v.p. 1987), Ctrl. Soc. Neurol. Rsch., Can. Congress Neurol. Scis. (hon.), Spanish Neurol. Soc. (hon. 1994), Sigma Xi, Alpha Omega Alpha (Merit award Northwestern U. Alumni Assn. 1986). Home: 4425 Wildwood Rd Dallas TX 75209-2801 Office: U Tex Southwestern Med Ctr Dallas TX 75235 Business E-Mail: rogerrosenberg@utsouthwestern.edu.

**ROSENBERG, RUDY,** chemical company executive; b. Feb. 26, 1930; came to U.S., 1949, naturalized, 1954; s. Hilaire and Frieda Rosenberg; m. Rose H. Wauters, Nov. 7, 1953; 1 child, Rudy. Student in classical studies, Atheneum Leon Lepage, Brussels, 1946. Buyer Lever Bros., Brussels, 1946-49; head biochem. divsn. Mann Rsch. Labs., N.Y.C., 1954-61, Gallard-Schlesinger, Carle Place, NY, 1961-75; pres. Accurate Chem. & Sci. Corp., Westbury, NY, 1975—. Prin., v.p. Leeches U.S.A. Ltd. Served with U.S. Army, 1951-53. Mem. Reticuloendothelial Soc. Internat. Clubs: Antique Automobile, Rolls Royce, Puppetry Guild Greater N.Y. Democrat.

**ROSENBERG, SAMUEL NATHAN,** French and Italian language educator; b. N.Y.C., Jan. 19, 1936; s. Israel and Etta (Friedland) R. AB, Columbia U., 1957; PhD, Johns Hopkins U., 1965. Instr. Columbia U., N.Y.C., 1960-61; lectr. Ind. U., Bloomington Ind 1962-65, asst. prof., 1965-69, assoc. prof., 1969-81, prof. dept. French and Italian, 1981-99, prof. emeritus, 2000—. Chmn. dept. French and Italian Ind. U., Bloomington, 1977—84; editor ENCOMIA jour. of Internat. Courtly Lit. Soc., 2005—. Author: Modern French CE, 1970, (with others) Harper's Grammar of French, 1983, (with W. Apel) French Secular Compositions of the 14th Century, 3 vols., 1970-72, (with H. Tischler) Chanter m'estuet: Songs of the Trouveres, 1981; translator: (with S. Danon) Ami and Amile, 1981, rev. edit., 1996, Lyrics and Melodies of Gace Brulé, 1985, (with H. Tischler) The Monophonic Songs in the Roman de Fauvel, 1991, Lancelor-Grail Cycle, vol. 2, 1993, Chansons des trouvères, 1995, Songs of the Troubadours and Trouvères, 1997; (with others) Early French Tristan Poems, 2 vols., 1998, (with C. Callahan) Les Chansons de Colin Muset, 2005, (with E. Doss-Quinby) The Old French Ballette, 2006. Pres. Mid-Am. Festival of the Arts, Inc., Bloomington, Ind., 1984-85. Woodrow Wilson Found. fellow, 1959-60; Fulbright fellow, 1960-61; Lilly Faculty fellow, 1986-87. Mem MLA, Am. Assn. Tchrs. French; mem. Medieval Acad. Am., Internat. Courtly Lit. Soc., Am. Literary Translators Assn. (bd. dirs. 2002—), Romance Philology Adv. Bd., Phi Beta Kappa (editor, Encomia, 2005-). Home: PO Box 1164 Bloomington IN 47402-1164 Business E-Mail: srosenbe@indiana.edu.

**ROSENBERG, SARAH ZACHER,** retired cultural organization administrator; b. Kelem, Lithuania, Jan. 10, 1931; came to U.S., 1938; d. David Meir Zacher and Rachel Korbman; m. Norman J. Rosenberg, Dec. 30, 1950; children: Daniel, Alyssa. BA in History, U. Nebr., 1970, MA in Am. History, 1973. Rsch. historian U. Mid-Am., Lincoln, Nebr., 1974-78, program developer dept. humanities, 1978-79, asst. dir. div. acad. planning, 1980-81, dir. program devel., 1981-82; exec. dir. Nebr. Humanities Coun., Lincoln, 1982-87, Nebr. Found. for Humanities, Lincoln, 1984-87, Am. Inst. for Conservation Hist. and Artistic Works, Washington, 1987-97, exec. dir. found., 1991-97; program officer, spl. cons. mus. div. NEH, Washington, 1987, external reviewer, 1981, 89; pvt. practice Potomac, Md., 1997—2004; ret., 2004. Lay participant long-range planning conf. Nebr. Bar Assn., Hastings, 1986. Co-editor: The Great Plains Experience: Readings in the History of a Region, 1978; contbr. articles to profl. jours. Action mem. Hadassah, Lincoln, 1961—87, Tifereth Israel Synagogue, Lincoln, 1961—87, Beth El Congregation, Besthesda, Md., 1988—2001, Kol Shalom Congregation, 2001—; bd. dirs. Sta. KUCV, affiliate Nat. Pub. Radio, Lincoln,

1986—87, Lincoln Cmty. Playhouse, Lincoln, 1986—87. NEH grantee, 1981, 86, merit awards, 1983, 87; Humanities Resource Ctr. grantee, Peter Kiewit Found., 1984. Mem. Am. Hist. Assn., Western Hist. Assn., Alpha Theta. Democrat. Home: 8102 Appalachian Ter Potomac MD 20854-4050 Personal E-mail: srosenb435@aol.com.

**ROSENBERG, SAUL ALLEN**, oncologist, educator; b. Cleve., Aug. 2, 1927; BS, Western Res. U., 1948, MD, 1953. Diplomate Am. Bd. Internal Medicine, Am. Bd. Oncology. Intern Univ. Hosp., Cleve., 1953—54; resident in internal medicine Peter Bent Brigham Hosp., Boston, 1954—61; research asst. toxicology AEC Med. Research Project, Western Res. U. 1948—53; asst. prof. medicine and radiology Stanford (Calif.) U., 1961—65, assoc. prof., 1965—79, chief divsn. oncology 1965—95, prof., 1970—95; prof. emeritus, 1995—; Am. Cancer Soc. prof. Stanford (Calif.) U., 1983—89, assoc. dean, 1989—92. Chmn. bd. No. Calif. Cancer Program, 1974—80. Contbr. articles to profl. jours. Served to lt. M.C. USNR, 1954—56. Master: ACP; fellow: Am. Coll. Radiology (hon.); mem.: Western Assn. Physicians, Western Soc. Clin. Rsch., Radiation Rsch. Soc., Calif. Acad. Medicine, Assn. Am. Physicians, Am. Soc. Clin. Oncology (pres. 1982—83), Inst. Medicine NAS, Am. Assn. Cancer Rsch., Am. Soc. Therapeutic Radiotherapy Oncology (hon.). Office: Stanford U Sch Medicine Div Oncology 269 Campus Dr Stanford CA 94305

**ROSENBERG, SEYMOUR**, psychologist, educator; b. Newark, Sept. 7, 1926; s. Morris and Celia (Weiss) R.; children: Harold Stanley, Michael Seth. BS, The Citadel, 1948; MA, Ind. U., 1951, PhD, 1952. Rsch. psychologist USAF, San Antonio, 1952-58, U. Kans., Lawrence, 1958-59, Bell Tel. Labs., Murray Hill, NJ, 1959-65; vis. prof. psychology Columbia U., NYC, 1965-66; prof. psychology Rutgers U., New Brunswick, NJ, 1966—2000, chmn. dept. psychology, 1981-83, 94-95, prof. emeritus psychology, 2001—. Adj. prof. Rutgers U. Med. Sch., 1974—2000; vis. scholar U. Leuven, Belgium, 1983, Belgium, 92, Univ. de Provence, France, 1990; panel mem. NSF, 1970—72. Cons. editor Jours. Personality Social Psychology, 1968-69; assoc. editor, 1970-73; contbr. articles to profl. jours. With USN, 1945—46. Grantee, NSF, 1965—90, NIMH, 1966—68; Rsch. scientist grantee, 1968—73, Social Sci. Rsch. Coun. fellow, 1973—74. Fellow APA; mem. Soc. Exptl. Social Psychology, Psychometric Soc., Classification Soc., NY Acad. Sci., Ea. Psychol. Assn. Home: 689 Canal Rd Somerset NJ 08873-7327 Office: Rutgers U Dept Psychology ED Livingston Campus New Brunswick NJ 08903 Business E-Mail: srpsych@rci.rutgers.edu.

**ROSENBERG, SHELI Z.**, investment company executive; Degree, Tufts U., Northwestern U. Atty. Cotton, Watt, Jones & King, 1966—70; mng. ptnr. Schiff Hardin & Waite, 1970—80; from gen. coun. to vice-chmn. Equity Group Investments, LLC, Chgo., 1980—2000, vice-chmn., 2000—. Bd. dirs. CVS Corp., Capital Trust, Cendant Corp., Manufactured Home Communities, Inc., Equity Residential Properties Trust, Equity Office Properties Trust, Ventas, Inc.; adv. bd. J.L. Kellogg Grad. Sch. Bus. N.W. Univ. Trustee Rush Presbyn. St. Luke's Med. Ctr., exec. com.; co-founder, pres. Ctr. for Exec. Women, J.L. Kellogg Grad. Sch. Bus., 2001—. Office: Equity Group Investments LLC 737 North Michigan Ave Ste 1405 Chicago IL 60611 E-mail: szr312@aol.com.

**ROSENBERG, SHELI ZYSMAN**, lawyer, finance company executive; b. N.Y.C., Feb. 2, 1942; d. Stephen B. and Charlotte (Laufer) Zysman; m. Burton X. Rosenberg, Aug. 30, 1964; children: Leonard, Marcy. BA, Tufts U., 1963; JD, Northwestern U., 1966. Bar: Ill. 1966. Ptnr. Schiff, Hardin & Waite, Chgo., 1973-80; exec. v.p., gen. counsel Equity Fin. Mgmt., Chgo., 1980-90, Equity Group Investments, Inc., Chgo., 1988-94, pres., CEO, 1994—, Equity Fin. and Mgmt. Co., Chgo., 1994—; prin. Rosenberg & Liebentritt, P.C., Chgo., 1995—. Bd. dirs. Gt. Am. Mgmt. & Investment, Chgo., 1994—; v.p. gen. counsel, 1985-90, sec., 1983-90; bd. dirs. CVS Corp. Ill.; trustee Equity Residential Properties Trust, Manufactured Home Cmtys., Inc.; mem. bd. trust Equity Office Properties. Bd. dirs., pres. Chgo. Network.

**ROSENBERG, SHIRLEY SIROTA**, publications executive; b. Bklyn. s. Charles and Donia (Rudoy) Sirota; m. Jerome D. Rosenberg; children: Jonathan, Hindy. BA, Bklyn. Coll. Mng. editor Bklyn. (N.Y.) Jewish Examiner, 1946—48, Washington (D.C.) Jewish Ledger, 1953—55; freelance writer, 1968—; contract writer-editor Dept. HEW, Washington, 1968-72; writer, editor Smithsonian Instn., Washington, 1972-77; sr. instr. George Washington U., 1979—99; pres. SSR, Inc., Washington, 1977—. Washington corr. Parent's mag.; cons. NSF, Nat. Task Force on Minorities, Women and the Handicapped in Sci. and Engring., Sci. Comm. Office R&D Office, EPA, Joseph P. Kennedy Inst., bd. dirs. Office of Commn., U.S. Holocaust Meml. Coun., Humanities mag., NEH, George Washington U. Pubs. Specialist Program, ARC Blood Program. Author: The First Oil Rush, 1967, How Children Grow, 1971, Code of Ethics and Professional Standards for Print Media Professionals, 1981, 92, A National Conversation on American Pluralism and Identity, 1995, Living is a Lifelong Process, 1995, Staying Connected: A Guide for Parents on Raising a Teenage Daughter, 2000, Mud, Muscles and Miracles, 1990; co-author: A Portrait of Leadership, A Fighter for Health: The Honorable Paul Rogers, 2005; editor-author: First Special Report on Alcohol and Alcohol Abuse, 1972, Forging Partnerships for Africa's Future, Facility Study, Bureau of Engraving and Printing, The Quest for the Therapeutic Institution, The Search for the Therapeutic Institution, Gender-Based Violence: Emerging Issues in Programs Serving Displaced Persons; contbr. articles to trade and profl. jours.; editor, coord. papers UN, World Bank, U.S. Govt Recipient numerous awards. Office Phone: 202-543-1800. E-mail: ssr@ssrinc.com.

**ROSENBERG, STANLEY DAVID**, psychologist, educator; b. NYC, Mar. 30, 1944; s. Milton I. and Miriam Rosenberg; m. Harriet Jane Rosenthal, June 5, 1966; children: Karen Beth Marks, Eric William. BS, cornell U., 1965; PhD, Yale U., 1968. Lic. psychologist NH, Vt. Assoc. prof. Dartmouth Med. Sch., Hanover, NH, 1975—81, prof. psychiatry, 1981—. Cons. in field. Author: The Cold Fire, 1976, Men at Midlife, 1981, The Mid-Life Transition; contbr. articles to profl. jours., chapters to books. Recipient Margaret Riggs award for Disting. Contbr., NH. Psychol. Orgn., 1992; grantee, Ittleson and van Amerigen Founds., 1972—74, 1985—88, NIH, 1983—88, Mellon Found., 1984, 1986—89, Rockefeller Ctr., 1989—90, NIMH, 1990—, UCLA, 1999—2000, Schering-Plough, 2001—04. Fellow: Soc. for Personality Assessment; mem.: Phi Kappa Phi. Home: 139 River Rd Lyme NH 03768 Office: DMS Dept Psychiatry 1 Medical Center Dr Lebanon NH 03756 Office Phone: 603-653-0740. Personal E-mail: stan.rosenberg@dartmouth.edu.

**ROSENBERG, STEVE**, secondary school educator; b. N.Y.C., July 30, 1956; s. Stanley and Carmen Rosenberg; m. Melanie Oey; children: Aaron David, Ian Alan. BA, Calif. State U., Fullerton, 1984. Cert. tchg. credential Calif. Tchr. Whitney HS, Cerritos, Calif., 1989—. Author: Modern World History; contbr. articles to profl. jours. Home: 13402 Rose St Cerritos CA 90703 Office: Whitney HS 16800 Shoemaker Ave Cerritos CA 90703 Office Phone: 562-926-5566 ext. 22355. Business E-Mail: esore@esore.org.

**ROSENBERG, STEVEN A.**, surgeon, researcher; BA, MD, Johns Hopkins U., Balt.; PhD in Biophysics, Havard U., Cambridge, Mass. Resident in surgery Peter Bent Brigham Hosp., Boston, 1970—74; chief surgery br Ctr. Cancer Rsch., Nat. Cancer Inst., NIH, Bethesda, Md., 1974—. Prof. surgery Uniformed Services U. of Health Sciences, George Washington U. Sch. Medicine and Health Sciences. Contbr. articles to profl. jours. Office: Ctr Cancer Rsch Surgery Br Bldg 10 Rm 2B42 10 Center Dr Bethesda MD 20892 Office Phone: 301-496-4164. Office Fax: 301-402-1738. E-mail: steven_rosenberg@nih.gov.*

**ROSENBERG, TERRY**, artist; b. Hartford, Conn. s. David Rosenberg and Evelyn Eaton. AA, Miami-Dade C.C., 1974; BFA, U. Miami, 1976; MFA, Alfred U., 1978. Artist, N.Y.C., 1978—. Vis. artist, lectr. in field. Exhibited in group shows at U.S. Art Now, Konstallen, Goteborg, Sweden, 1981, MIT,

Cambridge, Mass., 1982, Hillwood Art Mus., Brookville, NY, 1983, Whitney Mus. Am. Art, N.Y.C., 1984, Sao Paulo Bienal, 1985, Boston Mus. Fine Arts, 1987, Va. Mus. Fine Arts, 1991; author: Generatrix, 1995, (exhbn. catalog) Figuring Motion: Terry Rosenberg, 2002; Represented in permanent collections Bklyn. Mus. Art, Fine Arts Mus San Francisco, Graphische Sammlung Albertina, Vienna, Austria, Walker Art Ctr., Mpls. Recipient Masters award, Nebr. Arts Coun., 1996, Artists Design award, Bemis Ctr. Contemporary Arts, 1991; Individual Artists grantee, NY Found. Arts, 1989. Office: 96 Grand St # 3 New York NY 10013 Office Phone: 212-941-6215. E-mail: atrr@aol.com.

**ROSENBERG, THOMAS B.**, film producer, real estate company executive; BA, Univ. Wis.; JD, Univ. Calif., Berkeley. Atty pvt. pratice; co-founder Capital Assoc. Group real estate, Chgo., 1977—; founder, co-chair, CEO Lakeshore Entertainment Corp, Chgo., 1994—. Investment com. Capri Capital Adv., Chgo. Films: (exec. prodr.) The Commitments, 1991, A Midnight Clear, 1992, Pinocchio, 1994, The Road to Wellville, 1994, Kids in the Hall: Brain Candy, 1996, Box of Moon Light, 1996, Prince Valiant, 1997, Homegrown, 1998, Phoenix, 1998, 200 Cigarettes, 1999, Arlington Road, 1999, The Hurricane, 1999, Madhouse, 2004, Suspect Zero, 2004; (prodr.) 'Til There Was You, 1997, The Real Blonde, 1997, Polish Wedding, 1998, Passion of Mind, 2000, The Next Best Thing, 2000, Autumn in New York, 2000, The Gift, 2000, The Mothman Prophecies, 2002, The Human Stain, 2003, Underworld, 2003, Cantado dietro i paraventi, 2003, Wicker Park, 2004, Million Dollar Baby, 2004 (Academy of Motion Picture Arts and Sciences award for Best Picture, 2005). Home: 875 N Michigan Ave Ste 3430 Chicago IL 60611-1958 Office Phone: 312-335-2600. E-mail: info@lakeshoreentertainment.com.

**ROSENBERG, TINA**, reporter; b. Bklyn., 1958; BS, Northwestern U., 1981, MS, 1982. Fgn. policy editl. writer The New York Times, freelance writer New York Times mag., 1983-96, fgn. policy editl. writer, 1996—, mem. editl. bd.; adj. prof. internat. rels. Columbia U., N.Y.C. Vis. fellow Nat. Security Archive; former sr. fellow World Policy Inst., New Sch. U. Author: Children of Cain: Violence and the Violent in Latin America, The Haunted Land: Facing Europe's Ghosts After Communism (Pulitzer prize for general nonfiction, Nat. Book award, 1996); contbr. articles to publs. Recipient MacArthur Fellowship "genius" award. Office: NY Times Editl Bd 229 W 43rd St New York NY 10036*

**ROSENBERGER, BRYAN DAVID**, lawyer; b. Johnstown, Pa., Oct. 8, 1950; s. Clarence Haines and Ida Rae (Neiderheiser) Rosenberger; m. Barbara Leah Byer, July 4, 1977; children: Laura Michelle, Lisa Renee. BS, Juniata Coll., 1971; JD, Coll. of William and Mary, 1974. Bar: Pa 1974. Assoc. Eckert Seamans Cherin & Mellott, Pitts., 1974-82, ptnr., 1983—, chmn. corp. and bus. dept., 1992-98, mem. exec. com., 1994-98, also bd. dirs., chmn. bus. div., 2001—04. Active new leadership bd Pitts. Symphony Soc., 1990—98. Mem.: Allegheny County Bar Assn. Home: 1358 Oakledge Ct Upper Saint Clair PA 15241-3540 Office: Eckert Seamans Cherin & Mellott 600 Grant St Ste 4400 Pittsburgh PA 15219-2702 Office Phone: 412-566-6123. Business E-Mail: brosenberger@eckertseamans.com.

**ROSENBERGER, JANET THUMA**, retired elementary school educator; b. Marietta, Pa., Feb. 9, 1939; d. Benjamin E. and Mary Ellen (Engle) Thuma; m. Lyle L. Rosenberger, June 6, 1959; children: Kathie, Karen, Kyna Rosenberger. BS in Edn., Gwynedd Mercy, Gwynedd Valley, Pa., 1977; MS in Edn., Beaver Coll., Glenside, Pa., 1980. Cert. elem. educator, reading specialist. Tchr. 1st grade Souderton (Pa.) Area Sch. Dist., 1977—2003; ret., 2003. Avocations: hiking, gardening, theater, piano, reading. Office: Souderton Area Sch Dist 760 Lower Rd Souderton PA 18964-2094

**ROSENBERGER, MARGARET ADALINE**, retired elementary school educator, writer; b. Micanopy, Fla., Oct. 30; d. Eugene David and Lillian Adeline (Bauknight) Rosenberger. Student, Stetson U., 1946—48; BA in Edn., U. Fla., 1949, MEd, 1952. Drama sec. Nat. Youth Adminstrn., Gainesville, Fla., 1939—40; civil svc. clk. U.S. Army, Camp Blanding, Fla., 1940—46; tchr. J.J. Finley, Gainesville, 1949—52; prin., tchr. Micanopy Jr. H.S., 1952—55; gen. supr. Alachua County Schs., Gainesville, 1955—57, elem. supr., 1958—59; tchr. U.S. Army Dependents' Sch., Heidelberg, Germany, 1957—58; prin. Littlewood Elem. Sch., Gainesville, 1959—73, Prairie View Elem. Sch., Gainesville, 1973—82, ret., 1982; owner Rose Hill Publs. Mem. sch. adv. com. Prairie View Elem. Sch., 1975—82. Author: My God of Love, Mercy, Miracles and Angels, 1996, Secrets and Songs of Payne's Prairie, 1998, vol. 2, 2004—, A Teacher's Odyssey, 2001, My Pets and I, 1999, Poems for Children, 2001, My Angels and I, 2001, Spiritual Interpretations of God's Truths, 2002, The Birth and Growth of the Village, 2003, The Other Sides Where Love Knows No Color, 2005, numerous poems; co-author: Reflections of Light, 1995; co-author: (with Frances B. Head) A Lifetime of Humor, 2005; author, composer: St. Augustine Song; contbr. articles to local newspapers. Pres. Govs. Children's Commn., Gainesville, 1956—57; dir. The Village Chorus, Gainesville, 1987—; mem. Gainesville Schs. PTA, 1959—82, PTA Micanopy, 1952—55; Dem. candidate Fla. House Rep., 1974; pianist, organist Village Vespers on Sunday Evenings, 1990—; bd. dir. Foster Grandparents, Gainesville, 1974—76; v.p. bd. dir. No. Fla. Retirement Village, Inc., 1981, chmn. bd. dir., 1982—86, rep. bd. dirs., 1986—, chmn. bd. dir., historian, 1988—. Named Woman of Distinction for Alachua and Bradford Counties, 2005; recipient Disting. Alumna award, U. Fla., 2006. Mem.: Internat. Soc. Poets, Am. Soc. Composers, Authors & Pub., Micanopy Hist. Soc., Altrusa Internat. Club Gainesville (chmn. internat. com., chmn. newsletter, spkr. for programs), Order of Eastern Star, Delta Kappa Gamma (internat. soc. 1959—). Democrat. Baptist. Avocations: stamp collecting/philately, coin collecting/numismatics, book collecting, post card collecting, creative writing. Home: 410 SW Wacahoota Rd Micanopy FL 32667 Mailing: 8015 NW 28th Pl B 110 Gainesville FL 32606

**ROSENBLATT, ALBERT MARTIN**, state appeals court judge; b. NYC, Jan. 17, 1936; s. Isaac and Fannie (Dachs) R.; m. Julia Carlson, Aug. 23, 1970; 1 child, Elizabeth. BA, U. Pa., 1957; JD, Harvard U., 1960. Bar: NY 1961. Dist. atty. Dutchess County, NY, 1969-75, county judge NY, 1976-81; supreme ct. justice NY State Supreme Ct., 1982-89, chief adminstrv. judge, 1987—89, assoc. justice, appellate divsn., second dept., 1989-98; assoc. judge NY State Ct. Appeals, Poughkeepsie, NY, 1998—. Instr. judge N.Y. State, 1987-89; vis. prof., victorian studies dept., Vassar Coll., 1992-94; moderator N.Y. State Fair Trial Free Press Conf., 2000-06; instr. newly elected state supreme ct. judges and county judges; asst. dist. attys., 1974, 75; instr. law tng. N.Y. State Police Acad., 1997; lectr. Nat. Dist. Attys. Assn., 1968-74; teaching team mem. trial advocacy workshop Harvard Law Sch., 1998, 99; chmn. State-Fed. Jud. Coun., 2005—. Mem. bd. editors N.Y. State Bar Jour., 1992-99; former editor. Baker Street Jour.; contbr. articles on law to profl. jours. and popular mags. Bd. dirs. United Way Cmty. Chest, 1970; bd. dirs. Bardavon 1869 Opera House, Dutchess County Hist. Soc.; mem. adv. bd. Jewish Cmty. 1987—; pres. Hist. Soc. Cts. of State of N.Y., 2002—; mem. State-Fed. Jud. Coun., 2003—, chmn., 2005—; mem. U.S. Master's Maccabiah Team, 1997; With USAR, 1960-66. Mem. N.Y. State Bar Assn. (named Outstanding Prosecutor 1974, Outstanding Jud. Svcs. award 1994), N.Y. State Dist. Attys. Assn. (pres. 1974, Frank S. Hogan award 1987, Jud. Svcs. award 1994), Profl. Ski Instrs. Am. (cert. 1984—), Baker St. Irregulars Club (former assoc. editor Baker St. Jour.). Republican. Jewish. Avocations: cert. profl. assoc. ski instructor, squash. Home: 300 Freedom Rd Pleasant Valley NY 12569-5431 Office: 10 Market St Poughkeepsie NY 12601-3228 Address: State NY Ct Appeals 20 Eagle St Albany NY 12207-1095 Office Phone: 845-486-6444.

**ROSENBLATT, ALICE F.**, healthcare insurance company executive; With The New Eng., William M. Mercer, Inc., Mut. of NY; chief actuary, sr. v.p. HMO and grp. svcs. Blue Cross of Calif., 1987—89; sr. v.p., chief actuary Blue Cross/Blue Shield Mass., 1989—93; prin. health and welfare grp. Coopers & Lybrand, Boston; chief actuary, exec. v.p. integration planning and implementation Wellpoint Health Networks, Inc., 1996—2004; exec. v.p.

integration planning/implementation, chief actuary WellPoint, Inc. Commr. Medicare Payment Adv. Commn. Fellow: Soc. Actuaries (bd. dirs.); mem.: Am. Acad. Actuaries (bd. dirs.). Office: WellPoint Inc 120 Monument Cir Indianapolis IN 46204

**ROSENBLATT, JASON PHILIP**, literature and language professor; b. Balt., July 3, 1941; s. Morris D. and Esther (Friedlander) R.; m. Zipporah Marton, June 2, 1964; children: Noah David, Raphael Mark. BA, Yeshiva U., 1963; MA, Brown U., 1966, PhD, 1969. Assoc. prof. English U. Pa., Phila., 1968-74, Georgetown U., Washington, 1974-76, assoc. prof., 1976-83, prof. English, 1983—. Vis. lectr. English lit. Swarthmore (Pa.) Coll., 1972-73; cen. exec. com. Folger Inst./Folger Shakespeare Librr., Washington, 1976-88. Author: Torah and Law in "Paradise Lost", 1994, Renaissance England's Chief Rabbi: John Selden, 2006; co-editor: Not in Heaven: Coherence and Complexity in Biblical Narrative, 1991; mem. editl. bd. Milton Studies, 1992—; contbr. articles to scholarly publs. Recipient Virginia Graham Healey award, 1998-99; Guggenheim Found. fellow, 1977-78, NEH fellow, 1990-91, Folger Shakespeare Librr./NEH fellow, 1999-2000. Mem. MLA (del. assembly 1989-91, exec. com. div. religion and lit. 1982-86, exec. com. 17th century Eng. lit. 2002—), Milton Soc. Am. (exec. com. 1977-80, James Holly Hanford award 1989, v.p. 1998, pres. 1999), Milton Seminar, Phi Beta Kappa. Democrat. Jewish. Avocations: talmud study, music, swimming. Office: Dept English Georgetown Univ Box 571131 Washington DC 20057-1131 Office Phone: 202-687-7577. E-mail: rosenblj@georgetown.edu.

**ROSENBLATT, JOAN RAUP**, mathematical statistician; b. N.Y.C., Apr. 15, 1926; d. Robert Bruce and Clara (Eliot) Raup; m. David Rosenblatt, June 10, 1950. AB, Barnard Coll., 1946; PhD, U. N.C., 1956. Intern Nat. Inst. Pub. Affairs, Washington, 1946-47; statis. analyst U.S. Bur. of Budget, 1947-48; rsch. asst. U. N.C., 1953-54; mathematician Nat. Inst. Standards and Tech. (formerly Nat. Bur. Standards), Washington, 1955—, asst. chief statis. engring., 1963-68, chief statis. engring. lab., 1969-78, dep. dir. Ctr. for Applied Math., 1978-88; dep. dir. Computing and Applied Math. Lab., Gaithersburg, 1988-93, dir., 1993-95, guest rschr. Statis. Engring. Divsn., 1996—. Mem. com. on indsl. rels. Dept. Stats. Ohio State U., 1981-90; mem. adv. com. in math. and stats. USDA Grad. Sch., 1971—; mem. Com. Applied and Theoretical Stats., Nat. Rsch. Coun., 1985-88. Mem. editorial bd. Communications in Stats., 1971-79, Jour. Soc. for Indsl. and Applied Math., 1965-75, Nat. Inst. Stds. and Tech. Jour. Rsch., 1991-93; contbr. articles to profl. jours. Chmn. Com. on Women in Sci., Joint Bd. on Sci. Edn., 1963—64. Rice fellow, 1946, Gen. Edn. Bd. fellow, 1948-50; recipient Fed. Woman's award, 1971, Gold medal Dept. Commerce, 1976, Presdl. Meritorious Exec. Rank award, 1982. Fellow AAAS (chmn. stats. sect. 1982, sec. 1987-91), Inst. Math. Stats. (coun. 1975-77), Am. Statis. Assn. (v.p. 1981-83, dir. 1979-80, Founders award 1991), Washington Acad. Scis. (achievement award math. 1965); mem. AAUW, Royal Statis. Soc. London, Philos. Soc. Washington, Internat. Statis. Inst., Caucus Women Stats. (pres. 1982, treas.). Mem. math., Exec. Women Govt., Phi Beta Kappa, Sigma Xi (treas. Nat. Bur. Standards chpt. 1982-84). Home: 2939 Van Ness St NW Apt 702 Washington DC 20008-4628 Office: Nat Inst Stds and Tech 100 Bureau Dr Stop 8980 Gaithersburg MD 20899-8980 Business E-Mail: jrr@nist.gov.

**ROSENBLATT, MICHAEL**, internist, researcher, academic administrator, educator; b. Lund, Sweden, Nov. 27, 1947; s. Arthur Rosenblatt and Jean (Strosberg) Bialer; m. Patricia Ellen Regenbogen, Aug. 23, 1969; children: Anna Miriam, Adam Richard. AB summa cum laude, Columbia U., N.Y.C., 1969; MD magna cum laude, Harvard U., Cambridge, Mass., 1973. Diplomate Am. Bd. Internal Medicine. Intern then resident Mass. Gen. Hosp., Boston, 1973-75, clin. rsch. fellow in endocrinology and metabolism, 1975-77, chief endocrine unit, 1981-84; instr. in medicine Harvard U., Boston, 1976-78, asst. prof. medicine, 1978-82, assoc. prof. medicine, 1982-85; v.p. for biol. rsch. Merck Sharp & Dohme Rsch. Labs., 1984-87, v.p. for biol. rsch. and molecular biology, 1987-89, sr. v.p. rsch. West Point, Pa., 1989-92; dir. divsn. health sci. and tech. Harvard-MIT, 1992-98; Ebert prof. molecular medicine Harvard Med. Sch., Boston, 1992-98; chief divsn. bone and mineral metabolism Beth Israel Hosp., Boston, 1992—2000, 2002—. Faculty dean acad. programs Beth Israel Deaconess Med. Ctr., Harvard Med., 1996—2000, George R. Minot prof. med., 1996—2003; exec. dir. Carl J. Shapiro Inst. Edn. and Rsch. at Harvard Med. Sch. and Beth Israel Deaconess Med. Ctr., 1996—2000, pres., 1999—2001; dean, prof. physiology and medicine Tufts U. Sch. Medicine, 2003—. Editor: Atrial Natriuretic Factor Endocrinology and Metabolism Clinics of N.Am., 1987; contbr. numerous sci. articles on parathyroid hormone and calcium metabolism to leading sci. jours. Recipient Vincent du Vigneaud award Gordon Confs., Kingston, R.I., 1986, Fuller Albright award Am. Soc. for Bone and Mineral Rsch., 1986, citation Japan Endocrine Soc., Tokyo, Taiwanese Osteoporosis Soc., Tainan. Fellow AAAS; mem. The Endocrine Soc., Am. Soc. for Biochemistry and Molecular Biology, Am. Soc. for Clin. Investigation, Am. Soc. Bone and Mineral Rsch. (pres. 1997-98), Assn. Am. Physicians, Inter-Urban Clin. Club (pres. 1997-98). Office: Tufts U Sch Medicine 136 Harrison Ave Boston MA 02111-1800

**ROSENBLATT, PETER RONALD**, lawyer, former ambassador; b. NYC, Sept. 4, 1933; s. William and Therese (Steinhardt) Rosenblatt; m. Naomi Henriette Harris; children: Therese Sarah Browning, Daniel Harris, David Steinhardt. BA, Yale U., 1954, LLB, 1957. Bar: N.Y. 1959, D.C. 1969. Tchg. asst. history Yale U., New Haven, 1954—55; asst. dist. atty. N.Y. County, 1959—62; assoc. Stroock & Stroock & Lavan, N.Y.C., 1962—66; dep. asst. gen. counsel AID, Washington, 1966; mem. White House staff, Washington, 1966—68; jud. officer, dept. bd. contract appeals U.S. Post Office Dept., Washington, 1968—69; v.p., dir. EDP Technology, Inc., Washington, 1969—71; pvt. practice law Washington, 1969—71; spl. cons. to Senator Edmund S. Muskie, 1970—72; practice law Washington, 1972—77, 1981—91; founding ptnr. Heller & Rosenblatt, Washington, 1991—. Personal rep. of Pres. with rank amb. to conduct negotiations on future polit. status of Trust Ter. of Pacific Islands, Washington, 1977-81; mem. Mid. East study group Dem. Adv. Coun. Elected Ofcls., 1974-76; bd. dirs. MediSense, Inc., 1983-96. Sec., chmn. exec. com. Coalition for a Dem. Majority, 1973-77, pres., 1983-93; bd. dirs. Com. on Present Danger, 1976-77, 82-93, 04-; mem. U.S. Nat. Com. Pacific Econ. Cooperation, 1986, sec., 1987-03; bd. govs. Haifa (Israel) U., 1990-94, 98-; sec.-treas. Fund for Democracy and Devel., 1991-94, pres., 1994—; mem. adv. coun. Nixon Ctr., 1994—; mem. task force on fgn. policy Dem. Policy Commn., 1986; bd. govs. Am. Jewish Com., 1998—, v.p. 2005-, pres. D.C. chpt. 2003-05, bd. dirs. UN Watch, 2000—, chmn., bd. govs. Koppelman Inst. on Am. Jewish-Israeli Rels., 1999-02; bd. advisors Jewish Inst. Nat. Security Affairs, 2000—; mem. Nat. Security Initiative, 2001—. Postgrad. fellow, Tel-Aviv U., 1971. Mem. ABA, N.Y., D.C. Bar, Coun. Fgn. Rels. Jewish. Office: Heller & Rosenblatt 1101 15th St NW Ste 205 Washington DC 20005-5002 Office Phone: 202-466-4700. Personal E-mail: ffddprosenblatt@erols.com. E-mail: ffdd@erols.com.

**ROSENBLATT, ROGER**, writer; b. NYC, Sept. 13, 1940; m. Virginia Rosenblatt; children: Carl, Amy, John. PhD in English and Am. Lit., Harvard U.; doctorate (hon.), U. Md., Claremont Grad. Sch., U. Utah, Pace U., Brigham Young U. Briggs-Copeland prof. creative writing Harvard U., 1968-73; dir. edn. NEH, 1973-75; lit. editor The New Republic, 1975-78; columnist Washington Post, mem. editorial bd., 1976-79; essayist, sr. writer Time, 1980-88; essayist MacNeil/Lehrer News Hour, PBS, 1983—; columnist, editor-at-large Life mag., 1989-92; editor-at-large Time, The New, 1999—2001. Parsons Family Univ. prof. writing Southampton Coll., L.I. U. Author: Black Fiction, 1974, Children of War, 1983 (Robert F. Kennedy Book prize), Witness: The World Since Hiroshima, 1985, Life Itself: Abortion in the American Mind, 1992 (Melcher award), The Man in the Water, 1994, Coming Apart, 1997, Consuming Desires, 1999, Rules for Aging, 2000, Where We Stand, 2002, Anything Can Happen, 2003, Lapham Rising, 2006, (plays) Free Speech in America, 1991, And, 1992, Bibliomania, 1993, Ashley Montana Goes Ashore in the Caicos, 2005, (novel) Lapham Rising, 2006. Fulbright scholar, Dublin, Ireland, 1965; recipient numerous honors including two George Polk awards, George Foster Peabody award, Emmy award.

**ROSENBLATT, STEPHEN PAUL,** marketing and sales promotion company executive; b. N.Y.C., Feb. 13, 1935; s. Jack Aaron and Ruth (Kloth) R.; m. Dorothy Freedman, Apr. 7, 1962; children: Gregg, Amy, Robert. BEd, NYU, 1957. Tchr. art N.Y.C. Schs., 1957-58; art dir. Morse Internat., N.Y.C., 1958-65; v.p. L.C. Gumbinner Advt., N.Y.C., 1966-71; group mktg. dir. Norcliff Thayer, Tarrytown, NY, 1971-75; pres. BMS Mktg. Services, Inc., N.Y.C., 1975-89, The Promotion Group Inc. subs. Doctus PLC, N.Y.C., 1989-91, SPQR Inc., Yorktown Heights, NY, 1991-93, ret., 1993. Home: 1451 White Hill Rd Yorktown Heights NY 10598-3543

**ROSENBLOOM, BERT,** marketing educator, consultant, writer; b. Phila., Feb. 2, 1944; s. Max and Dora (Cohen) R.; m. Pearl Friedman, Aug. 18, 1968; children: Jack Alan, Robyn. BS, Temple U., 1966, MBA, 1968, PhD, 1974. Instr. mktg. Rider Coll., Trenton, NJ, 1968-72, asst. prof., 1972-74; asst. prof. mktg. Baruch Coll. CUNY, 1974-76; assoc. prof. Drexel U., Phila., 1976-80, prof., 1980-85, G. Behrens Ulrich prof. mktg., 1985-98, assoc. dean grad. programs, 1994-97, Rauth chair electronic commerce mgmt., 1999—2005, Rauth prof. mktg. mgmt., 2005—. Vis. scholar Higher Sch. Commerce Paris, 1993; cons. editor mktg. Random House, N.Y.C., 1977—; exec. dir. Safe Guard Sci. E-Commerce Mgmt. Ctr., 1999-2000, sr. rsch. fellow, 2000—; cons. in field; bd. dirs. Reality Landscaping Corp., McKee Real Estate Devel. Corp., RESHARE Corp.; vis. disting. prof. Hannon U., Japan, 2000; vis. disting. scholar U. St. Gallen, 2000; Disting. vis. fellow Sogang U., Korea, 2001; bd. dirs. Reshare Corp., 2004—; mem. adv. bd. Duttweiler Inst. Mktg. and Retailing. Author: Marketing Channels, 1978, 3d edit., 2003, Market Functions and the Wholesaler Distribution, 1987, Marketing Channels: A Management View, 5th edit., 1997, 6th edit., 1999, 7th edit., 2003, Retail Marketing, 1981, Direct Selling Channels, 1993, Wholesale Mktg. Channels, 1994; editor Jour. Mktg. Channels, 1989—, Jour. Consumer Mktg., Jour. Global Mktg., Jour. Acad. Mktg. Sci.; contbr. articles to profl. jours. Mem. E-Commerce Commn., Mayor Phila., 1999—. Named Disting. Erskine fellow U. Canterbury, New Zealand, 1986; recipient Outstanding Educator award Chapel of Four Chaplains, 1984, Nomura Fund Collaborative rsch. award U. Rykus, Japan, 1998; rsch. award Distbn. Rsch. and Edn. Found., 1986, rsch. award Direct Selling Found., 1986, 91, 96, Literati Club award for excellence, 2002; Nat. Assn. Wholesaler Distbrs. grantee, 1991; honored as disting. prof. Retail Mktg. Inst. of Australia, 1985. Fellow Acad. Mktg. Sci. (bd. govs. 1978-89); mem. Internat. Mgmt. Devel. Assn. (pres. 1992-94), Am. Mktg. Assn. (v.p. Phila. chpt. 1978-79), Beta Gamma Sigma. Office: Drexel U Sch Bus 32d and Market Sts Philadelphia PA 19104 E-mail: rosenbl@drexel.edu.

**ROSENBLOOM, DANIEL,** investment advisor, lawyer; b. N.Y.C., Feb. 11, 1930; s. Sol and Florence (Vogel) R. BA, U. Va., 1951, JD, 1954; LLM, NYU, 1960. Bar: Va. 1954, N.Y. 1956. Atty. Paskus, Gordon, and Hyman, N.Y.C., 1956—61; v.p., sec., gen. counsel Phila. and Reading Corp., N.Y.C., 1962—67; pntr. First Manhattan Co., N.Y.C., 1968—2002, sr. mng. dir., 2002—. Trustee Nat. Found. for Facial Reconstruction, N.Y. Univ. Med. Ctr., Univ. Va. Law Sch. Found. 1st bl. AUS, 1954—56. Mem. Sunningdale Country Club, Farmington Country Club, Harmonie Club, Atlantic Golf Club, River Club, Phi Alpha Delta, Phi Epsilon Pi. Office: First Manhattan Co 437 Madison Ave New York NY 10022-7001

**ROSENBLOOM, DAVID HARRY,** political science and law educator; b. N.Y.C., Aug. 27, 1943; s. Jerome and Rita R. BA, Marietta Coll., 1964, LLD (hon.), 1994; MA, U. Chgo., 1966, PhD in Polit. Sci., 1969. Asst. prof. U. Kans., Lawrence, 1969-71; fellow Am. Soc. Pub. Adminstrn. U.S. Civil Svc. Commn., Washington, 1970-71; vis. sr. lectr. Tel Aviv (Israel) U., 1971-73; asst. prof. U. Vt., Burlington, 1973-75, assoc. prof., 1975-78; vis. assoc. prof. Syracuse (N.Y.) U., 1978-79, prof., 1979—88, disting. prof., 1988-90, Am. U., Washington, 1990—. Bd. trustees Marietta Coll., 2003—; guest prof. pub. adminstrn. People's U., Beijing, 2003—, Northwest U., Xi'an, China, 2005—. Author: (Books) Federal Service and Constitution, 1971, Public Administration, 2004, 6th edit., Public Administration and Law, 1997, Building a Legislative-Centered Public Administration, 2000, Administrative Law for Public Managers, 2003. Mem. Clinton-Gore Transition Team, U.S. Office Pers. Mgmt., Washington, 1992. Recipient Charles Levine Meml. award for excellence and Disting. Rsch. award Am. Soc. for Pub. Administrn. and Nat. Assn. Schs. of Pub. Affairs and Administration, Washington, 1992, 93, Thomas Dye award for outstanding svc. Policy Studies Orgn., 1996, Dwight Waldo award for outstanding contbns. to lit. and leadership of Pub. Adminstrn., Am. Soc. Pub. Adminstrn., Washington, 1999, Louis Brownlow Book award Nat. Acad. Pub. Adminstrn., 2001. Fellow Nat. Acad. Pub. Adminstrn. Recipient John Gaus award for exemplary scholarship in joint tradition polit. sci. and pub. adminstrn. Am. Polit. Sci. Assn., 2001. Office: American U 4400 Massachusetts Ave NW Washington DC 20016-8001 Office Phone: 202-885-2361. Business E-Mail: rbloom@american.edu.

**ROSENBLOOM, DAVID LEE,** medical educator, director; b. New York, Mass., Mar. 3, 1944; s. Charles and Beatrice Schaeffer Rosenbloom; m. Alice E. Richmond, July 26, 1981; 1 child, Elizabeth Lara. BA, Colgate U., Hamilton, N.Y., 1965; PhD, MIT, Cambridge, 1970. Asst. prof. Hamilton Coll., Clinton, NY, 1970—73; dir. Parkman Ctr. Urban Affairs City of Boston, 1973—75, exec. asst. to Mayor, 1973—75, commr. health and hosps., 1975—83; v.p., pres. Health Data Inst., Lexington, Mass., 1984—87; chmn., CEO Cmty. Med. Alliance, Inc, Boston, 1989—93; from assoc. prof. to prof. Boston U. Sch. Pub. Health, 1991—; dir. Join Together, Boston, 1991—. Adj. lectr. Heller Sch. Brandeis U., Waltham, Mass., 1983—. Author: The Election Men, Professional Campaign Managers and American Democracy. Vice chair Spaulding Rehab. Network, Boston, 1983. Scholar, Am. Legion, 1961—65; Woodrow Wilson Grad. fellow, 1966, 1969—70. Mem.: APHA, Phi Beta Kappa. Democrat. Jewish. Achievements include patents pending for method of behavior change over a network. Office: Join Together 1 Appleton St Boston MA 02116 Office Phone: 617-437-1500. Office Fax: 617-437-9394. Business E-Mail: david@jointogether.org.

**ROSENBLOOM, H(ARRY) DAVID,** lawyer; b. N.Y.C., May 26, 1941; s. Milton M. and Rose (Gold) Rosenbloom; m. Carla L. Peterson, June 23, 1968; children: Sarah Alix, Julia Micol. AB, Princeton U., 1962; postgrad. (Fulbright scholar), U. Florence, Italy, 1962-63; JD, Harvard U., 1966. Bar: N.Y. 1967, DC 1968. Spl. asst. to Arthur J. Goldberg U.S. amb. UN, 1966-67; law clk. to Abe Fortas U.S. Supreme Ct., 1967-68; assoc. Caplin & Drysdale, Washington, 1968-72, pntr., 1972-77, 81—. Spl. asst. to dep. asst. sec. for tax policy Dept. Treasury, Washington, 1977, internat. tax counsel, 1978—81; lectr. Harvard U. Law Sch., 1984—87, 1990—93, 1995—96, 1999, Pub. Fin. Tng. Inst., Taipei, 1985—86, 1989, Stanford U. Law Sch. 1988, Inst. Tecnologico Autonomo d' Mex., 1993, 95, 97, Columbia U. Law Sch., 1997, U. Pa. Law Sch., 1998, U. Luigi Bocconi, Milan, 2001, 04, 05, So. African Tax Inst., U. Pretoria, 2002, NYU Law Sch., 2000—; dir. internat. tax program, 2002—; faculty law U. Sydney, 2001, 03, 05, 06. Home: 2948 Garfield Ter NW Washington DC 20008-3507 Office: 1 Thomas Cir NW Washington DC 20005-5802 Office Phone: 202-862-5037. Business E-Mail: hdr@capdale.com.

**ROSENBLOOM, LEWIS STANLEY,** lawyer; b. Fort Riley, Kans., Feb. 28, 1953; s. Donald and Sally Ann (Warsawsky) R.; children: Micah, Shaina. BA, Lake Forest Coll., 1974; JD with high honors, DePaul U., 1977. Bar: Ill. 1977, US Dist. Ct. (no. dist.) Ill. 1977, US Ct. Appeals (7th cir.) 1979, US Supreme Ct. 1983, US Ct. Appeals (9th cir.) 1987, US Ct. Appeals (3rd cir.) 1991. Sr. acct. Gale, Takahasi & Channon (now Ernst & Young), Chgo., 1973-74; law clk. to Hon. Robert L. Eisen U.S. Dist. Ct. (no. dist.) Ill., Chgo., 1976; assoc. Nachman, Munitz & Sweig, Ltd., Chgo., 1976-82, prin., 1982-87; pntr., co-chmn. involvency, bankruptcy & bus. reorgn. dept. Winston & Strawn, Chgo., 1987-93; pntr., vis. corp. reorgn. counsel McDermott, Will & Emery, Chgo., 1993—2006; pntr., chmn. Dept. Bankruptcy and Reorganization LeBoeuf, Lewis, Green & MacRae, LLP, Chgo., 2006—. Mem. bd. advisors to bankruptcy, comml. law advisor Bus. Laws, Inc., 1988—; lectr. in field. Contbr. articles to profl. jours. Mem. adv. com. and fin. subcom. Ill. Bd. Higher Edn., Springfield; mem. state edn. and legal aid subcom. Ill. Coun. on Children and Youth Welfare. Coll. Scholar Lake Forest Coll., 1973-74. Fellow Am. Coll. Bankruptcy (dir.); mem. ABA (bus. bankruptcy com. 1982—.

chmn. new and pending bankruptcy legis. com. 1982-85, chmn. transp. reorganizations com. 1985-88), Chgo. Bar Assn. (bankrupcy reorganization com., co-chmn. subcom. on retention and fees 1987-88). Office: LeBoeuf Lamb Greene & MacRae LLP Two Prudential Plaza 180 N Stetson Ste 3700 Chicago IL 60601 Business E-Mail: lrosenbloom@llgm.com.

**ROSENBLOOM, MOREY STEPHEN,** lawyer; b. Phila., Aug. 26, 1944; s. Howard and Esther (Medvene) R.; m. Marsha Riffkin, May 26, 1968; children: Brett, Eric. BS in Acctg., Temple U., 1966, JD, 1969. Bar: Pa. 1970, US Tax Ct., 1975, US Supreme Ct., 1980, NY, 2001. Law asst. to chief justice Pa. Supreme Ct., 1969-70; pntr. Blank Rome Comisly & McCauley, Phila., 1970—90; prin. CMS Co., 1990—95; ptnr. Blank Rome LLP, Phila., 1995—, chair, tax and fiduciary dept., 1996—2001, chmn. bus. dept., 2003—06. Adj. prof. law Temple U. Sch. Law, Phila., 1977-2000, Villanova Law Sch., 1999-2004; lectr., prof. Am. Coll., Bryn Mawr, Pa., 1978-90. Co-author: Tools and Techniques of Estate Planning, 11th edit., 1990, Funding Corporate Buy-Sell Agreements with Life Insurance, 1980, The Wait and See Buy Sell, 1978. Bd. visitors Temple U. Sch. of Law; bd. mem. Am. Friends of Hebrew U., Elwyn Jerusalem, Thomas Jefferson U. Cardiology Rsch. Found. Fellow Am. Coll. Trust and Estate Coun.; mem. ABA, Pa. Bar Assn. (past chmn. real property probate and trust law sect.), Phila. Bar Assn., Phila. Estate planning Coun. Office: Blank Rome LLP One Logan Sq Philadelphia PA 19103-6998 Office Fax: 215-832-5599. Business E-Mail: rosenbloom@BlankRome.com.

**ROSENBLUM, NORMA FRISCH,** lawyer; b. N.Y.C., Dec. 2, 1925; d. Jacob Frisch and Anna (Fox) Frisch Schwartz; m. Philip Rosenbloom, Oct. 31, 1946; children: David, James, Eric. BA, New Sch. Social Rsch., 1951; JD, Rutgers U., Newark, 1979. Bar: N.J. 1979, NY 1980. Mem. faculty, head dept. music Ranney Sch., Tinton Falls, N.J., 1962-74; chief law clk. Monmouth County (N.J.) Prosecutor's Office, 1979-80; assoc. Karasic & Karasic, P.C., Oakhurst, N.J., 1980-82; ptnr. Abrams, Gatta, Rosen & Rosenbloom, Ocean Twp., N.J., 1982-90, Abrams, Gatta, Rosen, Rosenbloom & Sevrin, P.C., 1990-92; of counsel Abrams, Gatta, Falvo & Sevrin, P.A., 1992-99; legal adv. Epiphany House Inc., Asbury Park, N.J., 1999—. Asst. county counsel Monmouth County, 1987-88; mem. N.J. Supreme Ct. Family Part Practice Com., 1997-98. Sec., mem. exec. bd. Temple Beth Miriam, Elberon, N.J., 1969-74; mcpl. leader Monmouth Beach (N.J.) Dem. Com., 1973-2004; del. Dem. Nat. Conv., 1976; freeholder rep. to Monmouth County Cmty. Action Program, poverty program, 1975-76; bd. dirs. Cen. Jersey Regional Health Planning Bd., 1973-75; trustee search com. Brookdale C.c., Lincroft, N.J., 1984-85; trustee Planned Parenthood Monmouth County, 1981-88. Recipient award for cmty. involvement Asbury Park-Neptune Youth Coun., 1970. Fellow Am. Acad. Matrimonial Lawyers; mem. ABA, N.J. Women Lawyers Assn. (pres. 1994-95), N.J. State Bar Assn. (mem. legis. com., trustee women in the profession sect.), Women Lawyers Monmouth County. Democrat. Jewish. Avocation: classical pianist. Home: 74 Thornbrooke Dr Shrewsbury NJ 07702 Office: Epiphany House 300 4th Ave Asbury Park NJ 07712-6006

**ROSENBLUM, BARRY NORTON,** physician; b. St. Louis, Jan. 30, 1956; m. Lisa Margaret Sklar, Nov. 29, 2003. MD, U. Mo., Kansas City, 1980. Resident St. Louis U. Sch. Medicine, 1980—85, fellow in facial plastic and reconstructive surgery, 1985—86; asst. clin. prof. Columbia U. Coll. Physicians, N.Y.C., 1985—88; asst. prof. St. Louis U. Sch. Medicine, 1988—91; attending physician Mo. Bapt. Med. Ctr., St. Louis, 1996—2002, pvt. attending physician, 2002—. Contbr. chapters to books, articles to profl. jours. Fellow: ACS. Republican. Avocations: automobile racing, motorcycling, antique gun collecting. Office: Suburban Surgical Associates Inc Ste 600D 3023 N Ballas Saint Louis MO 63105 Personal E-mail: bnrosenblum@msn.com. E-mail: bnr@ssainc.net.

**ROSENBLUM, CONSTANCE,** newspaper editor; Culture editor Phila. Inquirer; John Rockwell arts and leisure sect. editor NY Times, NYC, 1998, city sect. editor. Author: Gold Digger: The Outrageous Life and Times of Peggy Hopkins Joyce, 2000; contbg. editor: The Best of the City Section of the NY Times, 2005. Office: NY Times City Section 229 West 43rd St New York NY 10036-3959*

**ROSENBLUM, ESTELLE H.,** retired dean, nursing educator; b. Davenport, Iowa, Feb. 8, 1933; d. Dan and Cecil (Spiewak) Masters; m. Sidney Rosenblum, Aug. 30, 1953 (dec. 1988); children: Jay Douglas, Gail Rae, Paul Mitchell; m. Jack Grevey, Mar. 31, 1996; stepdaughter: Eileen Grevey Hillson. Student, U. Iowa, 1950—53; BSN, Wayne State U., Detroit, 1956; MA in Audiology, U. N.Mex., 1971, PhD, 1979; MSN, U. Tex., El Paso, 1981. Head nurse Northville (Mich.) State Hosp., 1956; head nurse, supr. Sister Kenny Polio/Rehab. Hosp., 1957-60; pub. health nurse Englewood County Health Dept., 1961-62; nursing supr. Bernalillo County Indian Hosp., Albuquerque, 1962-63, asst. dir. nursing, 1963-64; clin. tchr. U. N.Mex. Coll. Nursing, Albuquerque, 1964-65, inst. to prof., 1972-86, dean and prof. nursing, 1986-93, dean and prof. emerita, 1993—; sch. nurse West Mesa H.S., Albuquerque, 1967-69. Internat. nursing cons.; dir. ANA Approved CE program, Prof. Seminar Cons., 1979-89; spkr. Hong Kong Nurse Educators Soc., 1985; founder convenio U. N.Mex. and U. Mex., 1990, first nurse midwifery grad. program, U. N.Mex., 1989, first nurse practitioner program at grad. level, 1987. Author: Fundamentals of Hearing for Health Professionals, 1981; contbr. articles to profl. jours., chpts. to books. Bd. dirs. U. N.Mex. Found., 1996—, bd. sec. 2000-04, Nancy Floyd Haworth Breast Cancer Found., 1995—; docent City of Albuquerque, 1996—; chair recognition com. Jewish Cmty. Ctr., 1998—. USPHS grantee, 1989; Albuquerque Rotary Charitable Found. Clinton P. Anderson fellow; recipient Centennial Disting. Alumni award, U. N.Mex., 1989, Helene Fuld award to Coll. Nursing, U. N.Mex. 1987, Sigma Delta Tau Nat. Disting. Alumni award, 1988, State N.Mex. Gov.'s Disting. Svc. award, 1993, Estelle H. Rosenblum Thesis award U. N.Mex. Coll. Nursing, 1995, Nurse of the Yr. Awards "Legend of Nursing" award March of Dimes, 2002, Myrtle K. Aydelotte Dean's award U. Iowa Coll. Nursing, 2000; Rosenblum-Weiss Ctr. for Nursing Excellence in women and children's health care established at U. N.Mex., 2000. Univ. Iowa Coll. of Nursing Alumni award, 2004. Fellow Am. Acad. Nursing; mem. Am. Assn. Colls. of Nursing (emeritus, exec. devel. series 1988-92), Am. Colls. Nursing (bd. dirs. 1990-92), N.Mex. Nurses Assn. (pres. 1975), N.Mex. Health Resources (bd. dirs. 1986-88), The Rotary Club of Albuquerque (Harvest ball fundraiser 1994—), Sigma Theta Tau (founder, pres. Gamma Sigma chpt. 1974-76, Mentor award), Phi Kappa Phi.

**ROSENBLUM, HAL DAVID,** school psychologist; b. Bklyn., Oct. 14, 1973; s. Leslie and Diane Rochelle Rosenblum. BS, Bklyn Coll., 1996, MS in Edn., 1999. Psychologist Stanley S. Lamm Inst., Bklyn., 2000—05; sch. psychologist NYC Dept. Edn., Bklyn., 2005—. Mem.: APA (assoc.). Office Phone: 718-923-5189.

**ROSENBLUM, JAY ALAN,** neurologist; b. Newark, June 12, 1933; s. Irving and Peggy (Carpenter) R.; m. Judith Grandes, Sept. 1958 (div. 1965); children: Melissa, Shepherd, Todd; m. Sue Goldman Rosenblum, June 13, 1971; 1 child, Steven. AB with honors, U. Pa., 1954; MD, Wake Forest Med., 1958; GM, U. Pa., 1965. Diplomate Am. Acad. of Pain Mgmt., Am. Bd. Forensic Medicine; cert. neurorehabilitation physician. Dir. neurology Madison Ave Hosp., N.Y.C., 1980, N.Y. Infirmary Hosp., N.Y.C., 1980; clin. cons. in neurology N.Y. State Dept of Health, N.Y.C., 1985; instr. in neurology N.Y. Med. Coll., 1985; clin. asst. prof. neurology NYU Med. Sch., 1965, 1970—. Asst. vis. neurologist Bellevue Hosp., NYC; bd. dirs. Am. Bd. Forensic Medicine, Springfield, Mo., bd. adv. for profl. standing; dir. indsl. medicine seminar Coll. of Ins., NYC, 1988-89; moderator diagnosis and treatment back disorders Acad. of Medicine, NYC, 1991; lectr. in field; pres. med. bd. NY Infirmary-Beekman Downtown Hosp., 1982; mem. NY State Bd. for Profl. Med. Conduct, 2004. Contbr. articles to profl. publs. Task force of handicap vehicles Dept. Health, City of N.Y., 1985; impartial specialist-neurology U.S. Dept. Labor, 1985. Capt. U.S. Army, 1959-62. Fellow Am. Soc. Indsl. Medicine (pres. 1993), Am. Acad. of Infrared Imaging (pres. 1995); mem. Am.

Back Soc. (dir. neurothemograhy workshop 1989), NY County Med. Soc. (bd. dirs., chmn. bd. censors 2002). Office: 175 E 79th St New York NY 10021-0432 Office Phone: 212-249-7867.

**ROSENBLUM, JEFFREY IRA,** consulting economist; b. N.Y.C., Mar. 12, 1956; s. Charles and Sylvia Lilian (Silverstein) R.; m. Monica Rosales, Sept. 15, 2000. BS, SUNY Brockport, 1983; PhD, U. Tex., 1992. Analyst Pub. Utility Commn. Tex., Austin, 1986—91, asst. mgr., 1991—94; mgr. KPMG Peat Marwick LLP, N.Y.C., 1994—96, sr. mgr. Dallas, 1996—98, KPMG LLP (formerly KPMG Peat Marwick), Short Hills, NJ, 1999—2001, Arthur Andersen LLP, Roseland, NJ, 2001—02; pres. Monrosen, Inc., 2002—05; sr. mgr. Deloitte Tax LLP, Seattle, 2005—. Mem. Am. Econ. Assn., Law and Econs. Assn. Home: 11917 SE 198th Ct Renton WA 98058 Office: 925 4th Ave Ste 3300 Seattle WA 98104 Office Phone: 206-716-7158. Business E-Mail: jrosenblum@deloitte.com. E-mail: jeffr3@comcast.net.

**ROSENBLUM, JOHN WILLIAM,** finance educator; b. Houston, Jan. 1, 1944; s. H. William and Susan (Ullmann) R.; m. Carolyn Edith Jones, Sept. 12, 1964; children: J. Christopher, Kathryn, Nicholas. AB, Brown U., 1965; MBA, Harvard U., 1967, DBA, 1972. Instr. Harvard U. Bus. Sch., Boston, 1969-72, asst. prof., 1972-75, assoc. prof., 1975-79; prof. Darden Grad. Sch. Bus. Adminstrn., U. Va., Charlottesville, 1979-80, assoc. dean, 1980-82, dean, 1982-93, Tayloe Murphy prof., 1993—; dean Jepson Sch. Leadership Studies, U. Richmond, Va., 1996-2000. Bd. dirs. Chesapeake Corp., The Providence Jour. Co., Grantham, Mayo, Van Otterloo, Thomas Rutherford, Inc. Co-author: Strategy and Organization, 1973, (2d edit.), 1977, Cases in Political Economy-Japan, 1980. Bd. dirs. Landmark Vols., Tredeger Nat. Civil War Ctr., Jamestown-Yorktown Found., Inc., Atlantic Challenge, Charlottesville Symphony Orch., Farnsworth Art Mus. Mem. Phi Beta Kappa, Omicron Delta Kappa.

**ROSENBLUM, JUDITH A.,** law educator; b. Chgo., June 12, 1951; BA, U. Rochester, 1973; JD, University Mich., Ann Arbor, 1976. Atty. Gordon, Elden, Schlack, Glickson & Gordon, 1976—77; staff atty. Citr. Judicial Conduct Organs. American Judicature Soc., Chgo., 1977—83, staff atty. Ednl. Programs, 1977—80, sr. staff atty., 1980—83; legal writing instr. Northwestern U. Sch. Law, Chgo., 1984—98, acting dir. legal writing, 1992, 1995, asst. dir. legal writing, 1998—2000, academic support coord., 1996—, dir. comm. and legal reasoning. Contbr. articles to profl. jours. Mem.: Chgo. Bar Assn. Office: Northwestern U Sch Law 357 E Chicago Ave Chicago IL 60611 Office Phone: 312-503-8943. E-mail: j-rosenbaum2@law.northwestern.edu.

**ROSENBLUM, MARTIN JEROME,** ophthalmologist; b. N.Y.C., Apr. 7, 1948; s. Philip and Rita (Steppel) R.; m. Zina Zarin, May 31, 1975; children: Steven David, Richard James. BS, Bklyn. Coll., 1968; MD, U. Ariz., 1973; postgrad., Columbia U., 1977. Diplomate Am. Bd. Ophthalmology, Nat. Bd. Med. Examiners. Intern Cornell U., N.Y.C., 1973-74; resident N.Y. Med. Coll., 1975-78, instr., 1978-79; practice medicine specializing in eye surgery St. Petersburg, Fla., 1979—. Chief ophthalmology Edward White Hosp.; asst. clin. prof. ophthalmology, U.So. Fla.; attending surgeon St. Anthony's Bayfront Med. Ctr., Am. Soc. for Cataract and Refractive Surgery, Ctr. Spl. Surgery; med. dir. Suncoast Eye Clinic, Pa. Fellow ACS, Am. Acad. Ophthalmology; mem. AMA, Am. Soc. Ophthalmic Plastic and Reconstructive Surgery, Fla. Med. Assn., Fla. Soc. Ophthalmology, Pinellas County Med. Soc., Bayou Country Club. Republican. Jewish. Avocations: tennis, golf, travel, skiing. Office: 2200 16th St N Saint Petersburg FL 33704-3106 Home: 7676 Hunter Lane Pinellas Park FL 33782 Office Phone: 727-822-4729. E-mail: mjreye@aol.com.

**ROSENBLUM, MINDY FLEISCHER,** pediatrician; b. Bronxville, NY, June 5, 1951; d. Herman and Muriel (Gold) Fleischer; m. Jay S. Rosenblum, June 22, 1971; children: Meira, Tamar, Rafi, Rachel. BA, Yeshiva U., 1972; MD, Albert Einstein Coll., 1976. Diplomate Am. Bd. Pediat., Am. Bd. Pediatric Endocrinology. Intern in pediat. Bronx Mcpl. Hosp. Ctr., 1976-77, residency in pediat., 1977-79; fellow in pediatric endocrinology Children's Hosp. of Phila., 1981; asst. prof. U. Pa., Phila., 1981—95; attending physician Bryn Mawr (Pa.) Hosp., 1981—, Lankenau Hosp., Wynnewood, Pa., 1983—; clin. assoc. Children's Hosp. of Phila., 1995—. Fellow Am. Acad. Pediat.; mem. Phila. Pediat. Soc. (bd. dirs. 1988-92), Am. Diabetes Assn., Lawson Wilkins Pediatric Endocrine Soc. Office Phone: 610-642-9200. Personal E-mail: jmr101@comcast.net.

**ROSENBLUM, NANCY LIPTON,** political science professor; BA with high honors, Radcliffe Coll., 1969; PhD, Harvard Univ., 1973; LHD (hon.), Kalamazoo Coll., 1993. Asst. prof. Harvard Univ., 1973—77, assoc. prof., 1977—80; prof. Brown Univ., 1980—97; vis. prof. Harvard Univ., 1985; chair, Polit. Sci. dept. Brown Univ., 1989—95, Henry Merritt Wriston prof., 1997—2001, founder & dir., Stephen Robert Inst. for Study of Values, 1998—2000; Sen. Joseph Clark prof. of ethics in politics & govt. Harvard Univ., 2001—. Mem. exec. com. Conf. for Study of Polit. Thought, 1988—; rev. editor Political Theory, 1988—; mem. editl. bd., 1993—97; council mem. Am. Polit. Sci. Assn., 1991—93, Tocqueville Soc., 2001—; mem. vis. com. dept. Polit. Sci. Brandeis Univ., 1986, Univ. Mich., Ann Arbor, 1993, Queens Coll., 1993, Stanford Univ., 1994, Univ. Alta., Canada, 1995; mem. vis. com. Dept. Polit., Princeton Univ., 2002. Author: Membership & Morals: The Personal Uses of Pluralism in America, 1998, Another Liberalism: Romanticism and the Reconstruction of Liberal Thought, 1987, Bentham's Theory of the Modern State, 1978; editor: Obligations of Citizenship and Demands of Faith, 2000, Liberalism and the Moral Life, 1993; co-editor: Breaking the Cycles of Hatred, 2002, Civil Society and Government, 2002; contbr. articles to profl. jour., chapters to books. Bd. dir. Civil Liberties Union Mass., First Work Ctr., Provincetown, Mass. Recipient David Easton award, AP3A, 2002; Bunting Inst. Fellow, Radcliffe Coll., 1988—89. Fellow: Am. Acad. Arts & Sci. Office: Harvard University Littauer 318 Cambridge MA 02138 Office Phone: 617-384-5851. Business E-Mail: nrosenblum@latte.harvard.edu.

**ROSENBLUM, RICHARD MARK,** utilities executive; b. NYC, Apr. 28, 1950; s. Victor Sigmund and Julia K. R.; m. Michele E. Cartier, Aug. 30, 1979; children: Gialisa, Jeremy Scott. BS, MS, Rensselaer Poly. Inst., 1973. Startup engr. Combustion Engring., Inc., Windsor, Conn., 1973-76; engr. So. Calif. Edison Co., Rosemead, 1976-82; project mgr. San Onofre Nuclear Generating Sta., 1982-83, tech. mgr., 1983-84, nuclear safety mgr., 1984-86, mgr. quality assurance, 1986-89, mgr. nuclear regulatory affairs, 1989-93, v.p. engring. and tech. svcs., 1993-95, v.p. distbn., 1996-98, sr. v.p. T&D, 1998—2005; v.p. generation, chief nuc. officer Generation Bus. Unit, 2005—. N.Y. State Regents scholar, 1968-73. Office: 2244 Walnut Grove Ave Rosemead CA 91770-3714 Business E-Mail: richard.rosenblum@sce.com.

**ROSENBLUM, ROBERT H.,** art historian, educator; b. NYC, July 24, 1927; s. Abraham H. and Lily M. (Lipkin) Rosenblum; m. Jane Kaplowitz, June 23, 1977; children: Sophie Lila, Theodore Abraham. BA, Queens Coll., 1948; MA, Yale U., 1950; PhD, NYU, 1956; MA (hon.), Oxford U., 1972; ArtsD (hon.), Queens Coll., 1992. Mem. faculty U. Mich., Ann Arbor, 1955-56, Princeton U., 1956-66, Yale U., New Haven, 1966-67, NYU, 1967—, prof. fine arts, 1967—, Henry Ittleson Jr. Prof. Modern European Art. Vis. prof. Columbia U., 1960-61, 1963; adj. curator Guggenheim Mus., NYC, 1996—98, Stephen and Nan Swid Curator 20th-Century Art, 1998—. Author: Cubism and Twentieth Century Art, 1960, Transformations in Late Eighteenth Century Art, 1967, Ingres, 1967, Frank Stella, 1971, Modern Painting and the Northern Romantic Tradition, The International Style of 1800, 1976, Andy Warhol: Portraits of the 70s, 1979, 19th Century Art, 1984, The Dog in Art From Rococo to Post-Modernism, 1988, The Romantic Child From Runge to Sendak, 1989, Paintings in the Musee d'Orsay, 1989, The Jeff Koons Handbook, 1992, Andy Warhol Portraits, 1993, Mel Ramos: Pop Images, 1994, The Paintings of August Strindberg, The Structure of Chaos, 1995, On Modern American Art, 1999, 1900: Art at the Crossroads, 2000, Introducing Gilbert & George, 2004. Served with U.S. Army, 1945-46. Recipient Award for Disting. Contbr. to the Field of Art Criticism, Internat.

Assn. Art Critics/USA, 2005, Disting. Tchg. award, NYU, 2005. Fellow: Am. Acad. Arts and Scis.; mem.: Coll. Art Assn. (Frank Jewett Mather Award for distinction in art criticism 1981), Legion of Honor, L'Ordre Arts et Lettres (commandeur, chevalier). Office: NYU Dept Fine Arts Washington Sq New York NY 10003-6688

**ROSENBLUM, WILLIAM F., JR.,** lawyer; b. NYC, May 11, 1935; AB cum laude, Princeton U., 1957; JD, Columbia U., 1960. Bar: N.Y. 1961, U.S. Dist. Ct. (so. dist.) N.Y. 1965. Gen. atty. Stanley Warner Corp., 1964-66; assoc. Leon, Weill & Mahony, 1967-70, Finley, Kumble, Wagner & Heine, 1970-74; pvt. practice, 1975; v.p. legal affairs Rep. Nat. Bank N.Y., 1976-82; sr. v.p., dep. gen. counsel, corp. sec. Rep. N.Y. Corp., 1987—2001; sr. v.p., dep. gen. counsel HSBC USA Inc., 2000—01; mng. dir., gen. counsel NuVerse Advisors LLC, N.Y.C., 2001—. Mem.: ABA (mem. bus. law sect., mem. futures and derivatives regulation and pvt. investment cos. coms.), Assn. Bar City N.Y. (fgn. and comparative law UN com. 2000—04, investment mgmt. regulation com., banking law com., investment funds com.), N.Y. State Bar Assn. (mem. sect. internat. law, bus. law, futures and derivatives regulation 1990—). Office: Nuverse Advisors LLC 645 Fifth Ave New York NY 10022 Business E-Mail: wrosenblum@nuverse.com.

**ROSENBLUM, ZINA MICHELLE ZARIN,** psychology professor, marketing professional, researcher; b. N.Y.C., Mar. 4, 1949; d. Harry and Miriam (Bachrach) Zarin; m. Martin Jerome Rosenblum, May 31, 1975; children: Steven David, Richard James. BA magna cum laude, Queens Coll., 1971; MEd, Columbia U., 1973, MEd Counseling Psychology, 1973. Prof. psychology Marymount Manhattan Coll., N.Y.C., 1971—73; addictions counselor Manhattan Vets. Hosp., N.Y.C., 1971—73; project dir. BBD&O Advt., N.Y.C., 1973—74, Grey Advt., N.Y.C., 1974—75; supr. market rsch. Doyle Dane & Bernbach, N.Y.C., 1975—77, SSC& B, N.Y.C., 1977—78; dir. rsch. Hershey Co., Pa., 1978—79; administr. Suncoast Eye Clinic, St. Petersburg, Fla., 1979—97; prof. psychology St. Petersburg Coll., Seminole, Fla., 1997—. Sec. Nat. Coun. Jewish Women, Fla., 1980—81; docent Fla. Holocaust Mus., 2005—. Scholar, Columbia U., 1971; Nat. Merit scholar, Coll. Bd., 1970. Mem.: APA, Phi Beta Kappa. Office: Suncoast Eye Clinic Martin Rosenblum 2200 16th St North Saint Petersburg FL 33704 Office Phone: 727-822-4729. Personal E-mail: zcurl@aol.com.

**ROSENBLUTH, MORTON,** periodontist, educator; b. NYC, Sept. 28, 1924; s. Jacob and Eva (Bigeleissen) R.; m. Sylvia Fradin, July 2, 1946; children: Cheryl Bonnie, Hal Glen. BA, NYU, 1943, grad. program in periodontia, oral medicine, 1946, DDS, 1946. Diplomate Am. Bd. Periodontology. Intern Bellevue Hosp., N.Y.C., 1946-47, resident, 1947; individual practice dentistry N.Y.C., 1947-59; individual practice periodontia North Miami Beach, Fla., 1960—; individual practice periodontia, TMJ, implantology Bay Harbor Islands, Fla., 1995—. Periodontist Mt. Sinai Hosp., N.Y., Polyclinic Hosp. and Med. Sch. N.Y., Mt. Sinai Hosp., Miami Beach, Fla., Parkway Gen. Hosp.; chief dental dept. North Miami Gen. Hosp.; chmn. periodontia sect. Dade County Rsch. Ctr.; clin. assoc. prof. divsn. oral and maxillofacial surgery U. Miami Sch. Medicine; assoc. clin. prof. Southeastern U. Health Scis.; assoc. prof. Nova Southeastern U. Coll. Dental Medicine; lectr. throughout U.S.A., Israel, Mexico, Rome, Teheran, Bangkok, Hong Kong, Tokyo, Honolulu, Jamaica, Paris, London, Sicily, Budapest, Brussels, Luxembourg, South Africa and others; vis. lectr. U. Tenn. Dental Coll., NYU Dental Coll.; cons. VA Hosp., Miami. Contbr. articles to profl. jours. Mem. adv. bd. U. Fla. Coll. Dentistry; mem. profl. adv. bd. North Dade Children's Ctr., Hope Sch. Mentally Retarded Children; mem. sci. adv. com. United Health Found.; chmn. Dental divsn. United Fund of Dade County, Combined Jewish Appeal; nat. chmn. Hebrew U. Sch. Dental Medicine; bd. dirs. Health Planning Coun. South Fla.; pres. Condominium Assn.; bd. dirs. and bd. overseers Am. Friends of Hebrew U.; mem. med. adv. bd. Dade-Broward Lupus Found.; trustee Jewish Congregation, 1961-64. With AUS, 1943-46; capt. USAF, 1951-52. Recipient Maimonides award State of Israel, 1979. Fellow Am. Coll. Dentists, Internat. Coll. Dentists; mem. ADA, Am. Acad. Periodontology, Am. Assn. Hosp. Dental Chiefs, Am. Acad. Dental Medicine, Am. Soc. Advancement Gen. Anesthesia in Dentistry, Am. Soc. Periodontists, Fla. Soc. Periodontists, Northeastern Soc. Periodontists, Fla. Dental Soc. (chmn. coun. on legislation), Miami Dental Soc., Miami Beach Dental Soc., East Coast Dental Soc. (sec.-treas. 1968, pres. 1971-72), North Dade Dental Soc. (pres. 1963-64), Fedn. Dentaire Internat., Fla. Acad. Dental Practice Adminstrn., Alpha Omega (pres. 1978-78, internat. regent 1973-75, internat. editor 1975-77, internat. pres.-elect 1977-78, internat. pres. 1979, chmn. bd. Alpha Omega Found. 1985-90), Am. Dental Interfrat. Coun. (pres. 1981-82), Nocoma Club (pres. 1958-60), NYU Century Club (local chmn.), Jockey Club (bd. govs.), KP, Masons, Kiwanis (bd. dirs. 1965), Chaine Des Rotisseurs (Miami Beach charge de missions). Home: 20281 E Country Club Dr Apt # 1001 Aventura FL 33180 Office: 1048 Kane Concourse Bay Harbor Islands FL 33154-2000 Office Phone: 305-867-0005. Personal E-mail: periomort@aol.com.

**ROSENDAL, HANS ERIK,** retired meteorologist; b. Lyngby, Denmark, July 19, 1931; s. Kaj and Anna Katrine (Hansen) R.; m. Angela Karlos, Dec. 20, 1958; children: Erik P., Dana G., Paul A. BS, U. Wis., 1960; MS, U. Mich., 1965. Meteorologist U.S. Weather Bur., Washington, 1960-65; state climatologist Nat. Weather Svc., Madison, Wis., 1965-73, meteorologist Milw., 1973-74, Phoenix, 1974-76, Honolulu, 1976—2005; ret., 2005. Editor Mariners Weather Log, 1962-64. Recipient Gold medal U.S. Dept. Commerce, Honolulu, 1992. Fellow Am. Meteorol. Soc. (spl. award 1992). Lutheran. Home: 1242 Mokapu Blvd Kailua HI 96734-1847 E-mail: rosendalhe@aol.com.

**ROSENDHAL, JEFFREY DAVID,** federal agency administrator, educator, astronomer; b. Bklyn., June 21, 1941; s. Louis and Beulah (Goldsmith) R.; m. Sharon E. Katzman, Dec. 27, 1964 (div. Jan. 25, 1989); children: Martin Andrew, Rachel Lynn; m. Ellen R. Anderson, Feb. 14, 1992. BA, Williams Coll., 1962; MS, U. Ill., 1963; PhD, Yale U., 1968. Vis. asst. prof. astronomy U. Wash., Seattle, 1968-69; asst. prof. U. Wis., Madison, 1969-71, U. Ariz., Tucson, 1971-74; with NASA, Washington, 1974—2004, mgr. advanced programs and tech., astrophysics divsn., 1978-80, asst. assoc. administr. advanced planning Office Space Sci., 1980-81, asst. assoc. administr. sci. Office Space Sci., Applications, 1981-87, spl. asst. to assoc. administr. for space sci. and applications, 1987-89, 92-93, spl. asst. for policy Office Exploration, 1989-90, asst. dir. exploration (internat.) Office Aeronautics, Exploration and Tech., 1990-91, asst. dir. strategic planning Astrophysics Divsn. Office of Space Sci., 1993-96, asst. assoc. administr./edn. and outreach Office Space Sci., 1996-2001, edn. and pub. outreach dir. Office of Space Sci., 2001—04, asst. assoc. administr. for edn. programs Office of Edn., 2004. Vis. prof. internat. rels. George Washington U., 1988-89; mem. staff energy subcom. House Sci. Space and Tech. Com., 1992; vis. sr. scholar Nat. Air and Space Mus., 2005-06; cons., Jet Propulsion Lab., Univs. Space Rsch. Assn., Astron. Soc. Pacific, NASA, 2005—; dep. dir. U. Space Rsch. Assn. Nat. Ctr. Earth and Space Sci. Edn., 2006. Mem. editl. bd.: Jour. Brit. Interplanetary Soc., 1988—; contbr. articles to profl. jours. Recipient Team Achievement award European Space Agy., 1983, 85, 86, Presdl. award of Meritorious Exec. in Sr. Exec. Svc., 1987, 2001; NSF grantee, 1971, 72-73; NASA fellow Yale U., 1966-68; hon. Woodrow Wilson fellow, 1962. Fellow: AIAA (assoc.); mem.: Sr. Execs. Assn., Internat. Astron. Union, Internat. Acad. Astronautics, Royal Astron. Soc., Am. Astron. Soc. (divsn. planetary scis., hist. astronomy divsn.), Astron. Soc. Pacific (Klumpke-Roberts award 2006), Cosmos Club, Phi Beta Kappa. Achievements include discovery of the variability of the microturbulence in early-type high luminosity stars; direction of the selection of flight experiments for every major NASA scientific mission 1980-1988; development of strategic and implementation plans for incorporating education and the public understanding of science into space science research programs and missions; establishment of a national support network for space science education; creation of the largest single program in astronomy and space science education ever undertaken, an effort that is now reaching tens of millions of people every year. Home: 11446 Links Dr Reston VA 20190-4813 E-mail: jeffrosendhal@comcast.net.

**ROSENE, PAUL EARL,** music educator; b. Chgo., Ill., Mar. 26, 1930; s. Earl Nile and Dorothy Mae Rosene; m. Doris J. Mehrkens, Nov. 18, 1951; children: Richard, Cindy Mann. MusD Edn., U. of Ill., Champaign-Urbana, Illinois, 1968—76; Master degree in Edn. -Psychology and Music, Ill. State U., Normal, IL, 1955—57; BS in Music Edn., Ill. State Normal U., Normal, Illinois, 1947. Cert. master tchr. Ill.; supr. student tchg. in music Ill., master tchr. Music Educators Nat. Conf. Dir. of music edn. Saybrook (Ill.) Pub. Sch., Saybrook, Ill., 1951—52; supr. of music and dir. of bands Chenoa (Ill.) Pub. Schs., 1952—53; instructor band sch. USAF, Geneva, NY, 1953—54, bandsman French horn Dayton, Ohio, 1954—55, dir. of men's glee club, 1954—55; dir. of instrumental music Avon (Ill.) Pub. Schs., 1955—57; supr. of music and dir. of h.s. bands Pittsfield (Ill.) Pub. Schs., 1957—67; prof. of music edn. and supr. of student tchg. in music Ill. State U., Normal, 1967—90; music cons. handbells and choirchimes Malmark, Inc., Lady Lake, Fla., 1990—. USA pers. dir. Sch. Band/Chorus of Am., Bloomington, 1967—79. Author: (music book) Making Music With Choirchimes Instruments, 1982; author: (composer) (music techniques book) Making Music with Choirchimes Instruments - Advanced Method, 1986; composer (music for choirchimes): (music publ.) Pontifest, 1988; author: (techniques book) Special Effects for Choirchimes, 2003. Dir. of handbells Bethany Luth. Ch., Leesburg, Fla., 1990—; dir. Cen. Ill. Cmty. Band, Bloomington-Normal, 1979—90; dir. and founder Ill. State U. Handbells and Choirchime Ensembles, Normal, 1974—90. Staff sgt. band dir., instr. band sch. USAF, 1953—55. Mem.: Pittsfield Tchrs. Assn. (pres. 1960—67), Ill. Music Edn. Assn. (v.p. 1972—80, pres. dist. III 1972—84, Disting. Svc. Award 1991), Fla. Music Educators Assn., Nat. Assn. for Music Therapy (editor newsletter 1967—90), Music Educators Nat. Conf. (univ. contact Gt. Lakes divsn. 1979—84), Fla. Band Assn. (adjudicator 1994—). Republican. Lutheran. Avocations: Bible study, walking, reading, attending concerts, computer technology. Home: 216 Lake Griffin Rd Lady Lake FL 32159-3836 Office: Music Edn Cons 216 Lake Griffin Rd Lady Lake FL 32159-3836 Office Phone: 352-753-8304. E-mail: rosenebell@aol.com.

**ROSENFELD, ALBERT HYMAN,** science and medical writer; b. Phila., May 31, 1920; s. Samuel and Annie (Zeiffert) R.; m. Lillian Elizabeth Snow, Aug. 24, 1948; children: Robert, Shana. BA in History and Social Scis., N.Mex. State U., 1950, DLett (hon.), 1971. Freelance mag. writer, corr., Santa Fe, 1950-56; sci. editor Life mag., N.Y.C., 1956-69; mng. editor Family Health mag., N.Y.C., 1969-71; writer, prodr. Time-Life Video, N.Y.C., 1971-72; sci. editor, columnist Saturday Rev., N.Y.C., 1973-79; cons. on future programs March of Dimes Birth Defects Found., White Plains, NY, 1973—2005; adj. asst. prof. U. Tex. Med. Br., Galveston, 1973-98. Author: The Quintessence of Irving Langmuir, 1962, The Second Genesis, 1969, Prolongevity II, 1985; co-author: Responsible Parenthood, 1980; contbr. articles to profl. publs. Sgt. U.S. Army, 1942-45, ETO. Recipient award for leadership in med. journalism Lasker Found., 1967, Nat. Mag. award Columbia U., 1975, James P. Grady medal Am. Chem. Soc., 1981. Mem. World Future Soc., Nat. Assn. Sci. Writers, Authors Guild, Smithsonian Assocs., Hastings Ctr. Democrat. Jewish. Avocations: music, sketching, tennis, baseball, hiking. E-mail: alrosenf@westnet.com.

**ROSENFELD, ARTHUR F.,** federal official, lawyer; b. Allentown, Pa., 1944; m. Carla Toledo. BA, Muhlenberg Coll., 1970; MBA, Lehigh U., 1974; JD, Villanova U., 1979. Bar: D.C. 1979, U.S. Supreme Ct., U.S. Ct. Appeals (4th, 5th and D.C. cirs.). Labor atty. U.S. C. of C., Washington, 1979—84; atty. Hansell & Post, 1984—86; numerous positions including counsel for regulations divsn. employee benefits, spl. asst. to solicitor of labor, assoc. dep. sec. U.S. Dept. Labor, 1986—97; sr. labor advisor to chmn. James M. Jeffords Senate Com. Health, Edn., Labor and Pensions, 1997—2001; gen. counsel NLRB, 2001—05, acting gen. counsel, 2005—06; dir. Fed Mediation & Concilation Svc., Washington, 2006—. Fellow: The Coll. of Labor and Employment Lawyers. Office: Fed Mediation & Concillation Svc 2100 K St NW Rm 900 Washington DC 20427*

**ROSENFELD, ARTHUR H.,** physics professor, researcher; b. Birmingham, Ala., June 22, 1926; BS in Physics, Va. Poly. Inst., 1944; PhD in Physics, U. Chgo., 1954; DSc (hon.), U. Durham, Eng., 1983. Rsch. assoc. Inst. Nuclear Studies U. Chgo., 1954-55; rsch. assoc. Lawrence Berkeley Lab. U. Calif., Berkeley, 1955-57; asst. prof. to assoc. prof. U. Chgo., 1957-63; prof. physics U. Calif., Berkeley, 1963-94, dir. particle data group Lawrence Berkeley Lab., 1964-75, acting chmn. dept. computer sci., 1967-68, leader rsch. group A Lawrence Berkeley Lab., 1971-73, leader energy-efficient bldgs. rsch program Lawrence Berkeley Lab., 1975-83, vice chmn. energy and resources grad. program, 1986-94, dir. Ctr. Bldg. Sci. Lawrence Berkeley Lab., 1986-94, founder, acting dir. Calif. Inst. for Energy Efficiency, 1988-90, prof. emeritus, 1994—; sr. advisor to asst. sec. energy efficiency U.S. Dept. Energy, Washington, 1994-99; commr. Calif. Energy Comm., Sacramento, Calif., 2000—. Vis. prof. Coll. de France, Paris, 1976; co-founder Am. Coun. Energy-Efficient Econ., 1979, chmn., 1981-83, pres., 1984-90, bd. dirs., 1990-94; mem. steering com. advanced customer tech. test maximum energy efficiency Pacific Gas & Electric Co., 1989-98; mem. tech. adv. panel joint com. on energy regulation and environ. State of Calif., 1990-91; mem. Nat. Sci. and Tech. Coun., 1994—, civilian indsl. tech. com, 1994—, co-chmn. subcom. constrn. and bldg., 1994—. Author: (with E. Fermi and others) Nuclear Physics, 1949, Experimental Meson Spectroscopy, 1968, 3d edit., 1972, Supplying Energy Through Greater Efficiency: The Potential for Conservation in California's Residential Sector, 1983, A New Prosperity: The SERI Solar/Conservation Study, 1991, Scenarios of U.S. Carbon Reductions, Interlaboratory Working Group, 1997; contbr. articles, seminars to profl. jours., confs.; assoc. editor Jour. Computational Physics, 1964-73, Energy and Bldgs., 1979—, Energy, the Internat. Jour., 1985-91; editl. cons. Ency. of Applied Physics, 1988—. Mem. governing bd. Am. Inst. Physics, 1974-77; co-founder Am. Coun. for an Energy Efficient Economy, 1979, Ctr. for Energy and Climate Solution, Washington, DC; chmn. 1981-83, pres. 1984—, mem. adv. com. Calif. Legis. Joint Com. on Energy Regulation and Environ., 1990-91. Recipient Leo Szilard award for Physics in Pub. Interest, 1986, Sadi Carnot award for Energy Efficiency, US Dept. Energy, 1993, Star Energy Efficiency for outstanding contbn. in promoting energy efficiency Alliance to Save Energy, 1995, 2005 Enrico Fermi award, US Dept. Energy Fellow Am. Physical Soc. (sec., treas. divsn. particles and fields 1967-71, Leo Szilard award for physics in the pub. interest 1986); mem. NAS (panel on policy implications of greenhouse warm 1990—), Fedn. Am. Sci. (coun. 1964-72, 77-81, 83-87, 94-98, 2004—), Am. Inst. Physics (mem. governing bd. 1974-77). Achievements include co-developement of Ultra-Violet Water Works to purify water in villages and slums, 1996; studied under Enrico Fermi at U. Chgo. Office: Calif Energy Commn 1516 9th St Sacramento CA 95814 Office Phone: 916-654-4930. Business E-Mail: AHRosenfeld@LBL.gov.*

**ROSENFELD, ARTHUR HERBERT,** lawyer; b. Bklyn., May 24, 1930; s. Abraham and Sadie (Albert) R.; m. Lois E. Glantz, Apr. 15, 1956; children: Felicia Ann, Carolyn Jane, Sara Ellen. Student, St. Andrew's U., 1950-51; AB, Union Coll., Schenectady, 1952; JD, Harvard U., 1955; postgrad., CCNY, 1962-63. Bar: N.Y. 1955. Pres. Warren, Gorham & Lamont, Inc., N.Y.C., 1970-81, Internat. Thomson Profl. Pub., N.Y.C., 1981-84; chmn. bd. Rosenfeld, Emanuel Inc., Larchmont, NY, 1984-88; pres. Prentice Hall Tax & Profl. Ref., N.Y.C., 1988-89, Maxwell Macmillan Profl. and Bus. Reference Div., Englewood Cliffs, NJ, 1989-92; chmn. Arthur H. Rosenfeld Assocs., 1991—; Civic Rsch. Inst., Inc., 1992—. Mem. ABA, N.Y. State Bar Assn., Am. Assn. Pubs. (exec. coun. 1991). Harvard Club. Democrat.

**ROSENFELD, GERALD,** investment company executive, financial analyst; b. NYC, Dec. 29, 1946; s. Jack and Shirley (Ohrer) R.; m. Nancy P. Henenfeld, Jan. 18, 1970 (div. Dec. 1984); 1 child, Erica; m. Judith Ellen Zarin, May 26, 1985; 1 child, Jack. BCE, CCNY, 1968; M in Engring. Sci., CUNY, 1970; PhD, NYU, 1973. Instr. NYU, N.Y.C., 1970-73; assoc. prof. U. Md., Catonsville, 1973-76; mgr. analytical services McKinsey & Co., N.Y.C., 1976-79; assoc. Salomon Bros., Inc., N.Y.C., 1979-80, v.p., 1980-85, mng. dir., 1985-87, chief fin. officer, 1987-88; mng. dir. Bankers Trust Co., N.Y.C., 1988—92, Lazard Freres & Co., 1992—98; sr. mng. dir. NationsBanc

Montgomery Securities, 1998; mng. mem. G. Rosenfeld & Co., 1998—2000; CEO Rothschild North America, 2000—. Bd. dir. Resources Connection, ContiGroup Companies, Case Corp.; mem. adv. bd. Corpedia Edn. Mem. bd. overseers Stern Sch. Bus., N.Y. Univ., bd. dir., Jewish Theol. Sem.; mem. bd. adv. Lerner Sch. Bus., Univ. Del. Fellow: Am. Acad. Arts & Sci. Office: Rothschild North America 51st Fl 1251 Ave of the Americas New York NY 10020

**ROSENFELD, HARRY MORRIS,** editor; b. Berlin, 1929; s. Sam and Esther Rosenfeld; m. Anne Hahn, Feb. 28, 1953; children: Susan, Amy, Stefanie. BA, Syracuse U., 1952; postgrad., NYU, 1954, Columbia U., 1955-59. With N.Y. Herald Tribune, 1954-66, fgn. editor, 1962-66; mng. editor Herald Tribune News Svc., 1959-62; with Washington Post, 1966-78, fgn. editor, 1969; asst. mng. editor Met. News, 1970-74, Nat. News, 1974-76, Outlook/Book World, 1976-78; editor Times Union and Knickerbocker News, Albany, NY, 1978-88, L.A. Herald Examiner, 1985, The Times Union and Sunday Times Union, 1978-96; editor-at-large, columnist L.C. Times Union, Albany, NY, 1996—. Dir. daily Watergate coverage for Washington Post (newspaper award Pulitzer Gold medal for pub. svc.); vice-chmn. N.Y. Fair Trial Free Press Conf., 1985-98, vice chmn. emeritus, 1998—; co-chmn. N.Y. State Reporters Com. for Freedom of Press; mem. adv. com. Harvard Journalism Fellowship for Advanced Studies in Pub. Health; Pulitzer juror, 1987-88, 96, 97; chmn. Elder Network of the Capital Region. Commr. N.Y. State Regents Commn. on Libr. Svcs. Recipient Black United Front award, 1973, First Amendment award Anti-Defamation League-B'nai B'rith, L.A., Outstanding Alumni award, Syracuse U. Coll. of Arts and Scis., 1993, Media Responsibility award N.Y. State Martin Luther King Jr. Inst. for Non-Violence, 1993, Dr. Morton Berger Meml. award Maimonides Day Sch., 2005. Mem. Am. Soc. Newspaper Editors, N.Y. State AP Assn. (pres. 1983, 3d pl. column award 1983, 85, 1st pl. column award 1987), N.Y. State Soc. Newspaper Editors, Internat. Press Inst., UPI Fgn. News Com. (rep. for N.E.), Soc. Profl. Journalists (adv. bd. Albany chpt.), and 3 commns. on Cameras in the Cts. (adv. comm.). Office: Times Union PO Box 15000 Albany NY 12212-5000 Office Phone: 518-454-5450. Business E-Mail: hrosenfeld@timesunion.com.

**ROSENFELD, IRENE B.,** food products company executive; b. Bklyn., 1953; BA in Psychology, Cornell U, 1975, MS in Bus., 1977, PhD in Mktg. & Statistics, 1980. With Dancer, Fitzgerald Sample Advertising (now Saatchi and Saatchi), 1979—81, Kraft Foods Inc., 1981—2004, exec. v.p., gen. mgr., beverages divsn., 1991—94, exec. v.p., gen. mgr. desserts & snacks divsn., 1994—96; pres. Kraft Foods Canada, 1996—2004; group v.p. Kraft Foods Inc., 2000—04; pres. Kraft Food N. Am., 2003—04; chmn., CEO Frito-Lay Inc. (divsn. of PepsiCo Inc.), Plano, Tex., 2004—06; CEO Kraft Foods Inc., 2006—. Bd. dirs. AutoNation, Inc. Mem. YWCA Acad. Women Achievers; bd. trustees Cornell U. Named one of Most Powerful Women, Forbes Mag., 2006; recipient The Masters in Excellence award, Jewish Student Cmty. at Cornell Univ., 2005. Office: Kraft Foods Inc 3 Lakes Dr Northfield IL 60093*

**ROSENFELD, ISADORE,** cardiologist, educator; b. Sept. 7, 1926; arrived in U.S., 1958; s. Morris and Vera (Friedman) Rosenfeld; m. Camilla Master, Aug. 19, 1956; children: Arthur, Stephen, Hildi, Herbert. BS, McGill U., 1947, M.D.C.M., 1951, diploma in internal medicine, 1956, DSc (hon.), 1999; PhD (hon.), Tel Aviv U. Intern Royal Victoria Hosp., Montreal; resident Balt. City Hosp.; clin. asst. prof. medicine NY Hosp. Weil Cornell Med. Ctr., NYC, 1964—71, clin. assoc. prof., 1971—79, clin. prof., 1979—. Now hon. fellow; attending physician NY Hosp., NYC, 1989—, Meml. Sloan Kettering Cancer Ctr.; juror Lasker Sci. Awards, 1974—90; dir. Rsch. Am., 1990; Rossi Disting prof. clin. medicine NY Hosp. Weil Cornell Med. Ctr., 1993—; vis. prof. Baylor U. Coll. Medicine, 1982; mem. practicing physicians adv. coun. to U.S. Sec Health and Human Svcs., practicing physician, 1992—96; bd. overseers Cornell U. Med. Coll., 1980—; bd. vistors U. Calif. Sch. Medicine, Davis, 1983—; cons. NIH; invited lectr. in field. Physician; lectr. in field; TV commentator in field. Author: EKG and X-Ray in Diseases of the Heart, 1963, The Complete Medical Exam, 1978, Second Opinion, 1981, Modern Prevention, 1986, Symptoms, 1988, The Best Treatment, 1991, Doctor, What Should I EAT?, 1995, Dr. Rosenfeld's Guide to Alternative Medicine, 1997, Love Now-Age Later, 1999, Power to the Patient: The Treatment to Insist on When You're Sick, 2002, Dr. Isadore Rosenfeld's Breakthrough Medicine, 2004, Healing Breakthroughs, 2004, Dr. Isadore Rosenfeld's Breakthrough Health, 2005; med. cons.: Vogue mag., 1993—97, FOX News Channel, 1996—; contbg. editor: Parade mag., 1997—; health editor:, 1998—. Pres. Rosenfeld Heart Found., N.Y.C., 1979—82; mem. N.Y. Heart Assn., 1979—82; mem. nat. adv. commr. Harriman Inst. Advanced Study of Soviet Union, 1982—; mem. nat. adv. commr. increasing physical activity program Robert Wood Johnson Found. Recipient Vera award, The Voice Found., 1981, Inaugural award, N.Y. Heart Assn., Silver award for patient edn. and info., Nat. Health Info. Rsch. Chr., 1996, Citizen of the World award, U.N., 1999, Siver award, Nat. Health Info., 1999, Gold Triangle award, Am. Acad. Dermatology, Silver award, Nat. Mature Media awards, Dist. Med. Svc. award, Am. Physicians Fellowship, Merit award, Consumer Health Pub. Assn., Am. Consumer Publ. Assn. and Am. Consumer Publ. Corp, 2000, Advocacy award for impact on pub. opinion through the Media, Rsch. Am., 2001, Lifetime Achievement award, Found. Biomed. Rsch. Fellow: Am. Physician's Fellowship for Israel (hon. nat. pres. 1975—), N.Y. County Med. Soc. (bd. censors 1979—83, v.p. 1983—84, pres. 1984—85, bd. trustees 1985—), Royal Coll. Physicians Can., Am. Coll. Chest Physicians, ACP, Cornell Alumni Assn. (hon.). Jewish. Achievements include research in hypertension; angina pectoris; sudden cardiac death; arteriosclerosis. Office: 125 E 72nd St New York NY 10021-4250 Personal E-mail: irmd@earthlink.net. E-mail: irmd@mac.com.

**ROSENFELD, JOHN LANG,** geology educator; b. Portland, Oreg., July 14, 1920; s. James Wendel and Gladys (Lang) R.; m. Juanita Baker, Oct. 22, 1943; children: Susan Jane, John Lang. AB, Dartmouth Coll., 1942; AM, Harvard U., 1949, PhD, 1954. Asst. prof. geology Mo. Sch. Mines, U. Mo. Rolla, 1949—55; vis. asst. prof. geology Wesleyan U., Middletown, Conn., 1955—57; from asst. prof. to prof. geology UCLA, 1957—91, prof. geology emeritus, 1991—. Commr. Geol. and Natural History Survey, State of Conn., 1955-57. Contbr. numerous articles to profl. jours. Guggenheim fellow, 1963-64. Fellow Mineral. Soc. Am., Geol. Soc. Am.; mem. AAAS, Am. Geophys. Union, Nature Conservancy (life), Union Concerned Scientists. Office: UCLA Dept Earth And Space Scis Los Angeles CA 90095 Office Phone: 310-825-1505. E-mail: rosenfel@ucla.edu.

**ROSENFELD, JONATHAN D.,** lawyer; b. 1961; AB, Brandeis Univ., 1983; JD, Boston Univ., 1986. Bar: Calif. 1986, Conn. 1989, Mass. 1990. Ptnr., chmn. Labor dept. Wilmer Cutler Pickering Hale & Dorr, Boston. Office: Wilmer Cutler Pickering Hale & Dorr 60 State St Boston MA 02109 Office Phone: 617-526-6941. Office Fax: 617-526-5000. Business E-Mail: jonathan.rosenfeld@wilmerhale.com.

**ROSENFELD, LAWRENCE J. (LARRY),** lawyer; b. Bronx, NY, Aug. 25, 1950; BA magna cum laude, Queens Coll., CUNY, 1972; JD, Yale, 1975. Bar: Ariz. 1976, US Supreme Ct. 1981. Named one of Leading Lawyers, Ariz. Bus. Jour., 2006; named to Best Lawyers in Am., 2003—06, Chambers USA (Labor and Employment Law), 2005—06. Mem.: ABA, Maricopa County Bar Assn., Ariz. State Bar Assn. Office: Greenberg Traurig LLP Ste 700 2375 E Camelback Rd Phoenix AZ 85016-9000 Office Phone: 602-445-8502. Office Fax: 602-445-8100. Business E-Mail: rosenfeldl@gtlaw.com.

**ROSENFELD, NACHMAN,** plastic surgeon; b. Tel Aviv, Feb. 16, 1943; s. Pinhas and Sara Rosenfeld; m. Hennia Finkelstein; children: Dror, Iris. MD, Hebrew U., 1968. Board Certified Am. Bd. Plastic Surgery, 1978. Resident Albert Einstein Coll. Medicine, NYC, 1977, asst. clin. instr.; pvt. practice, 1977—. Fellow: Am. Coll. Surgeons; mem.: Am. Soc. for Asthetic Plastic Surgery, Am. Soc. Plastic Surgeons. Office: 871 5th Ave New York NY 10021

**ROSENFELD, ROBERT A.,** lawyer; BA in Pub. Affairs with highest distinction, George Washington U., 1971; BA with first class honors, Oxford U., 1973; JD cum laude, Harvard U., 1976. Bar: Calif., U.S. Ct. Appeals (7th cir.), U.S. Ct. Fed. Claims, U.S. Supreme Ct. Atty., shareholder Heller, Ehrman, White, & McAuliffe LLP, San Francisco, 1979—. Rhodes scholar, 1973. Office: Heller Ehrman 333 Bush St San Francisco CA 94104 Fax: 415-772-6268. Office Phone: 415-772-6609. E-mail: bob.rosenfeld@hellerehrman.com.

**ROSENFELD, ROBERT LEE,** psychiatrist; b. Chgo., Apr. 11, 1945; s. Joseph and Sonia Rosenfeld; children: Jonathan, Elizabeth. AB, Washington U., 1966; MD, U. Ill., Chgo., 1970. Diplomate gen. psychiatry and child/adolescent psychiatry Am. Bd. Psychiatry and Neurology. Consulting psychiatrist Chgo. Bd. Health and Mental Health, 1973—75; consulting child/adolescent psychiatry Lake County Mental Health, Waukegan, Ill., 1974—78, Ravenswood Hosp. Mental Health, Chgo., 1974—80, Orchard Ctr. for Mental Health, Skokie, Ill., 1976—78; consulting psychiatrist Sch. Dist. 69/74, Skokie, 1976—80; pvt. practice Winnetka, Ill., 1976—95, Northbrook, Ill., 1995—. Lectr. in field. Fellow: Am. Acad. Child/Adolescent, Am. Psychiat. Assn.; mem.: Phi Beta Kappa, Alpha Omega Alpha. Jewish. Avocations: yoga, travel, working out, reading. Office: 801 Skokie Blvd #212 Northbrook IL 60062 Office Phone: 847-564-1131. Office Fax: 847-498-3038.

**ROSENFELD, RONALD ALLEN,** federal agency administrator; b. 1939; married; 3 children. Grad., Wharton Sch. Bus., Harvard Law Sch. Dep. asst. sec. for single family housing US Dept. Housing & Urban Devel., Washington, 1989—91, gen. dep. asst. sec. housing, FHA commr.; dep. asst. sec. corp. fin. US Dept. Treasury, Washington, 1992—93; sec. commerce State of Okla., Oklahoma City, 1995—98; pres. Govt. Nat. Mortgage Assn. (Ginnie Mae) US Dept. Housing & Urban Devel., Washington, 2001—04; chmn. Fed. Housing Fin. Bd., Washington, 2004—. Office: Fed Housing Fin Bd 1625 Eye St NW Washington DC 20006*

**ROSENFELD, STEVEN B.,** lawyer; b. NYC, Apr. 12, 1943; s. Eugene David and Laura (Sipin) R.; m. Naomi Eve Winkler, Aug. 21, 1965; children: Kathryn Anne, Elizabeth Jane. BA, Columbia Coll., 1964; LLB, Columbia U., 1967. Bar: N.Y. 1967, D.C. 1984, U.S. Dist. Ct. (so. dist.) N.Y. 1969, U.S. Dist. Ct. (ea. dist.) N.Y. 1970, U.S. Ct. Appeals (2d cir.) 1971, U.S. Ct. Appeals (3d cir.) 1974, U.S. Ct. Appeals (Fed. cir.) 1978, D.C. 1979, U.S. Supreme Ct. 1979, U.S. Ct. Appeals (5th cir.) 1982, U.S. Ct. Appeals (6th and D.C. cirs.) 1984, U.S. Ct. Appeals (4th and 9th cirs.) 1987, U.S. Ct. Appeals (1st cir.) 1989, U.S. Ct. Appeals (10th cir.) 1991. Law clk. to Hon. Charles M. Metzner U.S. Dist. Ct. (so. dist.) N.Y., 1967-68; assoc. Rosenman & Colin, N.Y.C., 1968-71; dep. gen. counsel N.Y. State Commn. on Attica, N.Y.C., Batavia, NY, 1971-72; assoc. Paul, Weiss, Rifkind, Wharton & Garrison, N.Y.C., 1972-75, ptnr., 1976—. Lectr. Columbia U. Sch. Law, 1995—2002; chmn. Conflicts of Interest Bd. N.Y.C., 2002—. Contbr. articles to profl. jours. Bd. dirs. N.Y. Assn. New Ams., N.Y.C., 1973-95; trustee Dalton Sch., N.Y.C., 1988-94; trustee Putney Sch. Putney, Vt., 1995-01, N.Y. Theatre Workshop, 1996—; chair bd. visitors CUNY Law Sch., 2003—. Mem. N.Y. State Bar Assn. (ho. of dels. 1996-98), Assn. Bar City N.Y. (exec. com. 1992-96, v.p. 1998-99, past mem. various coms.), Legal Aid Soc. (pres. 1989-91, bd. dirs., exec. com. 1978-95). Democrat. Jewish. Avocations: opera music, chamber music, theater, tennis. Office: Paul Weiss Rifkind Et Al 1285 Ave of Americas New York NY 10019-6028

**ROSENFELD, STEVEN IRA,** ophthalmologist; b. N.Y.C., Nov. 18, 1954; s. Frederick and Pearl (Stern) R.; m. Lisa Allyson Klar, June 24, 1978; children: Michael, Julie. BA, Johns Hopkins U., 1976; MD, Yale U., 1980. Diplomate Am. Bd. Ophthalmology, Nat. Bd. Med. Examiners. Intern Yale-New Haven Hosp., 1980-81; resident Barnes Hosp., St. Louis, 1981-84; fellow Bascom Palmer Eye Inst., Miami, Fla., 1984-85; ptnr. in pvt. practice Delray Eye Assocs., Delray Beach, Fla., 1985—. Clin. instr. Bascom Palmer Eye Inst., 1985-90, asst. clin. prof., 1990-96, assoc. clin. prof., 1996—; assoc. examiner Am. Bd. Ophthalmology, Phila., 1993—. Author: The Eye in Systemic Disease, 1990, Lens and Cataract, 1996; contbr. articles to profl. jours. Recipient Harry Rosenbaum Rsch. award Washington U. Sch. Medicine, 1984; named one of Best Doctors in Am., 1996; Heed Ophthalmic Found. fellow, 1984. Fellow ACS, Am. Acad. Ophthalmology (chmn. B.C.S.C. section Lens and Cataract Surgery 2002—), Soc. Heed Fellows; mem. Castroviejo Corneal Soc., Eye Bank Assn. Am., Fla. Med. Assn., Fla. Soc. Ophthalmology, Assn. for Rsch. in Vision and Ophthalmology, Ocular Microbiology and Immunology Soc. Phi Beta Kappa, Alpha Omega Alpha. Avocations: tennis, golf, fly fishing, lacrosse. Office: Delray Eye Assocs 16201 South Military Trail Delray Beach FL 33484-6503 Office Phone: 561-498-8100.

**ROSENFELD, WALTER DAVID, JR.,** architect, writer; b. N.Y.C., May 30, 1930; s. Walter David and Florence (Romann) R.; m. Marilyn Smith, Oct. 15, 1954; children: John W., Sarah E., Susannah, Elizabeth A. AB, U. Pa., 1952; postgrad., Ind. U., 1953-54, Yale U., 1954-55, 57-60. Registered architect, Mass., N.H.: cert. constrn. specifier. Draftsman, specifier Perry Dean Stewart, Boston, 1960-67; architect, specifier, v.p., prin. The Architects Collaborative, Cambridge, Mass., 1967-86, also dir., 1980-84; cons. architect Walter Rosenfeld CSI, Newton, Mass., 1986—. Author: The Practical Specifier, 1985; contbg. editor Progressive Architecture mag., 1980-94; contbr. articles to profl. jours. Pres. Friends of Newton Free Libr., Mass., 1970-72; chmn. Newton Ward 1 Dem. Com., 1974-80; vice chmn. designer sel. com. City of Newton, 1976-86; bd. dirs. Mass. Audubon Soc., 1987-99, Mass. Audubon Coun., 01—. Mem. AIA, Constrn. Specifications Inst. (bd. dirs. Boston chpt. 1980-86, pres. Boston chpt. 1987-88), Boston Soc. Architects. Office: Walter Rosenfeld CSI PO Box 568 Edgartown MA 02539-0568 Personal E-mail: walrna@rcn.com

**ROSENFIELD, ALLAN,** medical educator, dean, obstetrician, gynecologist; b. Cambridge, Mass., Apr. 28, 1933; s. Harold Hermann and Beatrice (Garber) Rosenfield; m. Clare Starkie, July 31, 1966; children: Paul Allan, Jill Emilie. BA cum laude, Harvard U., 1955; MD, Columbia U., 1959. Diplomate Am. Bd. Ob-Gyn. Intern, surgical resident Beth Israel Hosp., Boston, 1959—61; resident in ob-gyn Boston Hosp. for Women (now Brigham and Woman's Hosp.), Boston, 1963—66; rep., med. advisor The Population Council and Ministry Pub. Health, Bangkok, 1967—73; asst. dir. tech. assistance div. Population Coun., N.Y., 1973—75; prof. ob-gyn Columbia U., NYC, 1975—88, prof. pub. health, 1975—86, DeLamar Prof. pub. health, 1986—, dir. ctr. for population and family health, 1975—88, acting chmn. dept. ob-gyn., 1984—86, dean Joseph Mailman Sch. Pub. Health, 1986—. Mem. Found. for AIDS Rsch.; chair NY State AIDS Adv. Coun. Contbr. articles to profl. jours. Bd. dirs. Kaiser Family Found., David and Lucile Packard Found. Capt. USAF, 1961—63. Fellow: ACOG; mem.: APHA, Inst. Medicine of NAS (several coms. and bds.). Jewish. Avocations: tennis, skiing, music. Home: 4 Crosshill Rd Hartsdale NY 10530-3014 Office: Columbia U Joseph Mailman Sch Pub Hlth 600 W 168th St New York NY 10032-3722 Office Phone: 212-305-3929.*

**ROSENFIELD, ANDREW M.,** lawyer, educator; b. Chgo., Sept. 20, 1951; s. Maurice and Lois (Fried) R.; m. Betsy Bergman, Sept. 10, 1978; children: Zachary William, Edwin Alexander, Betty Alana, Jake Leonard. BA with honors, Kenyon Coll., 1973; MA, Harvard U., 1978; JD cum laude, U. Chgo., 1978. Bar: Ill. 1978. Pres., founder Lexecon Inc., Chgo., 1977; adj. prof. Northwestern U. Law Sch., Chgo., 1985-86; lectr. in law U. Chgo., 1986—; founder, chmn UNext, 2000—; mng. ptnr. Gleacher & Co. LLC. Lectr. numerous law and bus. seminars. Mem. bd. trustees U. Chgo., 1996—; vice chmn. bd. trustees Art Inst. Chgo. Mem. Order of Coif. Clubs: Chicago, Standard (bd. dirs.1985—). Jewish. Home: 10 W Deerpath Rd Lake Forest IL 60045-2111 Office: U Chgo Law Sch 1111 E 60th St Chicago IL 60637 also: UNext Ste 455 111 N Canal St Chicago IL 60606 Office Phone: 773-702-9597. E-mail: rosenfield@unext.com.

**ROSENFIELD, JAMES HAROLD, SR.,** communications executive; b. Boston, July 18, 1929; s. Harold and Beatrice (Garber) R.; m. Nancy Lee Stenbuck, Oct. 19, 1952; 2 children. BA, Dartmouth Coll., 1952; D of Comml. Sci. (hon.), St. John's U., 1981. TV network sales exec. NBC, N.Y.C., 1954-57; advt. mgr. Polaroid Corp., Boston, 1956-59; v.p. mktg. Airequipt, Inc., New Rochelle, NY, 1959-65; TV account exec. CBS, Inc., N.Y.C., 1965-67, dir. daytime sales, 1967-70, v.p. Ea. sales, 1970-75, v.p. network sales adminstrn., 1975-77, v.p., nat. sales mgr., 1977, pres. TV Network Div., 1977-81; exec. v.p. CBS/Broadcast Group, N.Y.C., 1981-83, sr. exec. v.p., 1983-85; chmn., CEO John Blair Communications, Inc., N.Y.C., 1987-93; pres. JHR Assocs., Consulting, N.Y.C., 1993; mng. dir. Veronis, Suhler & Assocs., N.Y.C., 1994-98; pres. JHR & Assocs., 1998—. Bd. dirs. Salon Interactive, Inc., Global Vision-New Media, Columbia U. Sch. Pub. Health; bd. chmn. Entertainment Media Works, LLC, 2004—. Emeritus nat. bd. dirs. Jr. Achievement, Inc.; past alumni trustee Roxbury (Mass.) Latin Sch.; bd. dirs., former chmn. Adv. Coun. With Signal Corps, AUS, 1950-53. Fellow: Internat. Acad. TV Arts (life); mem.: Internat. Radio TV Soc. (past pres.). Business E-Mail: jimr@jhrandassociates.com.

**ROSENGART, TODD KENNETH,** cardiothoracic surgeon, researcher, neurosurgeon, consultant; b. Bklyn., Jan. 24, 1960; s. Martin Rosengart and Barbara Kodish; m. Debra Helen Rosengart, June 15, 1989; children: Michael, Eric. BS with distinction, Northwestern U., Evanston, Ill., 1981; MD with distinction, Northwestern U., Chgo., 1983. Diplomate Am. Bd. Surgery, Am. Bd. Thoracic Surgery. Intern in gen. surgery NYU Med. Ctr., N.Y.C., 1983-84, resident in gen. surgery, 1984-85, resident and chief resident in gen. surgery, 1987-89; med. staff fellow NIH, Bethesda, Md., 1985-87; asst. thoracic surgeon N.Y. Hosp., 1989-90, thoracic surgeon, 1990-91; instr. Cornell U. Med. Coll., N.Y.C., 1989-90, asst. prof. surgery, 1991-93, asst. prof. cardiothoracic surgery, 1993-97, assoc. prof. cardiothoracic surgery, 1997—; assoc. prof. cardiothoracic surgery Weill Med. Coll. Cornell U., N.Y.C., 1998—; assoc. attending cardiothoracic surgeon N.Y. Presbyn. Hosp., N.Y.C., 1997-99; chief cardiothoracic surg. Evanston (Ill.) Hosp., 1999—; assoc. prof. surgery Northwestern U. Med. Sch., 1999—. Sr. registrar Hosp. for Sick Children, London, 1991; asst. Harley St. Clinic, London, 1991; tchg. asst. NYU Med. Ctr., 1988-89; asst. attending surgeon Jamaica Hosp., 1993-96; United Hosp. Med. Ctr., 1994—; attending physician N.Y. Hosp. Med. Ctr. of Queens, 1995—; mem. Ctr. for Vascular Biology, 1996—; assoc. attending cardiothoracic surgeon N.Y. Hosp., 1997, N.Y. Presbyn. Hosp., 1998—; vis. assoc. prof. surgery Columbia U., 1997—; vis. assoc. attending surgeon Presbyn. Hosp., 1997—: manuscript reviewer, presenter, cons. in field. Editl. bd. Cardiac and Vascular Regeneration: Angiogenesis and Myogenesis, Basic th Therapeutic, 1999—; contbr. numerous articles to profl. publs., chpts. to books; patentee gene transfer therapy delivery devide and method, perfusion and occlusion device and method. Nat. Merit scholar, 1977; recipient rsch. award A.G. Morrow Soc., 1987, 97; grantee miles Labs., 1992—, N.Y. Heart Assn., 1994-97, Datascope Corp., 1995—, AccuLase, Inc., 1995—, St. Jude Med., 1996—, Picower Found., 1996—, U.S. Surg. Corp., 1996—, Thoracic Surgery Found. Rsch. and Edn. 1997-99, OrthoBiotech, 1997—, Baxter Healthcare Corp., 1998—, NIH, 1998—. Fellow ACS, Am. Coll. Cardiology (Ill. chpt. alternate councilor 2002—), Am. Coll. Chest Physicians; mem. AAAS, Am. Fedn. Clin. Rsch., Am. Heart Assn. (sci. coun. on cardiothoracic and vascular surgery, met. Chgo. bd. dirs. 2002—, coun. cardiovascular surgery and anesthesia exec. com. 2002—, coun. cardiovascular surgery and anesthesia chmn. memership and comm. com. 2003—, coun. cardiovascular surgery and anesthesia program 2003—, mem., mktg. and comm. com. 2004—), Am. Soc. Gene Therapy (cardiovascular scientific com. 2003—), Nat. Assn. for Bloodless Medicine and Surgery (bd. dirs. 1997—), Andrew Morrow Soc. Cardiac Surgeons, N.Y. Soc. Thoracic Surgery (membership com. 1994-97, chmn. membership com. 1998—, program com. 1994—, chmn. program com. 1997-99), Soc. Thoracic Surgeons, Soc. Univ. Surgeons, N.Y. Acad. Scis., 21st Century Cardiac Surg. Soc. (pres. 1998-2000, membership chmn. 1995-96, v.p. 1996-98), N.Y. Soc. Thoracic Surgery (chmn., membership com. 2001-2002, workforce health policy, reform and advocacy 2003—), Chgo. Cardiac Surgery Soc. (chmn. orgn. com. 2002, pres. 2003-2004), Spencer Soc. Surgeons, Alpha Omega Alpha, Phi Rho Sigma. Office: Evanston Northwestern Healthcare 2650 Ridge Ave Burch 100 Evanston IL 60201

**ROSENGARTEN, FRANK,** retired language educator, retired literature educator, writer; b. N.Y.C., June 13, 1927; s. Herbert and Clae Rosengarten; m. Lucille Vera Lindner, Mar. 4, 1979; m. Lillian Lebrecht Rosengarten, Apr. 27, 1959 (div. 1977); children: Philip, Daniel, Lydia. BA in English, Adelphi Coll., 1950; MA in English, Columbia U., 1951, PhD in Italian, 1962; MA in French, CUNY, 1998, PhD in French, 2000. Instr. Queens Coll., Flushing, NY, 1957—59, assoc. prof. Italian and Comparative Lit., 1967—92; instr. Adelphi U. Garden City, NY, 1957—59; instr. Italian Columbia U., N.Y.C., 1959—60; asst. prof. Case Western Res. U., Cleve., 1962—63, assoc. prof., 1964—67; prof. Italian and Comparative Lit. CUNY, N.Y.C., 1980—92; ret., 1992. Co-founder Rsch. Group on Socialism and Democracy, N.Y.C., 1983. Author: Vasco Pratolini:The Devel. of a Social Novelist, 1965, The Italian Antifascist Press, 1968, Silvio Trentin: Dall'interventismo alla Resistenza, 1980, The Writings of the Young Marcel Proust, 2001; editor: (publication) Rsch. Group on Socialism and Democracy, 1984—2001; co-editor: New Studies in the Politics and Culture of US Communism, 1993; editor: Antonio Gramsci: Letters from Prison, 1994; contbr. articles, essays in English and Italian. Seaman second class USN, 1945—46, Norfolk Va. Fellow NEH, 1967; grantee APS, 1965. Mem.: Adv. bd/The Brecht Forum, Columbia U Seminar on Modern Italian Hist., Modern Lang. Assoc. Achievements include research in co-founder of the Group on Socialism and Democracy. Home: 160 E 84th St Apt 7D New York NY 10028-2016 Personal E-mail: frosengart@aol.com.

**ROSENGREN, JOHN CHARLES,** lawyer; b. Ft. Benning, Ga., Apr. 23, 1946; s. Warren John Rosengren and Ann Mary (Burton) Paddock; m. Theresa Mary Kuoli, July 31, 1971 (children: John, Elizabeth, Philip. BA, Loras Coll., 1968; JD, Boston Coll., 1971. Bar: N.Y. 1972, U.S. Dist. Ct. (ea. and so. dists.) N.Y. 1972. Assoc. Ide & Haigney, N.Y., 1971-73, Alexander & Green, N.Y.C., 1973-78; counsel Frank B. Hall & Co., Briarcliff, N.Y. 1978-79; ptnr. Marks & Murase, N.Y.C., 1980-95; v.p., gen. counsel Arthur J. Gallagher & Co., Itasca, Ill., 1995—. Mem. ABA (subcom. on Ea. investment in the U.S.). Home: 26345 W Glenbarr Ln Barrington IL 60010-2864 Office: Arthur J Gallagher & Co The Gallagher Ctr 2 Pierce Pl Ste 100 Itasca IL 60143-1293

**ROSENHAUER, JAMES JOSEPH (JIM ROSENHAUER),** lawyer; b. Chgo., May 25, 1942; s. Norbert E. and Eleanor E. (Berg) R.; m. Vivian M. Garcia, June 11, 1966; 1 child, Christine. AB, Cath. U. Am., 1966; JD, Yale U., 1967. Bar: D.C. 1968. Assoc. Hogan & Hartson, Washington, 1967-74, ptnr., 1975—, head bus., fin. and tax group. Mem. ABA, DC Bar Assn., DC Bar, Internat. Bar Assn., Inter-Am. Bar Assn., TriBar Legal Opinion Com. Office: Hogan & Hartson Columbia Square 555 13th St NW Washington DC 20004-1161 Office Phone: 202-637-5641. Office Fax: 202-637-5910. E-mail: jjrosenhauer@hhlaw.com.*

**ROSENHAUS, DREW,** professional sports agent; b. 1966; BA, U. Miami, 1987; JD, Duke U., 1990. CEO Rosenhaus Sports Representation, Miami Beach, Fla. Co-author (with Don Yaeger): A Shark Never Sleeps: Wheeling and Dealing with the NFL's Most Ruthless Agent, 1988; film appearances include Jerry Maguire, 1996, Any Given Sunday, 1999. Office: Rosenhaus Sports Representation 6400 Allison Rd Miami Beach FL 33141 Office Phone: 305-936-1093. Fax: 305-864-3731.*

**ROSENHEIM, DANIEL EDWARD,** journalist, television news director; b. Chgo., Aug. 12, 1949; s. Edward W. and Margaret Morton (Keeney) R.; m. Christina J. Adachi, May 10, 1974 (div. 1979); m. Cindy Catherine Salans, June 20, 1980; children: Joseph Michael, James Salans, Nicholas Edward. BA, Wesleyan U., 1971. Factory worker, Pitts. and Chgo., 1972-77; reporter Sun-Jour., Lansing, Ill., 1977; bus./labor editor Hammond (Ind.) Times, 1977-80; bus. writer Chgo. Sun Times, 1980-82, spl. writer, 1982-84; bus.

writer Chgo. Tribune, 1984-85; econs. editor San Francisco Chronicle, 1985-87, city editor, 1987-94, mng. editor, 1994-96; news dir. KRON-TV, San Francisco, 1996-2000; dir. KPIX-TV, San Francisco, 2000—05, v.p. news, 2005—. Mem. adv. bd. News Lab, Project for Excellence in Journalism. Mem. Soc. Profl. Journalists, Radio and TV News Dirs. Assn., San Francisco Tennis Club. Avocations: tennis, golf, fly fishing. Office: KPIX-TV 855 Battery St San Francisco CA 94107 Office Phone: 415-765-8618. Personal E-mail: drosen7777@hotmail.com. Business E-Mail: rosenheim@kpix.cbs.com.

**ROSENHEIM, DONALD EDWIN,** electrical engineer; b. NYC, Mar. 23, 1926; s. Seymour Lawrence and Leah Rebecca (Rosenberg) R.; m. Judith Comfort Hyman, June 22, 1958; children— Micah Robert, Jay Aaron. BSEE magna cum laude, Poly. Inst. Bklyn., 1949; MS, Columbia U., 1957. Devel. engr. Servo Corp. Am., 1949-51; mem. rsch. staff IBM, 1951—, asst. dir. rsch. divsn., 1972-73. Dir. San Jose (Calif.) Rsch. Lab., 1973-83, dir. tech. coordination, 1983-84; asst. dir. Almaden Rsch. Ctr., San Jose, 1984-92 With USN, 1944—46. Fellow IEEE; mem. Tau Beta Pi, Eta Kappa Nu. Republican. Jewish. Home: 128 Smith Creek Dr Los Gatos CA 95030-2139 Personal E-mail: jdrosenheim@msn.com. E-mail: rosenheimjudydon@yahoo.com.

**ROSENHOUSE, MICHAEL ALLAN,** lawyer, editor, consultant, columnist; b. Chgo., Nov. 8, 1946; s. Seymour Samuel and Jeanne Mozette (Rosenthal) R. BA, Yale U., 1968; JD, U. Chgo., 1974. Bar: Ill. 1974, N.Y. 1982. Atty. pvt. practice, Rochester, NY. Mng. editor: Am. Jurisprudence, 2d edit., 1991—93, Am. Law Reports (Fed.), 1991—93; editor: (newsletter) Bank Employment Law Report, 1998—99; author: Recent Court. of Appeals Decisions Reflect Strict Interpretation of Procedure Requirements, 2003, Employment Law (Syracuse Law Rev.), 1998; columnist: The Daily Record, 2001—03. Bd. trustees Urban Choice Charter Sch., Rochester, NY, 2005. Mem.: ABA, N.Y. State Bar Assn., Monroe County Bar Assn. (co-chair Disability Labor and Employment Law Commn. 1998—99), U. Chgo. Club of Rochester (bd. dirs. 1999—2001), Yale Alumni Assn. (schs. com. 1997—), U. Chgo. Law Sch. Alumni Assn. (bd. dirs. 1977—80). Avocations: squash, tennis, golf. Office: 16 W Main St Rochester NY 14614 Office Phone: 585-232-8500.

**ROSENKER, MARK VICTOR,** federal agency chairman; b. Balt., Dec. 8, 1946; s. Stanley and Irene (Moss) R.; m. Heather Beldon. BA in Communications, U. Md., 1969, postgrad., 1970-71; grad., USAF Air Command and Staff Coll., 1990, USAF Air War Coll., 1996. Asst. to events producer, relief engr. ABC-TV News, Washington, 1968-69; dep. dir. radio and TV Com. Reelect Pres., Washington, 1972; staff asst. to sec. U.S. Dept. Interior, Washington, 1972-73; account exec. Daniel Edelman Pub. Relations, Inc., Washington, 1973-75; dir. comm. Am. Moped/Motorized Bicycle Assn., Washington, 1975; dep. press sec. Pres. Ford Com., Washington, 1976; v.p. Electronic Industries Alliance, Washington, 1977—99; asst. exec. dir. for external affairs United Network for Organ Sharing, 1999—2001; dep. asst. to Pres. The White House, Washington, 2001—02, dir. Mil. Office, 2001—02; mem. Nat. Transp. Safety Bd. (NTSB), Washington, 2003—, vice chmn., 2003—06, acting chmn., 2005—06, chmn., 2006—. Mem. bd. visitors Cmty. Coll. USAF, Maxwell, Ala., 1981-86; commr. Am. Battle Monument Commn., 1990-94 Active Campaign to Elect Reagan/Bush, Washington, 1980, 84, Campaign to Elect Bush/Quayle, 1988, 92—; sr. advisor Dole/Kemp Campaign, 1995-96, Bush/Cheney Campaign, 2000-01. 1st lt. USAF, 1969-72, maj. gen. USAFR, 1972—. Decorated Air Force Disting. Svc. medal USAF, Legion of Merit, Meritorious medal with oak leaf cluster, Air Force Commendation medal, Joint Svc. Achievement medal, Air Force Achievement medal with oak leaf cluster, Compliance award Am. Safe Boating Coun., 2005; recipient Chuck Docekal Meml. award, 1987, Am. Battle Monuments Commn. Meritious Svc. medal, 1994. Mem. Am. Soc. Assn. Execs., Greater Washington Soc. Assn. Execs., Res. Officers Assn. Club, Capitol Hill Club, Army Navy Club. Avocations: sailing, tennis, skiing, golf. Office: Nat Transp Safety Bd 490 L'Enfant Plaza SW Washington DC 20594

**ROSENKILDE, CARL EDWARD,** retired physicist; b. Yakima, Wash., Mar. 16, 1937; s. Elmer Edward and Doris Edith R.; m. Bernadine Doris Blumenstine, June 22, 1963 (div. Apr. 1991); children: Lauren Louise, Paul Eric; m. Wendy Maureen Ellison, May 24, 1992. BS in Physics, Wash. State Coll., 1959; MS in Physics, U. Chgo., 1960, PhD in Physics, 1966. Fellow Argonne (Ill.) Nat. Labs., 1966-68; asst. prof. math. NYU, 1968-70; asst. prof. physics Kans. State U., Manhattan, 1970-76, assoc. prof., 1976-79; physicist Lawrence Livermore (Calif.) Nat. Lab., 1979-93, lab. assoc., 1994-95, participating guest, 1995-97; chief scientist C.R. Sci., 1993-98; ret. Cons. Lawrence Livermore Nat. Lab., 1974-79; astronomy instr. Los Positas Coll., 1997; part-time instr. physics Bellarmine Coll. Prep., 1999-2000; full-time instr., 2000-04, Tchg. Opportunities Ptnrs. Sci., 2004—. Contbr. articles to profl. jours. Woodrow Wilson fellow, 1959-60. Mem.: NSTA, Math. Assn. Am., Accoustical Soc. Am., Am. Geophys. Union, Soc. Indsl. and Applied Math., Am. Astron. Soc., Calif. Math. Coun. C.C., Am. Assn. Physics Tchrs., Am. Phys. Soc., Sigma Xi, Phi Eta Sigma, Phi Kappa Phi, Phi Beta Kappa. Republican. Presbyterian. Achievements include research in nonlinear wave propagation in complex media, theoretical physics, fluid dynamics. Personal E-mail: carlrosenkilde@comcast.net.

**ROSENKRANTZ, BARBARA GUTMANN,** science and medicine historian; b. NYC, Jan. 11, 1923; d. James and Jeanette (Mack) G.; m. David P. Bennett, Sept. 5, 1942 (div.); 1 child, Louise; m. Paul Rosenkrantz, Apr. 19, 1950 (dec. 1986); children: Judith, Deborah; m. J. Nathaniel Marshall, 1988. AB, Radcliffe Coll., 1944: PhD, Clark U., 1970. Rsch. assoc. Harvard U., Cambridge, Mass., 1970-71, lectr., 1971-73, assoc. prof. history of sci., 1973-75, prof., 1975-93, prof. emeritus, 1993—, chmn. history of sci. dept., 1984-89, master Currier House, 1971-79, faculty admin'r. Arthur Dulitn Health and the State, 1972, (with William A. Koelsch) American Habitat, 1973; editor for history Am. Jour. Pub. Health, 1985-89. NIH research grantee, 1970-72; Rockefeller Found. fellow, 1979-80; Ctr. for Advanced Study in Behavioral Scis. fellow Stanford U., 1984, Inst. Medicine fellow; Sherman Fairchild Disting. Scholar, Calif. Inst. Tech., 1989. Fellow: Am. Acad. Arts and Scis., Mass. Hist. Soc.; mem.: Am. Hist. Assn., History of Sci. Soc., Am. Assn. for History of Medicine. Jewish. Office: Harvard U Dept History Sci Ctr 371 Cambridge MA 02138 Office Phone: 617-496-2239. Fax: 617-495-3344.

**ROSENKRANTZ, DANIEL J.,** computer science educator; b. Bklyn., Mar. 5, 1943; s. Harry and Ruth (Sirota) R.; m. Carole Jaffee, Aug. 2, 1969; children: Holly, Sherry, Jody, Andrew. BS, Columbia U., 1963, MS, 1964, PhD, 1967. With Bell Telephone Labs., Murray Hill, N.J., 1966-67; info. scientist GE Co. R & D Ctr., Schenectady, N.Y., 1967-77; prof. dept. computer sci. U. Albany-SUNY, 1977—2005, prof. emeritus, 2005—, dept. chair, 1993-85; prin. computer scientist Phoenix Data Systems, Albany, 1983-85. Author: (with P.M. Lewis II and R.E. Stearns) Compiler Design Theory, 1976. Fellow ACM (editor-in-chief jour. 1986-91, area editor for formal langs. and models of computation 1981-86, mem. spl. interest group on mgmt. of data, mem. numerous conf. coms., Sigmod Contbns. award 2001); mem. IEEE Computer Soc., ACM Spl. Interest Group on Automata and Computability Theory (sec. 1977-79). Office: U at Albany SUNY Dept Computer Sci Albany NY 12222-0001 Home: 6882 Milani St Lake Worth FL 33467-5902 Office Phone: 518-442-4274. Business E-Mail: djr@cs.albany.edu.

**ROSENKRANTZ, ROGER DANIEL,** writer, educator; b. NYC, Dec. 21, 1938; s. Arthur Bernard and Frances Maslow Rosenkrantz; m. Margaret Anne Foote, Aug. 7, 1964; 1 child, Kurt Jacob. BA, Oberlin Coll., 1960; PhD in Philosophy, Stanford U., 1968; PhD in Math., Dartmouth Coll., 1986. Asst. prof. CCNY and CUNY, 1967—72; vis. asst. prof. U. Western Ont., London, Ont., Canada, 1972; assoc. prof. U. SC, Columbia, 1972—74; prof., head dept. religion Va. Tech. U., Blacksburg, 1976—78. Author: Inference Method and Decision, 1977, Foundation and Applications of Inductive Problems,

1980; editor: Papers on Probability, Statistics and Statistical Physics, 1980. Mem.: Math. Assn. Am., Am. Math. Soc. Republican. Avocations: cross country skiing, tennis, canoeing, hiking. Home: 3 Tempy Ln Wayne ME 04284 Personal E-mail: rdrosenkrantz@aol.com.

**ROSENKRANTZ, STEVEN JAY,** lawyer; b. N.Y.C., Feb. 4, 1965; s. Michael and Rhona Sue (Dasheff) R. BA, Rutgers U., 1987, JD, 1991. Bar: Pa. 1994, DC 1996. Rsch. assoc. Fedn. Am. Scientists, Washington, 1993-94; rsch. asst. U.S. Dept. Justice, Washington, 1994-95; fgn. affairs specialist U.S. Arms Control & Disarmament Agy., Washington, 1995-99; spl. asst. office of undersec. state arms control U.S. Dept. State, Washington, 1998-2001, fgn. affairs officer Office of Missile Def. and space Policy, 2001—. Mem.: Mid. East Inst., Phi Beta Kappa. Avocations: history, classical music, fencing, reading, chess. Home: 1401 Blair Mill Rd Apt 1811 Silver Spring MD 20910-4875 Office: US Dept State Office Missile Def and Spa Washington DC 20520 Office Phone: 202-647-8140. Business E-Mail: rosenkrantzsj@state.gov.

**ROSENKRANZ, ROBERT BERNARD,** military officer; b. Paterson, NJ, Sept. 26, 1939; s. Irving Morton and Lucille (Kane) R.; m. Barbara Jean Larson, May 17, 1970; children: Stephen Robert, Deborah Anne, Diana Rebecca, Susan Leslie. BS, U.S. Mil. Acad., 1961; MA, U. Pa., 1969. Commd. 2d. lt. U.S. Army, 1961, advanced through grades to maj. gen., 1992, officer Fed. Republic of Germany, 1962-65, bn. exec. officer Republic of Korea, 1973-74, battery comdr. Vietnam, 1966-67, bn. and brigade comdr. Germany, 1977-79, 83-85; assoc. prof. U.S. Mil. Acad., West Point, NY, 1969-72; dir. soviet studies U.S. Army War Coll., Carlisle, Pa., 1981-83; sr. mil. asst. under sec. of def. Pentagon, Washington, 1986-88; dep. dir. Army Ops., Readiness and Mobilization U.S. Army Pentagon, Washington, 1988-89, dir. force programs, 1989-92; comdr. U.S. Army Optec, Washington, 1992-95; sr. v.p. range and logistics svcs. Dyncorp, Reston, Va., also Ft. Worth, 1995-2001; v.p. force mgmt. and logistics MPRI, Alexandria, Va., 2001—04; sr. v.p., gen. mgr. BeamHit, Columbia, Md., 2004—05; v.p. bus. devel. KEI Pearson Inc., Arlington, Va., 2005; pres. ITS, Dyncorp internat., Falls Church, Va., 2005—. Decorated Bronze Star, Air medal; recipient Superior Svc. medal U.S. Dept. Def., 1988, D.S.M., 1992, 95. Mem.: Nat. Def. Indsl. Assn., Internat. Test and Evaluation Assn., Assn. of the U.S. Army, Internat. Inst. Strategic Studies. Republican. Jewish. Avocations: jogging, reading, woodworking, golf, racquetball. Home: 3222 Wynford Dr Fairfax VA 22031-2828 Office Phone: 571-722-0238. E-mail: bob.rosenkranz@dyn-intl.com, rrosen007@aol.com.

**ROSENMAN, KENNETH D.,** medical educator; b. N.Y.C., Feb. 25, 1951; AB, Cornell U., 1972; MD, NY Med. Coll., 1975. Bd. cert. internal medicine; bd. cert. occupational and preventive medicine. Asst. prof. U. Mass., Amherst, 1979-81; dir. occupational and environ. health NJ Dept. Health, Trenton, 1981-86; pvt. practice Plainsboro, NJ, 1986-88; assoc. prof. Mich. State U., East Lansing, 1988-93, prof., 1993—. Office: Mich State U 117 W Fee Hall East Lansing MI 48824-1316 Office Phone: 517-353-1846. E-mail: rosenman@msu.edu.

**ROSENN, HAROLD,** lawyer; b. Plains, Pa., Nov. 4, 1917; s. Joseph and Jennie (Wohl) R.; m. Sallyanne Frank, Sept. 19, 1948; 1 child, Frank Scott. BA, U. Mich., 1939, JD, 1941; LLD, Coll. Misericordia, 1991. Bar: Pa. 1942, U.S. Supreme Ct. 1957. Ptnr. Rosenn & Rosenn, Wilkes Barre, Pa., 1948-54, Rosenn, Jenkins & Greenwald, Wilkes Barre, 1954-87, of counsel, 1988—. Mem. Pa. State Bd. Law Examiners, 1983-93, Pa. Gov.'s Justice Commn., 1968-73, Pa. Crime Commn., 1968-73, Fed. Jud. Nominating Com., Pa., 1977-79, Appellate Ct. Nominating Com., Pa., 1979-81; asst. dist. atty. Luzerne County, Pa., 1952-54. Chmn. United Jewish Appeal Campaign of Wyo. Valley, 1956, 1984, 2003, ARC, Wilkes-Barre, 1959, chair, 1963—65, life bd. dirs., 1991—; pres. Pa. Coun. on Crime and Delinquency, Harrisburg, 1969—71; chmn. United Way Campaign of Wyo. Valley, 1975, chmn. of bd., 1978—80; hon. mem., bd. dirs. N.E. Pa. Philharmonic, 2005; pres. Temple Israel of Wilkes Barre, 1972—74, chmn. bd., 1974—84, life bd. dir.; bd. dir. Coll. Misericordia, Dallas, Pa., 1976—86, emeritus, 1986—; bd. dir. Hoyt Libr., Kingston, Pa., 1971—78, Nat. Coun. on Crime and Delinquency, N.Y.C., 1969—71, Jewish Cmty. Ctr. Wilkes-Barre, 1964—66, Keystone State Games, Jewish Fedn. Bd. of Greater Wilkes-Barre, St. Vincent de Paul Soup Kitchen, 1987—2000; trustee Wilkes-Barre and Wyoming Valley Vets. Hosp. Fund, 2003; comdr. Post 395 Am. Legion, Kingston, 1948. Capt. USAAF, 1942—45, ETO. Decorated medal with 6 bronze stars, European combatant cross French Govt.; named Golden Key Vol. of Yr., United Way of Pa., 1989; recipient Erasmus medal, Dutch Govt., Disting. Svc. award in Trusteeship, Assn. Governing Bds., Univs. and Colls., 1990, Disting. Cmty. Svc. award, Greater Wilkes-Barre Soc. Fellows Anti-Defamation League, 1991, Clara Barton honor award, Wyo. Valley chpt. ARC, 1992, Lifetime Achievement award, United Way of Wyo. Valley, 1992, Outstanding Vol. Fundraiser award, Greater Pocono chpt. Nat. Soc. of Fundraising Execs., 1995, honoree, Wyo. Valley Interfaith Coun., 1986, Ethics Inst. N.E. Pa., 2001, 10 Gallon Blood Donor award, ARC, inductee, Jr. Achievement Hall of Fame for N.E. Pa., 1997, President's award, Luzerne County Bar, 2003. Mem. ABA, Pa. Bar Assn., Am. Judicature Soc., The Pa. Soc., B'nai B'rith (pres. Wilkes Barre 1952-53, Cmty. Svc. award 1976), U. Mich. Club N.E. Pa. (pres. 1946-76), Westmoreland Club (Wilkes-Barre), Huntsville Golf Club (Leh-man, Pa.). Republican. Jewish. Office Phone: 570-826-5645. Business E-Mail: hrosenn@rjlaw.com.

**ROSENNE, MEIR,** lawyer, federal agency administrator; b. Iasi, Romania, Feb. 19, 1931; arrived in Israel, 1944; s. Jacob and Mina Rosenhaupt; m. Vera Ayai, June 9, 1959; children: Mihal, Dafna. MA in Polit. Sci., Inst. Polit. Sci., Paris, 1953; LLB, Sorbonne, U. Paris, 1955, PhD in Internat. Law with honors, 1957; grad., Inst. Internat. Studies, Paris, 1953. In govt. service, Israel, 1953—; consul Israel Consulate, N.Y.C., 1967-69; sr. lectr. in polit. sci. U. Haifa, Israel, 1969-71; coordinator Atomic Energy Commn. Israel, 1969-71; chief legal adviser Fgn. Office Israel, Jerusalem, 1971-79; Israeli amb. to France, Paris, 1979-83; Israeli amb. to U.S. Washington, 1983-87; pres. State of Israel Bonds, N.Y., 1989-93; ptnr. Balter, Guth, Aloni & Co., Jerusalem, 1994—. Chmn. overseas com. Jerusalem Bank; bd. dirs. Israel Discount Bank Holding, Ltd. Contbr. articles to newspapers. Chmn. internat. bd. govs. Share-Zedek Hosp., Jerusalem, 1989—94. Sgt. Israeli Air Force, 1948—50. Named comdr., Nat. Order French Legion of Honor; recipient Harold Weil medal, NYU Sch. Law, Elie Wiesel award. Mem.: French Assn. Internat. Law, Am. Soc. Internat. Law, Israeli Bar Assn., Soc. Internat. Law, Internat. Law Soc. France, Internat. Club Washington. Avocations: volleyball, swimming. Office: Balter Guth & Aloni 23 Hillel St Jerusalem Israel Business E-Mail: mrosenne@bgalaw.co.il.

**ROSENOW, EDWARD CARL, III,** medical educator; b. Columbus, Ohio, Nov. 2, 1934; s. Oscar Ferdinand and Mildred Irene (Eichelberger) R.; m. Constance Donna Grahame, Sept. 7, 1957; children: Sheryl Lynn, Scott Edward. BS, Ohio State U., 1955, MD, 1959; MS in Medicine, U. Minn., 1969. Diplomate Am. Bd. Internal Medicine, Am. Bd. Pulmonary Diseases. Intern Riverside Meth. Hosp., Columbus, Ohio, 1959-60; resident in internal medicine Mayo Grad. Sch. Medicine, Rochester, Minn., 1960-65, clin. fellow in thoracic diseases, 1965-66; cons. in internal medicine (pulmonary diseases) Mayo Clinic, Rochester, 1966; instr. in medicine Mayo Grad. Sch. Medicine, Rochester, 1969-73; asst. prof. medicine Mayo Med. Sch., Rochester, 1973-77, assoc. prof. medicine, 1977-80, prof. medicine, 1980; chmn. divsn. pulmonary and critical care medicine, 1987-94; assoc. dir. internal medicine residency program Mayo Clinic, Rochester, 1977-79, program dir. internal medicine residency program, 1979-84, sec. Mayo staff, 1979; pres. Mayo staff, 1986; Arthur M. and Gladys D. Gray prof. medicine Mayo Clinic, Rochester, 1987-96, prof. emeritus, 1996—. Cons. NASA, Houston. Capt. M.C., U.S. Army, 1962-64. Recipient Alumni Achievement award Coll. Medicine Ohio State U., 1989, Disting. Mayo Clinician award, 1994, Henry S. Plummer Disting. Internist award, 1994, Karis award Mayo Clinic, 1996, Disting. Alumnus award Mayo Found., 1998; Edward W. and Betty Knight Scripps Professorship named in his honor Mayo Med. Sch., 1994, Edward C. Rosenow, III, Outstanding Subsplty. fellow award established in his honor;

inductee Sigma Chi Hall of Fame, 2005 Fellow ACP (gov. Minn. chpt. 1987-91, Ralph S. Claypoole Sr. award for Lifetime Dedication to Patient Care 1995, Minn. chpt. Laureate award 1994, Disting. Lectr. award 1996), Am. Coll. Chest Physicians (master fellow, editl. bd. CHEST 1973-78, editor spl. case reports 1975-90, com. on postgrad. med. edn. 1978-84, spl. program com. 1982, com. on undergrad. med. edn. 1981-82, co-chmn. sci. program com. internat. Coll. Chest Physicians meeting, Sydney, Australia, 1985, regent 1984-88, pres. elect 1988-89, pres. 1989-90, pres. Chest Found. 1998—, Endowed Hon. Lectr. in name 2004); mem. AMA, So. Minn. Med. Assn., Minn. Thoracic Soc., Am. Thoracic Soc., Sigma Xi. Office: Mayo Clinic Div Pulmonary Diseases 200 1st St SW Rochester MN 55905-0002 Office Phone: 507-284-2511. Business E-Mail: rosenow.edward@mayo.edu.

**ROSENOW, JOHN EDWARD,** foundation executive; b. Lincoln, Nebr., Sept. 15, 1949; s. Lester Edward and Lucille Louise (Koehler) R.; m. Nancy Kay Hadley; children: Matthew, Stacy. BS in Agrl. Engring., U. Nebr., 1971. Dir. of tourism Nebr. Dept. Econ. Devel., Lincoln, 1971-79, interim dept. dir., 1985; founder Nat. Arbor Day Found., 1972, exec. dir. million-mem. Lincoln and Nebraska City, 1979-94, pres., 1994—. Co-author: (book) Tourism: the good, the bad, and the ugly, 1979. Democrat. Mem. United Ch. of Christ. Office: Nat Arbor Day Found 211 N 12th St Lincoln NE 68508-1422 Office Phone: 888-448-7337.

**ROSENOW, MITCHELL PAUL,** sound recording engineer, studio owner, musician, music producer; s. Richard Vernon and Norma Mae Rosenow; m. Ronette Shaleen Dizmang, Nov. 25, 1983; 1 child, Francis (Frank) Vernon. GED, Manhattan Vocat. Tech. Sch., Kans., 1971. Sound sys. design engr. Silvertrain Sound, Lawrence, Kans., 1974—76; self-employed audio engr. Interlace Video, Sunflower Cablevision, HBO, Cinemax, NBC, ABC, CBS, ESPN, Fox, Raycom, Time Warner Cable, various Fortune 500 teleconfs. nationwide, Lee's Summit, Mo., 1975—; sound engr. various local bands Kansas City area, Kans., 1975—80; monitor engr. Amazing Rhythm Aces, Memphis, 1976; audio engr., music show prodr. Columbine Cablevision, Ft. Collins, Colo., 1980—81; rec. engr. Little Apple Studio, Manhattan, Kans., 1981—83; chief audio engr. Interlace Video, Lenexa, Kans., 1987—89. Cons. in rec. and live sound nationwide, 1987—; cons. in audio design TV remote facilities nationwide, 1987—. Rec. engr. (TV series) Bring It All Back Home (Cable Ace award, 1978); engineer: (DVD) Motivating Moves for People with Parkinson's (U. Continuing Edn. Assn. Nat. Outstanding Program award, 2004). Mem.: Audio Engring. Soc. (mem. Internat. Brotherhood Elec. Workers Local 53 radio and TV divsn.). Office Phone: 816-554-3782. Business E-Mail: kcmixman@aol.com.

**ROSENQUIST, JAMES ALBERT,** artist; b. Grand Forks, N.D., Nov. 29, 1933; s. Louis A. and Ruth C. (Hendrickson) R.; m. Mary Lou Adams, June 5, 1960; 1 child, John Adams; m. Melinda Thompson, Apr. 18, 1987; 1 child, Lily McLean. Attended, U. Minn., Art Students League, NYC, 1954-55; DFA (hon.), U. So. Fla., 1981, Bard Coll., 1997. Billboard painter A.H. Villepigue, Inc., NYC, 1957—59, Artkraft Strauss Sign Corp., NYC, 1957—59; lectr. Yale Sch. Art, 1964; artist in residence Aspen Inst. Humanist Studies, 1965. One-man shows include Green Gallery, N.Y.C., 1962, 64, Mus. Modern Art, 1963, Sperone Gallery, Turin, Italy, 1964, Sonnabend Gallery, Paris, 1964, 67, 68, Dwan Gallery, Los Angeles, 1964, Moderna Museet, Stockholm, 1965, 66, Castelli Gallery, N.Y.C., 1965, 66, 68, 69, 70, 73, 74, 78, 85, 88, 91, Mus. Modern Art, Turin, 1965, Nat. Gallery Can., Ottawa, Ont., 1968, Met. Mus. Art, N.Y.C., 1968, Max Protech, Washington, 1974, Nat. Gallery Victoria, Australia, 1978, Sable-Castelli Gallery, Toronto, 1978, Colo. State U., Ft. Collins, 1982, Castelli/Fergen/Corcoran, N.Y.C., 1982, Mayer Gallery, London, 1982, Mus. Contemporary Art, Houston, 1982, Whitney Mus. Am. Art, N.Y.C., 1982, Mus. Fine Arts, Houston, 1983, 88, U. South Fla., 1984, Butler Inst. Am. Art, 1988, Wetterling Gallery, Stockholm, 1989, Mus. Modern Art, Austin, Tex., 1990, Cen. Hall of Artists, Moscow, 1991, IVAM Centre Julio Gonzales, Valencia, Spain, 1991, Gagosian Gallery, N.Y.C., 1992, Leo Castelli Gallery, N.Y.C., 1993, Wetterling Teo Gallery, Singapore, 1994, Seattle Art Museum, 1995, Galerie Thaddaeus Ropac, Paris, 1997, Baldwin Gallery, Aspen, 1999, Salvador Dali Museum, Fla., 2000, Gagosian Gallery, N.Y.C., 2001, numerous others; exhibited in numerous group shows U.S. and, Europe, including 16 Ams. at, Mus. Modern Art, 1963, Artist and Object at, Guggenheim Mus., 1963, São Paulo, Brazil, 1967, Mus. Modern Art, Tokyo, 1967, Musée des Arts Decoratives, Palais Louvre, 1967, Haywood Gallery, London, 1969, Albright-Knox Gallery, Buffalo, 1971, Mus. Contemporary Art, Chgo., 1972, Met. Mus. Art, N.Y.C., 1969-70, Whitney Mus. Am. Art, N.Y.C., 1974, biennial, Whitney Mus. Am. Art, N.Y.C., 1981, including 16 Ams. at, Mayer Gallery, London, 1978, U. Mich. Mus., 1978, Fitzwilliam Mus., Cambridge, Eng., 1978, Bklyn. Mus., 1981, Va. Mus., Richmond, 1981, Haus der Kunst, 1982, Nat. Gallery Victoria, B.C., Can., 1982; represented in permanent collections Pasadena Mus., Modern Museet, Stockholm, Stadtlicht, Amsterdam, Holland, Whitney Mus., Albright-Knox Gallery, Mus. Modern Art, N.Y.C., Met. Mus. Art, N.Y.C., Nat. Gallery Can., Wallraf-Richartz Mus., Cologne, Germany, others; Biennial Exhbn. Prints, Nat. Mus. Modern Art, Tokyo 1968, 7th Internat Expn. Graphics, Moderna Gallery, Ljubliana, Yugoslavia 1967); painting of bomber F-111. Bd. dirs. Nat. Endowment for Arts. Recipient Norman Waite Harris award Chgo. Art Inst. 1963, Prix di Tella, Argentina 1965, Friend of Japan award, 1970, World Print award, 1983, Fla. Amb. of the Arts award, 1987, Golden Plate award Am. Acad. Achievement, 1988, Fla. prize, 1991, Skowhegan medal in painting, 1994, FCG Art award, 2002. Mem. Municipal Art Soc., N.Y.

**ROSENSAFT, LESTER JAY,** management consultant, lawyer; b. Leominster, Mass., Jan. 11, 1958; s. Melvin and Beatrice (Golombek) Rosensaft; m. Elizabeth Amanda Lahti, July 29, 1992 (div. 2004); 1 child, Mia Elisabeth. BS in Econs., Wharton Sch., U. Pa., 1978; JD, MBA, Case Western Res. U., 1981; LLM in Corp. Law with high honors, NYU, 1983. Bar: Ohio 1981, U.S. Dist. Ct. (no. dist.) Ohio 1982, U.S. Dist. Ct. (all dists.) N.Y. 1982, Mass. 1992. With Cons. to Mgmt., Inc., Cleve., N.Y.C., Boston, Hong Kong, 1977—, v.p., 1977—80, pres., 1980—83, chmn., 1983—85; pvt. practice specializing in corp. and comml. law Ohio, 1981—. Mem. Hall, Rosensaft & Yen, Cleve., Singapore, 1981—90; reorganization law fed. cts., Ohio, 1982—, NY, 1982—; pres., CEO Eljay Devel. Corp., 1985—86; chmn., CEO Logistix Ltd., 1987—90; ptnr. Sanctuary Assocs., Boston, 1988—89; pres., CEO Union Meat Co., East Hartford, Conn., 1989—90, also bd. dirs.; pres. Golub Enterprises II, Inc., 1989—90, also bd. dirs.; COO CCC Fin. Orgn., Cleve., 1992—95, also bd. dirs.; pres., CEO ASA Comm., Inc., N.Y.C., 1995—, also bd. dirs.; pres., CEO ASA Adminstrn., Inc., Chgo., 1999—, Greensboro, NC, 1999—, Toronto, 1999—, also bd. dirs.; mem. fin. and strategic planning com. ASA Acquisition Corp., also bd. dirs.; mem. ASA Mgmt. and Exec. Com., 1995—, ASA Investment Com., 1996—98; v.p. corp. devel. Paramount Sys. Design Group, Inc., N.Y.C., also vice chmn. bd. dirs.; v.p., CFO Chipurnoi Inc., Long Island City, NY, also bd. dirs.; v.p., CFO Kinnerton Industries, N.Y.C., London, 1983—85; vice chmn., gen. counsel GIOIA Couture, N.Y.C., Akron, Ohio, 1984—86, also bd. dirs.; chmn., CEO Invictus Ventures, Boston, 2005—; mem., bd. dirs. Aircraft Co., 2005—, Insight Edn., 2005—; bd. dirs. Insight Educators, Inc., The Anteraga Co. Co-author: Industrial Development Survey for City of Leominster, 1978; contbr. articles to profl. jours. Active Combined Jewish Philanthropies; participant 40th Anniversary II Pres.'s Mission, 1987; chmn. Region V Outreach Mission, 1988; vice chmn. Regional Campaign Leadership Mission, 1991; mem. Russian Resettlement Com., 1988—91, Maj. Gifts Gala Com., 1989; ednl. cons., advisor indsl. devel. and strategic urbanism; cons. federally funded biomed rsch. projects; bd. overseers Beth Israel Deaconess Hosp., 2003—, mem. Dreamday at Fenway planning com.; mem. planning com. Dreamday at Fenway, 2005; mem. exec. adv. coun. Keene State Coll. 1984—88; assoc. alumni trustee U. Pa., 1991—95, activist secondary com. ctrl. Mass., bd. govs. Cleve., 1992—95; mem. pres.'s soc. Beth Israel Deaconess Hosp., Boston, 2003—, mem. bd. overseers, mem. adv. bd. Transplant Ctr., mem. fin. and devel. com., bd. dirs., 2004—. Recipient Grand award, APEX, 1999, Best of Show award, ESMA, 1999, numerous ACE awards, Silver and Gold Quill awards, 1996—99, Cronite Cup award. Mem.: ABA, Coll. Firm Prins., Coun. Cons. Orgns., Inst. Mgmt. Cons. (cert.), Soc. Profl. Mgmt. Cons., Internat. Soc. Strategic Planning Cons., N.Y.C. Reorga-

nization Roundtable, Bankruptcy Lawyers Bar Assn., Assn. Bar City of N.Y., Ohio State Bar Assn., Greater Cleve. Bar Assn., Turnaround Mgmt. Assn., Assn. Corp. Growth, North Ctrl. Mass. C. of C. (indsl. devel. com. 1984—86), Belmont Country Club, Boca Pointe Golf and Racquet Club, Phi Alpha Delta (vice justice). Home: 640 Hammond St 102 Chestnut Hill MA 02467-2310 Personal E-mail: ljrosensaft@aol.com.

**ROSENSAFT, MENACHEM ZWI,** lawyer, writer, foundation administrator; b. Bergen-Belsen, Germany, May 1, 1948; arrived in U.S.A. 1958, naturalized, 1962; s. Josef and Hadassah (Bimko) Rosensaft; m. Jean Bloch, Jan. 13, 1974; 1 child, Joana Deborah. BA, MA, Johns Hopkins U., 1971; MA, Columbia U., 1975, JD, 1979. Bar: N.Y. 1980. Adj. lectr. dept. Jewish studies CCNY, 1972-74, professorial fellow, 1974-75; rsch. fellow Am. Law Inst., 1977-78; law clk. to judge U.S. Dist. Ct. (so. dist.) N.Y., N.Y.C., 1979-81; assoc. Proskauer, Rose, Goetz & Mendelsohn, N.Y.C., 1981-82, Kaye, Scholer, Fierman, Hays & Handler, N.Y.C., 1982-89; v.p. assoc. counsel Chase Manhattan Bank, N.Y.C., 1989-93; spl. counsel Hahn & Hessen, N.Y.C., 1994-95; sr. internat. counsel Ronald S. Lauder Found., N.Y.C., 1995-97; exec. v.p. Jewish Renaissance Found., Inc., N.Y.C., 1996-2000; ptnr. Ross & Hardies, N.Y.C., 2000—03, McGuire Woods LLP, N.Y.C., 2003; spl. counsel Van Der Moolen Specialists USA, LLC, NYC, 2004, sr. legal cousnel, 2004—05, gen. counsel, 2005—. Author: Moshe Sharett Statesman of Israel, 1966, Not Backward to Belligerency, 1969, (poetry) Fragments, Past and Future, 1968; editor: Bergen Belsen Youth Mag., 1965, Life Reborn, Jewish Displaced Persons 1945-1951, 2001, Columbia Jour. Transnational Law, 1978—79; co-editor (with Yehuda Bauer): (book) Anti-semitism: Threat to Western Civilization, 1988; contbg. editor: Reform Judaism, 1993—2002; contbr. articles to profl. jours.; chmn. editl. bd.: Holocaust Survivors' Memoirs Project, 2000—. Chmn. Internat. Network Children Jewish Holocaust Survivors, 1981—84, founding chmn., 1984—; nat. pres. Labor Zionist Alliance, 1988—91; chmn. comm. human rights World Jewish Congress, 1986—91, chmn. exec. com. Am. sect., 1986—90; mem. Gen. Coun. World Zionist Orgn., 1987—92; mem. U.S. Holocaust Meml. Coun., 1994—2004, chmn. content com., 1994—2000, chmn. collections and acquisitions com., 1996—2000, chmn. task force on procs. for com. on conscience, 1996, mem. exec. com., 1996—2003, chmn. governance com., 2001—02; bd. dirs., exec. com. Nat. Com. for Labor Israel, 1988—91, 1995—2001; mem. Am. Zionist Tribunal, 1988—90, chmn., 1990; sec. Am. Zionist Fedn., 1990—93; bd. dirs. Am. Jewish Joint Distbn. Com., 1988—91; mem. exec. com. Nat. Jewish Cmty. Rels. Adv. Coun., 1994—97; organizer, leader demonstration in Germany against Pres. Reagan's visit to Bitburg Cemetery and Bergen-Belsen concentration camp, 1985; del. meeting on recognition of Israel between five Am. Jews and leaders of Palestine Liberation Orgn. Stockholm, 1988; mem. N.Y.C. Holocaust Meml. Commn., 1982—96, chmn. collections com., 1987—89; mem. N.Y. County Dem. Com., 1981—85; mem. nat. adv. bd. United Synagogue Conservative Judaism, 1995—2002, also chmn. United Synagogue del. to Nat. Jewish Cmty. Rels. Adv. Coun., 1994—97; pres. Park Ave. Synagogue, 2003—, sec., 1988—2003, trustee, 1994—; chmn. Sherr Inst. Adult Jewish Studies, 1993—2002. Recipient Parker Sch. recognition of achievement with honors in internat. and fgn. law, 1979, Abraham Joshua Heschel Peace award, 1989, 400th Anniversary medal, City of Warsaw, 1999, commendation Jewish Heritage Week, Comptr. N.Y.C., 1999, Elie Wiesel Holocaust Remembrance award, Israel Bonds, 2003, Simon Rockower award for excellence in feature writing, 2006; Harlan Fisk Stone scholar, 1977—79. Mem.: ABA, Phi Beta Kappa. Home: 179 E 70th St New York NY 10021-5109 Office: Van Der Moolen Specialists USA LLC 29th Fl 45 Broadway New York NY 10006 Office Phone: 646-576-2790. Personal E-mail: mrosensaft@vdm-usa.com.

**ROSENSCHEIN, GUY RAOUL,** pediatric and visceral surgeon, airline pilot; b. July 28, 1953; s. Maurice and Caroline (Meller) R. MD, Lariboisiere-St. Louis, Paris, 1977. Qualified airline transport pilot; FAA-approved aviation med. examiner, flight instr. Intern Hosp. St-Louis, 1973-74, Hosp. Lariboisière, 1975-76; resident Hosp. de Paris, 1977-80, Hosp. Bretonneau, 1977-78, Hosp. Lariboisière, 1979-80, Hosp. de Monaco, Monte Carlo, 1980-81, Hosp. St. Vincent de Paul, Paris, 1981-82, attache, 1982-84, asst., 1984-86, asst. prof. pediat. surgery; chef de clinique U. Paris, 1984-86; attache Hosp. de Villeneuve St. Georges, 1987-94, C.H.S. Saine Anne, Paris, 1982-94; maitre de stage hospitalier Faculty Med. de Creteil, 1987-92; profl. transport instr., 1993; attending pediat. surgery Maimonides Med. Ctr., 1994-97, S.I. Univ. Hosp., 1994-2000, St. John's Regional Health Ctr., Springfield, Mo., 2000, N.W. Med. Ctr., Springdale, Ark., 2001—. Pilot, 1981; asst. clin. prof. of surger UAMS, U. Ark., 2003-. Author: Pancreatite non traumatique et non infectieuse de l'enfant, 1982. Capt., M.C., French Armed Forces, 1977. Mem. Nat. Assn. Flight Instrs., TE Flying Club (chief flight instr. 1995-2000). Office: 601 S Maple Springdale AR 72764 Home: PO Box 395 Springdale AR 72765-0395 Office Phone: 479-927-3100. Business E-Mail: Rosenschein@juno.com.

**ROSENSHINE, ALLEN GILBERT,** advertising agency executive; b. NYC, Mar. 14, 1939; s. Aaron and Anna (Zuckerman) R.; m. Suzan Weston-Webb, Aug. 31, 1979; children: Andrew, Jonathan. AB, Columbia Coll. 1960. Copywriter J.B. Rundle (advt.), NYC, 1962-65; copywriter Batten, Barton, Durstine & Osborn, NYC, 1965, copy supr., 1967, v.p., 1968, asso. creative dir., 1970, sr. v.p., creative dir., 1975-77, exec. v.p., 1977-80, pres., 1980-82, chief exec. officer, 1981-86, chmn., 1983-86, also dir., mem. exec. com.; pres., chief exec. officer BBDO Internat., NYC, 1984-86, also bd. dirs.; pres., chief exec. officer Omnicom Group, NYC, 1986-88; chmn., chief exec. officer BBDO Worldwide, NYC, 1989—2004, chmn., 2004—. Lectr. gen. studies Bklyn. Coll., 1961-65 Office: BBDO Worldwide Inc 1285 Avenue Of The Americas New York NY 10019-6028*

**ROSENSTEEL, GEORGE THOMAS,** physics professor, nuclear physicist; b. Balt., Sept. 30, 1947; s. Walter St. George and Marie Emily (White) R.; m. Tsetsa Dankova. BSc, U. Toronto, Ont., Can., 1973, PhD, 1975. Can. fellow NRC, 1976-78; prof. physics Tulane U., New Orleans, 1978—, chmn. dept., 1985-91. Vis. fellow Brit. Sci. and Engring. Coun., U. Sussex, Eng., 1986; vis. prof. Nat. Inst. Nuclear Theory, U. Washington, 1992, Inst. Theoretical Physics U. Gent, Belgium, 1999. Contbr. numerous articles to profl. jours. Delivered grad. sch. commencement address Tulane U., 1987; recipient 7 grants NSF, 1979—. Mem. Am. Phys. Soc., Am. Math. Soc., Sigma Xi (young scientist award 1987). Office: Tulane U Dept of Physics New Orleans LA 70118 Office Phone: 504-862-3174. Business E-Mail: george.rosensteel@tulane.edu.

**ROSENSTEEL WAY, NANCY ANN,** music educator; b. Johnstown, Pa., Feb. 7, 1960; d. Thomas Frederick and Dolores Ann Rosensteel; m. Scott Allen Way, Sept. 25, 1994; children: Alexander, Anne. BS in Music Edn., Ind. U. Pa., 1982; MusM in Choral Conducting, Hartt Sch. Music, 1987. Instr. St. Francis U., Loretto, Pa., 1987—90; asst. prof. music Mount Aloysius Coll., Cresson, Pa., 1991—. Dir. music Allegheny Highlands Regional Theatre, Ebensburg, Pa., 1981—92; chorus master Johnstown (Pa.) Symphony Orch., 1987—90; artistic dir. Blair Concert Chorale, Altoona, Pa., 1987—2004; mem. opera panel Pa. Coun. Arts, Harrisburg, Pa., 1988—89, mem. choral, 1988—89. Mem.: Chorus Am., Am. Choral Dirs. Assn., Pi Kappa Lambda. Roman Catholic. Office: Mount Aloysius Coll 7373 Adm Peary Hwy Cresson PA 16630 Office Phone: 814-886-6495. Business E-Mail: nway@mtolay.edu.

**ROSENSTEIN, NEIL,** surgeon, genealogist, researcher; b. Cape Town, South Africa, Oct. 31, 1944; came to US, 1969; s. Emanuel Boruchovich and Annie (Marine) R.; m. Mavis Joyce Naumann, Jan. 14, 1968; children: Joel, Ari, Moshe Baruch, Rafael Samuel, Jonathan Simcha. MD, U. Cape Town Med. Sch., 1967. Intern Tel Hashomer Hosp., Tel Aviv, 1968-69; surg. resident Mt. Sinai Hosp., Cleve., 1970—73, NYC, 1973—75; mem. surg. staff Trinitas, Elizabeth, NJ, 1975—, The Union Hosp., NJ, 2001—. Author: These Are the Generations, 1969, The Unbroken Chain, 1976, 90, The Margolis Family, 1984, The Gaon of Vilna and his Cousinhood, 1997, The Lurie Legacy: The House of Davidic Royal Descent, 2004, The Grandees of New Jersey: Naar, Baiz, Peixotto, Pretto and Seixas Families, 2006; co-author: From King David to Baron David—A Rothschild Saga, 1989, Avnei

Zikaron, 1999; editor: Latter Day Leaders, Sages and Scholars, 1982, The Feast and the Fast, 1984, Illustrated History of Union County, 2005. Founder, pres. Jewish Geneal. Soc., NYC, 1977-79; bd. dirs. YMHA, Union, NJ, 1990-2001; mem. adv. bd. Auschwitz Jewish Center Found., NYC, 1999—; founder, dir. Computer Ctr. for Jewish Genealogy; rep. to genealogy com. Ctr. for Jewish History bd. dirs. Yeshiva U., NY, 2001—; co-pres. synagogue Elmora Hills Minyan, 1994-2004, pres., 2005—. Mem. Med. Soc. NJ, Union County Med. Soc. NJ, AmeriGroup NJ, NJ (med. adv. com.). Republican. Jewish. Home: 185 Shelley Ave Elizabeth NJ 07208-1061 E-mail: Neil@Tali.com.

ROSENSTEIN, ROBERT ALAN, scientific consultant; b. Chgo., July 12, 1938; s. Milton W. and Gayle (Blacher) R.; 1 child, Daniel Jeremy. BS, U. Ill., 1961; PhD, Northwestern U., 1970. Aerospace technologist NASA Lewis Rsch. Ctr., Cleve., 1961-64; rsch. assoc. Inst. Theoretical Chem. Tech. U., Munich, 1970-72; cons. Chgo., 1972-76; sr. rsch. chemist Armak Rsch. Lab. (now Akzo Chemie USA), McCook, Ill., 1977-79; coatings engr. Fansteel/VR Wesson, Waukegan, Ill., 1979-80; application programmer Nuclear Data, Schaumburg, Ill., 1981; sci. cons., Glenview, Ill., 1982—. Cons. Internat. Union Pure and Applied Chemistry, Commn. on Solubility Data, 1978-87. Active Project Upward Bound, Northwestern U., 1968-69, Jewish Vocational Service Prof. Mgr. Tech. Program, Chgo., 1975-98. NIH predoctoral fellow, 1967. Mem. Am. Phys. Soc., U. Ill. Alumni Assn., Chgo. Pub. Sch. Alumni Assn. (founding mem.), Northwestern Alumni Assn., Chgo. Chemists Club (pres. 1986-87). Democrat. Jewish. Avocations: history, sightseeing, current events, wagnerian opera. Office Phone: 773-381-7166. E-mail: lightcone@illinoisalumni.org.

ROSENSTEIN, ROD J., prosecutor; b. Phila., Jan. 13, 1965; s. Robert Jacob and Gerry M. (Stoloff) R. BS in Econ., U. Pa., Phila., 1986; JD, Harvard U., 1989. Bar: Pa. 1989, D.C. 1992, Md. 2002, U.S. Ct. Appeals (D.C. cir.) 1990, U.S. Ct. Appeals (5th cir.) 1991, U.S. Ct. Appeals (9th cir.) 1992, U.S. Ct. Appeals (4th cir.) 1998, U.S. Ct. Appeals (8th cir.) 2003, U.S. U.S. Tax Ct. 2003, U.S. Ct. Appeals (1st, 2d, 10th and 11th cirs.) 2004, U.S. Supreme Ct. 2002. Law clk. to Hon. Douglas H. Ginsburg U.S. Ct. Appeals (D.C. cir.), Washington, 1989-90; trial atty. Pub. Integrity Sect., Washington, 1990-93; counsel to dep. atty. gen. U.S. Dept. Justice, Washington, 1993-94, spl. asst. crminal divsn., 1994-95, asst. US atty. dist. MD, 1997—2001, dep. asst. atty. gen. criminal matters, 2001—02, prin. dep. asst. atty. gen. tax divsn., 2002—05; US atty. (dist. Md.) US Dept. Justice, Baltimore, Md., 2005—; assoc. counsel Office Ind. Counsel, Washington, 1995—97. Office: US Attys Office 36 S Charles St 4th Fl Baltimore MD 21201*

ROSENSTOCK, LINDA, dean, medical educator; b. NYC, Dec. 20, 1950; m. Lee Bailey; children: Adam Lee, Matthew Lynn. AB in Psychology, Brandeis U., 1971; student, U. B.C., Vancouver, Can., 1971-72; MD, MPH, Johns Hopkins U., 1977. Diplomate Am. Bd. Internal Medicine, Am. Bd. Preventive Medicine; lic. physician and surgeon, Wash. Med. resident then chief resident U. Wash., Seattle, 1977-80, resident in preventive medicine, instr. medicine, 1980-82, asst. prof., 1982-83, 83-87, lectr. environ. health, 1982-83, adj. asst. prof., 1983-86, mem. grad. sch. faculty, 1985—, assoc. prof., 1987-93, prof. medicine and environ. health, 1993—94, also dir. programs, 1994; dir. Nat. Inst. Occupational Safety and Health, Washington, 1994—2000; dean UCLA Sch. of Pub. Health, 2000—, prof. environ. health sciences, 2000—; prof. medicine UCLA Sch. Medicine, 2000—. Dir. Harborview Med. Ctr., Seattle, 1981-87, acting sect. head, 1992-94; dir. Nat. Inst. Occupational Safety and Health, Washington, 1994—. Assoc. editor Internat. Jour. Occupational Medicine and Toxicology, 1991—; mem. editorial bd. Am. Jour. Indsl. Medicine, 1985-94, Jour. Gen. Internal Medicine, 1987-90, Environ. Rsch., 1987—, Western Jour. Medicine, 1990—; contbr. numerous articles to profl. jours. Mem. exec. bd. Physicians for Human Rights, 1990—; mem. occupl. health adv. bd. United Auto Workers GM, 1990-94, chair, 1993-94; mem. task force on pneumoconioses Am. Coll. Radiology, 1991-94; mem. external adv. panel Agrl. Health and Safety Ctr., 1992-93; mem. adv. com. Ctrs. for Disease Control, 1992-94; mem. com. to survey health effects of mustard gas and lewisite Inst. Medicine, 1992, mem. bd. health promotion and disease prevention, 1993-94; mem. bd. sci. counselors HHS, 1993-94, mem. exec. com. nat. toxicology program, 1994—; mem. med. adv. bd. Teamsters Internat., 1993-94. Recipient Upjohn Achievement award Harborview Med. Ctr., 1978, Jean Spencer Felton MD award Western Occupational Med. Assn., 1988, Environ. and Occupational Medicine award Nat. Inst. Environ. Health Scis., 1991-94; Robert Wood Johnson scholar, 1980-82, Henry J. Kaiser scholar, 1984-89. Fellow ACP (health promotion subcom. 1989-90, clin. practice subcom. 1990-91), Collegium Ramazzini; mem. APHA (chair membership com. 1983-85, chairperson occupational helath and safety sect. 1985-86, gov. coun. 1986-88), Am. Coll. Occupational Medicine (mem. jud. com. 1989-94), Am. Thoracic Soc. (com. health care policy and clin. practice 1990-93), Internat. Commn. Occupational Health (sci. com. epidemiology in occupational health 1989—), Soc. Gen. Internal Medicine (program planning com. 1987, Glaser award com. 1993-94), Western Assn. Physicians, Pacific Interurban Clin. Club. Office: UCLA Sch Pub Health 16-035 Ctr for Health Sciences Box 951772 Los Angeles CA 90095*

ROSENSTOCK, SUSAN LYNN, orchestra administrator; b. Bklyn., Nov. 2, 1947; BS, SUNY, Cortland, 1969; MBA, So. Meth. U., 1977, MFA, 1978. Asst. mgr. Columbus (Ohio) Symphony Orch., 1978-82; grants program dir., info. officer Greater Columbus Arts Coun., 1982-83, asst. dir. grants and adminstrn., 1983-84; dir. ann. giving and spl. events Columbus Symphony Orch., 1984-86, dir. devel., 1986-90, orch. mgr., 1990-98, gen. mgr., 1998—. Panelist Ohio Arts Coun. Music Panel, 1986, 87, NEA, 2002, Challenge Grants Panel, 1991, J.C. Penney Gold Rule Award Judges Panel, 1993, 94. Mem. Am. Symphony Orch. League (devel. dirs. steering com. nat. conf. 1987, 88), Nat. Soc. Fund Raising Execs. (program com. Ctrl. Ohio chpt. 1988-94, chmn. program com. 1993, 94, bd. dirs. 1993-95, treas. 1995). Office: Columbus Symphony Orch 55 E State St Columbus OH 43215-4203 E mail: ouonnr@columbusymphony.com

ROSENSTREICH, DAVID LEON, medical educator, immunologist, allergist; b. NYC, Nov. 16, 1942; s. Joseph S. and Gertrude (Tankenbaum) R.; m. Victoria Abokrek, June 13, 1965; children: Jonathan, Peter, Rebecca. BS in Chemistry, CCNY, 1963; MD, NYU, 1967. Intern, resident Bronx (N.Y.) Mcpl. Hosp. Ctr., 1967-69; clin. assoc. NIAID, NIH, Bethesda, Md., 1969-72; sr. investigator NIDR, NIH, Bethesda, 1972-78; vis. assoc. prof. Rockefeller U., N.Y.C., 1978-80; prof. medicine Albert Einstein Coll. Medicine, N.Y.C., 1980—, dir. div. allergy and immunology, 1980—. Dir. Bronx Asthma Project. Editor: Mitogens in Immunobiology, 1975, Cellular Functions in Immunity and Inflamation, 1980; assoc. editor Clin. Revs. in Allergy, 1987—, Annals of Allergy, 1994—. Comdr. USPHS, 1969-78. Fellow Am. Soc. Clin. Investigation, Am. Acad. Allergy and Immunology, Am. Coll. Allergy, Am. Assn. Physicians. Avocation: winemaking. Office: Albert Einstein Coll Med 1635a Poplar St Bronx NY 10461-1926 Office Phone: 718-405-8075. Business E-Mail: rosenstr@aecom.yu.edu.

ROSENSWEIG, DANIEL L., Internet company executive; BA, Hobart Coll., NY. Assoc. pub. PC Mag., 1992—94, v.p., pub. N.Y.C., 1994—96; pres. Ziff-Davis Internet Pub. Group, 1996-97; pres., CEO ZDNet, Inc., N.Y.C., 1997—2000; pres. CNET Networks, 2000—02; COO Yahoo!, Inc., Calif., 2002—. Office: Yahoo! Inc 701 First Ave Sunnyvale CA 94089

ROSENSWEIG, RONALD ELLIS, chemical engineer, consultant; b. Hamilton, Ohio, Nov. 8, 1932; s. Herman and Deana (Meisel) R.; m. Ruth Evelyn Cohen, Sept. 5, 1954; children—Scott Elliot, Beth Ellen, Perry Ethan. Chem. Engr., U. Cin., 1955; S.M., MIT, 1956, Sc.D., 1959. Asst. prof. dept. chem. engring. MIT, Cambridge, 1959-62; prin. scientist Avco Corp., Wilmington, Mass., 1962-69; pres., tech. dir., co-founder Ferrofluidics Corp., Burlington, Mass., 1969-73, also dir., 1969-85; rsch. assoc. Exxon Corp., Annandale, NJ, 1973-78; sr. rsch. assoc., 1978-85, sci. advisor 1985-95; internat. rsch. chair Blaise Pascal, Paris, 1996-98; rsch. affiliate MIT, 2004—. Vis. prof. U. Minn., Mpls., 1980, U. Chgo., 1990, Weizmann Inst. Sci., Israel, 1997. Author: Ferrohydrodynamics, 1985; contbr. articles to profl. jours.;

patentee in field Fellow NSF, MIT, 1955-56; recipient IR-100 awards Indsl. Rsch. Pubs., 1968, 69, 71; named Young Engr. of Yr., Avco Corp., 1966, Disting. Engring. Alumnus U. Cin., 1986. Mem. Nat. Acad. Engring., Am. Inst. Chem. Engrs. (Alpha Chi Sigma award for rsch. 1985), Am. Phys. Soc., Magnetic Fluids Conf., Internat. Steering Com. (chmn. 1977-92). Jewish. Home: 34 Gloucester Rd Summit NJ 07901-3023 Office Phone: 908-277-2846. E-mail: resosen@comcast.net.

ROSENTHAL, ALAN SAYRE, government official, lawyer; b. N.Y.C., Sept. 30, 1926; s. Morris S. and Elizabeth (Ralph) R.; m. Helen Miller, Sept. 8, 1951; children: Edward S., Susan L., Richard M., James M. AB, U. Pa., 1948; LL.B., Yale U., 1951. Bar: N.Y. 1952. Asst. in instrn. Yale U. Law Sch., 1950-51; law clk. to U.S. Circuit Judge Henry W. Edgerton, Washington, 1951-52; atty. appellate sect., civil div. Justice Dept., 1952-72, asst. chief, 1958-72; admnstrv. judge atomic safety and licensing appeal panel AEC (now Nuclear Regulatory Commn.), Washington, 1972-91, chmn., 1972-88; admnstrv. judge pers. appeals bd. GAO, Washington, 1991-96, chmn., 1992-94; admnstrv. judge atomic safety and licensing bd. panel Nuclear Regulatory Commn., Washington, 1999—. Mem. ethics panel Montgomery County Bd. Edn., 1987-93; lectr. law U Pa., 1981-83, Am. U., 1991-92. Pres. Kensington Elem. Sch. PTA, 1966-67; pres. North Chevy Chase Swimming Pool Assn., 1974-76; chmn. trustees Cedar Ln. Unitarian Universalist Ch., 1970-71; bd. dirs. Montgomery chpt. ACLU, 1967-69. Served with USAAF, 1944-46. Recipient John Marshall award Justice Dept., 1969, Disting. Svc. award Nuclear Regulatory Commn., 1988. Mem. Order of Coif, Phi Beta Kappa, Pi Gamma Mu, Delta Sigma Rho Home: 3203 Kent St Kensington MD 20895-3210 Personal E-mail: rsnthl@comcast.net.

ROSENTHAL, ALBERT JAY, advertising executive; b. Chgo., Sept. 30, 1928; s. Harry and Jennie (Comm) R.; m. Rhoda R. Rosenstein, June 18, 1950; children: Jayne, Michael, James, Nancy. BA, U. Ill., 1950. Reporter Transradio Press., Chgo., 1950-51; columnist Lerner Newspapers, Chgo., 1951-53; creative dir. Elliot, Jaynes & Baruch, Chgo., 1953-61; chmn. Albert Jay Rosenthal & Co., Chgo. and N.Y.C., 1961-85; chmn. Midwest div. HBM/Creamer-Albert Jay Rosenthal, Chgo., 1985-88, Della Femina, McNamee WCRS, Inc., Chgo., 1988-93; chmn. DFM/Tatham, Chgo., 1993; founder, pres. Franchising & Licensing World Ctr., Chgo., 1994-98; v.p. mktg., chief mktg. officer Terry Farms Inc., Wayzata, Minn., 1998—. Weekly columnist Franchising and You, Chgo. Sun-Times. Bd. dirs. Ill. Arts Alliance Found., Ill. Arts Alliance, Court Theatre U. Chgo.; mem. sustaining fund com. Ravinia Festival Assn.; mem. mktg. com. World Bus. Coun., Washington; vice chmn. Chgo. Internat. Film Festival; v.p. Gastro-Intestinal Rsch. Found. U. Chgo. Named one of Chgo. Ten Outstanding Young Men, Chgo. Jr. Assn. of Commerce, 1962, Advt. Man of Yr., Alpha Delta Sigma, 1978, Communicator of Yr., Jewish United Fund, 1988 Jewish. Home: 1110 N Lake Shore Dr Apt 32N Chicago IL 60611-1022

ROSENTHAL, ALBERT LESTER, dermatologist, educator; b. New Bedford, Mass., July 25, 1926; s. Myer and Ruth Naomi (Gourse) R.; m. Carol Ash, July 30, 1969; children: Robert, Jill, Bruce. BA magna cum laude, Tufts U., 1946, MD, 1951. Diplomate Am. Bd. Dermatology. Intern RI Hosp., Providence, 1951-52, asst. resident surgery, 1952-53; asst. resident dermatology Mass. Gen. Hosp., Boston, 1955-56; asst. in dermatology NYU, 1958-60; practice medicine specializing in dermatology Trenton, NJ, 1958—; attending dermatologist Mercer Hosp., 1958—, chief dermatologist, 1958-93; chief dermatology Helene Euld Hosp., 1973-85; assoc. in dermatology U. Pa., Phila., 1969-73; assoc. prof. dermatology Hahnemann Med. Coll., Phila., 1973-87, clin. prof. dermatology, 1987—; mem. staff Grad. Hosp. Pa., 1969-73, Hamilton Hosp., chief dermatologist, 1972-76. Contbr. numerous articles on dermatology to med. jours. Trustee Friend of the NJ State Mus., 1972—, chmn. bd. trustees, 1980-82, v.p. fine arts, 1978-80; gov. appointee adv. coun. NJ State Mus., 1994-2000, exec. com., 2001-; adv. bd. Princeton Sr. Resource Ctr., 1997—, exec. com.; adv. bd. Am. Festival Newark Mus., 1998-2002; mem. Mercer County Cultural and Heritage Commn., 1982-2000, chmn., 1984-2000; mem. Mercer County Open Space Preservation Commn., 1992-2000; founding mem. Leader's Soc. Dermatology Found., 1988; gov. appointee Bd. Trustees NJ State Mus., 2000—, exec. com. sec. 2002—. Served to capt., M.C., USAF, 1953-55. Mem. Am. Acad. Dermatology, Pa. Acad. Dermatology, Noah Worcester Dermatology Soc., Phila. Dermatology Soc. (pres. 1984-85), NJ Dermatology Soc., NJ Med. Soc., Mercer Med. Soc., AMA. Jewish. Office: 74 Franklin Corner Rd Lawrenceville NJ 08648-2102 E-mail: carosentha@aol.com.

ROSENTHAL, AMNON, pediatric cardiologist; b. Gedera, Israel, July 14, 1934; came to U.S., 1949, naturalized, 1959; s. Joseph and Rivka Rosenthal; m. Prudence Lloyd, July 22, 1962; children: Jonathan, Eben, Nathaniel. MD, Albany Med. Coll., 1959. Intern Buffalo Children's Hosp., 1959-60; resident in pediatrics Children's Hosp. Med. Center, Boston, 1960-62, resident in pediatric cardiology, 1965-68; asso. prof. pediatrics Children's Hosp. Med. Center and Harvard U. Med. Sch., Boston, 1975-77; prof. pediatrics C.S. Mott Children's Hosp., U. Mich., Ann Arbor, 1977—, assoc. dir. dept. pediatrics, 1989-92, dir. pediatric cardiology, 1977-97. Served to capt. M.C. USAF, 1962-65. Recipient Founders award, Am. Acad. Pediat., 2003, Disting. Svc. award, U. Mich., 2003; Amnon Rosenthal endowed professorship, 1994. Mem. Am. Acad. Pediatrics, Soc. for Pediatric Rsch., Am. Pediatric Soc., Am. Heart Assn., Am. Coll. Cardiology, Am. Bd. Pediatrics, Am. Bd. Pediatric Cardiology (chmn. 1987-88). Office: CS Mott Children's Hosp Ann Arbor MI 48109-0204 Office Phone: 734-936-6703. Business E-Mail: amnonr@umich.edu.

ROSENTHAL, ANDREW, newspaper editor; BA, Univ. Denver, 1978. Washington correspondent NY Times, 1987—92, Washington bur. editor, 1992—97, fgn. editor, 1997—2001, asst. mng. editor, 2001—03, deputy editorial page editor, 2003—. Office: The NY Times 229 W 43rd St New York NY 10036 3050*

ROSENTHAL, ARTHUR JESSE, publishing executive; b. N.Y.C., Sept. 26, 1919; s. Arthur J. and Grace (Ellinger) R.; m. Margaret Ann Roth, Dec. 12, 1975; children: James, Kathryn, Paul. BA, Yale U., 1941; postgrad., Harvard U. Bus. Sch., 1942. Spl. asst. to U.S. ambassador to Israel, Jerusalem, 1948; pres., editor in chief Basic Books, Inc., N.Y.C., 1949-72; dir. Harvard U. Press, Cambridge, 1972-90; pub. Hill and Wang, N.Y.C., 1990—. Founding trustee Bank St. Coll. Edn., 1952-68 Editorial bd.: Pub. Interest, Harvard Bus. Rev, Family Process, Yale U. Press. Trustee Austen Riggs Center, Stockbridge, Mass. Served to capt., M.I. U.S. Army, 1942-46. Mem.: Century Assn. (N.Y.C.); St. Botolph (Boston).

ROSENTHAL, DAN, retired director; b. NYC, July 9, 1940; m. Ann Rosenthal, Apr. 30, 1945. BA in Psychology, CUNY, 1968; PhD in Ednl. Psychology, U. Pitts., 1973. Asst. prof. of ednl. psychology Temple U. Philadelphia, Pa., 1973—79; dir. of instl. studies reports Richard Stockton Coll., Pomona, NJ, 1979—84; computer ctr. mgr. Miss. Coll., Clinton, Miss., 1984—94; assoc. dir., instl. rsch. and assessment Auburn U., Auburn, Ala., 1994—2004. Contbr. rsch. papers to profl. jours. Scholar Advanced Studies Seminar, Nat. Ctr. for Ednl. Stats., 1996, Coop. Systems Fellow Program, 1996. Mem.: Am. Ednl. Rsch. Assn., Friends Baldwin City Libr. (pres.), Health Care All Kansans (treas.). Avocations: physical fitness, nutrition. Home: 607 Parkside Ct Baldwin City KS 66006

ROSENTHAL, DOUGLAS EURICO, lawyer; b. N.Y.C., Feb. 12, 1940; s. Jacob and Edna Louise (Muir) R.; m. Erica Switzen Kremen, Nov. 12, 1967; children: Benjamin Muir, Rachel Elizabeth. BA summa cum laude, Yale U., 1961, LLB, 1966, PhD in Polit. Sci, 1970; postgrad., Oxford U., Eng., 1962; MA, Columbia U., 1963. Bar: NY 1968, DC 1980, US Dist. Ct. DC, US Dist. Ct. (so. and ea. dists.) NY, US Ct. Appeals (D.C. cir.), US Ct. Appeals (2d cir.), US Supreme Ct. 1976. Project dir. Russell Sage Found., NYC, 1968-70; assoc. Fried, Frank, Harris, Shriver & Jacobson, NYC, 1970-74; asst. chief fgn. commerce sect., antitrust divsn. Dept. Justice, Washington, 1974-77, chief, 1977-80; ptnr. Sutherland, Asbill & Brennan, Washington, 1980-88,

Coudert Bros., 1989-94, Sonnenschein, Nath & Rosenthal, LLP, Washington, 1994—2005, Constantine/Cannon P.C., Washington, 2005—. Adj. prof. Tokyo U. Law Sch., 1992; spkr. USIA, Australia, France, Eng., Can., Germany, Japan. Author: Lawyer and Client: Who's in Charge?, 1972, 2d rev. edit.; co-author: (with Donald I. Baker) US Dept. Justice Antitrust Guide for International Operations, 1977, (with William Knighton) National Law and International Commerce: The Problem of Extraterritoriality, 1982; co-editor (with Carl J. Green) Competition Regulation in the Pacific Rim, 1996. mem. bd. advisors Antitrust and Trade Regulation Report, 1989-; George Washington Jour. Internat. Law and Econ.; mem. editl. bd. CCH Merger Notification and Clearance in Can.; contbr. articles to profl. publs. Mem. Sedona Conf. Working Group on econs. and antitrust Inst. for Consumer Antitrust Studies, Loyola U., Chgo.; committeeman Nassau County (N.Y.) Dem. Party, 1963—65; lifetime mem. corp. Culinary Inst. Am.; mem. Brookings Roundtable on Trade and Investment; mem. trade and competition com. Internat. C. of C. Recipient Edward S. Corwin Nat. Award Am. Polit. Sci. Assn., 1971; Henry Fellow Balliol Coll., Oxford U., 1962, Nobel Internat. and Woodrow Wilson Fellow Columbia U., 1963. Mem. ABA (antitrust sect.), Coun. Fgn. Rels., Am. Law Inst. (life, adv. com. law governing lawyers), Confrerie des Chevaliers du Tastevin, Mory's Assn., Phi Beta Kappa. Jewish. Achievements include being lead attorney in 15 major international antitrust litigations. Office: 1627 Eye St NW Washington DC 20006 Office Phone: 202-204-3510. Business E-Mail: drosenthal@sonnenschein.com.

ROSENTHAL, EARL EDGAR, art history educator; b. Milw., Aug. 26, 1921; s. Edgar Ernst and Reneé (Wyler) R. BS, U. Wis. at, Milw., 1943; PhD, NYU, 1953; Doctor honoris causa, U. Granada, 1994. Asst. dir. Milw. Art Inst., also Layton Art Gallery, Milw., 1952-53; vis. lectr., dept. art history U. Chgo., from 1953, prof., 1968-91, prof. emeritus, 1991—. Author: The Cathedral of Granada, 1961; The Palace of Charles V in Granada, 1985, translated to Spanish 1988, Arquitectura imperial, 1988. Contbr. articles to profl. publs. Served to lt. (j.g.) USNR, 1943-46, PTO. Recipient Gold medal in Fine Arts King of Spain, 1989, medal of honor Fundación Rodríguez Acosta (Granada), 1989; Spanish govt. grantee, 1948-49; Fulbright grantee Italy, 1949-50; Fulbright grantee Spain, 1963-64; Guggenheim grantee Italy, 1963-64 Mem. Hispanic Soc. Am., Coll. Art Assn., Soc. Archtl. Historians (dir. 1957-58, 66-69), Academia de San Fernando (Madrid) (corr.), Academia de Bellas Artes (Granada) (corr.). Home: 203 Hutchcock Way Apt 214 Santa Barbara CA 93105

ROSENTHAL, EDWARD LEONARD, secondary school educator; b. Chgo., June 15, 1948; s. Irving H. and Nina (Kritchevsky) R.; m. Hilary Rosenberg, June 29, 1969; children: Rachel, Rebecca. BS in Sci. and Letters, U. Ill., 1969; MEd in Earth Sci., Northern Ill. U., 1972. Tchr. St. Joseph Sch., Dyer, Ind., 1969-70; tchr., golf coach Joliet Cath. HS, Ill., 1970-77; tchr., girls golf coach Naperville N. HS, Ill., 1977—. Chmn. United Multi Family Homeowners, Bolingbrook, Ill., 1974-75; v.p. Ill. Jr. Miss Program, Bolingbrook, 1985-87; trustee Village of Bolingbrook, 1975-81, mayor, 1981-85; bd. dirs. West Suburban Temple Har Zion, 1988-92. Named one of Outstanding Young Men Am., 1975, 82, Ill. Girls' Golf Coach Yr., 1988-89; elected to Ill. Golf Coaches Hall Fame, 1995; recipient Disting. Svc. award, 1974. Mem. NEA, Ill. Edn. Assn. 1999-2005, resolutions com. 2006-), Ill. Edn. Assn. (bd. dirs., 1992-98, 99-2005, exec. com. 1994-98, 2001-05, chmn. legis. com. 1987-90), Ill. Earth Sci. Assn., Nat. Sci. Tchrs. Assn., Ill. Girls' Golf Coaches Assn. (pres. 1985-88), Naperville Unit Edn. Assn. (1st v.p. 1990-95), Cmty. Assn. Inst. Ill. (bd. dirs. 1980-83), Ill. Jr. Golf Assn. (bd. dirs. 2001-06). Jewish. Avocation: golf. Home: 508 Clover Ln Bolingbrook IL 60440-1416 Office: Naperville N High Sch 899 N Mill St Naperville IL 60563-2909 E-mail: edrosenthal@hotmail.com.

ROSENTHAL, GERT, economist; b. Amsterdam, The Netherlands, Sept. 11, 1935; arrived in Guatemala, 1937; s. Ludwig and Florence (Koenigsberger) R.; m. Margit Uhlmann, Oct. 18, 1959; children: Caroline, Deborah, Jacqueline, Susan. BA, U. Calif., Berkeley, 1957, MA, 1958. Economist Nat. Planning Office, Guatemala, 1960-65; sr. ofcl. Ministry of Fin., Guatemala, 1966-67; sr. economist Secretariat of Cen. Am. Common Market, Guatemala, 1967-68; min. of planning Nat. Planning Office, Guatemala, 1969-70, 73-74; fellow Adlai Stevenson Inst. for Internat. Affairs, Chgo., 1971; coord. UN Tech. Assistance Project UN Conf. of Trade and Devel. Geneva, 1972; dir. Mex. office Econ. Commn. for Latin Am., Mexico City, 1975-85, dep. exec. sec. Santiago, Chile, 1986—87, exec. sec., 1988—97; rep. of Guatemala to the United Nations, 1999—2004. Author: Direct Foreign Investment in Central America, 1973; contbr. articles to profl. jours. Home: Residencial Santo Domingo Ste 5 Calle de los Duelos Antigua Guatemala Office Phone: 917-847-4821. Personal E-mail: grosenthal61@hotmail.com. Business E-Mail: grosenthal@un.int.

ROSENTHAL, HELEN NAGELBERG, county official, advocate; b. NYC, June 6, 1926; d. Alfred and Esther (Teichholz) Nagelberg; m. Albert S. Rosenthal, Apr. 10, 1949 (dec.); children: Lisa Rosenthal Michaels, Apryl Meredith Rosenthal Stuppler. BS, CUNY, 1948; MA. NYU, 1950; postgrad., Adelphia U., LI U., Lehman Coll., 1975. Cert. early childhood and gifted edn. tchr., NY, NJ, elem. and secondary tchr., Fla. Tchr. gifted students NY Bd Edn., Bklyn., 1949-77, 79-87, Baldwin Pub. Schs., NY, 1977-79; rep. community affairs County of Dade, Fla., 1988-92; ret., 1992; condo dir. Pembroke Pines, 1999—. Author: Criteria for Selection and Curriculum for the Gifted, 1977, Science Experiments for Young Children, 1982, Music in the Air...and in Our Minds. Dir. Condominium, 1989-91. Recipient Departmental award, 1948. Mem. Concerned Citizens for Educating Gifted and Talented (officer NYC chpt.), Assn. Gifted and Talented Edn. (NY chpt.), Am. Inst. Cancer Rsch., Bklyn. Coll. Alumni Assn. (pres. Broward-Dade chpt. 1995-96, v.p. membership 1996—).

ROSENTHAL, HOWARD LEWIS, political science professor; b. Wilkinsburg, Pa., Mar. 4, 1939; s. Arnold Sidney R. and Elinor (Kaufman) (Rosenthal) Lewis; m. Annie Regine Lunel, June 30, 1960 (div. Nov., 1967); children: Illia Rebecca, Jean Laurent; m. Margherita Guastoni Spampinato, Feb. 6, 1968; 1 son, Gil Guastoni. BS, MIT, 1960, PhD, 1964. Asst. prof. polit. sci. U. Calif.-Irvine, 1965-66; asst. prof. and assoc. prof. polit. sci. Carnegie-Mellon U., Pitts., 1966-71, prof., 1971-93; Roger Williams Straus prof. social scis. Princeton U, NJ, 1993—2005; prof. emeritus Princeton U., 2005—. Vis. prof. Hebrew U., Jerusalem, 1968-69, U. Calif., San Diego, 1976-77, MIT, Cambridge, 1989-90, U. Paris I, 1990, Walras-Pareto lectr. U. Lausanne, Switzerland, 1996; vis. grad. lectr. Fondation Nat. des Scis. Politiques, Paris, 1972-73; disting. vis. prof. Brown U., 2003—05. Author: Prediction Analysis of Cross Classifications, 1977, Analysis of Ordinal Data, 1977, Partisan Politics, Divided Government and the Economy, 1995, Flexible Integration: Towards a More Effective and Democratic Europe, 1995, The Realignment of National Politics and Income Redistribution, 1997, Congress: A Political-Economic History of Roll Call Voting, 1997, Credit Markets for the Poor, 2005, Polarized America: The Dance of Ideology and Unequal Riches, 2006; mem. editl. bd. Pub. Choice, Economics of Governance. Fellow NSF, 1969-92, 98-2003, Ford Found., 1972-73, Social Sci. Rsch. Coun., 1964-65, nat. fellow Hoover Instn., Stanford U., 1979-80; Sherman Fairchild disting. scholar Calif. Inst. Tech., 1982-83; fellow Internat. Ctr. for Econ. Rsch., Turin, Italy, 1991-93, Ctr. for Advanced Study in Behavioral Scis., 1991-92, 98-99, ECARE U. Libre de Brussels, 1995, Russell Sage Found., 2002-03, 2005-, John Simon Guggenheim Mem. Found., 2002-03. Fellow Am. Acad. Arts and Scis., 2002. Mem. Pub. Choice Soc. (Duncan Black award 1979), Am. Polit. Sci. Assn. (CQ Press award 1985). Office: Russell Sage Found 112 E 64th St New York NY 10021

ROSENTHAL, J. THOMAS, hospital administrator, medical educator; b. Richmond, 1949; BA, Johns Hopkins U.; MD, Duke U., 1974. Intern Johns Hopkins U., Balt., 1970; resident U. Va. Hosp., Charlottesville, Va., 1976, Lahey Clinic Found., Boston, 1980; exec. vice chmn. dept. surgery UCLA Sch. Medicine, 1991, prof. surgery/urology, 1993—, assoc. vice chancellor, 2003—; dir., vice provost UCLA Med. Group, 1996—; chief med. officer

UCLA Health Sys., 1999—; vice provost UCLA Med. Group Affairs. Office: UCLA Urology/David Geffen Sch Medicine Box 951731 14-214R CHS Los Angeles CA 90095-1731 Office Phone: 310-825-4686.

**ROSENTHAL, JAMES D.,** retired federal official, retired ambassador; b. San Francisco, Jan. 15, 1932; BA, Stanford U., 1954; student, Fgn. Svc. Inst., 1960—61, Nat. War Coll., 1974—75. With U.S. Fgn. Svc., 1956—90, adminstrv. officer Port of Spain, Trinidad and Tobago, 1958—60; polit. officer Saigon, Vietnam, 1961—65; mem. faculty U.S. Mil. Acad., 1965—67; internat. rels. officer Vietnam affairs Dept. State, 1967—70, dir. Vietnam, Laos and Cambodia affairs, 1975—77, dep. dir. mgmt. ops. Washington, 1986—90; mem. U.S. del. to Vietnam Peace Talks Paris, 1970—72; dep. chief of mission Bangui, 1972—74, Kuala Lumpur, Malaysia, 1977—79, Manila, Philippines, 1979—83; amb. to Guinea Conakry, 1983—86; exec. dir. Commonwealth Club of Calif., 1990—96. Personal E-mail: jrosent333@aol.com.

**ROSENTHAL, JANE,** film company executive; b. Providence, 1957; d. Martin and Jane. m. Craig Hatkoff; children: Juliana, Isabella. Student, Brown U.; BA, NYU, 1977. Rsch. staff CBS Sports, NY; editor program practices CBS Entertainment, 1977, program exec. miniseries L.A., 1978, assoc. dir. motion pictures for TV, 1979; v.p. feature prodn. Universal Studios, 1984—85; v.p. in charge of motion pictures and TV Walt Disney, 1985—87; v.p. in charge of movies and miniseries Warner Bros. TV, 1987—88; co-founder (with Robert DeNiro), ptnr. Tribeca Film Ctr., N.Y.C., 1989—; co-founder Tribeca Film Festival, N.Y.C., 2002. Prodr.: (films) Thunderheart, 1992, Night and the City, 1992, A Bronx Tale, 1993, Faithful, 1996, Marvin's Room, 1996, Wag the Dog, 1997, Analyze This, 1999, Entropy, 1999, Flawless, 1999, The Adventures of Rocky & Bullwinkle, 2000, Meet the Parents, 2000, Prison Song, 2001, Showtime, 2002, About a Boy, 2002, Analyze That, 2002, House of D, 2004, Stage Beauty, 2004, Meet the Fockers, 2004, Rent, 2005; (TV series) Tribeca, 1993; exec. prodr.: (films) Nine, 1996, The Repair Shop, 1998; (TV films) Witness to the Mob, 1998, Holiday Heart, 2000. Office: Tribeca Prodns 6th Fl 375 Greenwich St New York NY 10013*

**ROSENTHAL, JEFFREY M.,** lawyer; b. Poughkeepsie, NY, Aug. 14, 1951; BA in Econ., English, U. Pitts., 1973, MBA, 1974; JD, Rutgers U., Camden, 1982. Bar: NJ 1982, DC 1984, NY 2004. Shareholder, co-chair nat. fin. inst. practice group Greenberg Traurig LLP, Florham Park, NJ. Mem.: ABA (bus. law sect.), NJ State Bar Assn. (bd. dir.). Office: Greenberg Traurig LLP 200 Campus Dr PO Box 677 Florham Park NJ 07932 Office Phone: 973-360-7900. Office Fax: 973-301-8410. Business E-Mail: rosenthalj@gtlaw.com.

**ROSENTHAL, JOEL,** manufacturing executive; b. Ft. Worth, Oct. 25, 1946; s. Melvin and Jane (Hertzman) R.; m. Susan Ellman, Nov. 15, 1970; children: Jackie Ilene, Harold Joseph. BBA, No. Tex. State U., 1969. V.p. First Street Corp., Ft. Worth, 1969-72; mgr. Edison Jewelers & Distbrs., Ft. Worth, 1972-73; v.p. Yankton Sioux Industries, Wagner, S.D., 1973-81, pres., 1981-85; cons., Canton, S.D., 1985—; pres. Ctrl. Plains Tractor Parts, Sioux Falls, S.D., 1986—. Cons. econ. devel. State of S.D., Pierre, 1985-86; guest lectr. U. S.D., 2003. Chmn. S.D. Rep. Com., 1995-2003; mem. Electoral Coll., 1996, 2000; pres. City Coun., Wagner, 1978-83; trustee Carnegie Libr., Wagner, 1978-83; active Rep. Nat. Com., Washington, 1985-2003, S.D. Jud. Qualifications Commn., 1983-86, Pvt. Industry Coun., Pierre, 1985-86, SD Coun. of Econ. Advs., 2003. Named S.D. Vol. of Yr. Office of Gov., 1983. Republican. Jewish. Home: 6001 S Tomar Rd Sioux Falls SD 57013 Office: PO Box 1818 Sioux Falls SD 57101-1818 Office Phone: 605-334-0021.

**ROSENTHAL, JOEL HOWARD,** think-tank executive; b. Brookline, Mass., Apr. 28, 1960; s. Edward and Helen R.; m. Patricia Barney, Dec. 7, 1986; children: Sarah, David. BA, Harvard U., 1982; PhD, Yale U., 1988. Pres. Carnegie Coun. on Ethics and Internat. Affairs, N.Y.C., 1995—; adj. prof. N.Y.U., N.Y.C., 1996—. Co-dir. Carnegie Coun./Nat. War Coll. working group on Ethics and the Future of Internat. Conflict; coordinator Carnegie Coun.'s projects on Justice and the World Economy and Ethics and U.S. Fgn. Policy. Author: Righteous Realists, 1991; editor: Ethics and Internat. Affairs, 1990—, Ethics and Internat. Affairs: A Reader (2d edit.), 1999; contbr. articles to profl. jours. Co-dir. NEH 1994 Summer Faculty Inst. on Teaching Ethics and Internat. Affairs, U. Va.; charter author and 1st chmn. Internat. Ethics sect., Internat. Studies Assn. Office: Carnegie Coun 170 E 64th St New York NY 10021-7478

**ROSENTHAL, LARRY,** cosmetic dentist; b. NYC, 1948; married; 1 child. DDS, U. Pa. Sch. Dental Medicine, 1974. Dir. aesthetic continuum Baylor Coll. Dentistry, Dallas, Advanced Program, NYU, U. Ky. Coll. Dentistry; dir. Aesthetic Advantage Inc., Rosenthal Group Aesthetic Dentistry, NY. Spkr. in field. Named one of Top Cosmetic Dentists in NY, NY Mag., 2004; recipient Internat. Five-Star Diamond award, Am. Acad. Hospitality Sci. Mem.: Am. Acad. Cosmetic Dentistry (asst. editor, AACD Jour.). Achievements include print features in Vogue Mag., Elle, Glamour, Town & Country, New York Times, and Wall Street Jour; TV appearances on Weekend Today, The View, Access Hollywood. Office: Rosenthal Group Aesthetic Dentistry 30 E 76th St Ste 5B New York NY 10021 Office Phone: 212-794-9600. Office Fax: 212-794-3644.*

**ROSENTHAL, LEE H.,** federal judge; b. Nov. 30, 1952; m. Gary L. Rosenthal; children: Rebecca, Hannah, Jessica, Rachel. BA in Philosophy with honors, U. Chgo., 1974, JD with honors, 1977. Bar: Tex. 1979. Law clk. to Hon. John R. Brown U.S. Ct. Appeals (5th cir.), 1977-78; assoc. Baker & Botts, 1978-86, ptnr., 1986-92; judge U.S. Dist. Ct. (so. dist.) Tex., 1992—. Mem. Fed. Jud. Conf. Adv. Com. for Fed. Rules of Civil Procedure, 1996-2003, chair 2003-; chair 1999 Fifth Cir. Jud. Conf.; mem. Am. Law Inst., cons. group on transactional rules of civil procedure, adviser aggregate litigation project. Mem. bd. editors Manual for Complex Litigation, 1999—. Mem. vis. com. Law Sch. U. Chgo., 1983-86, 94-97, 99-2001; pres. Epilepsy Assn. Houston/Gulf Coast, 1989-91; trustee Briarwood Sch. Endowment Found., 1991-92; bd. dirs. Epilepsy Found. Am., 1993-98, DePelchin Children's Ctr., 1992-; bd. trustees Kinkaid Sch. Fellow Tex. Bar Found.; Mem. ABA, Texas Bar Assn., Houston Bar Assn. Office: US Dist Ct US Courthouse Rm 11535 515 Rusk St Houston TX 77002-2600

**ROSENTHAL, LUCY GABRIELLE,** writer, editor, educator; b. NYC; d. Henry Moses and Rachel (Tchernowitz) Rosenthal. AB, U. Mich., 1954; MS in Journalism, Columbia U., 1955; MFA, Yale Sch. Drama, 1961; postgrad. Writers Workshop, U. Iowa, 1965—68. Asst. editor Radiology mag., Detroit, 1955—57; free-lance editl. cons. various pub. houses, lit. agts. NYC, 1957—73; mem. admissions staff Writers Workshop U. Iowa, Iowa City, 1965—68; editor Book-of-the-Month Club, NYC, 1973—74, mem. editl. bd. judges, 1974—79, sr. editl. advisor, 1979—87. Mem. biography jury Pulitzer Prize, 1980; mem. bd. Am. Book Awards, 1981-82; adj. prof. English, NYU, 1986—; mem. guest faculty in writing Sarah Lawrence Coll., 1988-96, regular faculty writing, 1996—; lectr., adj. asst. prof. English, writing program Columbia U., 1990-96, Humanities faculty, 92nd St. YM/YWCA, 1987; fiction workshop The Writer's Voice, West Side YMCA, summer 1991; adj. prof. NYU Sch. Continuing Edn., 1988; mem. faculty Sarah Lawrence Ctr. for Continuing Edn., 1989, 90; instr. fiction writing course Art Workshop Internat., Assisi, Italy, summer 1993. Plays produced at Eugene O'Neill Meml. Theater Ctr., 1966, 67; author: The Ticket Out, 1983; editor: Great American Love Stories, 1988, The World Treasury of Love Stories, 1995, The Eloquent Short Story: Varieties of Narration, 2004; contbr. to Global City Rev., 1995; contbr. articles to various mags. and periodicals. Pulitzer fellow critical writing, 1968. Mem. Authors Guild, Authors League, Nat. Book Critics Circle, Women's Media Group (bd. mem. 1979-81), PEN, Phi Beta Kappa, Phi Kappa Phi. Office: Sarah Lawrence Coll Bronxville NY 10708 E-mail: lrosenth@slc.edu.

**ROSENTHAL, MICHAEL ROSS,** academic administrator, consultant; b. Youngstown, Ohio, Dec. 2, 1939; s. Samuel Herman and Frances Vance (Schlesinger) m. Linda Gabler, Sept. 6, 1963; children: Heidi, Erika, Nicolas Gabler. AB, Case Western Res. U., 1961; MS, U. Ill., 1963, PhD, 1965. Asst. prof. chemistry Bard Coll., Annandale, NY, 1965-68, assoc. prof. chemistry, 1968-73, prof. chemistry, 1973-84, assoc. dean acad. affairs, 1980-84; v.p. acad. affairs St. Mary's Coll. of Md., St. Mary's City, 1984-89; provost, dean faculty, prof. chemistry Southwestern U., Georgetown, Tex., 1989-96; dep. sec. Md. Higher Edn. Commn., Annapolis, 1996—99; spl. asst. to provost McDaniel Coll., Westminster, Md., 1999—, vis. prof., chair dept. chemistry, 2005—. Acad. cons., ind. and as rep. of Assn. Am. Colls. Author or co-author of numerous articles in jours. of inorganic chemistry and chem. edn. Chmn. Environ. Mgmt. Coun., Dutchess County, N.Y., 1978-84; founding chmn. Heritage Task Force for Hudson River Valley, 1980-84; pres., bd. dirs. Hudson River Heritage, N.Y., 1978-84; bd. dirs. Hudson River Rsch. Coun., 1976-84; teaching assoc. Danforth Found., 1980. Recipient Outstanding Cmty. Svc. award Dutchess County (NY) Legislature, 1980 Mem. Am. Chem. Soc., The Royal Society (Chemistry, London), Hudson River Environ. Soc., Sigma Xi, Phi Beta Kappa, Phi Lambda Upsilon Democrat. Office: McDaniel Coll 2 College Hill Westminster MD 21157 Office Phone: 410-857-2268. Business E-Mail: mrosenth@mcdaniel.edu. *Those of us who spend our professional lives as educators are subject to many pressures and influences - financial influences, political influences, intellectual influences. I try to remember that in the usually chaotic world of education the only really important thing is the welfare of the student.*

**ROSENTHAL, PHIL,** television producer, director, writer; b. 1960; s. Max and Helen Rosenthal; m. Monica Horan, Apr. 1990; 2 children. Supervising prodr., dir. (TV series) Coach, 1995—96, writer A Family for Joe, 1990, Baby Talk, 1991, The Man in the Family, 1991, Down the Shore, 1992, creator, writer, exec. prodr. Everybody Loves Raymond, 1996—2005 (Emmy award for Outstanding Comedy Series, 2003); actor: (films) Who Shot Patakango, 1990, Spanglish, 2004.

**ROSENTHAL, RICHARD JAY,** psychiatrist; b. N.Y.C., Jan. 12, 1939; s. Sam and Yvette Loraine (Kapelov) Rosenthal; m. Strawn Rosenthal, Nov. 10, 1984. BA, Cornell U., 1960; MD, Albert Einstein Coll. of Medicine, 1964. Diplomate Nat. Bd. Med. Examiners, Am. Bd. Psychiatry and Neurology. Resident in psychiatry Mt. Sinai Hosp., N.Y.C., 1968; clin. assoc. L.A. Psychoanalytic Inst., 1980; pvt. practice Los Angeles, 1970—; asst. clin. prof. psychiatry UCLA, 1971—2005; faculty L.A. Psychoanalytic Inst., 1984—; dir. inpatient gambling treatment program Westwood Hosp., 1990—93; chief of psychiatry CPC Westwood Hosp., L.A., 1992—93; supr. attending Cedars Sinai Med. Ctr., L.A., 1982—; co-dir. UCLA Gambling Studies Program, 2003—. Founder/pres. Calif. Coun. on Problem Gambling, 1986—99; com. on impulse disorders APA Task Force on DSM IV, 1988—93; com. on social and econ. impact of path. gambling Nat. Acad. Sci., 1998—99; vis. prof. psychiatry UCLA, 2005—. Contbr. chapters to books, articles to jours. Beit T'Shuvah Residential Treatment Ctr. L.A., 1992—94; adv. com. Little Hoover Commn. on Gambling in Calif., 1997; trustee Mus. Photog. Arts, San Diego. Lt. comdr. USN, 1964—70. Recipient Rsch. award, Nat. Coun. on Problem Gambling, 1993, Herman Goldman award, 1995, Robert Custer award, 2004. Fellow: Am. Psychiat. Assn. (life distng.); mem.: Internat. Dostoevsky Soc., So. Calif. Psychiat. Soc. (ethics com. 1992—), Inst. for the Study of Gambling and Comml. Gaming (adv. bd. 1993—), Am. Acad. Psychiatrists in Alcoholism and Addictions. Achievements include first controlled study of repetitive self mutilation(demonstrated progression and role of dissociation); author of current diagnostic criteria for pathological gambling; co-investigator on first genetic study of pathological gambling (demonstrating physiological predisposition); research establishing the legitimacy of the disorder; founding of California council on problem gaming, started first inpatient treatment program on the west coast, began UCLA gambling studies program, mentored researchers and clinicans. Avocations: photography, fly fishing. Office: 435 N Roxbury Dr Beverly Hills CA 90210 Office Phone: 310-278-3746.

**ROSENTHAL, ROBERT,** psychology professor; b. Giessen, Germany, Mar. 2, 1933; came to U.S., 1940, naturalized, 1946. s. Julius and Hermine (Kahn) R.; m. Mary Lu Clayton, Apr. 20, 1951; children: Roberta, David C., Virginia. AB, UCLA, 1953, PhD, 1956; PhD (hon.), U. Giessen, 2003. Diplomate clin. psychology Am. Bd. Examiners Profl. Psychology. Clin. psychology trainee Los Angeles Area VA, 1954-57; lectr. U. So. Calif., 1956-57; acting instr. UCLA, 1957; from asst. to assoc. prof., coordinator clin. tng. U. N.D. 1957-62; vis. assoc. prof. Ohio State U., 1960-61; lectr. Boston U., 1965-66; lectr. clin. psychology Harvard U., Cambridge, Mass., 1962-67, prof. social psychology, 1967-95, chmn. dept. psychology, 1992-95, Edgar Pierce prof. psychology, 1995-99, Edgar Pierce prof. emeritus, 1999—; disting. prof. U. Calif., Riverside, 1999—. Experimenter Effects in Behavioral Research, 1966, enlarged edit., 1976; (with Lenore Jacobson) Pygmalion in the Classroom, 1968, expanded edit., 1992, Meta-analytic Procedures for Social Research, 1984, rev. edit., 1991, Judgment Studies, 1987; (with others) New Directions in Psychology 4, 1970, Sensitivity to Nonverbal Communication: The Pons Test, 1979; (with Ralph L. Rosnow) The Volunteer Subject, 1975, Primer of Methods for the Behavioral Sciences, 1975, Essentials of Behavioral Research, 1984, 2d edit., 1991, Understanding Behavioral Science, 1984, Contrast Analysis, 1985, Beginning Behavioral Research, 1993, 5th edit., 2005, People Studying People: Artifact and Ethics in Behavioral Research, 1997, (with Ralph L. Rosnow and Donald B. Rubin) Contrasts and Effect Sizes in Behavioral Research: A Correlational Approach, 2000; (with Brian Mullen) BASIC Meta-analysis, 1985; editor: (with Ralph L. Rosnow) Artifact in Behavioral Research, 1969, Skill in Nonverbal Communication, 1979, Quantitative Assessment of Research Domains, 1980, (with Thomas A. Sebeok) The Clever Hans Phenomenon: Communication With Horses, Whales, Apes and People, 1981, (with Blanck and Buck) Nonverbal Communication in the Clinical Context, 1986, (with Gheorghiu, Netter and Eysenck) Suggestion and Suggestibility: Theory and Research, 1989, (with Harrigan and Scherer) Te New Handbook of Methods in Nonverbal Behavior Research, 2005 Recipient Donald Campbell award Soc. for Personality and Social Psychology, 1988, James McKeen Cattell Sabbatical award, 1995-96; co-recipient Golden Anniversary Monograph award Speech Comm. Assn., 1996; named Watson lectr. U. N.H., Lanzetta Meml. lectr. Dartmouth Coll., Bayer lectr. Yale Sch. Medicine, Foa lectr. Temple U., Disting. Alumni lectr. UCLA, Marschak lectr. UCLA; Guggenheim fellow, 1973-74, fellow Ctr. for Advanced Study in Behavioral Scis., 1988-89; sr. Fulbright scholar, 1972; recipient Gold Medal for Life Achievement in Sci. of Psychology Am. Psychol. Found., 2003. Fellow AAAS (co-recipient Sociopsychol. prize 1960, co-recipient Behavioral Sci. Rsch. prize 1993), APA (divsn. evaluation, measurement, and stats., co-recipient Cattell Fund award 1967, co-chmn. Task Force on Statis. Inference, Disting. Sci. award for applications of psychology, 2002, Disting. Sci. Contbns. award, 2002, divsn. evaluation, measurement and stats., others), Am. Psychol. Soc. (charter, James McKeen Cattell award 2001); mem. Soc. Exptl. Social Psychology (Disting. Scientist award 1996), Ea. Psychol. Assn. (Disting. lectr. 1989), Mid-we. Psychol. Assn., Mass. Psychol. Assn. (Disting. Career Contbn. award 1979), Soc. Projective Techniques (past treas.), Phi Beta Kappa, Sigma Xi. Office: U Calif Olmsted Hall Riverside CA 92521-0001 Office Phone: 951-827-4503.

**ROSENTHAL, ROBERT JON,** newspaper editor, journalist; b. NYC, Aug. 5, 1948; s. Irving and Ruth (Moss) R.; m. Inez Katherina von Sternenfels, Nov. 22, 1985; children: Adam, Benjamin, Amelia. BA, U. Vt., 1970. News asst. N.Y. Times, N.Y.C., 1970-73; reporter Boston Globe, 1974-79, Phila. Inquirer, 1979-82, Africa corr., Nairobi, Kenya, 1982-85, fgn. editor, Phila., 1986-91, city editor, 1991-93, asst. mng. editor, daily, 1993-94, assoc. mng. editor, 1994-96, exec. editor, 1996-98, editor, exec. v.p., 1998—2001; mng. editor, v.p. San Francisco (Calif.) Chronicle, 2002—. Recipient Third World Reporting award Nat. Assn. Black Journalists, 1983, Mag. award Overseas Press Club, 1985, Disting. Fgn. Corr. award Sigma Delta Chi, 1985, Mag. Writing award World Population Inst., 1986. Avocations: ice hockey, gardening, fishing, cooking. Office: 1 Stevens Ct Belvedere Tiburon CA 94920-1549

**ROSENTHAL, SEYMOUR JOSEPH,** artist, printmaker; b. N.Y.C., Aug. 14, 1921; m. Frances Aida Friedlander, Dec. 18, 1943. Lectr. in field. One-man shows include Suffolk Mus., Stony Brook, N.Y., ACA Gallery, 1969, Indpls. Mus. Art, East Hampton Jewish Ctr., L.I., N.Y., Suffolk Jewish Cmty. Ctr., Commack N.Y., Gallery ACA N.Y.; group shows include Bklun. Mus., N.Y.C., 1967, Huntington Hartford Mus., 1973, 75; represented in permanent collections Indpls. Mus. Art, Suffolk Mus., Stony Brook, Harry S. Truman Libr., Independence, Mo., Technion Bldg., Haifa, Israel, N.Y. Pub. Libr., Smithsonian Instn., Internat. Brotherhood Elec. Workers Local 3, N.Y.C., Met. Mus. Art, N.Y. print and drawing collection. With U.S. Army, WWII.

**ROSENTHAL, SHIRLEY LORD,** cosmetics magazine executive, novelist; b. London, Aug. 28; came to U.S., 1971; d. Francis J. and Mabel Florence (Williamson) Stringer; m. James Hussey; m. Cyril Lord; m. David Anderson; m. A. M. Rosenthal, June 10, 1987; children: Mark, Richard. Student, S.W. Essex Coll., London, 1948—50. Reporter London Daily Mirror; fiction editor Woman's Own, 1950-53; features editor Good Taste mag., 1953-56; features, fiction editor Woman and Beauty, 1956-59; women's editor Star Evening newspaper, 1959-60, London Evening Standard, 1960-63, London Evening News, 1963-68; beauty editor Harper's Bazaar, London, 1963-71, N.Y.C., 1971-73; beauty, health editor Vogue mag., Condé Nast Publs., N.Y.C., 1973-75; v.p. corp. rels. Colgate, Helena Rubinstein, N.Y.C., 1975-80; beauty dir. Vogue mag., 1980—95, contbg. editor, 1995—. Chairwoman media coun. The Am. Acad. Dermatology, 1995—; corp. v.p. content iBeauty.com, 1999—2002; enrichment advisor Silverson Cruises, 2004—. Syndicated Field columnist on beauty; author 3 beauty books; also novels: Golden Hill, 1982; One of My Very Best Friends, (Lit. Guild Selection), 1985; Faces, 1989; My Sister's Keeper, 1993, The Crasher, 1998. City commr. Craigavon City, No. Ireland, 1963-68. Address: 131 E 66th St New York NY 10021-6129 E-mail: Shirlord3@aol.com.

**ROSENTHAL, SOL,** lawyer; b. Balt., Oct. 17, 1934; s. Louis and Hattie (Getz) R.; m. Diane Myra Sackler, June 11, 1961; children: Karen Abby, Pamela Margaret, Robert Joel. AB, Princeton U., 1956; JD, Harvard U., 1959. Bar: Md. 1959, Calif. 1961. Law clk. to chief judge U.S. Ct. Appeals, 4th cir., Balt., 1959-60; assoc. Kaplan, Livingston, Goodwin, Berkowitz & Selvin, Beverly Hills, Calif., 1960-66, ptnr., 1966-74, Buchalter Nemer, L.A., 1974—96; of counsel Blanc, Williams, Johnston & Kronstadt, L.A., 1996-2000, Arnold & Porter, 2000—. Bd. dirs. Playboy Enterprises, Inc., Chgo.; arbitrator Dirs. Guild Am., L.A., 1976—, Writers Guild Am., L.A., 1976—, Ind. Film and TV Alliance, 1989—, SAG, L.A., 1992—; negotiator Writers Guild-Assn. Talent Agts., L.A., 1978—; mem. entertainment and large complex case panels Am. Arbitration Assn., 1997—. Founder Camp Ronald McDonald for Good Times, L.A., 1985; charter founder Mus. Contemporary Art, L.A., 1988. Fellow: Coll. Comml. Arbitrators, Am. Bar Found.; mem.: ABA, Beverly Hills Bar Assn. (pres. 1982—83), Acad. TV Arts and Scis. (bd. govs. 1990—92), L.A. Copyright Soc. (pres. 1973—74), Los Angeles County Bar Assn. (trustee 1981—82), Calif. Bar Assn., Phi Beta Kappa. Office: Arnold & Porter 777 S Figueroa St Ste 4400 Los Angeles CA 90017-5844 Office Phone: 213-243-4000. Business E-Mail: sol_rosenthal@aporter.com.

**ROSENTHAL, STEVEN SIEGMUND,** lawyer; b. Cleve., May 22, 1949; s. Fred Siegel and Natalie Josephine Rosenthal; m. Ilene Edwina Goldstein, Oct. 1, 1983; children: Alexandra M., Eliana D. AB, Dartmouth Coll., 1971; JD, Harvard U., 1974. Bar: Fla. 1974, D.C. 1975, U.S. Supreme Ct. 1978, Calif. 1983. Law clk. judge Malcolm R. Wilkey U.S. Ct. Appeals (D.C. cir.), 1974-75; assoc. Covington & Burling, Washington, 1975-80, Morrison & Foerster, Washington, 1980-81, ptnr., 1981-97, Cooper, Carvin & Rosenthal, PLLC, Washington, 1998-2001, Holland & Knight LLP, Washington, 2001—02, Kaye Scholer LLP, Washington, 2002—. Lawyer rep. Jud. Conf. D.C. Cir., 1981-83, 2004—; mem. adv. com. on procedures U.S. Ct. Appeals D.C. Cir., 2003—. Pres. Family and Child Svcs. Washington, 1986-88, trustee, 1978—. Mem. ABA, Am. Law Inst., Phi Beta Kappa. Republican. Office: Kaye Scholer LLP 901 Fifteenth St NW Ste 1100 Washington DC 20005-2327

**ROSENTHAL, SUSAN BARBARA,** retired librarian; b. Elberon Park, NJ, Apr. 7, 1946; d. Joseph and Anna (Warar) Rosenthal. BA, Montclair State Coll., 1967; MEd in Libr. Sci., U. Miami, 1973. Cert. media specialist, tchr., Fla., N.J. Tchr. Manasquan Bd. Edn. (N.J.), 1967-71; tech. svcs. libr. Oakland Park (Fla.) Libr., 1978-92, asst. dir., 1992-93, acting dir., 1993, ret. Author: (mag.) Galumph, 1965-67; contbr. A Micro Handbook for Small Libraries and Media Centers, 1983, 2d edit., 1986, 3d edit., 1991. Mem. Humane Soc., Broward County, Fla., 1981, WPBT-TV PBS sta., 1975-2000, So. Mus. Flight, 1997—, Friends of the Oakland Park Libr., 1998—, mem. luncheon com., 1999, mem. planning com., 1999; charter mem. Mus. of Discovery and Sci., 1989-96, U.S. Holocaust Meml. Mus., 1994—; donor Miami Book Fair Internat., 1990—, Cats Exclusive, Boca Raton (Fla.) Mus. Art, So. Poverty Law Ctr. Wall of Tolerance, Survivors of the Shoah Visual History Found., Friends of the Oakland Park Libr., Sierra Club, WPBT-TV PBS Sta., Am. Coming Together, Abandoned Pet Rescue, Becca's Closet, Black Box Voting, Broward House, Coconut Grove Arts Festival, Defenders of Wildlife, Delray Affair, others. Recipient St. Cloud Tchg. award Société d'Enseignement, St. Cloud, France, 1966, 2 awards Libr. Pub. Rels. Coun., winner, 1983, hon. mention, 1985, cert. appreciation U.S. Holocaust Meml. Mus., 1996, 2000. Mem. ALA, AARP, Nat. Alliance for Mentally Ill, Fla. Libr. Assn., Fla. Pub. Libr. Assn., Broward County Libr. Assn. (treas. 1981-83, continuing edn. com. 1980), Apple Libr. Users Group, Apple Computer Enjoyment Soc. (chpt. sec. 1984-87, corp. sec. 1985-89), Consumers Union, NFO Rsch., Wilderness Soc., World Wildlife Fund, Environ. Def. Fund, People for Ethical Treatment of Animals, Nat. Resources Def. Coun., Nature Conservancy, Nat. Wildlife Fedn., Mensa, actforchange.org, moveon.org, Procrastinators Club Am., Pi Delta Phi.

**ROSENTHAL, TIMOTHY MARK,** music educator; b. West Bend, Wis., Aug. 3, 1966; s. David Elmer and Doris Jean Rosenthal; m. Lizabeth Ann Rosenthal, Sept. 14, 1996; children: Taylor Jerome Cagle, Hayley Louise, Samuel David. MusB in Edn., U. Wis., Oshkosh, Wis., 1993. Commd. lt. U.S. Army, 1984, advanced through grades to staff sgt.; music educator Beloit (Wis.) Turner Schs., 1994—, dir. drama, 1994—. Avocations: acting, softball. Home: 3139 S Davis Dr Beloit WI 53511

**ROSENTHAL, TONY (BERNARD),** sculptor; b. Highland Park, Ill., Aug. 9, 1914; s. Nathan H. and Bessie (Baumgarden) R.; m. Halina Kotlowicz, Apr. 2, 1946 (dec. 1991); m. Cynthia Dillon, 1995. AB, U. Mich., 1936; student, Art Inst. Chgo., Cranbrook Acad. Arts; doctorate (hon.), Hofstra U., 1989. Exhbns. include Art Inst. Chgo., Met. Mus. Art, Mus. Modern Art, N.Y., Whitney Mus. Am. Art, N.Y.C., Pa. Acad. Fine Arts, Archtl. League, N.Y., Yale U., U. Ill., U. Nebr., 100 Biennale Exhbn., Sao Paulo, Brazil, Brussel's Fair, 1958, others; one man shows include San Francisco Mus, Western Mus. Assn. Travel Exhbn., Santa Barbara (Calif.) Mus., Long Beach (Calif.) Mus. Catherine Viviano Gallery N.Y., Kootz Gallery, N.Y.C., M. Knoedler & Co., Denise Rene Gallery, Paris, 1988, others; archtl. commn. include Temple Emanuel, Beverly Hills, Calif., 1955, IBM Bldg., 1958, Southland Ctr. Dallas, IBM Western Hdqrs., Los Angeles, Police Plaza, N.Y.C., Fullerton (Calif.) State Coll., Fin. Ctr. Pacific, Honolulu, Holocaust Meml., Buffalo, Metro-Rail Sta., Miami, S.E. Nat. Bank, Miami, Grove Isle, Miami, Met. Hosp., Phila., 1010 Lamar, Houston, Crantsrook Acad. Art, Bloomfield Hills, Mich., Steelpark, 400 E. 80th St, N.Y.C., Alamo, Astor Pl., N.Y.C., Rondo, 111 E. 59th St, N.Y.C., U. Ind., Hofstra U., N.Y., others; works in permanent collections Milw. Art Ctr., Ill. State U., Los Angeles County Mus., Long Beach, Lincoln (Mass.) Mus., Ariz. State Coll., Mus. Modern Art, Whitney Mus. Art, Albright Knox Art Gallery, Buffalo, U. Ill., NYU, Yale U., Middelheim Mus., Antwerp, Belgium, Guggenheim Mus., N.Y.C., Hofstra U. Fashion Inst. Art, N.Y.C., others; pvt. collections. Served with AUS, 1942-46. Recipient awards, prizes San Francisco Mus., 1950, Los Angeles City Exhbn., 1951, 52, Audubon Artists, N.Y., 1953, Pa. Acad. Fine Arts, 1953, Los

Angeles County Mus., 1950, 57, Santa Barbara Mus. Art, 1959, Art in Steel award Iron and Steel Inst., 1974-75, Disting. Alumni award U. Mich., 1977, Sculpture award Inst. Arts and Letters, N.Y.C., 1985. Mem. NAD, 1992- (Academician, 1994-)

**ROSENTHAL, WILLIAM J.,** lawyer; b. Balt., Nov. 4, 1920; s. Justin J. and Ray Marian (Stern) Rosenthal; m. Margaret Irwin Parker, July 4, 1956; children: Adriane Leigh, Jacqueline Rae, John Justin. AB, Johns Hopkins U., Balt., 1941; LL.B., U. Balt., 1950. Bar: Md. 1950. Adminstrv. asst. Office Price Adminstrn., Washington, 1941-42; assoc. Earle K. Shawe, Balt., 1951-67; ptnr. Shawe & Rosenthal (formerly Earle K. Shawe), Balt., 1967—. Lectr. U. Balt., 1952—56; mem. regional adv. coun. NLRB; vets. rep. Md. Constrn. Adv. Coun., 1946—49; lectr. NYU Conf. Labor Rels., 1981, Boston U. Labor Law Seminar, 1985; expert witness on labor law, legis. and congl. coms. Author: D-Day Through V-E Day; co-author: The Developing Labor Law; contbr. articles to profl. jours. Served to lt. USNR, 1942—46, ETO. Mem.: ABA, Balt. Bar Assn., Md. Bar Assn., Johns Hopkins Club, Suburban Club (bd. govs., pres.), Spiked Shoe Soc., Pi Delta Epsilon, Omicron Delta Kappa. Home: 8207 Cranwood Ct Baltimore MD 21208-1823 Office: Shawe & Rosenthal Sun Life Bldg Charles Center Baltimore MD 21201 Office Phone: 410-752-1040. Business E-Mail: rosenthal@shawe.com.

**ROSENWASSER, MIKE,** lawyer; b. Texarkana, Ark., 1946; BBA, U. Tex., 1968, JD, 1971. Bar: Tex. 1971, NY 1992. Ptnr., co-head Corp. Fin. & Securities Vinson & Elkins LLP, NYC. Office: Vinson & Elkins LLP 26th Fl 666 Fifth Avenue New York NY 10103 Office Phone: 212-237-0019. E-mail: mrosenwasser@velaw.com.

**ROSENZWEIG, CHARLES LEONARD,** lawyer; b. N.Y.C., Apr. 12, 1952; s. William and Frieda (Dechner) R.; m. Rya R. Mehler, June 14, 1975; children: Jessica Sara Newshel, Erica Danielle. AB cum laude, Princeton U., 1974; JD, NYU, 1977. Bar: N.Y. 1978, U.S. Dist. Ct. (ea. and so. dists.) N.Y. 1978, U.S. Ct. Appeals (7th cir.) 1980, U.S. Ct. Internat. Trade 1981, U.S. Ct. Appeals (2d cir.) 1985. Assoc. Graubard, Moskovitz et al, N.Y.C., 1977-85; ptnr. Rand Rosenzweig Radley & Gordon LLP, N.Y.C., 1987—. Mem. panel of neutrals comml. divsn. Supreme Ct. State N.Y. Internat. Law. and Politics. Chmn. bd. Jewish Cmty. Ctr., Harrison, 1998-2000. Mem. ABA (internat. law sect.), N.Y. State Bar Assn. (co-chair internat. litig. com. 1995-98, mem. exec. com. comml. and fed. litig. sect. 1995-2005), NYU Alumni Assn. (chmn. jour. internat. law and politics alumni 1985-87), Assn. Comml. Fin. Attys. Avocations: skiing, bicycling, scuba diving, languages. Home: 9 Hadley Rd Armonk NY 10504-2417 Office: Rand Rosenzweig et al 800 3rd Ave New York NY 10022 also: 50 Main St 12th Fl White Plains NY 10606 Office Phone: 212-687-7070. Business E-Mail: crosenzweig@randrose.com.

**ROSENZWEIG, MARK RICHARD,** psychologist, neuroscientist, educator; b. Rochester, NY, Sept. 12, 1922; s. Jacob and Pearl (Grossman) R.; m. Janine S.A. Chappat, Aug. 1, 1947; children: Anne Janine, Suzanne Jacqueline, Philip Mark. BA, U. Rochester, 1943, MA, 1944; PhD, Harvard U., 1949; doctorate (hon.). U. René Descartes, Sorbonne, 1980, U. Louis Pasteur, Strasbourg, France, 1998, U. Montreal, Can., 2006. Postdoctoral rsch. fellow Harvard U., 1949-51; asst. prof. U. Calif., Berkeley, 1951-56, assoc. prof., 1956-60, prof. psychology, 1960-91, assoc. rsch. prof., 1958-59, rsch. prof., 1965-66, prof. emeritus, 1991—, prof. grad. studies, 1994—. Vis. prof. biology U. Sorbonne, Paris, 1973-74; mem. U.S. nat. com. for Internat. Union Psychol. Sci., NRC and NAS, 1984-96. Author: Biologie de la Mémoire, 1976, (with A.L. Leiman) Physiological Psychology, 1982, 2nd edit., 1989, (with M.J. Renner) Enriched and Impoverished Environments: Effects on Brain and Behavior, 1987, (with D. Sinha) La Recherche en Psychologie Scientifique, 1988, (with W.H. Holtzman, M. Sabourin and D. Bélanger) History of the International Union of Psychological Science, 2000; editor: (with P. Mussen) Psychology: An Introduction, 1973, 2nd edit., 1977, International Psychological Science: Progress, Problems, and Prospects, 1992, (with A.L. Leiman and S.M. Breedlove) Biological Psychology, 1996, 3d edit., 2002, (with S.M. Breedlove and N.V. Watson) 4th edit., 2004; co-editor: (with E.L. Bennett) Neural Mechanisms of Learning and Memory, 1976, (with L. Porter) Ann. Rev. of Psychology, 1968-94, (with K. Pawlik) International Handbook of Psychology, 2000; contbr. articles to profl. jours. Served with USN, 1944-46. Recipient Disting. Alumnus award U. Rochester; Fulbright rsch. fellow; faculty rsch. fellow Social Sci. Rsch. Coun., 1960-61; rsch. grantee NSF, USPHS, Easter Seal Found., Nat. Inst. Drug Abuse. Fellow AAAS, APA (Disting. Sci. Contbn. award 1982, Disting. Contbn. award for Internat. Advancement of Psychology 1997), Am. Psychol. Soc.; mem. NAS, NAACP (life), Am. Physiol. Soc., Internat. Union Psychol. Sci. (hon. life, mem. exec. com. 1996—, v.p. 1980-84, pres. 1988-92, past pres. 1992-96), Internat. Brain Rsch. Orgn., Soc. Exptl. Psychologists, Soc. for Neurosci., Société Française de Psychologie, Sierra Club (life), Common Cause, Fulbright Assn. (life), Phi Beta Kappa, Sigma Xi. Office: U Calif Dept Psychology 3210 Tolman Hall Berkeley CA 94720-1650 Office Phone: 510-642-8986, 510-642-5292. Business E-Mail: memory@socrates.berkeley.edu.

**ROSENZWEIG, RICHARD STUART,** publishing company executive; b. Appleton, Wis., Aug. 8, 1935; s. Walter J. and Rose (Bahcall) R. BS, Northwestern U., 1957; Advanced Mgmt. Program, Harvard U., 1975. Credit rep. Dun & Bradstreet, Inc., 1958; with Playboy Enterprises, Inc., 1958—, exec. asst. to pres., 1963-73, sr. v.p., dir., 1973-82, dir. mktg., 1974-82, exec. v.p. publs. group, 1975-77, exec. v.p., head West Coast ops., 1977-80, exec. v.p. corp. affairs Los Angeles, 1980-82, exec. v.p., chmn. emeritus, 1982—; pres. Playboy Jazz Festivals, 1989—. Dir. I. Bahcall Industries, Appleton; exec. v.p. dir. 1973—) Playboy Enterprises; chmn. Alta Loma Entertainment, 2000—. Trustee L.A. Film Expn.; mem. 2d decade coun. Am. Film Inst.; bd. dirs. Mus. Contemporary Art, Chgo., Periodical and Book Assn. Am. Internat. Inst. Kidney Diseases of UCLA, Children of Night, Maple Ctr, Beverly Hills, mem., chmn. bd. UCLA Legis. Network, Town Hall of Calif.; adv. bd. West Hollywood Mktg. Corp., 1985—; bd. dirs. So. Calif. ACLU, 1985—; mem. Los Angeles County Mus.; apptd. to blue ribbon com. project West Coast Gateway. With AUS, 1957; chmn. Modern and Contemporary Art Coun. L.A. County Mus. of Art.; pres. Beverly Hills Cultural Ctr.; exec. com. Henry Mancini Inst.; v.p. Fraternity of Friends music Ctr.; dir. Variety Club So. Calif., West Hollywood C. of C; mem. UCLA Chancellor's Assocs., UCLA Royce 270; offcl. amb. Govt. Beverly Hills. Recipient Do-ers award, 1988, Beverly Hills medal Beverly Hills City Coun., 1993. Mem. Am. Mktg. Aslsn., L.A. Pub. Affairs Officers Assn., Pres.'s Cir., Beverly Hills C. of C. (bd. dirs., visitors' bur., v.p.), Beverly Hills Fine Art Commn. (chmn.), Beverly Hills Econ. Devel. Coun., Founders Circle of Music Ctr., Pub. Affairs Coun., Craft and Folk Art Mus., Pres.' Coun. and Contemporary Arts Coun. L.A. Mus. Contemporary Art, The Am. Cinematheque (groundbreaker), Beverly Hills Rotary Club, Acad. TV Arts and Scis. Office: Playboy Enterprises Inc 2706 Media Center Dr Los Angeles CA 90065-1733

**ROSES, ALLEN DAVID,** neurologist, educator; b. Paterson, N.J., Feb. 21, 1943; BS in Chemistry summa cum laude, U. Pitts., 1963; MD, U. Pa., 1967. Diplomate Am. Bd. Psychiatry and Neurology. Intern Hosp. of the U. Pa., Phila., 1967—68; resident in neurology N.Y. Neurol. Inst., Columbia U., N.Y.C., 1968—70; chief resident divsn. neurology Duke U. Med. Ctr., 1970—71; assoc. in medicine divsn. neurology, 1970—73, asst. prof. medicine divsn. neurology, 1973—76, assoc. prof. medicine divsn. neurology, 1976—79, asst. prof. biochemistry, 1977—89, prof. neurology dept. medicine, 1979—97, prof. neurobiology, 1989—97, Jefferson-Pilot Corp. prof. neurobiology and neurology, 1990—97, chief divsn. neurology dept. medicine, 1977—97; v.p., worldwide dir. genetics Glaxo Wellcome R&D, Research Triangle Park, NC, 1997—. Fellow Nat. Multiple Sclerosis Soc. Lab. Neurochemistry, Divsn. Neurology, Duke U. Med. Ctr. Lab. Virology, Divsn. Pediat. Neurology, Duke U. Med. Ctr., 1971-73, dir. Duke Neuromuscular Rsch. Clinic, 1974—; dir. neurosciences study program Sch. Medicine, 1975-85, investigator Howard Hughes Med. Inst., 1977-81, dir. Duke Muscular Dystrophy Assn. Clinic, 1979—, Joseph and Kathleen Bryan Alzheimer's Disease Rsch. Ctr., 1985—; cons. neurologist N.C. State Hosp.

Sys., Cherry Hosp., Goldsboro, 1973-76, N.C. State Hosp. Sys., Lenox Baker Hosp., Durham, 1971—; chmn. internat. sci. adv. com. Australian Neuromuscular Rsch. Inst., 1989-92; sci. adv. Cyprus Isnt. Neurology and Genetics. Assoc. editor Molecular and Cellular Neuroscis., 1989-94; mem. editl. bd. Amyloidosis Jour., 1993-96, Neurobiology of Disease, 1993—, Fondation Ipsen, Rsch. and Perspectives in Neuroscis., 1994—, Alzheimer's Rsch., 1995—, Contemporary Neurology, 1995—, Alezheimer's Disease Rev., 1995—; contbr. articles to profl. jours. Capt. USAFR, 1967-72. Recipient Rsch. Career Devel. award Nat. Inst. Neurol. and Communicative Disorders and Stroke, 1976, Best in the Triangle-Aerobics Instr. award Spectator Mag., 1986, Leadership in Excellence in Alzheimer's Disease award Nat. Inst. Aging, 1988, Met-Life Found. prize for outstanding med. rsch., 1994, Potamkin prize for Alzheimer's Disease Rsch., 1994, Internat. Alzheimer's Disease award Parke-Davis, 1996, award for muscular dystrophy rsch. Svc. Merchandise, 1997; Basil O'Connor Starter Rsch. grantee Nat. Found. March of Dimes. Fellow Am. Acad. Neurology; mem. Am. Soc. for Clin. Rsch., Am. Neurol. Assn. (trustee 1982-84, 96—), Assn. Univ. Profs. Neurology, Assn. Brit. Neurologists (hon. fgn. mem.), Muscular Dystrophy Assn. (genetics task force and rev. com. 1989—, med. adv. com. 1990—, nat. v.p. 1994—), Alzheimer's Assn. (med. sci. adv. com. 1989—, chair 1996—), Sigma Tau award 1990, Rita Hayward Gala award 1994), Phi Beta Kappa. Office: Glaxo Wellcome 5 Moore Dr Research Triangle Park NC 27709

**ROSE-SINGH, JUDITH ANGELLA,** elementary school educator; d. Roy Agustus Rose and Alice Francina Hunter; m. Oscar Dougal Singh, Dec. 30, 1987; children: Shelly-Ann Nicole Mittoo-Brown, Cecilia Maria Mittoo. AA in Primary Edn., Mico Coll., Jamaica, 1980; EdB in Sch. Adminstrn., U. of W.I., Kingston, Jamaica, 1990; MS in Edn., Fla. Internat. U., Miami, 1995; Ednl. Specialist in Math Edn., Fla. State U., 1999. Cert. elem. edn., ESOL, ednl. leadership Dept. of Edn./Fla. Music educator Tivoli Gardens H.S., Kingston, Jamaica, 1980—81; elem. educator Shortwood Practising Sch., St. Andrew, Jamaica, 1981—90; lectr. Passley Gardens Tchr.s' Coll. and Passley Gardens Agrl. Coll., Port Antonio, Jamaica, 1990—91; adj. prof. Fla. Meml. Coll., Miami, 1995—2001, Barry U., Miami Shores, Fla., 2001—; educator Miami-Dade County Pub. Schs., Miami, Fla., 1994—. Historian Jamaica Assn. of Dade Educators, Inc., Miami, Fla., 2004—. Contbr. articles to profl. jours. Bd. mem. JADE, Inc., Miami, Fla., 1994—2006. Recipient Cert. of Merit - Child Psychology and Devel., U. of the WI, 1989; grantee, Hewitt Packard, 2004. Mem.: Am. Ednl. Rsch. Assn., Dade County Sci. Tchrs. Assn. (corr.), Dade County Coun. of Tchr. of Math. (corr.), Phi Delta Kappa (corr.). Seventh Day Adventist. Avocations: reading, singing, music, travel. Home: 9476 Caribbean Blvd Miami FL 33189 Office Phone: 305-242-8340. E-mail: rosesinghj@dadeschools.net.

**ROSETT, ARTHUR IRWIN,** lawyer, educator; b. NYC, July 5, 1934; s. Milton B. and Bertha (Werner) R.; m. Rhonda K. Lawrence; children: David Benjamin, Martha Jean, Daniel Joseph. AB, Columbia U., 1955, LL.B., 1959. Bar: Calif. 1968, N.Y. State 1960, U.S. Supreme Ct. 1963. Law clk. U.S. Supreme Ct., 1959-60; asst. U.S. atty. So. Dist. N.Y., 1960-63; practice law N.Y.C., 1963-65; assoc. dir. Pres.'s Commn. on Law Enforcement and Adminstrn. Justice, 1965-67; acting prof. law UCLA, 1967-70, prof., 1970—. Author: Contract Law and Its Application, 1971, 6th edit. (with D.J. Bussell), 1999, (with D. Cressey) Justice by Consent, 1976, (with E. Dorff) A Living Tree, 1987. Served with USN, 1956-58. Mem. Am. Law Inst. Home: 641 S Saltair Ave Los Angeles CA 90049-4134 Office: UCLA Law Sch 405 Hilgard Ave Los Angeles CA 90095-1476 Business E-Mail: rosett@law.ucla.edu.

**ROSETT, DANIEL J.,** film company executive; Degree in bus. and econ., U. Calif., Santa Barbara, 1984. CPA. Mgr. MGM Peat Marwick; with Walt Disney Co., exec. dir. studio ops.; v.p., corp. controller MGM Studios, 1994—95, sr. v.p. fin. ops., 1995—98, exec. v.p. studio fin. and ops., 1998—2001, exec. v.p. mktg. and distribution, 2001—04; pres. United Artists, 2004—. Office: United Artists Corp 10250 Constellation Blvd Los Angeles CA 90067

**ROSEVEAR, CORA,** curator; b. N.Y.C. d. Kenneth White and Leslie Ferguson Rosevear. BA, Skidmore Coll., Saratoga Springs, N.Y.; grad., Courtauld Inst. Art, London. Assoc. curator painting and sculpture Mus. Modern Art, N.Y.C., 1988—. Mem.: Am. Assn. Mus. Curators, Internat. Coun. Museums, Am. Assn. Museums. Office: Mus Modern Art 11 W 53 St New York NY 10019 Office Phone: 212-708-9648.

**ROSHA, UZI,** lawyer; b. Tel Aviv, Dec. 11, 1968; arrived in U.S., 1999; s. Rachel and Yossi Rosha. JD, Tel Aviv U., 1998; LLM, Columbia U., 2000. Bar: N.Y. 2004, Israel 1998. Clk. Supreme Ct., Chief Justice, Jerusalem, 1998—99, Ministry of Justice, Jerusalem, 1998; compliance officer Bear Stearns & Co., N.Y.C., 2001—04; compliance mgr. Lehman Bros., N.Y.C., 2004—05; chief compliance officer Fulcrum Global Ptnrs., N.Y.C., 2005—. Chmn. Orgn. for Democracy and Equality, Tel Aviv, 1996—99; mem. moot trial assoc. prof. sociology Columbia U. Law Sch.; bd. dirs. ISEF, N.Y.C., 2005. Lt. Israeli Paratroopers, 1987—91. Scholar, Columbia U., Sch. of Law, 1999, Tel Aviv U., 1994, 1995, 1996, 1997. Mem.: Israeli Bar Assn. (assoc.), N.Y. State Bar Assn. (assoc.). Office: Fulcrum Global Ptnrs 535 Madison Ave New York NY 10022

**ROSHAN, DANIEL,** obstetrician, gynecologist; arrived in U.S., 1987; s. Mordechai Cohen and Mom Lea Roshan; m. Elana Roshan, Mar. 21, 1998; children: Jacqueline, Rebecca, Joshua, Ariel. BS, Pahlavi U., 1987; MD, Sackler U., Tel Aviv, Israel, 1992; grad., Johns Hopkins U. Diplomate Maternal Fetal Medicine Am. Bd. of Ob-gyn., 2001, cert. Am. Bd. of Ob-gyn, 1999. Asst. prof. NYU Sch. of Medicine, N.Y., 2000—; dir. perinatology svcs. NYU Med. Ctr./Tisch Hosp., NY, 2000—. Sec. Iranian-Am. Jewish Med. Assn., N.Y., 2003. Recipient America's Top Ob-gyn, SLD Industries, 2004. Fellow ACOG. Offcal NYU Program for Maternal Fetal Medicine 530 First Ave Ste 7N New York NY 10016 Office Phone: 212-263-3234. Office Fax: 212-263-0616. Business E-Mail: roshad01@med.nyu.edu.

**ROSHEL, JOHN ALBERT, JR.,** orthodontist; b. Terre Haute, Ind., Apr. 7, 1941; s. John Albert and Mary M. (Griglione) R.; m. Kathy Roshel; children: John Albert III, James Livingston, Angela Kay. BS, Ind. State U., 1963; DDS, Ind. U., 1966; MS, U. Mich., 1968. Individual practice dentistry specializing in orthodontics, Terre Haute, 1968—. Mem. ADA, Am. Assn. Orthodontists, Terre Haute U. of C., Terre Haute Country Club, Lions, Elks, K.C., Lambda Chi Alpha, Delta Sigma Delta, Omicron Kappa Upsilon. Roman Catholic. Home: 15 E Wedgeway Dr Terre Haute IN 47802-4983 Office: 4241 S 7th St Terre Haute IN 47802-4367 Personal E-mail: drjrosh@aol.com.

**ROSHKO, ANATOL,** aeronautical engineer; b. Bellevue, Alta., Can., July 15, 1923; arrived in U.S., 1950, arrived in U.S. 1950; married, 1957; 2 children. BSc, U. Alta, 1945; MS, Calif. Inst. Tech., 1947, PhD in Aero. Engring., 1952. Instr. math. U. Alta., 1945-46, lectr. engring., 1949—50; rsch. fellow Calif. Inst. Tech., Pasadena, 1952—55, asst. prof. to prof., 1955—85; acting dir. Grad Aero. Labs, Pasadena, 1985—87; Theodore von Karman prof. aeronautics Calif. Inst. Tech., Pasadena, 1985—, prof. emeritus, 1994—. Sci. liaison officer Office Naval Rsch., London, 1961-62; cons. McDonnell Douglas Corp., 1954-90, Rocketdyne Corp. Divsn., Rockwell Internat., 1984-90; founding dir. Wind Engring. Rsch. Inc., 1970; mem. Aero. & Space Engring. Bd., 1988-93. Recipient Timoshenko medal ASME, 1999; named to U. Alta. Alumni Wall of Recognition, 1998. Fellow AAAS, AIAA (Dryden Rsch. lectr. 1976, Fluid Dynamics award 1998), Am. Phys. Soc. (Fluid Dynamics prize 1987), Indian Acad. Scis. (hon.), Can. Aeronautics and Space Inst.; mem. NAS, ASME, NAE. Office: Calif Inst Tech Mail Sta 105-50 1201 E California Blvd Pasadena CA 91125-0001 Office Phone: 626-395-4484. E-mail: roshko@caltech.edu.

**ROSHOLT, ROBERT A.,** financial executive; b. Mar. 24, 1950; BA, St. Olaf Coll.; MBA, U. Rochester. Asst. v.p. Profit Planning Group First Chicago NBD Corp., Chgo., 1974-82, mem. Treasury Dept., 1982-87, head

Treasury Dept., sr. v.p., 1987; former CFO First Chgo. NBD Corp., Chgo.; exec. v.p. First Nat. Bank of Chgo.; exec. v.p., head of ops. AON Corp., Chgo., 2000—02; exec. v.p. fin. and investments Nationwide Fin. Svc., 2002—03, exec. v.p., chief fin. and investment officer, 2003—. Office: 1 Nationwide Pl Columbus OH 43215*

**ROSHONG, DEE ANN DANIELS,** dean, educator; b. Kansas City, Mo., Nov. 22, 1936; adopted d. Vernon Edmund and Doradell (Kellogg) Daniels, d. Ken Garner and Lucille Cronin Davidson; m. Richard Lee Roshong, Aug. 27, 1960 (div). BMusEd., U. Kans., Lawrence, 1958; MA in Counseling and Guidance, Stanford U., Calif. 1960; postgrad., Fresno State U., U. Calif., Berkeley; EdD, U. San Francisco, 1980. Counselor, psychometrist Fresno City Coll., 1961-65; counselor, instr. psychology Chabot Coll., Hayward, Calif., 1965-75, coord. counseling svcs. Livermore, Calif., 1975-81, asst. dir. student pers. svcs., 1981-89, Las Positas Coll., Livermore, Calif., 1989-91, assoc. dean student svcs., 1991-94, dean student svcs., 1991—2003, life coach, 2000—; counselor Experience Unltd., Pleasant Hill, Calif., 2004—; symposium organizer Calif. State U., East Bay, 2004—. Writer, coord. I, A Woman Symposium, 1974, Feeling Free to Be You and Me symposium, 1975, All for the Family Symposium, 1976, I Celebrate Myself Symposium, 1978, Person to Person in Love and Work Symposium, 1978, The Healthy Person in Mind and Spirit Symposium, 1980, Change Symposium, 1981, Sources of Strength Symposium, 1982, Love and Friendship Symposium, 1983, Self Esteem Symposium, 1984, Trust Symposium, 1985, Prime Time: Making the Most of This Time in Your Life Symposium, 1986, Symposium in Healing, 1987, How to Live in the World and Still Be Happy Symposium, 1988, Student Success is a Team Effort, Sound Mind, Sound Body Symposium, 1989, Creating Life's Best Symposium, 1990, Choices Symposium, 1991, Minding the Body, Mending the Mind Symposium, 1992, Healing through Love and Laughter Symposium, 1993, Healing Ourselves Changing the World Symposium, 1994, Finding Your Path Symposium, 1995, Build the Life You Want Symposium, 1996, Making Peace With Yourself and Your Relationships Symposium, 1997, Everyday Sacred Symposium, 1998, Wisdom of the Heart Symposium, 1999, Inner Wisdom Symposium, 2000, Second Half of Life Symposium, 2001, A Celebration of Life Symposium, 2003, Viewing Mental Health and Mental Illness From a Multi-Cultural Perspective Symposium, 2004, Promoting Mental Health in Multi-Cultural Settings Symposium, 2005, Building Bridges to Hope and Recovery: Healing Ourselves, Transforming the System Symposium, 2006; mem. cast TV prodns. Eve and Co., Best of Our Times, Cowboy; chmn. Falling Awake Symposium, 2002, Calif. C.C. Chancellor's Task Force on Counseling, Statewide Regional Counseling Facilitators, 1993-95, Statewide Conf. Emotionally Disturbed Students in Calif. C.C.s, 1982—, Conf. on the Under Represented Student in Calif. C.C.s, 1986, Conf. on High Risk Students, 1989. Author: Counseling Needs of Comunity College Students, 1980. Bd. dirs. Teleios Sinetar Ctr., Ctr. for Cmty. Dispute Resolution, 1998—, Pleasanton Youth Collaborative Bd., 1997-2002, Pleasanton Youth Master Plan Bd., 1998—; choir dir., 1996-99; pres. bd. Tri-Valley Unity Ch., 1998-2005, v.p. 2005, lay minister 2005, Tri-Valley Haven bd., 2000—, Calif. State U. East Bay Inst. Mental Illness and Wellness Edn. bd., 2000—, Ellis Life Coach Tng., 1999—, Interspiritual Mentor Tng. Program, 2005; title III activity dir. Las Positas Coll., 1995-99, dir. pace program, 1999-2003, dir. quest program, 2000-03. Mem.: Calif C.C. Counselors Assn. (exec. award 1986—87, award for Outstanding and Disting. Svc. 1986—87, Pleasanton Mayor's award 2000—01, 2002), Calif. Assn. C. C. (chmn. commn. on students svcs. 1979—84), Assn. Counseling and Devel., Nat. Assn. Women Deans and Counselors, Western Psychol. Assn., Assn. Humanistic Psychologists. Home and Office: 1856 Harvest Rd Pleasanton CA 94566-5456 Personal E-Mail: deeroshong@comcast.net.

**ROSHWALD, AVIEL ISAIAH,** history professor; b. Mpls., Mar. 19, 1962; s. Miriam Mindla Roshwald; m. Alene Moyer, Oct. 17, 1999. BA, U. Minn., 1980; PhD, Harvard U., 1987. Prof. history Georgetown U., Washington, 1991—. Author: Estranged Bedfellows: Britain and France in the Middle East during the Second World War, 1990, Ethnic Nationalism and the Fall of Empires: Central Europe, Russia & the Middle East, 1914-1923, 2001, The Eudrance of Nationalism: Ancient Poets and Modern Dilemmas, 2006; co-editor (with Richard Stites): European Culture during the Great War: The Arts, Entertainment, and Propaganda, 1914-1918, 1999. Jewish. Office: Georgetown U Dept History 37th and O Sts NW Washington DC 20057-1035 Office Phone: 202-687-6089.

**ROSICA, GABRIEL ADAM,** retired manufacturing executive, electrical engineer; b. NYC, Jan. 9, 1940; s. Gabriel J. and Elma (P.) R.; m. Bettina R. Nardozzi, Sept. 8, 1962; children: Gregory A., Julie Ann, Mark A. BA in Math. and Physics, Columbia U., 1962, BSEE, 1963; MSEE, Rensselaer Poly. Inst., 1966; MBA, Boston U., 1971. Registered profl. engr., Mass. Rsch. engr. United Aircraft Research Labs., East Hartford, Conn., 1963-67; mgr. electronic devel. The Foxboro (Mass.) Co., 1967-75, gen. mgr. U.S. div., 1975-77, v.p., 1977-80; pres., COO Modular Computer Sys., Inc., Ft. Lauderdale, Fla., 1980-82, pres., chmn., CEO, 1982-88; pvt. practice bus. cons. Boca Raton, Fla., 1988-91; sr. v.p. Elsag Bailey Corp., Pepper Pike, Ohio, 1991-92; exec. v.p. Bailey Controls Co., Wickliffe, Ohio, 1993-94; COO Bailey Control Co., Wickliffe, Ohio, 1994-96; sr. v.p. Keithley Instruments, Solon, Ohio, 1996-2001, exec. v.p., 2001—05, ret., 2005—. Chmn. engring. adv. coun. U. Fla., Gainesville, 1987-90; chmn. hi tech adv. coun. Coll. Boca Raton, Fla., 1987-90. Mem. Pres.'s Coun. Fla. Atlantic U., Boca Raton, 1987-91; trustee Nova U., Ft. Lauderdale, Fla., 1987-94. Recipient Boston U. Chair, 1971, Outstanding Young Engr. of Year award Mass. Soc. Profl. Engrs., 1974. Mem. IEEE (sr. mem.), Am. Electronics Assn. (bd. dirs. 1987, chmn Fla. bd. dirs. 1987-88), Fla. High Tech. and Industry Coun. Home: 35640 Spicebush Ln Solon OH 44139-5063 E-mail: gabe.rosica@att.net.

**ROSIER, DAVID LEWIS,** retired investment banker; b. Sioux City, Iowa, Mar. 22, 1937; s. Orel Lewis and Jewell May (Palmer) R.; m. Jackie Dodd, July 1965 (div. 1973); 1 child, Michele; m. Carol Mary Byre, Nov. 25, 1982 (dec. Sept. 1997); m. Rosemarie Dimino, Sept. 9, 1999 (div. Jan. 2004). BSBA, U. Denver, 1960. Registered investment assoc. V.p., mgr. mktg. Hertz Internat., Ltd., N.Y., 1970-71; regional v.p. Amtrak, N.Y., 1971-73; mng. ptnr. Rosier & Assocs., Ltd., San Diego, 1969—; sr. v.p. for strategic mktg. Am. Prins. Holdings, Inc., San Diego 1979-84; v.p., registered prin. Am. Diversified Equity Corp., Costa Mesa, Calif., 1984-85; pres. Glen Eagle, Inc., 1986-87; sr. v.p. Western Region Cozad Investment Svcs. Inc., San Diego, 1987-88; dir. corp. fin. Brookstreet Securities Corp., Irvine, Calif., 1993—2005; ret.; dir. fixed asset group U.S. Euro Securities, Inc. Global Investment Bank, 2005. Spkr. in field. Bd. dirs. Nautical Heritage Soc. (Hamburg award 1988). Mem. Oceanside Rotary (Paul Harris fellow, benefactor, pres., founder Rotary Club of Oceanside Found.), Kona Kai Internat. Yacht Club (commodore 1987), Internat. Order of the Blue Gavel (founder, past chmn. bd. trustees Humanities Found.), Phone Charities Internat. (founder, mng. mem. 1996-98), Nat. Investment Banking Assn. (bd. dirs. 2001-04), Golf Club of Calif. (bd. gov. 2005-). Home: 5114 Bella Collina St Oceanside CA 92056-1903 Office Phone: 760-732-3393. E-mail: daverosier@cox.net.

**ROSING, WAYNE,** information technology executive; Former mgr. Digital Equipment Corp., Data General; former dir. engring. Lisa and Apple II divsn. Apple Computer Inc.; exec. positions Sun Microsystems Inc., 1985—94; founder Sun Microsystems Lab.; former pres. FirstPerson Inc. (sub. of Sun Microsystems Inc.); former chief tech. officer, v.p. engring. Caere Corp.; v.p. engring. Google Inc., Mountain View, Calif., 2001—. Office: Google Inc 1600 Amphitheatre Pky Mountain View CA 94043 Office Phone: 650-623-4000. Office Fax: 650-618-1499.

**ROSINSKI, EDWIN FRANCIS,** medical educator; b. Buffalo, June 25, 1928; s. Theodore Joseph and Josephine M. (Wolski) R.; m. Jeanne C. Hueniger, Oct. 27, 1951; children: John T., Mary E., Sarah J. BS, SUNY, Buffalo, 1950; EdM, U. Buffalo, 1957, EdD, 1959. Prof. health scis. Med. Coll. Va., Richmond, 1959-66; dep. asst. sec. HEW, Washington, 1966-68; exec. vice chancellor U. Calif., San Francisco, 1968-72, prof., 1972-94; prof.

emeritus medicine & pharmacy, 1994—. Adv. Rockefeller Found., N.Y.C., 1962-67, WHO, Geneva, 1962-78, Imperial Com. Health, Tehran, Iran, 1974-77; cons. Stanford Research Inst., Menlo Park, Calif., 1975-79. Author: The Assistant Medical Officer, 1965; contbr. over 100 articles to profl. jours. Served with USAF, 1950-54. Recipient spl. citation HEW, 1968, Merrell Flair award, 1991; named disting. prof. Australian Vice Chancellors Office, 1974, disting. vis. prof. Tulane U., New Orleans, 1983, Alumni of Yr. SUNY, Buffalo, 2006. Fellow AAAS; mem. Assn. Am. Med. Colls. (Merrel Flair award), Am. Ednl. Research Assn., Soc. Health and Human Values (founding mem.), Calif. Pharmacists Assn. (hon.), Phi Delta Kappa. Roman Catholic. Avocation: physical fitness. Home: 80 Sotelo Ave San Francisco CA 94116-1423

**ROSKAM, CATHERINE S.,** bishop; b. May 30, 1943; m. Philip K. Roskam, Sept. 3, 1966; 1 child, Gemma. BA in theatre, Middlebury Coll., 1965; MDiv, Gen. Theol. Sem., NYC, 1984. Worked in theatre as an actress and prodr., NYC; ordained deacon, 1984, priest, 1984; asst. rector Holy Apostles Ch., NYC; priest-in-charge Holy Innocents' mission congregation, San Francisco; interim rector Ch. of Our Savior, Mill Valley, Calif.; diocesan missioner Episcopal Diocese of Calif., 1991—95; consecrated bishop, 1996; suffragen bishop Episcopal Diocese of NY, 1996—. Mem. exec. coun. Episcopal Ch. in the USA, 2000—; mem. Anglican Consultative Coun., 2001—; mem. bd. trustees Gen. Theol. Sem., NYC, vice chair, 2001—02. Office: Episcopal Diocese of NY 1047 Amsterdam Ave New York NY 10025 Office Phone: 212-316-7400. Office Fax: 212-316-7405.

**ROSKAM, JAN,** aerospace engineer; b. The Hague, The Netherlands, Feb. 22, 1930; arrived in U.S., 1957; s. Kommer Jan and Agatha (Bosman) Roskam; m. Janice Louise Thomas-Barron, Dec. 21, 1994. MA in Aerospace Engring., Tech. U. Delft, 1954; PhD in Aeros. and Astronautics, U. Wash., 1965. Asst. chief designer Aviolanda Aircraft Co., Netherlands, 1954-57; sr. aerodynamics engr. Cessna Aircraft Co., Wichita, Kans., 1957-59; sr. group engr. Boeing Co., Wichita and Seattle, 1959-67; prof. emeritus aerospace engring. U. Kans., Lawrence, 1967—; cons. to govt. and industry. Author: Airplane Flight Dynamics and Automatic Flight Controls, 2 vols., 1979; co-author: Airplane Aerodynamics and Performance, 1981, Airplane Design, Part I-VIII, 1986, Roskam's Airplane War Stories, 2002. Served to 1st lt. Royal Netherlands Air Force, 1954—56. Fellow: AIAA, Soc. Automotive Engrs.; mem.: Exptl. Aircraft Assn., U.S. Chess Fedn., Koninklijk Instituut van Ingenieurs, Royal Aero. Soc., Air Force Assn., Aircraft Owners and Pilots Assn., Omicron Delta Kappa, Sigma Gamma Tau, Tau Beta Pi, Sigma Xi. Office: U Kans 2004 Lea Hl Lawrence KS 66045-0001 Personal E-mail: roskam@sunflower.com. Business E-mail: roskam@darcorp.com.

**ROSKENS, RONALD WILLIAM,** management consultant, retired academic administrator; b. Spencer, Iowa, Dec. 11, 1932; s. William E. and Delores A.L. (Beving) R.; m. Lois Grace Lister, Aug. 22, 1954; children: Elizabeth, Barbara, Brenda, William. BA, U. No. Iowa, 1953, MA, 1955, LHD (hon.), 1985; PhD, U. Iowa, 1958; LLD (hon.), Creighton U., 1978, Huston-Tillotson Coll., 1981, Midland Luth. Coll., 1984, Hastings Coll. 1981; LittD (hon.), Nebr. Wesleyan U., 1981; PhD (hon.), Ataturk U., Turkey, 1987; DSc (hon.), Jayewardenepura U., Sri Lanka, 1991; LHD (hon.), U. Akron, 1987, Am. Coll. Greece, Athens, 1994, Kent State U., 2005. Lic. min. United Ch. of Christ (Congl. and E&R). Tchr. Minburn (Iowa) High Sch., 1954, Woodward (Iowa) State Hosp., summer 1954; asst. counselor to men State U. Iowa, 1956-59; dean of men, asst. prof. spl. edn. Kent (Ohio) State U., 1959-63, assoc. prof., then prof., 1963-72, asst. to pres., 1963-66, dean for adminstrn., 1968-71, exec. v.p., prof. ednl. adminstrn., 1971-72; chancellor, prof. ednl. adminstrn. U. Nebr., Omaha, 1972-76; pres. U. Nebr. System, 1977-89, pres. emeritus, 1989; hon. prof. East China Normal U., Shanghai, 1985; adminstr. USAID, Washington, 1990-92; pres. Action Internat., Inc., Omaha, 1993-96, Global Connections, Inc., Omaha, 1996—. Interim exec. officer Omaha Pub. Libr., 1996-98; mem. Bus.-Higher Edn. Forum, 1979-89, exec. com., 1984-87; mem. govtl. relations com. Am. Council Edn., 1979-83, bd. dirs., 1981-86, vice chair, 1983-84, chair, 1984-85; chmn. com. on financing higher edn. Nat. Assn. State Univs. and Land Grant Colls., 1978-83, vice chmn. com. on financing higher edn., 1983-84, chmn. com. on fed. student fin. assistance, 1981-87; mem. nat. adv. com. on accreditation and instl. eligibility U.S. Dept. Edn., 1983-86, chmn. bd. dirs., 1986; exec. bd. North Cen. Assn., 1979-84, chmn. exec. bd., 1982-84, pres., 1989-90; active Environ. Ams. Bd., 1991-92, Strategic Command Consultation Commn., 1993-96, Nat. Exec. Res. Corps, Fed. Office Emergency Preparedness, 1968-88; chmn. Omaha/Douglas Pub. Bldg. Commn., 1996—. Co-editor: Paradox, Process and Progress, 1968; contbr. articles profl. jours. Mem. Kent City Planning Commn., 1962-66; bd. dirs. United Ch. of Christ Bd. Homeland Ministries, 1968-74, Met. YMCA, Omaha, 1973-77, Mid-Am. council Boy Scouts Am., 1973-77, Midlands United Community Services, 1972-77, NCCJ, 1974-77, Omaha Rotary Club, 1974-77, 93—, Found. Study Presdl. and Congl. Terms, 1977-89, First Plymouth Congl. Ch., 1989-90, Midland Luth. Coll., 1993-2000, Coun. Aid to Edn., 1985-89, ConAgra Foods, Inc., 1993—, Russian Farm Cmty. Project, Capitol Fed. Found., Topeka, Kans., 1999—, The Silverstone Group, 2004—; trustee Huston Tillotson Coll., Austin, Tex., 1968-81, chmn., 1976-78, Joslyn Art Mus., 1973-77, Nebr. Meth. Hosp., 1974-77, 1st Ctrl. Congregational Ch., Brownell-Talbott Sch., 1974-77, Harry S. Truman Inst., 1977-89, Willa Cather Pioneer Meml. and Ednl. Found., 1979-87; pres. Kent Area C. of C., 1966; mem. Met. Commn. Coll. Found., 1993-96; min.-in-residence Countryside Cmty. United Ch. Christ, Omaha, 2003—. Decorated comdr.'s cross Order of Merit (Germany); recipient Disting. Svc. award Kent, Ohio, 1967, Brotherhood award NCCJ, 1977, Americanism citation B'nai B'rith, 1978, Legion of Honor, Order of DeMolay, 1980, gold medal Nat. Interfrat. Coun., 1987, Agr. award Triumph Agr. Expn., Omaha, 1989, Disting. Alumni Achievement award U. Iowa, 2004; named Nat. 4-H Alumnus, 1967, Outstanding Alumnus, U. No. Iowa, 1974, Midlander of Yr., Omaha World Herald, 1977, King Ak-Sar-Ben LXXXVI, 1980; named to DeMolay Hall of Fame, 1993; named Hon. Consul Gen. of Japan, 1999. Mem. AAAS, APA, AAUP, Am. Coll. Pers. Assn., Assn. Urban Univs. (pres. 1976-77), Am. Ednl. Rsch. Assn., Coun. on Fgn. Rels., Chief Execs. Orgn., Young Pres. Orgn., Scottish Rite (bd. dirs. Omaha coun. 1999-), Lincoln C. of C. (bd. dirs. 1989-90), Masons (33 deg.), Rotary (bd. dirs. Omaha 1974-77, pres. Kent, Ohio chpt., 1970-71), Phi Delta Kappa, Phi Eta Sigma, Sigma Tau Gamma (pres. grand coun. 1968-70, Disting. Achievement award 1980, Disting. scholar 1981), Omicron Delta Kappa (nat. pres. 1986-90, Found. pres. 1986-96). Home: 10849 N 58th Plz Omaha NE 68152 Office Phone: 402-399-0928.

**ROSKI, EDWARD P., JR.,** real estate developer, professional sports team executive; s. Edward P. Roski, III; m. Gayle Roski. BS in Fin. and Real Estate, U. So. Calif., 1962. Joined Majestic Realty Co., 1966, chmn., CEO; part owner Staples Ctr., LA Kings, LA Lakers; owner Silverton Hotel & Casino, Las Vegas, Nev. Bd. dirs. Comerica Bank, Calif., LA Sports & Entertainment Commn. Dir. Big Bros. of Greater L.A.; bd. govs. Natural History Mus. of L.A. County, Bowers Museum of Cultural Art; bd. trustees Loyola Marymount U., U. So. Calif.; bd. regents Loyola High School; founder Majestic Realty Found., 2002-. Served USMC, 1962—66. Named a Champions of Industry, Calif. Bus. Properties Assn., 2004; named one of Forbes' Richest Americans, 2006; recipient Partners with Youth award, Big Sisters of Greater Los Angeles and the Inland Empire, 2004, Woodrow Wilson award for Public Service, 2006. Mem. Explorers Club, Soc. Indsl. Realtors. Avocations: bicycling, mountain climbing. Office: Majestic Realty 13191 Crossroads Pkwy N 6th Fl City Of Industry CA 91746-3497 Office Phone: 562-948-4301. Business E-mail: eroski@majesticrealty.com.*

**ROSKIN, WILLIAM A.,** communications executive; BBA, City Coll. of NY, 1963; LLB, St. John's U. Sch. of Law, 1966; LLM, NY U. Grad. Sch. of Law, 1968. Staff, law dept. RCA Global Comm., Inc.; gen. counsel City NY Dept. Pers., City Svc. Commn., N.Y.C., 1971—76; v.p., labor rels. Warner Comm., 1976—86; sr. v.p., human resources Coleco Industries, Inc.,

1986—88; v.p. human resources, admin. Viacom, Inc., N.Y.C., 1988—92, sr. v.p., human resources, admin., 1992—2004, exec. v.p., 2004—. Office: Viacom Inc 1515 Bdwy New York NY 10036

**ROSKOSKI, JOHN,** religious studies educator, coach; b. Rahway, NJ, May 23, 1960; s. Charles Clement and Elaine Magdelene Roskoski; m. Tracy Ann Abrego, Apr. 23, 1995; children: Nicholas Thaddeus, Samuel John. BA in Religious studies, Seton Hall U., 1981, MA in Jewish-Christian studies, 1990; MA in Theology, New Brunswick Theol. Sem., 1986; MPhil in Theology, Fordham U., 2004; postgrad., Omega Bible Inst. and Sem. Cert. strength trng. instr. YMCA. Tchr. religion St. Michael's HS, Jersey City, 1982—83; instr. logic Middlesex CC, Edison, NJ, 1986; strength coach Bishop Ahr HS, Edison, 1984—89; tchr. religion Marist HS, Bayone, NJ, 1989—91; adj. prof. theol. St. Peter's Coll., Jersey City, 1992—. Contbr. articles to profl. jours. Mem.: Assn. Bibl. Rsch., Nat. Honor Soc., Theol. Honor Soc. Roman Catholic. Avocations: chess, walking sticks, coin collecting/numismatics, powerlifting. Home: 23 Morse Ave Edison NJ 08817 Personal E-mail: sampson95@optonline.net.

**ROSKOSKI, ROBERT, JR.,** biochemist, educator, author; b. Elyria, Ohio, Dec. 10, 1939; s. Robert and Mary R.; m. Laura Martinsek, Aug. 27, 1974. BS, Bowling Green State U., 1961; MD, U. Chgo., 1964, PhD, 1968. Asst. prof. U. Iowa, Iowa City, 1972-75, assoc. prof., 1975-79, vis. prof. Iowa City, 1993; prof. dept. biochemistry and molecular biology Health Scis. Ctr., La. State U., New Orleans, 1979—; Fred G. Brazda prof. Med. Ctr., La. State U., New Orleans, 1991—; founder, sci. dir. Blue Ridge Inst. for Med. Rsch., 2006—. Cons. biochemistry test com. Nat. Bd. Med. Examiners, 1981-84, 2003—, Assn. Internat. Cancer Rsch., Royal Soc. New Zealand; mem. merit rev. bd. for basic scis. VA, 1992-95; mem. rev. com. biol. scis. U. South Fla., 1992-95, biochemistry III study sect. NIH, 1996—97, biophysics (sec. 1994-96, pres. 1997), Coun. Acad. Scos., Greater New Orleans Soc. for Neurosci. (pres. 1982-83). Achievements include condr. research enzymology. Home: 221 Haywood Knolls Dr Hendersonville NC 28791-8717 also: PO Box 158 Horse Shoe NC 28742-0158 Office: 3754 Brevard Rd Ste 116A Box 19 Horse Shoe NC 28742-8814 Office Phone: 828-891-5637. E-mail: rrj@brimr.org.

**ROSKY, BURTON SEYMOUR,** lawyer; b. Chgo., May 28, 1927; s. David T. and Mary W. (Zelkin) R.; m. Leatrice J. Darrow, June 16, 1951; children: David Scott, Bruce Alan. Student, Ill. Inst. Tech., 1944-45; BS, UCLA, 1948; JD, Loyola U., L.A., 1953. Bar: Calif. 1954, U.S. Supreme Ct 1964, U.S. Tax Ct 1964; C.P.A., Calif. Auditor City of L.A., 1948- 51; with Beidner, Temkin & Ziskin (C.P.A.s), L.A., 1951-52; supervising auditor Army Audit Agy., 1952-53; practiced law L.A., Beverly Hills, 1954—; ptnr. Duskin & Rosky, 1972-82, Rosky, Landau & Fox, 1982-93, Rosky, Landau & Stahl, Beverly Hills, 1993-99; pvt. practice Beverly Hills, 1999—. Lectr. on tax and bus. problems; judge pro tem Beverly Hills Mcpl. Ct., L.A. Superior Ct.; mem. L.A. Mayor's Community Adv. Council. Contbr. profl. publs. Charter supporting mem. Los Angeles County Mus. Arts; contbg. mem. Assocs. of Smithsonian Instn.; charter mem. Air and Space Mus; mem. Am. Mus. Natural History, L.A. Zoo; supporting mem. L.A. Mus. Natural History; mem. exec. bd. So. Calif. coun. Nat. Fedn. Temple Brotherhoods, mem. nat. exec. bd.; mem. bd. govs. Loyola Sch. Law, L.A.; regent Coll. Art. Assn. Atty.-CPAs. With USNR, 1945-46. Walter Henry Cook fellow Loyola Law Sch. Bd. Govs. Fellow Jewish Chautauqua Soc. (life mem.); mem. Am. Arbitration Assn. (nat. panel arbitrators), Am. Assn. Attys.-CPAs (charter mem. pres. 1968), Calif. Assn. Attys.-CPAs (charter mem., pres. 1963), Calif. Soc. CPAs, Calif., Beverly Hills, Century City, Los Angeles County bar assns., Am. Judicature Soc., Chancellors Assocs. UCLA, B'nai B'rith, Tau Delta Phi, Phi Alpha Delta. Jewish (mem. exec. bd., pres. temple, pres. brotherhood). Club: Mason. Office: 8383 Wilshire Blvd Beverly Hills CA 90211-2410 Office Phone: 323-655-9757.

**ROSKY, THEODORE SAMUEL,** insurance company executive; b. Chgo., Apr. 14, 1937; s. Theodore and Lora Marie (O'Connell) R.; m. Jacqueline Reed, Apr. 19, 1958; 1 child, Laura Marie. BA, State U. Iowa, 1959. Various actuarial positions Conn. Gen. Life Ins. Co., Hartford, 1959-66, assoc. actuary, 1967-70, controller, 1970-73, 2d v.p., actuary, 1973, v.p., 1973-78; exec. v.p. Capital Holding Corp., 1978-84, exec. v.p., CFO, 1984-91, exec. v.p.; 1991-92; bd. dirs. Legend Funds, 1993-98, SBM Mut. Funds, 1995-97, SBM Certificate Co., 1996-98; fin. svcs. Dory L.P., 1998-99. Instr. State U. Iowa, 1958-59, U. Hartford, 1964-66, U. Conn., 1967-68. Active Mayor's Adv. Com. on Pub. Art, 1990—2005; mem. bd. pensions Evang. Luth. Ch. Am., 1974—82, 1984—87, 1989—95; bd. dirs. Hartford Coll. for Women, 1974—78, Macauley Theater, 1983—85, Louisville Fund for the Arts, 1980—97, Louisville Luth. Home, 1983—97, Louisville Orch., 1982—88, 1989—95, Ky. Opera, 1992—2001, Lincoln Found., 1992—2002, Actors Theatre of Louisville, 1995—, New Performing Arts, 1996—98, Oak and Acorn, 1995—2001, Glassworks Found., 2002—03, Pub. Radio Partnership, 2003—04, YMCA Safe Place, 2003—, Sch. Choice Scholarships, 2004—05. Recipient award Soc. Actuaries, 1958 Fellow Soc. Actuaries; mem. Am. Acad. Actuaries, Southeastern Actuaries Club. Republican. Lutheran. Home and Office: 2304 Speed Ave Louisville KY 40205-1642

**ROS-LEHTINEN, ILEANA CARMEN,** congresswoman; b. Havana, Cuba, July 15, 1952; arrived in US, 1959; d. Enrique Emilio and Amanda (Adato) Ros; m. Dexter Lehtinen; 2 children, 2 stepchildren. AA, Miami-Dade Community Coll., Fla., 1972; BA, Fla. Internat. U., 1975, MS, 1987. Fla. Ed. Acad., from 1978; mem. Fla. Ho. of Reps., Tallahassee, 1983—86, Fla. Senate, 1986—89, U.S. Congress from 18th Fla. dist., 1989—; mem. govt. reform com., internat. rels. com. Recipient Nat. Legis. award LULACH, 1999, Official of the Year, Youth Crime watch of Am., 2001. Republican. Episcopalian. Office: US Ho of Reps 2160 Rayburn Ho Office Bldg Washington DC 20515-0918 also: Dist Office Ste 100 9210 Sunset Dr Miami FL 33173

**ROSMAN, HOWARD S.,** cardiologist, educator; b. Detroit, Aug. 29, 1947; s. Carl and Mae S. Rosman; m. Sarine John-Rosman, Aug. 21, 1999; m. Nancy R Rosenhaus, Aug. 4, 1974 (div. Apr. 17, 1997); 1 stepchild, Akash D. Patel children: Sarah Z., Benjamin J., David A., John M BA, Harvard Coll., Cambridge, Mass., 1969; MD, U. Mich., Ann Arbor, 1975. Resident in internal medicine Emory U., Ga., 1978; vis. fellow cardiology Royal Postgraduate Med. Sch., London, 1979; fellowship in cardiovascular disease Emory U., Ga. 1981; sr. staff physician Henry Ford Health Sys., Detroit, 1982—99; sr. staff physician St John Hosp. and Med. Ctr., Detroit, 1999—. Clin. asst. prof. of medicine U. of Mich., Ann Arbor, Mich., 1983—88; assoc. chief divsn. of cardiology Henry Ford Health Sys., Detroit, 1987—99; clin. assoc. prof. of medicine U. of Mich., Ann Arbor, Mich., 1989—94; program dir. cardiology fellowship Henry Ford Hosp., Detroit, 1987—99; dir. of undergraduate med. edn., 1992—99; prof. of internal medicine Case Western Res. U., Cleveland, Ohio, 1999—99; mem. bd. of governors Henry Ford Health Sys., Detroit, 1997—99; councilor Am. Coll. of Cardiology, Mich. Chpt., Mich., 1999—2005; cardiology program dir. St John Hosp. and Med. Ctr., Detroit, 1999—; prof. of medicine Wayne State U., Detroit, 1999—. Pres. Am. Heart Assn., Metro Detroit, 2004—06. Recipient Outstanding Faculty Tchr., U. Mich. Med. Students, 1982 - 1994 (11 awards), Henry Ford Hosp. Residents, 1983 - 1999 (6 awards), Instr. of the Yr., St John Hosp. Cardiology Fellows, 1999 - 2005 (3 awards), Dept. of Internal Medicine Tchg. award, Wayne State U. Med. Sch., Medicine Faculty, 2003. Fellow: Am. Heart Assn., Am. Coll. of Cardiology. Office: St John Hosp and Med Ctr 22151 Moross #126 Detroit MI 48202 Office Phone: 313-343-4612. E-mail: howard.rosman@stjohn.org.

**ROSMAN, MICHAEL E.,** lawyer; BA in polit. sci. and econ. summa cum laude, U. Rochester, 1981; JD, Yale Law School, 1984. Assoc. Rosenman & Colin, New York City, 1984—93; gen. counsel Ctr. for Individual Rights, 1994—. Guest lecturer Washington Semester, American U. Office: Center for Individual Rights 1233 20th Street NW Suite 300 Washington DC 20036

**ROSNER, ANN** See SEAMAN, BARBARA

**ROSNER, JONATHAN LINCOLN,** physicist, researcher; b. N.Y.C., July 23, 1941; s. Albert Aaron and Elsie Augustine (Lincoln) R.; m. Joy Elaine Fox, June 13, 1965; children: Hannah, Benjamin. BA, Swarthmore Coll., 1962; MA, Princeton U., 1963, PhD, 1965. Research asst. prof. U. Wash., Seattle, 1965-67; vis. lectr. Tel Aviv U., Ramat Aviv, Israel, 1967-69; asst. prof. physics U. Minn., Mpls., 1969-71, assoc. prof., 1971-75, prof., 1975-82, U. Chgo., 1982—. Contbr. numerous articles to profl. and scholarly jours. Alfred P. Sloan fellow, 1971-73, Guggenheim fellow, 2002. Fellow Am. Phys. Soc. Democrat. Jewish. Avocations: fishing, hiking, skiing, amateur radio. Office: U Chgo Enrico Fermi Inst 5640 S Ellis Ave Chicago IL 60637-1433 Business E-mail: rosner@hep.uchicago.edu.

**ROSNER, M. NORTON,** diversified financial services company executive; b. Camden, N.J., Aug. 17, 1931; s. Adolph and Anne (Cotler) R.; m. M. Patricia Eskin, Oct. 18, 1953; children— Robert, Susan, Jan BS in Econs., U. Pa., 1953; MBA, U. Mich., 1965. From acct. to mgr. overhead standards RCA Corp., Camden, NJ, 1953-62; supr. methods and programs, then internal cons. forward model planning Ford Motor Co., Dearborn, Mich., 1962-66; asst. controller, then v.p. planning Singer Co., N.Y.C., 1966-70; treas., then v.p. fin. Popular Services, Passaic, NJ, 1970-72; dir. fin. planning, then asst. controller, then gen. mgr. GSD, then v.p. RE/GSD Xerox Corp., Rochester, NY, 1972-90; retired, 1990. Bd. dirs., treas. Parcel Post Assn., N.Y.C., 1970-71; dir. Harbinger, Stamford, Conn.; chmn. Xerox Realty Corp., Stamford. Vice chmn. Compeer, Inc., Rochester, N.Y., 1981-87, chmn., 1987-89; chmn. DP2, Rochester, 1985-87; bd. dirs., treas. Rochester Blue Cross-Blue Shield, 1987-89; dir. Palm Beach County Mental Health Assn., 1992, treas., 1993, v.p., 1994-95, pres., 1995-96; dir. JARC, 1992, v.p., 1993, pres., 1994-96. Recipient Nat. Vol. Action award Pres. U.S. Mem.: U. Mich.; U. Pa. Home: 3700 S Ocean Blvd Apt 408 Highland Beach FL 33487-3363

**ROSNER, ROBERT,** astrophysicist, educator; b. Garmisch-Partenkirchen, Bavaria, Germany, June 26, 1947; came to U.S., 1959; s. Heinz and Faina (Brodsky) R.; m. Marsha Ellen Rich, Sept. 5, 1971; children: Daniela Karin, Nicole Elise. BA, Brandeis U., 1969; PhD, Harvard U., 1976. Asst. prof. Harvard U., Cambridge, Mass., 1978-83, assoc. prof., 1983-86; astrophysicist Smithsonian Astrophys. Observatory, Cambridge, 1986-87; prof. U. Chgo. 1987—, William E. Wrather prof., 1998—; chief scientist Argonne Nat. Lab., 2002—05, dir., 2005—. Trustee Adler Planetarium, Chgo., 1989-98, chmn. dept. astronomy and astrophysics, 1991-97. Contbr. more than 190 articles to profl. jours. Woodrow Wilson fellow, 1969. Fellow Am. Phys. Soc., Am. Acad. Arts and Scis. (elected); mem. Am. Astron. Soc., Soc. Indsl. and Applied Math., Am. Geophys. Union, Norwegian Acad. Sci. and Letters (fgn. mem.). Home: 4950 S Greenwood Ave Chicago IL 60615-2816 Office: U Chicago Astrophysics 5640 S Ellis Ave Chicago IL 60637-1433 Business E-Mail: r-rosner@uchicago.edu.

**ROSNER, SHARON ELLEN,** actress, speech pathology/audiology services professional; b. Bklyn., Apr. 16, 1954; d. Herbert Paul and Linda (Kleiner) R. BS, Syracuse U., 1974; grad. program audiology, U. Ariz., 1975-76; MS, San Francisco State U., 1979; studied piano, San Francisco Conserv Music, 1979-84; acting degree, Drama Studio London, Berkeley, Calif., 1983. Audiologist Sonoma (Calif.) State Hosp., 1979-80; therapist Sch. for the Deaf, N.Y.C., 1984-86; speech-lang.-hearing specialist Home Therapists Assn., N.Y.C., 1988-93; tri-lingual cons., diagnostic/rehab. practitioner Comprehensive Network, N.Y.C., 1988-93; pvt. practice in speech, voice, comm. disorders and autism L.A., 1994—. Actor various off-Broadway and reg. theatre, film, TV, commls., and voiceovers; cons. Toward Rehab. Involvement by Parents of the Deaf (TRIPOD), L.A., 1993—; reader recorded books Jewish Guild for the Blind, N.Y.C., 1989-93; actor, dir., playmaking mentor Va. Ave. Project for At Risk Youth, L.A., 1996—. Actor: (solo theatrical piece) Family Matters: An Immigrant Memoir, 1986-91 (N.Y. Newsday Manhattan profile 1989); contbr. rsch. papers on psychophys. acoustics to profl. publs.; designer custom hearing protection for major rock bands; weekly columnist "Letters from L.A.," Athens, Greece; seminars on directing actors, faculty and film dept., N.Y. Coll., Athens, Greece, film dir's. and screenwriter's unions, Athens, Greece; dir. Theatre of the Deaf, Athens, Greece; journalist mags., Athens; tchr., actor, dir. workshops, Athens. Vol. Acad. Awards Silent Auction, AIDS Healthcare Found., L.A.; vol. John Huston Awards, Artists' Rights Found., L.A.; vol. Project Angel Food, L.A. Mem. AFTRA, SAG, Am. Speech-Lang.-Hearing Assn. (cert. of clin. competence), Actors Equity Assn., Women in Film (prodr. pub. svc. announcements 1994-96, vol. Crystal awards and Lucy awards), Ind. Feature Film Project/West (vol. programming), Women in Theater, Creative Women of the Arts. Avocations: piano, art, photography, weightlifting, yoga.

**ROSNOW, RALPH LEON,** psychologist, educator; b. Balt., Jan. 10, 1936; s. Irvin and Rebecca (Faber) R.; m. Mimi Quin Medinger, Aug. 12, 1963. BS, U. Md., 1957; MA, George Washington U., 1958; PhD, Am. U., 1962. Asst. prof. Boston U., 1963-67; assoc. prof. Temple U., Phila., 1967-70, full prof., 1970-2001; vis. prof. London Sch. Econs., 1973, Harvard U., Cambridge, Mass., 1978, 1988-89; Thaddeus Bolton prof. Temple U., 1982—2001, Thaddeus Bolton prof. emeritus, 2002—; dir. social and orgnl. psychology divsn. psychology, 1988-2000. Cons. editor jours. and encys. in psychology and comm.; cons. on rsch. methods and data analysis, 1976—. Author: Paradigms in Transition, 1981; author: (with Robert Rosenthal) The Volunteer Subject, 1975, Essentials of Behavioral Research, 2d edit., 1991, Contrast Analysis, 1985; author: Beginning Behavioral Research, 5th edit., 2005, People Studying People, 1997, Contrasts and Effect Sizes in Behavioral Research, 2000; author: (with Gary Fine) Rumor and Gossip, 1976; author: (with Mimi Rosnow) Writing Papers in Psychology, 7th edit., 2006; editor (with Robert Rosenthal): Artifact in Behavioral Research, 1969; editor: (with Marianthi Georgoudi) Contextualism and Understanding in Behavioral Science. Recipient George A. Miller award Soc. Gen. Psychology, 1999. Fellow: APA, AAAS, Am. Psychol. Soc.; mem.: Soc. Exptl. Social Psychology. Home: 177 Biddulph Rd Radnor PA 19087-4506

**ROSOFF, WILLIAM A.,** lawyer; b. Phila., June 21, 1943; s. Herbert and Estelle (Finkel) R.; m. Beverly Rae Rifkin, Feb. 9, 1970; children: Catherine D., Andrew M. BS with honors, Temple U., 1964; LLB magna cum laude, U. Pa., 1967. Bar: Pa. 1968, U.S. Dist. Ct. (ea. dist.) Pa. 1968. Law clk. to Hon. Abraham L. Freedman. U.S. Ct. Appeals (3d cir.), 1967-68; instr. U. Pa. Law Sch., Phila., 1968-69; assoc. Wolf, Block, Schorr & Solis-Cohen, Phila., 1969-75, ptnr., 1975-96, chmn. exec. com., 1987-88; also vice chmn. bd. dirs. Advanta Corp., Spring House, Pa., 1996—, pres., 1999—. Trustee RPS Realty Trust, 1990-96, Atlantic Realty Trust, 1996—; guest lectr. confs. and seminars on tax law; mem. tax adv. bd. Commerce Clearing House, 1983-94; mem. legal activities policy bd. Tax Analysts, 1978-95; mem. Little, Brown Tax Adv. Bd., 1994-96; chmn. bd. dirs. RMH Telsevcs., Inc., 1997-99. Editor U. Pa. Law Rev., 1965-67; mem. editl. bd. Jour. Partnership Taxation, 1983-2000; contbr. articles to profl. jours. Past mem. com. on law and social action Phila. coun. Am. Jewish Congress; bd. visitors Temple Fox Sch. Bus., 2005-. Fellow Am. Coll. Tax Counsel; mem. Am. Law Inst. (cons. taxation of partnerships 1976-78, assoc. reporter taxation of partnerships 1978-82, mem. adv. group on fed. income tax project 1982-, cons. taxation of pass-through entities 1995-2000), Order of Coif, Beta Gamma Sigma, Beta Alpha Psi. Office: PO Box 918 Spring House PA 19477-0918 Business E-Mail: wrosoff@advanta.com.

**ROSOVSKY, HENRY,** economist, educator; b. Danzig, Sept. 1, 1927; came to U.S., 1940, naturalized, 1949; s. Selig S. and Sophie (Rosovsky) R.; m. Nitza Brown, June 17, 1956; children— Leah, Judith, Michael. AB, Coll.

William and Mary, 1949, LL.D., 1976; A.M. (John E. Thayer scholar), Harvard U., 1953, PhD, 1959; L.H.D. (hon.), Yeshiva U., 1977, Hebrew Union Coll., 1978, Colgate U., 1979, Brandeis U., 1984; PhD (hon.), Hebrew U. of Jerusalem, 1982; LL.D. (hon.), Queen's U., Ont., 1984, U. Hartford, 1984, CUNY, 1986, U. Mass., 1986, Harvard U., 1998; DHL (hon.), Hebrew Coll., Brookline, Mass., 1987, NYU, 1993; DL, St. Mary's Coll. Md., 1989, Jewish Theol. Sem., 1995. From asst. prof. to prof. econs. and history U. Calif.-, Berkeley, 1958-65; chmn. Center Japanese and Korean Studies, 1962-65; prof. econs. Harvard U., 1965—, Walter S. Barker prof. econs., 1975-84, Geyser univ. prof., 1984-96, Geyser univ. prof. emeritus, 1996—; chmn. dept., 1969-72, dean Faculty Arts and Scis., 1973-84; assoc. dir. East Asia Research Center, 1967-69. Mem. Harvard U. Corp., 1985-97; vis. prof. Hitotsubashi U., Tokyo, 1957, Tokyo U., 1962, Hebrew U., Jerusalem, 1965; hon. dir. Japan Fund.; dir. emeritus Corning, Inc.; hon. prof. Centro U. Francisco, De Vitoria, Madrid, 1996. Author: Capital Formation in Japan, 1868-1940, 1961, Quantitative Japanese Economic History, 1961, (with K. Ohkawa) Japanese Economic Growth, 1973, The University: An Owner's Manual, 1990; editor: Explorations in Entrepreneurial History, 1954-56, Industrialization in Two Systems, 1966, Discord in the Pacific, 1972, (with H. Patrick) Asia's New Giant, 1976, (with P. Higonnet, D. Landes) Favorites of Fortune, 1991, (with S. Kumon) The Political Economy of Japan, Vol. 3: Cultural and Social Dynamics, 1992. Chmn. bd. trustees Am. Jewish Congress, 1975-88. Served to 1st lt. AUS, 1946-47, 50-52. Jr. fellow Soc. Fellows, 1954-57; recipient Schumpeter prize Harvard, 1963, Clark Kerr medal U. Calif., Berkeley, 1992. Fellow Am. Acad. Arts and Scis., Am. Philos. Soc.; mem. Am. Econ. Assn., Econ. History Assn., Assn. Asian Studies, Chevalier, Legion of Honor, Order of Sacred Treasure, Star (Japan). Office: Harvard Univ Loeb House 17 Quincy St Cambridge MA 02138-3805 Home: 130 Mount Auburn St Apt 506 Cambridge MA 02138 E-mail: hrosovsky@harvard.edu.

ROSOW, STUART L., lawyer; b. NYC, Mar. 28, 1950; s. Bernard and Lillian (Bonime) R.; m. Amy Berk Kuhn. AB cum laude, Yale U., 1972; JD cum laude, Harvard U., 1975. Law clk. to presiding justice U.S. Ct. Appeals (7th cir.), Chgo., 1975-76; assoc. Paul, Weiss et al, N.Y.C., 1976-79, Kaye, Scholer, Fierman, Hays & Handler, N.Y.C., 1979-84, ptnr., 1984-97, Proskauer Rose LLP, N.Y.C., 1997—. Adj. prof. Columbia Law Sch., N.Y.C., 1998—. Mem. ABA, N.Y. State Bar Assn., Assn. of Bar of City of N.Y. Office: Proskauer Rose LLP 1585 Broadway Fl 27 New York NY 10036-8299 Office Phone: 212-969-3150. Business E-Mail: srosow@proskauer.com.

ROSOWSKI, ROBERT BERNARD, manufacturing executive; b. Detroit, July 23, 1940; s. Bernard and Anna (Maciag) R.; m. Kathleen Patricia Bates, Aug. 26, 1961; children: John, Paul, Mary, Judith. BS, U. Detroit, 1962; MBA, Mich. State U., 1974. CPA Mich. Auditor, staff supr. Coopers and Lybrand, Detroit, 1962-71; fin. analyst Masco Corp., Taylor, Mich., 1971-73, controller, 1973-85, v.p., controller, 1985-96, v.p., controller and treas., 1996—2001, v.p., treas., 2001—. Bd. dirs. Detroit Cath. Ctrl. HS, 1999—, Detroit Cath. Ctrl. Alumni Assn., pres. 1999-2002; chmn. Oakwood Hosp. Found., 1990—; trustee Oakwood Healthcare System, 1997—. Mem. Am. Inst. CPA's, Mich. Assn. CPA's, Fin. Execs. Inst. Avocations: golf, fishing, boating, photography. Office: Masco Corp 21001 Van Born Rd Taylor MI 48180-1300 Office Phone: 313-792-6258. Business E-Mail: robert_rosowski@mascohq.com.

ROSS, ALLYNE R., federal judge; b. 1946; BA, Wellesley Coll., 1967; JD cum laude, Harvard Law Sch., 1970. Assoc. Paul, Weiss, Rifkind, Wharton & Garrison, 1971-76; asst. U.S. atty. U.S. Dist. Ct. (N.Y. ea. dist.), 2nd circuit, Brooklyn, 1976-83, chief, appeals div., 1983-86, magistrate judge, 1986-94, dist. judge, 1994—. Mem. Fed. Bar Coun., Bar Assn. City N.Y. Office: US Dist Ct Ea Dist NY 225 Cadman Plz E Rm 252 Brooklyn NY 11201-1818

ROSS, BARRY C., lawyer; BA, SUNY, Albany, 1971; JD magna cum laude, Brooklyn Law Sch. Bar: NY 1976. Ptnr., group co-leader Bryan Cave LLP, NYC. Office: Bryan Cave LLP 1290 Ave of the Americas New York NY 10104 Office Phone: 212-541-2255. E-mail: bcross@bryancave.com.

ROSS, BEVERLEY LONG, real estate broker; b. Reno, Sept. 1, 1940; d. John Clemons Long and Roma Lucille Barkman; m. Barry L. Ross, Oct. 2, 1959; children: J. Michael, Pamela Sue Roxane. BS, Calif. State U., Sacramento, 1970; grad., Realtors Inst. Cert. residential specialist, accredited buyer rep., Performance Mgmt. Network. Tchr. Washoe County Schs., Reno, 1961-64; homebound tchr. Prince Georges County, Oxon Hill, Md., 1972-73; kindergarten tchr. Raleigh Pre-Sch., N.C., 1974-75; owner Boise (Idaho) Pre-Sch., 1975-82; realtor United Realty, Boise, 1977-79; assoc. broker, ptnr. Treasure Valley Realty, Boise, 1979-92; broker, owner Bev Ross Realty, Boise, 1992—. Mem. foothill plans com. City of Boise, 1990—92; mem. source water assessment adv. com. Idaho Dept. Environ. Quality, Boise, 1998; mem. park impact fee adv. com. City of Boise, 2000—; elder, corp. pres. and treas. Southminster Presbyn. Ch., 1991—92, corp. pres., treas., 2001—03. Recipient Tribute to Women in Industry, Women's and Children's Alliance, 1999. Mem.: Women's Coun. Realtors (pres. 2000), Ada County Assn. Realtors (chair legis. com. 1991, dir. Ada County Realtors Found. 1999—2001, v.p. 2002, pres.-elect 2003, pres. 2004, Disting. Svc. award 1993, 2004), Idaho Assn. realtors (chair legis. com. 1992, state dir. continuing edn. task force 1997—98), Nat. Assn. Realtors, Soroptimist Internat. Boise (pres. 1988—89). Avocations: singing, reading, walking, travel. Office Phone: 208-345-7555. E-mail: bev@bevrossrealty.com.

ROSS, BRIAN ELLIOTT, news correspondent; b. Chgo., Oct. 23, 1948; s. Kenneth Earl and Shirley Louise (Johnston) R. BA, U. Iowa, 1971. Corr. KWWL-TV, Waterloo, Iowa, 1971, WCKT-TV, Miami, Fla., 1972-74; news corr. NBC News, Cleve. and NYC, 1974—94; chief investigative corr. ABC News, NYC, 1994—. Named to U. Iowa Journalism Sch. Hall of Fame, 1998; recipient Peabody award, 1974, 1992, DuPont-Columbia U. award, 1975, 1985, 1986, Sigma Delta Chi award, 1976, Nat. Headliner award, 1976—78, 1987, 2004, 2005, Robert F. Kennedy award, 1979, Emmy award, 1980, 1985, 1988, 1992, Overseas Press Club award, 1988, 1990, 1992, 1994, 1998, George M. Polk award, 1989, 1993, 1997, 1998, 2005, Sidney Hillman award, 1993, Outstanding Internat. Investigative Reporting award, Ctr. Pub. Integrity, 2005, Disting. Alumni award, U. Iowa, 2005. Office: ABC News 77 W 66th St New York NY 10023 Office Phone: 212-456-7612. E-mail: brian.e.ross@abc.com.*

ROSS, BRUCE SHIELDS, lawyer; b. LA, Feb. 1, 1947; s. Floyd and Mary Louise (Shields) R.; m. Janet G. Ross, Jan 27, 1968 (div. Jan. 1977); 1 child, Stephanie; m. Carol Burlingame, Apr. 2, 1977; children: Andrew, Tiffany. AB cum laude, Oberlin Coll., 1968; JD, U. Calif., Berkeley, 1971. Bar: Calif. 1971, U.S. Tax Ct. 1973, U.S. Dist. Ct. (ctrl. dist.) Calif. 1977; cert. specialist in estate planning, trust, probate law, Calif. Assoc. Nossman and Krueger, Los Angeles, 1971-73; from assoc. to ptnr. Poindexter & Doutre, Los Angeles, 1973-78; assoc. Alschuler & Grossman, Los Angeles, 1978, ptnr., 1979-84, Morrison & Foerster, Los Angeles, 1984—90, Ross, Sacks, and Glazier, LA, 1991—2001; exec. ptnr. Holland & Knight LLP, L.A. and Rancho Santa Fe, Calif., 2001—. Mem. adv. bd. Philip E. Heckerling Inst. on Estate Planning, U. Miami, 2000—, adj. prof. law, grad. program in estate planning, 2000—03; academician Internat. Acad. Estate and Trust Law; participant Temporary Judge Program, LA Mcpl. Ct., 1989—95; mem. panels; lectr. in field. Mem. U. Calif. Law Rev., 1969-71, note and comment editor 1970-71; author: Calif. Practice Guide: Probate, 1986-2004 (updated annually); co-editor Guidebook to the Calif. Rules of Prof. Conduct for Estate Planning, Trust and Probate Counsel, 1997; contr. articles to profl. jours. Fin. chmn. Boy Scouts Am., Glendale, Calif., 1984-85; trustee Pacific Asia Mus., Pasadena, Calif., 1983-1991, pres. 1988-1991; gov. The Webb Schs. of Calif., Claremont, 1987—. Mem. ABA (chair task force on state and local regulation, com. on exempt orgns., sect. taxation 1984-88, chair estate and trust litig. com. 1991-93, group chair litig. and controversy com. 1996-, mem. supervisory coun. 1997-2003, co-chair multijurisdictional practice com. 2000-02, sect. liaison to ethics 2000 comm. 1998-2000, real property, probate and trust law sect.), Los Angeles County Bar Assn. (exec. com. tax. sect. 1984-85,

exec. com. estates and trusts sect. 1994-97, exec. com. alternative dispute resolution sect. 1996-97), State Bar Calif. (mem. 1987-89, vice-chair 1989-90, chair 1990-91, advisor 1991-1994; fellow Am. Coll. Trust Trust and Estate Counsel (sec., treas., v.p. and pres.-elect 2001-05, pres., 2005, mem. bd. regents 1995-2001, 02—, mem. bd. exec. com. 2000-01, 02-). Democrat. Unitarian Universalist. Avocations: music, opera, swimming, stamp collecting/philately. Home: 430 Coutin Ln Glendale CA 91206-3103 Office Phone: 213-896-2400. Business E-Mail: bruce.ross@hklaw.com.

ROSS, CHARLES, artist; b. Phila., Dec. 17, 1937; s. Fred H. and Gertrude (Hill) R.; m. Elizabeth Ginsberg, 1977. AB in Math, U. Calif., Berkeley, 1960, MA in Sculpture, 1962. Exhibited in one-man shows: Dilexi Gallery, San Francisco, 1961, 65, 66, 68, Dwan Gallery, N.Y.C., 1968, 69, 71, Daytons Gallery 12, Mpls., 1968, John Weber Gallery, N.Y.C., 1972, 77, 79, 81, The Clocktower, N.Y.C., 1974, Utah Mus. Fine Arts, Salt Lake City, 1975, Mus. Contemporary Art, La Jolla, Calif., 1976, Chgo., 1976, Inst. Contemporary Art, Phila., 1977, Susan Caldwell Gallery, N.Y.C., 1977, MIT, 1977, Portland Center for Visual Arts, 1981, Sena Gallery, Santa Fe, 1991, Johnson Gallery U. N.Mex., 1992, Humphrey Gallery, N.Y.C., 1995, Mus. de Arte y Diseno Contemporaneo, San Jose, Costa Rica, 1996; exhibited in group shows: Archtl. League of N.Y., 1967, Albright Knox Art Gallery, Buffalo, 1967, Finch Coll., N.Y.C., 1967, Aldrich Mus., Ridgefield, Conn., 1967, Nelson Atkins Mus., Kansas City, 1968, Milw. Art Ctr., 1968, Whitney Mus., N.Y.C., 1969, Art Inst. Chgo., 1969, Art Gallery of Ont., Toronto, 1969, Galeriespilotes, Lausanne, Switzerland, 1970, Mus. Fine Arts, Boston, 1971, Indpls. Mus. Art, 1974, Neuberger Mus., SUNY, Purchase, 1975, Stadtisches Mus. Leverkusen, Germany, 1975, Phila. Coll. Art, 1977, Hirshhorn Mus., Washington, 1977, Old Customs House, N.Y.C., 1977, Mus. Natural History, N.Y.C., 1977, Leo Castelli Gallery, N.Y.C., 1978, Yale U. Art Gallery, 1978, Dartmouth Coll. Gallery, 1978, Aspen (Colo.) Ctr. for Visual Arts, 1980, Centre Georges Pompidou, Paris, 1980, Renwick Gallery, Smithsonian Instn., Washington, 1980, Mus. Contemporary Art, Chgo., 1981, MIT, Cambridge, 1981, Bard Coll., 1984, Light Gallery, N.Y.C., 1985, Venice Biennale, 1986, Differentes Natures la Defense, Paris, 1992, Achenvate Mus. History and Art, 1994, Richard Humphrey Gallery, N.Y.C., 1995, Kunsthallen Brandts Klaedefabrik, Odense, Denmark, 1996, SITE Santa Fe, 1996, NIT Intercomm. Ctr., Tokyo, 1997, Biennale de Lyon, France, 2000, Harwood Mus., Taos, N.Mex., 2005; commns. include: prism/solar spectrum skylight sculpture for Fed. Bldg, Lincoln, Nebr., 1976, U. Pa., 1977, Dietrich Found., Phila., 1979, Spectrum Bldg, Denver, 1980, Grand Rapids Art Mus., Mich., 1982, Towson State U., Md., 1983, Cumberland Rapid Transit Sta., Chgo., 1983, Linay Corp., Kansas City, Mo., 1985, Plaza of the Americas, Dallas, 1985, Wells Fargo Bldg., San Diego, 1986, San Francisco Internat. Airport, 1987, Anchorage Internat. Airport, 1987, Naugatuck Higher Edn. Ctr., Conn., 1990, Harvard Bus. Sch. Chapel, 1992, French Ministry of Culture Chateau d'Oiron, 1993, Cook Inst., Grand Rapids, Mich., 1996, Dwan Light Sanctuary, United World Coll., Montezuma, N.Mex., 1996, U.S. Fed. Courthouse, Tampa, 1998, Saitama (Japan) U., 1999, Kauffman Found., Kansas City, 2001, Nat. Mus. of the Am. Indian, Smithsonian Inst., Washington, D.C., 2004, Meiji U, Tokyo, 2004, Albuquerque Conv. Ctr., 2004, Highlands U., Las Vegas, 2005; represented in permanent collections Nelson Atkins Mus., Whitney Mus. Am. Art, Berkeley Art Mus., Indpls. Mus. Art, Butler Inst. Am. Art, Herbert F. Johnson Mus. Art Cornell U., GSA Art and Architecture Program, U. Pa., Dietrich Found., Grand Rapids Art Mus., Gen. Elec. Corp., City Chgo., Towson State U., Becton Dickinson Corp., Security Pacific Bank, Found. Chgo. N.Y.C., Wynne Jackson Inc., Albuquerque Mus., Linclay Corp., Witco Chem. Corp., City of San Diego, Walker Art Ctr., City of San Francisco, State of Alaska, Koll Co., Los Angeles County Mus. Art, Mus.de Arte y Diseno Contemporaneo, San Jose, Kunsthallen Brandts Klaedefabrik, Odense, Des Moines Art Ctr., French Ministry of Culture, Frederick A. Weisman Mus., Mpls., Harvard Bus. Sch., Mus. Fine Arts, Santa Fe, United World Coll., N.Mex., Saitama U., Japan, Kauffman Found., Kansas City, Meiji U., Tokyo, Nat. Mus. Am. Indian, Washington (Wash. Bldg. Congress award, 2005); works in progress include: Star Axis, architectonic earthwork/naked eye observatory atop a mesa in N.Mex. Author: Sunlight Convergence Solar Burn (Am. Inst. Graphic Arts award 1976); films Sunlight Dispersion, 1972, Solar Eclipse, 1972. Recipient Art and Architecture Collaborations award Boston Soc. Architects, 1993, Interfaith Forum on Religion, Art and Arch. Design award Harvard Bus. Sch. Chapel, 1993, award for distinction for artistic achievement Nat. Coun. Art Adminstrs., 1997. Office: Loic Malle 167 Blvd Haussmann 75008 Paris France Business E-Mail: malle.loic@wanadoo.fr. E-mail: info@staraxis.org. My work deals with the nature of light, time, and planetary motion.

ROSS, CHRISTINE MARIE, media coordinator, small business owner, disc jockey, educator; b. Dubuque, Iowa, Oct. 10, 1958; d. Harvey H. and Shirley A. Brimeyer; 1 child, Andrew Peter. Bachelors Degree, Clarke Coll., Dubuque, 1998. Owner, mgr. Chris' Gen. Store, Holy Cross, Iowa, 1983—2002; owner, mgr., disc jockey Criss Cross Prodns., Holy Cross, Iowa, 1991—; coll. prof. NE Iowa C.C., Peosta, 2000—; media coord. McGraw-Hill, Dubuque, 2005—. EMT Holy Cross Vol. Fire Dept., 1987—; leader Boy Scouts Am., Holy Cross, 1996—99; v.p. Holy Cross Athletic Club, 2000—02; sec./treas. Holy Cross Volleyball League, 2002; pres. Clarke Coll. Nontraditional Student Orgn., Dubuque. Recipient Howard and Gertrude Thompson award, Clarke Coll., 1996—97. Home: 884 Main St Holy Cross IA 52053

ROSS, CHRISTOPHER WADE STELYAN, diplomat; b. Quito, Ecuador, Mar. 3, 1943; parents Am. citizens; s. Claude G. Anthony and Antigone Andrea R.; m. Carol Geraldine Canning, Nov. 30, 1968 (div.); 1 child, Anthony Gordon. AB summa cum laude, Princeton U., 1965; cert., Mid. East Arab Studies, 1964; MA, Johns Hopkins U., 1967. Editl. asst. Mid. East Jour., Washington, 1965-68; instr. Arabic lang. Columbia U., N.Y.C., 1966, Princeton (N.J.) U., 1967; pub. affairs trainee USIA, 1968-69; jr. officer trainee Am. Embassy, Tripoli, Libya, 1969-70; dir. Am. Cultural Ctr. Fez, Morocco, 1970-73, press attache Am. Embassy, Beirut, 1973-76, pub. affairs officer Algiers, 1976-79, dep. chief mission and charge d'affaires, 1979-81; pub. affairs advisor Bur. Nr. East & South Asian Affairs Dept. of State, Washington, 1981-82, dir. regional affairs Bur. Nr. East & South Asian Affairs, 1984-85; exec. asst. to Under Sec. State for Polit. Affairs Washington, 1985-88; amb. Algeria, 1988-91, Syria, 1991-98; coord. counterterrorism Dept. State, Washington, 1998; spl. coord. pub. diplomacy, 2001—03; sr. adv. Bureau Internat. Info. Programs, 2003—04; spl. adv. Iraqi polit. affairs Bur. N.E. Affairs, 2004—; exec. dir. Search for Common Ground in Mid. East, 1999—2001; sr. advisor polit. affairs Coalition Provisional Auth., Baghdad, 2004. Chmn. bd. trustees Am. Sch. Algiers, 1978-80; hon. chmn., bd. trustees Damascus Cmty. Sch., 1991-98. Contbr. articles to profl. jour. Recipient Superior Honor award USIA, 1978, 83, Superior Honor award Dept. of State, 1988, Presdl. Meritorious Svc. award, 1983, 85, 89, 93, Disting. Honor award Dept. of State, 1997, Disting. Pub. Svc. medal Dept. Def., 2005. Mem. Coun. Fgn. Rels., Am. Fgn. Svc. Assn., Assn. Diplomatic Studies and Tng., Mid. East Inst., Mid East Studies Assn. N.Am., Royal Soc. Asian Affairs, Am. Inst. Maghrib Studies, Princeton Club. Greek Orthodox. Avocations: classic cars, bicycling. Personal E-mail: cwsross@starpower.net.

ROSS, CLARK GRANT, economics educator; b. Gloucester, Mass., June 24, 1950; s. Norman C. and Helen (Blecher) R. B.A., U. Pa., 1971; Ph.D., Boston Coll., 1975. Asst. prof. dept. econs. College of William and Mary, 1975-76; research scientist U. Mich., 1976-79; asst. prof. econs. Davidson Coll., N.C., 1979-83, assoc. prof., 1983—, chmn. dept., 1983—; cons. in field. Contbr. articles to profl. jours. Mem. Am. Econs. Assn., So. Econs. Assn. Roman Catholic. Home: RR 2 Box 283cc Davidson NC 28036-9802

ROSS, COLEMAN DEVANE, accountant, insurance company executive; b. Greensboro, NC, Mar. 18, 1943; s. Guy Matthews and Nancy McConnell (Coleman) R.; m. Carol Louise Morde, Aug. 26, 1965; children: Coleman, Jonathan, Andrew. BSBA, U. NC, 1965, postgrad., 1994, Grad. Sch. Banking of South, 1982—84, Am. Coll., 2004—; MA, Trinity Coll., 2006. CPA, CPCU, CLU, ChFC. With Price Waterhouse, 1965—99, ptnr., 1977—99; chmn., mng. ptnr. Nat. Ins. Svcs. Group, 1988-94; exec. v.p., CFO Trenwick

Group Ltd., 2000—02, Phoenix Cos., Inc., 2002—03. Bd. dirs. NCCI Holdings, Inc., Pan-Am. Life Ins. Co., Security Capital Assurance Ltd. Exec. bd. Conn. Rivers coun. Boy Scouts Am., 1978—, pres., 1985-88, bd. dirs. N.E. Region, 1988—, v.p., 1993-96, 2002—, pres. New England area, 1988-91, bd. dirs. Greater NY coun., 1994-2004; participant Leadership Greater Hartford, 1977; bd. visitors U. NC, 2001-05; bd. dirs. McLean Found., 2003-06. Recipient Silver Beaver award Boy Scouts Am., 1987, Silver Antelope award, 1991. Mem. AICPA (reins. auditing and acctg. task force 1979-85, rels. with actuaries com. 1982-85, ins. cos. com. 1985-88, acctg. stds. exec. com. 2002-05, property and liability ins. co. task force 2005—), NC Assn. CPAs, Nat. Assn. of Corp. Dirs., CFA Inst., Soc. Fin. Svc. Profls., CPCU Soc., Chartered Ins. Inst., Fin. Exec. Internat., Internat. Ins. Soc., NY Soc. Security Analysts (com. on improved corp. reporting 1999-2001, 05—), Inst. Mgmt. Accountants, Inst. Internal Auditors, Polytechnic Club, Carolina Club, Williams Club. Home: 318 W University Dr Chapel Hill NC 27516 Personal E-mail: coleman@colemanross.com.

ROSS, CONRAD HAROLD, art educator, writer; b. Chgo., Apr. 26, 1931; s. Julius A. and Pearl Felicia (Finkleman) R.; m. Janice L. Koenig, Apr. 10, 1954; children: Katherine, Joseph, Rachel. BFA, U. Ill., 1953; MFA, U. Iowa, 1959. Instr. La. Poly. Inst., Ruston, 1961-63; prof. Auburn (Ala.) U., 1963-97. Lectr. Kansas U., Lawrence, 1968; instr. Arrowmont Sch. Arts and Crafts, Gatlinburg, Tenn., 1983; artist-in residence U. Ga., Cortona, Italy, 1984; v.p. So. Graphics Coun., 1978-80; pres. Ala. Art League, Montgomery, 1978-80; dir. Auburn Works on Paper, 1981-87; owner Wycross Press; artist, painter. One man show includes Montgomery Mus. of Fine Arts, 1999. V.p. Mid South Unitarian Universalist Assn., 1995-98; pres. Unitarian Universalist Fellowship, Auburn, 1974. 1st lt. U.S. Army, 1954-55. Louis Comfort Tiffany Found. grantee, 1960. Democrat. Avocation: piano. Office: Wycross Press PO Box 2311 Auburn AL 36831-2311 Office Phone: 334-887-6836. Personal E-mail: jcro@bellsouth.net.

ROSS, DANIEL J.J., publishing executive; b. Albany, N.Y., June 2, 1943; AB, Hamilton Coll., 1966; MA, U. Fla., 1969. Prodn. mgr. U. Fla. Press, 1976-80; mktg. mgr. U. Ala. Press, 1980-85; asst. dir. Duke U. Press, 1985-89; editor-in-chief U. Nebr. Press, Lincoln, 1989-95, dir., 1995—2001; dir. editor-in-chief Univ. Ala. Press, 2001—. Office: 20 Rsch Dr Tuscaloosa AL 35487-0380 Office Phone: 205-348-5180. Business E-Mail: danross@uapress.ua.edu.

ROSS, DANIEL R., lawyer; b. Stamford, Conn., Oct. 20, 1941; s. Adrian E. and Ruth (Hill) R.; m. Faye Zerwekh. Aug. 15, 1965; children: Kevin S., Eric D., David W. SB, MIT, 1963; LLB, U. Pa., 1966. Atty. adviser to Hon. Theodore Tannenwald, Jr. U.S. Tax Ct., Washington, 1966-68; assoc. Drinker, Biddle & Reath, Phila., 1970-77, ptnr., 1977-98, Commons & Commons, Phila., 1998—2005, Ross & McCrea, 2005—. Presenter in field. Pres. bd. trustees First United Meth. Ch. Germantown, 1984-2004; bd dirs Smith Playground and Playhouses, Inc, 2003—. Capt. U.S. Army, 1968-70, Vietnam. Mem. ABA (chair com. on income of estates and trusts 1985-87, com. on govt. subcoms. 1988-91, taxation sect.). Avocations: bicycling, skiing, tennis, computers. Office: 7169 Germantown Ave 2d Fl Philadelphia PA 19119 Office Phone: 215-247-3550. Personal E-mail: danross@aol.com. Business E-Mail: dross@rossmccrea.com.

ROSS, DARIUS ALEXANDER, arbitrager and commodities trader, philanthropist; b. Laurel, Miss., July 16, 1965; s. Malachi and Alice Audrey (Rodgers) R.; m. Rose Mary Mitchell, Feb. 17, 1995 (div. Dec. 1996); children: Tomika, Alexander, T'mia; m. Linda Johnson, Sept. 17, 1998 (div. Dec. 1999). Student, Chicago State U., 1983-86, Wright Coll., 1984, Internat. Acad. Design, 1985, Lake Forest Coll., 1986, AMA Inst., 1992, World Trade Inst. of N.Y., 1992, U. Pa. Dirs. Inst., 1996-97, Harvard U. Dirs. Inst., 1997, Northwestern U., Evanston, Ill., 1997—, Kennesaw State U., U. Chgo., NYU, Columbia U., N.Y. Inst. Fin., Oxford-Templeton Inst., MIT; cert. divinity & ministry, Abaak Acad., 1999, cert. futurist studies, 1999. Cert. bus. broker, merger and acquisition intermediary cons., corp. valuation cons.; lic. real estate comml. broker and appraiser. Pres. Darius Ross Interest Ltd., 1989—, BG III MDW Holdings, 1989—, BG III Ohio Holding, 1989—, BG III Wis., 1989—, BG III Mich., 1989—. Bd. dirs. Rossfinaco, Darfin Holdings, Cacig Group, Creamie Inc., Tamco Holdings, Daril Holdings, Darmac Interest., Ross & Ross Assocs., Altimia Holdings, Tamco Industries, Cacicg Group, Tadar Investments, Rossco Equities, Macross Trading, Ross To Ross Assoc., Daalta Devels., Nelgui Holdings, Katdad Investments, Soumislau Holdings, The 79th St. Entertainment Group, Albaltal Internat., LLC, Macalicon Multi State Holdings, The Ross 7AM Agrl. Co., Dam 7AM Ross Co. Holdings Group LLC. Bd. dirs. Tilman Cmty. Health Clinic, 1997, N.Y.C. H.S. of Econs. and Fin. Benefit Bd./Bus. Adv. Bd., Chgo. Acad. of Performing Arts Benefit Bd.; active Jobs for Youths, 1991-96, George W. Ross African Am. Studies Award and Found., Target 79th St. Redevel. Group, Kennedy King Coll. Computer Info. Sys. Adv. Bd.; mem. Consolidated Corp. Found Of Lincoln Ctr., N.Y. Trust, Chgo. Symphony Orch. Assn., Rep. Senatorial Trust; bd. dirs. DA 7AM Ross Co. Found., Malalic Inst., NWO-3 Charity Trust, D. Alexamder Ross Ptnrs. Internat. LLC, Alexisal Internat. Edn. Charities. Recipient award Chgo. Directory of Apparel Mfrs., 1989; named Young Leader, S.W. Herald, 1989, N.Y. Times Heir Column, 1989, YEO/The Bridge Wealthy 100, 1990, Ace Young Entrepreneur of Yr., 1989, 90, YEO Entrepreneur Data Directory, 1993. Mem. ABA (assoc. mem.), NAFE, U.S. Postal Adv. Bd., Chgo. Postal Adv. Bd., Auburn Pk. Postal Adv. Bd., Hyde Pk. Postal Adv. Bd., Urban Bankers Assn., Turnabout Mgmt. Assn., Internat. Assn. Fin. Engrs., Treasury Mgmt. Assn., Chgo. Coun. Fgn. Rels., Am. Bus. Women's Assn. Nat. Assn. Women in Edn., Bus. Brokers Assn., Future Industry Assn., World Trade Assn., Nat. Cmty. Econ. Devel. Assn., Nat. Assn. Corp. Dirs. (sec. Chgo. chpt. 1997), N.Y. Stock Exch. Luncheon Club, Mid Day Club (Chgo.), Met. Club (Chgo.), Chgo. Merc. Exch Club, Midam Club of Chgo., Profl. Security Internat., World Super Projects Fedn., Execs. Club (Chgo.), Mpls. Athletic Club, Univ. Club of Mich. State U., Assn. for Corp. Growth, Nat. Assn. Corp. Treasurers, Coun. Instl. Investors, Nat. Black MBA Assn., Alliance of Bus. Brokers and Intermediaries, Assn. Midwest Bus. Brokers, East Manhattan C. of C., Midwest Assn. Family Bus. Owners, Am. Soc. Corp. Secs., Comml. Fin. Assn., Young Execs. Club, Forest Akers Golf Club, Ohio State U. Faculty Club, Chgo. Athletic Assn., Chgo. Symphony Orch. Assocs., U. R.I. Club, Wellesley Coll. Club, Nat. Bar Assn. Women Lawyers Divsn., Am. Bar Assn., Hispanic Nat. Bar Assn., U. Wash. Faculty Club, World Future Soc., Hispanic Nat. Bar Assoc., Women's Bar Assn., Women's Bar Assn. of DC, Nat. Assn. Women Lawyers, Nat. Assn. Women Execs., Chgo. Social Sports Club, Brown U. Faculty Club, Columbia Faculty HSE Club, U. Del. Faculty Club, U. Pa. Faculty Club, U. Louisville Faculty Club, U. Utah Nashville, Hofstra Faculty Club, Texas A&M Faculty Club, U. Texas Faculty Club, U. Wis. Faculty Club, U. Mo. Faculty Club, Harvard Club, Canebrake Golf Club, Polo Club, Powerboat Racing Club, Jai Alai Club, ATV Racing Club, Chariot Racing Club, U. Del. Faculty Club, U. Pa. Faculty Club. Republican. Roman Catholic. Avocations: tennis, soccer, golf, international travel, shooting. Office Phone: 212-414-7679. Personal E-mail: drspktoyou@yahoo.com.

ROSS, DARRIN, composer; Pres. Bad Boi Studios; composer, sound engr. Jam on Prodns., 1984—. Collaborator with Renee Harris Dance Party USA.; with Renee Harris 1 House Street. Recipient Philly's St. Buzz Producer of Yr. award, 1997.

ROSS, DAVID EDMOND, church official; b. Lewiston, Maine, Oct. 1, 1950; s. Rev. and Mrs. Lorne Arla Collins R.; m. Shirley Evelyn Godin, Aug. 19, 1972. BA in Theology cum laude, Berkshire Coll., 1973; MPA, U. Maine, 1989. Ordained to ministry Advent Christian Ch., 1975. Pastor State Road Advent Christian Ch., Presque Isle, Maine, 1973-91; exec. dir. Advent Christian Ch. Gen. Conf., Charlotte, NC, 1991—2003; sr. pastor Fellowship Advent Christian ch., Bethlehem, NC, 2003—. V.p. Maine State Conf. Advent Christian Chs., 1975-76, pres., 1976-91, 86-91; mem. exec. coun. Advent Christian Ch., 1981-90, long range strategy com., 1986—; seminar leader Am. Festival of Evangelism, Kansas City, 1981; dir. Northern Lights Youth

Choir, 1974-90. Exec. dir., CEO Advent Christian Gen. Conf., 1991—2003. Office: Fellowship Advent Christian Church 885 Icard Ridge Rd Taylorsville NC 28681 Office Phone: 828-495-8086. Personal E-mail: bethlehemshepherd@hotmail.com.

**ROSS, DEBRA BENITA,** marketing executive, jewelry designer; b. Carbondale, Ill., May 1, 1956; d. Bernard Harris and Marian (Frager) R. BS, U. Ill., 1978; MS, U. Wis., 1979. Dir. mktg. Ambion Devel., inc., Northbrook, Ill., 1983-89, Fitness Horizons, Inc., Northbrook, 1989-91, v.p. mktg., 1991-97; owner Benita Ross Designs, Northbrook, 1992—. Home: 1853 Mission Hills Ln Northbrook IL 60062-5760

**ROSS, DENNIS B.,** former diplomat; b. San Francisco, Nov. 26, 1948; married; 3 children. Grad, UCLA, 1970; PhD (hon.), Amherst Coll.; Jewish Theological Seminary, Syracuse U. Dep. dir. Office of Net assessment The Pentagon, 1982—84; exec. dir. Berkeley-Stanford program on Soviet internat. behavior, 1984—86; dir. Near East and South Asian affairs NSC; dep. dir. office net assessment The Pentagon, Washington; dir. policy planning office US Dept. State, Washington, 1988—92, spl. Middle East coord., 1997—2001; counselor and Ziegler disting. fellow Washington Inst. for Near East Policy, Washington. Spkr. in field; fgn. affairs analyst Fox News Channel; commentator Washington Post, NY Times, LA Times; chmn. Inst. Jewish People Policy Planning. Author: (book) The Missing Peace: The Inside Story of the Fight for Middle East Peace, 2004; contbr. articles to profl. jours. Recipient Presdl. Medal for Disting. Fed. Civilian Svc. Achievements include facilitation of Israeli-Jordan peace treaty; assisting the Israelis and Palestinians in reaching 1995 Interim Agreement; brokered Hebron Accord, 1997. Office: Washington Inst Near Fast Policy 1828 L St NW Ste 1050 Washington DC 20036

**ROSS, DENNIS E.,** retired automotive executive, retired lawyer; b. 1951; Bachelors, Law Degree, U. Mich. Tax legis. counsel, dep. asst. sec. Office Tax Policy U.S. Treasury Dept., 1986—89; tax ptnr. Davis Polk and Wardwell, NY, 1989—95; chief tax officer Ford Motor Co., Dearborn, Mich., 1995—2000, v.p., gen. counsel, 2000—05, ret., 2005. Office: Ford Motor The American Rd Whq Dearborn MI 48121

**ROSS, DIANA (DIANA ERNESTINE EARLE ROSS),** singer, actress, entertainer, fashion designer; b. Detroit, Mar. 26, 1944; d. Fred and Ernestine R.; m. Robert Ellis Silberstein, Jan. 1971 (div. 1976); children: Rhonda, Tracee, Chudney; m. Arne Naess, Oct. 23, 1985 (div. 2000, dec. 2004); children: Ross Arne, Evan Olaf. Pres. Diana Ross Enterprises, Inc., Anaid Film Prodns., Inc., RTC Mgmt. Corp., Chondee Inc., Rosstown, Rossville, music pub. Started in Detroit as mem. the Primettes; lead singer until 1969, Diana Ross and the Supremes; solo artist, 1969—; albums include Diana Ross, 1970, 76, Everything Is Everything, 1971, I'm Still Waiting, 1971, Lady Sings The Blues, 1972, Touch Me In The Morning, 1973, Original Soundtrack of Mahogany, 1975, Baby It's Me, 1977, The Wiz, 1978, Ross, 1978, 83, The Boss, 1979, Diana, 1981, To Love Again, 1981, Why Do Fools Fall In Love?, 1981, Silk Electric, 1982, Endless Love, 1982, Swept Away, 1984, Eaten Alive, 1985, Chain Reaction, 1986, Diana's Duets, 1987, Workin' Overtime, 1989, Red Hot Rhythm and Blues, 1987, Surrender, 1989, Ain't No Mountain High Enough, 1989, The Force Behind the Power, 1991, Stolen Moment: The Lady Sings... Jazz & Blues, 1993, Musical Memories Forever, 1993, The Remixes, 1994, A Very Special Season, 1994, Making Spirits Bright, 1994, Take Me Higher, 1995, Voice of Love, 1996, Gift of Love, 1996, The Greatest, 1998, The Real Thing, 1998, Every Day is a New Day, 1999, Love From...Diana Ross, 2001, The #1's, 2004, Complete Symphony, 2004, The Blue Album, 2006, I Love You, 2006; films include Lady Sings the Blues, 1972, Mahogany, 1975, The Wiz, 1978; NBC-TV spl., An Evening With Diana Ross, 1977, Diana, 1981, numerous others; TV movie Out of Darkness, 1994; author: Secrets of a Sparrow, 1993, Diana Ross: Going Back, 2002, Upside Down: Wrong Turns, Right Turns and the Road Ahead. Recipient citation V.P. Humphrey for efforts on behalf Pres. Johnson's Youth Opportunity Program, citation Mrs. Martin Luther King and Rev. Abernathy for contbn. to SCLC cause, awards Billboard, Cash Box and Record World as worlds outstanding singer, Grammy award, 1970, Female Entertainer Yr. NAACP, 1970, Cue award as Entertainer Yr., 1972, Golden Apple award, 1972, Gold medal award Photoplay, 1972, Antoinette Perry award, 1977, nominee as Best Actress Yr. Lady Sings the Blues Motion Picture Acad. Arts and Scis., 1972, Golden Globe award, 1972, BET (Black Entertainment Television) Walk Fame award, 1999, Heroes award, NARAS, NY Chpt., 2000; named to Rock and Roll Hall Fame, 1988. Office: c/o Motown Records 825 8th Ave New York NY 10019*

**ROSS, DONALD,** transportation executive; m. Nancy Ross; 3 children. From mgmt. trainee to br. mgr. Enterprise Rent-A-Car, St. Louis, 1964—71, corp. v.p., 1980—92, sr. exec. v.p., COO, 1992—2001, pres., 2001—, from mgmt. trainee to br. mgr. Kansas City, Mo., 1972—80; also bd. dirs. BJC auto. Centric Group, BJC Health Care, Mo. Bapt. Hosp. Bd. dirs. Mcpl. Theatre Assn., St. Louis; past bd. dirs. DeSmet Jesuit HS, Boys Hope/Girls Hope. Mem.: Boone Valley Golf Club (bd. dirs.). Office: Enterprise Rent a Car 600 Corporate Park Dr Saint Louis MO 63105-4211

**ROSS, DONALD, JR.,** language educator, academic administrator; b. N.Y.C., Oct. 18, 1941; s. Donald and Lea (Meyer) R.; m. Sylvia Berger (div.); 1 child, Jessica; m. 2d, Diane Redfern, Aug. 27, 1971; children— Owen, Gillian BA, Lehigh U., 1963, MA, 1964; PhD, U. Mich., 1967. Asst. prof. English U. Pa., Phila., 1967—70; prof. English U. Minn., Mpls., 1970—, dir. composition program, 1982—86, 2002—03, dir. Univ. Coll., 1984—89. Author: American History and Culture from the Explorers to Cable TV, 2000; co-author: Word Processor and Writing Process, 1984, Revising Mythologies: The Composition of Thoreau's Major Works, 1988; co-editor, contbr.: American Travel Writers, 1776-1865, 1997, American Travel Writers, 1850-1915, 1998; contbr. articles to profl. jours. Grantee Am. Coun. Learned Socs., 1976, 90, NSF, 1974, Fund for Improvement of Postsecondary Edn., 1982-85; recipient Disting. Teaching award U. Minn., 1992. Mem. MLA, Assn. for Computers and Humanities (exec. sec. 1978-88), Internat. Soc. for Travel Writing (exec. sec. 2001—). Office: U Minn Dept English 207 Lind Hall 207 Church St SE Minneapolis MN 55455-0152 Business E-Mail: rossj001@umn.edu.

**ROSS, DONALD EDWARD,** former academic administrator; b. Mineola, NY, June 29, 1939; s. Alexander Walker and Florence M. (Carville) R.; m. Helen Landgren, July 23, 1966; children: Ellen Ross Sarafian, Kevin McAndrew. BFA, NY Inst. Tech., 1962, LLD (hon.), 1978; MS, Hofstra U., 1970. Dean of students NY Inst. Tech., Old Westbury, 1962-68; co-founder, pres. Wilmington Coll., Del., 1967—77; pres., CEO Lynn U. (formerly Coll. of Boca Raton), Fla., 1971—2006. Chmn. adv. com. U.S. Army Command and Gen. Staff Coll. Bd. dirs. Fla. Endowment Fund, 1989—; trustee Boca Raton Community Hosp., 1990—; mem. governing bd. Philharmonic Orch. Fla., 1990—; mem. U.S. Mil. Screening Com. Named Industrialist of Yr. Greater Boca Raton C. of C., 1992, Man of the Yr., City of Hope; recipient Boy Scouts Am. Leadership Svc. award, Boca Raton award, 1991, LEAH Bridge Builder of the Year, 1999. Mem. Assn. Univ. Pres., Econ. Coun. of Palm Beach County, Royal Palm Yacht and Country, Loggerhead Club, Adirondack League Club, Old Forge Club, City (Boca Raton). Avocations: snowskiing, tennis, reading, travel, golf. Home: 7411 Floranada Addison Res Delray Beach FL 33484 Office Phone: 561-237-7782. E-mail: president@lynn.edu.*

**ROSS, DONALD K.,** lobbyist, environmental organization administrator, lawyer; Grad., Fordham Coll., NYU. Dir. Citizens Action Group; founding dir. NY Pub. Interest Rsch. Group; ptnr. Malkin & Ross, Albany, NY; CEO M&R Strategic Svcs.; chair Greenpeace Inc., Washington, DC, 2004—. Office: Greenpeace 702 H St, NW Washington DC 20001 also: M&R 2120 L St, NW Ste 400 Albany NY 12207 E-mail: dkross@mrss.com.

**ROSS, DONALD ROE,** federal judge; b. Orleans, Nebr., June 8, 1922; s. Roe M. and Leila H. (Reed) Ross; m. Janice S. Cook, Aug. 29, 1943; children: Susan Jane, Sharon Kay, Rebecca Lynn, Joan Christine, Donald Dean. JD, U. Nebr., 1948, LLD (hon.), 1990. Bar: Nebr. 1948. Practice law, Lexington, Nebr., 1948—53; mayor City of Lexington, 1953; ptnr. Swarr, May, Royce, Smith, Andersen & Ross, 1956—70; U.S. atty. Dist. Nebr. US Dept. Justice, 1953—56; gen. counsel Rep. Nat. Com., 1956—58; mem. Rep. Exec. Com. for Nebr., 1952—53; com. mem. Rep. Nat. Com., 1958—70, vice-chmn., 1965—70; judge US Ct. Appeals (8th Cir.), 1970—87, sr. judge, 1987—. Office: 5815 N 148th Plaza Omaha NE 68116

**ROSS, DOUGLAS,** lawyer; b. LA, July 12, 1948; s. Mathew and Brenda Butler (Boynton) R.; m. Lynne Rose Maidman, June 14, 1970. AB cum laude, Tufts U., 1970; JD with honors, George Washington U., 1973. Bar: Ohio 1973, D.C. 1980, U.S. Supreme Ct. 1976. Asst. atty. gen., antitrust sect. Office of Ohio Atty. Gen., Columbus, 1973-74; spl. asst. U.S. atty. Ea. Dist. Va., Alexandria, 1977; trial atty. antitrust divsn. U.S. Dept. Justice, Washington, 1975-82; atty. advisor Office of Legis. Affairs, 1984-86, Office of Legal Policy, 1987-89, Office Policy Devel., 1989-92; Supreme Ct. counsel Nat. Assn. Attys. gen., 1982-91. Ran advocacy project for states to enhance their effectiveness before Supreme Ct., 1982—91; operated clearinghouse on state constl. law, 1987—91; civil divsn. Appellate Staff U.S. Dept. Justice, Washington, 1992—94, Office of Consumer Litigation, 1994—2000, spl. counsel for agr. antitrust divsn., 2000—. Recipient Meritorious award Dept. Justice, 1979, Spl. Achievement award, 1984, 96, 97. Mem. Supreme Ct. Hist. Soc., D.C. Bar Assn., Supreme Ct. Opinion Network (bd. dirs. 1989-91), Arlington County Sports Commn. (chair aquatics com. 2004—), North Tract Master Plan Oversight Com. (chair indoor subcom. 2004—). Jewish. Home: 3153 19th St N Arlington VA 22201-5103 Office: US Dept Justice 950 Pennsylvania Ave NW Washington DC 20530-0001 Office Phone: 202-514-1874.

**ROSS, DREW,** music educator; b. Virginia Beach, Dec. 24, 1979; s. Charles and Laura Ross. MusB in Edn., George Mason U., 2002. Lic. tchr. Va. Band dir. Paramount Charter Acad., Kalamazoo, 2003—04, Chantilly (Va.) H.S., 2005—. Grad. intern, univ. bands asst. U. Va. Bands, Charlottesville, 2004—05; grad. asst. Western Mich. U., Kalamazoo, 2003—04; brass instr. Crossmen Drum and Bugle Corps, Allentown, Pa., 2002. Named Crossmen of Yr., Crossmen Drum and Bugle Corps, 2000, Mem. of Yr., Tarheel Sun Drum and Bugle Corps, 1997, 1999; recipient Disting. Svc. award, Crossmen Drum and Bugle Corps, 1999, 2001; Melton Music Tchg. fellow, George Mason U., 2000—02. Mem.: Music Educators Nat. Conf., Va. Music Educators Assn., Kappa Kappa Psi. Office: Chantilly HS 4201 Stringfellow Rd Chantilly VA 20151 Office Phone: 703-222-8107. Home Fax: 703-222-8197; Office Fax: 703-222-8197. Business E-Mail: drew.ross1@fcps.edu.

**ROSS, E. EARL,** small business owner; b. July 3, 1942; s. Edward Earl and Ruth Randles (Loewen) R.; m. Mary Donna Moore, May 31, 1964; 1 son, Damon Moore. BA in Psychology, Central Mo. State U., 1965; MA in Corrections, Webster U., 1976. Reporter Warrensburg (Mo.) Daily Star-Jour., 1965; social worker St. Louis County Welfare Div., Maplewood, Mo., 1966-68; assoc. dist. scout exec. Boy Scouts Am. St. Louis, 1968; dep. juvenile officer St. Louis County Juvenile Ct., Clayton, Mo., 1969-72; program dir. St. Louis County Detention Ctr., Clayton, Mo., 1972-99, asst. supt., 1978-99; CEO Golf-o-Gram, 1999—. Trainer statewide detention staffs; past pres. Historygram, Inc. Recipient Outstanding Detention Program award Nat. Council Juvenile and Family Ct. Judges, 1982. Mem. St. Louis County Juvenile Justice Assn., Am. Mgmt. Assn. Home: 15333 Appalachian Trl Chesterfield MO 63017-1939

**ROSS, EDWARD,** cardiologist; b. Fairfield, Ala., Oct. 10, 1937; s. Horace and Carrie Lee (Griggs) R.; m. Catherine I. Webster, Jan. 19, 1974; children: Edward, Ronald, Cheryl, Anthony. BS, Clark Coll., 1959; MD, Ind. U., 1963. Diplomate Am. Bd. Internal Medicine; cert. specialist in clin. hypertension Am. Soc. Hypertension. Intern Marion County Gen. Hosp., Indpls., 1963; resident in internal medicine Ind. U., 1964-66, 68, cardiology rsch. fellow, 1968-70, clin. asst. prof. medicine, 1970; cardiologist Capitol Med. Assn., Indpls., 1970-74; pvt. practice medicine, specializing in cardiology Indpls., 1974—. Staff cardiologist Winona Meml. Hosp., Indpls., chief cardiovascular disease, 2000-04, med. dir. cardiovascular svcs., 2000—, med. dir. cardiac cath lab, 2000—, chief interventional cardiology, 2000-04; staff Meth. Hosp., Indpls., chmn. cardiovasc. sect., 1989-96; chmn. cardiovasc. sect., dir. cardiovasc. ctr. Meth. Hosp., 1990-92; bd. dirs. Meth. Hosp. Heart-Lung Ctr., med. dir. cardiovasc. svcs., 1991-98; med. dir. cardiovascular svcs. Methodist Hosp., Indpls., Ind., 2000—; cardiac catheterization lab., 2000—, cardiovascular programs, Clarion Health Indpls., 2000—, cardiovascular svcs., Cardiac Cath. Lab., cardiovascular programs, Clarion Health Ptnrs., 2000-. Assoc. editor Angiology, Jour. Vascular Disease; sr. editor Jour. Vascular Medicine, 1983—. Mem. Ctrl. Ind. Health Planning Coun., 1972-73; bd. dirs. Ind. chpt. Am. Heart Assn., 1973-74, multiphasic screening East Side Clinic, Flanner Ho. of Indpls., 1968-71; med. dir. Nat. Ctr. for Health Svc. R&D, HEW, 1970; consumer rep. radiologic device panel health FDA, 1988-92; dir. hypertensive screening State of Ind., 1974; J.B. Johnson Cardiovasc. lectr. Nat. Med. Assn., 1991. Capt. MC, USAF, 1966-68. Recipient Lifetime Achievement award, Ctr. Leadership Devel., 2003, Leadership award, Indpls. Police Dept., 2005; scholar, Nat. Found. Health, 1955, Gorges Found., 1956; Woodrow Wilson fellow, 1959. Fellow Royal Soc. Promotion of Health (Eng.), Am. Coll. Angiology (v.p. fgn. affairs, sec. 1993—), Internat. Coll. Angiology, Am. Soc. of Angiology, Am. Coll. Cardiology, Assn. Black Cardiologists (mem. bd. dirs. 1990-94); mem. NAACP, AMA, Am. Soc. Contemporary Medicine and Surgery, Nat. Med. Assn. (coun. sci. assembly 1985-89), Ind. Med. Soc., Marion County Med. Soc., Am. Coll. Physicians, Am. Heart Assn., Ind. Soc. Internal Medicine (pres. 1987-89), Ind. State Med. Assn. (chmn. internal medicine sect. 1987-89), Ind. Med. Soc., Aesculapean Med. Soc., Hoosier State Med. Assn. (pres. 1980-84, 90-95), Urban League, Alpha Omega Alpha, Alpha Kappa Mu, Beta Kappa Chi, Omega Psi Phi. Methodist. Office Phone: 317-923-7849. Business E-Mail: eross@clarian.org.

**ROSS, EDWARD JOSEPH,** architect; b. Dec. 13, 1934; s. Miriam Ross; children: Linda Joy, Melissa Carol. Student, Boston Archtl. Ctr., 1952-55, 61-62, USAF Surveying Sch., 1955-56, Boston Soc. Civil Engrs., 1956-57, Carl Bolivar Structural Engr., 1962-63. Registered arch., Mass., Calif., N.Y., Fla., N.H., Vt., cert. Nat. Coun. Archtl. Registration Bds.; lic. constrn. supr. Mass., expert witness constrn. law. Draftsman, assoc. William W. Drummey, Architect, Boston, 1952-59; job capt., designer Drummey-Rosane-Anderson, Boston, 1959-64; projects arch. Maginnis & Walsh & Kennedy, Boston, 1964-69; v.p. William Nelson Jacobs Assocs., Inc., Boston, 1969-73; staff arch. Robert Charles Assocs., Inc. Archs., Boston, 1973-74; office mgr. Charles F. Jacobs Assocs., Inc., Cambridge, Mass., 1974-76; cons. arch. Linenthal, Eisenberg & Anderson, Boston, 1976-77; staff arch. Eisenberg Haven Assocs., Inc., Boston, 1977-78; chief arch., chief insp. Boston Housing Authority, 1978-83; prin. Edward J. Ross, AIA/FARA, Randolph, Mass., 1983-84; arch., sr. assoc., dir. constrn. adminstrn. Stull and Lee, Inc., Boston, 1984-91; pvt. practice Randolph, Stoughton, Mass., West Palm Beach, Fla., 1963—2000; consulting arch., contrn. adminstr., expert witness, 2000—. Mem. FCC Tech Plus. Mem. exec. bd. and ops. com. United Civic Orgn.; bd. dir. Linderhof Property Owners Assn., Knollsbrook Condominium Complex. Staff sgt. USAF, maj. Mass. Mil. Res. Fellow: Soc. Am. Registered Archs.; mem.: USO (New Eng. coun.), AIA, Boston Soc. Archs. (mem. housing com. 1982—86), Constrn. Specifications Inst., Mass. State Assn. Archs., Am. Arbitration Assn. (nat. panel 1965—), United Civic Orgn. (mem. exec. bd. and ops. com.), Assn. First Corps Cadets, Am. Assn. Ret. Persons, Air Force Assn. (pres. Boston chpt.), Mass. Air N.G. Hist. Assn., Mil. Hist. Soc. Mass., Oxford 100 Condominium Assn. (pres.), Linderhof Golf Course Site One Assn. (pres. 1980—86), Ancient and Hon. Arty. Co. Mass., Oxford Colony Club Century Village (v.p.), Ten of Us Club, Am. Legion, KP, Elks. Address: 201 Oxford 100 West Palm Beach FL 33417-1412 Office Phone: 561-615-6680. Fax: 561-686-6345.

**ROSS, E(DWIN) CLARKE,** association executive, educator; b. Balt., Sept. 21, 1948; s. Harry Edwin and Margaret Frances (Turner) R.; m. Elizabeth Christine Shannon, Mar. 26, 1988; 1 child, Andrew Clarke. BA, U. Md., 1970, MA, 1974; D of Pub. Adminstrn., George Washington U., 1981. Vol. VISTA, Washington, 1970-71; legis. asst. Nat. Assn. State Mental Health Program Dirs., Washington, 1971-72; from asst. dir. to dir. Govt. Rels. United Cerebral Palsy Assns., Washington, 1972-84; asst. prof. European region Troy State U., Weisbaden, Germany, 1984-86; asst. exec. dir. for fed. rels. Nat. Assn. State Mental Health Dirs., Washington, 1986-93, dep. exec. dir., 1993-95; exec. dir. Am. Managed Behavioral Healthcare Assn., Washington, 1995-98; dep. exec. dir. pub. policy Nat. Alliance for the Mentally Ill., Arlington, Va., 1998-2000; CEO Children and Adults with Attention Deficit/Hyperactivity Disorder, Landover, Md., 2000—. Adj. grad. faculty, Cen. Mich. U., Washington, 1983-84, 87-93, 99—; adj. assoc. prof. U. Md., College Park, 1992-95. Author: Managed Behavioral Health Care Handbook, 2001; contbr. articles to profl. jours. and chpts. to books; author: Endurance as a Virtue: Army of Northern Virginia Civil War Experiences. Vol. Com. for Legal Svcs., Washington, 1970-71; mem. U.S. Olympic Com. on Winter Sports for Disabled, Colo. Springs, Colo., 1983-84; mem. program com. Dem. Club, Annapolis, Md., 1984. Recipient Maternal and Child Health scholarship to Johns Hopkins U., State of Md., 1975. Mem. SAR, Am. Coll. Mental Health Adminstrn., Am. Soc. Pub. Adminstrn., Am. Polit. Sci. Assn., St. Andrew's Soc., Sovereign Mil. Order of Temple of Jerusalem, Beta Gamma Sigma (life). Presbyterian. Avocations: Scottish country dance, skiing, Scottish and U.S. history. Home and Office: 1718 Reynolds St Crofton MD 21114-2635 E-mail: clarke_ross@chadd.org.

**ROSS, EDWIN WILLIAM,** rubber company executive; b. Phila., May 28, 1938; s. Edwin Morrison and Frances Louise (Ort) R.; m. Dorothy Anne Reilly, Sept. 24, 1966; children: E. William Jr., Catherine Ross Conlin, James David. BS, Lehigh U., 1960. Chmn. bd., CEO Key Chems., Inc., Phila., 1965-87; pres., CEO Pelmor Labs., Inc., Newtown, Pa., 1989—2005; chmn. Pelseal Techs., LLC, Newtown, Pa., 1998—2005. Mem. adv. bd. Prime Bank, Ft. Washington, Pa., 1995—98. Deacon Bryn Mawr (Pa.) Presbyn. Ch., 1977-81, elder, 1985-91, trustee, 1997-2003, pres. bd. trustees, 2001-2003; bd. dirs. Main Line Adult Day Care Ctr., 1999. Recipient Alumni award Lehigh U. Alumni Assn., 1985. Mem. SAR, MidAtlantic Employers Assn. (chmn. 1995-96), Metal Finishing Suppliers Assn. (pres. 1986-88, 89-90, Munning award 1992), N.E. Phila. C. of C. (chmn. 1983), Lehigh U. Alumni Assn. (bd. dirs. 1997-2000), Swedish Colonial Soc., Sons. of the Revolution Soc., St. Andrew's Soc., Colonial Soc., Exch. Club (pres. Frankford-Phila. 1972), Phila. Country Club (pres. 1986-89). Republican. Avocations: downhill skiing, hunting, travel, golf. Office: Pelmor Labs Inc 401 Lafayette St Newtown PA 18940-0309 Office Phone: 215-968-3334. Personal E-mail: ewmross@hotmail.com.

**ROSS, ELLIOTT DANIEL,** neurologist, researcher; b. N.Y.C., Mar. 1, 1945; BA, MD, Boston U., 1968. Diplomate Am. Bd. Psychiatry and Neurology. Clin. fellow in neurology Med. Sch. Harvard U., Boston, 1972—75; asst. prof. neurology U. Tex. Southwestern Med. Ctr., Dallas, 1975—81; asst. prof. psychiatry, 1979—81; assoc. prof. neurology and psychiatry, 1982—88; prof., chmn. neurology, dept. neurosci. U. N.D., Fargo, 1988—96; prof. neurology U. Okla. Health Sci. Ctr., Oklahoma City, 1996—. Grainik disting. lectr. Soc. Biol. Psychiatry, 1985; Plenary lectr. Can. Coll. Neuropsychopharmacology, Vancouver, BC, Canada, 1986; chief neurol. svc. VA Med. Ctr., Fargo, 1990—96, dir. Ctr. Alzheimer's and Neurodigenerative Disorders, Oklahoma City, 1996—; dir. clin. rsch. program Neuropsychiatric Rsch. Inst., Fargo, 1990—96; dir. Ctr. Memory Loss and Dementia U. Okla. Health Sci. Ctr., 2000—. Author: Archives Neurology, 1979, 3d edit., 1981, Archives General Psychiatry, 1981, Brain and Language, 1988, 2d edit., 1997, Neuropsychiatry, Neuropsychology and Behavioral Neurology, 1994; assoc. editor:, 1993—2004. Lt. comdr. USN, 1970—72, Vietnam. Mem.: Behavioral Neurology Soc. (sec.-treas. 1981—91, pres. 1991—93), Internat. Neuropsychology Soc., Am. Neurol. Assn., Am. Acad. Neurology. Achievements include research in right hemisphere's role in language, affect and emotions; neurology of depression; acoustical analysis of affective prosody; different forms of amnesias. Office: OUHSC Dept Neurology PO Box 26901 Oklahoma City OK 73126-0901 Address: Alzheimer Ctr VAMC 11AZ 921 NE 13th St Oklahoma City OK 73104-5007

**ROSS, EUNICE LATSHAW,** retired judge; b. Bellevue, Pa., Oct. 13, 1923; d. Richard Kelly and Eunice (Weidner) Latshaw; m. John Anthony Ross, May 29, 1943 (dec. Jan. 1978); 1 child, Geraldine Ross Coleman. BS, U. Pitts., 1945, LLB, 1951. Bar: Pa. 1952. Atty. Pub. Health Law Rsch. Project, Pitts., 1951-52; atty. jud. asst., law clk. Ct. Common Pleas Allegheny County, Pitts., 1952-70, dir. family divsn., 1970-72, judge, 1972-96, Commonwealth Ct. Pa., 1997—2004. Adj. law prof. U. Pitts., 1967-73; mem. Bd. Jud. Inquiry and Rev., Commonwealth of Pa., 1984-89, Gov's Justice Commn., 1972-78; mem. orphan's ct. rules com. Supreme Ct. Pa., 1998—2005. Author: (with others) Survey of Pa. Public Health Laws, 1952, Justice, 1995, Lötschers of Latterbach, Mennonite Heritage Mag., 2003; co-author: Will Contests, 1992; contbr. articles to law publs. Mem. exec. com. bd. trustees U. Pitts., 1980—86, bd. visitors Law Sch., 1985—, bd. visitors Health Sch., 1986—98; mem. adv. bd. Animal Friends, Pitts., 1973—98; committeewoman for 14th ward, vice chmn. Pitts. Dem. com., 1972; bd. dirs. The Program, Pitts., 1983—87, Pitts. History and Landmarks Found., West Pa. Hist. Soc., West Pa. Conservancy. Named Girls Scouts Woman of Yr., Pitts. coun. Girl Scouts U.S.A., 1975, Alumni of Yr., U. Pitts. Law Sch., 2001; recipient Disting. Alumna award, U. Pitts., 1973, Medal of Recognition, 1987, Alumni award, U. Pitts. Sch. of Law, 2001, Susan B. Anthony award, Women's Bar Assn. Western Pa., 1993, Probate and Trusts award, 1994, cert. of achievement, Pa. Fedn. Women's Clubs, 1975, 1977. Mem.: ABA, Allegheny County Bar Assn. (vice chmn., exec. com. young lawyers sect. 1958—59), Pa. Trial Judges Conf., Scribes, Order of Coif. Home: 1204 Denniston Ave Pittsburgh PA 15217-1329 Personal E-mail: rossdent@comcast.net.

**ROSS, FRANK HOWARD, III,** management consultant; b. Charlotte, NC, Aug. 28, 1946; s. Frank Howard Jr. (dec.) and Alma (Richardson) R. (dec.); m. Beverly Hazel Ross, June 30, 1973 (div.); children: Martha McCausland, Frank Howard IV; m. Barbara Rydz-Roth, July 9, 2005; children: Ingrid Rydz, Veronica Anne, Karl Vincent. BS in Engring., N.C. State U., 1968. Cons. Fails & Assocs., Inc., Raleigh, N.C., 1968-73; ptnr. Ross-Payne & Assocs., Inc., Barrington, Ill., 1973—. Bd. dirs. Gilldorn Savs., Chgo., 1982-85, Brickman Industries, Inc., Chgo., 1980-90; CFO WRT, Inc., Chgo., 1993-95; pres., chmn. bd. dirs. Emerald Capital Investments, Inc., Barrington, 1993-97; adviser, spkr. on constrn. and fin.; bd. dirs. Sherman Plumbing, 1975-95. Author: More $ Through $ Management, 1975, MIS and You, 1978, Planning and Budgeting, 1979, Profit by Design, 1981, Pricing for Profit, 1983, Wealthbuilding, 1984, Equipment Cost Analysis, 1988, Survival in a Tight Economy, 1988, Associated Landscape Contractors of America Operating Cost Survey, 1989, 91, Cash Flow, 1989, Dealing with the Competition of the 90's, 1990, Designing Your Accounting System, 1991, Bidding in a Tight Market, 1992, Industry's Wage and Benefit Study, 1992, Financing Your Business, 1993, Pricing, 1994, 2d edit., 1997, How Low Can You Go?, 1995, Valuing Your Business, 1998, Posturing for Growth and Prosperity, 1999, My Executive Dashboard, 2004 Mem. Presbyn. Ch. Barrington. Mem. Inst. Mgmt. Cons., Barrington Hills Country Club, Haig Point Country Club, Sigma Alpha Epsilon. Home and Office: Ross Payne Assocs Inc 190 Kimberly Rd Barrington IL 60010-2017 Office Phone: 847-381-8939.

**ROSS, GARY EARL,** writing educator; b. Buffalo, Aug. 12, 1951; s. Earl Ross and Marlene (Edwards) Anderson; m. Katharyn Ellen Ketter, Dec. 23, 1970 (div 1993); children: Colleen, Timothy, David; m. Patrice Lynette Cox, Aug. 14, 1999; children: Cody, Madelynne. BA in English, SUNY, Buffalo, 1973, MA in Humanities, 1975. Cert. English tchr., N.Y. Secondary English tchr. Buffalo Pub. Schs., 1973-76, Canisius High Sch., Buffalo, 1976-77; writing instr. Ednl. Opportunity Ctr. SUNY, Buffalo, 1977—94, assoc. prof., 1994—2003, prof., 2003—. Writing instr. Upward Bound SUNY, Buffalo, summers 1980—, acting dir., summer 1984; presenter in field, U.S., Can., Europe, 1975—; reader various profl. fiction readings, 1985-; bd. mem. Just

Buffalo Literacy Ctr. Contbr. articles, short stories, poems, essays to profl. publs.; videographer Writers on Video, Buffalo Pub. Libr., 1989; author (book) Wheel of Desire, 2000, Dots, 2002, Shimmerville, 2002, (plays) Sleepwalker, 2002, Matter of Intent, 2005 (Edgar Allan Poe award for Play, Mystery Writers Am., 2006). Bd. mem. Umima Theatre Co. Local Incentive Funding Test fellow for fiction Buffalo Arts Coun., 1989; recipient Excellence award N.Y. State/United Univ. Professions, 1990, award of Yr. Arts Coun., 2003. Mem. Niagara Erie Writers (chmn. bd. dirs. 1987-89), Just Buffalo, Inc. (fiction resident 1987, 92, bd. dirs. 2003-), Mid-Atlantic Popular/Am. Culture Assn. (bd. mem.), United Univ. Professions, Assn. Tchg. Artists (bd. dirs. 2003-06). Avocations: computing, games, film history, contemporary literature. Office: SUNY EOC Buffalo 465 Washington St Buffalo NY 14203-1707 Office Phone: 716-849-6727 ext. 119. E-mail: geross@buffalo.edu.

**ROSS, GEORGE H.,** real estate company executive, lawyer; b. 1928; married; 2 children. Grad., BA, Bklyn. Coll.; JD, Bklyn. Law Sch. Bar: 1953. Worked with Donald Trump since 1974; with The Trump Orgn., NYC, 1996—, exec. v.p., sr. counsel. Lectr. Practicing Law Inst., Am. Mgmt. Assn., Learning Annex; adj. prof. NYU. Boardroom judge: (TV series) The Apprentice, 2004—; author (with Andrew James McLean): (book) Trump Strategies for Real Estate: Billionaire Lessons for the Small Investor, 2005. Achievements include development of major buildings in the NY area including 40 Wall Street, 100 Wall Street, Trump Tower, Chrysler building, and many hotels. Office: The Trump Orgn 725 5th Ave New York NY 10022-2519

**ROSS, GERALD FRED,** electrical engineering executive, researcher; b. N.Y.C., Dec. 14, 1930; s. Samuel Henry and Jenny (Saltzman) Rozansky; m. Vivian Ida Turkish, Dec. 24, 1953; children: Jayne T. Ross Kaufman, Steven A., Helene B. Ross Joseph. BEE, CCNY, 1952; MEE, Poly. U., 1955, PhD, 1963. Registered profl. engr., N.Y., Mass., Fla. Rsch. asst. U. Mich., Ann Arbor, 1952-53; sr. engr. W.L. Maxson Corp., N.Y.C., 1954-58; rsch. sect. head Sperry Gyroscope Co., Great Neck, L.I., NY, 1958-65; dept. mgr. Sperry Rsch. Ctr., Sudbury, Mass., 1965-81; chmn. Geospatial Sys. Inc. (formerly-ANRO Engring.), Sarasota, Fla., 1981—, Ana Lux Corp. 2002-. Pres., v.p., treas. Adams Pool Corp., Lexington, Mass., 1968-81. Capt. USAFR, 1953—. Contbr. author 3 books, 1986, 90, 93; contbr. numerous articles to profl. jours.; patentee in field. Fellow Polytechnic U. Fellow IEEE (life; K.C. Black Nerem Best paper award 1974, Pioneer award 2004), Nat. Acad. Engring. (life); mem. Electromagnetics Acad., Lexington Golf Club, Longboat Key Club, Sigma Xi (sr.), Tau Beta Pi, Eta Kappa Nu. Republican. Jewish. Avocations: golf, bridge. Office: GSI 1800 2d St Ste 730 Sarasota FL 34236-5971 Office Phone: 941-957-3080. Personal E-mail: drgfr@aol.com.

**ROSS, GERALD HARVEY,** family practice and environmental medicine physician; s. Henry Warburton and Norine Hazel (Bishop) Ross; m. Heather M. Pollett, Aug. 15, 1970; children: Graham D.P., Andrew W.J. BSc, Dalhousie U., 1969, MD, 1974. Diplomate Internat. Bd. Environ. Medicine, Am. Bd. Environ. Medicine. Med. dir. N.S. Environ. Medicine Clinic, Halifax, Canada, 1970—74; family medicine practice New Minas, Nova Scotia, Canada, 1974—87; med. staff, 1989—99; med. fellow Environ. Health Ctr., Dallas, 1987—89, med. staff, 1989—99; rsch. fellow Gerald H. Ross, M.D., P.L.L.C., Bountiful, Utah, 1999—2004. Mem. adv. com. Environ. Hypersensitivits Ont. Dept. Health, Toronto, 1989—94; rsch. fellow Breakspeare Hosp. for Environ. Medicine, Kings Langley, Hertfordshire, England, 1988—89. Co-author reports to Ont. Ministry of Health; contbr. chapters to books, articles to profl. jours.; scientific papers; mem. editl. bd. Internat. Jour. Hygiene and Environ. Health, 2001—03, Environ. Epidemiology and Toxicology, 1998—2001, mem. East Coast adv. com. The Med. Post, Toronto, 1978—94. Many leadership positions Ch. LDS, Dallas, 1988—99. Internat. fellow in environ. medicine, N.S. Dept. Health, 1987—89, Innovations in Edn. Utah grantee, 2003. Fellow: Royal Soc. Medicine (U.K.), Am. Acad. Environ. Medicine (pres. 1995—97, chair rsch. com. 1991—94, bd. dirs. 1993—98, Award of appreciation for serving as Pres. 1997); mem.: AMA, Assn. Am. Physicians and Surgeons, Am. Coll. Nutrition, Am. Coll. Occupl. and Environ. Medicine, Can. Soc. Environ. Medicine, Coll. Family Physicians Can., Am. Bd. Environ. Medicine (bd. govs. 1993—2004), Chem. Sensitivity Found. (bd. dirs.), Can. Med. Assn., Tex. Med. Assn. Mem. Lds Ch. Avocations: reading advances in science, reading mystery fiction, movies. Office: Gerald H Ross MD PLLC PO Box 115 Bountiful UT 84011

**ROSS, GLORIA JEAN,** artist; b. Terrell, Tex., June 24, 1943; d. John Frederick and Shirley Joe (West) Williams; m. Winston Byrd Ross, Aug. 24, 1963; 1 child, John Winston. BS, U. North Tex., 1965; MS, U. North Tex., 1981, MFA, 1983. Cert. tchr. Art tchr. West Springfield H.S., Fairfax, Va., 1967-70, Tucker (Ga.) H.S., 1970-72, Westminster Sch., Atlanta, 1972-73; art/adult edn. tchr. San Jose (Calif.) Sch. Sys., 1973-74, Virginia Beach (Va.) Schs., 1975; adult edn. dir. Denton (Tex.) Pub. Schs., 1983-85; program dir. Children's Arts and Ideas Found., Dallas, 1985-88; continuing edn. coord. Tex. Woman's U., Denton, 1988-90; freelance artist Plano, Tex., 1990—. One person shows include U. North Tex. Art Gallery, Denton, 1983, Irving Cultural Ctr., Tex., 1986, Trammel Crow Ctr. Gallery, Dallas, 1988, Tex. Woman's U., Denton, Tex., 1990, Eleven East Ashland, Phoenix, 1991, Wichita Falls (Tex.) Art Assn. Gallery, 1992, Del Rio (Tex.) Art Ctr., 1992; exhibited in group shows Irving (Tex.) Arts Ctr., 1985, Cedar Valley C.C., Cedar Hill, Tex., 1990, Paige-Hansen Art Gallery, Dallas, 1994, Arlington (Tex.) Mus. Art, 1995, Plano (Tex.) Cultural Arts Ctr., 1995, 96, Eastfield C.C., Mesquite, Tex., 1995; represented in collections Hyatt Hotel, Cancun, Mex., Renaissance Hotel, Washington, Harris Hosp., Ft. Worth, Bus. Interiors, Irving, EMSI, Dallas, Oracle Corp., Renaissance Hotel, Houston, The Mus. of Photography, Riverside, Calif., Pizza Inn Japan, Texins Credit Union, Richardson, Tex., Capital Mortgage, Ft Wroth, Northern Telecom, Newark Equitable Ins., Dallas, Ga. Street Hotel, Indpls., Fed. Depository Regional Office, Dallas, Harris Hosp., Ft. Worth, Butler and Binion, Dallas, Merrell, Dallas, Trinity Med. Ctr., Ft. Worth Gehad Investments, Dallas, Nat. Athletic Assn., Dallas, NCNB, Dallas, others. Founder, bd. mem. Dallas (Tex.) Women's Caucus for Art, 1983-90, first pres., 1983. Recipient Fellowship award Mid-Am. Arts Alliance, Kansas, Mich., 1992. Mem. So. Graphics Assn. Democrat.

**ROSS, HOWARD PHILIP,** lawyer; b. May 10, 1939; s. Bernard and Estelle (Maremont) Ross; m. Loretta Teresa Benquil, 1962 (div.); children: Glen Joseph, Cynthia Ann, Ryan Reeve; m. Jennifer Kay Shirley, 1984. BS, U. Ill., 1961; JD, Stetson Coll. Law, 1964. Bar: Fla. 1964, U.S. Ct. Appeals (5th cir.) 1965, U.S. Supreme Ct. 1969, U.S. Ct. Appeals (11th cir.) 1981, cert.: civil trial lawyer, bus. litigator. Assoc. Parker & Battaglia and predecessor firm, St. Petersburg, Fla., 1964-67; ptnr. Battaglia, Ross, Dicus & Wein, P.A., St. Petersburg, 1967—, pres., CEO, 1992-99, chmn. bd. dirs., 2000—. Lectr. Stetson Coll. Law, St. Petersburg, 1971—72, adj. prof., 1987. Author: Florida Corporations, 1979; co-author: Managing Discovery in Commercial and Business Litigation, 1993; contbr. articles to profl. jours. Hon. chair St. Petersburg br. Awards Banquet NAACP, 1995; bd. dirs. St. Petersburg Neighborhood Housing Svcs., Inc., 1997, legal counsel, 1997—, pres., 2000—02; bd. dirs. Cmty. Alliance, 1997—2002; chmn. subcom. Citizen Rev. Com. City of St. Petersburg, 1992—94, co-chair, 1994—97. Recipient Woman's Svc. League Best Groomed award, 1979, Fla. Bar Merit citation, 1974, Cmty. Svc. award, NAACP, 1998, Humanitarian award, YMCA of Tampa Bay, 1999, C.W. Bill Young Pinellas Pinnacle award, 2002, Disting. Alumni award, Stetson Lawyers Assn., 2006. Mem.: ABA, Am. Arbitration Assn. (roster of neutrals, large complex cases and comml. 2003—), St. Petersburg Bar Assn., Fla. Bar Assn. (chmn. civil trial certification com. 1993—94), St. Petersburg Area C. of C. (bd. govs. 1990—95, v.p. pub. affairs 1992—93, exec. com. 1992—95, v.p. membership 1993—94, counsel 1994—95, dean entrepreneurial acad. 1996—, treas. 2000—02, bd. govs. 2000—05, chmn.-elect 2002—03, chmn. of Yr. 1993—94). Republican. Jewish. Office: Battaglia Ross Dicus & Wein PA PO Box 41100 980 Tyrone Blvd N Saint Petersburg FL 33710-6382 Office Phone: 727-381-2300. Business E-Mail: hross@brdwlaw.com.

**ROSS, HUGH COURTNEY,** electrical engineer; b. Dec. 31, 1923; s. Clare W. and Jeanne F. Ross; m. Sarah A. Gordon (dec.); m. Patricia A. Malloy; children: John C., James G., Robert W. Student, Calif. Inst. Tech., 1942, San Jose State U., 1946-47; BSEE, Stanford U., 1950, postgrad., 1954. Registered profl. elec. engr., Calif. Instr. San Benito (Calif.) High Sch. and Jr. Coll., 1950-51; chief engr. vacuum power switches Jennings Radio Mfg. Corp., San Jose, Calif., 1951-62; chief engr. ITT Jennings, San Jose, Calif., 1962-64; pres. Ross Engring. Corp., Campbell, Calif., 1964—. Contbr. articles to profl. jours. Fellow IEEE (life) (chmn. Santa Clara Valley subsect. 1960-61); mem. Am. Vacuum Soc., Am. Soc. Metals. Achievements include patents in field. Avocations: electronics, electric autos, camping, ranching, solar power. Office: 540 Westchester Dr Campbell CA 95008-5012 Office Phone: 408-377-4621.

**ROSS, IVY,** apparel executive, artist; Completed programs in indsl. design, Syracuse U. Sch. Design; completed programs in jewelry design, Fashion Inst. Tech.; profl. mgmt. development program, Harvard Bus. Sch. Positions with Coach, Liz Claiborne, Calvin Klein, Swatch Watch, Victoria's Secret, Bausch & Lomb; sr. v.p., design Mattel, Inc.; exec. v.p., product design and development, Old Navy Brand Gap, Inc., 2004—. Lectr. and workshops on a variety of topics RI Sch. Design, Phila. Coll. Art, Fashion Inst. Tech., Cooper-Hewitt Mus. and the Montreal Visual Arts Ctr. Artist, metal work in jewelry (permanent collections) Smithsonian Inst., Victoria and Albert Mus. London, Cooper-Hewitt Mus. NY; contbr. chapters to books. Named one of 25 Masters of Innovation, BusinessWeek; recipient Women in Design award, Diamond Internat. award; Nat. Endowment for the Arts grant. Office: Gap Inc Old Navy Divsn 2 Folsom St San Francisco CA 94105*

**ROSS, JAMES OWEN,** education educator, researcher; b. Morganton, NC, Sept. 27, 1948; s. Owen and Vivian Chapman Ross; life ptnr. Charles Anthony Staley; 1 child, Juliana Adele. BFA, U. of NC at Greensboro, Greensboro, North Carolina, 1971; AM, Brown U., 1986, PhD, 2003. Prof. Ringling Sch. of Art and Design, Sarasota, Fla., 1974—75, Ctrl. Piedmont C.C., Charlotte, ND, 1976—80, Appalachian State U., Boone, NC, 1983—84, RISD, Providence, 1985—86, U. of Okla., 1987—88, Wentworth Inst. of Tech., Boston, 1990—91; tchg. fellow Brown U., 1990—92; prof. ND State U., 1991—92, Western Carolina U., 1992, U. of Memphis, 1995—96, East Tenn. State U., 1997—98. Building, Preliminary Design Windsor Locks Rapids Exhbn. Ctr. (Interior Design Educators Coun. Internat. Exhbn., Nashville, Tenn., 1995), building interior, Hynes Residence Libr. (Interior Design Educators Coun. Internat. Exhibit, Denver, Colo., 1996). Dem. nominee in NC state senate, 27th dist. NC Dem. Party, NC, 1996; vestry mem. St. Peter's Episcopal Ch., Charlotte, NC, 1981—82; represented bus. in hist. dist. Friends of Fourth Ward Hist. Dist., Charlotte, NC, 1979—82. Tchg. fellow, Brown U., 1990—91. Mem.: Internat. Interior Design Assn. (Presdl. Commendation 1999), AIA (assoc.), Soc. of Archtl. Historians (life). Democrat-Npl. Soc. Of Friends. Achievements include research in impact of nineteenth-century public health movement upon American architecture: Theories of Disease, Ventilation, and Sunlight, 1840-1944. Avocations: travel, back packing, swimming, gardening, cooking. Home: 132 Malbon's Mills Rd Skowhegan ME 04976 Personal E-mail: james.ross.g86@alumni.brown.edu.

**ROSS, JEAN M.,** think-tank executive; Grad., U. Calif., Santa Cruz; M in City and Regional Planning, U. Calif., Berkeley. Asst. rsch. dir. Svc. Employees Internat. Union, Washington; sr. cons. Assembly Human Svcs.; prin. cons. Assembly Revenue and Taxation Com.; exec. dir. Calif. Budget Project, Sacramento, 1994—. Mem. exec. com. Calif. Governance Consensus Project; bd. mem. Inst. on Taxation and Econ. Policy, Washington; mem. adv. com. Calif. Franchise Tax Bd.; spkr. in field. Contbr. articles to profl. jours. Sr. fellow, UCLA Sch. Pub. Policy and Social Rsch., 2000—01. Office: California Budget Project 1107 9th St Ste 310 Sacramento CA 95814-3608

**ROSS, JEANNE NMI,** psychologist; b. Chgo., Jan. 10, 1923; d. Joseph Pacwa and (Prendota) Tillie; m. Milton Jaeger (dec.); m. Gunther Rothenberg (dec.). BA with hons., U. Ill., 1952, MA, 1954; EdD, U. N.Mex., 1969. Lic. adminstr. Calif., 1977, Ariz., 1977, cert. sch. psychologist Calif., 1977. Tchr. Alamogordo (N.Mex.) Pub. Schs., 1954—55, Rantoul Pub. Schs., Ill., 1954—59; instr. So. Ill. U., Carbondale, Ill., 1960—63; clin. dir. N.Mex. Girl's Sch., Albuquerque, 1968—69; sch. counselor Albuquerque (N.Mex.) Pub. Schs., 1969—71; dir. project, head title III Am. Indian program Sacaton (Ariz.) Sch. Dist., 1972—73; sch. psychologist Vista (Calif.) Unified Sch. Dist., 1977—87, ret., 1987. Contbr. articles to profl. jours. Pvt. women's corps. U.S. Army, 1944—45. Recipient Chi Omega award, U. Ill., 1952, award, AAUW, 1967. Mem.: Calif. Ret. Tchrs. Assn., Phi Kappa Phi (scholarship 1952), Alpha Lambda Delta (scholarship 1950). Independent. Avocations: photography, painting, travel, theater, opera, music.

**ROSS, JEFF,** communications executive; b. Bronx, NY, May 13, 1950; s. Barbara Ross; m. Shareen Goon, May 26, 2001. BS in Biology, SUNY, Geneseo, NY, 1968—73. With William Morris Agy., Beverly Hills, Calif., 1980—82; personal mgr. Jeff Ross Entertainment, Inc., Sherman Oaks, Calif., 1982—. Blue ribbon emmy panel Acad. TV Arts & Sci., N. Hollywood, Calif., 1982—2001. Fundraiser Dem. Nat. Com., LA, 1994—98; bd. mem. Nat. Conf. Personal Mgrs., LA, 1984—86. Mem.: Baron Oaks Homeowners Assn. (pres. HOA 2002—05), Nat. Assn. Photoshop Profls., Ho. Blues Found., TV Acad. Arts & Scis., Sherman Oaks Homeowners Assn., UCLA Alumni Assn. Democrat-Npl. Avocations: photography, astronomy, sports. Home and Office: Jeff Ross Entertainment Inc 14560 Benefit St #206 Sherman Oaks CA 91403 Office Fax: 818-332-4023. Business E-Mail: jeff@jeffrossentertainment.com.

**ROSS, JEFFREY ALAN,** social studies educator; b. Sleepyfye, Minn., Dec. 18, 1968; s. Daniel Ross and Joan Schillar-Ross; children: Kassondra Ethan BS, U. Minn., Mankato, 1992. Tchr. social studies Sauk Ctr. Pub. Schs., Minn., 1992—. Coach football/basketball, 1992—. Sunday sch. tchr. Mem.: Sauk Ctr. Edn. Assn. (pres. 2001—02, 2006—). Lutheran. Avocations: sports, reading, travel, movies. Home: 936 Lilac Dr Sauk Centre MN 56378 Personal E-mail: jeffrbowe@hotmail.com.

**ROSS, JEFFREY C.,** mathematics educator, department chairman; BS in Math., Lynchburg Coll., Va., 1973—77. Math dept. chair Va. Episcopal Sch., Lynchburg, 1982—. Recipient Fulton Master Tchr. award, Va. Episcopal Sch., 1986, Smith Family award, 2002. Mem.: NCTM. R-Consevative. Methodist. Avocations: fishing, boating, camping, coaching. Office: Virginia Episcopal Sch 400 VES Rd Lynchburg VA 24503 Personal E-mail: brtrout549@hotmail.com. Business E-Mail: jross@ves.org.

**ROSS, JEFFREY S.,** lawyer; b. NYC, Mar. 7, 1951; AB with highest honors, U. Mich., 1972; JD, Stanford U., 1975. Bar: Calif. 1975, US Dist. Ct. (no. Calif. dist.), US Ct. Appeals (9th cir.), US Supreme Ct. Atty., pres. Friedman Ross & Hersh PC; ptnr. Pillsbury Winthrop Shaw Pittman, San Francisco. Mem.: San Francisco Barrister Club (bd. dirs. 1981—83, pres. 1983), Nat. Assn. Bar Presidents, San Francisco (bd. dirs. 1986—88, pres. 1997, Award of Merit 1990, 1998), Phi Beta Kappa, Phi Eta Sigma. Office: Pillsbury Winthrop Shaw Pittman 50 Fremont St San Francisco CA 94105 Office Phone: 415-983-1730. Office Fax: 415-983-1200. Business E-Mail: jeff.ross@pillsburylaw.com.

**ROSS, JERRY L.,** astronaut; b. Crown Point, Ind., Jan. 20, 1948; s. Donald J. and Phyllis E. Ross; m. Karen S. Pearson; 2 children. BS in Mech. Engring., Purdue U., West Lafayette, Ind., 1970; MS in Mech. Engring., Purdue U.; Grad. Test Flight Engr., USAF Test Pilot Sch., 1976; Dsc (hon.), Purdue U. Commd. 2d lt. USAF, 1970, ret., 2000; rschr. ramjet engring divsn. Air Force Aeropropulsion Lan, Wright-Patterson AFB, Ohio, 1972—74; lab. exec. officer, chief mgmt. ops. office Wright Patterson AFB Labs., Dayton, Ohio, 1974—75; flight test engr., supr. crew member. 6510th; Flight Test Engring. USAF, Edwards AFB, Calif., 1976—79; payload officer, flight controller Lyndon Johnson Space Center, Houston, 1979—80, chief vehicle integration test office; astronaut NASA, Houston, 1980—; chief astronaut NASA

Engring. and Safety Ctr. Named a Disting. Grad. of the USAF Test Pilot Sch.; recipient 13 NASA medals, Victor A. Prather award, Am. Astron. Soc., 1985, 1990, 1999, Defense Superior Svc. Medal with one Oak Leaf, Air Force Legion of Merit, Defense Meritorious Svc. Medal with 3 Oak leaf Clusters, Air Force Meritious Svc. Medal with one Oak Leaf, Outstanding Flight Test Eng. Award Class 75B. Mem.: Internat. Acad. Astronautics (corr.), Purdue Alumni Assn. (life), Assn. of Space Explorers (life). Achievements include seven space flights; over 1133 hours in space, including 58 hours, 18 minutes on nine space wks. Avocations: genealogy, stained glass, racquetball, woodworking, photography. Office: Astronaut Ctr NASA Johnson Space Ctr Houston TX 77058

**ROSS, JIMMY DOUGLAS,** retired military officer; b. Hosston, La., May 23, 1936; s. Horace Eugene and Lucile Marie (Pontious) R.; m. Patricia L. Cox., Dec. 18, 1955; children: Sabra, DiAnna, Tony. BS, Henderson State U., 1958; MA in Bus. Mgmt., Central Mich. U., 1975. Commd. 2d lt. U.S. Army, 1958, advanced through grades to 4 Star Gen., 1994, served comdr. co., bn., brigade levels, comdg. gen. 2d Support Command (Corps) VII Corps Nellingen, Germany, 1980-82; dir. transp., energy and troop support Office Dep. Chief of Staff for Logistics, U.S. Army, Washington, 1982-84; chief staff U.S. Army Materiel Command, Alexandria, Va., 1984-86; comdr. U.S. Army Depot System Command, Chambersburg, Pa., 1986-87; dep. chief of staff for logistics U.S. Army, Washington, 1987-92; commdg. gen. U.S. Army Materiel Command, Alexandria, Va., 1992-94; retired, 1994. Bd. dirs. VSE Engring. Co., Stanley Assoc., Inc., Armed Forces Svcs. Corp., Integrated Data Corp., Am. Ecology Corp.; chmn. Def. Industry Conf. Bd.; pres. bd. dirs. Indsl. Coll. of Armed Forces Assn.; pres., COO Cypress Internat., 2000-03; sr. logistics officer Cypress Internat., Inc., 2004. Dist. commr. Alpine dist. Boy Scouts Am., 1980-82; v.p., COO Biomed. Svcs., ARC Nat. Hdqrs., 1994-99; chmn. Army Sci. Bd.; pres. Buffalo Soldiers Meml. Fund Found., 2001; bd. dirs. Buffalo Soldiers Found., 2001. Decorated D.S.M. with oak leaf cluster, Legion of Merit, Bronze Star, Air medal. Fellow Assn. U.S. Army (sr.); mem. Am. Def. Indsl. Assn., Nat. Def. Transp. Assn., Armed Forces Benefit Assn. (bd. dirs.). Methodist. Home: 4981 Maple Glen Pl Lake Forest FL 32771 Office Phone: 703-549-5880. E-mail: jross27@cfl.rr.com.

**ROSS, JO ANN,** media buyer; b. Bklyn., June 8, 1953; d. James Patrick and Rita Marie (McDonnell) R.; m. Michael Edward Zelman, Nov. 3, 1984. BA in Govt. and Pub. Adminstrn., Am. U., Washington, 1975. Negotiator Boxell & Jacobs, NYC, 1980-84; supr. Young & Rubicam, NYC, 1984; sr. negotiator Bozell, Jacobs, Kenyon & Eckhardt, NYC, 1984-85, v.p., 1985-88; sr. v.p. Bozell, Inc., NYC, 1988-89; account exec. ABC TV Network, NYC, 1989; v.p. Olympic sales CBS, 1992—2002, pres. network sales, 2002—. Named one of Most Powerful Women in Entertainment, Hollywood Reporter, 2005; recipient Woman of Yr. award, Women in Sports and Events, 2005. Mem. Am. Assn. Advt. Agencies (broadcast and program com. 1988—). Avocations: ballet, exercise. Office: CBS 51 West 52nd St New York NY 10019*

**ROSS, JOHN,** physical chemist, educator; b. Vienna, Oct. 2, 1926; arrived in U.S., 1940; s. Mark and Anna (Krcmar) Ross; m. Virginia Franklin (div.); children: Elizabeth A., Robert K.; m. Eva Madarasz. BS, Queens Coll., 1948; PhD, MIT, 1951; D (hon.), Weizmann Inst. Sci., Rehovot, Israel, 1984, Queens Coll., SUNY, 1987, U. Bordeaux, France, 1987. Prof. chemistry Brown U., Providence, 1953—66, MIT, Cambridge, 1966—80, chmn. dept., 1966—71, chmn. faculty of Inst., 1975—77; prof. Stanford (Calif.) U., 1980—2001, chmn. dept., 1983—89, prof. emeritus, 2001—. Cons. to industries; mem. emeritus bd. govs. Weizmann Inst., 1971—. Author: Physical Chemistry, 1980, Physical Chemistry, 2d edit., 2000; editor: Molecular Beams, 1966; contbr. articles to profl. jours. 2nd lt. U.S. Army, 1944—46. Recipient medal, Coll. de France, Paris, Presdl. Nat. Medal of Sci., 1999, Austrian Cross of Honor for Sci. and Art, 1st class, 2002. Fellow: AAAS, Am. Phys. Soc.; mem.: NAS, Am. Chem. Soc. (Irving Langmuir Chem. Physics prize 1992, Peter Debye award in phys. chemistry 2001, Theodore William Richards medal 2004), Am. Acad. Arts and Sci. Home: 738 Mayfield Ave Stanford CA 94305-1044 Office: Stanford U Dept Chemistry Stanford CA 94305-5080 Office Phone: 650-723-9203. Business E-Mail: john.ross@stanford.edu.

**ROSS, JOHN, JR.,** cardiologist, educator; b. NYC, Dec. 1, 1928; s. John and Janet (Moulder) R.; children: Sydnie, John, Duncan; m. Lola Romanucci, Aug. 26, 1972; children: Adan, Deborah Lee. AB, Dartmouth Coll., 1951; MD, Cornell U., 1955. Intern Johns Hopkins Hosp., 1955—56; resident Columbia-Presbyn. Med. Center, NYC, 1960—61, NY. Hosp.-Cornell U. Med. center, 1961—62; chief sect. cardiovascular diagnosis cardiology br. Nat. Heart Inst., Bethesda, Md., 1962—68; prof. medicine U. Calif., San Diego, 1968—2000, also dir. cardiovascular div., 1968—91, rsch. prof. medicine, 2000—, disting. prof. medicine, 2003—; prof. cardiovascular research Am. Heart Assn. Western States Affiliate, 1984—99. Mem. cardiology adv. com. Nat. Heart, Lung and Blood Inst., 1975-78, task force on arteriosclerosis, 1978-80, adv. council, 1980-84; bd. dirs. San Diego Heart Assn.; vis. prof. Brit. Heart Assn., 1990. Author: Mechanisms of Contraction of the Normal and Failing Heart, 1968, 76, Understanding the Heart and Its Diseases, 1976; mem. editorial bd. Circulation, 1967-75, 80-88, editor in chief 1988-93, Circulation Research, 1971-75, Am. Jour. Physiology, 1968-73, Annals of Internal Medicine, 1974-78, Am. Jour. Cardiology, 1974-79, 83-88, Jour. Clin. Investigation, 1992-97, Italian Heart Jour., 1998-99, Jour. Cardiac Failure, 2000-05, Circulation Jour. Japan, 2000—; cons. editor Circulation, 1993-03; contbr. chpts. to books, sci. articles to profl. jours. Served as surgeon USPHS, 1956—63. Decorated grande ufficiale Order of Merit of Republic of Italy, 1998; recipient Ing. Enzo Ferrari prize for Enzo Ferrari, Modena, Italy, 1989, James B. Herrick award Coun. Clin. Cardiology Am. Heart Assn., 1990, Academic Mentorship award Am. Heart Assn., 2004. Master Am. Coll. Cardiology (v.p. trustee, pres. 1986-87, Disting. Scientist award 1990); fellow ACPM; mem. Am. Soc. Clin. Investigation (councillor), Am. Physiol. Soc., Assn. Am. Physicians, Cardiac Muscle Soc., Assn. Univ. Cardiologists, Assn. West. Physicians (councillor), Japanese Circulation Soc. (hon.). Home: 8599 Prestwick Dr La Jolla CA 92037 Office: U Calif Dept Med M # 0613B San Diego CA 92093

**ROSS, JOHN EMERSON,** public relations executive, writer; b. Mariemont, Ohio, Aug. 4, 1946; s. Simon Neely Ross and Margaret Forshoe; m. Katie Anders, May 11, 1969. Reporter Press-Chronicle, Johnson City, Tenn. 1969—70; dir. intermadin socsc er Tusculum Coll., Greeneville, Tenn. 1970—72; dir. pub. info. Plymouth (N.H.) State Coll., 1972—76, Dickinson Coll., Carlisle, Pa., 1983—86; dir. media rels. U. Miami, Coral Gables, Fla., 1983—86; dir. pub. rels. U. Cin., 1986—87; v.p. Halstead Comms., N.Y., 1987—93, sr. cons., 1993—2002; prin. RossWriters, Upperville, Va., 2003—. Bd. dirs. PASA, Washington. Co-author: North America's Greatest Fishing Lodges, 1997, rev. edit., 2000, North America's Greatest Big Game Lodges & Outfitters, 1999; author: Trout Unlimited Guide to America's 100 Best Trout Streams, 1999, rev. edit., 2005, Great Water Great Fish - The Worldwide Guide to Flyfishing, 1999, North America's Greatest Bird Hunting Lodges & Preserves, 2000, Public Relations & the Presidency: Strategies and Tactics for Effective Communications, 2001; co-editor: The Quotable Graduate, 2003; editor: Sports Afield, 1997, Sporting Classics, 1999; contbr. chapters to books, articles to profl. jours. Mem.: Ducks Unlimited, Trout Unlimited, Izarks Walder Hearsue Am. Home: PO Box 521 Upperville VA 20185

**ROSS, JOHN T.,** artist, educator; b. N.Y.C., Sept. 25, 1921; s. Ferdinand Joseph and Mary Agnes (Higgins) R.; m. Clare Romano; children: Christopher, Timothy. Student, Cooper Union Art Sch., 1939-48, BFA, 1975. Art dir. Pageant Mag., N.Y.C., 1946-48; mem. faculty New Sch. for Social Rsch., N.Y.C., 1957—; prof., chmn. dept. art Manhattanville Coll., Purchase, NY, 1964-86. Adj. prof. Yale U., New Haven, 1982; adj. faculty Columbia U., N.Y.C., 1983-85; art dir. Aquarius Press, N.Y.C., 1968-72; chmn. bd. Ctr. for Book Arts, N.Y.C., 1995-99; bd. dirs. Art Ctr. No. N.J., Englewood, 1966-67; fgn. svc. staff officer USIA, Romania and Yugoslavia, 1964. Writer-illustrator: (with Clare Romano) Complete Printmaker, 1972 (rev. 90), John Ross and Clare Romano: The Artists and the Book, 2001; exhibited works in

70 one-man shows at various galleries, 1950—; pub. artists books, 1971—; printmaker, artist-designer, 1950—; dir. High Tide Press, N.Y.C., 1991—. Chmn. adv. panel Cooper Union Art Sch., N.Y.C., 1967-69. Sgt. U.S. Army, 1943-46, Italy. Recipient Citation for profl. achievement Cooper Union Art Sch., 1966, Benjamin Clinedinst medal Artists Fellowship, 1992, others; Tiffany Found. grantee, 1954, McDowell Colony fellow, 1978, 82, 87. Mem. NAD, Century Assn. N.Y.C., Soc. Am. Graphic Artists (pres.), Ctr. for Book Arts N.Y.C., Typophiles N.Y.C., Grolier Club. Avocation: swimming. Mailing: PO Box 1122 New York NY 10159-1122 Office Phone: 212-533-5109. Personal E-mail: rossromano@aol.com.

**ROSS, JOSEPH COMER,** pulmonologist, educator, academic administrator; b. Tompkinsville, Ky., June 16, 1927; s. Joseph M. and Annie (Pinckley) R.; m. Isabelle Nevins, June 15, 1952; children: Laura Ann, Sharon Lynn, Jennifer Jo, Mary Martha, Jefferson Arthur. BS, U. Ky., 1950; MD, Vanderbilt U., 1954. Diplomate Am. Bd. Internal Medicine (bd. govs. 1975-81), with added qualifications in pulmonary disease. Intern Vanderbilt U. Hosp., Nashville, 1954-55; resident Duke U. Hosp., Durham, NC, 1955-57, rsch. fellow, 1957-58; from instr. medicine to prof. Ind. U. Sch. Medicine, Indpls., 1958-70; prof., chmn. dept. medicine Med. U. of S.C., Charleston, 1970-80; vis. prof. Vanderbilt U. Sch. Medicine, Nashville, 1979-80, prof. medicine 1981-99, prof. medicine emeritus, 1999—, assoc. vice chancellor for health affairs, 1982-99, assoc. vice chancellor for health affairs emeritus, 1999—. Mem. cardiovascular study sect. NIH, 1966-70, program project com., 1971-75; mem. adv. coun. Nat. Heart, Lung and Blood Inst., 1982-86; mem. ad hoc coms. NAS, 1966, 67; mem. Pres.'s Nat. Adv. Panel on Heart Disease, 1972; mem. merit rev. bd. in respiration VA Rsch. Svc., 1972-76, chmn., 1974-76. Mem. editorial bd. Jour. Lab. and Clin. Medicine, 1964-70, Chest, 1968-73, Jour. Applied Physiology,1968-73, Archives of Internal Medicine, 1976-82, Heart and Lung, 1977-86; contbr. articles to profl. jours. Bd. dirs. Nashville Ronald McDonald Ho., past pres.; bd. dirs. Agape, Leadership Nashville, v.p.; mem. adv. com. Davidson County Cmty. Health Agy.; active Tenn. Lung Assn.; elder Ch. of Christ. With U.S. Army, 1945—47. Fellow: ACP, Am. Coll. Cardiology, Am. Coll. Chest Physicians (gov. S.C. 1970–76, chmn. sci. program com. 1973, vice chmn. bd. govs. 1974—75, exec. coun. 1974—80, chmn. bd. govs. 1975—76, pres.-elect 1976—77, pres. 1977—78, chmn. by-laws com. 2002—04, bd. regents 2002—04); mem.: AMA (sect. on med. schs.), Am. Soc. Internal Medicine, So. Soc. Clin. Rsch., Am. Thoracic Soc. (nat. councillor 1972—76), S.C. Med. Soc., Ctr. Social Clin. Rsch., Assn. Profs. Medicine, Assn. Am. Physicians, Am. Soc. Clin. Investigartion, Am. Physiol. Soc., Am. Fedn. Clin. Rsch. (chmn. Midwest sect.), S.C. Lung Assn. (v.p. 1974—75), Phi Beta Kappa, Alpha Omega Alpha. Office: Vanderbilt U Med Ctr Oxford House Ste 212 Nashville TN 37232-0001 Personal E-mail: joseph.ross@comcast.net. Business E-mail: joseph.ross@vanderbiltmcmail.edu.

**ROSS, JUNE ROSA PITT,** biologist, educator; b. Taree, NSW, Australia, May 2, 1931; came to U.S., 1957; d. Bernard and Adeline Phillips; m. Charles Alexander, June 27, 1959. BSc with honors, U. Sydney, New S. Wales, Australia, 1953, PhD, 1959, DSc, 1974. Rsch. assoc. Yale U., New Haven, 1959—60, U. Ill., Urbana, 1960—65, Western Wash. U., Bellingham, 1965—67, assoc. prof., 1967—70, prof. biology, 1970—2003, prof. emeritus, 2004—, chair dept. biology, 1989—90. Pres. Western Wash. U. Faculty Senate, Bellingham, 1984-85; conf. host Internat. Bryozoology Assn., 1986. Author (with others): A Textbook of Entomology, 1982, Geology of Coal, 1984; editor (assoc.): Palaios, 1985—89; contbr. 150 articles to profl. jours. Recipient J. Wolfensohn Award of Excellence Sydney U. Grad. Union of N.Am., 1995, P. and R. Olscamp Outstanding Rsch. award Western Wash. U., 1986; NSF grantee. Mem.: Internat. Bryozoology Assn. (pres. 1992—95), The Paleontol. Soc. (councillor 1984—86, treas. 1987—93), Australian Marine Scis. Assn., U.K. Marine Biol. Assn. (life). Avocations: hiking, classical music. Office: Western Wash U Dept Biology Bellingham WA 98225-9160 Office Phone: 360-650-3634. E-mail: ross@fire.biol.wwu.edu.

**ROSS, KATHLEEN ANNE,** academic administrator; b. Palo Alto, Calif., July 1, 1941; d. William Andrew and Mary Alberta (Wilburn) Ross. BA, Ft. Wright Coll., 1964; MA, Georgetown U., 1971; PhD, Claremont Grad. U., 1979; LLD (hon.), Alverno Coll. Milw., 1990, Dartmouth Coll., 1991, Seattle U., 1992; LHD (hon.), Whitworth Coll., 1992; LLD (hon.), Pomona Coll., 1993; LHD (hon.), Coll. of New Rochelle, 1998; LLD (hon.), U. Notre Dame, 1999, Gonzaga U., 1999; LHD (hon.), Carroll Coll., 2003, Pacific Luth. U., 2004. Cert. tchr. Wash. Secondary tchr. Holy Names Acad., Spokane, Wash., 1964-70; dir. rsch. and planning Province Holy Names, Wash. State, 1972-73; v.p. acads. Ft. Wright Coll., Spokane, 1973-81; rsch. asst. to dean Claremont Grad. Sch., Calif., 1977-78; assoc. faculty mem. Harvard U., Cambridge, Mass., 1981; pres. Heritage U., Toppenish, Wash., 1981—. Cons. Wash. State Holy Names Schs., 1971-73; coll. accrediting assn. evaluator N.W. Assn. Schs. and Colls., Seattle, 1975—; dir. Holy Names Coll., Oakland, Calif., 1979—; cons. Yakama Indian Nation, Toppenish, 1975—; speaker, cons. in field. Author: (with others) Multicultural Pre-School Curriculum, 1977, A Crucial Agenda: Improving Minority Student Success, 1989; Cultural Factors in Success of American Indian Students in Higher Education, 1978. Chmn. Internat. 5-Yr. Convocation of Sisters of Holy Names, Montreal, 1981, 96; TV Talk show host Spokane Coun. of Chs., 1974-76; mem. Nat. Congl. Adv. Com. on Student Fin. Assistance, 2002-06. Named Yakima Herald Rep. Person of Yr., 1987, MacArthur fellow, 1997; recipient E.K. and Lillian F. Bishop Founds. Youth Leader of Yr. award, 1986, Disting. Citizenship Alumna award, Claremont Grad. Sch., 1986, Golden Aztec award, Wash. Human Devel., 1989, Harold W. McGraw Edn. prize, 1989, John Carroll awrd, Georgetown U., 1991, Holy Names medal, Ft. Wright Coll., 1981, Pres.'s medal, Estern Wash. U., 1994, First Ann. Leadership award, Region VIII Coun. Advancement and Support Edn., 1993, Wash. State Medal of Merit, 1995, Lifetime Achievement award, Yakima YWCA, 2001, numerous grants for projects in multicultural higher edn., 1974—. Mem. Nat. Assn. Ind. Colls. and Univs., Soc. Intercultural Edn., Tng. and Rsch., Sisters of Holy Names of Jesus and Mary-SNJM. Roman Catholic. Office: Heritage U Office of Pres 3240 Fort Rd Toppenish WA 98948-9562 Office Phone: 509-865-8600.

**ROSS, KEVIN MCANDREW,** academic administrator; m. Kristen Carr Ross; children: Ainsley, Graham. AB, Colgate U., 1994; MA in Liberal Arts, St. John's Coll., 1997; PhD in Higher Edn. Leadership and Policy, Vanderbilt U. Admissions officer, assoc. dir. admissions The Hill Sch., Pottstown, Pa., Avon Old Farms Sch., Conn.; asst. to pres. Wilmington Coll., Del.; assoc. dean Eugene M. and Christine E. Lynn Coll. Internat. Comm. Lynn U., Boca Raton, Fla., 1999, COO, 2004—06, pres., 2006—. Bd. dirs. Palm Beach Literacy Coalition. Office: Lynn U Office of Pres 3601 N Military Trail Boca Raton FL 33431 E-mail: kross@lynn.edu.*

**ROSS, LAINIE FRIEDMAN,** pediatrician; b. Manhasset, N.Y., May 1961; AB, Princeton U., Princeton, N.J., 1982; MD, U. Pa. Sch. of Medicine, Phila. Pa., 1986; PhD, Yale U., New Haven, Conn., 1996. Cert. Bd. Am. Bd. of Pediat., NC, 2002. Assoc. dir. Maclean Ctr. Clin. Med. Ethics U. Chgo., 1994—; prof. dept. pediat. medicine, history and philosophy social sci. and medicine U. Chgo., Chgo., 2000—. Author: Children, Families and Health Care Decision Making, 1998, Children in Medical Research, 2006. Fellow: Am. Acad. Pediat. (bioethics sect. exec. com. 1999—2005, mem. com. on bioethics 2004—). Office: Univ Chgo 5841 S Maryland Ave MC 6082 Chicago IL 60637 Office Phone: 773-702-0660. Office Fax: 773-834-5964. Business E-mail: lross@uchicago.edu.

**ROSS, LARRY,** sociologist, anthropologist, educator; s. Jonathan and Thelma Ross. BA, Case Western Res. U., Cleve., 1993; MA, PhD, U. of Missouri, 1999. Evaluation coord.; adj. rscht. grad. instr. U. of Mo., Columbia, 1993—2000; asst. prof. Anthropology U. of Nebr., Omaha, 2000—; assoc. prof. sociology and anthropology Lincoln U., Jefferson City, Nebr., 2004—. Rsch. assoc. The Cleve. Mus. of Natural History, 2001—03. Author: (book) African American Jazz Musicians in the Diaspora, 2003. Group study exch. amb. Rotary Internat., Cleve. Heights, Ohio, 1988—89. Recipient Award for Piano Performance, Internat. Assn. of Jazz Educators,

1990; The Chancellor's G. T. Ridgel Fellowship, U. of Missouri, 1996—99. Mem.: Am. Anthrop. Assn., Delta Kappa Epsilon Internat. Frat. (life; v.p. 1992—93). Office: Lincoln U 820 Chestnut St Omaha NE 65101

**ROSS, LEONARD LESTER,** anatomist, educator; b. NYC, Sept. 11, 1927; s. Aaron Theodore and Shirley (Smolen) R.; m. Marcella Gamel, June 23, 1951 (dec. Aug. 1995); children: Jane, Jill; m. Frances Robb, Nov. 12, 1998; 1 child, Jennifer. AB, NYU, 1946, PhD, 1954. Asst. prof. U. Ala. Med. Coll., 1954-57; assoc. prof. Cornell U. Med. Coll., 1957-69, prof., 1969-73; vis. prof. Cambridge U., 1967-68; prof., chmn. dept. anatomy Med. Coll. Pa., Phila., 1973-89, exec. v.p., Annenberg dean, 1989-93, pres. and Annenberg dean, 1993-94, provost and Annenberg dean Phila., 1993-96; provost Allegheny U., Phila., 1996-98. Exec. v.p. Allegheny Health, Edn. and Rsch. Found. Assoc. editor: Anat. Record, 1976. Served with M.C., U.S. Army, 1946-47. Recipient Lindback award for teaching, 1976; NIH sr. research fellow, 1967-68 Mem. Am. Assn. Anatomists (exec. com. 1984-88), Soc. Neurosci., Soc. Cell Biology, N.Y. Soc. Electron Microscopists (pres. 1975-76), Assn. Anatomy Chairmen (pres. 1983-84), AAUP (nat. council 1974-77), Sigma Xi. E-mail: rossll63@netscape.net.

**ROSS, LESA MOORE,** quality assurance professional; b. New Orleans, Jan. 25, 1959; d. William Frank and Carolyn West Moore; m. Mark Neal Ross, Nov. 30, 1985; children: Sarah Ann, Jacquelyne Caroline. BS in Engring., U. N.C., Charlotte, 1981; MBA in Quality and Reliability Mgmt., U. North Tex., 1991; MS in Reliability Engring., U. Md., 2004. Seismic qualification engr. Duke Power Co., Charlotte, N.C., 1981-82; quality assurance engr. Tex. Instruments Inc., Lewisville, Tex., 1982-91; compliance mgr. Am. Med. Electronics, Inc., 1992-93; owner Ross Quality Cons., 1993-95; customer quality assurance sect. mgr. Hitachi Semiconductor (Am.) Inc., 1995-96; v.p. quality Ross Networking Cons. Inc., Flower Mound, Tex., 1996—. Bd. dirs. Greater Lewisville YMCA, 2000—03. Recipient Nat. Sci. Found. Rsch. Grant, U. N.C., Charlotte, 1980. Mem. Am. Soc. Quality Control (cert. quality engr., quality auditor, reliability engr., cert. quality technician, cert. quality mgr., sec. Dallas sect. 1994-95, chair-elect Dallas sect. 1995-96, chair 1996-97), Zeta Tau Alpha (pres. 1984-85). Avocations: crafts, cross-stitching, reading, travel. Home and Office: 4925 Wolf Creek Trl Flower Mound TX 75028-1955 E-mail: Lross@rnc-inc.com.

**ROSS, MADELYN ANN,** academic administrator, newspaper editor; b. Pitts., June 26, 1949; d. Mario Charles and Rose Marie (Mangieri) R. BA, Indiana U. of Pa., 1971; MA, SUNY-Albany, 1972. Reporter Pitts. Press, 1972-78, asst. city editor, 1978-82, spl. assignment editor, 1982-83, mng. editor, 1983-93, Pitts. Post-Gazette, 1993—2005; assoc. vice chancellor U. Pitts., 2005—. Bd. dirs. PG Pub. Co.; instr. Community Coll. Allegheny County, 1974-81; Pulitzer Prize juror, 1989, 90. Mem. Task Force Leadership Pitts., 1985-92; v.p. Old Newsboys Charity Fund; bd. dirs. Dapper Dan Charity. Mem. Am. Soc. Newspaper Editors, Press Club of Western Pa. (pres.), Internat. Women's Forum. Democrat. Roman Catholic. Avocations: tennis, piano, organ. Office: U Pitts 424 Craig Hall Craig St Pittsburgh PA 15260

**ROSS, MALCOLM,** minerals consultant; b. Washington, Aug. 22, 1929; s. Clarence Samuel and Helen Hall (Frederick) R.; m. Daphne Dee Virginia Riska, Sept. 1, 1956; children: Christopher A., Alexander MacC. BS in Zoology, Utah State U., 1951; MS in Chemistry, U. Md., 1959; PhD in Geology, Harvard U., 1962. Rsch. mineralogist U.S. Geol. Survey, Washington, 1954-5, 61-74, Reston, Va., 1974-95, scientist emeritus, 1996—; minerals and health cons., 1999—. Prin. investigator lunar sci. program NASA, 1969—74. Author: Asbestos and Other Fibrous Minerals, 1988; contbr. over 100 articles to profl. jours. First lt. U.S. Army, 1952—54. Recipient Disting. Svc. award, U.S. Dept. Interior, 1986; grantee Fulbright Commn., Cyprus, 2000. Fellow Mineral. Soc. Am., Geol. Soc. Am., AAAS; mem. Am. Geophys. Union, Clay Minerals Soc., Can. Mineral Assn., Mineral Soc. Am. (bd. dirs. treas. 1976-80, v.p. 1990, pres. 1991, Pub. Svc. award, 1990). Republican. Congregationalist. Achievements include research in on asbestos and asbestos-related disease. Avocations: long distance bicycling, photography. Home: 1608 44th St NW Washington DC 20007-2025 Office Phone: 202-338-6572. E-mail: mrdrr@earthlink.net.

**ROSS, MARILYN J.,** language educator, communications educator; BA in Am. Studies, U. Miami, Fla., 1969, MA in Am. Studies, 1971, PhD in Higher Edn. Leadership, 1995. Asst. prof. English Fla. Meml. Coll., 1971-84, assoc. prof. English and mass comm. arts, 1985-94, prof. higher edn., 1995—. Founder mass comm. arts program Fla. Meml. Coll., 1980, coord. modern langs., 1999—; presenter Round Table Oxford U., Eng., 2005, others. Author: Success Factors of Young African American Males at a Historically Black College, 1998, Success Factors of Young African American Women at a Historically Black College, 2002; prodr. over 100 hrs. African Am., Caribbean and Hispanic programming, WLRN-TV. Recipient Outstanding Svc. award Vets. Club, 1979, Outstanding and Dedicated Svc. in Behalf of FMC award Miami Cable Access Corp., 1987, award Fla. Meml. Coll./Black Archives History and Rsch. Found. of South Fla., Inc., 1999. Mem. MLA, AAUW, Assn. Ednl. Leadership, Nat. Coun. Tchrs. English, Nat. Assn. African Am. Studies, Am. Studies Aassn., Epsilon Tau Lambda, Kappa Delta Pi, Phi Lambda Pi, Delta Theta Mu, Phi Kappa Phi, Phi Alpha Theta. Address: Unit F-602 1121 Crandon Blvd Apt F602 Key Biscayne FL 33149-2781 E-mail: ross1848@bellsouth.net.

**ROSS, MARION,** actress; b. Albert Lea, Minn. children: Jim, Ellen. Grad., San Diego State U. Performed with Globe Theatre, San Diego, LaJolla Summer Theatre; Broadway debut in Edwin Booth; starred in touring prodns. of Never Too Late, Barefoot in the Park, The Glass Menagerie, Long Days Journey Into Night, Love Letter, Steel Magnolias, Over The River and Through The Woods, Barefoot in the Park, film debut in Forever Female, 1953; on woman show A Lovely Light, 1988—; TV series include Life with Father, 1953-55, Paradise Bay, 1965-66, Happy Days, 1974-84, Love Boat, 1985-86 (2 Emmy nominations), Bklyn. Bridge, 1991-93 (Emmy nomination for lead actress in a comedy 1992, 93), Hidden in Silence, 1995, Evening Star, 1996, The Great War, 1996, The Third Twin, 1997, About Search, 1998, The Lake, 1998, Drew Carey Show, 1998, That 70's Show, 1998, Touched By an Angel, 1999 (Emmy nomination 1999), The Ladies and the Champ, 2001, The Gilmore Girls, A Family of Strangers. Office: Dale Olson & Assocs 7420 Mulholland Dr Los Angeles CA 90046-1306 Office Phone: 323-876-9331.

**ROSS, MATHEW,** medical educator; b. Boston, July 29, 1917; s. Abraham and Frances (Lampke) R.; m. Brenda Boynton, Dec. 24, 1946; children: Douglas Ross, Gail Ross, Craig Ross, Bruce Ross. BS, Tufts U., Medford, Mass., 1938, MD, 1942. Diplomate Am. Bd. Psychiatry and Neurology. Intern Kings County Hosp., N.Y.C., 1942-43; resident VA Med. Ctr., L.A., 1946-48, L.A. Psychoanalytic Inst., 1949-53; prof. Sch. Medicine UCLA, 1953-58, George Washington U., Washington, 1958-73; psychiat. adminstrn. U. Chgo., 1959; prof. Sch. Medicine Harvard U., Boston, 1963-73, Brown U., Providence, 1964-65, R.I. U., Providence, 1964-65, U. Calif., Irvine, 1974—; fellow Sch. Alcoholism U. Utah, 1977. Fulbright rsch. scholar U. Gronigen and U. Amsterdam, The Netherlands, 1962-63; med. dir. Am. Psychiat. Assn., Washington, 1958-62. Editor: Newsletter Am. Psychiat. Assn., 1958-62, Mental Hosp. & Community Psychiatry, 1958-62, PDE Scientific Journal, 1975-90. Sr. legislator State of Calif., 1985-86, sr. senator, 2002-2006; mem. Newport Beach (Calif.) Arts Commn., 1989-95; pres. Med. Soc. of Leisure World, 2000—. Maj. U.S Army, 1943-46, ETO. Fellow ACP (life), Am. Psychiat. Assn. (life), Am. Assn. Psychoanalysts, Am. Pub. Health Assn., So. Calif. Psychiat. Soc. (founding pres. 1953-60); hon. fellow Australia-New Zealand Royal Coll. Psychiatrists; mem. Soc. Med. Cons. to Armed Svcs. Home: Unit 164 24055 Paseo Del Lago Laguna Woods CA 92637-2675 Office Phone: 949-462-0232. E-mail: matross@att.net.

**ROSS, MATHEW P.,** lawyer; b. NYC, Aug. 2, 1964; BA, Syracuse U., 1986; JD, We. New England Coll., 1990. Bar: NY 1991, US Ct. Mil. Appeals 1991, US Dist. Ct. So. Dist. NY 1995, US Dist. Ct. Ea. Dist. NY 1995, US Dist. Ct.

No. Dist. NY 2004. Ptnr. Wilson, Elser, Moskowitz, Edelman & Dicker LLP, NYC. Capt. Judge Adv. Gen.'s Corps, 1991—94, Fort Eustis, Va. Mem.: Xavier Bar Assn., NY State Bar Assn. Office: Wilson Elser Moskowitz Edelman & Dicker LLP 23rd Fl 150 E 42nd St New York NY 10017-5639 Office Phone: 212-490-3000 ext. 2287. Office Fax: 212-490-3038. Business E-Mail: rossm@wemed.com.

**ROSS, MATTHEW,** lawyer; b. NYC, Dec. 28, 1953; s. Harvey and Cecile (Shelsky) R.; m. Susan Ruth Goldfarb, Apr. 20, 1986; children: Melissa Danielle, Henry Max, Thomas Frank. BS in Econs., U. Pa., 1975; JD, U. Va., 1978. Bar: NY 1979, U.S. Dist. Ct. (so. dist.) N.Y. 1979. Assoc. Cravath, Swaine & Moore, N.Y.C., 1978-84; prin., assoc. gen. counsel KPMG LLP, N.Y.C., 1984-90; prin., deputy gen. counsel Deloitte & Touche USA LLP, N.Y.C., 1990—. Mem. ABA (corp. law sect.), N.Y. State Bar Assn. (corp. banking and bus. law sect.), Assn. of Bar of City of N.Y. (corp. law com.), Beta Gamma Sigma. Avocations: basketball, golf, tennis, skiing. Home: 5 Barker Ln Scarsdale NY 10583-7507 Office: Deloitte & Touche USA LLP 1633 Broadway New York NY 10019-6708 Office Phone: 212-492-3898. Business E-Mail: mross@deloitte.com.

**ROSS, MICHAEL AARON,** lawyer; b. Newark, Sept. 15, 1941; s. Alexander Ash and Matilda (Blumenthal) R.; m. Leslie Gordon, June 26, 1976; children: Christopher Gordon, Alan Gordon. BA, Franklin and Marshall Coll., 1963; JD, Columbia U., 1966; MS in Econs., U. London, 1967. Bar: N.Y. 1968. Assoc., then prtnr. Shearman & Sterling, NYC, 1967-93; dep. gen. counsel Citigroup, NYC, 1993—2001; gen. counsel Citibank, NYC, 1998—2003, Citigroup Internat., 2002—03; counsel Wilmer Cutler Pickering Hale and Dorr LLP, NYC, 2004—05; with Blaqwell Legal Consulting, NYC, 2006—. Mem. ABA, N.Y. State Bar Assn., Am. Law Inst., New York County Lawyers Assn., Assn. Bar City of N.Y., Univ. Club. Office Phone: 646-746-8083. Personal E-Mail: mikeaross262@yahoo.com. Business E-Mail: michael.ross@blaqwell.com.

**ROSS, MICHAEL CHARLES,** lawyer; BA, U. Va., 1970, JD, 1977. Assoc. Latham & Watkins, 1977-85, ptnr., 1985-93; sr. v.p., gen. counsel, sec. Safeway Inc., Oakland, 1993—.

**ROSS, MIKE,** congressman; b. Texarkana, Ark., Aug. 2, 1961; m. Holly Ross; children: Sydney, Alex. BA in Political Sci., U. Ark., 1987. Owner Holly's Health Mart and Home Med. Equipment; area mgr. Fox Meyer Drug Co.; mem. Ark. Senate, 1990-2001, chair children and youth com.; mem. US Congress from 4th Ark. dist., Washington, 2001—; mem. com. on Energy and Commerce U.S. Ho. Reps.; chief of staff to Lt Gov. of Ark., 1985—89. Democrat. Methodist. Office: US Ho Reps 314 Cannon Ho Office Bldg Washington DC 20515-0404

**ROSS, MOLLY OWINGS,** jewelry designer, sculptor, small business owner; b. Ft. Worth, Tex., Feb. 5, 1954; d. James Robertson and Lucy (Owings) R. BFA, Colo. State U., 1976; postgrad., U. Denver, 1978-79. Graphic designer Amber Sky Illustrators and Sta. KCNC TV-Channel 4, Denver, 1977-79; art dir. Mercy Med. Ctr., Denver, 1979-83, Molly Ross Design, Denver, 1983-84; co-owner Deltex Royalty Co., Inc., Colorado Springs, Colo., 1981—, LMA Royalties, Ltd., Colorado Springs, 1993—; art dir., account mgr. Schwing/Walsh Advt., Mktg. and Pub. Rels., Denver, 1984-87, prodn. mgr., 1987-88; jewelry designer Molly O. Ross, Gold and Silversmith, Denver, 1988—. Coun. mem. feminization of poverty critical needs area coun. Jr. League Denver, 1989—90, chmn. children in crisis/edn. critical needs area, 1990—91, chmn. project devel. 1991—92, co-chmn. Done in a Day Cmty. Project 75th Anniversary Celebration, 1991—93, bd. dirs., 1993—94, co-chmn. project IMPACT, 1994—95, exec. v.p. external affairs, 1995—96, co-chmn. cmty. coalitions com., 1996—98; mem. steering com. Denver Urban Resources Partnership, 1995—2002, steering com. chmn., 1996—99; pres.-elect Jr. League Denver, 1989—99, pres., 1999—2000, mem. steering com. Internat. Conf. on Vol. Adminstrn., 2001—02; bd. dirs. Environ. Def. Regional Adv. Bd., 2003—; mem. nat. adv. bd. Am. Farmland Trust, 2005—; mem. Rachel's Network, 2005—; bd. dirs. ArtReach, 2001—; pres. Four Mile Hist. Pk. Vol. Bd., 1985—86; bd. dirs. Four Mile Hist. Pk. Assn., 1985—86, Hist. Denver, Inc., 1986—87, Denver Emergency Housing Coalition, 1989—90; co-founder, bd. dirs. Ctr. Ethics and Social Responsibility/PREP, 1994—2001, pres. bd. dirs., 1997—99, treas. bd. dirs., 1999—2000; bd. dirs. Jr. League Denver Found., 1998—2002, Excelsior Youth Ctr. Found., 2001—, Friends of Warren Village, 2000—01. Named Vol. of Month (March), Jr. League Denver, 1990, Vol. of Yr., Four Mile Hist. Pk., 1988; recipient Gold Peak Mktg. award-team design Am. Mktg. Assn., 1986, Silver Peak Mktg. award-team design Am. Mktg. Assn., 1986, Gold Pick award-art dir. Pub. Rels. Soc. Am., 1980-81, cert. Appreciation USDA, 1999, 2001. Mem. Natural Resources Def. Coun., Physicians for Social Responsibility, Am. Farmland Trust, Nat. Trust for Hist. Preservation, Environ. Def., Rachel's Network. Avocations: horseback riding, bicycling, hiking, backpacking, pastel drawing.

**ROSS, MONTE,** electrical engineer, researcher; b. Chgo., May 26, 1932; s. Jacob Henry and Mildred Amelia (Feller) R.; m. Harriet Jean Katz, Feb. 10, 1957; children: Karyn, Dianne. Ethan BS in Elec. Engring., U. Ill., 1953; MS, Northwestern U., 1962. Devel. engr. Chance Vought, Dallas, 1953-54; sr. electronics engr. Motorola, Chgo., 1955-56, project engr., 1957-59, assoc. dir. rsch., 1960-63; dir. rsch. Hallicrafters Co., Chgo., 1964-65; mgr. laser tech. McDonnell Douglas Astronautics Co., St. Louis, 1966-70, dir. laser comms.; program mgr. Laser Space Comms., 1971-87; pres. Ultradata Sys., Inc. (formerly Laser Data Tech.), St. Louis, 1987—2001, CEO, 2001—. Mem. alumni bd. dept. elec. and computer engring. U. Ill., 1985-90; guest lectr. various univs.; cons. NSF. Author: Laser Receivers, 1966; tech. editor Laser Applications Series, vol. 1, 1971, vol. 2, 1974, vol. 3, 1977, vol. 4, 1980; patentee in field. Chmn. Laser Mus. and Space Signal Obs., 1997—. Recipient St. Louis High Tech. Entrepreneur of Yr. award, 1995; McDonnell Douglas Corp. fellow, 1985. Fellow IEEE; mem. Internat. Laser Comms. Soc. (pres. 1988-89), Sigma Xi. Home: 19 Beaver Dr Saint Louis MO 63141-7901 Office: Ultradata Sys Inc 1240 Dielman Ind Ct Saint Louis MO 63132-2212 Business E-Mail: mross@ultradatasystems.com.

**ROSS, MURRAY LOUIS,** lawyer; b. Rochester, N.Y., Apr. 26, 1947; s. Charles Allen and Florence L. (Falk) R.; m. Linda Marie Wabschall, Dec. 26, 1970. AB in History, Lycoming Coll., 1969; JD, U. Toledo, 1972. Bar: Pa. 1976. Asst. to exec. v.p. Falk Machinery Inc., Rochester, 1972-74; asst. v.p. Phila. (Pa.) Stock Exch., 1975-78, dir. securities dept., 1978-79, dir. market surveillance, 1979-82, v.p., corp. sec., 1982—; exec. v.p. Shiffrin Selections, Ltd., 1994—. Corp. sec. Phila. (Pa.) Bd. Trade Inc., 1984—, Phila. (Pa.) Depository Trust Co., 1986—, Stock Clearing Corp. Phila., 1986—. Mem. ABA, Phila. Bar Assn., Securities Assn. of Phila. Avocations: wine, golf, ice hockey. Home: 1126 Woodstock Ln West Chester PA 19382-7244 Office: Phila Stock Exchange Inc 1900 Market St Lbby 4 Philadelphia PA 19103-3584

**ROSS, NELSON G.,** lawyer; b. Jan. 4, 1938; BA, Boston Univ., 1960; LLM, Boston Coll., 1964. Bar: Mass. 1964. Assoc. Ropes & Gray, Boston, 1967—76, ptnr., 1976—, head labor & employment dept. Contbg. editor: The Developing Labor Law. Pres. bd. trustees South Shore Conservancy; trustee Hingham Pub. Libr.; mem. Hingham Personnel Bd. Recipient Cushin-Gavin award, Boston Labor Guild, 2001. Mem.: ABA, Mass. Bar Assn., Boston Bar Assn. Office: Ropes & Gray 1 International Pl Boston MA 02110-2624 Office Phone: 617-951-7450. Office Fax: 617-951-7050. Business E-Mail: nelson.ross@ropesgray.com.

**ROSS, NORMAN ALAN,** publisher; b. Bklyn., Nov. 1, 1942; s. Robert E. and Bertha (Cohen) Ross; m. Leslie Ann Sandler, Oct. 10, 1969; children: Caroline Beth, Juliet Michelle. BBA, CCNY, 1964, postgrad., 1967-74. Prodn. mgr. Thomas Pub. Co., 1964-67; sys. analyst Reuben H. Donnelley Corp., 1968-70; project mgr. Holt Rinehart & Winston, 1971-73; pres. Clearwater Pub. Co., Inc., N.Y.C., 1973-88, Video Strategies USA, Inc.,

N.Y.C., 1981-84, Broadside Ltd. pub. Broadside Mag., 1983-87, Norman Ross Pub. Inc., 1987—2002, Acad. Microforms Inc., 1999—2003; exec. dir. Norman Ross Pub., subs. Proquest, 2003—; pres. Ross Pub., Inc., 2003—. Author: (book) Index to the Decisions of the Indian Claims Commission, 1973, Index to the Expert Testimony Before the Indian Claims Commission, 1973, Guide to Yiddish Children's Books from the Yivo Institute, 1989. Home: 392 Central Park W Apt 20-c New York NY 10025-5878 Office: Ross Pub Inc 250 W 57th St New York NY 10107 Office Phone: 212-765-8200. Business E-Mail: norman@rosspub.com.

ROSS, PATTI JAYNE, obstetrics and gynecology educator; b. Nov. 17, 1946; d. James J. and Mary N. Ross; m. Allan Robert Katz, May 23, 1976. BS, DePauw U., 1968; MD, Tulane U., 1972. Diplomate Am. Bd. Ob-Gyn. Asst. prof. U. Tex. Med. Sch., Houston, 1976—82, assoc. prof., 1982—98, prof., 1998—2004, dir. adolescent ob-gyn., 1976—, dir. student edn., dir. devel. dept. ob-gyn. Cons. in field; spkr. in field; appeared on Lifetime TV network. Contbr. articles to profl. jours. Mem. Rape Coun.; vol. Children's Miracle Network/Hermann's Children's Hosp.; Olympic torch relay carrier, 1996; founder Women's Med. Rsch. Fund, U. Tex. Med. Sch., Houston; bd. dirs. Am. Diabetes Assn., 1982—, Susan Komen Found. Recipient Patti Jayne Ross Professorship, 2004. Mem.: Profl. Women Execs., Orgn. Women in Sci., Am. Women's Med. Assn., AAAS, Soc. Adolescent Medicine, Assn. Profs. Ob-Gyn., Houston Ob-Gyn. Soc., Harris County Med. Soc., Tex. Med. Assn., River Oak Breakfast Club, Sigma Xi. Roman Catholic. Office: 6431 Fannin St #3278 Houston TX 77030-1501 Office Phone: 713-500-6431. Business E-Mail: patti.j.ross@mth.tmc.edu.

ROSS, PHILIP ROWLAND, retired library director; b. Indiana, Pa., Apr. 7, 1940; s. David Biddle and Miriam Elizabeth (Hill) R.; m. Elaine Lucille George, July 17, 1965; children: Mary Elizabeth, David Bruce. BA, Pa. State U., 1962; MSLS, U. Md., 1969. Postal fin. officer USAF, Tachikawa AFB Tokyo, 1963-65; chief data control and quality control Hdqrs. Air Force Systems Command, Andrews AFB, Md., 1965-68; asst. libr. acquisitions West Liberty (W.Va.) State Coll., 1969-86; dist. mgr. Wheeling (W.Va.) office First Investors Corp., 1986-89, divs. mgr. State of Ark. Little Rock, 1989-92; dir. Lonoke (Ark.) Prairie County Regional Libr. System, 1992-2000; ret., 2000. Founder, treas.-mgr. West Liberty (W.Va.) State Coll. Fed. Credit Union, 1977-82, chmn. bd., 1984-85; co-founder, bd. dirs., Lonoke County Mus., sec., 2005—; mem. Ark. On Line Network Adv. Com., Little Rock, 1993-96, Libr. Devel. Dist. State Coun., Little Rock, 1993-2000, vice chmn., 1996. Capt. USAF, 1962—68, maj. Res. USAF. Decorated various USAF medals and decorations. Mem.: AARP (chpt. v.p. 2003, pres. 2004—06), ALA, S.E. Libr. Assn., Ark. Libr. Assn. (membership com. 1994—95, conv. com. 1996, 1997), Assn. Ark. Pub. Librs. (treas.-sec. 1993, 1994, v.p., pres.-elect 1995, pres. 1996), Lonoke C. of C., Lions (pres. 2003—05), Am. Legion (life). Republican. Methodist. Avocations: reading, gardening, refinishing antique furniture. Home: 691 Wayne Elmore Rd Lonoke AR 72086-9126

ROSS, R. DALE, medical products executive; Founder, pres., CEO HMSS Inc., 1982—90; chmn., CEO US Oncology, Houston, 1992—. Office: US Oncology 16825 Northchase Dr Houston TX 77060*

ROSS, RANDOLPH ERNEST, investor; b. N.Y.C., Mar. 17, 1955; s. David Harvey and Pearl (Frandsen) R.; m. Joan Frances Healey, Apr. 2, 1982. AB in History, Brown U., 1977; MBA in Fin., Columbia U., 1981. CFA; comml. pilot FAA. Nat. editor Sta. WEAN Radio, Providence, 1977-79; rsch. analyst, asst. v.p. Kidder, Peabody & Co., Inc., N.Y.C., 1981-85; rsch. analyst First Manhattan Co., N.Y.C., 1985-86; portfolio mgr. Brundage, Story and Rose, N.Y.C., 1986-92; sr. portfolio mgr., v.p. Bankers Trust Co., N.Y.C., 1992-93; investment strategist, sr. v.p. Kidder, Peabody & Co. Inc., N.Y.C., 1993-94; pvt. investor Bklyn., 1994-96; mng. dir. Morgan Hill Corp., N.Y.C., 1996—2004; pvt. investor, 2004—. Mem. CFA Inst., N.Y. Soc. Security Analysts. Republican. Avocations: commercial pilot, sailing, trap and skeet shooting, architectural and urban history, fiction. Home: 111 Hicks St Ste 4A Brooklyn NY 11201-1638

ROSS, RICH, broadcast executive; b. NYC, Oct. 7, 1961; BA in internat. rels. and English, U. Pa., 1983; JD, Fordham U., 1986. Mgr. talent rels. Nickelodeon, 1990, v.p. talent rels., 1990—92, v.p. program enterprises, 1992—93; sr. v.p. devel. and prodn. FX Networks, 1993—96; sr. v.p. programming and prodn. Disney Channel, 1996—99, exec. v.p., gen. mgr. programming and prodn., 1999—2002, pres., 2002—04, Disney Channel Worldwide, 2004—. Bd. dirs. Cable in the Classroom. Office: Disney Channel 500 S Buena Vista St Burbank CA 91521

ROSS, RICHARD FRANCIS, veterinarian, educator, dean, microbiologist; b. Washington, Iowa, Apr. 30, 1935; s. Milton Edward and Olive Marie (Berggren) R.; m. Karen Mae Paulsen, Sept. 1, 1957; children: Scott, Susan D.V.M., Iowa State U., 1959, MS, 1961, PhD, 1965. Rsch. assoc. Iowa State U., Ames, 1959—61, asst. prof., 1962—65, assoc. prof., 1966—72, prof., 1972—, assoc. dir., assoc. dean Coll. Vet. Medicine, 1990—92, interim dean, 1992—93, dean Coll. Vet. Medicine, 1993—2000, interim dean, dean Coll. Agr., dir. Agr. Expt. Sta., 2000—02, prof. emeritus, 2004; oper. mgr. Vet. Lab. Inc., Remsen, Iowa, 1961—62; postdoctoral fellow NIAID, Hamilton, Mont., 1965—66. Sr. U.S. scientist Alexander von Humboldt Found., Bonn, Fed. Republic Germany, 1975-76; chmn. Internat. Rsch. Program on Comparative Mycoplasmology, 1982-86; pres. Iowa State U. Rsch. Found., Ames, 1984-86; Howard Dunne meml. lectr. Am. Assoc. Swine Practitioners, 1984; mem. adv. bd. Sec. Agr., 1996-99; mem. strategic planning task force USDA, 1997-99, mem. safeguarding task force, 2001-02, mem. implementation team, 2003—; bd. govs. ISU Found., 2004—. Contbr. numerous articles to profl. publs., 1963— Named Disting. Prof., Iowa State U., 1982, Hon. Master Pork Producer, Iowa Pork Producers Assn., 1995, recipient Faculty Citation Iowa State U. Alumni Assn., 1984, Beecham award for rsch. excellence, 1985, Howard Dunne Meml. award Am. Assoc. Swine Practitioners, 1988, Am. Feed Mfg. award for rsch., 1995, Sec. of Agr. award for personal and profl. accomplishment, 1996, Gamma Sigma Delta Merit award for disting. achievement in agr. 2002. Mem. Am. Coll. Vet. Microbiologists (diplomate, vice chmn. 1974-75, sec.-treas. 1977-83), Am. Soc. Microbiology (chmn. div. 1985-86), Internat. Orgn. Mycoplasmology (chair 1990-92, Bd. Dirs. award 2002), AVMA, AAAS, Osborn Research Club, Conf. Rsch. Workers in Animal Diseases (coun. mem., pres. 1992), Assn. Am. Vet. Med. Colls. (pres. 1997-98), Rotary Club. Republican. Lutheran. Avocations: fishing, gardening, walking, reading, history. Home: 4022 Stone Brooke Rd Ames IA 50010-2900 Personal E-Mail: rfross@iastate.edu.

ROSS, RICHARD FREDERICK, lawyer; b. Coral Gables, Fla., May 12, 1952; s. Norman and Jeanne (Gustafson) Ross; m. Carolyn Ross, June 30, 1985. BA magna cum laude, Mich. State U., 1974; JD, U. Detroit, 1977. Bar: Ariz. 1977; cert. real estate specialist Ariz. Bd. Legal Specialization. Atty. Cunningham, Goodson & Tiffany, Phoenix, 1977-81; founding ptnr. Storey & Ross, Phoenix, 1981-89; ptnr. Squire, Sanders & Dempsey LLP, Phoenix, 1989—, co-chmn., Real Estate & Hospitality Practice Group. Former bd. dirs. dean's coun. of 100 Ariz. State U. Coll. Bus., Tempe; former bd. dirs. Ctrl. Ariz. chpt. Am. Heart Assn., Phoenix; former bd. dirs. Phoenix Symphony, HomeBase Cmty. Youth Shelter, Phoenix, Terraco Properties (subs. Phoenix Meml. Hosp.), Phoenix. Mem. ABA (mem. hospitality com., mem. real property, probate and trust law), Internat. Soc. Hospitality Cons., Am. Hotel and Motel Assn., Urban Land Inst., Internat. Coun. Shopping Ctr., Valley Partnership. Office: Squire Sanders & Dempsey LLP Two Renaissance Sq 40 N Central Ave Ste 2700 Phoenix AZ 85004-4424 Office Phone: 602-528-4018. Office Fax: 216-479-8780. Business E-Mail: rross@ssd.com.

ROSS, RICHARD STARR, retired medical school dean, cardiologist, educator; b. Richmond, Ind., Jan. 18, 1924; s. Louis Francisco and Margaret (Starr) Ross; m. Elizabeth Starr, July 1, 1950; children: Deborah Starr, Margaret Casad, Richard McCracken. Student, Harvard U., 1942—44, MD cum laude, 1947; ScD (hon.), Ind. U., 1981; LHD (hon.), Johns Hopkins U.,

1994. Diplomate Nat. Bd. Med. Examiners, Am. Bd. Internal Medicine (subsplty. bd. cardiovasc. disease). Successively intern, asst. resident, chief resident Osler Med. Service, Johns Hopkins Hosp., 1947—54; research fellow physiology Harvard Med. Sch., 1952—53; instr. medicine Johns Hopkins Med. Sch., 1954—56, asst. prof. medicine, 1956—59, assoc. prof., 1959—65, assoc. prof. radiology, 1960—71, prof. medicine, 1965—, Clayton prof. cardiovascular disease, 1969—75; dir. Wellcome Research Lab., Johns Hopkins; physician Johns Hopkins Hosp.; dir. cardiovascular div. dept. medicine, adult cardiac clinic Johns Hopkins Sch. Medicine and Hosp., dir. myocardial infarction research unit, 1967—75; dean med. faculty, v.p. medicine Johns Hopkins U., 1975—90, dean emeritus, 1990—. Sir Thomas Lewis lectr. Brit. Cardiac Soc., 1969; John Kent Lewis lectr. Stanford U., 1972; bd. dirs. emeritus Johns Hopkins Hosp., Francis Scott Key Med. Ctr.; mem. cardiovasc. study sect., 1966—67, Nat. Heart and Lung Inst., 1965—69, chmn. cardiovasc. study sect., 1966—69, mem. tng. grant com., 1971—73, chmn. heart panel, 1972—73, adv. coun., 1974—78; mem. Inst. Medicine, 1975—; chmn. vis. com. Harvard Med. and Dental Sch., 1979—86; bd. overseers Harvard U., 1980—86. Editor: Modern Concepts Cardiovascular Disease, 1961—65, The Principles and Practice of Medicine, 17th-22nd edits., 1968—88; mem. editl. bd.: Circulation, 1968—74, mem. editl. com.: Jour. Clin. Investigation, 1969—73; contbr. numerous articles to profl. jours. Capt. M.C. U.S. Army, 1949—51. Named hon. fellow, UMDS, Guy's and St. Thomas's Hosps., London, 1996; recipient Flexner award, Assn. Am. Med. Coll., 1994, Pres.'s medal, Johns Hopkins U., 2005. Master: ACP; fellow: Am. Coll. Cardiology (Convocation medal 1990); mem.: Heart Assn. Md. (pres. 1967—68), Am. Heart Assn. (chmn. sci. sessions program com. 1965—67, chmn. publs. com. 1970—73, pres. 1973—74, dir. 1974—77, Gold Heart award 1976, Connor lectr. 1979, James B. Herrick award 1982), Assn. Univ. Cardiologists (councillor 1972—75), Am. Clin. and Climatol. Assn. (pres. 1978—79, councillor 1979—83, Metzger lecture 1986), Am. Soc. Clin. Investigation (councillor 1967—69), Sociedad Peruana de Cardiologie (corr.), Brit. Cardiac Soc. (corr.), Cardiac Soc. Australia and New Zealand (corr.), Assn. Am. Physicians, Am. Physiol. Soc., Am. Fedn. Clin. Rsch., Boylston Med. Soc., Elkridge Club, Interurban Club (pres. 1978), Peripatetic Club, Alpha Omega Alpha, Sigma Xi. Home: 830 W 40th St # 851 Baltimore MD 21211-2181 Office: Johns Hopkins U 1830 E Monument St Baltimore MD 21287 E-mail: rross@jhmi.edu.

ROSS, ROBERT DONALD, library director; b. N.Y.C., Mar. 28, 1931; s. William and Ceceile (Cross) Rosenfeld. BA, CCNY, 1954; postgrad., NYU, 1960—64, Columbia U., N.Y.C., 1968; MLS, Rutgers U., 1966. m. Madeleine Ladner, May 28, 1961; children: Jeffrey Laurence, Jodie Dianne. Ref. libr. Bklyn. Pub. Libr., 1965; reader svcs. libr., asst. prof. Suffolk County (N.Y.) C.C., 1966-69; dir. South Brunswick (N.J.) Pub. Libr., 1969-73, Ridgewood (N.J.) Pub. Libr., 1973-95. Adj. prof. Middlesex County C.C., NJ, 1973—76. Mem. exec. bd. South Brunswick Cmty. Coun., 1970-73, Human Rels. Coord. Coun., Ridgewood, 1988-94; mem. adv. com. Nat. Project Ctr. for Films and Humanities, N.Y.C., 1971-75; treas. Bergen-Passaic Regional Libr. Coop., 1987-88, mem. exec. bd., 1986-89; mem. Ridgewood Bicentennial Commn., 1975-76; treas. Temple Emanu-El, Reno, 1998-2000, bd. dirs., 2002-2003; bd. dirs. For the Love of Jazz, Reno, 1998-2000, docent Nev. Mus. Art, 2004—. Mem. ALA (chmn. discussion group com. fundraising and fin. devel. sect. libr. adminstrn. and mgmt. divsn. 1984-85), N.J. Libr. Assn. (libr. devel. com. 1977-93, chmn. edn. for librarianship com. 1982-83, govt. rels. com. 1982, 100th ann. com. 1988-91), Librs. South Middlesex (chmn. 1970-73), North Bergen Fedn. Librs. (chmn. dirs. coun. 1975), Bergen County Coop. Libr. Sys. (pres., treas. 1982-83, 86-87, exec. bd. computer consortium 1987-89, budget com. 1989-94), Ridgewood C. of C. (bd. dirs. 1983-93, treas. 1988-93), Soc. Valley Hosp. Ridgewood, Ridgewood Kiwanis (pres. 1982-83, treas. 1987-88, Disting. Club. Pres. award 1983). Home: 4910 Deer Pass Dr Reno NV 89509-0577

ROSS, ROBERT EVAN, bank executive; b. Alliance, Ohio, Sept. 22, 1947; s. James Jacob Ross and Eva Mae (Forsha) Bodo; m. Susan Margaret Burd, June 20, 1970; children: Margaret Mae, James William. BBA, Kent State U., 1970; MBA, U. Chgo., 1977. Advisor to fraternities, dean of men's office Kent (Ohio) State U., 1970-71; trainee, supt. of trainees Northern Trust Co., Chgo., 1971-73, jr. analyst, 1973-74, trust rep., 1974-77, trust officer, 1977-81, v.p., div. head for personal fin. planning, 1981-85; portfolio mgr., investment rep. Morgan Stanley, Chgo., 1985-89; pres. Northern Trust Bank in Winnetka, Ill., 1989-92; exec. v.p. Northern Trust Bank/Lake Forest, Ill., 1992-95, vice chmn., 1995-97, pres., CEO, 1997—2001; pres., CEO Northern Trust Bank-Ohio, 2001—04; sr. v.p. wealth strategies group No. Trust Co., 2004—06; mng. dir. pvt. banking Harris Bank, Chgo., 2006—. Bd. dirs. No. Trust Bank, Lake Forest, O'Hare, Ill., DuPage, Ill. Bd. dirs. The Camerata Singers of Lake Forest, Lake Forest Symphony, 1992-2001, Ragdale Found., 1999-2000, Cleve. Zool. Soc., 2003; bd. govs. Ill. St. Andrew Soc., 1998-2001; suburban chair United Way North Region, 1993—; mem. centennial commn. on identity, values and comm. Kent State U., 1998; trustee DePaul U., Chgo., Barat Coll. Edn. Found., Kent State U. Found., 2003. Avocations: sports, reading, stock market, painting. Office: No Trust Bank Lake Forest Deerpath And Bank Ln Lake Forest IL 60045

ROSS, ROBERT JOSEPH (BOBBY ROSS), college football coach; b. Richmond, Va., Dec. 23, 1935; s. Leonard Aloysius and Martha Isabelle (MMiller) R.; m. Alice Louise Bucker, June 13, 1959; children: Chris, Mary Catherine, Teresa, Kevin, Robbie. BA, Va. Mil. Inst., 1959. Tchr., head football coach Benedictine High Sch., Richmond, 1959-60; tchr., coach Colonial Heights (Va.) High Sch., 1962-65; asst. football coach Va. Mil. Inst., Lexington, 1965-67, Coll. William and Mary, Williamsburg, Va., 1967-71, Rice U., Houston, 1971-72, U. Md., College Park, 1972-73; head football coach The Citadel, Charleston, SC, 1973-77; head coach U. Md., College Park, 1982-87; head football coach Ga. Inst. Tech., Atlanta, 1987-91, asst. coach Kansas City (Mo.) Chiefs, 1978-82; head coach San Diego Chargers, 1992-96, Detroit Lions, 1997-2001, U.S. Mil. Acad., West Point, NY, 2003—. 1st lt. U.S. Army, 1960-62. Named Coach of Yr., Washington Touchdown Club, 1982, Kodak Coach of Yr., 1990, Bobby Dodd Coach of Yr., 1990, Bear Bryant Coach of Yr., 1990, Scripps-Howard Coach of Yr., 1990, Nat. Coach of Yr., CBS Sports, 1990, Coach of Yr., Walter Camp Football Found., 1990, NFL Coach of Yr. UPI, 1992, Pro Football Weekly, 1992, Pro Football Writers' Assn., 1992, Football News, 1992, Football Digest, 1992, Maxwell Football Club, 1992, AFC Coach of Yr. Kansas City 101 Banquet. Mem. Am. Football Coaches Assn., Coll. Football Assn. (coaching com. 1988-92). Roman Catholic. Office: US Military Acad Bldg 639 Howard Rd West Point NY 10996-1985

ROSS, ROBERT K., foundation administrator, physician; BA in Public Administration, M in Public Administration, MD, U. Penn. Clinical scholar U. Penn. Sch. of Medicine, 1988—90; former dir. Phila. Dept. of Health; former pediatrician Nat. Health Services Corps, Camden; former dir. Health and Human Services Agy., San Diego County, 1999—2000; pres., CEO Calif. Endowment, 2000—. Consultant Phila. Sch. Dist. Children's Health Initiative; mem. NJ Governor's Commn. on Health Care Costs, Nat. Vaccine Advisory Comm.; bd. mem. Nat. Marrow Donor Program; mem. President's Summit for America's Future. Bd. dirs. San Diego United Way, Jackie Robinson YMCA, Calif. Endowment. Recipient Youth Advocacy Humanitarian of Yr. award, Outstanding Community Svc. award, Volunteers of Am., Leadership award, Hosp. Council of San Diego, Health Administrator of Yr. Citation, Nat. Assn. of Health Svc. Exec. Mem.: Am. Acad. of Pediatrics. Office: Calif Endowment 1000 N Alameda St Los Angeles CA 90012*

ROSS, ROBINETTE DAVIS, publisher; b. London, May 16, 1952; d. Raymond Lawrence and Pearl A. (Robinette) Davis; m. William Bradford Ross, III, Mar. 16, 1979; children: Nellie Tayloe, William Bradford IV. Student, Am. U., 1977-78. Asst. to editor The Chronicle of Higher Edn., Washington, 1978, advt. mgr., 1978-82, advt. dir., 1983-88, assoc. pub., 1988-94, The Chronicle of Philanthropy, 1988-94; publ. The Chronicle of Higher Edn., Washington, 1994—; pub. The Chronicle of Philanthropy,

Washington, 1994—. Mem. Am. News Women's Club, City Tavern Club, Mt. Vernon Club. Episcopalian. Office: The Chronicle of Higher Edn 1255 23rd St NW Ste 700 Washington DC 20037-1146

ROSS, RODERIC HENRY, retired insurance company executive; b. Jamestown, N.Y., July 14, 1930; s. Edwin A. and Mary (Dornberger) R.; m. Patricia Johnson, Aug. 6, 1955; children: Timothy, Amy, Jane, Christopher. BA, Hobart Coll., 1952, LLD (hon.), 1979. CLU, ChFC. Gen. agt. Phila. Life Ins. Co., 1957-70, sr. v.p. mktg., 1972-73, pres., 1973-83, vice chmn., 1983-84; chmn., CEO Keystone State Life Ins. Co., Phila., 1985-2000; ret., 2001. Bd. dirs. PMA Capital Corp., Phila.; past chmn. Ins. Fedn. Pa.; dir. Intergroup Svcs. Corp., Malvern, Pa. Rector's warden St. David's Ch., Radnor, Pa., 1989-90; hon. trustee Hobart-William Smith Colls., Geneva, N.Y., 1972—, chmn. bd., 1983-88. Sgt. U.S. Army, 1952-54. Mem. Am. Soc. CLUs, Nat. Assn. Nat. Assn. Life Underwriters, Million Dollar Round Table (life), Union League (former dir.), Orpheus Club, St. David's Golf Club (Wayne, Pa.), Penna Soc., Pine Valley Golf Club (Clementon, N.J.). Republican. Episcopalian. Avocations: golf, tennis. Home: (Summer) PO Box 332 Bemus Point NY 14712-0332 Home: 770 Pugh Rd Wayne PA 19087 E-mail: rodnpatross@verizon.net.

ROSS, STAN, real estate company executive; b. 1939; Degree, Baruch Coll., 1956, LLD (hon.), 1999. Mng. ptnr. E&Y Kenneth Leventhal Real Estate Group; vice chmn. Real Estate Industry Svcs. Ernst & Young LLP, 1995—99; chmn. Lusk Ctr. U. So. Calif. LA, 1999—. Cons. Ernst & Young; bd. dirs. The Irvine Co., Forest City Enterprises, U. Judaism. Trustee Urban Land Inst., gov.; trustee Baruch Coll. Mem.: AICPA (mem. auditing standards bd.). Office: USC LuckCtr Real Estate 331 Ralph andGoldy Lewis Hall Los Angeles CA 90089-0626

ROSS, STANFORD G., lawyer, government official; b. St. Louis, Oct. 9, 1931; m. Dorothy Rabin, June 9, 1958; children: John, Ellen. AB with honors, Washington U., 1953; JD magna cum laude, Harvard U., 1956. Bar: D.C. 1969, Calif. 1956, N.Y. 1959. Assoc. Irell & Manella, L.A., 1956-57; tchg. fellow, rsch. asst. Harvard Law Sch., 1957-58; assoc. Dewey, Ballantine, Bushby, Palmer & Wood, N.Y.C., 1958-61; asst. tax legis. counsel U.S. Dept. Treasury, 1961-63; prof. law N.Y. U., 1963-67; White House staff asst. to Pres. Johnson, 1967-68; gen. counsel U.S. Dept. Transp., 1968-69; ptnr. Caplin & Drysdale, Washington, 1969-78; commr. Social Security Adminstrn., Washington, 1978-79; ptnr. Califano, Ross & Heineman, Washington, 1980-82, Arnold & Porter, Washington, 1983—2002. Pub. trustee Social Security Trust Funds, Washington, 1990-95; chmn. Social Security Adv. Bd., 1997-2002. Editor: Harvard Law Rev, 1954-56. Mem. ABA, Fed. Bar Assn., Internat. Fiscal Assn., Nat. Acad. Social Ins. Office: Arnold & Porter 555 12th St NW Washington DC 20004-1206

ROSS, STEPHEN M., real estate company executive; BS, U. Mich., 1962; JD, Wayne State U.; LLM in Taxation, NYU. Dir. Insignia Fin. Group, Inc.; founder, dir. Charter Mcpl. Mortgage Acceptance Co.; founder, chmn., CEO The Related Cos. LP, NYC. Dir. Juvenile Diabetes Found.; bd. trustees Solomon R. Guggenheim Mus.; trustee Jackie Robinson Found., Jewish Assn. for Svcs. for Aged. Named one of Forbes' Richest Americans, 2006. Mem.: Real Estate Board of NY (dir.). Office: The Related Cos LP 60 Columbus Cir New York NY 10023 Office Phone: 212-421-5333.*

ROSS, SUE HOISINGTON, elementary school educator, music educator; b. Silver Creek, N.Y., Sept. 30, 1951; d. Richard Leroy and Jeanne Marie Hoisington; 1 child, Michael Parrish Wilkerson. MusB in Edn., Shenandoah Conservatory Music, 1973; MusM with hons. in Edn., SUNY, Fredonia, N.Y., 1987. Cert. tchr. Va. N.Y. Tchr. elem. vocal music Loudoun County Pub. Schs., Leesburg, Va., 1973—76; tchr. vocal music Loudoun Country Day Sch., Leesburg, 1976—79; tchr. elem. vocal music Lakeshore Ctrl. Schs., Angola, NY, 1980—. Supr. student tchrs. Lake Shore Ctrl. Schs., 1980—; lectr. in field. Active MADD; mem. beautification program Lake Erie; vol. Erie County Rep. Com., Fornham, NY, 1983—85. Mem.: Nat. Assn. Music Educators, N.Y. State Sch. Music Assn. Republican. Office: Lake Shore Central Schools Beach Rd Angola NY 14006 Home: 2203 Pleasant Ave Lake View NY 14085 Office Phone: 716-549-2300. Personal E-mail: sucross51@aol.com.

ROSS, TERENCE P., lawyer; b. 1958; Grad. with honors, Stanford U., 1980; JD, U. Va. Sch. Law, 1983. Bar: Commonwealth Va., DC, NY, US Supreme Ct., US Ct. Appeals Fed. Circuit. Law clk. to Judge Roger Robb, US Ct. Appeals Dist. Columbia Circuit; assoc. Gibson, Dunn & Crutcher LLP, Washington, 1984—91, ptnr., 1991—. Adj. prof. George Mason U. Law Sch.; writer and spkr. in field on intellectual property topics; rsch. editor, mem. mng. bd. Va. Law Review. Author: Intellectual Property Law: Damages and Remedies, 2000. Mem. bd. visitors U. Va. Named to Magnificent Seven: IP's Best Young Trial Lawyers, IP Worldwide, 2002. Mem.: ABA (mem. steering com., mem. intellectual property lit. com.), DC Bar Assn. (chair annual develop. in intellectual property law forum). Office: Gibson Dunn & Crutcher LLP 1050 Conn Ave NW Washington DC 20036 Office Phone: 202-955-8664. Business E-Mail: tross@gibsondunn.com.

ROSS, TERRY D., lawyer; b. Glendale, Calif., Aug. 12, 1943; BA, U. Calif., Santa Barbara, 1965; JD, U. Calif. Hastings Coll. Law, 1968. Bar: Calif. 1969, U.S. Dist. Ct. (so. dist.) Calif. 1969, U.S. Dist. Ct. (ctrl. dist.) Calif. 1992, U.S. Dist. Ct. (no. dist.) Calif. 1999, U.S. Ct. Appeals (9th cir.) 1977, U.S. Supreme Ct. 1983. Ptnr. DLA Piper Rudnick Gray Cary US LLP, San Diego. Mem. panel arbitrators Am. Arbitration Assn. Note and comment editor Hastings Law Jour., 1967-68. Bd. dirs., mem. exec. bd., 1 st v.p. E. San Diego Co. YMCA. Mem. ABA (sect. litig.), State Bar Calif., San Diego County Bar Assn. (mem. arbitration panel, superior ct. com., client rels. com.) S D Marlin Club, 3DMB Boat and Ski Club, Phi Delta Phi. Office: DLA Piper Rudnick Gray Cary US LLP Ste 1700 401 B St San Diego CA 92101-4297 E-mail: tross@graycary.com, Terry.Ross@dlapiper.com.

ROSS, VIOLET BICA, retired elementary school educator, retired psychologist; d. Ellie A. and Anna (Muresan) Bica; m. L. Clayton Ross, Oct. 23, 1976 (dec.). BS, Mount Union Coll., 1944; MA, Kent State U., 1952. Tchr. Alliance Bd. Edn., 1945—53; psychologist Maple Heights Bd. Edn., Ohio, 1954—56, Cleveland Heights Bd. Edn., 1956—61, Shaker Heights Bd. Edn., Ohio, 1961—76; ret., 1976. Psychologist chair Kent Area Sch., 1959—60, nat. conventions. Named Dormitory at Mt. Union Coll. Bica-Ross Hall, 1999, Dormitory at Wash. Jefferson Coll. Bica-Ross Hall, 2004. Mem.: Kappa Delta, Kappa Delta Pi, Delta Kappa Gamma. Achievements include donations of scholarships to Mount Union College, Washington and Jefferson College. Avocations: reading, travel, golf. Home: 112 Royal Oak Dr Aurora OH 44202

ROSS, WALTER BEGHTOL, music educator, composer; b. Lincoln, Nebr., Oct. 3, 1936; s. Robert Thurber and Barbara Adeline (Ellis) R.; m. Marion Helen Wright, July 22, 1960; 1 child, Douglas Campbell. BA, U. Nebr., 1960, MusM, 1962; student, Torcuato Di Tella, Buenos Aires, 1965-66; D of Mus. Arts, Cornell U., 1966. Asst. prof. music CUNY, Cortland, 1966-67; prof. U. Va., Charlottesville, 1967—. Mem. judging panel symphonic awards ASCAP, 1978, Internat. Biennial Composition Contest, P.R., 1981, Va. chpt. Coll. Band Dir.'s Nat. Assn. Nat. Band Composition Contest, 1982, 88; bass Blue Ridge Chamber Orch., Charlottesville, 1992—. Composer over 100 works, including compositions for symphony orch., symphonic band, brass, chamber music, piano, voice, opera, theatre, and film; recs. include Clarinet Concerto for Piano and Orch., Wind Quintet, Nos. 2 and 3, Harlequinade for piano and wind quintet, Escher's Sketches, Concerto for Wind Quintet and String Orch., Piano Concerto, also others. Nominee Pulitzer Prize, 1973; recipient ASCAP award, 1974—, 1st prize Internat. Trombone Assn., 1982; grantee Am. Music Ctr., 1983; fellow Presser Found., 1958, 59, Orgn. Am. States, 1965, NEA, 1975. Democrat. Avocations: chess, cooking, amateur astronomy. Office: U Va Dept Music Charlottesville VA 22903 E-mail: wbr@virginia.edu.

**ROSS, WILBUR LOUIS, JR.,** investment banker; b. Weehawken, NJ, Nov. 28, 1937; s. Wilbur Louis and Agnes (O'Neill) R.; m. Judith Nodine, May 26, 1961 (div. 1995); children: Jessica, Amanda; m. Hilary Geary, Oct. 9, 2004. AB, Yale U., 1959; MBA with distinction, Harvard U., 1961. Assoc. Wood, Struthers and Winthrop, NYC, 1963-64; pres. Faulkner, Dawkins and Sullivan Securities Corp., NYC, 1964-76; sr. mng. dir. Rothschild, Inc., NYC, 1976-2000; CEO News Comms., Inc., NYC, 1996-98; chmn., chief investment officer Rothschild Recovery Fund, NYC, 1997-2000; chmn., CEO WL Ross & Co, LLC, NYC, 2000—. Bd. dirs Biocraft Labs Inc., Rutherford, NJ, FurVault Inc., NYC, Investors Ins. Co., Lawrence Harbor, NJ, Revere Copper and Brass Co., Stamford, Syms Corp., Secaucus, NJ, Am. Bankruptcy Inst., Washington, Allis Chalmers Corp., Milw., KTI Inc., RH Cement Co., Seoul, Korea, Tong Yang Life Ins. Co., Seoul, Kansai Sawayaka Bank, Osaka, Fresca Credit Card Co., Osaka; fin. advisor equity holders com. Texaco Co., A.H. Robins Co., Pub. Service NH; hon. econ. amb. from Korea to APEC Investment, Mont., 1999; chmn. Asia Recovery Fund L.P., WL Recovery Fund LP, Asia Co. Investment Ptnrs. L.P.; chmn. Clarent Hosp. Corp., Internat. Steel Group, Inc., Cleve., 2002—, Ohizumi Mfg. Co., Japan, 2003-, Burlington Industries, 2003-, Marquis Who's Who LLC, 2003-, Marquis Who's Who Inc., 2004-, Internat. Coal Group, 2004-, Internat. Textile Group, 2005—; dir. Nikko Elec. Co., Japan, Miltal Steel Co., Nev., Internat. Steel Group. Treas. NY State Dem. Com., 1980-83, Am. Fedn. Arts, 1993—, The New Mus., 1993—; vice chmn. Bklyn. Mus., 1981—; chmn. univ. coun. com. on art Yale U., 1983-88; chmn. NAD, N.Y.C., 1985—, Am. Art Forum, Smithsonian Instn., 1987—; trustee, vice chmn. Nat. Mus. Am. Art, Washington, 1986-91, chmn., 1991—; trustee, Mus. Am. Fin. History; trustee Sarah Lawrence Coll., 1986—, chmn. art gallery, 1984—; pres. Parrish Art Mus., 1991-95; chmn. NY Hist. Soc., 1993-94; bd. dirs Smithsonian Inst. Nat. Bd., 1994—, chmn. bd. 1995; nat. chmn. Smithsonian Bicentennial Celebration, 1996; trustee Gustave Hyde Ctr. Nat. Mus. Am. Indian, 2001—, Nat. Mus. Am. Fin. History; bd. dirs. Turnaround Mgmt. Assn., 2001—; chmn. Absolute Recovery Hedge Fund, Ltd., Hamilton, Bermuda, Taiyo Fund, 2003-, Japan Real Estate Recovery Fund, 2003-. With U.S. Army, 1961-63. Named one of Forbes' Richest Americans, 2006. Fellow Jonathan Edward Coll. of Yale U., Met. Mus. Art; mem. Fin. Analysts Fedn. (chartered), Century Assn., The Bus. Round Table, Bath and Tennis Club, Everglades Club, Harvard Bus. Sch. Club NY (bd. dirs.), Beach Club. Avocation: collecting art. Office: WL Ross and Co LLC 600 Lexington Ave New York NY 10022 Business E-Mail: wlross@wlross.com.*

**ROSS, WILLIAM DEE, JR.,** economist; b. Jackson, Miss., May 16, 1921; s. William Dee and Betty (Biggs) R.; m. Nell Triplett, July 25, 1944; 1 child, William Dee III. BA, Millsaps Coll., 1942; MA, Duke U., 1947, PhD, 1951. Economist U.S. Mil. Govt. for Germany, Berlin, 1945—46; instr. econs. Duke U., Durham, NC, 1946—49; assoc. prof. La. State U., Baton Rouge, 1949—54, prof. econs., 1954—56, dean Coll. Bus. Adminstrn., 1956—76; pres. Fin. Econs. Svcs., Inc., Baton Rouge, 1976—99, Ross Bus. Svcs., Inc., Baton Rouge, 2000—. Bd. dirs. Piccadilly Cafeterias Inc., others; dir. La. Hwy. Fin. Study, La. Legis. Coun., 1953-54; cons. Joint House-Senate Hwy. Com., La. Legislature, La. Dept. Hwys., 1955-56; lectr. exec. devel. programs Mich. State U., Ga. Inst. Tech., La. State U.; mem. dept. econs., fin. and adminstrn. Hwy. Rsch. Bd., Nat. Acad. Scis., Washington, 1957-64; mem. adv. coun. Tax Inst. Am., 1961-63. Author (with B.U. Ratchford) Berlin Reparations Assignment, 1947, Financing Highway Improvements in Louisiana, 1955, Business in a Free Society, 1966; contbr. articles to profl. jours. Bd. dirs. area coun. Boy Scouts Am. Served to 1st lt. USAAF, 1943-45. Mem. Am. Assn. Collegiate Schs. Bus., Am. Econ. Assn., So. Econ. Assn. (exec. com. 1960-62), Nat. Tax Assn. (exec. com. 1960-63, editl. com. Nat. Tax Jour. 1959-62), Am. Fin. Assn., So. Fin. Assn. (pres. 1962-63), Southwestern Social Sci. Assn., Omicron Delta Kappa, Beta Gamma Sigma. Lodges: Rotary. Methodist.

**ROSS, WILLIAM JARBOE,** lawyer; b. Oklahoma City, May 9, 1930; s. Walter John and Bertha (Jarboe) R.; m. Mary Lillian Ryan, May 19, 1962; children: Rebecca Anne Roten, Robert Joseph, Molly Kathleen Fritch. BBA, U. Okla., 1952, LLB, 1954; LHD (hon.), Oklahoma City U., 2005. Bar: Okla. 1954. Since practiced in Oklahoma City; asst. mcpl. counselor, 1955-60; mem. firm Rainey, Ross, Rice & Binns, 1960—, ptnr., 1965-99, of counsel, 2000—; chmn. bd. Ethics and Excellence in Journalism Found., Inasmuch Found. Mem. bd. visitors U. Okla. Coll. Law; bd. dirs Ethics and Excellence in Journalism Found., Inasmuch Found. Mem. Okla. Bar Assn., Okla. Heritage Assn., Newcomen Soc., Okla. City Golf and Country Club, Econ. Club, Fortune Club, Rotary, Phi Alpha Delta, Beta Theta Pi, KC Home: 6923 Avondale Ct Oklahoma City OK 73116-5008

**ROSS, WILLIAM WARFIELD,** lawyer; b. Washington, Oct. 3, 1926; s. W. Warfield and Vera Elfleda (Payne) R.; m. Jennie Fitch, Jan. 30, 1963; children— James, Mary, Billy; m. Nan Robertson, Sept. 25, 1999. AB St. John's Coll., Annapolis, Md., 1948; LL.B., Yale U., 1951. Bar: D.C. 1951. Legal asst. Exec. Office Pres. Harry S. Truman, 1952-53, Pres. Dwight D. Eisenhower, 1953; atty. appellate sect. civil div. Dept. Justice, Washington, 1954-57; asst. to solicitor FPC, Washington, 1957-59; ptnr. Wald, Harkrader & Ross, Washington, 1963-87, Pepper, Hamilton & Scheetz, Washington, 1987-91. Adj. prof. Cornell U. Grad. Sch. Bus. and Pub. Adminstrn., 1977-80; chmn. D.C. Council Common. on Bd. Appeals and Rev. of D.C. Govt., 1972 Chmn. Nat. Capital area ACLU, 1966-68; chmn. audit hearing panel Title I ESEA of 1965, 1976-80. Served with USN, 1945-46 Mem. ABA (chmn. sect. adminstrv. law 1978-79) Bar Assn. D.C. (chmn. adminstrv. law sect. 1968-69, gov. 1969-70), D.C. Bar, Fed. Bar Assn., Fed. Energy Bar Assn. (contbr. articles to jour.). Home: 4978 Sentinel Dr Apt 303 Bethesda MD 20816-3573 E-mail: eifraw@comcast.net.

**ROSSAVIK, IVAR KRISTIAN,** obstetrician, gynecologist; b. Stavanger, Rogaland, Norway, Nov. 3, 1936; came to U.S., 1982; s. Andreas and Bergit (Berge) R.; divorced; children: Line, Anne Britt, Kirsten, Solveig; m. Claudia Lagos, May 23, 1987; children: Claudia Kristina, Eevar Benjamin. MD, U. Oslo, 1962, PhD, 1982. Pvt. practice, medicine, Stavanger, 1974; asst chief, acting chmn. U. Tromsoe, Norway, 1974-76; clin. fellow Nat. Hosp. of Norway, Oslo, 1976-81, Norwegian Radium Hosp./U. Oslo, 1981-82; pvt. practice Oslo, 1977-82; rsch. assoc. prof. Baylor Coll. Medicine, Houston, 1983-86; assoc. prof. U. Okla., Oklahoma City, 1987-93, prof., 1993—2001; owner, cons. Clinica Guadalupana, 2001—. Inventor Rossavik Growth Equation, 1980; author: (textbook) Practical Obstetrical Ultrasound: With and Without A Computer, 1991 (Italian translation 1998). Lt. Royal Norwegian Navy, 1964-65. Lutheran. Avocation: computers. Office: Clinica Guadalupana 801 NW 23d St Oklahoma City OK 73106 Personal E-mail: iros@ionef.net.

**ROSSBACHER, LISA ANN,** academic administrator; b. Fredericksburg, Va., Oct. 10, 1952; d. Richard Irwin and Jean Mary (Dearing) R.; m. Dallas D. Rhodes, Aug. 4, 1978. BS, Dickinson Coll., 1975; MA, SUNY, Binghamton, 1978, Princeton U., 1979, PhD, 1983. Cons. Republic Geothermal, Santa Fe Springs, Calif., 1979-81; asst. prof. geology Whittier (Calif.) Coll., 1982-84, Calif. State Poly. U., Pomona, 1984-86, assoc. prof. geol. sci., 1986-91, assoc. v.p. acad. affairs, 1987-93, prof. geol. sci., 1991-93; v.p. acad. affairs, dean faculty Whittier (Calif.) Coll., 1993-95; dean of coll.; prof. geology Dickinson Coll., Carlisle, Pa., 1995-98; pres. So. Poly. State U., Marietta, Ga., 1998—. Vis. rschr. U. Uppsala, Sweden, 1984. Author: Career Opportunities in Geology and the Earth Sciences, 1983, Recent Revolutions in Geology, 1986; (with Rex Buchanan) Geomedia, 1988; columnist Geotimes, 1988—; contbr. articles to profl. jours. Recipient scholarship Ministry Edn. of Finland, Helsinki, 1984; grantee Sigma Xi, 1976, NASA, 1983-94. Fellow AAAS (geol. nominating com. 1984-87, chair-elect geology and geography sect. 1997-98, chair 1998-99, past chair 1999-00); mem. Geol. Soc. Am., Ga. Assn. Colls. (pres. 2005-06). Office: So Poly State U 1100 S Marietta Pkwy SE Marietta GA 30060-2855

**ROSSEL, CARY,** corporate financial executive; Student, Hebrew U. Jerusalem, So. Meth. U. Chief fin. officer Glazer's Wholesale Drug, 1991—. Mem.: Alcoholic Beverage Industry Elec. Data Inerchange Coun. (retail subcom. chair). Office: Glazers 14911 Quorum Dr Ste 400 Dallas TX 75254-7042

**ROSSELLINI, ISABELLA,** actress, model; b. Rome, June 18, 1952; d. Roberto Rossellini and Ingrid Bergman; m. Martin Scorsese, Sept. 1979 (div. Nov. 1982); m. Jonathan Wiedemann (div.); 1 child, Elettra Ingrid. Student, Finch Coll., 1972, New Sch. for Social Research, N.Y.C. Model for Lancôme cosmetics, 1982—95. Actor (films) A Matter of Time, 1976, Il Pap'occhio, 1980, The Meadow, 1982, White Nights, 1985, Blue Velvet, 1986, Siesta, 1987, Red Riding Hood, 1987, Tough Guys Don't Dance, 1987, Zelly and Me, 1988, Cousins, 1989, Wild at Heart, 1990, Les Dames Galantes, 1990, Death Becomes Her, 1992, The Pickle, 1992, Fearless, 1993, Wyatt Earp, 1994, Immortal Beloved, 1994, The Innocent, 1995, The Funeral, Crime of the Century, 1996, Big Night, 1996, The Real Blonde, 1998, Empire, 2002, Roger Dodger, 2002, The Tulse Luper Suitcases: The Moab Story, 2003, The Saddest Music in the World, 2003, The Tulse Luper Suitcases, Part 2: Vaux to the Sea, 2004, King of the Corner, 2004, Heights, 2004, The Feast of the Goat, 2005, The Architect, 2006; (TV films) The Last Elephant, 1990, Lies of the Twins, 1991; Don Quixote, 2000, Monte Walsh, 2003, Earthsea, 2004; (TV miniseries) The Odyssey, 1997, Merlin, 1998, The Impostors, 1998, Left Luggage, 1998; (TV series) Napoléon, 2002; (TV appearances) Friends, 1996, Chicago Hope, 1997, The Simpsons, 1999, Alias, 2004, 2005; writer (films) My Dad Is 100 Years Old, 2005; Author: Some of Me, 1997, In the Name of the Father, the Daughter and the Holy Spirits: Remembering Roberto Rossellini, 2006 Office: United Talent Agy 9560 Wilshire Blvd Ste 500 Beverly Hills CA 90212*

**ROSSELLO, PEDRO,** former governor; b. San Juan, P.R., Apr. 5, 1944; m. Maga Nevares, Aug. 9, 1969; children: Juan Oscar, Luis Roberto, Ricardo Antonio. BS, U. Notre Dame, 1966; MD, Yale U., 1970; MPH, U. P.R., 1981; LLD (hon.), U. Notre Dame, 1995, U. Mass., 1995. Intern straight surgery Beth Israel Hosp., Boston, 1970-71, resident gen. surgery, 1971-74; resident cardiac and burns Mass. Gen. Hosp., Boston, 1972; resident trauma San Francisco Gen. Hosp., 1973; sr. resident pediat. surgery Children's Hosp., Boston, 1974-75, chief resident, pediat. surgery-urology, 1975-76; instr. surgery Harvard Med. Sch., 1975-76; pvt. practice San Juan, 1976-82; asst. prof. surgery U. P.R., 1978-82, assoc. prof. surgery, 1982-92; dir. Dept. Health City of San Juan, 1985-87; chief surgery San Jorge Hosp., San Juan, 1989-92, med. dir., 1990; gov. PR, San Juan, 1993-2001. Legal gov. So. Regional Project Infant Mortality, 1993-95; chair So. States Energy Bd., 1995-96; chmn. So. Growth Policies Bd., 1999-2000; chair So. Tech. Coun., 1998-99, So. Internat. Trade Coun., 1998-99; mem. intergovtl. policy adv. com. U.S. Trade Rep., 1994-2001; pres. Coun. State Govts., 1998; mem. adv. coun. Welfare to Work Partnership; mem. Dem. Nat. Com.; bd. dirs. U.S.-Spain Coun.; mem. nat. adv. bd. Initiative and Referendum Inst. Contbr. articles to profl. jours. Mem P.R. Olympic Com., 1982-84, 87-88; v.p. New Progressive Party, 1988-91, pres., 1991-99; mem. exec. com. Edn. Commn. States, 1995-2000; bd. visitors emeritus Georgetown U. Law Ctr., Washington; del. Dm. Nat. Conv., Chgo., 1996, 2000. Capt. USNG, 1970-76. Recipient Pres.'s award U.S. Hispanic C. of C., 1996, Pres.'s award League of United Latin Am. Citizens, 1998, Rolex Achievement award, 1999. Mem. Nat. Govs. Assn. (host 1996 ann. meeting), So. Govs. Assn. (chair 1997-98), Dem. Govs. Assn. (chair 1998), P.R. Tennis Assn. (pres. 1982-84), Caribbean Tennis Assn. (pres. 1983-84), Alpha Omega Alpha. Avocations: jogging, tennis, ocean kayaking.

**ROSSEN, JORDAN,** lawyer; b. Detroit, June 13, 1934; s. Nathan Paul and Rebecca (Rizy) R.; m. Susan Friebert, Mar. 24, 1963 (div. June 1972); 1 child, Rebecca; m. M. Elizabeth Bunn, Jan. 3, 1981; children— N. Paul, Jordan David. BA, U. Mich., 1956; JD, Harvard U., 1959. Bar: Mich. 1960, N.Y. 1998, U.S. Dist. Ct. (ea. dist.) Mich. 1960, U.S. Dist. Ct. (ea. and so. dists.) N.Y. 1999, U.S. Ct. Appeals (6th cir.) 1966, U.S. Ct. Appeals (7th cir.) 1974, U.S. Ct. Appeals (D.C. cir.) 1984, U.S. Ct. Appeals (3rd cir.) 1987, U.S. Ct. Appeals (2d cir.) 2004, U.S. Supreme Ct. 1966. Assoc. Sullman, Elmer, Eames & Moody, Detroit, 1960-62; assoc. Sugar & Schwartz, Detroit, 1962-64; asst. gen. counsel UAW, Detroit, 1964-74, assoc. gen. counsel, 1974-83, gen. counsel, 1983-98; of counsel Meyer, Suozzi, English and Klein, N.Y.C., NY, 1998—; prof. labor studies Wayne State U., 2000—04. Vice pres. N.P. Rossen Agy., Inc., Detroit, 1960-83; gen. counsel Mich. Health & Social Security Research Inst., Inc., Detroit, 1965-83; dir. UAW Job Devel. & Tng. Corp., Detroit, 1984-90; mem. 6th Cir. Jud. Conf. Editor: Mich. Bar Labor Section Publication, 1961-64. Contbr. articles to profl. jours. Pres. Young Democrats, Mich., 1963-65; chmn. Americans for Democratic Action, Mich., 1966-68; chmn. Voter Registration Dem. Party, Mich., 1967. Recipient Human Rights award, City of Detroit, 1978. Mem.: Nat. Assn. Adminstrv. Law Judges, Coll. Labor and Employment Lawyers, Fed. Bar Assn., N.Y. Bar Assn., Mich. Bar Assn. Jewish. Office: 1350 Broadway Ste 501 New York NY 10018-7705 Office Phone: 212-763-7034. Business E-Mail: jrossen@msek.com.

**ROSSEN-KNILL, DEBORAH F.,** academic administrator, language educator; BA in fiction writing, U. Mich., 1982, MFA in fiction, 1985; PhD in English, U. Minn., 1995. Freelance writer Columbia Presbyn. Med. Ctr., N.Y.C., 1988; tech. and bus. writer Hansome Energy Sys., Inc., Linden, NJ 1986—90; tchg. asst. U. Mich., Ann Arbor, 1983—85, lectr., 1985—86, Madonna Coll., Livonia, Mich., 1986; Sch. Continuing Edn. Divsn. Degree Studies, Gen. Studies Program, NYU, 1987—88, adj. asst. prof., 1989; instr., program in composition and comm. U. Minn., Mpls., 1990—94, asst. coord. upper divsn. composition course, program in composition and comm., 1993—94; vis. scholar Inst. Rsch. in Cognitive Sci., U. Penn., 1994—95; adj. faculty, dept. English U. Penn., 1994—95; postdoctoral fellow Inst. Rsch. in Cognitive Sci., U. Penn., 1995—96; dir. writing program Phila. Coll. Textiles and Sci., 1996—98; dir. Writing Across the U. U. Penn., 1998—99, dir. Speaking Across the U., 1999; sr. lectr., dept. English U. Rochester, 2000—, dir. coll. writing program, 2000—, dean freshman, 2001—. Tchr. creative writing Huron Valley Women's Prison, Ypsilanite, Mich., 1979; co-coord. Guild House Readings, Ann Arbor, Mich., 1985; judge, Icarus contest in fiction, prose and art work NYU, 1988, evaluator bus. sch. essay exam, 88, student adv. gen. studies program, 88; chair, grad. student org. curriculum com. U. Minn., 1990—91, sec. NCTE Student Affiliation, 1991—92; v.p. Grad. Student Org., 1991—92; mem. composition group U. Minn., 1993—94; sec. linguistics panel MMLA, 1994, chair linguistics sessions on dialogue in fiction, 95; spkr. in field. Author: (short stories) Fox Bait, 1988, The Unreal Child, 1985, Booze an' Bo, 1984, co-author (with other) numerous scholary pubs.; co-author: (with others) numerous articles. Finalist, Mark Twain Sesquicentennial Fiction Contest, 1985; recipient P.E.O. Nat. Scholar award, 1994.

**ROSSER, ALVIN RAYMON,** artist; b. Port Clinton, Ohio, July 5, 1928; s. Samuel Webster and Reba Della Rosser; m. Barbara Emma Roth, June 10, 1953; children: Rachelle Karen, Jill Allyn. BFA, Ohio U., 1950, MFA, 1953; postgrad., Hans Hofmann Sch. of Art, N.Y.C., 1953-54. Comml. artist Mutual Broadcasting System, N.Y.C., 1954; art tchr. Chagrin Falls H.S., Ohio, 1955; instr. Lehigh U., Bethlehem, Pa., 1956—58; artists' rep. Gerard Agy., N.Y.C., 1958—60; art dir. Topper Toy Co., Elizabeth, NJ, 1961—62; scenic designer Harnick-Adams Prodns., N.Y.C., 1963—66; art tchr. Sparta Bd. of Edn., NJ, 1966—89. Exhibited in group shows at Ward Eggleston Gallery, N.Y.C., 1953, Roko Gallery, 1953, Koltnow Gallery, 1953—57, Cleve. Mus. Art, 1954, N.Y.C. Ctr., 1954, 1955, 1956, 1957, Jersey City Mus., 1959, Montclair Mus., 1967; artist (one-man shows) Ohio U., 1953, Lehigh U., 1955, Paper Mill Playhouse, N.J., 1960, featured artist N.J. State Fair, 2000, Artery Gallery, Milford, Pa., 2000—02; author: (short stories) A Lesson in Love, I Thought My Father was God, 2002. Trustee, v.p. Sussex County Arts Coun., Newton, NJ, 1970—76. Cpl. U.S. Army, 1950—52. Recipient Emerson Poetry award and 1st prize, Ohio U., 1954, Skylands Best in Show award, Sussex County Arts Coun., 1989, Skylands Select Best in Show award, 2001, Patrick-Claus award, 2003. Avocations: fishing, gardening, beekeeping, pool, ventriloquy. Mailing: PO Box 76 Sparta NJ 07871-0076

**ROSSER, ANNETTA HAMILTON,** composer; b. Jasper, Fla., Aug. 28, 1913; d. Carlos Calvin and Jermai Reuben (Gilbert) Hamilton; m. John Barkley Rosser, Sept. 7, 1935 (dec. Sept. 1989); children: Edwenna Merryday, John Barkley Jr. BM, Fla. State U., 1932. Cert. tchr. Fla. Tchr. music Kirby-Smith Jr. High Sch., Jacksonville, Fla., 1932-35; 1st violinist Santa

Monica (Calif.) Symphony, 1949-50; concertmaster Ithaca (N.Y.) Chamber Orch., 1948-56, Cornell Univ. Orch., Ithaca, 1948-56, soloist, 1957; 1st violinist Princeton (N.J.) Symphony, 1959-61; concertmaster Madison (Wis.) Symphony Orch., 1963-66, 1st violinist, 1967-82. Composer of over 100 vocal and instrumental compositions including Meditations on Cross, song cycle for 2 voices, flute and piano, 1976, An Offering of Song, book of 48 songs, 1977, Songs of a Nomad Flute, song cycle for soprano, flute and piano, 1978, Six Songs of the T'ang Dynasty for soprano and violin, 1983, Nocturne for violin and piano, 1989, Trio for flute, violin and piano, 1991, Scherzo for flute ensemble, 1991, (book of 21 songs) Another Offering of Song, 1998. Bd. dirs Madison Opera Guild, 1972-86, Madison Civic Music Assn., 1983-85; past pres. Madison Symphony Orch. League, Ithaca Federated Music Club, Ithaca Composers Club; bd. dirs. Madison Art Ctr., 1979-83, Madison Woman of Distinction, 1980, Madison Civics Club, 1976-79, pres., 1977-78; pres. Art League Madison Art Ctr., 1980-82, Univ. League Scholarship Benefit Concert of Rosser Compositions, U. Wis., MMadison, 2003. Recipient Sr. Svc. award Rotary Club, 1994; original music manuscripts and programs were added to archives of U. Wis.-Madison Music Libr., 1996. Mem. AAUW, Wis. Acad. Scis., Arts, and Letters, Univ. League, Univ. League Bird Study Group, Madison Club, Wis. Acad. Scis., Arts, and Letters, PEO, Phi Kappa Phi, Pi Kappa Lambda, Sigma Alpha Iota. Republican. Presbyterian. Avocations: Chinese snuff bottles, English brass rubbings, birding. Home: 4209 Manitou Way Madison WI 53711-3703

**ROSSER, EDWIN MICHAEL,** mortgage company executive; b. Denver, Oct. 11, 1940; s. Edwin Michael and Anne (Ratliff) R.; m. Keren Call, July 17, 1969; children: Kevin, William. BS, Colo. State U., 1964; MA, U. No. Colo., 1974. Cert. mortgage banker. Mktg. officer United Bank Mortgage, Denver, 1968-74; dir. nat. accounts PMI Mortgage Ins. Co., Denver, 1974-85; v.p. Moore Mortgage Co., Denver, 1985-87, Pacific First Mortgage Corp., Englewood, Colo., 1987-89; 1st v.p. 1st Nat. Bank, San Francisco, 1990-93; v.p. nat. accounts United Guaranty Corp., 1993—. Bd. dirs. Rocky Mtn. Women's Inst. Photographer represented in Denver Art Mus., The Buffalo in Winter, (1st place award 1981). Steering com. Blueprint for Colo., Govs. Unified Housing Task Force; mem. Colo. Housing Coun. (chmn. 1986-87); bd. dirs. Colo. State U. Found.; mem. adv. bd. Arapahoe County Open Space and Trails, 1999—; mem. Colo. Land Use Commn., 1999, Colo. State Housing Bd., 2003; bd. dirs. The Conservation Campaign, 2004. Fellow Soc. Mortgage Bankers; mem. Am. Planning Assn., Soc. of Cert. Mortgage Bankers (chmn.), Mortgage Bankers Assn. Am. (cert., bd. govs. 1986-90, state and local achievement award 1986, Ernest P. Schumacher award 1988, disting. svc. award 2003, Burton Wood Legis. Svc. award), Colo. Mortgage Bankers Assn. (bd. dirs. 1979-88, pres. 1986, adv. bd. trust for pub. land, E.C. Spelman award 1978, Lifetime Achievement award 1998), Colo. Assn. Commerce and Industry, Denver Nat. Soc. Real Estate Fin., Mus. Natural History, Denver C. of C., Rocky Mtn. Mutual Housing Assn. (bd. dirs.), Ctr. of Fin. Real Estate (bd. dirs.), Colo. State U. Alumni Assn. (nat. pres. 1985, bd. dirs. 1979-87, mem. found. bd. 1987-91, 93-2000, Honor Alumnus 1984, ha Sasso award Dept. Athletics 1993), Univ. Club, City Club Denver, Nat. Soc. for Real Estate Fin. (CRF designation 1997), Colo. State U. Henry Alumni (Svc. award 2000), Univ. Club, Alpha Sigma Gamma Republican. Roman Catholic. Avocations: photography, fly fishing. Home: 12478 E Amherst Cir Aurora CO 80014-3306 Office: United Guaranty Residential Ins Co 6312 S Fiddlers Green Cir Englewood CO 80111-4943 Personal E-mail: emrcmb@aol.com.

**ROSSER, ESSIE,** minister, counselor, marketing professional; b. Dawson, Ga., Apr. 15, 1939; d. James Andrews and Essie Louise Kimbrough; children: Evelyn Ellington, Augustus Reid, Anthony Reid, Lassels Reid. Student, Corp. Coll., 1968—69; AA, Onondaga C.C., Syracuse, N.Y., 1972; BA, Oswego State Coll., 1974; JD, Atlanta Law Sch., 1982; ThD, 1998; DD, Abotra Bible Inst. and Sem. Trained nursing technician Syracuse Meml. Hosp., NY, 1957—62; employment counselor, dir. People's Employment Agy., Syracuse, 1962—64, CEO, dir. job readiness/placement clients, writer manual Decatur, Ga.; cons. families/food plan Family Food Svs., Fulton, NY, 1964—68; sales dir., CEO Dependable Janitorial Svs., North Syracuse, NY, 1969—73; rsch. supr. Math., Inc., Dayton, Ohio, 1975—77; adminstrv. asst. psychology dept. Clark Coll., Atlanta, 1977—82; min., counselor drug deliverance/prevention counselor ch. Worldwide Word Ministries., Inc., Atlanta. Achievements include development of faith based deliverance programs; drug prevention curriculums beginning with pre-k child, extending through high school presently being established in faith based organizations engaging their help with the drug problem. Avocations: antiques, music, writing, travel. Home: 180 Gibson St Atlanta GA 30316-1453

**ROSSER, JAMES MILTON,** academic administrator; b. East St. Louis, Ill., Apr. 16, 1939; s. William M. and Mary E. (Bass) R.; 1 child, Terrence. BA, So. Ill. U., 1962, MA, 1963, PhD, 1969, LHD (hon.), 2003. Diagnostic bacteriologist Holden Hosp., Carbondale, Ill., 1961-63; rsch. bacteriologist Eli Lilly & Co., Indpls., 1963-66; coordinator Black Am. studies, instr. health edn. So. Ill. U., Carbondale, 1968-69, asst. prof. Black Am. studies dir., 1969-70, asst. to chancellor, 1970; assoc. vice chancellor for acad. affairs U. Kans., Lawrence, 1970-74, assoc. prof. edn., pharmacology and toxicology, 1971-74; vice chancellor dept. higher edn. State of N.J., Trenton, 1974-79, acting chancellor, 1977; pres., prof. health care mgmt. Calif. State U., Los Angeles, 1979—. Mem. tech. resource panel Ctr. for R&D in Higher Edn., U. Calif., Berkeley, 1974-76; mem. health maintenance orgn. com. Health Planning Coun., State of N.J., 1975-79; mem. standing com. on R&D bd. trustees Ednl. Testing Service, 1976-77; mem. steering com. and task force on retention of minorities in engring. Assembly of Engring. NRC, 1975-78; mem. Bd. Med. Examiners, State of N.J., 1978-79; vis. faculty Inst. Mgmt. of Lifelong Edn., Grad. Sch. Edn., Harvard U., 1979; mem. Calif. State U. Trustees Spl. Long Range Fin. Planning Com., 1982-87; mem. Am. Coun. on Edn., 1979—, AFL/CIO Labor Higher Edn. Coun., 1983—, Nat. Commn. Higher Edn. Issues, 1981-82; mem. The Calif. Achievement Coun., 1983-89, strategic adv. counc. Coll. and Univs. Systems Exch., 1988-91; bd. dirs. Am. Humanities Coun., So. Calif. Am. Humanics, Inc. Coun., United Calif. Bank, Edison Internat., Fedco, Inc.; task force on equality and fairness Texaco, 1999-2002. Author: An Analysis of Health Care Delivery, 1977. Mem. exec. bd., chmn. varsity scouting program LA area coun. Boy Scouts Am., 1980—; bd. dirs. Hispanic Urban Ctr., LA, 1979, LA Urban League, 1982-95, Cmty. TV of So. Calif., Sta. KCET, 1980-89, 98—, United Way, L.A., 1980-91, Orthopaedic Hosp., 1983-86, L.A. Philharm. Assn., 1986-99, Nat. Health Found., 1990-98; mem. Citizen's Adv. Coun. Congl. Caucus Sci. and Tech., 1983—; mem. performing arts coun./edn. coun. Music Ctr., 1984-99; minority bus. task force Pacific Bell, 1985-88; bd. govs. Nat. ARC, 1986-91, Mayor's Blue Ribbon Task Force on Drugs, City of L.A., 1988, LA Annenberg Met. Project, 1994-01; Nat. Adv. Coun. on Aging, 1989-93; trustee Woodrow Wilson Nat. Fellowship Found., 1993-04; bd. advisors Historically Black Colls. and Univs. and Minority Insts., Dept. Air Force, 1997-01; bd. dirs. Ams. for the Arts, 1991-04; mem. L.A. Adv. Alliance, Pasadena Tournament of Roses, 2000-03; mem. Action Forum on Diversity in the Engring. Workforce, Nat. Acad. Engring., 2000-04; mem. Calif. Coun. on Sci. and Tech., 1999—; mem. campaign adv. com. The Audubon Ctr. L.A., 2001-03; active Alliance for Coll. Ready Pub. Schs., 2001—, Calif. Cmty. Found., 2002—, L.A. World Affairs Coun., 2004; mem. 2020 vision com. SIU, 2002. NSF fellow, 1961; NDEA fellow, 1967-68; recipient award of recognition in Edn. Involvement for Young Achievers, 1981, Pioneer of Black Hist. Achievement award Brotherhood Crusade, 1981, Alumni Achievement award So. Ill. U., 1982, Friend of Youth award Am. Humanics, Inc., 1985, Leadership award Dept. Higher Edn. Ednl. Equal Opportunity Fund Program, 1989, Medal of Excellence Gold State Minority Found., 1990, Take Charge of Learning Success award Inst. for Redesign of Learning, 1995, The Educator Achievement award NSF, 1995, Nat. Svc. award L.A. Urban League, 1995, Edn. award Watts Found. Cmty. Trust, 1995, Humanitarian award Torrance Area C. of C., 2004. Mem. Calif. C. of C. (bd. dirs. 1993—), Alhambra C. of C. (bd. dirs. 1979—), Los Angeles C. of C. (bd. dirs. 1985-90), Am. Assn. State Colls. and Univs., Kappa Delta Pi, Phi Kappa Phi. Roman Catholic. Office: Calif State U LA Office of Pres 5151 State University Dr Los Angeles CA 90032

**ROSSER, JOHN BARKLEY, JR.,** economics professor; b. Ithaca, N.Y., Apr. 12, 1948; s. John Barkley and Annetta Louise (Hamilton) R.; m. Sue A. Vilhauer, Aug. 31, 1968 (div. 1979); children: Meagan Rebecca, Caitlin Elizabeth; m. Marina R. Vcherashnaya, May 24, 1987; 1 child: Alexandra Ashley. BA, U. Wis., 1969, MA, 1972, PhD, 1976. Project specialist Inst. Environ. Studies, Madison, Wis., 1972-75; planning analyst Dept. Natural Resources, Madison, 1975-76; prof. econs. James Madison U., Harrisonburg, Va., 1977—, Kirby L. Kramer Jr. chair of bus. adminstrn., 1996—. Author: From Catastrophe to Chaos: A General Theory of Economic Discontinuities, 1991, (with M.V. Rosser) Comparative Economics in a Transforming World Economy, 1996, 2nd edit., 2004, (with D. Colander and R.P.F. Holt) The Changing Face of Economics: Conversations with Cutting Edge Economists, 2004, Complexity in Economics, 2004; editor Jour. Econ. Behavior and Frgn., 2002-; contbr. articles to profl. jours Mem. Am. Econs. Assn., So. Econs. Assn., N.Y. Acad. Scis. Home: 236 Franklin St Harrisonburg VA 22801-4019 Office: James Madison Univ MSC0204 Dept Economics Harrisonburg VA 22807-0001 Office Phone: 540-568-3212. Business E-Mail: rosserjb@jmu.edu.

**ROSSER, RICHARD FRANKLIN,** educational association administrator, consultant; b. Arcanum, Ohio, July 16, 1929; s. Harold Arm and Margaret (Whitacre) R.; m. Donna Eyssen, Mar. 21, 1951; children— Eric, Carl, Edward. BA, Ohio Wesleyan U., 1951; MPA, Syracuse U., 1952, PhD, 1961. Joined USAF, 1952, advanced through grades to col.; 1968; prof. polit. sci. USAF Acad., Colorado Springs, Colo., 1959-73, head dept., 1967-73, ret., 1973; prof. polit. sci., dean Albion (Mich.) Coll., 1973-77; pres. DePauw U., Greencastle, Ind., 1977-86, chancellor, 1986; pres. Nat. Assn. Ind. Colls. and Univs., Washington, 1986-93; cons. in higher edn. pvt. practice, Racine, Wis., 1993—. Author: An Introduction to Soviet Foreign Policy, 1969, contbr. articles to profl. jours. Mem. univ. senate United Meth. Ch., 1980-84; mem. spl. commn. of Chief of Staff on Honor Code U.S. Mil. Acad., 1989; bd. visitors Air U., 1991-94; bd. trustees Ohio Wesleyan U., 1991—; mem. nat. adv. com. Instnl. Quality and Integrity, 1994—; co-chair Citizens for Librs., Grand Traverse County, 1995-96. Decorated Legion of Merit with oak leaf cluster. Mem. Phi Beta Kappa, Omicron Delta Kappa. Unitarian. Home and Office: 21 Twin Pond Rd Topsham ME 04086

**ROSSET, BARNET LEE, JR.,** publishing executive; b. Chgo., May 28, 1922; s. Barnet Lee and Mary (Tansey) R.; m. Joan Mitchell, 1950 (div. 1952); m. Hannelore Eckert, Aug. 1953 (div. 1957); 1 child, Peter; m. Cristine Agnini, Mar. 11, 1965 (div. 1979); children: Tansey, Beckett; m. Elisabeth Krug, 1980 (div. 1991); 1 child, Chantal. Ph.B., U. Chgo., 1947; BA New Sch. Social Research, N.Y.C., 1952. Pub., editor Grove Press, Inc., 1951-86, Evergreen Rev., 1957-73, Blue Moon Books, Inc., N.Y.C., 1987-98, Evergreen Rev. Inc., 1998—, Foxrock, Inc., 1995—. Served to 1st lt. Signal Corps AUS, 1942-46. Recipient Ninth Pub. citation PEN Am. Ctr., 1988, Poor Richard's award Small Press Ctr., 1999, Commandeur De L'Ordre Des Arts et Des Lettres, French Govt., 1999, Nat. Book Critics Cir. Lifetime Achievement award, 2001, Curtis Benjamin award Assn. Am. Pubs., 2001, 1st Ann. Hadada award Paris Rev., 2003. Mem. PEN, Overseas Press Club. Office: 61 4th Ave New York NY 10003-5204 Office Phone: 212-505-6880. Personal E-mail: evergreen@nyc.rr.com.

**ROSSETTI, ARMAND JOHN, JR.,** lawyer; b. Stoneham, Mass., Sept. 20, 1947; s. Armand John and Mary Liberty Rossetti; m. Patricia Ann Imbrici, Dec. 27, 1981; 1 child, Michael John. BS in Chemistry, Salem State Coll., 1970; JD, Mass. Sch. Law, 1993. Bar: Ma., NH. Med. lab. tech. Smith Kline and French, Boston, 1970—72; v.p. to pres. State Toxicology Svc., Inc., Boston, 1972—81; pvt. practice Andover and Middleton, Mass., 1999—. Cons. Med. Learning Channel, Walleslay, Mass. Author: Transcendence, 1995, Code Talkers, 1998. Avocation: music.

**ROSSETTINI, TIMOTHY JAMES,** music educator, director; b. Paterson, N.J., Nov. 20, 1980; s. Louis Joseph and Madeline Ruth Rossettini; m. Amanda J. West, May 20, 2006. MusB cum laude in Applied Percussion, James Madison U., 2003. Lic. tchr. music va., 2003. Dir. bands Denbigh H.S., Newport News, Va., 2004—. Mem.: Va. Band and Orch. Dirs. Assn. (mem. all-state percussion audition com. 2005—06). Office: Denbigh High School 259 Denbigh Boulevard Newport News VA 23608 Office Phone: 757-886-7700 1147. Office Fax: 757-872-6542. Business E-Mail: tim.rossettini@nn.k12.va.us.

**ROSSETTOS, NICHOLAS J.,** research and development company executive; AB in Econs., Princeton U.; MS in Acctg., Northeastern U., MBA. Dir. fin. and adminstrn. EnviroBusiness, Inc.; mgr. fin. Centerwatch (subs. Thomson CP); CFO Atlantic Tech. Ventures, Inc., N.Y.C., 2000—. Office: Atlantic Technology Ventures Inc 787 7th Ave New York NY 10019-6018

**ROSSI, ANTHONY GERALD,** lawyer; b. Warren, Ohio, July 20, 1935; s. Anthony Gerald and Lena (Guarnieri) R.; m. Marilyn J. Fuller, June 22, 1957; children: Diana L., Maribeth, Anthony Gerald III. BS, John Carroll U., 1957; JD, Cath. U. Am., 1961. Bar: Ohio 1961. Ptnr. Guarnieri & Secrest, Warren, 1961—; former acting judge Warren Municipal Ct. Mem. Mahoning-Shenango Estate Planning Coun., 1968—, past sec.; past pres. Warren Olympic Club; past bd. govs. Cath. U. Am. Law Sch. Coun.; past trustee Trumbull Art Guild, Warren Civic Music Assn. Capt. Transp. Corps, AUS, 1957-65. Mem. ABA, Ohio Bar Assn., Trumbull County Bar Assn. (exec. com. 1975—, pres. 1976-77), Am. Arbitration Assn., Ohio State Bar Found., Ohio Motorist Assn. (corp. mem., trustee 1980-86, 92-98), Wolf's Club, KC, Elks, Ohio Acad. of Trial Lawyers. Home: 2500 Hidden Lakes Dr NE Warren OH 44484-4159 Office: 151 E Market St Warren OH 44481-1102 Office Phone: 330-393-1584. E-mail: ganslaw@netdotcom.com.

**ROSSI, BARBARA,** economics professor; PhD in Econs., Princeton U., NJ, 2001. Asst. prof. economics Duke U., Durham, NC, 2001—. Contbr. articles to profl. jours. Fellow, Princeton U., 1996; grantee Office of Internat. Rsch. Rsch. grant, Duke U., 2006; scholar Invernizzi Scholarship, Bocconi U. (Italy), 1996; Trent Found. grant, Duke U., 2006, Office of Internat. Affairs grant, 2000, Ctr. for European Studies grant, 2005, Internat. Fin. Summer fellow, Princeton U., 1999—2000, Marco Fanno scholar, Mediocredito Ctrl., 1996. Fellow: European Area Bus. Cycle; mem.: Com. On Status Women In Econs. Profession, Econometric Soc., Am. Econ. Assn. Office: Duke U Social Science Building Durham NC 27705

**ROSSI, DINO J.,** former state legislator; b. Seattle, Oct. 15, 1959; s. John and Eve Rossi; m. Terry Rossi, 1987; children: Juliauna, Jake, Joseph, Jillian. BA in Bus. Mgmt., Seattle U., 1982. Mem. Wash. Senate, Dist. 5, Olympia, 1996—2003; mem. energy, tech., and telecom. com. Wash. Senate; mem. natural resources, parks and recreation com.; mem. ways and means com.; chmn., 2003; mem. capital budget subcom.; mem. joint com. on pension policy. Vol. Sr. Ctr.; co-founder Operation Homefront; past bd. dirs. Boys and Girls Club, Mountains to Sound Greenway Bd. Mem. Rotary (Issaquah). Republican.

**ROSSI, ENNIO C.,** internist, educator; b. Madison, Wis., Apr. 3, 1931; s. Joseph and Esther (D'Amelio) R.; m. Anna Maria Bianchi, June 22, 1957; children: Roberta, Marco. BA, U. Wis., 1951, MD, 1954. Diplomate Am. Bd. Internal Medicine. Intern Ohio State U. Hosps., 1954-55; resident medicine U. Wis. Hosps., 1958-61, fellow, 1961-63; instr. medicine Marquette U., Milw., 1963-64, asst. prof. medicine, 1964-66; assoc. prof. medicine Northwestern U., Chgo., 1966-72, prof. medicine, 1972-96, prof. emeritus, 1996—, chief hematology, 1967-84, chief transfusion medicine, 1984-96. V.p. med. affairs Life Source Blood Ctr., Glenview, Ill., 1988-93; vis. scientist Mario Negri Inst., Milan, 1977. Co-editor: Haemostasis and the Kidney, 1989; sr. editor: Principles of Transfusion Medicine, 1991, 2d edit., 1996. Capt. U.S. Army, 1956-58. Fulbright scholar, U.S. Dept. State, U. Rome, 1955; Nat. Heart, Lung Blood Inst. Transfusion Medicine Acad. awardee, 1983; WHO travelling fellow, 1985. Fellow ACP; mem. Am. Soc. Hematology, Am. Soc.

Pharmacology and Exptl. Therapeutics, Am. Assn. Blood Banks (chmn. acad. transfusion medicine com. 1988-93), Internat. Soc. Blood Transfusion. Home: 812 Oak St Apt 302 Winnetka IL 60093-2560

**ROSSI, GUIDO A(NTONIO),** mathematics professor, researcher; b. Moretta, Cuneo, Italy, Jan. 17, 1944; s. Giulio Cesare and Anna Maria (Ferraris di Celle) R.; m. Maria Emilia Zucchi, Mar. 27, 1978. Dr. in Math., U. Torino, Italy, 1967. Asst. U. Torino, 1969-82; asst. prof. Facoltà di Economia e Commercio, 1969-82, assoc. prof. math., 1982-86, prof. math. social scis. and econs., 1986, full prof., 1986—, prof. math. for fin., 1996. Dir. Inst. Math Finanziaria, 1974-81, 83-85, 1992-94, dir. dept. stats. and applied math. human scis., 1995-2003, coord. rsch. projects, 1986—; pres. U. Mgmt. d'Impresa Sch., 2002—, pres.bd. tchrs. actuarial scis., 2005-; prof. Scuola di Applicazione Italian Army, 1992—; mem. sci. bd. 3d A.F.I.R. Colloquium, 1993; mem. Internat. Sci. Com.; organizer FUR X conf.; bd. tchrs. doctorate program in math. for fin. markets joint Univs. Brescia, Milano, Torino, Pavia, 1991-2003, decision scis. U. Torino, 2003—. Contbr. articles to profl. and sci. jours. Served to lt. Italian Army, 1967-68, diplomated Sommelier, 1986. Decorated cavaliere dell'Ordine al Merito Civile di Savoia, 1990, comdr., 1996. Mem. Unione Matematica Italiana, Assn. per la Matematica Applicata alle Scienze Economiche Sociali (auditor 1977-89, 2002—, adminstr. 1990—2001), Assn. Italiana di Ricerca Operativa (auditor 1990—), Italian Order of Actuaries, Assn. Italiana Sommeliers, Assn. Museo Ferroviario Piemontese (pres. 1986-2005), Am. Math. Soc., European Math. Soc., Inst. Vienna Circ., Istituto Italiano dei Castelli-Internat. Burgen Institut, Fondo per l'Ambiente Italiano, Italian Fedn. Ferrovie Turistiche and Museali (cofounder, first pres. 1997-99), European Fedn. Mus. Tourist Railways (cofounder, bd. mem., 2003-); Clubs: I Neoteri (pres. 1990-92). Roman Catholic. Achievements include contributions to the foundations of probability, decision theory and financial decisions. Office: Dept Statistica & Matematica Applicata Piazza Arbarello 8 I-10122 Turin Italy E-mail: guido.rossi@unito.it.

**ROSSI, JOSEPH ANTHONY,** film and television make-up artist, educator; b. Providence, July 10, 1955; s. Michael Thomas and Jennie (Paolucci) R.; m. Christina Elliott; children: Michael Elliott, Sofia Rose. BS, R.I. Coll., 1977. Tchr. film and TV R.I. Coll., Providence, 1983-86, Salve Regina Coll., Newport, R.I., 1983—; owner, prin. Joe Rossi Makeup, Providence, 1977—, 1001 Faces, Providence, 1979—. Dept. head Underdog and Showtimes' Brotherhood. Make-up artist Pres. William Clinton and Hillary Rodham Clinton, v.p. Albert Gore, make-up artist on feature films War of the Worlds, Fever Pitch, The Last Shot, Stuck on You, Little Black Book, Moonlight Mile, Hanging By a Thread, Mona Lisa Smile, Goodbye, Hello, Shallow Hal, Osmosis Jones, Passionada, Prozac Nation, Me, Myself and Irene, Bye, Bye, America, David Mamet's State and Main, Thirteen Days, Lift, The Human Stain, Pink Floyd, Zoom, Crimestoppers 800, First Person, Saturday Night Live, Rivera Live, Wide World Sports, Nat. Geog. Lost Subs K-19, 2004, make-up artist Face the Nation, 60 Minutes, 1995 Skating Finals ABC-TV, Unsolved Mysteries, Providence, Face the Nation, 2004, Peter Jennings, Outside Providence, Universal feature Meet Joe Black, original design Philip Glass Opera, The Fall of the House of Usher and Genet's The Balcony, at the Bolshoi Theatre, Russia; contbr. chapters to books. Bd. dirs. R.I. State Coun. on Arts, 1996-2003. Home and Office: 137 Abbott Run Valley Rd Cumberland RI 02864-3249 Office Phone: 401-334-3436. E-mail: joe@rossimakeup.com.

**ROSSI, MARK ANTONY,** political consultant, writer; b. Jersey City, Apr. 3, 1965; s. Reynaldo and Florence Mary Rossi; m. Kimberly Jean Morgan, May 4, 2002. AAS in Polit. Sci., C.C. USAF, Ramstein, West Germany, 1989; BA in Polit. Sci., 1991, cert. in cmty. rels. civil svc., 1997. Polit. cons. Rep. Party, 1991—; dir. cmty. rels. HHS, Jersey City, 1995—99. Author: (non-fiction) The Intruder Bulletins: Dark Side of Technology, 2003, Mother Of All Machines, 2002, Sword Of Our Fathers: Essays on the Hardships of Writing, 2002, (fiction) Tracking The Beast, 2001, Grins of Divinity, 2001, (poetry) Persistence of Metaphor, 2001, (drama) Obscentities, 2000, (screenplays) Hellscape Three, 2002, Serpenthouse, 2003, (plays) Gear Fear, 1995, Cross, 1996, Thief in the Mist, 1997. Spkr. Ariz. Breakfast Club, 2000—02. Sgt. USAF, 1984—90. Named Pub. Employee of Yr., City of Jersey City, 1997; recipient Cold War Recognition cert., Dept. of Def., 1999, Essay of Yr. award, Very Spl. Arts N.J., 1997, N.J. Playwright of Yr. award, Bayonne Writer's Group of N.J., 1997. Mem.: Bioethics & Lit. Soc. (life), Am. Legion (corr.; pub. affairs 1999—2003). Avocations: theater, jazz. Home: 1773 E Gail DR Chandler AZ 85225-8714 Personal E-mail: markantonyrossi@yahoo.com.

**ROSSI, NORBERT GUIDO,** music educator; b. Tarentum, Pa., July 30, 1952; m. Debora Susan Shoop, June 2, 1973; children: Paul, Auralee. BA in choral music edn., Anerson Coll., 1974; MA in tchg., Grand Canyon U., 2002. Choral dir. Browning (Mont.) HS, 1974—76; music tchr. Bloomfield (Conn.) Mid. Sch., 1976—79; choral dir. Shelby (Mont.) HS, Mont., 1979—80, Cut Bank (Mont.) HS, 1980—89, Columbia Falls (Mont.) HS, 1989—2000, Walla Walla (Wash.) HS, 2000—. Composer: His Heart Sleeps, 1997. Mem.: Wash. Am. Choral Dirs. Assn. (rs chair 2000—), Music Educators Nat. Conf., Mont. Choral Dirs. Assn. (pres. 1993—95). Avocations: reading, hiking, fly fishing. Home: 186 Kimberly Ct Walla Walla WA 99362 Office: Walla Walla HS 800 Abbott Rd Walla Walla WA 99362 Office Phone: 509-527-3039. Office Fax: 509-527-3034. E-mail: nrossi@wwps.org.

**ROSSI, PETER HENRY,** sociology educator; b. N.Y.C., Dec. 27, 1921; s. Peter Maxim and Elizabeth (Porcelli) R.; m. Alice Schaerr, Sept. 29, 1951; children: Peter Eric, Kristin Alice, Nina Alexis. BS, CCNY, 1943; PhD, Columbia, 1951. Research asso. Bur. Applied Social Research, Columbia U., 1947- 51; asst. prof. Harvard U., 1951-55; prof. dept. sociology U. Chgo., 1955-67; dir. Nat. Opinion Research Center, 1960-67; prof. dept. social relations Johns Hopkins, 1967-74, chmn. dept., 1967-70; dir. research Center for Met. Planning and Research, 1972-74; prof. sociology, dir. Social and Demographic Research Inst., U. Mass., Amherst, 1974-92, Stuart A. Rice prof. sociology, dir., 1984-92, prof. emeritus, 1992—; faculty assoc. Chapin Hall U. Chgo., 1994—. Author: Why Families Move, 1956, The Politics of Urban Renewal, 1962, The Education of Catholic Americans, 1966, New Media and Education, 1967, Ghetto Revolts, 1970, Cities Under Siege, 1971, Evaluating Social Programs, 1972, Roots of Urban Discontent, 1974, Reforming Public Welfare, 1976, Prison Reform and State Elites, 1977, Evaluation: A Systematic Approach, 1979, Money, Work & Crime, 1980, After the Clean-up, 1980, Social Science and Natural Hazards, 1981, Measuring Social Judgements, 1982, Natural Hazards and Public Choice, 1982, Under the Gun, 1983, Applied Sociology, 1983, Without Shelter, 1989, Down and Out in America, 1989, Of Human Bonding, 1990, Just Punishments, 1997, Feeding the Poor, 1999; editor: Am. Jour. Sociology, 1957-58; assoc. editor: Am. Sociol. Rev, 1957-60, Am. Sociologist, 1964-66; editor: Social Sci. Research, 1972-89; contbr. articles to profl. and popular jours. Served with AUS, 1942-45. Recipient Alvah and Gunnar Myrdal award for contbns. to evaluation research, 1981; Commonwealth award for contbns. to sociology, 1985; faculty research grantee Social Sci. Research Council, 1959; Carnegie sr. fellow, 1965 Fellow Am. Acad. Arts and Scis.; mem. Am. Sociol. Assn. (sec. 1968-72, pres.-elect 1979-80, pres. 1980-81), Am. Evaluation Assn.

**ROSSI, RONALD ALDO,** sports association administrator, Olympic athlete; b. Bronx, N.Y., Dec. 2, 1956; s. Aldo D. and Jeanette (Morretta) R.; m. Susan Veltman, Mar. 26, 1983; children: Scott, Lauren. BEE, Manhattan Coll., 1978. Registered profl. engr., N.Y. Mem. computer ops. staff John Blair and Co., N.Y.C., 1978-83, communications engr., 1984; sports program dir. U.S. Luge Assn., Lake Placid, NY, 1984-85, exec. dir., 1985—. Com. mem. U.S. Luge Assn., 1978—, athlete's rep., 1980-83; com. mem. U.S. Olympic Com., Colorado Springs, Colo., 1989-90, 93-96. Mem. U.S. Olympic Luge Team, Sarajevo, Yugoslavia, 1984; mem. Olympic team staff, Calgary, Can., 1988, Albertville, France, 1992, Lillehammer, Norway, 1994, Nagano, Japan, 1998, Salt Lake City, 2002, Torino, Italy, 2006. Avocations: luge, golf, softball, movies, computers. Address: US Luge Association 57 Church St Lake Placid NY 12946-1805

**ROSSI, RUTH HARRIS,** special education educator; d. Everett Tomlinson Harris and Clora Ethel Stanley; m. Raymond Anthony Rossi, Feb. 26, 1977; children: Hillary Niles, Tess Virginia, Anthony John. BA, U. R.I., 1967, postgrad., 1973; EdM, Seattle U., 1995. Spl. ed. tchr. Lakota Mid. Sch., Federal Way, Wash., 1989—, spl. ed. dept. chair, 2002—. Mem. post-secondary transition adv. com. Federal Way Sch. Dist., 1999—. Treas. PTA, Woodmont East Sch., Federal Way, 1982, 1996, 1997; leader, membership facilitator CampFire, Kent, Wash., 1982—86; mem. customer adv. com. Puget Sound Power, Renton, Wash., 1983, 1984. Grantee, Federal Way Edn. Found., 2003. Mem.: Assn. for Supervision and Curriculum Devel., ACLU, Audubon Soc. Avocations: reading, walking, gardening, cooking, needle-point. Office: Lakota Mid Sch 1415 SW 314th St Federal Way WA 98023

**ROSSI, STEVEN B.,** newspaper publishing company executive; m. Rosemary; four children. BA, Ursinus Coll.; MBA, U. Pa., 1974. Gen. mgr., corp. controller IU Internat. Corp.; v.p., gen. mgr. Amerigas Indsl. Gases, 1988-91; v.p., CFO Phila. Newspapers Inc. Knight Ridder, Phila., 1987-88, sr. v.p. ops. Phila. Newspapers Inc., 1989-91, exec. v.p. Phila. Newspapers Inc., 1991-98, sr. v.p. ops. San Jose, Calif., 1998—2001, pres. newspaper div., 2001—04, sr. v.p., CFO, 2004—. Chmn. bd. dirs. Am. Music Theater Festival; bd. dirs. Univ. Arts. Mem. Pa. Newspapers Publ.'s Assn. (bd. dirs.). Office: Knight Ridder 50 W San Fernando St San Jose CA 95113-2429

**ROSSIDES, EUGENE TELEMACHUS,** lawyer, writer; b. N.Y.C., Oct. 23, 1927; s. Telemachus and Anna (Maravel) R.; m. Elinor Burcham (div.); 1 child, Gale; m. Aphrodite Macotsin, Dec. 30, 1961; children: Michael, Alexander, Eleni. AB, Columbia U., 1949, JD, 1952. Criminal law investigator Office of Dist. Atty., N.Y.C., 1952; assoc. Rogers & Wells, N.Y.C. 1954 56, 61-66, ptnr., 1966-69, 73-92, sr. counsel, 1993—; asst. atty. gen. State of N.Y., N.Y.C., 1956-58; asst. to undersec. Dept. Treasury, Washington, 1958-61, asst. sec., 1969-73. Bd. dirs. Sterling Nat. Bank, N.Y.C. Author: U.S. Import Trade Regulation, 2d edit., 1986, Foreign Unfair Competition, 3d edit., 1991, United States Import Trade Law, 1992, also articles; chief import editor Internat. Trade Reporter, Bur. Nat. Affairs, 1980—; editor: The Truman Doctrine of Aid to Greece: A Fifty-Year Retrospective, 1998, Doing Business in Greece, 1996, U.S. Rels. with Greece and Cyprus, 1990—. Mem. Grace Commn., Washington, 1981-82; chmn. nationalities div. Reagan Bush Com., Washington, 1980; campaign mgr. N.Y.C. Nixon for Pres. Com., 1968, Keating for Senator Com., N.Y. State, 1964; bd. dirs. Eisenhower World Affairs Inst., Washington, Am. Hellenic Inst. Capt. USAF, 1952-60. Recipient Medal for Excellence, Columbia U., 1972, Young Lawyer's award Columbia Law Sch. Alumni Assn., 1972, Silver Anniversary award NCAA, 1974, John Jay award Columbia Coll. Alumni Assn., 1994. Mem. ABA, N.Y. State Bar Assn., Fed. Bar Assn. Republican. Greek Orthodox. Avocations: tennis, photography. Home: 3666 Upton St NW Washington DC 20008-3125 Office: Clifford Chance Rogers & Wells LLP 2001 K St NW Washington DC 20006-1037

**ROSSINGTON, GARY,** musician; b. Jacksonville, Fla., Dec. 4, 1951; m. Dale Krantz, 1982; 2 children. Founding mem., guitarist Lynyrd Skynyrd, 1964—77, 1987—; co-founder The Rossington-Collins Band, 1980—82. Musician: (albums) (with Lynyrd Skynyrd) Pronounced Leh-Nerd Skin-Nerd, 1973, Smokes, 1973, Second Helping, 1974, Nuthin' Fancy, 1975, Gimme Back My Bullets, 1976, One More from the Road, 1976, Street Survivors, 1977, Southern by the Grace of God, 1988, Lynyrd Skynyrd 1991, The Last Rebel, 1993, Endangered Species, 1994, Freebird: The Movie, 1996, Southern Knights, 1996, Twenty, 1997, Lyve, 1998, Edge of Forever, 1999, Universal Masters Collection, 1999, Christmas Time Again, 2000, Vicious Cycle, 2003, (with The Rossington-Collins Band) Anytime, Anyplace, Anywhere, 1980, This is the Way, 1982. Named to Rock and Roll Hall of Fame, 2006. Office: Vector Mgmt PO Box 120479 Nashville TN 37212 also: Sanctuary Records 5226 Greens Dairy Rd Raleigh NC 27616-4612*

**ROSSINI, JOSEPH,** contracting and development corporate executive; b. New Rochelle, NY, Nov. 25, 1939; m. Antonia Rossini; children: Katherine, Anthony, Andrew. *Wife, Antonia Rossini, is a nationally recognized American wildlife artist, known for the 1995 Florida State Duck Stamp; she has received numerous awards. She received a BA from Stonybrook State University and an MA from New York University. She is a member of the New Rochelle Council on the Arts. Great-great Uncle Gioachino Rossini was the composer of the "William Tell Overture" and the "Barber of Seville," among other works. Father, Carmelo, was a contractor-builder in the United States and Canada. Brother, Frank, was a deep sea diver and soldier of fortune; he was one of the last Americans to leave Saigon at the end of the war.* Student, Fordham U., 1965—66, Iona Coll., 1972. Pres. Rossini Contracting Corp., Mt. Vernon, NY, 1963—; prin. Rossini Devel. Co., Monticello, NY, 1965—. Bd. dirs. Circuit Realty Corp., New Rochelle, 1970-71. Mem. planning bd. City of New Rochelle, 1986-92, mem. bldg. dept. adv. com., 1985; vol. instr. N.Y. State Dept. Environ. Conservation, Albany, 1968-95; vice chmn. New Rochelle Conservative Party, 1984-2001, chmn., 2001—; county committeeman Westchester County Conservative Party; pres., bd. trustees Beechwoods Cemetery, New Rochelle; dir. New Rochelle Neighborhood Revitalization Corp., 1993-96. With USN, 1959-61. Mem. NRA (benefactor life patron), Gen. Contractors Assn. N.Y., Constrn. Industry Coun. Westchester and Hudson Valley, Bldg. Trades Employers Assn., Soc. Explosives Engrs., Deep Founds. Inst., Young Ams. for Freedom, Am. Lauretana Assn., Mensa, Assoc. Gen. Contractors Am., Caths. in Constrn., Tin Can Sailors, Westchester County Firearm Owners Assn., N.Y. State Rifle and Pistol Assn., ASCE Constrn. Inst., Cath. League. Roman Catholic. Office: Rossini Contracting Corp 113 Edison Ave Mount Vernon NY 10550-5005 Office Phone: 914-664-4300. Personal E-mail: joe@rossinicontracting.com.

**ROSSITER, ALEXANDER, JR.,** publishing executive, editor; b. Elmira, N.Y. Mar 2, 1936; s. Alexander H. and Eleanor (Howell) R.; m. Sylvia Lee Vanlandingham, June 11, 1960; children: Alexander H. III, Jill Jarrell. BA, Rutgers U., 1958; postgrad., Emory U., 1959. With UPI, 1959-92; newsman Atlanta, 1959-61, Richmond, Va., 1961-63; bur. mgr. Cape Canaveral, Fla., 1963-73; sci. editor Washington, 1973-87; exec. editor, 1987-88; exec. editor, sr. v.p., 1988-91; editor, exec. v.p., 1991-92; asst. v.p., dir. news svc. Duke U., Durham, NC, 1992—2001, dir. com. Pratt Sch. Engrs., 2001—02, assoc. dean pub. affairs, 2003—. Mem. nat. adv. bd. Knight Ctr. for Specialized Journalism, Colleg Pk., Md., 1988-92; mem. adv. bd. Med. Journalism Program, U. N.C., Chapel Hill, 2000-04. Recipient Grady-Stack medal Am. Chem. Soc., 1987, other journalism awards. Mem. Nat. Assn. Sci. Writers, Edn. Writers Assn. Office: Duke U 305 Teer Bldg Box 90271 Durham NC 27708 *Enthusiasm is the key to success. Take on your education, your family responsibilities and your work with enthusiasm and good things will result.*

**ROSSITER, BRYANT WILLIAM,** chemistry consultant; b. Ogden, Utah, Mar. 10, 1931; s. Bryant B. and Christine (Peterson) R.; m. Betty Jean Anderson, Apr. 16, 1951; children: Bryant, Mark, Diane, Steven, Linda, Karen, Matthew, Gregory. BA, U. Utah, 1954, PhD, 1957. Researcher Eastman-Kodak Co., Rochester, NY, 1957-63, head color phys. chem. lab., 1963-70, dir. chemistry div., 1970-84, dir. sci. tech. devel., 1984-86; pres. Viratek Inc., Costa Mesa, Calif., 1986-89; sr. v.p. ICN Pharms., Costa Mesa, 1989-90; ret., 1990; pres., CEO WRECON, Inc., Laguna Hills, Calif., 1991-96, ret., 1996. Sr. editor John Wiley & Sons, N.Y., 1970—; chmn. bd. Nucleic Acid Rsch. Inst., Costa Mesa, 1987-88; trustee Eastman Dental Ctr., Rochester, 1973-93 (bd. pres. 1982-85); bd. dirs. Verax & Corp. Editor: (chem. treatises) Physical Methods of Chemistry (11 vols.), 1970-76, Physical Methods, (12 vols.), 1986—, Chemical Experimentation Under Extreme Conditions, 1979. Mem. rsch. adv. com. U.S. Agy. for Internat. Devel., Washington, chmn. rsch. adv. com., 1989-92; mem. panel on biosci. Pres. Coun. Advisors on Sci. and Tech., 1991; mem. adv. com. Cornell Internat. Inst. for Food, Agr. and Devel., 1991; presiding officer Ch. Jesus Christ Latter Day Saints, Ea. U.S. and Can., 1959-86, counselor presidency San Diego temple, 1998-2002. 1st lt. USAFR, 1951-58. Named Hon. Alumni Brigham Young U., Provo, Utah, 1982. Fellow AAAS, Am. Chemists (lectr. Fellows award 1988, Will Judy award Juanita Coll. 1978); mem. Internat. Union Pure and Applied Chemistry (chmn. U.S. nat. com., originator, chmn.

Chemical Rsch. Applied to World Needs com. 1975-87, chmn. Chemical Rsch. Applied to World Needs II The Internat. Conf. on Chemistry and World Food Supplies, 1982), Am. Chem. Soc. (chmn. internat. activities). Avocations: horseback riding, reading, fishing. Home and Office: 25662 Dillon Rd Laguna Hills CA 92653-5800 E-mail: bwr@ni.net.

**ROSSITER, ROBERT E.,** interior auto parts manufacturing executive; b. Detroit, 1946; BBA, Northwood U. With Lear Siegler Inc., 1971-87, former pres. seating div.; pres., chief oper. officer Lear Seating Corp., Southfield, Mich., 1987-2000, also bd. dirs.; CEO, pres. Lear Corp., Southfield, Mich., 2000—, Chmn., 2003—. Bd. dirs. Detroit Renaissance, Focus: HOPE, Detroit. Office: Lear Seating Corp 21557 Telegraph Rd Southfield MI 48034*

**ROSSKY, PETER JACOB,** chemistry professor, researcher; BA, Cornell U., 1971, MA, 1972; PhD in Chemical Physics, Harvard U., 1978. Postdoctoral rsch. SUNY-Stony Brook, 1978—79; prof. then George W. Watt Centennial prof. chemistry U. Texas, Austin, 1979—; dir. Inst. for Theoretical Chemistry, U. Texas, Austin. Editorial bd. mem. Accounts of Chemical Rsch., Chemical Physics Letters, Jour. of Chemical Physics, Jour. of Physical Chemistry, Theoretical Chemistry Accounts. Fellow: Am. Acad. Arts & Sciences. Office: U Texas Dept Chemistry & Biochemistry 1 University Station A5300 Austin TX 78712

**ROSS-LEE, BARBARA,** dean, educator; BS Biology and Chemistry, Wayne State U., M Tchr. Spl. Populations; grad., Mich. State U., 1973; DSc (hon.), N.Y. Coll. Osteo. Medicine; degree (hon.), Wilmington Coll., 2001. Legis. asst. Senator Bill Bradley; chmn. dept. family medicine, assoc. dean health policy Mich. State U. Coll. Medicine; dean Ohio U. Coll. Osteo. Medicine, 1993—2001; dean, v.p. health scis. and med. affairs N.Y. Coll. Osteo. Medicine, 2001—. Lectr. in field; dir. Osteo. Heritage Health Policy Fellowship Program; exec. dir. Inst. Nat. Health Policy and Rsch., NOMA (the osteo. affiliate NMA); mem. bd. dirs. Assn. Acad. Health Ctrs., Nat. Fund Med. Edn., Nat. Health Svs. Corps' Assn. Clinicians Underserved; trustee Found. Appalachian Ohio; participant confs. Contbr. more than 30 scholarly articles med. and health-care issues. Named to Ohio Women's Hall of Fame, 1998; recipient Magnificent 7 award, Bus. and Profl. Women/USA, 1993, Women's Health award, Blackboard African-Am. Nat. Bestsellers, Disting. Pub. Svc. award, Okla. State U. Coll. Osteo. Medicine, Walter F. Patenge medal pub. svc., Mich. State U. Coll. Osteo. Medicine, 2001. Fellow: Am. Osteo. Bd. Family Physicians; mem.: NIH (adv. com. rsch. on women's health), Future Primary Care (Inst. Medicine's com.), U.S. Dept. Health and Human Svs. (nat. adv. com. rural health), Appalachian Health Policy (Appalachian regional commn.'s adv. coun.), AACOM Bd. Govs. (chair-elect exec. coun.), AOA Bur. Profl. Edn., Trilateral Internat. Med. Workforce Group. Achievements include first to be an osteopathic physician to participate in the prestigious Robert Wood Johnson Health Policy Fellowship. Office: NY Coll of Osteopathic Med Old Westbury No Blvd Rockefeller Bldg Rm 107 Westbury NY 11568-8000 Office Phone: 516-686-3747. E-mail: brosslee@nyit.edu.

**ROSSMAN, RUTH SCHARFF,** artist, educator; b. Bklyn. d. Joseph and Elsie (Frankel) Scharff; m. Phillip Rossman; 1 dau., Joanne. Grad., Cleve. Inst. Art, 1934; BS, Case Western Res. U., 1934; postgrad., Kahn Inst. Art, 1947-50, UCLA, 1960. Art instr. Canton (Ohio) public schs., 1934-39, Canton Art Inst., 1937-45, Rustic Canyon Art Center, Los Angeles, 1978-81. One-woman shows at Heritage Gallery, L.A., 1963, 66, Canton (Ohio) Community Ctr., 1967, Marymount Coll., U. Judaism, 1980, L.A. Fedn. Bldg., 1981, 89, Platt Gallery, 1986, 93, 98, others; exhibited in group shows Mus. Modern Art, N.Y.C., Butler Mus., Washington and Jefferson Coll., Denver Mus., Space Mus., Mt. St. Mary's Coll., L.A., M.H. de Young Mus., San Francisco Mus. Art, Venice Art Walk, ann. 1981-94, 96-2000, Univ. Judaism, 1986, 93, Brand Art Gallery, 1987, Platt Gallery, 1998, others; represented in permanent collections Pa. Acad. Fine Arts, Phila., Brandeis-Bardin Inst., U. Redlands, Calif., Nat. Watercolor Soc., Ahmanson Collection, Rocky Mt. Nat., others; paintings included in book The California Romantics: Harbingers of Watercolor, 1987, Retrospective Art Exhibit U. Judaism Platt Gallery, 1998. Chair selection com. for Platt Gallery, U. Judaism, L.A., 1986—. Recipient purchase-cash awards Los Angeles All-City Art Exhbn. Mem. Nat. Watercolor Soc. (pres. 1974-75, juror 75th Ann. Exhbn. 1995).

**ROSSMANN, JACK EUGENE,** psychologist, educator; b. Walnut, Iowa, Dec. 4, 1936; s. Wilbert C. Rossmann and Claire L. (Mickel) Walter; m. Marilyn Martin, June 14, 1958; children: Ann, Charles, Sarah. BS, Iowa State U., 1958, MS, 1960; PhD, U. Minn., 1963. Lic. psychologist Minn. Asst. prof. Macalester Coll., St. Paul, 1964-68, assoc. prof., 1968-73, prof., 1973—, v.p. acad. affairs, 1978-86, chair dept. psychology, 1990-2000. Cons.-evaluator North Ctrl. Assn., 1975—; cons. Pers. Decisions Internat., Mpls., 1989—2000, Bush Found., 1993—; sr. advisor Spencer Found., 2004—. Author: (with others) Open Admissions at CUNY, 1975; contbr. articles to profl. jours. Bd. dirs. Twin City Inst. for Talented Youth, St. Paul, 1978-91; trustee United Theol. Sem., New Brighton, Minn., 1984-96; pres. Minn. Intercollegiate Athletic Conf., 2003—. 2d lt. U.S. Army, 1959. Mem.: AAUP (pres. Minn. conf. 1993—95), APA, Minn. Psychol. Assn. (treas. 2001, pres. 2003), Assn. Instl. Rsch., Am. Psychol. Soc. Home: 99 Cambridge St Saint Paul MN 55105-1947 Office: Macalester Coll 1600 Grand Ave Saint Paul MN 55105-1801 Office Phone: 651-696-6110. Business E-Mail: rossmann@macalester.edu.

**ROSSMANN, MICHAEL GEORGE,** biochemist, educator; b. Frankfurt, Germany, July 30, 1930; s. Alexander and Nelly (Schwabacher) R.; m. Audrey Pearson, July 24, 1954; children: Martin, Alice, Heather. BSc with honors, Polytechnic, London, 1951, MSc in Physics, 1953; PhD in Chemistry, U. Glasgow, 1956; DSc (hon.), U. Uppsala, Sweden, 1983, U. Strasbourg, France, 1984, Vrije U., Brussels, 1990, U. Glasgow, 1993, U. York, Eng., 1994, U. Quebec, 1998. Fulbright scholar U. Minn., 1956-58; research scientist MRC Lab. Molecular Biology, Cambridge, Eng., 1958-64; assoc. prof. biol. scis. Purdue U., West Lafayette, Ind., 1964-67, prof., 1967-78, Hanley Disting. prof. biol. scis., 1978—; prof. biochemistry, 1975—. Editor: The Molecular Replacement Method, 1972; contbr. more than 400 articles to profl. jours. Grantee NIH, NSF, HFSP; recipient Fankuchen award Am. Crystallographic Assn., 1986, Horwitz prize Columbia U., 1990, Gregori Arminoff prize Royal Swedish Acad. Sci., 1994, Stein & Moore award Protein Soc., 1994, Ewald prize Internat. Union Crystallography, 1996, Cole award Biophys. Soc., 1998, Elion award Internat. Soc. for Antiviral Rsch., 2000, Ehrlich and Darmstaedter prize Paul Erhlich-Fedn., 2001. Mem. Am. Soc. Biol. Chemists, Am. Chem. Soc., Biophys. Soc. (Cole award 1998), Am. Crystallographic Assn. (Fankuchen award 1986), Brit. Biophys. Soc., Inst. Physics., Chem. Soc. (U.K.), AAAS, NAS, Indian Nat. Sci. Acad., Royal Soc., Nat. Sci. Bd., Lafayette Sailing Club. Democrat. Home: 1208 Wiley Dr West Lafayette IN 47906-2434 Office: Purdue U Dept Biol Scis 915 W State St West Lafayette IN 47907-2054 Office Phone: 765-494-4911. Business E-Mail: mr@purdue.edu.

**ROSSO, JEAN-PIERRE,** electronics executive; b. Aix-les Bains, Savoie, France, July 11, 1940; Diploma in civil engring., Ecole Polytechnique, Lausanne, Switzerland, 1966; MBA, U. Pa., 1967. Mgr. fin. and adminstrn. Honeywell, Paris, 1969—70, dir. African divsn., 1970—71, sales dir., 1971—75; pres., CEO Rossignol Ski, Burlington, Vt., 1975—81; dir. gen. Rossignol SA, Voiron, France, 1980—81; v.p. bus. devel. Honeywell Europe SA, Brussels, 1981—85, pres., 1981—94; v.p., gen. mgr. Honeywell Med. Electronics, N.Y.C., 1983—85; group v.p. Honeywell Info. Systems, Mpls., 1985—87; pres., CEO Case Corp., Racine, Wis., 1994—99, chmn., 1996—99; former chmn., CEO CNH Global, 1999—. Mem. adv. com. Trade Policy and Negotiations, 2002—02; bd. overseers Wharton Sch.; bd. dirs. ADC Telecoms., Inc., Medtronic, Inc. Mem.: Bus. Roundtable. Avocations: golf, skiing. Office: Case Corp 700 State St Racine WI 53404-3392

**ROSSO DE IRIZARRY, CARMEN (TUTTY ROSSO DE IRIZARRY),** finance executive; b. Ponce, P.R., Feb. 9, 1949; d. Jorge Ignacio and Carmen Teresa (Descartes) Rosso Castain; m. Alfredo R. Irizarry Sile, Aug. 29, 1967. BBA, U. P.R., Rio Piedras. Vice pres. Alcay Inc., San Juan, P.R., 1972—, also bd. dirs.; v.p. J.I.C. Corp., M.I.C. Corp. Bd. dirs., now pres. bd. Construcciones Urbanas Inc., Internat. Fin. Corp.; organizer Best of Saks Fifth Avenue 1990-2000. Troop leader Girl Scouts U.S.A., 1977-80; bd. dirs. PTA, San Juan, 1978-81, 86-88; activities coord. Colegio Puertorriqueño Niñas, San Juan, 1987-88; judge Miss P.R. Pageant, San Juan 1987-88, 93, 94, 95, Miss World P.R. Pageant, San Juan, 1987-88, Miss World of P.R., 1990; pres. fundacion dept. Oncologia Pediatrica Hosp. Universitario Dr. Antonio Ortiz, 1990-2005; organizer Best of Saks Fifth Avenue Benefit, 1991, 92, 93, 94, 95, pres. 1992, 94, 96, 2005; com. mem. Make a Wish Found. Colleccion Alta Moda, 1994; mem. com. Muceo Ponce Gala, 1994; mem. com. Museo Ponce Coala, 1994; luminaria J.C. Penney, 1994; destellos de la Moda, 1994, 95-96, 2005; pres. Best of Saks 5th Avenue Benefit, 1990-96; organizer Fundacion Oncologica Escada Spring and Summer, 2003. Named to Ten Best Dressed List, San Juan Star, 1986-87, Hall of Fame of Ten Best Dressed, 1989; recipient luminaria J.C. Penney, 1994, Club Damas Medal, 2005. Fellow Assn. Porcelanas; mem. Union Mujeres Americanas, Club de Leones (Garden Hills, P.R., Lady of Yr. award 1978), Club Avico Dama, Caparra Country Club (pres. 1985-86), Club de Presidentas, Altrusas, Bankers Club, Club Civicos Damas (judge hat show 1989, in charge spl. events 1992), Mu Alpha Phi. Republican. Roman Catholic. Avocations: china painting, boating, water-skiing. Office: Internat Fin Corp PO Box 8486 Santurce San Juan PR 00910-0486

**ROSSOLIMO, ALEXANDER NICHOLAS,** management consultant; b. Paris, June 8, 1939; came to U.S., 1952; naturalized, 1958; s. Nicholas S. and Vera A. (Boudakovitch) R.; m. Meryl Louise Stowbridge, Sept. 10, 1977; children: Gregory, Katherine, Elizabeth. Student, Lycée Français of N.Y., 1955—57; BEE with honors, CUNY, 1962; MA in Applied Math., Harvard U., Cambridge, Mass., 1963; PhD in Applied Physics, Harvard U., 1973; MBA, MIT, Cambridge, 1973. Cert. in bus. French. Tchg. fellow Harvard U., 1963-65, rsch. asst., 1966-71; fin. analyst Péchiney, Paris, 1972; brand/advt. mgmt. The Clorox Co., Oakland, Calif., 1973-74; project leader The Boston Consulting Group, 1974-77; dir. planning and fin. analysis United Brands, Boston, 1977-80; sr. dir. Digital Equipment Corp., Maynard, Mass., 1980-92; pres. Strategy Assocs. Internat., Newton, Mass., 1992-94, pres., chief exec. officer, 1994—; co-founder, acting CEO, vp. bus. strategy and corp. devel. IntellectExchange Inc., 1999—2001; regional dir. F2 Intelligence Group LLC, Mpls., 2004—. Vis. fellow Harvard U., Cambridge, Mass., 1991-93; bd. dirs. ACG Internat., Chgo.; founding dir. Forum 128, Forum 99; bd. dirs. Ctr. for Security and Social Progress, Inc., chmn., 1998—; dir. Law Enforcement Assistance Found., 1999—; mem. bd. advisors Radia Techs. Corp., 2004-05. Contbr. numerous articles to bus. and internat. newspapers. Mem. search com. Ecole Bilingue, French-Am. Internat. Sch. of Boston, 1991-93; fund raiser Milton (Mass.) Acad., 1994-97, Phillips Exeter Acad., 1997—, Phillips Andover Acad., 2000—. Recipient award in elec. engring. Blonder-Tongue Co., N.Y.C., 1961, Belden prize, gold medal in math., 1960; NSF postgrad. fellow, 1962-63; ACG Dealmaker Challenge winner, 1995. Mem. Nat. Assn. Corp. Dirs., Bus. Execs. for Nat. Security, Boston Security Analysts Soc., Royal United Svcs. Inst. for Def. Studies (London), French Am. C. of C., Japan Soc. Boston, World Affairs Coun., Internat. Assn. of Macro-Engring. Socs. (mem. commn. on macro-engring.), Assn. for Corp. Growth Boston (chmn. 1995-96), Harvard Club Boston, Harvard Faculty Club, Toastmasters Internat. (pres.), Tau Beta Pi, Eta Kappa Nu. Avocations: jogging, tennis, foreign languages, professional organizations, theater. Office: Strategy Assocs Internat PO Box 207 Waban MA 02468-0002 Business E-Mail: arossolimo@yahoo.com.

**ROSSON, GLENN RICHARD,** building products and furniture company executive; b. Galveston, Tex., Aug. 17, 1937; s. John Raymond and Elsie Lee R.; m. Edwina Lucille Hart, June 2, 1956; children: Darrell Richard, Alex Mark. BBA, Tex. Tech U., 1959. C.P.A., Tex. Supr.; accountant Axelson div. U.S. Industries Inc., Longview, Tex., 1960-67, controller, 1968, group financial v.p. Dallas, 1969, group chmn., 1969-72, v.p., 1973-74, sr. v.p., 1974, exec. v.p., 1974-80, also dir.; pres. Rosson Investment Co., 1980—; chmn. bd. Yorktowne Inc., 1988—. Chmn. bd. dirs. Quality Product Finishing, Inc., 1998—. Mem. Am. Inst. C.P.A.s, Tex. Soc. C.P.A.s, Nat. Assn. Accts. (past nat. dir., past pres. E. Tex. chpt.), Assn. for Corp. Growth (past pres.). Clubs: Dallas Athletic, TBARM Raquet. Home: 11367 Drummond Dr Dallas TX 75228-1946 Office: 6060 N Central Expy # 560 Dallas TX 75206-5142 Office Phone: 214-891-6357. E-mail: rosson@gte.net.

**ROSSOUW, JACQUES E.,** preventive medicine physician, researcher; b. S. Africa, 1943; Former acting dir. Women's Health Initiative, NIH, Bethesda, Md.; lead project officer, Women's Health Initiative, Nat. Heart, Lung, and Blood Inst. NIH, Bethesda, Md. Named one of 100 Most Influential People, Time Mag., 2006. Achievements include performing studies concerning women's health in areas of menopause, estrogen replacement, calcium and vitamin D supplements, and high-fat diet, others. Office: Women's Health Init NHLBI-NIH PO Box 30105 Bethesda MD 20824-0105 Office Phone: 301-592-8573.*

**ROSSOW, WILLIAM BRIGANCE,** physics professor; b. Washington, Apr. 26, 1947; m. Lynne Margaret Kemen, June 7, 1974. BA in Physics/Math., Hanover (Ind.) Coll., 1969; MS in Physics, Cornell U., Ithaca, NY, 1972, PhD in Astronomy, 1975. Rsch. asst. Woods Hole (Mass.) Oceanog. Inst., 1968; tchg. asst. in physics Cornell U., Ithaca, NY, 1969—72, rsch. asst. in physics/astronomy 1972—75; vis. scientist Princeton (NJ) U. NOAA GFDL, 1975—78; phys. scientist NASA Goddard Inst. Space Studies, NYC, 1978—2006; adj. full prof. applied physics Columbia U., NYC, 1992—95; disting. prof. remote sensing CUNY, NYC, 2006—. Mem. working group data mgmt. radiation projects World Climate Rsch. Program, Geneva, 1982—98, mem. sci. steering group Global Energy and Water Expt., 1993—2001, mem. cloud sys. study sci. steering group Global Energy and Water Expt., 1995—, chmn. radiation panel, 2001—, mem. working group satellite matters, 2002—03, chmn. working group on data mgmt. and analysis Global Energy and Water Expt., 2002—, mem. observation and assimilation panel, 2005—; sec. Internat. Commn. Planetary Atmospheres and Their Evolution, 1984—89; mem. coun. long-term climate monitoring NOAA, 2002—05; mem. energy and water study sci. integration team NASA, 2003—, mem. user working groups eos distributed active archive centers, 1990—2002; mem. US Vice Pres.'s environ. task force US Govt., 1992—93. Co-author: (novels) Lear's Daughters: Reign of Fire, Wave and Flame. Recipient Group Achievement award for Pioneer Venus Sci. Team, NASA, 1980, Spl. Achievement award, 1983, 1987, NASA Exceptional Sci. Achievement medal, 1988, Group Achievement award to Galileo Project Team, NASA, 1998, Alumni Achievement award, Hanover Coll., 1986, Verner E. Suomi award, Am. Meteorol. Soc., 2005; fellow Am. Geophysical Union, 1998, Am. Meteorol. Soc., 2005. Fellow: Am. Meteorol. Soc. (mem. info. sys. com. 2002—04, mem. com. atmospheric radiation 1990—92, assoc. editor Jour. Climate 1995—), Am. Geophys. Union; mem.: Am. Astron. Soc., Planetary Soc. Office: CUNY City Coll Steinman Hall T-107 New York NY 10031 Office Phone: 212-650-5389. Office Fax: 212-650-8097. Business E-Mail: wbrossow@ccny.cuny.edu.

**ROSSUM, RALPH ARTHUR,** political science professor; b. Alexandria, Minn., Dec. 17, 1946; s. Floyd Arthur and June Marion (Carlson) R.; m. Constance Mary Brazina, Aug. 19, 1972; children: Kristin, Brent, Pierce. BA summa cum laude, Concordia Coll., 1968; MA, U. Chgo., 1971, PhD, 1973. Instr. Grinnell (Iowa) Coll., 1972-73; asst. prof. Memphis State U., 1973-77, assoc. prof., 1977-80, Loyola U., Chgo., 1980-83, assoc. dean grad. sch., 1981-82; dep. dir. bur. justice stats. U.S. Dept. Justice, Washington, 1983-84; Alice Tweed Tuohy prof. govt. Claremont (Calif.) McKenna Coll., 1984-88, v.p. and dean of faculty, 1988-91; pres. Hampden-Sydney (Va.) Coll., 1991-92; Salvatori Vis. prof. Claremont (Calif.) McKenna Coll., 1992-93, Salvatori prof. Am. Constitutionalism, 1994—; Fletcher Jones Prof. of Am. Politics U. Redlands, Redlands, Calif., 1993-94. Mem. adv. bd. Nat. Inst. Corrections, U.S. Dept. Justice, 1988-91; mem. Robert Presley Inst. Corrections Rsch. and Tng., State of Calif., 1988-91; dir. Rose Inst. of State and Local Govt.; mem. nat. bd. dirs. FIPSE, U.S. Dept. Edn., 2002—. Author: Federalism, the Supreme Court and the Seventeenth Amendment, 2001, others, Antonin Scalia's Jurisprudence: Text and Tradition, 2006; co-author: The American Founding, 1981, American Constitutional Law, 1983, 1987, 1991, 1995, 1999, 2003—, others; editor (sr.): Benchmark, 1983—86; book rev. editor:, 1986—91; contbr. 65 articles to profl. jours., chapters to books. Trustee Episcopal Theol. Sch., Claremont, 1987-91. Ford Found. fellow, 1968—72. Mem.: Am. Polit. Sci. Assn. Episcopalian. Office: Claremont McKenna Coll Dept Govt 850 Columbia Ave Claremont CA 91711-3901 Office Phone: 909-607-3392. Business E-Mail: ralph.rossum@claremontmckenna.edu.

**ROST, PETER,** pharmaceutical company executive; b. Bollebygd, Sweden, May 31, 1959; came to U.S., 1987; s. Siegfrid and Kathie (Zerne) Rost; m. Tina Forssten, Apr. 21, 1984; children: Maximilian Forssten, Sebastian Forssten. MD, U. Gothenburg, Sweden, 1984. Intern anesthesiology dept. Ea. Hosp., Gothenburg, 1984, practice medicine specializing in anesthesiology, 1984; pres., CEO Bus. Lit. Inc., Gothenburg, 1985-87; account supr., copywriter Grey Gothenburg, Gothenburg, 1985-87; med. dir. account supr. Maher Kaump & Clark, Inc., L.A., 1987-92; assoc. dir. med. edn. Lederle Labs. divsn. Am. Cyanamid Co., Wayne, NJ, 1992, dir. med. edn., 1993; product mgr. Lederle Labs. divsn. Am. Cyanimid Co., Wayne, NJ, 1993-94; mkt. planning mgr. Wyeth-Ayerst Internat., St. Davids, Pa., 1995, dir. mktg internal medicine products, 1995-96, dir. comml. ops. Europe, 1996-98; gen. mgr. Wyeth-Ayerst Global Pharma., Sweden, 1999—2001; v.p. endocrine care, global prescription bus. Pfizer, Peapack, NJ, 2001—. Chmn., chief exec. officer W. Swedish Model Group, Gothenburg, 1985. Author: Emergency Surgery, 1985, The Art of Driving a Car Free, 1985. Mem. AMA, Am. Coll. Physician Execs., Pharm. Advt. Coun. Office: Pfizer 100 Rte 206 N Peapack NJ 07977-8616 Home: 29 Great Hills Rd Short Hills NJ 07078 Personal E-mail: Rostpeter@hotmail.com.

**ROST, THOMAS LOWELL,** retired botany educator; b. St. Paul, Dec. 28, 1941; m. Ann Marie Ruhland, Aug. 31, 1963. BS, St. John's U., Collegeville, Minn., 1963; MA, Minn. State U., 1965; PhD, Iowa State U., 1971. Postdoctoral fellow Brookhaven Nat. Lab., Upton, NY, 1970-72; asst. to full prof. dept. botany U. Calif., Davis, 1972-82, faculty asst. to chancellor, 1982-83, prof., chmn. plant biology sect., 1994-96, assoc. dean divsn. biol. sci., 1996—2003, exec. assoc. dean, 2003—05; prof. emeritus. Cons. faculty of agronomy U. Uruguay, 1979, 89, 2005; vis. fellow Rsch. Soc. Biol. Sci., Canberra, Australia, 1979-80; vis. prof. U. Wroclaw, Poland, 1987, U. Exeter, Eng., 1993, Copenhagen U., 2003, Aristotte U., Thessalaniki, Greece, 2005. Co-author: Botany: A Brief Introduction to Plant Biology, 1979, Botany: An Introduction on Plant Biology, 1982; co-editor: Mechanisms and Control of Cell Division, 1977, Plant Biology, 1998, 2d edit., 2005; contbr. articles to profl. jours. Internat. pres. Gamma Sigma Delta, 2004—06. Served to capt. U.S. Army, 1965—67. Fellow Japan Soc. Promotion of Sci.; mem. Bot. Soc. Am., Soc. Exptl. Biology, Am. Inst. Biol. Sci. Democrat. Roman Catholic. Avocation: community theatre. Office: U Calif Sect Plant Biology Davis CA 95616-8537 Office Phone: 530-752-0628.

**ROST, WILLIAM JOSEPH,** chemist; b. Fargo, N.D., Dec. 8, 1926; s. William Melvin and Christine Ruth (Hamerlik) R.; m. Rita Cincoski, Sept. 15, 1951; children: Kathryn, Patricia, Carol. BS, U. Minn., 1948, PhD, 1952. From asst. prof. to prof. pharm. chemistry Sch. Pharmacy U. Kansas City, Mo., 1952-63; prof. pharm. chemistry Sch. Pharmacy U. Mo., Kansas City, 1963—. Co-author: Principles of Medicinal Chemistry, 1974, 3d rev. edit., 1988; contbr. articles profl. jours. Mem. Am. Pharm. Assn., Am. Chem. Soc., Sigma Xi, Kappa Psi, Rho Chi, Phi Lambda Upsilon. Office: U Mo Sch of Pharmacy Kansas City MO 64110 Home: 709 W 100th Ct Kansas City MO 64114

**ROSTEN, IRWIN,** writer, producer, director; Writer-producer news, pub. affairs Sta. KNXT-CBS, Los Angeles, 1954-60; dir. news, pub. affairs Sta. KTLA, Los Angeles, 1960-63; writer-producer, dir. Wolper Prodns., Inc., Los Angeles, 1963-67; chief documentary dept. MGM Studios, Culver City, Calif., 1967-72; pres. Ronox Prodns., Inc., Los Angeles, 1970-87. Writer-prodr.-dir. Nat. Geog. Soc. spls.: Splendid Stones, Elephant, Great Moments with National Geographic, The Thames, Mysteries of the Mind, Gold!, The Legacy of L.S.B. Leakey, The Volga, The Incredible Machine, Grizzly!, The Eerie World of Jacques-Yves Cousteau, National Parks: Playground or Paradise?, numerous other shows including Unsolved Mysteries, The Wolf Men, Ripley's Believe It or Not, Sports Illustrated, Trial by Wilderness, Hollywood: The Dream Factory, Kifaru: The Black Rhinoceros, Birds Do It, Bees Do It, Indestructible People, Journey Into Life, One Man's Noise: Stories of an Adventuresome Oceanographer, Tiger: Lord of the Wild, Celebrate the Century; video prodr. opening ceremonies 1984 Olympic Games, L.A., Interactive Multimedia: Columbus, Evolution/Revolution. Recipient Emmy award Acad. TV Arts and Scis.; recipient Writers Guild Am. award, Peabody award, Am. Med. Writers Assn. award, Christophers award, Ohio State U. award, Saturday Rev. award, CINE Golden Eagle award Mem. Writers Guild Am., Dirs. Guild Am., Acad. TV Arts and Scis., Internat. Documentary Assn.

**ROSTER, MICHAEL,** lawyer; b. Chgo., May 7, 1945; AB, Stanford U., 1967, JD, 1973. Bar: Calif. 1973, DC 1980. Ptnr. McKenna, Conner & Cuneo, LA, Washington, 1973—87, Morrison & Foerster, LA, Washington, 1987—93; gen. counsel Stanford (Calif.) U., 1993—2000; exec. v.p., gen. counsel Golden West Fin. Corp., Oakland, Calif., 2000—. Bd. dirs. Silicon Valley Bancshares, vice chmn., 1995—98; chmn. Encirq, 1998—2000, Insert Therapeutics, 2000—04, Fed. Home Loan Bank, San Francisco, 2005—. Contbr. articles to profl. jours. Bd. dirs. Pasadena Heritage, 1986—87. Lt. (j.g.) USN, 1969—71. Mem.: ABA (fin. svcs. com. 1981—, chmn. com. savs. instns. 1985—89, banking com. 1989—, vice chmn. 2005—), Calif. Bankers Assn., Am. Corp. Counsel Assn. (chmn. 2000—01), Calif. Bar Assn. (chmn. banking com. 1978—79), Stanford U. Alumni Assn. (chmn. 1992), LA Athletic Club. Office: Golden West Fin Corp 1901 Harrison Oakland CA 94612

**ROSTKER, BERNARD,** civilian military employee; m. Louise Cowen; children: David, Michael. BS in Econs. and Edn., NYU, 1964; M in Econs., Syracuse U., 1967, PhD in Econs., 1970. Economist Manpower Requirements Directorate Office of the Asst. Sec. of Def. for Sys. Analysis, 1968-70; rsch. economist RAND Corp., 1970-72, program dir. manpower per. and tng. program, 1972-77; prin. dep. asst. sec. for manpower and res. affairs USN, 1977-79, dir. Selective Svc., 1979-81, dir. navy mgmt. program Ctr. for Naval Analyses, 1981-83; dir. sys. mgmt. divsn. Sys. Rsch. and Applications Corp., 1983-84; program dir. force devel. and employment program RAND Corp. The Arroyo Ctr., 1984-90, assoc. dir., 1984-90; dir. Def. Manpower Rsch. Ctr. RAND Nat. Def. Rsch. Ctr., 1990-94; asst. sec. for manpower and res. affairs USN, 1994—98, spl. asst. to dep. sec. def. for Gulf War illnesses, 1996—; under sec. of the Army, 1998—2000; under sec. for pers. and readiness, 2000—. Office: Spl Asst Gulf War Illnesses Suite 901 Four Skyline Place 5113 Leesburg Pike Falls Church VA 22041

**ROSTOW, CHARLES NICHOLAS,** lawyer, educator; b. Geneva, Mar. 3, 1950; s. Eugene Victor and Edna (Greenberg) R.; m. Heyden White, Oct. 31, 1987; children: Theodore Isaac, Celia A.M. BA, Yale U., 1972, PhD, 1979, JD, 1982. Assoc. Shearman & Sterling, N.Y.C., 1982-85; spl. asst. to legal adviser Dept. State, Washington, 1985-87; dep. legal adviser NSC, Washington, 1987, spl. asst. to Pres., legal adviser, 1987—93; assoc. prof. Coll. of Law U. Tulsa, 1993—95, disting. rsch. prof. Coll. of Law, 1995—98; exec. dir. Mass. Office Internat. Trade and Investment, 1995-98; counsel and dep. staff dir. House Select Comm. on Nat. Security & Mil./Comm. Concerns with the PRC, 1998; staff dir. Senate Select Com. on Intelligence, 1999-2000; Charles H. Stockton prof. internat. law U.S. Naval War Coll., Newport, RI, 2001; gen. coun. U.S. Mission UN, N.Y.C., 2001—05; sr. counsel Rsch Found. of SUNY, 2005—06; univ. counsel, vice chancellor for legal affairs SUNY, 2006—.

Author: Anglo-French Relations 1934-36, 1984; editor: Akten zur deutschen auswaertigen Politik: 1918-1945, vols. XIV-XXI, 1980-83; contbr. articles to prof. jours. Hon. dir. John Goodwin Tower Ctr. for Polit. Studies, So. Meth. U.; nat. adv. bd. Am. Jewish Com. Mem. Assn. Bar City of N.Y., Coun. Fgn. Rels., Phi Beta Kappa, Cosmos Club, Yale Club (N.Y.C.), Elizabethan Club (New Haven). Jewish. Office: SUNY State Univ Plz Albany NY 12246 Office Phone: 518-443-5400. E-mail: nicholas.rostow@suny.edu.

**ROSTOW, ELSPETH DAVIES,** political science professor; b. NYC; d. Milton Judson and Harriet Elspeth (Vaughan) Davies; m. Walt Whitman Rostow, June 26, 1947 (dec. Feb. 2003); children: Peter Vaughan, Ann Larner. AB, Barnard Coll., 1938; AM, Radcliffe Coll., 1939; MA, Cambridge U., Eng., 1949; LHD (hon.), Lebanon Valley Coll.; LLD (hon.), Austin Coll., 1982, Southwestern U., 1988; LHD (hon.), Wheaton Coll., 2006. Mem. faculty various instns. Barnard Coll., N.Y.C. and MIT, Cambridge, 1939-69; mem. faculty U. Tex., Austin, 1969—, dean div. gen. and comparative studies, 1975-77, prof. govt., 1976—, dean Lyndon B. Johnson Sch. Pub. Affairs, 1977-83, Stiles prof. Am. studies, 1985-88, Stiles prof. emerita, 1988—. Mem. Pres.'s Adv. Com. for Trade Negotiations, 1978-82, Pres.'s Commn. for a Nat. Agenda for the Eighties, 1979-81; rsch. assoc. OSS, Washington, 1943-45; Geneva corr. London Economist, 1947-49; lectr. Air War Coll., 1963-81, Army War Coll., 1965, 68, 69, 78, 79, 81, Nat. War Coll., 1962, 68, 74, 75, Indsl. Coll. Armed Forces, 1961-65, Naval War Coll., 1971, Fgn. Svc. Inst., 1974-77, Dept. of State, Europe, 1973; bd. dirs. U.S. Inst. of Peace, vice chmn., 1991, chmn. 1991-92; co-founder The Austin Project, 1991; mem. Gov.'s Task Force on Revenue, Tex., 1991. Author: Europe's Economy After the War, 1948, (with others) American Now, 1968, The Coattailless Landslide, 1974; editor (with Barbara Jordan) The Great Society: A Twenty-Year Critique, 1986; columnist Austin Am. Statesman, 1985-92; contbr. articles to revs., poems to scholarly jours., newspapers, and mags. Trustee Nat. Acad. Pub. Adminstrn., 1989—95, Sarah Lawrence Coll., 1952—59, So. Ctr. for Internat. Studies, 1990—; bd. visitors and govs. St. Johns Coll., 1986—89; bd. dirs. Barnard Coll., 1962—66, Lyndon Baines Johnson Found., 1977—83, Salzburg Seminar, 1981—89, co-chair sr. fellows, 1997—2001; vis. scholar Phi Beta Kappa, 1984—85; bd. adv. to pres. Naval War Coll., Newport, RI, 1995—99; nat. advisor Commn. on Deliberative Polling, 1999—2001. Decorated Order of St. Joan D'Arc; named Fulbright lectr.; recipient Top Hand award, U. Tex. Ex-Students Assn., 1996, Presdl. citation, U. Tex., 1998, Disting. Alumna award, Barnard Coll., 1998, Dist. Svc. award, Tex. Exec., 2005, Disting. Svc. award, U. Tex., 2005, Civilian Svc. award, US Army, 2006; grantee, USIA, 1983—84, 1990. Mem.: Tex. Philos. Soc. (trustee 1989—95, 1997—2001), Headliners Found. (vice-chmn. 1996—2002), Phi Beta Kappa, Omicron Delta Kappa, Mortar Bd. (hon.), Phi Nu Epsilon (hon.). Home: 1 Wildwind Pt Austin TX 78746-2434 Office: U Tex PO Box Y University Station Austin TX 78713 Office Phone: 512-471-8909. Business E-Mail: elspeth.rostow@mail.utexas.edu.

**ROSTROPOVICH, MSTISLAV LEOPOLDOVICH,** conductor, musician, music director; b. Baku, Azerbaijan, Mar. 27, 1927; s. Leopold and Sofia (Fedotova) Rostropovich; m. Galina Pavlovna Vishnevskaya, 1955; children: Olga, Elena. Grad., Moscow Conservatory 1948; Mus D (hon.), Oxford, 1980; numerous hon. doctorate degrees. Faculty mem. Moscow Conservatory, 1953, prof., 1960; head cello and double-bass dept., formerly prof. Leningrad Conservatory; music dir., conductor Nat. Symphony Orch., Washington, 1977-94; hon. prof. Cuban Nat. Conservatory, 1960-78. Pres. Evian Internat. Music Festival. Debut as violoncellist, 1940; performer (world concert tours): Moscow Philharm. Orch.; recordings include with various artists Mstislav Rostropovich Melodiya Recordings, 1949—56, 1948—59, The Young Rostropovich: Rare Recordings, 1950—52, Schnittke's Cello Concerto No. 2, In Memorium, Return to Russia. Decorated Hon. Knight of Brit. Empire, Officer's Cross of Merit Fed. Republic Germany, Comdr. French Legion of Honor; named Musician of Yr., Music Am., 1987; recipient First prize, All-Union Competition of Musicians, 1945, Internat. Cellist Competitions, Prague, 1947, 1951, Internat. Cellist Competitions, Budapest, 1949, USSR State prize, 1951, Stalin prize, 1951, 1953, Lenin prize, 1963, Gold medal, Royal Philharm. Soc., Siemens prize, Sonning prize, Denmark, Grammy award, 1970, 1977, 1980, 1984, Life in Music prize, 1984, Albert Schweitzer Music award, 1985, Presdl. medal of Freedom, 1987, Ditson Condr.'s award, Columbia U., 1990, Four Freedoms award, Franklin and Eleanor Roosevelt Inst., 1992, Kennedy Ctr. hon., 1992, Imperial award, 1993, Wolf Prize in the Arts, 2004. Mem.: Acad. Arts of French Inst.-Forty Immortals, Union Soviet Composers, Am. Acad. Arts and Scis., Acad. of St. Cecilia, Rome (hon.), Brit. Royal Acad. Music (hon.). Mailing: Vishnevskaya-Rostopovich Found 1776 K St NW Ste 800 Washington DC 20006 also: Vishnevskaya-Rostropovich Found 1 Artilleriyskaya str Business-center Europa-Haus Ste 318-319 191104 Saint Petersburg Russia*

**ROSWELL, ROBERT H.,** former federal agency administrator; MD, U. Okla., 1975. Diplomate Am. Bd. Internal Medicine. Resident in internal medicine U. Okla. Sch. Medicine; mem. faculty various med. schs.; fellow in endocrinology and metabolism U. Okla. Sch. Medicine; various leadership positions VA facilities, VA Ctrl. Office, Washington; chief of staff VA med. ctrs., Birmingham, Ala., Oklahoma City; dir. Fla. and P.R. VA healthcare network, Bay Pines, Fla., 1995; exec. dir. Fed. Persian Gulf Vets. Coordinating Bd., 1994—99; under sec. health US Dept. Vets. Affairs, Washington, 2002—04. Served in U.S. Army, 1978—80, col. M.C. USAR.

**ROSZKOWSKI, JOSEPH JOHN,** lawyer; b. Pawtucket, RI, Aug. 11, 1938; s. Joseph J. and Anna T. Roszkowski; m. Geraldine J. Szpila, July 2, 1966. BA, Alliance Coll., 1960; JD, Marquette U., 1964. Bar: Wis. 1964, U.S. Dist. Ct. (ea. dist.) Wis. 1964, R.I. 1965. Ptnr. Zimmerman, Roszkowski & Brenner, Woonsocket, R.I., 1965—. Corporator Fogarty Hosp., North Smithfield, RI, 1976—88; counsel Landmark Med. Ctr., 1989—90; mem. R.I. Bd. Bar Examiners, 1996—2001; R.I. probate judge, 1996—2000, 2005—. Mem. Nat. Ski Patrol, RI, 1974—83; legal counsel R.I. Tuna Tournament, 1975    ; bd. dirs. R.I. Legal Svcs., Providence, 1974—87, Legal Aid Soc., Providence, 1985—; chair Town of Cumberland, 2000. Mem. ABA (ho. of dels. 1996-2003, state del. 2000-2001, 2003—, bd. govs. 2001, 2002, commr. Interest on Lawyers' Trust Accounts 1986-90, 2002—), R.I. Bar Found. (pres. 1990-95), R.I. Bar Assn. (pres. 1985-86), Am. Law Inst., Am. Judicature Soc., Fed. Tax Inst. New England (adv. com. 1985-86), R.I. Med. Examiners, U.S. Jaycees (nat. dir. 1968), Am. Acad. Hosp. Attys. Lodges: Rotary (pres. Cumberland, R.I. 1987). Avocations: skiing, sailing, gardening, tennis. Home: 1o Little St Cumberland RI 02864-1101 Office: Zimmerman Roszkowski & Brenner 1625 Diamond Hill Rd Woonsocket RI 02895-1541 E-mail: jroskow@aol.com.

**ROSZKOWSKI, STANLEY JULIAN,** retired federal judge; b. Boonville, N.Y., Jan. 27, 1923; s. Joseph and Anna (Christkowski) R.; m. Catherine Mary Claeys, June 19, 1948; children: Mark, Gregory, Dan, John. BS, U. Ill., 1949, JD, 1954. Bar: Ill. 1954. Sales mgr. Warren Petroleum Co., Rockford, Ill., 1954; ptnr. Roszkowski, Paddock, McGreevy & Johnson, Rockford, 1955-77; judge U.S. Dist. Ct. (we. dist.), Rockford, Ill., 1977-98; pres. First State Bank, Rockford, 1963-75, chmn. 1975—; mediator-arbitrator JAMS/ENDISPUTE, Chgo., 1998—. Chmn. Fire and Police Commn., Rockford, 1967-74, commr.; chmn. Paul Simon Com., 1972; active Adlai Stevenson III campaign, 1968-71; Winnebago County Citizens for John F. Kennedy, 1962, Winnebago County Dem. Cen. Com., 1962-64; bd. dirs. Sch. of Hope, 1960—; mem. Ill. Capital Devel. Bd., 1974—. With USAAF, 1943-45. Decorated Air medal with 2 oak leaf clusters.; recipient Pulaski Am. Heritage award Polish Am. Congress, Chgo., 1982 Mem. ABA, Ill. Bar Assn., Fla. Bar Assn., Winnebago County Bar Assn., Am. Coll. Trial Lawyers, Am. Judicature Soc., Assn. Trial Lawyers Am., Ill. Trial Lawyers Assns., Am. Arbitration Assn. (arbitrator), Fed. Judges Assn. (bd. dirs. 1988—). Business E-Mail: sjrassoc@aol.com.

**ROTBERG, EUGENE HARVEY,** investment banker, lawyer; b. Phila., Jan. 19, 1930; s. Irving Bernard and Blanche Grace (Levick) R.; m. Iris Sybil Comens; children— Diana Golda, Pamela Lynn. BS, Temple U., 1951; LL.B., U. Pa., 1954; PhD (hon.), Salem-Teikyo U., 1992. Chief counsel Office Policy

---

Research Securities and Exchange Commn., Washington, 1963-66; v.p.; treas. World Bank, Washington, 1969-87; exec. v.p. Merrill Lynch & Co., N.Y.C., 1987-90. Served with U.S. Army. Decorated King Leopold II medal (Belgium); recipient Disting. Svc. award Securities and Exch. Commn., 1968; named Alumnus of Yr., Temple U. Home: 7211 Brickyard Rd Potomac MD 20854-4808 Office: 1250 24th St NW Ste 350 Washington DC 20037-1124 Office Phone: 202-944-3810. E-mail: genebanker@aol.com.

**ROTBERG, IRIS COMENS,** social scientist; b. Phila., Dec. 16, 1932; d. Samuel Nathaniel and Golda (Shuman) Comens; m. Eugene H. Rotberg, Aug. 29, 1954; children: Diana Golda, Pamela Lynn. BA, U. Pa., 1954, MA, 1955; PhD, Johns Hopkins U., Balt., 1958. Research psychologist Pres.'s Commn. on Income Maintenance Programs, Washington, 1968-69, Office Planning, Research and Evaluation, Office Econ. Opportunity, Washington, 1970-73; dep. dir. compensatory edn. study Nat. Inst. Edn., Washington, 1974-77, dir. Office Planning and Program Devel., 1978-82; program dir. NSF, Arlington, Va., 1985-87, 89-91, 1993-96; tech. policy fellow Com. on Sci., Space and Tech., U.S. Ho. of Reps., Washington, 1987-89; sr. social scientist RAND, Washington, 1991-93; rsch. prof. edn. policy Grad. Sch. Edn. and Human Devel. George Washington U., Washington, 1996—. NSF fellow, 1956-58. Home: 7211 Brickyard Rd Potomac MD 20854-4808 Office Phone: 202-994-2735. Business E-Mail: irotberg@gwu.edu.

**ROTBERG, ROBERT IRWIN,** historian, political scientist, educator, academic administrator; b. Newark, Apr. 11, 1935; s. Louis and Mildred S. R.; m. Joanna H. Henshaw, June 17, 1961; children: Rebecca T.H., Nicola S.D., Fiona J.Y. AB, Oberlin Coll., 1955; MPA, Princeton U., 1957; DPhil, U. Oxford, 1960. Asst. prof. history, rsch. assoc. Ctr. for Internat. Affairs Harvard U., 1961-68, rsch. assoc. Ctr. for Internat. Affairs, 1968-95; rsch. dir. Twentieth Century Fund, 1968-71; prof. polit. sci. and history MIT, 1968-87; acad. v.p. for Arts, Scis. and Tech. Tufts U., Medford, Mass., 1987-90; pres. Lafayette Coll., Easton, Pa., 1990-93, World Peace Found., Cambridge, 1993—; coord. Inst. for Internat. Devel. Harvard U., 1993-99, dir. program on intrastate conflict Kennedy Sch., 1999—. Adj. prof. Kennedy Sch. Govt., Harvard U., 1993—; mem. coun. NEH, 1993-99; cons. Dept. State, 1968-73, Commrs. of Middlesex County, Mass., 1976-77. Author: A Political History of Tropical Africa, 1965, The Rise of Nationalism in Central Africa, 1965, Protest and Power in Black Africa, 1970, Joseph Thomson and the Exploration of Africa, 1971, Haiti: The Politics of Squalor, 1971, Africa and Its Explorers, 1971, The Black Homelands of South Africa, 1977, Black Heart: Gore-Browne and the Politics of Multiracial Zambia, 1978, Conflict and Compromise in South Africa, 1980, Suffer the Future: Policy Choices in Southern Africa, 1980, Imperialism, Colonialism and Hunger, 1982, Namibia: Economic and Political Prospects, 1983, South Africa and its Neighbors, 1985, The Founder: Cecil Rhodes and the Pursuit of Power, 1988, rev. edit. 2002, Africa in the 1990s and Beyond: Policy Opportunities and Choices, 1988, From Massacres to Genocide: The Media, Public Policy, and Humanitarian Crises, 1996, Vigilance and Vengeance: NGOs Preventing Ethnic Conflict in Divided Societies, 1996, Haiti Renewed: Political and Economic Prospects, 1997, Burma: Prospects for a Democratic Future, 1998, War and Peace in Southern Africa, 1998, Creating Peace in Sri Lanka, 1999, Peacekeeping and Peace Enforcement in Africa, 2000, Truth v. Justice, 2000, Patterns of Social Capital, 2001, Ending Autocracy, Enabling Democracy, 2002, State Failure and State Weakness in a Time of Terror, 2003, When States Fail: Causes and Consequences, 2004, Crafting the New Nigeria, 2004, Battling Terrorism in the Horn of Africa, 2005; editor Jour. Interdisciplinary History, 1970—. Chmn. Middlesex County Govtl. Rev. Task Force, 1972; v.p. Cambridge Civic Assn., 1969-72; mem. Lexington Town Meeting, 1973-90, 94—, Lexington Sch. Com., 1974-77; mem. Ciskel Commn., 1979-80; trustee World Peace Found., 1980—, Oberlin Coll., 1983—. Coun. Internat. Exch. Scholars, 1991-95. Rhodes scholar U. Oxford, 1960; Guggenheim fellow, 1970-71; Hazen Found. fellow, 1976-77. Fellow Royal Geog. Soc., Am. Acad. Arts and Scis.; mem. Am. Hist. Assn., African Studies Assn., Coun. on Fgn. Rels., Oberlin Coll. Alumni Assn. (pres. 1981-82). Office: World Peace Found Belfer Ctr 79 John F Kennedy St Cambridge MA 02138-5758 Office Phone: 617-496-2258. E-mail: robert_rotberg@harvard.edu.

**ROTCH, JAMES E.,** lawyer; b. Auburn, Ala., Mar. 26, 1945; s. Elroy B. and Martha (Ellisor) R.; m. Darlene Edwards, June 26, 1999; children: Jamison B., Susannah R., Amie L. Vaughn. BS, Auburn U., 1967, postgrad., 1967-68; JD, U. Va., 1971. Bar: Ala. 1971, U.S. Dist. Ct. (no. dist.) Ala. 1973. Rsch. asst. Office Instl. Rsch. Auburn (Ala.) U., 1967-68; clk. U.S. Judiciary System, Birmingham, Ala., 1971-72; assoc. Bradley Arant Rose & White LLP, Birmingham, 1971-76; ptnr. Bradley, Arant, Rose & White LLP, Birmingham, 1976—; administrv. ptnr., 1990-93; chmn. bd. dirs. Kaleidoscope Prodns., Inc. Mem. adv. com. Bioelastics Rsch. Ltd., Birmingham, 1992—, Gov.'s Task Force on Biotechnology, Ala., 1993. Author: The Birmingham Pledge. Pres. adv. com. Birmingham Mus. Art, 1989-92; bd. dirs. Operation New Birmingham, 1990-91, 95—, co-chmn. cmty. affairs com., mem. exec. com.; Coalition for Better Edn., Birmingham, 1990—; active Boy Scouts Am.; bd. dirs. Birmingham Com. for Olympic Soccer, 1994-96, Ala. Sports Found., 1994-98, Entrepreneurial Ctr. Inc., 1996—, chmn., 2002; mem. adminstrv. bd. Canterbury United Meth. Ch., 1991-93; chmn. Birmingham Pledge Found., 2000—; chmn. Birmingham Area Tech. Leadership Alliance. Capt. USAR, 1972-78. Named Communicator of Yr., Birmingham Bus. Jour., 2001; recipient Outstanding Achievement award, Operation New Birmingham, 1994, Liberty and Justice award, 2000, Key to Unlocking Door to Adversity award, Mercedes-Benz U.S. Internat., 2002. Mem. ALA, Auburn U. Bar Assn., Birmingham Bar Assn., Internat. Bar Assn., Ala. State Bar Assn. (Merit award 1999-2000), Leadership Birmingham, Leadership Ala. (bd. dirs. 1998—), Auburn Coll. Liberal Arts (adv. coun.), U. Va. Alumni Assn., Newcomen Soc., Birmingham Regional C. of C. (bd. dirs. 2001, vice chmn. for tech. devel. 2002, chmn.-elect 2003, chmn 2004, chmn. exec. com. 2005), Auburn U. Alumni Assn., Birmingham Venture Club (bd. dirs. 2001), Country Club of Birmingham, Turkey Club, Summit Club (charter), Kiwanis (sec. 1998-99). Methodist. Avocations: horses, bird hunting, cattle farming, golf. Office: Bradley Arant Rose & White LLP One Federal Pl 1819 5th Ave N Birmingham AL 35203 Office Phone: 205-521-8000. E-mail: jrotch@bradleyavant.com.

**ROTCHFORD, PATRICIA KATHLEEN,** lawyer, mediator; b. Chgo., Nov. 17, 1945; d. Charles E. Sr. and Mary (Rodde) R.; 1 child, John. BA with honors, Rosary Coll., River Forest, Ill., 1966; JD, No. Ill. U., 1979. Bar: Ill. 1979; cert. mediator/arbitrator, Mich.; Ill. Tchr. pub. schs., Schiller Park, Ill., 1966-76; sole practice Elmhurst, Ill., 1977-79; assoc. Shand, Morahan, Evanston, Ill., 1979-83; corp. counsel CNA Fin., Chgo., 1983-86; gen. counsel, v.p., corp. sec. MMI Cos., Bannockburn, Ill., 1986-87; gen. counsel, v.p., corp. sec. Inland Group, Northbrook, Ill., 1987-90; pvt. practice fin. and ins. legal counsel, Northbrook, 1990—. Bd. dirs. Notre Dame Corp., Chgo.; U.S. rep. ins. claims Lloyds of London; mediator. Author: (pamphlet) Handle Your Own Claims, 1983, (book) Women's Resource Guide, 1988, Women's Insurance and Financial Resource Guide, 1988. Counselor for battered women. Mem. ABA (mem. dispute resolution sect.), Mich. Bar, Womens Bar Assn. Ill. (active coms. and activities), Corp. Councils Am., Womens Exec. Network, Nat. Assn. for Women in Careers (nat. bd. dirs.), Spider. Office: Box 1261 Northbrook IL 60065-1261 E-mail: patkresq@msn.com.

**ROTE, NELLE FAIRCHILD HEFTY,** management consultant; b. Watsontown, Pa, May 23, 1930; d. Edwin Dunkel and Phebe Hill (Fisher) Fairchild; m. John Austin Hefty, Mar. 20, 1948 (div. June 1970); children: Harry E. Hefty, John B. Hefty, Susan E. Hefty DeBartolo; m. Keith Maynard Rote, Dec. 16, 1983 (dec. Aug. 1985). Student, Bucknell U., 1961, Williamsport Sch. of Commerce, 1968-69, Pa. State U., 1971-72, 83, Susquehanna U., 1970-76; account exec. Sta. WTGC Radio, Lewisburg, 1976-78; co-owner Colonial Printing Co., Lewisburg, 1978-83; temp. HATS-Temps, Lewisburg, 1986-89; artist, editor Create-A-Book, Inc., Milton, Fla., 1980-92; census crew leader, spl. svc. Dept. Commerce, Washington, 1990; cons. Create-A-Book, Inc., Gulf Breeze, Fla., 1991—99. Children's Playmate

---

Mag., 1942; author: McGruff and Me, 1999, My Christmas Wish, 1999, School Fun Book, 1999, My Fishing Adventure, 1999, Nurse Helen Fairchild, World War I, 1917-1918, 2006; contbr. articles to profl. jours.; exhibitions include Union County Libr., Lewisburg, 2003. Proofreader Lewisburg Bicentennial Commn., Lewisburg, 1976; charter mem. Women's Art Mus., Washington; charter sponsor Women in Mil. Svc. Meml., Arlington, Va., 1991; founder, donor Nelle Fairchild Rote Book Fund, Union County Libr.; editor, poet Holiday Newspaper Bus. Assn., Lewisburg, 1987. Recipient Humanitarian recognition, Tri-County Fedn. Women's Clubs, Pa., 1965, Grand prize in Cooking, Milton Std., 1966, Most Profl. Photo award, Lewisburg Festival Arts, 1980, Hon. Mention award, Women in Arts, Harrisburg, Pa., 1981, Photo Contest award, Congressman Allen Ertel, 1981, 2d pl. Photo award, Union County Fair, 1981, 3d pl. Photo award, 1981, Hon. Mention Photo award, Susquehanna Art Soc., 1981, Silver award for Poetry, World of Poetry, 1990. Mem.: DAR (nat. def. reporter Shikelimo chpt. 1989—95, sec. 1992—95, regent 1995—2001, vice chmn. Pa. State Soc. DAR women vets com. 1998—2001, vice-regent 2001—04, Prize for safety poster 1942), Soc. Profl. Journalists, Warrior Run Heritage Soc., Western Front Assn., Marine Corps League Aux. (life), Civic Club Lewisburg (v.p. 1994—97), Am. Legion Aux. (sgt.-at-arms 2003, Unit 182). Achievements include Initiator for renaming bridge in Watsontown, PA. to "Nurse Helen Fairchild Meml. Bridge" (a WWI Reserve Army Nurse relative), 2002. Home: 1015 St Paul St Lewisburg PA 17837-1213 Office Phone: 570-523-3741. Personal E-mail: elle12@ptd.net.

**ROTELL, CYNTHIA A.,** lawyer; BA, Barnard Coll., 1982; JD, Bklyn. Law Sch., 1990. Bar: Calif. 1990. With Latham & Watkins, L.A., 1990—, ptnr., 1997—. Mem.: L.A. County Bar Assn. (exec. com. bus. and corps. law sect.), State of Calif. Bar Assn. Office: Latham and Watkins LLC 633 W Fifth St Ste 4000 Los Angeles CA 90071

**ROTELLA, STEPHEN J.,** bank executive; BA, SUNY, Stony Brook, 1975; MBA, SUNY, Albany, 1978. Dir. mortgage products Shearson Lehman Bros.; with JP Morgan Chase, 1987—2005, COO Chase Home Fin., 1998—2001, exec. v.p., mem. exec. com., CEO Chase Home Fin., 2001—04; pres., COO Washington Mutual Inc., Seattle, 2005—. Mem. exec. com. Housing Policy Council Fin. Services Roundtable; bd. dir., mem. residential bd. gov. Mortgage Bankers Assn. Bd. dir. St. Barnabas Med. Ctr., NJ. Office: Washington Mutual Inc Washington Mutual Tower 1201 Third Ave Seattle WA 98101

**ROTENBERG, MANUEL,** physics professor; b. Toronto, Ont., Can., Mar. 12, 1930; came to U.S., 1946; s. Peter and Rose (Plonzker) R.; m. Paula Weissbrod, June 22, 1952; children: Joel, Victor. BS, MIT, 1952, PhD, 1956. Staff Los Alamos (N.Mex.) Nat. Lab., 1955-58; instr. physics Princeton (N.J.) U., 1958-59; asst. prof. U. Chgo., 1959-61; prof. applied physics U. Calif., San Diego, 1961-93, dean grad. studies and research, 1975-84, chmn. dept. elec. engring. and computer sci., 1988-93, rsch. prof., 1993—. Author: The 3-j and 6-j Symbols, 1959; founding editor: Methods of Computational Physics, 1963, Jour. of Computational Physics, 1962; editor: Biomathematics and Cell Kinetics, 1981. Fellow Am. Phys. Soc.; mem. AAAS, Sigma Xi. Office: U Calif San Diego La Jolla CA 92093-0407 Office Phone: 858-534-2726. Business E-Mail: rote@ucsd.edu.

**ROTENBERG, MARC STEVEN,** advocate, lawyer; b. Boston, Apr. 20, 1960; s. Michael and Karen (Sethur) R.; m. Anna Markopoulos; children: Chaz, Chloe. AB, Harvard Coll., 1982; JD, Stanford U., 1987; student, Georgetown U., 1994—. Bar: Mass. 1987, D.C. 1990. Teaching fellow Harvard U., Cambridge, Mass., 1982-88; exec. dir. Pub. Interest Computer Assn., Washington, 1983-84; instr. Stanford (Calif.) U., 1986-87; counsel Senate Jud. Com., Washington, 1987-88; dir. Washington office Computer Profls. for Social Responsibility, 1988-94; pres. Electronic Privacy Info. Ctr., Washington, 1994—. Adj. prof. law Georgetown Law Ctr., 1991—, Washington Coll. Law, 1997—; chmn. pub. interest registry, Privacy Internat., 2004-05; mem. adv. panels NSF, ABA, AAAS, ALA, Orgn. for Econ. Coop. and Devel., Paris, Austrian Inst. on Law and Policy, Salzburg. Author: Information Privacy Law, 2005; co-author: Intomation Privacy Law, 2003; editor: Technology and Privacy: The New Frontier, 1998; bd. editors Electronic Info. Law Reporter, Govt. Info. Quar., Computer Law and Security Report, Ency. Computer Sci.; contbr. articles to profl. jours. Ford Found. fellow internat. law, 1994; recipient 3rd Pl. U.S. Amateur Chess Championship, 1993, Law award World Tech. Network, 2002. Mem. ABA (Cyberspace Law Excellence award 2005), Assn. Computing Machines. Avocations: chess, basketball, german expressionism, record producing.

**ROTH, DALE DAVIS,** music educator, religious organization administrator; b. Williamston, SC, June 1, 1960; d. Carl Hampton and Marion Garrett Davis; m. Ronald D. Roth, June 11, 1988; children: Elizabeth, Garrett. MusB, Columbia Coll., 1982; MEd, Southern Wesleyan U., 2003. Tchr. cert. Columbia Coll., SC, 1982—; team evaluator SC, 1998; tchr. cert. Converse Coll., Spartanburg, SC, 1991. Piano, voice tchr. pvt. practice, 1982—; jv and varsity cheerleader coach Clinton H.S., 1982, prom advisor, 1986—; spring musical music dir., 1990—. Bible sch. dir. First Baptist Ch., Joanna, SC, 2001—. Mem.: SC Music Educators (region chair coord. 1999—), Music Educators Nat. Conf. Baptist. Avocations: knitting, baking. Home: 707 E Ferguson St Clinton SC 29325 Office: Clinton HS 800 N Adair St Clinton SC 29325 Business E-Mail: ddroth@laurens56.k12.sc.us.

**ROTH, DANIEL BENJAMIN,** lawyer, engineering company executive; b. Youngstown, Ohio, Sept. 17, 1929; s. Benjamin F. and Marion (Benjamin) R.; m. Joann M. Roth; children: William M., Jennifer A., Rochelle. BS in Fin., Miami U., Oxford, Ohio 1951; JD, Case-Western Res. U., 1956. Bar: Ohio 1956, U.S. Supreme Ct. 1960, D.C. 1983. Chmn. Roth, Blair, Roberts, Strasfeld & Lodge, LPA, Youngstown, 1969—; co-founder, chmn. Nat. Data Processing Corp., Cin., 1961-69; chmn., pres., CEO Torent, Inc., Youngstown, 1971—, Morrison Metalweld Process Corp., 1979-2003; vice chmn. McDonald Steel Corp., 1980—, Torent Oil & Gas Co., 1979—2002, Vaughn Indsl. Car & Equipment Co., 1988—2002. Bd. dirs. Gasser Chair Co. Profl. singer: appearances including Steve Allen Show, 1952. Bd. dirs. Youngstown Symphony, Stambaugh Auditorium; bd. dirs. Youngstown Playhouse, v.p., 1991-93; pres. Rodef Sholom Temple, Youngstown, 1982-84. 1st lt. USAF, 1951-53, lt. col. Res., ret. Recipient Mgr. of Yr. award Mahoning Valley Mgmt. Assn., 1989, Man of Yr. award Youngstown YWCA, 1995. Mem. ABA, DC Bar Assn., Ohio Bar Assn., Mahoning County Bar Assn., Lawyer-Pilots Bar Assn., Soc. Benchers of Case Western Res. U. Law Sch., Youngstown Club, Pelican Marsh Club (Naples, Fla.), Zeta Beta Tau (nat. v.p. 1964-66), Omicron Delta Kappa, Phi Eta Sigma, Tau Epsilon Rho. Jewish. Office: Roth Blair Roberts Strasfeld & Lodge 600 City Centre One Youngstown OH 44503-1514 Office Phone: 330-744-5211.

**ROTH, DARYL,** theater producer; b. NJ; m. Steven Roth, 1969; children: Amanda, Jordan. Student, NYU. Prodr.; owner Daryl Roth Prodns., N.Y.C.; owner Daryl Roth Theater, 1996—, DR2 Theater, 2002—. Co-anchor PBS show N.Y. Theatre Rev.; spkr. in field; guest lectr. Columbia U., NYU, Harvard Club, Women's Art Coalition. Prodr.: (N.Y. and London prodn.) Three Tall Women (Pulitzer prize, 1994), (Broadway prodn.) Twilight, Los Angeles.1992 (Tony nomination), Camping with Henry and Tom (Outer Critics Circle award, Lucille Lortel award), Defying Gravity, (off-Broadway) Snakebit, How I Learned to Drive (Best Play of Season, 1997, Pulitzer prize, 1998), Old Wicked Songs, 1996 (Pulitzer prize finalist for drama, 1996), Wit (Pulitzer prize for Drama, 1999), Bomb-itty of Errors; (plays) Closer Than Ever, 1987—1888, Nick & Nora, 1991, Proof, 2000—03 (Tony Award for Best Play, 2001), The Tale of the Allergist's Wife, 2000—02, Bea Arthur on Broadway, 2002, The Goat, or Who is Sylvia, 2002 (Tony Award for Best Play, 2002), Medea, 2002—03, Salome, 2003, Anna in the Tropics, 2003—04, Caroline, or Change, 2004—. Established (with husband) Roth Ctr. for Jewish Life, Dartmouth U., 1997; bd. dirs. Lincoln Ctr. Theater, Sundance Inst., Albert Einstein Coll. for Med. Rsch. Named award in her honor Daryl Roth Creative Spirit award, honored (with husband) with the Louis Marshall Award, Jewish Theological Seminary. Office: Daryl Roth Prodns 152 W 57th St Fl 21 New York NY 10019

**ROTH, ERIC,** screenwriter; 6 children. Student, Columbia U., UCLA. Screenplays include: The Stranger in 7A, 1972, The Nickel Ride, 1975, The Concorde - Airport '79, 1979, Suspect, 1987, Memories of Me, 1988 (with Billy Crystal), Mr. Jones, 1993, Forrest Gump, 1994 (Acad. award Best Adapted Screenplay), the Postman, 1997, The Horse Whisperer, 1998, The Insider (nominated for Acad., Golden Globe 1999), Munich, 2005; co-writer: (with Michael Mann) Ali, 2001. Office: care Creative Artists Agy 9830 Wilshire Blvd Beverly Hills CA 90212-1804*

**ROTH, ERIC M.,** lawyer; b. Bklyn., Jan. 16, 1954; BA with distinction in all subjects, Cornell U., 1974; JD, NYU, 1977. Bar: N.Y. 1978; U.S. Dist. Ct. (so., ea. dists.) N.Y. 1978, D.C. 1980; U.S. Supreme Ct. 1981; U.S. Ct. Appeals (2nd. cir.) 1984, (4th, 5th cirs.) 1985, (8th cir.) 1989, (11th cir.) 1995, (9th cir.) 1997. Law clk. to Hon. Lee P. Gagliardi U.S. Dist. Ct., 1977-79; atty. Wachtell, Lipton, Rosen & Katz, N.Y.C. Bd. dirs., former chmn. MFY Legal Svcs., Inc. Note and comment editor: NYU Law Review, 1976-77. Trustee NYU Sch. Law Found. Mem. ABA, N.Y. State Bar Assn., The D.C. Bar, Fed. Bar Coun., NYU Law Alumni Assn. Inc. (former mem. bd. dirs). Office: Wachtell Lipton Rosen & Katz 51 W 52nd St Fl 29 New York NY 10019-6150

**ROTH, GAYLE YVONNE,** elementary school educator; b. Goshen, Ind., Mar. 14, 1965; d. Lynn Devon Rheinheimer and Darlene Faye Mishler, James Wiley Mishler (Stepfather); m. Keith Alan Roth, Apr. 4, 1987; children: Anthony Lynn, Amber Nicole. BS, Ind. U., Ft. Wayne, 1986. Cert. elem. tchr. Ind. Tchr. grade 2 Prairie Heights Elem., LaGrange, Ind., 1988—. Grantee Einstein grant, Dekko Found., 2003; scholar, Middlebury Cmty. Classroom Tchrs. Assn., 1983. Mem.: Internat. Trotting and Pacing Assn. (assoc.), Midwestern Big Four (assoc.; exec. sec. 1995—), LaGrange Trottingbred Assoc. (assoc.; race sec. 1983—2005). Home: 8880W 350N Shipshewana IN 46565 Office: Prairie Heights Elemy Sch 0455S 1150E Lagrange IN 46761 Office Phone: 260-351-3214.

**ROTH, GEORGE STANLEY,** biochemist, researcher, physiologist; b. Honolulu, Aug. 5, 1946; s. George Frederick and Laura Ann (Zembrzuski) Roth; m. Mary Jane Fletcher, Mar. 11, 1972; children: Susan Marie, George William. BS, Villanova U., 1968; PhD, Temple U., 1971. Fellow Fels Rsch. Inst., Phila., 1971-72; staff fellow Gerontology Rsch. Ctr. NIH, Balt., 1972-76, rsch. chemist, 1976—, chief molecular physiology and genetics sect., 1984-99, sr. guest scientist, 2000—04; CEO Geroscience, Inc. (formerly Gerotech Inc.), 2000—; exec. dir. Am. Aging Assn., 2002—03. Vis. prof. Mehary Med. Coll., Nashville, 1983; Alpha Omega Alpha prof. U. P.R. Med. Sch., San Juan, 1986; chmn. Gordon Rsch. Conf. Biology of Aging, Oxnard, Calif., 1985; rsch. cons. George Washington U., 1977—82; Ben Cohen Meml. lectr. U. Mich., 1998; lectr. Med. Sci. Ctr. Student Sci. program, 1980; Sandoz lectr. gerontology, Basel, Switzerland, 84, Basel, 86, Basel, 92. Contbr. articles to profl. jours.; editor: Exptl. Gerontology, Exptl. Aging Rsch., Proc. Soc.Exptl. Biology and Medicine; co-editor: Chem. Rubber Co. Press Series in Aging, 1981—; mem. editl. bd. Ency. of Aging, 1987—. Co-dir. Ea. Harford County Civic Assn., Bel Air, 1981—88; v.p. Cmty. Coalition Harford County, Bel Air, Md., 1988—90, bd. dirs., 1990—92. Recipient Rsch. award, Am. Aging Assn., 1981, prize for gerontol. rsch., Sandoz Ltd., 1989, Third Age award, Internat. Assn. Gerontology, 1989. Spl. award, Balt. Longitudinal Study Aging, 1991, Equal Opportunity award, NIH, 1995, Merit award, 1996; Sigma Chi scholar, Miami U., Oxford, Ohio, 1989. Fellow: Gerontol. Soc. Am. (chair biol. scis. sect. 1975—76, chair rsch. com. 1978—79, chmn. fellowship com. 1986—87); mem.: Soc. Exptl. Biology and Medicine. Republican. Roman Catholic. Avocations: basketball, fishing, hiking, canoeing. Office: GeroSci Inc 1124 Ridge Rd Pylesville MD 21132

**ROTH, GREGORY EDWARD,** social studies educator; b. Canton, Ohio, May 1, 1949; s. Edward and Rosemary Roth; m. Connie May Roth, Sept. 1, 1973; children: William Martin, Jonathan Edward. BA, Malone Coll., Canton, 1972; postgrad., Bowling Green State U., Ohio, 1972—74; MA, U. Akron, Ohio, 1977. Permanent secondary edn. cert. Social studies tchr. Jackson Jr. High, Massillon, Ohio, 1976—77; tchr. Cuyahoga Falls Schs., Ohio, 1977—. Active First Friends Ch., Canton. Mem.: NEA, Ohio Edn. Assn., Cuyahoga Falls Edn. Assn. (exec. bd. mem. 1978—, v.p. 1994—96, pres. 1986—88, Lifetime Achievement award 2002). Republican. Evangelical. Home: 2826 Midvale Rd NW Canton OH 44708-1751 Office: Cuyahoga Falls HS 2300 Fourth St Cuyahoga Falls OH 44221

**ROTH, HADDEN WING,** lawyer, mediator, arbitrator; b. Oakland, Calif., Feb. 10, 1930; s. Mark and Jane (Haley) R.; m. Alice Becker, Aug., 1987; 1 child, Elizabeth Wing. AA, Coll. Marin, 1949; BA, U. Calif., Berkeley, 1951; JD, U. Calif., San Francisco, 1957. Bar: Calif. 1958, U.S. Dist. Ct. (no. dist.) Calif. 1958, U.S. Ct. Appeals (9th cir.) 1958, U.S. Supreme Ct. 1966. Atty. Calif. and fed. courts, 1957—; judge Municipal Ct., Marin County, Calif., 1966—70, Superior Ct. pro tem, Marin County, Calif., 1966—70; instr. Golden Gate Coll. Law, Calif., 1971—73; hearing officer Mendocino Coast Hosp., Petaluma Valley Hosp., Redbud Cmty. Hosp., Calif., 1981—92; arbitrator, 1990—; mediator, spl. master, 1990—. Judge Marin County Mcpl. Ct.; counsel Marin Muni Water Dist., County of Marin; Bolinas Pub. Utility Dist., Ross Valley Fire Svc., Tiburon Fire Protection Dist., Town of Corta Madera, Town of Ross, Town of San Anselmo; hearing officer dist. hosps.; lectr. at law Golden Gate Coll. Law. Chmn. Marin County prison task force, 1973; bd. dirs. Marin Gen. Hosp., 1964-66. Named Outstanding Citizen of Yr., Coll. Marin, 1972. Mem. ABA, Calif. Bar Assn., Marin County Bar Assn., Mediation Soc. San Francisco, Am. Assn. Ind. Investors, Nat. Assn. Securotoes Dealers, Nat. Arbitration Forum. Democrat. Avocations: running, weightlifting, reading. Office: PO Box 151567 San Rafael CA 94915 Office Phone: 415-479-5623. Personal E-mail: hwroth@pacbell.net.

**ROTH, HAROLD,** architect; b. St. Louis, June 30, 1934; s. Samuel and Dorothy (Yawitz) R.; m. Dvora Feigon, Dec. 6, 1959; children: Elizabeth, David. AB, Washington U., 1956; MArch, Yale U., 1957. Designer Warner Burns Toan & Lunde, N.Y.C., 1957; sr. designer Eero Saarinen & Assocs., Roche Dinkeloo & Assocs., Hamden, Conn., 1959-65; ptnr. Harold Roth—Edward Saad, Hamden, Conn., 1965-72; sr. ptnr. Roth & Moore Architects, New Haven, 1973—; critic archtl. design Yale U. Sch. Architecture, New Haven, 1964-98. Pres., trustee Perspecta, Yale Archtl. Jour. Trustee Long Wharf Theatre, New Haven, 1972-98, Conn. Trust for Hist. Preservation, 1993-90; pres. bd. trustees Conn. Architecture Found., 1990-93; bd. govs. Bldg. Stone Inst., 1999-2003; bd. regents Am. Arch. Found., 1999-2001; profl. advisor Western European Architecture Found., 2000—. Officer U.S. Army, 1957-59, Korea. Recipient Design award Nat. Coun. Religious Arch., 1970, 96, Design award New Haven Preservation Trust, 1978, 88, Tucker award Bldg. Stone Inst., 1983, 88, Honor award Concrete Reinforcing Steel Inst., 1983, Design award Portland Cement Assn., 1984, Design award Archtl. Record, 1970, 80, Design award AIA/ALA, 1983, Faculty Design award Assn. Collegiate Schs. of Arch., 1988, Healthcare Facilities Design award Boston Soc. Archs., 1992; fellow Pierson Coll., Yale U., 1978—. Fellow: AIA (chmn. nat. com. on design 1990, bd. dirs. 1992—94, sec. Coll. of Fellows 1998—99, vice-chancellor 2000, chancellor 2001, Design award Conn. 1974, 1978, 1983, 1986, 1989, 1990, 1993, 1997, 1998, Design award New Eng. 1968, 1984, 1992, 2001, N.Y. State Design award of merit 2000). Home: 37 Autumn St New Haven CT 06511-2220 Office: Roth and Moore Architects 65 Audubon St New Haven CT 06510-1205 Office Phone: 203-787-1166. Business E-mail: hroth@rothandmoore.com.

**ROTH, HARVEY PAUL,** retired publishing executive; b. NYC, Feb. 20, 1933; s. Lewis Theodore and Harriet (Wallow) R.; m. Tanya Cohen; children by previous marriage: Andrea Murner, Matthew Jay; stepchildren: Laura Meryl Becker, Matthew Robert Turetzky. AB, Bklyn. Coll., 1954; LL.B., N.Y. U., 1957. Bar: N.Y. bar 1959. Editor West Pub. Co., NYC, 1959-61; pres.

BFL Communications, Inc., Plainview, NY, 1961-76, Roth Pub., Inc., Great Neck, NY, 1976—2005, ret., 2005; chmn. Alcove Press, London, 1970-75, Nash Pub. Corp., LA, 1971-75. Served with U.S. Army, 1957-58. Personal E-mail: rothharvey@hotmail.com.

**ROTH, JAMES FRANK,** chemicals executive, chemist; b. Rahway, N.J., Dec. 7, 1925; s. Louis and Eleanor R.; m. Sharon E. Mattes, June 20, 1969; children by previous marriage: Lawrence, Edward, Sandra. BA in Chemistry, U. W.Va., 1947; PhD in Phys. Chemistry, U. Md., 1951. Research chemist Franklin Inst., Phila., 1951-53, mgr. chemistry lab., 1958-60; chief chemist Lehigh Paints & Chems. Co., Allentown, Pa., 1953-55; research chemist GAF Corp., Easton, Pa., 1955-58; with Monsanto St. Louis, 1960-80, dir. catalysis research, 1973-77, dir. process sci. research, 1977-80; corp. chief scientist Air Products and Chems., Inc., Allentown, 1980-91; indsl. cons., 1991—. Contbr. articles to profl. jours.; mem. editl. bd. Jour. Catalysis, 1976-85, Catalysis Revs., 1973-93, Applied Catalysis, 1981-85; editor for Ams., 1985-88, assoc. editor, 1988-95. With USN, 1943-46. Recipient Richard J. Kokes award Johns Hopkins U., 1977, Chem. Pioneer award Am. Inst. Chemists, 1986, Perkin medal Soc. Chem. Industry, 1988. Mem. NAE, Am. Chem. Soc. (St. Louis sect. St. Louis award 1975, E.V. Murphree nat. award 1976, Indsl. Chemistry award 1991), Catalysis Soc. N.Am. (E.J. Houdry award 1991), Catalysis Club of Phila. (award 1981). Inventor process biodegradable detergents, for acetic acid; U.S., fgn. patents in field. Home: 5440 Eagles Point Cir Apt 205 Sarasota FL 34231-9171

**ROTH, JAMES MICHAEL,** archivist; b. Greenfield, Mass., Apr. 7, 1971; s. Dennis James Roth and Elizabeth Bergere Dunbar; m. Wendy Joan Garpow, Sept. 9, 2000; 1 child, Sophia Grace. BA, Johnson State Coll., Vt., 1995; MA in History, U. NH, Durham, 1999; MSc in Libr. Scis., U. NC, Chapel Hill, 2001. Projectionist Inter State Theaters, Chatham, Mass., 1988—89; asst. mgr. Hoyts Movie Theaters, 1989—91; ordinary seaman Seafarer's Internat. Union, N.Y., 1992—93; archives specialist JFK Presdl. Libr., Boston, 2001—02, archivist, 2002—04; lead archivist JFK Presdl. Libr. and Mus., 2004—. Contbr. articles to profl. jour. Historic dist. commn. Town Plymouth, 2004—. Mem.: New Eng. Archivists (edn. com. mem. 2001—), Soc. Am. Archivists (dist. 1 rep. 2005—). Office: JFK Presdl Libr Columbia point Boston MA 02125

**ROTH, JANE RICHARDS,** federal judge; b. Phila., June 16, 1935; d. Robert Henry Jr. and Harriett (Kellond) Richards; m. William V. Roth Jr., Oct. 9, 1965; children: William V. III, Katharine K. BA, Smith Coll., 1956; LLB, Harvard U., 1965; LLD (hon.), Widener U., 1986, U. Del., 1994. Bar: Del. 1965, U.S. Dist. Ct. Del. 1966, U.S. Ct. Appeals (3d cir.) 1974. Adminstrv. asst. various fgn. service posts US Dept. State, 1956-62; assoc. Richards, Layton & Finger, Wilmington, Del., 1965-73, ptnr., 1973-85; judge U.S. Dist. Ct. Del., Wilmington, Del. 1985-91, US Ct. Appeals (3d Cir.), Wilmington, Del., 1991—2006, sr. judge, 2006—. Adj. faculty Villanova U. Sch. Law. Hon. chmn. Del. chpt. Arthritis Found.; bd. overseers Widener U. Sch. Law; bd. consultors Villanova U. Sch. Law; trustee Hist. Soc. Del. Recipient Nat. Vol. Service citation Athritis Found., 1982. Fellow Am. Bar Found.; mem. ABA, Fed. Judges Assn., Del. State Bar Assn. Republican. Episcopalian. Office: US Court of Appeals 3rd Cirt Lock Box 12 5100 Fed Bldg 844 King St Wilmington DE 19801-1790*

**ROTH, JOE,** motion picture company executive; b. NYC, June 13, 1948; m. Donna Roth. BA, Boston U. Prodn. assistant various commls. and feature films, San Francisco; also lighting dir. Pitchel Players, San Francisco; then producer L.A.; co-founder Morgan Creek Prodns., L.A., 1987-89; chmn. 20th Century Fox Film Corp., L.A., 1989-92; founder Caravan Pictures, L.A., 1992-94; chmn. Walt Disney Motion Pictures Group, Burbank, 1994—96, Walt Disney Studios, Burbank, 1996—2000; founder Revolution Pictures, 2000—. Bd. dirs. Pixar Studios, 2000—. Prodr. (films) Tunnel Vision, 1976, Our Winning Season, 1978, Americathon, 1979, Ladies and Gentlemen, the Fabulous Stains, 1981, Final Terror, 1983, The Stone Boy, 1984, Moving Violations, 1985, Off Beat, 1986, Where the River Runs Black, 1986, Streets of Gold, 1986, P.K. and the Kid, 1987, Young Guns, 1988, Skin Deep, 1989, Major League, 1989, Nightbreed, 1990, The Three Musketeers, 1993, Angels in the Outfield, 1994, Low Down Dirty Shame, 1994, Houseguest, 1995, The Jerky Boys, 1995, Heavyweights, 1995, Tall Tale, 1995, While You Were Sleeping, 1995, The Forgotten, 2004; exec. prodr. (films) Cracking Up, 1977, Bachelor Party, 1984, Revenge of the Nerds II: Nerds in Paradise, 1987, Dead Ringers, 1988, Renegades, 1989, Enemies: A Love Story, 1989, The Exorcist III, 1990, Pacific Heights, 1990, Angie, 1994, Before and After, 1996, Tears of the Sun, 2003, Daddy Day Care, 2003, Hollywood Homicide, 2003, Mona Lisa Smile, 2003, An Unfinished Life, 2005; dir. Streets of Gold, 1986, Coupe de Ville, 1990, America's Sweethearts, 2001, Christmas with the Kranks, 2004, Freedomland, 2006. Named one of 50 Most Powerful People in Hollywood, Premiere mag., 2002—05. Office: Pixar 1200 Park Ave Emeryville CA 94608*

**ROTH, JOHN REECE,** electrical engineer, educator, researcher, inventor; b. Washington, Pa., Sept. 19, 1937; s. John Meyer and Ruth Evangeline (Iams) R.; m. Helen Marie DeCrane, Jan. 14, 1972; children: Nancy Ann, John Alexander. BS in Physics, MIT, 1959; PhD, Cornell U., 1963. Engring. aide Aerojet-Gen. Corp., Azusa, Calif., 1957, 1958; aerospace engr. N.Am. Aviation, Canoga Park, Calif., 1959; prin. investigator NASA Lewis Rsch. Ctr., Cleve., 1963—78; prof. elec. engring. U. Tenn., Knoxville, 1978—2004, prof. emeritus, 2004—; hon. prof. U. Electronic Sci. and Tech. China, Chengdu, 1992—; prin. investigator Office Naval Rsch., Washington, 1980—89, Air Force Office Sci. Rsch., Washington, 1981—95, 2001—03, Army Rsch. Office, 1988—93, NASA Langley Rsch. Ctr., Hampton, Va., 1995—98, 2001—03, March Instruments, Inc., Concord, Calif., 1996—98, NSF, 2002—03. Cons. TVA, Chattanooga, 1982-84, BDM Corp., 1987-88, Tenn. Eastman, 1989-90, March Instruments, 1995-98, Procter & Gamble, 1996, 2000, Internat. Eco Scis., 1997-98, Environ. Elements Corp., 1997-00, Tetra Pak Suisse, 1998-00, Atmospheric Glow Techs., Inc., 1999-05, YTC-Am., Inc., 2005, Harrick Plasma, 2006; mem. NAS-NRC Com. on Aneutronic Fusion, 1986-87; hon. guest prof. Tsinghua U., Shenzhen campus, 2006-; spkr. at profl. meetings Author: Industrial Plasma Engineering, Introduction to Fusion Energy; contbr. articles to profl. jours. Sloan scholar, 1955-59; Ford fellow, 1961-62; recipient B. Otto and Katherine Wheeley award for Excellence in Tech. Transfer, 1999, NASA Inventor's award, 2004. Fellow IEEE, AIAA (assoc.); mem. Am. Phys. Soc., Am. Nuc. Soc. (exec. com. No. Ohio sect. 1975-78), Nuc. and Plasma Scis. Soc., Am. Soc. Engring. Edn., Knoxville Mus. Art, East Tenn. Soc. Archaeol. Inst. Am., Sigma Xi (pres. U. Tenn. Knoxville chpt. 1985-86). Achievements include 11 US patents. Home: 12359 N Fox Den Dr Knoxville TN 37934-3755 Office: U Tenn Dept Elec Computer Engring 409 Ferris Hall Knoxville TN 37996-2100 Office Phone: 865-974-4446. Business E-mail: jrr@utk.edu.

**ROTH, JOHN ROGER,** geneticist, biology educator; b. Winona, Minn., Mar. 14, 1939; s. Frederick Daniel and Louise Mae (Wirt) R.; m. Uta Goetz (div.); children: Katherine Louise, Frederick Phillip; m. Sherylynne Harris, Jan. 4, 1986. BA, Harvard U., 1961; PhD, John Hopkins U., 1965. From asst. prof. molecular biology to prof. molecular biology U. Calif., Berkeley, 1967-76; prof. biology U. Utah, Salt Lake City, 1976—2002; prof. sect. microbiology U. Calif., Davis, 2002—, chair sect. microbiology, 2003—. Recipient Disting. Prof. award, 1990, Rosenblatt award, 1990. Mem. NAS, Am. Soc. for Microbiology, Genetics Soc. Am. Office: Univ Calif Microbiology 314 Briggs Hall One Shields Ave Davis CA 95616

**ROTH, JONATHAN DEAN,** music educator; s. M. Dean and Doris M. Roth; m. Leah A. Merrill, Feb. 25, 1966; children: Will John Capozzi, Amanda Lee Capozzi, Laura Brooke Capozzi, Holly Kristin Capozzi, Nathanael Dean Capozzi, Samuel Ian Nathanael, Timothy Jonathan. MusB in Edn., Gordon Coll., Wenham, Mass., 1988; MusM, U Conn., Storrs, CT, 1999. Cert. in usic K-12 Maine, 2001. Music tchr. Hillsboro-Deering Sch. Sys., NH, 1988—98, Kittery Sch. Sys., Maine, 1998—. Men's ministry mem. Dover Bapt., NH, 2005—06. Mem.: Maine Music Edn. Assn. (assoc.). Independent. Baptist. Office Phone: 207-439-2572.

**ROTH, KENNETH,** human rights advocate; b. Elmhurst, Ill., Sept. 23, 1955; s. Walter and Muriel (Teitell) R.; m. Nina Brodsky, May 29, 1983; children: Lisa, Emma. BA magna cum laude, Brown U., 1977; JD, Yale U., 1980. Bar: N.Y. 1981. Law clk. to Judge Edward Weinfeld U.S. Dist. Ct. for So. Dist. N.Y., N.Y.C., 1980-81; assoc. Paul, Weiss, Rifkind, Wharton & Garrison, N.Y.C., 1981-83; from asst. U.S. atty. to chief appellate atty. criminal div. U.S. Atty.'s Office for So. Dist. N.Y., N.Y.C., 1983-87; assoc. counsel Office Ind. Counsel for Iran/Contra, Washington, 1987; dep. dir. Human Rights Watch, N.Y.C., 1987-93, exec. dir., 1993—. Editor, author numerous reports on human rights worldwide; contbr. articles to newspapers and mags. Mem. Assn. Bar City N.Y., Coun. Fgn. Rels. Office: Human Rights Watch 350 5th Ave Fl 34 New York NY 10118-3499

**ROTH, LANE,** communications educator; b. N.Y.C., Apr. 10; BA with nat. honors in German, NYU; MA, Fla. State U., 1974, PhD in Mass Comm., 1976. Camera operator Sta. WFSU-TV, Tallahassee, 1973-74; broadcast engr., producer-creator, writer, performer Sta. WFSU-FM, Tallahassee, 1974-76; co-host Sta. WNIN-TV, Evansville, Ind., 1976-77; asst. prof. radio-TV-film U. Evansville, 1976-78; asst. prof. comm. Lamar U., Beaumont, Tex., 1978-82, assoc. prof., 1982—. Bd. dirs. Mental Health Assn. of Jefferson County, pres., 1997, 98; writer, performer fund-raising promos, Sta. KVLU-FM, Beaumont, 1995—. Author: Film Semiotics, Metz, and Leone's Trilogy, 1983; contbr. articles to profl. mags., jours.; contbr. to acad. books. Bd. dirs. Mental Health Assoc. of Jefferson Co., 1993—. Recipient Regents Merit award for excellence in tchg., 1980, Mental Health Assn. award for dedicated leadership, 1999. Mem. Popular Culture Assn. Roman Catholic. Avocations: Jungian psychology, analysis of popular film and tv, singer-impressionist-songwriter. Office: Lamar U Dept Communications Beaumont TX 77710 Office Phone: 409-880-8152.

**ROTH, LAWRENCE MAX,** pathologist, educator; b. McAlester, Okla., June 25, 1936; s. Herman Moe and Blanche (Brown) R.; m. Anna Berit Katarina Sundstrom, Apr. 3, 1965; children: Karen Esther Hart, David Josef. BA, Vanderbilt U., 1957; MD, Harvard U., 1960. Diplomate Am. Bd. Pathology. Rotating intern U. Ill. Research and Ednl. Hosps., Chgo., 1960—61; resident in anat. pathology Washington U. Sch. Medicine, St. Louis, 1961—64; resident in clin. pathology U. Calif. Med. Ctr., San Francisco, 1967—68; asst. prof. pathology Tulane U. Sch. Medicine, New Orleans, 1968—71; assoc. prof. pathology Ind. U. Sch. Medicine, Indpls., 1971—75, prof., 1975—2002, prof. emeritus pathology, 2002—, dir. divsn. surg. pathology, 1971—2002. Series editor: Contemporary Issues in Surgical Pathology; mem. editl. bd. Am. Jour. Surg. Pathology, Human Pathology, Seminars in Diagnostic Pathology, Internat. Jour. Gynecol. Pathology, Endocrine Pathology; contbr. articles to med. jours. Served to capt. U.S. Army, 1965—67. Recipient James Harshman award, Ind. Assn. Pathologists, 1989. Mem. Am. Med. Assn. Investigative Pathologists, U.S. and Can. Acad. Pathology, Am. Soc. Clin. Pathologists, Coll. Am. Pathologists, Internat. Soc. Gynecol. Pathologists, Arthur Purdy Stout Soc. Surg. Pathologists, Assn. Dirs. Anatomic and Surg. Pathology. Home: 7898 Ridge Rd Indianapolis IN 46240-2538 Office: 635 Barnhill Dr Indianapolis IN 46202 Business E-Mail: lroth@iupui.edu.

**ROTH, LOREN H.,** psychiatrist; b. May 9, 1939; m. Ellen A. Roth; children: Jonathan, Alexandra, Elizabeth. BA in Philosophy, Cornell U., 1961; MD cum laude, Harvard U., 1966, MPH, 1972; postgrad., Am. U., 1972-73. Diplomate Am. Bd. Psychiatry and Neurology; lic. physician, Conn., Md., Mass., Pa. Med. intern Univ. Hosps., Western Res. U., Cleve., 1966-67; resident psychiatry Yale U., New Haven, 1969-70, Mass. Gen. Hosp., Boston, 1970-72; staff psychiatrist Ctr. for Studies Crime and Delinquency, NIMH, Rockville, Md., 1972-74; co-dir., dir. law and psychiatry program Western Psychiat. Inst. and Clinic/U. Pitts., 1974—, chief adult clin. svcs., 1983-87, 88-89, chief clin. svcs., 1989-95, co-dir., dir. law and psychiatry program, 1974-94; vice-chmn. dept. psychiatry U. Pitts., 1988-97, acting prof., 1974-78, assoc. prof., 1978-82, prof., 1982—; v.p. for managed care U. Pitts. Med. Ctr., 1993-97; assoc. vice chancellor for edn., health scis. U. Pitts. Sch. Medicine, 1995-97, assoc. sr. vice chancellor health scis., 1997—; sr. v.p., quality care U. Pitts. Med. Ctr. Health Sys., 2003—, chief med. officer, 1997—. Med. staff Presbyn.-Univ. Hosp., Pitts., 1983—; gen. med. officer Fed. Penitentiary, Lewisburg, Pa., 1967-69; William E. Schumacher disting. lectr. Maine Dept. Mental Health and Mental Retardation, Portland, 1982; mem. commn. on mentally disabled ABA, Washington, 1987; cons. law and psychiatry Dept. Welfare, Commonwealth Pa., 1974; cons. reviewer, site visitor crime and delinquency sect. NIMH, 1977; examiner Am. Bd. Psychiatry and Neurology, 1985. Author: (with others) Informed Consent: A Study of Decisionmaking in Psychiatry, 1984; editor: (with others) Psychiatry, Social, Epidemiologic and Legal Psychiatry, Vol. 5, 1986; contbr. articles to profl. jours., chpts. to books; editorial bd. Criminology, 1974-78, Law and Human Behavior, 1980-85, Internat. Jour. Law and Psychiatry, 1980-88, Behavioral Scis. and the Law, 1987-95; assoc. editor Am. Jour. Psychiatry, 1982-90; cons. editor Criminal Justice and Behavior, 1982-85. Lt. comrd. USPHS Res., 1967—. Recipient Steve Allen award United Mental Health, Inc., 1990; grantee NIMH, 1979, 80-81, 89, Founds. Fund for Rsch. in Psychiatry, 1980-82. Fellow Am. Psychiat. Assn. (Isaac Ray award 1988), Am. Coll. Utilization Rev. Physicians, Am. Coll. Psychiatrists; mem. AMA, Am. Acad. Psychiatry and Law (pres. 1983-84), Group for Advancement Psychiatry (com. on psychiatry and law 1979-80, chmn. 1981-84), Am. Soc. Criminology, Am. Soc. Law and Medicine (bd. dirs. 1982-85), Internat. Acad. Law and Mental Health (bd. dirs.), Am. Psychopath. Assn., Phi Beta Kappa, Phi Kappa Phi. Home: 6820 Edgerton Ave Pittsburgh PA 15208-2803 Office: U Pitts Med Ctr Forbes TWR 200 Lothrop St Ste 11016 Pittsburgh PA 15213-2546 Office Phone: 412-647-4860. E-mail: rothlh@upmc.edu.

**ROTH, MARJORY JOAN JARBOE,** special education educator; b. Ranger, Tex., May 24, 1934; d. James Aloysius and Dorothy Knight (Taggart) Jarboe; m. Thomas Mosser Roth, Jr., Dec. 22, 1959; children: Thomas Mosser III, James Jarboe. BA in English, Rice U., 1957; MEd in Ednl. Adminstrn., U. N.C., Greensboro, 1981. Cert. tchr.-specific learning disabilities, middle grades lang. arts and social studies, intermediate grades, adminstr.-prin., N.C. Tchr. 4th grade Houston Ind. Sch. Dist., 1957-60; specific lang. disabilities instr. Forsyth Tech. C.C., Winston-Salem, N.C., 1976-77; specific learning disabilities tchr. Forsyth Country Day Sch., Winston-Salem, 1977-80; tchr. 5th grade Winston-Salem/Forsyth County Schs., 1982-83, specific learning disabilities tchr. Mt. Tabor High Sch., 1983-86; part time instr. English and Learning Disabilities Forsyth Tech. C.C., 1986-90; founding pres., prin. Greenhills Sch., Winston-Salem, 1990—. Co-author, co-editor Greenhills News. Sunday Sch. dir., tchr. Galloway Meml. Episcopal Ch., 1960-70, pres., treas., sec. Churchwomen, 1963-74; treas. Elkin Jr. Woman's Club, 1962; chmn. Elkin Heart Fund Drive, 1968; bd. dirs. Hugh Chatham Hosp. Auxillary, 1968, Friends of the Elkin Pub. Libr. 1968-74, chmn., 1970-72, chmn., exhibits chmn. summer reading program; pres. South Surry Heart Assn., 1969; mem. Churchwomen of St. Paul's Episcopal Ch., Winston-Salem, 1982—, Fiddle and Bow Folk Music Soc., Winston-Salem, 1992—. Recipient June Lyday Orton award for outstanding svc. in the field of dyslexia, 1997; Forsyth fellow NEH, 1985; grantee in field. Fellow Acad. Orton-Gillingham Practitioners and Educators; mem. ASCD, Children with Attention Deficit Disorder (profl. adv. bd. N.C. Triad chpt 1990-96), Learning Disability Assn. N.C. (sec., bd. dirs. 1981-86), Internat. Dyslexia Assn. (sec., bd. dirs. Carolinas br. 1981-85, founding pres. N.C. br. 1987-91, bd. dirs. 1987-96, nat. nominating com. 1992-94). Internat. Multisensory Structured Lang. Edn. Coun., Inc. (bd. dirs. 2000-03, 05—, mem. coun. 1995—). Republican. Avocations: tennis, hiking, folk music. Home: 940 Fox Hall Dr Winston Salem NC 27106-4431 Office: Greenhills Sch 1360 Lyndale Dr Winston Salem NC 27106-9739 Office Phone: 336-924-4908.

**ROTH, MICHAEL,** lawyer; b. N.Y.C., July 22, 1931; s. Philip Arthur and Mollie (Breitenbach) R.; m. Jeany Macoir, Nov. 24, 1957; 3 children BA, Yale Coll., 1953; JD, Columbia U., 1956, M. Internat. Affairs, 1964. Bar: N.Y. 1956. Law assoc. Stroock & Stroock & Lavan, N.Y.C., 1956-63; ptnr. Roth, Carlson, Kwit & Spengler, N.Y.C., 1964-74; chmn. N.Y. State Liquor Authority, N.Y.C., 1974-77; ptnr. Shea & Gould, N.Y.C., 1979-89; of counsel

Katten, Muchin, Rosenman, N.Y.C., 1989—. Mem. U.S. del. to UN Population Commn., 1969; Rep.-Conservative candidate for N.Y. State atty. gen., 1978; mem. Pres.' Task Force on Internat. Pvt. Enterprise, 1983-84, Pres.' Commn. on Mgmt. AID Programs, 1991-92. Mem. Sunningdale Country Club (Scarsdale, N.Y.). Republican.

**ROTH, MICHAEL I.**, communications executive, lawyer; b. Bklyn., Nov. 22, 1945; s. Harry A. and Sally (Kutin) R.; m. Carole A. Snofsky, Aug. 10, 1968; children— Barrie, Marc, Andrew BS, CCNY, 1967; JD, Boston U., 1971; LL.M., NYU, 1973. Bar: N.Y. 1971. CPA: N.Y. 1973, Conn. 1973. With Coopers & Lybrand, NYC, 1969-76; ptnr. Stamford, Conn., 1976-82; exec. v.p. corp. fin., tax and adminstrn. Primerica Corp. (formerly Am. Can Co.), Greenwich, Conn., 1982-87, exec. v.p., 1987, chief fin. officer, 1987-88; exec. v.p., chief fin. officer MONY Fin. Svcs., NYC, 1989-91; pres., COO, MONY-Mut. Ins. Co., NYC, 1991-94, chmn. bd. dirs., CEO, 1994—2004; bd. dir. Interpublic Group, NYC, 2002—, chmn., 2004—, CEO, 2005—. Bd. dirs. Pitney Bowes Corp., Gaylord Entertainment Mem. leadership com. Lincoln Ctr. for Performing Arts; bd. dirs. Child Guidance Ctr., Stamford, 1984-85, Baruch Coll. Fund, Enterprise Found., Partnership for NYC; trustee Temple BethEl, Stamford, 1984-85 Mem. Am. Inst. CPA's, Conn. Soc. CPA's, Stamford Tax Assn. (pres. 1981-82) Office: Interpublic Group 1114 Ave of the Americas New York NY 10036*

**ROTH, MICHAEL S.**, academic administrator, art educator; BA, Wesleyan U.; MA, Princeton U., Phd in history. H.B. Alexander Prof. Humanities & Cultural Studies Claremont Grad. Sch.; assoc. dir. Getty Rsch. Inst., chmn. Rsch. & Edn. Dept.; pres. Calif. Coll. Arts, San Francisco 2000—. Author: Freud: Conflict & Culture, 1998; curator (exhibitions) Sigmund Freud: Conflict & Culture, Libr. Congress, 1998; author: Looking for L.A.: Architecture, Film, Photography & Urban Landscape, 2001, Disturbing Remains: Memory, History, & Crisis in Twentieth Century, 2001. Office: Office of the President California College of the Arts 1111 Eighth St San Francisco CA 94107

**ROTH, PAUL BARRY**, dean, educator, emergency medicine physician; b. Glen Ridge, NJ, Oct. 7, 1947; s. Jerome M. and Selma (Leitner) R. BS, Fairleigh Dickinson U., 1969, MS, 1972; MD, George Washington U., 1976; postgrad., U. N.Mex., Albuquerque, 1976-79. Resident in family practice U. N.Mex. Sch. Medicine, Albuquerque, 1976—79; owner, pres. EMS of N.Mex., Albuquerque, 1978-82; owner, mem. of bd. Heights Urgent Care Ctr., Albuquerque, 1980-82; dir. divsn. emergency medicine dept. family, cmty. and emergency medicine U. N.Mex. Sch. Medicine, Albuquerque, 1982-91, prof. emerg. med., 1991—, chair dept. emergency medicine, 1991-93, interim chief med. officer, 1992—93, interim dean, 1994—95, dean, 1994—; interim dir. U. N.Mex. Med. Ctr., Albuquerque, 1994—95; med. dir. disaster medicine Nat. Disaster Med. Sys.; exec. v.p. U. N.Mex. Health Sci. Ctr., 2005—. Chair disaster com. U. N.Mex. Med. Ctr. Contbr. articles to Annals of EM, Current Practice of EM-Disaster Medicine, Jour. of AMA. Recipient Outstanding Individual Svc. award Nat. Disaster Med. Sys., 1986. Fellow Am. Coll. Emergency Physicians (chair sect. on disaster medicine, 1991-92), Am. Acad. Family Practice; mem. AMA, Soc. for Acad. Emergency Medicine, Am. Coll. Physician Execs., Am. Acad. Family Physicians. Office: HSC Sch Medicine Adminstrn MSC08 4720 1 University of New Mexico Albuquerque NM 87131-0001 Office Phone: 505-272-2321. Business E-Mail: PRoth@salud.unm.edu.

**ROTH, PAUL NORMAN**, lawyer; b. NYC, May 4, 1939; m. Ellen Joan Lipp, May 24, 1964; children: Stefanie H., Jessica A. AB cum laude, Harvard U., 1961, LLB magna cum laude, 1964. Bar: NY 1967, US Ct. Appeals (2 nd cir.) 1966, US Dist. Ct. (So. and Ea. Dists.) NY 1967, US Supreme Ct. 1975. Assoc. Cleary, Gottlieb, Steen & Hamilton, NYC, 1965-69; ptnr., Corp. Practice Area Schulte Roth & Zabel LLP, NYC, 1969—. Spkr. in field. Trustee Ctrl. Synagogue, NYC, 1987-95; bd. dirs. Citizens for NYC, 1999—. Fulbright fellow, Netherlands, 1965. Fellow NY Bar Found.; mem. ABA (chair com. pvt. investment entities), Nat. Assn. Securities Dealers (legal adv. bd. 1999-2003), Lawyers Alliance for NY (bd. dirs. 1999-2002), NY State Bar Assn., Assn. of Bar of City of NY (com. on securities regulation 1982-85, chmn. 1989-92), Harvard Law Sch. Assn. NY (trustee 1987-90, v.p. 1992-93, pres. 1999—2001), Century Country Club, Phi Beta Kappa. Office: Schulte Roth & Zabel LLP 919 Third Ave New York NY 10022-4774 also: Healthcoat House 20 Savile Row London W1S 3PR England Office Phone: 212-756-2450. Fax: 212-593-5955. E-mail: paul.roth@srz.com.

**ROTH, PHILIP MILTON**, writer; b. Newark, Mar. 19, 1933; s. Herman and Bess (Finkel) R.; m. Margaret Martinson, Feb. 22, 1959 (dec. 1968); m. Claire Bloom, Apr. 29, 1990 (div. June 1994). Student, Rutgers U., 1950-51; AB, Bucknell U., 1954; MA, U. Chgo., 1955. Tchr. English U. Chgo., 1956-58; faculty Iowa Writers Workshop, 1960-62; writer in residence Princeton U., 1962-64; adj. prof. U. Pa., 1967-77; disting. prof. Hunter Coll. CUNY, 1989-92. Author: Goodbye, Columbus, 1959 (Nat. Book award for Fiction, 1960), Letting Go, 1962, When She Was Good, 1967, Portnoy's Complaint, 1969, Our Gang, 1971, The Breast, 1972, The Great American Novel, 1973, My Life as a Man, 1974, Reading Myself and Others, 1975, The Professor of Desire, 1977, The Ghost Writer, 1979, A Philip Roth Reader, 1980, Zuckerman Unbound, 1981, The Anatomy Lesson, 1983, The Prague Orgy, 1985, Zuckerman Bound, 1985, The Counterlife, 1987 (Nat. Book Critics Circle award for fiction, 1988), The Facts: A Novelist's Autobiography, 1988, Deception, 1990, Patrimony, 1991 (Nat. Book Critics Circle award for biography/autobiography 1992), Operation Shylock: A Confession, 1993 (PEN-Faulkner award for fiction, 1993), The Conversation of the Jews, 1993, Sabbath's Theater, 1995 (Nat. Book award for fiction, 1995), American Pastoral, 1997 (Pulitzer prize for fiction, 1998), I Married A Communist, 1998 (Amb. Book award of English-Speaking Union), The Human Stain, 2000 (PEN-Faulkner award for fiction, 2000, Prix Medicis Etranger, 2000), The Dying Animal, 2001, Shop Talk: A Writer and His Colleagues and Their Work, 2002, The Plot Against America, 2004 (Book Sense Honor Book for adult fiction, 2005), Everyman, 2006; works pub. in Harper's, New Yorker, Epoch, Commentary, others; reprints in Best Am. Short Stories of 1956, 59, 60. O'Henry Prize Stories of 1960 Recipient prize for fiction Paris Rev., 1958, Nat. Inst. Arts and Letters award, 1960, Daroff award Jewish Book Coun. Am., 1960, Medal of Honor for Lit., Nat. Arts Club, 1991, Karel Capek prize Czech Republic, 1994; Guggenheim fellow, 1959-60, Rockefeller fellow, 1966.

**ROTH, RICHARD**, news correspondent; b. NYC, Apr. 27, 1949; married; 1 child. BA with honors, Union Coll., Schenectady, NY, 1970; MA, Columbia U., 1972. With CBS News, 1972—, bur. chief, corr. Moscow, 1976—74, fed. corr. Washington, 1976—81, corr. Rome, 1981—86, NYC, 1986—90, LA, 1990—94, London, 1998—, NBC News, London, 1994—98. Reporter, substitute anchor (TV series) CBS Evening News, contbr. 48 Hours, corr. (documentaries) 48 Hours on Crack Street, 1986. Co-recipient Edward R. Murrow award, Radio-TV News Dirs. Assn. & Found., George Foster Peabody award, 2 Emmy awards; recipient David Kaplan award, Overseas Press Club, 2006. Office: CBS News Broadcasting House 566 Chiswick High Rd London W4 5XS England Office Phone: 020 89872829.*

**ROTH, ROBERT**, lawyer, journalist; s. Andrew and Sarah Roth. BA cum laude, Bklyn. Coll., 1974; JD, Ind. U., 1977. Bar: NY 1980. V.p., gen. counsel Andrew Roth and Sons, Inc., Bklyn., 1980—; corr., contbg. photographer UPI, NYC, 1980—96; aviation analyst Fox News Channel, 1999—2000. Photojournalist (news photograph) Statue of Liberty Centennial (UPI Pictures of the Yr., 1989), lead correspondent (series of television news reports) Crash of Egyptair Flight 990. Mem. young fellows The Frick Collection, NYC, 2003. Recipient Sam Castan Meml. award Excellence Journalism, Bklyn. Coll., 1974. Mem.: NY Press Club, NY County Lawyers Assn. Avocation: travel. Office: Andrew Roth and Sons Inc PO Box 190293 Brooklyn NY 11219-3736 Office Phone: 718-851-1416.

**ROTH, ROBERT A.**, newspaper executive; b. Upper Darby, Pa., Mar. 19, 1947; s. Robert Raymond and Ruth Lorrayne (Jonas) R. BA magna cum laude, Carleton Coll., 1969; postgrad., U. Chgo., 1969-71. Co-founder Chgo. Reader, 1971, 1971-94, editor, 1975-90; pres. Chgo. Reader, Inc., 1974—, Washington Free Weekly, Inc., 1982—. Dir. Inst. for Alternative Journalism, San Francisco 1983-89, Raw Vision, Ltd., London, 1991—, Stonington (Maine) Sea Products, Inc., 2002—. Co-founder Intuit: The Ctr. for Intuitive and Outsider Art, Chgo., 1991, pres., 1991-96, bd. dirs., 1991—; trustee Carleton Coll., Northfield, Minn., 1994-98. Recipient Alumni Disting. Achievement award Carleton Coll., 1989, Donald J. Cowling Cup, 2002; named to Esquire Register, Esquire mag., 1984; named among Who's Who in Chgo. Bus., Crain's Chgo. Bus., 1990, 91, 92, 93, 94, 95, 96. Mem. Assn. Alternative Newsweeklies (pres. 1983-87). Avocations: folk and outsider art, architecture. Office: Chgo Reader 11 E Illinois St Chicago IL 60611-5652 Business E-Mail: broth@chicagoreader.com.

**ROTH, ROBERT EARL**, ecologist, educator; b. Wauseon, Ohio, Mar. 30, 1937; s. Earl Jonas and Florence Lena (Mahler) R.; m. Carol Sue Yackee, Aug. 8, 1959; children: Robin Earl, Bruce Robert. BS, Ohio State U., 1959, BS in Secondary Sci. Edn., 1960, MS in Conservation Edn., 1960; PhD in Environ. Edn., U. Wis., 1969. Supr. conservation edn. Ethical Culture Schs., N.Y.C., 1961-63; naturalist, sci. tchr. Lakeside Sch., Spring Valley, NY, 1963-65; instr. No. Ill. U., Oregon, 1965-67; asst. prof. Ohio State U., Columbus, 1969-73, assoc. prof., 1973-78, prof. environ. edn. and sci. edn., 1978-2001, prof. emeritus, 2001—, chmn. divsn., 1973-84, coord. office internat. affairs, 1985-89, asst. dir. sch. sec. Sch. Natural Resources, 1989-93, acting dir. Sch. Natural Resources, 1993-94, assoc. dir., 1994-2001, state extension specialist Environ. Edn., 1993-2001. Rsch. & devel. assoc. Mosely & Assocs., Columbus, 1986-89; project cons. NARMA project, U.S. Agy. internat. Devel., Santo Domingo, Dominican Rep., 1982-87; cons. Richard Trott & Assocs., 1988-90, Kinzelman & Kline, 1990-2001, Midwest consortium Internat. Activity, 1995; evaluator Montclair State U., N.J. Sch. Conservation, 1999; workshop leader Carribean Conservation Assn., Bridgetown, Barbados, 1981-83; vis. scholar Indonesian Second U. Devel. project, Jakarta, 1988; AID lectr., Thesolonika, Greece, 1992; bd. supr. Franklin Soil & Water Conservation Dist., 2003-05. Exec. editor Jour. Environ. Edn., 1974-91 (Pub.'s prize 1970); contbr. articles to profl. jours. Committeeman Boy Scouts Am., 1983-86; adv. coun. McKeever Environ. Learning Ctr., Pa., 1977-83. Named vis. scholar, Uganda Makerere U., 1989, Pacific Cultural Found., Taipei, Taiwan, 1989, 1999, 2001; recipient Pomerene Tchg. Enhancement award, Ohio State U., 1986, 1995, Environ. Edn. award, Ohio Alliance for the Enrivon., 1992, Outstanding Advising award, Coll. Food Agrl. and Environ. Scis., 1996. Mem.: Sch. Nat. Resource Alumni Assn. (inducted hon. 100), Nat. Sci. Tchrs. Assn. (life), N.Am. Assn. Environ. Edn. (life; bd. dirs. 1972—82, pres. 1977—78, Walt Jeske award 1988, Outstanding Contbns. to Rsch. award 2000). Avocations: swimming, canoeing, camping, fishing, travel. Home: 570 Morning St Columbus OH 43085-3775 E-mail: roth.3@osu.edu.

**ROTH, ROBERT HOWARD**, psychologist; b. Newark, Jan. 15, 1933; s. Max and Marion (Gurkewitz) R.; m. Estelle Goldstein, June 16, 1957; children: Lisa C., Neil A. BS, Juilliard Sch., N.Y.C., 1953; MA, Columbia U., 1956, EdD, 1960. Lic. psychologist, N.Y., N.J. Instr. Union Coll., Cranford, N.J., 1959-60, Newark State Coll., Union, N.J., 1960-63; asst. prof. Hunter Coll. CUNY, N.Y.C., 1963-65; assoc. prof. Newark State Coll., Union, N.J., 1965-68, chmn. psychology dept., 1967-71; prof. psychology Kean U., Union, 1968—. Cons. Marlboro (N.J.) Psychiat. Hosp., 1982-97; pvt. practice clin. psychology Madison Med. Ctr. Editor: Contemporary Studies in Psychopathology, 1983, Contemporary Studies in Personality, 1986, Explorations in Mental Disorders, 1987, Personality Structures and Functions, 1989, Psychopathologies and Treatments, 1991, Ego, Self, Person, Context, 1992, 2d edit., 1996, Tempest in the Mind, 1994. Fellow Am. Orthopsychiatric Assn.; mem. APA, AAAS, N.Y. Acad. Scis., N.J. Acad. Scis. (chmn. psychology sect. 1971-73). Home: 111 Gallinson Dr New Providence NJ 07974-2723

**ROTH, SANFORD IRWIN**, pathologist, educator; b. McAlester, Okla., Oct. 14, 1932; s. Herman Moe and Blanche (Brown) R.; m. Kathryn Ann Corliss, Sept. 3, 1961; children: Jeffrey Franklin, Elisabeth Francyne, Gregory James, Suzannah Joan. Student, Vanderbilt U., 1949-52; MD, Harvard U., 1956. Intern Mass. Gen. Hosp., Boston, 1956-57, resident in pathology, 1957-60, pathologist, 1962-75, Armed Forces Inst. Pathology, 1960-62; asst. prof. Med. Sch. Harvard U., 1962-69, assoc. prof. Med. Sch., 1969-75; pathologist, prof., chmn. dept. Coll. Medicine U. Ark., Little Rock, 1975-81; prof. Med. Sch. Northwestern U., Chgo., 1981—2000, asst. dean admissions, 1998-2000, prof. emeritus, 2000—; chief lab. svc. VA Lakeside Med. Ctr., Chgo., 1981-86. Attending pathologist Northwestern U. Hosp., 1981-2001; vis. prof. pathology Harvard Med. Sch., 2001—; cons. in pathology Mass. Gen. Hosp., 2001—. With M.C. U.S. Army, 1960-62. Mem. AMA, AAAS, Coll. Am. Pathology, U.S.-Can. Acad. Pathology, Soc. for Investigative Dermatology, Mass. Med. Soc. Home: 169 Tisquantum Rd Chatham MA 02633-2578 Office: Fruit St Boston MA 02114 Office Phone: 508-945-2995. Business E-Mail: sroth@northwestern.edu. E-mail: sroth@partners.org.

**ROTH, SARAH EVE**, occupational safety professional; b. West Allis, Wis., Mar. 10, 1971; d. Douglas Fred and Rene'e Alice Roth. BS in Edn., U. of Wis., Whitewater, 1994. Sales assoc. K-Mart, Burlington, Wis., 1988—94; safety asst. Velvac, Inc., New Berlin, Wis., 1993; safety intern Johnson Controls, Inc, Milw., 1994; corp. safety adminstr. Schweiger Industries, Inc., Jefferson, Wis., 1994; tech./product specialist Lab Safety Supply, Janesville, Wis., 1994—; tax specialist H & R Block, Janesville, 1999—2003; comml. print model Janesville, 1997—. Program com. chairperson Jefferson County Area Safety Network, Jefferson, 1994; founder, owner Princess Specialty Gifts, 2001— Author: (book) Moments in Time, 2000. Mem.: Am. Soc. Safety Engrs. (pub. commn. dir. 1994, nodnl chair 1995). Avocations: writing, dance, piano, weightlifting, golf. Home: 1521 Excalibur Dr Janesville WI 53546 Office: Lab Safety Supply 401 South Wright Rd Janesville WI 53546 Personal E-mail: sarahroth310@hotmail.com. Business E-Mail: s.roth@labsafety.com.

**ROTH, SOL**, rabbi; b. Rzeszow, Poland, Mar. 8, 1927; came to U.S., 1934, naturalized, 1939; s. Joseph and Miriam (Lamm) R.; m. Debra H. Stitskin, Nov. 26, 1957; children: Steven, Michael (dec.), Sharon. BA, Yeshiva U., 1948; MA, Columbia U., 1953, PhD, 1966; D in Divinity (hon.), Yeshiva U., 1977. Rabbi Yeshiva U. Theol. Sem., 1950. Ordained rabbi Orthodox Jewish Congregations, 1950; pres. Rabbinical Council Am., 1980-82, N.Y. Bd. Rabbis, 1976-79; chmn. Israel Commn. Rabbinical Council Am., 1976-78; dean Chaplaincy Sch., N.Y. Bd. Rabbis, 1976-79; Samson R. Hirsch prof. dept. philosophy Yeshiva U., N.Y.C. Rabbi Jewish Ctr. Atlantic Beach, N.Y., 1956-86; rabbi Fifth Ave Synagogue, 1986-2003, rabbi emeritus, 2003—; pres. Rabbinical Coun. Am., 1980-82, Religious Zionists Am., 1991-94 Author: Science and Religion, 1967, The Jewish Idea of Community, 1977, Halakhah and Politics: The Jewish Idea of a State, 1988 (Samuel Belkin Meml. Lit. award 1989), The Jewish Idea of Culture, 1997; editor: Morasha. Recipient award Synagogue Adv. Council United Jewish Appeal, 1975; named Rabbi Dr. Sol Roth Chair in Talmud and Contemporary Halakha established at Yeshiva U., 1989. Jewish. Home: 201 E 62nd St New York NY 10021-8026 Office: Yeshiva U Dept Philosophy 500 W 185th St Dept New York NY 10033-3299 Personal E-mail: rothsol@aol.com.

**ROTH, STEVEN**, real estate company executive; AB, Dartmouth Coll., 1962, MBA with highest distinction, 1963. With Kenilworth Assoc., NJ, 1975—79; co-founder, mng. gen. ptnr. Interstate Properties, 1979—; CEO, chmn. bd. Vornado Realty Trust, NYC, 1989—; CEO Alexander's Inc. 1995—, chmn., 2004—. Bd. dir. Amos Tuck Sch., Dartmouth Coll. 1981—87; trustee Whitney Mus. Am. Art, NYC, Intrepid Mus. Found., NYC; bd. dir. Jewish Theol. Seminary Am., NYU Sch. Med. Found. With USAR. Named one of Forbes' Richest Americans, 2006. Office: Vornado Realty Trust 888 Seventh Ave New York NY 10019 also: Alexander's Inc 210 Rte 4 E Paramus NJ 07652 Office Phone: 212-894-7000.

**ROTH, TERENCE VINCENT**, surgeon; b. Milw., Jan. 19, 1942; BS, Marquette U., Milw., 1964; MD, Med. Coll. Wis., 1968. Diplomate Am. Bd. Surgery. Intern U. Ky., Lexington, 1968-69; resident gen. surgery Cleve. Clinic, 1969-73; surgeon West Allis Meml. Hosp., St. Francis Hosp., St. Luke's Hosp., Elmbrook Meml., Wis., 1973—; pvt. practice. Mem. ACS, AMA, A.S.G.S., Soc. Laparoendoscopic Surgery, Wis. A.C.S., Wis. Surg. Soc. Office: 2424 S 90th St Ste 408 West Allis WI 53227-2455 Office Phone: 414-328-8640.

**ROTH, THOMAS**, marketing executive; Grad., Western Mich. U. With Tarkenton and Co., Atlanta; founder HR Skills divsn. Nat. Edu. Tng. Group, 1988-92; dir. product devel. Wilson Learning Corp., Eden Prairie, Minn., 1981-88, v.p. product mgmt. in global R & D, 1992-94, v.p. product mgmt. and tng. group, 1994-99, v.p. global cons., 1999—. Cons. IBM, AT&T, Ford Motor Co., Pfizer, E.I. DuPont, Gen. Electric, Oracle, Dow Chem., Lucent, Tex. Instruments, Colgate-Palmolive, Honeywell, others; spkr. in field. Co-author: Creating the High Performance Team, 1987. Office: Wilson Learning Corp Warehouse 8000 W 78th St #175 Minneapolis MN 55439-2536

**ROTH, TIM**, actor; b. London, May 14, 1961; m. Nikki Butler, 1993; children: Timothy, Cormac. With Glasgow Citizen's Theatre, The Oval House, The Royal Ct. Appeared in play Metamorphosis; films include The Hit, 1985, A World Apart, 1988, The Cook, the Thief, His Wife and Her Lover, 1990, Vincent and Theo, 1990, Rosencrantz and Guildenstern Are Dead, 1991, Jumpin' at the Boneyard, 1992, Reservoir Dogs, 1992, Bodies, Rest and Motion, 1993, Pulp Fiction, 1994, Rob Roy, 1995 (Acad. award nominee for best supporting actor 1996), Little Odessa, 1995, Four Rooms, 1995, No Way Home, 1996, Everyone Says I Love You, 1996, Hoodlum, 1997, Gridlock'd, 1997, Animals, 1997, Deceiver, 1998, The Legend of the Pianist on the Ocean, 1998, Vatel, 1999, Leggenda del pianista sull'oceano, 1998, The Million Dollar Hotel, 2000, Lucky Numbers, 2000, Planet of the Apes, 2001, Invincible, 2001, The Musketeer, 2001, Emmett's Mark, 2002, Whatever We Do, 2003, To Kill a Mockingbird, 2003, With It, 2004, Silver City, 2004, New France, 2004, The Beautiful Country, 2004, Dark Water, 2005, Jumpshot, 2005, The Last Sign, 2005, Don't Come Knocking, 2005, Even Money, 2006; TV movies include Meantime, Made in Britain, Metamorphosis, Murder in the Heartland, 1993; dir.: The War Zone, 1998; TV guest appearance Tales From the Crypt, 1989. Office: Ilene Feldman Agy 8730 W Sunset Blvd Ste 490 Los Angeles CA 90069-2248*

**ROTH, WILLIAM H.**, insurance company executive; BSc, Indiana U., MBA in fin. and acctg. CPA. With WellPoint Health Networks; sr. v.p. e.bus. ops. WellPoint; sr. v.p. Blue Cross of Calif., 1998—2000; head of regional ops. UNICARE; cons. Deloitte & Touche; sr. v.p., consumer markets Aetna Inc., 2001—. Office: Aetna Inc 151 Farmington Ave Hartford CT 06156

**ROTH, WILLIAM JOSEPH**, dermatologist; s. James Charles and Elizabeth Roth. BS in Biol. Sci., Stony Brook U., N.Y., 1981, PhD in Molecular Pathology, 1986, MD, 1990. Diplomate Am. Acad. of Dermatology, 1994, Dermatologist / dermatologic surgery / photomedicine Watson Clinic LLP, Lakeland, Fla., 1994—, dir., 2003—04. Asst. clin. prof. Dept. of Dermatology and Cutaneous Surgery, U. South Fla., Tampa, 1997—. Contbr. articles to profl. jours. Grantee rsch. grantee, NIH, 1981—86. Fellow: Fla. Soc. of Dermatologic Surgery; mem.: Am. Soc. for Mohs Surgery, Am. Soc. of Dermatologic Surgery, Fla. Soc. of Dermatology and Dermatologic Surgery, Am. Mensa. Office: Watson Clinic LLP 1600 Lakeland Hills Blvd Lakeland FL 33805

**ROTH, WILLIAM MCKINLEY**, psychologist; b. Phila., Jan. 24, 1945; s. William M. and Ethel M. Roth; m. Ledjie Baird Roth (div.); m. Gretchen O. Roth. BA in journalism, Penn. State U., 1966, Ba in psychology, 1966; MA in psychology, Temple U., 1969. Lic. profl. psychologist Pa., 1977, cert. sch. psychologist and pupil svcs. superv. Dir. employment and tng. Southco Inc., Concordville, Pa., 1969—72; supr. of pupil svcs. Del. County Intermediate Unit, Morton, Pa., 1973—2003. Prvt. practice, Exton, Pa., 1977—; crisis coord. Del. County Sch., Media, Pa., 1985—2003. Contbr. articles various profl. jours. Pres. Pa. Psychology Assn. Sch. Divsn., Harrisburg, Pa., 1980—81; reader, narrator Pa. Assn. For the Blind, Phila., 1970—75. Mem.: Pa. Psychological Assn. (pres., sch. disvsn. 1980—81). Avocation: films rsch. Home: 608 Pancoast Ln Downingtown PA 19335 Office: William M Roth Psychologist 300 N Pottstown Pike Exton PA 19341 Office Phone: 610-518-6970. Office Fax: 610-518-6970. E-mail: broth124@comcast.net.

**ROTH, WILLIAM STANLEY**, hospital foundation executive; b. NYC, Jan. 12, 1929; s. Sam Irving and Louise Caroline (Martin) R.; m. Hazel Adcock, May 6, 1963; children: R. Charles, W. Stanley. AA, Asheville-Biltmore Jr. Coll., N.C., 1948; BS, U. N.C., Asheville, 1950. Dep. regional exec. Nat. coun. Boy Scouts Am., 1953-65; exec. v.p. Am. Humanics Found., 1965-67; dir. devel. Bethany Med. Ctr., Kansas City, Kans., 1967-74; exec. v.p. Geisinger Med. Ctr. Found., Danville, Pa., 1974-78; found. pres. Bapt. Med Ctrs., Birmingham, Ala., 1978—. Sec. Western Med. Systems, Cherokee Cmty. Homes, Cullman Sr. Housing, Dekalb Sr. Housing, Limestone Sr. Housing, Oxford Sr. Housing. Editor: Torch and Trefoil, 1960—61. Mem.-at-large Nat. coun. Boy Scouts Am., 1972-86; chmn. NAHD Ednl. Fund, 1980-82; ruling elder John Knox Kirk, Kansas City, Mo., Grove Presbyn. Ch., Danville, Pa. Recipient Silver award United Meth. Ch., 1970, Mid-West Health Congress, 1971; Seymour award for outstanding hosp. devel. officer, 1983, 60 Yr. Vet. award Boy Scouts Am., 2001. Fellow Assn. for Healthcare Philanthropy (int. pres. 1975-76); mem. Nat. Soc. Fund Raising Execs. (pres. Ala. chpt. 1980-82, nat. dir. 1980-84, mem. ethics bd. 1993-2000, advanced cert fund raising exec., Outstanding Fund Raising Exec., Ala. chpt. 1983), Mid-Am. Hosp. Devel. Assn. (pres. 1973-74), Mid-West Health Congress (devel. chmn. 1972-74), Am. Soc. for Health are Mktg. and Pub. Rels., Ala. Soc. for Sleep Disorders, Ala. Heart Inst., Ala. Assn. Healthcare Philanthropy (pres. 1991-93, chmn. bd. 1993-94), Ala. Planned Giving Coun. (bd. dirs. 1991-2000, pres. 1994-95), Alpha Phi Omega (nat. pres. 1958-62, dir. 1950—. Nat. Disting. Scv. award 1962), Delta Upsilon (pres. N.C. Alumni 1963-65), Rotary (pres. club 1976-77), Relay House, Summit Club, Green Valley Club (bd. govs.), Elks, Order of the Arrow (Nat. Disting. Svc. award 1958), Order of Holy Grail, Order of Golden Fleece. Home: 341 Laredo Dr Birmingham AL 35226-2325 Office: 3500 Blue Lake Dr Ste 101 Birmingham AL 35243-1908 Office Phone: 205-979-8285. Personal E-mail: billroth1@aol.com.

**ROTHBERG, ABRAHAM**, writer; b. NYC, Jan. 14, 1922; s. Louis and Lottie (Drimmer) R.; m. Esther Conwell, Sept. 30, 1945; 1 son, Lewis Josiah. AB, Bklyn. Coll., 1942; MA, U. Iowa, 1947; PhD, Columbia U., 1952. Chmn. editorial bd. Stateside (mag.), N.Y.C., 1947-49; instr. English, creative writing Columbia U., N.Y.C., 1948; instr. English, humanities Hofstra Coll., Hempstead, NY, 1947-51; prof. English St. John Fisher Coll., 1973-83, chmn. dept. English, 1981-82; disting. writer-in-residence, vis. prof. Wichita State U., 1985. Editor-in-chief Free Europe Press, N.Y.C., 1952—59, East Europe Mag., 1952—59; mng. editor George Braziller, Inc., N.Y.C., 1959, New Leader mag., N.Y.C., 1960—61; cons. editor New Jewish Ency., 1960—62; writer, editl. con.; European corr. Nat. Observer, Washington, Manchester (Eng.) Guardian, 1962—63; sr. editor Bantam Books, Inc., N.Y.C., 1966—67; cons. editor The New Union Prayer Book, N.Y.C., 1975. Author: Abraham, Eyewitness History of World War II, 1962, The Thousand Doors, 1965, The Heirs of Cain, 1966, The Song of David Freed, 1968, The Other Man's Shoes, 1969, The Boy and the Dolphin, 1969, The Sword of the Golem, 1971, Aleksandr Solzhenitsyn: The Major Novels, 1971, The Heirs of Stalin: Dissidence and the Soviet Regime, 1953-1970, 1972, The Stalking Horse, 1972, The Great Waltz, 1978, The Four Corners of the House, 1981, The Holy Warriors, 2005, A Beast in View, 2005, Pinocchio's Sister: A Feminist Fable, 2005, The Torii Gate, 2005, The Former People, 2006, numerous short stories, essays and poems; editor: U.S. Stories, 1949, Flashes in the Night, 1958, Anatomy of a Moral, 1959, A Bar-Mitzvah Companion, 1959, Great Adventure Stories of Jack London, 1967; contbr. articles to profl. jours. Served in AUS, 1943-45. Recipient John H. McGinnis Meml. award for short story,

1970, John H. McGinnis Meml. award for essay, 1973—74, Lit. award, Friends of Rochester Libr., 1980; Ford Found. fellow, N.Y.C., 1951—52. Home: 340 Pelham Rd Rochester NY 14610-3355

**ROTHBERG, GERALD**, editor, publishing executive; b. Bklyn., Oct. 29, 1937; s. Abraham and Pauline Rothberg; m. Glenda Fay Morris, June 18, 1970 (div. 1988); children: Laura, Abigail. BA, Bklyn. Coll., 1960; postgrad., Dickinson Law Sch., 1962. Spl. projects editor Esquire (mag.), 1963-66; owner, editor, pub., founder Circus (mag.), N.Y.C., 1966—; owner, founder, editor Sci. and Living Tomorrow, 1980—, Who's In, 1981; founder, editor Sports Mirror mag., 1983—, MGF mag., 1985—; Country Mirror mag., 1994—. Author: (novels) Composition 36, 1993, The Six-Hour Song, 1994, Redeeming Esau, 1995, The Esau Swindle, 2003, The Golem Code, 2004, Saturday Books, 2006. Mem. Periodical and Book Assn. Am. (pres.) Office: Circus Mag 1275 1st Ave Ste 256 New York NY 10021 Office Phone: 212-242-4902. Personal E-mail: circusmag@aol.com.

**ROTHBERG, GLENDA FAY MORRIS**, lawyer; b. Rome, Ga., Aug. 7, 1946; d. Glenn Howell and Fay (Givens) Morris; m. Gerald Rothberg, June 18, 1970 (div. Jan. 1989); children: Laura, Abigail. AB, Randolph-Macon Woman's Coll., 1968; JD, Benjamin Cardozo Law Sch., 1985. Bar: N.Y. 1986, U.S. Dist. Ct. (so. and ea. dists.) N.Y. 1987, U.S. Supreme Ct. 1990. Law guardian juvenile rights divsn. Legal Aid Soc., N.Y.C., 1988-91; pvt. practice N.Y.C., 1992—. Faculty dir. Inst. for not-for-profit Mgmt. Columbia Bus. Sch., N.Y.C., 1994-98. Vol. Manhattan Mediation Ctr., N.Y.C., 1996-99; chair legal com. N.Y.C. Comptr. Task Force on Open Adoption, 1999-2001 Fellow Am. Bar Found.; mem ABA, Assn. of Bar of City of N.Y. (com. chair 1996-99, mem. coun. on children 1999-2002). Office: Ste 400 363 Seventh Ave New York NY 10001 E-mail: gmrlaw@aol.com.

**ROTHBERG, MOREY DAVID**, historian, editor; b. Phila., Apr. 5, 1951; s. Herman Jacob and Dorothy Slotkin Rothberg. BA, U. Md., 1973; MA, PhD, Brown U., 1982. Pers. mgmt. specialist U.S. Office Pers. Mgmt., Washington, 1982—86; dir. John Franklin Jameson papers project Am. Hist. Assn., Washington, 1984—94; editor Comptr. Currency, Washington, 1999—. Editor: (documentary edit.) John Franklin Jameson and the Development of Humanistic Scholarship in America (3 vols.). Founding pres. Wash. Guitar Soc., Silver Spring, Md., 1992—94. J. Franklin Jameson fellow, Am. Hist. Assn. and Libr. of Congress, 1983—84. Mem.: Orgn. Am. Historians (assoc.), Am. Hist. Assn. (assoc.), Phi Beta Kappa. Home: Unit A 10801 Amherst Ave Silver Spring MD 20902 Office Phone: 202-874-6211.

**ROTHBERG-BLACKMAN, JUNE SIMMONDS**, retired nursing educator, psychotherapist; b. Phila., Sept. 4, 1923; d. David and Rose (Protzel) Simmonds; m. Jacob Rothberg, Sept. 7, 1952 (dec. Feb. 2001); children: Robert Rothberg, Alan Rothberg; m. Stanley F Blackman, May 27, 2002 (dec. July 2005). Diploma in nursing, Lenox Hill Hosp., 1944; BS, N.Y. U., 1950, MA, 1959, PhD (NIH fellow), 1965; Diploma in Psychotherapy and Psycho-analysis, Adelphi U., Inst. for Advanced Psychol. Studies, 1987. USPHS traineeship N.Y. U., 1957-59; sr. public health nurse Bklyn. Vis. Nurse Assn., 1951-53; prin. investigator in nursing, homestead study project Goldwater Hosp. and N.Y. U., 1959-61; instr. N.Y. U., 1964-65, asst. prof., 1965-68, assoc. prof., 1968-69, project dir. grad. program rehab. nursing, 1966-69, prof., 1969-87, prof. emeritus, 1987—; dean Adelphi U., Garden City, NY, 1969-85, v.p. acad. adminstrn., 1985-86; pvt. practice West Hempstead, NY, 1993-97. Pres. David Simmonds Co. Inc., Med. Supply Co., 1982-89; dir., chmn. compensation com. Quality Care, Inc.; cons. region 2 Bur. Health Resources Devel., HHS.; audit com. Ipco Corp. (formerly Sterling Optical Corp.), 1991; cons., spkr. in field. Contbr. articles to profl. jours. Mem. pres.'s coun. N.Y. U. Sch. Edn., 1973-75; treas. Nurses for Polit. Action, 1971-73; trustee Nurses Coalition for Action in Politics, 1974-76; bd. visitors Duke Med. Ctr., 1970-74; mem. governing bd. Nassau-Suffolk Health Systems Agy., 1976-79; leader People-to-People Internat. med. rehab. del. to People's Republic of China, 1981; mem. com. for the study pain disability and chronic illness behavior Inst. Medicine, 1985-86, com. on ethics in rehab. Hastings Ctr., 1985-87; trustee Paget's Disease Found., 1987-89. Recipient Disting. Alumna award NYU, 1974, recognition award Am. Assn. Colls. Nursing, 1976, Achievers award Ctr. for Bus. and Profl. Women, 1980 Fellow Am. Acad. Nursing (governing coun. 1980-82); mem. Nat. League Nursing (exec. com. coun. of baccalaureate and higher degree programs 1969-73), Am. Nurses Assn. (joint liaison com. 1970-72), Commn. Accreditation of Rehab. Facilities, Am. Congress Rehab. Medicine (pres. 1977-78, chmn. continuing edn. com. 1979-86, 34th Ann. John Stanley Coulter Meml. lectr. 1984, Gold Key award 1984, Edward W. Lowman award 1990), Am. Assn. Colls. Nursing (pres. 1974-76), L.I. Women's Network (pres. 1980-81), Kappa Delta Pi, Sigma Theta Tau, Pi Lambda Theta. Achievements include having June S. Rothberg collection in Nursing Archives, Mugar Meml. Library, Boston U. Home and Office: 3941 Redondo Way Boca Raton FL 33487 Personal E-mail: stanleyb2@aol.com.

**ROTHBLATT, DONALD NOAH**, urban and regional planner, educator; b. NYC, Apr. 28, 1935; s. Harry and Sophie (Chernofsky) R.; m. Ann S. Vogel, June 16, 1957; children: Joel Michael, Steven Saul. BCE, CUNY, 1957; MS in Urban Planning, Columbia U., 1963; Diploma in Comprehensive Planning, Inst. Social Studies, The Hague, 1964; PhD in City and Regional Planning, Harvard U., 1969. Cert. Am. Inst. Cert. Planners; registered prof. engr., NY. Planner NYC Planning Commn., 1960-62, NY Housing and Redevel. Bd., 1963-66; research fellow Ctr. for Environ. Design Studies, Harvard U., Cambridge, Mass., 1965-71; tchg. fellow, instr., then asst. prof. city and regional planning Harvard U., 1967-71; prof. urban and regional planning, chmn. dept. San Jose (Calif.) State U., 1971—. Lady Davis vis. prof. urban and regional planning Hebrew U., Jerusalem and Tel Aviv U., 1978; vis. scholar Indian Inst. Archs., New Delhi, 1979, Shandong Province, China, 1996, U. Lodz, Poland, 2000, Paris Regional Transp. Authority, France, 2002, Greater London Authority, Eng., 2003, Sydney (Australia) Regional Orgn. of Couns., 2004, Toronto Urban Devel. Svcs., Can., 2005; elected to Coll. Fellows of Am. Inst. Cert. Planners, 2006; vis. scholar, rsch. assoc. Inst. Govtl. Studies, U. Calif., Berkeley, 1980—; cons. to pvt. industry and govt. agys. Author: Human Needs and Public Housing, 1964, Thailand's Northeast, 1967, Regional Planning: The Appalachian Experience, 1971, Allocation of Resources for Regional Planning, 1972, The Suburban Environment and Women, 1979, Regional-Local Development Policy Making, 1981, Planning the Metropolis: The Multiple Advocacy Approach, 1982, Comparative Suburban Data, 1983, Suburbia: An International Assessment, 1986, Metro-politan Dispute Resolution in Silicon Valley, 1989, Good Practices for the Congestion Management Program, 1994, Activity-Based Travel Survey and Analysis of Responses to Increased Congestion, 1995, An Experiment in Sub-Regional Planning: California's Congestion Management Policy, 1995, Estimating the Origins and Destinations of Transit Passengers from On/Off Counts, 1995, Changes in Property Values Induced by Light Transit, 1996, Comparitive Study of Statewide Transportation Planning Under ISTEA, 1997, North American Metropolitan Planning Reexamined, 1999, Govern-ment Performance Measures Linking Urban Mass Transportation With Land Use and Accessibility Factors, 2000, Best Practices in Developing Regional Transportation Plans, 2001, Comparative Study of U.S. Metropolitan Trans-portation Planning, 2004; editor: National policy for Urban and Regional Development, 1974, Regional Advocacy Planning: Expanding Air Transport Facilities for the San Jose Metropolitan Area, 1975, Metropolitan-wide Advocacy Planning; Dispersion of Low and Moderate Cost Housing in the San Jose Metropolitan Area, 1976, Multiple Advocacy Planning: Public Surface Transportation in the San Jose Metropolitan Area, 1977, A Multiple Advocacy Approach to Regional Planning: Open Space and Recreational Facilities for the San Jose Metropolitan Area, 1979, Regional Transportation Planning for the San Jose Metropolitan Area, 1981, Planning for Open Space and Recreational Facilities in the San Jose Metropolitan Area, 1982, Regional Economic Development Planning for the San Jose Metropolitan Area, 1984, Planning for Surface Transportation in the San Jose Metropolitan Area, 1986, Expansion of Air Transportation Facilities in the San Jose Metropolitan Area, 1987, Provision of Economic Development in the San Jose Met. Area, 1988, Metropolitan Governance: American/Canadian Intergovernmental Perspec-tives, 1993, Metropolitan Governance Revisited, 1998; contbr. numerous articles to profl. jours.; dir.: Pub. TV series Sta. KTEH, 1976. Mem. adv. coun. Bay Area Met. Transp. Commn., 1995—. Served to 1st lt. C.E. US Army Corps of Engrs., 1957—59. Rsch. fellow John F. Kennedy Sch. Govt. Harvard U., 1967-69; William F. Milton rsch. fellow, 1970-71; faculty rsch. grantee, NSF, 1972-82, Calif. State U., 1977-78; grantee Nat. Inst. Dispute Resolution, 1987-88, Can. Studies Enrichment Program, 1989-90, Can. Studies Rsch. Program, 1992-93, Univ. Rsch. and Tng. Program grantee Calif. Dept. Transp., 1993-97; recipient Innovative Tchg. award Calif. State U. and Coll., 1975-79; co-recipient Best of West award Western Ednl. Soc. for Tele-communication, 1976; recipient award Internat. Festival of Films on Archi-tecture and Planning, 1983, Meritorious Performance award San Jose State U., 1986, 88, 90, 96-2001. Mem.: AAUP, Architecture and Urban and Regional Planning (chmn. 1973—75), Calif. Edn. Com. Architecture and Landscape, Internat. Fedn. Housing and Planning, Planners for Equal Opportunity, Am. Planning Assn., Assn. Collegiate Schs. of Planning (pres. 1975—76). Office: San Jose State U Dept Urban & Regional Planning San Jose CA 95192-0185 *My basic view is that we should try to develop ourselves fully and help others do the same, so that we will be able to live in harmony with, and contribute to, our world community.*

**ROTHCHILD, DONALD SYLVESTER**, political science professor; b. N.Y.C., Aug. 11, 1928; s. Sylvester Edward and Alice Levy Rothchild; m. Edith White, Apr. 23, 1954; children: Derek Edward, Maynard White. BA with high honors, Kenyon Coll., 1949; MA, U. Calif., Berkeley, 1954; PhD, Johns Hopkins U., 1958. From instr. to assoc. prof. Colby Coll., Waterville, Maine, 1957-65; prof. U. Calif., Davis, 1965—; faculty rsch. lectr., 1997, fellow Washington Ctr., 2000—01, 2003, disting. prof., 2003—. Vis. Ful-bright lectr. Makerere U., Kampala, Uganda, 1962—64; sr. lectr. U. Nairobi, Kenya, 1966—67; internat. adv. bd. Africa Today, 1968—, Internat. Nego-tiation, 1995—; vis. Ford prof. U. Zambia, Lusaka, 1970—71; vis. prof. U. Ghana, Legon, 1975—77, Legon, 1985, U. Calif., Berkeley, 2002; professo-rial lectr. Johns Hopkins U., Washington, 1993, Washington, 95, Washington, 2001, Washington, 03; vis. scholar Brookings Instn., 1992—93; vis. scholar Ctr. Internat. Security and Cooperation U. Stanford, 1998—99; mem. steering com. Inst. Global Conflict and Cooperation, 2003—06. Author: Racial Bargaining in Independent Kenya, 1973, Managing Ethnic Conflict in Africa, 1997; co-author: Sovereignty as Responsibility, 1996; co-editor: The Inter-national Spread of Ethnic Conflict, 1998, Ending Civil Wars: The Implemen-tation of Peace Agreements, 2002, Sustainable Peace: Power and Democracy After Civil Wars, 2005, Africa-U.S. Relations: Strategic Encounters, 2006; editor: Jour. Nationalism and Ethnic Politics, 1994—; contbr. articles to profl. jours. Internat. observer mission Carter Ctr., Ghana, 1992; rapporteur Friedrich Ebert Found., Kampala, 1993; Hubert H. Humphrey spkr. Alumni Assn. Conf., Accra, Ghana, 1994. Sgt. U.S. Army, 1950—52. Disting. Am. Specialist grantee, USIA, Thika, Kenya, 1993, Peace fellow, U.S. Inst. Peace, Washington, 1994—95. Mem.: Internat. Studies Assn., Internat. Studies Assn., African Studies Assn., Am. Polit. Sci. Assn., Internat. Polit. Sci. Assn. (pres. rsch. com. 1988—94). Democrat. Avocations: opera, theater, ballet. Home: 208 W 8th St Davis CA 95616-3637 Office: Univ Calif Dept Polit Sci 1 Shields Ave Davis CA 95616-8682 Office Phone: 530-752-2636. Business E-Mail: dsrothchild@ucdavis.edu.

**ROTHENBERG, ALAN DAVID**, lawyer; b. Newark, Nov. 30, 1947; s. John F. and Ruth (Parent) R.; m. Karen Lynn (Jacobson) R.; m. May 17, 1970; children: Scott Michael, Kelli Brooke. BA, Franklin and Marshall Coll., 1970; JD, U. Md., 1975. Bar: Md. 1976, Md. 1975, U.S. Dist. Ct. Md. 1976. Atty. I.C.C., Washington, 1975-96; pvt. practice Rockville, Md., 1975—. Bd. dirs. U.S. Premier Fed. Credit Union, Washington. Author: Landlord Tenant Handbook, 1974. With U.S. Army N.G., 1970-72. Mem. Md. Bar Assn., Md. Trial Lawyers Assn., Montgomery County Bar Assn. Avocations: skiing, tropical fish. Home: 1721 Sunrise Dr Potomac MD 20854-2667 Office: 401 N Washington St Ste 500 Rockville MD 20850-2225 Office Phone: 301-424-7224. E-mail: adrothenberg@hotmail.com.

**ROTHENBERG, ALAN I.**, lawyer, professional sports association execu-tive; b. Detroit, Apr. 10, 1939; m. Georgina Rothenberg; 3 children. BA, U. Mich., 1960, JD, 1963. Bar: Calif. 1964. Assoc. O'Melveny & Myers, LA, 1963—66; ptnr. Manatt Phelps Rothenberg & Phillips, LA, 1968—90, Latham & Watkins, LA, 1990—2000; instr. sports law U. So. Calif., 1969, 1976, 1984, Whittier Coll. Law, 1980, 1984; pres., gen. counsel LA Lakers and LA Kings, 1967—79, LA Clippers Basketball Team, 1982—89; pres. U.S. Soccer Fedn., Chgo., 1990—98; founder, past chmn., trustee Maj. League Soccer, 1993—; chmn. Premier Partnerships, 1st Century Bank, LA, 2002—. Bd. dir. Calif. Pizza Kitchen Inc., 2006—, Arden Realty Inc., Zenith Nat. Corp.; mem. exec. com. CONCACAF. Bd. dirs., pres. Constl. Rights Found., 1987—90; soccer commr. 1984 Olympic Games; chmn., pres., CEO 1994 World Cup Organizing Com., 1990—94. Mem.: NBA (bd. govs. 1971—79, 1982—89), ABA, N.Am. Soccer League (bd. govs. 1977—80, Major League Soccer mgmt. com. 1994—), LA Bar Assn., LA County Bar Assn., State Bar Calif. (pres. 1989—90), Order of Coif. Office: 1st Century Bank Ste 1400 1875 Century Park E Los Angeles CA 90067*

**ROTHENBERG, ALBERT**, psychiatrist, educator; b. NYC, June 2, 1930; s. Gabriel and Rose (Goldberg) R.; m. Julia C. Johnson, June 28, 1970; children: Michael, Mora, Rina. AB, Harvard U., 1952; MD, Tufts U., 1956. Diplomate Am. Bd. Psychiatry and Neurology. Intern Pa. Hosp., Phila., 1956-57; resident in psychiatry Yale U., West Haven (Conn.) VA Hosp., 1957-58, Grace-New Haven Hosp., 1958-59, Yale Psychiat. Inst., New Haven, 1959-60, chief resident, 1960-61; practice medicine specializing in psychiatry New Haven, 1960-61, 1963-75; chief neuropsychiatry Rodriguez U.S. Army Hosp., San Juan, P.R., 1961-63; practice medicine specializing in psychiatry Farmington, Conn., 1975-79, Stockbridge, Mass., 1979-94, Chatham, NY, 1994—2006, Canaan, NY, 2006—, Great Barrington, Mass., 1994-98; dir. rsch. Austen Riggs Center, Stockbridge, Mass., 1979-94. Asst. dir. Yale Psychiat. Inst., 1963-64, sr. staff mem., 1964-83; mem. staff Yale-New Haven Med. Ctr., West Haven VA Hosp., U. Conn. Health Ctr., Farmington; cons., mem. editorial bd. various jours. in psychiatry and psychology; instr. dept. psychiatry Yale U. Sch. Medicine, 1960-61, 63-64, asst. prof., 1964-68, assoc. prof., 1968-74, clin. prof., 1974-84; prof. psychiatry U. Conn. Sch. Medicine, Farmington, 1975-79, dir. residency tng., 1976-78, dir. clin. svcs., 1975-78; prin. investigator Studies in the Creative Process, 1964—; vis. prof. Pa. State U., 1971, adj. prof., 1971-78; vis. prof. dept. Am. studies Yale U., 1974-76, U. Capetown Med. Sch., South Africa, 1999, Saltpêtrière Hosp., Paris, 1999; lectr. dept. psychiatry Harvard U. Med. Sch., 1982-86, clin. prof., 1986—; researcher in psychotherapy. Author: (with B. Greenberg) Index of Scientific Writings on Creativity: Creative Men and Women, 1974, Index of Scientific Writings on Creativity: General 1566-1974, 1976; (with C.R. Hausman) The Creativity Question, 1976; The Emerging Goddess: The Creative Process in Art, Science and Other Fields, 1979; The Creative Process of Psychotherapy, 1988; Adolescence: Psychopathology, Normality, and Creativity, 1990; Cre-ativity and Madness: New Findings and Old Stereotypes, 1990, Living Color, 2001; contbr. articles to profl. jours. Researcher on creativity in the arts, sci. and tech. Served with M.C. U.S. Army, 1961-63. Recipient Tufts Med. Alumni award 1956, Rsch. Scientist Career Devel. award NIMH 1964, 69, Golestan Found. award 1991, 92, Kovler award MESAB, 1999; Guggenheim Meml. fellow 1974-75, Ctr. Adv. Study in Behavioral Studies fellow 1986-87, Netherlands Inst. for Adv. Study in Humanities and Social Scis. fellow, 1992-93. Fellow Am. Psychiat. Assn. (disting. life), Am. Coll. Psychoana-lysts; mem. AAAS, Mass. Psychiat. Soc., Am. Soc. Aesthetics, Rapaport-Klein Group, Sigma Xi. Democrat. Achievements include research in the creative process, schizophrenia, anorexia nervosa, and psychotherapy. Home: PO Box 1001 52 Pine Ridge Rd Canaan NY 12029-3101 Business E-Mail: albert_rothenberg@hms.harvard.edu.

**ROTHENBERG, ELEANORE**, psychotherapist; d. Max and Dora (Kaplan) Dubin; children: David, Michael, Seth. BA cum laude, Bklyn. Coll., 1955; MPA, N.Y.U., 1969, PhD, 1975; MSW, Yeshiva U., N.Y.C., 1992 Cert. group psychotherapist Am. Group Psychotherapy Assn.; LCSW Office of Professions N.Y. State Edn. Dept. Exec. dir. N.Y.C. Profl. Standards Rev.

Orgn., 1974—80; dir. stds. and evaluation N.Y.C. HHC, 1981—83; social worker Cmty. Living Corp., Mt. Kisco, 1992—94; founder, exec. dir. and group leader Sibling Ctr. Sisters and Brothers of People with Disabilities, N.Y.C., 1994—. Chair bd. dir. Sibling Ctr., N.Y.C.; adj. asst. prof. Columbia U. Sch. Pub. Health, 1980—2001; lectr. New Sch. U., 1984—86; preceptor King's Fund Coll., London, 1980; pro bono psychotherapist N.Y. Disaster Counseling Coalition, 2001—; conducted psychotherapy group with 9/11 survivors, NYC, 2002; conducted 9/11 commemorative art exhibit Am. Group Psychotherapy Assn./N.Y. Times/9/11 Fund, N.Y.C., NY, 2002—04; presenter to workshops and confs.; book reviewer. Contbr. scientific papers, articles to profl. jours. Vol. Physicians Social Responsibility, 1980. Fellow, NIH, 1965—75; grantee, W.T. Grant Found., 2002—03, Pettus Found., 2004. Mem.: Ea. Group Psychotherapy Soc. (co-chair mentoring com. 2002—), Am. Group Psychotherapy Assn., NYU Alumni Assn., Bklyn. Coll. Alumni Assn. Democrat. Jewish. Avocations: drawing, skiing, kayaking, cooking, dancing. Office: Sibling Ctr 525 E 89th St #4C New York NY 10128 also: 180 E 79th St Ste 1C New York NY 10021 Office Phone: 212-831-5586.

**ROTHENBERG, ELLIOT CALVIN**, lawyer, writer; b. Mpls., Nov. 12, 1939; s. Sam S. and Claire Sylvia (Feller) R.; m. Sally Smalying; children: Sarah, Rebecca, Sam. BA summa cum laude, U. Minn., 1961; JD, Harvard U. (Fulbright fellow), 1964. Bar: Minn. 1966, U.S. Dist. Ct. Minn. 1966, D.C. 1968, U.S. Supreme Ct. 1972, N.Y. 1974, U.S. Ct. Appeals (2d cir.) 1974, U.S. Ct. Appeals (8th cir.) 1975. Assoc. project dir. Brookings Inst., Washington, 1966-67; fgn. svc. officer, legal advisor U.S. Dept. State, Washington, 1968-73; Am. Embassy, Saigon; U.S. Mission to the UN; nat. bur. Anti-Defamation League, N.Y.C., 1973-74; legal dir. Minn. Pub. Interest Rsch. Group, Mpls., 1974-77; pvt. practice law Mpls., 1977—. Adj. prof. William Mitchell Coll. Law, St. Paul, 1983—; faculty mem. several nat. comm. law and First Amendment seminars. Author: (with Zelman Cowen) Sir John Latham and Other Papers, 1965, The Taming of the Press: Cohen v. Cowles Media Co., 1999, The Taming of the Press, 1999; co-author: Defending the First, 2005, Whose First Amendment?, 2005; contbr. articles to profl. and scholarly jours. and books, newspapers, popular mags. State bd. dirs. YMCA Youth in Govt. Program, 1981-84; v.p. Twin Cities chpt. Am. Jewish Com., 1980-84; mem. Minn. Ho. of Reps., 1978-82, asst. floor leader (whip), 1981-82; pres., dir. North Star Legal Found., 1983—; legal affairs editor Pub. Rsch. Syndicated, 1986—; briefs and oral arguments published in full Landmark Briefs and Arguments of the Supreme Ct. of the U.S., Vol. 200, 1992; mem. citizens adv. com. Voyageurs Nat. Pk., 1979-81. Recipient Legis. Evaluation Assembly Legis. Excellence award, 1980, Vietnam Civilian Svc. medal U.S. Dept. State, 1970, North Star award U. Minn., 1961; Fulbright fellow, 1964-65. Mem. ABA, Minn. Bar Assn., Harvard Law Sch. Assn., Am. Legion, Mensa, Phi Beta Kappa. Jewish. Office: 3010 Hennepin Ave S Ste 231 Minneapolis MN 55408-2614 Personal E-mail: srothenbe@aol.com.

**ROTHENBERG, JEROME**, writer, literature educator; b. NYC, Dec. 11, 1931; s. Morris and Estelle (Lichtenstein) R.; m. Diane Brodatz, Dec. 25, 1952; 1 son, Matthew. BA, CCNY, 1952; MA, U. Mich., 1953; LittD (hon.), SUNY, Oneonta, 1997. With Mannes Coll. Music, N.Y.C., 1961—70. Vis. prof. U. Calif., San Diego, 1971, 77-84, U. Wis.-Milw., 1974-75, San Diego State U., 1976-77, U. Calif., Riverside, 1980, U. Okla., Norman, 1984; vis. Aerol Arnold prof. English U. So. Calif., 1983; vis. writer in residence SUNY, Albany, 1986, prof. English SUNY, Binghamton, 1986-88; prof. visual arts and lit. U. Calif., San Diego, 1989—, chmn. visual arts, 1990-93; head, creative writing, 1994-95. Poet, freelance writer, 1956—; author: numerous books of poetry and prose including Between, 1967, Technicians of the Sacred, 1968, Poems for the Game of Silence, 1971, Shaking the Pumpkin, 1972, America a Prophecy, 1973, Revolution of the Word, 1974, Poland/1931, 1974, A Big Jewish Book, 1978, A Seneca Journal, 1978, Vienna Blood, 1980, Pre-Faces, 1981, Symposium of the Whole, 1983, That Dada Strain, 1983, New Selected Poems, 1986, Khurbn, 1989, Exiled in the Word, 1989, The Lorca Variations I-VIII, 1990, Apres le jeu de silence, 1991, The Lorca Variations (complete), 1993, Gematria, 1994, An Oracle for Delfi, 1995, Poems for The Millennium, vol. 1, 1995, Seedings, 1996, The Book, Spiritual Instrument, 1996, Poems for the Millennium, Vol. 2, 1998, A Paradise of Poets, 1999, A Book of The Book, 2000, The Case for Memory, 2001, Livre de Temoignage, 2002, A Book of Witness, 2003, María Sabina, 2003, Writing Through: Translations and Variations, 2004, A Book of Concealments, 2004, 25 Caprichos after Goya, 2004, The Burning Babe, 2005, China Notes & The Treasures of Dunhuang, 2006; editor, pub. Hawk's Well Press., N.Y.C., 1958-65, Some/Thing mag., 1966-69, Alcheringa: Ethnopoetics, 1970-76, New Wilderness Letter, 1976-86. Served with AUS, 1953-55. Recipient award in poetry Longview Found., 1960, Am. Book award, 1982, PEN Ctr. USA West award, 1994, 02, PEN Oakland Josephine Miles award, 1994, 96, Alfonso el Sabio award for translation San Diego State U., 2004, Poetry in Transl. award PEN Am. Ctr., 2004; Wenner-Gren Found. grantee-in-aide for rsch. in Am. Indian poetry, 1968; Guggenheim fellow in creative writing, 1974; NEA poetry grantee, 1976. Mem. PEN Am. Ctr., New Wilderness Found., World Poetry Acad. Office: care New Directions 80 8th Ave New York NY 10011-5126 Office Phone: 760-436-9923. Personal E-mail: jrothenberg@cox.net. Business E-Mail: jrothenb@ucsd.edu.

**ROTHENBERG, KAREN H.**, dean, law educator; BA magna cum laude, Princeton U., 1973, MPA, 1974; JD, U. Va., 1979. Faculty mem. U. Md. Sch. Law, 1983—, founding dir. Law & Health Care Prog., Marjorie Cook Prof. Law, interim dean, 1999—2001, dean, 2001—. Assoc. Covington and Burling, Washington, DC; pres. Am. Soc. Law, Medicine and Ethics; asst. to dir. Office Rsch. on Women's Health, NIH, 1995—96. Co-editor-in-chief Jour. Law, Medicine, and Ethics; co-editor: Women and Prenatal Testing: Facing the Challenges of Genetic Technology; contbr. articles to profl. jours. Named one of Md. Top Women, Daily Record; recipient Joseph Healey Health Law Tchr.'s award, Am. Soc. Law, Medicine and Ethics, 1996, Md. Leadership in Law Award, 2003. Mem.: ABA (coordinating group on bioethics and the law), NIH (sect. on prenatal care, recruitment & ret. of women in clin studies, sect. on ethical, legal and social implications of genetics), Nat. Inst. Child & Human Develop. (adv. coun.), Nat. Action Plan Breast Cancer, Ethics in Reproduction (nat. adv. bd.), Inst. Medicine's Com. (sect. legal and ethical issues for inclusion of women in clin. stud.). Office: U Md Law Sch Dean's Office 500 W Baltimore St Baltimore MD 21201 Office Phone: 410-706-2041. Fax: 410-706-4045. Business E-Mail: krothenberg@law.umaryland.edu.

**ROTHENBERG, LARAINE S.**, lawyer; b. Bklyn., Feb. 20, 1947; BA, U. Pa., 1967; JD, Columbia U., 1971. Bar: N.Y. 1972. Atty. Proskauer Rose LLP, 1974—90; ptnr. McDermott, Will & Emery, N.Y.C., 1990—94, Fried Frank Harris Shriver & Jacobson LLP, N.Y.C., 1994—. Contbr. articles to profl. jour. Bd. dir. Wallace Found., Pig Iron Theatre Co.; mem. bd. vis. Columbia Law Sch. Recipient Tax Mgmt. Disting. Author award, 1997, Women of Power and Influence award, NOW-NYC, 2002, Disting. Svc. medal, Columbia U. Alumni Fedn., 2003, award for outstanding pro bono svc., Legal Aid Soc., 2005. Mem. N.Y. State Bar Assn. (mem. exec. com. 1981-89, co-chmn. continuing legal edn. 1988-89, problems of the profession 1987-88, chmn. employee benefits com. 1985-86, co-chmn. 1984-85, chmn. exempt orgns. com. 1982-84, mem.-at-large com. 1981-82), Assn. Bar City N.Y. (mem. taxation of corporations com. 1990—, chmn. spl. com. on employee benefits 1987-88, mem. taxation com. 1979-82), Internat. Bar Assn., Internat. Fiscal Assn.; founding mem. Alumnae Columbia Law Sch. Office: Fried Frank Harris Shriver & Jacobson LLP 1 New York Plz New York NY 10004 Business E-Mail: rothela@friedfrank.com.

**ROTHENBERG, LINDA ANN**, science educator; b. NYC, May 11, 1956; d. John and Muriel Angus; m. Thomas Charles Rothenberg, Apr. 23, 1977; children: Mark, Jason. BA in Elem. Edn., Queens Coll., 1978, MS in Spl. Edn., 1982. Cert. early childhood edn. tchr. Fla. Bd. Edn., elem. edn. tchr Fla. Bd. Edn. Sci. tchr. Hernando County Sch. Bd., Spring Hill, Fla., 2004—, elem. tchr., 1988—; dist. sci. fair dir., 1995—2004, tchr. trainer ESL, 1993—98, exceptional student educator, 1988—; adj. instr. St. Leo's Coll., Dade City, Fla., 1994; elem. tchr. NYC Bd. Edn., 1978—88. Chmn. Pine Grove Sch. Adv. Bd., Brooksville, Fla., 1990—92. V.p. Springstead H.S.

Band Boosters, Spring Hill, Fla., 2001—03; chmn. of charity events Nature Coast Corvettes, Spring Hill, 2003; support group leader Internat. Waldenstrom's Macroglobulin Anemia Found., 2004—. Grant, Hernando County Edn. Found., 2004. Mem.: Nat. Sci. Teachers Assn. Achievements include established Hands On Sci. Mus. for Children at Pine Grove Elem. Sch; established first science lab for Westside Elementary School. Avocations: painting, music, swimming. Office: Westside Elem Sch 2400 Applegate Dr Spring Hill FL 34609

**ROTHENBERG, PAMELA V.,** lawyer; b. Ft. Knox, Ky., Dec. 11, 1958; BA in History summa cum laude, Tufts U., 1981; JD, Northwestern U., 1984. Bar: Ill. 1984, DC 1985. Assoc Rudnick & Wolfe, Chgo., 1984—85, Lane & Edson PC, Washington, 1985—86; assoc & prin. David, Hagner, Kuney & Davison, Washington, 1986—98; mem. Womble Carlyle Sandridge & Rice PLLC, Washington, 1998—, co-mng. mem. Washington, DC office, 2004—. Mem.: ABA, Women's Bar Assn. of DC, Phi Beta Kappa. Office: Womble Carlyle Sandridge & Rice PLLC 7th Fl 1401 Eye St NW Washington DC 20005 Office Phone: 202-857-4422. Office Fax: 202-261-0022. Business E-Mail: prothenberg@wcsr.com

**ROTHENBERG, PETER JAY,** lawyer; b. NYC, Apr. 3, 1941; s. Max and Judith (Berkowitz) R.; m. Laraine H. Silver, Aug. 29, 1970; children: Daniel, Jason. AB, Harvard U., 1961, LLB, 1964. Bar: N.Y. 1965, U.S. Tax Ct. 1969. Dep. counsel judiciary sub. com. on jud. machinery U.S. Senate Com., Washington, 1965-66; assoc. Paul, Weiss, Rifkind, Wharton & Garrison, N.Y.C., 1969-73, ptnr., 1974—, coordinator, tax dept. Served to capt. U.S. Army, 1966-69. Mem. N.Y. State Bar Assn. (exec. com. tax sect. 1979-87), Assn. Bar City N.Y. (tax com. 1977-79, com. on taxation of internat. transactions 1990-93), Internat. Fiscal Assn. Democrat. Jewish. Home: 895 Park Ave New York NY 10021-0327 Office: Paul Weiss Rifkind Wharton & Garrison Ste 417 1285 Avenue Of The Americas Fl 21 New York NY 10019-6028 Fax: 212-373-2004. E-mail: prothenberg@paulweiss.com.

**ROTHENBERG, ROBERT PHILIP,** public relations counselor; b. NYC, June 5, 1936; s. Robert Edward and Lillian Babette (Lustig) R. BA, Cornell U., 1956; MS, Boston U., 1958. With publicity dept. Columbia Pictures Corp., N.Y.C., 1959-60; asst. to pres., pub. rels. dir. Harry N. Abrams Pub. Co., N.Y.C., 1960-62; press sec. to gubernatorial candidate William R. Anderson Tenn., 1962; with Rowland Co., N.Y.C., 1963-70, v.p., 1965-67, sr. v.p., 1967-70; ptnr., exec. v.p. Robert Marston and Assocs., N.Y.C., 1970-88, sr. exec. v.p., 1978-88, also bd. dirs.; ptnr., pres. Marston and Rothenberg Pub. Affairs, Inc., and Washington, 1977-88; chmn., pres. Rothenberg Pub. Rels. Comms. Counsel, N.Y.C., 1988—; v.p. Medbook Publs., Inc., 1995—2004; dir. pub. rels. BigChange Networks, LLC, Washington and N.Y.C., 1998—2004. Sr. cons. The Lund Group, Inc. Trustee Mus. of Holography, N.Y.C.; bd. dirs. Found. to Save African Endangered Wildlife, World Rehab. Fund, N.Y.C., 1982-98, Amas Musical Theatre, Inc., 2002-03; assoc. Nat. Park Found.; counselor Am. Bus. Cancer Rsch. Found., Southport, Conn.; fellow Met. Mus. of Art, 1990—; pres., chmn., bd. trustees St. Bartholomew's Preservation Found., 1992-95; mem. Blue Hill Troupe, Ltd. With USAFR, 1959-65. Mem. Internat. Soc. Poets, Pride and Alarm Soc., Harriman Soc. of ARC, English-Speaking Union, Anchor Soc., DeWitt Clinton Soc., Players Club Unitarian Universalist. Home and Office: 400 E 54th St Apt 29B New York NY 10022-5169

**ROTHER, JOHN,** association executive, lawyer; b. Springfield, Mo., Apr. 18, 1947; s. Charles C. and Eleanor J. (Morrison) R. BA with honors, Oberlin Coll., 1969; JD with honors, U. Pa., 1975. Bar: Pa. 1975, D.C. 1977. Appellate litigator NLRB, Washington, 1975-77; counsel Senator Jacob Javits U.S. Senate labor & human resources commn., Washington, 1977-81; staff dir., chief counsel spl. commn. on aging U.S. Senate, Washington, 1981-84; policy and strategy dir. AARP, Washington, 1984—. Chair Generations United; vice chair Nat. Quality Forum; founding mem. Nat. Acad. Social Ins., Corp. for Nat. Service. Named One of 150 Who Make A Difference, Nat. Jour., Washington, 1986. Mem. D.C. Bar, Gerontol. Soc. Am. Office: AARP 601 E St NW Washington DC 20049-0001 E-mail: jrother@aarp.org.

**ROTHERHAM, ANDREW J.,** not-for-profit administrator, consultant; s. James A. Rotherham and Barbara M. LaRock, James LaRock (Stepfather) and Beverly Thierwechter (Stepmother); m. Julie Lynne Lusher, July 21, 2001; children: Elizabeth Rose, Susan Shenandoah. BA in Polit. Sci., Va. Tech. U., 1994; MEd., U. Va., 2000. Policy specialist Am. Assn. Sch. Administrs., Arlington, Va., 1996—98; dir. 21st Century Schs. Project Prog. Policy Inst., Washington, 1998—99, dir. edn. policy, 2000—05; spl. asst. to pres. domestic policy The White House, Washington, 1999—2000; co-dir. Edn. Sector, Washington, 2005—. Sr. fellow Prog. Policy Inst., 2005—; chmn. bd. Nat. Coun. Tchr. Quality, Washington, 2003—05; bd. dirs. Charter Sch. Leadership Coun., Washington; trustee Cesar Chavez Pub. Charter H.S. Pub. Policy, Washington, 2003—. Co-editor: 3 Books; contbr. articles to profl. jours., newspapers and mags. Active Va. State Bd. Edn., Richmond, Va., 2005—. Named Outstanding Young Alumni, Coll. Arts and Scis. Va. Tech. U., 2005. Home: 750 Montei Drive Earlysville VA 22936 Personal E-mail: arotherham@educationsector.org.

**ROTHERMEL, DANIEL KROTT,** lawyer, bank executive; b. West Reading, Pa., Mar. 21, 1938; s. Daniel Grim and Ruth Elizabeth (Krott) R.; m. Sarah Finch, July 9, 1960; children: Anne, Daniel F., K. Melissa. BS, Pa. State U., 1960; JD, Am. U., 1966. Bar: D.C. 1967. Acct. Lukens Steel Co., Coatesville, Pa., 1960-61; pvt. practice Reading, Pa., 1966-68; atty. Carpenter Tech. Corp., Reading, 1968-70, resident counsel, 1970-78, asst. sec., 1972-73, sec., 1973-88, v.p., gen. counsel, sec., 1978-88; pres., chief exec. officer Cumru Assocs. Inc., Reading, Pa., 1989—. Bd. dirs. Sovereign Bank, Sovereign Bancorp, Inc., lead dir., chmn. exec. com. Mem. Inst. Cmty. Affairs, Pa. State U., 1974-78; bd. dirs Berks County chpt ARC, 1987 86; mem., chmn. adv. bd. Berks campus Pa. State U., 1982—97; ch. lay leader. Lt. USNR, 1961-66. Mem. ABA, D.C. Bar Assn., Am. Soc. Corp. Secs., U.S. C. of C., Pa. C. of C., Reading-Berks C. of C., Rotary. Republican. Lutheran. Home: 20 Glenbrook Dr Reading PA 19607-9645 Office: Cumru Assocs Inc PO Box 6573 Reading PA 19610-0573

**ROTHERT, ANTHONY EDWARD,** lawyer, director; b. Dubuque, Iowa, Apr. 28, 1970; s. Ronald Hugh and Lucille Veronica (Scanlan) Rothert. BA, St. Louis U. Coll. of Arts and Sciences, 1988—92; MSW, St. Louis U. Sch. of Social Svc., 1992—93; JD, St. Louis U. Sch. of Law, 1993—96. Bar: Mo. 1996, Ill. 1997, U.S. Dist. Ct. (so. dist.) Ill. 2004, U.S. Dist. Ct. (we. and ea. dists.) Mo. 2006, U.S. Ct. Appeals (8th cir.) 2004, U.S. Supreme Ct. 2001. Med. social worker LAB Home Health Care, St. Louis, 1994—95, BJC Health Systems, St. Louis, 1995—95; asst. state's atty. Madison County State's Atty., Edwardsville, Ill., 1996—99; instr. Sanford-Brown Coll., St. Louis, 1999—2006; atty. Land of Lincoln Legal Assistance Found., Alton, Ill., 1999—2006, 2000; Legal Advocacy Svc., Guardianship and Advocacy Commn., Alton, Ill., 2000—06; legal dir. ACLU Ea. Mo., 2006—. Mem. com. on mental health law Ill. Bar Assn., Springfield, Ill., 2002—, mem. com. on supreme ct. rules, 2002—, mem. com. on sogi, 2004—. Mem. com. Law Related Edn. for Pub., 2005—; bd. dirs. Phoenix Crisis Ctr., Granite City, Ill., 1998—2004; mem. Ill. Guardianship Assn., 2004—, Cmty. Alternatives, 2006—. Recipient M.S.W. Student of the Yr., NASW - Ea. Mo., 1993. Mem.: Am. Constitution Soc., Ill. Bar Assn., Am. Messanic, Alpha Sigma Nu, Phi Beta Kappa. Avocations: travel, reading, writing. Office: ACLU EM 4557 Laclede Ave Saint Louis MO 63108 Office Phone: 618-474-5503. Office Fax: 618-474-5517. Personal E-mail: tonyr@charter.net. Business E-Mail: tony@aclu-em.org. E-mail: arothert@gac.state.il.us.

**ROTHERT, MARILYN L.,** dean, educational nurse; b. June 4, 1939; married; 3 children. BSN cum laude, Ohio State U., 1961; MA in Ednl. Psychol., Mich. State U., 1979, PhD in Ednl. Psychol., 1980. RN, Mich. Staff nurse Univ. Hosp., Columbus, Ohio, 1961; instr. sch. nursing Hurley Hosp., Flint, Mich., 1961-66; asst. instr. sch. nursing Mich. State U., East Lansing, 1967-77, grad. asst. dept. community health sci., 1977-80, asst. prof. Coll.

Human Medicine, 1980-82, asst. prof., dir. lifelong edn. Coll. Nursing, 1982-84, asst. prof. Coll. Human Medicine, 1982-84, assoc. prof., dir. lifelong edn. Coll. Nursing, 1984-88, assoc. prof. Coll. Human Medicine, 1984-86, prof., dir. lifelong edn. Coll. Nursing, 1988-92, prof., assoc. dean outreach and profl. devel., 1992-96, prof., dean Coll. Nursing, 1996—. Cons. No. Ill. U., Ohio State U., Mich. State Dept. Natural Resources, Can. Nurses Assn., Mich. Judicial Inst., Med. Coll. Va., U. Wash., Kirtland Coll., Anderson Coll. Contbr. articles to profl. jours. Co-chmn. Capitol Health Event, 1987-88; mem. worksite health subcom. Mich. Dept. Pub. Health; mem. State 4-H Health Com. Coop. Extension Svc., 1972-75, 82—; mem. med. adv. com. Mich. Civil Svc. Health Screening Unit, 1984. Mem. ANA (mem. coun. continuing edn., nurse researchers), Mich. Nurses Assn. (chmn. continuing edn. adv. com. 1989), Soc. for Med. Decision Making, The Brunswik Soc., Soc. for Judgment and Decision Making, Soc. for Rsch. in Nursing Edn., Midwest Nursing Rsch. Soc., Am. Pub. Health Assn., Nat. Ctr. for Health Edn., Nat. League for Nursing, Mich. State U. Faculty/Profl. Women's Assn. (bd. dirs. 1989—), Capitol Area Dist. Nurses Assn. (mem. nom. com. 1984-86, continuing edn. com. 1984), Phi Kappa Phi. Office: Mich State U Coll Nursing A-230 Life Sci Bldg East Lansing MI 48824

**ROTHFELD, MICHAEL B.,** theatrical producer, investor; b. N.Y.C., May 19, 1947; m. Ella M. Foshay, May 22, 1970; 2 children. BA, Columbia U., 1969, MS, MBA, Columbia U., 1971, cert. internatl fellows program, 1971. With Time, Inc., 1971-76, assoc. editor Fortune N.Y.C., 1971-74; asst. to chmn. bd. dirs., CEO Time Inc., N.Y.C., 1974-76; with Salomon Bros., N.Y.C., 1976-83, v.p., 1979-83, The First Boston Corp., N.Y.C., 1983-84, mng. dir., 1985-89; gen. ptnr. Bessemer Ptnrs. and Bessemer Holdings, 1989-97, ltd. ptnr., 1997-98. Chmn. bd. dirs. Graphic Controls Corp., 1995-98; bd. vis. Columbia Coll., 1998—, vice chmn. 2002-05, chair, 2005—, bd. adv. Knight-Bagheot program in fin. journalism Grad. Sch. Journalism, 1996—, trustee, 2005—; chmn. Redfields, LLC, Eagle Prodns., LLC, N.Y.C. Prodr. Gore Vidal's The Best Man, 2000 (winner Drama Desk award, Outer Critics Circle award, Tony nomination). Office: Eagle Productions LLC 200 E 69th St New York NY 10021

**ROTHFIELD, LAWRENCE I.,** microbiology educator; b. NYC, Dec. 30, 1927; s. Joseph and Henrietta (Brown) R.; m. Naomi Fox, Sept. 18, 1953; children: Susan Anne, Lawrence, Jane, John. BA, Cornell U., 1947; MD, NYU, 1951. Intern, then resident Bellevue, Presbyn. hosps., N.Y.C., 1951-53, 55-57; successively instr., clin. asst. prof., asst. prof. NYU Sch. Medicine, 1957-64; from asst. prof. to assoc. prof. Albert Einstein Coll. Medicine, N.Y.C., 1964-68; prof. U. Conn. Sch. Medicine, Farmington, 1968—, chmn. dept. microbiology, 1968-80. Mem. molecular biology rev. panel NIH, 1970-75, microbiology and immunology adv. com. Pres.'s Biomed. Rsch. Panel, 1975, molecular biology rev. panel NSF, 1979-83; mem. microbial physiology and genetics rev. panel NIH, 1990-94, chairperson, 1991-93. Author: Structure and Function of Biological Membranes, 1972; mem. editorial bd. Jour. Membrane Biology, 1969-83, Jour. Biol. Chemistry, 1974-80. With M.C. U.S. Army, 1953-55. Mem. Am. Soc. Biol. Chemists, Am. Soc. Microbiology (chmn. microbial physiology div. 1975). Home: 540 Deercliff Rd Avon CT 06001-2859 Office: U Conn Health Center Farmington CT 06032 Office Phone: 860-679-3581. Business E-Mail: lroth@neuron.uchc.edu.

**ROTHFIELD, NAOMI FOX,** physician; b. Bklyn., Apr. 5, 1929; d. Morris and Violet (Bloomgarden) Fox; m. Lawrence Rothfield, Sept. 18, 1953; children: Susan, Lawrence, John, Jane. BA, Bard Coll., 1950; MD, NYU, 1955. Intern Lenox Hill Hosp., N.Y.C., 1955-56; instr. NYU Sch. Medicine, 1956-62, asst. prof., 1962-68; assoc. prof. U. Conn. Sch. Medicine, Farmington, 1968-72, prof., 1972—, chief divsn. rheumatic diseases, 1972—99. Contbr. chpts. to books, articles to med. jours. Bd. dirs. Conn. Choral Artists, 1999—. Mem. Am. Soc. Clin. Investigation, Am. Rheumatism Assn., Assn. Am. Physics. Jewish. Home: 540 Deercliff Rd Avon CT 06001-2859 Office: U Conn Sch Medicine Divsn Rheumatic Diseases Farmington CT 06030-0001 Office Phone: 860-679-3604. E-mail: rothfield@nso.uchc.edu.

**ROTHKOPF, ARTHUR J.,** association executive; b. NYC, May 24, 1935; s. Abraham and Sarah (Mehlman) Rothkopf; m. Barbara Sarnoff, Dec. 25, 1958; children: Jennifer, Katherine. AB, Lafayette Coll., 1955; JD, Harvard U., 1958. Bar: N.Y. 1959, D.C. 1967. Atty. U.S. Dept. Treasury, NYC, 1958—60, SEC, Washington, 1960—63; assoc. tax legis. counsel U.S. Dept. Treasury, Washington, 1963—66; ptnr. Hogan & Hartson, Washington, 1967—91; gen. counsel U.S. Dept. Transp., Washington, 1991—92, dep. sec., 1992—93; pres. Lafayette Coll., Easton, Pa., 1993—2005, pres. emeritus, 2005—; sr. v.p. U.S.C. of C., 2005—. Bd. dirs. Ins. Svcs. Office, Inc., Jersey City, Bristol West Holdings; sr. v.p. U.S. C. of C.; mem. Sec. of Edn.'s Commn. on Future of Edn., 2005. Trustee Fed. City Coun., Washington, 1983—91, Smithsonian Nat. Mus. Am. History; past chair bd. dirs. Coun. Higher Edn. Accreditation; bd. dirs., past chmn. Assn. Ind. Colls. and Univs. Pa. Mem.: The Pa. Soc. (pres.), Univ. Club (N.Y.C.), Harvard Club of NYC, Chevy Chase Club, Met. Club of Washington. Jewish. Office: 1615 H St NW Washington DC 20062 Office Phone: 202-463-5359. Business E-Mail: ajrothkopf@uschamber.com.

**ROTHLISBERGER, RODNEY JOHN,** music educator; b. Bottineau, N.D., May 13, 1940; s. Forrest John and Ellen Rothlisberger; m. Gay Elaine Mohr, Dec. 20, 1975 (div.). BA, St. Olaf Coll., Northfield, Minn., 1962; MA, Eastman Sch. Music, Rochester, N.Y., 1967; DMusA, U. Colo., Boulde, 1978. Anacortes Washington Pub. Schs., 1962-64; organist, choirmaster U.S. Mil. Acad., West Point, NY, 1965-67; instr. Bowdoin Coll., Brunswick, Maine, 1967-70; instr. Melbourne (Australia) HS, 1973-75; prof. Berea (Ky.) Coll., 1976-77; instr. Concordia Coll., Moorhead, Minn., 1979-81, Moorhead Pub. Schs., 1989-95; prof. Minn. State U., Moorhead, 1995—, chmn. music dept., 2002—05. Active Civic Opera Bd., 1996—2002; bd. dir. Fargo-Moorhead Symphony, 2004—05, bd. dirs. Luth. Brotherhood, Moorhead, 1988—2002, Red River Boy Choir, Moorhead, 1984—2000, Arts Coun. Fargo-Moorhead, 1985—89. With U.S. Army, 1965—67. Recipient Achievement award, Lake Agassiz Arts Coun., 1987. Mem.: Am. Guild Organists (dean Red River Valley chpt. 1985—87, Minn. state chmn. 1995—2002, chmn. nat. com. membership 1994—2000), Music Educators Nat. Conf., Am. Choral Dirs. Assn., Nat. Assn. Tchrs. Singing. Presbyterian. Avocation: reading. Home: 1021 River Dr Moorhead MN 56560-3369 Office: Minn State U Moorhead 1104 7th Ave S Moorhead MN 56563-0002 Office Phone: 218-477-2966. Business E-Mail: rothlisb@mnstate.edu.

**ROTHMALER, PETER ANTELL,** mathematician, educator; b. Bklyn., July 9, 1939; s. Oswald Rothmaler and Fanny Dorothea Antell; m. Ann Vellaire, June 25, 1966. BA in Math. with honors, Hamilton Coll., 1961; MA, U. Mich., 1962. Math. instr. Coll. DuPage, Glen Ellyn, Ill., 1979—. Mem.: Assn. Christians in Math. Scis., Math. Assn. Am. Messianic Jewish. Avocations: chess, astronomy, baseball, nature. Home: 69 Wilcox Ave Elgin IL 60123 Office: Coll DuPage 425 Fawell Blvd Glen Ellyn IL 60137

**ROTHMAN, BARBARA I.,** elementary school educator; b. Blue Earth, Minn., Feb. 1, 1943; d. Alger M. and Gladys I. Myers; m. Sheldon Rothman, June 27, 1970 (div. 1997); 1 child, Trevor D. BA, Calif. U., 1965; MA, U. San Francisco, 1978; Early Childhood Cert., U. Calif., Irvine, 1973. Nat. bd. cert. early childhood 1997, cert. tchr. early childhood edn., adminstrv. svcs. credtial 1999. Seminar presenter Bur. of Edn. and Rsch., Bellevue, Wash., 1988—; tchr. Nueva Day Sch., Hillsbourough, Calif., 1969-70; self-employed pub. Irvine, Calif., 1983—; kindergarten tchr., mentor tchr. Newport-Mesa Unified Sch. Dist., Newport Beach, Calif., 1966—2002, prim. elem. sch., 2002—; prin. Lincoln Elem. Sch., 1990—2004. Author: Free To Be Just 4 Years Old, 1983, Free To Be Just 5 Years Old, 1983, Free To Be Just 5, 1990, Companion, 1990, Free To Be Pattern Book, 1991. Active mem. Nat. P.T.A. (Phoebe Apperson Hearst Outstanding Educator award 1988), Calif. P.T.A. (special recognition 1988); bd. dirs. Newport-Mesa Schs. Foundl. Recipient Career Achievement award, 1987. Mem. Calif. Reading Assn., Calif. Kindergarten Assn., Delta Kappa Gamma (Outstanding Educator award 1990). Home: 19462 Sierra Raton Rd Irvine CA 92603-3825

**ROTHMAN, BARBARA KATZ,** sociology educator; b. NYC, June 21, 1948; d. Marcia Katz Berken; m. Herschel M. Rothman; children: Daniel Colb, Leah Colb, Victoria Colb. BA, Bklyn. Coll., 1969, MA, 1972; PhD, NYU, 1979. Prof. sociology CUNY, 1979—. Author: Recreating Motherhood, 1989, The Tentative Pregnancy, 1986, In Labor: Women and Power in the Birthplace, 1982, Of Maps and Imaginations: Genetic Thinking and The Meaning of Life, 1998, The Book of Life, 2000, Weaving a Family: Untangling Race and Adoption, 2005; editor: Ency. of Childbearing, 1993. Mem. Soc. for Study of Social Problems (pres. 1993-94). Office: CUNY Sociology Dept 55 Lexington Ave New York NY 10010-5518 Office Phone: 646-387-4470. Business E-Mail: bkatzrothman@gc.cuny.edu.

**ROTHMAN, BERNARD,** lawyer; b. NYC, Aug. 11, 1932; s. Harry and Rebecca (Fritz) R.; m. Barbara Joan Schaeffer, Aug. 1953; children: Brian, Adam, Helene. BA cum laude, CCNY, 1953; JD, NYU, 1959. Bar: N.Y. 1959, U.S. Dist. Ct. (ea. and so. dists.) N.Y. 1962, U.S. Ct. Appeals (2d cir.) 1965, U.S. Supreme Ct. 1966, U.S. Tax Ct. 1971. Assoc. Held, Telchin & Hell, 1961-62; asst. U.S. atty. Dept. Justice, 1962-66; assoc. Edward Gettinger & Peter Gettinger, 1966-68; ptnr. Schwartz, Rothman & Abrams, P.C., 1968-78, Ferster, Bruckman, Wohl, Most & Rothman, LLP, N.Y., 1978-98, Law Offices of Bernard Rothman, N.Y.C., 1999—2004; coun. Sankel, Skurman & McCartin, LLP, 2004—. Acting judge Village of Larchmont, 1982-88, dep. Village atty., 1974-81, former arbitrator Civil Ct., N.Y.C., family disputes panel Am. Arbitration Assn.; guest lectr. domestic rels. and family law on radio and TV, also numerous legal and mental health orgns. Author: Loving and Leaving-Winning at the Business of Divorce, 1998; co-author: Family Law Syracuse Law Rev. of N.Y. Law, 1992, Leaving Home, Family Law Review, 1987, Put Your Kids First, Am. Bar Assn. Family Adv. Quar., 2000; contbr. articles to profl. jours. Mem. exec. bd., past v.p. Westchester Putnam coun. Boy Scouts Am., 1975—; past mem. nat. coun., 1977-81; mem. adv. com. N.Y. State PEACE, 1994—; pres. Congregation B'nai Israel, 1961-63, B'nai Brith, Larchmont chpt., 1981-83. Recipient Silver Beaver award Boy Scouts Am. Wood Badge award. Fellow Am. Acad. Matrimonial Lawyers (bd. govs. N.Y. chpt. 1986-87, 91-93), Interdisciplinary Forum on Mental Health and Family Law (co-chair 1986-97); mem. ABA (family law sect., contbr. Family Advocate Quar.), N.Y. State Bar Assn. (exec. com. family law sect. 1982—, co-chmn. com. on mediation and arbitration 1982-88, 93-99, chair com. on parent edn. 2004—, com. on legis. 1978-88, com. on child custody 1985-88, com. alt. dispute resolution), Assn. of Bar of City of N.Y. (women in the cts. com. 1996-99), N.Y. State Magistrate Assn., Westchester Magistrate Assn., N.Y. Rd. Runners Club, Limousine 6 Track Club. Democrat. Office: 143 B Harris Hills Somers NY 10589 Office Phone: 212-682-2288. E-mail: divorcelawyer@att.net.

**ROTHMAN, DAVID J.,** historian, educator; b. NYC, Apr. 30, 1937; s. Murray and Anne (Beier) R.; m. Sheila Miller, June 26, 1960; children: Matthew, Micol. BA, Columbia U., 1958; MA, Harvard U., 1959, PhD, 1964. Asst. prof. history Columbia U., N.Y.C., 1964-67, assoc. prof., 1967-71, prof., 1971—; Bernard Schoenberg prof. social medicine, dir. Ctr. for Study of Society and Medicine. Fulbright-Hayes prof. Hebrew U., Jerusalem, 1968-69, India, 1982; vis. Pinkerton Prof. Sch. Criminal Justice, State U. N.Y., at Albany, 1973-74; Samuel Paley lectr. Hebrew U., Jerusalem, 1977; Mem. Com. for Study of Incarceration, 1971-74; co-dir. Project on Community Alternatives, 1978-82; chmn. adv. bd. on criminal justice Clark Found., 1978-82; mem. bd. advisors The Project on Death in Am., Open Soc. Inst., 1995-2000, trustee; mem. bd. trustees Open Soc. Inst., 1996—, pres. Inst. on Medicine as a Profession, 2003—. Author: Politics and Power, 1966, The Discovery of the Asylum, 1971; co-author: Doing Good, 1978, Conscience and Convenience: The Asylum and its Alternatives in Progressive America, 1980; (with Sheila M. Rothman) The Willowbrook Wars, 1984; Strangers at the Bedside, 1991, Beginnings Count: The Technological Imperative in American Health Care, 1997; editor: The World of the Adams Chronicles, 1976, (with Sheila M. Rothman) On Their Own: The Poor in Modern America, 1972, The Sources of American Social Tradition, 1975, (with Stanton Wheeler) Social History and Social Policy, 1981, (with Norval Morris) The Oxford History of the Prison, 1995, (with Steven Marcus and Stephanie Kiceluk) Medicine and Western Civilization, 1995, (with Sheila M. Rothman) The Pursuit of Perfection, 2003, Trust Not Enough. Recipient Albert J. Beveridge prize Am. Hist. Assn., 1971. Mem. Am. Hist. Assn., N.Y. Acad. Medicine, Phi Beta Kappa. Office: Columbia U Coll Physicians and Surgeons Ctr Study Soc and Medicine 630 W 168th St New York NY 10032-3702

**ROTHMAN, HENRY ISAAC,** lawyer; b. Rochester, N.Y., Mar. 29, 1943; s. Maurice M. and Golde (Nusbaum) R.; m. Golda R. Shatz, July 3, 1966; children: Alan, Miriam, Cheryl, Suri. BA, Yeshiva U., 1964; JD, Cornell U., 1967. Bar: NY 1967. Trial atty. SEC, NYC, 1967-69; ptnr. Booth, Lipton & Lipton, NYC, 1969-87, Parker, Chapin, Flattau & Klimpl, NYC, 1987-2000, Jenkens & Gilchrist Parker Chapin LLP, NYC, 2001—05, Troutman Sanders LLP, NYC, 2005—. Bd. dirs. Camp Morasha, Lake Como, Pa., 1982-06, vice chmn., 1992-00; bd. dirs. Assn. of Jewish Sponsored Camps, Inc., 1986-00; bd. dirs. Yeshiva U. High Schs., N.Y.C., 1984-99, vice chmn. bd., 1990-91, chmn. bd., 1992-95; v.p. Manhattan Day Sch., N.Y.C., 1985-96, bd. dirs.; assoc. v.p. Orthodox Union, N.Y.C., 1990-00, v.p., 2001—; vice chmn. bd. dirs. Azrieli Grad. Sch. Jewish Edn. and Administrn., 2000—. Mem. ABA (com. on fed. regulation of securities), Assn. Bar City NY, Yeshiva U. Alumni Assn. (pres. 1986-88, hon. pres. 1988-90). Office: Troutman Sanders LLP The Chrysler Bldg 405 Lexington Ave New York NY 10174-0002 Office Phone: 212-704-6000. Business E-Mail: henry.rothman@troutmansanders.com.

**ROTHMAN, HOWARD JOEL,** lawyer; b. NYC, July 10, 1945; BA, CCNY, 1967; JD, Bklyn. Law Sch., 1971; LLM, NYU, 1972. Bar: N.Y. 1972. From assoc. to ptnr. Marshall, Bratter, Greene, Allison & Tucker, N.Y.C., 1972—82; ptnr. Rosenman & Colin LLP N.Y., 1982—97, Kramer, Levin, Naftalis & Frankel LLP, N.Y.C., 1997—. Mem. adv. panel Commr. Fin. of City of N.Y., 1981-83. Author prof. books and articles. Mem. ABA (corp. tax. com. 1977-87, income from real property com. 1980—), Internat. Bar Assn., N.Y. State Bar Assn. (exec. com. tax sect. 1999-2000, corp. tax com. 1979-87, partnerships com. 1979—, N.Y.C. tax matters com. 1977—, income from real property com. 1987—), Bur. Nat. Affairs (real estate jour. 1984—, tax mgmt. adv. bd. 1979—), Alliance for Young Artists and Writers (bd. dirs.), Poetry Soc. Am. (bd. dirs.), N.Y. Found. for Arts (bd. dirs.).

**ROTHMAN, JAMES EDWARD,** cell biologist, educator; b. Haverhill, Mass., Nov. 3, 1950; BA summa cum laude, Yale U., 1971; PhD in Biochemistry, Harvard U., 1976; D h.c., U. Regensburg, 1995. U. Geneva, 1997. Fellow MIT, Cambridge, 1976-78; asst. prof., dept. biochemistry Stanford (Calif.) U., 1978—81, assoc. prof., 1981—84, prof., 1988—84; E.R. Squibb prof. molecular biology Princeton (N.J.) U., 1988—91; Paul Marks chair Sloan-Kettering Inst., N.Y.C., 1991—2003, chmn. program in cellular biochemistry and biophysics, 1991—2003, vice chmn., 1994—2003; prof. physiology, head ctr. chem. biol. Columbia U., 2003—. Editl. bd. Molecular and Cellulat Biology, 1982—84; chmn. Gordon Conf. on Molecular Membrane Biology, 1983; bd. editors Science, 1984—89; editl. com. Ann. Review Biochemistry, 1985—90, assoc. editor, 2003; editl. bd. Cell, 1984—94; study sect., Molecular Cytology NIH, 1990—94, coun., Nat. Inst. Digestive and Kidney Diseases, 1997—99; Devel. Therapeutics Review Group Nat. Cancer Inst., 1997—98; bd. sr. editors Jour. Clin. Investigation, 2002—. Recipient Eli Lily award for Fundamental Rsch. in Biol. Chemistry, 1986, Passano Young Scientist award, 1986, Alexander Von Humboldt award, 1989, Heinrich Wieland prize, 1990, Rosenstiel award in Biomedical Sciences, 1994, V.D. Mattia award, 1994, Fritz Lipmann award, 1995, Mayor's award for Excellence in Sci. and Tech., 1995, Gairdner Found. Internat. award Gairdner Found., 1996, King Faisal Internat. prize in Sci., 1996, Harden medal, 1997, Feodor Lynen award, 1997, Jacobaeus prize, 1999, Heineken prize, 2000, Otto-Warburg medal, 2001, Albert Lasker award for Basic Medical Rsch., Lasker Found., 2002, Louisa Gross Horwitz prize of Columbia U., 2002; Fellow Andrew W. Mellon, 1979-1982; scholar Dreyfus Found. Teacher, 1981-86; commd. as a Kentucky Col. by Gov. State of Kentucky, 1997. Fellow: Am. Acad. of Arts and Sciences, NAS (Richard Lounsbery award

1997); mem.: European Molecular Biology Orgn. (foreign assoc. 1995), Inst. Medicine, NAS. Office: Columbia U Russ Berrie Med Sci Pavilion 1150 St Nicholas Ave Rm 520 New York NY 10032 Office Phone: 212-851-5565. Business E-mail: jr2269@columbia.edu.*

**ROTHMAN, MELVIN L.,** retired judge; b. Montreal, Que., Can., Apr. 6, 1930; s. Charles and Nellie (Rosen) R.; m. Joan Elizabeth Presant, Aug. 4, 1954; children: Ann Elizabeth, Claire Presant, Margot Sneyd. BA, McGill U., 1951, B.C.L., 1954. Bar: Que. 1954. Practice law, Montreal, 1954-71; mem. Phillips, Vineberg, Goodman, Phillips & Rothman; judge Superior Ct., Dist. of Montreal, 1971-83, Ct. Appeal of Que., 1983—2005; dep. judge Supreme Ct. N.W. Territories, 1977—2005. Named Queen's Counsel. Mem. Jr. Bar of Montreal (pres. 1963-64), Bar of Montreal (council 1964-65), Institut Philippe Pinel (sec., dir. 1965-70). Home: 487 Argyle Ave Westmount PQ Canada H3Y 3B3 E-mail: melvin.rothman@sympatico.ca.

**ROTHMAN, PAUL ALAN,** publishing executive; b. Bklyn., June 26, 1940; s. Fred B. and Dorothy (Regosin) R.; m. Mary Ann Dalson, July 28, 1966 (div. 1992); m. Carol Ann Liske, Sept. 17, 1999; children: Deborah, Diana. BA, Swarthmore Coll., 1962; JD, U. Mich., 1965; LLM in Taxation, NYU, 1967. Bar: NY 1965. Assoc. Dewey, Ballentine, Busby, Palmer & Wood, NYC, 1965-67; v.p. Fred B. Rothman & Co., Littleton, Colo., 1967-85, pres., 1985-2000; chmn. bd. Colo. Plasticard, Littleton, 1983-95; owner LoDo Law Books, Denver, 1998—. Editor: Mich. Law Rev., 1963—65. Home: 1801 Wynkoop St Apt 708 Denver CO 80202-1196 Office: LoDo Law Books 1701 Wynkoop St Union Sta # 300 Denver CO 80202 Office Phone: 720-904-5145. E-mail: parothman@yahoo.com.

**ROTHMAN, RUSSELL L.,** medical educator; b. New Hyde Park, N.Y., Oct. 22, 1970; s. Matthew and Carole Rothman; m. Alice Rothman, Mar. 15, 1998; 1 child, Jacob Cameron. BS, Duke U., Durham, N.C., 1992, MD, 1996—96, M in Pub. Policy, 0196. Lic. internal medicine Am. Bd. of Internal Medicine, pediats. Am. Bd. of Pediats. Resident Duke U. Med. Ctr., Durham, 1996—2000; Robert Wood Johnson clin. scholar U. N.C., Chapel Hill, 2000—02; asst. prof. Vanderbilt U., Nashville, 2002—. Contbr. articles to profl. jours. Recipient K23 Career Devel. award, NIH, NIDDK, 2005—10, Clear Health Comm. Rsch. award, Pfizer Clear Health Comm. Inititiave, 2004—06, Diabetes Rsch. Pilot and Feasability award, NIH, NIDDK, 2004—06, Milton Halmolsky award for outstanding rsch. 2003. Fellow: Am. Acad. of Pediats. (NovoNordisk Clin. Rsch. award 2004—07); mem.: ACP, Soc. of Gen. Internal Medicine (presenter), Am. Diabetes Assn. Achievements include research in role of health literacy; adolescents with type 2 diabetes. Office: Vanderbilt Med Ctr Ste 6000 MCE Nashville TN 37232-8300 Office Phone: 615-322-5000.

**ROTHMAN, STEVEN MARK,** pediatric neurologist, neuroscientist; b. Chgo., Oct. 15, 1948; s. Albert Rothman and Muriel Trifshik; m. Lynne Barbara Kipnis, Mar. 16, 1980; children: Kate Kipnis, Jonathan Daniel, Daisy, Belfast. MD, SUNY Upstate Med. U., 1973. Cert. in neurology with spl. competence in child neurology Am. Bd. Psychiatry & Neurology, Chgo., 1979. Asst. prof. pediat. neurology Wash. U. Sch. Medicine, St. Louis, 1980—88, 1988—92, Stein prof. devel. neurology, 1992—. Dir. dept. of neurology St. Louis Children's Hosp., 1992—2004. Contbr. articles to profl. jours. Mem.: Am. Epilepsy Soc. (chair. neuroscience spl. interest group 2003—06), Can. Neurol. Assn. (hon.). Achievements include patents for cooling cerebral cortex for epilepsy. Office: Washington U 660 South Euclid Box 8111 Saint Louis MO 63110 Office Phone: 314-454-6084.

**ROTHMAN, STEVEN R.,** congressman; b. Englewood, NJ, Oct. 14, 1952; div.; 2 children. BA in Polit. Philos., Syracuse U., NY, 1974; JD, Washington U. Sch. Law, St. Louis, 1977. Bar: NJ 1977, NY 1984. Atty. Miller, Hochman, Meyerson and Schaeffer, Esquires, 1978—80, Steven R. Rothman, Esquire, Englewood, NJ, 1980—93; mayor Englewood, NJ, 1983—89; judge Bergen County Surrogate Ct., NJ, 1993-96; mem. US Congress from 9th NJ dist., 1997—; mem. appropriations com., asst. Dem. whip. Gen. counsel NJ Young Dems., 1981-82; treas. Bergen County Dem. Party, 1982; Dem. nominee for Bergen County Freeholder, 1989; bd. dirs. Jewish Cmty. Ctr. on the Palisades, 1990-92, United Jewish Cmty. of Bergen and North Hudson. Recipient Humane Legislator of Yr. Am. Humane Assn., 2000, Legislator of Yr., Nat. Orgn. to Insure Sound-Controlled Environment, 2001, David Bodian Meml. award, Internat. Post-Polio Task Force, 2002, Human award, Am. Jewish Com. Mem.: NJ Trial Lawyers Assn., Assn. Trial Lawyers Am., Bergen County Bar Assn., NJ Bar Assn., ABA. Democrat. Jewish. Office: US Ho Reps 2303 Rayburn Ho Office Bldg Washington DC 20515 Office Phone: 202-225-5061.*

**ROTHMEIER, STEVEN GEORGE,** merchant banker, investment company executive; b. Mankato, Minn., Oct. 4, 1946; s. Edwin George and Alice Joan (Johnson) R. BBA, U. Notre Dame, 1968; MBA, U. Chgo., 1972. Corp. fin. analyst Northwest Airlines, Inc., St. Paul, 1973, mgr. econ. analysis, 1973-78, dir. econ. planning, 1978, v.p. fin., treas., 1978-82, exec. v.p., treas., dir., 1982-83, exec. v.p. fin. and administrn., treas., dir., 1983, pres., chief operating officer, 1984, pres., chief exec. officer, 1985-86, chmn., chief exec. officer, 1986-89, also bd. dirs.; pres. IAI Capital Group, Mpls., 1989-93; chmn., CEO Great No. Capital, St. Paul, 1993—. Bd. dirs. Arvin Meriter Inc., Gencorp, Precision Castparts, Waste Mgmt., Inc.. Am. Coun. on Germany, German Marshal Fund. Chmn. St. Agnes Found. Decorated Bronze Star. **Mem.** Mpls. Club. Chgo. Club. Republican. Roman Catholic. Office: Great Northern Capital 332 Minnesota St Ste W2900 Saint Paul MN 55101-1377 *Success is not an accident; it is a habit. Success is the result of desire, dedication, sacrifice, mental toughness, hard work—and prayer. And you are not successful until you can share your success with others.*

**ROTHROCK, LINDSEY NICHOLE,** lawyer; b. Richmond, Ind., Nov. 19, 1978; d. Dale Ray Croley and Robin Lynn Lotich. Scott D. Lotich (Stepfather); m. Michael David Rothrock, July 16, 2005. BA in Psychology (hon.), Ind. U., Bloomington, 2001; JD, DePaul U. Coll. Law, Chgo., 2004. Law clk. Goldstein, Fishman, Bender & Romanoff, Chgo., 2002—04; atty. Burns, Figa & Will, PC Greenwood Village, Colo., 2004—. Sr. law student DePaul Tech., Intellectual Property Clinic, Chgo., 2003—04; legal writing and analysis tchr. asst. DePaul U. Coll. Law, 2002—03. Project site mgr. Chgo. Cares, 2002—03; vol. judge U. of Denver Sturm Coll. Law, 2005—. Recipient Ctr. for Computer-Assisted Legal Instrn. Legal Writing and Analysis award, DePaul U. Coll. Law, 2002. Mem.: ABA, Douglas Elbert County Bar Assn., Colo. Bar Assn., Blue Key Nat. Hon. Soc., Golden Key Nat. Honor Soc., Liberal Arts Mgmt. Program, Nat. Honors Soc., Alpha Lambda Delta, Phi Eta Sigma, Order of Omega Greek Honor Frat. (life), Phi Beta Kappa (life), Alpha Xi Delta (life; pres. 1999—99). Office: Burns Figa & Will PC 6400 S Fiddler's Green Cir Ste 1000 Greenwood Village CO 80111 Office Phone: 303-796-2626. E-mail: lrothrock@bfw-law.com.

**ROTHSCHILD, AMALIE RANDOLPH,** filmmaker, film producer, film director, photographer; b. Balt., June 3, 1945; d. Randolph Schamberg and Amalie Getta (Rosenfeld) R. BFA, R.I. Sch. Design, 1967; MFA in Motion Picture Prodn., NYU, 1969. Spl. effects staff in film and photography Joshua Light Show, Fillmore E. Theatre, N.Y.C., 1969-71; artist-photographer represented by Staley-Wise Gallery N.Y.C., 2004. Still photographer TWA Airlines Pub. Rels. Dept., Village Voice newspaper, Rolling Stone mag., Newsweek mag., After Dark, N.Y. Daily News, others, 1968-72; co-founder, ptnr. New Day Films, distbn. coop., 1971—; owner operator Anomaly Films Co., N.Y.C. 1971—; co-founder Assn. Ind. Video and Filmmakers, Inc., N.Y.C., 1974-78; instr. in film and TV, NYU Inst. of Film and TV, 1976-78; cons. in field to various organizations including Youthgrant Program of Nat. Endowment for Humanities, Washington, 1973-76. Exhibitions include Soho Triad Fine Arts Gallery, 1997, 2000, 2002, Gomez Gallery, 1998, 2000, VH-1 Mus. First Gallery, 1999, Govinda Gallery, 2001, Snap Galleries, Birmingham, Eng., 2005, SACI, Florence, Italy, 2005, Tate Gallery, Liverpool, England, 2005, Holden Luntz Gallery, 2005, Redferns Music Picture Gallery, London, 2006; (film): Woo Who? May Wilson, 1969, It

Happens to Us, 1972, Nana, Mom and Me, 1974, Radioimmunoassay of Renin, Radioimmunoassay of Aldosterone, 1973, Conversations with Willard Van Dyke, 1981, Richard Haas: Work in Progress, 1984, Painting the Town: The Illusionistic Murals of Richard Haas, 1990 (Emily award Am. Film and Video Festival 1990); editor: Doing It Yourself, Handbook on Independent Film Distribution, 1977; author: Live at the Fillmore East: A Photographic Memoir, 1999; licensed photograph collections include Corbis/Bettmann Archive, 1994—, Star File Photo Agy., 1997- Mem. Cmty. Planning Bd. 1, Borough of Manhattan, N.Y.C., 1974-86. Recipient spl. achievement award Mademoiselle mag., 1972; Ind. filmmaker grant Am. Film Inst. 1973; film grantee N.Y. State Coun. on the Arts, 1977, 85, 87, Nat. Endowment Arts, 1978, 85, 87, Md. Arts Coun., 1977, Ohio Arts and Humanities Couns., 1985. Mem.: AIVF, Ind. Documentary Assn., NY Women in Film, Univ. Film and Video Assn. Democrat. Address: 135 Hudson St New York NY 10013-2102 also: Via Carrand 22 Florence 50133 Italy E-mail: a.rothschild@agora.it.

**ROTHSCHILD, BRIAN JAMES,** marine biologist, educator; b. Newark, Aug. 14, 1934; s. Daniel Leslie and Dorothy Goodman Rothschild; m. Susan L. Brunenmeister, Feb. 2, 1980; children: Elise, Jessica. BS, Rutgers U., New Brunswick, N.J., 1957; Master's, U. Maine, Orono, 1959; PhD, Cornell U., Ithaca, N.Y., 1962. Chief skipjack-yellowfin tuna ecology program Bur. Comml. Fisheries Honolulu Biol. Lab., 1962—67, acting dep. area dir. Bur. Comml. Fisheries, 1967—68, sr. scientist Bur. Comml. Fisheries, 1968; assoc. prof. Coll. Fisheries, Fisheries Rsch. Inst., and Ctr. Quantitative Scis. in Forestry, Fisheries and Wildlife U. Wash., 1968—71, prof. Coll. Fisheries, Fisheries Rsch. Inst., and Ctr. Quantitative Scis. in Forestry, Fisheries and Wildlife, 1971—72, dir. Nat. Oceanic and Atmospheric Adminstrn., Seattle, 1971—72, dir. SW fisheries ctr., nat. marine fisheries svc. La Jolla, Calif., 1972—76, acting dir. extended jurisdiction planning staff nat. marine fisheries svc. Washington, 1976, dir. office policy devel. and long range planning nat. marine fisheries svc., 1976—78, sr. policy advisor and sr. scientist office of the adminstrn., 1978—80; prof. ctr. environ. and estuarine studies Chesapeake Biol. Lab. U. Md., Solomons, 1980—95; dean Intercampus Grad. Sch. Marine Scis. and Tech. U. Mass., 2000—05, dean Sch. Marine Sci. and Tech. North Dartmouth, 1995—. Author: Dynamics of Marine Fish Populations. Recipient Career Achievement award, Am. Inst. Fishery Rsch. Biologists, 2003. Fellow: AAAS, Am. Inst. Fishery Rsch. Biologists; mem.: Oceanography Soc., Am. Geophys. Union, Am. Fisheries Soc., Sigma Xi. Office: Sch Marine Science and Technology 706 South Rodney French Blvd New Bedford MA 02744 Office Phone: 508-999-8193. Office Fax: 508-999-8197. Business E-Mail: brothschild@umassd.edu.

**ROTHSCHILD, DONALD PHILLIP,** retired lawyer, arbitrator; b. Mar. 31, 1927; s. Leo and Anne (Office); m. Ruth Eckstein, July 7, 1950; children: Nancy Lee, Judy Lynn Hoffman, James Alex. AB, U. Mich., 1950; JD summa cum laude, U. Toledo, 1965; LLM, Harvard U., 1966. Bar: Ohio 1966, D.C. 1970, U.S. Supreme Ct. 1975. R.I. 1989. Tchg. fellow Harvard U. Law Sch., Cambridge, Mass., 1965—66; instr. solicitor's office U.S. Dept. Labor, Washington, 1966—67; prof. law George Washington U. Nat. Law Ctr., Washington, 1966—89, prof. emeritus, 1989; prof. law N.Y. Law Sch., 1989—96; ret., 1996. Vis. prof. U. Mich. Law Sch., Ann Arbor, 1976; dir. Consumer Protection Ctr., 1971—. Inst. Law and Aging, Washington, 1973—89, dir. for Cmty. Justice, Washington, 1974—78, Nat. Consumers League, Washington, 1981—87; v.p. Regulatory Alternatives Devel. Corp., Washington, 1982—; cons. Washington Met. Coun. Govt., 1979—82; counsel Tillinghast, Collins & Graham, Providence, 1989—95, chair human resource group. Author: From the Cockpit of the Rubaiyat, 2002; co-author: Consumer Protection Text and Materials, 1973, Collective Bargaining and Labor Arbitration, 1979, Fundamentals of Administrative Practice and Procedure, 1981; contbr. articles to profl. jours. Chmn. bd. dirs. D.C. Citizens Complaint Ctr., Washington, 1980; mayoral appointee Adv. Com. on Consumer Protection, Washington, 1979—80. Recipient Cmty. Svc. award, Television Acad., Washington, 1981. Mem.: ABA, D.C. Bar Assn., Am. Arbitration Assn., Fed. Mediation and Conciliation Svc., Nat. Acad. Arbitrators, Nat. Assn. Coll. and Univ. Attys. (Brown U.), Fed. Trade Commn. Adv. Coun., Phi Kappa Phi. Jewish. Office: Donald P Rothchild Esq Cataoms Walk Unit C8 601 Periwinkle Way Sanibel FL 33957 Personal E-mail: dpchild@earthlink.net.

**ROTHSCHILD, GITA F.,** lawyer; b. 1950; BA, George Washington U., 1971; MS, Boston U., 1972; JD cum laude, Temple U. Sch. of Law, 1977. Bar: NJ 1977, NY 1984, US Ct. of Appeals, Second & Third Circuits, US Supreme Ct. Ptnr., insurance group McCarter & English, Newark. Chmn., dist. V fee arbitration com. NJ Supreme Ct., 1984—88; mem. Am. Law Inst., Defense Rsch. Inst.; faculty mem. Defense Trial Academy, 1996; ed. bd. mem. NJ Lawyer, 1996—99. Mem.: ABA, Internat. Assn. of Defense Counsel, Essex County Bar Assn., NJ State Bar Assn. Office: McCarter & English Four Gateway Ctr 100 Mulberry St Newark NJ 07102 Office Phone: 973-639-5959. Office Fax: 973-624-7070. Business E-Mail: grothschild@mccarter.com.

**ROTHSCHILD, JENNIFER ANN,** artist, educator; b. Mesa, Ariz., Aug. 16, 1948; d. Joe Dean and Frances Ann (McFarland) Johnston; m. Harry Ronald Rothschild, Feb. 14, 1981. Diploma, El Camino Jr. Coll., 1968; BA in Art Edn., Calif. State U., 1970. Cert. secondary sch. tchr., Calif, Arts and crafts specialist City of Hawthorne (Calif.) Parks and Recreation, 1966-67; portrait artist Disneyland, Anaheim, Calif., 1970-74; secondary sch. art tchr. Orange (Calif.) Unified Schs., 1972-80; freelance custom apparel designer Honolulu, 1982-94; sculptor, artist, 1994—. One woman show at Roy's Honolulu, 2001, Art Centre Gallery, Honolulu, 1997. Studio 1 Gallery, 2004; corp. artist Arts of Paradise Gallery, Honolulu, 1997—; exhibited in show at City of Manhattan Beach, Calif., 1966, Assn. of Hawaii Artists, 1996—, in book Encyclopedia of Living Artists, 10th edit., 1997. Bd. dirs. Hawaii Tennis Patrons, Honolulu, 1996—, Assn. of Hawaii Artists Show chairwoman, 2002. Recipient scholarship Chouinard Sch. Art Inst., 1965-66, 1st Place Stamp Design award Easter Seals, 1995-96, Hokele Artists award Hawaiian Airlines, 1996, Most Unique Art award Assn. of Hawaii Artists Aloha Show, 1997. Fellow Nat. Mus. Women in Arts; mem. AAUW. Honolulu Art Acad., Assn. Hawaii Artists (v.p. 1996-97, pres. 1999-2001), Hawaiian Pacific Tennis Assn. (rules chmn. 1997), mem. Windward Art Guild, 2002, Nat. League of Am. Pen Women, Hon., chapter, Alpha Omicron Pi. Republican. Presbyterian. Avocations: reading, writing, painting, sculpting, carving. E-mail: onoaloha@hawaii.rr.com.

**ROTHSCHILD, MARY ANN,** music educator; b. June 10, 1952; Student, U. N.W. Fla.; AA, Okallosa Walton, 1979; student, conservatory, Canberra, Australia, 1980—82; BA, U. N.Mex., 1985. Cert. (hon.) Calif. Music Tchrs. Assn. Music tchr. Composer Daughter of Zion I, 1990, Daughter of Zion II, 1994, La Chayim, 1997. Pres. Right to Life, Albuquerque, 1987-89. Mem. Music Tchrs. Nat. Assn. (sec. local chpt. Montgomery, Ala., 1981-88, Redlands, Calif., 1988-90, Palm Beach County, Fla., 1994-96, v.p. 1996-98, pres. 1998-99), Women's Algow (v.p. 1985-87, pres. 1987-89). Republican. Home: 1433 SE Cambridge Dr Port Saint Lucie FL 34952-5410 Office Phone: 561-398-6808. Personal E-mail: csom@bellsouth.net.

**ROTHSCHILD, MATTHEW,** editor; b. Grad. Univ. Past editor Multinational Monitor; assoc & mng editor The Progressive, 1983—94, editor, 1994—. Host Progressive Radio; co-founder & Dir The Progressive Media Project. Office: The Progressive 409 E Main St Madison WI 53703

**ROTHSCHILD, MICHAEL,** economics professor; b. Chgo., Aug. 2, 1942; s. Edwin Alfred and Ann (Meyer) R.; m. Linda Preiss, Sept. 7, 1969 (div. 1991); m. Lynn Kay Greenberg, May 1, 1994; children: David, Daniel. BA, Reed Coll., 1963; MA, Yale U., 1965; PhD, MIT, 1969. Asst. prof. econs. Harvard U., 1969-73; lectr. Princeton U., 1972-74, assoc. prof., 1974-75, prof., 1975-76; then prof. U. Wis., Madison, 1976-83; prof. U. Calif.-San Diego, 1983-95, divisional dean social scis., 1985-95; dean Woodrow Wilson Sch. Pub./Internat. Affairs Princeton U., 1995—2002, prof. econs. and pub. affairs, 2002—. Editor: (with Peter Diamond) Uncertainty in Economics, 1978, (with Charles T. Clotfelder) Studies of Supply and Demand in Higher

Education, 1993. Guggenheim fellow, 1978-79. Fellow AAAS, Am. Acad. Arts and Scis., Econometric Soc., Am. Econ. Assn. (disting.). Office: Woodrow Wilson Sch Princeton U Hl Princeton NJ 08544-1013

**ROTHSCHILD, WILLIAM BARON,** psychiatrist, educator; b. Calif. s. Edward A. and Jane Rothschild; m. Debra D. Rothschild; 1 child, Cameron. MD, Univ Of Calif At San Francisco, San Francisco, 1968—72; BS, U. Calif. 1969. Diplomate Am. Bd. Psychiatry And Neurology, 1978. Resident Mass. Mental Health Ctr., Boston, 1972—75; asst. clin. prof. psychiatry Med. Sch. Tufts U., 1975—80; staff psychiatrist South Shore Mental Health Ctr., Quincy, Mass., 1975—2003, Brockton (Mass.) VA Med. Ctr., 1975—. Instr. psychiatry Med. Sch. Harvard U., Boston, 1975—. Mem.; Nat. Assn. VA Physicians, Am. Psychiat. Assn., Phi Beta Kappa. Office: Brockton VA Med Ctr 940 Belmont St Brockton MA 02301 Office Phone: 508-583-4500 62343. Personal E-mail: sayhey@att.net.

**ROTHSTEIN, ANNE LOUISE,** academic administrator, educator; b. Bklyn., Feb. 15, 1943; d. William and Rose Mary (Smith) R. BS, Bklyn. Coll., 1963; MA, Tchrs. Coll. Columbia, N.Y.C., 1965, EdD, 1970. Tchr. Erasmus Hall High Sch., Bklyn., 1963-64, Fort Hamilton High Sch., Bklyn., 1964-64; lectr. Hunter Coll. in the Bronx, N.Y., 1965-68; instr., prof. Lehman Coll., Bronx, 1968—, dept. chair, 1980-93, assoc. dean, 1983-93, assoc. provost/dir. for sponsored program devel., 1993-98. Dir. Lehman Ctr. for Sch./Coll. Collaboratives, Bronx, 1988—; grant specialist for sch./coll. programs, 1985—; small sch. developer, 1999—. Editor, pub. Motor Skills: Theory into Practice, 1976-87; chair editorial bd. Strategies, 1986-92; author: Research and Statistics, 1985, Motor Learning: Basic Stuff, 1987. Grantee in field. Fellow Rsch. Consortium Am. Alliance, Am. Alliance for Health, Physical Edn., Recreation and Dance; mem. Nat. Assn. for Sport and Physical Edn., Nat. Assn. for Girls and Women in Sport, Assn. for Supervision and Curriculum Devel., Am. Ednl. Rsch. Assn. Avocations: computers, grants consulting. Home: PO Box 3007 Newtown CT 06470-3007 Office: Lehman Coll Bedford Park Blvd W Bronx NY 10468 Office Phone: 718-960-8569. Personal E-mail: arothstein@aol.com. Business E-Mail: anne.rothstein@lehman.cuny.edu.

**ROTHSTEIN, BARBARA JACOBS,** federal judge; b. Bklyn., Feb. 3, 1939; d. Solomon and Pauline Jacobs; m. Ted L. Rothstein, Dec. 28, 1968; 1 child, Daniel BA. Cornell U., 1960; LL.B., Harvard U., 1966. Bar: Mass. 1966, Wash. 1969, U.S. Ct. Appeals (9th cir.) 1977, U.S. Dist. Ct. (we. dist.) Wash. 1971, U.S. Supreme Ct. 1975. Pvt. practice law, Boston, 1966-68; asst. atty. gen. State of Wash., 1968-77; judge Superior Ct., Seattle, 1977-80, Fed. Dist. Ct. Western Wash., Seattle, 1980—, chief judge, 1987-94, dir. Fed. Jud. Ctr., 2003—. Faculty Law Sch. U. Wash., 1975-77, Hastings Inst. Trial Advocacy, 1977, N.W. Inst. Trial Advocacy, 1979—; mem. state-fed. com. U.S. Jud. Conf., chair subcom. on health reform; dir. Fed. Jud. Ctr.; bd. dirs. Inst. Jud. Adminstrn., NYU Sch. Law. Recipient Matrix Table Women of Yr. award Women in Communication, Judge of the Yr. award Fed. Bar Assn., 1989; King County Wash. Women Lawyers Vanguard Honor, 1995 Mem. Am. Judicature Soc. (mem. commn.), Nat. Assn. Women Judges, Fellows of the Am. Bar, Am. Law Inst. (bd. dirs.), Wash. State Bar Assn., Am. Law Inst., Phi Beta Kappa, Phi Kappa Phi. Office: Fed Jud Ctr 1 Columbus Cir NE Washington DC 20002-8003

**ROTHSTEIN, FRED C.,** health facility administrator; b. Cleve. m. Jackie Rothstein; 2 children. BA, Miami U., Oxford, Ohio; MD, Chgo. Med. Sch. U. Health Scis., 1976. Bd. cert. pediatrics and pedatric gastroenterology. Pediat. internship Cleve. Metro Gen. Hosp., Ohio, 1976—77, Rainbow Babies & Children's Hosp., Ohio, 1976—77, pediat. residency, 1977—79, pediat. gastroenterology fellowship, 1979—81, chief divsn. pediat. gastroenterology, practicing physician, pediat. gastroenterologist, pres., CEO; dir. dept. pediatrics, sr. v.p. med. affairs Mt. Sinai Med. Ctr., Cleve.; sr. v.p. clin. integration U. Hosps. Health System, Cleve., 1996—2002, acting pres., CEO, 2002—03; pres., CEO U. Hosps. Cleve., 2003—. Asst. prof. pediatrics Case Western Reserve U.; bd. trustees Ctr. Health Affairs (CHA), 2004, Geauga Regional Hosp., Chardon, Ohio, 1997; bd. dirs. BioEnterprise. Contbr. more than 60 peer-reviewed abstracts, articles, and book chapters on issues concerning pediatric gastroenterology. Mem.: N.Am. Soc. Pediat. Gastroenterology and Nutrition, Am. Gastroenterological Assn., Am. Acad. Pediatrics, Am. Coll. Gastroenterology. Office: Univ Hosps Cleve 11100 Euclid Ave Cleveland OH 44106 Office Phone: 216-844-6217.*

**ROTHSTEIN, GERALD ALAN,** investment consultant; b. Bklyn., Oct. 18, 1941; s. Manuel and Gertrude (Buxbaum) R.; m. Cynthia Bea Pincus, June 11, 1967; children: Michael Neil, Lori Pamela, Meryl Patricia. BBA, City Coll. N.Y., 1962; MBA, U. Pa., 1965. 1st v.p. Shearson Hammill & Co., N.Y.C., 1966-74, Shearson Hayden Stone, N.Y.C., 1974-75; v.p. William D. Witter, Inc., N.Y.C., 1975-76; from v.p. to internat. investment banker Oppenheimer & Co., N.Y.C., 1976—95, internat. investment banker, 1995—2004; mng. dir. internat. money mgmt. CIBC World Markets, N.Y.C., 1998—2004; cons. Marshepaug Advisors, 2004—. Trustee Ctr. Social and Emotional Edn., NYC. Mem. N.Y. Soc. Security Analysts, CFA Inst. Personal E-mail: gerald.rothstein@verizon.net.

**ROTHSTEIN, LAURA,** dean, law educator; BA, U. Kans., 1971; JD, Georgetown U. Law Ctr., 1974. Asst. prof. law Ohio No. U., 1976—79, dir. admissions, 1978—79; assoc. prof. law W.Va U., 1980—84, prof. law, 1984—86, U. Houston, 1985—96, assoc. dean Student Affairs, 1988—93, Law Found. prof. 1996—2000, assoc. dean Grad. Studies and Spl. Progs., 1999—2000; prof. law Brandeis Sch. Law, U. Louisville, 2000—, dean, 2000—. Vis. assoc. prof. law U. Pitts., 1979—80; staff atty. Dept. Justice, Antitrust Div., Washington, DC, 1974—75, Ohio State Atty. Gen., Antitrust Sec., 1975—76, Devel. Disabilities Law Project, U. Pitts. Sch. Law, 1979—80; affiliated Appalachian Rsch. & Defense Fund, Inc., Charleston, W.Va., 1980—85; assoc. dir. devel. Health Law and Policy Inst., U. Houston, 1997—2000. Editor: Health Law News, 1993—98; contbr. articles to law jours. Bd. mem. Urban Montessori Sch., Louisville, 2001—; adv. bd. mem. Children's Organ Transplant Assn., 2000—. Mem.: ABA (mem. Diversity Com. 2002—), Soc. Am. Law Tchrs., Brandeis Inns Ct., Ky. Bar Assn., Ky. Bar Found., Louisville Bar Assn., River Oaks Women's Breakfast Club. Office: Louis D Brandeis Sch Law U Louisville Wilson W Wyatt Hall 2301 S Third St Louisville KY 40292 Office Phone: 502-852-6879. Office Fax: 502-852-0862. E-mail: laura.rothstein@louisville.edu.

**ROTHSTEIN, PAUL FREDERICK,** lawyer, educator; b. Chgo., June 6, 1938; BS, Northwestern U., 1958, LLB, 1961. Bar: Ill. 1962, D.C. 1967, U.S. Supreme Ct. 1975. Instr. U. Mich Law Sch., 1963; assoc. prof. law U. Tex., 1964-67; mem. Surrey, Karasik, Gould & Greene, Washington, 1967-70; prof. Georgetown U. Law Ctr., Washington, 1970—; spl. counsel U.S. Senate Jud. Com. Subcom. on Criminal Laws and Procedures, 1975-77; spl. counsel U.S. Ho. of Reps. Jud. Com. Subcom. on Criminal Law, 1980. Cons. Treasury, 1967-74, HEW, 1970, Commrs. on Uniform State Laws, 1969-75, Nat. Acad. Scis., 1976-77, 95-96, D.C. Law Revision Commn., 1976-78; spkr., coord. numerous legal edn. seminars for judges and lawyers, 1970—. Author: Evidence in a Nutshell, 1970, 2d edit., 1981, 3d edit., 1997, Understanding the New Federal Rules of Evidence, 1973, 74, 75, Federal Rules of Evidence with Practice Comments and Annotations, 1978, 2d edit., 1981, 3d edit., 2001, Cases, Materials and Problems in Evidence, 1986, 2d edit., 1998; contbr. articles on various legal matters to profl. jours.; editor-in-chief Northwestern U. Law Rev., 1960-61. Recipient U. Iowa Legal Edn. award 1974, Disting. Pub. Svc. award Crime Victims Compensation Bd., 1978; other civic and profl. awards; Fulbright scholar, Oxford, Eng., 1962-63. Mem. Fed. Bar Assn. (chmn. fed. rules of evidence com. 1974-77, Disting. Svc. award 1975, nat. coun. 1976-80, chmn. continuing legal edn. com. 1980), D.C. Bar (continuing legal edn. bd. 1980—), ABA (chmn. rules of evidence and criminal procedure com., criminal justice sect. 1984-88), Assn. Am. Law Schs. (sec. evidence sect. 1976, chmn. 1977), Nat. Assn. Criminal Injuries Compensations Bds. (sec. 1977-80), Internat. Assn. Criminal Injuries Compensation Bds. Office: Georgetown U Law Ctr 600 New Jersey Ave NW Washington DC 20001-2022

**ROTHSTEIN, SAMUEL,** librarian, educator; b. Moscow, Jan. 12, 1921; arrived in Can., 1922, naturalized, 1929; s. Louis Israel and Rose Rothstein; m. Miriam Ruth Teitelbaum, Aug. 26, 1951; children: Linda Rose, Sharon Lee. BA, U. B.C., 1939, MA, 1940, LLD, 2004; grad. student, U. Calif., Berkeley, 1941-42, grad. student, 1946-47, BLS, 1947; postgrad., U. Wash., 1942—43; PhD (Carnegie Corp. fellow 1951-54), U. Ill., 1954; DLitt, York U., 1971. Teaching fellow U. Wash., 1942-43; prin. libr. asst. U. Calif., Berkeley, 1947; mem. staff U. B.C. Libr., Vancouver, 1947-51, 54-62; acting univ. libr. U. B.C., Vancouver, 1961-62, prof. libr. sci., 1961—86, prof. emeritus, 1986—, dir. Sch. Librarianship, 1961-70. Vis. prof. U. Hawaii, 1969, U. Toronto, 1970, 79, Hebrew U., Jerusalem, 1973; mem. Commn. Nat. Plan Libr. Edn., 1963—; mem. assoc. com. sci. info. Nat. Rsch. Coun. Can., 1962-69; councillor B.C. Med. Libr. Svc., 1971; mem. exec. com. Pacific divsn. Can. Jewish Congress, 1962-69, internat. House Assn. B.C., 1959-60; mem. Can. Adv. Bd. Sci. and Tech. Info.; mem. cabinet Combined Jewish Appeal of Greater Vancouver, 1992-95; pres. Vancouver Pub. Libr. Trust, 1987-88. Author: The Development of Reference Services, 1955, (with others) Training Professional Librarians for Western Canada, 1957, The University-The Library, 1972, Rothstein on Reference..., 1989; also articles.; co-editor: As We Remember It, 1970. Life mem. bd. dirs. Jewish Cmty. Ctr. of Greater Vancouver, pres., 1972-74; bd. dirs. Jewish Fedn. of Greater Vancouver, 1993-2000. Recipient ALISE award Assn. Library Info. Sci. Edn., 1987, Beta Phi Mu award ALA, 1988. Mem. Can. Libr. Assn. (hon. life), Assn. Am. Libr. Schs. (pres. 1968-69), Can. Assn. Libr. Schs. (hon. life, pres. 1982-84), ALA (coun. 1963-69, Beta Phi Mu award 1988), B.C. Libr. Assn. (hon. life, pres. 1959-60, Helen Gordon Stewart award 1970), Pacific N.W. Libr. Assn. (pres. 1963-64, hon. life), Can. Libr. Assn. (hon. life, coun. 1958-60, Outstanding Svc. to Librarianship award 1986), Bibliog. Soc. Can. (coun. 1959-63), Can. Assn. Univ. Tchrs. Home: 1416 W 40th Ave Vancouver BC Canada Personal E-mail: sammir@shaw.ca. Business E-mail: samuelr@interchange.ubc.ca.

**ROTHWELL, ELAINE B.,** artist; b. Mpls., May 8, 1926; d. Frederick Roscoe and Stella Frances (LaVallee) Bartholomew; m. William Stanley Rothwell, May 10, 1946; children: Suzanne, Amy Verrett, Wendy Rothwell-Lopez, Bart. BFA, San Jose State U., 1966; pvt. study, Woodbury Graphic Studio, Los Altos, Calif., 1975-76, Amaranth Intaglio Workshop, Los Altos, 1985. *Rothwell was first known for her series of 14 etchings using chess imagery and chess positions. This series was featured in a cover story in Chess Life Magazine in March 1979. Her 1983 Spiritus Loci series of eight etchings forms a cartographical puzzle. Her later series, Art History Mysteries, 1994, Mad Meg Amok, 1997, Inklings, 1999, Seasons of Romance, 2006 and Moons, 2005, are online at www.artbyrothwell.com. By means of figure ground ambiguities and enigmatic images, Rothwell's etchings baffle the viewers' eyes with games of visual discovery.* One-woman shows include Triton Mus. Art, Santa Clara, Calif., 1976, Palo Alto Civic Ctr., Calif., 1977, Stanford Art Spaces, Stanford U., Calif., 1985, 1988, 1989, West Valley Art Mus., Surprise, Ariz., 1996, Roseville Arts Ctr., Calif., 2003, exhibited in group shows at Carnegie Art Ctr., North Tonawanda, N.Y., 1995, 1996, N.J. Ctr. Visual Arts Internat., Summit, 1997, 1998, Brand Libr. and Art Ctr., Glendale, Calif., 1996, Internat. Exhbn. Art League Manatee County, Fla., 1996, Nat. Soc. Artists, 1997, Am. Color Print Soc., 1997, Grand Exhbn. Nat. Competition, Akron, Ohio, 1998, Printwork '98, Barrett Ho., Poughkeepsie, N.Y., 1998, 73d Ann. Internat. Print Competition/Print Ctr., Phila., 1999, Manhattan Arts Internat., 1999, Chautauqua Nat. Exhbn. Am. Art, 1999, No. Colo. Ann. Nat. Exhbns., 1999, 2000, Stage Gallery, Merrick, N.Y., 2000, Pacific Prints, Palo Alto, Calif., 2006, retrospective exhbns., Gallery 9, Los Altos, Calif., 2002, Gallery II, Nevada City, Calif., 2002. Represented in permanent collections Newberry Libr., Chgo., Triton Mus. Art, Santa Clara, West Valley Art Mus., Brand Libr. Art Ctr., Glendale, Crocker Mus., San Francisco. Mem.: Am. Color Print Soc., Nat. Mus. Women in Arts (charter), Crocker Art Mus., Crocker Art Mus., Auburn Old Town Gallery, Triton Mus. Art. Home and Office: 3030 Eagles Nest Auburn CA 95603-5918

**ROTHWELL, TIMOTHY,** pharmaceutical executive; b. London, Jan. 8, 1951; came to u.s., 1966; s. Kenneth Gordon Rothwell and Jean Mary (Stedman) Davey; m. Joanne Claire Fleming; children: Tiffany, Heather. BA, Drew U., 1972; JD, Seton Hall U., 1976; LLM, NYU, 1979, exec. MBA, 1983. With Sandoz Pharms., East Hanover, NJ, 1972—, patent atty., 1974-77, patent and trademark counsel, 1980-82, mng. ops. planning and adminstrn., 1982-84, dir. mktg. ops., 1984-85, exec. dir. field ops., 1985-86, v.p. field ops., 1986-87, pres. profl. bus. ops., 1987-88, corp. v.p., chief oper. officer, 1989—91; sr. v.p. sales and mktg. Squibb, Princeton, NJ, 1991; v.p. global mktg. and sales Burroughs-Wellcome, 1992; pres., CEO Sandoz Pharm. Corp., 1995; pres. pharm. op. Rhone-Poulenc Rorer Inc., 1996, pres., bd. dirs., 1996-97; exec. v.p., pres. pharm. ops. Pharmacia Corp., NJ, 1998—2002; pres., CEO Sanofi-Synthelabo N.Am., 2002—, Sanofi-Aventis U.S., 2004—. Bd. dirs. PhRMA; trustee Somerset Med. Ctr., Healthcare Inst. NJ; found. bd. dirs. U. Medicine and Dentistry of NJ. Mem. NJ State Bar Assn., NY State Bar Assn., Am. Soc. Pharmacy Law, Nat. Health Care Quality Coun., Am. Found. Pharm. Exec. (bd. dirs.), NJ Patent Law Assn. (pres. 1986), Health Inst. NJ. Avocations: stamp collecting/philately, soccer, golf, tennis.

**ROTHWELL, WENDY,** biology educator; b. Milw., Wis., Aug. 9, 1957; d. William and Elaine Rothwell; m. Alberto Lopez, June 24, 2000. BA in Music (emphasis on Composition), San Jose State U., Calif., 1988, BS in Molecular Biology, 1992; PhD in Molecular, Cell & Devel. Biology, U. Calif., Santa Cruz, 1992—98. Sheet metal mechanic Hewlett Packard, Palo Alto, Calif., 1980—91; post-doctoral rschr. U. Calif., Santa Cruz, 1998—2000, lectr. molecular, cell and devel. biology, 1998—2004; instr., exptl. methods U. Calif. Ext., Cupertino, 2005—; gen. biology instr. Foothill Coll., Los Altos, 2006—06; lectr. biomolecular engring. U. Calif., Santa Cruz, 2005—. Recipient Excellence in Tchg. award, Ctr. for Tchg. Excellence, U. Calif., Santa Cruz, 2001—02. Avocation: playing the saxophone. Office: Univ Calif 210 Engring 2 Santa Cruz CA 95064 Office Phone: 831-459-1623.

**ROTI, THOMAS DAVID,** judge; s. Sam N. and Theresa S. (Salerno) R.; m. Donna Sumichrast, 1972; children: Thomas S., Kyle D., Rebecca D., Gregory J BS, Loyola U., Chgo., 1967, JD cum laude, 1970. Bar: Ill. 1970, U.S. Dist. Ct. (no. dist.) Ill. 1971, U.S. Ct. Appeals (7th cir.) 1971. Sr. law clk. to Judge Frank McGarr, U.S. Dist. Ct. No. Dist. Ill., 1971-72; assoc. Arnstein, Gluck & Lehr, Chgo., 1972-73; Boodell, Sears et al, Chgo., 1973-75; asst. gen. counsel Dominick's Finer Foods, Inc., Northlake, Ill., 1975-77, v.p., gen. counsel, 1977-97; judge Cir. Ct. Cook County, 2000—. Mem. nat. conf. lawyers and econs. com. Food Mktg. Inst., Washington, 1987—97; trustee Nat. Conf. Cmty. and Justice, 1995—2000; legis. com. Ill. Retail Mchts. Assn., Chgo., 1987—97. Trustee Joint Civic Com. Italian Ams., Chgo., 1986-95; mem. Chgo. Coun. EDU-CARE Scholarship Program, 1988; dir. Chgo. Clean Streak, 1990-97. Maj., Qartermaster Corps, USAR, 1967-83 Recipient Am. Jurisprudence award, 1970, Alumni Assn. award Loyola U., 1970. Mem. ABA, Ill. Bar Assn., Ill. Judges Assn. (bd. dirs. 2005), Chgo. Bar Assn., N.W. Suburban Bar Assn. (bd. govs. 2006-, co-chair civil practice com.), Justinian Soc. Lawyers, Cath. Lawyers Guild Chgo. (bd. govs., dir. 2004—). Phi Alpha Delta, Alpha Signa Nu Roman Catholic. Office: 2121 Euclid Ave Rolling Meadows Il 60008 Business E-mail: tdroti@cookcountygov.com

**ROTNER, PHILIP R.,** lawyer; b. Chgo., Feb. 6, 1947; m. Janet Rotner. AB, U. Calif., 1969; JD, Harvard U., 1972. Bar: Ill. 1972, Mass. 1973, Calif. 1975, N.Y. 1996. Litig. assoc. Gaston, Snow, Motley & Holt, Boston, 1973—74, assoc., 1974—80; ptnr. McCutchen, Doyle, Brown & Enersen, San Francisco, 1981—95; gen. counsel Deloitte & Touche USA LLP, Broadway, NY, 1995—2005; ptnr. Mayer, Brown, Rowe & Maw LLP, Chgo., 2005—. Vis. faculty Law Sch. Trial Advocacy Program Harvard U., 1990, 93; spkr. in field. Office: Mayer Brown Rowe & Maw LLP 71 S Wacker Dr Chicago IL 60606 Home: 1040 North Lake Shore Dr Apt 33C Chicago IL 60611 E-mail: protner@mayerbrownrowe.com.

**ROTOLO, SUSAN (SUZE),** artist; b. N.Y.C., Nov. 20, 1943; d. Joachim Peter and Mary Teresa Rotolo; m. Enzo Bartoccioli; 1 child, Luca. Tchr. bookmaking; workshop leader in field. Illustrator, designer textiles, compact disc cover art, scenery and props for theater, Laugh the Blues Away Cookbook, 2001; solo exhbns. at Jefferson Market Libr., N.Y.C., 1997, 98, 99, NYU Casa Italiana Gallery, 1998, Donnell Libr. Ctr., N.Y. Pub. Libr., 2000, Ctr. for Book Arts, N.Y.C., 2001, 05; art exhibited in shows including Galleria Todini, Perugia, Italy, Ctr. for Book Arts, N.Y.C., ARC Gallery, Chgo., Spring Studio, N.Y.C., Columbia Coll. Gallery, Chgo., N.Y. State Mus., Albany, Left Bank Gallery, Bennington, Vt., Art Acad. Cin., Nat. Guild Bookworkers Traveling Exhbn., Harper Collins Exhbn. Space, N.Y.C., Corcoran Gallery, Washington, Nat. Mus. Women in Arts, Washington, Md. Fedn. Art, Balt., Medlalia Gallery, N.Y.C., many others; artist one-of-a-kind sculptural books; included in Book Arts Collection of L.I. U., Bklyn. Mus., Nat. Mus. Women in the Arts, Washington, Mus. Modern Art, Franklin Furnace, N.Y.C.; art appears in books pub. by Lark Books, Davis Publs.; featured in Somerset Studio Mag., 2005, other nat. and internat. art publs.; appearance (TV shows) No Direction Home: Bob Dylan, PBS. Recipient Spl. Mention award for tech. expertise combined with creative risk, Appearances and West Village Coalition for Parks and Playgrounds, 1995, First Pl. Jury prize Valdosta (Ga.) Fine Arts Gallery, Valdosta (Ga.) U. Mem. Ctr. for Book Arts, Am. Craft Coun., Guild of Bookworkers. Avocations: art, music, reading. Office: Suzart 682 Broadway New York NY 10012-2320 Office Phone: 212-254-5591. E-mail: suzarte@verizon.net.

**ROTT, STEPHEN ROSS,** biologist, educator; s. Clarence and Kathy Rott (Stepmother); m. Cindy Kuykendall, Apr. 4, 2004; children: Jennifer Stephannie Purvis, Jason Stewart, Bryan Nathanial. BS, Purdue U., 1968; MEd, Ind. U., 1974. Tchr. Cardinal Ritter HS, Indpls., 1968—74, Carmel (Ind.) HS, 1974—. Recipient Clean Air award, Cleaner Air Com. Indpls., 1990. Mem.: NEA (assoc.), Nat. Assn. Biology Tchrs. (assoc.), Ind. State Tchrs. Assn. (assoc.), Ind. Assn. Biology Tchrs. (life), Sierra Club (assoc.). Avocations: hiking, woodworking, gardening. Office: Carmel Clay Schs 520 E Main Carmel IN 46032 Office Phone: 317-846-7721. Personal E-mail: srott@ccs.k12.in.us.

**ROTTEN, JOHNNY See LYDON, JOHN**

**ROTTENBERG, CLAIRE J.,** writer, educator; d. Berthold and Helen Rottenberg. BA, CUNY, Flushing, 1968; MEd, U. of Cin., 1971; EdD, Ariz. State U., 1991. Cert. tchr. edn. sci., spl.edn., early childhood State of Israel, 1997. Tchr. lang. and hearing impaired N.Y.C. Pub. Schs., 1971—74, Memphis City Schs., 1974—76, Tempe City Schs., Tempe, Ariz., 1976—88; asst. prof. edn. U. of Southwestern La., Lafayette, 1991—92, Kennesaw State U., Kennesaw, 1992—97; lectr. English linguistics Bar-Ilan U., Ramat Gan, Israel, 1999—2002, lectr. English as a fgn. lang., 2000—05. Author: (book) Great Readings in Research (NEA); contbr. articles to profl. jours. Avocations: computers, travel. Personal E-mail: daniyh21@yahoo.com.

**ROTTER, ANDREW JON,** history educator; b. Madison, Wis., June 13, 1953; m. Padma A. Kaimal, June 24, 1984; children: Sophie, Phoebe. BA in History, Cornell U., 1975; MA in History, Stanford U., 1976, PhD in History, 1981. Instr. Stanford U., Palo Alto, 1979; vis. asst. prof. Calif. State U., Chico, 1980-81; asst. prof. St. Mary's Coll. Calif., 1981-84, 85-86; vis. asst. prof. Colgate U., 1986-87, asst. prof., 1988-90, assoc. prof., 1990—98, prof., 1998—; asst. prof. Vanderbilt U., 1987-88. Author: The Path to Vietnam: Origins of the American Commitment to Southeast Asia, 1987, Comrades at Odds: The United States and India, 1947-1964, 2000; editor: Light at the End of the Tunnel: A Vietnam War Anthology, 1999; contbr. articles, rev. essays, book revs. to profl. jours. James Birdsall Weter fellow Stanford U., 1979-80, Stanford U. Ctr. for Rsch. Internat. Studies fellowship, 1980, Gandhi Peace Found. fellowship, 1984-85, Sr. Rsch. fellowship Am. Coun. Learned Socs., 1990-91, Picker Rsch. fellowship Colgate U., 1990-91; Albert J. Beveridge Rsch. grantee Am. Hist. Assn., 1984, Rsch. grantee Harry S. Truman Libr. Inst., 1987; recipient David M. Potter award Stanford U. Dept. History, 1978-79. Mem. Am. Hist. Assn., Orgn. Am. Historians, Soc. for Historians of Am. Fgn. Rels. Home: 9 W Pleasant St Hamilton NY 13346-1203 Office: Colgate U Dept History 13 Oak Dr Dept History Hamilton NY 13346-1383

**ROTTER, PAUL TALBOTT,** retired insurance executive; b. Parsons, Kans., Feb. 21, 1918; s. J. and LaNora (Talbott) R.; m. Virginia Sutherlin Barksdale, July 17, 1943; children: Carolyn Sutherlin, Diane Talbott. BS summa cum laude, Harvard U., 1937. Asst. mathematician Prudential Ins. Co. of Am., Newark, 1938-46; with Mut. Benefit Life Ins. Co., Newark, 1946—, successively asst. mathematician, asso. mathematician, mathematician, 1946-59, from v.p. to exec. v.p., 1959-80, ret., 1980. Mem. Madison Bd. Edn., 1958-64, pres., 1959-64; Trustee, mem. budget com. United Campaign of Madison, 1951-55; mem. bd., chmn. advancement com. Robert Treat council Boy Scouts Am., 1959-64. Fellow Soc. Actuaries (bd. govs. 1965-68, gen. chmn. edn. and exam. com. 1963-66, chmn. adv. com. edn. and exam. 1969-72), Phi Beta Kappa Soc.; mem. Brit. Inst. Actuaries (assoc.), Am. Acad. Actuaries (v.p. 1968-70, bd. dirs., chmn. edn. and exam. com. 1965-66, chmn. rev. and evaluation com. 1968-74), Asso. Harvard Alumni (regional dir. 1965-69), Actuaries Club N.Y. (dir. 1967-68), Harvard Alumni Assn. (v.p. 1964-66), Am. Lawn Bowls Assn. (pres. SW divsn.). Clubs: Harvard N.J. (pres. 1956-57); Harvard (N.Y.C.); Morris County Golf (Convent, N.J.); Joslyn-Lake Hodges Lawn Bowling (pres. 1989-90). Home: 18278 Canfield Pl San Diego CA 92128-1002

**ROTTERDAM, PAUL ZWIETNIG,** artist, retired art educator; b. Neustadt, Austria, Feb. 12, 1939; s. Peter and Emilie Rotterdam; m. Rebecca S. Littlejohn; 1 child, Charlotte Zwietnig-Rotterdam. PhD, U. Vienna, Austria, 1967 Vi. Inst. Harvard U., Cambridge, Mass., 1960—88. Vis. prof. U. Tex., San Antonio, 1979, Akademie der bildwolen Kneuste, Vienna, 1996. Subject of book Worklist 1953-2005 (Carl Aigner), 2005; contbr. Address: PO Box 952 North Blenheim NY 12131 E-mail: paulzr@midtel.net.

**ROTTMAN, ELLIS,** public information officer; b. Balt., Apr. 5, 1930; s. Abraham Isaac and Sadie (Harris) R.; m. Carol Parker Donovan, May 30, 1965; children—Marcus, Lisa, Jason, Adam. BS, U. Md., 1952. Assoc. editor Army Times Pub. Co., Washington, 1956-59; editor, dir. pub. relations Am. Fedn. Govt. Employees, AFL-CIO, 1959-65; pub. info. officer U.S. Post Office Dept., 1966-69; editor Manpower mag. Dept. Labor, 1969-75; editor, publs. dir. FDA, Rockville, Md., 1975-78; public info. dir. Labor-Mgmt. Services Adminstrn. Dept. Labor, 1978-84; pub. info. officer Office Sec. of Labor, 1984-94. Served with AUS, 1952-54. Recipient Journalism award Internat. Labor Press Assn., AFL-CIO, 1959, 60, 61, 62, 64; award merit Fed. Editors Assn., 1974, 75, 77, 78 Jewish. Home: 901 N Belgrade Rd Silver Spring MD 20902-3247 Office: 2nd St And Constitution Ave NW Washington DC 20210-0001

**ROTUNDA, ADAM MICHAEL,** dermatologist; b. Mineola, N.Y., Aug. 2, 1974; s. Robert and Josephine Rotunda; m. Thuy Nguyen, July 20, 1997; 1 child, Tia Linh. BS in Nutritional Scis. summa cum laude with honors, Cornell U., Ithaca, N.Y., 1996; MD valedictorian, SUNY Downstate Med. Sch., Bklyn., 2001. Bd. Cert. Am. Bd. Dermatology, 2005. Intern St. Vincent's Hosp., N.Y.C., 2001—02; resident Divsn. Dermatology UCLA Sch. Medicine, LA, 2002—05, clin. prof., 2006—; mohs micrographic surgery and cutaneous oncology fellowship Bennett Surgery Ctr., Santa Monica, 2005—06. Contbr. articles to profl. jours. Named Article Incentive Program Competition winner, Calif. Dermatologic Surgery Rev., 2006; recipient Alumni Svc. award, SUNY Downstate Health Sci. Ctr., 2001, Lifetime Membership award, Downstate Student Ctr., 2001. Mem.: L.A. Met. Dermatologic Soc., Calif. Soc. Dermatology and Dermatologic Surgery, Pacific Dermatologic Assn., Am. Soc. Dermatologic Surgery, Am. Coll. of Mohs Micrographic Surgery and Cutaneous Oncology, Am. Acad. Dermatology. Achievements include invention of Methods and related compositions for reduction of fat and skin tightening. Personal E-mail: arotunda@hotmail.com.

**ROTUNDA, DONALD THEODORE,** public relations consultant; b. Blue Island, Ill., Feb. 14, 1945; s. Nicholas and Frances (Manna) R. BA, Georgetown U., 1967; MA, London Sch. Econs., 1968, PhD, 1972. Analyst NASA, Washington, 1972; lectr. in econs. U. DC, 1973; legis. asst. Ho. of Reps., Washington, 1974-76, economist budget com., 1977; mgmt. analyst Office Mgmt. and Budget, Washington, 1977-81; cons., 1981-82; mgr. editorial svcs. United Technologies Corp., Hartford, Conn., 1982-87, Pepsico, Inc., Purchase, NY, 1987-89, Union Carbide Corp., Danbury, Conn., 1989-90; dir. editorial svcs. Martin Marietta, Bethesda, Md., 1990-92; cons. pub. rels., 1992—. Contbr. numerous articles to Washington Post, New Republic, Saturday Rev. Roman Catholic. Home: 4431 Klingle St NW Washington DC 20016-3578 Office Phone: 202-966-4855. Personal E-mail: donaldrotunda@verizon.net.

**ROTUNDA, RONALD DANIEL,** law educator, consultant; b. Blue Island, Ill., Feb. 14, 1945; s. Nicholas and Frances (Manna) R.; children: Nora, Mark. AB magna cum laude, Harvard U., 1967, JD magna cum laude, 1970. Bar: N.Y. 1971, U.S. Ct. Appeals (2d cir.) 1971, U.S. Ct. Appeals (D.C. cir.) 1971, U.S. Ct. Appeals (7th cir.) 1990, U.S. Supreme Ct. 1974, Ill. 1975. Law clk. U.S. Ct. Appeals (2d cir.), 1970-71; assoc. Wilmer, Cutler & Pickering, Washington, 1971-73; asst. majority counsel Watergate Com., U.S. Senate, Washington, 1973-74; spl. cons. Office of Ind. Counsel, Washington, 1997-99; asst. prof. U. Ill. Coll. Law, Champaign, 1974-77, assoc. prof., 1977-80, prof., 1980-93, Albert E. Jenner, Jr. prof. of law, 1993—2002; found. prof. law George Mason U., Arlington, Va., 2002—06, prof., 2006—; spl. counsel Dept. Def., 2004—05. Vis. prof. law European U. Inst., Florence, Italy, 1981, U. Ala., 1999; mem. profl. responsibility exam. com. Nat. Conf. Bar Examiners, 1980-87; constl. advisor Supreme Nat. Coun. Cambodia, 1993; cons. Supreme Ct. Moldova, 1996, vis. sr. fellow in constnl. studies Cato Inst., 2000. Author: (with Morgan) Problems and Materials of Professional Responsibility, 1976, 9th edit., 2006; (with Nowak and Young) Constitutional Law, 1978, (with Nowak) 2d edit., 1983, 7th edit., 2004, Modern Constitutional Law: Cases and Materials, 1981, 7th edit., 2003, (with Nowak) Treatise on Constitutional Law, 4 vols., 2d edit., 1992, (with Nowak) vols., 3d edit., 1999, Legal Ethics, 2002, 2d edit., 2002, 3rd. edit, 2005. Fulbright research scholar, Italy, 1981, Venezuela, 1986. Fellow Am. Bar Found. (life), Ill. Bar Found. (life); mem. Am. Law Inst. Roman Catholic. Office: George Mason Univ Law Sch 3301 Fairfax Dr Arlington VA 22201 Business E-mail: rrotunda@gmu.edu.

**ROUB, BRYAN R(OGER),** electronics executive; b. Berea, Ohio, May 1, 1941; s. Bernard Augustus and Pearl Irene (Koeblitz) R.; m. Judith Elaine Penman, June 19, 1965; children: Paul, Bradley, Michael. Student, Ohio Wesleyan U., 1959-62; BS, Ohio State U., 1966; MBA, U. Pa., 1978. Mem. audit staff Ernst & Ernst, Cleve., 1966-70; asst. contr. Midland-Ross, Cleve., 1970-73, contr., 1973-81, v.p. 1977-81, sr. v.p., 1981-82, exec. v.p. fin., 1982-84; sr. v.p. fin. Harris Corp., Melbourne, Fla., 1984-93, sr. v.p., CFO, 1993—2006. Bd. dirs. Fairchild Semicondr.; mem. fin. coun. II Machinery and Allied Products Inst., Washington, 1977-84, coun. I, 1984—2004, vice chmn., 1994-95, chmn., 1996-98; mem. conf. bd. coun. CFOs, 1993-96. Mem. adv. coun. Coll. Adminstry. Scis., Ohio State U., 1978-81; mem. citizen's adv. coun. Westlake (Ohio) Schs., 1981-83; trustee Alcoholism Svcs. Cleve., 1982-84; mem. devel. bd. St. John's Hosp., 1983-84; pres. Westridge Homeowners' Assn., 1977; dir., treas. Tortoise Island Homeowners' Assn., 1988-90; bd. dirs. Easter Seal Soc. of Brevard County, 1993-98. Mem. AICPA, Ohio Soc. CPAs, Fin. Execs. Inst. (treas. N.E. Ohio chpt. 1976-78, bd. dirs. 1980-81, 83-84, v.p. 1981-82, pres. 1982-83, bd. dirs. Orlando chpt. 1984—, v.p. 1985-86, pres. 1986-87, nat. bd. dirs. 1987-90, area v.p. 1990-91, chmn. budget and fin. com. 1988-89, chmn. planning com. 1995-97, v.p. at large 1997-99, vice-chmn. 1999-2000, chmn. 2000-01, office of chmn. 1997-2002), Fin. Execs. Rsch. Found. (trustee 1994-97, 1999-2000), Westwood Country Club, Eau Gallie Yacht Club (bd. govs., treas. 1990-92), Suntree Country Club. Address: 10280 S Tropical Trail Merritt Island FL 32952-6919 Personal E-mail: brrathome@aol.com.

**ROUDEBUSH, JAMES GORDON,** career military officer; B of Medicine, U. Nebr., 1971, MD, 1975; M in Pub. Health, U. Tex., San Antonio, 1983; attended, Aerospace Medicine Primary Course, Brooks AFB, Tex., 1980, Tri-Service Combat Casualty Care Course, Fort Sam Houston, 1981; attended by seminar, Air War Coll., 1988; attended, Inst. for Fed. Health Care Executives, George Washington U., Washington, DC, 1989; student, Nat. War Coll., Fort Lesley J. McNair, Washington, DC, 1991—92; attended, Exec. Mgmt. Course, Def. Sys. Mgmt. Coll., Fort Belvoir, Va., 1993. Commd. 2d lt. USAF, 1972, advanced through grades to lt. gen., 2006; resident in family practice Wright-Patterson USAF Med. Ctr., Wright-Patterson AFB, Ohio, 1975-78; physician in family practice, flight surgeon USAF Hosp., Francis E. Warren AFB, Wyo., 1978-82; resident in aerospace medicine USAF Sch. of Aerospace Medicine, Brooks AFB, Tex., 1982—84; chief of aerospace medicine 81st Tactical Fighter Wing, RAF Bentwaters, England, 1984-86, comdr., 1986-88, 36th Tactical Fighter Wing Hosp., Bitburg AB, Germany, 1988-91; vice comdr. Human Systems Ctr., Brooks AFB, Tex., 1992—94; command surgeon U.S. Ctrl. Command, MacDill AFB, Fla., 1994-97, Pacific Air Forces, Hickam AFB, Hawaii, 1997-98; comdr. 89th Med. Group, Andrews AFB, 1998-2000; command surgeon U.S. Transp. Command and Hdqs. Air Mobility Command, Scotts AFB, Ill., 2000—01; dep. surgeon gen. USAF, Bolling AFB, Washington, DC, 2001—06, surgeon gen., 2006—. Decorated Legion of Merit with oak leaf cluster, Def. Superior Svc. Mmdal with oak leaf cluster, Meritorious Svc. medal with two oak leaf clusters, Air Force Commendation medal, Joint Meritorious Unit award, Air Force Outstanding Unit award with oak leaf cluster, Nat. Def. Svc. Medal with bronze star, Southwest Asia Svc. medal with bronze star, Air Force Overseas Long Tour Ribbon with oak leaf cluster, Air Force Longevity Svc. award Ribbon with silver oak leaf cluster, Small Arms Expert Markmanship Ribbon, Air Force Training Ribbon, Chief Physician Badge, Chief Flight Surgeon Badge. Mem. Soc. of USAF Flight Surgeons, Aerospace Med. Assn., Internat. Assn. of Mil. Flight Surgeons Pilots, Assn. of Mil. Surgeons of the U.S., Air Force Assn., Am. Coll. of Preventive Medicine, Am. Coll. of Physician Execs., AMA.*

**ROUDENKO, SVETLANA,** mathematics professor; PhD, Mich. State U., 2002. Asst. rsch. prof. Duke U., Durham, NC, 2002—05; asst. prof. Ariz. State U., Tempe, 2004—. Analysis Program grantee, NSF, 2004—06. Office: Ariz State U Dept Math Tempe AZ 85287-1804

**ROUECHE, JOHN EDWARD, II,** education educator, director; b. Sept. 3, 1938; s. John Edward and Mary (Harris) R.; m. Suanne Davis; 1 stepchild, Robin Sue Maca; children by previous marriage: Michelle Renee, John Edward III. BA, Lenoir Rhyne Coll., Hickory, N.C., 1960, LittD, 2001; LHD, Lenoir Rhyne Coll., 2001; MA, Appalachian Coll., Boone, N.C., 1961; PhD, Fla. State U., 1964. Dean Gaston Coll., Gastonia, NC, 1964-67; assoc. rsch. educator UCLA, 1967-69; dir. jr. coll. divsn. Nat. Lab. Higher Edn., 1968-71; assoc. prof. edn. Duke U.; prof. edn., dir. c.c. leadership program U. Tex., Austin, 1971—, Sid W. Richardson regents chair, 1987—. Mem. chancellor's coun. U. Tex., 1990—, U. Tex. Littlefield Soc., 1992—; lectr. Earl Pullias lectr. U. So. Calif., 1992, Coll. Bd. Disting. Lectr. N.Y.C., 1993, Frances Crain Cook Disting. Lectr. U. Tex., 1994; internat. adv. bd. Gt. Am. Res. Ins. Co., 1988-94; co-chair Nat. Adv. Bd. for C.C.s, Invest Learning Corp., 1993-96; chair nat. adv. com. Kaplan Ednl. Partnerships, 1995-98; La Platica Disting. lectr. Ariz. State U., 1999; chmn. nat. adv. bd. 3-D Internat., 2000-. C.C. editor Jossey-Bass Publs., 1971-82; editor Creative Teaching Series, Media Systems Corp., 1980-85; mem. editl. bd. C.C. Times, C.C. Jour., 1990-94, others; author 35 books, including Profiles of Excellence in America's Schools, 1986, Access with Excellence, 1987, Shared Vision, 1989, Teaching as Leading, 1990, Under-representation: A Question of Diversity, 1991, Between a Rock and a Hard Place, 1993, The Company We Keep, 1995, Strangers in Their Own Land: Part Time Faculty, 1995, Embracing the Tiger: The Effectiveness Debate and the Community College, 1997, High Stakes, High Performance: Making Remedial Education Work, 1999, In Pursuit of Excellence: The Community College of Denver, 2001, Practical Magic: On the Front Lines of Teaching Excellence, 2003, Opting for Opportunity: Entrepreneurship in the Community College, 2005; contbr. over

150 articles and monographs. Pres. Doss Sch. PTA, 1974-75; chmn. bd. N.W. Hills United Meth. Ch., 1973-76. Recipient Disting. Svc. award Nat. Coun. Univs. and Colls., 1984, Disting. Rsch. Publ. award, 1990, 93, 95, 97, Outstanding Alumnus award Appalachian State U., 1979, Disting. Grad. award Fla. State U., 1981, Tchg. Excellence award U. Tex., 1982, Outstanding Rschr. award, 1985, Excellence award for outstanding learned article U.S. Edn. Press Assn., 1983, Disting. Rsch. award Nat. Assn. Devel. Edn. 1984-86, Disting. Rsch. Publ. award Nat. Coun. Student Devel., 1987, Disting. Rsch. award Nat. Coun. Staff, Program, and Orgn. Devel., B. Lamar Johnson Nat. Leadership award League for Innovation in the Cmty. Coll., 1988, Disting. Svc. & Leadership award CCP, INC., 1993, Disting. Faculty award U. Tex., 1994, Disting. Rsch. award Interassn. Student Devel. Orgns., 1995, Chancellor's Leadership award State of Ala., 1995, Career Rsch. Excellence award U. Tex., 1998, Disting. Grad. award Lenoir-Rhyne Coll., 2000; named lifetime amb. for N.C., 1978; Kellogg fellow, 1962-64, Disting. Internat. Leadership award Govt. of South Africa, 2000, 01, Disting. Nat. Svc. award Nat. Coun. Instrnl. Adminstrs., 2001, Disting. Leadership award Tex. Assn. Cmty. Colls., 2003 Star Leadership award Nat. Hispanic Border Inst., 2005, Mirabeau Lamar award Assn. Tex. Colls. and Univs., 2005. Mem. Am. Assn. Cmty. and Jr. Colls. (bd. dirs. 1989-94, Nat. Leadership award 1986, Disting. Rsch. award coun. colls. and univs. 1990, 94, 96, dist. rsch. sr. scholar award 1994, 96, nat. student devel. inter-assn. rsch. award 1995-96), Am. Assn. Higher Edn., Coun. Univs. and Colls. (past pres., bd. dirs.), Phi Beta Kappa, Phi Delta Kappa. Home: 4700 Lookout Mountain Cv Austin TX 78731-3654 Office: U Tex Austin One University Sta D5600 Austin TX 78712-0378 Office Phone: 512-471-7545. Business E-Mail: roueche@mail.utexas.edu.

**ROUGHGARDEN, JOAN E.,** biology professor; b. Paterson, NJ, Mar. 13, 1946; BS in Biology, U. Rochester, NY, 1968, AB with highest honors in Philosophy, 1968; MS/PhD in Biology, Harvard U., Cambridge, Mass., 1971. Asst. prof., instr. biology U. Mass., 1970—72; prof. biol. scis. and geophysics Stanford U., Calif., 1972—. Dir., founder Stanford U. Earth Systems Prog., 1992—99; vis. rsch. fellow Merton Coll., U. Oxford, 1994; mem. sci. adv. bd. Pacific Ocean Conservation Network, Calif., 1997—99, Channel Islands Nat. Marine Sanctuary, Santa Barbara, Calif., 1999—2001; ctr. fellow Nat. Ctr. Ecol. Synthesis and Analysis U. Calif., Santa Barbara, 1998. Contbr. articles to profl. jours.; mem. editl. bd.: Theoretical Population Biology, 1975—86, Oecologia, 1979—82, Am. Naturalist, 1984—89; author: Theory of Population Genetics and Evolutionary Ecology: An Intro., 1979, Anolis Lizards of the Caribbean: Ecology, Evolution and Plate Tectonics, 1995, Primer of Ecol. Theory, 1998, Evolution's Rainbow: Diversity, Gender and Sexuality in Nature and People, 2004 (Stonewall prize for nonfiction, Am. Libr. Assn., 2005); co-author: Sci. of Ecology, 1987; co-editor: Perspectives in Ecol. Theory, 1989. Grantee Guggenheim Found. fellowship, 1985. Fellow: Am. Acad. Arts & Scis. Office: Dept Biol Scis Stanford U Stanford CA 94305-5020 E-mail: joan.roughgarden@stanford.edu.*

**ROUHANI, SHAHROKH,** civil engineering environmental educator, consultant; b. Tehran, Iran, Mar. 28, 1956; came to U.S., 1974; s. Aboutorab and Parirokh (Garakani) R.; m. Firouzeh Yekta, Aug. 18, 1983; children: Nina, Shiva. BSCE, U. Calif., Berkeley, 1978, BA in Econs., 1978; SM in Engring., Harvard U., 1980, PhD in Environ. Scis., 1983. Registered profl. engr., Ga. Asst. prof. Ga. Inst. Tech., Atlanta, 1983-90, assoc. prof. civil engring., 1990-96; sr. cons. Dames & Moore, Atlanta, 1990-95; pres. New Fields, Inc., Atlanta, 1995—. NSF vis. scientist Ctr. Geostats., Paris Sch. of Mines, 1987-88; expert mem. ASTM, EPA, U.S. Geol. Survey, Dept. Def. Geostats. Standardization Com., 1991-96. Co-author: Ground Water, 1991; contbr. articles to profl. publs., chpts. to books, also numerous reports, papers in field. Mem. ASCE (award 1991, chmn. nat. ground water hydrology 1991, chmn. task com. on geostatis. techniques in geohydrology 1987-89, sec. water resources com. Ga. sect. 1988, spl. session organizer 1989, 90, contact mem. task com. 1988-90, symposium organizer 1991), Am. Geophys. Union (assoc. editor Water Resources Rsch. 1989-94), Internat. Water Resources Assn., Am. Water Resources Assn., N.Am. Coun. on Geostats., Internat. Geostatis. Assn., Phi Beta Kappa, Tau Beta Pi, Chi Epsilon, Sigma Chi. Office: Newfields Inc 1349 W Peachtree St NW Ste 2000 Atlanta GA 30309-2926 Office Phone: 404-347-9050. Business E-Mail: srouhani@newfields.com.

**ROUINTREE, JAMES PAUL,** retired music educator; b. West Plains, Mo., Sept. 24, 1933; s. Aubrey Thadeus and Helene Elizabeth Rouintree; m. Patricia Earle Thompson, Feb. 19, 1955; children: Kevin Paul, Darren Ray. B.Mus.Edn., Drury Coll., Springfield, Mo., 1954; MS in Music Edn., U. Ill., Urbana, 1962; EdD in Music Edn., U. Ill., 1975. Cert. K-12 tchr. Mo., Ill. K-12 tchr., dir. vocal and instrumental music Mountain View (Mo.) Pub. Schs., 1957—61; dir. bands Edison Jr. H.S./Champaign H.S., Ill., 1961—69; faculty instrumental music Anderson U., Ind., 1969—98; condr. Anderson Symphony, 1971—72; dir. music Arrow Hts./West Anderson Ch. of God, 1971—85; condr. Anderson U. Wind Ensemble, 1969—98; ret., 1998. Choir dir. Glenstone Bapt. Sch., Springfield, 1952—53; trombonist 326th and Armed Forces Radio Jazz Band, Ft. Leonardwood, Mo., 1954—57; prin. trombone Anderson Symphony Orch., 1973—91. Condr., dir. Anderson Cmty. Band, 1975—85. With U.S. Army, 1954—57. Mem.: Coll. Band Dirs. Nat. Assn., Internat. Trombone Assn., Music Educators Nat. Conf., Kappa Kappa Psi, Alpha Lambda Chi. Republican. Ch. Of God Anderson. Avocations: gardening, farming. Home: 2239 Tartan Rd Anderson IN 46012

**ROUKEMA, MARGARET SCAFATI,** congresswoman; b. West Orange, N.J., Sept. 19, 1929; d. Claude Thomas and Margaret (D'Alessio) Scafati; m. Richard W. Roukema, Aug. 23, 1951; children: Margaret, Todd (dec.), Gregory. BA with honors in History and Polit. Sci. Montclair State Coll., 1951, postgrad. in history and guidance, 1951-53; postgrad. program in city and regional planning, Rutgers U., 1975. Tchr. history, govt., public schs., Livingston and Ridgewood, N.J., 1951-55; mem. U.S. Congress from 7th N.J. dist., Washington, 1981—83, U.S. Congress from 5th N.J. dist., Washington, 1983—2003; vice chair fin. svcs. com., chair housing and community opportunity subcom.; mem. banking com., edn. and the workforce com. Vice pres. Ridgewood Bd. Edn., 1970-73; bd. dirs., co-founder Ridgewood Sr. Citizens Housing Corp.; chairwoman Fin. Inst. and Consumer Credit Sub. Com. U.S. Congress; sponcer Family Med. Leave U.S. Congress; lectr. Rutgers Univ. Trustee Spring House, Paramus, N.J.; trustee Leukemia Soc. No. N.J., Family Counseling Service for Ridgewood and Vicinity; mem. Bergen County (N.J.) Republican Com.; NW Bergen County campaign mgr. for gubernatorial candidate Tom Kean, 1977; bd. mem. Children's Aid and Family Svcs., The Red Cross, Ramapo Coll. Mem. Bus. and Profl. Women's Orgn. Clubs: Coll. of Ridgewood, Ridgewood Rep. Republican. *I have served in several roles in my life. Wife, mother, teacher, public servant. All are personally rewarding; each affords the opportunity to help others in need and to enrich the lives of those around you. As a member of Congress, I find the most rewards are in the knowledge that I can truly make a difference and improve the lives of thousands of people. The challenges are frequently insurmountable, but the rewards are incalculable.*

**ROULAC, STEPHEN E.,** real estate consultant; b. San Francisco, Aug. 15, 1945; s. Phil Williams and Elizabeth (Young) R.; children: Arthur, Fiona. BA, Pomona Coll., 1967; MBA with distinction, Harvard Grad. Sch. Bus. Administrn., 1970; JD, U. Calif., Berkeley, 1976; PhD, Stanford U., 1978. CPA, Hawaii. Asst. constrn. supt., foreman, adminstr. Roulac Constrn. Co., Pasadena, Calif., 1963-66; rsch. asst. Econs. Rsch. Assocs., L.A., 1966-67; assoc. economist Urbanomics Rsch. Assocs., Claremont, Calif., 1967; acquisition auditor Litton Industries Inc., Chgo., Beverly Hills, 1967-68; tax cons. Lybrand, Ross Bros. and Montgomery, L.A., 1968; cons. to constrn. group and corp. planning dept. Owens-Corning Fiberglas Corp., Toledo, 1969-70; CEO Questor Assocs., San Francisco 1972-83; chmn. nat. mgmt. adv. svcs. Kenneth Leventhal & Co., 1983-84; pres. Stephen E. Roulac & Co., 1985-86; mng. ptnr. Roulac Group of Deloitte Haskins & Sells (Deloitte & Touche), 1987-91; CEO The Roulac Group, Larkspur, Calif., 1992—. Strategic fin. econ. and transactions cons. Roulac Capitol Mkt. Strategies, Roulac Capitol Flows; expert witness, preparer econ. analyses for legal matters including civil trial of Irvine Co., Jewell et. al. vs. Bank of Am., Tchrs. vs. Olympia &

York, Calif. Legis., Calif. Corps. Dept., Midwest Securities Commrs. Assn., Nat. Assn. Securities Dealers, SEC, Dept. of Labor, HUD; advisor to investment arm of Asian country, Calif. Pub. Employees Retirement System, U.S. Dept. Labor, numerous others; adj. prof. Tex. A&M U., 1986, U. Chgo., 1985, UCLA, 1983-84, Stanford Grad. Sch. Bus., 1970-79, Pacific Coast Banking Sch., 1978, Hastings Coll. Law, 1977-78, U. Calif., Berkeley, 1972-77, Calif. State U., 1970-71, Northeastern U., 1969-70; keynote speaker, instr. continuing edn. sessions, program chmn., corps., orgns. Author: Real Estate Investments Digest: Principles and Applications, 1972, Case Studies in Property Development, 1973, Syndication Landmarks, 1974, Tax Shelter Sale-Leaseback Financing: The Economic Realities, 1976, Modern Real Estate Investment: An Institutional Approach, 1976, (with Sherman Maisel) Real Estate Investment and Finance, 1976 (1976 Bus. Book of Yr. The Libr. Jour.); editor-in-chief, pub. Calif. Bicyclist, 1988-95, Tex. Bicyclist, 1989-94, Roulac's Strategic Real Estate, 1979-89; columnist Forbes, 1983, 84, 87, 92, 93, Intuition Network, Ctr Real Estate Rsch. Nortwestern U., Nat. Bureau Real Estate Rsch., New Leaders, World 2000, NACORE/ARES Corp. Rsch. Found., Mystery Sch.; mem. editorial adv. bd. Am. Real Estate and Urban Econs. Assn. Jour., 1977-81, Housing Devel. Reporter, 1978-80, Fin. Edn. Jour., 1976-70, Jour. Housing Rsch., 1996—, Jour. Real Estated Edn. and Practice, 1996—, Jour. Real Estate Lit., 1996—, Jour. Property Valuation and Investment, 1992—, Real Estate Workouts and Asset Mgmt., 1992—; assoc. editor Real Estate Rev., 1993—; editor Jour. Real Estate Rsch., 1992—; contbg. editor Real Estate Law Jour., 1973-78, Real Estate Rev., 1973-75; spl. issue editor Calif. Mgmt. Rev., 1976; editor: Real Estate Syndication Digest, 1971-72, Notable Syndications Sourcebook, 1972, Real Estate Securities and Syndication: A Workbook, 1973, Due Diligence in Real Estate Transactions, 1974, Real Estate Venture Analysis, 1974, Real Estate Securities Regulation Sourcebook, 1975, Questor Real Estate Investment Manager Profiles, 1982, Questor Real Estate Securities Yearbook, 1980-85, Retail Giants and Real Estate, 1986, Roulac's Top Real Estate Brokers, 1984-88, (monograph) Ethics in Real Estate; contbr. articles to profl. jours., newspapers; cassettes; frequent appearer on TV shows including MacNeil/Lehrer Newshour, 1986, Cable News Network, 1987, ABC TV, 1987, KCBS Radio, 1986, WABC Radio, Dallas, 1986. Mem. real estate adv. com. to Calif. Commr. Corps., 1973, Calif. Corp. Commr.'s Blue Ribbon Com. on Projections and Track Records, 1973-74; mem. adv. bd. Nat. Bicycle Month, League of Am. Wheelmen, Ctr. for Real Estate Rsch. Kellogg Grad. Sch. Mgmt., Northwestern U. Named Highest Instr. Student Teaching Evaluations, Schs. Bus. Adminstrn., U. Calif., Berkeley, 1975-76; named to Pomona Coll. Athletic Hall of Fame, 1981; W.T. Grant fellow Harvard U., 1969-70,; George F. Baker scholar Harvard Grad. Sch. Bus. Adminstrn., 1970; Stanford U. Grad. Sch. Bus. fellow, 1970-71. Mem. Strategic Mgmt. Soc., Am. Acad. Mgmt., Am. Fin. Assn., Am. Planning Assn, European Real Estate Soc., Internat. Real Estate Soc., Inst. Mgmt. Cons., ISSSEEM, Soc. Sci. Exploration, Am. Real Estate and Urban Econs. Assn., Intuition Network (bd. dirs.), World Future Soc. (exec. com. and adv. bd. World 2000), Am. Econ. Assn., Am. Real Estate Soc. (pres. 1995-96, award for best paper presented in ann. meeting, 1995, 96), Noetic Sci., Nat. Bur. Real Estate Rsch. (founder, bd. dirs.), Harvard Club N.Y., L.A. Adventures Club. Avocations: art, antiquarian books, reading, bicycling. Office: The Roulac Group 709 5th Ave San Rafael CA 94901-3202

**ROULEAU, R. MICHAEL,** retail executive; Co-founder, pres. Office Warehouse; exec. v.p. store ops. Lowe's, 1992-95, pres. contractor yard divsn., 1995-96; CEO Michaels Stores, Inc., Irving, Tex., 1996—, pres., 1997—. Office: Michaels Stores Inc 8000 Bent Branch Dr Irving TX 75063

**ROUMAN, JOHN CHRIST,** classics educator; b. Tomahawk, Wis., May 1, 1926; s. Christ and Soteria (Dedes) R. BA in Greek, Carleton Coll., 1950; MA in Greek, Columbia U., 1951; student, Rutgers U., 1951-53, U. Kiel, Germany, 1956-57, U. Minn., Mpls., 1959-60; PhD in Classics, U. Wis., 1965. German tchr. Seton Hall Preparatory Sch., South Orange, NJ, 1954-56; ancient history tchr. Malverne (N.Y.) High Sch., 1957-59; tchg. asst. in ancient history U. Wis., Madison, 1960-61, rsch. asst. in ancient history, 1961-65; rsch. asst. in Greek epigraphy Inst. Advanced Study, Princeton, NJ, 1962-63; asst. prof. classics U. N.H., Durham, 1965-71, assoc. prof., 1971-91, prof., 1991—, prof. classics emeritus, 1999, co-chmn. Spanish and classics depts., mem. adv. bd. Prof. John C. Rouman classical lectr. series, 1997—. Examiner N.H. State Bd. Edn. in Latin and Greek, 1979-80; judge Warren H. Held Jr. Exam-Contests in Latin and Mythology, 1988—; cons. Nat. Classical Greek Examination, 1980; presenter, lectr. in field; mem. adv. bd. Christos and Mary Papoutsy Disting. Endowed Chair in Bus. Ethics, N.H. Coll./So. N.H. U., 2000—03; exec. bd. Hellenic Soc. PAIDEIA, NH, 2001. Active Colovos Rd. Com., 1981-82. With USN, 1944-46. Fulbright scholar U. Kiel, 1956-57; recipient Disting. Tchg. award U. N.H. Alumni Assn., 1985, Pericles award Am. Hellenic Ednl. Progressive Assn. and Daus. of Penelope, 1993, Profile of Svc. award U. N.H. Aumni Assn., 2000; Prof. John C. Rouman Classical Lecture Series named in his honor. Mem. Am. Classical League (rep. to TCNE at ann. meeting 1978, mem. fin. com. 1984-93, treas. 1982-83, contbg. editor newsletter, 2005—), Am. Philol. Assn. (Nat. Excellence in Tchg. Classics award, 1991), Archaeol. Inst. Am., Classical Assn. Can., Classical Assn. New Eng. (mem. exec. com. at-large 1981-84, mem. nominating com. 1983-84, 86-87, pres. 1987-88, Barlow-Beach award 1991, mem. ad hoc com. on elections and appointments), Medieval Acad. Am., Modern Greek Studies Assn., Nat. Assn. Advisors Health Professions, NH Classical Assn. (mem. exec. com. 1965—, chair nominating com. 1986—), Strafford County Greco-Roman Found. (pres. 1978—), Vergilian Soc. Am., Carleton Coll. Alumni Assn. (Alumni award for Dist. Achievement 2000), Phi Kappa Theta (faculty advisor, 1982—, chmn. nat. bd., 1993-94, nat. found. 1993—, Man of Achievement award 2000, Chpt. Advisor award 2002). Independent. Greek Orthodox. Personal E-mail: Jrouman@comcast.net.

**ROUMANI-DENN, VIVIENNE RACHEL,** library and information scientist, consultant; d. Josef and Elisa Tammam Roumani; m. Morton M. Denn; children: Aryeh B. Bourkoff, Dania T. Matheos, Natan D. Bourkoff. BA, Simmons Coll., Boston, 1971; MLS, U. Md., College Park, 1984; M in Adminstrv. Sci., Johns Hopkins U., Balt., 1990. Head interlibrary loan Libr. of Congress, Washington, 1989—90; head interlibrary loan and document delivery svcs. U. Calif., Berkeley, 1990—93, earth scis. and maps libr., 1993—97, Judaica libr., 1997—99; founding dir. libr. and archives Am. Sephardi Fedn., NYC, 1999—2000, exec. dir., 2000—03; pres. VR Consulting, NYC, 2003—. Author: (online publication) The Last Jews of Libya, 1999, (documentary film), 2006; contbr. chapters to books, articles to profl. jours. Exec. bd. Oakland (Calif.) Hebrew Day Sch., 1996—99, U. Calif. Berkeley Hillel, 1996—99, Ctr. for Jewish Living and Learning, Berkeley, 1996—99, Jewish Inst. Pitigliano, Italy, Washington, 2000, Friends of Gerona, Spain, NYC, 2000—00. Office: VR Consulting 140 Riverside Dr New York NY 10024 Office Phone: 917-957-4132. Business E-Mail: vroumani@nyc.rr.com.

**ROUMBOS, MARIA K.,** elementary school educator; b. Flushing, NY, Nov. 22, 1970; d. Kostas J. and Alexandra K. Roumbos; m. Mark A. Cichon, July 2, 1995; children: Michael Roumbos Cichon, Marissa Roumbos Cichon. BS in Elem. Edn. summa cum laude, Adelphi U., 1991, MA in Secondary Edn. in Math. summa cum laude, 1993. Cert. tchr. early childhood edn., elem. edn., math. edn. Tchr. St. Nicholas Ch. Sch., Flushing, NY, 1986—, asst. dir., 1990—; tchr. Floral Park-Bellerose Sch. Dist., 1991—. Tutor in field, NY, 1991—2001. Recipient Pres.'s Achievement award, Queens Coll., 1989, Honors in Sci. and Math cert. merit, Soc. Women Engrs., 1991, Merit award, N.Y.C. Assn. Tchrs., 1988, Scholastic Achievement award, N.Y. Gov.'s Com., 1991, Merit award, Hellenic U. Club of N.Y., 1993, Outstanding Achievement award, Greek Lang. Inst., 1988, Internat. award for Striving for Peace on Earth, N.Y. Dist. of Kiwanis, 1987; Paul Douglas scholar, Empire State Challenger scholar, United Fedn. Tchrs. scholar, N.Y. State scholar. Mem.: Inst. for Math. and Sci. Studies (life), Internat. Baccalaureate Scholars (life), Nat. Honor Soc. (life; chpt. co-pres. 1987—88), Kappa Delta Pi (life). Democrat. Greek Orthodox. Avocations: reading, photography, painting, arts-n-crafts, gardening.

**ROUNDS, MICHAEL,** governor; b. Huron, S.D., Oct. 24, 1954; m. Jean Rounds; 4 children. Degree in Polit. Sci., SD State U., Brookings. Former ptnr. Fischer, Rounds & Assocs., Inc., part owner; state senator Dist. 24, 1991—2001; senate majority leader State of S.D., gov., 2003—. Bd. pres. Oahe YMCA; v.p. Home and Sch. Assn. St. Joseph Sch.; pres. Pierre-Ft. Pierre Exch. Club. Mem.: Ducks Unlimited, Knights of Columbus, Pierre Elks Lodge. Republican. Roman Catholic. Avocations: racquetball, hunting, boating, camping. Office: Office of Gov 500 E Capitol Ave Pierre SD 57501 Office Phone: 605-773-3212. Office Fax: 605-773-5844.*

**ROUNDTREE, JACQUELINE WASHINGTON,** public relations executive, government official, consultant; b. Rock Hill, S.C., Dec. 19, 1949; d. Jack H. Washington and Mary (Washington) McGhee; m. Joe L. Bolder, Oct. 17, 1969 (div. 1983); m. Eugene V.N. Roundtree, Nov. 12, 1983; 1 child, Mary Margaret. B.A., Howard U., 1971, Ph.D., 1975, J.D., 1990. Reporter, editor Washington Star, 1969-78; part-time coll. instr. Howard U., Washington, 1975-81; spl. asst. sec. Dept. Commerce, Washington, 1978-80; dep. chief pub. affairs Minority Bus. Devel. Agy., Washington, 1980-82; regional pub. affairs officer HUD, Boston, 1983—; pub. relations cons. United Community Planning Corp. Boston, 1982-83, All-Stainless Corp., Hingham, Mass., 1982—, APR Co., 1985—, ptnr., 1985-89. Bd. dirs. Urban League Guild Eastern Mass., 1982-87; Md. state commr. Internat. Women's Yr., 1977-78; vol. United Way Mass. Bay, 1990—; bd. dirs. Mass. Assn. for Mental Health, 1985—, chmn. communications com., 1984—; citizens adv. com. Mass. Probation Commn., 1986—; trustee South Shore Natural Sci. Ctr., 1988—; corporator Boston Children's Mus., 1989—. Recipient Balt./Washington Newspaper Guild Front Page award for news series, 1972; named Outstanding Employee, HUD, 1985, 89. Mem. Women in Communications (bd. dirs., newsletter editor 1985), Howard U. Alumni Club, Alpha Kappa Alpha, Gamma Sigma Sigma (Alumnus of Yr. 1981). Republican. Baptist. Avocations: reading, writing; golf. Office: HUD 451 7th St SW Washington DC 20410

**ROUNICK, JACK A.,** lawyer, clothing retail executive; b. Phila., June 5, 1935; s. Philip and Nettie (Brownstein) Rounick; m. Noreen A. Garrigan, Sept. 4, 1970; children: Ellen, Eric, Amy, Michelle. BBA, U. Mich., 1956; JD, U. Pa., 1959. Bar: Pa. 1960, US Dist. Ct. (ea. dist.) Pa. 1960, diplomate: Am. Coll. Family Trial Lawyers. Spl. asst. atty. gen., 1963-71; ptnr. Israelit & Rounick, 1960-67, Moss & Rounick, 1968-69, Moss, Rounick & Hurowitz, Norristown, Pa., 1969-72, Moss & Rounick, Norristown, 1972-73, Pechner, Dorfman, Wolffe, Rounick and Cabot, Norristown, 1973-87; v.p., gen. counsel Martin Lawrence Ltd. Edits., Inc., 1987-93, dir., 1984—95; asst. sec., dir. Deb Shops, Inc., 1974—; counsel to firm Wolf Block, Schorr & Solis-Cohen LLP, 1997—2006; counsel Flamm, Boroff & Bacine, P.C., Blue Bell, Pa., 2006—. Author: Pennsylvania Matrimonial Practice, 6 vols., 1982; editor: Pa. Family Lawyer, 1980—87; bd. editors Family Adv. Fin. chmn. Pa. Young Reps., 1964—66, treas., 1966—68, chmn., 1968—70. Recipient Boss of Yr. award, Montgomery County Legal Secs. Assn., 1970, cert. of appreciation, Pa. Bar Inst., 1980. Fellow: Am. Acad. Matrimonial Lawyers (pres. Pa. chpt. 1982—84, gov. 1983—85, v.p. 1985—87, chmn. bd. rev. 1997—98), Internat. Acad. Matrimonial Lawyers; mem.: FLS, ABA (coun. family law sect. 1982—87, coun. 2000—03), Scope and Correlation Com. (chmn. 2005—06), Family Adv. (bd. editors), Am. Coll. Family Trial Lawyers (licentiate), Montgomery Bar Assn., Pa. Bar Assn. (past chmn. family law sect. 1978—80, Spl. Achievement award 1979—80), Friends of Hebrew U. (bd. dirs. 1987—93, nat. coun. trustees 1987—93, pres. Phila. chpt. 1988—91, v.p. 1990—91, bd. trustees 1987—2006). Republican. Jewish. Office: 794 Penllyn Pike Blue Bell PA 19422 Office Phone: 267-419-1504. Business E-Mail: jrounick@flammlaw.com.

**ROUNSAVILLE, KEITH EUGENE,** lawyer; b. Ancon, Panama, Aug. 6, 1945; s. William Russell Rounsaville and Dorothy Naletta Chambers; m. Linda Ann White, Feb. 14, 1976 (div. Oct. 1, 1994); m. Karla Rae Spaulding, May 24, 2000; children: Keith Chambers, David William. BA with honors, Yale U., 1967; JD cum laude, Columbia U., 1970. Cert.: Fla. Bar (in antitrust and trade regulation), bar: Calif. 1971, DC 1972, Fla. 1974. Assoc. O'Melveny & Myers LLP, LA, 1970; shareholder Trenam, Kemker, Scharf, Barkin, Frye, O'Neill & Mullis, P.A., Tampa, Fla., 1974—2000, Stearns Weaver Miller Alhadeff & Sitterson, P.A., Tampa, 2000—02; shareholder, chmn. antitrust dept. Akerman Senterfitt, Orlando and Tampa, Fla., 2002—. Chmn. Rough Riders dist., Gulf Ridge coun. Boy Scouts Am., Tampa, 1991—92, dist. commr., 1990—91; pres. Rotary Club of Tampa Bay, Tampa, 1994—95, sec., 1993—94. Capt. JAGC USMC, 1971—73, Vietnam. Named Rotarian of the Yr., Rotary Club of Tampa Bay, 1992; named one of The Best Lawyers in Am. Antitrust Law, Fla., 2006; named to America's Leading Lawyers for Bus., for Antitrust Law, Chambers USA, 2003—06; recipient Dist. award of Merit, Boy Scouts Am., 1991, Harlan Stone Fiske scholar, Columbia U. Sch. of Law. Mem.: ABA (mem. Sherman Act com. sect. antitrust law 1974), Fla. Bar (chmn. and vice chmn. antitrust com. 1984—92, exec. coun., bus. law sect. 1984—92), Am. Law Inst. Avocations: hiking, international travel. Office: Akerman Senterfitt 420 South Orange Ave Ste 1200 Orlando FL 32801-4904 Office Phone: 407-423-4000. Office Fax: 407-843-6610. Business E-Mail: keith.rounsaville@akerman.com.

**ROUNTREE, ASA,** lawyer; b. Birmingham, Ala., Aug. 9, 1927; s. John Asa and Cherokee Jemison (Van de Graaff) Rountree; m. Elizabeth Rhodes Blue, Aug. 11, 1951 (dec.); m. Helen Hill Updike, Oct. 10, 1998. AB, U. Ala., 1949; LLB, Harvard U., 1954. Bar: Ala. 1954, U.S. Dist. Ct. (no. dist.) Ala. 1954, U.S. Ct. Appeals (5th cir.) 1955, N.Y. 1962, U.S. Dist. Ct. (so. dist.) N.Y. 1963, U.S. Ct. Appeals (2d cir.) 1963, U.S. Supreme Ct. 1972. Assoc. Cabaniss & Johnston, Birmingham, Ala., 1954-60, ptnr., 1960-62; assoc. Debevoise & Plimpton, N.Y.C., 1962-63, ptnr., 1963-91; spl. counsel Maynard, Cooper, & Gale, P.C., Birmingham, 1991—. Bd. dirs. U. Ala. Law Sch. Found. With U.S. Army, 1945—46, lt. U.S. Army, 1951—53. Mem.: ABA (chmn. litig. sect. 1980—81), Am. Coll. Trial Lawyers, Am. Law Inst., Assn. Bar City of N.Y., N.Y. State Bar Assn., Ala. Bar Assn., Am. Bar Found., Mountain Brook Club (Birmingham), River Club (N.Y.C.). Episcopalian. Office: Maynard Cooper Gale PC 2400 AmSouth/Harbert Plz 1901 6th Ave N Birmingham AL 35203-2618 Home: 8 Cross Creek Dr Birmingham AL 35213

**ROUPE, JAMES PAUL,** accountant; b. Havre de Grace, Md., Apr. 20, 1957; s. Paul Clyde and Shirley Louise (Trivette) R. AA, Harford C.C., Bel Air, Md., 1977; BS, Towson State U., 1979. CPA, Md. Mgmt. asst. Loyola Fed. Savings and Loan, Balt., 1979—81; asst. treas. Legum Chevrolet-Nissan, Balt., 1983—89; contr. Bob Bell Chevrolet/Nissan, Inc., Balt., 1989—92, corp. sec.-treas., 1992—; Bob Bell Chevrolet of Bel Air (Md.) Inc., 1992—, Bob Bell of Upper Marlboro (Md.), L.C., 1992—95. Recipient Bus. Mgmt. Excellence award Nissan Motor Corp., 1990-2005. Mem. AICPA, Md. Assn. CPAs, Chevrolet Coun. Bus. Acctg. Mgrs. Republican. Baptist. Office: Bob Bell Chevrolet Nissan 7900 Eastern Blvd Baltimore MD 21224-2125

**ROURKE, MICKEY (PHILIP ANDRE ROURKE JR.),** actor; b. Schenectady, NY, Sept. 16, 1956; m. Debra Feuer, 1981 (div. 1989); m. Carre Otis, June 26, 1992 (div. Dec. 1998). Profl. boxer, 1991—95; gym owner Shapiro, West Hollywood. Actor (films) including 1941, 1979, Heaven's Gate, 1980, Fade to Black, 1980, Body Heat, 1981, Diner, 1982 (Nat. Soc. of Film Critics award best supporting actor 1982), Rumblefish, 1983, The Pope of Greenwich Village, 1984, Year of the Dragon, 1985, Eureka, 1985, 9 1/2 Weeks, 1985, Angel Heart, 1987, A Prayer for the Dying, 1987, Barfly, 1987, Homeboy (also screenwriter), 1988, Johnny Handsome, 1989, Wild Orchid, 1990, The Desperate Hours, 1990, Harley Davidson and the Marlboro Man, 1991, White Sands, 1992, F.T.W., 1994, Fall Time, 1995, Exit in Red, 1996, Bullets, 1996, The Rainmaker, 1997, Love in Paris, 1997, Double Team, 1997, Buffalo '66, 1997, Thursday, 1998, Shergar, 1999, Shades, 1999, Out in Fifty, 1999, The Animal Factory, 2000, Get Carter, 2000, The Pledge, 2001, Spun, 2002, Masked and Anonymous, 2003, Once Upon a Time in Mexico, 2003, Man on Fire, 2004, Sin City, 2005, Domino, 2005; (TV movies) Act of Love, 1980, City in Fear, 1980, Rape and Marriage: The Rideout Case, 1980, Thicker Than Blood, 1998. Avocation: motorcycling.

**ROUS, STEPHEN NORMAN,** urologist, educator; b. N.Y.C., Nov. 1, 1931; s. David H. and Luba (Margulies) R.; m. Margot Woolfolk, Nov. 12, 1966; children: Benjamin, David. AB, Amherst Coll., 1952; MD, N.Y. Med. Coll., 1956; MS, U. Minn., 1963. Diplomate: Am. Bd. Urology. Intern Phila. Gen. Hosp., 1956-57, resident, 1959-60, Flower-Fifth Ave. and Met. Hosp., N.Y.C., 1957-59, Mayo Clinic, Rochester, Minn., 1960-63; practice medicine specializing in urology San Francisco, 1963-68; assoc. prof. urology N.Y. Med. Coll., N.Y.C., 1968-72, assoc. dean, 1970-72; prof. surgery, chief div. urology Mich. State U., East Lansing, 1972-75; prof., chmn. dept. urology Med. U. S.C., Charleston, 1975-88; urologist-in-chief Med. U. S.C. and County hosps., Charleston, 1975-88; editorial dir. Norton Med. Books div. W.W. Norton and Co., 1988-94, editorial cons., 1994—; clin. prof. surgery Uniformed Svcs. U. of Health Scis., Bethesda, Md., 1992-2001; clin. prof. surgery, urology Brown U. Med. Sch., 2006—. Adj. prof. urology Med. U. S.C., 1988-99, prof. emeritus, 1999—; adj. clin. prof. surgery Dartmouth Med. Sch., 1988-91, prof. surgery (urology), 1991-2001, prof. surgery emeritus, 2001—; staff urologist Dartmouth-Hitchcock Med. Ctr., 1991-99; cons. urologist Saginaw VA Hosp., 1971-75, Charleston VA Hosp., 1975-88; hon. cons. St. Peter's Hosp., London, 1981-82; sr. vis. fellow Inst. Urology, London, 1981-82; mil. cons. in urology USAF Surgeon Gen., 1982-85; chmn. alumni devel. com. Mayo Clinic, 1979-82; hon. staff The Exeter Hosp., N.H., 1988—; nat. bd. visitors N.Y. Med. Coll., 1988-97; chief urology VA Med. Ctr., White River Junction, Vt., 1991-2001; mem. reparative justice bd. Vt. Dept. Corrections, 2004; urologist VA Med. Ctr., Providence, 2005— Author: Understanding Urology, 1973, Urology in Primary Care, 1976, Spanish edit., 1978, Russian edit., 1979, Urology: A Core Textbook, 1985, 2d edit., 1996, The Prostate Book, 1988, latest rev. edit., 2001, (with Judge Hiller B. Zobel) Doctors and the Law: Defendants and Expert Witnesses, 1993, (with Dr. Pamela Ellsworth) The Little Black Book of Urology, 2001; editor Urology Ann., 1987-97, Stone Disease: Diagnosis and Management, 1987; mem. editl. bd. Mil. Medicine, 1984-94; contbr. articles to med. jours. Mem. East Lansing (Mich.) Planning Commn., 1974-75; vestryman, jr. warden All Saints Episcopal Ch., East Lansing, 1973-75, lay reader, mem. diocesan com. on continuing edn., 1975-86; vestryman St. Michael's Episc. Ch., 1979-82, Charleston, S.C., chmn. every mem. canvas, 1979-80, chmn. lay readers, 1983-86; mem. fin. com., lay reader Christ Episc. Ch., Exeter, N.H., 1989-91; lector St. Thomas Episc. Ch., Hanover, N.H., 1991—; vestryman, 1992-96, stewardship chmn., 1992-94; jr. warden 1994-96; chalicist, lector, del. to diocesan conv. Trinity Ch., Newport, R.I, 2006—; mem. selectman's alt. Hampton Falls Planning Bd., 1989-91; alt. mem. Zoning Bd. Adjustment, Hanover, 1997-2000; bd. trustees, Nat. Hypertension Assn., N.Y.C., 2001—; bd. dirs. Med. Sci. Techs. Inc., Newport News, Va., 2001—. Col. USAFR, 1981-85, col. USAR, 1985-2000, col. AUS, ret., 2001—. Recipient "A" designator in urology, U.S. Army Surgeon Gen., 1986. Fellow ACS, Am. Acad. Pediatrics; mem. AMA, Soc. Univ. Urologists, Internat. Soc. Urology, Am. Urol. Assn., Nat. Urologic Forum, Soc. Pediatric Urology, Brit. Assn. Urol. Surgeons, German Urol. Assn. (hon.), Mayo Alumni Assn. (v.p. 1979-81, pres. 1983-85), Army and Navy Club (Washington), Lotos Club (N.Y.C.), Dartmouth Club of N.Y.C., Sigma Xi, Alpha Omega Alpha (hon.). Home: 421 Bellevue Ave #2A Newport RI 02840 Personal E-mail: stephen.n.rous@dartmouth.edu.

**ROUSE, CHRISTOPHER CHAPMAN, III,** composer, educator; b. Balt., Feb. 15, 1949; s. Christopher Chapman Jr. and Margery (Harper) Rouse; m. Ann Jensen, Aug. 28, 1983; children: Jillian, Alexandra, Adrian 1 stepchild, Angela. MusB, Oberlin Conservatory, 1971; MFA, DMA, Cornell U., 1977; DMus (hon.), Oberlin Coll., 1996, SUNY, Geneseo, 2000. Asst. prof. composition U. Mich., Ann Arbor, 1978—81, Eastman Sch. Music, Rochester, NY, 1981—85, assoc. prof. composition, 1985—91, prof. composition, 1991—2002; mem. faculty Juilliard Sch., 1997—. Composer-in-residence Balt. Symphony Orch., 1986—89, Schleswig Holstein Festival, 1989, Helsinki Biennale, 1997, Tanglewood Music Ctr., 1997, Pacific Music Festival, 1998, Aspen Music Festival, 1999—; writer numerous musical subjects; historian rock music. Composer for numerous renowned soloists and ensembles, including Yo-Yo Ma, Evelyn Glennie, Emanuel Ax, Dawn Upshaw, Cho-Liang Lin, Charles Castleman, James VanDemark, Jan de Gaetani, Leslie Guinn, Sharon Isbin, Carol Wincenc, William Albright, Soc. New Music, Blackearth Percussion Group, Boston Pops, Boston Musica Viva, Aspen Music Festival, Chamber Music Soc. Lincoln Ctr., N.Y. Internat. Festival of Arts, Chamber Music Am., New Eng. Conservatory Music, Nonesuch Records, orchestral works programmed by Berlin, Helsinki, Stockholm, NYC, Israel, Netherlands, Buffalo, L.A., Rochester Philharms., Orch. Nat. de France, Orch. de Paris, Residentie, Concertgebouw, Vienna & Zurich Tonhalle, New Zealand, Philharmonia, also Vienna, BBC, Berlin, Montreal, Chgo., Boston, St. Louis, Detroit, Balt., Nat., Pitts., Houston, Denver, Milw., Cleve., Minn., Phila., Oakland, Cin., Atlanta, N.J., Utah, Indpls., Memphis, San Francisco, Dallas, Göteboro U., Bournemouth symphony orchs, also The Netherlands, Finnish, Frankfurt, Moscow, Austrian, Flemish, BBC and NHK Tokyo Radio Orchs., commd. composer Atlanta Symphony, Phila. Orch., N.Y. Philharm., L.A. Philharm., Balt. Symphony, Houston Symphony, Minn. Orch., London Symphony, Cleve. Orch., Detroit Symphony, St. Louis Symphony, Boston Pops, Rochester Philharm., Cleve. Quartet, NYC Ballet. Recipient awards, Guggenheim Found., League Composers/ISCM, NEA, Rockefeller Found., Am. Music Ctr., Warner Bros. Record Co., Koussevitzky Found., BMI and Pitney Bowes, Friedheim 1st prize, Kennedy Ctr., 1988, Pulitzer prize for music, 1993, Grammy award, 2002. Mem.: Am. Acad. Arts and Letters (Acad. award 1993). Office: Juilliard Sch 60 Lincoln Center Plz New York NY 10023

**ROUSE, DORIS JANE,** physiologist, research scientist; b. Greensboro, N.C., Oct. 3, 1948; d. Welby Corbett and Nadia Elizabeth (Grainger) R.; m. Blake Shaw Wilson, Jan 6, 1974; children: Nadia Jacqueline, Blair Eliza[illegible]. BA in Chemistry, Duke U., 1970, PhD in Physiology and Pharmacology, 1980. Tchr. sci. Peace Corps, Tugbake, Liberia, 1970-71; rsch scientist Burroughs Wellcome Co., Rsch. Triangle Park, NC, 1971-76; sr. physiologist Rsch. Triangle Inst., Durham, 1976-83, dir. chmt., 1980-2000, also dir. NASA tech. application team, 1980-2000, dir. TB Tech. Transfer Program, 1999—, dir. Global Health, 2001—; portfolio project mgr. Global Alliance for Tb Drug Devel., 2002—. Adminstr. ANSI Tech. Adv. Group for Wheelchairs, N.Y.C., 1982-86; adj. asst. prof. U. N.C. Sch. Medicine, 1983-92; chair Instl. Rev. Bd., Profl. Devel. Award com., chair salary com. Rsch. Triangle Inst.; mem. adv. bd. Assistive Tech. Rsch. Ctr., 1994-96; portfolio project mgr. Global Alliance for TB Drug Devel., 2002—, bus. adv. Healthspot, 2004-05. Mem. adv. bd. Assn. Retarded Citizens, Arlington, Tex., 1981—88, Western Gerontology Soc., San Francisco, 1982—85; bd. dirs. Simon Found., Chgo., 1983—95; mem. spl. rev. com. small bus. applications Nat. Forum on Tech. and Aging; mem. fund steering com. Academy Venture, 2000—04. Recipient Group Achievement award NASA, 1979, 2000, President's award, RTI, 2003, 05. Mem: Am. Soc. Microbiology, Assn. Fed. Tech. Transfer Execs., Licensing Execs. Soc., Rehab. Engring. Soc. N.Am. (chmn. wheelchair com. 1981—86). Home: 2410 Wrightwood Ave Durham NC 27705-5802 Office: Research Triangle Inst PO Box 12194 Durham NC 27709-2194 Office Phone: 919-541-6980. Personal E-mail: drouse@nc.rr.com. Business E-Mail: rouse@rti.org.

**ROUSE, LEO E.,** dean, dental educator; Grad., Howard U. Coll. Dentistry, 1973; postgrad. studies in comprehensive dentistry, Watson Army Hosp., 1976—78. Assoc. dean clinical affairs Coll. Dentistry, Howard U., chmn. dept. clinical dentistry, interim dean, 2003—04, dean, 2004—. Examiner cons. and mem. exam. devel. com. N.E. Regional Bd. Dental Examiners. With U.S. Army, 1972—97, comdr. and COO U.S. Army, 1995—97, US Army Dental Command, ret. col., 1997—. Recipient Alumni Achievement award, Howard U. Coll. Dentistry, 1997. Fellow: Am. Coll. Dentists; mem.: ADA, Am. Assn. Dental Examiners, Am. Dental Edn. Assn., Nat. Dental Assn., Omicron Kappa Upsilon. Office: Howard Univ Coll Dentistry 600 W St NW Washington DC 20059 Office Phone: 202-806-0440. Business E-Mail: lrouse@howard.edu.*

**ROUSE, RICHARD HUNTER,** historian, educator; b. Boston, Aug. 14, 1933; s. Hunter and Dorothee (Hüsmert) R.; m. Mary L. Ames, Sept. 7, 1959; children: Thomas, Andrew, Jonathan. BA, State U. Iowa, 1955; MA, U. Chgo., 1957; PhD, Cornell U., 1963. Mem. faculty UCLA, 1963—, prof. history, 1975—. Assoc. dir. Ctr. Medieval and Renaissance Studies, 1966-67, acting dir., 1967-68; dir. Summer Inst. in Paleography, 1978, chair grad. coun., 1989-90; adv. bd. Hill Monastic Manuscript Libr., St. John's U., Collegeville, Minn., Ambrosiana Microfilm Library, Notre Dame (Ind.) U., Corpus of Brit. Medieval Libr. Catalogues, Brit. Acad. Author: Serial Bibliographies for Medieval Studies, 1969, (with M.A. Rouse) Preachers, Florilegia and Sermons: Studies on the Manipulus Florum of Thomas of Ireland, 1979; (with others) Texts and Transmission, 1983; (with C.W. Dutschke) Medieval and Renaissance Manuscripts in the Claremont Libraries, 1986; (with M.A. Rouse) Cartolai, Illuminators and Printers in Fifteenth-Century Italy, 1988; (with L. Bataillon and B. Guyot) La Production du livre universitaire au moyen age, exemplar et pecia, 1988; (with others) Guide to Medieval and Renaissance Manuscripts in the Huntington Library, 1989; (with M. Ferrari) Medieval and Renaissance Manuscripts at the University of California, Los Angeles, 1991; (with M.A. Rouse and R.A.B. Mynors) Registrum de libris doctorum et auctorum veterum, 1991; (with M.A. Rouse) Authentic Witnesses: Approaches to Medieval Texts and Manuscripts, 1991; (with M.A. Rouse) Manuscripts and Their Makers: Commercial Book Producers in Medieval Paris 1200-1500, 2 vols., 2000, (with M.A. Rouse) Henry of Kirkestede, Catalogus de libris autenticis et apocrifis, 2004; co-editor: Viator: Medieval and Renaissance Studies, 1970-; mem. editorial bd. Medieval and renaissance manuscripts in Calif. libraries, Medieval Texts, Toronto; Medieval Texts, Binghamton, Library Quar., 1984-88, Speculum, 1981-85, Revue d'histoire des Textes, 1986-, Cambridge Studies in Paleography and Codicology, 1990-98; press, (with M.A. Rouse) Catalogue of Medieval and Renaissance Manuscripts in the Beinecke Rare Book and Manuscript Library Yale University, 1984-, Filologia MedioLatina, 1994-, Manuscripta, 2000—, Utrecht Studies in Medieval Literacy, 2000—, Litterae Caelestes, 2005— Am. Coun. Learned Socs. fellow, 1972-73, vis. fellow All Souls Coll., Oxford, 1978-79, Guggenheim fellow, 1975-76, Rosenbach fellow in bibliography U. Pa., 1976, NEH fellow, 1981-82, 84-85, 94-96, Inst. for Advanced Studies fellow Jerusalem, 1991; J.R. Lyell reader in bibliogrphy U. Oxford, 1991-92; vis. fellow Pembroke Coll., U. Oxford, 1992, Pembroke Coll., U. Cambridge, 2000-01. Fellow Royal Hist. Soc., Medieval Acad. Am.; mem. Medieval Acad. Pacific (councillor 1965-68, pres. 1968-70), Medieval Acad. Am. (councillor 1977-80), Comité international de paléographie (treas. 1985-90), Comité international du vocabulaire des institutions et de la communication intellectuelles au moyen age, 1987—, Societa internazionale per lo studio del medioevo latino, 1988—. Home: 11444 Berwick St Los Angeles CA 90049-3416 Office: Dept History U Calif Los Angeles CA 90024 Office Phone: 310-825-4610. Business E-Mail: rouse@history.ucla.edu.

**ROUSE, ROSCOE, JR.,** retired librarian, educator; b. Valdosta, Ga., Nov. 26, 1919; s. Roscoe and Minnie Estelle (Corbett) R.; m. Charlie Lou Miller, June 23, 1945; children: Charles Richard, Robin Wells. BA, U. Okla., 1948, MA, 1952; MALS, U. Mich., 1958, PhD, 1962; student (Grolier Soc. scholar), Rutgers U., 1956. Bookkeeper C & S Nat. Bank, Valdosta, Ga., 1937-41; draftsman R.K. Rouse Co. (heating engrs.), Greenville, SC, 1941-42; student asst. U. Okla. and Rice U., 1947-48; asst. librarian Northeastern State Coll., Tahlequah, Okla., 1948-49, acting librarian, instr. library sci., 1949-51; circulation librarian Baylor U., 1952-53, acting univ. librarian, 1953-54, univ. librarian, prof., 1954-63, chmn. dept. library sci., 1956-63; dir. libraries State U. N.Y. at Stony Brook, L.I., 1963-67; dean libr. svcs., prof. Okla. State U., Stillwater, 1967-87, univ. libr. historian, 1987-92, chmn. dept. libr. edn., 1967-74; ret., 1987. Vis. prof. U. Okla. Sch. Library Sci., summer 1962, N. Tex. State U., summer 1965; acad. library cons.; pub. dir. Seretean Wellness Ctr., Okla. State U., 2002—; mem. AIA-Am. Library Assn. Library Bldg. Awards Jury, 1976; bd. dirs. Fellowship Christian Libr. and Info. Specialists; in retirement, volunteers writing and photography for local newspaper. Author: A History of the Baylor University Library, 1845-1919, 1962; editor: Okla. Librarian, 1951-52; co-author: Organization Charts of Selected Libraries, 1973; A History of the Okla. State U. Library, 1992; contbr. articles, book revs., chpts. to publs. in field. Bd. dirs. Stillwater Pub. Librs., 1989-92, chmn., 1990-92. 1st lt. USAAF, 1942-45. Decorated Air medal with 4 oak leaf clusters; recipient citation Okla. State Senate, 1987, Rotary Outstanding Achievement award, 1996; named in 150 Prominent Individuals in Baylor's History. Mem. ALA (life, mem. coun. 1971-72, 76-80, 83-84, 84-88, chmn. libr. orgn. and mgmt. sect. 1973-75, planning and budget assembly 1978-79, coun. com. on coms. 1979-80, bldgs. and equipment sect. exec. bd. 1979-80, chmn. bldgs. for coll. and univ. librs. com. 1983-85, chmn. nominating com. libr. history roundtable 1993-94), AARP, (sec. local chpt. 1998-2000), Okla. Libr. Assn. (life, pres. 1971-72, ALA coun. rep. 1976-80, 83-84, OLA Disting. Svc. award 1979, Spl. Merit award 1987), S.W. Libr. Assn. (chmn. coll. and univ. div. 1958-60, chmn. scholarship com. 1968-70), Internat. Fedn. Libr. Assns. (standing com. on libr. bldgs. and equipment 1976-88), Assn. Coll. and Rsch. Librs. (chmn. univ. librs. sect. 1969-70, mem. exec. bd. and rep. to ALA Coun., 1971-72), U. Mich. Sch. Libr. Sci. Alumni Soc. (pres. 1979-80, Alumni Recognition award 1988), mem. Alumni Found. Com., 1992-94, Payne County Ret. Educators Assn. (v.p., pres. elect 1991-92, pres. 1992-93), Okla. State U. Emeriti Assn. (pres. 2000-01), Okla. Hist. Soc. (com. on Okla. Higher Edn. mus. 1985—, pub. dir. 2002—), Stillwater Rotary Club (pres. 1980-81, Rotarian of Yr. 1999, editor Rotary Weekly bulletin, various coms., pub. dir. 1998—), Beta Phi Mu, Archons of Colophon. Baptist (chmn. bd. deacons 1973). *It is sometimes a hidden influence in our lives which drives us toward a set goal. We ourselves may not recognize the real source of that urge to fulfill a dream. Only after many years was I able to look back and discern the factors in my youth that pushed me toward my goal of attaining a good education. They grew out of the influence that the Great Depression had on my early life. Because of that experience the preparation for a career became my first goal in life, yet the ways and means for achieving it were virtually nonexistent. It was to be, however, and I was fortunate to realize that goal. It causes me to think now that perhaps the degree of determination and endurance one possesses is paced more by adverse condition than by times of comfort and ease.*

**ROUSE, TERRIE SUZITTE,** museum director; b. Youngstown, Ohio, Dec. 2, 1952; d. Eurad and Florence (Wilcox) Rouse; 1 child, Malcom Adam Rouse-West. BA, Trinity Coll., 1974; MS in Profl. Studies, Cornell U., 1977; cert. in internat. affairs, Columbia U., 1979, MA, 1979. Mgr. curator Adam Clayton Powell St. Office Bldg., N.Y.C., 1979-81; sr. curator Studio Mus. Harlem, N.Y.C., 1981-86; dir. mus. N.Y. Transit Mus., Bklyn., 1986—91; dir. Calif. Afro-Am. Mus., 1991—93; artistic exec. dir. Atlanta Ballet, 2002—03; exec. v.p., dir. museums Union Sta., Kansas City, 2005—. Advisor Bellevue Hosp. Art Bd., 1981—. Contbr. articles to profl. jours. Mem. Conf. Mil. Transp. Ofcls. Named Outstanding Young Women Am., 1981—83. Mem.: Am. Assn. Mus. (assessor 1981—). Avocations: sewing, reading, doll collecting. Personal E-mail: trouse3008@aol.com.

**ROUSE, WILLIAM ARTHUR, JR.,** education educator; b. New Bern, N.C., June 14, 1964; s. William Arthur and Sheila (Merritt) Rouse; m. Tracy Sumrell, June 21, 1995; children: Chandler, Taylor. BS, East Carolina U., 1987, EdS, 1998, EdD, 2004. Tchr. Pitt County Schs., Greenville, NC, 1987—96, asst. prin., 1996—98, prin., 1998—2005; asst. prof. dept. ednl. leadership East Carolina U., Greenville, 2005—. Author: (jour.) A Comparison of Business Education Students Achievement: National Board Certified Teachers vs. Non-National Board Certified Teachers, 2006. Mem.: So. Regional Coun. Ednl. Adminstrs., Nat. Assn. Secondary Sch. Assn. Supervision and Curriculum Devel. Home: 675 Gatewood Dr Winterville NC 28590 Office: East Carolina Univ Speight Bldg 102-E Greenville NC 27858-4353 Business E-Mail: rousew@ecu.edu.

**ROUSH, GLENN A.,** state senator; m. Ardith Roush. Served in Mont. Ho. of Reps., 1981—84, State Senate, 1999—; ret. Mont. Power Co.; Dem. senator dist. 8 Mont. State Senate, 1998—, mem. bus. and industry com., mem. energy and telecom. com., legis. com. and mem. coms. on coms. com., chmn. natural resources com. With U.S. Army. Democrat. Home: PO Box 185 Cut Bank MT 59427-0185

**ROUSH, JOHN A.,** academic administrator; b. Wisconsin; m. Susie Miller Roush; children: Luke, Mark. B in English, Ohio U.; M, M, D, Miami U., Ohio. Grad. asst. football coach to exec. asst. to pres. Miami U., Ohio; exec. asst. to pres. U. of Richmond, 1982—90, v.p. planning, 1990—98; pres. Centre Coll., Danville, Ky., 1998—. Mem. Coun. of Pres., Assn. of Gov. Bds., Nat. Assn. Independent Coll. & Univ.; treas. Assn. Presbyn. Coll. & Univ., 2002—03. Contbr. articles to profl. jours. Capt. U.S. Army. Office: Centre Coll 600 W Walnut St Danville KY 40422 Office Phone: 859-238-5200. E-mail: jroush@centre.edu.*

**ROUSH, NADINE MARIE,** elementary school educator; b. Elmhurst, Ill., Sept. 25, 1957; d. Donald Raymond and Roberta Helen (Foulis) Stoike; m. Jan Alan Roush, Dec. 17, 1977. BA, Purdue U., West Lafayette, Ind., 1982; MS, Purdue U., 1986. Facilitator gifted K-12 Ft. Larned Unified Sch. Dist. #495, Larned, Kans., 1982—84; tchr. grade 4 Avon Upper Elem., Ind., 1984—85; facilitator gifted K-12 Lafayette Sch. Corp., 1985—86; tchr. grades 4/5 Vinton Elem. Sch., Lafayette, 1986—90, tchr. 4/5, 1992—95; tchr. grade 5 Edgelea Elem. Sch., Lafayette, 1991—92, Earhart Elem. Sch., Lafayette, 1995—. Mem. adv. bd. Grad. Profl. Devel. Purdue U. Coll. Edn., West Lafayette, 2002—06. Author: Get Moving! The Transportation Activity Book, 1984; contbg. author: Preparing a Professional Portfolio, 2005. Mem. Feast of Hunters Moon com. Tippecanoe County Hist. Assn., Lafayette, 1995—2002. Recipient Crystal Apple for Outstanding Tchg. award, Purdue U., 1996, Golden Apple for Tchg. award, Greater Lafayette C. of C., 1989; Democratic Citizenship fellow, James F. Ackerman Ctr. Mem.: Ind. Coun. Social Studies (bd. dirs. 1997—2001, named Disting. Educator of Yr. 2004), Internat. Reading Assn., Nat. Coun. Social Studies, Delta Kappa Gamma. Home: 2356 N 600 W Frankfort IN 46041 Office: Earhart Elem Sch 3280 S 9th St Lafayette IN 47909

**ROUSSAKIS, PETER ELLWOOD,** minister, publisher; b. Bridgeport, Conn., Oct. 16, 1946; s. Charles and Dorothy Roussakis; m. Phyllis Ann Berkshire, Oct. 31, 1970; children: Alex, Aaron. BSc, So. Conn. State U., 1968, MSc, 1973; M in Ch. Music, So. Bapt. Theol. Sem., 1973; D in Ministry, Austin Presbyn. Theol. Sem., 1986; MST, Boston U., 1991; PhD, Grad. Theol. Found., 1998. Elem. sch. tchr. Trumbull Pub. Schs., Conn., 1968—71; min. music and edn. Brethren Ch., New Lebanon, Ohio, 1973—75; assoc. pastor First United Meth. Ch., Shelby, Ohio, 1977—80; asst. prof. ch. music Southwestern U., Georgetown, Tex., 1980—86; pastor First Bapt. Ch., Hampton, NH, 1986—89; pastor, min. of music Cmty. Ch. Alton, NH, 1989—98; pastor First Brethren Ch., Burlington, Ind., 2000—. Editor Meetinghouse Press, Burlington. Author: (religion text) Classic Worship: With Brethren in Mind, 2005, Confessing the Compendium: Praying the Lord's Prayer as Confessing Faith, 2005. Mem.: Nat. Assn. Brethren Ch. Elders, Hymn Soc. of US and Can. Mem. The Brethren Church. Avocation: collecting antique records. Home and Office: PO Box 246 Burlington IN 46915 Office Phone: 765-566-3265. E-mail: jsbaklava@sbcglobal.net, meetinghousepress@sbcglobal.net.

**ROUSSEAU, EUGENE ELLSWORTH,** musician, music educator, consultant; b. Blue Island, Ill., Aug. 23, 1932; s. Joseph E. and Laura M. (Schindler) R.; m. Norma J. Rigel, Aug. 15, 1959; children: Lisa-Marie, Joseph. B of Mus Edn., Chgo. Mus. Coll., 1953; MusM, Northwestern U., 1954; student, Paris Conservatory of Music, 1960-61; PhD in Music Lit. and Performance, U. Iowa, 1962. Instr. Luther Coll., 1956-59; asst. prof. Cen. Mo. State Coll., 1962-64; prof. music Ind. U., Bloomington, 1964-88, disting. prof. music, 1988—; prof. U. Minn., 2000—. Guest prof. U. Iowa, 1964, Hochschule fur Musik, Vienna, Austria, 1981-82, Ariz. State U., 1984, Prague Conservatory Music, 1985, Showa Coll. Music, 1996, 98, Tokyo Coll. Music, 1997, Paris Conservatory, 1997, Munshino Acad. Music, Tokyo, 2000; tchr. U. Wis.-Ext., 1969—; R&D of saxophone mouthpieces; music arranger; svc. on numerous acad. coms.; tchr. 1st course in saxophone Mozarteum in Salzburg, Austria, 1991—; mem. jury Munich Internat. competitions, 1987, 90, 2001, pres. of juries, 1991-92; first solo saxophonist to perform on Prague Spring Festival, 1993; mem. jury Can. Nat. Music competition, 1994; juror Japan Wind and Percussion Competition, 1997; v.p. jury Adolphe Sax Internat. Competition, Belgium, 1998; guest artist prof. Villa Musica, Mainz, 1998, 2000; faculty saxophone Ticino Music, Lugano, 2001, 02, 03; chief cons. saxophone R&D Yamaha corp., 1972-92; soloist Hammanmmtsu Wind Instrument Festival; faculty ann. master class Vancouver C.C.; host World Saxophone Congress XIII, U. Minn., Mpls., 2003; recorded for Deutsche Grammophon, 1971; guest faculty Am. Band Coll., 2000, 03, 06; adjudicator Thailand Internat. Composition Competition, 2006. Worldwide concert saxophonist; Carnegie Hall debut, 1965; author: Marcel Mule: His Life and the Saxophone, 1982, Saxophone High Tones, 1978, revised 2d edit., 2003, Method for Saxophone (2 vols.), 1975; performer 1st solo saxophone recitals, several European cities, 1st Am. solo saxophone performance in Japan, 1984; 1st to record concert saxophone on compact disc (Delos); radio broadcasts in Berlin, Bremen, London, Montreal, Ostrava, Paris, Prague, Toronto, Vienna; saxophone recs. for Deutsche Gramophon, Golden Crest, Coronet, Delos, Liscio, ALM, McGill and RIAX; CD rec. with Belgian RAF Band; numerous world premieres of composition written for him. Instr., asst. band leader 25th Infantry Div. U.S. Army, 1954-56. Named Hon. Prof. Music, Prague Conservatory, 1993, Braga Inst., Italy, 2001; recipient Edwin Franko Goldman award, Am. Bandmasters Assn., 1995, Disting. Alumni award, U. Iowa, 1996; grantee, Fulbright Found., 1960—61, Rsch. and Exchange Bd., 1985, NEA, 1986. Mem. N Am. Saxophone Alliance (pres. 1978-80), Comite Internat. de Saxophone (pres. 1982-85), Coll. Music Soc., Clarinet and Saxophone Soc. (U.K.), Music Tchrs. Nat. Assn. (Tchr. of Yr. award for Ind. 1993), Fulbright Assn. (life), World Saxophone Congress (co-founder 1969, pres. organizing com. 2000--). Office Phone: 612-624-3875. E-mail: rouss007@umn.edu.

**ROUSSEAU, IRENE VICTORIA,** artist; children: Douglas, Scott. BA, Hunter Coll., N.Y.C.; MFA, Claremont (Calif.) Grad. Sch., 1969; PhD, N.Y. U., 1977. Tenured prof. William Paterson Coll., Wayne, NJ, 1970-74. Spkr. in field. Exhbns. include Betty Parsons Gallery, N.Y.C., Claremont Colls., State Mus. Sci. and Industry, L.A., Morris Mus. Arts and Scis., Morristown, N.J., The Bronx Mus. of Art, Galleri Sci. Agnes, Copenhagen/Roskilde, Denmark, Sculptors 5, Madison, N.J., Edmund Sci. Co., Barrington, N.J., AT&T World Hdqrs., Basking Ridge, N.J., N.J. Ctr. for Visual Arts, The Brotherhood Synagogue Holocaust Meml. Gramercy Pk. (mosaic), N.Y.C., 1986, 1st Internat. Art Biennale, Malta, 1995, U. Lausanne (Switzerland), 1997, Internat. Biennale Malta, 1997 (awards), Am. Inst. Archs., N.Y., 1998, Southwestern Coll., Kans., 1999, Lausanne, Switzerland, 2001, BRIDGES, Internat. Joint Conf., 2003, Math. Soc. France and Ministry of Culture Exhbn., 2004-05, Internat. Interdisciplinary Conf., Athens, Greece, 2005, Renaissance Banff, Alb., Can., 2005, travelling exhibit, Soc. Math. France and The Min. Culture, 2005, Yellow Bird Gallery, Newburg, N.Y., 2005; artist in residence Program Greece, 2000, Internat. Coll. Internat. Soc. Art, Math., Architecture, Freiburg, Germany, 2002, Internat. Conf. Connections in Math., Music, Art, Sci., and Arch., Granada, Spain, 2003, Internat. Soc. Arts, Math., and Arch. and BRIDGES (Math. Connections in Art, Music, and Sci.) Internat. Joint Conf., Granada, Spain, Inst. Math. Scis. Banff Ctr., Can. Math.Soc., Banff Internat. Rsch. Sta.; one woman shows Weston Gallery Sch. Arch., Newark, 2003, N.J. Inst. Tech. Sch. Arch., 2003, Weston Art Gallery Sch. Arch. NJIT, Newark, 2004; traveling exhibit Math. Soc., 2005; contbr. articles and works of art to jours., books and catalogues. Recipient seven 1st prize awards for creative work in N.J., ER Squibb and Sons Sculpture award, AIA N.J. Presentation Design award, 1995, Internat. Art Biennale Malta Installatin award, 1997, Traveling Exhibit throughout Europe and Middle East and Africa of Winners of the 1997 Biennale in Malta, 1997-99. Mem. AIA (profl. affiliate N.J., N.Y., chmn. architecture dialogue com. Presentation award 1995), Internat. Sculptors Assn., Am. Abstract Artists (exhbn. chmn. 1978-79, pres. 1979-82), Fine Arts Fedn. (bd. dirs.), Coll. Art Assn., Women's Caucus on Art (conf. spkr.), Phi Delta Kappa. Home: 41 Sunset Dr Summit NJ 07901-2322 Personal E-mail: mosaicartforms@comcast.net.

**ROUSSEAU-VERMETTE, MARIETTE,** artist; b. Trois-Pistoles, Que., Can., Aug. 29, 1926; d. Joseph-Herve and Corrinne (Belanger) Rousseau; m. Claude Vermette, Nov. 29, 1952; children: Marc, Jerome. Student, Ecole des Beaux Arts du Que., 1944-48, Studio Dorothy Liebes, San Francisco, 1948-49, Oakland Coll. Arts and Crafts, 1948-49; studied different tapestry techniques in Europe, 1952, 58. Head dept. fibre, visual arts Banff (Alta.) Sch. Fine Arts, Canada, 1979—85. Solo exhbns. include: Musée des Beaux-Arts de Montréal, 1961, Galerie Camille Hébert, Montréal, 1964, New-Design Gallery, Vancouver, B.C., 1964, Galerie Godard-Lefort, Montréal, 1969, Musée du Québec, 1972, Marlborough-Godard Gallery, Toronto, 1974, Centre Culturel Canadien, Paris, 1974, Centre Culturel Canadien, Brussels, 1974, Winnipeg (Man.) Art Gallery, 1976, Grace Borgenicht Gallery, N.Y., 1977, Galerie Alice Pauli, Lausanne, Switzerland, 1978, Brown Grotta Gallery, Wilton, Conn., 1993-2001, Galerie Bernard, Montreal, Can., 2004—, numerous others; group shows include: Nat. Gallery of Can., 1959, Biennale Internationale de la Tapisserie, Lausanne, Switzerland, 1962, 65, 67, 71, 77, Triennale de Milan, 1968, Mus. Modern Art, N.Y.C., 1968-69, Art Gallery of Windsor, Ont., 1977, 81, Musée d'Art Contemporain, Montréal, Mus. Modern Art, Kyoto, Japan, 1977, Mus. Modern Art, Tokyo, 1978, Musée d'Art Contemporain de Montréal, 1979, Biennale, Lodz, Poland, 1981, numerous others; theatrical works include: Théâtre Maisonneuve, Place des Arts, Montréal, 1967, Theatre of the Can. Ctr. of Arts, Ottawa, 1965-68, The JFK Ctr. for Performing Arts, Washington, 1970, Group de la Place Royal, 1968, 69, 73; permanent collections include: Nat. Gallery of Can., Art Gallery of Charlottetown, Can. Pavilion, Osaka, Japan, Québec Pavilion, Osaka, Palais de Justice, Montréal, Mus. Modern Art, Kyoto, Met. Mus., N.Y.C., Chgo. Art Mus., numerous others. Decorated officer Order of Can.; Can. Coun. grantee, 1968; recipient Honor certificate in Conférence Canadienne des Arts, 1974. Subject of numerous articles and books. Office: 373 Rue Morin Saint-Adele PQ Canada J8B 2P8

**ROUSSEL, LEE DENNISON,** economist; b. NYC, May 15, 1944; d. Ethan Allen and Frances Isabel (Ferry) Dennison; m. Andre Homo Roussel, Sept. 6, 1980; children: Cecilia Frances, Stephanie Anne. AB, Wellesley Coll. 1966; MA, Northeastern U., 1974. Mgmt. intern U.S. Dept. HEW, 1966-68; with Planning Office Commonwealth of Mass., 1968-70; exec. dir. Gov.'s Commn. Citizen Participation, Boston, 1973; with Boston area office U.S. Dept. HUD, 1970-78; fgn. svc. officer USAID, 1978-99, with housing and urban devel. office Washington and Tunis, 1978-82, chief housing and urban devel. office for C.Am. Honduras, 1982-87, asst. dir. office housing and urban programs Washington, 1987-91, country rep. for Czech and Slovak Fed. Rep., 1991-92, country rep. for Czech Rep., 1993-94; min. counselor, U.S. rep. to devel. assistance com. OECD, Paris, 1994-99; sr. advisor USAID, Panama, 1999—2002, chief, exec. mgmt. human resources, 2004—05, mgmt. advisor Office of Econ. growth, 2006—. Episcopalian. Home: 2333 N Oak St Falls Church VA 22046 E-mail: leeroussel@hotmail.com.

**ROUSSELOT, PETER FRESE,** lawyer, consultant; b. NYC, Jan. 7, 1942; s. Louis Marcel and Evelyn Valdez (Hastrup) R.; m. Mary Dumesnil, Cobb, Nov. 22, 1979; children: Laura Rodman, Richard Frese, Anne Stewart, Louise Dierks. BA summa cum laude, Yale U., 1963; LLB, Harvard U., 1966. Bar: US Dist. Ct. DC 1967, US Ct. Appeals (DC cir.) 1967, US Ct. Appeals (3d cir.) 1993, US Supreme Ct. 1970. Assoc. Hogan & Hartson, Washington, 1966-74, ptnr., 1975-94, mem. exec com., 1986-88; mng. dir. corp. affairs So. Pacific Rail Corp., Washington, 1994-97; ind. internat. railroad cons., 1997—. Asst. to nat. co-chmn. Citizens for Robert F. Kennedy, Washington, 1968; del. Dem. Nat. Conv., 2004; chair Arlington County Dem. Com., Va., 2006-. Mem. Yale Club Washington, Phi Beta Kappa. Democrat. Episcopalian. Avocations: tennis, hiking, photography. Office: 3182 Key Blvd Arlington VA 22201-5065 Office Phone: 703-276-1584. E-mail: pfrou@aol.com.

**ROUSSOS, LOUIS ABLEN,** statistician, psychology professor; b. Norfolk, Va., Feb. 19, 1955; s. Christos Constantine and Silvia Martha (Amrod) Roussos; m. Gabriella Lucia Smith, July 14, 1990; children: Gina Patience, Elias Isaiah, Joseph Christos, Silvio Christopher. BS in Engring., Old Dominion U., 1977, MS in Engr. Mechanics, 1980; MS in Stats., U. Ill., Champaign, Ill., 1990, PhD in Psychology, 1995. Registered profl. engr., Va., 1978. Aero. rsch. engr. Langley Rsch. Ctr. NASA, Hampton, Va., 1980—87; adj. prof. Tidewater C.C., Va. Beach, Va., 1987—88; rsch. Law Sch. Admission Coun., Newtown, Pa., 1995—2001; chief psychometrician Prime Assessment, Champaign, 2001—02; asst. prof. Dept. of Ed. Psych. U. Ill., Champaign, Ill., 2002—. Adj-prof. Bucks County C.C., Newtown, 2000—01. Mem. editl. bd.: Psychology in the Schools Jour., 2005—; contbr. articles to profl. jours. Recipient Tech. Brief award, NASA, 1981, Disting. Dissertation award, APA, 1999; fellow, NASA, 1977—78; grantee, Ednl. Testing Svc., 2002—05, NASA, 1984—85, MBTI Rsch. Adv. Bd., 1993, NSF, 2002—03, Univ. Ill. Rsch. Bd., 2004—05. Ednl. Testing Svc., 1997—99; scholar, Consulting Engrs. Coun. Va., 1976. Mem.: Nat. Coun. Measurement in Edn. (award 2005, Outstanding Dissertation award 1997), Am. Ednl. Rsch. Assn., Psychometric Soc., Tau Beta Pi. Achievements include development of HCA/CCPROX nonparametric dimensionality estimation software; invention of GAMESTATS technique for determining statistical mastery cut-off criteria; development of software for simulating skills-diagnosis data; discovery of the population parameter for the Mantel-Haenszel DIF statistic; development of software to calculate the M-H DIF parameter; discovery of integral equations for the DETECT population parameter; development of software for calculating the DETECT population parameter; software for modeling and simulating multidimensional item response data; invention of method for modeling non-viscous damping in a finite element model; development of software for evaluating DIF in a Computerized Adaptive Testing (CAT) setting; invention of invented new techniques for evaluating internal validity for skills diagnosis models. Home: 2010 Silver Court West Urbana IL 61801 Office: Univ of Ill Dept of Educational Psych 1310 South Sixth Street Champaign IL 61820 Office Phone: 217-333-1428. Office Fax: 217-244-7620. Personal E-mail: gandlroussos@juno.com. Business E-Mail: roussos@uiuc.edu.

**ROUSU, MATTHEW C.,** economics professor; b. Meriden, Conn., June 25, 1976; s. Jeanne R. and James W. Nelson (Stepfather); m. Amanda E. Green. May 17, 1999; children: Jacob T. Allison V. BSBA, U. SD, Vermillion, 1998; PhD, Iowa State U., Ames, 2002. Rsch. economist RTI Internat., Research Triangle Park, NC, 2002—04; asst. prof. econs. Susquehanna U., Selinsgrove, Pa., 2004—. Cons. for govt. and other projects. Contbr. articles to profl. jours. Drama ministries Christ United Meth. Ch., Selinsgrove, Pa., 2005—06. Mem.: Am. Econs. Assn. (assoc.), Am. Agrl. Econs. Assn. (assoc.). Methodist. Avocations: poker, travel, golf. Home: 34 Woodlynn Dr Selinsgrove PA 17870 Office: Susquehanna University 514 Steele Hall Selinsgrove PA 17870 Office Phone: 570-372-4186.

**ROUSUCK, J. WYNN,** theater critic; b. Cleve. Mar. 19, 1951; d. Morton I. and Irene Zelda (Winograd) R. BA summa cum laude, Wellesley Coll., 1972; MS, Columbia U., 1974. Assoc. editor, program guide, Sta. WCLV-FM, Cleve., 1972-73; theater and film reviewer Cleve. Press, 1973; gen. assignment arts reporter Balt. Sun, 1974-84, theater critic, 1984—. Instr. English Goucher Coll., Towson, Md., 1981; master critic O'Neill Critics Inst., Waterford, Conn., 1990—; theater critic Md. Pub. TV., 1986; faculty Nat. Endowment for Arts Journalism Inst. in Theater U. So. Calif., 2005; spkr. in field. Recipient Dog Writers Assn. Am. awards 1977, 79, Md. chpt. 1st Place Arts Reporting award Soc. Profl. Journalists, 1993, Front Page award Disting. Criticism Washington-Balt. Newspaper Guild, 1997, 99, 2002, Bill Pryor Meml. grand prize for writing, 1999, Bernie Harrison Meml. award for commentary, 2002; NEH journalism fellow U. Mich., 1979-80, fellow O'Neill Critics Inst., 1982. Mem. Balt. Bibliophiles (bd. dirs. 1982-83), Octavo Plus, Walters Art Gallery, Balt. Wellesley Club (pres. 1978-79). Jewish. Avocations: rare books, art. Office: The Baltimore Sun 501 N Calvert St Baltimore MD 21278-0001

**ROUTE, CANDACE,** elementary school educator; d. Hubert Lee and Julianne Jackson; m. Leslie Ray Route, Dec. 28, 1974; 1 child, Brian. EdB, Tex. Tech U.- Lubbock, 1972; Med, East Tex. State U., Commerce, 1985. Cert. kindergarten tchr. Tex., 1972. Kindergarten tchr. Hale Ctr. ISD, Tex., 1972—73, Dallas ISD, 1973—74, Gibert ISD, Ariz., 1978—81, North Lamar ISD, Paris, 1981—85, Kerrville ISD, Tex., 1993—97, Harlandale ISD, San Antonio, 1997—2001, reading tchr., 2001—03, reading coach, 2003—; ednl. cons. Region VIII Edn. Svc. Ctr., Mt. Pleasant, Tex., 1985—89, Region XII Edn. Svc. Ctr., Waco, Tex., 1989—90; adminstrv. asst. Ingram ISD, Tex., 1991—92; reading coach Harlandale Ind. Sch. Dist., San Antonio, 2003—. Early childhood cons. Dept. Human Resources, Paris, 1974—78; owner/ednl. cons. A Child's Garden of Learning, Kerrville, Tex., 1992—93. Recipient Ednl. Achievements award, Notable Women Tex., 1985. Mem.: Tex. Fedn. Tchrs., Kappa Delta Pi. Independent. Avocations: architecture, antiques. Home: 610 Mello Oak San Antonio TX 78258 Office Phone: 210-977-1580.

**ROUTH, DONALD K. (DONALD KENT ROUTH),** psychologist, educator; b. Oklahoma City, Mar. 3, 1937; s. Ross Holland and Fay (Campbell) R.; m. Marion Starbird Wendler, Sept. 10, 1960; children: Rebecca Ann (dec.), Laura Diane. BA, U. Okla., 1962; PhD, U. Pitts., 1967; BA in History, Fla. Gulf Coast U., 2006. Diplomate Am. Bd. Profl. Psychology. Asst. prof. psychology and pediatrics U. Iowa, Iowa City, 1967-70, prof., 1977-85; assoc. prof. psychology Bowling Green State U., Ohio, 1970-71; assoc. prof. U. N.C., Chapel Hill, 1971-77; prof. psychology and pediat. U. Miami, Coral Gables, Fla., 1985—2002, prof. emeritus, 2002—. Chmn. behavioral medicine study sect. NIH, 1983-85 Editor Jour. Pediatric Psychology, 1976-82, Jour. Clin. Child Psychology, 1987-91, Jour. of Abnormal Child Psychology, 1992-98, Am. Jour. on Mental Retardation, 1998-2002, Internat. Clin. Psychologist, 2001—04; contbr. numerous articles to profl. jours., books Pres. Eno River Unitarian Universalist Fellowship, 1976-77; vol. faculty Fla. Gulf Coast U., 2002—05. Recipient award for disting. contbn. Soc. Pediatric Psychology, 1981, Presdl. award, 1988; Rsch. Psychologist of Yr. award Fla. Psychol. Assn., 1987, Reconocimiento, El Colegio Nacional de Psicologis de Mex., 1999, Disting. Alumni award Okla. Mil. Acad., 2004. Mem. APA (pres. div. child, youth and family svcs., 1984, pres. div. on mental retardation 1987, pres. divsn. clin. psychol. 1998), Internat. Soc. Clin. Psychology (founder, pres. 1998-99), Disting. Profl. Contbns. to Clin. Psychology (sect. on clin. child psychology 1989, div. clin. psychology, 1992, Nicholas Hobbs award div. child youth and family svcs., 1996, Edgar A. Doll award divsn. mental retardation and devel. disabilities 2001). Democrat. Home: 20131 Seagrove St #402 Estero FL 33928 E-mail: drouth@miami.edu.

**ROUTSON, CLELL DENNIS,** manufacturing executive; b. Elkhart, Ind., Oct. 8, 1946; s. Clell Dean and Olene Maize (Replogle) Routson; m. Paula Leone McLallin, Sept. 2, 1967 (div. June 1988); children: Clell Dustin, Courtney Trevor; m. Suzann Kay Bron, 1995 (div. Aug. 1998). BSBA, Ball State U., Muncie, Ind., 1971. With Proctor & Gamble, Cin., 1971-74; nat. sales mgr. Palmer Instruments, Inc., Cin., 1974-76; with Nordson Corp., Amherst, Ohio, 1976-81, MCC Powers, Cleve., Chgo., Singapore, 1981-86; sales mgr., v.p., pres. Burgess, Inc., Freeport, Ill., 1986-89; mgr. mktg. and sales, v.p. sales and mktg. Kloppenberg & Co., Englewood, Colo., 1990-92; v.p. ops., gen. mgr. T.E.I. Engineered Products, Englewood, 1992-96; pres. (one-yr. contract) Bailco Svc. Corp., Englewood, 1996-97; pres. Composite Tek, Boulder, Colo., 2000—. Mng. dir. Resource Dynamics, Singapore, Chgo., and Denver, 1985-86, 96-99. Contbr. articles to profl. jours. Bd. dirs. Mountain Area Pregnancy Ctr., 2003—. Mem. Mountain Area Pregnancy Ctr. (bd. dirs. 2003), Dallas Tower Club. Republican. Baptist. Office Phone: 303-250-0929. Personal E-mail: croutson@earthlink.net. Business E-Mail: cdr@compositetek.com.

**ROUTSON, SUSAN HUTCHINS,** secondary school educator, consultant, peer counseling specialist; b. Cin., May 13, 1943; d. Ralph Pearson and Sarah Minabelle (Abbott) Hutchins; m. Ronald Irving Routson, Oct. 7, 1967; children: Sarah Mary, David Patrick. BS in Math. and Biology, Purdue U., 1965; MS in Microbiology/Clin. Pathology, Mich. State U., 1967. Cert. secondary math. and biology tchr., Ind.; cert. non-profit bd. trainer; cert. peer program educator; cert. trainer, Nat. Assn. Peer Programs, 2003. Researcher Miami U., Oxford, Ohio, 1968; apt. mgr. Miami U. Student Housing, Oxford, 1969-74; substitute tchr. Richmond (Ind.) Community Schs., 1976—; coord. vol. tutors, 1978-80; bus. mgr. Richmond Cotillion, 1983-87; dir. Peer Info. Ctrs. for Teens, 1986—; trainer Planning Programs for Young Adolescents, 1989—. Adult educator Girl Scouts U.S.A., 1978—; svc. unit mgr., 1983—87; program dir. Richmond YWCA, 1986—95; state bd. dirs. Ind. Youth Adv. Program, 1989—2000, pres., 1992—2000; bd. dirs. Nat. Youth Adv. Program, 1989—2000; mem. state dept. of edn. svc. learning com. Mem. Nat. Peer Helper Assn., 1992—; Richmond Sch. Supt.'s Adv. Com., 1975—88, Greater Richmond Progress Com. Edn., Child Care, Teen Pregnancy and Substance Abuse Task Forces, 1986—91; mem. agy. dirs. coun. United Way, 1995—, pres., 1998—2001; mem. Ind. Coun. on Adolescent Pregnancy, bd. dirs., 1991—96, v.p., 1993—96; founding bd. mem. DIPLOMAS, 1993—, pres., 2000—; founding pres. Ind. Peer Programs Assn., 2002—; mem. steering com. Safe Schs./Healthy Schs., 2003; mem. exec. bd. Treaty Line Girl Scouts U.S.A., Richmond, 1976—88, pres., 1990—96. Named Vol. of Yr., Whitewater Valley United Way, 1986, Exemplary Youth Orgn. Creator, Lilly Endowment, 1988, Leadership Assoc., 1992, Pres. Bush Vol. Action Leader, 1991; recipient Thanks Badge, Treaty Line Girl Scouts USA, 1984, Peer Program of Yr. award, Nat. Assn. Peer Programs, 2002, First Cert. Peer Program award, 2002; Journey Fellow Lilly Endowment, 2005. Mem. Children's Def. Fund, So. Poverty Law Ctr., Nature Conservancy, Nat. Assn. for Edn. of Young Children, Internat. Altrusa (scholarship chair 1996-, Woman of Achievement 2002), Nat. Assn. Curriculum Devel., Delta Kappa Gamma (pres. 1996-2002), Alpha Phi (pres. Richmond chpt. 1985-90). Republican. Roman Catholic. Home: 4566 Smyrna Rd Richmond IN 47374-9659 Office: Richmond High Sch 380 Hub Etchison Pkwy Richmond IN 47374

**ROUVAS, SAKAS,** singer, gymnast; b. Island of Corfou, Greece, Jan. 5, 1974; Signed by Polygram, 1991. Represented Greece in pole vault Hellenic Nat. Team; rep. Greece Eurovision Song Contest, 2004. Performer: Thessaloniki Song Festival, (TV) Athen 2004-Die Gala, 2004, singer 6 albums, 4 single albums; notable guest appearences Fort Boyard, 2002, 20h10 pétantes, 2003, Hallo Deutschland, 2004, Leute heute, 2004, Bettina S., 2004. Recipient Best New Singer, Best Song, and Best Stage Performance, Hellenic Music Awards (four years in a row), 3rd Place for song "Shake it", Eurovision Song Contest, 2004. He played a role in reconciliation efforts with Turkey. In 1997, he performed on stage with Turkish singer Barat Kud in a concert in UN-controlled territory on Cyprus. For this he was awarded the International Ipeksi prize for understanding and cooperation. Mailing: Polygram Records Inc 185 Miles Ave Akron OH 44306-1606 E-mail: sakis@sakisrouvas.com

**ROUVELAS, EMANUEL LARRY,** lawyer; b. Seattle, Sept. 10, 1944; s. Larry E. and Mary (Derezes) R.; m. Marilyn S. Edmunds, Jan. 23, 1967; children: Eleftherios, Mary. BA, U. Wash., 1965; JD, Harvard U., 1968, AMP, 1996. Bar: Ill. 1968, D.C. 1973. Assoc. Kirkland & Ellis, Chgo., 1968-69; counsel U.S. Senate Com. on Commerce, Washington, 1969-73; chief counsel U.S. Senate Mcht. Marine and Fgn. Commerce Subcoms., Washington, 1969-73; chmn., ptnr. Preston, Gates, Ellis & Rouvelas Meeds, Washington, 1974—; advisor to two Presdl. transitions and bi-partisan congl. caucus; bd. dirs. Am. Comml. Lines, 2005-, chmn. nominating governance com., 2005-. Regent Am. Architectural Found., 2005—. Office: Preston Gates Ellis Et Al 1735 New York Ave NW Washington DC 20006-5209 Office Phone: 202-628-1700.

**ROUZE, JEFFREY ALAN,** real estate executive; b. Rockford, Ill., Feb. 5, 1952; s. Robert Lloyd and Ellen Erma (Korpi) R. BBA in Real Estate Fin., U. Wis., 1974, MS in Bus. and Real Estate, 1977. Lic. real estate broker, Wis.; notary pub., Wis. Exec. mgmt. trainee Grootemaat Corp., Milw., 1977-79; real estate cons. CUNA Mut. Ins. Soc., Madison, Wis., 1979-84, real property and mortgage mgr., 1984-93, sr. asset mgr., 1994—2001; pres. Hollywood Econ.

Alliance, 2002—; ptnr. Hollywood Devel. LLC, L.A., 2001—. Treas. Strollers Theatre, Ltd., Madison, 1985-89; bd. dirs. Hollywood (Calif.) Entertainment Dist., 1998-99, 2005—, Hollywood Historic Trust, 2000—; treas. St. Paul's Luth. Ch., Santa Monica, Calif., 2002—; bd. dirs. Hollywood Neighborhood Coun., 2003—; bd. dirs. Hollywood Heritage, 2003—. Mem. Nat. Assoc. Corp. Real Estate Execs. (master corp. real estate), Inst. Real Estate Mgmt. (cert. property mgr.), Mortgage Bankers Assn. Am., Urban Land Inst., Coml. Investment Real Estate Inst., Hollywood C. of C. (treas. 2002—). Address: 530 S Barington Ave No 307 Los Angeles CA 90049 Office Phone: 310-451-6719. E-mail: jarouze@earthlink.net.

**ROVE, KARL CHRISTIAN,** federal official; b. Denver, Dec. 25, 1950; s. Louis C. (Jr.) and Reba Louise (Wood) Rove; m. Valerie Wainright Rove, July 10, 1976 (div. Jan. 1980); m. Darby Tara Hickson, Jan. 25, 1986; 1 child, Andrew Madison. Student, U. Utah, 1969—71, U. Md., 1972, George Mason U., 1973—75, U. Tex., 1977. Exec. dir. Coll. Rep. Nat. Com., Washington, 1971—73; spl. asst. to chmn. George Bush Nat. Com., Washington, 1973—75, exec. asst. to co-chmn. Richard Obenshain, 1975, also mem. RC exec. com., 1971—75; fin. dir. Va. Rep. Com., Richmond, 1976; dir. Fund for Ltd. Govt., Houston, 1977—79; dep. dir. Gov. William P. Clements Jr. Com., Houston, 1979—80; dir. Tex. Victory Com., Austin, 1980; spl. asst. for adminstrn., dep. exec. asst. to Gov. State of Tex., Austin, 1980—81; pres. Karl Rove & Co., Austin, 1981—99; polit. advisor and chief strategist George W. Bush gubernatorial and presdl. campaigns, 1993—2001; sr. advisor to Pres. The White House, Washington, 2001—, asst. to the Pres. & dep. chief of staff for policy, 2005—. Pres. U.S. Youth Coun., Washington, 1975—77, chmn., 1973—77, selection panel, 1973—77; regent Tex. Woman's U., Denton, 1981—83, East Tex. State U., 1990—91; treas. Tex. Women's Employment and Edn. Program, Austin, 1981—83; mem. regional selection panel White House Fellows Commn., 1987—90. Mem. spl. com. on governance Tex. Higher Edn. Coord. Bd., 1989—91; bd. dirs. Tex. Bus. Hall of Fame, 1987—88; mem. Bd. for Internat. Broadcasting, 1991—; bd. visitors McDonald Obs., 1993—. Named one of 100 Most Influential People of 2005, Time mag. Mem.: Barton Creek Country Club (Austin). Office: The White House 1600 Pennsylvania Ave NW 1st Fl W Wing Washington DC 20500

**ROVELSTAD, GORDON H.,** dentist, researcher; b. Elgin, Ill., May 19, 1921; s. Henry Randolph and Margot Helen (Greenhill) R.; m. Barbara Jean Johnson, Apr. 8, 1945; children: Craig Gordon, Martha Kay, Andrew Todd. Student, St. Olaf Coll., 1939-41; DDS, Northwestern U., Chgo., 1944, MSD, 1948, PhD, 1960; DSc (hon.), Georgetown U., 1970. Diplomate Am. Bd. Pediatric Dentistry. Asst. prof. pediatric dentistry Northwestern U., Chgo., 1946-53; head dental dept. Children's Meml. Hosp., Chgo., 1948-53; ensign USNR, 1943, advanced through grades to capt. Camp Peary, Va., 1945-46; with USNTC, Camp Peary, Va., 1954-59; dir. rsch. U.S. Naval Dental Sch. Bethesda, Md., 1960-65; officer in charge U.S. Naval Dental Rsch. Inst., Gt. Lakes, Ill., 1965-69; dir. rsch. USN Dental Corp., Washington, 1969-74; ret., 1974; asst. dean, prof. U. Miss. Sch. Dentist, Jackson, 1974-80; exec. dir. Am. Coll. Dentists, Gaithersburg, Md., 1981-94, exec. dir. emeritus, 1994—; pres. William J. Gies Found., Gaithersburg, Md., 1982-98, pres. emeritus, 1998—. Hon. bd. dirs. William J. Gies Found. for Advancement of Dentistry, Am. Dental Edn. Assn., 2003—. Contbr. articles to profl. jours. Fellow Am. Coll. Dentists (pres., v.p.), Internat. Coll. Dentists, N.Y. Acad. Sci., N.Y. Acad. Dentists; mem. ADA, Am. Acad. Pediatric Dentistry (pres., v.p.), Internat. Assn. Dental Rsch. (pres., v.p., sec.), Rotary Internat., Sigma Xi. Avocations: miniatures, music, golf, fishing. Home: 5400 Vantage Point Rd Apt 706 Columbia MD 21044-2663

**ROVELSTAD, MATHILDE V(ERNER),** retired library and information scientist, educator; b. Germany, 1920; came to U.S., 1951. m. Howard Rovelstad, 1970. PhD, U. Tubingen, 1953; MS in L.S, Catholic U. Am., 1960. Prof. libr. sci. Cath. U. Am., 1960-90, prof. emeritus, 1990—; ret., 1990. Vis. prof. U. Montreal, 1969 Author: Bibliotheken in den Vereinigten Staaten, 1974; translator Bibliographia, an Inquiry into its Definition and Designations (R. Blum), 1980, Bibliotheken in den Vereinigten Staaten von Amerika und in Kanada, 1988; contbr. articles to profl. jours. Research grantee German Acad. Exch. Svc., 1969, Herzog August Bibliothek Wolfenbüttel, Germany, 1995. Mem. Internat. Fedn. Libr. Assns. and Instns. (standing adv. com. on libr. schs. 1975-81), Assn. for Libr. and Info. Sci. Edn. Home: Apt HR-T35 719 Maiden Choice Ln Catonsville MD 21228-6231 Office: Cath U Am Sch Libr & Info Sci Washington DC 20064-0001

**ROVEN, ALFRED NATHAN,** surgeon; came to the U.S., 1949. BA in Psychology, Calif. State U., Northridge, 1969; MD, U. So. Calif., 1977. Diplomate Am. Bd. Plastic and Reconstructive Surgery, Am. Bd. Otolaryngology. Resident in otolaryngology U. So. Calif., 1977-82; clin. chief plastic surgery Cedars Sinai Med. Ctr., L.A., 1989-91; resident in plastic and reconstructive surgery U. N.C., 1982-84; clin. chief burns Cedars Sinai Med. Ctr., L.A., 1990-92, clin. chief hands, 1990-92. Qualified med. examiner State of Calif., 1985. Contbr. articles to jours. Avocation: reading. Office: 5757 Wishire Blvd 6 Los Angeles CA 90036 Office Phone: 323-937-7733.

**ROVER, EDWARD FRANK,** foundation administrator, lawyer; b. Oct. 4, 1938; s. Frederick James and Wanda (Charkowski); m. Maureen Wyer, June 15, 1968; children: Elizabeth, Emily, William. AB, Fordham U., 1961; JD, Harvard U., 1964. Bar: N.Y. 1964, U.S. Tax Ct. 1968, U.S. Dist. Ct. (so. dist.) N.Y. 1975, U.S. Supreme Ct. 1994. Assoc. White & Case, N.Y.C., 1964-71, ptnr., 1972—2004, of counsel, 2004—; pres. Dana Found., N.Y.C., 2004—. Bd. dirs. Markel Found., N.Y.C., Cranshaw Corp., Harvard-Mahoney Neurosci. Inst., Boston, Rumsey-Cartier Found., Geneva, Charles A. Dana Found., N.Y.C., pres. Bd. dirs. Waterford Sch., Sandy, Utah, Dana-Farber, Boston, Norton Simon Art Mus., L.A.; sec. Solomon R. Guggenheim Found., NY. Mem. Assn. Bar City N.Y., Century Assn., Scarsdale Golf Club, Harvard Club, Univ. Club. Home: 1111 Park Ave New York NY 10128-1234 Office: Dana Found 745 Fifth Ave Ste 900 New York NY 10151 Office Phone: 212-223-4040. Business E-Mail: erover@dana.org.

**ROVINE, ARTHUR WILLIAM,** international arbitrator; b. Phila., Apr. 29, 1937; s. George Isaac and Rosanna (Lipsitz) R.; m. Phyllis Ellen Hamburger, Apr. 7, 1963; children: Joshua, Deborah. AB, U. Pa., 1958; LLB, Harvard U., 1961; PhD, Columbia U., 1966. Bar: D.C. 1964, N.Y. 1984. Assoc. Curtis, Mallet-Prevost, Colt & Mosle, N.Y.C., 1964—66; asst. prof. Cornell U., Ithaca, NY, 1966—72; editor Digest of U.S. Practice in International Law U.S. Dept. State, Washington, 1972—75, asst. legal adviser, 1975—81, first agt. of U.S. Govt. to Iran-U.S. Claims Tribunal The Hague, Netherlands, 1981—83; of counsel Baker & McKenzie, N.Y.C., 1983—85, ptnr., 1985—2005. Adj. prof. law Georgetown U., Washington, 1977-81; vis. lectr. law Yale U., 1998; adj. prof. law Fordham U., 2005—; dir. internat. arbitration confs. Fordham Law Sch.; arbitrator in internat. and other matters. Author: The First Fifty Years: The Secretary-General in World Politics, 1920-1970, 1970; editor: Digest of U.S. Practice in International Law, 1973, 74; co-editor: The Case Law of the International Court of Justice, 1968, 1972, 1974, 1976; bd. editors Am. Jour. Internat. Law, 1977-87; also articles on internat. law and arbitration. Mem. panel on settlement of transnat. bus. disputes, N.Y. panel Ctr. for Pub. Resources; chmn. law subcom. of internat. adv. coun. on profl. edn. Coun. on Internat. Ednl. Exch.; mem. Com. on Fgn. Rels. Mem. ABA (chmn. internat. law sect. 1985-86, del. to Ho. of Dels. 1988-90), Am. Soc. Internat. Law (cert. of merit 1974, exec. coun. 1975-77, v.p. 1998-99, pres. 2000-02), U.S. Coun. for Internat. Bus. (arbitration com.), Am. Arbitration Assn., Internat. Ctr. for Dispute Resolution (panel of arbitrators), Assn. Bar City N.Y. (arbitration com.), London Ct. Internat. Arbitration. Home: 215 East 68th St New York NY 10021 Office Phone: 212-891-3550. E-mail: arthur.w.rovine@bakernet.com.

**ROVINSKY, JOSEPH JUDAH,** obstetrician, gynecologist; b. Phila., Sept. 4, 1927; s. Israel and Sarah (Blackman) R.; m. Judith S. Levin, June 24, 1964; children: Audrey, John, Jill, Michael, Paul, David. BA, U. Pa., 1948, MD, 1952. Diplomate Am. Bd. Ob-gyn. Intern U. Pa. Hosp., Phila., 1952-53; resident in ob-gyn Mt. Sinai Hosp., N.Y.C., 1953-58; practice medicine specializing in ob-gyn, 1958—; chmn. dept. ob-gyn City Hosp. Center,

Elmhurst, NY, 1964-74; prof. ob-gyn Mt. Sinai Sch. Medicine, N.Y.C., 1969-74; prof., chmn. dept. ob-gyn Sch. Medicine Health Scis. Center, SUNY, Stony Brook, 1975-79, prof., 1975-89; chmn. dept. ob-gyn L.I. Jewish Med. Center, 1973-92; prof. ob-gyn: Albert Einstein Coll. Medicine, 1989-94; dir. dept. ob/gyn. Sound Shore Med. Ctr. of Westchester, New Rochelle, 1992—. Mem. obstetric adv. com. N.Y.C. Dept. Health, 1964-92. Author: Medical, Surgical and Gynecological Complications of Pregnancy, 1961, 2d edit., 1965; editor: Davis' Gynecology and Obstetrics, 1968-73. Served to capt., M.C. USAF, 1964-66. Mem. ACS, Am. Coll. Obstetricians and Gynecologists, Am. Soc. Reproductive Medicine, Am. Uro-Gynecologic Soc., N.Y. Acad. Medicine, N.Y. Obstetrical Soc., N.Y. Gynecol. Assn., Med. Soc. State N.Y. Jewish. Office: Sound Shore Med Ctr Westchester 16 Guion Pl New Rochelle NY 10801-5500

**ROVIRA, LUIS DARIO,** state supreme court justice; b. San Juan, PR, Sept. 8, 1923; s. Peter S. and Mae (Morris) R.; m. Lois Ann Thau, June 25, 1966; children: Douglas, Merilyn. BA, U. Colo., 1948, LL.B., 1950. Bar: Colo. 1950. Justice Colo. Supreme Ct., Denver, 1979-95, chief justice, 1990-95, ret., 1995. Mem. Pres.'s Com. on Mental Retardation, 1970-71; chmn. State Health Facilities Council, 1967-76; arbiter and mediator Jud. Arbiter Group, Denver. Trustee Temple Buell Found. With AUS, 1943-46. Mem. ABA, Colo. Bar Assn., Denver Bar Assn. (pres. 1970-71), Colo. Assn. Retarded Children (pres. 1968-70), Alpha Tau Omega, Phi Alpha Delta. Clubs: Athletic (Denver), Country (Denver). Home: 4810 E 6th Ave Denver CO 80220-5137 Office: Judicial Arbiter Group 1601 Blake St Denver CO 80202 Office Phone: 303-572-1919.

**ROVIT, RICHARD LEE,** neurosurgeon; b. Boston, Apr. 3, 1924; s. Samuel and Frances (Ehrenberg) R.; m. Barbara Sayre Margolis, Mar. 29, 1953; children: Sandra Amy Golze, Adam John, Hugh Russel. Grad., U. Mich., 1944; MD, Jefferson Med. Coll., 1950; MSc, McGill U., 1961. Diplomate Am. Bd. Neurol. Surgery (dir. vice chmn. 1986-92). Intern in surgery Beth Israel Hosp., Boston, 1950-51; resident, then chief resident Mass. Gen. Hosp., Boston, 1951-55; USPH fellow in neurology The Nat. Hosp., London, 1956; sr. fellow in neurosurgery Lahey Clinic, Boston, 1957; fellow in neurophysiology and EEG Montreal (Can.) Neurol. Inst., 1958-59; prof. clin. neurosurgery NYU, 1967—; chmn. neurosurgery St. Vincent's Hosp. and Med. Ctr., N.Y.C., 1967-92; prof. neurosurgery N.Y. Med. Coll., Valhalla, 1990—. Editor, author: Trigeminal Neuralgia, 1991; contbr. articles to profl. jours. Trustee Sarah Neuman divsn. Jewish Home and Hosps., N.Y.C., 2004-. Lt. USN, 1952-54. Fellow ACS (v.p. 1994-95), Am. Assn. Neurol. Surgeons (v.p. 1980-81); mem. N.Y. Soc. Neurosurgeons (pres. 1974-76, 79-80), Soc. Neurol. Surgeons, Fairview Country Club (Greenwich, Conn.), Harvard Club of N.Y. Avocations: golf, running. Home: 42 Brite Ave Scarsdale NY 10583-2309 Office: Manhattan Neurosurg 153 W 11th St New York NY 10011-8305 Office Phone: 212-604-7767.

**ROVNER, ILANA KARA DIAMOND,** federal judge; b. Riga, Latvia, 1938; arrived in U.S., 1939; d. Stanley and Ronny (Medalje) Diamond. AB, Bryn Mawr Coll., 1960; postgrad., U. London King's Coll., 1961, Georgetown U., 1961—63; JD, Ill. Inst. Tech., 1966; LittD (hon.), Rosary Coll., 1989, Mundelein Coll., 1989; DHL (hon.), Spertus Coll. of Judaica, 1992. Bar: Ill. 1972, U.S. Dist. (no. dist.) Ill. 1972, U.S. Ct. Appeals (7th cir.) 1977, U.S. Supreme Ct. 1991, Fed. Trial Bar (no. dist.) Ill. 1982. Jud. clk. U.S. Dist. Ct. (no. dist.) Ill., Chgo., 1972—73; asst. U.S. atty. U.S. Atty.'s Office, Chgo., 1973—77, dep. chief of pub. protection, 1975—76, chief pub. protection, 1976—77; dep. gov., legal counsel Gov. James R. Thompson, Chgo., 1977—84; dist. judge U.S. Dist. Ct. (no. dist.) Ill., Chgo., 1984—92; cir. judge U.S. Ct. Appeals (7th cir.), Chgo., 1992—. Mem. Gannon-Proctor Commn. on the Status of Women in Ill., 1982—84; mem. civil justice reform act adv. com. 7th Cir. Ct., Chgo., 1991—95, mem. race and gender fairness com., 1993—; mem. fairness com. U.S. Ct. Appeals (7th cir.), 1996—, mem. gender study task force, 1995—96; mem. jud. conf. U.S. Com. Ct. Adminstrn. Case Mgmt., 2000—. Ctrl. and East European law initiative vol. ABA, 1997—; trustee Bryn Mawr Coll., Pa., 1983—89; mem. bd. overseers Ill. Inst. Tech./Kent Coll. Law, 1983—; trustee Ill. Inst. Tech., 1989—; mem. adv. coun. Rush Ctr. for Sports Medicine, Chgo., 1991—96; bd. dirs. Rehab. Inst. Chgo., 1998—; bd. visitors No. Ill. Coll. Law, 1992—94; vis. com. Northwestern U. Sch. Law, 1993—98, U. Chgo. Law Sch., 1993—96, 2000—03; chair Ill. state selection com. Rhodes Scholarship Trust, 1998—2000. Named Today's Chgo. Woman of the Yr., 1985, Woman of Achievement, Chgo. Women's Club, 1986; named one of 15 Chgo. Women of the Century, Chgo. Sun Times, 1999; named to Today's Chgo. Women Hall of Fame, 2002; recipient Spl. Commendation award, U.S. Dept. Justice, 1975, Spl. Achievement award, 1976, Ann. Nat. Law and Social Justice Leadership award, League to Improve the Cmty., 1975, Ann. Guardian Police award, 1977, Profl. Achievement award, Ill. Inst. Tech., 1986, ORT Women's Am. Cmty. Svc. award, 1987—88, commendation def. of prisoners com., Chgo. Bar Assn., 1987, Svc. award, Spertus Coll. of Judaica, 1987, Ann. award, Chgo. Found. for Women, 1990, Louis Dembitz Brandeis medal for Disting. Legal Svc., Brandeis U., 1993, 1st Woman award, Valparaiso U. Sch. Law, 1993, Hebrew Immigrant Aid Soc. Chgo. 85th Anniversary honoree, 1996, Arabella Babb Mansfield award, Nat. Assn. Women Lawyers, 1998, award, Chgo. Attys. Coun. of Hadassah, 1999, First Woman award, Chgo. Bar Assn. Alliance for Women and Women's Bar Assn. Ill., 2000, Georgetown U. Law Ctr., 2001, Chgo. Hist. Soc. Trailblazers Award, 2003, Lifetime Achievement award, Decalogue Soc. Lawyers, 2004, Vanguard award, Chgo. Bar Assn. and Lesbian and Gay Bar Assn. Chgo., 2004, Thurgood Marshall Career Achievement award, Assn. Corp. Counsel Chgo. chpt., 2005, Hero of Liberty award, Nat. Liberty Mus., 2005, Inaugural Judge Abraham Lincoln Marovitz Mentoring award, Chgo. Bar Assn. and Found. Lend-a-Hand Program, 2005. Mem.: Chgo. Bar Assn. (Justice John Paul Stevens award 2005), Jewish Judges Assn. Ill. (Lifetime Achievement award 2004), Decalogue Soc. of Lawyers (citation of honor 1991, Merit award 1997), Chgo. Coun. Lawyers, Women's Bar Assn. Ill. (ann. award 1989, 1st Myra Bradwell Woman of Achievement award 1994, 1st Woman award (in conjunction with Chicago Bar Assn. Alliance for Women) 2000), Fed. Judges Assn., Fed. Bar Assn. (mem. selection com. Chgo. chpt. 1977—80, treas. 1978—79, sec. 1979—80, 2d v.p. 1980—81, 1st v.p. 1981—82, pres. 1982—83, v.p. 7th cir. 1983—84, v.p. 7th cir. 1984—85), Kappa Beta Pi, Phi Alpha Delta (hon.). Office: 219 S Dearborn St Ste 2774 Chicago IL 60604-1803

**ROVNER, MICHAL,** video artist, photographer; b. Tel Aviv, Nov. 7, 1957; BA in cinema/television and philosophy, Tel Aviv U., 1981; BFA (hon.), Bezalel Acad. Art. Co-founder Camera Obscura Art Sch., Tel Aviv, 1978. Permanent Collections: Mus. Modern Art, Metrop. Mus. Art, Guggenheim Mus., Whitney Mus. American Art, NYC, Art Inst Chgo., Mus. of Contemporary Art, Chgo., Los Angeles County Mus. Art, Mus. Fine Arts Houston, Corcoran Gallery Art, Washington, D.C., Israel Mus., Jerusalem, MACRO: Museo d'arte contemporanea Rome, Musée de l'Elysée, Lausanne, Tel Aviv Mus.; Commissioned Works: Installation Tel/Hill (mural), Colonnade House, Tel Aviv, 95; Installation Co-Existence (several murals overhanging Syrian-African break); Construct Process-Artist's Mus., Mitzpe-Ramon, Israel, 95; Exhibitions: Sky Line, Tel Aviv Mus. Art, 88.; Video installations include: Overhang, Chase Manhattan Bank on Park Ave. NYC, 2000; Overhanging, Stedelijk Mus., Amsterdam, 1999; Mutual Interest, Tate Gallery, London, 1997, Stedelijk Mus., Amsterdam, 1997 and P.S.1, NYC, 1999; Over 40 solo exhibitions in video and film including: Tel Aviv Mus. Art, 90, Maison Cult Mercier, Montreal, 91, Art Inst Chgo. 93 & Israel Mus. Jerusalem, 94, Michal Rovner: The Space Between, Whitney Mus. of American Art, 2002, Against Order? Against Disorder?, Israeli Pavilion at the 50th Internat. Art Exhibition, Venice Biennale, 2003, Michal Rovner in stone, PaceWildenstein Gallery, 2004. Office: PaceWildenstein Gallery 32 E 57th St 2nd Fl New York NY 10022

**ROWAN, HENRY M.,** electrical engineer; b. Raphine, Va. m. Betty Rowan. BS in Elec. Engring., MIT. Founder, chmn. Inductotherm Industries, Inc., Rancocas, N.J. Patentee in field. Glassboro (N.J.) State Coll. renamed in his honor, 1992. Mem. NAE. Achievements include research in frequency tripler circuit utilizing the third harmonic component of transformers, stabilized controlled rectifyer circuit having inductive load and induction heating systems for efficiently melting metals. Office: Inductotherm Industries Inc PO Box 157 10 Indel Ave Rancocas NJ 08073-0157

**ROWAN, HERMAN T.,** art educator, artist; b. NYC, July 20, 1923; s. Charles and Hannah Rosen; m. Helen June Rowan (div.); m. Terri Deane Rowan, Sept. 15, 1968; children: Nathaniel, Samuel. BS, Kans. State U., 1950; MFA, State u. Iowa, 1952. Prof. U. Minn., Mpls., 1963—. Author: (retrospective exhbn.) U. Minn., 1992; exhibitions include Joan of Art Gallery, Mpls., 2006. Sgt. Air Corps U.S. Army, 1941—45, ETO. Home: 1915 19th Ave NE Minneapolis MN 55418

**ROWAN, RICHARD G.,** academic administrator; BS, Furman U.; MEd, EdS, Ga. State U.; D of Design (hon.), Nottingham Trent U., Eng. Pres., co-founder Savannah (Ga.) Coll. Art and Design, 1978—2000, chancellor, 2000—01. Mem. Savannah adv. bd. Bank of Am. Recipient Oglethorpe award, Freedom award NAACP; named to Hon. Order Ky. Cols. Mem. Savannah C. of C. (pres., bd. dirs.). Office: Savannah Coll Art & Design Office of the Chancellor PO Box 3146 Savannah GA 31402-3146

**ROWAN, RICHARD LAMAR,** business management educator; b. Guntersville, Ala., July 10, 1931; s. Leon Virgle and Mae (Williamson) R.; m. Marilyn Walker, Aug. 3, 1963; children: John Richard, Jennifer Walker. AB, Birmingham-So. Coll., 1953; postgrad., Auburn U., 1956-57; PhD, U. N.C., 1961. Instr. Auburn (Ala.) U., 1956-57, U. N.C., Chapel Hill, 1958-59, 60-61; lectr. U. Pa., Phila., 1961-62, asst. prof., 1962-66, asso. prof. industry, 1966-73, prof. industry, 1973—. Dir. indsl. research unit, 1989-91; co-dir. Ctr. for Human Resources, 1991—; visitor to Faculty Econs. and Politics Cambridge (Eng.) U., 1972; pvt. sector advisor U.S. State Dept. Com. on Internat. Investment and Multinational Enterprises, OECD, 1982-89; chmn. Labor Relations Council, 1985—. Author: (with H.R. Northrup) The Negro and Employment Opportunity, 1965, Readings in Labor Economics and Labor Relations, 5th edit., 1984, The Negro in the Steel Industry, 1969, The Negro in the Textile Industry, 1970, (with others) Studies of Negro Employment, 1970, Educating the Employed Disadvantaged for Upgrading, 1972, Collective Bargaining: Survival in the 1970's, 1972, Opening the Skilled Construction Trades to Blacks, 1972, The Impact of Government Manpower Programs, 1975, International Enforcement of Union Standards in Ocean Transport, 1977, The Impact of OSHA, 1978, Multinational Bargaining Attempts: The Record, the Cases, and the Prospects, 1980; (with H.R. Northrup) Employee Relations and Regulations in the 80s, 1982; (with others) Multinational Union Organizations in the Manufacturing Industries, (with D.C. Campbell) The Multinational Enterprises and the OECD Industrial Relations Guidelines, 1984, Trade Union Clout Erodes, But For How Long?, 1985, Employee Relations Trends and Practices in the Textile Industry, 1986; contbr. articles to profl. jours. Mem. personnel com. Del. Valley Settlement Alliance, 1966-68. Served with Transp. Corps U.S. Army, 1953-56. Recipient Disting. Alumni award, Birmingham-So. Coll., 2000. Mem. Indsl. Rels. Rsch. Assn. (sec. Phila. 1964-65), Acad. Internat. Bus. Democrat. Episcopalian. Home: 113 Blackthorn Rd Wallingford PA 19086-6046 Office: U Pa Wharton Sch 3733 Spruce St Philadelphia PA 19104-6301 Office Phone: 610-565-0409.

**ROWAN, WILLIAM HAMILTON, JR.,** computer science educator; b. Nashville, Tenn., May 8, 1933; s. William Hamilton and Elizabeth (Lowry) R.; m. Sarah Conley, June 9, 1973; children: Elizabeth, Bill. BE, Vanderbilt U., 1955; PhD, N.C. State U., 1965. Registered profl. engr., Tenn. Jr. engr. Boeing Airplane Co., Seattle, 1955-57; instr. of mechanics Vanderbilt U., Nashville, 1959-60; electronics engr. Tenn. State Hwy. Dept., Nashville, 1960-61; grad. student civil engring. N.C. State U., Raleigh, NC, 1961-64; asst. prof. math. Vanderbilt U., Nashville, 1964-67; assoc. prof. and chmn. computer sci. dept., 1967-71, prof. computer sci., 1971-95, prof. computer sci. emeritus, 1996—. Staff couns. AVCO Corp. aerostructures divsn., Nashville, 1965-70; pres., CEO, On-Line Computing, Inc., Nashville; bd. dirs. On-Line Data, Inc., Nashville, 1974-85. Co-editor: (book) Application of Finite Element Methods in Civil Engineering, 1969; co-author: (book) Computer Methods of Structural Analysis, 1970. 1st lt. U.S. Army, 1957-59. Recipient fellowship grant Ford Found., N.C. State U., Raleigh, 1961-64. Mem. IEEE, Am. Soc. for Engring. Edn., Assn. for Computing Machinery, Phi Kappa Phi, Tau Beta Pi. Avocation: golf. Office: Vanderbilt Univ Box 1679 Sta B Nashville TN 37235 E-mail: whrfl@att.net.

**ROWAND, AARON,** professional baseball player; b. Aug. 29, 1977; Studied, Cal. State Fullerton. Outfielder Chgo. White Sox, 2001—05, Phila. Phillies, 2005—. Achievements include world series champion, 2005. Office: Citizens Bank Ballpark One Citizens Bank Way Philadelphia PA 19148*

**ROWARK, MAUREEN,** fine arts photographer; b. Edinburgh, Midlothian, Scotland, Feb. 28, 1933; came to U.S., 1960, naturalized, 1970; d. Alexander Pennycook and Margaret (Gorman) Prezdpelski; m. Robert Rowark, May 3, 1952 (div. July 1965). 1 child, Mark Steven. Student, Warmington Bus. Coll., Royal Leamington Spa, Eng., 1950-51, Royal Leamington Spa Art Sch.; diploma, Speedwriting Inst., N.Y.C., 1961; AS in Edn., St. Clair County Community Coll., Port Huron, Mich., 1977, AA, 1978. Supr. record reading Nevin D. Hirst Advt., Ltd., Leeds, England, 1952-55; publicity asst. Alvis Aero Engines, Ltd., Coventry, England, 1955-57; adminstrv. asst. Port Huron Motor Inn, 1964-66; adminstrv. asst. pub. rels. dept. Geophysics and Computer Svcs., Inc., New Orleans, 1966-68; sales mgr. Holiday Inn, Port Huron, 1968-70; adminstrv. asst. Howard Corp., Port Huron, 1971-73; sales and systems coord. Am. Wood Products, Ann Arbor, Mich., 1973-74; systems coord. Daniels & Zermack Architects, Ann Arbor, 1974; systems coord., cataloger fine arts dept. St. Clair County Community Coll., Port Huron, 1976-79; freelance fine arts photographer Port Huron, 1978—. Photographer Patterns mag. front cover, 1978, Erie Sq. Gazette, 1979, Bluewater Area Tourism Bur. brochure, 1989, 92, 93, 97, 2000, 01, Corns Castle, Lexington, 2002, Port Huron, Can. Legion, Wyo., Ont. Br., 1987, 88—; Grace Episcopal Ch. Mariner's Day, Port Huron, 1987, 92-2001, Homes mag., 1989. Photographer (one-woman shows) Grace Episcopal Ch., 1995, Port Huron Mus., 1995, St. Clair River Remedial Action Plan, 1995 (Best in Landscape Category), Mich. Waterways Coun. Girl Scouts Exhibit, 1996; Exhibited in group shows at Ea. Mich. Internat. Juried Exhbn., 2000, 1981—98 (Award of Excellence, 1982, 1983, Best Photography award, 1995, 1996, 1997), Our Town Juried Exhbn., 1997, St. Clair County C.C., 1983, 1986 (Award of Excellence, 1986), Gallery Lambton, Sarnia, Ont., Can., 1983—92 (Best Photography, 1988), 1994, 1996—97, 2000, Bluewater Bridge, 1988, Kaskilaaksontie, Finland, 1991 (Par Excellence award), Swann Gallery, Detroit, 1996, St. Clair (Mich.) Art Gallery, Genesis Gallery, Lexington, Mich., others, Represented in permanent collections Royal Can. Legion, Wyo. Br. Centaph, Capac State Bank, Grace Episcopal Ch., Thomas Edison Inn, Port Huron Hosp., Front Cover Good Health News; costume design, manufacture and modelling Bluewater Art Assn., 2000—01, photographer Bluewater Percussion Brochure, 2001; author short stories. Cons., buyer interior decor Grace Episcopal Ch., 1994; active Port Huron Mus., 1978; founder Bluewater les Chapeaux Rouge chpt. Red Hat Soc., 2001—; prodr. dir. calendar We Can Still Make Waves, 2005; prodr., designer parade float Rotary Internat., 2005 (1st pl. award). Recipient hon. mention Gallery Lambton, Sarnia, 1981, 2d pl. memoir writing women's history month St. Clair County C.C., 1999; winner 2d and 3d place awards Times Herald Newspaper, 1988, 1st place juried photography award Port Huron Art Festival, 1997, 1st place St. Patrick's Day Parade Float, 2005, 1st place Rotary Internat. Day Parade Float, 2005. Mem. St. Clair County C.C. Alumni Assn., Phi Theta Kappa, Lambda Mu. Democrat. Episcopalian. Avocations: costumes and interior design, travel, theater, memoir writing. Home and Office: 3512 Walnut St Port Huron MI 48060 Office Phone: 810-989-9192. E-mail: ha-penerth-of-tar@prodigy.net.

**ROWDEN, MARCUS AUBREY,** lawyer, retired government agency administrator; b. Detroit, Mar. 13, 1928; s. Louis and Gertrude (Lifsitz) Rosenzweig; m. Justine Leslie Bessman, July 21, 1950; children: Gwen, Stephanie. BA in Econs. U. Mich., Ann Arbor, 1950, JD with distinction, 1953. Bar: Mich. 1953, D.C. 1978. Trial atty. Dept. Justice, 1953-58; legal advisor U.S. Mission to European Communities, 1959-62; solicitor, assoc. gen. counsel, gen. counsel AEC, 1965-74; commr., chmn. U.S. NRC, Washington, 1975-77; ptnr. Fried, Frank, Harris, Shriver and Jacobson, Washington, 1977—. With U.S. Army, 1946—47. Decorated officer Order Legion of Honor Republic of France; Recipient Disting. Service award AEC, 1972 Mem. ABA, Fed. Bar Assn., Mich. Bar Assn., DC Bar Assn., Internat. Nuc. Law Assn., Order of Coif. Home: 7937 Deepwell Dr Bethesda MD 20817-1927 Office: Fried Frank Harris Shriver and Jacobson 1001 Pennsylvania Ave NW Washington DC 20004-2505 Office Phone: 202-639-7070.

**ROWE, AUDREY,** paralegal; b. Albuquerque, June 26, 1958; d. James Franklin Ringold and Geneva Doris (Jennings) Robinson. A in Specialized Bus. in Acctg., ICS Ctr. for Degrees, Scranton, Pa., 1988, A in Specialized Bus. in Fin., 1989; BSBA, Century U., 1991, MBA, 1995, cert. paralegal studies, 1996, A in Specialized Bus. in Paralegal Studies, 1999. Svc. rep. Mountain and Southwestern Bell Telephone Co., Albuquerque, Houston, 1978-83; clk., carrier U.S. Postal Svc. PS05, Bellaire, Sugar Land, Tex., 1983-86; supr. mails U.S. Postal Svc. EAS15. Sugar Land, 1986-87; officer-in-charge U.S. Postal Svc. EAS 18, Rosharon, Tex., 1987; from supr. mails EAS 15 to gen. supr. mails EAS 17 U.S. Postal Svc., Houston, 1987-89; relief tour supt. U.S. Postal Svc. EAS 21 (Detail Assignment), Houston, 1989; mgr. gen. mail facility U.S. Postal Svc. EAS22 (Detail Assignment), Capitol Heights, Md., 1989-90; mgr. mail processing U.S. Postal Svc. EAS21, Charlottesville, Va., 1990-91; MSC dir. city ops. U.S. Postal Svc. EAS23 (Detail Assignment), Roanoke, Va., 1991; mgr. gen. mail facility U.S. Postal Svc. EAS24, Washington, 1991-96; plant mgr. U.S. Postal Svc. EAS25, Dulles, Va., 1992; pvt. contractor, paralegal, 1996-98; paralegal Lenox, Biddinger & Conrad, P.C., Woodbridge, Va., 1997-99, Wilson Strickland & Benson P.C., Atlanta, 1999-2000, Chamberlain, Hrdlicka, White, Williams & Martin, 2000—03, Holland & Knight, LLP, 2003—. Mem. Nat. Fedn. Paralegal Assn., Nat. Assn. Legal Assts. Avocations: piano, violin, reading. Personal E-mail: allrowe@aol.com.

**ROWE, BOBBY LOUISE,** art educator; b. Montgomery, Ala., Feb. 15, 1930; d. Herbert and Louise (Barbaree) R. AB, Montevallo U., 1950; MA, Columbia U., 1959; PhD, Fla. State U., 1974. Cert. tchr. K-12 and jr. coll., Fla. Supr. student tchrs. U. Fla. Coll. Edn., Gainesville; assoc. prof. art edn. Mid. Tenn. State U., Murfreesboro; art edn. dir. Cleve. State U.; art curriculum specialist Palm Beach County Sch. Bd., West Palm Beach, Fla. Fiber artist, computer imagist, digital photographer, writer; lectr., presenter in field. Contbr. articles to profl. jours. Mem. Nat. Art Edn. Assn., Am. Edn. Rsch. Assn., Alpha Delta Kappa. E-mail: artrowe711@msn.com.

**ROWE, BONNIE GORDON,** music company executive; b. Buford, Ga. May 3, 1922; s. Bonnie Gordon and Alma (Poole) R.; m. Mary Wilburta Shidler; 1 child, Sharon Lynn; m. Gloria Lucille Fairfax, Feb. 17, 1962 (div.); 1 child, Susan Rebecca. Student, Ga. Evening Coll., 1939-41, U. Wichita, 1948-49, Ga. State Coll., 1949-52. Traffic mgr. Bonanza Air Lines, Las Vegas, 1946-48, music tchr., 1948-52; owner Rowe Accordion Distbg. Co., Rowe Accordion Ctr., Atlanta, 1952-56, Atlanta Music Pub. Co., 1956—, B. Rowe Music Co., Atlanta, 1957—. Pres.-treas. B. Rowe Enterprises, Inc., 1973—. Bd. dir. Sandtown Found., Atlanta. Lt. col. USAAF, World War II, ETO. Decorated Air medals with three oak leaf clusters. Mem.: Nat. Assn. Music Mchts., Atlanta Fedn. Musicians (life), The Mil. Order of the World Wars (past comdr. Atlanta chpt.), Internat. Platform Assn., Sandtown Civitan Club (pres., past pres. Met. Atlanta Coun., lt. gov.), Air Force Assn., Res. Officers Assn., Travelers Protective Assn., 781st Bomb Squadron Assn. (465th bomb group WWII), Atlanta C. of C., Mil. Officers Assn. Am., Southea. Accordion Assn. (past pres.), Dobbins AFB Officers Club, Elks (exalted ruler 1987, 1988, 1989, past pres. past exalted rulers assn., past state organist Ga. Elks Assn., trustee Union City), Am. Legion, Georgia Delta Phi. Home: 5085 Erin Rd SW Atlanta GA 30331-7810 Office: 6102 Mableton Pkwy Mableton GA 30126-4302 Office Phone: 770-948-8403. Personal E-mail: brga30331@aol.com.

**ROWE, CHARLES ALFRED,** artist, graphics designer, educator; b. Great Falls, Mont., Feb. 7, 1934; s. Alfred Lewis and Alice Lillian (Ledbetter) R.; m. Eugenia Dean, July 5, 1958; children: Allison Rene, Jon Garner, Dorian Leigh. Student, Mont. State U., 1952—53, So. Meth. U., 1956—57, U. Chgo., 1959—60; BFA, Sch. Art Inst., Chgo., 1960; MFA, Tyler Sch. Art, 1968. Prin. Charles Rowe Advt., Chgo., 1957-60; graphic designer Am. Can Co., Bellwood, Ill., 1960-62, Abrams-Bannister Engraving, Inc., Greenville, SC, 1962-64; prof. art U. Del., Newark, 1964-97, emeritus prof., 1997—. One-man shows include Tyler Sch. Art, Phila., 1968, Mickelson Gallery, Washington, 1970, 1974, C.M. Russell Mus., Great Falls, 1972—73, 1981, 1992, Pleiades Gallery, N.Y.C., 1977, 1981, Vision of La Herradura, Almuñecar, Spain, 1988, USAF exhbn. Soc. Illustrators, N.Y.C., 1991, 2004, West Chester (Pa.) U., 1992, Soc. Illustrators, N.Y.C., 1993, 2004, exhibited in group shows at C.M. Russell Mus., 1974, 1976, 1978, 1980, 1982—83, 1986—91, Am. Painters in Paris, 1976, Monac-Western Art Exhibit, Spokane, Wash., 1977—78, Easton (Md.) Waterfowl Festival, 1981—82, USAF Nat. Collection, 1987, 1989, 1991, USAF exhbn. Soc. Illustrators, N.Y.C., 1989, Our Own Show, Soc. Illustrators, 1990—96, 1998—2000, 2003—06, Atrium Gallery, 1995, 1996, One Small Step, NASA, U. Del., Newark, 1995, Our Own Show, Soc. Illustrators, N.Y.C., 2002—04, Art and Antiques, Wilmington, Del., 2005, over 220 other exhbns., Represented in permanent collections U. Del., Mont. State Collection, Mont. State U., Del. State Collection, Libr. Congress, Washington, Great Falls Pub. Schs., Michael Landon Prodns., Calif., Meredith Corp., Des Moines, Collection Knissel, Austria, Star Showers Found., Graveson-en-Provence, France, Archives Victoria and Albert Mus., London, artists USAF Nat. Collection, Washington, Jacqueline Pierson, Nice, France, artists USAF Nat. Collection, Washington, Banco de Granada, Spain, NASA Space Mus., Hauptman and Greenwood Collections, N.Y.C., Vera Haas, Dallas Jerry Pinkney, Croton-On Hudson, Baker, Honolulu, fabric designer Galleon Fabrics, Inc., N.Y.C., Jones of N.Y., Saks Fifth Ave., Bush Collection, Swampscott, Mass., Steele Collection, Big Fork, MT, Jordan Baker, Kevin Kilner, Hollywood, Calif., 1987, Kevin Kostner Collection, 1997, designer graphics Mont. State Arts Coun., Del. state duck stamp, 1981. With inf. U.S. Army, 1954-56. Ctr. for Advanced Study fellow, 1981-82; grantee U. Del., 1964-79, Nat. Endowment for Arts and Humanities, 1972-73, U. Del. Bicentennial, 1976. Mem. Soc. of Illustrators (N.Y.C.). Home: Chapel Hill 133 Aronimink Dr Newark DE 19711-3802 E-mail: CharlesRoweStudio@comcast.net. *In my paintings and other artforms I strive for perfection, uniqueness, and a special inner beauty, but more than that, I try to create art that has a universal quality. This universality makes an artform communicate beyond a specific locale, continent or a limited time reference. All great works of art have this special element regardless of when they were created.*

**ROWE, DAVID LEE,** financial advisor; b. Colorado Springs, Colo., Jan. 30, 1954; s. Prentiss Eldon and Jo Ann (Osborn) R.; m. Elizabeth Webb, June 21, 1986; children: Schuyler Jourdan, Thomas Prentiss. BA, U. Colo., 1976; Master's degree, Johns Hopkins U., 1979; MBA, NYU, 1995. Asst. to undersec. U.S. Dept. Commerce, Washington, 1979—80; analyst Commodities Rsch. Inst., N.Y.C., 1980—81; fin. advisor Merrill Lynch, N.Y.C., 1981—83, Prudential Wachovia Securities, N.Y.C., 1983—, sr. v.p., asst. br. mgr., 1997—. Mem. cmty. ministry coun. St. Bartholomew's Ch., N.Y.C., 1987-96, mem. vestry, 1997—2005, treas., 2000—05; bd. dirs. 133 E. 80th St. Corp., 1999—; adv. bd. Health Advocates Older People, 2003—; bd. dirs. Quogue Jr. Theatre Troupe, 2006—. Home: 133 E 80th St New York NY 10021-0317 Office: Wachovia Securities 625 Madison Ave New York NY 10022-1801 Office Phone: 212-303-8738. Personal E-mail: cujhunyu@yahoo.com. Business E-mail: david.l.rowe@wachoviasec.com

**ROWE, DAVID WINFIELD,** lawyer; b. Chgo., Nov. 7, 1954; s. Bernard John and Gertrude Katherine (Johnson) R.; m. Martha Lynn Plott, June 12, 1977; children: Daniel, Peter. BA, Davidson Coll., 1976; PhD in Psychology, U. Tenn., 1981; JD, U. Mich., 1987. Bar: Colo. 1987, Nebr. 1989, U.S. Dist. Ct. Colo. 1987, U.S. Dist. Ct. Nebr. 1989, U.S. Ct. Appeals (10th cir.) 1987, U.S. Ct. Appeals (8th cir.) 2004, U.S. Supreme Ct. 2006. Vis. asst. prof.

Davidson (N.C.) Coll., 1981-82; mental health worker Peninsula Psychiat. Hosp., Louisville, Tenn., 1982-84; instr. dept. psychology U. Tenn., Knoxville, 1982-84; assoc. Gorsuch, Kirgis, Campbell, Walker & Grover, Denver, 1987-89; NIMH postdoctoral fellow in law and psychology U. Nebr., Lincoln, 1989-91; assoc. and ptnr. Kinsey, Ridenour, Becker & Kistler, Lincoln, Nebr., 1991—2005; ptnr. Kinsey, Rowe, Becker & Kistler, LLP, Lincoln, 2006—. Mem. interim study group on care Health and Human Svcs. com. Nebr. State Legislature, 1990-91; adj. prof. psychology U. Nebr., Lincoln, 1992-94; bd. dirs., past treas. Lincoln Attention Ctr. for Youth; mem. The Mediation Ctr., Detention Ctr. Adv. Bd., 2003-. Author: (with others) Dimensions of Child Advocacy: Advocating for the Child in Protection Proceedings, 1990, Children Under Three in Foster Care, 1991. Exec. com. Lancaster County Rep. Com., 1991-97, chmn., 1993-95; bd. dirs. Lincoln-Lancaster Mental Health Found., 1993-, v.p., 1995-96, pres., 1996-97; mem. Ctrl. Com. Nebr. Rep. Com., 1993-97; bd. dirs. The Arc of Lincoln Lancaster County, 2003-; deacon Westminster Prebyn. Ch., 1996-99. Mem. ABA, Nebr. Bar Assn. (alternative dispute resolution com. 1990—2000), Cornhusker Kiwanis (pres. Lincoln 1997-98). Office: Kinsey Rowe Becker & Kistler LLP 121 S 13th St#601 PO Box 85778 Lincoln NE 68501-5778 Office Phone: 402-438-1313. E-mail: drowe@krbklaw.com.

**ROWE, ERNEST RAS,** education educator, academic administrator; b. Hot Springs, Ark., July 19, 1933; s. Stephen Paul and Emma Leathia (Martin) R.; m. Carla True Dirk, May 27, 1995. BS with distinction, Ariz. State U., 1955, MEd, 1962, EdD, 1965; postgrad., Gonzaga U., 1975, Dublin City U., Ireland, 1989. Tchr. Madison Sch. Dist., Phoenix, 1960-61, Garden Grove (Calif.) Unified Sch. Dist., 1964-66; cons. spl. edn. Ariz. Dept. Pub. Instrn., Phoenix, 1966-67; asst. prof. Idaho State U., Pocatello, 1967-70, assoc. prof., 1970-74, prof. edn., 1974-95, interim chmn. dept. edn., summer 1992; adminstrv. intern Cen. Adminstrn., 1982-83, 94-95. Vis. prof. edn. Calif. State U., Long Beach, summer 1965; adv. mem. Idaho Task Force on Higher Edn., 1982-83; gov. apptd. Idaho commr. to Edn. Commn. of the States, 1979-93, rep. to steering com., 1989-93; elected chmn. Idaho State U. Faculty Senate, 1970, 71-72, 86-87. Contbr. articles to profl. jours. Bd. dirs. Bannock Meml. Hosp., 1975-78; mem. Idaho Bd. Medicine pre-litigation panel for malpractice hearings, 1980-95. 1st lt. U.S. Army, 1955-57. Mem.: AAUP, Am. Inst. Parliamentarians (gov. N.W. region 1992—94, univ. parliamentarian), Nat. Soc. Study Edn., Kyrene Corridor Club, Rotary (pres. Pocatello, Idaho club 1981—82, asst. dist. gov. 1998—99, Ariz. pres. Chandler Club 2002—03), Masons, Phi Kappa Phi (pres. 1972—73, 1987—88). Episcopalian. Avocations: exercise, music, travel, photography. Home: 678 N Poplar Ct Chandler AZ 85226-6801 E-mail: errcyrano@cox.net. *Initiative and responsibility are cornerstones of a meaningful personal and professional life. Sadly they are missing in much of contemporary society. Apathy, the absence of civility and self-indulgence appear most prominently at the turn of the century and thus far in the 21st century.*

**ROWE, G. STEVEN,** state attorney general; m. Amanda Rowe; 4 children. BS, US. Mil. Acad.; MBA, U. Utah; JD, U. Maine. Mem. Dist. 30 Maine Ho. of Reps., 1993-95, mem. Dist. 35, 1995—2001; litigation counsel UNUM-Provident; atty. gen. State of Maine, 2001—. Mem. Pine Tree Legal Assistance, Inc. With U.S. Army, with USAR. Mem.: N.E. Legis. Assn. on Prescription Drug Prices, Maine Econ. Growth Coun. Democrat. Office: Office of Atty General State House Station 6 Augusta ME 04333 Office Phone: 207-626-8800.*

**ROWE, HAHN,** composer; Composer: (albums) The New Body, performer with Mimi, with Moby, with David Byrne, Foetus, with Syd Straw, with Swans, with True Mori, Michael Brook, with many others; composer: (films) Clean Shaven, The Transformation, Black Kites, Spring Forward.

**ROWE, HARRISON EDWARD,** electrical engineer; b. Chgo., Jan. 29, 1927; s. Edward and Joan (Golden) R.; m. Alicia Jane Steeves, Feb. 10, 1951; children: Amy Rogers, Elizabeth Joanne, Edward Steeves, Alison Pickard. BS in Elec. Engring., Mass. Inst. Tech., 1948, MS, 1950, Sc.D., 1952; M of Engring. (hon.), Stevens Inst. Tech., 1988. Mem. tech. staff Radio Research Lab., Bell Labs., Holmdel, NJ, 1952-84; Anson Wood Burchard prof. elec. engring. Stevens Inst. Tech., Hoboken, NJ, 1984-93, prof. emeritus, 1993—. Vis. lectr. U. Calif., Berkeley, 1963, Imperial Coll., U. London, 1968; mem. Def. Sci. Bd. Task Force, 1972-74 Author: Signals and Noise in Communication Systems, 1965, Electromagnetic Propagation in Multi-Mode Random Media, 1999; assoc. editor: IEEE Trans. on Communication, 1974-76; contbr. articles to profl. jours.; patentee in field. Served with USN, 1945-46. Co-recipient Microwave prize, 1972, David Sarnoff award, 1977. Fellow IEEE; mem. Monmouth Symphony Soc., Navesink Country Club, Sigma Xi, Tau Beta Pi, Eta Kappa Nu. Clubs: Shrewsbury Sailing and Yacht, Appalachian Mountain. Unitarian Universalist. Home: 9 Buttonwood Ln Rumson NJ 07760-1045 Office Phone: 732-747-0356. Business E-Mail: harrisonrowe@comcast.net.

**ROWE, HERBERT JOSEPH,** retired trade association executive; b. Granite City, Ill., Mar. 25, 1924; s. Herbert Bernard and Maude (Klein) R.; m. Ann Muter, Dec. 2, 1950; children: Douglas H., Stephen F., James D., Edith L., Allen. Student, U. Tex., 1942—43, Purdue U., 1943—44; BS in Mktg., U. Ill., 1948; LittD (hon.), London Inst. for Applied Rsch., 1975. With Edward Valves, Inc. (subs. Rockwell Mfg. Co.), 1948—50, Muter Co., Chgo., 1952—71, v.p., 1957—64, pres., 1964—71, treas., 1964—67, chmn. bd., 1965—71, also dir., 1957—71; pres., treas. dir. Wescoil Co., 1964—66, Tri-Axial Corp., 1966—67; v.p., treas. Gen. Magnetic Corp., 1965—67, chmn. bd., dir., 1967—70, Pemcor, Inc., Westchester, Ill., 1971—75; assoc. adminstr. external affairs NASA, 1975—78; sr. v.p. Electronic Industries Assn., 1978—89; chmn. Famro Corp., 1989—90; pres. Internat. Electronics Fedn., 1989—90. Sec.-treas. Englewood Elec. Supply Wis., Inc., 1972-75, Rahr's Inc., 1972-75; pres. Enclave of Naples, Inc., 1992-94, treas., 1994-96; pres. Rowe Corp., 1994-97; treas. Quality wholesale Foods of S.W. Fla., 1994-96. Pres. Pokagon Trails coun. Boy Scouts Am., 1964-66, pres. Calumet coun., 1966-68, region 7 exec. com., 1966-72, vice chmn., 1971-72, bd. dirs. East Ctrl. region, 1972-75, nat. program com., 1970-78, 90-94, nat. Cub Scout com., 1970-80, chmn., 1990-94, S.E. regional exec. com., 1975-78, So. regional exec. bd., 1993—, bd. dirs. Nat. Capital Area coun., 1978-90, adv. bd., 1990-94, exec. bd. S.W. Fla. coun., 1992—, nat. exec. com., exec. bd., 1990-95, nat. adv. bd., 1995—; membership chmn. Nat. Eagle Scouts Assn., 1976-80; corp. campaign chmn. Chgo. Met. Crusade Mercy, 1964-68, chmn. Bd. Edn. Caucus, Flossmoor, Ill., 1962; bd. dirs. Flossmoor United Party, 1963-68; mem. U. Ill. Found., 1967—; adv. com. U. Ill. Coll. Commerce and Bus. Adminstrn., 1968-78, 97-2002; bd. dirs. Electronic Industries Found., 1974-94; adv. bd. Air and Space Mus., Smithsonian Inst., 1975-78; active Moorings Presbyn. Ch., Naples, Fla. With USMCR, 1942-46, 50-52. Recipient Silver Beaver award Boy Scouts Am., 1966, Silver Antelope award, 1969, Silver Buffalo award, 1997; NASA team award Bicentennial Expo on Sci. and Tech., Exceptional Svc. medal, 1978, Baden-Powell fellow World Scout Found., 1992. Mem. AIAA, AAAS, Electronic Industries Assn. (hon., bd. dirs. 1967-69, bd. govs. 1969-75, exec. com. parts divsn. 1966-75, vice chmn. parts divsn. 1970-74, chmn. 74-75, bd. dirs. consumer electronics divsn. 1972-75, chmn. world trade com. 1968-70, vice-chmn. 1970-73, chmn. membership and service com. 1972-74, Disting. Svc. award 1989), Am. Loudspeaker Mfrs. Assn. (v.p., dir. 1967-68, pres., bd. dirs. 1968-70), Assn. Electronic Mfrs. (bd. dirs. 1970-73), Nat. Space Club, Nat. Space Inst., Am. Acad. Polit. Social Sci., Am. Soc. Assn. Execs. (vice chmn. internat. sect. 1986-87, chmn. 1987-88), US Naval Inst., Field Mus. Natural History, European Soc. Assn. Execs., Greater Washington Soc. Assn. Execs., Naples Coun. World Affairs (bd. dirs. 2003-05), Explorers Club, Chgo. Art Inst., Am. Legion, Chaine des Rôtisseurs, L'Ordre Mondial, Internat. Wine and Food Soc. (pres. Naples br. 2001-), English-Speaking Union (pres. Naples chpt. 1996—, nat. dir. 1997—, regional vice chmn. 2000-03, chmn. 2003-), Conservancy, S.W. Fla. Inc., Forum Club S.W. Fla. (bd. dirs. 2000-03), Naples Press Club (bd. dirs. 1998-2000), Royal Poinciana Golf Club, Naples Yacht Club, Circumnavigators Club, Beta Gamma Sigma, Alpha Phi Omega, Sigma Chi (dir. Kappa Kappa corp. 1954-75, sec. 1971-73, pres. 1973-75, Charles J.

Kiler award 1975, Grand Consul's citation 1976, Significant SIG award 2006). Home: 4601 Gulf Shore Blvd N Apt 12 Naples FL 34103-2214 Personal E-mail: hrowe13@comcast.net.

**ROWE, JOHN WALLIS (JACK ROWE),** insurance company executive, health facility administrator; b. Jersey City, June 20, 1944; s. Albert Wallis and Elizabeth (Lynch) R.; m. Valerie Ann DelTufo, Aug. 10, 1968; children: Meredith, Abigail, Rebecca. BS with honors, Canisius Coll., 1966; MD with distinction, U. Rochester, 1970. Diplomate Am. Bd. Internal Medicine, Am. Bd. Nephrology. Resident in internal medicine Harvard Med. Sch., Beth Israel Hosp., Boston, 1970-72; clin. assoc. Nat. Inst. Child Health and Human Devel., Balt., 1972-74; rsch., clin. fellow Harvard Med. Sch., Mass. Gen. Hosp., Boston, 1974-75; from instr. to prof. Harvard Med. Sch., Boston, 1976-88; pres. Mt. Sinai Sch. Medicine, N.Y.C., 1988-99, Mt. Sinai Hosp., N.Y.C., 1988-98; prof. geriatrics & medicine Mt. Sinai Sch. Medicine and Mt. Sinai Hosp., N.Y.C., 1988—; CEO Mt. Sinai-NYU Med. Ctr. and Health Sys., N.Y.C., 1998-2000; pres. Aetna Inc., Hartford, Conn., 2000—02, CEO, 2000—06, chmn., 2001—. Chmn. bd. trustees U. Conn., 2003—; mem. Medicare Payment Adv. Com., 1997-2004; trustee Ctr. for Advancement of Health. Editor: Health and Disease in Old Age, 1982, Geriatric Medicine, 1988, Handbook of the Biology of Aging, 1990, Geriatric Neurology, 1991; author: Successful Aging, 1998; contbr. articles to jours. in field. Lt. comdr. USPHS, 1972-74. MacArthur Found. grantee, 1985-98. Mem. NAS Inst. Med., Am. Acad. Arts & Scis., Gerontol. Soc. Am. (pres. 1988), Am. Fedn. for Aging Rsch. (pres. 1988), N.Y. Yacht Club, Century Assn. Roman Catholic. Avocation: sailing. Office: Aetna 151 Farmington Ave Hartford CT 06156 Office Phone: 860-273-4455. Business E-Mail: RoweJW@aetna.com.

**ROWE, JOHN WILLIAM,** utilities executive; b. Dodgeville, Wis., May 18, 1945; married; 1 son. BS, U. Wis., 1967, JD, 1970. Bar: Wis. 1970, Ill. 1970, U.S. Supreme Ct. 1979, Pa. 1982. Assoc. Isham, Lincoln & Beale, Chgo., 1970-77, ptnr., 1978-80; counsel to trustee Chgo. Milw. St. Paul & Pacific R.R., Chgo., 1979-80; v.p. law Consol. Rail Corp., Phila., 1980-82, sr. v.p. law, 1982-84; chief exec. officer Cen. Maine Power Co., Augusta, 1984-89; pres., CEO New Eng. Elec. System, Westboro, Mass., 1989-98, former bd. dirs.; chmn., pres., CEO Unicom Corp. & Commonwealth Edison Co., 1998-2000; pres., co-CEO Exelon Corp., Chgo., 2000—03, chmn., pres., CEO, 2003—. Bd. dirs. UnumProvident Corp., Fleet Boston Fin., Wis. Ctrl. Tranp. Co.; of counsel to trustees Chgo., Milw., St. Paul, Pacific Railroad Co. Bd. trustees Art Inst. Chgo., Chgo. Hist. Soc., Field Mus., Wis. Alumni rsch. Found., Am. Enterprise Inst., Ill. chpt. Nature Conservancy; vice-chmn. Edison Electric Inst.; nat. trustee Northwestern U.; past pres. USS Constitution Mus.; past chmn. Mass. Bus. Roundtable. Mem. Econ. Club. Chgo., Comml. Club Chgo. (civic com.), Order of the Coif, Phi Beta Kappa. Home and Office: Unicom Corp Ten S Dearborn St # 37 Chicago IL 60603*

**ROWE, LARRY LINWELL,** lawyer, former state senator; b. Bluefield, W.Va. m. Julia Beury; 3 children. BA, W.Va. U., 1970, MPA, JD, W.Va. U., 1976. Bar: W.Va. 1976, U.S. Dist. Ct. (so. dist.) W.Va. 1976, U.S. Ct. Appeals (4th cir.) 1978, U.S. Supreme Ct. 1992. Staff counsel W.Va. Housing Devel. Fund, Charleston, 1976-77; sr. law clk. to Hon. K. K. Hall U.S. 4th Cir. Ct. Appeals, Charleston, 1978-79; pvt. practice Charleston, 1980—. Adj. prof. law U. Charleston, 1980—81. Bd. dirs. W.Va. Artists & Craftsmen's Guild, Charleston, 1980—84, Cedar Lakes' Mountain State Arts & Crafts Fair, Ripley, 1981—82; chmn., mem. Legal Aid Soc. Charleston, 1981—84; pres. W.Va. Dance Theatre, Charleston, 1981—82; hearing examiner W.Va. Bd. Regents, Charleston, 1985—89, W.Va. Bd. Medicine, Charleston, 1987—88; mem. W.Va. Ho. of Del., 1997—2000, W.Va. Senate, 2001—05. W.Va. Bd. Regents scholar, W.Va. U. Coll. Law, 1974—76, Cato scholar, 1974—76. Mem.: Phi Beta Kappa, Order of Coif. Democrat. Office: 4200A Malden Dr Charleston WV 25306-6442 Office Phone: 304-925-1333. Business E-Mail: larrylrowe@larrylrowe.com.

**ROWE, MARIELI DOROTHY,** media literacy education consultant, organization executive; b. bonn, Germany, Aug. 13; came to U.S., 1939; m. John Westel Rowe; children: Peter Willoughby, William Westel, Michael Delano. BA, Swarthmore Coll., Pa.; postgrad., U. Colo., Boulder, 1990; MA, Edgewood Coll., Madison, Wis., 1990. Interim exec. dir. Friends of Sta. WHA-TV, Madison, Wis., 1976; exec. dir. Nat. Telemedia Coun., Madison, 1978—. Project assoc. Loyola U., Chgo., 1989—92; bd. dirs. Sta. WYOU, Madison. Co-prodr., author TV documentary Kids Meet Across Space, 1983; editor Telemedium, Jour. of Media Lit., 1980—. Co-founder, bd. dirs., pres. Friends of Pub. Stas. WHA-TV, radio, Madison, 1968-78; v.p. bd. Nat. Friends of Pub. Broadcasting, N.Y. and Washington, 1970-76; pres., v.p. bd. Wis. Coun. and Am. Coun. for Better Broadcasts, Madison, 1963-75; commr. Gov.'s Blue Ribbon Commn. on Cable Comm., Wis., 1971-73; bd. dirs. Broadband Telecomm. Regulatory Bd., Madison, 1978-81. Recipient Spl. Recognition award Am. Coun. Better Broadcasts, 1981, Spl. award Joint Congress and World Meeting on Media Lit., Spain, 1995, Meritorious Svc. award Alliance for Media Literate Am., 2003, 50th Anniversary Lighting the Way Toward a Media Wise World award Nat. Telemedia Coun., 2003. Mem. Soc. Satellite Profls. Internat. (charter), Internat. Visual Lit. Assn., Zeta Phi Eta (1st v.p. 1992, pres. 1993, Marguerite Garden Jones award 1989). Unitarian Universalist. Avocations: skiing, hiking, travel, music. Home: 1001 Tumalo Trl Madison WI 53711-3024 Office Phone: 608-218-1182. Personal E-mail: ntelemedia@aol.com.

**ROWE, MARY P.,** organizational ombudsman, management educator; b. Chgo., Feb. 18, 1936; married; children: Katherine, Susannah, Timothy. BA in History, Swarthmore Coll., 1957; PhD in Econs., Columbia U., 1971; LLD (hon.), Regis Coll., 1975. With World Council of Chs./Office of UN High Commr. for Refugees, Salzburg and Vienna, Austria, 1957-58; research asst. Nat. Bur. Econ. Research, N.Y.C., 1961; economist planning bd. Office of Gov., V.I., 1962-63; free-lance cons. Nigeria, 1963-66, Boston, 1967-69; cons., sr. economist with Ctr. for Ednl. Policy Research, Harvard U. Harvard U., Cambridge, Mass., 1970, cons., sr. economist with Abt Assocs., 1970, tech. dir. early proj. 1971-72, cons. economist with Abt Assocs., 1971; dir. Carnegie Corp. Grant Radcliffe Inst., Cambridge, 1972; spl. asst. to pres., ombudsperson MIT, Cambridge, 1973—, adj. prof. Sloan Sch. Mgmt., 1985—. Mem. steering com., program on negotiations Harvard U., 1995—. Mem. editorial bd. Negotiation Jour., 1985—, Alternative Dispute Resolution Report, 1987-90; contbr. articles to profl. jours. Trustee Cambridge Friends Sch., 1969-75; mem. bd. advisors Brookline Children's Ctr., 1971-76; mem. Cambridge Friends Meeting and Com. on Clearness, 1971-78, New Eng. Concerns Com., 1973—, Mass. Policy Adv. Com. on Child Abuse/Neglect, 1977-79, Mass. State Youth Council, 1978-83; mem. Mass. State Employment and Tng. Council, 1975-83, chair, 1980-83; mem. nat. adv. Com. Black Women's Ednl. Policy and Research Network Project/Wellesley Coll. Ctr. for Research on Women, 1980-83; bd. dirs. Bay State Skills Commn., 1980-81, Wellesley Women's Research Ctr., 1984-87; sec. bd. dirs. Bay State Skills Corp., 1981-90; mem. panel on employment disputes Ctr. for Pub. Resources, 1986—. Recipient Meritorious Civilian Svc. award Dept. of Navy, 1993. Mem. Soc. Profls. in Dispute Resolution (chair com. on ombudspersons 1982-92, employment disputes), Calif. Caucus Coll. and Univ. Ombudsmen, Univ. and Coll. Ombudsman Assn., Ombudsman Assn. (co-founder, 1982, pres. 1985-87, program on negotiation steering com. 1995—, Disting. Neutral Ctr. for Pub. Resources 1990—, convenor, presenter at confs.). Office: MIT 10-213 77 Massachusetts Ave Cambridge MA 02139

**ROWE, MELINDA GRACE,** public health service officer; b. Decatur, Ala., Aug. 18, 1953; m. Dana Calvin Craig Jr., Jan. 1, 1994. MD, U. Ala., 1978, MPH, 1985, MBA, 1987. Bd. cert. Am. Bd. Pediatrics, Am. Bd. Preventive Medicine. Pediatrics intern U. Ky., Lexington, 1978-79; pediatrics resident Lloyd Nolan Hosp., Fairfield, Ala., 1979-81; physician Columbus (Miss.) Children's Clinic, 1981, pvt. practice, Winfield, Ala., 1982-84; preventive medicine resident U. Ala., Birmingham, 1984-85; asst. state health officer Pub. Health Area III, Pelham, Ala., 1985-95; dir. health Jefferson County Health Dept., Louisville, 1995—2001; dir. health officer Savannah (Ga.) Lance Health, 2001—03; commr. of health Lexington Fayette County Health Dept., Lexington, Ky., 2003—. Asst. prof. U. Ala., Birmingham, 1988—, U.

Louisville, 1995—. Bd. dirs. Cahaba River Soc., Birmingham, 1988—95, U. Ala.-Birmingham Nat. Alumni Soc., 1988—93, Health Ky., Goodwill Industries; bd. dirs. Wilderness Road coun. Girl Scouts U.S., Lexington, 2006—. Mem.: Lexington Med. Soc., Ga. Med. Assn., Ky. Health Depts. Assn. (v.p.), Louisville/Jefferson County Primary Care Assn. (bd. dirs.), Jefferson County Med. Soc., Ky. Pediat. Soc., Ky. Pub. Health Assn. (pres.-elect), Ky. Med. Assn., Rotary of Lexington. Methodist. Avocations: reading, walking, travel, music. Home: 3557 Cornwall Dr Lexington KY 40503-4150 Office Phone: 859-288-2300. Business E-Mail: melinda.rowe@ky.gov.

**ROWE, MICHAEL DUANE,** artist; b. Lykens, Pa., Nov. 5, 1947; m. Kathryn Jean Branoff. Student, Art Inst. Pitts., 1971-72. Exhibited in shows at Art Assn. Harrisburg, Pa., 1985, 86, 87, State Mus. Pa., 1986, 87, Doshi Gallery, Harrisburg, 1987, Cheltenham (Pa.) Art Ctr., 1989, 92, Delaplaine Art Ctr., Frederick, Md., 1989 (1st prize 1989), 90, 91, Immaculata (Pa.) Coll., 1990, U. of the Arts, Phil., 1990, Butler Inst. of Am. Art, Youngstown, Ohio, 1990, 92, Phila. Art Alliance, 1990, Alternative Mus., N.Y.C., 1990, 91, 95, Spaces, Cleve., 1991, Alexandria (La.) Art Mus., 1991, Pa. State U., 1992, Allentown (Pa.) Mus. Art, 1992, Muhlenberg Coll., Allentown, 1992 (award 1992), Michael Stone Gallery, Washington, 1992, Ea. N.Mex. U., 1992, Del. Ctr. for Contemporary Arts, Wilmington, 1993, Laguna Gloria Art Mus., Austin, Tex., 1993, Silvermine Art Guild Exhibit, New Cannan, Conn., 1993, Pa. State U., Univ. Park, 1993, East Tenn. U., Johnson City, 1994, Chrysler Mus., Norfolk, Va., 1994, Davidson (N.C.) Coll. Visual Arts Ctr., 1995, Southern Alleghenies Mus. of Art, 1995, Loretto, Pa., 1996, 97, 99, Susquehanna Art Mus., Harrisburg, Pa., 1998. Whitaker Ctr., Harrisburg, 1999, 2000; represented in permanent collection So. Alleghenies Mus., Loretto, Pa. Grantee Art Matters, Inc., 1988; Pa. Coun. of the Arts fellow, 1993. Episcopalian. Avocations: running, travel, reading. Home: 814 Meadow Ln Camp Hill PA 17011-1545 Business E-mail: krowe@state.pa.us.

**ROWE, PETER A.,** columnist; b. Walnut Creek, Calif., Sept. 7, 1955; s. Raymond Alan and Marion (Green) R.; m. Lynn Huston, Aug. 13, 1977; children: Kyle, Reid, Alec. BA in History, U. Calif., Berkeley, 1977, BA in Journalism, 1977; MSJ, Northwestern U., 1981. Reporter Argus, Fremont, Calif., 1977-80, Va.-Pilot, Norfolk, 1981-84, San Diego Union, 1984-87, asst. features editor, 1987-88, features editor, 1988-92; columnist San Diego Union-Tribune, 1992—. Gannett fellow Northwestern U., 1980-81, Jefferson fellow, 2006; Fulbright scholar, 2003. Mem.: Nat. Soc. Newspaper Columnists (pres. 2000—02). Roman Catholic. Office: San Diego Union Tribune PO Box 120191 San Diego CA 92112-0191 Office Phone: 619-293-1227. Business E-Mail: peter.rowe@uniontrib.com.

**ROWE, PETER GRIMMOND,** architecture educator, researcher; b. Wellington, New Zealand, June 28, 1945; arrived in U.S., 1969; s. Leslie Grimmond and Dorothy Olive (Perkins) Rowe; m. Lauretta Vinciarelli, Oct. 18, 1993; 1 child, Anthony. BArch, Melbourne (Australia) U., 1969; MArch in Urban Design, Rice U., 1971; AM (hon.), Harvard U., 1986. Adj. assoc. prof. human ecology U. Tex. Health Sci. Ctr., Houston, 1977—85; assoc. prof. Sch. Arch./Sch. Pub. Health Rice U., 1977—85, dir. Sch. Arch., 1981—85; prin. Environ. Planning and Design, Houston, 1985—87; dir. urban designs programs Grad. Sch. Design Harvard U., 1985—90, Raymond Garbe prof. arch. and urban design Grad. Sch. Design, 1987—, chmn. dept. urban planning and design Grad. Sch. Design, 1988—92, dean faculty design, 1992—2004; hon. prof. Xi'an U. Arch. and Tech., 1999—. Bd. mem. Can. Arch. Ctr., 1995—; mem. U.S. Gen. Svcs. Adminstrn., Pub. Bldgs. Svc. Nat. Register of Peer Profls., 1996—98; hon. cons. Chair Com. on Arch. Melbourne U., 1997—98, 2002; chmn. rev. com., faculty arch. and town planning Technion U., Israel, 1997; chmn. Dean's Cir., Sch. Arch. Rice U., 1998—2001, mem. Dean's Cir., 2001; mem. ctr. artery corridor adv. group task force City of Boston, 1999—; jury mem. Olympic Village Competition, Athens, Greece, 2000; sr. advisor urban planning and design City of Wenzhou, China, 2000—; jury mem. West Kowloon Reclamation Concept Plan Competition, Hong Kong, 2001—02. Author: Principles for Environmental Management, 1978, Design Thinking, 1987, Making a Middle Landscape, 1991, Modernity and Housing, 1993, Civic Realism, 1997, Asia Modern, 1998, Projecting Beruit, 1998; co-author: Modern Urban Housing in China: 1840-2000, 2001, Architectural Encounters with Essence and Form in Modern China; co-editor: Yi-Ti-Laing-Yi Zhi Jian: Redevelopment in Suzhou, China, 1997, Shan Shiu City: Urban Development in Wenzhou, China, 2001, Environments of Opportunity: Redevelopment on the Waterfront of Las Palmas de Gran Canaria, Spain, 2001; pub., mem. editl. bd.: Harvard Design Mag., 1997—. Fellow: Inst. for Urban Design; mem.: Am. Planning Assn., Boston Soc. Archs. (hon.), Urban Land Inst. (assoc.). Office: Harvard U Grad Sch Design 48 Quincy St Cambridge MA 02138-3000

**ROWE, RICHARD EDWIN,** lawyer; b. Mt. Vernon, Ohio, July 24, 1944; s. William B. and Letha (Mason) Rowe; m. Sally Braun, June 27, 1967; children: Gregory B., Katherine M. BSBA, W.Va. U., 1966, JD, 1969. Bar: W.Va. 1969, U.S. Dist. Ct. W.Va. 1969, U.S. Ct. Appeals (4th cir.) 1973, U.S. Supreme Ct. 1980, N.C. 2001. Assoc. Wilson, Frame & Rowe, Morgantown, W.Va., 1969-78; ptnr. Goodwin & Goodwin, Charleston, W.Va., 1978—. Democrat. Methodist. Avocations: pottery, photography, collecting. Home: RR 2 Box 209A Cottageville WV 25239-9518 Office: Goodwin & Goodwin 300 Summers St Ste 1500 Charleston WV 25301 Office Phone: 304-346-7000. Business E-Mail: rer@goodwingoodwin.com.

**ROWE, RICHARD HOLMES,** lawyer; b. Waltham, Mass., Jan. 2, 1937; s. Robert C. Rowe and Roberta (Holmes) Hayes; m. Sylvia C. Barrow, Aug. 23, 1963; children: Elizabeth C., Dorothy H., Christopher H. AB, Bates Coll., 1957; JD, Harvard U., 1964. Bar: DC 1965, NY 1980. Atty., exec. SEC, Washington, 1964-69, 70-79; v.p. Shareholders Mgmt. Co., LA, 1969-70; ptnr. Proskauer Rose Goetz & Mendelsohn, Washington, 1979—. 1st lt. USMCR, 1957-60. Mem. ABA, FBA, DC Bar Assn., Assn. Bar City of NY Democrat. Office: Proskauer Rose LLP 1001 Pennsylvania Ave NW Ste 400 Washington DC 20004-2537 Office Phone: 202-416-6820. Business E-Mail: rowe@proskauer.com.

**ROWE, RICHARD R.,** on-line information and management services company executive; b. Burlington, Iowa, Apr. 14, 1933; s. Charles Ronald and Elva Margaret (Gilliland) R.; children: Katherine, Susannah, Timothy, Christopher, Jonathan. BA in Psychology, UCLA, 1955; S.T.B. in Psychology of Religion, Boston U., 1958; PhD in Psychology, Columbia U., 1963. Cert. and lic. psychologist, Mass. Dir. test devel. and research West African Exams. Council, 1963-67; assoc. dean Grad. Sch. Edn., Harvard U., Cambridge, Mass., 1967-73; dir. program in clin. psychology and pub. practice Harvard U., 1967-73; v.p. Am. Inst. for Research, Cambridge, 1973-79; pres., chief exec. officer The Faxon Co., Westwood, Mass., 1979-93; founder, chmn., pres., CEO RoweCom, Inc. (acquired by Divine, Inc. in 2001), 1994—2003; dir. Internat and Information Services Dept. Dean for America campaign, 2003—04. Chmn. Serials Industry Systems Adv. Com.; mem. State Bd. edn., Mass., 1990-95, chmn., Mass. Edn. Reform Implementation Task Force, 1993—. Pres. Statewide Adv. Council to Office for Children, Mass., 1980-87, chmn., 1983-87; mem. K-12 computer literacy com. Mass. High Tech Council, 1983-84; spl. adviser Mass. Legis. Com. on Ednl. Excellence, 1983-84; mem. Mass. Legis. Commn. Early Edn., 1988—. Mem. Am. Psychol. Assn., ALA, Library and Info. Tech. Assn. Clubs: Harvard (N.Y.C.).

**ROWE, SANDRA MIMS,** editor; b. Charlotte, NC, May 26, 1948; d. David Lathan and Shirley (Stovall) Mims; m. Gerard Paul Rowe, June 5, 1971; children: Mims Elizabeth, Sarah Stovall. BA, East Carolina U., Greenville, N.C., 1970; postgrad., Harvard U., 1991. Reporter to asst. mng. editor The Ledger-Star, Norfolk, Va., 1971-80, mng. editor, 1980-82, The Virginian-Pilot and The Ledger Star, Norfolk, Va., 1982-84, exec. editor, 1984-86, v.p., exec. editor, 1986-93; editor The Oregonian, Portland, 1993—. Mem. Pulitzer Prize Bd., 1994-2003, chair, 2003. Bd. visitors James Madison U., Harrisonburg, VA., 1991-95; chair journalism adv. bd. Knight Found.; mem. adv. bd. The Poynter Inst., Medill Sch. Journalism, Northwestern U.; chair bd. visitors Knight Fellowships, Stanford U. Recipient George Beveridge Editor of Yr. award Nat. Press Found., 2003; named Woman of Yr. Outstanding Profl.

Women of Hampton Rds., 1987; inducted into Va. Journalism Hall of Fame, 2000. Mem. Am. Soc. Newspaper Editors (pres., bd. dirs. 1992-99), Va. Press Assn. (bd. dirs. 1985-93). Episcopalian. Office: The Oregonian 1320 SW Broadway Portland OR 97201-3499

**ROWE, SHERYL ANN,** librarian; b. Stephenville, Tex., Sept. 29, 1946; d. Horace Milton and Letha Faye (Hensley) Hughes; m. Darrell Vanoy Rowe, Nov. 27, 1969; children: Jason Burt, Shelley Jean. BA in English, Tarleton State U., Stephenville, 1967; MS in Libr. Sci., Tex. Women's U., Denton, 1986. Cert. tchr. secondary edn. Tchr. Lake Worth H.S., Tex., 1967—69, Aledo H.S., Tex., 1967—73, 1978—84, libr., 1984—. Mem. ALA, Tex. Libr. Assn., Region XI Librs. Assn. (treas. 1984—). Office: Aledo HS 1000 Bailey Ranch Rd Aledo TX 76008-4407 Office Phone: 817-441-8711. Business E-Mail: srowe@aledo.k12.tx.us.

**ROWE, THOMAS (THOMAS DOC ROWE),** engineer, researcher; Founder Tarco Research, Redding, Calif., 1977—. Co-invented and co-created (with builder, designer Dennis Dusty Kasier), the first Dolphin Submarine or VASH (Variable Attitude Submersible Hydrofoil-11ft long, made with tough carbon fiber with a layer of Kevlar, 200 to 600 horsepower inboard engine, giving a surface speed in excess of 170 mph, with an underwater speed of 70mph, it runs on both gasoline, alcohol and fuel cells. The design was conceived in 1974, development began October, 1988); first prototype, Noland Won made it's first historic flight on September 7, 1992 at Oak Bottom Marina on Whiskeytown lake in Northern California, it became the first lighter than water vehicle to ever successfully fly underwater; credited to be the first human to pilot an underwater craft in excess of 100 mph, a record achieved in the bionic dolphin in 1995; co-developer (with Rob Innes) of a new marine leisure craft concept that looks like and simulates the movement of a dolphin (bionic dolphin-Sweet Virgin Angel-100 horsepower, prop-driven mammal is piloted from a cockpit encased by an F16 canopy and can be driven at speeds exceeding 50 kmh and made to perform like a dolphin. Completed in 2001; famous bionic dolphin appeared in Austin Powers Goldmember. Office: Tarco Research 11020 Myrtlewood Dr Redding CA 96003-7680 Business E-Mail: docvash@aol.com.

**ROWE, THOMAS DUDLEY, JR.,** law educator; b. Richmond, Va., Feb. 26, 1942; s. Thomas Dudley and Georgia Rosamond (Stripp) R.; m. Susan Fletcher French, Jan. 5, 2001. BA, Yale U., 1964; MPhil, Oxford U., Eng., 1967; JD, Harvard U., 1970. Bar: D.C. 1971, N.C. 1976. Law clk. to assoc. justice Potter Stewart U.S. Supreme Ct., Washington, 1970-71; asst. counsel administrv. practice subcom. U.S. Senate, Washington, 1971-73; assoc. Miller, Cassidy, Larroca & Lewin, Washington, 1973-75; assoc. prof. Duke U. Sch. Law, Durham, NC, 1975-79, prof., 1979-96, Elvin R. Latty prof., 1996—, assoc. dean for rsch., 1981-84, sr. assoc. dean acad. affairs, 1995-96. Vis. prof. Georgetown U. Law Ctr., Washington, 1979—80, U. Mich. Law Sch., Ann Arbor, 1985, U. Va. Law Sch., Charlottesville, 1991, UCLA Law Sch., 2002, 04; Straus Disting. vis. prof. Pepperdine U. Sch. Law, 2006; atty. Munger, Tolles & Olson, L.A., 1991; adv. com. on rules of civil procedure U.S. Jud. Conf., 1993—99. Co-author: Federal Courts in the 21st Century: Cases and Materials, 1996, 2002, Civil Procedure, 2004; contbr. articles to profl. jours. Fellow U.S. Dept. Justice, Washington, 1980-81; Rhodes scholar, 1964-67; recipient Disting. Teaching award Duke Bar Assn., 1985. Mem. ABA, Am. Law Inst. Democrat. Office: Duke U Sch Law Durham NC 27708-0360 Office Phone: 919-613-7099. Business E-Mail: trowe@law.duke.edu.

**ROWE, WILLIAM DAVIS,** finance company executive; b. Hibbing, Minn., June 5, 1937; s. Richard Lawrence and Alicia (Davis) R.; m. Bobbie Grace Childress, Apr. 20, 1963; children— Lisa, William BA in Psychology, U. Minn, 1959, postgrad. in indsl. relations and bus. adminstrn., 1960; grad. exec. devel. program, Northeastern U., 1975; grad. Advanced Mgmt. Program, Harvard U., 1980. Dir. personnel, adminstrn. EDP Control Data Corp., Mpls., 1964-70; with Comml. Credit Co. subs. Control Data Corp, 1971-84, 85—; sr. v.p. consumer group Balt., 1975-81; sr. v.p. consumer realty services, 1981-83; sr. v.p. consumer banking services, 1983-84; v.p. market devel. Computer Service Co., Control Data Corp., Mpls., 1984; sr. v.p., chief adminstrv. officer Comml. Credit Co., Balt., 1985-87; pres. Enterprise Bank Network Bank Svcs. Co., Atlanta, 1988-91; exec. mng. dir., vice chmn. Foster Ptnrs. Inc., Peat Marwick Alliance Co., 1991—; pres., COO Foster Ptnrs., 2001—. Bd. dirs. Fla. Corp.; co-owner Spirit of West Land Co., Glenwood Springs, Colo., 2001—; lectr. in field Mem. Mayor's Vol. Council of Equal Opportunity, Balt.; trustee St. Paul's Sch. for Girls, Brooklandville, Md., 1981—; bd. dirs. Boy Scouts Am., Take Stock in Children, 1996—. Served to capt. USMC, 1960-63. Mem. Am. Fin. Services Assn. (bd. dirs. and mem. exec. com. 1980-84, consumer banking adv. com. 1983-84), Am. Mgmt. Assn. (pres.'s roundtable 1976) Republican. Avocations: hunting, skiing, cattle ranching. E-Mail: browe@spiritwestland.com.

**ROWE, WILLIAM JOSEPH,** internist; b. Cin., Oct. 31, 1927; s. Alvin Harold and Ida Claire (Omansky) R.; m. Mary Elaine Kenkel, Apr. 16, 1955. BS, U. Cin., 1950, MD, 1954. Diplomate Am. Bd. Internal Medicine. Asst. clin. prof. medicine Med. U. Ohio, Toledo, 1962—93; chmn. dept. medicine St. Vincent's Hosp., Toledo, 1979-83; chief adv. com. cardiac rehab. N.W. Ohio Heart Assn., Toledo, 1981-83. Del. citizen amb. program to China People to People, 1988. Contbr. articles to profl. jours., including Acta Astronautica, Lancet, Circulation. Capt. USAF, 1955-57. Fellow Brit. Interplanetary Soc.; mem. Nat. Space Soc. Republican. Achievements include describing only the second space syndrome, the Apollo 15 Space Syndrome; first to describe mechanisms for endothelial injuries of cardiovascular systems complicating extraordinary unremitting endurance exercise on earth or secondary to too little exercise and microgravity. Avocations: tennis, running, writing, travel. Home: 1485 Bremerton Ln Keswick VA 22947 Personal E-Mail: rowerun@aol.com.

**ROWE, WILLIAM L. S.,** lawyer; b. Martinsville, Va., Mar. 31, 1948; s. Mason Cole Rowe and Catherine (Thomas) Showalter; m. Carol Lawhorne, June 6, 1970 (div. 1991); children: William L. S. Rowe, Jr., Benjamin C., Susannah B.; m. Pamela-Jean Love, Feb. 29, 1992. BA, Washington & Lee Univ., Va., 1970; JD, Univ. Va., 1973. Bar: Va. 1973, U.S. Dist. Ct. E.D Va., U.S. Ct. Appeals (4th cir.), U.S. Claims Ct., U.S. Tax Ct. Assoc. Hunton & Williams, Richmond, Va., 1973-1980, ptnr., 1980—. Special tax counsel, Va. Mfg. Assn.; general counsel Greater Richmond Community Found. 1990—; speaker in the field. Contbr. articles to profl. jours. Bd. gov., trustee, Greater Richmond Community Found., 1979-91, bd. dirs. REB Found., Massey Found., 1980-89. Fellow Am. Coll. of Tax Counsel; mem. ABA, Va. State Bar (bd. trustees sect. on taxation 1988-90), Va. Bar Assn. (chmn. com. on taxation 1985-87), Richmond Bar Assn., Va. State C. of C. (chmn. tax com. 1994—). Avocations: fly fishing, wild flowers, gardening. Office: Hunton & Williams Riverfront Plz East Tower PO Box 1535 Richmond VA 23218-1535

**ROWELL, BARBARA CABALLERO,** retired academic administrator; b. New Orleans, Sept. 5, 1922; d. Albert Henry Wischnewske (stepfather) and Antoinette (Angelo) Caballero; m. J.C. Rowell, Dec. 17, 1941; children: Jerrie Carlene, Kerry Gene, Ricky Ray. AA in Bus. Adminstrn., Okaloosa Walton. Coll.; BA in Social Scis., U. West Fla. Exec. sec. Bishop Enterprises, Ft. Walton Beach; office mgr. and real estate property mgr. Fred Cooke Real Estate, Ft. Walton Beach, Fla.; adminstrv. sec. to v.p. Okaloosa Walton Coll., Niceville, Fla. Leader brownie scouts Girl Scouts U.S., cub scouts Boy Scouts Am.; bd. dirs., curriculum com. U. West Fla. Ctr. for Life Long Learning; chair univ svc. com., pres., began Writing Lab; originator, implementor U. West Fla. Tutor Program, Career Fair, started scholarship program, Proctor Program; curriculum com. U. West Fla.Ctr. for Lifelong Learning, presenter S.E. Conf. Insts. of Learning in Retirement, Charleston, S.C.; gov.'s campaign vol.; state legislature campaign vol.; active Ctr. for Life Long Learning, U. West Fla. Mem. AAUW, DAV Aux., Order of Ea. Star (past matron). Avocations: travel, reading, gardening, dance.

**ROWELL, EDWARD MORGAN,** retired foreign service officer, educator; b. Oakland, Calif., Oct. 13, 1931; s. Edward Joseph and Mary Helen (Mohler) Rowell; m. Lenora Mary Wood, Aug. 23, 1957; children: Edward Oliver, Karen Elizabeth Schuler, Christopher Douglas. BA in Internat. Relations, Yale U., 1953; postgrad., Stanford U., 1964-65, Stanford Bus. Sch., 1970-71. Fgn. service insp. U.S. Dept. State, Washington, 1971-74; dep. dir., econ. officer Office Iberian Affairs, Washington, 1974-75; dep. dir. Office West European Affairs, Washington, 1975-76, dir., 1977-78; minister-counselor U.S. Embassy, Lisbon, Portugal, 1978-83; dep. asst. sec. Bur. Consular Affairs, Washington, 1983-85; U.S. amb. to Bolivia La Paz, 1985-88; U.S. amb. to Portugal Lisbon, 1988-90; U.S. amb. to Luxemburg, 1990-94; sr. assoc. Global Bus. Access, Ltd., 1994—. Mem. adv. bd. Portuguese-Am. Leadership Coun. U.S.; mem. Cleveland Park Congregational Ch. Washington, 1956—; trustee Cleveland Park Ch., 2000—03; bd. dirs. Luso-Am Develop Found., 1988—90. With U.S. Army, 1953—55. Decorated grand cross Bolivian Condor of the Andes, grand cross Luxembourg Oaken Crown; recipient State Dept. Superior Honor award, 1983, 1991, Presdl. Honor Award, 1988; grantee, Una Chapman Cox Found., 1984; Yale U. scholar, 1949—52, U. Calif. fellow, 1953. Mem.: Diplomatic & Consular Officers Ret. (gov. 2001—, treas. 2005—), Arena Stage Assocs., Yale Univ. Alumni Assn., Stanford Univ. Alumni Assn., Wash. Inst. Foreign Affairs (membership com. 1999—), Assn. Diplomatic Studies & Training (pres. 1997—2001, treas. 2005—), Am. Foreign Svc. Assn. (v.p. 1995—97), Am Acad. Diplomacy (bd. dirs. 2002—, chmn. audit com. 2006—), Cosmos Club. Avocations: photography, tennis, music. Home: 5414 Newington Rd Bethesda MD 20816-3316 Personal E-Mail: edmrowell@aol.com.

**ROWELL, LESTER JOHN, JR.,** retired insurance company executive; b. Cleve., Apr. 2, 1932; s. Lester John and Frances Laureen (Corbett) R.; m. Patricia Ann Loesch, Jan. 16, 1953 (div. Sept. 1970); children: Deborah, Cynthia, Gregory, Maureen, Diane; m. Carol Ann Jankowski, Sept. 26, 1970. BS, Pa. State U., 1955; grad. Advanced Mgmt. Program, Harvard U. Bus. Sch., 1971. CLU. Second v.p., field mgmt. Mut. Life Ins. Co. N.Y., N.Y.C. 1969-70, v.p agys., 1970-72, v.p. sales, 1972-78, sr. v.p., 1978-80; exec. v.p. Provident Mut. Life Ins. Co., Phila., 1980-84, pres., 1984-86, pres., chief oper. officer, 1987, pres., chief exec. officer, 1991-93, chmn., pres., chief exec. officer, 1993-96; ret. Bd. dirs. Pa. State U., The PMA Group. Capt. USMC, 1953-62. Recipient Alumni award Pa. State U., 1972, Disting. Alumni award Pa. State U., 1988; Alumni Fellow Pa. State U., 1987. Republican. Personal E-mail: budrowell@aol.com.

**ROWELL, VICTORIA,** actress; b. Portland, Maine, May 10, 1960; m. Tom Fahey (div.); 2 children. Attended, Sch. Am. Ballet. Dancer Am. Ballet Theatre, Dance Theatre Harlem, Am. Ballet Theatre II. Actor: (TV series) The Young and the Restless, 1990—98, 2000, 2002— (Outstanding actress in daytime drama series, NAACP Image award, 2006), As the World Turns, 1988, The Cosby Show, 1989—90, The Fresh Prince of Bel-Air, 1990, Herman's Head, 1991, 1993, Deadly Games, 1995, Diagnosis Murder, 1997, Family Law, 2001; (TV films) Full Eclipse, 1993, Secret Sins of the Father, 1994, Feast of All Saints, 2001, Without Warning, 2002, A Town Without Pity, 2002; (films) Leonard Part 6, 1987, The Distinguished Gentleman, 1992, Dumb and Dumber, 1994, One Red Rose, 1995, Barb Wire, 1996, Eve's Bayou, 1997, Dr. Hugo, 1998, Secrets, 1998, A Wake in Providence, 1999, Fraternity Boys, 1999, Black Listed, 2003, Motives, 2004, Midnight Clear, 2005, A Perfect Fit, 2005. Mem.: Sigma Gamma Rho. Mailing: c/o CBS Television City 7800 Beverly Blvd Los Angeles CA 90036*

**ROWEN, ANDREW S.,** lawyer; b. Seattle, 1954; BA, U. Calif., Berkeley, 1976; JD, Harvard U., 1979. Bar: NY 1980. Assoc. Sullivan & Cromwell, NYC, now ptnr. fin. institutions and coord. insurance practice area. Mem.: ABA, NYC Bar Assn. (com. on insurance law). Office: Sullivan & Cromwell 125 Broad St Fl 28 New York NY 10004-2489 Office Phone: 212-558-4000. Office Fax: 212-558-3588. Business E-Mail: rowena@sullcrom.com.

**ROWEN, HARVEY ALLEN,** investment company executive; b. Chgo., Sept. 21, 1943; BS in Acctg., UCLA, 1964; JD, U. Calif., Berkeley, 1967; MBA in Mktg. & Fin., NYU, 1981. Bar: Calif., D.C., N.Y. Pvt. practice, Beverly Hills, Calif., 1967-68; counsel Securities & Exch. Commn., Washington, 1968-71, Com. Energy & Commerce, U.S. Congress, Washington, 1971-75; sr. cons. SRI Internat. (formerly Stanford Rsch. Inst.), Palo Alto, 1975-77; asst. to pres. Merrill Lynch, Pierce, Fenner & Smith, Inc., N.Y.C., 1977-80, v.p. corp. planning, 1980-81, Merrill Lynch & Co., Inc., N.Y.C., 1981-83, v.p. banking devel., banking divsn., 1983-84; exec. v.p. Merrill Lynch Bank & Trust Co., N.Y.C., 1984-85, pres., 1985-88; chmn. trust com. Merrill Lynch Trust Co., N.Y.C., 1987-90; prin. Harvey Rowen & Assocs., Newport Beach, Calif., 1990-91; pres., CEO The Charles Schwab Trust Co., S.F., 1992—; sr. v.p. Schwab Instl. Svcs. to Corps. Charles Schwab & Co., Inc., 1992—. Mem. dean's adv. bd. Haas Sch. Bus., U. Calif., Berkeley; lectr. in field. Author: The Securities Acts Amendments of 1975, 1975, The Securities Acts Amendments of 1975: A Legislative History, 1976, The Emerging Financial Services Industry, 1983; author: (with others) The Deregulation of the Banking and Securities Industries 305, 1979; mem. editorial adv. bd. Banking Expansion Reporter. Mem. ABA (bus. sect., banking com., fed. regulation securities com., chmn. product and svc. devels. subcom. of com. devels. in investment svcs. 1985-87), Am. Bankers Assn., Calif. Bankers Assn., Calif. Bar Assn. Office: The Charles Schwab Trust Co 1 Montgomery St Fl 7 San Francisco CA 94104-4505

**ROWEN, HENRY STANISLAUS,** retired economist, former federal agency administrator; b. Boston, Mass., Oct. 11, 1925; s. Henry S. and Margaret ISabelle (Maher) Rowen; m. Beverly Camille Griffiths, Apr. 18, 1951; children: Hilary, Michael, Michael, Christopher, Sheila Jennifer, Diana Louise, Nicholas. BS, MIT, 1949; M in Philosophy, Oxford U., Eng., 1955. Economist Rand Corp., Santa Monica. Calif. 1950—61, pres. 1967—77; dep. asst. sec. internat. security affairs US Dept. Def., Washington, 1961—64; asst. dir. Bur. Budget, 1965—66; prof. pub. policy Stanford (Calif.) U., 1972—95, prof. emeritus, 1995—, dir. pub. policy program, 1972—75; sr. fellow Hoover Inst., Stanford, Calif., 1983—; Edwin B. Rust prof. pub. policy Stanford (Calif.) U., 1986—95, dir. Asia/Pacific Rsch. Ctr., 1997—2001; asst. sec. internat. security affairs US Dept. Def., Washington, 1989—91. Chmn. nat. intelligence coun. CIA, Washington, 1981—83; chmn. US Dept. Energy Task Force on the Future of Sci. Programs, 2002—03; mem. Commn. on the Intelligence Capabilities of the US Regarding Weapons of Mass Destruction, 2004. Co-author (with R. Imai): Nuclear Energy and Nuclear Proliferation, 1980; co-author: (with C. Wolf Jr.): The Future of the Soviet Empire, 1987; editor: Options for U.S. Energy Policy, 1977, Behind East Asian Growth, 1998; co-editor (with C. Wolf Jr.): The Impoverished Superpower, 1990; co-editor: (with C. Lee, W. Miller, M. Hancock) The Silicon Valley Edge, 2001; contbr. articles to profl. jours. Chmn. chief naval ops. exec. panel USN, Washington, 1972—81, mem. exec. panel, 1983—89, 1991—93; mem. Def. Sci. Bd. US Dept. Def., 1983—89; chmn. Def. Policy Bd., 1991—94. With USN, 1943—46, PTO. Mem.: Internat. Inst. Strategic Studies. Republican. Roman Catholic.

**ROWEN, MARSHALL,** radiologist; b. Chgo. s. Harry and Dorothy (Kasnow) R.; m. Helen Lee Friedman, Apr. 5, 1952; children: Eric, Scott, Mark. AB in Chemistry with highest honors, U. Ill., Urbana, 1951; MD with honors, U. Ill., Chgo., 1954, MS in Internal Medicine, 1954. Diplomate Am. Bd. Radiology. Intern Long Beach (Calif.) VA Hosp., 1955; resident in radiology Los Angeles VA Hosp., 1955-58; practice medicine specializing in radiology Orange, Calif., 1960—. Chmn. bd. dirs. Moran, Rowen and Dorsey, Inc., Radiologists, 1969—2002; asst. radiologist L.A. Children's Hosp., 1958; assoc. radiologist Valley Presbyn Hosp., Van Nuys, Calif., 1960; dir. dept. radiology St. Joseph Hosp., Orange, 1961—2004, v.p. staff, 1972; dir. dept. radiology Children's Hosp. Orange County, 1964—2002, chief staff, 1977—78, v.p., 1978—83, v.p., trustee, 1990—91, 1993—98, 2000—06; asst. clin. prof. radiology U. Calif., Irvine, 1967—70, assoc. clin. prof., 1979—82, clin. prof. radiology and pediat., 1976—2006, pres. clin. faculty assn., 1980—81; trustee Choc. Padrinos; sec. Choco Health Svcs., 1987—89, v.p., 1990—93, trustee, 1995—, Found. Med. Care Orange County,

1972—76, Calif. Commn. Adminstrn. Svcs. Hosp., 1975—79, Profl. Practice Systems, 1990—92, Med. Splty. Mgrs., 1990—2004, St. Joseph Med. Corp., 1993—98; v.p. Found. Med. Care Children's Hosp., 1988—89; v.p., sr. v.p. St. Joseph Med. Corp. IPA, 1995—98; sr. v.p. Orange Coast Managed Care Svcs., 1995—98, Paragon Med. Imaging, 1993—2003, Calif. Managed Imaging, 1994—2006, Alliance Premier Hosps., 1995—96; chmn. bd. dirs. Children's Healthcare Calif., 1995—2002, hon. chmn., bd. dirs., 2003—06; corp. mem. Blue Shield Calif., 1995—2002; mem. physician's rev. com. Blue Cross Calif., 1996—2006, mem. Blue Shield coun. advisors, 2001—06; trustee Children's Hosp. at Mission, 2004—06. Mem. editorial bd. Western Jour. Medicine; contbr. articles to med. jours. Founder Orange County Performing Arts Ctr., mem. Laguna Art Mus., Laguna Festival of Arts, Opera Pacific, South Coast Reportory, Am. Ballet Theater, World Affairs Coun. Served to capt. M.C., U.S. Army, 1958-60. Recipient Rea sr. med. prize U. Ill, 1953; William Cook scholar U. Ill., 1951, Friend of Children award Children's Hosp. Guild, 1995, Charley award Children's Hosp., 1996. Fellow Am. Coll. Radiology; mem. AMA, Am. Heart Assn., Soc. Nuclear Medicine (trustee 1961-62), Orange County Radiol. Soc. (pres. 1968-69), Calif. Radiol. Soc. (pres. 1978-79), Radiol. Soc. So. Calif. (pres. 1976), Pacific Coast Pediatric Radiologists Assn. (pres. 1971), Soc. Pediatric Radiology, Calif. Med. Assn. (chmn. sect. on radiology 1978-79), Orange County Med. Assn. (chmn. UCI liaison com. 1976-78), Cardioradiology Soc. So. Calif., Radiol. Soc. N.Am., Am. Roentgen Ray Soc., Am. Coll. Physician Execs., Soc. Chmn. Radiologists Children Hosp., Center Club, Sports Club (Irvine), Phi Beta Kappa, Phi Eta Sigma, Omega Beta Phi, Alpha Omega Alpha. Office: 1201 W La Veta Ave Orange CA 92868-4213 Office Phone: 714-771-8171. Personal E-mail: romarsh@aol.com.

**ROWEN, RUTH HALLE,** musicologist, educator; b. N.Y.C., Apr. 5, 1918; d. Louis and Ethel (Fried) Halle; m. Seymour M. Rowen, Oct. 13, 1940; children: Mary Helen Rowen, Louis Halle Rowen. BA, Barnard Coll., 1939; MA, Columbia U., 1941, PhD, 1948. Mgmt. ednl. dept. Carl Fischer, Inc., N.Y.C., 1954-63; assoc. prof. musicology CUNY, 1967-72, prof., 1972—, mem. doctoral faculty in musicology, 1967—. Author: Early Chamber Music, 1948, reprinted, 1974; (with Adele T. Katz) Hearing-Gateway to Music, 1959, (with William Simon) Jolly Come Sing and Play, 1956, Music Through Sources and Documents, 1979, (with Mary Rowen) Instant Piano, 1979, 80, 83, Symphonic and Chamber Music Score and Parts Bank, 1996; contbr. articles to profl. jours. Mem. ASCAP, Am. Musicol. Soc., Music Library Assn., Coll. Music Soc., Nat. Fedn. Music Clubs (nat. musicianship chmn. 1962-74, nat. young artist auditions com. 1964-74, N.Y. state chmn. Young Artist Auditions 1981, dist. coord. 1983, nat. bd. dirs. 1989-2000, rep. UN 1991-2000), N.Y. Fedn. Music Clubs (pres.), Phi Beta Kappa Home: 115 Central Park West At 25D New York NY 10023-4153 *Opportunity grows with each constructive thought.*

**ROWLAND, ALLEN R.,** former retail executive; b. June 1944; With Albertson's, Boise, 1971, various positions to sr. v.p. various cities, 1971-96; pres., COO Smith's Food & Drug Ctrs., 1996-97; pres., CEO, dir. Winn-Dixie Stores, Inc., Jacksonville, Fla., 1999—2003; owner Sun Chase Air Charter Svc., Rowland Interest.

**ROWLAND, ANGELA KAY,** education educator, consultant; b. Chillecothe, Ohio, Sept. 11, 1970; d. Cecil Clement Rowland and Sandra Kay Sparks. BA in Psychology, W.Va. U., 2002, MA in Corp. and Orgn. Comm., 2004. Cert. notary pub., tng. and devel. specialist. Asst. to exec. dir. W.Va. Conservation Agy., Charleston, 1993—97; desktop publ. specialist Ohio Univ., Athens, 1997—2000; records asst. W.Va. U., Parkersburg, 2001—02, English prof., 2004—; proct. speech, English and psychology Wash. State CC, 2005—. Trainer, spkr. stress mgmt. Wash. Co. Pub. Defender, Marietta, Ohio, 2004. Author: (poetry) Rays of Light Anthology, 1997 (Bronze medal, 1997), (short stories) Into the Mist Anthology, 2001 (Editor's Choice, 2001). Tchr. Literary Vols., Parkersburg, W.Va., 1994—99; mem. Nat. Dem. Comm., Parkersburg, W.Va., 1996—97; bd. dirs. Good Samaritan Low-Income Health Clinic, 2005—. Mem.: W.Va. Assn. Notary Publics. Avocations: writing, swimming, reading. Home: 2306 Pennsylvania Ave Parkersburg WV 26101 Personal E-Mail: rowland@wirefire.com.

**ROWLAND, ARTHUR RAY,** librarian; b. Hampton, Ga., Jan. 6, 1930; s. Arthur and Jennie (Goodman) R.; m. Jane Thomas, July 1, 1955; children: Dell Ruth, Anna Jane. AB, Mercer U., Macon, Ga., 1951; M. Librarianship, Emory U., 1952; postgrad., Oxford U., 1989. Circulation asst. Ga. State Coll. Library, 1952, circulation librarian, 1952-53; librarian Armstrong Coll., Savannah, Ga., 1954-56; head circulation dept. Auburn U. Library, 1956-58; librarian, assoc. prof. library sci. Jacksonville U., 1958-61, Augusta Coll., 1961-76, prof., libr., 1976-91, libr. emeritus 1991—. Lectr. libr. edn. U. Ga., 1962-66; trustee Augusta-Richmond County Pub. Libr., 1980-93, pres. bd. trustees, 1983-85, v.p. bd., 1988-91; trustee Augusta Regional Libr., chmn., 1984-85; trustee East Cen. Ga. Regional Libr., 1987-93, chmn., 1988-91; chmn. Gov.'s Conf. on Ga. Librs. and Info. Svcs., 1977; del. White House Conf. on Librs. and Info. Sci., 1979; cons. on librr. mgmt. to Govt. of Indonesia, 1986. Author: Bibliography of the Writings of Georgia History, 1966, A Guide to the Study of Augusta and Richmond County, Georgia, 1967, (with Helen Callahan) Yesterday's Augusta, 1976, (with James E. Dorsey) A Bibliography of the Writings on Georgia History 1900-1970, rev. edit., 1978, (with Marguerite F. Fogleman) Reese Library Genealogical Resources, 1988, supplement, 1990, Goodman Cousins, 1988, Rowland Cousins, 1990, New Guide to the Study of Augusta, 1990, Index to City Directory of Augusta, Georgia, 1841-1879, 1991, More Goodman Cousins, 1993, My Fair Grandmother, 1994, Distant Cousins, The Huguenots Connecting Rowland, Bulloch, de Bourdeaux, DeVeaux and Roosevelt Families of S.C., N.C. and Ga., 1995, The Bessent Family of Georgia, 1995, Reeves Family of Georgia, 1996, Descendants of Wiley Reeves, 1996, Rowland-Huckaby Connections, 1996, Georgia Almanac, 1996, Rowland Family of Virginia, North Carolina and Georgia and Beyond, 1998, Atkinson Family in Virginia, 1998, Ancestors of David Jackson, 1998, Ancestors of Rachael Hines Lewis, 1998, Ancestors of Elizabeth Proctor in Virginia and England, 1998, Ancestors of Martha Whitehead, 1998, Wiley Reeves, His Descendants and Ancestors, 1999, John Rowland, Immigrant, 2000, Reeves Family in England, Virginia, North Carolina, Georgia and Beyond, 2000, The Mississippi Branch of the Rowland Family, 2000, Ancestors and Connections of Dunbar Rowland, 2000, Printing in Louisville, 2000, Confederate Printing in Augusta, Ga., 2000, Goodman Family of N.C., Ga. and Beyond Their Cherokee Indian Heritage, 2000, Hillhouse Family of Wash., Ga., 2000, Printing in Wash., Ga., 2000, Jacob Martin Hugenot of Charleston, S.C., 2000, John Gensel of Charleston, S.C., 2000, Bessent Family, 2000, Rowland Family in Ga., 2000, Printers of Augusta, Georgia, 1786-1900, 2003, Printing in Milledgeville, Georgia, 2003, Preliminary Checklist of Penfield, Georgia Imprints, 2003, A Preliminary Checklist of Georgia Imprints, 1763-1860, 2003, Civil War Marriages Richmond County, Georgia, 2004, Grocers, Butchers, Baker and Others, 2004, 1890 Census of Augusta and Richmond County Georgia, 2004, Citizens of Augusta and Richmond County, Georgia During the Civil War, 2005, Confederate Soldiers From Augusta and Richmond County, Georgia, 2005, Name Index to Augusta Georgia City Directories 1880-1891, 2006, others; editor: Reference Services, 1964, Historical Markers of Richmond County, Georgia, rev. edit., 1971, The Catalog and Cataloging, 1969, The Librarian and Reference Service, 1977, Reminiscences of Augusta Marines, 1985; supervising editor (with Heard Robertson) Jour. Archibald Campbell, 1981; contbr. to profl. jours. V.p. Jones Assn. Trustees and Friends, 1989-91. With USN, 1948-49. Recipient Nix-Jones award for disting. service Ga. Library Assn., 1981, Town and Gown award Augusta Coll. Alumni Assn., 1985. Mem. ALA, Am. Assn. State and Local History, Bibliog. Soc. Am., Southeastern Libr. Assn. (hon. life, exec. bd. 1971-72), Ga. Libr. Assn. (hon. life, 2d v.p. 1965-67, 71-73, 1st v.p., pres.-elect 1973-75, pres. 1975-77, chmn. budget com. 1977-79, adv. to pres. 1979-83, 85-92), Civil. Savannah River Area Libr. Assn. (past pres., editor union list of serials 1967), Duval County Libr. Assn. (past v.p.), Nat. Geneal. Soc., Ga. Geneal. Soc., N.C. Geneal. Soc., S.C. Geneal. Soc., Augusta Geneal. Soc., Richmond County Hist. Soc. (curator 1964-91, pres. 1967-69, founder, editor Richmond County History), Huguenot Soc. S.C. Ga. Hist. Soc. (curator emeritus), Ga. Bapt.

Hist. Soc., Nat., Young Men's Libr. Assn. (v.p. 1988-91), Ga. Trusts for Hist. Preservation, Hist. Augusta (trustee emeritus), Soc. Ga. Archivists, Kappa Phi Kappa. Baptist. Address: 172 Adamsville Spring Rd North Augusta SC 29860-7748

**ROWLAND, DAVID JACK,** retired academic administrator; b. Columbus, Ohio, June 17, 1921; s. David Henry and Ethel (Ryan) R.; m. Mary Ellen Stinson, Apr. 8, 1944; children: David Allen, Ryan Stinson, Sue Ellen Rowland Summers. BS, Ohio U., 1949; MA, U. Ala., 1951; LittD (hon.), Athens State Coll., 1967; LLD (hon.), Jacksonville State U., 1969. Pres. Walker Coll., Jasper, Ala., 1956-88, chancellor, 1988-95; interim pres. U. Ala./Walker Coll., 1995-96; ret., 1996. Bd. dirs. First Nat. Bank, Jasper, first Comml. Bancshares, Birmingham, Ala.; chmn. Ala. ACT Bd., Tuscaloosa, 1968—; real estate developer. Wildlife columnist and illustrator. Chmn. Jasper Indsl. Bd., 1987—; commr. Ala. Mining commn., Jasper, 1976—; mem. Ala. Employer Guard Res. commn., Birmingham, 1988—; trustee Walker Coll.; chmn. adv. bd. Jasper Salvation Army; vice chmn. Walker County Human Resource Coun. Col. U.S. Army, 1942-46, ATO. Decorated Legion of Merit; recipient Silver Beaver award Boy Scouts Am., 1972; named to Ala. Sr. Citizen Hall of Fame. Mem. Res. Officers Assn. (pres. Jasper chpt.), Summit Club, Met. Dinner Club, Rotary (pres. Jasper 1967-68, Paul Harris fellow), Masons, Ala. Silver Hair Legislature. Avocations: tree farmer, growing christmas trees, wildfowl carver. Home: 1000 Valley Rd Jasper AL 35501-4925

**ROWLAND, DIANE,** health facility administrator, researcher; b. Bridgeport, Conn., Oct. 14, 1948; m. Brian L. Biles, Sept. 17, 1977. BA, Wellesley Coll., 1970; MPA, U. Calif., L.A., 1973; SCD, Johns Hopkins U., 1987. Mem. staff U.S. House Rep., Washington, 1983—91; assoc. dir. Commonwealth Fund Commn. on Elderly People Living Alone, Balt., 1985—91; assoc. prof. Johns Hopkins U., Balt., 1987—93; exec. v.p. Kaiser Family Found., Washington, 1993—. Exec. dir. Kaiser Commn. on Future of Medicaid, Washington, 1991—98, Kaiser Commn. on Medicaid & the Uninsured, Washington, 1998—; pres. Assn. Health Svc. Rsch., Washington, 2000; mem. Sec. Task Force on Infant Mortality, Washington, 2000—. Contbr. articles to profl. jours. Fellow Brookdale Nat. fellow, Brookdale Found., 1987. Mem.: Inst. Medicine, 2004. Greek Orthodox. Avocations: travel, reading, sailing. Office: Henry J Kaiser Family Found 1330 G Street NW Washington DC 20005

**ROWLAND, ESTHER E(DELMAN),** retired dean; b. NYC, Apr. 12, 1926; d. Abraham Simon and Ida Sarah (Shifrin) Edelman; m. Lewis P. Rowland, Aug. 31, 1952; children: Andrew, Steven, Joy Rosenthal. BA, U. Wis., 1946; MA, Columbia U., 1948, MPhil, 1984; cert. in bioethics, Columbia U./Albert Einstein, 1996. Instr. in polit. sci. CCNY, 1947-51, Mt. Holyoke Coll., South Hadley, Mass., 1948-49; dir. health professions adv. bd. U. Pa., Phila., 1971-73; adviser to pre-profl. students Barnard Coll., NYC, 1974-79, dean for pre-profl. students, 1980-93, assoc. dean studies, 1989-95; ret., 1995—. Proofreader Monthly Review, N.Y.C., 1997-2003. Mem. exec. com. Nat. Emergency Civil Liberties Com., N.Y.C., 1975-90; mem. exec. com. Women's Counseling Project, 1981-86. Mem. N.E. Assn. Health Professions Advisers (exec. com. 1973-74), N.E. Assn. Pre Law Advisors (exec. com. 1981-83, 85-86), Neurol. Inst. Aux., N.Y.C. Found. Sr. Citizens (ombudsman 1997-99), Aux. Am. Acad. Neurologists (exec. bd. 1999-2001). Home: 404 Riverside Dr New York NY 10025-1861 E-mail: eerowland@gmail.com.

**ROWLAND, FRANK SHERWOOD,** chemistry professor; b. Del., Ohio, June 28, 1927; m. Joan Lundberg, 1952; children: Ingrid Drake. Jeffrey Sherwood. AB, Ohio Wesleyan U., 1948; MS, U. Chgo., 1951, PhD, 1952, DSc (hon.), 1989, Duke U., 1989, Whittier Coll., 1989, Princeton U., 1990, Haverford Coll., 1992, Clark U., 1996, U. East Anglia, 1996; LLD (hon.), Ohio Wesleyan U., 1989, Simon Fraser U., 1991, U. Calgary, 1997; laurea honoris causa, U. Urbino, Italy, 1998; DSc, Carleton Coll., 1998, Gustavus Adolphus Coll., 1997, Occidental Coll., 1998, Kanagawa Univ., Japan, 1999, LaTrobe U., Australia, 2000, U. Waterloo, Can., 2001, Ohio State U., 2002. Instr. chemistry Princeton (N.J.) U., 1952—56; prof. chemistry U. Kans., 1956—58, assoc. prof. chemistry, 1958—63, prof. chemistry, 1963—64, U. Calif., Irvine, 1964—, dept. chmn., 1964—70, Aldrich prof. chemistry, 1985—89, Bren prof. chemistry, 1989—94, Donald Bren rsch. prof., chemistry, 1994—. Humboldt sr. scientist Fed. Republic Germany, 1981; chmn. Dahlem (Germany) Conf. on Changing Atmosphere, 1987; vis. scientist Japan Soc. for Promotion Sci., 1980; co-dir. western region Nat. Inst. Global Environ. Change, 1989—93; del. Internat. Coun. Sci. Unions, 1993—98; fgn. sec. NAS, 1994—2002; lectr., cons. in field; mem. ozone commn. Internat. Assn. Meteorology and Atmospheric Physics, 1980—88, hon. life mem., 1996, mem. commn. on atmospheric chemistry and global pollution, 1979—91; mem. acid rain peer rev. panel U.S. Office of Sci. and Tech., Exec. Office of White House, 1982—84; mem. vis. com. Max Planck Inst., Heidelberg and Mainz, Germany, 1982—96; ozone trends panel mem. NASA, 1986—88; chmn. Gordon Conf. Environ. Scis.-Air, 1987; mem. Calif. Coun. Sci. Tech., 1989—95; mem. exec. com. Tyler Prize, 1992—. Contbr. articles to profl. jours. Named to, GTE Acad. All-Am. Hall of Fame, 2000; recipient numerous awards including, John Wiley Jones award, Rochester Inst. Tech., 1975, Disting. Faculty Rsch. award, U. Calif., Irvine, 1976, Profl. Achievement award, U. Chgo., 1977, Billard award, N.Y. Acad. Sci., 1977, Tyler World Prize in Environ. Achievement, 1983, Global 500 Roll of Honor for Environ. Achievement, UN Environment Program, 1988, Dana award for Pioneering Achievements in Health, 1987, Silver medal, Royal Inst. Chemistry U.K., 1989, Wadsworth award, N.Y. State Dept. Health, 1989, medal, U. Calif. Irvine, 1989, Japan prize in Environ. Sci., 1989, Dickson prize, Carnegie-Mellon U., 1991, Albert Einstein prize, World Cultural Coun., 1994, Nobel Prize in chemistry, 1995, Alumni medal, U. Chgo., 1997, Nevada medal, 1997, Gold medal, Acad. Athens, 2003; fellow Guggenheim Found., 1962, 1974. Fellow: AAAS (pres.-elect 1991, pres. 1992, chmn. bd. dirs. 1993), Am. Geophys. Union (Roger Revelle medal 1994), Am. Phys. Soc. (Leo Szilard award for physics in pub. interest 1979); mem.: NAS (co-DATA com. 1977—82, com. atmospheric scis. solar-terrestial com. 1979—83, sci. com. on problems environment 1986—89, bd. environ. studies and toxicology 1986—91, com. on atmospheric chemistry 1987—89, Infinite Voyage film com. 1988—92, Robertson Meml. lectr. 1993, chmn. com. on internat. orgns. and programs 1993—2002, chmn. office of internat. affairs 1994—2002, coun. 1994—2002, co-chmn. interacad. panel 1995—2000, mem. exec. com. 2000—02), Royal Soc. Eng., Academia Bibliotheca Alexandrinae, Inst. Medicine, Am. Philos. Soc., Am. Meteorol. Soc., Korean Acad. Sci. Tech. (fgn. sec.), European Acad. Arts, Scis. and Humanities, Am. Chem. Soc. (chmn. divsn. nuclear sci. and tech. 1973—74, chmn. divsn. phys. chemistry 1974—75, E.F. Smith lectureship 1980, Orange County award 1975, Tolman medal 1976, Zimmerman award 1980, Environ. Sci. and Tech. award 1983, Esselen award 1987, Peter Debye Phys. Chem. award 1993), Am. Acad. Arts and Scis., Sigma Xi, Phi Beta Kappa. Office: Dept Chemistry U Calif Irvine 571 Rowland Hall Irvine CA 92697-2025 E-mail: rowland@uci.edu.

**ROWLAND, HOWARD RAY,** mass communications educator; b. Eddy County, N.Mex., Sept. 9, 1929; s. Lewis Marion and Ursula Kewne (Hunt) R.; m. Meredith June Lee, Apr. 19, 1951; children: Runay Ilene Olson, Rhonda Lee Fisher. B in Journalism, U. Mo., 1950; MS in Journalism, So. Ill. U., 1959; PhD, Mich. State U., 1969. Feature writer Springfield (Mo.) Newspapers, Inc., 1954; newspaper editor Monett (Mo.) Times, 1954-55; editl. writer So. Ill. U., Carbondale, 1959. Prof. So. Ill. U. (Minn.) State U., 1959-86, asst. dean, 1986-87, 88-90; dir. Ctr. for British Studies, Alnwick, Eng., 1987-88, 90-91. Emeritus prof. St. Cloud State U., 1991—; cons. Conf. of Campus Ombudsmen, Berkeley, 1971; recorder Seminar on Fund Raising, Washington, 1985; bibliographer Higher Edn. Bibliography Yearbook, 1987. Author: American Students in Alnwick Castle, 1990, St. Cloud State University—125 Years, 1994, Big War, Small Town, 2003; editor: Effective Community Relations, 1980; sect. editor: Handbook of Institutional Advancement, 1986; author book revs. Chair All-Am. City Com., St. Cloud, 1973-74. With U.S. Army, 1951-53. NDEA doctoral fellow Mich. State U., 1967-69; recipient Appreciation award Mayor of St. Cloud, 1974, Disting. Svc. award Coun. for Advancement and Support Edn., 1985. Mem. Soc. of Profl.

Journalists (Minn. chpt. pres. 1963-64, dep. dir. 1965-67), Coun. for Advancement and Support of Edn. (dist. 5 chair 1977-79, Leadership award 1979), Phi Delta Kappa (Mich. State U. chpt. pres. 1968-69, St. Cloud State Univ. chpt. pres. 1978-79). Presbyterian. Avocations: writing, fishing, travel, photography, antiques. Home: 29467 Kraemer Lake Rd Saint Joseph MN 56374-9646 *Striving to achieve is more rewarding than striving for acclaim. Achievement brings personal satisfaction more fulfilling than recognition.*

**ROWLAND, JAMES RICHARD,** electrical engineering educator; b. Muldrow, Okla., Jan. 24, 1940; s. Richard Cleveland and Imogene Beatrice (Angel) R.; m. Jonell Condren, Aug. 24, 1963 (dec. May 1991); children: Jennifer Lynn, Angela Janel; m. Mary Anderson, Jan. 2, 1995. BSEE, Okla. State U., 1962; MSEE, Purdue U., 1964, PhD in Elec. Engring., 1966. Registered profl. engr., Okla. Instr. Purdue U., West Lafayette, Ind., 1964-65; from asst. to assoc. prof. Ga. Inst. Tech., Atlanta, 1966-71; from assoc. to full prof. Okla. State U., Stillwater, 1971-85; prof., chmn. dept. elec. and computer engring. U. Kans., Lawrence, 1985-89, prof., 1985—. Cons. Lockheed-Ga. Co., Marietta, 1966-71, U.S. Army Missile Command, Huntsville, Ala., 1969-79, Sandia Nat. Labs., Albuquerque, 1979, Puritan-Bennett, Lenexa, Kans., 1992. Author: Linear Control Systems, 1986; mem. editorial adv. bd. Computer and Elec. Engring., 1971-98; co-contbr. 60 articles to profl. jours. Fellow IEEE (edn. soc. pres. 1982-83, Centennial medal 1984, edn. soc. Achievement award 1986, edn. conf. award 1988, Region 5 Oustanding Educator award 1995, Svc. award 2002), Am. Soc. Engring. Edn. (dir. grad. div. 1987-89, Midwest sec. chair 2001-02), Eta Kappa Nu (dir. 1989-91), Kiwanis. Republican. Baptist. Avocations: golf, gardening. Home: 2424 Free State Ct Lawrence KS 66047-2831 Office: U Kans Dept Elec Engring & Computer Sci 2001 Eaton Hall Lawrence KS 66045 Office Phone: 785-864-8822. E-mail: jrowland@eecs.ku.edu.

**ROWLAND, KELLY (KELENDRIA TRENE ROWLAND),** singer; b. Atlanta, Ga., Feb. 11, 1981; With Destiny's Child, 1992—2005; solo career, 2005—. Singer (with Destiny's Child): (albums) Destiny's Child, 1998, The Writing's on the Wall, 1999, Survivor, 2001 (Am. Music award for Favorite Pop Album, 2002), 8 Days of Christmas, 2001, Destiny Fulfilled, 2004 (Am. Music award for Favorite R&B Album, 2005), (songs) No, No, No, 1997, Say My Name, 1999 (2 Grammy awards, 2001, MTV Video Music award for Best R&B Video, 2000), Get on the Bus, 1999, Bills Bills Bills, 1999, Bug-A-Boo, 1999, Jumpin' Jumpin', 2000, Independent Woman, 2000, Survivor, 2001 (Grammy award, Best R&B Performance, 2002, MTV Video Music award for Best R&B Video, 2001), Bootylicious, 2001, Emotion, 2001, Lose My Breath, 2004, Soldier, 2005; singer: (solo career) (albums) Simply Deep, 2002, (songs) Stole, 2002, Can't Nobody, 2003, Train on a Track, 2003; singer: (with Nelly) Dilemma, 2002 (Grammy award for Best Rap/Sung Collaboration, 2003); actor: (films) Freddy vs. Jason, 2003. Recipient Favorite R&B Group, Am. Music Awards, 2001, 2002, 2005, BET award for Best Female Group, 2001, NAACP Image award for Outstanding Duo or Group, 2001, 2005, 2006, Choice Pop Group, Teen Choice Awards, 2001, Brit award for Best Internat. Group, 2002, World's Best-Selling Group, World Music Awards, 2002, World's Best-Selling Pop Group, 2002, 2006, World's Best-Selling R&B Group, 2002, 2006, Best-Selling Female Group of All Time, 2006. Address: 1505 Hadley Houston TX 77002 Office Phone: 713-772-5175.*

**ROWLAND, KYLA FAYE,** musician; b. LaFollette, Tenn., Aug. 11, 1945; d. William Kyle and Eulalia Faye Martin; m. Bobby Dwayne Mullins, Mar. 1, 1991;; children: Shellie Allyson Kinard, Barry Nelson. Songwriter WORD Music, Nashville, 1976—84, Gt. RM Pub., Morristown, Tenn., 1984—95; spkr. Kyla Rowland Ministries, Morristown, Tenn., 1990—; pres., author, songwriter My Abby Pub., Morristown, Tenn., 1990—; author, songwriter Daywind Records, Nashville, 2001—; radio host, syndicated program Everyday Life, Tenn., 2003—. Coord. Pigeon River Revival, Pigeon Forge, Tenn., 2001—. Author: Between Me And The Storm, Girl Talk; composer: (southern gospel song) There Rose A Lamb (Dove Award and Singing News Song Of Yr., 1993). Republican. Baptist. Avocations: cooking, reading. Office: My Abby Publishing LLC PO Box 11 Morristown TN 37815 Personal E-mail: kyla72@hotmail.com.

**ROWLAND, LANDON HILL,** diversified holding company executive; b. Fuquay Springs, N.C., May 20, 1937; s. Walter Elton and Elizabeth Carr (Williams) R.; m. Sarah Fidler, Dec. 29, 1959; children: Sarah Elizabeth, Matthew Hill, Joshua Carr. BA, Dartmouth Coll., 1959; LL.B., Harvard U., 1962. Bar: Mo. Assoc. Watson, Ess, Marshall & Enggas, Kansas City, Mo., 1962-70, ptnr., 1970-80; v.p. Kansas City So. Industries, Inc., 1980-83, pres., chief oper. officer, 1983-86, pres., chief exec. officer, 1987—, also bd. dirs.; pres., chief exec. officer Kansas City So. Ry. Co., 1990-91, chmn., 1990—. Lectr. antitrust law U. Mo. Kansas City; chmn. DST Systems, 1983—. Co-author West's Mo. Practice Series. Trustee Midwest Rsch. Inst., Kansas City, Mo.; chmn. bd. dirs. Swope Ridge Health Care Ctr.; bd. dirs. Lyric Opera of Kansas City, Am. Royal, Jacob L. & Ella C. Loose Found.; chmn. Met. Performing Arts Fund. Mem. ABA, Mo. Bar Assn., Phi Beta Kappa. Clubs: Kansas City Country, Kansas City, River. Home: Ever Glades Farm 12717 NE Mt Olivet Rd Kansas City MO 64166-1236 Office: Ever Glades Fin 920 Main St #204 Kansas City MO 64105-2008

**ROWLAND, LEWIS PHILLIP,** neurology educator, editor, clinical investigator; b. Bklyn., Aug. 3, 1925; s. Henry Alexander and Cecile (Coles) Rowland; m. Esther Edelman Rowland, Aug. 31, 1952; children: Andrew Simon, Steven Samuel, Joy Rosenthal. BS, Yale U., 1945, MD, 1948; PhD (hon.), U. Aix-Marseilles, France, 1986, U. Padua, 1996. Diplomate Am. Bd. Psychiatry and Neurology. Intern New Haven Hosp., 1949-50; asst. resident NY Neurol. Inst., 1950-52, fellow, 1953; clin. assoc. NIH, Bethesda, Md., 1953-54; practice rsch. medicine, specializing in neurology NYC, 1954-67, Phila., 1967-73, NYC, 1973—; asst. neurologist Montefiore Hosp., NYC, 1954-57; vis. fellow Nat. Inst. Med. Rsch., London, 1956; from asst. prof. to prof. neurology Columbia Coll. Physicians and Surgeons, 1957-67, prof. dept. neurology, 1973—, chmn. dept. neurology, 1973-98; prof., chmn. dept. neurology U. Pa. Med. Sch., 1967-73; from asst. neurologist to attending neurologist Presbyn. Hosp., 1957-67; co-dir. Neurol. Clin. Rsch. Ctr., 1961-67, dir. neurology svc., 1973-98, attending neurologist, 1973—, pres. med. bd., 1991-94. Cons. Harlem Hosp., 1973—; mem. med. adv. bd. Myasthenia Gravis Found., pres., 1971-73; med. adv. bd. Muscular Dystrophy Assocs., Nat. Multiple Sclerosis Soc., NYC Multiple Sclerosis Soc., 1977-92, Com. to Combat Huntington's Disease; chmn. med. adv. bd. NYC Multiple Sclerosis Soc. 1977-92; pres. Parkinson's Disease Found., 1979-; mem. tng. grants com. Nat. Inst. Neurol. Disorders and Stroke, NIH, 1971-73, bd. sci. counselors, 1978-83, chmn., 1981-83, mem. nat. adv. coun., 1986-90, cons. to dir., 2000-01; hon. adv. Motor Neuron Rsch. Ctr., Columbia U., 2005-. Mem. editl. bd. Archives of Neurology, 1968-76, Advances in Neurology, 1969—, Italian Jour. Neurol., 1977—99, Handbook of Clin. Neurology, 1982—, New Eng. Jour. Medicine, 1990-2000, Med. Letter, 1990-97, Jour. Neurol. Sci., 1991—, Jour. Neuromuscular Disorders, 1991-97, Clin. Neurosci., 1995-98; editor-in-chief Neurology, 1977-87, Neurology Today, 2001—; assoc. editor Medlink, 1995—. With USNR, 1942—44, with USPHS, 1953—54. Mem. Am. Neurol. Assn. (pres. 1980, hon. mem 1989—), Inst. Medicine, Nat. Acad. Sci. (elected 1996), Am. Acad. Neurology (pres.-elect 1987-89, pres. 1989-91, hon. mem. 1997—), Phila. Neurol. Soc. (pres. 1972), Assn. Rsch. Nervous Mental Disease (pres. 1969, trustee 1976—, v.p. 1980, chmn. bd. trustees 1992-98), Assn. Univ. Profs. Neurology (sec. 1971-74, pres. 1978), Am. Acad. Neurol. Found. (pres. 1996, chair bd. trustees 1997-99, trustee 1999—), Ea. Pa. Multiple Sclerosis Soc. (chmn. med. adv. bd. 1969-73); hon. mem. Neurol. Socs. France, Poland, Can., Europe, Italy, Gt. Britain, Spain, Japan. Home: 404 Riverside Dr New York NY 10025-1861 Office: Columbia U Med Ctr Neurological Inst 710 W 168th St New York NY 10032-2603 Office Phone: 212-305-8551. Business E-Mail: lpr1@columbia.edu.

**ROWLAND, PLEASANT T.,** toy company executive, publisher; m. Jerry Frautschi. Grad., Wells Coll., 1962. Elem. tchr. Mass., Calif., Ga. and N.J.; TV news reporter, anchor KGO-TV, San Francisco; v.p. Boston Ednl. Rsch.

Co., 1971-78; pub. Children's Mag. Guide, 1981-89; creator Am. Doll Collection, 1985; founder, pres. Pleasant Co. (sold to Mattel and renamed American Girl, Inc.), 1986—98; vice chmn. Mattel, Inc., 1998—2000. Founder Pleasant T. Rowland Found., Aurora Found. LLC. Named one of 12 Outstanding Entrepreneurs, Inst. Am. Entrepreneurs, 1990, one of Am.'s Top 50 Women Bus. Owners, Working Women mag., 1993-98; recipient Best and Brightest in Mktg. award Advt. Age, 1993, Mem. Internat. Women's Forum, Com. of 200.*

**ROWLAND, RALPH THOMAS,** retired architect; b. Elizabeth, N.J., Oct. 10, 1920; s. Thomas Aloysius and Anna Frances (McQuaid) R.; m. Bernice Barbara Cannizzo, Sept. 7, 1946; children: Glenn Thomas, Mark Louis, Roy Joseph, Lisa Rowland Majewski. Student, Manhattan Coll., 1937-38, Columbia U., 1945-49. Archtl. field supr., specifier Voorhees Walker Foley & Smith, N.Y.C., 1945-50; specifier, project mgr. Sargent Webster Crenshaw & Folley, Watertown, N.Y., 1951-53; pvt. practice Hamden, Conn., 1954-56; field supr. Fletcher Thompson, Inc., Bridgeport, Conn., 1954-56, project mgr., 1957, 65-73, asso., 1963-73, v.p., 1973-81, dir. archtl. research, 1981-85, adv. coun., 1994-98. Chmn. Conn. Bldg. Code Standards Com., 1978-82; vice chmn. Conn. State Codes and Standards Com., 1982-86; cons. in field. Editorial chmn.: Conn. Architect Mag., 1966-74; project mgr. design, St. Vincents Med. Center, Bridgeport, Conn. Mem. Cheshire Planning Commn., 1966-72, chmn., 1967-68; pres. Hamden C. of C., 1964, New Eng. Bldg. Code Assn., 1989; mem. Cen. Naugatuck Valley Regional Planning Agy., 1966-74, chmn., 1969; mem. Cheshire Democratic Town Com., 1960-70, treas., 1963-69; mem. Conn. Archtl. Sch. Task Force, 1987-88. With USN, 1942-45. Fellow AIA; mem. AIA Conn. (past pres.), AARP (pres. Cheshire chpt. 1995-97), Conn. Bldg. Ofcls. Assn., Cheshire C. of C. Roman Catholic. Home: 201 N Rolling Acres Rd Cheshire CT 06410-2119

**ROWLAND, ROBERT ALEXANDER, III,** lawyer; b. McAllen, Tex., Apr. 27, 1943; s. Robert Alexander Jr and Marguerite (Gerry) Rowland; m. Victoria Nalle, Apr. 2, 1977; children: Julia Marie, Emily Nalle. BS, Tex. A&M U., 1966; JD, George Washington U., 1972. Bar: Tex. 1972, U.S. Dist. Ct. (so. dist.) Tex. 1973, U.S. Ct. Appeals (5th cir.) 1973, U.S. Supreme Ct. 1976, U.S. Dist. Ct. (no. dist.) Tex. 1979, U.S. Dist. Ct. (we. dist.) Tex. 1982, U.S. Dist. Ct. (ea. dist.) Tex. 1983. Law clk. U.S. Ct. Appeals (5th cir.), Houston, 1973-74; assoc. Vinson & Elkins, Houston, 1975-81; ptnr. Susman, Godfrey & McGowan, Houston, 1982—88; mng. dir. Johnson and Gibbs, Houston, 1988-91; ptnr. Hutcheson & Grundy, LLP, Houston, 1992-94; chmn., CEO Associated Counsel of Am., 1995—; ptnr. Roach & Rowland, Houston, 2005—. Bd. dirs. Vol. Ctr., Houston, 1975—84, pres., 1982—83; founding mem., bd. dirs. Tex. Accts. and Lawyers for Arts, 1979—92, pres., 1989—91; devel. coun. Sch. Liberal Arts Tex. A&M U., 1992—, steering com., 1995—, devel. coun. George Bush Sch. Govt. and Pub. Svc., 2004—; trustee Houston Pks. Bd. Endowment Fund, 2002—; chmn. endowment com. Houston Audubon Soc., 2006—; co-chmn. Mayor's Transition Com. for Parks, City of Houston, 1992—94; candidate for State Rep., Tex. Legis. Dist. 134, Rep. Primary, 2002; fin. com. Harris County Rep. Party, 2003—, chmn., 2005—; bd. dirs. United Reps. of Harris County, 2002—; Rep. precinct chmn. Harris County Precinct, 2003—05; active Mission Outreach coun. Christ Ch. Cathedral, 2002—05, chmn., 2004—05, co-chmn., grants subcom., 2005—06, chmn. grants subcom., 2006—; bd. dirs. Houston Pks. Bd., 1993—2005, chmn., 2003—05; bd. dirs. Contemporary Art Mus. Houston, 1974—80, 1991—94; bd. dirs. Sarah Campbell Blaffer Gallery of Art U. Houston, 1989—94; bd. dirs. Tex. Opera Theater, 1988—89; mem. bd. trustees Nat. Recreation and Pk. Assn., 1992—95; bd. dirs. Cultural Arts Coun., Houston, 1981—86, Pk. People Inc., 1979—2001, pres., 1991—92, endowment com. chmn., 1994—2004; bd. dirs. Compass, 2006—; mem. quality of life adv. com. Greater Houston Partnership, 2006—, co-chair parks and open spaces com., 2006—. Capt. U.S. Army, 1966—69, Vietnam. Fellow: Tex. Bar Found., Houston Bar Found.; mem.: Houston Young Lawyers Assn. (bd. dirs. 1975—79, pres. 1978—79), State Bar Tex., Houston Bar Assn. (dir. 1979—88, sec., chmn. law and art com. 1984—85, 2d v.p. 1985—86), C Club (program chmn. exec. com. 2005, exec. com. 2005—, membership chmn. 2006), Coronado Club, River Oaks Country Club, Phi Delta Phi. Episcopalian. Home: 2010 Chilton Rd Houston TX 77019-1502 Office: Associated Counsel Am Inc Ste 125 4605 Post Oak Pl Houston TX 77027-9744 Office Phone: 713-840-7100. Personal E-mail: rob@robrowland.com. Business E-Mail: rob@associatedcounsel.com.

**ROWLAND, THEODORE JUSTIN,** physicist, researcher; b. Cleve., May 15, 1927; s. Thurston Justin and Lillian (Nesser) R.; m. Janet Claire Millar, June 28, 1952 (div. 1967); children: Theodore Justin, Dawson Ann, Claire Millar; m. Patsy Marie Beard, Aug. 21, 1968. BS, Western Res. U., 1948; MA, Harvard U., 1949, PhD, 1954. Rsch. physicist Union Carbide Metals Co., Niagara Falls, NY, 1954-61; prof. phys. metallurgy U. Ill., 1961-92, asst. dean Coll. Engring., acting assoc. dean Grad. Coll., 1990-91, prof. emeritus, 1992—; pres., dir. Materials Cons., Inc. Cons. physicist, 1961—; cons. metallurgist, 1976—. Editor 2 books; author monograph; contbr. articles to profl. jours. Fellow Am. Phys. Soc.; mem. AIME, AAAS, AAUP, Phi Beta Kappa, Sigma Xi. Achievements include initial verification of charge density waves in dilute alloys; original contributions to theory and experiment in nuclear magnetic resonance in metals. Home: 805 Park Lane Dr Champaign IL 61820-7613 Office: U Ill Dept Materials Sci and Engring 1304 W Green St Urbana IL 61801-2920 Business E-Mail: trowland@uiuc.edu.

**ROWLANDS, DAVID THOMAS,** pathology educator; b. Wilkes-Barre, Pa., Mar. 22, 1930; s. David Thomas and Anna Jule (Morgan) R.; m. Gwendolyn Marie York, Mar. 1, 1958; children: Julie Marie, Carolyn Jane. MD, U. Pa., 1955. Diplomate: Am. Bd. Pathology, Am. Bd. Allergy and Immunology. Intern Pa. Hosp., Phila., 1955-56; resident Cin. Gen. Hosp., 1956-60; asst. prof. U. Colo., 1962-64, Rockefeller U., 1964-66; assoc. prof. Duke U., Durham, NC, 1966-70; prof. pathology U. Pa., Phila., 1970-82, chmn. dept. pathology, 1973-78; prof. medicine, 1979-82; prof., chmn. dept. pathology U. So. Fla., Tampa, 1982-91, assoc. dean, 1983-84, prof. pediatrics, 1986-91; med. dir. Lifelink Tissue Bank, 1991-93. Mem. editorial bd.: Am. Jour. Pathology, 1971-81, Developmental and Comparative Immunology, 1977-79. Served with USNR, 1960-62. Recipient Lederle Med. Faculty award U. Colo., 1964, Jacob Ehrenzeller award Pa. Hosp., 1976 Mem. Am. Assn. Pathologists, Internat. Acad. Pathology, Am. Assn. Clin. Pathology, Am. Assn. Immunologists, Coll. Am. Pathologist, Arthur Purdy Stout Soc. Presbyterian. Home: 13804 Cypress Village Cir Tampa FL 33618-8406

**ROWLANDS, GENA,** actress; b. Madison, Wis., June 19, 1936; d. Edwin Merwin and Mary Allen (Neal) R.; m. John Cassavetes, Apr. 9, 1954 (dec. Feb. 3 1989); 4 children. Student, U. Wis., Am. Acad. Dramatic Art, NYC. Theatrical appearance include The Middle of the Night, 1956; Actress: (films) including The High Cost of Loving, 1958, Lonely Are The Brave, 1962, A Child is Waiting, 1963, Spiral Road, 1962, Faces, 1968, At Any Price, 1970, Minnie and Moscowitz, 1971, A Woman Under the Influence, 1974 (Golden Globe award for Best Motion Picture Actress in a Drama, 1975), Two Minute Warning, 1976, Opening Night, 1977, The Brinks Job, 1978, One Summer Night, 1979, Gloria, 1980, Tempest, 1982, Love Streams, 1983, Light of Day, 1987, Another Woman, 1988, Once Around, 1990, Ted and Venus, 1991, Night on Earth, 1992, Silent Cries, 1993, Parallel Lives, 1994, Anything for John, 1995, Something to Talk About, 1995, The Neon Bible, 1995, Enfants de Salaud, 1996, Unhook the Stars, 1996, Hope Floats, 1997, She's so Lovely, 1997, The Mighty, 1997, Paulie, 1998, The Weekend, 1999, Taking Lives, 2004, The Notebook, 2004, The Skeleton Key, 2005, (TV movies) A Question of Love, 1978, Strangers, 1979, Thurday's Child, 1983, Early Frost, 1984, The Betty Ford Story, 1987 (Emmy award for Outstanding Lead Actress in a Miniseries or Special, 1987, Golden Globe award for Best Performance by an Actress in a TV Film, 1988), Montana, Face of a Stranger, 1991 (Emmy award, Leading Actress in a Mini-Series or Special, 1992), Parallel Lives, 1994, Best of Friends for Life, 1996, Ljuset häller mig sällskap, 2000, Color of Love: Jacey's Story, 2000, Wild Iris, 2001, Hysterical Blindness, 2002, (Emmy award best supporting actress in TV movie, 2003), Charms for the

Easy Life, 2002, The Incredible Mrs. Ritchie, 2003 (Daytime Emmy award for Outstanding Performer in a Family Special, 2004); numerous other TV appearances. Mem. Actors Equity Assn., Screen Actors Guild, AFTRA, Am. Guild Variety Artists.

**ROWLES, MICHAEL G.,** lawyer; b. Evanston, Ill. m. Maureen Rowles; children: Meagan, Caitlin, Camryn. JD, U. Ill. With Burke, Bosselman & Weaver, Chgo., Jenner & Block, 1993—95, Paige Polin Busch & Boatwright, San Diego, 1995—96, Zevnik Horton Guibord McGovern Palmer & Fognani, 1996; gen. counsel, sr. v.p., sec. Entravision, 2000—06; exec. v.p., gen. counsel Live Nation, Inc., 2006—. Office: Live Nation Inc 9348 Civic Ctr Dr Beverly Hills CA 90210*

**ROWLETT, RALPH MORGAN,** archaeologist, educator; b. Richmond, Ky., Sept. 11, 1934; s. Robert Kenny and Daisy (Mullikin) R.; m. Elsebet Sander-Jorgensen, Aug. 25, 1963 (div. Jan. 1986); children: Rolf R. Arvid, Erik Kenneth; m. Elizabeth Helen Dinan, Apr. 21, 1989 (div. Oct. 1995); 1 child, Helen Holly; m. Magda Mircea, 2005. Student, U. Ky., 1952-53; BA summa cum laude, Marshall U., 1956; postgrad., U. London, 1962-63; PhD, Harvard U., 1968. Instr. anthropology U. Mo., Columbia, 1965-67, asst. prof., 1967-69, assoc. prof., 1969-75, prof., 1975—. Postdoctoral fellow Ghent U., 1969; vis. prof. Bucuresti U., 2005. Co-author: Neolithic Levels on the Titelberg, Luxembourg, 1981, Meeting Anthropology Phase to Phase, 2000; anthropology editor Random House Unabridged Dictionary of English, 1980—; editor: Horizons and Styles, 1993, Horizons and Styles in West Eurasiatic Archaeology; developer thermoluminescence dating of flint, 1972; co-developer electron spin resonance dating of flint, 1981. 1st lt. arty., U.S. Army, 1956-58. Decorated officer Legion de Merit (Luxembourg); named Ky. col., 1976; grantee NSF, 1973-75, 76-79, 82-83, Earthwatch, 1985-88, Svc. Archeologique de Neuchatel, 1989, British Coun., 1993, Acad. of Romania, 1996, Internat. Rsch. and Exch. Bd., 1997. Fellow Am. Anthrop. Assn.; mem. AAAS, Archaeol. Inst. Am., Soc. Am. Archaeology, Societe Prehistorique de Luxembourg, Societe Archeologique Champenoise, English Heritage, Palomino Horse Breeders Assn., Sigma Xi. Green Party. Mem. Christian Ch. (Disciples of Christ). Home: Hollywell Hill 1197 State Road Ww Fulton MO 65251-5106 Office: Univ Mo Dept Anthropology Columbia MO 65211-0001 Office Phone: 573-882-4731. E-mail: rowlettR@missouri.edu.

**ROWLETTE, HENRY ALLEN, JR.,** social worker, counseling psychologist; b. Phila., July 8, 1947; s. Henry Allen Sr. and Ophelia Alberta (Kilson) R.; m. Geraldine Lee Stevens, Mar. 1972 (div. Mar. 1986); children: Cessandra N., Deaeon D., Christiene A.; m. Carolyn Rowlette; 1 child, Janetta M.; m. Ann Laura Rowe, Mar. 19, 1989. BA, Cheyney State Coll., 1970; MEd, Boston U., 1981; MSW, Temple U., 1988; PhD, Suffield Coll. and U., 2003. Cert. sch. social worker, NJ; lic. clin. social worker; diplomate Am. Psychotherapy Assn., Nat. Bd. Cognitive Behavioral Therapists; ordained minister Bapt. Ch. Cardiac monitor technician Bapt. Med. Ctr., Little Rock, 1982-83; mental health technician The Horsham Clinic, Ambler, Pa., 1984; psychiat. technician The Lower Bucks Hosp., Bristol, Pa., 1984; mental health technician The Helene Fuld Med. Ctr., Trenton, NJ, 1988-90, psychiat. social worker, 1988-92; profl. sch. social worker The Willingboro Sch. Dist., NJ, 1990—96. Dist. crisis intervention team Willingboro Sch. Dist., 1994-96; therapist The NJ State Prison, Trenton, 1996-98, The Southwoods State Prison, Bridgeton, NJ; clinician Kennedy Meml. Health Ctr., Cherry Hill, NJ, 1998—, The Lumberton Schs./Sch. Social Worker, Lumberton, NJ, 1998; behavioral cons. Founds. Behavioral Health, Willow Grove, Pa., 1999; mental health technician The Children's Hosp. Phila., 1999-2000. Clin. social worker Phila. Prison System, 2000; mem. NAACP, Trenton, 1990. With US Army, 1971-79. Mem. NASW, Am. Assn. Christian Counselors, Omega Psi Phi (Delta Upsilon chpt.), Phi Delta Kappa (Trenton chpt.), Am. Psychotherapy Assn., Nat. Bd. Cognitive Behavioral Therapists, Nat. Bd. Addiction Examiners, Nat. Assn. Forensic Counselors. Democrat. Baptist. Avocations: fishing, reading, computer technology/games. Home: 18 Foxchase Dr Burlington NJ 08016-3044 Office Phone: 609-953-5608. Personal E-mail: drhrowlettejr@comcast.net.

**ROWLEY, BEVERLEY DAVIES,** sociologist; b. Antioch, Calif., July 28, 1941; d. George M. and Eloise Davies; m. Richard B. Rowley, Apr. 1, 1966 (div. 1983). BS, Colo. State U., 1963; MA, U. Nev., 1975; PhD, Union Inst., 1983. Social worker Nev. Dept. Pub. Welfare, Reno, 1963—65, Santa Clara County Dept. Welfare, San Jose, Calif., 1965—66; field dir. Sierra Sage coun. Camp Fire Girls, Sparks, Nev., 1966—70; program coord. divsn. health scis. Sch. Medicine U. Nev., 1976—78, program coord., health analyst office rural health, 1978—84, acting dir. office rural health, 1982—84; exec. asst. to pres. Med. Coll. of Hampton Rds., Norfolk, Va., 1984—87; rsch. mgr. Office Med. Edn. Info. AMA, Chgo., 1987—88, dir. dept. data systems, 1988-91; dir. med. edn. Maricopa Med. Ctr., Phoenix, 1991—99; pres. Med. Edn. and Rsch. Assocs., Inc., Phoenix, Chgo., 1999—, Med. Edn. & Rsch. Assocs., Tempe, Ariz., 1999—; vis. prof. Ariz. State U. East, Mesa, 1999—2000, profl. and personal coach, 2004—; pres., exec. dir. Maricopa Med. Found., Phoenix, 2004—. Various positions as adj. prof. and lectr. in health scis. U. Nev. Sch. of Medicine, 1972-75; lectr. dept. family and cmty. medicine U. Nev., 1978-84, asst. dir., evaluator Health Careers for Am. Indians Programs, 1978-84; cons. Nev. Statewide Health Survey, 1979-84; interim dir. Health Max, 1985-86; asst. prof. dept. family and cmty. medicine Med. Coll. of Hampton Rds., Norfolk, Va., 1985-87. Editor of five books; contbr. numerous articles to profl. jours. Mem. Am. Sociol. Assn., Nat. Rural Health Assn. (bd. dirs. 1986-88), Assn. Behavioral Sci. and Med. Edn. (pres. 1986), Assn. Am. Med. Colls. (exec. coun. 1993-95), Coun. Acad. Scis. (adminstrv. bd. 1992-97), Assn. Hosp. Med. Edn. (bd. dirs. 1997—), Delta Delta Delta. Achievements include development of three computer systems including AMA-FREIDA; four internet-based educational programs for physicians. Avocations: hiking, skiing, gardening, sewing, ceramics. Office: MERA Inc 1903 E Sarah Ln Tempe AZ 85284-3430 E-mail: BDR@MERAInc.com.

**ROWLEY, CYNTHIA,** apparel designer; b. Barrington, Ill. Grad., Art Inst. of Chicago. Designer Cynthia Rowley, Inc., 1983—; owner, designer Cynthia Rowley Boutiques, NYC, Chicago, Los Angeles and Japan, Swellco (subsidiary of Cynthia Rowley, Inc.). Work featured in Vogue, Elle, W, Harper's Bazaar, Glamour, New York Times, In Style, Elle Décor, French Vogue. Co-author: Swell: A Girl's Guide to the Good Life, 1999, Home Swell Home, 2002, Swell Holiday, 2003, The Swell Dressed Party, 2005. Recipient New Fashion Talent award, Council of Fashion Designers of Am., 1994. Office: Cynthia Rowley Inc 376 Bleecker St New York NY 10014*

**ROWLEY, GEOFFREY HERBERT,** management consultant; b. Harrow, Middlesex, Eng., Nov. 10, 1935; came to U.S., 1962; s. Herbert and Muriel Jessie (Nicolls) R. BA, Bristol U., Eng., 1958; cert. indsl. adminstrn., Glasgow U., Scotland, 1962; MBA, Harvard U., 1964. Purchasing officer Pirelli Ltd., London, 1958-61; rsch. assoc. Assn. for Internat. Rsch., Inc., Cambridge, Mass., 1964-68, v.p., 1968—2002, cons. in expatriate compensation, 1964—. Lectr. in field; dir. U. Bristol Found., Inc. Contbr. articles to profl. jours. Served with Royal Navy, 1953-55. Mem. Am. Compensation Assn., Inst. for Human Resources, Brit. Ins. Mgmt., Harvard Club. Home: 11 Berkeley Pl Cambridge MA 02138-3411 Office Phone: 617-251-3023. E-mail: GH.Rowley@verizon.net, GHRowley@aol.com.

**ROWLEY, GLENN HARRY,** lawyer; b. Hyannis, Mass., May 16, 1948; s. Harold Frederick and Olive Nellie (Jones) R.; 1 child, Brewster Westgate. BBA, U. Mass., 1970; JD with cum laude, Western New Eng. Coll., 1980. Bar: Mass. 1980, U.S. Dist. Ct. Mass. 1980, U.S. Tax Ct. 1981, cert.: Nat. Elder Law Found./ABA (elder law atty.). Staff mem. Cape Cod Planning and Econ. Devel. Commn., Barnstable, Mass., 1975-76; staff, estate planning tax dept. Coopers and Lybrand, Springfield, Mass., 1980-81; legal assoc. Roberts and Farrell, West Chatham, Mass., 1982-84; ptnr. Roberts, Farrell & Rowley, West Chatham, 1984-97; pvt. practice Chatham, Mass., 1997—. Cons. Local Citizen Scholarship Trusts, Harwich and Chatham, Mass., 1985—. Contbr. (weekly news column) The Enterprise, others; contbr. articles to profl. jours. Founding mem. Brewster (Mass.) Conservation Trust, 1984; elected mem. Brewster Hist. Dist. Com., 1975; adv. bd. The May Inst., The Cape Cod

Writers Ctr., Inc. With USN, 1971-74, Iceland. Recipient Am. Jurisprudence awards Lawyers Co-op. Pub. Co., 1978, 79. Mem. Mass. Bar Assn., Ocean Edge Exec. Club, Profl. Writers of Cape Cod, Cape Cod Estate Planning Coun., Nat. Acad. Elder Law Attys., Phi Delta Phi. Avocations: travel, writing. Home: Annaniases Knoll/Sheep Pond Brewster MA 02631 Office: The Marketplace PO Box 1489 26 George Ryder Rd S West Chatham MA 02669 Office Phone: 508-945-1000. E-mail: glennh.rowley@verizon.net.

**ROWLEY, HOWARD A.,** neurologist, radiologist, educator; b. Joliet, Ill., May 26, 1958; s. Willard G. and Monna M. Rowley; m. Carol A. Diamond; children: Anne R., Paul A., Joseph H. MD, Wash. U., St. Louis, Mo., 1980. Diplomate Am. Bd. Radiology, 1993, Am. Bd. Psychiatry and Neurology, 1991, lic. in neuroradiology Am. Bd. Radiology, 1997. Joseph Sackett prof. radiology U. Wis., Madison, Wis., 1999—, chief neuroradiology, 1999—. Achievements include development of advanced methods in stroke imaging and intervention. Office: University of Wisconsin 600 Highland Ave Box 3252 Madison WI 53792-3252 Office Phone: 608-265-8310.

**ROWLEY, JANET DAVISON,** physician; b. NYC, Apr. 5, 1925; d. Hurford Henry and Ethel Mary (Ballantyne) Davison; m. Donald A. Rowley, Dec. 18, 1948; children: Donald, David, Robert, Roger. PhB, U. Chgo., 1944, BS, 1946, MD, 1948; DSc (hon.), U. Ariz., 1989, U. Pa., 1989, Knox Coll., 1991, U. So. Calif., 1992, St. Louis U., 1997, St. Xavier U., 1999, Oxford U., Eng., 2000, Lund U., Sweden, 2003, Dartmouth U., 2004. Diplomate Am. Bd. Med. Genetics. Rsch. asst. U. Chgo., 1949—50; intern Marine Hosp., USPHS, Chgo., 1950—51; attending physician Infant Welfare and Prenatal Clinics Dept. Pub. Health, Montgomery County, Md., 1953—54; rsch. fellow Levinson Found., Cook County Hosp., Chgo., 1955—61; clin. instr. neurology U. Ill., Chgo., 1957—61; USPHS spl. trainee Radiobiology Lab. The Churchill Hosp., Oxford, England, 1961—62; rsch. assoc. dept. medicine and Argonne Cancer Rsch. Hosp. U. Chgo., 1962—69, assoc. prof. dept. medicine and Argonne Cancer Rsch. Hosp., 1969—77, prof. dept. medicine and Franklin McLean Meml. Rsch. Inst., 1977—84, Blum-Riese Disting. Svc. prof., dept. medicine and dept. molecular genetics and cell biology, 1984—, Blum-Riese Disting. Svc. prof. dept. human genetics, 1997—, interim dep. dean for sci. biol. scis. divsn., 2001—02. Bd. sci. counsellors Nat. Inst. Dental Rsch., NIH, 1972—76, chmn., 1974—76; mem. Nat. Cancer Adv. Bd., Nat. Cancer Inst., 1979—84, Nat. Adv. Coun. for Human Genome Rsch. Inst., 1999—2004; adv. com. Frederick Cancer Rsch. Facility, 1983—84; bd. sci. counsellors Nat. Human Genome Rsch. Inst., NIH, 1994—99, chmn., 1994—97; adv. bd. Howard Hughes Med. Inst., 1989—94, MD Anderson Cancer Ctr., 1998—2005; vis. com. dept. applied biol. scis. MIT Corp., 1983—86; bd. sci. cons. Meml. Sloan-Kettering Cancer Ctr., 1988—90; adv. com. Ency. Britannica U. Chgo., 1988—96; W. Jack Stuckey Jr. lectr. Tulane Career Ctr., 1996; Presdl. Symposium Am. Soc. Pediatric Hematology/Oncology, 1995; lectr. in field; mem. coun. adv. Internat. Geneminica Rsch. Inst., 2004—; mem. sci. adv. bd. Meml. Sloan-Kettering Cancer Ctr., 2004, Translational Genomics Rsch. Inst., Phoenix., 2004—; mem. sci. and med. adv. bd. Calif. Inst. Regenerative Medicine, 2005—. Co-founder, co-editor: Genes, Chromosomes and Cancer, mem. editl. bd.: Oncology Rsch., Cancer Genetics and Cytogenetics, Internat. Jour. Hematology, Genomics, Internat. Jour. Cancer, Leukemia, past. mem. editl. bd.: Blood, Cancer Rsch., Hematol. Oncology, Leukemia Rsch.; contbr. chapters to books, articles to profl. jours. Adv. com. for career awards in biomed. scis. Burroughs Wellcome Fund, 1994—98; selection panel for Clin. Sci. award Doris Duke Charitable Found., 2000—02, 2006; mem. Pres.'s Adv. Coun. on Bioethics, 2001—; mem. med. rsch. material command leukemia program U.S. Army, 2002—04; mem. adv. com. McDonnell Found. Program for Molecular Medicine in Cancer Rsch., 1988—98; adv. bd. Leukemia Soc. Am., 1979—84; selection com. scholar award in biomed. sci. Lucille P. Markey Charitable Trust, 1984—87; trustee Adler Planetarium, Chgo., 1978—; med. adv. bd. G&P Charitable Found., 1999—. Co-recipient Charles Mott prize, GM Cancer Rsch. Found., 1989; named Chicagoan of Yr., Chgo. mag., 1998; recipient First Kuwait Cancer prize, 1984, Esther Langer award, Ann Langer Cancer Rsch. Found., 1983; A Cressy Morrison award in natural scis., N.Y. Acad. Scis., 1985, Past State Pres. award, Tex. Fedn. Bus. and Profl. Women's Clubs, 1986, Karnofsky award and lecture, Am. Soc. Clin. Oncology, 1987, Antoine Lacassagne Lique prize, Nat. Francaise Contre le Cancer, 1987, King Faisal Internat. prize in medicine (co-recipient), 1988, Katherine Berkan Judd award, Meml. Sloan-Kettering Cancer Ctr., 1989, Steven C. Beering award, U. Ind. Med. Sch, 1992, Robert de Villiers award, Leukemia Soc. Am., 1993, Kaplan Family prize for cancer rsch. excellence, Oncology Soc. Dayton, 1995, Cotlove award and lecture, Acad. Clin. Lab. Physicians and Scientists, 1995, Nilsson-Ehle lecture, Mendelian Soc. and Royal Physiographic Soc., 1995, Gairdner Found. award, 1996, medal of honor, Basic Sci. Am. Cancer Soc., 1996, Nat. Medal of Sci., 1998, Lasker award for clin. scis., 1998, Woman Extraordinaire award, Internat. Women's Assocs., 1999, Golden Plate award, Am. Acad. Achievement, 1999, Women Achieving Excellence award, YWCA of Met. Chgo., 2000, Philip Levine award, Am. Soc. Clin. Pathology, 2001, Emile M Chamot award, State Microscopy Soc. Ill., 2001, Mendel medal, Villanova U., 2003, Benjamin Franklin medal, Am. Philos. Soc., 2003, Dist. Alumni Award, U. Chgo., 2003. Fellow: AAAS (nominating com. 1998); mem.: NAS (chmn. sect. 41 1995—99, mem. com. 2004), Chgo. Network, Inst. Medicine (coun. 1988—90), Cancer Rsch. (lectr. 2003), G.H.A. Clowes Meml. award 1989, Charlotte Friend award 2003, Dorothy P. Landon award 2005), Am. Soc. Hematology (lectr. Millenium Symposium 1999, Presdl. Symposium 1998, Dameshek prize 1982, Ham-Wasserman award 1995, Henry M. Stratton medal 2003), Genetical Soc., Am. Soc. Human Genetics (pres.-elect 1992, pres. 1993, Allen award and lectr. 1991, Disting. Sci. lectr. 2003), Am. Philos. Soc., Am. Acad. Arts and Scis. (nominating com. 1998), Alpha Omega Alpha, Sigma Xi (William Proctor prize for sci. achievement 1989). Episcopalian. Home: 5310 S University Ave Chicago IL 60615-5106 Office: U Chgo 5841 U Maryland Ave Rm 2115 Chicago IL 60637-1463 Office Phone: 773-702-6117. Business E-Mail: jrowley@medicine.bsd.uchicago.edu.

**ROWLEY, MAXINE LEWIS,** retired home economics and consumer educator, retired department chairman; b. Provo, Utah, Sept. 23, 1938; d. Max Thomas Lewis and Illa Lewis Sanford; m. Arthur William Rowley, Sept. 23, 1960; children: Anne, Jenefer. BA (Ford Found. scholar), Brigham Young U., 1960, PhD in Edn. Adminstrn., 1989; BS, U. Utah, 1974; MA, Utah State U., 1980. Promotion writer Sta. ABC KCPX-TV, 1960; extension home economist USDA, 1961; mgmt. trainee Deseret Book Co., Salt Lake City, 1969; dept. chair Patricia Stevens Career Coll., Salt Lake City. 1970; chair consumer and homemaking dept. Sand Ridge Jr. H.S. Weber Sch. Dist., Roy, Utah, 1975, learning experience designer, 1976-78; consumer and home econs. faculty Utah State U., Logan, 1978-79; spl. appointee to Utah State U. by the Utah State Bd. Edn., 1978-86; interim Gladys Chalkley Brannegan Am. Home Econ. Assn., 1993; chair dept. family life and home econs. Brigham Young U., 1988, 1999—2002; ret., 2002. Instrumental writer Utah State U. Found., 1979; mem. faculty Brigham Young U., 1979; mem. women's legis. coun. State of Utah, 1992—2005. Author: NCFR Public Policy Handbook, 1997; (filmstrips, texts and tchrs. guide) CHECS, 1979; (curriculum guide) Operation: Free Enterprise, 1982, Curriculum of Food Sci., Nutrition, vol. I, 1990, vol. II, 1992, vol. III, 1993; co-author: Legacy, vol. I, 1998. Active ward, stake and region positions Ch. of Jesus Christ of Latter-day Saints; leader 4-H Club, coun. mem.; adv. leader Girl Scouts U.S.A., Young Homemakers; active State Text Book Evaluation Com., 1978-86, U. Utah Evaluation Com., 1979; edn. and rsch. com. Am. Cancer Soc., State of Utah, 1993-94. Named Outstanding Leader Am. Edn., 1976, Nat. Tchr. of Yr., 1977, Outstanding Tchr. in Dept., Brigham Young U., 1984-94, Outstanding Voccat. Edn. Leader, State of Utah, 1996, Nat. Honor Roll in vocat. edn. Nat. Assn. Vocat. Family and Consumer Scis., 1999. Mem.: NEA, Internat. Fed. Home Econ. (nat. officer), Am. Edn. Rsch. Assn. (Nat. chair, HERSIG 2001—03), Utah Assn. Family and Consumer Scis. (disting. svc. award 2003), Worldwide Orgn. Women (women's legis. coun. State of Utah 1998—2004, internat. bd. dirs. 1999—2003), Utah Home Economics Tchrs. (nat. chmn. public rels. and legis. coms 1978). Home Econs. Edn. Assn., Am. Edn. Rsch. Assn. (nat.chair Home Econs. Related Spl. Interest Group 2000—03, marriage, family &

human devel. dept. 2002—), County Welfare Com., Utah Edn. Assn. (award for womens awareness task force project 1976), Utah Nutrition Coun. (chair 1995), Utah Coun. for Improvement Edn., Utah Vocat. Assn., Utah Home Econs. Assn., Am. Vocat. Assn., Am. Assn. Family and Consumer Scis. (nat. v.p., bd. dirs., chair ann. meeting, bd. liaison publs. 1995—97, nat. com. publs. 1999—), Am. Home Econs. Assn. (contbr., author yearbook 1984, Nat. Leadership award 1993), Nat. Assn. Vocat. Home Econs. Tchrs., Ellen H. Richards Cir., Spurs, White Key (pres. 1960), Alpha Delta Kappa, Gamma Phi Omicron, Phi Kappa Phi, Kappa Omicron Nu (advisor 1980—2005, Nat. award of excellence 1999, nat. endowment honoree 1989, nat. leadership endowment 2001). Home: 9801 Lampton Cir South Jordan UT 84095-9211

**ROWLEY, PETER TEMPLETON,** pediatrician, educator; b. Greenville, Pa., Apr. 29, 1929; s. George Hardy and Susan Mossman (Templeton) R.; m. Carol Stone, Mar. 19, 1967; children: Derek Stone, Jason Templeton. AB magna cum laude, Harvard U., 1951; MD, Columbia U., 1955. Diplomate: Am. Bd. Internal Medicine. Intern med. service N.Y. Hosp.-Cornell Med. Center, 1955-56; clin. assoc. Nat. Inst. Neurol. Disease and Blindness, NIH, 1956-58; asst. resident, then resident Harvard Med. Service, Boston City Hosp.; asst. in medicine Harvard U. Med. Sch. and researcher Thorndike Meml. Lab., 1958-60; hon. research asst. dept. eugenics, biometry and genetics Univ. Coll., U. London, 1960-61; postdoctoral fellow dept. microbiology NYU Sch. Medicine, 1961-63; asst. prof. medicine Stanford U., 1963-70; assoc. prof. medicine pediatrics and genetics U. Rochester, 1970-75, prof. medicine, pediatrics, genetics and microbiology, 1975—, prof. oncology, 1991—, chmn. div. genetics, 1990—; physician, pediatrician Strong Meml. Hosp., 1970—. Mem. N.Y. State Exec. and Adv. Coms. on Genetic Disease, 1979—; WHO vis. scholar Inst. Biol. Chemistry, U. Ferrara, Italy, 1970. Editor (with M. Lipkin Jr.): Genetic Responsibility: On Choosing Our Children's Genes, 1974; co-editor: Genetic Testing. With USPHS, 1956-58. Recipient Excellence in Teaching award U. Rochester Class of 1976, 1973; NRC fellow, 1960-63; Buswell research fellow, 1970-71, 71-72 Fellow ACP, Am. Coll. Genetics; mem. Am. Fedn. Clin. Rsch., Am. Soc. Hematology, Am. Soc. Human Genetics (social issues com. 1980-89, program com. 1993-96), N.Y. State Health Rsch. (sci. bd. 1997—). Office: U Rochester Med Sch Div Genetics PO Box 641 601 Elmwood Ave Rochester NY 14642-0001 Business E-Mail: peter_rowley@urmc.rochester.edu.

**ROWLING, J.K. (JOANNE KATHLEEN ROWLING),** writer; b. Gloucestershire, England, July 31, 1965; d. Peter and Anne Rowling; m. Jorge Arantes, Oct. 16, 1992 (div. Nov. 30, 1993); 1 child, Jessica; m. Neil Murray, Dec. 26, 2001; children: David, Mackenzie. BA in French & Classics, Exeter U., 1986; LittD (hon.), Napier U., 2000, Dartmouth Coll., 2000, U. Exeter, 2000; degree (hon.), U. St. Andrews, 2000, U. Edinburgh, 2004; LLD (hon.), Aberdeen U., 2006. Former rsch. Amnesty International; teacher Scotland, 1990—94. Author: (novels) Harry Potter and the Philosopher's Stone, 1997 (Children's Book of the Year, British Book Awards, 1998, Gold Winner, Smarties Book Prize, 1997, Birmingham Cable Children's Book Award, Young Telegraph Paperback of the Year, Sheffield Children's Book Award, Sorcieres Prix, 1999, Premio Cento per la Letteratura Infantile, 1998), Harry Potter and the Sorcerer's Stone (U.S. title), 1998 (Anne Spencer Lindbergh Prize in Children's Literature, 1998, ABBY Award, American Booksellers Assoc., 1999), Harry Potter and the Chamber of Secrets, 1998 (Gold Winner, Smarties Book Prize, 1998), Harry Potter and the Prisoner of Azkaban, 1999, Harry Potter and the Goblet of Fire, 2000, Quidditch Through the Ages, 2001, Fantastic Beasts & Where to Find Them, 2001, Harry Potter and the Order of the Phoenix, 2003, Harry Potter and the Half-Blood Prince, 2005 (Quills award for Book of Yr., 2005, Brit. Book of Yr. award, 2006). Named Officer of the Most Excellent Order of the British Empire (O.B.E.) by Charles, Prince of Wales, No. 2 on the list, "British Top 50 Movers and Shakers", BBC 3, Amazon.com's No. 1 of Top 10 authors, 1995—2005; named one of Most Powerful Women, Forbes mag., 2005. Office: Christopher Little Literary Agency 10 Eel Brook Studios 125 Moore Park Rd London SW6 4PS England

**ROWLINGSON, JOHN CLYDE,** anesthesiologist, physician, educator; b. Syracuse, N.Y., Aug. 3, 1948; s. John Winthrop and Genevieve Estelle (Mahan) R.; m. Rosemary Colette Laney, Oct. 26, 1974 (div. 1992); children: Kristen, Andrew; m. Karen Wheeler, Aug. 4, 2001; stepchild, Isaac. BS, Allegheny Coll., 1970; MD, SUNY, Buffalo, 1974. Intern Millard Fillmore Hosp., Buffalo, 1974-75; resident in anesthesiology U. Va., Charlottesville, 1975-77; fellow in anesthesia pain mgmt. U. Va. Med. Ctr., 1977-78; asst. prof. anesthesiology U. Va. Sch. Medicine, Charlottesville, 1978-82, assoc. prof., 1982-86, prof., 1986—, Cosmo A. DiFazio prof. anesthesiology, 2005. Assoc. dir. Pain Mgmt. Ctr., U. Va. Health Sci. Ctr., 1978-79, dir., 1980-98, dir. acute pain svc., 1987—. Author: Regional Anesthesia, 1984; co-editor: Handbook of Critical Care Pain Management, 1993. Recipient Nils Lofgren award ASTRA, 1999; Nat. Inst. Handicapped Rsch. fellow, 1983-87, Pain fellow 1977-78. Fellow Am. Coll. Anesthesiology; mem. Am. Soc. Anesthesiologists, Am. Soc. Regional Anesthesia (rsch. grantee 1977, pres. 1996-97), Am. Pain Soc., Internat. Assn. Study of Pain, Am. Acad. Pain Medicine (editl. bd. Anesthesia Analg 1996—, Reg. Anesthesia and Pain Medicine, 1997—), Va. Soc. Anesthesiology (sec, treas. 2005-). Methodist. Avocations: running, tennis, skiing, biking. Home: 5606 Lake Tree Ln Crozet VA 22932 Office: U Va Hlth Sys Health Sci Ctr Anesthesiology PO Box 800710 Charlottesville VA 22908-0710 Office Phone: 434-924-2283. Business E-Mail: jcr3t@virginia.edu.

**ROWNY, MICHAEL J.,** communications executive; b. Tokyo, Apr. 10, 1950; s. Edward L. Rowny; m. Melissa Blake. Student, U. Pa., Phila., 1968-70; BS, MIT, 1972; JD, Georgetown U., 1977. Profl. staff mem. U.S. Senate Fin. Com., Washington, 1974-78; asst. to ambassador Spl. Trade Rep., Geneva, Switzerland, 1978-79; dep. staff dir. The White House, Washington, 1979-80; v.p., sec. Avenir Group, Inc., Washington, 1981; v.p. strategic planning and ventures Bendix Corp., Southfield Mich. 1981-83; sr v p fin MCI Communications, Washington, 1983-86; CEO Hermitage Holding Co., Washington, 1986-89; pres., pres. CEO Ransohoff Co., Hamilton, Ohio, 1989-92; exec. v.p., CFO ICF Kaiser Internat., Vienna, Va., 1992-94; exec. v.p. MCI Communications Corp., Washington, 1994-99; bd. dirs. Step 9 Software Corp., Fairfax. Bd. dirs. Avenir Group, Inc., Bloomfield Hills, Mich.; chmn. bd. dirs. Embratel, Rio de Janeiro.

**ROWSON, SEBASTIAN,** engineering executive; s. Norman William and Josette Eva Rowson. MS in Fundamental Physics, U. Paris Sud Orsay, 1995, MS in Elecs., Sensors, and Integrated Circuits, 1996, PhD in Physics, 2000. Rsch. engr. UCLA, 2000—00; sr. engr. Ethertronics, San Diego, 2000—02, dir. tech. transfer, 2002—04, dir. R & D, 2004—. Contbr. articles to profl. jours. Mem.: IEEE (assoc.). Achievements include patents for antenna technology. Office: Ethertronics Inc 9605 Scranton Rd Ste 300 San Diego CA 92121 Office Phone: 858-550-3826.

**ROY, ABHRA,** plasma engineer, researcher; b. Calcutta, India, Sept. 21, 1966; m. Kuhu Banerjee, Aug. 4, 1972. PhD in Mech. Engring., Indian Inst. Tech., Kharagpur, India, 1998. Post doctoral rsch. scientist SUNY, Stony Brook, NY, 1998—2000; rsch. engr. CFD Rsch. Corp., Sunnyvale, Calif., 2000—. Reviewer Jour. Heat Transfer; contbr. articles to profl. jours. Recipient Univ. Gold medal, Jadavpur U., Calcutta, India, Mem. Sigma Xi (life). Achievements include help in designing world's largest diameter silicon tube growth system. Office: 2880 Lakeside DR STE 226 Santa Clara CA 95054-2821 Home: 1485 De Rose Way Unit 227 San Jose CA 95126 Personal E-mail: abhra_roy@yahoo.com. Business E-mail: aro@cri-cfd-na.com.

**ROY, BISWADEV,** scientist; s. Mahadev Prasad and Aruna Roy; m. Saswati Datta, Dec. 29, 2000; children: Piyali, Arko. PhD, Jadavpur U., Calcutta, India, 1995. MSEE, U. Ctrl. Fla., 2000. Sr. grad. rsch. asst. Sch. Elec. Engring. and Computer Sci. U. Ctrl. Fla., Orlando, Fla., 1997—99; vis. scientist UMBC, 1999—2000; sr. rsch. meteorologist Sci. Sys. and Applications, Inc., Greenbelt, Md., 2000—03; phys. scientist Nat. Exposure Rsch. Lab. US EPA, Rsch. Triangle Park, NC, 2003—. Sr. grad. rsch. asst. Sch. of EE and Computer Sci., U. of Ctrl. Fla., Orlando, 1997—99. Guest lectr. on remote sensing NC State U., Sch. of Marine, Earth and Atmospheric Sci., Raleigh, 2004—06. Recipient Group Achievement award, Nat. Aeronautics and Space Adminstrn., USA, 2002. Mem.: IEEE Geoscience and Remote Sensing Soc., Am. Inst. of Aeronautics and Astronautics, Nat. Geog. Avocations: travel, music, cooking, aerospace. Home: 504 Willingham Rd Morrisville NC 27560-7477 Office Phone: 919-541-5338. Office Fax: 919-541-1379. Personal E-mail: broy1@nc.rr.com. E-mail: roy.dev@epa.gov.

**ROY, CHRISTOPHER MARVIN,** elementary school educator; b. Grand Rapids, Minn., Jan. 4, 1977; s. Michael Henry Roy and Marlene Marie Eichorn; m. Sonyia Marie Brohman, Mar. 15, 2003. BS in Elem. Edn., Bemidji State U., Minn., 1998; M in Elem. Edn., No. Ariz. U., 2005. Second grade tchr. Coyote Canyon Sch., Bullhead City, Ariz., 1999—. Home: 5079 Silver Bullet Dr Fort Mohave AZ 86426

**ROY, DAVID TOD,** literature educator; b. Nanking, China, Apr. 5, 1933; s. Andrew Tod and Margaret (Crutchfield) R.; m. Barbara Jean Chew, Feb. 4, 1967. AB, Harvard U., 1958, AM, 1960, PhD, 1965. Asst. prof. Princeton U., 1963-67; assoc. prof. U. Chgo., 1967-73, prof., 1973—99, prof. emeritus, 1999—, chmn. com. on Far Eastern Studies, 1968-70, chmn. dept. Far Eastern Langs. and Civilizations, 1972-75. Author: Kuo Mo-jo: The Early Years, 1971; contbr.: How to Read the Chinese Novel, 1990, Minds and Mentalities in Traditional Chinese Literature, 1999; co-editor: Ancient China: Studies in Early Civilization, 1978; translator: The Plum in the Golden Vase or Chin P'ing Mei, vol. 1, 1993, vol. 2, 2001, vol. 3, 2006. Served with U.S. Army, 1954-56. Ford Found. fellow, 1958-60, Jr. fellow Harvard Soc. Fellows, 1960-63, fellow Fulbright-Hays Commn., 1967, Chgo. Humanities Inst. fellow, 1994-95; grantee Am. Coun. Learned Socs., 1976-77, NEH, 1983-86, 95-96. Mem. Am. Oriental Soc., Assn. for Asian Studies. Clubs: Quadrangle (Chgo.). Democrat. Home: 5443 S Cornell Ave Chicago IL 60615-5603 Office: U Chgo 1050 E 59th St Chicago IL 60637-1559 Business E-Mail: davidroy@uchicago.edu.

**ROY, DELLA MARTIN,** materials science educator, researcher; b. Merrill, Oreg., Nov. 3, 1926; d. Harry L. and Anna (Cacka) Martin; m. Rustum Roy, June 8, 1948; children: Neill R., Ronnen A., Jeremy R. BS, U. Oreg., 1947; MS, Pa. State U., 1949, PhD, 1952. Various rsch. positions Pa. State Univ., Univ. Park, 1952—60, sr. rsch. assoc. geochemistry, 1960—62, sr. rsch. assoc. materials sci. engring., 1962—69, assoc. prof. materials sci. engring., 1969—75, prof. materials sci. engring., 1975—92, prof. emeritus materials sci., 1992—. Cons. in field; chmn. status of cement, concrete materials adv. bd., Washington, 1977—80; spl. adv. concrete durability NRC. 1985—. Editor: Instructional Modules in Cement Science, 1985, Jour. Cement & Concrete Rsch., 1971—; contbr. articles to profl. jours. Fellow: AAAS, Am. Concrete Inst. (Keynote address 1980, Can. Ctr. Mineral and Energy Tech. award 1989), Mineral. Soc. Am., Inst. Concrete Tech. (hon.), Am. Ceramic Soc. (trustee 1990—, Jeppson Medal award 1982, Copeland award 1987, Bleininger award 2004); mem.: NAS (exec. com., transp. bd. 1991—), Internat. Acad. Ceramics, Nat. Acad. Engring. (acad. adv. bd. 1989—, membership policy com. 2001—), Coun. Materials Rsch. Soc. (chmn. cement symposia 1980—81, 1986—88, trustee 1988—90), Friends of Health (mem. bd.). Democrat. Office: Pa State U Hastings Rd 110 Materials Rsch Lab University Park PA 16802 Business E-Mail: dellaroy@psu.edu.

**ROY, ELMON HAROLD,** minister; b. Russell Springs, Ky., Dec. 17, 1924; s. Leslie C. and Olza (Gosser) R.; m. Retha Adkins; children: Joel, Michael. BA in Theology, So. Missionary Coll., 1953; MA, Belin U., 1958, Spalding U., 1970; PhD in Theology, Pacific We. U., 1966; postgrad., Andrews Theol. Seminary, 1974; LLD, Coll. St. Thomas, 1982. Ordained to ministry, 1959. Assoc. pastor, Bucyrus, Ohio, 1955-56, Akron, Ohio, 1956-57; pastor East Liverpool, Ohio, 1957-60, Coudersport, Pa., 1960-64, Huntsville, Ala., 1964-65, Louisville, 1965-71; chaplain Pleasant Grove Hosp., Louisville, 1971—75; pastor Springfield, Ohio, 1975-85, Wooster, Ohio, 1985-88; chaplain Louisville, 1989—. Cons. religious liberty, 1983-88; chaplain Jefferson County Ct. Author: In Remembrance of Redemption, 1996, Courage for Hospital Days 1973, Earth's Coming Events, 1968, Israel's Early Leaders, 1984, Moments of Meditation, 1975, The Word for These Times, 1988, Morning is Coming, 1989, Something to Live By, 1958, Prescription for Personal Peace, 1995, Decisions Determine Destiny, 1994; contbr. numerous articles to mags. Pres. South Oldham Ch. Coun., 1971-72; mem. Ohio conf. bd. edn., 1985-88. With USN, 1943-46. Recipient Outstanding Cmty. Svc. award Pleasant Grove Hosp., Commrs. Commendation award Wayne County, Ohio Senate Commendation award, Gov.'s Outstanding Kentuckian award; decorated six battle stars, knight Sovereign Order of St. John of Jerusalem, Knights of Malta, Hospitallers, comdr. Star of Peace Fedn. des Combattants En Europe, Tenn. Col., Ky. Adm., Croix De Guerre, Cross of Valor, Royal Afghanistan Order of Crown of Amanullah, Order of Polonia Restituta, Orderu Virtuti Militari, Philippine Presdl., City Philipine Liberation medal; named hon. citizen of Tenn., hon. sheriff Clark County, Ohio, hon. Ky. Sec. of State, Ky. Amb.; named to Order Ky. Cols. Fellow Philos. Soc. Gt. Britain, Huguenot Soc., Royal Soc. Arts; mem. SAR (chaplain Louisville-Thruston chpt. 1974-75), Am. Acad. Religion, Ky. Hist. Soc., Order Founders and Patriots of Am., East Liverpool Ministerial Assn. (sec., treas. 1960), Coudersport Ministerial Assn. (v.p. 1971-72), Soc. Ky. Pioneers, Mil. Order Fgn. Wars. Address: 2417 W Highway 22 Crestwood KY 40014-9481 Office Phone: 502-241-1939.

**ROY, HEMANT KUMAR,** gastroenterologist, researcher; b. Calcutta, West Bengal, India, Dec. 30, 1964; s. Hirendra and Meena Roy; m. Urbi Ghosh, Dec. 30, 1993; children: Priya, Anjuli. BS, Vanderbilt U., Nashville, 1985; MD, Northwestern U., Chgo., 1989. Asst. prof. U. Nebr. Med. Ctr., Omaha, 1995—2002; assoc. prof. Northwestern U., Evanston, Ill., 2002—. Dep. editor: Archives Internal Medicine. Recipient Career Devel. award, Am. Soc. Clin. Oncology, 1996—99; grantee, Glaxo Inst. Digestive Health, 1997, NIH, 2004—. Mem.: Am. Coll. Gastroent. (rsch. com. 2000). Achievements include research in light scattering as a screening test for colon cancer. Office: Evanston Northwestern Healthcare G208 2650 Ridge Ave Highland Park IL 60035 Office Phone: 847-570-3115.

**ROY, KEVIN,** newscaster; b. Chgo. BA in Broadcast Journalism summa cum laude, U. Mo., Columbia, 1990. Anchor and reporter KCRG-TV, Cedar Rapids, Iowa, 1990—92; weekend anchor and reporter WHAS-TV, Louisville, 1992—93; Washington corr. Belo Broadcasting Bur., 1993—95; weekend anchor and investigative reporter KGW-TV, Portland, Oreg., 1995—98; reporter WLS-TV, Chgo., 1998—, co-anchor Weekend Morning News, 2002—. TV journalist Son of Suicide, 2001 (Best News Series Emmy, 2001, Silver Dome award Best Series, 2001, nat. media award of Mental Health Assn. of Mentally Ill in Ill., 2001, Gold Bell Media award, Mental Health Assn. of Ill., 2001), AIDS in Africa: The Lost Generation, 2002 (Best Hard News Feature Emmy, 2002), (news segment) Frank Lloyd Wright, 2001 (AP Ill. honors, 2001). Vol. Loving Outreach to Survivors of Suicide Cath. Charities, Chgo.; bd. mem. Mental Health Assn. of Ill. Recipient Best Reporter Individual Excellence on Camera Emmy, NATAS, 2001, Individual Excellence in News Writing Emmy, 2002. Mem.: AFTRA, NATAS. Office: WLS-TV 190 N State St Chicago IL 60601 Office Phone: 312-750-7577. E-mail: kroy@sbcglobal.net.

**ROY, MICHELLE E.,** musician, information technology consultant; b. Lewiston, Maine, Dec. 15, 1969; d. Leonard A. and Joyce B. Roy; m. Andrew Jocuns, Aug. 15, 1997 (div. Sept. 25, 2006). BA, Swarthmore (Pa.) Coll., 1992; MusM, Ind. U., 1994. Data warehouse support analyst MIT, Cambridge, 1996—2000; tech. lead cons. Buchanan & Edwards, Inc., Alexandria, Va., 2000—. Musician: (music performance) Deuce, Tresorino; musician: (harpsichord soloist) bach sinfonia. Mem.: Chamber Music Am. (assoc.), Early Music Am. (assoc.). Democrat. Personal E-mail: meroyinc@yahoo.com.

**ROY, PATRICK,** retired professional hockey player; b. Quebec City, Que., Can., Oct. 5, 1965; m. Michèle Piuze (div.); children: Jonathan, Frederick, Jana. Goaltender Montreal Canadiens, 1984—95, Colo. Avalanche, 1995—2003; v.p. hockey operations Quebec Remparts, QMJHL, 2003—, owner, gen. mgr., head coach, 2005—. Named to All-Rookie Team, NHL, 1986, Second All-Star Team, 1988, 1991, First All-Star Team, 1989, 1990, 1992, Sporting News All-Star Team, 1989, 1990, 1992, Colo. Sports Hall of Fame, 2004; recipient Conn Smythe Trophy as Playoff MVP, 1986, 1993, 2001, William M. Jennings Trophy, 1987—89, 1992, 2002, Vezina Trophy, 1989, 1990, 1992, Trico Goaltender award, 1989, 1990. Achievements include being a member of Stanley Cup Champion Montreal Canadiens, 1986, 1993, Colo. Avalanche, 1996, 2001; setting the record with most NHL wins by a goaltender; setting the record for most NHL playoff wins by a goaltender with 151. Office: Quebec Remparts Colisée Pepsi 250 boulevard Wilfrid-Hamel Quebec City PQ G1L 5A7 Canada*

**ROY, PAUL EMILE, JR.,** county official; b. Sumter, S.C., Dec. 18, 1942; s. Paul Emile and Harriette Orvilla (Sorenson) R.; m. Patricia Jane Stariha, July 2, 1977; children: Lisa Anne, Jennifer Jo AA, Grand Rapids Jr. Coll., 1963; student, Universidad de las Americas, Mexico City, 1963—64, Instituto Mexicano-Norteamericano de Relaciones Culturales, 1964—65; BA, Aquinas Coll., Grand Rapids, 1967; MA, U. Americas Escuela de Graduados, Mexico City, 1968; postgrad., U. Mich., 1977—79; MBA, Calif. Coast U., 1994. Asst. prin., instr. Spanish Muskegon Cath. Ctrl. H.S., Mich., 1971—75; dir. employment and tng. Muskegon/Oceana Consortium County of Muskegon, 1975—87, dir. employment and tng., 1988—95, dir. employment and tng. and facilities mgmt., 1995—2003, dir. pub. facilities, 2003—. Mem. Mich. Com. for Devel. of Romance Lang. Performance Objectives; adult edn. adv. com. Muskegon Pub. Schs.; appointee Mich. Youth Employment Coun.; v.p. regional adv. coun. U.S. Dept. Labor, 1981; mem. City of Muskegon Local Devel. Funding Authority, 1988—, Downtown Devel. Authority, 1988—, City of Whitehall (Mich.) Local Devel. Funding Authority, 1988—, Muskegon Econ. Growth Alliance Edn. Com.; bd. dirs. United Way, 1998-2004, campaign chmn., 1986-88, Pacesetter award, 1987; bd. dirs. YMCA, 1999-2001; cons. U.S. Dept. Labor, Washington, Mich. Dept. Labor, Lansing, Gov.'s Office Manpower, Ind., U. Mich., Ann Arbor, various pvt. cos., non-profit orgns Mem. Am. Assn. Tchrs. Spanish and Portuguese, Mich. Assn. Tchrs. ESL, Mich. Assn. Employment and Tng. Dirs. (pres. 1980-81), Mich. Employment and Tng. Inst. (founding bd. dirs. 1980-81), Nat. Assn. Counties (employment steering com.), Nat. Assn. County Employment and Tng. Adminstrs. (nat. bd. dirs. 1979-80, nat. chmn. orgnl. resources com. 1981) Avocations: golf, travel, reading, theater. Office: Muskegon Cty Dept Employment & Tng 1611 Oak Ave Muskegon MI 49442-2405

**ROY, PRABIR KUMAR,** physicist; arrived in US, 2002, permanent resident, 2004; s. Narayan Chandra and Khuku (Datta) R.; m. Chandana Nipay, Apr. 22, 1996. BS in Physics with honors, Chittagong U., Bangladesh, 1986, MS in Physics, 1987; PhD, Osaka U., Japan, 1998. Rsch. fellow Inst. Laser Engring., Suita, Japan, 1994—98; rsch. scientist Omachron Sci. Inc, Hampton, Ont., Canada, 1998—2001; postdoctoral rschr. La. Tech U., Ruston, La., 2001—02; postdoctoral physicist Lawrence Berkeley Nat. Lab., 2002—03, term physicist scientist, 2003—06, sr. sci. assoc., 2006—. Organizing sec. Chittagong Sci. Coun., 1986-92. Exec. editor Shandhan sci. jour., 1984-87, mem. editl. bd., 1990-91; contbr. over 100 sci. articles to profl. publs. Monbusho scholar Japanese Govt., 1995—; rsch. fellow Ministry of Sci. and Tech., Dhaka, Bangladesh, 1994. Mem. AAAS, Am. Phys. Soc., Inst. Laser Engring., CSIR. Home: 10944 San Pablo Ave Apt 235 El Cerrito CA 94530 Office: Lawrence Berkeley Nat Lab 1 Cyclotron Rd MS #47R-0112 Berkeley CA 94720 Office Phone: 510-495-2616. Business E-Mail: pkroy@lbl.gov.

**ROY, RANJA,** mathematician, educator; b. Kolkata, West Bengal, India, Aug. 13; d. Deba Prasanna and Dipali Roy; children: Sohini Upadhyay, Kushal Roy Upadhyay. PhD, Binghamton U., 1993—98. Vis. asst. prof. Millersville U., Pa., 1998—99, Union Coll., Schenectady, NY, 1999—2001; asst. prof. NY Inst. Tech., Old Westbury, NY, 2001—. Contbr. scientific papers. Mem.: Am. Math. Soc. (corr.). Home: 6 Lewis Ln Port Washington NY 11050

**ROY, ROB J.,** biomedical engineer, anesthesiologist, educator; b. Bklyn., Jan. 2, 1933; m. Carole Ann Apmann, Aug. 1, 1959 (div.); children: Robert Bruce, David John, Bruce Glenn; m. Judith Anne Webb, Oct. 6, 1996. BSEE, Cooper Union, N.Y.C., 1954; MSEE, Columbia U., 1956; DEngSc, Rensselaer Poly. Inst., 1962; MD, Albany (N.Y.) Med. Coll., 1976. Profl. engr., N.Y.; diplomate Am. Bd. Anesthesiology. Prof. elec. engrin. dept. Rensselaer Poly. Inst., Troy, N.Y., 1962; prof. elec. engring. dept., 1980—, head biomed. engring. dept., 1985-94; prof. anesthesiology Albany (N.Y.) Med. Ctr., 1979—. Author: State Variables for Engineers, 1965, 2d edit., 1998; author over 200 papers in field. Mem.: IEEE (life), Am. Soc. Anesthesiologists, Sigma Xi. Office: Albany Med Ctr Dept Anesthesiology 47 New Scotland Ave Albany NY 12208-3412 E-mail: royr@rpi.edu, robjroy@att.net.

**ROY, ROBERT RUSSELL,** toxicologist; b. Mpls., Sept. 14, 1957; s. Rudolph Russell and Arlene Charlotte (Miller) R.; m. Barbara Jane Richie, Oct. 10, 1987; children: Andrew, Katherine. BA cum laude, Augsburg Coll., 1980; MS, U. Minn., 1986, PhD, 1989. Bd. cert. in toxicology. Toxicologist, project mgr. Pace Labs., Inc., Mpls., 1989-90; toxicologist Minn. Dept. Health, Mpls., 1990-93, Minn. Regional Poison Ctr., St. Paul, 1990-97; team leader, toxicology specialist 3M, St. Paul, 1997—, sr. toxicology specialist, 2000—. Lectr. U. Minn., Mpls., 1986-90, Midwest Ctr. Occupl. Health and Safety, St. Paul, 1990—, instr., 1989; adj. assoc. prof. U. Minn., 1993—; grad. faculty toxicology and pub. health U. Minn.; adj. asst. prof. emergency medicine Oreg. Health Sci. U., Portland. Active Mt. Carmel Luth. Ch. Coun., Mpls., 1983-85. Mem. Soc. Toxicology, Am. Indsl. Hygiene Assn., Delta Omega. Home: 6301 Oxbow Bend Chanhassen MN 55317-9110 Office: Corp Toxicology 3 M Ctr Bldg 220-6E-03 Saint Paul MN 55144-1000 Business E-Mail: rroy@mmm.com.

**ROY, ROBERT WILLIAM,** artist, educator; b. Worcester, Mass., Oct. 7, 1945; s. Vincent Charles and Rita Marie R.; m. Laurie Jean Zephir, Aug. 1, 1981; children: Patrick Zephir, Roy. BFA magna cum laude, U. Mass. Amherst, 1969; MFA, Yale U., 1971. Instr. Sch. of the Worcester Art Mus. 1972-81; prof., chair painting dept. Montserrat Coll. of Art, Beverly, Mass., 1988—. Adj. instr. Mount Wachusett C.C., Gardner, Mass., 1982-98, mem. adv. bd., 1997—; vis. lectr. U. Lowell, Mass., 1982-83, Worcester State Coll., 1986-87; vis. critic Smith Coll., Northampton, Mass., 1983, vis. artist, U. Southern Maine, 2002, Artist-in-residence, Burren Coll. Art, Ireland, 2004. Exhibited in group shows at most recently Montserrat Coll. Art, 2000, Danforth Mus. Art, 2001, The European Biennial of Contemporary Art, Frankfurt, Germany, 2002, Ben Shahn Galleries, William Paterson U., Wayne, N.J., 2002, The Liverpool (Eng.) Biennial, 2002, U. Galleries, Ill. State U., Normal, Ill., 2003, River Gallery, Ipswich. Mass., 2003, Schitkamp Gallery, Clark U., Worcester, Mass., 2003, Art Gallery, U. N.H., Durham, 2004, Art Complex Mus., Duxbury, Mass., 2004, U. Alberta, Edmonton, Can., 2004, U. W. Ga., Carrolton, Ga., 2004, Ontario Coll. of Art, Toronto, Can., 2004, Print Gallery, U. the Arts, Phila., 2004, HallSpace, Boston, 2005, Boston U., 2005, Housatonic Mus. Art, Bridgeport, Conn., 2005, Art Gallery, Gordon Coll., Wenham, Mass., 2006, Danforth Mus. Art, 2006, one-man shows include Montserrat Coll. Art, 2000, U. So. Maine, 2002, HallSpace, Boston, 2005, Danforth Mus. Art, 2006, Represented in permanent collections Mus. Modern Art, N.Y.C., Danforth Mus. Art, Trenton State Coll., Art Complex Mus., Duxbury, Mass., Housatonic Mus. Art, Bridgeport, Conn. Recipient Ture Bengtz Meml. prize, 2005; fellow Yale U., Norfolk, Conn., 1968, Mass. Artists Found., Boston, 1977; Ford Found. Faculty grantee, 1976, 78, 80, Cornelia Faculty Fellow, 2003. Mem. L.A. Printmaking Soc., Coll. Art Assn. N.Y.C., Boston Printmakers, Southern Graphics Coun. Home: 95 Regan St Gardner MA 01440-4015 Office: Montserrat College of Art 23 Essex St # Beverly MA 01915-4508 Business E-Mail: rroy@montserrat.edu.

**ROY, RUSTUM,** citizen scientist; b. Ranchi, India, July 3, 1924; came to U.S., 1945, naturalized, 1961; s. Narendra Kumar and Rajkumari (Mukherjee) R.; m. Della M. Martin, June 8, 1948; children: Neill, Ronnen, Jeremy. BSc with honors, Patna U., India, 1942, MSc, 1944; PhD, Pa. State U., 1948; DSc (hon.), Tokyo Inst. Tech., 1987, Alfred U, 1993. Research asst. Pa. State U., 1948-49, mem. faculty, 1950—, prof. geochemistry, 1957—, prof. solid state, 1968—, chmn. solid state tech. program, 1960-67, chmn. sci. tech. and soc. program, 1977-84, dir., 1984-89, dir. materials research lab., 1962-85, Evan Pugh prof., 1981—, Evan Pugh prof. solid state emeritus, 1999—; sr. sci. officer Nat. Ceramic Lab., India, 1950; mem. com. mineral sci. tech. Nat. Acad. Scis., 1967-69, com. survey materials sci. tech., 1970-74; exec. com. chem. div. NRC, 1967-70, nat. materials adv. bd., 1970-77, mem. com. radioactive waste mgmt., 1974-80, chmn. panel waste solidification, 1976-80, chmn. com. USSR and Eastern Europe, 1976-81. Mem. com. material sci. and engring. NRC, 1986-89; mem. Pa. Gov.'s Sci. Adv. Com.; chmn. materials adv. panel Gov.'s Sci. Adv. Com., 1965-80; mem. adv. com. on engring. NSF, 1968-72, adv. com. to ethical and human value implications sci. and tech., 1974-76, adv. com. div. materials rsch., 1974-77; Hibbert lectr. tech. and religion U. London, 1979; cons. to industry; mem. adv. com. Coll. Engring., Stanford U., 1984-86; internat. sci. lectr. NRC, 1991-92; rsch. prof. materials Ariz. State U., 1999—; vis. prof. medicine U. Ariz., 1999—. Author: Honest Sex, 1968, Crystal Chemistry of Non-metallic Materials, 1974, Experimenting with Truth, 1981, Radioactive Waste Disposal, Vol. 1, the Waste Package, 1983, Lost at the Frontier, 1985; founding editor-in-chief: Materials Rsch. Bull., 1966—. Jour. Materials Edn., 1980-2000, Bull. Sci. Tech. and Soc, 1981-2000, Materials Rsch. Innovations, 1997—; contbr. over 1000 articles to profl. jours., 25 patents in field. Chmn. bd. Dag Hammarskjold Coll. 1973-75; chmn. ad hoc com. sci., tech. and ch. Nat. Coun. Chs., 1966-68; bd. dirs. Kirkridge Retreat, 1958-80, chmn., 1978-80; founder, chmn. bd. Friends of Health; chmn. bd. Campaign for Better Health. Sci. policy fellow Brookings Instn., 1982-83; recipient Ellis Island medal of hon., 1996; named to Order of the Rising Sun with Gold Rays status in Japanese Emperor's birthday honors list, 2002. Fellow: AAAS (chmn. chemistry sect. 1985), Mineral. Soc. Am. (award 1957), Am. Phys. Soc., Indian Acad. Scis. (hon.), Am. Ceramic Soc. (Sosman lectr. 1975, Orton lectr. 1984, disting. life, Educator of Yr. 1993); mem.: U.S. Nat. Acad. Engring., Materials Rsch. Soc. (pres. 1976, founder), Am. Soc. Engring. Educators (Centennial medal 1993, Hall of Fame 1993), Am. Ceramic Soc. (Petroleum Rsch. Fund award 1960, Dupont award for Chem. of Materials 1993), Fine Ceramics Assn. Japan (Internat. award), Ceramic Soc.Japan (hon. Centennial award 1991), Mineral Soc. Am., Fedn. Materials Socs. (Nat. Materials Advancement award 1991), Russian Acad. Scis. (elected fgn.), Engring. Acad. Japan (elected fgn.), Indian Nat. Sci. Acad. (elected fgn.), Royal Swedish Acad. Engring. Scis. (elected fgn.). Home: 500 E Marylyn Ave Apt 124 State College PA 16801-5312 Office: 102 Materials Research Lab University Park PA 16802-4800 Office Phone: 814-865-3421. Business E-Mail: rroy@psu.edu. *My major responsibility to the increasingly unified world culture, as a scientist supported largely by the public, is to integrate into its emerging radically pluralist yet globally unifying Religion, the insights from Science and the impact of Technology on the human condition. As a Christian Radical Pluralist, I am committed to presenting to my fellow humans—expecially all non-scientists, from Presidents and CEOs to the person in the street—an accurate picture of the whole truth about my scientific "advances" and those of others—their limited and ambivalent nature and their relatively minor position in the sum total of human concerns.*

**ROY, SITESH RANEN,** pediatrician, allergist, immunologist, educator; s. Ranen Bimoloananda and Sumita Ranen Roy; m. Hemangi Sitesh Roy, May 0, 1997. Grad., D.G. Ruparel Coll., Mumbai, India, 1990; MBBS, Seth G. S. Med. Coll., Bombay, India, 1990—96. Cert. Am. Bd. Pediat., 2000, Am. Bd. Allergy & Immunology, Am. Bd. Med. Specialities, 2003. Pediat. residency U. Ill., Chgo., 1997—2000; fellowship pediat. allergy and immunology Nat. Jewish Med. and Rsch. Ctr., U. Colo., Denver, 2000—02; asst. prof., pediat. & medicine U. Miss. Med. Ctr., Jackson, 2002—. Dir., pediatric allergy & immunology clinic Jackson Med. Mall. Contbr. papers to profl. jours. and pubs. Named one of Best Doctors in Am., 2005—06. Fellow: Am. Acad. Pediat., Am. Acad. Allergy Asthma and Immunology; mem.: Am. Coll. Allergy, Asthma and Immunology. Avocations: hiking, travel, bicycling. Office: Univ Miss Med Ctr 2500 N State St Jackson MS 39216-4505 Office Phone: 601-984-5249.

**ROY, SUDIPTA D.,** education educator; b. Bolani, Orissa, India, Aug. 28, 1970; d. Sabita Ranjan and Sati Dutta Roy. MS, Calcutta U., India, 1991; PhD, Indira Gandhi Int. Devel. Rsch., Mumbai, India, 2000; MBA, Gov.'s State U., Univ. Pk., Ill., 2004. Economist Indsl. Devel. Bank India, Mumbai, 1996—2000; cons. Asian Devel. Bank, Philippines, 2001, Nat. Stock Exch., Mumbai, 2000—03; adj. instr. Gov.'s State U., 2005—; asst. prof. Kankakee CC, Ill., 2006—. Contbr. papers to profl. jours. and pubs. Avocations: reading, coin collecting/numismatics, ping pong/table tennis, badminton. Office: Kankakee CC PO Box 888 River Rd Kankakee IL 60901

**ROYAL, BRENDA CAMPBELL,** biology educator; b. Cookeville, Tenn., Aug. 21, 1957; d. Lloyd W. and Myrtle Owen Campbell; children: Julie Michelle, Emily Ruth. BS, Mid. Tenn. State U., Murfreesboro, 1980, MS, 1982. Instr. biology LaVergne H.S., Tenn., 1988—94; tchr. advanced placement biology Hume-Fogg Acad. Magnet H.S., Nashville, 1994—. Curriculum cons. Ctr. Sci. Outreach, Vanderbilt U., Nashville, 2004—06; instr. biology Freewill Bapt. Bible Coll., 2002—04; cons. advanced placement biology Coll. Bd., 2004—. Author: AP Biology Professional Development Workshop Materials. Tchr. sr. adult women's class First Bapt. Ch., Smyrna, Tenn., 2004—06. Recipient Outstanding Biology Tchr. Yr., Nat. Assn. Biology Tchrs., 2005; grantee, PENCIL Found., 1995, 2002. Mem.: Nat. Sci. Tchrs. Assn., Nat. Assn. Biology Tchrs. Baptist. Achievements include Siemens Advanced Placement Instructor for TN, 2006. Avocations: running, writing, baking, travel. Home: 400 E Gresham Drive Smyrna TN 37167 Office: Hume-Fogg Academic Magnet High School 700 Broadway Nashville TN 37203 Office Phone: 615-291-6300. Personal E-mail: brendafcr@aol.com. E-mail: brenda.royal@mnps.org.

**ROYAL, DARRELL K.,** university official, retired football coach; b. Hollis, Okla., July 6, 1924; s. Burley Ray and Katy Elizabeth (Harmon) R.; m. Edith Marie Thomason, July 26, 1944; children: Marian (Mrs. Abraham Kazen III) (dec.), Mack, David (dec.). BS in Bus, U. Okla., 1950. Former head football coach, then dir. athletics U. Tex., now asst. to univ. pres. Author: Darrell Royal Talks Football, 1963. Recipient Horatio Alger award, 1996, Contbns. to Coll. Football award Nat. Coll. Football Award Assn., 2002; named Coach of Yr., Football Coaches Assn., 1963, 70, Tex. Sports Writers, 1961, 63, 69, 70, Southwesterner of Yr., 1961, 62, 63; named to U. Tex. Longhorn Hall of Fame, 1976, Tex. Sports Hall of Fame, 1976, Jim Thorpe Okla. Hall of Fame, 1977, Nat. Football Hall of Fame, 1983, Coach of Decade for 1960's, ABC; Darrell K. Royal Meml. Football Stadium, U. Tex. named in his honor, 1996; inducted into Southwestern Bell Cotton Bowl Hall of Fame, 1998, Okla. Heritage Soc. Hall of Fame, 2000; football field at Hollis H.S. named in his honor, 2003. Mem.: Delta Upsilon. Presbyterian. Office: U Tex SRH2 101 D1100 Austin TX 78712

**ROYAL, HENRY DUVAL,** nuclear medicine physician, educator, director; b. Norwich, Conn., May 14, 1948; BS, Providence Coll., 1970; MD, St. Louis U., 1974. Diplomate Am. Bd. Internal Medicine; Am. Bd. Nuclear Medicine. Intern R.I. Hosp., Providence, 1974, resident in internal medicine, 1975-76; resident in nuclear medicine Harvard Med. Sch., Boston, 1977-79; from assoc. to staff physician Barnes Hosp., St. Louis, 1987—; from assoc. to cons. staff physician Children's Hosp., St. Louis, 1987—; prof. nuclear medicine Washington U., St. Louis, 1993—; exec. dir. Am. Bd. Nuc. Medicine, St. Louis, 2004—. Co-team leader health effects sect. Internat. Atomic Energy Agy. Internat. Chernobyl Project, 1990; mem. com. on assessment of CDC radiation studies NRC/NAS, 1993-98; mem. sci. com. 1 and 4 Nat. Coun. on Radiation Protection and Measurements, 1993—; mem. coun. Nat. Coun. on Radiation Protection, 1996—, bd. dirs., 2000-05; adv. com. environ. hazards Vets., 1997—; bd. dirs. Am. Bd. Med. Specialities, 2005—. Contbr. articles to profl. jours. Mem.: Soc. Nuc. Medicine (v.p. 2002, pres. 2003), Alpha Omega Alpha. Office: W Pavilion B Rm 961 Box 8223 Washington Univ 660 S Euclid Ave Saint Louis MO 63110 Office Phone: 314-362-2809. Business E-Mail: royalh@mir.wustl.edu.

**ROYAL, NANCY B.,** primary school educator; b. Newnan, Ga., Mar. 27, 1949; d. Harold C. and Jewell (Stephens) Batchelor; m. Mayo H. Royal Jr., Aug. 15, 1970; children: Amanda Elizabeth, Molly Cole. BSEd, Ga. Coll., 1971; MEd, Ga. State U., 1978; EdS, West Ga. Coll., 1986. Cert. early childhood edn. Second grade tchr. Jo Wells Elem. Sch., Hapeville, Ga., 1970-71; kindergarten tchr. Columbia Drive Bapt. Sch., Decatur, Ga., 1972-75, Indian Creek Bapt. Sch., Stone Mountain, Ga., 1975-77, Meml. Drive Presbyterian Sch., Stone Mountain, 1978-80; first grade tchr. Elm St. Elem. Sch., Newnan, Ga., 1980-83, kindergarten tchr. 1980-96, prin. 1999—2003; fed. programs coord. Coweta County Schools, 2003—. Active State Reading Textbook Adoption Com., 21st Century Consortium Edn.; presenter edn. workshops. Treas. Newnan Jr. Svc. League, chairperson selection com. christmas program; pre-sch. Sunday sch. tchr. Newnan First Bapt. Ch., 1980—, children's choir dir., mem. stewardship com., chair weekday ministries com. Recipient Presdl. Excellence in Math. award 1992, Disting. Alumni award Ga. State U., 1993; named Atlanta Jour.-Constitution's Honor Tchr., 1989, Ga. Tchr. of Yr., 1993, Nat. Educator award Milken Family Found., 1995. Mem. Alpha Delta Kappa, Phi Kappa Phi, Phi Delta Kappa, Ga. Coun. Tchrs. Math. Mailing: PO Box 280 Newnan GA 30264 Business E-Mail: nancy.royal@cowetaschools.net.*

**ROYAL, WILLIAM HENRY,** retired real estate developer, architect; b. Jackson, Tenn., Dec. 16, 1924; s. Joe Henry and Millie Earline (Anderson) R.; m. Odell Peebles, June 16, 1943; children: William H. Jr., Frederick E., Diana, Carolyn M., Wanda II. Diploma, Chicago Tech. Coll., 1939; student, MIT, 1969, '73, U. Neb., 1971-76, U. Minn., 1974-76. Reg. architect, Ill., Mo. Architect, engr. U.S. Army Engr. Dist., Detroit, 1957-61, gen. architect St. Paul, 1959-62, supr. architect Chgo., 1962-70, gen. architect Omaha, Neb., 1970-73; architect, job captain Ellerbe & Co., St Paul, 1962; cons. FREBO, U.S. Postal Svc., St. Paul, 1973-77; constr. mgr. H.Q. U.S. Postal Svc., Washington, 1977-80; pres. William H. Royal & Assoc., Inc., Lake St. Louis, Mo., 1987—2002, Chgo., 1995-97, St. Louis Airport Devel. Corp., 1988-89; v.p. Steelgrade Corp., Clayton, Mo., 1991-93; sec.-treas. Am. Community Telecomms. System, Inc., Ferguson, Mo., 1992-97; pres. Royal King Constrn. Co., St. John, Mo., 1995-97. Author: (tng. manual) Architect Engineer Contracts, 1970; editor: Master Planning, Kinloch Redevelopment, 1987. Steward, United Meth. Ch., Omaha, 1970-73; urban cons. United Meth. Ministries, Omaha, 1970-73, Youth Coord., United Meth. Ch., Omaha, 1971-73; mem. Douglas County Parole Bd., Omaha, 1971-72. Recipient Commendation U.S. Postal Svc., Washington, 1976, Svc. award, 1980, letter of Appreciation, 1982; nominee Rockefeller Pub. Svc. award, U.S. Postal Svc., St. Paul, 1976. Avocations: computer programming, fishing, travel. Home: 1 Berry Ct Lake Saint Louis MO 63367-1921 Office: William H Royal & Assocs 1 Berry Ct Lake Saint Louis MO 63367-1921 Office Phone: 636-561-2735.

**ROYALL, MARY-JULIA C.,** church organist, historian; b. Donalds, S.C., Dec. 30, 1925; d. John McCants Campbell and Cordelia Bearden; m. Jervey DuPré Royall, Sept. 18, 1949; children: Julia C., Anne DuPré. BA, Erskine Coll., 1945; MA, U. S.C., 1948, performers cert. in organ, 1953. With Salem Coll. Organ Acad.; mem. staff Brevard Music Camp, 1946; music tchr. Montreat (N.C.) H.S. and Coll., 1946—47; pvt. piano tchr., 1953—66; dir. h.s. glee club Moultrie H.S., Mt. Pleasant, SC, 1960—62, Coll. Prep. Sch., Charleston, 1972—74; organist St. Mary's Cath. Ch., Charleston, 1979—. Author: Mt. Pleasant S.C.: The Victorian Village, 1997, Mt. Pleasant, S.C.: The Friendly Town, 2001. Historian Town of Mt. Pleasant, 1996—; mem. com. Charleston County SC Nat. Heritage Corridor, 1995—98; mem. Mt. Pleasant Presbyn. Ch., 1950—; pres. Confederate Meml. Assn., Mt. Pleasant, 1984—, Christ Ch. Parish Preservation Soc., Mt. Pleasant, 1994—. Named Tree Farmer of Yr., S.C., 1982—83; named to Order of the Gavel, Town of Mt. Pleasant, 1996; recipient Robert N. Pryor Svc. award, Confederation of Local Hist. Socs., S.C., 1997, Outstanding So. Citizen award, Sons of Confederate Vets., 2003. Mem.: S.C. Forestry Assn., Organ Hist. Soc. (editor newsletter S.C. chpt. 1979—84), Am. Guild Organists (S.C. state chmn., mem. Charleston chpt.). Home: 349 Bay View Acres Mount Pleasant SC 29464

**ROYBAL-ALLARD, LUCILLE,** congresswoman; b. Boyle Heights, Calif., June 12, 1941; d. Edward Roybal; m. Edward T. Allard; 4 children. BA in Speech, Calif. State U., L.A., 1965. Former mem. Calif. State Assembly, 1987—93; mem. U.S. Congress from 34th Calif. dist., 1993—; mem. appropriations com.; mem. Ho. Com. on Standards of Official Conduct. Recipient Madre y Mujer award, Kimberly-Clark, 2006. Democrat. Office: Ho of Reps 2330 Rayburn Bldg Washington DC 20515-0534 also: 225 E Temple St Ste 1860 Los Angeles CA 90012

**ROY-BURMAN, PRADIP,** molecular biology and virology educator; b. Comilla, Bengal, India, Nov. 12, 1938; came to U.S., 1963; s. Prafulla Nath and Mrinalini (Barman) Roy-Burman; m. Sumitra Ghosh, Nov. 26, 1963. BSc. with honors, Calcutta (India) U., 1956, MSc., 1958, PhD, 1963. Rsch. assoc. dept. biochemistry Sch. of Medicine U. So. Calif., L.A., 1963-66, Dernham sr. rsch. fellow in oncology Am. Cancer Soc., 1966-71, asst. prof. dept. biochemistry, 1967-72, assoc. prof. dept. pathology and biochemistry, 1972-78, prof. dept. pathology and biochemistry and molecular biology, 1978—, vice chmn. dept. pathology, 1987—2003. Interim chmn. dept. molecular microbiology and immunology, U. So. Calif., L.A., 1995-97; mem. pathology B study sect., NIH, 1990-94, 99-2003, reviewers res., 1994-98, 2005—, ad hoc mem. sci. tech. rev. bd. for biomed. behavioral rsch. facilities NCRR, NIH, 1997—, prostate cancer rsch. program review panel, Dept. of Def. 2001—; chmn. NIH, ad hoc mem. TPM study negiton 2006—, NCI RO1 Emphasis Rev. Panels, 1998—, European Comm. Program, 2006-05; chmn. symposium internat. congress biochem. molecular biology, 1994, co-chmn. symposium internat. cancer congess, 1994, chmn. workshop on pathogenesis of animal retrovirus, session immune interaction, 1996, 5th Internat. Symposium Hormonal Carcinogenesis, 2006; spkr. in field. Author (with others) books; contbr. articles to profl. jours.; book reviewer; inventor novel transcription regulatory elements for gene transfer vectors, mouse models for human prostate cancer, others; mem. editl. bd. Hematological Oncology, 1987—97, Cancer Biology and Therapy, 2001—. Rsch. grantee Am. Cancer Soc., NIH, Am. Diabetes Assn., Whitehall Found., Martell Found. Mem. Am. Soc. for Microbiology, Am. Soc. for Biol. Chemists and Molecular Biology, Am. Assn. Cancer Rsch., Am. Soc. Investigative Pathology, Internat. Assn. for Comparative Rsch. on Leukemia and Related Diseases. Democrat. Hindu. Avocations: writing, hiking, golf. Office: Keck Sch Of Medicine HMR 210B 2011 Zonal Ave Los Angeles CA 90033 Office Phone: 323-442-1184. Business E-Mail: royburma@usc.edu.

**ROYCE, BARRIE SAUNDERS HART,** physicist, researcher; b. Eng., Jan. 10, 1933; came to U.S., 1957, naturalized, 1978; s. Vincent Pateman Hart and Kathlene (Saunders) R.; m. Dominique J.M. Vallee, May 7, 1964; children: Vincent Rene Hart, Marc Edward Hart. BSc in Physics, King's Coll., U. London, 1954, PhD, 1957. Rsch. assoc. Carnegie Inst. Tech., 1957-60, Princeton U., 1960-61, mem. faculty, 1961—2003, prof. applied physics and materials scis., 1978—2003, prof. emeritus, 2003—, acting dean grad. affairs Sch. Engring. and Applied Sci., 2003—04; master of Dean Mathey Coll., 1986-94. Mem. editl. adv. bd. Jour. Photoacoustics, to 1984. Mem. Princeton Borough Zoning Bd. Adjustment, 1980-93, chair, 1993—. Grantee NSF, Air Force Office Sci. and Rsch., Army Rsch. Office. Mem. Am. Phys. Soc., Sigma Xi. Office: Princeton U D416 Duffield Hall Eq Princeton NJ 08544-0001 E-mail: bshroyce@princeton.edu.

**ROYCE, ED (EDWARD RANDALL ROYCE),** congressman; b. LA, Oct. 12, 1951; m. Marie Porter. BA, Calif. State U., Fullerton. Tax mgr. Southwestern Portland Cement Co.; mem. Calif. Senate, 1983-93, U.S. Congress from 40th Calif. dist. (formerly 39th), 1993—; mem. banking and

fin. svcs. com., internat. rels. com. Vice chmn. Public Employment and Retirement Com.; mem. Bus. and Profs. com., Indsl. Rels. com.; legis. author, campaign co-chmn. Proposition 15 Crime Victims/Speedy Trial Initiative; author nation's 1st felony stalking law, bill creating Foster Family Home Ins. Fund, legis. creating foster parent recruitment and tng. program; mem. Banking and Fin. Svcs. Com., Internat. Rels. Com. Named Legis. of Yr. Orange County Rep. Com., 1986, Child Adv. of Yr. Calif. Assn. Svc. for Children, 1987. Mem. Anaheim C. of C. Republican. Office: US Ho Reps 2202 Rayburn Ho Office Bldg Washington DC 20515

**ROYCE, PAUL CHADWICK,** healthcare administrator; b. Mpls., July 2, 1928; BA, U. Minn., 1948, MD, 1952; PhD, Case Western Res. U., 1959. Diplomate Am. Bd. Internal Medicine. Intern U. Chgo. Clinics, 1952-53; fellow NSF Case Western Res. U., Cleve., 1953-54, 56-58, Upjohn fellow, 1958-59; resident internal medicine Bronx Mcpl. Hosp., N.Y., 1959-61; asst. prof. of medicine Albert Einstein Coll. of Med., N.Y.C., 1961-69; sr. staff endocrinologist Guthrie Clinic, Sayre, Pa., 1970-81; assoc. prof. of medicine Hahnemann Med. Sch., Phila., 1973-81; emeritus prof. medicine Med. Coll. Pa./Hahnemann U., 1996—; dean and prof. clin. sci. and physiology Sch. Medicine U. Minn., Duluth, 1981-87; sr. v.p., clin. dir. Monmouth Med. Ctr., Long Branch, NJ, 1987-94; med. dir. The Segal Co. N.Y., 1995-98; prin. Royce Assocs., Atlantic Highlands, NJ, 1995—; tutor Writing Ctr., Monmouth U., NJ, 2001—05. Producer, host TV prgram Doctors on Call, 1983-87 (Nat. Friends of Pub. Broadcasting Hill award 1987). Lt. USNR, 1954-56. Mem. Am. Physiol. Soc., Fedn. Am. Scientists, Physicians for Social Responsibility, Sigma Xi, Alpha Omega Alpha. Avocations: skiing, bicycling, canoeing.

**ROYCE, RAYMOND WATSON,** lawyer, rancher, citrus grower, investor; b. West Palm Beach, Fla., Mar. 5, 1936; s. Wilbur E. and Veda (Watson) R.; m. Catherine L. Setzer, Apr. 21, 1979; children: Raymond, Steven, Nancy, Kathryn, Ryan. BCE, U. Fla., 1958, JD, 1961. Bar: Fla. 1961, U.S. Dist. Ct. (so. dist.) Fla. 1961, U.S. Ct. Appeals (5th cir.) 1961, U.S. Ct. Appeals (11th cir.) 1981. With Scott, Royce, Harris & Bryan P.A., Palm Beach, Fla., 1962-99; pres. Scott, Royce, Harris, Bryan, Barra and Jorgensen, P.A., Palm Beach Gardens, Fla., 1982-99; ptnr. Holland & Knight LLP, West Palm Beach, 1999—. Bd. govs. No. Palm Beach Improvement Dist., 1995-99. Mem. Fla. Bar (bd. govs. 1974-78), Fla. Blue Key, Phi Delta Phi. Democrat. Presbyterian. Home: 5550 Whirlaway Rd Palm Beach Gardens FL 33418-7735 Office: Holland and Knight LLP 222 Lakeview Ste 1000 West Palm Beach FL 33401-4027 Office Phone: 561-650-8316.

**ROYCE, STANTON,** motivational speaker, consultant, marketing professional, sales executive; b. Steubenville, Ohio, June 1, 1950; m. Melanie Espinosa, 1984. Student, Franciscan U., Steubenville, 1973; AS in Elec. Engring., Jefferson C.C., Steubenville, 1983; BS in Psychology, U. Cin., 1991; MBA, U. Phoenix, 1994. Night club entertainer, hypnotist, Wintersville, Ohio, 1970-73; mgr. Liberty Fin. Corp., Columbus, Ohio, 1973-76, Bally Mfg., Steubenville, 1976-79; pres. Cmty. Interfaith Svcs., Steubenville, 1979-83; dir. engring. May Co., Youngstown, Ohio, 1983-84; dir. ops. LaSalle Ptnrs., Chgo., 1984-93; mgr. Core Resources, Inc., Cin., 1993-94; pres. Royce Personal Devel., Hamden, Conn., 1994—, Extreme Achievers Inc. Author: The Salesman's Quick & Easy Success System, 1993, Million Dollar Persuasion, 1994, Encyclopedia of Sales Techniques, 1995, Billion Dollar Success Secrets, 1996, Billion Dollar Power Persuasion, 1997, Rejectionproof Selling, 1999, Recessionproof Selling, 2001, Overcoming Rejection, 2002, Failure isn't a Four Letter Word, 2003. Founder, 1st pres. Alternatives to Living in Violent Environments, Jefferson County, 1980-81; victims asst. counselor Jefferson County Cmty. Mental Health Ctr., Steubenville, 1977-79; mem. disaster comms. ARC, Jefferson County, 1965-77. Mem., officer Nat. Spkrs. Assn., Alpha Sigma Kappa Honor Soc. Avocations: hiking, mountain biking, travel. Office: Achievers Tower 7605 Via de Calma NE Albuquerque NM 87113-1306

**ROYCHOWDHURY, ABHIJIT,** chemist, entrepreneur; s. Ranjan Kumar and Usha Roychowdhury; m. Rumita Roychowdhury, Apr. 23, 2000; 1 child, Ayona. PhD, Ctrl. Drug Rsch. Inst./Agra U., Lucknow, and Agra, India, 1997. Postdoctoral fellow U. Fla., Gainesville, 1999—2004; rsch. assoc. U. Ala., Birmingham, 2004—05; asst. rsch. chemist So. Rsch. Inst., Birmingham, 2005—. Rsch. asst. dept. biotech., New Delhi and Conrad, Va., 1992—96. Spkr. BWW, Birmingham, 2003. Recipient Youth Leadership award, Rotary Club Internat., Kanpur, India, 1986; State Govt. Merit scholar, Ministry of Edn., Allahabad, India, 1984—86, sr. rsch. fellow, CSIR, New Delhi, 1996—98. Mem.: Uttar Pradesh Assn. for Advancement of Sci. and Tech., Indian Soc. Chemists and Biologists, Am. Chem. Soc., Indian Coun. Chemists (life). Achievements include research in functionalized and non-standard nucleosides; C-nucleoside with a non-standard hydrogen bonding pattern; synthesis of heterocycle annealed amino acids; novel methodologies for heterocycle synthesis, cycloaddition and free radical reactions. Office Phone: 205-581-2603.

**ROYCHOWDHURY, VWANI,** electrical engineer, educator; PhD in Elec. Engring., Stanford U., Calif., 1989. Mem. faculty sch. elec. and computer engring. Purdue U., 1991—95, assoc. prof., 1995—96; mem. faculty to prof. elec. engring. UCLA, 1996—. Mem. faculty biomedical engring. interdepartmental prog. UCLA. Contbr. articles to sci. jours.; co-author: Theoretical Advances in Neural Computation and Learning, 1994, Discrete Neural Computation: A Theoretical Found., 1995. Recipient Best Paper award, IEEE Transactions on Neural Networks, 1999. Achievements include patents in field. Office: Elec Engring Dept UCLA 56-125B Engring IV Bldg Box 951594 Los Angeles CA 90095-1594 E-mail: vwani@ee.ucla.edu.*

**ROYCROFT, HOWARD FRANCIS,** lawyer; b. Balt. Sept. 9, 1930; s. Howard T. and Bessie (Weaver) R.; m. Barbara Lee Seal, Mar. 20, 1954; children: Suzanne Carol Roycroft Soderberg, Nancy Lee Roycroft Branigan. BA, U. Md., 1953; LLB, Georgetown U., 1958. Bar: D.C. 1958. Mem. firm Hogan & Hartson, Washington, 1958, ptnr., 1965-87, exec. com., 1970-73, counsel, 1987—. Dir. United TV, Inc., 1982—2001, U TV San Francisco, Inc., 1983—; mng. ptnr., dir. WIJY, Inc., Hilton Head, SC, 1989—97; lectr. Howard U. Sch. Law, 1973—74; guest lectr. U. Tex., 1980; mem. Met. Washington Bd. Trade. Bd. dirs. YMCA Met. Washington, 1974-76. 1st lt. USMC, 1953-55. Mem. ABA, Va. Bar Assn., Fed. Comm. Bar Assn., Bar Assn. D.C., Nat. Broadcasters Club, Barristers, Aircraft Owners and Pilots Assn., Nat. Acad. TV Arts & Scis., Broadcast Pioneers, Alexandria Rotary Club, Bryce Mountain Ski and Country Club (dir., pres. 1974-87), Mt. Vernon Country Club, Old Dominion Boat Club, Washington Tennis Patrons Club, Army-Navy Club, Chaine des Rotisseurs Gastronome Club, Skull Creek Yacht Club, Kappa Alpha, Beta Kappa, Delta Theta Phi. Republican. Methodist. Office: Hogan & Hartson 555 13th St NW Ste 800E Washington DC 20004-1161 E-mail: HRoycroft@netscape.com.

**ROYER, KATHLEEN ROSE,** pilot; b. Pitts., Nov. 4, 1949; d. Victor Cedric and Lisetta Emma (Smith) Salway; m. Michael Lee Royer, June 6, 1971 (div. Aug. 1975). Student, Newbold Coll., 1968-69; BS, Columbia Union Coll., 1971; MEd, Shippensburg U., 1974; student, Lehigh U., 1974-75. Cert. tchr. Pa. Music. Music tchr. Harrisburg (Pa.) Sch. Dist., 1971-77; flight instr. Penn-Air, Inc., Altoona, Pa., 1977; capt. asst. chief pilot Air Atlantic Airlines, Centre Hall, Pa., 1977-80; capt., chief pilot Lycoming Air Svc., Williamsport, Pa., 1980-81; govs. pilot Commonwealth of Pa., Harrisburg, 1981-87; flight engr. Pan-Am, N.Y.C., 1987-91; pilot, 1st officer B737 United Airlines, Chgo., 1992-96, 1st officer B767 N.Y.C., until 1996, Washington, 1996-99; flight officer B747-400 JFK Internat. Airport, Jamaica, NY, 1999—2001, capt. Airbus 320, 2001—, airbus line check airman, 2005—. Frist woman pilot/engr. crew mem. on 747 Pan Am. Airlines, 1989—91, chief pilot, cons. Mem.: UAL-Airline Pilot Assn. (coord. critical incident stress program 1994—96), Flight Engrs. Internat. Assn. (scheduling rep. 1989, scheduling dir. 1990, 1st vice chmn. bd. adjustments 1993, v.p. dir. scheduling 1991—92), Internat. Soc. Women Airline Pilots, Whirley Girls (Washington), 99's (local chair Ctrl. Pa. chpt. 1987—92). Republican. Avocations:

owner/flying 1965 Cessna 180, golf, music, reading. Home: 34 Lazy Eight Dr Daytona Beach FL 32128 Office: San Francisco Intl Airport San Francisco CA Personal E-mail: royer17@bellsouth.net.

**ROYER, TOM A.,** entomologist, educator; b. Cherokee, Iowa; s. Don and Dorothy Royer; m. Joleen Royer; children: Kelly, Kevin. BS, Iowa State U., Ames, 1973—78; MS, S.D. State U., Brookings, 1980—83; PhD, Tex. A&M U., College Station, 1987—90. Ext. specialist U. Ill. Coop. Ext. Svc., Edwardsville, 1991—92, ext. educator, 1992—97; asst. prof. Okla. State U., Stillwater, 1997—2003, assoc. prof., 2003—. Contbr. chapters to books. Mem.: Soc. Southwestern Entomologists (pres.-elect 2004—), Entomol. Soc. Am. (chair, sect. E 2002—03), Gamma Sigma Delta, Sigma Xi, Phi Kappa Phi. Office: Okla State Univ 127 NRC Stillwater OK 74078 Office Phone: 405-744-5531. E-mail: tom.royer@okstate.edu.

**ROYHAB, RONALD,** journalist, editor; b. Lorain, Ohio, Oct. 6, 1942; s. Halim Farah and Elizabeth Della (Naiser) R.; m. Roberta Lee Libb, Apr. 20, 1969; children: David Libb, Aaron Nicholas. Reporter Lorain Jour., 1966—69; reporter spl. assignment Scripps Howard Cin. Post, 1971—72; investigative reporter Scripps Howard Cleve. Press, 1972—75; chief bur. Scripps Howard Ohio Bur., Columbus, 1975—78; asst. mng. editor Scripps Howard News Svc., Washington, 1978—81; mng. editor Scripps Howard El Paso Herald Post, 1981—83; asst. mng. editor Scripps Howard Pitts. Press, 1983—92; assoc. editor Pitts. Post Gazette, 1992—93; mng. editor Toledo Blade, 1993—97, exec. editor, 1997—; v.p. Toledo Blade Co., 2004—. Bd. dirs. Toledo Blade Co. With USAR, 1964-70. Decorated Knight Order St. Ignatius of Antioch; recipient 7 awards for Excellence Cleve. Newspaper Guild, 1972-75, Spl. Sect. awards Pa. Newspaper Pubs. Assn., 1985, 86, 88, Benjamin C. Bradlee Editor of the Yr. award Nat. Press Found. 2005; named to DeMolay Legion of Honor, 1997; Am. Polit. Sci. Assn. fellow, 1970-71. Mem. Am. Soc. Newspaper Editors, AP Soc. Ohio (pres. 2000-01), Ohio Newspaper Assn., Toledo Press Club (pres. 2002-03). Eastern Orthodox. Home: 27262 Fort Meigs Rd Perrysburg OH 43551-1230 Office: Toledo Blade 541 N Superior St Toledo OH 43660-0002 Office Phone: 419-724-6161. Personal E-mail: royhab@theblade.com.

**ROYLE, DAVID BRIAN LAYTON,** television producer, journalist; arrived in U.S., 1974; s. J. H. L. and J. M. D. Royle; m. Cornelia Boardman Service; children: William Brian Layton, Richard John Boardman. BA cum laude, U. N.C., 1978; MA, U. Minn., 1985. Journalist Northcliffe Newspapers, Stoke-on-Trent, England, 1979-82; news producer Ctrl. Ind. TV, Birmingham, England, 1982-83; producer Inside Story, N.Y.C., 1984-86; prodr. New Atlantic Prodns., N.Y.C., 1986-89; pres. David Royle Prodns., N.Y.C., 1989—. Dir. Russian Archive, 1992—97; prodr. Wall St. Jour. TV, 1995; sr. prodr. Nat. Geog. TV, Washington, 1996—98, exec. prodr. 1998—2005, sr. v.p. prodn., 2000—04, exec. v.p. prodn., 2004—05; exec. v.p. programming and prodn. Smithsonian Networks, 2006—. Prodr.: (TV films) Rupert Murdoch: Press Baron Who Would Be King, PBS, 1985 (Emmy nomination), Assignment Africa, PBS, 1986 (Emmy nomination), Senator Sam, PBS, 1988 (Ohio State award, Cine Golden Eagle), Inside Gorbachev's USSR, PBS, 1989 (George Polk award, DuPont-Columbia U. Gold Baton); prodr.: (TV films) American Detective in Russia, ABC, 1992; prodr.: (TV films) The Eagle and The Bear, ABC/A&E, 1993 (Cine Golden Eagle), Dr. Frank, PBS, 1994 (Cine Golden Eagle, Regional Emmy award), TV Nation, NBC/BBC, 1994 (Prime Time Emmy award), Emerging Powers: Brazil, PBS/NHK Japan, 1996, Inside Base Camp, Nat. Geog. Channel, 2001 (Emmy award, 2001), Liberia, America Dream?, 2004 (Edward R. Murrow award, duPont-Columbia U. Silver Baton); (TV series) Target: Mafia, 1993, Trauma: Life and Death in the E.R., TLC, 1996, Nat. Geographic Explorer, TBS, 1999— (6 Emmy awards, Emmy nominations), Taboo, 2002—04, National Geographic's Most Amazing Moments, 2004—05. Gov. Clifton Coll., Bristol, England, 1997—. Named Hon. Citizen, Mpls., 1983; recipient Excellence award, U. Minn. Sch. Journalism & Mass Comm., 2000; scholar, Rotary Internat., 1983; Morehead scholar, 1974—78, NJ Arts fellow, 1995. Mem.: NATAS, Writers Guild, Soc. Profl. Journalists, U. N.C. Alumni Assn. (bd. dirs. 2005—). Avocations: running, sailing, photography, reading. Office: Smithsonian Networks Washington DC

**ROYSTER, LYNN CHRISTINE,** academic administrator, educator; b. Balt., Md., Aug. 23, 1947; d. Kenneth Frederick and Dorothy Charlotte Umpleby; m. Michael James Royster, Aug. 10, 2002; children: Patrick Bart Holaday, Brett Christine Holaday. BA, U. of Mich., Ann Arbor, 1969; MA, Prescott (Ariz.) Coll., 1993; JD, George Wash. U., Washington, 1975; PhD, Union Inst. and U., Vt., 1990. Bar: Washington 1976, Tex. 1979, N.J. 1986, Ill. 1987. Dir. chronic illness initiative DePaul U., Sch. for New Learning, Chgo., 2003—. Atty. Lorance and Thompson, Houston, 1978—83; adj. faculty Prescott Coll., 1993—96; vis. faculty DePaul U. Sch. for New Learning, 1997—2006. Contbr. articles to profl. jours. and books. Dir. Lake Forest (Ill.) Lake Bluff Parent Coun., 1988—89; vice chair CFIDS Assn. of Am., Charlotte, NC, 2004—06; bd. sec. Chronic Fatigue Syndrome, Fibromyalgia, and Chem. Sensitivity Coalition of Chgo., 2003—06; trustee Prescott Coll., 1995—96; bd. sec. Touchstone Theatre, Lake Forest, Ill., 1987—89. Mem.: Chi Omega. Avocations: mediation, writing, weightlifting. Office: DePaul Univ Sch for New Learning 25 E Jackson Blvd Chicago IL 60611 Office Fax: 312-321-9665. Business E-Mail: lroyster@depaul.edu.

**ROZANSKI, MORDECHAI,** historian, university dean; b. Lodz, Poland, July 4, 1946; came to U.S., 1968; s. Louis and Bertha R.; m. Bonnie Gail Asher, May 30, 1970; 1 child, Daniel K. BA, McGill U., 1968; postgrad. Columbia U., 1970, New Asia Coll., 1971-72; PhD, U. Pa., 1974. Instr. history U. Pa., Phila., 1969-71; assoc. prof. Asian history Berry Coll., Rome, Ga., 1974 76; asst. prof. Asian history dir. Office of Internat. Edn. and rgn. area studies program Pacific Luth. U., Tacoma, 1976-82; assoc. dean for internat. studies Adelphi U., Garden City, N.Y., 1982-84, assoc. provost, 1984-86; dean Coll. Liberal Arts, Fairleigh Dickinson U., Teaneck, N.J., 1986-89, v.p. for academic affairs, 1989-1991, provost, Wagner Coll., Staten Island, 1991-1993, pres. U. of Guelph, Ontario, 1993-2003, pres., Rider U., Lawrenceville, 2003-; dir. programs Nat. Council on Fgn. Langs. and Internat. Studies, 1983-86. Trustee, World Affairs Council, Seattle, 1978-81; vice chmn. Nat. Com. on Internat. Studies and Program Adminstrs., 1979-80; chmn. Pacific N.W. Internat./Intercultural Edn. Consortium, 1979-82. Que. Province fellow, 1967; Wilson Meml. scholar, 1968; U. Pa. fellow, 1968-71; Am. Hist. Assn. Am.-East Asian Relations fellow, Columbia U., 1970; Can. Council doctoral fellow, 1971-73; U.S. Office of Edn. research grantee, 1977; Lilly Found. fellow Stanford U., summer 1978. Author: Manual of World History, 1975; Guide to U.S. State Papers on China, 1979; editor-in-chief Am.-East Asian Relations Newsletter, 1980-83; contbr. articles to profl. publs. Office: Rider Univ 2083 Lawrence Rd Lawrenceville NJ 08648-3099*

**ROZARIO STEWART, GWENDOLYN MICHELLE,** elementary school educator; b. San Francisco, Dec. 13, 1954; d. James Calhoun and Annette Marie Miller; m. Stephen Michael Stewart, Jan. 1, 2000; children: Alicia Marie Rozario, Alexander Rozario Jr. BA, U. San Francisco, 1977; M in pub. admin., Coll. of Notre Dame, 1989; D in edn., U. San Francisco, 1995. Vice principal San Lorenzo (Calif.) Unified Sch. Dist., 1992-93; tchr. Martin Luther King Jr. Mid. Sch., Madera, Calif., 1993—2001; adj. faculty Merced Cmty. Coll., Merced, Calif., 1994—98; mentor tchr. Martin Luther King Jr. Mid. Sch., Madera, Calif., 1994—2000; principal Fresno United Alternative Edn., Fresno, Calif., 2000—01; tchr. Westside Intermediate Sch., Los Banos, Calif., 2001—04; English tchr. Los Banos (Calif.) HS, 2004—. Grant writing cons. self employed, Madera, Calif., 1992—; summer sch. principal Los Banos HS, 2006. Author: An Analysis of New Teacher Introduction Program in Madera Unified School District, 1995. Recipient Cmty. Svc. award, Martin Luther King Jr. Sch., 1991, Disting. Tchr. award, Madera Unified Sch. Dist. Com., 1994. Mem.: The Link, Inc., Fresno Cpt. (recording sec. 2004—05), Nat. Soc. of Philanthropy, Madera County Food Bank (recording sec. 1999—2005). Avocations: writing poetry, exercise, reading, jazz. Office Phone: 559-474-6341.

**ROZBRUCH, S. ROBERT,** orthopedist, researcher; b. Bklyn., Sept. 2, 1965; s. Max and Frieda Rozbuch; m. Yonina Jacobs, July 2, 1989; children: Jason, Elizabeth. BA magna cum laude, U. Pa., 1985; MD in Rsch. with honors, Cornell U. Weill Med. Coll., 1990. Resident orthop. Hosp. Spl. Surgery, N.Y.C., 1990—95; fellow Internat. Ctr. Limb Lengthening, Balt. 1998—99; pres. S. Robert Rozbruch MD, PC, N.Y.C., 1999—; now chief limb lengthening svc. Hosp. Spl. Surgery, N.Y.C., dir. Inst. Limb Lengthening and Reconstruction, 2002—; asst. attr. orthop. surgery Weill Med. Sch. Cornell U., 2002—. Treas. Limb Lengthening and Reconstruction Soc., 2002—, bd. dir. 2002. Author: Fractures of the Knee in Clin. Orthop., 2000, Orthop. Knowledge Update-Trauma 3, 2003; contbr. articles to profl. jours. Bd. trustees Temple Israel Ctr., White Plains, NY, 2002—. Recipient Neer award, Am. Shoulder and Elbow Surgeons, 1991. Fellow: Am. Acad. Orthop. Surgeons; mem.: Orthop. Trauma Assn. Achievements include first to founder Limb Lengthening and Reconstruction program at Hosp. Spl. Surgery, N.Y.C. Avocations: gardening, exercise. Office: Hosp Spl Surgery 535 E 70th St New York NY 10021 Office Phone: 212-606-1415. Business E-Mail: rozbruchsr@hss.edu.

**ROZEK, THOMAS M.,** health facility administrator; Pres. Children's Hosp. of Mich.; sr. v.p. Detroit Med. Ctr.; pres. & CEO Miami Children's Hosp., 1999—. Bd. trustees Fla. Hosp. 2001; bd. dirs. Children's Trust of Miami-Dade County, 2003. Office: Miami Children's Hosp 3100 SW 62nd Ave Miami FL 33155

**ROZELL, WILLIAM BARCLAY,** lawyer; b. Ossining, NY, Mar. 30, 1943; s. William M. and Doris M. (Mittenmaier) R.; m. Susan Kai Wylie, Oct. 4, 1969; m. Susan Marie Walker, Dec. 5, 1975; children: Rebecca, Mariah. BSc in Engring., Brown U., 1965; JD, Cornell U., 1968. Bar: Ohio 1969, N.Y. 1969, U.S. Dist. Ct. (so. dist.) N.Y. 1970, U.S. Dist. Ct. (ea. dist.) N.Y. 1971, Alaska 1972, U.S. Dist. Ct. Alaska 1972, U.S. Supreme Ct. 1976, U.S. Ct. Appeals (9th cir.) 1977. VISTA atty. Office Econ. Opportunity, Chgo. and Columbus, Ohio, 1968—69; assoc. White & Case, N.Y.C., 1969—72, Faulkner, Banfield, Doogan & Holmes, Juneau, Alaska, 1972—74, ptnr., 1975—81, mem. firm, 1981—98; pvt. practice Juneau, 1998—. Bd. dirs. Alaska Legal Services Corp., 1974-77. Fellow Am. Bar Found.; mem. ABA, Alaska Bar Assn. (gov. 1976-82, pres. 1980-81), Alaska Bar Found. (trustee 1984-2001), Juneau Bar Assn., Order of Coif. Office: PO Box 20730 Juneau AK 99802-0730 Office Phone: 907-586-0142.

**ROZEN, JEROME GEORGE, JR.,** entomologist, researcher, curator; b. Evanston, Ill., Mar. 19, 1928; s. Jerome George and Della (Kretchmar) R.; m. Barbara L. Lindner, Dec. 18, 1948; children: Steven George, Kenneth Charles, James Robert. Student, U. Pa., 1946-48; BA, U. Kans., Lawrence, 1950; PhD, U. Calif.-Berkeley, 1955. Entomologist in taxonomy U.S. Dept. Agr., 1956-58; asst. prof. entomology Ohio State U., 1958-60; assoc. curator dept. entomology Am. Mus. Natural History, N.Y.C., 1960-65, curator hymenoptera, 1965—, chmn. dept. entomology, 1960-71, dep. dir. research, 1972-86. Field expdns. in U.S., Europe, Mex., Trinidad, Argentina, Chile, Brazil, Peru, Venezuela, Morocco, Pakistan, Republic of South Africa, Namibia, Israel, Egypt, Kyrgzstan, Turkey; adj. prof. CUNY, 1968—; mus. assoc. Univ. Kans. Nat. History Mus. and Biodiversity Rsch. Ctr., 2004—. Contbr. numerous sci. articles on bees (Apoidea) and beetles (Coleoptera). Fellow AAAS; mem. Am. Inst. Biol. Scis., Entomol. Soc. Am. (editor misc. publs. 1959-60), Soc. Study of Evolution, Soc. Systematic Biology, N.Y. Entomol Soc. (pres. 1964-65), Washington Entomol. Soc., Pacific Coast Entomol. Soc., Kans. Entomol. Soc., Orgn. Biol. Field Stas. (pres. 1990), Internat. Soc. Hymenopterists (co-organizer, Bee Course, 1999-). Home: 55 Haring St Closter NJ 07624-1709 Office: Am Mus Natural History Central Park West New York NY 10024-5192 Office Phone: 212-769-5466. Business E-Mail: rozen@amnh.org.

**ROZENBERG, LANA,** cosmetic dentist; b. 1968; DDS, U. Pacific Sch. Dentistry, 1994. Dir. Dental Day Spa, NY. Named one of NY Top Cosmetic Dentists, NY Mag., 2002, 2004. Avocations: boating, golf, skiing, tennis, financial investments. Office: Dental Day Spa 45 W 54th St - Ste 1B New York NY 10019 Office Phone: 212-265-7724. Business E-Mail: office@rozenbergdds.com.*

**ROZETT, ROBERT BERNARD,** library director, historian; b. Summit, NJ, Apr. 21, 1956; s. George Robert and Thelma Frumkin Rozett; m. Shoshana Cohen, May 29, 1985; children: Tamar, Naomi, Hadas, Michael. B, Rutgers U., 1978; M, Hebrew U., Jerusalem, Israel, 1981, PhD, 1987. Lectr. Yad Vashem, Jerusalem, 1981—87, co-curator hist. exhibit, 1990—92, libr. dir., 1993—. Author: Approaching the Holocaust, Texts and Contexts, 2005; editor: Facts on File Encyclopedia of the Holocaust, 2000; editor: (assoc. editor) Encyclopedia of the Holocaust, 1988—91; editor: The Holocaust, Frequently Asked Questions, 2005; contbr. articles numerous articles about the Holocaust, Bibliographical Essay The Holocaust Encyclopedia, 2001, chapters to books. Recipient Phi Beta Kappa, Rutgers U., 1978, Phi Alpha Theta, 1978. Mem.: Israel Hist. Soc. Office: Yad Vashem Mount of Remembrance Jerusalem 91034 Israel Office Phone: 972-2-6443531. Office Fax: 972-2-6443443. Business E-Mail: robert.rozett@yadvashem.org.il.

**ROZIN, BORIS.** mathematician, researcher; b. Kiev, Ukraine, Mar. 31, 1964; arrived in U.S., 2001; s. Naum and Alla Rozin; m. Natali Zvoleiko, Apr. 2, 1999; 1 child, Miriam. MS in Computer En gring., Vinnitsa (Ukraine) State Technol. U., 1989. Assoc. prof. dept. of applied math. and computer scis. Vinnitsa State Technol. U., 1989—98. Contbr. articles to profl. jours. Fellow: Internat. Club of Golden Sect. (assoc.). Judaism. Achievements include research in theory of asynchronous cell division; theory of Binet formulas for Fibonacci and Lucas p-numbers; continuous functions for the Fibonacci and Lucas p-numbers. Personal E-Mail: rozinb@yahoo.com.

**ROZMAN, GILBERT FRIEDELL,** sociologist, educator; b. Mpls., Feb. 18, 1943; s. David and Celia (Friedell) R.; m. Masha Dwosh, Jan. 25, 1945; children: Thea Dwosh, Noah Dwosh. BA, Carleton Coll., Northfield, Minn., 1965; PhD (Woodrow Wilson fellow 1965-66), Princeton U., 1971. Mem. faculty Princeton U., 1970—, prof. sociology, 1979—, Musgrave prof. sociology, 1992—. mem. com. studies Chinese civilization Am. Council Learned Socs., 1975-80; mem. U.S.-USSR Bi-Nat. Commn. Humanities and Social Scis., 1978-86, IREX Univ. Coun., 1998-2001. Author: Urban Networks in Ch'ing China and Tokugawa Japan, 1973, Urban Networks in Russia, 1750-1800, and Premodern Periodization, 1976, Population and Marketing Settlements in Ch'ing China, 1982, A Mirror for Socialism: Soviet Criticisms of China, 1985, The Chinese Debate About Soviet Socialism 1978-85, 1987, Japan's Response to the Gorbachev Era, 1985-1991: A Rising Superpower Views a Declining One, 1992, Northeast Asia's Stunted Regionalism: Bilateral Distrust in the Shadow of Globalization, 2004; co-author: The Modernization of Japan and Russia, 1975; editor: The Modernization of China, 1981, Soviet Studies of Premodern China: Assessments of Recent Scholarship, 1984, Japan in Transition: From Tokugawa to Meiji, 1986, The East Asian Region: Confucian Heritage and Its Modern Adaptation, 1991, Dismantling Communism: Common Causes and Regional Variations, 1992, Russia and East Asia: The 21st Century Security Environment, 1999, Japan and Russia: The Tortuous Path to Normalization, 1949-1999, 2000, Korea at the Center: Dynamics of Regionalism in Northeast Asia, 2006. Guggenheim fellow, 1979-80; grantee NSF, NEH, Social Sci. Rsch. Coun., Nat. Coun. for Soviet and E. European Studies, U.S. Inst. Peace, Woodrow Wilson Internat. Ctr. Mem. Assn. Asian Studies, Am. Sociol. Assn., Am. Assn. Advancement Slavic Studies. Home: 20 Springwood Dr Trenton NJ 08648-1048 Office: Princeton U 149 Wallace Hall Princeton NJ 08544-0001 E-mail: grozman@princeton.edu.

**ROZMAN, JAMES D.,** school system administrator, minister; b. Lynwood, Calif., Sept. 5, 1950; s. Clyde A. and Mae A. Rozman. AA, Coll. San Mateo, 1970; BS, We. Bapt. Coll., Salem, Oreg., 1977; MDiv, Talbot Theol. Sem., La Mirada, Calif., 1981; D of Ministry, Biola U. La Mirada, Calif., 1989; grad., USAF Acad. Instr. Sch., 1984, USAF Squadron Officer Sch., 1988, Air Command and Staff Coll., 1994, USAF Air War Coll., 1996; cert. wing chaplain course, Air U., Maxwell AFB, 2001. Cert. in clin. pastoral edn., 1998. Commd. USAF, 1980, advanced through ranks to lt. col., installation chaplain Holloman AFB, N.Mex., 1981-84, installation staff chaplain Sondrestrom Air Base, Greenland, 1984-85, protestant chaplain Travis AFB, Calif., 1985-87, Tactical Air Command site chaplain Griffiss AFB, N.Y., 1987-89, sr. protestant chaplain San Vito dei Normanni, Italy, 1989-91, protestant chaplain Langley AFB, Va., 1991-94, sr. protestant chaplain Tinker AFB, Okla., 1994-97, sr. parish chaplain Travis AFB, 1998—2001, wing chaplain L.A. AFB, Calif., 2001—04; clin. pastoral edn. resident Walter Reed Army Med. Ctr., Washington, 1997-98. Acting sr. chaplain, USAF Chapel Team, Apr. 1995 Oklahoma City Bombing Rescue Effort, Tinker AFB, Okla. Mem. VFW (life), Mil. Chaplains Assn. (life), Air Force Assn. (life), Air Force Sgts. Assn. (life), Mil. Officer Assn. Am. (life), Assn. Clin. Pastoral Edn., Assn. Calif. Sch. Adminstrs., Internat. Assn. Christian Sch. Adminstrs., Internat. Assn. Christian Early Educators, Biola U. Alumni Assn., We. Bapt. Coll. Alumni Assn., Am. Legion. Republican. Baptist. Avocations: walking, travel, swimming, reading. Office: 2545 Rebecca Lynn Way Santa Clara CA 95050-5583 Home: 2454 Rebecca Lynn Way Santa Clara CA 95050-5583 Office Phone: 408-768-0784. Personal E-Mail: therozman@juno.com.

**ROZOF, PHYLLIS CLAIRE,** lawyer; b. Flint, Mich., Aug. 3, 1948; d. Eugene Robert and Loveta Lucille Greenwood; m. Robert James Rozof, July 17, 1970 (dec. Oct. 1995); children: Nathan, Zachary. AB with high distinction, U. Mich., 1970, JD magna cum laude, 1977. Bar: Mich. 1977, Fla. 1978. Assoc. Honigman Miller Schwartz and Cohn, Detroit, 1977-81, ptnr., 1982—. Mem. Comml. Real Estate Women Detroit (pres. 1992-93). Office: Honigman Miller Schwartz & Cohn LLP 2290 1st National Bldg Detroit MI 48226 Office Phone: 313-465-7532. Business E-Mail: prozof@honigman.com.

**ROZOFF, JONATHAN MARK,** legal consultant; b. Chgo., Aug. 7, 1963; BA, Brown U., 1985; MBA, U. Pa., 1990. Intern US Senator Claiborne Pell, Washington, 1982; analyst The MAC Group, Inc., Cambridge, Mass., 1985—88, Hong Kong, 1985—88; v.p. Cornerstone Rsch., NYC, 1990—.

**ROZZELL, SCOTT ELLIS,** lawyer; b. Texarkana, Tex., Apr. 12, 1949; s. George M. and Dora Mae (Boyett) Rozzell; children: Stacey Rozzell Murphree, Kimberly Marie. BA, So. Meth. U., 1971; JD, U. Tex., 1975. Bar: Tex. 1975, U.S. Dist. Ct. Tex. (so. dist.) 1975, U.S. Dist. Ct. Tex. (no. dist.) 1977, U.S. Ct. Appeals (1st, 3d, 9th cirs.) 1977, U.S. Ct. Appeals (5th and D.C. cirs.) 1976. Assoc. BakerBotts, LLP, Houston, 1975-82, ptnr., 1983-94, sr. ptnr., 1995-2000; exec. v.p., gen. counsel, corp. sec. CenterPoint Energy, Inc., Houston, 2001—; exec. v.p., gen. counsel, corp. sec., bd. dir. Tex. Genco Holdings Inc., 2003—04. Mem. State of Tex. Aircraft Pooling Bd., 1997-2002; devel. bd. U. Tex. Health Sci. Ctr. Houston, 1992-2003; mem. Tex. Commn. for Lawyer Discipline, 2001-03, chair 2002-03; bd. advisors Houston C.C. Sys., 2004-. Bd. dirs. Manned Space Flight Edn. Found., Inc., 1997—, vice chair 2000—, Tex. Aviation Hall of Fame, 2001—; vice-chmn., 2006—, Cancer Counseling Inc., Houston, 1991-92; mem. so. regional adv. bd. Inst. Internat. Edn., 2002—; chmn. Assn. Electric Cos. Tex., 2006—. Fellow Tex. Bar Found. (sustaining life), Houston Bar Found. (sustaining life, bd. dirs. 1991-93, chair 1993), Am. Bar Found. (life); mem. ABA, State Bar Tex. (bd. dirs. 1997-2000), Houston Bar Assn. (bd. dirs. 1991-95, pres. 1996-97), Fed. Energy Bar Assn., Houston Young Lawyers Assn. (bd. dirs. 1978-82, pres. 1983-84), Coronado Club, Houstonian. Republican. Presbyterian. Avocation: flying vintage military aircraft. Office: CenterPoint Energy Inc 1111 Louisiana 47th Floor PO Box 4567 Houston TX 77210-4567 Home: 8 N West Oak Dr Houston TX 77056 Office Phone: 713-207-1502. Business E-Mail: scott.rozzell@centerpointenergy.com.

**RUAN, LIAN JIN,** library director; arrived in U.S., 1986; d. Yong-dong Jin and Jin-xiu Dai; m. Zhong-jin Ruan, June 24, 1987; children: Gordon J., George J. BA in World History, Peking U., 1984; MA in African History, UCLA, 1988; MLS, U. Ill., 1990. Rsch. info. specialist Ill. Fire Svc. Inst., Champaign, 1990—99, dir., head libr., 1999—. Newspaper cataloger Ill. State Hist. Libr., Springfield, 1990, manuscript cataloger, 90; libr. cons. Champaign Fire Dept., 1990—. Contbr. articles to profl. jours. Recipient Chancellor's Academic Profl. Excellence award, U. Ill. Mem.: ALA (mem. Illinet network adv. coun. 2003—), Spl. Libr. Assn. (downstate bd. dirs. Ill. chpt. 2002—04, Diversity Leadership Develop. award 2003), Chinese Heritage Assn. (vice prin. chinese sch. 1998—99, prin. chinese sch. 1999—2000, bd. dirs. 2000—03). Internat. Fire Libr. Consortium (adv. com. 1997—2001). Office: Ill Fire Svc Inst Univ Ill 11 Gerty Dr Champaign IL 61820 Office Phone: 217-265-6107. Business E-Mail: lruan@fsi.uiuc.edu.

**RUAN, WEIHUA,** mathematician; b. Canton, Gangdong, China, June 10, 1958; s. Wanghan Ruan and Ruiyu Zhao; m. May Meiliang Wu, June 18, 1989; children: Joseph Y., Ellynna S. PhD, N.C. State U., Raleigh, 1988. Assoc. prof. math. Purdue U. Calumet, Hammond, Ind., 1995—2001, prof. math., 2001—. Edn. and rsch. Purdue U. Calumet, Hammond, Ind., 1990—. Deacon. Achievements include development of new theories in mathematical biology and mathematical physics. Office: Purdue Univ Calumet Hammond IN 46323 Office Phone: 219-989-2271. E-mail: ruanw@calumet.purdue.edu.

**RUANE, KRISTA,** TV food stylist; b. Phila. BFA, Washington U., St. Louis; attended, French Culinary Inst., NY. Sr. food stylist Food Network. Food stylist Mario Batali, Rick Bayless, Food Network, All My Children, ABC, Isaac Mizrahi Show, Today Show, NBC, Last Holiday, Paramount Pictures, Food Network Kitchens Cookbook, Food Network Kitchens Making it Easy cookbook. Office: 575 1oth St 2 Brooklyn NY 11215 Office Phone: 718-810-4516.*

**RUB, TIMOTHY F.,** museum director; b. NYC, Mar. 9, 1952; s. Louis Rub and Marguerite (Gustafson); m. Sally Rub; children: Peter, Katharine. BA in Art History, Middlebury Coll., 1974; MA in Art History, NYU, 1979; MBA, Yale U., 1987; postgrad., Harvard U., 1998. Curatorial intern Met. Mus. Art, 1983; lectr. art and archtl. history Cooper-Hewitt Mus./Parsons Sch. Design, Stevens Inst. Tech., 1979-84; guest curator Bronx Mus. Arts, NY, 1985-86; curator Cooper-Hewitt Mus., NYC, 1983-87; assoc. dir. Hood Mus. Dartmouth Coll., Hanover, NH, 1987-91, dir., COO, 1991-2000; dir. Cin. Art Mus., 2000—06; dir., CEO, Cleve. Mus. Art, 2006—. Avocation: gardening. Office: Cleveland Mus Art 11150 East Blvd Cleveland OH 44106

**RUBAN, LILIA,** education educator, researcher; b. Altin-Topkan, Leninabad, Tajikistan, Nov. 5, 1970; arrived in U.S., 1995; d. Mikhail Fyodorovich and Anna Ivanovna Ruban; m. Dennis Charles Lincoln, July 19, 1997; children: Nicholas Lincoln children: Michael Lincoln. BS in Fgn. Langs., Odessa State U., 1993, MS in Romance-Germanic Philology, 1994; PhD in Ednl. Psychology, U. Conn., 2000. Rsch. Ctr. on the Gifted and Talented, Storrs, Conn., 1995—2000; asst. prof. curriculum and instrn. U. Houston, 2000—. Fed. grants reviewer U.S. Dept. Edn., Washington, 2001—02; rsch. faculty Urban Talent Rsch. Inst. Mem. editl. bd.: Jour. Classroom Interaction, 2000—, Rev. in Higher Edn., 2004—; contbr. chapters to books, articles to profl. jours. Named Mem. of the Oxford Round Table on Spl. Edn., Oxford Round Table, Oxford, Eng., 2004; recipient Outstanding Paper award, S.W. Ednl. Rsch. Assn., 2002, Rsch. Excellence award, Coll. Edn. U. Houston, 2005. Mem.: World Coun. for Gifted Children, Am. Ednl. Rsch. Assn. (Disting. Paper award 2003), Tex. Assn. for Gifted and Talented (mem. Tex. 2015 Gifted Inst. 2003—03), Nat. Assn. for Gifted Children (chmn. rsch. and evaluation divsn. 2005—, Dissertation award 1999, Doctoral Student of the Yr. 2000). Avocations: gardening, cooking, travel, museums, languages. Home: 19210 Dianeshire Dr Spring TX 77388-5919 Office: Univ Houston 256 Farish Hall Houston TX 77204-5027 Office Phone: 713-743-3311. Home Fax: 281-288-5879; Office Fax: 713-743-4900. Business E-Mail: lruban@uh.edu.

**RUBARDT, PETER CRAIG,** conductor, educator; b. Oakland, Calif., Aug. 7, 1958; s. Kenneth and Betty (Maspero) R.; m. Hedi Salanki; children: Daniel, Vivienna. BA, U. Calif., Berkeley, 1981; M of Music, SUNY, Stony Brook, 1984; student, Hochschule fur Musik, Vienna, 1984-86; D Mus. Arts, Julliard Sch., 1989. Prof., conductor SUNY, Purchase, 1989-90, Rutgers U., New Brunswick, NJ, 1991-96; resident conductor N.J. Symphony, Newark, 1990-93; assoc. conductor Syracuse (N.Y.) Symphony, 1993-97; music dir., condr. Greater Pensacola (Fla.) Symphony Orch., 1997—. Guest conductor various orchs. Condr. rec. Bach Concerti, 1998. Fullbright fellow USIA, 1984-86; Bruno Walter scholar, Julliard Sch., 1986-88. Mem. Am. Symphony Orch. League, Condrs. Guild. Democrat. Home: 8774 Thunderbird Dr Pensacola FL 32514 Office: Pensacola Symphony Orch PO Box 1752 Pensacola FL 32598-1752 Office Phone: 850-435-2533.

**RUBBERT, PAUL EDWARD,** retired engineering executive; b. Mpls., Feb. 18, 1937; s. Adolf Christian and Esther Ruth Rubbert; m. Mary Parpart, Oct. 6, 1958 (div. 1985); children: Mark, David, Stephen. BS with high distinction, U. Minn., 1958, MS in Aero. Engring., 1960; PhD in Aerodyn., MIT, 1965. Rsch. engr. The Boeing Co., Seattle, 1960-62, 65-72, unit chief aerodyns rsch., comml. airplane group, 1972—, tech. fellow, 1989; ret. Cons. NASA, 1989—, aeronautics adv. com., aerospace rsch. and tech. subcoms.; corp. vis. com. MIT, 1990—; served on various coms. Nat. Rsch. Coun. Panel; aerodyns. cons. GM; speaker in field. Contbr. articles to profl. jours. Recipient Arch T. Colwell Merit award Soc. Automotive Engrs., 1968, Wright Brothers Lectureship in Aeronautics Am. Inst. of Aeronautics and Astronautics, 1994 Fellow AIAA (Outstanding Tech. Mgmt. award Pacific Northwest sect., disting. lectr., assoc. editor jour., past mem. fellow selection com., dir., chmn. various workshops and coms.), Royal Aero. Soc.; mem. NAE. Achievements include three patents in field.

**RUBEL, ERIC A.,** lawyer; b. Hempstead, N.Y., July 12, 1960; s. Ralph and Josephine Rubel; m. Susan Rubel, Jan. 20, 1991; children: Alexander, Molly. BA cum laude, Middlebury Coll., 1982; JD with highest honors, George Washington U., 1985. Bar: D.C., Pa. Law clk. to Hon. Jane Restani U.S. Ct. Internat. Trade, N.Y.C., 1985-86; assoc. Arnold & Porter, Washington, 1986—92, ptnr., 1993—94; gen. counsel U.S. Consumer Product Safety Commn., Washington, 1994-97; ptnr., Consumer Product Safety Group Arnold & Porter, Washington, 1997—. Mem. ABA (vice chair sect. adminstrv. law and regulatory practice 1997-98), Order of Coif. Office: Arnold and Porter 555 12th St NW Washington DC 20004-1206 Office Phone: 202-942-5749. Office Fax: 202-942-5999. Business E-Mail: eric.rubel@aporter.com.

**RUBEL, MATTHEW EVAN,** retail executive; b. Ft. Lauderdale, Fla., Nov. 29, 1957; s. Stanley Bernard and Isabell Rubel. BS in Journalism, Ohio U., 1979; MBA, U. Miami, 1980. Pres. splty. store div. Revlon Inc., N.Y.C., 1988; pres., CEO Pepe Jeans USA; exec. v.p. J. Crew Group, 1994—99, CEO Popular Club Plan, 1994—99; chmn., CEO Cole Haan, 1999—2005; pres., CEO Payless ShoeSource, Inc., 2005—. Avocations: tennis, boating. Office: Payless ShoeSource 3231 SE 6th Ave Topeka KS 66607*

**RUBELL, DONALD,** gynecologist, hotel executive, art collector; m. Mera Rubell; children: Jason, Jennifer. Named one of Top 200 Collectors, ARTnews Mag., 2004, 2005, 2006. Avocation: collector of contemporary art. Mailing: The Rubell Art Collection 95 NW 29th St Miami FL 33127

**RUBELLO, DAVID JEROME,** artist; b. Detroit, Sept. 3, 1935; s. Ludovico and Girolama (Trupiano) R.; m. Mary Anne Keithan, Oct. 14, 1978. BFA, Am. Acad. Art, Rome, 1961; MFA, U. Mich., 1972; cert., Acad. Fine Art, Copenhagen, 1966. Lect. art U. Mich., Ann Arbor, 1973—74; asst. prof. art Pa. State U., University Park, 1974-80; assoc. prof. art Towson (Md.) State U., 1980-81; assoc. prof. U. Mich., Ann Arbor, 1988-90. One man shows include Cade Gallery, Royal Oak, Mich., 1987; exhibited in group shows at Detroit Inst. Art, 1987, GMB Gallery Internat., Bloomfield Hills, Mich., 1991, Kresge Art Inst., 1989, Kalamazoo Art Inst., 1990, 91, Photo Nat. 2, Ella Sharp Mus., Jackson, Mich., BBAA, Birmingham, Mich., Arts Coun., Traverse City, Mich., 1995-96, Patrimonio Invitational Wayne State U., Detroit, 1996. Ann. Celebrate Mich. Artists P.C. Art Ctr., Rochester, 1994, 95, 96, Art Ctr., Mt. Clemens, Mich., 1997, Crative Art Ctr., Pontiac, Mich., 1997; exhibited Null Dimension, Fulda, Germany, 1988, Systematica Constructive Art, Madrid, 1989, B4 Pub. Invitational, London, 1990, Archive 90s, Amsterdam and London, Konkrete Miniatures Invitational, Amsterdam, 1991, Planet Art Gallery, Capetown, South Africa, 1999, Detroit Focus, 2000; contbr. articles to profl. jours. including The Structurist, 1999, 2002. Recipient awards for art work; featured professional artist profile B&W Fine Art Photography Mag., June 2001.

**RUBEN, ALAN MILES,** law educator; b. Phila., May 13, 1931; s. Maurice Robert and Ruth (Blatt) R.; m. Betty Jane Willis, May 23, 1965. AB, U. Pa., 1953, MA, JD, U. Pa., 1956. Bar: Pa. 1957, Ohio 1972. Law clk. Supreme Ct. Pa., 1956-58; pvt. practice Phila. 1958-65; assoc. counsel Aetna Life & Casualty Co., Hartford, Conn., 1965-69; corp. counsel Lubrizol Corp., Cleve., 1969-70; prof. Cleve.-Marshall Coll. Law, Cleve. State U., 1970—2003, prof. emeritus, 2003—; adv. prof. law Fudan U., Shanghai, People's Republic of China, 1993—; dep. to city solicitor Phila., 1958-61; dep. atty. gen. State of Pa., 1961-65; spl. counsel to U.S. Senate Subcom. on Nat. Stockpile, 1962; commentator Higher Edn. Issues Sta. WCLV-FM, Cleve., 1975-87. Mem. nat. panel labor arbitrators Nat. Acad. Arbitrators, Fed. Mediation and Conciliation Svc. and Am. Arbitration Assn., Ohio State Employment Rels. Bd.; lectr. law U. Conn. Law Sch., 1968; vis. prof. law FuDan U., Shanghai, Peoples Republic of China, 1988-89; cons. Shanghai Law Office for Fgn. Economy and Trade, Peoples Republic of China, 1991-94. Author: The Constitutionality of Basic Protection for the Automobile Accident Victim, 1968, Unauthorized Insurance: The Regulation of the Unregulated, 1968, Arbitration in Public Employee Labor Disputes: Myth, Shibboleth and Reality, 1971, Illicit Sex of Campus: Federal Remedies for Employment Discrimination, 1971, Model Public Employees Labor Relations Act, 1972, Sentencing the Corporate Criminal, 1972, Modern Corporation Law, supp. edit., 1978, An American Lawyer's Observations on the Inauguration of the Shanghai Stock Exchange, 1989, Ohio Limited Partnership Law, 1992-2002, Practice Guides, Ohio Limited Liability Company, Law, 1995; co-editor: How Arbitration Works, 1997, editor-in-chief 6th edit., 2003; contbr.: With an Eye to Tomorrow: The Future Outlook of the Life Insurance Industry, 1968, The Urban Transportation Crisis: The Philadelphia Plan, 1961, Philadelphia's Union Shop Contract, 1961, The Administrative Agency Law: Reform of Adjudicative Procedure and the Revised Model Act, 1963, The Computer in Court: Computer Simulation and the robinson Patman Act, 1964. Bd. dirs. U.S. Olympic Com., 1968-73; chmn. U.S. Olympic Fencing Sport Com., 1969-73; pres. U.S. Fencing Assn., 1968-73; capt. U.S. Pan-Am. Fencing Team, 1971, U.S. Olympic Fencing Team, 1972; bd. dirs. Legal Aid Soc. Cleve., 1973-77; trustee Cleve.-San Jose Ballet, 1999-2001. Winner Internat. Inst. Edn. Internat. Debate Championship, 1953; recipient Harrison Tweed Bowl and Am. Law Inst. prizes Nat. Moot Ct. Competition, 1955; named Guggenheim scholar, 1949-53, Fulbright scholar FuDan U., Shanghai, 1993-94. Fellow Coll. Labor and Enployment Lawyers, Inc.; mem. ABA, Ohio Bar Assn. (corp. law and profl. responsibility com.), Cleve. Bar Assn. (Securities Law Inst. 1995-2002), Assn. Am. Law Schs. (chmn. sect. law and edn. 1976-78), Internat. Indsl. Rels. Rsch. Assn., Internat. Soc. Labor Law, Internat. Bar Assn., Union Internat. Des Avocats, Internat. Law Assn., AAUP (pres. Ohio conf. 1974-75), Rowfant Club, Phi Beta Kappa, Pi Gamma Mu. Home: 9925 Lake Shore Blvd Bratenahl OH 44108-1052 Office: Cleveland Marshall Coll Law Cleve State U 1801 Euclid Ave Cleveland OH 44115 Office Phone: 216-687-2310. Business E-Mail: alan.ruben@law.csuohio.edu.

**RUBEN, GARY A.,** marketing and communications consultant; b. Cochem, Germany, Jan. 1, 1924; came to U.S., 1939, naturalized, 1943; s. Jules and Erna (Hirsch) R.; m. Irene Jehle, Aug. 12, 1962; 1 child, Monique L. Student, Acad. Comml. Art, Indpls., 1940-41. With advt. dept. Indpls. News, 1940-41; advt. mgr. Greater Indpls. Amusement Corp., 1941-42; pres. Ruben Advt. Agy., Indpls., 1948-68; chmn. bd. Ruben, Montgomery & Assos., 1968-76; pres. Prestige Program Sales Inc., 1973-76, Gary A. Ruben Inc. (advt. and mktg. cons.), Indpls., 1976—. Past lectr. advt. and bd. fellows Northwood Inst.; past pres. Nat. Fedn. Advt. Agys., 1971. Hon. trustee Indpls. Children's Mus. With Combat Engrs. AUS, 1943-46. Paul Harris fellow Rotary Internat. Mem.: Ind. Broadcast Pioneers. Office: 7370-D Lions Head Dr Indianapolis IN 46260 *It was years ago, in the late 30's in Vienna, that the cry "Lebensraum" echoed across yet another land. And, a family, judged comfortable by most standards, scattered to the four winds, leaving behind all things material, but salvaging the will to survive and to commence once again in a new land. To a boy in his teens and still dressed in European-style short pants upon arrival in this country, the emotion, the sights, the sounds, and the smells were overwhelming and exciting to say the least...so began another chapter in my life. In the ensuing years, I learned the true meaning of individual freedom. And while the echoes of Vienna have become dim, that dim sound will continue to remind me that all worthwhile things in life are earned—not given, and even in adversity, there is opportunity.*

**RUBEN, IDA GASS,** state senator; b. Washington, Jan. 07; d. Sol and Sonia E. (Darman) Gass; m. L. Leonard Ruben, Aug. 29, 1948; children: Garry, Michael, Scott, Stephen. Del. Md. Ho. of Dels., Annapolis, 1974-86; mem. Md. Senate, Annapolis, 1986—, majority whip, 1995-99, pres. pro-tem, 2000—. Chair Montgomery County House Delegation, 1981-86, Montgomery County Senate Delegation, 1987—; mem. house econ. matters com., 1974-85, house ways and means com., 1985-86, legis. policy com., 1991—, vice-chair senate budget and taxation com., 1997-99, joint budget and audit com., 1991—, exec. nominations com., 1991—, joint protocol com., 1991—, chair, senate budget and tax., subcom. on pub. safety, transp., econ. devel. and natural resources, 1995-99, mem. joint com. on spending affordability, 1995—, mem. capital budget subcom., 1995—; mem. Gov.'s Motor Carrier Task Force, 1989—; conv. chair Nat. Order Women Legislators, 1980. Chair Women Legislators Caucus Md., 1982-84; trustee Adventist Health Care Mid-Atlantic, Takoma Park, Md.; bd. dirs. Ctrs. for Handicapped, Silver Spring, Md.; former internat. v.p. B'nai Brith Women. Recipient Cert. Appreciation Ctrs. for Handicapped, 1987, Meritorious Svc. award Safety and Survival, 1989, Cover Those Trucks award AAA Potomac, 1989, Leadership Laurel award Safety First Club Md., 1989, Woman of Valor award B'nai B'rith Women, 1991, Pub. Affairs award Planned Parenthood Md., 1992, ESOL support recognition Montgomery County Pub. Schs., 1992, Appreciation award Fraternal Order Police, 1992, John Dewey award Montgomery County Fedn. Tchrs., 1992, ARC of Md., 1992, Safety Leader award Advocates for Hwy. and Auto Safety, 1993, Disting. Svc. award Gov.'s Commn. Employment of People with Disabilities, 1993, award Faculty Guild U. Md. for support of faculty and univ., 1993, Sincere Appreciation award for commitment to Md.'s youth Md. Underage Drinking Prevention Coalition, 1994, Faithful Svc. to citizens Montgomery County award Montgomery County Assn. of Realtors, 1994; named Most Effective Pub. Ofcl. by residents of Silver Spring, 1990, one of 100 Most Powerful Women in Washington Metro Area by Washingtonian Mag., 1994, 97, Legislator of Yr. award Nat. Commn. Against Drunk Driving, 1995, Legislator of Yr. award Montgomery County Med. Soc., 1995, Carmen S. Turner Achievement in Cmty. Svc. award Montgomery County Dept. Transp., 1995, Safety Leader award Advocates for Hwy. and Auto Safety, 1996, Legislator of Yr. award AAA, Potomac, Md., 1997, Vince and Larry award Md. Com. for Safety Belt Use, 1997, Legislative Leadership award Montgomery County, 1998, Leadership award Olney Theater Ctr., 1998, Legislator of Yr. award Greater Montgomery County C. of C., 1999, Hwy. Safety Herd award Advocates for Hwy. and Auto Safety, 1999, One of Md.'s Top 100 Women, The Daily Record, 1994, 97, 2001, 03, Am. Lung Assn. Appreciation award in protecting youth from tobacco industry, 2000, Olney Theater honoree contbns. Olney Theatre and arts in Md., 2000, Pub. Policy Leadership award Am. Cancer Soc., 2002; M.A.D.D. Award of Exellence, 2002, Disting. Pub. Svc. award Am. Lung Assn. of Md., 2003, Disting. Legislator award Md. Impaired Driver Coalition, 2003, S. Robert Cohen award Jewish Found. Group Homes, 2004, Arts Stars award Montgomery Coll., 2004, others; named to Washington, Md., Del., Pa. Svc. Sta. Assn. Hall of Fame, 1994, Suburban Md. Transp. Priorities outstanding leadership in transp. pub. policy adminstrn., 2000; Md. Coll. Art and Design honoree, 2000. Mem. Coun. State Govts. (com. on suggested legislation), Hadassah. Democrat. Jewish. Home: 11 Schindler Ct Silver Spring MD 20903-1329 Office: Md State Senate 422 Miller Senate Office Bldg 11 Bladen St Annapolis MD 21401-8012 Office Phone: 301-858-3634. Business E-Mail: ida_ruben@senate.state.md.us.

**RUBEN, JEFFREY M.,** finance company executive, lawyer; b. 1963; BS, Pa. State U.; JD, Temple U. Bar: Pa. 1990. Assoc. Klehr, Harrison, Harvey, Brantzburg & Ellers; joined Am. Bus. Fin. Svcs., Bala Cynwyd, Pa., 1992; sr. v.p.; exec. v.p., gen. counsel, 1998—. Mem. ABA.

**RUBEN, LAWRENCE,** real estate developer, real estate company executive, lawyer; b. Bklyn., Sept. 28, 1926; s. Irving and Minnie (Sruelif) R.; m. Selma Belfer, Dec. 20, 1952 (dec. 2002); children: Richard Gordon, Lenore Denise, Rochelle Gail Ruben Kivell; m. Jan Gottlieb, Dec. 5, 2004. BA, NYU, 1949; LLB, Bklyn. Law Sch., 1951. Bar: N.Y. 1952. Gen. practice law, N.Y.C., 1952-53; pres. Ru-Min Constrn. Co., N.Y.C., 1953-54; exec. v.p. Belco Petroleum Corp., N.Y.C., 1954-64, dir., 1954-85; v.p. Fundamental Bldg. Corp., 1952—; pres. Randall Devel. Co., Aragon Devel. Corp., Lawrence Ruben Co., Inc.; ptnr. Lexington Madison Co., Tower Plaza Assocs., Devonshire Assocs., Boylston Ptnrs., Devonshire Constrn. Co. Inc., Lawrence Assocs., Granite Ptnrs., Inc., Harper-Lawrence; pres. Washington Mgmt. Corp. Mem. adv. NYU Real Estate Inst.; mem. Rockefeller U. Coun.; med. ctr. adv. bd. NY UJA; bd. Govs. Am. Jewish Com. Patron Albert Einstein Coll. Medicine; sponsor Grad. Sch. Sci.; bd. dirs. Cardoza Sch. Law at Yeshiva U.; chmn. United Jewish Appeal, Scarsdale, N.Y., 1974-75; mem. pres.'s coun. Meml. Sloan Kettering Cancer Ctr. With AUS, 1945-46. Mem. ABA, Fenway Golf Club, Boca Rio Golf Club, Harmonie Club. Office: 600 Madison Ave New York NY 10022-1615

**RUBEN, RICHARD S.,** lawyer; b. Bklyn., Jan. 21, 1950; BS magna cum laude, U. So. Calif., 1972; JD, UCLA, 1975. Bar: Calif. 1975. Ptnr. Pillsbury Winthrop Shaw Pittman LLP, Costa Mesa, Calif., mem. mng. bd., 1999—2003, ptnr. Litigation practice, sr. So. Calif. trial atty., 2005—. Adj. prof. Whittier Coll. Law Sch. Mem. Order of the Coif. Office: Pillsbury Winthrop Shaw Pittman 7th Fl 650 Town Center Dr Costa Mesa CA 92626 Office Phone: 714-436-6800. Office Fax: 714-436-2800. Business E-Mail: richard.ruben@pillsburylaw.com.

**RUBEN, ROBERT JOEL,** pediatric otorhinolaryngologist, educator; b. NYC, Aug. 2, 1933; s. Julian Carl and Sadie (Weiss) R.; children: Ann, Emily, Karin, Arthur. AB, Princeton U., 1955; MD, Johns Hopkins U., 1959. Intern Johns Hopkins Hosp., Balt., 1959-60, resident, 1960-64, dir. neurophysiology lab., div. otolaryngology, 1958-64; practice specializing in pediatric otorhinolaryngology N.Y.C., 1964—; asst. prof. otorhinolaryngology N.Y. U. Sch. Medicine, 1966-68; mem. staff hosps. Montefiore Med. Ctr., Bronx Med. Hosp. Ctr., N. Cen. Bronx Hosp., Montefiore Med., Jacobi Hosp., Bronx, NY, Children's Hosp. at Montefiore; prof., chmn. Montefiore Med. Ctr., Bronx Mcpl. Hosp. Ctr., N. Cen. Bronx, Bronx, 1979-99; prof. Montefiore Med. Ctr., Bronze Mcpl. Hosp. Ctr., N. Cen. Bronx, Bronx, NY, 1999—; prof. pediatrics Albert Einstein Coll. Medicine, Bronx, 1983—; assoc. prof. otorhinolaryngology N.Y.C., 1968-70, prof., chmn. dept. otolaryngology, 1970-98, prof. dept. otolaryngology, 1970—, mem. emeritus dept. otolaryngology, 1998—, disting. univ. prof., 1998—; prof. pediatrics Albert Einstein Coll. Medicine and Montefiore Med. Ctr., 1983—. Chmn. Nat. Com. for Rsch. and Neurol. and Communicative Disorders, pres., 1982-84; bd. dirs. Am. Bd. Otolaryngology-Head and Neck Surgery, 1989—; chmn. ENT devices com. FDA, 1993-96. Editor-in-chief: Internat. Jour. Pediatric Otorhinolaryngology, 1979—. Bd. dirs. N.Y. League Hard of Hearing, 1969-75, 76-85, Ctr. for Book Arts, 2006—; bd. dirs. Friends of Princeton U. Libr., chair, 2001-05. Served to surgeon USPHS, 1964-66. Recipient Rsch. award Am. Acad. Ophthalmology and Otolaryngology, 1962, Edmund Prince Fowler award Am. Rhinological-Laryngological-Otological Assn., 1973, Gold medal Best Didactic Film, IX World Congress Otorhinolaryngology, 1977, Pres.'s award Am. Acad. Otolaryngology-Head and Neck Surgery, 1992, Johns Hopkins U.

Soc. of Scholars, 1993, George E. Schambaugh Otology prize, 1996, Merit award Am. Otological, 2004, Sylvian Tchg. award, Senta, 2005, Presdl. citation Trio, 2005. Fellow ACS, N.Y. Acad. Medicine; mem. AMA, Am. Assn. Anatomists, Audiology Study Group N.Y. (pres. 1964-66), Acoustical Soc. Am., Am. Acad. Ophthalmology and Otolaryngology, Soc. Univ. Otolaryngologists, Am. Otol. Soc. (sec.-treas. rsch. fund 1979—, award of merit 2004), Soc. for Ear, Nose and Throat Advances in Children (pres. 1973), Assn. for Rsch. in Otolaryngology (pres. 1985-86), Am. Acad. Pediat. (chmn. otol. bronchoesphology 1983-85), Am. Soc. Pediat. Otolaryngology (historian 1986-95), Am. Soc. Pediat. Otolaryngologists (historian 1986-93, pres.-elect 1993-94, pres. 1994-95), Internat. Fedn. Otolaryngol. Socs. (chmn. com. on pediat. otolaryngology 2004—), Nat. Inst. Deafness and Other Comm. Disorders (adv. coun. 1989-93), Am. Laryngol. Soc., Grolier Club (mem. coun. 2005—), Explorers Club. Home: 1025 5th Ave Apt 12C S New York NY 10028-0134 Office: Montefiore Med Ctr 111 E 210th St Bronx NY 10467-2401 Office Phone: 718-920-2484. E-mail: ruben@aecom.yu.edu.

**RUBEN, ROBERT JOSEPH,** lawyer; b. N.Y.C., Apr. 9, 1923; m. Audrey H. Zweig, Nov. 20, 1949; children: Pamela, James. BS, Columbia U., 1943; MA, Harvard U., 1948; LL.B., Fordham U., 1953. Bar: N.Y. 1954. Exec. trainee Chase Nat. Bank, N.Y.C., 1948-49; economist, 1949-53; assoc. Milbank, Tweed, Hope & Hadley, N.Y.C., 1953-55; assoc., then ptnr. Shea & Gould, N.Y.C., 1955-90; sec. Gen. Battery Corp., Reading, Pa., 1963-73, Fiat Metal Mfg. Co., Inc., Plainview, N.Y., 1961-64, Filtors, Inc., East Northport, N.Y., 1961-64, Trans-Industries, Inc., 1969-2001, dir., 2001—06; asst. sec. Elgin Nat. Industries, 1975-88. Asst. Judge City Ct., Rye, N.Y., 1977-90; arbitrator Nat. Assn. Securities Dealers, 1990—, Pacific Stock Exch., 1992—, Am. Arbitration Assn., 1990—, N.Y. Stock Exch., 1994—. Trustee Rye Hist. Soc.; bd. dirs. Carver Center, Port Chester, N.Y., 1972-90. Served with AUS, 1943-46. Decorated Combat Inf. medal. Mem. AM, N.Y. State Bar Assn., Assn. Bar of City of N.Y., Harvard Club (N.Y.C.), Harvard-Radcliffe Club So. Calif., Columbia U. Club So. Calif., Beta Gamma Sigma, Zeta Beta Tau. Home: 21285 Amora Mission Viejo CA 92692-4930

**RUBENFELD, JED,** law educator; AB, Princeton U., 1980; JD, Harvard U., 1986. Law clk. for Judge Joseph T. Sneed US Ct. of Appeals (9th cir.), 1986—87; assoc. Wachtell, Lipton, Rosen & Katz, 1987—89; asst. US atty. US Atty.'s Office, So. Dist. NY, 1989—90; assoc. prof. Yale U., New Haven, 1990—94, prof. law, 1994—, Slaughter prof., 2000—. US rep. Coun. of Europe's Commn. on Democracy through Law. Author: Freedom and Time, 2001. Office: Yale Law Sch PO Box 208215 New Haven CT 06520 E-mail: jed.rubenfeld@yale.edu.

**RUBENFELD, STANLEY IRWIN,** lawyer, director, mediator, arbitrator; b. NYC, Dec. 7, 1930; s. George and Mildred (Rose) R.; children: Lise Susan, Kenneth Michael, Andrew James, Victoria Louise, Alexandria Elizabeth; m. Madeleine Conway, Nov. 5, 2000. BA, Columbia U., 1952, JD, 1956. Bar: N.Y. 1956. Practice law, N.Y.C., 1956—2002, 1965-68; assoc. Shearman & Sterling, 1956-65, ptnr. Paris, 1965-68, N.Y.C., 1968-93, of counsel, 1994—2002. Arbitrator and mediator NASD; mediator U.S. Fed. Ct., IRS Panel, CPR Panel; arbitrator NYSE, Internat. C. of C.; South Shore Music, Inc. Editor-in-chief Columbia Law Rev., 1955-56; contbr. articles to profl. jours. Past pres. Port Washington (N.Y.) Cmty. Chest; former bd. dirs. Residents for a More Beautiful Port Washington. Lt. (j.g.) USNR, 1952-54. Stone scholar, 1951-52, 54-55, 55-56; Rockefeller Found. grantee, 1955 Mem. ABA, N.Y. State Bar Assn. (tax sec., past chmn. fgn. activities com., reorgn. corp.), Assn. Bar City N.Y. (past chmn. com. on recruitment lawyers), Nat. Assn. Law Placement (past bd. dirs., exec. com.), Columbia U. Law Sch. Alumni Assn. (bd. visitors, adviser, past bd. dirs.), Columbia Coll. Alumni Assn., Tax Club (past chmn.), Phi Delta Phi, Tau Epsilon Phi (past pres.). Office Phone: 203-253-1053. E-mail: srubenfeld@optonline.net.

**RUBENS, SIDNEY MICHEL,** physicist, consultant; b. Spokane, Wash., Mar. 21, 1910; s. Max Zvoln and Jennie Golda (Rubinovich) R.; m. Julienne Rose Fridner, May 11, 1944; 1 child, Deborah Janet. BS, U. Wash., 1934, PhD, 1939. Instr. U. So. Calif., L.A., 1939—40; rsch. assoc. UCLA, 1940—41; physicist Naval Ordnance Lab., Washington, 1941—46, Engring. Rsch. Assocs., St. Paul, 1946—52; mgr. physics Univac divsn. Sperry Rand, St. Paul, 1958—61, dir. rsch., 1961-66, staff scientist, 1969—71, dir. spl. projects, 1971—75, cons., 1975—81; tech. advisor Vertimag Sys. Corp., 1981—, Advanced Rsch. Corp., Mpls., 1986—. Lectr. U. Pa., 1960-61; mem. adv. subcom. on instrumentation and data processing NASA, 1967-69; mem. panel on computer tech. NAS, 1969. Author: Amplifier and Memory Devices, 1965; contbg. author: Magnetic Recording—The First Hundred Years, 1999. Hon. fellow U. Minn., 1977—. Fellow IEEE (Magnetic Soc. info. storage award 1987, Millennium medal 2000); mem. AAAS, N.Y. Acad. Scis., Am. Phys. Soc., Am. Geophys. Union, Acad. Applied Sci., Minn. Acad. Sci., Am. Optical Soc., Phi Beta Kappa, Sigma Xi, Pi Mu Esilon. Achievements include patents in magnetic material and devices. Office: Advanced Research Corporation 4459 White Bear Pkwy Saint Paul MN 55110-7626

**RUBENSKY, MITCHELL,** band director; b. Bronx, Mar. 12, 1954; s. Herman H. and Norma Rubensky. MusB in Percussion, Manhattan Sch. Music, 1978; MusM, Herbert H. Lehman Coll., Bronx, 1984. Dir. music Frank D. Whalen Jr. HS, Bronx, 1982—2001; band dir. Bronx HS of Sci., 2001—. Chmn. student and tchr. programming Frank D. Whalen Jr. HS, 1995—2001. Recipient Prins. Pride of Music award, NYC Bd. Edn., Dist. 11, 1987, Edni. Svc. award, Assn. Jewish Profls., 2001, Edni. Leadership award, Jewish Tchrs. Cmty. Chest, 2004. Avocation: antique stereos. Office: Bronx HS Science 75 W 205th St Bronx NY 10468 Office Phone: 718-817-7700 ext. 517. E-mail: mir312@aol.com.

**RUBENSTEIN, ARTHUR HAROLD,** academic administrator, educator, dean, internist; b. Johannesburg, Dec. 28, 1937; arrived in U.S., 1967; s. Montague and Isabel (Nathanson) R.; m. Denise Hack, Aug. 19, 1962; children: Jeffrey Lawrence, Errol Charles. MB BCh, U. Witwatersrand, 1960, DSc (hon.) in Medicine, 2002. Diplomate Am. Bd. Internal Medicine. Intern, then resident Johannesburg Gen. Hosp., 1961, 63-65, 66-67; fellow in endocrinology Postgrad. Med. Sch., London, 1965-66; fellow in medicine U. Chgo., 1967-68, from asst. prof. to assoc. prof., 1968-74, prof., 1974-97, Lowell T. Coggeshall prof. med. sci., 1981-97, assoc. chmn. dept. medicine, 1975-81, chmn., 1981-97; attending physician Mitchell Hosp., U. Chgo., 1968-97; dean, CEO, Gustave L. Levy disting. prof. Mt. Sinai Sch. Medicine, N.Y.C., 1997—2001; exec. v.p., dean U. of Pa. Health Sys., Sch. of Med., Phila., 2001—. Mem. study sect. NIH, 1973-77, Hadassah Med. Adv. Bd., 1986-95, adv. coun. Nat. Inst. Arthritis, Metabolism and Digestive Diseases, 1978-80; chmn. Nat. Diabetes Adv. Bd., 1982, mem., 1981-83. Mem. editl. bd. Diabetes, 1973-77, Endocrinology, 1973-77, Jour. Clin. Investigation, 1976-81, Am. Jour. Medicine, 1978-81, Diabetologia, 1982-86, Diabetes Medicine, 1987-91, Annals of Internal Medicine, 1991-96, Medicine, 1992—; contbr. articles to profl. jours. Mem. Gov.'s Sci. Adv. Coun. State of Ill. 1989-96. Recipient David Rumbough Meml. award Juvenile Diabetes Found., 1978. Master ACP (John Phillips Meml. award 1995); fellow South African Coll. Physicians, Royal Coll. Physicians (London), N.Y. Acad. Medicine; mem. Am. Soc. for Clin. Investigation, Am. Diabetes Assn. (Eli Lilly award 1973, Banting medal 1983, Solomon Berson Meml. lectr. 1985), Brit. Diabetes Assn. (Banting lectr. 1987), Endocrine Soc., Am. Fedn. Clin. Rsch. Ctrl. Soc. Clin. Rsch. (v.p. 1988, pres. 1989), Assn. Am. Physicians (treas. 1984-89, councillor 1993-94, v.p. 1994-95, pres. 1995-96), Am. Bd. Internal Medicine (bd. govs. 1985-93, exec. com. 1990-93, chmn. 1992-93), Residency Rev. Com., Am. Acad. Arts and Scis., Am. Acad. Medicine (coun. 1991-96), Assn. Profs. Medicine (councillor 1991-94, v.p. 1994-95, pres. 1995-96, Robert Williams award 1997), Assn. Am. Med. Colls. (mem. coun. of deans adminstrv. bd. 2002—), Assn. Am. Acad. Health Ctrs. (chmn. bd. dirs. 2005—), Am. Clin. Climatology Assn. Office: U Penn School Med 295 John Morgan Bldg 3620 Hamilton Walk Philadelphia PA 19104 Office Phone: 215-898-6796. Business E-Mail: ahrdean@mail.med.upenn.edu.

**RUBENSTEIN, ATOOSA BEHNEGAR,** editor-in-chief; b. Iran, 1973; arrived in U.S., 1978; m. Ari Rubenstein, 1998. BA in Polit. Sci., Barnard Coll., 1993. Fashion asst., assoc. fashion editor, fashion edit to sr. fashion editor Cosmopolitan Mag., 1993—95; founding editor-in-chief CosmoGirl! mag., 1998—2003; editor-in-chief Seventeen Mag., 2003—. Office: Seventeen Mag 1440 Broadway 13th Fl New York NY 10018 Office Phone: 917-934-6601. Office Fax: 917-934-6650.*

**RUBENSTEIN, BERNARD,** orchestra conductor; b. Springfield, Mo., Oct. 30, 1937; s. Milton and Evelyn Marion (Friedman) R.; m. Ann Warren Little, Aug. 28, 1961; children: Tanya, Stefan Alexei. B.Mus. with distinction, Eastman Sch. Music, U. Rochester, 1958; M.Mus., Yale U., 1961. Assoc. prof. conducting, dir. orch. orgns. Northwestern U., Evanston, Ill., 1968-80; music dir. San Juan Symphony, Durango, Colo., 1997—2001, Farmington, N.Mex., 1997—2001, Fargo-Moorhead Symphony, 2003—. Asst. condr. R.I. Philharm. Orch., 1961-62; condr. music dir. Santa Fe Symphony Orch., 1962-64; condr. Greenwood Chamber Orch., Cummington, Mass., 1968-79; asst. condr. Stuttgart Opera, 1966-68; condr. music dir. Music for Youth, Milw., 1970-80; assoc. condr. Cin. Symphony Orch., 1980-86; music dir. Tulsa Philharm., 1984-96, condr. laureate, 1996—; music dir. San Juan Symphony, 1997-2001; guest condr. numerous orchs. including Milw. Symphony Orch., St. Paul Chamber Orch., Guadalajara Symphony Orch., Berlin Radio Orch., Frankfurt Radio Orch., Grant Park Orch., Chgo., die reihe, Vienna, Austrian Radio Orch., Eastman Philharm., Halle Symphony Orch., E. Ger., Warsaw Philharm., St. Louis Little Symphony, W. German Radio Orch., Palazzo Pitti Orch. Florence, Italy, Frankfurt Opera, Thououenstler Orch., Vienna, S.W. German Radio Orch., Baden-Baden, Jerusalem Symphony, Anchorage, Hamilton, Ont., Hartford Conn., L.A. Chamber Orch., Austin (Tex.) Symphony, Am. Composers Orch. N.Y.C., Nat. Opera of Mongolia, Cuban Nat. Symphony, Havana, Orquesta de Oriente, Santiago de Cuba. Winner internat. conducting competition Serate Musicale Fiorentine, 1965; Fulbright scholar, 1964-66; recipient Charles Ditson award Yale U., 1961, Martha Baird Rockefeller award, 1966-68 Mem. Am. Symphony Orch. League, Condrs. Guild. Office: 1070 Governor Dempsey Dr Santa Fe NM 87501-1078 E-mail: baton@ix.netcom.com.

**RUBENSTEIN, DAVID AARON,** military officer, healthcare administrator; b. Rockville Centre, N.Y., Nov. 23, 1954; s. Robert R. and Mona Sydney (Feder) R.; m. Patricia Barrier, Mar. 18, 1978; children: Sarah Elizabeth, William Robert. BS in Health Edn., Tex. A & M U., 1977; MHA, Baylor U., 1989; M of Mil. Arts and Sci., Command and Gen. Staff Coll., 1990. Commd. 2d lt. U.S. Army, 1977, advanced through grades to brig. gen., 2006, med. platoon leader 3d inf. div. Germany, 1977—79, ops. officer 3d med. battalion, 1979—80, pers. officer 307th med. battalion Ft. Bragg, NC, 1981—82, co. comdr., 1982—83, mil. instr. Acad. of Health Scis. Ft. Sam Houston, Tex., 1984—87, grad. student, 1987—88, adminstrv. resident William Beaumont Army Med. Ctr. Ft. Bliss, Tex., 1988—89, grad. student Command and Gen. Staff Coll. Ft. Leavenworth, Kans., 1989—90; adminstrv. asst. Office of the Army Surgeon Gen. Army Med. Svc. Corps, Washington, 1990—92; chief coordinated care Army Hosp., Ft. Belvoir, Va., 1992—93; hosp. comdr. 18th Mobile Army Surg. Hosp., Ft. Lewis, Wash., 1996—96; grad. student Army War Coll., Carlisle Barracks, Pa., 1996—97; dep. comdr. Eisenhower Army Med. Ctr., Ft. Gordon, Ga., 1997—99; hosp. comdr. 21st Combat Support Hosp., Ft. Hood, Tex., 1999—2001, Bosnia-Herzegovina, 1999—2000; cmdr. Landstuhl Regional Med. Ctr., Germany, 2001—03; chief of staff Europe Regional Med. Commd., 2003—04; cmdr. 30th Med. Brigade, 2004; asst. surgeon gen., 2005. Pres. Health Orgn. Network, El Paso, Tex., 1989, asst. surgeon gen. force sustainment, 2005; pres. Healthcare Execs. Ctrl. Savannah River Area, 1998-99; participant U.S. Army seminar Baylor U., Ft. Sam Houston, 1989. *As the Commanding General (CEO) for Europe Regional Medical Command, a two-hospital, 28 health clinic healthcare system, Brigadier General Rubenstein is responsible for all health care provided and managed by the Army in Germany and in 92 European countries. He recently received designation as an Honorary Healthcare Graduate Professor for Baylor University. He previously served as a Governor on the American College of Healthcare Executives' Board of Governors. The college is a 30,000 member professional society dedicated to the excellence of healthcare executives. He served as healthcare administration consultant to the Army Surgeon responsible for developing excellence in Army healthcare administration.* Author leadership seminar; reviewer books Lehigh U. Press, 1990, Mil. Rev. Jour., Mil. Medicine; contbr. articles to profl. jours. Religious lay leader Office of the Jewish Chapel, Ft. Bragg, 1982-83, Ft. Bliss, 1988-89, Ft. Leavenworth, 1989-90, Bosnia-Herzegovina, 1999-2000; fund drive coord. United Fund, Ft. Leavenworth, 1989; vol. Muscular Dystrophy Assn., Washington, 1990-91. Decorated Legion of Merit; recipient Fed. Healthcare Leadership award, 2003. Fellow: Am. Coll. Healthcare Execs. (regent 2000—02, gov. 2002—; Regent's award 1993); mem.: VFW, Assn. of U.S. Army, Am. Hosp. Assn., Assn. Mil. Surgeons of U.S. Republican. Jewish. Avocations: flying, running, history, reading. Office Phone: 210-221-6411. Business E-Mail: david.rubenstein@us.army.mil.

**RUBENSTEIN, DONALD P.,** lawyer; b. New Rochelle, NY, Apr. 6, 1958; BA magna cum laude, U. Pa., 1980; JD, Cornell U., 1985. Bar: Calif. 1985. Assoc. Bronson, Bronson & McKinnon, San Francisco, 1985—92, non-equity ptnr., 1992—93, equity ptnr., 1993—98; ptnr. Crosby Heafey Roach & May (combined with Reed Smith in 2003), San Francisco, 1998—2003, Reed Smith LLP, San Francisco, 2003—. No. Calif. practice group leader litig. group. Mem.: ABA, Bar Assn. San Francisco, State Bar Calif. Office: Reed Smith LLP Two Embarcadero Ctr Ste 2000 San Francisco CA 94111 Office Phone: 415-659-5946. Office Fax: 415-391-8269. Business E-Mail: drubenstein@reedsmith.com.

**RUBENSTEIN, EDWARD,** physician, educator; b. Cin., Dec. 5, 1924; s. Louis and Nettie Rubenstein; m. Nancy Ellen Millman, June 20, 1954 children: John, William, James. MD, U. Cin., 1947. House staff Cin. Gen. Hosp., 1947—50; fellow May Inst., Cin., 1950; sr. asst. resident Ward Med. Svc., Barnes Hosp., St. Louis, 1953—54; chief of medicine San Mateo County Hosp., Calif., 1960—70; assoc. dean postgrad. med. edn., prof. medicine Stanford (Calif.) U., 1971—, emeritus, active. Faculty Stanford Photon Rsch. Lab.; affiliated faculty Stanford Synchortron Radiation Lab., 1971—; maj. materials facilities com. NRC, 1984—85, Nat. Steering Com. 6 GeV Electron Storage Ring, 1986—. Author (textbook): Intensive Medical Care; editor: Synchrotron Radiation Handbook, 1988, vol. 4, 1991, Synchrotron Radiation in the Biosciences, Molecular Medicine; mem. editorial bd.: Sci. Am., Inc., 1991—94; editor (textbook): Sci. Am. Medicine, 1978—94; editor: (series) Molecular Cardiovascular Disease, 1995, Molecular Oncology, 1996, Molecular Neuroscience, 1998. With USAF, 1950—52. Named Disting. Scientist, SvrroMed, Inc., 2003; recipient Kaiser award for outstanding and innovative contbns. to med. edn., 1989, Albion Walter Hewlett award, 1993. Master: ACP (Laureate 2002); fellow: AAAS, Royal Soc. Medicine; mem.: Am. Clin. and Climatol. Assn., Soc. Photo-Optical Engrs., Western Assn. Physicians, Calif. Acad. Medicine, Inst. Medicine, APS, Alpha Omega Alpha. Achievements include research in mechanisms of autoimmunity, dysfunction of the choroid plexus and cerebrospinal fluid circulatory system, synchrotron radiation, nonprotein amino acids, and molecular chirality. Office: Stanford Med Ctr Dept Medicine Stanford CA 94305

**RUBENSTEIN, HOWARD JOSEPH,** public relations executive; b. NYC, Feb. 3, 1932; s. Samuel and Ada (Sall) R.; m. Amy Forman, Dec. 17, 1959; children: Roni, Richard, Steven. AB, U. Pa., 1953; student law, Harvard, 1953; LL.B. (Dean's scholar), St. Johns Sch. Law, 1959, LLD (hon.), 1990. Bar: NY 1960. Pres. Rubenstein Assocs., Inc. pub. rels. cons., N.Y.C., 1954—; asst. counsel judiciary com. U.S. Ho. of Reps.; mem. Gov.'s Fgn. Claims Commn., 1961-62; cons. joint legis. com. child care needs NY, 1965-66; adviser SBA, 1965-66. Mem. Gov.'s Com. on Sale of World Trade Ctr., 1981, Mayor's Com. on Holocaust Commemoration, 1981—, NY State Task Force on Energy Conservation, Dept. Housing, 1981-83, Mayor's Coun. Econ. Bus. Advisors, 1991-93; co-chmn. Holocaust Commn., 1993—; v.p. Jewish Cmty. Rels. Coun., 1988-94, advisor, 1995—; past dir. Brownsville

Boys Club; bd. dirs. Provide Addict Care Today, Police Athletic League, NY chpt. March of Dimes; active U.S. Internat. Coun., 1977-81, Commn. on Status of Women, 1982-89. NYC Commn. Operation Welcom Home, 1991; mem. Mayor's Bus. Adv. Coun., 1996—; advisor NY Commn. on Status of Women, 1995—; comm. advisor Gov.'s Coun. Jerusalem 3000, 1996-01; bd. dirs. Albert Einstein Coll. Medicine, 1997—; bd. govs. Jewish Cmty. Rels. Coun., 1999—; exec. com. Real Estate Bd. NY, 1985—, NYC & Co., 2001—, Partnership for NYC, 2004—. Mem. Assn. Better N.Y. (mem. exec. com. 1972—), Phi Beta Kappa, Beta Sigma Rho. Jewish (dir. congregation). Home: 993 5th Ave New York NY 10028-0105 Office: Rubenstein Assoc Inc 1345 Avenue Of The Americas New York NY 10105-0302 Office Phone: 212-843-8080.

**RUBENSTEIN, JACOB SAMUEL**, rabbi; b. Rosenheim, Germany, July 17, 1949; came to U.S., 1951; s. David and Eva (Bergman) R.; m. Deborah Powell, Sept. 1, 1969; children: Shira, Daniel, Jonathan, Yoheved. BA, Hebrew U., Jerusalem, 1972; MA, Harvard U., 1976. Ordained rabbi, 1972. Chief justices Ashkenazic and Sephardic Rabbinic Cts., Jerusalem, 1972; rabbi Congregation Beth Sholom, Milford, Mass., 1975-77, Providence, 1977-84, Young Israel of Scarsdale, N.Y., 1984—. Trustee Westchester Jewish Conf., White Plains, 1986-98; vice chmn. rabbinic adv. bd. N.Y. United Jewish Appeal Fedn., 1990-92, exec. officer Westchester Rabbinical Coun., 1986—; vice chmn. Nat. Rabbinic Cabinet of United Jewish Appeal, N.Y.C., 1990-93; pres. Westchester (N.Y.) Bd. Rabbis, 1990-93; nat. chmn. United Jewish Appeal-Rabbinic Cabinet, 1993-95, pres., 1995-96; pres. Rabbinical Coun. of Am., 1997-99, hon. pres. 1999-2000. Contbr. to: Rabbinical Council of America Sermon Manual, 1982, 84, 85, 87-88, 91-92, HaDarom, Torah for Today, 1990, Theological and Halaknic Reflections on the Holocaust; mem. Congl. Acad. Rev. Bd., 1986-89. Mem. Blue Ribbon Panel on Anti-Bias Crime, Westchester County-White Plains, N.Y., 1988; mem. adv. bd. Washington Inst. for Jewish Leadership and Values, 1988. Recipient City of Peace award Israel Bonds, 1978, Dr. and Mrs. Abraham Stern Svc. award Yeshiva U., 1983, Rabbinical Leadership award Ohr Hameir Theol. Sem., 1985, Rabbinic Svc. award United Jewish Appeal, 1987, Samuel W. and Rose Hurowitz award United Jewish Appeal Fedn., 1993, Ohev Torah award Ariel Am. Friends of Midrasha, 1995, award Nat. United Jewish Appeal, 1993, Orthodox Union Nat. Rabbinical Leadership Centennial medallion, 1999. Mem. Rabbinical Coun. Am. (exec. bd., chmn. legis. and pub. affairs coms. 1985-97), Religious Zionists Am., Inst. for Pub. Affairs (chmn. rabbinical adv. com. 1990-93), Bet Din of Am., The Orthodox Jewish Caucus. Office: Young Israel of Scarsdale 1313 Weaver St PO Box 103H Scarsdale NY 10583-8603 *Physical and social forces govern my life. But in the area of moral freedom, no matter how strong and overwhelming the limitations and mysteries, I can be sovereign, and under the burden of conditioning and conflict motivate my life.*

**RUBENSTEIN, JEROME MAX**, lawyer; b. St. Louis, Feb. 16, 1927; s. Jacob J. and Anne (Frankel) R.; m. Judith Hope Grand, July 31, 1954; children— Edward J., Emily Rubenstein Muslin, Sarah H. AB, Harvard U., 1950, LLB, 1955. Bar: Mo. 1956, U.S. Dist. Ct. (ea. dist.) Mo. 1956, U.S. Ct. Appeals (8th cir.) 1956. Mem. English lit. faculty U. So. Philippines, Cebu, 1950-51; law clk U.S. Dist. Ct., St. Louis, 1955-56; assoc. Lewis, Rice, Tucker, Allen & Chubb, St. Louis, 1956-64, Grand, Peper & Martin, St. Louis, 1964-65, ptnr., 1965-66; jr. ptnr. Bryan Cave, St. Louis, 1966-67, ptnr., 1968-97, of counsel, 1998—. Dir. Commerce Bank, N.A. Bd. dirs. Independence Ctr., St. Louis, 1985-88, The Arts and Edn. Coun. Greater St. Louis, 1991-99. Served with USN, 1945-46. Bd. dirs. Independence Ctr., St. Louis, 1985. Served with USN, 1945-46 Mem. ABA, Mo. Bar Assn., St. Louis Bar Assn., Mo. Athletic Club, Harvard Club of St. Louis (pres. 1982-83, bd. dirs. 1983-90). Jewish. Avocations: jogging, tennis. Home: 7394 Westmoreland Dr Saint Louis MO 63130-4240 Office: Bryan Cave 1 Metropolitan Sq Ste 3600 Saint Louis MO 63102-2750

**RUBENSTEIN, JOSHUA SETH**, lawyer; b. Bklyn., Aug. 5, 1954; s. Seth and Elaine (Freedman) Rubenstein; children: Mary-Jane, Kenan, Rebecca, Marlena, Isaac. BA magna cum laude, Columbia U., 1976, JD, 1979. Bar: NY 1980, NJ 1980, US Dist. Ct. (ea. and so. dist.) NY 1980, US Dist. Ct. NJ 1980, US Tax Ct. 1986. Assoc. Fried, Frank, Harris, Shriver & Jacobson, N.Y.C., 1979—82, KMZ Rosenman LLP, 1982—88; ptnr. KMZ Rosenman LLP (now Katten, Muchin Rosenman, LLP), 1989—, mem. mgmt. com., 1994—98, chmn., 1998—2002, chmn. trusts and estates dept., 1995—; mng. ptnr. Katten Muchin Rosenman LLP, N.Y.C., 2002—, Charlotte, NC, 2002. Mem. adv. com. surrogate's ct. Office Ct. Adminstrn., 1997—; mem. adv. coun. Law Sch. Trusts, Wills and Estate Planning Columbia U., 1997—; lectr. in field. Author: Answer Guide New York Surrogate's Court, 2004; contbr. articles to legal publ. Dir., sec. Irvington Inst. Med. Rsch., 1991, treas., 1991—92. sec., 1992—93, co-pres., 1993—94, pres., 1994—2000, vice-chmn., 2000—; mem. legis. com., mem. devel. com., mem. bd. governance com., mem. Madeleine Borg com., chmn., mem. exec. com., 1994—; mem. profl. adv. com. Lincoln Ctr., NY Philharm., Mus. Modern Art, Met. Mus. Art, Columbia U., Columbia U. Law Sch., Mus. Art and Design; chmn. estates and trust splty. group, chmn. splty. group task force, mem. exec. com. lawyers divsn. United Jewish Appeal-Fedn., 1989—99; trustee Jewish Bd. Family and Children's Svc., 1991, v.p., 1998—. Named Best Lawyers in NY, NY Mag.; recipient James H. Fogelson award, Lawyer's divsn. United Jewish Appeal Fedn., 1993, Trusts and Estate Lawyers award, 2001. Fellow: NY State Bar Found. (regent), Am. Coll. Trusts and Estate Counsel (mem. state laws com.); mem.: ABA, Soc. Trust and Estate Practitioners, Internat. Acad. Estate and Trust Law (academician 1997—), Assn. Bar City of NY, NJ Bar Assn. (real property and probate sect., mem. adv. com. rels. legis. and exec. brs.), NY State Bar Assn. (vice chmn. legis. com. 1988, chmn. 1988—91, co-chmn. ad hoc com. rev. proposals EPTL adv. com. N.Y. State 1991—, mem.-at-large exec. com. 1992—95, liaison to legis. policy com. 1995—, treas. 1997—98, sec. 1998—99, chair elect 1999—, chair 2000—01, trust and estate law sect. Pres.'s Pro Bono Svc. award 1991, Exec. Com. award 1992, 1995, 1996), Practising Law Inst. (mem. estate adv. com., lectr. 1984—), Hadassah estate planning seminar faculty and adv. bd. 1993—), Phi Beta Kappa. Democrat. Jewish. Office: Katten Muchin Rosenman LLP 575 Madison Ave New York NY 10022-2511 Office Phone: 212-940-7150. E-mail: joshua.rubenstein@kattenlaw.com.

**RUBENSTEIN, LEONARD**, engineering company executive; b. NYC, June 18, 1931; s. William and Sylvia (Jaffe) R.; m. Reva Scharf, Jan. 1951 (div. 1960); m. Geraldine Marilyn Porper, Aug. 14, 1965 (dec. Sept. 2000); children: Alan, Elaine, Philip, Ruth, Jennie. BS in Physics, Poly. Inst. N.Y., 1964. Registered profl. engr. NY, NJ, Del., Ga. Equipment engr. We. Elec., NYC, 1957-66; elec. engr. Gibbs & Hill, NYC, 1966-69; chief engr. Kiegl Lighting, NYC, 1969-72; project mgr. Stone & Webster, NYC, 1972-87; pres., prin. Rubenstein Engring. PC, NYC, 1975—; v.p. engring. Laramore Douglas & Popham, NYC, 1988-90; v.p., dir. engring. Gibbs & Hill, NYC, 1990-92; pres., prin. David Internat., 1990—; markter NPS, Florham Pk., NJ, 1992-95. Devel., pipeline project, Costanza, Romania, Trieste, Italy. Contbr. articles to profl. publs. Chmn. Walt Whitman Ind. Dems., Bklyn., 1966-68, chmn. West Bklyn. Ind. Dems., 1964-66; bd. dir. NY Gilbert & Sullivan Players, NYC, 1993—; chmn., bd. dirs. 450 West End Corp, 1984-88; mem. bd. mngr. McBurney YMCA, 1988-97. With US Army, 1951-53. Mem. IEEE (sr., chmn. NY sect. 1995-96, asst. editor Today's Engr. 1997-98, Region I award 1985, 94, 96), NSPE, Soc. Mfg. Engr. (charter mem. Vision Soc., sr. mem. Robotics Internat.), Power Engring. Soc. (chmn. NY/LI chpt. 1984-85). Achievements include development of first large scale waterless power plant; design of first commercial power plant using air stored in salt mine. Avocations: handball, music. Home and Office: 8 W 65th St New York NY 10023 E-mail: repl@nyc.rr.com.

**RUBENSTEIN, PAMELA SILVER**, manufacturing executive; b. Lansing, Mich., May 12, 1953; d. Neil M. and Leah Rebecca (Coffman) Silver; m. Alec Robert Rubenstein. BA in Linguistics, U. Mich., 1974; MA in teaching English to spkrs. of other langs., Columbia U. Tchrs. Coll., 1976; MA in Linguistics, U. Ill., 1978, doctoral studies in linguistics, 1978-80. Instr. Columbia U. Tchrs. Coll., N.Y.C., 1976, U. Ill., Urbana, 1978, libr. Linguistic

Dept., 1978-79; asst. libr. Ill. State Geol. Survey, 1979-80; tchr. Congregation Temple Israel, Springfield, Ill., 1980-81; adminstr., tchr. Springfield Bd. Jewish Edn., 1981-82; instr. Comm. Divsn. Lincoln Land C.C., Springfield, 1981-82; tchr. Cmty. Hebrew Sch., Charleston, SC, 1982-83; instr. The Citadel and Coll. of Charleston, 1983; legal sec. Gibbs & Holmes, Charleston, 1984, May, Oberfell & Lorber, South Bend, Ind., 1984-88; instr. U. Notre Dame, Ind., 1987; tchr. Triton Sch. Corp., Bourbon, Ind., 1988-89; v.p., asst. treas. Allied Splty. Precision, Inc., Mishawaka, Ind., 1989—2005, CEO, owner, 2005—. Contbr. articles to profl. jours. Mem. Temple Beth-El Sisterhood, South Bend, Ind., 1987—. Mem.: Nat. Tooling and Machining Assn. (mem. edn. team, audit team 2005—, bd. mem., Mich. chpt. 2004—), Hadassah (life). Office: Allied Splty Precision Inc 815 E Lowell Ave Mishawaka IN 46545-6480 Office Phone: 574-255-4718. Business E-Mail: pam.rubenstein@aspi-nc.com.

**RUBENSTEIN, STEVEN PAUL**, newspaper columnist; b. LA, Oct. 31, 1951; s. Victor Gerald and Florence (Fox) R.; m. Caroline Moira Grannan, Jan. 1, 1989; children: William Laurence, Anna Katherine. BA, U. Calif. Berkeley, 1977. Reporter L.A. Herald Examiner, 1974-76, San Francisco Chronicle, 1976-81, columnist, 1981—. Office: San Francisco Chronicle 901 Mission St San Francisco CA 94103-2905

**RUBENSTEIN, WILLIAM S.**, lawyer; b. NYC, 1955; BA, Fairleigh Dickinson U., 1978; JD cum laude, Benjamin N. Cardozo Sch. Law, 1981. Bar: NY 1981. Co-head, banking/savings and loans mergers and aquisitions Skadden, Arps, Slate, Meagher & Flom LLP, NYC. Notes and comment editor: Cardozo Law Rev., 1981. Office: Skadden Arps Slate Meagher & Flom LLP 4 Times Sq New York NY 10036 Office Phone: 212-735-2642. Office Fax: 212-735-2000. Business E-Mail: wrubenst@skadden.com.

**RUBERG, ROBERT LIONEL**, surgery educator; b. Phila., July 22, 1941; s. Norman and Yetta (Wolfman) R.; m. Cynthia Lief, June 26, 1966; children: Frederick, Mark, Joshua. BA, Haverford Coll., Pa., 1963; MD, Harvard U., 1967. Diplomate Am. Bd. Surgery, Am. Bd. Plastic Surgery. Instr. surgery U. Pa., Phila., 1972-75; asst. prof. Ohio State U., Columbus, 1975-81, assoc. prof., 1981-88, prof., 1988—. Bd. dirs. Am. Bd. Plastic Surgery, 1991-97, vice-chair, 1996-97; chmn. curriculum com. Coll. Medicine, Ohio State U., 1984-97; chief plastic surgery Ohio State U. Hosps., 1985—. Plastic Surgery Ednl. Found. research grantee, 1976, 78. Fellow ACS; mem. Am. Assn. Plastic Surgeons, Assn. Acad. Chairmen of Plastic Surgery (pres. 1994-95), Plastic Surgery Edn. Found. (pres. 2000-01). Avocation: bicycling. Home: 100 Walnut Woods Ct Gahanna OH 43230-6200 Office: N325-B Means Hall 1654 Upham Dr Columbus OH 43210

**RUBIN, ALAN A.**, pharmaceutical and biotechnology consultant; b. NYC, July 10, 1926; s. Harry and Gertrude R.; m. Helen M. Feinstein; children: Jeffrey, Ronald, Howard. BS, NYU, 1950, MS, 1953, PhD, 1959. Pharmacologist Schering Corp., Bloomfield, N.J., 1954-64; dir. pharmacology Endo Labs., Garden City, N.Y., 1964-70, v.p. rsch., 1970-74; dir. rsch. DuPont Pharms., Wilmington, Del., 1974-82, dir. sci. info. and tech., 1982-87; dir. licensing tech. DuPont Merck Pharms., Wilmington, Del., 1987-91; pres. ARA Assoc., Rockland, Del., 1991—. Bd. dirs. Redox Pharms., Greenvale, N.Y. Editor: Search for New Drugs, 1972, New Drugs: Discovery and Development, 1978; contbr. articles to profl. jours. With U.S. Army, 1944-46. Mem. AAAS, Am. Soc. Pharmacology and Exptl. Therapeutics, Soc. Exptl. and Biol. Medicine. N.Y. Acad. Sci. Home: 207 Hitching Post Dr Wilmington DE 19803-1914 Office: ARA Assoc PO Box 244 Rockland DE 19732-0244 Personal E-mail: alannar@msn.com.

**RUBIN, ALBERT LOUIS**, internist, nephrologist, educator; b. Memphis, May 9, 1927; s. Malcolm M. and Sarah Anne (Bryan) R.; m. Carolyn M. Diehl, Sept. 28, 1953; 1 child, Marc. Student, Williams College, 1944-45, MIT, 1945-46; MD, Cornell U., 1950. Diplomate Am. Bd. Internal Medicine. Intern Bellevue Hosp., N.Y.C., 1950-51, resident internal medicine, 1951-54, fellow nephrology, 1954-55, physician-in-charge, 1953-61; established investigator Am. Heart Assn., N.Y.C., 1958-63; dir. Rogosin Labs., Cornell U. Med. Coll., N.Y.C., 1963—, The Rogosin Kidney Ctr., N.Y.C., 1971—, The Rogosin Inst., N.Y.C., 1989—; prof. biochemistry, surgery, medicine Cornell U. Med. Coll., N.Y.C., 1969—; surgeon The N.Y. Hosp., N.Y.C., 1969—. Com. on sci. and tech. aspects of processing materials in space NRC, NYC; dir. affiliations and patient referrals N.Y. Hosp.-Cornell Med. Ctr., 1977-80; bd. dirs., bd. incorporators neurosci. rsch. program MIT. Author: Physical Diagnosis: A Textbook and Workbook in Methods of Clinical Examination, 1972, Humoral Aspects of Transplantation, 1976, Manual of Clinical Nephrology, 1980; cons. editor Am. Jour. Medicine, Time mag., 1959-94. With USN, 1944-45. Recipient Hoeing award Nat. Kidney Found., 1982. Mem. ACP, AAAS, Am. Soc. for Artificial Internal Organs, Transplantation Soc., Sigma XI. Home: 220 Allison Ct Englewood NJ 07631-4301 Office: The Rogosin Inst 505 E 70th St 2d Fl Rm 230 New York NY 10021-9809 Business E-Mail: rubina@mail.rockefeller.edu.

**RUBIN, ARKADY**, biostatistics and data management researcher, executive; b. St. Petersburg, Russia, Jan. 29, 1955; s. Mikhail Rubin and Mikhalina Rubina. BS in econ., Inst. of Nat. Economy, 1972—76, PhD, 1983—86. Prin. biostatistician Johnson & Johnson, Raritan, NJ, 1991—98; assoc. dir. biostatistics Pfizer, NYC, 1998—2003; exec. dir., biostatistics and data mgmt. NovaDel Pharma, Flemington, NJ, 2003—. Contbr. articles to profl. jours. Recipient Corp. award for the design of the low dose contraceptive clin. program, Johnson & Johnson, 1997. Mem.: Am. Statis. Assn. Achievements include design of clinical program for the contraceptive patch currently marketed as Evra; clinical program Norvasc/Lipitor combination pill (trade name Caduet); clinical program for the low-dose oral contraceptive currently marketed as Ortho Tri-Cyclen Lo; patents for Ortho Tri-Cyclen Lo. Office: NovaDel Pharma 25 Minneakoning Rd Flemington NJ 08822 Home: 964 Concord Way Branchburg NJ 08853-4173 E-mail: arubin@novadel.com.

**RUBIN, ARTHUR HERMAN**, retired academic administrator; b. NYC, Aug. 14, 1927; s. Samuel and Bessie (Moritt) R.; m. Janice Levy, Apr. 9, 1950 (div. 1965); children: Renee Ellen, Linda Joy; m. Audrey M. Schmidt, July 1, 1973. BS, NYU, 1950, MA, 1951. Adminstrv. asst. to asst. dean Sch. Edn. NYU, 1947-54, lab. asst. bus. edn. dept., 1950-54, instr., 1954-56, program dir. grad. students orgn., 1954-63, dir. tours, 1955-58, coord. summer sessions activities, 1959-64, dir. Bur. Pub. Occasions, 1963-74, asst. v.p. pub. occasions, 1974-75, dir. extramural affairs Coll. Dentistry, 1976, assoc. dean adminstrn., 1976-80, adj. asst. prof. behavioral scis. and cmty. health, 1976-80, dir. alumni rels. Sch. of Med., 1980-95, dir. spl. events med. ctr., 1988-95; cons. to Office Alumni Rels. NYU Sch. Medicine, 1995-2000; cons. to Office Spl. Events, NYU Med. Ctr., 1995-2000, ret., 2000. Tchr. Patrick Henry Jr. High Sch., N.Y.C., 1949-58; acting asst. prin. Robert F. Wagner Jr. High Sch., N.Y.C., 1958-63; cons. in field. Trustee Agnew Found., 1967—; mem. Great Valley coun. Girl Scouts U.S., 2005—; mem. exec. bd., sec. Harris York Condominium Assn., 1998—99, mem. exec. bd., treas., chmn coms., 2001—06. Recipient NYU Presdl. citation, 1971, GSO award, 1980, Ernest O. Melby award Sch. Edn. Alumni Assn., 1976, citation Bus. Edn. Assn. Met. N.Y., 1976, Sesquicentennial award NYU Alumni Fedn., 1982, Meritorious Svc. award, 1985, dir. Emeritus citation, 1992. Mem. Ea. Bus. Tchrs. Assn. (chmn. exhibits 1953-74, exec. bd. 1969-71, pres. 1972-73, award 1974), Bus. Edn. Assn. Met. N.Y. (exec. bd. 1962-83), Nat. Bus. Edn. Assn. (exec. bd. 1972-74, conv. mgr. 1974-92, Disting. Svc. award 1992, Cert. of Appreciation 1992), N.Y. Acad. Pub. Edn. (bd. dirs. 1979-98, pres. 1992-94), NYU Edn. Alumni Assn. (v.p. 1961-62, 64-67), NYU Club (bd. govs. 1972-78, 79-89, v.p. 1985-86, chmn. bd. 1986-87), Delta Pi Epsilon Rsch. Found. Inc. (bd. dirs. 1990-92), Delta Pi Epsilon (Svc. awards Alpha chpt. 1971, 81). Home: 2605 Houghton Lean Macungie PA 18062-9506

**RUBIN, ARTHUR LEONARD**, systems engineer, mathematician; s. Herman and Jean Estelle Rubin; m. Ronni Petitt, July 10, 1987. PhD, Calif. Inst. of Tech., 1978. Programmer Purdue U. Computer Ctr., West Lafayette, Ind., 1971—72; sr. engr. Jet Propulsion Lab., Pasadena, Calif., 1973—82; sr. mem.

tech. staff Aerojet ElectroSystems, Azusa, Calif., 1982—86; programmer cons. Fin. News Network, Los Angeles, 1987—90; contract programmer IdealSoft, Alhambra, Calif., 1987—89; engring. specialist - software Beckman Instruments, Brea, Calif., 1990—95; rsch. engr. sr. staff Lockheed Martin, Goodyear, Ariz., 1996—2000; prin. sys. engr. Raytheon, Fullerton, Calif., 2000—. Contbr. scientific papers. Recipient 4th Pl., USA H.S. Math. Olympiad, 1972; Putnam fellow, 1970—73. Mem.: IEEE, Math. Assn. of Am., Mensa (life; area sec. 1976—78). Libertarian. Jewish. Achievements include patents pending for methods and apparatus for evaluating operational integrity of a data processing system using moment bounding. Avocation: filksinging (science fiction folksinging). Office: Raytheon 1801 Hughes Dr Fullerton CA 92833 Office Phone: 714-446-4218. Personal E-mail: ronnirubin@sprintmail.com.

**RUBIN, AVIEL DAVID**, computer science educator, writer; b. Manhattan, Kans., Nov. 8, 1967; BS in Computer Sci. (hon.), U. Mich., Ann Arbor, 1989, MSE in Computer Sci., Engring., 1991, PhD in Computer Sci., Engring., 1994. Tchg. asst. U. Mich., 1988—93; programmer, Meyers Corners Lab IBM, Poughkeepsie, NY, 1989; programmer Great Lakes Software Co., Howell, Mich., 1989; mem., cryptography and network security rsch. group Bellcore, 1990; adj. prof. NYU, 1995—99; mem., secure systems rsch. dept. AT&T Labs-Rsch., 1997—2002; assoc. prof., dept. computer sci. John Hopkins U., 2003—04, prof., dept. computer sci., 2004—; tech. dir. John Hopkins U. Info. Security Inst., 2003—. Vis. prof. École Normale Supérieure, Paris, 1999; bd. dir. USENIX Orgn., 2000—04; mem. AT&T Internet Intellectual Property Review, 1999—2001, Govt. Infosec Sci. and Tech. Study Group on Malicious Code, 1999—2000, DARPA Info. Sci. and Tech. Study Group, 2003—06, Security Peer Review Group of the Fed. Voting Assistance Program's Secure Electronic Registration and Voting Experiment Project, 2003—04; mem. steering group ISOC Symposium on Network and Distributed System Security, 2001—04; mem. adv. bd. Info. Security and Cryptography Book Series, 2001—06; mem. exec. com. DIMACS workshop series with spl. focus on network security, 2002—04; mem. technical adv. boards, including Tablus, Site Advisor, Neopath Networks, Hx Technologies, Fortify Software, Bodymedia, Authentica and Arbor Networks; invited spkr. in field; panelist in field. Author: (books) White-hat Security Arsenal, 2001, Brave New Ballot: The Battle to Safeguard Democracy in the Age of Electronic Voting, 2006; co-author: Web Security Sourcebook, 1997, Peer-to-Peer, 2001, Firewalls and Internet Security: Repelling the Wily Hacker, 2nd edit., 2003; contbr. chapters to books, articles to profl. jours.; refereed conf. and jour. publs., mem. editl. bd. Bellcore Security Update Newsletter, 1995—96, Jour. of Privacy Tech., 2004—06, co-editor Electronic Newletter of the IEEE Technical Com. on Security & Privacy, 1998, assoc. editor Electronic Commerce Rsch. Jour., 1999—2002, mem. for Computing Machinery Transactions on Internet Tech., 2002—05, IEEE Security & Privacy Mag., 2003—, IEEE Transactions on Software Engring., 2005—06, guest editor Communications of the Assn. for Computing Machinery, Spl. Issue on Wireless Networking Security, 2003, guest co-editor IEEE Security & Privacy Mag., Spl. Issue on Electronic Voting Security, 2004, IEEE Computer, Securing the High-Speed Internet, 2004, mem. editl. and adv. bds. Internat. Jour. Info. and Computer Security, 2004—06. Election judge, Baltimore County; dir. ACCURATE, A Ctr. for Correct, Usable, Reliable, Auditable and Transparent Elections, funded by Nat. Sci. Found. Co-recipient Co-author of Best Student Paper, Building Systems that Flexibly Control Downloaded Executable Content, 6th USENIX UNIX Security Symposium, 1996, Best Paper award & Best Student Paper award, The Design and Analysis of Graphical Passwords, 8th USENIX Security Symposium, 1999, Best Paper award, A Robust, Tamper-Evident and Censorship-Resistant Web Publishing System, 9th USENIX Security Symposium, 2000, Best Student Paper award, Security Analysis of a Cryptographically-Enabled RFID Device, 14th USENIX Security Symposium, 2005; named Baltimorean of Yr., Baltimore Mag., 2004; recipient Index on Censorship Freedom of Expression award for the Best Circumvention of Censorship for the Publius project, 2001, Pioneer award, Electronic Frontiers Found., 2004. Achievements include patents in field. Avocations: pool, golf, tennis, soccer, piano. Office: John Hopkins U Whiting Sch Engring Dept Computer Sci Office NEB 224 3400 N Charles St Baltimore MD 21218-2681 Office Phone: 410-516-8177. Office Fax: 443-264-2406. Business E-Mail: rubin@jhu.edu.*

**RUBIN, BENJAMIN ARNOLD**, microbiologist, immunologist, medical educator, researcher; b. NYC, Sept. 27, 1917; s. Eli and Helen Sarah (Arenoff) R.; m. Mae Koenig, Aug. 31, 1951. BS, CCNY, 1937; MS, Va. Polytech. Inst. & State U., 1938; PhD, Yale U., 1947. Asst. dir. Circle Analytical Lab., N.Y.C., 1938-40; chief lab. and radiology U.S. Army C.E., Nfld., also Cen. Am., 1940-44; asst. chief microbiologist Scherly Rsch. Lab., Lawrenceburg, Ind., 1944; rsch. asst. Yale U., New Haven, 1944-47; chief microbiologist Broockhaven Nat. Lab., L.I., 1947-52, Syntex, Mexico City, 1952-54; prof. pub. health and preventitive medicine Coll. of Medicine Baylor U., Houston, 1954-60; mgr. biol. rsch. Wyeth, Radnar, Pa., 1960-84; rsch. prof. Phila. Coll. Osteo. Medicine, 1984-95; ret. Cons. GE, Valley Forge, Pa., 1972-80, U.S. Congressional com. energy and commerce, 1976-80, biological applications of space. Contbr. over 150 articles to sci. jours. Named to Inventors Hall of Fame, 1992; recipient John Scott award and medal, 1982, Proctor medal Phila. Drug Exchange, 1993; named Inventor of Yr., 1985. Achievements include invention of bifurcated needle in Smallpox eradication program. Home: 50 Belmont Ave Apt 601 Bala Cynwyd PA 19004-2428 Office: Phila Coll Osteo Medicine 4150 City Ave Philadelphia PA 19131-1610

**RUBIN, CATHY ANN**, retired secondary school educator; b. Denver, July 17, 1948; d. Harry Phillip and Charlotte Ruth (Brinig) R. BA, Colo. State U., 1970; MA, U. No. Colo., 1971. Cert. tchr. Colo. Tchr. Adams County Dist. 50 Schs., Westminster, Colo., 1971-72; tchr. educationally handicapped Jefferson County Pub. Schs., Golden, Colo., 1972-98. Typist, bookkeeper Kenmark-Shaw's Jewelers, Denver, 1966—. Sec.-treas. Hillel Found., 1979-81; fundraiser Women's Am. Orgn. for Rehab. through Tng., Denver, 1979—; bookkeeper Religious Coalition for Abortion Rights, Denver, 1982-90; vol. TV PBS sta., Denver, 1978, Muscular Dystrophy Assn., Colo. AIDS Project; vol. usher DCTC, 1999—; vol. for the blind and dyslexic, 2005-. Democrat. Jewish. Avocations: music, reading, sailing, knitting, needlepoint. Home: 3500 S Ivanhoe St Denver CO 80237-1123

**RUBIN, CHANDA**, professional tennis player; b. Lafayette, La., Feb. 18, 1976; d. Edward and Bernadette Rubin. Grad., Episcopal Sch. Acadiana, 1993. Mem. USTA Jr. Devel. Team, 1989, USTA Nat. Team, 1990; prof. tennis player, 1991—. Mem. U.S. Pan Am. Team, 1995, U.S. Fed Cup Team, 1995—97, 1999, 2003—04, U.S. Olympic Team, Atlanta, 1996, U.S. Women's Olympic Tennis Team, Athens, 2004. Founder The Chanda Rubin Found. Recipient 3 U.S. Jr. Titles; winner U.S. nat. title and Rolex Orange Bowl 12s crown, 1988; named Most Improved Female Player, Tennis Mag., 1995, Female Athlete of Yr., U.S. Tennis Assn., 1995, Most Caring Athlete, USA Weekend Mag., 1997; finalist (with Testud) U.S. Open.; winner 7 Career Singles titles and 10 Career Doubles titles, WTA Tour. Office: USTA 70 W Red Oak Ln White Plains NY 10604-3602 also: Advantage International 1751 Pinnacle Dr Ste 1500 Mc Lean VA 22102-3833

**RUBIN, CHARLES ALEXIS**, writer; b. L.A., Dec. 4, 1953; s. Herbert Bernard and Jacqueline (Bashor) R.; m. Doris Sara Villalobos, July 23, 1978; 1 child, Daniel Charles. BA in English magna cum laude, San Francisco State U., 1978, MA in English, 1980. Communications supr. Am. Protective Services, Oakland, Calif. 1982-83; assoc. editor Personal Computing mag., San Jose, 1983-84; free-lance writer Oakland, 1984—; sr. assoc. Waterside Assocs., Fremont, Calif., 1986-87; sr. analyst Internet Rsch. Group, Los Altos, Calif., 1999-2002; sr. strategist Gallagher Pub. Rels., Alameda, Calif., 2000—02; ptnr. Gallagher Group Pub. Rels., Alameda, Calif., 2002—04, Story Comm., Oakland, Calif., 2004—. Editorial com. Televisual Market Strategies, Saratoga, 1985-86. Author: The Endless Apple, 1984, Thinking Small: The Buyer's Guide to Portable Computers, 1984, Appleworks: Boosting Your Business with Integrated Software, 1985, Command Performance: Appleworks, 1986, Microsoft Works, 1986, Macintosh Hard Disk Management, 1988, Running Microsoft Works, 1990, The Macintosh Bible

(What Do I Do Now?), 1990, The Macintosh Bible Guide to System 7, 1991, The Macintosh Bible Guide to File Maker Pro, 1991, The Macintosh Bible Guide to Clarisworks, 1993, The Little Book of Computer Wisdom, 1994, Guerrilla Marketing Online Weapons, 1996, Guerrilla Marketing Online, 1997, Managing Your Business with Quickbooks, 1998, Running Microsoft Word 2000, 1999. Democrat. Jewish. Home: 1053 Tahiti Ln Alameda CA 94502-6911 Business E-Mail: charlie@storypr.com.

**RUBIN, DAVID LEE,** humanities educator, critic, editor; b. Indpls., Sept. 30, 1939; s. Ira Bertram and Jeanne Iva (Gamso) R.; m. Carolyn Dettman, June 12, 1965; 1 child, Timothy Craig. BA, U. Tenn., 1962; cert., U. Paris, 1963; MA, U. Ill., 1964, PhD, 1967. Instr. French U. Ill., Urbana, 1966-67; asst. prof. U. Chgo., 1967-69, U. Va., Charlottesville, 1969-74, assoc. prof., 1974-82, prof. French, 1982-2001, mem. Fulbright selection com., 1996—, mem. com. on comparative lit., 1997-2001, prof. emeritus, assoc. univ. seminar program, 2001—; seminar dir. Folger Inst., 1989. Chair poetry bd. Va. Quar. Rev., 2003—; Great Books discussion leader Jefferson Inst. Lifelong Learning, U. Va., 2001-; assoc. ctr. advanced studies U. Va., 1979, 80-81, 87, 93, 99-2000; pub., editor-in-chief Rookwood Press, 1992—; cons. PMLA Can. Coun., Etudes littéraires françaises, NEH, numerous univ. presses; lectr., spkr. in field. Author: Higher Hidden Order, 1972, The Knot of Artifice, 1981, A Pact with Silence, 1991; editor: The Selected Poetry and Prose of John T. Napier, 1972, La poésie française du premier 17e siècle, 1986, 2d edit., 2006, Sun King, 1991; co-editor: La Cohérence Intérieure, 1977, Convergences, 1989, The Ladder of High Designs, 1991, The Fulbright Difference, 1993; founding editor Continuum, 1989-93, EMF: Studies in Early Modern France, 1994-2002, EMF Critiques, 1994-2002, Rookwood Texts, 1997—, Rookwood Reprints, 2002—; mem. editl. bd. Purdue Studies in Romance Literatures, 1975-2001, Oeuvres et Critiques, 1976-2001, French Rev., 1986 94; Am. corr. Cahiers Maynard, 1973-2001, Cahiers Tristan L'Hermite, 1989-2001; contbr. articles to profl. jours., chpts. to books. U.S. State Dept. Fulbright fellow, 1963—64, fellow, Woodrow Wilson Found., 1963—64, Guggenheim Found., 1980—81, Hewlett fellow, summer, 1997, The Shape of Change: Studies in Honor of David Lee Rubin, 2002. Mem. MLA, ACLU, Phi Beta Kappa. Avocations: reading, exercise. Home: 520 Rookwood Pl Charlottesville VA 22903-4734 Personal E-mail: dlr93039@yahoo.com.

**RUBIN, DONALD BRUCE,** statistician, educator, research and development company executive; b. Washinton, Dec. 22, 1943; s. Allan A. and Harriet Rubin; m. Kathryn M. Kazarow; children: Scott Wilk, Paul Stuart. AB magna cum laude, Princeton U., 1965; MS, Harvard U., 1966, PhD, 1970. Rsch. statistician Ednl. Testing Svc., Princeton, NJ, 1971-75, chmn. stats., 1975-79, sr. statis. advisor, 1979-81; pres. Datamatrics Rsch. Inc., Waban, Mass., 1981—; prof. U. Chgo., 1982-84, Harvard U., Cambridge, Mass., 1984—, chmn. stats., 1985-94, 2000—, John L. Loeb Prof. Stats., 2002—. Author: Handling Nonresponse in Sample Surveys by Multiple Imputation, 1980, Multiple Imputation for Nonresponse in Surveys, 1987, classic edit., 2004; author: (with others) Incomplete Data in Sample Surveys (Vol. 2): Theory and Bibliography, 1983; co-author: (with R.J.A. Little) Statistical Analysis With Missing Data, 1987, 2d edit., 2002, (with A. Gelman, J. Carlin, H. Stern) Bayasian Data Analysis, 1995, 2d edit., 2003, (with R. Rosenthal and R. Rosnow) Contrasts and Effect Sites in Behavioral Research: A Correlational Approach, 2000, Matched Sampling for Causal Effects, 2006; co-editor: (with P.W. Holland) Test Equating, 1982; contbr. over 300 articles to profl. jours. Recipient Parzen prize for statis. innovation, 1996; Woodrow Wilson Grad. fellow, 1965; NSF Grad. fellow, 1965, 68, John Simon Guggenheim fellow, 1977-78. Fellow AAAS (chmn. stats. 1992), Am. Statis. Assn. (editor jour. 1980-82, dir. 1980-82, statistician of yr. Boston chpt. 1995, Chgo. chpt. 2000, S.S. Wilks medal 1995), Inst. Math. Stats. (coun. mem. 1990-92, 99-2001, Fisher lectr. 2004); mem. NAS (com. on nat. stats. 1989-92, mem. panel on confidentiality data 1989-92, panel on bilingual edn. 1990-92, working group on statis. analysis of com. on basic rsch. in behavioral and social scis. 1985-86, panel statis. in 21st century 1995, other coms.), AAAS, Am. Acad. Arts and Sci., Biometric Soc., Internat. Assn. Survey Statisticians, Internat. Statis. Inst., Psychometric Soc., Royal Statis. Soc. Office: Harvard U Dept Statistics Cambridge MA 02138 E-mail: rubin@stat.harvard.edu.

**RUBIN, DOROTHY MOLLY,** language educator, writer; b. NYC, Feb. 11, 1932; d. Harry and Clara (Schweller) Schleimer; m. Arthur I. Rubin, Aug. 24, 1950; children: Carol Anne, Sharon Anne. Student, CUNY, 1949—51; BA, Rutgers U., 1959, MEd, 1961; PhD in Ednl. Psychology, Johns Hopkins U., 1968. Tchr. N.J. pub. schs., 1959—62; asst. prof. Coppin State Coll., Md., 1962—63, Towson State Coll., Md., 1963—66; adj. prof. Rollins Coll., Fla., 1968—69; assoc. prof. Ewing Coll. N.J., 1969—73, prof., 1973—. Cons.harper & Row, 1983; cons., spkr., columnist. Author: Teaching Elementary Language Arts, 1975, 6th edit., 2000, Gaining Word Power, 1978, 7th edit., 2006, The Vital Arts-Reading and Writing, 1979, Reading and Learning Power, 1980, 3d edit., 1991, The Teacher's Handbook of Reading-Thinking Exercises, 1980, The Primary-Grade Teacher's Language Arts Handbook, 1980, The Intermediate Grade Teacher's Language Arts Handbook, 1980, Gaining Sentence Power, 1981, The Teacher's Handbook of Primary-Grade Reading/Thinking Exercises, 1982;: Vocabulary Expansion, 1982, A Practical Approach to Teaching Reading, 1982, 2d edit., 1993, Diagnosis and Correction in Reading Instruction, 1982, 4th edit., 2002, Teaching Reading and Study Skills in Content Areas, 1983:; 2d edit., 1991, Writing and Reading: The Vital Arts, 2d edit., 1983, Power English: Basic Language Skills for Adults, 1989, rev. edit., 1990, Power Vocabulary: Basic Vocabulary for Adults, 1992—93, Comprehension Strategies for an Integrated Language Arts Classroom, 1994, Mind Bind, Moon Master, Quick Scramble, endl. video games, Comprehension Strategies for an Integrated Language Arts Classroom, 1994, Teaching Elementary Language Arts: An Integrated Approach, 1995, 5th edit., 2000, Power Reading: Reading and Thinking Strategies for Adults, 1995, Phonics: Skills and Strategies in a Balanced Reading Program, 1998, Levels 1-4, Comprehension Skills and Strategies in a Balanced Reading Program, 1998, Vocabulary Skills and Strategies in a Blaanced Reading Program, 1998, Your Child Can Succeed in School: 100 Common-Sense Answers to Frequently Asked Questions, 1999, Writing and Thinking Skills: Sentence Writing, 2000, Writing and Thinking Skills: Paragraphs and Composition, 2000, Word Meaning & Reasoning Levels 1-3, 2000, Writing and Thinking Skills: Fun With Writing, 2001, One Year of Words: College Vocabulary Enhancement, 2004, Grammar and Usage: Simplified, 2005, (audio) Passport to Power English, 1987; contbr. articles to profl. jours.; syndicated columnist Word Games, columnist The Times, Trenton, N.J., Asbury Park (N.J.) Press. Recipient profl. awards. Mem.: Phi Kappa Phi, Nat. Coun. Tchrs. English, Internat. Reading Assn., Pi Lambda Theta, Kappa Delta Pi. Home and Office: 917 Stuart Rd Princeton NJ 08540-1212 E-mail: arthurirubin@netscape.net.

**RUBIN, EDWARD,** law educator, dean; AB, Princeton U., 1969; JD, Yale U., 1979. Curriculum planner NYC Bd. Edn., 1970—76; law clk. to Hon. Jon O. Newman US Ct. Appeals (2nd cir.), 1979—80; assoc. Paul, Weiss, Rifkind, Wharton & Garrison, NYC; acting prof. U. Calif. Sch. Law, 1982—87, assoc. dean, 1989—92, prof., 1987—96, Richard W. Jennings Professor, 1996—98; prof. U. Pa. Law Sch., Phila., 1998—2005, Theodore K. Warner, Jr. prof. law, 2003—05; dean & John Wade-Kent Syverud prof. law Vanderbilt U. Law Sch., Nashville, 2005—. Contbr. articles to law jours.; author: Beyond Camelot: Rethinking Politics and Law for the Modern State, 2005; co-author (with Malcolm Feeley): Federalism: A Theoretical Inquiry, 2005. Mem.: ABA, Am. Law Sch. Office: U Vanderbilt Law Sch Office of the Dean 131 21st Ave South Rm 290 A Nashville TN 37203-1181 Office Phone: 615-322-9800. Office Fax: 215-573-2025, 615-322-5151. E-mail: ed.rubin@vanderbilt.edu.

**RUBIN, EDWARD M.,** geneticist, medical researcher; b. NYC, Jan. 17, 1951; BA in Physics, U. Calif. San Diego; MD, U. Rochester Med. Ctr., 1980; PhD in Biophysics, U. Rochester. Cert. Clin. Genetics, 1987. Intern, pediatrics U. Calif. San Francisco, 1980—81, resident, med. genetics 1981—82, genetics fellow, 1983—87, assoc. prof.; rsch. assoc. Howard Hughes Med. Inst.; interim dir. US Dept. Energy Joint Genome Inst., 2002—03, dir.,

2003—; joined Lawrence Berkeley Nat. Lab., 1988, head, genome sciences dept., 1998, dir., genomics divsn., genome sciences dept., sr. scientist, 2003—. Active in US and internationally Human Genome Project; co-chair Cold Spring Harbor Genome Sequencing and Biology Mtg.; scientific chair Internat. Human Genome Orgn. Office: Lawrence Berkeley Nat Lab Mailstop 84-171 1 Cyclotron Road Berkeley CA 94720 also: JGI Production Genomics Facility 2800 Mitchell Dr Walnut Creek CA 94598 Business E-Mail: emrubin@lbl.gov.*

**RUBIN, ELLEN,** educational coordinator; d. Jack and Mary Elizabeth Rubin; m. Rami Gertler, Oct. 4, 1979 (div.). MS in Spl. Edn., Bank St. Coll. Edn., NYC, 1976. Cert. spl. edn. N-6 NY, 1977. Asst. tchr. Hellen Keller Services for the Blind (formerly Indsl. Home for the Blind), NYC, 1966—68; rehab. tchr. Lighthouse for the Blind, Haifa, Israel, 1969—70; ednl. program coord. George Simmons Rehab. Ctr. for the Blind, Ministry Welfare, Beersheva, Israel, 1970—79; ednl. counselor Ben Gurion U. of the Negev, Beersheva, 1979—80; ednl. programming counselor Assn. for the Advancement of the Blind and Retarded, Inc. Jamaica, NY, 1981—82; spl. educator Early Intervention Programs, Guild for Exceptional Children, Bklyn., 1982—83; instr., cons., advisor Computer Ctr. for Visually Impaired People, Baruch Coll., NYC, 1983—2004; coord. disability programs Ednl. Equity Concepts, Inc., NYC, 1983—2004; part-time coord. internat. exch. programs Mobility Internat. USA, Eugene, Oreg., 1996—. Lectr. Sch. Occupl. Therapy, U. Hosp., Hadassah Med. Ctr., Jerusalem, 1974—79; team lectr. Haifa U., Natanya, Israel, 1977—78; lectr. Ministry Welfare, Beersheva, 1978—80; adv. panel mem. Commrs. Adv. Panel for the Office Spl. Edn. Svcs., NY State Edn. Dept., Albany, 1982—97; adv. com. mem. Quality Improvement Ctr. for Diabilities, NYU, NYC, 1984—2001; adv. coun. mem. Interagency Coordinating Coun., NY State Health Dept., Albany, NY, 1988—92; bd. dirs. Creative Adaptations for Learning, Great Neck, NY, 1990—; cons./adv. com. mem. Programs and Svcs. for People With Disabilities, Lincoln Ctr. for the Performing Arts, NYC, 1993—; testing coord. Touch Graphics, Inc., NYC, 1996—; trainer in accessibility features Assn. Sci. and Tech. Ctrs., Washington, 1998—2004; cons. Smithsonian Instn., Washington, 1999—; guest lectr. mus. edn. Bank St. Coll. Edn., NYC, 2001—; Ams. with Disabilities Act cons. Wildlife Conservation Soc., NY Aquarium, Bklyn., 2002—03. Contbr. articles to profl. jours. Advisor disability adv. com. Taxi and Limousine Commn., NYC, 1996—2006; cmty. liaison Beth Israel Methadone Clinic, NYC, 2000—04. Recipient Cmty. Svc. award, Jewish Guild for the Blind, 1993, Access Builder award, Baruch Coll., CUNY, 2003. Personal E-mail: ellenr@panix.com.

**RUBIN, EMANUEL LEO,** musicologist, composer; b. Pitts., July 9, 1935; s. Abe and Elsie Rubin; m. Serene Werner, June 17, 1956; children: Diane, Faith Ellen, Jonathan Mitchell. BFA in Music Performance, Carnegie-Mellon U., Pitts., 1957; EdMusB in Music Edn., Carnegie-Mellon U., 1957; MFA in Composition, Brandeis U., Waltham, Mass., 1960; PhD in Musicology, U. of Pitts., 1968. Prof. of music history and Judaic studies U. Mass., Amherst, 1985—. Composer: (songs) Sonata for Flute and Piano, Sonata for Oboe and Piano, Shirei nashim al milchama: Four Hebrew Songs for Voice and Piano, Psalm 150 for Choir (SATB) and Organ, Three Diversion for Four Horns, Three Nursery Rhyme Settings for Chorus and Jazz Combo, Canzona for Large Brass Ensemble and Five Percussion, O die Schornsteine: Song for Voice and Viola, For Herself: Song for High Voice and Piano, Trombonius-a-um: Four Pieces for Three Trombones, Triptych: Three Ballet Scenes (Dilemma of George Morgan), For Herself, 2006, Concerto for French Horn and Orchestra, 2006, Different Windows, 2006, others; author: The English Glee in the Reign of George III: Participatory Art Music for an Urban Society, 2003, John Travers' Canzonets of 1746: Critical and Performing Edition, 2005; co-author (with John H. Baron): Music in Jewish History and Culture, 2006; editor: A Collection of Catches, Canons, and Glees (The Warren Collection), 1970; contbr. articles to profl. jours., chapters to books. Eccles Rsch. fellow, The Brit. Libr., 2001, John Hay fellow, U. of London, 2001, Rsch. Travel grantee, NEH, 1990, various other grants, various agencies, 1968—99. Mem.: Soc. for Am. Music, Soc. for Jewish Music, Am. Musicol. Soc. Office: University of Massachusetts Amherst MA 01003 Office Phone: 413-545-4697. E-mail: erubin@music.umass.edu.

**RUBIN, E(RWIN) LEONARD,** lawyer; b. Chgo., Jan. 11, 1933; s. Samuel and Frances Birdie (Rabin) R.; m. Stephanie Siegel, Mar. 4, 1961 (div. Dec. 1981); children: Matthew, Suzanne; m. Audrey Gay Holzer, May 8, 1983; children: Margot, Bette. Student, U. Ill., Urbana, 1948-51; AB, U. Miami, 1956, JD, 1959. s. N.Y. 1960, Ill. 1962, U.S. Dist. Ct. (no. dist.) Ill. 1962, U.S. Ct. Appeals (7th cir.) 1990, U.S. Ct. Appeals (5th cir.) 1998, U.S. Supreme Ct. 2004. Assoc. Hays, St. John A&H, N.Y.C., 1960—62, Devoe, Shadur, Mikva, Chgo., 1962—65; gen. counsel Playboy Enterprises, Inc., Chgo., 1965—78; ptnr. E. Leonard Rubin Law Offices, Chgo., 1978—81, Epton, Mullin & Druth Ltd., Chgo., 1981—86, Brinks, Hofer, Gilson & Lione, Chgo., 1986—96, Gordon & Glickson, LLC, Chgo., 1996—2002, Sachnoff & Weaver, Ltd., Chgo., 2002—. Adj. prof. U. Ill., Northwestern U. Law Sch., Loyola U. Sch. Law, John Marshall Law Sch. Pres. Lawyers for Creative Arts, Chgo., 1983-85; bd. dirs. Wisdom Bridge Theatre, Chgo., 1983-85; mem., bd. dirs. Appletree Theater of Highland Park. Cpl. U.S. Army, 1953-5, ETO. Mem. ABA, Ill. Bar Assn., Chgo. Bar Assn. (bd. mgrs. 1983-85, chmn. various coms., dir. Christmas Spirits Satire Show 1965-99), Union Internat. Des Avocats (pres. intellectual property commn. 1997-2000), Copyright Soc. Am. (trustee, past pres. midwest chpt.). Jewish. Home: 270 Sunset Dr Northfield IL 60093-1047 Office: Sachnoff & Weaver Ltd 10 S Wacker Dr 40th Fl Chicago IL 60606 Office Phone: 312-207-1000. Business E-Mail: elrubin@sachnoff.com.

**RUBIN, GABRIEL REVI,** psychiatrist; b. Bklyn., Feb. 9, 1927; s. Samuel and Augusta Gertrude (Katz) R.; m. Janis Lyn Millstein, June 23, 1988. BA, NYU, 1946; MD, Hahnemann Med. Coll., 1950. Diplomate Am. Bd. Psychiatry and Neurology. Resident psychiatrist Bellevue Hosp., N.Y.C., 1953-54, Pilgrim State Hosp., Brentwood, L.I., N.Y., 1954-56; clin. asst. psychiatrist Hillside Hosp., Queens, N.Y., 1956-58; chief psychiat. in-patient and outpatient svcs. Elmhurst (Queens, N.Y.) Gen. Hosp., 1958-60; med. dir. Fifth Ave Ctr. for Counseling and Psychotherapy, N.Y.C., 1960-76; chmn. faculty Met. Inst. Psychoanalytic Studies, N.Y.C., 1960-76; adj. psychiatrist Beth Israel Hosp. Med. Ctr., N.Y.C., 1960—; asst. attending psychiatrist Roosevelt Hosp., N.Y.C., 1963—; clin. assoc. psychiatrist Mt. Sinai Med. Coll., N.Y.C., 1980—. Attending psychiatrist Forest Hills Gen. Hosp., Kew Gardens Gen. Hosp., Hillcrest Gen. Hosp., Blvd. Hosp., Astoria Gen. Hosp., Whitestone Gen. Hosp., Deepdale Gen. Hosp., Howard Park Hosp., Queens, 1958—. Hike leader Appalachian Mountain Club, N.Y.C., 1986—. 1st lt. USAF, 1951-53, Korea. Fellow N.Y. Acad. Medicine (life), N.Y. Acad. Sci. (life); mem. Island Peer Rev. Orgn., N.Y. County Peer Rev. Orgn., Bronx County Peer Rev. Orgn., Am. Contract Bridge League (life master). Avocations: piano, hiking, tennis, biking, bridge. Office: 200 E 71st St #18A New York NY 10021-5147 Personal E-mail: gabrielrubinmd@aol.com.

**RUBIN, GERALD MAYER,** biochemistry educator; b. Boston, Mar. 31, 1950; s. Benjamin H. and Edith (Weisberg) R.; m. Lynn S. Mastalir, May 7, 1978; 1 child, Alan F. BS, MIT, 1971; PhD, Cambridge U., Eng., 1974, ScD, 2002. Helen Hay Whitney Found. fellow Stanford U. Sch. Medicine, Calif., 1974-76; asst. prof. biol. chemistry Sidney Farber Cancer Inst.-Harvard U. Med. Sch., Boston, 1977-80; staff mem. Carnegie Instn. of Washington, Balt., 1980-83; John D. MacArthur prof. genetics U. Calif., Berkeley, 1983—. Investigator Howard Hughes Med. Inst., 1987—, v.p. biomed. rsch., 2000-01, v.p., dir. planning Janelia Farm Campus, 2001-03; v.p. dir. Janelia Farm Rsch. Campus, 2003—. Recipient Young Scientist award Passano Found., 1983, U.S. Steel Found. award Nat. Acad. Scis., 1985, Eli Lilly award in biochemistry Am. Chem. Soc., 1985, Genetics Soc. Am. medal, 1986. Mem. NAS, Inst. of Medicine, Am. Acad. Arts and Scis. Office: Janelia Farm Rsch Campus Howard Hughes Med Inst 19700 Helix Dr Ashburn VA 20147-2408 Business E-Mail: rubing@jfrc.hhmi.org.

**RUBIN, GERROLD ROBERT,** advertising executive; b. Evanston, Ill., Mar. 31, 1940; s. Bennie George and Anita (Perich) R.; m. Barbara Ann Nieman, Sept. 5, 1962; children: John, Ann. BS in Radio, TV, Film, Northwestern U., 1962. Account exec. Leo Burnett Advt., Chgo., 1962-67, account supr. Toronto, Ont., 1967-68; Needham, Harper Steers, Chgo., 1968-73, account dir. Los Angeles, 1973-78; mgmt. rep. Needham, Harper & Steers, Chgo., 1978-81, pres., CEO Los Angeles, 1981-86, Rubin, Postaer & Assocs., Santa Monica, Calif., 1986—. Bd. dirs. Country Music Assn., Nashville, 1983—. Presbyterian. Office: Rubin Postaer & Assocs 2525 Colorado Ave Santa Monica CA 90404

**RUBIN, HARRY MEYER,** software industry executive; b. NYC, Dec. 21, 1952; s. Martin J. and Helene Rubin; m. Cathy Hemery, May 26, 1990; children: Gabriella, James. BA, Stanford U., 1974; MBA, Harvard U., 1976. Investment banker Wertheim & Co., Inc., NYC, 1976-77; fin. mgr. Am. Airlines, Inc., NYC, 1977-79; dir. fin. planning-entertainment, electronics groups RCA Corp., NYC, 1979-81; CFO RCA Videodiscs, RCA Home Video, RCA Cable RCA Entertainment Group, NYC; v.p. strategic planning RCA Corp., NYC, group v.p. fin. and bus. affairs RCA entertainment ops., 1981-86; gen. mgr. Home Video Gen. Electric Co., 1986-87; v.p., gen. mgr. home video div. NBC, Inc., 1988-93; exec. v.p. GT Interactive Software Corp., 1994-98; pres. GT Interactive Internat., 1998-2000; pres. internat. Infogrames, Inc., 2000-01; sr. exec. v.p. and head of worldwide pub. Atari Inc., 2001—05, COO, 2004—05; chmn. Henmead Enterprises, Inc., 2005—06. Dir. Image-Metrics plc; dir., co-head exec. com. RCA/Columbia Pictures Worldwide Video; founding ptnr. Samuel Adams Beer; founding dir. Arts & Entertainment Network. Mem.: 22 Club, Phi Beta Kappa. Avocations: travel, foreign languages. Home: 784 Park Ave New York NY 10021-3553 Personal E-mail: harry.rubin@gmail.com.

**RUBIN, HERBERT,** lawyer; b. Lisbon, Conn., June 4, 1918; s. Simon and Rose (Berko) R.; m. Rose Luttan, July 6, 1941; children: Barbara, Caroline, Donald. AB, CCNY, 1938; JD, NYU, 1942. Bar: N.Y. 1942, U.S. Dist. Ct. (so. and ea. dists.) N.Y. 1951, U.S. Supreme Ct. 1956, U.S. Ct. Appeals (2d, 3d, 4th, 6th, 9th, 10th, 11th and D.C. cirs.). Assoc. Newman & Bisco, 1942; faculty NYU Law Sch., 1946-50, 57-62; prof. creditors' rights Rutgers U. Law Sch., 1949-57; pvt. practice, 1946-56; ptnr. Sereni, Herzfeld & Rubin, and successor Herzfeld & Rubin, N.Y.C., 1956—, sr. ptnr., 1968—. Instr. mil. law U.S. Army, 1944-46; prof. constl. law L.I.U., 1963-68; trustee North Shore L.I. Jewish Hosp. Editor-in-chief NYU Law Rev., 1940-41; bd. editors N.Y. Law Jour., 1971—; contbr. articles to profl. jours. Mem. N.Y. State Banking Bd., 1975-85, N.Y. State Jud. Selection Com., 1975-83, Sen. Moynihan's Jud. Selection Com., 1982-2000, Sen. Schumer's Jud. Selection Com., 1999—, City Charter Revision Commn., 1998-2001; trustee Am. Assn. Jewish Lawyers and Jurists. 1st lt. Signal Corps, AUS, 1942-46. Recipient award, NCCJ, 1967, United Jewish Appeal, 1968, 1997, Israel Bonds, 1973, NYU Law Assn. award, 1987, Judge Weinfeld award, NYU, 1992, Vanderbilt award, 1999. Fellow Am. Bar Found.; mem. ABA (mem. coun. N.Y. state), N.Y. State Bar Assn., Queens County Bar Assn. (pres. 1970), Assn. Bar City Of N.Y., Fed. Bar Coun., Jewish Lawyers Guild (award 2001). Office: Herzfeld & Rubin 40 Wall St Fl 54 New York NY 10005-2301 Office Phone: 212-471-8500. Office Fax: 212-232-6610. Business E-Mail: hrubin@herzfeldrubin.com.

**RUBIN, JEFFREY WAYNE,** lawyer; b. Syracuse, N.Y., Oct. 10, 1950; s. Harold and Ida Rubin. BA, SUNY, Binghamton, 1971; JD, Syracuse U., 1977. Bar: N.Y. 1978, U.S. Dist. Ct. (so. and ea. dists.) N.Y. 1978, U.S. Supreme Ct. 1991. Assoc. Guggenheimer & Untermyer, N.Y.C., 1978-82, Squadron, Ellenoff, Plesent & Sheinfeld, N.Y.C., 1982-85, ptnr., 1985—2002, Hogan & Hartson LLP, 2002—. Mem. ABA (bus. law sect.). U.S. Army. Mem. of Bar of City of N.Y. Office: Hogan & Hartson L L P 875 3rd Ave New York NY 10022 Office Phone: 212-918-8224. Business E-Mail: jwrubin@hhlaw.com.

**RUBIN, JOEL EDWARD,** manufacturing executive; b. Cleve., Sept. 5, 1928; s. Morris and Pearl (Jacobs) R.; m. Lucille Schutmaat, Dec. 18, 1953; children: Brian G., Jennifer L., Rebecca R. BS, Case Inst. of Tech., 1949; MFA, Yale U., 1951; PhD, Stanford U., 1960. Exec. v.p. Kliegl Bros. Lighting, NYC, 1954-85; prin. cons. Joel E. Rubin & Assocs., NYC, 1985-93; prin. cons. theater planning Artec Cons. Inc., NYC, 1993—2005; prin. cons. Joel E. Rubin & Assoc., NYC, 2005—. Co-author: Theatrical Lighting Practice 1954; author: Technological Development of Stage Lighting 1960. Member Coll. of Fellows of Am. Theatre, John F. Kennedy Ctr. for the Performing Arts, Washington. Recipient Golden Triaga, Prague Quadrennial, 1987, Zlatou medal, 1991, 1st time award Bus. Com. for the Arts, Forbes Mag., 1987; recipient Founders' award US Inst. for Theatre Tech., 1972, 79, Nat. award, 1990, Lifetime hon. membership award, 1996, Spl. citation, 1996; Dr. Joel E. Rubin Founder's award named in his honor US Inst. Theatre Tchrs., 2000; Internat. Student Rsch. grants established in his honor US Inst. Theatre Tchrs., 2000; nominee Entertainment Design Lifetime Achievement in Lighting, 2005 Fellow Am. Theatre Assn. (v.p. 1961-63), US Inst. of Theatre Technology (pres. 1963-64); mem. Am. Nat. Theatre Acad. (bd. dirs. 1971-75), Internat. Theatre Inst. of the US (bd. dirs. 1975-79), Nat. Coun. of Arts and Govt. (bd. dirs. 1975-79), Internat. Orgn. Theatre Architects and Scenographers (US chmn., rep. 1968-98, pres. 1971-79, Gold medal award 1996), Illuminating Engring. Soc. Avocations: collecting books, stage design, lincolniana. Home: 24 Edgewood Ave Hastings On Hudson NY 10706-2024 Office: Joel E Rubin and Assoc 119 W 57th St Ste 820 New York NY 10019 Office Phone: 212-757-5646. Personal E-mail: booksjoel@aol.com.

**RUBIN, KARL COOPER,** mathematics educator; b. Urbana, Ill., Jan. 27, 1956; s. Robert J. and Vera (Cooper) R. AB, Princeton U., 1976; MA, Harvard U., 1977, PhD, 1981. Instr. Princeton (N.J.) U., 1982-83; mem. Inst. Advanced Study, Princeton, 1983-84; prof. Columbia U., NYC, 1989 90; asst. prof. math. Ohio State U., Columbus, 1984-87, prof., 1987-97; prof. math. Stanford (Calif.) U., 1997—. Contbr. articles to Inventiones Math. Recipient Presdl. Young Investigator award NSF, 1985; NSF postdoctoral fellow, 1981, Sloan fellow, 1985, Guggenheim fellow, 1994. Mem. Am. Math. Soc. (recipient Cole Prize, 1992), Phi Beta Kappa. Achievements include rsch. on elliptic curves, Tate-Shafarevich groups, Birch and Swinnerton-Dyer conjecture, Iwasawa theory and p-adic L-functions. Office: Stanford U Dept Math Stanford CA 94305-2125

**RUBIN, KENNETH ALLEN,** lawyer; b. Rockville Centre, N.Y., Nov. 24, 1947; s. Albert Alton and Marion (Osterweis) R.; m. Susan Kurman, Sept. 14, 1980; children: Jennifer, Kelly. BS, Cornell U., 1969, MS, 1971, JD, 1973. Bar: D.C. 1974, N.Y. 1974, U.S. Ct. Appeals (D.C. crct.) 1974, U.S. Ct. Appeals (5th crct. 1975, U.S. Ct. Appeals (4th, 9th and 10th crct.) 1976, U.S. Ct. Appeals (3d, 8th and 11th crcts.) 1986, U.S. Supreme Ct. 1992. Trial atty. Dept. Justice, Washington, 1973-74; sr. ptnr. Morgan, Lewis & Bockius LLP, Washington, 1974—. Adj. prof. USDA Grad. Sch., Washington, 1977-85, U. Ala., Huntsville, 1978-91, Antioch U., Washington, 1978; lectr. Cornell U., Ithaca, N.Y., 1979—. Author: What the Business Executive Needs To Know about U.S. Environmental Laws and Liabilities, 1991, (manual) A Tidal Wave of Lawsuits and Regulations Flood the Once-Placid Waters of Drinking Water Utilities, 2000, Oil Spill Reporting Manual, 2002. Mem. adv. com. Cornell Ctr. for Environment. Mem. ABA, Am. Water Works Assn., Swiss Club Washington, Cornell Club Washington. Office: Morgan Lewis & Bockius LLP 1111 Pennsylvania Ave NW Washington DC 20004 E-mail: karwaterlawyer@aol.com.

**RUBIN, LAWRENCE GILBERT,** physicist, science administrator; b. Bklyn., Sept. 17, 1925; s. Harry E. and Ruth (Feirberg) R.; m. Florence Ruth Kagan, Feb. 11, 1951; children: Michael G., Richard D., Jeffrey N. Student, Cooper Union, N.Y.C., 1943, 46-47; BS in Physics, U. Chgo., 1949; MA in Physics, Columbia U., 1950. Staff mem., physicist research div. Raytheon Co., Waltham, Mass., 1950-64; group leader Nat. Magnet Lab., MIT, Cambridge, Mass., 1964-78, divsn. head high magnetic field facility, 1978-93; advisor to high magnetic field facility, 1994-95; vis. scientist MIT, 1996—. Mem. NAS adv. panel Nat. Bur. Standards, 1976-82, 85-90; bd. dirs. Lake

Shore Cryotronics, Inc., Columbus, Ohio; gen. chmn. 6th Internat. Temperature Symposium, Washington, 1982, 7th Internat. Temperature Symposium, Toronto, 1992, 8th Internat. Temperature Symposium, Chgo., 2002; chmn. adv. com. Physics Today Buyers' Guide; contbg. editor Physics Today; organizer, mgr. Am. Phys. Soc. Tutorial program, 1993-2003. Mem. editl. bd. Rev. Sci. Instruments, 1968-70, 79-81; contbr. articles to physics jours. With U.S. Army, 1943-46, ETO. Fellow IEEE (life, chmn. Keithley award com. 2002-04), Am. Phys. Soc. (organizer and 1st chmn. instrument and measurement sci. group 1985). Jewish. Home: 1504 Centre St Newton Center MA 02459-2447 Office: MIT Bldg NW14 1209 170 Albany St Cambridge MA 02139-4208 Office Phone: 617-253-5517. Business E-Mail: lrubin@mit.edu.

**RUBIN, LEONARD SIDNEY,** physiologist, educator, researcher; b. New York, N.Y., Aug. 27, 1922; s. Hyman Hersh and Toba Rubin; m. Blanche Rubin, Mar. 30, 1950; children: Beth S., Joshua T., Matthew M. BS Chemistry, CUNY, New York, NY, 1943; PhD Neuroscience, NY Univ., New York, NY, 1950. Instr. NY Univ., New York, NY, 1943—44, rsch. assoc., 1950—53; chief psychophysiology br. Med. Labs, Army Chem. Corps., Edgewood, 1953—57; assoc. prof. Univ. Pa. Sch. of Medicine, Philadelphia, 1960—81; rsch. cons. Childrens Hosp. of Phila., Philadelphia, 1960—65; prof. Temple Univ. Med. Coll., Philadelphia, 1970—75; rsch. cons. St. Christopher's Hosp. for Children, 1964—67; cons., behavioral toxicology FDA, 1976—81; prof. Phila. Coll. of Med., Philadelphia, 1982—92; cons. biostatistics Cellcor Corp., Boston, 1988—92; prof., physiology/pharmacology Phila. Coll. of Osteo. Med., Philadelphia, 1981—. Armed forces nrc com. on vision, Washington, 1956—57; armed forces nrc com. on bioacoustics, Washington, 1956—57. Editl. cons. Jour. Studies on Alcohol, Jour. Nervous and Mental Disease, Psychophysiology, Psychopharmacologia, Am. Jour. Psychiatry. US Army, 1944—46. Recipient Social Sci. Rsch. Award, Inst. of Math., Stanford U., 1955, A.E. Bennet Award, Soc. of Biol. Psychiatry, 1961; scholar Fgn. Exch. Scholar, NAS, Yugoslavia, 1974. Fellow: Am. Psychol. Soc., Soc. of Biol. Psychiatry, Am. Psychol. Assn.; mem.: Soc. for Psychophysiological Rsch., Acad. of Psychosomatic Medicine, Sigma Xi. Jewish. Avocations include author, In Numerous Research Journals, 1952-1996. Avocation: studying philosophy, art, and music. Home: 706 Powder Mill Lane Wynnewood PA 19096-4035

**RUBIN, LEWIS J.,** physician, researcher; b. New York, NY, Aug. 5, 1950; s. Theodore and Erna Rubin; m. Juanita Rose Brooks; children: Lauren, Rose Sheelah, Jai Sheelah. MD, Albert Einstein Coll. of Medicine, 1972—75. Am. Bd. Internal Medicine ABIM/ Wash., DC, 1978. Prof. medicine U. Calif. San Diego, 1999—. Fellow: ACP, Am. Coll. Chest Physicians, Am. Heart Assn., Royal Coll. Physicians UK; mem.: Am. Soc. Clin. Investigation. Achievements include basic and clinical research in cardiopulmonary diseases, leading to drug developments and new treatments. Home: 6404 Avenida Wilfredo La Jolla CA 92037 Office: U Calif San Diego Med Ctr 9300 Campus Point Drive #7381 La Jolla CA 92037-7381 Office Phone: 858-657-8700. Business E-Mail: ljrubin@ucsd.edu.

**RUBIN, LOUIS DECIMUS, JR.,** retired language educator, writer, publishing executive; b. Charleston, S.C., Nov. 19, 1923; s. Louis Decimus and Janet (Weinstein) R.; m. Eva M. Redfield, June 2, 1951; children: Robert Alden, William Louis. Student, Coll. of Charleston, 1940-42, LittD (hon.), 1989; AB, U. Richmond, 1946, LittD (hon.), 1972; MA, Johns Hopkins U., 1949, PhD, 1954; LittD (hon.), Clemson U., 1986, U. of the South, 1991, U. N.C. at Asheville, 1993, U. N.C., Chapel Hill, 1995. Instr. Johns Hopkins U.; editor Hopkins Rev., 1950-54; fellow criticism Sewanee Rev., 1953-54; exec. sec. Am. Studies Assn., asst. prof. Am. civilization U. Pa., 1954-56; assoc. editor Richmond (Va.) News Leader, 1956-57; assoc. prof. English Hollins Coll., 1957-60, prof., chmn. dept., 1960-67; prof. English U. N.C., 1967-73, Univ. Disting. prof., 1973-89, prof. emeritus, 1989—. Editor Hollins Critic, 1963-68; vis. prof. history La. State U., 1957; Fulbright lectr. U. Aix-Marseille, 1960; lectr. Breadloaf Writer's Conf., 1961; vis. prof. U. N.C., 1965, Harvard U., 1969; lectr. Am. studies seminars Kyoto (Japan) U., 1979; founder, pub., editl. dir. Algonquin Books Chapel Hill, 1982-91. Author: Thomas Wolfe: The Weather of His Youth, 1955, No Place on Earth, 1959, The Golden Weather, 1961, The Faraway Country, 1963, The Teller in the Tale, 1967, The Curious Death of the Novel, 1967, George W. Cable, 1969, The Writer in the South, 1972, William Elliott Shoots A Bear, 1975, Virginia: A History, 1977, The Wary Fugitives, 1978, Surfaces of a Diamond, 1981, A Gallery of Southerners, 1982, The Even-Tempered Angler, 1983, The Edge of the Swamp, 1989, The Algonquin Literary Quiz Book, 1990, The Mockingbird in the Gum Tree, 1991, Small Craft Advisory, 1991, The Heat of the Sun, 1995, Babe Ruth's Ghost, 1996, Seaports of the South, 1998, A Memory of Trains, 2000, An Honorable Estate, 2001, My Father's People, 2002, Where The Southern Cross the Yellow Dog: On Writers and Writing, 2005; editor: Southern Renascence, 1953, The Lasting, South, 1957, Teach the Freeman: R.B. Hayes and the Slater Fund for Negro Education, 1959, The Idea of an American Novel, 1961, South: Modern Southern Literature in Its Cultural Setting, 1961, Bibliographical Guide to the Study of Southern Literature, 1969, The Comic Imagination in American Literature, 1973, The Literary South, 1978, The American South, 1980, The History of Southern Literature, 1985, An Apple for My Teacher, 1987, A Writer's Companion, 1995, The Quotable Baseball Fanatic, 2000; co-editor: So. Lit. Jour., 1968-89; contbr. articles to periodicals. Served with AUS, 1943-46. Guggenheim fellow, 1958-59, fellow Am. Coun. Learned Socs., 1964, Fulbright fellow, Oliver Max Gardner award, Mayflower award, Disting. Virginian award, NC award for Lit., 1992, R. Hunt Parker Meml. award for lifetime contributions to NC lit. heritage, Academy award in Lit., Am. Acad. of Arts and Letters, 2004, Ivan Sandrof Lifetime Achievement award, Nat. Book Critics Cir., 2005, John Tyler Caldwell award for the Humanities, 2005. Fellow So. Writers (chancellor 1991-93); mem. Soc. Study So. Lit. (pres. 1975-76), Phi Beta Kappa. Address: 42 Speyside Cir Pittsboro NC 27312

**RUBIN, MARTIN N.,** meeting planner, consultant; b. NYC, Aug. 9, 1928; s. Max and Esther (Chernow) R.; m. Shirley Anne Rubin, Aug. 22, 1954 (div. Aug. 1964); m. Karen Anne O'Brien, Sept. 21, 1981. AB, U. Mich.; AM, Miami U.; Oxford, Ohio; PhD.; Sussex U. Eng. Lic. psychologist. With Dayton (Ohio) Sch. System, 1951-60, West Alexandria (Ohio) Sch. System, 1961-63; instr. Wright State U., Dayton, 1961-63; with Devereux Found., Pa., N.Y. Dept. Corrections, Bklyn., 1971-73, Council for Retarded Children, Albany, NY, 1973-75; prin. M. Rubin & Co., Inc., Mount Vernon, NY, 1975—. Author: Developmentally Disabled, 1965. Candidate Dem. State Legis., 1982; adv. bd. Mt. Vernon Mental Health Bd., 1985. Master's degree scholar Miami U., 1958; Guidance Inst. grantee Miami U., 1959. Fellow Am. Assn. Mental Deficiency (pres. 1967); mem. Soc. Assn. Execs. (bd. dirs. 1985—). Lodges: Masons (sr. warden 1983). Avocations: dance, singing. Office Phone: 914-664-4120. Personal E-mail: loukob@aol.com.

**RUBIN, MELVIN LYNNE,** ophthalmologist, educator; b. San Francisco, May 10, 1932; s. Morris and May (Gelman) R.; m. Lorna Isen, June 21, 1953; children: Gabrielle, Daniel, Michael. AA, U. Calif., Berkeley, 1951, BS, 1953; MD, U. Calif., San Francisco, 1957; MS, State U. Iowa, 1961. Diplomate Am. Bd. Ophthalmology (bd. dirs. 1977-83, chmn. 1984). Intern U. Calif. Hosp., San Francisco, 1957-58; resident in ophthalmology State U. Iowa, 1958-61; attending surgeon Georgetown U., Washington, 1961-63; asst. prof. surgery U. Fla. Sch., Gainesville, 1963-66, assoc. prof. ophthalmology, 1966-67, prof. ophthalmology, 1967—97, prof. emeritus, 1997—, chmn. dept. ophthalmology, 1978-95, eminent scholar, 1989-97, eminent scholar emeritus, 1997. Author: Studies in Physiological Optics, 1965, Fundamentals of Visual Science, 1969, Optics for Clinicians, 1971, 2d edit., 1974, 25th ann. edit., 1995, The Fine Art of Prescribing Glasses, 1978, 3d edit., 2000; editor: Dictionary of Eye Terminology, 1984, 5th edit., 2006, Eye Care Notes, 1989, revised edit., 2001, Taking Care of Your Eyes, 2003; cons. editl. bd. Survey Ophthalmology; contbr. more than 100 articles to profl. jours. Co-founder Citizens for Pub. Schs., Inc., 1965, ProArteMusica Gainesville, Inc., 1969, pres., 1971-73; mem. Thomas Ctr. Adv. Bd. for the Arts, 1978-84, nat. sci. adv. bd. Helen Keller Eye Rsch. Found., 1989-96; bd. dirs. Hippodrome State Theater, 1981-87, Friends of Photography Ansel Adams Ctr., 1991-97, U. Fla. Found., 2005-; trustee U. Fla. Performing Arts Ctr.,

1995—2004; chmn. nat. art coun. U. Fla. Harn Mus. Art, 2005—. With USPHS, 1961-63. Recipient Best Med. Book for 1978 award Am. Med. Writers Assn., 1979, Shaler Richardson award for svc. to medicine Fla. Soc. Ophthalmology, 1995; M.L. Rubin Ann. Lectureship established in his honor by Fla. Soc. of Ophthalmology, 1993. Fellow ACS, Am. Acad. Ophthalmology (sec., dir. 1978-92, pres. 1988, Sr. Honor award 1987. Guest of Honor 1992), Found. Am. Acad. Ophthalmology (bd. trustees, 1988-95, chmn., 1992-94), Joint Commn. on Allied Health Pers. in Ophthalmology (Statesman of Yr. award 1987); mem. Assn. Rsch. in Vision and Ophthalmology (trustee 1973-78, pres. 1979), Retina Soc., Macula Soc., Club Jules Gonin, N.Y. Acad. Sci., Fla. Soc. Ophthalmology, Am. Ophthal. Soc. (coun. 1998-2002), Pan Am. Soc. Ophthalmology, Ophthalmic Photographers Soc., Alachua County Med. Soc., Fla. Med. Assn., AMA (editorial bd. Archives of Ophthalmology 1975-85), Sigma Xi, Alpha Omega Alpha., Phi Kappa Phi. Office: U Fla Med Ctr PO Box 100284 Gainesville FL 32610-0284 Office Phone: 352-846-2132. Business E-Mail: mrubin@eye.ufl.edu.

**RUBIN, MICHAEL,** lawyer; b. Boston, July 19, 1952; m. Andrea L. Peterson, May 29, 1983; children: Peter, Eric, Emily. AB, Brandeis U., 1973; JD, Georgetown U., 1977. Bar: Calif. 1978, U.S. Dist. Ct. (no. dist.) Calif. 1978, U.S. Ct. Appeals (9th cir.) 1978, U.S. Ct. Appeals (5th, 7th, 10th cirs.) 1982, U.S. Supreme Ct. 1984, U.S. Ct. Appeals (D.C. cir.) 1984, U.S. Ct. Appeals (11th cir.) 1987. Teaching fellow Law Sch. Stanford (Calif.) U., 1977-78; law clerk to Hon. Charles B. Renfrew U.S. Dist. Ct. (no. dist.) Calif., San Francisco, 1978-79; law clerk to Hon. James R. Browning U.S. Ct. Appeals (9th cir.), San Francisco, 1979-80; law clerk to Hon. William J. Brennan, Jr. U.S. Supreme Ct., Washington, 1980-81; assoc. Altshuler & Berzon, San Francisco, 1981-85, ptnr., 1985-89, Altshuler, Berzon, Nussbaum, Berzon & Rubin, San Francisco, 1989-2000, Altshuler, Berzon, Nussbaum, Rubin & Demain, San Francisco, 2000—. Office: Altshuler Berzon Nussbaum Rubin & Demain 177 Post St Ste 300 San Francisco CA 94108-4700 Office Phone: 415-421-7151. E-mail: mrubin@altshulerberzon.com.

**RUBIN, MICHAEL G.,** sports internet company executive; Student, Villanova U. Founder KPR Sports Internat. (changed name to Global Sports Inc. in 1997), 1991; chmn., pres., CEO GSI Commerce (changed name in 2002 from Global Sports Inc.), King of Prussia, Pa., 1995—; co-pres. GSI Commerce, 2004—05. Featured in The Wall St. Jour., USA Today, People Mag., CNBC, CNN. Named Entrepreneur of Yr., Ernst and Young, Entrepreneur of Yr., Inc. Mag. Office: GSI Commerce 935 1st Ave King Of Prussia PA 19406-1342 Fax: 610-265-2866.*

**RUBIN, MICHAEL HARRY,** lawyer, educator; b. Baton Rouge, Jan. 13, 1950; s. Alvin B. and Janice (Ginsberg) R.; m. Ayan J. (Liss), June 11, 1972; children: Bethany, Gillian. BA with honors, Amherst Coll., 1972; JD, La. State U., 1975. Bar: La., 1975; U.S. Ct. Appeals (5th Cir.) 1975; U.S. Dist. Ct. (Mid., Ea. and We. Dists.) La., 1976; U.S. Supreme Ct., 1982. Ptnr. Sanders, Downing, Kean, and Cazedessus, Baton Rouge, 1975—83, Rubin Curry Colvin & Joseph, Baton Rouge, 1983—93, McGlinchey and Stafford, Baton Rouge, 1993—. Adj. prof. La. State U. Law Sch., 1976—, Tulane Law Sch., 1976—. Co-author and author 12 books, numerous law rev. articles. Recipient Gold medal award, Atlanta Found. for the Improvement of Justice, Burton award, Libr. of Congress, 2003. Mem.: ABA (vice chair, real property sect. ethics and professionalism Com.), La. State Bar Found., Baton Rouge Bar Found. (past pres.), La. Law Inst. (active mem., com. on revisions to La. lending law and procedure), Baton Rouge Bar Assn. (past pres.), Anglo-Am. Real Property Inst., Am. Law Inst. (mem. adv. com., restatement of the law of property-mortgages, mem., adv. com., restatement of the law of property - joint ownership), Am. Coll. Mortgage Attys., Am. Coll. Comml. Fin. Lawyers, Am. Acad. Appellate Lawyers, Nat. Conf. Bar Pres. (mem. exec. coun.), Am. Coll. Real Estate Lawyers (treas., bd. gov.), La. State Bar Assn. (past pres., pres.), U.S. Fifth Cir. Bar Assn. (past pres., bd. gov.), So. Conf. Bar Pres. (pres.). Office: McGlinchey Stafford PLLC One American Pl 14th Fl Baton Rouge LA 70825 Office Phone: 225-383-9000, 225-382-3623. Office Fax: 225-343-3076. Business E-Mail: mrubin@mcglinchey.com.

**RUBIN, PATRICIA LEE,** art historian; BA summa cum laude, Yale U., 1976; MA with distinction, Courtauld Inst., 1978; PhD, Harvard U., 1986. Mem. I Tatti Adv. Com., 1996—; reader Cambridge U. Press, 1996—, Yale U. Press, 1996—; acting dir. Harvard U. Ctr. for Renaissance Studies, 1997; cons. BBC, 1995—99; external examiner Manchester U.; adv. bd. Medici Archive Project; spkr. in field; conf. presenter. Mem. editl. bd. Art History, 1995—96, 1996—99, Renaissance Studies, 1995—99; exhbn. revs. editor 1995—96, 1996—99; contbr. articles to profl. jours. Recipient Eric Mitchell prize for Giorgio Vasari Art and History, 1996. Mem.: Ente Raccolta Vinciana, Soc. for Renaissance Studies (coun. mem. 1995—99). Office: Courtauld Inst Art Somerset House Strand London WC2R ORN England

**RUBIN, PHYLLIS GETZ,** health association executive; b. N.Y.C., Aug. 6, 1937; d. Joseph and Sylvia (Rosenberg) Getz; m. James Milton Rubin, Oct. 28, 1961; children: Felicia Sue, Andrea Faith. BA, Syracuse U., 1959; MA, Columbia U., 1961, Adelphi U., 1975. Physical edn. tchr. Hicksville (N.Y.) Pub. Schs., 1959-93; bd. dirs., pres. Assoc. Am. Acad. Allergy, Asthma and Immunology; owner JP Med Fit, 1997—. Producer: (video) Aerobic Dancercise for Children, 1987. Bd. dir. COPAY, Great Neck, N.Y., 1986-91; v.p., sec. Pierpont Condominium Bd., 1986-90. Recipient Founder's Day award PTA, 1986. Mem.: N.Y. State Alliance for Health, Phys. Edn., REcreation and Dance (program spkr. 1984, 85, 93, v.p. Nassau zone 1987—2000, Zone Svc. award 1993). Avocations: tennis, reading, meditation, golf. Office Phone: 516-972-2342. E-mail: jpmedfit@aol.com.

**RUBIN, RHEA JOYCE,** library consultant; b. Chgo., June 14, 1950; d. Harold and Edith (Botkin) B.; m. Lawrence Berman, June 7, 1975; 1 child. Hannah Rubin Berman. BA, U. Wis., 1972, MA, 1973. Dir. Prog. Regional Library for The Blind and Handicapped, Salem, 1976—78; libr. Nat. Coun. Aging, Inc., Washington, 1978—80; cons. Rubin Cons., Oakland, Calif. 1980—. Author: Using Bibliotherapy, 1978, Bibliotherapy Sourcebook, 1978; (with others) Challenge of Aging, 1983, (with others) Let's Talk About It: A Planners Manual, 1984, Working With Older Adults, 1987, 2d edit., 1988, 3d edit., 1990, Of a Certain Age: A Guide to Contemporary Fiction Featuring Older Adults, 1990, Intergenerational Library Programs: A How to Do It Manual, 1993, (with others) Librarian Inside: A Practical Guide for Prison Librarians, 1995, Humanities Programming: A How to Do It Manual, 1997, Defusing the Angry Patron: A How to Do It Manual, 2000, Planning Library Services for People with Disabilities, 2001, Demonstrating Results: Using Outcome Measurement, 2006; book reviewer Libr. Jour.; contbr. articles to profl. jours. Recipient Show Monroe award, 1992, Exceptional Svc. award, ASCLA, 1993, 2006. Mem. ALA (chair numerous com. 1972—, Shaw award 1980). Office: 5860 Heron Dr Oakland CA 94618-2628 Office Phone: 510-339-1274. E-mail: rhea@rheajoyceerubin.org.

**RUBIN, RICHARD ALLAN,** lawyer; b. NYC, June 19, 1942; s. Louis Max and Ruth Ann (Goldman) R.; m. Susan Deborah Levitt, June 18, 1966; children: Karen, Jill. BS, Queens Coll., 1964; JD, Bklyn. Law Sch., 1967; LLM, NYU, 1968. Bar: N.Y. 1967. Assoc. Schwartz and Frank, NYC, 1968—69, Javits and Javits, NYC, 1969—71; ptnr. Wolf Haldenstein Adler Freeman Herz & Frank, NYC, 1972—76, Parker Chapin LLP, NYC, 1977—2000, Jenkens & Gilchrist, Parker Chapin LLP, NYC, 2001—05, Troutman Sanders LLP, NYC, 2005—. Lectr. Am. Mgmt. Assn., N.Y. State Bar Assn., N.Y.C. Bar Assn. Mem. ABA. Office Phone: 212-704-6130. Business E-Mail: rrubin@troutmansanders.com.

**RUBIN, RICK (FREDERICK JAY RUBIN),** record producer; b. Long Beach, NY, Mar. 10, 1963; s. Mickey and Linda (Tomberg) Rubin. BFA, NYU, 1985. Owner, founding pres. Def Jam Recordings, NYC, 1984—88, Am. Recordings (formerly Def Am. Recordings), LA, 1988—. Composer: (songs) I Need a Beat, 1985, Rock the Bells, 1985, I Can't Live Without My Radio, 1985, Can You Rock It Like This, 1985, Fight for Your Right, 1986,

Brass Monkey, 1986, It's Tricky, 1986, My Adidas, 1986, New Style, 1986, No Sleep Till Brooklyn, 1986, She's On It, 1986, Bite the Bullet, 1986, Raising Hell, 1986, You & Me, 1987, Goin' Back to Cali, 1987, That's a Lie, 1988, Cold Chillin' in the Spot, 1989, Jack the Ripper, 1989, Hemp Rally, 1993, Kaught in da Ak, 1993, It's a New Style, 1996, 4,3,2,1, 1997, State to State, 1997, Nowhere to Run, 1998, Squirrels, 1999, Super Dee Jay, 1999, 99 Problems, 2004, Busted in the Hood, 2004, Chavas, 2004; prodr.: (albums) Beavis & Butthead Experience, 1993, Working Class Hero: A Tribute to John Lennon, 1995, Chef & Friends: The Songs of South Park, 1998, Chef Aid: The South Park Album, 1998, Mr. Hankey's Christmas Classics, 1999, Essential Roy Orbison, 2006, (Slayer) Hell Awaits, 1985, Reign in Blood, 1986, South of Heaven, 1988, Seasons in the Abyss, 1990, Decade of Aggression, 1991, Divine Intervention, 1994, Serenity in Murder, 1995, Undisputed Attitude, 1996, Diabolus in Musica, 1998, God Hates Us All, 2001, Soundtrack to the Apocalypse, 2003, (Run-D.M.C.) King of Rock, 1985, Raising Hell, 1986, Tougher Than Leather, 1988, Together Forever, 1991, Greatest Hits, 2002, (LL Cool J) Radio, 1985, Walking with a Panther, 1989, All World, 1996, (Beastie Boys) Licensed to Ill, 1986, Sounds of Science, 1999, Solid Gold Hits, 2005, (The Cult) Electric, 1987, Electric Mixes, 1989, Wildflower, 1990, Pure Cult, 1993, Love Removal Machine, 1994, High Octane Cult, 1996, Rare Cult, 2000, (Danzig) Danzig, 1988, Danzig II: Lucifuge, 1990, Danzig III: How the Gods Kill, 1992, Dirty Black Summer, 1992, Thrall: Demonsweatlive, 1993, Danzig 4, 1994, (Andrew Dice Clay) Andrew Dice Clay, 1990, Day the Laughter Died, 1990, Dice Rules, 1990, 40 Too Long, 1993, (Red Hot Chili Peppers) Blood Sugar Sex Magik, 1991, Give It Away, 1991, What Hits!?, 1992, Plasma, 1994, One Hot Minute, 1995, Under the Covers, 1998, Californication, 1999, Live Rare Remix Box, 1999, One Hot Minute, 1999, Road Trippin', 2001, By the Way, 2002, Greatest Hits, 2003, Phenomenon, 2006, Stadium Arcadium, 2006, (Mick Jagger) Wandering Spirit, 1993, (Tom Petty & the Heartbreakers) Greatest Hits, 1993, Playback, 1995, Songs & Music from She's the One, 1996, Anthology, 2000, (Tom Petty) Wildflowers, 1994, You Don't Know How it Feels, 1994, (Joan Jett & the Blackhearts) Flashback, 1994, (Johnny Cash) American Recordings, 1994, Unchained, 1996, American III: Solitary Man, 2000, Love, 2000, Murder, 2000, American IV: The Man Comes Around, 2002, Unearthed, 2003, My Mother's Hymn Book, 2004, Legend of Johnny Cash, 2005, American V: A Hundred Highways, 2006, (Johnny Cash & Willie Nelson) VH1 Storytellers, 1998, (Nine Inch Nails) Further Down the Spiral, 1995, Downward Spiral, 2004, (Donovan) Sutras, 1996, Try for the Sun, 2005, (Sheryl Crow) Globe Sessions, 1998, Sweet Child O'Mine, 1999, (System of a Down) System of a Down, 1998, Sugar, 1999, Chop Suey, 2001. Toxicity, 2001, Steal This Album!, 2002, Hypnotize, 2005, Mezmerize, 2005, (Rage Against the Machine) Renegades, 2000, Live at the Grand Olympic Auditorium, 2003, (Paloalto) Paloalto, 2000, Sonny, 2000, Heroes & Villains, 2003, (Aerosmith) Young Lust, 2001, O, Yeah!, 2002, Gold, 2005, (Krishna Das) Breath of the Heart, 2001, Door of Faith, 2003, (Audioslave) Audioslave, 2002, Doesn't Remind Me, 2005, Out of Exile, 2005, (Jay-Z) Black Album, 2003, (Jay-Z & Linkin Park) Collision Course, 2004, (Limp Bizkit) Eat You Alive, 2003, Results May Vary, 2003, Greatest Hitz, 2005, (The Mars Volta) De-Loused in the Comatorium, 2003, Intertiatic ESP, 2004, Televators, 2004, (Neil Diamond) 12 Songs, 2005, (Ozzy Osbourne) Prince of Darkness, 2005, (Dixie Chicks) Taking the Long Way, 2006; exec. prodr. (Public Enemy) Yo! Bum Rush the Show, 1987, It Takes a Nation of Millions to Hold Us Back, 1988, Power to the People & the Beats, 2005, (Shakira) Don't Bother, 2005, Fijación Oral, Vol. 1, 2005, Oral Fixation, Vol. 2, 2005, (Sir Mix-A-Lot) Mack Daddy, 1992, Chief Boot Knocka, 1994, Jump On It, 1996, Return of the Bumpasaurus, 1996; prodr.: (soundtracks) Krush Groove, 1985, Less Than Zero, 1987, Marked for Death, 1990, Cool World, 1992, Wayne's World, 1992, Coneheads, 1993, Judgment Night, 1993, Last Action Hero, 1993, Party Girl, 1995, Mortal Kombat, 1996, Twister, 1996, I Know What You Did Last Summer, 1997, Jackie Brown, 1997, Private Parts, 1997, Can't Hardly Wait, 1998, Small Soldiers, 1998, Big Daddy, 1998, Human Traffic, 1999, Blair Witch 2, 2000, Heavy Metal 2000, 2000, Little Nicky, 2000, Scream 3, 2000, Jackass, 2001, Shallow Hal, 2001, Scorpion King, 2002, Spider-Man, 2002, Osbourne Family Album, 2002, Collateral, 2004, Kill Bill Vol. 2, 2004, Resident Evil: Apocalypse, 2004, Spider-Man 2, 2004, One Tree Hill, Vol. 2, 2006, Underworld: Evolution, 2006; actor: (films) Krush Groove, 1985, Men Don't Leave, 1990; writer, dir., actor (films) Tougher Than Leather, 1988. Named Hot Prodr. of Yr., Rolling Stone Mag., 1988; recipient Joel Weber award, New Music Seminar, 1990, Best Visionary award, Esquire Esky Music Awards, 2006. Office: American Recording 22301 Mulholland Hwy Calabasas CA 91302 Office Phone: 818-223-8030.

**RUBIN, ROBERT EDWARD,** diversified financial services company executive, former secretary of the treasury; b. NYC, Aug. 29, 1938; s. Alexander and Sylvia (Seiderman) R.; m. Judith Leah Oxenberg, Mar. 27, 1963; children: James Samuel, Philip Matthew. AB in Econ. (summa cum laude), Harvard U., 1960; postgrad., London Sch. Econs., 1960-61; LLB, Yale U., 1964; DHL (hon.), Yeshiva U., 1996. Bar: N.Y. 1965. Assoc. Cleary, Gottlieb, Steen & Hamilton, N.Y.C., 1964-66, Goldman, Sachs & Co., N.Y.C., 1966-70, ptnr., 1971, mem. mgmt. com., 1980, vice chmn., co-COO, 1987-90, co-sr. ptnr., co-chmn., 1990-92; asst. to Pres. for econ. policy The White House, Washington, 1993-95; dir. The Nat. Econ. Coun., Washington, 1993—95; sec. US Dept. Treasury, Washington, 1995-99; chmn. exec. com., mem. Office of the Chmn. Citigroup Inc., NYC, 1999—; vice chmn., dir., chmn. exec. com. Coun. Fgn. Relations, Washington, 2003—: Mem. Pres.'s Adv. Com. for Trade Negotiations, Washington, 1980-82, mem. adv. com. on tender offers SEC, Washington, 1983, Gov.'s Commn. on Trade Competitiveness, 1987, regulatory adv. com. N.Y. Stock Exch., 1988-90, adv. com. internat. capital markets Fed. Res. Board N.Y., 1989-93, Securities and Exch. Commn. Market Oversight and Fin. Svcs. Adv. Com., 1991-93, Gov.'s Adv. Panel on Fin. Svcs., 1988-89; ptnr., bd. dirs. N.Y.C. Partnership Inc., 1991-93; bd. dirs. Ctr. for Nat. Policy, 1982-93, vice chmn.; 1984; bd. dirs. N.Y. Futures Exch., N.Y.C. 1979-85, Chgo. Bd. Options Exch. Inc., 1972-76, Ford Motor Co., 2000-06; bd. trustees Mt. Sinai Hosp., 1977, vice chmn.; 1986; trustee Sta. WNET-TV, 1985-93, Carnegie Corp. of N.Y., 1990-93; mem. Mayor's Coun. Econ. Advisors, 1990, Gov.'s Coun. on Fiscal and Econ. Priorities, 1990-92; mem. advisory bd., Insight Venrure Partners, 2000- Author (with Jacob Weisberg): In an Uncertain World: Tough Choices from Wall Street to Washington, 2003 (named one of Ten Best Bus. Books, Bus. Week, 2003). Trustee Am. Ballet Theatre Found., N.Y.C., 1969-93; trustee Collegiate Sch., 1978-84; mem. bd. overseers' com. to visit econs. dept. Harvard U., 1981-87, com. on univ. resources, 1987-92; mem. fin. com. N.Y. campaign Mondale for Pres., 1983-84; mem. investment adv. coun. N.Y.C. Pension Fund, 1980-89; chmn. Dem. Cong. Dinner, Washington, 1982; Dems. for the 80s, 1985-89, Dems. for the 90s, 1989-90; chmn. N.Y.C. host com. 1992 Dem. Conv., 1989-92; mem. Commn. Nat. Elections. Recipient award Nat. Assn. Christians and Jews, N.Y.C., 1977, Disting. Leadership in Govt. award Columbia Bus. Sch., 1996, Euromoney Mag. award Fin. Min. Yr., 1996, Medal for High Civic Svc. award Citizens' Budget Com., 1997, Fgn. Policy Assn. medal, 1998, "Chmn." award Washington Greater Boys/Girls Clubs, 1998, Intrepid Sea Air Space Mus. award, 1998, Jefferson award Am. Inst. Pub. Svc., 1998, Award of Merit Yale U., 1998, Global Leadership award UN Assn., 1998, Paul Tsongas award, 1998. Mem. Phi Beta Kappa, Harvard Club (N.Y.C.), Century Country Club (Purchase, N.Y.). Democrat. Jewish. Office: Citigroup Inc 399 Park Ave 3d Fl New York NY 10043-0001*

**RUBIN, ROBERT JOSEPH,** internist, consultant, nephrologist; b. Bklyn., Feb. 7, 1946; s. B. Norman and Suzanne (Fried) R.; m. Fran Auerbach, June 14, 1970; children: Elyse Beth, David Jon. AB, Williams Coll., 1966; MD, Cornell U., 1970. Diplomate Am. Bd. Internal Medicine, Nephrology. Intern New England Med. Ctr. Hosps., Boston, 1970-71, resident, 1971-72, 74-76; epidemic intelligence officer, respiratory disease and spl. pathogens, divsn. viral diseases Ctr. for Disease Control, 1972-74; asst. dean govt. affairs Tufts U., 1979-84, assoc. prof. medicine, 1984-. Chief renal divsn. Lemuel Shattuck Hosp., Boston, 1979-81; asst. sec. planning and evaluation U.S. HHS, Washington, 1981-84; clin. assoc. prof. Georgetown U., Washington, 1984-95, clin. prof., 1995—; exec. v.p. ICF, Inc., 1984-88; pres. Health and Scis. Internat., 1988-92, Lewin ICF Inc., 1992, Lewin-VHI, Inc., 1992-96, Lewin Group, 1996-99, CEO, 1999-2001. Contbr. articles to profl. jours. With

USPHS, 1972-74, asst. surgeon gen., 1981-84. Robert Wood Johnson Health Policy fellow, 1977 Mem. ACP, AMA, Am. Soc. Nephrology, Internat. Soc. Nephrology, Mass. Med. Soc., Kenwood Club, Potomac Club, Williams Club, Phi Beta Kappa. Republican. Jewish.

**RUBIN, ROBERT SAMUEL,** lawyer; b. Cin., Apr. 25, 1954; s. Carl B. and Gloria W. R.; m. Virginia K. Carson, May 14, 1980; children: John C., Claire W., Elizabeth K. LLB, U. Wales, Aberystwyth, Eng., 1976; JD, U. Cin., 1979. Bar: Ohio 1979, U.S. Dist. Ct. (so. dist.) Ohio 1979. Assoc. Brown, Cummins & Brown, Cin., 1979-82, Porter, Wright, Morris & Arthur, Cin., 1982-88, partner, 1988-92; ptnr. Cohen Todd Kite & Stanford, Cin., 1992—. Mem. arbitration rules com. U.S. Dist. Ct. (so. dist.) Ohio 1984, fed. mediation panel, 1990—; lectr. Nat. Bus. Inst., 1994, 99; mem. oversight adv. bd. Lunken Airport, 2000-04, chmn. bd. dirs., 2001-04. Author: Fundamentals of Commercial Lending Law. Mem. cmty. initiatives com., cert. com. United Way and Cmty. Chest, 1995-97. Mem. Ohio Bar Assn., Cin. Bar Assn., U. Cin. Coll. Law Alumni Assn. (trustee 1988-90), Univ. Club. Home: 3693 Kroger Ave Cincinnati OH 45226-1931 Office: Cohen Todd Kite & Stanford 1200 Chiquita Ctr 250 East 5th St Cincinnati OH 45202-3174

**RUBIN, ROBERT SAMUEL,** investment banker; b. Boston, Sept. 22, 1931; s. Jesse Abraham and Rose (Solomon) R.; m. Martha Lucy Adams, Dec. 15, 1956; children: Rebecca, David, James, Nathaniel. BA, Yale U., 1953; MBA, Harvard Coll., 1955. With Lehman Bros., 1958-70, ptnr., 1967-70; mng. dir., bd. dirs. Lehman Bros. Kuhn Loeb, Inc., N.Y.C., 1970-84; mng. dir. Salomon Smith Barney, Inc., N.Y.C., 1989—2001; sr. v.p. Bank One (now J.P. Morgan Chase), 2002—. Chmn Bklyn. Mus.; bd. dir. St. Anne's Sch. 2d lt. U.S. Army, 1955—58. Home: 218 Columbia Hts Brooklyn NY 11201-2105 Office: JP Morgan Chase 320 Park Ave New York NY 10022

**RUBIN, ROBERT TERRY,** psychiatrist, researcher, educator; b. LA, Aug. 26, 1936; s. Joseph Salem and Lorraine Grace (Baum) R.; m. Lynne Esther Mathews, Mar. 10, 1962 (div. Dec. 1980); children: Deborah, Sharon, Rachel; m. Ada Joan Mickas, Jan. 18, 1985. AB in premedical studies, UCLA, 1957; MD, U. Calif., San Francisco, 1961; PhD in physiology, U. So. Calif., 1977. Diplomate Am. Bd. Psychiatry and Neurology. Intern Phila. Gen. Hosp., 1961-62; resident in psychiatry Sch. Medicine UCLA, 1962-65, asst. prof. psychiatry, 1965-71, prof. psychiatry, 1972; prof. Pa. State U., Hershey, 1972-93; prof. neuroscis. Coll. Medicine Drexel U., Pitts., 1992—2006, prof. psychiatry, dir. Ctr. Neurosci. Rsch. Allegheny Campus, 1992—2005; prof. psychiatry UCLA Sch. Medicine, 2005—; chief dept. psychiatry & mental health VA Greater LA Healthcare System, 2005—. Cons. Naval Health Rsch. Ctr., San Diego, 1969-70; mem. Brain Rsch. Inst. UCLA, 1969—89; assoc. dir. Pitts. Tissue Engring. Initiative, 1994-2000; trustee Kinsey Inst. Sex Rsch., Ind. U., 1986-90. Contbr. articles to profl. jours. With USNR, 1967—69. Recipient Rsch. Sci. Devel. awards NIMH, 1972-77, Rsch. Scientist award, 1982, 87, 93. Fellow: AAAS, Am. Coll. Psychiatrists, Am. Psychiat. Assn.; mem.: Internat. Soc. Psychoneuroendocrinology (pres. 1984—87). Avocations: swimming, bagpiping. Office: VA Greater LA Healthcare System Dept of Psychiatry 116A 11301 Wilshire Blvd Los Angeles CA 90073 Office Phone: 310-268-3319. Business E-Mail: robert.rubin@va.gov.

**RUBIN, ROBERTA GAIL,** retired pathologist; b. Bklyn., Apr. 2, 1934; d. Victor and Pearl Bernard R.; m. Walter D'Uill; children: Leon Jesse, Victoria Roslyn. MD, SUNY, Bklyn., 1958. Pathologist Chilton Meml. Hosp., Pompton Plains, N.J., 1968-98; dir. lab. Livingston (N.J.) Cmyt. Hosp., 1987-88; assoc. pathologist Bronx Lebanon Hosp. Ctr., 1967-68; staff pathologist Maimonides-Coney Island Med. Ctr., Bklyn., 1964-67; dir. MDS Lab., Wayne, NJ, 1973—89; ret., 1989. Clin. instr. pathology SUNY, Bklyn., 1964-67, Albert Einstein Sch. Medicine, Bronx, 1967-68. Sec., treas. bd. Morris Area Cmty. Fedn., Whippany, N.J., 1989—. Fellow: Coll. Am. Pathologists; mem.: N.J. Soc. Pathologists (bd. dirs. 1989—2001), Found. Am. Med. Women's Assn. (treas. 2001—), Nat. Coun. Women's Health (pres. 1999—2001), Am. Women's Hosp. Assn. (chmn. 1993—), Am. Med. Women's Assn. (v.p. fin. 1993, Camille Mermod award 1995). Avocations: doll art collector, cosmology, reading. Home: 10 Woodland Ave Glen Ridge NJ 07028

**RUBIN, SAMUEL HAROLD,** internist, consultant; b. N.Y.C., July 24, 1916; s. Joseph and Esther (Goldfarb) R.; m. Audrey Arndt, Nov. 20, 1943; children: James E., David A. AB, Brown U., 1938; MD, St. Louis U., 1943; MS, U. Chgo., 1957; DSc (hon.), N.Y. Med. Coll., 1997. Diplomate: Am. Bd. Internal Medicine. Intern Jewish Hosp., St. Louis, 1943-44; resident St. Louis U. Group Hosp., 1944-45, St. Mary's Hosp., Kansas City, Mo., 1945-46; practice medicine Asbury Park, NJ, 1948-61; vol. faculty mem. N.Y. Med. Coll., 1948-61, assoc. prof. dept. medicine, 1962-65, prof., 1965—, dir. Inst. Human Values in Med. Ethics, 1984-86; chief med. service N.Y. Med. Coll.-Met. Hosp. Center, 1966-71, assoc. dean, 1971-72, exec. dean, 1972-74, dean, v.p. acad. affairs, 1975, provost, dean, 1977-83, provost, dean emeritus, 1983—, cons., 1983—. Mem. bd. trustees St. Clares' Hosp., N.Y.C., 1985-2000, N.Y. Med. Coll., 1988-94. Contbr. articles to med. jours. With M.C. AUS, 1946-48. NIH program dir. grantee, 1966-71 Fellow A.C.P.; mem. N.Y. Acad. Sci. Home: 425E Heritage Hills Dr Somers NY 10589-1912

**RUBIN, SANDRA MENDELSOHN,** artist; b. Santa Monica, Calif., Nov. 7, 1947; d. Murry and Freda (Atliss) Mendelsohn; m. Stephen Edward Rubin, Aug. 6, 1966. BA, UCLA, 1976, MFA, 1979. Instr. Art Ctr. Coll. Design, Pasadena, Calif., 1980, UCLA, 1981. One-woman exhbns. include L.A. Louver Gallery, 1982, 92, 2003, L.A. County Mus. Art, 1985, Fischer Fine Arts, London, 1985, Claude Bernard Gallery, NYC, 1987; group exhbns. include L.A. County Mus. Art, 1977, 82, 83, L.A. Mcpl. Art Gallery, 1977, 83, 93, L.A. Contemporary Exhbns., 1978, L.A. Inst. Contemporary Arts, 1978, Newport Harbor Art Mus., Newport Beach, Calif., 1981, Odyssia Gallery, NYC, 1981, Nagoya (Japan) City Mus., 1982, Long Beach (Calif.) Mus. Art, 1982, Brooke Alexander Gallery, NYC, 1982, Laguna Beach (Calif.) Mus. Art, 1982, Jan Baum Gallery, L.A., 1984, San Francisco Mus. Art, 1986, Claude Bernard Gallery, NYC, 1986, Struve Gallery, Chgo., 1987, Boise (Idaho) Mus., 1988, Judy Youen's Gallery, London, 1988, Tatistscheff Gallery, Inc., Santa Monica, Calif., 1989, Tortue Gallery, Santa Monica, 1990, Contemporary Arts Forum, Santa Barbara, Calif., 1990, San Diego Mus. Art, 1991, Fresno (Calif.) Met. Mus., 1992, Jack Rutberg Fine Arts, L.A., 1993, San Jose Mus. Art, 2003, Pasadena Mus. Calif. Art, 2004. Recipient Young Talent Purchase award L.A. County Mus. Art, 1980; Artist's Fellowship grant NEA, 1981, 91. Avocations: gardening, exercise, reading, singing. E-mail: smr@pacific.net.

**RUBIN, SETH ISAIAH,** psychologist; b. Alexandria, La., Mar. 6, 1945; BA, Northwestern U., 1966, MA, 1968, PhD in Psychology, 1971. Diplomate in psychoanalysis and analytical psychology; cert. profl. qualification in psychology; lic. psychologist, Pa., Calif., Ariz.; Mass. Outpatient psychology fellow Hosp. U. Pa., 1978-80; tng. candidate, diploma candidate C.G. Jung Inst., Zurich, 1982-87; instr. dept. psychology Northwestern U., 1969-70; asst. prof. dept. psychology U. Ill. at Chgo. Circle, 1970-72; asst. rsch. prof. dept. psychiatry Med. Coll. Pa., 1974-75; asst. prof. dept. rsch. medicine, 1976-77, asst. prof. dept. ob-gyn., 1976-83, clin. assoc. dpet. psychiatry, 1987-88, clin. assoc. prof./clin. assoc prof. psychology in psychiatry, 1987-92; allied health profl. Phila. Psychiat. Ctr., 1988-92; allied health affiliate, clin. psychologist Calif. Pacific Med. Ctr., 1994—2004. Adj. prof. Union Grad. Sch., 1989-96, Calif. Sch. Profl. Psychology, Berkeley/Alameda, 1992—; vis. prof. psychology Saybrook Inst., 1994-95; lectr. in field; dir. James Goodrich Whitney Clinic, C.G. Jung Inst. San Francisco, 2004. Contbr. articles to profl. jours. Fellow Am. Coll. Advanced Practice Psychologists, Internat. Coll. Prescribing Psychologists; mem. APA, Internat. Assn. for Analytical Psychology, Am. Soc. Clin. Psychopharmacology, Assn. Grad. Analytical Psychologists of the C.G. Jung Inst., San Francisco Jung Inst. (dir., James Goodrich Whitney Clin.), Soc. for Psychotherapy Rsch., othrs. Office: 2019 A Webster St San Francisco CA 94115-2329 Office Phone: 415-771-5115. E-mail: sirseth@well.com.

**RUBIN, STANLEY CREAMER,** television producer, film producer; b. N.Y.C., Oct. 8, 1917; s. Michael Isaac and Anne (Creamer) R.; m. Elizabeth Margaret von Gerkan (actress Kathleen Hughes), July 25, 1954; children: John, Chris, Angela. Michael. Student, UCLA, 1933-37, BA, 2006. Writer Universal Studios, Universal City, Calif., 1940-42, Columbia Pictures, Los Angeles, 1946-47; writer, producer NBC-TV, Burbank, Calif., 1948-49; theatrical film producer various studios, 1949-55, Rastar Prodns., Columbia Pictures, 1988-91; TV producer CBS-TV, Los Angeles, 1956-59, Universal Studios, Universal City, 1960-63, 20th Century-Fox, Los Angeles, 1967-71, MGM Studios, Culver City, Calif., 1972-77; pres. TBA Prodns., Los Angeles, 1978—. Producer theatrical films including The Narrow Margin, 1950, My Pal Gus, 1950, Destination Gobi, 1951, River of No Return, 1952, Promise Her Anything, 1966, The President's Analyst, 1967, Revenge, 1989; co-producer White Hunter, Black Heart, 1990; TV prodns. include G.E. Theatre, 1959-63, Ghost and Mrs. Muir, 1968-69, Bracken's World, 1969-71; writer, producer TV film The Diamond Necklace, 1948 (Emmy award 1949); producer TV films including Babe, 1975 (Hollywood Fgn. Press Golden Globe award, Christopher medal), And Your Name is Jonah, 1978 (Christopher medal 1979), The Story of Satchel Paige, 1980 (Image award 1981); exec. producer TV prodn. Escape from Iran: The Canadian Caper, 1981. Producer spl. programming Dem. Nat. Conv., San Francisco, 1984, Columbia Pictures and Rastar Prodns., 1988-91. 1st lt. USAAF, 1942-46. Mem. Writers Guild Am. (dir. 1941-42), Producers Guild Am. (bd. dirs. 1968-74, pres. 1974-79, v.p. 1987-94, bd. dirs. 1994-2000), Acad. Motion Picture Arts and Scis., Acad. TV Arts and Scis. (bd. govs. 1971, 73), Phi Beta Kappa. Home and Office: 8818 Rising Glen Pl Los Angeles CA 90069-1222 E-mail: tbaprez@aol.com. *I'm still too young to sum up my life, but here's a thought in progress: Stay curious.*

**RUBIN, STEPHEN CURTIS,** gynecologic oncologist, educator; b. Phila., May 24, 1951; s. Alan and Helen (Metz) R.; m. Anne Loughran, May 30, 1985; children: Michael, Elisabeth. BS, Franklin & Marshall U., 1972; MD, U. Pa., 1976. Diplomate Am. Bd. Ob-gyn. (dir. divsn. gynecol. oncology 2005—), Nat. Bd. Med. Examiners. Intern in ob-gyn. U. Pa. Hosp., Phila., 1976—77, residency in ob-gyn., 1977—80, fellow in gynecologic oncology, 1980—92; asst. prof. ob-gyn. Med. Coll. Pa., Phila., 1982-85, dir. surg. gynecology, 1982-85, chief gynecol. oncology, 1984-85; asst. mem. gynecol. staff Meml. Sloan-Kettering Hosp., N.Y.C., 1985—90, assoc. mem., 1990—93; asst. prof. ob-gyn Cornell U. Med. Coll., 1985—90, assoc. prof., 1990—93; prof. ob-gyn., chief gynecologic oncology U. Pa., Phila., 1993—, Franklin Payne prof., gyn. oncology, 2003—. Editor: Ovarian Cancer, Cervical Cancer, Chemotherapy of Gynecologic Cancer, Uterine Cancer; contbr. over 250 articles to profl. publs. Recipient Career Devel. award Am. Cancer Soc., 1987, Boyer award Meml. Sloan-Kettering; grantee Nat. Cancer Inst., 1991, 96, 98, 99. Mem. ACS, ACOG, Am. Soc. Clin. Oncology, Soc. Gynecol. Oncologists (Pres.'s award 1993), Am. Gynecol. and Obstet. Soc., Soc. Gynecologic Investigation, Soc. Pelvic Surgeons, Gynecol. Cancer Found. (Karin Smith award 1996). Office: U Pa Med Ctr 3400 Spruce St Philadelphia PA 19104-4206 Office Phone: 215-662-3326.

**RUBIN, STEPHEN D.,** food products executive; BBA, JD, U. Wis. Pres. Vita Food Products, Inc., Chgo., 1982—, dir., 1982—, chmn. bd. Office: Vita Food Products Inc 2222 W Lake St Chicago IL 60612

**RUBIN, STEPHEN EDWARD,** publishing executive, editor, journalist; b. NYC, Nov. 10, 1941; s. Irving and Evelyn (Halprin) R. BA, NYU, 1965; MS, Boston U., 1966. Editor UPI, N.Y.C., 1966-69; freelance writer N.Y.C., 1969-82; founder, dir. Writers Bloc, N.Y.C., 1976-82; editor Vanity Fair Mag., N.Y.C., 1982-83; exec. editor Bantam Books, N.Y.C., 1984-85, v.p., editorial dir., 1985-88, sr. v.p., editor-in-chief adult fiction and non-fiction, 1987-88, sr. v.p., pub., editor-in-chief adult fiction and non-fiction, 1988-90; pres., pub. Doubleday divsn. Bantam Doubleday Dell Pub. Group, N.Y.C., 1990-95; chmn., CEO Bantam Doubleday Dell Internat. Divsn., London, 1995-98; pres., pub. Doubleday Divsn. Bantam Doubleday Dell Pub. Group (now Doubleday Broadway Group), N.Y.C., 1998—. Author: The New Met in Profile, 1974 Recipient Annual Prize, UJA-Fedn. NY pub. divsn., 2005. Avocations: listening to musical performances, collecting records, tapes and cds, reading, exercising. Office: Random House Inc 1745 Broadway New York NY 10019

**RUBIN, STEVEN D.,** lawyer; b. June 1, 1960; BA in Economics, Tulane U., 1982; JD with honors, U. Fla., 1986. Bar: Fla. 1986. Assoc. Stearns, Weaver, Miller, Weissler, Alhadeff & Sitterson, 1986—91, shareholder, 1991—2000, dir., 1998—2000; sr. v.p., gen. counsel Telergy, Inc., 2000—01, Ivax Corp., Miami, 2001—. Office: Ivax Corp 4400 Biscayne Blvd Miami FL 33137 Office Phone: 305-575-6000. Office Fax: 305-575-6055. E-mail: steven_rubin@ivax.com.

**RUBIN, THEODORE ISAAC,** psychiatrist, writer; b. Bklyn., Apr. 11, 1923; s. Nathan and Esther (Marcus) R.; m. Eleanor Katz, June 16, 1946; children: Jeffrey, Trudy, Eugene. BA, Bklyn. Coll., 1946; MD, U. Lausanne, Switzerland, 1951; grad., Am. Inst. Psychoanalysis, 1964. Resident psychiatrist Los Angeles VA Hosp., 1953, Rockland State Hosp., NY, 1954, Bklyn. State Hosp., 1955, Kings County Hosp., NY, 1956; chief psychiatrist Women's House of Detention, NYC, 1957; mem. faculty Downstate Med. Sch., NY State U., 1957-59; pvt. practice NYC, 1956—. Tng. and supervising psychoanalyst Am. Inst. for Psychoanalysis of Karen Horney Clinic and Ctr.; mem. faculty Am. Inst. Psychoanalysis, 1962—; pres. emeritus bd. trustees Am. Inst. Psychoanalysis. Author: Jordi, 1960, Lisa and David, 1961, Sweet Daddy, 1963, In The Life, 1964, Platzo and the Mexican Pony Rider, 1965, The Thin Book by a Formerly Fat Psychiatrist, 1966, The 29th Summer, 1966, Cat, 1966, Coming Out, 1967, The Winner's Note Book, 1967, The Angry Book, 1969, Forever Thin, 1970, Emergency Room Diary, 1972, Doctor Rubin Please Make Me Happy, 1974 Shrink, 1974, Compassion and Self-Hate, An Alternative to Despair, 1975, Love Me, Love My Fool, 1976, Reflections in a Goldfish Tank, 1977, Alive and Fat and Thinning in America, 1978, Reconciliations, 1980, Through My Own Eyes, 1982, One to One, Understanding Personal Relationships, 1983, Not to Worry, The American Family Book of Mental Health, 1984, Overcoming Indecisiveness, 1985, Lisa and David, The Story Continues, 1986, Miracle at Bellevue, 1986, Real Love, 1990, Child Potential, 1990, Anti-Semitism: A Disease of the Mind, 1990, Little Ralphie and The Creature, 1998; mem. editl. bd. Am. Jour. Psychoanalysis; also articles, columns.; co-writer (TV movie) Lisa and David, 1998. Served as officer USNR, World War II. Recipient Adolf Meyer award, Assn. Improvement Mental Health, 1963. Fellow Am. Acad. Psychoanalysis; mem. NY County Med. Soc., Am. Psychiat. Assn., Assn. Advancement Psychoanalysis, Authors Guild, Contemporary Authors, Writers Guild East. Office: 141 E 55th St Ste 9B New York New York 10022 Office Phone: 917-301-4889.

**RUBIN, VERA COOPER,** astronomer, researcher; b. Phila., July 23, 1928; d. Philip and Rose (Applebaum) Cooper; m. Robert J. Rubin, June 25, 1948; children: David M., Judith S. Young, Karl C., Allan. BA in Astronomy, Vassar Coll., 1948; MA, Cornell U., 1951; PhD, Georgetown U., 1954, DHL (hon.), 1997; DSc (hon.), Creighton U., 1978, Harvard U., 1988, Yale U., 1990, Williams Coll., 1993, U. Mich., 1996, Ohio State U., 1998, Smith Coll., 2001, Grinnell Coll., 2002, Ohio-Wesleyan U., 2004, Princeton U., 2005. From rsch. assoc. to asst. prof. Georgetown U., Washington, 1955-65; physicist U. Calif., LaJolla, 1963-64; astronomer Carnegie Inst., Washington, 1965—2001, sr. fellow, dept. terrestrial magnetism, 2001—. Chancellor's Disting. prof. U. Calif., Berkeley, 1981; vis. com. Harvard Coll. Obs., Cambridge, Mass., 1976—82, 1992—2002, Space Telescope Sci. Ins., 1990—92; Beatrice Tinsley vis. prof. U. Tex., 1988; Commonwealth lectr. U. Mass., 1991; Yunker lectr. Oreg. State U., 1991; Bernhard vis. fellow Williams Coll., 1993; Oort vis. prof. U. Leiden, The Netherlands, 1995; lectr. in field, Chile, Russia, China, Armenia, India, Japan, Europe; trustee Assoc. Univs., Inc., 1993—96; mem. Press. Commn. to Select U.S. Nat. Medal Sci. Awardees, 1995—98, chair, 1997—98; Pres.'s disting. visitor Vassar Coll., 1987; Halley lctr. Oxford Univ., 1997; bd. dirs. Research Corp., 2002—; adv. bd. Lowell Observatory. Assoc. editor: Astrophys. Jour. Letters, 1977—82, mem. editl. bd.: Sci. Mag., 1979—87, mem. sr. editl. bd.; 2001—, co-author several peer reviewed research papers. Named to Nat. Sci. Bd., 1996—2002; recipient U.S. Nat. Medal of Sci., 1993, Jansky Lectureship, Nat. Radio Astronomy Observatory, 1994, Gold medal, Royal. Astorn. Soc. London, 1996, Weizmann Women and Sci. award, 1996, Helen Hogg prize, Can. Astron. Soc., 1997, John Scott Award, City of Phila., 2001, Peter Gruber Internat. prize in cosmology, 2002, Bruce medal, Astron. Soc. of Pacific, 2003. Mem.: NAS (space sci. bd. 1974—77, chair sect. on astronomy 1992—95, James Craig Watson medal 2004), AAAS, Am. Philos. Soc., Assn. Univ. Rsch. in Astronomy (trustee 1973—76, 1994—96), Pontifical Acad. Scis. (Gold medal), Internat. Astron. Union (pres. commn. on galaxies 1982—85, chair U.S. nat. commn. 1999—2001), Am. Astron. Soc. (coun. 1977—80, Henry Norris Russell prize lectr. 1994), Phi Beta Kappa (scholar 1982—83). Democrat. Jewish. Achievements include being the first women permitted to observe at Palomar Observatory in California in 1965; being the first women since 1828 to receive the Gold Medal of the Royal Astronomical Society in London. *As an observational astronomer, it is my aim to obtain data of highest quality in order to answer questions concerning the universe in which we live. In spite of our enormous ignorance, each day offers exciting opportunities to learn a little more. This is the real joy of doing science.*

**RUBIN, ZICK,** psychology professor, writer, lawyer; b. NYC, Apr. 29, 1944; s. Eli and Adena Rubin; m. Carol Moses, June 21, 1969; children: Elihu James, Noam Moses BA, Yale U., 1965; PhD, U. Mich., 1969; JD, Harvard U., 1988. Bar: Mass., 1988. Asst. to assoc. prof. Harvard U., Cambridge, Mass., 1969—76; Louis and Frances Salvage prof. social psychology Brandeis U., Waltham, Mass., 1976—89; law clk. chief judge U.S. Ct. Appeals (1st cir.), 1988—89; assoc. Palmer & Dodge, Boston, 1990—93, counsel, 1994—2001; of counsel Hill & Barlow, Boston, 2001 03; prin. Law Office of Zick Rubin, Boston, 2003—. Chmn. com. behavioral scis. Yale U. Coun., New Haven, 1981-86; mem. Adams Papers adminstrv. com. Mass. Hist. Soc., 2001—. Author: Liking and Loving, 1973, Children's Friendships, 1980; co-author: Psychology, 1993; editor: Doing Unto Others, 1974, Relationships and Development, 1986; contbg. editor: Psychology Today, 1980-85; editorial bd.: Harvard Law Rev., 1986-88. Recipient Socio-Psychol. prize AAAS, 1969, Nat. Media award Am. Psychol. Found., 1980; grantee NSF, NIMH, Ford Found., Social Sci. Research Council, Found. Child Devel.; named one of Boston's top lawyers, Boston Mag. 2002. Mem. ABA, Nat. Assn. Coll. and Univ. Lawyers, Copyright Soc. USA, Boston Bar Assn., Am. Psychology-Law Soc., Authors Guild, Phi Beta Kappa. Clubs: Elihu (New Haven). Jewish. Office Phone: 617-965-9425. Business E-Mail: zrubin@zickrubin.com.

**RUBINFIEN, LEO H.,** photographer, filmmaker; b. Chgo., Aug. 16, 1953; Student, Reed Coll.; BFA, Calif. Inst. Arts, 1974; MFA, Yale U., 1976. Instr. in photography Swarthmore Coll., 1977, Sch. Visual Arts, N.Y.C., 1978-87; assoc. prof. art Fordham U., 1981-87; represented by Robert Mann Gallery, N.Y.C.; mem. faculty Gallatin Sch., NYU, 2001—. Mem. grad. faculty Sch. of Visual Arts, NYU, 2002—; vis. lectr. Cooper Union, 1982; vis. prof. Nusashino Fine Arts U., Tokyo, 2002. One man shows include Castelli Gallery, N.Y., 1981, Fraenkel Gallery, San Francisco, 1982, 86, Robert Mann Gallery, N.Y.C., 1994, 2001, Met. Mus. Art, N.Y.C., 1992, Sakai Art Forum, Tokyo, 1993, Cleve. Mus. Art, 1994, Seattle Art Mus., 1994, Robert Mann Gallery, N.Y.C.; exhibited in group shows at Internat. Ctr. Photography, N.Y., 1981, Inst. Contemporary Arts, London, 1981, San Francisco Mus. Modern Art, 1981, George Eastman House, Rochester, N.Y., 1981, Corcoran Gallery, Washington, 1981, Mus. Modern Art, N.Y., 1984, Met. Mus. Art, 2001, Tokyo Met. Mus. Photography, 2002; dir., co-author (film) The Money Juggler, 1988, My Bed in the Leaves, 1990; author: (books) A Map of the East, 1992, 10 Takeoffs 5 Landings, 1994, Shomei Tomatsu: Skin of the Nation, 2004, (essays) A Love-Hate Relations, Artforum, 1978, Investigations of a Dog, 1999, Guesses About the Work of Wu Yiming, 1999, The Poetry of Plain Seeing, 2000, Perfect Uncertainty, 2001, The Mask Behind the Face, 2004. Fellow Guggenheim Found., 1982-83, Asian Cult Coun., 1984, Internat. Ctr. Advanced Studies, 1998—, Japan Found., 2002, Asian Cult. Coun., 2002 Home: 145 Nassau St Apt 11c New York NY 10038-1514 Personal E-mail: oscawana@earthlink.net.

**RUBINI, GAIL,** education director; b. Washington, Dec. 6, 1950; d. Milton and Frances Kagan; m. Conrad Gleber; children: John Patrick, David Conrad. BA, UCLA, 1972; MFA, R.I. Sch. Design, 1976; MBA, U. Ill., Chgo., 1981. V.p. fin. Artist Prodn. Press, Chgo., N.Y.C., 1976—; adminstr. grants City of Chgo., 1979-80; edn. dean Ctr. for Media Arts, N.Y.C., 1981-86; dir. edn. SCS Bus. and Tech. Inst., N.Y.C., 1986—. Author: Darkroom Dynamics. Recipient grant Polaroid Corp., 1979-81, Ill. Arts Council, 1980, Nat. Endowment for Arts, 1982. Office: Gleber Printing 225 Varick St New York NY 10014-4304

**RUBIN-KATZ, BARBARA,** sculptor, human services manager; b. Springfield, Mass., May 3, 1931; d. Samuel and Jane (Freeman) Kurn; m. Emanuel Rubin, Mar. 27, 1955 (div. Dec. 1984); children: Raphael, Jonathan, Daniel, Rebecca; m. Robert Nathan Katz, June 15, 1986. BA, U. Ariz., 1952; MSW, Simmons Coll., 1955; MPH, Columbia U., 1977; postgrad. in Sculpture Studies, Phila. Coll. Art, 1981-85. Rschr. Bellevue Hosp., N.Y.C., 1970-75; health svcs. coord. Fedn. Jewish Agencies, N.Y.C., 1977-79, assoc. dir. planning Phila., 1979-84; sculptor Brookline, Mass., 1985—. Prin. works include sculpture at Mass. Gen. Hosp., Villa Campana, Tucson, Worcester Poly. Inst., Regency Park, Brookline, Mass, Temple Emanuel, Tucson, St. Elizabeth's Hosp., Brighton, Mass.; exhibited in group shows at Copley Soc. Boston shows, 1990—, New Eng. Sculptors Assn. shows, 1987—, The Roxbury Latin Sch., 1991, Jr. League Boston Decorator's Showhouse, Walpole, Mass., 1994, Faneuil Hall, Boston, 1994, Prestige Gallery, Danvers, Mass., 1995, Michael Allen Gallery, Brookline, Mass., 1996, Festival Arts, Newton, 1997, Curtis Gallery, Lenox, Mass., 1997, 98, Worcester Poly. Inst. 1997-98 Bradford (Mass.) Coll. 1999; contbr. articles to profl. jours Mem. Copley Soc. Boston (Copley Artist award 1992), New Eng. Sculptor's Assn. (bd. dirs. 1993), Brookline Coun. for Arts and Humanities. Home: 1731 Beacon St Apt 1403 Brookline MA 02445-5329 Personal E-mail: kate@wpi.edu.

**RUBINO, JOHN ANTHONY,** management and human resources consultant; b. Port Chester, N.Y., Nov. 22, 1956; s. Angelo J. and Ann (Posillipo) R.; m. Cynthia C. Corica, Nov. 9, 1980; 1 child, Sean Anthony. BA in Psychology magna cum laude, Wagner Coll., 1978; MBA with distinction, Pace U., 1985. Cert. compensation profl. Convention svc. mgr. Waldorf-Astoria Hotel, N.Y.C., 1978-80; compensation analyst County of Westchester, White Plains, N.Y., 1980-82; sr. compensation analyst Anaconda-Ericsson, Inc., Greenwich, Conn., 1982-83; compensation mgr. ASEA, Inc., White Plains, N.Y., 1983-84 Sterling Drug, Inc., N.Y.C., 1984-87; dir. exec. compensation The Equitable Life Insur. Co., N.Y.C., 1987-93; sr. mgr. human resources cons. Ernst & Young, N.Y.C., 1993-96; pres. Rubino Cons. Svcs., Pound Ridge, N.Y., 1996—. Author: Developing Compensation Programs, 1990, Communicating Compensation Programs, 1992; contbr. articles to profl. jours. Mem. Am. Compensation Assn. (course developer, instr., course leader, guest speaker 1988—), Am. Mgmt. Assn. (course developer, instr., course leader, guest speaker 1988—), Soc. for Human Resource Mgmt. (guest spkr. 1999—). Avocations: performing renaissance music, poetry, golf. Home and Office: Rubino Cons Svcs 29 Conant Valley Rd Pound Ridge NY 10576-1815 Office Phone: 914-533-5310. Personal E-mail: rubinocs@aol.com.

**RUBINO, VICTOR JOSEPH,** academic administrator, lawyer; b. NYC, Dec. 25, 1940; s. Joseph V. and Olympia (Gayda) R.; 1 child, Victor Gayda. BA in Govt., Cornell U., 1962, LLB, 1965. Bar: N.Y. 1965, U.S. Dist. Ct. (so. dist.) N.Y. 1969. Staff atty. Westchester Legal Svcs., White Plains, NY, 1968-71; assoc. Squadron Ellenoff Plesent & Lehrer, N.Y.C., 1971; treas., program officer Council on Legal Edn., N.Y.C., 1971-79; assoc. dir. Practising Law Inst., N.Y.C., 1979-83, exec. dir., 1983—. Democratic candidate for N.Y. State Assembly, 1970; chmn. Rye (N.Y.) Human Rights Commn., 1975-76. Served to capt. U.S. Army, 1966-68. Mem. ABA, Assn. Bar City N.Y. Office: Practising Law Inst 810 7th Ave Fl 26 New York NY 10019-5818 Office Phone: 212-824-5701. Business E-Mail: vrubino@pli.edu.

**RUBINSON, HOWARD ALAN,** physician; b. Bklyn., Aug. 24, 1949; s. Samuel and Hilda (Cohen) R.; m. Carol Berman, May 16, 1976; children: Roger, Abby. AB, Cornell U., 1971; MD, Hahnemann Med. Coll., Phila., 1975. Diplomate Am. Bd. Radiology. Radiology instr. Sch. Medicine U. Miami, Fla., 1979-81, asst. prof. radiology Fla., 1981-84; mem. attending staff North Beach Hosp., Ft. Lauderdale, Fla., 1984-89, North Ridge Med. Ctr., Ft. Lauderdale, Fla., 1989—, Hollywood (Fla.) Med. Ctr., 1998—, Parkway Regional Med. Ctr., 2001—; attending staff Holy Cross Hosp., Ft. Lauderdale, Fla., 2004—, Mercy Hosp., Miami, Fla., 2005—. Contbr. articles to profl. jours. Mem. Am. Coll. Radiology, Am. Soc. Emergency Radiology, Soc. Breast Imaging, Radiol. Soc. N.Am., Am. Roentgen Ray Soc., Soc. Thoracic Radiology, South Fla. Radiol. Soc. (pres. 1996-97), Fla. Radiol. Soc., Fla. Med. Assn., Broward County Med. Assn. Office: Ste 120 2900 N Military Tr Boca Raton FL 33431 Personal E-mail: hrubinson@comcast.net.

**RUBINSTEIN, AARON,** lawyer; b. NYC, Nov. 15, 1950; s. Jacob and Golda Rubinstein; m. Carri Sue Zogan, Mar. 3, 1974; children: David Michael, Joanne. BA magna cum laude, Cornell U., 1972; JD, NYU, 1975. Bar: NY 1976, US Dist. Ct. (so. and ea. dists.) 1976, US Supreme Ct. 1986. Assoc. Kaye, Scholer LLP, NYC, 1975-84, ptnr., 1985—, chair Litig. Dept. and Securities and Derivatives Litig. Mem. ABA, NY State Bar Assn., Assn. of Bar of City of NY, Order of Coif. Office: Kaye Scholer LLP 425 Park Ave New York NY 10022-3506 Office Phone: 212-836-8412. E-mail: arubinstein@kayescholer.com.

**RUBINSTEIN, ERNEST,** librarian, educator; b. Queens, N.Y., July 11, 1952; s. Jack and Jeanne Rubinstein; life prtnr. Paul Glassman. BA, Brandeis U., 1974; AMLS, U. Mich., 1977; MTS, Harvard U., 1979; MA, Hebrew Union Coll., 1985; PhD, Northwestern U., Evanston, Ill., 1995. Indexer H.W. Wilson Co., Bronx, NY, 1984—88; editor Am. Theological Libr. Assn., Chgo., 1988—90; reference libr. North Park Coll., Chgo., 1990—94; libr. Interchurch Ctr., N.Y.C., 1994—2005; libr. theol. Drew U., Madison, NJ, 2005—. Asst. adj. prof. humanities NYU, N.Y.C., 1995—; adj. faculty New Sch., N.Y.C., 2001—; book reviewer Publs. Weekly, N.Y.C., 1999—2001. Author: (non-fiction) Episode of Jewish Romanticism, 1999; contbr. articles to mags. Vol. peer counselor Horizons, Chgo., 1992—94, Aids Pastoral Care Network, Chgo., 1992—94. Mem.: Am. Acad. Religion. Jewish. Home: 200 Cabrini Blvd Apt 42 New York NY 10033 Office: Drew Univ Libr Madison NJ 07940 Personal E-mail: ehr3@nyu.edu.

**RUBINSTEIN, EVA (ANNA),** photographer; b. Buenos Aires, 1933; d. Arthur and Aniela (Mlynarska) R.; m. William Sloane Coffin Jr., 1956 (div. 1968); children: Amy, Alexander (dec.), David. Ballet tng., Paris, N.Y.C., Calif., 1938-53; student. Scripps Coll., 1950-51, UCLA, 1952-53; student in photography, Lisette Model, 1969, Jim Hughes, 1971, Ken Heyman, 1970, Diane Arbus, 1971. Lectr. numerous workshops, seminars, confs.; instr. photo seminars Lodz Film Sch., Poland, 1986, 87. Dancer, actress: off-Broadway and Broadway, including original prodn. The Diary of Anne Frank, 1955-56; European dance tour, 1955; one-person shows of photographs include Underground Gallery, N.Y.C., 1972, Dayton Art Inst., Ohio, 1973, Arles Festival, France, 1975, Canon Photo Gallery, Amsterdam, 1975, Neikrug Gallery, N.Y.C., 1975, 79, 81, 82, 85, La Photogalerie, Paris, 1975, Friends of Photography, Carmel, Calif., 1975, Galerie 5.6, Ghent, Belgium, 1976, Gallery Trochenpresse, Berlin, 1977, Frumkin Gallery, Chgo., 1977, Galeria Sinisca, Rome, 1979, Hermitage Found. Mus., Norfolk, Va., 1982, Photographers Gallery, London, 1983, Galerie Forum Labo, Arles, France, 1983, Galerie Nicephore, Lyon, France, 1983, Image Gallery, Madrid, 1984, Muzeum Sztuki, Lodz, Poland, 1984, Il Diaframma/Canon Gallery, Milan, 1984, A.R.P.A. Gallery, Bordeaux, 1984, Chateau d'Eau, Toulouse, France, 1985, Galerie Demi-Teinte, Paris, 1985, Associated Artist Photographers galleries in Warsaw, Krakow, Lodz, Katowice and Gdansk, Poland, 1985-86, Foto/Medium/Art Gallery, Wroclaw, Poland, 1986, Visions Gallery, San Francisco, 1986, Canon Galerie, Paris, 1986, Salone Internat. SICOF, Milan, 1987, St. Krzysztof Gallery, Lodz, 1987, L'Image Fixe, Lyon, 1988, Artotheque, Grenoble, 1988, Neikrug Photographic, N.Y.C., 1989, Heuser Art Ctr. Gallery, Bradley U., Peoria, Ill., 1989, 3-os Encontros da Imagem, Braga, Portugal, 1989, Bibliotheque Nat. Galerie Colbert, Paris, 1989, Galerie Picto-Bastille, Paris, 1989-90, Portfolio Gallery, London, 1990, Vaison-La-Romaine, France, 1990, Hist. Mus. of City of Lodz, 1990, Galerie Artem, Quimper, France, 1993, Galerie F.N.A.C. Etoile, Paris, 1994, other F.N.A.C. galleries (France, Belgium, Spain), 1994-97, Galerie Augustus, Berlin, 1995, L'Imagerie, Lannion, France, 1995, Zacheta Gallery, Warsaw, 1996, Salon of Modern Art B.W.A., Bydgoszcz, Poland, 1997, Galleries of Polish Insts., Sofia, Bulgaria, Berlin, Moscow, Bratislava, Slovakia, I. Beszkova Gallery, Plewen, Bulgaria, 1997, Hungarian Mus. Photographic Art, Budapest, 1997, LTF Gallery, Lodz, Poland, 1998, Konfrontacje Fotograficzne, Gorzow Wielopolski, Poland, 1998, Centrum Kultury Zamek, Poznan, Poland, 1998, Mus. Regionalny, Wrzesnia, Poland, 1998, Galeria Korytarz, Jelenia Gora, Poland, 1998, Galeria Foto-Medium-Art, Wroclaw, Poland, 1998, Galeria Pusta, Centrum Kultury, Katowice, Poland, 1998, Teatr Wielki, Lodz, Poland, 2000, Gallery Europa Club, NY, 2003, Château de la Petite, Malmaison, France, 2004, Alliance Française, N.Y.C., 2006; numerous group shows since 1971 including most recently Zacheta Gallery, Warsaw, 2002, Lodz Photographic Soc., 2002, Polish/Am.Photographers, Polish Consulate, NY, 2003, Gutman Libr., Harvard, 2003, Floating Found. Photography, N.Y., 2004, XL, La Collection Photographique du Musée d'Arles, 2005; represented: in permanent collections Library of Congress, Washington, Met. Mus. Art, N.Y.C., Bibliotheque Nationale, Paris, Musee Reattu, Arles, France, Kalamazoo Inst. Arts, Israel Mus., Jerusalem, Fotografiska Museet, Stockholm, Muzeum Sztuki, Lodz, Poland, Histo Mus. of City of Lodz, others; author: Eva Rubinstein, 1974, Eva Rubinstein, I Grandi Fotografi, 1983, 2 ltd. edit. portfolios with introductions by John Vachon andAndré Kertész, Lodz: Brief Encounters, 1998, Eva Rubinstein: Fotografie 1967-1990, 2003; contbr. photographs in various books, mags., profl. jours. *Making photographs is my way of exploring the questions that keep me alive by ever leading to further questions.*

**RUBINSTEIN, FREDERIC ARMAND,** lawyer; b. Antwerp, Belgium, Apr. 20, 1931; came to U.S., 1942; s. Samuel N. and Sieffe (Warrenreich) R.; m. Susan August, Dec. 24, 1968; 1 child, Nicolas Eric August Rubinstein. BA, Cornell U., 1953, JD, 1955. Bar: N.Y. 1955. Assoc. Law Offices of I. Robert Feinberg, N.Y.C., 1955-60, Guggenheimer & Untermyer, N.Y.C., 1960-65, ptnr., 1965-85, Kelley Drye & Warren LLP, N.Y.C., 1985—. Vice chmn. zoning & planning com. Local Community Bd. # 6, N.Y.C., 1980-86. Mem. ABA (bus. law sect., emerging growth ventures subcom., chmn. 1988-96). Office: Kelley Drye & Warren LLP 101 Park Ave New York NY 10178-0002 Office Phone: 212-808-7581.

**RUBINSTEIN, JOSEPH HARRIS,** education educator; b. N.Y.C., Oct. 5, 1936; s. Morris M. and Anne (Roslofsky) R.; m. Heike Buechler, Aug. 12, 1968; children: Mark Philip, Sara Erika. AB, N.Y.U., 1960, MS, 1964, PhD, 1969. Assoc. rsch. scientist N.Y.U., 1969-71, asst. prof., biology, 1971-72; dir. maths. and sci. curriculum Open Court Publ. Co., La Salle, Ill., 1972-79, cons., 1979-84; prof. Coker Coll., Hartsville, S.C., 1984—, chmn. dept. edn., 1984-99. Author: Realmath, 1975, 2d edit. 1989, 3d edit. 1999, Math Explorations and Applications, 1998, 2d edit., 2003, Real Science, 1999, SRA Real Math, 2006. With U.S. Army, 1955-58. Mem. Nat. Coun. Tchrs. Math., Nat. Sci. Tchrs. Assn., N.Y. Acad. Scis., Sigma Xi. Jewish. Home: 414 Laurel Oak St Hartsville SC 29550-3712 Office: Coll Ave Coker College Hartsville SC 29550-3797 Business E-Mail: jrubinstein@coker.edu.

**RUBINSTEIN, MOSHE FAJWEL,** engineering educator; b. Miechow, Poland, Aug. 13, 1930; came to U.S., 1950, naturalized, 1965; s. Shlomo and Sarah (Rosen) R.; m. Zafrira Gorstein, Feb. 3, 1953; children: Iris, Dorit. BS, UCLA, 1954, MS, 1957, PhD, 1961. Designer Murray Erick Assos. (engrs. and archs.), L.A., 1954-56; structural designer Victor Gruen Assos., L.A., 1956-61; asst. prof. UCLA, 1961-64, assoc. prof. dept. engring., 1964-69, prof., 1969—, chmn. engring. sys. dept., 1970-75, program dir. modern engring. for execs. program, 1965-70. Cons. Pacific Power & Light Co., Portland, Oreg., Northrop Corp., U.S. Army, NASA Rsch. Ctr., Langley, Tex.

Instruments Co., Hughes Space System Divsn., U.S. Army Sci. Adv. Com., Kaiser Aluminum and Chem. Corp., IBM Corp., TRW. Author: (with W.C. Hurty) Dynamics of Structures, 1964 (Yugoslavian transl. 1973), Matrix Computer Analysis of Structures, 1966 (Japanese transl. 1974), Structural Systems, Statics Dynamics and Stability, 1970 (Japanese transl. 1979), Patterns of Problem Solving, 1975, (with K. Pfeiffer) Concepts in Problem Solving, 1980, Tools for Thinking and Problem Solving, 1986; IEEE Press Videotapes; Models for People Driven Quality, 1991, Quality through Innovation, 1991, Creativity for Ongoing Total Quality, 1993, Relentless Improvement, 1993, (with I.R. Firstenberg) Patterns of Problem Solving, 2d edit., 1995, (with I.R. Firstenberg) The Minding Organization, 1999 (Portuguese/Japanese transl. 2000, Spanish/Chinese/Russian transls. 2001). Recipient Disting. Tchr. award UCLA Acad. Senate, 1964, Western Electric Fund award Am. Soc. Engring. Edn., 1965, Disting. Tchr. trophy Engring. Student Soc., UCLA, 1966; Sussman prof. for disting. visitor Technion-Israel Inst. Tech., 1967-68; named Outstanding Faculty Mem., UCLA Engring. Alumni award, 1979, Outstanding UCLA Civil Engring. Alumni award, 1990, Outstanding Faculty Mem., State of Calif. Command Coll., 1987, 88, 89, 94, 95; Fulbright-Hays fellow, Yugoslavia and Eng., 1975-76; voted one of UCLA's Top 20 Profs. of the Century. Mem. ASCE, Am. Soc. Engring. Edn., Seismol. Soc. Am., Sigma Xi, Tau Beta Phi. Achievements include research in use of computers in structural systems, analysis and synthesis; problem solving and decision theory; creativity and innovation in the orgn. Home: 10488 Charing Cross Rd Los Angeles CA 90024-2646 Office: UCLA Sch Engring & Applied Sci Los Angeles CA 90024 Office Phone: 310-825-7731. Business E-Mail: mrubinst@ucla.edu.

**RUBIN-VEGA, DAPHNE,** actress; b. Panama City, Panama, Nov. 18, 1969; m. Tommy Costanzo, 2002; 1 child. LHD (hon.), Kean U., 2005. Mem. Pajama Party (pop trio), DRV (rock band). Actress (films) The Occultist, 1987, I Like It Like That, 1994, Lotto Land, 1995, Wild Things, 1998 (Blockbuster award best supporting actress in a suspense thriller), Flawless, 1999, Skeleton Woman, 2000 (Best Actress in a feature film, NY Independent Film and Video Festival), Justice, 2003, Virgin, 2003, Alchemy, 2005, Life on the Ledge, 2005, (TV series) NY Undercover, 1996, Hey Joel, 2003, (Broadway plays) Rent, 1996—97 (Theatre World award best actress in musical, Tony award nomination best actress in a musical, Drama Desk award nomination), (plays) Rocky Horror Picture Show, 2001, Anna in the Tropics, 2004 (Tony award nomination best featured actress in a play), Two Sisters and a Piano, Gum, Between Us (Outstanding Female Performance Rutgers U.), The House of Bernarda Alba, 2006, Everything's Turning into Beautiful, 2006. Mailing: c/o Cathexis Inc ATTN Juan Azize PO Box 778 New York NY 10013 E-mail: daphnespeaks@att.net.*

**RUBLE, AMANDA L.,** elementary school educator; b. Sandusky, Ohio, Nov. 30, 1973; d. Daniel and Cynthia Matter; m. Eric Ruble; 1 child, Lauryn. BS in Edn., Bowling Green U., Ohio, 1997, MEd in Gifted and Talented, 2001. Nat. bd. cert. adolescent social studies. Tchr. Gibsonburg (Ohio) Exempted Village Schs., 1998—2000, Stamm Elem. - Fremont (Ohio) City Schs., 2000—. Office: Stamm Elem Sch 1038 Miller St Fremont OH 43420

**RUBLE, BERNARD ROY,** minister, educator, personnel director, labor relations consultant; b. Greensburg, Ind., Apr. 4, 1923; s. Jesse Emery and Marietta (Ward) Ruble; m. Mary Helen Rullman, Dec. 22, 1946; children: Barry Reece, Blane Rodney. BS, Ind. U., Bloomington, 1949; postgrad. transactional analysis, Midwest Inst. Human Understanding, 1972—75. Asst. mgr. Morris 5 and 10 Stores, Greensburg, Ind., 1941; store keeper Public Svc. Co., Ind., Greensburg, 1941—43; asst. mgr. pers. Kroger Co., Cin., 1949—51, mgr. pers. Madison, Wis., 1951—56, Ft. Wayne, Ind., 1956—58, Cleve., 1958—73, mgr. labor rels. Erie mktg. area Solon, Ohio, 1973—84; faculty Kroger Edn. Ctr., Cin., 1978—84. Educator Cleve. State U., trustee Meat Cutters Health and Welfare Fund, 1971—79, Retail Clks. Union Health and Welfare Fund, Akron, 1970—88, No. Ohio Hospice Coun., 1981—84. Active United Appeal Greater Cleve., Cmty. Chest Greater Cleve., Met. Health Planning Corp., Ohio; hosp. vol. Vis. Nurses Assn., Ohio, Home Health Care, Washington, Hospice Western Reserve, Washington; adv. com. Washington, 1977—78; v.p. trustee Urban League Greater Cleve., 1968—75; trustee Cmty. Health Found., Ohio, Greater Cleve. Interchurch Coun., 1993—99; bd. dirs. N.E. Ohio Hosp. Coun.; team rep. B.R. Ruble Racing, Burton, Ohio. With USAC, 1943—45. Mem.: Chesterland Ministerial Assn., Indsl. Rels. Rsch. Assn. (pres.), Cleve. Pers. Assn., Am. Soc. Pers. Adminstrn. (charter), Soc. Advancement Mgmt. (trustee Madison chpt. 1952—55), Photog. Soc. Am., Sertoma (trustee Madison 1952—56, Ft. Wayne 1957—58, charter), Masons, Alpha Kappa Psi. Home and Office: 8644 Ranch Dr Chesterland OH 44026-3132 Office Phone: 440-729-4691. E-mail: brr3x@sbcglobol.net.

**RUBLE, RONALD MERLIN,** humanities and theater communications educator; b. Shelby, Ohio, July 4, 1940; s. Eldred Roy and Dessie Cedelia (Shaw) Briner; m. Nancy Kay Dillon, Aug. 29, 1970 (div. Apr. 1976); children: Eric Douglas, Kristofer Philip. BA, Otterbein Coll., 1962; MA, Bowling Green State U., 1966, PhD, 1975. Site coord. Arts Unltd. Firelands Coll. of Bowling Green U., Huron, Ohio, 1989-92, instr. speech and theater, 1970-75, program dir. speech and theater, 1979-88, asst. prof. speech and theater, 1976-79, chmn. dept. humanities, 1976-80, assoc. prof. humanities and theater, 1979-98, tchg. artist Arts Unltd., 1987-89, assoc. prof. emeritus humanities, 1998—; bus. mgr., play dir. Huron Playhouse Bowling Green U., 1966-78, 2002—03; artistic dir. Caryl Crane Children's Theatre, Huron, 1990—. Co-chmn. Arts in the Parks Festival, North Ctrl. Ohio Arts Coun., Sandusky, 1976-78, v.p. bd. dirs., 1977-78; theater cons. Caryl Crane Children's Theatre, Sandusky, 1984-90. Site play The Gingerbread lady, 1978 (1st place N.W. region Ohio Cmty. Theatre Assn. 1978); contbr. poems, short story to profl. publs; playwright. Unit commr. Erie dist. of Firelands coun. Boy Scouts Am., Huron, 1984-87, mem. troop rev. bd., 1985-96, merit badge counselor Firelands dist. Heart of Ohio coun., Vermilion, Ohio, 1984—; elder 1st Presbyn. Ch., Huron, 1988-90, 95-97. Recipient Outstanding Educator in Arts award Ohio Ho. of Reps., 1975, Outstanding Young Man of Am. award Nat. Jaycees, 1977, Outstanding Cmty. Svc. award Huron C of C., 1983, 84, 85, Outstanding Leader award Firelands Area Coun. Boy Scouts Am., 1988, Scouter's Key award, 1987, Scouter of the Yr. award Troop 31, 1985, Marcellus F. Cowdery Educator of Yr. award Erie County C. of C., 1998. Mem. Am. Alliance Theatre Edn., Drama League, Ohio Theatre Alliance, Am. Film Inst., Ohio Humanities Coun., Internat. Soc. of Poets (disting.), Nat. Authors Registry, Poets Guild, Acad. of Am. Poets. Avocations: creative writing, concerts, plays, yardwork. Home: 729 Taylor Ave Huron OH 44839-2522 Office: Bowling Green State U Firelands Coll 1 University Dr Huron OH 44839-9719

**RUBLEY, CAROLE A.,** state legislator; b. Bethel, Conn., Jan. 18, 1939; d. George B. and Evelyn M. (Maloney) Drumm; m. C. Ronald Rubley, Aug. 25, 1962; children: Lauren M. Rubley Simpson, Stephen R., Kristin Rubley Vaughan. BA in Biology, Albertus Magnus Coll., 1960; MS in Environ. Health, West Chester U., 1988. Tchr. biology Danbury (Conn.) High Sch., 1960-62, Waltham (Mass.) High Sch., 1962-63; real estate salesperson Henderson-Dewey, Wayne, Pa., 1976-81; solid waste coord. Chester County Health Dept., West Chester, Pa., 1981-88; environ. cons. Environ. Resources Mgmt., Exton, Pa., 1988-92; mem. Pa. Ho. Reps., Valley Forge, 1992—. Mem. environ. resources, energy, consumer affairs, fin. and children and youth com. House of Reps.; mem. Pa. 21st Century Environ. Commn.; former chair energy and elec. utilities com. NCSL, task force on protecting Democracy. Author: (with others) Leading Pennsylvania into 21st Century, 1990. Chmn. Ea. Chester County Regional Planning Commn., 1976-85; vice chmn. planning commn. Tredyffrin Twp., Berwyn, Pa., 1976-86, mem. bd. suprs., 1987-92; bd. dirs. Pa. Resources Coun., exec. v.p., 1988-92. Recipient Outstanding Legislator award, Pa. Planning Assn., 2004. Mem. LWV (pres. Upper Main Line chpt. 1976-78, Involved Voter of Yr. award 1993), Pa. Environ. Coun., Green Valleys Assn., Open Land Conservancy. Republican. Roman Catholic. Avocations: aerobics, tennis, hiking, reading, travel. Home: 621 Vassar Rd Wayne PA 19087-5312 Office Phone: 610-640-2356. Business E-Mail: carole.rubley@verizon.net.

**RUBNITZ, MYRON ETHAN,** pathologist, educator; b. Omaha, Mar. 2, 1924; s. Abraham Srol and Esther Molly (Jonich) R.; m. Susan Belle Block, Feb. 9, 1952; children: Mary Lu Rubnitz Roffe, Peter, Thomas (dec.), Robert. BSc, U. Nebr., 1945; MD, U. Nebr., Omaha, 1947. Diplomate Am. Bd. Pathology. Intern Mt. Sinai Hosp., Cleve., 1947-48; fellow Mt. Sinai Hosp., N.Y.C., 1948-49; resident in pathology Michael Reese Hosp., Chgo., 1949-51; pathologist VA Hosp., Hines, Ill., 1953-56, chief labs., 1956-93, cons., 1993—; assoc. path. pathology Loyola U. Med. Sch., Maywood, Ill., 1963-70, prof., 1970-99, prof. emeritus, 1999—. Adj. prof. Ill. State U., Normal, 1979-96, 2003—, U. St. Francis, Joliet, Ill., 1989—, Ea. Ill. U. Charleston, 1991—, Western Ill. U., Macomb, 1991—; clin. instr. Augustana Coll., Rock Island, Ill., 1991—. Chmn. candidates com. Village Caucus, Winnteka, Ill., 1969-70; bd. dirs. Chgo. Commons Assn., 1968—, North Shore Sr. Ctr., 1998—; mem. New Trier High Sch. Caucus, Winnetka, 1972-74. With AUS, 1943-46, PTO; 1st lt. M.C., U.S. Army, 1951-53. Fellow Am. Soc. Clin. Pathologists, Coll. Am. Pathologists; mem. Internat. Acad. Pathology, Assn. VA Pathologists (pres. 1982-84), Chgo. Pathology Soc., Lake Shore Country Club (Glencoe, Ill.), Mich. Shores Club (Wilmette, Ill.). Avocations: electronics, tennis, travel. Home: 979 Sheridan Rd Winnetka IL 60093 Personal E-mail: northfieldoc@juno.com.

**RUBOCKI, MELANIE GOEDEKER,** lawyer; BA, U. Pa., Phila., 1993, BS in Bus., 1993; JD, U. Notre Dame, South Bend, Ind., 1997. Bar: Idaho, Ill. Atty. Perkins Coie LLP, Boise, Idaho, 2004—. Office: Perkins Coie LLP 251 E Front St Ste 400 Boise ID 83702 Office Phone: 208-343-3434. Office Fax: 208-343-3232. Business E-Mail: mrubocki@perkinscoie.com.

**RUBOTTOM, GEORGE MILTON,** foundation administrator, chemist; b. London, Mar. 19, 1940; s. Alphonso Milton and Lorna Annie Rubottom. AB, Middlebury Coll., 1962; PhD, MIT, 1967. Lectr. Bucknell U., Lewisburg, Pa., 1968—70; asst. prof. U. PR, Rio Piedras, 1970—75; assoc. and full prof. U. Idaho, Moscow, 1975—84; sr. program dir. in chemistry NSF, Arlington, Va., 1984—. Exec. sec. edn., human resources com. Nat. Sci. Bd., Washington, 1987—2000; mem. dir.'s rev. bd. NSF, Arlington, 1987—2000. Author: (book) Academic Excellence: The Sourcebook, 2001; reviewer: jour. Jour. Org. Chem., Tetrahedron, Tetrahedron Letters. Scuba instr. YMCA, Washington, 1994—. Grantee, NIH, 1973—78, Petroleum Rsch. Fund, 1971—72, 1979—81; Postdoctoral fellow, NIH, 1967—68. Mem.: Am. Chem. Soc., Sigma Xi, Phi Kappa Phi, Phi Beta Kappa. Achievements include research in new methods for the oxidation of C-C double bonds; new methods for the preparation and cleavage of cyclopropanols. Business E-Mail: grubotto@gmail.com.

**RUBRIGHT, JAMES ALFRED,** paperboard and packaging company executive; b. Phila., Dec. 17, 1946; s. James Alfred and Helen Lucille (Evans) R. (deceased); m. Mary Elizabeth Angelich, Dec. 30, 1987; children: Noah Michael, Benjamin James, Jami Anne, Nathaniel Drew, James McCurdy, William Angelich. BA, Yale U., 1969; JD, U. Va., 1972. Bar: Ga. 1972. Ptnr. King & Spalding, Atlanta, 1972-94; sr. v.p., gen. counsel Sonat Inc., Birmingham, 1994-97; pres. So. Natural Gas Co. subs. Sonat Inc., Birmingham, 1997-98; exec. v.p. Sonat Inc., Birmingham, 1998-99; chmn., CEO Rock-Tenn Co., Norcross, Ga., 1999—. Office: Rock-Tenn Co 504 Thrasher St Norcross GA 30071-1914

**RUCCHIN, STEVE,** professional hockey player; b. Thunder Bay, Ont., Can., July 4, 1971; BS, U. Western Ontario. Center Mighty Ducks of Anaheim, 1994—2005, NY Rangers, 2005—06, Atlanta Thrashers, 2006—. Office: Atlanta Thrashers Centennial Tower 101 Marietta St NW Ste 1900 Atlanta GA 30303*

**RUCCI, ANTHONY JOSEPH,** health care products and services executive; b. Youngstown, Ohio, Sept. 19, 1950; BS, Bowling Green State U., 1972, MA, 1976, PhD in Inds I and Organizational Psychology. 1978. Asst. dir., pers. adminstr. Mahoning County Mental Health and Retardation Bd., Youngstown, Ohio, 1972-74; cons., grad. student Bowling Green (Ohio) State U., 1974-78; cons. LWFW Inc., Dallas, 1978-79; pers. planning specialist Baxter Internat. Inc., Deerfield, Ill., 1979-80, mgr. pers. planing, 1980-85; v.p. orgn. and human resource planning Am. Hospital Supply Corp. Am. Hosp. Supply Corp., 1985-86; sr. v.p. human resources Baxter Internat. Inc., Deerfield, Ill., 1986-92. Instr. Bowling Green State U., 1974-78, Davis Jr. Coll., 1975-77, U. Tex. at Dallas, 1979, U. Ill., Chgo. Cir., 1981, Lake Forest Grad. Sch. Mgmt., 1983; invited speaker confs., socs., forums, seminars; mem. White House Fellows Regional Selections Panel, Chgo., 1988, 89. Cons. editor, mem. editorial bd. Jour. Applied Psychology, 1982-86; assoc. editor Human Resource Planning Jour., 1989; editorial reviewer Jossey-Bass Pub. Co., 1991; contbr. articles to profl. jours. Mem. Chancellor's Exec. Adv. Bd., U. Ill. at Chgo.; bd. dirs. Lake Forest Grad. Sch. Mgmt., 1984-87; mem. Human Resource Mgmt. Adv. Bd. U. Mich. Sch. Bus. Adminstrn. Mem. APA, The Bus. Roundtable (bd. dirs., employee rels. com.), Adv. Coun. on Human Resources Mgmt. of the Conf. Bd. (bd. dirs.), Coun. on Orgn. and Mgmt. of the Conf. Bd. (bd. dirs.), Soc. Indsl./Organizational Psychology, Human Resource Planning Soc. (bd. dirs. 1986-90), Human Resource Mgmt. Assn. Chgo. (bd. dirs. 1986-89), Antaean Soc., Sigma Xi, Omicron Delta Kappa.

**RUCH, DAVID S.,** orthopedist, surgeon; m. Susan G. Ruch; children: David S. Jr., John Charles, Michael R. MD, Bowman Gray Sch. Medicine, Winston-Salem, NC, 1988. Diplomate Am. Bd. Orthopaedic Surgery, 1996. Prof. Duke U. Med. Ctr., Durham, NC, 2005—; prof. orthopaedic surgery Wake Forest U. Sch. Medicine, Winston-Salem, 2004—05. Dir. hand, upper extremity and microvascular surgery fellowship program Duke U. Med. Ctr., 2005—. Mem.: Am. Orthopaedic Assn. Office: Duke U Med Ctr Box 3466 Durham NC 27710 Office Phone: 919-668-5259. Office Fax: 919-668-5476.

**RUCHKIN, VLADISLAV,** psychiatrist; b. Arkhangelsk, Russia, Dec. 1, 1969; s. Vladimir Ruchkin and Margarita Ruchkina; m. Irina Karpuck, July 12, 1995. MD, Arkhangelsk State Inst., Russia, 1993, Candidate of Med. Scis., 1997; PhD, Umea U., Sweden, 1998. Diplomate Russian Bd. Psychiatry and Neurology 1994. Forensic psychiatrist Regional Ctr. Forensic Psychiatry, Arkhangelsk, Russia, 1994—99; asst. prof. No. State Med. U., Arkhangelsk, 1999—. Assoc. dir. rsch. Rehab. Ctr. Abandoned Children, Arkhangelsk, Russia, 1995—99; post doctoral fellow Yale Child Study Ctr., 2000—02, assoc. dir. internat. child mental health program, 2000—, asst. dir. rsch. tng. program, 2000—02, assoc. rsch. scientist, 2003—05, asst. prof. adj., 2005—. Contbr. numerous articles to profl. jours. Sgt. Anti-Aircraft, 1988—89, Belarus. Mem.: Am. Assn. Child and Adolescent Psychiatry, European Assn. for Forensic Child and Adolescent Psychiatry, Psychology, and Allied Professions (bd. mem. 1999—). Avocations: reading, music. Office: Yale Child Study Ctr 230 S Frontage Rd New Haven CT 06520-7900 Business E-Mail: vladislav.ruchkin@yale.edu.

**RUCK, ROSEMARIE ULISSA,** retired social worker, freelance/self-employed writer; b. Buffalo, Aug. 24, 1939; d. Stanley Joseph Ren and Bertha Sosnowski; m. Donald Neal Ruck, Nov. 8, 1958; children: Theresa Dorene Ruck Novak, Donna Rose Ruck Seyler, Michael Donald. AS, Genesee C.C., 1970—72; BS, SUNY Brockport Coll., 1972—75. Chemical Dependency Counselor Pk. Ridge Unity Health Sys. & Brockport Coll., NY, 1999, Basic Reading and ESL Tutor Literacy Volunteers of Am., Inc., NY, 1984. Sr. caseworker/counselor Assn. for Retarded Citizens, Batavia, NY, 1975—79; dir. Literacy Volunteers of Am. - Genesee County Chpt., Batavia, NY, 1983—89. Exec. dir. Literacy Volunteers of Am. - Orleans County Chpt., Albion, NY, 1989—98; chem. dependency counselor Pk. Ridge- Unity Health Sys., Rochester, NY, 1998—99; social worker Lakeside Beikirch Care Ctr., Brockport, NY, 1999—2002; writer Freelance -, Holley, NY, 2002—. Mem. of Genesee c.c. steering com. Genesee County Legislature, Batavia, NY, 1967—68; mem. of com. responsible for devel. of Genesee county registry Genesee County Inter-Agy. Coun., Batavia, NY, 1975—77; grant writer & mem. of program com. for domestic violence program YWCA, Batavia, NY, 1980—81; mem. of steering com. for regional action phone Genesee County Inter-agency Coun., Batavia, NY, 1985—86; mem. of steering com. for vol.

connection registry United Way of Genesee County, Batavia, NY, 1983—84; program chair person YWCA, Batavia, NY, 1980—82; voluneer leadership chairperson Young Women's Christian Associaiton, Batavia, NY, 1983—84; strategic planning com. chairperson United Way of Ea. Orleans County, Albion, NY, 1999—2001. Recipient Friends of Edn., Albion Ctrl. Sch. Bd. of Edn., 1991, Recognition of Outstanding Leadership, Literacy Volunteers of Am. - Genesee County Chpt., 1989, Literacy Volunteers of Am. - Orleans County Chpt., 1992, 1993, 1994, 1995, 1996, 1997, 1998, Genesee County Chpt. of Assn. for Retarded Citizens, 1979, Quality Recognition award, Lakeside Beikirch Care Ctr., 2001. Mem.: Literacy Volunteers of Am., Holley's Writers Club. Catholic. Achievements include Revived rural literacy organization and became number one in national organizations from over 450 affiliates; development of first workplace literacy program in Western NY state. Avocations: reading, writing, travel, art, exercise. Home: 5314 Upper Holley Rd Holley NY 14470 Personal E-mail: ruruck@juno.com.

**RUCKELSHAUS, WILLIAM DOYLE,** investment company executive, former federal agency administrator; b. Indpls., July 24, 1932; s. John K. and Marion (Doyle) R.; m. Jill Elizabeth Strickland, May 11, 1962; children: Catherine Kiley, Mary Hughes, Jennifer Lea, William Justice, Robin Elizabeth. BA cum laude, Princeton U., 1957; LL.B., Harvard U., 1960. Bar: Ind. 1960. Atty. Ruckelshaus, Bobbitt & O'Connor, Indpls., 1960-68; dep. atty. gen. State of Ind., 1960-65, chief counsel Office of Atty. Gen., 1963-65; minority atty. Ind. Senate, 1965-67; mem. Ind. Ho. of Reps., 1967-69, majority leader, 1967-69; asst. atty. gen. civil divsn. US Dept. Justice, Washington, 1969-70; adminstr. EPA, Washington, 1970-73, 1983-85; acting dir. FBI, Washington, 1973; dep. atty. gen. U.S. Dept. Justice, Washington, 1973; mem. firm Ruckelshaus, Beveridge, Fairbanks & Diamond, Washington, 1974-76; sr. v.p. law and corp. affairs Weyerhaeuser Co., Tacoma, 1976-83; pres. William D. Ruckelshaus Assocs., 1985-88; mem. firm Perkins Coie, Seattle, 1985-88; chmn. bd., CEO Browning-Ferris Industries, Inc., Houston, 1988-95, chmn., 1995—99; founder, prin. also bd. dirs. Madrona Investment Group, LLC, 1996—; strategic dir. Madrona Venture Group, Seattle, 1999—; chmn. World Resources Inst., Washington D.C., 1999—. Bd. dirs. Cummins Engine Co., Nordstrom, Inc., Weyerhaeuser Co., Inc., Vykor, Inc. Rep. nominee for U.S. Senate, Ind., 1968; apptd. by Pres. Clinton to serve as U.S. envoy to Pacific Salmon Treaty with Can., 1997-98; mem., Pres. Council on Sustainable Devel., 1993-97; commr. Commn. on Ocean Policy, 2001-; chmn. Salmon Recovery Funding Bd., Wash. Mem. World Resource Inst. (chmn. 1998—), Fed. Bar Assn., Ind. Bar Assn., D.C. Bar Assn., Indpls. Bar Assn. Office: Madrona Investment Group LLC 1000 2nd Ave Ste 3700 Seattle WA 98104-1053 Office Phone: 206-674-3008. E-mail: bill@madrona.com.

**RUCKENSTEIN, ELI,** chemical engineering professor; b. Botosani, Romania, Aug. 13, 1925; arrived in U.S., 1969; m. Velina Rothstein, May 15, 1948; children: Andrei, Lelia. BSChemE, Poly. Inst., Bucharest, Romania, 1949, PhD, 1967; PhD (hon.), Tech. U., Bucharest, 1993. Prof. Poly. Inst., Bucharest, 1949—69; vis. prof. U. London, 1969; NSF sr. scientist Clarkson Coll. Tech., Potsdam, NY, 1969—70; prof. U. Del., Newark, 1970—73, SUNY, Buffalo, 1973—81, disting. prof., 1981—. Vis. Humbolt prof. Bayreuth U., Germany, 1986; Gulf vis. prof. Carnegie Mellon U., Pitts., 1988—89; disting. lectr. U. Waterloo, 1985, U. Mo., 1983; Fair Meml. lectr. U. Okla., 1987; Colburn Symposium lectr. U. Del., 1988, Robert L. Pigford meml. lectr., 99; Van Winkle lectr. U. Tex., 1989; Berkeley lectr., 97; Robert A. Welch Found. lectr., 97; Barnett F. Dodge disting. lectr. Yale U., 1998. Contbr. articles to profl. jours. Named Merk Disting. lectr., Rutgers U., 1992; recipient Nat. award, Romanian Dept. Edn., 1958, 1964, Tchg. award, 1961, George Spacu award, Romanian Acad. Sci., 1963, Sr. Humbolt award, Alexander von Humbolt Found., 1985, Creativity award, NSF, 1985, Nat. Medal of Sci., 1998. Mem.: AIChE (Alpha Chi Sigma award 1977, Walker award 1988, Founders award 2002), NAE (Founders award 2004), Am. Chem. Soc. (Kendall award 1986, Jacob F. Schoellkopf medal 1986, Langmuir Disting. Lectr. award 1994, E.V. Murphree award 1996). Office: SUNY Dept Chem Engring 303 Furnas Hall Buffalo NY 14260-4200 Business E-Mail: feaeliru@buffalo.edu.

**RUCKER, DARIUS,** musician; b. Charleston, SC, May 13, 1966; m. Beth Leonard, 2000; 1 child. Albums with Hootie & the Blowfish include: Cracked Rear View, 1994 (two Grammy awards 1995), Fairweather Johnson, 1996, Musical Chairs, 1998, Take 2, 2000, Hootie & the Blowfish, 2003, Looking for Lucky, 2005, Live in Charleston, 2006; solo albums include: Back to Then, 2002. Home: 2519 Devine St Columbia SC 29205-2407*

**RUCKER, DONALD W.,** emergency physician, educator, consultant; b. Montreal, Que., Can. came to U.S., 1960; s. Klaus G. and Daisy Rucker. AB, Harvard U., 1977; MD, U. Pa., 1981; MBA, Stanford U., 1987, MS, 1988. Diplomate Am. Bd. Internal Medicine, Am. Bd. Emergency Medicine. Product mgr. Datamedic, Waltham, Mass., 1988-93; emergency physician Beth Israel Hosp., Boston, 1990—2000; instr. Med. Sch. Harvard U., Boston, 1992—2000; v.p., chief med. officer Siemens Med. Solutions, 2000—. Emergency physician Univ. Pa. Health System, 2000—. Fellow Am. Coll. Emergency Physicians. also: 51 Valley Stream Pkwy Malvern PA 19355-1406

**RUCKER, MARGARET RICKENBACKER,** psychologist, special education educator; b. Simpsonville, S.C., July 2, 1972; d. Douglas Randolph and Emily Gressette Rucker. BS, Coll. of Charleston, 1994; EdS, Citadel, 2002. Cert. tchr. S.C. Bd. Edn., Nat. Cert. Sch. Psychologist Nat. Assn. Sch. Psychologists. Spl. edn. tchr. Calhoun County Sch. Dist., St. Matthews, SC, 1994—97, Charleston County Sch. Dist., 1997—99; sch. psychologist Cherokee County Sch. Dist., Gaffney, 2001—05. Contbr. articles to profl. jours. Mem.: Nat. Assn. Sch. Psychologists (award 2004), Palmetto State Tchrs. Assn. Avocations: kayaking, reading, hiking. Home: 648 Cotton Branch Dr Boiling Springs SC 29316

**RUCKER, RICHARD DOUGLAS, JR.,** emergency physician; b. May 3, 1947; m. Helen Regina Mostue Hannula, Jan. 15, 1977; children: Brigit-Mary Irene Hannula, Seth Benjamin Hannula, Michael Jacob, Joshua Preiss. BA in Liberal Arts, U. Ariz., 1969, MS in Zoology, 1970; MD, George Washington U., Washington, 1975; PhD in Surgery, U. Minn., 1994. Diplomate Am. Bd. Emergency Medicine, Am. Bd. Surgery, Am. Bd. Thoracic Surgery, lic. Nat. Bd. Med. Examiners, Minn., Mo., Mass., N.D.; cert. BLS instr., ACLS instr., Pediat. Advanced Life Support instr., Advance Trauma Life Support instr. Intern in gen. surgery U. Minn., Mpls., 1975—76, resident in gen. surgery, 1976—83; resident in thoracic surgery Washington U., St. Louis, 1986—87, Boston U., 1987—88; emergency medicine physician Midway Hosp., St. Paul, 1978—81, St. John's Hosp., St. Paul, 1978—81, Divine Redeemer Hosp., St. Paul, 1983—86; trauma surgeon St. Paul Ramsey Hosp., St. Paul, 1983—86; cardiothoracic surgeon numerous hosps., St. Paul, 1989—92; emergency medicine physician hosps., Mpls., 1992; cardiovascular and thoracic surgeon Dakota Heartland Hosp., Fargo, ND, 1992—96; emergency medicine physician hosps., Bloomington, Minn., 1996—. From lab. asst. to grad. tchg. asst. U. Ariz., Tucson, 1968—71; physician with hosp. privileges Unity Hosp., Fridley, Minn., 1996—, Mercy Hosp., Anoka, Minn., 1996—, Fairview Ridges Hosp., Bloomington, Minn., 1999—, Meth. Hosp., St. Louis Park, Minn., 1996—, Healteast Hosps., 2002—; clin. asst. prof. surgery U. N.D. Sch. Medicine, 1993—96. Contbr. chpts. to books and articles to profl. jours. Lt. USAR, 1970—78. Recipient award, SAR, 1966, Res. Officers Assn., 1967, Assn. U.S. Army, 1968, Svc. award, Phi Delta Epsilon Med. Soc., 1973—74, Rsch. award, HEW, 1972, NIH, 1978—81, Resident Rsch. award, Assn. Acad. Surgeons, 1981; Rsch. grant, Washington Heart Assn., 1973. Fellow: Am. Acad. Emergency Medicine, Am. Coll. Emergency Medicine, Am. Coll. Cardiology, Am. Coll. Chest Physicians (assoc.), Am. Coll. Surgeons (assoc.); mem.: Am. Coll. Exec. Physicians, Aldo R. Castaneda Soc. Pediat. Cardiovascular Surgery, Ramsey County Med. Soc., Am. Coll. Emergency Physicians, Minn. Med. Soc., Alpha Epsilon Delta, Beta Beta Beta, Phi Eta Sigma. Office: Emergency Physicians Profl Assn 7301 Ohms Ln Ste 650 Edina MN 55439-4000 Home: 330 Woodlawn Ave Saint Paul MN 55105-1240 Office Phone: 952-835-9880. Office Fax: 952-835-4403. E-mail: RDRuckerJr@aol.com, RDRuckerJr@comcast.net.

**RUCKER, RICHARD NEAL,** retired protective services official, emergency medical technician, director; b. Canton, Ohio, Sept. 16, 1945; s. Mason Samual and Wilma Pansy Rucker; m. Linda Mae Hicks, Apr. 13, 1968; children: Linda Denise McFarland, Stacy Elizabeth, Paula Renee, Richard Andrew, Heidi Suzanne, Kristine Dannell, Michael David, Brittany Alexandra. Dep. insp. gen. Ohio Insp. Gen. Office, Columbus, 1998—2001; maj. Ohio State Hwy. Patrol, Columbus, 1972—98; ret. State dir. EMS State Govt., Columbus, Ohio, 2001—. Bd. chmn. Wesleyan Ch., Galloway, Ohio, 1997—2005. With USN, 1965—67. Decorated Navy letter of Recognition US Navy. Achievements include patents for Candle Safety Device Patent. Avocations: golf, gardening. Office: Ohio EMS 1970 West Broad St Columbus OH 43223 Office Phone: 614-995-4752. Office Fax: 614-995-7012. E-mail: rnrucker@dps.state.oh.us.

**RUCKER, ROBERT D.,** state supreme court justice; b. Canton, Ga. married; 3 children. BA, Ind. U., 1974; JD, Valparaiso Sch. of Law, 1976; LLM, U. Va., 1998. Dep. prosecuting atty., Lake County, Ind.; city atty. City of Gary, Ind.; pvt. practice East Chicago; judge Ind. Ct. of Appeals, 1991—99; justice Ind. Supreme Ct., Indpls., 1999—. Former vice chmn. Ind. Commn. for Continuing Legal Edn. Bd. dirs. Legal Svcs. of N.W. Ind. Decorated Vietnam Vet. Fellow: Indianapolis Bar Foundation; mem.: ABA, Nat. Bar Assn. (exec. com. mem. Judicial Council), Ind. Judges Assn., Am. Judicature Soc. Office: Ind Supreme Ct State House Rm 312 200 W Washington St Indianapolis IN 46204-2798*

**RUCKER, THOMAS LEE,** physicist; PhD in Analytical Chemistry, U. Tenn., Knoxville, 1988. Mgr. radiol. assessment and protection SAIC, Oak Ridge, Tenn., 1988—; rsch. assoc. Oak Ridge Nat. Lab. Mem.: Am. Chem. Soc., Health Physics Soc. (local councilman 2005). Office: Science Applications International Corp PO Box 2501 Oak Ridge TN 37831-2501 Office Phone: 865-481-2993.

**RUCKMAN, ROGER NORRIS,** pediatric cardiologist; b. Washington, Dec. 15, 1944; s. Norris Elliott and Eugenia (Campbell) R.; m. Kathleen Anne Smith; children: Robert, Karen, Stephen, Jonathan. BA in Chemistry, Williams Coll., Williamstown, Mass., 1966; MD, U. Va., 1970. Cert. in Pediat. 1976, in Pediatric Cardiology 1979. Intern Peter Bent Brigham Hosp., 1970-71; resident Med. Ctr. Hosp. of Vermont, 1973-75; fellow in cardiology Children's Hosp., Boston, 1975-77; asst. prof. pediatrics U. Nebr., Omaha, 1977-79, George Washington U., Washington, 1980-82, assoc. prof. pediatrics, 1982-90, prof. pediatrics, 1990—; pediatric cardiologist Children's Hosp. Nat. Med. Ctr., Washington, 1980—, chmn. cardiology, 1986-89. Contbr. articles to profl. jours. Served to capt. U.S. Army, 1971-73. Recipient Disting. Service award, Am.-Korea Found., 1972; NIH grantee, 1982—. Fellow Am. Acad. Pediatrics, Am. Coll. Cardiology; mem. Am. Heart Assn., Teratology Soc., Soc. Pediatric Research, Columbia Country Club (Chevy Chase, Md.). Republican. Presbyterian. Avocations: tennis, golf. Office: CNMC Dept Cardiology 111 Michigan Ave NW Washington DC 20010-2916 Office Phone: 202-884-2020. Business E-Mail: rruckman@cnmc.org.

**RUD, ANTHONY GORDON, JR.,** education educator; b. Pittsfield, Mass., Jan. 10, 1953; s. Anthony Gordon and Marianne (Ellis) R.; m. Rita Marian Long, Aug. 6, 1983; 1 child, Rachel Anne Elizabeth. AB, Dartmouth Coll., 1976; MA, Northwestern U., 1979, PhD, 1982. Asst. dir. admissions Dartmouth Coll., Hanover, N.H., 1982-86; fellow, sr. fellow N.C. Ctr. for Advancement of Teaching, Cullowhee, 1986-94; assoc. dean Purdue U., West Lafayette, Ind., 1994—2001, prof., 2001—. Editor, author: A Place for Teacher Renewal, 1992, The Educational Conversation, 1995. Office: Purdue U EDST BRNG 100 N University St West Lafayette IN 47907-2098 E-mail: rud@purdue.edu.

**RUDA, HOWARD,** lawyer, finance company executive; b. N.Y.C., Sept. 7, 1932; s. Menahem and Lucy (Gillenson) R.; m. Leah E. Zeliger, Sept. 22, 1963; 1 child, Amy. BA, CCNY, 1954; JD, Columbia U., 1959. Bar: N.Y. 1959, U.S. Dist. Ct. (so. and ea. dists.) N.Y. 1959. Assoc., then ptnr. Laporte & Meyers, N.Y.C., 1959-63; staff atty., then gen. counsel Meinhard Comml. Corp., N.Y.C., 1963-68; with C.I.T. Group Holdings, Inc., N.Y.C., 1968-87, asst. gen. counsel, 1968—; gen. counsel, v.p., dir. C.I.T. Corp., C.I.T. Leasing Corp., N.Y.C., 1973-84; counsel Hahn & Hessen, N.Y.C., 1987—. Lectr. Practicing Law Inst., Banking Law Inst.; dir. Am. Bankruptcy Inst., 1982-91; arbitrator Am. Arbitration Assn. Editor: Asset Based Financing, Jour. of Bankruptcy Law and Practice. Served with U.S. Army, 1954-56. Fellow Am. Bar Found., Am. Coll. Comml. Fin. Lawyers (regent 1992-95); mem. ABA (chmn. equipment financing com. 1982-85, chmn. ad hoc bulk sales com. 1987-90), Am. Law Inst., Phi Beta Kappa. Jewish. Home: 8 Mirrielees Rd Great Neck NY 11021-2928 Office: Hahn & Hessen 488 Madison Ave New York NY 10022 Office Phone: 212-478-7265. Business E-Mail: hruda@hahnhessen.com.

**RUDACILLE, SHARON VICTORIA,** medical technician; b. Ranson, W.Va., Sept. 11, 1950; d. Albert William and Roberta Mae (Anderson) Rudacille. BS cum laude, Shepherd Coll., 1972. Med. technologist VA Ctr., Martinsburg, W.Va., 1972—. Instr. Sch. Med. Tech., 1972—76, assoc. coord. edn., 1976—77, edn. coord., 1977—78, quality assurance officer clin. chemistry, 1978—80, lab. svc. quality assurance and edn. officer, 1980—84, clin. chemistry sect. leader, 1984—86, staff med. technologist, 1986—94, supervisory med. technologist, 1994—95, sr. med. technologist, 1995—; adj. faculty mem. Shippensburg (Pa.) State Coll., 1977—78, Shepherd Coll., 1977—78. Mem.: Shepherd Coll. Alumni Assn., W.Va. Soc. Med. Technologists, Am. Soc. Clin. Pathologists, Am. Soc. Med. Tech., Sigma Pi Epsilon. Bapt. Home: PO Box 14 Ranson WV 25438-0014

**RUDAVSKY, DAHLIA C.,** lawyer; b. NYC, Sept. 9, 1951; d. Benjamin Zev and Malka B. (Liben) R.; m. Robert R. Jampol, Oct. 31, 1971; children: Malka, Noah. BA magna cum laude, Yale U., 1972; JD, Calif., Berkeley, 1978. Bar: Calif. 1979, Mass. 1980, U.S. Dist. Ct. (no. dist.) Calif. 1979, U.S. Dist. Ct. Mass. 1981, U.S. Ct. Appeals (1st cir.) 1984, U.S. Supreme Ct. 1990. Assoc. Angoff, Goldman, Manning, Pyle, Wanger & Hiatt, Boston, 1980-84, Avery & Friedman, Boston, 1984-86, McDonald Noonan & Kaplan, Newton, Mass., 1986-88; ptnr. Shilepsky, Messing & Rudavsky, P.C., Boston, 1988-93, Messing and Rudavsky, P.C., Boston, 1993—, Messing, Rudavsky & Weliky PC, Boston. Cons. in field. Named one of top Boston lawyers, Boston Mag., 2004; recipient Georgina Smith Award, AAUP, Washington, 1990. Mem. AFL-CIO (lawyers coordinating com., nat. adv. bd. 1983-84), Nat. Lawyers Guild, Mass. Bar Assn. Fluent in french & hebrew. Office: Messing Rudavsky & Weliky PC 50 Congress St Boston MA 02109 E-mail: drudavsky@mrwemploymentlaw.com

**RUDCZYNSKI, ANDREW B.,** academic administrator, medical researcher; b. Nottingham, England, Sept. 7, 1947; came to U.S., 1951; s. Richard B. and Krystyna Z. R.; m. Andrea Skalny, Oct. 16, 1976 (div. Oct. 1990); children: Christina, Thomas. BSc in Biology/Biochemistry, McGill U., 1969; PhD in Immunology, Syracuse U., 1974; MBA in Adminstrn., So. Ill. U., 1984. Prin. investigator scrub typhus project divsn. Rickettsiology U.S. Army Med. Rsch. Infectious Diseases, Ft. Detrick, Md., 1974—76; rsch. assoc. dept. biology Mich. Cancer Found., Detroit, 1976-77, rsch. scientist dept. immunology, unit chief immunology unit Breast Cancer Prognostic Study, 1977-80; asst. dir. Office Rsch. and Grants U. Md. Eastern Shore, Princess Anne, 1980-83; extramural assoc. Office Extramural Rsch. and Tng., Office of Dir. NIH, 1981-82; asst. dir. Office Rsch. & Sponsored Programs Rutgers U., Piscataway, NJ, 1983-84, dir., 1984-99; asst. v.p. rsch. adminstrn., 1985-93, assoc. v.p. rsch. policy and adminstrn., 1993-99; assoc. v.p. fin., exec. dir. rsch. svcs. U. Pa., Phila., 1999—. Field reader strengthening devel. instns. program U.S. Dept. Edn., 1990; mem. Chancellor's task force instrn. and rsch. infrastructure support N.J. Dept. Higher Edn., 1992. Contbr. articles, abstracts to profl. jours. Capt. U.S. Army Med. Svc. Corps, 1974-76. Recipient traineeship award NSF, 1969-71; predoctoral fellow NIH, 1973-74. Mem. AAAS, Nat. Coun. Univ. Rsch. Adminstrs. (profl. devel. com. 1988-90, region II program com. 1989-90, chmn. region II 1990-92, nat. program com. 1994-95), Coun.

Govtl. Rels. (fed. mgmt. devel. com. 1989-90, bd. dirs. 1998-2003, tech. transfer and ethics com. 1998-99, chair rsch. compliance and adminstrn. com. 1999-2003), Beta Gamma Sigma, Sigma Xi. Roman Catholic. Home: 2033 Rodman St Philadelphia PA 19146-1359 Office: Univ Pa Office Rsch Svcs 3451 Walnut St Ste P-221 Philadelphia PA 19104-6205 Office Phone: 215-573-9249. Business E-Mail: abrude@pobox.upenn.edu.

**RUDD, D(ALE) F(REDERICK),** chemical engineering professor; b. Mpls., Mar. 2, 1935; m. Sandra C. Coryell, 1964; children: Karen, David. BS, U. Minn., 1956, PhD in Chem. Engring., 1960. Asst. prof. chem. engring. U. Mich., Ann Arbor, 1960-61; from asst. prof. to prof. U. Wis., Madison, 1961-94, Schlicter emeritus prof. chem. engring., 1994—. Co-author: Strategy of Process Enging., 1968, Process Synthesis, 1973, Strategy of Pollution Control, 1977, Petrochemical Tech. Assessment, 1981, Microkinetics of Heterogeneous Catalysis, 1993. Named J.S. Guggenheim fellow, 1970; recipient Allan P. Colburn award, 1971. Mem. Nat. Acad. Engring., 1978. Achievements include contributions to the knowlege of process engineering. Personal E-mail: daleandsandy@yahoo.com.

**RUDD, DAVID WILLIAM,** management consultant, chemical engineer, consultant; b. Floral Park, N.Y., Dec. 31, 1931; s. Edward Lynn and Joanna (McSorley) Rudd; m. Harriet Fay Sart, Aug. 8, 1953; children: Rebecca, Rachel. BA in Chemistry, Colby Coll., 1953; MS in Phys. Chemistry, Northeastern U., 1962. Rsch. chemist Monsanto Chem. Co., Everett, Mass., 1956-58, Kendall Co., Walpole, Mass., 1958-60, Metal Hydrides, Beverly, Mass., 1960-62; sr. staff engr. Western Electric Co., North Andover, Mass., 1969-78; mem. rsch. staff Engring. Rsch. Ctr., Princeton, NJ, 1978-80; co-founder, dir. David W. Rudd Assocs., mfg. cons., 1985—. Iso-9000 auditor, 1993; co-owner cert. tree farm, Sumner, Maine. Vol. tutor program Mass. Pub. Sch., Lawrence, 1991. With 7th Cav. U.S. Army, 1953—55. Co-recipient Malcolm Baldrige Nat. Quality award, with AT&T's Transmission Divsn., 1992; recipient Engring. Excellence award, Western Electric Co., 1969, C. B. Sawyer Meml. award, 1974, Vol. Tutoring Program award, AT&T, 1991, Lucent Tech. Patent award, 1999. Mem.: We. Electric Engring. Excellence Soc. (pres. 1977—83), Svc. Corp Ret. Execs., Tel. Pioneers Am. (life), Western Foothills Heritage Trust, McLaughlin Found., Sumner Hist. Soc. (bd. dirs. 1996—). Achievements include research in surface chemistry, permeability of metals to hydrogen, rocket propellant synthesis infrared method of Q evaluation synthetic quartz, crystal growth, printed circuit tech., metal joining; computer-integrated mfg. techniques, statis. quality control, soldering tech., environ. modifications of mfg. processes, ISO 9,000 auditor; patents for for growth of synthetic quartz; research in infra red analysis of quartz; computer control of synthetic quartz crystal growth process. Home: 489 Valley Rd Sumner ME 04292-3402 Office Phone: 207-388-2362. Personal E-mail: davhar@megalink.net.

**RUDD, NICHOLAS,** investor, consultant; b. NYC, Mar. 18, 1943; s. Emmanuel and Lucie Lia Rudd; m. Judith Carol Anderson, 1995; children: Alexis Henry, Kenneth Charles. BA, Columbia U., 1964, MBA, 1967. Mem. staff Ford Motor Co., N.Y.C., 1964-65, Young & Rubicam Inc., N.Y.C., 1968-99, sr. v.p. mgmt. svcs., 1980-90, chief info. officer, 1990-95; chief knowledge officer Wunderman Cato Johnson, N.Y.C., 1996-99; prin. Venture Mgmt. Svcs., Inc., 1999—2003, Anderson Rudd Co., 2003—; mktg. chair Stamford Symphony Orch., 2003—. Dir. emeritus Nat. Choral Coun., chmn., 1993-95, Veritas Therapeutic Cmty. Found.; bd. dirs. Columbia U. Club NY, A Better Chance of Westport; mem. com. TEAM Westport. Mem. Beta Gamma Sigma. Office: 20 Sea Spray Rd Westport CT 06880

**RUDD, RICKY,** race car driver; b. Chesapeake, Sept. 12, 1956; m. Linda Rudd; 1 child, Landon. Profl. race car driver NASCAR, 1975—, team owner, driver, 1993—. Named Winston Cup Rookie of Yr., 1977, winner, Riverside, 1983, Banquet Frozen Foods 300, 1989, Bud at the Glen, 1990, TranSouth 500, 1991, Peek Antifreeze 500, 1992, Miller Genuine Draft 400, 1993, Slick 50 300, 1994, Dura Lube 500, 1995, Winston Cup, 1996, AC Delco 400, 1996, Miller 500, 1997, Brickyard 400, 1997, NAPA Autocare 500, 1998, 9th in NASCAR standings, 1995. Office: c/o NASCAR PO Box 2875 Daytona Beach FL 32120-2875

**RUDDY, FRANK,** lawyer, retired ambassador; b. NYC, Sept. 15, 1937; s. Francis Stephen and Teresa (O'Neil) Ruddy; children: Neil, David, Stephen. AB, Holy Cross Coll., 1959; MA, NYU, 1962, LLM, 1967; LLB, Loyola U., New Orleans, 1965; PhD, Cambridge U., Eng., 1969. Bar: D.C., N.Y., Tex., U.S. Supreme Ct. Faculty Cambridge U., 1967-69; asst. gen. counsel USIA, Washington, 1969-72; sr. atty. Office of Telecomm. Policy, White House, Washington, 1972-73; dep. gen. counsel USIA, Washington, 1973-74; counsel Exxon Corp., Houston, 1974-81; asst. adminstr. AID (with rank asst. sec. state) Dept. State, Washington, 1981-84; U.S. ambassador to Equatorial Guinea, 1984-88; gen. counsel U.S. Dept. Energy, Washington, 1988-89; v.p. Sierra Blanca Devel. Corp., Washington, 1989-92; ptnr. Ruddy & Muir, Washington, 1998—2004, Sale & Quinn, Washington, 2004—. Vis. scholar Johns Hopkins Sch. Advanced Internat. Studies, 1990—94; dep. chmn. UN Referendum for Western Sahara, 1994. Author: International Law in the Enlightenment, 1975; editor: American International Law Cases (series); editor in chief Internat. Lawyer; contbr. articles to legal jours. Bd. dirs. African Devel. Found., Washington, 1983-84, Human Life Internat., 1999—; mem. Coun. of Am. Ambs., Washington, 1988—. Served with USMCR, 1956-61 Mem.: ABA (chmn. treaty compliance sect. 1991—93), Hague Acad. Internat. Law Alumni Assn., Internat. Law Assn., Am. Soc. Internat. Law, Dacor House, Cosmos Club (Washington), Knights of Malta. Republican. Roman Catholic. Office: Sale & Quinn Fifth Fl 910 16th St NW Washington DC 20006 Office Phone: 202-872-4712. Personal E-mail: fruddy@hotmail.com. Business E-Mail: globalltd@earthlink.net.

**RUDDY, JAMES W.,** lawyer; b. 1949, AB, U. Mich., 1971, JD, Wayne State U., 1973. Bar: Wash. 1974, Mich. 1974. Trial atty. Safeco Corp., 1974—76, corp. counsel, 1976—84, assoc. gen. counsel, 1984-89, v.p., gen. counsel, 1989—92, sr. v.p., gen. counsel, 1992—. Office: Safeco Corp Safeco Plz T 22 Seattle WA 98185-0001

**RUDE, BRIAN DAVID,** utilities company executive; b. Viroqua, Wis., Aug. 25, 1955; s. Raymond and Conelee (Johnson) R.; m. Karen Thulin; children: Erik, Nels. BA magna cum laude, Luther Coll., 1977; MA, U. Wis., Madison, 1994. Mem. Wis. Assembly, Madison, 1982-84, Wis. Senate, Madison, 1984-2000; pres. Wis. State Sen., 1993-96, 98. With corp. comms. The Trane Co., La Crosse, Wis., 1981-85; dir. external rels. Dairyland Power Coop.; bd.dirs. Fortress Bank of Westby. Mem. LaCrosse C. of C., Lions, Sons of Norway, Norwegian-Am. Hist. Assn. (vice-chmn.), WWTC Found. (chmn., pres.), Rotary. Republican. Lutheran. Avocations: reading, gardening, travel, fishing. Home: 307 Babcock St PO Box 367 Coon Valley WI 54623-0367 Office: 3200 East Ave S PO Box 817 La Crosse WI 54602 Office Phone: 608-788-4000. Personal E-mail: bdr@dairynet.com.

**RUDE, LARA PEIRCE,** special education educator; d. Thomas and Deborah Peirce; m. Peter Rude, Apr. 3, 2004; 1 child, Ethan Thomas. BA, Wittenberg U., 1993; MEd, Westminster Coll., 2002. Spl. edn. tchr. Ecker Hill Mid. Sch., Park City, Utah, 1995—. Office: Ecker Hill Mid Sch 2465 W Kilby Rd Park City UT 84098 Office Phone: 435-645-5610. E-mail: lrude@pcschools.us.

**RUDEE, MERVYN LEA,** engineering educator, researcher; s. Mervyn C. and Hannah Rudee; m. Elizabeth Eager, 1958; children: Elizabeth Diane, David Benjamin. BS, Stanford U., 1958, MS, 1962, PhD, 1965. Asst. prof. materials sci. Rice U., Houston, 1964-68, assoc. prof., 1968-72, prof. materials sci., 1972-74; prof. U. Calif. San Diego, La Jolla, 1974—, founding provost Warren Coll., 1974-82, founding dean Sch. Engring., 1982-93, coord. grad. program on materials sci., 1994-99, faculty athletic rep., 1999—; interim dean engring. U. Calif., Riverside, 1995-97. Vis. scholar Corpus Christi Coll., Cambridge, Eng., 1971-72; vis. scientist IBM Thomas J. Watson Rsch. Ctr., Yorktown Heights, N.Y., 1987; dir. fellows program Calif. Coun.

on Sci. and Tech., 1999-2000. Pres., bd. trustees Mus. Photographic Art, San Diego, 1995-96; trustee The Burnham Inst., 1998—2004, The Glen Canyon Inst., 1999—, The San Diego River Park Found., 2003-. Lt. (j.g.) USN, 1958-61. Guggenheim fellow, 1971-72. Fellow AAAS; mem. Microscopy Soc. Am., Materials Rsch. Soc., Tex. Soc. Electron Microscopy (hon., pres. 1966), Sigma Xi, Tau Beta Pi. Office: U Calif San Diego Dept Elec & Computer Engring La Jolla CA 92093-0407 Office Phone: 858-534-8998. Business E-Mail: rudee@ucsd.edu.

**RUDEL, JULIUS,** conductor; b. Vienna, Mar. 6, 1921; came to U.S., 1938, naturalized, 1944; s. Jakob and Josephine (Sonnenblum) R.; m. Rita Gillis, June 24, 1942 (dec. May 1984); children: Joan, Madeleine, Anthony Jason. Student, Acad. Music, Vienna; diploma in conducting, Mannes Coll. Music, 1942; diploma hon. doctorates, U. Vt., 1961, U. Mich., 1971; doctorates hon. causa, Pace Coll., Manhattan Coll., 1994, Mannes Coll. Music, 1994, Manhattanville Coll., 1994, Manhattan Sch. Music, 1996. With N.Y. City Opera, 1943-79, debut, 1944, gen. dir., 1957-79, 3rd St. Music Sch. Settlement, 1945-52, mus. dir. Chautauqua Opera Assn., 1958-59, Caramoor Festival, Katonah, N.Y., 1964-76, Cin. May Festival, 1971-72, Kennedy Ctr. Performing Arts, 1971-75; music advisor Wolf Trap Farm Pk., 1971, Phila. Opera, 1978-81; condr. Spoleto (Italy) Festival, 1962-63; music dir. Buffalo Philarm. Orch., 1979-85, debut as condr. Met. Opera, 1978, San Franciso Opera, 1979, Vienna State Opera, 1976, Royal Opera, Covent Garden, 1984, Rome Opera, 1987, Opera de la Bastille, 1992, Teatro Colon, Buenos Aires, 1992, Royal Danish Opera, Copenhagen, 1993, L.A. Opera, 1995; condr. Am. premiere of Braunfels's Die Vogel at Spoleto Festival USA, 2005; dir. prodn.: Kiss Me Kate, Vienna Volksoper Opera, 1956; prin. ghest condr. Palm Beach Opera, 2003; guest condr. Chgo. Symphony, Phila. Orch., N.Y. Philharm., Boston Symphony, Detroit Symphony, Israel Philharm., Paris Opera, Munich Opera, Hamburg State Opera, Vienna State Opera, other symphonic, operatic orgns. in U.S. and Europe. Decorated Croix du Chevalier in arts and letters France; recipient gold medal Nat. Arts Club, 1958, citation Nat. Assn. Am. Composers and Conductors, 1958, citation Nat. Fedn. Music Clubs, 1959, Ditson award Columbia, 1959, Page One award in music Newspaper Guild, 1959, hon. insignia for arts and sci. Govt. of Austria, 1961, Handel medallion for music City N.Y., 1965, citation Nat. Assn. Negro Musicians, 1965, citation Nat. Opera Assn., 1971, comdr.'s Cross German Order Merit, 1967, hon. lt. Israeli Army, 1969, Julius Rudel award for young condrs., Pan Am./Pan African award for humanism, 1981, Peabody award, 1985, Disting. Achievement award Kurt Weill Found., 2000. Office: c/o Shuman Assocs 120 W 58th St Apt 8D New York NY 10019-2126 Office Phone: 212-315-1300.

**RUDELIUS, WILLIAM,** marketing educator; b. Rockford, Ill., Sept. 2, 1931; s. Carl William and Clarissa Euclid (Davis) R.; m. Jacqueline Urch Dunham, July 3, 1954; children: Robert, Jeanne, Katherine, Kristi. BS in Mech. Engring., U. Wis., 1953; MBA, U. Pa., 1959, PhD in Econs., 1964. Program engr., missile and space vehicle dept. Gen. Electric Co., Phila., 1956-57, 59-61; sr. research economist North Star Research Inst., Mpls., 1964-66; lectr. U. Minn., Mpls., 1961-64, asst. prof. mktg. Coll. Bus. Adminstrn., 1964, assoc. prof., 1966-72, prof., 1972—. Co-author: (with W. Bruce Erickson) An Introduction to Contemporary Business, 1973, rev. 4th edit., 1985, (with Eric N. Berkowitz, Roger A. Kerin and Steven W. Hartley) Marketing, 1986, rev. 8th edit., 2006, (with Roger A. Kerin and Steven W. Hartley) Marketing: The Core, 2004; (with Krzysztof Przybytowski, Roger A. Kerin and Steven W. Hartley) Marketing na Przykladach, 1998; (with others) Mapketkht, 1st Russian edit., 2001; contbr. articles to profl. jours. Served USAF, 1954—55. Home: 1425 Alpine Pass Minneapolis MN 55416-3560 Business E-Mail: rudelius@umn.edu.

**RUDENSTINE, NEIL LEON,** former academic administrator, educator; b. Ossining, NY, Jan. 21, 1935; s. Harry and Mae (Esperito) R.; m. Angelica Zander, Aug. 27, 1960; children: Antonia Margaret, Nicholas David, Sonya. BA, Princeton U., 1956; BA (Rhodes Scholar), Oxford U., 1959, MA, 1963; PhD, Harvard U., 1964. Instr. dept. English Harvard U., Cambridge, Mass., 1964-66, asst. prof., 1966-68; assoc. prof. English Princeton (N.J.) U., 1968-73, prof. English, 1973-88, dean of students, 1968-72, dean of Coll., 1972-77, provost, 1977-88, provost emeritus, 1988—; exec. v.p. Andrew W. Mellon Found., N.Y.C., 1988-91; pres. Harvard U., Cambridge, Mass., 1991-2001, pres. emeritus, 2001—. Chair bd. ArtStor, A.W. Mellon Found., 2001—. Author: Sidney's Poetic Development, 1967, Pointing Our Thoughts, 2001; (with George Rousseau) English Poetic Satire, 1972; (with William Bowen) In Pursuit of the PhD, 1992. Trustee Princeton U., N.Y. Pub. Libr., Cucatull Inst. Art, London, Goldman Sachs Found., The Barnes Found., Am. Acad. in Berlin. 1st lt. arty. U.S. Army, 1959—60. Hon. fellow New Coll./Oxford U., Emmanuel Coll./Cambridge U. 1991. Fellow Am. Acad. Arts and Scis.; mem. Am. Philos. Soc., Coun. on Fgn. Rels., Com. for Econ. Devel. Office: Art Stor AW Mellon Found 151 E 61st St New York NY 10021 Office Phone: 212-500-2419. Business E-Mail: nlr@mellon.org, nlr@artstor.org.

**RUDER, DAVID STURTEVANT,** government official, lawyer, educator; b. Wausau, Wis., May 25, 1929; s. George Louis and Josephine (Sturtevant) R.; m. Susan M. Small; children: Victoria Chesley, Julia Larson, David Sturtevant II, John Coulter; stepchildren: Elizabeth Frankel, Rebecca Wilkinson. BA cum laude, Williams Coll., 1951; JD with honors, U. Wis., 1957, LLD, 2002. Bar: Wis. 1957, Ill. 1962. Of counsel Schiff Hardin & Waite, Chgo., 1971—76; assoc. Quarles & Brady, Milw., 1957—61; assit. prof. law Northwestern U., Chgo., 1961—63, assoc. prof., 1963—65, prof., 1965—2005, William W. Gurley meml. prof. of law, 1994—2005; emeritus, 2005—; assoc. dean Law Sch. Northwestern U., Chgo., 1965—66, dean Law Sch., 1977—85; chmn. Securities and Exch. Commn., Washington, 1987—89; ptnr. Baker & McKenzie, Chgo., 1990—94, sr. counsel, 1994—99. Cons. Am. Law Inst. Fed. Securities Code; planning dir. Corp. Counsel Inst., 1962-66, 76-77, com. mem., 1962-87, 90—; adv. bd. Ray Garrett Jr. Corp. and Securities Law Inst., 1980-87, 90—; vis. lectr. U. de Liege, 1967; vis. prof. law U. Pa., Phila., 1971; faculty Salzburg Seminar, 1976; mem. legal adv. com. bd. dirs. N.Y. Stock Exch., 1978-82; mem. com. profl. responsibility Ill. Supreme Ct., 1978-87; adv. bd. Securities Regulation Inst., 1978—, chmn., 1994-97; bd. govs. Nat. Assn. Securities Dealers, 1990-93, chmn. Legal Adv. Bd., 1993-96; Arbitration Policy Task Force, 1994-97; trustee Fin. Acctg. Found., 1996-2002, Internat. Acctg. Stds. Com. Found., 2000-05; mem. Internat. Acctg. Stds. Com. Strategy Working Party, 1997-99, chmn. Securities and Exch. Commn. Hist. Soc., 1999-04; chmn. Mut. Fund Dirs. Forum, 1999—. Editor-in-chief: Williams Coll. Record, 1950-51, U. Wis. Law Rev, 1957; editor: Proc. Corp. Counsel Inst, 1962-66; contbr. articles to legal periodicals. 1st lt. AUS, 1951-54. Fellow Am. Bar Found.; ABA (sec. bus. law 1970—, coun. 1970-94, com. chmn., mem. various coms.), Chgo. Bar Assn., Wis. Bar Assn., Am. Law Inst., Order of Coif, Comml. Club of Chgo., Lawyers Club Chgo., Gargoyle Soc., Phi Beta Kappa, Phi Delta Phi, Zeta Psi. Home: 325 Orchard Ln Highland Park IL 60035-1939 Office: Northwestern U Sch Law 357 E Chicago Ave Chicago IL 60611 Office Phone: 312-503-8444.

**RUDER, JOHN REGAN,** physician; b. Colorado Springs, Colo., Oct. 23, 1947; s. Ralph Emerson and Rosemary Pierron (Regan) R.; m. Sheri Dee Rigby, July 6, 1985; children: Elizabeth, Lindsey, John. BA, Dartmouth Coll., 1969, MD, 1977. Intern in surgery U. N.Mex. & Affiliated Hosps., 1977-78; med. dir. Navajo Reservation, 1977-78; resident in surgery Dartmouth-Hitchcock Med. Ctr., 1978-81; resident in plastic and reconstructive surgery U. Utah, 1981-83, asst. clin. prof. plastic & reconstructive surgery Salt Lake City, 1986-90; chief plastic & reconstructive surgery VA Hosp., Salt Lake City, 1986-90; clin. instr. hand & upper extremity surgery Loma Linda (Calif.) U., 1990-91; v.p. Hand Surgery Assocs., Arlington Heights, Ill., 1991—. Co-author: (chpts.) Injuries and Rehabilitation of the Upper Extremity, 1998, Upper Extremity Compressive Neuropathies, 1998. Mem. ACS, Am. Soc. for Surgery of the Hand, Am. Soc. of Plastic and Reconstructive Surgery, Am. Assn. Hand Surgery, Alpha Omega Alpha. Office: Hand Surgery Assocs 515 W Algonquin Rd Ste 120 Arlington Heights IL 60005-4440 Office Phone: 847-956-0099.

**RUDER, TIA L.,** music educator; d. Judy K and Duane F Ruder. MusB cum laude in Edn., Wichita State U., 1992, MusB cum laude in Performance, 1992, BA cum laude, 1993, MusM in Edn., 1999. K-12, Vocal and Instrumental Music Kans. State Bd. of Edn., 1992, nat. bd. cert. in early adolescent and young adult. Instrumental music tchr. Wichita Pub. Schools, Kans., 1992—. Summer instrument cleaning and repair Wichita Pub. Schools, Kans., 2000—05; asst. dir. all-city band Wichita Pub. Schs., 1993—; pvt. music tchr., Wichita, 1992—2003; soprano soloist and instrumental music dir. Mt. Vernon Presbyn. Ch., Wichita, Kans., 1992—2001; summer sch. tchr. Oakley Pub. Schools, Oakley, Kans., 1992—97, Wichita Pub. Schools, 2000—04. State forensics championships adjudicator Kans. State H.S. Activities Assn., Wichita, 1992—2005. Recipient Honors Program Grad., Wichita State U., 1992, Mortar Bd. Scholar, 1991; U. Leader Scholar, 1992—96. Mem.: NEA, Kans. Bandmasters Assn., Fedn. of Teachers, Kans. Music Educators Assn., Music Educators Nat. Conf. Avocations: cooking, home improvement, science fiction, theater. Personal E-mail: tiaruder@email.com.

**RUDER, WILLIAM,** public relations executive; b. NYC, Oct. 17, 1921; s. Jacob L. and Rose (Rosenberg) R.; m. Betty Cott, May 23, 1980; children: Robin Ann, Abby, Brian, Michal Ellen, Eric. BSS., City Coll., N.Y., 1942. With Samuel Goldwyn Prodns., 1946-48; pres. Ruder & Finn, Inc., N.Y.C., 1948-80, William Ruder Inc., 1981—. Asst. sec. commerce, 1961-62; Tobe lectr. Harvard Grad. Sch. Bus., 1962; mem. grad. adv. bd. City Coll. N.Y., Baruch Sch. Bus., N.Y.C.; cons. State Dept.; bd. dirs. W.P. Carey & Co., Inc.; trustee Continuum Health Ptnrs., Inc. Author: The Businessman's Guide to Washington. Bd. dirs. Bus. Com. for Arts, Jewish Bd. Guardians, Chamber Music Soc. Lincoln Ctr., Fund for Peace, Project Return Found.; exec. com. United Way Am.; trustee, chmn. Manhattanville Coll., Purchase, N.Y., 1974-75; trustee Com. for Econ. Devel., St. Lukes/ Roosevelt Hosp.; bd. overseers Wharton Sch. U. Pa.; mem. pres.'s coun. Meml. Sloan-Kettering Cancer Ctr.; chmn. bd. ACCESS. Capt. USAAF, 1941-45. Mem. UN Assn. U.S.A. (nat. policy panel dir., trustee com. for econ. devel.). Home: PO Box 230 East Hampton NY 11937 Office: Ruder Finn Inc 301 E 57th St New York NY 10022-2900

**RUDERMAN, WARREN,** chemist; b. NYC, Jan. 7, 1920; s. Jack and Mollie (Ettin) R.; m. Carol Carver Schmied, June 15, 1945; children: Barbara, Clifford, William, Genevieve. PhD, Columbia U., 1949. Rsch. scientist, lectr. in chemistry Columbia U., N.Y.C., 1947-54; pres., founder Isomet Corp., Oakland, NJ, 1954-73; founder, chmn., CEO, pres. INRAD Inc., Northvale, NJ, 1973—2000; founder, pres. INCRYS, Demarest, NJ, 2002—. Fellow N.Y. Acad. Scis.; mem. Am. Chem. Soc., Am. Phys. Soc., Optical Soc. Am. Republican. Office: INCRY Inc 45 Duane Ln Demarest NJ 07627 Office Phone: 201-768-0403. E-mail: warrud@optonline.net.

**RUDICK, A. JOSEPH,** research and development company executive; BA in Chemistry, Williams Coll., 1979; MD, U. Pa., 1983. Ptnr. Assoc. Ophthalmologists PC, NY, 1988—; co-founder Healthdesk Corp., 1993, dir., 1993—98; v.p. Paramount Capital, Inc., 1994—98; founder Optex (subs. Atlantic Tech. Ventures, Inc.), Channel (subs. Atlantic Tech. Ventures, Inc.), Atlantic Tech. Ventures, Inc., bus. cons., 1997—98, pres., 1999—2000, dir., 1999—, 2000—.

**RUDIGER, LANCE WADE,** secondary school educator; b. Bklyn., Mar. 27, 1948; s. H.F. and Muriel Marie (Staudermann) R.; 1 child, Heidi. BS in Chemistry, SUNY, Albany, 1976, MEd, St. Lawrence U., 1982. Cert. tchr. N.Y. Tchr. chemistry Potsdam H.S., 1982—, chmn. dept. sci., 1992—1. Adj. prof. Canton (N.Y.) Coll. Tech., Mater Dei Coll., Ogdensburg, N.Y., Empire Coll., Albany, 1986—; tchr. Inst. Chem. Edn.-Sci. demonstration; bd. dirs., treas. St. Lawrence Valley Tchrs. Learning Ctr., Canton; sci. coord. Upward Bound St. Lawrence U.; program com., bd. dirs. N.Y. Assn. State Computers & Tech. in Edn.; writer for N.Y. State Regents chemistry core curriculum; mem. N.Y. State Part D Performance Regents Test Devel. Com.; reviewer chemistry tchr. cert. exam N.Y State; mem. SED Regents Benchmark Commn.; item writer NYS Chem. Regents; mem. NYSED-McGraw Hill Chemistry Regents Anchor Com.; mem. h.s. chemistry exam com. Am. Chem. Soc., 2005 Co-author: Chemistry Environment, 1990; editor, reviewer Activ Chemistry. Bd. dirs. March of Dimes N.Y. State, Syracuse, N.Y. State chemistry regional and state coord. mentor; mem. environ. mgmt. bd. St. Lawrence County, 1997-, edn. com. chair, 1999-, vice chair, 2003-; mem. bd. examiners Nat. Coun. Accreditation Tchr. Edn., 2001—. Recipient Newmast award NASA, 1987, Dreyfus Master Tchr. award, 1989, Fulbright Symposium award Australia, 2002; grantee NSTA-FDA, 2003, Am. Chem Soc., Woodrow Wilson Found., Binghamtom U. Step Program, St. Lawrence Valley Tchrs. Ctr., 1991-98, Sweetwater Found., Miami U. (Ohio), 1995, Johns Hopkins Space Grant Consortium, Wright Ctr. for Aerospace and Space Engring., Reynolds Metals Excellence in Edn., 1990-94, Cornell U. Sci. Workshop, IRIS; named solar sys. amb. Jet Propulsion Lab., NASA. Mem. Nat. Sci. Tchrs. Assn. (local leader, manuscript review adv. panel The Sci. Tchr., sci. safety com. 2000, webwatchers 2001, Exxon BaP key leader and North Country liaison, mem. reports com.), Nat. Radio Astronomy Obs. (assoc., mentor astronomy workshop), Am. Astron. Soc. (tchr. resource agent 1996-98, Leadership Workshop award 1998), Sci. Tchrs. Assn. N.Y. State (bd. dirs. 1990—, chmn. sect. 1992—, fin. com. 2000—, grant com. chair, presenter at convs. 1988—; hospitality chair ann. conf. NYSC & TE 1996, 98, 2000, bd. dirs.), North Country Conservation Edn. Assn. (life), USCG Acad. Nat. Parents Assn. (bd. dirs. 1997-98), N.Y. State Tchr. Cert. Exam Adv. Com., Canton Club, Lions (past pres. Waddington, N.Y., Pres.'s award, bd. dirs. Canton, pres. 1997-98, treas. 1998-99, v.p. 1999-2003), Potsdam Kiwanis (charter, bd. dirs. 1989-91), Phi Delta Kappa (rsch. dir., v.p. program 1999, v.p. membership, pres. 2001—, Phi Delta Kappan 2004, Gerald Read travel scholar 2004). Home: 54 Court St Canton NY 13617-1159 Office: Potsdam High School Leroy St Potsdam NY 13676-1798 E-mail: lrudiger@aol.com.

**RUDIN, ANNE,** retired mayor, nursing educator; b. Passaic, NJ, Jan. 27, 1924; m. Edward Rudin, June 6, 1948; 4 children. BS in Edn., Temple U., 1945, RN, 1946; MPA, U. So. Calif., 1983; LLD (hon.), Golden Gate U., 1990. RN, Calif. Mem. faculty Temple U. Sch. Nursing, Phila., 1946-48; mem. nursing faculty Mt. Zion Hosp., San Francisco, 1948-49; mem. Sacramento City Council, 1971-83; mayor City of Sacramento, 1983-92; ind. pub. policy cons. Pres. LWV, Riverside, 1957, Sacramento, 1961, Calif., 1969-71; Calif. Elected Women's Assn., 1973—; trustee Golden Gate U. 1993-96; mem. adv. bd. U. So. Calif., Army Depot Reuse Commn., 1992-94; bd. dirs. Sacramento Theatre Co., 1992-99, Japan Soc. No. Calif., Sacramento Symphony, 1993-96, Calif. Common Cause, 1993 -96, Sacramento Edn. Found., 1993-2006; v.p. Sacramento Traditional Jazz Soc. Found.; pres. bd. dirs. Natomas Basin Conservancy; foreman Sacramento County Grand Jury, 2000-01. Recipient Women in Govt. award U.S. Jaycee Women, 1984, Woman of Distinction award Sacramento Area Soroptimist Clubs, 1985, Civic Contbn. award LWV Sacramento, 1989, Woman of Courage award Sacramento History Ctr., 1989, Peacemaker of Yr. award Sacramento Mediation Ctr., 1992, Regional Pride award Sacramento Mag., 1993, Humanitarian award Japanese Am. Citizen's League, 1993, Outstanding Pub. Svc. award Am. Soc. Pub. Adminstrn., 1994, Cmty. Svc. Recognition award, Japanese Am. Citizens League, 1999, Contbr. to Pub. Art award Am. Soc. for Pub. Admin., 2004, Robert T. Malsui award Pub. Svc., Town & Country Dem. Club, 2005; named Girl Scouts Am. Role model, 1989; named to Sacramento Traditional Jazz Soc. Hall of Fame, 2000. Mem.: Calif. Med. Alliance (Mem. of Yr. 2005).

**RUDIN, SCOTT,** film and theatre producer; b. NYC, July 14, 1958; Prodn. asst., asst. to theatre prodrs. Kermit Bloomgarden and Robert Whitehead; casting dir. motion pictures and theatre, prodr. with Edgar Scherick, exec. v.p. prodn. 20th Century Fox, 1984-86, pres. prodn., 1986-87; founder Scott Rudin Prodns., 1990—. Prodr. (films) Mrs. Soffel, 1984, Pacific Heights, 1990, Regarding Henry, 1991, Little Man Tate, 1991, The Addams Family, 1991, Life With Mikey, 1993, The Firm, 1993, Searching for Bobby Fischer, 1993, Sister Act 2, 1993, Addams Family Values, 1993, I.Q., 1994, Nobody's Fool, 1994, Sabrina, 1995, Clueless, 1995, Up Close and Personal, 1996, Ransom, 1996, Marvin's Room, 1996, The First Wives Club, 1996, In and Out, 1997, Twilight, 1998, The Truman Show, 1998, A Civil Action, 1998, Wonder Boys, 1999, Rules of Engagement, 1999, Brokeback Mountain, 1999, Angela's Ashes, 1999, Bringing Out the Dead, 1999, Sleepy Hollow, 1999, Rules of Engagement, 2000, Zoolander, 2001, The Royal Tenenbaums, Changing Lanes, 2002, The Hours, 2002, The Stepford Wives, 2004, The Manchurian Candidate, 2004, The Village, 2004, I Heart Huckabees, 2004, Life Acquatic with Steve Zissou, 2004, Closer, 2004, Freedomland, 2006, Failure to Launch, 2006; exec. prodr. (films) Flatliners, 1990, Sister Act, 1992, Jennifer Eight, 1992, South Park: Bigger, Longer and Uncut, 1999, Team America: World Police, 2004, Lemony Snicket's A Series of Unfortuante Events, 2004, Wild Tigers I Have Known, 2006; (TV movies) Revenge of the Stepford Wives, 1980, He Makes Me Feel Like Dancing, 1983 (Outstanding Children's Program Emmy award 1982, Feature Documentary Acad. award 1984); (theatre) Passion, 1994 (Best Musical Tony award 1994), Indiscretions, 1995, Hamlet, 1995, Seven Guitars, 1995, Skylight, 1997, A Funny Thing Happened on the Way to the Forum, 1996, On the Town (with the N.Y. Shakespeare Festival), 1997, The Chairs, 1998, The Judas Kiss, 1998, (London) Closer, 1998, The Blue Room, 1998, Closer, 1999, Amy's View, 1999, Wide Guys, 1999, Copenhagen, 1999 (Tony Award); (off broadway) Stupid Kids, 1998, The Most Fabulous Story Ever Told, 1999, Shaft, 2000. Named one of 50 Most Powerful People in Hollywood, Premiere mag., 2002—06. Office: Scott Rudin Prodns c/o Starr & Co 350 Park Ave 9th Fl New York NY 10022 also: Scott Rudin Prodns Inc c/o Star & Co LLC 850 Third Ave 15th Fl New York NY 10022*

**RUDKIN, GEORGE HENRY,** plastic surgeon; b. Wilmington, Del., July 29, 1964; s. George Osborne and Helene Rita (De Sanctis) R. BA in Natural Sciences, Johns Hopkins U., 1986; MD, Columbia U. Coll. Physicians and Surgeons, 1990. Diplomate Am. Bd. Surgery, 1997, Am. Bd. Plastic Surgery, 1999. Intern, gen. surgery UCLA Med. Ctr., 1990—91, resident, gen. surgery, 1991—96, resident, plastic surgery, 1996-98, hosp. appt., asst. prof., divsn. plastic & reconstructive surgery, 1999—; chief, plastic surgery W. LA VA Med. Ctr. Co-investigator for the active VA Merit Review Grant: Molecular Mechanism of Bone Regeneration: Role of BMP-2, 2002—06. Author several textbook chapters; contbr. numerous publications in peer-reviewed plastic surgery literature. Recipient VA Career Develop. award, 1998—2001. Fellow, Am. Coll. Surgeons; mem. Am. Soc. Plastic & Reconstructive Surgeons, Plastic Surgery Rsch. Coun., Calif. Soc. Plastic Surgeons, Alpha Omega Alpha, Phi Beta Kappa. Office: UCLA Cosmetic Surgery Ctr UCLA Divsn Plastic & Reconstructive Surg 200 UCLA Medical Plz Ste 465 Los Angeles CA 90095-6960 Office Phone: 310-825-5510. Office Fax: 800-825-2752, 310-206-7579.*

**RUDLEY, LLOYD DAVE,** psychiatrist; b. Phila., Aug. 7, 1955; s. John Frank and Ida (Rothman) R. BA summa cum laude, U. Pa., 1977; MD, Hahnemann U., 1981. Diplomate Am. Bd. Psychiatry and Neurology. Resident in psychiatry Med. Coll. Pa., Phila., 1981-85; pvt. practice Phila. 1985—, Elmer, NJ, 1986—; staff psychiatrist N.E. Cmty. Mental Health Ctr., Phila., 1985-87, Counseling Program N.J., Marlton, 1987-88; attending psychiatrist Hosp. U. Pa., Phila., 1985—. Attending psychiatrist Inst. of Pa. Hosp., Phila. Psychiat. Ctr.; cons. psychiatrist Horizon Ho, Phila, 1989—; mem. med. adv. bd. Juvenile Diabetes Found., Phila., 1986—. Mem. jr. com. Scheie Eye Inst., Phila., 1985—. Mem. AMA, Am. Psychiat. Assn., Pa. Psychiat. Soc., Pa. Med. Soc., Philadelphia County Med. Soc. (mental health subcom. 1988—, Janssen clin. scholar 1994), Phi Beta Kappa. Republican. Avocation: collecting maps.

**RUDLOFF, UDO,** surgeon, researcher; b. Schweinfurt, Bavaria, Germany, Apr. 16, 1969; arrived in US, 2002; s. Herbert and Helga (Gall) Rudloff. PhD, German Cancer Rsch. Ctr., Heidelberg, 1994; MD, Ruprecht Karls U., Heidelberg, Germany, 1997. Rsch. fellow German Cancer Rsch. Ctr., Heidelberg, 1991—94, European Molecular Biology Labs., Heidelberg, 1993; ho. officer dept. surgery and orthop. Zomba Ctrl. Hosp., Malawi, 1997—98; ho. officer U. Hosp. Aintree, Liverpool, England, 1999, Leicester Gen. Hosp., England, 1999—2000, Hinchingbrooke Hosp., Huntington, England, 2000, Dewsbury Dist. Hosp., England, 2000—01; registrar Guy's and St. Thomas' Hosp., London, 2001—02; ho. officer North Shore - LI Jewish Health Sys., Manhasset, NY, 2002—05, NYU Sch. Medicine, NYC, 2005—. Contbr. Archives Gynecology and Obstetrics, Basel, Switzerland, 2002—06. Contbr. articles to numerous profl. jours. Recipient Academic Exch. Travel award, German Rsch. Found., 1991, GFM Young Talent award, Soc. Advancement Rsch. in Molecular Biology, Heidelberg, Germany, 1995; scholar, German Acad. Scholarship Found., 1994—97, Scholarship Found. Roman Cath. Ch., 1994. Mem.: Royal Coll. Obstetricians and Gynecologists. Achievements include characterization of a new, essential class of polymerase I-specific transcription factors named TAFs; research in DNA binding properties. Office: NYU 462 First Ave 15N1 BHC New York NY 10016 Office Phone: 212-263-7302. Personal E-mail: udo_rudloff@hotmail.com. E-mail: rudlou01@med.nyu.edu.

**RUDLOFF, WILLIAM JOSEPH,** lawyer; b. Bonne Terre, Mo., Feb. 19, 1941; s. Leslie W. and Alta M. (Hogenmiller) R.; m. Rita Howton, Aug. 5, 1965; children: Daniel, Andrea, Leslie, Susan. AB, Western Ky. U., 1961; JD, Vanderbilt U., 1965. Bar: Ky. 1965, Tenn. 1965, U.S. Supreme Ct. 1975, U.S. Ct. Appeals (sixth cir.) 1981. U.S. magistrate Western Dist. Ky., 1971-75. NDEA fellow U. Nebr., 1961-62, U. Ky. fellow. Fellow: Ky. Bar Found. (life; charter); mem.: Ky. Workplace Injury Law and Advocacy Group, Internat. Acad. Litigators (diplomate), Ky. Acad. Trial Attys., Am. Coll. Legal Medicine, Trial Attys. Am., Am. Bd. Trial Advocates. Office: 553 E Main St Bowling Green KY 42101-2256 Home: 1138 Cedarwood Way Bowling Green KY 42104 Office Phone: 270-781-7754. Personal E-mail: w.rudloff@ccol.net.

**RUDMAN, ILENE H.,** psychotherapist; d. Lillian and Isadore Hillman; 1 child, Jonah Louis. MPA, Harvard U., 1978; MA in Counseling Psychology, Lesley U., 1989. Cert. spiritual psychology Concord Inst., 1994; mediation Cmty. Dispute Settlement Ctr., 1999. Manpower specialist US Dept. Labor, Washington, 1966—71; employment and tng. specialist Commonwealth of Mass., Boston, 1971—75; fed. women's program coord. U.S. Dept. Health Edn. and Welfare, Boston, 1975—81; co-founder Rodgers and Rudman, Brookline, Mass., 1981—83; dir. spl. projects Bay State Skills Corp and Transitional Employment Enterprises, Boston, 1983—87; program coord. -outreach Lesley U., Cambridge, Mass., 1987—88; career counselor Mt. Wachusetts C.C., Gardner, Mass., 1989—90, Radcliffe Career Svc., Cambridge, Mass., 1990—96; pvt. practice career coach, counselor and psychotherapist Watertown and Maynard, Mass. Author: (poetry) Vegetarian Woes (New Eng. Poets and Writers prize, 2003). Co-chair worshsip com. First Parish Stow and Acton, Stow, Mass. Pub. Mgmt. fellow, U.S. Dept. Pers. Mgmt., 1977—78. Mem.: APA (assoc.), Career Counselors Consortium. Avocations: fiber arts, photography, poetry. Office: Ilene H Rudman 173 Mount Auburn St Watertown MA 02472 Office Phone: 617-924-0303.

**RUDMAN, JEFFREY B.,** lawyer; b. Cambridge, Mass., May 1, 1948; s. Stanley H. and Dorothy (Braidy) R.; m. Susan Victoria Fried, Aug. 25, 1986; children: Samuel Newland, Nicholas Braidy. AB, Columbia U., 1970; BA, Oxford (Eng.) U., 1972; JD, Harvard U., 1975. Bar: Mass. 1975, U.S. Dist. Ct. Mass. 1975, U.S. Ct. Appeals (1st cir.) 1977. Assoc. Hale and Dorr, Boston, 1975-80, ptr. 1980-83, sr. ptnr. 1983—2004; ptnr., co-chmn. Securities dept., mem. Litigation dept. Wilmer Cutler Pickering Hale and Dorr, Boston, 2004—. Trustee Boston Pub. Libr., Boston Mus. Project, former trustee Boston Pub. Libr. Found.; sec. New Eng. & N.J. Rhodes Scholarship Selection Coms., 1985—; former mem. cmty. adv. bd. WGBH. Rhodes scholar, 1970-72. Mem. Mass. Bar Assn., Boston Bar Assn., Phi Beta Kappa, St. Botolph Club Home: 1 Adams St Charlestown MA 02129-3433 Office: Wilmer Cutler Pickering Hale and Dorr 60 State St Boston MA 02109-1816 Office Phone: 617-526-6912. Office Fax: 617-526-5000. Business E-Mail: jeffrey.rudman@wilmerhale.com.

**RUDMAN, JOAN ELEANOR,** artist, educator; b. Owensburg, Ind., Oct. 7, 1927; d. William Hobart and Elizabeth Joaquin (Edington) Combs; m. William Rudman, June 9, 1951; children: Mary Beth, Pamela Ann. BA, Mich. State U., 1949, MA, 1951. Tchr. Arlington Jr. and H.S., Poughkeepsie, NY, Rippowam H.S., Stamford, Conn., North Branch Club, West Dover, Vt.; artist, demonstrator Round Hill Cmty. House, Greenwich; artist-in-residence So. Vt. Arts Ctr., Manchester, Peony Festival at Hildene, Manchester, 2000; jury of selection Hudson Valley Art Assn., 1971—, pres. 2000; selection and awards juror 2d Bergen County Mus. Open Mems. Juried Awards-Allied Artist, NY; dir. Watercolor Workshops, Greenwich; liaison t0 Metro Mus. Catharine Lorillard Wolfe Art Club; watercolor lectr. and demonstrator tri-state area.; juried show, 1996—2002; guest spkr., guest lectr. 2-day workshop Vt. Watercolor Soc., Chester; watercolor juror Walter Brooks Meml. Watercolor Show, Rowaton, Conn. One-woman shows include Burning Tree Country Club, Greenwich, Town and Country Club, Hartford, Conn., U. Conn., Stamford, Conn. Valley Art Gallery, New Milford, So. Vt. Arts Ctr., Manchester, The Nathaniel Witherall Gallery, Greenwich, Burke Rehab. Ctr. White Plains, N.Y.; exhibited in group shows at Wadsworth Antheneum, 1970, Mus. of Am. Art, New Britain, Conn., So. Vt. Art Ctr., Manchester, 1980-81, Nature Ctr., Westport, Conn., 1979-80, Mus. Fine Arts, Springfield, Mass., 1977, Wadsworth Antheneum, 1970, Mus. Am. Art, New Britain, Conn., Nat. Arts Club Open Show, 1969, 78-79, 81-82, Salmagundi Club, N.Y.C., 1978-80, 82, Am. Watercolor Soc., N.Y.C., 1974, 77, 82, Nat. Acad. Design, 1986, 94, W.C. Founder's Show, Art Soc. Old Greenwich, 1999, Walter Brooks Meml. Watercolor Show, Rowayton, Conn., 2000; represented in permanent collection Kresge Mus., East Lansing, Mich., others; contbr. chpts. to books. Art dir. Round Hill Cmty. Guild; active North Stamford Congl. Ch., asst. assoc. curiator of healing through Art at Christ Ch., Greenwich; charter mem. Nat. Mus. Women in the Arts, Washington. Recipient Nat. Art League awards, 1969, 71, 72, 73, Art Soc. Old Greenwich award, 1989, 94, 99, Windsor Newton award, 1982, YWCA Greenwich Contemporary Women's Art Exhibit award, 1985, Best in Show award Art Soc. Old Greenwich, 1991, 1st Prize Graphics award Art Soc. Old Greenwich, 1994, 2nd Prize award Watercolor, Vol. of Yr. plaque, 1997. Mem. NAD, AAUW (New Canaan chpt.), Am. Watercolor Soc. (bd. dirs., asst. editor newsletter), Acad. Artists, Inc., Hoosier Salon (awards 1975-76), Am. Artists Profl. League (50th Nat. Exhbn. award 1978), Hudson Valley Art Assn. (pres. 2000—, bd. dirs., publ. rels. editor, designer catalog and brochure, awards 1970, 80—, pres.), Conn. Watercolor Soc. (award 1978), Conn. Artists 33, Whiskey Painters Am. (award 1978), Conn. Women Artists, Catharine Lorillard Wolfe Art Club (chmn. 1989-90, co-chair 1994, v.p. 1992-94, awards 1989-90), Pen and Brush (award 1977-78, 97), Nat. League Am. Pen Women (awards 1967, 69, 76-87, treas. 1990—), Nat. Press Club, Columbia U. Alumni Club (hon.), Nat. Soc. DAR (mem. Stamford chpt., historian, good citizens chair), Mich. State Alumni Club, Delta Phi Delta (hon.), Phi Kappa Phi (hon.), Alpha Xi Delta. Republican. Home: 274 Quarry Rd Stamford CT 06903-5004

**RUDMAN, PAUL LEWIS,** lawyer, former state supreme court justice; b. Bangor, Maine, Mar. 26, 1935; s. Abraham Moses and Irene (Epstein) R.; m. Inez Lee Kolonel, Oct. 8, 1961; children Andrew Isaac, Carole Sue. AB, Yale Coll., 1957; JD, George Washington U. Sch. Law, 1960. Bar: Maine 1960, D.C. 1960; U.S. Dist. Ct. Maine, 1961. Ptnr. Rudman & Winchell, Bangor, 1960-92; justice Maine Supreme Jud. Ct., Bangor, 1992—2005; atty. Rudman & Winchell LLC, Bangor, 2005—. Ct. liaison Bd. Overseers of Bar, Media & Courts Com.; chair Jud. Education Com., Sentence Review Panel; mem. Jud. Advisory Bd., AEI-Brookings Jud. Education Program. Capt. Maine Air NG, 1960-66. Office: Rudman & Winchell LLC PO Box 1401 84 Harlow St Bangor ME 04402*

**RUDMAN, SOLOMON KAL,** magazine publisher; b. Phila., Mar. 6, 1930; s. Benjamin and Lena (Holtzman) R.; m. Lucille Steinhauer, June 29, 1958; 1 child, Mitchell. BS in Edn., U. Pa., 1951; MS in Edn., Temple U., 1957; LHD (hon.), Holy Family U., Phila., 2002, U. Arts, 2003, LHD (hon.), 2005, PhD (hon.), 2006. Chmn. dept. spl. edn. Franklin D. Roosevelt Sch., Bristol Twp., Pa., 1960-68; pub. premier record/ radio trade Fri. Morning Quarterback, Cherry Hill, Pa., 1968—. Bd. dirs. Variety Club, NARAS, Crime Commn., Pa., NJ, Del.; co-host Merv Griffin TV Show, 1981-82; music expert Today Show, 1981-82, Tomorrow Show, 1981-82, Tom Snyder TV Show; host Phila. Franklin Inst. Sci. and Fels Planetarium mobile sci. programs, entertainment shows to Phila.-N.J. Sr. Citizens' homes, children's and vets. hosps.; co-host, talent booker Easter Seals Telethon; creator h.s. jazz piano competition U. the Arts, Phila., e-books for the recording industry; created Kal and Lucille Rudman Inst. for Entertainment Industry Pub.; (mag.) MQB (Modern QB) for Modern Rock Music; prodr. CD's of advance hits N.Am. radio stas.; launched music trade mag. Pro QB, launched Q-Beatl; created 50 billboards for Mothers In Charge. Bd. dirs. Phila. Broadcast Pioneers; sponsor carillon bells Ave. of Arts, Phila., TV cameras Temple U. Sch. Comm., alert systems Phila. police dog cars, Franklin Inst. Travelling Sci. Show to Phila. elem. schs., Citizens' Crime Commn., 1st ann. classical piano HS competition, Chestnut Hill Coll., 100th Anniversary Jewish Fedn. Phila., Franklin Inst. Time Capsule, Phila., Jewish Fedn. Atrium, Phila.; co-sponsor purchase and distbn. of dictionaries to Phila. Elem. Sch. pupils (in memory of Ennis Cosby), Robotics Competition Phila. HS, NJ United Cerebral palsy Marathon Dance, Rutgers U.; co-sponsor Succeeding By Reading Program; active Phila. Middle Schs., Jewish Book week, Phila. Ave. of Arts., Newspapers In Edn., others; founder Kal and Lucille Rudman Inst. for Entertainment Studies, Drexel Hill, U. Coll. Media Arts and Design, Phila., 1974; grad. FBI Cmty. Outreach. Recipient Lifetime Achievement award Phila. Music Conf., Lifetime Music Achievement award Delaware Valley Music Poll., Presdl. Citation, Citizens Crime Com., Plaque on Walk of Fame, Ave. of the Arts, Enforcement award Nat. Marines, Radio Milestone award to Phila. Radio Legends, March of Dimes; named to Broadcast Pioneers Hall of Fame Phila.; named Penndelphia Humanitarian of Yr., Humanitarian of Yr. Nat. Sunshine Fedn. Mem. Phila. Music Alliance (bd. dirs.), Nat. Activities Panel (bd. dirs.), NARAS (bd. dirs.), Masons (cmty. svc. award, Grand Master), Phila. Police Commrs. Club (named hon. dep. police commr.). Achievements include helping to create Music Theater Dept. at U. Arts, Phila; creating the 1st Police Athletic League, Abington, Pa. Office: Friday Morning Quarterback 1930 Marlton Pike E Cherry Hill NJ 08003-2150

**RUDMANN, BRENT L.,** museum director, educator; b. Fullerton, Calif., Nov. 11, 1972; s. Jerry Lee and Bari Lynn Rudmann; m. Kristina Mary Gundersen, July 10, 1999. AA, Irvine Valley Coll., Calif., 1994; BA, San Marcos State U., Calif., 1997; MA in Pub. History and Tchg., U. San Diego, 2005. Master's lic. one hundred ton ship USCG, 2004. Coord. II Dana Point Ocean Inst., Calif., 2000—04; mus. mgr. hist. and cultural affairs Zwaanendael Mus., Lewes, Del., 2004—; adj. faculty Del. State U., Georgetown, 2005—. Author: (ednl. program) Carry On Mr. Bowditch, 2003, Revenue Cutter Service, 2003. Coord. tall-ship festival 375th Com., Lewes, 2005—06; sea scout leader Ship 198, Milton, Del., 2005—06. Fellow, U. San Diego, 1997—98; scholar, Orange County Tchrs. Fed. Credit Union, 1994. Master: Del. Marine Archeol. Soc. (corr.; chair 2005—06); mem. Nat. Maritime Hist. Soc. (assoc.), San Diego Maritime Mus. (assoc.), Assn. State and Local History (assoc.). Home: 17304 Pine Water Dr 3 Lewes DE 19958 Office: Zwaanendael Mus 102 Kings Hwy Lewes DE 19958 Personal E-mail: theodon1@aol.com.

**RUDNER, SARA,** dancer; b. Bklyn., Feb. 16, 1944; d. Henry Nathaniel and Jeannette (Smolensky) R.; 1 child, Edward Eli Rudner Marschner. AB in Russian Studies, Barnard Coll., 1964; MFA in Choreography, Bennington Coll., 1999. Dancer Sansardo Dance Co., N.Y.C., 1964-65, Am. Dance Co. at Lincoln Ctr., N.Y.C., 1965, Shakespeare Festival Touring Children's Show, N.Y.C., 1966; featured dancer Twyla Tharp Dance Found., N.Y.C., 1966-85; artistic dir., dancer Sara Rudner Performance Ensemble, N.Y.C., 1977—; guest dancer Joffrey Ballet, N.Y.C., 1973, Pilobolus Dance Theatre, N.Y.C., 1975, Lar Lubovitch Dance Co., N.Y.C., 1975-76; guest lectr., choreographer grad. dance dept. UCLA, 1975. Dir. dancer Sarah Lawrence Coll.; tchr. master workshop NYU Theater Program, 1988-90; pres., artistic dir. Heart Dance, Inc. Choreographer: Palm Trees and Flamingoes, 1980, Dancing for an Hour

or So, 1981, Minute by Minute, 1982, Eight Solos, 1991, Heartbeats, Inside Out, 1993; (with Jennifer Tipton and Dana Reitz) Necessary Weather, 1994; (with Rona Pondick, Robert Feintuch and Jennifer Tipton) Mine, 1996, Alley Theater-The Greeks part I and II, 1997, Heartbeat/mb with Christopher Janney and Mikhail Barysnikov, 1998. Choreographer Dancing-on-View St. Mark's Ch., N.Y.C., 1999, Santa Fe Opera. Grantee Creative Artists Pub. Svc. Program, N.Y., 1975-76, N.Y. State Coun. on Arts, 1975-78, Nat. Endowment for Arts, 1979-81, 91-92, 94-97; Guggenheim fellow, 1981-82; recipient N.Y. Dance and Performance award, 1984. Business E-Mail: srudner@slc.edu.

**RUDNICK, IRENE KRUGMAN,** lawyer, educator, former state legislator; b. Columbia, SC, Dec. 27, 1929; d. Jack and Jean (Getter) Krugman; m. Harold Rudnick, Nov. 7, 1954 (dec.); children: Morris, Helen Gail. AB cum laude, U. S.C., 1949, JD, 1952. Bar: (S.C.) 1952. Individual practice law, Aiken, SC, 1952—; now ptnr. Rudnick & Rudnick; instr. bus. law U. S.C., Aiken, 1962—; tchr. Warrenville Elem. Sch., 1965-70; supt. edn. Aiken County, 1970-72; mem. S.C. Ho. of Reps., 1972—78, 1980—84, 1986—94. Pres. Adath Yeshurun Synagogue; active Aiken County Dem. Party, S.C. Dem. Party; hon. mem. Aiken Able-Disabled. Recipient Citizen of Yr. award, 1976-77, Bus. and Profl. Women's Career Woman of Yr., 1978, 94, Aiken County Friend of Edn. award, 1985, 93, Outstanding Legis. award Disabled Vets., 1991, Citizen of Yr. award Planned Parenthood, 1994, Sertoma Svc. to Mankind award, 1996, Pickens Salley So. Woman of Distinction award, 2005; named Aiken County C. of C. Woman of Yr., 2005. Mem. AAUW, Aiken Able-Disabled (hon.), Aiken Hist. Soc., Hist. Aiken Found., Alpha Delta Kappa, Order Eastern Star, Hadassah Sisterhood, Am. Legion Aux. Office: PO Box 544 135 Pendleton St NW Aiken SC 29801-3859 Office Phone: 803-648-2565.

**RUDNICK, JAMIE,** geneticist, research scientist; d. James and Jackie Rudnick. BS in Biology, U. Nebr., Lincoln, 2001; PhD in Wildlife Genetics, Purdue U., West Lafayette, Ind., 2006. Zookeeper Folsom Children's Zoo, Lincoln, 1997—2001; conservation assoc. Brookfield Zoo, Ill., 2006—. Author and co-author sci. papers in field. Recipient All Am. Scholar award, 1999, Lynn Fellowship award, Purdue U., 2001. Mem.: Am. Genetic Assn., Am. Zoo and Aquarium Assn., Am. Ornithologists' Union. Office: Chgo Zoological Soc Brookfield Zoo 3300 Golf Rd Brookfield IL 60513 Business E-Mail: jarudnic@brookfieldzoo.org.

**RUDNICK, LEWIS G.,** lawyer; b. May 31, 1935; AB with honors, Univ. Ill., Urbana-Champaign, 1957; MBA, Columbia Univ., 1960; JD, Northwestern Univ., 1964. Bar: Ill. 1964, US Dist. Ct. (no. dist. Ill.) 1964. Ptnr., Franchise & Distribution practice group DLA Piper Rudnick Gray Cary, Chgo. Gen. counsel Internat. Franchise Assn. Edn. Found.; mem. Ill. Franchise Adv. Bd.; mem. gov. com. ABA Forum on Franchising, 1977—84, chmn., 1981—83. Editor: Jour. of Internat. Franchising & Distribution Law; contbr. articles to profl. jours. Mem.: ABA, Internat. Franchise Assn. (counsel). Office: DLA Piper Rudnick Gray Cary Suite 1900 203 N LaSalle St Chicago IL 60601-1293 Office Phone: 312-368-4055. Office Fax: 312-630-7312. Business E-Mail: lewis.rudnick@dlapiper.com.

**RUDNICK, PAUL DAVID,** lawyer; b. Chgo., May 15, 1940; s. Harry Louis and Cele (Gordon) R.; m. Hope Korshak, June 13, 1963; children: William A., Carolyn. BS, Tulane U., 1962; JD cum laude, Northwestern U., 1965. Bar: Ill. 1965, Colo. 1994, U.S. Dist. Ct. (no. dist.) Ill. Assoc. Schiff, Hardin & Waite, Chgo., 1965-66; ptnr. Piper Rudnick, Chgo., 1966-99, sr. counsel, 2000—04; sr. counsel, Real Estate practice DLA Piper Rudnick Gray Cary, Chgo., 2005—. Editor Northwestern U. Law Rev., 1964-65; co-editor, author: Illinois Real Estate Forms, 1989. Mem. Pitkin County Colo. Planning and Zoning Commn. Mem. Am. Coll. Real Estate Lawyers, Internat. Found. for Employee Benefit Plans, Order of Coif. Office: DLA Piper Rudnick Gray Cary Suite 1900 203 N La Salle St Chicago IL 60601-1293 Office Phone: 312-368-4060. Office Fax: 312-630-7353. Business E-Mail: paul.rudnick@dlapiper.com.

**RUDO, MILTON,** retired manufacturing executive; b. Balt., Jan. 17, 1919; s. Saul E. and Bertha (Berkowitz) R.; m. Roslind Mandel, Mar. 27, 1943; children: Stephanie Ellen, Neil Dennis. BA, Johns Hopkins U., 1940; AMP, Harvard U., 1964. Various positions Brunswick Corp., Skokie, Ill., 1940-66, corp. v.p., pres. Bowling divsn. Chgo., 1966-74, group v.p. recreation bus., 1974-84, ret., 1984, cons. to the CEO, 1984-87; dir., cons. to the CEO Donlen Leasing Corp., Skokie, 1986-90. Pres. Nat. Bowling Hall of Fame and Mus., 1979. Capt. AUS, 1942-45, ETO. Recipient ann. award N.Y. Mktg. Club, 1960, Industry Svc. award, 1973; named to Bowling Hall of Fame, 1984. Mem. Nat. Bowling Coun. (pres. 1972), Briarwood Country Club (Deerfield, Ill.), Hamlet Country Club (Delray Beach Fla.). Home (Summer): 1755 Lake Cook Rd Highland Park IL 60035 Home (Winter): 712 Pine Lake Delray Beach FL 33445

**RUDOFF, SHELDON,** lawyer; b. Bklyn., May 29, 1933; s. Raphael and Goldie (Gorelick) R.; m. Hedda Muller, Nov. 22, 1964; children: Shaindy, Sara, Simone. BA cum laude, Yeshiva Coll., 1954; JSD cum laude, NYU, 1958; ordination, RIETS, 1957. Bar: N.Y. 1958, U.S. Dist. Ct. (so. and ea. dists.) N.Y. 1958, U.S. Supreme Ct. 1978. Ptnr. Shatzkin, Cooper & Rudoff, N.Y.C., 1970-84, Labaton Sucharow & Rudoff, N.Y.C., 1984—; pres. Union Orthodox Jewish Congregation Am. 1990-94, hon. pres., 1994—; pres. Beth Din Am., 1996—2003, hon. pres., 2003—. V.p. Yeshiva Coll. Alumni, N.Y.C., 1962-64; pres. Young Israel West Side, N.Y.C., 1969-72; sec. Orthodox Union, 1972-76, v.p., 1976-78, sr. v.p., 1978-84, chmn. bd., 1984-90, pres. 1990-94; trustee Fedn. Jewish Philanthropies, 1980-91, United Jewish Cmtys. Recipient Pres.'s award Orthodox Union, N.Y.C., 1972, Nat. Leadership award Nat. Conf. Synagogue Youth, N.Y.C., 1974, Kesser Shem Tov award Orthdox Union, 1995. Mem. ABA, N.Y State Bar Assn. Assn Bar City N.Y. (transp. com. 1976—). Office: Labaton Sucharow & Rudoff 100 Park Ave New York NY 10017-5516 Office Phone: 212-907-0700. E-mail: srudoff@labaton.com.

**RUDOLPH, ABRAHAM MORRIS,** pediatrician, educator; b. Johannesburg, Republic of South Africa, Feb. 3, 1924; s. Chone and Sarah (Feinstein) Rudolph; m. Rhona Sax, Nov. 2, 1949; children: Linda, Colin, Jeffrey. MBBCh summa cum laude, U. Witwatersrand, Johannesburg, 1946, MD, 1951; D (hon.), Rene Descartes U., Paris, 1996. Instr. Harvard Med. Sch., 1955—57, assoc. pediat., 1957—60; assoc. cardiologist in charge cardiopulmonary lab. Children's Hosp., Boston, 1955—60; dir. pediatric cardiology Albert Einstein Coll. Medicine, 1960—66, prof. pediat., assoc. prof. physiology, 1962—66; vis. pediatrician Bronx Mcpl. Hosp. NY. Ctr., N.Y.C., 1960—66; prof. pediat. U. Calif. San Francisco, 1966—94, prof. physiology, 1974—88, Neider prof. pediatric cardiology, prof. ob-gyn and reproductive scis., 1974—94, chmn. dept. pediat., 1987—91, prof. pediatr. emeritus, 1994—; practice medicine, specializing in pediatric cardiology San Francisco. Mem. cardiovasc. study sect. NIH, 1961—65; mem. nat. adv. heart coun., 1968—72; established investigator Am. Heart Assn., 1958—62; career scientist Health Rsch. Coun., N.Y.C., 1962—69; Harvey lectr. Oxford (Eng.) U., 1984; inaugural lectr. 1st Nat. Congress Italian Soc. Perinatal Medicine, 1985. Editl. bd. Pediat., 1964—70, Circulation, 1966—74, 1983—88, assoc. editor Circulation Rsch., 1970, Pediatric Rsch., 1970—77; editor: Rudolph's Pediatrics, Rudolph's Fundamentals of Pediatrics; contbr. articles to profl. jours. Recipient Merit award, Nat. Heart, Lung and Blood Inst., 1986, Arvo Yllpo medal, Helsinki 1987, 2000, Jonxis medal, Children's Hosp. Groningen, 1993, Nils Rosen von Rosenstein award, Swedish Pediat. Soc., 1999, Pollin prize for pediat. rsch., N.Y. Presbyn. Hosp., Columbia U. Coll. Physicians and Surgeons, 2005. Fellow: AAAS, Am. Assn. Adv. Sci., Royal Coll. Physicians (London), Royal Coll. Physicians (Edinburgh); mem.: Am. Heart Assn. (Rsch. Achievement award 1991, Founding Disting. Scientist award 2003), Am. Pediatric Soc. (coun. 1985—92, v.p. 1992—93, pres. 1993—94, Howland award 1999), Soc. for Pediatric Rsch. (coun. 1961—64), Soc. for Clin. Investigation, Am. Phys. Soc., Am. Acad. Pediat. (past chmn. sect. on cardiology, E. Mead Johnson award for rsch. in pediat. 1964, Borden award 1979, Lifetime Med. Edn. award 1992, Joseph St. Geme leadership

award Pediat. 1993, Founder award, cardiology sect. 2001, Pollin Pediatric Rsch. prize 2005), NAS Inst. Medicine. Office: U Calif Cardiovascular Rsch Inst Calif Rm M1331 Box 0544 San Francisco CA 94143-0544 Business E-Mail: abraham.rudolph@ucsf.edu.

**RUDOLPH, ANDREW HENRY,** dermatologist, educator; b. Detroit, Jan. 30, 1943; s. John J. and Mary M. Rudolph; children: Kristen Ann, Kevin Andrew. MD cum laude, U. Mich., 1966. Diplomate Am. Bd. Dermatology. Intern Univ. Hosp., U. Mich. Med. Ctr., Ann Arbor, 1966-67, resident dept. dermatology, 1967-70; pvt. practice medicine specializing in dermatology, 1972—. Asst. prof. dermatology Baylor Coll. Medicine, Houston, 1972-75, assoc. prof., 1975-83, clin. practice, 1983—; chief dermatology svc. VA Hosp., Houston, 1977-82; mem. staff Meth. Hosp., Tex. Children's Hosp., St. Luke's Episcopal Hosp. Mem. editl. bd. Jour. Sexually Transmitted Diseases, 1977-85; contbr. to med. publs. Served as surgeon USPHS, 1970-72. Regent's scholar U. Mich., 1966. Fellow Am. Acad. Dermatology; mem. AMA, Am. Dermatol. Assn., Tex. Med. Assn., Harris County Med. Soc., Houston Dermatol. Soc. (past pres.), Tex. Dermatol. Soc., Skin Cancre Found., Am. Venereal Disease Assn. (past pres.), Mich. Alumni Assn. (life), Alpha Omega Alpha, Phi Kappa Phi, Phi Rho Sigma, Theta Xi. Office: 6560 Fannin St Ste 724 Houston TX 77030-2768

**RUDOLPH, FREDERICK,** history professor; b. Balt., June 19, 1920; s. Charles Frederick and Jennie Hill (Swope) R.; m. Dorothy Dannenbaum, June 18, 1949; children: Marta R. MacDonald, Lisa R. Cushman. BA, Williams Coll., 1942, Litt.D., 1985; MA, Yale U., 1949, PhD, 1953; LHD, U. Rochester, 1994, Wilkes U., 1998. Instr. history Williams Coll., 1946-47; asst. instr. Yale, 1949-50; mem. faculty Williams Coll., 1951—, prof., 1961—; Mark Hopkins prof. history, 1964-82, emeritus, 1982—, chmn. Am. civilization program, 1971-80. Williams Coll. marshal, 1978-87; vis. lectr. history and edn. Harvard U., 1960, 61; vis. prof. Sch. Edn., U. Calif.-Berkeley, 1983; mem. commn. plans and objectives Am. Council Edn., 1963-66; mem. study group on postsecondary edn. Nat. Inst. Edn., 1980-83; mem. com. on baccalaureate degrees Assn. Am. Colls., 1981-85; vis. assoc. Ctr. Studies in Higher Edn., U. Calif.-Berkeley, 1983 Author: Mark Hopkins and the Log, 1956, rev. edit. 1996, The American College and University: A History, 1962, rev. edit., 1990 (Japanese translation, 2003), Curriculum: A History of the American Undergraduate Course of Study Since 1636, 1977, rev. edit., 1993; editor: Essays on Education in the Early Republic, 1965, Perspectives: A Williams Anthology, 1983; exec. editor: Change, 1980-84, cons. editor, 1985-92. Founding mem. Berkshire County Hist. Soc., 1962, v.p., 1962-66, pres., 1966-68, bd. dirs., 1974-76; trustee Hancock-Shaker Cmty. Inc., 1974-91, Wyoming Sem., 1976-79, Bennington Mus., 1985-95; bd. dirs. Armand Hammer United World Coll. Am. West, 1993-2005. Capt. AUS, 1942-46. Guggenheim fellow, 1958-59, 68-69; recipient Frederic W. Ness award Assn. Am. Colls., 1980, Rogerson cup Williams Coll., 1982, Disting. Svc. award Wyo. Seminary, 1986. Mem. AAUP, Nat. Acad. Edn., Mass. Hist. Soc. (fellow), Am. Hist. Assn., Am. Studies Assn., Phi Beta Kappa. Democrat. Home: PO Box 515 Williamstown MA 01267-2800

**RUDOLPH, GILBERT LAWRENCE,** lawyer; b. LA, Aug. 23, 1946; s. Martin and Marion R.; Susan Ilene Fellenbaum, Sept. 18, 1983; children: Samara Lisa, Felicia Beth. BA, Ariz. State U., 1967; postgrad., Am. U., Washington, 1967-69; JD, U. Cin., 1973. Bar: D.C. 1973, U.S. Dist. Ct. D.C. 1974, U.S. Ct. Appeals (D.C. cir.) 1974, Ariz. 1975, U.S. Dist. Ct. Ariz. 1975, Calif. 1979. Assoc. Streich, Lang, Weeks & Cardon, P.A., Phoenix, 1975-78; ptnr. Gilbert L. Rudolph, P.C., Phoenix, 1978-87; sr. mem. O'Connor, Cavanagh, Anderson, Killingsworth & Beshears, P.A., Phoenix, 1987-99; shareholder, co-chair fin. instn. practice group Greenberg Traurig LLP, Phoenix, 1999—. Lectr. on lending issues. Bd. dirs. Temple Chai, 2002—, Make-A-Wish Found. of Am., 1984—89, Aid to Adoption of Spl. Kids, Ariz., 1995—2003. Fellow Am. Coll. Consumer Fin. Svcs. Lawyers; mem. ABA (com. on consumer fin. svcs. bus. law sect. 1981—, com. on comml. fin. svcs. 1989—, mem. com. on uniform comml. code 1992—), Conf. on Consumer Fin. Law (governing com. 1986—). Republican. Jewish. Office: Greenberg Traurig LLP Ste 700 2375 E Camelback Rd Phoenix AZ 85016 Office Phone: 602-445-8206. E-mail: rudolphg@gtlaw.com.

**RUDOLPH, HEIDI ANNE JANTZ,** mathematician, educator; d. Marilyn Lois Clasen and Charles Raymond Jantz, Nancy Jantz (Stepmother); m. James Gordon Rudolph, Oct. 11, 1986; children: Jessica Raye, Jay Gardner. BA, Wittenberg U., 1985; MEd, John Carroll U., 1990. Cert. tchr. Ohio, 1985. Tchr. math. Huber Heights City Schs., Ohio, 1985—86, Orange City Schs., Pepper Pike, Ohio, 1987—. Tchr. lead team Orange City Schs., Pepper Pike, Ohio, 2004—; cheerleading advisor Orange Athletic Dept., Pepper Pike, Ohio. Presenter (math teacher/presenter) Parametrics can be fun!, Interact with TI Interactive, Cabri Jr. for Geometry, Study Cards for Beginners, Study Cards, Cabri Jr and Collaboration. Choir mem. The Ch. in Aurora, Ohio, 2000—05. Mem.: Nat. Coun. of Tchrs. of Math.

**RUDOLPH, JAMES ROBERT,** psychologist; b. Albuquerque, Mar. 1, 1957; s. Anita Jean and Robert John Rudolph; life ptnr. John Chester Gonsiorek. BA in Psychology, Sociology, U. N. Mex, 1980, MA in Spl. Edn., 1981; PhD in Counseling Psychology, Lehigh U., 1988. Lic. psychologist Minn. Bd. of Psychology, 1990, registered Nat. Register of Health Svc. Providers in Psychology, 1999, Diplomate Am. Bd. of Profl. Psychology, 2000, cert. profl. qualification in psychology Assn. of State and Provincial Psychology Bds., 2001. Spl. edn. tchr. Albuquerque Pub. Schs., 1982—83; psychiat. crisis counselor Mt. Tom Inst. for Human Svcs., Holyoke, Mass., 1988; psychotherapist Constance Bultman Wilson Ctr. for Adolescent Psychiatry, Faribault, Minn., 1988—90, physician's assoc., 1990; adj. asst. prof. St. Mary's Coll. Grad. Ctr. Mpls. 1990—93; pvt. practice Mplsn, 1992—2002; clin. dir. dir. of profl. tng. Carver County Mental Health Program, Waconia, Minn., 1991—; adj. faculty Capella U., Mpls., 2004. Clin. adj. faculty Minn. Sch. of Profl. Psychology, Mpls., 1992—2000; practice sample reviewer. oral exam mentor, examiner counseling psychology Am. Bd. of Profl. Psychology, Mpls., 2001—. Contbr. articles to profl. jours., chapters to books. Recipient Certificates of Excellence in Clin. Supervision, Minn. Sch. of Profl. Psychology, 1990's. Mem.: APA, Chi Sigma Iota. E-mail: jamesrudolph@mn.rr.com.

**RUDOLPH, LAVERE CHRISTIAN,** library director; b. Jasper, Ind., Dec. 24, 1921; s. Joseph Frank and Rose (Stradtner) R. AB, DePauw U., 1948; B.D., Louisville Presbyn. Sem., 1951; PhD, Yale, 1958; student, U. Zurich, Switzerland, 1960; M.L.S., Ind. U., 1968. Ordained to ministry Presbyn. Ch., 1950; pastor in Ind. and Conn., 1950-54; mem. faculty Louisville Presbyn. Sem., 1954-69, prof. ch. history, 1960-69; lectr. history U. Louisville, 1965-69; rare books bibliographer Van Pelt Library U. Pa.; head tech. services Lilly Library, Ind. U., 1970-78, curator of books, 1978-86, librarian emeritus, 1987—. Author: Hoosier Zion, 1963 (Thomas Kuch award Ind. U. Writers Conf. 1964), Story of the Church, 1966, Francis Asbury, 1966, Indiana Letters, 1979, Religion in Indiana, 1986, Hoosier Faiths, 1995. Served to capt. USAAF, 1940-46. Mem.: Am. Soc. Ch. History, Phi Beta Kappa. Democrat. Home: 2455 Tamarack Trail apt 101 Bloomington IN 47408 Office: Ind U Library Bloomington IN 47405

**RUDOLPH, MAYA,** actress, comedienne; b. Gainesville, Fla., July 27, 1972; d. Richard and Minnie (Riperton) Rudolph. BA in photography, U. Calif., Santa Cruz, 1994. Former backup singer The Rentals. Actor: (TV series) Saturday Night Live, 2000—, City of Angels, 2000, (guest star) Chicago Hope, 1996—97.; (TV films) The Devil's Child, 1997, True Love, 1999; (films) Gattaca, 1997, Chuck & Buck, 2000, Duets, 2000, Duplex, 2003, 50 First Dates, 2004, A Prairie Home Companion, 2006, Idiocracy, 2006.*

**RUDOLPH, SCOTT,** pharmaceutical executive; b. 1958; s. Arthur Rudolph. Dir., chmn. of bd., CEO NBTY, Inc., Bohemia, NY, 1986—. Past chmn. of bd. dirs. Dowling Coll., Long Island, NY, 1997—2000; vice chmn. Dowling Coll. Bd., 2004—. Office: NBTY PO Box 9001 Bohemia NY 11716-9001*

**RUDOLPH, SHAY JEANETTE,** music educator, musician; b. So. Weymouth, Mass., Sept. 29, 1977; d. Steven Arthur and Cynthia Rudolph. MusB, Boston U., 1995—99, MusM, 2003—05. Cello instr. Norwood Pub. Schools, Mass., 2000—; chamber music instr. Greater Boston Youth Symphony Orchestras, 2001—; cellist Plymouth Philharm. Orch., Plymouth, Mass., 1999—2005, Indian Hill Symphony, Littleton, Mass., 2001—, Back Bay Players, Boston, 1999—, Rudolphs Cello/Piano Duo, Norwood, Mass., 1989—; cello soloist Pky. Concert Orch., Westwood, Mass., 1991. Recipient String Dept. award, Boston U., 1999. Mem.: Pi Kappa Lambda. Personal E-mail: s23jr02@yahoo.com.

**RUDOLPH, WALLACE MORTON,** law educator; b. Chgo., Sept. 11, 1930; s. Norman Charles and Bertha (Margolin) R.; m. Janet L. Gordon, Feb. 14, 1964 (div. Jan. 1998); children: Alexey, Rebecca, Sarah; m. Mimi Longworth, Mar. 22, 1998; children: Haille, Bryon. BA, U. Chgo., 1950, JD, 1953. Bar: Ill. 1953, U.S. Ct. Mil. Appeals 1954, U.S. Supreme Ct. 1954, Nebr. 1962, Wash. 1978. Rsch. assoc. Ford Found., 1953-54, Ford Found. (Project in Law and Behavior Sci.), 1954-55; instr. U. Chgo. Law Sch., 1959; assoc. Antonow & Fink, Chgo., 1960-61; asst. prof. law U. Nebr., Lincoln, 1961-63, assoc. prof., 1963-64, prof., 1965-76, U. Puget Sound Sch. Law, 1976-94, dean, 1976-80; prof. Seattle U. Sch. Law, 1994—; prof. law Fla. A&M U. Law Sch., 2006. Vis. prof. law U. Wis., 1980-81, U. Ill., 1984; chair excellence in law Memphis State U. Law Sch., 1991; mem. Commrs. Uniform State Law, 1973-77; judge Ct. Indsl. Rels., Nebr., 1975-77; mem. Wash. Jud. Coun. and COm. II, 1976-80. Pub. Employment Rels. Commn., Wash., 1977-97; dean U. Orlando, 1997-98. Author: Handbook for Correctional Law; contbr. articles to profl. jours.; author: Model Criminal Procedure Code, 1975, Model Sentencing and Corrections Act, 1978, Amicus Curiae Brief, Wash. State Supreme Ct, 1979. Bd. dirs. LIMIT, 1992-94, Nebr. chpt. ACLU, 1956-57; mem. Nebr. Dem. Contact Com., 1973-74, 75-76; chmn. Firt Congl. Dist. Dem. Party, 1975-76; mem. exec. com. Unitarian Ch., Lincoln, 1965-67. With JAGC, U.S. Army, 1954-57. Mem. AAUP, ABA, Soc. Criminology, Am. Law Inst., Am. Arbitration Assn. Office Phone: 321-284-4480. Personal E-mail: wmr337@hotmail.com.

**RUDOLPHSEN, WILLIAM M.,** retail executive; BS in Acctg., Marquette U.; MBA, DePaul U. With Walgreen Co., Deerfield, Ill., 1977—, dir. 3d party acctg., 1995—98, divisional v.p. acctg., contr., 1998—2004, sr. v.p., CFO, 2004—. Office: Walgreen Co 200 Wilmot Rd Deerfield IL 60015*

**RUDOY, HERBERT L.,** lawyer; b. 1942; m. Carole Rudoy; children: Jennifer, Michael. BA, Duke U., 1964; JD, Northwestern U., 1967. Atty. Interperformances Inc., Chgo. Bd. dirs. Sports Lawyers Assn. Mem.: Ill. Bar Assn. Office: Herbert L Rudoy Ltd 230 W Superior #510 Chicago IL 60610 also: Interperformances Inc 230 W Superior #510 Chicago IL 60610 Office Phone: 312-266-2525, 312-654-1717. Business E-mail: chisport@aol.com.

**RUDSTEIN, DAVID STEWART,** law educator; b. Leeds, Eng., Sept. 27, 1946; BS, U. Ill., 1968, LL.M., 1975; JD, Northwestern U., 1971. Bar: Ill. 1971, U.S. Supreme Ct. 1977. Teaching asst. U. Ill. Coll. Law, 1971-72; law clk. to Justice Walter V. Schaefer Supreme Ct. Ill., Chgo., 1972-73; asst. prof. law Ill. Inst. Tech.-Chgo. Kent Coll., 1973-76, assoc. prof., 1976-79, prof., 1979—, assoc. dean, 1983-87. Author: Double Jeopardy, 2004, (with C.P. Erlinder and D. Thomas) Criminal Constitutional Law, 1990. Mem. ABA, Chgo. Coun. Lawyers, Order of Coif. Office: Ill Inst Tech-Chgo 565 W Adams St Chicago IL 60661-3613 Office Phone: 312-906-5354. E-mail: drudstei@kentlaw.edu.

**RUDY, DAVID ROBERT,** physician, educator; b. Columbus, Ohio, Oct. 19, 1934; s. Robert Sale and Lois May (Arthur) R.; m. Rose Mary Sims; children by previous marriage: Douglas D., Steven W., Katharine L. Rudy Hoffer, Hunter A. Elam. BSc, Ohio State U., 1956, MD, 1960; MPH, Med. Coll. Wis., 1995. Diplomate Am. Bd. Family Practice, Am. Bd. Preventive Medicine. Intern Northwestern Meml. Hosp., Chgo., 1960-61; resident in internal medicine Ohio State U. Hosp., 1963-64; resident in pediatrics Children's Hosp., Columbus, Ohio, 1964; pvt. family practice Columbus, 1964-75; dir. residency program Riverside Meth. Hosp., Columbus, 1975-85; dir. family practice residency Monsour Med. Ctr., Jeannette, Pa., 1985-88; dir. residency Bon Secours Hosp., Grosse Pointe, Mich., 1988-91; prof., chmn. Finch U. Health Scis., Chgo. Med. Sch., Dept. Family Preventive Medicine, 1991-95, 97—; prof. Pomerene chair family medicine Ohio State U., 1995-97. Editor, contbr. (textbook) Family Medicine for the House Officer; author: Family Medicine Q & A: NMS Series; contbr. articles to profl. jours. Capt. flight surgeon MC. USAF, 1961—63; col. USAFR (ret.). Recipient USAF Commendation medal. Fellow Am. Acad. Family Physicians; mem. AMA, Ill. State Med. Assn. Republican. Office: Chgo Med Sch Finch U Clinic 3333 Green Bay Rd North Chicago IL 60064-3037

**RUDY, ELLEN BEAM,** nursing educator; b. Moundsville, W.Va., May 5, 1936; d. William Henry and Mary Ellen Beam; m. Theodore Rudy, June 13, 1959; children: Richard, Alan, William. BSN, Ohio State U., 1958; MPA, U. Dayton, 1974; MSN, U. Md., 1977; PhD, Case Western Res. U., 1980. Cmty. health staff nurse Columbus (Ohio) Pub. Health Nursing Svc., 1958-60; supr. in-svc. instr. Henry County Hosp., New Castle, Ind., 1960-66; emergency room staff nurse St. Elizabeth Med. Ctr., Dayton, Ohio, 1970-73; instr. critical care Johns Hopkins Hosp., Balt., 1975-76; assoc. prof., program dir. Kent (Ohio) State U. Adult Program, 1978-84; adminstrv. assoc. U. Hosp. Cleve., 1985-90; assoc. prof., chmn. MSN Case Western Res. U., Cleve., 1985-88, prof., chair acute care nursing, 1988-90, assoc. dean rsch., 1990-91; dean, prof. U. Pitts. Sch. Nursing, 1991-2005. Author: (with others) Critical Care Nursing, 1992 (Am. Jour. Nursing Book of Yr. 1993); contbr. articles to profl. jours. Grant reviewer NIH Nursing Student Sect., Washington, 1990-93; provider expert testimony Senate Appropriations Com., Washington, 1993, Health Care Forum, Washington, 1993. Edward J. and Louise Mellen Endowed Chair in Acute Care Nursing, 1989-91; fellow Am. Acad. Nursing, 1988; rsch. grantee NIH Nat. Ctr. for Nursing Rsch., 1989-91, 91-94. Mem. ANA, AACN, Am. Heart Assn., Nat. Kidney Found. (co-chair critical care task force 1988-91), Coun. Nurse Researchers. Office: Univ Pitts Sch Nursing 350 Victoria Building Pittsburgh PA 15261-2403 Home: 7815 Lydia Dr Lewis Center OH 43035-8076

**RUDY, FRANK R.,** pathologist; b. Harrisburg, Pa., Jan. 23, 1949; s. Burton B. and Blanch T. (Rhoads) R.; m. Debra R. Bromberg, Dec. 27, 1970; children: Allison, Nicole. BA, Franklin & Marshall Coll., 1970; MD, U. Pitts., 1974. From assoc. pathologist to chmn. lab. Polyclinic Hosp., Harrisburg, 1979-95; chmn. Pinnacle Health Lab., Harrisburg, 1996-99, vice-chmn. 2000—. Regional mem. Commn. for Lab. Accreditation, 1996—2002; pres. Pathology Assocs. Ctrl. Pa., Harrisburg, 1997—. Author: Uropathology, 1989, Principles and Practices of Surgical Pathology; contbr. articles to profl. jours. Fellow Coll. Am. Pathology, Am. Soc. Clin. Pathologists; mem. Internat. Acad. Pathology, Am. Pathology Found., U.S. Acad. Pathology, Canadian Acad. Pathology. Avocation: scuba diving. Office: Pinnacle Health Labs Med Scis Bldg 100 S 2d St PO Box 8700 Harrisburg PA 17105-8700 Business E-Mail: frudy@pinnaclehealth.org.

**RUDY, KATHLEEN VERMEULEN,** small business owner; b. Grand Rapids, Mich., Dec. 29, 1931; d. John Weston and Geneva (Swiet) Vermeulen; m. Fredrick Albers Yonkman, June 9, 1953 (div. Sept. 1980); children: Sara Yonkman Davis, Margriet Yonkman Finnegan, Nina Yonkman Tower; m. Raymond Bruce Rudy, Nov. 14, 1981. BA, Hope Coll., 1953. Owner Kate's Antiques, 1974—2000. Editor mag. Jr. League of Boston, 1960's, Scarsdale Jr. League, 1960's. Bd. dirs. Jr. League of Boston, 1960s, Greenwich Cmty. for Human Svcs., 1970s-80s, Neighbor to Neighbor, Greenwich, 1980-98; trustee Hope Coll., 1986-96; chmn. Mary Fund com. Ladies Golf Tournament, 1985; mem. Women's Nat. Rep. Club, N.Y.C., 1995—; bd. govs., 1997-2004, 06—; mem. Hope Coll. Pres.'s Task Force, 1997-99; treas. Women's Nat. Rep. Club, 2000-02, chmn. nominating com. 2000—, 2d v.p., 2002-04, mem. internat. affairs com., 2004—. Mem. Jr. League of Phoenix, Greenwich Country Club, Boulders Golf Club (Scotts-

dale), Dorset Field Club, Doubles Club, Kappa Alpha Theta. Republican. Congregationalist. Avocations: tennis, golf, antiques, travel, art. Home and Office: 37 Lismore Ln Greenwich CT 06831-3741 E-mail: RayRudy@worldnet.att.net.

**RUDY, MONICA ELAINE,** small business owner, music educator; b. Goshen, Ind., June 18, 1976; d. John C. and Rebecca Lee Pappas; m. John Ervie Rudy, Sept. 5, 1998; 1 child, Clara Isabella. BA, Ohio State U., Columbus, 2000. Cert. tchr. Wiggles N' Tunes. Owner Monica Rudy's Music Studio, Grove City, Ohio, 1998—; pvt. instr. music. Musician: Pappas Family Recorder Quartet, 2002. Mem. Christian edn. bd. S.W. Grace Brethren Ch., Grove City, Ohio, 2001—, mem. missions bd. 2001—, coord.children's worship, 2004—, tchr., 2005—. Mem.: Nat. Guild Piano Teachers (assoc.), Ohio Music Tchrs. Assn. (assoc.), Music Tchrs. Nat. Assn. (assoc.). Avocations: music, gardening, reading, interior decorating, painting. Office: Monica Rudy's Music Studio 3214 Angela Dr Grove City OH 43123

**RUDY, RAYMOND BRUCE, JR.,** retired food company executive; b. L.A., Apr. 24, 1931; s. Raymond Bruce and Wrena Margaret (Higgins) R.; m. Kathleen Vermeulen; children: Bruce Rudy, Alice M.R. Price, Barbara R. Frith. BS, UCLA, 1953; MBA, Xavier U., Cin., 1960. Brand mgr. Procter & Gamble, Cin., 1956-62; product mgr. Hunt-Wesson Foods, Fullerton, Calif., 1962-63; group v.p. Gen. Foods Corp., White Plains, NY, 1963-79; pres. Oroweat Foods Co. subs. Continental Grain Co., N.Y.C., 1979-83; chmn., pres. Arnold Foods Co., Inc., Greenwich, Conn., 1984-86; pres. Affiliates of Best Foods subs. CPC Internat., Englewood Cliffs, NJ, 1987-89; ret., 1989; chmn., CEO, New Hampton, Inc., 1993-94; dep. chmn. Snapple Natural Beverages, Inc., 1992-94; mng. dir. J.W. Childs Assoc., 1995—; chmn. Personal Care Group, Inc., 1996-98. Chmn. Beltone Electronics Corp., 1997-2000, Internat. Diverse Foods, 1998-99, Empire Kosher Poultry, Inc., 1997-2000, Am. Safety Razor, 2000-05, Hartz Mountain Corp., 2001-04, The Meow Mix Co., 2002-03, The Sunny Delight Beverage Co., 2004—; bd. dirs. Pinnacle Foods Corp., Widmer Bros. Brewing, Inc. With U.S. Army, 1954—56. Mem. Greenwich Country Club, Dorset Field Club, The Links, The Boulders. Congregationalist.

**RUDY, YORAM,** biomedical engineer, biophysicist, educator; b. Tel Aviv, Feb. 12, 1946; arrived in U.S. 1973; s. Nahum and Yaffa (Krinkin) R. BSc, Technion/Israel Inst. Tech., Haifa, 1971, MSc in Physics, 1973; PhD in Biomed. Engring., Case Western Res. U., 1978. Asst. prof. dept. biomed. engring. Case Western Res. U., Cleve., 1981-86, assoc. prof., 1986-89, prof., 1989—2004, prof. dept. of physiology and biophysics, 1991—2004, prof. dept. medicine, 1992—2004, dir. cardiac bioelectricity rsch./tng. ctr., 1994—2004; Fred Saigh disting. prof. engring., prof. biomed. engring., cell biology and physiology, medicine, radiology and pediat. Washington U., St. Louis, 2004—, dir. Cardiac Bioelectricity and Arrhythmia Ctr., 2004—. Vis. prof. Technion/Israel Inst. Tech., 1982-83, U. Parma, Italy, 1986-87, U. Utah, Salt Lake City, 1990, Tel Aviv U., 1991, Russian Acad. of Scis., St. Petersburg, 1997, U. Berne, Switzerland, 1998, Johns Hopkins U., 2005, Columbia U., 2005; cardiovascular and pulmonary study sect. NIH, 1984-88; lectr., spkr. in field. Mem. editl. bd. Jour. Electrocardiology, Jour. Cardiovasc. Electrophysiology, Cardiovasc. Rsch., Cardiac Electrophysiology Rev.; Heart Rhythmn Jour. contbr. articles to profl. jours. Grantee NIH, 1985—, Am. Heart Assn., 1990-95, NSF, 1987-94; recipient Gordon K. Moe Prof. award, 1997, NIH-Nat. Heart, Lung and Blood Inst. Merit award, 1998. Fellow IEEE, Am. Physiol. Soc., Am. Inst. Med. and Biol. Engring., Am. Heart Assn., Heart Rhythm Soc., Biomed. Engring. Soc. (Disting. Lectr. award 2001); mem. NAE, Biophys. Soc. Achievements include development of a novel imaging modality for non-invasive imaging of cardiac electrical events from electrical potentials measured on the body surface (electrocardiographic imaging, ECGI), of theoretical models of cardiac excitation at the cellular, sub-cellular and tissue levels; elucidation of the cellular mechanisms of cardiac arrhythmias and the role of tissue architecture in arrhythmogenesis. Office: Washington U St Louis Cardiac Bioelectricity Ctr 290 Whitaker Hall Campus Box 1097 Saint Louis MO 63130-4899

**RUE, DOUGLAS MICHAEL,** solutions engineer; b. Pensacola, Fla., Apr. 9, 1964; s. Barbara J. Rue; m. Andra O'Neal, 1995; 1 child, Christian Michael Rue. AA in Bus., Pensacola (Fla.) Jr. Coll., 1984, AA in Computer Sci., 1984; BS in Computer Sci. cum laude, St. Augustine's Coll., 1988; MS in Telecomms., DePaul U., 1990. Cert. Adtran Data Sales Solutions, 2004. Data sys. analyst Internat. Paper, Memphis, 1990-91, project analyst, 1991-94; tech. cons. Sprint, Universal City, Calif., 1994—98, sr. tech. cons. Universal City, Calif., Jacksonville, Fla., 1998—2000; sr. sales engr. Teleglobe Bus., Atlanta, 2000; solutions engr. Global Crossing Telecom., 2000—01, US LEC Telecom., Memphis, 2004—, solutions engr. CMAC Charlotte, NC, 2003—04; account exec. Allegiance Telecom., 2001—02, Network Telephone, Atlanta. Adj. prof. telecom. sys. adminstrn., DeVry U., Pomona, Calif., 1995, adj. prof. telecom. enterprise networks design and data comm., 2002-03. Active Habitat for Humanity, 1999; with U.S. Army Res., 1985-91. Office: 3150 Lenox Park Blvd Ste 417 Memphis TN 38115 Personal E-mail: douglasrue@aol.com

**RUEB, SHEREE A.,** social services administrator; b. Lincoln, Nebr., Aug. 23, 1960; d. Larry Hawkins. Annette Hawkins; m. Brent G. Rueb, July 7, 1985. BA, Hastings Coll., 1979—83; MA, Wichita State U., 1991. V.p. Mental Health Assn. South Ctrl. Kans., Wichita, 1991—95; state dir. Green Thumb, In.c, Arlington, Va., 1995—97; dir. sr. work experience ARC, Wichita, 1997—. Adv. bd. Reno County Workforce, Hutchinson, Kans., 1998—; bd. dirs. Kans. Workforce Investment, Hays, 1997—; adv. bd. Sedgwick County Workforce Partnership, Wichita, 1998—. Vice chair Older Workers Task Force State of Kans., 1997—. Mem.: Harvey County Archl. Assn. (sec., treas. 1995—, pres. 1996—98). Avocation: historic architecture, historic preservation. Office: ARC Midway KS Chpt 707 N Main Wichita KS 67203

**RUECKERT, ROLAND RUDYARD,** retired virologist, educator; b. Rhinelander, Wis., Nov. 24, 1931; s. George Leonard and Monica Amelia (Seiberlich) R.; m. Ruth Helen Ullrich, Sept. 5, 1959; 1 child, Wanda Lynne. BS in Chemistry, U. Wis., 1953, PhD in Oncology, 1960. Fellow Max Planck Inst. for Biochemistry, Munich, 1960-61, Tübingen, Fed. Republic Germany, 1961-62; asst. rsch. virologist virus lab. U. Calif., Berkeley, 1962-65; asst. prof. biophysics lab. U. Wis., Madison, 1965-69, assoc. prof. biophysics lab., 1969-73; prof. Inst. for Molecular Virology, Madison, 1973-85, dist. rsch. prof., 1985-96, prof. emeritus, 1996-97. Mem. viology study sect. NIH, Bethesda, Md., 1981-85; pres. Am. Soc. Virology, 1989-90. With U.S. Army, 1953-55. Recipient William D. Stovall award, U. Wis., 1953, Marie Christine Kohler award U, Oneida County Tree Farmer of the Yr., 2001. Achievements include research in dodecahedral model for picornavirus structure and assembly, molecular biology of picornaviruses (polio 8 common cold), structure 8 biology of small insect viruses, mechanism of neutralization by antibodies and antivirals. Home: 2234 W Lawn Ave Madison WI 53711-1952 Office Phone: 608-262-6949. Business E-Mail: rrruecke@facstaff.wisc.edu.

**RUEDA, LEOPOLDO M.,** entomologist, research scientist; PhD, NC State U., Raleigh, 1984. Med. entomologist NC Pub. Health Pest Mgmt., Raleigh; asst. prof. U. Philippines, Los Banos, Laguna, Philippines, 1984—88; vis. scientist NC State U., Raleigh, 1988—91; rsch. entomologist Tenn. State U., Nashville, 1991—93; NC State U., 1993—94; capt., med. entomologist US Army, Ft. Sam Houston, Tex., 1994—98; rsch. entomologist Walter Reed Army Inst. Rsch., Silver Spring, Md., 2001—. Sci. adviser Internat. Found. Sci., Stockholm, 1988—. Author: (scientific research) Entomopathogenic Nematodes; contbr. numerous sci. articles to profl. jours. Chmn. Philippine Am. Folk Arts of RTP, Raleigh, 1999—2000. Capt. U.S. Army, 1994—98, Silver Spring, Md. Tropical Medicine fellow, SE Asian Mininsters Edn. Orgn., 1977, Tropical Biology fellow, 1977, NC State U., 1981—84, Phi Sigma Honor Soc. of Biology, 1978—79. Mem.: AAAS, Mid-Atlantic Mosquito and Vector Control Assn., Am. Soc. Tropical Medicine and Hygiene, Soc. Nematologists, Soc. Invertebrate Pathology, Soc. Vector Ecology, Am. Mosquito Control Assn., Entomol. Soc. Am. Roman Catholic.

Achievements include research in taxonomically described and named new species of mosquitoes, calliphorid flies, and macrochelid mites. Office: Walter Reed Army Inst Rsch Wrbu/Si 4210 Silver Hill Rd Suitland MD 20746 Office Phone: 301-238-1075. Office Fax: 301-238-3168. E-mail: ruedapol@si.edu.

**RUEDENBERG, KLAUS,** theoretical chemist, educator; b. Bielefeld, Germany, Aug. 25, 1920; came to U.S. 1948, naturalized, 1955; s. Otto and Meta (Wertheimer) R.; m. Veronika Kutter, Apr. 8, 1948 (dec. Jan. 2004); children: Lucia Meta, Ursula Hedwig, Annette Veronika, Emanuel Klaus. Student, Montana Coll., Zugerberg, Switzerland, 1938-39; licence es Scis., U. Fribourg, Switzerland, 1944; postgrad., U. Chgo., 1948-50; PhD, U. Chgo., Switzerland, 1950; PhD (hon.), U. Basel, Switzerland, 1975, U. Bielefeld, Germany, 1991, U. Siegen, 1994. Research assoc. physics U. Chgo., 1950-55; asst. prof. chemistry, physics Iowa State U., Ames, 1955-60, assoc. prof., 1960-62, prof., 1964-78, disting. prof. in sci. and humanities, 1978-91, disting. prof. emeritus, 1991—, sr. chemist Ames Lab., U.S. Dept. Energy, 1964-91, assoc., 1991—. Prof. chemistry Johns Hopkins, Balt., 1962-64; vis. prof. U. Naples, Italy, 1961, Fed. Inst. Tech., Zurich, 1966-67, Wash State U. at Pullman, 1970, U. Calif. at Santa Cruz, 1973, U. Bonn, Germany, 1974, Monash U. and CSIRO, Clayton, Victoria, Australia, 1982, U. Kaiserlautern, Germany, 1987; lectr. univs., rsch. instns. and sci. symposia, 1953—. Contbr. articles to profl. jours.; assoc. editor: Jour. Chem. Physics, 1964-67, Internat. Jour. Quantum Chemistry; Chem. Physics Letters, 1967-81, Lecture Notes in Chemistry, 1976-2003, Advances in Quantum Chemistry, 1987-2004; editor-in-chief Theoretica Chimica Acta, 1985-97; hon. editor Theoretical Chemistry Accounts, 1997—. Co-founder Octagon Center for the Arts, Ames, 1966, treas., 1966-71, also bd. dirs. Guggenheim fellow, 1966-67; Fulbright sr. scholar, 1982. Fellow: AAAS, Internat. Acad. Quantum Molecular Scis., Am. Inst. Chemists, Am. Phys. Soc.; mem.: AAUP, Am. Chem. Soc. (Midwest award 1982, Nat. Award in Theoretical Chemistry 2002), Phi Lambda Upsilon, Sigma Xi.

**RUEF, JOHN SAMUEL,** clergyman; b. Chgo., Jan. 24, 1927; s. John E. and Leota A. (Rice) R.; m. Jane Margraves Holt, Oct. 11, 1951; children: Marcus, Adam, Seth, Sarah. AB, U. Chgo., 1945; BD, Seabury-Western, 1950, STM, 1955, DD, 1975; ThD, Harvard U., 1960. Faculty mem. Berkeley Div. Sch., New Haven, 1960—71; pres. Nashotah (Wis.) House, 1974—85; chaplain Chatham (Va.) Hall, 1985—93; rector Pruden Parish, Chatham, 1993—2005. Author: Understanding the Gospels, 1967, The Gospels and Teachings of Jesus, 1967, The First Letter of Paul to Corinth, 1977. Home: PO Box 1143 Chatham VA 24531-1143 E-mail: revruef@gamewood.net.

**RUEGG, DONALD GEORGE,** retired rail transportation executive; b. LaJunta, Colo., Sept. 11, 1924; s. George Albert and Cecilia Corrine (Decker) R.; m. Ruth Carson, June 27, 1946 (dec. 1963); m. Mary Ann Eichelberger, June 24, 1964. BA, Dartmouth Coll., 1947; MBA, U. Chgo., 1972. Sec. to trainmaster, trainmaster's clk. Atchison, Topeka & Santa Fe Ry. Co., 1942—50, traveling car agt. Chgo., 1950—51, transp. inspector, 1951—52; safety supr. Atchison Topeka & Santa Fe Ry. Co., Emporia, 1952—53, trainmaster, 1953—68; asst. to v.p. info. sys. Atchison, Topeka & Santa Fe Ry. Co., Topeka, 1968—69, asst. to v.p. operation, 1969—72, gen. mgr. L.A., Topeka, 1968—69, asst. to v.p. info. sys. Atchison, Topeka & Santa Fe Ry. Co., Topeka, 1968—69, asst. to v.p. operation, 1969—72, gen. mgr. L.A., 1972—73, asst. v.p. ops., 1973—78, v.p. ops., 1978—83, exec. v.p., 1983—86; ret., 1986. Personal E-mail: donruegg@aol.com.

**RUEGGEBERG, ERNA M.,** nursing consultant, nursing administrator, researcher; b. Balt., Aug. 31, 1924; d. Frederick Carl and Selma Augusta (Heimann) Rueggeberg. BSN, U. Colo., 1947; MA in Ednl. Adminstrn., U. Chgo., 1958; DHL (hon.), Carthage Coll., 1985. RN, Ill. Dept. Profl. Regulation. Staff nurse U. Colo. Med. Ctr.-Colo. Gen. Hosp., Denver, 1947—49, Denver Gen. Hosp., 1949, head nurse pediats., 1949—52; acting supr. pediats. U. Colo. Sch. Nursing, 1952—53; instr. pediats. Sch. Nursing U. Colo., Boulder and Denver, 1953—56; instr. pediat. nursing U. Kans. Sch. Nursing, Lawrence and Kansas City, 1955—56, asst. chair, assoc. prof., 1956—60; asst. head, asst. prof. Cen. Mo. State Coll., Warrensburg, Mo., 1960—61, head, asst. prof., 1961—63; dir. chmn., dir. basic nursing edn. Lutheran Gen., Park Ridge, Ill., 1963—88; ret., 1988. Adviser Alumni Assn. Luth. Gen. and Deaconess Hosp. Sch. Nursing, Park Ridge, 1988—; coordinating coun. rep. Health Careers Coun. Ill., mem. adv. bd., bd. and exec. com., 1965—68. Commd. min. Stevens Ministry Program, St. Louis, 1991. Recipient Spiritus Christi award, Concordia Coll., 1981, Sr. award for outstanding health manpower achievement, Health Careers Coun. Ill., 1968. Mem.: ANA, AAUP, North Suburban Assn. for Health Resources (chmn. nursing and allied health edn. allied health edn. 1973), Ill. Coun. Hosp. Schs. Profl. Nursing, Nat. League for Nursing, Internat. Coun. Nurses, U. Colo. Sch. Nursing Alumni Assn. (membership dir. 1978—), Assoc. Alumni U. Colo. (membership dir. 1947—), U. Chgo. Alumni Assn. (life; membership dir. 1958—), Pi Lambda Theta (life; Chgo. chpt.). Lutheran. Avocations: gardening, gourmet cooking, travel, planned tours. Home: PO Box 363 Mount Prospect IL 60056-0363

**RUEGGER, PHILIP T., III,** lawyer; b. Plainfield, NJ, Oct. 14, 1949; s. Philip T. Jr. and Gloria Marie (McLaughlin) R.; m. Rebecca Lee Huffman, Aug. 3, 1974; children: Sarah, Britt, Michael. AB magna cum laude, Dartmouth Coll., 1971; JD, U. Va., 1974. Bar: N.Y. 1975. Assoc. Simpson Thacher & Bartlett, NYC, 1974-81, ptnr., 1981—, ptnr., exec. com., 1993—, head corp. dept., 2002—, chmn. exec. com., 2004—. Bd. dirs. Henry St. Settlement. Mem. Assn. Bar City NY, Henry St. Settlement (mem. bd.). Manursing Island Club (Rye, NY), Apawamis Club (Rye), Phi Beta Kappa. Office: Simpson Thacher & Bartlett 425 Lexington Ave New York NY 10017-3954 Office Phone: 212-455-3220. Business E-Mail: pruegger@stblaw.com.

**RUEGSEGGER, DONALD RAY, JR.,** radiological physicist, educator; b. Detroit, May 29, 1942; s. Donald Ray and Margaret Arlene (Elliot) R.; m. Judith Ann Merrill, Aug. 20, 1965 (div.); children: Steven, Susan, Mark, Ann; m. Patricia Ann Mitchell, Oct. 16, 1999. BS, Wheaton Coll., 1964; MS, Ariz. State U., 1966, PhD (NDEA fellow), 1969. Diplomate Am. Bd. Radiology. Radiol. physicist Miami Valley Hosp., Dayton, Ohio, 1969—, chief med. physics sect., 1983—. Physics cons. X-ray dept. VA Hosp., Dayton, 1970-73; adj. asst. prof. physics Wright State U., Fairborn, Ohio, 1973-74, clin. assist. prof. radiology, 1976-81, clin. assoc. prof. radiology, 1981—, group leader in med. physics, dept. radiol. scis. Med. Sch., 1978-85. Mem. AAAS, Am. Assn. Physicists in Medicine (pres. Ohio River Valley chpt. 1982-83, co-chmn. local summer sch. arrangements comm. 1986), Am. Coll. Radiology, Am. Coll. Med. Physics (founding chancellor), Am. Phys. Soc., Ohio Radiol. Soc., Health Physics Soc. Home: 6252 Donnybrook Dr Centerville OH 45459-1837 Office: Radiation Therapy Miami Valley Hosp 1 Wyoming St Dayton OH 45409-2722 Office Phone: 937-208-4058. E-mail: drruegsegger@mvh.com.

**RUEHL, MERCEDES,** actress; b. Queens, NY, Feb. 28, 1948; BA in English, Coll. of New Rochelle; studied acting with Uta Hagen, Tad Danielewski. Appearances include (theatre) Vanities, 1977-78, Billy Irish, 1980, Much Ado About Nothing, Misalliance, Androcles and the Lion, Tartuffe, Medea, 1980-82, Three Sisters, 1982-83, The Day They Shot John Lennon, 1982-83, Flirtation, 1983, June Moon, 1983-84, Monday After the Miracle, 1983-84, Coming of Age in Soho, 1985, The Marriage of Bette and Boo, 1985, I'm Not Rappaport, 1985 (Obie Award, Village Voice, 1985), American Notes, 1988, Other People's Money, 1989, Lost in Yonkers, 1991 (Tony award, 1991, Drama Desk award, 1991, Outer Critics Circle award 1991), The Shadow Box, 1994 (Tony nominee - Featured Actress in a Play, 1995), The Rose Tattoo, 1995, Woman Before a Glass, 2005 (Obie award, Village Voice, 2005); (film) The Warriors, 1979, Four Friends, 1981, Heartburn, 1986, 84 Charing Cross Road, 1987, Leader of the Band, 1987, The Secret of My Success, 1987, Radio Days, 1987, Big, 1988, Married to the Mob, 1988, Slaves of New York, 1989, Crazy People, 1990, Another You, 1991, The Fisher King, 1991 (Academy award Best Supporting Actress 1991), Lost in Yonkers, 1993, Last Action Hero, 1993, Rosanna's Grave, 1996, Out of the Cold, 1999, More Dogs Than Bones, 1999, The Minus Man, 1999, What's Cooking, 2000, Spooky House, 2000; (TV movie) Indictment: The McMartin Trial, 1995, Subway Stories: Tales From the Underground,

1997, Gia, 1997, Mary Kay Letourneau Story: The All-American Girl, 2000, The Lost Child, 2000, The Amati Girls, 2000, Guilt by Association, 2002; (TV mini-series) Widows, 2002, (TV series) Frazier, 1996, Spooky House, 1999. Recipient Nat. Film Critics Circle award, 1988, Clarence Derwent award, 1989.

**RUEHLE, CHARLES JOSEPH,** pathologist, military officer; b. May 26, 1943; s. John Donald and Alta (Brown) R.; m. Nellie Backus, Aug. 5, 1972 (div.). DVM, Iowa State U., 1967; MD, U. Iowa, 1973; MS, 1973. Diplomate Am. Bd. Preventive Medicine, Am. Bd. Pathology. Commd. 2d lt. USAF, 1964; advanced through grades to col., sr. flight surgeon, 1984; chief flight surgeon, 1987; chief Vet. Svc., Grissom AFB, Ind., 1967-69; resident in aerospace medicine Brook AFB, Tex., 1973-75; resident in pathology Wilford Hall USAF Med. Ctr., Lackland AFB, Tex., 1975-79; with div. aerospace pathology Armed Forces Inst. Pathology, Washington, 1979-88; chief div. aerospace pathology, 1982-85; chmn. dept. forensic scis., 1985-88; sec. Joint COm. Aviation Pathology, 1984-88; exec. asst. to fed. air surgeon FAA, Washington, 1988—93, sr. aviation med. examiner, 1996—; mgr. appeals & special projects branch, 1993—2003, prin. liasion, 2004—; spl. asst. fed. Surgeon, 2003—. Adj. asst. prof. prevetive medicine Uniformed Services U. Health Scis. lectr. aerospace pathology; cons. USAF Sugeon Gen., 1987; chmn, Airliner Cabin Environ. Report Team, 2002- Fellow Am. Soc. Clin Pathologists, Aerospace Med. Assn.; mem. Am. Acad. Forensic Scis. AMA, USAF Flight Surgeons, Nat. Sojourners, Assn. Mil. Surgeons U.S., Internat. Soc. Air Safety Investigators, Air Force Assn., Alpha Zeta, Gamma Sigma Delta, Omega Tau Sigma (gov. 1967-75). Republican. Presbyterian. Home: 1000 Lower Pindell Rd Lothian MD 20711-2704 Office: Fed Air Surgeon FAA 800 Independence Ave SW Washington DC 20591-0001 Office Phone: 202-493-4580. E-mail: charles.ruehle@faa.gov.

**RUEMMLER, KATHRYN H.,** prosecutor; b. Richland, Wash., 1972; BA cum laude, U. Wash., Seattle, 1993; JD, Georgetown U., 1996. Def. atty. Zuckerman Spaeder LLP, Washington; litig. atty. Latham & Watkins, Washington; prosecutor, US Atty's Office US Dept. Justice, Washington, 2001—. With Enron Task Force, US Dept. Justice, 2003—, dep. dir., 2005—.*

**RUESINK, ALBERT WILLIAM,** biologist, plant sciences educator; b. Adrian, Mich., Apr. 16, 1940; s. Lloyd William and Alberta May (Foltz) R.; m. Kathleen Joy Cramer, June 8, 1963; children: Jennifer Li, Adriana Eleanor. BA, U. Mich., 1962; MA, Harvard U., 1965, PhD, 1966. Postdoctoral fellow Swiss Fed. Inst. Tech., Zurich, 1966-67; prof. biology Ind. U., Bloomington, 1967—, spl. asst. to Pres. for Faculty Rels., 1999—2005. Recipient Amoco Teaching award Ind. U., 1980 Mem. AAUP (pres. chpt. 1978-79, 90-91), Am. Soc. Plant Physiologists, Bot. Soc. Am. Democrat. Mem. United Ch. of Christ. Home: 2605 E 5th St Bloomington IN 47408-4286 Office: Ind U Dept Biology 1001 E 3d St Bloomington IN 47405 Office Phone: 812-855-5555. Business E-Mail: ruesink@indiana.edu.

**RUESTERHOLZ, VIRGINIA P.,** telecommunications industry executive; m. Kevin Ruesterholz; 2 children. B in Chem. Engring., Stevens Inst. Tech., 1983; MS in Telecom. Mgmt., Bklyn. Poly. Inst., 1991. Mgr. NY Tel., 1984, market area v.p., gen. mgr. svc. delivery and field ops., 1993; v.p. complex installation and maintenance for network svcs. Bell Atlantic, v.p. ops. assurance, sr. v.p. wholesale markets; pres. Verizon Ptnr. Solutions Verizon Comm., pres. Verizon Telecom. Mem. bus. and tech. bd. Stevens Inst. Tech. Bd. dirs. Manhattan Theater Club. Recipient 40 Under 40 award, Crain's NY Bus., Rising Star award, NY Women's Agenda. Mem.: Edwin A. Stevens Soc. (chair). Office: Verizon Comm 140 West St New York NY 10007*

**RUETTER, GUNTER H.,** surgeon; b. Worms on Rhine, Germany, Apr. 19, 1953; s. Elli Ruetter; 1 child, Jan-Frederik H. MD, U. Heidelberg, 1982; PhD, German Cancer Rsch. Ctr., 1989. Medical License State of Baden-Wuerttemberg, Germany, 1982, Specialist in Emergency Medical Services (EMS) Hesse Med. Assn., Germany, 1987, Specialist in Sports Medicine Hesse Med. Assn., Germany, 1988, Specialist in Surgery (general and trauma surgery) Hesse Med. Assn., Germany, 1989, Qualified Surgeon in Chief for Emergency Medical Services (EMS) Baden-Wuerttemberg Med. Assn., Germany, 1990. Sci. asst. German Cancer Rsch. Ctr., Heidelberg, Germany, 1976—82; resident surgeon, gen. surgery St. Franziska Stift Krankenhaus, Bad Kreuznach, Germany, 1983; sr. surgeon U. Hosp. for Surgery, Marburg, 1984—89; resident surgeon, plastic surgery and hand surgery St. Marien Krankenhaus, Siegen; med. dir. Paul Hartmann Corp., Heidenheim; gen. mgr. Serapharm, Inc., Muenster; pres. Monitoring Force Group, Washington, 1995—. Lectr. Ortenberg Med. Sch., Marburg, Germany, 1991—89; cons., def. and disaster medicine Ind., Washington, 2002—; lectr., med. entrepreneurship and clin. rsch. C of C., Germany; lectr. Netherlands Def. Coll., The Hague, Netherlands, 2004—; student, european master in disaster medicine program U. of Ea. Piedmont, Novara, Italy, 2005—; col. (med. corps) Joint Med. Svc. Air Forces Reserves, Bonn, Germany, 2002—; br. chief (r), joint med. svc. res. forces Ministry of Def., Bonn, 2005—; chmn. Joint Med. Res. Forces Orgn., Bonn, 2004—; del. Interallied Confederation of Med. Res. Officers, Brussels, 2004—; lectr. U. Marburg, Med. Sch., Germany, 1994—99, Acad. of the German Armed Forces Joint Med. Svc., Munich, 2004—. Contbr. articles to profl. jours. Founding mem. German Am. Bus. Coun., Washington, 2005. Col. Joint Med. Svc. Air Force Res., 2002, Bonn, Germany. Recipient diploma, German Assn. for Sports Medicine, 1998. Master: Initialled Confederation of Med. Res. Officers (del. 2004), Joint Med. Res. Forces Orgn. (chmn. 2004); mem.: World Assn. for Disaster and Emergency Medicine, German Natural Scientists and Physicians Assn., German Disaster Medicine Assn., German Assn. for Trauma Surgery, German Assn. for Surgery, German Assn. for Mil. Medicine and Pharmacy, US C. of C., DC C. of C., Assn. of Mil. Surgeons of the US, German Exec. Round Table, Am. German Bus. Club, German Rsch. Forces Assn., Army and Navy Club, Wash., German Officers Club, Wash., German Atlantic Coun. Office: Monitoring Force USA Inc 888 Seventeenth Street NW Washington DC 20006-332 Office Phone: +1 (202) 296 5699. Office Fax: +1 (202) 296 2609.

**RUETTGERS, MICHAEL CADET,** electronics executive; b. Muskogee, Okla., Dec. 11, 1942; s. John J. and Florence J. (Nunn) Ruettgers; m. Maureen Lee Sanders, July 12, 1969; children: Polly K., Christopher M., Abigail G. BS, Idaho State U., 1964; MBA, Harvard U., 1967. Engring. planner LTV Aerospace Co., Detroit, 1964—68; bus. area mgr. Raytheon Co., Lexington, Mass., 1968—81; sr. v.p., gen. mgr. Keane Inc., Boston, 1981—86; COO TFS Inc., Chelmsford, Mass., 1987—88; pres., COO EMC Corp., Hopkinton, Mass., 1988—2000, CEO, 1992—2001, chmn., bd. dirs., 2004—. Bd. dirs. Keane Inc., TFS Inc., Raytheon Corp. Republican. Roman Catholic. Avocations: hunting, fishing. Office: EMC Corp 171 South St Hopkinton MA 01748-2222*

**RUFF, KENNETH,** management consultant, information technology manager; BS in Computer Sci. and Elec. Engring., U. South Fla., 1986, post grad. Mgmt. cons. FPL Corp., Miami, Fla., 1987—89; managing dir. N.Am. network Telerate, Jersey City, 1989; mgmt. cons. Sandoz, East Hanover, NJ, 1989; mgmt. cons. N.Y. and Tex. IBM, 1986, 1987, 1993; mgmt. cons. GTE, Dallas, 1993, AT&T Solutions, Bridgewater, NJ, 1995, Tokio Marine, N.Y.C., 1995—96, Chase Manhattan Bank, N.Y.C., 1991, 1992, 1997, 2000, Merril Lynch, Princeton, NJ, 1999; project manager Cendant Car Rntal Group, Garden City, N.Y. and Parsippany, NJ, 2000—04; design architect and mgmt. cons. Bank of Am., 2004—05; mgmt. cons. JP Morgan Pvt. Bank, 2005—. Address: 970 Va St Dunedin FL 34697: 22 Elm St Huntington NY 11743-3678

**RUFF, LINDY,** professional hockey coach; b. Warburg, Alta., Canada, Feb. 17, 1960; m. Gaye Ruff; children: Brett, Eryn, Brian and Madeleine (twins). Defenseman Lethbridge Broncos, 1976—79, Buffalo Sabres, 1979-89, NY Rangers, 1989-91; player/asst. coach Rochester Americans, 1991-92, San Diego Gulls; asst. coach Fla. Panthers, 1993—97; head coach Buffalo Sabres, 1997—. Vol. Children's Hosp., Buffalo, Muscular Dystrophy Assn. Named

Buffalo Sabre's Rookie of the Yr., 1980; recipient Jack Adams Award, 2006. Avocations: fishing, boating, golf. Office: c/o Buffalo Sabres HSBC Arena 1 Seymour H Knox III Plz Buffalo NY 14203-3096*

**RUFF, ROBERT LOUIS,** neurologist, physiologist, researcher; b. Bklyn., Dec. 16, 1950; s. John Joseph and Rhoda (Alpert) R. BS summa cum laude, Cooper Union, 1971; MD summa cum laude, U. Wash., 1976, PhD in Physiology, 1976. Diplomate Am. Bd. Neurology and Psychiatry. Asst. neurologist N.Y. Hosp., Cornell Med. Sch., N.Y.C., 1977—80; asst. prof. physiology and medicine U. Wash., Seattle, 1980—84; assoc. prof. neurology Case We. Res. Med. Sch., Cleve., 1984—92, prof. neurology and neuroscis., 1993—, residency dir., neurology dept., 1994—2003, vice chair neurology dept., 1995—2004; chief dept. neurology Cleve. VA Med. Ctr., 1984—2003, chief phys. medicine and rehab. svc., 1998—2000, mgr. rehab. and spinal cord injury and disorder product line, 1999—2003; med. dir. Functional Elec. Stimulation Ctr., Cleve., 2000—; chief Spinal Cord Injury and Dysfunction Svc., Cleveland VA Med. Ctr., 2003—05; dir. neurology and acting rehab. rsch. svc. Office R & D Dept. VA Ctrl. Office, Washington, 2004—; nat. dir. neurology Dept. Vet. Affairs, Washington, 2005—. Adv. Child Devel. and Mental Retardation Ctr., Seattle, 1980-84, Burien Devel. Disability Ctr., Wash., 1982-84; mem. med. adv. bd. Muscular Dystrophy Assn., Seattle, 1984, NE Ohio chpt. Multiple Sclerosis Soc., 1986—; mem. adv. bd. for Neurology Dept. Vets. Affairs, 1989—; mem. study sect. for rehab. career devel. awards; chmn. med. adv. bd. N.E. Ohio chpt. Myasthenia Gravis Found., 1987—, trustee, 1993—, nat. med. adv. bd., 1988—, grant and fellowship com., 1990—. Assoc. editor: Neurology, 1994—96, mem. editl. bd.:, 1996—97, assoc. editor: Jour. Rehab. Rsch. and Devel., 2000—, ad hoc reviewer: various profl. and sci. jours., mem. editl. bd.: Jour. Rehab. and Devel., 1999—; contbr. articles to profl. jours., chapters to books. Nat. bd. dir. Myasthenia Gravis Found., Doctor's award, 2002. Recipient Tchr. Investigator award NIH; NSF fellow, 1971; NIH grantee, Muscular Dystrophy Assn. grantee, Dept. Vets. Affairs, Rsch. Enhancement Advanced Ctr. awards, 1999—, Dr. award Myasthenia Gravis Found. Am., 2002; NY State Regents med. scholar, 1971. Fellow Am. Heart Assn. (stroke coun.), Am. Acad. Neurology (scientific issues com., legis. action com.); mem. AMA, IEEE, Am. Paraplegia Soc., Am. Soc. Neuro-Rehab., Am. Physics Soc., Neurosci. Soc., Biophys. Soc., Am. Neurol. Assn., N.Y. Acad. Sci., Am. Geriatrics Soc., Am. Physiol. Soc., Sigma Pi Sigma (v.p. 1970-71), Alpha Omega Alpha (v.p. 1975-76). Home: 935 Richmond Rd Lyndhurst OH 44124 Office: VA Med Ctr 10701 East Blvd Ste 128W Cleveland OH 44106-1702 Business E-Mail: robert.ruff@med.va.gov.

**RUFFA, ANTHONY ARMAND,** mechanical engineer; s. Anthony R. and Joan R. Ruffa; m. Geraldine S. Skuches, June 30, 1984; children: Elizabeth C., A. Joseph. BS in mech. engring., U. Md., 1981; PhD, Yale U., 1990. Mech. engr. Elec. Boat Divsn. Gen. Dynamics, Groton, Conn., 1981—85; mech. engr. Naval Undersea Warfare Ctr., Newport, RI, 1985—. Adj. prof. physics U. R.I. Named NAVSEA Scientist of Yr., Naval Sea Sys. Command, 2000. Mem.: Am. Soc. Mech. Engrs., Assn. Scientists and Engrs. (Profl. Achievement award 2003). Achievements include 30 U.S. Patents, with 10 pending and others in preparation. Office: Naval Undersea Warfare Center 1176 Howell Street Newport RI 02841 Business E-Mail: ruffaaa@npt.nuwc.navy.mil.

**RUFFALO, MARK,** actor; b. Kenosha, Wis., Nov. 22, 1967; m. Sunrise Coigney, June 2000; children: Keen, Bella. Actor: (films) Rough Trade, 1993, A Song For You, 1993, There Goes My Baby, 1994, Mirror, Mirror 2:Raven Dance, 1994, A Gift From Heaven, 1994, Mirror, Mirror III: The Voyeur, 1995, The Dentist, 1996, The Last Big Thing, 1996, Blood Money, 1996, Safe Men, 1998, 54, 1998, A Fish in the Bathtub, 1999, Ride with the Devil, 1999, You Can Count on Me, 2000, Committed, 2000, Life/Drawing, 2001, The Last Castle, 2001, XX/XY, 2002, Windtalkers, 2002, My Life Without Me, 2003, View From the Top, 2003, In the Cut, 2003, Eternal Sunshine of the Spotless Mind, 2004, 13 Going On 30, 2004, Collateral, 2004, Just Like Heaven, 2005, Rumor Has It..., 2005, All the King's Men, 2006; (TV films) On the 2nd Day of Christmas, 1997, Houdini, 1998; (TV series) The Beat, 2000; (films) The Destiny of Marty Fine, 1996; writer: films The Destiny of Marty Fine, 1996; exec. prodr., actor: (films) We Don't Live Here Anymore, 2004; (Broadway plays) Awake and Sing!, 2006. Office: William Morris Agy One William Morris Pl Beverly Hills CA 90212*

**RUFFIN, DAVID ALISTON,** secondary school educator, entertainer; b. Roanoke, Va., Mar. 3, 1951; s. William Carl and Lona Botwright Ruffin; m. Sarah Mary Schenk, June 15, 1996; children: Carrie Lona Ruffin Bauers, Aliston Edward, Andrew David stepchildren: Mary Alice Wafer Younger, John Scott Wafen. BA in Theatre Prodn., Bob Jones U., 1976. Lic. radio broadcaster. Social studies and theatre tchr. Azle (Tex.) H.S., 1992—; entertainment dir. Hawkwook Medieval Faire, Roanoke, Tex., 1996—2001; entertainer The Bilge Pumps, Grand Prairie, Tex., 2001—. Prodr., dir., founder Popcorn Players, Azle, 1995—2004; co-founder, dir. U.S. Karate and Self Def., Ft. Worth; pres. bd. Hip Pocket Theatre, Ft. Worth, 2004—. Author: (plays) A Doctor in the House, Drama, 2004. Pres. Azle Arts Assn., 1997—99. Mem.: ACLU, Hist. Presevation Soc., Live Theatre League Tes. non-profit theaters. Avocation: woodworking.

**RUFFIN, HERBERT GEORGE, II,** history professor; b. Sacramento, Aug. 17, 1969; s. Herbert George and Sadie Mae Ruffin; m. Veronia Tanya Ruffin, Dec. 18, 2004. AS in Social sci., San Jose City Coll., Calif., 1995; BA in Am. History, U. Calif., Santa Cruz, 1997; MA in Am. History, Claremont Grad. U., 2005, student in Am. History, 2003—; cert. in African Studies, Claremont U., 2004. Cert. computer numerical control machining specialist UAW-Labor Employment and Tng. Corp., Calif., 1991. Tchg. asst. San Jose City Coll., Calif., 1994—95, counseling asst., 1997, vis. prof., 1999—99, supply coord. Smithsonian Instn., Ctr. for Folklife and Cultural Heritage, Washington, 1998—99; web technician Claremont Grad. U., Calif., 1999—2003; tchg. asst. Pitzer Coll., Claremont, Calif., 2000; rsch. assist. Claremont Coll., Calif., 2001—04; vis. prof. Chaffey Coll., Rancho Cucamonga, Calif., 2002, Claremont McKenna Coll., Calif., 2003—05. Cons. folklife festival Smithsonian Instn., Ctr. for Folklife and Cultural Heritage, Washington, 1999—2000; intern Smithsonian Instn., Program in African Am. Culture, Nat. Mus. of Am. History, Washington, 2000, coord. and asst. program developer, 2000—01; cons. African Americans in West conf. Claremont Grad. U., Calif., 2001. Author: (multimedia) Africans on the North American Frontier, 1528-1864; multimedia, Priesthood and Ritual in Ghana: 10th MEHU Anniversary Celebration, 1987-1997, Priesthood and Ritual in Ghana: Musama Disco Christo Church Diamond Jubilee, 1922-1997; author: (multimedia cd) FundaMentals: Part One, A RUFF Assessment of Hip-hop History and Culture, 1965-1986; contbr. multimedia - smithsonian institution; rap album, Who Am I?: Songs From the Ruffunk Experience, multimedia, Ontario Community University Program (OCUP), for Ontario, Pitzer College, CGU, and HUD partnership, Black Graduate Students Association Online, multimedia - pomona college, Latin American Studies at Pomona College Online, multimedia, School of Politics and Economics at CGU; author: (multimedia) African Diaspora Central, (multimedia - smithsonian institution) A Quest for Freedom: The Black Experience in the American West; book reviewer: numerous books. Recipient Outstanding Social Sci./Family Studies Achiever award, San Jose-Evergreen C.C. Dist., 1994-1995, Martin Luther King scholarship, San Jose City Coll., 1994-1995, Leadership Opportunity Award scholarship, U. Calif., 1995-1997, Edn. Abroad award, U. Calif. Edn. Abroad Program, 1996-1997, Acad. Excellence award for African-Am. Student Life, U. Calif., 1996, 1997, Minority Student Internship Program award, Smithsonian Instn., 1997, 2000; Victor Atkins fellowship, Claremont Grad. U., 2001-2002, John McGuire fellowship, 2003-2004. Mem.: Black Grad. Students Assn. (sec. 2002—04), Western Hist. Assn., Assn. for Study of Afro-Am. Life and History, Am. Hist. Assn. Achievements include student activist leader instrumental in desegregating Claremont Graduate University and fighting hate crimes. Avocations: researching history and current affairs, working out, video gaming (sports and strategy games), multimedia production, rebuilding classic Mustang. Personal E-Mail: herbert.ruffin@cgu.edu.

**RUFFIN, JOHN,** federal agency administrator, researcher; b. New Orleans, June 29, 1943; s. Wesley and Olivia Ruffin; m. Angela Beverly, Aug. 24, 1968; children: John Wesley, Meeka Dionne, Beverly Alaina. BS, Dillard U., 1965; MS, Atlanta U., 1967; PhD in systematic and devel. biology, Kans. State U., 1971; postgrad., Harvard U., 1975-77. Instr. biology So. U., Baton Rouge, 1967-68; asst. prof. biology Atlanta U., 1971-74; assoc. prof. Ala. A&M U., Huntsville, 1974-75; prof. biology, chmn. dept. NC Ctrl. U., Durham, 1978—90, dean Coll. Arts and Sciences, 1986—90; assoc. dir. rsch. on minority health NIH, 1990—2001; dir. Nat. Ctr. on Minority Health and Health Disparities, NIH, 2001—. Adv. bd. NC Bd. Sci. and Tech., 1983—; chmn. MARC study sect. NIH, Bethesda, Md., 1979-81, com. mem. MARC study sect., 1984-87. Grantee NIH, 1976; Cabot Research fellow, 1976; recipient Presdl. Meritorious Rank Award, 1998. Mem. AAAS, Botanical Soc. Am., NC Acad. Sciences, Assn. Southeastern Biologists, Assn. Environ. and Exptl. Botany. Office: Nat Ctr Minority Health and Health Disparities 6707 Democracy Blvd Ste 800 Bethesda MD 20892-5465 Office Phone: 301-402-1366. Office Fax: 301-402-7040. E-mail: ruffinj@ncmhd.nih.gov.*

**RUFFIN, JULIAN EDWARD,** marriage and family therapist, educator; b. Rocky Mount, N.C., Mar. 10, 1949; s. Julian Foxhall and Hazel Lee Ruffin; m. Anne Marie Sinclair, May 12, 1979; children: Andrew, Adam, Alex. BA, Wake Forest U., 1971; MDiv, So. Seminary, Louisville, 1974; PhD, U. S.C., 1982. Lic. marriage and family therapist S.C. Mental health counselor Dept. Mental Health, Columbia, SC, 1975—80; dir. child and adolescent svcs., 1980—93; dir. psychosocial program Children's Cancer Ctr., Columbia, 1993—. Pvt. practice family therapy, Columbia, 1982—; mental health cons. USPHS for Head Start, 1989—91, S.E. Regional Ctr. for Drug-Free Schs., 1989—91. Contbr. articles to profl. jours. Asst. scout master Boy Scouts Am., Columbia, 1991—; v.p. bd. S.C. Youth Workers Assn., 1982—84; mem. S.C. adv. bd. Nat. Dropout Prevention, 1987—90; mem. adv. coun. for child protection Benedict Coll., Columbia, 1987—89. Named one of Outstanding Young Men in Am., 1984; recipient Outstnading Contbns. to Children and Families award, Richland County Dept. Social Svcs., 1986, Disting. Svc. award, Mental Health Assn. Mid-Carolina, 1988, Robert Beatty Meml. award, S.C. Youth Workers Assn., 1985. Mem.: APA, Assn. Marriage and Family Therapists. Democrat. Methodist. Avocations: skiing, water-skiing, golf, tennis, backpacking. Home: 3601 Monroe St Columbia SC 29205 Office: Childrens Cancer Ctr 7 Richland Medical Pk Columbia SC 29203 Office Phone: 803-434-3520.

**RUFFING, ANNE ELIZABETH,** artist; b. Bklyn. d. John Paul and Ruth Elizabeth (Price) Frampton; m. George W. Ruffing, Mar. 29, 1967; 1 dau., Elizabeth Anne. BS, Cornell U., 1964; postgrad., Drexel Inst. Tech., 1966. One-woman exhbns. include, IBM, 1966, Hall of Fame, Goshen, N.Y., 1971, group exhbns. include, Internat. Women's Arts Festival, World Trade Center, N.Y.C., 1975-76, Berkshire Mus., Pittsfield, Mass., 1965, 76, Cooperstown (N.Y.) Mus., 1969; represented in permanent collections, Met. Mus. Art, Bklyn. Mus., Library of Congress, Harvard U., Smithsonian Instn., N.Y. Hist. Soc. Johnston Hist. Mus., Atwater Kent Mus., Albany Inst. History and Art, Whitney Mus. Am. Art, Boston Public Library. Recipient 1st place Eric Sloane award, 1974; Internat. Women's Year award Internat. Women's Art Festival, 1976 Address: 1031 Lewis Farm Rd Zebulon NC 27597

**RUFFNER, FREDERICK G., JR.,** book publisher; b. Akron, Ohio, Aug. 6, 1926; s. Frederick G. and Olive Mae (Taylor) R.; m. Mary Ann Evans, Oct. 8, 1954; children: Frederic G. III, Peter Evans. BS, Ohio State U., 1950. Advt. Jim Robbins Co., Royal Oak, Mich., 1950-52; research mgr. Detroit Detroit Corp., 1953-54; pres. Gale Research Co., Detroit, 1954-87, Omnigraphics, Inc., 1987—. Editor: Ency. of Assns, 1956-68, Code Names Dictionary, 1963, Acronyms and Initialisms Dictionary, 1965, Allusions Dictionary, 1985; pub. Gold Coast Mag., 1992—; patentee in field. Bd. dirs. Friends of Detroit Pub. Libr., pres., 1975-76; mem. exec. bd. Detroit coun. Boy Scouts Am., 1974—, v.p., 1976-82; pres. Coun. for Fla. Librs., 1979—; trustee Bon Secours Hosp., Grosse Pointe, Mich., 1980-81; v.p. Etruscan Found., Florence, Italy, 1980—; pres. Mich. Ctr. for the Book, 1990, Literary Landmarks Assn., Gold Coast Jazz Soc., Ft. Lauderdale, 1992—; bd. dirs., v.p. Ohio State U. Found., Bonnet House, Ft. Lauderdale, 1992. 1st lt. AUS, 1944-46. Decorated Bronze Star, Combat Inf. award; recipient Centennial award Ohio State U., 1970, Benjamin Creativity award Assn. Am. Pubs., 1985, Career medal Ohioana Libr. Assn., 1988, Lifetime Achievement award Am. Libr. Trustees Assn., 1992; named to Entrepreneurs Hall of Fame, Nova U. Mem. Am. Antiquarian Soc., ALA (hon. life), Am. Mgmt. Assn., Am. Assn. Mus., Detroit Hist. Soc., Am. Hist. Print Collectors Soc., Bibliog. Soc. Am., Sierra Club, Pres. Assn., Audubon Soc., Am. Name Soc., Early Am. Industries Assn., Nat. Press Club (Washington), Ephemera Soc., Johnny Appleseed Soc., Navy League, Newcomen Soc., Cen. Bus. Dist. Assn. Detroit (vice-chmn. 1985-87), Jazz Forum (Grosse Pointe Farms, Mich.), Nat. Trust Hist. Preservation, Fairfield Heritage Soc., Archives Am. Art, Pvt. Librs. Assn., Friends Ft. Lauderdale Pub. Libr. (pres. 1974-78), Phileas Soc. (pres. 1985—), Ohio State U. Club (pres. Detroit club 1958, nat. chmn. Ohio State U. campaign, 1985-88), Masons, Shriners, Book Club, Detroit Athletic Club, Econ. Club, Prismatic Club (pres. 1990), Fontenada Soc. (pres. 1990-91), Detroit Club, Country Club Detroit, Ocean Reef Club, Grosse Pointe Yacht Club, Coral Ridge Yacht Club, Lauderdale Yacht Club, Princeton Club, Salmagundi Club, Grolier Club, Century Assn., Marco Polo Club, Faculty Club Ohio State U., Old Club, Commonwealth Club (San Francisco), Grosse Pointe Club, Wawetonong Club, Tau Kappa Epsilon. Republican. Presbyterian. also: 1000 Flamingo Isle Dr Fort Lauderdale FL 33301-2670 also: 901 E Las Olas Blvd Fort Lauderdale FL 33301-2320 Address: Omnigraphics Inc 615 Griswold St Detroit MI 48226-3415 Home: 17111 E Jefferson Ave Apt 18 Grosse Pointe MI 48230-1942

**RUFFO, MICHAEL,** painter; b. S.I., Mar. 9, 1954; s. Thomas Anthony and Marie (Papa) Ruffin; m. Lorelei Ann Perez, July 5, 1975. BFA, Sch. Visual Arts, N.Y.C., 1991. Exhibited in group shows at Salmagundi Club, 1992—93, 1995—99, Agora Gallery, 1998—99, World Fine Art, 1999, Knickerbocker Gallery, 1999, Hiram Blauvelt Mus., 1999, Nexus Gallery, 1999—2001, NYU, 2000, Green County Coun. Arts, 2002, Gordon Green Gallery, 2002, Mountaintop Gallery, 2003—04, Bklyn. Waterfront Artists Coalition Silver Anniversary Show, 2005, Bklyn. Waterfront Artists Coalition, 2006, Represented in permanent collections U.S. Dept. State, Bklyn. Waterfront Artists Coalition. Recipient Excellence award, Manhattan Arts Internat. Competition, 1997—98, 1999. Mem.: Bklyn. Waterfront Artists Coalition, Nurture Art (reigstry), Orgn. Ind. Artists, N.Y. Artists Equity Assn. Roman Catholic. Achievements include patents for lockable lid support. Personal E-Mail: mruffo@verizon.net.

**RUFFOLO, ROBERT R.,** research and development company executive; b. Yonkers, N.Y., Apr. 14, 1950; married; 3 children. BS in Pharmacology, Ohio State U., 1973, PhD in Pharmacology, 1976. Rsch. scientist and chmn. cardiovascular rsch. com. Lilly Rsch. Labs., 1977—83; various rsch. positions SmithKline Beecham Pharm., 1983—2000; exec. v.p., pharm. rsch. and devel. Wyeth Rsch., 2000—02; sr. v.p. Wyeth Pharm. No. Am., 2002—; pres. Wyeth Rsch., 2002—. Adj. prof. dept. pharmacology McGill U. Sch. Medicine, Montreal, Canada, 1982—89; sci. rev. cons. NIH, Nat. Inst. on Drug Abuse, 1984; adj. prof. divsn. pharmacology Ohio State U. Coll. Pharmacy, Columbus, 1989—; mem. site visit com. U. Chgo., Nat. Heart, Lung and Blood Inst., 1988; adj. prof. dept. pharmacology Baylor U. Sch. Medicine, Houston, 1990—; mem. subcom. for receptor nomenclature and drug classification: adrenoceptors Internat. Union for Pharmacology, 1990—, mem. com. for receptor nomenclature and drug classification; bd. visitors U. Wis. Sch. Pharmacy, Madison, 1993—96. Named disting. vis. prof., U. Houston, 1994, Malone-Booker lectr. in pharmacology, Howard U., 1995, Chief Sci. Officer of Yr., Pharm. Achievement awards, 2004; recipient fellowship, Am. Found. for Pharm. Edn., 1973—76, PRAT fellowship, Nat. Ints. of Gen. Med. Scis., 1977—78, Cert. of Appreciation, FDA, Com. for Advanced Sci. Edn., 1989, Albert Szentgyorgy medal, 1997, Lorenzini Gold medal, Lorenzini Med. Sci. Found., 1999. Mem.: SAG, Am. Soc. for Pharmacology and Exptl. Therapeutics (chmn. symposium of peripheral alpha-adrenergic receptors 1983, mem. program com. 1984—89, chmn., organizer 1990, mem. subcom. on pharmacology in industry 1990—92, mem. nomination com. 1992—93, mem. com. on indsl.-acad. rels. 1993—94, sec.-treas. 1994—97, mem. in. com. 1994—97, coun. mem. 1994—97, mem. investment subcom. 1995—96, chmn. fin. com. 1995—96, mem. Sollman Award selection com. 1997, coun. mem. 1999—, Travel award 1981, 1984, John Jacob Abel award 1988, John V. Croker lectr. 1998), Brit. Pharmacol. Soc., Fedn. of Am. Socs. Exptl. Biology (mem. publs. com. 1989—). Soc. Critical Care Medicine, Mid-Atlantic Pharmacology Soc., Phi Kappa Phi. Office: Wyeth Rsch Pharm R&D 500 Arcola Rd Collegeville PA 19426 also: Wyeth Pharmaceuticals 5 Giralda Farms Madison NJ 07940

**RUFRANO, GLENN,** real estate company executive; Co-chmn. The Peabody Group; ptnr., pres., COO, CFO The O'Connor Group, 1983—2000; CEO New Plan Excel Realty Trust, N.Y.C., 2000—. Bd. dirs. TrizecHahn Corp.; adj. prof. NYU Real Estate Inst. Mem.: Nat. Assn. Real Estate Investment Trusts (bd. govs.), Internat. Coun. Shopping Ctrs., Urban Land Inst. Office: New Plan Excel Realty Trust 1120 Ave of the Americas New York NY 10036

**RUFUS, NANCY G.,** secondary school educator; b. Cleve., Aug. 19, 1949; d. Nicola G. and Elabeth Angelo Gentile; m. Joseph G. Rufus (dec.); children: Susan, Jodie. BS, Kent State U., Ohio, 1972. Cert. tchr. Ohio. Tchr. Hudson (Ohio) Schs., 1976—84; tchr., chmn. dept. Our Lady of the Elms, Akron, Ohio, 1986—. Mem.: Nat. Coun. Social Studies, Toastmasters (pres. Hudson chpt.).

**RUGABER, WALTER FEUCHT, JR.,** retired publishing executive, academic administrator; b. Macon, Ga., Nov. 29, 1938; s. Walter Feucht and Edith Almeda (Maynard) R.; m. Sally Sanford, Oct. 6, 1962; children—Leslie, Christopher, Mark BS, Northwestern U., 1960. Corr., editor N.Y. Times, 1965—78; v.p., exec. editor Greensboro Daily News & Record, NC, 1978—82; pres., pub. The Roanoke Times, Va., 1982—2000; pres. Landmark Pub. Group, 1995—99; interim pres. Hollins U., Roanoke, Va., 2001—02; presdl. fellow Va. Tech. U., 2003—. Mem. Pulitzer Prize Bd., 1990-99. Bd. dirs. United Way of Roanoke Valley, Va., 1982—88, Roanoke Sympony Soc., 1985—91, pres., 1986—88; trustee Hollins U., 1993—2002, 2004—. Mem. Am. Newspaper Pubs. Assn., Am. Soc. Newspaper Editors, So. Newspaper Pubs. Assn. E-mail: wrugaber@swva.net.

**RUGGIERO, DAVID L.,** music educator, accountant; s. Elide M. and Lorenzo Ruggiero. B in Bus. Adminstrn., Bryant U., 1985; M in Edn., Lesley U., 2003. Cert. music pre-K-9 profl. Mass., 2004, music 5-12 profl. Mass., 2004. Music tchr. pre-k to 1 Medfield Pub. Schs., Mass., 2003—; music educator k-5 Newton Pub. Schs., Mass., 2000—01; sr. auditor State RI Auditor Gen., Pawtucket, RI, 1985—99; music tchr. Sharon Pub. Schs., Mass., 2001—02. Avocation: skiing. Office Phone: 508-359-5135.

**RUGGIERO, KENNETH JOSEPH,** psychologist; b. Lewiston, NY, Jan. 28, 1972; s. Kathleen Ann and Kenneth Joseph Ruggiero; m. Deana Irene Burbee, June 29, 2002; 1 child, Justin Kenneth. PhD, W.Va. U., 1996—2001. Lic. in clin. psychology SC, 2004. Rschr. Med. U. S.C. Charleston, 2001—; asst. prof., 2003—. Recipient Psychiatry Golden Apple award for Outstanding New Tchr., Med. U. SC, 2002, Cir. of Excellence in Tchr. award, 2004, Faculty Mentorship Excellence award, 2005. Mem.: Assn. for Advancement of Behavior Therapy (pres., disaster and trauma sig; chair, pub. edn. com. 2002—05, Student Rschr. award 1999). Office: Med Univ of South Carolina 165 Cannon St 3rd Floor Charleston SC 29403 Office Phone: 843-792-2945. Office Fax: 843-792-3388. E-mail: ruggierk@musc.edu.

**RUGGIERO, MATTHEW JOHN,** bassoonist; b. Phila., Sept. 18, 1932; s. Pompeo and Theresa (Ciampa) R.; m. Nancy Cirillo, Apr. 2, 1961; children: Eleanor, Claudia, Lisa. Diploma, Curtis Inst. Music, 1957; AA, Harvard U., 1982, BA cum laude, 1984, MA, 1987; PhD, Boston U., 1993. Second bassoonist Nat. Symphony Orch., Washington, 1957-60; asst. prin. bassoonist Boston Symphony Orch., 1961-89; prin. bassoonist Boston Pops Orch., 1974-89; ret., 1989. Mem. faculty Boston U., 1963—, New Eng. Conservatory Music, 1963—. Served with U.S. Army, 1954-57. Boston U. Profs. Program scholar and fellow, 1989.

**RUGGLES, RUDY LAMONT, JR.,** international security advisor; b. Evanston, Ill., Nov. 11, 1938; s. Rudy Lamont and Ruth (Cain) R.; m. Cecelia Ann Consorte, July 20, 1974 (div. 1996); m. Nancy Orbison, June 1965 (div. 1972); m. Sara Joyce Silbernagel, Feb. 3, 1998; children— Rudy, Christopher, Daniel, Andrew. BA, Harvard U., 1960, MBA, 1966. Sr. assoc. physicist IBM Rsch. Labs., Poughkeepsie, NY, 1960-64; corp. planning cons. corp. hdqrs. IBM, Armonk, NY, 1966-71; sr. mem. profl. staff Hudson Inst., Croton-on-Hudson, NY, 1971-75, pres., 1975-79, also dir.; prin. Cresap, McCormick & Paget, Inc., 1979-82; ptnr. The Phila. Mgmt. Cons. Group, Inc., 1982—; mng. dir. New China Group, Inc., 1982—. Chmn. residential solicitation United Fund, Pound Ridge, N.Y., 1969; mem. parents com. St. Paul's Sch., Concord, N.H.; dir. Danbury Hosp. and Danbury Hosp. Devel. Fund, Conn., 1978—; med. affairs com.; chmn. fin. com. Pound Ridge Community Ch., 1969-70; bd. dirs. Harry Frank Guggenheim Found., 1982—; bd. visitors Sch. Langs. and Linguistics Georgetown U.; trustee New Canaan Country Sch.; charter mem. bd. trustees The Newberry Libr., Chgo.; mem. Ridgefield (Conn.) Drug and Alcohol Commn.; mem. steering com. Ridgefield Coalition Against Alcohol and Substance Abuse; treas., bd. dirs. Nat. Coun. Alcoholism and Drug Dependence; chmn. bd. dirs. Midwestern Conn. Coun. on Alcoholism, adv. bd. Founders Hall; bd. advisors Founders Hall, Ridgefield Sr. Ctr.; mem. bd. visitors Orgn. for Tropical Studies, Duke U. With C.E., U.S. Army, 1962. Recipient John Carroll Disting. medal, Georgetown U., hon. cert. Order of Lenin, Russian Nat. Acad. Sci. Fellow Explorers Club; mem. Hudson Inst. (hon.), N. Am. Soc. Corp. Planning (dir. 1966-72), Internat. Inst. Strategic Studies, Internat. Map Collectors Soc., James Caird Soc., Ends of the Earth (hon.), Hummingbird Soc. (life), Harvard Club N.Y.C., Carnegie Club at Skibo Castle, Sigma Xi.

**RUGGLES, SANDRA WAUGH,** biophysicist; BS in Physics, U. Calif., San Diego; PhD in Biophysics, U. Calif., San Francisco, 2002. Co-founder Quicksilver Genomics, Inc., 2000, Catalyst Biosciences, Inc., 2002; postdoctoral rschr. U. Calif., San Francisco, 2002—. Named one of Top 100 Young Innovators, MIT Tech. Review, 2004. Office: Catalyst Biosciences Inc 209 Utah Ave South San Francisco CA 94080

**RUGMAN, ALAN MICHAEL,** international business educator; b. Bristol, Eng., June 9, 1945; arrived in Can., 1968, naturalized, 1973; s. Kenneth M. and Dorothy Irene Rugman; m. Helen Scruton, 1970; 1 child, Andrew. BA in Econs. with honors, U. Leeds, Eng., 1966; MSc in Econ. Devel., U. London, 1967; PhD in Econs., Simon Fraser U., Can., 1974; MA, Oxford U., Eng. 1998. Lectr. econs. U. Winnipeg, Manitoba, Canada, 1970—73, asst. prof. econs., 1973—78, assoc. prof. econs., 1978—80; rsch. prof. fin. Concordia U., Montreal, Canada, 1979—80; assoc. prof. bus. adminstrn. Dalhousie U., Halifax, NS, Canada, 1980—82, prof., 1982—87; dir. Ctr. Bus. Studies, 1980—87; prof. internat. bus. U. Toronto, 1987—98; rsch. dir. Ont. Internat. Bus. Ctr., 1988—92; Thames Water fellow in strategic mgmt. Templeton Coll., U. Oxford, 1998—2001, assoc. fellow, 2001—; prof. internat. bus., bus. econs., public policy Indiana U.; L. Leslie Waters Chair Internat. Bus. Kelley Sch. Bus., Indiana U.; dir. IU CIBER. Outside advisor on free trade, fgn. investment, internat. competitiveness two Canadian prime ministers, 1986—93; mem. internat. trade advisory com. Govt. of Can., 1986—88; cons. private sector companies, rsch. inst., govt. agencies; vis. prof. Columbia U., 1978—79, Columbia Bus. Sch., Ctr. for internat. Affairs, Harvard U., 1984, London Sch. Bus., 1985, U. Hawaii, 1988, U. Alberta, 1988, UCLA, MIT, Warwick Bus. Sch., U. Paris-La Sorbonne; mem. editorial bd. Strategic Mgmt. Jour., Acad. Mgmt. Executive, Jour. Internat. Bus. Studies, numerous other profl. jours. Author: International Diversification and the Multinational Enterprise, 1979, Multinationals in Canada: Theory, Performance and Economic Impact, 1980, Inside the Multinationals: The Economics of Internal Markets, 1981, Outward Bound: Canadian Direct Investment in the United States, 1987, Multinationals and Canada: United States Free Trade, 1990, The Theory of Multinational Enterprises, 1996, Multinational Enterprises and Trade Policy, 1996, International Business, 2000, 2003, The End of Globalization, 2000, 2001, Leadership in International Business Education and Research, 2003, Free Trade in the Americas, 2004, North American Economic and Financial Integration, 2004, The Regional Multinationals, 2005, International Business: Firm and Environment, 1985, Megafirms: Strategies for Canada's Multinationals, 1985, Administered Protection in America, 1987, Global Corporate Strategy and Trade Policy, 1990, International Business, 1985, 1995, Environmental Regulations and Corporate Strategy, 1999, Multinationals as Flagship Firms: Regional Business Networks, 2000, Analysis of Multinational Strategic Management, 2005; editor: New Theories of the Multinational Enterprise, 1982, Multinationals and Technology Transfer: The Canadian Experience, 1983, International Business in Canada, 1989, Research In Global Strategic Management, 1990, 1991, Foreign Investment and North American Free Trade, 1994; co-author, co-editor: Multinationals and Transfer Pricing, 1985, co-editor: Business Strategies and Free Trade, 1988, The Oxford Handbook of International Business, 2001, The World Trade Organization in the New Global Economy, 2001, Real Options and International Investment, 2005, Internationalization, International Diversification and the Multinational Enterprise, 11, 2005, European-American Trade and Financial Alliances, 2005, International Business, 2006; referee manuscripts for numerous profl. jours.; reviewer manuscripts for numerous pubs.; lectr. to profl. confs.; contbr. over 200 articles to profl. jours, chapters to books, book revs. to profl. jours. Grantee Soc. Scis. and Humanities Rsch. Coun. Can., 1983, 1984. Fellow: Royal Soc. Arts, Acad. Internat. Bus. (v.p. 1989—90, pres. 2004—06), Massey Coll. (sr.); mem.: Am. Econ. Assn., Acad. Mgmt., North Am. Econ. Fin. Assn. (bd. dirs. 1979—91, pres. 1984). Office: Ind Univ Kelley Sch Bus BU 752 1309 E 10th St Bloomington IN 47405

**RUGO, STEVEN ALFRED,** architect; b. Washington, June 1, 1953; s. Alfred Joseph and Lena (Aubrey) R.; m. Mary Lourie Blackett, Nov. 11, 1978 (div. Jan. 1983); m. Laura Secord de Frise, June 25, 1988; children: Peter William, Aubrey Secord. Student, Ripon Coll., 1971-73, Harvard U., 1973; BArch, Syracuse U., 1976. Assoc. firms Booth/Hansen, Booth Nagle & Hartray, Booth & Nagle, Chgo., 1976-81; pvt. practice architecture Rugo/Raff Ltd., Chgo., 1982—. Assoc. bd. mem. Rush Presbyn., St. Lukes Med. Ctr., Chgo., Art Inst. Chgo. Mem. AIA, Met. Planning Coun., Chgo. Archtl. Club, Southeast Ravenswood Assn., Racquet Club, Saddle and Cycle, Arts Club, Spring Island Club. Episcopalian. Avocations: painting, printmaking. Office: 20 W Hubbard St Chicago IL 60610-4623

**RUGOFF, RALPH,** curator; BA in Semiotics, Brown U. Pew Arts Journalism fellow Columbia U., NYC; rsch. fellow Goldsmiths Coll., London; dir. Calif. Coll. Arts Wattis Inst. for Contemporary Art, San Francisco, 2000—, founding chair Curatorial Practice Program. Guest lectr. Royal Coll. Art; guest lectr., Goldsmith Coll. U. London, U. Calif., LA, Otis Art Inst., Art Ctr., Pasadena, Calif. Contbr. articles to profl. journals and magazines; curator (exhibitions) Just Pathetic, Am. Fine Arts Gallery, NY and Rosamund Felsen Gallery, LA, 1990—92, Scene of the Crime, Armand Hammer Mus. and Cultural Ctr., LA, 1997, At the Threshold of the Visible: Minuscule and Small-Scale Art 1964-1996, 1997—99, The Greenhouse Effect, Serpentine Gallery and Nat. History Mus., London, 2000, Sudden Glory: Sight Gags and Slapstick in Contemporary Art, CCA Wattis Inst., 2002, Capp Street Project: 20th Anniversary Exhbn., 2003, Baja to Vancouver: The West Coast and Contemporary Art, 2004, Monuments for the USA, 2005, Irreducible: Contemporary Short Form Video, 2005. Recipient Ordway prize, Penny McCall Found., 2005. Office: Wattis Inst for Contemporary Art California College of Arts 1111 Eighth St San Francisco CA 94107*

**RUH, EDWIN,** ceramic engineer, consultant, researcher; b. Westfield, NJ, Apr. 22, 1924; s. Harry John and Martha A. (Grasing) R.; m. Elizabeth J. Mundy, June 14, 1952; children: Edwin Jr., Elizabeth Jeanne. BS in Ceramic Engring. with honors, Rutgers U., 1949, MS in Ceramic Engring., 1953, PhD in Ceramics, 1954. Registered profl. engr., Pa. Rsch. engr. Harbison Walker Refractories Co., Pitts., 1954-57, asst dir. rsch., 1957-70; dir. rsch. Harbison Walker Refractories Div. Dresser Ind., Pitts., 1970-73, dir. advanced tech., 1973-74; v.p. rsch. Vesuvius Crucible Co., Pitts., 1974-76; adj. prof. Carnegie Mellon U., Pitts., 1976-84; rsch. prof. Rutgers U., New Brunswick, NJ, 1984—94. Pres. Ruh Internat., Inc., Pitts., 1976-2003. Author: Refractories for the Chemical Process Industries, 1984; editor Metallurgical Transactions, 1979-84; author chpts. to books; contbr. articles to profl. jours. With U.S. Army, 1943-46, ETO. Fellow: Am. Ceramic Soc. (disting. life mem., pres. 1985—86, Founders award Phila. sect. 1989, Bleininger award Pitts. sect. 1990); mem.: AIME, AAAS, Keramos (nat. pres. 1970—72, Greaves-Walker Roll of Honor 1976), Australasian Ceramic Soc., Acad. Ceramics (prof.), Iron and Steel Soc., Minerals, Metals and Materials Soc., Ceramic Assn. NJ (pres. 1991—92, Ann. award 1988), Nat. Inst. Ceramics Engrs. (P.A.C.E. award 1963, Greaves-Walker award 1999). Republican. Presbyterian. Avocations: antiques, antique autos. Home: 892 Old Hickory Rd Pittsburgh PA 15243-1112 Office Phone: 412-561-6994. E-mail: edemruh@adelphia.net.

**RUHL, MARY B.,** lawyer; BA, Wilson Coll., 1971; MA, U. Wis., 1973, JD, 1977. Bar: Calif. 1977, Wis. 1977. With Latham & Watkins, L.A., 1977—, ptnr. Mem.: Wis. State Bar Assn., Calif. State Bar Assn. Office: Latham and Watkins LLP 633 W Fifth St Ste 4000 Los Angeles CA 90071

**RUHL, SARAH,** playwright; b. 1974; m. Tony Charuvastra; 1 child, Anna Beatrice Ruhl Charuvastra. BA in English, Brown U., 1997, MFA in Playwriting, 2001. Author: (plays) Melancholy Play, 2002, Eurydice, 2003, Late: A Cowboy Song, Orlando, 2003, The Clean House, 2004 (Susan Smith Blackburn Prize, 2004, Pulitzer Prize finalist, 2005), Dead Man's Cell Phone, 2005, Passion Play: A Cycle, 2005. Recipient Helen Merrill award, 2003, Whiting Writers' award, 2003; Kennedy Ctr. Fellow, Sundance Theatre Lab., 2000, MacArthur Fellow, John D. and Catherine T. MacArthur Found., 2006. Office: c/o Bruce Ostler Bret Adams Ltd Artists' Agency 448 W 44th St New York NY 10036*

**RUHM, THOMAS FRANCIS,** retired lawyer; b. Bridgeport, Conn., June 8, 1935; s. Herman David and Martica (Sturges) R.; m. Michele Wood, Oct. 5, 1974; children: Wendy Sturges, Thomas Wood. BA, Yale U., 1957; JD, Havard U., 1962. Bar: N.Y. 1963, U.S. Dist. Ct. (so. and ea. dists.) N.Y. 1964, U.S. Ct. Appeals (2d cir.) 1969. Assoc. Shearman & Sterling, N.Y.C., 1962-70; asst. gen. counsel Bessemer Securities Corp., N.Y.C., 1970-96, v.p., 1981-96; ret., 1996. Chmn. legal aspects venture capital investing Practicing Law Inst., NY and San Francisco, 1979-81; lectr. on venture capital NYU Grad. Sch., 1986-90, Concordia Coll., Bronxville, NY, 1999-2001; expert on fed. securities law, venture capital legal matters, investment tax policy, Fed. Res. monetary policy; witness during 1980s fed. tax hearings; adj. prof. fin. St. John's U., 2000-03, Concordia Coll, 2005. Contbg. author Technology and Economic Policy, 1986; author: (bi-monthly newsletter) Fed. Reserve Monetary Policy, 1997—; contbr. articles to profl. jours. Commr. upper div. Eastchester (NY) Youth Soccer League, 1990-91, coach, 1985-91, dir. coaching 1995-94; sr. warden Christ Ch., Bronxville, NY, 1991-94; chmn. fin. com. 1982-1986, Vestry mem., 1981-1986 and 1990-1994, past v.p. and treas. Bronxville Sch. PTA; treas., bd. dir. Friends of Bronxville Pub. Libr., 1997-2000; mem. Quogue (NY) Cultural Com., 1998-2003; treas. Quogue Hist. Soc., 2003; mem. Blue Hill Troupe, Ltd., 1972—. Lt.(jg) USNR, 1957—59, lt. US Naval Res., 1961—64. Mem. Naval Order of U.S., N.Y. Commandery, St. Andrew's Soc., Am. Scottish Found., Univ. Club N.Y.C. (mem. coun. 2000—2004), Bronxville Field Club, Quogue Field Club, Quogue Beach Club, Men's Book Club (Bronxville), Geezer Bridge (Bronxville). Republican.

**RUHNKE, TIMOTHY R.,** zoologist, educator; b. Beatrice, Nebr., Oct. 15, 1963; s. Robert F. and Loretta L. Ruhnke; m. Alice M. Moritz; children: Michael R., Luke Alexander. PhD, U. Conn., 1993. Prof. zoology W.Va. State U., Institute. Partnership for Enhancing Expertise in Taxonomy Program grantee, NSF, 2001—06. Mem.: Helminthological Soc. Wash., Am. Soc. Parasitology. Achievements include discovery of 22 new species of platyhelminths. Office: WVa State U Dept Biology H101 Institute WV 25112 Office Phone: 304-766-3210. Business E-Mail: ruhnketr@wvstateu.edu.

**RUI, YONG,** research and development company executive; b. Tianjin, China; s. Fusheng Rui and Hanzhu Yao; m. Dongqin Feng. PhD, U. Ill., Urbana-Champaign, 1999. Rschr. Microsoft Rsch., Redmond, Wash., 1999—2005; tech. asst. to pres. Microsoft China R&D Group, Beijing, 2006—. Co-chmn. various confs. Mem. editl. bd.: Internat. Jour. Multimedia Tools and Applications; contbr. chapters to books, over 15 articles to profl. jours. Fellow, U. Ill., 1997. Mem.: ASCE (editor jours.), IEEE (editor jours.). Achievements include 34 patents or patents pending; first to introducing relevance feedback into image retrieval.

**RUINA, JACK PHILIP,** electrical engineer, educator; b. Rypin, Poland, Aug. 19, 1923; arrived in U.S., 1927, naturalized, 1932; s. Michael and Nechuma (Warshaw) R.; m. Edith Elster, Oct. 26, 1947; children: Ellen, Andrew, Rachel. BEE, CCNY, 1944; MEE, Poly. Inst. Bklyn., 1949, DEE, 1951. Rsch. fellow Microwave Rsch. Inst., Poly. Inst. Bklyn., 1948-50; from instr. to assoc. prof. elec. engring. Brown U., 1950-54; rsch. assoc. prof. coordinated sci. lab. U. Ill., 1954-59, rsch. prof. elec. engring., 1959-63; prof. elec. engring. MIT, 1963—, v.p. for spl. labs., 1966-70. U.S. observer Antarctica, 1964; on leave to U.S. Govt., 1959-63, pres. Inst. Def. Analysis, 1964-66; dep. for rsch. to asst. sec. air force, 1959-60; asst. dir. for def. rsch. and engring. Office Sec. Def., 1960-61; dir. Advanced Rsch. Projects Agy., Dept. Def., 1961-63; mem. panel Presdl. Sci. Adv. Commn., 1963-72, sci. adv. bd. USAF, 1964-67, adv. bd. and panels for Dept. Def., HEW, Dept. Transp., ACDA, Office Tech. Assessment, NSF, NSC, 1963—; mem. gen. adv. com. ACDA, 1969-74; sr. cons. Office Sci. and Tech. Policy, The White House, 1977-80; chmn. com. on environ. decision making NAS, 1974-77; bd. dirs. Mitre Corp. Recipient Fleming award, 1962, Disting. Alumnus award Poly. Inst. Bklyn., 1970, One Hundred and Twenty Fifth Anniversary medal CCNY, 1973. Fellow IEEE, AAAS, Am. Acad. Arts and Scis.; mem. Internat. Sci. Radio Union. Office: MIT Dept Elec Engring 292 Main St Cambridge MA 02142-1014 Home: 130 Mount Auburn St Apt 409 Cambridge MA 02138-5779 E-mail: ruina@mitre.org.

**RUIZ, CARLOS LEON,** nuclear scientist, physicist; b. El Paso, Sept. 21, 1943; s. Pedro Luis and Maria Elida Ruiz; m. Cynthia Ann Stuart, Aug. 2; children: Christopher Leon, Theresa Ann. BS, U. Tex., El Paso, 1966; MS, U. Kans., 1969, PhD, 1975. Rsch. assoc. La. State U., Baton Rouge, 1974—76, sr. rsch. assoc., 1976—78; mem. tech. staff Sandia Nat. Lab., Albuquerque, 1981—96, prin. mem. tech. staff, 1996—. Vis. asst. prof. La. State U., Baton Rouge, 1979—81. Coach, referee Am. Youth Soccer Assn., Albuquerque, 1981—88. Recipient Nova award, Lockheed-Martin, Albuquerque, 2004. Mem.: Toastmasters Internat. Achievements include being an inventor in the field of nuclear physics. Avocation: guitar. Office: Sandia Nat Labs PO Box 5800 Albuquerque NM 87185 Office Phone: 505-845-7550. E-mail: clruiz@sandia.gov.

**RUIZ, COOKIE,** performing company executive; BA in English, Spanish, Wright St. U., Dayton, Ohio. Cert. Fund Raising Executive, 2002. Pres. Jr. League, Austin, Tex.; dir. fund devel. Ballet Austin, 1996-97, gen. mgr., 1997—99, exec. dir., 1999—. Recipient American Red Cross Clara Barton Medal of Honor. Mem.: bd. Austin Convention & Visitors Bureau, Assoc. of Fundraising Professionals, bd. trustees, Dance USA. Office: Ballet Austin 3002 Guadalupe St Austin TX 78705-2818

**RUIZ, HECTOR DE JESUS,** information technology executive; b. Piedras Negras, Mex. B of Elec. Engring., M of Elec. Engring., U. Tex., Austin; D in Elecs., Rice U., 1973. Various positions Tex. Instruments, Dallas; pres. Motorola's Semiconductor Products Sector; COO Advanced Micro Devices, Inc., Sunnyvale, Calif., 2000—02, pres., 2000—06, CEO, 2000—, chmn. bd. dirs., 2004—. Bd. dirs. Eastman Kodak Co., Semiconductor Indus. Assn. Apptd. by Pres. Adv. Com. Trade Policy and Negotiations; mem. Govs. Task Force Econ. Growth; apptd. by Gov. G.W. Bush Tex. Higher Edn. Coord. Bd.; mem. adv. coun. Coll. Engring. U. Tex.; mem. adv. bd. Tsinghua Sch. of Econ. and Mgmt.; Nat. Sec. Telecommunications Adv. Com. Named one of 50 Most Important Hispanics in Tech. & Bus., Hispanic Engr. & Info. Tech. mag., 2005; named to, Hispanic Engr. Nat. Awards Conf. Hall of Fame, 2000; fellow, Internat. Engring. Consortium, 2002. Mem.: Hispanic Profl. Engrs. (apptd. bd. dirs.). Office: Advanced Micro Devices Inc 1 AMD Pl Sunnyvale CA 94088*

**RUIZ, MACEDONIO,** entomologist; b. De tamazula, Mexico, Dec. 4, 1961; arrived in US, 1988; s. Macedonio and Enedina (Sanchez) Ruiz; m. Gloria Ruiz, Feb. 24, 1990; children: Favio, Alex, Emilia. BS in Agronomy, U. Guadalajara, 1985. Cert. entomologist Md., Mass.; advanced level integrated pest mgmt. in indsl., institutional and residential specialist U. Purdue, 1998. Tchr., sr. rschr. depts. entomol. and botany U. Guadalajara, Autlan, 1985—88; pest control adv. Entomol. Sys. Inc., Corona, Calif., 1992—93; svc. specialist, entomologist Steritech Group, Inc., Charlotte, NC, 1993—. Cons. Discovery Pl., Charlotte, 2001—. Recipient Integrated Pest Mgmt. Profl. in Urban and Indsl. Entomology award, Purdue U., 1998. Mem.: Entomol. Soc. Am. Democrat. Roman Catholic. Avocations: coin collecting/numismatics, Tae Kwon Do, soccer. Home: 14926 Bridle Trace Ln Pineville NC 28134 Office: Steritech Group Inc 7600 Little Ave Charlotte NC 28226 Office Phone: 704-541-5660. Office Fax: 704-541-6051. Personal E-mail: mruiz44@bellsouth.net.

**RUIZ, OLGA,** lawyer, educator; b. Hialeah, Fla., Dec. 21, 1969; d. Aniceto A. and Otilia A. Ruiz. BA in Polit. Sci., Fla. Internat. U., 1989; JD, U. Miami, 1992. Bar: Fla. 1992, U.S. Dist. Ct. (so. and mid. dists.) Fla. 1993, U.S. Ct. Appeals (11th cir.) 1996. Assoc. Blaxberg, Grayson & Singer P.A., Miami, Fla., 1993; atty., law clk. U.S. Magistrate Linnea R. Johnson, Miami, 1993, 95; pvt. practice law Miami, 1993-98, 2002—; assoc. Law Offices of Stephen A. Papy, Miami, 1995-96; asst. dist. legal counsel Fla. Dept. Children and Families, Miami, 1997-98, 2000—01; ptnr. Metcalfe & Metcalfe, Miami, 1998—2000; atty. Blaxberg, Grayson, Kukoff & Segal, P.A., 2001, Office of Jose M Quinon, P.A., 2001—02. Prof. debtor-creditor law Rollins Coll., Tampa, Fla., 1994, 95. Vol. teen ct. judge Teen Ct., Tampa, 1994-95; vol. lawyer Put Something Back Pro Bono Project Dade Bar, Miami, 1996—; bd. mem. Am. Cancer Soc. New Directions, Miami, 1996-97; guardian ad litem Dade County, Miami, 1996-97. Mem. ABA, Dade County Bar Assn., Concerned Matrimonial Lawyers, Juvenile Justice Attys. Assn. Republican. Avocations: reading, aerobics with weights, cooking, ice skating, belly dancing. Office: 1401 Brickell Ave Ste 510 Miami FL 33131 Office Phone: 305-416-0550. Business E-Mail: ruizatty@bellsouth.net.

**RUIZ, PEDRO,** psychiatrist; b. Cuba, Dec. 31, 1936; MD, U. Paris VI, 1964. Intern Jackson Meml. Hosp., Miami, Fla., 1965, resident in psychiatry, 1966-68; prof. psychiatry U. Tex./Houston Health Sci. Ctr., 1969—. Mem.: Am. Psychiat. Assn. (v.p., asst. Assn. Social Psychiatry (pres. 2000—02), Am. Coll. Psychiatrists (pres. 2000—01), Am. Bd. Psychiatry and Neurology (past pres.). Office: U Tex-Houston Health Sci Ct Mental Sci Inst 1300 Moursund St Houston TX 77030-3406 Office Phone: 713-500-2799. Business E-Mail: pedro.ruiz@uth.tmc.edu.*

**RUIZ, PEDRO JAVIER,** education educator; b. San Juan, PR, July 16, 1959; s. Pedro J. Ruiz and Carmen M Gonzalez; life ptnr. Thomas G. Clark, Oct. 25, 1957. BS in Psychology, Cath. U. PR, Ponce, 1982; MS in Bilingual Spl. Edn., Garden City, NY, 1993; PhD in Bilingual Edn., NYU, 2003. Mgr., avp Citibank NA, Internat. Pvt. Banking, NYC, 1982—91; bilingual spl. edn. tchr. Dist. 75/Citywide Programs, NYC, 1991—95; coord., project mas, title vii N.Y.C. Bd. of Edn.-Ctrl. Office, 1996—97; asst. dir. Dist. 75/Citywide Programs-Ctrl. Office, NYC, 1997—99; adminstr. k-12, bilingual, ESL Mt. Vernon City Sch. Dist., NY, 1999—2005; coord. NY State Edn. Dept., Office Bilingual Edn. and Fgn. Lang. Studies, Albany, 2005—. Dir. Bilingual Spl. Edn. Acad., NYC, 1996—97; past-pres. NY State Assn.

Bilingual Edn., NYC, 2001—02; exec. bd. mem. Nat. Assn. Bilingual Edn., Washington, 2004—, pres., 2005—. Recipient Svc. Excellence Award for Outstanding Performance, Citibank NA, 1985, Remunda Cadoux Leadership in Fgn. Lang. Supervision Award, NY State Assn. of Fgn. Lang. Tchrs., 2004, 2005 Dissertation award, Nat. Assn. for Bilingual Edn., 2005, Ednl. Leadership Scholarship Project award, Dr. Ramon S. Velez award, Nat. P.R. Day Reader, 2006; fellow Ph.D. - Fed. - Title VII Fellowship, NY U., NY, 1995-1998; scholar Masters Program in Bilingual Sgl. Edn., NYC Bd. Edn., 1991-1993. Mem.: NY State Assn. Bilingual Edn., Nat. Assn. Bilingual Edn., Latino Children Ednl. Network, Coun. for Exceptional Children, Assn. Supervision and Curriculum Devel. Democrat. Roman Catholic. Avocations: furniture restoration, travel, reading, gardening. Home: 729 Belvidere Ave Plainfield NJ 07062 Office Phone: 518-474-8775. Personal E-mail: pedrojruiz@aol.com.

**RUIZ, RAMÓN EDUARDO,** history professor; b. Sessions Ranch, Calif., Sept. 9, 1921; s. Ramon and Dolores (Urueta) R.; m. Natalia Marrujo, Oct. 14, 1944; children— Olivia, Maura. BA, San Diego State Coll., 1947; MA, Claremont Grad. Sch., 1948; PhD, U. Calif., Berkeley, 1954. Asst. prof. U. Oreg., Eugene, 1955-57, So. Meth. U., Dallas, 1957-58; prof. Smith Coll., Northampton, Mass., 1958-69; prof. Latin Am. history U. Calif. at San Diego, 1969-91, prof. emeritus, 1991—, chmn. dept. history, 1971-76, chmn. divsn. humanities, 1972-74; mem. project grant com. NEH, 1972-73, 75-77, dir. pub. programs divsn., 1979-80; Ralph Chase lectr. San Angelo State U., 2000. Vis. prof. Facultad de Economia, Univ. de Nuevo Leon, Mexico, 1965-66, Coll. de Sonora, Mexico, summer 1983, Pomona Coll., 1983-84, Coll. de Michoacan, Mexico, summer 1986, 87, Univ. Nacional Autonoma de Mexico, fall 1992; scholar-in-residence Colegio de la Frontero Norte, Mexico, 1994-96; MacArthur Found. nominator, 1981-82; mem. project grant com. Ford Found. Author: Cuba: The Making of A Revolution, 1968 (One of Best History Books, Book World Washington Post 1968), Mexico: The Challenge of Poverty and Illiteracy, 1963, An American in Maximillians's Mexico, 1865-1866, 1959; (with James D. Atwater) Out From Under; Benito Juarez and Mexico's Struggle for Independence, 1969; (with John Tebbel) South by Southwest: The Mexican-American and His Heritage, 1969, Interpreting Latin American History, 1970, Labor and the Ambivalent Revolutionaries: Mexico, 1911-23, 1975, The Mexican War: Was it Manifest Destiny?, 1963, The Great Rebellion: Mexico, 1905-1924, 1980 (Hubert C. Herring prize), The People of Sonora and Yanqui Capitalists, 1988, Triumphs and Tragedy: A History of the Mexican People, 1992 (named One of Five Best History Books 1991-92, L.A. Times, Gold Medal award Commonwealth Club San Francisco 1993, History Book Club selection); (with Olivia Teresa Ruiz) Reflexiones Sobre la Identidad de los Pueblos, 1996, On the Rim of Mexico: Encounters of the Rich and Poor, 1998, Memories of a Hyphenated Man, 2003. Served to lt. USAAF, 1943-46. William Harrison Mills traveling fellow in internat. rels., 1950; John Hay Whitney Found. fellow, 1950; Fulbright fellow Mex., 1965-66; fellow Ctr. for Advanced Study in Behavioral Scis., 1984-85, Rockefeller Resident, Bellagio Study Ctr., 2003, Ena H. Thompson lectureship, Pomona Coll., 1995; recipient Am. Philos. Soc. grant in aid, 1959, Nat. medal Humanities Pres. U.S., 1998. Mem. Am. Hist. Assn. (Beveridge prize com. 1974-76), Conf. Latin Am. History, Chicano-Latino Faculty Assn. U. Calif. (pres. 1989-91), Phi Beta Kappa, Sigma Delta Pi. Home: PO Box 1775 Rancho Santa Fe CA 92067-1775

**RUIZ, VANESSA,** judge; b. San Juan, P.R., Mar. 22, 1950; d. Fernando and Irma (Bosch) Ruiz-Suria; married; m. David E. Birenbaum, Oct. 22, 1983; stepchildren: Tracy, Matthew. BA, Wellesley Coll., 1972; JD, Georgetown U., 1975. Bar: D.C. 1972. Assoc. Fried, Frank, Harris, Shrives & Kampelman, Washington, 1975—83; sr. mgr., counsel Sears World Trade Inc., Washington, 1983—87; founding ptnr. Sloan, Lehner & Ruiz, Washington, 1987—89; ptnr. Pepper, Hamilton & Scheetz, Washington, 1989—91; dep. corporation counsel, legal counsel div. D.C., Washington, 1991—93, prin. dep. corporation counsel, 1993—94, corporation counsel, 1994; assoc. judge D.C. Ct. of Appeals, Washington, 1994—. Spkr. in field; adjunct prof. Georgetown U. Co-author: Europe Without Frontiers: A Lawyers' Guide, 1989. Recipient Judge of the Yr. award, Hispanic Bar Assn., 2001. Mem.: ABA, Hispanic Bar Assn., DC, Am. Law Inst., Coun. for Ct. Excellence, Nat. Assn. Women Judges (pres.-elect), Inter-Am. Bar Assn. Office: DC Ct of Appeals 500 Indiana Ave NW Fl 6 Washington DC 20001-2131 Office Fax: 202-626-8868.*

**RUIZ-BRAVO, NORKA,** federal agency administrator; B in biology, Goucher Coll., Towson, Md., 1975; M in biology, Yale U., PhD in biology, 1983. Post-doctoral fellow in physiol. chemistry Johns Hopkins U.; postdoctoral fellow in biochemistry and molecular biology U. Tex. MD Anderson Cancer Ctr., mem. faculty, 1983—89, Baylor Coll. Medicine, Houston, 1983—89; sci. rev. adminstr. Office Rev. Activities Nat. Inst. Gen. Med. Sciences, NIH, 1990, program dir. Divsn. Genetics and Biology, 1992, acting dep. dir. Divsn. Minority Opportunities in Rsch., spl. asst. Office Extramural Activities; sci. rev. adminstr. Nat. Ctr. Human Genome Rsch., NIH; dep. dir. Divsn. Cancer Biology Nat. Cancer Inst., NIH, 1997—98, acting dir. Divsn. Cancer Biology, 1998—99; dep. assoc. dir. extramural activities Nat. Inst. Gen. Med. Sciences, NIH, 1999—2000, assoc. dir. extramural activities, 2000—03; dep. dir. extramural rsch. NIH, 2003—. Mem.: AAAS, Soc. Devel. Biology, Am. Soc. Cell Biology. Office: NIH 9000 Rockville Pike Bethesda MD 20892 Office Phone: 301-496-1096. Office Fax: 301-402-3469. E-mail: nb9b@nih.gov.

**RUIZ GUTIERREZ, CARLOS HUMBERTO,** professional soccer player; b. Guatemala City, Sept. 15, 1979; m. Laura Ruiz Gutierrez; children: Andrea, Samantha. Mem. CSD Municipal, Guatemala Football League; forward LA Galaxy, Major League Soccer, 2002—. Mem. Guatemala Nat. Team, 2001—. Named MLS Player Month (two times), Major League Soccer, 2003, MLS Player Week (three times), 2002, MLS MVP, 2002. Achievements include tied for league goals in goals (15 goals), Major League Soccer, 2003. Office: L A Galaxy 18400 Avalon Blvd Ste 200 Carson CA 90746-2181

**RUIZ MADAS, YESENIA,** educational counselor; b. Bklyn., Oct. 17, 1976; d. Federico and Margarita Ruiz, Adrian Feliciano (Stepfather); m. Timothy C. Madas, May, 5, 2001. BA, Mercy Coll., NY, 2000, MS, 2003. Job coach Lifespire, NY, 1994—99; social worker St. Christopher's Inc., NY, 2000; academic advisor Mercy Coll., Bronx, NY, 2001—04; student devel. specialist Brookdale C.C., Lincroft, NJ, 2004—. Mem. vol. rels. com. Habitat for Humanity. Recipient Humanitarian award, Jane Addams Vocat. H.S., 1994. Mem.: NJ Edn. Assn., NJ CC Counselors Assn. Roman Catholic. Avocations: reading, sewing, carpentry, bicycling, oragami. Office: Brookdale Community College 765 Newman Springs Rd Lincroft NJ 07738 Office Phone: 732-224-2556. Business E-Mail: ymadas@brookdalecc.edu.

**RUIZ-VARGAS, YOLANDA,** finance educator; b. Mayagüez, P.R., Apr. 24, 1968; d. Samuel Ruiz and Isabel Vargas. BSBA cum laude, U. P.R. Mayagüez, 1990, MBA, 1994; PhD, U. of Tex., Edinburg, 2000. Acctg. officer Calzados HQ, Inc, Mayagüez, 1990—93; planner trainee Cutler Hammer of PR, Cabo Rojo, PR, 1994; tchg. asst. U. of Texas-Pan Am., Edinburg, 1996—99; instr. U. P.R., Mayagüez, 1994—96, asst. prof., 2000—03, assoc. prof., 2003—, assoc. dean for rsch. and grad. affairs, 2004—. Co-coordinator UPR- Ctr. for Profesional Enhancement, Mayagüez, PR, 2002—02; faculty rep. Grad. Coun. - UPR Mayagüez, Mayagüez, PR, 2001—03; faculty advisor 2002 PhD. Project Fin. Doctoral Students Assn. Conf., San Antonio, —, 2001 PhD. Project Fin. Doctoral Students Assn. Conf., Toronto, Canada; liaison 2000 PhD Project Fin. Doctoral Students Assn. Conf., Dallas. Spkr. planning com. mem. 1999 PhD Project Fin. Doctoral Students Assn. Conf., Orlando; mem. 2002 FMA Ann. Meeting Program Com., San Antonio; vis. asst. prof. Tex. A&M Internat. U., Laredo, 1999—2000. Scholar acad. scholar, U. P.R., 1996—2000. Mem.: Am. Fin. Assn., Internat. Coun. for Small Bus., Fin. Mgmt. Assn. Internat., Alpha Delta Kappa, Beta Gamma Sigma. Avocations: reading, travel. Office: U PR COBA - PO Box 9009 Mayaguez PR 00681-9009 Business E-Mail: yruiz@caribe.net. E-mail: yruiz@uprm.edu.

**RUKEYSER, M.S., JR.,** television consultant, writer; b. N.Y.C., Apr. 15, 1931; s. Merryle Stanley and Berenice (Simon) Rukeyser; children: Jill Victoria, Patricia Bern. Student. U. Va., 1948-52. Reporter Albany (N.Y.) Times-Union, 1949, Internat. News Service, N.Y.C., 1951; TV publicist Young & Rubicam, Inc., N.Y.C., 1952-57; with NBC, 1958-80, 81-88, dir. news info. Washington, 1962, v.p. press and publicity N.Y.C., 1963-72, v.p. corp. info., 1972-74, v.p. pub. info., 1974-77, exec. v.p. pub. info., 1977-80, 81-84, exec. v.p. corp. communications, 1984-88; v.p. comm. Newsweek Inc., 1980-81; sr. v.p. GTG Entertainment, 1988-90; pres. Rukeyser Communications, N.Y.C., 1990—. Sr. fellow Freedom Forum Media Ctr., 1991-92. Author (with Grant Tinker): Tinker in Television: From General Sarnoff to General Electric, 1994. With U.S. Army, 1953—54. Office: Ste 1213 616 Clearwater Park Rd West Palm Beach FL 33401-6250 Personal E-mail: budruk@gmail.com.

**RUKEYSER, ROBERT JAMES,** manufacturing executive; b. New Rochelle, NY, June 26, 1942; s. Merryle Stanley and Berenice Helene (Simon) R.; m. Leah A. Spiro, July 26, 1964; children: David Bern, Peter Lloyd. BA, Cornell U., 1964; MBA with distinction, NYU, 1969. Bond analyst Dun & Bradstreet, NYC, 1964-65, Standard & Poors, NYC, 1965-66; mktg. rep. data processing div. IBM, NYC, 1967-72, regional mktg. staff, 1973-74, mktg. mgr., 1974-76, corp. mgr. internal comm. and editl. programs Armonk, NY, 1976-79; mgr. comm. ops. Franklin Lakes, NJ, 1979-81; pub. affairs dir., asst. to chmn. Fortune Brands, Inc. (formerly Am. Brands, Inc.), NYC, 1981-83, v.p. pub. affairs, asst. to chmn., 1983-85, v.p. office products Old Greenwich, Conn., 1986-87, v.p. ops., 1987-89, sr. v.p. corp. affairs, 1990-99. Bd. dirs. Fortune Brands (formerly Am. Brands Inc.); mgmt. cons. and author, 2000-. Vice chmn., chair fin. com., mem. exec. com. The Hole in the Wall Gang Camp.; treas., bd. dir., Assn. of Hole in the Wall Camps.

**RUKEYSER, WILLIAM SIMON,** journalist; b. NYC, June 8, 1939; s. Merryle Stanley and Berenice (Simon) R.; m. Elisabeth Mary Garnett, Nov. 21, 1963; children: Lisa Rukeyser Burn, James William. AB, Princeton U., 1961; rsch. student, Cambridge U., Eng., 1962—63; LittD (hon.), Maryville Coll., 2002. Copyreader Wall St. Jour., 1961-62, staff reporter Europe, 1963-67; assoc. editor Fortune Mag., 1967-71, mem. bd. editors, 1971-72; founding mng. editor Money mag., N.Y.C., 1972-80; mng. editor Fortune mag., 1980-86; dir. internat. bus. devel. Time Inc., 1986-88; editor in chief, exec. v.p. Whittle Communications, Knoxville, Tenn., 1988-91; chmn., CEO, Whittle Books, Knoxville, 1991-94; pres. William Rukeyser, Inc., Knoxville, 1994—; editl. dir. Corporate Board Member mag., 1998—; contbg. editor CNN, 1995-97. Commentator Good Morning America, ABC-TV, 1978-85, CBS Radio Stas. News Svc., 1979-86; mem. nat. adv. coun. Maryville (Tenn.) Coll., 1998—; mem. adv. bd. Ctr. of Inquiry in Liberal Arts Wabash Coll., Crawfordsville, Ind., 2001—. Jud. com. Union County (NJ) Med. Soc., 1977-80; co-chair capital campaign Nat. Mental Health Assn., 1984-85; liaison com. U. Tenn. Med. Ctr., 1992-99; vice chmn. U. Health Sys. Inc., 1999—; chmn. bd. dirs. Knoxville Jazz Orch., 2001—. Mem.: Univ. Press Club (alumni adv. bd. Princeton chpt. 2005—). Office: 1001 First Tennessee Plz Knoxville TN 37929 Personal E-mail: wsr@finehand.com.

**RULAND, MILDRED ARDELIA,** retail executive, retail buyer; b. Draketown, Ga., Aug. 11, 1918; m. Harry Morse Ruland, Aug. 19, 1947; children: Hal Morse, Judy Lee Ruland Rigas. BS, West Ga. Coll., 1966. Elem. tchr., New London, Conn., 1947-48, Atlanta, 1948-51, Rome, Ga., 1951-81; mgr. McBrayer Bros. Furniture Co., Rome, 1981—. Rosenwald Found. scholar, 1941-42. Mem. NEA, Nat. Fedn. Ind. Bus. (corr. sec. 1975—), Ga. Edn. Assn. (del. 1964-74), Ga. Home Furnishings Assn., Twickham Garden Club, Rome Pride Assn., Rome C. of C., Alfa Delta Kappa. Republican. Baptist. Avocations: dance, swimming, bowling, hiking, singing.

**RULAND, RICHARD EUGENE,** literature educator, critic, historian; b. Detroit, May 1, 1932; s. Eugene John and Irene (Janette) R.; m. Mary Ann Monaghan; children: Joseph, Michael, Paul, Susan; m. Birgit Noll. BA, Assumption Coll. U. Western Ont., Can., 1953; MA, U. Detroit, 1955; PhD, U. Mich., 1960. Instr., then asst. prof. English and Am. studies Yale U., New Haven, 1960-67, Morse rsch. fellow, 1966-67; prof. English and Am. lit. Washington U. St. Louis, 1967—, chmn. dept. English, 1969-74; chmn. comparative lit. program, 1993-94. Vis. Bruern prof. Am. lit. Leeds (Eng.) U., 1964-65; vis. Fulbright prof. U. Groningen, The Netherlands, 1975, Sch. of English and Am. Studies U. East Anglia, Eng., 1978-79; vis. disting. prof. Am. lit. Coll. of William and Mary, 1980-81. Author: The Rediscovery of American Literature: Premises of Critical Taste, 1900-1940, 1967, America in Modern European Literature: From Image to Metaphor, 1976, (with Malcolm Bradbury) From Puritanism to Postmodernism: A History of American Literature, 1991 (paperback 1992), translation into Czech and Hungarian, 1997; editor: Walden: A Collection of Critical Essays, 1967, The Native Muse: Theories of American Literature, Vol. I, 1972, 76, A Storied Land: Theories of American Literature, Vol. II, 1976; contbr. articles to profl. jours. Guggenheim Rsch. fellow, 1982-83. Mem. Assn. Depts. English (pres. 1974). Avocation: jazz musician. Office: Washington U Dept English Saint Louis MO 63130

**RULE, ANN,** author; 4 children. Degree in English, U. Washington, 1958, PhD in Humane Letters, Willamette U., 2004, postgrad. in police sci. Former policewoman, Seattle; speaker on subject of serial killers. Author (non-fiction books): The Stranger Beside Me, 1980, The I-5 Killer, Want-Ad Killer, Lust Killer, Beautiful Seattle, 1984, Small Sacrifices, 1987, If You Really Loved Me, 1991, Everything She Ever Wanted, 1992, (novel) Possession, 1983, A Rose for Her Grave, 1993, You Belong to Me, 1994, Dead by Sunset, 1995, A Fever in the Heart, 1995, Green River, Running Red, 2004, Kiss Me Kill Me: And Other True Cases, 2004; exec. prodr. ABC mini-series Small Sacrifices, 1989 (Peabody award), NBC mini series Dead by Sunset, 1995, CBS mini-series And Never Let Her Go, 2000, USA Network mini-series The Stranger Beside Me, 2003; contbr. over 1400 articles to newspapers and mags. including True Detective, Cosmopolitan, and others. Vol. Seattle Crisis Clinic. Recipient: Washington State Governor's award. Address: PO Box 98846 Seattle WA 98198-0846

**RULE, CHARLES FREDERICK (RICK RULE),** lawyer; b. Nashville, Apr. 28, 1955; s. Frederick Charles and Mary Elizabeth (Malone) R.; m. Ellen Friedland, May 13, 1976 BA, Vanderbilt U., 1978; JD, U. Chgo., 1981. Bar: U.S. Ct. Appeals. (D.C. cir.) 1983. Law clk. U.S. Ct. Appeals (fed. cir.), Washington, 1981-82; spl. asst. to asst. atty. gen. Antitrust div. Dept. Justice, Washington, 1982-83, dep. asst. atty. gen. policy planning, 1984-85, acting asst. atty. gen., then dep. asst. atty. gen. regulatory affairs, 1985-86, asst. atty. gen., 1986-89; ptnr. Covington & Burling, Washington, 1989-2001, Fried, Frank, Harris, Shriver & Jacobson LLP, Washington, 2001—. Legal, econ. analyst Lexecon, Inc., Chgo., 1979-80 Mem. Bar of D.C. Ct. Appeals, Phi Beta Kappa, Phi Eta Sigma. Republican. Presbyterian. Office: Fried Frank Harris Shriver & Jacobson LLP 1001 Pennsylvania Ave Nw Washington DC 20004-2505 Office Phone: 202-639-7300. Business E-Mail: ruleri@ffhsj.com.

**RULE, SHEILA,** editor; m. Gerald Boyd (div.). BA in Journalism, Univ. Mo., 1972. Reporter St. Louis Post-Dispatch, 1972—77; from reporter to fgn. corr., Nairobi, London NY Times, NYC, 1977—94, sr. editor, career devel., 1994—. Bd. dir. UN Assn. NY. Bd. dir. Good Shepherd Services, NYC. Office: Career Devel NY Times 229 W 43rd St New York NY 10036 Office Phone: 212-556-4143. Office Fax: 212-556-4401.*

**RULIS, CHRISTOPHER C.,** lawyer; b. Cheswick, Pa., Apr. 15, 1956; s. Casmer Rulis and Margaret Thimons; m. Lisa Ross, Sept. 26, 1992; children: Marisa, Amanda. BA, Indiana U., Pa., 1978; JD, U. Akron, 1981. Bar: U.S. Supreme Ct., Pa. Supreme Ct., U.S. Tax Ct, Allegheny County Ct. Common Pleas. Assoc. atty. Brandt, Milnes, Rea, Pitts., 1983—90, Rothman Gordon P.C., Pitts.; vice mayor O'Brien, Rulis, Bochicchio, Sosso, LLC, Pitts., 1996—2005. Spl. master Allegheny County Ct. Common Pleas, 1996—. Mem. Gov.'s Club, Harrisburg, Pa., 1996—2000. Fellow, Million Dollar

Advocate's Forum, 1997—. Fellow: Acad. Trial Lawyers; mem.: Pa. Defense Inst., Allegheny County Bar Assn., Pa. Bar Assn. Republican. Roman Catholic. Home: 2762 Brunton Ct Allison Park PA 15101 E-mail: crulis@orbslaw.com.

**RULIS, RAYMOND JOSEPH,** manufacturing executive, consultant; b. New Britain, Conn., June 2, 1924; s. James Alexander and Eva (Ragauskas) R.; m. Thelma Pelchat, June 16, 1949 (dec.); children: Elaine, Jeffery, Catherine, Elizabeth, Amy, Daniel, Jean; m. Virginia Kleene, Oct. 9, 1999. BSME, U. Conn., 1949; postgrad., U. Conn., Ohio State U., Northeastern U., 1949-58; student, Fed. Exec. Inst., Charlottesville, Va., 1976. Devel. engr. Hamilton Standard, U.T.C., Windsorlocks, Conn., 1951-55; mgr. fuel controls Lycoming Textron, Stratford, Conn., 1955-59; mgr. controls and accessories GE, Lynn, Mass., 1959-62; successively program mgr. sert spacecraft, chief spacecraft engr., chief launch vehicle engr., chief engring design, program mgr. QCSEE program NASA Lewis Rsch. Ctr., Cleve., 1962-81; v.p. rsch. and devel. Textron Turbocomponents Group, Walled Lake, Mich., 1981-92; cons., 1992—. Cons. Joint FAA/NASA Civil Aero Rsch. Document Study, 1972, Cruise Missile PRogram, 1977-78, C-17 Aircraft Source Selection Bd., 1978, Tri-Svcs. Propulsion Group, 1976-78; chmn. Conf. on Short Haul Systems, NASA, 1976; mem. exec. coun. Aerospace Industries Tech. Coun., 1988-89. Contbr. articles to profl. jours.; patentee in field. Chmn. Boy Scouts Am. Fund Drives, Cleve., 1976-78; mem. Coun. on World Affairs, Cleve., 1976-81. With U.S. Army, 1943—46. Decorated Combat Infantryman's badge, Bronze Star medal, Purple Heart. Mem. Am. Helicopter Soc. (chmn. tech. session 1970), AIAA (chmn. tech. session 1965), Detroit Engring Soc., KC. Roman Catholic. Avocation: golf. Office: RJR Cons 9 Outpost Ln Hilton Head Island SC 29928-3820

**RULISON, JOSEPH RICHARD,** investment advisor; b. Syracuse, NY, May 14, 1956; s. Laurence M. and Catherine (Fox) R.; m. Karen Richards, Sept. 6, 1980; children: Elizabeth, Mallorie, Morgan, Abigail. BA, St. John Fisher Coll., 1978, LLD (hon.), 2006; D (hon.), St. John Fisher Gallery, 2006. Account exec. Prudential-Bache Securities, Rochester, NY, 1982—84; investment exec. Tucker Anthony & R.L. Day, Inc., 1984—89; ptnr., exec. v.p. Marsh Capital Mgmt., 1989—96; pres., CEO Rulison & Co., Inc., 1996—2001; founder, gen. mgr. Muniflow, 2001—; market exec., sr. v.p. cash flow solutions Bank of Am., 2005—, market pres., 2005—, market exec., cash flow solutions, 2005—. Trustee, past chmn. bd. trustees, past pres., hon. trustee Geva Theatre; chmn. bd. trustees St. John Fisher Coll.; former treas. Monroe County Rep. Com.; chmn. County Monroe Indsl. Devel. Agy., Monroe County Greater Outdoor Sports Facility-Frontier Field, Monroe County Mid-Sized Arts Com.; past councilman Brighton Town Bd.; past mem. Brighton Planning Bd., Master Plan Com., Archtl. Rev. Bd.; vice-chmn. Empire Zone of Monroe County; bd. dirs. Monroe County Water Authority Mem. Genesee Valley Club (former gov., house chmn.), Oak Hill Country Club, The Oldfield Club. Roman Catholic. Avocations: politics, theater, art, wine, golf. Office: Bank America NY7-144-02-02 1 East Ave Rochester NY 14638 Business E-Mail: joseph.r.rulison@bankofamerica.com.

**RUMAKER, MICHAEL,** writer, language educator; b. Phila., Mar. 5, 1932; s. Michael Joseph and Winifred Marvel Rumaker. Degree in writing (hon.), Black Mountain Coll., 1955; MFA, Columbia U., 1970. Lectr. writing New Sch. for Social Rsch., NYC, 1967-71; tchr. writer, mem. intellectual resources pool Tappan Zee H.S., Orangeburg, NY, 1965-69; instr. writing workshops Rockland Ctr. for Arts, West Nyack, NY, 1975-78; adj. lectr. Rockland C.C. Suffern, NY, 1978-87; writer-in-residence CCNY, CUNY, 1969-71, adj. prof., 1985—98. Author: (novels) The Butterfly, 1962, English edit., 1968, Russian edit., 2002, A Day and a Night at the Baths, 1979, German edit., 1997, My First Satyrnalia, 1981, To Kill a Cardinal, 1992, Pagan Days, 2000, (non-fiction) An Immodest Proposal, 2004, (short stories) Gringos and Other Stories, 1967, 2nd edit., 1991, German edit., 1968, English edit. (Exit 3), 1966, (memoir) Robert Duncan in San Francisco, 1996, Black Mountain Days, 2003, (poems) Pizza Selected Poems, 2005, The Fairies are Dancing All Over the World, 2006, (plays) Queers (Schwul), 1970, 2004, (poem) The Fairies Are Dancing All Over the World, 2006. Mem. Nat. Writers Union. Literary Agent: Harold Ober Assocs 425 Madison Ave Rm 1001 New York NY 10017-1183 Business E-Mail: mr6213@tco.com.

**RUMBAUGH, CHARLES EARL,** arbitrator, mediator, educator, lawyer; s. Max Elden and Gertrude Maude (Gulker) R.; m. Christina Carol Pinder; children: Eckwood, Cynthia, Aaron, Heather. BS, UCLA, 1966; JD, Calif. Western Sch. Law, 1971; cert. in advanced mgmt., U. So. Calif., 1993. Bar: Calif. 1972, U.S. Dist. Ct. (cen. dist.) Calif. U.S. Ct. Appeals (9th cir.), U.S. Supreme Ct. Engr. Westinghouse Electric Corp., Balt., 1966-68; legal counsel Calif. Dept. of Corps., L.A., 1971-77, Hughes Aircraft Co., L.A., 1977-84, asst. to corp. dir. contracts, 1984-89, asst. to corp. v.p. contracts, 1989-95; corp. dir. contracts/pricing Lear Astronics Corp., 1995-97; pres. Ctr. for Conflict Resolution, 1998-99; pvt. practice in pvt. dispute resolution as arbitrator, mediator, pvt. judge, dispute resolution cons. Former EEOC mediator, adminstrv. law judge; mem. arbitration and mediation panels ArbitrationWorks, 1994—2002, Franchise Arbitration & Mediation, Inc., L.A. County Superior Ct., Santa Barbara County Superior Ct., member panel pvt. alt. dispute resolution neutrals U.S. Ct. Fed. Claims; armed svcs. bd. of contract appeals panel of pvt. alt. dispute resolution neutrals, DLA panel of dispute neutrals, also settlement officer U.S. Dist. Ct.; alternative dispute resolution panel World Bank; adj. prof. Calif. State U.; lectr. Naval Postgrad. Sch. and U. Calif.; spkr. in field. Mem. editl. bd. Nat. Contract Mgmt. Jour., 1996-00; contbr. articles to profl. jours. Counselor Boy Scouts Am., L.A.; mem. City of Palos Verdes Estates (Calif.) Citizen's Planning Com., 1986-90; judge pro tem LA County Superior Ct., L.A., 1991-2000. Fellow: Nat. Contract Mgmt. Assn. (pres. L.A./South Bay chpt. 1991—92, nat. dir. 1992—93, nat. v.p. southwestern region 1993—95, founder, chmn. alt. dispute resolution com., cert. profl. contracts mgr., nat. bd. advisors, Fellow of Yr. award 1994, Nat. Achievement award 2001); mem.: FBA (pres. Beverly Hills chpt. 1992—93), ABA (founder fed. contracts dispute resolution com. dispute resolution sect, forum on franchising, forum on constrn. industry, pub. contract law sect., mem. constrn. claims com., internat. law sect., vice chair strategic alliance com.), Inst. Supply Mgmt. (former chmn. fed. acquisitions, subcontract mgmt. group), Am. Arbitration Assn. (arbitrator, mediator), Christian Legal Soc., Aerospace Industries Assn. (dispute procurement techniques com. 1987—88, 1993—94), Soc. Profls. in Dispute Resolution (chmn. internat. sector com. 1996—2000, past bd. dir., L.A. chpt.), State Bar Calif. (vice chmn. ADR com. 2001—04, chmn. franchise law com. 2002—03, Wiley W. Manual pro bono award 1992), Nat. Def. Indsl. Assn. (vice-chmn. west coast legal subcom. 1994—2000, procurement planning com. 1994—), Calif. Dispute Resolution Coun. (cons. to qualifications com. 1997—99). Avocations: camping, skiing, jogging, equestrian. Office: PO Box 2636 Rolling Hills CA 90274 E-mail: adroffice@rumbaugh.net.

**RUMBAUGH, JEFFREY ARLIN,** neurologist, neuroscientist; b. Lansing, Mich., Jan. 8, 1971; s. Stanley A. and Marcia L. Rumbaugh; m. Y. Nan Park, May 25, 1996. BS, Haverford Coll., Pa., 1993; MS, U. Rochester, N.Y., 1996, PhD, 1998, MD, 2000. Lic. physician Md., 2004, diplomate Am. Bd. Psychiatry and Neurology, 2005. Intern Johns Hopkins U., Balt., 2000—01, resident neurology, 2001—03, chief resident neurology, 2003—04, asst. prof. neurology Divsn. Neuroimmunology and Neuro-Infectious Diseases, 2004—. Founder, dir. neuroimmunolgy, neuro-infectious disease consult svc. Johns Hopkins U., 2004—. Contbr. articles to profl. jours. Mem. humanism in medicine com., Rochester, 1999—2000; vol. outreach for AIDS awarenes Students Rochester, 1993—2000. Recipient Analytical Chemistry award, Am. Chem. Soc., 1993, Travel award, Am. Soc. Clin. Investigation, 2006; fellow, Elmer Stotz Found., 1995, Louis and Molly Wok Found., 1996, Elmer Stotz, 1995, Louis and Molly Wok, 1996, NIH Genetics, 1996, E. H. Hooker, 1997; scholar, U. Rochester, 1993. Achievements include discovery of a possible new host defense mechanism involving matrix metalloproteinases and viral proteins; research in several new biochemical mechanisms involved in DNA replication and repair; a possible biochemical pathway involved in HIV replication. Avocation: running. Office: Johns Hopkins University 600 N Wolfe Street Baltimore MD 21287 Office Phone: 443-287-4656. Office Fax: 410-502-8075.

**RUMBAUGH, JOHN R.,** health facility administrator, military officer; BA in Bus., Grove City Coll., Pa., 1982; MBA, Golden Gate U., San Francisco, 1989; MA in Nat. Security, Naval War Coll., 2003. Commd. ens. USN, 1962, advanced through grades to capt., health care adminstr., 1983—94; exec. commd. officer 3d Med. Battalion, Okinawa, Japan, 1994—97; staff officer Office of Sec. of Def., Washington, 1997—2000; dir. adminstrn. Naval Hosp., Guantanamo Bay, Cuba, 2000—02; strategic med. planner US Ctrl. Command, Tampa, Fla., 2003—05; bridage comdr. Uniformed Svcs. U., Bethesda, Md., 2005—. Fellow: Am. Acad. Med. Adminstrs. (diplomate in healthcare adminstrn. 1997, statesman in healthcare adminstrn. 1997); mem.: Am. Coll. Managed Care Adminstrs., USN Med. Found. Home: PO Box 34612 Bethesda MD 20827

**RUMBAUGH, MAX ELDEN, JR.,** professional society administrator; b. Ada, Okla., Dec. 11, 1937; s. Max E. and Gertrude (Gulker) R.; m. Joan E. Brockway; children: Maria Rumbaugh Gross, Max E. III. BS in Engring., U.S. Mil. Acad., 1960; MS in Engring. Scis., Purdue U., 1965, MBA, 1972. Instr. Purdue U., West Lafayette, Ind., 1964-65; corp. officer Midwest Applied Sci. Corp., West Lafayette, 1965-72; chief engr. advanced tech. Switzer div. Wallace-Murray Corp., Indpls., 1972-77. dir. research, 1977-81; mgr. engring. activities div. Soc. Automotive Engrs., Warrendale, Pa., 1981-84, v.p., asst. gen. mgr., 1984-86, exec. v.p., 1986—2002, exec. v.p. emeritus, 2002—; pres. Performance Rev. Inst., 1991—2001. Pres. Soc. Rsch. Adminstrs. Internat., 1973-74; chmn. Ind. sect. Soc. Automotive Engrs., 1978-79; bd. dirs., exec. com. Am. Nat. Standards Inst., NYC, 1986-02; bd. dirs. Intelligent Transp. Soc. Am., 1992-04, mem. exec. com., 1998-04, Scottsdale Sister Cities Assn., 2006—; internat. spkr. Automotive Engring., 1997-. Author mag. column Focus, 1986-2002. Bd. dirs. Jr. Achievement Western Pa., Pitts., 1986-98, YMCA, North Hills, Pitts., 1985-94, Scottsdale Sister Cities, 2006—; sec. Intelligent Transp. Soc. Am. Bd. Dirs., 2000-04. 1st lt. U.S. Army, 1960—63. Mem. ASME, Am. Soc. Assn. Execs., Coun. Engring. and Sci. Soc. Execs. (bd. dirs. 1990-97, sec. 1993-94, v.p. 1994-95, pres. 1995-96), Soc. Automotive Engrs. of China (hon.), Soc. Automotive Engrs. of India (hon.), Russian Internat. Acad. Engring., Intelligent Transp. Soc. Am. (bd. dirs. 1992-03, sec. 2000-03, chmn. fin. com. 2000-03), Russian Acad. Quality Problems, Rotary (bd. dirs. 1982-84, 93-97, v.p. 1994-95, pres. 1995-96, chmn. youth exch. 2003-). Avocations: skiing, photography. Home: 8731 E San Pablo Dr Scottsdale AZ 85258- Office: Soc of Automotive Engrs Inc 400 Commonwealth Dr Warrendale PA 15086-7511 Office Phone: 480-991-3059.

**RUMBELL, MARY BETH,** secondary school educator; b. Detroit, June 29, 1955; d. Harold D. and Ruth M. Parks; m. Michael H. Rumbell, July 15, 1978; children: John Michael Harold, Daniel Edward Charles. BA, Wayne State U., Detroit, 1995. Cert. CE and CB 7-12 State of Mich. Tchr. Acad. Sacred Heart, Bloomfield Hills, Mich., 1997—. Advisor Nat. Honor Soc. (Wansboro chpt.), Bloomfield Hills, 2001—; tchr. mentor chair Acad. Sacred Heart, 2005—. With USAR, 1974—77. Democrat. Avocations: golf, reading, dogs. Office: Acad Sacred Heart 1250 Kensington Rd Bloomfield Hills MI 48304-3029 Home: 21689 Albion Farmington Hills MI 48336

**RUMBELOW, ROBERT WESLEY,** composer, conductor, director; s. Arthur Ray and Virginia Marie Rumbelow; m. Linda Scott, June 6, 1992; children: Wesley Robert, Katarina Scott. Dr. Musical Arts, U.Rochester - Eastman Sch. of Music, NY, 1996. Dir. of wind ensemble activities Columbus State U., Ga., 1996—. Consulting and clinics Ind., Columbus, Ga., 1996—. Composer: (concert works / art music) Many Different Works. Usher, sound, deacon First Presbyn., Columbus, Ga., 2000—05. Named Sir Georg Solti Conducting Competition Winner, John Philip Sousa Found., 2004. Mem.: CBDNA, GMEA, NBA, ASOL, Conductors Guild. Office: Columbus State Univ 4225 University Ave Columbus GA 31907-5645 Office Phone: 706-649-7252. Personal E-mail: rumbelow.robert@colstate.edu.

**RUMBLEY, PHILIP LEE,** music educator, musician, photographer; b. Alice, Tex., Jan. 8, 1956; s. Jack Edward and Rose Mary Rumbley; m. Karen Gay Stevens, Feb. 14; 1 child, Philip Prescott. BA in visual arts, U. Tex., 1981. Photographer T.B. Butler Publ. Co., Tyler, Tex., 1984—90, U. Tex. Health Ctr., Tyler, Tex., 1990—; adj. faculty music Tyler Jr. Coll., Tex., 2000—. Contract musician, 1989—. Author: (jour article) Am. Jour. Medicine, 1991, several oral presentations. Recipient First Pl. Sports Photography, United Press Internat., 1984, Outstanding Achievement, 1985, Second Pl. News Photography, N.E. Tex. Press Assn., 1986, Third Pl. News Photography, 1987, Katie award News Reporting, Dallas Press Club, 1988, Outstanding Vol. award, Tex. Asthma Camp. Mem.: Tex. Music Educators Assn., Bio-Commn. Assn. (past pres.), Tex. Press Assn., Nat. Press Photographers Assn. Home: 1810 S Sneed Tyler TX 75701 E-mail: phil.rumbley@uthct.edu.

**RUMBOUGH, STANLEY MADDOX, JR.,** industrialist; b. N.Y.C., Apr. 25, 1920; s. Stanley Maddox and Elizabeth (Colgate) R.; m. Nedenia Hutton, Mar. 23, 1946 (div. 1966); children: Stanley H., David P. (dec.), Nedenia Colgate; m. Margaretha Wagstrom, Dec. 21, 1967 (div. 1990); m. Janna Herlow, Mar. 19, 1990. AB, Yale U., 1942; postgrad. in bus. adminstrn., NYU, 1947-51. Vice pres.-dir. Willis Air Service, Teterboro, NJ, 1946-47; v.p., dir. White Metal Mfg. Co., Hoboken, NJ, 1945-61, pres., 1960-61; pres., dir. Metal Container Corp., 1950-59, Am. Totalisator, Balt., 1956-58; chmn. bd. Extrusion Devel. Corp., 1959-61; co-founder, chmn. bd. Elec. Engring. Ltd., 1960-69; chmn. bd. Wallace Clark & Co., 1962-69; co-founder, dir. Trinidad Flour Mills, 1961-72; co-founder Jamaica Flour Mills, 1963-66; dir. Dart Industries. Spl. asst. to sec. Dept. Commerce, 1953; spl. asst. White House charge exec. br. liaison, 1953-55; founder Washington D.C. Tennis Patrons Found. Chmn. U.S. Com. for UN, 1957-58; co-founder Citizens for Eisenhower, 1951; vice chmn. Citizens for Eisenhower-Nixon Com., 1952; bd. dirs. Young Pres. Orgn., 1958-65, 69-80; trustee Young Pres. Found., 1957-70, pres., 1962-65; bd. dirs. N.Y. World's Fair Corp., 1961-70, Nat. Conf. on Citizenship, 1973—2003, Population Resource Ctr., 1978-92, Planned Parenthood of Palm Beach Area, 1979-95, Planned Parenthood Fedn. Am., 1981-84, Kravis Ctr. Performing Arts; bd. dirs. Palm Beach Civic Assn., chmn. 2005—, co-chmn., 1997-2005; trustee Libr. for Presdl. Papers, 1966-70, Internat. House, 1959—. Fgn. Policy Assn., 1961-70, Am. Health Found., 1972-76; bd. dirs. Art Family of Fla., 1983-95. Capt. USMCR, 1942-46. Decorated Air medal (8), D.F.C. (2). Mem. Chief Execs. Orgn., World Pres.'s Orgn. (founding), Young Pres.'s Orgn. (founding), Def. Orientation Conf. Assn., Racquet and Tennis Club, Internat. Lawn Tennis Club, Maidstone Club, Seminole Club, Bath and Tennis Club, Everglades Club, Nat. Golf Links Am. Club, Zeta Psi. Republican. Home: 655 Island Dr Palm Beach FL 33480-4744 Office: 44 Cocoanut Row Ste B103 Palm Beach FL 33480-4069

**RUMLER, ROBERT HOKE,** agricultural products executive, consultant, retired trade association administrator; b. Chambersburg, Pa., Apr. 4, 1915; s. Daniel Webster and Jennie (Sellers) R.; m. Frances Jeannette Montgomery, June 7, 1939 (dec. 1983); children: Craig M., Karen A. Loden; m. Hazel Miller-Karper, Aug. 23, 1986 (dec. 1998). BS, Pa. State U., 1936. Asst. county agt. U. Mo., 1936-37; county agri. agt. Pa. State U., 1937-45; asst. mgr., editor agrl. promotion divsn. E. I. duPont de Nemours & Co., Inc., Wilmington, Del., 1945-48; exec. sec., COO, Holstein-Friesian Assn. Am., 1948-53, 53-75, exec. sec., CEO, 1975-81, exec. chmn., 1981-82, chmn. emeritus, 1982—. Pres. Holstein-Friesian Svcs., Inc., 1968-81; agribus. cons., 1982—; hon. mem. Holstein-Friesian de Mex. (C.A.); bd. dirs., chmn. Vt. Nat. Bank, Vt. Fin. Svcs., Inc., 1957-88; mem. U.S./USSR Joint Com. Agrl. Cooperation; past chmn. U.S. Agrl. Export Devel. Coun., FAS-USDA; mem. coordinating group Nat. Coop. Dairy Herd Improvement program USDA, 1964-80; mem. agrl. policy adv. com. USTR/USDA Multilateral Trade Negotiations, 1973-87, mem. agrl. tech. adv. com., 1987-95. Contbg. editl. writer Holstein World. Trustee Ea. States Expn., trustee emeritus, 1993—; trustee Assoc. Industries Vt.; past bd. dirs. Internat. Stockmans Ednl. Found.;

chmn. adv. bd. Pa. State U., Mont Alto, 1988-98, chmn. 1990-94, emeritus 1998, Centennial fellow, 2004; bd. advisors Pa. State U., Harrisburg, 1990-94. Recipient Disting. award Nat. Dairy Herd Improvement Assn., 1974, Disting. Svc. award Nat. Agrl. Mktg. Orgn., 1977, Cert. of Appreciation, USDA, 1982, Disting. Svc. award Holstein Assn., 1985; named Disting. Alumnus, Pa. State U., 1978, Coll. Agr., 2000, Dairy Industry Man of Yr., World Dairy Expo, 1979, Headliner-of-Yr. Livestock Publs. Coun., 1995, Internat. Person of Yr. World Dairy Expo, 1996, 1st Disting. Alumnus AZ Frat., Pa. State U., 1996; Centennial fellow Pa. State Mont Alto Campus, 2004; named to Internat. Livestock Hall of Fame, 1987; Robert H. Rumler scholarship founded in his name. Fellow Agr. Adventures; mem. Purebred Dairy Cattle Assn. (dir., exec. com.), Nat. Soc. Livestock Record Assns. (past pres., dir., Disting. Svcs. award 1981), Am. Dairy Sci. Assn. (Disting. Svc. award 1977), Agri-Bus. Found. (All-Time Gt. award 1981), Nat. Dairy Shrine (Dairy Hall of Fame 1976), N.E. Master Farmers Assn. (hon. master farmer 1999, Pa. Farm Bur. Disting. Svc. to Agr. award 1999), U.S. Animal Health Assn., Kiwanis, Masons, Elks, Alpha Zeta (hon. roll 1997), Gamma Sigma Delta. Mem. United Ch. of Christ. Home: 937 Wallace Ave Chambersburg PA 17201-3884 Personal E-mail: bobrumler@pa.net.

**RUMMEL, HAROLD EDWIN,** travel company executive, retail executive; b. Youngstown, Ohio, Oct. 4, 1940; s. Harold Edward and Florence Louise (Hill) R.; children: Timothy B., Jonathan S., Briana. BS, U. Fla., 1963. Writer, editor President's coun., Fla., 1958-70; polit. campaign mgr. various state and congressional campaigns, Tallahassee, 1971-79; sr. v.p. Fla. Fed. Saving Bank, St. Petersburg, Fla., 1979-86; pres., CEO Rummel Co. including The Rummel Real Estate Group, Inc., HardwareUSA.net, St. Petersburg, Fla., 1986—2003, Woodland Bay Group Inc., Mobile, Ala., 1986—2003, Rummel Group Inc., 1986—2003, Global Quest, Inc., Sahara Quest. Active in civic and polit. orgns. Democrat. Avocations: nature, wildlife photography, travel. Home: 1002 Charleston St Mobile AL 36604 Office Phone: 727-204-1187. Personal E-mail: rumgroup@bellsouth.net.

**RUMMEL, ROBERT WILAND,** aeronautical engineer, writer; b. Dakota, Ill., Aug. 4, 1915; s. William Howard and Dora (Ely) R.; m. Marjorie B. Cox, Sept. 30, 1939; children: Linda Kay, Sharon Lee, Marjorie Susan, Robert Wiland, Diana Beth. Diploma in Aero. Engring., Curtiss Wright Tech. Inst. Aerosci., 1935. Stress anaiyst Hughes Aircraft Co., Burbank, Calif., 1935-36, Lockheed Aircraft Corp., Burbank, 1936; draftsman Aero Engring. Corp., Long Beach, Calif., 1936. Nat. Aircraft Co., Alhambra, Calif., 1936-37; chief engr. Rearwin A/C & Engines, Inc., Kansas City, Kans., 1937-42; chief design engr. Commonwealth A/C, Inc., Kansas City, 1942-43; v.p. engring. Trans World Airlines, Inc., Kansas City, Mo., 1943-59, v.p. planning and rsch., 1959-69, v.p. tech. devel., 1969-78; pres. Robert W. Rummel Assocs., Inc., Mesa, Ariz., 1978-87; aerospace cons., 1987—. Commnr. Presdl. Commn. Space Shuttle Challenger Accident, 1986; chmn. nat. rsch. coun. Aero Space Engring. Bd. Fellow Inst. Aero. Scis., Soc. Automotive Engrs.; mem. NAE. Masons (32 deg.), Shriners. Home and Office: 1189 Leisure World Mesa AZ 85206-3067 Office Phone: 480-396-9030. Personal E-mail: rwrummel@aol.com.

**RUMP, MARJORIE,** library director; b. St. Joseph, Missouri, Jan. 19, 1919; d. Edward August and Adeline Amelia Gummig; m. John S. Rump, July 25, 1943 (dec. Sept. 29, 1996); children: Jack, Susan, Marilyn. BA, U. Redlands, Calif., 1941; MLS, U. So. Calif., 1957. Book buyer Sierra Book Store, Bakersfield, Calif., 1953—66; libr. Kern County Libr., Bakersfield, Calif., 1961—66, Ea. Bakersfield H.S., Calif., 1966—68; br. supr. to dep. dir. Kern County Libr., Bakersfield, Calif., 1968—88, dep. dir., 1988—2001. Mem. bd. Kern County Cmty. Found., Bakersfield, Calif., 1995—; ptnr. Easter Hill Assocs., 1996; trustee Conf. of Calif. Hist. Soc. Trust, Stockton, Calif., 1998—, Rocky Heights, LLC, 2001—. Editor: Inside Historic Kern, 1982; contbr. articles in the California Historian, 1997. Recipient Citizen's Recognition Award, City of Bakersfield, 1983, Jubilee Medallion, U. Redlands, 1984, Soroptimist Women of Distinction Award, Soroptimist Internat., 1990. Mem.: Petroleum Prodn. Pioneers, Conf. Calif. Hist. Soc. (pres. 2000—02), Am. Soc. Pub. Adminstr. (pres. 1980, Doubenmeir Award for Pub. Adminstrn 1979), Kern County Hist. Soc. (pres. 1981), Soroptimist Internat., Bakersfield (pres. 1978—79), Greater Bakersfield C. of C., Wakayama Sister City (treas. 1984—94). Presbyterian. Avocations: gardening, travel. Home: 3000 Elmwood Bakersfield CA 93305

**RUMSCHITZKI, DAVID SHELDON,** chemical engineering educator; BS in Chem. Engring. and Math., Cooper Union, 1978; MS in Chem. Engring., U. Calif., Berkeley, 1979, PhD in Chem. Engring., 1984. Process engr. Stauffer Che. Co., Dobbs Ferry, NY, summer 1978; rsch. engr. Mobil R&D Corp., Paulsboro, NJ, summer 1984; asst. prof. dept. chem. engring. CCNY, 1983-84, 85-89, assoc. prof., 1990-96, prof., 1997—2004, Herbert G. Kayser prof. chem. engring., 2004—. Vis. scientist Max Planck Inst. fur Biophys. Chemistry, Gottingen, Germany, 1985, dept. molecular biology Rsch. Inst. Scripps Clinic, La Jolla, Calif., 1988-89, dept. biophysics Rohr U. Bochum, Germany, 1996-97. Alexander von Humboldt fellow, 1996-97; recipient Frederick Urban Meml. scholarship for excellence in chem. engring., 1978, Harry W. Reddick Fund prize and medal for math., 1978, Standard Oil Co. fellowship, 1978, 79, Presdl. Young Investigator award NSF, 1987-93, Best Papter award ASME Bioengring. Divsn., 1995-96, Melville medal ASME, 1996. Mem. Sigma Pi Sigma, Tau Beta Pi, Sigma Xi. Office: Dept Chem City Coll NY 140th St Convent Ave New York NY 10031 E-mail: David@che.ccny.cuny.edu.

**RUMSEY, VICTOR HENRY,** electrical engineering educator emeritus; b. Devizes, Eng., Nov. 22, 1919; s. Albert Victor and Susan Mary (Norman) R.; m. Doris Herring, Apr. 2, 1942; children: John David, Peter Alan, Catherine Anne. BA, Cambridge U., 1941, DSc in Physics, 1972; DEng, Tohoku U., Japan, 1962. With U.K. Sci. Civil Service, 1941-48; asst. to assoc. prof. Ohio State U., 1948-54; prof. U. Ill., 1954-57, U. Calif., Berkeley, 1957-66, prof. elec. engring. and computer scis. San Diego, 1966-87, prof. emeritus, 1987—, dept. chmn., 1977-81. Author: 1 book in field; contbr. articles to profl. jours.; patentee in field. Recipient George Sinclair award Ohio State U., 1982, John Kraus Antenna award IEEE Antennas and Propagation Soc., 2004) (Guggenheim fellow. Fellow IEEE (Morris Liebman prize, John Kraus award Antennas and Propagation), Union Radio Scientifique Internationale, Internat. Astron. Union; mem. Nat. Acad. Scis. Home: 1171 Bohemian Ln Occidental CA 95465-9115

**RUMSFELD, DONALD HENRY,** secretary of defense; b. Chgo., July 9, 1932; AB, Princeton U., 1954; degree (hon.), De Paul U. Coll. Commerce, Ill. Coll., Lake Forest Coll., Park Coll., Tuskegee Inst., Nat. Coll. Edn., Bryant Coll., Claremont Grad. Sch., Calif., Ill. Wesleyan U., RAND Grad. Sch., Hampden-Sydney Coll. Adminstrv. asst. to Rep. David Dennison U.S. Ho. of Reps., 1957-59, mem. staff Rep. Robert Griffin, 1959; investment broker A.G. Becker & Co., Chgo., 1960-62; mem. U.S. Ho. of Reps. from 13th Ill. dist., Washington, 1963—69; dir. Office of Econ. Opportunity & asst. to the Pres. The White House, Washington, 1969—70, counsellor to the Pres., 1970—73, dir. Cost of Living Coun., 1971—73; U.S. amb. & permanent rep. to NATO US Dept. State, Brussels, 1973-74; chair transition to the presidency of Gerald R. Ford The White House, Washington, 1974, chief of staff, 1974-75; sec. US Dept. Def., Washington, 1975—77, 2001—; pres., CEO G.D. Searle & Co., Skokie, Ill., 1977-85, chmn. CEO, 1985; spl. presdl. amb. to Mid. East The White House, 1983-84; sr. advisor William Blair & Co., Chgo., 1985-90; chmn., CEO General Instrument Corp., Chgo., 1990-93; chmn. bd. dirs. Gilead Scis., Inc., Foster City, Calif., 1997—2001. Mem., Gen. Advisory Com. on Arms Control & advisor to the govt. on nat. security affairs, 1983-84, US Joint Advisory Commn. on US/Japan Relations, 1983-84, Nat. Commn. on Pub. Svc., 1987-90, Nat. Econ. Commn., 1988-89, Commn. on US/Japan Relations, 1989-91; spl. presdl. envoy on the Law of the Sea Treaty, 1982-83, sr. advisor to the Pres. panel on Strategic Systems, 1983-84, chmn. U.S. Commn. to Assess the Ballistic Missile Threat to the U.S., 1998; commr. U.S. Fed. Trade Deficit Rev. Commn., 1999-2000; U.S. Commn. to Assess Nat. Security Space Mgmt. & Orgn., 2000; bd. visitors, Nat. Def. U., 1988-92. Aviator, flight instructor USN, 1954—57 USNR, 1957—75. Recipient

Disting. Eagle Scout award, 1975, Presdl. Medal of Freedom, The White House, 1977, Outstanding Chief Exec. Officer in the Pharmaceutical Industry award, 1980, George Catlett Marshall award, 1984, Woodrow Wilson award, 1985, Dwight David Eisenhower medal, 1993, James H. Doolittle award, 2003, Ronald Reagan Freedom award, 2003, Gerald R. Ford medal, 2004. Republican. Office: US Dept Defense 1000 Defense Pentagon Washington DC 20301-1000 Office Phone: 703-692-7100.*

**RUNCO, MARIO, JR.,** astronaut, Earth scientist, meteorologist, spacecraft window engineer, information technology manager; b. Bronx, NY, Jan. 26, 1952; s. Mario and Filomena (Ragusa) Runco; m. Susan Kay Friess; 2 children. BS in Meteorology and Phys. Oceanography, CCNY, 1974, DSc (hon.), 1999; MS in Atmospheric Physics, Rutgers U., New Brunswick, NJ, 1976. Rsch. hydrologist US Geol. Survey, LI, NY, 1976—77; state trooper NJ State Police, 1977—78; commd. ensign USN, 1978; rsch. meteorologist Naval Rsch. Lab., Monterey, Calif., 1978—81; watch and meteorol. officer USS Nassau (LHA-4), 1981—83; lab. instr. Naval Postgrad. Sch., Monterey, 1984—85; commdg. officer Oceanographic Unit USNS Chauvenet, 1985—86; fleet environ. svcs. officer Naval Pacific Meterology and Oceanography Command, Pearl Harbor, Hawaii, 1986—87; astronaut NASA Johnson Space Ctr., Houston, 1987—; mission specialist Space Shuttles Atlantis (STS-44), 1991, Space Shuttle Endeavour (STS-54), 1993, Space Shuttle Endeavour (STS-77), 1996; space shuttle flight software avionics lab. test pilot Lyndon B. Johnson Space Ctr. NASA, Houston, 1987—92, capsule communicator Mission Control Ctr. (CAPCOM), 1989—94, lead sci. and utilization Internat. Space Sta. Sci. Window/Window Rsch. Facility, 1993—, Earth and planetary scientist, 1994—, project mgr. Lunar Habitation Sys. project, 2004—, lead spacecraft window optical requirements, 2005—. Decorated Def. Superior Svc. medal NASA, Def. Meritorious Svc. medal, Exceptional Svc. medal, Three Space Flight medals, Two Navy Sea Svc. Deployment Ribbons, Navy Battle Efficiency Ribbon, Navy Achievement medal, Navy Pistol Expert medal; recipient Class of 1938 Athletic Svc. award, CCNY, 1973, Townsend Harris medal, 1993, John Cardinal Spellman award, Cardinal Hayes HS, 1993. Achievements include three space flights, 551 hours in space and one 4.5 hour spacewalk, and designation as Naval Surface Warefare Officer. Avocations: ice hockey, antique cars, collecting toy trains, model railroads, baseball. Office: Human Exploration Sci Office NASA Lyndon B Johnson Space Ctr 2101 NASA Rd 1 Houston TX 77058-3696

**RUND, DOUGLAS ANDREW,** emergency physician; b. Columbus, Ohio, July 20, 1945; s. Carl Andrew and Caroline Amelia (Row) Rund; m. Sue E. Padavana, 1980; children: Carie, Emily, Ashley. BA, Yale U., 1967; MD, Stanford U., 1971. Lic. physician Ohio, diplomate Nat. Bd. Med. Examiners, Am. Bd. Family Practice, Am. Bd. Emergency Medicine. Intern U. Calif. San Francisco-Moffett Hosp., 1971—72; resident in gen. surgery Stanford U., 1972—74, Robert Wood Johnson Found. clin. scholar in medicine, 1974—76; med. dir. Mid-Peninsula Health Svc., Palo Alto, Calif., 1975—76; clin. instr. dept. medicine and preventive medicine Stanford U. Med. Sch., 1975—76; assoc. prof., dir. divsn. emergency medicine Ohio State Coll. Medicine, 1982—87, dir. emergency medicine residency program, assoc. prof. dept, 1976—87, prof., chmn. dept. preventive medicine, 1988—90, prof., chmn. dept. emergency medicine, 1990—, prof., interim chmn. dept. family medicine, 1994—95, assoc. dean, 2001—; pres. Ohio State Univ. Physicians, 2002—. Attending staff Ohio State U. Hosps., 1976—; med. dir. CSCC, Emergency Med. Svcs. Dept.; pres. Internat. Rsch. Inst. Emergency Medicine; sr. rsch. fellow NATO: Health and Med. Aspects of Disaster Preparedness, 1985—87; vis. epidemiology and injury control U. Edinburgh, Scotland, 1987; working group, emergency and critical care in space NASA, 2001—; bd. dirs. Am. Bd. Emergency Medicine, 1988—97, sr. editor in tng. exam., 1989—, pres., 1995—; pres., chmn. bd. dirs. Physicians of the Ohio State U. (POSU), 2002—; med. dir. Worthington Fire Dept. Author: Triage, 1981, Essentials of Emergency Medicine, 1982, 2d edit., 1986, Emergency Radiology, 1982, Emergency Psychiatry, 1983, Environmental Emergencies, 1985; editor: Emergency Medicine Ann., 1983—84, Emergency Medicine Survey, Annals of Emergency Medicine, Annals of Emergency Medicine Symposium, 1986; editor: (in chief) Ohio State Series on Emergency Medicine, Emergency Medicine Observer, 1986—87; mem. editl. bd.: Physician, Sports Medicine, Emergency Med. Svcs.; co-author: Family Medicine Priciples and Practice, 1978, 2d edit., 1983; contbr. articles to profl. jours. Recipient Faculty Tchg. award, Ohio State U., 1999, Douglas A. Rund Disting. Faculty award, Dept. Emergency Medicine, 2003. Fellow: Am. Coll. Emergency Physicians (task force on substance abuse and injury control, Outstanding Contbn. to Edn. award 1992); mem.: IAAA, Internat. Soc. for Emergency Med. Svcs. (med. dir.), Columbus Med. Forum (pres. 1993—), Soc. Acad. Emergency Medicine (chmn. internat. com. 1991—), Assn. Acad. Chairs Emergency Medicine (pres. 1992—93), Nat. Inst. on Alcohol Abuse and Alcoholism, Alpha Omega Alpha. Office: Ohio State U 146 Means Hall 1654 Upham Dr Columbus OH 43210-1240

**RUND, REX BENJAMIN,** church administrator, music director; b. Urbana, Ill., Aug. 20, 1960; s. Benjamin Joseph and Marie Theresa Rund; m. Cathy Berns Rund, Mar. 19, 1988; children: Jacob Simon, Emma Sophie, Marian Rose. B in Music Edn., Ea. Ill. U., 1984, MA, 1985. Peace corps vol. US Peace Corps, Leogane, Haiti, 1985—87; grad. asst. Ea. Ill. U., Charleson, 1988—88; asst. headmaster Salzburg Internat. Prep. Sch., Salzburg, Austria, 1989—91; mid. sch. coord. & tchr. Danube Internat. Sch., Vienna, 1991—95; music tchr. Marshall Cmty. Schs., Ill., 1995—97; dir. of music and liturgy Our Lady of Mt. Carmel Ch., Ind., 1997—. Leadership bd. Nat. Assn. of Pastoral Musicians Indpls. Chpt., Indpls., 1998—2000. Composer: (liturgical songs) O God, You are My Rock, 1998, God's Caring Love Makes the Difference, 2002, As a Family, We Build God's Kingdom, 2003, Color the World with the Light of Christ, 2004, Journey with Jesus, 2005. Co-founder, mission trip leader, and translator Our Lady of Mt. Carmel, St. Antoine Haiti Parish Twinning Program, Ind. Recipient Disting. Young Alumnus award, Ea. Ill. U., 1988, Villa Grove H.S. Hall of Fame Charter Mem., Villa Grove H.S., 1988, Peace Corps Vol. of the Yr. award for Ams. and Caribbean, US Peace Corps, 1987; scholar Warner Presdl. award, Ea. Ill. U., 1983, Talented Student award, 1981—84. Mem.: Choristers' Guild, Am. Choral Dirs. Assn., Nat. Assn. of Pastoral Musicians. Roman Catholic. Avocations: running marathons, travel. Office: Our Lady of Mt Carmel Ch 14598 Oakridge Rd Carmel IN 46032 Office Phone: 317-663-4007. Office Fax: 317-846-3475. E-mail: rundr@olmc1.org.

**RUNDBACK, JOHN H.,** radiologist, interventional radiology director; b. NYC, Apr. 3, 1963; s. Robert Joseph Rundback and Hazel Greenberg-Rundback; m. Lili Spierer, Oct. 29, 1988; 1 child, Matthew. BA in Chemistry magna cum laude, CUNY, Bklyn., 1983; MD, SUNY, Downstate, 1987. Diplomate Am. Bd. Radiology (examiner 2004), Am. Bd. Angiography and Interventational Radiology. Intern St. Vincent's Hosp. and Med. Ctr., NYC, 1987—88; resident in diagnostic radiology Beth Israel Med. Ctr., NYC, 1988—92, chief resident, 1991—92; fellow in interventional radiology Washington Hosp. Ctr., 1992—93; assoc. attending radiologist Muhlenberg Hosp. Ctr., Bethlehem, Pa., 1993—95, Westchester Med. Ctr., Valhalla, NY, 1995—2001, Danbury Hosp., Conn., 2000—01, Lawrence Hosp., Bronxville, NY, 2001—05, NY Presbyn., NYC, 2001—05; dir. interventional radiology Holy Name Hosp., Teaneck, NJ, 2005—. Asst. prof. radiology and surgery, dir. clin. rsch. Vascular Health Ctr. NY Med. Coll., Valhalla, 1995—2001, assoc. prof., 2000—01; assoc. prof. clin. radiology, dir. clin. rsch. vascular and interventional radiology Coll. Physicians and Surgeons Columbia U., NYC, 2001—05, adj. assoc. prof., 2005—; councilor clin. trials divsn. SIR Found., 2004—; cons. Rex Med.; chmn. cordis endovascular CYPHER adv. bd. Johnson & Johnson; mem. med. adv. bd. Medicines Co.; mem. sci. adv. bd. Boston Scientifics Corp., Cryovascular Inc.; presenter in field. Mem. editl. bd.: Jour. Vascular and Interventional Radiology, 2004—, reviewer, 1997—2000, 2002—04, Jour. Cardiovasc. Medicine; guest editor: Techniques Vascular and Interventional Radiology; contbr. articles to profl. jours. Recipient Sadek K. Hilal Faculty Rsch. award, Columbia Presbyn. Med. Ctr. Radiology, 2003; grantee, Am. Biosciences, Nuvelo, European Union, Medtronic, Inc., Boston Scientifics, Inc., others. Fellow: Soc. Vascular Medicine and Biology, Am. Heart Assn., Soc. Cardiovasc. and Interventional Radiology; mem.: Soc.

Interventional Radiology Found. (bd. dirs. 2000—, chair cooperative alliance interventional rsch. clin. trials network 2003—), Cardiovasc. and Interventional Radiology Soc. Europe, NY State Roentgen Ray Soc., Am. Coll. Radiology, Radiol. Soc. N.Am., Phi Beta Kappa. Achievements include research in hemodynamic effects and target renal parenchymal damage during protected renal angioplasty using a temporary occulsive device in a pig model or renal artery stenosis; RENAISSANCE genesis renal artery stent trial. Office: Holy Name Hosp Interventional Radiology 718 Teaneck Rd Teaneck NJ 07666 Office Phone: 201-833-3310. Office Fax: 201-541-5910. Business E-Mail: rundback@mail.holyname.org, jr2041@columbia.edu.

**RUNDELL, ARDEN GRABKE,** musician; b. Chico, Calif., Dec. 16, 1961; d. Harold Salisbury and Lois Jean Grabke; m. Robert Glenn Rundell, Aug. 7, 1994; 1 child, Miriam. BA in Psychology, Western Wash. U., 1985, MBA, 1986; PhD in Bus. Adminstrn., Ariz. State U., 1995. Compensation/benefits adminstr. Spacelabs Med., Redmond, Wash., 1986—88; benefits adminstr. Children's Hosp., Seattle, 1989—90; rsch./tchg. asst. Ariz. State U., Tempe, 1990—95; adj. prof. bus. N.W. Coll., Kirklan, Wash., 1996—98; project cons. fin. Bank Am., Seattle, 1997—2000. Violinist Beaverton (Oreg.) Chamber Symphony, 1996—97, Bellevue (Wash.) Philharm., 1997—; statistics instr. U. Phoenix, 2005—. Co-author: Handbook of Human Resource, 1995. Violinist Eastside Foursquare Ch., Kirkland, 2000—. With N.G. U.S. Army, 1980—86. Scholar, Western Wash. U., 1985—86. Mem.: Acad. Mgmt. Democrat. Pentacostal. Avocations: music, computer languages, astronomy, physics. Home: 6521 SE Couger Mt Way Bellevue WA 98006

**RUNDELL, ORVIS HERMAN, JR.,** psychologist, educator; b. Oklahoma City, June 16, 1940; s. Orvis Herman and Virginia Reid (George) R.; m. Jane Shannon Brians, June 25, 1966; children: Leslie Jane, Anne Reid. BS, U. Okla., 1962, MS, 1972, PhD, 1976. Lab. mgr. Okla. Ctr. Alcohol and Drug-Related Studies, Oklahoma City, 1969-76, staff scientist, 1974—. Asst. prof. psychiatry and behavioral scis. U. Okla. Health Sci. Center, 1976—; dir. clin. physiology and sleep disorders ctr. Columbia Presbyterian Hosp., Oklahoma City, 1982-2001; clin. dir. Diagnostic Sleep Ctr. of Dallas, 1989-93; ptnr. Sleep Medicine Assocs., 1994—, Sleep Assocs., 2000—, Sleep Remedies, LLC, 2002—; dir. Columbia Sleep Ptnrs. Program, 1996-2001; clin. dir. The Sleep Clinic, Oklahoma City, 2000—, Sleep Labs PRN, 2001—; cons. in field; instl. rev. bd. U. Okla. Health Sci. Ctr., 1989-2001. Contbr. articles to profl. jours., chpts. in books; asst. editor Alcohol Tech. Reports, 1976-90; cons. editor Psychophysiology, 1974-2001. Bd. dirs. Hist. Preservation, Inc., Oklahoma City, 1978-90. With USAR, 1963-69. Grantee, Nat. Inst. Drug Abuse, Nat. Inst. Alcohol Abuse and Alcoholism. Fellow Am. Acad. of Sleep Medicine; mem. N.Y. Acad. Scis., Psi Chi, Phi Gamma Delta. Home: 431 NW 20th St Oklahoma City OK 73103-1918 Office: 5530 N Francis Oklahoma City OK 73118 Office Phone: 405-767-6970. Office Fax: 405-879-1949. Personal E-mail: zzzs@cox.net.

**RUNDIO, LOUIS MICHAEL, JR.,** lawyer; b. Chgo., Sept. 13, 1943; s. Louis Michael Sr. and Germaine Matilda (Pasternack) R.; m. Ann Marie Bartlett, July 10, 1971; children: Matthew, Melissa. BS in Physics, Loyola U., Chgo., 1965, JD, 1972. Bar: Ill. 1972, U.S. Dist. Ct. (no. dist.) Ill. 1972, U.S. Ct. Appeals (7th cir.) 1974, U.S. Dist. Ct. (ea. dist.) Mich. 1983. Assoc. McDermott, Will & Emery, Chgo., 1972-77, ptnr., 1978—. Served to 1st lt. U.S. Army, 1965-68, Vietnam. Mem. ABA, Chgo. Bar Assn. Home: 676 Skye Ln Barrington IL 60010-5506 Office: McDermott Will & Emery 227 W Monroe St Ste 3100 Chicago IL 60606-5096

**RUNDLE, JOHN BELTING,** physicist, researcher; b. Somerville, N.J., Aug. 31, 1950; s. David Bradford and Dorothy (Belting) R.; m. Marie Cardoza, July 27, 1974; children: Paul Belting, Daniel Edgar. Student, U. Ill., 1968-69, 74; BS in Engring., Princeton U., 1972; MS, UCLA, 1973, PhD, 1976. Postdoctoral fellow UCLA, 1976-77; research scientist Sandia Nat. Labs., Albuquerque, 1977-90; physicist Lawrence Livermore (Calif.) Nat. Lab., 1990-93; prof. physics, civil & environ. engring. and geol. dir. U. Colo., 1993—2002; dir. Colo. Ctr. for Chaos and Complexity, 1993—, Ctr. for Computer Sci. Engring., Univ. Davis, 2002—. Vis. assoc. Calif. Inst. Tech., Pasadena, 1981-84; cons. various govtl. agys, 1980—; mem. Nat. Acad. Scis. NRC com. on Geodesy, 1986-90, chmn., 1988-90, mem. Nat. Acad. Scis. NRC Panel on Modeling in the Earth Scis., 1989-91, NASA geophysics sci. working group, 1986—; vis. scholar dept. physics Boston U., 1988-89; chmn. evaluation panel So. Calif. Earthquake Ctr. NSF, 1990; disting. vis. scientist JPL, 1997—. Contbr. articles to profl. jours. Grantee NASA, NSF, Dept. Energy. Mem. Am. Geophys. Union, Seismol. Soc., Am. Phys. Soc., Am. Soc. Natural Philosophy, Princeton Club (v.p. 1985), Sigma Xi, Phi Beta Kappa, Tau Beta Pi, Phi Eta Sigma. Achievements include research in statistical mechanics of high dimensional complex nonlinear threshold systems; simulations of earthquake, neural network and other threshold systems. Office: U Colo Colo Ctr Chaos Complexity Ekeley S236 Boulder CO 80309-0001 Fax: 303-492-5070. E-mail: rundle@cires.colorado.edu.

**RUNDLETT, ELLSWORTH TURNER, III,** lawyer; b. Portland, Maine, Jan. 12, 1946; s. Ellsworth Turner II and Esther (Stevens) R.; m. Lisa Warren, Oct. 25, 1964 (div. June 1967); 1 child, Ellsworth Turner IV; m. Jamie Donnelly, June 7, 1982 (div. 1986); m. Marilyn DeJenzano, Aug. 17, 1994. AB cum laude, Bowdoin Coll., 1968; JD, U. Maine, 1973. Bar: Maine 1973, U.S. Dist. Ct. Maine 1973, U.S. Ct. Appeals (1st cir.) 1973; cert. civil trial specialist, Nat. Bd. Trial Advocacy; diplomate Nat. Coll. Advocacy. Bowdoin Coll. intern U.S. Senate, Washington, 1967; law clk. Superior Ct. Maine, Portland, 1972-73; asst. corp. counsel City of Portland, 1973-76; ptnr. Childs, Rundlett, Fifield, Shumway and Altshuler, Portland, 1980—. Author: Maximizing Damages in Small Personal Injury Cases, 1991; contbr. legal articles to Maine Bus. Digest, 1978-84. Pres. Pine Tree Alcohol Treatment Ctr., Windham, Maine, 1978-80; trustee Portland Players, Inc., South Portland, Maine, 1977-84, pres., 1985-87. Mem ATI & Cumberland County Bar (justice 1983-84, 86-87), v.p. 1988-90, pres. 1990), Maine Bar Assn. (bd. govs. 1991—), Maine Trial Lawyers Assn. (pres. 2000-01), U. Maine Law Alumni (bd. dirs. 1984-87, v.p. 1988, pres. 1989, bd. govs. 1991—), Cumberland Club, Portland Club (bd. govs. 1983-86), Bowdoin Club of Portland (pres. 1978). Office: Childs Rundlett & Fifield 257 Deering Ave Portland ME 04103-4858 Office Phone: 207-773-0275. Business E-Mail: derry@maine.rr.com.

**RUNGE, DONALD EDWARD,** food wholesale company executive; b. Milw., Mar. 20, 1938; s. Adam and Helen Teresa (Voss) R.; divorced; children: Roland, Richard, Lori. Grad., Spencerian Coll., Milw., 1960. Fin. v.p. Milw. Cheese Co., Waukesha, Wis., 1962-69; dir. Farm House Foods Corp., Milw., 1966-89, pres., 1966-89, CEO, treas., 1984-89, chmn., pres., 1985-89; chmn., CEO Retailing Corp. Am., Milw., 1982-89; CEO, treas. Drug Sys. Inc., Milw., 1984-89; chmn. Drug Sys. Inc. (now Retailing Corp. of Am.), Milw., 1985-89; pres. TDC, 1987-89; chmn., pres. Runge Industries, Gen. Growth, Inc., 1989—. Bd. dirs. Convenient Food Mart, CasaBlanca Industries, Inc., City of Industry, Calif., Palm Beach Opera, 1992—; sec. The Diana Corp., Milw., 1985-86, treas. 1986—, pres. 1987-96; chmn. Economy Dry Goods Co. Inc.; treas. Fairbanks Farms Inc.; chmn., CEO Internat. Diamond Exch., LLC, 2006—. Adventist. Address: 111C Palm Point Cir Palm Beach Gardens FL 33418-4032 Office Phone: 561-625-4844. *I believe there is very little in life that cannot be accomplished if a person truly wants to attain the goal.*

**RUNGE, JEFFREY WILLIAM,** federal agency administrator; b. 1955; m. Ginny Runge; children: Emily, Will. B.A. U. South; MD, U. S.C., 1981. Diplomate Am. Bd. Emergency Medicine. Resident Charlotte Meml. Hosp. and Med. Ctr., 1984; faculty emergency medicine residency Carolinas Med. Ctr., Charlotte, NC, 1984; dir. Carolinas Ctr. Injury Prevention and Control; adminstr. Nat. Hwy. Traffic Safety Adminstrn. US Dept. Transp., Washington, 2001—05; chief med. officer US Dept. Homeland Security, Washington, 2005—, acting under sec. for sci. & tech., 2006—. Mem.: N.C. Med. Soc. (spkr.), N.C. Coll. Emerency Physicians (past pres.), Am. Coll. Emergency Physicians (trauma care and injury control com., rsch. com.). Office: US Dept Homeland Security 3801 Nebraska Ave Washington DC 20393

**RUNGE, KAY KRETSCHMAR,** library director; b. Davenport, Iowa, Dec. 9, 1946; d. Alfred Edwin and Ina (Paul) Kretschmar; children: Peter Jr., Katherine. BS in History Edn., Iowa State U., Ames, 1969; MLS, U. Iowa, 1970. Pub. svc. libr. Anoka County Libr., Blaine, Minn., 1971-72; cataloger Augustana Coll., Rock Island, Ill., 1972-74; dir. Scott County Libr. Sys., Eldridge, Iowa, 1974-85, Davenport (Iowa) Pub. Libr., 1985—2001, Des Moines Pub. Libr., 2001—. V.p. Quad-Cities Conv. and Visitors Bur., 1992—97, Quad-Cities Grad. Study Ctr., 1992—2001, Downtown Davenport Devel. Corp., 1992—2000, Hall of Honor Bd., Davenport Ctrl. H.S., 1992—95, Brenton Bank Bd., 1995—2001, Wells Fargo Bank Bd., 2001; steering com. Quad-Cities Vision for the Future, 1987—91, Humanities Iowa, 1993—2000, chair, 1998—99; bd. govs. Iowa State U. Found., 1991—; citizens adv. coun. Iowa State U., 1998—2000, Leadership Iowa, 1998—99; adv. bd. U. Iowa Sch. Libr. Sci., 1999—, adj. prof., 2000—01; devel. bd. Iowa State U. Found., 2000—; active Greater Des Moines Leadership, 2002—03; dean's adv. bd. Liberal Arts and Sci. Coll. Iowa State U., 2000—; bd. regents Iowa Pub. Radio Exec. Coun., 2005—; bd. dirs. River Ctr. for Performing Arts, Davenport, 1983—97, Iowa State U. Rsch. Pk., 1998—2000, Hamilton/Kaplan U., 2002—, Davenport One, Downtown Devel., 2000—01, Des Moines Operation Downtown, 2004—; chmn. bd. dirs. Am. Inst. Commerce, 1989—98. Recipient Svc. Key award Iowa State U. Alumni Assn., 1979, ALA/ALTA Nat. Advocacy Honor Roll award, 2000, Des Moines Women of Influence award, 2004, Carrie Chapman Catt Pub. Involvement award Iowa State U., 2006; named Quad City Panhellenic Woman of Yr., 1998. Mem. ALA (chmn. libr. adminstrs. and mgrs. div., fundraising sect. 1988, bd. dirs., Exhibits Round Table 2003—), Iowa Libr. Assn. (pres. 1983, Mem. of Yr. award 2000), Pub. Libr. Assn. (bd. dirs. 1990-99, pres. 2000-01), Iowa Edn. Media Assn. (Intellectual Freedom award 1984), Alpha Delta Pi (alumni state pres. 1978). Lutheran. Address: 126 Forest Rd Davenport IA 52803 Office Phone: 515-283-4288.

**RUNK, FRED J.,** retired insurance company executive; CFO Am. Fin. Group, Inc., Cin. Office: American Financial Group Inc 1 E 4th St Cincinnati OH 45202 Office Fax: (513) 579-2113.

**RUNKEL, PHILLIP M.,** archivist; b. Waukesha, Wis., Nov. 4, 1946; s. Joseph E. and Lydia R. Runkel. BA, Carroll Coll., 1969; MA, Marquette U., 1972; MLS, Peabody Coll., 1973. Archivist Marquette U., Milw., 1977—. Author: Alfred Lunt and Lynn Fontanne: A Bibliography, 1978; editor: Dorothy Day and the Catholic Worker Movement: Centenary Essays, 2001. Iraq Peace Team del. Voices in the Wilderness, Baghdad, 2003. Mem.: Midwest Archives Conf., Soc. Am. Archivists. Home: Apt 121 100 Corina Blvd Waukesha WI 53186 Office: Marquette Univ Archives 1355 W Wisconsin Ave Milwaukee WI 53233 Office Phone: 414-288-5903. Office Fax: 414-288-6709. E-mail: phil.runkel@marquette.edu.

**RUNKLE, BEATRIZ PAMELA,** medical educator, pediatrician; AB, Radcliffe Coll., Cambridge, Mass., 1969; MD, Georgetown U., 1975. Diplomate Am. Bd. Pediat., 1983. Resident pediat. Georgetown Univ. Med. Ctr., 1975—79; fellow neonatal-perinatal medicine Univ. Miami, 1980—83; asst. prof. pediat. Emory U. Sch. Medicine, Atlanta, 1983—86; clin. asst. prof. pediat. Georgetown U. Sch. Medicine, Washington, 1986—; neonatologist Va. Hosp. Ctr., Arlington, 1986—, med. dir. nurseries, 1991—2004. Fellow: Am. Acad. Pediat. Office: Va Hosp Ctr 1701 N George Mason Dr Arlington VA 22205 Office Phone: 703-558-6675.

**RUNKLE, ETHEL MONA,** artist; b. Davenport, Iowa, Dec. 4, 1921; d. Louis and Agnes (Jungjohann) Behrens; m. Karl Ehresman Runkle, Jan. 25, 1947; children: Carol Ann, Richard Louis. Grad., Shimer Coll., Ill., 1942; student, St. Ambrose Coll., Davenport, Iowa, 1943, Chgo. Art Inst., 1945, N.Y. Sch. Interior Design, 1955. Illustrator Rock Island (Ill.) Arsenal, Huntington Hist. Soc. Color, San Diego, 1942-44; stewardess United Air Lines, Chgo., 1944-46; craft dir. Westbury (N.Y.) Country Club, 1967; owner, operator Polynesian Fashions, Huntington, N.Y., 1967-71, The Woodshed, Escondido, Calif., 1975-77; art dir. Holland-Am. Lines, Seattle, 1986-87; artist San Diego, 1983—. Operator Hawaii Condo Rentals, San Diego, 1964—; art demonstrator San Marcos Art Assn., Calif., 1987, Escondido Art Assn., Calif., 1987, La Jolla Art Assn., La Jolla, Calif., 1986, So. Calif. Executed mural, 1987; represented in pvt. artist collections; exhibited in Nat. Watercolor Soc., L.A., 1987. Historian Clipped Wings, San Diego, 1985-86, Lloyd Harbor Hist. Assn., N.Y., 1966-71, Huntington Hist. Soc., N.Y., 1963-71, Soc. Preservation L.I. Antiquities, N.Y., 1967-70. Recipient Pres.'s Citation of Merit, Nat. Soc. Paint Casein & Acrylic, N.Y., 1988, Am. Watercolor Soc., Am. Soc. Marine Painters, San Bernadino Art Mus., award Escondido Art Assn., 1987. Mem.: Nat. Watercolor Soc. (cert., regional rep.), San Diego Watercolor Soc. (pres.), North County Vallecitos Art Assn. (pres.), Am. Soc. Marine Artists (bd. dirs.). Republican. Lutheran. Avocations: marine biology, snorkeling, travel, reading, history.

**RUNKLE, MARTIN DAVEY,** library director; b. Cin., Oct. 18, 1937; s. Newton and Ilo (Neal) R.; m. Nancy Force, Aug. 7, 1965; children: Seth, Elizabeth. BA, Muskingum Coll., 1959; MA, U. Pitts., 1964, U. Chgo., 1973. Library systems analyst U. Chgo., 1970-75, head cataloging librarian, 1975-79, asst. dir. tech. services, 1979-80, dir. library, 1980—2004. Sr. lectr. grad. library sch. U. Chgo., 1977-90. Fulbright grantee, 1965-67. Mem. ALA. E-mail: mrunkle183@comcast.net.

**RUNKLE, ROBERT CHARLES,** physicist; b. New Hartford, N.Y., July 30, 1976; s. Robert Eugene and Elizabeth Jean Runkle; m. Lauren Caslin, Sept. 22, 2001. BA, PhD, U. N.C., Chapel Hill, 2003. Rsch. physicist Pacific N.W. Nat. Lab., Richland, Wash., 2003—. Mem.: IEEE, Am. Phys. Soc. Office: Pacific NW Nat Lab 902 Battelle Blvd Richland WA 99352 Office Phone: 509-376-9216.

**RUNNALLS, DAVID,** think-tank executive; BA, U. Toronto, 1966; MIA, Columbia U., 1968. Sr. advisor Internat. Devel. Rsch. Ctr., UN Devel. Program; dir. Environment and Sustainable Devel. Program Inst. for Rsch. on Pub. Policy; pres., CEO Internat. Inst. for Sustainable Devel., Winnipeg, Man., Canada, 1999—, also bd. dirs. Bd. mem. China Coun. Working Group on Trade and Environment, Internat. Inst. for Environment and Devel., London, World Environment Ctr., N.Y.C., Pollution Probe; Can. bd. mem. IUCN; bd. mem. World Conservation Union; com. chair World Conservation Congress, Montreal, Canada, 1996. Office: Internat Inst for Sustainable Devel 6th Fl 161 Portage Ave East Winnipeg MB Canada R3B 0Y4

**RUNNELLS, BARBARA ANN,** technologist; b. Rush City, Minn., Dec. 21, 1956; d. Rudolph Anthony and Dorothy Carol Marolt; m. Gerry William Runnells, June 23, 1984; children: Amy JoAnn, Stacy Marie, Lisa Lynn. BA in med. tech., Coll. St. Scholastica, 1979. Cert. ASCP MT. Phlebotomist St. Mary's Hosp., Duluth, Minn., 1978—79; generalist, x-ray and EKG Mercy Hosp., Moose Lake, Minn., 1979—82; generalist Burlington Med. Ctr., Iowa, 1982—87, microbiologist, 1987—89, generalist, 1989—99, chemist, 1999—2000; generalist St. River Med. Ctr., Burlington, 2000—. Recipient Outstanding Vol., Girl Scouts U.S., Shining Trail Coun., Burlington, 2002. Mem.: ASCP. Democrat. Roman Catholic. Achievements include Developing a Point of Care Standards for Great River Med. Ctr. and lab. Avocations: scrapbooks, sports, crafts, quilting. E-mail: Brunne@Lisco.com.

**RUNNELS, BRIAN DAVID,** music educator; b. Freeport, Tex., June 25, 1957; s. Bruce Leland and Billie Jo (Price) R.; m. V. Beth Latham, Feb. 25, 1978; childlren: Emily, Daniel, Betsy. B Music Ed., Houston Bapt. U., 1981; M Music, Southwestern Bapt. Theol. Sem., Ft. Worth, 1985; D Musical Arts, U. Mo., Kansas City, 1992. Assoc. prof., chair dept. music Bemidji (Minn.) State U., 1995—2005; prof., chair dept. music Murray (Ky.) State U., 1995—2005; dean Coll. Arts and Humanities Houston Bapt. U., 2005—. Asst. condr. Houston Youth Symphony, 1979-81, Kansas City Civic Orch., 1985-87; condr. Burlington Civic Symphony, 2006—. Contbr. articles to profl. jours. Bd. dirs., v.p. for prodns. Murray Civic Music Assn., 1995—; bd. dirs. Kansas City Civic Orch., 1985-87, Headwaters Cmty. Music Ctr., Bemidji, Minn.,

1992-95, Minn. Alliance for Arts in Edn., Mpls., 1990-95. Named to Outstanding Young Men of Am., 1985. Mem. Coll. Music Soc., Tex. Assn. Deans Liberal Arts and Scis. (sec.), Music Educators Nat. Conf., Phi Mu Alpha Sinfonia, Sigma Alpha Iota, Pi Kappa Lambda. Baptist. Avocations: golf, computers. Home: 17119 Driver Ct Sugar Land TX 77478-4682 Office: Houston Bapt U 7502 Fondren Rd Houston TX 77074 Business E-Mail: brunnels@hbu.edu.

**RUNNELS, DAVID G.,** lawyer; b. Woodbridge, Eng., 1961; BBA with high honors in Fin., U. Tex., 1983, JD with honors, 1986. Bar: Tex. 1986. Ptnr., Energy Transactions Andrews Kurth LLP, Houston, mem. mgmt. com. Mem.: Tex. Gen. Counsel Forum (bd. dir.), Houston Bar Found. (bd. dir.), Tex. Young Lawyers, State Bar Tex., Phi Delta Phi. Office: Andrews Kurth LLP 600 Travis St Ste 4200 Houston TX 77002-3090 Office Phone: 713-220-4161. Office Fax: 713-238-7191. Business E-Mail: drunnels@andrewkurth.com.

**RUNNICLES, DONALD,** conductor; b. Edinburgh, Scotland, Nov. 16, 1954; Student, Edinburgh U., Cambridge U., London Opera Ctr.; DMus (hon.), U. Edinburgh, 1995. Music dir., prin. condr. San Francisco Opera, 1992—; prin. condr. NY Orch. of St. Luke's. Repetiteur Nat. Theatre, Mannheim, Germany, 1980—, Kapellmeister, 1984—, prin. condr., Hanover, 1987—, numerous appearances with Hamburg Staatsoper, former gen. music dir. Stadtische Buhnen, Freiburg/Breisgau, appearances with Met. Opera include Lulu, 1988, The Flying Dutchman, 1990, The Magic Flute, condr. Vienna Staatsoper, 1990—91, Sonome, 1996, debut Don Giovanni, Glyndebourne, 1991, Salzburg Festival, 1996, condr. London Symphony Orch., La Scale Milan Freischutz, Orch. Paris, Israel Philharm., Rotterdam Philharm., Seattle Symphony, Pitts. Symphony, St. Louis Symphony, Chgo. Symphony, San Francisco Symphony, Cleve. Orch., New World Symphony, Bavarian Radio Symphony, Billy Budd and the Ring, Vienna State Opera, 2001, Katya Kabanova, San Francisco, 2002, Schoenberg's Gurrelieder, London Proms, 2002, Tristan und Isolde, BBC Symphony Orch., 2002—03, (world premier) Doctor Atomic, John Adams, 2005, rec. artist Hansel and Gretel, Gluck's Orphée with San Francisco Opera Orch., 1995, Tannhäuser-Bayreuth Festspick, 1995, Harvey Milk with San Francisco Opera, 1996, Mozart Requiem, 2005—, opened Edinburgh Festival, 1994, 1996. Recipient Officer of Brit. Empire. Office: San Francisco Opera War Meml Opera House 301 Van Ness Ave San Francisco CA 94102-4509*

**RUNOWICZ, CAROLYN DILWORTH,** physician; b. Willimantic, Conn., May 1, 1951; d. S. Robert and Aline (Bergeron) Dilworth. BA, U. Conn., 1973; MD, Jefferson Med. Coll., 1977. Diplomate in ob-gyn. and gynecol. oncology Am. Bd. Ob-Gyn. Resident in ob-gyn. Mt. Sinai Hosp., NYC, 1977-81, fellow gynecol. oncology, 1981-83; instr., dir. divsn. ob-gyn. Albert Einstein Coll. Medicine, NYC, 1983-88, asst. prof. dept. ob-gyn., 1988-93, assoc. prof., 1993—98; dir. gynecologic and oncology, divsn. ob-gyn. Our Lady of Mercy, Bronx, NY, 1988; prof., dir. gynecol. oncology dept. ob-gyn. Montefiore Med. Ctr., NYC, 1998—2001; prof. Columbia U. Coll. Physicians and Surgeons, 2001—03; vice chmn. ob-gyn. St. Luke's Roosevelt Hosp., 2001—03; dir. Carole and Ray Neag Comprehensive Cancer Ctr., prof. ob-gyn., NE chair exptl. oncology U. Conn. Health Ctr., Famington, NY, 2003—. Presdl. appointee Nat. Cancer Adv. Bd., 2004—, chair, 2006—; lectr. in field. Author: Menopause Book, 1994, To Be Alive, 1995, Woman and Cancer, 1999, Answer to Cancer, 2004; contbr. chapters to books, articles to profl. jours. Galloway fellow Sloan Kettering Meml. Hosp., NYC, 1980. Fellow: Am. Coll. Ob-Gyn.; mem.: AMA, ACS (pres. 2005), Am. Gynecol. Club, Am. Cancer Soc. (pres. 2005—06), NY Obstet. Soc., Am. Gynecol. Obstetrics Soc., Soc. Gynecologic Oncologists, Am. Med. Women's Assn. Office: U Conn Health Ctr 263 Farmington Ave Farmington CT 06032 Office Phone: 860-679-2809. Business E-Mail: crunowicz@uchc.edu.

**RUNQUIST, LISA A.,** lawyer; b. Mpls., Sept. 22, 1952; d. Ralf E. and Violet R. BA, Hamline U., 1973; JD, U. Minn., 1976. Bar: Minn. 1977, Calif. 1978, U.S. Dist. Ct. (ctrl. dist.) Calif. 1985, U.S. Supreme Ct. 1995. Assoc. Caldwell & Toms, L.A., 1978-82; ptnr. Runquist & Flagg, L.A., 1982-85; pvt. practice Runquist & Assocs., L.A., 1985-99, 2005—, Runquist & Zybach LLP, L.A., 1999—2005. Mem. adv. bd. Exempt Orgn. Tax Rev., 1990—, Calif. State U. L.A. Continuing Edn. Acctg. and Tax Program, 1995—. Editor-in-chief bd.: ABA Bus. Law Today, 1994—2002; author: The ABCs of Nonprofits, 2005; contbr. chapters to books. Recipient Outstanding Lawyer award, ABA Bus. Law Sect., 1999. Mem. ABA (bus. law sect. coun. 1995-99, com. on nonprofit corps. 1986—, chair 1991-95, subcom. current devels. in nonprofit corp. law 1989—, chair 1989-91, subcom. rels. orgns. 1989—, chair 1987-91, 95-98, subcom. legal guidebook for dirs. 1986—, subcom. model nonprofit corp. act, partnerships and unincorp. bus. orgns. com. 1987—, sec. of taxation exempt orgns. com. 1987—, subcom. religious orgns. 1989—, chair 1995-97, 2005—, state regulation of securities com. 1988-99, ad hoc com. info. tech. 1997-2003, chmn., 1997-98, co-chmn. 1998-2002, sect. liaison to tech. coun. 1997-2000, co-chmn. subcom. non-exempt orgns. 1997-2003, corp. laws com. 1999-2005, subcom. guidebook for dirs. of closely held corps. chair 2000-04, liaison ALI/ABA principles of law of nonprofit orgns. project 2003—, standing com. solo and small firm practitioners 2004-05, co-chair state and local regulation subcom. 2003-05), Calif. Bar Assn. (bus. law sect., nonprofit and unincorp. orgns. com. 1985-92, 93-96, 97—, chair 1989-91, 2006—), Christian Legal Soc., Ctr. Law and Religious Freedom, Christian Mgmt. Assn. (dir. 1983-89). Office: 17554 Community St Northridge CA 91325 Office Phone: 818-760-8986. Business E-Mail: lisa@runquist.com.

**RUNTE, ALFRED,** environmental historian, consultant; b. Binghamton, N.Y., Apr. 16, 1947; s. Paul and Erika Runte; m. Christine Ann Salo, June 9, 1984. BA, SUNY, Binghamton, N.Y., 1969; MA, Ill. State U., 1971; PhD, U. Calif., Santa Barbara, Calif., 1976. Lectr. history and environ. studies U. Calif., Santa Barbara, 1976—78; fellowship specialist Smithsonian Instn., Washington, 1978—79; asst. dir., asst. prof. environ. studies Baylor U., Waco, Tex., 1979—80; asst. prof. history U. Wash., Seattle, 1980—87, adj. asst. prof. environ. studies, 1980—87; freelance cons. Seattle, 1987—. Pk. tng. technician, ranger historian Nat. Pk. Svc., Yosemite National Park, Calif., 1980—83; centennial nat. forests historian U. S. Forest Svc., Washington, 1989—91; bd. dirs. Ctr. Study of Environ., Santa Barbara; bd. trustees Nat. Parks and Conservation Assn., Washington, 1991—97; spkr. in field; freelance radio commentator. Author: Allies of the Earth: Railroads and the Soul of Preservation, Trains of Discovery: Western Railroads and the National Parks, 4 edits., National Parks: The American Experience, 3 edits., Public Lands, Public Heritage: The National Forest Idea, Yosemite: The Embattled Wilderness; mem. editl. bd.: Fundação O Boticário de Proteção à Natureza, 2002—, U. Alaska Press, 1992—96; contbr. over 300 articles to profl. jours. Recipient Frederick K. Weyerhaeuser award, Forest History Soc., 1978; fellow, Nat. Trust for Hist. Preservation and Colonial Williamsburg, Inc., 1971, Resources for Future, Inc., 1973—74; grantee, 1986; Herbert E. Kahler Rsch. fellowship, Ea. Nat. Pk. and Monument Assn., 1987. Mem.: Wash. Assn. R.R. Passengers, Nat. Assn. R.R. Passengers (nat. bd. dirs. 1974—82). Democrat. Presbyn. Avocations: travel, reading, gardening. Home and Office: 7716 34th Avenue NE Seattle WA 98115-4805 Office Phone: 206-525-3608. Home Fax: 206-526-5451. Personal E-Mail: alfred_runte@msn.com.

**RUNTE, ROSEANN,** academic administrator; b. Kingston, NY, Jan. 31, 1948; arrived in Can., 1971, naturalized, 1983; d. Robert B. and Anna Loretta O'Reilly; m. Hans-Rainer Runte, Aug. 9, 1969. BA summa cum laude, SUNY, New Paltz, 1968; MA, U. Kans., 1969, PhD, 1974; DLitt (hon.), Acadia U., 1989, Meml. U., 1990, U. Vest Timisoara, 1996, U. Arad, 2001; Assoc. (hon.), Moraine Valley C.C., 2003. Lectr. Bethany Coll., W.Va., 1970—71; lectr. adult studies St. Mary's U., Halifax, N.S., Canada, 1971—72; from lectr. to assoc. prof. Dalhousie U., Halifax, N.S., Canada, 1972—83, asst. dean, 1980—82, chmn. dept. French, 1980—83; pres. U. Sainte-Anne, Pointe-de-l'Eglise, N.S., Canada, 1983—88; prin. Glendon Coll., Toronto, Canada, 1988—94; pres. Victoria U., 1994—2001, Old Dominion U., 2001—. Bd. dirs. Banque Nat., Va. Advanced Carrier and Shipbldg. Integration Ctr., Le Groupe Jean Coutu, Va. Inst. Devl. Indsl. authority. Author: Brumes Bleues, 1982, Faux-Soleils, 1984, Birmanie Blues, 1993; editor: Studies in 18th Century Culture, vols. VII, VIII, IX, 1977—79, A Canadian in Love, 2000,

The Passionate Mind, 2000; lit. rev. editor: French Rev., 1988—94; editor: Lit. Rsch., 1994—97; co-editor: Man and Nature, 1982, Le Development Regional, 1986—87, From Orality to Literature, 1991, Lectures Canadiennes, 1993, Visions of Beauty, 1995, The Foundation for International Training: 25 Years of International Development, 2001; co-translator: Local Development, 1987; mem. editl. bd. Purdue Romance Lang. Series, 2001—. V.p. Can. commn. UNESCO, 1991—92, pres., 1992—96; vice-chair exec. bd. Found. for Internat. Tng., 1994—95, chair bd., 1995—2000; internat. adv. bd. Expo 2000, 1995—2000; v.p. Assn. Internat. des études québecoises, 1999—2001; mem. Internat. Women's Forum, 1998—; chair comm. internat. edn. Am. Coun. on Edn., 2004—06; chair accreditation com. visit NCAA, 2004—; commr. Southeastern Accreditation Commn., 2004—; chair Gottschalk Prize Com., 1994; chair publs. com. Hannah Found., 1989—92; vice-chair bd. Gardiner Mus., 1994—2001; chair prix du salon Livre Com., 1998; hon. life mem. UNESCO, 2003; bd. dirs. Assn. Med. Svcs., 1989—92; adv. bd. Nat. Libr., 1984—91; bd. dirs. Urban League, United Way, Va. Stage Co., Second Wind Dance Co., Hampton Roads Partnership, Greater Norfolk Corp. Decorated Order of Can., Ordre du Mérite France, Order Acad. Palmes; recipient Fr. Coppée award, French Acad., 1989, Queen Elizabeth Jubilee medal, 2002, Woman of Distinction award, Zonta Group, 2004, Environ. award, Norfolk Environment Commn., 2004, WFXN Trailblazer award, 2004, Lighthouse award, Elizabeth River Project, Tidewater Humanitarian award, Nat. Conf. Cmty. and Justice, 2006, Women of Distinction award, YWCA, 2006, Humanitarian award, NCCJ, 2006, Billbro award Servant Leadership, 2006; Regents scholar, SUNY, 1965, Title IV grantee, NDEA, 1968. Fellow: Royal Soc. Can., Soc. Study Values in Edn., World Acad. Arts and Scis.; mem.: Royal Coll. Physicians and Surgeons (exec. com. 1998—2002), Soc. for Study Higher Edn. (bd. dirs. 1988—90), Can. Soc. 18th Century Studies (pres. 1975—76), Atlantic Soc. 18th Century Studies (pres. 1972—76), Can. Fedn. Humanities (pres. 1982—84), Internat. Assn. of Comparative Lit. (treas. 1989—91, sec. 1991—94), Internat. Soc. 18th Century Studies (assoc. treas. 1983—87), World Parliament of Cultures, Club of Rome (exec. com. 1999—2006), Knights of Malta (grande dame 1991—), Phi Delta Kappa, Delta Kappa Gamma. Home: 5000 Edgewater Dr Norfolk VA 23508 Office: Old Dominion U Norfolk VA 23529 Office Phone: 757-683-3159. E-mail: rrunte@odu.edu.

**RUNTSCH, CLARENCE FREDERICK,** sculptor; b. Verdigre, Nebr., Mar. 13, 1923; s. Albert and Anna Marie (Czekay) R.; m. Alice Jean McCabe, Aug. 2, 1947 (div. Mar. 1977); 1 child, Teresa Ann Runtsch Duffett. Student, Texas A&M, 1942, Cumming Sch. of Art, Des Moines, 1946-48, Drake U., 1947, Kansas City Art Inst., 1948-50; BFA, U. Kansas City, 1950; student, Kansas City Art Inst., 1950-51; MFA, Univ. Tennessee, 1956. Artist/designer Mus. Natural History, Kansas City, 1951-52; illustrator Civil Svc., U.S. Army, Kansas City, 1952-54; chief designer Am. Mus. Atomic Energy, Oak Ridge, Tenn., 1954-76. Artist/sculptor ltd. edits. and commns., 1951—; principal works include collections at Smithsonian Inst., 1961, U.S. Marine Corps. Mus., 1993, Buffalo Bill Hist. Ctr., 2000, art in corp. and pvt. collections, U.S., Switzerland, Germany. Tech. Sgt. USMC, 1942-46. Recipient 5 Combat Stars USMC, Presdl. Unit Citation. Mem. Am. Soc. Arms Collectors, Smoky Mountain Gun Collectors (charter life mem., pres. 1964), Oak Ridge Art Ctr. (dir. 1956-59), Sertoma (charter pres. 1966—), Southeastern Antique Arms Collectors (charter life mem., dir. 1977—), Free and Accepted Masons (life mem.), Elks. Avocations: collecting and researching antique weapons, collecting indian beadwork. Home: 101 E Vanderbilt Dr Oak Ridge TN 37830-6113

**RUNYAN, CHARLES KENT,** education educator; b. Cape Girardeau, Mo., Oct. 20, 1950; s. Charles Shelby and Jean Murrill Runyan; m. Linda Sue Stear, Sept. 2, 1972; children: Charles Keith, Jaime Lynn Peterson, Jonathon Scott. BS in Lang. Arts, Marshall U., 1972, MA in Ednl. Adminstrn., 1974; EdD in Ednl. Leadership, W.Va. U., 1988. Tchr., coach Hurricane (W.Va.) H.S., 1972—89; prof. curriculum and instrn. Pittsburg (Kans.) State U., 1989—. Mem. steering com. Kansas City (Kans.) Tchg. Fellows, Kansas City, 1998—; co-dir. Kans. Tchr./Mentor Acad., 2000—; dir. Putnam City Induction Program, Winfield, W.Va., 1986—88; presenter in field; cons. numerous sch. dists. and higher edn. instns.; adj. asst. prof. Marshall U.; mem. nat. task force Nat. Coun. State Classrooms for 21st Century; mem. various coms. Kans. State Dept. Edn. Author: Developmental Induction Programs, 1991, Restructuring the American School, 1997; contbr. articles to profl. jours. Pres. Pittsburg Unified Sch. Dist. Bd. Edn., 1997—98; chmn. bd. dirs. Kans. Tchrs. Credit Union, Pittsburg, 2000—. Named Tchr. of Yr., Putnam C. of C., 1989. Mem.: NEA, Assn. Tchr. Educators, Midwest Ednl. Rsch. Assn., Phi Delta Kappa (pres., chpt. del., Svc. Key 1998, Ednl. Leadership award 1989). Avocations: basketball, golf. Home: 2203 S Homer Pittsburg KS 66762 Office: Pittsburg State U 117 Hughes Hall Pittsburg KS 66762 E-mail: krunyan@pittstate.edu.

**RUNYON, KEITH LESLIE,** lawyer, editor; b. Louisville, Oct. 3, 1950; s. Leslie Thomas and Marjorie Fillmore (Fisher) R.; m. Amelia Payne Sweets, Dec. 29, 1979; children: Amelia Brown Payne, Keith Leslie Jr. Student, U. London, 1971; BA cum laude, U. Louisville, 1972, JD, 1982. Staff writer Courier-Jour., Louisville, 1972-77, staff atty., 1984-86; staff atty., assoc. editor Louisville Times and Courier Jour., 1977-86, forum editor, 1986-90; editl. page editor, 1990-92; editor opinion pages, 1992-96; opinion editor, 1996—. Moderator Ky. Author Forum, 1996-. Editor: The Forum and Book Editor, 2001—. Nat. bd. dirs. English-Speaking Union U.S., N.Y., 1976-79, pres. Ky. br., Louisville, 1986-87; pres., dir. U Louisville Alumni Assn., 1987-93; mem. exec. com. Louisville com. on fgn. rels., 1985-87; Leadership Louisville, 1990-91; clk. Session Calvin Presbyn. Ch., Louisville, 1986-88; mem. St. Francis in the Fields Ch., Harrods Creek, Ky.; bd. dirs. Walden Theatre, Louisville, 1999-2001; mem. alumni bd. U. Louisville Brandeis Sch. of Law, 2001—. Recipient William E. Leidt award The Episc. Ch. of U.S., 1975, Roy Howard award (shared) Scripps Howard Journalists Nat. for Pub. Svc., 1976; named Alumnus of Yr., U. Louisville, 1991, disting. alumnus U. Louisville Sch. Law, 1996; Ctr. Fgn. Journalists fellow, 1993, Bingham fellow, 1995-96. Mem. ABA, Ky. Bar Assn., Louisville Bar Assn., Nat. Conf. Edit. Writers (editor The Masthead, 1994-96), Soc. Profl. Jours. (Outstanding Editl. Writing award, 1983, 84, 85, Outstanding Criticism award 1997, 98). Home: Nitta Yuma Harrods Creek KY 40027 Office: Courier-Jour and Louisville Times Co 525 W Broadway Louisville KY 40202-2206 Business E-Mail: krunyon@courier-journal.com.

**RUOFF, A. LAVONNE BROWN,** language educator; b. Charleston, Ill., Apr. 10, 1930; d. Oscar and Laura Alice (Witters) Brown; m. Milford Anthony Prasher, Aug. 19, 1950 (div. 1964); m. Gene W. Ruoff, June 10, 1967; children: Stephen Charles, Sharon Louise(dec.). Student, U. Ill., Chgo., 1948—50; BS in Edn., Northwestern U., Evanston, Ill., 1953, MA in English, 1954, PhD in English, 1966. Instr. to asst. prof. Roosevelt U., Chgo., 1961—66; asst. prof. English U. Ill., Chgo., 1966—69, assoc. prof., 1969—81, prof., 1981—94, prof. emerita, 1994. Interim dir. D'Arcy McNickle Ctr. for Am. Indian History, Newberry Libr., 1999-2000; editor Am. Indian Lives series U. Nebr. Press, Lincoln, 1985—; mem. Am. Lit. com. Internat. Exch. of Scholars, Washington, 1987-90, chair, 1989-90; NEH dir. Summer Seminars for Coll. Tchr. on Am. Indian Lit., 1979, 83, 89, 94. Author: American Indian Lit., 1990; Lit. of the Am. Indian, 1990; editor: The Moccasin Maker, 1987, 2d edit., 1998; Wynema, 1997; From the Deep Woods to Civilization and Indian Boyhood, 2001; (with Jerry W. Ward, Jr.) Redefining Am. Lit. History, 1990; (with Donald Smith) Life, Letters and Speeches of George Copway, 1997. Bd. dir. Am. Indian Coun. Fire Chgo., 1980-88. Recipient Lifetime Achievement award Before Columbus Found., 1998, Lit. MLA and Assn. for Study of Am. Indian Lits. award for Outstanding Contbr., 1993; MELUS award for Outstanding Contbn. to Multiethnic Lit., 1986; named Writer of Yr. for Annotation/Bibliography, Wordcraft Circle of Native Writers and Storytellers, 1999; Writer of Yr. for Series Editing Am. Indian Lives; Svc. award Wordcraft Cir. of Native Writers, 2003; NEH fellow, 1992-93, U. Ill. Chgo. Inst. for Humanities fellow, 1990-91; NEH Rsch. Divsn. grantee, 1981. Mem.: MLA (chair discussion group Am. Indian lit. 1990, chair lit. of people of color com. 2000—01, exec. coun. 2002—05, del. assembly organizing com. 2004—05, radio com.

2006—, award for lifetime scholarly achievement 2002), Multi Ethnic Studies Europe and the Ams., Assn. for Study of Am. Indian Lits., Multi-Ethnic Lit. in the U.S., Am. Studies Assn. Personal E-mail: lruoff@uic.edu.

**RUOTSALA, JAMES ALFRED,** historian, writer; b. Juneau, Alaska, Feb. 17, 1934; s. Bert Alfred and Eva (Karppi) E.; m. Janet Ann Whelan, July 31, 1987; stepchildren: Theresa Cowden, Douglas Whelan, Peggy MacInnis, Michael Whelan, Bruce Whelan, Charlene Rhodes. Student, U. Md., 1960—61, Basic Officers Sch., Maxwell AFB, 1964, Air U., 1985; AA, U. Alaska, Kenai, 1990; BA in Photography, Shaftesbury U., 1997, MA in Journalism, 2001. Asst. divsn. mgr. Macmillan Pub. Co., 1964-80; mgr. Denny's Restaurants, 1980-82; dir. mktg. and sales Air Alaska, 1982-89; state security supr., lt. Knightwatch Security, Juneau, 1990-96; ret., 1996. Archival dir. Alaska Aviation Heritage Mus., 1987-90. Author: Lockheed Vegas in Southeast Alaska, 1980, We Stand Ready, 1986, Eielson, Father of Alaskan Aviation, 1986, Pilots of the Panhandle, The Early Years 1920-1935, 1997, Alaska Wings, 2002, Alaskans Stood Ready, 2002; Alaska's Aviation Heritage Air Alaska newspaper; contbr. articles to profl. jours. Journalist 1st class USN, 1951-56; sgt. U.S. Army, 1958-64; 1st sgt. USAR, 1983-94; ret. USAR, 1994; col. Alaska State Def. Force, 1985-98, ret. Decorated Korean Svc. medal with 2 combat stars, Korean Presdl. unit citation, UN Svc. medal, Nat. Def. Svc. medal, Vietnam Svc. medal, Meritorious Svc. medal with 2 oak leaf clusters, Army Commendation medal with 4 oak leaf clusters; recipient USAF Brewer Aerospace award, Grover Leoning award, Paul E. Garber award, 1984-85, State of Alaska Gov.'s Cert. Appreciation, 1983, Mayor's Pub. Svc. award, Anchorage, 1985, Commendation from Gov. of Alaska, 1993, 94, 18th Session Alaska Legis. Cert. Recognition, 1993, 94, Cert. of Appreciation, Pres. Bill Clinton, 1994. Mem.: Am. Aviation Hist. Soc., Aviation and Space Writers Assn., Pioneers of Alaska (sec. 1988, v.p. 1989, pres. 1990, Igloo 33, treas. 1994—95, pres. 2002—, Igloo 6, Cert. Appreciation 1988, Alaskan of Yr. award 2000), Am. Legion (historian, post 25 commdr. 2002—04), Res. Officers Assn. (pub. affairs officer 1985—), VFW (sr. vice comdr. 1995, post quartermaster 1996—99, sr. vice comdr. 2000, post comdr. 2001—02), U.S. Naval Inst., Ret. Officers Assn., Masons. Lutheran. Home: 2723 John St Juneau AK 99801-2020 Personal E-mail: jruotsala@gci.net.

**RUPAUL, (ANDRE CHARLES),** model, singer; b. San Diego, Nov. 17, 1960; Driver luxury car business, 1978-82; on-air reporter Manhattan Cable, England; first face of M.A.C., M.A.C. Cosmetics, 1995. Albums include Freak Sex, 1985, RuPaul is Supermodel of the World, 1993, Foxy Lady, 1996, Star Booty, 1997, Ho Ho Ho, 1997, Red Hot, 2004, Workout, 2005; formed groups RuPaul and the U-Hauls, Wee Wee Pole; appearances include (TV) The Am. Music Show, (TV movie) A Mother's Prayer, 1995; (films) Crooklyn, 1994, Wigstock: The Movie, 1995, To Wong Foo, Thanks for Everything! Julie Newmar, 1995, Smoke, 1995, Red Ribon Blues, 1995, The Brady Bunch Movie, 1995, Blue in the Face, 1995, A Very Brady Sequel, 1996, Fled, 1996, An Unexpected Life, 1998, EDtv, 1999, But I'm a Cheerleader, 1999, Rick & Steve the Happiest Gay Couple in the World, 2000, The Eyes of Tammy Jane, 2000, The Truth About Jane, 2000, For the Love of May, 2000, Who is Cletis Tout?, 2001, Skin Walker, 2004, Zombie Prom, 2006; (video) B-52's Love Shack; co-host (with Michelle Visage) WKTU morning radio show, NYC, 1996; host The Rupaul Show, VH1, 1997. Recipient Vito Russo Entertainer Yr., Gay and Lesbian Alliance Against Defamation, 1999. Office: C/O Tommy Boy Records 902 Broadway Fl 13 New York NY 10010-6002*

**RUPEKA, ROBERT W.,** court administrator; b. Youngstown, Ohio; s. Robert E. and Donna J. Rupeka. BA in Polit. Sci./Mgmt., Case Western Res. U., 1993; MBA, Youngstown State U., 2005. Cons. Prodigal Media Co., Youngstown, Ohio, 1993-94; adminstr. Mahoning County Clk. of Cts., Youngstown, 1994-2000; ct. adminstr. Mahoning County Common Pleas Cts., Youngstown, 2000—06; v.p. Econ. Cmty. Devel. Inst., Youngstown, 2006—. Media/polit. cons., Youngstown, 1993-99. Mem., v.p. Mahoning County Alcohol and Drug Addiction Svcs. Bd., Youngstown, 1998-2001. Mem. Ohio Assn. for Ct. Adminstrn., Mahoning/Shenango Case Western Res. U. Alumni Assn. (pres. 1999-2000). Office: ECDI 20 W Federal St Youngstown OH 44503 E-mail: rrupeka@ecdi.org.

**RUPERT, DONALD WILLIAM,** lawyer; b. Clearfield, Pa., Oct. 15, 1946; s. Donald Lee and Dorothy Mae (Bonsall) R.; m. Patricia A. Rupert, June 21, 1969. BS in Chemistry, Miami U., Ohio, 1968; JD, Washburn U., Topeka, 1976. Bar: Tex. 1976, Ill. 1978, U.S. Ct. Appeals (Fed. cir.) 1978, U.S. Dist. Ct. (so. dist.) Tex. 1977, U.S. Ct. Appeals (7th cir.) 1981, U.S. Dist. Ct. (no. dist.) Ill. 1979, U.S. Supreme Ct., 1992. Assoc. Arnold, White & Durkee, Houston, 1976-78, Kirkland & Ellis, Chgo., 1978-83, ptnr., 1983-86; ptnr. Neuman, Williams, Anderson & Olson, Chgo., 1986-90; founding ptnr. Roper & Quigg, 1990-93; ptnr. Keck, Mahin & Cate, Chgo., 1993-96; ptnr. Mayer, Brown, Rowe & Maw, LLP, Chgo., 1996—; cons. USAF, Dayton, Ohio, 1974-81. Contbr. articles to profl. jours. Served to capt. USAF, 1968-74. Miami U. Undergrad. Rsch. fellow, 1967, Grad. Rsch. fellow, 1968. Mem. ABA, Am. Intellectual Property Law Assn., Tex. Bar Assn., Phi Kappa Phi. Democrat. Presbyterian. Home: 2310 Marcy Ave Evanston IL 60201 Office: Mayer Brown Rowe & Maw LLP 71 S Wacker Dr Chicago IL 60606

**RUPERT, ELIZABETH ANASTASIA,** retired dean; b. Emlenton, Pa., July 12, 1918; d. John Hamilton and Eva Blanche (Elliott) R. Diploma, Altoona Sch. Commerce, 1936; BS in Edn., Clarion State Coll., 1959; MSLS, Syracuse U., 1962; PhD, U. Pitts., 1970. Sec. Quaker State Oil Refining Corp., 1939-56; tchr., libr. Oil City Area Schs., 1959-61; libr. Venango campus Clarion (Pa.) U., 1961-62, prof. Sch. Libr. Sci., 1962-70, dean Sch. Libr. Sci., Coll. Libr. Sci., 1971-85; prof. emeritus, 1994. Interim pres. Clarion U., spring, 1977; acct. William Rupert Mortuary, Inc., 1948—88. Author: Pennsylvania Practicum Program for School Librarians: An Appraisal, 1970; mem. ad hoc edit. com. Pa. Media Guidelines, Pa. Dept. Edn., 1976, author (with others) Encyclopedia of Library and Information Science, 1984. Bd. dirs. Knox Pub. Libr., 1991-97; mem. Abscurf; mem. numerous bds. and couns. Church of God. Recipient Disting. Faculty award Clarion U. Alumni Assn., 1976, Disting. Svc. award, 1986, Disting. Alumni award, 1987, Zonta Internat. Women of Achievement award, 1987. Mem. Beta Phi Mu, Pi Gamma Mu. Republican. Home: PO Box H Knox PA 16232-0608

**RUPERT, HOOVER (LYNN HOOVER RUPERT),** minister, writer; b. Madison, N.J., Nov. 3, 1917; s. Lynn Hoover and Hazel L. (Linabary) R.; m. Hazel Pearl Senti, June 22, 1941; children— Susan (Mrs. William Newbry), Elizabeth (Mrs. Warren W. Wright). AB, Baker U., 1938; A.M., Boston U., 1940, M.Div. cum laude, 1941; student (summers), Garrett Bibl. Inst. and Northwestern U., 1942, Union Theol. Sem., 1943; D.D., Adrian Coll., 1952, Baker U., 1966; L.H.D., Millikin U., 1974. Ordained to ministry Methodist Ch., 1940; asst. pastor First Meth. Ch., Baldwin, Kans., 1936-38, St. Mark's Meth. Ch., Brookline, Mass., 1938-41; pastor Thayer-St. Paul, Kans., 1941-43, First Ch., Olathe, Kans., 1943-45; dir. youth dept. Gen. Bd. Edn. Meth. Ch., Nashville, 1945-50; pastor 1st Meth. Ch., Jackson, Mich., 1950-59, 1st United Meth. Ch., Ann Arbor, Mich., 1959-72, Kalamazoo, 1972-83; faculty dept. religion Fla. So. Coll., Lakeland, 1983-89; adj. faculty Wesley Theol. Sem., Washington, 1989-93. Dean Meth. Meth. Pastors Sch., 1959-65; mem. Jud. Coun. United Meth. Ch., 1968-88, sec., 1976-88, sec. emeritus, 1988; chaplain Epworth Summer Assembly, Ludington, Mich., 1984-98; Bible lectr. Asbury Meth. Village, 1990-2004. Author: Prayer Poems on the Prayer Perfect, 1943, Christ Above All (editor), 1948, Youth and Evangelism, 1948, Youth and Stewardship, rev. edit., 1960, Your Life Counts (editor), 1950, What Methodists Believe, rev. edit., 1959, John Wesley and People Called Methodists 1953, I Belong, 1954, And Jesus Said, 1960, Enjoy Your Teen-Ager, 1962, A Sense of What is Vital, 1964, The Church in Renewal, 1965, Divine Demands: God's Commandments, 1966, My People are Your People, 1968, Where is thy Sting?, Christian Perspectives on Death, 1969, What's Good About God?, 1975 God Will See You Through, 1976, An Instrument of Thy Peace, 1982, The High Cost of Being Human, 1986, Why Didn't Noah Swat Both Mosquitoes, 1993, Up to Your Armpits in Alligators, 1996; writer, syndicated weekly mag. column Accent on Living; newspaper feature Talking to Teens; other publs., periodicals, and newspapers. Trustee

Bronson Hosp., 1972-88, Adrian Coll., 1952-67, Asbury Meth. Village, 1996-2000; pres., bd. dirs. Youth for Understanding, 1970-83, Ann Arbor United Fund, YMCA-YWCA. Recipient Distinguished Alumnus award Boston U., 1969; Lucinda Bidwell Beebe fellow Boston U., 1941 Mem. World Meth. Council, Nat. Council Chs., Mark Twain Soc. Nat. Forensic League, Pi Kappa Delta, Alpha Psi Omega. Lodges: Mason, Rotary (Paul Harris fellow 1983), Chi Rho. Home: 403 Russell Ave Gaithersburg MD 20877-2811

**RUPP, GEORGE ERIK,** international relief organization executive; b. Summit, N.J., Sept. 22, 1942; s. Gustav Wilhelm and Erika (Braunoehler) R.; m. Nancy Katherine Farrar, Aug. 22, 1964; children: Katherine Heather, Stephanie Karin. Student, Ludwig Maximilians U., Munich, Germany, 1962-63; AB, Princeton U., 1964; BD, Yale U., 1967; post grad., U. Sri Lanka, Peradeniya, 1969-70; PhD, Harvard U., 1972. Ordained to ministry Presbyn. Ch. USA, 1971; faculty fellow in religion, vice chancellor Johnston Coll., U. Redlands, Redlands, Calif., 1971-74; asst. prof. Harvard Div. Sch., Harvard U., Cambridge, Mass., 1974-76, assoc. prof., 1976-77, prof., dean, 1979-85; prof., dean acad. affairs U. Wis., Green Bay, 1977-79; prof., pres. Rice U., Houston, 1985-93, Columbia U., NYC, 1993—2002; pres. Int. Rescue Comm., NY, 2002—. Bd. dir. Com. for Econ. Devel., Inst. Internat. Edn., InterAction. Author: Christologies and Cultures: Toward a Typology of Religious Worldviews, 1974, Culture Protestantism: German Liberal Theology at the Turn of the Twentieth Century, 1977, Beyond Existentialism and Zen: Religion in a Pluralistic World, 1979, Commitment and Community, 1989, Globalization Challenged: Conviction, Conflict, and Community, 2006; contbr. articles to profl. jour. Recipient Alexander Hamilton medal, Columbia U., 2002, Centennial medal for contbn. to soc., Harvard U. Grad. Sch. Arts and Scis., 2004, Gold medal, Nat. Inst. Social Scis., 2005, Woodrow Wilson award, Princeton U., 2006; Danforth Grad. fellow, 1964—71. Mem.: AAAS, Soc. Values in Higher Edn., Coun. Fgn. Rels., Am. Acad. Religion. Office: International Rescue Committee 122 East 42nd Street New York NY 10168

**RUPP, JOSEPH D.,** metal products executive; BS Metallurgical Engineering, U. MO. With Olin Corp., 1972—, v.p., manufacturing and engineering, 1985—96; pres. Olin Brass, Olin Corp., 1996—2001; v.p. Olin Corp., 1996—2001, exec. v.p., operations, 2001—02, pres. CEO, 2002—, chmn., 2005—. Office: c/o Olin 190 Carondelet Plaza Clayton MO 63105*

**RUPP, KALMAN,** economist; b. Budapest, Hungary, Apr. 7, 1948; s. Kalman and Ethel Rethy Rupp; m. Kathryn Schiavone Nelson, Oct. 22, 2004; children: Kristen Schiavone, Erin Schiavone; m. Agnes Romhanyi (div.); children: Susan, Judith. PhD, U. Econs., Budapest, Hungary, 1971, Columbia U., N.Y., 1982. Rsch. analyst Cent. Statis. Bur., Budapest, Hungary, 1971—72; rsch. fellow Inst. Econs. Hungarian Acad. Scis., Budapest, 1972—75; postdoctoral fellow Albert Einstein Coll. of Medicine, N.Y., 1978—79; sr. economist Westat, Rockville, Md., 1980—88, U.S. GAO, Washington, 1988—90, U.S. DHHS, Washington 1990—95, U.S. Social Security Adminstrn., Washington, 1995—. Rsch. cons. European Ctr. Social Welfare Tng. and Rsch., Vienna, 1975—76; lectr. Columbia U., N.Y., 1979, rsch. analyst, 1979—80. Author: Entrepreneurs in Red: Structure and Organizational Innovation in the Centrally Planned Economy, 1983, The Youth Labor Force, 1945-1995: A Cross-National Analysis, 1981 (named Disting. Book in Labor Econs., Princeton U., 1982); author and editor: Paying for Results in Vocational Rehabilitation: Will Provider Incentives Work for Ticket to Work?, 2003, Growth in Disability Benefits: Explanations and Policy Implications, 1998; contbr. articles to profl. jours. Recipient Commissioner's citation, Commr. Social Security, 1998, 2001, Excellence in Fed. Career award, Fed. Exec. Bd., 2001; fellow, NIMH, 1978; grantee, Ford Found., 1976. Mem.: Am. Econ. Assn., Soc. Govt. Economists (bd. mem. 1990—91), Nat. Acad. Social Ins. Achievements include design of first large-scale randomized social experiment to study effects of vocational rehabilitation on social security disability insurance beneficiaries; research in the economics of the Social Security Administration's disability programs; design of the methodology of randomized social experiments; one of the first to use administrative record data for policy evaluations. Office: Social Security Administration 500 E Street SW Suite 930 Washington DC 20254 Office Phone: 202-358-6216. Business E-Mail: kalman.rupp@ssa.gov.

**RUPP, RALPH RUSSELL,** retired audiologist, educator, author; b. Saginaw, Mich., Apr. 12, 1929; s. Martin Carl and Veronica Marie (Riethmeier) R. BA, U. Mich., 1951, MA, 1952; PhD, Wayne State U., 1964. Speech and hearing cons. Detroit Pub. Schs., 1955-60; exec. dir. Detroit Hearing and Speech Center, 1960-62; assoc. in audiology Henry Ford Hosp., Detroit, 1962-65; prof. audiology U. Mich., Ann Arbor, 1965-89; coord. audiology Eastern Mich. U., 1985-93, cons. in audiology, 1994—, U. Mich., 1994—2006, ret., 2006. Cons. St. Joseph Mercy Hosp., Ann Arbor, Ann Arbor VA Hosp., Mott Children's Health Ctr., Flint, Mich., Pontiac (Mich.) Gen. Hosp., U. Mich. Health Svcs.; pres. Detroit Hearing Ctr., 1966. Author: (with James Maurer) Hearing and Aging: Tactics for Intervention, 1979, (with Kenneth Stockdell) Speech Protocols in Audiology, 1980; contbr. articles to profl. jours. Served with Med. Service Corps, U.S. Army, 1953-55. Named Disting. Alumnus, Saginaw High Sch., 1981, Outstanding Grad., Wayne State U. Fellow Am. Speech, Lang. and Hearing Assn. (Editor's award); mem. Acad. Rehab. Audiology (past editor Jour.), Mich. Speech and Hearing Assn. (pres. 1954, Disting. Service award, past editor Jour, honor award). Home: 3163 Plymouth Rd Ann Arbor MI 48105-3203

**RUPP, SHERON ADELINE,** photographer, educator; b. Mansfield, Ohio, Jan. 14, 1943; d. Warren Edmund Rupp and Frances (Hanson) Christian. BA in Sociology and Psychology, Denison U., 1965; MFA in Photography, U. Mass., 1982. Teaching asst. in photography Hampshire Coll., Amherst, Mass., 1981; instr. photography Northfield (Mass.) Mt. Hermon Sch., 1982-83, U. Mass., Amherst, 1984, Holyoke (Mass.) Community Coll., 1986, 87-88; vis. asst. prof. photography Hampshire Coll., 1985, 87; vis. lectr. photography Amherst (Mass.) Coll., 1994. Guest artist, lectr. Boston Mus. Sch., Portland (Maine) Sch. Art, NYU, U. Mass., Deerfield (Mass.) Acad., Hartford Sch. Art/U. Hartford-Conn., Springfield Mus. Fine Arts, Mass., Bard Coll, N.Y., Mass. Coll. Art, Boston; others; guest lectr. Carpenter Ctr., Harvard U., Cambridge, Mass., 2000. One-woman shows include Tisch Sch. Arts NYU, 1987, Portland Sch. Art, 1989, Hart Gallery, Northampton, Mass., 1992, O.K. Harris Gallery, N.Y.C., 1992, Cleve. Mus. Art, 2000; two-person shows include Columbus (Ohio) Mus. Art, 1997—98, Springfield (Mass.) Tech. C.C., 1997; Exhibited in group shows at Mus. Modern Art, N.Y.C., 1991, 1999—, Springfield Mus. Fine Art, 1993, U. Mass., Amherst, 1993, Dirs. Guild, L.A., 1994, Manchester (N.H.) Inst. Arts and Scis., 1995, Weber State U., Utah, 1995, Grand Ctrl. Terminal, N.Y.C., 1995, Photog. Resource Ctr. 3d Biennial, Boston, 1995, DeCordova Mus., Lincoln, 2000—, Smithsonian Arts and Scis., Washington, 2001, Denison U. Art Gallery, Granville, Ohio, 2002, Around the House, A.N. Bush Gallery, Salem, Oreg., 2002, Boston Mus. Fine Arts, 2002—03, Guild Hall, East Hampton, N.Y., 2003, Smith Coll. Mus. Art, Northampton, Mass., 2004, Represented in permanent collections De Cordova Mus., Mus. Modern Art, N.Y.C., Fogg Art Mus. at Harvard U., Hallmark Collection of Photography, Kansas City, Columbus Mus. Art, The J. Paul Getty Mus., L.A., Mus. Fine Arts, Boston, Rose Art Mus. Brandeis U., Mead Art Mus. Amherst Coll., Smith Coll. Mus. Art, Danforth Mus. Art, Springfield Tech. C.C. Found., Carpenter Ctr. for Visual Arts Harvard U., The Smithsonian, Corcoran Galley of Art, Washington; photographs (including cover photo) in Double-Take Mag., winter 1998. Bd. dirs. Zone Art Ctr., 1987-94. Recipient Mass. Fellowship award in photography Artist Found., 1984, 87; visual artist fellow Nat. Endowment for the Arts, 1986, 94, Guggenheim fellow, 1990. Avocations: hiking, bicycling, writing. Home and Office: 364 Hatfield St Apt C Northampton MA 01060-1541 also: 3 The Lope Haydenville MA 01039 E-mail: sheron@crocker.com.

**RUPPAR, PETER GEOFFREY,** lawyer; b. Washington, July 15, 1944; s. Albert H. and Evelyn (Jurgensen) R.; m. Barbara Koenig; children: Andrea Lynn, Sharon Elaine. BS, Cornell U., 1966; JD, SUNY, Buffalo, 1973. Bar: N.Y. 1974, U.S. Dist. Ct. (we. dist.) N.Y. 1974. Confidential law asst. appellate div. 4th dept. N.Y. State Supreme Ct., Buffalo, 1973-76; assoc.

Duke, Holzman, Yaeger & Photiadis, Buffalo, 1975-80, ptnr., 1980—. Presenter in field. Contbr. articles to profl. jours. Assoc. mem. Erie County Local Emergency Planning Com., Buffalo, 1989-90. 1st lt. U.S. Army, 1966-69. Mem. NY State Bar Assn. (exec. com. environ. law sect., co-chair task force on agrl. environ. law), Erie County Bar Assn. (chmn. environ. law com. 1987-90). Republican. Office: Duke Holzman Yaeger & Photiadis 1800 Main Place Tower Buffalo NY 14202-3789 Office Phone: 716-855-1111. Business E-Mail: pruppar@dhyplaw.com.

RUPPE, ARTHUR MAXWELL, retired lawyer; b. Boone, N.C., Dec. 15, 1928; s. Arthur Monroe and Floye (Robinson) Ruppe; m. Ruth Marie Ledford; children: Ruth Carol, Sharon Marie, Arthur Maxwell, Jr., Susan Lunette. AA, Gardner Webb Coll., 1947; AB, U. N.C. Law Sch., 1950, LLB, JD, 1952. Bar: N.C. 1952, U.S. Dist. Ct. (ea. dist. N.C.) 1955, U.S. Ct. Mil. Appeals 1968, cert.: (mediator). Asst. staff, judge adv. U.S. Army, Ft. Bragg, NC, 1952—55; sole practice Fayetteville, NC, 1955—98; mediator, 1997—2003; ret., 2003. Served to 1st lt. U.S. Army, 1952—55. Mem.: ABA, Cumberland County Bar Assn. (pres. 1982—83), 12th Jud. Dist. Bar Assn., N.C. Bar Assn. (patron), K.P. Democrat. Baptist. Avocations: travel, reading, investing. Home: 336 Summertime Rd Fayetteville NC 28303-4658

RUPPENTHAL, KARL M., author, educator; b. Russell, Kans., Oct. 5, 1917; s. John P. and Viola (Whitaker) Ruppenthal; m. Irja Alice Autio, May 30, 1942 (dec. Mar. 1999); children: Sara, Stephen, Brian; m. Josephine Mason, Nov. 18, 2000. AB, U. Kans., 1939, LL.B., 1941, JD, 1968; MBA, U. Calif.-Berkeley, 1950; PhD, Stanford U., 1959. Bar: D.C., Kans., U.S. Tax Ct., U.S. Ct. Appeals (9th cir.), U.S. Supreme Ct. Reporter Russell County News, 1934-35; owner bookstore and restaurant, 1940-41; pilot TWA, 1942-68; UPS Found. prof., dir. Centre Transp. Studies U. B.C., Vancouver, 1971-84. Mem. TWA/ALPA System Bd. Adjustment, 1947-49; exec. v.p. Airline Pilots Assn., 1950; prof., dir. transp. mgmt. program Stanford, 1958-69, dir. European logistics mgmt. program, summers, 1969-71; Ryder prof. transp. U. Miami (Fla.), 1970; founder, editor Farwest Press Ltd.; dir. Aero Air, Inc., Hazleton Labs., Hazleton Nuclear Sci., Karloid Corp.; cons. Can. Ministry Transport, Am. Airlines, AllItalia, C.P. Air, Saudi Arabian Airlines, VASP, TWA, Air Transport Assn., Ethiopian Air Lines, Pacific Western Airlines, NASA, Boeing Co., World Bank, Govts. of Alta. and B.C. Author: Regulation, Competition and the Public Interest, Case Problems in Air Transportation, Canada's Ports and Waterborne Trade; founder, editor: Logistics and Transp. Rev.; cons. editor New Can. Ency.; contbg. editor The Nation, Ency of Mgmt. Pres. Palo Alto Friends of Library, 1952-58; mem. Palo Alto City Council, Calif., 1953-59, Unitarian-Universalist Ch. of Berkeley; pres. Karl and Alice Ruppenthal Found. Arts. Stanford Sloan fellow; recipient Nathan Burkham award in copywright law; Wilton Park fellow. Fellow Chartered Inst. Transport; mem. NAS (com. mem.), Acad. Logistics (founding), Am. Econ. Assn., Indsl. Relations Research Assn., Transp. Research Forum, Canadian Transp. Research Forum, Am. Judicature Soc., Am. Arbitration Assn. (nat. panel), Peninsula Funeral Soc. (founding bd. dirs.), Univ. Club, Masons, Phi Beta Kappa, Sigma Phi Epsilon, Beta Gamma Sigma. Home: 820 Euclid Ave Berkeley CA 94708

RUPPERSBERGER, CHARLES ALBERT, III, (DUTCH RUPPERSBERGER), congressman; b. Balt., Jan. 31, 1946; s. Charles Albert Jr. and Margaret (Wilson) R.; m. Kay Murphy, Dec. 28, 1968; children: Charles Albert, Jill Ann. BA, U. Md., 1967; JD, U. Balt., 1970. Bar: Md. 1972, US Supreme Ct. 1977. Social worker Balt. City Schs., 1967-69; claims adjuster US Fidelity and Guaranty Co., Balt., 1969-70; law clk. to presiding justice Balt. County Cir. Ct., Towson, 1970-72; asst. state's atty. Balt. County State's Atty., Towson, 1972-80; ptnr. Ruppersberger, Winter, Clark & Mister, Timonium, Md., 1980—94; mem. US Congress from 2nd Md. dist., 2003—. Chief of investigation div. State's Atty.'s Office, Towson, 1972-80; liaison Balt. County Police Dept. and Md. State Police, 1973-80. Coach, v.p. Cockeysville (Md.) Recreation Council, 1978—; campaign mgr. for senator Francis X. Kelly, Annapolis, Md., 1980-85; councilman Balt. County Council, 1985-94; legal council Balt. County Athletic League; pres. Topfield condominium Assn., Cockeysville, 1975-78, Greater Timonium Community Council, 1980—, co-chmn. fundraising U. Hosp.; bd. dirs. Timonium (Md.) Meth. Ch., 1984—. Recipient Appreciation award Balt. County Order of Fraternal Police, 1977, Cert. of Appreciation Balt. County Police, 1979; named one of Outstanding Young Marylanders Jaycees, 1979. Mem. Md. Bar Assn. (grievance com.), Balt. County Bar Assn. (chmn. bench-bar com.), Nat. Coll. Dist. Attys. (advisor 1974-80), U. Md. Alumni Assn. (v.p.), US Lacrosse Team. Lodges: Masons. Democrat. Methodist. Office: US Ho Reps 1630 Longworth Ho Office Bldg Washington DC 20515-2002

RUPPERT, JOHN LAWRENCE, lawyer; b. Chgo., Oct. 7, 1953; s. Merle Arvin and Loretta Marie (Ford) R.; m. Katharine Marie Tarbox, June 5, 1976. BA, Northwestern U., 1975; JD, U. Denver, 1978; LLM in Taxation, NYU, 1979. Bar: Colo. 1978, U.S. Dist. Ct. Colo. 1978, Ill. 1979, U.S. Tax Ct. 1981. Assoc. Kirkland & Ellis, Denver, 1979-84, ptnr., 1984-88, Ballard, Spahr, Andrews & Ingersoll, Denver, 1988-96; shareholder Brownstein Hyatt Farber & Strickland, P.C., Denver, 1996—. Lectr. U. Denver Coll. Law, fall 1984-92; adj. prof. law grad. tax program, 1993-94; sec. Capital Assocs., Inc., 1989-96; sec. Brothers Gourmet Coffees, Inc., 1995-2000; assoc. sec. Renaissance Cosmetics, Inc., 1996-98; sec. Skillset Software, Inc., 2000-01; asst. sec. Rhythms NetConnections Inc., 2000-01. Contbr. articles to profl. jours. Mem. ABA, Colo. Bar Assn. (mem. exec. coun. tax sect. 1985-89), Denver Bar Assn. Office: Brownstein Hyatt & Farber 410 17th St Fl 22D Denver CO 80202-4402 Office Phone: 303-223-1170. Personal E-Mail: jruppert53@comcast.net. Business E-Mail: jruppert@bhf-law.com.

RUPPERT, JOSEPH ALPHONSUS, music educator, language educator; b. Balt., Oct. 4, 1920; s. George John Ruppert and Anna Mary McGowan. BA, Cath. U., Washington, 1947; MA, Pitts. U., Pitts., 1962; D in Mus. Arts, Cath. U., Washington, 1970. Tchr. Ctrl. Cath. H.S., Pitts., 1947—62, St. John's Coll., Washington, 1962—70, Dade Pvt. Sch., Miami, Fla., 1971, Bishop Walsh H.S., Opa-Looka, Fla., 1972; postal clk. U.S. Post Office, Miami, Fla., 1974—86, ret., 1986. Contbr. articles to profl. jours. Mem. Pitts. Diocesan Liturgical Commn. Roman Catholic. Avocation: music. Home: 5921 Daybreak Ter Baltimore MD 21206

RUSCH, GERALD ALLEN, financial consultant; b. Milw., July 8, 1937; s. Herman A. and Martha H. (Gebauer) R.; m. Joan R. Ruehlman, Dec. 29, 1961; children: Susan, Heidi. BA, U. Wis., 1960. Area rep. Wis. Heart Assn., Milw., 1960-61, Tex. Heart Assn., Austin, 1961-63; commr. cons. Wis. Telephone, Milw., 1963-74; sole proprietor Rusch Ins., Eau Claire, Wis., 1974—; fin. rep., 1974—. Contbr. articles to mags. 1st lt. USAR, 1960-67. Named Agent of Yr. Eau Claire Gen. Agents and Mgrs. Assn., 1980. Mem. Nat. Assn. Fin. Profls., Million Dollar Roundtable, Phi Sigma Epsilon. Avocations: photography, walking, reading, classical music. Office: Northwestern Mut Fin Network 4233 Southview Dr Ste 1 Eau Claire WI 54701 Home (Winter): 14071 Brant Point Cir #621 Fort Myers FL 33919 Home (Summer): 4224 W Robin Meadows Ln Eau Claire WI 54701

RUSCH, THOMAS WILLIAM, manufacturing executive; b. Alliance, Nebr., Oct. 3, 1946; s. Oscar William and Gwen Falerne (Middleswart) R.; m. Gloria Ann Sutton, June 20, 1968 (div. Oct. 1979); children: Alicia Catherine, Colin William; m. Lynn Biebighauser, Jan. 17, 1981. BEE, U. of Minn, 1968, MSEE, 1970, PhD, 1973; MS in Mgmt. of Tech., U. Minn., 1993. Sr. physicist cen. rsch. 3M Co., St. Paul, 1973-77, rsch. specialist cen. rsch., 1977-79; project scientist phys. electronics div. Perkin Elmer Corp., Eden Prairie, Minn., 1979-83, sr. project scientist phys. electronics div., 1983-85, lab mgr. phys. electronics div., 1985-87, product mgr. phys. electronics div., 1987-88, sr. product mgr. phys. electronics div., 1988-93; v.p. product devel. Chorus Corp., St. Paul, 1993-94; pres. Creekside Techs. Corp., Plymouth, Minn., 1994—; co-founder Xoft MicroTube, Inc., Plymouth, 1998, chief tech. officer Fremont, Calif., 2001—02; prin. engr. Xoft, Inc., 2002—. Editor: X-rays in

Materials Analysis, 1986; co-author: Oscillatory Ion Yields, 1977; patentee in field. Recipient IR100 award for transfer vessel Rsch. and Devel. mag., 1981, IR100 award for energy analyser, 1985. Office: 49000 Milmont Dr Fremont CA 94538

RUSCH, VALERIE WILLIAMS, thoracic surgeon; b. NYC, Oct. 16, 1951; AB in Biochemistry, Vassar Coll., 1971; MD, Columbia U., 1975. Diplomate Nat. Bd. Med. Examiners, Am. Bd. Surgery, Am. Bd. Thoracic Surgery. Intern in gen. surgery U. Wash., Seattle, 1975-76, resident in gen. surgery, 1975-80, resident in cardiothoracic surgery, 1980-82; faculty assoc. dept. of thoracic surgery M.D. Anderson Cancer Ctr., Houston, 1982-83; thoracic surgeon Harborview Med. Ctr., Seattle, 1983-86, assoc. staff mem., 1986-89; thoracic surgeon Group Health Coop. of Puget Sound, Seattle, 1983-84; chief cardiothoracic surgery VA Hosp., Seattle, 1986-87; thoracic surgeon Univ. Hosp., Seattle, 1983-89; mem. courtesy med. staff Pacific Med. Ctr., Seattle, 1987-89; assoc. attending surgeon thoracic svc. Meml. Sloan-Kettering Cancer Ctr., N.Y.C., 1989-94, attending surgeon, 1994—, chief thoracic surgery, 2000—. Asst. prof. div. cardiothoracic surgery U. Wash., 1983-88, assoc. prof., 1988-89; asst. mem. divsn. clin. rsch. Fred Hutchinson Cancer Rsch. Ctr., Seattle, 1985-89; assoc. mem. Meml. Hosp., Meml. Sloan-Kettering Cancer Ctr., N.Y.C., 1989-94, mem., 1994—; assoc. prof. surgery Cornell U. Med. Coll., N.Y.C., 1989-95, prof. surgery Cornell U. Med. Coll., 1995—; mem. cancer clin. investigations rev. com. Nat. Cancer Inst., 1991-98. Mem. editl. bd. Jour. Thoracic and Cardiovasc. Surgery, 1992-, Jour. Clin. Oncology, 2004-; contbr. articles to profl. publs.; author abstracts in field. Grantee NIH, 1985-89, Deknatel Corp., 1986-87, Bard Electro Med. Systems, 1989, NeoRx Corp., 1989-90, Pfizer Corp., 1995-98. Fellow ACS (mem. bd. govs. 2002-), Am. Coll. Chest Physicians; mem. Am. Assn. Thoracic Surgery (mem. coun. 2006-), Soc. Thoracic Surgeons, Assn. Acad. Surgery, Soc. Surg. Oncology (mem. com. tng. 1993-95, mem. edn. com. 1993-95), Am. Soc. Clin. Oncology (mem. program com. 1993, 96, bd. dirs. 2002-05), Am. Thoracic Soc., NY Cancer Soc., Internat. Assn. Study of Lung Cancer, Am. Med. Women's Assn., Am. Bd. Thoracic Surgery (mem. bd. dirs. 2003-), Henry Harkins' Surg. Soc., M.D. Anderson Assocs., Gen. Thoracic Surg. Club, Alpha Omega Alpha. Office: Meml Sloan-Kettering Cancer Thoracic Surgery Svc 1275 York Ave New York NY 10021-6094 Office Phone: 212-639-8695. Business E-Mail: ruschv@mskcc.org.

RUSCH, WILLIAM GRAHAM, religious organization administrator; b. Buffalo, Dec. 23, 1937; s. William Godfrey and Hope (French) R.; m. Thora Joan Ellefsen, Sept. 2, 1967. BA, SUNY, Buffalo, 1959, MA in Classical Langs., 1960; MDiv, Luth. Theol. Sem., Phila., 1963; PhD, Oxford (Eng.) U., 1965; DD (hon.), Yale U., 1995. Ordained to ministry Evang. Luth. Ch., 1966. Assoc. pastor Evang. Luth. Ch. of the Holy Trinity, N.Y.C., 1966-68; asst. prof., chmn. dept. classical langs. Augsburg Coll., Mpls., 1968-71; assoc. exec. dir. div. Theol. Studies Luth. Coun. in the USA, 1971-78; adj. prof. The Gen. Theol. Sem., N.Y.C., 1978-82, 95; exec. dir., asst. to Bishop Evang. Luth. Ch. in Am., Chgo., 1987-96; dir. Commn. on Faith and Order Nat. Coun. of Chs. of Christ USA, N.Y.C., 1996-2001; exec. dir. Found. for Faith and Order, N.Y.C., 2001—. Vis. lectr. Waterloo Luth. Theol. Sem., 1969; adj. prof. theology Fordham U., N.Y.C., 1984-86, Luth. Theol. Sem., Phila., 1998—, St. John's Disting. prof., 2002-03; prof. Angelicum Pontificia U. San Tommaso, Rome, 2005-; mem. cen. com. World Coun. Chs., 1991-98, mem. standing com. faith and order commn., 1991—; adj. faculty Yale Div. Sch., 1999—; scholar-at-large Graymoor Ecumenical Inst., 2002-03; Jean-Marie Tillard disting. prof. Angelicum Pontificia U., San Tommaso, Rome, 2005-2006. Author: The Trinitarian Controversy, Ecumenism: A Movement Toward Church Unity; contbr. articles to profl. jours. Samuel Trexler fellow of N.Y. Synod Luth. Ch. in am., 1964, 65. Mem. Am. Acad. Religion, Am. Soc. Christian Ethics, Am. Soc. Ch. History, Internat. Assn. Coptic Studies. Lutheran. Avocations: book collecting, chess, tennis. Office: Found for Faith and Order 77 Park Ave New York NY 10016 Personal E-Mail: ruschgrif@worldnet.att.net.

RUSCHA, EDWARD, artist; b. Omaha, Dec. 16, 1937; m. Danna Knego, 1967; children: Edward Joseph. Studied at, Chouinard Art Inst., Los Angeles, 1956-60. Numerous vis. artist positions including UCLA, 1969-70; US Rep., Venice Biennale, 2005. Author: Twentysix Gasoline Stations, 1962, Various Small Fires, 1964, Some Los Angeles Apartments, 1965, The Sunset Strip, 1966, Thirtyfour Parking Lots, 1967, Royal Road Test, 1967, Business Cards, 1968, Nine Swimming Pools, 1968, Crackers, 1969, Real Estate Opportunities, 1970, Records, 1971, A Few Palm Trees, 1971, Colored People, 1972, Hard Light, 1978; noted for numerous graphite, gunpowder and pastel drawings, over 200 limited-edit. prints; producer, dir.: films Premium, 1970, Miracle, 1974; began showing works, Ferus Gallery, LA, 1963; first internat. show Galerie Rudolf Zwirner, Cologne, Germany,1968; works include (paintings) Standard Station, Amarillo, Tex., 1963; Annie, 1963, Smash, 1963, Electric, 1964, (mural) Miami-Dade Pub. Library, Fla., 1985; one-man exhbns. include Minn. Inst. Arts, 1972, Nigel Greenwood Ltd., London, 1970, 73, 80, Leo Castelli Gallery, N.Y.C., (10 shows) 1973—, Albright-Knox Art Gallery, Buffalo, 1976, Stedelijk Mus. Amsterdam, 1976, Ft. Worth Art Mus., 1977, San Francisco Mus. Modern Art, 1982, Whitney Mus. Am. Art, 1982, Vancouver Art Gallery, 1982, Contemporary Arts Mus., Houston, 1983, Los Angeles County Mus. Art, 1983, James Corcoran Gallery, Los Angeles, 1985, Gagosian Galleries, Chelsea, 2002, Beverly Hills, 2003, also others; exhibited in group shows at 64th Whitney Biennial, 1987, Centre Pompidou, Paris, 1989, Mus. Boymans—van Beuningen, Rotterdam, The Netherlands, 1990, Ghislaine Hussenot, Paris, 1990, Fundacio Caixa, Barcelona, Spain, 1990, Serpentine Gallery, London, 1990, Mus. Contemporary Art, L.A., 1990-91, Robert Miller Gallery, N.Y.C., 1992, Thaddaeus Ropac, Salzburg, Austria, 1992; represented in permanent collections including Mus. Modern Art, Los Angeles County Mun. Art. Whitney Mus. Hirshhorn, Washington, Miami-Dade Pub. Libr., Denver Pub. Libr., J. Paul Getty Mus., L.A., also others; restrospective of works on paper J. Paul Getty Mus., L.A., 1998; paintings exhibited, Gagosian Gallery, Beverly Hills, 1999, Metro Plots, N.Y., 1999; retrospective of career Hirshhorn Mus., 2000, Sculpture Garden, Washington, D.C., 2000, Mus. Contemporary Art, Chgo., Miami Art Mus., Modern Art Mus., Ft. Worth, Tex. Trustee Mus. Contemporary Art, L.A. Guggenheim fellow; Nat. Endowment Arts grantee. Fellow: Am. Acad. Arts & Sci.; mem.: Am. Acad. Arts and Letters (mem. dept. art). Office: 90 Gagosian Gallery 980 Madison Ave New York NY 10021-1848 also: 35 S Venice Blvd Venice CA 90291

RUSCHE, MARK C., lawyer; b. Marietta, Ga., Jan. 19, 1959; BA, Furman Univ., 1981; JD cum laude, Univ. SC, 1985. Bar: Ga. 1986. Ptnr., leader, real estate, fin. and investment group Alston & Bird LLP, Atlanta. Bd. of editors Comml. Leasing Law & Strategy. Mem.: Order of Coif. Office: Alston & Bird LLP One Atlantic Ctr 1201 W Peachtree St NW Atlanta GA 30309-3424 Office Phone: 404-881-7281. Office Fax: 404-253-8798. Business E-Mail: mark.rusche@alston.com.

RUSCHER, CHARLES B., finance educator, consultant; b. Freeport, N.Y., July 22, 1956; s. Thomas E. and Barbara A. B. Ruscher; m. Dianne S. Witters, Oct. 26, 1957; 1 child, Kristin R. BA in Bus. Adminstrn., Bridgewater Coll., 1978; grad., Campbell U., 1987; MBA, James Madison U., 1989; grad., East Carolina U., 1989; PhD in Fin., U. Ariz., 1999. Plant contr., fin. acct. Am. Brands, Crozet, Va., 1979—83; bus./personal fin. planner Am. Express Fin. Svcs., Charlottesville, Va., 1983—85; comml. loan/trust officer 1st Am. Bank Va., Harrisonburg, 1985—90; fin. instr. James Madison U., Harrisonburg, 1990—92; fin. cons. U. Ariz., Tucson, 1992—95; fin. prof. James Madison U., Harrisonburg, 1995—99, U. Ariz., Tucson, 1999—; fin. cons., interim CFO Ardext Techs., Tucson, 2001. Fin. cons. Cruscher Fin. Cons. Svcs., Tucson, 1990—; dir. Small Bus. Devel. Ctr. Bd., Tucson, 1990—; trainer Intrados Internat. Mgmt. Group, Fed. Fin. Instns. Exam. Coun., 1991. Dir. Bridgewater (Va.) Coll. Estate Planning Bd., 1986—87; panelist Bus. Devel. Fin. Corp. Summit, Tucson, 2000. Fellow: Eller Entrepreneurship Ctr.; mem.: Fin. Mgmt. Assn. Internat. (faculty advisor 1990—), Beta Gamma Sigma

(treas. 1992). Avocations: travel, hiking, reading, reading financial journals and books. Home: 5789 N Camino Del Sol Tucson AZ 85718 Office: U Ariz Dept Fin McClelland Hall 315R Tucson AZ 85721 E-mail: ruscher@bpa.arizona.edu.

RUSCIO, KENNETH PATRICK, academic administrator, political science professor; b. Red Bank, NJ; BA, Washington and Lee U., 1976; MPA, Syracuse U., 1979, PhD, 1983. Asst. prof. social sci. and policy studies Worcester Polytechnic Inst., 1985—87; asst. prof. politics Washington and Lee U., 1987—94, dean Freshman, 1987—94, assoc. dean Williams Sch. Commerce, Econs. and Politics, 1991—98, assoc. prof., 1994—2000, prof., 2000—02, acting assoc. dean, 2001—02, pres., 2006—; dean Jepson Sch. Leadership Studies, U. Richmond, 2002—06. Contbr. articles to profl. jours. Mem.: Am. Conf. of Academic Deans, Assn. Am. Colls. and Univs., Internat. Leadership Assn., Am. Polit. Sci. Assn. Office: Washington and Lee U Office of Pres Lexington VA 24450-0303*

RUSCONI, PAOLO, pediatric cardiologist; arrived in U.S., 1989; s. Camillo Rusconi and Enrica Bodega. MD, U. Pavia, Italy, 1982. Lic. cardiology U. of Milan, pediats. Am. Bd. Pediats., pediat. cardiolgy Am. Bd. Pediat. Cardiology, Flex, cert. Fgn. Med. Grad. Exam. in Med. Sci. Intern Ospedale di Lecco, 1982—83; cardiology resident Ospedali Riuniti di Bergamo, Italy, 1984—87; rsch. fellow Brompton Hosp., London, 1987—88; sr. ho. officer in pediats. Riverside Health Authority, London, 1988—89; pediat. resident Riley Hosp. Children Ind. U. Med., Indpls., 1990—93; pediat. cardiology fellow U. Miami, Fla., 1993—96, asst. prof. pediats., 1996—2006; assoc. prof. pediats. Miller Sch. Medicine U. Miami, 2006—. Med. dir. pediat. heart failure and cardiac transplant Miller Sch. of Medicine, U. of Miami, 1996—. Contbr. scientific papers to profl. jours. Lt. Italian Med. Corps., 1983—84. Mem.: Am. Coll. of Cardiology, Internat. Soc. of Heart and Lung Transplantation. Roman Catholic. Achievements include development of new treatment in the management of heart failure in children. Office: Univ of Miami PO Box 016960 (R-76) Miami FL 33101 Office Phone: 305-585-8115. Office Fax: 305-324-6012. Business E-Mail: p.rusconi@miami.edu.

RUSH, ANDREW WILSON, artist; b. Detroit, Sept. 24, 1931; s. Harvey Ditman and Mary Louise (Stalker) R.; m. Jean Cochran, Apr., 1957; children: Benjamin, Samuel, Joseph, Margaret; m. Ann Woodin, Oct., 1978. B.F.A. with honors, U. Ill., 1953; M.F.A., U. Iowa, 1958. Asso. prof. art U. Ariz., 1959-69; co-dir. Rockefeller Found. Indian Arts Project, 1960-64; vis. artist, artist-in-residence Ohio State U., 1970, U. Ark., 1972, Colo. Coll., 1973-74; resident mem. Rancho Linda Vista, Community of the Arts, Oracle, Ariz., 1969—; founder, dir. The Drawing Studio, Tucson, 1992—. One-man shows include Carlin Galleries, Ft. Worth, 1973, Graphics Gallery, Tucson, 1972, 75, Tucson Art Inst., 1984, Cruzitas Gallery, San Antonio, 1996, U. Ariz. Mus. Art, 2003, Davis-Dominguez Gallery, Tucson, 2003; exhibited in group shows at World's Fair, N.Y.C., 1964, USIS exhbns., Europe, Latin Am., 1960-65; represented in permanent collections Libr. of Congress, Uffizzi Mus., Dallas Mus., Ft. Worth Mus., Seattle Mus., Free Libr., Phila.; illustrator: Andrew Rush on Oliver Wendell Holmes, 1973, Rule of Two (Ann Woodin), 1984, Voice Crying in the Wilderness (Edward Abbey), 1990, Ask Marilyn, 1992 (pub. art winner 1995), Voice of the Borderlands, 2005; designer The Tucson Gateway Project, 1998 Served with USMC, 1953-55. Fulbright grantee, 1958-59 Address: Rancho Linda Vista O M Star Rte 2360 Oracle AZ 85623 E-mail: awrush@earthlink.net.

RUSH, AUGUSTUS JOHN, psychiatrist, educator; b. Glen Ridge, N.J., Dec. 15, 1942; s. Augustus John Jr. and Helen Rush; 1 child, Matthew; m. Dee Miller, May 31, 1986; 1 child, Augustus John III. AB in Biochemistry cum laude, Princeton U., 1964; MD, Columbia U., 1968. Intern Northwestern U., Chgo., 1968-69; resident U. Pa., Phila., 1972-75; asst. prof. U. Okla. Health Scis. Ctr., Oklahoma City, 1975-78; assoc. prof. U. Tex. Southwestern Med. Ctr., Dallas, 1978-83, Betty Jo Hay prof., 1983-88, Betty Jo Hay Disting. Chair in Mental Health, 1988—. Author: Beating Depression, 1983; co-author: Cognitive Therapy of Depression, 1979, Cognitive Therapy of Depressed Adolescents, 1994; editor: Short-Term Psychotherapies for Depression, 1982; co-editor: Depression: Basic Mechanisms Diagnosis and Treament, 1986—; assoc. editor Biol. Psychiatry, 1994-97, sr. editor, 2004-. Fellow Am. Psychiat. Assn., Am. Coll. Psychiatrists, Am. Coll. Neuropsychopharmacology; mem. Soc. for Psychotherapy Rsch. (pres. 1984-85), Soc. for Biol. Psychiatry (sec.-treas. 1990-94, v.p. 1994, pres. 1996-97, treas. 1998-). Office: Ste 834 6363 Forest Park Rd Dallas TX 75390-9086 Office Phone: 214-648-4601. Business E-Mail: john.rush@utsouthwestern.edu.

RUSH, BOBBY L., congressman; b. Albany, Ga., Nov. 23, 1946; m. Carolyn Rush; 5 children. BA in Polit. Sci., Roosevelt U., 1974; MA in Polit. Sci., U. Ill., 1992; MA in Theology, McCormick Theolocal Seminary, 1998. Fin. planner Sanmar Fin. Planning Corp.; assoc. dean Daniel Hale Williams U.; ins. agent Prudential Ins. Co.; city alderman Chgo., 1984-93; dem. committeeman Chgo. 2nd ward, 1984, 88, Central Ill., 1990; dep. chmn. Ill. Dem. Party, 1990; mem. US Congress from 1st Ill. Dist., 1993—. Chmn. Environ. Protection, Energy and Pub. Utilities com., Budget and Govt. Operations com., Capitol Devel. com., Hist. Landmark Preservation Com.; mem. Commerce com. Former mem. Student Non-Violent Coordinating com.; founder Ill. Black Panther Party; past coord. Free Breakfast for Children, Free Med. Clinic. With US Army, 1963-68. Recipient Ill. Enterprise Zone award Dept. Commerce and Community, Operation PUSH Outstanding Young Man award, Henry Booth House Outstanding Community Svc. award, Outstanding Bus. and Profl. Achievement award South End Jaycees, Chgo. Black United Communities Disting. Polit. Leadership award; named one of Most Influential Black Americans, Ebony mag., 2006. Democrat. Office: US Ho Reps 2416 Rayburn Ho Office Bldg Washington DC 20515-1301 Office Phone: 202-225-4372. Office Fax: 202-226-0333.*

RUSH, CURT STEFAN, lawyer; b. 1955; BA in Philosophy, Hunter Coll., 1981; JD cum laude, Bklyn. Law Sch., 1984. Bar: NY 1985. Assoc. Shereff, Friedman, Hoffman & Goodman, P.A., NYC; corp. counsel Image Bank, Inc., 1990—93, Globe Comm. Corp., Boca Raton, Fla., 1993—96; gen. counsel Global DirectMail Corp., Port Washington, NY; sec. Systemax, Inc., Port Washington, NY, 1996—; gen. counsel, 1996—. Office: Systemax Inc 11 Harbor Park Dr Port Washington NY 11050 Office Phone: 516-608-7000. Office Fax: 516-625-0038.

RUSH, DOMENICA MARIE, health facilities administrator; b. Gallup, N.Mex., Apr. 10, 1937; d. Bernardo G. and Guadalupe (Milan) Iorio; m. W. E. Rush, Jan. 5, 1967. Diploma, Regina Sch. Nursing, Albuquerque, 1958. RN N.Mex.; lic. nursing home adminstr.; cert. legal nurse cons., 2004. Charge nurse, house supr. St. Joseph Hosp., Albuquerque, 1958-63; dir. nursing Cibola Hosp., Grants, 1963-64; supr. operating room, dir. med. seminars Carrie Tingley Crippled Children's Hosp., Truth or Consequences, N.Mex., 1964-73; adminstr. Sierra Vista Hosp., Truth or Consequences, 1974-88, pres. 1989—90; clin. nursing mgr. U. N.Mex. Hosp., 1994-99; adminstr. Nor-Lea Hosp., Lovington, N.Mex., 1990-94; with regional ops. divsn. Presbyn. Healthcare Svcs., Albuquerque, 1994—, regional ops., 1994—2003; adminstr. Sierra Vista Hosp., Truth or Consequences, N.Mex., 1995—2003; regional adminstr. Presbyn. Healthcare Svcs., 2003—04; founder Rush Health Consulting Svc., 2004—; adminstr. Trans Health, Inc., Albuquerque, 2006—; intern adminstrn. and spl. projects Presbyn. Healthcare Svcs., Albuquerque, 2005. Bd. dirs. N.Mex. Blue Cross/Blue Shield, 1977-88, chmn. hosp. relations com., 1983-85, exec. com. 1983—; bd. dirs. Region II Emergency Med. Svcs. Originating bd. SW Mental Health Ctr., Sierra County, N.Mex., 1975; chmn. Sierra County Personnel Bd., 1983—. Recipient Frank Gabriel award N.Mex. Hosp. Health Svc. Assn., 2003, Govenor's award Emergency Med. Svcs., 2003, Govs.award for Outstanding Woman, N. Mex., 2004; Named Lea County Outstanding Woman, N.Mex. Commn. on Status of Women, Woman of Yr. for Lea County, N.Mex.; 1993. Mem. Am. Coll. Health Care Adminstrs., Sierra County C. of C. (bd. dirs. 1972, 75-76, svc. award 1973, Businesswoman of the Yr. 1973-74), N.Mex. Hosp. Assn. (bd. dirs., sec.-treas., pres.-elect, pres. 1977-88, pres. 1980-81, exec. com. 1980-83, 84-85, recipient meritorius svc. award 1988), N.Mex. So. Hosp.

Coun. (sec. 1980-81, pres. 1981-82), Am. Hosp. Assn. (N.Mex. del. 1984-88, regional adv. bd. 1984-88). Republican. Roman Catholic. Avocations: raising thoroughbred horses, cooking. Home: 1100 N Riverside Dr Truth Or Consequences NM 87901-9789 Office Phone: 505-740-2334. Personal E-mail: brush@zianet.com. E-mail: domrush@gmail.com.

**RUSH, DORIE MAE,** nursing educator; b. Assiniboia, Sask., Can., May 3, 1970; d. June and Steve Yorga (Stepfather); m. Tark Morgan Rush, Mar. 22, 2003; children: Hailey Madison Caragata, Stone Morgan, Brooke Ashlyn Caragata, Austin Talon. DON, Sask. Inst. Applied Arts and Sci., Regina, 1990; BSN, U. Phoenix, Tucson, 2003; postgrad., U. Phoenix, Yuma, Ariz., 2004—. Cert. inpatient OB, NCC, Ariz., fetal monitoring, NCC, Ariz. Unit-based educator Yuma Regional Med. Ctr., 2000—, resource coord., 1997—2000, staff nurse, 1993—97; OB flight nurse Suncare Air Ambulance, Yuma, 1999—2000; part-time Ariz. Western Coll., Yuma, 2002—. Fetal monitor instr. Assn. Women's Health Obstetric and Neonatal Nurses, Yuma, 2003—. Author: (poster presentation) Dynamic New Grad Orientation to Labor and Delivery. Named Yuma's Best Nurse, City of Yuma, 2002. Mem.: AWHONN. Office: Yuma Regional Med Ctr 2400 S Ave A Yuma AZ 85364-7127 Office Phone: 928-336-3020. Home Fax: 928-329-7706; Office Fax: 928-336-7453. Personal E-mail: dmrush@adelphia.net. E-mail: drush@yumaregional.org.

**RUSH, GEOFFREY,** actor; b. Toowomba, Queensland, Australia, July 6, 1951; m. Jane Menelaus, 1988; children: Angelica, James. diploma, LittD, U. Queensland. Actor: (plays) Wrong Side of the Moon, 1971, Lock Up Your Daughters, 1972, Assault With a Deadly Weapon, 1972, Twelfth Night, 1972, 1983, 1984, Ruling Class, 1972, You're a Good Man Charlie Brown, 1972, Puss in Boots, 1972, Juno and the Paycock, 1973, Expresso Bongo, 1973, National Health, 1973, The Imaginary Invalid, 1973, Suddenly at Home, 1973, Aladdin, 1973, Hamlet on Ice, 1973, Godspell, 1974, The Rivals, 1974, The Philanthropist, 1974, Present Laughter, 1974, Jack and the Beanstalk, 1975—77, King Lear, 1978, 1988, Point of Departure, 1978, Clowneroonies, 1978, Waiting for Godot, 1979, On Our Selection, 1979, Teeth and Smiles, 1980, Revenger's Tragedy, 1981, No End of Blame, 1982, You Can't Take It With You, 1981, A Midsummer Night's Dream, 1982, 1983, Mother Courage, 1982, Silver Lining, 1982, The Prince of Homburg, 1982, Royal Show, 1983, Blood Wedding, 1983, Netherwood, 1983, 1984, The Marriage of Figaro, 1983, Pal Joey, 1983, The Blind Giant is Dancing, 1983, Sunrise, 1983, Benefactors, 1986, On Parliament Hill, 1987, Shepherd on the Rocks, 1987, The Winter's Tale, 1987, Tristram Shandy-Gent, 1988, Les Enfants du Paradis, 1988, The Importance of Being Earnest, 1988, 1990—91, 1992, Troilus & Cressida, 1989, The Diary of a Madman, 1989, 1990, 1992 (Variety Club award for Stage Actor of yr., 1989, Sydney Theatre Critics Cir. award for Most Outstanding Performance, 1989, Victorian Green Rm. award for Best Actor, 1990), Marat/Sade, 1990, The Comedy of Errors, 1990, The Government Inspector, 1991, Uncle Vanya, 1992, The Dutch Courtesan, 1993, Oleanna, 1993, Hamlet, 1994, 1995; (films) Hoodwink, 1980, Starstruck, 1981, Twelfth Night, 1985, On Our Selection, 1994, Five Easy Pizzas, 1994, Children of the Revolution, 1996, Shine, 1996 (BAFTA award Best Actor, 1997, Golden Globe award for Best Performance in Motion Picture, 1997, Screen Actors Guild award for Outstanding Performance, 1997, Oscar award for Best Actor, 1997), Oscar & Lucinda, 1997, Shakespeare in Love, 1998 (BAFTA award Best Supporting Actor, 1999), Elizabeth, 1998, Mystery Men, 1999, House on Haunted Hill, 1999, Quills, 2000 (NY Film Critics Online award for best actor, 2000), The Tailor of Panama, 2001, Lantana, 2001, Frida, 2002, The Banger Sisters, 2002, Swimming Upstream, 2003, Ned Kelly, 2003, Finding Nemo (voice), 2003, Pirates of the Caribbean: The Curse of the Black Pearl, 2003, Intolerable Cruelty, 2003, The Life and Death of Peter Sellers, 2004 (Golden Globe award for best actor miniseries or TV movie, 2005, Screen Actors Guild Award for best actor in a TV movie or miniseries, 2005, Emmy award for outstanding lead actor in a miniseries or a movie, 2005), Munich, 2005, Candy, 2006, Pirates of the Caribbean: Dead Man's Chest, 2006; (TV series) Consumer Capers, 1979—81, Menotti, 1980—81, The Burning Piano, 1992, Mercury, 1996; dir.: (plays) Clowneroonies, 1978—80, Animal Acts, 1984—86, Teen Ages, 1984—86, Carols-By-Lazerlight, 1984—86, The 1985 Scandals, 1986, Pearls Before Swine, 1986, Pell Mell, 1986, 1987, 1988, The Merry Wives of Windsor, 1987, The Popular Mechanicals, 1987, 1988, 1992, Les Enfants du Paradis, 1989, The Wolf's Banquet, 1989, Popular Mechanicals, 1992, Aristophane's Frogs, 1992; co-translator The Government Inspector, 1991, writer (with George Whaley) (TV film) Clowning Around, 1992, (with John Clarke) (play) Aristophane's Frogs, 1992, Call Me Sal, 1996, Children of the Revolution, 1997, Les Misérables, 1998. Office: Creative Artists Agy 9830 Wilshire Blvd Beverly Hills CA 90212-1804*

**RUSH, HERMAN E.,** television executive; b. Phila., June 20, 1929; s. Eugene and Bella (Sacks) R.; m. Joan Silberman, Mar. 18, 1951; children: James Harrison, Mandie Susan. BBA, Temple U., 1950. With Ofcl. Films, 1951-57; owner Flamingo Films, 1957-60; with Creative Mgmt. Assocs., NYC, 1960-71, pres. TV divsn., 1964-71, exec. v.p parent co., dir., 1964-71; ind. prodr., 1971-75; prodr. Wolper Orgn., 1975-76; pres. Herman Rush Assocs., Inc. (Rush-Flaherty Agy. subs.), 1977-78, Marble Arch TV, LA, 1979-80, Columbia Pictures TV, Burbank, Calif., 1980-87; chmn., CEO Coca-Cola Telecom., 1987-88, Rush Assocs., Inc., Burbank, 1988—; Katz/Rush Entertainment Group, Beverly Hills, Calif., 1990-96, New Tech. Entertainment, LLC, Beverly Hills, 1996—, Internet Content Provider East Cap. Fin. Corp., chmn. emeritus; mng. ptnr. Media Consulting Assocs. CEO Infotainment Internat., Inc.; pres., chmn. Royal Animated Art, Inc.; Entertainment Industries Coun.; co-owner, exec. prodr. The Montel Williams Talk Show, 1991-2006; mem. bd. advisors Smart Video Techs., Inc.; CEO Creative Conteal Providers, LLC Trustee Sugar Ray Robinson Youth Found., 1967-75; pres. Retarded Infant Svcs., N.Y.C., 1957-63; bd. dirs. U.S. Marshall's Svc. Found., Just Say No Found.; conferee White House Conf. for a Drug Free America, 1987, 88. Mem. Acad. TV Arts and Scis., Hollywood Radio and TV Soc., Producers Caucus. Clubs: Friars, Friman. Office: Rush Entertainment Group 2222 Ave of the Stars Los Angeles CA 90067 Office Phone: 310-553-6145. Personal E-mail: hermanrush@aol.com.

**RUSH, JAMES EDWARD,** retired information scientist; b. Warrensburg, Mo., July 18, 1935; s. Alexander Edward Rush and Verna Lavena Pollock; m. Delores Ann Lee, June 9, 1958; children: Susan Diane Wittenauer, Pamela Elaine, Adam Jay, Jennifer Lee. BS in Chemistry and Math., Ctrl. Mo. State U., 1957; PhD, U. of Mo., 1962. Asst. editor, organic index editing dept. Chem. Abstracts Svc., Columbus, Ohio, 1962—65, asst. head, chem. info. procedures dept., 1965—67, tech. liaison officer, 1967—68; adj. prof., libr. and info. sci. U. of Ill., Ill., 1980—83; pres. James E. Rush Assocs., Inc., Powell, Ohio, 1969—88; exec. dir. PALINET, Phila., 1988—99; adj. prof., coll. of info. sci. and tech. Drexel U., Phila., 2000—; asst. prof., computer and info. sci., 1969—73 adj. prof., computer and info. sci., 1973—85; dir. R&D Online Computer Libr. Ctr., Inc., Dublin, Ohio, 1973—80; dir. of rsch. Online Computer Libr. Ctr., 1980; adj. prof., libr. and info. sci. U. of South Fla., Tampa, 1992—97. Del., Pa. gov.'s conf. on libr. and info. svcs. Office of the Gov., Harrisburg, 1990; chair, bd. of dirs. Pa. Preservation Consortium, Phila. Author: (book) Information Retrieval and Documentation in Chemistry, Guide to Information Science, (eight-volume set of books) Library Systems Evaluation Guide, Vols. 1-8, (update service (serial) Microcomputers for Libraries: Product Review and Procurement Guide, (book) Optical Disk Storage: Technology and Applications, Information Science and Technology: An Introduction. With Army N.G., 1952—60. Mem. Am. Chem. Soc. (chmn. divsn. of chem. lit. 1973), Am. Soc. for Info. Sci. and Tech. (pres. 1994—95, gen. chmn. 1980—82). Independent-Republican. Presbyterian. Avocations: construction, woodworking, gardening, photography. Home: 673 Old Eagle School Rd Wayne PA 19087-2042 Home Fax: none. Personal E-mail: rush_jamese@hotmail.com.

**RUSH, JEFFREY, JR.,** former federal agency administrator; b. Kansas City, Kans. m. Dawn Rush; 2 children. B, Baker U.; JD, George Mason U. Criminal investigator USDA, Hyattsville, Md., 1971—75, with supervisory criminal

---

investigation Kansas City, Mo., 1975—78, asst. regional inspector gen. Chgo., 1978—80, regional inspector gen., 1980—83, dep. asst. insp. gen., 1983—94; acting insp. gen. Peace Corp, 1993; insp. gen. USAID, 1994—99, US Dept. Treasury, Washington, 1999—2004. With U.S. Army, 1968—71. Mem.: ABA, DC Bar Assn., Va. State Bar Assn.

**RUSH, JULIA ANN HALLORAN (MRS. RICHARD HENRY RUSH),** artist, writer; b. St. Louis, Oct. 25, 1927; d. Edward Roosevelt and Flavia Hadley (Griffin) Halloran; m. Richard Henry Rush, Aug. 15, 1956; 1 child, Sallie Haywood. Student Washington U., St. Louis, 1945-47; B.A., George Washington U., 1949. One-woman shows: Fort Amador Officers Club, Panama Canal Zone, El Panama Hotel, Panama, George Washington U., Statler Hotel, Roosevelt Hotel, Washington, Newspaper Women's Club, Washington, Waukegan Library, Ill., Epworth Heights Hotel, Ludington, Mich.; exhibited in group shows: Panama Art League, Corcoran Gallery; represented in permanent collections: U. Panama; also pvt. collections; model John Robert Powers Agy., 1950; sec.-treas., dir. N.Am. Acceptance Corp., 1956-58; v.p. Rush and Halloran Inc., 1957-58, ptnr., 1954-57; research asst. to husband's bi-weekly newsletter Art/Antiques Investment Report, 1973—; articles in Wall St. transcript, 1971—. Illustrator: Antiques As An Investment (author Richard H. Rush), 1968; research asst.: Investments You Can Live With and Enjoy (author: Richard H. Rush), 1974, 2d edit., 1975, 3d edit., 1976; Photographer: Automobiles as an Investment, 1982; Investing in Classic Cars, 1984. Recipient 1st prize (Panama) Newspaper Women's Club, 1953; First Prize Panama Art League, 1953. Mem. DAR, Nat. League Am. Penwomen, Florence Crittenton Circle (rec. sec. 1968-69), Kappa Kappa Gamma. Club: Washington, Royal Palm Yacht (No. Ft. Myers, Fla.), Boca West Golf and Country (Boca Raton, Fla.)

**RUSH, KATHY LYNN,** education educator; d. Charles Fenton Norrad and Beryl Alexandria Tracy; m. Thomas Jay Norrad, June 3, 1988; 1 child, Kessia Naomi. BN, U. of NB, Can., 1978; MS, Queen's U., Can., 1985; PhD, Ga. State U., Atlanta, 2000. Lic. Licensure, Nurses Assn. of NB, New Brunswick, Can., 1978, State Bd. of Nursing, S.C., 2001. Lectr., prof. U. of NB, Fredericton, Canada, 1984—2000; prof. U. of S.C. Upstate, Spartanburg, 2001—. Rschr. U. of S.C. Upstate, Spartanburg, 2001—, chairholder of Mary Black Palmetto professorship, 2001—04. Author: (book chpt.) The Encyclopedia of Elder Care: The Comprehensive Resource on Geriatric and Social Care, Geriatric Nursing Research Digest, (jour. article) Jour. of Professional Nursing, Western Journal of Nursing Research. Recipient Sigma Theta Tau Internat. Honor Soc. of Nursing, Ga. State U., Epsilon Alpha Chpt., 2001. Mem.: Instl. Rev. Bd., Spartanburg Regional Med. Ctr., So. Nursing Rsch. Soc., Nat. League for Nursing (jour. reviewer 2005—), Mu Rho Chpt. of Sigma Theta Tau. Office: Univ of South Carolina Upstate 800 Univ Way Spartanburg SC 29303 Office Phone: 864-503-5449.

**RUSH, KEVIN ARLAND,** music educator; b. Franklin, Pa., July 29, 1983; s. Terry Arland and Emily Darlene Rush. MusB, Westminster Coll., 2005. Cert. profl. tchr. music K-12 Pa. Music educator, Clarion County, Pa., 2005—. Sr. organist, choir dir. Good Hope Luth. Ch., Oil City, Pa., 2004—. Mem.: Pa. Music Educators Assn., Phi Kappa Tau, Mu Pi Epsilon (chaplain 2003—). Republican. Presbyterian. Home: 11211 Rt 68 Rimersburg PA 16248

**RUSH, NORMAN,** author; b. San Francisco, Oct. 24, 1933; s. Roger and Leslie (Chessé) R.; m. Elsa Scheidt; children: Jason, Liza. BA, Swarthmore Coll., 1956. Dealer antiquarian books, 1960-78; instr. English, history Rockland C.C., Suffern, NY, 1973-78; co-dir. Peace Corps, Botswana, 1978-83; freelance writer, 1983—. Author: Whites, 1986, Mating, 1991 (Nat. Book award for fiction 1991, Internat. Fiction prize Irish Times and Aer Lingus 1992), Mortals, 2003. Recipient Rosenthal award Nat. Acad. and Inst. Arts and Letters, 1987; fellow Nat. Endowment for Arts, 1986, Guggenheim fellow, 1987, Bellagio residency fellow Rockeller Found., 1990. Mem. PEN Am. Ctr.

**RUSH, RICHARD HENRY,** finance company executive, educator, writer; b. NYC, Mar. 6, 1915; s. Henry Frederick and Bessie (Vreeland) R.; m. Julia Ann Halloran, Aug. 15, 1956; 1 dau., Sallie Haywood. *Dr. Rush is the great grandson of Philip Freneau, The Poet of the American Revolution who is credited as having saved the country from monarchy through his publication of the National Gazette. He is the great grandnephew of General Phil Kearny, Civil War general and New Jersey's most prominent soldier. The grandnephew of America's first Consul General and Minister to Japan, Townsend Harris, who through his determined negotiating of the American Japanese trade treaty, signed in 1858, opened Japan to trade with the west. Harris, before going to Japan, founded the free College of the City of New York as President of the New York Board of Education.* BA summa cum laude, Dartmouth Coll., 1937, MCS, 1938; MBA with highest distinction, Harvard U., 1941, DCS (Littauer fellow), 1942. Chief economist, chmn. planning com. All Am. Aviation (U.S. Air), 1943—45; dir. aviation U.S. Bur. Fgn. and Domestic Commerce, 1945—46; dir. aircraft divsn. Nat. Security Resources Bd., 1948—51; Washington rep. to J. Paul Getty, 1951—52; ptnr. Rush & Halloran, 1953—58; pres., chmn. bd. N.Am. Acceptance Corp., Atlanta, Washington, 1956—59; owner Richard H. Rush Enterprises, Greenwich, Conn., Washington, 1953—73; prof., chmn. dept. finance and investments Sch. Bus. Adminstrn., Am. U., Washington, 1967—70, Sch. Bus. Adminstrn. Am. U., Washington, 1977—79. Author: Art as an Investment, 1961, A Strategy of Investing for Higher Return, 1962, The Techniques of Becoming Wealthy, 1963, Antiques as an Investment, 1968, The Wrecking Operation: Phase One, 1972, Investments You Can Live With and Enjoy, 1976, Techniques of Becoming Wealthy, 1977, Automobiles as an Investment, 1982, Selling Collectibles, 1982, Collecting Classic Cars for Profit and Capital Gain, 1984, Collector Cars: Classics for the New Century, 2001; contbr. over 700 articles to newspapers, mags. and profl. jours.; editor series of books on starting businesses for U.S. Dept. Commerce; contbg. editor Wall St. Transcript, 1971-97, Art/Antiques Investment Report, 1972-97. Trustee, exec. com. Finch Coll., 1968-72. Recipient Pres.'s med., CCNY, 1997. Mem. AAUP, Am. Mktg. Assn. (chmn. sci. com.), Am. Econ. Assn., Am. Statis. Assn., Internat. Platform Assn., Harvard Club N.Y.C., Royal Palm Yacht Club (Ft. Myers), Phi Beta Kappa, Phi Kappa Phi, Omicron Delta Kappa. Episcopalian.

**RUSH, RICHARD R.,** academic administrator; Pres. Calif. State U. Channel Islands, Camarillo. Office: Calif State U Channel Islands 1 University Dr Camarillo CA 93012 Business E-Mail: richard.rush@csuci.edu.

**RUSH, W. MARVIN,** trucking executive; children: W.M. (Rusty), Robin. CEO, chmn. Rush Enterprises Inc., San Antonio, 1965—2006, chmn., 2006—; founder World Wide Tires, several leasing companies, insurance agy., fin. co., nursing parent. Office: Rush Enterprises Inc PO Box 34630 San Antonio TX 78265-4630*

**RUSHDIE, SALMAN,** writer; b. Mumbai, June 19, 1947; s. Anis Ahmed and Negin (Butt) R.; m. Clarissa Luard, 1976 (div. 1987); child, Zafar; m. Marianne Wiggins, 1988 (div. 1993); m. Elizabeth West (div.); child, Milam; m. Padma Parvati Lakshmi, Apr. 17, 2004. Student, Cathedral Sch., Bombay; MA in History with honors, King's Coll., Cambridge U., Eng., 1968. Hon. prof. MIT. Author: Crimus, 1975, Midnight's Children, 1981 (Booker prize for fiction, 1981, English Speaking Union Literary award, 1981, James Tait Black Meml. prize, 1982, Booker of Bookers spl. award, 1993), Shame, 1983 (Prix de Meilleur Livre Etranger, 1984), The Jaguar Smile: A Nicaraguan Journey, 1987, The Satanic Verses, 1988 (Whitbread award 1988, shortlist Booker prize for fiction, 1988, German Author Yr. award, 1988), Is Nothing Sacred? (Herbert Read Meml. lectr. 1990), Haroun and the Sea of Stories, 1990 (Writer's Guild prize for children's fiction 1991), Imaginary Homelands, 1991, East, West, 1994, The Moor's Last Sigh, 1995 (Whitbread Novel award, 1995, Brit. Book awards Author of Yr., 1995, shortlist Booker prize, 1995), Burning Your Boats: The Collected Short Stories, 1996, The Ground Beneath Her Feet, 1999, Fury, 2001, Shalimar the Clown, 2005 (shortlist Whitbread Novel award, 2005). Recipient: Kurt Tucholsky prize, 1992, Prix

---

Colette, 1993, State Prize for European Lit., 1994, Aristeion Lit. prize, 1996, Mantova Lit. prize, 1997, Budapest Grand prize lit., 1998, Commandeur de l'Ordre des Arts et des Lettres, 1999, Freedom of the City, Mexico City, 1999. Fellow Royal Soc. Lit. Address: Author Mail Random House UK 20 Vauxhall Bridge Rd London SW1V 2SA England*

**RUSHER, MARY NASH KELLY,** lawyer; b. Norfolk, Va., May 25, 1958; BA in Polit., German, magna cum laude, Wake Forest Univ., 1980; JD, Univ. Va., 1984. Bar: NC 1985. Law clk., Hon. John D. Butzner, Jr. U.S. Court of Appeals, 4th Cir., 1984—85; with Hunton & Williams LLP, Raleigh, NC, 1985—, ptnr., capital fin., real estate, 1993—, and mem. exec. com., 2002. Mem.: ABA, NC Bar Assn., Nat. Assn. Bond Lawyers, Mortar Board, Omicron Delta Kappa, Phi Beta Kappa, Order of Coif. Office: Hunton & Williams LLP Ste 1400 421 Fayetteville St Mall Raleigh NC 27601 Office Phone: 919-899-3066. Office Fax: 919-899-3160. Business E-Mail: mnrusher@hunton.com.

**RUSHER, WILLIAM ALLEN,** writer, commentator, columnist; b. Chgo., July 19, 1923; s. Evan Singleton and Verna (Self) R. AB, Princeton U., 1943; JD, Harvard U., 1948; DLit (hon.), Nathaniel Hawthorne Coll., 1973. Bar: N.Y. 1949. Assoc. Shearman & Sterling & Wright, N.Y.C., 1948-56; spl. counsel fin. com. N.Y. Senate, 1955; assoc. counsel internal security subcom. U.S. Senate, 1956-57; pub., v.p. Nat. Review mag., N.Y.C., 1957-88, also bd. dirs.; Disting. fellow The Claremont Inst., 1989—. Mem. Adv. Task Force on Civil Disorders, 1972. Author: Special Counsel, 1968, (with Mark Hatfield and Arlie Schardt) Amnesty?, 1973, The Making of the New Majority Party, 1975, How to Win Arguments, 1981, The Rise of the Right, 1984, The Coming Battle for the Media, 1988; editor: The Ambiguous Legacy of the Enlightenment, 1995; columnist Universal Press Syndicate, 1973-82, Newspaper Enterprise Assn., 1982—; played role of Advocate in TV program The Advocates, 1970-74. Chmn., bd. dirs. Media Rsch. Ctr., Washington, 2001—, Nat. Rev. Bd., 1957-88, 90—; bd. advisors Ashbrook Ctr., Ashland, Ohio, past chmn.; past vice chmn. Am. Conservative Union; past trustee Pacific Legal Found., Sacramento. Served as 2d lt. to capt., USAAF, 1943-45, India-Burma Theater. Recipient Disting. Citizen award NYU Sch. Law, 1973. Mem. ABA, Univ. Club (N.Y.C. and San Francisco), Met. Club (Washington). Anglican. Home and Office: 1661 Pine St Apt 933 San Francisco CA 94109

**RUSHFORTH, ANN FAY,** artist, art educator; b. Tampa, Fla., July 17, 1944; d. Robert George Rushforth and Alla Petrovna Riordan; m. Reid Johnson Perryman, May 13, 2000; m. John William Semko, Nov. 11, 1971 (div.); 1 child, Tao Alexandre Semko. BA, George Wash. U., 1966—66; MFA, Antioch U., 1980. Asst. to dir. of film and broadcasting Smithsonian Instn., Washington, 1967—68; adminstrv. asst. Am. Craft Council-Bennington Exhbns., Bennington, Vt., 1972; asst. mgr. Am. Craft Council-Rhinebeck Exhbns., Rhinebeck, NY, 1973—74; dir. pub. rels. Scope Gallery, Torpedo Factory, Alexandria, Va., 1975, pres., 1976—77, bd. dirs., 1978; chmn. dept. art Stoneridge H.S., Bethesda, Md., 1981—84; v.p. Foundry Gallery, Washington, 1986; dir. Pavo Real Gallery, Washington, 1987—88; gallery dir. Arise Gallery of Asian Art and Antiques, Washington, 1988—90; spl. projects photographer Woodrow Wilson Ho. Mus., Washington; arts instr. Duke Ellington Sch. of Arts, Washington, 1990—91, Visual Systems, Rockville, Md., 1991, Fillmore Art Ctr., Washington, 1991; executive dir. The Art Barn Assn., Washington, 1991—93; freelance master paintings copyist Nat. Gallery of Art, Washington, 1993—94; arts instr., 2005—. Rep. Dupont Cir. Consortium of Galleries, Washington, 1986; art instr. Md. Coll. of Art and Design, Dept. Continuing Edn., Rockville, 1990—91; dir., devel. officer R St. Gallery, Washington, 1992—93; conservator, appraiser Artsserve, Ltd., Newnan, 1995—; co-founder Contemporary Arts Alliance, Newnan, 2003—; art instr. The Pottery Wheel, Newnan, Ga., 2005—. Dir.: Carrollton Arts Guild Exhbns.; art critic: Eyewash Newpaper, 1990—91; editor: (exhibition catalog) Sculpture to Touch: For the Sight Impaired, 1987, Md. Craft Coun. News, 1976—78; Wash. Post Mag., 1977, Woodrow Wilson House Mus. Annual Report, Nat. Trust Hist. Preservation, 1987, Greater Chattanooga Artists, The Bureau, 1999, CABIA Arts Calendar, 1999, one-woman shows include Everson Mus. Art Gallery, Syracuse, NY, 1978, Montpelier Cultural Ctr., Md., 1981, Foundry Gallery, Washington, DC, 1986, In Town Gallery, Chattanooga, 2000, exhibited in group shows at NE Juried Exhbn. 12, Rhinebeck, NY, 1974—77, Frederick Wholesale Fair 3, Md., 1975—77, Fairtree Gallery, NYC, 1976, Inc. Gallery, 1976, Concepts Gallery, Ridgewood, NJ, 1976, Scope Gallery, Alexandria, Va., 1976 (Best in Show), 1977, 1984, Montgomery Coll. Gallery, Rockville, Md., 1977, US Govt. Svc. Adminstrn. Invitational Exhbn., Washington, DC, 1977, Westlake Gallery, White Plains, NY, 1977, 1980, 1983, Coqui Galleries, Westport, Conn., 1977, 1978, 1979, Fredericksburg Gallery of Modern Art, Va., 1977, Jelly Mill Gallery, Manchester, Vt., 1981, Md. Nat. Capitol Park and Planning Commn., 1980, VAC Gallery, Columbia, Md., 1981, Visual Arts Ctr., 1982, WWAC Gallery, Washington, DC, 1982, 1985, 1985, 1986, Nat. Capital AMCCAP Festival, 1984 (Second Place, Hon. Mention in Sculpture), 1993, Design Ctr., 1984, Art League Gallery, Alexandria, 1985, Art Barn Gallery, Washington, DC, 1985, 1992, 1992, 1993, Signature Galleries Invitational, Boston and Hyannis, Mass., 1985, Concepts '85, Margate, NJ, 1985, Martin Luther King Libr. Gallery, Washington, DC, 1986, R St. Gallery, 1989, Rockland Ctr., Ellicott City, Md., 1989, Foundry Gallery, Washington, DC, 1989, Jackson Sch. Studios, 1990, 1991, 1992, 901 E St. Gallery, 1991, 1993, Capital Arts Inc. Georgetown Visitation Sch., 1992, 1993, Georgetown Holiday Inn, 1992, The Spy Club, 1993, Universal N. Gallery, 1993, 1993, Washington Project for the Arts, 1993, Jackson Art Ctr., Studio #21, 1993, Gallery West, Alexandria, 1993, Corcoran Sch. Gallery, Washington, DC, 1993, Avery Gallery, Atlanta, Ga., 1995, Blair Voltz Exhbns., Atlanta, 1997, The Stalls, Bennett St., 1997, Grandview Gallery, 1997, Waterhouse Pavilion, Chattanooga, 1998, AVA Gallery, 1998, 1999, Urban Art Inst., 2000, Panoply Showhouse, Newnan, Ga., 2001, Tenn. Valley Art Mus., Tuscumbia, Ala., 2002, Arts Clayton Gallery, Jonesboro, Ga., 2002, Atlanta Arts Club, 2002, Forum Gallery at Defoor Centre, Atlanta, 2002, 2004, Atlanta Coll. Art, Coweta County, Ga., 2003, Keptever Gallery, Peachtree City, Ga., 2004, Mandeville Gallery, Carrollton, Ga., 2004, Jackalope's Gallery, Carrollton, 2004, MECCA Festival for the Arts, 2004, Carrollton Artists Guild, 2004, Carrollton Arts Ctr., 2005, exhibitions include HMR Engring. Inc., Alexandria, 1993, Meml. Hosp. Foyer, Chattanooga, 1999, UTC Faculty Club, 1999, Ga. State Fair, Perry, 2004, prin. works include St. John the Wonderworker, Patron St. Altarpiece and Icon of St. Brigid, Abess & Healer, St. John the Wonderworker Ea. Orthodox Ch., Atlanta, 1996, Christus Rex, Ceramic bas Relief Altarpiece, St. Paul's Episc. Ch., Newnan, 2006. Lector St.Paul's Episcopal Ch., Newnan, 2004—06. Mem.: Am. Ceramic Soc. Potter's Coun. Womens Caucus for Arts, Portrait Soc. Atlanta (edn. dir. 2005), Nat. Coun. Edn. for Ceramic Arts, Newnan-Coweta Artist Assn., Carrollton Artist Guild (exhbn. dir. 2005). Libertarian. Episcopalian. Avocations: physical fitness, dog shows, travel, art history. Office Phone: 678-634-6360. E-mail: annfayrushforth@hotmail.com.

**RUSHFORTH, BRENT N.,** lawyer; BA, Stanford Univ., 1964, MA, 1966; JD, Univ. of Calif., Boalt Hall School of Law, 1969. Bar: Dist. of Columbia, Calif. Atty., shareholder Heller, Ehrman, White, & McAuliffe LLP, Washington, managing shareholder.

**RUSHING, DEBRA FARROW,** pharmacist; b. Indpls. d. Glenn Vernon and Betty Jean Farrow; m. David Earnest Rushing, Oct. 3, 1992 (dec. June 2002); children: Amber Marie, Dustin David, Zachary Glenn. BS in Pharmacy, Butler U., 1978. Resident pharmacy Ind. U. Hosp., Indpls., 1981—82; staff pharmacist Ind. U. Hosp., Indpls., 1978—81; supr. pharmacy, 1982—83; staff pharmacist, 1983—2005, Clarian N. Med. Ctr., Carmel, Ind., 2005—. Mem.: Ind. Pharmacists Alliance, Am. Soc. Clin. Pharmacy, Am. Soc. Health Sys. Pharmacists. Republican. Methodist. Avocations: reading, bicycling, decorating, scrapbooking. Home: 14505 Dublin Dr Carmel IN 46033 Office: Clarian North Med Ctr 11700 N Meridian St Carmel IN 46032 Office Phone: 317-688-2774. Business E-Mail: drushing@clariannorth.com.

**RUSHING, JOHN ALAN,** business educator; s. Thomas Jefferson and Mary Emma Rushing; m. Sherre Lynn Garvin, Nov. 23, 1963; children: John Alan Jr., Laura Ann. M internat. bus. adminstrn., Nova U., 1990; D in Bus. Adminstrn., Nova Southeastern, 2001. Pres. Kiwi Rsch. and Devel., Ft. Lauderdale, Fla., 1987–89; adj. faculty Broward C.C., Davie, Fla., 1992–99; corp. sec. Geep Corp., Oxford, Miss., 1989–2005; asst. prof. Barry U., Miami Shores, Fla., 1999–2003, asst. dean for academic affairs, 2003—, regional dir., 2006—. Author: Adventure Capital, 2001. Chair bus. devel. Davie C. of C., Davie, Fla., 1997, chair edn. conf., 1999, mem., 1990–99. Mem.: Am. Soc. of Devel., Acad. of Internat. Bus., Sigma Beta Delta Internat. Bus. Honor Soc., Gold Key Honor Soc. Avocation: radio controlled boats and airplanes. Office: Barry U 305 John Knox Rd Tallahassee FL 32303 Office Phone: 850-385-2279. Office Fax: 850-385-7576. Business E-Mail: jrushing@mail.barry.edu.

**RUSHING, PHILIP DALE,** retired social worker; b. Carbondale, Ill., Mar. 15, 1932; S. Paul and Beulah Myrl (Benton) R.; m. Linda North, July 5, 1958 (div. July 1964); 1 child, Lisa Anne Rushing Burrow; m. Rosalie Anne Sturm, Aug. 20, 1966. BA, So. Ill. U., 1958; MSW, Washington U., St. Louis, 1960. Diplomate Am. Bd. Clinical Social Workers; LCSW Ill. Child welfare worker Ill. Dept. Pub. Welfare, Salem, East St. Louis, 1958-60, child welfare supr. East St. Louis, 1960-63; field rep. Nat. Assn. for Retarded Children, Dallas, Denver, 1963-65; dir. social svcs. A.L. Bowen Children's Ctr., Harrisburg, Ill., 1965-68; asst. zone dir. for mentally retarded Ill. Dept. of Mental Health, Harrisburg, 1968-74; regional coord. for devel. disabilities Ill. Dept. of Mental Health & Devel. Disabilities, Marion, 1974-83; social work adminstr. Choate Mental Health & Devel. Ctr., Anna, Ill., 1983-95; ret., 1995. Adj. asst. prof. So. Ill. U. Rehab. Inst., Carbondale, Ill., 1968-78; bd. dirs. Southeastern Ill. Pastoral Counseling Ctrs., chmn. pers. com., 1996-98. Bd. deacons First Presbyn. Ch., Harrisburg, 1974-77, bd. trustees, 1978-80, bd. elders, 1980-83, 96-98, 2003-06. With USN, 1951-55, Korea Fellow Am. Assn. on Mental Retardation (life, chmn. social work divsn. Ill. chpt. 1973-74); mem. NASW (chmn. East St. Louis Ill. chpt. 1962). Home: 6542 Hwy 13 W Harrisburg IL 62946-4142 Personal E-mail: pr.rushing@juno.com.

**RUSHING, TONNIE AUSTIN PAGE,** musician, educator; b. Hartwell, Ga., Mar. 6, 1940; d. George Wilson and Ruth Smith Page; m. Roger Kendall Vichery, June 18, 1960; children: George Kendall, Carol Page; m. Charles Maynard Rushing, Aug. 18, 1979; stepchildren: Joan E., Brian C., Susanne E. BS in Edn., Athens State Coll., Ga., 1973; cert. in Computer Tech., Trident Tech. Coll., 1992, Sylvan Learning Ctr., 1996; cert. in Sign Lang., Trident Tech. Coll., 1997. Musician, Ga., 1958—; prin. owner Opus 11 George Bed & Breakfast, 1988—97; afternoon activities dir. O'Quinn Preschool-Kindergarten, 2001. Dir. music Summer Stock Theater, Morristown, Tenn., 1969; music educator Covenant Sch. Fine Arts Enrichment, 1976—79; music dir. Young Charleston Theatre Co., 1988, 96; mem. founding com. Covenant Fine Arts Enrichment Sch., Decatur, 1976; mem. adv. com. Coun. Arts John C. Calhoun State Coll., Decatur. Singer: North Ala. Charleston Symphony, St. Micheal's Ch., Grace Episc. Ch., Choir Eng. Tour, 1981—2002; musician: French Protestant Ch., 1988—96; author: Huguenots and the Legacy, 1994; dir.: (recording) Huguenot Psalter, 1991; jacket cover Huguenot Psalter, 1991. Pres Decatur (Ala.) Civic Chorus; vol. Crisis Ctr. Mental Health Ctr., Decatur, 1971—79; mem. comprehensive planning com. City Hartwell, Ga., 2003; bd. dirs. Preservation Soc., 2004, Hart County Hist. Soc. 2004; music asst. 2d Presbyn. Ch., Charleston, SC, 1988; sect. leader St. Michaels Ch., Charleston, 1998—2001; elder Hartwell 1st Presbyn. Ch., 2004; bd. dirs. Charleston (S.C.) Symphony Orch. Chorus and Chamber Choir. Mem.: PTA, Am. Guild Organists, Presbyn. Assn. Musicians, Charleston (S.C.) County Med. Auxillary, Nat. assn. Mental Illness, Hartwell Women's Club, Sigma Alpha Iota. Republican. Home: 175 E Johnson St Hartwell GA 30643 Personal E-mail: cmandtpr@hartcom.net.

**RUSHNELL, SQUIRE DERRICK,** television executive, writer; b. Adams Center, N.Y., Oct. 31, 1938; s. Reginald Grant and Erica Mifanwy Redwood Sedgemore (Squire) R.; children: Robin Tracy, Hilary Adair, Squire Grant Sedgemore. Student, Syracuse U., 1956-60. Disc jockey Stas. WOLF, WEN and WFBL, Syracuse, NY, 1958-61. Sta. WTRL, Bradenton, Fla., 1961-62; exec. prodr. Sta. WBZ AM-TV, Boston, 1962-67; program dir. KYW News-Radio, Phila., 1968; exec. prodr. Kennedy & Co. Sta. WLS-TV, Chgo., 1969-71, program dir., 1971-73; v.p. programs ABC-owned TV stas., N.Y.C. 1973-74; v.p. children's TV ABC Entertainment Network, N.Y.C., 1974-78; v.p. Good Morning Am. and children's programs ABC-TV Network, N.Y.C. 1978-81, v.p. long range planning and children's TV, 1981-87; v.p. late night and children's TV ABC Entertainment, N.Y.C., 1987-89; pres. Rushnell Comm. & Pub. Inc., 1990-96; pres., CEO GoodLife TV Network, Washington, 1996—2001; motivational spkr., 2001—. Author: The Kingdom Chums Greatest Stories, 1986, When God Winks: How the Power of Coincidence Guides Your Life, 2001, When God Winks on Love, 2004, When God Winks at You, 2006; co-author: Broadcast Programming, 1981, Broadcast/Cable Programming, 1985, rev. edit., 1989, 1993. Recipient Emmy awards, 1975-88, TV Critics Circle award, 1976, all for outstanding children's TV programming, Am. Children's TV Festival award, 1985, 87. Mem. NATAS, Nat. Acad. Arts and Scis., Internat. Radio and TV Soc., Action for Children's TV (award for outstanding children's TV programming). Office Phone: 508-939-8510. Business E-Mail: squire@whengodwinks.com.

**RUSHTON, ALAN R.,** physician, medical researcher, historian; b. Oak Park, Ill., Mar. 10, 1949; s. Raymond H. and D. Loree (Swan) R.; m. Nancy Spencer, May 5, 1973; children: Andrew, Daniel. AB in Chemistry, Earlham Coll., 1971; PhD in Genetics, U. Chgo., 1975, MD, 1977. Diplomate Am. Bd. Pediatrics, Am. Bd. Med. Genetics. Resident, intern Yale U.-New Haven (Conn.) Hosp., 1977-80; physician Hunterdon Med. Ctr., Flemington, NJ, 1980—; assoc. clin. prof. pediatrics Robert Wood Johnson Med. Sch., New Brunswick, NJ, 1980—. Lectr. genetics Princeton (N.J.) U., 1980-84; adj. prof. Med. U. Ams., Nevis, West Indies. Author: Genetics and Medicine in the United States 1800-1922, 1994. Fellow Am. Acad. Pediatrics, Am. Coll. Med. Genetics, N.Y. Acad. Medicine, Royal Soc. Medicine; mem. Am. Assn. History Medicine, History Sci. Soc. Office: Hunterdon Pediatric Assocs 6 Sand Hill Rd Ste 202 Flemington NJ 08822-4600 Office Phone: 908-788-6468. E-mail: arrdoc@aol.com.

**RUSI, EDUARD,** engineering educator; b. Korca, Albania, Nov. 17, 1978; s. Nihat and Flutur Rusi. Grad. in Elec. Engring., U. Wis. Tchr. asst. U. Wis., Manitowoc, Wis., 2002—04. Project outreach leader Campus Crusade for Christ, Tirana, Albania, 1998—2000. Mem.: U. Wis. Alumni Assn., Phi Theta Kappa Honor Soc. Home: 2302 University Ave Apt 114 Madison WI 53726 Personal E-mail: rusi@wisc.edu.

**RUSIE, RUTH LOUISE,** special education educator; b. Russiaville, Ind., Oct. 13, 1918; d. Volna Ernest and Mamie Audrey (Gallion) Ritz; m. Horace Robert Rusie, June 28, 1941; children: James Frederick, David Robert, John Lindley. BA, DePauw U., 1940; MS, Ind. U., 1972. Elem. sch. tchr. Met. Sch. Dist. Martinsville (Ind.), 1958-72, spl. reading tchr., 1972-80; coord. Martinsville Literacy Coalition, 1982—. Mem. Ind. Right-to-Read Com., 1975-78; mem. adv. bd., participant Reading is Fundamental, Martinsville, 1992-96. Composer music for elementary students The Stupid Thief, 1972. Bd. dirs. Martinsville Edn. Found., 1991—; bd. dirs. Cmty. Found. of Morgan County, 2001—, v.p., 2005; bd. dirs. People Respecting Individuality and Diversity in Everyone (P.R.I.D.E.), 1997—; co-pres., 2002—, Cmty. Concerts N.Y.C., 1994—, co-pres., 2003—; bd. dirs., treas. Morgan County Pub. Libr., Martinsville, 1984-2001; mem. com. on food Habitat for Humanity, Martinsville, 1997—; mem. Martinsville Arts Coun., 1981—; dir., 1981—; driver cancer patients ARC, Martinsville, 1981-2000; dir., 1986-92; dir. vol. desk Morgan County Meml. Hosp., Martinsville, 1982-94; driver Meals-On-Wheels, Martinsville, 1985—; grand marshall Morgan County Fall Foliage Festival Parade, Martinsville, 1993; adv. bd. United Way Ctrl. Ind., 2003-2004, mem. solutions coun., 2004—; elder Presby. Ch., 2004—; trustee Morgan County Pub. Libr. Found., 2004—; treas. 2006; mem. edn. devel. program Morgan County Habitat for Humanity, 2004—; bd. dirs. NBA, 2004—. Named Citizen of Yr., Kiwanis, 1990, 2004, Rotary, 1993; recipient

Cmty. Spirit award, H.S. Nat. Honor Soc., 1992, Mayor's award for literacy, Mayor and City Ofcls., 1993, Excellence of Cmty. Svc. award, DAR, 1995, Ind. Jefferson award, Am. Inst. Pub. Svc./Indpls. Star, 1996, Svc. to Mankind award, Morgan County Sertoma Club, 2002, S.W. Ind. Dist. Sertoma Internat., 2003, Leadership award, ABC Channel 6, Indpls., 2006. Mem. Martinsville Woman's Club (pres. 1957-59), Martinsville Literary Club, Coterie (pres. 1986-88), Monday Afternoon Art Club, Foxcliff Golf Club (pres. 1981-82), Kappa Kappa Kappa (pres. 1956-57, province officer 1957-59). Presbyterian. Avocations: reading, bell and singing ch. choirs, bridge, opera, theater.

**RUSKAI, MARY BETH,** mathematics professor; b. Cleve., Feb. 26, 1944; d. Michael J. and Evelyn (Gortz) R. BS, Notre Dame Coll., Cleve., 1965; MA, PhD, U. Wis., 1969. Battelle fellow in theoretical physics U. Geneva, 1969-71; rsch. assoc. in math. MIT, Cambridge, Mass., 1971-72; rsch. assoc. in physics U. Alta., Edmonton, Can., 1972-73; asst. prof. math. U. Oreg., Eugene, 1973-76; asst. prof. U. Lowell, Mass., 1977-82, assoc. prof. Mass., 1982-86, prof. dept. math. Mass., 1986—2002, emeritus, 2002—, pres. faculty senate Mass., 1990-91; rsch. prof. Tufts U., 2003—. Sci. scholar Bunting Inst., Cambridge, Mass., 1983-85; rsch. prof. MSRI, Berkeley, 2002; vis. prof. Rockefeller U., N.Y.C., 1980-81, U. Vienna, Austria, 1981, Rome, 1988, Ga. Tech., Atlanta, 1997, Walton vis. prof. Dublin Inst. Tech., 2003; faculty rsch. assoc. Naval Surface Warfare Ctr., Silver Springs, Md., 1986; vis. prof. math. U. Mich., Ann Arbor, 1991-92; vis. mem. Courant Inst. Math. Sci., NYU, 1988-89; cons. Bell Labs., Murray Hill, N.J., 1972, 83, 88-89; conf. dir. NSF/CBMS Conf. on Wavelets, 1990; Flora Stone Mather vis. prof. Case Western Res. U., Cleve., 1995; vis. prof. Ga. Inst. Tech., 1997, U. Reims, France, 1998, Tech. U. Berlin, 2000; cons. Microsoft Rsch., 1999. Editor-in-chief Wavelets and Their Applications, 1990-92; mem. editl. bd. Notices of Am. Math. Soc., 1994-99, Jour. Math. Physics, 2001-; mem. editl. adv. bd. Internat. Jour. Quantum Chemistry, 1996-2000; contbr. articles to profl. jours. NSF predoctoral fellow, 1965-69; recipient NSF Career Advancement award, 1988-89. Fellow AAAS (symposium organizer 1991, 94, nominating com. math. sect. 1991-94, mem.-at-large math. sect. 2004—); mem. Internat. Union Pure & Applied Physics (vice chair commn. on math. physics, U.S. liaison com. 1999-2005), Internat. Assn. Math. Physicists, Am. Math. Soc. (reviewer, session chmn., com. 1987—, com. chmn., coun. mem. at-large 1998-2000), Math. Assn. Am. (com.), Am. Phys. Soc. (reviewer), Assn. Women in Math., Assn. Women in Sci. (pres. New Eng. chpt. 1986-87), Appalachian Mountain Club (Boston; winter leader 1979-97), Sigma Xi. Office: Tufts U Dept Math Medford MA 02155 E-mail: marybeth.ruskai@tufts.edu.

**RUSKIN, JOSEPH RICHARD,** actor, director; b. Haverhill, Mass., Apr. 14, 1924; s. Ely and Betty Edith (Chaimson) Schlafman; m. Barbara Greene; 1 child, Alicia. Grad., Carnegie Inst. Tech., 1949. Founder Rochester (N.Y.) Arena Theatre, 1949-52. Actor N.Y. stage plays, 1952-58, Theatre Group, UCLA, Mark Taper Forum, 1959—, (films) Fall of Legs Diamond, 1959, Magnificient Seven, 1960, Escape from Zahrein, 1963, Robin and the Seven Hoods, 1965, Prizzi's Honor, 1985, Longshot, 1987, Indecent Proposal, 1992, Spider-Man, 1994, (voice) Star Trek: Insurrection, 1998, King Cobra, 1999, The Scorpion King, 2002; regular appearances various TV programs, 1952—; TV appearance: Alias, 2002; dir. Houston Alley, 1965-69; freelance dir., 1969—. Served with USNR, 1943-46. Mem. AFTRA, SAG, Actors Equity Assn. (nat. coun.). Home: 1326 Devon Ave Los Angeles CA 90024-5346

**RUSKIN, ROBERT STERLING,** educational association administrator; b. Washington, Nov. 27, 1945; s. Robert Edward and Thelma (Gipe) R.; m. Rebecca Lynne Wilson, Aug. 11, 1967; 1 child, Brant Edward. BA, Washington Coll., Chestertown, Md., 1967; MA, W.Va. U., 1969, PhD, 1971. Lic. psychologist Va., D.C. Prof. dept. psychology Georgetown U., Washington, 1971-86, chmn. dept. psychology, 1976-85, dir. Ctr. for Personalized Instrn., 1977-80, dir. Teaching Resource Ctr., 1985-86; chief psychol. assessor leadership devel. U. Md., College Park, 1984—; prin. investigator and project dir., consortium univs. rsch fellows program U.S. Army Rsch. Inst., Washington, Alexandria, 1985—; nat. rsch. fellow U.S. Dept. Edn., Washington, 1986-87; affiliate prof. psychology George Mason U., Washington, 1989—; prin. investigator Consortium & Office of Substance Abuse Prevention, Washington, 1990-93; dir. programs and rsch. Consortium of Univs. of Washington Metro. Area, 1987-88, v.p., 1989—. Psychol. cons. DuPont Corp., Seaford, Del., 1986-88; psychol. cons. Consortium of Univs. of D.C., 1984—; cons. in field; rep. of U.S. to UNESCO Planning Meeting, Paris, 1979. Co-author: Behavioral Instruction: An Evaluative Review, 1977; editor manuscript: Consortium Research Fellows Program; editor The Jour. of Personalized Instrn., 1975-81, Revista a Tecnologia Educativa, 1976-83. Battelle Inst. Disting. Acad. Rsch. fellow U.S. Army Rsch. Inst., 1984-86. Fellow APA, Am. Psychol. Soc. (charter); mem. AAAS, D.C. Psychol. Assn., Va. Psychol. Assn., Psi Chi. Methodist. Avocations: golf, fishing. Home: 309 W Alex Ave Alexandria VA 22302 Office: Consortium of Univs of Wash 1 Dupont Cir NW Washington DC 20036-1110 E-mail: robert.ruskin@ari.army.mil.

**RUSLING, BARBARA N(EUBERT),** real estate broker; b. St. Louis, Nov. 27, 1945; d. Ralph L. and Rosemary (Stroot) Neubert; m. Randolph H. Wieser, Apr. 23, 1966 (div. Nov. 1983); children: Keith, Steve, Eric; m. Robert Best Rusling, Aug. 2, 1985 (dec. Oct. 2004). BA, Vanderbilt U., 1966; postgrad., Baylor U., 1975. Lic. real estate broker, cert. justice of the peace. Appraisal intern Smith Real Estate, Waco, Tex., 1975; resident real estate broker Sanger Suburban Realty, Waco, 1975-81, sales mgr., 1981-83; pres., gen. mgr. Coldwell Banker Hallmark Realty, Waco, 1983-99; with Coldwell Banker Jim Stewart, Realtors, 1999—; commr. Tex. Gen. Svcs. Commn., 1997—2002; trustee Tex. State Tech. Coll., 2002—. Mem. from dist. 57 Tex. State Ho. Reps., 1995-97. Chmn. bd. dirs. YWCA, Waco, 1976—79; dir. Leadership Waco Program, 1986—87; various positions Hist. Waco Found.; bd. dirs. Waco Civic Theatre, treas., 1999—2001; bd. dirs. Family Counseling Ctr., 1991—96, United Way, 1992—98, Family Abuse Ctr., 1993—2002, 2004—, Waco BBB, 1994—99; Justice of the Peace, 2004—. Mem.: Waco C. of C. (bd. dirs. 1990—93), Waco Bd. Realtors (past bd. dirs., Salesman of Yr. 1979), Realtors Nat. Mktg. Inst. (cert.), Tex. Assn. Realtors (edn. com., strategic planning com. 1983—95, realtor lawyer com. 1985—93), Am. Heart Assn. (McLennan County bd. dirs. 1997—, pres. 1999—2000), Kappa Delta. Home: 1635 Meandering Way China Spring TX 76633-2905 Office: Coldwell Banker 500 N Valley Mills Dr Waco TX 76710-6007 Office Phone: 254-776-0000. Personal E-mail: brusling@aol.com.

**RUSMISEL, STEPHEN RAYMOND,** lawyer; b. NYC, Jan. 27, 1946; s. R. Raymond and Esther Florence (Kutz) R.; m. Beirne Donaldson, Sept. 6, 1980 (div. Jan. 1984); 1 child, Margo Alexander; m. Melissa J. MacLeod, Aug. 24, 1985 (div. Oct. 1996); children: Benjamin William, Eric Scot Kunze, Erin Lea Kunze; m. Teresa R. Paterniti, June 28, 1997; 1 child. Sarah J. Lamendola. AB, Yale U., 1968; JD, U. Va., 1971. Bar: NY 1972. US Ct. Appeals (2d cir.) 1974, US Dist. Ct. (so. dist.) NY 1975. Assoc. Winthrop, Stimson, Putnam & Roberts, NYC, 1971-80, ptnr., 1980-2000, Pillsbury Winthrop Shaw Pittman LLP, NYC, 2001—. Aux. officer Bedminster Twp. Police, NJ, 1976—. Mem. Practicing Law Inst., Am. Arbitration Assn. (arbitrator 1996—), Far Hills Polo Club (Annandale, NJ), Ausable Club (St. Huberts, NY), Phi Delta Phi. Republican. Avocations: flying, carpentry, gardening, poetry. Home: Shad-owline Farm Bedminster NJ 07921 Office: Pillsbury Winthrop Shaw Pittman LLP 1540 Broadway New York NY 10036-4039 Office Phone: 212-858-1000. Business E-Mail: stephen.rusmisel@pillsburylaw.com.

**RUSODIMOS, IASON,** mathematics professor; b. Panama, Nov. 25, 1954; arrived in U.S., 1973; s. Constantino and Ioanna Rusodimos. BSEE, Ga. Tech., Atlanta, 1976, MSEE, 1977, MS in Math., 1982, MS in Physics, 1984. Prof. math. Ga. Perimeter Coll., Atlanta, 1984—. Mem.: Am. Phys. Soc., Soc. for Indsl. and Applied Math., Am. Math. Soc., Math. Assn. Am. Home: PO Box 29398 Atlanta GA 30359

**RUSS, EDMOND VINCENT, JR.,** marketing professional; b. Washington, Feb. 14, 1944; s. Edmond V. and Thayer Kennedy (Thompson) R.; m. Tena Marie Loveland, Dec. 26, 1982; children: Jamie Russ Solanics, E.V. Russ III, Christina T. Russ, Cory S. Russ. BA, Kent State U., Ohio, 1966; MBA, U. Pitts., 1967. Dir. mktg. Borg-Warner Ednl. Systems, Niles, Ill., 1969-74; v.p. mktg. Rusty Jones Inc., Chgo., 1974-83; gen. mgr. Signed, Sealed and Delivered, Melrose Park, Ill., 1983-86; v.p. mktg. Merchant Network Inc., Chgo., 1986-90; dir. mktg. Am. Appraisal Assocs., Milw., 1990-93, Pricewaterhouse Coopers, 1993-2001; ptnr., chief mktg. officer Grant Thornton LLP, 2001—. Mem. Am. Mktg. Assn., Assn. Acctg. Marketers, Bus. Mktg. Assn., Strategic Mgmt. Assn., Vintage Sports Car Drivers Assn., Porsche Club Am. Avocations: tennis, community theater, sports car racing. E-mail: planetera@comcast.net.

**RUSS, FENEE L.,** principal, consultant; d. Charles and Hassie Russ. BA in Bus. Adminstr. and Mktg., Clark-Atlanta U., 1991; MS in Ednl. Leadership, Nova Southeastern U., 1998, EdD, 2005. Cert. profl. educator Fla. Dept. Edn., 1993. Tchr. Sch. Dist. Palm Beach County, West Palm Beach, Fla., 1993—98, asst. prin., 1998—. Named Tchr. of Yr., Boca Raton Rotary Club, 1995; recipient, Palm Beach County Vocat. Assn., 1995. Mem.: LWV, AAUW (assoc.), Nat. Mus. Women Arts (assoc.), Toastmasters Internat. (assoc.), Phi Delta Kappa (assoc.). Avocations: piano, reading, travel. Office: Sch Dist PBC/Eagles Landing 19500 Coral Ridge Dr Boca Raton FL 33498 Office Phone: 561-470-7022.

**RUSS, JOANNA,** author; b. N.Y.C., Feb. 22, 1937; d. Everett and Bertha (Zinner) R. BA English high honors, Cornell U., 1957; MFA Playwriting and Dramatic Lit., Yale U., 1960. Lectr. English Cornell U., 1967—70, asst. prof., 1970—72; asst. prof. English Harpur Coll. SUNY Binghamton, 1972—75; asst. prof. English U. Colo., 1975—77; assoc. prof. English, U. Wash., 1977—90, prof., 1984—90. Author: Picnic on Paradise, 1968, And Chaos Died, 1970, The Female Man, 1975, We Who Are About To, 1977, Kittatinny: A Tale of Magic, 1978, The Two of Them, 1978, On Strike Against God, 1980, The Adventures of Alyx, 1983, The Zanzibar Cat, 1983, How To Suppress Women's Writing, 1983, Extra (Ordinary) People, 1984, Magic Mommas, Trembling Sisters, Puritans and Perverts: Feminist Essays, 1985, (collection) The Hidden Side of the Moon, 1987, To Write Like a Woman, 1995, (nonfiction) What Are We Fighting For, 1998; also numerous short stories Mem. Sci. Fiction Writers Am. (Nebula award Best Short Story 1972, Hugo award for Best Novella 1983)

**RUSSACK, JOHN A.,** federal official; Grad., U. Kans., 1970, Nat. War Coll., 1991. Dep. to assoc. dir. of crit. intelligence for military support CIA, exec. asst. to dep. dir., military dep. dir. nonproliferation ctr., dep. asst. dir. for collection, dep. chief external ops., cover divsn. for counterintelligence; dir. office of intelligence US Dept. Energy, Washington, 2003—05; program mgr. Information-Sharing Environment Office Dir. Nat. Intelligence, Washington, 2005—.

**RUSSE, CONRAD THOMAS CAMPBELL,** accountant; b. Bethesda, Md., July 15, 1954; s. Frederick William Jr. and Constance Oakman (Fagan) R.; m. Deborah Joyce Thompson, June 14, 1980; children: Thomas Campbell, Catherine Alexandra, Caroline Saunders. BS, Duke U., 1977; MBA, Ga. State U., 1982. CPA, Ga., Tenn., N.C. Estimator Advance Builders, Inc., Smyrna, Ga., 1978; contractor B&B Drywalls, Marietta, 1979-81; acct. Evans, Snyder & Co., Atlanta, 1981-82; tax acct. Peat Marwick Mitchell & Co., Charlotte, N.C., 1982-85, Ernst & Whinney & Co., Chattanooga, 1985-86; tax mgr. Costello, Strain & Co, CPAs, Chattanooga, 1986-89; prin. Thomas C. Russe, CPAs, Chattanooga, 1989—. Bd. dirs. treas. Visually Impaired Tng. and Learning Ctr., Chattanooga, 1988-93, Chattanooga Tax Practitioners, 1987-95. Membership chmn. Cherokee Area coun. Boy Scouts Am., Chattanooga, 1987, 88; bd. dirs. Allegro Dance Theater, 1990-92; bd. dirs. Small Bus. Devel. Ctr., 1995—. English Speaking Union scholar, 1972-73. Mem. N.C. Assn. CPAs, Ga. Soc. CPAs (mem. taxation com. 1993—, tax forum com. 1995—), Tenn. Soc. CPAs (taxation com. 1990, 92, tax liaison com. 1992-95, small bus. com. 1999), Chattanooga Estate Planning Coun. Chattanooga Area C. of C. (seminars chmn. small bus. coun. 1987, 88, steering com. small bus. coun. 1989-95), CPA Club (bd. dirs. 1991-92), CPA-Atty. Forum (pres. 1992-94), Chattanooga Civitan Club. Episcopalian. Avocations: reading, antique refinishing, biking. Home: PO Box 4322 Chattanooga TN 37405-0322

**RUSSEL, WILLIAM BAILEY,** engineering educator; b. Corpus Christi, Tex., Nov. 17, 1945; m. 1972; 2 children. BA, Rice U., 1969, MS in Chem. Engring., 1969; PhD in Chem. Engring., Stanford U., 1973. NATO fellow applied math. Cambridge U., 1973-74; from asst. prof. to assoc. prof. chem. engring. Princeton U., NJ, 1974-83, prof. NJ, 1983—, chmn. dept. chem. engring. NJ, 1987-96, dir. Materials Scis. Inst. NJ, 1996-98, dean graduate sch. NJ, 2002—. Olaf A. Hougen prof. U. Wis., 1984 Mem.: Materials Rsch. Soc., Am. Chem. Soc., Soc. Rheology (pres. 2001—03, Bingham award 1999), NAE, AIChE (William H. Walker award 1992). Office: Princeton U 205 Nassau Hall Princeton NJ 08544 E-mail: graddean@princeton.edu.

**RUSSELL, ALLAN DAVID,** lawyer; b. Cleve., May 6, 1924; s. Allan MacGillivray and Marvel (Codling) R.; m. Lois Anne Robinson, June 12, 1947, m. Patricia A. Ellis, March 8, 2003; children: Lisa Anne, Robinson David, Martha Leslie BA, Yale U., 1945, LLB, 1951. Bar: N.Y. 1952, Conn. 1956, Mass. 1969, U.S. Supreme Ct. 1977. Atty. Sylvania Electric Products, Inc., N.Y.C., 1951-56, div. counsel Batavia. NY, 1956-65; sr. counsel 1965-71; sec., sr. counsel GTE Sylvania Inc., Stamford, Conn., 1971-76; asst. gen. counsel GTE Svc. Corp., 1976-80, v.p., assoc. gen. counsel, 1980—83; pvt. practice Redding, Conn., 1983—2004. Sec., dir. mktg. subs. Sylvania Entertainment Products Corp., 1961-67; sec. Wilbur B. Driver Co/Dist. leader Rep. Party, New Canaan, Conn., 1955-56; sec. bd. dirs. Youth Found., Inc., 1981-83, bd. dirs., 1985-2001, pres., 2000-01; mem. planning commn., Redding, Conn., 1987-89; mem. Redding Bd. Ethics, 1990-96, chmn., 1992-96; warden Christ Ch. Parish, Redding, 1987-89; bd. dirs. Mark Twain Libr., 1988-94, 2002-2004, v.p., 1988-89, pres., 1990-92 With USAAF, 1943—46. Mem. SAR, assn. of Bar of City of N.Y., Conn. Bar Assn. (exec. com. corp. counsel sect. 1986-90), Am. Soc. Corp. Secs., St. Nicholas Soc., Collie Club Am. Found., Inc. (v.p., dir. 1986-89, pres. 1989-90), Soc. Colonial Wars, Yale Alumni Assn. (sec. local chpt. 1953-56), Yale Club of Danbury (pres. 1990—), Phi Delta Phi Home: 33 Old Field Hill Rd Unit #32 Southbury CT 06488-3837

**RUSSELL, ALLEN STEVENSON,** retired metal products executive; b. Bedford, Pa., May 27, 1915; s. Arthur Stainton and Ruth (Stevenson) R.; m. Judith Pauline Sexauer, Apr. 5, 1941. BS, Pa. State U. 1936. MS, 1937, PhD, 1941. With Aluminum Co. Am., 1940-82, assoc. dir. rsch., 1973-74; v.p. Alcoa, Pa., 1974-78; v.p. sci. and tech. Pitts., 1978-81; v.p., chief scientist, 1981-82. Adj. prof. U. Pitts., 1981-86 Contbr. articles to profl. jours.; patentee in field. Named IR-100 Scientist of Yr., 1979; Pa. State U. alumni fellow, 1980; K.J. Bayer medalist, 1981; recipient chem. Pioneer award Am. Inst. Chemists, 1983 Fellow Am. Soc. Metals (Gold medal 1982), AIME (James Douglas gold medal 1987), Am. Inst. Chemists; mem. NAE (coun. 1978-84), Am. Chem. Soc., Sigma Xi. Republican. Presbyterian. Home: 27 Meadowlark Ln Hilton Head Plantation Hilton Head Island SC 29926 Personal E-mail: alsrus@msn.com.

**RUSSELL, ANDREW BENJAMIN,** historian, educator; b. Oxnard, Calif., June 27, 1960; s. Leonard Russell and Sylvia Bergdal; m. Tona Hughes (div.); m. Rose T. Díaz, Jan. 14, 2001. BA in History, U. Nev., Las Vegas, 1988, MA in History, 1996; PhD in History, Ariz. State U., Tempe, 2003. Seasonal park ranger Nev. Divsn. State Parks. Spring Valley, 1988—90; svc. worker Las Vegas Convention Authority, 1991—95; tchg. asst. U. Nev., Las Vegas, 1994; tchg. assoc. Ariz. State U. Tempe, 1996—98; part-time instr. Albuquerque Tech. Vocat. Inst./Cmty. Coll. (now Ctrl. N.Mex. CC), 1999—2003; history instr. Albuquerque TVI/Cmty. Coll., 2003—. Rsch. historian Ariz. Humanities Coun., Phoenix, 1997; vol. rschr. Ariz. Am. Indian Movement,

Phoenix, 1998; presenter in field. Contbr. chapters to books. Recipient Phoenix One Hundred award, City of Phoenix, 1997; grantee, Civil Liberties Pub. Edn. Fund., 1998—99. Mem.: SW Oral History Assn., Albuquerque Hist. Soc. (bd. dirs. 2004—), Oral History Assn. (workship facilitator 1997—, nominating com. 2005.) Achievements include research in Japanese-American history. Avocations: guitar, songwriting, camping, travel. Business E-Mail: aruss@comcast.edu.

**RUSSELL, ANNE M.,** editor-in-chief; Editor book divsn. Billboard Publ.; editor Photo Dist. News; reporter Adweek; assoc. editor Am. Photographer; sr. editor Working Women; asst. editor Folio: Pub. News, editor-in-chief, 1992—97, Living Fit, 1997—99, Vegetarian Times, 1999; editl. dir. Fox TV's Health Network, Shape mag., 2001—03, editor-in-chief, 2003—. Office: Shape 21100 Erwin St Woodland Hills CA 91367*

**RUSSELL, ANNE WRENN,** property manager; b. Greensboro, NC, Mar. 2, 1934; d. Oscar Ivey and Lucy (Lula) Elinor (Wright) Wrenn; children: Elinor Russell Ball, Martha Anne Russell Martin, John Leon, Barbara Russell Richardson. BA in French, U. NC, Chapel Hill, 1956. Cert. N.C. Real Estate Bd., paralegal Atlanta Paralegal Inst., 1991. Camp counselor, Mass., 1954; with acctg. dept. Bank Greensboro, 1955; sec. Meth. Bd. Edn., Durham, NC, 1957—59; real estate sales person Geraci and Preston, Greensboro, 1991—92; property mgr. Wrenn-Zealy Properties, Inc., Greensboro, 1992—. Active Greensboro Opera Guild, Greensboro Opera Co., 1981—90; opera chorus mem. Greensboro Opera Co., 1981—85; active Greensboro Symphony Guild, 1981—90; com. correspondent Ch. Missions, 2005—; bd. mem. Ea. Music Festival, Greensboro, 1985—86. Mem.: U. N.C. Greensboro Musical Arts Guild (bd. mem. 2003—), English Speaking Union, Greensboro Choral Soc. (mem. steering com.), U. N.C. Chapel Hill Alumni Assn. (life), Greensboro Hist. Book Club (life). Republican. Methodist. Avocations: piano, singing, painting, sewing, tennis. Office: Wrenn-Zealy Properties 1403 Sunset Dr Greensboro NC 27408 Office Phone: 336-272-3183. Personal E-mail: nannebird@hotmail.com.

**RUSSELL, ANNIKA RENEE,** secondary school educator, financial consultant; d. Sondra Kay and Steve Lynn Russell. BA, Dakota Wesleyan U., 1996; MEd, U. Nebr., Lincoln, 2002. Lic. Securities SD, 2003. HS tchr., coach Sanborn Ctrl. Sch., Forestburg, SD, 1996—2005, Wessington Springs Schs., SD, 2005—; fin. rep. Primerica Fin. Svcs., Mitchell, SD, 2000—. Tech. instr. cons. State of SD, Spearfish, 1998—99; SD team coach Internat. Sports Specialist, Inc., North Logan, Utah, 1999—. Youth group leader United Meth. Ch., Mitchell, SD, 1999—2001. Mem.: ACTE, NEA, ASCD, SD Edn. Assn., SD Volleyball Coaches Assn., SD Coaches Assn., Nat. Bus. Edn. Assn. Methodist. Avocations: running, reading, crafts, skiing, biking. Home: 301 W 12th Ave Mitchell SD 57301

**RUSSELL, ATTIE YVONNE,** academic administrator, pediatrics educator, dean; b. Washington, Aug. 10, 1923; d. George and Kathleen L. (Milliner) Werner; m. Rex Hillier, Apr. 19, 1954 (dec.); m. Henry J. Russell, 1960 (div. 1971); children: Richard Russell, Margaret Jane Russell-Harde; m. Harry F. Camper, Sept. 2, 1984. BS, Am. U., 1944; PhD, State U. Iowa, 1952; MD, U. Chgo., 1958. Intern Phila. Gen. Hosp., 1958-59; resident in pediatrics Bronx Mcpl. Hosp., NY, 1960-61, Del. Hosp., Wilmington, 1962-63; dir. maternal and child health, crippled children's svcs. Del. State Bd. Health, Dover, 1963-68; asst. dean community health affairs, assoc. prof. pediatrics U. Cin. Coll. Medicine, 1968-71; clin. assoc. prof. pediatrics Med. Coll. Pa., Phila., 1966-68, 71-74; dep. dir. div. pub. health State of Del., Dover, 1971-74; dir. Santa Clara Valley Med. Ctr., San Jose, Calif., 1974-79; assoc. dean, clin. prof. pediatrics, family medicine Stanford U. Sch. Medicine, Calif., 1974-79; dir. USPHS Hosp., Boston, 1979-81, Balt. City Hosps., 1981-82; asst. v.p. community affairs, prof. pediatrics U. Tex. Med. Br., Galveston, 1982-87, asst. v.p. student affairs, dean students, prof. pediatrics, 1987-92, clin. prof. pediatrics, 1992—. Reviewer Coun. for Internat. Exchange of Scholars, Washington, 1987-94; dir. III Symposium on Health and Human Svcs. in the U.S.-Mex., Brownsville, 1988; mem. sci. coun. Am. Fedn. for Aging Rsch., Inc., 1983-86. Contbr. articles and abstracts to profl. jours. Mem. budget com. United Way, Galveston, 1982-84; mem. Mayor's Adv. Com. for Sr. Citizens and Handicapped Persons for the City of Galveston, 1983-85; bd. advisors Galveston Hist. Found., 1983-88; mem. Com. for Coop. Action Planning, 1983-88, Houston-Galveston Health Promotion Consortium, 1983-88, Injury Control Prevention (Houston), 1984-89, aging programs adv. com. Houston-Galveston Area Coun., 1985-92. Recipient Disting. Alumni award Am. U., 1984. Fellow Am. Acad. Pediatrics, Am. Pub. Health Assn.; mem. AMA, Am. Coll. Preventive Medicine, Am. Physiol. Soc., Mass. Med. Soc., Tex. Med. Assn., Galveston C. of C. (legis. com. 1983-88), Order of Eastern Star, Sigma Xi, Alpha Omega Alpha.*

**RUSSELL, BEVERLY ANN,** librarian, writer; b. Riverside, Calif., Jan. 15, 1947; d. James and Hazel M. Russell. BA in Polit. Sci., Calif. State U., 1971, MLS, 1973. Libr. asst. Riverside Pub. Libr., 1974—75; asst. libr. U. Calif., 1975—76; office asst. Calif. State Dept. Rehab., L.A., 1976—77; libr. technician Magnavox Rsch. Labs., Torrance, Calif., 1976—83; libr. asst. Burbank (Calif.) Unified Sch. Dist., 1985—86; office technician Social Svcs. Dept., Van Nuys, Calif., 1988—92; libr. Pleasant Valley State Prison, Coalinga, Calif., 1994—. Co-author (poetry) Roots & Wings, 1986, Three Women Black, 1988. Mem.: Alpha Kappa Alpha. Avocations: writing, poetry. Home: 250 Truman St #250 Coalinga CA 93210 Office: Pleasant Valley State Prison PO Box 8500 Coalinga CA 93210-8500 Office Phone: 559-935-4900.

**RUSSELL, BILL,** former professional basketball team executive, former professional basketball player; b. Monroe, La., Feb. 12, 1934; Grad., San Francisco State Coll., 1956. Player, Boston Celtics Profl. Basketball Club, 1956-69, coach, 1966-69; sportscaster ABC-TV, 1969-80, CBS-TV, 1980-83; coach NBA Seattle Supersonics, 1973-77, Sacramento Kings, 1987-88, v.p. basketball ops., then exec. v.p., 1988-89. Mem. U.S. Olympic Basketball Team (Gold medal), 1956 Appeared in: TV series Cowboy in Africa; also commis.; co-host: The Superstars, ABC-TV, 1978-79; Author: Second Wind: Memoirs of an Opinionated Man, 1979. Inducted into Basketball Hall of Fame, 1974; mem. 11 NBA championship teams. Office: c/o Retired Players Assn 30 Kennedy Plz Providence RI 02903-2329

**RUSSELL, C. EDWARD, JR.,** lawyer; b. Portsmouth, Va., Aug. 19, 1942; BA, Hampden-Sydney Coll., 1964; LLB, Washington & Lee U., 1967. Bar: Va. 1967. Law clk. to Hon. John A. MacKenzie U.S. Dist. Ct. (ea. dist.) Va., 1967-68; atty. Kaufman & Canoles, Norfolk. Mem. ABA (bus. law sect., real property, probate and trust law sect.), Va. State Bar (bus. law sect., real property sect.), Va. Bar Assn. (bus. law sect., real estate sect., chmn. young lawyers sect. 1977), Omicron Delta Kappa, Phi Alpha Delta. Office: PO Box 13368 Norfolk VA 23506-0368 Office Phone: 757-624-3108. E-Mail: cerussell@kaufcan.com.

**RUSSELL, CAROL ANN,** personnel service company executive; b. Detroit, Dec. 14, 1943; d. Billy and Iris Koud; m. Victor Rojas (div.). BA in English, CUNY-Hunter Coll., 1993. Registered employment cons. Various positions in temp. help cos., N.Y.C., 1964-74; v.p. Wollborg-Michelson, San Francisco, 1974-82; co-owner, pres. Russell Staffing Resources, Inc., San Francisco and Sonoma, 1983-98; ret.; co-founder HR 24/7, 1998. Media guest, spkr., workshop and seminar leader in field; host/cmty. prodr. Job Net program for TCI Cable T.V. Pub. Checkpoint Newsletter; feature writer/columnist The Slant; contbr. articles to profl. publs. Founding v.p. The Friends of the Frank Lloyd Wright Civic Ctr. Libr. Marin County; vice chair Sonoma County Commn. on Status of Women, 2003—06; mem. cmty. action com. Sonoma County Commn. on Human Rights; founding cmty. prodr. Northbay Pride Music Festival, 2005—; bd. dirs Sonoma County Libr. Found., 2003—. Named to Inc. 500, 1989—90. Mem. Am. Women in Radio and TV, No. Calif. Human Resources Coun., Calif. Women Human Resource Mgmt., Calif. Assn. Pers. Cons. (pres. Golden State chpt. 1984-85), Calif. Assn. Temp. Svcs., Bay Area Pers. Assn. (pres. 1983-84), Pers. Assn. Sonoma County, Scowrers and Molly

Maguires (bd. dirs., editor The Herald), Sherlock Holmes Soc. London, Nat. Women's Polit. Caucus (comms. chair Marin chpt. 2002, pres. Marin chpt. 2003). Office Phone: 707-669-0009. Personal E-mail: incloverdale@comcast.net.

**RUSSELL, CHARLES HARRY,** music educator, restaurant manager; b. Flint, Mich., Oct. 7, 1962; s. Harry Charles and Sandra Kay Russell; m. Pamela Rene Flewelling, Aug. 20, 1983; children: Alena, Angela, Charles. BA, U. Michigan, Flint, Michigan, 1992; MusB in Edn., U. Michigan, Flint, 2002. Sr. asst. restaurant mgr. Taco Bell, Flint, 1987—; trumpet tchr. Herter Music Ctr., Flint, 1997—. Composer: (music) Your Memory Will Live, 1991, If Only, 1990. Recipient Eagle Scout, Boy Scouts of Am., 1980. Mem.: Mich. Band and Orch. Assn., Music Educator Nat. Conf. Home: 4379 Regency Rd Swartz Creek MI 48473 Personal E-mail: cruss9999@aol.com.

**RUSSELL, CHARLES WILLIAM, III,** communications executive, writer; b. Hollywood, Calif., Feb. 18, 1953; s. Charles Willam Russell, Jr. and Shirley Louise Russell; m. Jeanette Marie Joslin, Mar. 26, 1982; children: Charles Murray, William Storm. BA, Loyola Marymount U., LA, 1975, MA, 1979. Cert. Media Mgmt. U. So. Calif. Annenberg Sch. for Comm., 1985. Scriptwriting UCLA, 1979. Pub. rels. mgr. Getty Oil Co., LA, 1982—87; sr. writer-prodr. Walt Disney Imagineering, Glendale, 1988—99; v.p. interactive strategy Young & Rubicam Advt., Irvine, 2000—01; pres. Chick Russell Comm., Pasadena, Calif., 2002—. Prodr., writer (museum exhibit) U-boat 505, Chgo. Mus. Sci. and Industry. Action! An Adventure in MovieMaking, Chgo. Mus. Sci. and Industry (Am. Mus. Assn. Outstanding Achievement, 2005, TEA Thea Award, 2005), (website) Lincoln Car Website, Mercury Car Website, (theme park) Tokyo DisneySea (TEA Thea Award, 2002), (zoo expansion) Fort Worth Zoo Texas Wild (TEA Thea Award, 1995), (museum) Mus. of the American West. Eagle scout Boy Scouts of Am., Hollywood, 1967. Recipient Golden Quill award, Internat. Assn. Bus. Communicators, 1985, Silver Screen award, Internat. Indsl. Film Festival, 1984. Mem.: Assn. for Pub. History, TEA, Western Mus. Assn., Am. Assn. Museums.

**RUSSELL, CHARLIE L.,** writer; b. Monroe, La., Mar. 10, 1932; s. Charlie L. and Katie O. Russell; children: Katheryn K., Joshua E. BS in English, U. San Francisco, 1959; MSW, NYU, 1966; MFA, U. Calif., San Diego, 1986. Author: (play) Five on the Black Hand Side, 1969, (film script) Five on the Black Hand Side, 1972 (Image award, NAACP, 1972), (novels) The Worthy Ones, 2002. With U.S. Army, 1953—55, Korea. Home: 1413 Neilson St Berkeley CA 94702 E-mail: charlierussell@attbi.com.

**RUSSELL, CHARLOTTE SANANES,** biochemistry professor, researcher; b. NYC, Jan. 4, 1927; d. Joseph and Marguerite (Saltiel) Sananes; m. Joseph Brooke Russell, Dec. 20, 1947; children: James Robert, Joshua Sananes. BA, Bklyn. Coll., 1946; MA, Columbia U., 1947, PhD, 1951. Asst. prof. chemistry CCNY, N.Y.C., 1958-68, assoc. prof., 1968-72, prof., 1972—, prof. emerita, 2001—. Peer reviewer NSF, NIH; ad hoc reviewer sci. jours. including Jour. Bacteriology, Biochemistry. Contbr. articles to profl. jours. Mem. AAAS, Am. Soc. Biochemistry and Molecular Biology, Am. Chem. Soc., Amnesty Internat., Sigma Xi. Office: CCNY Dept Chemistry 138th St & Convent Ave New York NY 10031 Office Phone: 212-650-6681. Business E-Mail: chrcc@sci.ccny.cuny.edu.

**RUSSELL, CHRISTOPHER JOHN,** secondary school educator, music educator; b. Milw., Nov. 3, 1972; s. Robert Arthur and Barbara Ann Russell. BS, Northwestern Coll., 1996; MA in Music Edn., U. St. Thomas, 2001; PhD, U. Minn., 2006. Tchr. mid. sch. music Carol Morgan Sch., Santo Domingo, Dominican Republic, 1996—97; tchr. vocal music Park High Sch., Cottage Grove, Minn., 1997—. Mem.: Am. Choral Dirs. Assn., Minn. Music Educators Assn., Nat. Assn. Music Edn. Conservative. Avocations: motorcycling, weightlifting, softball, bicycling. Office: Park High Sch 8040 80th St S Cottage Grove MN 55016

**RUSSELL, DANA C.,** information technology executive, accountant; BS in Acctg., MS in Acctg., Weber State U. CPA Utah. With WordPerfect, Iomega, Price Waterhouse; various financial positions Novell, Inc., Waltham, Mass., 1994—, v.p. fin., corp. controller, 2003—06, treas., 2005—06, interim CFO, 2006—. Office: Novell Inc 404 Wyman St Ste 500 Waltham MA 02451*

**RUSSELL, DAVID L.,** federal judge; b. Sapulpa, Okla., July 7, 1942; s. Lynn and Florence E. (Brown) R.; m. Dana J. Wilson, Apr. 16, 1971; 1 child, Sarah Elizabeth BS, Okla. Bapt. U., 1963; JD, Okla. U., 1965. Bar: Okla. 1965. Asst. atty. gen. State of Okla., Oklahoma City, 1968-69, legal adviser to gov., 1969-70; legal adviser Senator Dewey Bartlett, Washington, 1973-75; U.S. atty. for Western dist. Okla. Dept. Justice, 1975-77, 81-82; ptnr. Benefield & Russell, Oklahoma City, 1977-81; judge U.S. Dist. Ct. (we. dist.) Okla., Oklahoma City, 1982—, chief judge, 1994—2002. Lt. comdr. JAGC, USN, 1965-68. Selected Outstanding Fed. Ct. Trial judge Okla. Trial Lawyers Assn., 1988, The Jour. Record award Okla. County Bar Assn., 2005. Mem. Okla. Bar Assn., Fed. Bar Assn. (pres. Oklahoma City chpt. 1981), Order of Coif (alumnus mem.), Jud. Conf. US (mem. exec. com. 2003-06). Republican. Methodist. Office: US Dist Ct US Courthouse 200 NW 4th St Oklahoma City OK 73102-3026 Office Phone: 405-609-5100.

**RUSSELL, DAVID O.,** film director, film producer, scriptwriter; b. N.Y.C., N.Y., Aug. 20, 1958; m. Janet Grillo. Grad., Amherst Coll., 1981. Dir., writer, prodr. (films) Bingo Inferno, 1987, I Heart Huckabees, 2004, dir., writer, exec. prodr. Spanking the Monkey, 1994, dir., writer Flirting with Disaster, 1996, Three Kings, 1999; dir.: (films) Hairway to the Stars, 1990; exec. prodr.: Anchorman: The Legend of Ron Burgundy, 2004, Wake Up, Ron Burgundy: The Lost Movie, 2004; prodr.: The Slaughter Rule, 2002; actor: Adaptation, 2002; dir., prodr. (documentaries) Soldier's Pay, 2004. Office: Apt 2B 250 W 99th St New York NY 10025-5442

**RUSSELL, DAVID W.,** molecular geneticist; BA in Biology, U. Tex., Austin, 1975; PhD in Chemistry, U. NC, Chapel Hill, 1980. Damon Runyon Cancer Rsch. Found. postdoctoral fellow U. British Columbia, 1980—82; mem. faculty U. Tex. Southwestern Med. Ctr., Dallas, 1982—90, prof. dept. molecular genetics, 1990—, Eugene McDermott disting. chair molecular genetics, 1992—. Contbr. articles to profl. jours.; mem. editl. bd.: Cell Metabolism, Trends in Biochemical Scis., assoc. editor: Jour. Biol. Chemistry. Recipient Rsch. Career Devel. award, NIH, 1984, Louis N. Katz award, Am. Heart Assn., 1985, Kilby Sci. Place award, Tex. Instruments, 1993, Adolph Windhaus prize, Falk Found., Germany, 2002. Fellow: NAS; mem.: Am. Soc. Mass Spectrometry, Endocrine Soc. (Ernst Oppenheimer award 1999), Am. Soc. Biol. Chemistry, AAAS. Office: Dept Molecular Genetics U Tex Southwestern Med Ctr 5323 Harry Hines Blvd Dallas TX 75390 E-mail: david.russell@utsouthwestern.edu.

**RUSSELL, DAVID WILLIAMS,** lawyer; b. Lockport, N.Y., Apr. 5, 1945; s. David Lawson and Jean Graves (Williams) R.; m. Frances Yung Chung Chen, May 23, 1970; children: Bayard Chen, Ming Rennick. AB, Dartmouth Coll., 1967, MBA, 1969; JD cum laude, Northwestern U., 1976. Bar: Ill. 1976, Ind. 1983. English tchr. Talladega Coll., Ala., 1967; math. tchr. Lyndon Inst., Lyndonville, Vt., 1967-68; asst. to pres. for planning Tougaloo Coll., Miss., 1969-71, bus. mgr., 1971-73; law clk. Montgomery, McCracken, Walker & Rhoads, Phila., 1975; with Winston & Strawn, Chgo., 1976-83; ptnr. Klineman, Rose, Wolf & Wallack, Indpls., 1983-87, Johnson, Smith, Pence, Densborn, Wright & Heath, Indpls., 1987-99, Bose McKinney & Evans, Indpls., 1999—2004, Harrison & Moberly, Indpls., 2004—. Cons. Alfred P. Sloan Found., 1972-73; dir. Found. for Internat. Svcs., 1985—, sec., 1985-88, pres. 1988-89; U.S. Dept. Justice del. to U.S. China Joint Session on Trade, Investment & Econ. Law, Beijing, 1987; leader Ind. Products Trade Fair, Kawachinagano, Japan, 1996; lectr. Ind. law Ind. Gov.'s Trade Mission to Japan, 1986, internat. law Ind. CLE Forum, 1986-96, 2000-03, chms. 1987, 89, 91, 2001-03; adj. prof. internat. bus. law Ind. U., 1993-95; nat. selection com. Woodrow Wilson Found. Adminstrv. Fellowship Program, 1973-76; vol. Lawyers for Creative Arts, Chgo., 1977-83; dir. World Trade

Club of Ind., 1987-93, 2005—, v.p., 1987-91, pres., 1991-92; dir. Ind. Swiss Found., 1991-2002; dir. Writer's Ctr., Indpls., 1999—, treas., 2001—; dir. Asian Am. Alliance, 1999—, treas., 2006—; dir. Indpls. (Ind.) Peace Games, Inc., 2000—, Friends of Taiwan Assn., Inc., 2001—, Advance Ind. Found, 2005—; dir. Ind. Soviet Trade Consortium, 1991-99, sec., 1991-92; v.p., bd. dirs. Ind. Sister Cities, 1988—; dir. Internat. Ctr. Indpls., 1988-92, v.p. 1988-89; Ind. dist. enrollment dir. Dartmouth Coll., 1990-99; dir. Carmel Sister Cities, 1993—, v.p. 1995-96, pres. 1997-99, chmn., 1999—; v.p., gen. coun. Lawrence Durrell Soc., 1993—; internat. adv. bds. Supply Chain & Global Mgmt. Acad. Kelley Grad Sch. Bus., Ind. U., 2001—; mem. internat. adv. bd. Ind. U. Law Sch., 2003—, Ind. Econ. Devel. Corp. 2005—; bd. advisors Ctr. for Internat. Bus. Edn. and Rsch. Krannert Grad. Sch. Mgmt. Purdue U., 1995—; dir., v.p., gen. coun. Global Crossroads Found., Inc., 1995-2003; mem. bd. arbitrators NASD, 1999—; dir. Ind. Dist. Export Coun., 1999—, chmn. 2005-. Named Hon. fellow, Ctr. for Internat. Legal Studies, 2002—, Internat. Bus. Person of Yr., World Trade Club of Ind., 2002, Sagamore of the Wabash, 2002, Ind. Super Lawyer, Ind. Monthly Mag. and Ind. Law and Politics, 2004, 2005, 2006; Adminstrv. fellow, Woodrow Wilson Found., 1969—72, David Williams Russell Day named in his honor, Jan. 15, 2002, Indpls. Mem. ABA, ACLU, Ill. Bar Assn., Ind. Bar Assn. (vice chmn. internat. law sect. 1988-90, treas. 2002-, chmn. 1990-92, 2002-04, co-chmn. written publs. com. 1997-99), Indpls. Bar Assn., Dartmouth Lawyers Assn., Indpls. Assn. Chinese Ams., Chinese Music Soc., Dartmouth Club of Ind. (sec. 1986-87, pres. 1987-88), Internat. Bar Assn., Zeta Psi. Presbyterian. Home: 10926 Lakeview Dr Carmel IN 46033-3937 Office: Harrison & Moberly LLP 2100 First Ind Plz 135 N Pennsylvania St Indianapolis IN 46204-2400 Office Phone: 317-639-4511. Business E-Mail: drussell@h-mlaw.com.

**RUSSELL, ELBERT WINSLOW,** neuropsychologist; b. Las Vegas, N.Mex., June 4, 1929; s. Josiah Cox and Ruth Winslow Russell; children from previous marriage Gwendolyn Marie Harvey, Franklin Winslow, Kirsten Nash, Jonathan Nash; m. Sally Lynn Kolitz, Apr. 2, 1989. BA, Earlham Coll., Richmond, Ind., 1951; MA, U. Ill., 1953; MS, Pa. State U., 1958; PhD, U. Kans., 1968. Lic. psychologist Florida, 1973. Clin. psychologist Warnersville (Pa.) State Hosp., 1959-61; clin. neuropsychologist VA Med. Ctr., Cin., 1968-71, dir. neuropsychology lab. Miami, Fla., 1971-89, rsch. psychologist, 1989—. Adj. prof. Nova U., Ft. Lauderdale, 1980-87, U. Miami Med. Sch., 1980-94, U. Miami, 1979—. Author: (with C. Neuringer and G. Goldstein) Assessment of Brain Damage, 1970; (with R.I. Starkey) Halstead Russell Neuropsychology Evaluation System (manual and computer program), 1993, rev. 2001; contbr. articles to profl. jours. Recipient Life Time Achievement award, Am. Bd. Psychol. Assessment, 1999, Halstead award, Reitan Soc., 2000. Fellow APA, Am. Psychol. Soc., Nat. Acad. Neuropsychology; mem. Sigma Xi. Democrat. Mem. Soc. Of Friends. Home: 6091 SW 79th St Miami FL 33156-2944 Office: 9350 S Dixie Hwy Ph 3 Miami FL 33156-2944 Office Phone: 305-670-2284. Personal E-mail: ewr@bellsouth.net.

**RUSSELL, FINDLAY EWING,** physician; b. San Francisco, Sept. 1, 1919; s. William and Mary Jane (Findlay) R.; m. Janet Louise Thiel. Feb. 14, 1950; children: Christa Ann, Sharon Jane, Robin Emily, Constance Susan, Mark Findlay. BA, Walla Walla Coll., Wash., 1941; MD, Loma Linda U., Calif., 1950; postgrad. (fellow), Calif. Inst. Tech., 1951-53; PhD, U. Santa Barbara, Calif., 1974, LLD (hon.), 1989. Intern White Meml. Hosp., Los Angeles, 1950-51; practice medicine specializing in toxinology and toxicology Los Angeles, 1953—; mem. staff Los Angeles County-U. So. Calif. Med. Center, Loma Linda U. Med. Center, U. Ariz. Med. Ctr.; physiologist Huntington Inst. Med. Research, 1953-55; dir. lab. neurol. research Los Angeles County-U. So. Calif. Med. Center, 1955-80; mem. faculty Loma Linda U. Med. Sch., 1955—; prof. neurology, physiology and biology U. So. Calif. Med. Sch., 1966-81; prof. pharmacology and toxicology U. Ariz. Health Scis. Coll. Pharmacy, 1981—. Cons. USPHS, NSF, Office Naval Rsch., WHO, U.S. Army, Walter Reed, USAF, Brooks AFB. Author: Marine Toxins and Venomous and Poisonous Marine Animals, 1965, Poisonous Marine Animals, 1971, Snake Venom Poisoning, 1980; co-author: Bibliography of Snake Venoms and Venomous Snakes, 1964, Animal Toxins, 1967, Poisonous Snakes of The World, 1968, Snake Venom Poisoning, 1983, Bibliography of Venomous and Poisonous Marine Animals and Their Toxins, 1984, Venomous and Poisonous Marine Invertebrates of the Indian Ocean, 1996; editor: Toxicon, 1962-70. Served with AUS, 1942-46. Decorated Purple Heart, Bronze Star; recipient award Los Angeles County Bd. Suprs., 1960; award Acad. Medicine Buenos Aires, 1966; Skylab Achievement award, 1974; Jozef Stefan medal Yugoslavia, 1978; U.S. State Dept. medallion, 2006. Fellow A.C.P., Am. Coll. Cardiology, Royal Soc. Tropical Medicine, N.Y. Acad. Scis.; mem. Internat. Soc. Toxinology (pres. 1962-66, Francisco Redi medal 1967), Royal Soc. Medicine, Am. Soc. Physiology, Western Soc. Pharmacology (pres. 1973) Office: U Ariz Health Scis Coll Pharmacy Pharm/Tox Tucson AZ 85721 Office Phone: 520-626-4047.

**RUSSELL, FRANCIA,** ballet director, educator; b. LA, Jan. 10, 1938; d. W. Frank and Marion (Whitney) R.; m. Kent Stowell, Nov. 19, 1965; children: Christopher, Darren, Ethan. Studies with, George Balanchine, Vera Volkova, Felia Doubrouska, Antonina Tumkovsky, Benjamin Harkarvy; student, NYU, Columbia U.; degree (hon.), Seattle U., 2003. Dancer, soloist N.Y.C. Ballet, 1956-62, ballet mistress, 1965-70; dancer Ballets USA/Jerome Robbins, N.Y.C., 1962; tchr. ballet Sch. Am. Ballet, N.Y.C., 1963-64; co-dir. Frankfurt (Fed. Republic Germany) Opera Ballet, 1976-77; dir., co-artistic dir. Pacific N.W. Ballet, Seattle, 1977—; dir. Pacific N.W. Ballet Sch., Seattle. Affiliate prof. of dance U. Wash. Dir. staging over 100 George Balanchine ballet prodns. throughout world, including Russia and China, 1964—. Named Woman of Achievement, Matrix Table, Women in Comm., Seattle, 1987, Gov.'s Arts award, 1989, Dance Mag. award, 1996, Brava award Women's U. Club, 2003. Mem. Internat. Women's Forum. Home: 2833 Broadway E Seattle WA 98102-3935 Office: Pacific NW Ballet 301 Mercer St Seattle WA 98109-4600

**RUSSELL, FRANK ELI,** retired newspaper publishing executive; b. Kokomo, Ind., Dec. 6, 1920; s. Frank E. and Maude (Wiggins) R.; children: Linda Carole Russell Atkins, Richard Lee, Frank E. III, Rita Jane Russell Eagle, Julie Beth Russell; m. Nancy M. Shover, Oct. 5, 1991. AB, Evansville Coll., 1942; D. Ind. U., 1951; LLD (hon.), U. Evansville, 1985; HHD (hon.), Franklin Coll., 1989. Bar: Ind. 1951; CPA, Ind. Ptnr. George S. Olive & Co., Indpls., 1947-53; exec. v.p. Spickelmier Industries, Inc., Indpls., 1953-59; bus. mgr. Indpls. Star & News, 1959-77; v.p., gen. mgr. Ctrl. Newspapers, Inc., Indpls., 1977-79, pres., 1979-95, chmn., bd. dirs., 1996-98; ret., 1998; also bd. dirs. Ctrl. Newsprint; pres. Bradley Paper Co., also bd. dirs. Past chmn. adv. bd. mem. Indpls. TV Assn., Inc.; trustee retirement trust Ctrl. Newspapers, Inc.; chmn. retirement com. Hoosier State Press. Bd. dirs. Ariz. Cmty. Found., 1992-96, Eiteljorg Mus., 1994—; trustee, chmn. bd. Nina Mason Pulliam Charitable Trust, 1997—. Recipient Life Salvation award Salvation Army, 1989, Disting. Alumni award Ind. U. Sch. Law, 1989, Life Trustee award U. Evansville, 1991, Ralph D. Casey award, 1997. Mem. ABA, AICPA, Ind. Bar. Assn., Indpls. Bar Assn. (past bd. dirs., past treas.). Ind. Assn. CPAs (past dir.), Tax Execs. Inst. (past pres.), Ind. Assn. Credit Mgmt. (dir., v.p.), Inst. Newspaper Controllers and Fin. Officers (dir., past pres.), Ind. Acad. Ind. Assn. Colls., Midwest Pension Conf. (ind. chpt.), Newspaper Advt. Bur. (bd. dirs.), Salvation Army (life mem. award), Columbia Club, Meridian Hills Country Club, Masons, Shriners, Order of Coif, Phi Delta Phi, Sigma Alpha Epsilon. Methodist. Office: Nina Mason Pulliam Charitable Trust 135 N Pennsylvania St Ste 1200 Indianapolis IN 46204-1956

**RUSSELL, GEORGE HAW,** video production company executive; b. Neosho, Mo., May 22, 1945; s. Kenneth L. and Marjorie (Haw) R.; m. Suzanne Bennett, June 1, 1967; children: Margaret Anne, Marjorie Jane, Karen Lee, George Andrew. BA, La. State U., 1967. Exec. Ednl. Video Network, Huntsville, 1990—; ptnr. Sam Houston Group Ltd. Liability Partnership, Huntsville, 1991—. Prodr. ednl. videos Nombres et Couleurs, 1988 (Silver Apple award 1988), Napoleon, 1989 (Silver Apple award 1989), Bullfight, 1990, The French Revolution, 1990; exec. prodr. Spain's Historic Cities, 1992, Munich's Oktoberfest, 1992, The New Nutriton Pyramid, 1992,

The Visual Language of Design, 1992, Florence, 1993, Joan of Arc, 1993, New Food Guide Pyramid, 1993, Cleaning and Maintaining Your VCR, 1993, Arts and Crafts of Mexico, 1993, Understanding Geysers and Hot Springs, 1993, Thoreau at Walden Pond, 1993, French Markets, 1993, Great Zimbabwe, 1993. Bd. govs. Tex. Com. on Natural Resources, Dallas, 1979—; bd. dirs. Gibbs-Powell House Mus., Huntsville, Natural Area Preservation Assn. Dallas; chmn. forest practices Lone Star Sierra Club, Austin, Tex., 1984—; chmn. Fed. Forest Reform, Washington, D.C., 1991—. 1st lt. U.S. Army, 1971-74. Recipient sgt. achievement award Sierra Club, San Francisco 1985, chpt. conservation award 1987, environ. heroes for centennial 1991; named Citizen of Month, Huntsville Item 1988. Democrat. Methodist. Avocations: environmental advocacy, historic building restoration, collecting antiques and folk art. Home: 1409 19th St Huntsville TX 77340-5056 Office: Ednl Video Network 1401 19th St Huntsville TX 77340-5057 Office Phone: 936-295-5767. Personal E-mail: ghr@cyberclone.net.

**RUSSELL, IRWIN EMANUEL,** lawyer; b. N.Y.C., Jan. 24, 1926; m. Suzanne Russell, Nov. 15, 1968. BS in Econs., U. Pa., 1947; JD, Harvard U., 1949. Bar: N.Y. 1949, Calif. 1971. Atty. office chief counsel Wage Stabilization Bd., Washington, 1951-53; pvt. practice N.Y.C., 1954-71; founder, chmn., dir. RAI Rsch. Corp., Hauppage, NY, 1954-91; exec. v.p., treas., dir. The Wolper Orgn., Inc., L.A., 1971-76; pvt. practice Beverly Hills, Calif. 1977—; bd. dirs. The Walt Disney Co., 1987—2001. With USAAF, 1944-45. Home: 10590 Wilshire Blvd Apt 1402 Los Angeles CA 90024-4563 Office: 9401 Wilshire Blvd Ste 760 Beverly Hills CA 90212-2933 Office Phone: 310-777-3630. Business E-Mail: ierussell@pacbell.net.

**RUSSELL, JAMES ALVIN, JR.,** college administrator; b. Lawrenceville, Va., Dec. 25, 1917; s. Dr. James Alvin and Nellie M. (Pratt) R.; m. Lottye J. Washington, Dec. 25, 1943; children: Charlotte Justyne, James Alvin III. BA, Oberlin Coll., 1940; BS, Bradley U., 1941, MS, 1950, spl. insts.: EdD, U. Md., 1967; spl. insts., Wayne U., U. Mich., U. Ill., NSF. Prof. div. engring., also prof. edn. div. grad. studies Hampton Inst., 1950-71; pres. St. Paul's Coll., Lawrenceville, 1971-81; dir. instructional programs and student services Va. C.C. System, 1981-82; chmn. div. prof. studies W.Va. State Coll., 1982-86, acting pres., 1986-87, exec. asst. to pres., 1987-88; pres. So. W.Va. C.C., 1988-89, ret., 1989. Pres. Peninsula Council Human Relations, 1961-65. United Negro Coll. Fund fellow, 1966-67. Mem. IEEE, Am. Soc. Engring. Edn., Am. Assn. Univ. Adminstrs., Am. Vocat. Assn., Am. Tech. Edn. Assn., Nat. Assn. Indsl. Tech., Am. Assn. for Higher Edn., Nat. Assn. for Equal Opportunity in Edn., Brunswick C. of C., Sigma Pi Phi, Alpha Kappa Mu, Iota Lambda Sigma, Omega Psi Phi. Home: 811 Grandview Dr Dunbar WV 25064-1175 E-mail: Drjarusdun@aol.com.

**RUSSELL, JAMES BENJAMIN,** microbiologist, educator, research scientist; s. Lincoln A. and Mary M. Russell; 1 child, Aaron T. BS, Cornell U., Ithaca, NY, 1973; MS, U. Calif., Davis, 1974, PhD, 1978. Asst. prof. U. Ill., Urbana, 1978—81; rsch. microbiologist Agrl. Rsch. Svc., USDA, Ithaca, 1981—; prof. Cornell U., Ithaca, 1981—. Author: Rumen Microbiology and Its Role in Ruminant Nutrition, 2002; contbr. more than 200 articles, revs. to profl. publs., chpts. to books. Named North Atlantic Area Scientist of Yr., USDA, 1993, 2005; recipient Outstanding Tchr. award, U. Ill., 1981, Am. Feed Industry award, USDA, 1993, 2005. Fellow: Am. Acad. Microbiology; mem.: Am. Soc. Animal Sci., Am. Dairy Sci. Assn., Am. Soc. Microbiology. Achievements include patents for rumen fluid for calves to prevent needless diarrhea; patents pending for carbonated cow manure to kill pathogenic bacteria. Avocation: swimming. Office Phone: 607-255-4508.

**RUSSELL, JAMES BRIAN,** broadcast executive, media consultant; b. Hartford, Conn., Jan. 30, 1946; s. Seymour and Marian (Kamins) R.; m. Kathleen Anne Schardt, Dec. 28, 1968; children: Theodore, Jennifer, Kimberly. BA in Journalism, Am. U., 1968; postgrad. Wharton Sch. Bus., U. Pa.; postgrad., Stanford U. News dir. Sta. WPIK-AM, Arlington, Va., 1965-66; editor, anchorman Sta. WAVA-AM/FM, Washington, 1966-68; editor, corr. UPI, Washington, Cambodia and Vietnam, 1968-71; from reporter to exec. prodr. All Things Considered Nat. Pub. Radio, Washington, 1971-78; sta. dir., sr. v.p. programming Stas. KTCA/KTCI-TV, Mpls./St. Paul, 1978-88; v.p. nat. prodns., exec. prodr. Marketplace U. So. Calif., L.A., 1988-97; v.p. nat. Radio and GM Marketplace Prodns., L.A., 1997-99; sr. v.p. Minn. Pub. Radio, Am. Pub. Media & GM Marketplace Prodns., L.A., 2000—06; pres. Jim Russell Prodns., 2006—. Cons. Corp. Pub. Broadcasting, Nat. Endowment Arts, Sta. WNET-TV, N.Y.C., Sta. WGBH-TV, Boston, Nat. Pub. Radio, Am. Pub. Radio, Pub. Radio Internat., Am. Documentary Consortium, The Learning Channel, The Pacific Rim Consortium, Internat. Pub. TV Conf., Audible, Inc.; adv. bd. Assoc. Press Broadcasters, 2002-. Columnist pub. broadcasting's Current newspaper. Mem. prison visitor program AMICUS, St. Paul, 1984-85. Postgrad. fellow in journalism U. Mich.; recipient Nat. Headliner award 1972, 74, Ohio State award 1973, 75, duPont Columbia awards Columbia U., 1979, 81, 97, Peabody award 2001, Nat. TV Emmy award Acad. TV Arts and Scis., 1989, William Kling award for Innovation and Entrepreneurship, 1998, Mo. Honor medal for disting. svc. in journalism, 2000. E-mail: jim@programdoctor.com.

**RUSSELL, JAMES WEBSTER, JR.,** editor, columnist; b. Shreveport, La., Nov. 30, 1921; s. James Webster and Aline (Faulk) R.; m. Jean Buck, June 29, 1949 (dec. Sept. 2002); children: Nancy Russell Dearr, Eileen Russell Goure; m. Sylvia Swogger Sheldon, Aug. 17, 2004. BA, La. State U., 1942. Fla. mgr. Internat. News Service, 1946-51; bur. chief UPI, Tallahassee, 1951-52; regional editor U.P.I., Atlanta, 1953-57; asst. city editor Miami (Fla.) Herald, 1957-58, bus.-fin. editor, 1958-74, fin.-econ. columnist, 1974—99. Guest lectr. U. Miami, Fla. Internat. U., Miami-Dade Community Coll., La. State U. Contbr. articles to: Fla. Trend, Times of London, N.Y. Times, Gentlemen's Quar. Trustee Fla. So. Coll. Served with USAAF, 1942-45. Recipient Englt award Invest-In-Am. Club., 1976; decorated Air medal with eleven oak leaf clusters; inducted La. State U. Sch. of Mass Comms. Hall of Fame, 1998. Mem. Soc. Am. Bus. Writers, Lambda Chi Alpha, Sigma Delta Chi. Republican. Methodist (chmn. ch. council on ministries 1971-72). Home: 4800 SW 64th Ct Miami FL 33155-6133

**RUSSELL, JEFFREY BURTON,** historian, educator; b. Fresno, Calif., Aug. 1, 1934; s. Lewis Henry and Ieda Velma (Ogborn) R.; m. Diana Emily Mansfield, June 30, 1956; children: Jennifer, Mark, William, Penelope. AB, U. Calif., Berkeley, 1955, A.M., 1957; PhD, Emory U., 1960. Asst. prof. U. N.Mex., Albuquerque, 1960-61; jr. fellow Soc. of Fellows, Harvard U., Cambridge, Mass., 1961-62; mem. faculty U. Calif., Riverside, 1962-75, prof. dept. history, 1969-75, assoc. dean grad. div., 1967-72; dir. Medieval Inst., Michael P. Grace prof. medieval studies U. Notre Dame, South Bend, Ind., 1975-77; dean grad. studies Calif. State U., Sacramento, 1977-79; prof. history U. Calif., Santa Barbara, 1979—, prof. religious studies, 1994—. Author: Dissent and Reform in the Early Middle Ages, 1965, Medieval Civilization, 1968, A History of Medieval Christianity: Prophecy and Order, 1968, Religious Dissent in the Middle Ages, 1971, Witchcraft in the Middle Ages, 1972, The Devil: Perceptions of Evil from Antiquity to Primitive Christianity, 1977, A History of Witchcraft: Sorcerers, Heretics, and Pagans, 1980, Medieval Heresies: a Bibliography, 1981, Satan: The Early Christian Tradition, 1981, Lucifer: The Devil in the Middle Ages, 1984, Mephistopheles: The Devil in the Modern World, 1986, The Prince of Darkness, 1988, Ruga in Aevis, 1990, Inventing the Flat Earth: Columbus and the Historians, 1991, Dissent and Order in the Middle Ages, 1992, A History of Heaven: The Singing Silence, 1997, Essays in Honor of Jeffrey B. Russell, 1998, Paradise Mislaid: How We Lost Heaven and How We Can Regain It, 2006; contbr. articles to profl. jours. Fulbright fellow, 1959-60; Am. Council Learned Socs. grantee, 1965, 70; Social Sci. Research Council grantee, 1968; Guggenheim fellow, 1968-69; Nat. Endowment for Humanities sr. fellow, 1972-73 Fellow Medieval Acad. Am.; mem. Am. Soc. Ch. Histor Am. Acad. Religion, Astron. Soc. Pacific. Home: 4798 Calle Camarada Santa Barbara CA 93110-2053 Office: U Calif Dept History Santa Barbara CA 93106 E-mail: russell@history.ucsb.edu.

**RUSSELL, JEFFREY SCOTT,** engineering educator; b. Alliance, Ohio, June 14, 1962; s. Ronald Francis Russell and Georgia Ann (Charleston) Holmes; m. Vicki Carolina Radford, Aug. 17, 1985; children: Nicole Lynne, Jacob Thomas, Matthew David, Rachel Marie. BS, U. Cin., 1985; MS, Purdue U., 1986, PhD, 1988. Grad. tchg. asst. Purdue U., West Lafayette, Ind., 1985-87, grad. rsch. asst., 1987-88, postdoctoral rsch. assoc., 1988-89; from asst. to assoc. prof. civil engring. U. Wis., Madison, 1989—. Lectr. Tex. A&M U., College Station, 1988—, U. Tex., Austin, 1992—, U. Wis. Madison Ext., 1990—. Editor Jour. Mgmt. in Engring., 1996—. Mem. Wis. Right to Life, Madison, 1989-94; project coord. U. Wis. Coll. Testament Distbn., Gideon's Internat., Madison West Camp, 1990—; dir. evangelistic ministries First Ch. of Nazarene, Madison, 1992-93. Recipient Presdl. Young Investigator award NSF, 1990, Edmund Friedman Young Engr. award for profl. achievement, 1993. Mem. ASCE (assoc., sec. constrn. div. 1989-92, Collingwood Prize 1991, Outstanding Profl. Civil and Environ. Engring. 1991, Walter L. Huber Civil Engring. Rsch. prize 1996, bd. dirs. 1998—), Am. Assn. Cost Engrs. (assoc.), Am. Soc. Engring. Edn., Constrn. Mgmt. Assn. Am., Sigma Xi, Tau Beta Pi. Achievements include identification of causes of constrn. contractor failure; devel. of analytical models to assist in predicting contractor failure prior to contract award. Office: U Wis-Madison 2304 Engring Hall 1415 Johnson Dr Madison WI 53706-1607

**RUSSELL, JOHN FRANCIS,** retired librarian; b. Mt. Carmel, Ind., Apr. 30, 1929; s. David Freeman and Bertha (Major) R.; m. Edith Raymond Hyde, June 27, 1953; 1 child, Anne Marie. BA, DePauw U., 1951; postgrad., Ind. U., 1951-52; MA, Johns Hopkins U., 1954; student, Cath. U. Am., summer 1955; MS, Grad. Sch. Libr. Sci./Drexel, U., 1977. Tchr. English Park Sch. Balt., 1954-75, chmn. dept., 1957-75; tchr. speech. dir. Ira Aldridge Players Morgan State Coll., fall 1965-66; tchr. drama Loyola Coll., 1964, 66. Editor: The Secondary School Theatre, 1972-74. Pres. Tchrs.'s Assn. Ind. Sch. Balt. Area, 1960-62, adv. bd., 1966-67, chmn. com. on English, 1966-68; exec. com. Assn. Ind. Md. Sch., 1967-68; dir., costumer Johns Hopkins U. Playshop, 1963-64; lectr. Lecture Group, Woman's Club Roland Park, others, 1964—; bd. dirs. Balt. area coun. World Federalists U.S.A., 1961-67, vice chmn., 1964-67, nat. exec. coun., 1963-65; bd. dirs. Ctr. Stage, 1964-77; dir. Blvd. Players, pres., 1960-67; dir. Pasadena Little Theatre, v.p., 1979-83, pres., 1983-85, 2d v.p., 1990—; dir. Center Stage Players, New Image Theatre, Theatre Network of Houston, U.S.A. Theatre, Actors Conservatory Tex., v.p., 1990-91, Glenbrook United Meth. Ch. Drama Ministry; bd. dirs. Unicorn Sch. Acting, 1996-2003, v.p., 1997-2003; adv. com. Am. H.S. Theatre Festival, 1975; mem. adminstrv. bd. St. Mark's United Meth. Ch., 1957-67, Towson United Meth. Ch., 1967-77, First United Meth. Ch., Houston, 1980-89; adminstrv. coun., vice-chmn. Glenbrook United Meth. Ch., 1997, chmn. pastor-parish rels. com., 1998, lay del., 1999, 2000, 03, 04, lay leader 1999—; sec. Festival Angels, 1982-2001 (Outstanding Svc. award 1991); cmty. vol. svcs. com., ARC, 1985-90; comprehensive volunteerism adv. com., Sheltering Arms, 1986-89. Recipient Nat. Citation of Merit Am. Shakespeare Festival, 1961, Theatre Goddess award U.S.A. Theatre, 1998, Critics Choice award Houston Post, 1984; certs. of appreciation Sheltering Arms, 1986-89, cert. of recognition, 1988. Mem. Am. Assn. Cmty. Theatre, Harris County Heritage Soc., Am. Film Inst., Drama League, Am. Theatre Assn. (v.p. Mid-Atlantic dist. 1967-68, pres. 1968-69, nat. dir. 1970-73, Mid-Atlantic chpt. award for achievement and contbn. to theatre 1973), Secondary Sch. Theatre Assn. (v.p. devel. 1974-75), Tex. Non-Profit Theatre, Nat. (bd. dirs. 1969), Md. Coun. Tchrs. English (pres. 1969-70), Capital Area Media Educators Orgn. (exec. com. 1970-73, screening chmn. 1971-73), ALA, Tex. Libr. Assn. (audiovisual chmn. conv. planning com. 1981), Coun. Info. and Referral Svcs. (newsletter editor 1984-86), Tex. Alliance Info. and Referral Svcs. (conv. speaker 1981, 83, 84, 85), Alliance of Info. and Referral Svcs. (conv. speaker 1985), Houston Pub. Libr. Staff Assn. (pres. 1981-82), Literacy Vols. Am. (sec. Houston 1984-87, adv. bd. 1989-91, 95-96, bd. dirs. 1992-95, chmn. program com. 1991-93), Reading, Edn. and Devel. Coun. (recruitment chmn., exec. com. 1984-86), Cultural Arts Coun. of Houston/Harris County, Park Pl. Civic Club (exemplary svc. award 1991), AARP (bd. dirs. chpt. 1172 1998—, v.p. 1999-2000, 01-02, pres. 2003-04), Phi Beta Kappa, Phi Eta Sigma, Beta Phi Mu. Home: 7817 Grove Ridge Dr Houston TX 77061-1405 E-mail: jrussell10@houston.rr.com.

**RUSSELL, JOHN JOSEPH,** English educator; b. Orange, NJ, Dec. 4, 1949; s. James Francis and Catherine Mary Russell. BA, Seton Hall U., 1973; MA, U. Chgo., 1979, Seton Hall U., 1982; PhD, Fordham U., 1991. Asst. prof. English Union County Coll., Cranford, NJ, 1991—97, assoc. prof. English, 1997—2005, sr. prof. English, 2005—. Author: (book) Hamlet and Narcissus, 1995. Office: Union County Coll 1033 Springfield Ave Cranford NJ 07016 E-mail: russell@ucc.edu.

**RUSSELL, JOHN S.,** contract research organization executive; b. 1954; BA, U. N.C., 1977; MA, Columbia U., 1978; JD, Harvard U., 1985. Editor trade books dept. Houghton Mifflin Co., N.Y.C., 1978—82; atty. Research Triangle Park, NC, 1986—98; exec. v.p., gen. counsel, sec. Quintiles Transnational, Research Triangle Park, NC, 1998—. Author: Favorite Sons, 1992 (Sir Walter Raleigh award for fiction, 1993). Chmn. Opera Co. N.C. Office: Quintiles Transnational Riverbirch Bldg PO Box 13979 4709 Creekstone Dr Ste 200 Research Triangle Park NC 27709

**RUSSELL, JOSEPH ALLEN,** engineer, consultant; b. Lompoc, Calif. s. Clark Earl and Nanice Mercedis (Poett) Russell; m. Nancy Bolson, July 3, 1971 (div. 1981); children: Elizabeth, Rosalind; m. Reevah Simon, July 18, 1999. Student, Allen Hancoc Coll., Santa Maria, Calif., 1968-70, Calif. Polytechnic Inst., San Luis Obispo, Calif., 1970-71. Registered profl. engr., Calif. Electro optical engr. Electro Optical Industries, Santa Barbara, Calif., 1971-73; designer, field engr. Stearns/Roger, Denver, 1973-74; instrumentation and controls engr. C.F. Braun, Alhambra, Calif., 1974-76; technician, sys. engr. Fairchild Energy, Ft. Fairfield, 1988; project engr. G.W.F. Power Sys., Walnut Creek, Calif. 1989-92; chief telescope engr. Mt. Wilson Obs., Pasadena, Calif., 1992—2003. Tech. expert for profl. engring. test Price & Assocs., Pomona, Calif., 1991. Candidate state sen. Libertarian Party, West L.A., 1985. Achievements include patent for storage ring fusion energy generator. Office: De La Guerra Power Inc PO Box 41955 Los Angeles CA 90041-0955

**RUSSELL, JOYCE ANNE ROGERS,** retired librarian; b. Chgo., Nov. 6, 1920; d. Truman Allen and Mary Louise (Hoelzle) Rogers; m. John VanCleve Russell, Dec. 24, 1942; children: Malcolm David, John VanCleve. BA, Adelphi Coll., 1937; BS in Chemistry, U. Ky., 1942; M.L.S., Rosary Coll., 1967; postgrad., Rutgers U., 1970-71. Research chemist Sherwin Williams Paint Co., Chgo., 1942-45; reference librarian Chicago Heights (Ill.) Pub. Library, 1959-61; librarian Victor Chem. Works, Chicago Heights, 1961-62; lit. chemist Velsicol Chem. Corp., Chgo., 1964-67; chemistry librarian U. Fla., Gainesville, 1967-69, interim assoc. prof., 1967-69; librarian Thiokol Chem. Corp., Trenton, N.J., 1969-73; supr. library operations E.R. Squibb Co., Princeton, N.J., 1973-80. sr. research info scientist, 1980-91. Mem. library adv. commn. Mercer Community Coll., 1979—; adv. asso. Rutgers U. Grad. Sch. Library and Info. Scis., 1978— Editor: Bibliofile, 1967—69; contbr. articles to profl. jours. Mem. PTA, 1950-66; den mother Cub Scouts, 1952-59. Mem. Spl. Libraries Assn. (sec., dir., v.p., pres. Princeton-Trenton 1971, 75-80), Am. Chem. Soc. (bus. mgr., sec., dir. Trenton sect. 1969-78), AAUW, Mortar Board, Beta Phi Mu, Sigma Pi Sigma, Chi Delta Phi, Pi Sigma Alpha. Home: 1189 Parkside Ave Trenton NJ 08618-2625

**RUSSELL, KENNETH CALVIN,** metallurgical engineering educator; b. Greeley, Colo., Feb. 4, 1936; s. Doyle James and Jennie Frances (Smith) R.; m. Charlotte Louise Wolf, Apr. 13, 1963 (div. 1978); children: David Allan, Doyle John. Met.E., Colo. Sch. Mines, 1959; PhD, Carnegie Inst. Tec., 1963. Engr. Westinghouse Rsch. and Devel. Ctr., 1959-61; NSF postdoctoral fellow Physics Inst., U. Oslo, 1963-64; assoc. prof. metallurgy M.I.T., Cambridge, 1964-69, assoc. prof., 1969-78, prof. metallurgy, 1978—, prof. nuc. engring., 1979—. Contbr. articles to profl. publs. Served as 2d lt. U.S. Army, 1959-60.

**RUSSELL, KERI,** actress; b. Fountain Valley, Calif., Mar. 23, 1976; Actress in films: Honey, I Blew Up the Kids, 1992, Dead Man's Curve, 1998, Mad About Mambo, 2000, We Were Soldiers, 2002, The Upside of Anger, 2005; TV series include: MMC, 1989, Mickey Mouse Club, 1991-93, Emerald Cove, 1993, Daddy's Girls, 1994, Malibu Shores, 1996, Roar, 1997, Felicity, 1998-2002 (Golden Globe for Best Performan by an Actress in a TV series 1999); TV films include: MMC in Concert, 1993, Clerks, 1995, The Babysitter's Seduction, 1996, The Lottery, 1996, When Innocence is Lost, 1997, Eight Days a Week, 1997, Cinderelmo, 1999; TV guest appearances include: Boy Meets World, 1993, Married...with Children, 1987, 7th Heaven, 1996, Roar, 1997. Winner Golden Globe for best performance by an actress in a TV series for Felicity, 1999. Office: The Gersh Agy 232 N Canon Dr Beverly Hills CA 90210-5302

**RUSSELL, KURT VON VOGEL,** actor; b. Springfield, Mass., Mar. 17, 1951; s. Bing Oliver and Louise Julia (Crone) R.; m. Season Hubley, Mar. 17, 1979 (div.), 1 son, Boston; 1 son (with Goldie Hawn), Wyatt Russell. Student, pub. schs. Profl. baseball player, 1971-73; co-head (with Goldie Hawn, Kate Hudson, Oliver Hudson) Cosmic Entertainment, 2003. Actor in numerous films including The Absent Minded Professor, 1961, It Happened at the World's Fair, 1963, Follow Me Boys, 1966, The One and Only Genuine Original Family Band, 1968, The Horse in the Grey Flannel Suit, 1968, The Computer Wore Tennis Shoes, 1970, The Barefoot Executive, 1971, Fools' Parade, 1971, Now You See Him Now You Don't, 1972, Charley and the Angel, 1972, Superdad, 1974, The Strongest Man in the World, 1975, Used Cars, 1980, Escape from New York, 1981, The Thing, 1982, Silkwood, 1983, Swing Shift, 1984, The Mean Season, 1985, The Best of Times, 1986, Big Trouble in Little China, 1986, Overboard, 1987, The Winter People, 1988, Tequila Sunrise, 1988, Winter People, 1989, Tango and Cash, 1989, Backdraft, 1991, Unlawful Entry, 1992, Captain Ron, 1992, Tombstone, 1993, Stargate, 1994, Executive Decision, 1996, Escape from L.A., 1996 (also writer, producer), Breakdown, 1997, Soldier, 1998, 3000 Miles To Graceland, 2001, Vanilla Sky, 2001, Interstate 60, 2002, Dark Blue, 2002, Miracle, 2004, Sky High, 2005, Dreamer: Inspired by a True Story, 2005, Poseidon, 2006; TV series include Travels with Jamie McPheeters, 1963-64, The New Land, 1974, The Quest, 1976; TV movies include Search for the Gods, 1975, The Deadly Tower, The Quest (pilot), 1975, Christmas Miracle in Caulfield USA, 1977, Elvis, 1979, Amber Waves, 1980; prodr. (films) Escape from L.A., 1996; exec. prodr. (TV films) 14 Hours, 2005; TV guest appearances include The Fugitive, Daniel Boone, Gilligan's Island, Lost in Space, The FBI, Love American Style, Gunsmoke, Hawaii Five-O. Served with Calif. Air N.G. Recipient numerous auto racing trophies, 10 baseball awards, 5 acting awards, 1 golf championship. Mem. Profl. Baseball Players Assn., Stuntman's Assn. Achievements include being the World championship Class Modified Stock, 1959 Race of Champions, Las Vegas. Office: Creative Artists Agy 9830 Wilshire Blvd Beverly Hills CA 90212-1825*

**RUSSELL, LAURA WIMBERLY,** artist; b. Rapid City, S.D., Aug. 17, 1949; d. Charles Leslie Wimberly and Peggy (Whitehead) Minier; m. Michael L. Russell, Aug. 21, 1971 (dec. Feb. 1986). BA in Creative Studies, U. Calif., Santa Barbara, 1970; MA, San Jose State U., 1974. Art tchr., Cusco, Peru; founder, dir. The Mobile Art Studio (now Ayllu Yapaychay), Cusco, 1991—, Mus. Andean Children's Art, Cusco, 1999. One-woman shows William Sawyer Gallery, San Francisco, 1976, Art Mus. South Tex., Corpus Christi, 1980, Watson de Nagy Gallery, Houston, 1988, Watson/Willour Gallery, Houston 1981, U. Redlands, Calif., 1982, Contemporary Arts Mus., Houston, 1983, Hadler/Rodriguez Gallery, Houston, 1983, 84, Canancuhua Gallery, Corpus Christi, 1985, Southwest Tex. U., 1985, Fuller Goldeen Gallery, Houston, 1987, 88, Berman Gallery, Palo Alto, Calif., 1988, Butler Gallery, 1989, 90, Kimpton Gallery, San Francisco, 1991, Lew Allen Gallery, Santa Fe, 1991, Brian Gross Fine, San Francisco, 1992, 93, 96, Inst. Cultural Peruano Nonteamericana, Lima, Peru, 1993, Ctr. de Estudios Andinos, Cusco, Peru, 1994, 95, Ricardo Paloma Cultural Ctr, Lima, 2004 Fellow NEA, 1981. Home: 110 De La Costa Ave Santa Cruz CA 95060-6321 Studio: 2537B Mission St Santa Cruz CA 95060-5751

**RUSSELL, MARJORIE ROSE,** manufacturing executive; b. Welcome, Minn., Sept. 3, 1925; d. Emil Frederick and Ella Magdalene (Sothman) Wohlenhaus; m. Kenneth Kollmann Russell, Sept. 15, 1947 (dec. May 1971); children: Jennie Rose, Richard Lowell, Laura Eloise, James Wesley. Student, Northwestern Sch., Mpls., 1944-45, St. Paul Bible Inst., 1946-47. Cook U. Minn., Mpls., 1943-45; maintenance person U. Farm Campus/N.W. Schs., St. Paul, 1945-46; clk. Kresge Corp., Mpls., 1945; cook, waitress, mgr. Union City Mission Bible Camp, Mpls., 1944-47; caterer for v.p. Gt. No. R.R., St. Paul, 1947; custodian Old Soldiers Home, St. Paul, 1946; nurse Sister Elizabeth Kenney Polio Hosp., St. Paul, 1946; seamstress Hirsch, Weis, White Stag, Pendleton, Mayfair, Portland, Oreg., 1960-72; owner, operator, contract mgr., creative designer The Brass Needle, Portland, 1972—. Contractor Forrester's Sanderson Safety, Scotsco, Nero & Assocs., Gara Gear, Portland, 1972—, Columbia Sportswear; tchr. Indo Chinese Cultural Ctr., Portland, 1982; mfr. of protective chaps and vests for the Pacific Northwest Logging industry. Designer, producer Kisn Bridal Fair, 1969; composer: He Liveth in Me, 1968; prodr. Safety Chaps for Loggers. Sec. Model Cities Com., Portland, 1969; com. mem. Neighborhood Black Christmas Parade, Portland, 1970; custume designer Local Miss Jr. Black Beauty Contest, Portland, 1973; nominating com. Nat. Contract Mgmt. Assn., Portland, 1978; mem. nominating com. Multi-Cultural Sr. Adv. Com., 1988-91. Mem. NAFE, Urban League, Urban League Guild (historian 1991-92), Am. Assn. Ret. Persons, Nat. Contract Mgmt. Assn. Democrat. Mem. United Ch. of Christ. Avocations: music, swimming, painting, gardening, arts. Home: 4115 SE Monroe St Portland OR 97222-5955

**RUSSELL, MARK,** comedian; b. Buffalo, Aug. 23, 1932; s. Marcus Joseph and Marie Elizabeth (Perry) Ruslander; m. Alison Kaplan, Dec. 17, 1978; children: Monica, John, Matthew. Student, George Washington U., 1952; LittD, Union Coll., 1987; LHD, Canisius Coll., 1988; LHD (hon.), Goucher Coll., 1990; LLD (hon.), D'Youville Coll., 2004. Lectr., public speaker. Polit. comedian, featured performer Shoreham Hotel, Washington, 1961-81; prin. Mark Russell Comedy Spls., Pub. Broadcasting Svc., 1975—, Mark Russell's 25th Anniversary Special, 2000 (Silver Telly award 2000); host Mark Russell's England, PBS-TV, 1988, Mark Russell's Irish Fling, 1993, Mark Russell's Great Ala. Trek, 1994, Mark Russell's Tour de France, 1995, Mark Russell's Vita Italia, 1996; co-host NBC's Real People, 1979-84; regular contbr. Good Morning Am., ABC-TV, Inside Politics Weekend, CNN; author: Presenting Mark Russell, 1980; syndicated columnist via Tribune Media Svcs., 1975. Mem. father's day coun., Washington. With USMC, 1953—56. Recipient Mark Twain award Internat. Platform Assn., 1980, 86, 4th Ann. Lucy award Shea's Buffalo, 1992, Nat. Humor Treasure award Nat. Humor Conf., 1995, SOAR St. Elizabeth Ann Seton award Washington, 1995, Washingtonian of the Yr. Washingtonian Mag., 1996, Disting. Washingtonian award Univ. Club, 2001, Theodore Roosevelt Exemplary Citizenship award T. R. Inaugural Site Found., 2005; named Father of Yr., Am. Diabetes Assn. 2005 Mem. AFTRA, Am. Fedn. Musicians. Office: PO Box 9904 Washington DC 20016-8904 Office Phone: 202-362-5045. E-mail: mail@markrussell.com.

**RUSSELL, MARY E.,** medical products executive, cardiologist; b. Jan. 9, 1955; MD, Chgo. Med. Sch., 1984. Faculty mem. Harvard Sch. of Pub. Health, Harvard Med. Sch., Brigham and Women's Hosp., Mass. Gen. Hosp.; med. dir. CV cons. Parexel Internat.; v.p. cardiovascular clin. affairs Boston Sci. Corp., Natick, Mass., 2000—01, v.p. clin. affairs internat., 2001—04, sr. v.p., chief med. officer cardiovascular clin. scis., 2004, sr. v.p. clin. & regulatory, chief med. officer, 2004—. Office: Boston Sci Corp One Boston Scientific Pl Natick MA 01760-1537 Office Phone: 508-650-8000.*

DuPont fellow, 1961-62; NSF fellow, 1962-63 Mem.: Metallurgical Soc. Am. Inst. Mining, Metallurgical and Petroleum Engrs., Am. Phys. Soc. Office: MIT Rm 13-5050 Cambridge MA 02139 Office Phone: 617-253-3328. E-mail: kenruss@mit.edu.

**RUSSELL, MARY RHODES,** state supreme court justice; b. Hannibal, Mo., July 28, 1958; d. Cleveland Jerome and Mary Elisabeth (Stewart) Rhodes; m. James Lowell Russell, Nov. 25, 1995. BA in Mass. Comms., BS in Home Econs., Truman State U., 1980; JD, U. Mo., Columbia, 1983. Bar: Mo. 1983, Ill. 1984, U.S. Dist. Ct. (ea. dist.) 1984, U.S. Supreme Ct. 1992. Administv. asst. Mo. Senate, Jefferson City, 1980-83, law clk., 1983-84; prtnr. Clayton & Rhodes, Hannibal, 1984-95; judge Mo. Ct. Appeals (ea. dist.), St. Louis, 1995—2004, Mo. Supreme Ct., 2004—. Author: Enforcement of Discovery Sanctions, 1994. Bd. dirs. Commn. on Ret., Removal and Discipline of Judges, St. Louis, 1994-95, Matthews-Dickey Boys & Girls Club; mem. urban campout project Girl Scouts USA, St. Louis, 1996; mem., past pres. PEO, Hannibal, 1993-95, Jefferson City, 1995—. Recipient Equal Justice award Legal Svcs. Ea. Mo., 1994, Citation of Merit award U. Mo. Sch. Law, 1997; Henry Toll fellow, 1997. Mem. Bar Assn. St. Louis (chair bench/bar rels. 1996-97), Woman Lawyers Assn. St. Louis, Nat. Assn. Women Judges, Kansas City Met. Bar Assn., Mo. Lawyer Trust Account Found. (vice chmn., bd. dirs. 1990-95), Rotary (program chmn. 1996-97). Episcopalian. Avocations: cardinal baseball, travel, cooking. Office: Supreme Ct Mo PO Box 150 Jefferson City MO 65102 Office Phone: 573-751-6880. Business E-Mail: mary.russell@courts.mo.gov.*

**RUSSELL, MARYANNE,** photographer; Grad., NYU; student, Internat. Ctr. Photography. Staff photographer Time Inc.; owner Maryanne Russell Photography Inc., 1986—. Photographer (works appeared at) Acad. Art Coll., San Francisco, Lobet Gallery, NYC, Grant Gallery, Chelsea Art Gallery, (group exhbns.) Sephora's Flagship store. Mem.: Am. Soc. Media Photographers, NY Women in Comm. (Liz Hoover award 1994). Achievements include photography clients AT&T, Christian Dior, HBO, NY Giants, Paramount Pictures, People mag., Time Warner Inc., Viacom, and many others. Office: Maryanne Russell Photography Inc 230 E 52nd St Ste 1B New York NY 10022 Office Phone: 212-308-8722.

**RUSSELL, MICHAEL JAMES,** lawyer; Cert. in German, U. Vienna, 1979; BA summa cum laude, Gettysburg Coll., 1980; MA, JD, Vanderbilt U., 1984. Bar: Pa. 1984, DC 1985, U.S. Supreme Ct. 1995. Atty. USDA, Washington, 1984-85; majority counsel subcom. on juvenile justice senate judiciary com. U.S. Senate, Washington, 1985-86, minority gen. counsel subcom. on constn., 1987, legis. dir. to Senator Arlen Specter, 1987-90; senate staff mem. Congrl. Crime Caucus, 1987-90; dep. dir. Nat. Inst. Justice U.S. Dept. Justice, Washington, 1990-93, acting dir., 1993-94; pres. Russell & Assocs., Washington, 1994-96; sr. pub. safety advisor Corp. Nat. Svc., Washington, 1994-96; dep. chief of staff to Senator Ben Nighthorse Campbell, Washington, 1996—2001; dep. asst. sec. for policy and budget (enforcement) U.S. Dept. Treasury, Washington, 2001—03; staff dir. govt. affairs subcom. on fin mgmt., the budget and internat. security U.S. Senate, Washington, 2003—. Office: 446 Hart Senate Office Bldg Washington DC 20510

**RUSSELL, NAS'NAGA R.,** illustrator; b. Dayton, Ohio, Apr. 13, 1941; s. Willard George and Kathryn Louise (Pangborn) R.; m. Harriet Ann Russell, June 1967 (div. 1973); 1 child, Jamie Noelle; m. Barbara Jane Mullins, Sept. 14, 1984. Grad. h.s. Mgr. AAAirlines, Ft. Worth, 1970-74; writer Harper & Rowe, N.Y.C., 1974-75; owner, dir. Art Gallery, Kettering, Ohio, 1979-83. Dir., owner Nas'Naga Enterprises, Inc. Pro., Centerville, Ohio, 1980-83; lectr., spkr. in field. Author, illustrator: Indians' Summer, 1975, Western Writers of America, 1975-1980, Dayton's Society of Painters and Sculptors, 1978-1980, Faces Beneath The Grass, 1979, Darker Side of Glory, 2000; columnist Western Mag., Oslo, Norway, 1976-79; co-author: Poetry Anthology, 2004. Airlines rep. Okla. for Indian Opportunity, Tex., 1970—74; steering com. Newark state mound project Ohio Hist. Soc., 2000. With USN, 1959—63. Recipient Humanitarian Svc. award Oklahomians for Indian Opportunity, Norman, Okla., 1973, United Cerebeal Palsy, Dayton, 1984, Outstanding Artistic Achievement award Green County Ohio, Xenia, 1975. Avocations: archery, painting, research. Home: 3000 B E Main St #359 Columbus OH 43209

**RUSSELL, PAUL EDGAR,** electrical engineering educator; b. Roswell, N.Mex., Oct. 10, 1924; s. Rueben Matthias and Mary (Parsons) R.; m. Lorna Margaret Clayshulte, Aug. 29, 1943; children: Carol Potter, Janice Russell Cook, Gregory. BSEE, N.Mex. State U., 1946, BSME, 1947; MSEE, U. Wis., 1950, PhDEE, 1951. Registered elec. engr., Ariz. From instr. to asst. prof. elec. engring. U. Wis., Madison, 1947-52; sr. engr., design specialist Gen. Dynamics Corp., San Diego, 1952-54; from prof. to chmn. elec. engring. dept. U. Ariz., Tucson, 1954-63; dean engring. Kans. State U., Manhattan, 1963-67; prof. Ariz. State U., Tempe, 1967-90; dir. engring. Ariz. State U. West, Phoenix, 1985-88; dir. Sch. Constrn. and Tech. Ariz. State U., Tempe, 1988-90. Cons. in field, 1954—; programs evaluator, mem. engring. commn. Accreditation Bd. for Engring. and Tech., N.Y.C., 1968-81. Contbr. articles to jours. and chpts. to books. Served as sgt. U.S. Army, 1944-46. Recipient Disting. Service award N.Mex. State U., 1965. Fellow IEEE (life, chmn. Ariz. sect. 1960), Accreditation Bd. Engring. and Tech.; mem. Am. Soc. Engring. Educators. Home: 5902 E Caballo Ln Paradise Valley AZ 85253 Office Phone: 480-948-0716.

**RUSSELL, PAUL FREDERICK,** lawyer; b. Kansas City, Mo., Feb. 3, 1948; s. Walter Edward and Dorothy Marie (Sickels) R.; m. Kerry Diann Anderson, June 2, 1973; children: Philip, Erin, Shannon, Kelsey, Scott. BA, Northwestern, 1970; JD cum laude, U. Mich., 1973. Bar: Ill. 1973, U.S. Dist. Ct. (no. dist.) Ill. 1973. Assoc. Vedder, Price, Kaufman & Kammholz, Chgo., 1973-79, ptnr., 1980—. Mem. ABA, Chgo. Bar Assn., Ill. State Bar Assn., Univ. Club (Chgo.), Mich. Shores Club. Office: Vedder Price 222 N La Salle St Chicago IL 60601-1003 Office Phone: 312-609-7740. Business E-Mail: prussell@vedderprice.com

**RUSSELL, PAUL SNOWDEN,** surgeon, educator; b. Chgo., Jan. 22, 1925; s. Paul Snowden and Carroll (Mason) R.; m. Allene Lummis, Sept. 24, 1952; children— Katherine Swift, Paul Snowden, Allene, Laura Rice. PhB, U. Chgo., 1944, BS, 1945, MD, 1947; MA (hon.), Harvard U., 1962. Diplomate Am. Bd. Surgery, Am. Bd. Thoracic Surgery. From surg. intern. to resident Mass. Gen. Hosp., 1948-56, asst. surgery, 1957-60, chief gen. surg. svcs., 1962-69, chmn. com. on rsch., 1973-76; postdoctoral fellow USPHS, 1954-55; from tchg. fellow to clin. assoc. surgery Harvard Med. Sch., 1956-60, John Homans prof. surgery, 1962-98, John Homans Disting. prof. surgery, 1998—; assoc. prof. surgery Columbia Coll. Phys. and Surg., 1960-62; assoc. attending surgeon Presbyn. Hosp., NYC, 1960-62; assoc. vis. surgeon Francis Delafield Hosp., NYC, 1960-62, 1972-94. Mem. com. tissue transplantation NRC-Nat. Acad. Scis., 1963-71, com. trauma, 1963-68; ad hoc com. to study clin. investigation and edn. in USN, 1971-73; allergy and immunology study sect. USPHS, 1963-65, chmn. allergy and immunology study sect. B, 1965-67; mem. transplantation and immunology com. Nat. Inst. Allergy and Infectious Diseases, 1967-69, chmn., 1970; mem. com. on cancer immunotherapy Nat. Cancer Inst., 1974-79. Contbr. papers in field.; Editorial bd.: Archives Surgery, 1963-72, Surgery, 1963-71, Transplantation, 1965-79, Annals of Surgery, 1966—, Transplantation Procs., 1966—, Jour. Immunology, 1977-80. Trustee Pine Manor Coll., Chestnut Hill, Mass., 1963-76, Groton Sch., 1964-79, The Conservation Law Found., 1997—; bd. dirs. Boston Fulbright Com., 1968, pres., 1980—; vice chmn. bd. govs., trustee corp. Jackson Lab. With USAF, 1951-53. Fellow AAAS, ACS, Royal Soc. Medicine, Am. Acad. Arts and Scis., Assn. Immunologists, NY Acad. Scis., Mass. Med. Soc., New Eng. Surg. Soc., Boston Surg. Soc. (pres. 1994), Soc. Univ. Surgeons, Soc. Exptl. Biology and Medicine, Halsted Soc., Whipple Soc., Internat. Soc. Surgery, Am. Surg. Assn., Transplantation Soc. (pres. 1970), Polish Acad. Sci. (fgn.), Sigma Xi. Home: 10 Longwood Dr Apt 148 Westwood MA 02090 Office: Dept Surgery Mass Gen Hosp Boston MA 02114 Office Phone: 617-726-2801.

**RUSSELL, PEGGY TAYLOR,** soprano, educator; b. Newton, N.C., Apr. 5, 1927; d. William G. and Sue B. (Cordell) Taylor; m. John B. Russell, Feb. 23, 1953; children: John Spotswood, Susan Bryce. MusB in Voice, Salem Coll., 1948; MusM, Columbia U., 1950; postgrad., U. N.C., Greensboro, 1977; student, Am. Inst. Music Studies, Austria, 1972, student, 1978; student of

Clifford Bair, Nell Starr (hon.), Salem Coll., Winston-Salem, N.C.; student of Edgar Schofield, Chloe Owen, N.Y.C.; student opera-dramatics, Boris Goldovsky, Southwestern Opera Inst.; student of Ande Andersen, Max Lehner, Graz, Austria. Mem. faculty dept. voice Guilford Coll., Greensboro, NC, 1952—53, Greensboro Coll., 1971—72; pvt. tchr. voice Greensboro, 1963—. Co-founder, v.p. sales, mktg. Russell Textiles, Inc., Greensboro, 1988; vis. instr. in voice U. N.C., Chapel Hill, 1973—77; founding artistic dir., gen. mgr. Young Artists Opera Theatre, Greensboro, 1983, staged and produced 18 operatic prodns., 1983—91; gues lectr. opera workshop U.N.C., Greensboro, 1990—91; lectr. opera Friends of Weymouth, Southern Pines, NC, 1994; lectr. on music history and opera, High Point, NC, Ctr. Creative Leadership, Greensboro, 1979—80, 1st Presbyn. Ch., 1982. Singer: debut in light opera as Gretchen in The Red Mill, 1947; singer: (debuts) Rosalinda in Die Fledermaus, 1949, Lola in Cavalleria Rusticana, 1951, Violetta in La Traviata, 1953, Fiordiligi in Cosi fan Tutte, 1956; singer: Marguerite in Faust, 1967, First Lady in The Magic Flute, 1972, mem. Greensboro Orotario Soc., 1955—59; singer: (soprano soloist) The Messiah, 1952, 1958, The Creation, 1955, Solomon, 1958, Presbyn. Ch. of the Covenant, 1968—71; singer: guest appearances Sta. WFMY-TV, 1958—62; singer: (soprano soloist) Greensboro Symphony Orch., 1964, 1980, Ea. Music Festival Orch., 1965, Greensboro Civic Orch., 1980; singer: (soloist in numerous recitals). Judge Charlotte Opera Guild Auditions, 1994; mem. Friendship Force of Guilford County, Netherlands, 1985, Germany, 1987; bd. dirs. Music Theater Assocs., Greensboro Friends of Music, N.C. Lyric Opera, Piedmont Opera Theatre. Grantee N.C. Arts Coun. and NEA, 1991. Mem.: Piedmont Triad Coun. Internat. Vis. (Appreciation award Nat. Coun. Internat. Visitors 1994), N.C. Symphony Soc., Civic Music Assn. (chmn. 1963—64), Atlanta Opera Guild, Broadway Theater League (chmn. 1961—63), Symphony Guild (dir. 1977—78), Greensboro Music Tchrs. Assn. (pres. 1966—67), Music Educators Nat. Conf., N.C. Fedn. Music Clubs (dir. 1956—58), Nat. Assn. Tchrs. of Singing (state gov. 1976—82, coord. Regional Artist Contest 1982—84), Ctrl. Opera Svc., Nat. Opera Assn. (chmn. regional opera com. 1985—91, judge vocal competition auditions 1991, 1992, 1994, chmn. trustees Cofield Endowment 1991), Weathersoon Art Mus. Guild, English Speaking Union (bd. dirs. Greensboro chpt., chmn. Shakespeare competition 1995), Guilford County Planning/Devel. Office (Forecast 2015 com.), Greensboro Preservation Soc., Greensboro City Club. Home: 3012 W Cornwallis Dr Greensboro NC 27408-6730

**RUSSELL, RICHARD DONCASTER,** geophysics educator, academic administrator; b. Toronto, Ont., Can., Feb. 27, 1929; s. Richard Douglas and Ada Gwennola (Doncaster) R.; m. Virginia Ann Reid Clippingdale, Aug. 11, 1951; children: Linda Jean, Morna Ann, Mary Joyce. BA, U. Toronto, 1951, MA, 1952, PhD, 1954. Asst. prof. physics U. Toronto, 1956-58, prof., 1962-63; assoc. prof. physics U. B.C., Vancouver, Canada, 1958-62, prof. geophysics, 1963-91, prof. emeritus, 1991—, head dept. geophysics, 1968-72, head dept. geophysics and astronomy, 1972-79, dean sci., 1978-81, assoc. dean sci., 1980-83, assoc. v.p. acad., 1983-86. Sec.-gen. Inter-Union Commn. on Geodynamics, 1976—80; profl. geoscientist. Author (with John Arthur Jacobs and J. Tuzo Wilson): Physics and Geology International Series in the Earth Sciences, first edit., 1959, Physics and Geology McGraw-Hill International Series in the Earth and Planetary Science, 2d edit., 1973; author: (with Ronald McCunn Farquhar) Lead Isotopes in Geology Interscience, 1960. Fellow Royal Soc. Can.; mem. Am. Geophys. Union, Can. Geophys. Union (J. Tuzo Wilson medal 1992). Home: 226-4955 River Rd Delta BC Canada V4K 4V9

**RUSSELL, RICHARD OLNEY, JR.,** cardiologist, educator; b. Birmingham, Ala., July 9, 1932; s. Richard Olney and Louise (Taylor) R.; m. Phyllis Hutchinson, June 15, 1963; children: Scott Richard, Katherine Hutchinson, Meredith Cooper, Stephen Wilbon. AB cum laude, Vanderbilt U., 1953, MD, 1956. Diplomate Am. Bd. Internal Medicine, 1964, Am. Bd. Cardiovascular Disease, 1967. Intern Peter Bent Brigham Hosp., Boston, 1956-57, resident, 1959-60, 63-64; fellow in cardiology Med. Coll. Ala., Birmingham, 1960-62, instr., 1962-63; instr. medicine U. Ala., Birmingham, 1964-65, asst. prof., 1965-70, assoc. prof., 1970-73, prof., 1973-81, clin. prof., 1981—; pvt. practice medicine specializing in cardiology Birmingham, 1981—. Mem. Jefferson County Bd. Health, 1977—81, chmn., 1979. Author: (with Charles Edward Rackley) Hemodynamic Monitoring in a Coronary Intensive Care Unit, 1974, 2d rev. and enlarged edit., 1981, Coronary Artery Disease: Recognition and Management, 1979, (with others) Radiographic Anatomy of the Coronary Arteries: An Atlas, 1976, Acute Ischemic Syndromes in American College of Cardiology Self Assessment Program, 1993; mem. editl. bd. Circulation, 1976-80, Am. Jour. Cardiology, 1977-82, Heart and Lung, 1978-83, Chest, 1978-83, Ala. Jour. Med. Scis, 1977-80, Jour. Am. Coll. Cardiology, 1987-90; sect. editor for Case Studies for Cardiosource for Am. Coll. Cardiology, 2001-06, assoc. editor, 2006—; contbr. articles to profl. jours. Distbn. com. Greater Birmingham Found., 1984-90; exec bd. Birmingham area coun. Boy Scouts Am., 1987-1998, v.p., 1990-96, coun. commr., 1996-98; vice chmn. Vulcan dist., 1988-89, chmn., 1989-91, bd. dirs. S.E. region, 1990-92, bd. dirs. southern region, 1992—; bd. dirs. Ctrl. Ala. United Way, 1988-92; mem. Newcomen Soc., 1988—; chmn. exec. com. Birmingham Bapt. Med. Ctr., Montclair, 1995, pres.-elect med. staff, 1998-99, pres. 1999-2000; chmn. Nat. Eagle Scout Assn. Scholarship Com. So. Region, 2001-03; asst. coun. commr. Greater Ala. coun. Boy Scouts Am., 1998-2000, coun. commr., 2001-04, v.p. bd., 2006; mem. Am. Bd. Cardiovasc. Disease, 1991-96. Capt. U.S. Army. Decorated Commendation medal; recipient Dist. Award of Merit, Boy Scouts Am., 1991, Silver Beaver award, 1990, Disting. Eagle Scout, 1999, Silver Antelope award 2001; NIH rsch. fellow, 1966-67. Fellow: ACP, Am. Coll. Cardiology (bd. govs. 1978—81, trustee 1984—85, 1989—94, ann. sci. session program chmn. 1994, disting. fellowship 2001, Ala. chpt. named lectureship in honor); mem.: Med. Assn. State Ala. (spkr. house counselors dels. 1989—94, Laureate award 1999), Birmingham Soc. Internists (pres. 2001—03), Birmingham Cardiovascular Soc. (pres. 1983), Jefferson County Med. Soc. (v.p. 1982, pres. 1984), So. Soc. Clin. Investigation, Am. Fedn. Clin. Rsch., Am. Coll. Chest Physicians (bd. regents 1985—91), Am. Heart Assn. (pres. Ala. affiliate 1975—76, v.p. so. region 1986—87, task force on practice guidelines 1998—2000), Royal Soc. Medicine, NY Acad. Scis., Kiwanis (Brimingham sec. 1984—85, disting. pres. 1994—95), Leadership Birmingham, Omicron Delta Kappa, Alpha Omega Alpha, Phi Beta Kappa. Home: 4408 Kennesaw Dr Birmingham AL 35213-1826 Office: Ala Heart Inst 880 Montclair Rd 1st Fl Birmingham AL 35213 E-mail: rrussell@cvapc.com.

**RUSSELL, ROBERT HILTON,** Romance languages and literature educator; b. Oak Park, Ill., Dec. 26, 1927; s. Melvin Alvord and Gladys (Hilton) R.; m. June Adele Thayer, Oct. 27, 1956. AB, Knox Coll., 1949; A.M., Harvard U., 1950, PhD, 1963; A.M., Dartmouth Coll., 1968. Instr. Romance langs. and lits. Dartmouth Coll., 1957-61, asst. prof., 1961-63, assoc. prof., 1963-67, prof., 1967-91, prof. emeritus, 1991—. Vis. prof. Spanish, U. San Diego, 1989, 90, 91, Knox Coll., 1993; guest lectr. Trinity Coll., Dublin, 1967, U. Salamanca, 1977, U. Leeds, 1978, Oxford U., 1978, U. P.R., 1987. Author: The Christ Figure in Misericordia, 1968; translator: Our Friend Manso, 1987. Corporate mem. United Ch. Bd. Homeland Ministries, 1963-69; N.H. del. Gen. Synod, United Ch. Christ, 1973, 75; corporator Internat. Inst. in Spain. Mem. MLA, Asociación Internacional de Hispanistas, Asociación Internacional de Galdosistas, Phi Beta Kappa. Democrat. Home: 17 Willow Spring Cir Hanover NH 03755-2901 Office: 6072 Dartmouth Hall Hanover NH 03755-3511

**RUSSELL, ROBIE GEORGE,** lawyer; b. Moscow, Idaho, July 7, 1948; s. George Robie Russell and Jean Ray (Atkinson) O'Reilly; m. Nancy Kay Olson, May 31, 1975; children: George Robie, Erin Kay. BS in Polit. Sci., Pub. Adminstrn., U. Idaho, 1972, cert. in Pub. Adminstrn., 1974, JD, 1978. Bar: Idaho 1979, U.S. Dist. Ct. Idaho 1979, U.S. Ct. Claims 1980, U.S. Ct. Appeals (9th cir.) 1980, U.S. Tax Ct. 1981, U.S. Ct. Appeals (fed. cir.) 1985, U.S. Supreme Ct. 1985, Wash. 1991. Dep. atty. gen. State of Idaho, Boise, 1979-81, sr. dep. atty. gen., div. chief, 1981-86; regional adminstr. region 10 U.S. EPA, Alaska, Idaho, Oregon, Wash., 1986-90; pres. Environ. Property Mgmt., Inc., Bainbridge Island, Wash., 1991-93; of counsel Ryan Swanson &

Cleveland, Seattle, 1993-94; atty. Russell & Assocs., Seattle, 1995—. Counsel Idaho Sec. of State, Boise, 1982-86. Contbg. author: Idaho Media Law Handbook, 1986; editor: Idaho Cities Mag., 1974-75, (newsletter) Local Govt. Legal News, 1981-86; contbr. articles to profl. jours. Pres., treas. Lincoln Day Assn., Boise, 1979-86; vice-chmn. Selective Svc. Bd., Boise, 1983-86; chmn., vice-chmn. Ada County Reps., Boise, 1984-86; chmn. Combined Fed. Campaign, 1988; mem. Puget Sound Fed. Exec. Bd., 1986-90; mem. Am. Ctr. Internat. Leadership, Soviet Union/Poland delegation, 1989; active Boy Scouts Am. Named one of Outstanding Young Men in Am., 1980—. Mem. ABA, Idaho State Bar Assn., Wash. State Bar Assn. (CLE com.), Boise Bar Assn., Idaho County Bar Assn., Nat. Inst. Mcpl. Law Officers, Assn. Idaho City Attys. (sec., treas. 1981-86, founder), Assn. Idaho Cities (advisor 1981—, Boyd Martin award 1985), Phi Alpha Delta, U. Idaho Alumni Assn. (bd. dirs. 1973-74), Sons and Daus. Idaho Pioneers, U. Idaho Vandal Scholarship Fund (Moscow, Idaho) (chpt. pres., bd. dirs. 1975—, nat. v.p. 1987-89, nat. pres. 1989-90, Vandal Booster of Yr. 1985). Republican. Avocations: stamp collecting/philately, fishing, gardening, music, lit. Home: PO Box 10667 Bainbridge Island WA 98110-0667 Office: Russell & Assocs 76 S Main St Seattle WA 98104-2514

**RUSSELL, ROBIN J.,** broadcast executive; Sr. exec. v.p., gen. mgr. Columbia TriStar Home Entertainment; sr. exec. v.p., gen. mgr. bus. Sony Pictures Home Entertainment. Office: Sony Pictures Home Entertainment 10202 West Washington Blvd Culver City CA 90232*

**RUSSELL, RODNEY E.,** school system administrator; b. Knoxville, Tenn., Feb. 3, 1964; s. Howard Wade and Lucille Annette Russell; m. Jamie Renee Humphrey, Apr. 7, 1990; 1 child, Daniel Thomas. BS, East Tenn. State U., 1986; EdS, Lincoln Meml. U., Harrogate, Tenn., 1997; EdD, Trevecca Nazarene U., Nashville, 2005. Supr. staff devel. and extended learning Knox County Schs., Knoxville, 2003—, evening alternative sch. prin., 2005—06. Non-daycare facility mgr. Boys Club of Knoxville, 1985—87; lang. devel. specialist Knox County Schs., 1987—91, tchr. 4th grade, 1989—96, sci. specialist, 1996—2003; min. of youth Smithwood Bapt. Ch., Knoxville, 1999—. Bd. dirs. Tenn. Staff Devel. Coun., Tenn., 2000—06. Named Tchr. of the Yr. Bldg. Level, Tenn. Dept. of Edn., 1993; named to Leadership Edn. Class, Knoxville C. of C., 1993; recipient Beacon in the Classroom award, Apple Computers, 1994, 21st Century grant for computer tech., Knox County Schs., 1992; grantee, Jr. League of Knoxville, 1995. Mem.: NEA (assoc.), NSTA (assoc.), Tenn. Staff Devel. Coun. (assoc.; bd. dirs. 2000—06), Nat. Staff Devel. Coun. (assoc.; co-chair conf. exhibits 2004—06), Phi Delta Kappa, Pi Lambda Theta. Baptist. Achievements include research in impact of content reading strategies impact on achievement; development of new teacher academy and mentor program for teachers in Knox County. Avocations: golf, swimming, skiing. Home: 4910 Shannon Run Drive Knoxville TN 37918 Office: Sarah Simpson Prof Dev Center 810 Tipton Avenue Knoxville TN 37918 Office Phone: 865-579-8018 1051. Home Fax: 865-579-8191; Office Fax: 865-579-8191. Personal E-mail: russell_rodney@bellsouth.net.

**RUSSELL, SABIN,** newswriter; m. Ashley Wolff; 2 children. Grad., Yale U., 1974. Writer Venture Mag., Electronic News, various cmty. newspapers Vermont and NH; med. writer San Francisco Chronicle. Recipient Sci. in Soc. Journalism award, Nat. Assn. Sci. Writers, Inc., 2001; grantee, Kaiser Family Found. Primary responsibilities include coverage of science and health policy, focusing on topics such as HIV/AIDS, bioterrorism, SARS, West Nile virus, mad cow, and other infectious diseases. Office: San Francisco Chronicle 901 Mission St San Francisco CA 94103-2988 Office Phone: 415-777-8447. Office Fax: 415-896-1107. Business E-Mail: srussell@sfchronicle.com.*

**RUSSELL, SUE ANN,** clinical psychologist; b. Connersville, Ind., Apr. 14, 1949; d. Hugh B. Russell and Martha Jane Meyer. BS, U. Colo., 1971; MDiv, Abilene Christian U., 1981; PhD in Clin. Psychology, U. N.D., 1992. Intern Psychol. Svcs. Ctr. U. N.D., Grand Forks, 1986-92; intern Stone Ctr. Wellesley Coll., Wellesley, 1991-92; rsch. psychologist women's drinking project U. N.D., Grand Forks, 1986-92; pvt. practice Grand Forks, 1993—. Founding fellow Jean Baker Miller Tng. Inst. of Wellesley Coll., 1996. Contbr. articles to profl. jours. Missionary to Tonga Tribe, Africa, 1972—74. Fellowship Nat. Inst. on Alcohol Abuse and Alcoholism Nat. Inst. of Mental Health, 1991-92, Nat. Rsch. Svc. award 1988-91; pre-doctoral rsch. fellow Stone Ctr. of Wellesley Coll., 1991-92. Mem. Am. Psychol. Assn., N.D. Psychol. Assn., Assn. of Prevention and Cruelty to Animals Avocations: American Eskimo dogs, creating wildlife sanctuary and natural prairie habitat on 290 acres. Office: 628 7th Ave S Ste B Grand Forks ND 58201-4854 Office Phone: 701-746-8737.

**RUSSELL, TERRENCE JOSEPH,** lawyer; b. Jacksonville, Fla., Sept. 26, 1944; AA, St. Leo Coll., 1964; BA, U. Fla., 1966; JD, Fla. State U., 1968. Bar: Fla. 1969. Law clk. to Hon. W.O. Mehrtens U.S. Dist. Ct. (so. dist.) Fla., 1969; atty. Ruden, McClosky, Smith, Schuster & Russell, P.A., Ft. Lauderdale, Fla. Mem. appellate restructure commn. Fla. Supreme Ct., 1985—86, mem. nominating com., 1994—, chmn. nominating com., 1997, 98; mem. Fed. Magistrate's merit selection panel, 1985; vice-chmn. 17th Jud. Cir. Nominating Com., 1982—84, chmn., 1985—86; mem. spl. com. representation of death sentenced inmates Fla. Bar, bd. govs., 1987—91, pres., 2001—02. Bd. govs. Nova U. Law Sch., 1981, chmn., 1993—97; bd. dirs. Broward County Legal Aid Svcs., 1985—86. Mem.: ATLA, ABA (ho. of dels. 2000—04, sects. litig., legal edn.), Fla. Bar Found. (bd. dirs. 1992—98, pres. 2004—), Fla. State U. Law Sch. Alumni Assn. (pres. 1985), Am. Bd. Trial Advs., Am. Bar Found., Acad. Fla. Trial Lawyers (coll. diplomates), Broward County Trial Lawyers Assn., Broward County Bar Assn. (chmn. spl. com. legal malpractice ins. 1978, bar-bench liaison com. 1978, jud. selection and tenure com. 1978—79, exec. com. 1980, 1981, pres. 1984—85), Gold Key, Delta Theta Phi. Office: Ruden McClosky et al PO Box 1900 Fort Lauderdale FL 33302-1900 Office Phone: 954-527-2460. Business E-Mail: terrence.russell@ruden.com.

**RUSSELL, THEODORE EMERY,** diplomat; b. Madras, India, Nov. 21, 1936; s. Paul Farr and Phyllis Hope (Additon) R.; m. Sara Mather (Stedman) Russell, Sept. 3, 1960; children: Douglas Richmond Russell, Richard Mather Russell. BA, Yale U., 1958; MA, Fletcher Sch. Law & Diplomacy, 1960, MALD, 1961; sr. tng., Nat. War Coll., 1980—81. Fgn. svc. officer Dept. State, Italy, Czechoslovakia, Washington, 1963-80, dep. office dir. (EUR/RPE) Washington, 1981-83; dep. chief mission Copenhagen, 1983-87, Prague, Czechoslovakia, 1987-91; dep. asst. adminstr. for internat. activities EPA, Washington, 1992-93; amb. to Slovak Republic Bratislava, Slovakia, 1993-96; dep. comdt. internat. affairs Army War Coll., Carlisle, Pa., 1996-99; dir. internat. rels. MHz Networks, 2001—03; internat. security affairs cons., 2001—. Adj. fellow CSIS. Founding chmn. Friends of Slovakia. Mem. Army-Navy Club, Fgn. Svc. Assn., Nat. War Coll. Alumni Assn. Avocations: hiking, fishing, history. Home and Office: 1833 Briar Ridge Ct Mc Lean VA 22101-4233

**RUSSELL, THERESA LYNN,** actress; b. San Diego, Mar. 20, 1957; d. Jerry Russell Paup and Carole (Mall) Platt; m. Nicholas Jack Roeg, Feb. 12, 1986; children: Statten Jack, Maximilian Nicolas Nextus. Appeared in films including The Last Tycoon, 1976, Straight Time, 1978, Bad Timing, 1980, Eureka, 1984, Razor's Edge, 1984, Insignificance, 1985, Aria, 1987, Black Widow, 1987 (Nat. Assn. Theater Owners award 1985), Track 29, 1988 (Newcomer of Yr. award), Physical Evidence, 1989, Impulse, 1990, Cold Heaven, 1991 (Best Actress award Viareggio Film Festival 1991), Whore, 1991, Kafka, 1991, Thicker Than Water, 1992, The Trade Off, 1993, (narrator) Being Human, 1993, Flight of the Dove, 1994, Grotesque, 1995, The Proposition, 1995, A young connecticut Yankee in King Arthur's Court, 1995, Public Enemies, 1996, The Proposition, 1997, Running Women, 1998, Wild Things, 1998, Luckytown, 2000, The Believer, 2001, The House Next Door, 2002, Project Viper, 2002, Passionada, 2002, Now & Forever, 2002, Save It for Later, 2003, Chinaman's Chance, 2006; TV movies Blind Ambition, 1979, Later, 1983, Women's Guide to Adultery, 1993, Hotel Paradise, 1995, Once You Meet a Stranger, 1996, Trade Off, 1996, Earth vs. the Spider, 2001, Love Comes

Softly, 2003, Blind Injustice, 2005, Empire Falls, 2005; (TV miniseries) Blind Ambition, 1979; guest appearances Nash Bridges, 2000, Law & Order: Criminal Intent, 2006; BBC radio play Double Indemnity, 1993.*

**RUSSELL, THOMAS WILLIAM FRASER,** chemical engineer, educator; b. Moose Jaw, Saskatchewan, Can., Aug. 5, 1934; s. Thomas D. and Evelyn May (Fraser) R.; m. Shirley A. Aldrich, Aug. 1956; children: Bruce, Brian, Carey. BChe, U. Alta., Canada, 1956; MChe, U. Alta., 1958; PhD, U. Del., 1964. Registered profl. engr., Del. Rsch. engr. Rsch. Coun. of Alta., Edmonton, Alberta, Canada, 1956—58; process design engr. Union Carbide Can., Montreal, Quebec, Canada, 1958—61; Allan P. Colburn prof. of chem. engring. U. Del., Newark, Del., 1961—; acting dean Coll. of Engring., U. Del., 1978—79; dir. Inst. of Energy Conversion, U. Del., 1979—95; chmn. Dept. Chem. Engring., U. Del., 1986—91; vice provost for rsch. U. Del., 2000—05. Cons. E.I. duPont de Nemours & Co., Inc., Wilmington, Del., 1968—. Author 2 books; contbr. articles to profl. jours., patentee in field. Recipient award, NAE, 1990 to present, 3M Lectureship award, Am. Soc. of Engring. Edn., 1984, Thomas H Chilton award, AIChE, Wilmington Sect. 1988. Mem. NAE, Am. Inst. Chem. Engring. (Thomas H. Chilton award 1988, Chem. Engring. Practice award 1987), Am. Chem. Soc., Am. Soc. Engring. Edn. (3M Lecture award chem. engring. divsn. 1984). Achievements include patents for method for the manufacture of thin film solar cells; method for the continuous deposition by vacuum deposition; first to development of a continuous process for the manufacture of thin film solar modules. Avocations: hiking, skiing, windsurfing. Office: U DE Dept Chem Engring Newark DE 19716 Office Phone: 302-831-1714. Personal E-mail: russell@che.udel.edu.

**RUSSELL, WALTER DALLAS, JR.,** diversified financial services company executive; b. Culver City, Calif., Oct. 31, 1979; s. Walter Dallas and Leann Marie Russell. BBA in Fin., U. Houston, 2005. Sr. mgr. MRG, Inc., Houston, 2000—03; escrow officer Land Am. Ptnrs. Title, 2003—. Mem.: AARP (assoc.), Am. Mensa. Office Phone: 713-426-4949. Personal E-mail: drussell2028@yahoo.com.

**RUSSELL, WILLIAM EDWARDS, IV,** educational association administrator, researcher; b. N.Y. s. Cutler (Stepfather); m. Barbara Jean Pratico, May 23, 1993; children: Billy, Christina Danielle. BA in Econs., DePauw U., 1985; BS in Psychology, U. Conn., 1989; MPhil, Columbia U., 1996, PhD, 2000. Dir. R&D, Greenwich Assocs., Conn., 1996—. Mem. Nat. Coun. of Measurement in Edn., 1992—. Recipient Pub. Svc. award, Ind. Ret. Persons, 1989, Excellence in Edn. award, Alpha Sigma Lambda, 1992, Academic Achievement award, Delta Kappa Epsilon, 1994. Fellow: Ivy Club; mem.: Am. Ednl. Rsch. Assns., Mensa. Achievements include development of Greenwich Quality Index. Avocations: sailing, golf. Office: Greenwich Assocs 8 Greenwich Office Pk Greenwich CT 06831 Office Phone: 203-625-5034. Office Fax: 203-629-1200. Business E-Mail: brussell@greenwich.com.

**RUSSELL, WILLIAM JOSEPH,** educational association administrator; b. Boston, Sept. 23, 1941; s. Stanley Whiteside and Helen Rita R.; m. Frances Marie Chapdelaine, June 25, 1967; 1 son, Scott David. BS, Boston Coll., 1963; M.Ed., Northeastern U., 1966; PhD, U. Calif., Berkeley, 1971. Head math. dept. Oceana, Pacifica, Calif., 1966-71; asst. for ed. and profl. affairs Am. Ednl. Research Assn., Washington, 1971-73, dep. exec. dir., 1973-74, exec. dir., 1974—2002. Ad. bd. Edn. Resource Info. Center Ednl. Testing Center, Princeton, N.J., 1975-87; exec. officer Nat. Council on Measurement in Edn., Internat. Assn. Computing in Edn., 1987-89. Editor: Ednl. Researcher, 1979-90. Mem. Am Ednl. Research Assns., Phi Delta Kappa. Roman Catholic. Home: 1443 Creekside Ct Vienna VA 22182-1701 Office: AERA 1230 17th St NW Washington DC 20036-3078 Personal E-mail: billfran@lycos.com.

**RUSSELL, WILLIAM STEVEN,** finance executive; b. Evanston, Ill., Aug. 5, 1948; s. John W. and Lillian H. Russell; m. Susan M. Hanson, Aug. 20, 1972. BS, So. Ill. U., 1970. CPA, Ill. Sr. staff auditor Arthur Andersen & Co., Chgo., 1972-76; acctg. mgr., controller, asst. sec. and treas. Lawter Internat., Inc., Northbrook, Ill., 1976-86, treas., sec., 1986-87, v.p. fin., treas. and sec., 1987-96, pvt. investor, 1996—. Served with U.S. Army, 1970-72. Mem. Am. Inst. CPA's, Beta Alpha Psi, Beta Gamma Sigma. Roman Catholic. Home and Office: 51 Park Lane Park Ridge IL 60068-2834

**RUSSERT, TIMOTHY JOHN,** broadcast journalist, broadcast executive; b. Buffalo, May 7, 1950; m. Maureen Orth; 1 child, Luke. BA, John Carroll U., 1972; JD, Cleve. State U., 1976. Bar: NY, DC. Spl. counsel US Senate, 1977—82; counselor NY Gov.'s Office, 1983—84; with NBC News, 1984—; moderator, mng. editor Meet the Press, 1991—; anchor The Tim Russert Show CNBC, 1994—; sr. v.p., Washington bureau chief NBC News. Nat. polit. analyst Today program and NBC Nightly News with Tom Brokaw; supr. NBC News Today program live broadcasts from Rome, 1985; overseer prodn. prime time spl. A Day in the Life of Pres. Bush, 1990, A Day in the Life of Pres. Clinton, 1993; has covered 8 U.S./Russian Summits, Geneva, Malta, Washington, Moscow, Vancouver; lectr. at more than 30 univs. Author: Big Russ and Me: Father and Son-Lessons of Life, 2004, Wisdom of Our Fathers: Lessons and Letters from Daughters and Sons, 2006. Recipient Alumni Spl. Achievement award, Cleve.-Marshall Coll. Law, Pres.'s medal, Trocaire Coll., John Peter Zenger award, N.Y. State Bar Assn., 1992, Disting. Grad. award, Nat. Cath. Educator's Assn., 1995, Spl. Achievement Alumni medal, John Carroll U., Joan S. Barone award, 2000, Annenberg Center's Walter Cronkite award, 2000, Edward R. Murrow award overall excellence in TV journalism, 2001, News Media award, VFW, 2005, The Cath. Acad. Comm.'s Gabriel award, 2005, Am. Legion Journalism award, Congl. Medal of Honor Soc. Journalism award, Allen H. Neuhart award excellence in journalism, David Brinkley award excellence in communication, Emmy coverage Pres Reagan's funeral, Golden Plate award, Acad. Achievement. Fellow: Comm. European Cmtys. Office: NBC News Meet the Press 4001 Nebraska Ave NW Washington DC 20016-2733

**RUSSETT, BRUCE MARTIN,** political science professor; b. North Adams, Mass., Jan. 26, 1935; s. Raymond Edgar and Ruth Marian (Martin) R.; m. Cynthia Margaret Eagle, June 18, 1960; children: Margaret Ellen, Mark David, Lucia Elizabeth, Daniel Alden. BA magna cum laude, Williams Coll., 1956; diploma in econs., Cambridge (Eng.) U., 1957; MA, Yale U., 1958, PhD, 1961; PhD (hon.), Uppsala U., 2002. Instr. MIT, Cambridge, 1961-62; asst. prof., then assoc. prof. Yale U., New Haven, 1961-68, prof., 1968—, Dean Acheson prof. internat. rels. and polit. sci., 1985—, chair dept. polit. sci., 1990-96, dir. UN studies, 1993—2006. Vis. prof. Columbia U., 1965, U. Mich., 1965-66, U. Libre Brussels, 1969-70, U. N.C., 1979-80, Richardson Inst., London, 1973-74, Netherlands Inst. Advanced Study, 1984, Tel Aviv U., 1989, U. Tokyo, 1996, Harvard U., 2001; prin. cons. pastoral letter on peace Nat. Conf. Cath. Bishops, Washington, 1981-83; co-dir., secretariat ind. working group Future of the UN, 1993-96. Author: World Handbook of Political and Social Indicators, 1964, What Price Vigilance?, 1970 (Kammerer award Am. Polit. Sci. Assn. 1971), Interest and Ideology (with E. Hanson), 1975, Controlling the Sword, 1990, Grasping the Democratic Peace, 1993, The Once and Future Security Council. 1997, (with John Oneal) Triangulating Peace, 2001, (with Francis Oakley) Governance, Accountability, and the Future of the Catholic Church, 2004, (with Alex Mintz) New Directions for International Relations, 2005, Purpose and Policy in the Global Community, 2006, others; editor: Jour. Conflict Resolution, 1972—; contbr. articles to profl. jours. Grantee NSF, 1964, 65, 69, 77, 79, 85, 88, 89, 90, 95, 98, Ford Found., 1993, 94, 97, John and Catherine MacArthur Found., 1988, 91; Fulbright-Hays fellow, Belgium and Israel, 1969, 89; John Simon Guggenheim Found. fellow, 1969, 77; German Marshall Fund fellow, 1977. Fellow Am. Acad. Arts and Scis.; mem. AAUP, Am. Polit. Sci. Assn. (coun. 1984-86), Internat. Studies Assn. (pres. 1983-84), Peace Sci. Soc. Internat. (pres. 1977-79). Avocations: tennis, classical music, skiing. Home: 70 Martin Ter Hamden CT 06517-2333 Office: Yale U Dept Polit Sci PO Box 208301 New Haven CT 06520-8301 Office Phone: 203-432-5233. E-mail: bruce.russett@yale.edu.

**RUSSI, GARY D.,** academic administrator; BSc, Southwestern Oklahoma State U., 1969; PhD, U. Kansas, 1972. With U.S. Army various mgmt. positions, 1969—92; tchr., rsch. asst. Kansas U., 1969; various positions such as project coord. and v.p., rsch. and strategic planning et al. Drake U., 1973—93; v.p. acad. affairs Oakland U., 1993—95, interim pres., 1995—96, pres. Rochester, Mich., 1996—. Contbr. articles to profl. jours.; author book reviews. Mem. bd. Automation Alley, Oakland County Bus. Roundtable; bd. trustees Citizens Rsch. Coun. of Mich., Crittenton Hosp.; chair, bd. dirs. Rochester Hills Strategic Planning Process; pres. coun. Mid-Continent Athletics Conf.; chair, bd. dir. Mich. Virtual U. Recipient Rho Ci Soc. undergrad. rsch. award, Southwestern Oklahoma State U., 1969, Merck Rsch. award, 1996, Disting. Alumni award, 1998, George Wibby Athletic award, Oakland U., 2002. Office: Oakland U 204 Wilson Hall Rochester MI 48309-4401 E-mail: russi@oakland.edu.

**RUSSIANO, JOHN See MILES, JACK**

**RUSSIN, JONATHAN,** lawyer, consultant; b. Kingston, Pa., Oct. 30, 1937; s. Jacob S. and Anne (Wartella) R.; m. Antoinette Stackpole, Oct. 6, 1962; children: Alexander, Andrew, Benjamin, Jacob. BA, Yale U., 1959, LLB, 1963. Bar: DC 1964. Guide interpreter Am. Nat. Exhibit, Moscow, 1959; rsch. asst. Law Faculty U. East Africa, Dar es Salaam, Tanganyika, 1961-62; regional legal adviser for Caribbean AID, 1967-69; ptnr. Kirkwood, Kaplan, Russin & Vecchi, Santo Domingo, Dominican Republic, 1969-74, Washington, 1974-78, Kaplan Russin & Vecchi, Madrid, 1978-81, Washington, 1981-92; ptnr., dir. Russian practice group Russin & Vecchi, Moscow, 1992—. Washington rep. for Moscow Patriarchate of Russian Orthodox Ch.; convener adv. coun. Inst. for European, Russian and Eurasian Studies, George Washington U.; mem. adv. bd. Caribbean Am. Directory; trustee St. Nicholas Cathedral, Washington, St. Vladimir's Orthodox Theol. Sem., Crestwood, N.Y., 1985-93; legal adviser Orthodox Ch. in Am. Contbr. articles to profl. jours. Bd. dirs. Nat. Coun. Internat. Visitors, Washington, 1987—93. Fund for Democracy and Devel., Washington, 1993—, MUCIA Global Edn. Group, Inc., 1996—2000, Delphi Internat., Washington, 1988—2000, Dominican Am. Cultural Inst., Santo Domingo, 1988—92. Recipient Order of St. Vladimir, Moscow Patriarchate, Russian Orthodox Ch., 1991. Mem.: Russian Assn. Internat. Law, DC Bar, Yale Club Washington, Yale Club NY, Inter-Am. Bar Assn., ABA. Office: 1000 Potomac St NW 5th Fl Washington DC 20007-3501 Office Phone: 202-822-6100. E-mail: jonathan.russin@russinvecchi.com.

**RUSSO, ALEXANDER PETER,** artist, educator; b. Atlantic City, June 11, 1922; s. Peter Joseph and Lillian Mary (Soma) R.; 1 child, Eugenie. Student. Pratt Inst., 1940-42, Swarthmore Coll., 1946-47; S.S., Bard Coll., 1947; B.F.A. (Breevort-Eickenmeyer fellow), Columbia U., 1952; postgrad., Acad. Fine Arts, Rome, 1952-54. Inst. Advanced Fine Arts, 1977-79. Instr. New Orleans Acad. Art, 1948-49; asst. prof. art U. Buffalo, 1955-58; instr. in graphic design Parsons Sch. Design, 1958-60; chmn. dept. drawing and painting Corcoran Sch. Art, 1961-70, chmn. faculty, acting dean, 1967-70; lectr., thesis adv. George Washington U., 1961-70; prof. Hood Coll., Frederick, Md., 1970-90, prof. emeritus, 1990—, chmn. dept. art, 1970-87. Vis. guest prof. art Instituto Allende, San Miguel de Allende, Mexico, 1993-94; panelist Md. State Coun. Arts, Balt., 1981-82; reviewer art programs Md. State Bd. Edn., 1981—; guest art critic Southampton Press, N.Y., 1989, 91; cons. in field. One-man shows include Corcoran Gallery Art, Washington, 1946, 64, Chiurazzi Gallery, Rome, 1953, Cavallino Gallery, Venice, Italy, 1954, U. So. Ill., 1955, Frank Rehn Gallery, N.Y.C., periodic exhbns., 1954-74, Phoenix II Gallery, Washington, 1983, Ingber Gallery, N.Y.C., 1983, Washington Gallery Art, 1963, Franz Bader Gallery, Washington, 1967, Internat. Monetary Fund, Washington, 1968, 79, Agra Gallery, Washington, 1971, Benson Gallery, Bridgehampton, L.I., 1976, Phoenix Fine Arts, Frederick, 1981, Benton Gallery, Southampton, N.Y., 1985, 86, 88, 90-91, Arlene Bujese Gallery, East Hampton, N.Y., 1994-95, 97-98, to 2006, Hood Coll., Frederick, Md., 1991, Western Md. Coll., Westminster, 1991, Bell Gallery, Seattle, 1991-92, Gettysburg (Pa.) Coll., 1989, Nabi Gallery, N.Y.C., 2006; group exhbns. include Salon de la Marne, Paris, 1945, Met. Mus. Art, N.Y.C., 1948, Bordighera Internat., Italy, 1953-54, Mus. Modern Art, Madrid, 1953, Sala di Esposizione delle Biblioteca Americano, Rome, 1953, Whitney Mus. Am. Art, N.Y.C., 1960, Mus. Modern Art, N.Y.C., 1969, Guild Hall, East Hampton, N.Y., 1976, East Hampton Avant-Garde, A Salute to the Signa Gallery, 1990, NAS, Washington, 1984, Bell Gallery, Seattle, 1990, Illustrator's Club, N.Y.C., 1991, Armory Exhbn., N.Y.C., 1991, Inst. Alleude, San Niguel de Allende, Mex., 1994, Fulbright Assoc. 20th Anniv. Art Exhibition, 1997, Josh Kligerman Gallery, San Miguel de Allende, Mex., 1994; represented in permanent collections Albright-Know Gallery, Buffalo, Columbia U., N.Y.C., Delgado Mus. Art, New Orleans, Corcoran Gallery Art, Fiat Automobile Co., Rome, Nat. Collection Smithsonian Inst., Washington, Fed. Ins. Deposit Corp., Washington, Gettysburg Coll. Pa.; author: Profiles on Women Artists, 1985, The Challenge of Drawing, 1986, (poetry) Vignettes, 1996. Served with USNR, 1942-46. Fellow Guggenheim Found., 1947-48, 49-50,Edward McDowell Found., 1956, Hood Coll. Hodson teaching fellow, 1983; Fulbright grantee for painting and research, Rome, 1952-54, U.S.-Indo Subcommn. on Edn. and Culture grantee, India, 1984. Office: PO Box 1377 Wainscott NY 11975-1377 also: Arlene Bujese Dealer 40 Whooping Hollow Rd East Hampton NY 11937-2400 Office Phone: 631-324-4914. *Success is an equivocal matter. "Outward success", no doubt, is meaningful and necessary to most people in terms of fulfilling goals or for some similar reason. "Interior success" is more difficult to achieve, for it means the labor of a developing soul, and, more often than not, the relinquishing of what most would consider to be "material success." Whatever I have achieved in the way of outward or material success, therefore, is but a minute reflection of that which I wish to achieve on the spiritual level. There is a long way to go.*

**RUSSO, ANTHONY,** film director; b. Cleve. Cordir., writer, prod, with Joe Russo (films) Pieces, 1997, The Kiss, 2001, Co-dir., writer, with Joe Russo Welcome to Collinwood, 2002, You, Me and Dupree, 2006, co-dir. with Joe Russo (TV series) Lucky, 2002, Arrested Development, 2003 (Emmy award Outstanding Directing for a Comedy Series, 2004), co-dir., exec. prod. with Joe Russo LAX, 2004, What About Brian, 2006—. Office: c/o Jason Burns United Talent Agy 9560 Wilshire Blvd #500 Beverly Hills CA 90212 also: c/o Section 8 Films 10866 Wilshire Blvd #1100 Los Angeles CA 90024*

**RUSSO, ANTHONY JOSEPH,** public relations professional; b. N.Y.C., Oct. 23, 1953; s. Lucio and Tina (Iarossi) R. BA cum laude, Alfred U., 1974; MA, Columbia U., 1975; PhD, Claremont Grad. Sch., 1982. Asst. to chmn. Mocatta Metals, NYC, 1982-83; account exec. Gavin Anderson and Co., NYC, 1983-85; sr. account exec. Adams and Reinhart, NYC, 1985; dir. corp. rels. Geto and DeMilly, NYC, 1985-86; v.p. Cameron Assocs., NYC, 1986-88; CEO Euro RSCG Life PR and Noonan Russo, NYC, 1998—; chmn. Madison Life Scis. Mem. editl. bd.: Jour. Comml. Biotech., Bio People. Bd. dirs. March of Dimes, Target Autism Genome. Mem. APA, Pub. Rels. Soc. Am., Psi Chi. Democrat. Office: Euro RSCG Life PR 200 Madison Ave 7th Fl New York NY 10016 also: Euro RSCG Life PR Paris 2 Allee de Longchamp 92281 Suresnes France also: 4370 La Jolla Village Dr San Diego CA 92130 also: Euro RSCG Life PR 11 Great Newport St London WC2H 7JA England E-mail: tong.russo@euoorscg.com.

**RUSSO, CHERYL JEAN,** elementary school educator, special education educator; d. Allen William and Charlene Linnea Carlsen; m. Sirio Robert Russo, Aug. 11, 1996; stepchildren: Angela Russo Fitzpatrick, Dominick. BA, Carthage Coll., Kenosha, Wis., 1978; MS in Edn., No. Ill. U., DeKalb, 1985. Spl. edn. resource tchr. Schafer Elem., Lombard, Ill., 1978—79; Jackson Mid. Sch., Villa Park, Ill., 1978—79; resource tchr. Schafer Elem. Sch., Lombard, Ill., 1979—82, self-contained primary LD, 1982—85; self-contained LD/BD, Jefferson Jr. H.S., Villa Park, Ill., 1983—91; instr. No. Ill. U., DeKalb, 1985—96; 4th grade tchr. Artmore Elem., Villa Park, Ill., 1991—. Mem. curriculum com. Sch. Dist. #45, Villa Park, Ill., 1997—2002, sch. leadership team, steering com. 1987—90, grade level chairperson, 1997—2000; dir., facilitator numerous grants. Coord., vol. U.S. Amateur Golf Tournament, 1995; mem. Salem United Meth. Ch., Barrington, Ill., 1960—97, LaGrange Meth. Ch., Ill., 1997—. Recipient grant, U. Ill., 2004—. Mem.: ASCD, Ill. Reading Assn., Internat. Reading Assn., Coun. for Exceptional Children, Kappa Delta Pi. Democrat. Methodist. Avocations: reading, travel, gardening, photography, antiques. Office: Sch Dist #45 Villa Park 225 S Harvard Villa Park IL 60181 Office Phone: 630-530-6255. E-mail: russo7@ameritech.net.

**RUSSO, CHRIS,** radio personality; b. NY, 1966; m. Jeanne Russo. BA, Rollins Coll. Morning sports anchor WKIS, Orlando, Fla.; weekend sports talk show host WMCA, NYC; sports talk show host WFAN-AM 66, NYC, 1989—. Co-host (radio shows) Mike & the Mad Dog, 1989—, The Huddle; co-author (with Allen St. John): Mad Dog 100: The Greatest Sports Arguments of All Time, 2003, Mad Dog Hall of Fame: The Ultimate Top-10 Rankings of the Best in Sports, 2006. Co-recipient Marconi Radio award for Major Market Personality of Yr., Nat. Assn. Broadcasters, 2000. Office: WFAN-AM 34-12 36th St Astoria NY 11106 Office Phone: 718-706-7690.

**RUSSO, GUY J.,** financial services company executive; Sr. v.p. fin. and info. services CommunityAmerica Credit Union, Lenexa, Kans. Named one of Premier 100 IT Leaders, Computerworld, 2005. Office: CommunityAmerica Credit Union 9777 Ridge Dr Lenexa KS 66219*

**RUSSO, IRMA HAYDEE ALVAREZ DE,** pathologist; b. San Rafael, Mendoza, Argentina, Feb. 28, 1942; came to U.S., 1972; d. Jose Maria and Maria Carmen (Martinez) de Alvarez; m. Jose Russo, Feb. 8, 1969; 1 child, Patricia Alexandra. BA, Escuela Normal MTSM de Balcarce, 1959; MD, U. Nat. of Cuyo, Mendoza, 1970. Diplomate Am. Bd. Pathology. Intern Sch. Medicine Hosps., Argentina, 1969-70; resident in pathology Wayne State U. Sch. Medicine, Detroit, 1976-80. Rsch. asst., instr. Inst. Histology and Embryology Sch. Medicine U. Nat. of Cuyo, 1963-71, assoc. prof. histology Faculty Phys., Chem. and Math. Scis., 1970-72; rsch. assoc. inst. Molecular and Cellular Evolution U. Miami, Fla., 1972-73; rsch. assoc. exptl. pathology lab. divsn. biol. scis. Mich. Cancer Foun., Detroit, 1973-75, rsch. scientist, 1975-76, vis. rsch. scientist, 1976-82, asst. mem., pathologist, 1982-89, assoc. rsch. mem., 1989-91, co-dir. pathology reference lab., 1982-86, chief exptl. pathology lab., 1989-91; co-dir. Mich. Cancer Found. Lab. Svcs., 1986-91; mem. Fox Chase Cancer Ctr., 1991—, active staff mem. dept. surgery med. scis. divsn., 2004—; dir. anatomic pathology Am. Oncologic Hosp. Dept. Pathology, 1991-92; dir. Lab. Svcs., 1992-94; chief molecular endocrinology sect. Breast Cancer Rsch. Lab. Fox Chase Cancer Ctr., 1994—; chief resident physician dept. pathology Wayne State U. Sch. Medicine, 1978-80, asst. prof., 1980-82; mem. staff Harper-Grace Hosps., Detroit, 1980-82; adj. prof. Pathology and Cell Biology Jefferson Sch. Medicine/Thomas Jefferson U., 1992—, chairperson Basic Breast Biology Study Sect. U. Calif. Breast Cancer Program, 1997, mem. endocrinology panel peer rev. com. breast cancer rsch. program U.S. Army R & D Command, 1994, 95, 96, 2002, 03, chairperson endocrinology peer rev. com., 1996; ad-hoc mem. biochem. endocrinology study sect. NIH, DHHS, 1994, metabolic pathology study sect., 1996-97; mem. European Commn. Cancer Prevention, 1994—; mem. bd. sci. counselor, sec. health and human svcs. Nat. Toxicology Program Bd., 1994-98; mem. Internat. Life Scis. Inst.-Risk Sci. Inst. Mammary Working Group, 1992—; pres., founder League of Women Against Cancer, Rydal, Pa., 1994—; guest lectr. dept. obstetrics Sch. Medicine U. Nat. of Cuyo, 1965-71; mem. resource devel. subcommittee of the profl. advisory com., Latinas Living Beyond Breast Cancer, 2000—; mem. Breast Cancer Res. Sci. Review Panel, N.J.commr. on cancer rsch., Trenton, N.J., 1997, 2000. Editor-in-chief Jour. Women's Cancer, 1997—; contbr. articles to profl. jours. Rockefeller grantee, 1972-73; Nat. Cancer Inst. grantee, 1978-81, 84-87, 94-99, 2003—, Am. Cancer Soc. grantee 1988-89, 91-94, U.S. Army Med. R&D Command grantee, 1994-93, 2003—; recipient Shannon award Nat. Cancer Inst./NHHSS, 1992-94, Gold medal Inst. U. Dexeus, Barcelona, Spain, 2000. Mem. AAAS, Soc. Española Senología y Patología Mamaria, Nat. Cancer Inst. (breast cancer working group, breast cancer program 1984-88), Nat. Alliance Breast Cancer Orgns. (med. adv. bd. N.Y.C. chpt. 1986—), Ea. Coop. Oncology Group, Coll. Am. Pathologists, Am. Soc. Clin. Pathologists, Am. Assn. Cancer Rsch., Am. Assn. Clin. Chemistry, Internat. Coll. Physicians and Surgeons, Women in Cancer Rsch., The Endocrine Soc., Internat. Assn. Against Cancer, Sigma Xi, Food Quality Protection Act, Sci. Review Bd., Fed. Insecticide Fungi and Rodenticide Act, Adivsory Panel, EPA. Roman Catholic. Office: Fox Chase Cancer Ctr 333 Cottman Ave Philadelphia PA 19111 Office Phone: 215-728-4781. Personal E-mail: Lowac@msn.com. Business E-Mail: Irma.Russo@fccc.edu.

**RUSSO, JOE,** film director; b. Cleve. married. Co-dir., writer, prod, with Anthony Russo (films) Pieces, 1997 (Best Actor award, Am. Film Inst.), The Kiss, 2001, co-dir., writer with Anthony Russo Welcome to Collinwood, 2002, You, Me and Dupree, 2006, co-dir. with Anthony Russo (TV series) Lucky, 2002, Arrested Development, 2003 (Emmy award Outstanding Directing for a Comedy Series, 2004), co-dir., exec-prod. with Anthony Russo LAX, 2004, What About Brian, 2006—. Office: c/o Jason Burns United Talent Agy 9560 Wilshire Blvd #500 Beverly Hills CA 90212 also: c/o Section 8 Films 10866 Wilshire Blvd #1100 Los Angeles CA 90024*

**RUSSO, JOSE,** pathologist; b. Mendoza, Argentina, Mar. 24, 1942; came to U.S., 1971; s. Felipe and Teresa (Pagano) R.; m. Irma Haydee, Feb. 8, 1969; 1 child, Patricia Alexandra. BS, Agustin Alvarez Nat. Coll., 1959; MD, U. Nat. Cuyo, 1967. Instr. Inst. Gen. and Exptl. Pathology Med. Sch., Mendoza, 1961-66; asst. prof. Inst. Histology and Embryology, 1967-71; Rockefeller Found. postdoc. fellow Inst. Molecular and Cellular Evolution U. Miami, 1971—73; chief exptl. pathology lab. Mich. Cancer Found., Detroit, 1973-81; assoc. clin. prof. pathology Wayne State U., Detroit, 1979-91, chmn. dept. pathology, 1981-91; chmn. dept. pathology, sr. mem. Fox Chase Cancer Ctr., Phila., 1991-94; sr. mem., dir. Breast Cancer Rsch. and Environ. Ctr., 1994—; dir. med. outreach and minority affairs, sci. dir. League of Women Against Cancer. Mem. Mich. Cancer Found., 1982-91; adj. prof. pathology Jefferson Sch. Medicine, U. Pa. Sch. Medicine, Phila. Author: Tumor Diagnosis by Electron Microscopy, vol. 1, 1986, vol. 2, 1988, vol. 3, 1990, Immunocytochemistry in Tumor Diagnosis, 1985, Molecular Basis of Breast Cancer, 2004; editor-in-chief Jour. of Women's Cancer; contbr. over 380 articles to profl. jours USPHS grantee, 1978, 80, 84, 88, 90, 93-95, 98, 2000, 02, grantee Am. Cancer Soc., 1982, Dept. of Def., 1999-2003; NRC Argentina fellow. 1967-71 Mem. Am. Assn. Cancer Rsch., Am. Soc. Cell Biology, Soc. Exptl. Biology and Medicine, Tissue Culture Assn., Am. Soc. Clin. Pathology, Internat. Acad. Pathology, Am. Coll. Pathology, Sigma Xi Roman Catholic. Office Phone: 215-728-4782. Business E-Mail: j_russo@fccc.edu.

**RUSSO, LORRAINE,** humanities educator; b. N.Y.C., Dec. 10, 1949; d. Salvatore and Rosalie Betty Russo. BS in Edn., Mills. Coll. Edn., N.Y.C., 1971; MA in Edn., NYU, 1974, Hunter Coll., 1987. Cert. tchr., N.Y.; lic. in esthetics, N.Y. Ins. underwriter Home Ins. Co., N.Y.C., 1972-73; elem. edn. tchr. Miraculous Medal Sch., Ridgewood, N.Y., 1973-77, St. Bartholomew Sch., Elmhurst, N.Y., 1978-83; tchr. Immaculate Heart Sch., N.Y.C., 1983-85; tchr. arts and crafts Jr. H.S. 10, Astoria, N.Y., 1985-86; English tchr./ESL Newtown H.S., Elmhurst, 1986—, SAT/PSAT supr. Princeton-Ednl. Testing Svc., 1991—2002; tchr. skin care Lia Schorr Skin Care Inst., N.Y.C., NY. Mayoral candidate vol. Kenna Rep. Club, Astoria, 1989-93. With USAR, 1975-79. Recipient Cert. of Appreciaiton, Ednl. Testing Svc., 1996. Avocation: antiques. Home: 21-50 33d Rd Long Island City NY 11106 E-mail: rus480@aol.com.

**RUSSO, MARISA N.,** media consultant; b. Fullerton, Calif., Mar. 4, 1969; d. Ralph and Nelia (Burdi) Russo. B, Calif. State U., 1992. Sales assoc. The Broadway, Brea, Calif., 1985—95; tchr. Bennett Reed Sch., Inglewood, Calif., 1996—2000; regional cons. McGraw Hill, Calif., 2000—02, nat. cons. Calif., 2002—. Speaker various ednl. confs. Mem.: One, IRA. Democrat. Roman Cath. Home: 11381 Parkfield Ct Riverside CA 92505

**RUSSO, PATRICIA F.,** telecommunications company executive; b. Trenton, NJ, June 12, 1952; m. Frank Russo. BA, Georgetown U., 1973; postgrad. in advanced mgmt., Harvard U., 1989; DEng (hon.), Steven Inst. Tech.; D in

Entrepreneurial studies (hon.), Columbia Coll., SC. Sales and mktg. mgmt. exec. IBM, 1973-81; with AT&T (now Lucent Techs. Inc.), 1981; pres., Bus Comm. Sys. Unit AT&T (now Avaya Inc.), 1992-96; pres., COO Eastman Kodak Co., 2000—02; exec. v.p. strategy bus. devel. and corp. ops. Lucent Techs. Inc., Murray Hill, NJ, 1997-99, exec. v.p., CEO svc. provider networks Warren, NJ, 1999—2000, pres., CEO Murray Hill, NJ, 2002—03, chmn., CEO, 2003—. Bd. dirs. Lucent Techs. Co., 2002—, Schering-Plough Corp., NJ Mfrs. Ins. Co., Avaya Inc.; chair Nat. Security Telecom. Adv. Com. 2004—. Bd. dirs. Georgetown U.; mem. Network Reliability Interoperability Coun.; mem. appointed by Gov. James McGreevey NJ Commn. on Jobs Growth and Econ. Develop. Named one of 100 Most Powerful Women in Bus., Fortune mag., 1998—2006, 100 Most Influential People, Time mag., 2006, 10 Most Powerful Women in NJ Bus., Star-Ledger, 2006. Office: Lucent Techs Inc 600 Mountain Ave New Providence NJ 07974*

**RUSSO, PAUL M.,** electronics executive; B in engring., McGill U.; MEE, U. California, Berkeley, PhD Computer Sci. and Electrical Engring. Mem. of the technical staff, head Microsystems Rsch., RCA, Princeton, NJ, 1970—80; sr. mgr. Indsl. Electronics Grp., General Electronics (GE), Charlottesville, Va., 1980—83; gen. mgr. Microelectronics Ctr. in Rsch., Triangle Park, NC, 1983—85; founder, CEO, dir. Genesis Microchip Inc., 1987—2000, chmn., 1987—2001; founder, pres., CEO, chmn. Silicon Optix, San Jose, Calif. Outside dir. ATI Technologies. Office: Silicon Optix Hdqs 2025 Gateway Pl Ste 360 West San Jose CA 95110 Office Phone: 1-408-487-9290. Office Fax: 1-408-487-9298.*

**RUSSO, RENE,** actress; b. Burbank, Calif., Feb. 17, 1954; m. Dan Gilroy, Mar. 14, 1992; 1 child, Rose. Fashion model Eileen Ford Agy. Actor: (films) Major League, 1989, Mr. Destiny, 1990, One Good Cop, 1991, Freejack, 1992, Lethal Weapon 3, 1992, In the Line of Fire, 1993, Major League 2, 1994, Outbreak, 1995, Get Shorty, 1995, Tin Cup, 1996, Ransom, 1996, Buddy, 1997, Lethal Weapon 4, 1998, The Thomas Crown Affair, 1999, The Adventures of Rocky and Bullwinkle, 2000, Showtime, 2002, Big Trouble, 2002, Two for the Money, 2005, Yours, Mine and Ours, 2005, (TV series) Sable, 1987-88. Address: 8046 Fareholm Dr Los Angeles CA 90046

**RUSSO, RICHARD,** writer; b. Johnstown, NY, July 15, 1949; m. Barbara Marie Russo; children: Emily, Kate. BA, U. Ariz., 1967, Ph.D, 1979, MFA, 1980. Writer, Camden, Maine; prof. english Colby Coll., Waterville, Maine, 1991—96. Author: Mohawk, 1994, The Risk Pool, 1994, Nobody's Fool, 1994, Straight Man, 1998, Empire Falls, 2002 (Pulitzer Prize Fiction, 2002, named Best Novel of Yr. Time Mag., 2002), The Whore's Child, 2003; writer: (films) Twilight, 1998; (TV films, teleplay) The Flamingo Rising, 2001; Brush with Fate, 2003; exec. prodr., writer: (films) The Ice Harvest, 2005.*

**RUSSO, ROY LAWRENCE,** retired electronics engineer; b. Kelayres, Pa., Nov. 6, 1935; s. Peter John and Mary (Fudge) R.; m. Elizabeth Jean Tautkus, Dec. 26, 1959; children: Mark, Keith, Aileen, Linda. BSE.E., Pa. State U., 1957, MSE.E., 1959, PhDE.E., 1964. Asst. prof. elec. engring. Pa. State U., University Park, 1964-65; mgr., staff mem. IBM Research, Yorktown Heights, NY, 1965-77, mem. research staff, 1983-85, mgr. design automation lab., 1985-94; sr. engr. Gen. Tech. div. IBM, Hopewell Junction, 1977-81, mgr. strategy, 1981-82; cons. prof. elec. engring Stanford U., 1982-83; retired, 1994. Editor-in-chief IEEE Computer Soc., 1983-85; co-inventor ink jet printer correction system. Treas. St. Patrick's Ch., Yorktown Heights, 1975-77. Recipient Invention Achievement award IBM, 1978, Outstanding Contbn. award IBM, 1968, 89, Outstanding Writing award Pa. State U., 1967 Fellow IEEE (dir. computer divsn. 1989); mem. IEEE Computer Soc. (pres. 1986-87, Svc. award, Centennial medal 1984, Richard E. Merwin award 1992), Eta Kappa Nu.

**RUSSO, THOMAS ANTHONY,** lawyer; b. NYC, Nov. 6, 1943; s. Lucio F. and Tina (Iarossi) R.; m. Nancy Felipe, June 18, 1966 (div. 1974); m. Janice Davis, June 10, 1977 (div. 1979); m. Marcy C. Appelbaum, June 16, 1985; children: Morgan Danielle and Alexa Anne (twins), Tyler James. BA, Fordham U., 1965; MBA, JD, Cornell U., 1969. Bar: NY 1970, U.S. Ct. Appeals (2d cir.) 1971, U.S. Dist. Ct. (so. and ea. dists.) NY 1971, U.S. Ct. Appeals (7th cir.) 1982. Staff atty. SEC, Washington, 1969—71; assoc. Cadwalader, Wickersham & Taft, N.Y.C., 1971—75; dir. divsn. trading and markets Commodity Futures Trading Commn., Washington 1975—77; ptnr., mem. mgmt. com. Cadwalader, Wickersham & Taft, N.Y.C., 1977—92; vice chmn., chief legal officer, mem. exec. com. Lehman Bros., N.Y.C., 1993—. Mem. bd. dirs. SIA; vice-chmn. bd. trustees, mem. exec. com. Inst. Fin. Markets; trustee, chmn. exec. com., mem. devel. vision and outreach com., mem. exec. compensation com., mem. scholar rescue fund com., mem. scholar rescue fund selection com. Inst. Internat. Edn.; mem. adv. com. SEC Hist. Soc.; vice chmn. nat. bd. trustees, fin. com., mem. exec. com., mem. nominating com., chmn. pension investment com. March of Dimes; mem. monitoring com. The Group of Thirty; mem. US Coun. Internat. Bus.; mem. Cornell U. Coun., internat. adv. com. Fed. Res. Bank NY. Author: Regulation of the Commodities Futures and Options Markets; co-author: Regulation of Brokers, Dealers and Securities Markets with Supplement; mem. editl. bd. Jour. Fin. Regulation and Compliance, Futures and Derivatives Law Report; practitioner bd. advisors Stanford Jour. Law, Bus. and Fin. Named to Hall of Fame, Futures Industry Assn., 2003. Mem.: ABA, Fgn. Policy Assn., D.C. Bar Assn., Assn. Bar City NY (chmn. com. commodities regulations 1981—82, chmn. internat. law subcom. of the com. on commodities regulation 1984—85), Econ. Club NY, Fellows of Phi Beta Kappa Soc. Office: Lehman Bros Inc 745 7th Ave 31st Fl New York NY 10019-6801 Business E-Mail: trusso1@lehman.com.

**RUSSO, VINCENT JOSEPH,** surgeon; b. Phila., Apr. 15, 1939; s. Joseph Vincent Russo and Yolanda Italia D'Ambrosio; m. Sheila Kay Roos, June 8, 1963; children: Teresa, Joseph, Katrina, Anita. AB, Columbia U., 1960; MD, Boston U., 1964, MPH, 1983. Diplomate Am. Bd. Surgery. Staff surgeon Anna Jaques Hosp., Newburyport, Mass., 1971-88; clin. instr. surgery Harvard Med. Sch., Boston, 1984-98; med. dir. Blue Cross/Blue Shield, Methuen, Mass., 1990-98; sr. staff surgeon Lawrence (Mass.) Gen. Hosp., 1990-2000; med. dir. Ea. Mass. Health Ctrs., 1999—2000; clin. instr. Sch. Medicine Boston U., 2001—04; seaterm ship's physician Mass. Maritime Acad., 2001—. Cons. surgeon Manchester (N.H.) VA Med. Ctr., 1985-98; pres. Essex North Med. Soc., Newburyport, 1988-89, 2002-04; dist. 3 med. examiner Essex County, 1986—; ship's doctor Mass. Maritime Acad. 2001—. Bd. trustees, corporator, mem. auditing com. Newburyport Savings Bank, 1987—; mem. UNICO, Andover, Mass., 1994-97. Lt. cmdr. USN, ships surgeon USS Forrestal Aircraft Carrier, 1969-71; chmn. bd. selectmen Town of Newbury, Mass, 2004—; field rep., surveyor Joint Commn. on Accreditation of Health Orgns., 2004—; commr. mosquito control Commonwealth of Mass., 2005—; chmn. auditing com. Newburyport Five Cents Savings Bank, 2006—; corporator Anna Jaques Hosp., Newburyport, Mass., 1985—. Lt. col. U.S. Army, 1990-91, Desert Storm. Fellow ACS (councilor Mass. chpt. 1995-98); mem. AMA, Soc. Am. Gastrointestinal Endoscopic Surgeons, Mass. Med. Soc. (legis. com. 1990—, del. 2000—), Boston Surg. Soc., Essex North Dist. Med. Soc. (exec. com. 1986—, pres. 2002-04), Rotary (sr. active), Mass. Med. Soc. (reference com. 2002-04, bd. trustees 2004—), U.S. Naval Inst. Roman Catholic. Avocations: theater, downhill skiing, automobiles, swimming, symphony. E-mail: vjrusso@massmed.org.

**RUSSOMANNO, DAVID JAMES,** electrical engineer, educator; b. Newark, Feb. 10, 1964; s. James A. Russomanno and Jimmie Nell Jediny; m. Theresa Lynn Hollingsworth, Nov. 21, 1963; 1 child, Evan David. B of Elec. Engring., Auburn U., Ala., 1986; PhD, U. S.C., Columbia, 1993. Prof., chair elec. and computer engring. U. Memphis, 1993—. Contbr. articles to profl. jours. Recipient Herff Coll. of Engring. Outstanding Faculty Tchg. award, U. Memphis, 2005, Herff Coll. of Engring. Outstanding Faculty Rsch. award, 2006; DuPont Grad. fellowship, Dupont Corp., 1990, Ballard Trust professorship, U. Memphis/Ballard Trust, 2003. Mem.: IEEE (Memphis sect. chair 2000—01). Achievements include Principal Investigator on National Science Foundation Grants; Principal and Co-Principal Investigator on DOD Con-

tracts and Grants; design of Object-Inference Framework (funded by Inter-graph Corp.). Office: Dept of Elec and Computer Eng 206 Engring Sci Memphis TN 38152 Office Phone: 901-678-3253. Office Fax: 901-678-5469. E-mail: drussmnn@memphis.edu.

**RUSSONIELLO, JOSEPH PASCAL,** lawyer, dean; b. Jersey City, Oct. 12, 1941; s. Sabin G. and Justine B. (Terraciano) Russoniello; m. Moira F. Ward, Aug. 29, 1969. B in Social Sci., Fairfield U., 1963; JD, NYU, 1966. Bar: N.J. 1967, Calif. 1969. Spl. agt. FBI, Washington, 1966—67; dep. dist. atty. City and County San Francisco Dist. Atty. Offices, 1969—75; assoc. Cooley Godward Castro Huddleson & Tatum, San Francisco, 1975—78; ptnr. Cooley Godward L.L.P., San Francisco, 1978—82, 1990—2001, sr. counsel, 2002—; U.S. atty. U.S. Dept. Justice (no. dist.) Calif., San Francisco, 1982—90. Pres., bd. dirs. San Francisco Law Sch., 1996—2001, dean, 2002—; ana.yst Sta. KTVU-Ch. 2, Oakland, 1994—. Pres. Northgate Cottages, Napa, Calif., 1988—, Silverado Property Owners Assn., 2004—; v.p. Mid-Pacific region Nat. Italian Am. Fedn., 1996—99; mem. nat. rev. bd. U.S. Conf. Cath. Bishops, 2004—; chmn. Caths. Truth and Justice, San Francisco, 1991—. Named Alumni of the Yr., Pub. Sector, NYU Law Sch., 1991; recipient Man of the Yr. award, NIAF, 1986, St. Thomas More Soc., San Francisco, 2000, Italian Am. Cmty. Svc. Agy., San Francisco, 2004, Assumpta award, Trustees St. Mary's Cathedral, 2000, Papal Pro Ecclesia medal, 2000, Landsman award, 2005. Fellow: Am. Coll. Trial Lawyers; mem.: Am. Law Inst., Am. Bd. Trial Lawyers (adv.), McFetridge Inn of Ct. (barrister). Republican. Avocations: tennis, golf, reading, saxophone. Office: Cooley Godward LLP 101 California St 5th Fl San Francisco CA 94111-5800 Office Phone: 415-693-2014. Business E-Mail: Russonielloj@cooley.com.

**RUSSOTTO, PAUL,** artist, educator; b. NYC, May 28, 1944; s. John and Margaret Russotto; m. Ellen Russotto, Aug. 30, 1969; children: Vita, Luca. Student, Art Students League, N.Y.C., 1962-63. Painting and drawing instr. MFA program Parsons Sch. Design, N.Y.C., 1978—80, N.Y. Studio Sch. Drawing, Painting and Sculpture, N.Y.C., 1980—82, Vt. Studio Ctr., Johnson, 1985—, Internat. Sch. Art, Montecastello di Vibio, Italy, 1993, 94; painting and drawing instr. Beijing (China) Art Ins., 1987—88, Shanghai (China) Art Mus., 1987—88; painting and drawing instr., MFA program Pa. Acad. Fine Arts, Phila., 1997, SUNY, Binghamton, 1997, Nat. Acad. Design, N.Y.C., 1999—2000. One-man shows include Forty-year Drawing Survey 1960-2000, traveling to U.N.C. and Italy, exhibited in group shows at Mus. Chateau de Rochefort-en-Terre, Brittany, France, 1995, Omaggio a Marino Marini, Venice, Florence, Rome, Paris, 2000, Heckscher Mus. Fine Art, Huntington, N.Y., 2000, 8 Artisti da New York, Florence, Rome, Montecatini Terme, Italy, 2001, Angeli, Rome, Florence, Montecatini Terme, Venice, Romania, 2001—02, Omaggio a Magnelli, Italy, France, Romania, 2005, numerous others, Represented in permanent collections Met. Mus. Art, N.Y.C., Heckscher Mus. Fine Art, GE Corp., Novartis Corp., East Hanover, N.J., Mus. of Art, Bates Coll., Lewiston, Maine, N.Y. Pub. Libr., Tokai Bank, Chgo. Asheville (N.C.) Art Mus., Bklyn. Mus. Art, Accademia d'Arte Moderna Dino Scalabrino, Montecatini Terme, Italy, Ciba-Geigy, Circolo La Scaletia, Matera, Italy, City of Todi, Italy. Recipient Purchase award, AAAL, N.Y.C., 1997, Found. award, Rochefort-en-Terre Found., 1995. Mem.: Nat. Acad. Design (cert. of merit 1996, Palmer Meml. prize 2000, Henry Ward Ranger award 2001). Office: P O Box 385 Canal St Sta New York NY 10013-0385

**RUST, EDWARD BARRY, JR.,** insurance company executive, lawyer; b. Chgo., Aug. 3, 1950; s. Edward Barry Sr. and Harriett B. (Fuller) R.; m. Sally Buckler, Feb. 28, 1976; 1 child, Edward Barry III. Student, Lawrence U., 1968-69; BS, Ill. Wesleyan U., 1972; JD, MBA, So. Meth. U., 1975. Bar: Tex. 1975, Ill. 1976. Mgmt. trainee State Farm Ins. Cos., Dallas, 1975-76, asst. v.p. Bloomington, 1976, sr. atty., 1976-78, asst. v.p., 1978-81, v.p., 1981-83, exec. v.p., 1983-85, pres., CEO, 1985—87, CEO, chmn., 1987—. Pres. and bd. dirs. State Farm Investment Mgmt. Corp., State Farm Internat. Services, Inc., State Farm Cos. Found.; bd. dirs. exec. and investment coms. State Farm Annuity and Life Ins. Co., State Farm Mut. Automobile Ins. Co., State Farm Life Ins. Co., State Farm Fire and Casualty, State Farm Gen. Trustee Ill. Wesleyan U., 1985—; mem. adv. coun. Grad. Sch. Bus. Stanford U., 1987-94; mem. bus. adv. coun. Coll. Commerce and Bus. Adminstrn. U. Ill. Mem. Am. Enterprise Inst., Bus. Roundtable (chmn. edn. task force), Tex. State Bar Assn., Ill. Bar Assn., Am. Inst. Property and Liability Underwriters (trustee 1986-96), Ins. Inst. Am. (trustee 1986-96), Ins. Inst. for Highway Safety (vice chmn.), Nat. Alliance of Bus. (chmn. 1998—), Ill. Bus. Roundtable (chmn. 1998—), Bus. Advisory Coun. Univ. Ill. Coll. Commerce and Bus. Admin. Office: State Farm Ins Cos 1 State Farm Plz E-12 Bloomington IL 61710-0001*

**RUST, JOHN HOWSON, JR.,** lawyer, state legislator; b. May 21, 1947; s. John Howson and Laura Jeanne (Johnson) R.; m. Susan Byrne, Aug. 15, 1970; children: John W., Thomas A., Robert B. BA, U. Va., 1969, JD, 1972. Bar: Va. 1972, U.S. Dist. Ct. (ea. dist.) Va. 1973, U.S. Ct. Appeals (4th cir.) 1975, U.S. Supreme Ct. 1976. Mem. firm Rust & Rust, P.C. Mem. Ho. of Dels., Commonwealth of Va., 1980-82, 97-2001. Office: PO Box 460 10370 Main St Fairfax VA 22030-0460 Office Phone: 703-273-0583. E-mail: johnhr@erols.com.

**RUST, JOHN PHILIP,** economist, educator; b. Milw., Wis., May 23, 1955; s. Donald Roland and Lois May Rust; m. Deborah Fairleigh Minehart, Aug. 26, 2000; 1 child, Lauren. PhD, MIT, 1983. Prof. economics U. Wis., Madison, 1983—95, Yale U., New Haven, 1995—2001, U. Md., College Park, 2001—. Founder Technoluddites, Inc. Home: 106 Park Valley Rd Silver Spring MD 20910 Office: U Md 3105 Tydings Hall College Park MD 20742 Office Phone: 301-405-3489. Business E-Mail: jrust@gemini.econ.umd.edu.

**RUST, NEIL W.,** lawyer; b. Haslemere, Surrey, Eng., Aug. 14, 1957; BS, U. of London, 1978, LLB, 1985; JD, U.of Penn., 1987. Bar: California, Associate of the Royal School of Mines, London. With White & Case LLP, 1987—. Named Atty. of Yr., Calif. Lawyer Mag., 2002; named one of 12 Dealmakers of Yr., Am. Lawyer Mag., 2004. Office: c/o White & Case 633 West Fifth St ste 1900 Los Angeles CA 90071

**RUST, PATRICIA JOAN,** television executive; b. LA, Sept. 24, 1958; d. William Evans Jr. and Jacquelyn (Knox) R. BA, UCLA, 1978, postgrad., 1978-80, 87-89; student, Am. Film Inst. Writer, producer PBS, LA, 1978-79, creator, host On Cue; corr. ABC-TV, LA, 1979-82; pres. Patricia Rust Prodns., LA, 1982—. Host, writer, creator, producer numerous syndicated spls., 1982-89; writer, producer comedy shows and spls. ABC, NBC, CBS and PBS; spkr. in field. Film and TV writer, story editor: including network comedy spls., TV movies, episodes; author: The King of Skittledeedoo, 1999, 2d edit., 2001 (Parents' Choice award winning literacy book); assoc. editor: Prodrs. Guild Mag., 1990—; contbr. L.A. Times Kids Page. Pres., founder, The Rust Found. for Literacy, 1999—; founder JackietheAngel.net, 1999, PowerforKids.com, 2000. Recipient Golden Mike award Radio and TV News Assn., Hollywood, 1984, Humanitarian Book award for best children's book, 2001; named Best Network Comedy Writer NBC, 1990; winner comedy writing competition Am. Film Inst., 1989. Mem. NATAS, Hollywood Radio and TV Soc., Producers Guild, Writers Guild Am., Am. Film Inst., Daily Bruin Alumni Assn. (pres.), Caucus for Writers, Prodr. and Dir. Office: Patricia Rust Prodns # 924 12021 Wilshire Blvd # 924 Los Angeles CA 90025-1206 E-mail: patricia@powerforkids.com.

**RUST, STEPHEN THOMAS,** geriatrician; s. Thomas F. and Marcia J. Rust; m. Elaine Marie Davie, Sept. 27, 1977; children: Nathaniel S., Erin E., Laura N., Ellen M. BA in Biology, Earlham Coll., 1980; MD, Ind. U., 1984. Cert. in Internal Medicine ABIM, 1987, in Geriatric Medicine ABIM, 1992, in Hospice and Palliative Medicine Am. Bd. Hospice and Palliative Care, 2003, Med. Dir. in Long Term Care Am. Med. Dirs. Assn., 2001. Chief resident of internal medicine Ball Meml. Hosp., Muncie, Ind., 1987—88; group practice internal medicine and geriat. Maine Coast Meml. Hosp., Ellsworth, 1988—97, med. dir., intensive care unit, 1989—93, exec. com. mem., 1993—97, med. staff pres., 1993—95; med. dir. geriatric assessment team Parkview Med. Ctr., Pueblo, Colo., 1997—2004; physician geriatric med.

group Geriatric Medicine Assocs., Denver, 2004—05; continuing care phy-sician Colo. Permanente Med. Group, Aurora, 2005—. Med. dir. Minnequa Med. Ctr., Pueblo, Colo., 1999—2004, Covenant Village, Westminster, Colo., 2004—; in-patient hospice physician Fuente de Vida, Pueblo, 2003—04; adv. com. mem. Sangre de Christo Hospice and Palliative Care, Pueblo, 2003—05; mem. papim mgmt. clin. effectiveness team St. Anthony Hosps., Denver, 2004—05. Fellow: ACP (life Fellowship award 1998, Fellowship 1998); mem.: AMA (Physicians Recognition award 1987—). Mem. Society Of Friends. Office: Kaiser Permanente 2550 S Parker Rd Ste 400 Aurora CO 80014

**RUST, WILLIAM DAVID, JR.,** retired structural engineer; b. Washington, Oct. 11, 1931; s. William David and Anna Mae (Lyles) R.; m. Eunice Charles Williams, Oct. 24, 1953; children: Diann Yvonne Rust-Tierney, Cheryl Frances, William Douglas. BS in Civil Engring., Howard U., 1954; postgrad., Cath. U. Am., 1956-57; MS in Engring., George Washington U., 1962; postgrad., U. Va., 1973-74. Registered profl. engr., Mass. Naval architect Phila. Naval Shipyard, 1954; structural engr. U.S. Gen. Svcs. Adminstrn., Washington, 1956-92; ret. 1992. Lectr. civil engring. Fed. City Coll. (now U. D.C.), Washington, 1973; mem. com.Interagency Seismic Safety, Washing-ton, 1978-90, ASCE, Found. and Excavation Stds., N.Y.C., 1978-95, AISC, Steel Specification Simplification, Chgo., 1980-81; mem. coms. Fed. Constrn. Coun., Washington, 1978-90. Pack com. chmn. Boy Scouts Am., Washington, 1968; clk. session Northminster Presbyn. Ch., Washington, 1972; commr. genn. assembly Presbyn. Ch. U.S., Ft. Worth, 1973. Lt. C.E., U.S. Army, 1954-56. Fellow ASCE; mem., NSPE, Structural Stability Rsch. Coun. (mem.-at-large), Tau Beta Pi (life). Achievements include administration of development of first nationwide microfilming of design and construction drawings system for the U.S. General Services Adminstration. Home: 7600 Alaska Ave NW Washington DC 20012-1469 E-mail: w.rustjr@worldnet.att.net.

**RUSTHOVEN, PETER JAMES,** lawyer; b. Indpls., Aug. 12, 1951; s. Richard and Henrietta (Iwema) R.; children from previous marriage: Julia Faith, David James; m. Linda C. Bennett, Dec. 28, 1987; children: Mark Bennett, Matthew Boyd. AB magna cum laude, Harvard U., 1973, JD magna cum laude, 1976. Bar: Ind., 1976. Assoc. Barnes, Hickam, Pantzer & Boyd, Indpls., 1976-81; assoc. counsel to Pres. of U.S., White House, Washington, 1981-85; of counsel Barnes & Thornburg, Indpls., 1985-86, ptnr., 1987—. Counsel Presdl. Commn. on Space Shuttle Challenger Accident, 1986; spl. cons. U.S. Atty. Gen.'s Adv. Bd. on Missing Children, 1988; adj. fellow Hudson Inst., 1989-91, adj. sr. fellow, 1991—; sr. fellow Ind. Policy Rev. Found., 1991—; bd. advisors Indpls. Lawyers Chpt. Federalist Soc., 1993—; mem. nat. practitioners coun., 1995—. Contbr. monthly column The Am. Spectator mag., 1973-79; mem. bd. editors Harvard Law Rev., 1974-76, case editor, 1975-76; contbr. articles to nat. mags. Bd. dirs. Ednl. Choice Charitable Trust, 1994—, Legal Svcs. Orgn. Indpls., 1977-79; precinct committeeman Marion County Rep. Ctrl. Com., Indpls., 1978-81; state media dir. Ind. Reagan for Pres. Com., 1979-80, Ind. Reagan-Bush Com., 1980; speechwriter nat. Reagan for Pres. Campaign, 1980; mem. legal policy adv. bd. Washington Legal Found., 1989—, transition counsel's office Bush-Cheney Presdl. Transition, 2001; candidate for Rep. nomination for U.S. Senate, Ind., 1998. Grantee Inst. Politics, Harvard U., 1972. Mem. Ind. Bar Assn., Indpls. Bar Assn., Phi Beta Kappa. Roman Catholic. Avocations: golf, contract bridge, baseball memorabilia collecting. Office: Barnes & Thornburg 1313 Merchants Bank Bldg 11 S Meridian St Ste 1313 Indianapolis IN 46204-3535 Office Phone: 317-231-7289. Business E-Mail: peter.rusthoven@btlaw.com. E-mail: peter.rusthoven@hotmail.com.

**RUSTIN, RUDOLPH BYRD, III,** surgeon, educator; b. Charleston, S.C., May 14, 1957; s. Rudolph Byrd and Mary Pringle (Herrin) R.; m. Sandra Lee Talbott, Nov. 28, 1985; children: Jonathan, Jeffrey. BS in Chemistry cum laude, Hampden Sydney Coll., 1979; MD, Med. U. S.C., 1983. Diplomate Am. Bd. Surgery, Am. Bd. Colon and Rectal Surgery. Intern Cleve. Clinic Found., 1983-84, resident, 1984-88, chief resident gen. surgery, 1987-88, fellow, 1988-89; private practice colon rectal surgery Charleston, 1989—; clin. assoc. surgery Med. U. S.C., Charleston, 1989—. Active staff Roper Hosp., Charleston, St. Francis Xavier Hosp.; med. dir. Commun-i-Care, 2002; presenter in field. Fellow ACS, Am. Soc. Colon Rectal Surgeons, Southeastern Surgical Congress; mem. Med. Soc. S.C., S.C. State Med. Assn., S.C. Med. Assn. (del.), So. Med. Assn., Charleston County Med. Soc., Phi Beta Kappa. Office: 125 Doughty St Ste 770 Charleston SC 29403-5764

**RUT, WANDA E.,** artist, educator, writer; b. Lwow, Poland, Jan. 5, 1923; arrived in U.S., 1976, naturalized; d. Adam Edmunt and Langmoier Anna Binder; m. Roman Smoleniec, 1977 (dec. 1979); m. Tadewsz Rut, 1958 (div. 1968); 1 child, Tomasr. BA in Textile Design, Inst. Indsl. Arts, Lwow, Poland, 1943; BA in Econs., Sch. Higher Edn. in Econ., Wroclaw, Poland, 1950; MFA, Acad. Fine Arts, Warsaw, Poland, 1957; student, Polish Acad. Scis., 1975. Chmn. Art Tchg. Divsn. Polish Assn. Artists and Designers, Warsaw, 1966—75; coord. Tailoring Mus. Fashion and Modeling Sch., Warsaw, 1975; editor art column Polish-Am. Weekly Newspaper, N.Y., 1978—80; art dir. Polish Inst. Arts and Scis., N.Y., 1983; cons. Polish Mus. Found., Port Washington, NY, 1984; art therapist N.Y., NY, 1984—85; freelance clothing designer. Tchr. various schs., Poland; costume designer Motion Picture Studios, Wroclaw, Opera House, Prague, Czech Republic; bd. jurors Artist Craftsmen of N.Y., 1980—82. One-woman shows include 40 shows in various international cities including, Avery Fisher Hall Lincoln Ctr., N.Y.C., N.Y., 1977, Suffolk County Hist. Mus., Riverhead, L.I., N.Y., 1978, Mus. of Sci. and Industry, LA, Calif., 1979, Guild Hall Mus., Moran Gallery, East Hampton, N.Y., 1977, Cepelia Salons, San Francisco, Calif., 1977, Inter-church Ctr., N.Y.C., N.Y., 1980, Pen & Brush Club, 1980 (1st prize, 1980), Donnell Libr., 1984, exhibited in group shows at Student Art Show, Moscow, Russia, 1953 (award, 1953), numerous others totalling near 100, exhibitions include Polish Art Weaving, Dresden, East Germany, 1969 (award, 1969), Tchrs. Head Club, Warsaw, Poland, 1973 (award, 1973), Internat. Book & Press Clubs, Poland, 1974 (award, 1974), Womanart Gallery, N.Y.C., N.Y., 1978 (1st prize, 1978), Slavic-Am. Cultural Assn., 1983 (award, 1983), numerous others, Represented in permanent collections Polish Inst. Arts and Scis., N.Y.C., N.Y., Old Warsaw (Poland) Gallery, Alexandria, Va., Polish Mus. Found., Port Washington, N.Y., Slavic Gallery, Glen Cove, N.y., Mus. Textile Industry, Lodz, Poland, Sport Mus., Warsaw, Poland, Brno, Czech. Republic, Stockholm, Sweden, Parliament of Polish People's Republic, Warsaw, Poland, Phys. Edn. Ctr., Cairo, Egypt, City Coun. of Warsaw and Wroclaw, Nat. Tchrs. Club, Warsaw, Poland, Forum Hotel. Recipient 1st prize, Cepelia Art Contest, Warsaw, Poland, 1976, Polish Art Competition, Doylestown, Pa., 1977. Achievements include invention of cylindrical loom enabling weaving in the round. Avocations: poetry, writing. Home: 1660 NE 191 St Apt 402 North Miami Beach FL 33179 Office: Am Inst Polish Culture 1440 79th St Causeway Ste 117 Miami Beach FL 33141

**RUTA, THOMAS V.,** professional sports team executive, accounting executive; married. BS summa cum laude, Fordham U., 1966; MBA with distinction, Pace U.; postgrad. in law, Fordham U. CPA, N.Y., N.J., Minn. Founding ptnr. Behan, Ling & Ruta CPAs, P.C., N.Y.C., now chmn.; pres.; ltd. ptnr. Pitts. Penguins; mem. Hockey Holdings & Mgmt. Group. Office: 475 Park Ave S 31st Fl New York NY 10016 Office Phone: 212-695-7003. Business E-Mail: truta@blrcpaspc.com.

**RUTAN, BURT (ELBERT LEANDER RUTAN),** aircraft designer, aircraft company executive; b. Portland, Oreg., June 17, 1943; s. George and Irene R. BS in Aero. Engring., Calif. State Polytech. U., 1965; attended, Space Tech. Inst., Calif. Inst. Tech.; attended academic portion of Aerospace Rsch. Pilots Sch., Edwards Air Force Base. Flight test project engr. Air Force Flight Test Ctr., Edwards AFB, Calif., 1965-72; dir. Bede Test Ctr., Kans., 1972-74; pres. Rutan Aircraft Factory, Mojave, Calif., 1974—; founder, CEO Scaled Composites Inc., Mojave, Calif., 1982—; v.p. Beech Aircraft, 1985. Designer more than 100 aircraft including BD-5J jet (world's smallest private jet aircraft), VariViggen, VariEze (a stall-proof kit airplane with a propeller at the back and winglets on the nose), Solitaire, Defiant, Raytheon Beechcraft

Starship, Proteus (high altitude long endurance aircraft being used for everything from cellular communications to suborbital space launches), Boomerang, Virgin Atlantic GlobalFlyer (set a world record for the first solo, non-stop, non-refueled circumnavigation of the world, piloted by Steven Fossett, 2005), White Knight (an airborne launch aircraft) and other kits; designer Voyager aircraft (a superlight plane that could carry 10 times its weight in fuel, first to fly around-the-world without stopping, refueling in 1986); company made history with first private manned mission to space in SpaceShipOne (a two-passenger, high altitude research rocket); Space-ShipOne achieved two record flights (broke 62.5-mile barrier) and won the Ansari X prize on October 4, 2004; SpaceShipOne donated to Smithsonian Inst. on October 6, 2005; pilot for EZ-Rocket (XCOR), which made a record-setting point-to-point flight, departing from Mojave California Space-port and gliding onto a neighboring airport in California City in 2005. Recip. Spirit of St. Louis medal, Am. Soc. Mech. Engrs., 1987, Best Design award, Exptl. Aircraft Assn.; Air medal, 1970, Stan Szik design contbn. trophy, 1972, EAA Outstanding New Design, 1975-76, 78; Dr. August Raspet Meml. award, 1976, ABC World News Tonight Person of the Week, 1986, Collier trophy for ingenious design and devel., Nat. Aeronautic Assn., 1986, Presdl. Citizens medal for design/develop. of the voyager "around-the-world" air-craft, 1986, FAI gold medal for Voyager Constrn., 1987, medal for the City of Paris, 1987, NASA langley Rsch. Ctr. dirs. award, 1987, Soc. of NASA Flight Surgeons, W. Randolph Lovelace award 1987, medal of Outstanding Achieve-ment and disting. leadership, 1987, Soc. of exptl. test pilots, 1987, Aviation Man of the Yr, 1987, Lindbergh Eagle award, 1987, USAF 40th anniversary award, 1987, The City of Genoa, Italy, Christopher Columbus Internat. Communications medal, 1987, British gold medal, 1987, Outstanding En-gring. achievement awards, 1988, Franklin medal, 1987, Disting. inventor award 1988, Meritorious Svc. award, 1988, Internat. Aerospace Hall of Fame Honoree, 1988, medal of achievement, 1989, Crystal Eagle award, 1989, Meritorious Civilian Svc. medal, 1989, Leroy Randle Grumman medal, 1989, Structures, Structural Dynamics and Materials award AIAA, 1991, Bus. Leader in Aerospace, Scientific Am., 2003, Ansari X prize, 2004, NAS Award in Aero. Engring., 2005; co-recipient with Paul Allen, Smithsonian's Nat. Air and Space Mus. Trophy, 2005; named Innovator of Yr., R&D Mag., 2004; named one of 100 Most Influential People of 2005, Time mag., Rave award in indsl. design, WIRED, 2005. Mem. NAE, Exptl. Aircraft Assn., Soc. Exptl. Test Pilots, Am. Inst. Aeronautics & Astronautics (recipient Reed Aeronautics award, 2001), Soc. Flight Test Engrs., Acad. Model Aeronautics, Internat. Order Characters, Aircraft Owners and Pilots Assn.; Fellow Am. Acad. Arts & Sciences Holds 3 US patents: Grizzly wide-chord flap suspension system; variable geometry high lift system incorporated in the Beech Starship (foreign patents also held); Rutan Model 115 Starship configuration (foreign patents also held). Office: Scaled Composites Inc Mojave Airport 1624 Flight Line Mojave CA 93501-1663 Office Phone: 661-824-4541. Office Fax: 661-824-4174.*

**RUTAN, CHARLES R.,** musician; b. May 10, 1966; s. Frank and Peggy (Hendry) Rutan; m. Catherine Mayer, May 29, 1999; children: Gwendolyn, Sophia. MusB in Composition summa cum laude, U. Arts, Phila., 1992; postgrad. in music instrn., Chestnut Hill Coll., 1994; postgrad., Piping Ctr., Glasgow, Scotland, 1998. Cert. tchr. Pa. CEO, founder Bagpipes FAO and Zampoqnari Filadelfia, Phila.; mgr., prin. oboist Chestnut Hill Orch. Per-formed for Pres. George Bush, Mrs. Tom Ridge, Queen Noor, Regent of Jordan; opened for Rod Stewart Trump Taj Majal, Atlantic City; piper MiGaea Yacht; prin. bagpipe Reading Symphony Orch.; performed USMC, U.S. Army and USN Ceremonies, Guiness Stout and U.S. Airways Promo-tions, Tom Polis Golf Classic; featured on various TV programs, mags., newspapers, including Phila. Weddings, Modern Bride mags.; ABC, NBC, CBS, CNN, FOX, Finnish Nat. TV, Irish Am. Newspaper; ceremonial piper retirement ball for Phila. Episcopal Bishop; piper installation ceremonies Phila. Archdiocesan parishes, Presbytery ofcls., organ dedication ceremonies; performer Irish Uilleann (Union) Pipes, World Bagpipes, Villanova Coll. of Engr., 2004—04, EMS Today Conv., Bingshangm Realestate Conv. Com-poser (symphonic music): 3 symphonies, numerous choral works, works for bagpipes. Mem.: ASCAP (spl. composer award 1994), Friends of Scotland's Classic Malts, Music Educators Nat. Conf., Eastern U.S. Pipeband Assn., Am. Fedn. Musicians, Internat. Double Reed Soc. Office Phone: 800-544-4028.

**RUTANEN, ROY STEWART,** producer, television personality; b. Putnam, Conn., July 1, 1947; s. Phyllis Morse Rutanen; children: Rene, Jade Babey, Jessica Smith, Sarah. BA, U. Mass., 1998. TV reporter, anchor Sta. KENS-TV, San Antonio, 1982-87; TV reporter Sta. KMOL-TV, Tex., 1987-88; anchor, reporter Sta. XTRA-TV, San Diego, 1988-89; writer, prodr., dir. Electronic Scribe, Southbridge, Mass., 1990-2000; talk-show host Sta. WESO-TV, Southbridge, 1998-99, Sta. 13-10 WORC-TV, Worcester, Mass., 1999—. Dir. opers. Artist Devel. Complex, Southbridge, Mass. Author, narrator (documentary) Holy Ground, 1996; (video) welcome to Strubridge, 1999; author, prodr. (documentary) Reflections of Belchertown, 2000; Writer, prodr. Rehabilitative Resources, Inc., 2000 (Telly award 2001). Active Am. Cancer Soc., Southbridge, 1999. With U.S. Army, 1966-69. Recipient 2d pl. Tex. AP, 1982, Best Feature award Soc. Profl. Journalists, 1984, award of Honor Tex. Safety Assn., 1984, Media award of the Yr., 1986, 2 Golden Mike awards, 1988, 2 Telly awards, 1996. Home and Office: 901 N Woodstock Rd Southbridge MA 01550 Fax: 508-764-3572. E-mail: royr2000@juno.com.

**RUTENBERG, JIM,** journalist; Reporter New York Daily News, 1996—99, NY Observer, 1999, The New York Times, 2003—. Author: (articles) Critics Say Coverage Helped Lead to War, 2003, Shaping Reactions - After First Debate, Both Sides Work Hard to Sway Perceptions, 2004, Mayor Seeking Major Changes at Ground Zero, 2005. Office: The New York Times 229 W 43rd St New York NY 10036*

**RUTENBERG-ROSENBERG, SHARON LESLIE,** retired journalist; b. Chgo., May 23, 1951; d. Arthur and Bernice (Berman) Rutenberg; m. Michael J. Rosenberg, Feb. 3, 1980; children: David Kaifel and Jonathan Reuben (twins), Emily Mara. Student, Harvard U., 1972; BA, Northwestern U., 1973, MSJ, 1975; cert. student pilot. Reporter-photographer Lerner Home News-papers, Chgo., 1973—74; corr. Medill News Svc., Washington, 1975; reporter-newsperson, sci. writer UPI, Chgo., 1975—84; ret., 1984. Inter-viewer: exclusives White House chief of staff, nation's only mother and son on death row; others. Vol. Chgo.-Read Mental Health Ctr. Recipient Peter Lisagor award for exemplary journalism in features category, 1980, 81; Golden Key Nat. Adv. Bd. of Children's Oncology Svc. Inc., 1981; Media awards for wire svc. feature stories, 1983, 84, wire svc. news stories, 1983, 84, all from Chgo. Hosp. Pub. Rels. Soc. Mem. Profl. Assn. Diving Instrs., Nat. Assn. Underwater Instrs., Hon. Order Ky. Cols., Hadassah, Sigma Delta Chi, Sigma Delta Tau Home: 745 Marion Ave Highland Park IL 60035-5123

**RUTER, ALLAN J.,** literature and language educator; b. Grundy Center, Iowa, May 28, 1954; s. Eugene T. and Thelma Okones Ruter; m. Jill Lynne Mussay, July 2, 1983; children: Karl Allan, Edward Eike. B of Spl. Studies, Cornell Coll., 1976; MA in Tchg., Northwestern U., Evanston, Ill., 1978, MA in english, 1997. Asst. to dean of students Lake Forest Coll., Ill., 1976—77; instr. of English Glenbrook Acad. for Internat. Studies, Ill.; co-dir., instr. of English Glenbrook North H.S., Northbrook, Ill., 2005—; instr. of English Glenbrook South H.S., Glenview, Ill., 1977—2005, coord. of pub. info., 1980—81, asst. instrnl. supr. of English, 1984—99, instr. of history, 1984—90, sch. accreditation team chair, 2000—05; instr. of humanities Northwestern U. Ctr. for Talent Devel., Evanston, Ill., 1998—2000. Leader/trainer/designer Glenbrook Peer Counseling Program, Glenview/Northbrook, Ill., 1982—2003; ednl. travel leader Am. Coun. for Internat. Studies, Boston, 1992—; editl. cons. Wonderlic Pers. Inventory, Inc., Libertyville, Ill., 1995—95; product devel. cons. Scott Foresman Co., Glenview, Ill., 1997—97; cert. trainer Ctr. for Performance Assessment, Denver, 2002—05; consulting writer McDougal Littell, Inc., Evanston, Ill., 2005—. Author: (poetry) 1964: The Hardy Boys, 1984, (non-fiction) A Short History of Wellsburg, Iowa (Archived in the State Hist. Libr. of Iowa, 1976), (travel writing) Guernica: Home at Last, 1994; contbr. articles to profl. jours. Vice-chair Glenview Sch. Dist. 34 Caucus, Ill., 1989—93; bd. dirs. Glenview

Soccer Club, Ill., 1996—99; appearance commn. Village of Glenview, Ill., 2002—05, downtown plan commr., 2005—; Independence Day Celebration commr. Glenview Pk. Dist., Ill., 2002—04; planning com. Village Glenview, 2005—; exec. bd. mem., youth ministries bd. chair, choir mem., confirmation instr., lector, substitute organist Glenview Cmty. Ch., Ill., 1981—; exec. bd. mem. Cornell Coll. Alumni Assn., Mount Vernon, Iowa, 2002—. Recipient Outstanding Tchr. award, U. Chgo., 1989; Summer Seminar fellow, NEH, 1987, 1991, Ind. Study fellowship, Coun. for Basic Edn., 1990, Columbia U. Summer Seminar fellow, Gilder-Lehrman Inst., 2005. Mem.: ASCD, Glen-brook Edn. Assn. (v.p. 2003—05), Nat. Coun. of Teachers of English (conv. presenter 1983—2004, commn. on lit. 1994—97, com. instrnl. tech. 1992—95), Rotary (Glenview, Ill.) (hon.), Phi Delta Kappa. United Church Of Christ. Avocations: gardening, travel, running. Home: 2349 Fir St Glenview IL 60025 Office: Glenbrook North HS 2300 Shermer Rd North-brook IL 60062 Office Phone: 847-509-2433. Personal E-mail: aruter@comcast.net. Business E-mail: aruter@glenbrook.k12.il.us.

**RUTFORD, ROBERT HOXIE,** geologist, educator; b. Duluth, Minn., Jan. 26, 1933; s. Skuli and Ruth (Hoxie) R.; m. Marjorie Ann, June 19, 1954; children: Gregory, Kristian, Barbara. BA, U. Minn., 1954, MA, 1963, PhD, 1969; DSc (hon.), St Petersburg State Tech U., Russia, 1994. Football and track coach Hamline U., 1958-62; rsch. fellow U. Minn., 1963-66; asst. prof. geology U. S.D., 1967-70, assoc. prof., 1970-72, chmn. dept. geology, 1968-72, chmn. dept. physics 1971-72; dir. Ross Ice Shelf Project U. Nebr., Lincoln, 1972-75; dir. divsn. Polar Programs NSF, Washington, 1975-77; vice chancellor for research and grad. studies, prof. geology U. Nebr., 1977-82, interim chancellor, 1980-81; pres., prof. geoscis. U. Tex., Dallas, 1982-94, Excellence in Edn. Found. prof. of geoscis., 1994—. US del. to Sci. Com. on Antarctle Rsch., 1986-02, v.p., 1996-98, pres., 1998-02, exec. com., 2002-04, hon mem, 2004—; chmn. NRC Polar Rsch. Bd., 1991-95; bd. trustees Geol. Soc. Am. Found., 2005-; bd. govs. US Corp., 1988—, Arctic Inst. N.Am., Mem. editl. bd. Issues in Sci. and Tech., 1991-94. Trustee Baylor Coll. Dentistry, 1989-96. 1st lt. U.S. Army, 1954-56. Recipient Antarctic Svc. medal, 1964, Disting. Svc. award NSF, 1977, Ernie Gunderson award for svc. to amateur athletics S.D. AAU, 1972, Outstanding Achievement award U. Minn., 1993, "M" Club Lifetime Achievement award, 1995, Commemorative medal Polish Acad. Scis., 2004. Fellow Geol. Soc. Am.; mem. Antarctican Soc. (pres. 1988-90), Arctic Inst. N.Am. (mem. bd. govs. US corp. 1996-), Explorers Club, Am. Polar Soc. (hon.), Philos. Soc. Tex., St. Petersburg Acad. Engring. (Russia), Tex. Acad. Sci., Sigma Xi. Lutheran. Office: Univ Tex Dallas Geosciences Program Richardson TX 75083-0688 Office Phone: 972-883-6470.

**RUTGARD, LORRAINE LEVIN,** hearing impaired educator; b. Chgo., May 29, 1925; d. Sam and Rhea (Schneiderman) Levin; m. Meyer David Rutgard, July 4, 1947; children: Marlan Beth Globerson, Jeffrey Jay. BA, U. Wis., 1946; MA in Spl. Edn., Northeastern Ill., U. 1974. Social worker Hebrew Immigrant Aid Soc. (HIAS), Chgo., 1946-50; tchr. Chgo. Bd. Edn., 1959-72; adminstr. pvt. practice physician Med. Office, Skokie, Ill., 1972-81; ret., 1981. Vol. St. Mary's/Westside Food Bank Alliance, Area Agy. on Aging; docent West Valley Art Mus.; mem. Planned Parenthood; charter mem. Holocaust Mus., Washington. Mem. NOW, Hadassah, Temple Beth Shalom and Sisterhood (mem. CARE com.). Avocations: yoga, hiking, aerobics, snorkeling, sports.

**RUTH, JAMES PERRY,** financial planner; b. Washington, Feb. 27, 1946; s. Robert Walker and Virginia Null Ruth; m. Kathleen McHugh, Aug. 10, 1968; children: Heather Lynn, Michael James. BS in Bus. and Public Adminstrn., U. Md., 1970; postgrad., Am. Coll., Bryn Mawr, 1971-83. CLU, CFP, chartered fin. cons. agt., Northwestern Mutual Life Ins. Co., Washington, 1967-74. Gen. agt. Indpls. Life, Rockville, Md., 1974-82; partner Fox, Ruth & Middledorf, Rockville, 1975-82; mgr. Mfrs. Fin. Svcs., Rosslyn, Va., 1982-84; pres. Potomac Fin. Group, 1984—. Contbr. articles to profl. publs.; quoted in N.Y. Times, U.S. News and World Report, USA Today, others. Past pres. Jelleff Boys' Club; past pres. Montgomery County Police Boys' and Girls' Club; chmn. bd. dirs. Asbury Meth. Village Found. Named Outstanding Young Man Am., U.S. Jaycees, 1979. Mem. Nat. Assn. Ins. and Fin. Advisors (pres. Md. chpt. 1995-96), Nat. Assn. Securities Dealers, Suburban Md. Assn. Ins. and Fin. Advisors (past pres., H.L. Meyer Meml. award 1980), Fin. Planning Assn., Suburban Md. Estate Planning Coun. (past pres.), Million Dollar Round Table. Lutheran. Home: 508 Lawson Way Rockville MD 20850 Office: Ste 420 18310 Montgomery Village Ave Gaithersburg MD 20879-3553 Business E-Mail: jruth@pfgroup.org.

**RUTH, RODNEY,** musician, music consultant, contractor, educator; b. Robesonia, Pa., Sept. 12, 1934; s. Herbert J. and Pearl (Rentz) R.; m. Gloria Mae Kauffman, Nov. 14, 1953; 1 child, Tiffany Tunisia. MusB, Manhattan Sch. Music, 1960; MA, Columbia U., 1964. Freelance musician; music cons., contractor Meadowlands Sports Complex, various theaters and performing arts ctrs., individual conductors and performers, bands, orchs., festivals, N.J., N.Y., Pa., 1957—; tchr. Paterson (N.J.) Bd. Edn., 1961-98. Performed with USAF Band, 1953-57; music contractor for world premiers (musicals) Lucifer, Laugh a Little, Cry a Little, Shoemakers Holiday, Love Games, Las Vegas Laugh-In '75. Scholar Manhattan Sch. Music, N.Y.C., 1958-60. Mem. Nat. Edn. Assn., Music Educators Nat. Conf., Am. Fedn. Musicians. Avoca-tions: travel, gardening, golf. Home and Office: Rod Ruth Music 129 Schuyler Rd Allendale NJ 07401-1836 Office Phone: 201-327-7374. E-mail: rodruthmusic@aol.com.

**RUTH, SEBASTIAN A.,** performing company executive; b. Ithaca, NY, July 18, 1975; s. David and Linda Frank Ruth; m. Minna Choi Ruth, June 25, 2004. BA, Brown U., 1997. Exec. artistic dir. Cmty. Music Works, Provi-dence, 1997—, Violinist Providence String Quartet, Providence, 1997—, Boston Philharmonic, Boston, 1998—2002. Adv. bd. mem. City of Providence, Arts Dept., Providence, 2003—. Avocations: gardening, bicycling. Office: Cmty Music Works 1392 Westminster St Providence RI 02909 Office Phone: 401-861-5650.

**RUTHBERG, MILES N.,** lawyer; BA summa cum laude, Yale Univ., 1973; JD magna cum laude, Harvard Univ., 1976. Bar: DC 1979, Calif. 1979. Law clk. Justice Thurgood Marshall, US Supreme Ct., Judge Carl McGowan, US Ct. of Appeals, DC Cir.; former nat. chair, securities litigation and profl. liability practice group Latham & Watkins, former global dept. chair, litigation dept., exec. com. mem. Bd. governors Assn. of Bus. Trial Lawyers. Developments editor Harvard Law Rev., 1976; author: numerous articles in profl. publications. Mem.: ABA, DC Bar Assn., Calif. State Bar Assn. Office: Latham & Watkins Ste 4000 633 W Fifth St Los Angeles CA 90071-2007

**RUTHENBERG, KIRK R.,** lawyer; b. Blue Island, Ill., Dec. 31, 1952; BA, U. Ill., 1975; JD, Georgetown U., 1979. Bar: Ill. 1979, DC 1989, Md. 1991, US Dist. Ct. No. Dist. Ill. 1979, US Dist. Ct. DC 1991, US Dist. Ct. Dist. Md. 1992, US Ct. Appeals 4th Cir. 1993. Named ptnr. Sonnenschein Carlin Nath & Rosenthal (now Sonnenschein Nath & Rosenthal LLP), Chgo., 1986, now ptnr. Washington, head DC litig. & bus. regulation practice group. Office: Sonnenschein Nath & Rosenthal LLP Ste 600, E Tower 1301 K St NW Washington DC 20015 Office Phone: 202-408-6410. Office Fax: 202-408-6399. Business E-Mail: kruthenberg@sonnenschein.com.

**RUTHERFORD, BOYD KEVIN,** federal agency administrator; BA, Howard U., 1979; MA, JD, U. So. Calif., 1990. Atty. analyst Bankers Trust Co., 1979—81; mktg. rep. Data Control Corp., 1981—86; sr. acct. exec. Telenet Comm. Corp., 1986—87; litigation assoc. Carlsmith Wickman Case Mukai & Ichik, 1990—91; atty. Daihatsu Am., Inc., 1991—92; of counsel Mitsubishi Motor Sales of Am., Inc., 1992—94; assoc. Van Ness Feldman, P.C., 1994—98, Tydings & Rosenberg, LLP, 1998—2000; delegate Rep. Party Nat. Convention, 2000; dir. bus. devel. Kelly Law Registry, 2000—01; assoc. adminstr. office enterprise devel. Gen. Svcs. Adminstrn., 2001—03, assoc. adminstr. office performance improvement, 2002—03; acting sec. Md.

Dept. Gen. Svcs., 2003, sec., 2003—06; asst. sec. departmental adminstrn. USDA, 2006—. Office: USDA S Agr Bldg 1400 Independence Ave SW Rm 209A Washington DC 20250 Office Phone: 202-720-3291.*

**RUTHERFORD, GEORGE WILLIAMS, III,** preventive medicine physi-cian; b. San Diego, Apr. 6, 1952; s. G. Williams and Anna Gwyn (Dearing) R.; m. Lisa Anderson, Aug. 24, 1974 (div. 1984); children: Alicia Gwyn, George Williams IV; m. Mary Workman, Feb. 23, 1985; children: Alexandra Catherine, Anne Elizabeth Martha, Hugh Thomas Gwyn, Amanda Frances Julia. AB in Classics, Stanford U., 1974, BS in Chemistry, 1975, AM in History, 1975; MD, Duke U., 1978. Diplomate Am. Bd. Pediat., Am. Bd. Preventive Medicine, Nat. Bd. Med. Examiners. Intern in pediat. U. Calif. Med. Ctr., San Diego, 1978-79; resident in pediat. U. Calif. Med. Ctr., Hosp. for Children, San Diego, 1979-80; resident Hosp. for Sick Children, Toronto, 1980-81; chief resident Children's Hosp. and Health Ctr., San Diego, 1981-82; EIS officer div. viral diseases, divsn. field svcs Epidemiology Office Ctrs. for Disease Control, Atlanta, 1982-84; dir. divsn. immunization, acting dir. divsn. tropical disease N.Y.C. Dept. Health, 1983-85; med. epidemiologist AIDS program Ctrs. for Disease Control, San Francisco Dept. Pub. Health, 1985-87; from med. dir. to dir. AIDS office San Francisco Dept. Pub. Health, 1986-90; chief, infectious disease br. and state epidemiologist Calif. Dept Health, Berkeley, 1990-92, dep. dir. prevention svcs. and state epidemiologist, 1992-95, state health officer, 1993-95; assoc. dean adminstrn., prof. epidemiology/health adminstrn. Sch. Pub. Health, U. Calif., Berkeley, 1995-97; prof. epidemiology and preventive medicine U. Calif., San Fran-cisco, 1997—, dir. Inst. Global Health, 2004—. Transport physician Chil-dren's Hosp. and Health Ctr., San Diego, 1981; clin. asst. prof. pediatrics Emory U., Atlanta, 1982-83, Cornell U., N.Y.C. 1984-85, U. Calif., San Francisco, 1986 92, asst. clin. prof. epidemiology and biostats., 1987-92, family and cmty. medicine, 1988-90; assoc. adj. prof. epidemiology, biostats. and pediatrics, 1992-95, adj. prof., 1996—; assoc. clin. prof. cmty. health u. Calif., Davis, 1991-95; cons. Pan-Am. Health Orgn., S.Am., 1986-89, Ctrs. Disease Control, Atlanta, 1987—, WHO, 1988-90. Contbr. numerous articles to profl. jours., chpts. to books; co-translator cardiology teaching manual, other Spanish med. articles; editor in chief Calif. Morbidity, 1990-92; mem. editl. bd. Calif. AIDS Update, 1988—, Current Issues in Pub. Health, 1993-97; referee: AIDS, 1988—, Am. Jour. Pub. Health, 1989—, Brit. Med. Jour., 1994—, Internat. Jour. Epidemiology, 1991—, Jour. Acquired Immune Deficiency Syndrome, 1989—, New Eng. Jour. Medicine, 1989—, Western Jour. Medicine, 1989—. Mem. numerous profl. adv. coms., task forces, etc. which aid govt. and charitable orgns. in work against infectious disease, especially AIDS. Capt. USPHSR, 1982—. Fellow Am. Acad. Pediatrics; mem. APHA, Am. Assn. for History of Medicine, Am. Soc. Tropical Medicine and Hygiene, Bay Area Communicable Disease Exch., Calif. Med. Assn., Infectious Disease Soc. Am., No. Calif. Pub. Health Assn., Internat. AIDS Soc., Soc. for Epidemiol. Rsch., Assn. State and Territorial Health Ofcls. Republican. Episcopalian. Avocation: tennis. Office: U Calif San Francisco Global Health Inst Ste 1200 50 Beale St San Francisco CA 94105 Office Phone: 415-597-8200. E-mail: grutherford@psg.ucsf.edu.

**RUTHERFORD, JIM,** professional sports team executive; b. 1948; 1 child, Andrea. Goalie Detroit Red Wings, 1970—71, 1973—80, 1982—83, Pitts. Penguins, 1971—73, Toronto Maple Leafs, 1980—81, LA Kings, 1981—82; dir. hockey ops Compuware Sports Corp., 1982-94; gen. mgr. Windsor Spitfires, Ont., 1984-88, head coach Ont., 1986-87; dir. hockey ops. Detroit Ambassadors, 1989-91, coach, dir. hockey ops., 1991-92, Detroit Jr. Red Wings (formerly Ambassadors), 1992-94; COO KTR Hockey Ltd. Partner-ship, Hartford, Conn., 1994—; pres., gen. mgr., COO Carolina Hurricanes (formerly Hartford Whalers), 1994—. Mem. Team Can. hockey world championships, Vienna, 1977, Moscow, 79; player rep. 5 seasons Red Wings. Named Exec. of Yr., Can. Hockey League, 1993, Ont. Hockey League, 1994, The Hockey News, 2002. Achievements include being the general manager of Stanley Cup Champion Carolina Hurricanes, 2006. Office: Carolina Hurri-canes 1400 Edwards Mill Rd Raleigh NC 27607-3624*

**RUTHERFORD, JOHN,** sheriff; b. Sept. 2, 1952; m. Patricia Rutherford; 2 children. Grad., Fla. State U. Uniformed patrolman City of Jacksonville, Fla., sergeant, lt. patrol and detective divsn., dir. region five criminal justice tng. ctr., capt., chief svcs., chief traffic and spl. ops., chief patrol, dir. corrections, 1995—2003, sheriff, 2003—. Achievements include created several programs within Jacksonville including Justice and the Revolving Door, Operation Showdown, and Anti-Litter. Office: 501 E Bay St Rm 303 Jacksonville FL 32202 Office Phone: 904-630-2134. Office Fax: 904-630-4741.

**RUTHERFORD, JOHN SHERMAN, III, (JOHNNY RUTHERFORD),** professional race car driver; b. Coffeyville, Kans., Mar. 12, 1938; s. John Sherman and Mary Henrietta (Brooks) R.; m. Betty Rose Hoyer, July 7, 1963; children: John Sherman, Angela Ann. Student, Tex. Christian U., 1956. Profl. race car driver, 1959-94; ret., 1994; driver super-modified race cars, sprint cars, stock cars, midgets, sports cars, Indy cars, Trans-Am cars and formula 5000. Mem. Indy Car Racing Inc.; dir. spl. events Indy Racing League, 1995—; pace car driver for Championship Auto Racing Teams, 1992-95; auto racing cons. Pennzoil Products-Racing Divsn.; lectr. in field. Author: (auto-biography) Lone Star J.R., 2000; host: TV show The Racers; race commen-tator TV show, NBC, ESPN, CBS, ABC; appeared in numerous TV commercials; art work included in traveling exhbn. Art and Athletes; TV and radio pub. services messages for Nat. Safety Council, Calif. Hwy. Patrol, U.S. Marines, Muscular Dystrophy Assn., Cystic Fibrosis Assn., Boy Scouts, Camp Fire, Jewel Charity, Shriner's Hosp., Tex. Soc. to Prevent Blindness, Air N.G. Hon. state chmn. Am. Cancer Soc., Tex., Tarrant County Soc. to Prevent Blindness, Emergency Medicine Found., Ft. Worth Kidney Assn., Ft. Worth Burn Ctr.; Ind. chmn. Am. Heart Assn.; hon. mem. bd. dirs. Tex. Opera Speedway Children's Charities, 1998—. CARA Charities, 2000--; bd. dirs. Indy HOF and Oldtimers, 2002—. With USMC Rea. 1977— Named Ft. Worth Newsmaker of Yr., 1974, Driver of Yr. Sport Mag., 1976, Driver of Yr. Auto Race Writers and Broadcasters Am., 1974, 80, Olsonite Driver of Yr., 1980, Corvette Challenge's Sportsman of Yr., 1988, Motorsports amb., 1993; recipient Jim Clark award, 1969, Extra Mile award, 1973, Jim Malloy award, 1974, Eddie Sachs award, 1975, Louie Meyer award, 1992; chosen for Internat. Race of Champions, 1974, 76-79, 84, chosen Fast Masters, 1993; named to Tex. Sports Hall of Fame, 1981, Indy 500 Hall of Fame, 1987, Boys Clubs Am.'s Celebrity Hall of Fame, 1987, Tex. Auto Racing Hall of Fame, 1988, Nat. Sprint Car Hall of Fame, 1995, Internat. Motorsports Hall of Fame, 1996, Tex. Motorsports Hall of Fame, 2003, Philanthropy Hall of Fame, 2006. Mem. Fedn. Internat. Automobile, Internat. Motors Sports Assn., Exptl. Aircraft Assn., Warbirds of Am., Confederate Air Force, Internat. Aerobatic Club, League Auto Racing (sec., bd. dirs.), Championship Drivers Assn. (bd. dirs.), Nat. Rifle Assn., Air Force Assn., Air Power Coun., Blue Angels Assn., Ft. Worth Boat Club, Shady Oaks Country Club, Speedway Club, Lions. Achievements include winning 27 championship-car races; winner Indianapo-lis 500, 1974, 76, 80, second place, 1975; set new world's record for stock cars, Daytona Beach, Fla., 1963; set record at Indpls. 500, 1973; at Mich. Internat. Raceway, 1984; U.S. Auto Club Nat. Sprint Car champion, 1965; Nat. Driving champion USAC and CART, 1980; oldest driver (48) to win a 500 mile Indy Car Race, 1986. Personal E-mail: bettyr4tx@msn.com. *I am a firm believer in the fact that a person can do anything in this world he or she wants to as long as you have desire. People have to set goals, things to achieve. No one ever remembers who finished second. Luck is where preparation meets opportunity.*

**RUTHERFORD, MARY LOUISE MANLOVE,** artist; b. Nashville, May 2, 1929; d. William Robert and Mayme (Escue) Manlove; m. Samuel Kenneth Rutherford, Dec. 20, 1952; children: Samuel Kenneth Jr., Kate, Susan. BA, Vanderbilt U., 1951, MA, 1972. Lectr. art history. Exhibited oil paintings on canvas in local and regional shows and galleries. Avocations: reading, travel, ballroom dancing.

**RUTHERFORD, PAUL HARDING,** physicist; b. Shipley, Yorkshire, Eng., Jan. 22, 1938; came to U.S., 1965, naturalized, 1976; s. Joseph William and Annie (Harding) R.; m. Audrey Jones Irvine, Oct. 31, 1959; children—

Andrea Christine, Julia Irvine. BA, Cambridge U., Eng., 1959, MA, PhD, Cambridge U., Eng., 1963. Research asso. Princeton (N.J.) U. Plasma Physics Lab., 1962-63, mem. research staff, 1965-68, research physicist, 1968-71, sr. research physicist, 1971-99, head theoretical div., 1972-80, dep. asso. dir. for research, 1978-80, asso. dir. research, 1980-95. Chair tech. adv. com. Internat. Thermonuclear Exptl. Reactor, 1992-99; rsch. assoc. U.K. Atomic Energy Authority Culham (Berkshire, Eng.) Lab., 1963-65; lectr. astrophys. scis. Princeton U. Co-author: (with R.J. Goldston) Introduction to Plasma Physics, 1995; mem. editl. bd. Physics of Fluids, 1973-75, Nuc. Fusion, 1980-99. Recipient E.O. Lawrence award U.S. Dept. Energy, 1983, Disting. Career award Fusion Power Assocs., 1998. Fellow Am. Phys. Soc. Home: 10 Burr Dr Princeton NJ 08540-1950 Office: Plasma Physics Lab PO Box 451 Princeton NJ 08543-0451 Business E-Mail: prutherford@pppl.gov.

**RUTHERFORD, ROBERT BARRY,** vascular surgeon; b. Edmonton, Alta., Can., July 29, 1931; s. Robert Lyon and Kathleen Emily (Gunn) R.; m. Beulah Kay Folk, Aug. 20, 1955; children: Robert Scott, Lori Jayne, Holly Anne, Trudy Kay, Jay Wilson. BA in Biology, Johns Hopkins U., 1952, MD, 1956. Emeritus prof. surgery U. Colo., Denver, 1996—. Editor: (texts) Management of Trauma, 1968, 4 edits., Vascular Surgery, 1978, 6th edition, 2005, An Atlas of Vascular Surgery, Vol. 1, 1993, Vol. 2, 1998, Decision Making in Vascular Surgery, 2001; editor quar. rev. Seminars in Vascular Surgery. Fellow ACS, Royal Coll. Surgeons Glasgow, Soc. for Vascular Surgery (disting. fellow); mem. Phi Beta Kappa, Alpha Omega Alpha. Republican. Unitarian Universalist. Avocations: skiing, biking, wind surfing, sailing. Home: 14337 Dorsal St Corpus Christi TX 78418 Home (Summer): 345 Small Shore Trl Oakland ME 04963-4317

**RUTHERFORD, SUZANNE L.,** geneticist; b. Oil City, Pa., Sept. 7, 1968; d. Donald E. and Marilyn F. Rutherford; m. Carlos G. Klink, Aug. 8, 1998. BA, Reed Coll., Portland, 1984; PhD, U. Calif., San Diego, 1994. Asst. mem. Fred Hutchinson Cancer Rsch. Ctr., Seattle, 2000—05, assoc. mem., 2005—. Affiliate dept. biology, molecular and cellular biology program U. Wash.; cons. Sequonom, San Diego, 2001—02. Contbr. articles to profl. jours.; mem. editl. bd.: BioEssays, 2002—, PLoS ONE, 2006—. Fellow, U. Chgo.; grantee, NIH, 2002—; scholar, Damon Runyon Cancer Rsch. Fund, 2002—05. Mem.: AAAS, Genetics Soc. Am. Achievements include discovery of evidence for and formulated the 'Hsp90 capacitor hypothesis', a potential molecular mechanism for rapid morphological evolution in response to environmental change. Office: Fred Hutchinson Cancer Research Center 1100 Fairview Ave N Seattle WA 98109-1026 Office Phone: 206-667-5026. E-mail: srutherf@fhcrc.org.

**RUTHERFORD, THOMAS TRUXTUN, II,** state legislator, municipal official; b. Columbus, Ohio, Mar. 3, 1947; s. James William and Elizabeth Whiting (Colby) R.; m. Linda Sue Rogers, Aug. 28, 1965 (div.); 1 child, Jeremy Todd. BBA, U. N.Mex., 1970, JD, 1982. Page, reading clk. N.Mex. State Legislature, 1960-65; mem. N.Mex. Atty. Gen. Environ. Adv. Commn., 1972; radio broadcaster Inc. KOB Radio and TV, 1963-72; mem. N.Mex. Senate, Albuquerque, 1972-96, majority whip, 1978-88. Chmn. rules com. N.Mex. State Senate, chmn. econ. devel. and new tech. interim. com., mem. sci. and new tech. oversight com., majority fl. leader, 1996; pres. Rutherford & Assocs., Albuquerque, 1978—83; pvt. practice, Albuquerque, 1983—; gen. counsel Nat. Fraternal Order of Police, 1996—2001; commr., chair Bernalillo County Commn., 1996—2004; lobbyist The Rutherford Group, 1996—; bd. dirs. Hispano C. of C., Kirtland Partnership Com., Albuquerque Econ. Devel., Camp Sierra Blanca Youth Detention Ctr., N. Mex. Bus. Weekly Top 100 Power Brokers, 1996—2004; past chmn. Albuquerque Cable TV Adv. Bd.; mem. S.W. Regional Energy Coun., N.Mex. Gov.'s Commn. on Pub. Broadcasting; bd. dirs., v.p. Rocky Mountain Corp. for Pub. Broadcasting; mem. Am. Coun. Young Polit. Leaders; del. mission to Hungary, Austria, Greece, 1983; mem. Fgn. Trade Adv. Com. Bd. Econ. Devel. and Tourism; trade del. People's Republic of China, 1985; local govt. del. Switzerland, 2001. Mem. Leadership N.Mex. Class of 2004; bd. dirs. Nat. Assn. Counties, N.Mex. Assn. Counties. N.Mex. Broadcasting Assn. scholar, 1970. Home: 1016 monroe NE Albuquerque NM 87110

**RUTHERFORD, VICKY LYNN,** special education educator; b. Florence, SC, Sept. 12, 1947; BS, Hampton U., 1969, MA, 1971; PhD, Mich. State U., 1991. Certr. tchr. French, spl. edn., reading specialist, Va., tchr. spl. edn., S.C. Social worker day care Hampton (Va.) Dept. Social Svc., 1970-72; reading therapist, asst. dir. dir. Bayberry Reading Clinic, Hampton, 1973-77; tchr. reading, English, counselor York County Schs., Yorktown, Va., 1977-85; staff advisor, asst. to course coord. Mich. State U., East Lansing, 1985-90; tchr. autism/emotionally impaired Florence (S.C.) Dist. 1 Sch. Sys., 1996—2004; tchr. emotionally impaired Long Beach Unified Sch. Dist., 2004—. Instrnl. designer: Addiction Severity Index #1, 1987, #2, 1988, Managing a Diverse Workforce, 1990; designer, trainer: Project Teach, 1991; designer, developer: (video) Camp Takona Summer Experience, 1992. Bass guitarist, Sunday sch. sec., youth worker, Sun. sch. supt. Progressive Ch. of Jesus, Florence, 1992-98, Greater Zion Tabernacle Apostolic Ch., Florence, 1998-2004, City of Refuge Gardena, Calif., 2004-. Fellow Mich. Dept. Edn., 1987-89. Mem. Internat. Reading Assn. Office: Rogers Mid Sch 365 Monrovia Ave Long Beach CA 90803

**RUTHERFORD, WILLIAM B.,** corporate financial executive; BS in Acctg., U. Tampa. With HCA Inc., 1986—, chief fin. officer ea. group Nashville, 1996—. Office: HCA Inc 1 Park Plz Nashville TN 37203

**RUTHERFORD, WILLIAM DRAKE,** investment executive; b. Marshalltown, Iowa, Jan. 14, 1939; s. William Donald and Lois Esther (Drake) R.; m. Janice W. Rutherford, Feb. 4, 1965 (div. Mar. 1982); children: Wayne Donald, Melissa Drake; m. Karen Anderegg, Jan. 2, 1994. BS, U. Oreg., 1961; LLB, Harvard U., 1964. Bar: Oreg. 1964, U.S. Dist. Ct. Oreg. 1966. Assoc. Maguire, Kester & Cosgrave, Portland, Oreg., 1966-69; house counsel May & Co., Portland, 1969-70; pvt. practice, 1970-71, McMinnville, Oreg., 1971-84; mem. Oreg. Ho. of Reps., Salem, 1977-84; state treas. State of Oreg., Salem, 1984-87; chmn. Oreg. Investment Coun., Salem, 1986-87; exec. v.p., dir. U.S. and Australia ops. ABD Internat. Mgmt. Corp., N.Y.C., 1987-88, pres., chief exec. officer, bd. dirs., 1988-89; pres., bd. dirs. Societé Gen. Touche Remnant, 1990-93; dir. spl. projects Metallgesellschaft Corp., N.Y.C., 1994-95; mng. dir. Macadam Capital Ptnrs., Portland, 1995-96; CEO Fiberboard Asbestos Compensation Trust, Portland, 1997; prin. Rutherford Investment Mgmt. LLC, 1998—. Chmn. bd. dirs. Metro One Telecomms. Author: Who Shot Goldilocks?, 2006. Trustee The Nature Conservancy, 2005—; bd. dirs. Portland Opera Assn., 1995—99; mem. investment bd. Oreg. Cmty. Found. Recipient Contbn. to Individual Freedom award ACLU, 1981 Mem. Nat. Assn. State Treas. (exec. v.p. 1985, 86, pres. western region 1985, 86), Nat. Assn. State Auditors, Comptr. and Treas. (exec. com. 1987). Office: 10300 S W Greenburg Rd Ste 115 Portland OR 97223 Office Phone: 503-452-1210. Business E-Mail: WRutherford@rutherfordinvestment.com.

**RUTHERFURD, JOHN,** financial information company executive; LLB, Harvard Law Sch., 1966; AB, Princeton U., 1962. V.p., chief of staff Chase Info. Svcs. Group, 1980—85; founder Interactive Data Corp., 1968, pres., 1985—89, 1990—95; exec. v.p. Dun & Bradstreet Fin. Info. Svcs., 1989—90; mng. dir., new bus. develop. Moody's Investors Svc., NYC, 1995-96, chief adminstr. officer, 1996-98, pres., 1998—2000; pres., CEO Moody's Corp., NYC, 2000—, chmn., 2003—. Office: Moodys Corp 99 Church St New York NY 10007

**RUTHERGLEN, GEORGE A.,** law educator; b. Portland, Oreg., Sept. 12, 1949; s. John Alfred and Helen Kathleen (Bero) R.; m. Jessica Rosalind Feldman, Apr. 25, 1975; children: Susannah Kathleen, Michael Francis. AB, U. Calif., Berkeley, 1971, JD, 1974. Bar: Va. 1979, US Dist. Ct. We. Va. 1980, US Ct. Appeals 4th Cir. 1980, US Supreme Ct. 1988. Law clk. to Hon. J. Clifford Wallace US Ct. Appeals 9th Cir., San Diego, 1974-75; law clk. to justices William O. Douglas and John Paul Stevens US Supreme Ct., Washington, 1975-76; asst. prof. U. Va. Sch. Law, Charlottesville, 1976—80,

assoc. prof., 1980—82, prof., 1982—, now John Barbee Minor disting. prof. law, Edward F. Howrey rsch. prof. Supervising atty. Post-Conviction Assistance Project, 1980—; cons. standing com. on fed. jud. improvements ABA, Chgo., 1988-89. Author: Major Issues in the Federal Law of Employment Discrimination, 1983, 87, 96, Employment Discrimination Law: Visions of Equality in Theory and Doctrine, 2001; co-author with J. Jeffries, Jr., P. Karlan & P. Low) Civil Rights Actions: Enforcing the Constitution, 3rd edit., 2000. Mem. Order of Coif, Phi Beta Kappa. Democrat. Office: U Va Sch Law 580 Massie Rd Charlottesville VA 22903-1789 Office Phone: 434-924-7015. E-mail: gar3h@virginia.edu.

**RUTHMAN, THOMAS ROBERT,** manufacturing executive; b. Cin., May 24, 1933; s. Alois H. and Catherine (Gies) R.; m. Audrey J. Schumaker, Mar. 17, 1979; children: Thomas G., Julia C., Theresa K. Grad., LaSalle U. 1970. With Ruthman Pump and Engring. Inc. (formerly Ruthman Machinery Co.), Cin., 1953—, gen. mgr., 1964-70, v.p., 1970-74, pres., 1974—, pres., owner, 1981—. Pres. Gusher Pumps, Inc., Fulflo Spltys. Co., Gusher Pumps of New Castle, Cin., Williamstown (Ky.), Dry Ridge, Calif.; pres., owner, dir. Great Lakes Pump & Supply, Mich.; owner BSM Pump Corp, North Kingston, R.I., Negel Pump Co.; pres., owner Birmingham (Eng.) Pump Supply, Ruthmann Pumpen, GMBH, Germany. Office: 1212 Streng St Cincinnati OH 45223-2643

**RUTHVEN, JOHN A.,** wildlife artist; b. Cin., 1924; m. Judy Ruthven; 1 child, Kevin. Student, Cin. Art Acad., Jack Storey Ctrl. Acad. Comml. Art. Opened comml. art studio, 1946; founder Wildlife Internationale Inc., 1971; major exhibits include Famous Figureheads Series, Nat. Mariner Mus., Washington, Cin. Mus. Natural History, 1994, Artist of Am. exhbn., Denver, Leigh Yawkey Woodson Mus., Wausau, Wis., Soc. Animal Artists nat. tours, 1992—2000, Hiram Blauvelt Art Mus., Oradell, NJ, Rory Tory Peterson Inst. Natural History, Jamestown, NY, 1998, 2004—05, The Smithsonian Instn.'s Preservation and Rsch. Ctr., 1998; major commissions include Procter & Gamble, Cin. Bengals, John Deere & Co., WILDS Internat. Ctr. for the Preservation of Wild Animals, Armco Steel Corp., Bankers Life & Casualty, Mead Corp., Colonial Williamsburg, Classical Music Hall of Fame. Co-author, illustrator (with William Zimmerman) Top Flight Speed Index to Waterfowl of N.Am., 1965, paintings featured in (books) An Instrument of Your Peace, Eyes of Tenderness, John A. Ruthven, In the Audubon Tradition. Served USN, WWII. Named Winner of Fed. Duck Stamp competition for "Redhead Ducks", 1960, Artist of Yr., Ducks Unlimited, 1972, First Ohio Duck Stamp/Print Artist, 1982, 25th Anniversary Artist, Trout Unlimited, 1984, First Ohio Animal Stamp/Print Artist, 1988, Pacific Flyaway Artist, Ducks Unlimited, 1989; recipient Irma Lazarus Award for sustained arts excellence, Ohio Gov.'s Awards for the Arts, 2001, Nat. Medal of Arts, 2004. Mem.: Soc. Animal Artists (past pres.), Nat. Audubon Soc., Am. Ornithological Assn., Cin. Bird Club, Outdoors Writers Assn. Achievements include painting unveilings at The White House, Hermitage Mus., St. Petersburg, Russia, Pres.'s Palace, Philippines, for Crown Prince Henri, Luxemborg, Neil Armstrong Space Mus., Ohio State Capital Rotunda. Office: Wildlife Internationale Inc 202 E Grant Ave PO Box 59 Georgetown OH 45121

**RUTKOFF, ALAN STUART,** lawyer; b. Chgo., May 31, 1952; s. Roy and Harriet (Ruskin) R.; m. Mally Zoberman, Dec. 22, 1974; children: Aaron Samuel, Jordana Michal, Robert Nathaniel. BA with high distinction, U. Mich., 1973; JD magna cum laude, Northwestern U., 1976. Bar: Ill. 1976, U.S. Dist. Ct. (no. dist.) Ill. 1976, U.S. Ct. Appeals (7th cir.) 1977, U.S. Ct. Appeals (3d cir.) 1978, U.S. Supreme Ct. 1981, U.S. Ct. Appeals (5th cir.) 1983, U.S. Ct. Appeals (8th cir.) 1990, U.S. Dist. Ct. (we. dist.) Wis. 1996, U.S. Ct. Appeals (6th cir.) 2003. Assoc. Altheimer & Gray, Chgo., 1976-80; ptnr. Kastel & Rutkoff, Chgo., 1980-83, Holleb & Coff Ltd., Chgo., 1983-84, McDermott Will & Emery LLP, Chgo., 1984—, gen. coun., 2005—. Pres. N. Suburban Synagogue Beth El, Highland Pk., Ill., 1999-2001. Mem. ABA, Chgo. Bar Assn., Order of Coif. Home: 801 Timberhill Rd Highland Park IL 60035-5148 Office: McDermott Will & Emery LLP 227 W Monroe St Ste 4400 Chicago IL 60606-5096 Office Phone: 312-984-7751. Business E-Mail: arutkoff@mwe.com.

**RUTKOFF, PETER M.,** humanities educator; b. NYC, June 5, 1942; s. Harry Rutkoff and Minnie Kronstadt; m. D. Elder, Jan. 1, 2005; children: Joshua, Rebekah. BA, St. Lawrence U., 1964; PhD, U. Pa., Phila., 1971. Robert Oden prof. of Am. studies Kenyon Coll., Gambier, Ohio, 1971—. Departmental chair Kenyon Coll., Gambier, 1999—2005. Author: (fiction and nonfiction) New York Modern: The Arts and the City (Best Book, Ohio Acad. of History, 2002), (novel) Shadow Ball: A Novel of Basball and Chicago. Recipient Disting. Faculty Tchg. award, Kenyon Coll., 2004. Home: PO Box 328 Gambier OH 43022 Office: Kenyon Coll Wing Center Gambier OH 43022 Office Phone: 740-427-5317. Personal E-Mail: rutkoff@kenyon.eud. Business E-Mail: rutkoff@kenyon.edu.

**RUTKOVE, SEWARD BRIAN,** neurologist, educator, neuroscientist; b. Bklyn., May 18, 1964; s. Lowell Jay and Edith (Botwinick) R.; m. Elena Ruehr, Sept. 2, 1989. BA, Cornell U., Ithaca, N.Y., 1985; MD, Columbia U., N.Y., 1989. Diplomate Am. Bd. Psychiatry and Neurology, 1996, spl. qualification in clinical neurophysiology Am. Bd. Psychiatry and Neurology, 1997. Internship, residency, internal med. St Joseph Mercy Hosp., Ann Arbor, Mich., 1989—91; residency in neurology Brigham and Women's Hosp., Boston, 1991—94, fellowship in clinical neurophysiology, 1994—95; neurologist Beth Israel Deaconess Med. Ctr., Boston, 1995—2003; assoc. prof. neurology Med. Sch. Harvard U., Boston, 2003—; chief Divsn. Neuromuscular Disease Dept. Neurology Beth Israel Deaconess Med. Ctr., Boston, 2004—. Contbr. articles to profl. jours. Grantee, NIH, 2003, 2005. Mem. Am. Acad. Neurology, Physicians for Nat. Health Plan. Achievements include development of electrical impedance myography-a new approach to evaluating muscle and nerve diseases; novel approaches to using temperature for the evaluation of peripheral nerve diseases. Avocations: double bass, piano, skiing. Office: Beth Israel Deaconess Medical Center 330 Brookline Avenue TCC-810 Boston MA 02446 Office Phone: 617-667-8130. Business E-Mail: srutkove@bidmc.harvard.edu.

**RUTKOWSKI, DUANE JOSEPH,** social studies educator; b. Phila., Aug. 20, 1956; s. Edward Joseph and Dorothy Lucille Rutkowski. BA, U. Pa., 1978; postgrad., U. Arts, 1978—82. Dean students, tchr. social studies Performing Arts Sch., Phila., 1978—89; dir. music, organist, dir. choir St. Laurentius Ch., 1968—, tchr. 7th grade social studies, music, lang. arts, 1990—. Asst. dir. Acad. Boys Choir, Phila., 1976—89; guest soloist, organist various area chs., 1990—. Chmn. pastoral coun., fundraiser St. Laurentius Ch., Phila., 1993—. Named Tchr. of Yr., Fox 29 TV Sta. Phila., 1992, 1993, Celebrate Fishtown Assn., Phila., 1998, Fishtown Civic Assn., Phila., 2005; recipient Tchg. Excellence award, Phila. (Pa.) Flag Day Assn., 2005. Mem.: Met. Opera Guild, Nat. Cath. Educators Assn., Phila. Flag Day Assn. Roman Catholic. Avocations: travel, gourmet cooking. Home: 2651 E Huntington St Philadelphia PA 19125 Office: St Laurentius Sch 1612 E Berks St Philadelphia PA 19125 Office Phone: 215-423-8834.

**RUTLEDGE, CHARLES OZWIN,** pharmacologist, educator; b. Topeka, Oct. 1, 1937; s. Charles Ozwin and Alta (Seaman) R.; m. Jane Ellen Crow, Aug. 13, 1961; children: David Ozwin, Susan Harriett, Elizabeth Jane, Karen Ann. BS in Pharmacy, U. Kans., 1959, MS in Pharmacology, 1961; PhD in Pharmacology, Harvard U., 1966. NATO postdoctoral fellow Gothenburg (Sweden) U., 1966-67; asst. prof. U. Colo. Med. Ctr., Denver, 1967-74, assoc. prof., 1974-75; prof., chmn. dept. pharmacology U. Kans., Lawrence, 1975-87; dean, prof. Pharmacology Purdue U., West Lafayette, Ind., 1987—2002, exec. dir. Discovery Park, 2001—05, interim vice provost rsch., 2002—05, v.p. rsch., 2005—. Contbr. articles on neuropharmacology to profl. jours. Grantee NIH, 1970-87. Mem. AAAS, Am. Soc. Pharmacology and Exptl. Therapeutics (councillor 1982 84, sec.-treas. 1990-93, pres. 1996-97), Am. Assn. Coll. Pharmacy (chm. biol. scis. sect. 1983-84, chmn. coun. faculties 1986-87, chmn. coun. deans 1993-94, com. implement change pharm. edn. 1989-92, pres. 1996-97), Soc. for Neurosci., Am. Pharm. Assn.

Avocations: gardening, skiing. Home: 40 Brynteg Est West Lafayette IN 47906-5643 Office: Purdue U Hovde Hall Rm 338 610 Purdue Mall West Lafayette IN 47907-2040 Office Phone: 765-494-6209. Business E-Mail: chipr@purdue.edu.

**RUTLEDGE, EDWARD K.,** mortgage broker; b. Winfield, Ill., Feb. 1, 1972; s. John K. and Nancy Ann D. Rutledge; m. Katherine Collins Horne, Nov. 13, 1999; children: Elizabeth Thorne, Eleanor Stone. BS, Miami U., 1994. Fin. mgr. LaSalle Nat. Trust, Chgo., 1994—96; global products coord. ABN AMRO Asset Mgmt., Amsterdam, 1996—99; mgr. Charter Cons. Chgo., 2000—03; v.p. Draper and Kramer, Chgo., 2003—. Mem. Trout Unlimited, Atlantic Salmon Fedn., Ruffed Grouse Soc., Chgo. Coun. on Fgn. Rels., Chgo.; steering com. Chgo. Opera Theater, Chgo., 2005. Recipient Eagle Scout, Boy Scouts of Am., 1986. Mem.: SAR, Friends of Downtown, No. Ill. Comml. Assn. Realtors (com. chair), CCIM, Mensa, Pinewood Club, Tavern Club (bd. dirs. 2005), U. Club Chgo., Casino, Phi Gamma Delta. Avocations: fishing, hunting, skiing, scuba diving, travel. Office: Draper and Kramer 33 W Monroe Ste 1900 Chicago IL 60603 Office Phone: 312-795-2511. Business E-Mail: rutledge@draperandkramer.com.

**RUTLEDGE, JOANNE,** artist, consultant; b. Indpls., Dec. 17, 1941; d. Edward John and Dorothy Louise (Bachelor) Underwood; m. Kenneth Clay Smith, Sept. 7, 1963 (div. May 1990); children: Elizabeth, Kenneth Clay, Jr., Andrew; m. Mark Alan Rutledge, July 31, 1993. RN, St. Vincent's Sch. Nursing, Indpls., 1962; BSN, Ind. U., Indpls., 1979. RN Ind. Staff RN Children's Hosp., Washington, 1962—63, St. Vincent's Hosp., Indpls., 1963—64, Women's Hosp. Spl. Care Nursery, Indpls., 1990—97; nurse cons. Hosp. Care for Indigent Ind. State Program, Indpls., 1995—. Exhibitions include Ind. State Fair, Ind. Heritage Arts, Southside Art League Regional Show. Docent Indpls. Mus. Art, 1983—; reading tutor Kiwanis Project, 2002—; active various coms. Children's Mus. Guild, 1975—; Indpls. Athletic Club Art Bd. Found., 1990—. Recipient Billy Cothran Landscape award, Indpls. Art Ctr., 1985. Mem.: Ind. Plein Art Painters Assn., Stutz Artist's Assn., Ind. Artist's Club (assoc.), Proctor Club (pres. 1994—95). Roman Catholic. Avocations: travel, photography, hiking, attending concerts and theater, scuba diving. Home: 1019 W 75th St Indianapolis IN 46260-3408 Office: Ind Hosp Care for the Indigent 402 W Washington St Indianapolis IN 46204

**RUTLEDGE, KATHERINE BURCK,** artist; b. La., Mar. 16, 1949; d. Cyril Büsing and Sarah Marlette Burck; m. Clayton Fenton Rutledge, Apr. 24, 1982. BFA, La. State U., 1971; postgrad., New Orleans Acad. Fine Arts, 1988—90. Represented in permanent collections McIlhenny Collection of Natural Sci., La. State U., New Orleans Zoo. Fellow La. State Mus. Natural Sci., Baton Rouge, 1979—82. Scholar, Audubon Soc., Baton Rouge Chpt., 1980. Mem.: The Pocahontas Found., Magna Carta Dames, Jamestown Soc. (life). Republican. Avocations: gardening, birdwatching. Home: 238 Ship Dr Baton Rouge LA 70806

**RUTLEDGE, MARY ELIZABETH,** cultural organization administrator; b. Denver, Oct. 20, 1923; d. Frederick Edwin Tibbetts and Mary Frances Tibbetts-Wallace, Robert John Wallace (Stepfather); m. Albert Francis Rutledge, May 1, 1948 (dec.); children: John, James, Frances. BA in Sociology, Wells Coll., 1945. Field mgr. Seal Ohio Girl Scout Coun., Columbus, 1967—80, publs. mgr., 1980—95; exec. staff Assn. Girl Scouts, 1968—. Editor Cook Book for a Water Tank, Cook Book for Hunger. Instr., trainer CPR Am. Red Cross, Am. Heart Assn.; with Columbus Girl Scout Coun., 1967—95; mem. Diocesan Coun. Cath. Women, Columbus, 1960—; pres. Diocesan Coun. of Coun. Women, Columbus, 1984—86. Mem.: Norwester Women's Club (pres. 2001—), Ft. Monroe Wines Club (v.p., officer 1956), St. Agatha Womens Club (pres. 1966). Roman Catholic. Avocations: gardening, cooking, travel.

**RUTLEDGE, PETER J.,** federal agency administrator; b. Somerville, NJ, June 19, 1949; BSME, Rutgers U., 1971; M Indsl. Engring., Tex. A&M U., 1974; M Sci. Reliability Engring., U. Md., 1993, PhD in Reliability Engring., 1997. Mech. engr. Delaval Steam Turbine Co., Trenton, NJ, 1972; safety engr. Army Materiel Command Intern Tng. Ctr., Texarkana, Tex., 1972—74, Picatinny Arsenal, Dover, NJ, 1974—75; chief engring. br. safety office Army Materiel Command, Alexandria, Va., 1975—83; tech. advisor Dir. Army Safety, the Pentagon, Washington, 1983—85; dep. dir. occupl. safety and health Safety and Occupl. Health Policy Directorate Office of Sec. of Def., Washington, 1985—88; with NASA, Washington, 1988—; dir. space flight SMA divsn., 1996—97, dir. enterprise safety and mission assurance divsn. Office Safety and Mission Assurance, 1997—. Office: NASA Hdqrs Mail Code Q 300 E St NW Washington DC 20546-0579

**RUTLEDGE, ROGER KEITH,** lawyer; b. Knoxville, Tenn., Dec. 27, 1946; s. Perkins P. and Jean Mac (Karnes) R.; m. Lily Mee Kin Hee, June 6, 1970; children: Amelia Leilani, Sarah Elizabeth. BA in History with honors, U. N.C., 1968; JD cum laude, Am. U., 1977. Bar: Tenn. 1977, U.S. Dist. Ct. (we. dist.) Tenn. 1978, U.S. Supreme Ct. 1982. Served in U.S. Peace Corps, Nepal, 1968-70; fgn. service officer U.S. Dept. State, Washington and Italy, 1971-76; ptnr. Rutledge & Rutledge, Memphis, 1977—. Pres. Jabez Burns, Inc., 1998-99; sec., treas. R-Track Tech., Inc. Editor fiction Carolina Quar., 1967-68; assoc. editor Am. U. Law Rev., 1976-77. Mem. campaign com. Albert Gore Jr. U.S. Senate, Shelby County, 1984, for pres. campaign, 1988, 2000; bd. chmn. United Meth. Neighborhood Ctrs., Inc., 1992. Mem. ABA, Tenn. Bar Assn., Memphis Bar Assn. (editor Bar Forum 1986, asst. editor 1987). Democrat. Methodist. Office: Rutledge & Rutledge 1053 W Rex Rd Memphis TN 38119-3819 *Notable cases include: Fite vs. First Tenn. Prodns. Credit Assn., which involved age discrimination in employment, 1988; Capital Tool & Mfg. vs. Maschinenfabrik Herkules, which involved trade secret law and internat. injunction, 1988.*

**RUTSALA, VERN A.,** poet, writer, language educator; b. Feb. 5, 1934; s. Ray Edwin and Virginia Mae (Brady) R.; m. Joan Merle Colby, Apr. 6, 1957; children: Matthew, David, Kirsten. BA, Reed Coll., 1956; MFA, U. Iowa, 1960. Instr. Lewis and Clark Coll., Portland, 1961-64, asst. prof., 1964-69, assoc. prof., 1969-76, prof., 1976—2004. Vis. prof. U. Minn., Mpls-1968-69, Bowling Green (Ohio) State U., 1970; vis. writer Idaho, Moscow, 1988, Redlands (Calif.) U., 1979; chmn. English dept. Lewis and Clark, Portland, 1986-89, MWC/Pacific MFA program, 2005. Author: The Window, 1964, Laments, 1975, The Journey Begins, 1976, Paragraphs, 1978, Walking Home from the Icehouse, 1981, Backtracking, 1985, Ruined Cities, 1987, Selected Poems, 1991, Little-Known Sports, 1994, Greatest Hits: 1964-02, 2002, A Handbook for Writers, 2004, The Moment's Equation, 2004, How We Spent Our Time, 2006. With U.S. Army, 1956-58. Guggenheim Found. fellow, 1982-83, NEA fellow, 1975, 79, Masters fellow Oreg. Arts Commn., 1990; recipient Carolyn Kizer prize Western Oreg. State Coll., 1988, N.W. Poets prize N.W. Rev., 1975, Hazel Hall award Oreg. Inst. Lit. Arts, 1992, Juniper prize U. Mass. Press, 1993, Duncan Lawrie prize Arvon Found., 1994, Carolyn Kizer prize, 1997, Richard Snyder prize, 2004, Akron Poetry prize, 2004, Kenneth O. Hanson award, 2005; finalist Nat. Book award, 2005. Mem. AAUP, AWP, PEN, Poetry Soc. Am. Avocations: drawing, painting, sports.

**RUTSKY, LESTER,** retired textiles executive; writer; b. N.Y.C., May 23, 1924; s. Samuel and Bess (Millman) Rutsky; m. Elaine Selesnik, Aug. 30, 1959. Student viola, Stuyvesant House, 1935—37, Christadora House, 1937—38. Co-writer (songs) You're Gonna be Sorry; contbr. articles to profl. jours.; author: numerous poems. Recipient Paul Elliot Meml. award, Poetry Soc. Mich., 1982, 1st pl., Ind. State Poetry Soc., Poetry Clubs Ind. Democrat. Avocations: painting, violin, piano.

**RUTSTEIN, DAVID W.,** lawyer, food products executive; b. NYC, July 7, 1944; s. David and Mazie (Weissman) R.; m. Rena E. Bergsmann, July 19, 1967; children: Sara E., Charles B. BA, U. Pa., 1966; JD with honors, George Washington U., 1969. Bar: Pa. 1969, D.C. 1969. Dep. atty. gen., Pa., 1969-70; ptnr. firm Danzansky, Dickey, Tydings, Quint & Gordon, Washington,

1970-78; sr. v.p., gen. counsel Giant Food, Inc., Washington, 1978—2000; of counsel Bus. Transactions, Mergers & Acquisitions practices Venable LLP, Washington, 2001—. Bd. dirs., chmn., treas. Washington Met. Bd. Trade, Fed. City Coun. Bd. dirs., pres. Washington Hebrew Home for Aged (Hyman Goldman award), 1989-91; mem. exec. com. Fed. City Coun.; chmn. Agnes and Eugene Meyer Found., Wash. Met. Bd. Trade; trustee Greater Washington Rsch. Ctr. Named Washingtonian of the Year, Washingtonian Mag.; recipient award for Disting. Svc. to Washington Theater Cmty., KPMG. Mem. D.C. Bar Assn., Washington Met. Area Corp. Counsel Assn. (pres. 1986). Jewish. Home: 9 Greentree Ct Bethesda MD 20817-1440 Office: Venable Law Firm 575 7th St NW Washington DC 20004-1601 Office Phone: 202-344-4000. Office Fax: 202-344-8300. Business E-Mail: dwrutstein@venable.com.

**RUTSTEIN, ELEANOR H.,** psychologist; b. N.Y., Dec. 26, 1933; d. Louis Morris and Sarah Rutstein; m. Gilbert Sussman, Aug. 17, 1971; 1 child, Susanna Beth Sussman. BA in psychology summa cum laude with honors, Cornell U., Ithaca, NY, 1955; MA with honors, Boston U., 1956; PhD in Clin. Psychology, NYU, 1970. Lic. psychologist 1971. Training fellow Rsch. Ctr. for Mental Health, N.Y., 1965—66; psychologist Bronx Psychiatric Ctr., Bronx, NY, 1966—70; clin. psychologist Beth Israel Hosp., N.Y., 1970—72; clin. asst. prof. Cornell Univ. Med. Coll., White Plains, NY, 1980—89; vis. asst. prof. Albert Einstein Coll. of Medicine, Bronx, NY, 1987—91; adj. clin. supr. Yeshiva Univ., Bronx, NY, 1991—; pvt. practice New Rochelle, NY, 1971—. Contbr. scientific papers pub. to profl. jour. Group facilitator Group Mothers of Pre-Schoolers, recently div. woman, White Plains, 1976—; mem. Move On, 2004—. Mem.: APA, N.Y. State Psychol. Assn., Psi Chi, Phi Kappa Phi, Phi Beta Kappa. Democrat. Avocations: piano, photography, theater, music, gourmet cooking. Home and Office: 597 Pinebrook Blvd New Rochelle NY 10804 Office Phone: 914-576-4866. Personal E-mail: eleanorhrutstein@aol.com.

**RUTSTEIN, REBECCA ANNE,** painter; b. Phila., June 25, 1971; Studied art history and studio art, Wash. U., St. Louis, 1989—90; BFA, Cornell U., 1993; MFA, U. Pa., 1997. Artist-in-residence Vt. Studio Ctr., Johnson, 1997, Banff Centre for the Arts, Canada, 2003, 2004. Solo exhibitions include Painting and Drawings, Tjaden Gallery, Ithaca, NY, 1993, Painting and Collages, Morgan Print Gallery, U. Pa., Phila., 1996, Small Works/Sacred Spaces, 1997, Recent Works, Lockjaw Gallery, Phila., 1999, Paintings, Drawings & Illuminations, 2000, Erasure, Tribes Gallery, NYC, 2000, Second Skin, In Rare From Gallery, Lambertville, NJ, 2000, Shifting Images, Bridgette Mayer Gallery, Phila., 2002, Love & Subduction, 2004, Underworld, Fleisher Art Meml., Phila., 2002, Breaking Boundaries, Phila. Mus. Art Mus. Restaurant, 2004, Canopy Adventures, List Gallery, Swarthmore Coll., PA, 2004. Bd. dirs. Grad. Sch. Fine Arts (now Sch. Design) Assn. U. Pa., 2001—04. Named Degree Marshall (Valedictorian), Fine Arts Dept., Cornell U., 1993; recipient Piero Dorazio Color Award, Grad. Sch. Fine Arts, U. Pa., 1996, Charles Addams Meml. Prize, 1997, Natvar Bhavsar Prize for group exhbn. East/West Visions In Between, Arthur Ross Gallery, Phila., 1997; Overseers Scholar Fellowship, U. Pa., 1995—96, Artist's Grant, Vt. Studio Ctr., 1997, Pew Fellowship in the Arts, 2004.

**RUTSTEIN, SEDMARA ZAKARIAN,** piano educator, concert pianist; b. Kazan, Russia, Oct. 18, 1937; came to U.S., 1974; d. Suren and Ekaterina (Todorovskaya) Zakarian; m. Alexander Rutstein, Aug. 29, 1958; 1 child, Alla. D in Music, Leningrad State Conservatory, USSR, 1961, diploma (hon.), 1959. Prof. Leningrad State Conservatory, 1961-73; artist-in-residence Grinnell (Iowa) Coll., 1974—76; prof. Oberlin (Ohio) Conservatory, 1976—. Recording artist, classical piano music XVIII through XX centuries, 1972—. Grantee Oberlin Coll., 1984-98. Mem. Am. Music Tchrs. Assn. Avocations: reading, music, travel. Home: 226 N Prospect St Oberlin OH 44074-1035 Office: Oberlin Coll Conservatory of Music Oberlin OH 44074 Office Phone: 440-775-8250. Business E-Mail: sedmara.z.rutstein@oberlin.edu.

**RUTSTEIN, STANLEY HAROLD,** apparel retailing company executive; b. Wilkes-Barre, Pa., July 1, 1941; s. Sydney D. and Bessie H. (Cohen) R.; m. Jo Ella Rutstein; children— Wendy Sue, Michael Scott, Lynne Elizabeth. Student, Wilkes Coll., 1959-61; grad., Advanced Mgmt. Program, Harvard U., 1975. Buyer Barbara Lynn Stores, Inc., N.Y.C., 1961-63; buyer, then mdsg. mgr. Casual Corner div. U.S. Shoe Corp., Enfield, Conn., 1963-71, pres., 1971-76; pres., cons., dir. U.S. Shoe Corp., Cin., 1976-79; pres. Commonwealth Trading, Inc., Stoughton, Mass., 1979-85, Chadwick's of Boston Ltd., 1983-85; cons. Commonwealth Trading, Inc., 1985—; pres. Trim Trends, Inc., Boston, 1986-87, chmn., 1987—, chief exec. officer, pres. Narragansett Clothing Co., Tiverton, RI, 1987-90, also bd. dirs.; bd. dirs. Reynolds Bros. Inc., 1989-95; pres., CEO S/J Designs Inc., 1989—2002, DBA, Northeast Knitters, Wagner Realty, Bradenton, Fla., 2002—. Bd. dirs. The Icing, Inc., Sycamore Shops, Inc. Bd. dirs. Ptnrs. for Disabled Youth, 1992. Mem. Young Pres. Orgn. Office: Wagner Realty 3639 Cortez Rd West Bradenton FL 34210 Home: The Water Club 1281 Gulf of Mexico Dr #203N Longboat Key FL 34228 Office Phone: 941-727-2800, 941-539-8313. E-mail: nextmoveboston@aol.com.

**RUTTAN, VERNON WESLEY,** agricultural economist, educator; b. Alden, Mich., Aug. 16, 1924; s. Ward W. and Marjorie Ann (Chaney) R.; m. Marilyn M. Barone, July 30, 1945; children: Lia Marie, Christopher, Alison Elaine, Lore Megan. BA, Yale U., 1948; MA, U. Chgo., 1950, PhD, 1952; LLD (hon.), Rutgers U., 1978; D Agrl. Sci. (hon.), U. Kiel, Germany, 1986, Purdue U., 1991. Economist TVA, 1951-54; prof. agrl. econs. Purdue U., 1954-63; staff economist President's Council Econ. Advisers, 1961-63; economist Rockefeller Found., 1963-65; head dept. agrl. econs. U. Minn., St. Paul, 1965-70, Regent's prof., 1986-99, Regent's prof. emeritus, 2000—. Pres. Agrl. Devel. Council, N.Y.C., 1973-77 Author (with Y. Hayami): Agricultural Development: An International Perspective, 1971, 1985; author; U.S. Development Assistance Policy, 1996, Technology, Growth and Development, 2001, Social Science Knowledge and Economic Development, 2003, Is War Necessary for Economic Growth, 2006. Recipient Alexander von Humboldt award, 1985. Fellow AAAS, Am. Acad. Arts and Scis., Am. Agrl. Econs. Assn. (pres. 1971-72, Publ. award 1956, 57, 62, 66, 67, 71, 79, 85, 97); mem. NAS. Home: 1666 Coffman St Apt 112 Saint Paul MN 55108-1326 Office: Dept Applied Econs U Minn Saint Paul MN 55108 Business E-Mail: vruttan@umn.edu.

**RUTTENBERG, CHARLES BYRON,** lawyer; b. Reading, Pa., Nov. 16, 1922; s. Abraham David and Mollie Belle (Rabinowitz) Ruttenberg; m. Arden Honore Suk, July 29, 1955; children: Victoria Arden, Valerie Honore, Alexandra Anne. Student, Yale U., New Haven, Conn., 1941—42; BA, U. Va., Charlottesville, 1946; LLB, U. Pa., Phila., 1949. Bar: DC. With Covington & Burling, Washington; gen. counsel NSF, Washington, Nat. Found. Arts Humanities, Washington, 1949-69; ptnr. Arent, Fox, Kintner, Plotkin & Kahn, Washington, 1969—; fed. mediator US Dist. Ct., 1998—, DC Superior Ct., 2000—. Chmn. legis. bus., mem. exec. com., bd. dirs., gen. counsel Greater Washington Bd. Trade, 1983—92, Nat. Assn. Rec. Merchandisers, Video Software Dealers Assn., 1985. Editor, mem. mng. bd.: U. Pa. Law Rev., 1947—49. Gen. counsel Nat. Opera Inst., 1985—95; co-chmn. U. Pa. Law Sch. Alumni Fund, Washington, 1983—91; chmn. lawyers com. DC Commn. Arts, 1972—75; gen. counsel People to People Music Program, Washington, 1970—91; trustee, gen. counsel Wolf Trap Found. Performing Arts, Vienna, Va., 1981—91, Nat. Inst. Music Theatre, Washington, 1969—90; gen. counsel, bd. dirs. Am. Film Inst., 1969—91; trustee, mem. exec. com. U. DC, 1990—94; bd. dirs., pres. Cosmos Club Hist. Preservation Found., 1987—; bd. dirs., v.p., exec. com. Iona Sr. Svcs., 1997—; bd. dirs. Washington Area Lawyers for the Arts, 1984—95, Greater Washington Rsch. Ctr., 1980—95; mem. adv. bd. DC Lottery, 2002—. With USAF, 1942—46, capt. USAFR, 1946—55. Recipient Outstanding Svc. awards, US Govt., 1967, 1968. Mem.: ABA, Arts Internat. (gen. counsel), U. Pa. Law Alumni Assn. (pres. 1967—71, bd. dirs. 1967—78), Washington Athletic Club (bd. govs. 1969—74), Mitchell Lane Club, St. Alban's Club, Cosmos Club (bd. mgmt. 2000—03, gen. counsel 2003—06, v.p. 2006—, Disting. Svc. award 2005), Phi Beta Kappa. Home: 4735 Butterworth Pl NW Washington DC

20016-4459 Office: Arent Fox Kintner Plotkin & Kahn 1050 Connecticut Ave NW Ste 500 Washington DC 20036-5303 Office Phone: 202-857-6082. Personal E-mail: cbruttenberg@aol.com. Business E-Mail: ruttenbc@arentfox.com.

**RUTTENBERG, FRANK Z.,** lawyer; b. San Antonio, June 4, 1954; BBA, U. Tex., 1976; JD, St. Mary's U., 1979; LLM in Taxation, NYU, 1982. Bar: Tex. 1979. Lawyer Strasburger & Price, L.L.P., San Antonio; ptnr. Bracewell & Patterson, San Antonio, 1999—. Office: Bracewell & Giuliani One Alamo Ctr 106 S Saint Marys St Ste 800 San Antonio TX 78205-3603 Office Phone: 210-299-3467. Business E-Mail: frank.ruttenberg@bracewellgiulianillc.com.

**RUTTENCUTTER, BRIAN BOYLE,** manufacturing company executive; b. Long Beach, Calif., June 15, 1953; s. Wayne Andrew and Florence Mae (Heckman) F.; m. Marilyn Ruth Grubb, Sept. 9, 1978; children: Christi Anne (dec.), Melissa Lyn. BS in Bus. Adminstrn. and Acctg., Biola U., 1976; MBA, Calif. State U., Long Beach, 1983. Cert. mgmt. acct. Controller Fuller Theol. Sem., Pasadena, Calif., 1976-80; dir. gen. acctg. Air Calif., Newport Beach, 1980-84; corp. controller PBS Bldg. Systems, Inc., Anaheim, Calif., 1984-88, v.p. fin. and adminstrn., 1988-93; CFO, v.p. fin. For Better Living, Inc., and The Quikset Orgn., Auburn and Irvine, Calif., 1993-95; v.p. fin., CFO, bd. dirs. Phillips Industries Inc., Commerce, Calif., 1996—2003; CFO ABC Window Co., Inc., Ontario, Calif., 2004—05, pres., CEO, 2005—. Chmn., vice chmn., fin. commn. City of Irvine, Calif., 1990—94, vice-chmn. cmty. svcs. commn., 1996—98; active Drivers for Hwy. Safety, Irvine, 1986; trustee Fin. Execs. Rsch. Found., 2004—; v.p. Greater Irvine Rep. Assembly, 1990, treas., 1991; bd. dirs. Grace Brethren Ch., Long Beach, 1978—80, Woodbridge Cmty. Ch., Irvine, 1986—88, 1991—92, vice chmn., 1991, chmn., 1992 Mem. Inst. Cert. Mgmt. Accts., Inst. Mgmt. Accts., Fin. Execs. Internat. (past pres., chpt. bd. dirs., nat. bd. dirs., area v.p.), Assn. Corp. Growth (chpt. bd. dirs., chpt. pres., v.p., treas., pres.-elect). Republican. Avocations: tennis, golf, flying stunt kites, performing contemporary christian music. Home: 1071 Castlerock Ln Cowan Heights CA 92705-6110

**RUTTER, FRANCES TOMPSON,** retired publisher; b. Arlington, Mass., Apr. 12, 1920; d. Harold F. and Mildred F. (Wheeler) Tompson; m. John H. Ottemiller, Mar. 24, 1943; children: Joan Tompson Gillum, John Tompson Ottemiller; m. William D. Rutter, Oct. 26, 1970. AB magna cum laude, Pembroke Coll., Brown U., 1941; postgrad., Mt. Holyoke Coll., 1942—43. Res. book librarian Brown U., 1941-42; annotator ship's papers John Carter Brown Library, Providence, 1944-45; librarian Sci. Service, Washington, 1944-45; ptnr. Shoe String Press, Hamden, Conn., 1952-58; sec., treas. Shoe String Press, Inc., 1958-68, pres., treas., 1968-80, also bd. dirs.; sec.-treas., dir. Tompson-Malone, Inc., book mfrs., 1967-80; pres., treas., dir. Tompson & Rutter, Inc., 1980-89; ret., 1989. V.p. class 1941 Pembroke Coll., 1967-73, 76-91, pres., 1973-76, head class agt., 1979-85, bequests and trust chmn., 1979-90, 40th reunion gift com., 1980, co-chair 50th reunion gift com., 1990-91, 55th reunion gift com., 1995-96; spl. projects adv. panel N.H. Commn. on Arts, 1980-84; mem. natural resources com. Grantham, 1980; mem. Grantham Planning Bd., 1981-87, sec., 1981-83, chmn., 1985-87; chmn. Grantham Recycling Com., 1988-89, Grantham Hist. Soc., 1992-96, Habitat for Humanity-Kearsarge/Sunapee chpt., 1989-94; mem. Diocesan Altar Guild Bd., 1990-93, sec., 1991-92; vol. Mary Hitchcock Meml. Hosp. Aux., 1991-2003; mem. vestry St. Paul's Episc. Ch., 1997-2000, jr. warden, 1998-2000; assoc. Holy Cross Monastery, West Park, N.Y. Mem. Friends of Fernald Libr. of Colby-Sawyer Coll., ACLU (life), LWV (editor newsletter 1987-89), Assoc. Alumni Brown U. (bd. dirs. 1981-83), Nicholas Brown Soc., Pembroke Ctr. Assocs. (coun. 1984-86), Soc. for Preservation N.H. Forests, Episcopal Peace Fellowship, Phi Beta Kappa. Episcopalian. Home: Apt 203 Valley Terrace 2820 Christian St White River Junction VT 05001 Personal E-mail: franbill@valley.net.

**RUTTER, JEREMY BENTHAM,** archaeologist, educator; b. Boston, June 23, 1946; s. Peter and Nancy Kendall (Cornstock) Rutter; m. Sarah Robbins Herndon, Jan. 31, 1970; children: Benjamin Ryerson, Nicholas Kendall. BA in Classics with honors, Haverford Coll., 1967; PhD in Classical Archaeology, U. Pa., 1974; MA, Dartmouth Coll., 1993. Vis. asst. prof. dept. classics UCLA, 1975-76, from asst. prof. to prof. dept. classics, 1976—, prof. humanities, 2001—, chmn. dept. classics, 1992-98, 2003—. Participant excavations, Germany, 1966, Italy, 1968—69, Greece, 1972—75, Greece, 1977, Greece, 78, Greece, 1980—81, Greece, 1984—86, Greece, 1988—89, Greece, 1991—; mem. numerous coms. Am. Sch. Classical Studies, Athens. Author: Lerna III: The Pottery of Lerna IV, 1995; mem. editl. adv. bd. Hesperia, Am. Jour. Archaeology; contbr. articles, revs. to profl. jours. With U.S. Army, 1969—71, Vietnam. Woodrow Wilson fellow, 1967—68, NDEA fellow, U. Pa., 1968—69, 1971—73, NEH Rsch. grantee, 1979—81, Travel grantee, Am. Coun. Learned Socs., 1982, Sr. Faculty grantee, 1985—86, 1991—92, 2001—02. Mem.: Classical Assn. New Eng., Archeol. Inst. Am. (mem. numerous coms., Olivia James Traveling fellow 1974—75), Am. Schs. Oriental Rsch., Phi Beta Kappa. Home: 47 Eagle Rdg Lebanon NH 03766-1900 Office: Dept Classics Dartmouth College Hanover NH 03755-3506 Office Phone: 603-646-2910. E-mail: jeremy.rutter@dartmouth.edu.

**RUTTER, MARSHALL ANTHONY,** lawyer; b. Pottstown, Pa., Oct. 18, 1931; s. Carroll Lennox and Dorothy (Tagert) R.; m. Winifred Hitz, June 6, 1953 (div. 1970); m. Virginia Ann Hardy, Jan. 30, 1971 (div. 1992); children: Deborah Frances, Gregory Russell, Theodore Thomas; m. Terry Susan Knowles, Dec. 19, 1992. BA, Amherst (Mass.) Coll., 1954; JD, U. Pa., 1959. Bar: Calif 1960. Assoc. O'Melveny & Myers, Los Angeles, 1959-64, Flint & MacKay, Los Angeles, 1964-67, ptnr., 1967-72, Rutter Hobbs & Davidoff, Los Angeles, 1973—. Bd. dirs. Ojai Festivals Ltd., 2001, treas., 2004—. Gov. The Music Ctr. of L.A. County, 1978-86, 89-92; bd. dirs. Music Ctr. Operating Co., 1992-96; bd. dirs. Chorus Am., Washington, 1987-96, pres., 1993-95; bd. dirs. L A Master Chorale Assn., 1964 , pres. 1990-92, chmn. 1992-96, vice chmn., 1996-2001; vestryman All Saints Ch., Beverly Hills, Calif., 1983-86, 88-90. Mem. ABA, Assn. Bus. Trial Lawyers (bd. dirs. 1980-82), L.A. County Bar Assn., Beverly Hills Bar Assn., Century City Bar Assn., English-Speaking Union (various offices L.A. chpt. 1963-91), L.A. Jr. C. of C. (bd. dirs. 1964-67). Democrat. Episcopalian. Avocations: classical and choral music, golf, stamp collecting/philately. Home: 1045 S Orange Grove Blvd Apt 10 Pasadena CA 91105-1795 Office: Rutter Hobbs & Davidoff Ste 1700 1901 Ave of Stars Los Angeles CA 90067-6018 Fax: 310-286-1728. Office Phone: 310-286-1700. Business E-Mail: mrutter@rutterhobbs.com.

**RUTTER, MICHAEL LLEWELLYN,** child psychology educator; b. Brummanna, Lebanon, Aug. 15, 1933; arrived in Eng., 1936; s. Llewellyn Charles and Winifred Olive (Barbar) Rutter; m. Marjorie Heys, Dec. 27, 1958; children: Sheila Carol, Stephen Michael, Christine Anne. MB, BChir, U. Birmingham, Eng., 1955, MD with honors, 1963; diploma in psychol. medicine, U. London, 1961; degree (hon.), U. Leiden, 1985, Cath. U., 1990, U. Birmingham, 1990, U. Edinburgh, 1990, U. Chgo., 1993, U. Minn., 1993, U. Ghent, 1994; degree, U. Warwick, 1999, U. East Anglia, 2000, U. North London, 2000, U. York, 2005, U. Oxford, 2005. Various tchg. positions in pediat., neurology, internal, 1955-58; registrar then sr. registrar Maudsley Hosp., London, 1958-62; mem. sci. staff MRC Social Psychiatry Rsch. Unit, London, 1962-65; sr. lectr. then reader U. London Inst. Psychiatry, 1966-73, prof. child psychiatry, 1973-98, hon. dir. MRC Child Psychiatry unit, 1984-98, with Social Genetic and Devel. Psychiatry Rsch. Ctr., 1994—98; prof. devel. psychopathology Inst. Psychiatry, 1998—. Nuffield med. traveling fellow Albert Einstein Coll. Medicine, N.Y.C., 1961-62; fellow Ctr. for Advanced Study in Behavioral Scis., Stanford, Calif., 1979-80; hon. prof. U. Amsterdam, 2001. Author: Helping Troubled Children, 1975, Maternal Deprivation Reassessed, 2nd edit., 1981, (with H. Giller) Juvenile Delinquency: Trends & Perspectives, 1983, (with M. Rutter) Developing Minds: Challenge and Continuity Across the Lifespan, 1993, (with H. Giller, A. Hagell) Antisocial Behavior by Young People, 1998, (with T. Moffitt, A. Caspi and P. Silva) Sex Differences in Antisocial Behavior: Conduct Disorder, Delinquency and Violence in the Dunedin Longitudinal Study, 2001, (with M. Tienda) Ethnicity and Cansa Mechanisms, 2005; co-editor: Autism: A

Reappraisal of Concepts and Treatment, 1978, Stress, Risk and Resilience In Children and Adolescents: Processes, Mechanisms and Interventions, 1994, Development Through Life: A Handbook For Clinicians, 1994, Psychosocial Disorders in Young People: Time Trends & Their Causes, 1995, Antisocial Behavior by Young People, 1998, Child and Adolescent Psychiatry, 4th edit., 2002, Ethnicity and Casual Mechanisms, 2005, Genes & Behavior: Nature-Nurture Interplay Explained, 2006; editor: Scientific Foundations of Developmental Psychiatry, 1980, Developmental Neuropsychiatry, 1983. Recipient Goulstonian lectr. award, Royal Coll. Physicians, 1973, rsch. award, Am. Assn. Mental Deficiency, 1975, Salmon lectr. award, N.Y. Acad. Medicine, 1979, C. Anderson Aldrich award, Am. Acad. Pediat., 1981, Adolf Meyer ward lectr. award, APA, 1985, Disting. Sci. Contbn. award, 1995, Castilla del Pino prize for achievement in psychiatry, Spain, 1995, Lifetime Achievement award, IMFAR, 2002, G. Stanley Hall award, APA, 2003, Marmor award, 2003, Arnold Lucius Gesell prize, 2004, Bronfenbrenner award, 2005, Camille Cosby World of Children award, 2005; fellow, Royal Soc., 1987; Belding travelling scholar, 1963, Rock Carling fellow, 1979. Fellow Royal Soc. Medicine (London, hon.), Royal Coll. Pediat. and Child Health (hon. founding fellow 1996), Royal Coll. Psychiatrists (London, hon.), Kings Coll. London, Brit. Acad.; mem. AAAS (fgn. hon.), Internat. Soc. Rsch. in Child and Adolescent Psychiatry (pres. 1997-99), U.S. Nat. Acad. Edn. (fgn. assoc.), Brit. Pediat. Assn. (hon.), Assn. Child Psychology and Psychiatry (chmn. 1973-74), Brit. Psychol. Soc. (hon. fellow), Am. Acad. Child Psychiatry (hon. membership), NAS (fgn. assoc. Inst. Medicine, Sarnat Internat. prize in mental health 2001), Soc. Rsch. in Adolescence (John P. Hill award for excellence in theory devel. and rsch. 1992), Soc. Rsch. Child Devel. (pres. 1999-2001), Inst. Child Health (London, hon. fellow 1996), Internat. Acad. Rsch. in Learning Disabilities, Academia Europaea (founding mem.), Acad. Med. Scis. (founder, clin. v.p.). Home: 190 Court Ln London SE21 7ED England Office: SGDP Rsch Centre P080 Inst Psychiatry DeCrespigny Park London SE5 8AF England Office Phone: 44 2078480882. Business E-Mail: j.wickham@iop.kcl.ac.uk.

**RUTTER, NATHANIEL WESTLUND,** geologist, educator; b. Omaha, Nov. 22, 1932; s. John Elliot and Karleen (Ludden) R.; m. Mary Marie Munson, Sept. 11, 1961; children: Todd, Christopher. BS, Tufts U., 1955; MS, U. Alaska, 1962; PhD, U. Alta., 1965, DSc honoris causa, 2001. Geologist Venezuelan Atlantic Refining Co., 1955-58; research scientist Geol. Survey Can., Calgary, Alta., 1965-74, head urban projects sect. Ottawa, Ont., 1974; environ. advisor Nat. Energy Bd., Ottawa, 1974-75; assoc. prof. dept. geology U. Alta., Edmonton, 1975-77, 77-80, prof., chmn. dept., 1980-89, 77-96, prof. dept. atmospheric scis., 1996-97, univ. prof., 1997—, assoc. dean. faculty sci.; pres. Can. nat. com. Internat. Geol. Correlation Program, UNESCO, 1996-97. Pres. Internat. Union Quaternary Rsch. Congress, 1982-87; mem. Internat. Geosphere-Biosphere Program: A Study of Global Change, 1988-94; mem. rsch. com. Can. Global Change Program, 1992-94; chmn. global change com. INUQA, 1991-95; hon. prof. Chinese Acad. Sci., Beijing, 1994—; disting. lectr. Sigma Xi, 1995-97; mem. sci. bd. Internat. Union of Geol. Scis.-UNESCO, 1997—. Contbr. numerous articles to profl. jours.; assoc. editor Arctic, Geosci. Can. Quaternary Rsch.; mem. editl. bd. Quaternary Sci. Revs., Quaternary Rsch., Estonia Jour. Sci., Arctic; editor-in-chief Quaternary Internat. Named Officer Order of Can., 2001; recipient Queen's Golden Jubilee medal, 2003, Alberta Centennial medal, 2005; grantee Natural Scis. and Engring. Rsch. Coun. Can., grantee Energy, Mines and Resources. Fellow Royal Soc. Can.; mem. Assn. Profl. Engrs., Geologists and Geophysicists of Alta., Internat. Union Quaternary Rsch. (v.p. 1982-87, pres. 1987-91, hon. 1999), Can. Quaternary Assn. (v.p. 1981-82, Johnston medal 1997), Geol. Soc. Am. (mgmt. bd. dirs. quaternary geol. and geomorphology divsn. 1982-84, Disting. Career award 2003), Geol. Assn. of Can. (J. Willis Ambrose medal 1998), Internat. Assn. Quaternary Rsch. (hon.), Explorer's Club, Cosmos Club. Home: Rural Route 3 Stony Plain AB Canada T7Z 1X3 Office: U Alta Dept Earth & Atmospheric Scis Edmonton AB Canada T6G 2E3 Office Phone: 780-492-3085. E-mail: nat.rutter@ualberta.ca.

**RUTTER, WILLIAM J.,** biochemist, educator; b. Malad City, Idaho, Aug. 28, 1928; s. William H. and Cecilia (Dredge) R.; m. Jacqueline Waddoups, Aug. 31, 1951 (div. Nov. 1969); children: William Henry II, Cynthia Susan; m. Virginia Alice Bourke, 1972 (div. 1978). BA, Harvard U., 1949; MA, U. Utah, 1950; PhD, U. Ill., 1952. USPHS postdoctoral fellow U. Wis., Madison, 1952-54, Nobel Inst., Stockholm, 1954-55; from asst. prof. to prof. biochemistry, dept. chemistry U. Ill., 1955—75; prof. biochemistry and genetics U. Wash., 1975—79; Hertzstein prof. biochemistry U. Calif., San Francisco, chmn. dept. biochemistry and biophysics, 1979—82, dir. Hormone Research Inst., 1983-89. Co-founder, Chiron Corp., 1981, chmn. bd. dirs., 1981-99, chmn. emeritus, 1999-; mem. USPHS Biochemistry and Nutrition Fellowship Panel, 1963-66; cons. physiol. chemistry study sect. NIH, 1967-71; mem. basic sci. adv. exec. com. Nat. Cystic Fibrosis Research Found., 1969-74, chmn., 1972-74, pres.'s adv. council, 1974-75; exec. com. div. biology and agr. NRC, 1969-72; mem. developmental biology panel NSF, 1971-73; mem. biomed. com. Los Alamos Sci. Lab., 1972-75; pres. Pacific Slope Biochem. Conf., 1972-73; mem. bd. sci. counselors Nat. Inst. Environ. Health Scis., 1976—; mem. adv. com. biology div. Oak Ridge Nat. Lab., 1976-80; adv. bd. Oak Ridge Nat. Lab. and Martin-Marietta Energy Systems, 1984-87; basic research adv. com. Nat. Found., 1976—; bd. dirs. Keystone Life Sci. Study Ctr., Meridian Instruments, 1982-88, Hana Biologics, 1980-83; sci. adv. bd. German Ctr. Molecular Biology, U. Heidelberg, 1983—, AMGEN, 1979-81; panel sci. advisors Internat. Ctr. Genetic Engring. and Biotechnology, 1984—; mem. bd. overseers Harvard U., 1990-96, special commn. NSF, 1992, sci. adv. bd. FDA, 1993; chmn., CEO, Synergenics, LLC. Asso. editor: Jour. Exptl. Zoology, 1968-72; editor: PAABS Revista, 1971-76, Jour. Cell Biology, 1976-78, Archives Biochemistry and Biophysics, 1978—, Developmental Genetics, 1979—; editorial bd. various jours; contbr. articles to profl. jours. Served with USNR, 1945; bd. trustee, Carnegie Institution Washington. Guggenheim fellow, 1962-63; recipient Heins award for Tech. and Econ., 1995, Jacob Heskel Gabbay award in Biotechnology and Medicine, 1999, Bower award for Bus. Leadership, Franklin Inst., 2000, Biotechnology Heritage award, 2003. Mem. Am. Soc. Biol. Chemists (treas. 1970-76, mem. editorial bd. jour. 1970-75), Am. Soc. Cell Biology, Am. Chem. Soc. (Pfizer award enzyme chemistry 1967), Am. Soc. Developmental Biology (pres. 1975-76), NAS., Am. Acad. Arts and Sciences. Achievements include patents for; patents pending for: Office: Univ Calif Hormone Rsch Inst San Francisco CA 94143-0001 also: Chiron Corp 4560 Horton St Emeryville CA 94608-2916 Home: 1 Market St San Francisco CA 94105-1521*

**RUTTINGER, GEORGE DAVID,** lawyer; b. Detroit, Jan. 17, 1948; s. George Jacob and Margaret Mary (Smith) R.; m. Camille Ann Larson, Oct. 4, 1975; children: Jacob Charles, David Hayes, Philip George. AB with high distinction and honors, U. Mich., 1970, JD magna cum laude, 1973. Bar: Calif. 1975, D.C. 1975, U.S. Dist. Ct. D.C. 1975, U.S. Dist. Ct. Md. 1987, U.S. Ct. Appeals (D.C. and 4th cirs.) 1984, U.S. Ct. Appeals (1st cir.) 1988, U.S. Supreme Ct. 1984, U.S. Dist. Ct. (ea. dist.) Mich. 1995, U.S. Ct. Appeals (6th cir.) 1996, U.S. Ct. Appeals (3d cir.) 1999, U.S. Ct.Appeals (9th cir.) 2002. Law clk. to Hon. Malcolm R. Wilkey U.S. Ct. Appeals, Washington, 1973-74; assoc. Latham & Watkins, L.A., 1974, Crowell & Moring LLP (formerly Jones, Day, Reavis & Pogue), Washington, 1975-79, ptnr., 1980—. Author: (with others) Containing Legal Costs: ADR Strategies for Corporations, Law Firms and Government, 1988; contbr. articles to profl. jours. Fellow Am. Bar Found. Office: Crowell & Moring LLP 1001 Pennsylvania Ave NW Fl 10 Washington DC 20004-2595 Office Phone: 202-624-2670. Business E-Mail: gruttinger@crowell.com.

**RUTZ, RICHARD FREDERICK,** physicist, researcher; b. Alton, Ill., Feb. 9, 1919; s. Erwin William and Esther Norma (Brooks) R.; m. Mary Lamsom Lambert, June 10, 1945; children— Frederick R., Carl R., William L. BA, Shurtleff Coll., Alton, Ill., 1941; MS, State U. Iowa, 1947. Staff mem. Sandia Corp., Albuquerque, 1948-51; mem. staff, mgr. IBM T.J. Watson Sr. Rsch. Ctr., Yorktown Heights, NY, 1951-87. Contbr. articles to profl. jours.; patentee semicond. devices With U.S. Maritime Svc., 1941-42, USAAF, 1942-46. Fellow IEEE; mem. Am. Phys. Soc. Home: 601 Horizon Pl Apt 204 Grand Junction CO 81506 E-mail: rfrutz@frontier.net.

**RUUD, CLAYTON OLAF,** engineering educator; b. Glasgow, Mont., July 31, 1934; s. Asle and Myrtle (Bleken) R.; children: Kelley Astrid, Kirsten Anne; m. Paula Kay Mannino, Feb. 24, 1990. BS in Metallurgy, Wash. State U., 1957; MS in Materials Sci., San Jose State U., 1967; PhD in Materials Sci., U. Denver, 1970. Registered profl. engr., Calif., Colo. Asst. remelt metallurgist Kaiser Aluminum & Chem. Corp., Trentwood, Wash., 1957-58; devel. engr. Boeing Airplane Co., Seattle, 1958-60; mfg. rsch. engr. Lockheed Missiles & Space Corp., Sunnyvale, Calif., 1960-63; rsch. engr. FMC Corp., San Jose, 1963-67; sr. rsch. scientist U. Denver, 1967-79; prof. indsl. engring. Pa. State U., University Park, 1979—. Founder, developer, and co-director of quality and manufacturing management masters degree Pa. State U.; cons. in field; bd. dirs. Denver X-Ray Inst. Inc., Altoona, Pa. Editor series: Advances in X-Ray Analysis, Vol. 12-22, 1970-80, Nondestructive Character of Materials, Vol. 1-6, 1983-1996; editor X-Ray Spectometry, 1975-87; editl. com. Nondestructive Testing and Evaluation, 1991-1995; contbr. chpts. to books. Chmn. Nat. Acad. Sci. Safe Drinking Water Com., Washington, 1976-78. Recipient IR 100 award, 1983, Gov.'s New Product Award, Pa. Soc. Profl. Engrs., 1988. Fellow ASM Internat. (chmn. Resid. Stress Conf. 1989-91); mem. Internat. Ctr. for Diffraction Data, Soc. Mfg. Engrs., Metall. Soc. of AIME. Achievements include patents in x-ray analysis and residual stress measurement; invention of fiber optic based position sensitive scintillation X-ray detector, instrument for simultaneous stress and phase composition measurement; development of an X-ray diffraction instrument for manufacturing process quality control. Office: 9116 East Sprague Ave #336 Spokane WA 99206-3601 Business E-Mail: cor1@psu.edu.

**RUURS, MARGRIET,** writer; m. Kees Ruurs; children: Alexander, Arnout. MEd, Simon Fraser U., 1998. Author Boyds Mills Press, Tundra Books, Fitzhenry & Whiteside, Whitecap Books; guest lectr. Iowa Writing Project. Spkr. in field. Author: (book) Emma's Eggs (Storytellers World Honor Title), A Pacific Alphabet, When We Go Camping, Wild Babies, Emma at the Fair, A Mountain Alphabet, My Librarian is a Camel, Animal Alphabed, Emma & The Coyote (Silver Seal, Mr. Christie award), Emma's Cold Day, (novels) Big Little Dog, Logan's Lake, (educational text) The Power of Poems, (book of poetry) Virtual Maniac. Recipient Storytellers World Honor Title, Internat. Reading Coun., 1997, Presdl. Award for Reading & Tech., Internat. Reading Assn., 2005. Mem.: Writers Union of Can., Can. Soc. of Children's Authors and Illustrators, Soc. of Children's Book Writers and Illustrators, Internat. Reading Assn. Home: Box 2 Shedd OR 97377 Personal E-mail: margriet@margrietruurs.com.

**RUVIELLA-KNORR, JEANNE L.,** music educator, consultant, clinician; d. Jean and Marion Post Ruviella; m. H. Richard Knorr, May 26, 1962 (div. Dec. 24, 1993); children: Richard Post Knorr, Michelle Renee Mitchell. MusB, Boston U., 1962; MA, U. So. Calif., 1966; PhD, U. Md., 2004. Cert. advanced profl. cert. tchg. Md., Dalcroze cert. Longy Sch., Dalcroze-Orff-Kodaly cert. Manhattan Sch. Music. Music tchr. L.A. Pub. Schs., 1962—66, Burlington Pub. Schs., Vt.; prof. music edn. Shelton Coll., Cape Canaveral, Fla., 1968—74; music tchr., cons. Anne Arundel County Pub. Schs., Severna Park, Md., 1974—79; prof. music edn. Towson (Md.) U., 1979—97, prof. emerita, 1997—; prof. music edn. Frostburg (Md.) State U., 1999—2000; tchr. music Harford County Schs., Abingdon, Md., 2000—06, Clinician Towson U., 1994—, developer Grad. Dalcroze-Orff-Kodaly Cert. program, co-dir. Dalcroze-Orff-Kodaly Cert. program, 1981—97, adj. faculty Dalcroze-Orff-Kodaly Cert. program, 1997—; cons. in field. Contbg. author: music series Share the Music, Grades 7-8, 1996—2005, Music and You, Grades 7-8, 1989—2005, co-compiler: keyboard proficiency packet for Towson U., rev. Leader women's support groups Chapelgate Ch., Marriottsville, Md., 2000—. Mem.: Md. Music Educators Assn., Music Educators Nat. Conf. (clinician 1983—87, 2000). Avocations: travel, music. Personal E-mail: ruviella@comcast.net.

**RUWE, ROBERT PAUL,** federal judge; b. OH, 1941; Grad., Xavier U., 1963; JD, No. Ky. U., 1970. Spl. agent intelligence divsn. IRS, US Dept. Treasury, Washington, 1963—70, chief counsel, 1970-87; judge U.S. Tax Ct., Washington, 1987—2002, sr. judge, 2002—. Office: US Tax Ct 400 2nd St NW Washington DC 20217-0002

**RUXIN, PAUL THEODORE,** lawyer; b. Cleve., Apr. 14, 1943; s. Charles and Olyn Judith (Koller) R.; m. Joanne Camy, May 25, 1965; children: Marc J., Sarah. BA, Amherst Coll., 1965; LLB, U. Va., 1968. Bar: Ill. 1968, U.S. Dist. Ct. (no. dist.) Ill. 1968, U.S. Ct. Appeals D.C. 1972. Assoc. Isham, Lincoln & Beale, Chgo., 1968—73, ptnr., 1974—77; ptnr., chmn. energy utilities sect. Jones Day, Cleve., 1977—2005, of counsel, 2006—. Mem. editl. com. Yale U. edit. Boswell Papers, 2003—. Mem. Hudson Archtl. and Hist. Bd. Rev., 1981-87; mem. bd. govs. Folger Shakespeare Libr., 1999—; exec. bd. Greater Cleve. Boy Scouts Am., 1978-90; bd. dirs. Cleve. chpt. ARC, 1991-97. Mem. ABA, Bar Assn. Greater Cleve., Fed. Energy Bar Assn. (com. chmn. 1981), Chgo. Bar Assn., Rowfant Club, Caxton Club, Grolier Club, Chgo. Lit. Club. Office: Jones Day 77 W Wacker Dr Fl 35 Chicago IL 60601-1662 also: 901 Lakeside Ave Cleveland OH 44114-1116 Office Phone: 312-782-3939. E-mail: paultruxin@jonesday.com.

**RUXIN, ROBERT H.,** lawyer; b. 1953; Grad. with honors, Princeton U.; JD with honors, Harvard Law Sch. V.p. and gen. counsel Kazmaier Assoc., Inc., 1986—. Venue legal counsel Foxboro Stadium, World Cup, 1994; mng. dir. NCAA Internat., 1992—98; guest commentator Nat. Pub. Radio; bd. mem. Sports Lawyers Assn.; dir. Princeton Assn. New England, Jewish Major Leaguers, Inc. Author: An Athletes Guide to Agents, 2004. Avocations: coaching baseball, coaching basketball, coaching soccer. Office: 12100 Sunset Hills Rd Ste 130 Reston VA 20190 Office Phone: 703-437-4377.

**RUYLE-HULLINGER, ELIZABETH SMITH (BETH RUYLE),** municipal financial advisor, consultant; b. Oct. 26, 1946; d. Daniel Lester and Mae (Coley) Smith; m. Craig Harlan Hullinger, Oct. 24, 1985; children: Leigh Ann Ruyle, Clint (dec.), Bret AA, St. Petersburg Jr. Coll., 1966; BA English, U. Fla., 1968; MPA, U. Ga., 1975. Rsch. asst. Emory U., Atlanta, 1969—70; health planner Met. Coun. for Health, Atlanta, 1960—72; coord. govtl. rels. Atlanta Regional Commn., 1972—76, coord. govtl. affairs, 1976—78; exec. dir. South Suburban Mayors' and Mgrs. Assn., East Hazel Crest, Ill., 1978—2000; pres. Chgo. Southland Econ. Devel. Alliance, 1990—2000; exec. v.p., dir. Ehlers & Assocs., Lisle, Ill., 1988—. Exec. dir. South Towns Agy. Risk Mgmt., 1980-98, South Towns Area Benefits Coop., 1983-89, South Towns Bus. Growth Corp., 1983-90; cons. Planning Devel. Svc., Tinley Park, Ill., 1986—Contbr. articles to profl. and devel. mags Mem. World's Fair Adv. Com., Chgo., 1986, Met. Planning Coun., 1990-2000, Cook County Tax Reform adv. coun., South Suburban Arts Coun., 1987, Coun. Urban Econ. Devel., 1986; adv. coun. Urban Innovations, Chgo., 1995-2000, Chgo. Assembly Project, 1995-2000; mem. Regional Partnership, 1985-2000; bd. dirs. South Suburban Hosp., 1987-96, mem. governing coun., 1993-2000; bd. dirs. Fin. Cmty. Devel. Corp., 1998-2000 Mem. Internat. City Mgmt. Assn., Ill. City Mgmt. Assn., Met. City Mgrs. Assn., Ill. Govtl. Fin. Officers Assn., Ill. Tax Increment Assn., Lambda Alpha Methodist. Home: 17255 66th Ct Tinley Park IL 60477-3501 Office: Ehlers & Assocs 550 Warrenville Rd Ste 220 Lisle IL 60532-5500 Office Phone: 630-271-3330. Business E-Mail: bruyle@ehlers-inc.com.

**RUYTER, NANCY LEE CHALFA,** dance educator; b. Phila., May 23, 1933; d. Andrew Benedict Chalfa and Lois Elizabeth (Strode) McClary; m. Ralph Markson (div.); m. Hans C. Ruyter, Dec. 7, 1968 (dec. Jan. 1998). BA in History, U. Calif., Riverside, 1964; PhD in History, Claremont Grad. Sch., 1970. Tchr. theater dept. Pomona Coll., 1965-72; instr. dance program U. Calif., Riverside, 1974-76, acting chair dance program, 1974-75; instr. dance dept. UCLA, 1976; instr. phys. edn. dept. Orange Coast Coll., 1976-77; asst. prof. dept. phys. edn. and dance Tufts U., 1977-78; asst. prof. phys. edn. dept. Calif. State U., Northridge, 1978-82; from asst. prof. to full prof. dance dept. U. Calif., Irvine, 1982—, assoc. dean Sch. Fine Arts, 1984-88, 95-96, chair dept. dance, 1989-91. Presenter in field. Appeared with Jasna Planina Folk Ensemble, 1972-77, 78-79, Di Falco and Co., 1955-57; choreographer, dir. numerous coll. dance prodns.; contbr. articles, revs. to profl. publs.; author:

Reformers and Visionaries: The Americanization of the Art of Dance, 1979, The Cultivation of Body and Mind in Nineteenth-Century American Delsartism, 1999. Mem. Am. Soc. Theatre Rsch., Bulgarian Studies Assn., Congress on Rsch. in Dance (bd. dirs. 1977-80, 2003-, pres. 1981-85), Folk Dance Fedn., Internat. Fedn. Theatre Rsch., Soc. Dance Rsch., Soc. Ethnomusicology, Soc. Dance History Scholars (steering com. 1980-81), Spanish Dance Soc., Theatre Libr. Assn. Office: U Calif Dept Dance Irvine CA 92697-2775 Office Phone: 949-824-7284. Business E-Mail: nlruyter@uci.edu.

**RUZEK, SHERYL KENDRA BURT,** healthcare educator, sociologist; b. French Camp, Calif., June 15, 1945; d. Frederick Dent and DeEtta Hamsher Burt; m. James Richard Griesemer, July 15, 1989; 1 child, Jennifer Yael. MPH, U. Calif. Sch. Pub. Health, Berkeley, 1980—82; PhD, U. Calif., Davis, 1968—77. Continuing edn. specialist U. Calif., San Francisco 1977—81, adj. assoc. prof. sociology, 1983—85; prof. pub. health and women's studies Temple U., Phila., 1985—, acting dean Grad. Sch., 2000—02, co-dir. Ctr. for Women's Health Rsch., Leadership and Advocacy, 2005—. Chair bd. dir. Coalition Med. Rights Women, San Francisco, 1979—80; vice-chair bd. trustees Emer. Care Rsch. Inst., Plymouth Meeting, Pa., 1998—; bd. mem. and co-chair com. health comm. Coun. Accredited MPH Programs, Washington, 2000—; mem. working group on health comm. Office Disease Prevention and Health Promotion U.S. Dept. Health and Human Svcs., Rockville, Md., 2003—. Author: The Women's Health Movement. Feminist Alternatives to Medical Control, 1978; contbg. editor: Women's Health: Complexities and Differences, 1997; co-editor (with Irving Zola): Health, Society and Policy Series; contbr. chapters to books, reviews, articles to profl. jours. Mem. rsch., policy and advocacy com. Maternity Care Coalition, Phila., 1989—2000; coun. mem. Trinity-Lansdowne United Meth. Ch., 2000—. Recipient Gt. Tchr. award, Temple U., 1996, citation Devel. Primary Care, Kiev, Ukraine, Am. Internat. Health Alliance and U.S. AID, 1999—2004; fellow, NSF, 1968—70, Nat. Heart Blood and Lung Inst., 1981—83, Temple U., 1988, 1994, 1996; grantee, Fund Improvement of Post-Secondary Edn., 1983—86, Carnegie Found. and Am. Sociol. Assn., 1975, NIH Nat. Heart, Blood & Lung Inst., 1984—86, U.S. Office Edn., 1990—93, Pa. State Dept. Health, 2004—. Mem.: APHA, Nat. Women's Health Network (charter mem.). Unitarian Universalist. Avocations: gardening, vintage dancing. Office Phone: 215-204-3718. E-mail: sruzek@temple.edu.

**RYABY, JAMES THOMAS,** pharmaceutical executive, cellular biologist; b. Passaic, NJ, Nov. 5, 1958; s. John Peter and Louise Ryaby; children: John Peter, Eloise Helle. PhD, Mt. Sinai Sch. Medicine, NY, 1991. Dir. rsch. OrthoLogic Corp, Phoenix, 1991—97, v.p. rsch. and clin. affairs Tempe, Ariz., 1997—2003, sr. v.p. rsch. and clin. affairs, chief sci. officer, 2003—. Contbr. articles to profl. jours. Recipient Best Presentation award, Internat. Soc. for Fracture Repair, 1994. Mem.: Internat. Bone and Mineral Soc., Am. Acad. Orthop. Surgeons, Orthop. Rsch. Soc., Am. Soc. for Bone and Mineral Rsch. Achievements include research in fracture and bone repair. Avocations: fishing, tennis, skiing, food and wine. Home: 9721 N 118th Way Scottsdale AZ 85259 Office: OrthoLogic Corp 1275 W Washington St Tempe AZ 85281 Office Phone: 602-286-5326. Office Fax: 602-926-2617. Business E-Mail: jryaby@olgc.com.

**RYALL, JO-ELLYN M.,** psychiatrist; b. Newark, May 25, 1949; d. Joseph P. and Tekla (Paraszczuk) R. BA in Chemistry with gen. honors, Rutgers U., 1971; MD. Washington U., St. Louis, 1975. Diplomate Am. Bd. Psychiatry and Neurology. Resident in psychiatry Washington U., St. Louis, 1975-78, psychiatrist Student Health, 1978-83, asst. prof. clin. psychiatry, 1983—2003, assoc. prof. clin. psychiatry, 2003—. Inpatient supr. Malcolm Bliss Mental Health Ctr., St. Louis, 1978-80, pvt. practtice medicine specializing in psychiatry, St. Louis, 1980—. Bd. dirs. Women's Self Help Ctr., St. Louis, 1980. Fellow: APA (pres. ea. Mo. dist. br. 1983-85, sect. coun. AMA 1986—99, dep. rep. to assembly 1994—97, rep. 1997—2001, chair bylaws com. 2000—03, dep. rep. area 4 2001—06, rep. area 4 2006); mem.: AMA (alt. del. Mo. 1988—90, 1993—94, del. 1995—, mem. coun. on constn. bylaws 1998—2006, vice chair 2002—04, chair 2004—06), Manic Depressive Assn. St. Louis (chmn. bd. dirs. 1985—89), Mo. State Med. Assn. (vice spkr. ho. of dels. 1986—89, spkr. 1989—92), St. Louis Met. Med. Soc. (del. to state conv. 1981—86, councilor 1985—87, v.p. 1989, del. to state conv. 1993—), Am. Med. Women's Assn. (pres. St. Louis dist. br. 1981—82, regional gov. VIII 1986—89, pres. St. Louis dist. br. 1992, spkr. ho. of dels. 1993—96), Washington U. Faculty Club. Office: 12166 Old Big Bend Rd Ste 210 Saint Louis MO 63122 Office Phone: 314-909-0121.

**RYAN, ALLAN ANDREW, JR.,** lawyer, director, educator, writer; b. Cambridge, Mass., July 3, 1945; s. Allan Andrew and Anne (Conway) Ryan; m. Nancy Foote, June 30, 1978; children: Elizabeth, Andrew. AB, Dartmouth Coll., 1966; JD magna cum laude, U. Minn., 1970. Bar: DC 1972, Mass. 1985. Law clk. to assoc. justice Byron R. White U.S. Supreme Ct., 1970-71; assoc. Williams, Connolly & Califano, Washington, 1974-77; asst. to Solicitor Gen. U.S., Washington, 1977-80; dir. office of spl. investigations, Dept. Justice, Washington, 1980-83, spl. asst. to atty. gen., 1983; pvt. practice law, 1983-85; with office of gen. counsel, Harvard U., 1985—2001; dir. intellectual property Harvard Bus. Sch., 2001—. Presenting counsel Internat. Commn. Inquiry on Kurt Waldheim, London, 1988; adj. prof. Boston Coll. Law Sch., 1989—, Harvard U., 1997—. Author: Quiet Neighbors: Prosecuting Nazi War Criminals in America, 1984; pres., editor-in-chief: Minn. Law Rev., 1969—70. Mem. exec. com. New Eng. region Anti-Defamation League, 1990—, mem. nat. commn., 2004—; chair Ctr. Civil Rights and Pub. Policy, 2003—; bd. dirs. Facing History and Ourselves Nat. Found., 1985—92; mem. adv. bd. Holocaust and human rights rsch. project Boston Coll. Law Sch., 1984—. Capt. USMC, 1971—74. Recipient Internat. Human Rights award, Anti-Defamation League, 1986, Leadership award, 1997, 2005. Mem.: ABA, Boston Bar Assn. Office: Harvard Bus Sch Publ 60 Harvard Way Boston MA 02163 Office Phone: 617-783-7849. Business E-Mail: allan_ryan@harvard.edu.

**RYAN, ANTONY L.,** lawyer; b. July 21, 1971; BA summa cum laude, Yale Univ., 1992; JD magna cum laude, Harvard Univ., 1995. Bar: Mass. 1995, NY 1997. Law clk., Hon. Judith W. Rogers US Ct. of Appeals, DC Cir.; assoc. Cravath Swaine & Moore LLP, NYC, 1996—2003, ptnr., litig., 2003—. Supervising editor Harvard Law Rev. Mem.: Fed. Bar Coun. Am. Inn of Ct., Phi Beta Kappa. Office: Cravath Swaine & Moore LLP Worldwide Plz 825 Eighth Ave New York NY 10019-7475 Office Phone: 212-474-1296. Office Fax: 212-474-3700. Business E-Mail: aryan@cravath.com.

**RYAN, ARTHUR FREDERICK,** insurance company executive; b. Bklyn., Sept. 14, 1942; s. Arthur Vincent and Gertrude (Wingert) R.; m. Patricia Elizabeth Kelly; children: Arthur, Kelly Ann, Kevin, Kathleen. BA in Math., Providence Coll., 1963, D (hon.) of bus. adminstrn., 1994; student, Am. Coll., 1963—65; LHD (hon.), Dowling Coll.; DSc, NJ Inst. Tech., 2005. Area mgr. Control Data Corp., Washington, 1965-72; project mgr. data processing divsn. Chase Manhattan Corp., NYC, 1972-73, 2d v.p., 1973-74, v.p., 1974—77, sr. v.p., 1977—82, exec. v.p., 1978-82, exec. v.p. corp. ops. and systems, 1982—84, exec. v.p. individual banking, 1984, head worldwide retail bank, 1984—90, vice chmn., 1985—90, pres., COO, 1990—94; pres., CEO, chmn. Prudential Ins. Co. Am., Newark, 1994—99; (Prudential Ins. Co. Am. incorporated to become Prudential Fin., Inc., 1999); pres. Prudential Fin., Inc., Newark, 1999—, pres., CEO, chmn., 2000—. Bd. dirs. Regeneron Pharmaceuticals, 2003—. Bd. trustees Providence Coll., 1992—, NY Presbyn. Hosp.; nat. bd. Local Initiatives Support Coalition; bd. dirs. New Am. Schools; co-chair Achieve, Inc., NJ United for Higher Sch. Standards, NJ Performing Arts Ctr. Lt. U.S. Army, 1963—65. Co-recipient (with wife) Pelican award for Corp. and Cmty. Leadership, St. Vincent's Coal., 2001, (with wife) Inaugural Cmty. Leadership award, NJ Performing Arts Ctr. Women's Bd. Assn., 2002; recipient Nat. Alumni Personal Achievement Award, Providence Coll., 75th Anniversary Alumni Service Award, Diamond Anniversary Award, Keeper of the Dream award, Nat. Action Network, 2000, Patterson Award, United Negro Coll. Fund/The Coll. Fund, 2000, Pub. Svc. award, NJ State CofC,

2001, Medal of Life award, PIUS XII Found., 2001, Cir. of Life Award, Million Dollar Round Table Found., 2002. Mem.: Am. Bankers Assn. Office: Prudential Fin Inc Prudential Plaza 24th Fl 751 Broad St Newark NJ 07102-3714*

**RYAN, B.J.,** professional baseball player; b. Bossier City, La., Dec. 28, 1975; Attended, SW La. Univ. Relief pitcher Cincinnati Reds, 1999, Balt. Orioles, 1999—2005, Toronto Blue Jays, 2005—. Office: Rogers Centre One Blue Jays Way Toronto M5V 1J1 Canada*

**RYAN, CANDACE I.,** writer, director, editor; d. Lilburn Terry and Maureen Adell Ryan; children: Elizabeth Maureen Solomon, Virginia Violet Hildenbrand. AA in human rels., Bridgeport U., 1978. BA in journalism, Rice U., 1965—68. Human Relations-Death & Life. Abused Woman & Children of CT, 1978. Adv. bd. Barrington Rev. of the Arts, Westport, Conn., 1976—85; councilor Inner Cities Volunteers of CT., Stamford, Conn., 1976—89; asst dir. & advisor CT. Commn. on the Arts, Westport, Conn., 1977—89. Roving writer Family & Moral Issues, Sacremento, Calif., 1993—. Author: Detecting! The Midnight Tattler, over 20 novels, 14 short stories. Travel industry rep. State Dept. Amb. of Peace, India, Africa, China, numerous countries, Madagascar, 1978—89; sec. World Wildlife Found., San Diego, 1990—93; asst. advisor Women & Children Outreach Org., Sacramento, 1991—2003; asst. editor Wolferts Retreat Ctr. for the Arts, Stamford, Conn., 1980—90. Recipient Journalism Excellence, Fairfield U., 1982, 6 Poetry awards, 1976—2004; Louis Webber grant, Century Acceptance Assoc., 1990—92. Fellow: Mystery Writers Assoc. (corr.; sr. writer 2000); mem.: Beta Corp. Agy. Consortium (v.p. 1981—91), US Travel Industry (rep. China 1984, Israel 1985, France 1986), Quota Club Internat. (sec. 1984—88), Eagles Club of Am. (corr.; mem. 2000, Volunteers above and Beyond the Call of Duty 2001). Republican. Bapt. Achievements include research in Human Relations-Death & Survivors. Avocations: writing, reading, camping, travel. Home: 1419 Eckman Ave Chula Vista CA 91911 Office: Ghost & Creative Writers Co 1419 Eckman Ave Chula Vista CA 91911

**RYAN, CAROL J.,** educational administrator; b. Niagara Falls, N.Y., June 13, 1939; d. Samuel Battaglia and Josephine Latona; m. John W. Ryan, Sept. 17, 1960; children: James, Kathleen, John Jr., Michael. BA, Niagara Univ. 1960; MEd, George Mason U., 1980. Cert. reading specialist emotional distbr., mental retardation K-12, specific lang. disabilities pre-K-12. Special edn. cons. Mass. Dept. of Youth Svcs., Worcester, Mass., 1982—84; edn. liaison Bureau of Instl. Schs., Westboro, Mass., 1986—87; edn. coord. Univ. Mass Med. Ctr., Westboro, Mass., 1987—98; edn. dir. Found. Sch., Alexandria, Va., 1998—2003, Largo, Md., 2003—. Mem.: Coun. of Exceptional Children. Office: The Found Sch 1330 McCormick Dr Largo MD 20774

**RYAN, CLARENCE AUGUSTINE, JR.,** biochemistry professor; b. Butte, Mont., Sept. 29, 1931; s. Clarence A. Sr. and Agnes L. (Duckham) R.; m. Patricia Louise Meunier, Feb. 8, 1936; children: Jamie Arlette, Steven Michael (dec.), Janice Marie, Joseph Patrick (dec.). BA in Chemistry, Carroll Coll., 1953; MS in Chemistry, Mont. State U., 1956, PhD in Chemistry, 1959; PhD (hon.), Wash. State U., 2005. Postdoctoral fellow in biochemistry Oreg. State U., Corvallis, 1959-61, U.S. Western Regional Lab., Albany, Calif., 1961-63; chemist USDA, Albany, 1963-64; asst. prof. biochemistry Wash. State U., Pullman, 1964-68, assoc. prof., 1968-72, prof., 1972—, Charlotte Y. Martin disting. prof., 1991—, chmn. dept. agrl. chemistry, 1977-80, fellow Inst. Biol. Chemistry, 1980—. Faculty athletics rep. to PAC-10 & NCAA Wash. State U., 1991-94, 96-97; vis. scientist dept. biochemistry U. Wash., 1981; vis. scientist Harvard U. Med. Sch., 1982, Bert and Natalie Vallee vis. prof., 1997; res. adv. bd. Kemin Industries, Des Moines, 1981—, Plant Genetics, Davis, Calif., 1987-89; rsch. adv. bd. Frito-Lay, Inc., Dallas, 1982, Plant Genetic Engring. Lab., N.Mex. State U., Las Cruces, 1986-89, Noble Found., 1996-2002; mem. NRC rev. bd. Plant Gene Exptl. Ctr., Albany, 1990-93; mgr. biol. stress program USDA Competitive Grants Program, Washington, 1983-84; former mem. adv. panels for H. McKnight Found., Internat. Potato Ctr., Lima, Peru, Internat. Ctr. Genetic Engring. and Biotech., New Delhi, Internat. Ctr. Tropical Agr., Cali, Colombia, Internat. Tropical Agr., Ibandan, Africa; mem. grant rev. panels NSF, USDA, DOE, NIH; co-organizer Internat. Telecom. Symposium on Plant Biotech.; mem. adv. bd. Bert and Natalie Vallee Found., Harvard Med. Sch., 1997-2000; bd. dirs. New Biology, San Francisco. Mem. editl. bd. several biochem. and plant physiology jours.; contbr. articles to profl. publs., chpts. to books; co-editor 2 books Trustee Carroll Coll., Helena, Mont., 1998-2002; mem. rsch. adv. bd. Danforth Plant Sci. Ctr., St. Louis, 1998-2005. Grantee USDA, NSF, NIH, Rockefeller Found., McKnight Found.; recipient Merck award for grad. rsch. Mont. State U., 1959, Alumni Achievement award Carroll Coll., 1986, Pres.'s Faculty Excellence award in rsch. Wash. State U., 1986; named to Carroll Coll. Alumni Hall of Fame, 1981, Carroll Coll. Basketball Hall of Fame, 1982; named 1 of 100 centennial disting. alumni Mont. State. U., 1993; Career Devel. grantee NIH, 1964-74, non-resident fellow Noble Found., 1996-2002. Fellow Am. Acad. Microbiology; mem. AAAS, NAS (elected 1986), Am. Chem. Soc. (Kenneth A. Spencer award 1992), Am. Soc. Plant Physiologists (Steven Hales prize 1992), Am. Soc. Exptl. Biology, Biochem. Soc., Am. Peptide Soc., Internat. Soc. Chem. Ecology (Silverstein-Simione award 1997), Internat. Soc. Plant Molecular Biology (bd. dirs.), Phytochem. Soc. N.Am., Nat. U. Continuing Assn. (Creative Programming award 1991), Phi Kappa Phi (Recognition award 1976). Democrat. Avocations: fishing, basketball, golf, ice skating. Office: Wash State Univ Inst Biol Chemistry Pullman WA 99164-0001 Office Phone: 509-335-3304. Personal E-mail: cabudryan@hotmail.com.

**RYAN, CYNTHIA RHOADES,** lawyer; b. Wilmington, Del., Feb. 6, 1954; d. Harry Edris and Patricia Irene (Dux) Rhoades; m. John G. Christfield, Aug. 6, 1977 (div. 1984); m. Matthew C. Ryan, Oct. 10, 1993. BA in Polit. Sci., U. Del., 1976; JD, Widener U., 1979. Bar: Del. 1979, U.S. Supreme Ct. 1989. Dep. atty. gen. State of Del., Wilmington, 1979-85; staff counsel permanent subcom. investigations U.S. Senate, Washington, 1985-87; trial atty. criminal div. U.S. Dept. Justice, Washington, 1987-88, sr. atty. DEA, 1988-91, assoc. chief counsel internat. law sect., 1991-96; chief counsel Office of the Chief Counsel, Drug Enforcement Administrn., 1996—. Mem. ABA, Del. Bar Assn., Internat. Assn. of Chiefs of Police, Alpha Sigma Alpha. Avocations: sports, gardening, gourmet cooking, piano, tenor banjo. Business E-Mail: cynthia.r.ryan@usdoj.gov.

**RYAN, DANIEL JOHN,** university administrator; b. Buffalo, June 5, 1960; s. Michael E. and Joan F. R.; m. Sandra Suffoleto, Aug. 19, 1989. BA in Pol. Sci., Canisius Coll., Buffalo, 1982, MS in Edn., 1992; PhD in Edn., SUNY, Buffalo, 1997. Fin. cons. First Albany Corp., Buffalo, 1982-84; confidential investigator County of Erie, Buffalo, 1984-87; econ. mkt. analyst City of Buffalo, Buffalo, 1987-90; asst. dir. career planning Canisius Coll., Buffalo, 1990-97, asst. dean students svcs., 1997—; dir. career planning and placement SUNY, Buffalo. Lectr. Buffalo and Erie County Pub. Libr., Buffalo, 1990—; dir. career planning and placement SUNY Buffalo. Author: A Job Search Handbook for People with Disabilities. Pres. Univ. Dist. N. Buffalo Civic Assn., Buffalo, 1990-91; v.p. Kiwanis Club of N. Buffalo, 1987-88; vice chmn. City of Buffalo rep. Com., 1989-91, sec. 1993-95; chmn. Delaware Ward Rep. Com., 1985-91. Recipient Edward A. Parish award, Ea. Assn. Colls. and Employers. Mem. Nat. Assn. Student Personnel Administrn.(region II Outstanding New Profl.), N. Buffalo Community Devel. Corp., Assn. for Higher Edn. and Disabilities. Republican. Avocations: reading, raquetball. E-mail: dryan@buffalo.edu.

**RYAN, DAVID ALAN,** systems analyst; b. Cin., Nov. 13, 1961; s. James Patrick and Virginia Ann (Stewart) R. BS, Wright State U., 1983; MS, Tex. A&M U., 1988. Statistician U.S. Bur. of Census, Washington, 1988-92, computer specialist, 1992—. Vol. math. modeling Soil Conservation Svc., Washington, 1991-96; math. and probability vol. Washington Opera, 1992—; data entry/programming vol. Opera Am., Washington, 1990-91; hist. rschr. Gasby's Tavern Mus., Alexandria, Va., 1991-94; mem. Bravo! for the Washington Opera, 1991-95. Recipient Vol. Svc. award Soil Conservation Svc., 1992, 93. Mem. Am. Statis. Assn., Capitol PC Users Group, Ballston-

Va. Square Civic Assn. (exec. com. 1995—, sec. 1996—, NCAC rep. 1997-98), The Washington Opera Guild, The Washington Opera Camerata, The DC Wagner Soc. Achievements include building a supercomputer at home in 2000. Avocations: classical music, ethnomusicology, history, geography, travel. Office: Bur of Census/CES Ste 208 Washington Plz II Washington DC 20233-6300

**RYAN, DAVID THOMAS,** lawyer; b. Torrington, Conn., Apr. 18, 1939; s. Edward John and Margaret (Murphey) R.; m. Dale Anderson, Aug. 21, 1965; children: Rachael Anderson, Conor Anne. BS, U. Md., 1961; LLB, Georgetown U., 1965. Bar: Conn. 1966, U.S. Dist. Ct. Conn. 1967, U.S. Ct. Appeals (2d cir.) 1969, U.S. Ct. Appeals (fed. cir.) 1982, U.S. Claims Ct. 1983, U.S. Supreme Ct. 1992. Ptnr. Cooney, Scully & Dowling, Hartford, Conn., 1966-77, Robinson & Cole, Hartford, 1977—. Fellow Am. Coll. Trial Lawyers; mem. Am. Bd. Trial Advs., Conn. Trial Lawyers Assn. (bd. dirs.). Home: 126 Westerly Ter Hartford CT 06105-1117 Office: Robinson & Cole 280 Trumbull St Ste 26 Hartford CT 06103-3509 Office Phone: 203-275-8200. E-mail: dryan@rc.com.

**RYAN, DELORIS KAY,** elementary school educator; b. Fredericksburg, Iowa, Nov. 18, 1951; d. Lester Ernest and Marion Marie (Mellmann) Mahlstedt; m. Steven Joseph Ryan, July 23, 1977; children: Elizabeth Marie, Angela Kay, Rebecca Rose. BA, Upper Iowa U., 1974; postgrad., U. Iowa, 1976-82, Drake U., 1990; MA, Viterbo Coll., 1995. Nat. bd. cert. mid. childhood generalist 2003. Elem. tchr. M-F-L Schs., Monona, Iowa, 1974-76, Washington (Iowa) Community Schs., 1976-85, South Tama (Iowa) County Schs., 1988—, fourth grade coord., dept. head, 1989—. Ctrl. com. mem. Nat. Assessment of Writing Guidelines, 1992; team leader Reading First, 2002—; instr. Edn. dept. Buena Vista U., 2002—. Mem, NEA, AAUW (vp Washington chpt. 1980), Iowa Edn. Assn., Bus. and Profl. Women (pres. Washington chpt. 1982, Washington Woman of Yr. 1981), Washington Edn. Assn. (treas. 1977-79), South Tama Edn. Assn. (pres. 1992-93, 2003—), LeGrand Libr. Bd. (pres. 1992-1998). Democrat. Lutheran. Avocations: sewing, cooking, travel. Home: 603 Willow Ln Le Grand IA 50142

**RYAN, DENNIS NEIL,** lawyer; b. Enid, Okla., Oct. 10, 1945; BA, Iowa State U., 1967; JD, So. Meth. U., 1974. Bar: Tex. 1974, admitted to practice: US Supreme Ct., US Ct. Appeals (5th Cir.), US Dist. Ct. (No. Dist.) Tex., US Dist. Ct. (Ea. Dist.) Tex. Law clk. to Hon. William M. Taylor Jr. US Dist. Ct. (No. Dist.) Tex., 1974-76; atty. Jackson & Walker LLP, Dallas; ptnr., Litig. Andrews Kurth LLP, Dallas, mem. mgmt. com. Capt. USAF, 1968—71. Mem.: Dallas Bar Assn., Tex. Assn. Def. Counsel, State Bar Tex., ABA (Litig. Sect., Bus. Law Sect.). Office: Andrews Kurth LLP 1717 Main St Ste 3700 Dallas TX 75201 Office Phone: 214-659-4428. Office Fax: 214-659-4791. Business E-Mail: dryan@andrewskurth.com.

**RYAN, EDWARD F.,** lawyer; b. Chgo., Sept. 14, 1943; BA magna cum laude, U. St. Thomas, 1965; JD, Georgetown U. Law Ctr., 1968. Bar: Ill. 1968, Fla. 1984, US Dist. Ct. (No. Dist. Ill.), US Ct. Appeals (7th, 8th, 11th cirs.), US Supreme Ct. Ptnr. Holland & Knight LLP, Chgo., mem. dir. com. Lectr. in the field. Fellow: Am. Bar Found.; mem.: Fla. Bar, ABA, Chgo. Bar Assn. Office: Holland & Knight LLP 131 S Dearborn St 30th Fl Chicago IL 60603 Office Phone: 312-578-6552. Business E-Mail: edward.ryan@hklaw.com.

**RYAN, EDWARD W.,** economics professor; b. Plainfield, NJ, Aug. 23, 1932; s. Edward A. and Helen R. (Shannon) R.; m. Georgian Hurley, Dec. 17, 1966; children: Sarah, Jennifer. BS, U. Pa., 1955; MA, Duke U., 1957; LHD (hon.), Manhattanville Coll., 2003. Lectr. Fordham U., N.Y.C., 1956-57; instr. Iona Coll., New Rochelle, NY, 1958-60; Ryan-Bacardi prof. econs. Manhattanville Coll., N.Y.C., 1958—, Doc. of Humane Letters (L.H.D.), 2003. Dir. Econ. Freedom Inst. Author: In the Words of Adam Smith: The First Consumer Advocate, 1990, Liberty, Virtue and Happiness: The Story of Economic Freedom in America, 2000. Mem.: Econ. History Assn., Assn. Pvt. Enterprise Edn., Am. Econ. Assn. Roman Catholic. Home: 25 Jefferson Rd Scarsdale NY 10583-6411 Office: Manhattanville College 2900 Purchase St Purchase NY 10577-2132 E-mail: edwryan1@aol.com.

**RYAN, ELLEN BOUCHARD,** psychology professor, gerontologist; b. Holyoke, Mass., 1947; arrived in Can., 1982; d. Raoul Rosario and Etiennette Marie Bouchard; m. Patrick J. Ryan, July 12, 1969; children: Lorraine Yvette, Dennis Patrick, Kevin Myles. BA, MA, Brown U., 1968; PhD, U. Mich., 1970. From asst. prof. psychology to prof. U. Notre Dame, 1970—82, chmn. dept., 1978-82; prof. psychiatry McMaster U., Hamilton, Ont., Canada, 1982—, dir. Ctr. for Gerontol. Studies, 1985-95, prof. gerontology, 1987—. Editor: Attitudes Toward Language Variation, 1982, Language Communication and The Elderly, 1986, Intergenerational Communication, 1994, Language Attitudes, 1994, Communication, Aging and Health, 1996. Grantee NICHD, 1972-75, NSF, 1976-79, Nat. Inst. Edn., 1979-82, Natural Scis. and Engring. Rsch., 1983-89, Gerontol. Rsch. Coun. of Ont., 1983-85, Ont. Ministry Health, 1986-89, Soc. Sci. and Humanities Rsch. Coun., 1986—. Fellow APA, Gerontol. Soc. Am., Can. Psychol. Assn.; mem. Internat. Assn. of Lang. and Social Psychology, Can. Assn. Gerontology. Home: 71 Sulphur Springs Rd # 14 Ancaster ON Canada L9G 5C1 Office: McMaster U Dept Psychiatry 1200 Main St W Hamilton ON Canada L8N 3Z5 Office Phone: 905-525-9140 ext. 24449. Business E-Mail: ryaneb@mcmaster.ca.

**RYAN, FRANCIS WILLIAM,** history educator, coach, dean; b. Chester, Pa., Mar. 2, 1946; s. John Joseph and Anne Ryan; children: Jennifer Lynn, Colleen Marie. BA, Duke U., Durham, N.C.; Cert. Tchr., Immaculata U., Malvern, Pa. Tchr. history, coach St. James HS, Chester, Pa., 1968—70, Malvern Prep., Pa., 1970—74, tchr. history, coach, dean students, athletic dir.; tchr. history, coach Chester H S, Ohio, 1974-78, Named to Hall of Fame Del. County Old Timers, 1994, Wall of Fame, Malvern Corp., 2003, Wall of Honor, St. James H.S., 2005. Home: 406 Municipal Dr Thorndale PA 19372 Office: 484-595-1100 ext. 3509. E-mail: fryan@malvernprep.org.

**RYAN, FRANK HARRY,** plastic surgeon; b. May 21, 1960; BS, U. Mich., 1982; MD, Ohio State U. Coll. Of Medicine, 1986. Surgical residency Cedars-Sinai Med. Ctr., U. Missouri & UCLA Med. Ctr., 1986—94; plastic surgeon priv. practice, Beverly Hills, 1994—. Mem. adv. bd. A. Craig Matthias Found. Founder Bony Pony Ranch Found., Malibu. Avocations: boating, fishing, golf, tennis. Office: 9675 Brighton Wy Ste 340 Beverly Hills CA 90210 also: Bony Pony Ranch Found 9663 Santa Monica Blvd Ste 785 Beverly Hills CA 90210 Personal E-Mail: fhrmd@aol.com.

**RYAN, GEORGE WILLIAM,** manufacturing executive; b. Sinking Springs, Ohio, Oct. 13, 1939; s. Winson Mark and Mary Edith (Smalley) R.; 1 child: Gina Kristin. Student, Wilmington Coll., 1962. Process engr. B.F. Goodrich Co., Marietta, Ohio, 1962-66; product dev. mgr. Chrysler Corp., Sandusky, Ohio, 1966-70; asst. tech. mgr. Inmont Corp., Toledo, 1970-72; tech. mgr. Occidental Petroleum, Burlington, NJ, 1973; owner Ryan Devel. Corp., Peebles, 1973-88; prin. Ironwood Valley Ranch, Ohio, 1986—. Substitute tchr. Adams County Sch. Dist.; cons. Hooker Chem. Corp., Burlington, NJ, 1973; expert Internat. Exec. Svc. Core. Bd. dirs., pres. Missionary Evang. Ch. of Christ; active Adams County Workforce Commn.; mem. Rep. Inner Cir. Mem. Soc. Plastic Engrs., Peebles Ind. Inc. (sec., treas., bd. dirs., 1984-88). Republican. Office Phone: 937-587-2266. E-mail: rydevryan@aol.com.

**RYAN, HALFORD ROSS,** speech educator; b. Anderson, Ind., Dec. 29, 1943; AB, Wabash Coll., 1966; MA, U. Ill., 1968, PhD, 1972. Prof. Washington and Lee U., Lexington, Va., 1970—. Author: FDR's Rhetorical Presidency, 1988, Harry Emerson Fosdick, 1989, Henry Ward Beecher, 1990, Classical Communication for the Contemporary American Presidency, 1992, Harry S. Truman, 1993; editor: Oratorical Encounters, 1988, Inaugural Addresses of Twentieth-Century American Presidents, 1993, U.S. Presidents as Orators, 1995; also articles. Recipient awards Eleanor Roosevelt Inst., 1979, Herbert

Hoover Inst., 1986, Maurice Mednick Found., 1991; Rockefeller Theol. fellow, 1967. Mem. Speech Communication Assn. Office: Washington and Lee U Robinson Hall Lexington VA 24450 Office Phone: 540-458-8812.

**RYAN, HAROLD MARTIN,** judge; b. Detroit, Feb. 6, 1911; s. Martin and Ida Ryan; m. Lilliana Wargnier, Sept. 4, 1944; children: Kathleen, Nancy, Harold Jr., John, Theresa. Student, Mich. State U., 1930-31; JD, U. Detroit, 1935. Bar: Mich. 1935, U.S. Supreme Ct. 1935. Atty., 1935—; asst. pros. atty. Wayne County, Detroit, 1942-45; state senator Mich. 1st Dist., Lansing, 1948-61; U.S. congressman 14th Congrl. Dist. Mich., Washington, 1961-65; cir. ct. judge Wayne County, Detroit, 1978-85. With USAFR, 1961-66. Recipient Pres.'s Outstanding Svc. award, U. Detroit, 2005. Democrat. Roman Catholic. Avocations: golf, football, history. Home: 28601 Little Mack Ave Saint Clair Shores MI 48081-3012

**RYAN, J. BRENDAN,** advertising executive; BA in History, Fordham U.; MBA, Wharton U. V.p. mktg. Citibank; product mgmt. Gen. Foods; head account mgmt. dept., bd. dirs. OMW, NYC; with Ogilvy & Mather; pres., CEO Foote Cone & Belding NY, 1991—96; CEO FCB Worldwide, NYC, 1996—2004, chmn., 1996—. Bd. dirs. FreshDirect, 2006—. Mem. Citizens Crime Commn., NYC; bd. dirs. Citymeals-On-Wheels, Regis H.S., exec. com. The Quills. Office: Foot Cone & Belding 100 W 33rd St #5 New York NY 10001-2921 Office Phone: 212-885-3000. Office Fax: 212-885-2803.*

**RYAN, J. BRUCE,** healthcare management consulting executive; b. Southbridge, Mass., Mar. 28, 1944; s. Charles J. and Doris (Olney) R.; m. Sarah E. Pattison, Aug. 16, 1993. BSBA in Fin., U. Mass., 1972, MSBA, 1975; MA in Econs., U. Wash., 1976, Regional v.p. Amherst Assocs. Inc., Atlanta, 1976—85; exec. v.p. Jennings Ryan & Kolb, Inc., Atlanta, 1985—2005; CFO Cross Country Cons., 2002—05; pres. JBR Cons. Inc., 2005—. Contbr. articles to profl. jours. With U.S. Army, 1968-70. Mem. Healthcare Fin. Mgmt. Assn. (Helen M. Yerger/L. Van Seawell best article award 1990), Fin. Mgmt. Assn. Avocation: sailing. Home: 1060 Kentucky Ave NE Atlanta GA 30306-3534

**RYAN, JAMES,** insurance company executive; b. Pitts., Jan. 21, 1937; s. Martin Charles and Lucy Elizabeth (Misklow) r.; m. Marlene Sullivan Ryan, Jan. 27, 1973. BA, U. Pitts., U. Louisville. Cert. ins. wholesaler. Chmn. Market Finders Ins. Corp., Louisville, 1972—. Com. chmn. Am. Assn. Mng. Gen. Agts., 1988-89; pres. Ky. Lloyd's Assn., 1985—; bd. dirs. Nat. Assn. Profl. Surplus Lines Office, Inc., 1983-86; pres. Ky. Surplus Lines Assn., Louisville, 1988-89; mem. adv. coun. Essex Ins. Co., 1991-93, Am. Equity Ins. Co., Scottsdale, Ariz., 1999. Pub. in Best Rev., 1995. Ky. Thoroughbred Owners & Breeders, Inc., Hon. Order of Blue Goose Internat., Kosair Shrine Temple, Hon. Order of Ky. Col. Named Adv. Coun. Colony Ins. Co., Glen Allen, Va., 1991-93, Hamilton Ins. Co., 1993, Cardinal Ins. Co., 1991-93. Mem. Profl. Ins. Agts., Ind. Ins. Agts. Assn., Am. Assn. Mng. Gen. Agts. (cert., chmn. adv. com. 1991-92, bd. dirs. 1994-96, v.p. zone 2 1995-96, pres.-elect 1996-97, pres. 1997-98), Nat. Assn. Profl. Surplus Lines Offices (chmn. legis. com. 1988-89, Published Best Rev. 1995), Am. Assn. of Gen. Agts. Republican. Roman Catholic. Avocations: breeding and racing thoroughbred horses, golf. Office Phone: 502-423-1800. E-mail: jryan@mfic.com.

**RYAN, JAMES C.,** theater educator; b. Omaha, Nebr., Dec. 2, 1955; s. Thomas Edward Ryan and Marilyn Rita Curran; m. Sylvia Nell Watkins, May 17, 1980; children: Michael Watkins, Colin Patrick. BS in Edn., U. Okla., Norman, 1991. Cert. tchr. Okla. Dept. Edn. Theatre tech. Firehouse Dinner Theatre, Omaha, Nebr., 1972—74; tech. asst. U. Nebr., Lincoln, 1974—78; designer Inspiration Point Drama Camp, Eureka Springs, Ark., 1980; freelance theatre designer Norman, Okla., 1980—90; tchr. West Mid. HS, Norman, 1992—97, Norman N. HS, 1997—. Chair, nomination com. Okla. Speech, Theatre, Communication Assn., 2001—; dist. com. W. Okla. Forensic League, 2002—; divsn. coord. Cameron U. Summer Speech Camp, Lawton, 2003—. Dir.: (plays) A Thousand Cranes, 2000 (state champion), Caucasian Chalk Cir. Named Diamond Coach, Nat. Forensic League, Charlene Barton Coach of Yr., W. Okla. NFL Dist., 2003, Disting. Speech, Theatre & Debate Tchr., Nat. Fedn. HS Activity Assns., 2005; recipient Presdl. Scholars Tchr. of Excellence award, U.S. Dept. Edn., 2004.

**RYAN, JAMES JOSEPH,** retired lawyer; b. Cin., June 17, 1929; s. Robert J. and Marian (Hoffman) R.; m. Mary A. Noonan, Nov. 25, 1954; children: Kevin, Timothy, Nora, Daniel. AB, Xavier U., 1951; JD, U. Cin., 1954. Bar: Ohio 1954. Tchr. assoc. Northwestern U., Chgo., 1954-55; ptnr. Dolle, O'Donnell & Cash, Cin., 1958-75, Taft, Stettinius & Hollister, Cin., 1971-99. Lectr. U. Cin. Coll. Law, 1960-65. Chmn. Health Planning Assn. Ohio River Valley, Cin., 1978-85; bd. dirs. Hamilton County Bd. of Mentally Retarded, 1968-80; trustee Resident Home for Mentally Retarded, 1980-97, St. Francis-St. George Hosp. Devel. Coun., 1989-99. Mem. ABA, Ohio Bar Assn., Cin. Bar Assn., Queen City Club, Western Hill Club. Republican. Roman Catholic. Avocations: reading, sports. Home: 5316 Cleves Warsaw Pike Cincinnati OH 45238-3602 Office: 1800 Firstar Tower 425 Walnut St Cincinnati OH 45202-3923

**RYAN, JAMES LEO,** federal judge; b. Detroit, Nov. 19, 1932; s. Leo Francis and Irene Agnes Ryan; m. Mary Elizabeth Rogers, Oct. 12, 1957; children: Daniel P., James R., Colleen M. Hansen, Kathleen A. LLB, U. Detroit, 1956, LLD (hon.), 1986, BA, 1992; LLD (hon.), Madonna Coll., 1976, Detroit Coll., 1978, Thomas M. Cooley Law Sch., Lansing, Mich., 1986. Atty. Waldron, Brennan & Maher, 1960—62; pvt. practice Redford Twp., Mich., 1962—66; Justice of peace 1963—66; judge 3d Cir. Ct. of Mich., 1966—75; justice Mich. Supreme Ct., 1975—86; judge U.S. Ct. Appeals (6th cir.), 1985—2000, sr. judge, 2000—. Faculty Nat. Jud. Coll., Reno; adj. faculty, bd. dirs. Ave Maria Sch. Law; adj. prof. Thomas M. Cooley Law Sch., 1979—85; U. Detroit, 1974—. Contbr. articles to profl. jours. Capt. JAGC USNR, 1954—92, ret. mil. judge USNR. Mem.: USNR Lawyers Assn., Detroit Bar Assn., Fed. Bar Assn., State Bar Mich., Fed. Judges Assn., K.M., K.C. Office: US Ct Appeals US Courthouse 231 W Lafayette Blvd Detroit MI 48226-2700*

**RYAN, JAMES WALTER,** physician, medical researcher; b. Amarillo, Tex., June 8, 1935; s. Lee W. and Emma E. (Haddox) R.; children: James P.A., Alexandra L.E., Amy J.S. AB in Polit. Sci., Dartmouth Coll., 1957; MD, Cornell U., 1961; D.Phil., Oxford U., Eng., 1967. Diplomate Nat. Bd. Med. Examiners. Intern, Montreal (Que.) Gen. Hosp., McGill U., 1961-62, asst. resident in medicine, 1962-63; USPHS research asso. NIMH, NIH, 1963-65; guest investigator Rockefeller U., N.Y.C., 1967-68, asst. prof. biochemistry, 1968; investigator Howard Hughes Med. Inst., 1968—71; assoc. prof. medicine U. Miami (Fla.) Sch. Medicine, 1968-79, prof. medicine, 1979-95, mem. vasc. biology ctr., 1995-00; prof. anesthesiology, pharmacology and toxicology Med. Coll. Ga., Augusta, 1995-00; sr. scientist ntGen, 2000—; chief scientist Ryogen, LLC, 2005—. Sr. scientist Papanicolaou Cancer Rsch. Inst., Miami, 1972-77; hon. med. officer to Regius prof medicine Oxford U., 1965-67; vis. prof. Clin. Rsch. Inst. Montreal, 1974; mem. vis. faculty thoracic disease divsn., dept. internal medicine Mayo Clinic, 1974; vis. prof. Montreal Gen. Hosp./McGill U., 1985. Contbr. numerous articles on biochem. rsch. and pathology to sci. jours.; patentee in field. Rockefeller Found. travel awardee, 1962; William Waldorf Astor traveling fellow, 1966; USPHS spl. fellow, 1967-68; Pfizer travelling fellow, 1972; recipient USPHS Rsch. Career Devel. award NIH, 1968, Louis and Artur Luciano award for research of circulatory diseases McGill U., 1984-85. Mem. AAAS, Am. Physiol. Soc., Am. Chem. Soc., Biochem. Soc., Am. Soc. Biochemist and Molecular Biology, Am. Heart Assn. (mem. coun. cardiopulmonary diseases 1972—, coun. for high blood pressure rsch. 1976—), Microcirculatory Soc., Oxford and Cambridge Club (London), Sigma Xi. Baptist. Home: 3047 Lake Forest Dr Augusta GA 30909-3027 Office: ntGen Ryogen LLC 3047 Lake Forest Dr Augusta GA 30909

**RYAN, JANE FRANCES,** corporate communications executive; b. Bronxville, NY, Nov. 1, 1950; d. Bernard M. and Margaret M. (Griffith) R.; m. Kevin Horan, Dec. 26, 1982; 1 child, Kevin. BS in Journalism, Ohio U., 1972; MBA in Mktg., Golden Gate U., 1990. Asst. promotion mgr. Fawcett Publs., Greenwich, Conn., 1972-75; mktg. coordinator Fawcett Mktg. Services div. CBS, Greenwich, Conn., 1975-78; dist. sales mgr. CBS Publs., San Francisco, 1978; prodn. mgr. Cato Inst., San Francisco, 1979-81; account supr. Bus. Media Resources, Mill Valley, Calif., 1981-90, dir. mktg. svcs., 1990-93; dir. publs. RAND Corp., Santa Monica, Calif., 1993—. Office: RAND 1700 Main St Santa Monica CA 90401-3297

**RYAN, JASON MICHAEL,** lawyer; b. Wharton, Tex., Oct. 30, 1975; m. Megan A. Ryan, Dec. 30, 2000. BBA with honors, U. Tex., 1998, JD with honors, 2001. Bar: Tex. 2001, US Ct. Appeals (5th cir.), US Dist. Ct. (So. Dist.) Tex. Assoc. Baker Botts LLP, Houston, 2001—; reserve officer USN, 2005—. Editor-in-chief Am. Jour. Criminal Law; contbr. articles to law jours. Mem.: ABA, Mil. Officers Assn. of Am., Houston Mil. Affairs Com., Houston World Affairs Coun. (coun. cabinet), Houston Vol. Lawyers Program (bd. dirs.), Pro Bono Coll. of State Bar Tex., Houston Young Lawyers Assn. (bd. dirs.), Houston Bar Found., Houston Bar Assn. (co-chair LegalLine Com.), Energy Bar Assn. (v.p. Houston Chap., mem. Alternative Dispute Resolution Com.), Alpha Phi Omega. Office: Baker Botts LLP One Shell Plaza 910 Louisiana St Houston TX 77002 Office Phone: 713-229-1820. Office Fax: 713-229-2820. Business E-Mail: jason.ryan@bakerbotts.com. E-mail: jason.m.ryan@navy.mil.

**RYAN, JENNY REBEKA,** lawyer; b. Tuscaloosa, Ala., Nov. 9, 1973; JD, U. Ala., Tuscaloosa, 1999. Cert.: Ala. Bar Assn. (Guardian ad Litem) 2004. Law clk. Judge John Bush, Wetumpka, Ala., 1999—2000, Ala. Ct. Criminal Appeals, Montgomery, 2000—01; staff atty. US Dist. Ct., Mid. Dist. of Ala., Montgomery, 2001—02; assoc. Douglas J. Fees, PC, Huntsville, Ala., 2002—04; of counsel Crownover & Standridge, Tuscaloosa, 2004—. Active mem. Tuscaloosa Children's Theatre, 2004—06. Mem.: TCT Guild (assoc.). D-Liberal. Methodist. Avocations: theater, singing, politics, current events, reading. Office: Crownover & Standridge 2600 7th St Tuscaloosa AL 35401 Office Fax: 205-349-1779. Personal E-Mail: jryanlaw@hotmail.com.

**RYAN, JOAN,** food company executive; BS in Acctg., U. Ill. CPA, Ill. With Price Waterhouse Co., Baxter Healthcare Corp., Kewaunee Sci. Corp.; divsn. contr., CFO NutraSweet Co.; v.p. fin., CFO Ameritech Small Bus. Svcs., 1995-98, Alliant Foodservice, Inc., Deerfield, Ill., 1998-2000; CFO, Tellabs, Inc., Lisle, Ill., 2000—03; sr. v.p., CFO SIRVA, Inc., Westmont, Ill., 2003—. Bd. dirs. Fed. Signal Corp. Bd. dirs. Boys and Girls Club Chgo.

**RYAN, JOHN DUNCAN,** lawyer; b. Portland, Oreg., Dec. 20, 1920; s. Thomas Gough and Virginia Abigail (Hadley) R.; m. Florence A. Ryan, Jan. 30, 1970 (dec. 1987); m. Virginia Kane Wilson, June 15, 1996 BS, Fordham U., 1943; JD, Lewis & Clark Coll., Portland, 1950. Bar: Oreg. 1950. Pvt. practice, Portland, 1950—. Adj. instr. Northwestern Sch. Law Lewis & Clark Coll., 1953-70 Author: (poems) Expressions, 1993, Expressions II, 1995, No Road without a Turning, 2005, (book) Expressions, 1988, 1999, Cooking with John Ryan, 2002 Sgt. Air Corps, U.S. Army, 1942-46, ETO Recipient St. Thomas More award Catholic Lawyers for Social Justice, 1993 Mem. ABA (Oreg. del. 1985-93, chmn. spl. com. on law & literacy 1991-93), ATLA, Am. Coll. Trial Lawyers, Oreg. State Bar (bd. govs. 1963-67), Oreg. Trial Lawyers Assn. (Trial Lawyer of Yr. 1993), Multnomah County Bar Assn. (Professionalism award 1997), Washington County Bar Assn Home and Office: 503 SW Colony Dr Portland OR 97219-7763

**RYAN, JOHN JOSEPH,** physician; b. Columbus, Ga., Sept. 5, 1957; s. Joseph Vincent and Annie Elizabeth R.; m. Sonia Francisca Ryan, Nov. 17, 1984; children: Annie, Joseph, Catherine. BS in Med. Tech., Columbus (Ga.) State U., 1978; MD, U. Autonoma Nuevo Leon (Mex.), 1990. Diplomate Am. Bd. Family Practice. Intern Anderson Family Practice, Anderson, SC, 1991—92, resident, 1991—94; physician Lowry's Family Medicine, Chester, SC, 1994—98; pvt. practice Chester, 1998—. Bass Chester Cmty. Chorus; coach Ryans Raiders Youth Soccer Alliance, Chester, SC. Fellow: Am. Acad. Family Practice; mem.: S.C. Acad. Family Practice, S.C. Med. Assn., AMA (med. assoc.), Rotary, KC (Grand Knight). Roman Catholic. Avocations: fishing, golf, gardening.

**RYAN, JOHN MICHAEL,** secondary school educator; b. Warwick, N.Y., Aug. 24, 1951; s. John and Ann Ryan; m. Jeanne M. Ryan, Aug. 17, 1974; children: James, Michael, Kelly, Tara. BS in Social Scis., Murray State U., Ky., 1974; EdM in Adminstrn., Plymouth State Coll., N.H., 1983. Tchr. social sci. Greenwood Lake Schs., NY, 1974—78, Vernon Sch. Dist., NJ, 1978—. Exec. bd. N.J. Soccer Coaches Assn., 1983—2001, pres., 1998—2001. Named to N.J. Coaches Hall of Fame, 1998; grantee, Freeman Found., 2006. Mem.: Nat. Soccer Coaches Assn. Am. Avocations: fly fishing, hiking, history. Home: 250 Frenchtown Rd Milford PA 18337 Office: Vernon Twp HS PO Box 800 Vernon NJ 07462

**RYAN, JOHN MORGAN,** lawyer; b. Glen Ridge, NJ, May 18, 1936; AB, Dartmouth Coll., 1958; LLB, U. Va., 1963. Bar: Va. 1964. Lectr. at law Marshall-Wythe Sch. Law Coll. William and Mary, 1976-86; ptnr. Vandeventer Black LLP, Norfolk, Va.; gen. counsel Va. Internat. Terminals, Inc. Trustee Contemporary Art Ctr. Va.; chair Arts and Humanities Commn., Va. Beach, Va.; bd. dirs. Children's Health Sys., Inc., Greater Norfolk Corp. Fellow: Va. Law Found. (mem. coun.), Am. Bar Found., Am. Coll. Trial Lawyers; mem.: ABA (labor rels., litigation sect.), So. Conf. Bar Pres., Nat. Conf. Bar Pres., Va. State Bar, Norfolk-Portsmouth Bar Assn., Maritime Law Assn. US (bd. dirs. 2005—), Va. Bar Assn. (pres. 1988), S.E. Admiralty Law Inst., James Kent Am. Inn of Ct. (past pres.), 4th Cir. Jud. Conf., Maritime Law Assn. (legis. com.). Office: Vandeventer Black LLP 500 World Trade Ctr Norfolk VA 23510-1679 Office Phone: 757-446-8600. Business E-Mail: jryan@vanblk.com.

**RYAN, JOHN R.,** academic administrator, career military officer; m. Diane L. Ackerman; children: Tricia, Kelly, Julie. Graduate, USN Acad., 1967; MSc in Adminstrn., George Washington U., 1975. Enlisted USN, 1968, advanced through grades to vice adm.; naval aviator Patrol Squadron 8, 1969-72; various assignments Naval Acad., 1972-75; served on USS Nimitz, 1975-77; adminstrv. officer Commander Patrol Wing Five, 1977-80; ops. officer Patrol Squadron Twenty-Six, 1980-81; various assignments Patrol Squadron Eleven, 1981-83, Office of Chief of Naval Ops., 1983-85; military asst. to exec. sec. Immediate Office of Sec. Defense, 1985-86; comdr. Patrol Squadron Thirty-One, Moffett Field, 1986-87; exec. asst. to dep. chief naval ops. Office of Chief of Naval Ops., 1987-88; comdr. Patrol Wing Ten, Moffett Field, 1988-90; various assignments U.S. Pacific Command, 1990-93; comdr. patrol wings US Pacific Fleet/Commdr., Anti-Submarine Warfare Forces, U.S. Pacific Fleet, 1993-95; commdr., maritime surveillance and reconnaissance force, us sicth fleet commdr., fleet air mediterranean/commdr. Maritime Air Forces, 1995-98; supt. USN Acad., 1998—2002; pres. SUNY Maritime Coll., 2002—04; interim pres. SUNY, Albany, 2004; acting chancellor SUNY Sys., 2005, chancellor, 2005—. Decorated D.S.M., Legion of Merit with two gold stars, Meritorious Svc. medal with two gold stars. Office: SUNY Sys Adminstrn Chancellor's Office State University Plaza Albany NY 12246*

**RYAN, JOHN WILLIAM,** academic administrator; b. Chgo., Aug. 12, 1929; s. Leonard John and Maxine (Mitchell) R.; m. D. Patricia Goodday, June 20, 1949; children: Kathleen Elynne Ryan Acker, Kevin Dennis Mitchell, Kerrick Charles Casey. BA, U. Utah, 1951; MA, Ind. U., 1958, PhD; D Pub. Adminstrn., Nat. Inst. Devel. Adminstrn., Thailand, 1991; DLitt (hon.), U. St. Thomas, 1977; LLD (hon.), Ind. U., 1988. U. Notre Dame, 1978, Oakland City Coll., 1981, St. Joseph Coll., 1981, Hanover Coll., 1982, DePauw U., 1983, Manchester Coll., 1983, U. Evansville, 1985, Wabash Coll., 1986, Ind. U., 1988, U. Md., 1994, SD State U., 2005, S.Dakota State U., 2004. Rsch. analyst Ky. Dept. Revenue, Frankfort, 1954-55; vis. rsch. prof. U. Thammasat, Bangkok, 1955-57; asst. dir. Inst. Tng. for Pub. Svc. Ind. U., 1957-58;

successively asst. prof., assoc. prof. polit. sci., assoc. dir., Bur. Govt. U. Wis., 1958-62; exec. asst. to pres., sec. of univ. U. Mass., Amherst, 1964-65, chancellor Boston, 1965-68; v.p. acad. affairs Ariz. State U., 1963-65; v.p., chancellor regional campuses Ind. U., Bloomington, 1968-71, pres., 1971-87, pres. emeritus, 1987—; prof. emeritus, 1996-95; prof. pub. and environ. affairs, 1981-95, prof. emeritus, 1995—; cons. AID, 1991-92; chancellor SUNY, Albany, 1996—2000, chancellor emeritus, 2000—; hon. prof. Moscow State U., 1999. Interim pres. Fla. Atlantic U., 1989, U. Md., Balt., 1994; bd. dirs. Ind. U. Found., chmn. 1972-87; chmn. Nat. Adv. Bd. on Internat. Edn. Programs, 1985-89; chancellor SUNY System, 1996-2000. Contbr. articles to profl. jours. Bd. govs. Pub. Broadcasting Svc., 1973-82; bd. visitors Air U., 1974-81; chmn. Air Force Inst. Tech Subcom., 1976-81; mem. univ. adv. com. Am. Coun. Life Ins.; bd. dirs. Corp. Community Coun., 1976; mem. nat. adv. coun. Pan Am. Games, 1985; mem. adv. bd. Assocs. for Religious and Intellectual Life, 1984—; active United Way Ind. Centennial Commn. Mem. Am. Soc. Pub. Adminstrn. (pres. Ind. chpt. 1969-70, nat. chpt. 1972-73, nat. coun. from 1970, Ind. Soc. Chgo. (non-resident v.p. from 1976, Am. Polit. Sci. Assn., Assn. Asian Studies, Am. Coun. Edn., Assn. Am. Univs. (chmn. 1981-82), Nat. Acad. Public Adminstrn., Nat. Acad., Explorers Club, Adelphia (hon.), Columbia Club (Indpls.), Skyline Club, Cosmos Club (Washington), Athenaeum (London), KC, Equestrian Order of Holy Sepulchre, Elks, Phi Kappa Phi, Phi Alpha Theta, Pi Sigma Alpha, Beta Gamma Sigma, Kappa Sigma (worthy grand master 1985-87). Office: Ind U SPEA 415 1315 E 10th St Bloomington IN 47405-1701 Office Phone: 812-855-5780. Personal E-mail: chancem123@aol.com. Business E-Mail: ryan@indiana.edu.

**RYAN, JOHN WILLIAM,** educational association administrator; b. Manchester, NH, Sept. 16, 1937; s. William Charles and Mary Ann (Marcoux) R.; m. Carol Jean Battaglia, Sept. 17, 1960; children: James, Kathleen, John, Michael. AB, St. Anselm Coll., 1959; MA, Niagara U., 1960; PhD, St. John's U., 1965. Asst. prof. history Gannon U., Erie, Pa., 1965-66; edn. specialist, div. grad. programs U.S. Office Edn., Washington, 1966-68, regional coordinator, grad. acad. programs, 1968-70; dir. univ. relations Univ. Assos., Inc., Washington, 1970-72; asst. to pres., sec. Council of Grad. Schs. in U.S., Washington, 1972-80; exec. v.p. Renewables Research Inst., Annandale, Va., 1980-81; exec. dir. Worcester (Mass.) Consortium Higher Edn., 1981-89, N.H. Coll. and Univ. Coun., Manchester, 1989-93; cons.; exec. dir. Mass. Vet. Med. Assn., Marlborough, Mass., 1995-98; cons., 1998—. Contbr. articles to profl. jours. Bd. dirs. No. Va. C.C., 1999—, Loudoun Healthcare, Inc., 2000—, Loudoun County Econ. Devel. Commn., 2000. Personal E-mail: jwryan@belmontcc.com.

**RYAN, JOSEPH,** lawyer; b. Seattle, Feb. 11, 1942; s. John Joseph and Jane (Wing) R.; m. Mary Katherine Gavin, Aug. 10, 1963; children: Michael Gavin, Kathleen Ann, Jennifer Jo. BA, U. Washington, 1964; JD, Columbia U., 1967. Bar: Calif. 1968, U.S. Supreme Ct. 1983, D.C. 1983. Ptnr. O'Melveny & Myers, L.A., 1976—93, mng. ptnr., 1993—94; sr. v.p., gen. counsel Ritz-Carlton Hotel Co., LLC, Atlanta, 1994—; exec. v.p., gen. counsel Marriott Internat., Inc., Washington, 1994—. Tchr., lectr. N.Y. Law Jour. Author: Stating Your Case: How To Interview for a Job as a Lawyer, 1982, Take or Pay Contracts: Alive and Well in California, vol. 192, 1987, Current Investment Banking Activities in the United States, vol. 2, #15 M&A Report, 1988; co-author (with Lorin Fife) The Urban Lawyer, 1987; contbr. articles to law pubs. Bd. dirs. Pasadena Playhouse, L.A., 1981-92, Planetary Soc., Pasadena, 1981, Westridge Sch., L.A., 1982-91, Natural History Mus. Los Angeles County, 1988-93. Capt. U.S. Army, 1968-70. Mem. ABA, N.Y. Bar Assn., L.A. County Bar Assn., D.C. Bar Assn., Calif. Bar Assn., Nat. Assn. Bond Lawyers (legis. com.). Republican. Roman Catholic. Avocations: running, biking, camping, hunting and fishing, boating. Home: 10836 Alloway Dr Potomac MD 20854-1503 Office: Marriott Internat Inc 10400 Fernwood Rd Bethesda MD 20817

**RYAN, JOSEPH W., JR.,** lawyer; b. Phila., June 24, 1948; s. Joseph W. Sr. and Marie R. (Hillgrube) R.; m. Mary Pat Law, Sept. 11, 1971; children: Caitlin, Joseph W. III. BA, St. Joseph's U., 1970; MA, Villanova U., 1971; JD, U. Va., 1978. Bar: Ohio 1978, U.S. Supreme Ct. 1982. Ptnr. Porter Wright Morris & Arthur LLP, Columbus, Ohio, 1978—. Lectr. Sch. Dentistry Ohio State U., Columbus, 1982-89, CLE Inst., 1984—; trial acad. faculty Internat. Assn. Def. Counsel, Boulder, Colo., 1994, dir.-elect, 2005-06, dir. 2006—. Author: Use of Demonstrative Evidence, 1985; assoc. editor Litigation News, 1986—, editor in chief, 2000-02. Trustee Columbus Zool. Assn., 1980-90; bd. dirs. Columbus Speech and Hearing Ctr., 1988-99, pres., 1995-96. Mem. ABA (sec. litig., co-chair publs. divsn.), Ohio State Bar Assn., Columbus Bar Assn., Internat. Assn. Def. Counsel, Am. Arbitration Assn. (panel of arbitrators). Republican. Roman Catholic. Office: Porter Wright Morris & Arthur 41 S High St Ste 30 Columbus OH 43215-6101 Office Phone: 614-227-2000. Business E-Mail: jryan@porterwright.com.

**RYAN, JOYCE ETHEL,** writer, artist; b. Atlanta, Aug. 29, 1949; m. Jim Cyril Klar, Apr. 5, 1975 BFA, U. Ga., 1972. Instr. Marsh Draughon Coll., Atlanta, 1972—73; mgr. retail store Army & Air Force Exch. Svc., Dallas, 1974; illustrator U.S. Army Logistics Ctr., Ft. Lee, Va., 1975—77; mgr. graphics Ecosystems Internat., Millersville, Md., 1980—82; dir. freelance art studio Seoul, 1983—85; pres. Butterfly Books, Ariz., 1985—. Instr. Cochise Coll., Sierra Vista, 1986 Illustrator, author: Seoul Sketches, 1985, Scenes of Southern Arizona, 1986, Seoul Travel Guide, 1987, Traveling with Your Sketchbook, 1990, The Happy Camper's Gourmet Cookbook, 1992, Calligraphy: Elegant and Easy, 1994, Drawing at Home, 1996, America's Best Cheesecakes, 1998, Fifty Years of Excellence: Texas Watercolor Society, 1999, America's Best RV Cookbook, 2003; contbr. to RV America mag., 2003— Mem.: Art Ctr. Corpus Christi, San Antonio Watercolor Group. Avocations: drawing, painting. Office Phone: 210-494-0077. Personal E-mail: texaswavelady@hotmail.com.

**RYAN, JUDITH W.,** geriatrics nurse, educator; b. Waterbury, Conn., Dec. 8, 1943; d. James Patrick Ryan and Edna (Swanson) Billings. BS, U. Conn., 1965; MS, Boston U., 1967; PhD, U. Md., 1984. RN, Md., Conn.; cert. adult nurse practitioner ANCC. Instr. U. Conn., Storrs, 1967-69; asst. prof. Ind. U., Purdue U., Indpls., 1969-73. U. Md., Balt., 1973-82, dir. primary care adult nurse practitioner cert. program, dept. medicine, supportive care project, 1985-87, asst. prof. sch. nursing, 1987-95, asst. prof., 1976-82; clin. dir. EverCare, Balt., 1995-99; pres. Nurse Practitioners and Cons., P.C. of Prime Health Group, 2000—. Arbitrator Health Claims Arbitration Program, Md., 1976—; bd. mem. Md. Bd. Nursing, Balt., 1991-98, pres., 1993-96; trustee Md. Nurses Assn. Polit. Action Com., Balt., treas., 1989-91. Contbr. articles to profl. jours. Named Distinguished Practitioner Nursing, Nat. Acad. Practice, 1984-99. Mem. Am. Coll. Nurse Practitioners, Md. Nurses Assn. (2d v.p. 1986-88), Nurse Practitioner Assn. Md., Sigma Theta Tau, Phi Kappa Phi. Office: 20 New Plant Ct Ste 204 Owings Mills MD 21117 Home: 1514 Woodside Ave Baltimore MD 21227 Office Phone: 410-654-8602. Personal E-mail: jwryan128@comcast.net.

**RYAN, KELLI LORRAINE,** ballerina, educator; b. Merced, Calif., June 26, 1957; d. Howard Fredrick Burley Adcock and Lorraine Cervantes-Adcock; m. Riley Ray Ryan III, May 1, 1999; 1 child, Victoria Alyn Bommarito Salda. M. in Psychology, San Jose State U., 1988. Ballerina Vaganova Choreographic/Kirov Ballet, USSR, 1977, Paris Opera Ballet, France, 1977, Diplomat of Elem., Intermediate and Advanced Cecchetti Syllabus Cecchetti Coun. Am., Calif., 1970, cert. hypnotherapist A.C.H.E., Calif., 1988. Instructress ballet/jazz for the deaf Berkley Sch. for Deaf, 1972—74; corps de ballet San Francisco Ballet, 1975—82; soloist Ballet Lausanne, Brussels, 1976—77; artistic dir. Alameda Dance Repertory Theater, Calif., 1977—82; soloist Ballet de Toscano, Florence, Italy, 1998—99; vol. instructress, ballet/movement for the developmentally disabled Calif., 1982—. Regional del. Nat. Dance Week, Calif., 2003—; mem. Nat. Dance Assn., Reston, Va. 2004—, Am. AAHPERD, Reston, 2004—. Solo performer (TV spl. - ballet) Isadora by Bejart); oil painting series for Vatican Coll., As It Is In Heaven (In the Vatican's permanent collection, 1998), watercolor series (aquarelli), Garden in the Rain (In the Vatican's permanent collection, 1999); ballerina

(performance L.A. Times Book Fest) Celebrate Nat. Dance Week. Mem. Atwater C. of C.; chmn. bd. Am. Ballet Conservatory, Atwater, Calif., 2003—05. Recipient Commendation of Pub. Svc., U.S. Congress, 18th Dist., 2004, cert. of recognition, Merced County Bd. Suprs., 2004. Mem.: Internat. Dance Coun., Kiwanis (Greater Atwater). Conservative. Catholic. Achievements include founding American Ballet Conservatory; creation of tax-exempt ballet/music/art conservatory which provides scholarships to Central Calif.'s dance, art, music, photography, writing students; creating a ballet school which provides a comprehensive ballet conservatory education regardless of students ability to pay; development of method of instructing toddlers in Ballet and foreign languages; a no fail smoking cessation method. Home: 1301 Fruitland Ave Atwater CA 95301 Office: American Ballet Conservatory 1175 Broadway Atwater CA 95301 Office Phone: 209-356-1401. Office Fax: 209-357-8812. Personal E-mail: kellryan@pacbell.net.

**RYAN, KENNETH EUGENE,** engineer; b. Guilford, N.Y., Apr. 3, 1936; s. Julian Nichols and Irene M. Ryan; m. Nancy Race, Aug. 29, 1959; children: Patrick, Kathleen, Timothy, Maureen. BS, Cornell U., 1958, MS, 1959. Registered profl. engr., N.Y. With various mobile equipment mfrs., 1959-66; rsch. assoc. Cornell U., Ithaca, N.Y., 1966-69; sr. project engr. Raymond Corp., Greene, N.Y., 1969—. Chmn. Zoning Bd. Appeals, Oxford, N.Y., 1973-83; chmn. com. North Guilford (N.Y.) Ch., 1989-91; mem. Oxford Planning Bd., 1970—; chmn. Chenango County Planning Bd., 2003—. Mem. NSPE, ASME, Soc. Exptl. Stress Analysis. Achievements include patents in field. Avocation: photography. Home: 221 Ryan Rd Oxford NY 13830-9801

**RYAN, KENNETH J.,** immunologist, educator; MD, U. Wash., 1966. Cert. pathologist. Mem. staff Univ. Med. Ctr., Tuscon; prof. pathology, microbiology, immunology U. Ariz. Coll. Medicine, 1972—, dean acad. affairs Tuscon, 2002—04, interim dean, 2002—04. Avocations: golf, tennis. Office: U Ariz Sch Medicine Rm 2205 PO Box 245017 1501 N Cambell Ave # C 206 Tucson AZ 85724-0002

**RYAN, KEVIN V.,** prosecutor, lawyer; married; 2 children. BA in History, Dartmouth Coll.; JD, U. San Francisco. Prosecutor Alameda County Dist. Atty.'s Office; judge San Francisco Mcpl. Ct., 1996—98; mem. San Francisco Superior Ct., 1999, presiding judge criminal divsn.; US atty. (no. dist.) Calif. US Dept. Justice, 2002—. Bd. dirs. No Calif. High Intensity Drug Trafficking Area Working Group; mem. Pres. Bush's Corp. Fraud Task Force; apptd. mem. subcom. Controlled Substances and Terrorism and Nat. Security, appointed to Jud. Coun.'s Exec. Legis. Action Network, Chief Justice of Calif. Supreme Ct.; appointed to Criminal Law Planning Com. of Calif. Continuing Jud. Studies Program, Governing Com. of Calif. Ctr. for Jud. Edn. and Rsch.; appointed to Adult Probation Dept.'s Oversight Com., Presiding Judge for Cts.; mem. exec. com. San Francisco Superior Ct.; mem. exec. com. Am. Inn of Cts., U. San Francisco Sch. Law; bd. govs. U San Francisco Law Soc.; bd. trustees Schs. of Sacred Heart, San Francisco; mem. faculty Intensive Trial Advocacy Program, U. San Francisco Sch. Law; lectr. in field. Recipient Mcpl. Ct. Trial Judge of Yr., San Francisco Trial Lawyers' Assn. 1998. Office: US Attys Office No Dist Calif 450 Golden Gate Ave San Francisco CA 94102*

**RYAN, KEVIN WILLIAM,** virologist, clinical research administrator; b. Ft. Dodge, Iowa, Dec. 8, 1952; s. Joseph Michael Ryan and Etoile Evelyn Werth; m. Mary Ellen Lyman, June 1, 1974; children: Matthew Lyman, Mark Joseph. BS, U. Iowa, 1978; PhD, U. Mich., 1984. Staff fellow Nat. Inst. Allergy and Infectious Diseases, NIH, Bethesda, Md., 1984-86; rsch. asst. dept. virology and molecular biology St. Jude Children's Rsch. Hosp., Memphis, 1986-89, asst. mem., 1989-98; asst. prof. pathology U. Tenn. Coll. Medicine, Memphis, 1994-98; sci. rev. adminstr. Nat. Inst. Allergy and Infectious Diseases, NIH, Rockville, Md., 1998-2000; program officer virology vaccine and prevention rsch. prog. divsn. AIDS, Nat. Inst. Allergy and Infectious Diseases, NIH, Bethesda, Md., 2000—05; deputy chief Prevention Scis. Br., 2001—02, chief, 2002—05, lead program officer grant-supported internat. clin. rsch. in HIV/AIDS prevention, 2001—05; mem. working group NIAID, Comprehensive Internat. Program for Rsch. in AIDS (CIPRA), 2001—05; dep. dir. pediatrics, adolescent and maternal AIDS, Ctr. for Rsch. for Mothers and Children, Nat. Inst. Child Health and Human Devel., NIH, Rockville, Md., 2005—. Prin. investigator Nat. Inst. Allergy and Infectious Diseases, 1992—98; lead program officer HIV prevention trials network HPTN, 2002—05; govt. project officer HIV Network Prevention Trials Internat. (HIVNET) Master Contract for AIDS Rsch. NIAID, 2002—04; NIAID Rep. HPTN Prevention Leadership Group, 2002—05; dep. chief Pediat., Adolescent and Maternal AIDS br. Ctr. for Rsch. Mothers and Children, Nat. Inst. of Child Health and Human Devel., NIH, 2005—; lead NICHD program officer Adolescent Medicine Trials Network, 2005—, Women and Infants HIV Transmission Study, 2005—; program officer Pediatric HIV-AIDS Cohort Study, 2005—. Contbr. articles to profl. jours., chpts. to tech. manuals. Fellow postdoctoral Mich. Cancer Inst., U. Mich., 1982. Mem.: Am. Soc. for Microbiology. Roman Catholic. Avocations: woodworking, golf. Office: Nat Inst Child Health and Human Devel PAMA 6100 Executive Blvd Rockville MD 20852-0001 Business E-Mail: kr90p@nih.gov.

**RYAN, L. THOMAS, JR.,** lawyer; b. Binghamton, N.Y., Feb. 10, 1952; s. Lawrence T. and Rita Ryan; children: L. Thomas III, Michael I. BS, U. Ala., Tuscaloosa, 1975, JD, 1978. Bar: Ala. 1979, U.S. Dist. Ct. (no. dist.) Ala. 1979, U.S. Ct. Appeals (11th cir.) 1985. Assoc. Lammons Bell & Sneed, Huntsville, Ala., 1978-80; ptnr. Ryan & Robins, Huntsville, 1980-84, Simpson Hamilton & Ryan, Huntsville, 1984-87, Hamilton & Ryan, Huntsville, 1987-89; owner The Ryan Law Firm, Huntsville, 1989—. Bd. dirs. Nat. Children's Advocacy Ctr., Huntsville, 1984-88; bd. dirs., pres. Foster Children's Alliance, Huntsville, 1988-90; bd. dirs. Lawyer Referral and Info. Svc. Madison County, Ala., Huntsville, 1992—. Mem. Am. Acad. Estate Planning Attys., Nat. Acad. Elder Law Attys., Masons, Elks, Eagles. Democrat. Roman Catholic. Avocations: reading, boating, computers, golf. Office: The Ryan Law Firm 2319 Market Pl SW Ste B Huntsville AL 35801-5250

**RYAN, L. TIMOTHY,** chef, educator, academic administrator; b. Pitts. m. Lynne Ryan; 2 children. BS, U. New Haven; MBA, U. New Haven Sch. Bus. Adminstrn.; graduated, Culinary Inst. Am., 1977; EdD, U. Pa., Pa. Graduate Sch. Edu., Phila. Cert. Master Chef 1985. Asst. chef Ben Gross' Restaurant, Irwin, Pa.; exec. chef La Normande, Pitts.; joined Culinary Institute Am., Hyde Park, NY, 1982, exec. v.p., v.p. edu., dir., culinary edu., dept. head, culinary edu., chef-instructor, pres., 2001—. Developer Am. Bounty Restaurant. Author: The Culinary Olympics Cookbook, 1984, 1988, New Professional Chef, Techniques of Healthy Cooking, An American Bounty; editl. adv. com. mem.: Cheers, Seafood Bus., Take Out Bus. magazines, former chmn. editl. coun.: Nat. Culinary Review; contbr. to videos and television shows. Named to Am. Acad. Chefs, 1990; recipient Gold medals, Pitts. Culinary Arts Salon, 1981, Eastern Regional Olympic Tryouts, 1982, Gourmet Fair, Japan, 1983, Honor Roll Am. Chefs, Food & Wine magazine, 1983, Chef Yr. award, Am. Culinary Fedn., 1998, Presdl. medal, Am. Culinary Fedn., Mem.: Cooks Societies, 1998, Hon. Doctorate Foodservice medallion, N.Am. Assn. Food Equipment Manufacturers, Grand prize of show, Internat. Feinschmecker Parade, Austria. Mem.: Am. Culinary Fedn. (Pitts. chpt. bd. dirs. 1981—82, pub. rels. chair 1982—83, apprenticeship chair, Mid-Hudson chpt. 1982—84, culinary com. 1983—, team capt.) U.S. culinary team 1984, master chef com. 1985—, team capt., U.S. Team, Culinary World Cup Competition 1986, team capt., U.S. culinary team 1988, N.E. v.p. 1991—93, nat. pres. 1995—96, chmn. bd. 1996—97, team mgr., U.S. team, Salon Culinaire Mondial 1987, team mgr., U.s. team, Internat. World Culinary Arts Festival, four Gold Medals and World Championship (Hot Food Competition), Internat. Culinary Competition, Germany 1988, two team Gold medals, Salon Culinaire Mondial, Basel, Switzerland 1987, Team grand prize, Culinary World Cup Competition, Luxembourg 1986, Team medal for culinary excellence, Salon Culinary Art, NY 1985, Two gold medals and silver cup, Internat. Culinary Competition, Germany 1984). Achievements include launching the world's first bachelor's

degree program in Culinary Arts Management and Baking and Pastry Arts Management; developing a highly successful publishing program; expanding the continuing education programs. Office: Culinary Inst Am 1946 Campus Dr Hyde Park NY 12538-1499

**RYAN, LEO VINCENT,** business educator; b. Waukon, Iowa, Apr. 6, 1927; s. John Joseph and Mary Irene (O'Brien) Ryan. BS, Marquette U., 1949; MBA, DePaul U., 1954; PhD, St. Louis U., 1958; postgrad., Catholic U. Am., 1951-52, Bradley U., 1952-54, Northwestern U., 1950; LLD, Seton Hall U., 1988; DHL, Ill. Benedictine U., 1997. Joined Order Clerics of St. Viator, Roman Cath. Ch., 1950. Faculty Marquette U., Milw., 1957-65, dir. continuing edn. summer sessions, coord. evening divsns., 1959-65, prof. indsl. mgmt., 1964; prof., chmn. dept. mgmt. Loyola U., Chgo., 1965-66; dep. dir. Peace Corps, Lagos, Nigeria, 1966-67, dir. Western Nigeria Ibadan, 1967-68; asst. superior gen. and treas. gen. Clerics of St. Viator, Rome, 1968-69, dir. edn. Am. province Arlington Heights, Ill., 1969-74; pres. St. Viator H.S., 1972-74; dean, prof. mgmt. U. Notre Dame Coll. Bus. Adminstrn., Ind., 1975-80; dean DePaul U. Coll. Commerce, 1980-88, prof. mgmt., 1980-99; Wicklander prof. ethics DePaul U., 1993-94; prof. emeritus, 1999. Dir. Peace Corps tng. programs Marquette U., 1962-65; adj. prof. human devel. St. Mary's Coll., Winona, Minn., 1972-74; sch. bd. Archdiocese Chgo., 1972-75, vice-chmn., 1973-75, nat. edn. com. US Cath. Conf., 1971-75, exec. com., 1973-75; nat. adv. bd. Benedictine Sisters Nauvoo, 1973-83; nat. adv. coun. SBA, 1982-85, vice-chmn. minority bus., 1982-85, exec. com. Chgo. chpt., 1982-84; vis. prof. U. Ife, Ibadan, 1967-68,; chmn. trust audit com. First Bank-Milw., 1980-85, chmn. audit and exam. coms., 1985-90, adv. coun., 1991-93; bd. dirs. Henricksen & Co., Inc.; fin. commn. Clerics of St. Viator, 1978-, provincial chpt., 1985-91, 2001-03, devel. adv. bd. 1996-2001, new foundations com. 1996-98, alt. mem., 1997-2001, provincial coun., 2001-03, coord. coun., U.S., Belize, Columbia, 2001-03, comprehensive devel. coun., 2004; Fulbright prof. Adam Mickiewicz U., Poland, 1993-95; vis. prof. Helsinki Sch. Econs., 1992-2002, Polish-Am. Ctr., U. Lodz, 1998, Poznan Acad. Econs., 1991, 1999—; co-chair bus. and profit. com. Archdiocese of Chgo. Sesquetennial Com. Out Reach Divsns. Ctrl. Planning Group, 1993-94; vis. prof. Notre Dame, 2000, Helsinki Sch. Econs., 2000; vis. scholar U. St. Thomas, Houston, 2006; mem. adv. bd. Sch. Bus. U. Kiev, Ukraine, 2001; vis. adv. bd. DePaul U. Gallery and Mus., 2005—; vis. rsch. scholar U. St. Thomas, Houston, 2006. Author: Human Action in Business, 1996, Etyka Biznesu, 1997, 4th edit., 2000, From Autarcy to Market: Polish Economics and Politics, 1945-1995, 1998, 2d edit., 1999, Students Focus on Business Ethics, 2000, Praxiology and Pragmatism, 2002, Poland: A Transformational Appraisal, 2003; mem. editl. bd. Internat. Jour. Value Based Mgmt., 1983-2003, Bus. Ethics Quar., 1983-2004, European Bus. Jour., 1990-2002, Mid Atlantic Jour. of Bus., 1990-2002, European Jour. Econs. Fin. and Adminstrv. Studies, 2006, Clerics of St. Viator Quar. Mem. Pres.'s Com. on Employment Handicapped, 1959-65, Wis. Gov.'s Com. on Employment Handicapped, 1959-65, Wis. Gov.'s Com. on UN, 1961-64, Burnham Park Planning Commn., 1982-88; bd. dir. Ctr. Pastoral Liturgy U. Notre Dame, 1976-79; trustee Lake Forest Grad. Sch. Mgmt., 1989-91, St. Mary of Woods Coll., 1978-81, Cath. Theol. Union, U. Chgo., 1992-95, Divine Word Coll., 1997-2006; regent Seton Hall U., 1981-87, mem. acad. affairs com., 1981-87, chmn., 1983-87; dir. Ctr. for Enterprise Devel., 1992-95; elected fellow St. Edmunds Coll. Cambridge U., 1992—; mem. Cath. Commn. Intellectual and Cultural Affairs, 1992—, Cath. Campaign for Am., 1994-98; bd. dir. Internat. Bus. Ethics Inst., Am. Grad. Sch. Internat. Mgmt., 1995-97; mem. adv. com. Mgmt. Edn. in Poland, U. Md., College Park, 1995-2000; mem. Iowa Gov. Heartland Leadership Coun., 2003—. Recipient Freedom award Berlin Commn., 1961, chieftaincy title Asoju Atoaja of Oshogbo Oba Adenle I, Yorubaland, Nigeria, 1967, B'nai B'rith Interfaith award, Milw., 1963, Disting. Alumnus award Marquette U., 1974, DePaul U., 1976, Tchr. of Yr. award Beta Alpha Psi, 1980, Centennial Alumni Achievement award Marquette U., 1981, Boland Meml. Disting. Alumni award, St. Louis, 1989, Disting. Alumni and Bicentennial awards Jesuit Bus. Schs., 1989, Pres.' award St. Viator H.S., 1992, Medal of Merit Adam Mickiewicz U., 1995, Excellence in Tchg. award Adam Mickiewicz U., 1997, Ill. Ernst and Young Entrepreneur Supporter award, 1999, Vincentian U. Ethics Scholar award, 2000, Centennial award Dominican U. Sch. Bus., 2002; Brother Leo V. Ryan award named in his honor Cath. Bus. Edn. Assn., 1962; Ryan Scholars in Mgmt. established in his honor DePaul U., 1989, Outstanding Svc. award, 1991-93, Commerce Alumni award of merit, 1997; DePaul Creativity Ctr. named in his honor, 1997, trustee; named hon. life chmn. Nat. Adv. Com., Ryan Creativity Ctr., Creative Cutting Edge award, 1999; Ryan Scholarship named in his honor St. Viator H.S., 1992, Lion award, 1997, trustee, 2000-01, gov., 2001-03; named Man of Yr. Jr. C. of C., Milw., 1959, Marquette U. Bus. Adminstrn. Alumni Man of Yr., 1974; named Disting. Vis. Term Prof. Seton Hall U., 2001, Alumnus of Yr., St. Patrick Grade and H.S., Waukeon, Iowa, 2006; Milw. Bd. Realtors traveling fellow, 1964, Nat. Assn. Purchasing Agts. faculty fellow, 1958, German Am. Acad. Exch. Coun. fellow, 1983, Presdl. fellow Am. Grad. Sch. Internat. Mgmt., 1989, vis. scholar, 1995, Malone fellow in Islamic studies, Bahrain and Saudi Arabia, 1990, fellow Kosciuszko Found. Adam Mickiewicz U., 1990; scholar-in-residence Mgmt. Sch. Imperial Coll. Sci. and Tech. U. London, 1989; vis. scholar U. Calif., Berkeley, 1989; USIA Acad. Specialists grantee, Poland, 1991-93; fellow St. Edmund's Coll. Cambridge U., 1992; named vis. rsch. fellow Von Hugel Inst., 1992-93; scholar-in-residence Am. Grad. Sch. Internat. Mgmt., 1995; guest scholar Kellogg Inst. Internat. Studies U. Notre Dame, 1997; vis. rsch. scholar U. St. Thomas, Houston, 2006. Mem. Cath. Bus. Edn. Assn. (nat. pres. 1960-62, nat. exec. bd. 1960-64), Assn. Sch. Bus. Ofcls. (com. 1965-67), Am. Assembly Collegiate Schs. Bus. (com. internat. affairs 1977-84, chmn. 1981-84, bd. dirs. 1981-87, program chmn. 1979-80, exec. com., chmn. projects/svc. mgmt. com. 1984-86), Am. Fgn. Svc. Assn., Am. Assn. Profl. Ethics (bd. dir. 1996-98), Am. Philat. Soc., Allamakee County Hist. Soc. (charter life), Acad. Internat. Bus., Acad. Mgmt. (social issues div., chmn. membership com. 1990-91), Ancient Order of Hibernians, Nat. Returned Peace Corps Assn., Atomic Vets. Assn., August Derleth Soc., Chgo. Area Return Peace Corps Vols., Econ. Club Chgo., Chgo. Coun. Fgn. Rels., Coun. Fgn. Rels. (diplomat cir. 1998), European Bus. Ethics Network Poland (hon. 1998), Soc. Bus. Ethics (mem. exec. com. 1991—, pres. 1993-94, adv. bd. 1995-97), Assn. Social Econs. (life), Iowa Hist. Soc., Iowa Postal History Soc., Iowa Heartland Leadership Coun., Fulbright Assn. (life), Internat. Assn. for Bus. and Soc. (founder), Internat. Soc. for Bus., Econs. and Ethics (charter), Internat. Trade and Fin. Assn. (founder, bd. dir. 1989-92, 96-98, v.p membership 1991-92, 96-97), Internat. Learned Soc. Praxiology, (hon. life, internat. adv. bd. praxiology ann.), Polish Inst. Arts and Scis. in Am., Postal History Soc., Polish Am. Historical Assn, DePaul Inst. Bus. and Profl. Ethics (founder 1984, bd. mem. 1984-94, mus. adv. com. 2005—), Founders award 1999), USS Mt. McKinley Reunion Assn. (life, hon. chaplain AGC-7 1989-96, Disting. Svc. award 1991, 96), Friends of Nigeria, Alpha Sigma Nu, Alpha Kappa Psi (bd. dir. found. 1985-91, vice-chmn. 1987-91, chmn. scholarship com. 1987-91, chmn. devel. cent. 1987, exec. com. 1990-91, Bronze Disting. Svc. award 1949, Silver Disting. Svc. award 1958, Recognition medal, 2001), Beta Alpha Psi, Beta Gamma Sigma (co-chair 75th Anniversary com. Ill., faculty advisor DePaul chpt. 1986-92), Century Travel Club (Silver award), Delta Mu Delta, Pi Gamma Mu, Tau Kappa Epsilon. Office Phone: 847-870-4903. Personal E-mail: leovryan@aol.com. E-mail: leovryan@viatorians.com

**RYAN, LEONARD EAMES,** judge; b. Albion, N.Y., July 8, 1930; s. Bernard and Harriet Earle (Fitts) R.; m. Ann Allen, June 18, 1973; 1 child, Thomas Eames Allen-Ryan. Grad., Kent Sch., 1948; AB, U. Pa., 1954; JD, NYU, 1962. Bar: D.C. 1963, N.Y. 1963, U.S. Ct. Appeals (D.C. cir.) 1963, U.S. Dist. Ct. (so. and ea. dists.) N.Y. 1965, U.S. Ct. Appeals (2nd cir.) 1966, U.S. Supreme Ct. 1967. Field engr. constrn. U.S. Steel Fairless Works, Morrisville, Pa., 1951-52; reporter Upper Darby (Pa.) News, 1954; newsman AP, Pitts., Phila., Harrisburg, N.Y.C., 1955-62; reporter, spl. writer on law N.Y. Times, 1962-63; info. adviser corp. hdqrs. IBM, N.Y.C., 1963; trial atty. firm Perrell, Nielsen & Stephens, N.Y.C., 1964-66; trial atty. civil rights div. Dept. Justice, Washington, 1966-68; asst. to bur. affairs CBS News, N.Y.C., 1968; program officer Office Govt. and Law, Ford Found., N.Y.C., 1968-74; pvt. practice law, cons. pub. affairs, N.Y.C., 1974-91; v.p., sec. W. P. Carey & Co., Inc., N.Y.C., 1977—82; impartial hearing officer Edn. for All

Handicapped Children Act of 1975, 1976-91; per diem adminstrv. law judge N.Y. State Agys., 1976-91; hearing examiner N.Y. State Family Ct., 1980-81; apptd. U.S. adminstv. law judge, 1991; adminstv. law judge Office Hearings and Appeals, San Rafael, Calif., 1991—93, Phila., 1993-94, N.Y.C., 1994—. Arbitrator Small Claims Ct., N.Y.C., 1974-84; bd. dirs. Community Action for Legal Svcs. Inc., N.Y.C., 1971-77, vice-chmn., 1975-77; co-chmn. Citizens Com. to Save Legal Svcs., N.Y.C., 1975-76; bd. dirs. Lower East Side Svc. Ctr., N.Y.C., 1977-89. Author: (with Bernard Ryan Jr.) So You Want to Go Into Journalism, 1963; contbr. articles to profl. jours. Served with USAR, 1950-57. Mem. Am. Judicature Soc., Assn. of Bar of City of N.Y., N.Y. State Bar Assn., St. Elmo Club (Phila.), Heights Casino (Bklyn.). Home: 32 Orange St Brooklyn NY 11201-1634 Office: 111 Livingston St Brooklyn NY 11201-5078 .

RYAN, LISA KATHLEEN, environmental and medical science educator; b. Morgantown, W.Va., July 9, 1958; d. Richard Stoetzer and Ellen Stewart Wagner; m. Gill Diamond, Aug. 31, 1997; m. Niall Patrick Ryan, Oct. 3, 1981 (dec. Oct. 1, 1993); children: Allison Kathleen, Michael Richard Diamond, Sara Elana Diamond. BS in microbiology, Penn State U., University Pk., 1976—80; MS in med. microbiology, W.Va. U. Med. Sch., Morgantown, 1980—83; PhD in toxicology, U. Pitts. Grad. Sch. of Pub. Health, 1986—92. Rsch. biologist, immunotoxicology br. U.S. EPA, Rsch. Triangle Pk., NC, 1995—2000; asst. prof., dept. of pathology UMDNJ-New Jersey Med. Sch., Newark, 2000—03; asst. prof. dept. oral biology UMDNJ-N.J. Dental Sch., Newark, 2003—. ORD regional sci. advisor, EPA region 2, U.S. EPA Office of Sci. Policy, Washington, 1998—2000; rsch. fellow in medicine Mass. Gen. Hosp./Harvard Med. Sch., Boston, 1992—95. Contbr. articles to profl. jours. Recipient Re-entry to Rsch. Supplemental award, NIH NIAID, 2000—03, Individual Nat. Rsch. Svc. award, NIH NHLBI, 1994—97; Rsch. Grant Co-Investigator, 2003—, Student Rsch. award, Allegheny-Erie Regional Chpt. of the Soc. of Toxicology, 1991, Devel. of an ELISA for Endotoxin Detection, Hyclone Diagnostics/Travenol Laboratories, 1981—82. Mem.: AAAS, Sigma Xi, Am. Conf. of Govtl. Indsl. Hygenists, Am. Thoracic Soc., Am. Soc. for Microbiology, Soc. for Leukocyte Biology, Am. Assn. Immunologists, Soc. Toxicology. Achievements include patents for polymyxin agarose-lipopolysaccharide antigen and associated method. Avocations: swimming, ice skating, piano, clarinet, skiing. Office: UMDNJ-New Jersey Dental Sch Dept Oral Biology 185 South Orange Ave Newark NJ 07101 Office Phone: 973-972-2624. Business E-Mail: ryanlk@umdnj.edu.

RYAN, LUCILLE FRANCIS See LAWLESS, LUCY

RYAN, MARIANNE ELIZABETH, lawyer; b. Ft. Knox, Ky., Nov. 15, 1964; d. John L. and Frances J. (McIntosh) R. BA, Trinity Coll., 1986; JD, Yale U., 1991; MS in Info., U. Mich., 2003. Bar: Ill. 1991, U.S. Dist. Ct. (no. dist.) Ill. 1991. Assoc. Pattishall, McAuliffe, Newbury, Hilliard & Geraldson, Chgo., 1991—93; internet editor Law Jour. EXTRA! The N.Y. Law Pub. Co., N.Y.C., 1994—95; rsch. scholar Nat. Ctr. for Philanthropy and Law NYU Sch. Law, 1996—99; coord. tech. Americorps/Project F.I.R.S.T., N.Y.C., 1999—2000; VISTA svc. leader Americorps/Ohio Campus Compact, Yellow Springs, 2000—01; resident fellow Lloyd Hall Scholars Program, U. Mich., Ann Arbor, 2002—03; Cmty. Info. fellow Alliance for Cmty. Tech., 2002—; mem. behavioral sci. instl. rev. bd., 2006—. Adj. prof. trademark and copyright law John Marshall Law Sch., Chgo., 1993. Exec. editor Yale Jour. on Regulation. Recipient Margaret Mann award, Sch. of Info., U. Mich., 2003; Olin fellow, U. Mich. Law Sch., 2004—05, Rackham Regents' fellow, U. Mich., 2004—, Jacob Javits fellow, U.S. Dept. Edn., 2005—, Margaret Dow Towsley scholar, U. Mich., 2001—02, USA Funds Access to Edn. scholar, 2005—, Microsoft summer fellow, U Mich., 2002. Mem.: Soc. Philosophy and Tech., Internat. Soc. Ethics and Info. Tech., Assn. Internet Rschrs., Assn. Practical and Profl. Ethics, Phi Beta Kappa. Home: 1150 Paddock Pl Apt 107 Ann Arbor MI 48108 Business E-Mail: meryan@umich.edu.

RYAN, MARK ANTHONY, architect, lawyer; b. Council Bluffs, IA, Sept. 6, 1964; s. Paul Elmer and Darreline Kay (Wyland) Ryan; m. Shelli Ann Hagerbaumer, Sept. 26, 1992. BA in Architecture with distinction, Iowa State U., Ames, 1987; JD summa cum laude, Creighton U., Omaha, 2003. Registered profl. arch., Wis.; bar: Iowa, 2003, Nebr. 2004, U.S Patent and Trademark Office 2005. Project arch. U.S. Army C.E., Omaha, 1987-90, arch., security engr., 1990-91, environ. project mgr., 1991-96; owner, arch. Ryan Designs, Omaha, 1987—; project mgr. Bovis Constrn. Corp. and Bovis Lend Lease, Omaha, 1997-2000; CEO Ad Hoc Comm. Resources, LLC, Omaha, 1999—, gen. counsel, 2004—; pvt. law practice Ryan Patent Law, 2004—. Bd. advisors Fitness Plus, Council Bluffs, Iowa, 1990—92; expert witness, Iowa, Nebr., 1991—; law clk. West Corp., 2002; intern law clk. U.S. Dist. Ct., Nebr., 2003. Chmn. City Devel. Commn., Council Bluffs, Iowa, 1992; trustee San. and Improvement Dist. No. 142, Douglas County, Nebr., 1995—96. Scholar, State of Iowa, 1982; Valentino scholar, 2001, Lane Found. scholar, 2002, Abrahams scholar, 2002. Mem.: ABA, AIA (sec. S.W. Iowa sect. 1991, treas. 1992, v.p. 1993, pres. 1994—96), Nat. Bar Assn., Omaha Bar Assn., Nebr. State Bar Assn., Iowa Bar Assn., Golden Key, Phi Delta Phi, Tau Sigma Delta, Phi Kappa Phi. Avocations: architecture, bicycling, aquatics, tennis. Office: Ryan Patent Law 9030 Raven Oaks Dr Omaha NE 68152-1759 Business E-Mail: mark@adhoccr.com.

RYAN, MARLEIGH GRAYER, language educator; b. NYC, May 1, 1930; d. Harry and Betty (Hurwick) Grayer; m. Edward Ryan, June 4, 1950; 1 child, David Patrick. BA, NYU, 1951; MA, Columbia U., 1956, PhD, 1965; Cert., East Asian Inst., 1956; postgrad., Kyoto U., 1958-59. Research assoc. Columbia U., NYC, 1960-61, lectr. Japanese, 1961-65, asst. prof., 1965-70, assoc. prof., 1970-72; vis. asst. prof. Yale U., New Haven 1966-67; assoc. prof. U. Iowa, Iowa City, 1972-73, prof., 1973-81, chmn. dept., 1972-81; prof. Japanese SUNY, New Paltz, 1981-98, dean liberal arts and scis., 1981-90, prof. emeritus, 1999—; assoc. in rsch. Reischauer Inst. for Japanese Studies, Harvard U., Cambridge, Mass., 1999—, chair study group on Asian Am. Lit., 2000—02; retirement study group leader Harvard Inst. Learning, 2003—06. Vice chmn. seminar on modern Japan, Columbia U., 1984-85, chmn., 1985-86; co-chmn. N.Y. State Conf. on Asian Studies, 1986, editor, 1993-99, mem. exec. com., 1993-96, sec., 1993-99, co-chmn., 1998. Co-author: (with Herschel Webb) Research in Japanese Sources, 1965; author: Japan's First Modern Novel, 1967, The Development of Realism in the Fiction of Tsubouchi Shoyo, 1975; assoc. editor: Jour. Assn. Tchrs. Japanese, 1962-71, editor, 1971-75. East Asian Inst. fellow Columbia U., 1955; Ford Found. fellow, 1958-60; Japan Found. fellow, 1973, Woodrow Wilson Ctr. Internat. Scholars fellow, 1988-89; recipient Van. Am. Disting. Book award Columbia, 1968 Mem. MLA (sec. com. on teaching Japanese Lang. 1962-68, mem. del. assembly 1979-87, mem. exec. com. div. Asian lit. 1981-86), Assn. Tchrs. Japanese (exec. com. 1969-72, 74-77), Assn. Asian Studies (bd. dirs. 1975-78, N.E. asian coun. 1975-78, coun. of confs., 1993-96), Midwest Conf. Asian Studies (pres. 1980-81) Personal E-mail: marleighryan@earthlink.net. *Studying the most difficult language in the world has taught me patience and tact. One learns what it is to sit completely still at the Japanese No theatre and absorb wondrous sights and sounds in an atmosphere of absolute peace. Discovering the stillness in movement is perhaps the most important lesson we in the West can derive from our Asian experience.*

RYAN, SISTER MARY JEAN, health facility executive; LHD, Webster U., 1994, U. Mo., St. Louis, 2003, Lindenwood U., 2003. Pres., CEO SSM Health Care, 1986—. Presenter in field. Co-author: CQI and the Renovation of an American Health Care System: A Culture Under Construction, 1997. Mem. Excellence in Mo. Found.; chair Taking Care/A Health Forum for Women Religious, Madison, Wis.; bd. dirs. Inst. for Healthcare Improvement, United Way of Greater St. Louis; sec. Hawthorn Found. of Mo.; mem., treas., bd. dirs. St. Louis Regional Chamber and Growth Assn.; bd. dirs SSM Health Care of Okla., SSM Health Care of Wis., SSM Health Care-St. Louis. Named one of 20 Disting. Women/St. Louis Area, 25 Most Influential Women in Bus. in St. Louis; recipient Brotherhood/Sisterhood award, Nat. Conf. Cmty. and

Justice, Gov.'s Quality Leadership award, State of Mo., Corp. that Makes a Difference award, Internat. Women's Forum. Office: SSM Health Care Sys Inc 477 N Lindbergh Blvd Saint Louis MO 63141

RYAN, MEG (MARGARET MARY EMILY ANN HYRA), actress, film producer; b. Fairfield, Conn., Nov. 19, 1961; m. Dennis Quaid, Feb. 14, 1991 (div. July 16, 2001); 1 child, Jack Henry; 1 adopted child, Daisy True. Student, NYU. Established Fandango Films (then called Prufrock Pictures), 1994—2000. Mem. of jury Festival Internat. de Cannes, 2003. Appearences include (TV) One of the Boys, 1982, As The World Turns, 1982-84, Wild Side, 1985, (films) Rich and Famous, 1981, Amityville 3-D, 1983, Top Gun, 1986, Armed and Dangerous, 1986, Innerspace, 1987, Promised Land, 1987, D.O.A., 1988, The Presidio, 1988, When Harry Met Sally, 1989, Joe Versus the Volcano, 1990, The Doors, 1991, Prelude to a Kiss, 1992, Sleepless in Seattle, 1993, Flesh and Bone, 1993, When a Man Loves a Woman, 1994, Restoration, 1994. I.Q., 1994, French Kiss, 1995 (also prodr.), Two for the Road, 1996 (also prodr.), Courage Under Fire, 1996, Addicted to Love, 1997, Anastasia (voice), 1997, City of Angels, 1998, Hurlyburly, 1998, You've Got Mail, 1998, Hanging Up, 2000, Proof of Life, 2000, Kate & Leopold, 2001, In the Cut, 2003, Against the Ropes, 2004; prodr. Lost Souls, 2000, Desert Saints, 2002; exec. prodr. Northern Lights, 1997, The Wedding Planner, 2001. Vol. CARE humanitarian orgn. Recipient Golden Apple award Hollywood Women's Press Club, 1989, Woman of Yr. award Hasty Pudding Theatricals, 1994, ShoWest Conv. Actress of Yr. award, 1999, Am. Comedy Award, 1990, 1994, Women in Film Crystal Award, 1995; named one of the Top 100 Movie Stars of All Time, Empire (UK) Magazine, 1997, The Most Powerful People in Hollywood, Premiere (USA) Magazine, 1999, Most Powerful People in Hollywood, Entertainment Weekly's, 1998. Office: Creative Artists Agy 9830 Wilshire Blvd Beverly Hills CA 90212*

RYAN, MELBAGENE T., retired food service and nutrition director; b. Arkadelphia, Ark., Jan. 6, 1927; d. Horace Samuel and Eunice Bridges (Moorman) Tull; m. Wayne Stuart Ryan, Dec. 26, 1954. BS in Edn., Henderson U., 1948; M in Edn., Tex. Women's U., 1951. Tchr. Eudora Pub. Schs., Ark., 1948-52; dir. food services Tex. Christian U., Ft. Worth, 1952-53, Tex. Women's U., 1953-58; dir. food and nutriton service Irving Ind. Sch. Dist., Tex., 1958-85. Project dir. to develop stds. excellence with a self study and evaluation Tex. Sch. Food Svc. Assn., 1985-88; cons. in field. Co-author and project dir.: (with others) Youth Advisory Council Resource Manual, 1978-79, Effective Food Service Management Using Computers, 1982. With child nutrition Tex. Sch. Food Svc. Assn., Washington, 1974-79; with legis. Am. Sch. Food Svc. Assn., Irving, 1980-85; mem. Denton Co. Hist. Commn., 1997—, Denton Co. Courthouse-on-the Square Mus., chmn. 1998—; mem. adv. bd. Lake Forest Good Samaritan Village, 1998—, Tex. Woman's U. Centennial Celebration, 2001, planning com., 1998-99, Denton Good Samaritan Village, 2003; chmn. Bayless Selby House Mus., 2002—. Recipient Food Facilities Design award Instns. Volume Feeding Awards Program, New Orleans, 1977, Trend Setter award, North Tex. Brokers Assn., Dallas, 1978; Melbagene Ryan Scholarship named in her honor by Dallas Profl. Friends, 1985. Mem. Denton Dietetic Assn. (pres. 1977-78), Tex. Dietetic Assn., Am. Dietetic Assn. (chmn. joint com. 1979-82), Tex. Sch. Food Svc. Assn. (pres. 1975-76, nutrition edn. 1975), Am. Sch. Food Svc. Assn. (conf. com. 1977-78, 1982-83), Tex. Women's U. Alumni Assn. Methodist. Home and Office: 1121 Ryan Rd Denton TX 76210-5539

RYAN, MICHAEL D., state supreme court justice; BA, St. John's U., Collegeville, Minn., 1967; JD, Ariz. State U., 1977. Dep. county atty. Maricopa County Atty.'s Office, 1977—85; judge pro tempore Superior Ct. State of Ariz., Maricopa County, 1985—86, judge Maricopa County, 1986—96, assoc. criminal presiding judge Maricopa County, 1993—96; judge Ariz. Ct. Appeals, Divsn. 1, 1996—2002, vice chief judge, 2001—02; justice Ariz. Supreme Ct., 2002—. Chair Scottsdale Jud. Appts. Adv. Bd., 1999—2002; vice chair Ariz. State Bar Task Force on Persons with Disabilities, 2002—; mem. Maricopa County Resource Site Team for Ctr. for Sex Offender Mgmt., 1996—2000, Ariz. Atty. Gen.'s Capital Case Commn., 2000—02; mem. adv. com. Nat. Ctr. for State Cts., Ctr. for Effective Pub. Policy, also State Justice Inst.'s Nat. Solutions Project, 2003—; chair Ariz. Supreme Ct. Com. on Keeping Record, 2004—. Infantry platoon comdr. USMC, 1968, Vietnam. Recipient Semper Fi award, First Marine Divsn. Assns., Phoenix chpt., 2001, Outstanding Alumnus award, Ariz. State Univ. Coll. Law, 2003, Disting. Achievement award, 2003, James A. Walsh Outstanding Jurist award, State Bar Ariz., 2005. Mem.: State Bar of Arizona (Judicial award of Excellence 2001), Maricopa County Bar Assn. (bd. dirs. 1987—91, 1997—2002, chair task force recruitment and retention of women and minorities 1997—2004, Henry S. Stevens Judge of the Yr. award 2001). Office: Ariz Supreme Ct 1501 W Washington Phoenix AZ 85007-3231*

RYAN, MICHAEL LOUIS, controller; b. Corning, Iowa, Feb. 22, 1945; s. Leo Vincent and Elda May (Lawrence) R AAS Constrn. Tech., Iowa State U., 1985; BS Acctg., Drake U., 1972. CPA, Iowa, Wyo. Acct. Ernst & Ernst, Des Moines, 1972—75, Becker, Herrick & Co., Pueblo, Colo., 1975—78; pvt. practice acctg. Gillette, Wyo., 1979—81; acct. Karen M. Moody, CPA, Sheridan, Wyo., 1981—85; contr. T-C Investments, Inc., Sheridan, 1985—; ptnr. WHG Partnership, Sheridan, 1991—; v.p. Bosley-Ryan Constrn., Inc., Sheridan, 1993—. With spl. forces U.S. Army, 1966-68, Vietnam Mem. AICPA (tax divsn.), Wyo. Soc. CPA, Am. Legion (fin. officer 1977-83), Lodge (sec. Sheridan club 1982-90, pres. 1989), Phi Kappa Phi, Beta Alpha Psi, Beta Gamma Sigma Democrat. Roman Catholic. Home: 735 Canby St Sheridan WY 82801-4907 Office: 566 Turner Ln Sheridan WY 82801 E-mail: mkryan@wavecom.net.

RYAN, NOLAN, former professional baseball player; b. Refugio, Tex., Jan. 31, 1947; s. Lynn Nolan and Martha (Hancock) Ryan; m. Ruth Elsie Holdruff, June 26, 1967; children: Reid, Reese, Wendy. Student: Alvin Jr. Coll., 1966—69. Pitcher N.Y. Mets, N.Y.C., 1966—71, Calif. Angels, 1972—79, Houston Astros, 1980—88, Texas Rangers, 1989—93; cattle rancher, China Grove, Ray and Gonzalvez Tex.; owner The Bass Inn, Waterfront Steakhouse and Grill, Express Bank (sold to First Community Capital in 2002); owner, Texas league farm club team The Round Rock Express, Round Rock, Tex.; investor, ptnr. The Express Bank of Texas, Round Rock, Tex., 2003—. Commr. Tex. Parks and Wildlife Commn., 1995—2001, vice chmn., 1995—97. Author (with Steve Jacobson): Nolan Ryan: Strike-Out King, 1975; author: (with Bill Libby) Nolan Ryan: The Other Game, 1977; author: (with Joe Torre) Pitching and Hitting, 1977; author: (with Harvey Frommer) Throwing Heat: The Autobiography of Nolan Ryan, 1988; author: (with Tom House) Nolan Ryan's Pitcher's Bible, 1991; author: (with Jerry Jenkins) Miracle Man: Nolan Ryan, The Autobiography, 1992; author: (with others) Kings of Hill, 1992. Founder, bd. dirs. The Nolan Ryan Found.; bd. dirs. The Justin Cowboy Crisis Fund, Texas Water Found., Natural Resources Found., Tex. With AUS, 1967. Named Am. League Pitcher of Yr., Sporting News, 1977; named to All-Star Team, Am. League, 1972, 1973, 1975, 1979, Nat. League, 1981, 1985, Baseball Hall of Fame, 1999. Achievements include holding over 50 Major League records including most seasons pitched (27), most strikeouts (5,714) and most no-hit games (7). Office: Round Rock Express 3400 E Palm Valley Blvd Round Rock TX 78664

RYAN, PATRICK G., diversified financial services company executive, director; b. Milw., May 15, 1937; m. Shirley Welsh, Apr. 16, 1966; children: Patrick Jr., Robert J., Corbett M. BS, Northwestern U., 1959. Sales agt. Penn Mut., 1959-64, Pat Ryan & Assocs. Chgo., 1964-71; chmn., pres. Ryan Ins. Group Inc., Chgo., 1971-82; pres., chief exec. officer Combined Internat. Corp. (now Aon Corp.), Northbrook, Ill., 1982—, bd. dirs., 1982—; pres., CEO Aon Corp., Chgo., 1990—2005, chmn., 1990—. Bd. dirs. Sears Roebuck and Co., Chgo., Tribune Co., Chgo. Life trustee, past chmn., Rush Univ. Med. Ctr., Chgo.; chmn., trustee Northwestern U.; past trustee Field Mus. Natural History, Chgo. Recipient Lifetime Achievement award, The Review-Worldwide Reinsurance, 2005, Internat. Exec. of the Yr., Brigham Young Univ., 2002, Golden Plate award, Acad. of Achievement, 2002; named to Chgo. Bus. Hall of Fame. Mem., past pres., Econ. Club Chgo. Office: Aon Corp Aon Ctr 200 E Randolph St Chicago IL 60601*

RYAN, PATRICK M., lawyer; m. Barbara E. Ryan; children: Michael, Jason, Megan. BA, U. Okla., 1967, JD, 1969. Bar: Okla., U.S. Dist. Ct. (we. and ea. dists.) Okla., U.S. Ct. Appeals (10th cir.), U.S. Ct. Mil. Appeals, U.S. Supreme Ct. Ptnr. Crowe & Dunlevy, Oklahoma City, 1974—81; pres., dir. Ryan, Geister & Whaley, Oklahoma City, 1982—95; U.S. atty. for western dist. Okla. Office of U.S. Atty., Oklahoma City, 1995—99; pvt. practice Ryan & Whaley, 1999—. Editor: Okla. Law Rev. Trustee World Neighbors, 1994—97; active St. John the Bapt. Chat. Ch., Edmond, Okla. With JAGC USAF, 1969—74. Recipient Leadership award, Okla. County Bar Assn., 1989. Fellow: Internat. Acad. Trial Lawyers, Am. Coll. Trial Lawyers (mem. Okla. state com. 1990—95), Okla. Bar Found. (v.p. 1978, 1980); mem.: ABA, Okla. Bar Assn. (gov. bd. govs. 1990—93, mem. young lawyers sect.), Order of Coif. Office: 119 N Robinson Ave Ste 900 Oklahoma City OK 73102-4617

RYAN, PATRICK MICHAEL, lawyer; b. Chgo., May 26, 1944; s. Edward Michael and Kathleen Teresa (Crimmins) R.; m. Holly Ann Daleske, Aug. 31, 1968; children: Rebecca Eileen, Brendan Patrick, Abigail Christine, Lucas Christopher. BA, St. Mary's Coll., Winona, Minn., 1966; JD, Marquette U., 1969. Bar: Wis. 1969. Law clk. Wis. Supreme Ct., Madison, 1969-70; ptnr. Quarles & Brady LLP, Milw., 1970—2001, chmn., mng. ptnr., 2002—. Dir. and officer several pvt. bus. corps. Mem. ABA, Wis. Bar Assn., Milw. Bar Assn., University Club. Avocations: reading, sports. Home: 363 Huntington Dr Cedarburg WI 53012-9507 Office: Quarles & Brady LLP 411 E Wisconsin Ave Ste 2550 Milwaukee WI 53202-4497 Office Phone: 414-277-5000. E-mail: pmr@quarles.com.

RYAN, PAUL, congressman; b. Janesville, Wis., Jan. 29, 1970; s. Paul and Betty Ryan; m. Janna Ryan; 3 children. BS in Econs. and Polit. Sci., Miami U., Ohio, 1992. Aide Staff of US Senator Bob Kasten of Wis., Washington; econ. adv., speechwriter Empower Am., Jack Kemp, Bill Bennett, Washington; legis. dir. US Senate, Washington; mktg. cons. Ryan Inc., Ctrl., Janesville; mem. US Congress from 1st Wis. dist., 1999—, mem. ways and means com., mem. joint econ. com., mem. budget com. Defeated former Kenosha City Coun. Pres. Lydia Spottswood in 1998 to succeed two-term Rep. Mark Neumann, who ran unsuccessfully for the Senate. Mem. Janesville YMCA, Janesville Bowmen Inc. and Ducks Unlimited. Republican. Roman Catholic. Office: US Ho Reps 1113 Longworth Ho Office Bldg Washington DC 20515 Office Phone: 202-225-3031.*

RYAN, RAY DARL, JR., academic administrator; b. Joliet, Ill., Dec. 2, 1945; s. Ray D. and Oral Ada (Smiley) R.; m. Marianne Rossetto, Aug. 28, 1965; children: Kimberley, Kristin, Matthew. BS, U. Wis., Menomonie, 1970, MEd, U. Mo., 1973, EdD, 1975; Doctorate (hon.), Tomsk (Siberia) Poly. U., 1992. Cert. vocat./tech. tchr., adminstr., chief sch. officer. Dep. supt. pub. instrn. Nev. Dept. Edn., Carson City; dep. supt. spl. programs Ariz. Dept. Edn., Phoenix, state dir. vocat. educator; exec. dir. Ctr. Edn. and Tng. for Employment Ohio State U., Columbus, assoc. dean rsch., internat. affairs. Bd. dirs., vice-chair Coun. Ednl. Devel. and Rsch., pres., CEO Nat. Occup. Testing Inst., 1999. Mem. OTT, ASTD, Phi Delta Kappa, Epsilon Pi Tau, Omicron Tau Theta. Office: NOCTI 500 N Bronson Ave Big Rapids MI 49307

RYAN, RAYMOND D., retired steel company executive, insurance company executive; b. Big Timber, Mont., Feb. 7, 1922; s. Robert Allen and Elsie (Beery) R.; m. Eunice Dale Burnett, Jan. 17, 1943; children: Raymond Brant, Brenda Ruth, Ronald Dale. BA, U. Mont., 1948, JD (hon.), 1970; LLM, NYU, 1949. Bar: Mont. 1948. Various fin. officer positions U.S. Steel and subsidiaries in U.S. and Venezuela, 1949-75; v.p., treas. U.S. Steel, 1975-83; pres. The Evergreen Group Inc., Stamford, Conn., 1984-94, chmn., 1995-96, Evergreen Benefits Inc., 1996-99, The Money Suite Co., Missoula, Mont., 1999—. With mil. police AUS, 1943-45, ETO. Mem. ABA, Met. Club (N.Y.C.), Phi Sigma Kappa, Phi Delta Phi. Home: PO Box 160601 Big Sky MT 59716-0601 Office Phone: 406-995-3397. Personal E-mail: rayd@moneysuite.com. *Although luck and ambition are the basis of many apparently successful careers, true success comes from hard work, ethical relationships, dedication, and a willingness to accept responsibility.*

RYAN, REGINA CLAIRE (MRS. PAUL DEUTSCHMAN), editor, literary agent; b. NYC, June 19, 1938; d. Edward F.X. and Kathryn Regina (Gallagher) R.; m. Paul Deutschman, Apr. 11, 1970 (widowed, 2002). BA, Trinity Coll., 1960; postgrad., New Sch. for Social Research, 1960-61, N.Y. U. Film Sch., 1961, N.Y. U. Grad. Sch. English, 1962-63. Copywriter trainee, sec. J. Walter Thompson Co., N.Y.C., 1960-64; asst. to mng. editor Alfred A. Knopf, Inc., N.Y.C., 1964-67, editor, 1967-75; editor-in-chief, v.p. Gen. Books div. Macmillan Pub. Co., N.Y.C., 1975-76; pres. Regina Ryan Pub. Enterprises, Inc., N.Y.C., 1976—. Co-author: Janice LaRouche's Strategies for Women at Work, 1984, 1987. Active Larchmont-Mamaroneck Young Reps., 1960-64; campaign worker, speech writer mayoralty campaign, Larchmont, 1962, 64; mem. Manhattan Women's Polit. Caucus, 1972-74; mem. com. Jimmy Carter Presdl. Campaign; mem., chmn. Sherman Dem. Town Com., Conn., 1985-86; mem. Jewish Cmty. Ctr. for Sherman, 1998-2001; Justice of the Peace, Sherman, 1986-96. Mem. PEN Am. Ctr., Women's Media Group, Agent's Roundtable, Internat. Women's Com. on Human Rights, AARP, Linnaean Soc., N.Y. Audubon Soc., N.Y. Mycological Soc., Vet. Feminists Am. Democrat. Home and Office: 251 Central Park W New York NY 10024-4134

RYAN, RICHARD, ambassador; Irish rep. to UN, N.Y.C., 1998—. Office: Permanent Mission Ireland to UN One Dag Hammarskjold Plz 885 Second Ave 19th Fl New York NY 10017-2201

RYAN, RON, former professional sports team executive, consultant; b. Welland, Ont., Can. m. Jill Ryan; children: Doug, Susan, Kaitland, Tenley. Grad., Colby Coll., 1962; EdM, U. Pa., 1964. With athletic depts., coach Merrimack Coll., Colgate U.; head coach New Eng. Whalers, 1973-74, 74-75, gen. mgr., 1975-78; exec. dir. World Hockey Assn., 1978-80; pres. PRISM New Eng., 1981; vice pres., gen. mgr. SportsChannel New Eng., 1983-87, SportsChannel Fla., 1987-88; exec. v.p. Phila. Flyers, 1988—91, COO, 1991—2003, pres., 2003—06, cons., 2006—. Office: c/o Philadelphia Flyers 3601 S Broad St Philadelphia PA 19148*

RYAN, SHEILA A., retired dean, nursing educator; Diploma in nursing, Creighton Meml. St. Joseph's Hosp. Sch. Nursing, 1967; BSN, U. Nebr., 1969; MSN in Psychiat. Nursing, U. Calif., San Francisco, 1971; PhD in Clin. Nursing Rsch., U. Ariz., 1981. Asst. prof. nursing Creighton U., Omaha, 1971—76, dean nursing, 1977—86; dean Sch. Nursing, dir. Med. Ctr. Nursing U. Rochester, NY, 1986—99; prof., Charlotte Peck Lienemann and Alumni Disting. Chair Coll. Nursing U. Nebr. Med. Ctr., Omaha. Fellow: Am. Acad. Nursing; mem.: Inst. for Healthcare Improvement, Nat. League Nursing (treas. 1993, pres. 1998), Sigma Theta Tau. Med. Nursing (treas.-sec.), Am. Internat. Health Alliance (bd. dirs. 1999—). Office: UNMC Coll Nursing Rm 4030 985330 NE Medical Ctr Omaha NE 68198-5330

RYAN, SHELLI ANN, public relations executive; b. Blair, Nebr., Dec. 8, 1968; d. Gorlyn Lew and Ruthie Ann Hagerbaumer; m. Mark Anthony Ryan, Sept. 26, 1992. BS, Bellevue U., 1992; MPA, U. Okla., 1997. Accredited Pub. Rels., Pub. Rels. Soc. Am. Mgr. mktg. svcs. Electronic Display Sys., Grand Island, Nebr., 1988-90; mktg. rep. Keeler/Raynor/Hinz, Bellevue, Nebr., 1990-92; mktg. coord. Accent Svc. Co., Omaha, 1992-95; corp. comm. specialist Applied Comm., Inc., Omaha, 1995-96; prin. Ryan Designs, Omaha, 1996-98; pres. Ad Hoc Comm. Resources, Omaha, 1999—. Media spokesperson Am. Heart Assn., Omaha, 1990-95; pub. rels. judge Jr. Achievement, Omaha, 1990, 96. Recipient 40 under 40 award Midlands Bus. Jour., 2002; named Woman Yr. Am. Women's Bus. Assn., Omaha, 1996, Gold Citation of Excellence, Am. Mktg. Assn., 2004, Best of Show and Pinnacle award Am. Mktg. Assn., 2002, Profl. Achievement award Am. Women's Assn., 2005, Bronze award Vision awards League Am. Comms. Profls., 2005.

Mem. Pub. Rels. Soc. Am. (sec. 1998, treas. 1997, pres. 2001, dir. 1996—), Am. Bus. Women's Assn. (pres. 1995-96, Profl. Achievement award 2005). Avocations: weightlifting, bicycling. Home: 9030 Raven Oaks Dr Omaha NE 68152-1759

**RYAN, STEPHEN JOSEPH, JR.,** ophthalmologist, educator; b. Honolulu, Hawaii, Mar. 20, 1940; s. S.J. and Mildred Elizabeth (Farrer) Ryan; m. Anne Christine Mullady, Sept. 25, 1965; 1 child, Patricia Anne. AB, Providence Coll., 1961; MD, Johns Hopkins U., 1965. Intern Bellevue Hosp., N.Y.C., 1965—66; resident Wilmer Inst. Ophthalmology, Johns Hopkins Hosp., Balt., 1966—69, chief resident, 1969—70; fellow Armed Forces Inst. Pathology, Washington, 1970—71; instr. ophthalmology Johns Hopkins U., Balt., 1970—71, asst. prof., 1971—72, assoc. prof., 1972—74; Grace and Emery Beardsley prof. ophthalmology Keck Sch. Medicine, U. So. Calif., LA, 1974—, chmn. dept. ophthalmology, 1974—95, dean, 1991—2004, sr. v.p. for med. care, 1993—2004, Grace and Emery Beardsley Chair in Ophthalmology, med. dir. Doheny Eye Inst. (formerly Estelle Doheny Eye Found.), 1977—86, pres. Doheny Eye Inst., 1987—, chief of staff Doheny Eye Hosp., 1985—88; acting head ophthalmology divsn. dept. surgery Children's Hosp., 1975—77. Mem. adv. panel Calif. Med. Assn., 1975—. Editor (with M.D. Andrews): A Survey of Ophthalmology--Manual for Medical Students, 1970; editor: (with R.E. Smith) Selected Topics on the Eye in Systemic Disease, 1974; editor: (with Dawson and Little) Retinal Diseases, 1985; editor: (with others) Retina, 1989; editor:, 2000, 4t edit., 2005; assoc. editor Ophthalmol. Surgery, 1974—85, mem. editl. bd.: Am. Jour. Ophthalmology, 1981—, Internat. Ophthalmology, 1982—, Retina, 1983—, Graefes Archives, 1984—; contbr. articles to med. jours. Recipient cert. of merit, AMA, 1971, Louis B. Mayer Scholar award, Rsch. to Prevent Blindness, 1973, Rear Adm. William Campbell Chambliss USN award, 1982, Mildred Weisenfeld Award for Lifetime Achievement in Vision Rsch., Fight for Sight, 2000. Mem.: AMA, Inst. Medicine NAS, Jules Gonin Club, Rsch. Study Club, Nat. Eye Care Project, Retina Soc., Macula Soc., Pan-Am. Assn. Microsurgery, L.A. Acad. Medicine, Pacific Coast Oto-Ophthal. Soc., Los Angeles County Med. Assn., Calif. Med. Assn., L.A. Soc. Ophthalmology, Assn. Univ. Profs. of Ophthalmology, Pan-Am. Assn. Ophthalmology, Am. Ophthal. Soc., Am. Acad. Ophthalmology and Otolaryngology (award of Merit 1975), Wilmer Ophthal. Inst. Residents Assn., Soc. Scholars of Johns Hopkins U. (life). Office: 1450 San Pablo St Los Angeles CA 90033 Business E-Mail: sryan@doheny.org.

**RYAN, STEPHEN M.,** lawyer; s. Alex L. Ryan and Lynda A. Turner; m. Christine M. Ryan, Dec. 31, 1988; children: Travis A., Caroline A., Taylor R. BA, U. Tex., 1988; JD with honors, U. Mich., 1997. Bar: Tex. 1997. B-52 navigator/electronic warfare officer USAF, 1988—94, active duty law student Ann Arbor, Mich., 1994—97, asst. staff judge adv. Barksdale AFB, La., 1997—2002; atty. Nathan Sommers Jacobs & Gorman, Houston, 2002—05, LeBoeuf Lamb, Greene, & MacRae LLP, Houston, 2005—; staff judge adv. 147th Fighter Wing, Tex. Air N.G., Houston, 2002—. Maj. USAF, 1988—2002, lt. col. Tex. ANG, USAFR, 2004—. Decorated Achievement medal USAF, Air medal U.S. Ctrl. Command, Commendation medal USAF, Meritorious Svc. medal; recipient Corpus Juris Secundum award, Torts, 1995. Mem.: Res. Officers Assn., VFW, Delta Sigma Phi. Roman Catholic. Avocations: scouting, world travel, aviation. Office: LeBoeuf Lamb Greene & MacRae LLP 1000 Main St Ste 2550 Houston TX 77002 Office Phone: 713-287-2000. Office Fax: 713-287-2100. Business E-Mail: smryan@llgm.com.

**RYAN, SUSAN MAGNESS,** librarian, educator; b. Takoma Park, Md., May 27, 1958; d. Donald Eaton and Shirley Anne Magness; m. Edward Timothy Ryan, Sept. 1, 1984; 1 child, Shannon Kelsey BS, Fla. State U., 1981, MS, 1982; MLS, UCLA, 1989. Intelligence officer CIA, Washington, 1983-84; assoc. dir. libr. Stetson U., DeLand, Fla., 1989—. Author: Downloading Democracy: Government Information in an Electronic Age, 1996; contbg. author: Government CD-ROMs: A Practical Guide to Searching Electronic Databases, 1994; mem. editl. bd. Jour. Govt. Info., 1993-96, column editor, 1994-96; contbr. articles to profl. jours. Bd. dir. coun. advisors for Sch. Libr. and Info. Studies, Fla. State U., Tallahassee, 1995-97. Mem. ALA (Catharine J. Reynolds award for rsch., govt. docs. round table 1996), Fla. Libr. Assn. (chairperson govt. docs. caucus 1992-93), Ctrl. Fla. Libr. Consortium (chairperson govt. docs. interest group 1991-92), Fla. Assn. Coll. and Rsch. Librs. (exec. bd. 2002-2005). Office: duPont-Ball Libr Campus Unit 8418 Deland FL 32723

**RYAN, THOMAS F.,** lawyer; b. Detroit, Nov. 4, 1943; BS, Ferris State U., 1965; JD magna cum laude, Wayne State U., 1971. Bar: Ill. 1972, US Ct. of Appeals (7th cir.) 1972, US Dist. Ct. (no. dist.) Ill. 1972, U.S. Supreme Ct. 1978. Joined Sidley & Austin (now Sidley Austin Brown & Wood), Chgo., 1972—; now ptnr. antitrust and bus. counseling Sidley Austin Brown & Wood, Chgo., mem. exec com. Mem. adv. com. on cir. rules 7th Fed Ct. Appeals. 1st lt. U.S. Army, 1966-68. Fellow Am. Coll. Trial Lawyers; mem. Chgo. Bar Assn. (mem. jud. evaluation com.), 7th Cir. Bar Assn. (bd. govs. 1986-89, 2nd v.p. 1990-91, pres. 1991-92). Office: Sidley Austin Brown & Wood LLP Bank One Plz 10 S Dearborn St Chicago IL 60603 Office Phone: 312-853-5817. Office Fax: 312-853-7036. Business E-Mail: tryan@sidley.com.

**RYAN, THOMAS JOHN,** cardiologist; b. Manhasset, N.Y., Dec. 19, 1928; s. Mark J. Ryan and Margaret M. Rooney; m. Nancy Therese Cooney, June 12, 1954; children: Kathie Steinberg, Amy, Beth Ryan Walter, Thomas John Jr., Paula, Jennifer Brown. BA, Holy Cross Coll., Worcester, Mass., 1950; MD, Georgetown Med., Washington, DC, 1954. Diplomate Nat. Bd. of Med. Examiners Pa., 1954, cert. Am. Bd. of Internal Medicine Pa., 1962, Subspecially Bd. Cardiovascular Disease Pa. Chief cardiology St. Elizabeth's Hosp., Boston, 1961—71; instr. in medicine Harvard Med. Sch., Boston, 1961—71; asst. prof. of medicine Tufts Med. Sch., Boston, 1963—68, assoc. prof. medicine, 1968—71; chief cardiology Boston U. Med. Ctr., Boston, 1971—94; prof. medicine Boston U. Sch. of Medicine, Boston, 1971—, sr. cons. in cardiology, chief emeritus, 1994—. Author: (265 articles pub.) In Peer Reviewed Med. Jours., 24 book chpts. in medical texts. Advisor Dept. of Pub. Health, Boston, 1979—96, med. N.Y. State adv. com. N.Y.C., 1991—2003; med. adv. panel Tech. Assessment Group-Blue Cross, Chgo., 2001—03. Capt. Med. Corps. U.S. Army, 1955—57, Ft. Banks, Mass. Recipient Disting. Leadership award, Am. Heart Assn., 1980, Paul Dudley White award, 1982, Alpha Omega Alpha, Nat. Med. Honor Soc., 1985, Lawrence B. Ellis Lectureship, Harvard Med. Sch., 1986, Gold Heart award, Am. Heart Assn., 1991, The Best Doctors in Am., Woodward/White, Inc., 1994, James B. Herrick award, Coun. on Clin. Cardiology, Am. Heart Assn., 1996, The Stokes Lectureship, Irish Cardiac Soc. Royal Coll. of Physicians and Surgeons, Dublin, Ireland, 1996, Chairman's award, Am. Heart Assn., 2001; fellow Fullbright Scholar, Fullbright Com., Washington, DC, 1990—91, Fogarty Sr. Internat. Fellowship, Oxford U., 1990—91. Master: Am. Coll. Cardiology (bd. govs. 1980—83, bd. trustees 1986—93, Disting. Fellowship award 1998), ACP; fellow: European Soc. Cardiology, Soc. Geriatric Cardiology, Irish Cardiac Soc. (hon.); mem.: NIH (mem. cardiology adv. com. 1990), Am. Heart Assn. (pres. 1984—86), Am. Bd. Internal Medicine (mem. subspecialty bd. cardiovasc. medicine 1986—92), Cardiovasc. Health Initiative Developing Countries (mem. sci. adv. com.), Internat. Health, Inst. Medicine (mem. bd. 1995—98), InterAm. Soc. Cardiology (pres. 1992—95), Assn. Profs. Cardiology, Assn. Univ. Cardiologists, New Eng. Cardiovasc. Soc. (pres. 1973), Roxbury Soc. Med. Improvement, Am. Fedn. Clin. Rsch., Am. Clin. and Climatol. Assn., Mass. Med. Soc. Independent. Roman Catholic. Achievements include early contributor to development of coronary arteriography and the conduct of randomized clinical trials and is internat. recognized as an authority on ischemic heart disease. Avocations: history of western civilization and medicine, classical music, sailing, skiing, golf. Office: Boston U Sch Medicine 88 East Newton St Boston MA 02118 Business E-Mail: thomas.ryan@bmc.org.

**RYAN, THOMAS L.,** funeral company executive; BBA, U. Tex. CPA PricewaterhouseCoopers, 1988—96; fin. mgmt. positions Service Corp. Internat., Houston, 1996—2000, CEO European ops., 2000—02, pres. & COO, 2002—05, pres. & CEO, 2005—. Mem.: Young Presidents Org. Office: Service Corporation Internat 1929 Allen Pkwy Houston TX 77019*

**RYAN, THOMAS M.,** drug store chain executive; b. 1953; Pharmacist CVS Corp., Woonsocket, RI, from 1975, numerous managerial positions v.p. pharmacy ops., sr. v.p. pharmacy, exec. v.p. pharmacy, exec. v.p. stores; pres., CEO CVS Pharmacy, Inc. (then part of Melville Corp.), Woonsocket, RI, from 1993; vice chmn., COO CVS Corp., 1996—98, pres., CEO, 1998—, chmn., 1999—. Bd. dirs. Fleet Fin. Group, Reebok Internat. Ltd., Yum Brands!, Inc.; bd. trustees Healthcare Leadership Coun. Office: CVS Corp One CVS Dr Woonsocket RI 02895*

**RYAN, TIMOTHY J.,** congressman; b. Niles, Ohio, July 16, 1973; s. Rochelle Ryan. Student, Youngstown State U., 1991—92; BA in Polit. Sci., Bowling Green State U., 1995; JD, Franklin Pierce Law Ctr., Concord, NH, 2000. Congl. aide Staff of US Rep. James A. Traficant of Ohio, 1995—97; intern Trumbull County Prosecutor's Office; mem. Ohio State Senate from 32nd dist., Columbus, 2001—02, US Congress from 17th Ohio dist., 2003—, mem. armed svcs. com., mem. edn. and the workforce com., co-chair Mfg. Caucus. Trustee Found. Extended. Recipient Legis. Leadership award on Domestic Mfg., US Bus. and Industry Coun., 2004, Friend of Nat. Pks. award, Nat. Pks. Conservation Assn., 2005. Mem. KC, Sons Italy, Internat. Narcotic Enforcement Officers Assn., Ancient Order Hibernians, Elks. Democrat. Office: US Ho Reps 222 Cannon Ho Office Bldg Washington DC 20515 Office Phone: 202-225-5261.*

**RYAN, TIMOTHY PATRICK,** investment company executive; BS in Mgmt. cum laude, Suffolk U., Boston, 1990. Fund acct. State St. Bank & Trust, Boston, 1990—92; analyst to sr. analyst John Hancock Advisors, 1992—96; sr. statistical analyst Putnam Investments, 1996—97; attribution analyst Fidelity Mgmt. and Rsch., 1997—2000, mgr., attribution analyst, 2000—03, dir., attribution analyst, 2004—05; v.p., performance mgmt. Hartford Investment Mgmt., 2005—. Adv. bd. mem. Jour. of Performance Measurement, 2001—; founder and owner Ryan Tax Prep & Advisory, 1995—2005. Editor: Portfolio Analysis, 2006, author 6 articles to profl. jours. Co-recipient Top Reviewer, Jour. of Performance Mgmt., 2002, 2003, 2004, 2005; recipient Article of Yr. award, Dietz award for Performance Measurement Lit., 2004. Mem.: Golden Key. Achievements include design of reading curriculum of CFA Institute's CIPM Expert exam. Avocations: reading, carpentry, golf.

**RYAN, TOM,** reporting applications platform company executive; BS in Computer sci., San Francisco State U.; MBA in Internat. Bus., U. Notre Dame de Namur. Sr. mgmt. positions at Informix, Illustra, Oracle and Amdahl; dir. customer support Actuate Corp., South San Francisco, Calif., 1997—2002, CIO, sr. v.p. customer svc., 2002—. Mem. adv. bd. AppMail, San Mateo County Cmty. Coll. Dist. Computer Sci. Divsn. Office: Actuate Corp 701 Gateway Blvd South San Francisco CA 94080-7084 Office Phone: 650-837-2000. Office Fax: 650-827-1560.

**RYAN, UNA SCULLY,** health science association administrator, medical educator; b. Kuala Lumpur, Malaysia, Dec. 18, 1941; d. Henry and Amy (Yee) Scully; m. Allan Dana Callow, May 26, 1989; children: Tamsin Randlett, Amy Jean Susan Ryan. BSc in Zoology, Chemistry & Microbiology, Bristol (Eng.) U., 1963; PhD in Cell Biology, Cambridge (Eng.) U., 1968. Fellow dept. biology U. Va., Charlottesville, 1964-66; fellow dept. medicine U. Miami, Fla., 1966-67, adj. asst. prof. biology Fla., 1968-71; dir. lab. for ultrastructure studies Howard Hughes Med. Inst., Miami, 1967-71; from instr. to assoc. prof. medicine U. Miami Sch. Medicine, 1967-80, prof. medicine, 1980-89; sr. scientist Papanicolaou Cancer Rsch. Inst., Miami, 1972-77; rsch. prof. surgery Washington U. Sch. Medicine, St. Louis, 1990—; dir. health scis. Monsanto Co., St. Louis, 1990-93; pres., CEO T Cell Scis., Needham, Mass., 1993-98; rsch. prof. medicine Boston U. Sch. Medicine, 1993—; pres., CEO AVANT Immunotherapeutics, Needham, Mass., 1998—. Dir. course W. Alton Jones Cell Sci. Ctr., 1979-81; dir. Hybridoma Facility, U. Miami, 1986-89; chair local organizing com. Internat. Coun. on Thrombosis and Hemostasis, 1984; chair Rev. Com. for Extracellular Matrix Interactions in Lung, 1983; chair various revs. NHLBI; chair Mass. Biotech. Coun., 2004-06; mem. various rev. and adv. coms. Author: J. Tissue Culture Methods, 1987, Pulmonary Endothelium in Health Disease, 1987, Endothelial Cells, 1988, Vascular Endothelium: Receptors and Transduction Mechanisms, 1989; editor: Tissue & Cell, 1981-87; rev. editor In Vitro, 1986; reviewer profl. jours.; contbr. articles to profl. jours. UK state scholar, 1960, Country Major scholar, 1960; D.S.I.R. rsch. fellow, 1964, 65, Ethel Sargant Rsch. fellow, 1964-65, Sci. Rsch. Coun. fellow, 1966; recipient Louis and Artur Lucian award for rsch. in circulatory diseases, 1984, Merit award Nat. Heart, Lung and Blood Inst., 1986, Lillie award Woods Hole, Marine Bill, Lab., 1989, Order of Brit. Empire, 2002. Mem. Am. Soc. Cell Biology, Soc. Neurosci., Tissue Culture Assn., Internat. Soc. Heart Rsch., Am. Heart Assn. (coun. on basic rsch., coun. on circulation, cardiopulmonary coun.), Am. Physiol. Soc., Am. Microcirculatory Soc., European Soc. Microcirculation, Am. Thoracic Soc. (dir. course on culture of pulmonary endothelial cells), Internat. Soc. Applied Cardiovascular Biology, N.Y. Acad. Scis., Fla. Soc. Electron Microscopy, Sigma Xi. Office: AVANT Immunotherapeutics 119 4th Ave Needham MA 02494-2725

**RYAN, VINCE,** lawyer; b. Houston, Aug. 12, 1947; m. Teresa Pamela Rodriguez; 3 children. BA in English, U. Houston, 1969, JD, 1974; MA in History, Rice U., 1979. Bar: Tex. 1974. Assoc. James Patrick Smith, 1974—75, Thomas P. Duncan, Houston, 1975—76, Smith and Conner, Houston, 1976—79, Watrous, Joyce and Ryan, Houston, 1980—81; divsn. chief commrs. ct. divsn. Office of Harris County Atty., Houston, 1981—83, first asst., 1984—88; of counsel Sinex & Stephenson, Houston, 1988—95; regional mng. atty. Calame Linebarger, Houston, 1996—98; of counsel Linebarger Goggan, Houston, 1998—2004, Travis Law Firm, Houston, 2004—. Dir. legal rsch. svc. U. Houston; adj. faculty U.S. Army Command and Gen. Staff Coll., 1988—. Mem. Dist. C Houston City Coun., 1988—94; alt. City of Houston rep. Houston-Galveston Area Coun., 1989—94; pres. Region 14, Tex. Mcpl. League, 1993—94; bd. dirs. Panama Canal Commn., 1995—99. With U.S. Army, 1969—72, Vietnam, with U.S. Army, 1990, lt. col. USAR. Grad. fellow, 1977—78, Rsch. fellow, 1978—79. Mailing: 3720 Blue Bonnet Houston TX 77025 Office: Travis Law Firm Ste 900 2700 Post Oak Blvd Houston TX 77056-5707

**RYAN, WILLIAM,** executive; B in Psychology, MEd. Ptnr. Neuhaus Ryan Wong, South San Francisco.

**RYAN, WILLIAM FRANCIS,** priest; b. Renfrew, Ont., Can., Apr. 4, 1925; s. William Patrick Ryan and Helen Mary Doneg BA, Montreal U., 1951; MA in Labor Rels., St. Louis U., 1953; postgrad., Heythrop Coll., Oxon, Eng.; STL, St. Albert Coll., Louvain, 1958; PhD in Econs., Harvard U., 1964. Ordained priest Roman Catholic Ch., 1957. Asst. prof. econs. Loyola Coll., Montreal, Que., Canada, 1963-65; nat. dir. Social Justice Office Can. Conf. Cath. Bishops, Ottawa, Ont., 1964-70, gen. sec., 1984-90; founding dir. Ctr. of Concern, Washington, 1970-78; nat. supr. Jesuit Order, Toronto, Ont., Canada, 1978-84; chancellor Sch. Theology Regis Coll., Toronto, 1978-84; vis. sr. rsch. fellow Can. Inst. for Internat. Peace and Security, Ottawa, 1990-91; chair on Cath. social thought St. Paul U., Ottawa, 1991-92; 2001dir. Jesuit Project on Ethics in Politics, Ottawa, 1992. Exec. sec. Inter-religious Peace Colloquium, Washington 1975-78; bd. dirs. Roncalli Internat. Found., Montreal, 1979-83, North/South Inst., Ottawa, 1979-91; spl. advisor to Internat. Devel. Rsch. Ctr., Ottawa, 1993-2000; coord. Jesuit Ctr. for Social Faith and Justice, 1997—; lectr. in field. Author: The Clergy and Economic Growth in Quebec, 1966, Culture, Spirituality and Economic Development—Opening a Dialogue, 1995, Our Way of Proceeding, in the Lab, The Temple and The Market: Reflections at the Intersection of Science,

Religion and Development, 2000; co-author: Religious as Contemplatives in the 80's, 1984, The Lab, The Temple and The Market: Expanding the Conversation, 2001; translator: The Primacy of Charity in Moral Theology, 1961; co-editor: Globalization and Catholic Social Thought--Present Crisis, Future Hope, 2005; subject of biography Faith and Freedom—The Life and Times of Bill Ryan sj, by Jamie Swift and Bob Chodos, 2002; contbr. articles to profl. jours. Mem. Am. Econs. Assn. Roman Catholic. Avocations: hiking, skiing. Office: 169 Sunnyside Ave Ottawa ON Canada K1S 0R2 Office Phone: 613-730-4569, 613-730-6029 ext. 2. Personal E-Mail: wfxrsj@web.ca.

**RYAN-GRIFFITH, MARY KATE,** special education educator; b. Balt., Oct. 9, 1957; d. Charles Ambrose Ryan and Elizabeth Joan Ebert; m. George Vintin Griffith Jr., June 29, 1991; 1 child, Virginia Elizabeth Griffith; m. Ronald Hemmerick, Apr. 24, 1982 (div. 1988). BS, Vanderbilt U., 1980; MA, Gallaudet U., Washington, 1984. Cert. advanced profl. M.d. Interpreter, tutor Montgomery County Pub. Schs., Wheaton, Md., 1986—87, spl. edn. instrln. asst. Rockville, Md., 1987—89, 3d-4th gr. tchr. Tacoma Park, Md., 1989—91, spl. edn. tchr. Gaithersburg, Md., 1991—2005, Leiderman Mid. Sch., Silver Spring, Md., 2005—. Presenter in field. Contbr.: textbook Exceptional Children - An Introduction to Special Education, 2003, 2005. Pres. Lovettsville Cmty. Ctr., Va., VSA Arts Bd., 2000; mem. Lovettsville ES PTO, Va., Resnik E.S. PTA, Gaithersburg, Va. Named Outstanding Woman of Loudoun County, Loudoun Commn. on Women, 2003, Outstanding Spl. Educator, PTA Mont. chpt. Mem.: NEA, Coun. for Exceptional Children, Md. State Tchr.'s Assn., Delta Kappa Epsilon. Achievements include being named Ms. Wheelchair, Md., 1987. Avocations: performing with very special arts, drawing, making jewelry, writing, stained glass. Home: 12942 Axline Rd Lovettsville VA 20180

**RYAN-HALLEY, CHARLOTTE MURIEL,** oncology clinical specialist, family practice nurse practitioner; b. Beedeville, Ark., Sept. 2, 1939; d. Eugene Sanford and Edith Elizabeth (Goforth) Breckenridge; m. Alexander Halley; children: Russell Kent Ryan, Cary Randall Ryan, Molly Reneé Ryan Nankervis. BSN cum laude, Calif. State U., Fresno, 1991, MSN, clin. specialist, 1997. RN Calif., cert. pub. health nurse, cert. advanced oncology nurse. Psychiat. technician Porterville (Calif.) State Hosp., 1959-67; tchr. developmentally disabled Ariz. Tng. Ctr., Coolidge, 1967-71; Montessori tchr. Tucson, 1972-77; tchr. developmentally disabled Heartland Opportunity Ctr., Madera, Calif., 1977-79; med. office mgr. office of orthopedic surgeon, Madera, 1979-83, office mgr., x-ray technician, 1983-87; staff nurse in oncology St. Agnes Med. Ctr., Fresno, 1991—99, 2002—06; oncology clin. nurse specialist Kaweah Delta Hosp., Visalia, Calif., 1999—2002. Instr. nursing dept. Calif. State U., Fresno, 1992-93, 95-98; clin. instr. paradigm nursing program Fresno City Coll., Fresno, Calif., 2003-05; nursing instr. Coll. Sequoias Visalia, Calif., 2005, 06; Calif. nurse del. to China, People to People Am. Program, 2005. Treas. Hospice of Madera County, 1990-92, bd. dirs., 1992; peer counselor Calif. State U., Fresno, 1989-91; pres. bd. dirs. Easter Seals Soc., Madera, 1981. Mem. Nat. Oncology Nursing Soc. (on-line forum moderator, item writer cert. test 1998-2002), Nightingale Soc., Golden Key, Sigma Theta Tau (chmn. pub. com., editor MUNEWS newsletter 1994-95). Republican. Avocation: reading. Office Phone: 559-458-3222. Personal E-Mail: rx4hugs@aol.com.

**RYANS, JOHN KELLEY, JR.,** marketing educator; s. John Kelley and Alta Mae Ryans; m. Cynthia Collis, Jan. 5, 1957. AB in Journalism, U. Ky., 1954; MS in Bus. Adminstrn., U. Tenn., 1958; DBA, Ind. U., 1965. Asst. prof. mktg. U. Md., College Park, 1964—68; assoc. prof. mktg. U. Ky., Lexington 1968—69; prof. mktg. Kent State U., Ohio, 1970—94, Bridgestone prof., 1994—2003, emeritus Bridgestone prof., 2003—; Good chair global strategy Bowling Green State U., Ohio, 2003—04. Vis. prof. internat. bus. Columbia U., NYC, 1977; cons. in field. Co-author (with D. Peebles): The Management of International Advertising, 1983; co-author: (with W. Shanklin) Marketing High Technology, 1984, Thinking Strategically, 1985, Essentials for Marketing High Technology, 1987; co-author: (with J. Baker and D. Howard) International Business Classics, 1988; co-author: Marketing Strategy for New Europe, 1990; co-author: (with S. Paliwoda) International Marketing Reader, 1995; co-author: India Business, 2002, author 11 other books. 1st lt. USAF, 1955—57. Named Disting. Scholar, Kent State U., 1999, Ohio Commodore, Gov. of Ohio, 2000; recipient 12-yr, award, No. Ohio US Dist. Export Coun., 2002. Fellow: Acad. Internat. Bus.; mem.: Am. Mktg. Assn. Found., Cleve. World Trade Assn. (bd. dirs. 1972—2006). Avocations: sports, writing, travel, cruises. Office: Kent State U Coll Bus Dept Mktg Kent OH 44240 Personal E-mail: jkryans@juno.com.

**RYBAK, ILYA A.,** neuroscientist, biophysicist, educator; b. Odessa, Ukraine, May 24, 1949; s. Alexander O. and Yelizaveta I. Rybak; m. Marina Gabay, Oct. 22, 1981; children: Vadim, Alexander. MSEE, Odessa Poly. U., Ukraine, 1975; PhD in Biophysics, St. Petersburg State U., Russia, 1988. Prof. Sch. Biomedical Engring. Drexel U., Phila., 1999—.

**RYBAK, R. T.,** mayor; m. Megan O'Hara; 2 children. BA polit. sci. and comm., Boston Coll., 1978. Gen. mgr. WCCO TV & WCCO Radio; v.p. Internet Broadcast Sys.; pub., mgr., bus. ops. Twin Cities Reader; mayor City of Minneapolis, Minn., 2001—. Founder, mem. bd. Save the Water in Mpls.; served Minn. Soc. Architects, Night of the Penguin, Hennepin Ave. Adv. Com., Adv. Fedn. Minn., Eiji Oue Inaugural Com.; coach Little League Baseball, Youth Soccer; vol. reader Minn. Pub. Sch.; co-coord. Bill Bradley for Pres., 2000; co-chair Tony Bouza for Gov., 1994; bd. dir. Residents Opposed to Airport Racket. Democrat. Office: City Hall Rm 331 350 S Fifth S Minneapolis MN 55415 Office Phone: 612-673-2700. Office Fax: 612-673-2305.*

**RYBCZYK, JOSEPH ANTHONY,** physicist, researcher, writer, inventor; b. Phila., Oct. 19, 1935; s. Frank Rybczyk and Isabella Slivak; life ptnr. Dolores Brannan; m. Ruth Diane Menendez, Dec. 30, 1955 (div.); children: Brian Keith, Deborah Gale, Karen Marie. Tech. diploma, DeVry Inst. Tech., Chgo., 1976. Tech. cert. USAF, Air Training Command, Francis E. Warren Air Force Base, Cheyenne, Wyo., 1956, NASA cert. instr./examiner George C. Marshall Space Flight Ctr., Huntsville, Ala., 1965. Various positions Lockheed Martin Tactical Def. Systems, Horsham, Pa., 1959—96; ind. rschr. in theoretical physics, 1996—. Author: Millennium Theory of Relativity, With USAF, 1955—59. Achievements include research in theory of natural motion; millennium theory of relativity; time and energy; the laws of acceleration; time and energy, inertia and gravity; millennium relativity velocity composition; relativistic motion perspective; millenium relativity acceleration composition; integrated relativisitc velocity and acceleration compostion; millennium theory of inertia and gravity; the four principal kinetic states of material bodies; patents for encoding printing device, 1978; man-powered propulsion device, 1986. Personal E-Mail: jrybczyk@comcast.net.

**RYBCZYNSKI, WITOLD MARIAN,** architect, educator, writer; b. Edinburgh, Scotland, Mar. 1, 1943; arrived in Can. 1953; s. Witold Kasimir and Anna Jadwiga (Hofman) Rybczynski; m. Shirley Hallam, Nov. 15, 1974. Diploma, Loyola Coll., Montreal, 1960; B.Arch., McGill U., 1966, M.Arch., 1972, DSc (hon.), 2002. Pvt. practice architecture, Montreal, 1970-82; research assoc. McGill U., Montreal, 1972-75, asst. prof. architecture, 1975-80, assoc. prof., 1980-86, prof., 1986-93; Meyerson prof. of Urbanism U. Pa., 1994—. Cons. UN, Manila, 1976, Internat. Devel. Rsch. Ctr., Ottawa, 1977, Banco de Mex., 1979—80; sr. fellow Design Futures Inst., 2003; mem. Meml. and Mus. Cons. Group. Author: Paper Heroes: A Review of Appropriate Technology, 1980, Taming the Tiger: The Struggle to Control Technology, 1983, Home: A Short History of an Idea, 1986, The Most Beautiful House in the World, 1989, Waiting in the Weekend, 1991, Looking Around: A Journey Through Architecture, 1992, A Place for Art, 1993, City Life: Urban Expectation in a New World, 1995, A Clearing in the Distance, 1999 (J. Anthony Lukas Book Prize, Christopher award), One Good Turn, 2000, The Look of Architecture, 2001, The Perfect House, 2002; contbg. editor: Saturday Night, 1990—2001; contbg. author Booknotes: Stories from American History, mem. adv. bd. Ency. Americana; founding editor: Wharton Real Estate Rev., 1996—; Slate, 2005—. Mem. adv. coun. Inst. Classical Archs.,

2003—; mem. adv. bd. Chgo. Humanities Festival, 2003—; advisor Libr. Am. Landscape History, 2002—; mem. U.S. Commn. Fin. Arts, 2004—. Recipient QSPELL Lit. prize for nonfiction, 1988, 1989, Prix Paul-Henri Lapointe, 1988, Progressive Arch. Design award, 1991, Jurzykowski Found. award, 1993, Athaneum Lit. prize, 1997, 2001, Christopher award 2000, J. Anthony Lukas prize, 2000; Ballard Real Estate scholar, 1994—95. Fellow: AIA (hon.). Office: Sch Design Meyerson Hall Philadelphia PA 19104 Office Phone: 215-573-0985. Business E-Mail: rybczyns@design.upenn.edu.

**RYBERG, WILLIAM A.,** orchestra executive; BMus, Western Wash. State U., 1980; MMus, Ind. U., 1983. Teller, loan officer, br. mgr., regional mgr. Ranier Nat. Bank; v.p., area mgr. West One Bank, Tacoma; v.p., dist. mgr. Key Bank, Wash., 1993-96; exec. dir. Bellingham (Wash.) Festival of Music, 1996-98; pres. Grand Rapids (Mich.) Symphony, 1998—2004, Oreg. Symphony Orch., Portland, 2004—. Office: 921 SW Wahington Ste 200 Portland OR 97205

**RYCHLAK, JOSEPH FRANK,** psychologist, educator; b. Cudahy, Wis., Dec. 17, 1928; s. Joseph Walter and Helen Mary (Bieniek) R.; m. Lenora Pearl Smith, June 16, 1956; children: Ronald, Stephanie. BS, U. Wis., 1953; MA, Ohio State U., 1954, PhD, 1957. Diplomate Am. Bd. Examiners in Profl. Psychology. Asst. prof. psychology Fla. State U., Tallahassee, 1957-58, Washington State U., Pullman, 1958-61; assoc. prof., then prof. psychology St. Louis U., 1961-69; prof. psychology Purdue U., West Lafayette, Ind., 1969-83, interim dept. head, 1979-80; prof. Loyola U. Chgo., 1983-99, Maude C. Clarke prof. humanistic psychology, 1983—, prof. emeritus, 1999—. Dir. Human Relations Ctr., Pullman, Wash., 1958-61; research cons. AT&T, 1957-82. Author: The Psychology of Rigorous Humanism, 1977, 2d edit., 1988, Discovering Free Will and Personal Responsibility, 1979, A Philosophy of Science for Personality Theory, 2d edit., 1981, Personality and Life Style of Young Male Managers, 1982, (with N. Cameron) Personality Development and Psychopathology, 2d edit., 1985, Artificial Intelligence and Human Reason: A Teleological Critique, 1991, Logical Learning Theory: A Human Teleology and Its Empirical Support, 1994, In Defense of Human Consciousness, 1997, The Human Image in Postmodern America, 2003; assoc. editor Psychotherapy: Theory, Rsch. and Practice, 1965-76, Jour. Mind and Behavior, 1985-94. With USAF, 1946-49. Named Outstanding Contbr. to Human Understanding, Internat. Assn. Social Psychiatry, 1971. Fellow Am. Psychol. Assn. (div. 24 pres. 1977-78, 86-87), Am. Psychol. Soc.; mem. Soc. Personality Assessment, Phi Beta Kappa. Roman Catholic. Home: 12974 Abraham Run Carmel IN 46033 Office Phone: 317-816-0073. E-mail: lenorary@aol.com. *From my father I learned to have a sense of purpose, work hard, and assume responsibility. From my mother I learned not to take myself too seriously, and to realize that my achievements are never entirely up to me.*

**RYDALCH, ANN,** federal agency administrator, former state senator; m. Vernal Rydalch. BS in Business Educ., Idaho State U. Mem. Idaho Senate, 1983—1990, chmn. Fed. Lab. Consortium Tech. Transfer, 2001-, state repr. Idaho, 2004-. Past mem. Idaho Bicentennial Commn.; former vice chmn. Idaho Republican Com. Office: ID Natl Energy & Envrn Lab PO Box 1625 MS 3810 2525 N Fremont Ave Idaho Falls ID 83415-3810

**RYDÉN, BENGT GUNNAR,** retired stock exchange executive; b. Stockholm, Oct. 30, 1936; s. Gunnar H. and Ragnhild L. (Soederbaum) Rydén; m. Monica I.H. Tillberg, May 18, 1961. MBA, Stockholm Sch. Econs., 1960, PhD, 1972. Dep. chief economist Fedn. Swedish Industries, Stockholm, 1965-66; editor-in chief Swedish "Veckans Affärer", Stockholm, 1971-73; chief exec. Ctr. Bus. and Policy Studies, Stockholm, 1974-84, Stockholm Stock Exch., 1985-98, exec. chmn., 1998-99; vice chmn. Swedish Acctg. Stds. Coun., 1989—2002; ret., 2002. Chmn. Internat. Fedn. Stock Exchs., 1995—97, Mus. Nat. Antiquities, Sweden, 1998—2005, Hallvarsson & Halvarsson AB, Sweden, 1999—, Seventh Swedish Nat. Pension Fund, 1999—, Pantor Engring. AB, 2000—; bd. dirs. Found. Fin. Rsch., Sweden, Svenskt Rekonstruktionskapital AB, Sweden, 2003—, Autobalance Svenska AB, 2004—; mem. Com. of Wise Men on the Regulation of European Securities Mkts., 2000—01, Govt. Commn. on Restoration Pub. Trust in Bus., 2002—04. Fellow, Indsl. Inst. Econ. and Social Rsch., 1966—70. Fellow: Swedish Acad. Auditing, Royal Swedish Acad. Engring. Scis. Business E-Mail: bengt.ryden@halvarsson.se.

**RYDEN, KENT C.,** social studies educator; b. Neenah, Wis., Oct. 25, 1959; s. Robert and Suzanne Barnes Ryden. BA, Carroll Coll., 1981; MA, U. Conn., 1984; PhD, Brown U., 1991. Assoc. prof. U. So. Maine, Portland, Maine, 1994—, dir. Am. and New Eng. Studies Program, 1994—. Author: Landscape with Figures: Nature and Culture in New England, Mapping the Invisible Landscape: Folklore, Writing, and the Sense of Place. Mem.: Assn. Study Lit. and Environ., Am. Studies Assn. (Ralph Henry Gabriel prize 1991). Office: University of Southern Maine PO Box 9300 Portland ME 04104-9300 Office Phone: 207-780-4941. Office Fax: 207-780-5553. Business E-Mail: kryden@usm.maine.edu.

**RYDER, DONALD J.,** military career officer; b. Haverstraw, N.Y. m. Lisa Jones; children: Brock, Donald Jr. BS in Edn., N.E. La. U.; MS in Mgmt., Fla. Inst. Tech.; grad., US Army Command and Gen. Staff Coll.; US Army War Coll. Commd. officer US Army, 1971, advanced through grades to brig. gen., various positions, platoon leader, 501st mil. police co., 1st armored divsn. Ansbach, Germany, comdr., 463d mil. police co. (EG) Fort Leonard Wood, Mo., S-4, 16th mil. police brigade Fort Bragg, NC, S-3 503d Mil. Police Bn. Ft. Bragg, NC, corrections staff officer HQ TRADOC Ft. Monroe, Va., exec. officer, dep. chief of staff for pers. adminstrn., S-3 18th Mil. Police Brigade V (US) Corps Frankfurt, Germany, dep. brigade comdr. 18th Mil. Police Brigade V (US) Corps, comdr. 93d Mil. Police Bn. V (US) Corps, comdr. 118th Base Support Bn., comdr. 14th Mil. Police Brigade, 21st Theater Army Area Mannheim, Germany, provost marshal gen.; sec. of the gen. staff US Army Europe and Seventh Army, Heidelberg, Germany, exec. officer to the comdr. in chief, dep. comdg. gen. 21st Theater Army Area Command Kaiserslautern, Germany; dep. comdg. gen. US Army Chem. and Mil. Police Ctrs. and Ft. McClellan, Ala., 1998-99; comdt. US Army Mil. Police Sch., Ft. Leonard Wood, Mo., 1999—, Fort McClellan, Ala., 1999—, Army Criminal Investigation Divsn., 2002—. Decorated Legion of Merit with two oak leaf clusters, Bronze Star, Meritorious Svc. medal with oak leaf cluster, Army Commendation medal with three oak leaf clusters, S.W. Asia Svc. medal with two campaign stars, Armed Forces Svc. medal, Humanitarian Svc. medal, NATO medal.

**RYDER, EDMUND CAMPION,** art history professor; b. Nishinomiya, Japan, Nov. 27, 1962; arrived in U.S., 1964; s. Donald Vincent and Reiko Shimazaki Ryder. BA cum laude, N.Y. U., N.Y.C., 1998, MA, post grad., N.Y. U., N.Y.C., 2001—. Adj. prof. N.Y. U., N.Y.C., 2001, Kean U., 2003. Byzantium: Faith and Power 1261-1557, 2004, author: (catalogues) Pilgrimage to Saint Catherine's, 2004, Trésors du Monasère Sainte-Catherine, Mont Sinai Egypte, 2004. Fellow, Dunbarton Oaks, Harvard U., 2006; grantee, A.G. Leventis Found., 2006; Jane and Morgan Whitney Fellow, Met. Mus. Art, 2004—05. Mem.: Byzantine Studies Conf., Coll. Art Assn.

**RYDER, EDWARD FRANCIS,** secondary school educator; b. Lynn, Mass., Mar. 25, 1931; s. Edward W. and Theresa (Callahan) R. BSBA, Salem State U., Winston-Salem, N.C., 1954, EdM in Edn., 1973; EdM in Bus. Edn., Boston U., 1956. Cert. tchr., Mass. Bus. tchr. North Quincy (Mass.) H.S., 1968—98. Owner, pub. Sunnyside Pub. Co., 1975—. Author: The Art of Playing Bingo and Winning Consistently, 1980, The Art of Entering Sweepstakes and Winning Consistently, 1981, How To Save a Fortune Using Refunds and Coupons, 1983, How to Unlock the Secrets of Winning and Good Luck, 1983, How You Can Achieve Total Success Through Self-Hypnosis, 1984, Where to Buy Everything Wholesale--A Book of Lifetime Savings, 1984, A Guide to Over 1,000 Things You Can Get--For Free!, 1984, The Art of Betting Horses and Winning Consistently, 1985, Blackjack: How to Play and Win Like an Expert, 1985, Hot Dice! How to Leave the Table a

Winner, 1986, Winning Secrets of a Poker Master, 1986, Picking Winners at the Harness Races, 1987, Winning Consistently at the Greyhound Races, 1987, Lucky Slots!! How to Beat the Casino Bandits, 1988, Secrets of Winning at Casino Roulette, 1988, Keno: The Art of Playing and Winning, 1989, How to Play and Win at Casino Baccarat, 1989, Secrets of Winning at Video Poker, 1990, Winning Secrets of a Master Sports Bettor--Football, 1991, Winning Secrets of a Master Sports Bettor--Basketball, 1992, Winning Secrets of a Master Sports Bettor--Baseball, 1992; all publs. updated, 1997. Roman Catholic. Home: 28 Sunnyside Rd Lynn MA 01905-1105 Office: Sunnyside Pubs 51 Willow St # 165 Lynn MA 01901-1108 Office Phone: 781-595-4742. Personal E-mail: gambleandwin@verizon.net.

**RYDER, HARL EDGAR,** economist, educator; b. Mt. Vernon, Ill., July 11, 1938; s. Harl Edgar and Pearl (Kirkpatrick) R.; m. Mary Irene Kingsolver, June 30, 1970; children: Jonathan Harl, David Eugene, Benjamin James. AA, Mt. Vernon Community Coll., 1958; BA, U. Ill., 1960, MS, 1961; PhD, Stanford U., 1967. Asst. prof. econs. Brown U., Providence, 1965-69, assoc. prof., 1969-73, chmn. dept. econs., 1974-81, prof., 1973—2005, prof. emeritus, 2005—. Office: Brown Univ Dept Econs 64 Waterman St Providence RI 02912-9079 E-mail: harl_ryder@brown.edu.

**RYDER, HENRY CLAY,** lawyer; b. Lafayette, Ind., Feb. 18, 1928; s. Raymond Robert and Mina Elizabeth (Arnold) R.; m. Ann Sater Clay, Nov. 29, 1952 (dec.); children: David C., Sarah Paige Hugon, Anne Ryder O'Keefe; m. Velma Iris Dean, Aug. 27, 1976 BS, Purdue U., 1948; LLB, U. Mich., 1951; LLD, Hanover Coll., 1998. Bar: Mich. 1951, Ind. 1952, U.S. Dist. Ct. (so. dist.) Ind. 1953, U.S. Ct. Appeals (7th cir.) 1957, U.S. Supreme Ct. 1981. Assoc. Buschmann, Krieg, DeVault & Alexander, Indpls., 1953-57, ptnr., 1957-60, Roberts & Ryder and successor firms, Indpls., 1960-86, Barnes & Thornburg (merger), Indpls., 1987-95, of counsel, 1996—. Pres. Ind. State Symphony Soc. Inc., 1979-82, bd. dirs., 1972-91, trustee, 1991—; chmn. United Way of Greater Indpls., 1984; vice chmn. Greater Indpls. Progress Com., 1979-86, chmn., 1987-89, mem. exec. com., 1979-2000, trustee Purdue U., 1983-89; trustee Hanover Coll., 1979-2003, chmn., 1988-98; bd. dirs. Hist. Landmarks Found. of Ind., 1985-96, chmn., 1992-95; bd. dirs. Purdue Rsch. Found., 1990-2006; hon. v.p. Nat. Soc. Chgo.; mem. cmty. bd. IUPUI U. Libr., 1998—, chmn. 2003-04; bd. govs. Heartland Film Festival, 2000—04. Lt. U.S. Army, 1951-53. Recipient Jefferson award Indpls. Star, 1983, Whistler award Greater Indpls. Progress Com., 1989; Sagamore of the Wabash, 1984; named Man of Yr., B'nai B'rith Soc., 1984, Ind. Acad., 1992, Lifetime Achievement award Nat. Soc. Fund Raising Execs., 1999, Spirit of Philanthropy award Ind. U. Purdue U. Indpls., 2005. Fellow: Ind. Bar Found., Am. Bar Found.; mem.: ABA, Indpls. Bar Assn., Ind. Bar Assn., Ind. C. of C. (bd. dirs. 1991—94), Purdue U. Alumni Assn. (pres. 1975—77, Alumni Svc. award 1982, Citizenship award 1989), Columbia Club Found. (trustee 1990—), Indpls. Lit. Club (pres. 2004—05), Kiwanis (Downtown Indpls. pres. 1983, Civic award 1981), Columbia Club (bd. dirs. 1987—90, sec. 1988, Benjamin Harrison award 1983, Columbian of Yr. award 2002), USAC Benevolent Found. (bd. dirs., pres. 1999—), USAC Properties (sec., bd. dirs. 1986—), U.S. Auto Club (bd. dirs. 1982—, Pres.'s award 1989, Eddie Edenburn award 2000), Lawyers Club of Indpls. (pres. 1966). Republican. Presbyterian. Office: Barnes & Thornburg 11 S Meridian St Indianapolis IN 46204-3535 Office Phone: 317-231-7521.

**RYDER, RANDALL TAYLOR,** nuclear medicine technologist, director; b. New Orleans, Apr. 10, 1963; s. Dewey and Nelwyn Ryder; m. Amanda L Middlesbrooks, July 25, 1992; children: Kristin, Taylor. BS in Electronic Engring. Tech., Northwestern State U., Natchitoches, La., 1990, BS in Radiologic/Nuc. Medicine Tech., 1995. Cert. medicine technologist, La., lic. radiographer La., cert., nuc. cardiology technologist. Nuc. medicine technologist Willis Knighton Health Systems, Shreveport, La., 1995—97; tech. dir. nuc. cardiology Cardiovasc. Consultants LLP, Shreveport, La., 1997—. State health policy liaison Soc. Nuc. Medicine, Reston, Va., 2003—; founder, pres. N.W. La. Nuc. Medicine Working Group, 2005—, NW La. Nuc. Medicine Working Group, 2005—. Musician: (performance musician) Concert. Adult Sunday edn. Southside Bapt., Mansfield, La., 1999—2003; mem. music com. Southside Bapt. Ch., Mansfield, La., 2000—03; mem. Grove Hill Cematery, Mansfield, La., 1995—2003. Mem.: Am. Soc. of Nuc. Cardiology, Soc. of Nuc. Medicine, Tau Kappa Epsilon (life; pres. 1993—94). Southern Baptist. Avocations: travel with family, music/concerts, collections. Office: Cardiovascular Cons LLP PO Box 32388 Shreveport LA 71133

**RYDER, TEREASA KAI,** retired protective services official; b. Lansing, Mich., Aug. 1, 1960; d. Donald C. Patterson and Carole Dae Swain; divorced; 1 child, Erik Zar. AA, Lansing Cmty. Coll., 1990; student, Siena heights U., 1999—. EMT, Mich.; cert. fire svc. instr. Mich. Firefighters Tng. Coun. Firefighter, engr., paramedic, EMT Lansing Fire Dept., 1985-99. Fire svc. instr. Lansing C.C., 1996-01; instr. Lansing Fire Dept., 1996-99; cons., instr. Mich. State U., East Lansing, 1999-00; tutor Grand Rapids Pub. Sch., 2003-04. Founder Meridian Residents Responsible Govt., Haslett, Mich., 1996-97. Recipient Cert. Recognition, Mayor Terry McKane, City of Lansing, 1986. Avocations: drawing, writing, walking, reading, knitting.

**RYDER, WINONA (WINONA LAURA HOROWITZ),** actress; b. Winona, Minn., Oct. 29, 1971; d. Michael and Cynthia (Istas) Horowitz. Founder Roustabout Studios, 1999. Films include: Lucas, 1986, Square Dance, 1987, Beetlejuice, 1988, Great Balls of Fire, 1989, Heathers, 1989, Edward Scissorhands, 1990, Mermaids, 1990, Welcome Home, Roxy Carmichael, 1990, Night On Earth, 1992, Bram Stoker's Dracula, 1992, Age of Innocence, 1993 (Golden Globe for Best Supporting Actress, 1994, Academy award nominee, Best Supporting Actress, 1993), The House of the Spirits, 1994, Reality Bites, 1994, Little Women, 1994 (Acad. Awd. nom., Best Actress), How to Make An American Quilt, 1995, Looking for Richard, 1993, The Crucible, 1996, Boys, 1996, Alien Resurrection, 1997, Celebrity, 1998, Girl, Interrupted, 1999, Autumn in New York, 1999, Lost Souls, 2000, Mr. Deeds, 2002, S1mOne, 2002, The Day My God Died (narrator), 2003, The Heart Is Deceitful Above All Things, 2004, The Darwin Awards, 2006, A Scanner Darkly, 2006. Named one of Top Players Under 35, People mag., 1996; named to Hollywood Walk of Fame, 2000.*

**RYDHOLM, RALPH WILLIAMS,** advertising executive; b. Chgo., June 1, 1937; s. Thor Gabriel and Vivian Constance (Williams) R.; m. Jo Anne Beechler, Oct. 5, 1963; children: Kristin, Erik, Julia. BA, Northwestern U., 1958, postgrad. in bus. adminstrn, 1958-59; postgrad. Advanced Mgmt. Program, Harvard U., 1982. Acct. trainee, copywriter Young & Rubicam Advt., Chgo., 1960-63; copywriter Post-Keyes-Gardner Advt., Chgo., 1963, E. H. Weiss Advt., Chgo., 1963-65; copy group head BBDO Advt., Chgo., 1965-66; with J. Walter Thompson Advt., Chgo., 1966-86, creative dir., v.p., 1969-76, exec. creative dir., 1976-80, sr. v.p., 1972-80, exec. v.p., dir., 1980-86; exec. v.p., chief creative officer, dir. Ted Bates Worldwide, N.Y.C., 1986-87; mng. dir., chmn. mgmt. com., chief creative officer, chmn., CEO, EURO RSCG Tatham Advt., Chgo., 1987-98; bd. dirs. Euro RSCG, USA; pres. R2 Cons., 1999—; spl. counsel J. Walter Thompson, 1999-2000. Bd. dirs., ops. com., chmn. creative com., vice chmn., 1996, chmn., 1997-98; Am. Assn. Advt. Agys. guest spkr. Ad Age Workshop, 1969, 77, 86, Adweek Seminar, 1993, CLIO awards, 1995; keynote spkr. Stephen B. Kelly Awards, 1993, CEBA Awards, 1997; chmn. CEBA Awards, 1997. Mem. assoc. bd. Newberry Libr. Assn., Friends com. Northwestern U.; bd. dirs., adv. coun. leadership coun. Chgo. Pub. Edn. Fund; Prin. for a Day Chgo. Pub. Schs., 1998—2005; bd. dirs. PRO AD PAC, 1998—; former chmn. bd. dirs. Am. Scandinavian Coun.; dir. Am. Assn. Advt. Agys. Found., 1997—99; cons. Exec. Svc. Corp., 2000—. Staff sgt. USAF, 1959—65. Recipient Clio awards, Internat. Broadcast award, Lion awards, Cannes Film Festival, Addy awards; named one of Top 100 Creative Ad People Ad Daily, 1972, Advt. Exec. of Yr. Adweek, 1991, Best Man in Advt. McCalls and Adweek, 1992; named to Creative Leader Hall of Fame, Wall St. Jour., 1994. Mem. ASCAP, Am. Advt. Fedn. (Silver medal Lifetime Svc. 1997), Chgo. Advt. Fedn., Chgo. Com. Coun. on Fgn. Rels., Saddle and Cycle Club, Econ. Club Chgo. (bd. dirs. 1996-98), Northwestern Club Chgo., Harvard Club Chgo., Harvard Club

N.Y.C., Execs. Club Chgo., Tavern Club, Club Internat., Carlton Club, Chikaming Country Club (Mich.), Dunes Club (Mich.), Lost Dunes Club (Mich.), Internat. Club, Hon. Order Ky. Cols., Openlands, Friends of the Parks, Friends of Chgo. River, Fernwood, Art Inst. Chgo., Lincoln Park Zoo, Phi Delta Theta Office Phone: 312-280-7726. Personal E-mail: rydholm@aol.com.

**RYERSON, LISA M.,** academic administrator; BA in English cum laude, Wells Coll., Aurora, N.Y., 1981; MS, SUNY. Asst. dir. admissions Wells Coll., Aurora, NY, 1981—84, assoc. dean of students, 1984—87, dean of students, 1991—94, v.p. to exec. v.p., 1994—95, pres., 1995—. Vice chair bd. of mng. dir. Ind. Coll. Funf of N.Y.; chair exec. bd. Pub. Leadership Edn. Network, Washington; bd. mem. Women's Coll. Coalition, Washington. Mem. exec. com. Cayuga County C. of C., Auburn, NY. Office: Wells Coll 170 Main St Aurora NY 13026

**RYERSON, PAUL SOMMER,** lawyer; b. Newark, Oct. 2, 1946; s. Robert Paul and Audrey Mae (Sommer) R.; m. Susan Jean Duckrow, Aug. 7, 1971 (div. Apr. 1995); children: James Sommer, Jill Carin; m. Kenswynn Black, Jan. 26, 2002. BA, Wesleyan U., 1968; JD, Columbia U., 1971. Bar: N.Y. 1972, D.C. 1972, U.S. Ct. Appeals (D.C. cir.) 1973, U.S. Dist. Ct. D.C. 1973, U.S. Supreme Ct. 1976, U.S. Ct. Appeals (5th cir.) 1979, U.S. Ct. Appeals (4th cir.) 1980. Law clk. to judge Jack B. Weinstein U.S. Dist. Ct. ea. dist. N.Y., 1971-72; assoc. Arnold & Porter, Washington, 1972-79, ptnr., 1980-89, Jones Day, Washington, 1989—. Contbr. articles to profl. publs. Mem. ABA, D.C. Bar Assn. Home: 5809 Nicholson Ln North Bethesda MD 20852-5719 Office: Jones Day 51 Louisiana Ave NW Washington DC 20001-2113 Office Phone: 202-879-3939. E-mail: psryerson@jonesday.com.

**RYERSON, WILLIAM NEWTON,** non profit organization executive; b. Phila., Mar. 9, 1945; s. W. Newton and Jean (Hamilton) R.; m. Leta C. Finch, Dec. 6, 1975. BA, Amherst Coll., 1967; M.Phil., Yale U., 1971. Dir. student intern program Population Inst., Washington 1971-73, dir. youth and student div., 1973-79; dir. devel. Planned Parenthood Southeastern Pa., Phila., 1979-81; assoc. dir. Planned Parenthood No. New Eng., Burlington, Vt., 1981-86; pres. Ryerson & Assocs., fundraising counsel, Shelburne, Vt., 1986-2000; exec. v.p. Population Comm. Internat., NYC, 1986-98; pres. Population Media Ctr., Shelburne, Vt., 1998—. Co-author: Population Activist's Handbook, 1974, Communicating Sustainability, 2000, Entertainment-Education and Social Change-History, Research and Practice, 2003. NASA trainee in biology, Yale U., 1967-70. Mem.: Phi Beta Kappa, Sigma Xi (assoc.). Home: PO Box 580 Shelburne VT 05482-0580 Office: PO Box 547 Shelburne VT 05482-0547 Office Phone: 802-985-8156. Business E-Mail: ryerson@populationmedia.org.

**RYLAND, WALTER H.,** lawyer; b. Richmond, Va., Jan. 23, 1943; s. John William and Evelyn (Quillin) R.; m. Madelaine Aerni, July 10, 1976; children: Mark Vanley, Caroline Aerni. BA, Washington & Lee U., 1965, LLB, 1967. Chief dep. atty. gen. Office of the Atty. Gen. of Va., Richmond, 1978-82; ptnr. Williams, Mullen, Christian & Dobbins, Richmond, 1983—. Counselor, Va. Mus. Fine Arts, Richmond, 1983—; pres. J. Sargeant Reynolds Found., Richmond, 1990. Co-editor: Racial Preferences in Government Contracting (Nat. Legal Ctr. for the Pub. Interest), 1993. Sec. bd. trustees Washington Internat. U. Va., 1989-91; bd. dirs. Coun. for Am. First Freedom, Richmond, 1988-92; pres. Theatre Va., Richmond, 1987-88; sec. Communication Disorders Found., Richmond, 1986-88; chmn. Cultural Art Ctr. at Glen Allen Found. Mem. ABA, Va. Bar Assn., Richmond Bar Assn. Office: Williams Mullen Clark & Dobbins 2 James Ctr 1021 E Cary St Richmond VA 23219-4000

**RYLANDER, HENRY GRADY, JR.,** mechanical engineering educator; b. Pearsall, Tex., Aug. 23, 1921; married; 4 children. BS, U. Tex., 1943, MS, 1952; PhD in Mech. Engring., Ga. Inst. Tech., 1965. Design engr. Steam Div., Aviation Gas Turbine Div., Westinghouse Elec. Corp., 1943-47; from asst. to assoc. prof. mech. engring. U. Tex., Austin, 1947-68, research scientist, 1950, prof. mech. engring., 1968—, Joe J. King prof. engring., 1980—. Cons. engr. TRACOR, Inc., 1964-69; founding dir. Ctr. for Electromechanics, U. Tex., 1977-85, chmn., mech. engring. dept., 1976-86. Named Disting. Grad. Coll. Engring., U. Tex., Austin, 1989. Fellow ASME (Leonardo da Vinci award 1985); mem. ASME. Office: U Tex Coll Engring C2200 Austin TX 78712 Office Phone: 512-471-3044. Business E-Mail: hgr@mail.utexas.edu.

**RYLANDER, ROBERT ALLAN,** financial service executive; b. Bremerton, Wash., Apr. 8, 1947; s. Richard Algot and Marian Ethelyn (Peterson) R.; children: Kate, Erik, Meagan. BA in Fin., U. Wash., 1969; postgrad., U. Alaska, 1972-74. Controller Alaska USA Fed. Credit Union, Anchorage, 1974-77, mgr. ops., 1977-80, asst. gen. mgr., 1980-83, exec. v.p., COO, 1983—; pres., CEO Alaska Option Svcs. Corp., Anchorage, 1983—97, Alaska USA Trust Co., Anchorage, 1997—2004. Chmn. Alaska USA Mortgage, Inc., Anchorage, 1992—, Alaska Option Svcs. Corp., Anchorage, 1997—; bd. dirs. Alaska USA Ins. Brokers, Anchorage, Alaska USA Found., Alaska USA Trust Co. Served to capt. USAF, 1969-74. Avocations: audio electronics, music, home theater. Home: PO Box 220587 Anchorage AK 99522-0587 Office: Alaska USA Fed Credit Union PO Box 196613 Anchorage AK 99519-6613 Business E-Mail: r.rylander@alaskausa.org.

**RYLANT, CYNTHIA,** writer; b. Hopewell, Va., June 6, 1954; d. John Tune and Leatrel (Rylant) Smith; 1 child, Nathaniel. BA, U. Charleston, 1975; MA, Marshall U., 1976; MLS, Kent State U., 1981. English instr. Marshall U., Huntington, W.Va., 1979-80, U. Akron, Ohio, 1983-84; children's libr. Akron (Ohio) Pub. Libr., 1983. Part-time lectr. Northeast Ohio Univs. Coll. Medicine, Rootstown, Ohio, 1991—. Author: (picture books) When I Was Young in the Mountains, 1982 (Caldecott Honor book, 1983, English Speaking Union Book-Across-the-Sea Amb. of Honor award, 1984), Am. Book award nom. 1982), Miss Maggie, 1983, This Year's Garden, 1984, Waiting to Waltz: A Childhood (verse), 1984 (Nat. Coun. for Social Studies Best Book, 1984), A Blue-Eyed Daisy (in U.K. as Some Year for Ellie), 1985 (Children's Book of Yr., Child Study Assn. Am., 1985), The Relatives Came, 1985 (Horn Book Honor book, 1985, Children's Book of Yr., Child Study Assn. Am., 1985, Caldecott Honor book, 1986), Every Living Thing (stories), 1985, A Fine White Dust, 1986 (Newbery Honor book, 1987), Night in the Country, 1986, Birthday Presents, 1987, Children of Christmas (in U.K. as Silver Packages and Other Stories), 1987, All I See, 1988, A Kindness, 1989, Mr. Grigg's Work, 1989, Soda Jerk (verse)1990, A Couple of Kooks (stories), 1990, Appalachia: The Voices of Sleeping Birds, 1991 (Boston Globe/Horn Book Honor book for nonfiction, 1991), Best Wishes, 1992, An Angel for Solomon Singer, 1992, Missing May, 1992 (Newbery Medal, 1992), The Dreamer, 1993, I Had Seen Castles, 1993, The Everyday Books, 1993, The Old Lady Who Named Things, 1996, Whales, 1996, Bookshop Dog, 1996, Blue Hill Meadows, 1997, Poppleton, 1997, Poppleton and Friends, 1997, Cat Heaven, 1997, Blue Hill Meadows and the Much-Loved Dog, 1997, Scarecrow, 1998, Bear Day, 1998, Tulip Sees America, 1998, Poppleton Everyday, 1998, Poppleton Forever, 1998, Bird House, 1998, Islander, 1998, Bless Us All, 1999, Cobble Street Cousins in Aunt Lucy's Kitchen, 1998, Bunny Bungalow, 1999, Cookie-Store Cat, 1999, Poppleton in Spring, 1999, Cobble Street Cousins: Some Good News, 1999, Cobble Street Cousins: Special Gifts, 1999, Poppleton in Fall, 1999, Give Me Grace, 1999, Heavenly Village, 1999, Poppleton Through and Through, 2000, Wonderful Happens, 2000, Thimbleberry Stories, 2000, Let's Go Home, 2000, Little Whistle, 2000, In November, 2000, Poppleton Has Fun, 2000, Little Whistle's Dinner Party, 2001, Little Whistle's Medicine, 2001, Ticky-Tacky Doll, 2001, The Great Gracie Chase, 2001, Poppleton in Winter, 2001, Summer Party, 2001, Good Morning Sweetie Pie and Other Poems for Little Children, 2002, Old Town in the Green Groves, 2002, Wedding Flowers, 2002, Long Night Moon, 2004, (Mr. Putter and Tabby series) Walk the Dog, 1994, Bake the Cake, 1994, Pour the Tea, 1994, Pick the Pears, 1995, Fly the Plane, 1997, Row the Boat, 1997, Toot the Horn, 1998, Take the Train, 1998, Paint the Porch, 2000, Feed the Fish, 2001, (The High-Rise Private Eyes series) Case of the Climbing Cat, 2000, Case of the Missing Monkey, 2000, The Case of the Puzzling Possum, 2001, The Case of the Troublesome Turtle, 2001, (Henry and Mudge series)

Henry and Mudge, 1987, Henry and Mudge in Puddle Trouble, 1990, Henry and Mudge Take the Big Test, 1991, Henry and Mudge in the Green Time, 1992, Henry and Mudge under the Yellow Moon, 1992, Henry and Mudge in the Sparkle Days, 1993, Henry and Mudge and the Forever Sea, 1993, Henry and Mudge Get the Cold Shivers, 1993, Henry and Mudge and the Happy Cat, 1994, Henry and Mudge and the Bedtime Thumps, 1991, Henry and Mudge and the Long Weekend, 1992, Henry and Mudge and the Wild Wind, 1992, Henry and Mudge and the Careful Cousin, 1994, Henry and Mudge and the Best Day of All, 1995, Henry and Mudge in the Family Trees, 1997, Henry and Mudge and the Sneaky Crackers, 1998, Henry and Mudge and the Starry Night, 1998, Henry and Mudge and Annie's Good Move, 1998, Henry and Mudge and the Snowman Plan, 1999, Henry and Mudge and Annie's Perfect Pet, 1999, Henry and Mudge and the Funny Lunch, 1999, Henry and Mudge and the Tall Tree House, 1999, Henry and Mudge and Mrs. Hopper's House, 1999, Henry and Mudge and the Great Grandpas, 1999, Henry and Mudge and a Very Special Merry Christmas, 1999, Henry and Mudge and the Wild Goose Chase, 1999, Henry and Mudge and the Big Sleepover, 1999, Henry and Mudge and the Tumbling Trip, 1999, Henry's Puppy Mudge Has a Snack, 2001, Henry's Puppy Mudge Takes aBath, 2001, Henry and Mudge and the Great Grandpas, 2005 (Am. Libr. Assn.'s Theodor Seuss Geisel Medal, 2006). Office: Simon & Schuster Children's 4th Floor 1230 Ave of The Americas New York NY 10020*

**RYLES, GERALD FAY,** investor, finance company executive; b. Walla Walla, Wash., Apr. 3, 1936; s. L. F. and Janie Geraldine (Bassett) R.; m. Ann Jane Birkenmeyer, June 12, 1959; children— Grant, Mark, Kelly. BA, U. Wash., 1958; MBA, Harvard U., 1962. With Gen. Foods Corp., White Plains, NY, 1962—66, Purex Corp., Ltd., Lakewood, Calif., 1966-68; cons. McKinsey & Co., Inc., Los Angeles, 1968-71; with Fibreboard Corp., San Francisco, 1971-79, v.p., 1973-75, group v.p., 1975-79; with Consol. Fibres, Inc., San Francisco, 1979-88, exec. v.p., 1979-81, pres., dir., 1981-86, chief exec. officer, 1986-88; cons. Orinda, Calif., 1988-90; with Interchecks Inc., 1990-92, pres., CEO, 1990-92; bus. exec., pvt. investor, 1992-94; chmn. bd., CEO Microserv, Inc., Kirkland, Wash., 1994—2001, chmn. bd., 2001—03. Bd. dirs Halifax Corp., Giant Campus, Inc., Zumiez, Inc. Capt. U.S. Army, 1958-66. Mem.: Harvard Bus. Sch. Assn., U. Wash. Alumni Assn. Republican. Episcopalian. Home: 127 3rd Ave Apt 301 Kirkland WA 98033-6177 Personal E-mail: g.ryles@verizon.net.

**RYMAN, ROBERT TRACY,** artist; b. Nashville, May 30, 1930; s. William Tracy and Nora (Boston) R.; m. Lucy Lippard, 1961 (div. 1966); children: Ethan, Ryman; m. Merrill Wagner, Jan. 31, 1969; children: William Tracy, George Corydon. Exhibited one man shows: Paul Bianchini Gallery, 1967, Solomon R. Guggenheim Mus., NYC, 1972, Kunsthalle, Basel, Switzerland, 1975, Palais des Beaux-Arts, Brussels, 1974, Stedelijk Mus., Amsterdam, Netherlands, 1974, Whitechapel Gallery, London, 1977, Centre Pompidou, Paris, 1981, Sidney Janis Gallery, NYC, 1981, Kunsthalle, Dusseldorf, Germay, 1982, Bonnier Gallery, NYC, 1983, Daniel Weinberg Gallery, LA, 1983, Galerie Maeght LeLong, Paris, 1984, Rhona Hoffman Gallery, Chgo., 1985, Leo Castelli Gallery, NYC, 1986, Galerie Maeght LeLong, NYC, 1986, Pace Gallery, NYC, 1990, DIA Art Found., NYC, 1988-89, Konrad Fischer Gallery, Dusseldorf, Fed. Germany, 1987, Pace Gallery, NY, Tate Gallery, London, MMA, N.Y., San Francisco Mus. Modern Art, Walker Arts Ctr., Mpls., Whitney Mus. Am. Art, 1999-2000, Richard Gray Gallery, NYC, 2001-02, James Cohan Gallery, 2001-02; group shows: Biennal Whitney Mus. Am. Art, NYC, 1977, Tokyo, Japan Art Assn., 2005, mem. AAAL, Am. Acad. Arts and Scis., Mcpl. Art Soc. NY (bd. dirs. 1991—). Studio: 637 Greenwich St New York NY 10014-3306 *There is never a question of what to paint, but only how to paint. The "how" of painting is the image.*

**RYMAR, JULIAN W.,** manufacturing executive, director; b. Grand Rapids, Mich., June 29, 1919; m. Margaret Macon Van Brunt, Dec. 11, 1954; children: Margaret Gibson, Gracen Macon, Ann Mackall. Student, Grand Rapids Jr. Coll., 1937—39, U. Mich., 1940—41, Wayne State U., 1948—52, Rockhurst Coll., 1952—53, Naval War Coll., 1954—58. Entered as aviation cadet USN, 1942; comdg. officer Naval Air Res. Squadron, 1957—60, staff air comdr., 1960—64; advanced through grades to cept. USN, 1964; chmn. bd., CEO, dir. Grace Co., Belton, Mo., 1955—90; chmn. bd. dirs. Shock & Vibration Rsch. Inc., 1956—66; chmn. bd., CEO Bedtime Story Fashions. Bd. dirs. Am. Bank & Trust. Mem. Kans. City Hist. Soc.; adv. bd. dirs. St. Joseph Hosp.; trustee Missouri Valley Coll., 1969—74; pres. Rymar Found.; active Sch. Am. Rsch., Inst. Am. Arts, Mus. N.Mex. Found., Spanish Colonial Art Soc.; active various positions Episcopal Ch.; bd. dirs. Bros. of Mercy, St. Luke's Hosp. Mem.: Soc. Profl. Journalists, Friends of Art (exec. bd. 1971—74, pres., chmn. bd. govs.), Spanish Colonial Arts Soc., Mus. Indian Arts and Culture, Mus. Internat. Folk Art, Mus. Fine Arts, Mus. N.Mex. Found., Santa Fe Symphony, Soc. Fellows of Nelson Gallery Found. (exec. bd. 1972—77), Mil. Order World Wars, Navy League U.S. (pres. 1959—60, dir. 1960—70), Rockhill Homes Assn. (v.p.), Sch. Am. Rsch., Inst. Am. Indian Art, Quiet Birdman Club, Arts Club of Washington, Press Club, Univ. Mich. Club, Sigma Delta Chi. Episcopalian. Personal E-mail: rymarvb@nets.com.

**RYMER, ILONA SUTO,** artist, retired art educator; b. NYC, Dec. 1, 1921; d. Alexander and Elizabeth (Komaromy) Suto; m. Robert Hamilton Rymer, Mar. 27, 1944 (dec. Dec. 1999); children: Thomas Parker, Shelley Ilona. BA, Long Beach State U., 1953, MA, 1954. Tchr., cons. Long Beach (Calif.) Sch. Dist., 1953-56; tchr. Orange (Calif.) Sch. Dist., 1956-58; tchr., cons. Brea (Calif.)-Olinda Sch. Dist., 1958-80; ind. artist, designer Graphic House Studio, Solvang, Calif., 1980—, Stampa-Barbara, Santa Barbara, Calif., 1990—. Lectr. folk art Brea Sch. Dist., 1975—80; co-founder and mem. Gallery Los Olivos, pres, 1993—. Author: (instrn. book) Folk Art U.S.A., 1975 (Proclamation City of Brea, 1975); art editor, feature writer, illustrator: Arabian Conneciton mag., 1985—86; needlepoint designer Backstictch Store, Solvang, Calif., 1982—83; one-woman shows include Liberty Bell Race Track, Pa., 1970, Gallery Los Olivos, Calif., 2004, exhibited in group shows at Dennas Mus. Ctr., Northwestern Mich. Coll., 2001, Nat. Exhbn. Am. Watercolor, 2002, Adirondack's Nat. Exhbn. of Am. Watercolors, Old Forge, N.Y., 2002—, commission, pres. Reagan's portrait on his stallion, Reagan Libr., Simi Valley, Calif., Khemosabi and Ruth, 1995. Artist and donor City of Solvang, Calif., 2005. Recipient 1st pl. Seminar award, Rex Brandt, 1961, Affiliate award, Laguna Art Mus., 1967, Best of Watercolor award, Orange County Fair, 1969, Bicentennial trip to France, Air France, 1975, Proclamation for Tchg., City of Brea, 1980, Theme award, Santa Barbara County Fair, 1991. Mem.: Mendocina Art Assn., Collage Artists Am., Artist Guild Santa Ynez Valley, Ctrl. Coast Art Assn., Santa Barbara Art Assn., Calif. Gold Coast Watercolor Soc. (signature). Presbyterian. Studio: 1887 Augustenburg Pl Solvang CA 93463 Personal E-mail: ilonarymer@comcast.net.

**RYMER, JON T.,** federal agency administrator; b. Apr. 2, 1955; m. Debra Rymer; 1 child, Thomson. BA, U. Tenn., 1981; MBA, U. Ark., 1996. Exec. v.p. First Am. Nat. Bank (now AmSouth Bank), Knoxville and Nashville, 1981—92, Boatman's Bank Ark. (now Bank of Am.), Little Rock, 1992—97; dir., practice leader assurance based adv. svcs. KPMG LLP, Chgo. and Cinn., 1997—2004; acting insp. gen. FDIC, 2004—06, insp. gen., 2006—. Served with U.S. Army. Mem.: Inst. Internal Auditors, Am. Legion. Office: FDIC 3501 Fairfax Dr Rm E9070 Arlington VA 22226

**RYMER, MARILYN MOLLMAN,** neurologist, researcher; b. St. Louis, Apr. 16, 1944; d. Henry Edward and Verna May Mollman; m. Robert Andrew Rymer, June 7, 1970; children: Michael Robert, Susan Rymer Beesley. MD, Washington U., St. Louis, 1970. Diplomate Am. Bd. Psychiatry and Neurology. Med. dir. St. Luke's Mid Am. Brain and Stroke Inst., Kansas City, 1993—; Edward T. Matheny Jr. Mo. endowed chair in neurosci. U. Mo. Kansas City Sch. Medicine, 1999—. Bd. dirs. VHA, Inc., Irvine, Tex., 1998—2003. Lt. USN, 1970—71. Fellow, St. Luke's Hosp. Found., 2006. Fellow: Am. Stroke Assn. Office: St Luke's Hosp 4401 Wornall Rd Kansas City MO 64111 Office Phone: 816-932-9847.

**RYMER, PAMELA ANN,** federal judge; b. Knoxville, Tenn., Jan. 6, 1941; AB, Vassar Coll., 1961; LLB, Stanford U., 1964; LLD (hon.), Pepperdine U., 1988. Bar: Calif. 1966, U.S. Ct. Appeals (9th cir.) 1966, U.S. Ct. Appeals (10th cir.), U.S. Supreme Ct. Dir., polit. rsch. and analysis Goldwater for President Com., 1964; v.p. Rus Walton & Assoc., Los Altos, Calif., 1965—66; assoc. Lillick McHose & Charles, L.A., 1966—75, ptnr., 1973—75, Toy and Rymer, L.A., 1975—83; judge U.S. Dist. Ct. (cen. dist.) Calif., L.A., 1983—89, U.S. Ct. Appeals (9th cir.), L.A., 1989—. Faculty The Nat. Jud. Coll. 1986-88; mem. com. summer edn. programs Fed. Jud. Ctr., 1987-88, mem. com. appellate judge edn., 1996-99; chair exec. com. 9th Cir. Jud. Conf., 1990; mem. com. criminal law Jud. Conf. U.S., 1988-93, Ad Hoc com. gender-based violence, 1991-94, fed.-state jurisdiction com., 1993-96; mem. commn. on structural alternatives Fed. Cts. Appeals, 1997-98. Mem. editorial bd. The Judges' jour., 1989-91; contbr. articles to profl. jours. and newsletters. Mem. Calif. Postsecondary Edn. Commn., 1974-84, chmn., 1980-84; mem. L.A. Olympic Citizens Adv. Commn.; bd. visitors Stanford U. Law Sch., 1986-99, trustee, 1991-2001, chair, 1993-96, exec. com., chmn. bd. trustees com. acad. policy, planning and mgmt. and its ad. hoc. com. athletics., chmn. bd. visitors Sch. Law, 1987—; bd. visitors Pepperdine U. Law Sch., 1987—; mem. Edn. Commn. of States Task Force on State Policy and Ind. Higher Edn., 1987-89, Carnegie Commn. Task Force Sci. and Tech. Jud. and Regulatory Decisionmaking, 1990-93, Commn. Substance Abuse Coll. and Univ. Campuses, 1992-94, commn. substance abuse high schs. Ctr. Addiction and Substance Abube Columbia U.; bd. dirs. Constnl. Rights Found., 1985-97, Pacific Coun. Internat. Policy, 1995—, Calif. Higher Edn. Policy Ctr., 1992-97; Jud. Conf. U.S. Com. Fed.-State Jurisdiction, 1993, Com. Criminal Law, 1988-93, ad hoc com. gender based violence, 1991-94; chair exec. com. 9th cir. jud. conf., 1990-94. Recipient Outstanding Trial Jurist award L.A. County Bar Assn., 1988; named David T. Lewis Disting. Jurist-in-Residence U. Utah, 1992. Mem. ABA (task force on civil justice reform 1991-93, mem. coord. com. agenda civil justice reform in Am. 1991), State Bar Calif. (antitrust and trade regulation sect., exec. com. 1990-92), L.A. County Bar Assn. (chmn. antitrust sect. 1981-82, mem. editl. bd. The Judges Jour. 1989-91, mem. com. professionalism 1988—, numerous other coms.), Assn. of Bus. Trial Lawyers (bd. govs. 1990-92), Stanford Alumni Assn., Stanford Law Soc. Soc. Calif., Vassar Club So. Calif. (past pres.). Office: US Ct Appeals 9th Cir US Court of Appeals Bldg 125 S Grand Ave Rm 600 Pasadena CA 91105-1621*

**RYN, CLAES GÖSTA,** political science professor; b. Norrköping, Sweden, June 12, 1943; permanent resident of U.S., 1979, naturalized, 2002; s. Gösta Karl and Cecilia Edit (Blom) R.; m. Marianne Carin Tedhagen, Aug. 30, 1969; children: Charlotte, Viveka, Elisabet. MA, Uppsala U., Sweden, 1967, postgrad., 1969—71, Syracuse U., 1968—69; PhD, La. State U., 1974. Asst. prof. politics Cath. U. Am., Washington, 1974-78, assoc. prof. politics, 1978-82, prof. politics, 1982—, asst. dean Sch. Arts and Scis., 1977-79, chmn. dept. politics, 1979-85. Adj. prof. govt. Georgetown U., 2002—; vis. assoc. prof. U. Va., Charlottesville, 1981; co-founder, chmn. Nat. Humanities Inst., Washington, 1984—; referee, evaluator NEH, Dept. Edn., USIA, pubs., jours., others; dir. various confs. and lecture series; mem. Richard M. Weaver fellowship selection com., 1980—; faculty sponsor Earhart Found., 1989—; awards com. Ingersoll Prizes, 1990; Salvatori doctoral fellowship selection com. Intercollegiate Studies Inst., 1990—; lectr. series Peking U., May 2000; appearances on TV and radio. Author: (with Bertil Häggman) Nykonservatismen i USA, 1971, Democracy and the Ethical Life, 1978, 2d rev. edit., 1990, Will, Imagination and Reason, 1986, 2d rev. edit., 1997, Individualism och gemenskap, 1986, The New Jacobinism, 1991, Unity Through Diversity (in Chinese), 2001, A Common Human Ground, 2003, America the Virtuous, 2003; editor: Humanitas, 1992—; co-editor (with George Panichas), author (with others), Peter Viereck an Conservatism, 2005, Irving Babbitt in Our Time, 1986; editor, author introduction for other volumes; contbr. articles to profl. jours.; mem. editl. bd. Modern Age, 1981—, Marknadsekonomisk Tidskrift, Sweden, 1986-92, This World, 1992—; editl. columnist Svenska Dagbladet, Sweden, 1996—. Mem. vestry St. Francis Episcopal Ch., Potomac, Md., 1986-88. Served with Swedish Army, Royal Life Company I 4 Regt., 1963, Signal Corps, 1967-68. Rsch. fellow Earhart Found., 1980-81, 87-88, Wilbur Found., 1980-81, 90, 93-94, others; Disting. Fgn. scholar Peking U., 2000; recipient award King of Sweden, 1983, Will Herberg award Disting. Faculty Svc. Intercollegiate Studies Inst., 2003; named Outstanding Grad. Prof., Cath. U. Am., 1992. Mem. Phila. Soc. (trustee 1999, 2d v.p. 2000-01, pres. 2001-02). Episcopalian. Home: 10008 Crestleigh Ln Potomac MD 20854-1820 Office: Cath Univ Am Dept Politics Washington DC 20064-0001

**RYNKIEWICZ, STEPHEN MICHAEL,** journalist; b. Sheboygan, Wis., Oct. 20, 1955; s. Walter Paul and Ruth Catharine (Van Hercke) R.; m. Brenda Gail Russell, Sept. 27, 1986. BA, U. Wis., 1976. Various staff assignments Chgo. Sun-Times, 1979-97, real estate editor, 1990-97; Internet prodr. Chgo. Tribune, 1997—. Pres. Ill. Freedom of Info. Coun., 1991-93; mem. profl. faculty Columbia Coll., Chgo., 1998. Pres. Chgo. Headline Club, 1991-92, treas., 2001-02; chmn. Peter Lisagor Awards for Exemplary Journalism, 2002—; sec. Headline Club Found., 2004—. Recipient Web site award, NAREE, 1997—2000, Editor, Pub. Best Newspaper Classified Site award, 2000, Online Journalism award for pub. svc., 2002, Peter Lisagor award in Bus. Reporting, 2003. Mem. Soc. Profl. Journalists (regional dir. 1992-95, sec. treas. 1995-96, membership chair 1997-98, diversity chair 1996-97), Nat. Soc. Real Estate Editors (bd. dirs. 1999-2000), Sigma Delta Chi Found. (bd. dirs. 1995-96). Office: Ste 400 435 N Michigan Ave Chicago IL 60611-4001

**RYNN, NATHAN,** physics professor, consultant; b. NYC, Dec. 2, 1923; s. Meyer and Rose (Wolkerwiczer) Rynkowsky; m. Glenda Brown, June 24, 1989; children by previous marriage: Jonathan, Margaret, David. BSEE, CCNY, 1944; MS, U. Ill., 1947; PhD, Stanford U., 1956. Rsch. engr. RCA Labs., Princeton, NJ, 1947-52; rsch. asst. Stanford U., Palo Alto, Calif., 1952-56, rsch. assoc., 1958; mem. tech. staff Ramo-Woolridge, L.A., 1956-57; supr. Huggins Labs., Menlo Park, Calif., 1957-58; rsch. staff physicist Princeton U., 1958-65; prof. physics U. Calif.-Irvine, 1965-94, prof. physics emeritus, rsch. prof. physics, 1994—. Vis. prof. Ecole Polytechnique Fed. of Lausanne, Switzerland, 1984-90, Ecole Polytechnique, Paris, and other European univs. and labs., 1973-80; indsl. sci. advisor/cons., 1964—; com. mem. Plasma Sci. Com. Nat. Rsch. Coun.; founder and leader plasma physics rsch. facility (the Q-Machine). Contbr. articles and revs. to profl. jours. With USN, 1944-46. Grantee NSF, U.S. Dept. Energy, Air Force Geophys. Lab.; Fulbright sr. fellow, 1978. Fellow Am. Phys. Soc., IEEE, AAAS; mem. Sigma Xi. Office: U Calif Dept Physics & Astronomy Irvine CA 92697-4575 Office Phone: 949-824-5944. Business E-mail: nrynn@uci.edu.

**RYSKAMP, CHARLES ANDREW,** museum director, educator; b. East Grand Rapids, Mich., Oct. 21, 1928; s. Henry Jacob and Flora (DeGraaf) R. AB, Calvin Coll., 1950; MA, Yale U., 1951, PhD, 1956; postgrad., Pembroke Coll., Cambridge U., 1953-54; Litt.D., Trinity Coll., Hartford, 1975; L.H.D., Union Coll., 1977. Nathan Hale fellow Yale U., 1954-55; instr. English Princeton U., 1955-59, asst. prof., 1959-63, assoc. prof., 1963-69; curator English and Am. lit. Univ. Library, 1967-69, prof., 1969—. Procter & Gamble faculty fellow, 1958-59; jr. fellow Coun. of Humanities, 1960-61, John E. Annan preceptor, 1961-64; dir. Pierpont Morgan Libr., N.Y.C., 1969-87, dir. emeritus, fellow (hon.), 1997—; dir. Frick Collection, 1987-97, dir. emeritus, fellow (hon.), 1997—; dir. vis. Inst. Advanced Study, Princeton, 1997-99; exhbn. of collection of drawings Pierpont Morgan Libr., 2001; adv.

bd. Skowhegan Sch. Painting and Sculpture, Pvt. Papers of James Boswell, Yale U.; vis. com. dept. drawings and printed books Pierpont Morgan Libr. Coun. and Libr. Com., Frick Collection; bd. adv. Princeton U. Art Mus. Author: William Cowper of the Inner Temple, Esq, 1959, William Blake, Engraver, 1969; editor: (with F.A. Pottle) Boswell: The Ominous Years, 1963, The Cast-Away, 1963, Wilde and the Nineties, 1966, William Blake: The Pickering Manuscript, 1972, (with J. King) The Letters and Prose Writings of William Cowper, vol. I, 1979, vol. II, 1981, vol. III, 1982, Vol. IV, 1984, Vol. V, 1986, (with R. Wendorf) The Works of William Collins, 1979, (with J. Baird) The Poetical Works of William Cowper, vol. I, 1980, vols. II-III, 1995, (with J. King) William Cowper: Selected Letters, 1989, Report to the Fellows of the Pierpont Morgan Library, vols. 16-21, 1969-89, Charles Ryskamp and Friends, 1999, (with Scott Westrem) The Works of John Chalkhill, 1999, Of Cabbages and Kings, 2004. Trustee, exec. com. Mus. Broadcasting, 1977-87; trustee John Simon Guggenheim Meml. Found., Libr. of Am.; trustee emeritus Corning Mus. Glass, Amon Carter Mus.; past vis. com. dept. paintings conservation Met. Mus. Art; patron William Blake Trust; bd. mgrs. Lewis Walpole Libr., Yale U.; bd. dirs. v.p. Gerard B. Lambert Found.; past v.p. Frederick R. Koch Found.; trustee Venetian Heritage. Decorated Order St. John of Jerusalem, comdr. Order Orange Nassau, The Netherlands, officer Order Leopold II, Belgium, comdr. Order of Falcon, Iceland; recipient Peter Stuyvesant award Dutch Am. West-India Co., 1987, Gold medal Holland Soc., 1991. Mem. Am. Philos. Soc., Museums Coun. N.Y.C. (past v.p.), Keats-Shelley Assn. Am. (past v.p.), Master Drawings Assn. (past pres.), Met. Opera Assn. (bd. adv., chmn. arts and archives com.), Drawing Soc. (nat. com.), Am. Assocs. Royal Nat. Theatre, Bibliog. Soc. Am., Acad. Am. Poets, Am. Antiquarian Soc., Assn. Art Mus. Dirs. (past pres.), NY Geneal. and Biog. Soc. (spl. corr.), Neuropathy Assn. (nat. adv. coun.), Cowper Soc., Assn. Internat. Bibliophilie (com. of Honor), Found. French Mus. (adv. bd.), Wordsworth Rydal Mount Trust, Grolier Club, Century Assn., Lotos Club, Knickerbocker Club, Elizabethan Club (New Haven), Roxburghe Club (London)

**RYU, DOJIN,** chemist, educator; PhD, U. Nebraska, Lincoln, 1993—97. Rsch. asst. prof. U. Nebr., 2001—04, adj. prof., 2004—; asst. prof. Tex. Woman's U., Denton, 2004—. Competitive Rsch. grant, USDA-NRICGP, 2005—. Mem.: IFT, Assn. Ofcl. Analytical Chemists, Internat. Assn. Food Protection, Sigma Xi, Phi Tau Sigma. Office: Texas Woman's Univ 304 Administration Dr Denton TX 76204 Office Fax: 940-898-2634. Business E-Mail: dryu@mail.twu.edu.

**RYU, JAE,** hydrologist; s. Wonyol Ryu and Bokson Kim; m. Yookyung Lee, Aug. 31, 2002; 1 child, Jimin. Doctorate, U. Wash., Seattle, 2006. Registered profl. engr., Wash., 2004. Rsch. assoc. U. Wash., Seattle, 2002—06; hydrologist Nat. Drought Mitigation Ctr., Lincoln, Nebr., 2006—. Mem.: ASCE (assoc.). Office Phone: 206-290-6851. Business E-Mail: jhryu@u.washington.edu.

**RYU, KYOO-HAI LEE,** physiologist; b. Seoul, Republic of Korea, Sept. 5, 1948; came to U.S., 1972; d. Hee Soon and Jung Ock Lee; m. David Tai-Hyung Ryu, May 13, 1978; children: Eugenia, Christina, John. BS, Yonsei U., Seoul, 1971; PhD, U. Minn., 1981. Postdoctoral fellow U. Minn., Mpls., 1980-81, staff scientist, 1981-82; sr. rsch. assoc. Wright State U., Dayton, Ohio, 1985-91; adminstr. Ohio Ctr. of Cosmetic Surgery, Bellefontaine, Ohio, 1991—. Home: 15 Bexley Ave Springfield OH 45503-1103 Office Phone: 937-390-3277. Personal E-mail: kyoo@ryunet.com.

**RYU, MANHO,** application developer; b. Sochungdo, Kyungido, Korea, Mar. 23, 1957; arrived in U.S., 1983; s. Bongoh Ryu and Youngah No; m. Michelle M. Ryu, May 28, 1960; children: Angie L., Jason C. BS in Computer Sci., Abilene Christian U., Tex., 1986; BS in Applied Math., U. Tex. at Dallas, Richardson, 1988; MS in Applied Math., U. Tex. at Dallas, 1993; MS in Computer Sci., Kennedy-Western U., Boise, Idaho, 1992; PhD in Computer Sci., Kennedy-Western U., 1996. Computer operator Electrospace Systems, Richardson, 1988; lead programmer Info. Mgmt. Group, Plano, Tex., 1989—90; analyst, systems supr. Epsilon Data Mgmt., Inc., Dallas, 1990—92; mgr. MIS dept. MB Direct, Inc., Dallas, 1992—93; dir. IS dept. Skyking Freight Sys., Dallas, 1993—94; sr. software engr. Spectra Vision Inc., Richardson, 1994—97, Estech Systems, Plano, 1997—98; sr. software devel. engr. Alcatel USA, Inc., Plano, 1998—. Author: (software) Clean Man TXU, Cash Man TXU. Mem.: IEEE, Assn. Computing Machinery, Math. Assn. Am. Home: 7902 Bow Ct Frisco TX 75035 Office: Alcatel USA Inc 3400 W Plano Pkwy Plano TX 75075 Office Phone: 972-477-9660. Personal E-mail: mmryu@yahoo.com.

**RYU, WOONG HWAN,** electrical engineer; b. Incheon, Republic of Korea, May 24, 1971; s. Jewan Ryu and Sim Kim; m. Jung Seok Park, June 22, 1996; children: Young Jin, Erin Angella. BS, Kwangwoon U., Seoul, 1994; MSc, Korea Advanced Inst. Sci. and Tech., Daejeon, 1997, PhD, 2001. Assoc. engr. Samsung Electronics, Kyungki-Do, Republic of Korea, 1997—2001; vis. assoc. rsch. fellow Gintic Inst. Mfg. Tech., Singapore, 2000—01; analog engr., staff Intel Corp., Folsom, Calif., 2001—. Contbr. articles to profl. jours., scientific papers to profl. confs. Tchr., counselor Open Door Social Welfare Ctr., Seoul, 1990—97. Mem.: IMAPS (assoc.), IEEE (assoc.). Achievements include patents pending for voltage plane with high impedance link; patents for clock distribution module of digital system using RF interconnection (also Korean patent). Office: Intel Corp 1900 Prairie City Rd Folsom CA 95630-9599 Home: 7023 Orofino Dr El Dorado Hills CA 95762-5565 Personal E-mail: whryu00@orgio.net. E-mail: woong.hwan.ryu@intel.com.

**RYUN, JAMES RONALD,** congressman; b. Wichita, Kans., Apr. 29, 1947; m. Anne Carol Snider; 4 children: Ned, Drew, Catharine, Heather. BA, U. Kansas. Founder, pres. Jim Ryun Sports, Inc.; mem. US Congress from 2nd Kans. dist., 1996—, comm. on armed services, comm. on the budget, comm. on financial services. Participant Olympic Games, 1964, 68, 72. Recipient Silver medal 1500 meter run Olympic Games, 1968; held world record in the mile, 1500 meters, 800 yards. Republican. Office: US Ho Reps 1110 Longworth Ho Office Bldg Washington DC 20515-1602 also: Topeka Dist Office Ste 100 800 SW Jackson Topeka KS 66612-1205*

**RZEPKOWSKI, JAMES EDWARD,** state agency administrator; b. Annapolis, Md., Mar. 8, 1971; s. Walter Jerome and Veronica Catherine (Gnacyk) R.; m. Laura E. Green, Aug. 23, 1997; 1 child, Brian Myer. BA, U. Md., 1993. Computer aide Nat. Security Agy. U.S. Dept. Defense, 1988-89; office mgr. Md. Dept. Housing and Cmty. Devel., 1990; legis. intern to Sen. John A Cade Md. State Senate, 1992; state del. dist. 32 State of Md., 1995—2003; ins. office rep. State Farm Ins. Agy., 1993—; assoc. dep. sec. Md. Dept. Bus. and Econ. Devel., 2003—. Adminstrv. asst. Crofton Convalescent Ctr., 1991; cashier Latelas Discount Liquors, 1992-93. State mem. Md. State Rep. Ctrl. Com., Annapolis, 1992; ofcl., player intramural sports U. Md.; pastoral coun. Cath. Student Ctr., 1992-93. Recipient Legis. Leadership award, The ARC of Md., 2000, Legislator of Yr. award, Anne Arundel County C. of C., 1996. Mem. K.C., Md. Medallion Soc. (charter), Eta Epsilon Alumni Assn. (pres. 1994—), Phi Beta Kappa, Omicron Delta Kappa, Alpha Lambda Delta, Golden Key, Pi Kappa Phi. Office: 217 E Redwood St Baltimore MD 21202 Home: 8109 Huntmaster CT Glen Burnie MD 21061-6343

**RZEZNIK, JOHNNY,** singer, musician; b. Buffalo, Dec. 5, 1965. Lead singer, guitarist Goo Goo Dolls, 1985—. Guitarist: (albums) First Release, 1987, Goo Goo Dolls, 1987, singer, guitarist: (albums) Jed, 1989, Hold Me Up, 1990, Superstar Car Wash, 1993, Boy Named Goo, 1995, Dizzy Up the Girl, 1998, Gutterflower, 2002, Let Love In, 2006, (songs) Iris, City of Angels soundtrack, 1998 (nominated for three Grammy Awards.), I'm Still Here, Treasure Planet soundtrack, 2002; guest appearance (TV series) Charmed, 2000, (albums) Birdland (with the Yardbirds), 2003; singer, composer: (TV series) Good Morning Miami, 2002. Recipient Artist of Yr. (with Goo Goo Dolls), Radio Music Awards, 2005. Office: Warner Brothers Records 3300 Warner Blvd Burbank CA 91505

**SA, JULIE (SHIA RI XIANG),** former council woman, former mayor, real estate developer; b. Korea, Dec. 15, 1950; came to U.S., 1973, naturalized, 1982; married. Degree in Polit. Sci., Dong-A U., Korea. Owner restaurant chain, China Doll; councilwoman City of Fullerton, Calif., 1992-94, 96-99, mayor, 1994-95; founder Golden Age World, Inc., Republic of Korea. Rep. bd. Orange County Sanitation Dists.; rep. to Tri-City Park Authority, City of Fullerton. Mem. Fullerton C. of C., Orange County Korean C. of C., Orange County Chinese C. of C.

**SA, PING,** statistician, educator; PhD in Stats., U. S.C., 1990. Asst. prof. stats. U. North Fla., Jacksonville, 1991—96, assoc. prof. stats., 1996—2004, prof. stats., 2004—. Contbr. articles to profl. jours.

**SAAB, DEANNE KELTUM,** real estate broker, appraiser; b. Allentown, Pa., Jan. 27, 1945; d. James A. and Agnes G. (Hanzlik) S. BA, Cedar Crest Coll., 1966; MS, U. Calif., Santa Barbara, 1973; realtors cert., Pa. State U., 1978. Cert. appraiser Assoc. Appraisal Inst., Pa., 1991; cert. sales profl. Nat. Assn. Home Builders, 1994. Tchr. Ojai (Calif.) Unified Sch. Dist., 1966-74; pvt. practice Allentown, 1978—; owner Heritage Gardens, Allentown, 1981—; pres., treas. DeAnne & Assoc., Inc., Allentown, 1987—. Co-founder, treas. performance group Lehigh Valley Folk Music Soc., 1996. Mem. AAUW (various offices, Best State Newsletter award 1987), Nat. Assn. Realtors, Pa. Assn. Realtors, Allentown Lehigh Valley Assn. Realtors, Cedar Crest Coll. Alumnae Assn. (class rep., various offices), Lehigh Valley Guild Craftsmen (various offices). Avocations: gourd, herbal crafting, painting, folk music performance. Home and office: 1360 Dorney Ave Allentown PA 18103-9731 Personal E-mail: dksaab@ptd.net.

**SAAB, MAUREEN WILSON,** social worker, consultant; b. Lackawanna, NY, Nov. 7, 1940; d. Martin Francis Wilson and Alice Joan Conmy; m. Richard Joseph Saab, June 12, 1965; children: Alice Joan, Joseph Richard, Bridget Jane Saab Van Sickle. BA, Marymount Coll., 1962; MSW, SUNY, Buffalo, 1964. Family counselor Family Svc. Soc., Buffalo, 1964—66; sch. social worker Zenia (Ohio) Schs., 1974; devel. dir. Nichols Schs., Buffalo, 1989—95; devel. coord. Arts Coun. Buffalo and Erie County, Buffalo, 1996—98; devel. cons. Buffalo, 1995—2000. Pres. Jr. League Buffalo, 1983—84; pres., chmn. bd. Hibert Coll., Hamburg, NY, 1999—2000; vice chmn. United Way of Buffalo and Erie County, 1986—88; vice chair cmty. bd. WNED, Western N.Y. Pub. Broadcasting Assn.; mem. cmty. bd. Theodore Roosevelt Inaugural Site; trustee Nichols Sch. Bd., Hibert Coll.; mem. SUNY Buffalo Friends of Sch. Architecture; vol. Albright-Knox Fine Arts Acad.; bd. dirs. Hopevale Home for Girls; mem. alumnae bd. Marymount Coll.; chair, pres. Presbyterian Homes and Sr. Care Found. Recipient Gloria Gaines award, Marymount Coll., Tarrytown, NY, 1997, Pres.' medal, Hilbert Coll., 2002, Susan Reid Greene Russell award, Jr. League Buffalo, 2004. Mem.: Garret Club (bd. dirs. 1998—2001). Roman Catholic. Avocations: reading, golf, walking. Home: 47 Hallam Rd Buffalo NY 14216

**SAAD, FATHY ZAKI,** medical association administrator, physician; b. Cairo, Dec. 6, 1941; s. Zaki Zolta and Monira Saad; m. Samira Shenoda, Apr. 25, 1970; children: Ihab, Irene. Med. degree in surgery, medicine, Ain Shams U., Cairo, 1967; MPH, U. So. Fla., 1991. Med. dir. Daimler-Chrysler-Corp., Ind. Foundry, 1999—2001, Indsl. Med. Ctr. Lakeland, Fla., 2001—02, Rogers State Prison, Med. Coll. Ga., Reidsville, 2002—. Med. practitioner Nigerian Med. Coun., Lagos, Nigeria, 1973—84; chief med. officer Ondo Gen. Hosp., Ondo State, Nigeria, 1977—84; med. fellow in occupl. and environ. medicine U. South Fla., 1998. Cert. med. rev. officer, 2001—. Named People's Dr., His Royal Majesty, The Ele Kole Ikole, Ekiti, Ondo State, Nigeria, 1983; recipient Appreciation of Svc., U. South Fla., 1993. Mem.: APHA, AMA, Am. Soc. Addiction Medicine, Am. Coll. Occupl. and Environ. Medicine. Republican. Avocation: reading. Office: Rogers State Prison Med Coll Ga 200 Rogers Rd Reidsville GA 30453

**SAAD, GERMAINE H.,** business management educator, researcher; b. Bany-Suef, Egypt, Nov. 26, 1944; d. Hozayen and Helpis Saad; m. Ayoub Barsoum Ayoub, Feb. 5, 1972; 1 child, Mariane Ayoub; 1 child, Sameh Ragheb. B in Comm., Cairo U., Guiza, Egypt, 1964, MBA, 1970; MA, U. Pa., 1978, PhD, 1980. Demonstrator and educator Cairo U., Egypt, 1964—74; instr. U. Pa., Phila., 1975—78, 1978—80; prof. Ain-Shams U., Cairo, 1980—86, CUNY, N.Y.C., 1982—84, Widener U., Chester, Pa., 1986—. Cons. Ctrl. Agy. for Orgns. and Adminstrns., Cairo, 1984—86; mem. editl. bd. Jour. Mgmt. Systems, Arlington, Va., 1989—95, Bus. Jour., New Haven, 1991—. Contbr. more than 45 articles to profl. jours. Vol. Abington Meml. Hosp., Pa., 1999; bd. dirs. St. George Orthodox Ch., Norristown, Pa., 1997—2002. Christian-Orthodox. Avocations: painting, travel, artwork. Home: 1847 Watson Road Abington PA 19001 Office: Widener U One University Place Chester PA 19013 E-mail: germaine.h.saad@widener.edu.

**SAAD, MICHAEL D.,** lawyer; b. Zanesville, Ohio, 1941; BS, Ohio State U., 1963, JD summa cum laude, 1966. Bar: Ohio 1966. Law clk. to Chief Justice Ohio State Supreme Ct.; ptnr. Squire, Sanders & Dempsey LLP, Columbus, Ohio, co-chmn., Real Estate & Hospitality Practice Group. Bd. dir. Ohio Housing Coun. Recipient Founder's Award, Ohio Capital Corp., 2002. Mem.: Order of Coif, Columbus Bar Assn. (fin. institutes com., real estate com., bankruptcy com.), Ohio State Bar Assn., Devel. Com. Ctrl. Ohio, ABA. Office: Squire Sanders & Dempsey LLP 1300 Huntington Ctr 41 South High St Columbus OH 43215-6197 Office Phone: 614-365-2735. Office Fax: 614-365-2499. Business E-Mail: msaad@ssd.com.

**SAADA, ADEL SELIM,** civil engineer, educator; b. Heliopolis, Egypt, Oct. 24, 1934; came to U.S., 1959, naturalized, 1965; s. Selim N. and Marie (Chahyne) S.; m. Nancy Helen Hernan, June 5, 1960; children: Christiane Mona, Richard Adel. Ingénieur des Arts et Manufactures, École Centrale, Paris, 1956; MS, U. Grenoble, France, 1959; PhD in Civil Engring., Princeton U., 1961. Registered profl. engr., Ohio. Engr. Société Dumez, Paris, 1959; research assoc. dept. civil engring. Princeton (N.J.) U., 1961-62; asst. prof. civil engring. Case Western Reserve U., Cleve., 1962-67, assoc. prof., 1967-72, prof., 1973—, chmn. dept. civil engring., 1978-98, Frank H. Neff prof. civil engring., 1987. R.J. Carroll Meml. lectr. Johns Hopkins U., 1990; cons., lectr. soil testing and properties Waterways Expt. Sta. (C.E.), Vicksburg, Miss., 1974-79; cons. to various firms, 1962—. Author: Elasticity Theory and Applications, 1974, 2d edit., 1993; contbr. numerous articles on soil mechanics and foundation engring. to profl. jours. Recipient Telford Prize Instn. of Civil Engrs., U.K., 1995, Disting. Leadership award Cleve. Tech. Socs., 2001. Fellow ASCE (named Outstanding Civil Engr. of Yr. Cleve. sect. 1992); mem. Internat. Soc. Soil Mechanics, ASTM, One Two One Athletic Club. Achievements include invention of pneumatic analog computer and loading frame. Home: 3342 Braemar Rd Shaker Heights OH 44120-3332 Office: Case Western Res U Dept Civil Engring Case Sch Engring Cleveland OH 44106 Office Phone: 216-368-2427. Business E-Mail: axs31@case.edu.

**SAADA, JACQUES,** legislator; b. Tunis, Tunisia, Nov. 22, 1947; married; 4 children. BA in Applied Linguistics, U. Que.; grad., McGill U. Pres. Polytrad Ltee, 1977—97; CEO B&B Translation, 1978—93; mem. Canm. Parliament, 1997—; parliamentary sec. to the solicitor gen. Can., 1998—2000; dep. govt. whip, 2001—03; min. responsible for Dem. reform, 2003—; leader Govt. House Commons, 2003—. Chair St. Lawrence Protestant Sch. Bd., 1987—90. Office: House of Commons Ottawa ON Canada K1A 0A6 also: Ste 115B 7400 Taschereau Blvd Brossard PQ Canada J4W 1M9

**SAADEH, CONSTANTINE KHALIL,** internist, medical educator, health facility administrator; b. Beirut, Sept. 6, 1957; came to U.S., 1982; s. Khalil Constantine and Angel Janet (Iskendaran) S.; m. M. Celeste Gaylor; 2 children: MacKenzie. BS in Biology-Chemistry, Am. U. Beirut, 1978, MD, 1982. Diplomate Nat. Bd. Med. Examiners, Am. Bd. Internal Medicine. Am. Bd. Allergy and Immunology, Am. Bd. Internal Medicine, Am. Bd. Rheumatology, Am. Bd. Geriatrics, Am. Acad. Pain Mgmt. Intern U. Miami, Jackson Meml. Hosp., Fla., 1982-83, resident in medicine Fla., 1983-85; fellow in clin. immunology Baylor Coll. of Medicine, Houston, 1985-87;

---

fellow in rheumatology U. Colo. Health Sci. Ctr., Denver, 1987-88, instr. dept. internal medicine, 1988-89; acting chief med. svc. VA Med. Ctr., Amarillo, Tex., 1989, med. svc. staff physician, 1989—; asst. prof. dept. internal medicine Tex. Tech U. Health Scis. Ctr., Amarillo, 1989-91, assoc. prof. internal medicine and pediatrics, dir., 1991—, regional chair internal medicine, dir. residency program, 1992-98, assoc. prof. dept. microbiology and immunology, 1992—, clin. prof. dept. microbiol./immun., internal med., pediats., 1998—; pvt. practice Allergy ARTS, Amarillo, Tex.; pres. Amarillo Ctr. for Clin. Rsch., 2000—. Chief medicine N.W. Tex. Hosp., Amarillo, 1999-2001; lectr. in field. Contbr. articles to profl. jours. Fellow ACP, Am. Acad. Allergy and Immunology, Am. Coll. Rheumatology; mem. AMA, So. Med. Assn. (chmn. rheumatology sect. 1996-97, sec. internal medicine sect. 1997-99, assoc. councilor 1998-99). Home: 3000 S Hughes St Amarillo TX 79109-3515 Office: 1901 Medi Park Ste 2050 Amarillo TX 79106-2109 also: Allergy ARTS Ste 2050 Amarillo TX 79106 Office Phone: 806-353-7000. Business E-Mail: aarts@allergyarts.com.

**SAADEH, SHERIF NABIL,** gastroenterologist, hepatologist, researcher; b. Amman, Jordan, Nov. 29, 1969; s. Nabil Ibrahim Saadeh and Helen Aziz Ibrahim; m. Claudia-Aghareed Jamal Haddad, July 17, 1971; children: Celina, Omar, Kareem. MBBS, U. Jordan Faculty Medicine, MD, 1993. Cert. Am. Bd. Internal Medicine, 1999, diplomate Am. Bd. Ethical Physicians, 2002, cert. gastroenterology Am. Bd. Med. Subspecialties, 2003. Staff gastroenterologist/hepatologist Baylor U. Med. Ctr., Dallas, 2003—. Author: (article) Am. Jour. Gastroenterology, 1998, Cleve. Clin. Jour. Medicine, 1999, (article med. publ.) Hepatology Jour., 2001, Gastroenterology Jour., 2002, (med. publ.) Alimentary, Pharmacology & Therapeutics, 2003, (article) Practical Gastroenterology Jour., 2003, (reviews) Gastroenterological Disorders, 2004. Recipient Poster of Distinction, Digestive Disease Week, 2002, Rsch. award, North Am. Conf. Gastroenterology Fellows, 2002, fellowship Am. Bd. Hosp. Physicians, 2002, America's Top Physician award, Consumer's Rsch. Coun. Am., 2003; grantee medical rsch. grant-subinvestigator, Nat. Insts. Health, 2001, medical rsch. grant, Cleve. Clinic Hepatology Inst., 2001. Mem.: Am. Coll. Gastroenterology, Crohn's & Colitis Found. Am., Am. Bd. Hosp. Physicians, Am. Coll. Ethical Physicians, Am. Liver Found., AMA, Am. Soc. Gastrointestinal Endoscopy, Am. Gastroenterol. Assn., Am. Assn. Study Liver Diseases. Office: Baylor Univ Med Ctr 3500 Gaston Ave, 4 Roberts Dallas TX 75246 Office Phone: 214-820-1636. Office Fax: 214-820-8168. Business E-Mail: sherifs@baylorhealth.edu.

**SAAL, HOWARD MAX,** clinical geneticist, pediatrician, educator; b. NYC, Aug. 20, 1951; s. Josef and Ester S.; m. Cara Tina Schweitzer, May 3, 1987; 1 child, Rebecca. BS, U. Mass., Amherst, 1973, MS, 1975; MD, Wayne State U., 1979. Intern pediatrics U. Conn. Med. Ctr., 1979-80; resident pediatrics U. Conn. Health Ctr., 1980-82; fellow med. genetics U. Wash. Sch. Medicine, 1982-84; dir. cytogenetics U. Conn. Health Ctr., Farmington, 1984-87; vice chmn. med. genetics Children's Nat. Med. Ctr., Washington, 1987-93, head clin. genetics Cin., 1993—. Asst. prof. pediats. George Washington U., Washington, 1987-93, assoc. prof. pediats., 1993; assoc. prof. clin. pediats. U. Cin. Sch. Medicine, 1993—, prof. pediats., 2000—. Contbr. articles to profl. jours. Mem. med. adv. com. Nat. Neurofibromatosis Found., N.Y.C., 1987-93; mem. health profl. adv. com. March of Dimes, Arlington, Va., 1991-93; bd. dirs. Capital Area March of Dimes, 1993. Tng. grantee NIH, 1979-82. Fellow Am. Acad. Pediats. (chmn. exec. com. for sect. on genetics and birth defects 1999-2003, com. genetics 2003—), Am. Coll. Med. Genetics; mem. Am. Soc. Human Genetics, Soc. Craniofacial Genetics (sec.-treas. 1990-96), Accredidation Coun. for Grad. Med. Edn. (med. genetics residency com). Avocation: photography. Home: 3715 Monets Ln Cincinnati OH 45241-3847 Office: Cin Childrens Hosp Med Ctr 3333 Burnet Ave Cincinnati OH 45229-3026 Office Phone: 513-636-4760. Business E-Mail: saalhm@cchmc.org.

**SAALFELD, FRED ERICH,** science educator, researcher; s. Eric Arthur and Milla (Kessler) S.; m. Elizabeth Renner, Nov. 22, 1958; 1 child, Fred E. Jr. (dec.). BS cum laude, So. East Mo. State U., 1957; MS in Phys. Chemistry, Iowa State U., 1959, PhD in Phys. Chemistry, 1961. Instr. Iowa State U., Ames, 1961—62; chemist Naval Rsch. Lab, Washington, 1962—63, head mass spectrometry sect., 1963—74, head phys. chem. br., 1974—76, supt. chem. divsn., 1976—82; chief scientist Office Naval Rsch., London, 1979—80, dir. rsch. Arlington, Va., 1982—87, dir., 1987—93, dep. chief naval rsch., tech. dir., 1993—98, exec. dir., tech. dir., 1998—2002; sr. fellow Potomac Inst. for Policy Studies, 2002—; disting. rsch. prof. Ctr. for Tech. and Nat. Security Policy Nat. Def. U., 2003—04. Author more than 500 publications, reports, presentations on applications of mass spectrometry to fields of combustion, laser, environ. analysis. Recipient Disting. Rank awards U.S. Pres., Washington, 1989, 96, Meritorious Rank award U.S. Pres., Washington, 1986, Robert Conrad award Soc. USN, Washington, 1988, Disting. Civilian Svc. award Sec. of Def./Dept. Def., 1999; named Fed. Exec. of Yr., Fed. Exec. Inst., Washington, 1991, named Fred E. Saalfed award for lifetime achievement in sci., Chief Naval Rsch., 2001. Fellow AAAS, Potomac Inst. Policy Studies (sr.); mem. Am. Chem. Soc. (councilor 1973-89), Am. Soc. Mass Spectrometry (sec. 1970-74), Combustion Inst., Chem. Soc. Washington (pres. 1972). Achievements include provision for science base for life support systems used in enclosed environments; development of educational programs used by USN for scientist training. Office Phone: 703-887-2197. Personal E-mail: fsaalfeld@cox.net.

**SAAM, ROBERT HARRY,** human resources specialist, consultant; b. Toledo, Mar. 7, 1947; s. Robert J. and Dorothy H. (Kinney) Saam; m. Pamela Soder, Oct. 30, 1982; children: Robert C., Cara B., Stacia J. BA, U. Toledo, 1970; MS in Ednl. Psychology, U. Wis., 1993. Investigative supr. Ohio Civil Rights Commn., Cleve., 1973—76; councillator U.S. EEO Commn., Cin., 1976—79; mgr. labor rels. Internat. Minerals and Chems., Mundelein, Ill., 1979—85; dir. human resources svcs. Rexnord, Inc., Brookfield, Wis., 1985—87; v.p., owner Thompson Cons. Ltd. Brookfield, 1987, 2000; v.p. Lee Hecht Harrison, Brookfield, 2000—. Contbr. articles to profl. jours. Mem.: Am. Assn. Counseling and Devel. Home and Office: 646 N 77th St Milwaukee WI 53213-3512 Business E-Mail: Rob.Saam@LHH.com.

**SAARI, DONALD GENE,** mathematician, department chairman, economist; b. Ironwood, Mich., Mar. 9, 1940; s. Gene August and Martha Mary (Jackson) S.; m. Lillian Joy Kalinen, June 11, 1966; children: Katri, Anneli. BS, Mich. Technol. U., 1962; PhD, Purdue U., 1967, DSc (hon.), 1989, U. Caen, France, 1998, Mich. Tech. U., 1999. Research astronomer Yale U., New Haven, 1967-68; prof. dept. math. Northwestern U., Evanston, Ill., 1968-2000, prof. econs., 1988-2000, Pancoe prof. math., 1995-2000, chmn. dept., 1981-84; prof. U. Nanjing (China), 1995; disting. prof. econ., math U. Calif., Irvine, 2000—, dir. Ctr. for Decision Analysis, 2002—05, dir. Inst. Math. Behavioral Sci., 2003—. Cons. Nat. Bur. Standards, Gaithersburg, Md., 1979-86, Commn. 9, Internat. Astron. Union, 1985-91; nat. com. math. Nat. Rsch. Coun., 1997-2003, chair 2001-03, math./sci. edn. bd., 2001—, Bd. Internat. Sci. Orgns., 2001-03, NRC com. on Internat. Inst. Applied Sys. Analysis, 2004—; chair trustees Math. Sci. Rsch. Inst., 2004—. Assoc. editor Jour. Econ. Behavior and Orgn., 1988-94, Celestial Mechanics and Dynamical Astronomy, 1989-97, Econ. Theory, 1990—, Social Choice and Welfare, 1997—, Qualitative Theory of Dynamical Sys., 1999—, Positivity, 2000—. Recipient Duncan Black award, Pub. Choice Soc., 1991, Chauvenet prize Math. Assn. Am., 1995, Ford prize Math. Assn. Am., 1985, Allendorfer award Math. Assn. Am., 1999; Guggenheim fellow, 1988-89. Fellow AAAS, Am. Acad. Arts and Scis.; mem. NAS, Am. Math. Soc. (chief editor bull. 1999-2005, mem. coun. 1999-2005), Am. Astron. Soc., Soc. Indsl. and Applied Math. (editor jour. 1981-88), Econometric Soc. Office: U Calif Inst Math Behavorial Scis SSPA 2119 Irvine CA 92697-5100 Office Phone: 949-824-5894. Business E-Mail: dsaari@uci.edu.

**SAATHOFF, MYRA KATHLEEN,** orthoptist; b. San Antonio, Mar. 17, 1943; d. Richard Byron and Mildred Katherine Coghlan; m. Oliver Kenneth Saathoff, Aug. 25, 1962; children: Denise Stephenson, Kristine Elise Gregoire. Student, Sam Houston State U., 1961—62; cert., Baylor U., 1964. Cert. orthoptist Am. Orthoptic Coun. Cert. orthoptist and ophthalmic technologist Dr. Whitney G. Sampson, Houston, 1964—65; chief cert. orthoptist John

---

Sealy Hosp., 1966—68; cert. orthoptist and ophthalmic technician Dr. William Phelps, Dallas, 1969—74, Dr. James G. Keatts, Pasadena, Tex., 1975—79; substitute tchr. sci. and nursing dept. Spring Ind. and Klein Ind. Sch. Dists., Spring, Tex., 1980—85; cert orthoptist and ophthalmic technician, contact lens technician Dr. Philip D. Scott, Houston, 1982—84; cert orthoptist and ophthalmic technician, surg. asst., contact lens technician Dr. Timothy Doucet, Conroe, Tex., 1985; cert. orthoptist and ophthalmic technician Drs. Richard Ruiz, Charles Garcia and Rosa Tang, Houston, 1986—88; faculty and low vision coord. Univ. Eye Assocs., 1986—2002; clin. dir. continuing edn. in low vision Hermann Eye Ctr., Houston, 1988—2002; ret., 2002. Contbr. articles to profl. jours. Adv. for visually impaired Delta Gamma Sorority, Houston, 1986—2002. Recipient honor cert., Am. Orthoptic Coun. and Am. Assn. Cert. Orthoptists, 1992. Mem.: Am. Assn. Cert. Orthoptists (life). Republican. Methodist. Achievements include patent for methods of treating migraine headaches. Avocations: scouting, crafts, animal caregiving. Home: 3010 Oak Forest Dr Houston TX 77018

**SAATY, THOMAS LORIE,** science educator; b. Mosul, Iraq, July 18, 1926; s. David Saaty and Dola Hayali; m. Bernadine Lucia Wearner; children: Linda, Michael, Emily; m. Rozann Waldron; children: John, Daniel. BA, Columbia Union Coll., 1948; MSc in Physics, Cath. U. Am., 1949; MA in Math., Yale U., 1951, PhD in Math., 1953; attended, U. Paris, 1952-53. Sci. analyst, submarine def. Melpari, Inc., 1953—54; sci. analyst, ops. evaluation group MIT, 1954-57; sci. analyst Navy Mgmt. Office, 1957-58; sci. liaison officer US Embassy, London, 1958-59; dir. advanced planning Office Naval Rsch., Washington, 1959-61, head math. br., 1961-63; sci. analyst Arms Control and Disarmament Agy., Washington, 1963-69; exec. dir. Conf. Bd. Math. Scis., Washington, 1965-67; prof. grad. groups ops. rsch., social sys. scis., grad. groups applied math., energy mgmt. and power, peace sci., civil engring., decision scis. Wharton Sch., U. Pa., Phila., 1969-79, chair, grad. groups ops. rsch., 1969—71; prof. chair., philosophy of sci., ops., decision scis. and artificial intelligence, math., sociology Joseph M. Katz Grad. Sch., Sch. Engring., U. Pitts., 1979—. Cons. govts., France, Egypt, Sudan, Kuwait, Tanzania, China, Indonesia, UN, 1958—; cons. bus., Westinghouse, US Steel, RCA, Woods Gordon Can., R.J. Reynolds, Ford Found., Am. Cyanimid, Colonial Penn Ins., Pan Am. Airlines, Monsanto, Conoco, N.Am. Rockwell, Xerox, Kodak, Martin Marietta, IBM, Booz Allen Applied Rsch., Logistics Mgmt. Inst., Urban Inst., Electric Power Rsch. Inst., NASA, AID, LEAA, NIH, Nat. Bur. Stds., Bur. of Census, Dept. Def., Dept. Air Force; invited lectr., 1972-76. Author: Mathematical Methods of Operations Research (with Japanese and Russian transls.), 1959, Elements of Queueing Theory with Applications (with Russian, Spanish, and German transls.), 1961, Modern Nonlinear Equations, 1967, reprinted edit., 1982, Mathematical Models of Arms Control and Disarmament (Russian transls.), 1968, Optimization in Integers and Related Extremal Problems (Russian transls.), 1970, Topics in Behavioral Mathematics, 1973, The Analytic Hierarchy Process (Russian, Portuguese, and Chinese transls.), 1980, revised edit., 1996, Decision Making for Leaders; The Analytical Hierarchy Process for Decisions in a Complex World (French, Indonesian, Spanish, Korean, Arabic, Persian, Thai transls.), 1982, rev. edit., 2000, Fundamentals of Decision Making with the Analytic Hierrchy Process, 1994, rev. edit., 2000, The Analytic Network Process: Decisions Making with Dependence and Feedback, 1996, rev. edit., 2001, Decision Making with Dependence and Feedback: The Analytic Network Process (ANP) and SuperDecisions Software, Guide, Manual, and Examples, 1997, The Brain, Unraveling the Mystery of How it Works: The Neural Network Process, 2000, Creative Thinking, Problem Solving & Decision Making, 2001, Theory and Applications of the Analytic Network Process, 2005; (with J. Bram) Nonlinear Mathematics, 1964, reprinted edit., 1981, (with R. Busacker) Finite Graphs and Networks (Japanese, Russian, German and Hungarian transls.), 1964-65, (with George B. Dantzig) Compact City (Russian transls.), 1973, (with Paul C. Kainen) The Four-Color Problem; Assaults and Conquest, 1977, reprinted edit. 1986, (with L. Klein) The Unthinkable and the Possible in the Middle East, 1975, (with Joyce Alexander) Thinking with Models, 1981, (with Luis G. Vargas) The Logic of Priorities; Applications in Business, Energy, Health, and Transportation), paperback edit., 1991, (with Kevin P. Kearns) Analytical Planning; The Organization of Systems (Russian transls.), 1985, paperback edit., 1991, (with Joyce Alexander) Conflict Resolution; The Analytic Hierarchy Process, 1989, (with Larry W. Boone) Embracing the Future, 1990, (with Luis G. Vargas) Prediction, Projection and Forecasting, 1991, (with Ernest H. Forman) The Hierarchon-A Dictionary of Hierarchies, 1993, (with L.G. Vargas) Decision Making in Economic, Political, Social and Technological Environments: The Analytic Hierarchy Process, 1994, (with L.G. Vargas) Models, Methods, Concepts and Applications of the Analytic Hierarchy Process, 2000, (with M. Ozdemir) The Encyclicon, 2005; editor, Lectures on Modern Mathematics, vols. I, II, III, Japanese trans., 1964-65, (with F.J. Weyl) The Spirit and Uses of the Mathematical Sciences, 1969; inventor multi-criteria decision making process: Analytic Hierarchy Process; reviewer: Math. Revs., 1954-75; editor, originator, Newsletter Math. Scis., 1965-67; assoc. editor: Naval Rsch. Quar., Jour. Ops. Rsch., 1958-63, Nonlinear Analysis with Applications, Socio-Economic Planning Scis., Internat. Jour. Sys., Measurement and Decisions, Jour. Math. Modeling, Info. Tech. and Decision Making, Jour. Multi-Criteria Decision Analysis, Jour. Sys. Sci. and Sys. Engring., internat. Jour. Orgnl. Analysis, Applied Math. Letters; contbr. 250 papers in field. Recipient award Inst. Mgmt. Scis., 1977, Gold medal Internat. Soc. Multicriteria Decision Making, 2000; named Alumnus of Yr. award Columbia Union Coll., 1982; established Thomas L. Saaty prize in Math. and Mgmt., 1982. Fellow AAAS; mem. NAE, NAS. Math. Assn. Am. (Lester R. Ford prize 1973), Am. Math. Soc., Ops. Rsch. Soc. Am., Internat. Inst. for Strategic Studies, World Future Soc., Internat. Peace Sci. Soc., Internat. Acad. Mgmt. (elected mem.), Beta Gamma Sigma. Mem. Soc. Of Friends. Achievements include development of the mathematical theory of the Analytic Network Process for decisions with dependence and feedback to decisions with benefits opportunities, costs, and risks; research in neural networks and how the synthesis of firing of neurons is intimately related to decision making using ratio and proportion. Office: U Pitts 322 Mervis Hall Pittsburgh PA 15260-7503 Office Phone: 412-648-1539. E-mail: saaty@katz.pitt.edu.

**SAAVEDRA, ABELARDO,** school system administrator; b. Feb. 18, 1951; m. Myrna Saavedra; children: Lisa, Elizabeth. BS, Texas A&I Univ., 1972, MS, 1974; PhD in sch. admin., Univ. Michian. Teacher Corpus Christi Pub. Schools, asst. prin., prin., admin.; dist. supt. Houston Pub. Schools, 2001, exec. dep. supt., 2002—04, supt., 2004—. Adj. prof. Univ. Houston, Texas A&M Univ.; mem. Gov. Task Force Juvenile Justice. Chmn. bd. Greater Houston Chapter Red Cross, March of Dimes; with WorkSource Bd. Dir. Recipient state and national recognition for development and adoptio of "real-world academic standards" in all grade levels. Mem.: Tex. Bus. Edn. Coalition (co-chmn.), South Tex. Ed. Research and Develop. Ctr. Office: Houston Independent Sch Dist 3830 Richmond Ave Houston TX 77027 Office Phone: 713-892-6300, 713-892-6061.

**SAAVEDRA, CHARLES JAMES,** retired banker; b. Denver, Nov. 2, 1941; s. Charles James and Evangeline Cecilia (Aragon) S.; m. Ann Helen Taylor, 1967; children: Michael, Kevin, Sarah. BSBA. Regis U., Denver, 1963; postgrad., U. Calif., San Francisco. 1964-66. V.p. Western States Bankcard Assns., San Francisco, 1969-77; dir. info. systems World Airways, Inc., Oakland, Calif., 1977-79; v.p. computer svcs. First Nationwide Bank, San Francisco, 1979-83; sr. v.p. Wells Fargo Bank, San Francisco, 1983-92, Union Bank Calif., San Francisco, 1992—2005; ret., 2006. Instr. Programming & Systems Inst., San Francisco, 1968-69; lectr. Am. Mgmt. Assn., 1984—. Pres. Richt Direction Project Contra Costa County; bd. dirs. No. Calif. Family Ctr. With USNR, 1963-64. Mem. Data Processing Mgrs. Assn. (bd. dirs., chmn. program com. 1981), Am. Nat. Stds. Inst., Am. Bankers Assn., San Francisco Jaycees, Commonwealth Club Calif., Lake Lakewood Assn., Alpha Delta Gamma. Home: 210 Lakewood Rd Walnut Creek CA 94598-4826

**SABA, SHOICHI,** electronics executive, director; b. Tokyo, Feb. 28, 1919; Grad., Imperial U., Tokyo, 1941. With Toshiba Corp., Tokyo, 1942-87, mng. dir., 1972-74, exec. v.p., 1974-76, sr. exec. v.p., 1976-80, pres., CEO, 1980-86, chmn., exec. officer, 1986-87, adviser to bd., 1987—2005, sr. exec.

adviser, 2005—; pres. Japanese Indsl. Stds. Com., 1994—2001. Chmn. nat. bd. govs. Nat. Scout Assn. Japan, 1994—; chmn., bd. trustees Internat. Christian U., 1998-2004. Office: Toshiba Corp 1-1 Shibaura 1-chome Minato-ku Tokyo 105-8001 Japan

**SABA, WALTER PEDRO,** health products executive; b. Lima, Peru, Apr. 29, 1955; came to U.S., 1991; s. Elias S. and Gabriela E. (Salomon) S.; m. Flor D. Giusti, Dec. 4, 1980; children: Elias G., Paulina T. Diploma in Film Studies, Conservatoire Libre de Cinema, Paris, 1977; M in Health Sci. Johns Hopkins U., 1993. Video producer Cath. U. of Peru, Lima, 1978-88; inf. coord. Nat. Program on AIDS, Lima, 1988-91; program officer Johns Hopkins U., Balt., 1993-97, sr. program officer, 1997—. Recipient Global Media award The Population Inst., Washington, 1996, Silver Apple award Nat. Ednl. Media Network, Oakland, Calif. 1996. Mem. Am. Pub. Health Assn. Office: Johns Hopkins U 1615 Thames St Baltimore MD 21231-3492 Office Phone: 410-537-1847. Personal E-mail: waltersaba@msn.com. E-mail: wsaba@jhpiegd.net.

**SABAN, HAIM,** investment company executive, television producer; b. Alexandria, Egypt, 1944; arrived in Israel, 1952, arrived in France, 1975, arrived in USA, 1983; m. Cheryl Saban, 1987; children: Ness, Tanya. TV series composer, 1975—95; chmn., CEO Saban Entertainment, LA, 1988—97, Fox Family Worldwide, LA, 1997—2001, Saban Capital Group, Inc., LA, 2001—; founder Saban Music Group, LA, 2002—. Dir. DirectTV Group, Inc., El Segundo, Calif.; bd. regents U. Calif., 2002—; founder Saban Ctr. Middle East Policy Brookings Inst., Washington, 2002, trustee. Composer: (TV series) Heathcliff, He-Man & the Masters of the Universe, The Littles, Inspector Gadget, Mister T, Punky Brewster, Kissyfur, Rainbow Brite, She-Ra: Princess of Power, MASK, Popples, The Real Ghost Busters, Zoobilee Zoo, Dennis the Menace, Maxie's World, Beverly Hills Teens, C.O.P.S., Dragon Quest, The Super Mario Bros. Super Show!, Samurai Pizza Cats; exec. prodr.: (TV series) Kidd Video, 1984—87, Rambo, 1986, Mighty Morphin' Power Rangers, 1993—96, V.R. Troopers, 1994, Sweet Valley High, 1994—98, Power Rangers Zeo, 1996—97, Big Bad Beetleborgs, 1997, Breaker High, 1997—98, Power Rangers Turbo, 1997, Beetleborgs Metallix, 1997, Diabolik, 1997, Power Rangers in Space, 1998, Mystic Knights of Tir Na Nog, 1998, Power Rangers Lost Galaxy, 1999, Power Rangers Lightspeed Rescue, 2000, Power Rangers Time Force, 2001; (films) Mighty Morphin' Power Rangers: The Movie, 1995, Turbo: A Power Rangers Movie, 1997, Rusty: A Dog's Tale, 1998, Addams Family Reunion, 1998; (TV films) The Phantom of the Opera, 1990, Casper: A Spirited Beginning, 1997, Casper Meets Wendy, 1998; writer (TV series) Around the World in 80 Dreams, 1992. Active in Israeli Cancer Rsch. Fund, John Wayne Cancer Inst., U. Tel Aviv, Nat. Park Found., United Friends of the Children, Children's Hosp. LA, Milken Cmty. High Sch. Served in Israeli Def. Force. Named one of Forbes' Richest Americans, 2006. Office: Saban Capital Group Ste 1050 10100 Santa Monica Blvd Los Angeles CA 90067 Office Phone: 310-557-5100.*

**SABAN, NICK,** professional football coach; b. Fairmont, WV, Oct. 31, 1951; m. Terry Saban; 2 children. BA business, Kent State, 1973, MA sports administration, 1975. Grad. asst. Kent State U., 1973—74, head coach, 1975—76, Syracuse U., 1977, West Virginia U., 1978—79, Ohio State U., 1980—81, U.S. Naval Academy, 1981; asst. coach Houston Oilers, 1988—89; head coach Toledo U., 1990; asst. coach Cleve. Browns, 1991—94; head coach Mich. State U., 1995—2000, Louisiana State U. 2000—05, Miami Dolphins, 2005—. Founder Nick's Kids. Achievements include coaching the NCAA Nat. Champion LSU Tigers, 2003. Office: c/o Miami Dolphins 7500 SW 30th St Davie FL 33314*

**SABAT, ROBERT HARTMAN,** magazine editor; b. Newark, Aug. 28, 1957; s. Charles and Marilyn Ruth (Hartman) S.; m. Jessica Schilling Fine, Oct. 15, 1989; children: Nathaniel, Olivia. BA, Brandeis U., 1980. Mng. editor Penthouse mag., NYC, 1986—91, Connoisseur mag., NYC, 1991—92, Lear's mag., NYC, 1994—94, Interview mag., NYC, 1994—95, Smart Money mag., NYC, 1995—99, exec. editor, 1999—2002; dep. editor US Weekly mag., NYC, 2002—03; mng. editor GQ mag., NYC, 2003—04; news editor Wall St. Jour., NYC, 2004—. Office: The Wall St Jour 200 Liberty St New York NY 10281 Personal E-mail: robertsabat@hotmail.com.

**SABATASSO, JARED RAY,** music educator; b. Pitts., Mar. 7, 1982; s. Daniel B. and Sherry D. Sabatasso. MusB in Edn., Ctrl. Meth. U., 2004. Music educator Newburg R-II Schs., Mo., 2004—05, Waynesville H.S., Waynesville, 2005—. Mem.: Mo. Music Educators Assn., Mo. Bandmasters Assn. (corr.), Mo. Educators Nat. Conf. (assoc.), Phi Mu Alpha (life). Home: 20580 Hwy 28 Dixon MO 65459 Office: Waynesville High Sch 200 GW Ln Waynesville MO 65583 Office Phone: 573-774-6401 ext. 2115. Personal E-mail: jrsabatasso@yahoo.com. E-mail: jsabatasso@waynesville.k12.mo.us.

**SABATINI, DAVID DOMINGO,** cell biologist, biochemist; b. Bolivar, Argentina, May 10, 1931; came to U.S., 1961; m. Zulema Lena Sabatini, 1960; children: Bernardo L., David M. MD. U. Litoral, Rosario, Argentina, 1954; PhD in Cell Biology, Rockefeller U., 1966. Instr., lectr., assoc. prof. cell biology Inst. Gen. Anatomy and Embryology, U. Buenos Aires, 1957-60; dir. admissions Sch. Medicine U. Buenos Aires, 1957-60; Rockefeller Found. fellow Sch. Medicine Yale U., 1961-63; rsch. assoc. cell biol. lab Rockefeller U., NYC, 1961-63, from asst. prof. to assoc. prof. cell biology, 1966-72; prof., chmn. dept. cell biology Sch. Medicine NYU, 1972-74, Frederick L. Ehrman prof., chmn. dept. cell biol. Sch. Med., 1975—; dir. MD-PhD program, 1987-97. Wendell Griffith Meml. lectr. St. Louis U., 1977; Mary Peterman Meml. lectr. Meml.-Sloan Kettering Inst., N.Y., 1977; 25th Robert J. Terry lectr. Wash. U., 1978; 3d ann. Keith R. Porter lectr. cell biology, 1994; vis. prof. Coll. France, Paris, 1986, George Washington U., 1986; 7th Ann. Kenneth F. Naidorff Meml. lectr. Columbia U., 1989; fellow Nat. Acad. Medicine, Argentina, 1956; UNESCO fellow Biophysics Inst., Rio de Janeiro, 1957; Pfizer traveling fellow, 1972; mem. molecular biology study sect. NIH, 1973-77, chmn., 1976-77; mem. bd. basic biology Nat. Rsch. Coun., 1986-89. Editor Jour. Cell Biology, 1971—, Jour. Cellular Biochemistry, 1980-84, Molecular & Cellular Biology, 1980-82, Procs. NAS USA 1985—, Biol. Cell, 1986—, Current Opinions Cell Biology, 1990—; mem. editl. bd. Procs. NAS, 1993-96. Mem. sci. adv. com. Irma T. Hirshcl Charitable Trust, 1979-85; bd. dirs. Pub. Health Rsch. Inst., 1980-88; bd. sci. dirs. Jane Coffin Childs Meml. Fund, 1980-86, Nat. Inst. Diabetes Digest Kidney Disease, 1982-86; sci. adv. com. Robert Wood Johnson Found. Minority Med. Faculty Devel. Program, 1987—, Human Frontier Sci. Program, 1991—, chair molecular grants, 1994—; mem. sci. rev. com. Pew Internat. Fellows Program, 1990—; med. adv. bd., 1989-93, internat. program, 1994—; mem. sci. adv. com. Inst. d'Embryologie Cellular Mol., Coll. France, 1994—; Ctr. Adv. Biotech. and Medicine, 1996—; mem. Alfred P. Sloan Jr. award selection com. GM Cancer Rsch. Found., 1996—. Recipient Samuel Roberts Noble Rsch. Recognition award, 1980. Fellow AAAS, Am. Acad. Microbiology, NY Acad. Sci.; mem. NAS (chmn. cell and devel. biology sect. 1994-96), Am. Soc. Cell Biology (pres. 1978-79, coun. mem. 1974-77, E. B. Wilson award 1986), Harvey Soc. (pres. 1985-86, pres. 1986-87), Argentine Med. Assn. (hon.), French Acad. Sci. (fgn. assoc.), Charles Leopold Mayer prize 1988, grande médaille, 2003), Am. Soc. Biol. Chemistry, Am. Soc. Microbiology, NY Soc. Electron Microbiology (pres. 1971), Am. Assn. Anatomy (chair cell biology, neurobiology, exec. coun. 1992—), Inst. Medicine. Business E-mail: david.sabatini@med.nyu.edu.

**SABATINI, NELSON JOHN,** healthcare executive; b. Rochester, N.Y., Jan. 20, 1940; s. John R. and Ida M. (Ceconi) S.; m. Marilyn Jean Gromala, Jan. 19, 1963; children—John Nelson, Michael Christopher Student, Lewis Coll., Lockport, Ill., 1958-62; BA in Psychology, George Washington U., 1971, postgrad. Claims rep. Social Security Adminstrn., Chgo., 1962-65, various positions Balt., 1965-79, dep. dir. disability programs, 1979-81, exec. asst. to commr., 1981-82, assoc. commr., 1982—, dep. commr., 1983-88; dep. sec. health and conservat hygiene State of Md., 1988, sec. health and mental hygiene, 1991—95, 2003—05; v.p. Univ. Md. Med. Systems, 1995, exec. v.p. 1995—2003; CEO Sabatini Cons. Group, 2005—. Named Disting. Mary-

lander of Yr. 1993; recipient Sec.'s cert. HHS, 1975; Commr.'s citation Social Security Adminstrn., 1977, 81; Presdl. Merit Rank award Pres. of U.S., 1984 Roman Catholic. Avocations: sailing, tennis. Office Phone: 443-827-3332. Business E-mail: sconsultinggroup@comcast.net.

**SABATINI, SANDRA,** physician; b. N.Y.C., Dec. 1, 1940; BS in Chemistry, Millsaps Coll., 1962; MS in Pharmacology, Marquette U., 1966; PhD in Pharmacology, U. Miss., 1968; MD in Internal Medicine, Tex. Med. Sch., 1974. Lic. physician, Ill., Tex. Intern in medicine U. Ill. Hosp., Chgo., 1974-75; asst. prof. U. Tex. Med. Sch., San Antonio, 1968-70; assoc. dir. U. Ill. Hosp., Chgo., 1977-78; asst. prof. U. Ill. Coll. of Medicine, Chgo., 1977-83, assoc. prof. medicine and physiology, 1983-84; attending physician in nephrology VA, Chgo., 1977-84; med. dir. Dialysis Unit U. Ill., Chgo., 1978-84; prof. internal medicine and physiology Tex. Tech. U. Health Sci. Ctr., Lubbock, 1985—, chmn. dept. physiology, 1993-96; attending physician in nephrology U. Med. Ctr., Lubbock, 1985—. Lab. instr. Millsaps Coll., Jackson, Miss., 1961-62; instr. pharmacology Bapt. Hosp. Sch. Nursing, Jackson, 1966-68; merit rev. mem. NSF, 1987, 91, 92; rev. mem. several orgns. including Chgo. Heart Assn., 1984, NIH, 1983, 86, 89-93, 96, Nat. Kidney Found., 1987, 89—, Am. Heart Assn., 1981-84, others; cons. U.S. Med. Licensing Exam/Nat. Bd. Med. Examiners, Step 1 Physiology Test Com., 1996-99. Editl. referee Am. Jour. Kidney Disease, Am. Jour. Physiology, Am. Jour. Nephrology, Annals of Internal Medicine, others; mem. editl. bd. Am. Jour. Nephrology, 1989-93, Seminars in Nephrology, 1984—; co-editor Am. Jour. Kidney Diseases, 1997—; author numerous publs. and abstracts in field; contbr. articles to profl. jours. Bd. dirs. YWCA of Lubbock, 1994-99; mem. Leadership Tex., 1994. Predoctoral fellowship grantee Marquette U., 1963-66; pub. health predoctoral fellow U. Miss. Med. Sch., 1967-69, gen. medicine sci. rsch. grantee U. Tex. Med. Sch., 1976-77, post-grad. fellow Karolinska Inst., Swedish Med. Coun., 1971, 73, NIH grantee, 1979-82, 84-99, Chgo. Heart Assn. grantee-in-aid, 1979-85, 99; grantee Nat. Eye Inst., 1979-80; recipient Banes Charitable trust award U. Ill., 1984-85, U.S. Olympic com. Rsch. Foudn., 1986-87; recipient Outstanding Alumnus award Tex. Med. Sch., 1994, numerous other awards in field. Fellow: ACP; mem.: AAUP, AAAS, ADA (hon.), Lubbock Arts Alliance, Leadership Tex. Alumnae Assn., Nat. Kidney Found. West Tex. (bd. dirs. 1993—99, Outstanding Vol. 1995, 2001, Disting. Svc. award 1996), Nat. Kidney Found. (numerous offices including chmn. several coms.), Italian-Am. Nephrologists, Inc., Internat. Soc. Nephrology, Ill. Kidney Found., Ctrl. Soc. Clin. Rsch., So. Soc. Clin. Rsch. (councillor 1997—99, pres.-elect 1999, pres. 2000), Assn. Chairs Dept. Physiology (councillor 1995—97), Am. Soc. Renal Biochemistry and Metabolism (pres.-elect 1994), Am. Soc. Pharmacology and Exptl. Therapeutics, Am. Soc. Nephrology, Am. Physiol. Soc., Am. Heart Assn., Am. Fedn. Med. Rsch., Lubbock Women's Club, Rotary Internat. Office: Tex Tech U Health Sci Ctr 3601 4th St Lubbock TX 79430-0001

**SABATINO, THOMAS JOSEPH, JR.,** lawyer; b. Norwich, Conn., Dec. 3, 1958; s. Thomas J. and Germaine (Clement) S.; m. Joan Kathryn Turnbull, June 4, 1983. BS cum laude, Wesleyan U., Middletown, Conn., 1980; JD, U. Pa., 1983. Bar: Mass. 1983, Ill. 1985, Calif. 1989. Assoc. Testa, Hurwitz & Thibeault, Boston, 1983-85, Coffield Ungaretti Harris & Slavin, Chgo., 1985-86; corp. counsel Baxter Healthcare Corp., Deerfield, Ill., 1986-90; pres., CEO Secure Med. Inc., Mundelein, Ill., 1990-92; assoc. gen. counsel Am. Med. Internat., Dallas, 1992-93, v.p., gen. counsel, 1993-95; v.p., assoc. gen. counsel Tenet Healthcare Corp., Dallas, 1995-97; v.p., assoc. gen. counsel, asst. sec. Baxter Healthcare Corp., Deerfield, Ill., 1997—2004, sr. v.p., 1997—2004; exec. v.p., gen. counsel Schering-Plough Corp., Kenilworth, NJ, 2004—. Office: Baxter Healthcare Corp One Baxter Pkwy Deerfield IL 60015

**SABATO, LARRY JOSEPH,** political science professor, director; b. Norfolk, Va., Aug. 7, 1952; s. N.J. and Margaret F. (Simmons) S. BA, U. Va., 1974; postgrad., Princeton U., 1974-75; DPhil, Oxford U., 1977. Lectr. politics New Coll. Oxford U., 1977-78; Robert Kent Gooch prof. politics U. Va., Charlottesville, 1978—, founder dir. Ctr. for Politics, 1998—. Guest scholar Brookings Instn., 1980; Thomas Jefferson vis. prof. Downing Coll., Cambridge U., 1982. Author: The Rise of Political Consultants: New Ways of Winning Elections, 1981, Goodbye to Goodtime Charlie: The American Governorship Transformed, 1983, PAC Power: Inside the World of Political Action Committees, 1984, The Party's Just Begun: Shaping Political Parties for America's Future, 1988, Feeding Frenzy: How Attack Journalism Has Transformed American Politics, 1991, American Government: Roots and Reform, 1992, Dirty Little Secrets: The Persistence of Corruption in American Politics, 1996, Midterm Madness: The Elections of 2002, 2002, Toward the Millennium: The Elections of 1996, 1997, Overtime! The Election 2002, Thriller, 2001, Get In The Booth: A Citizen's Guide to the 2004 Election, 2004, Divided States of America: The Slash and Burn Politics of the 2004 Presidential Election, 2005, Get in the Booth! A Citizen's Guide to the 2006 Election, 2006. Danforth fellow, 1975; Kellog fellow, 1983; Rhodes scholar; recipient Thomas Jefferson award U. Va., 2001. Mem. Am. Polit. Sci. Assn., Phi Beta Kappa. Office: U Va Dept Politics 240 Cabell Charlottesville VA 22904

**SABAT-RIVERS, GEORGINA,** Latin American literature educator; b. Santiago, Oriente, Cuba; came to U.S., 1962; d. José and Balbina (Mercadé) Sabat; m. Armando A. Guernica (div.); children: Armando A., Antonio J., Rodolfo M., Georgina M.; m. Elias L. Rivers, Sept. 19, 1969. MA in Romance Langs., Johns Hopkins U., 1967, PhD in Romance Langs., 1969. Instr. U. Oriente, Santiago de Cuba, 1956-61; asst. prof. Georgetown Visitation Coll., Washington, 1962-63, Western Md. Coll., Westminster, 1963-69, assoc. prof., 1969-73, prof., 1973-78, chair dept., 1974-78; assoc. prof. SUNY, Stony Brook, 1978-86, prof., 1986—, chair dept., 1981-84. Vis. prof. U. Calif., Irvine, 1989, U. Iowa, Iowa City, 1994, UNAM, Mexico City. Author: El Sueño de Sor Juana Inés de la Cruz: tradiciones literarias y originalidad, 1976, Sor Juana Inés de la Cruz Inundación castellada, 1982, Literatura Femenina conventual: Sor Marcela de San Félix Hija de Lope, 1992, others; mem. editl. bd. Colonial L.Am. Rev., 1990—, Calíope, En busca de Sor Juana, 1998, others; contbr. articles to profl. jours. Fellow NEH, 1984-85, Fulbright, 1987; Soviet Union Internat. Rsch. and Exch. Bd. grantee, 1986, Summer seminar grantee NEH, 1995. Fellow Am. Philos. Soc.; mem. MLA (editl. bd. 1987-90), AAUW. Internat. Internat. Revista Iberoamericana Lit. (editl. bd. 1987-90). Home and Office: 1532 Zoreta Ave Coral Gables FL 33146-2433 Personal E-mail: elias-n-georgina@worldnet.att.net.

**SABAU, CARMEN SYBILE,** retired chemist; b. Cluj, Romania, Apr. 24, 1933; naturalized U.S. citizen; d. George and Antoinette Marie (Chiriac) Grigorescu; m. Mircea Nicolae Sabau, July 11, 1956; 1 child, Isabelle Carmen. MS in Inorganic and Analytical Chemistry, U. C.I. Parhon, Bucharest, Romania, 1955; PhD in Radiochemistry, U. Fridericiana, Karlsruhe, Fed. Republic of Germany, 1972. Chemist Inst. Atomic Physics, Bucharest, Romania, 1956—74, Joint Inst. of Nuclear Rsch., Dubna-Moscow, 1974—75, Argonne (Ill.) Nat. Lab., 1976-98; ret., 1998. Author: Ion-exchange Theory and Applications in Analytical Chemistry, 1967; contbr. articles to profl. jours. Active Romanian World Coun.; del. NGO/DPI Conf. on Human Rights. Internat. Atomic Energy Agy. fellow, 1967-68, Humboldt fellow, 1970-72. Mem. Am. Romanian Acad. Arts and Sci., Internat. Soc. Intercomm. of New Ideas, Alexander von Humboldt Assn. Am., Alpha Friends of Antiquity, Rocky Mountain MLA. Home: 689 Banbury Way Bolingbrook IL 60440-1057 Personal E-mail: carmen_sabau@hotmail.com.

**SABB, ANNMARIE LOUISE,** retired chemist; b. New Brunswick, NJ, Sept. 21, 1942; d. Frank John and Marianne Previte; m. Frederick Joseph Sabb, Aug. 1, 1965; children: Frederick William, Jacqueline Marie. BA, Douglass Coll., New Brunswick, N.J., 1964; MS, Rutgers U., 1978; PhD, Princeton U., 1986. Sci. info. chemist FMC Corp., Balt., 1965—68; rsch. chemist Am. Cyanamid, Princeton, NJ 1969—74; sr. scientist Ayerst Rsch., Princeton, NJ, 1986—88; sr. rsch. scientist Wyeth-Ayerst Rsch., Princeton, NJ, 1989—90, prin. scientist, 1991—2001; prin. rsch. scientist Wyeth Rsch., Princeton, NJ, 2002—06; ret., 2006. Grad. coll. faculty fellow Princeton U., NJ, 1992—93;

conf. chair, co-organizer Strategic Rsch. Inst., N.Y.C., 1997—99; grant reviewer NIH, Washington, 1999—2001; sci. adv. bd. Inst. for the Study of Aging, NYC, 1999—2005; editl. adv. bd. Bentham Sci. Publishers, Hilversum, Netherlands, 2002—05; panelist careers in sci. and lab. rsch. Princeton U., 2005; cons., reviewer, spkr. in field. Editor: Current Topics in Medicinal Chemistry; contbr. articles to profl. jours. Recipient Patent award, Wyeth-Ayerst Rsch., 1997—2005. Mem.: Soc. for Neuroscience, Am. Chem. Soc. (pres. of Princeton sect. 1990—91, Phoenix award 1991), Sigma Xi, Iota Sigma Pi, Phi Beta Kappa. Achievements include patents for antidementia agents, drugs for neurological illness, antipsychotic agents, others; discovery of heterocyclic ring system with activity at the human 5-HT2C receptor drugs for schizophrenia; patents for 1,4 diazocino, 7,8,1-hi indole derivatives as antipsychotic and anti obesity agents; research in treatment of psychiatric disorders using 5-HT2C agonist. Office Phone: 609-737-9388. Personal E-mail: annmarie_sabb@yahoo.com.

**SABBATH, JOSEPH WATERS,** academic administrator; b. Paterson, N.J., May 24, 1969; s. George E. and Therese G. Sabbath; m. Laurie Anne Sabbath, Apr. 20, 1970; children: Samantha, Joseph. BA, St. Bonaventure U., N.Y., 1991; MA in Edn., St. Peter's Coll., Jersey City, N.J., 2004; JD, Quinnipiac U., Hamden, Conn., 1995. Cert.: N.J. Adminstrv. Office of the Cts. (mediation and conciliation skills), bar: N.J. 1996; cert. prin., supr. N.J., tchr. social studies N.J., tchr. elem. edn. N.J., tchr. law enforcement N.J. Tchr. Paterson (N.J.) Pub. Schs., 2000—04; edn. adminstr. Passaic County Tech. Inst., Wayne, NJ, 2004—. Atty. Joseph W. Sabbath, Atty. at Law, Clifton, NJ, 1996—. Mem. planning bd. East Rutherford (N.J.) Planning Bd., 1998—2000; mem. Mayor's Youth Outreach Task Force, Paterson, NJ, 2000—03; pro bono atty. N.J. Admin Office of the Cts., Paterson, 1996—2006. Recipient Corpus Juris Secundum award, West Pub. Corp, 1994—95, Am. Jurisprudence award, Lawyers Coop. Pub., 1994, Robert L. Clifford Am. Inn of Ct. del. scholarship, Robert L. Clifford Am. Inn of Ct., 1997—99. Mem.: N.J. Coun. for the Social Studies (corr.), N.J. Bar Assn. (corr.), N.J. Social Studies Supr.'s Assn. (corr.), N.J. Prins. and Suprs. Assn. (corr.), Kappa Delta Pi. Independent. Roman Catholic. Avocations: golf, skiing, hiking, exercise. Office Phone: 973-389-2017.

**SABBATINI, MARCELLO,** journalist, motor sports weekly director; b. Teramo, Abruzzo, Italy, Oct. 20, 1926; s. Ezio and Norina (Guerrieri) S.; m. Maria Pia Fiore, Jan. 23, 1956. Student Faculty of Law, U. Rome, 1945-49. Head sports Il Paese, Rome, 1949-54, Paese e Paese/Sera, Rome, 1954-58; dir. Autorama, Rome, 1959-60; head sports Telesera, Rome, 1960-61, chief staff, 1961-62; asst. editor Corriere dello Sport, Rome, 1963-65; dir. Automondo, Milan, 1965; direttore zesponsabile Autosprint, Bologna, Italy, 1966—81, gen. mgr., 1969-81, Motosprint, Bologna, 1976-81, Rombo, Rombo TV, Bologna, 1981-90; anchorman weekly motormagazine TV Cuore Rosso di TLRC, Modena, 2003—04; anchor Processo F.1 weekly TV show ODEON-TV, 2005. Editor news articles in field. Recipient numerous awards. Roman Catholic.

**SABBATINI, PAUL,** gynecologist, obstetrician; MD, U. Miss. Cert. med. oncologist NY. Assoc. attending physician Meml. Sloan-Kettering Cancer Ctr., N.Y.C., 1996—. Office: Meml Sloan-Kettering Cancer Ctr 1275 York Ave New York NY 10021 Office Phone: 212 639 6423.

**SABEL, BRADLEY KENT,** lawyer; b. Charleston, Ill., Oct. 6, 1948; s. Walter Bernard and Charlotte (Ahlstrom) Sabel; m. Nancy Jean Parker, Apr. 4, 1984. BA, Vanderbilt U., 1970; JD, Cornell U., 1975; MS in Bus. Policy, Columbia U., 1983. Bar: NY 1976. Atty. Fed. Reserve Bank NY, NYC, 1975-80, asst. counsel, 1980, asst., asst. counsel, 1981-85, assoc. counsel, 1985-87, counsel, 1988-93, counsel, v.p., 1993-94; counsel Shearman & Sterling, NYC, 1994-97, prin., 1997—. Contbr. articles to profl. jours. Bd. dirs., treas. NY Chamber Orch., NYC, 1985—87. With U.S. Army, 1970—72. Mem.: N.Y.C. Bar Assn. (chmn. banking law com.). Home: 2 Midland Gdns Apt 4E Bronxville NY 10708-4727 Office: 599 Lexington Ave Fl C2 New York NY 10022-6030 Office Phone: 212-848-8410. E-mail: bsabel@shearman.com.

**SABEL, CHARLES FREDERICK,** law educator; b. Dec. 1, 1947; AB summa cum laude, Harvard U., 1978, PhD in Govt., 1978. Rsch. assoc. Max Planck Institut, Germany, 1976; Ford Internat. asst. prof. of social sci. MIT, Cambridge, Mass., 1977—84, assoc. prof. social and polit. sci., 1984—87, prof., 1987—90, Ford Internat. Prof. of social sci., 1990—95; prof. law and social sci. Columbia U. Law Sch., NYC, 1995—. Author: Work and Politics: The Division of Labor in Industry, 1982, Local Partnerships and Social Innovation: Ireland, 1996, Learning by Monitoring, 2002; co-author: The Second Industrial Divide: Possibilities for Prosperity, 1984, A Constitution of Democratic Experimentalism, 2002, Can We Put an End to Sweatshops?, 2002. Office: Coulmbia Law Sch 435 W 116th St, Rm 533 New York NY 10027 Office Phone: 212-854-2618. Office Fax: 212-854-7946. E-mail: csabel@law.columbia.edu.

**SABELHAUS, MELANIE R.,** government agency administrator; b. Cleve. m. Bob Sabelhaus; 2 children. BS in Journalism, Ohio U. With IBM, 1972—86; founder, CEO Exclusive Interim Properties Ltd., Balt., 1986—97; v.p. global sales Bridgestreet Accommodations, 1997—98; dep. adminstr. SBA, Washington, 2002—. Co-chair Nat. Summit on Women in Philanthropy; bd. dirs. United Way, Alzheimer's Assn. of Ctrl. Md. Recipient Outstanding Vol. Fundraiser of the Yr. award for Md., Assn. of Fundraising Profls., 2002.

**SABELLA, ERNIE,** actor; b. Westchester, Sept. 19, 1949; s. Robert and Lorraine (Gladding) Sabella; m. Lulie Newcomb, July 29, 1983. BFA, U. Miami, 1972. Actor: (Broadway plays) The Robber Bridegroom, 1976, Carmelina, 1977, Little Johnny Jones, 1982, Guys and Dolls, 1992, A Funny Thing Happened on the Way to the Forum, 1996, Chicago, 1996, Man of La Mancha, 2002, Sweet Charity, 2005; (films) City Heat, 1984, Tough Guys, 1986, Fright Night II, 1988, Going Under, 1990, Faith, 1990, (voice) The Lion King, 1994, Quiz Show, 1994, (voice) Stand By Me, 1995, Roommates, 1995, (voice) Timon & Pumbaa's Wild Adventures: Hanging with Baby, 1997, Timon & Pumbaa's Wild Adventures: Grub's On, 1997, Timon & Pumbaa's Wild Adventures: Don't Get Mad, Get Happy, 1997, Timon & Pumbaa's Wild Adventures: Live and Learn, 1997, In & Out, 1997, Mousehunt, 1997, (voice) Timon & Pumbaa's Wild Adventure: True Guts, 1998, Timon & Pumbaa's Wild Adventure: Quit Buggin' Me, 1998, The Lion King II: Simba's Pride, 1998, The Out-of-Towners, 1999, Mickey's Magical Christmas: Snowed In at the House of Mouse, 2001, (voice) The Lion King III: Hakuna Matata!, 2004, Behind the Legend: Timon, 2004,; (TV films) Copacabana, 1985, Just My Imagination, 1992, Annie, 1999; (TV series) It's Your Move, 1984, Perfect Strangers, 1986, Roxie, 1987, A Fine Romance, 1989, Saved By the Bell, 1991, (voice) Timon & Pumbaa, 1995, Encore! Encore!, 1998, One Saturday Morning, 2001, House of Mouse, 2001. Roman Catholic. Avocations: golf, opera. Mailing: c/o Gage Group 14724 Ventura Blvd Ste 505 Sherman Oaks CA 91403*

**SABER, ALAN A.,** surgeon; arrived in U.S., 1992; s. Abb A. and Sue A. Saber; m. Dalia D. Saber; children: Sara S. children: Jason S., Angie S. MD, Alexandria U., 1984, MChir, 1988. Surg. resident Mt. Sinai Sch. Medicine, N.Y.C., 1993—95, surg. rsch. fellow, 1997—99, surg. resident, 1997—99, chief surg. resident, 1999—2000; clin. fellow minimally invasive surgery Cleve. Clinic Fla., Ft. Lauderdale, 2000—01; asst. prof. surgery Mich. State U., Kalamazoo, 2001—; chief sect. minimally invasive surgery, 2001—. Dir. bariatric surgery Mich. State U., 2001—. Author: (book) eMEDICINE; reviewer Jour. Investigative Surgery, 2001—. Fellow: ACS, Am. Soc. Bariatric Surgery (assoc.); mem.: Am. Soc. Gastrointestinal Endoscopic Surgeons. Achievements include research in minimally invasive surgery, bariatraic surgery, computer tomographic mapping of anatomical landmarks during laparoscopy surgery. Avocations: fishing, swimming, reading. Office: Michigan State Univ 1000 Oakland Dr Kalamazoo MI 49008 E-mail: saber@kcms.msu.edu.

**SABERS, RICHARD WAYNE,** state supreme court justice; b. Salem, S.D., Feb. 12, 1938; s. Emil William and Elrena Veronica (Godfrey) S.; m. Colleen D. Kelley, Aug. 28, 1965 (dec. Feb. 1998); children: Steven Richard, Susan Michelle, Michael Kelley; m. Ellie Schmitz, June 9, 2000. BA in English, St. John's U., Collegeville, Minn., 1960; JD, U. S.D., 1966. Bar: S.D. 1966, U.S. Dist. Ct. S.D. 1966, U.S. Ct. Appeals (8th cir.) 1983. From assoc. to ptnr. Moore, Rasmussen, Sabers & Kading, Sioux Falls, SD, 1966-86; justice SD Supreme Ct., Pierre and Sioux Falls, 1986—. Mem. editorial bd. U. S.D. Law Rev., 1965-66. State rep. March of Dimes, Bismarck, N.D., 1963; bd. dirs. St. Joseph Cathedral, Sioux Falls, 1971-86; trustee, bd. dirs. O'Gorman Found., Sioux Falls, 1978-86; active sch. bd. O'Gorman High Sch., Sioux Falls, 1985-86. Lt. U.S. Army, 1960—63. Named Outstanding Young Religious Leader, Jaycees, Sioux Falls, 1971. Mem. ABA, S.D. Bar Assn., Inst. Jud. Adminstrn., St. John's Alumni Assn. (pres. Sioux Falls chpt. 1975-91). Republican. Roman Catholic. Avocations: tennis, skiing, sailing, sports, wood carving. Office: SD Supreme Ct 500 E Capitol Ave Pierre SD 57501-5070 Home: 5218 S Sweetbriar Ct Sioux Falls SD 57108-2855 Office Phone: 605-367-5926.*

**SABERSKY, ROLF HEINRICH,** mechanical engineer; b. Berlin, Oct. 20, 1920; came to U.S., 1938, naturalized, 1944; s. Fritz and Berta (Eisner) S.; m. Bettina Sofie Schuster, June 16, 1946; children: Carol, Sandra. BS, Calif. Inst. Tech., 1942, MS, 1943, PhD, 1949. Devel. engr. Aerojet Gen. Co., 1943-46, regular cons., 1949-70; asst. prof. Calif. Inst. Tech., Pasadena, 1949-55, asso. prof., 1955-61, prof. mech. engrng., 1961-88, prof. emeritus, 1988—. Cons. various indsl. orgns. Author: Engineering Thermodynamics, 1957, Fluid Flow, 4th edit., 1999; contbr. articles to profl. jours. Fellow ASME (Heat Transfer Meml. award 1977, 50th anniversary award Heat Transfer Div 1988); mem. Sigma Xi, Tau Beta Pi. Home: 1135 Calle De Los Amigos Santa Barbara CA 93105-5467 Office: Calif Inst Tech Divsn Engring & Applied Sci Pasadena CA 91125-0001 E-mail: sabersky@cox.net.

**SABETI, PARDIS CHRISTINE,** researcher; b. Tehran, Iran, Dec. 25, 1975; BS, MIT, Cambridge, 1997; MS, U. Oxford, 1998, DPhil, 2002; MD summa cum laude, Harvard Med. Sch., Boston, 2006. Grad. rsch. fellow U. Oxford, 1997—2000; post-doctoral fellow genomics and infectious disease Broad Inst. of MIT and Harvard, Cambridge, Mass., 2003—. Corp. mem., bd. trustees MIT Corp., Cambridge, Mass., 1999—2004. Musician (writer, singer): (five-song cd) Headlight Waves (Billboard Songwriting Contest Hon. Mention, 2006). Named Trailblazer, Sci. Spectrum Mag., 2006; fellow, Paul and Daisy Soros Fellowships, 2001—03, L'Oreal For Women in Sci., L'Oreal U.S.A., 2004, Damon Runyon Cancer Rsch. Found., 2004—; Scholarship, Rhodes Trust, 1997—2000. Mem.: ASCAP (assoc.), MIT Bioengring. Vis. Com. (assoc.). Achievements include discovery of Novel method to identify natural selection in the genome. Office: Broad Inst of MIT and Harvard 7 Cambridge Ctr Cambridge MA 02142 Business E-Mail: pardis@broad.mit.edu.

**SABEY, RICHARD HOMER,** retired graphics designer; b. Chgo., Nov. 20, 1923; s. Lawrence Henry Sabey and Irene Bernadina Weyers; m. Eleanor Elaine Janssen, 1946; children: Kaaren, Kristin, Richard, Delle, John, Charles, Elaine, Douglas. Student, Art Inst. Chgo., Harrison Acad. Applied Art, Chgo. Acad. Fine Art, Am. Acad. Fine Art, Chgo. Artist Bielefield Studios/Robert Snyder & Assocs., Chgo., 1948—63; v.p. sales Handelan-Pedersen, Inc., Chgo., 1963—88; rep. Sec. of State of Ill., Chicago Hts., 1998—2003. Founder, founder Vets. Meml. Legion Post Scholarship; sponsor Boy Scouts Am.; mgr. Little League teams. Sgt. USAF, 1943—46. Mem.: VFW (life), Danish Brotherhood in Am., Am. Legion (past comdr., past chaplain), 9th Bombing Group Assn., 20th Air Force Assn., Air Force Assn. Republican. Lutheran. Avocations: painting, drawing, reading, airplane model building. Home: 214 Airport Rd Apt E217 North Aurora IL 60542

**SABHERWAL, SANJIV,** finance educator; b. Bhopal, India; BTech, Indian Inst. Tech., New Delhi, 1987; MBA, U. Miami, Coral Gables, 1990; PhD in Mgmt., Ga. Inst. Tech., Atlanta, 2000. Asst. prof. fin. U. R.I., Kingston, 2000—04, U. Tex., Arlington, 2004—. Contbr. articles to periodicals, to academic jours. Recipient Academic Excellence cert., U. Miami, 1990; grantee, Govt. of India, 1983—88; scholar, Ctr. Internat. Bus. Edn. Ga. Tech., 2000. Mem.: Ea. Fin. Assn. (mem. program com. 2002), Fin. Mgmt. Assn. (mem. program com. 2004). Office: U Tex at Arlington 701 S West St Arlington TX 76010 Office Phone: 817-272-5520.

**SABIN, JORGE A.,** emergency physician, consultant; Degree with hons., Miami Dade Coll., Fla.; MD, PhD, Duke U., N.C. Diplomate Am. Bd. Urgent Care Medicine, lic. physician S.C. Chief med. officer Saluda Lake Med. Ctr., Greenville, SC; pres. Ambulatory Medicine Assocs., LLC, Greenville, SC. Prof. health sci. Miami-Dade Coll., Fla., 1999—2000; cons. in field. Contbr. columns in newspapers. Recipient Disting. Educator Recognition award, Miami-Dade Coll. Mem.: Assn. Am. Physicians and Surgeons (life), Assn. Emergency Physicians (life). Avocations: hiking, kayaking, bicycling, scuba diving, music. Office Phone: 864-294-1800. Business E-Mail: jorge@sabinmd.com.

**SABIN, WILLIAM ALBERT,** writer; b. Paterson, N.J., May 29, 1931; s. David and Esther (Goodman) S.; m. Marie Frances Noonan, May 31, 1958; children—Margaret, John, Katherine, Christopher, James BA in English, Yale U., 1952, MA in English, 1956. Pub. bus. and office edn. McGraw Hill Book Co., N.Y.C., 1973-78, editor in chief bus. books, 1979-86, pub. bus. books, 1987-90. Author: The Gregg Reference Manual, 10th edit., 2004; co-author: College English: Grammar and Style, 1967. Served as cpl. U.S. Army, 1952-54, ETO Home: 540 Fogler Rd Bristol ME 04539-3101 Office Phone: 207-563-3266.

**SABISTON, DAVID COSTON, JR,** surgeon, educator; b. Onslow County, N.C., Oct. 4, 1924; s. David Coston and Marie (Jackson) S.; m. Agnes Foy Barden, Sept. 24, 1955; children: Anne Sabiston Leggett, Agnes Sabiston Butler, Sarah Coston. BS, U. N.C., 1944; MD, Johns Hopkins U., 1947; DSc (hon.), U. Madrid. Successively intern, asst. resident, chief resident surgery Johns Hopkins Hosp., Balt., 1947—53; successively asst. prof., assoc. prof., prof. surgery Johns Hopkins U. Med. Sch., Balt., 1955—64; Howard Hughes investigator Johns Hopkins Med. Sch., Balt., 1955—61; Fulbright rsch. scholar U. Oxford, England, 1960; rsch. assoc. Hosp. Sick Children, U. London, 1961; James B. Duke prof. surgery, chmn. dept. Duke Med. Sch., Durham, NC, 1964—94, chmn. dept. thoracic surgery, 1964—94; chief of staff Duke U. Med. Ctr., Durham, 1994—96, dir. internat. programs, 1996—. Chmn. Accreditation Coun. for Grad. Med. Edn., 1985—86. Editor: Textbook of Surgery, Essentials of Surgery, Atlas of General Surgery, Atlas of Cardiothoracic Surgery, A Review of Surgery; co-editor: Gibbon's Surgery of the Chest, Companion Handbook to Textbook of Surgery; chmn. editl. bd.: Annals of Surgery, mem. editl. bd.: Annals Clin. Rsch., ISI Atlas of Sci.: The Classics of Surgery Libr., Surgery, Gynecology and Obstetrics, Jour. Applied Cardiology, Jour. Cardiac Surgery, World Jour. Surgery. Capt. M.C., AUS, 1953—55. Named named Disting. Physician, U.S. Va., 1995; recipient Career Rsch. award, NIH, 1962—64, N.C. award in Sci., 1978, Disting. Achievement award, Am. Heart Assn. Sci. Coun., 1983, Michael E. DeBakey award for Outstanding Achievement, 1984, Significant Sigma Chi award, 1987, Coll. medalist, Am. Coll. Chest Physicians, 1987. Mem.: ACS (chmn. bd. govs. 1974—75, pres. 1975—82, chmn. bd. regents 1982—84, pres. 1985—86), James IV Assn. Surgeons (bd. dirs. U.S. chpt.), Soc. Internat. De Chirurgie, Soc. Thoracic Surgeons Gt. Britain and Ireland, Soc. Surg. Chairmen (pres. 1974—76), Johns Hopkins U. Soc. Scholars, Soc. Surgery Alimentary Tract, Soc. Thoracic Surgery, Surg. Biology Club II, Halsted Soc., Soc. Univ. Surgeons (pres. 1968—69), Soc. Vascular Surgery (v.p. 1967—68), Internat. Soc. Cardiovasc. Surgery, Soc. Clin. Surgery, Am. Assn. Thoracic Surgery (pres. 1984—85), Soc. Surg. Assn., Am. Surg. Assn. (pres. 1977—78, sec. 1969—73, pres. 1973—74), Inst. Medicine of NAS, Am. Bd. Surgery (chmn. 1971—72, diplomate), Philippine Coll. Surgeons (hon.), Surg. Congress Assn. Espanola de Cirujanos (hon.), French Surg. Assn. (hon.), Japanese Coll. Surgeons (hon.), Brazilian Coll. Surgeons (hon.), Colombian Surg. Soc. (hon.), German Surg. Soc. (hon.), Royal Australasian Coll. Surgeons (hon.),

Royal Coll. Surgeons Ireland (hon.), Royal Coll. Physicians and Surgeons Can. (hon.), Asociación de Cirugía del Litoral (Argentina) (hon.), Royal Coll. Surgeons Eng. (hon.), Royal Coll. Surgeons Edinburgh (hon.; editl. bd. jour.), Phila. Acad. Surgery (hon.). Ill. Surg. Soc. (hon.), University Club, Cosmos Club (Washington), Alpha Omega Alpha (Disting. Tchr. award 1992), Phi Beta Kappa. Office: Duke U Med Ctr PO Box 2600 Durham NC 27715-2600 Home: 622 Cedar Club Cir Chapel Hill NC 27517-7215

**SABL, JOHN J.,** lawyer; b. L.A., June 16, 1951; AB with distinction, Stanford U., 1973, JD, 1976. Bar: Calif. 1976, Ill. 1977. Assoc. Sidley & Austin, Chgo., 1977-83; ptnr. Sidley Austin Brown & Wood, Chgo., 1983-97, 2000—; exec. v.p., gen. counsel, sec. Conseco, Inc., Carmel, Ind., 1997-2000. Editorial bd. Stanford U. Law Review, 1974-75, assoc. mng. editor, 1975-76. Mem. ABA, Calif. Bar Assn., Ill. Bar Assn., Chgo. Bar Assn. (chmn. securities law commn. 1985-86), Phi Beta Kappa. Office: Sidley & Austin Bank One Plz 10 S Dearborn St Chicago IL 60603 E-mail: jsabl@sidley.com.

**SABLAN, DAVID J.,** marketing professional, political organization worker; Pres. D.J. Sabian and Co., 1999—; chmn. Rep. Party Guam, 2000—. Vice chmn. Guam State Coun. Vocat. Edn., 1988—90, chmn., 1991—94; mem. Gov.'s Task Force Tourism, 1987—89. Office: Guam Republican Party Chmn PO Box 2846 Hagatna GU 96932

**SABLE, BARBARA KINSEY,** retired music educator; b. Astoria, NY, Oct. 6, 1927; d. Albert and Verna (Rowe) Kinsey; m. Arthur J. Sable, Nov. 3, 1973. BA, Coll. Wooster, 1949; MA, Tchrs. Coll. Columbia U., N.Y.C., 1950; DMus, U. Ind., 1966. Office mgr., music dir. Sta. WCAX, Burlington, Vt., 1954; instr. Cottey Coll., 1959-60; asst. prof. N.E. Mo. State U., Kirksville, 1962-64, U. Calif., Santa Barbara, 1964-69; prof. music U. Colo., Boulder, 1969—, prof. emeritus, 1992—. Author: (novels) The Vocal Sound, 1982; contbr. poetry and short stories to lit. jours. Mem.: Colo. Music Tchrs. Assn., AAUP, Nat. Assn. Tchrs. Singing (past state gov., assoc. editor bull.). Democrat. Avocation: poetry. Home: 3430 Ash Ave Boulder CO 80305-3432 Office: U Colo PO Box 301 Boulder CO 80309-0301 Business E-Mail: bks@sable-boulder.com.

**SABLE, ROBERT ALLEN,** gastroenterologist; b. Bklyn., June 21, 1948; s. Benjamin and Sara S.; m. Valerie P. Kaplan Kopelman, July 1, 1969 (div. Mar. 1982); 1 child, Jesse; m. Ellen Sue Finer, May 29, 1982; children: Scott, Eric. BS, MIT, 1969; MD, Albert Einstein U., 1973. Bd. cert. in internal medicine, gastroenterology and geriatrics Am. Bd. Internal Medicine. Staff physician N.Y. Telephone Co. Mid Manhattan Med. Dept., N.Y.C., 1978-81; physician Riverdale Gastroenterology Cons., Bronx, NY, 1981—. Chief gastroenterology St. Barnabas Hosp., Bronx, 1982-2003, pres. med. bd., 1985-90; pres. divsn. coun. Montefiore Med. Ctr., 2001-03, pres. med. staff, 2005—. Contbr. articles, reports, revs. to profl. jours. Fellow ACP, Am. Coll. Gastroenterology; mem. AMA, Am. Gastroenterologic Assn., Am. Soc. for Gastrointestinal Endoscopy. Avocations: stamp collecting/philately, coin collecting/numismatics. Office: Riverdale Gastroenterol Con 3765 Riverdale Ave Bronx NY 10463-1845 Office Phone: 718-549-4267. Personal E-mail: ra.sable@verizon.net.

**SABLIK, MARTIN JOHN,** research physicist; b. Bklyn., Oct. 21, 1939; s. Martin C. and Elsie M. (Fuzia) S.; m. Beverly Ann Shively, Nov. 26,1965; children: Jeanne, Karen, Marjorie, Larry. BA in Physics, Cornell U., 1960; MS in Physics, U. Ky., 1965; PhD, Fordham U., 1972. Jr. engr. The Martin Co., Orlando, Fla., 1962-63; instr. half-time U. Ky., Lexington, 1963-65; rsch. assoc. Fairleigh Dickinson U., Teaneck, NJ, 1965-67, instr. physics, 1967-72, asst. prof., 1972-76, assoc. prof., 1976-80; sr. rsch. scientist Southwest Rsch. Inst., San Antonio, 1980-87, staff scientist, 1987—. Local chmn. Intermag. Conf., San Antonio, 1995; mem. adv. bd. Conf. on Properties and Applications of Magnetic Materials, 1990—, Workshop on advances in Measurement Techniques and Instrumentation for Magnetic Properties Determination, 1994, Magnetic Materials, Measurements and Modeling Symposium, 1996, Magnetic Materials, Measurements and Microstructure Symposium, 1998, Symposium Magnetic Materials for Magnetoelectronic Devices, 2000; mem. exec. bd. Topical Group on Magnetism and Its Applications, 1996-97; mem. program com., assoc. editor Intermag 2000, Toronto. Mem. editl. bd.: Nondestructive Testing and Evaluation, 1989—; contbr. articles to profl. jours.; mem. editl. bd.: IEEE Transactions on Magnetics, 2002—, assoc. editor:, 2003—. Recipient Imagineer award Mind Sci. Found., 1989. Fellow Am. Soc. Nondestructive Testing (chmn. So. Tex. sect. 1983-84, 2001-02); mem. IEEE (sr.), Am. Phys. Soc. Roman Catholic. Office: SW Rsch Inst PO Box 28510 San Antonio TX 78228-0510 Office Phone: 210-522-3342. E-mail: msablik@swri.org.

**SABLOFF, JEREMY ARAC,** archaeologist; b. NYC, Apr. 16, 1944; s. Louis and Helen (Arac) S.; m. Paula Lynne Weinberg, May 26, 1968; children: Joshua, Saralinda. AB, U. Pa., 1964; MA, PhD, Harvard U., 1969. From asst. prof. to assoc. prof. Harvard U., Cambridge, Mass., 1969—76; assoc. prof. anthropology U. Utah, Salt Lake City, 1976-77; curator anthropology Utah Mus. Natural History, Salt Lake City, 1976-77; prof. anthropology U. N.Mex., Albuquerque, 1978-86, chmn. dept., 1980-83; Univ. prof. anthropology and the history and philosophy of sci. U. Pitts., 1986-94, chmn. dept. anthropology, 1990-92; Charles K. Williams II dir. U. Mus., U. Mus. Term prof. anthropology U. Pa., Phila., 1994—2004, prof. anthropology, curator Mesoamerican archaeology, 1994—2004, Edmund J. and Louise W. Kahn endowed term prof. social scis., curator Mesoamerican archaeology, 2004—05, Christopher H. Browne disting. prof. anthropology, curator Mesoam. archaeology, 2004—. Sr. fellow for Pre-Columbian Studies, Dumbarton Oaks, 1986-92, chmn. 1989-92. Author: (with G.R. Willey) A History of American Archaeology, 1974, 2d edit., 1980, 3d edit., 1993, Excavations at Seibal: Ceramics, 1975, (with C.C. Lamberg-Karlovsky) Ancient Civilizations: The Near East and Mesoamerica, 1979, 2d edit. 1995, (with D. A. Freidel) Cozumel: Late Maya Settlement Patterns, 1984, The Cities of Ancient Mexico, 1989, rev. edit., 1997, The New Archaeology and the Ancient Maya, 1990, (with G. Tourtellot) The Ancient Maya City of Sayil: The Mapping of a Puuc Region Center, 1991; editor(with C.C. Lamberg-Karlovsky) The Rise and Fall of Civilizations, 1974, (with C.C. Lamberg-Karlovsky) Ancient Civilization and Trade, 1975, (with W.L. Rathje) A Study of Changing Pre-Columbian Commercial Systems, 1975, American Antiquity, 1977-81, (with G.R. Willey) Scientific American Readings in Pre-Columbian Archaeology, 1980, Simulations in Archaeology, 1981, Supplement to the Handbook of Middle American Indians: Archaeology, 1981, Archaeology: Myth and Reality: A Scientific American Reader, 1982, Analyses of Fine Paste Ceramics, 1982, (with D. Meltzer and D. Fowler) American Archaeology: Past and Future, 1986, (with E.W. Andrews V) Late Lowland Maya Civilization: Classic to Postclassic, 1986, (with J.S. Henderson) Lowland Maya Civilization in the Eighth Century A.D., 1993, Tikal: Dynasties, Foreigners, and Affairs of State, 2003 Pres. Kolb Found., 1995-2004; chair Smithsonian Coun., 1999-2001, chair sci. adv. commn., 2001-03; bd. mgrs. Sch. Am. Rsch. Grantee Nat. Geog. Soc., 1972-74, NSF, 1983-88, 2004—, NEH, 1990-91 Fellow AAAS (sec. H. chair 1994-95), Am. Anthrop. Assn., Soc. Antiquaries London; mem. NAS, Am. Philos. Soc., Soc. Am. Archaeology (pres. 1989-91), Am. Acad. Arts and Sci., Internat. Soc., Comparative Study of Civilizations, Sigma Xi Office: U Pa Mus Archaeology and Anthropology 33d and Spruce Sts Philadelphia PA 19104-6324

**SABO, MARTIN OLAV,** congressman; b. Crosby, ND, Feb. 28, 1938; s. Bjorn O. and Klara (Haga) S.; m. Sylvia Ann Lee, June 30, 1963; children: Karin, Julie. BA cum laude, Augsburg Coll., Mpls., 1959; postgrad., U. Minn., 1961-62. Mem. Minn. Ho. Reps. from 57B Dist., 1960-78, minority leader Dem.-Farmer-Labor party, 1969—73, speaker, 1973-78; mem. US Congress from 5th Minn. Dist., 1979—; chmn. Dem. Study Group; dep. majority whip 96th to 103rd Congresses; mem. permanent select com. on intelligence 102d Congress; chmn. Ho. Budget Com. 103d Congress; ranking minority mem. house budget com. 104th-106th Congress, mem. standards of official conduct com., appropriations com., ranking minority mem. subcom. on homeland security. Former mem. Nat. Adv. Commn. on Intergovtl. Rels.; past pres. Nat. Legis. Conf.; bd. regents Augsburg Coll. Mgr., player Dem.

Congl. Baseball Team, 1987—. Recipient Disting. Alumni citation Augsburg Coll., Arms Control Leadership award Employees Union, Local 113, SEIU, AFL-CIO; named One of 200 Rising Young Leaders in Am. Time mag., 1974; Man of Yr. Mpls. Jr. C.of C., 1973-74, One of Ten Outstanding Young Men of Yr. Minn. Jr. C. of C., 1974; inducted Scandinavian Am. Hall of Fame, 1994. Mem. Nat. Conf. State Legis. Leaders (past pres.). Democrat. Office: 2336 Rayburn Bldg Washington DC 20515-2305 Office Phone: 202-225-4755.

**SABOUSKY, RICHARD ANTHONY,** adult education educator; b. Oil City, Pa., Mar. 15, 1961; s. Robert Michael and Helen Pauline Sabousky. BS, Clarion U. Pa., 1984, MS, 1986; PhD, Kent State U., 1996. Cert. tchr. mentally and physically handicapped Pa. Tchr. Riverview Intermediate Unit, Shippenville, Pa., 1985—92; mem. faculty Clarion U. Pa., 1992—. Cons. Youth Alternatives, Oil City, Pa., 2001—, AC Valley Sch. Dist., St. Petersburg, Pa., 2002—, Mars (Pa.) Home for Youth, 2002—. Author: (chpt.) Transition Planning for Secondary Students with Disabilities, 2001. Recipient Disting. Alumni award, Clarion U. Venango Campus, 2002. Mem.: Coun. Exceptional Children. Home: 17 W Sixth St Oil City PA 16301 Office: Clarion U Pa 840 Wood St Sped Ctr Oil City PA 16301 E-mail: sabousky@clarion.edu.

**SABSAY, DAVID,** library director, consultant; b. Waltham, Mass., Sept. 12, 1931; s. Wiegard Isaac and Ruth (Weinstein) S.; m. Helen Glenna Tolliver, Sept. 24,1 966. BA, Harvard U., 1953; BLS, U. Calif., Berkeley, 1955. Circulation dept. supr. Richmond (Calif.) Pub. Library, 1955-56; city libr. Santa Rosa (Calif.) Pub. Library, 1956-65; dir. Sonoma County Library, Santa Rosa, 1965-92; libr. cons., 1992—. Coordinator North Bay Coop. Library System, Santa Rosa, 1960-64; cons. in field, Sebastopol, Calif., 1968—. Contbr. articles to profl. jours. Commendation, Calif. Assn. Library Trustees and Commrs., 1984. Mem. Calif. Library Assn. (pres. 1971, cert. appreciation 1971, 80), ALA. Clubs: Harvard (San Francisco). Home: 667 Montgomery Rd Sebastopol CA 95472-3020 E-mail: dsabsay@sonic.net.

**SABSHIN, MELVIN,** psychiatrist, educator, health science association administrator; b. N.Y.C., Oct. 28, 1925; s. Zalman and Sonia Sabshin; m. Edith Goldfarb, June 12, 1955; 1 child, James K; m. Marion Bennathan, Sept. 17, 2000. BS, U. Fla., Gainesville, 1944; MD, Tulane U., New Orleans, 1948. Diplomate Am. Bd. Psychiatry and Neurology. Assoc. dir. Michael Reese Hosp. Psychosomatic and Psychiat. Inst., Chgo., 1953-61; prof., head dept. psychiatry U. Ill. Coll. Medicine, Chgo., 1961-74; med. dir. Am. Psychiat. Assn., Washington, 1974-98; ret. Author Depression, 1960, Psychiatric Ideology, 1961; Normality, 1978; Normality and Life Cycle, 1984 With U.S. Army, 1944. Recipient Bowen award Am. Coll. Psychiatrists, 1978, Disting. Psychiatrist award, 1985 Mem.: Am. Coll. Psychiatrists (pres. 1974—75). Home: 2801 New Mexico Ave NW Washington DC 20007-3921

**SABY, JOHN SANFORD,** physicist, consultant; b. Ithaca, N.Y., Mar. 21, 1921; s. Rasmus S. and Maude Emily (Sanford) S.; m. Mary Elizabeth Long, June 9, 1945; children: Arthur D., Thomas S., Joseph A., Jean E. BA, Gettysburg Coll., Pa., 1942, ScD, D. (hon.), 1969; MS, Pa. State U., 1944, PhD, 1947. Lab. instr. Gettysburg Coll., 1940-42; instr. Cornell U., 1947-50; with Gen. Electric Co., 1951-82, mgr. semicondr./solid state Syracuse, NY, 1954-56, mgr. lamp phenomena research Cleve., 1956-82; cons., 1982—; mem. vis. com. biol. and phys. scis. Case Western Res. U., chmn., 1969. Co-author: Principles of Transistor Circuits, 1953; patentee in field. Fellow: IEEE (past com. officer); mem.: Cleve. Assn. Rsch. Dirs. (pres. 1963—64), Am. Phys. Soc., Nat. Assn. Watch and Clock Collectors, Phi Sigma Kappa, Phi Kappa Phi, Sigma Xi, Phi Beta Kappa. Home: 600 Carolina Village Rd # 295 Hendersonville NC 28792-3898

**SACCHETTI, SUSANNE LOUISE,** librarian; d. Russell and Susan Kerrigan; m. John Sacchetti. BA, Richard Stockton Coll., Pomona, NJ, 2001; MLS, Drexel U., Phila., 2005. Libr. Galloway Twp Pub. Schs., Galloway, NJ, 2002—03, Hamilton Twp Pub. Schs., Mays Landing, NJ, 2003—04; libr. specialist Atlantic Cape CC, Mays Landing, 2004—05, court house libr., 2005—. Contbr. poetry to jours. Mem.: NEA, ALA, NJ Edn. Assn., NJ Libr. Assn., Nat. Scholars Honor Soc. (life).

**SACCHI, TERRENCE J.,** cardiologist; b. Bklyn., July 16, 1952; m. Rita Sacchi; children: Terrence, Alexandra. BS in Biology magna cum laude, Fairfield U., 1972; MD, Albany U. 1976. Bd. cert. Am. Bd. Internal Medicine, Am. Bd. Cardiovasc. Disease; lic. physician, N.Y. Intern in internal medicine St. Vincent's Hosp. and Med. Ctr., N.Y.C., 1976-77, resident in internal medicine, 1977-79; fellow in cardiovasc. disease Georgetown U. Med. Ctr./Washington VA Hosp., Washington, 1979-81; interventional cardiology fellow Mercy Hosp., Des Moines, 1987; clin. instr. dept. medicine SUNY Health Scis. Ctr., Bklyn., 1982-85, clin. asst. dept. medicine 1985—; assoc. attending divsn. cardiology St. Vincent's Hosp. and Med. Ctr., N.Y.C., 1982—; physician-in-charge coronary care unit L.I. Coll. Hosp., Bklyn., 1986—, physician-in-charge catheterization lab. divsn. cardiology 1991—, chief divsn. cardiology dept. medicine, 1991—, med. dir. N.Y. Ctr. for Bloodless Medicine and Surgery, 1998—, vice-chmn. dept. internal medicine, 1998—. Asst. attending divsn. cardiology Maimonides Med. Ctr., Bklyn., 1988—; presenter in field. Contbr. numerous articles to med. jours., including New Eng. Jour. Medicine, Chest, Annals of Thoracic Surgery. Fellow Am. Coll. Chest Physicians, Coun. Clin. Cardiology, Am. Heart Assn., Am. Coll. Cardiology, N.Y. Cardiol. Soc.; mem. ACP, Med. Soc. Kings County, Alpha Omega Alpha. Office: Terrence J Sacchi Md 506 6th St Brooklyn NY 11215-3609 Fax: 718-780-1619.

**SACCO, DAVID J.,** neurosurgeon; b. Boston; m. Jodi Sacco. Degree in bioChemistry and cell biology, U. Calif, San Diego; MD, Loyola U, Chgo. Lic. physician Tex., Mass. Intern in gen. surgery, resident in neurol. surgery U. Ky.; fellow in pediat. Children's Hosp. Boston/Harvard Med. Sch.; clin. asst. prof. neurol. surgery U. Tex. Southwestern Med. Sch., Dallas; attending neurosurgeon Children's Med. Ctr. Dallas, Med. City Dallas Hosp., Tex. Scottish Rite Hosp. for Children. Presenter in field. Contbr. articles to profl. jours. Mem.: Alpha Omega Alpha. Office: Children's Med Ctr-Neurol Surgery 1935 Motor St Dallas TX 75235

**SACCO, JOHN MICHAEL,** accountant; b. NYC, Oct. 17, 1952; s. Anthony Carmine and Angelina (Pellegrino) Sacco. BS, St. John's U., 1974. CPA. Staff acct. Price Waterhouse & Co., NYC, 1974-75; semi-sr. acct. Seidman & Seidman, CPAs, White Plains, NY, 1976-77; sr. acct. Diamond Internat. Corp., NYC, 1977-79, Burns Internat. Security Svcs., Inc., Briarcliff Manor, NY, 1979-81; acctg. mgr. Burns Integrated Sys., Inc., Briarcliff Manor, NY, 1981-83; pvt. practice White Plains, NY, 1978—. Mem.: AICPA, NY Soc. CPA (mem. peer rev. com., mem. bus. valuations com., cooperation with bankers and credit grantors, mem. acctg. and auditing com., mem. acctg. & rev. svcs. com.). Republican. Roman Catholic. Home: 197 Upper Shad Rd Pound Ridge NY 10576-2237 Office: 110 Corporate Park Dr White Plains NY 10604 Office Phone: 914-253-8757. Business E-Mail: jmsaccocpa@verizon.net.

**SACCOCCIO, JACQUELINE,** artist; b. Providence, 1963; BFA in painting, RI Sch. Design, 1985; MFA in painting, Sch. of the Art Inst. of Chgo., 1988; student, L'Universita per Stranieri, Perugia, Italy, 1990. Adj. faculty RI Sch. Design. Solo exhibitions incl. Lauren Wittels Gallery, NYC, 1997, White Columns, NYC, 2001, Portage, Galerie Michael Neff, Frankfurt, Germany, 2003. Edward L. Ryerson Traveling Fellowship, 1988, Fulbright-Hays Found. Grant/Miguel Vinciguerra award, 1990—91, John Simon Guggenheim Meml. Found. Fellowship, 2000, Harold M. English/Jacob H. Lazarus-Met. Mus. Art Rome Prize Fellowship, Am. Acad. in Rome, 2005. Mem.: Coll. Art Assn.

**SACHA, ROBERT FRANK,** osteopath, educator; b. East Chicago, Ind., Dec. 29, 1946; s. S. Frank John and Ann Theresa S.; m. Linda T. LePage, 1988; children: Joshua Jude, Josiah Gerard, Anastasia Levon, Jonah Bradley.

BS, Purdue U., 1969; DO, Chgo. Coll. Osteo. Medicine, 1975; PharmD, Creighton U., 2004. Diplomate Am. Bd. Pediatrics, Am. Bd. Allery and Immunology. Pharmacist, asst. mgr. Walgreens Drug Store, East Chicago, Ind., 1969-75; intern David Grant Med. Ctr., San Francisco, 1975-76, resident in pediatrics, 1976-78; fellow in allergy and immunology Wilford Hall Med. Ctr., 1978-80; staff pediatrician, allergist Scott AFB (Ill.), 1980-83; practice medicine specializing in allergy and immunology Cape Girardeau, Mo., 1983—. Assoc. clin. instr. St. Louis U., 1980—; clin. instr. Purdue U., 1971-72, Pepperdine U., 1975-76, U. Tex.-San Antonio, 1978-80, assoc. clin. instr. So. Ill. U. Pres., Parent Tchrs. League; bd. gov. Chgo. Osteopathic Medicine. Maj. AF. USAF, 1975-83, comdr. USNR. Named one of Top Pediatricians 2002-2003, Pediatric Allergy, Immunology. Fellow Am. Coll. Allergy, Am. Coll. Chest Physicians, Am. Acad. Pediatrics, Am. Acad. Allergy-Immunology, Am. Assn. Cert. Allergists; mem. ACP, AMA, Am. Acad. Allergy, Assn. Mil. Allergists, Am. Coll. Emergency Physicians, Mil. Surgeons and Physicians. Republican. Lutheran. Office Phone: 573-334-1969. E-mail: bsacha@charter.net.

**SACHAR, DAVID BERNARD,** gastroenterologist, educator; b. Urbana, Ill., Mar. 2, 1940; s. Abram Leon and Thelma (Horwitz) Sachar; m. Joanna Maud Belford Silver, Aug. 29, 1961; children: Mark Benson, Kenneth Hulbert Belford(dec.). BA magna cum laude, Harvard Univ., 1959, MD cum laude, 1963. Cert. Am. Bd. Internal Medicine, diplomate Am Bd. Gastroenterology. Intern Beth Israel Hosp., Boston, 1963-65, resident in internal medicine, 1967-68; asst. chief clin. rsch. Pakistan SEATO Cholera Rsch. Lab., Dhaka, Bangladesh, 1965-67; resident in gastroenterology Mt. Sinai Hosp., NYC, 1968-70; instr. to prof. medicine Mt. Sinai Sch. Medicine, NYC, 1970-92, first Burrill B. Crohn prof. medicine, 1992-99, Arnold P. Gold Found. prof. medicine, 2005—; dir. divsn. gastroenterology Mt. Sinai Hosp., NYC, 1983-99, vice chmn. dept. medicine, 1992-99, dir. emeritus, 1999—, Arnold P. Gold Found. prof. medicine, 2005—. Co-chmn. work group on inflammatory bowel disease NIH, 1973—75; expert adv. panel gastroenterology and nutrition U.S. Pharmacopeial Conv., 1980—85; co-founder, sec., treas. Burrill B. Crohn Rsch. Found., NYC, 1984—; chmn. rsch. devel. com. Nat. Found. Ileitis and Colitis, 1984—89; K. H. Koster meml. lectr. Danish Soc. Gastroenterology, 1992; mem. Gastroenterology Leadership Coun. Task Force Fellowship Curriculum, 1994; internat. state art lectr. Falk Symposia, Germany, 1996; twentieth ann. Norman Tanner meml. lectr. St. George's Hosp. Med. Sch., London, 1997; internat. state art lectr., Belgium, 98, Brit. Soc. Gastroenterology, 1998, World Congresses Gastroenterology, Austria, 1998, Turkish Soc. Gastroenterology, 1998, World Congresses Gastroenterology, Italy, 1999, Hungarian Soc. Gastroenterology, 1999, Hellenic Soc. Gastroenterology, 1999; chmn. GI adv. bd. Solvay Pharm., Inc., 2000—02; internat. state art lectr. Falk Symposia, Germany, 2000—02; 25th ann. Nana Svartz meml. lectr., Örebro, Sweden, 2000; co chmn. 40th ann. post grad. course Portuguese Soc. Gastroenterology, 2000; internat. state art lectr., Italy, 01, Portuguese Soc. Gastroenterology, 2003; mem. GI adv. com. FDA, 2004—, chmn., 2005—. Editor: seven books and monographs on gastroenterology; contbr. chapters to books, over 220 articles to profl. journals. Trustee Bangladesh Coun. Asia Soc., NYC, 1972—75, Englewood Cliffs Bd. Edn., 1973—75. Capt. USPHS. Recipient Jacobi Medallion for Disting. Achievement, Mt. Sinai Alumni Assn., 1994, Alexander Richman Commemorative award for Humanism in Medicine, 1996, Norman Tanner medal, St. George's Hosp. Med. Sch., 1997, Gold Headed Cane award, 1997. Master: Am. Coll. Gastroenterology (mem. program dir. com. 1991, Henry Baker Presdl. Lectr. 1989, Berk/Fise clin. achievement award 2005); fellow: ACP, Am. Gastroent. Assn. (first chmn. clin. tchg. project 1984—90, mem. nominating com. 1993—94, chmn. immuno inflammatory disorders sectional nominating com. 1995, Disting. Educator Award 1996); mem.: Gold Humanism Honor Soc., Internat. Orgn. Study of Inflammatory Bowel Disease (first Am. elected chmn. 1989—92, chmn. task force clin. phenomics 1992—), Crohn's and Colitis Found. Am. (mem. grant rev. com. and coun. 1990—94, Disting. Svc. Award 1991, N.Y. Gov. Medal 1992), Brazilian Soc. Gastroenterology (patron 2003), Internat. Guild Miniature Artisans (trustee 2004—), Alpha Omega Alpha, Phi Beta Kappa. Achievements include co developer of oral rehydration therapy for diarrhea; development of resources and standards for clin. tchg. in gastroenterology; established Joanna and David B. Sachar International Award and Visiting Professorship in Inflammatory Bowel Disease. Office: Mt Sinai Med Ctr One Gustave L Levy Pl New York NY 10029 Business E-Mail: david.sachar@mountsinai.org.

**SACHAR, HOWARD MORLEY,** history educator; b. St. Louis, Feb. 10, 1928; s. Abram Leon and Thelma (Horwitz) S.; m. Eliana Steimatzky, July 23, 1964; children: Sharon, Michele, Daniel. BA, Swarthmore Coll., 1947; MA, Harvard U., 1950, PhD, 1953; LHD (hon.), Hebrew Union Coll. Jewish Inst. Religion, 1996. Instr. history U. Mass., 1953-54; dir. dir. Hillel Found. UCLA, 1954-57, Hillel Found., Stanford (Calif.) U., 1959-61, Hiatt Inst. in Israel, 1961-64; assoc. prof. history George Washington U., Washington, 1964-66, prof. history and internat. affairs, 1966—2004, prof. emeritus, 2004—. Author: The Course of Modern Jewish History, 1958, Aliyah, 1961, From the Ends of the Earth, 1964, The Emergence of the Middle East, 1969, Europe Leaves the Middle East, 1972, A History of Israel, 1976, The Man on the Camel, 1980, Egypt and Israel, 1981, Diaspora, 1985, A History of Israel Vol. II, 1987; A History of the Jews in America, 1992, Farewell España, 1994, Israel and Europe, 2000, Dreamland: Europeans and Jews in the Aftermath of the Great War, 2003, A History of the Jews in the Modern World, 2005, gen. editor Rise of Israel: A Documentary History, 1988; contbr. articles to NY Times, Washington Post, Commentary, others. Charles Brown fellow, 1957-58; NEH fellow, 1970-71; recipient Nat. Jewish Book award, 1976, 81. Mem. Am. Hist. Assn., Am. Jewish Hist. Soc., Phi Beta Kappa. Democrat. Jewish. Office: Elliot Sch Internat Affairs Emeriti George Washington U 1957 E St NW Washington DC 20052 Office phone: 301-942-7595. Office Fax: 202-994-6231. Business E-Mail: sachar@gwu.edu.

**SACHAR, LOUIS,** writer; b. East Meadow, N.Y., Mar. 20, 1954; married, 1985; 1 child. Student, Antioch Coll.; BA, U. Calif., Berkeley, 1976; JD, Hastings Coll. Law, San Francisco, 1980. Part-time atty. Author: (children's books) Sideways Stories From Wayside School, 1978 (1979 Children's Choice Book), Johnny's in the Basement, 1981, Someday Angeline, 1983, Sixth Grade Secrets, 1987, There's A Boy in the Girls' Bathroom, 1987, The Boy Who Lost His Face, 1989, Wayside School is Falling Down, 1989, Dogs Don't Tell Jokes, 1991, Marvin Redpost: Kidnapped at Birth?, 1992, Marvin Redpost: Is He a Girl?, 1993, Marvine Redpost: Why Pick on Me?, 1993, Alone in His Teachers' House, 1994, Wayside School Gets a Little Stranger, 1995, Holes, 1998 (Newbery award, finalist Nat. Book Award), Class President, 1999, Stanley Yelnat's Survival Guide to Camp Green Lake, 2003. Winner 1999 Newberry medal for Holes. Mem. Soc. Children's Book Writers and Illustrators, Authors Guild. Office: c/o Farrar Straus & Giroux 19 Union Sq W New York NY 10003-3304 Mailing: c/o Ellen Levine Trident Media Group Fl 36 41 Madison Ave New York NY 10010

**SACHATELLO-SAWYER, BONNIE LYNN,** education educator, director; m. Joseph Edward Sawyer. BA, Vanderbilt U., Nashville, Tenn., 1982—86; MA, U. Richmond, Va., 1987—90; EdD, Montana State U., Bozeman, 1989—96. Asst. dir. edn. Mus. of the Rockies, Bozeman, 1989—91, divsn. head, programs, 1992—2000; dir., Native Waters Mont. State U., Bozeman, 2000; exec. dir. Hopa Mountain, Inc., Bozeman, 2005—. Pres. REAL Experiences, Inc., Bozeman, 2000—. Author: (book) Lewis and Clark, 1997, Exploring the Planets, 1999, Adult Museum Programs, 2002.

**SACHDEO, AMIT,** dentist, educator; b. Allahabad, India, Feb. 07; s. Jogesh and Kiran Sachdeo. B in Dental Sci., Magadh U., 1997; MS, U. Bristol, 2000; postgrad., Harvard U., 2002—. CAD-CAM Training, Nobel Biocare, 2005, Esthetic Dentistry NY U., 2002, Human Participant Protections for Research Teams Nat. Cancer Inst., 2005, Cpr Am. Heart Assn., 2004, Public Oral Health Glasgow University-UK, 2001. Chief dental resident Sir Ganga Ram Hosp., India, 1997—98; resident Bristol Dental Sch., Bristol, England, 1999—2000; rsch. fellow-public oral health Glasgow U., Scotland, 2000—01; resident NYU, NYC, 2001—02; fellow Harvard U., Boston, 2002—. Contbr. articles to profl. jours. Fellow, Acad. Prosthodontics, 2005;

grantee, ACP/P&G, 2004; scholar, Straumann, 2003. Mem.: ARC (life), Internat. Acad. Dental Rsch., Am. Acad. Dental Rsch., Am. Acad. Cosmetic Dentistry (life), Acad. Osseointigration (life), Am. Coll. Prosthodontists (life). Achievements include research in Biofilm formation in the Edentulous. Avocations: swimming, skiing, reading, rollerblading, writing, horseback riding. Home: 1191 Boylston St Apt 59 Boston MA 02215 Office: Harvard U Dental Sch 188 Longwood Ave Boston MA 02115 Home Fax: 617-432-0901. Personal E-mail: amit_sachdeo@hsdm.harvard.edu.

**SACHER, CHARLES PHILIP,** lawyer; b. Bklyn., Sept. 5, 1939; s. Hans P. and Mary Carmel (O'Reilly) S.; m. Dorothy Anne Cronin, June 16, 1962; children: Charles, John, Richard. BBA in Acctg., U. Notre Dame, 1961, JD, 1964. Bar: Fla. 1964. Assoc. Saunders, Curtis, Ginestra & Gore, Ft. Lauderdale, Fla., 1966-69, ptnr., 1970-97; shareholder Sacher Martini & Sacher P.A., Coral Gables, 1998—. Capt. U.S. Army, 1964-66. Mem. ABA (Tax Sect.), Fla. Bar Assn. (Tax Sect.). Office: Sacher Martini & Sacher PA 2655 S Le Jeune Rd Ste 1101 Coral Gables FL 33134-5802 Office Phone: 305-448-3900. Personal E-mail: cps@sachmarlaw.com

**SACHER, STEVEN JAY,** lawyer; b. Cleve., Jan. 28, 1942; s. Albert N. and Cecil P. (Chessin) S.; m. Colleen Marie Gibbons, Nov. 28, 1970; children: Alexander Jerome, Barry Elizabeth, William Paul. BS, U. Wis., 1964; JD, U. Chgo., 1967. Bar: D.C. 1968. Assoc. solicitor Employee Retirement Income Security Act U.S. Dept. Labor, Washington, 1974-77; spl. counsel com. on labor and human resources U.S. Senate, Washington, 1977-79, gen. counsel, 1980-81; ptnr. Pepper Hamilton, Washington, 1982-88; shareholder Johnson & Gibbs, Washington, 1988-94; ptnr. Kilpatrick Stockton LLP, Washington, 1994—. Adj. prof. law Georgetown U. Law Ctr., 1977; co-chair sr. editors Employee Benefits Law and Annual Supplements, Bur. Nat. Affairs, Washington, 1991-2000. Mem. adv. bd. BNA Pension and Benefits Reporter; mem. editorial bd. Benefits Law Jour., Jour. Pension Planning and Compliance. Founding mem. ERISA Roundtable, Washington. Fellow Coll. Labor and Employment Lawyers, Am. Coll. Employee Benefits Counsel (charter); mem. ABA (mgmt. co-chmn. com. on employee benefits, sect. on labor and employment law 1988-91, chmn. prohibited trans. subcom., com. on employee benefits, sect. on taxation 1986-91), D.C. Bar Assn. Office: Kilpatrick Stockton LLP 607 14th St NW Ste 900 Washington DC 20005 Office Phone: 202-508-5840. Business E-Mail: ssacher@kilpatrickstockton.com.

**SACHS, ALAN ARTHUR,** lawyer; b. Bklyn., Feb. 7, 1947; s. Herman and Clara Sachs; m. Marilyn Mushlin, May 19, 1974; children: David Henry, Stephen Edward. BA, Columbia U., 1967; JD, Harvard U., 1970. Bar: NY 1971, Wis. 1983, Mo. 1989. Law clk. to judge U.S. Dist. Ct. (ea. dist.) N.Y., 1970-71; assoc. Cleary, Gottlieb, Steen & Hamilton, N.Y.C., 1971-79, Paskus, Gordon & Hyman, N.Y.C., 1979-81; sec., gen. counsel The Trane Co., LaCrosse, Wis., 1981-85; sr. v.p., gen. counsel, sec. Edison Bros. Stores Inc., St. Louis, 1985—2001; ptnr. Haar & Woods, LLP, St. Louis, 2001—. Mem.: ABA, Bar Assn. Met. St. Louis (chmn. bus. law sect.). Office: Haar & Woods LLP 1010 Market St Saint Louis MO 63101 Office Phone: 314-241-2224.

**SACHS, DAVID HOWARD,** surgeon, immunologist, educator; b. N.Y.C., Jan. 10, 1942; s. Elliot and Elsie (Hurvitz) S.; m. Kristina Olsson, Mar. 15, 1969; children: Michelle, Jessica, Karin, Teviah. AB, Harvard U., 1963; DES, U. Paris, 1964; MD, Harvard U., Boston, 1968. Intern in surgery Mass. Gen. Hosp., Boston, 1968-69, resident in surgery, 1969-70, dir. transplantation biology rsch. ctr. surgery dept., 1991—; chief immunology br. Nat. Cancer Inst., Bethesda, Md., 1982-90; prof. surgery and immunology Harvard U. Med. Sch., 1991—. Capt. PHS, 1970-91. Recipient Roche Ernest Hodge Meml. award, Am. Soc. Transplantation, 2005. Avocations: gardening, fishing, windsurfing, skiing. Office: Mass Gen Hosp East Bldg 149-9019 13th St Boston MA 02129

**SACHS, GEORGE,** biology professor, physician; b. Austria; BSc, U. Edinburgh, 1957, MB, ChB, 1960, DSc, 1980; MD, U. Gothenburg, 1987. Instr. Albert Einstein Coll., 1961—62; rsch. assoc. Columbia U., 1962—63; asst. prof. medicine and physiology U. Ala., Birmingham, 1963—65, assoc. prof., 1965—70, prof., 1970—82, dir. membrane biology, 1974—82; prof. medicine and physiology, Wilshire chair in medicine UCLA, 1982—, co-dir. ctr. ulcer rsch. and edn., 1987—2002, dir. membrane biology lab., 1987—; sr. med. investigator VAGLAHS, LA, 1984—99, staff physician, 1999—. Contbr. articles to profl. jours. Named Dr. Norman Frankel Scholar, U. Chgo., 2005, Evans Scholar, Boston U., 2005; recipient Beaumont Prize in Gatroenterology, Am. Gastroenterological Assn., 1985, Hoffman LaRoche award, 1982, Gairdner award, Gairdner Found., 2004, Ismar Boas Vorlesung Medal, German Gastroenterological Assn., 1992, others. Office: UCLA 405 Hilgard Ave Los Angeles CA 90095 Office Phone: 310-268-3923. E-mail: gsachs@ucla.edu.*

**SACHS, JEFFREY DAVID,** economist, educator; b. Detroit, Nov. 5, 1954; s. Theodore and Joan Sachs; m. Sonia Ehrlich Sachs; children: Lisa, Adam, Hannah. BA summa cum laude, Harvard U., 1976, MA in Econs., 1978, PhD in Econs., 1980; degree (hon.), St. Gallen U., Switzerland, 1990, Lingnan Coll. Hong Kong, 1998, Varna Econs. U., Bulgaria, 2000, Iona Coll. N.Y., 2000. Prof. internat. trade Harvard U., Cambridge, Mass., 1984—2002; prof. sustainable devel. Columbia U., NYC, 2002—, dir. Earth Inst., 2002—. Dir. Harvard Inst. Internat. Devel. Harvard U., 1995—99; chmn. commn. on macroecons. and health WHO, 2000—01; dir. Ctr. for Internat. Devel. Harvard U., 1998—2002; spl. advisor to sec. gen. Kofi Annan UN, N.Y.C., 2002—; cons. in field. Co-author: Macroeconomics in the Global Economy, 1992; author: Poland's Jump to the Market Economy, 1993, The End of Poverty: Economic Possibilities for Our Time, 2005, Development Economics, 1997, Macro Economics in the Global Econ., 2003, The End of Poverty: Economic Possibilities of Our Times, 2005. Named one of 100 Most Influential People of 2005, Time mag. Mem.: Inst. Medicine. Office: The Earth Inst at Columbia Univ 314 Low Libr MC 4327 535 West 116th St New York NY 10027 Office Phone: 212-854-8704.

**SACHS, JOHN PETER,** carbon company executive; b. Duesseldorf, Germany, 1926; married. BAChemE, Ill. Inst. Tech., 1948, MAChemE, 1950, PhDChemE, 1952. Various mgmt. positions in research and devel., engring. and ops. Union Carbide Corp., 1951-66; v.p. ops. then group v.p. Great Lakes Carbon Corp., N.Y.C., 1966-78; pres., chief exec. officer Gt. Lakes Carbon Corp., N.Y.C., 1978-86; chmn. bd., dir. Gen. Refractories Co., 1978-85; mng. ptnr. J.P. Sachs Assocs., Mgmt. Cons., New Canaan, Conn., 1987—99. Trustee Fairfield U., 1978-92; bd. dirs. Kneissl-Dachstein 1992-2004, Peridot, 1989-98. Mem. Am. Inst. Chem. Engrs. (pres. 1985) Home and Office: JP Sachs Assocs 67 Dunning Rd New Canaan CT 06840-4009

**SACHS, KATHERINE STEIN,** art historian; m. Keith L. Sachs. Grad., Univ. Pa., 1969. Rsch. coord. Phila. Mus. Art. Mem. contemporary collector's com. Harvard Univ. Art Museums; council mem. Tate Internat.; chmn. bd. gov. Ferkauf Grad. Sch. Psychology, Yeshiva Univ.; mem. Trustees Council Penn Women, 2000—; chmn. bd. overseers Inst. Contemporary Art, Univ. Pa., 1998—. Named one of Top 200 Collectors, ARTnews Mag., 2004, 2005, 2006. Avocation: Collector of Contemporary Art. Mailing: Philadelphia Museum of Art Benjamin Franklin Pkwy Philadelphia PA 19130

**SACHS, KEITH L.,** manufacturing executive; m. Katherine Stein. Grad., Univ. Pa., 1967; PhD (hon.), Hebrew Univ., Jerusalem, 2003. Chmn. Saxco Internat. Inc., Horsham, Pa. Trustee Phila. Mus. Art; chmn. bd. Am. Friends of Hebrew Univ. Named one of Top 200 Collectors, ARTnews Mag., 2004, 2005, 2006. Avocation: Collector of Contemporary Art. Office: Saxco International Inc 200 Gibraltar Rd Ste 101 Horsham PA 19044-2333

**SACHS, LEO,** geneticist, educator; b. Leipzig, Germany, Oct. 14, 1924; s. Elijah and Louise (Lichtblau) S.; m. Pnina Salkind; 4 children. BSc, U. Wales, Bangor, 1948; PhD, Trinity Coll. Cambridge U., 1951; DHC (hon.), Bordeaux U., 1985; MD (hon.), Lund U., 1997. Rsch. scientist John Innes

Inst., 1951-52; mem. sci. staff Weizmann Inst. Sci., Rehovot, Israel, 1952—, prof., chmn. genetics dept., 1962—, Otto Meyerhof prof. molecular biology, 1968. Mem. Israeli Acad. Sci. and Humanities, 1975; hon. fellow U. Wales, Bangor, 1999. Contbr. articles to sci. jours. Recipient Israel prize for natural sci., 1972; named Fogarty Internat. scholar NIH, 1972, Harvey Lecture, 1972; recipient Rothschild prize in biol. scis., 1977, Wolf prize in medicine, 1980, Bristol-Myers award for disting. achievement in cancer rsch., 1983, Royal Soc. Wellcome Found. prize, 1986, Sloan prize GM Cancer Rsch. Found., 1989, Warren Alpert prize Harvard Med. Sch., 1997, Emet prize in life scis., 2002. Fellow Royal Soc., 1997; mem. U.S. Nat. Acad. Scis. (fgn. assoc. 1995), Academia Europaea (fgn. mem.), Internat. Cytokine Soc. (hon. life 2001). Office: Weizmann Inst Sci Dept Molecular Genetics Rehovot 76100 Israel Business E-Mail: leo.sachs@weizmann.ac.il.

**SACHS, MARILYN STICKLE,** writer, educator, editor; b. N.Y.C., Dec. 18, 1927; d. Samuel and Anna (Smith) Stickle; m. Morris Sachs, Jan. 26, 1947; children: Anne, Paul. BA, Hunter Coll., 1949; MSLS, Columbia U., 1953. Children's libr. Bklyn. Pub. Libr., 1949-60, San Francisco Pub. Libr., 1961-67. Author: Amy Moves In, 1964, Laura's Luck, 1965, Amy and Laura, 1966, Veronica Ganz, 1968, Peter and Veronica, 1969, Marv, 1970, The Bears' House, 1971 (Austrian Children's Book prize 1977, Recognition of Merit award George C. Stone Ctr. for Children's Books 1989), The Truth About Mary Rose, 1973 (Silver Slate Pencil award 1974), A Pocket Full of Seeds, 1973 (Jane Addams Children's Book Honor award 1974), Matt's Mitt, 1975, Dorrie's Book, 1975 (Silver State Pencil award 1977, Garden State Children's Book award 1978), A December Tale, 1976, A Secret Friends, 1978, A Summer's Lease, 1979, Bus Ride, 1980, Class Pictures, 1980, Fleet Footed Florence, 1981, Hello...Wrong Number, 1981, Call Me Ruth, 1982 (Assn. Jewish Librs. award 1983), Beach Towels, 1982, Fourteen, 1983, The Fat Girl, 1984, Thunderbird, 1985, Underdog, 1985 (Christopher 1986), Baby Sister 1986, Almost Fifteen, 1987, Fran Ellen's House, 1987 (award Bay Area Book Reviewers Assn. 1988, Recognition of Merit award George C. Stone Ctr. for Children's Books 1989), Just Like A Friend, 1989, At the Sound of the Beep, 1990, Circles, 1991, What My Sister Remembered, 1992, Thirteen, 1993, Ghosts in the Family, 1995, Another Day, 1997, Suprise Party, 1998, Jo Jo & Winnie, 1999, Jo Jo & Winnie Again, 2000, The Four Ugly Cats in Apartment 3D, 2002, Lost in America, 2005, First Impressions, 2006; co-editor: (with Ann Durell) Big Book for Peace, 1990 (Calif. Children's Book award 1991, Jane Addams Children's Book prize 1991); reviewer San Francisco Chronicle, 1970—. Mem. PEN, ACLU, Sierra Club, Authors' Guild. Democrat. Jewish. Avocations: reading, walking, baseball. Home: 733 31st Ave San Francisco CA 94121-3523

**SACHS, MURRAY B.,** audiologist, educator; BS in Elec. Engring., MIT, 1962, MS in Elec. Engring. and Auditory Physiology, 1964, PhD in Elec. Engring. and Auditory Physiology, 1966. Teaching asst., dept. elec. engring. MIT, 1962-64, instr. dept. elec. engring., 1964—66; rsch. scientist US Navy Underwater Sound Lab., New London, Conn.; postdoctoral fellow U. Cambridge, 1968—69; asst. prof. biomedical engring. John Hopkins U. Sch. Medicine, Balt., 1970—74, assoc. prof. biomedical engring., 1974—80, prof. biomedical engring., 1980—, prof. neuroscience, 1981—, prof. otolaryngology-head and neck surgery, 1983—, dir. Ctr. Hearing Sci., 1986—91, Massey prof., dir. Whitaker Biomed. Engring. Inst., 1991—. Mem. com. comm. and control Internat. Union Pure and Applied Biophysics, 1975—80; mem. comm. disease panel and basic sci. task force Nat. Inst. Neurol. and Communicative Disorders and Stroke, NIH, 1977—78, chmn. communicative disease rev. com., 1977—79, ad hoc adv. com., 1979—86; ad hoc prog. project adv. com. Kresge Hearing Rsch. Inst., U. Mich., 1982—; sci. program adv. com. Nat. Inst. Neurol. and Communicative Disorders and Stroke, NIH, 1984—86; ad hoc prog. project adv. com. (cochlear implants), dept. otolaryngology-HNS U. Iowa Sch. Medicine, 1984—93; investigator Jacob Javitz Neuroscience, 1985; ad hoc program project adv. com., cochlear implant program MIT, 1986—; bd. scientific counselors Nat. Ctr. for Rsch. Resources, NIH, 1995—. Contbr. articles to profl. publs.; edit. bd. Hearing Rsch., 1978—. Lt. USNR, 1966—68, US Navy Underwater Sound Lab., New London, Conn. Named Whitaker Disting. Lectr., Biomedical Engring. Soc., 2000; recipient von Bekesy medal, Acoustical Soc. Am., 1998, Merit award, Assn. for Rsch. Otolaryngology, 1999. Fellow: AAAS (chmn. acad, coun. 1994); mem.: NAE, Assn. for Rsch. in Otolaryngology (coun. mem. 1982—), Am. Acad. Otolaryngology-HNS (rsch. com. 1986—), Am. Inst. for Med. and Biol. Engring. (founding fellow 1992, chair-elect, Coll. Fellows 1996—97), NAS (com. on hearing and bioacoustics 1985—88, Inst. Medicine 1990), Eta Kappa Nu, Tau Beta Pi, Sigma Xi. Office: Johns Hopkins U Sch Medicine 720 Rutland Ave Baltimore MD 21205-2109 Office Phone: 410-955-3131. Office Fax: 410-955-0549. Business E-Mail: msachs@bme.jhu.edu.

**SACHS, RICHARD GREGORY,** cardiologist; b. Orange, NJ, Mar. 5, 1941; m. Barbara Sachs; children: Eric, Chris, Kevin, Liz, Blair. MD, Georgetown U. Sch. Medicine, Washington, DC, 1966. Diplomate Am. Bd. Internal Medicine, Am. Bd. Cardiovascular Disease. Intern, medicine Georgetown Hosp., Washington, 1966-67, resident, cardiology, 1967-68; fellow, cardiology Emory U. Hosp., Atlanta, 1968-70, Inst. Cardiology, London; mem. staff Overlook Hosp., Summit, NJ, Morristown Meml. Hosp., NJ; clin. instr. Columbia Physicians and Surgeons; pvt. practice cardiology Summit, NJ. Recipient Lifetime Achievement award for Med. Svc., Overlook Hosp., Summit, NJ, 2006. Fellow Am. Coll. Cardiology; mem. FCCAHA. Office: Summit Med Group 129 Summit Ave Summit NJ 07901 also: Summit Med Group 95 Madison Ave Morristown NJ 07960*

**SACHS, SAMUEL, II,** museum director; b. N.Y.C., Nov. 30, 1935; s. James Henry and Margery Sachs; m. Susan McAllen (div.); children: Katherine, Eleanor; m. Jerre S. Hollander (div.); 1 child, Alexander; m. Elizabeth M. Gordon; 1 child, Hadley Elizabeth. BA cum laude, Harvard U., 1957; MA, NYU Inst. Fine Arts, 1962. With Mpls. Inst. Arts, 1958-60; asst. dir. U. Mich. Mus. of Art, Ann Arbor, 1963-64; chief curator Mpls. Inst. Arts, 1964-73, dir., 1973-85, Detroit Inst. Arts, 1985-97; dir., CEO Frick Collection, N.Y.C., 1997—. Bd. dirs. Internat. Com. on Fine Arts, Art Mus. Image Consortium, IFAR, NINCH, Japan Soc. Decorated knight 1st class Order North Star (Sweden); Order of Dannebrog (Denmark). Mem. Am. Assn. Museums, Assn. Art Mus. Dirs., Century Assn., Harvard Club. Home: 1112 Park Ave # 16B New York NY 10128-1235 E-mail: sachs@frick.org.

**SACHS, SHARONA,** internist, researcher; d. Eugene Sachs and Norma Fertziger. BA in English Lit. cum laude, U. Pa., 1983; MD summa cum laude, SUNY, 1988. Diplomate Am. Bd. Internal Medicine, lic. physician N.Y., Tex., S.C. Intern in internal medicine Duke U. Med. Ctr., 1988—89, resident in internal medicine, 1989—91; fellow divsn. hematology and oncology Hosp. of U. Pa., 1991—92; fellow divsn. respiratory medicine and critical care Duke U. Med. Ctr., 1992—95; mng. editor Le Jacq Pub., Inc., N.Y.C., NY, 1983—86; asst. prof. pulmonary medicine U.S.C. Sch. of Medicine, 1995—96; asst. prof. divsn. pulmonary and critical care U. Tex., Southwestern Sch. of Medicine, 1996—98, SUNY, Sch. of Medicine, Stony Brook, 1998—. Dir. Lung Cancer Evaluation Ctr., L.I. Cancer Ctr., Stony Brook Univ. Hosp., 2000—, med. quality assurance com., 2000, med. dir. Med. Step-Down Unit, 2001—03, clin. resource mgmt. com., 2001—02, patient safety com., 2002—03, search com., cardiology chair, 2002—04, oncology leadership coun., chmn. Palliative Care Program Devel., 2003; quality mgmt. assurance com. radiology svcs. Dallas VA Med. Ctr.; spkr. in field. Reviewer: Jour. Aerosol Medicine; contbr. articles to profl. jours. Recipient David K. Miller prize in medicine, SUNY, Janet M. Glasgow citation, Buffalo Found. scholarship; Rsch. fellow, NIH. Mem.: Soc. Critical Care Medicine, Am. Coll. Chest Physicians, Am. Thoracic Soc., Alpha Omega Alpha. Office Phone: 631-444-2981. Business E-Mail: ssachs@notes.cc.sonsb.edu.*

**SACHTLER, WOLFGANG MAX HUGO,** chemistry professor; b. Delitzsch, Germany, Nov. 8, 1924; arrived in US, 1983; s. Gottfried Hugo and Johanna Elisabeth (Bollmann) S.; m. Anne-Lore Luise Adrian, Dec. 9, 1953; children: Johann Wolfgang Adriaan, Heike Kathleen Julia, Yvonne Rhea Valeska. Diplomchemiker, Tech. U., Braunschweig, Ger., 1949; Dr.rer.nat. (Ph.D), 1952. Research chemist Kon-Shell Lab., Amsterdam, Netherlands,

1952-71, dept. head, 1972—83; extraordinary prof. chemistry U. Leiden, Netherlands, 1963-83; V.N. Ipatieff prof. Northwestern U. Evanston, Ill., 1983-96; chmn. Gordon Research Conf. Catalysis, NH, 1985. Rideal lectr. Faraday div. Royal Soc. Chemistry, 1981; F. Gault lectr., 1991. Mem. editl. bd. Jour. Catalysis, 1976-88, Applied Catalysis, 1983-87, Catalysis Letters, 1987—, Advances in Catalysis, 1987—, Catalysis Today, 1996—, Catalysis Reviews, 1997—; contbr. numerous articles to sci. jours. Recipient Deutsche Gesellschaft Mineraloel und Kohle Kolleg award, 1991. Fellow AAAS; mem. Royal Netherlands Acad. Scis., Internat. Congress Catalysis (pres. coun. 1992-96), Royal Dutch Chem. Soc. (hon. mem. catalysis divsn.), Am. Chem. Soc. (E.V. Murphee award 1987, Petroleum Chemistry award 1992), Catalysis Soc. N.Am. (Robert L. Burwell award 1985, E. Houdry award 1993). Home: 2141 Ridge Ave Apt 2D Evanston IL 60201-2788 Office: Northwestern U 2137 Sheridan Rd Evanston IL 60208-0001 Office Phone: 847-475-8607. Business E-Mail: wmhs@northwestern.edu.

**SACK, EDGAR ALBERT**, electronics company executive; b. Pitts., Jan. 31, 1930; s. Edgar Albert and Margaret Valentine (Engelmohr) S.; m. Eugenia Ferris, June 7, 1952; children: Elaine Kimberley, Richard Warren. BS, Carnegie-Mellon U., 1951, MS, 1952, PhD, 1954. Dept. mgr. Westinghouse Rsch. Lab., Pitts., 1960-63; engring. mgr. Westinghouse Microelectronics, Balt., 1963-65, ops. mgr., 1965-67, divsn. mgr., 1967-69; div. v.p. Gen. Instrument Corp., Hicksville, NY, 1969-73, group v.p., 1973-77, sr. v.p., 1977-84; pres., CEO Zilog Inc., Campbell, Calif., 1984-98, also chmn. bd. dirs.; pres. Productivity Assocs., Coronado, Calif.; founder, chmn. CDT, Inc., San Jose, Calif., 1998-99. Bd. dirs. Enfo-Web, Inc., Mountainview, Calif. LXi, Inc., Mountainview; vis. com. elec. engring. dept. Carnegie-Mellon U. 1969-74; mem. indsl. adv. coun. SUNY, Stony Brook, 1979-83; mem. adv. com. on solid state electronics Poly. Inst. Tech., 1981-83. Author: Forward Controllership Business Management System, 1989, 2nd edit., 1993, Development of the Coronado Shores-A History, 2005; patentee in field. Mem. Action Com. L.I, 1982-84; bd. dirs. Coronado Shores Assn. # 7, 2000-06, landscaping and recreational com., 2000-, chair, 2002-03, treas., 2004-06; mem. Sharp Coronado Hosp. Aux.; sec. San Diego Imperial Coun. of Vols., 2002; bd. dirs. Coronado Hosp. Found., 2003-04, chair projects and allocations com., 2004. Recipient 2nd Ann. Hammerschlag Disting. Lectr. award Carnegie Mellon U., 1995. Fellow IEEE, Poly. Inst. Tech.; mem. Semicondr. Industry Assn. (dir. 1982-85), Carnegie Mellon Alumni Assn. (Merit award 1981), Eta Kappa Nu (Outstanding Young Elec. Engr. 1959), Huntington Yacht Club (vice comdr. 1977), Tau Beta Pi (finalist San Francisco Entrepreneur of Yr. award 1991), Phi Kappa Phi. Home and Office: 1780 Avenida Del Mundo Unit 404 Coronado CA 92118-4011 Personal E-mail: esack@pacbell.net.

**SACK, GEORGE HENRY, JR.**, molecular geneticist; b. Balt., Apr. 17, 1943; s. George Henry and Sophia Ann (Philippi) S. BA, Johns Hopkins U., 1965, MD, 1968, PhD, 1974. Diplomate Bd. Med. Genetics, Bd. Med. Examiners. Intern Johns Hopkins Hosp., Balt., 1968-69, asst. resident, 1969-70, fellow genetics, 1975-76; rsch. fellow Johns Hopkins Sch. Medicine, Balt., 1970-73; asst. prof. dept. medicine Johns Hopkins U., Balt., 1976-84, assoc. prof. dept. medicine and biol. chemistry, 1984—; molecular biologist Kennedy Inst., Balt., 1982-93, dir. exec. health program, 1996—. Contbr. articles to profl. jours. Maj. USAR, 1973-75. Andrew W. Mellon scholar Johns Hopkins U., 1976, Kennedy Found. scholar, 1982-85. Fellow Am. Coll. Med. Genetics; mem. AMA, AAAS, Am. Soc. Human Genetics, Phi Beta Kappa. Office: Johns Hopkins Hosp Outpatient Ctr 601 N Caroline St Baltimore MD 21287-0005 Office Phone: 410-955-2374. Business E-Mail: gsack@jhmi.edu.

**SACK, ROBERT DAVID**, federal judge, law educator; b. Phila., Oct. 4, 1939; s. Eugene J. and Sylvia I. (Rivlin) Sack; BA, U. Rochester, 1960; LLB, Columbia U., 1963. Bar: N.Y. 1963. Law clk. to judge Fed. Dist. Ct. of N.J., 1963—64; assoc. Patterson, Belknap & Webb, N.Y.C., 1964—70; ptnr. Patterson, Belknap, Webb & Tyler, N.Y.C., 1970—86, Gibson, Dunn & Crutcher, N.Y.C., 1986-98; sr. assoc. spl. counsel U.S. Ho. of Reps. Impeachment Inquiry, 1974; judge U.S. Ct. Appeals (2d cir.), 1998—. Lectr. Practising Law Inst., 1973—97, Columbia U. Law Sch., 2001—. mem. bd. visitors, 2000—; adv. bd. Media Law Reporter. Author: Libel, Slander, and Related Problems, 1980, 2d edit., 1994, CD-ROM edit., 1995, Sack on Defamation-Libel, Slander, and Related Problems, 3d edit., 1999; co-author: Advertising and Commercial Speech, a First Amendment Guide, 1999; contbr. articles to profl. jours. Chmn. bd. dirs. Nat. Council on Crime and Delinquency, 1982—83; trustee seminars on media and society Columbia U. Sch. Journalism, 1985—92, N.Y.C. Commn. on Pub. Info. and Comm., 1995—98; v.p., bd. dirs. William F. Kerby and Robert S. Potter Fund. Fellow: Am. Bar Found.; mem.: ABA (bd. govs. forum com. on comm. law 1980—88), Assn. Bar City N.Y. (chmn. comm. law com. 1986—89). Office: US Circuit Ct for 2d Circuit 40 Foley Sq New York NY 10007-1502

**SACK, ROBERT DAVID**, geography professor; PhD, U. Minn., 1971. Clarence J. Glacken prof. geography U. Wis. Madison, 1994—, John Bascom prof. geography, 1997—, prof. Integrated Liberal Studies. Contbr. articles to profl. jours., chapters to books; author: Conceptions of Space in Social Thought: A Geog. Perspective, 1980, Human Territoriality: Its Theory and Hist., 1986, Place, Modernity, and the Consumer's World: A Relational Framework for Geog. Analysis, 1992, Homo Geographicus: A Framework for Action, Awareness, and Moral Concern, 1997, A Geog. Guide to the Real and the Good, 2003; editor: Progress: Geog. Essays, 2002. Recipient Hilldale award, Social Studies, 1993, Honors award, Disting. Rsch., Assn. Am. Geographers, 1994; grantee John Simon Guggenheim Meml. Found. fellowship, 1975—76, Fulbright Sr. Rsch. fellowship, 1979—80. Fellow: Am. Acad. Arts & Scis. Office: Dept Geography U Wis 550 N Park St Madison WI 53706-1404 E-mail: rdsack@facstaff.wisc.edu.*

**SACK, SEYMOUR**, nuclear scientist; b. 1929; BS in physics, MS in physics, PhD in physics, Yale U. Scientist Lawrence Livermore Nat. Lab., 1955—90, lab. assoc., 1990—. Specialist in nuclear weapon design; participant JASON (study on maintaining nuclear stockpile under a comprehensive test ban), 1995. Recipient Fleet Ballistic Missile Achievement award, Strategic Systems Program, US Navy, 1997, Enrico Fermi award, US Dept. Energy, 2003. Office: Lawrence Livermore Nat Lab 7000 East Ave Livermore CA 94550

**SACK, SYLVAN HANAN**, lawyer; b. Phila., Dec. 26, 1932; s. Isidore F. and Mollye (Bellmore) S.; m. Ellen L. Foreman, Aug. 13, 1972; children: Reuben H., Sara I. MS in Bus. Adminstrn, Pa. State U., 1956; JD, U. Balt., 1964. Bar: Md. 1964, U.S. Tax Ct. 1967, U.S. Supreme Ct. 1970; C.P.A. Md. With U.S. Treasury Dept., IRS, 1956—66; pvt. practice Balt., 1967—; assoc. counsel Safety First Club of Md., 1975—78, spl. counsel, 1979—; asst. city solicitor City of Balt., 1978—79. Gov. Md. chpt. Retinitis Pigmentosa Found., 1974-75 Contbr. articles to profl. jours. Chmn. Indsl. Toxicology NIOSH Function, 1977, Occupational Disease Forum, 1979, OSHA and Diseases in Workplace Seminar, 1981. Mem. Fed. Bar Assn. (gov. chpt. 1968—, chmn. bd. govs. 1970. chmn. environ. law program 1984), ABA (chmn. subcom. sect. taxation 1972-75), Md. Bar Assn., Assn. Trial Lawyers Am.; mem. Md. Trial Lawyers Assn. (lectr. toxic torts 1983 conv.) Office Phone: 410-484-1484.

**SACKETT, BARNARD (BARNEY)**, actor, film producer, director, scriptwriter; Personal mgr. Bret Morrison "The Shadow" of Mutual Network Blue Coal Radio, jazz artist Sylvia Syms, 1950; press agt. summer stock co. Quarterdeck Theatre, Atlantic City, N.J., 1952—55; drama critic, celebrity interviewer Sta. WDAS and Metromedia WIP, Phila., 1953—68; owner/operator Wayne Ave. Playhouse, Phila., 1957—69, Aarde Cinema and Sackett's Screening Room, Phila., 1970—73; liaison/coord. pvt. fin. placements West Hollywood, Calif. Opened TV prodn. agy. Empire State Bldg., N.Y.C., Knickerbock Hotel, Hollywood, Calif., Banker's Securities Bldg., Phila., 1947; writer, prodr., dir. first TV live action film prodn. The Closed Affair Dumont TV Closed Circuit, N.Y.C., 1948; writer, prodr., dir. comedy series The Penn Family WFIL-TV, 1949; concert impresario, 49; dir., prodr. all-star

mil. prodn. Death of a Salesman, Earle Theatre, Phila., 1952; originator/operator Silent Movie Nickelodeon Theater, N.Y.C.; film actor Eroticon, Bad Girls Go To Hell; personal rep. Erlanger Theater, New Locust Theatre; entertainment dir. Carlos 'n Charlies Night Club, Hollywood. Writer, prodr., dir.: (weekly musical comedy) What a Show; Playtime; (weekly satirical soap opera) Rough in the E.T.; (weekly TV series) The Gypsy Markoff Show; Bret Morrison and Lucille Manner Musical Review; Rehearsal with Maggie Teyte; talent coord.: United Nations Musical Review; presenter: concerts Acad. of Music, Witherspoon Concert Hall; presenter: (concerts) Town Hall; writer, prodr.: (films) Eroticon; All Men Are Apes; Nickelodeon Days; Sweet Smell of Sex. Mem. Hollywood C. of C., Beverly Hills C. of C., West. Hollywood C. of C. Served with U.S. Army, 1943—45, WWII. Achievements include designing world's only three-stage musical theatre, Music-Go-Round Playhouse; interviewed hundreds of famous people from world of sports, theater, film and politics including Debbie Reynolds, Joan Crawford, Sugar Ray Robinson, Bette Davis, Charlton Heston, Otto Preminger, Alfred Hitchcock, Gary Cooper, John Wayne, Sammy Davis, Jr., Henry Fonda, and Hedy Lamarr; exclusive on-stage celebrity interviewer for Stanley Warner Motion Picture Theatres, Phila.; writer, prodr., dir. 71st Annual Easter Sunrise Svc. Office: 1311 N Fairfax Ave Ste 15 West Hollywood CA 90046 Office Phone: 323-851-8842. E-mail: promethean@sbcglobal.net.

**SACKETT, SUSAN DEANNA**, writer; b. NYC, Dec. 18, 1943; adopted d. Maxwell and Gertrude Selma (Kugel) S. BA in Edn., U. Fla., 1964, MEd, 1965. Tchr. Dade County Schs., Miami, Fla., 1966-68, L.A. City Schs., 1968-69; asst. publicist, comml. coord. NBC-TV, Burbank, Calif., 1970-73; asst. to Gene Roddenberry, creator Star Trek, 1974-91; prodn. assoc. TV series Star Trek: The Next Generation, 1987-91, writer, 1990-91. Lectr. and guest spkr. Star Trek convs. in U.S., Eng., Australia, 1974-. Author, editor: Letters to Star Trek, 1977; co-author: Star Trek Speaks, The Making of Star Trek--The Motion Picture, 1979, You Can Be a Game Show Contestant and Win, 1982; Say Goodnight Gracie, 1986; author: The Hollywood Reporter Book of Box Office Hits, 1990, 2d edit., 1996, Prime Time Hits, 1993, Hollywood Sings, 1995, Inside Trek: My Secret Life with Star Trek Creator Gene Roddenberry, 2002. Mem. ACLU, Writers Guild Am., Nat. Writers Union, Am. Humanist Assn., Humanist Soc. Greater Phoenix (pres. 2000—), Mensa, Sierra Club, Am. Humanist Assn. (bd. dirs. 2005—). Democrat.

**SACKHEIM, ROBERT LEWIS**, aerospace engineer, educator; b. NYC, May 16, 1937; s. A. Frederick and Lillian L. (Emmer) S.; m. Babette Freund, Jan. 12, 1964; children: Karen Holly, Andrew Frederick. BSChemE, U. Va., 1959; MSChemE, Columbia U., 1961; postgrad., UCLA, 1966—72. Project engr. Comsat Corp., El Segundo, Calif., 1969-72; project mgr. TRW, Redondo Beach, Calif., 1964-69, sect. head, 1972-76, dept. mgr., 1976-81, mgr. new bus., 1981-86, lab. mgr., 1986-90, dep. ctr. dir., 1990-93, ctr. dir., 1993-99; asst. dir, chief engr. for space propulsion systems Marshall Space Flight Ctr, NASA, Huntsville, Ala., 1999—2006; adj. prof. mech. and aerospace engring. U. Ala., Huntsville, 2006—; ind. cons. in space and launch vehicles and propulsion sys. and tech. Instr. UCLA engring. ext., 1986, Continuing Engring. Edn., U. Ala., Huntsville, 2001; mem. adv. bds. NASA, Washington, 1989—; mem. peer rev. bd. various univs. and govtl. agys., 1990—; mem. Nat. Rsch. Coun./Aeronautics and Space Engring. Bd., 1994—; mem. NRC com. propulsion evaluation, 2003; mem. various NASA investigation teams; guest lectr. various univs. and AIAA short courses. Author: Space Mission Analysis and Design, 1991, Space Propulsion Analysis and Design, 1994, Space Launch and Transportation Systems, 2004; contbr. chpt. to book, more than 250 articles to profl. jours., confs. Mem. adv. bd. L.A. Bd. Edn., 1990-92; fund raiser March of Dimes, L.A., 1970-90, YMCA. San Pedro, Calif., 1974-86. Capt. USAF Reserve, 1960-63. Recipient 16 Group Achievement awards NASA, 1970, 78, 86, 2000, 2001, 2003, 2005, Sustained Svc. award AIAA, 2000, medal for outstanding tech. leadership NASA, Propulsion Outstanding Contbns. award French Acad. Aero/Astro., 2002, NASA/Dir.'s commendation, 2003, Presdl. Rank award for disting. fed. civil svc., 3 ann. TRW Chmn. awards, TRW PAtent of Yr. award, 1992, Govs. award for disting. svc. state Ala., 2004. Fellow AIAA (chmn. com. 1980-83, chmn. L.A. sect. 1997, chmn. Ala./Miss. sect. 2000, 2001, J.H. Wyld Propulsion award 1992, Shuttle Flag award 1984, Martin Schilling award 2001, Hermann Oberth award 2002, Holgar Toftoy award 2003), Internat. Acad. Astronautics, Nat. Acad. Engring., Sigma Xi. Achievements include patents in field. Office: Marshall Space Flight Ctr Huntsville AL 35812 Office Phone: 256-824-5121. Business E-Mail: bob.sackheim@nasa.gov, sackheir@uah.edu.

**SACKLER, MORTIMER D.A.**, pharmaceutical executive; BA, MD, Harvard U.; MBA, NYU. Founder, chmn., co-CEO Purdue Pharma LP; bd. mem. eMagin Corp. Bd. trustees Solomon R. Guggenheim Mus. Office: Purdue Pharma LP One Stamford Forum 201 Tresser Blvd Stamford CT 06901 Home: 15 E 62nd St New York NY 10021 Office Phone: 203-588-8000.

**SACKMANN, INGE-JULIANA**, astrophysicist; b. Schönau, Germany, Feb. 8, 1942; came to U.S., 1971; d. Emil Sackmann and Lilly Stelter; m. Robert Frederick Christy, Aug. 4, 1973; children: Ilia Juliana Lilly Christy, Alexandra Roberta Christy. BA, U. Toronto, Ont., Can., 1963, MA, 1965, PhD, 1968. Postdoctoral fellow U. Göttingen, Germany, 1968-69, Max-Planck-Inst. for Physics and Astrophysics, Munich, 1969-71; rsch. assoc. U. Hamburg Obs., Germany, 1971, Jet Propulsion Labs., Pasadena, 1974-76; rsch. fellow Calif. Inst. Tech., Pasadena, 1971-74, sr. rsch. fellow, 1976-81, faculty assoc., 1981—. Recipient Zonta Club award in math. and physics, 1961-62, Math. and Physics Soc. prize, 1962-63, AAAS award in math. and physics, 1962-63, McLennan prize in math. and physics, 1963-64, Loudon Gold medal in math. and physics, 1963-64, Chant award, 1963-64, Alexander von Humboldt award, 1970-71; co-recipient B'nai B'rith award, 1961-62; 1st alumni scholar U. Toronto, 1959-60, 60-61, Ont. scholar, 1959-60, 1st Alumni scholar, 1962-63, Phi Beta scholar, 1962 64, Nat. Rsch. Coun. Coun w/schp 1963-64, 64-65, 66-67, 68-69, 69-70; U. Toronto Open fellow, 1965-66. Mem. Internat. Astron. Union, Am. Astron. Soc., Orgn. of Women in Sci. Achievements include scientific findings in carbon creation, preditions of lively future of the sun. Home: 1230 Arden Rd Pasadena CA 91106-4146 Office: U Calif Inst Tech 1201 E California Blvd Pasadena CA 91125-0001 E-mail: ijsekrl@caltech.edu.

**SACKS, CHARLES BERNARD**, psychiatrist, educator; b. Cleve., May 14, 1939; s. Jerry and Frances (Shifrin) S.; m. Lora Jane Glickman, May 2, 1993; children: Eliza, Aaron. BA, Ohio State U., 1961, MD, 1965. Staff psychiatrist Washington Vets. Hosp., 1971-77; asst. clin. prof. Georgetown U., Washington, 1971—; staff psychiatrist Reston Clinic. Fairfax City, Md., 1976-77, Drug Treatment Adminstrn., Washington, 1971-72. Washington Free Clinic, 1971-73, Arlington & Fairfax City Hosp., 1977-88, Group Health Assocs., Washington, 1984-86; psychiatrist pvt. practice, McLean Va., 1977—; Greenbelt, Md., 1977—; dir. Chevy Chase Psychiat. Clinic, Washington, 1987-89; Mt. Vernon Mental Health Ctr., 1994—. Maj. U.S. Army, 1969-71. Decorated Bronze medal with Oak Leaf Cluster. Mem. Am. Psychiat. Assn. Avocations: sailing, photography, music, reading, sports. Office: 6201 Greenbelt Rd College Park MD 20740-2354 also: 1313 Vincent Pl Mc Lean VA 22101-3615 Office Phone: 703-821-1017.

**SACKS, HERBERT SIMEON**, psychiatrist, educator, consultant; b. NYC, Nov. 29, 1926; s. Maxwell Lawrence and Anne (Edelstein) S.; m. Helen Margery Levin, Dec. 26, 1948; children— Eric Livingston, Katharine Bird, Douglas Lowell, Russell Avery AB magna cum laude, Dickinson Coll., 1948; MD, Cornell U., 1952. Diplomate Am. Bd. Psychiatry and Neurology and subspecialty Child and Adolescent Psychiatry. Clin. assoc. Western New Eng. Psychoanalytic Inst., New Haven, 1955-63; intern in pediatrics Yale-New Haven Med. Ctr., 1952-53; jr. asst. resident in psychiatry Yale Psychiat. Inst., 1953-54; sr. asst. resident in psychiatry, USPHS fellow Yale-New Haven Med. Ctr. psychiat. out patient dept., 1954-55; USPHS fellow in child psychiatry Yale U. Child Study Ctr., 1955-57; clin. dir. Mid-Fairfield Child Guidance Ctr., Norwalk, Conn., 1957-59; cons. Expt. in Internat. Living, Putney, Vt., 1962-69; sr. cons. U.S. Peace Corps, Washington, 1962-69; cons. AID, U.S. Dept. State, Office of Sahel, West Africa, 1974-84, Neurosci.

Consultation Group, Grosse Point Farms, Mich., 1984-94; clin. prof. child and adolescent psychiatry Child Study Ctr., Yale U. Sch. Medicine, New Haven. Co-investigator, co-dir. Senegal River pilot health research program, New Haven and West Africa, 1976-78, co-investigator, co-dir. health sector, design team Senegal River integrated devel. project, 1981-83; vis. lectr. Yale Coll., 1969-71; mem. com. reviewers Dept. Commerce Nat. Bur. Standards, Inst. for Computer Scis. and Tech., Washington, 1975-77; mem. exec. com. Nat. Commn. on Confidentiality of Health Records, 1975-80 Author: Hurdles: The Admissions Dilemma in American Higher Education, 1978; contbg. author chpts. in books, articles on confidentiality, juvenile justice, higher edn., issues of youth in transition, other topics; author monographs Mem. Conn. Juvenile Justice Commn., Hartford, 1975-80; bd. advisors Dickinson Coll., Carlisle, Pa., 1980-85. Served to lt. (j.g.) U.S. Navy, 1944-46; PTO Fellow AMA, ACPO, Am. Psychiat. Assn. (trustee 1988-94, v.p. 1994-96, pres. 1997-98), Am. Acad. Child and Adolescent Psychiatry, Am. Orthopsychiat. Assn., Am. Coll. Psychiatrists; mem. Conn. Psychiat. Soc. (pres. 1976-77), Conn. Coun. Child and Adolescent Psychiatrists (pres. 1972-73), World Fedn. for Mental Health, Phi Beta Kappa. Avocations: farming, photography, fishing, lawn bowling. Home: 110 Laurel Rd New Haven CT 06515-2426 Office: 260 Riverside Ave Westport CT 06880-4804 also: Yale U Child Study Ctr PO Box 207900 New Haven CT 06520-7900 Office Phone: 203-227-0996.

**SACKS. IRA STEPHEN**, lawyer; b. NYC, Dec. 6, 1948; s. Marvin Leonard and Mildred (Finkelstein) S.; m. Deborah DiNolfo; children: James, Jennifer, Allison, Gillian. BS, MIT, 1970; JD, Georgetown U., 1974. Bar: N.Y. 1975, U.S. Dist. Ct. (so. and ea. dists.) N.Y. 1975, U.S. Ct. Appeals (2d cir.) 1975, U.S. Ct. Appeals (3d cir.) 1984, U.S. Supreme Ct. 1985, U.S. Ct. Appeals (9th cir.) 1986, U.S. Ct. Appeals (11th cir.) 1987, U.S. Ct. Appeals (D.C. and fed. cirs.) 1993. Assoc. Kaye, Scholer, Fierman, Hays & Handler, N.Y.C., 1974-82, ptnr., 1983-87, Fried, Frank, Harris, Shriver & Jacobson, N.Y.C., 1988—2003, Gursky and Ptnrs., N.Y., NY, 2003—05, Dreier LLP, N.Y.C., 2005—. Contbr. articles to profl. jours. NSF fellow, 1970. Mem. ABA, Supreme Ct. Hist. Soc., N.Y. State Bar Assn., Assn. of Bar of City of N.Y. Democrat. Jewish. Avocations: tennis, skiing. Home: 105 Old Colony Rd Hartsdale NY 10530-3610 Office: Dreier LLP 499 Park Ave New York NY 10022 Office Phone: 212-652-3730. Business E-Mail: isacks@dreierllp.com. E-mail: isacks@aol.com.

**SACKS, OLIVER WOLF**, neurologist, writer; b. London, July 9, 1933; Came to U.S., 1960; s. Samuel and Muriel Elsie (Landau) S. BA, U. Oxford, 1954; MA, BM, BCh, Middlesex Hosp., London, 1958; DHL (hon.), Georgetown U., 1990, Coll. Staten Island, CUNY, 1991; DS (hon.), Tufts U., 1991, N.Y. Med. Coll., 1991; DS (hon.), Med. Coll. Pa., 1992, Bard Coll., 1992, U. Turin, 2003. Intern in medicine, surgery and neurology Middlesex Hosp., 1958-60; rotating intern Mt. Zion Hosp., San Francisco 1961-62; resident in neurology UCLA, 1962-65; I.D. fellow in neuropathology and neurochemistry Albert Einstein Coll. Medicine, N.Y.C., 1965-66, instr. neurology, 1966-75, asst. prof., 1975-78, assoc. prof., 1978-85, clin. prof. neurology, 1985—. Adj. prof. psychiatry NYU, 1992-; sci. advisor Inst. Music and Neurologic Function, Beth Abraham Hosp., 1995-; cons. neurologist Comprehensive Epilepsy Ctr., Mt. Sinai Med. Ctr., 1999-; cons., speaker, lectr. in field; hon. lectureships in field. Author: Migraine, 1970, Awakenings, 1973, rev. paperback edit., 1990 (Hawthornden prize 1975), A Leg To Stand On, 1984, The Man Who Mistook His Wife for a Hat, 1985, Seeing Voices: A Journey into the World of the Deaf, 1989 (Mainichi Pub. Culture award 1996), An Anthropologist on Mars, 1995 (George S. Polk award for mag. reporting 1994, Nat. Assn. Sci. Writers award 1994, Esquire Apple Waterstone's Book of Yr. 1995), The Island of the Color Blind, 1996, Uncle Tungsten, 2001, Oaxaca Jour., 2002. Bd. mem. N.Y. Bot. Garden. Recipient Oskar Pfister award APA, 1988, Harold D. Vursell Meml. award Am. Acad. and Inst. Arts and Letters, 1989, Communicator of Yr. Royal Nat. Inst. Deaf, 1991, Lewis Thomas prize Rockefeller U., 2002, Sloan Found. award, 2002, Pub. Comm. award NSF, 2004; Guggenheim fellow, 1989, others. Fellow Am. Acad. Arts and Scis., Am. Acad. Arts and Letters, NY Acad. Scis. (hon.); mem. Am. Acad. Neurology (presdl. citation 1991), Am. Fern Soc., Am. Neurological Assn. (hon.), Assn. Brit. Neurologists (hon.), Brit. Pteridological Soc., NY Mineralogical Club, NY Stereoscopic Soc., Soc. Neurosci., NY Inst. Humanities, Alpha Omega Alpha. Office: 2 Horatio St Apt 3G New York NY 10014-1638

**SACKS, PATRICIA ANN**, librarian, consultant; b. Allentown, Pa., Nov. 6, 1939; d. Lloyd Alva and Dorothy Estelle (Stoneback) Stahl; m. Kenneth LeRoy Sacks, June 27, 1959. AB, Cedar Crest Coll., 1959; MS in Libr. Sci., Drexel U., 1965. News reporter Call-Chronicle, Allentown, 1956-59, 61-63; reference libr. Cedar Crest Coll., Allentown, 1964-66, head libr., 1966-73; dir. librs. Muhlenberg and Cedar Crest Colls., Allentown, 1973-94; dir. libr. svcs. Cedar Crest Coll., 1994; sr. fellow Lehigh Valley Assn. Ind. Colls., 1994-97, Ctr. Agile Ptnrs. in Edn., 1997-98; info. svcs. cons., 1998—. Del. On Line Computer Library Ctr. Users Council, Columbus, Ohio, 1977-84; cons. colls./health care orgns., libr. orgns. 1981—. Author: (with Whildin Sara Lou) Preparing for Accreditation: A Handbook for Academic Librarians, 1993; mem. editl. bd. Jour. Acad. Librarianship, 1982-84. Mem. United Way Lehigh Valley Coms., 1993—97; trustee Cedar Crest Coll., 1985—89; bd. dirs John and Dorothy Morgan Cancer Ctr., 1994—96; mem. cmty. concert bd. Allentown, Pa., 2003—. Named Outstanding Acad. Woman, Lehigh Valley Assn. for Acad. Women, 1984, Muhlenberg Coll. Outstanding Adminstr., 1987, Alumni Tricorn awrd Muhlenberg Coll., 1989, Alumnae Achievement award Cedar Crest Coll., 1994. Mem. ALA (chmn. copyright com. 1985-87), Assn. Coll. and Rsch. Librs. (chmn. stds. and accreditation com. 1976-78, 81-84), Lehigh Valley Assn. Ind. Colls. (chmn. librs. sect. 1967-81, 88-92), AAUW, LWV, Wildlands Conservancy, Appalachian Mountain Club (Echo Lake naturalist 1997—), Phi Alpha Theta, Phi Kappa Phi, Beta Phi Mu. Democrat. Home: 2007 Fairfield Dr Allentown PA 18103 3413 Personal E-mail: sackspa@ptd.net.

**SACKS, ROBERT A.**, lawyer; b. Long Beach, NY, 1957; AB, Harvard U., 1979; JD, U. Tex., 1982. Bar: NY 1983, Calif. 1990. Assoc. Sullivan & Cromwell, NYC, 1984—90, ptnr. litig. LA, 1990—, now ptnr.-in-charge LA office. Mem.: ABA. Office: Sullivan & Cromwell 1888 Century Pk E Los Angeles CA 90067-1725 Office Phone: 310-712-6600. Office Fax: 310-712-8800. Business E-Mail: sacksr@sullcrom.com.

**SACKS, TEMI J.**, public relations executive; b. Phila. d. Jule and Adeline (Levin) S. BA, Temple U. Pubs. editor Del. Valley Regional Planning Commn., Phila.; comms. assoc. Fedn. Jewish Agys., Phila.; exec, v.p., mng. dir. consumer and healthcare divsns. Lobsenz-Stevens Inc., N.Y.C.; exec. v.p., dir. nat. healthcare practice Shandwick, N.Y.C.; sr. v.p. Noonan-Russo, N.Y.C.; pres. T.J. Sacks & Assocs. Inc., N.Y.C. Mem. Healthcare Businesswomen's Assn., Healtcare Mktg. Assn., Women Execs. in Pub. Rels. Avocations: painting, skiing, jewelry design, antiques. Office Phone: 212-787-0787. Personal E-mail: tjsacks@tjsacks.com.

**SACKSTEDER, THOMAS MICHAEL**, corporate financial executive, entrepreneur, writer; b. Dayton, Ohio, July 20, 1950; s. Harry Pius and Mary Kay (Liebhardt) S.; m. Teresa Ann Nevius, Oct. 12, 1968 (div. Sept. 1980); children: Lori Ann, Kristi Marie, Julie Kay. Student, Sinclair Community Coll., 1968-72, Wright State U., 1972-73, Grand Valley State Coll., 1978-79, Lourdes Coll., 1994-95. Installer Western Electric, Dayton, 1969-70; sales rep. Smith Corona Mcht., Dayton, 1969-70; office mgr. Indsl. Machinery, Dayton, 1970-71; advisor Bell Pub. Rels., Dayton, 1972-73; sales mgr. Washington Nat. Ins., Dayton, 1974-81, Am. Fidelity Assurance Co., 1981-95; gen. ptnr. Innovative Benefits Resource Ltd., 1995—. Gen. ptnr., Annuity Compliance Specialists, ptnr., Christopher Blake Family Wellness Assn., benefits cons. Ind. State Tchrs. Assn. Ins. Trust, Indpls., 1986-91. Bd. dirs. Mental Health Assn., Dayton, 1971-75, Good Samaritan Mental Health Ctr., 1972-75; campaign mgmt. for polit. candidates and issue oriented policies, 1972—. Mem. Ohio Assn. Sch. Bus. Ofcls. (legis. com. 1993-95), Assn. of Sch. Bus. Ofcls., Natl. Tax Shelter Annuity Assn., Employers Counc. on Flexible Compensation, Natl. Assn. of Life Underwriters, Buckeye Assn. Sch.

Adminstrs., Jaycees, Kiwanis. Roman Catholic. Avocations: golf, swimming, writing, research, martial arts. Address: Innovative Benefits Resource Ltd Annuity Compliance Specialists PO Box 70 Holland OH 43528-0070 E-mail: tom.sacksteder@Ibracs.com.

**SACKTON, FRANK JOSEPH,** public affairs educator; b. Chgo., Aug. 11, 1912; m. June Dorothy Raymond, Sept. 21, 1940. Student, Northwestern U., Evanston, Ill., 1936, Yale U., New Haven, Conn., 1946, U. Md., College Park, 1951—52; BS, U. Md., 1970; grad., Command and Gen. Staff Coll., 1942, Armed Forces Staff Coll., 1949, Nat. War Coll., 1954; MPA, Ariz. State U., 1976, DHL (hon.), 1996. Mem. 131st Inf. Regt., Ill. N.G., 1929-40; commd. 2d lt. U.S. Army, 1934, advanced through grades to lt. gen., 1967; brigade plans and ops. officer (33d Inf. Div.), 1941, PTO, 1943-45; div. signal officer, 1942-43; div. intelligence officer, 1944; div. plans and ops. officer, 1945; sec. to gen. staff for Gen. MacArthur Tokyo, 1947-48; bn. comdr. 30th Inf. Regt., 1949-50; mem. spl. staff Dept. Army, 1951; plans and ops. officer Joint Task Force 132, PTO, 1952; comdr. Joint Task Force 7, Marshall Islands, 1953; mem. gen. staff Dept. Army, 1954-55; with Office Sec. Def., 1956; comdr. 18th Inf. Regt., 1957-58; chief staff 1st Inf. Div., 1959; chief army Mil. Mission to Turkey, 1960-62; comdr. XIV Army Corps, 1963; dep. dir. plans Joint Chiefs Staff, 1964-66; army general staff mil. ops., 1966-67; comptroller of the army, 1967-70; ret., 1970; spl. asst. for fed./state relations Gov. Ariz., 1971-75; chmn. Ariz. Programming and Coordinating Com. for Fed. Programs, 1971-75; lectr. Am. Grad. Sch. Internat. Mgmt., 1973-77; vis. asst. prof., lectr. public affairs Ariz. State U., Tempe, 1976-78; founding dean Ariz. State U. Coll. Public Programs, 1979-80; prof. public affairs Ariz. State U., 1980—, finance educator, v.p. bus. affairs, 1981-83, dep. dir. intercollegiate athletics, 1984-85, dir. strategic planning, 1987-88. Contbr. articles to public affairs and mil. jours. Mem. Ariz. Steering Com. for Restoration of the State Capitol, 1974-75, Ariz. State Personnel Bd., 1987-83, Ariz. Regulatory Coun., 1981-93. Decorated D.S.M., Silver Star, also Legion of Merit with 4 oak leaf clusters, Bronze Star with 2 oak leaf clusters, Air medal, Army Commendation medal with 1 oak leaf cluster, Combat Inf. badge. Mem.: Ariz. Acad. Public Adminstrn., Army-Navy Club (Washington), Arizona Country Club (Phoenix), Pi Alpha Alpha (pres. chpt. 1976—82). Home: 12000 N 90th St Unit 3072 Scottsdale AZ 85260-8643 Office: Ariz State U Sch Pub Affairs Tempe AZ 85287-0603 Business E-Mail: frank-sackton@asu.edu.

**SACLARIDES, THEODORE JOHN,** colon and rectal surgeon, educator; b. Clearwater, Fla., Oct. 12, 1956; s. Constantine Peter and Evelyn (Tsangaris) Saclarides; m. Elena Economou, July 12, 1980; children: Kathryn, Stephanie, Constantine, Alexandra, Theodora. BA, Vanderbilt U., 1978; MD, U. Miami, 1982. Asst. prof. to assoc. prof. of surgery Rush U., Chgo., 1985—, head, colorectal surgery, 1991—. Editor: The Female Pelvic Floor, 1996, Common Surgical Problems, 2002, Surgical Oncology, 2003. Office: Rush U 1653 W Congress Chicago IL 60612 Office Phone: 312-942-6519. Office Fax: 312-942-2867.

**SACOFF, ROBERT W.,** lawyer; m. Mary Colnon; children: Colin, Lydon. BA, U. Notre Dame, 1969; JD, Northwestern U. Sch. Law, 1973. Bar: Ill. Ptnr. Pattishall, McAuliffe et al., Ill., 1987—. Chair, sect. intellectual property law ABA, Chgo., 2003—04; pres. AIPPI US, 2004—. Office: Pattishall McAuliffe et al 311 S Wacker Dr Chicago IL 60606 Office Phone: 312-554-7934. Office Fax: 312-554-8015. Business E-Mail: rws@pattishall.com.

**SACRIPANTI, PETER JOHN,** lawyer; b. 1955; BA summa cum laude, Fordham U., 1982; JD, Pace U., 1984. Fed. prosecutor U.S. Dept. Justice; ptnr., mem. firm exec. mgmt. com. McDermott Will & Emery LLP. Recipient Ellis Island Medal Hon., 2001. Mem.: N.J. Bar Assn., D.C. Bar Assn., N.Y. Bar Assn. Office: McDermott Will & Emery LLP 50 Rockefeller Plz 11th Fl New York NY 10020-1605 Office Phone: 212-547-5583. Office Fax: 212-547-5444. Business E-Mail: psacripanti@mwe.com.

**SADAN, MARK,** photographer, film producer, artist; AA, Am. Acad. Dramatic Arts, N.Y.C., 1963; MFA, NYU, 1969; MEd, U. Mass., Amherst, 1974. Pres., dir. Kiva Film, N.Y., Mass., 1969—75; prodr., dir. short films Sesame St., 1969—72; dir., photo film unit Anti Poverty Program, N.Y.C., 1966—67. Cineprobes, 1969—73, The Mus. of Modern Art, N.Y.C., 1970—72, artist (films) Rosebud, Laughing Bear, Ann Arbor Film Festival, 1965—68, prodr., dir. Ecology Probe Planet Earth 74, The New Norway 81, photographer (books) Meditations of the Blessed Beauty, Tablet of Carmel, 1990—93; one-man shows include Nat. Photo Gallery, Riga, Latvia, 1989—90, Golden Lands, Golden Dreams, 2004, Mus. of New Art, 2005, Nat. Mus. of Dance and Hall of Fame, 2004—, exhibitions include Am. Mus. Dance, 2000—02; contbr. photographs pub. to profl. jour. Recipient Medal of Excellence for Photographic Art, Latvian Nat. Photographic Soc., 1990, Cine Golden Eagle, Cine Film Awards, 2003. Mem.: Sunday Photo Group (dir., lectr. 1982—2004), Film Video Workshop (founder, dir. 1969—74). Avocations: dance, photography, swimming, travel, movies. Home: PO Box 207 Ossining NY 10562 Office Phone: 914-762-0219. Personal E-mail: marksadan13@hotmail.com.

**SADAO, SHOJI,** architect; b. Los Angeles, Jan. 2, 1927; s. Riichi and Otatsu (Kodama) S.; m. Tsuneko Sawada, Apr. 8, 1972. B.Arch., Cornell U., 1954; Fulbright scholar, Waseda U., Tokyo, 1956-57. Designer Geodesics, Inc., Raleigh, N.C., 1954-56; job capt. Edison Price, Inc., N.Y.C., 1959-64; v.p. Fuller & Sadao (P.C.), Long Island City, N.Y., 1965—. Assoc. prof. archtl. design Sch. Architecture and Environ. Design, SUNY, Buffalo, 1976-77. Works include Dymaxion World Map, 1954; co-designer works include, U.S. Pavilion at Montreal Expo 67. Trustee Isamu Noguchi Found., Long Island City, N.Y., 1967—, exec. dir., 1989-2003; trustee Buckminster Fuller Inst. With AUS, 1945-49. Mem.: The Century Assn., Japan Soc. Address: Fuller & Sadao 33-38 10th St Long Island City NY 11106-4926

**SADDLEMYER, ANN (ELEANOR SADDLEMYER),** humanities educator, critic, theater historian; b. Prince Albert, Sask., Can., Nov. 28, 1932; d. Orrin Angus and Elsie Sarah (Ellis) S. BA, U. Sask., 1953, DLitt, 1991; MA, Queen's U., 1956, LLD (hon.), 1977; PhD, U. London, 1961; DLitt (hon.), U. Victoria, 1989, McGill U., 1989, Windsor U., 1990, U. Toronto, 1999, Concordia U., 2000. Lectr. Victoria Coll., BC, 1956-57, instr. BC, 1960-62, asst. prof. BC, 1962-65; assoc. prof. U. Victoria, 1965-68, prof. English, 1968-71, Victoria Coll. U. Toronto, 1971-95; prof., dir. Grad. Ctr. for Study of Drama, U. Toronto, 1977-79, 85-86, prof. emerita Dept. English, Comparative Lit., 1995—; sr. fellow Massey Coll., 1975-88, master, 1988-95, master emerita, 1995—; Berg prof. NYU, 1975. Adj. prof. U. Victoria; dir. Hedgerow Press; mem. heritage adv. commn. North Saanich, 2004—06. Dir. Theatre Plus, 1972-84; dir. Colin Smythe Pubs.; author: (with Robin Skelton) The World of W.B. Yeats, 1965, In Defence of Lady Gregory, Playwright, 1966, Synge and Modern Comedy, 1968, J.M. Synge Plays Books One and Two, 1968, Lady Gregory Plays, 4 vols., 1970, Letters to Molly: Synge to Maire O'Neill, 1971, Letters from Synge to W.B. Yeats and Lady Gregory, 1971, Collected Letters of John Millington Synge, Vol. I, 1983, vol. II, 1984, Theatre Business, The Correspondence of the First Abbey Theatre Directors, 1982, (with Colin Smythe) Lady Gregory Fifty Years After, 1987, Early Stages: Theatre in Ontario, 1980-1914, 1990, J.M. Synge: The Playboy of the Western World and Other Plays, 1995; (with Richard Plant) Later Stages: Theatre in Ontario, 1914-1970s, 1997, Becoming George--The Life of Mrs. W.B. Yeats, 2002; co-editor Theatre History in Canada, 1980-86, Selected Irish Drama, 1972-82, English Studies in Can., 1973-83, Themes in Drama, 1974-93, Shaw Ann., 1977—, Research in the Humanities, 1976-90; Irish Univ. Rev., 1970—, Yeats Ann., 1982-86; Studies in Contemporary Irish Lit., 1986—, Irish Studies Rev., 1997—; contbr. articles to profl. jours. Recipient Brit. Acad. Rose Mary Crawshay award, 1986, Disting. Svc. award Province of Ont., 1985, U. Toronto Alumni award of excellence, 1991, award yeats Soc. NY 2001; named Disting. Dau. of Pa., 1992, Woman of Distinction in Letters, Toronto, YWCA, 1994; Officer of Order of Can., 1995; Can. Coun. scholar, 1958-59, fellow, 1968, Guggenheim fellow, 1968, 77, sr. rsch. fellow Connaught, 1985. Fellow Royal Soc. Can., Royal Soc. Arts; mem. Internat.

Assn. Study Irish Lit. (chmn. 1973-76), Assn. Can. Theatre Rsch. (pres. 1976-77), Can. Assn. Irish Studies, Assn. Can. Coll. and Univ. Tchrs. English. Home: 10876 Madrona Dr North Saanich BC Canada V8L 5N9 Personal E-mail: saddlemy@uvic.ca.

**SADDLER, DONALD EDWARD,** choreographer, dancer; b. Van Nuys, Calif., Jan. 24, 1920; s. Elmer Edward and Mary Elizabeth (Roberts) Saddler. Student, Los Angeles City Coll., 1939; dance pupil of, Carmalita Maracci, Anton Dolin, Anthony Tudor, Madame Anderson Ivantzova. Mem. Ballet Theatre, NYC, 1940-43, 46-47; asst. dir., then artistic dir. Harkness Ballet, NYC, 1964-70. Exec. v.p. Rebekah Harkness Found., 1967—69; mem. exec. bd. Internat. Ballet Corp., 1979; prodr. Delacorte Theatre NY Dance Festival; guest artist Valerie Bettis Co. Dancer Grand Canyon Suite, 1937, High Button Shoes, 1947, Dance Me a Song, 1950, Bless You All, 1950, The Song of Norway, 1951, Winesburg, Ohio, 1958, The Golden Round, 1960, The Castle Period, 1961, Happy Birthday, Mr. Abbot!, 1987, with Ballet Theatre, NYC Bluebeard, Billy the Kid, Swan Lake, Aurora's Wedding, Les patineus, Lilac Garden, Gala Performance, Romeo and Juliet, Peter and the Wolf, Follies, 2001; dir.: (TV films) Holiday Hotel, 1950; choreographer theatre Blue Mountain Ballads, 1948, Wish You Were Here, 1952, Wonderful Town, 1952, John Murray Anderson's Almanac, 1953, Tobia la Candida Spia, 1954, La patrona di raddio di luna, 1955, Shangri-La, 1956, Buona notte Bettina, 1956, L'adorabile Giulio, 1957, Winesburg, Ohio, 1958, This Property is Condemned, 1958, Un trapezio per Lisistrata, 1958, When in Rome, 1959, Un mandarino per Teo, 1959, Dreams of Glory, 1961, Milk and Honey, 1961, Sophie, 1963, Morning Sun, 1963, To Broadway, With Love, 1964, No, No, Nanette, 1971, Much Ado About Nothing, 1972, Fanfare Gala, 1973, Good News, 1973, Tricks, 1973, The Merry Wives of Windsor, 1974, Miss Moffat, 1974, A Midsummer Night's Dream, 1975, A Doll's House, 1975, A Gala Tribute to Joshua Logan, 1975, Rodgers and Hart, 1975, The Robber Bridegroom, 1975, 1976, Koshare, 1976, Vaudeville, 1976, Dear Friends and Gentle Hearts, 1976, Icedancing, 1978, The Grand Tour, 1979, A Long Way to Boston, 1979, Happy New Year, 1980, Hey Look Me Over!, 1981, Pardon, Monsieur Moliere, 1982, On Your Toes, 1983, The Loves of Anatol, 1985, The Golden Land, 1985, Broadway, 1987, The Student Prince, 1987, Teddy and Alice, 1987, My Fair Lady, 1993, tours The Boys from Syracuse, Aida, La Perichole, The Merry Widow, Tropicana, We Take This Town, 1962, Knickerbocker Holiday, 1971, No, No, Nanette, 1971—73, Good News, 1973—74, Hellzapoppin', 1976—77, On Your Toes, 1984, (films) April in Paris, 1952, By the Light of the Silvery Moon, 1953, Young at Heart, 1954, The Main Attraction, 1963, The Happy Hooker, 1973, Radio Days, 1987, (TV films) Holiday Hotel, 1950, (TV series) The Perry Como Show, 1956, Canozionissima, 1959—60, Bell Telephone Hour, 1961—64, (TV films) Much Ado About Nothing, 1973, (TV miniseries) Tony Award Broadcasts, 1973, 1975—78, 1983, Verna: U.S.O. Girl, 1978; dir., choreographer tour Oh, Kay!, 1978, dir., choreographer theatre Wonderful Town, 1955, A Celebration for Sir Anton Dolin, 1984, 100 Years of Performing Arts at the Met., 1984, Kiss Me Kate, 1989, Am. Ballet Theatre's 40th Anniversary, Tribute to Lucille Lortel, Tribute to Richard Rodgers, Merman-Martin Gala, Tribute to Cy Coleman, An Evening with Kurt Weill, Jo Sullivan in Concert, Tribute to George Abbott, Tribute to Lerner and Loewe, Stratford Shakespeare Festival Gala, Am. Guild of Musical Artists 100th Anniversary Gala, dir., choreographer operas Bitter Sweet, Weiner Blut, Abduction from the Seraglio, Washington Opera Follies; dir.(theatre): Berlin to Broadway with Kurt Weill, 1972, George Abbott...A Celebration, 1976, Life with Father, 1982, I Hear Music...of Frank Loesser and Friends, 1984, State Fair Music Hall, 1957, 1959, Carousel Theatre, 1958, Stratford Shakespeare Festival, 1979; prodr.(theatre): The Sol Hurok Birthday Gala, 1973, The 30th Anniversary of City Center Theatre, 1975, (with Martin Feinstein): The Pre-Inaugural Ballet-Opera Gala, 1981,: The Dance Collection Gala, 1972, The 35th Anniversary of the Am. Ballet Theatre, 1975, The Cynthia Gregory Gala. Recipient Dance Mag. award, 1984, Lifetime Achievement award, Theatre Development Fund, 2001, Living Legend of Dance award, Dance Libr. Israel, 2001, Capezio Dance award, 2006. Address: Coleman-Rosenberg Apt 5D 155 E 55th St New York NY 10022-4051*

**SADE, DONALD STONE,** anthropology educator; b. Charleston, W.Va., July 17, 1937; s. Samuel and Charlotte Tracy (Stone) S.; m. Bonita Diane Chepko, Dec. 24, 1971 (div. Feb. 1994); children: Irony Cuervo del Norte, Omen Ondatra; m. Kerry L. Knox, Nov. 24, 1994. Grad., N.Y. State Ranger Sch., 1957; student, Hamilton Coll., 1957-60; AB, U. Calif., Berkeley, 1963, PhD, 1966. Instr. anthropology Northwestern U., Evanston, Ill., 1965-66, asst. prof., 1966-70, assoc. prof., 1970-75, prof., 1975-95, sr. lectr., 1995—97; scientist-in-charge Cayo Santiago, U. P.R., 1970-77; prof. emeritus Northwestern U., 1997—. Founder, pres. North Country Inst. for Natural Philosophy, Inc., Mexico, N.Y., 1980—. Sr. author: Basic Demographic Observations on Free-Ranging Rhesus Monkeys, 3 vols., 1985; editor: The North Country Naturalist, Vol. 1, 1987. Recipient Merit cert., Eastman Sch. Music., 2002, 2005; grantee, NSF, 1967—2006. Mem. Animal Behavior Soc., Guild Am. Luthiers, Nature Conservancy, Adirondack Mountain Club, Adirondack Coun., Classical Guitar Soc. Upstate NY. Office: North Country Inst for Natural Philosophy Inc 18 Emery Rd Mexico NY 13114-3311...and all I've done for want of wit, to memory now I can't recall. (Irish ballad).

**SADE, (HELEN FOLASADE ADU),** singer, lyricist; b. Ibadan, Nigeria, 1959; d. Adebisi Adu and Anne. BA, St. Martin's Coll. of Art, London, 1979. Mem. band Sade; recording artist Epic, A Division of Sony Music, N.Y.C. Albums include Diamond Life, 1984, Promise, 1985, Stronger Than Pride, 1988, Love Deluxe, 1992, The Best of Sade, 1994, Lovers Rock, 2000, Lovers Live, 2002; singles include Smooth Operator, 1984. Recipient Grammy award Best New Artist, 1986, Best R&B duo or group performance for "No Ordinary Love", 1994.

**SADEGH, ALI M.,** mechanical engineering educator, researcher, consultant; b. Tehran, Iran, Sept. 1, 1950; came to U.S., 1974; s. Saleh S. Mir-Mohamad-Sadegh and Asam Lotfi; m. Guita Miremadi, July 10, 1980; children: Mietra, Cameron, Mona, Jasmin, David. BSME, Arya-Mehr U. Tech., Tehran, 1972; MSME, Mich. State U., 1975, PhD in Mechanics, 1978; postgrad., U. Mich., 1979. Registered profl. engr., Mich.; cert. mfg. engr. Design engr. Nat. Radio engring. sect., Tehran, 1972-74; rsch. and teaching asst. Mich. State U., East Lansing, 1975-78; asst. prof. Arya-Mehr U. Tech., 1979-81; vis. asst. prof. Mich. State U., 1981-82; asst. prof. CUNY, N.Y.C., 1982-87, assoc. prof., 1987-91, prof., 1991—, chmn. dept. mech. engring., 1992-96, tchr. courses in solid mechanics, design and CAD/CAM. Cons. Devel. Iranian Heavy Industries, Tehran, 1979-81; tech. cons. AC Rochester Gen. Motors Co., 1986-92; forensic engr., 1990—; cons. and presenter in field. Contbr. over 120 articles to profl. jours.; 10 patents in field. U. Mich. scholar, Ann Arbor, 1978-79; recipient 46 Rsch. awards NSF, AT&T Found., PSC-CUNY, others. Fellow ASME (Best Paper award 1994, Melville medal 1993), Soc. Mfg. Engrs. (chmn. chpt. 320); mem. Am. Acad. Mechanics, Biomed. Engrs. Soc., Sigma Xi. Achievements include patents in field. Home: 787 Oneida Trl Franklin Lakes NJ 07417-2216 Office: CUNY Dept Mech Engring 140th St and Convent Ave New York NY 10031 Office Phone: 212-650-5203. Business E-Mail: sadegh@ccny.cuny.edu.

**SADEGHI-NEJAD, ABDOLLAH,** pediatrician, educator; b. Meshed, Iran, Apr. 29, 1938; s. Abdolhossein and Azizeh (Jabbari) S-N.; m. Marion M. Marquardt, Jan. 26, 1974; children: Nathan R., Adrienne R. BA, Beloit Coll., 1960; MS in Pathology, U. Chgo., 1964, MD, 1964. Diplomate Am. Bd. Pediatrics. Intern then resident U. Chgo., 1964-67; fellow pediatric endocrinology Tufts-New Eng. Med. Ctr., Boston, 1967-69, U. Calif., San Francisco, 1969-70; from asst. prof. to prof. pediatrics Tufts-New Eng. U., Boston, 1970—; chief pediatric endocrinology and metabolism divsn. New Eng. Med. Ctr., Boston, 1989—. Author and co-author books and articles. Mem. town meeting Town of Brookline, Mass., 1987-2001, 2005—, mem. adv. com., 1993-99; founder, mem. Friends of Lost Pond. Fellow Am. Acad. Pediatrics; mem. Am. Pediatric Soc., Am. Diabetes Assn., Endocrine Soc., European Soc. Pediatric Rsch., Lawson Wilkins Pediat. Endocrine Soc., Soc. Pediat. Rsch. Office: Tufts-New Eng Med Ctr 750 Washington St Boston MA 02111-1526

**SADER, CAROL HOPE,** former state legislator; b. Bklyn., July 19, 1935; d. Nathan and Mollie (Farkas) Shimkin; m. Harold M. Sader, June 9, 1957; children: Neil, Randi Sader Friedlander, Elisa Sader Waldman. BA, Barnard Coll., Columbia U., 1957. Sch. tchr. Bd. Edn., Morris, Conn., 1957-58; legal editor W. H. Anderson Co., Cin., 1974-78; freelance legal editor Shawnee Mission, Kans., 1978-87; mem. Kans. Ho. of Reps., 1987-94. Chair Ho. Pub. Health and Welfare Com., 1991-92; chair Joint Ho. and Senate Com. on Health Care Decisions for the 90's, 1992; vice chair Ho. Econ. Devel. Com., 1991-92; policy chair Ho. Dem. Caucus, 1993-94; appointee Kans. jud. qualifications commn. Kans. Supreme Ct., 1995-2004; apptd. Kans. Racing and Gaming Commn., 2003-, chmn., 2005—, Kans. State Bd. Healing Arts, 2003—. Pres. LWV, Johnson County, 1983—85; mem. State of Kans. LWV Bd., 1986—87; pres. Johnson County Found. Aging, 2002—04; mem. Johnson County Charter Commn., 1999; mem. exec. bd. Johnson County C.C. Found., 2000—03; mem. adv. group Kans. Gov.'s B.E.S.T. Team, 2002—; cmty. adv. com. Kans. REACH Found., 2003—; Dem. candidate for Kans. Lt. Gov., 1994; mem. Jewish Cmty. Rels. Bd., 1999—; chmn. bd. trustees Johnson County C.C., Overland Park, Kans., 1984—86, trustee, 1981—86; bd. dirs. United Cmty. Svcs. of Johnson County, Shawnee Mission, 1984—92, Jewish Vocat. Svc. Bd., 1983—92, House of Menuha, 1998—99, Appleseed Found. Kans., 1999—2001, Midwest Ctr. Holocaust Edn., 1999—2004, 2006—, exec. bd., 1999—2004, 2006—; chmn. Kans. State Holocaust Commn., 1991—94; pres. MAINstream Coalition, 1995—97, vice chair, 1998—2003; v.p. Kans. Advocates for Better Care, 1998—2001. Recipient Trustee award Assn. of Women in Jr. and C.C., 1985, awards Kans. Pub. Transit Assn., 1990, AARP, 1992, Assn. Kans. Theater, 1992, Nat. Coun. Jewish Women, 1992, Kans. Assn. Osteo. Medicine, 1992, Kans. Chiropractic Assn., 1992, United Com. Svcs. Johnson County, 1992, Disting. Pub. Svcs. award Johnson County, 1993, Hallpac Kans. Pub. Svc. award Hallmark Cards, Inc., 1993, Eddie Jacobsen award B'nai B'rith, 1994, Cmty. Svc. award House of Menuha, 1998, The Pillar award Greater K.C. Women's Political Caucus, 2003, Stand-Up, Speak-Out award Mainstream Coalition, 2003. Republican. Democrat. Avocations: landscape, theater, travel. Home: 8612 Linden Dr Shawnee Mission KS 66207-1807

**SADICK, NEIL SCOTT,** dermatologist; b. Bronx, NY, June 1, 1951; s. Harry and Shirley (Tompkins) Sadick; 1 child, Sydney Kamin. BA, SUNY, Binghamton, 1973; MD, SUNY, Syracuse, 1977. Diplomate Am. Bd. Internal Medicine, 1980, Am. Bd. Dermatology, 1983, Am. Acad. Cosmetic Surgery, 2000, Am. Bd. Hair Restoration Surgery, 2001. Pvt. practice, NYC, 1983—; mem. adv. bd. Dermatologic Soc. Greater NY, 1994—; clin. prof. dermatology Cornell U, Monroe Coll. Surg. advisor Archives Dermatology. Author: (book) Your Hair, Helping to Keep It, 1994; asst. editor (jour.) Jour. Am. Acad. Dermatology, 1994—; author: (book) Sclerotherapy of Varicose Veins, 1996; asst. editor (jour.) Jour. Aesthetic and Cosmetic Surgery,—. Mem.: Am. Soc. Dermatological Surgery (bd. dirs.), Am. Cancer Soc. (summer fellow 1977), Manhattan Met. Dermatology Soc. (pres. 1995—96), NY Acad. Medicine, Dermatology Found. (vice chmn. 1993—), Am. Soc. Cosmetic Surgery (bd. dirs.,), Am. Acad. Dermatology (adv. bd. 1995—), Dermatologic Soc. Greater NY (adv. bd. 1994, pres. 1995—96), Am. Coll. Phlebology. (pres. 2002—04, bd. dirs., Jobst award 1990), LI Dermatology Soc. Avocations: tennis, travel, antique pens. Office: 911 Park Ave New York NY 10028 Office Phone: 212-772-7242. Business E-Mail: nssderm@sadickdermatology.com.

**SADIK, MARVIN SHERWOOD,** art historian, consultant, retired museum director; b. Springfield, Mass., June 27, 1932; s. Harry Benjamin and Florence (Askinas) S. AB magna cum laude, Harvard U., 1954, A.M., 1960; D.F.A. (hon.), Bowdoin Coll., Brunswick, Maine, 1978. Curatorial asst. Worcester (Mass.) Art Mus., 1955-57; curator Mus. Art Bowdoin Coll., 1961-64, dir., 1964-67, Mus. Art U. Conn. at Storrs, 1967-69, Nat. Portrait Gallery, Washington, 1969-81. Author: Colonial and Federal Portraits at Bowdoin College, 1966, The Drawings of Hyman Bloom, 1968, The Paintings of Charles Hawthorne, 1968, Edith Halpert and the Downtown Gallery, 1968, The Life Portraits of John Quincy Adams, 1970, Christian Gullager: Portrait Painter to Federal America, 1976, Portraits of George Bellows, 1981; co-author: American Portrait Drawings, 1980. Decorated knight Order Dannebrog Denmark; recipient Detur prize Harvard Coll., 1952, Maine State Art award, 1975, gold medal for exceptional svc. Smithsonian Instn., 1981; Harris fellow, 1957-61; Barr fellow, 1957-61; fellow Belgian Art Seminar, 1956. Fellow Pierpont Morgan Library; mem. Am. Antiquarian Soc., Colonial Soc. Mass. (corr.) Clubs: Century Assn., Grolier. Home: PO Box 6360 Scarborough ME 04070-6360 Office Phone: 207-885-9644.

**SADIK, NAFIS,** United Nations administrator; b. Jaunpur, India, Aug. 18, 1929; d. Iffat Ara and Mohammad Shoaib; m. Azhar Sadik, 1954; 5 children. Student, Loretto Coll., Calcutta, India, Dow Med. Coll., Karachi, Pakistan, Johns Hopkins U., LHD (hon.), 1989, Brown U., 1993, Duke U., 1995; LLD, Wilfrid Laurier U., 1995; DSc (hon.), U. Mich., 1996, Claremont U., 1996; LHD (hon.), Philippines U., 1997; DSc (hon.), Long Island U., 1997; LHD (hon.), Nepal Tribhuvan U., 1998; DSc, Tulane U., 1999. Intern ob-gyn. City Hosp., Balt., 1952-54; civilian med. officer in charge of women's and children's wards various Pakistani armed forces hosps., 1954-63; resident physiology Queens U., Kingston, Ont., Can., 1958; head health sect. Planning Commn. on Health and Family Planning, Pakistan, 1964; dir. planning and tng. Pakistan Ctr. Family Planning Coun., 1966-68, dep. dir.-gen., 1968-70, dir.-gen., 1970-71; tech. advisor UN Fund for Population Activities, 1971-72, chief programme divsn., 1973-77, asst. exec. dir., 1977-87, exec. dir., 1987—; under-sec.-gen. UN, 1987—. Sec.-gen. Internat. Conf. on Population and Devel., 1994, Sec. for Internat. Devel. (pres. 1994-97). Writings include: Population: National Family Planning Programme in Pakistan, 1968, Population: the UNFPA Experience, 1984, Population Policies and Programmes: Making a Difference: Twenty-five Years of UNFPA Experience, 1994, Lessions learned from Two Decades of Experience, 1991, Making a Difference: Twenty-Five Years of UNFPA Experience, 1994; contbr. articles to profl. jours. Recipient Hugh Moore award; Paul Harris fellow Rotary, 1997. Fellow Royal Coll. Ob-Gyn. Avocations: bridge, reading, theater, travel. Office: UN Population Fund 220 E 42nd St Fl 19 New York NY 10017-5806

**SADINENI, SURESH BABU,** research scientist; b. Ongole, Andhra Pradesh, India, Aug. 22, 1975; s. RamaRao and Ramanamma Sadineni; m. Padmaja Chilukuri, May 22, 2003; 1 child, Saanvi. PhD, U. Nebr., Las Vegas, 2005. Grad. tchg. asst. dept. mech. engring. U. Nev., Las Vegas, 2001—02, grad. rsch. asst. dept. mech. engring., 2002—05, rsch. faculty dept. mech. engring., 2005. Mem.: Am. Nuclear Soc. Achievements include development of Code to Predict Transient Behavior of a Nuclear Reactor Coupled to an Accelerator. Home: Apt 104 4386 Escondido St Las Vegas NV 89119 Office: U Nev Dept Mech Engring 4505 Maryland Pkwy Las Vegas NV 89154 Office Phone: 702-895-1331. Personal E-mail: sbsadineni@yahoo.com.

**SADINSKY, RACHAEL,** curator, art appraiser; b. Elmira, N.Y., Feb. 28, 1958; MA, U. Del., Newark, Del., 1985; diploma in Appraisal Studies, NYU, 2004. Curator collections Arnot Art Mus., Elmira, NY, 1987—94; curator collections and exhibitions Art Mus. U. Ky., Lexington, Ky., 1995—2004. Author: A Collector's Vision: The 1910 Bequest of Matthias H. Arnot. Andelot fellowship, U. Del., 1983. Mem.: Am. Assn. Mus., Coll. Art Assn. Office Phone: 859-266-0576.

**SADLER, DAVID G(ARY),** manufacturing executive; b. Iowa City, Mar. 14, 1939; s. Edward Anthony and Elsie June (Sherman) S.; m. Karen Sadler; children: Michael Robert, Katherine Louise. Student, St. Ambrose Coll., 1957—59; BS in Indsl. Adminstrn. and Prodn., Kent State U., 1961. Various mgmt. positions Ford Motor Co., Lorain, Ohio, 1962—67, Sperry-New Holland, Lebanon, Ohio, 1967—71; mgr. mfg. Allis Chalmer, Springfield, Ill., 1971—72; dir. mfg. Purolator, Inc., Fayetteville, NC, 1972—73; v.p. mfg. farm equipment and ops. truck divsn. White Motor Co., Eastlake, Ohio and Chgo., 1973—78; corp. v.p. mfg. Massey Ferguson Ltd., Toronto, Ont., Canada, 1978—80. Internat. Harvester, Chgo., 1980—81, sr. v.p. ops. staff, 1981—82, v.p. bus. devel., 1982, pres. diversified group, 1982—83, pres. internat. group, 1983—85; pres. AMI, Inc., Chgo., 1985—86; vice chmn.,

CEO Savin Corp., Stamford, Conn., 1986, chmn., CEO, 1986—89, also bd. dirs.; pres. Asset Mgmt. Internat., Westport, Conn., 1989—95; chmn., CEO Rowe Internat., Grand Rapids, Mich., 1995—2000, also bd. dirs., 2000—01; CEO Merisel, Inc., El Segundo, Calif., also bd. dirs.; chmn., CEO, bd. dirs. Global Motorsport Group, Inc., Morgan Hill, Calif., 2002—04. Bd. dirs. greater Chgo. Safety Coun., 1981-84,Hellmold Assocs. Opportunity Fund II. Roman Catholic. Home: 751 Bradford Farms Ln NE Grand Rapids MI 49525-3348 E-mail: davidsadler@comcast.net.

**SADLER, ROBERT E., JR.,** bank executive; b. Miss. Grad., Wash. and Lee U., Lexington, Va.; MBA, Emory U. Various nat. and internat. positions Chemical Bank, 1970—83; joined M&T Bank, 1983, pres., 1996—2003, chmn., 2003—05; exec. v.p. M&T Nat. Bank; pres., CEO M&T Bank Corp., 2005—; CEO M&T, 2005—. Mem. bd. Security Mutual Life Ins. Co., NY, Del. N. Companies, Inc., Gibraltar, 2004—. Bd. managers Buffalo Soc. Natural Sciences. Mem.: Fin. Services Roundtable. Office: M&T Bank Corp One M&T Plaza Buffalo NY 14203-2399*

**SADLER EDEPLI, KIRSTEN,** biologist, educator; b. Lewiston, Maine, Sept. 30, 1968; d. William Alan and Sylvia Ruth Sadler, Sallie Inglis Sadler (Stepmother); m. Levent Edepli, May 5, 2001; 1 child, Emre Knight Edepli. BA, Mt. Holyoke Coll., South Hadley, Mass., 1990; MMSc, Harvard Med. Sch., Boston, 1994; PhD, Harvard U., Cambridge, Mass., 1998. Asst. prof. Bosphorus U., Istanbul, Turkey, 1998—2001; post-doctoral fellow MIT, Cambridge, Mass., 2002—05; asst. prof. Mt. Sinai Sch. Medicine, N.Y.C., 2006—. Dir. summer camp and enrichment program Project Duzce, Turkey, 1999—2000. Mem.: AAAS, Am. Assn. Study of Liver Disease, Am. Gastrological Assn., Soc. Devel. Biology. Episcopalian. Office: Mount Sinai Sch Medicine 1 Gustave L Levy Pl Box 1020 New York NY 10029 Office Phone: 212-749-2847.

**SADLO, KENNETH LOUIS,** poet, writer; b. St. Louis, Oct. 16, 1969; s. Kenneth Edward Sadlo, Mary Ann Cherrick. Student, St. Louis U., 1988—89, Lincolnland C.C., Springfield, Ill., 1991—92. Author: (CD) The Sound of Poetry, 2001, The Silence Within, 2001, The Best Poems and Poets of 2001, 2002. Liaison Quincy U. "The Falcon", Ill., 1992—93. Scholar John J. McDaniel scholar, 1984—88. Home: 11733 Lindemere Des Peres MO 63131 Office Phone: 314-821-8057. Personal E-mail: ksadlo01@yahoo.com.

**SADOCK, BENJAMIN JAMES,** psychiatrist, educator; b. NYC, Dec. 22, 1933; s. Samuel William and Gertrude S.; m. Virginia Alcott, Oct. 20, 1963; children: James William, Victoria Anne. AB, Union Coll., 1955; MD, N.Y. Med. Coll., 1959. Rotating intern Albany (N.Y.) Hosp., 1959-60; resident Bellevue Psychiat. Hosp., N.Y.C., 1960-63; instr. psychiatry Southwestern Med. Sch., Dallas, 1964-65, N.Y. Med. Coll., N.Y.C., 1965-67, asst. prof., 1967-71, assoc. prof., 1972-74, prof., 1975-80, dir. student health psychiatry, 1980—; prof. psychiatry NYU Sch Medicine, 1981-99, Menas S. prof. psychiatry, 2000—, vice chmn. dept. psychiatry, 1984—, faculty scholar, 2000—. Attending physician Lenox Hill Hosp.; attending psychiatrist Tisch Univ. Hosp. of NYU Med. Ctr., Bellevue Hosp.; cons. psychiatrist Franklin Delano Roosevelt VA Hosp., 1970-78, U.S. Dept. State, 1980-81, P.R. Inst. Psychiatry, 1976-80; examiner Am. Bd. Psychiatry and Neurology, 1970-80; mem. conf. on recert. Am. Bd. Med. Spltys.-Am. Psychiat. Assn., 1974; mem. Commn. on Continuing Edn. in Psychiatry, NIMH-Am. Psychiat. Assn., 1974-75. Co-author: Comprehensive Group Psychotherapy, 1971, 3d edit., 1993, The Sexual Experience, 1976, Comprehensive Textbook of Psychiatry, 8th edit., 2005, Pocket Handbook of Clinical Psychiatry, 1991, 4d edit., 2005, Comprehensive Glossary of Psychiatry and Psychology, 1991, Pocket Handbook of Drug Treatment in Psychiatry, 1992, 4t edit., 2005, Pocket Handbook of Psychiatric Emergency Medicine, 1993, Pocket Handbook of Primary Care Psychiatry, 1996; contbr. articles on psychiat. edn., individual and group psychotherapy, diagnosis and treatment of psychiat., sexual disorders to med. jours.; contbr. to Ency. Americana. Fellow Am. Psychiat. Assn. (treas. N.Y. County dist. br. 1973-76, mem. conf. on psychiatry and med. edn. 1967), N.Y. Acad. Medicine, A.C.P.; mem. AMA, Med. Soc. County and State N.Y., Am. Group Psychotherapy Assn., World Psychiat. Assn., Psychiat. Soc. N.Y. Med. Coll. (founder, pres. 1975-79), N.Y. Med. Coll. Alumni Assn. (gov. 1965-90), NYU-Bellevue Psychiat. Soc. (pres. 1981—), Alpha Omega Alpha. Office: 4 E 89th St New York NY 10128-0636 also: NYU Med Ctr 550 1st Ave New York NY 10016-6402 E-mail: bjs6@nyu.edu.

**SADOCK, GEOFFREY J.,** English professor; b. NYC, Sept. 30, 1942; s. Jules Bertero and Rosabelle Johnston Sadock; m. Karen Nauta, Sept. 4, 1971; 1 child, Katharine Cordelia Johnston Sadock. BA with honors, Bklyn. Coll., NYC, 1964; MA, Tufts U., Medford, Mass., 1966; PhD, Brown U., Providence, 1973. Instr. Fairleigh-Dickinson U., Madison, NJ, 1971—72; prof. Bergen CC, Paramus, NJ, 1972—. Dir. honors program Bergen C.C., Paramus, NJ, 1996—2001. Contbr. articles to profl. jours. Recipient Presidential Recognition award, SGC, 2004; fellow CCNY Grad. Ctr., NYC, 1991; Mid-Career fellow, Princeton U., 1994. Mem.: ALSC, NAS, NJCEA, NEA, KC, US English, English First, Internat. Walter Pater Soc., Victorian Soc. Am. Avocations: Victorian architecture and restoration, antique lighting. Home: 67 West Shore Ave Dumont NJ 07628

**SADOFF, JOAN HANDLEMAN,** film producer, social worker; b. Detroit, Feb. 25, 1938; d. Joseph and Sally Handleman; m. Robert Leslie Sadoff, June 21, 1959; children: Debra, David, Julie, Sherry. BS, U. Minn., 1959; MEd, Temple U., 1971, MSW, 1979. Clin. social worker Norristown (Pa.) State Hosp., 1977—78, Bartram HS for Human Svc., Phila., 1978—79, Family Svc. Phila., 1977, Northwestern Inst., Ft. Washington, Pa., 1980—92. Prodr.: (documentaries) Philadelphia, MS-Untold Stories, 1994 (Best Video for Edn., 1995); prodr.: (documentaries) Standing on My Sisters' Shoulders, 2001 (13 awards, appeared in 28 film festivals), Mem. adv. bd. LaSalle U., Phila. 1996—; bd. dirs., co-chmn. forum com. Cheltenham (Pa.) Twp. Adult Sch., 1996—; bd. dirs. Rittenhouse Sq. Com. fundraiser for Phila. Orch., Phila., 2003—, Cmty. Women's Edn. Project, Phila., 2002—, Inst. So. Jewish Life, Jackson, Miss., 2000—, Jewish Joint Distn. Com., NYC, 2003—. Named Social Worker of Yr., Phila. chpt. NASW, 2005; recipient Gallery of Success award, Temple U., 2004, Alumni Fellow award, Temple U. Sch. Social Adminstrn., 2004, Making a Difference for Women award, Soroptimist, 2005. Home: 441 Wingate Rd Huntingdon Valley PA 19006 Personal E-mail: joansadoff@aol.com.

**SADOFF, ROBERT LESLIE,** psychiatrist, educator; b. Mpls., Feb. 8, 1936; s. Max and Rose C. (Karroll) S.; m. Joan A Handleman, June 21, 1959; children: Debra, David, Julie, Sherry. BA, U. Minn., 1956, BS, 1957, MD, 1959; MS, UCLA, 1963. Intern L.A. VA Hosp., 1959—60; resident in psychiatry UCLA, 1960—63; asst. prof. psychiatry Temple U., Phila., 1966—72; clin. prof. U. Pa., Phila., 1972—; pvt. practice Jenkintown, Pa., 1965—. Lectr. law Villanova U., 1972-85. Author (with Marvin Lewis) Psychic Injuries, 1975, Forensic Psychiatry, 1975, 2d edit., 1988, Legal Issues in the Care of Psychiatric Patients, 1982, Violence and Responsibility, 1988, (with Robert I. Simon) Psychiatric Malpractice, 1992; editor: Psychiatric Clinics of North America, 1984. Bd. dirs. Joseph T. Peters Inst., Phila., 1980-92. Capt. M.C., U.S. Army, 1963-65. Recipient Earl Bond award U. Pa., 1979, VII ann. Nathaniel Winkelman award Phila. Psychiat. Ctr., 1988, Manfred Guttmacher award, 2993, Isaac Ray award, 2006. Fellow: Am. Coll. Legal Medicine, Am. Psychiat. Assn. (Manfred Guttmacher award 1993); mem.: Internat. Acad. Law and Mental Health (Philippe Pinel award 1995), Internat. Soc. for Philos. Enquiry (mentor 1987—), Am. Acad. Psychiatry and Law (pres. 1971—73), Am. Coll. Psychiatrists, Am. Red Magen David for Israel (nat. mem. 1986—2001). Avocation: collecting antique books in law and medicine. Office: The Pavilion Ste 326 261 Old York Rd Jenkintown PA 19046 Office Phone: 215-887-6144. E-mail: bobsadoff@aol.com.

**SADOH, GODWIN SIMEON,** music educator; b. Lagos, Nigeria, Mar. 28, 1965; arrived in US, 1994; s. Anthony Sadoh and Taiwo Akinsanya. BA in Piano Performance and Composition, Obafemi Awolowo U., Ile-Ife, Nigeria, 1988; MA in Ethnomusicology, U. Pitts., 1998; MusM in Organ Performance,

---

U. Nebr., 2000; MusD in Organ Performance and Composition, La. State U., 2004. Lectr. Dept. Music Obafemi Awolowo U., Ile-Ife, 1988—94; tchg. asst. U. Pitts. 1994—96; part-time faculty Sch. Music U. Nebr., Lincoln, Nebr., 1998—2000; music faculty Baton Rouge Coll., 2003—06; asst. prof. music LeMoyne-Owen Coll., Memphis, 2006—, coord. Sacred Music Program, 2006—, dir. concert choir, 2006—. Organist, choir dir. Eko Boys' HS, Lagos, 1980—82, St. Stephen's Episc. Ch., Wilkinsburg, Pa., 1996—98; assoc. dir. music ministries First United Meth. Ch., Lincoln, Nebr., 1999—2000; founder and dir. Ile-Ife (Nigeria) Choral Soc., Nigeria, 1980—90; organist Cathedral Ch. Christ, Lagos, Nigeria, 1980—90. Author: The Organ Works of Fela Sowande: Cultural Perspectives, 2005, Intercultural Dimensions in AYO Bankole's Music, 2006; composer: Nigerian Suite No. 1 for Organ Solo (ASCAP PLUS Award, 2004), Impressions from an African Moonlight, The Misfortune of a Wise Tortoise for Organ and Narrator, 2005, Nigerian Suite No. 2 for Organ Solo, 2005, (songs) Ope Lo Ye O, 2006, Open Your Mouth, 2006, A Bi Jesu, 2006, Ose Jesu, 2006, Lord Send Your Power, 2006, (hymn book) E Korin S'Oluwa (Sing Unto The Lord): Fifty Indigenous Church Hymns from Nigeria, 2005, Kabiyesi Hosana, 2005, Ise Oluwa, 2005, Ose Baba, 2005, Gbo Ohun Awon Angeli, 2005, Akoi Wata Geri, 2005, Keresimesi Odun de, 2005, Five African Marches for Organ Solo, 2006, Five African Dances for Organ Solo, 2006, 25 preludes on Yoruba Ch. Hymns for Organ; contbr. articles to profl. jours. Organist, choirmaster Eko Boys' H.S., Lagos, Nigeria, 1980—82; preacher St. Stephen's Episc. Ch., Wilkinsburg, Pa., 1996—98, Christ Luth. Ch., Lincoln, 1999—2000; vis. preacher Redeeming The Time Ministries Internat., Baton Rouge. Scholar, La. State U., 2000—03, U. Pitts., 1997; Dora Dean Emerson Meml. Music fellowship, Sch. Music, U. Nebr., Lincoln, 1998, Alvin Hatton Organ scholarship, 2000—03. Mem.: Musicological Soc. Nigeria, Soc. Ethnomusicology, Am. Guild Organists (scholarship 1998—2000), Organ Hist. Soc., The Hymn Soc., Nat. Assn. Composers, USA, Am. Soc. Composers, Authors and Publishers (See Honor's awards 2004, Plus award 2005, 2006), The Coll. Music Soc. Evang. Achievements include first African to earn a doctorate degree in organ performance from any institution in the world. Avocations: cooking, movies, travel. Business E-Mail: gsadoh1@lsu.edu.

**SADOVE, STEPHEN IRVING,** retail executive; b. Washington, July 25, 1951; s. A. Robert and Harriet (Tenenbaum) S.; m. Karin Sadove; children: Stacy, David, Laurie. BA, Hamilton Coll., 1973; MBA, Harvard U., 1975. Asst. product mgr. desserts divsn. Gen. Foods Corp., White Plains, N.Y., 1975-76, assoc. product mgr., 1976-77, product mgr., 1977-80, group product mgr., 1980-82, category mgr., 1982-84, mktg. mgr., 1984-86, bus. unit mgr. meals divsn., 1986-88, v.p., gen. mgr., 1988-89, exec. v.p., gen. mgr. desserts divsn., 1989-91; pres. Clairol, Inc., Stamford, Conn., 1991-96, Bristol-Myers Squibb Beauty Care, Stamford, 1996-97, Bristol-Myers Squibb Beauty Care and Nutritionals, Stamford, 1998—2001; vice-chmn. Saks Inc., N.Y.C., 2002—. Bd. dirs. Saks Inc., Ruby Tuesday Inc. Trustee Hamilton Coll., Hazelden. Avocations: tennis, golf, reading, arts. Office: Saks Inc 12 E 49th St New York NY 10017 Home: 7 Hickory Pine Ct Purchase NY 10577

**SADOW, HARVEY S.,** healthcare company executive; b. N.Y.C., Oct. 6, 1922; s. Nat. and Frances Donna (Saveth) S.; m. Sylvia June Riber, Dec. 22, 1944 (div. 1966); children: Harvey Jr., Suzanne Gail, Todd Forrest, Gay Summer; m. Jacqueline Lucille Clavel, Jan. 24, 1969 (div. 1993); 1 adopted child, Daniel Jean Marie; m. Mary Morrissey McSwiggan, July 13, 1995. BS, Va. Mil. Inst., Lexington, 1947; MS, U. Kans., 1949; PhD, U. Conn., 1953, DSc (hon.), 2000. Intelligence officer CIA, Washington, 1951-53; assoc. dir. rsch. Lakeside Labs., Inc., Milw., 1953-56; med. rsch. cons. Milw., 1956; dir. clin. rsch. U. Vitamin & Pharm. Corp., N.Y.C., 1957-64, v.p R & D, 1964-68; sr. v.p. scientific affairs USV Pharm./Revlon Corp., N.Y.C., 1969-71; pres, CEO Boehringer Ingelheim, Ltd. (named changed to Boehringer Ingelheim Pharms., Inc. 1984), Ridgefield, Conn., 1971-88, Boehringer Ingelheim Corp., Ridgefield, 1984-88, chmn. bd., 1988-90. Chmn. bd. Roxane Labs., Inc., Columbus, Ohio, 1981-88, Boehringer Ingelheim Animal Health, Inc., St. Joseph, Mo., 1981-88, Henley Co., N.Y.C., 1986-88, U. Conn. Rsch. and Devel. Corp., Storrs, 1984-87; bd. dirs. Anika Therapeutics, Inc., Trega Biosics., Inc., chmn. 2000-01, Cortex Pharms., Inc., Irvine, Calif., chmn. bd., 1991-99; bd. dirs. Cholestech Corp., Hayward, Calif., chmn. bd. 1992-2000; adv. bd. Salk Inst. Biotechnology-Indsl. Assocs., Inc., La Jolla, 1988-90; chmn. bd. dirs. Acacia Biosics. Inc., 1996-99, Rosetta Inpharmatics, Inc., 1999-2001. Co-author: Oral Treatment of Diabetes, 1967; contbr. articles to profl. jours. Bd. dirs. Pharm. Mfrs. Assn., 1983-90; chmn. Pharm. Mfrs. Assn. Found., 1988-90; bd. dirs. Comm. Bd. Higher Edn., Hartford, 1977-83, Govs. Tech. Adv. Bd., Hartford, 1984-87; mem. Conn. Commn. on Bus. Opportunity, Def. Diversification and Indsl. Policy, 1991-93; mem. bd. visitors Va. Mil. Inst., Lexington 1987—, pres. bd. 1991-95; chmn. bd. Conn. Law Enforcement Found., Hartford, 1981-86, 92-97, U. Conn. Found., Storrs, 1984-87; chmn., pres.' coun. Am. Lung Assn., N.Y.C., 1986-87, York Sch., Monterey, Calif., 1988-89; trustee Conn. Coll., Groton, 1991-96, Aldrich Mus. Contemporary Art, Ridgefield, Conn., 1991-98. Capt. U.S. Army, 1943—46. Decorated Disting. Svc. Cross, Fed. Republic of Germany, 1987; recipient Univ. medal U. Conn., 1987, Citizen of Yr. Conn. Chief of Police Assn., 1988, Recognition award Nat. Hypertension Assn., 1990, Humanitarian award Am. Lung Assn. Conn., 1993, Disting. Svc. award Conn. Innovations, Inc., 1996, Va. Mil. Inst. Found, 1998. Mem. Am. Soc. for Clin. Pharmacology and Therapeutics, Am. Fedn. for Clin. Rsch., Am. Diabetes Assn., Danbury C. of C. (Abraham Ribicoff Community Svc. award City of Danbury 1987, bd. dirs. 1978-81), Union League (N.Y.C.), Masons, Sigma Xi, Sigma Pi Sigma, Phi Lambda Upsilon. Avocations: art collecting, photography, music, writing. Personal E-mail: hssadow@aol.com.

**SADOWAY, DONALD ROBERT,** materials science educator; b. Toronto, Mar. 7, 1950; s. Donald Anthony and Irene Mary (Romanko) S.; m. Sandra Lynn Mary Babij, Sept. 8, 1973 (div. Sept. 1996); children: Steven, Laryssa, Andrew; m. Anne Marie Mazur, Jan. 4, 1997 (div. June 2003) m. Ronaeoa Rosenberg, Dec. 19, 2004. BASc, U. Toronto, 1972, MASc, 1973, PhD, 1977. Cert. in chem. metallurgy. Asst. prof. materials engring. MIT, Cambridge, 1978-82, assoc. prof., 1982-92, materials chemistry, 1992—, MacVicar faculty fellow, 1995—2005, John F. Elliott prof. of chem. metallurgy, 1999—. Assoc. editor Jour. Materials Rsch., 1995-2005; contbr. over 125 articles on electro and phys. chemistry to profl. jours.; patentee in field, U.S., Can., and Europe. Recipient Grad. Student Coun. Tchg. award MIT, 1982, 84, 87, 88, 93, Prof. T.B. King Meml. award dept. materials sci. and engring. undergrad. students MIT, 1986, Bose award, 1997; NATO postdoctoral fellow Nat. Rsch. Coun. Can., 1977, AT&T Faculty fellow in indsl. ecology, 1993-95. Mem. AAAS, Minerals, Metals and Materials Soc., Electrochem. Soc., Internat. Soc. Electrochemistry, Materials Rsch. Soc., Norwegian Acad. Tech. Sci. (elected). Office: MIT # 35-213 77 Massachusetts Ave Cambridge MA 02139-4307 Office Phone: 617-253-3487. E-mail: dsadoway@mit.edu.

**SADOWSKI, CAROL JOHNSON,** artist; b. Chgo., Mar. 20, 1929; d. Carl Valdamar Johnson and Elizabeth Hilma (Booth) Johnson Chellberg; m. Edmund Sadowski, July 9, 1949; children: Lynn Carol Mahoney, Christie Sadowski Cortez. AAS, Wright Coll., Ill., 1949. Tchr. art Malverne H.S., NY, 1968-69; artist Valley Stream, NY, 1968-76, Hollywood, Fla., 1976—. Guest spkr. Mus. Art, Ft. Lauderdale, Fla., 1991; Libr. League, Oakland Park, 1985; Boca Raton, Fla. Mus., others; TV appearances on WCGB, Gainesville; WSVN, Miami; Storer and Hollywood Cable; Artist Guild, Boca Raton Mus.; Broward C.C., Hollywood Fla. One woman shows include Mus. Fla. History, Tallahassee, 1984-85, 87; Hist. Mus. South Fla., Miami, 1986; Thomas Ctr. Arts, Gainesville, Fla., 1985, 87; Elliott Mus., Stuart, Fla., 1987; Hemingway Mus. and Home, Key West, Fla., 1986; I.G.F.A. Fishing Hall of Fame Mus., Dania, Fla., 1999, Alliance Francaise de Miami, 1995; commd. painting St. Agustin Antigua Found.; St. Augustine, Fla., 1985, Atlantic Bank, Ft. Lauderdale, Fla., Bonnet House Fla. Trust, Ft. Lauderdale, Hollywood Art & Culture Ctr., Hemingway Mus., San Francisco de Paula, Presdl. Palace, Havana, Tropical Art Gallery, Naples, Fla., 1981-83, Tequesta (Fla.) Art Gallery, 1985-89, Gingerbread Square Gallery, Key West, Fla., Wally Findlay Galleries, Inc., Palm Beach and N.Y.C., DeBruyne Fine Arts Gallery, Naples, 1998—, Patricia Cloutier Gallery, Tequesta, Fla., 1992-. Mem. Ft. Lauderdale Mus. Art; Hollywood Art and Culture Ctr. Recipient Hemingway

---

medal, Ernest Hemingway Mus., Cuba, 1990; appreciation award City of Hollywood; Chgo. Art Inst. scholar; Salmagundi Club N.Y. scholar. Mem. Internat. Platform Assn., Broward Art Guild, Fla. Hist. Assn., Ernest Hemingway Soc., Chopin Found., Am. Inst. for Polish Culture, Alliance Francaise de Miami, Women in the Arts Nat. Mus. (charter mem.), Nat. Women's History Mus. (charter mem.). Avocations: travel, bicycling, swimming, reading. Home: 1480 Sheridan St Apt B 17 Hollywood FL 33020-2295 Office Phone: 954-925-7482. Personal E-mail: esadowski@msn.com. *I try to do my best at what I love to do; not for money or fame, but for self satisfaction.*

**SADOWSKI, PETER T.,** lawyer; b. Warsaw, Oct. 30, 1954; came to U.S., 1968; s. Fryderyk and Maria (Jaklinska) S.; m. Denise A. Decker, Oct. 13, 1979; children: Katherine, Rachel. BA, St. Louis U., 1976; JD, St. Louis U. Law Sch., 1979. Asst. atty. gen. Mo. Atty. Gen.'s Office, Jefferson City, 1979-81; ptnr. The Stolar Partnership, St. Louis, 1981-96; shareholder Goldberg, Katz, Sadowski & Croft, St. Louis, 1996—99; exec. v.p., gen. counsel Fidelity Nat. Fin. Inc., Jacksonville, Fla., 1999—. Chmn. bd. dirs. greater needs com. YMCA, St. Louis, 1995—.

**SADOWSKY, MICHAEL J.,** microbiologist, educator; married; 2 children. BS, U. Wis., Madison, 1977; MS in Biology/Microbiology, U. Wis., Oshkosh; PhD in Microbiology, U. Hawaii, 1983. Rschr. McGill U. 1983—85; molecular biologist Allied Corp.; biologist Nitrogen Fixation and Soybean Genetics Lab. USDA-ARS, Beltsville, Md.; asst. prof. Dept. Soil Sci. and Microbiology U. Minn., St. Paul, 1989, prof. Dept. Soil, Water, and Climate and Biotechnology Inst., dir. grad. studies Microbial Engring. Program, U. McKnight Disting. prof., 2005—. Co-creator Agricultural Microbe Genomes Confs. Editor: (jour.) Applied and Environ. Microbiology; assoc. editor Symbiosis and Microbes and the Environment; contbr. articles to profl. jours. NSF Grant, 2003. Fellow: Am. Acad. Microbiology; mem.: Am. Soc. Microbiology (Region V Coord. and Branch Archivist). Avocations: woodworking, amateur radio electronics. Office: U Minn 439 Borlaug Hall 1991 Upper Buford Cir Saint Paul MN 55108 Office Phone: 612-625-1244. Office Fax: 612-625-2208. E-mail: sadowsky@soils.umn.edu.*

**SADR, ANN,** psychotherapist, educator; d. John Jacob Levine and Rosemary Agnes Earley; m. Farrokh S. Sadr, June 27, 1972; children: Mark, Patrick, Kathleen, David. BSN, Marquette U., 1969; MS in Counseling and Human Resources, Chestnut Hill Coll., Pa., 2000; MA in Clin. Psychology, Widener U., 2002, D in Clin. Psychology, 2004. Staff nurse Hines (Ill.) VA Hosp., 1969—71; instr. South Chicago Hosp. Sch. Nursing, 1971—73; staff nurse East Orange (NJ) VA Hosp., 1971—75; psychotherapist Michael G. Perovich & Assocs., Allentown, Pa., 2000—. Adj. asst. prof. Widener U., Chester, Pa., 2004—. Mem.: APA, Am. Group Psychotherapy Assn., Soc. for Personality Assessment, Pa. Psychol. Assn., Phila. Area Group Psychotherapy Assn. (bd. dirs. 2004—05). Roman Catholic. Office: Dr Michael G Perovich & Assocs 1150 Glenlivet Dr Ste A18 Allentown PA 18106 Office Phone: 610-395-1696. Office Fax: 610-395-1697.

**SADR, REZA,** mechanical engineer, educator; s. Jamal and Tahereh Sadr; m. Mahsa Sadr; children: Mahdi S., Hadi S. PhD, U. Utah, 2002. Rsch. engr. Ga. Tech. U., Atlanta, 2002—. Mem.: ASME, APS. Achievements include research in electrososmotic flow and micro/nano fluids. Office: Georgia Institute of Technology 771 Ferst Dr Atlanta GA 30332 Office Phone: 404-385-2828.

**SADRAIE, HAMID REZA,** civil engineer, researcher; PhD, U. Minn., 2006. Rsch. asst. U. Minn., Mpls., 2002—. Home: 425 13th Ave SE #1301 Minneapolis MN 55414 Office: U Minn 500 Pillsbury Dr SE Minneapolis MN 55455 Office Phone: 612-624-7500. Office Fax: 612-626-7750. Business E-Mail: sadra002@umn.edu.

**SADRAMELI, MOJTABA SEYED,** chemical engineer, researcher; b. Esfahan, Iran, Apr. 26, 1957; arrived in U.S., 2003; s. Abolfazl and Shamsi Sadrameli; m. Zohreh JahanFardian, June 18, 1982; children: Saeed, Mohsen. BS, Sharif U. Tech.; PhD, U. Leeds, England, 1988. Rschr. Iranian Petrochemical Co., Tehran, Iran, 1990—2003; prof. Tehran (Iran) Mech. U., 1988—2003; vis. prof. Dept. Chem. Engring. U. Fla., Gainesville, Fla., 2003—05; rsch. assoc. U. ND, Grankd Forks, ND, 2006—. Office: Chemical Engineering Department University of Florida Gainesville FL 32611 Business E-Mail: m.sadrameli@gmail.com.

**SADRUDIN, MOE,** humanitarian organization executive; b. Hyderabad, India, Mar. 3, 1943; arrived in U.S., 1964; m. Azmath Qureshi, 1964; 3 children. BSME, Osmania U., Hyderabad, 1964; MS in Indsl. Engring., NYU, 1966; IE, MBA, Columbia U., 1970. Cons. project engr. Ford, Bacon & Davis, N.Y.C., 1966; staff indsl. engr. J.C. Penney, N.Y.C., 1966-68; sr. cons. Drake, Sheahan, Stewart & Dougall, N.Y.C., 1968-70, Beech-Nut Inc. subs. Squibb Corp., N.Y.C., 1970-72; founder, pres. Azmath Constrn. Co., Englewood, NJ, 1972-77; crude oil cons., fgn. govt. rep., 1977—88; pres. A-One Petroleum Co., Fullerton, Calif., 1985—95; chmn., CEO, Universal Humanitarian Found., Fullerton, 1989—. Govt. advisor Puerto Rico, 1980-82, Dominica, 1983-84, St. Vincent, 1981-82, Kenya, 1983-84, Belize 1984-85, Costa Rica 1983-86, Paraguay 1984-87. Chmn. Universal Humanitarian Found., 1989—; active LA World Affairs Coun. Mem.: Internat. Platform Assn. Address: Universal Humanitarian Found 2656 Camino Del Sol Fullerton CA 92833-4806 Office Phone: 714-526-0633. Personal E-mail: unihumfound@aol.com. *Personal philosophy: I learned from a young age that acquisition of knowledge, developing honesty and integrity and service to humanity in the form of charity, love and struggle to help the poor and needy, are the main foundation stones of a successful life. I believe that acquisition of wealth is only a means to an end and not an end in itself. With accumulation of wealth, one has to care for the underprivileged and try to improve their lot.*

**SADYKOVA, VERA PHILIPPOVNA,** librarian, educator; b. Dneprostroy, Zaporozhie, Ukraine, Mar. 4, 1933; arrived in Kazakhstan, 1947; d. Yabtchenko and (Phesik) Philipp; m. Albert Sadykov, May, 13, 1956; children: Aleksey, Gennady. Grad., Kazakh State U., Alma-Ata, 1957, Inst. Culture, Leningrad, Russia, 1966. Cert. libr., philologist. Libr. Sci. and Tech. Libr. Kazakhstan, Almaty, 1960-62, asst. dir., 1964-65, dir., 1965-88, chief libr., 1988-94, mgr. sci.-methodical dept., 1962-64, 94—, instr. advanced courses, 1962—, head sci. resrch. sector, 1998. Instr. advanced courses Kazakh State Inst. Sci. and Tech. Info., Almaty, 1962—, Sci. and Tech. Libr. Ctr. Profl. Devel., Kazakhstan, Kirgizia, Tadzhikistan, Uzbekistan, 2000-. Author brochures; mem. editl. bd. Nautchnie i Technitcheskie Biblioteki, 1990-91, New Jour. Libr. World, 2002.; contbr. articles to profl. jours. Mem. presidium Trade Unions Com. of State Instns. Ofcls., Almaty, 1971-86. Recipient medals and hon. degree Honoured Worker of Kazakh Soviet Socialist Republic, Presidium of Supreme Soviet USSR, 1970, 83, 84, bronze medals Exhbn. Econ. Achievements of USSR, 1969, 74, 81. Avocations: collecting books, gardening. Office: Sci & Tech Libr Kazakhstan S Mukanov 223B 050026 Almaty Kazakhstan Office Phone: 68-28-70. E-mail: rntbb@nursat.kz, orb@os.kz.

**SAEED, FAIZA J.,** lawyer; BA with highest distinction, U. Calif. Berkeley, 1987; JD magna cum laude, Harvard Law Sch., 1991. Bar: NY 1992, Calif. 1993, DC 1993. Assoc. Cravath, Swaine & Moore LLP, 1991—98, ptnr., corp., 1999—. Named Young Global Leader, World Econ. Forum, 2006; named one of 45 Under Forty-Five, Am. Lawyer, 2003, Top 40 Lawyers Under 40, Nat. Law. Jour., 2005. Mem.: Harvard Law Sch. Vis. Com., Calif. State Bar Assn., Internat. Bar Assn., ABA, NY State Bar Assn., Assn. Bar City of NY, Phi Beta Kappa. Office: Cravath Swaine & Moore LLP Worldwide Plaza 825 Eighth Ave New York NY 10019-7475 Office Phone: 212-474-1454. Office Fax: 212-474-3700. Business E-Mail: fsaeed@cravath.com.

**SAEGER, JAMES SCHOFIELD,** history professor, writer; b. Columbus, Ohio, Aug. 19, 1938; s. James Louttit and Elizabeth (Schofield) Saeger; divorced; children: James P., Edwin S. BA, Ohio State U., 1960, MA, 1963,

PhD, 1969. V.p., dealer Jim Saeger Rambler Co., Columbus, Ohio, 1960—62; instr. history NC State U., Raleigh, 1965—67; from instr. to assoc. prof. history Lehigh U., Bethlehem, Pa., 1967—85, prof. history, 1985—. Co-dir. Gipson Inst. for 18th Century Studies, Bethlehem, 1979—91. Author: The Chaco Mission Frontier, 2000. Mem.: Conf. on Latin Am. History (com. mem. 0991—2005), Soc. Mil. History, Am. Hist. Assn. Avocations: golf, fishing, hiking, bicycling. Home: 239 Uncas St Bethlehem PA 18018 Office: Dept History Maginnes Hall 9 W Packer Ave Bethlehem PA 18015 Office Phone: 610-758-3366.

**SAEGER, REBECCA,** advertising executive; B in Psychology and Polit. Sci., Muhlenberg Coll., 1976; MBA, U. Pa., 1980. Various positions including sr. v.p., group dir. for Lever Bros. and Am. Express Ogilvy & Mather, NY, 1980—91; sr. v.p., group mgmt. supr., dir. account mgmt. Foote, Cone & Belding, San Francisco, 1991—97; exec. v.p. advt. and brand mktg. svcs Visa USA, 1997—2001; exec. v.p. brand mgmt. and mktg. comm. Charles Schwab Corp., San Francisco, 2004—. Mem. exec. mgmt. com. Visa USA. Mem. mktg. com. San Francisco Symphony; mem. adv. bd. World Congress Sports. Mem.: Assn. Nat. Advertisers (bd. dirs.). Office: The Charles Schwab Corp 101 Montgomery St San Francisco CA 94104

**SAEKS, ALLEN IRVING,** lawyer; b. Bemidji, Minn., July 14, 1932; m. Linda J. Levin; 1 child, Adam Charles. BS in Law, U. Minn., 1954, JD, 1956. Bar: Minn. 1956, U.S. Dist. Ct. Minn. 1956, U.S. Ct. Appeals (8th cir.) 1957, U.S. Ct. Appeals (fed. cir.) 1959, U.S. Supreme Ct. 1959, U.S. Ct. Appeals (11th cir.) 1997; cert. civil trial specialist. Asst. U.S. atty. Dept. Justice, St. Paul, 1956-57; assoc. Leonard Street and Deinard, Mpls., 1960-63, ptnr., 1964—. Adj. prof. law U. Minn. Law Sch., 1960-65; chmn. Lawyer Trust Acct. Bd., Interest on Lawyers Trust Accounts, 1984-87; nat. bd. dir. Equal Justice Works. Chmn. Property Tax Com., 1986—87; pres. Jewish Cmty. Rels. Coun of Minn. and the Dakotas, 1994—96; bd. dirs. Citizens League, Mpls., 1984—87, Equal Justice Works, Washington, 2002—. 1st lt. JAGC U.S. Army, 1957—60. Named one of Best Lawyers Am., 2006; recipient City of Mpls. award, 1996, Lifetime Commitment award, Cardozo Soc., 2001. Fellow Am. Bar Found. (life); mem. ABA (commn. on interest on lawyers trust accts. 1990-93), Minn. State Bar Assn. (ethics task force, 2003, Pres. award 2003), Fund for the Legal Aid Soc. (chmn. 1997-98, Law Day Testimonial award 1996), Hennepin County Bar Assn. (pres. 1983-84), Order of Coif, Phi Delta Phi. Office: Leonard St and Deinard 150 S 5th St Ste 2300 Minneapolis MN 55402-4238 Business E-Mail: ais1548@leonard.com.

**SAEKS, RICHARD EPHRAIM,** engineering executive; b. Chgo., Nov. 30, 1941; s. Morris G. and Elsie E. S. BS, Northwestern U., 1964; MS, Colo. State U., 1965; PhD, Cornell U., 1967. Registered profl. engr., Tex. Elec. engr. Warwick Mfg. Co., Niles, Ill., 1961-63; asst. prof. dept. elec. engring. U. Notre Dame, 1967-71, assoc. prof., 1971-73; assoc. prof. depts. elec. engring., math. Tex. Tech U., Lubbock, 1973-77, prof., 1977-79, Paul Whitfield Horn prof. elec. engring., math. computer sci, 1979-83; prof., chmn. elec. engring. Ariz. State U., 1983-88; dean Armour Coll. Engring. Ill. Inst. Tech., 1988-91, Motorola prof., 1991-92; v.p. engring. Accurate Automation Corp., 1992-2000, chief tech. officer, 2000—. Cons. Research Triangle Inst., 1978-80, Marcel Dekker Inc., 1978-80. Author: Generalized Networks, 1972, Resolution Space Operators and Systems, 1973, Interconnected Dynamical Systems, 1981, System Theory: A Hilbert Space Approach, 1982; contbr. articles to profl. jours.; Editor: Large-Scale Dynamical Systems, 1976, Rational Fault Analysis, 1977, The World of Large Scale Systems, 1982. Recipient Disting. Faculty Research award Tex. Tech U., 1978 Fellow: AIAA, IEEE, IEEE Systems Men and Cybernetics Soc. (pres. 1998—99, Joseph G. Wohl Outstanding Career award 2004). Achievements include patents in field. Office Phone: 423-894-4646. Business E-Mail: richard@saeks.org.

**SAENGER, BRUCE WALTER,** consulting firm executive; b. Hanover, N.H., July 16, 1943; s. Werner Hugo and Natalie Bertha (Brown) S.; m. Cheryl Jeanne Bouchard, Nov. 6, 1976. BA, Pa. State U., 1969; postgrad., Am. Coll., Bryn Mawr, Pa., 1979, Coll. Fin. Planning, Denver, 1980. CPCU; ChFC; CLU. Agt. Nationwide Ins., Lansdale, Pa., 1969-73, dist. sales mgr. Springfield, Mass., 1973-75, Am. Mut. Braintree, Mass., 1975-77; dir. mktg. Bankers LIfe & Casualty, Chgo., 1977-78; pres., founder Sales Tng. Techniques, Southboro, Mass., 1979-81, The Saenger Orgn., Medway, Mass., 1981—2004. Mem. faculty Notre Dame U., South Bend, Ind., 1977-78, Northeastern U., Boston, 1984-92; mem. RHU Commn., Washington, 1979-81; dir. Northeastern U. Inst., Boston, 1985-93; mem. Mass. Ins. Dept. Continuing Edn. Rev. Com., 1985—; program dir. U. Del. Ins. Program, 1989-91; accdd. cons. Mass. Soc. Lic. Ins. Advisers, 1995—; cons. in field. Author: Series 6 Study Book, 1983, Series 22 Study Book, 1984, Tax Shelter Market Guide, 1985, Marketing Mutual Funds, 1985, also articles. Bd. dirs. Lansdale Gen. Hosp., 1971-73, New Directions Theater Co., 1988-91; mem. Medway Bus. Coun., 1989-94, pres., 1990-92. With U.S. Army, 1960-66. Recipient Ednl. Achievement award Profl. Ins. Agts. Assn., 1983, Alumni Achievement award Pa. State Alumni Assn., 2005; named Outstanding Fin. Exec. of Yr., Fin. Mgmt. Assn., 1993. Fellow Soc. CLUs (ednl. adv., bd. dirs. 1987-91), Soc. CPCUs (ednl. adv.), Life Mgmt. Inst. (Outstanding Lectr. award 1984); mem. Internat. Assn. Fin. Planners (ednl. adv., bd. dirs. 1986-92, pres. 1989-91), Internat. Assn. for Fin. Planning (chmn. bd. dirs. 1990-92), Soc. Cert. Ins. Counselors, Life Underwriters Assn., Inst. CFP (v.p. edn., bd. dirs. 1990-91), Mass. Assn. Health Underwriters (pres. 1992-93, Boston Bus. Ethics award 2001), Pa. State U. Alumni Soc. (bd. dirs. 1990-92), Republican, Roman Catholic. Avocation: skiing. Home: 1 Village Rd PO Box 304 Waterville Valley NH 03215-1018 Office: Saenger Consulting Group 6 Village Rd PO Box 350 Waterville Valley NH 03215 Office Phone: 603-236-3300. Business E-Mail: bsaenger@saengerconsulting.com.

**SAENZ, CECILIA SONIA,** education educator; d. Justo Valdez and Ruth Martinez Molina; m. Lloyd Neal Smith, Sept. 14, 1984; 1 child, Michael Robert. BS, Sam Houston U., 1964; MEd, U. Houston, 1975; student, Tex. So. U., 1989; PhD Capella U., 2005—. Adminstrv. cert. 1977, supt. cert. Ariz., Tex., 2003. Second grade tchr. Houston I.S.D., 1972—78, prin., 1978—98, dir. dist. 13, 1989—91; asst. supt. Phoenix Elem. Sch. Dist. 1, Phoenix, 1998—2003; master tchr. U. Houston, 1974—78; prof. online U. Phoenix, 2004—. Prin. ACET (Assn. Compensating Edn.) Conf., Houston, 1995—98; state mem. Tex. Sch. Improvement Initiative Tex. Edn. Agy., 1997—99; asst. supt. Proposition 301 P.E.S.D., Phoenix Elem., Phoenix, 2002—03; dir./cons. Montessori Magnet Program Com., Phoenix, 2003; spkr. and presenter in field. Lobbyist Phoenix Elem., 2002—03, advocate/legis., 2003, spirit program coord., 2003. Named Helping Schs. Outstanding Prin., Tex. Soc. Cert. Pub. Accountants, 1996, Houston Prin. of Yr., Cert. Pub. A Schs., 1996; recipient Tex. Prin. of Yr., 1996, Best Prin. in Tex. award, 1997, Hispanic Prin. of Yr., Houston Independetn Sch. Dist., 1996, Tex. Assn. Hispanic Adminstrv. Exemplary Educator award, Houston Independent Sch. Dist., 1998, Edn. Recognition award, Tex. Assn. Hispanic Adminstrs., 1998, Spirit 2006 award, City of Phoenix, 2004. Mem.: Tex. Retirement System, Ariz. Sch. Adminstr., Am. Assn. U. Women. Democrat. Roman Catholic. Achievements include created, developed, structured Montessori Program for public schools; implemented school improvement process "Eight Steps" as trainer; initiated school reform process "Success for All" Alignment. Avocations: hiking, camping, gardening, travel, tree triming. Office Fax: 623-572-4219. Personal E-Mail: soniamaui@aol.com.

**SAENZ, MICHAEL,** college president; b. Laredo, Tex., Oct. 25, 1925; s. C.A. and Pola R. Saenz; m. Nancy Elizabeth King; children: Michael King, Cynthia Elizabeth. BS in Acctg. with honors, Tex. Christian U., 1949, MEd, 1952; PhD in Econs., U. Pa., 1961. Dep. collector IRS, Ft. Worth, Dallas, 1949-52; adminstr. United Christian Missionary Soc., Bayamon, PR, 1954-57, 59-65, exec. sec Indpls., 1965-71; acad. dean Laredo (Tex.) Jr. Coll., 1971-74; pres. N.W. campus Tarrant County Coll., Fort Worth, Tex., 1975—. Founder Nat. Comml. Coll. Ministy. Hispanic Coun., 1985, bd. dirs., 1985—, pres., 1989-91; founder, co-dir. Nat. Hispanic Leadership Inst., 1989—; trustee Tex. Christian U., Brite Div. Sch., 1973-2001. Bd. dirs. Civic Ballet of Laredo, Ft. Worth chpt. NCCJ, Juliette Fowler Homes, Dallas; chmn. Aztec dist., dir. Gulf Coast coun. Boy Scouts Am., 1971-75; gov. Career Devel. Ctr., Arlington,

Tex.; chmn. Laredo's Bicentennial Com., 1973-76; trustee, bd. dirs. United Way Ft. Worth, 1979-88; mem., vice moderator gen. bd. Christian Ch. (Disciples of Christ), 1991-93. Mem. Am. Assn. Cmty. Colls. (bd. dirs. 1991-94), Commn. Internat. Edn. Am. Coun. Edn., Tex. Jr. Coll. Tchrs. Assn., Tex. Assn. Jr. Coll. Instructional Adminstrs., Am. Acad. Polit. and Social Scis., Urban Ministries in Higher Edn., Civic Music Assn. Laredo, Rotary. Home: 4427 Tamworth Rd Fort Worth TX 76116-8127 Office: Tarrant County Coll NW Capmus 4801 Marine Pkwy Fort Worth TX 76179 E-mail: michael.saenz@teed.edu.

**SAFADI, M. OUSSAMA,** engineering educator; arrived in U.S., 1978; BSE, Calif. State U. Northridge, 1982; MSE, UCLA, 1985, PhD in Civil Engring., 1991. Lectr. UCLA, 1991—95; sr. lectr. U. So. Calif., LA, 1991—. Pres. Applied Math. and Engring. Rsch. Industry of Calif., L.A., 1991—. Home: PO Box 24344 Los Angeles CA 90024 Office Phone: 310-288-3431. Business E-Mail: safadi@usc.edu.

**SAFARS, BERTA** See FISZER-SZAFARZ, BERTA

**SAFER, JOHN,** artist; b. Washington, Sept. 6, 1922; s. John M. and Rebecca (Herzmark) S.; m. Joy Scott; children: Janine Whitney, Thomas. AB, George Washington U., 1947; LLB, Harvard U., 1949. Chmn. NationsBank/DC, 1980-92; chmn. exec. com. Fin. Gen. Bankshares, 1977-80; bd. dirs. Nat. Air and Space Mus., The Shakespeare Guild, Materia. Represented in permanent collections at Balt. Mus. Art, Corocoran Gallery Art, Dayton Art Inst., Frederik Meijer Sculpture Gardens, Folger Shakespeare Libr., Nat. Air and Space Mus., Washington Tennis Ctr., High Mus. Art, Atlanta, Milw. Mus. Art, Harvard Law Sch., Harvard Bus. Sch., Hofstra U., Mayo Clinic, Jacksonville, Fla., Phila. Mus. Art, San Francisco Mus. Art, Duke U. Med. Ctr., Embry-Riddle Aero. U., Georgetown U., George Washington U., Williams Coll., Scripps Rsch. Inst., Daniel Webster Coll., Am. Hosp., Paris, Embassy of U.S., London, Nassau, Beijing, New Delhi, Fayetteville (NC) Mus. Art, Nat. Jewish Mus., Nat. Peace Inst., Ponce (PR) Mus. of Art, UN, N.Y.C., corps. including Celanese Corp., NY, Crown Equipment Corp., New Bremen, Ohio, First Union Bank of Md., Bank of Am. Ctr., Norfolk, Va., Gen. Mills Corp., Mpls Rosemont Co., Atlanta, West Chase Corp., Houston, Nat. Air Traffic Controller, numerous others; author: John Safer, Sculptor, Art in Flight, 1990, The Sculpture of John Safer, 1982 1st lt. USAAF, 1942-46. Mem.: Cosmos, Burning Tree, Harvard, Woodmont (Washington), Lyford Cay (Nassau), Linville Ridge (N.C.). Office: PO Box 6720 Mc Lean VA 22106-6720 Office Phone: 703-276-7766. Personal E-Mail: johnsafer@aol.com.

**SAFF, EDWARD BARRY,** mathematics professor, dean; b. N.Y.C., Jan. 2, 1944; s. Irving H. and Rose (Koslow) Saff; m. Loretta Singer, July 3, 1966; children: Lisa Jill, Tracy Karen, Alison Michelle. BS with highest honors, Ga. Inst. Tech., 1964; PhD, U. Md., 1968. Asst. prof. U. Md., 1968; post-doctoral rschr. Imperial Coll., London, 1968-69; from asst. prof. to assoc. prof. math. U. S. Fla., 1969—76, prof., 1976-86, disting. rsch. prof., 1986—2001, dir. Ctr. Math. Svcs., 1978-83, dir. Inst. Constructive Math., 1985—2001, dir. Ctr. Constructive Approximation, 2001—04; exec. dean Coll. Arts and Sci. Vanderbilt U., Nashville, 2004—. Sr. vis. fellow Oxford U., 1978; hon. prof. Zhejiang Normal U. Author (with A. D. Snider): Fundamentals of Complex Analysis, 1976, 3d edit., 2003; author: (with A. W. Goodman) Calculus, Concepts and Calculations, 1981; author: (with A. Edrei and R. S. Varga) Zeros of Sections of Power Series; author: (with V. Totik) Logarithmic Potentials with External Fields, 1997; author: (with R. K. Nagle) Fundamentals of Differential Equations, 1993, Fundamentals of Differential Equations and Boundary Value Problems, 1993; author: (with D. S. Lubinsky) Strong Asymptotics for External Polynomials Associated with Weights on R, 1988; editor: Jour. Approximation Theory, 1990—; editor: (with R. S. Varga) Pade and Rational Approximation: Theory and Applications, 1977; editor: Cambridge U. Press, 1995—2001, Founds. Comp. Math., 1999—2004; editor-in-chief: Constructive Approximation Jour., 1983—, Computational Methods and Function Theory Jour., 2001—. Recipient Chancellor's Rsch. award, Vanderbilt U., 2005; fellow, Fulbright Found., 1968—69, Guggenheim Found., 1978; grantee, NSF, 1970—72, 1980—. Mem.: Math. Assn. Am., Am. Math. Soc., Sigma Xi. Office: Ctr Constructive Approximation Vanderbilt U Dept Math Nashville TN 37240 Office Phone: 615-322-7360. Business E-Mail: ed.saff@vanderbilt.edu.

**SAFFAR, JEAN-MARC,** healthcare consultant; b. Paris, May 1, 1965; s. Max and Michele S.; m. Claudia Moss, Feb. 13, 1994; children: Etty, Charles. MD, Paris Sch. Medicine, 1991, BS in Biostats., 1995; MS in Health Policy, Dauphine Sch. Mgmt., Paris, 1995; PhD in Pub. Health, Amiens Sch. Medicine, France, 1997; MS in Healthcare Mgmt., Harvard U., 1997; MBA, U. Mich., 2000. Internist Paris Hosp., 1991-93; pub. health rschr. Regional Health Obs., Amiens, France, 1994-96; sr. cons. KPMG Peat Marwick, Boston, 1997-98; sr. mgr. A.T. Kearney, Cambridge, Mass., 1998—2002. Cons. in field. Lt. French Army, 1993-94. Mem. French Med. Bd., French Assn. Pub. Health Profls., Harvard Club N.Y., U. Mich. Bus. Sch. Alumni Assn., Harvard Alumni Assn. Avocations: video editing, french movies, backgammon, skiing. Home: 1365 York Ave #12E New York NY 10021 Office: True North Capital 375 Park Ave Ste 2309 New York NY 10152 E-mail: jean-marc.saffar@post.harvard.edu.

**SAFFELS, ANNA WAYNE BROTHERS,** retired mathematician, educator; b. Gallant, Ala., Nov. 6, 1928; d. Homer Ervin and Bertie Galloway Brothers; m. George Aaron Saffels (dec.); children: Michael Aaron, Elisabeth Anne. BS in Secondary Edn., Jacksonville State U., 1949; MA in Secondary Edn., U. Ala., Birmingham, 1973. Cert. tchr. Ala., 1949. Tchr. Ivalee Sch., Attalla, Ala., 1949—53, 1956—61, 1964—66; tchr. math. Etowah H.S., Attalla, Ala., 1966—86, ret., 1986. Pres. Etowah County Classroom Tchrs. Assn., 1967—68. Pianist Ivalee Bapt. Ch., 1950—2006, Sunday sch. tchr., 1950—97, dir. sr. activities, 2000—06. Nominee Jacksonville State Tchr. Hall of Fame, 1972, Presdl. award for excellence in math. tchg. Mem.: NEA, Ala. Edn. Assn., Alpha Delta Kappa (past pres. Ala. Alpha Xi chpt.), Kappa Delta Pi. Avocations: genealogy, stamp collecting/philately, photography, music, flower gardening. Home: 3194 Hwy 77 Attalla AL 35954-7140 Personal E-Mail: awbsaffels@aol.com.

**SAFFIOTTI, UMBERTO,** pathologist; b. Milan, Jan. 22, 1928; came to U.S., 1960, naturalized, 1966; s. Francesco Umberto and Maddalena (Valenzano) S.; m. Paola Amman, June 21, 1958; children: Luisa M., Maria Francesca. MD cum laude, U. Milan, 1951, splty. diploma occupational medicine cum laude, 1957. Intern Inst. Pathol. Anatomy U. Milan, 1951-52, asst. to chmn. occupational medicine, chief lab. pathology, Inst. Occupational Medicine, 1956-60, fellow Inst. Gen. Pathology, 1957-60; rsch. assn. oncology, rsch. assoc. Chgo. Med. Sch., 1952-55, from asst. prof. to prof. oncology, 1960-68; mem. staff Nat. Cancer Inst., Bethesda, Md., 1968—, assoc. dir. carcinogenesis, 1968-76, chief lab. exptl. pathology, 1974-98, acting head Registry of Exptl. Cancers, 1988-98; scientist emeritus, 1998—; adj. prof., Environ. & Occ. Hlth. The George Washington U., Washington, 2000—. Mem. pathology B study sect., NIH, 1964-68; former mem. various adv. coms. govt. agys.; mem. cancer prevention com. Internat. Union Against Cancer, 1959-66, panel on carcinogenicity, 1963-66; chmn. ad hoc com. evaluation low levels environ. carcinogens HEW, 1969-70. Co-editor books; contbr. articles to profl. jours. Bd. dirs. Rachel Carson Trust, 1976-79. Recipient Career Devel. award NIH, 1965-68, Superior Svc. Honor award HEW, 1971, Pub. Interest Sci. award Environ. Def. Fund, 1977, Spl. Recognition award USPHS, 1980 Fellow NYAS; mem. AAAS, Am. Assn. Cancer Rsch. (pres. Chgo. chpt. 1966-67), Am. Soc. Investigative Pathology, Soc. Toxicology, Sigma Xi. Democrat. Home: 5931 Winnemg Rd Bethesda MD 20816-2259 Office: NIH Nat Cancer Inst 6116 Executive Blvd Rm 7212 Bethesda MD 20892-8314 Business E-Mail: saffiotti@nih.gov.

**SAFFIR, HERBERT SEYMOUR,** structural engineer, consultant; b. N.Y.C., Mar. 29, 1917; s. A.L. and Gertrude (Samuels) S.; m. Sarah Young, May 9, 1941; children: Richard Young, Barbara Joan. BSCE cum laude, Ga. Inst. Tech., 1940. Registered profl. engr., Fla., N.Y., Tex., P.R., Miss.; lic. land

surveyor, Fla. Civil engr. TVA, Chattanooga, 1940, NACA, Langley Field, Va., 1940—41; structural engr. Ebasco Svcs., N.Y.C., 1941—43, York & Sawyer & Fred Severud, N.Y.C., 1945; engr. Waddell & Hardesty, Cons. Engrs., N.Y.C., 1945—47; asst. county engr. Dade County, Miami, Fla., 1947—59; cons. engr. Herbert S. Saffir, Coral Gables, Fla., 1959—. Adj. prof. civil engring. Coll. Engring., U. Miami, 1964—; adviser civil engring. Fla. Internat. U., 1975-80; cons. on bldg. codes Govt. Bahamas, cons. on engring. in housing to UN; chmn. Met. Dade County Unsafe Structures Bd., 1977-92; mem. Bldg. Code Evaluation Task Force after Hurricane Andrew; mem. Am. Nat. Stds. Inst. Commn. Bldg. Design Loads, Nat. Adv. Group on Glass Design, Dade County Bldg. Code Com. 1993-96; cmty. rels. com. U. Miami/Coral Gables, 1993-96; reviewer for NSF; bd. adjustment City of Coral Gables, 1994-97, budget bd., 1997-2001; evaluation panel Biltmore, 1982-83; cons., presenter in field Author: Housing Construction in Hurricane Prone Areas, 1971, Nature and Extent of Damage by Hurricane Camille, 1972, Evaluation of Structural Damage Caused by Hurricanes, 1993; contbg. author: Wind Effects on Structures, 1976, Hurricane! Coping with Disaster, 2002; editor: Wind Engr., 1986-92; editor Manual of Wind Damage Investigation; contbr. articles to profl. jours.; designer Saffir/Simpson hurricane scale. With N.Y. Guard, 1942-43, AUS, 1943-44, WWII. Recipient Outstanding Svc. award Fla. Profl. Engrs., 1954, Pub. Svc. award Nat. Weather Svc., 1975, Disting. Svc. award Nat. Hurricane Conf., 1987; named Miami Engr. of Year, 1978, 94, Gov.'s Design award, 1986, Gov. Gilchrist award for Profl. Excellence, 1988, Albert H. Friedman Cmty. Svc. award, 1992, Engring. award Nat. Hurricane Conf., 1997; named to Ga. Tech. Engring. Hall of Fame, 1995; named Herbert S. Saffir Miami-Dade Permitting and Inspection Ctr. in his honor, 2002 Fellow Fla. Engring. Soc. (award for outstanding tech. achievement 1973, Cmty. Svc. award 1980, Lifetime Achievement award 2003, disting. engr. award 2003), Coll. Engrs. P.R. (Disting. Engr. award 2002); mem. ASCE (hon., past pres., sec., aerodynamics com. 1983—, mem. mitigation of wind damage com. 1985—, chmn. com. on damage investigation 1989—, mem. com. A7 on design loads for bldgs. 1972—), Soc. Am. Mil. Engrs., Am. Concrete Inst., ASTM (mem. com. performance bldg. constrn.), Internat. Assn. for Bridge and Structural Engring., Colegio de Ingenieros P.R., Am. Meterol. Soc., Am. Arbitration Assn., Wind Engring. Rsch. Coun. (past bd. dirs., Svc. award 1990), Am. Assn. for Wind Engring., Coral Gables C. of C. (bd. dirs., past pres., past chmn.), Tau Beta Pi, Chi Epsilon (hon.). Clubs: Country of Coral Gables. Home: 4818 Alhambra Cir Coral Gables FL 33146-1643 Office: Consulting Engineers 350 Sevilla Ave Ste 108 Coral Gables FL 33134-6617 Office Phone: 305-444-2611.

**SAFFIR, LEONARD,** public relations executive; b. N.Y.C., Apr. 19, 1930; s. Abraham and Gertrude S.; m. Patricia Roemer (div. 1980); children: Andrew, Michelle; m. Wendy McConaughy (div. 1992); 1 child, Samantha; m. Eleanor Unger, 1997. Student, Syracuse U., 1948-51. Editor, bur. chief Internat. News Service, Dallas, Tokyo, 1953-58; producer Eng., Australia, Asia, 1958-60; ptnr. Haft, Saffir, Siegel Pub. Relations & Advt., N.Y.C. 1960-62; asst. pub. N.Y. Standard, 1962-63; cons. Ferdinand Marcos, 1964; pub. Latin Am. Times, N.Y.C., 1965; exec. v.p. Franchises Internat., N.Y.C., 1965-69; press sec., chief of staff to Senator James Buckley U.S. Senate, Washington, 1970-76; pub., editor The Trib, N.Y.C., 1977-78, The Sun, Bridgehampton, NY, 1978-84; exec. v.p. Porter/Novelli, N.Y.C., 1984-90; pres. Jay DeBow & Ptnrs., N.Y.C., Fla., 1989-90, Leonard Saffir & Assocs. Pub. Rels., 2000—; investigative reporter, columnist Lake Worth Herald, 2001—03. CEO Adventures One, 1998-2000, Celebrity Stores.com, 1998-2000. Author: Power Public Relations, 1992, Power Public Relations: How to Master the New PR, 2000, PR on a Budget, 2006. Campaign mgr. Marchi for Mayor, N.Y.C., 1973, Buckley for Senator, N.Y., 1976. Served as sgt. USMC, 1951-53. Recipient Silver Anvil and Big Apple awards Pub. Rels. Soc. Am., Mayor's award City of N.Y., others. Mem. Authors Guild, Overseas Press Club (pres. 1988-89). Home: 6137 Rainbow Circle Lake Worth FL 33463 Personal E-Mail: lenpr@bellsouth.net.

**SAFFOLD, MONROE,** science educator, consultant; b. Lexington, Miss., Apr. 12, 1948; s. Monroe, Sr. and Dixie Saffold; m. Patricia-Jean Cole Saffold, Mar. 17, 1974; children: Nicole Patrice, Brian Keith. BS, U. Ill., Chgo., 1973, MS, 1983; MA, North Park Seminary, Chgo., 2005. Cert. tchr. Ill. Fitness instr., youth activities counselor Duncan YMCA, Chgo., 1966—71; tchr. biology and earth sci. Chgo. Pub. Schs., 1973—; fitness instr., youth activities and sports NCAA, NYSP Program, U. Ill., Chgo., 1974—85; instr. natural sci., biology and physics Ctrl. YMCA Coll., Chgo., 1976—78; instr. exercise and physiology U. Ill., Chgo., 1977—78; prof. anatomy and physiology Triton Coll., River Grove, Ill., 1989—. Cons. Robert Morris Coll. Adv. Bd., Chgo., 2005—. Guest (TV appearance) WMAQ-Channel 5 News, sports, 1991. Motiviational spkr. Lincoln's Challenge Acad., Rantoul, Ill., 1998—99; found. mem. Loretto Hosp. Found., Chgo., 2004—; motiviational spkr. Christian Heritage Acad., Northfield, Ill., 2005; pastor, Bible tchr. Camp Grow Ministries, Markesan, Wis., 2005—06. Mem.: Am. Fedn. Tchrs., Chgo. Tchrs. Union. Avocations: swimming, reading, bicycling, piano, exercise. Home: 14 Forest Ave River Forest IL 60305 E-Mail: monroesaffold@comcast.net.

**SAFFORD, FLORENCE VIRAY SUNGA,** travel agent, consultant; b. Masantol, Pampanga, Luzon, Philippines, Mar. 19, 1932; came to U.S., 1953; d. Filomeno Garcia and Dominga (Viray) Sunga; m. Francis Ingersoll Safford, Aug. 4, 1979; children: H. Robert, Erlinda Ann, Ruben Michael. BS in Edn. Adamson U., Manila, 1952; student Hotel Mgmt. and Polit. Sci., Kapiolani C.C., Honolulu, 1975; student. Am. Travel Sch., Honolulu, 1977. Tchr. Cecilio Apostles Elem. Sch., Manila, 1949-51, St. Michael Acad., Masantol, 1951-52; social worker Cath. Social Svc., Honolulu, 1970-77; cons. Travel Cons. of the Pacific, Honolulu, 1977—; social worker Kapiolani C.C., Honolulu. Mem. exec. bd. dirs. Oahu Cmty. Coun., 1994—; elected to Neighborhood Bd., 1982—84, 1993—95; apptd. by mayor of Honolulu to Ethics Commn., 1986—95; v.p. Marbella Home Owners Assn. at Summerlin Resorts, 2001—; bd. dirs., del. Summerlin Resorts Homeowners Assn., 2004—; bd. dirs. C. of C. of Hawaii. Named Most Outstanding Leader of the Community, Filipino Jaycees of Honolulu, 1976. Mem.: Aloha Bus. and Profl. Women's Club (treas., Outstanding award 1981—89), Filipino C. of C. of Hawaii (treas., bd. dirs. 1994, Outstanding award 1991—92), Women's Cmty. Action League of Hawaii (pres. 1972—2001, Outstanding Pres. 1992). Republican. Roman Catholic. Avocation: dance. also: 10849 Carbonia Ct Las Vegas NV 89144-4508

**SAFFRAN, KALMAN,** entrepreneur, venture capitalist; b. Boston, Dec. 28, 1947; s. Max and Marion (Patick) S. BA, Northeastern U., 1971; postgrad., MIT, 1971-72. Lic. real estate broker, Mass. Mgr. sys. MIT, 1972-76; corp. cons. United Brands Co., Boston, 1977-78; CEO Monitrex Corp., Boston, 1977-82; pres. Kalman Saffran Assocs., Inc., Newton, Mass., 1978—2000; bd. advisers Prism Venture Ptnrs. Bd. advisors Blackstone Bank and Trust Co., Boston; mem. network implementation panel U.S. Energy Research and Devel. Adminstrn., Washington, 1975-76; mem. computer com. MIT Lab. for Nuclear Sci., 1975-76. Mem. Data Processing Mgmt. Assn., Assn. Computing Machinery, Soc. for Info. Mgmt., IEEE, Mensa. Republican. Jewish. Home: 1564 Commonwealth Ave W Newton MA 02465-2806 Office: Kalman Saffran Assocs Inc PO Box 66033 Newton MA 02466-0001 Office Phone: 617-527-2000.

**SAFFURI, KHALED AHMAD,** cultural organization executive; b. Beirut, July 28, 1956; came to U.S., 1981; s. Ahmad Hasan Saffouri and Siham Sihani; m. Jenifer Ann Hall, Aug. 28, 1994 (div. Aug. 1997). BA in Bus. Adminstrn., USIA, Calif., 1985; MA in Mgmt., U. Redlands, Calif., 1987. Dir. Mid. East affairs Am.-Arab Anti-Discrimination Com., Washington, 1987-90; asst. exec. dir. Nat. Assn. Arab-Americans, Washington, 1990-93, Am. Muslim Coun., Washington, 1994-97; exec. dir. Am. Task Force for Bosnia, Washington, 1992-98, Islamic Inst., Washington, 1998—. Co-author: (book) Islam and Free Market, 1998. Moslem. Office: Islamic Inst Found 1920 L St NW Ste 200 Washington DC 20036-5036

**SAFIAN, GAIL ROBYN,** public relations executive; b. Bklyn., Dec. 12, 1947; d. Jack I. and Harriet S.; m. Jay Mark Eisenberg, Jan. 6, 1979; children: Julia, Eric. BA, SUNY, Albany, 1968; MBA, NYU, 1982. Reporter Albany (N.Y.)-Knickerbocker News/Times-Union, 1969, Athens (Ohio) Messenger, 1969-71; pub. relations asst. Mountainside Hosp., Montclair, N.J., 1971-74; dir. pub. relations Riverside Hosp., Boonton, N.J., 1974-78; consumer affairs coordinator Johnson & Johnson Personal Products Div., Milltown, N.J., 1978-79; v.p., group mgr. Harshe Rotman & Druck, N.Y.C., 1979-82; exec. v.p., dir. Health Care Div. Ruder Finn & Rotman, N.Y.C., 1982-84; v.p., mgr. client services Burson-Marsteller, N.Y.C., 1984-86; v.p., group mgr. health care Cohn & Wolfe, N.Y.C., 1986-90; exec. v.p., gen. mgr. MCS, Summit, N.J., 1990-94; pres. Safian Comm. Inc., Maplewood, N.J., 1994—. Mem. devel. com. Cancer Care, N.Y.C., 1985—. Recipient MacEachern award Am. Hosp. Assn., 1974, Communications Award Internat. Assn. Bus. Communicators, 1976, Creativity in Pub. Rels. award Inside PR, 1992, 93, Big Apple award 2005 Mem. Healthcare Businesswomen's Assn. (mem. bd. dirs.), N.Y. Acad. Scis., Women in Comm. (Clarion award 1974). Jewish. Home and Office: Safian Comm Inc 31 Hickory Dr Maplewood NJ 07040-2107 E-mail: gsafian@safianhealth.com.

**SAFIAN, KEITH FRANKLIN,** hospital administrator; b. Bklyn., June 22, 1950; s. Jack I. and Harriet S. (Cohen) S.; children: Elizabeth Anne, Alexander William. BS in EE and Indsl. Engring., SUNY, Buffalo, 1972; MBA, U. Pa., 1974. Asst. dir. Kings County Hosp. Ctr., Bklyn., 1974-76; asst. adminstr. NYU Med. Ctr., N.Y.C., 1977-80, assoc. adminstr., 1981-84, sr. assoc. adminstr., 1984-85; adminstr. St. John's Episcopal Hosp., Far Rockaway, NY, 1985-89; pres., CEO Phelps Meml. Hosp. Ctr., Sleepy Hollow, NY, 1989—. Bd. dirs. Addabbo Family Health Ctr., Arverne, N.Y., 1987-89, Rockaway Devel. and Revitalization Corp., Far Rockaway, 1988-89; bd. dirs. The ExcelCare Sys., Bronxville, N.Y., 1993-99, chmn. 1995-98; bd. dirs. No Met. Hosp. Assn., Newburgh, N.Y., 1989—, mem. exec. com., 1993-98, 2000-05, chmn., 1996, 2003, treas., 2001, vice chmn. 2002. Fellow Am. Coll. Healthcare Execs.; mem. Hosp. Adminstrs. Club of N.Y., Health Care Assn. N.Y. State (trustee 1996-98, 2003-05). Home: 16 Brokaw Ln Great Neck NY 11023-1160 Office: Phelps Memorial Hosp 701 N Broadway Tarrytown NY 10591-1096 Office Phone: 914-366-1001. Business E-Mail: phelpsceo@pmhc.us.

**SAFIAN, ROBERT L.,** executive editor; b. Mount Vernon, N.Y., Apr. 20, 1964; m. Mary Safian; children: Matthew, Nicholas. BA in History magna cum laude, Brown U., 1987. Summer intern, then reporter, then exec. editor The Am. Lawyer, 1987—94; sr. editor, then articles editor SmartMoney, 1994—97; head personal fin. coverage divsn. Fortune, 1997—98; mng. editor Money Mag., N.Y.C., 1998—2004; exec. editor Time mag., N.Y.C., 2004—. Tchr. legal affairs reporting Columbia U. Sch. Journalism, 1993—96; guest lectr. Harvard Law Sch., 1993. Named one of 40 Under 40, Crain's N.Y. Bus. Office: Time Inc Rockefeller Ctr New York NY 10020-1393

**SAFIAN, SHELLEY CAROLE,** advertising executive; b. Bklyn., May 29, 1954; d. Jack Israel and Harriet Sara (Cohen) S. BFA, Parsons Sch. Design, 1975; MA, U. Phoenix, 2002. Cert. coding specialist; in health svcs. mgmt. Keller Grad. Sch. Bus., 2005. Asst. art dir. Axelrod and Assocs., N.Y.C., 1975-77; art dir. Sta. WDBO-TV-AM/FM, Orlando, Fla., 1978-80; owner, pres. Safian Comm. Svcs., Inc., Winter Park, Fla., 1981—, Bonté Sportswear, Winter Park, Fla., 1993-97; chair allied health dept. Herzing Coll., Winter Park, Fla., 2004—. Mem. adv. com. Career Edn., Orange County, Fla., 1981—88, chmn., 1982—83; adj. prof. Internat. Acad. Design and Tech., 2000—; adj. prof. City Coll., Casselberry, Fla., 2000—. Author: Insurance Coding & Electronic Claims for the Medical Office, 2005. Exec. producer/dir. March of Dimes Telethon, Orlando, 1984; bd. dirs. Boy Scouts Am., 1987-91; exec. dir. United Cerebral Palsy Telethon, Orlando, 1982-83; pub. rels. liaison United Cerebral Palsy, Orlando, 1983-84; founder Career Dir. for Deaf, Orlando, 1985; trustee, pub. rels. chair Nat. Multiple Sclerosis Soc., 1991-92, bd. dirs., 1990, 91. Recipient 1st pl. Addy awards Orlando ADvt. Fedn., 1981, 87, 88, 89, 1st pl. Addy award, 2d pl. awards, merit awards, 1982, 84, 85, 87, 88, Nat. Telly award Bronze Statue, 1988, Up and Coming award Price Waterhouse/Orlando Bus. Jour., 1988, Pro-Mark 1st pl. awards Fla. Coun. Shopping Ctrs., 1989, 90, merit award, 1990, Telly award Bronze finalist, 1989, 91; named Tchr. of the Quarter, 2001. Mem. Broadcast Promotion and Mktg. Execs. Assn. (Silver Medalion 1983, nat. finalist 2 Silver Microphone awards 1986, 87), Broadcast Designer's Assn. (bd.d irs. 1980-82), Am. Women in Radio and TV (bd. dirs. 1980-81). Republican. Avocation: horseback riding.

**SAFIRE, WILLIAM,** journalist, foundation administrator; b. NYC, Dec. 17, 1929; s. Oliver C. and Ida (Panish) M.; m. Helene Belmar Julius, Dec. 16, 1962; children: Mark Lindsey, Annabel Victoria. Student, Syracuse U., 1947—49. Reporter NY Herald Tribune Syndicate, 1949-51; corr. WNBC-WNBT, Europe and Mid. East, 1951; radio-TV prodr. WNBC, NYC, 1954-55; v.p. pub. rels. Tex McCrary, Inc., 1955-60; pres. Safire Pub. Rels., Inc., 1960-68; sr. White House speechwriter Pres. Richard Nixon, Washington, 1969-73; polit. columnist NY Times, Washington, 1973—2005; columnist On Language, NY Times Mag., 1979—. Trustee Syracuse U.; chmn. Dana Found. Author: The Relations Explosion, 1963, Plunging into Politics, 1964, Safire's Political Dictionary, 1968, rev. edit., 1972—78, Before the Fall, 1975, Full Disclosure, 1977, Safire's Washington, 1980, On Language, 1980, What's the Good Word?, 1982, I Stand Corrected, 1984, Take My Word for It, 1986, Freedom, 1987, You Could Look It Up, 1988, Language Maven Strikes Again, 1990, Fumblerules, 1990, Coming to Terms, 1991, The First Dissident, 1992, Lend Me Your Ears, 1992, 1998, 2004, Good Advice on Writing, 1992, Quoth the Maven, 1993, Safire's New Political Dictionary, 1993, In Love with Norma Loquendi, 1994, Sleeper Spy, 1995, Watching My Language, 1997, Spread the Word, 1999, Scandalmonger, 2000, Let a Simile Be Your Umbrella, 2001, No Uncertain Terms, 2003, The Right Word, 2004; co-author (with Leonard Safir): Good Advice on Writing, 1982, Words of Wisdom, 1989, Leadership, 1990. Mem. Pulitzer Bd., 1995-2004. With AUS, 1952-54. Recipient Pulitzer prize for Disting. Commentary, 1978. Republican. Office: The Dana Foundation 900 15th St NW Washington DC 20005 Business E-Mail: wsafire@dana.org.

**SAFIRSTEIN, ROBERT LOUIS,** nephrologist, medical educator, medical researcher; BA in Chemistry, Bklyn Coll., 1965; MD, U. Cin., 1969. Diplomate Nat. Bd. Med. Examiners, 1970, Am. Bd. Internal Medicine, 1974. Internship pediat. Columbia Presbyn. Hosp., NYC, 1969—70; fellowship nephrology US Public Health Sys., Staten Island, NY, 1970—72; residency internal medicine Mt. Siani Sch. Medicine, NYC, 1972—74; rsch. assoc. dept. physiology Yale U. Sch. Medicine, Conn., 1974—77; asst. prof. or medicine Mt. Sinai Sch. of Medicine, NYC, 1977—87; assoc. prof. medicine Mt. Sinai Sch. Medicine, 1987—92; dir. nephrology, prof. medicine U. Tex. Med. Br., Galveston, Tex., 1992—99; chief U. Ark. Med. Scis., Little Rock, 1999—, exec. vice chair, 1999—; chief medicine Ctrl. Ark. Vets. Healthcare Sys., Little Rock, 1999—. Med. dir. Hemodialysis Unit Tex. Dept. Justice, Huntsville, Tex., 1997—99. Editor: The Metabolic Syndrome and Acute Renal Failure, A Festschrift in Honor of Thomas E. Andreoli, Kidney Internat., 2005—; contbr. chapters to books. Grantee, Nat. Inst. of Health, 2000—06, Vets. Adminstrn., 2005—, NIH, 2006—, 2006—, Am. Heart Assn., 2006—. Mem.: Internat. Soc. Nephrology, Am. Soc. Nephrology, Am. Physiol. Soc., Assn. Profs. Medicine. Achievements include patents for regulation of the P21 gene and uses thereof. Avocations: hiking, bicycling. Office: Central AR Veterans Healthcare System 4300 West 7th Street Little Rock AR 72205 Office Phone: 501-257-5866. Office Fax: 501-257-5867. Business E-Mail: safirsteinrobertl@uams.edu.

**SAFIZADEH, M. HOSSEIN,** finance educator; BBA, Iran Inst. Banking; MBA, PhD, Okla. State U. Prof. ops. and strategic mgmt. dept. Carroll Sch. Mgmt., Boston Coll., 1997—, interim dean, 2003—. Editl. bd. mem. Prodn. and Ops. Mgmt. Office: Boston Coll Carroll Sch Mgmt Fulton Hall 454A 140 Commonwealth Ave Chestnut Hill MA 02467 Office Phone: 617-552-0476. Business E-Mail: hossein.safizadeh.1@bc.edu.

**SAFKA, JIM,** information technology executive; BS Accounting, U. So. Ca.; MBA, J.L. Kellogg School of Management, Northwestern U. Mgr. Alberto-Culver, Inc., Warner Bros., Paramount Pictures; with Intuit; v.p. E*Trade, 1997—2002; v.p., gen. mgr. e-commerce AT&T Wireless, 2002—04; CEO Match.com, 2004—. Office: Match.com 3001 George Bush Hwy Ste 100 Richardson TX 75082*

**SAFLEY, JAMES ROBERT,** lawyer; b. Cedar Rapids, Iowa, Sept. 19, 1943; s. Robert Starr and Jean (Engelman) S.; m. Dianne Lee McInnis; children: Anne Michele, Jamie Leigh. BA, U. Iowa, 1965; JD, Duke U., 1968. Bar: Minn. 1968, U.S. Ct. Appeals (4th, 5th, 6th, 7th, 8th, 9th and 11th cirs.), U.S. Supreme Ct. Law clk. U.S. Dist. Ct. Minn., Mpls., 1968-69; assoc. Robins, Kaplan, Miller & Ciresi, Mpls., 1969-74, ptnr., 1974—. Mem. adv. coun. Women's Intercollegiate Athletics, U. Minn., 1988-94; mem bd. visitors Duke Law Sch., 2004—. Mem. ABA, Minn. State Bar Assn. (antitrust sect. chmn. 1985-87), Hennepin County Bar Assn., Duke Law Alumni Assn. (bd. dirs. 2001-03), Phi Beta Kappa. Office: Robins Kaplan Miller & Ciresi 2800 LaSalle Pla 800 Lasalle Ave Ste 2800 Minneapolis MN 55402-2015 Office Phone: 612-349-8274.

**SAFONOV, MICHAEL GEORGE,** electrical engineering educator, consultant; b. Pasadena, Calif., Nov. 1, 1948; s. George Michael and Ruth Garnet (Ware) S.; m. Nancy Kelshaw Schorn, Aug. 31, 1968 (div. Oct. 1983); 1 child, Alexander; m. Janet Sunderland, Feb. 25, 1985; 1 child, Peter. BSEE, MSEE, MIT, 1971, EE, 1976, PhDEE, 1977. Electronic engr. Air Force Cambridge Rsch. Lab., Hanscom AFB, Mass., 1968-71; rsch. asst. MIT, Cambridge, 1975-77; prof. elec. engring. U. So. Calif., L.A., 1977—, assoc. chmn. dept., 1989-93, vice chmn. engring faculty coun., 2001—02, chmn. engring. faculty coun., 2003—04. Vis. scholar Cambridge (Eng.) U., 1983-84, Imperial Coll., London, 1987, Calif. Inst. Tech., Pasadena, 1990-91; cons. Honeywell Systems and Rsch. Ctr., Mpls., 1978-83, Space Systems div. TRW, Redondo Beach, Calif., 1984, Northrop Aircraft, Hawthorne, Calif., 1985-91, also numerous others. Author: Stability and Robustness of Multivariable Feedback Systems (hon. mention Phi Beta Kappa 1981); co-author: (book and software) Robust-Control Toolbox, 1988; assoc. editor IEEE Trans. on Automatic Control, 1985-87, Internat. Jour. Robust and Nonlinear Control, 1998-93, Sys. and Control Letters, 1995—. Awards com. chair Am. Automatic Control Coun., 1993-95. Lt. (j.g.) USNR, 1972-75. Rsch. grantee Air Force Office Sci. Rsch., 1978—, NSF, 1982-84. Fellow IEEE; mem. AIAA (sr.), Common Cause. Republican. Office: U So Calif Dept EE Sys MC 2563 3740 McClintock Ave # 310 Los Angeles CA 90089-2563 Office Phone: 213-740-4455. Business E-Mail: msafonov@usc.edu. *Consider first only the very simplest problem--but strive for a representation of the simplest problem that generalizes.*

**SAFRA, JOSEPH,** bank executive; s. Joseph Safra. Co-owner Safra Group; chmn., CEO Banco Safra S.A., Sao Paulo, Brazil; chmn. Safra Nat. Bank NY. Mem. adv. bd. Wharton U. Pa.; chmn. bd. dirs. Banque Jacob Safra (Suisse) S.A. Contbr. New Ctr. Brazilian Studies Oxford U., Hazon Yeshaya Soup Kitchens. Named one of World's Richest People, Forbes Mag., 2000—04. Bank holdings span the Caribbean, New York and Europe and include Safra Bank NY, Banque Safra Luxembourg and First Internat. Bank Israel. Office: Safra Nat Bank NY 546 5th Ave New York NY 10036

**SAFRO, MILLICENT,** small business owner, decorative arts scholar, writer; Co-owner Tender Buttons, N.Y.C. and Chgo., 1964—. Lectr., appraiser in field; collector, dealer antique buttons. Co-author: Buttons, 1991; contbr. articles to mags., periodicals; exhibitions include Cooper-Hewitt Mus., N.Y.C., Smithsonian Instn., Washington, Atheneum, La Jolla, Calif., L.A. County Mus. Art, Henry Flagler Mus., Palm Beach, Fla., Shiseido Art Gallery, Tokyo. Avocation: dealer and collector of antique buttons. Office: Tender Buttons 143 E 62d St New York NY 10021 Office Phone: 212-980-3540.

**SAFT, STUART MARK,** lawyer; b. NYC, Feb. 17, 1947; s. Stanley and Dorothy (Ligerman) S.; m. Stephanie C. Optekman, June 6, 1970; children: Bradley S., Gordon D. BA, Hofstra U., 1968; JD, Columbia U., 1971. Bar: N.Y. 1972, Fla. 1975, U.S. Dist. Ct. (so. dist.) N.Y. 1975, U.S. Supreme Ct. 1990. Ptnr. Wolf Haldenstern Adler Freeman & Herz, N.Y.C., 1988—. Chmn. bd. dirs. Coun. of NY Coops., NYC, 1981-; chmn. Nat. Coop. Bank, NYC Workforce Investment Bd.; chmn. bd. dirs., CEO Pvt. Industry Coun. NYC, 1994-2000; bd. dirs. Nat. Assn. Housing Coops. Author: Commercial Real Estate Forms, 3 vols., 1987, Commercial Real Estate Transactions, 1989, Commercial Real Estate Workouts, 1991, Real Estate Development: Strategies for a Changing Market, 1990, Commercial Real Estate Leasing, 1992, Real Estate Investor's Survival Guide, 1992, Commercial Real Estate Financing, 1993, Commercial Real Estate Forms, 3d edit., 8 vols., 2001, Commercial Real Estate Transactions, 2d edit., 1995, Commercial Real Estate Workouts, 2d edit., 1996; contbg. editor: The Real Estate Finance Jour., 1989—; contbr. articles to profl. jours. Capt USAR, 1968—76. Mem. ABA, Am. Coll. Real Estate Lawyers, N.Y. Bar Assn., Fla. Bar Assn. Office: Wolf Haldenstern Adler Freeman & Herz 270 Madison Ave New York NY 10016-0601 Office Phone: 212-545-4710. Business E-Mail: saft@whafh.com.

**SAFYER, STEVEN MICHAEL,** medical association administrator, educator; b. New York, NY, Feb. 16, 1949; MD, Albert Einstein Coll. of Med., 1982. Cert. internal medicine. Intern Montefiore Med. Ctr., Bronx, NY, 1978—82, resident, 1983—85, v.p. med. affairs, 1997, sr. v.p., chief med. officer, 1998—; assoc. prof., dept. medicine Albert Einstein Coll. Medicine, 1987—, assoc. prof., dept. epidemiology & population health, 1987—; Office: MMC Centennial Bldg 111 E 210 St 4th Fl Bronx NY 10467*

**SAGAL, KATEY,** actress; b. L.A., Jan. 19, 1954; d. Boris Sagal and Sara Zwilling; m. Jack White, 1993 (div. 2000), m. Kurt sutter, Oct. 2, 2004. Student, Calif. Sch. of the Arts. Former back-up singer for various performers including Bob Dylan, Etta James; (with Bette Midler) former mem. The Harlettes. Actress: (stage prodns.) Martha Rose and the Miners, 1982, My Beautiful Lady, (TV series) Mary, 1986, Imagine That, 2002, (TV movie) The Failing of Raymond, 1971, Mother Goose Rock 'n' Rhyme, 1990, She Says She's Innocent, 1991, Trail of Tears, 1995, Mr. Headmistress, 1998, Chance of a Lifetime, 1998, God's New Plan, 1999, Smart House, 1999, (films) Maid to Order, 1987, The Good Mother, 1988, Following Tildy, 2002; regular (TV series) Married...With Children, 1987-97, (voice) Recess, 1997, (voice) Futurama, 1999, Tucker, 2000, 8 Simple Rules...for Dating My Teenage Daughter, 2002—. Mem. Actors' Equity Assn., Screen TV and Radio Artists. Office: Progressive Artists Agy Inc 400 S Beverly Dr Ste 216 Beverly Hills CA 90212-4404

**SAGAN, M. J.,** architectural firm executive; m. Craig L. Haft; children: Nicholas, Claire, Owen. BA in Architecture, Pa. State U., 1982. Lic. NY, NJ, Conn., cert. NCARB. Assoc., staff designer George F. Henschel, Jr., AIA, 1982—83; assoc./project arch. Becker, Becker & Lamont, Inc., New Canaan, Conn., 1983—84; assoc. Shope Reno Wharton Assoc., Greenwich, Conn., 1984—88; sr. assoc. Anderson/Schwartz Arch., N.Y.C., 1988—96; v.p. Anderson Architecture, NYC, 1996—2006; pres. MJ Sagan Architecture, 2006—. Exhibitions include Negotiating Domesticity/ The Greenwich Arts Coun., 2003, Princeton Pub. Libr., 2003. Recipient EDRA/Places Design award, 2003, Bldg. Team Project of the Yr.- Grand award, 2003, Good Design is Good Bus. award, 2002, Project award, Hudson River Pk., 2002, Gold award, 1994, Wallpaper Mag. Design award, 2004, AIA NJ, 2005, numerous other awards, AIA and others. Several selected publications from 1986-2002 in mag. such as: Arch. Record, House & Garden, The New York Times, Interior Design, Vogue, Diseno Interior 70, House Beautiful, Abitare, and Record Interiors. Business E-Mail: admin@mjsaganarchitecture.com.

**SAGAWA, YONEO,** horticulturist, educator; b. Olaa, Hawaii, Oct. 11, 1926; s. Chikatada and Mume (Kuno) S.; m. Masayo Yamamoto, May 24, 1962 (dec. Apr. 1988); children: Penelope Toshiko, Irene Teruko. AB, Washington U., St. Louis, 1950, MS, 1952; PhD, U. Conn., Storrs, 1956. Postdoctoral rsch. assoc. biology Brookhaven Nat. Lab., Upton, NY, 1955—57, guest in biology, 1958; asst. prof., then assoc. prof. U. Fla., 1957—64; dir. undergrad. sci. ednl. rsch. participation program NSF, 1964; cons. biosatellite project NASA, 1966—67; prof. horticulture U. Hawaii, 1964—; dir. Lyon Arboretum, 1967—91; assoc. dir. Hawaiian Sci. Fair, 1966—74, dir., 1967—68; rsch. assoc. in biology U. Calif., Berkeley, 1970—71; rsch. assoc. Bishop Mus., Honolulu, 1992—, Bot. Rsch. Inst. of Tex., 1993—Hawaii Tropical Bot. Garden, 1995—; external assessor U. Pertanian, Malaysia, 1994—. Mem. Internat. Orchid Commn. on Classification, Nomenclature and Registration; fellow Inst. voor Toepassing van Atoomenergerie in de Landbouw, U. Agr., Wageningen, The Netherlands, 1979-80; mem. sci. adv. bd. Nat. Tropical Bot. Garden, Kauai, Hawaii; consultant Las Cruces Bot. Garden, Costa Rica; cons. FAO, Singapore, 1971, USAID-Agribus. Assistance Program, Vols. in Overseas Coop. Assistance, UN Devel. Program-UN Internat. Short Term Adv. Resources; dir. Hawaii Tropical Bot. Garden; hon. scientist Rural Devel. Adminstrn., Republic of Korea, 1996—; cons. Fiji-N.Z. Bus. Coun., 1996, 97, 98, 99, 2000; cons. IRETA, Samoa, 1997, 98, 2003, 06; cons. Nat. Hort. Rsch. Inst., Suwon, Republic of Korea, 1998, 2000. Editor: Hawaii Orchid Jour., 1972-99, Pacific Orchid Soc. Bull., 1966-71; mem. editl. bd. Allertonia, 1976; mem. editl. adv. bd. Jour. Orchid Soc. India, 2002—; contbr. numerous articles to profl. jours. Trustee Friends of Honolulu Bot. Gardens, 1973-99. Recipient Disting. Svc. award South Fla. Orchid Soc., 1968, Grand prize for Poster, 1st Nagoya Internat. Orchid Show, 1990, Cert. of Achievement Garden Club Am., 1995, Digest Doer's Profile, 2000, Gold award Hawaii Orchid Growers Assn., 1996; grantee Am. Orchid Soc., Atomic Energy Commn., NIH, HEW, Inst. Mus. Svcs., Stanley Smith Hort. Trust, Honolulu Orchid Soc. Fellow Am. Orchid Soc. (hon. life, Gold medal for outstanding contbns and svcs. 1999); mem. AAAS, Internat. Assn. Hort. Sci., Am. Assn. Hort. Sci., Am. Inst. for Biol. Scis., Bot. Soc. Am., Hawn Bot. Soc. (past v.p.), Internat. Assn. Plant Tissue Culture, Internat. Palm Soc., Am. Anthurium Soc. (hon. life), Pacific Orchid Soc. (trustee 1994), Kaimuki Orchid Soc. (hon. life), Honolulu Orchid Soc. (hon., life), Lyon Arboretum Assn. (trustee 1974-91), Garden Club Honolulu (hon., life), Aloha Bonsai Club, Sigma Xi, Gamma Sigma Delta, Phi Kappa Phi (past pres., v.p. councillor U. Hawaii chpt.). Democrat. Office: U Hawaii TPSS St John Rm 102 3190 Maile Way Honolulu HI 96822-2279 Fax: 808-956-3894. Business E-Mail: yoneo@hawaii.edu.

**SAGE, ANDREW GREGG CURTIN, II,** retired brokerage house executive; b. Bryn Mawr, Pa., Mar. 11, 1926; s. Henry W. and Eleanor (Purviance) S.; m. Sara Wakefield, Sept. 29, 1956; children: Andrew Gregg Curtin III, Sally. Mem. staff DeCoppet & Doremus (odd lot stock house), N.Y.C., 1946-47, Sage & Co., N.Y. Stock Exchange Specialists, N.Y.C., 1947-48; assoc. Lehman Bros., N.Y.C., 1948-60, gen. ptnr., 1960-68, mng. ptnr., 1969, pres., 1970-73, vice chmn., 1973-77, mng. dir., 1977-82, Lehman Bros. Kuhn Loeb, Inc., 1977-82, Shearson Lehman Bros., Inc., 1982-87, sr. cons., 1987-90; pres., CEO, dir. Robertson CECO Corp., Boston, 1992-93, chmn. bd. dirs., 1994—, Chgo. Bd. dirs. Tom's Foods, Am. Superconductor Corp.; pres., treas. Sage Land Devel. Co.; pres., bd. dirs. Sage Capital Corp. Served with USAAF, 1944-46. Home: PO Box 1432 Wilson WY 83014-0937 Office Phone: 307-733-3100. Personal E-mail: andysage@earthlink.net.

**SAGE, ANDREW PATRICK, JR.,** systems engineering and management educator; b. Charleston, SC, Aug. 27, 1933; s. Andrew Patrick and Pearl Louise (Britt) S.; m. LaVerne Galhouse, Mar. 3, 1962; children: Theresa Annette, Karen Margaret, Philip Andrew. BS in Elec. Engring, The Citadel, 1955; SM, MIT, 1956; PhD, Purdue U., 1960; DEng (hon.), U. Waterloo, Can., 1987, Dalhousie U., Halifax, Nova Scotia, Can., 1997. Registered profl. engr., Tex. Instr. elec. engring. Purdue U., 1956-60; assoc. prof. U. Ariz., 1960-63; mem. tech. staff Aerospace Corp., Los Angeles, 1963-64; prof. elec. engring. and nuclear engring. scis. U. Fla., 1964-67; prof., dir. Info. and Control Scis. Corp. So. Methodist U., Dallas, 1967-74; head elec. engring. dept. So. Meth. U., 1973-74; Quarles prof. engring. sci. and systems U. Va., Charlottesville, 1974-84, chmn. dept. chem. engring., 1974-75, chmn. dept. engring. sci. and systems, 1977-84, assoc. dean, 1974-80; First Am. Bank prof. info. tech. George Mason U., Fairfax, Va., 1984—, assoc. v.p. for acad. affairs, 1984-85, dean Sch. Info. Tech. and Engring., 1985-96, univ. prof., founding dean emeritus, 1996—. Cons. Martin Marietta, Collins Radio, Atlantic Richfield, Tex. Instruments, LTV Aerospace, Battelle Meml. Inst., TRW Sys., NSF, Inst. Def. Analyses, Planning Rsch. Corp., MITRE, Engring. Rsch. Assocs., Software Productivity Consortium; gen. chmn. Internat. Conf. on Sys., Man and Cybernetics, 1974, 87; mem. spl. program panel on sys. sci. NATO, 1981-82; trustee, cons. Ctr. Naval Analysis, 1990-94. Author: Optimum Systems Control, 1968, 2d edit., 1977, Estimation Theory with Applications to Communications and Control, 1971, System Identification, 1971, An Introduction to Probability and Stochastic Processes, 1973, Methodology for Large Scale Systems, 1977, Systems Engineering: Methodology and Applications, 1977, Linear Systems Control, 1978, Economic Systems Analysis, 1983, System Design for Human Interaction, 1987, Information Processing in Systems and Organizations, 1990, Introduction to Computer Systems Analysis, Design, and Applications, 1989, Software Systems Engineering, 1990, Decision Support Systems Engineering, 1991, Systems Engineering, 1992, Systems Management for Information Technology and Software Engineering, 1995, Handbook of Systems Engineering and Management, 1999, Introduction to Systems Engineering, 2000; assoc. editor IEEE Transactions on Systems Sci. and Cybernetics, 1968-72; editor: IEEE Transactions on Systems, Man and Cybernetics, 1972-98; assoc. editor: Automatica, 1968-81; editor, 1981-96; mem. editl. bd. Systems Engring, 1968-72, IEEE Spectrum, 1972-73, Computers and Elec. Engring., 1972, Jour. Interdisciplinary Modeling and Simulation, 1976-80, Internat. Jour. Intelligent Sys., 1986—, Orgn. Sci., 1994-2002; editor Elsevier North Holland textbook series in sys. sci. and engring., 1970-88, John Wiley textbook series on sys. engring. and mgmt., 1989—; co-editor-in-chief Jour. Large Scale Sys.: Theory and Applications, 1978-88, Info. and Decision Technologies, 1988-94, Info. and Sys. Engring., 1995-96; editor in chief Sys. Engring., 1998—; co-editor in chief Info., Knowledge and Sys. Mgmt., 1999—; contbr. articles to profl. jours. Recipient Norbert Wiener award, 1980, Joseph G. Wohl career award, 1991, Superior Pub. Svc. award Sec. of the Navy, 1994; Case Centennial scholar, 1980, Award Washington Soc. of Engrs., 1996. Master: IEEE Sys./Man and Cybernetics Soc. (pres. 1984—85); fellow: AAAS (chmn. sect. M 1990), IEEE (life M. Barry Carlton award 1970, Centennial medal 1984, Outstanding Contbn. award 1986, Donald G. Fink prize 1994, Simon Ramo medal 2000), Internat. Coun. on Sys. Engring. (Pioneer award 2002); mem.: NAE, Inst. for Ops. Rsch. and Mgmt. Sci., Washington Soc. Engrs. (award 1996), Am. Soc. Engring. Edn. (Frederick Emmonds Terman award 1970, Centennial cert. for exceptional contbn. 1993), Internat. Fedn. Automatic Control (Outstanding Svc. award), Inst. Mgmt. Scis., Tau Beta Pi, Eta Kappa Nu (eminent mem. award 2002), Sigma Xi. Home: 8011 Woodland Hills Ln Fairfax VA 22039-2433 Office: George Mason U Sch Info Tech Fairfax VA 22030-4444 Office Phone: 703-993-1506. Business E-Mail: asage@gmu.edu.

**SAGE, C. J.,** literature and language professor, editor, writer; m. J. P. Dancing Bear, Oct. 26, 2001. MFA in Creative Writing, San Jose State U., 2003. Instr. English and creative writing De Anza Coll., Cupertino, Calif., 2004—, Hartnell Coll., Salinas, 2004—. Poetry editor Nat. Poetry Rev., Felton, Calif., 2003—. Author poetry. Recipient James D. Phelan Lit. Award, 2000, 2001, Marjorie McLaughlin Folendorf award for Outstanding Achievement in Creative Writing, 2001, prize, Acad. Am. Poets, 2002. Mem.: Acad. Am. Poets. Office Phone: 408-864-8999 ext. 3094. E-mail: professorcjsage@yahoo.com.

**SAGE, WEBSTER LEGENE, JR.,** ophthalmologist; b. St. Louis, Oct. 12, 1925; s. Webster LeGene and Alice Virginia (Gollehon) S.; m. Claudine New, May 20, 1952 (dec. June 1986); children: Bryan LeGene, Evan Webster; m. Shirley Barr, Jan. 2, 1988. BS, U. Ariz., 1949; MD, Baylor U., 1953. Diplomate Am. Bd. Ophthalmology. Intern Good Samaritan Hosp., Phoenix; resident Loma Linda (Calif.) U.; pvt. practice Phoenix, 1956—. Chmn. dept. ophthalmology Good Samaritan Hosp., Phoenix, 1960-62, St. Joseph's Hosp., Phoenix, 1971-72; cons. Ariz. Bd. Med. Examiners, Phoenix; owner Surg.

Eye Ctr. Ariz., Phoenix, 1985—. Chmn. bd. of elders and deacons Camelback Christian Ch., Scottsdale, Ariz. Maj. U.S. Army, 1962-64. Fellow ACS (life), Am. Acad. Ophthalmology, Internat. Coll. Surgeons; mem. Ariz. Ophthalmological Soc. (pres. 1963-64), Phoenix Ophthalmological Soc. (pres. 1967-68), Kiwanis Club, Paradise Valley Country Club, Phoenix Country Club. Avocations: travel, photography. Home: 8210 N Charles Dr Paradise Valley AZ 85253-2405 Office: 5133 N Central Ave Ste 100 Phoenix AZ 85012-1438

**SAGE-GAVIN, EVA MARIE,** retail executive; b. Boston, Sept. 26, 1958; d. Ross Francis and Theresa Veronica (Bufalo) S.; m. Dennis Gavin. BS in Indsl. Relations, Cornell U., 1980. Affirmative action personnel specialist Xerox Corp., Washington, 1980-81; compensation analyst Xerox Corp, Rochester, N.Y., 1981-82, sales recruiter Boston, 1982, employment mgr., 1983, systems mktg. rep., 1983-85; personnel mgr. Xerox Corp., L.A., 1985—86; human resources mgr. Xerox Corp, Irvine, Calif., 1986; dir. human resources Pepsi Co., 1991, v.p. corp. human resources, Taco Bell; sr. v.p. human resources Disney Consumer Products, 1997—2000, Sun Microsystems, Inc., 2000—03; exec. v.p. human resources Gap Inc., 2003—. Mem. career adv. bd. Emmanuel Coll., Boston, 1983-85. Named one of Top 25 Most Powerful Women in HR, HR Exec. mag., 2005. Mem. Am. Soc. Personnel Adminstrn., Women in Mgmt., Xerox Women's Network (edn. com. 1988), Kappa Kappa Gamma. Democrat. Roman Catholic. Avocations: skiing, travel, boating, sailing, aerobics. Office: Gap Inc 2 Folsom St San Francisco CA 94105 Office Phone: 650-952-4400. Office Fax: 415-427-2553.

**SAGEN, HARRY BRADLEY,** education educator; b. Waukegan, Ill., July 29, 1936; s. Harry Edvin Sagen and Loraine Marie Bradley; m. Teresa Kaye Blair, Dec. 22, 1984; children: Lance Blair, Deborah, Kathleen Thorne. BA with honors, Grinnell Coll., 1957; PhD, U. of Minn., 1962. Instr. U. of Minn., 1959—61; asst. dir., instl. rsch. U. of Ill., 1961—64; vis. prof. US Mil. Acad., West Point, NY, 1969—80; prof. of higher edn. U. of Iowa, 1964—98. Sr. lectr. Warsaw U., 1993; higher edn. planning specialist Nat. Manpower and Edn. Project, 1997; vis. fulbright prof. Yonsei U., Seoul, 1999; cons. World Bank, Baku, Azerbaijan, 2002, Tribhuvan U., Kathmandu, Nepal, 2002, Ministry of Edn., Columbo, Sri Lanka, 2003, U. Bucharest, 2004, Odessa State Tech. U., 2005, Hue U., 2006. Contbr. articles to profl. jours. Mem. Partners Adv. Coun., Iron Range Resources Agy., Eveleth, Minn., 2004—; bd. dirs. Laurentian Ednl. Ventures, Ely, Minn., 2002—. Recipient Commanders award for Civilian Svc., US Mil. Acad., 1980. Fellow: Soc. for Values in Higher Edn.; mem.: Am. Assn. of Higher Edn. (life; bd. of dirs. 1973—76), Phi Beta Kappa. Dfl. Congregational. Avocations: canoeing, cross country skiing. Home: 13667 Deer RD Ely MN 55731

**SAGER, DONALD JACK,** librarian, consultant, retired publishing executive; b. Milw., Mar. 3, 1938; s. Alfred Herman and Sophia (Sagan) Sager; m. Sarah Ann Long, May 23, 1987; children: Geoffrey, Andrew. BS, U. Wis., Milw., 1963; MSLS, U. Wis., 1964. Sr. documentalist AC Electronics divsn. GM, Milw., 1958-63; teaching asst. U. Wis., Madison, 1963-64; dir. Kingston (N.Y.) Pub. Libr., 1964-66, Elyria (Ohio) Pub. Libr., 1966-71, Mobile Pub. Libr., 1971-75, Pub. Libr. Columbus and Franklin County, Ohio, 1975-78; commr. Chgo. Pub. Libr., 1978-81; dir. Elmhurst Pub. Libr., Ill., 1982-83, Milw. Pub. Libr., 1983-91; pub. Highsmith Press, Ft. Atkinson, Wis., 1991-2000; pres., CEO Gossage Sager Assocs. LLC, N.Y.C., 2000—. Secy Online Computer Library Ctr, 1977—78, disting vis scholar, 1982; chmn investment comt PLA Pub Library, 1985—89, chmn mus comt, 1989—91, mem hist comt, 1993—95, chmn PLA nat conf comt, 1986—88; bd dirs Coun Wis Libraries, 1982—91, Urban Libraries Coun, 1985—93, secly, 1991—93; adj faculty Univ Wis, Milwaukee, 1984—91; consult in field. Author: Reference: A Programmed Instruction, 1970, Binders, Books and Budgets, 1971, Participatory Management, 1981, The American Public Library, 1982, Public Library Administrators Planning Guide to Automation, 1983, Managing the Public Library, 1984, Small Libraries, 1992, 3d rev. edit., 2000; co-editor: Urban Library Management Trends, 1989; contbg. editor: Public Libraries, 1990—2000; contbr. articles to profl. jours. Pres Milwaukee Civic Alliance, 1990—91; chmn Milwaukee United Way Campaign, 1984; pres Milwaukee Westown Assn, 1987—90; treas. Congl. Ch. Deerfield, Ill., 2002—05, bd. dirs., 2005—; bd dirs Goethe House, 1985—91. With AUS, 1956—58. Mem.: ALA (councilor-at-large 1995—2003, policy monitoring comt, awards comt, chmn core values task force, Joseph Lippincott award 2005), Library Admin Asn Wis (chmn 1987—88), Wis Library Asn Found (chmn 1986—88), Wis Library Asn, Chicago Book Clin, Ill Library Asn, Pub Library Asn (pres 1982—83, bd dirs, vpres, pres-elect), Exchange Club Milwaukee (pres 1988—89). Office Phone: 312-961-5536. Business E-Mail: dsager@gossagesager.com.

**SAGER, PHILIP TRAVIS,** pharmaceutical executive, cardiologist, researcher; b. NYC, Jan. 23, 1956; s. Clifford Julius and Ruth (Levy) Sager; m. Linda Sager. BS in Chemistry and Biology, MIT, 1977; MD, Yale U., 1982. Diplomate Am. Bd. Internal Medicine, Am. Bd. Cardiology, Am. Bd. Cardiac Electrophysiology. Resident, fellow in cardiology and cardiac electrophysiology Yale U., New Haven, 1982—88; asst. prof. medicine Sch. Medicine, U. So. Calif., LA, 1989—90; dir. electrophysiology, 1988-90, dir. Pacemaker Ctr., 1988-90; asst. prof. medicine Sch. Medicine, UCLA, 1990-96, assoc. prof. medicine, 1996—2001; dir. cardiac electrophysiology West L.A. VA Med. Ctr., 1990—2001; sr. dir., U.S. lead physician Astrazeneca Inc., Wilmington, Del., 2004—, med. sci. sr. dir., 2005—, exec. dir., curriculum vitae devel. and global quality tchg. strategy leader, 2006—; dir. cardiac rsch. Schering-Plough Rsch. Inst., 2001—; clin. prof. medicine UMDNJ Med. Sch., 2002—. Mem. cardiology adv. com. VA, Washington, 1990-94; cons. electrophysiology ACGME, Chgo., 1995-01; vis. prof. Kern Med. Ctr., Bakersfield, Calif., 1991, 94, U. Iowa Sch. Medicine, 1994, Northwestern U. Sch. Medicine, 1994, Yale U. Sch. Medicine, 1995, U. Calif., San Francisco, 1996; topic leader, ICH Expert Working Group on the Clin. Quality Tchg. Initative, 2002-05; mem. ICH E 14 Implementation Group, 2005-; chair Internat. DIA-FDA-HRS Quality Tchg. Conf., 2006; exe. com. mem. FDA Duke Critical Pathway Initiative; cons. pharm. cos.; lectr. in field. Contbr. chpts. to books, numerous articles to profl. jours.; reviewer sci. jours. and sci. mags. Recipient many rsch. grants, including Am. Heart Assn., 1996. Fellow ACP, Am. Heart Assn., Am. Coll. Cardiology, Heart Rhythm Soc.; mem. Am. Fedn. Clin. Rsch., Nat. Assn. Pacing and Electrophysiology (program dirs. com. 1992-01, govt. com. 1994-01, co-chair program dirs. com. 1997-01), Phi Beta Kappa, Alpha Omega Alpha. Avocations: travel, bicycling, scuba diving, reading history, movies. Office: AstraZeneca 1800 Concord Pike PO Box 15437 Wilmington DE 19850-5437 Office Phone: 302-885-5669. Personal E-mail: psager@alum.mit.edu.

**SAGER, WILLIAM FREDRICK,** retired chemistry professor; b. Glencoe, Ill., Jan. 22, 1918; s. Fred Anson and Alta (Stansbury) S.; m. Marilyn Olga Williams, Dec. 26, 1941; children: Karen Louise Sager Dickinson, Judith Lynn Sager Peyton), Kathryn Gwen Sager Potts. BS in Chemistry, George Washington U., 1939, MA in Organic Chemistry, 1941; PhD in Organic Chemistry, Harvard U., 1948. Research chemist The Texas Co., 1941-45; prof. chemistry George Washington U., 1948-65, U. Ill.-Chgo., 1965-86, prof. emeritus, 1986—, chmn., 1965-80. Cons. to govt. and industry, 1952—. Founder, pres. Sager Innovations, Inc. Patentee (U.S. patents on every saving devices). Recipient Disting. Service award U. Ill. Alumni Assn., 1985; Guggenheim fellow, 1954-55. Mem. Am. Chem. Soc., Sigma Xi, Alpha Chi Sigma. Home: 101 Clyde Morris Blvd Ormond Beach FL 32174 Office: Dept Chemistry U Ill-Chicago Chicago IL 60680

**SAGERHOLM, JAMES ALVIN,** retired naval officer; b. Uniontown, Pa., Dec. 23, 1927; s. Frithiof Norris and Margaret Blocher S.; m. Margaret Ann Herrlich, June 7, 1952; children— Lisa Marie, Ann Denise, Jeannine Louise, Mark Christian BS, U.S. Naval Acad., 1952. Commd. ensign U.S. Navy, 1952, advanced through grades to vice admiral, 1983, exec. officer USS Sproston, 1961—63, navigator USS Seadragon, 1965, exec. officer blue crew USS Mariano G. Vallejo, 1966-67, comdg. officer gold crew USS Kamehameha, 1968-71, head gen. purpose warfare forces group Office of Chief Naval Ops., 1971, dep. exec. dir. Chief Naval Ops. Exec. Panel, 1972, exec. sec. Chief Naval Ops. Exec. Bd., 1973, comdr. Naval Intelligence Support

Ctr. Washington, 1974-75, dep. dir. naval intelligence Chief Naval Ops., 1975-76, comdr. South Atlantic Force, U.S. Atlantic Fleet, 1976-78, dir. Office of Program Appraisal, Office of Sec. Navy, 1978-81, chief naval edn. and tng. Pensacola, Fla., 1983-85; exec. dir. Pres. Fgn. Intelligence Adv. Bd. White House, Washington, 1981-82; ret., 1985. Chmn. bd. dirs. Piedmont Environ. Coun., 1987-89; v.p. for nat. affairs Gen. George C. Marshall Home Found., 1990-91. Trustee Balt. Polytech. Inst. Found., 2000-03, U.S. Naval Acad. Found., 2005—. Decorated D.S.M., Legion of Merit, Meritorious Service medal; named Disting. Alumnus, Balt. Poly. Inst. Mem. Naval Submarine League, U.S. Naval Inst., K.C. Roman Catholic. Avocations: golf, civil war history. Home: 414 Rockfleet Rd Unit 102 Timonium MD 21093-7582

**SAGET, BOB,** actor, comedian, writer, television director; b. Phila., May 17, 1956; m. Sherri Kramer, 1982 (div. 1997); children: Aubrey, Lara, Jenny. Grad. film studies, Temple U., 1978. Host 2002 Winter Olympics. Appeared at Carnegie Hall, Las Vegas, Atlantic City, The Comedy Store, The Improv, Calif.; actor (stage) Privilege, 2005; (films) Critical Condition, 1986, 1998, Half Baked, 1998, Dumb and Dumberer: When Harry Met Llody, 2003; (TV) Full House, 1987-95, Raising Dad, 2001-02, (voice) How I Met Your Mother, 2005-; actor, exec. prodr. Father and Scout, 1994, Jitters, 1997; dir., exec. prodr. For Hope, 1997; co-host The Morning Program, 1986; host, writer: America's Funniest Home Videos, 1989-97; dir., actor, writer: HBO Comedy Hour: In The Dream State; dir. Dirty Work, 1998, Mind of the Married Man, 2001; dir., actor Becoming Dick, 2000. Address: Brillstein/Grey Entertainment 9150 Wilshire Blvd Ste 350 Beverly Hills CA 90212-3453

**SAGGIO, JOSEPH JOHN,** dean; b. Dayton, Ohio, Apr. 9, 1959; s. Joseph Charles and Shirley Ann Saggio; m. Nancy Jo Saggio, Oct. 27, 1984; children: Rachelle Lynn, Leah Nicole. BA, Calif. State U., Fresno 1981; MA, Asuza Pacific U., Asuza, Calif., 1985; M.A., Vanguard U., Costa Mesa, Calif. 1994; EdD, Ariz. State U., Tempe, 2000; Mgmt. Devel. Program, Harvard Grad. Sch. Edn. 2003. Ordained minister Assemblies of God, 1984. Assoc. pastor First Assembly of God, Palmdale, Calif., 1982—85; sr. pastor Mountain Christian Life Ch., Crestline, Calif., 1986—93; acad. dean Am. Indian Coll., Phoenix, 1994—2006, dean instn. assessment, 2006—; adj. prof. Assemblies of God Theol. Sem., Springfield, Mo., 2003—. Contbr. articles to profl. jours., chapters to books and book reviews. Republican. Avocations: music, singing, travel, writing. Office: Am Indian Coll 10020 N 15th Ave Phoenix AZ 85021-2199 Business E-Mail: jsaggio@aicag.edu.

**SAGURTON, WILMA,** retired secondary school educator, musician, historian; b. Mendham, NJ, Feb. 19, 1916; d. David Minard and Nanna Mae (Mockridge) Lewis; m. James R. Sagurton, Sept. 24, 1937; children: Joan, Frances Seigle, James, David. BA bio., chem., music and geology, Montclair, 1937; diploma math, Seton Hall, 1950; MA teaching Handicapped, Montclair State, 1971. Asst. bio. tchr. Montclair State U., 1936—37; tchr. sci. Bd. Of Edn., Bloomfield, 1937—62; tchr. elementary Bd. of Edn., Passaic, 1962—65; tchr. Sceep (Inner City), Newark, 1960—; organist, choir dir. Catholic Church, Mendham, 1950—63; tchr. piano private, 1940—; ret., 1980. Founder Mus. of Old Randolph, Randolph, NJ, 1985—. Co-author: Lewises of Combs Hollow, 1985; author: And then there was Lighting, 2002, Fireplace Cooking with Recipes, 2004. Local historian Mendham Township, 1984—; sec. Auxiliary Engine Company, Mendham, NJ, 1965; lectr. Nat. Register of historic sites, 1990—. Recipient Local Historian of the Yr., Heritage Com., 1991, Outstanding Vol. Cmty Svc. award, Mendham Twp., Athletic Letter, Fencing, Montclair State, 1933—37. Mem.: Chester Historical Soc., N.J. Retired Tchrs. Assn., Brookside Engine Co. No. 1 Auxiliary (life), John Ralston Historical Assn., CRAFTS, Garden Club (life; sec. 1989—91), Kappa Delta Pi. Democrat. Episcopalian. Avocations: music, photography, piano, historic preservation, public speaking. Home: 159 Mountainside Rd Mendham NJ 07945

**SAH, CHIH-TANG,** electrical and computer engineering educator; b. Beijing, Nov. 10, 1932; s. Adam Peng-tung and Shu-shen Huang; m. Linda Chang, Nov. 29, 1959; children: Dinah W.Y., Robert L.Y. *Father Adam Pen-tung Sah was first President of Amoy (Xiamen) University of China (1937-1944), and first Secretary General of Academia Sinica (1944-1949). He was a prolific textbook author in freshman physics, calculus, junior electrical circuits and senior electrical machines, and visiting professor at Massachusetts Institute of Technology, Stanford University and Ohio State University. Mother Shu-shen Huang was Chinese Olympian in 1930. Wife Linda Chang was recipient of Barat Cup and graduated magna cum laude at Barat College in 1958. Daughter Dinah Sah was head of Neuroscience department at Signal Pharmaceuticals, and Biogen, Inc. Now with Alnylam Pharmaceuticals, Inc. Son Robert is Director of Cartilage Tissue Engineering Laboratory at University of California at San Diego and vice chair of bioengineering department.* BS Physics, U. Ill., 1953, BSEE, 1953; MSEE, Stanford U., 1954, PhD, 1956; D honoris causa, U. Leuven, Belgium, 1975; Doctorate (hon.), Nat. Chaotung U., Taiwan, 2004. Research assoc. Stanford Electronics Lab., Palo Alto, Calif., 1956—59; sr. mem. tech. staff Shockley Transistor Corp., Palo Alto 1956—59; head, mgr. physics dept Fairchild Semiconductor Lab., Palo Alto, 1959-64; prof. physics and elec. engring. U. Ill., Urbana, 1962-88, dir. Ill. Solid State Electronics Lab.; Pittman Eminent Scholar chair, grad. research prof., chief scientist Coll. Engring. U. Fla., Gainesville, 1988—; hon. prof. Peking U., 2003, Tsnghua U., 2003. Cons. Jet Propulsion Lab., Dept. Energy, Pasadena, Calif., 1976-85, Harry Diamond Lab., Washington, 1974-75, IBM Corp., N.Y, numerous other electronics firms 1964-88; advisor Intel Corp., Oreg., Calif., other semicondr. mfrs., 1988—; program dir. 1st generation Si VLSI tech. Fairchild Corp., 1959-64. Author: Fundamentals of Solid-State Electronics, 1991, Transistor Reliability in Fundamentals of Solid-State Electronics—Solution Manual, 1996; editor Internat. Series Advances in Solid-State Electronics and Tech., 1991—; contbr. 300 articles to profl. jours. Recipient first high tech. award Asian American Mfg. Assn., 1982; named 1 of 1000 World's Most Cited Scientists Inst. Sci. Info., 1965-78. Fellow IEEE (life, IRE Browder J. Thompson prize 1963, J.J. Ebers award 1980, Jack Morton award 1989), U.S. Semiconductors Industry Assn. (U. Rsch. award, 1998, com. 100 Pioneer Recognition award, 2002, Disting. Lifetime Achievement award Chineese Inst. Engrs. USA, 2003), AAAS, Am. Physical Soc., Franklin Inst. (life fellow, Cert. of Merit award 1975); mem. Nat. Acad. Engring., Academia Sinica Taiwan (academician), Chinese Acad. Scis. (academician). Achievements include development of complementary metal-oxide semiconductor circuit (CMOS), 1962; Si P-N junction diode phenomena Sah-Noyce-Shockley Theory, 1957; MOS/transistor compact models, Sah, Pao, Jie, 1964-66, 96, 05-; invention of deep-level transient spectroscipy Sah, Tasch, Yau, 1966-71; DCIV diagnosis for deep-submicron transistor design and reliability Sah, Cai, Wang, Jie, 1995-. Office: 2716 NW 20th St Gainesville FL 32605-2999 Personal E-mail: tom_sah@msn.com.

**SAHA, ARUN KUMAR,** engineering educator, researcher; b. Gauripur, Assam, India, May 7, 1967; s. Ramani Mohan and Arati Saha; m. Mira Saha, Apr. 26, 1970; 1 child, Arunima. B Mech. Engring., Gauhati U., Assam, India, 1990; M Mech. Tech., Indian Inst. Tech., Kanpur, India, 1994; PhD, Indian Inst. of Tech. Kanpur, India, 1999. Lectr. Jorhat Engring. Coll., Jorhat, Assam, India, 1992; asst. exec. engr. Oil & Natural Gas Corp., Sibsagar, Assam, India, 1993; post doctoral rsch. assoc. SUNY, Stony Brook, NY, 1999—2000, La. State U., Baton Rouge, 2000—. Contbr. chapters to books, articles to profl. jours. and confs. (Best Paper Award, 2000). Avocations: painting, art, gardening.

**SAHA, SAMAR KANTI,** electronics engineer, educator; arrived in U.S., 1981; s. Phani Bhusan and Mahamaya Saha. PhD, Gauhati U., India, 1981; MS in Engring. Mgmt., Stanford U., Calif., 1992. Asst. prof. elec. engring. So. Ill. U., Carbondale, 1982—84; sr. product engr. Nat. Semiconductor, Santa Clara, Calif., 1984—90; staff engr., R & D LSI Logic Corp., Santa Clara, 1990—92; prin. engr. tech. CAD Nat. Semiconductor, Santa Clara, 1992—95; prin. engr., advanced devel. Tex. Instruments, Santa Cruz, 1995—97; mgr., tech. CAD Philips Semiconductors, San Jose, 1997—2000; mgr., tech. modeling Silicon Storage Tech., Inc., Sunnyvale, 2000—06; sr. mgr. Synopsys Inc., 2006—. Contbr. scientific papers to profl. jours. Recipi-

ent Outstanding Achievement, Analog Divsn. Nat. Semiconductor, 1988, Tchg. Contbn., EE Dept., U. Nev. Las Vegas, 2002. Mem.: IEEE (mem. compact modeling com. 2001—04, chmn. compact modeling com. 2005—, guest editor). Achievements include patents in field; research in scaling considerations for high performance 25 nm metal-oxide-semiconductor field-effect transistors; effects of inversion layer quantization on channel profile engineering for nMOSFETs with 0.1 m channel lengths; development of efficient approach for integrated circuit fabrication technology. Home: 286 Aspenridge Dr Milpitas CA 95035 Office Phone: 650-584-2894. Personal E-mail: samar@ieee.org.

**SAHAI, HARDEO,** medical statistics educator; b. Bahraich, India, Jan. 10, 1942; m. Lillian Sahai, Dec. 28, 1973; 3 children. BS in Math., Stats. and Physics, Lucknow U., India, 1962; MS in Math., Banaras U., Varanasi, India, 1964; MS in Math. Stats., U. Chgo., 1968; PhD in Stats., U. Ky., 1971. Lectr. math. and stats. Banaras U., Varanasi, India, 1964—65; asst. stats. officer Durgapur Steel Plant, West Bengal, India, 1965; statistician Rsch. and Planning divsn. Blue Cross Assn., Chgo., 1966; statis. programmer Cleft Palate Ctr. U. Ill., 1967; statis. programmer Chgo. Health Rsch. Found., 1968; mgmt. scientist Mgmt. Sys. Devel. Dept. Burroughs Corp., Detroit, 1971—72; from asst. prof. to prof. dept. math. U. P.R., Mayaguez, 1972—82; vis. rsch. prof. Dept. Stats. and Applied Math. U. Ceara, Brazil, 1978—79; sr. rsch. statistician Travenol Labs., Inc., Round Lake, Ill., 1982—83; chief statistician U.S. Army Hqrs., Ft. Sheridan, Ill., 1983—84; sr. math. statistician U.S. Bur. Census Dept. Commerce, Washington, 1984—85; sr. ops. rsch. analyst Def. Logistics Agy. Dept. Def., Chgo., 1985—86; prof. Dept. Biostats. and Epidemiology U. P.R. Med. Scis., San Juan, 1986—. Cons. P.R. Univ Cons., P.R. Driving Safety Evaluation Project, Water Resources Rsch. Inst., Travenol Labs., Campo Rico, P.R., U.S. Bur. Census, Washington, Lawrence Livermore Nat. Lab., Calif., others; vis. prof. U. Granada, Spain, U. Veracruzana, Mex., patrimonial prof. stats., 1997—; vis. prof. U. Nacional de Colombia, U. Nacional de Trujillo, Peru, 1993-94, hon. prof. stats., 1994—; adj. prof. dept. math. U. P.R. Natural Scis. Faculty, 1995—; Patrimonial prof. stafs U. Veracruzana, 1997—. Author: Statistics and Probability: Learning Module, 1984; author: (with Jose Berrios) A Dictionary of Statistical Scientific and Technical Terms: English-Spanish and Spanish-English, 1981, (with Wilfredo Martinez) Statistical Tables and Formulas for the Biological Social and Physical Sciences, 1996, (with Anwer Khurshid) Statistics in Epidemiology: Methods, Techniques and Applications, 1996, (with Satish C. Misra and Amwer Khurshid) Quotations on Probability and Statistics with Illustrations, 2004, (with Anwer Khurshid) A Pocket Dictionary of Statistics, 2000, (with Mohammad I. Ageel) The Analysis of Variance: Fixed, Random and Mixed Models, 2000, (with Mario M. Ojeda) A Glossary of Statistical, Sciebtfic and Technical Terms: English-Spanish, 2004, (with Lucas López Segovia and Hector W. Colón-Rosa) A Glossary of Medical Epidemiologic and Demographic Statistics: English-Spanish, 2003, (with Mario M. Ojeda) Un Manual de Distribuciones t, x2y F Centrales y No Centrales, 2000, (with Mario M. Ojeda) A Glossary of Computer and Management Terms: English/Spanish, 2004, (with Mario M. Ojeda) Comparisons of Approximations to the Percentiles of Noncentral t, x2 and F Distributions, 2001, (with A. Khurshid) Pocket Dictionary of Statistics, 2001, (with Mario M. Ojeda) Analysis of Variance for Random Models, Vol. 1: Balanced Data and Vol. 2: Unbalanced Data, 2004; mem. editl. bd. Sociedad Colombiana de Matematicas, P.R. Health Scis. Jour.; contbr. editor Current Index to Stats.; reviewer Collegiate Microcomputer, Comm. in Statistics, Indian Jour. Stats., Jour. Royal Statis. Soc. (series D, The Statistician), New Zealand Statistician, Biometrics, Can. Jour. Stats., Technometrics, Problems, Resources and Issues in Math. Undergrad. Studies; contbr. more than 150 articles and papers to profl. and sci. jours.; numerous articles to tech. mags. Active Dept. Consumer Affairs Svcs. Commonwealth of P.R., San Juan, Dept. Anti-Addiction Svcs., Commonwealth of P.R., San Juan., Inst. of AIDS, Municipality of San Juan, VA Med. Ctr. of San Juan, Caribbean Primate Rsch. Ctr., Ctr. Addiction Studies Caribbean Ctrl. U. Recipient Dept. Army Cert. Achievement award, 1984, U. Ky. Outstanding Alumnus award, 1993, medal of honor U. Granada, 1994, plaque of honor U. Nacional de Trujillo, 1994; fellow Coun. Sci. and Indsl. Rsch., 1964-65, U. Chgo., 1965-68, Harvard U., 1979, Fulbright Found., 1982; U.P. Bd. Merit schol., 1957-59, Govt. India Merit scholar, 1959-64; grantee NSF, 1974-77, NIMH, 1987-90, 91—, NIDA, 1991—. Fellow AAAS, Am. Coll. Epidemiology, Inst. Statisticians (charter statistician), Inst. Math. and Its Applications (charter mathematician), N.Y. Acad. Scis., Royal Statis. Soc.; mem. Internat. Statis. Inst., Internat. Assn. Tchg. Stats., Soc. Epidemiol. Rsch., Inst. Math. Stats., Bernouilli Soc. for Math. Stats. and Probability, Internat. Biometric Soc., Am. Soc. for Quality Control, Am. Stats. Assn., Japan Statis. Soc., Can. Statis. Soc., Inter-Am. Statis. Inst., Internat. Assn. Statis. Computing, Sch. Sci. and Math. Assn., Sigma Xi. Avocations: religious studies, philosophy, reading, gardening. Home: Urb Mayaguez Terrace 7083 Calle B Gaudier Texidor Mayaguez PR 00682-6617 E-mail: hsahai@hotmail.com.

**SAHAKIAN, LILLIAN ZAROUHI,** artist, designer; d. Archak Agapov Sahakian and Mariam Zarouhi Zahrbhanelian-Sahakian. Secretarial pool First Nat. City Bank, N.Y.C., 1954—55; sec., sales & mktg. Walker Mktg. Corp., Racine, Wis., 1958—59; typist, purchasing Kollsman Instrument Corp., Elmhurst, NY, 1963—70; supv. stenographer City Hosp. Ctr., 1974—78; exec. sec. Racine/Kenosha Cmty. Action Agy., 1979—80, Butter Buds Corp., Racine, 1989—91; mktg. specialist Johnson Internat., Inc., Racine, 1994—2003. Oil portrait - copy, Victor Choque (2nd Prize, 1955), exhibition, Early Oil Paintings-American Artist, Smithsonian, 1957, altar piece, Madonna & Child, St. Sarkis Ch., 1960, graphite rendering, Viet Nam Refugees - Grandmother & Grandson, 1964, watercolor painting, After Matisse, 1990, graphics logo, Lili Archak Studios, 2004, lifestyle interior designs, Interior Designs LLC. Choir mem. St. Hagop Ch., Wis., 1958—59. Scholar Entrepreneurial Incentive award, State of Wis., 2004. Mem.: NAMI Racine (bd. dirs. 1985—2006), Soc. for Tech. Comm., Kenosha Art Assn., Am. Inst. Graphic Artists (assoc.). Independent. Avocations: reading, do it yourself home repairs, research on the internet & other, computer generated art, cooking. Office: Lili Archak Studios LLC 1117 Saxony Dr Racine WI 53402 Office Phone: 262-898-9351.

**SAHANI, DUSHYANT V.,** radiologist, educator; b. Nagpur, MS, India, June 2, 1969; arrived in U.S., 1999; s. Vasudeo H. and Sulochana V. Sahani; m. Nita N. Nagpal, Feb. 26, 1995; 1 child, Vyoma. MB BS, P.D.M. Med. Coll., 1992; DMRD, Tata Cancer Hosp., 1995, MD, 1996; D. Nat. Bd., 1996. House officer Pediat. Centenar Hosp., Mumbai, India, 1992; house officer Medicine Masina Gen. Hosp., Mumbai, 1992-93; clin. asst., clin. assoc. P.D. Hinduja Hosp., Mumbai, 1996—98; rsch. fellow, clin. fellow Mass. Gen. Hosp., Boston, 1999—2002; clin. instr. Harvard Med. Sch., Mass. Gen. Hosp., Boston, 2002—; dir. computed tomography Mass. Gen. Hosp., 2004—. Contbr. articles to profl. jours.; reviewer: articles in field; contbr. chpts. in books. Recipient First Time Presenter award, Soc. Gastrointestinal Radiology, 2002, Wylie Dodd award, 2005, cum laude, Soc. Computed Body Tomography and MR, 2005. Fellow: Radiol. Soc. N.Am. (Rsch. Trainee award 2001), Am. Roentgen Ray Soc. (Bronze medal 2002, 2003). Avocations: reading, kayaking. Home: 5 Stone Rd Arlington MA 02474 Office: Mass Gen Hosp 55 Fruit St Boston MA 02114

**SAHELIJO, LEONARDO,** geneticist, researcher; b. Rokko Hyogo, Japan, Aug. 24, 1957; Med. dir. Abbott Labs., Abbott Park, Ill., 2001—, BASF Pharma, Almere, Netherlands; er physician Middlesborough, England, Harderwijk, Netherlands; physician Amsterdam, Netherlands.

**SAHID, JOSEPH ROBERT,** lawyer; b. Paterson, NJ, Feb. 14, 1944; s. Joseph James and Helen (Vitale) Sahid; m. Serra Yavuz; children: Annunziata, Joseph, Olivia. BS, Rutgers U., 1965; LLB, U. Va., 1968. Bar: NY 1973, US Dist. Ct. NY, US Ct. Appeals (2d and 3d cirs.), US Supreme Ct. Staff mem. Nat. Commn. Causes Prevention Violence, Washington, 1968-69; cons. Pres.'s Commn. Campus Unrest, Washington, 1970; assoc. Cravath, Swaine & Moore, NYC, 1972-77, ptnr., 1977-93, cons., 1994-97; ptnr. Barrack, Rodos & Bacine, NYC, 1995—96; pvt. practice NYC, 1996—. Mediator US Dist. Ct. (so. dist.) NY, NY Civil Ct.; arbitrator NY cts., Nat.

Assn. Securities Dealers. Author: (book) Rights in Concord, 1969; co-author: Law and Order Reconsidered, 1969; contbr. articles to profl. jours. Lt. USCG, 1968—72. Mem.: ABA, NY County Lawyers Assn. (arbitrator), NY State Bar Assn. (profl. discipline com.), Bar Assn. City NY (profl. discipline com. 2001—03, profl. responsibility com., coun. children com., legal referral svc., profl. discipline com. 2006—, mem. coop. condo mediation project). Address: 845 3rd Ave Fl 20 New York NY 10022-6601 Office Phone: 212-308-5930. E-mail: sahid@nysbar.com.

**SAHINER, MEHMET ALPER,** physics professor, researcher; PhD, Rutgers U., New Brunswick, 1999. Sr. scientist Evans Analytical Group, East Windsor, NJ, 1999—2003; asst. prof. Seton Hall U., South Orange, 2003—. Recipient Cottrell Coll. award, Rsch. Corp., 2005—; grantee, NSF, 2004—06. Mem.: Internat. XAFS Soc., Materials Rsch. Soc., Am. Phys. Soc. Achievements include research in High Tc superconductors structural characteization, High-k dielectrics, semiconductors. Office: Seton Hall Univ Dept Physics 400 S Orange Ave South Orange NJ 07079 Office Phone: 973-761-9060.

**SAHLEM, JAMES ROBERT,** law librarian; b. Buffalo, Feb. 21, 1948; s. Lee M. and Mildred A. (Hibschweiler) S.; m. Susan Mary Schifferli, Aug. 9, 1969; children: Steven, Andrea, Gregory. BS in Mgmt., Canisius Coll., 1970, MSEd, 1995; MLS, SUNY, Buffalo, 1971, ASC, 1985; MS in Edn., Canisius Coll., 1995. Cert. pub. libr. profl., N.Y. State Edn. Dept. Libr. trainee Bus. Labor Dept. Buffalo-Erie County Pub. Libr., Buffalo, 1970-71; libr. I Mobile Librs. Buffalo-Erie County Pub. Libr., Buffalo, 1971-74; libr. II Amherst Pub. Librs., Williamsville, N.Y., 1974-78; libr. III, dir. North Park Crane Brs., Buffalo, 1978-81; prin. law libr. NY State Supreme Ct. Libr. Buffalo, 1981—. Cons. Lippes, Silverstein et al, Buffalo, 1985—. Co-author: (with Jo Ann M. Wahl and Kevin Bauer) Powers of the New York Court of Appeals 1952-1993 Supplement, 1994. Sec., We. N.Y. Libr. Resources Coun. Mem. Am. Assn. Law Librs. (bd. dirs. Upstate N.Y.), Buffalo Curling Club (officer 1985-89), N.Y. State Unified Cts. Law Librs. (pres.). Avocations: curling, gardening. Office: NY State Supreme Ct Libr Buffalo 77 W Eagle St Buffalo NY 14202-3408

**SAHLENE,** singer; b. Soderhamn, Sweden, 1976; Rep. for Estonia Eurovision Song Contest, 2002. Child actress (TV series) The Children of Bullerbyn; singer: (albums) 12 Steps Down the Avenue, 1997, It's Been A While, 2003. Recipient 3rd Place for the song "Runaway", Eurovision Song Contest, 2002. Mailing: Comino Productions Inc 1648 10th Ave Brooklyn NY 11215 E-mail: sahlene@sahlene.com.

**SAHOTA, AMRIK,** medical researcher, educator, lab administrator; s. Sadhu Milkhy and Rao Kaur; m. Nirmala Thapar; children: Aneil, Jessica. BS in Biochemistry, Bath U., 1974; MS in Medicinal Chemistry, Loughborough U., 1976; PhD in Med. Genetics, Guy's Hosp. Med. Sch., London U., 1980. Diplomate in clin. molecular genetics Am. Bd. Med. Genetics; chartered biologist U.K. Postdoctoral fellow dept. molecular scis. Aston U., Birmingham, England, 1980—83; biochemist dept. hematology Gen. Hosp., Birmingham, England, 1983—85; rsch. assoc. dept. biology Ind. U., Bloomington, Ind., 1985—87; lab. dir. dept. med. and molecular genetics Ind. U. Med. Sch., Indpls., 1988—99; prof. genetics Rutgers U., Piscataway, NJ, 1998—; lab. dir. dept. pathology Robert Wood Johnson U. Hosp., New Brunswick, NJ, 2001—. Cons. Indpls.-Marion County Forensic Sci. Lab., 1991—98; adj. prof. dept. pathology Robert Wood Johnson Med. Sch., U. Medicine and Dentistry, NJ, 2001—05, clin. prof., 2005—. Contbr. articles to sci. jours.; editor conf. procs. Adminstr. India Cmty. Ctr., Indpls., 1996; com. mem. Boy Scouts, Indpls., 1992—95; asst. troop leader with activities and transp. Girl Scouts, Indpls., 1997—99, Hillsborough, NJ, 2000—02; communicator Hillsborough Twp. Bd. of Edn., NJ, 2002. Fellow: Royal Coll. Pathologists U.K., Inst. Biology U.K., Am. Coll. Med. Genetics; mem.: AAAS, N.Y. Acad. Scis., Internat. Soc. for Nephrology, Assn. Molecular Pathology, Soc. for Study of Inborn Errors of Metabolism, Brit. Soc. Human Genetics, Am. Soc. Human Genetics, Am. Assn. Clin. Chemistry. Achievements include research in Genetic basis of kidney stone disease. Avocations: travel, reading, health and fitness. Office: Rutgers Univ Dept Genetics Life Scis Bldg 145 Bevier Rd Piscataway NJ 08854-8082 E-mail: sahota@biology.rutgers.edu.

**SAHR, MORRIS GALLUP,** financial planner; b. Schenectady, Nov. 28, 1928; s. Nathan and Esther (Gallup) S.; m. Sarah Diane Eisenberg, Dec. 23, 1956; children: Evelyn, David, Janet. AB, U. Oreg., 1951, MA, 1953; PhD, Calif. Open U., Oakland, 1978. Cert. fin. planner, registered fin. cons. Pres. Deposit Mgmt. Svc., Inc., Charlottesville, Va., 1978—. Author: Nine Ways to Beat the High Cost of College, 1999, Annuity Owners' Mistakes, 2002; co-author: Your Book of Financial Planning, 1983, Encyclopedia of Financial Planning, 1984, The Financial Planner, 1986, Financial Planning Can Make You Rich, 1987. Chmn. Fairfax County Health Council, Va., 1964-68; del. White House Conf. on Aging, 1980, U.S. Congl. Adv. Bd., 1984-87; bd. dirs. Fairfax Indsl. Devel. Authority, 1985-95; adjudicator Am. Arbitration Assn., 1988-99; del. to China, People to People Amb. Program, 2000. Recipient award Danforth Found.; named 1 of Top 200 Planners in U.S., Money Mag.; hon. fellow Kennedy Libr., 1985; Paul Harris fellow, 1989. Mem. Internat. Assn. Fin. Planning (founder, 1st pres. Metro Washington chpt.), Inst. Cert. Fin. Planners (nat. govt. affairs com.), Am. Assn. Practicing Fin. Planners (past pres.), Internat. Assn. of Registered Fin. Cons., Rotary (pres. Fairfax 1984-85, Srs. Project Internat. award). Home and Office: 1289 Courtyard Dr Charlottesville VA 22903 Office Phone: 434-970-2277. Personal E-mail: morey-dms@adelphia.net.

**SAHRAKORPI, SEPPO,** physicist, researcher; s. Matti Ls and Sirpa Sahrakorpi; life ptnr. Renate Harrison. MSc, Tampere U. of Tech., 1996, PhD with commendation, 2001. Rsch. asst. Tampere U. of Tech., 1996—2001; rsch. assoc. Northeastern U., Boston, 2002—. Sci. computing cons. Advanced fiei Compoutation Cu., Northeastern U., 2002—. 2d lt. Finnish mil., 1991—92. Fellow, Vilho, Yrjo and Kalle Found., Finland, 1999—2000, Tampere U. of Tech. Found., 2000; grantee, Vilho, Yrjo and Kalle Found., Finland, 2002, The Acad. of Finland, 2001—02; scholar, Found. for Advancement of Tech., Finland, 1997—98, Vilho, Yrjo and Kalle Found., Finland, 1998, Jenny and Antti Wihuri Found., Finland, 2000. Mem.: Am. Phys. Soc., European Phys. Soc., Finnish Phys. Soc. Achievements include research in fermiology and angle-resolved photoemission of high-temperature superconductors. Personal E-mail: seppo.sahrakorpi@iki.fi.

**SAIBLE, STEPHANIE IRENE,** magazine editor; b. Mobile, Ala., Sept. 11, 1954; d. Lewis J. Slaff and Phoebe-Jane (Berse) Meiss. Student, Va. Commonwealth U., 1972—75. Editorial asst. Woman's World Magazine, Englewood, NJ, 1980—81, service copywriter, 1981—83, assoc. articles editor, 1983—84, articles editor, 1984—85, sr. editor features dept., 1985—86, sr. editor services dept., 1986, now editor-in-chief, 1994—. Contbr. articles to Woman's World, Modern Bride, New Body, Celebrity Beauty, Trim and Fit, Ladies Home Jour. Named Wonder Woman of the Yr., Bus. Jour., N.J., 1986. Mem.: Women in Comms. Office: Woman's World Mag 270 Sylvan Ave Englewood Cliffs NJ 07632-2521*

**SAIDA, TOYOYASU,** chemical and biochemical engineer; b. Tokyo, Jan. 18, 1935; came to U.S., 1985; s. Tameo and Fukiko Saida; m. Mariko Itano, Jan. 16, 1960; children: Tetsuo, Miyoko Asahi, Takashi Saida. BS, U. Tokyo, 1958. Registered profl. engr., Japan. Ops. engr. Toyo Gas Chems. Corp., Niigata, Japan, 1958-59; rschr. Tokyo Inst. of Tech., 1959-61; rsch. engr. Mitsui-Toatsu Chems. Ltd., Yokohama, Japan, 1961-69, chief rsch. engr., 1969-78; mgr. process rsch. divsn. Toyo Engring. Corp., Mobara, Japan, 1978-84, adv. bd. mem. Chiba, Japan, 1984-85; v.p. BW Biotec, Inc. Chgo., 1985-86; gen. mgr. Hazarmacorp Rsch. Ctr., Tsukuba, Japan, 1987-95; mng. dir. Saida & Assocs., Sheffield, Ill., 1997—. Author: Handbook of Membrane Technology, 1978, Handbook of Bioprocess, 1985, Cellulose, 1986. Recipient Excellent Invention of Yr. Sci. and Tech. Agy., 1965. Mem. Am. Chem. Soc., Soc. of Chem. Engrs., Japan. Achievements include invention of innovative new synthetic method of urea, large scale manufacturing process of single cell protein from n-paraffin, fuel alcohol manufac-

---

turing process from lignocellulosics, volume reduction method of radioactive wastes with liquid phase oxidation. Home and Office: 431 Kelburn Rd Apt 315 Deerfield IL 60015-4367 E-mail: tomsaida@aol.com.

**SAIDI, PARVIN,** hematologist, medical educator; b. Teheran, Iran, Mar. 21, 1932; came to U.S., 1946; d. Ahmad and Fatemeh (Ashouri) S.; m. Allahverdi Farmanfarmaian, May 27, 1958; children: Dellara Farmanfarmaian Terry, Kimya Farmanfarmaian Harris. BS, Smith Coll., Northampton, Mass., 1952; MD, Harvard U., 1956. Diplomate Am. Bd. Internal Medicine, subspecialty hematology and med. oncology. Intern medicine UCLA Med. Ctr., 1956-57; resident internal medicine U. Calif., San Francisco, 1957-59; NIH rsch. fellow hematology U. Calif. Hosps. and Children's Med. Ctr., San Francisco, 1959-61, 63-64; asst. prof. medicine U. Medicine & Dentistry N.J.-Rutgers Med. Sch., New Brunswick, 1968-71, assoc. prof., 1971-74; prof. U. Medicine & Dentistry N.J.-Robert Wood Johnson Med. Sch., New Brunswick, 1974—, chief divsn. hematology and oncology, dept. medicine, 1972—, Robert Wood Johnson U. Hosp., New Brunswick, 1981—, Melvyn H. and AB Motolinsky chair hematology, 2000—. Cons. internist, hematologist, oncologist St. Peter's Med. Ctr., New Brunswick, Douglass Coll., Rutgers U., New Brunswick, VA Hosp., Lyons, N.J., Muhlenberg Hosp., Plainfield, N.J., Princeton (N.J.) Med. Ctr.; dir. Melvyn H. Motolinsky Lab. Hematology Rsch., N.J. Regional Comprehensive Hemophilia Care Program; mem. Gov.'s Adv. Coun. on AIDS; chmn. N.J. Regional Comprhensive Hemophilia Care Program Adv. Bd.; chmn. HHS region II Comprehensive Hemophilia Diagnostic and Treatment Ctrs., 1984-85, 89-90, 94-95, 99-2000; chmn. med. adv. bd. Hemophilia Found. N.J.; mem. med. adv. exec. com. N.J. Blood Svcs. Cons. editor Am. Jour. Medicine; contbr. articles to profl. jours. Recipient disting. svc. award for rsch. in leukemia Melvyn H. Motolinsky Rsch. Found., 1977, Humanitarian award Hemophilia Assn. No. N.J., 1978. Fellow ACP (mem. sci. program com. N.J. region), Acad. Medicine N.J.; mem. Am. Soc. Hematology (edn. com.), N.J. Hemophilia Assn. (chmn. med. adv. com., spl. award, Dr. L. Michael Kuhn Meml. award 1996), Coop. Oncology Group N.J. (exec. com., chairperson subcom. on lymphoma), Am. Heart Assn. (coun. on thrombosis), Am. Fedn. Clin. Rsch., Royal Soc. Medicine (affiliate), Am. Soc. Clin. Oncology, World Fedn. Hemophilia, Alpha Omega Alpha, Phi Beta Kappa, Sigma Xi. Office: Robert Wood Johnson Med Sch 1 Robert Wood Johnson Pl New Brunswick NJ 08901-1928

**SAIDI, REZA F,** researcher; b. Lexington, Ky., Jan. 10, 1970; MD, Tehran U. of Med. Sciences, Iran, 1997. Medical Doctor Am. Bd. of Surgery, 2006. Surgery resident Providence Hosp. And Med. Ctr., Southfield, Mich., 2001—06; transplant fellow Mass. Gen. Hosp., Boston, 2006—. Rsch. fellowship, Howard Hughes Med. Inst., 1995. Fellow: Am. Soc. Transplant Surgeons (assoc.); mem.: Am. Assn. for Cancer Rsch., Am. Hepato-Pancreato-Biliary Assn. (assoc.), Am. Coll. Surgeons (assoc.). Achievements include research in expression of interferon receptors in pancreatic cancer; effects of steroids on liver ischemia/reperfusion injury. Office: Providence Hosp and Med Ctr 16001 West Nine Mile Road Southfield MI 48075

**SAIF, LINDA J.,** veterinary scientist, virologist, immunologist; BA, Coll. Wooster, 1969; MA, Ohio State U., 1971, PhD in Microbiology/Immunology, 1976; PhD (hon.), Ghent U., Belgium, 2003. Prof. OARDC Ohio State U. Wooster, 1979—, disting. univ. prof., 2002—. Contbr. articles to profl. jours. Mem.: NAS. Office: Food Animal Health Rsch Program OARDC/OSU 1680 Madison Ave Wooster OH 44691

**SAIFER, MARK GARY PIERCE,** pharmaceutical executive; b. Phila., Sept. 16, 1938; s. Albert and Sylvia (Jolles) S.; m. Phyllis Lynne Trommer, Jan. 28, 1961 (dec.); children: Scott David, Alandria Gail; m. Merry R. Sherman, June 26, 1994. AB, U. Pa., 1960; PhD, U. Calif., Berkeley, 1966. Acting asst. prof. zoology U. Calif., Berkeley, 1966, fellow, 1967-68; sr. cancer rsch. scientist Roswell Park Meml. Inst., Buffalo, 1968-70; lab. dir. Diagnostic Data Inc., Palo Alto, Calif., 1970-78; v.p. DDI Pharms., Inc., Mountain View, Calif., 1978-94, Oxis Internat., Inc., 1994-95; v.p., sci. dir. Mountain View Pharms., Inc., Menlo Park, Calif., 1996—, also bd. dirs. Lectr., expert witness in field. Author, patentee in field:, mem. editl. bd.: Current Pharm. Biotechnology Jour. Mem. AAAS (life), Am. Assn. Pharm. Scientists, Parenteral Drug Assn. Office: Mountain View Pharms Inc 3475 Edison Way Ste S Menlo Park CA 94025-1821 E-mail: saifer@mvpharm.com.

**SAIKI, KIM,** professional golfer; b. Inglewood, Calif., Jan. 24, 1966; Degree in pub. admin., U. Calif. Winner Wegmans Rochester LPGA Championships, 2004. Four-time All-PAC 10 honoree; NCAA All-Am., 1986; winner Jr. World Championships, USGA Jr. Girls Championships; five-time winner Players West Golf Tour; two-time winner Futures Tour. Achievements include earning 20 career top-ten finishes. Avocations: fitness, cooking, music. Office: c/o LPGA 100 International Golf Dr Daytona Beach FL 32124-1092

**SAIKI, PATRICIA (MRS. STANLEY MITSUO SAIKI),** federal agency administrator, congresswoman; b. Hilo, Hawaii, May 28, 1930; d. Kazuo and Shizue (Inoue) Fukuda; m. Stanley Mitsuo Saiki, June 19, 1954; children: Stanley Mitsuo, Sandra Saiki Williams, Margaret C., Stuart K., Laura H. BA, U. Hawaii, 1952. Tchr. U.S. history Punahou Sch., Kaimuki Intermediate Sch., Kalani High Sch., Honolulu, 1952-64; sec. Rep. Party Hawaii, Honolulu, 1964-66, vice chmn., 1966-68, 82-83, chmn., 1983-85; rsch. asst. Hawaii State Senate, 1966-68; mem. Hawaii Ho. of Reps., 1968-74, Hawaii State Senate, 1974-82, 100th-101st Congresses from 1st Hawaii dist.; mem. Pres.'s Adv. Coun. on Status of Women, 1969-76; mem. Nat. Commn. Internat. Women's Yr., 1969-70; commr. We. Interstate Commn. on Higher Edn.; fellow Eagleton Inst., Rutgers U., 1970; fellow Inst. of Politics, Kennedy Sch. Govt., Harvard U., 1993; del. dirs. Bank of Am. Hawaii, Landmark flyat on Corp. Internat. Asset Recovery Corp.; mem. nat. selection com. Innovations in Am. Govt., Ford Found., Harvard U., 1999-2002. Mem. Kapiolano Hosp. Aux.; sec. Hawaii Rep. Com., 1964-66, vice chmn., 1966-68, chmn., 1983-85; del. Hawaii Constl. Conv., 1968; alt. del. Rep. Nat. Conv., 1968, del., 1984, Rep. nominee for lt. gov. Hawaii, 1982, for U.S. Senate, 1990, for gov. Hawaii, 1994; mem. Fedn. Rep. Women; trustee Hawaii Pacific Coll.; past bd. govs. Boys and Girls Clubs Hawaii; mem. adv. coun. ARC; bd. dirs. Nat. Fund for Improvement of Post-Secondary Edn., 1982-85; past bd. dirs. Straub Med. Rsch. Found., Honolulu, Hawaii's Visitors Bur., Honolulu, Edn. Commn. of States, Honolulu, Hawaii Visitors Bur., 1983-85; trustee U. Hawaii Found., 1984-86, Hawaii Pacific Coll., Honolulu; bd. govs. East West Ctr., 2003-. Republican. Episcopalian. Avocation: golf. Home: 784 Elepaio St Honolulu HI 96816-4710 E-mail: pfsaiki@cs.com.

**SAILER, RACHEL ANN,** secondary school educator; b. Cedar Falls, Iowa, May 26, 1951; d. Charles Herbert and Sarah Bronwen Pinkham; m. John Jacob Sailer, Oct. 26, 1950; children: Amy Bronwen, Jacob Thomas. BA, U. No. Iowa, Cedar Falls, 1974; MLS, Hallins U., Roanoke, Va., 1999. Lic. collegiate profl. tchr. Va. Rsch. asst. Inst. Philosophy and Pub. Policy, College Park, Md., 1980—83; mktg. assoc. Mill Mountain Theatre, Roanoke, Va., 1983—86; tchr. drama Salem H.S., 1986—. Actress in cmty. and profl. local prodns. Tchr. Christ Episcopal Ch., 2000—; vol. Interfaith Hospitality, 2000—; bd. mem. Shortimers Cmty. Theatre, Roanoke, Va., 1985—88, Character Counts, 2005—. Named Tchr. of Yr., Salem City Schs., 2004—05. Mem.: Va. Edn. Assn. Democrat. Office: Salem HS 400 Spartan Dr Salem VA 24153-5090 Home: 2435 Berkley Ave SW Roanoke VA 24015 Office Phone: 540-387-2437.

**SAIN, CHARLES (HACK SAIN),** civil engineer, surveyor; b. New Market, Ala., Jan. 20, 1923; s. Will Oris and Clayta (Speck) Sain; m. Marie Myers, Aug. 8, 1942; children: Charles R., Elizabeth Lester Stockdale, Ann Marie Hays; m. Helen Weil, Mar. 18, 2000. BSCE, U. Fla., 1949. Registered profl. engr., Ala., Ariz., Colo., Conn., Fla., Ga., Ill., Ind., Iowa, Kans., Ky., La., Minn., Miss., N.J., N.Y., N.C., Okla., Pa., S.C., S.D., Tenn., Vt., Va., W.Va., Wis. V.p. engring. Moss-Thornton Co., Inc., Leeds, Ala., 1946-59; gen. mgr. Vecellio & Grogan, Beckley, W.Va., 1960-64; v.p engring. A.E. Burgess Co.,

---

Inc., Birmingham, Ala., 1964-67; pres. Charles H. Sain Assocs., Birmingham, 1968-89, Sain South Engring., Birmingham, 1978-89; CEO, chmn. bd. dirs. Sain Assocs., Inc., Birmingham, 1989—. Bd. visitors civil engring. dept. Coll. Engring. U. Ala., Birmingham; lectr. Auburn U., 1971, 72. Author: (with others) Standard Handbook for Civil Engineers, 1968, 4th edit., 1996; contbr. articles to profl. jours. Bd. dirs. State of Ala. Toll Bridge Authority, 1970-74; city engr. City of Vestavia Hills, Ala., 1976-88, City of Homewood, Ala., 1976-80; vice chmn., bd. dirs. Ala. Bapt. Retirement Ctrs., Montgomery, 1986-93; mem. Vestavia Hills, Ala. Bd. Zoning Adjustment, 1986-90; vice chmn. Jefferson County Bd. Zoning Adjustment, 1986—; mem. Vestavia Hills Bapt. Ch., 1991—, deacon. Lt. U.S. Army, 1944-46. Named Engr. of Yr. Ala., Engring. Found. Coun. U. Ala.-Birmingham, 1999. Mem. NSPE, ASCE (program chmn. Ala. chpt. 1966, equipment maintenance com. 1958-78, Life Achievement award), Am. Soc. Mil. Engrs., Internat. Platform Assn., Internat. Coun. Shopping Ctrs. (water quality com., environ. site assessment com., lectr., Disting. Svc. award 1996), Birmingham C. of C. (environ. ethicc com., lectr.), Tau Beta Phi, Sigma Tau. Avocations: golf, reading. Office: Sain Assocs Inc 244 W Valley Ste 200 Birmingham AL 35209-3616 E-mail: hsain@sain.com.

**SAINER, ARTHUR,** writer, theater educator; b. NYC, Sept. 12, 1924; s. Louis and Sadie (Roth) S.; m. Maryjane Treloar, Apr. 18, 1981; children: Douglas M., Stephanie M., Jane M., Ross M. BA, Washington Sq. Coll., N.Y.C., 1946; MA, Columbia U., 1948. Tchr. C.W. Post Coll., Bennington Coll., Vt., 1967-69, Adelphi U., Garden City, NY, 1974-75, S.I. Community Coll., 1974-75; faculty Wesleyan U., Middletown, Conn., 1977-80, Hunter Coll., N.Y.C., 1980-81; assoc. prof. theatre Middlebury Coll., Vt., 1981-83; theater faculty New Sch. for Social Rsch., N.Y.C., 1985—, SUNY, Albany, 2004—, Sarah Lawrence Coll., Bronxville, NY, 1990—2002; play dir. Boat Sun Cavern Middlebury Coll., Vt., 1983; drama critic Village Voice, N.Y.C., 1961—; play dir. Lord Tom Goldsmith at Theatre for New City, N.Y.C., 1979, Witnesses at Open Space, N.Y.C., 1977, Poor Man Rich Man, Theatre for the New City, 1992. Reporter Nat. Endowment for Arts, Washington, 1979—82. Editor: Village Voice, 1962; author: (plays) The Children's Army Is Late, 1974, Carol in Winter Sunlight, 1977, After the Baal-Shem Tov, 1979, Images of the Coming Dead, 1980, Sunday Childhood Journeys to Nobody at Home, 1984 (Berman award, 1984), Cruising Angel, 1984, The Celebration Reclaimed, 1993—95, The Burning Out of 82, 1997, Jews and Christians in the End Zone, 2000 (Nat. Found. for Jewish Culture award, 2006), The Potter's Wheel: To Repair the Soul, 2003, The People Impeach the Bushes, 2004, Conversions and Assassins, 2005, (criticisms) The Sleepwalker and the Assassin, 1964, The New Radical Theatre Notebook, 1975, 1997, Zero Dances, 1998; repor. Panelist Vt. Council on the Arts, Montpelier, 1982, 83; panelist N.Y. State Council on the Arts, 1976-78. Ford Found. grantee, 1979, 80; recipient grant Office for Advanced Drama Research, U. Minn., 1967, award for Grab Your Hat John Golden Found., 1946 Address: 59 Railroad Pl #304 Saratoga Springs NY 12866-2161 Personal E-mail: asainer@earthlink.net. *From the Burning Out of 82: Francis: But finally, who is going to do my work? No one is going to do it. Lev: Each will do his work. But in the end only God's work amounts to anything. Francis: And does that make you happy? Lev: It makes me useful.*

**SAINI, SIMARJEET SINGH,** electronics engineer; b. Mandi, India, Apr. 12, 1975; s. Balbir Singh Saini and Satish Kaur; m. Manpreet Kaur, Dec. 2, 2001; 1 child, Hardit Singh. PhD, U. Md., College Park, 2001. Lead rschr. Covega, Jessup, Md., 2000—04, lead app engr., 2005—; dir. optoelectronics Altanet Comm., Greenbelt, Md., 2004—05. Cons. BSNL, Jallandhar, Punjab, India, 1994—96; cons. r&d Potomac Optronics, Seoul, 2005—. Vol. Jainath, Patiala, Punjab, India, 2004—06. Recipient Disting. Rschr., ECE, U. Md., 2000; Army Rsch. Lab fellow, U.S. Army Rsch. Lab, 1996—97, Ednl. scholar, SPIE, 2000. Mem.: IEEE. Achievements include patents for resonant coupling for tapered waveguides; design of broadband gain chips for tunablelasers; patents for resonant coupling between waevguides over tapers; highly efficient semiconductor optical devices; patents pending for non-uniform current distribution for increased performance of SOA; method for parametric discrimination in fiber bragg grating sensors; design of highest performing semiconductor optical amplifiers in the world; research in highest sensitivity fiber bragg sensors for chemical and biological sensors; discovery of PARC, a new platform for monolithic integration of photonic devices; design of highest power super-luminiscent diode; first to rural area network for Punjab using TDMA system and frequency hopping. Home: 6110 Good Hunters Ride Columbia MD 21045 Office Phone: 240-456-7224. Personal E-mail: simarjeet.saini@gmail.com.

**SAINT, EVA MARIE,** actress; b. Newark, July 4, 1924; d. John Merle and Eva Marie (Rice) S.; m. Jeffrey Hayden, Oct. 28, 1951; children: Darrell, Laurette. BA, DFA, Bowling Green State U., 1946; student, Actors Studio, 1950. Appeared in various radio and TV dramatic shows, N.Y.C., 1947—; theater roles include The Trip to Bountiful, 1953 (Outer Circle Critics award, N.Y. Drama Critics award 1953), The Rainmaker, 1953, Winesburg, Ohio, 1970, The Lincoln Mask, 1972, Summer and Smoke, 1973, Desire Under the Elms, 1974, The Fatal Weakness, 1976, Candida, 1977, Mr. Roberts, First Monday in October, 1979, Duet for One, 1982-83, The Country Girl, 1986 (L.A. Dramalogue award 1986), Death of a Salesman, 1994, Love Letters, 1994-2005, On the Divide, 2004, Touch the Names, 2005; appeared in films On the Waterfront, 1954 (Acad. Award for best supporting actress 1955), That Certain Feeling, 1956, Raintree Country, 1957, A Hatful of Rain, 1957, North by Northwest, 1959, Exodus, 1961, All Fall Down, 1962, 36 Hours, 1963, The Sandpiper, 1964, The Russians are Coming, The Russians are Coming!, 1965, Grand Prix, 1966, The Stalking Moon, 1969, Loving, 1970, Cancel My Reservation, 1972, Nothing in Common, 1986, Marietté in Ecstacy, 1995, I Dreamed of Africa, 2000, Because of Winn-Dixie, 2005, Don't Come Knocking, 2005 (feature film) Superman Returns, 2006; TV dramas include The Macahans, 1976 (Emmy nom.), The Fatal Weakness, 1976, Taxi!!, 1978 (Emmy nom.), A Christmas to Remember, 1978, When Hell Was in Season, 1980, The Curse of King Tut's Tomb, The Best Little Girl in the World, 1981, Splendor in the Grass, 1981, Love Leads the Way, 1983, Jane Doe, 1983, Fatal Vision, 1984, The Last Days of Patton, 1986, A Year in the Life, 1986, Breaking Home Times, 1987, I'll Be Home for Christmas, 1988, Voyage of Terror: The Achille Lauro Affair, 1990, People Like Us, 1990 (Emmy award 1990), Palomino, 1991, Kiss of the Killer, ABC, 1992, My Antonia, 1994, After Jimmy, 1996, Too Say Goodbye, 1997, Titanic, 1997; (documentary) Primary Colors: The Story of Corita, 1991; (with Bill Moyers) Children in America's Schools, 1997, Papa's Angels, 2000, Open House, TV-CBS, 2003.

**ST. AMAND, PIERRE,** geophysicist; b. Tacoma, Wash., Feb. 4, 1920; s. Cyrius Z. and Mable (Berg) St A.; m. Marie Pöss, Dec. 5, 1945; children: Gene, Barbara, Denali, David. BS in Physics, U. Alaska, 1948; MS in Geophysics, Calif. Inst. Tech., 1951, PhD in Geophysics and Geology, 1953; Dr. honoris causa, U. De Los Altos, Tepatitlan, Mex., 1992. Asst. dir. Geophys. Lab., U. Alaska, also head ionospheric and seismologic investigations, 1946-49; physicist U.S. Naval Ordnance Test Sta., China Lake, Calif., 1950-54, head optics br., 1955-58; head earth and planetary sci. div. U.S. Ordnance Test Sta., 1961-78, cons. to tech. dir., head spl. projects office, 1978-88; fgn. service with ICA as prof. geol. and geophys. Sch. Earth Scis., U. Chile, 1958-60; originator theory rotational displacement Pacific Ocean Basin. Pres. Saint-Amand Sci. Services; adj. prof. McKay Sch. Mines, U. Nev., U. N.D.; v.p., dir. Covillea Corp.; v.p., dir. tech. Muetal Corp.; cons. World Bank, Calif. Div. Water Resources, Am. Potash & Chem. Co., OAS; mem. U.S. Army airways comms. sys., Alaska and Can., 1942-46; cons. Mexican, Chilean, Argentine, Philipines, Can., Rhodesian govts.; mem. Calif. Gov.'s Com. Geol. Hazards; mem. com. magnetic instruments Internat. Union Geodesy and Geophys., 1954-59, Disaster Preparation Commn. for L.A.; charter mem. Sr. Exec. Svc.; led drought relief expdns., India, The Philippines, Mex., Okinawa, Japan; rep. fed. emergency com. for LA (Calif.), USN. Adv. bd. GeoScience News; contbr. 100 articles to scientific jours. Chmn. bd. dirs. Ridgecrest Regional Hosp.; chmn. bd. dirs. Indian Wells Valley Airport Dist.; pres., dir. Indian Wells Valley Water Dist.; v.p. bd. dirs. Kern County Acad. Decathlon; mem. water resources bd. Kern County. Decorated knight

Mark Twain, Mark Twain Jour.; recipient cert. of merit OSRD, 1945, cert. of merit USAAF, 1946, letter of commendation USAAF, 1948, Spl. award Philippine Air Force, 1969, Diploma de Honor Sociedad Geologica de Chile, Disting. Civilian Svc. medal USN, 1968, L.T.E. Thompson medal, 1973, Thunderbird award Weather Modification Assn., 1974, Disting. Pub. Svc. award Fed. Exec. Inst., 1976, Meritorious Svc. medal USN, 1988, Disting. Alumnus award U. Alaska, 1990; Fulbright rsch. fellow France, 1954-55. Fellow AAAS, Geol. Soc. Am., Earthquake Engr. Rsch. Inst.; mem. Am. Geophys. Union, Weather Modification Assn., Am. Seismol. Soc., Sister Cities (Ridgecrest-Tepatitlan) Assn. (pres.), Rotary (past pres., Paul Harris fellow), Footprinters Internat. (mem. grand bd., pres.), Sigma Xi. Achievements include patents in photometric instrument, weather and ordnance devices, pvt. pilot multi-engine-instruments; identified Denali: Fairweather Faults in Alaska and Canada, Atacama Fault in Chile. Home and Office: 1748 W Las Flores Ave Ridgecrest CA 93555-8635 Office Phone: 760-375-0481. Personal E-mail: st-amand@ridgecrest.ca.us.

**SAINT-AMAND, PIERRE NEMOURS,** humanities educator; b. Port-Au-Prince, Haiti, Feb. 22, 1957; came to U.S., 1978; s. Nemours and Carmen (Clerveaux) Saint-A. BA, U. Montreal, 1978; MA, Johns Hopkins U., 1980, PhD, 1981. Asst. prof. Yale U., New Haven, 1981-82, Stanford U., Calif., 1982-86; assoc. prof. Brown U., Providence, 1986-90, prof., 1990—, Francis Wayland prof., 1996—. Vis. prof. Harvard U., Cambridge, Mass., 1992, U. Iowa, Iowa City, 2001. Author: Diderot, Le Labyrinthe de La Relation, 1984, Séduire Ou La Passion des Lumières, 1986, Les Lois de L'Hostilité, 1992, The Libertine's Progress, 1994, The Laws of Hostility, 1996; editor: Diderot, 1984, Le Roman au Dix-huitième siècle, 1987, Autonomy in the Age of the Enlightenment, 1993, Thérèse philosophe, 2000, Confession d'une jeune fille, 2005. Fellow Stanford Humanities Ctr., 1985-86, John Simon Guggenheim Meml. Found., 1989; decorated chevalier dans l'Ordre des Palmes académiques, 2001. Office: Brown U PO Box 1961 Providence RI 02912-1961

**SAINT-ANTOINE, PAUL HEWITT,** lawyer; b. Washington, 1964; AB summa cum laude, Kenyon Coll., 1986; JD, Columbia Univ., 1989. Bar: Pa. 1989, NJ 1989. Joined Drinker Biddle & Reath LLP, Phila., 1989, ptnr., litig. dept., head, antitrust practice group. Editor-in-chief Federal Antitrust Guidelines for the Licensing of Intellectual Property, Origins and Applications, 2nd ed., ABA. Named a Harlan Fiske Stone Scholar. Mem.: ABA, Pa. Bar Assn. Office: Drinker Biddle & Reath LLP One Logan Sq 18th & Cherry Sts Philadelphia PA 19103-6996 Office Phone: 215-988-2990. Office Fax: 215-988-2757. Business E-Mail: paul.saint-antoine@dbr.com.

**ST. ANTOINE, THEODORE JOSEPH,** retired law educator, arbitrator; b. St. Albans, Vt., May 29, 1929; s. Arthur Joseph and Mary Beatrice (Callery) S.; m. Elizabeth Lloyd Frier, Jan. 2, 1960; children: Arthur, Claire, Paul, Sara. AB, Fordham Coll., 1951; JD, U. Mich., 1954; postgrad., U. London, 1957—58. Bar: Mich. 1954, Ohio 1954, DC 1959. Assoc. Squire, Sanders & Dempsey, Cleve., 1954; assoc., ptnr. Woll, Mayer & St. Antoine, Washington, 1958-65; assoc. prof. law U. Mich. Law Sch., Ann Arbor, 1965-69, prof., 1969—81, Degan prof., 1981-98, Degan prof. emeritus, 1998—, dean, 1971-78. Pres. Nat. Resource Ctr. for Consumers of Legal Svcs., 1974—78; mem. pub. rev. bd. UAW, 1973—, chmn., 2000—; spl. counselor on workers' compensation Gov. of Mich., 1983—85; chmn. UAW-GM legal svcs. plan, 1983—95; reporter Uniform Law Commrs., 1987—92; mem. discipline bd. Mich. Atty., 1999—2005, vice chmn. discipline bd., 2000—02, chmn. discipline bd., 2002—05; life mem. Clare Hall, Cambridge (Eng.) U. Co-author: (with R. Smith, L. Merrifield, C. Craver and M. Crain) Labor Relations Law: Cases and Materials, 4th edit., 1968, 11th edit., 2005; editor: The Common Law of the Workplace: The Views of Arbitrators, 2d. edit., 2005; contbr. articles to profl. jours. Bd. dirs. Nat. Workrights Inst., 2005—. 1st lt. JAGC U.S. Army, 1955—57. Fulbright grantee, U. London, 1957—58. Mem. ABA (past sec. labor law sect., coun. 1984-92), Am. Bar Found., State Bar Mich. (chmn. labor rels. law sect. 1979-80), Nat. Acad. Arbitrators (bd. govs. 1985-88, v.p. 1994-96, pres. 1999-2000), Internat. Soc. Labor and Social Security Law (U.S. br. exec. bd. 1983—, vice chmn. 1989-95), Am. Arbitration Assn. (bd. dirs. 2000—), Nat. Workrights Inst. (bd. dirs. 2005-), Labor and Employment Rels. Assn., Coll. Labor and Employment Lawyers, Order of Coif (life). Democrat. Roman Catholic. Home: 1421 Roxbury Rd Ann Arbor MI 48104-4047 Office: U Mich Law Sch 625 S State St Ann Arbor MI 48109-1215 Office Phone: 734-764-9348. Business E-Mail: tstanton@umich.edu.

**SAINT ARNAULT, DENISE MARIE,** education educator, researcher; life ptnr. Deborah Roels, May 20, 1989; children: Angela Slag, Jeffrey Allen Slag. PhD, Wayne State U., Detroit, 1990—98. RN Mich., 1980. Assoc. prof. Mich. State U., East Lansing, 2000—. Grantee Rsch. grant, NIMH, 2005. Office: B510-B West Fee Hall Fee Rd East Lansing MI 48824 Business E-Mail: saintarn@msu.edu.

**ST. CLAIR, CLIFFORD MARK,** music educator; b. Memphis, Oct. 3, 1958; s. Phillip Morrison and Nancy Louise St. Clair; m. Shairi Lynn Wick, July 19, 1980; children: Raleigh Eugene, Lindsay Joy, Graeme Phillip, Brittany Noel, Abigail Anne. BA in Music Edn., Bethel Coll., 1980; MS in Music Edn., U. Ill., 1993. Cert. tchr. Iowa, 2001. Band dir. Sherburn Pub. Schools, Minn., 1984—88, Martin County West Pub. Schools, 1988—2001, Sheldon Cmty. H.S., Iowa, 2001—. Coach, referee regional commr. 1186 Am. Youth Soccer Orgn., Sherburn, Minn., 1995—2001, coach, referee, regional commr. 1446, 2004—; charter mem. and deacon Crossroads Cmty. Ch., Sheldon, 2002—05. Mem.: Internat. Trumpet Guild, Iowa Bandmasters Assn., Am. Band Assn., Music Educators Nat. Conf. Evangelical Christian. Avocations: soccer coach, soccer referee. Office: Sheldon Community High School 1700 E Fourth St Sheldon IA 51021 Office Phone: 712-324-2501. E-mail: cstclair@sheldon.k12.ia.us.

**ST. CLAIR, DONALD DAVID,** lawyer; b. Hammond, Ind., Dec. 30, 1932; s. Victor Peter and Wanda Small; m. Sergine Anne Oliver, June 6, 1970 (dec. June 1974); m. Beverly Joyce Tipton, Dec. 28, 1987. BS, Ind. U., 1955, MS, 1963, EdD, 1967; JD, U. Toledo, Ohio, 1992. Bar: Ohio 1992, U.S. Dist. Ct. (no. dist.) Ohio 1993, U.S. Supreme Ct., 1996. Assoc. prof. Western Ky. U. Coll. Edn., Bowling Green, 1967-68, U. Toledo, 1968-77, prof., 1977-92; atty., ptnr. Gazand, Bollinger, & St. Clair, Oregon, Ohio, 1992-97; pvt. practice Law Offices Donald D. St. Clair, Toledo, 1997—. Mem. Ohio Coun. Mental Health Ctrs., Columbus, 1978-79; dir. honors programs U. Toledo. Author: (poetry) Daymarks and Beacons, 1983, Impressions from an Afternoon in a Paris Courtroom, 1998; contbr. articles to profl. jours. Organizer Students Toledo Organized for Peace, 1970-71; mem. Lucas County Dem. Party, 1990—. With U.S. Army, 1955-57. Mem. ABA, AAU (nat. bd. dirs. 1973-74), Am. Inns of Ct., Ohio Bar Assn., Toledo Bar Assn., Ohio Acad. Trial Lawyers, Toledo Power Squadron (comdg. officer 1981), Bay View Yacht Club, Ohio Criminal Def. Lawyers Assn., Lucas County Bar Assn., Maumee Valley Criminal Def. Lawyers Assn., Ottawa County Bar Assn., Masons (32 degree), Shriners, Ancient Order Friars, Phi Alpha Delta. Office: PO Box 23185 Toledo OH 43623-0185 Personal E-mail: stclairlaw@attglobal.net.

**ST. CLAIR, GLORIANA STRANGE,** librarian, dean; b. Tonkawa, Okla., Dec. 13, 1939; d. Glen Leroy and Doris Mildred (Furber) Strange. BA in English, U. Okla., 1962, PhD in Literature, 1970; MLS, U. Calif., Berkeley, 1963; MBA in Mgmt., U. Tex., San Antonio, 1980. Rsch. asst. U. Calif, Berkeley, 1962-63; asst. libr., 1963-65; cataloguer U. Okla., Norman, 1965-68; supervising libr. San Antonio Pub. Libr., 1980-84; head acquisitions divsn. Tex. A&M U. Librs., College Station, 1984-87, humanities bibliographer, 1985, head pers. ops., 1986; asst. dir. tech. automation and adminstrv. svc. Kerr Libr., Oregon State U., Corvallis, 1987-90; assoc. head info. access svcs. Pa. State U. Lib
rs., University Park, 1990-98; dean univ. libr. Carnegie Mellon U., Pitts., 1998—. Editor Coll. & Rsch. Librs., 1990-96, Jour. Academic Librarianship, 1996—. Bd. dirs. Towers Condo. Bd., State College, 1993-94; mem. vestry, mem. book discussion group St. Andrew's Episcopal Ch., State College, 1991-98; examiner Pa. Quality Leadership, 1994. Sr. fellow UCLA, 1991. Mem. Assn. Coll. and Rsch. Librs. (chair editl.

adv. bd. 1990-96). Home: 154 N Bellefield Ave Apt 45 Pittsburgh PA 15213-2640 Office: Univ Librs Carnegie Mellon U 4909 Frew St Pittsburgh PA 15213-3890 Office Fax: 412-268-2793.*

**ST. CLAIR, HELAINE DENISE,** language educator; b. Newark, N.J., Jan. 23, 1952; d. Alex Alan and Ceil Rosalie Collins; m. Wayne St. Clair, June 14, 1975; children: Craig Eric, Alexis Rochelle. BA in Spanish, Adelphi U., 1974; BA in Spanish Ling., Fla. Atlantic U., 1975. Cert. Teacher N.Y., N.J., Pa. Tchg. asst. Fla. Atlantic U., Boca Raton, 1974—75; Spanish tchr. Shenendehowa Ctrl. Sch., Clifton Park, NY, 1984—. Mem.: Capital Orgn. Lang. Tchrs., N.Y. Assn. Fgn. Lang. Tchrs. Avocations: cooking, travel, exercise. Home: 3427 E Lydius St Schenectady NY 12303 Office: Shenendehowa High School Rt 146 Clifton Park NY 12065 Office Phone: 518-881-0310. Business E-Mail: stclhela@shenet.org.

**ST. CLAIR, JEFFREY,** editor; Editor CounterPunch mag; contbg editor In These Times. Author: A Pocket Guide to Environmental Bad Guys, Al Gore: a user's manual. Office: CounterPunch Magazine PO Box 228 Petrolia CA 95558

**ST. CLAIR, JESSE WALTON, JR.,** retired savings and loan association executive; b. Phila., Jan. 15, 1930; s. Jesse Walton and Susan Elizabeth (Leath) St. C.; m. Elizabeth Anne Bartlett, Oct. 6, 1951; children: Jesse Walton III, Susan Elizabeth, Bruce Bartlett, Anne Leath. BA, Coll. of William and Mary, 1951; MBA, U. Pa., 1958; postgrad., Harvard U., 1968. Trainee Fed. Res. Bank, Phila., 1955-57; with Girard Trust Bank, Phila., 1957-78, asst. treas., 1960-64, asst. v.p., 1964-67, v.p., 1967-70, sr. v.p., 1970-75, exec. v.p., 1976-78; pres., chief exec. officer First Nat. Bank of Allentown (Pa.), 1978-82; chmn., chief exec. officer Wilmington Savs. Fund Soc., 1982-90, ret., 1990. Trustee emeritus endowment fund Coll. William and Mary; former mem. exec. bd. Delmarva coun. Boy Scouts Am.; past trustee Wesley Coll. With USN, 1951-55. Mem. Wilmington Country Club, Theta Delta Chi. Republican. Methodist. Home: 4011 Springfield Ln Greenville Wilmington DE 19807

**ST. CLAIR, NIKÉ ENIKO,** music educator, conductor; d. Laszlo Simor; m. Kevin St. Clair, Mar. 13, 2002. ABD, U. So. Calif., LA, 2001. Music tchr., choral condr. Westridge Sch., Pasadena, Calif., 2000—05; profl./roster singer LA Master Chorale, Los Angeles, Calif., 2002—; music dir. First United Meth. Ch., Redondo Beach, Calif., 2003—05. Prof. Azusa Pacific U., Calif., 2002—; adj. prof. Santa Monica Coll., Calif., 2003—; vis. instr. Redlands U., Redlands, Calif., 2005—. Dir. Manzanar Youth Choir. Mem.: So. Calif. Kodaly Educators Assn. (solfege instr. 1999—), Orgn. Am. Kodaly Educators, Am. Choral Dirs. Assn., Am. Guild Musical Artists. Avocations: swimming, cross country skiing, hiking. Office Phone: 909-793-2121 ext. 3277.

**ST. CLAIR, THOMAS McBRYAR,** mining and manufacturing company executive; b. Wilkinsburg, Pa., Sept. 26, 1935; s. Fred C. and Dorothy (Renner) St. C.; m. Sarah K. Stewart, Aug. 1, 1959; children— Janet, Susan, Carol. AB, Allegheny Coll., 1957; MS, MIT, 1958; grad. advanced mgmt. program, Harvard U. With Koppers Co., Inc., Pitts., 1958-88, asst. to gen. mgr. engring. and constrn. div., 1966-69, comptroller, asst. treas., 1969-78, pres. Engineered Metal Products Group, 1978-83, v.p., asst. to chmn., 1983-84, v.p., treas., chief fin. officer, 1984-88; sr. v.p., chief fin. officer Phelps Dodge Corp., Phoenix, 1989-99; retired, 1999. Bd. dirs. Pitts. Theol. Sem. Mem. Fin. Execs. Inst., Duquesne Club (Pitts.). Presbyterian.

**ST. CLAIR, FRANK ARTHUR,** lawyer; b. Charlotte, N.C., June 16, 1949; BS, MIT, 1972; JD, NYU, 1975. Bar: Tex. 1975, U.S. Dist. Ct. (no. dist.) Tex. 1985; bd. cert. in comml. real estate law. Assoc. James H. Wallenstein, Dallas, 1975-78; v.p. Wallenstein & St. Claire, Dallas, 1978-81; pres. Frank A. St. Claire, P.C., Dallas, 1981-84; ptnr. St. Claire & Case, P.C., Dallas, 1984-88, pres., 1988-93; chmn. bd. Sunbelt Empire Title Co., Dallas, 1983-88; pres. St. Claire & Assocs., Dallas, 1993—; chmn. real estate section Godwin & Carlton, P.C., Dallas, 1994-96; ptnr., chmn. real estate sect. Strasburger & Price, L.L.P., Dallas, 1996-2000; pres. StClaireNet, 2001—. Author: Texas Condominium Law, 1986; co-author: Texas Real Estate Guide, 2000; contbr. articles to profl. jours. Ofcl. del. Dallas to Baltic Legal Conf., Riga, Latvia, 1990. Mem. Am. Coll. Mortgage Attys. (chmn. pubs. com. 1998—, mem. programs com. 1998—), Tex. Bar Assn. (study of uniform condominium act com., legis. liaison com. 1981-85, vice chmn. 1981-82, chmn. 1982-85, chmn. condominium and coop. housing com. 1985-89, title ins. com., mem. coun. real estate, probate and trust coun. 1991-95, treas. 1996-97, sec., chair-elect 1997-98, chair 1998-99), Dallas Bar Assn., Cmty. Assn. Inst. (bd. dirs. Dallas-Ft. Worth chpt. 1984-85, 87-89, pres.-elect 1989-90), Real Estate Fin. Exec. Assn. (assoc. sec. 1996-97), Real Estate Coun., Am. Coll. Real Estate Lawyers (planning com. 1990-98, chmn. practice tech. com. 1993-96, mem. common interest ownership com. 1986-98, alternative dispute resolution com. 1993-95), Tex. Coll. Real Estate Attys. (chmn. projects com. 1991-92, bd. dirs. 1994-98), Internat. Assn. of Attys. and Execs. in Corp. Real Estate (website com. 1997-2001). Episcopalian.

**ST. CYR, MARGARET ANN (PEGGY ST. CYR),** writer; b. Phila., May 1, 1932; d. Thomas Russell Reiling and Margaret Mary Cannon; m. Raymond Paul St. Cyr, May 14, 1952; children: Mary Louise, Sharon Ann, Margot Elizabeth, Daniel Paul, Mark Dennis. AA, Mesa CC, Ariz., 1977. Sec. to asst. contr. U. Pa. Hosp., Phila., 1965—67; sec. to chmn. dept. pathology Woman's Med. Coll., Phila., 1967—74; exec. sec. to asst. supt. Mesa Pub. Schs., 1969—81; advt. coord. Latter-day Sentinel, Phoenix, 1981—82; profl. writer, 1982—. Spkr. Family History Soc. Ariz. Author: From Conversion to Commitment, 1996, One Fold, One Shepherd, 1999. Sec. MARC Bd., Mesa, 1969—70, Mesa Constn. Week Com., 1972—74; co-founder East Falls Human Rels. Com., Phila., 1966; pres. PTA, 1965, 1966; sec. Dist. 29 Reps., Mesa, 1996, 4th vice chmn., 1997, 2d vice chmn., 1998, 1st vice chmn., 1999; precinct committeeman Dist. 18 Reps., 1994—. Served with Women's Army Corps U.S. Army, 1950—51. Named Vol. of Yr., Maricopa County Reps., 1997; recipient, Chapel of 4 Chaplains, Phila., 1967, cert. appreciation, Maricopa County Reps., 1996, Lincoln Day award, 1999, Best Makeup award, Tempe Little Theatre, 1976, Best Actress, 1976, Best Makeup, 1977, Best Dir., 1977, Most Contbn. Mem., 1977, Best Actress, 1978. Mem. Lds Ch. Avocations: acting, singing, choir directing. Home: 724 S Kachina Mesa AZ 85204 Personal E-mail: pete724x@aol.com.

**SAINT-DONAT, BERNARD JACQUES,** finance company executive; b. Avignon, France, May 22, 1946; came to U.S., 1971; s. Jean Eugene and Paule Louise (Chastan) S.; m. Ingrid Claire Armstrong, June 6, 1986. PhD in Sci., U. Paris, 1973. Rsch. fellow Harvard U., 1971-74; asst. prof. Columbia U., N.Y.C., 1974-76; assoc. prof. Yale U., New Haven, 1976-81; assoc. Lehman Bros., N.Y.C., 1981-84; v.p. Shearson Lehman Bros., N.Y.C., 1984-86, sr. v.p., 1986-89; mng. gen. ptnr. Knox Parthers, N.Y.C., 1989-93; mng. dir. CCF, N.Y.C., 1993-95, Credit Agricole Lazard Fin. Products, N.Y.C., 1995-96, Lazard Frères & Co. N.Y.C., 1996—2001, Lehman Bros., N.Y.C., 2001—04; pres. Saint-Donat & Co. Bd. dirs. New Haven Sister Cities, Inc.; mem. overseas vis. com. for maths. Harvard U. Author: Toroidal Embeddings, 1975; contbr. articles to profl. jours. Fellow Berkeley Coll., Yale U. Mem. Elizabethan Club (New Haven), Yale Club. Roman Catholic. Home: 1755 York Ave New York NY 10128 Office: 420 Lexington Ave Ste 300 New York NY 10170 Office Phone: 646-472-5036. Personal E-mail: bernard@saintdonat.com.

**ST. FLORIAN, FRIEDRICH GARTLER,** architect, educator; b. Graz, Austria, Dec. 21, 1932; came to U.S., 1967, naturalized, 1973; s. Friedrich and Anna Maria (Prassl) G.; m. Livia Campanella, Jan. 12, 1967; children: Alisia, Ilaria. M in Architecture, U. Graz, 1958; MS in Architecture, Columbia U., 1962; PhD in Fine Arts (hon.), RI Coll., 2005, Brown U., 2006. Instr. architecture Columbia U., N.Y.C., 1962-63; asst. prof. R.I. Sch. Design, Providence, 1963-70, assoc. prof., 1974-77; principal architect Friedrich St.Florian Architect, Providence, 1978—; prof. architecture R.I. Sch. Design,

1980—2004, prof. emeritus, 2004—, chmn. div. archtl. studies, 1977-78, dean of architecture, 1978-88, chief critic European Honors Program, 1991-93. Vis. asso. prof. MIT, Cambridge, 1970-71, 74-75 Works exhibited Nat. Inst. Architects, Rome, 1967, 14th Triennale, Milan, 1968, Moderna Museet, Stockholm, 1969, Hayden Gallery, MIT, 1973, Mus. Modern Art, N.Y.C., 1975, 96, 2002, Drawing Ctr., N.Y.C., 1979, Walker Art Ctr., Mpls., 1980, Georges Pompidou Ctr., Paris, 1994, Centre de Cultura Contemporania, Barcelona, 1994, Biennale di Venezia, 1996, Inst. d' Art Contemporain, Villeufranne, 2000, Kunsthalle Frankfurt, 2003. Recipient Nat. Endowment for Arts award, 1972-73, 76-77, 79, 26th ann. Progressive Architecture Mag. award, 1979; Ctr. for Advanced Visual Studies fellow MIT, 1970-77, Rome Prize fellow, fellow Am. Acad. in Rome, 1985, Fulbright fellow; named to RI Coll. Hall Fame, 2005. Mem. AIA. Design architect for the National World War II Memorial, Washington, D.C. Office: Friedrich St Florian AIA 112 Union St Providence RI 02903 Office Phone: 401-831-8400. Business E-Mail: friedrich@fstflorian.com.

**ST. GEORGE, ELAINE,** art educator; b. Wilkes Barre, Pa., Mar. 11, 1948; d. John and Hilda St. George; m. Jeffrey Michael Roblyer (div.); children: Ginevra Gwen Wilson, Julia Gia Roblyer. BFA, U. Miami, 1970, MEd, 1972; MFA, U. NC, 1972. Prof. Broward CC, Darie, Fla., 1979—99; art tchr. Broward County Sch. Bd., Ft. Lauderdale, Fla., 1988—92; Prof. Palm Beach CC, Lakworth, Fla., 1999—. Restoration appraiser Harvey Brown Ins. Agy., Delray Beach, Fla., 2004—. Paintings, original printmaking, pastel drawings, one-woman shows include Bailey Hall Broward CC, 1966. Mem.: Broward Ctr. Performing Arts, NYC Mus. Modern Art, Boca Raton Mus. Art, Ft. Lauderdale Mus. Art. Republican. Avocations: deep sea diving, tennis, horseback riding. Home and Office: 5095 Van Buren Rd Delray Beach FL 33484

**ST. GERMAIN, FERNAND JOSEPH,** retired congressman; b. Blackstone, Mass. s. Andrew Joseph and Pearl (Talaby) St. Germain; m. Rachel O'Neill, Aug. 20, 1953 (dec.); children: Laurene, Lisette. PhB in Social Sci, Providence Coll., 1948, LLD, 1965; LLB, Boston U., 1955; JSD (hon.), Suffolk U., 1976; DCL (hon.), Our Lady of Providence Sem., 1968; DBA (hon.), Bryant Coll., 1981; D in Pub. Svc. (hon.), Roger Williams Coll., 1981; LLB, Brown U., 1985. Bar: R.I. 1956, Fed. 1957, U.S. Supreme Ct. 1983. Mem. R.I. Ho. of Reps., 1952-60, 87th to 100th Congresses from 1st R.I. Dist., 1961-1989, chmn. house com. on banking fin. and urban affairs, 1980-88; ret., 1988. Served with AUS, 1949-52. Recipient Silver Shingle award for disting. public service Boston U. Sch. Law Alumni Assn., 1981, Alumni award disting. pub. service Boston U. Sch. Law, 1982 Mem. ABA, R.I., Bar Assn. Fed. Bar Assn., alumni assns. Our Lady of Providence Sem., Providence Coll., Boston U. Law Sch., Am. Legion. Democrat.

**ST. GERMAIN, SHARON MARIE,** writer; b. Mpls., Nov. 14, 1938; d. John Benjamin and Esther Lenoria Vandermyde; m. Donald Joseph St. Germain, June 17, 1961; children: Kim, Michael, Beth. BE, Hamline Univ., St. Paul, Minn., 1960. Co-dir. Writers Unlimited, White Bear Lake, Minn., 1969—; writing tchr. Hamline Univ., St. Paul, 1978—84, Mpls. Cmy. & Tech. Coll., Mpls., 1981—, Century Coll., White Bear Lake, Minn., 1994—, Cmty. Edn. programs, Mpls., St. Paul, Rochester Cmty. Edn., Minn., 1997—, St. Cloud Cmty. Edn., Minn., 1997—. Writer-in -the-sch. Mid. Sch., Mpls., St. Paul, 1980—85; faculty presenter Midwest Writers Conf., River Falls, Wis., 1979; guest spkr. pub. sch., libr. and writing organizations, Mpls., St. Paul, 1980—. Author: (childrens book) The Terrible Fight, 1990, several children's books; contbr. mag. story Boys' Life, 1975, sport series book Highlights for Children, 1975, articles to numerous profl. jours. Mem.: So. of Children's Book Writers and Illustrators, Writers Unlimited, World Wildlife Fund, Minn. Sr. Fedn., Am. Assn. of Retired People. Avocations: reading, travel, bicycling, swimming. Home: 2555 Upper Afton Rd Maplewood MN 55119 E-mail: donstg@netzero.com.

**SAINT-GIRARD, CHRISTIAN,** theater director, actor, educator, choreographer, theater producer; b. N.Y.C., May 29, 1954; s. Victoria J. Walter. Student, U. Oslo, 1972, Fordham U., 1972-74, Stella Adler Conservatory, N.Y.C.; studied with Uta Hagen and H. Berghof, HB Studios, N.Y.C.; studied dance, Joffrey Ballet; studied dance, Am. Ballet Theatre; also others. Dir. Merry-Go-Round Playhouse, Auburn, NY, 1990-92; dir. edn. Polka Dot Playhouse, Bridgeport, Conn., 2002; artistic dir. Playhouse-on-the-Green, Bridgeport, Conn. 2002. Mem. bd. advisors Actor's Outlet Theatre Ctr., N.Y.C., 1981-85, chmn. steering com., 1982-83; pres., producing artistic dir. Prodrs'. Assn. Real Theatre for Youth, Darien, Ct., 1986-87; tchr. workshops and classes; guest instr. acting and auditioning for mus. theatre and dance at profl. studios, including Actor's Outlet Theatre, Manhattan Theatre Workshop, N.Y.C., Studio at Once Upon a Time Prodns., Inc., N.Y.C., Phil Black's Dance Studio, N.Y.C., Darien Dance Ctr., Darien Arts Coun., Conn. Conservatory for Performing Arts, Workshop Prodns., Inc., Stratford (Conn.) Acad. Dance, Conn. Dance, Newtown (Conn.) Ctr. for Performing Arts, Showbiz Kids, Conn.; performer on Broadway in A Chorus Line, Grease, Shenandoah; on nat. tours in Camelot, A Light Night Music, Oliver!, title role in Pippin; performer in stock and dinner theatre in Funny Girl, Hello Dolly!, The King & I, Cabaret; also appeared in TV pilots, feature films, commls. and operas. Author: (with Viveca Lindfors) (play) Three Boards and A Passion, 1981; librettist (mus. play) Alice in Wonderland, 1985, (ballet) The Red Shoes, 1987; dir., choreographer Singin' in the Rain, She Loves Me, 42d Street, Cabaret, Mame, Into the Woods, Camelot, Applause, My Fair Lady, Unsinkable Molly Brown, Hello, Dolly!, Shenandoah, Music Man, Gypsy, Forty Carats, Chicago, On the Town, Twelfth Night, Cinderella, A Touch of Spring, West Side Story, Annie, Snow White, Pinocchio, Hansel and Gretel, Sleeping Beauty, The Magic Flute, Arsenic and Old Lace, Babes in Toyland, also others; choreographer Paint Your Wagon, Oklahoma, South Pacific, Fame Mem. SAG, AFTRA, Actors Equity Assn., Cath. Actors Guild. Roman Catholic. Avocations: painting, sketching, tennis. E-mail: CSGDirchor@aol.com.

**SAINT-JACQUES, BERNARD,** linguistics educator; b. Montreal, Que., Can., Apr. 26, 1928; s. Albert and Germaine (Lefebvre) Saint-J.; m. Marguerite Fauquenoy. MA, Sophia U., Tokyo, 1962; MS, Georgetown U., 1964; Doctorat as Lettres et Scis. Humaines, Paris U., 1975. Asst. prof. linguistics U. B.C., Vancouver, Canada, 1967—69, assoc. prof., 1969-78, prof., 1978-90, prof. emeritus, 1991—; prof. Aichi U., Japan, 1990—2003. Mem. U.S. Citizen Amb. Program. Author: Structural Analysis of Modern Japanese, 1971, Aspects sociolinguistiques du bilinguisme canadien, 1976, Language and Ethnic Relations, 1979, Japanese Studies in Canada, 1985, Studies in Language and Culture, 1995; editor: Intercultural Communication Studies, 1998; co-editor: Contrasting Political Institutions, 1997, (with M. Iwasaki) Democratic Viability in Politics, 2000. Leave fellow Can. Council, 1974; profl. fellow Japan Found., 1981; research fellow French Govt., 1982, Ohira Programme, Japan, 1983 Fellow Royal Soc. Can. Acad., Internat. Acad. Intercultural Rsch.; mem. Linguistic Soc. Am., Can. Soc. Asian Studies, Can. Linguistics Assn., Sietar Japan. Office Phone: 604-987-6319. Personal E-mail: bsaintj@telus.net.

**ST. JOHN, ADRIAN, II,** retired army officer; b. Ft. Leavenworth, Kans., Nov. 16, 1921; s. Adrian and Marie (McMahon) St John; m. Petronella Elizabeth Durham, Jan. 19, 1943 (dec. 1982); children: Adrian III (dec.), Brian; m. Florence Tucker Parrish, Jan. 29, 1998. BS, U.S. Mil. Acad., 1943; MA, U. Va., 1951; MPA, Am. U., 1981; postgrad., Army War Coll., 1960, U. Hawaii, 1963, Am. U., 1977-82. Commd. 2d lt. U.S. Army, 1943, advanced through grades to maj. gen., 1969; co. comdg. officer 15th Cav. U.S. Army, Europe, 1943—45; intelligence staff officer U.S. Army, Berlin, 1945—47; China desk officer gen. staff Washington, 1951—53, bn. comdg. officer 3d Bn., 31st Inf. Regt. Korea, 1954, comdr. 73d Tank Bn. Korea, 1955; mem. faculty Command and Gen. Staff Coll., Ft. Leavenworth, 1956—59; faculty adviser Iranian Def. Coll., 1959; S.E. Asia plans officer G3, U.S. Army-Pacific, 1960—64; long range plans br. Strategic Div., Orgn. Joint Chiefs of Staff, Washington, 1964—66; chief Surface P & O Div. J3, USMACV, Vietnam, 1966—67; comdg. officer 14th Armored Cav. Regt., Germany, 1967—69; asst. div. comdr. 4th Armored Div., Europe, 1969-70; chief

Strategic Plans and Policy Div. J5, Orgn. Joint Chiefs of Staff, Washington, 1970-71; dir. plans gen. staff U.S. Army, Washington, 1971-72; comdg. gen. 1st Armored Div., Europe, 1972-74; vice dir. joint staff Joint Chiefs of Staff, 1974-76; ret., 1976; mem. adv. council on internat. security affairs Republican Nat. Com., 1977-80; del. Va. State Rep. Conv., 1980, 81; sr. mil. adv. U.S. Negotiating Del. Mut. Balanced Force Reductions, Vienna, 1982—87; Joint Chiefs of Staff rep. U.S. Del. Conventional Stability Talks, Vienna, 1987-88, negotiations on Conventional Armed Forces, Europe, 1989-92. Del., presenter Congress Arms Control Mid. East, Delphi, Greece, 1994; U.S. del. World Helicopter Championships, Moscow, 1994, Oreg., 1996; chmn. operational working group internat. conf. on arms control in Mid. East, Jordan, 1994; mem. advance party OSCE to prepare for elections, Bosnia, 1997; presenter plaques signed by Sec. of Def. to Australian authorities in 6 cities during ceremonies commemorating VJ Day, 1995; supr. parliamentary elections, Bosnia, 1997. Co-chmn. orchestral benefit ball Austrian Embassy, 1993, 1994; supr. Mcpl. Election Commn., Bosnia, 2000; participant in Conf. on Application European Arms Control Negotiations to Pakistan-India Situation, U.K., 2001; election supr. Kosovo, 2001. Decorated D.S.M. with oak leaf cluster, Silver Star, Legion of Merit with 3 oak leaf clusters, Bronze Star with V device, Joint Svc. Commendation medal, Army Commendation medal with oak leaf cluster, Joint Meritorious Unit award, French Croix de Guerre with silver star, Vietnamese Gallantry Cross with palm; recipient European Comdr. in Chief's Individual Project partnership award, 1968, Presdl. award Disting. Citizen, 1993, Dept. State Superior honor award, 1989, 91, Sec. of Def. medal for disting. pub. svc., 1992, medal as disting. grad. U.S. Mil. Acad., 1998. Mem. Am. Security Coun., Am. Fgn. Affairs Coun., Heritage Found., World Affairs Coun., Leadership Inst. Roman Catholic. Office: 9110 Belvoir Woods Pkwy Apt 118 Fort Belvoir VA 22060-2717 E-mail: sinjenii@verizon.net. *There are no limits to the heights man can reach so long as he cares not who gets the credit.*

**ST. JOHN, ANTHONY PAUL,** retired manufacturing executive; b. Washington, Jan. 13, 1937; s. Sterling St. John and Beulah Marston; m. Myra Grace Cornfeld, Oct. 30, 1959; children: James Sterling, Ivy Kemp Harley, Mary Marston. JD, U. Va., Charlottesville, 1960; postgrad., Harvard U., Boston, 1979. Bar: Md. 1961. Atty. Amco Steel Corp., Balt., 1960—61, Nat. Labor Rels. Bd., Balt., 1961—65; asst. G.C., asst. v.p. law, v.p. union rels. Bethlehem Steel Corp., 1965—84; v.p. employee rels. Chrysler Corp., Auburn Hills, Mich., 1985—93. Adj. prof. Lehigh U., Bethlehem, 1993, 95; bd. dirs. Qualitech Steel Corp., 1999—2000. Bd. dirs. Moravian Acad., Bethlehem, 1978—85; chmn. Greater Detroit Alliance Bus., 1989—90; chmn. indsl. rels. com. Motor Vehicles Mfrs., 1990—92; bd. dirs. Henry Ford Hosp. NE, Bloomfield Hills, Mich., 1992, Red Cross of So. Mich., Detroit, 1989—92, Kids Peace Hosp., Bethlehem, 1993—95, Detroit C. of C., 1989—90, Muhlenberg Evening Coll., 1997—98. 1st lt. U.S. Army, 1961—68. Mem.: Sanctuary Golf Club (chmn. legal com.), Saucon Valley Country Club. Republican. Avocation: golf. Home: 1556 Sancon Valley Rd Bethlehem PA 18015 Address: 2957 Wilfert Rd Sanibel FL 33957 E-mail: saintmyty@earthlink.net.

**ST. JOHN, BRIDGETTE ALAYNE,** secondary school educator; b. New Orleans, Aug. 26, 1958; d. William Armand St. John Sr. and Patricia Meynier St. John. BA in Secondary Edn., La. Tech. U., 1981; MS in Math., Loyola U., New Orleans, 1991. Educator St. Rita's Sch., Harahan, La., 1981—85, Livaudais Jr. High, Terrytown, La., 1985—93, East Jefferson H.S., Metairie, La., 1994—. Ninth grade class sponsor Livaudais Jr. High, Terrytown, La., 1986—94; key club faculty advisor East Jefferson H.S., Metairie, 1994—, sophmore/jr. class sponsor, 1996—2000. Mem.: Dawn Busters Kiwanis Club. Office: East Jefferson HS 400 Phlox Ave Metairie LA 70001

**ST. JOHN, EDWARD P.,** social sciences educator; b. Napa, Calif., July 11, 1950; s. Wesley V. and Gladys L. St. John; m. Angela Collins, Feb. 21, 1981; children: Denis W., Liam E. BS, U. Calif., Davis, 1972, EdM, 1974; EdD in Adminstrn., Planning and Social Policy, Havard U., 1977. Prof. edn. U. Dayton, Ohio, 1996—97; prof. edl. leadership and policy studies Ind. U., Bloomington, 1998—2004; Igo Henderson prof. edn. Ctr. for the Study of Higher and Postsecondary Edn., U. Mich., Ann Arbor, 2005—. Contbr. numerous articlese to profl. jours. Recipient Leadership award, Assn. for the Study of Higher Edn., 2002, Robert P. Huff Golden Quill award, Nat. Assn. Student Fin. Aid Adminstrs., 1993; grantee, Ind. Commn. for Higher Edn. and Lumina Found. for Edn. grantee, 2002—; Lumina Found. for Edn. grantee. Mem.: Assn. for Study of Higher Edn. (bd. mem. 2001—03). Roman Catholic. Achievements include research that has examined the impact of federal and state education policies on changes in educational opportunity. Office: Ind Univ Sch of Edn 201 Rose Ave Bloomington IN 47405-1006 Personal E-mail: edstjohn@umich.edu.

**ST. JOHN, HENRY SEWELL, JR.,** utility company executive; b. Birmingham, Ala., Aug. 18, 1938; s. H. Sewell and Carrie M. (Bond) St. John; m. J. Ann Morris, Mar. 7, 1959; children: Sherri Ann, Brian Lee, Teresa Lynn, Cynthia Faye. Student, David Lipscomb Coll., 1956—58, U. Tenn., 1958—59, U. Ala., 1962—64. Engring. aide Ala. Power Co., Enterprise, 1960—62, Birmingham, 1962—66; asst. chief engr. Riviera Utilities, Foley, Ala., 1966—71; sec.-treas., gen. mgr., 1972—2001. Chmn. Baldwin County unit Am. Cancer Soc., 1977; treas. Christian Care Ctr. Inc., 1981—; Deacon Foley Ch. of Christ, 1975—82; elder, 1983—; bd. dirs. AGAPE of Mobile, 1977—80; bd. dirs., pres. South Baldwin Civic Chorus, 1979—82; bd. dirs. Baldwin County Econ. Devel. Alliance, 1997—2001, exec. com., 1999—2001, sec., 1998—99, treas., 1999—2001, chmn., 2000—01. Mem.: IEEE (life), Chevrolet Nomad Assn. (bd. dirs. 1991—2002, v.p. 1993—2002), South Baldwin C. of C. (dir. 1972—75, pres. 1974, dir. 1981—90, 1992—95, amb. 2002—), Pub. Gas Assn. Ala. (bd. dirs. 1987—88), Am. Pub. Power Assn. (com. legis. and resolutions 1972—2001, chmn. State of Ala. mem. com. 1982—2001, com on coms. 1997—2001, bd. dirs. 1997, 2001, exec. com. 1999—2000, chmn. nat. membership com. 1999—2000, chmn. bylaws com. 2000—01, Kramer-Preston Pub. Svc. award 2002), United Mcpl. Distbrs. Group (bd. dirs. 1972—2001), Electric Cities Ala. (bd. dirs. 1983—2001, exec. com. 1989—2001, vice chmn. 2000—01, chmn. 2001, Heritage award 2005), Ala. Mcpl. Electric Authority (vice chmn. 1981—83, bd. dirs. 1981—2001, chmn. 1984—2001), Mcpl. Electric Utility Assn. Ala. (exec. com., dir. 1971—85), Ala. Consumer-Owned Power Distbrs. Assn. (chmn. 1974—75, sec.-treas. 1980, vice chmn. 1981, chmn. 1982—83), S.E. Electric Reliability Coun. (assoc.), South Ala. Power Distbrs. Assn. (life; chmn. 1973—74), Nat. Corvette Mus., Nat. Corvette Owners Assn., Azalea City Classic Chevy (bd. dirs., exec. com. 1989—99, v.p. 1992, 1996—99), Gulf Shores Golf (dir. 1974—75), Foley Quarterback (sec.-treas. 1984—85), Classic Chevy, Internat. (life). Home: PO Box 1817 Foley AL 36536-1817 Personal E-mail: stjohn@gulftel.com.

**ST. JOHN, JULIE,** mortgage company executive; BA in English, U. Mich.; MBA, Fla. State U. CPA, Fla. Prin. Arthur Young & Co.; v.p. info. systems Residence Inn divsn. Marriott; joined Fannie Mae, Washington, 1990, sr. v.p. mortgage bus. tech., now exec. v.p., chief info. officer enterprise systems and ops. divsn. Mem. exec. bd. Boys & Girls Club of Greater Washington. Named one of Premier 100 IT Leaders, Computerworld, 2005. Mem.: AICPA, Women of Washington, Women in Housing and Fin. Office: Fannie Mae 3900 Wisconsin Ave NW Washington DC 20016-2892*

**ST. JOHN, ROBERT,** chef, writer; m. Jill St. John; 2 children. BS in Hospitality Mgmt., U. Southern Miss. Owner, exec. chef Purple Parrot Co., Hattiesburg, Miss.; owner, pres. New South Restaurant Grp., LLC., 1997—. Former pres., chmn. bd. of Miss. Restaurant Assoc.; bd. of dir. Miss. Art Commn., Miss. Mus. of Art; former bd. mem. Hattiesburg Civic Commn.; bd. of dir. Am. Wild Shrimp Coun.; chef's coun. Chef's for Humanity, 2005—; adv. bd. Hospitality Mgmt. Dept. U. Southern Miss.; founder Purple Parrot Co. Scholarship. Author: A Southern Palate, Deep South or How to Survive in a Southern Kitchen Without A Can of Cream of Mushroom Soup, Nobody's Poet, My South; writer food/humor column, 27 newspapers, host cooking show, WDAM. Named Miss. Restaurateur of Yr., 1996, Miss. Chef, Miss. Mag.; named one of South's Hottest Chefs, Y'All mag. Mem.:

Miss. Tourism Assoc., James Beard Found., Southern Foodways Alliance, Am. Culinary Assoc., Nat. Restaurant Fedn., Eta Sigma Delta (hon.). Office: New South Restaurant Grp LLC 3810 Hardy St Hattiesburg MS 39402 Office Phone: 888-315-6774. Office Fax: 601-264-0681.*

**ST. JOHN, TERRI,** secondary school educator; b. Battle Creek, Mich., July 17, 1953; d. Donald George and Virginia Beth Kelley. AA, Kellogg CC, 1975; BA, U. Central Fla., 1981; MA in Edn., U. Sarasota, 1995, EdD, 2001. Cert. tchr. Fla. Tchr., debate coach Forest Hill HS, West Palm Beach, Fla., 1983—85; tchr., theatre dir. Lake Weir HS, Ocala, Fla., 1985—89; tchr., debate coach Lake Highland Prep Sch., Orlando, Fla., 1991—97, Sarasota (Fla.) HS, 1997—. Presenter in field. Supporter St. Labre Indian Sch., Ariz., 2001—, Mayo Clinic Rsch., Minn., 2002—. Named Diamond Coach, Nat. Forensic League, 2005, Regional Coach of Yr., Fla. Forensic League Region III, 2005. Mem.: ASCD, Fla. Forensic League (v.p. ops. 2004—, 2d v.p. 2000—, mem. com. 2003—, named Region III Coach of Yr. 2005, 2006, named State Coach of Yr. 2006), Cath. Forensic League, Fla. Comm. Assn., Nat. Comm. Assn., Nat. Coun. Tchrs. English. Avocations: movies, golf, reading, theater. Office: Sarasota HS 1000 S Sch Ave Sarasota FL 34237 Business E-Mail: terri_st_john@sarasota.k12.fl.us.

**ST. JOHN, TERRY NOEL,** art educator; b. Sacramento, Calif., Dec. 24, 1934; s. Walter Oliver and Harmina Rose St. John; children: Walter, Noel. BA, U. Calif., 1958; MFA, CCA, 1966. Art instr. La. Polt Tech Inst., Ruston, La., 1966—68; assoc. curator Oakland Mus., Calif., 1969—90; art instr. U. Calif., Santa Cruz, Calif., 1978—90; prof. of art Notre Dame, Belmont, La., 1990—2000, art prof. emeritus, 2000. Author: (catalogue) Society of Six, 1972; exhibitions include Hacett Freedman Gallery, San Francisco. Avocation: world art centers. Personal E-mail: japlomic@pacbell.net.

**ST. JULIEN, THAIS MARY,** soprano, musician; d. George W. St. Julien Jr. and Rosemary Gloria Bourda. Pvt. vocal studies, Charles Paddock, New Orleans, 1973—81, Virginia Mac Watters, Bloomington, Ind., 1978—81, Norma Newton, Houston, 1981—88, Andrea von Ramm, New Orleans, 1986; pvt. recorder studies, Milton G. Scheuermann, Jr., 1975—80; apprentice, Des Moines Metro Opera Festival, Indianola, Iowa, 1987; Opera Workshop, Loyola U. New Orleans, 1977—78; Baroque performance practice, Skip Sempe, 1995. Asst. season ticket sales mgr. New Orleans Opera Guild, 1974—77; ensemble singer New Orleans Musica da Camera, 1974—78, principle vocal soloist, 1978—, asst. music dir., 1980—91, asst. instrument builder, 1981—, co-artistic dir., 1991—; founder/dir. Vox Feminae (women's vocal ensemble), 1994—, chief adminstr., 1999—; mgr. single ticket sales New Orleans Philharm. Orch., 1977—79; founder, soloist Banquette Opera, New Orleans, 1979—84; founding mem., calligrapher Scriptease Calligraphy, New Orleans, 1980—92; founding mem. soloist Ezcudanta (voice/guitar duo), New Orleans, 1982—85; part- time libr. technician Tulane U., Maxwell Music Libr., New Orleans, 1989—2005. Musical advisor Hermann Grima Ho. Mus., New Orleans, 1980—84; sec., adv. bd. Entergy Arts Bus. Ctr., New Orleans, 1997—2002; adv. bd. New Orleans Internat. Music Colloquium, 1998—2001; musical advisor Musica Antiqua, Albany, Oreg., 1998—2005; founding dir. music series Belle Alliance Hist. Plantation, Donaldsonville, La., 2002—; bd. pres. New Orleans Musica da Camera, New Orleans; instr. vocal masterclass S.W. Mo. State U.; presenter in field; founding artistic dir. Thursdays at Twilight Concert Series New Orleans Bot. Garden, 2003—. Musician (co-dir.): (albums) Satires, Desires and Excesses: Songs from the Carmina Burana, Natus Est: A Christmas Celebration, The Cross of Red: Music of Love and War from the Time of the Crusades, Maiden, Mother, Muse: The Women of the Cantigas of Alfonso X, Les Motets d'Arras: Songs and Dances of Medieval Arras, The Play of Robin and Marion, A Christmas Offering (Early Music Am./Millenium of Music Nat. Radio Competition, 1996), Natus Est, 1994, 1995, Now Make We Mirthe; musician: (co-dir., host) Alone of All Her Sex; musician: A Voice Still Heard, Early Jewish Music, (radio spl.) Praises from the Heart, Tristan et Iseult, on Cathedral, Court and Countryside Series, 1981; musician: (dir.) (albums) Medee; musician: Moonrise, Circles, Tristan et Iseult, on Cathedral, Court and Countryside Series, 1982, The Garden of Love; hist. music adv. (films) Interview with the Vampire; musician: Creole Cameos: Music of New Orleans Creoles of Color, Performances throughout the U.S.; prodr.(co-host): Continuum-WWNO2, Continuum; editor, contbr.: newsletter The Cypher (Am. Guild Organists, New Orleans); contbr. articles to profl. jours. Founding mem., pres. bd. dirs. St. Charles Ave. Com., New Orleans, 1972—75. Named Vis. Artist in Residence with Musica da Camera, The Hist. Shrine of Our Lady of Prompt Succor, New Orleans, 1989—; recipient Lifetime Achievement award, Gambit Newspaper, Tribute to the Classical arts, 1997, Pioneer in Preservation Honor award, Hist. Dist. Landmarks Commn., 1997, Cert. of Appreciation in Thankfulness for Contributions to the City, City of New Orleans, 2001. Mem.: Soc. Am. Magicians (v.p. local assembly), La. Partnership for the Arts, Southeastern Medieval Assn., Entergy Arts Bus. Ctr., Am. Musicological Soc., Knights of Slights, Internat. Brotherhood Magicians (pres. local ring), Mensa. Avocations: magic, reading, drawing, photography. Office: New Orleans Musica da Camera 1035 Eleonore St New Orleans LA 70115 Business E-Mail: mdc@nomdc.org.

**SAINT LAURENT, YVES (HENRI DONAT MATHIEU),** couturier; b. Oran, Algeria, Aug. 1, 1936; s. Charles Mathieu and Lucinne-Andree (Wilbaux) Saint L. Student, Lycée d'Oran. Worked with Christian Dior, 1954-57, successor, 1957-60. Adminstr. Société Yves Saint Laurent, 1962—. Costume designer (ballets) Cyrano de Bergerac, 1959, Adage et Variations, Notre-Dame de Paris, 1965, Delicate Balance, 1967, Sheherezade, 1973, (films) The Pink Panther, 1962, Belle de Jour, 1967, La Chamade, 1968, La Sirène du Mississippi, 1969, L'Affaire Stavisky, 1974; stage sets and costumes Spectacle Zizi Jeanmaire, 1961, 63, 68, Les Chants de Maldoror, 1962; costume designer for Mariage de Figaro, 1964; illus. La Vilaine Lulu, 1967; exhbns. include Met. Mus. Art N.Y. 1983, Beijing Mun, Fine Arts 1985, Musée des Arts de la Mode, Paris, 1986, Ho. Painters USSR, 1986, Hermitage Mus., St. Petersburg, 1987, Art Gallery NSW, Sydney, 1987, Sezon Mus., Tokyo, 1990. Recipient Neiman-Marcus award for fashions, 1958, Oscar from Harper's Bazaar, 1966, Internat. award Coun. Fashion Designers Am., 1982, Lifetime Achievement award, 1999, Best Fashion Designer Oscar, 1985; named Chevalier de la Légion d'Honneur, 1995, promoted de la Légion d'Honneur. Office: 5 ave Marceau 75116 Paris France*

**ST. LOUIS, MARTIN,** professional hockey player; b. Laval, Que., Can., June 18, 1975; m. Heather St. Louis; 1 child. Grad., U. Vt., 1997. Profl. hockey player Cleve. Lumberjacks (IHL), 1997—98, Calgary Flames, 1998—2000, Tampa Bay Lightning, 2000—. Mem. Team Can., World Cup of Hockey, 2004. Named to NCAA East First All-Am. Team, 1995—97, NHL All-Star Team, 2003, 2004; recipient Lester B. Peterson award, 2004, Hart Meml. Trophy, 2004. Achievements include being a member of Stanley Cup Champion Tampa Bay Lightning, 2004; being a member of World Cup Champion Team Canada, 2004. Office: c/o Tampa Bay Lightning 401 Channelside Dr Tampa FL 33602

**ST. MARTIN, CHARLOTTE,** trade association administrator; b. 1945; BS, U. North Tex., 1967. Office mgr. to rep. James M. Collins U.S. Ho. of Reps., 1970; mgr. sales and catering The Fairmount Dallas, 1971—77; dir. sales and mktg. Loews Anatole Hotel, Loews Corp., 1977—82, pres. and CEO, 1989—95; regional v.p. sales and mktg. Loews Hotels, Loews Corp., 1982—87, exec. v.p. sales and mktg., 1996—2005; pres. Dallas Convention and Visitors Bur., 1987—89; pres., CEO Charlotte St. Martin Enterprises 2005—06; exec. dir. League of Am. Theatres and Producers, Inc., 2006—. Office: League Am Theatres and Producers Inc 226 W 47th St New York NY 10036-1487 Office Phone: 212-764-1122. Office Fax: 212-398-2409. E-mail: league@broadway.org.*

**ST. PATRICK, MATTHEW,** actor; b. Phila., Mar. 16, 1979; Actor: (TV series) General Hospital, 1997, All My Children, 1998—2000, Six Feet Under, 2001—; TV appearances include NYPD Blue, 1996, 1998, Beverly Hills 90210, 1997, Mad TV, 2002, 2003.

**ST. PIERRE, GEORGE ROLAND, JR.,** materials scientist, engineering executive, educator; b. Cambridge, Mass., June 2, 1930; s. George Rol and Rose Ann (Levesque) St. P.; m. Roberta Ann Hansen, July 20, 1956; children: Anne Renee, Jeanne Louise, John David, Thomas George; m. Mary Elizabeth Adams, Dec. 11, 1976; m. Gretchen Ann Butrick, June 29, 2001; 1 child, Victoria Harr. BS, MIT, 1951, ScD, 1954; DSc (hon.), Ohio State U., 1998. Rsch. metallurgist Inland Steel Co., 1954-56; faculty Ohio State U., 1956—, prof. metall. engring., 1957-88, assoc. dean Grad. Sch., 1964-66, chmn. metall. engring., 1983-88, chmn. mining engring., 1985-92; dir. Ohio Mineral Rsch. Inst., 1984-92, prof., chmn. material sci. and engring., 1988-92, Presdl. prof., 1988-92, chmn., disting. u. prof. emeritus, 1992—; chief scientist Materials Directorate, Wright-Patterson AFB, 1995-96. Cons. in field; vis. prof. U. Newcastle, NSW, Australia, 1975; adv. com. materials sci. MIT, 1990-97; adv. bd. Argonne Nat. Lab., 1994-99. Editor: Physical Chemistry of Process Metallurgy, Vols. 7 and 8, 1961, Advances in Transport Processes in Metallurgical Systems, 1992, Transactions Iron and Steel Soc., 1994—; contbr. articles to profl. jours. Bd. dirs. Edward Orton Jr. Ceramic Found., 1989-92. With USAE 1956-57. Recipient Milton (Mass.) Clarence Boylston Sci. prize, 1947; MacQuigg award, 1971; Alumni Disting. Tchr. award, 1978; named Disting. scholar Ohio State U., 1988, Presdl. prof. Ohio State U., 1988. Fellow Minerals, Metals & Materials Soc., AIME (bd. dirs. 1988-91, 93-96, Educator award 1996), Am. Soc. Materials Internat. (Bradley Stoughton Outstanding Tchr. award 1961, Gold medal 1987, Albert E. White award 1997); mem. Am. Inst. Mining Metall. and Petroleum Engrs. (Mineral Industry Edn. award 1987), Iron and Steel Soc. (Elliott lectr. 1994), Am. Contract Bridge League (gold life master), Faculty Club (pres. 1990-92), Sigma Xi. Home: 4906 Stonehaven Dr Columbus OH 43220 Office: Ohio State U Dept Materials Sci/Engring 2041 N College Rd Columbus OH 43210-1124 Office Phone: 614-893-5287. Personal E-mail: gstpierr@columbus.rr.com.

**SAINT-PIERRE, GUY,** engineering executive; b. Windsor Mills, Que. Can., Aug. 3, 1934; s. Armand and Alice (Perra) Saint-P.; m. Francine Garneau, May 4, 1957; children: Marc, Guylaine, Nathalie. B in Applied Sci. in Civil Engring., Laval U., 1957; diploma, Imperial Coll., London, 1958; MSc, U. London, 1959; LLD (hon.), Concordia U., 1992; degree (hon.), Coll. Militaire Royal de Saint-Jean, 1993; DSc (hon.), Laval U., 1992; degree in Applied Sci. (hon.), Sherbrooke, 1994; DSe (hon.), Montreal U.; degree (hon.), Ottawa U., 2002. Registrar, Corp. Engrs. Que., 1964-66. V.p. Acres Que., 1967-70; minister of edn. Govt. Que., 1970-72, of industry and commerce, 1972-76; asst. to pres. John Labatt Ltd., Montreal, 1977—88, sr. v.p., 1977—88; pres., COO Ogilvie Mills Ltd., Montreal, 1977—88; pres., CEO, bd. dirs. The SNC-Lavalin Group Inc., 1989-96; chmn. bd. The SNC-Lavalin Group, Inc., 1996—2002; dir. Royal Bank of Can., 1990—2004, chmn. bd., 2001—04. Chmn. Bus. Coun. Nat. Issues, 1995—97; dir. Alcan Inc., 1995—, GM of Can. 1995—2004, Inst. Rsch. Public. Policy, 2003—. Gov. Conseil du Patronat de Que. Served as officer C.E. Can. Army, 1959—64. Decorated companion Order of Can.; named Canada's CEO of Yr., 1994, Canada's Internat. Exec. of Yr., 1996; recipient Sir John Kennedy Medal, 1993, Can. Engrs. Gold Medal award Can. Coun. Profl. Engrs., 1996; Engring. Inst. of Can.; inducted into Can. Bus. Hall of Fame, 2001. Mem.: Order Engrs. Que., Can. Mfrs. Assn. (chmn. bd., pres. 1987), Engring. Inst. Can., Montreal O. of C., Coun. Can. Unity (v.p.), Hermitage Club, Mt. Bruno Club, Mt. Royal Club, Can. Club Montreal (gov. 1985). Liberal. Roman Catholic. Office: Royal Bank of Canada 1 Pl Ville Marie PO Box 6001 Montreal PQ H3C 3A9 Canada Business E-Mail: guy.saint-pierre@rbc.com.

**ST. PIERRE, MICHAEL A.,** lawyer; b. Great Falls, Mont., May 29, 1955; BA magna cum laude, Boston Coll., 1977; JD, Suffolk U., 1980. Bar: R.I. 1980, Mass. 1980, U.S. Dist. Ct. R.I. 1981, U.S. Ct. Appeals (1st cir.) 2001, U.S. Supreme Ct. 1988. Law clk. to Chief Justice, R.I. Supreme Ct., 1980—81; asst. town solicitor Town of North Kingstown, 1980—84; atty. Revens, Revens & St. Pierre, Warwick, RI. Mem. Workers Compensation Bench Bar Com., 1991—, chmn., 1994—97; mem. disciplinary bd. R.I. Supreme Ct., 1997—. Mem.: ABA, R.I. Bar Assn. (Ho. of Dels. 1993—, meetings com. 1993—, exec. com. 1997—, pres. 2002—03), R.I. Trial Lawyers Assn. (young lawyers adv./clerkship com. 1987—92), Assn. Trial Lawyers Am., Fed. Bar Assn. Office: Revens Revens and St Pierre 946 Centerville Rd Warwick RI 02886

**ST. PIERRE, RONALD LESLIE,** public health and medical educator, academic administrator; b. Dayton, Ohio, Feb. 2, 1938; s. Leslie Frank and Ruth Eleanor (Rhoten) St.P.; m. Joyce A. Guilford, Apr. 1, 1961; children: Michele Christine, David Bryan. BS, Ohio U., 1961; M.Sc., Ohio State U., 1962, PhD, 1965. Instr. anatomy Ohio State U., Columbus, 1965-67, asst. prof., 1967-69, assoc. prof., 1969-72, prof., 1972—2002, chmn. dept. anatomy, 1972-81, assoc. v.p. health scis., 1981-83, sr. assoc. v.p. health scis. and acad. affairs, 1983—2002, assoc. dean Coll. Medicine and Pub. Health, 1987-96, vice dean Coll. of Medicine and Pub. Health, 1996-2000, exec. vice dean, 2000—02, interim dean pub. health, 1999—2002, assoc. v.p., prof. emeritus, 2002—, spl. asst. to sr. v.p. health scis., 2002—06; assoc. dir. Cancer Rsch. Ctr., 1974-78; acting provost, v.p. for acad. affairs Capital U., Columbus, 2006—. Vis. research assoc. Duke U., 1966-67; cons. Battelle Meml. Inst., Columbus, Ohio. Contbr. articles to profl. jours. Chmn. Ohio Gov.'s Com. on Employment of Handicapped, 1970-78; mem. state assoc. com. Presdl. Commn. Employment of Handicapped, 1970-78, chmn., 1971-72; mem. planning and adv. council White House Conf. on Handicapped Individuals, 1975-78; mem. Columbus Mayor's Com. on Internat. Yr. of Disabled. Recipient Lederle Med. Faculty award, 1968-71, prize for basic research South Atlantic Assn. Obstetricians and Gynecologists, 1968, Outstanding Individual award Ohio Rehab. Assn., 1969, Gov.'s award for community service, 1973, Coll. Medicine and Mental Health Alumni Faculty Tchg. award, Ohio State U. Coll. Medicine, 2002, Univ. Disting. Svc. award, 2003 Mem Am Auth Anatomists, Am. Assn. Immunologists. Am. Soc. Exptl. Biology and Medicine, Sigma Xi (pres. Ohio State chpt. 1979-80) Republican. Presbyterian. Home: 8586 Button Bush Ln Westerville OH 43082-8675 Office Phone: 614-747-7205. Business E-Mail: st-pierre.1@osu.edu.

**SAISSELIN, REMY GILBERT,** fine arts educator; b. Moutier, Bern, Switzerland, Aug. 17, 1925; came to U.S., 1938, naturalized, 1944; s. Paul A. and Jeanne (Nydegger) S.; m. Nicole M. Fischer, May 31, 1955; children: Anne, Juliet, Peter. BA, Queens Coll., 1951; MA, U. Wis., Madison, 1952, MA in French, 1953, PhD, 1957. Asst. prof. French Western Res. U., Cleve., 1956-59; asst. curator publs. Cleve. Mus. Art, 1959-65; prof. French lit. U. Rochester, N.Y., 1965-70; prof. fine arts N.Y., 1970-87; prof. humanities Hobart & William Smith Coll., 1987-90. Asst. editor: Jour. Aesthetics and Art Criticism, 1959-62; author: Taste in Eighteenth Centruy France, 1965, Rule of Reason and Ruses of the Heart, 1970, Literary Enterprise in XVIII Century France, 1979, The Bourgeois and the Bibelot, 1984, The Enlightenment Against the Baroque, 1992; exhbns. landscapes, still lifes, and abstractions in France, 1997. Served with U.S. Army, 1944-46. Guggenheim fellow, 1972-73 Mem. Phi Beta Kappa. Home: Route de Sancerre 18220 Saint Ceols France

**SAITO, FRANK KIYOJI,** import and export firm executive; b. Tokyo, Feb. 28, 1945; s. Kaoru and Chiyoko S.; m. Elaine Tamami Karasawa, Feb. 22, 1975; children: Roderic Kouki, Lorine Erika. LLB, Kokugakuin U., 1967. With import dept. Trois Co. Ltd., Tokyo, 1967-68; founder import/export dept. Three Bond Co., Ltd., Tokyo, 1968-71; sales mgr. Kobe Mercantile, Inc., San Diego, 1971-76; pres. K&S Internat. Corp., San Diego, 1976-94; K&S Techs., Inc., San Diego, 1997—. Office: 9710 Scranton Rd Ste 150 San Diego CA 92121-1771

**SAITO, ROBERT SHUNICHI,** writer, poet; b. Alameda, Calif., Sept. 9, 1933; s. Sam Shunji Saito and Yayeko Umegawa; m. Naida Cervantes, Dec. 7, 1966. Cert., Coronado Sch. Fine Arts, 1980. Enlisted USN, 1955, advanced through grades to chief petty officer, 1971, pers. officer USS Camden, 1972-75, ret., 1975. Pres. Mega Travel Inc., La Mesa, Calif., 1983-84. Author of poetry, short stories. Recipient 1st Pl. award for Batik, Coronado Art Assn., 1977. Roman Catholic. Avocations: batik art, photography, fishing, walking, tai-chi.

**SAIZAN, PAULA THERESA,** management consultant; b. New Orleans, Sept. 12, 1947; d. Paul Morine and Hattie Mae (Hayes) Saizan; m. George H. Smith, May 26, 1973 (div. July 1976). BS in Acctg. summa cum laude, Xavier U., 1969. CPA Tex. Sys. engr. IBM, New Orleans, 1969—71; acct., then sr. acct. Shell Oil Co., Houston, 1971—76, sr. fin. analyst, 1976—77, fin. rep., 1977—79, corp. auditor 1979—81, treasury rep., 1981—82, sr. treasury rep., 1982—86; asst. treas. Shell Credit Inc., Shell Leasing Co., Shell Fin. Co., Houston, 1986—88, sr. pub. affairs rep., 1988—89, sr. staff pub. affairs rep., 1990—91, program mgr., 1991—96, sr. program mgr., 1996—97, mgr. constituent rels. and edn. support, 1997—2000, mgr. nat. and cmty. outreach, 2000—03, mgr. stakeholder mgmt., 2003—04, sr. advisor corp. affairs, 2005; pres. PTBS, Inc., Houston, 2005—. Bd. dirs. Greater Houston Conv. and Visitors Bur., Xavier U.; vice-chair Nat. Coun. Negro Women, Inc.; adv. bd. Sch. Engring, Tex. So. U.; del. White House Conf. on Small Bus., 1995. Mem. AICPA, NAACP (bd. dirs., trustee spl. contribution fund), Tex. Soc. CPA, Leadership Houston, LWV Houston, Xavier U. Alumni Assn., Nat. Assn. Black Accts., Links Inc., Nat. Coun. Garden Clubs (life), Nat. Congress Black Women, Alpha Kappa Alpha, Phi Gamma Nu, Kappa Gamma Phi. Roman Catholic. Home: 7601 Oak Fern Houston TX 77040-4407 Office: PTBS Inc Ste 1000 5740 W Little York Rd Houston TX 77091 Personal E-mail: ptbs3@aol.com.

**SAJAK, PAT,** television game show host; b. Chgo., Oct. 26, 1946; m. Lesly Brown, Dec. 31, 1989, 2 children. Student, Columbia Coll., Chgo. Newscaster WEDC-Radio, Chicago, IL; disk jockey WNBS-Radio, Murray, Ky., 1971—72; staff announcer, public affairs program host, weatherman WSM-TV, Nashville, 1972—77; weatherman, host The Sunday Show, LA, 1977-81; host Wheel of Fortune, 1981—, The Pat Sajak Show, 1989-90, Pat Sajak Weekend, 2003—. Film appearances include: Airplane II: The Sequel, 1982, Jack Paar is Alive and Well, 1987; NBC television specials, host, The Thanksgiving Day Parade, The Rose Parade. Served with U.S. Army, Vietnam. Recipient 3 Emmys, People's Choice award, star on Hollywood Walk of Fame.

**SAKA, TUNA,** technology educator; b. Edremit, Turkey, Oct. 22, 1960; arrived in U.S., 1980; s. Oguz Saka and Nese Alpman; m. Oya Saka (div.); children: Serkan, Selin. AAS in Civil Tech., Hudson Valley C.C., 1985; BPS in Arch., SUNY, Buffalo, 1986, MArch, 1988. Assoc. prof. Pa. Coll. Tech., Williamsport, 1996—. Author: (textbook) Autocad for Architecture, 2000. Recipient AIA Scholarship award, 1986, R. Buckminster Fuller award, SUNY-Buffalo, 1987. Avocations: photography, technology, travel. Home: Apt C8 106 Carpenter St Muncy PA 17756-Pa Office: Pa Coll Tech 1 College Ave Williamsport PA 17701

**SAKAC, SISTER ANN,** college administrator. Pres., Mount St. Mary Coll., Newburgh, N.Y. Office: Mt St Mary Coll Office of the President Powell Ave Newburgh NY 12550-3494

**SAKAGUCHI, TAKEHIRO,** healthcare educator, researcher; b. Tokyo, July 1, 1947; s. Takeichi and Kimiko (Aota) Sakaguchi; m. Sanae Sakaguchi, Mar. 21, 1974. M of Hygiene, Kitasato U., Tokyo, 1972; D Med. Sci., St. Marianna U. Sch. Medicine, Kawasaki, Japan, 1985. Lectr. dept. pub. health Kitasato U., 1972-80; asst. prof. dept. hygiene St. Marianna U. Sch. Medicine, 1980-96, assoc. prof. dept. hygiene, 1996-97; prof. dept. life sci. Kawamura Coll., Tokyo, 1997-2000; prof. dept. human environment Kawamura Gakuen Woman's U., Abiko, Japan, 2000—. Lectr. Chuo U., Tokyo, 1988-97, Shizuoka (Japan) U., 1997-99, Nippon Dental U., Tokyo, 1998—, Azabu U., 2005—, Chuo U. Grad. Sch., Tokyo, 2006—. Contbr. articles to profl. jours. including Toxicology and Environ; Health. Mem. AAAS, NSSK (sub-chief dir. 2002—), Japanese Soc. Hygiene (councilor 1987—), Japan Soc. Occupl. Health (councilor 1990-96), Japanese Soc. Pub. Health (councilor 1993-96, 2002--), Japanese Assn. Infectious Diseases (councilor 1997—), Japanese Soc. Bacteriology, Soc. Phys. Fitness, Nutrition and Immunology (dir. 2004—), N.Y. Acad. Scis. Avocation: travel. Office: Kawamura Gakuen Woman's Univ 1133 Sageto Chiba 270-1138 Japan E-mail: t.sakagu@kgwe.ac.jp.

**SAKAI, KIYOKO,** artist; b. Osaka, Japan, Oct. 24, 1938; Osaka, Japan, m. Keizo Sakai, Nov. 7, 1965; children: Miyako, Alisa. BA, Doshisha U., Kyoto, Japan, 1961; postgrad., Art Students League, N.Y.C., 1973—78. Exhibited in one woman shows at Cottage Gallery, NJ, Move 21, Osaka, Kanner Kurzan Mus., NY, Myung Sook Lee Gallery, NY, Osaka Prefecture Cmtemporary Art Ctr., Japan, Drew U., NJ, Atrium Gallery, NJ, 2003, Haworth Mcpl. Libr., NJ, 2005; exhibited in group shows at Bergen Mus. Art and Sci., NJ, Inst. Superiore Per Industrio Artistiche, Urbino, Italy, Newark Mus., First Presbyn. Ch. Gallery, Edgewater, NJ, 2004, Cambridge Artists Cooperative Craft Gallery, 2005; permanent collections include Deloitte, Haskins and Sells, NJ, Zen Studies Soc., NY, NY Stock Exch. Recipient award Bergen Mus. Juried Show, Ramapo Coll. Juried Show, Art Showcase award. Manhattan Art Internat., Manhattan Art Internat.; Kenneth Hayes Miller Meml. scholar Art Student League of N.Y. Mem. Art Student League NY (life). Avocations: music, dance, literature. Personal E-mail: ksakai807@hotmail.com. E-mail: ksakai807@mindspring.com.

**SAKAI, NAOKI,** literature and language professor; s. Haruyoshi and Katsuko Sakai; m. Gail Pattemore Clarke, July 31, 1976; children: Andrew Pattemore, Haruyoshi. BA, Tokyo U., 1971; MA, U. Chgo., 1980, PhD, 1983. Asst. prof. U. Chgo., 1984—87, Cornell U., Ithaca, NY, 1988—91, assoc. prof., 1990—96, prof., 1997—. Sr. editor Traces, Ithaca, 1996—2003; chair William Riley Parker prize com. MLA Am., NYC, 2004—05. Recipient Disting. Lecturership award, German Am. Academic Coun., 1998, Shinghan Disting. Prof. award, Yonsei U., 2006. Office: Cornell Univ 386 Rockefeller Hall Ithaca NY 14853

**SAKAI, RICHARD,** motion picture and television executive, producer; b. San Francisco, Jan. 28, 1954; s. Hisasi Quintus and Jean Misako S.; childern: Benjamin, Timothy, Reilly. BA, UCLA, 1977, MFA, 1980. Pres. Gracie Films, Culver City, Calif., 1984—. Prodr. (film) Jerry Maguire, Bottle Rocket, As Good As It Gets, (TV) Simpsons. Mem. Acad. TV Arts and Scis. (6 Emmys), Acad. Motion Picture Arts and Scis. (nominated), PGA, ACLU. Office: Gracie Films 10202 Washington Blvd Culver City CA 90232-3119

**SAKAI, TOSHIHIKO,** engineer; b. Nagoya, Aichi, Japan, July 17, 1943; s. Saichi and Yoshie (Taguchi) S.; m. Junko Fukuoka, Oct. 7, 1971; children: Eiji, Kenji; m. Natsuko Kamei, Nov. 25, 1989; children: Rei, Rui. B.Sc., Nagoya Inst. Tech., Japan, 1967; M.Sc., Ga. Inst. Tech.; 1970; PhD, U.M.I.S.T., U.K., 1974. Assoc. engr. Toyota Ctrl. R. & D. Labs., Inc., Aichi, Japan, 1967-75, rschr., 1975-84, sr. rschr., 1984-95. Mgr. tech. secretariat Toyota Ctrl. R & D Labs., Inc., Aichi, 1982—89, CEO staff, 1991—95, gen. mgr., 1989—95; councilor Tsuchiya Co. Ltd., Nagaya, Japan, 1995; dir., bd. dirs. Overseas Ops., 1995—2000; sr. mng. dir. NIC Corp. (Venture Capital), Nagoya, Japan, 2001—; exec. v.p., COO Techno Search, Inc., Nagoya, 2004—. Contbr. articles to profl. jours.; inventor and patentee in field. Submit referee Textile Machinery Soc. Japan. Fellow Textile Inst. (UK); mem. Soc. Fiber Sci. and Tech. Japan, Soc. Automotive Engr., The NPO Rsch. Assn. New Industry Creation (sr. mn. dir. 2001—), Nagoya Jr. Chamber (exec. v.p. 1982). Avocations: travel, driving, golf. Home: City Corp B1003 Ueda 3-1501 Tenpaku Nagoya 468-0051 Japan Office: Techno Search Inc Nagryn Cof C Ind Bldg 10F Sakae 2-10-19 Naka Nagoya 460-0008 Japan Office Phone: +81-52-205-3021. Business E-mail: sakai@techno-search.com.

**SAKAI, YU,** pathologist; b. Osaka, Japan, July 10, 1966; s. Kunisuke and Kazuko Sakai; m. Masako Kondo, June 10, 2000. MD, Nat. Def. Med. Coll., Tokorozawa, Japan, 1991; PhD, Juntendo U., Bunkyo-ku, Japan, 2002. Jr. resident Nat. Def. Med. Coll., Tokorozawa, 1991—93, sr. resident, 1995—; physician Japan Self Def. Force Fukuoka Hosp., Kasuga, Fukuoka, Japan, 1993—94; pathologist Japan Self Def. Forces Ctrl. Hosp., Setagaya-ku, Tokyo, 1994—95, 1997—2005, Japan Self Def. Forces Sapporo Gen. Hosp., Japan, 2005—. Fellow: Japanese Soc. Pathology; mem.: Japanese Soc. Lab.

Medicine, Japanese Soc. Clin. Cytology. Avocation: fishing. Office: Dept Pathol Japan Self Def Forces Sapporo Gen Hosp 12-1-32 Hiragishi 1Jo Toyohira-ku Sapporo 062-0931 Japan Personal E-mail: zwq04043@nifty.ne.jp.

**SAKAMOTO, KATSUYUKI,** retired academic administrator, psychologist, educator; b. LA, Oct. 24, 1938; m. Edna Christine Sakamoto; children: David Katsu, Bryce Yoshio. BA in Psychology, Calif. State U., Fresno, 1961, MA in Psychology, 1968; PhD in Exptl. Social Psychology, So. Ill. U., Carbondale, 1971; postgrad., Carnegie Mellon U., 1984. Acting dir. Army Edn. Ctr., Munich, 1962-63; dir. social svcs. Salvation Army, Fresno, Calif., 1964-66; assoc. prof. psychology Keuka Coll., Keyka Park, N.Y., 1971-78; prof. social psychology Ea. Oreg. State Coll., La Grande, 1978-85, assoc. dean, then acting dean, 1980-82, 84, assoc. dean acad. affairs, 1982-85; prof. psychology Ind. U. East, Richmond, 1985-91, vice chancellor for acad. affairs, 1985-90, spl. asst. to chancellor, 1990-91; prof., chancellor Calif. Sch. Profl. Psychology, Alameda, 1991-98, ret., 1998. Lectr. So. Ill. U., 1970-71; vis. prof. SUNY, Binghamton, 1973; adj. prof. Alfred (N.Y.) U., 1972-76, Nazareth Coll. Rochester, N.Y., 1975-78, Eisenhower Coll., Seneca Falls, N.Y., 1975-77; evaluator Western Assn. Schs. and Colls., 1991—; commr.-at-large North Ctrl. Assn. Colls. and Schs., 1989-91, educator, cons., 1986-91; mem. exec. bd. for study ctrs. in Japan, China and Korea, campus dir. Oreg. Sys. Higher Edn., 1980-85; bd. visitors Newark (N.Y.) Devel. Ctr., 1975-77; presenter in field. Contbr. articles to profl. jours. Bd. dirs. troop 119 Boy Scouts Am., Richmond, 1986-91, Project 100001, Townsend Cmty. Ctr., Richmond, 1987-89, Alameda Girls Club, Inc., 1992—, Asian Cmty. Mental Health Svcs., 1991—, Found. for Ednl. Excellence, Alameda, 1993—; pres., bd. dirs. Whitewater Opera Co., Richmond, 1987-91, Leadership Wayne County, Richmond, 1988-91; cons. teaching mini-grant program Richmond Cmty. Schs., 1988-91; mem. citizens adv. bd. Wayne County Sheriff's Dept., 1989-91. Mem. APA, Am. Assn. for Higher Edn., Am. Assn. State Colls. and Univs., Am. Assn. Univ. Adminstrs. (nat. v.p. 1990-92, bd. dirs. Found. 1991—), Am. Assn. for Higher Edn. (founding mem. Asian Am. caucus), Asian Am. Psychol. Assn. (treas., membership officer 1983-91, pres. 1988-91), Calif. Psychol. Assn., Nat. Assn. Acad. Affairs Adminstrs., Nat. Coun. Schs. Profl. Psychology, Rotary (bd. dirs. Alameda 1993—). Home: 5000 S Centinela Ave Apt 109 Los Angeles CA 90066-6947 Office: Calif School Of Prof Psychology 1 Beach St Ste 100 San Francisco CA 94133-1221

**SAKAMOTO, NORMAN LLOYD,** state legislator, civil engineer; b. Honolulu, May 22, 1947; s. Shuichi and Fusa (Hayashi) S.; m. Penelope A. Hayasaka, July 12, 1970; children: David H., Gregory F., Katherine E. BSCE, U. Hawaii, 1969; MSCE, U. Ill., 1970. Registered profl. engr., Calif., Hawaii; lic. spl. inspector, Hawaii; lic. contractor, Hawaii. Engr. storm drain City of L.A., 1970-71, engr. streets and frwys., 1972-73; engr. hydrology C.E., 1971-72; v.p. S & M Sakamoto, Inc., Honolulu, 1973-85; pres. SC Pacific Corp., Honolulu, 1985—; mem. Hawaii Senate, Dist. 15, Honolulu, 1996—. Bd. dirs. Bldg. Industry Assn., Honolulu, spl. appointee, 1991-92, pres.-elect, 1993, pres., 1994; bd. dirs. City Contractors Assn., Honolulu; trustee Home Builders Inst. 1993-96; del. White House Conf. on Small Bus., 1995; co-chair Hawaii Congress on Small Bus. Scoutmaster Honolulu area Boy Scouts Am., 1989-92, asst. scoutmaster, 1993—; elected to Hawaii State Senate, Dist. 15, 1996—; mem. Aliamanu Clubhouse adv. bd. Boys and Girls Club; mem. Edn. Commn. of the States. Named Remodeler of Month Bldg. Industry Assn., 1990, 91, 96, Remodeler of Yr., 1991, Legislator of Yr., Bldg. Industry Assn., 2003, Legislator of Yr., Friends of the Libr., 2004; recipient Excellence award U. Hawaii, 2005, Charles Dick Medal of Merit, Nat. Guard Assn. US, 2005. Mem. ASCE, Nat. Assn. Home Builders, Internat. Fellowship Christian Businessmen, Nat. Fedn. Ind. Bus. (Guardian of Small Bus. award 1999), Constrn. Industry Legis. Assn., C. of C. Evangelical. Office: SC Pacific Corp 3210-A Koapaka St Honolulu HI 96819

**SAKAMOTO, RONALD RIKIO,** lawyer, construction executive; b. Honolulu, Oct. 2, 1951; s. Richard Tadashi and Hideko Sakamoto; m. Marie Kanno, Jan. 14, 2006; 1 child, Aaron Naoyuki. B in Econs. with distinction, Whitman Coll., 1973; JD, U. Hawaii, 1979. Bar: Hawaii 1979. Atty. Damon Key Char & Bocken, Honolulu, 1979—89, Char Sakamoto Ishii Lum and Ching, Honolulu, 1989—2006, pres., 2004—; v.p. Tileco Inc., Kapolei, Hawaii, 1983—, also bd. dirs. Business and prod. mgr., assoc. editor U. Hawaii Law Rev. Chair Friends William S. Richardson Sch. Law, Honolulu, 1982—87; bd. dirs. Hawaii Lupus Found., Inc., Honolulu, 1988—93, Hawaii Health Found., Honolulu, 1996—2006; sect. referee adminstr. sect. 7 Am. Youth Soccer Orgn., 2005—06; mem. rev. adv. com. U. Hawaii Sch. Law, Honolulu, 1980—93; nat. referee commn. Am. Youth Soccer Orgn., Hawthorne, Calif., 2005—06, regional referee adminstr. region 178 Honolulu, 2003—05; pres. Assn. Apt. Owners 855 Olokele, Honolulu, 1980—81. Named Referee of the Yr. Region 178, Am. Youth Soccer Orgn., 2002, Referee Instr. of the Yr. Sect. 7, 2005; M.M. Scott scholar, Hawaiian Trust, 1969—73. Mem.: ABA, Hawaii State Bar Assn. (chmn. bus. law sect. 1985, chmn. tax sect. 1994—95), William S. Richardson Sch. Law Alumni Assn. (bd. dirs. 1979—85). Office: Char Sakamoto Ishii Lum and Ching 841 Bishop St # 850 Honolulu HI 96813 Office Phone: 808-522-5133.

**SAKHNOVICH, LEV ARONOVICH,** mathematics educator, researcher; b. Lugansk, Ukraine, Feb. 24, 1932; naturalized, US, 2005; s. Aron and Donja (Bycova) S.; m. Olena Melnychenko, Feb. 21, 1954; children: Alexander, Anna. Tchr's diploma, Pedagogical Inst., Odessa, Ukraine, 1953; PhD in Math., U. Kharkov, Ukraine, 1958, DSc degree, 1960. Lectr. Pedagogical Inst., Ismael, Ukraine, 1956—57; prof. Tech. Inst., Odessa, Ukraine, 1957—64, Acad. Comm., Odessa, 1964—99, Chmn. dept. math. Tech.-Sci. Soc., Odessa, 1981—; vis. mem. Courant Inst. Math. Sci. Author, reviewer Russian Math. Survey, 1980; author Algebra Analysis Survey, 1993, Integral Equations with Difference Kernels on Finite Intervals, 1996, Interpolation Theory and its Applications, 1997, Spectral Theory of Canonical Differential Systesm, 1999; editor: Matrix and Operator Valued Functions, 1994; contbr. articles to profl. jours. Recipient prize Moscow Math. Soc., 1962; grantee Soros, 1993-99. Mem.: Am. Math. Soc. Home: 735 Crawford Ave Brooklyn NY 11223 E-mail: lev.sakhnovich@verizon.net.

**SAKIC, JOE (JOSEPH STEVE SAKIC),** professional hockey player; b. Burnaby, B.C., Canada, July 7, 1969; m. Debbie Sakic. Capt. Que. Nordiques, 1991—95; with Colo. Avalanche, 1995—. Mem. Team Can., World Cup of Hockey, 1996, 2004, Team Can., Olympic Games, Nagano, Japan, 1998, Salt Lake City, 2002. Named to NHL All-Star game, 1990—94, 1996, 1998, 2000—02, 2004; recipient Conn Smythe Trophy, 1996, Hart Trophy, 2001, Lester B. Pearson Award, 2001, Lady Byng Trophy, 2001, MVP Award, NHL All-Star game, 2004. Achievements include being a member of Stanley Cup Champion Colorado Avalanche, 1996, 2001; being a member of gold medal winning Canadian Hockey Team, Salt Lake City Olympic Games, 2002; being a member of World Cup Champion Team Canada, 2004. Office: c/o Colo Avalanche 1000 Chopper Cir Denver CO 80204-5809

**SAKIEWICZ, NICK,** professional sports team executive; b. Passaic, N.J. m. Isabel Sakiewicz; 1 child, Nick Jr. Grad., U. New Haven. Soccer player F.C. Nantes, French 1st Divsn., 1982, N.Y. Arrows, Major Indoor Soccer League, 1983, F.C. Belenenses, Portuguese 1st Divsn., 1984; sales mgr. TIF Instruments, Miami, Fla., 1985-90; zone mgr. Agy. Svcs., Inc., Atlanta, 1990, dir. sales Tampa, Fla., v.p. sales & mktg. Bell; asst. coach, goalkeeper coach Coll. Boca Raton (Fla.), 1987; goalkeeper coach Southeast Region, Olympic Devel. Program, 1985-89, Fla. Youth Soccer Assn., 1985-89; dir., then v.p. Providian Bancorp, San Francisco, 1995; past v.p. exec. sales Major League Soccer; pres., gen. mgr. Tampa Bay Mutiny, Major League Soccer, 1996-2000; gen. mgr. N.Y.-N.J. Metro Stars, Major League Soccer, East Rutherford, N.J., 2000—. Office: NY-NJ Metro Stars 3rd Fl 1 Harmon Plz Fl 3 Secaucus NJ 07094-2803

**SAKOIAN, LORRAINE J.,** secondary school educator; b. Pa., Feb. 28, 1965; d. Gerald and Ruthann Beaver; m. Mark S. Sakoian, Aug. 4, 1984; children: Michael, Mark, Jon. BA, U. Pitts., 1986; MA, Regent U., 1988. Cert. tchr. Pa. Tchr. Greater Works Acad., Monroeville, Pa., 1986—88; social

studies tchr. Conestoga Christian Sch., Morgantown, Pa., 2000—04, Twin Valley HS, Elverson, Pa., 2004—. Presenter in field. Regional and state judge Nat. History Day, Pa., 2004. Mem.: Global Assn. Tchrs. Econ., Pa. Coun. Social Studies Tchrs., Nat. Coun. Social Studies Tchrs. Office: Twin Valley High Sch 4897 N Twin Valley Rd Elverson PA 19520

**SAKOPOULOS, ANDREAS GEORGE,** cardiac and vascular surgeon; b. Viareggio, Italy, Sept. 4, 1962; s. George Sakopoulos and Paola Tognetti; m. Lisa Hinz. MD, U. Pisa, Italy, 1989. Diplomate Am. Bd. Cardiac, Vascular, Thoracic Surgery. Cardiothoracic surgeon Glendale (Calif.) Meml. Hosp., 2000—03, Verdugo Hills Hosp., La Canada, Calif., 2001—03, Glendale Adventist Hosp., 2001—03, St. Helena (Calif.) Hosp., 2003—, med. dir. ICU, 2003—; cardiothoracic surgeon Ukiah (Calif.) Valley Hosp., 2004—. Mem. bd. dirs. St. Helena Hosp. Found., 2001—. Contbr. articles to profl. jours. Youth soccer coach, Pasadena, Calif., 2000—03, St. Helena, 2003—; youth baseball coach Pasadena, 2000—. Recipient Socrates award, Ind. U. Sch. Medicine, Indpls., 1996. Fellow: ACS; mem.: Napa Valley Med Soc. (rep., mem. exec. com. 2003—). Office: 6 Woodland Rd Ste 304 Saint Helena CA 94574

**SAKS, GENE,** theater and film director, actor; b. NYC; Began career as an actor off-Broadway at Provincetown Playhouse and the Cherry Lane Theatre; played in: Auden's Dog Beneath the Skin, E.E. Cummings' Him, Molière's The Bourgeois Gentilhomme; appeared on Broadway in Mr. Roberts, South Pacific, Middle of the Night, The Tenth Man, A Shot in the Dark, Love and Libel, A Thousand Clowns; debut as dir. on Broadway Enter Laughing, 1963; dir. stage plays Nobody Loves an Albatross, 1964, Half a Sixpence, 1964 (Tony nominee Best Dir. Musical), Generation, 1965, Mame, 1966 (Tony nominee Best Dir. Musical), Same Time, Next Year, 1975 (Tony nominee Best Dir. Play), California Suite, 1972, I Love My Wife (best dir. of Musical award Drama Desk, Tony), 1977, Brighton Beach Memoirs (best dir. award, Tony), 1983, Biloxi Blues (best dir. of play award, Tony), 1985, The Odd Couple (female version), 1985, Broadway Bound, 1986, A Month of Sundays, 1987, Rumors, 1988, Lost in Yonkers, 1991 (Tony nominee Best Dir., Outer Critics Cir. award), Jake's Women, 1992, Barrymore, 1997, Mr. Goldwyn, 2001, Remembering Tennessee, 2001; dir. films Barefoot in the Park, The Odd Couple, Cactus Flower, Last of the Red Hot Lovers, Mame, Brighton Beach Memoirs, A Fine Romance; dir. TV movie Bye, Bye Birdie, 1995; appeared in films including a Thousand Clowns, Prisoner of Second Avenue, Lovesick, The One and Only, The Goodbye People, 1986, Nobody's Fool, 1994, IQ, 1994. Recipient George Abbott award for lifetime achievement in the theatre, 1990; elected to Theatre Hall of Fame, 1991. Mem. Stage Dirs. and Choreographers (pres.).

**SAKS, JUDITH-ANN,** artist; b. Anniston, Ala., Dec. 20, 1943; d. Julien David and Lucy-Jane (Watson) S.; m. Haskell Irvin Rosenthal, Dec. 22, 1974; 1 child, Brian Julien. Student, Tex. Acad. Art, 1957-58, Mus. Fine Arts, Houston, 1962, Rice U., 1962; BFA, Tulane U., 1966; postgrad., U. Houston, 1967. Curator student art collection U. Houston, 1968-72; artist Am. Revolution Bicentennial project Port of Houston Authority, 1975-76. Solo shows include Alley Gallery, Houston, 1969, 2131 Gallery, Houston, 1969; group shows include Birmingham (Ala.) Mus., 1967, Meinhard Galleries, Houston, 1977, Galeire Barbizon, Houston, 1980, Park Crest Gallery, Austin, 1981, Margolis Gallery, 2005, 06; represented in permanent collections including L.B. Johnson Manned Space Mus., Clear Lake City, Tex., Harris County Heritage Mus., Windsor Castle, Smithsonian Instn.; comms. include Pin Oak Charity Horse Show Assn., Roberts S.S. Agy., New Orleans, Cruiser Houston Meml. Rm., U. Houston. Recipient art awards including 1st prize for water color Art League Houston, 1969, 1st prize for graphics, 1969, 1st prize for sculpture, 1968, Nat. 1st place award for original print DAR/Am. Heritage Com., 1987, Nat. 1st place award for acrylic painting, DAR, 2000, Tex. award for Acrylic, 2003, 06, Nat. 3rd place award for painting, 2003, Nat. 3rd prize for acrylic, 2005, Tex. State 1st prize for drawing DAR, 2002, Shofar award, 2003, Outstanding Svc. award Boy Scout Troop 806, 2002, Tex. award for art, 2005. Mem. Art League Houston, Houston Mus. Fine Arts, DAR (chpt. curator 1983-85, 93-95, contbr. Tex. sesquicentennial drawing for DAR mag., rec. sec. 2001-03, libr. 2003-2005, counselor, 2005—, Tex. Best Chpt. Chmn. award 2003, 06, Tex. award for art 2003, Tex. State 1st prize acrylic 2004, 2005, Tex. Cert. award for acrylic 2006), Daus. Republic of Tex., Magna Charta Dames.

**SAKS, STEPHEN HOWARD,** accountant, health organization executive; b. Phila., May 16, 1941; s. Samuel and Edythe (Edelman) S.; m. Ruth Workman, Dec. 22, 1963; children: Amy Meryl, Brian Eric, Joshua Marc. BS in Econs., U. Pa., 1962. CPA, Pa. Staff acct. to ptnr. Peat, Marwick, Mitchell & Co., Phila., 1962-78; ptnr. Laventhol & Horwath, Phila., 1978-91; CFO Northeastern Health Sys., Phila., 1991—2001, Neumann Med. Ctr., Phila., 1992-98, Elkins Park Hosp., Pa., 2002—03; exec. dir. John F. Kennedy Meml. Hosp., Phila., 1998-99; v.p. fin. Cooper Health Sys., Camden, NJ, 1999—2001; interim CFO Whitman-Walker Clinic, Washington, 2004; dir. Shechtman Marks Devor PC, Phila., 2005—. Bd. dirs. Jewish Family and Children's Agy, Phila. 1979-88; treas. Jewish Employment and Vocat. Svc., Phila., 1984-88; chmn. bd. overseers Gratz Coll., Melrose Pk., Pa., 1987-90; pres. Beth Sholom Men's Club, Elkins Pk., Pa., 1987-90. Mem. AICPA, Pa. Inst. CPAs, Healthcare Fin. Mgmt. Assn. (advanced). Democrat. Avocations: community activities, travel. Office Phone: 215-496-9339. Personal E-mail: shsaks@verizon.net. E-mail: ssaks@smd-pc.com.

**SAKUGAWA, JUNE ELIZABETH,** music educator; b. Buffalo, June 13, 1953; d. Joseph Bernard Feldmeyer and Anna Mary Stresing; m. Edward Chokin Sakugawa, Apr. 19, 1997. A in Applied Sci. in Music, Onondaga C.C., Syracuse, N.Y., 1973; MusB in Music Edn., Fredonia State U. Coll., NY, 1975; M in Music Edn., U. No. Colo., 1994. Lic. educator Nev. Orch. dir., gen. music tchr. Holland Patent (N.Y.) Ctrl. Sch. Dist., 1975—76; orch. dir. Sch. Dist. 9-R, Durango, Colo., 1977—81; music tchr. St. Andrew Luth. Sch., Denver, 1981—84, Jefferson County Sch. Dist., Lakewood, Colo., 1984—85; orch. dir. Clark County Sch. Dist., Las Vegas, 1985—. Bd. dirs. Colo. String Tchrs. Assn., Denver, 1979—81. Vol. Las Vegas Basset Hound Rescue. Nominee Disney Am. Tchr. award, 2001, 2004; recipient superior performance ratings for mid. sch. orch., Clark County Mid. Sch. Orch. Festivals, 1985—2005. Mem.: NEA, Nev. State Educators Assn., Music Educators Nat. Conf., Am. String Tchrs. Assn. Avocations: colored pencil and graphite art, astronomy, scrapbooks. Home: 1268 Lime Point St Las Vegas NV 89110-5908 Office: Mike O'Callaghan Mid Sch 1450 Radwick Las Vegas NV 89110-5908 Office Phone: 702-799-7340 ext 4063. Office Fax: 702-799-8850. Personal E-mail: ejbassetlovers@aol.com. E-mail: jes335@interact.ccsd.net.

**SAKURADA, YUTAKA,** retired chemist; b. Kyoto, Jan. 1, 1933; s. Ichiro and Chiyoko (Okumura) S.; m. Keiko Sugimoto, May 10, 1960; children: Kazuhiro, Akihiro. BS, Kyoto U., 1956, MS, 1958, PhD, 1966. Rsch. fellow Cen. Rsch. Lab. Kuraray Co. Ltd., Kurashiki, Japan, 1958-62, 64-66; internat. fellow Stanford Rsch. Inst., Menlo Pk., Calif., 1962-64; tech. rep. N.Y. Office Kuraray Co. Ltd., N.Y.C., 1968-71; mgr. Med. Bus. Devel. Div. Kuraray, Osaka, Japan, 1974-77, gen. mgr. Med. Bus. 1977-88, gen. mgr. Corp. Rand D Div., 1988-89; mng. dir. Kuraray Plastics Co. Ltd., Osaka, 1989-91. Vice chmn. Japanese Soc. Biomaterials, Tokyo, 1987—96; pres. Haemonetics, Japan, 1991—2001, chmn. and CEO, 2001—05; pres. Haemonetics Japan/Asia, 2003—05, chmn., 2005—06; ret. Recipient Technology award The Soc. Polymers, 1984, Japanese Chem. Soc., 1985. Achievements include development of ethylene vinyl alcohol copolymer hollow fiber for hemo-dialyzer; development of dental adhesives. Home: GM Ebisunomori 1304 4-23-6 Ebisu Shibuya-ku Tokyo 150-0013 Japan Personal E-mail: ysakurada@star.ocn.ne.jp.

**SAKUTA, MANABU,** neurologist, educator; b. Ichikawa, Japan, Oct. 31, 1947; s. Jun and Shizuko (Tsuji) Sakuta; m. Yuko Fukushi, June 17, 1973; children: Akiko, Junko, Ken-Ichi. MD, U. Tokyo, 1973, PhD, 1978; MS in Neurology, U. Minn., 1981. Diplomate Japanese Bd. Neurology, Japanese Bd. Internal Medicine. Asst. dept. neurology U. Tokyo, 1980, lectr. dept. neurology, 1984—; from rsch. fellow dept. neurology to asst. prof. U. Minn.,

Mpls., 1980—82; head dept. neurology Japanese Red Cross Med. Ctr., Tokyo, 1982-2000; prof. Japanese Red Cross Women's Coll. Nursing, Tokyo, 1983-85, instr., 1986-88; lectr. dept. medicine U. Kobe, 1990—; prof. dept. neurology Kyorin U., Tokyo, 2000—, chmn., 2000—, chmn. 1st internal medicine, 2002—. Cons. Nakayama Hosp., Ichikawa, Japan, 1980—. Contbr. articles to profl. jours. Chmn. bd. trustees Japanese Soc. Tobacco Control, 2006—. Fellow: Royal Soc. Medicine (London); mem.: AAAS, Japanese Soc. Tobacco Control (pres. 2006—, chmn. 2006—), Am. Acad. Neurology, Japanese Soc. Autonomic Nervous Sys. (coun.), Japanese Soc. Sarcoidosis (coun.), Japanese Soc. Cerebrovascular Disease (coun.), Japanese Soc. Clin. Neurophysiology, Japanese Soc. Diabetology, Japanese Soc. Neurology (pres. Kanto br. 1984, mem. coun. Kanto br. 1984—, mem. coun. 1985—, mem. editl. bd. 1988—), Japanese Soc. Internal Medicine (pres. Kanto br. 1992), N.Y. Acad. Sci., Japanese No Smoking Soc. (chmn. bd. trustees 2006—), Tetsumon Club, U. Minn. Alumni Club, Chevalier du Tastevin (Burgundy), Chevalier Club (pres. internat. com. 1995—), Clin. Neurology Club. Democrat. Buddhist. Address: 71-7-504 Ichigaya-Yakuoji Shinjuku Tokyo 162 Japan Office Phone: 0422 47 5511. Personal E-mail: sakuta@shimkei.jp.

**SALACUSE, JESWALD WILLIAM,** lawyer, educator; b. Niagara Falls, NY, Jan. 28, 1938; s. William L. and Bessie B. (Buzzelli) S.; m. Donna Booth, Oct. 1, 1966; children: William, Maria. Diploma, U. Paris, 1959; AB, Hamilton Coll., 1960; JD, Harvard U., 1963. Bar: NY 1965, Tex. 1980. Lectr. law Ahmadu Bello U., Nigeria, 1963-65; assoc. Conboy, Hewitt, O'Brien & Boardman, NYC, 1965-67; assoc. dir. African Law Ctr., Columbia U., NYC, 1967-68; prof., dir. Rsch. Ctr., Nat. Sch. Adminstrn., Zaire, 1968-71; Mid. East regional advisor on law and devel. Ford Found., Beirut, 1971-74, rep. in Sudan, 1974-77; vis. prof. U. Khartoum, Sudan, 1974-77; vis. scholar Harvard Law Sch., 1977-78; prof. law So. Meth. U., Dallas, 1978-86, dean, 1980-86; dean, prof. internat. law Fletcher Sch. Law and Diplomacy, Tufts U., Medford, Mass., 1986-94, Henry J. Braker prof. comml. law, 1994—. Fellow Inst. Advanced Legal Studies, U. London, 1995; vis. prof. Ecole Nat. Ponts et Chaussées, Paris, 1990-95, Inst. Empressa, Madrid, 1995, U. Bristol, U. London Sch. Oriental and African Studies, 1995—2003; cons. Ford Found., 1978-82, 93, US Dept. State, 1978-80, UN Ctr. on Transnat. Corps., 1988—, Harvard Inst. Internat. Devel., 1990—, Asia Found., 1992, Harvard Law Sch./World Bank Laos Project, 1991-93; with Sri Lanka fin. sector project ISTI/US AID, 1993-94; lectr. Georgetown U. Internat. Law Inst., 1978-94, Panam. U., Mexico City, 1981; chmn. com. on Mid. Ea. law Social Sci. Rsch. Coun., 1978-84; chmn. Asia Tigers Fund Inc., 2005—, Coun. Internat. Exch. Scholars, 1987-91, India Fund Inc., 2005—, Emerging Markets Income Funds. I & II; bd. dirs. Inc., Global Ptnrs. Income Fund, Inc., Salomon Bros. Worldwide Income Fund, Inc., Emerging Markets Floating Rate Fund, Inc., Mcpl. Ptnrs. Funds I & II, Salomon Bros. High Income Funds I & II, Salomon Bros. 2008 Worldwide Dollar Govt. Term Trust, Mcpl. Ptnrs. Funds I & II; trustee Southwestern Legal Found., 1992-2004, Am. U. Paris, 1993-97; pres. Internat. Third World Legal Studies Assn., 1987-91; chmn. inst. Transnat. Arbitration, 1991-93; pres. Assn. Profl. Schs. Internat. Affairs, 1988-89; Fulbright disting. chair in comparative law, Italy, 2000; pres. Internat. Ctr. for Settlement Investment Disputes Arbitration Tribunal, 2004—. Author: (with Kasunmu) Nigerian Family Law, 1966, An Introduction to Law in French-Speaking Africa, Vol. I, 1969, Vol. II, 1976, (with Steng) International Business Planning, 1982, Making Global Deals-Negotiating in the International Marketplace, 1991, The Art of Advice, 1994, (video course) Negotiating in Today's World, 1995, The Wise Advisor, 2000, The Global Negotiator, 2003, Leading Leaders, 2005; contbr. articles to profl. jours. Mem. ABA, Dallas Bar Found. (trustee 1983-86), Coun. on Fgn. Rels., Am. Law Inst., Am. Soc. Internat. Law, Cosmos Club (Washington). Home: 10 Rogers St Cambridge MA 02142-4755 Office: Tufts U Fletcher Sch Law-Diplomacy Medford MA 02155 Office Phone: 617-627-3633. Business E-mail: jeswald.salacuse@tufts.edu.

**SALADINO, FRANK S.,** music educator; b. Smithtown, N.Y., June 13, 1972; s. Emanuel Frank Saladino and Lena DiTraglia; m. Lisa Marie Scudder-Saladino; children: Brett, Emanuel, Damian. BA in Performance, SUNY, Stony Brook, 1996; MS in Edn., Dowling Coll., Idle Hour, N.Y., 1999; post grad. in History and Lit., Fivetowns Coll., Dix Hills, N.Y., 2006—. Tchr. music St. Peters by the Sea Day Sch., Bay Shore, NY, 1998—2000, Northport Sch. Dist., 2000—01, Connet Quot Sch. Dist., Ronkonkana, 2001—. Music dir. Connet Quot Sch. Dist., Ronkonkana, NY, 2001—, stage crew advisor, 2004—. Office: Ronkonkoma Mid Sch 501 Peconic St Ronkonkoma NY 11779-7172 Home: 128 Villa Ave Deer Park NY 11729 Office Phone: 631-467-6000.

**SALAFSKY, IRA S.,** pediatrician, educator; b. Chgo., June 26, 1938; s. Mandel B. and Jeanette P. (Pritikin) Salafsky; m. Verena Zeller, Sept. 20, 1965 (div. June 1993); children: Niklaus, Anna Susan. AB, Dartmouth Coll., 1960; MD, Northwestern U., 1965. Diplomate Am. Bd. Pediat., Am. Bd. Med. Genetics. Intern Passavant Meml. Hosp., Chgo., 1965—66; resident in pediat. Children's Meml. Hosp., Chgo., 1966—68; physician North Suburban Pediat., Evanston, Ill., 1970—; assoc. prof. pediat. Northwestern U. Med. Sch., Chgo., 1970—; fellow Children's Meml. Hosp., Chgo., 1970—72. Genetics cons. Shriners Hosp. for Children, Chgo., 1972—. Contbr. articles to profl. jours. Capt. USAF, 1968—70. Fellow: Am. Acad. Pediat., Am. Coll. Med. Genetics (founding); mem.: Internat. Soc. Prenatal Diagnostics. Avocations: running, tennis, skiing, bicycling. Office: North Suburban Pediat 2530 Ridge Evanston IL 60201 Office Phone: 847-869-0892. Office Fax: 843-869-1070. Business E-mail: i-salafsky@northwestern.edu.

**SALAH, SAGID,** retired nuclear engineer; b. Seoul, Sept. 2, 1932; came to U.S., 1954; s. Galim and Faiza (Sultan) Salahutdin; m. Ravile Almakay, Apr. 2, 1966; children: Shamil, Kamil, Safiye. BChemE, U. Fla., 1958, MS in Nuclear Engring., 1960, PhD in Nuclear Engring., 1964. Nuclear engr. AEC, Bethonda, Md., 1964-66; sr. design engr. Westinghouse Astronuclear Lab., Large, Pa., 1966-70; sr. sys. engr. Westinghouse Nuclear Energy Sys., Pitts., 1970-73; mem. sys. safety engring. staff U.S. Nuclear Regulatory Commn., Bethesda, 1973-93; ret., 1993. Nuclear engring. cons. Oak Ridge (Tenn.) Inst. Nuclear Studies, 1963, 64; instr. U. Md., College Park, 1973-76. Contbr. articles to Nuclear Sci. and Engring. Youth coach Nat. Capital Soccer League, Vienna, Va., 1975-85. Mem. Am. Nuclear Soc. (emeritus, reviewer trans. papers 1972), Sigma Tau. Moslem. Achievements include measurements of neutron energy spectra in heterogeneous media using differential and integral methods, neutron energy spectra measurements and analysis in intermediate spectra reactors, three-dimensional transient analysis of boron dilution in PWR reactors. Home: 9302 Kilport Ct Vienna VA 22182-3426 Personal E-mail: srsalah@cox.net.

**SALAHUDDIN, AHMAD,** civil engineer, educator; b. Anbala, India, Sept. 19, 1941; arrived in Zimbabwe, 1987; s. Ahmad Chaudhary Shamsuddin and Sultanta Mahmuda. BSCE, Panjab U., Lahore, Pakistan, 1961; MSc in Civil Engring., Columbia U., 1967; PhD in Structural Engring., Concordia U., Montreal, Can., 1971. Design engr. cons. industry, Pakistan, 1961-65; rsch. assoc., asst. prof. Concordia U., Montreal, 1971-73, 77-81; specialist cons. Can., 1973-85, 81-83; assoc. prof. U. Bahrain, 1983-85; dir. Can. Inst. Tech. Edn., 1985-87; prof. engring. U. Zimbabwe, Harare, 1987—. Editor specifications draft Standards Assn. Zimbabwe, 1993—; coord. indsl. cons. Civil Engring. U. Zimbabwe, 1994—; mem. sci. com. Internat. Symposium Design of Structures, Germany, 1996; mem. African Structural Engring. Edn. Forum, Johannesburg, South Africa, 1996. Contbr. articles to profl. jours. Fulbright-Hays fellow, Washington, 1965-67. Mem. ASCE, Internat. Assn. Shell and Spatial Sturctures, Internat. Assn. Bridge and Structural Engring. Avocations: scientific reading and writing, listening to music, computer technology. Home: 6 Montagu Ct 142 Josiah Chinamano Ave Harare Zimbabwe Office: U Zimbabwe Civil Engring Dept PO Box MP167 Mount Pleasant Harare Zimbabwe Office Phone: 263-4-303211 ext. 1387. Personal E-mail: ahmadzw@yahoo.com. Business E-mail: salahuddin@eng.uz.ac.zw.

**SALAK, ANN M.,** literature and language professor, department chairman; d. Charles E. and Helen A. Salak. AB, John Carroll U., Cleve., 1972, MA, 1976. Instr. English and instrnl. asst. Cuyahoga CC, Cleve., 1972—82; instr.

English Cleve. State U. Developmental Edn., 1982—92, Pierce Coll. Fort Stellacoom, Lakewood, Wash., 1992—96, Pierce Coll. Puyallup, 1996—, chair bus. and humanities divsn., 1999—. Author: Improve Your Sentences, 1995. Bd. mem. Valley Arts United, Puyallup, Wash., 2004—06, exec. bd. mem., 2006—. Mem.: Wash. Cmty. and Tech. Coll. Humanities Assn. Democrat. Avocations: writing, photography, hiking, camping. Home: 5720 86th Ave NW Gig Harbor WA 98335 Office: Pierce Coll Puyallup 1601 39th Ave SE Puyallup WA 98374

**SALAM, DEBERA JEAN,** accounting company executive; b. Milw., Apr. 1, 1957; d. Leonard John Stadler and Joanne (Allen) Huberty; 1 child, Anthony Robert Ellington. Student, Marquette U., 1974-76, U. Houston, 1985-86. Cert. payroll profl. Payroll adminstr. Vetco Offshore, Houston, 1979-80; payroll mgr. Oncor Corp., Houston, 1980-83, Waukesha-Pearce Corp., Houston, 1983-87; mgmt. cons. Automatic Data Processing, Roseland, N.J., 1987-90; pres., owner Payroll Support Assocs., Houston, 1990—97; sr. mgr. Ernst & Young LLP, Houston, 1997—. Bd. advisors Warren Gorham & Lamont, Alexandria, Va., 1990—; pub. speaker on payroll compliance and adminstrn. matters; expert witness FMC vs. U.S., 1994. Author: Principles of Payroll Administration, 18th edit., 2003, Payroll Practitioners Compliance Handbook, 13th edit., 2003, (home study course) Mastering Payroll, 12th edit., 2003; editor-in-chief Propub. Publs., 1989-98. Mem. Am. Soc. Payroll Mgmt. (dir. fed. compliance 1990-95), Am. Payroll Assn. (pres. Houston chpt. 1986-87, spl. achievement award 1987, cert.), Am. Inst. Profl. Bookkeepers (mem. bd. advisors 1988—). Office: 1401 McKinney Houston TX 77010

**SALAM, GOHAR AZAM,** physician, director; s. Muhammad Abdul and Zafar Salam; m. Asifa Gohar Bari, May 15, 1995; children: Sameed Ahmed, Mazeez Ahmed. MD, Dow Med. Coll., Karachi, Pakistan, 1992; DO, NY Coll. Of Osteo. Medicine, Old Westbury, 2000. Diplomate Am. Bd. Of Family Medicine, 1995. Attending physician emergency rm. Standish Cmty. Hosp., Standish, Mich., 1994—96, dir. rural health clinic, emergency rm., 1997; attending physician emergency rm. Greenville Hosp., Jersey City, 1997—99; asst. dir., family practice residency program Saginaw Coop. Hospitals Inc., Saginaw, Mich., 2000—01; capt. USAR, Atlanta, 2001—; physician and founder Vitreoretinal Cons. Ft. Wayne, Ind., 2005—; staff physician Parkview Hosp., Luth. Hosp., Ft. Wayne, 2005—. Surg. retina fellow, vis. lectr. Ind. U. Sch. of Medicine, 2004—05, clin. lectr., dept. of ophthalmology, 2005—; chief resident, dept. of ophthalmology North Shore U. Hosp., NYU Sch. of Medicine, Manhasset, 2003—04, resident, dept. of ophthalmology, 2001—03; faculty devel. fellow Faculty Devel. Inst., U. Mich., Ann Arbor, 2000—01; asst. prof., dept. of family medicine Mich. State U., Sch. of Human Medicine, Saginaw, Mich., 2000—01; chief resident, clin. instr., dept. of family medicine Saginaw Coop. Hosp., Mich. State U. Sch. of Human Medicine, 1994—95; resident, clin. instr., dept. of family medicine Mich. State U. Sch. of Human Medicine, 1992—94. Author: (review book) Ophthalmology Board Review; contbr. articles to profl. jours. Recipient Excellence in Rsch. Resident award, Am. Soc. of Cataract and Refractive Surgeons- Storm Eye Inst., 2004, Who's Who in Executives and Professionals, 2004—05, Thomas J. Zuber award for Excellence in Tchg., Saginaw Coop. Hospitals, Mich. State U. Coll. of Human Medicine, 2001, Louise E. Zeile award for Outstanding Jr. Resident, 1994; Merrill Grayson fellowship, Dept. of Ophthalmology, Ind. U. Sch. of Medicine, 2004. Mem.: AMA, Assn. of Rsch. in Vision and Ophthalmology, Am. Acad. of Ophthalmology. Home: 615 Tawny Ct Huntertown IN 46748 Office: Vitreoretinal Cons of Ft Wayne 3978 New Vision Dr Fort Wayne IN 46845 Office Phone: 260-483-9500. Personal E-mail: goharsalam@yahoo.com.

**SALAMA, C. ANDRE TEWFIK,** electrical engineering educator; b. Heliopolis, Egypt, Sept. 27, 1938; arrived in Can., 1957; s. Tewfik and Sarine (Bigio) S.; m. Rhoda R. Kurtz, Dec. 19, 1974. BASc with honours, U. B.C., Vancouver, Can., 1961, MASc, 1963, PhD, 1966. Registered profl. engr., Ont. Mem. sci. staff Bell No. Rsch., Ottawa, Ont., Canada, 1966-67; asst. prof. elec. engring. U. Toronto, Ont., 1967-70, assoc. prof. Ont., 1970-77, prof. Ont., 1977-92, univ. prof. Ont., 1992—. Chmn., bd. dirs. Can. Microelectronics Corp., Kingston, Ont., 1984-98; program leader, bd. dirs. Micronet, Toronto, 1990—. Mem. editorial bd. Solid State Electronics, 1982-2000; contbr. over 300 articles to sci. jours. Recipient Izaak Walton Killam Meml. prize, 1994, Outstanding Lifetime Achievement award, Can. Semiconductor Tech. Conf., 2003, NSERC Lifetime Achievement award, 2004, Recognition award Rsch. Excellence and Outstanding Leadership Network Cures of Excellence, 2004; Info. Tech. Assn. Can. and Natural Scis. and Engring. Rsch. Coun. fellow U. Toronto, 1989-90. Fellow IEEE (assoc. editor Trans. on Cirs. and Systems 1987-89, Millenium medal 2000), Royal Soc. Can., Can. Acad. Engring.; mem. Electrochem. Soc., Assn. Profl. Engrs. Ont. Avocations: swimming, sailing, scuba diving, horseback riding, reading. Office: U Toronto Dept Elec Engring Toronto ON Canada M5S 1A4 Office Phone: 416-978-8658.

**SALAMON, LESTER MILTON,** political science professor; b. Pitts., Jan. 11, 1943; s. Victor William Salamon and Helen (Sanders) Weiss; m. Lynda Anne Brown, June 27, 1965; children: Noah, Matthew. BA in Econs. and Pub. Policy, Princeton U., 1964; PhD in Govt., Harvard U., 1971. Instr. dept. polit. sci. Tougaloo Coll., Miss., 1966-67; asst. prof. Vanderbilt U., Nashville, 1970-73; assoc. prof. policy scis. and polit. sci. Duke U., Durham, NC, 1973-80, dir. Ctr. for Urban and Regional Devel., 1973—77; dep. assoc. dir. U.S. Office Mgmt. and Budget, Washington, 1977-79; dir. Ctr. for Governance and Mgmt. Rsch., Internat. Washington, 1980-86; prof., dir. Inst. for Policy Studies, Johns Hopkins U., Balt., 1987-97, dir. Ctr. Civil Sector Studies, 1997—. Author: America's Nonprofit Sector: A Primer, 1992, The Emerging Sector: Nonprofit Organizations in Comparative Perspective, 1994, Partners in Public Service: Government Nonprofit Relations in the Modern Welfare State, 1995, Defining the Nonprofit Sector: A Cross-National Analysis, 1996, International Guide to Nonprofit Law, 1997, The Resilient Sector, 2003; editor: Beyond Privatization, 1989, Human Capital and America's Future, 1991, Global Civil Society, 1998, The Tools of Government, A Guide to The New Governance, 2002, The State of Non-Profit America, 2002, Global Civil Society, 2004; mem. editl. bd. Adminstrn. and Soc., 1985—, Voluntas, 1988—, Nonprofit and Voluntary Sector Quar., 1990—, Pub. Adminstrn. Rev., 2000—. Mem. experts com. to ind. sector panel on nonprofit sector Nat. Acad. Pub. Adminstrn. Panel, EPA; mem. Balt. City Planning Commn., 1987—95; mem. adv. com on voluntary fgn. aid USAID; chmn. bd. dirs. Cmty. Found. of Chesapeake. Recipient Laverne Burchfield award Am. Soc. Pub. Adminstrn., 1977, Disting. Book award Assn. of Rschrs. on Nonprofit Orgns. and Vol. Action, Disting. Book award Ind. Sector, 2002, Disting. Achievement award Assn. Rschrs. on Nonprofit Orgns. and Vol. Action, 2004. Mem. Internat. Soc. Third Sector Rsch. (vice chmn. 1991-95), Nat. Acad. Pub. Adminstrn., Social Sci. Rsch. Coun. (nonprofit field com.). Avocations: tennis, swimming, carpentry, sailing. Home: 903 Lynch Dr Arnold MD 21012-1504 Office: Johns Hopkins U Inst Policy Studies 3400 N Charles St Baltimore MD 21218-2680 Office Phone: 410-516-5463. Business E-mail: lsalamon@jhu.edu.

**SALAMON, LINDA BRADLEY,** English literature educator; b. Elmira, N.Y., Nov. 20, 1941; d. Grant Ellsworth and Evelyn E. (Ward) Bradley; divorced; children: Michael Lawrence, Timothy Martin. BA, Radcliffe Coll., 1963; MA, Bryn Mawr Coll., 1964, PhD, 1971; Advanced Mgmt. Cert., Harvard U. Bus. Sch., 1978; D.H.L., St. Louis Coll. Pharmacy, 1993. Lectr., adj. asst. prof. Eng., Dartmouth Coll., Hanover, NH, 1967-72; mem. faculty lit. Bennington Coll., Vt., 1974-75; dean students Wells Coll., Aurora, NY, 1975-77; exec. asst. to pres. U. Pa., Phila., 1977-79; assoc. prof. English Washington U., St. Louis, 1979—88, prof., 1988-92, dean Coll. Arts and Scis., 1979-92; prof. English George Washington U., Washington, 1992—. Mem. faculty Bryn Mawr Summer Inst. Women, 1979—99; dean Columbian Coll. Arts and Sci., Washington, 1992—95, interim v.p. acad. affairs, 1995—96. Author, co-editor: Nicholas Hilliard's Art of Limning, 1983; co-author: Integrity in the College Curriculum, 1985; contbr. numerous articles to literary and profl. jours. Bd. dirs. Am. Assn. Colls., vice chmn., 1985, chmn., 1986; bd. dir. Greater St. Louis council Girl Scouts U.S.A.; trustee Coll. Bd., St. Louis Coll. Pharmacy. Fellow Radcliffe Inst., 1973-74, Folger

Shakespeare Libr., 1986, NEH Montaigne Inst., 1988, Fulbright fellow, Taiwan, 2003, Ringler fellow Huntington Libr., 2004; Am. Philos. Soc. Penrose grantee, 1974. Mem.: MLA, Cosmos Club, Phi Beta Kappa. Office: George Washington U Dept of Eng Rome Hall 760 801 22D St NW Washington DC 20052-0001 Business E-mail: lbs@gwu.edu.

**SALAMON, MYRON BEN,** physicist, educator, dean; b. Pitts., June 4, 1939; s. Victor William and Helen (Sanders) S.; m. Sonya Maxine Blank, June 12, 1960; children— David, Aaron. BS, Carnegie-Mellon U., 1961; PhD, U. Calif., Berkeley, 1966. Asst. prof. physics U. Ill., Urbana, 1966-72, assoc. prof., 1972-74, prof., 1974—, program dir. Materials Research Lab., 1984-91, assoc. dean. Coll. Engring., 2000—06; dean natural sci. and math. U. Tex., Dallas, 2006—. Vis. scientist U. Tokyo, 1966, 71, Tech. U. Munich, Fed. Republic Germany, 1974-75; cons. NSF; Disting. Vis. Prof. Tsukuba (Japan) U., 1995-96. Editor: Physics of Superionic Conductors, 1979; co-editor: Modulated Structures, 1979; divisional assoc. editor: Phys. Rev. Letters, 1992-96; contbr. sci. papers to profl. jours. Recipient Alexander von Humboldt Sr. U.S. Scientist award, 1974-75; NSF coop. fellow, 1964-66; postdoctoral fellow, 1966; A.P. Sloan fellow, 1972-73; Berndt Matthias scholar Los Alamos Nat. Lab., 1995-96; visiting scientist CNRS and Inst. Laue-Langevin Grenoble, France, 1981-82. Fellow Am. Phys. Soc. Office: U Ill Coll Engring 1308 W Green St Urbana IL 61801-9013 Office Phone: 972-883-2416. E-mail: salamon@utdallas.edu.

**SALAMON, RENAY,** real estate broker; b. NYC, May 13, 1948; d. Solomon and Mollie (Friedman) Langman; m. Maier Salamon, Aug. 10, 1968; children: Mollie, Jean, Leah, Sharon, Eugene. BA, Hunter Coll., 1969. Licensed real estate borker, N.J. Mgr. office Customode Designs Inc., N.Y.C., 1966-68; co-owner Salamon Dairy Farms, Three Bridges, NJ, 1968-86; assoc. realtor Max. D. Shuman Realty Inc., Flemington, NJ, 1983-85; pres., chief exec. officer Liberty Hill Realty Inc., Flemington, NJ, 1985—. Cons. Illva Saronna Inc. (Illva Group), Edison, N.J. 1985—; real estate devel. joint venture with M.R.F.S. Realty Inc. (Illva Group), 1986—; bd. dirs. Anderson House. Mem. Readington twp. Environ. Commn., Whitehouse Sta., N.J., 1978-87, N.J. Assn. Environ. Commrs., Trenton, 1978—; fundraiser Rutgers Prep. Sch., Somerset, N.J., 1984-95; bd. dirs. Hunterdon County YMCA, 1987-95, Anderson House, 2000-04; mem. N.J.-Israel Commn., 1999—; bd. trustees Rutgers Prep. Sch., 2000—; chair Hunterdon County Bd. Social Svc., 2002, 2004; chair Hunterdon County Health and Human Svcs. Commn., 2004—. Named N.J. Broker Record. Forbes Inc., N.Y.C. 1987. Mem.: Realtors Land Inst. Republican. Jewish. Office: Liberty Hill Realty Inc 415 US Highway 202 Flemington NJ 08822-6021 Office Phone: 908-782-1919.

**SALAMON, RICK,** secondary school educator, department chairman; b. St. Louis, Nov. 1, 1945; s. Anthony Richard and Eugenia Ann (Theodorow) S.; m. Marilyn Ayres, Feb. 17, 1988; children: Gayle Michelle, Julie Ann. BS, U. Mo., 1967, MA, 1971; MAT, Webster Coll., 1974. Tutor, program planner Human Devel. Corp., Columbia, Mo., 1970-71; tchr. Pattonville Sch. Dist., Maryland Heights, Mo., 1971-73, Wellston (Mo.) Sch. Dist., 1973-74; tchr., dept. chair Wentzville (Mo.) Sch. Dist., 1974-99. Bd. dirs. Sch. and Coll. Commn., Jefferson City, Mo., 1984-87. 1st lt. U.S. Army, 1967-70. Mem. NEA (Mo. bd. dirs. 1979-86, pres. Wentzville chpt. 1977-78, 79-80, 91-93), Nat. Coun. Social Studies Educators, Am. Film Inst., Soc. Am. Baseball Rsch. (bd. dirs. Bob Broeg chpt., chpt. pres. 1991-92, Nat. Conv. chair 1992, nat. bd. dirs. 1994-98, nat. convention com. chair 1994-98), Am. Hosta Soc., Am. Hemerocallis Soc., St. Louis Sports Collectors Club (pres. 1980-81). Democrat. Avocations: collecting baseball, music and movie memorabilia, collecting books, film archivist and collector. Personal E-mail: ncksalamon@charter.net.

**SALAMONE, JOSEPH CHARLES,** polymer chemistry professor; b. Bklyn., Dec. 27, 1939; s. Joseph John and Angela (Barbagallo) S.; children: Robert, Alicia, Christopher. BS in Chemistry, Hofstra U., 1961; PhD in Chemistry, Poly. Inst. N.Y., 1967. NIH postdoctoral fellow U. Liverpool, England, 1966-67; rsch. assoc., Horace H. Rackham postdoctoral fellow U. Mich., Ann Arbor, 1967-70, adminstrv. sec., 1968-70; asst. prof., then assoc. prof. chemistry U. Mass., Lowell, 1970-76, prof., 1976-90, prof. emeritus, 1990—, dean Coll Sci., 1978-84, Disting. Rsch. fellow, 1984-90, chmn. dept. chemistry, 1975-78. Pres. Optimers Inc., Lowell, 1985-99; bd. dirs. Rochal Industries, Inc., Boca Raton, Fla.; cons. editor CRC Press, Inc., Boca Raton, 1992-97; v.p. chem. rsch. Bausch and Lomb, 1997-2000, v.p. rsch., 2000-2005, v.p. and spl. adv., 2006. Author 2 books, 2 encys.; mem. editl. bd. Polymer, 1976-94, Jour. Macromolecular Sci.-Chemistry, 1985-2003, Progress of Polymer Sci., 1987-2002, ChemTech, 1995-99; adv. bd. Jour. Polymer Sci., 1974—; editor-in-chief Polymeric Materials Ency., 1993-97; contbr. over 170 articles to profl. jours.; holder 150 U.S. and internat. patents. Recipient Disting. Alumnus award Poly. Inst. N.Y., 1984, Herman F. Mark award for Recognition of Work in Applied Tech., Poly. U., 2005. Fellow Am. Inst. Med. and Biol. Engring. (chmn. industry coun.); mem. Am. Chem. Soc. (chmn. divsn. polymer chemistry 1982, Indsl. Chemistry award 2004), Polymer Sci., Am. Acad. Ophthalmology (assoc.), Pacific Polymer Fedn. (sec., treas. 1988-90, dep. v.p. 1991-92, v.p., 1993, pres. 1994-95), Soc. Biomaterials (Clemson award for applied rsch.). Office Phone: 585-338-8119. Business E-mail: joe_salamone@bausch.com.

**SALAND, DEBORAH,** psychotherapist, educator; b. Val Dosta, Ga., July 25, 1954; d. Charles and Audrey (Horan) Gianniny. B in Profl. Studies, Barry U., 1990, MSW, 1992; D in Psychology, So. Calif. Sch. Profl. Studies, 1996. Lic. clin. social worker, Fla.; cert. addictions profl.; cert. master addiction specialist; diplomat Am. Psychotherapy Assn.; cert. forensic sentence mitigation specialist; cert. forensic addictions specialist; cert. group psychotherapist. Substance abuse counselor Spectrum Programs, Ft. Lauderdale, Fla., 1974—79; owner Obsession in Time, Miami, Fla., 1984-89, clin. dir. Interphase Recovery, Miami, 1988—89; substance abuse counselor Transitions Recovery, Miami, 1989—91; clin. dir. level II Pathways Treatment, Miami; pvt. practice Inst. Human Potential, Miami, 1993—; founder Eating Disorder Tex. Program, 1997—. Lectr. Addiction Trainsin Inst. U. Miami, 1992, mem. faculty, 1993—; clin. supr. Transitions Recovery, Miami, 1993—; Treatment Resources, Miami, 1993-94; adj. faculty N.Y. Inst. Tech., Boca Raton, Fla., 1997—; dir. Am. Family Eating Disorder Tract, 1997-98. Contbr. articles to profl. jours. Named Spl. Alumni Barry U., 1996. Mem. NASW, APA, Am. Group Psychotherapy Assn. (clin.). Med. Psychotherapist Am. (assoc. clin.) Nat. Bd. Cert. Counselors (counselor), Broward County Mental Health Assn. Office: Inst Human Potential 19501 NE 10th Ave Ste 305 Miami FL 33179-3502 Office Phone: 305-653-1716.

**SALANS, CARL FREDRIC,** lawyer; b. Chicago Heights, Ill., Mar. 13, 1933; arrived in France, 1972; s. Leon and Jean (Rudnick) Salans; m. Edith Motel, Sept. 26, 1956; children: Eric Lee, Marc Robert, Christopher John. AB, Harvard U., 1954; BA, Cambridge U., Eng., 1956, MA, 1958, LLB, 1958; JD, U. Chgo., 1957. Bar: Ill. 1958, D.C. 1973, U.S. Supreme Ct. 1972, (admitted in France as conseil juridique) 1974, (admitted in France as avocat) 1992. With State Dept., 1959-72, dep. legal adviser, 1966-72; practice law Paris, 1972—; ret. ptnr. Salans & Assocs., Paris, 1978—. Legal adviser U.S. del. Vietnam Peace Talk, Paris, 1968—71; vice-chmn. ICC Internat. Ct. Arbitration; arbitrator internat. cases; arbitrator U.S.-Iran Claims Tribunal, The Hague; mem. editl. bd. ICC Arbitration Bulletin. Mem.: ABA (chmn. com. East-West trade and investment 1975—82), London (Eng.) Ct. Internat. Arbitration, Swiss Arbitration Assn., Am. Arbitration Assn. (panel arbitrators), Am. Soc. Internat. Law, Am. C. of C. in France (bd. dirs. 1977—87, chmn. laws and pub. affairs com. 1980—85). Home: 18 Ave Raphael 75016 Paris France Office: Salans & Assocs 9 Rue Boissy d'Anglas 75008 Paris France Office Phone: 33 1 42 68 48 00. E-mail: csalans@salans.com.

**SALANS, LESTER BARRY,** physician, research scientist, educator; b. Chicago Heights, Ill., Jan. 25, 1936; s. Leon K. and Jean (Rudnick) S.; m. Lois Audrey Kapp, Dec. 21, 1958; children: Laurence Eliot, Andrea Eileen. BA, U. Mich., 1957; MD with honors, U. Ill., 1961. Internal medicine intern Stanford U. Med. Ctr., 1961, resident, 1962-64; USPHS postdoctoral and spl. fellow Rockefeller U., 1964-67, asst. prof., 1967-68; asst. prof. medicine

Dartmouth Coll., 1968-70, assoc. prof., 1970-77; assoc. dir. diabetes, endocrinology, metabolism, also chief lab. cellular metabolism and obesity Nat. Inst. Arthritis, Metabolism and Digestive Diseases, NIH, Bethesda, Md., 1976-81; adj. prof. Dartmouth Coll., 1978-79; dir. Nat. Inst. Arthritis, Diabetes, Digestive and Kidney Diseases, NIH, 1981-84; adj. prof. Rockefeller U., 1984—; v.p., head preclin. rsch. Sandoz Rsch. Inst., 1985-92; dean Mt. Sinai Sch. Medicine, 1984, prof. internal medicine, 1984-85, clin. prof. medicine, 1987—; v.p. scientific and acad. affairs Sandoz Rsch. Inst., 1993-97; pres. LBS Advisors, Inc., 1997—; prin. BioPharmAnalysis LLC, 2001—, Biopharmanalysis, LLC, 2001; adj. prof. dept. medicine Columbia U. Med. Ctr., 2005—. Adj. prof. Rockefeller U., 1985—2001; vis. prof. U. Geneva, Switzerland, 1974—75; dir. Forest Labs., 1998—; mem. adv. bd. Naomi Berrie Diabetes Ctr. Columbia-Presbyn. Hosp., N.Y.C., 1999—; adj. prof. medicine dept. medicine cool physicians and surgeons Columbia U. Med. Ctr., 2005—. Contbr. articles on insulin, diabetes mellitus, obesity to profl. jours., textbooks. Recipient NIH Rsch. Career Devel. award, 1972-76, NIH Dir. award, 1980, Juvenile Diabetes Fedn Pub. Svc. award, 1979 Fellow ACP; mem. AAAS, AAAS, Am. Soc. Clin. Investigation, Am. Fed. Clin. Rsch., Am. Diabetes Soc., Am. Diabetes Assn. (Charles H. Best award 1985), Endocrine Soc., Assn. Am. Physicians, Am. Soc. Clin. Nutrition. Office: 767 Fifth Ave Ste 11-64 11th fl New York NY 10153

SALANT, JONATHAN D., reporter; b. NYC, Feb. 15, 1954; s. Harry and Claire Leatrice (Weinstock) S.; m. Joan Friedenberg; 1 child, Isaac. BA in Polit. Sci., SUNY, Stony Brook, 1976; MS in Journalism, Columbia U., 1978. Reporter Bergen Record, Hackensack, NJ, 1976-78, Miami Herald, 1978-81; st. capitol reporter Albany (N.Y.) Times Union, 1981-84, Syracuse Herald Jour., 1984-87; Washington reporter Syracuse Newspapers, 1987-94; reporter Congressional Quar., 1994-97, AP, 1997—2004, Bloomberg News, 2004—. Contbg. editor: Capital Region mag., 1986—89; Washington editor: Empire State Report, 1997—2001. Contbr. U.S. Holocaust Mus., Washington, 1994—, United Jewish Appeal Fedn. Greater Washington, 1988—; sec. Standing Com. of Corr., Washington, 1991-92; mem. B;nai Israel Congregation, Rockville, Md. Recipient Reporting awards AP, 1984-85, 89-91, Syracuse Press Club, 1984-87, 89, 91; Paul Miller fellowship Freedom Forum, 1988-89. Mem. Nat. Press Club (speakers com. chair 1992-93, profl. affairs com. chair 1993-95, reporting awards 1990, 92, chair Freedom of Press com. 1996; forums com. vice-chmn. 1997, bd. govs. 1998—, vice chmn. 2001, chmn. 2002, treas. 2004, v.p. 2005, pres. 2006), Soc. Profl. Journalists (sec. of chpt. 1991-92, v.p. 1992-93, pres. D.C. chpt. 1993-94), Am. Polit. Items Collectors. pres., Regional Reporters Assn., 1992. Jewish. Avocations: political button collector, softball and baseball coach. Home: 5504 Thornbush Ct Bethesda MD 20814 Office: Bloomberg 1399 New York Ave Washington DC 20005 E-mail: jds15@aol.com.*

SALANT, RICHARD FRANK, mechanical engineer, educator; b. N.Y.C., Sept. 4, 1941; s. Joseph and Augusta (Dick) S.; m. Barbel Lang, Sept. 9, 1962; children: Scott M., Stephanie. BS, MS, MIT, 1963, ScD, 1967. Registered profl. engr., Ga. Asst. prof. U. Calif. Berkeley, 1966-68; asst. prof., assoc. prof. MIT, Cambridge, 1968-72; mgr. fluid mech. and heat transfer Borg-Warner Rsch. Ctr., Des Plaines, Ill., 1972-87; prof., chair tribology rsch. group Ga. Inst. Tech., Atlanta, 1987—; Ga. Power Disting. prof., 2001—. Cons. fluid sealing tech., Atlanta, 1987—. Assoc. editor Jour. Tribology, 1993-99, Jour. Fluids Engring., 1984-87; contbr. articles to profl. jours.; patentee in field. Fellow ASME (Henry R. Worthington medal 1996, Machine Design award 2003), Soc. Tribologists and Lubrication Engrs. (Edmond E. Bisson award 2000, Frank P. Bussick award 2002, 05). Home: 1138 Manning Farms Ct Dunwoody GA 30338-2648 Office: Ga Inst Tech Sch Mech Engring Atlanta GA 30332-0405 Business E-Mail: richard.salant@me.gatech.edu

SALAS, GUILLERMO, biologist, educator, medical technician; b. Santa Barbara, Chihuahua, Mexico, June 23, 1959; arrived in U.S., 1972; s. Cristino and Irene Salas; m. Rosa Isela Sanchez, Aug. 16, 1985; children: Joel, Omar. BS in Med. Tech., U. Tex., El Paso, 1982, MS, 1996. Cert. med. tech. Am. Soc. for Clin. Pathology, 1982. Med. technologist chemistry dept. Pathlab - Nichols Inst. Reference Lab., El Paso, 1982—88; med. technologist microbiology dept. Corning - Quest Diagnostics Reference Lab., El Paso, 1988—99; biomedical rsch. asst. U. Tex., El Paso, 1999—2001, clin. microbiology instr., 2001—03; biol. sciences instr. Pk. U., El Paso, 1999—2000, El Paso C.C., 1997—. City coord. World Wide Marriage Encounters (Hispanic version), El Paso, 2001—03. Mem.: Am. Soc. for Microbiology (assoc.), Am. Soc. for Clin. Pathology (assoc.). Roman Catholic. Avocations: reading, swimming, racquetball, softball, scuba diving. Home: 2081 Shadow Ridge Dr El Paso TX 79938 Office: El Paso Community College PO Box 20500 El Paso TX 79998-0500 Office Phone: 915-831-7106. Personal E-mail: gisal3733@aol.com. Business E-Mail: gsalas18@cp.epcc.edu.

SALAS, MAX, pediatrician, educator; MD, Nat. U. Mex., Mexico City, 1964. Diplomate Am. Bd. Pediats., 1969, Am. Bd. Pediatric Endocrinology, 1986. Rotating intern St. Luke's Hosp., St. Paul, 1963—64; resident in pediat. Children's Hosp., Boston, 1965—67, Sheffield, England, 1967—68; fellow in pediatric endocrinology Pitts. Children's Hosp., 1977—79, North Shore Univ. Hosp., Manhasset, NY, 1979—80; assoc. prof. pediat. UMDNJ/Robert Wood Johnson Med. Sch., New Brunswick, NJ, 1980—. Office: St Peters Univ Hosp 254 Easton Ave New Brunswick NJ 08901-1977 Office Phone: 732-745-8574. Personal E-mail: dr.maxsalas@comcast.net.

SALAS, RANDALL NOUEL, automotive company executive; b. Willemstad, Curazao, Venezuela, Oct. 20, 1945; s. Herbert and Claire (Nouel) S.; m. Silvia M. Mago, Feb. 16, 1974; children: Maria Silvia, Claudia Isabella. Student, Santiago de León, Caracas, Venezuela, 1965; BS in Indsl. Engring., Cath. U., Caracas, 1971, BA in Journalism, 1976. Pilots coordinating engr. Gen. Motors de Venezuela, Caracas, 1971-73, methods engr., 1973-76, gen. supply products facilitator, 1976-78, products facility mgr., 1978-80, prodn. mgr., 1980-81, dir. personnel, 1981-86, dir. personnel and pub. govtl. relations, v.p., 1987-97; human resources and pub. rels. v.p. Orinoco Iron-Sivensa, Caracas, 1997—. Bd. dirs. Camara Automotriz de Venezuela, Caracas. Named to Labor Merit Order 1st Degree, Ministry of Labor, 1987. Mem. Col. Engrs. Venezuela, Assn. Venezolana de Ejecutivos, Nat. Assn. Indsl. Relations Execs. Clubs: Lagunita Country (Caracas). Roman Catholic. Avocation: reading. Office: Sivensa Av Venezuela Torre America Piso 14 Bello Monte Caracas 1060 Venezuela Address: c/o SDP (OI) 14505 Commerce Way Ste 700 Miami Lakes FL 33016-1514 Office Phone: 212-707-6285. Business E-Mail: rsalas@orinoco-iron.com.

SALAT, CRISTINA, writer; b. NYC; Student, L.I. U. Founder Shark Prodns., 1998—, Kulana Affordable Artists Sanctuary, Hawaii, 1999—. Freelance editor, 1987—; author, editor, manuscript cons., workshop facilitator, 1985—. Author: Living in Secret, 1993, Alias Diamond Jones, 1993, Min Mors Koereste hedder Janey, 1995, Peanut's Emergency, 2002; contbr. to anthologies including Sister/Stranger, 1993, Am I Blue, 1994, Once Upon A Time, 1996, Higher Learning, 2001; contbr. to popular publ. Office Phone: 808-985-9055. E-mail: discoverkulana@yahoo.com.

SALAVERRIA, HELENA CLARA, retired language educator; b. May 19, 1923; d. Blas Saturnino and Eugenia Irene (Izaguirre) S. AB, U. Calif., Berkeley, 1945, secondary tchg. cert., 1946; MA, Stanford U., 1962. H.S. tchr., 1946-57; asst. prof. Luther Coll., Decorah, Iowa, 1959-60; prof. Spanish Bakersfield (Calif.) Coll., 1961—83, chmn. dept., 1973-80; ret., 1983. Mem. srs. adv. group on Cuesta Coll. Cmty. Svcs. Mem. AAUW (edn. com.), NEA, Calif. Fgn. Lang. Tchrs. Assn. (dir. 1976-77), Kern County Fgn. Lang. Tchrs. Assn. (pres. 1975-77), Union Concerned Scientists, Natural Resources Def. Coun., Calif. Tchrs. Assn. (chpt. sec. 1951-52), Yolo County Coun. Retarded, Soc. Basque Studies in Am., RSVP, Amnesty Internat., Common Cause, Sierra Club, Prytanean Alumnae, U. Women of Cambria, U. Calif. Alumni Assn., Stanford U. Alumni Assn., Friends of the Cambria Libr. Democrat. Home: PO Box 63 Cambria CA 93428-0063

SALAZAR, JOHN PAUL, lawyer; b. Albuquerque, Feb. 6, 1943; s. Henry Houghton and Anita (Chavez) Salazar; m. Terri J. Bestgen, June 12, 1967; children: Monique Michelle, John Paul, Stephen Houghton. BA, U. N.Mex., 1965; JD, Stanford U., 1968. Bar: N.Mex. 1968, U.S. Dist. Ct. N.Mex. 1968, U.S. Ct. Appeals (10th cir.) 1968, U.S. Supreme Ct. 1979. Dir. Rodey, Dickason, Sloan, Akin & Robb, P.A., Albuquerque, 1968—, mem. exec. com., 1984—86, mng. dir., west side office, 1985—88, chmn., environ. law sect., 1989—92, mem. exec. com., 1992—93, chair, environ. and natural resources dept., 1992—95, mem. exec. com., 1999—, chair, bus. dept., 2000—. Bd. visitors Stanford U. Law Sch., Calif., 1973—76; state campaign chmn. Jeff Bingaman for Atty. Gen., 1978, Jeff Bingaman for U.S. Sen., 1982, 88, 94, 2000; mem. presdl. search com. U. N.Mex., 1989—90; mem. Albuquerque Econ. Forum, past chair, gov. affairs com., 1990—96, past mem. bd. dirs., 1991—94, past vice chair, 1992—93; former hon. Cmdr. Field Command Def. Nuc. Agy., Kirtland AFB. Sr. editor N.Mex. Environ. Law Handbook, 1990, 2d edit., 1991, 3d edit., 1993. Former bd. dirs. N.Mex. Symphony Orch.; former mem. Easter Seal Soc.; vice chmn. City of Albuquerque Charter Revision com., 1970—71; mem. Albuquerque Unity, 1971—73; chmn. N.Mex. Disting. Pub. Svc. Awards Coun., 1986, 1987; chmn. city affairs com. Greater Albuquerque C. of C., 1972, v.p. govtl. affairs, 1973, pres.-elect, 1974, pres., 1975; mem. Presbyn. Hosp. Ctr. Assocs.; bd. dirs. Albuquerque Hispano C. of C., 2000—, vice-chair, 2001—04, chair, 2005. Mem.: ABA (environ. aspects of real estate transactions com., land use regulation com., real property, probate & trust law sect., land use planning & zoning com., state & local govt. sect.), Albuquerque Armed Forces Adv. Assn., U. N.Mex. Alumni Assn. (bd. dirs. 1979—85, exec. com. 1982—85, pres. 1983—84), Nat. Assn. Indsl. and Office Parks (govs. bus. adv. coun. 1991—94, past mem. N.Mex. border commn., past chair com. border devel. and internat. trade, mem. exec. com.), N.Mex. State Bar Assn. (former mem. jud. selection com., mem. Real Property, Probate and Trust sect., mem. Pub. Law sect., mem. Natural Resources, Energy and Environ. Law sect., former sec., treas. Young Lawyers sect.), Albuquerque Bar Assn. (former mem. jud. selection com., former dir.). Roman Catholic. Office: Rodey Dickason Sloan Akin & Robb PA PO Box 1888 Albuquerque NM 87103-1888 Office Phone: 505-768-7220. Office Fax: 505-768-7395. Business E-Mail: jsalazar@rodey.com.

SALAZAR, JOHN T., congressman; b. Alamosa, Colo., July 21, 1953; m. Mary Lou Salazar; children: Jesus, Esteban, Miguel. BSBA, Adams State Coll., 1981; class III grad., Colo. Agrl. Leadership Program, 1993; grad., Rapport Leadership Program, 1997. Owner & operator El Rancho Salazar; state rep. dist. 62 Colo. Ho. of Reps., Denver, 2002—04, mem. agr., livestock and natural resources, and info. and tech. coms.; mem. U.S. Congress from 3d Colo. dist., 2005—; mem. Agriculture com. and Transp. and Infrastructure U.S. Ho. Reps. Youth work group co-coord. Mi Esperanza Mentoring Program; chair seed export com. Colo Cert. Seed Growers; commr. Colo. State Agrl. Commn.; bd. dirs. Gov.'s Econ. Devel. Adv. Bd., Rio Grande Water Conservation Dist.; youth leadership athletic dir. St. Joseph's Parish. Served U.S. Army, 1973—76. Democrat. Roman Catholic. Office: US Ho Reps 1531 Longworth Ho Office Bldg Washington DC 20515-0603 also: Dist Office Ste 702 225 N 5th St Grand Junction CO 81501 Office Phone: 202-225-4761. Office Fax: 202-226-9669.*

SALAZAR, KEN LEE (KENNETH LEE SALAZAR), senator, former state attorney general; b. Alamosa, Colo., Mar. 2, 1955; s. Henry and Emma Salazar; m. Hope Hernandez; 3 children. BA in Polit. Sci., Colo. Coll., 1977; JD, U. Mich., 1981; LLD (hon.), Colo. Coll., 1993. Bar: Colo. 1981, U.S. Dist. Ct. Colo. 1981, U.S. Ct. Appeals (10th cir.) 1981, U.S. Supreme Ct. 1999. Farmer, rancher, Conejos County, Colo.; law clk. to atty. gen. State of Colo., Denver, 1979, chief legal counsel to gov., 1986—90, exec. dir. Dept. Natural Resources, 1990—94, atty. gen., 1999—2005; assoc. Sherman & Howard, Denver, 1981—86; dir. Parcel, Mauro, Hultin & Spaanstra, Denver, 1994—98; US Senator from Colo., 2005—. Gov.'s rep. State Bd. Equalization, Denver, 1990; mem. com. agr., nutrition, and forestry US Senate. com. energy and natural resources, com. veterans affairs, spl. com. ethics, spl. com. aging. Mem. Israel Friendship League, 1986—89; chair Great Outdoors Colo., Denver, 1993—94, Rio Grande Compact Commn., 1995—97, Sangre de Cristo Land Grant Commn., 1993—95; mem. Colo. Water Conservation Bd., Denver, 1990—, City and County of Denver Ethics Panel, 1993; gov.'s rep. State Bd. on Property Tax Equalization, 1987—91; del. Soviet-Am. Young Leadership Dialogue, 1984; mem. adv. com. Colo. U. Sch. Law Natural Resources Law Ctr., 1989—92; mem. Western Water Policy Rev. Adv. Commn., 1995—97; bd. dirs. Denver Cmty. Leadership Forum, 1988, Servicios de la Raza HUD 202 Project, 1985—89, chair, 1986. Recipient Friend of the First award, Colo. Press Assn., Profiles in Courage award, Conf. West Atty. Generals, Judge Learned Hand Human Relations award, Am. Jewish Com. Colo. Chapter, 2001; scholar Juan Tienda. Mem.: ABA, Am. Judicature Soc., Hispanic Bar Assn. (ABA task force on opportunities for minorities in legal profession, bd. dirs. 1986—87), Denver Bar Assn. (2d v.p. 1989, chair policy-cmty. rels. subcoms. 1982—84), Colo. Bar Assn. (bd. govs. 1989—90, task force to assess the legal profession 1986). Democrat. Roman Catholic. Avocations: basketball, outdoor activities, politics. Office: US Senate B40A Dirksen Senate Office Bldg Washington DC 20510 also: District Office Ste 450 2300 15th St Denver CO 80202-1184 Office Phone: 202-224-5852, 719-328-1100. Office Fax: 719-328-1129, 202-228-5036. E-mail: attorney.general@state.co.us.*

SALAZAR, LUIS, management consultant, lawyer; BA, Drew U., Madison, NJ, 1989; JD, Columbia U., NYC, 1992; MBA, U. Miami, Coral Gables, Fla., 2004. Assoc. Cole Schotz Meisel Forman & Leonard, Hackensack, Fla., 1992—97; shareholder Greenberg Traurig, Miami, Fla., 1997—. Pres. Latino Turnaround and Insolvency Network, Miami, 2002—. Mem.: Am. Bankruptcy Inst. Achievements include Drafter, Privacy Policy Enforcement in Bankruptcy Act of 2001. Office: Greenberg Traurig 1221 Brickell Ave Miami FL 33131 Office Phone: 305-579-0751. Office Fax: 305-962-5751. E-mail: salazarl@gtlaw.com.

SALAZAR-CARRILLO, JORGE, economics professor; b. Jan. 17, 1938; arrived in U.S., 1960; s. Jose Salazar and Ana Maria Carrillo; m. Maria Eugenia Winthrop, Aug. 30, 1959; children: Jorge, Manning, Mario, Maria Eugenia. BBA, U. Miami, 1958; MA in Econs., U. Calif. Berkeley, 1964; cert. in econ. planning, U. Calif., 1964, PhD in Econs., 1967. Sr. fellow, non-resident staff mem. Brookings Instn., Washington, 1965—. Dir., mission chief UN, Rio de Janeiro, 1974—80; prof. econs. Fla. Internat. U., Miami, 1980—, chmn. dept. econs., 1980—89; dir. Ctr. Econ. Rsch. & Edn.; former mem. coun. econ. advisors State of Fla.; advisor USIA; former advisor, contbg. editor Libr. of Congress, Washington; chmn. program com. Hispanic Profs. of Econs. and Bus.; cons. econs. AID, Washington, 1979—; former coun. mem. Internat. Assn. Housing, Vienna, 1981—; former exec. bd. Cuban Am. Nat. Coun., Miami, 1982—; bd. dirs. pres. Fla. chpt. Insts. of Econ. and Social Rsch. of Caribbean Basin, 1983—, U.S.-Chile Coun., Miami, 1984—, Fla.-Brazil Inst. Co-author: Trade, Debt and Growth in Latin America, 1984, Prices for Estimation in Cuba, 1985, The Foreign Debt and Latin America, 1983, External Debt and Strategy of Development in Latin America, 1985, The Brazilian Economy in the Eighties, 1987, Foreign Investment, Debt and Growth in Latin America, 1988, World Comparisons of Incomes, Prices and Product, 1988, Comparisons of Prices and Real Products in Latin America, 1990, The Latin American Debt, 1992, International Comparisons of Prices, Output and Productivity, 1996, Capital Markets, Growth and Economic Policy in Latin America, 1999, Growth in Latin America in the 1990s, 2000, Macroeconomics, 2001, Social Christian Doctrine and Econ. Devel., 2002; author: Wage Structure in Latin America, 1982, Oil and Development of Venezuela During the Twentieth Century, 1994. Fellow, Brit. Coun., London, 1960, Georgetown U., Washington, 1961—62, OAS, Washington, 1962—64, Brookings Instn., Washington, 1964—65. Mem.: Collegium of Cuban Economists (1st v.p.), Cuban Banking Study Group (dir.), Assn. for Study Cuban Economy (former mem. exec. com.), Nat. Assn. Forensic Economists, Internat. Assn. Energy Economists, Nat. Assn. Cuban Am. Educators (exec. com.), N.Am. Econs. and Fin. Assn., Econometric Soc. Latin Am., Am. Econ.

SALAZAR-TIO, RAFAEL, physicist, researcher; b. Lima, Peru, Sept. 3, 1971; s. Salazar-Andia Miguel and Carmen Lidda Tio-Negri; m. Elizabeth Blancas-Medina, June 10, 1996; 1 child, Mariajose Salazar-Blancas. MS in Physics, Nat. U. San Marcos, Lima, Peru, 1995; PhD in Physics, U. Balear Island, Palma de Mallorca, Spain, 2000; degree in Fin., Wash. U., St. Louis, Mo., 2005. Asst. prof. U. Balearic Islands, Palma de Mallorca, Spain, 1998—2000; rsch. assoc. Tech. U. Eindhoven, Eindhoven, Netherlands, 2000—02; assoc. prof. Nat. U. San Marcos, Lima, Peru, 2003—03; rsch. assoc. Washington U., St. Louis, 2003—06; sr. scientist Chevron, San Ramon, Calif., 2006—. Contbr. articles to profl. jours. Fellow, AECI, Spain, 1995, 2000; scholar, 1995—98. Office: Chevron ETC D 2332 6001 Bollinger Canyon Rd San Ramon CA 94583 Office Phone: 925-842-3122. E-mail: rswz@chevron.com.

SALBY, MURRY L, atmospheric and oceanic sciences professor; s. Harry Salby; 1 child, Alon M. PhD, Ga. Tech. Prof. dept. atmospheric and oceanic scis. U. Colo., Boulder, 1984—. Office: Univ Colo Stadium Rm 255 Boulder CO 80309 Office Phone: 303-492-6487.

SALCEDO, JOSE RODOLFO, nephrologist; b. Guadalajara, Jal, Mex., June 15, 1945; came to U.S., 1971; s. Rodolfo Salcedo-Moreno and Sara (Contreras) Moya; m. Uma T. Salcedo, Nov. 8, 1974; children: Nicholas A., Jonathan E. BA, U. Guadalajara, 1964, MD, 1970. Diplomate Am. Bd. Pediatrics, Pediatric Nephrology. Resident Martland Hosp., Newark, 1971-74; fellow in nephrology Children's Hosp., Washington, 1974-76, acting dir. pediatric nephrology, dir. dialysis unit, 1976-87, vice chmn., 1978—87; dir. pediatric nephrology divsn. N.J. Med. Sch., Newark, 1987-96; chief pediat. nephrology St. Joseph's Children's Hosp., Paterson, NJ, 1996—; assoc. prof. clin. pediats. and medicine U. Medicine and Dentistry NJ. Contbr. chpts. in books and articles to profl. jours. Office: St Joseph's Children's Hosp 703 Main St Paterson NJ 07503-2621 E-mail: salcedoj@sjhmc.org

SALCETTI, MARIANNE, newswriter, educator; d. Robert Anthony Salcetti and Mary Jane Lusher; m. Michael Mrkvicka, May 21, 1977 (div. Mar. 1985); 1 child, Jacob Gene Mrkvicka; m. Dale Rhines, Mar. 18, 1989 (div. June 1995); 1 child, Amalia Margaret Rhines. BA in Polit. Sci., Ohio State U., 1972, MA in Journalism, 1975; PhD in Mass. Comm., U. Iowa, 1992. Editor Franklinton News, Columbus, Ohio, 1974—76; beat reporter Chillicothe (Ohio) Gazette, 1976—77; investigative and health reporter Colorado Springs Gazette Telegraph, 1977—78; editor, co-owner The Weekly News, Johnson County, Iowa, 1980—82; instr. U. Iowa Sch. Journalism and Mass Comm., Iowa City, 1982—87; adj. faculty John Carroll U. and Ursuline Coll., Cleve., 1988—89; asst. prof. dept. comm. John Carroll U., Cleve., 1990—2000; contbg. writer The Cleve. Free Times, 1995—98; spl. projects editor The Garden City (Kans.) Telegram, 2000—02; comm. cons. Water Preservation Com., Finney County, Kans., 2002; investigator-rschr. Rebein & Bangerter, Attys. at Law, Dodge City, 2002—. Editl. radio commentator KSUI/WSUI, 1984—87; Presdl. election commentator WHK, Cleve., 1992; legis. prodr.-reporter State Capitol Update High Plains Pub. Radio, 2003; asst. prof. journalism Keene (N.H.) State Coll., 2003—; lectr. and presenter in field. Contbr. articles to profl. jours. V.p. Greater Cleve. Labor History Soc., 1997—99. Recipient Investigative Reporting award, Inland Daily Press Assn., 1977, Best News Story of the Yr. award, Iowa Press Assn., 1980, Silver Gavel award, ABA, 1981, Nat. Scholar award, Gannett Found., 1986, 1st pl. consumer reporting, Ohio Soc. Profl. Journalists, 1998, 2nd pl. best explanatory journalism, 1998, two honorable mentions, Enterprise News, 2001, honorable mention, Spot News, 2001, Bus. Reporting, 2002; Grauel Faculty fellow, John Carroll, 1995, John F. Murray Dissertation Rsch. grantee, George Meany Meml. Archives, AFL-CIO, 1987. Mem.: Kappa Tau Alpha. Avocations: reading, kayaking, gardening. Home: 272 South St Troy NH 03465 Office: Keene State Coll 229 Main St Keene NH 03435 Office Phone: 603-358-2724. Business E-Mail: msalcetti@keene.edu.

SALCH, STEVEN CHARLES, lawyer, mediator, arbitrator; b. Palm Beach, Fla., Oct. 25, 1943; s. Charles Henry and Helen Louise (Alverson) S.; m. Mary Ann Prim, Oct. 7, 1967; children: Susan Elizabeth, Stuart Trenton. BBA, So. Meth. U., 1965, JD, 1968. Bar: Tex. 1968, U.S. Dist. Ct. Tex. 1969, U.S. Dist. Ct. (so. dist.) Tex. 1969, U.S. Dist. Ct. (ea. dist.) Tex. 1972, U.S. Ct. Appeals (5th cir.) 1969, U.S. Ct. Appeals (fed. cir.) 1982, U.S. Ct. Fed. Claims, 1982. Assoc. Fulbright & Jaworski, Houston, 1968-71, participating assoc., 1971-75, ptnr., 1975—. Mem. panel of disting. neutrals CPR Inst. Co-author: Tax Practice Before the IRS, 1994; contbr. articles to legal jours. Pres. Tealwood Owners Assn., 1982—83, Meml. H.S. PTA, 1985—86; hon. life mem. Tex. PTA, 1986—; mem. devel. bd. U. Tex. Med. Br., Galveston, 2002—; adv. dir. 1894 Grand Opera House Soc., 2002—, co-chmn. adv. bd., 2004—05. Mem.: ABA (coun. dir. 1985—88, vice chair tax sect. 1988—91, chair tax sect. 1996—97), Houston Bar Found., Am. Bar Found., Internat. Fiscal Assn., Am. Coll. Tax Counsel (regent 5th cir. 1999—2006, sec.-treas. 2006—), Am. Law Inst., Fed. Bar Assn., Houston Bar Assn., State Bar Tex., Theodore Tannenwald Foundation (trustee 2000—), Colonial Williamsburg Found., Menard Soc., Pelican Club Galveston, Yacht Club, Houston Downtown Club, Galveston Country Club, Order of Coif, Phi Delta Phi, Phi Eta Sigma, Beta Alpha Psi. Presbyterian. Home: 4600 Caduceus Pl Galveston TX 77551-5719 Office: PO Box 3870 Galveston TX 77552 Office Phone: 713-651-5433. Business E-Mail: ssalch@fulbright.com. Set goals for yourself. Unless you know where you are and where you want to be in life, you will not be able to map a plan to accomplish your goals.

SALCUDEAN, MARTHA EVA, mechanical engineer, educator; b. Cluj, Romania, Feb. 26, 1934; arrived in Can., 1976, naturalized, 1979; d. Edmund and Sarolta (Hirsch) Abel; m. George Salcudean, May 28, 1955; 1 child, Septimiu E. BEng, U. Cluj, 1956, postgrad., 1962; PhD, U. Brasov, Romania, 1969; DSc (hon.), U. Ottawa, Ont., Can., 1992, U. B.C., Can., 2001. Mech. engr. Armatura, Cluj, 1956-63; sr. rsch. officer Nat. Rsch. Inst. Metallurgy, Bucharest, 1963-75; part-time lectr. Inst. Poly., Bucharest, 1967-75; sessional lectr. U. Ottawa, 1976-77, from asst. prof. to assoc. prof. to prof., 1977-85; prof., head dept. mech. engring. U. B.C., Vancouver, 1985-93, assoc. v.p. rsch., 1993-96, acting v.p. rsch. pro-tem, 1995, Weyerhausen Indsl. Rsch. chair computational fluid dynamics, 1996—2002, prof., Weyerhausen indsl. chair emerita dept. mech. engring., 2002—. Mem. grant selection com. for mech. engring. Natural Scis. and Engring. Rsch. Coun. Can.; mem. Nat. Adv. Panel to Min. Sci. and Tech. on advanced indsl. materials, Can., 1990; mem. governing coun. NRC; mem. def. sci.e adv. bd. Nat. Def.; chair Sci. Coun. B.C. Contbr. numerous articles to profl. jours. Decorated Order of B.C., 1998; recipient Gold medal B.C. Sci. Coun., Killam Rsch. prize U. B.C.; Rsch. Coun. Can. grantee, 1978—, Commemorative medal 125th anniversary Can. Confederation, 1993, Julian C. Smith medal Engring. Inst. Can., 1994-95, Meritorious Achievement award Assn. Profl. Engrs. & Geoscientists B.C., 1996, Killam Meml. prize engring., 1998. Fellow CSME, Can. Acad. Engring., Royal Soc. Can.; mem. ASME, Assn. Profl. Engrs. Ont., Order of Can. (apptd. officer 2004). Home: 1938 Western Pkwy Vancouver BC Canada V6T 1W5 Office Phone: 604-822-2732. Business E-Mail: msal@mech.ubc.ca.

SALDANA, LISA, psychology professor, consultant; d. Steven Graham Saldana Sr. BA, Reed Coll., Portland, Oreg., 1990—94; MA, U. Mo., Columbia, 1998, PhD, 1994—2003. Psychology intern La Rabida Children's Hosp., Chgo., 2001—03; asst. prof. Family Svcs. Rsch. Ctr., Med. U. S.C., Charleston, 2003—. Clin. cons. MST Svcs., Charleston, 2005—; faculty scholar Ctr. for Health Econ. & Policy Studies, Med. U. S.C., Charleston, 2005—; grant reviewer Substance Abuse & Mental Health Svcs. Adminstrn., 2005; editl. reviews Jour. of Child and Adolescent Substance Abuse, Child Maltreatment, Jour. of Pediatric Psychology; Jour. of Clin. Child and Adolescent Psychology, Families, Systems and Health; expert rater U. Rochester Med. Ctr., 2006—; presenter in field, 1994—. Author: (article)

Journal of Clinical Child and Adolescent Psychology (Clinician's Rsch. Recognition, 2006); contbr. over 25 papers to profl. jours. and pubs., chapters to books. Mentor Med. U. S.C., Charleston, 2003; vol. Angel Covers, Boulder, Colo., 2004; vol., sponsor, mentor Galilee Primary & Secondary Sch., Nairobi, Kenya, 2005; coord., dir. Family Svcs. Rsch. Project, Charleston, 2005. Recipient Cir. of Excellence award, Med. U. S.C., 2005—06, Family Rsch. Consortium, NIMH, 2005; grantee Ridgel fellowship, U. Mo.-Columbia, 1994—98, Minority Rsch. award, NIMH, 2004—, Agy. for Healthcare Rsch. & Quality, 2004—05, Annie E. Casey Found., 2005—. Mem.: APA, Soc. Pediatric Psychology, Assn. Behavior Analysis, Internat. Soc. Traumatic Stress Studies, Am. Profl. Soc. on Abuse of Children. Office: Family Svcs Rsch Ctr Med Univ SC 67 President St-Ste CPP PO Box 250861 Charleston SC 29425 Office Fax: 843-876-1808. Business E-Mail: saldanal@musc.edu.

**SALDANA, MANUEL E., JR.,** school system administrator; b. Findlay, Ohio, Aug. 24, 1945; s. Manuel and Sulema Saldana; m. Anna Laura Mendiola, Nov. 28, 1968; children: Manuel III, Richard Joseph, Ross Anthony, Jenna Sabrina. AA, SW Tex. Jr. Coll., 1965; BS, Sul Ross State U., 1967; M in Edn., Our Lady of the Lake U., 1978. Cert. Mid-Mgmt. in Edn. Tex. Edn. Agy. Math tchr. South San Antonio (Tex.) Ind. Sch. Dist., 1967—73, dir. data processing, 1973—76, asst. prin., 1976—82; dir. fed. programs Asherton (Tex.) Ind. Sch. Dist., 1982—83; math. tchr. Carrizo Springs (Tex.) Cert. Ind. Sch. Dist., 1983—84, asst. prin., 1984—89, prin., 1991—95, dir. fed. programs, 1995—; prin. Pearsall (Tex.) Ind. Sch. Dist., 1989—90. Dir. Even Start Family Literacy, Carrizo Springs; grant coord. Carrizo Springs (Tex.) Cert. Ind. Sch. Dist., nurse coord. Dir.(grant coordinator): Even Start Family Literacy Program (monetary award) 2003. Commn. Housing Authority, Carrizo Springs, 2002—04; bd. mem. City Planning Bd., Carrizo Springs, 2000—02. Fellow Math Summer Inst., Tex. So. U.; Houston, Tex., 1970; Ednl. grant, NSF, 1965-1967. Mem.: Tex. Elem. Prin., Supr. Assn. (corr.). Democrat-Npl. Roman Cath. Avocations: eucharistic minister, gardening, reading, tennis, landscaping. Home: 201 S 18th St Carrizo Springs TX 78834 Office: Carrizo Springs Cert Ind Sch Dist 300 N 7th Carrizo Springs TX 78834 Office Phone: 830-876-3505 1201. Office Fax: 830-876-3619. Business E-Mail: msaldana@cscisd.net.

**SALDANHA, JOHN,** biologist, director; s. Charles and Maisie Saldanha. BSc, Kingston Poly., Kingston-on-Thames, London, 1973; MSc, Reading U., England, 1974, PhD, 1980. Postdoctoral rsch. asst. Withington Hosp., Manchester, England, 1980—83; postdoctoral rsch. fellow Sch. Medicine Royal Free Hosp., London, 1984—87; resaerch fellow Med. Sch. St. Mary's Hosp., London, 1987—90; prin. scientist Nat. Inst. Biol. Standards and Control, South Mimms, England, 1990—2002; exec. dir. infectious diseases Can. Blood Svcs., Ottawa, Ont., Canada, 2002—05; dir. sci. affairs, blood screening Roche Molecular Sys., Pleasanton, Calif., 2005—. Office Phone: 925-730-8230.

**SALDINGER, ANNE GRENN,** cultural organization administrator, psychologist; m. Erez Saldinger, Oct. 11, 1981; children: Adva, Ari. BA in Psychology, U. Calif., Santa Cruz, 1976; BSW, Tel Aviv U., 1981; M in Counseling, Notre Dame de Namur, Belmont, Calif., 1991; PhD in Psychology, Wright Inst., Berkeley, Calif., 1998. Program facilitator Charlla Found., San Francisco, 1977; intern Pardesia Psychiatric Hosp., Netanya, Israel, 1980; social worker, counselor Galilee Cmty. Clinic, Nahariya, Israel, 1983; psychology fellow Stanford U. Counseling and Psychol. Svcs., 1995; exec. dir. Bay Area Holocaust Oral History Project, San Mateo, Calif., 1998—. Author: Life in a Nazi Concentration Camp, 2001. Office: Bay Area Holocaust Oral History Project 1700 Alameda de las Pulgas San Mateo CA 94403 Office Phone: 650-570-6382. E-mail: info@bahohp.org.

**SALDIVAR, ENRIQUE,** bioengineer, researcher; b. Mexico City, May 10, 1960; s. Pedro Saldivar Cadena and Alicia Salazar Flores; m. Adrienne Jane Sardella, Nov. 7, 1992; children: Cassandra Lane, Evan Valentine. MD, Universidad La Salle, 1983; MS, Universidad Autonoma Metropolitana, 1987; PhD, U. Calif., San Diego, 1992. Asst. prof. The Scripps Rsch. Inst., La Jolla, Calif., 1998—, sr. rsch. assoc., 1995—98, rsch. assoc., 1993—95; sr. scientist La Jolla Bioengring. Inst., 2003—. Mem. Whitaker Inst. Biomed. Engring., La Jolla, 1997—; vis. scholar U. Calif., San Diego, 2001—; founder Rainmaker Tech., Santee, Calif., 2001—. Contbr. articles to profl. jours. Recipient Nat. Instrumentation prize, Mexican Soc. Physiol. Scis., 1987, U. Merit medal, Universidad Autonoma Metropolitana, Mex., 1987; scholar, CONACYT, 1985—87, 1988—91, UCSD, 1991—92, Short-Term Invitation fellow for Rsch. in Japan, Japan Soc. for the Promotion of Sci., 1998, grantee, NIH, 1998—2003. Achievements include description and analysis of platelet interaction with surface bound proteins under flow; development of currently worldwide used tecnique to measure forming thrombus volume based on confocal microscopy. Office: La Jolla Bioengring Inst 505 Coast Blvd S La Jolla CA 92037 Business E-Mail: enrique@ljbi.org.

**SALE, GEORGE EDGAR,** pathologist; b. Missoula, Mont., Apr. 18, 1941; s. George Goble and Ruth Edna (Polleys) S.; m. Joan M. Sutliff, 1989; children: George Gregory Colby, Teo Marie Jonsson. AB, Harvard U., 1963; MD, Stanford U., 1968. Intern U. Oreg., Portland, 1968-69; sr. asst. surgeon USPHS, Albuquerque, 1969-71; resident in pathology U. Wash., Seattle, 1971-75, instr. pathology, 1975-78, asst. prof., 1978-81, assoc. prof., 1981-88, prof., 1988—. Asst. mem. faculty clin. divsn. Hutchinson Cancer Ctr., Seattle, 1975-88, assoc., 1988-91, mem., 1991—. Author, editor: Pathology of Bone Marrow Transplantation, 1984, Pathology of Transplantation, 1990. Mem. AAAS, Internat. Acad. Pathology, Coll. Am. Pathologists, Am. Assn. Investigative Pathologists, Physicians for Social Responsibility. Office: Fred Hutchinson Cancer Rsh Ctr G1-309 1100 Fairview Ave N Seattle WA 98109 1417 Office Phone: 206-200-1352 Business E-Mail: gsale@fhcrc.org

**SALE, LLEWELLYN, III,** lawyer; b. St. Louis, May 19, 1942; s. Llewellyn Jr. and Kathleen (Rice) S.; m. Cynthia Jean Bricker, Aug. 17, 1968 (div. Apr. 1995); children: Allyson J., Eryn E. AB cum laude, Yale U., 1964; LLB cum laude, Harvard U., 1967. Bar: Mo. 1967, U.S. Dist. Ct. (ea. dist.) Mo. 1967, U.S. Tax Ct. 1982, U.S. Ct. Claims 1985. From assoc. to ptnr. to mng. ptnr. Husch & Eppenberger, St. Louis, 1967-88; ptnr. Bryan Cave LLP, St. Louis, 1988—2004, of counsel, 2005—. Bd. dirs. Washington U. Child Guidance Clinic, St. Louis, 1978-80, Mental Health Assn. St. Louis, 1988-89. Mem. ABA, Bar Assn. Met. St. Louis (chmn. law econs. subcom. 1982), Noonday Club. Avocations: spectator sports, jogging. Office: Bryan Cave 211 N Broadway Ste 3600 Saint Louis MO 63102-2733 Office Phone: 314-259-2649. Business E-Mail: lsale@bryancave.com.

**SALE, MERRITT,** classicist, educator, comparatist; b. New Haven, Nov. 27, 1929; s. William Merritt and Helen (Stearns) S.; m. Marilyn Mills, June 13, 1953 (div. Oct. 1967); children: Elizabeth, David; m. Anne Perkins, May 18, 1991. BA, Cornell U., 1951, MA, 1954, PhD, 1958. Engr. U.S. Metals Co., Carteret, NJ, 1951-52; instr. in classics Yale U., New Haven, 1957-58; asst. prof., assoc. prof. Washington U. St. Louis, 1958-75, chmn. classics dept., 1961-69, prof. classics and comparative lit., 1975—, chmn. comparative lit. dept., 1981-90. Author: Sophocles' Electra: Commentary with Introduction and Translation, 1970, Existentialism and Euripides, 1977, Homer and the Roland, 1993, The Government of Troy, 1995, The Oral-Formulaic Theory Today, 2006. Recipient Founder's Day award for Excellence in Teaching Washington U., 1978 Mem. Am. Philol. Assn., London Inst. for Classical Studies Home: 2342 Albion Pl Saint Louis MO 63104-2524 Personal E-mail: aperkins@midwest.net.

**SALE, TOM S., III,** financial economist; b. Haynesville, La., July 27, 1942; s. Thomas and Mary Belle (Fagg) S.; divorced; children: Jennifer Elizabeth, Sarah Elaine. BA, Tulane U., 1964; MA, Duke U., 1965; PhD, La. State U., 1972. CFA. Faculty mem. La. Tech. U., Ruston, 1965—75, prof. econs., 1975—98, ret., 1998. Head dept. econs. and fin. La. Tech. U., 1974-86, 90-95, dir. grad. studies Coll. Adminstrn and Bus., 1988-89; fin. cons. Contbr. articles to profl. jours. Mem. Southwestern Fin. Assn. (pres. 1985-86), CFA

Inst. (exam. com. 1983-92, curriculum com. 1993-2004), Fedn. Bus. Disciplines (v.p. 1988-89, pres. 1989-90), CFA Soc. Dalla Fort Worth, Omicron Delta Kappa, Omicron Delta Epsilon. Episcopalian. Home: PO Box 1365 Ruston LA 71273-1365 Personal E-mail: tomsale3@cox.net.

**SALEH, BRIAN BEHROOZ,** aerospace transportation executive; b. Tehran, Iran, Apr. 25, 1939; came to U.S., 1959; m. Farideh Navidi, May 12, 1983. BSEE, Northrop U., Inglewood, Calif., 1967; MBA, Golden Gate U., San Francisco, 1973; instr. credential, Calif. Design engr. radio frequency cirs. Space Systems/Loral, Palo Alto, Calif., 1970—, mgr. GOES Comm. Subsys., 1974-76, program engr. NATO-III Satellite, 1976-79, mgr. Insat Program Engring., 1979-85, mgr. GOES Spacecraft Engring., 1985-91, mgr. GOES Spacecraft, 1991-92, dir. GOES Prodn. Program, 1992-95, dir. Telstar Program, 1995-97, sr. dir. Fixed Svc. Satellite Programs, 1997-98, sr. dir. common products and planning, 1998, sr. exec. dir. CD Radio Program, 1998-99, v.p. program mgmt., 1999—2002; pres. Aerospace Tech., San Jose, Calif., 2002—. Recipient Telstar 5 Program Mgmt. award, Loral Skynet, GOES I-M Project Group Achievement award, NASA, 2002. Personal E-mail: brian@saleh.com.

**SALEH, JOHN,** lawyer; b. O'Donnell, Tex., June 29, 1928; s. Nahum and Arslie S. BBA, U. Tex., 1950, JD with honors, 1952; cert. U.S. Army Judge Advocate Sch., U. Va., 1953. Bar: Tex. 1952, U.S. Ct. Mil. Appeals, 1953, U.S. Tax Ct. 1954, U.S. Dist. Ct. (no. dist.) Tex. 1956, U.S. Ct. Appeals (5th cir.) 1960, U.S. Supreme Ct. 1961, D.C. 1982. Pvt. practice, Lamesa, Tex., 1954—. Tchg. instr. legal rsch. writing U. Tex. Sch. Law, 1950-52 Mem. editl. bd. Tex. Law Rev., 1951-52. Mem. ABA, ATLA, Tex. Law Rev. Assn. (life), Tex. Bar Assn. (spl. com. to study rev. code criminal procedure 1969-71), D.C. Bar Assn., Tex. Trial Lawyers Assn., Tex. Bar Found., Order of the Coif, The Million Dollar Advocates Forum, Phi Delta Phi. Home: 605 Doak Odonnell TX 79351 Office: 502 N 1st St Lamesa TX 79331-5406 Office Phone: 806-872-2171.

**SALEH, PAUL N.,** telecommunications industry executive; BSEE, MSEE, Univ. Mich., MBA in Fin. with distinction. Various leadership positions to treas. Honeywell, 1985—96; sr. v.p., treas., CFO Walt Disney Co., 1997—2001; exec. v.p., CFO Nextel Commn. (merged with Sprint), 2001—05; CFO Sprint Nextel Corp., Reston, Va., 2005—. Bd. dir. Wolf Trap Found. Named best CFO in telecom svcs./wireless sector, Institutional Investor mag., 2004, 2005; named one of 100 Most Influential People in Fin., Treasury & Risk Mgmt. mag., 2005. Office: Sprint Nextel Corp 2001 Edmund Halley Dr Reston VA 20191*

**SALEM, BAKR IBRAMIM,** cardiologist; b. Jordan, Oct. 1, 1944; came to U.S., 1974; MB ChB, Cairo U., 1967. Diplomate Am. Bd. Internal Medicine, Am. Bd. Cardiovascular Diseases. Intern St. Luke's Hosp., St. Louis, 1974-75, resident in medicine, 1978-79, mem. staff; resident in medicine St. Mary's Health Ctr., St. Louis, 1975-76; fellow in cardiology St. Luke's Episcopal Hosp., Houston, 1976-78; pvt. practice Chesterfield, Mo. Fellow ACP, Soc. Cardiac Angiography and Intervension, Am. Coll. Cardiology, Am. Coll. Chest Physicians. Office: 222 S Woods Mill Rd Ste 500 Chesterfield MO 63017-3625 Office Phone: 314-205-6699.

**SALEM, DOROTHY CARLSON,** social sciences educator, history professor; b. Dayton, Ohio, Jan. 29, 1946; d. Donald R. and Ethel (Carlson) Mayer; m. Thomas Coopland (dec. 1967); m. Thomas Gregory Salem, Oct. 21, 1932; children: Kelle Ann, Beth Marie, Jennifer Lynn. AS, Cuyahoga Community Coll., Cleve., 1969; BA, Cleve. State U., 1971, MA, 1972; PhD, Kent State U., 1985, cert. in instrnl. design, 2001. Teaching asst. history Cleve. State U., 1971-72, adj. prof. history, 1985—; lectr. Cuyahoga Community Coll., Cleve., 1972-75, from asst. prof. to prof. social sci. women's studies, 1975-85, prof. social sci. and history, 1985—, dir. Inst. on Human Rels., 1985-89. Cons. multicultural curriculum and women's studies Cleve. Pub. Schs., 1987—. Author: To Better Our World, 1990; editor: African American Women: A Biographical Dictionary, 1993, The Journey, 1997; contbr. articles to profl. jours. Mem. adv. bd. Displaced Homemakers Network, Cleve., 1987—; bd. mem. Children's Support Rights, 1987-96. Recipient Besse award for tchg. excellence Cuyahoga C.C. Found., 1985, Nat. Teaching Excellence award Nat. Inst. Staff and Orgn. Devel., 1989, Disting. Alumnae award Cleve. State U., 1990, Ohio Prof. of Yr., Carnegie Found., 2002, Women of Profl. Excellence award YWCA, 2003; grantee NEH, 1992, 2003. Mem. Am. Hist. Assn., Nat. Women's Studies Assn., Ohio Acad. History, So. Assn. Women Historians. Democrat. Lutheran. Avocations: walking, gardening. Office: Cuyahoga Community Coll 2900 Community College Ave Cleveland OH 44115-3123 Office Phone: 216-987-4515. Personal E-mail: dorothysalem@yahoo.com.

**SALEM, GEORGE RICHARD,** lawyer; b. Jacksonville, Fla., Dec. 24, 1953; s. Kamel Abraham and Margaret Virginia (Bateh) S.; m. Rhonda M. Ziadeh, June 28, 1980; children: James George, Jihan Camille, Laila Suad, Sarah Rose. BA, Emory U., 1975, JD, 1977; LLM, Georgetown U., 1984. Bar: Ga. 1978, Fla. 1979, DC 1981. Ptnr. Thompson, Mann & Hutson, Washington, 1977-85; dep. solicitor U.S. Dept. Labor, Washington, 1985-86, solicitor of labor, 1986-89; ptnr., head of Middle East and US Dept. of Labor practices group Akin, Gump, Strauss, Hauer & Feld, Washington, 1990—2004; ptnr. AG Solutions, Law Offices of George R. Salem, 2005—; strategic advisor DLA Piper Rudnick Gray Cary, 2005—. Bd. dirs. Overseas Pvt. Investment Corp. Contbr. articles to profl. jours. Nat. exec. dir. ethnic voters div. Reagan Bush '84; bd. dirs. United Palestinian Appeal, Inc., 1981-85, 86—; co-founder, mem. Arab Am. Inst., Jan.-Mar., 1985, Dec. 1986—, chmn. bd. dirs., 1999—; chmn. Arab-Ams. for Bush-Cheney, 2000; mem. Am. Arab Anti-Discrimination Com. 2000-03, chmn. Arab-Ams. for Bush-Quayle '88, '92; adv. bd. Search for Common Ground in the Mid. East, 2001—; exec. adv. bd. Mid. East Inst., 2002—; bd. dirs. Am. Com. on Jerusalem, 1995—, Emory Law Sch. Coun., 2000-2002, Emory Bd. Govs., 1997-2001. Recipient Ellis Island Medal of Honor, 1992. Fellow College of Labor and Employment Lawyers; mem. ABA (labor and employment law sect.), Ga. Bar Assn. (labor rels. div.), Fla. Bar Assn. (labor rels. div.), DC Bar Assn. (labor rels. div.), Nat. Assn. Arab Ams. (bd. dirs. 1987, pres. 1992-94), Am. Ramallah Club (pres. DC chpt. 1984, Wash. rep. 1982-84), Am. Ramallah Fedn. (chmn. human rights com., Washington rep. 1982-84), Arab Am. Rep. Fedn. (chmn. 1985), Century Club Nat. Rep. Heritage Groups Coun., Delta Theta Phi, Omicron Delta Kappa. Mem. Eastern Orthodox Christian Ch. Office: Ste 200 1200 Nineteenth St NW Washington DC 20036 Office Phone: 202-887-1140. Office Fax: 202-887-5550. Business E-Mail: gsalem@georgesalem.com.

**SALEM, KAREN E.,** information technology executive; BS in indsl. engring., Penn. State U.; MBA, U. Cin. Sr. cons. Anderson Consulting; dir. bus. solutions Burger King; v.p. info. tech. Rexall Sundown; IT head AFC Enterprises; sr. v.p. and CIO Corning Cable Sys.; former sr. v.p. and CIO Winn-Dixie Stores, Inc., Jacksonville, Fla., 2002, Ingram Micro, 2005. Office: Ingram Micro PO Box 25125 1600 E St Andrew Pl Santa Ana CA 92799-5125

**SALEM, RICHARD ALLEN,** mediator; b. NYC, Aug. 15, 1930; s. Louis H. and Catherine (Levy) S.; m. Greta Waldinger, June 26, 1955; children: Susanne, Peter, Erica. BA in Sociology, Antioch Coll., 1953; MS in Journalism, Columbia U., 1957. Reporter Washington Post, 1957-59; editor, publ. Washington SBIC Newsletter, 1960-62; spl. asst. to dep. dir. for investment Small Bus. Adminstrn., Washington, 1963-64, assoc. dir. Office of Equal Opportunity, 1964-67, regional dir., 1967-68; Midwest dir. Cmty. Rels. Svc. U.S. Dept. Justice, Chgo., 1968-82; pres. Conflict Mgmt. Initiatives, Evanston, Ill., 1982—. Adj. prof. Loyola U., Chgo., 1986-90; mediator Wounded Knee Takeover, 1972, Skokie-Nazi Conflict, 1980. Co-author: Students Guide to Mediation and Law, 1987, Ctr. for Pub. Resources award, 1987; mem. editl. bd. Chgo. Reporter, 1996-2004, Jour. Mediation and Applied Conflict Analysis, 2005—; editor: Witness to Genocide - the

Children of Rwanda, 2000; contbr. articles to profl. jours. Bd. dirs. Housing Options for Mentally Ill, Evanston, 1997-2004, Found. Self-Sufficiency Ctrl. Am., 2000—; sec. World Mediation Forum, 1997-2002. With U.S. Army, 1953-55. Recipient Outstanding Performance award, U.S. Sr. Exec. Svc., 1980. Mem. Soc. Profls. in Dispute Resolution (2d v.p. 1988, bd. dirs. 1982-89, Mary Parker Follett award 1993). Home and Office: 1225 Oak Ave Evanston IL 60202-1220

**SALEM, THOMAS ERIC,** electrical engineer, educator; s. William Fredrick and Marjorie Marie Salem; m. Karen B. Tymann, May 14, 1994; children: Madelyn Grace, Eric Timothy, Benjamin Thomas. BS in Engring., Grove City (Pa.) Coll., 1988; MSEE, The U. Ala., 1993, PhD, 1996. Registered profl. engr., Pa., 1997. Project engr. E.I. Dupont DeNemours & Co., Aiken, SC, 1988—89, Westinghouse Savannah River Co., Aiken, 1989—95; asst. prof. engring. Pa. State U., Mont Alto, Pa., 1996—98, Elizabethtown (Pa.) Coll., 1998—2002; asst. prof. elec. engring. U.S. Naval Acad., Annapolis, Md., 2002—. Rsch. engr. U.S. Army Rsch. Lab., Adelphi, Md., 2004—, U.S. Naval Rsch. Lab., Washington, 2002—03; adj. lectr. Pa. State U., Harrisburg, Pa., 2000—01; sr. staff engr. ATC Diversified Electronics, Lancaster, Pa., 1999—2000; prin. electronics engr. TB Wood's Inc., Chambersburg, Pa., 1997—98. Recipient George Westinghouse Signature Excellence award, Westinghouse Savannah River Co., 1989, Westinghouse Total Quality Achievement award, 1991. Mem.: IEEE. Office: United States Naval Academy Maury Hall Mail Stop 14B 105 Maryland Av Annapolis MD 21402 Office Phone: 410-293-6178. Business E-Mail: salem@usna.edu.

**SALEMBIER, VALERIE BIRNBAUM,** publishing executive; b. Teaneck, N.J. d. Jack and Sara (Gordon) Birnbaum; m. Paul J. Block, Dec. 9, 1990. BA, Coll. New Rochelle, 1973. Advt. dir. Ms. Mag., N.Y.C., 1976-79, assoc. pub., 1979-81; pub. Inside Sports Mag., N.Y.C., 1982; sr. v.p. advt. USA Today, 1983-88; pub. TV Guide, Radnor, Pa., 1988; pres. N.Y. Post, N.Y.C., 1988—90; pub. Family Circle Mag., N.Y.C., 1991-93; v.p. advt. N.Y. Times, 1993-95; v.p., pub. Esquire Mag., 1996—2003; sr. v.p., pub. Harper's Bazaar, N.Y.C., 2003—. Lectr. in field. Author: (book) Rotissereie League Baseball, 1982; freelance mag. writer:. Chmn. N.Y.C. Police Found.; bd. dirs., past pres. Nat. Alliance Breast Cancer Orgns., former bd. dirs.; bd. dirs., past pres. Beneficial Orgn. Aid Ex-Fighters; former trustee Ctrl. Synagogue, Coll. New Rochelle; trustee N.Y.C. Sports Devel. Corp. Mem.: Women in Comm., Com. 200, Womens Forum. Office: Harpers Bazaar 1700 Broadway New York NY 10019

**SALENTINE, THOMAS JAMES,** pharmaceutical executive; b. Milw., Aug. 8, 1939; s. James Edward and Loretta Marie S.; m. Susan Anne Sisk, Apr. 16, 1966; children: Anne Elizabeth, Thomas James Jr. BS in Acctg., Marquette U., Milw., 1961. CPA, Ind., Wis. Sr. audit mgr. Price Waterhouse, Milw., 1961-74; dir. corp. acctg. Ward Foods Inc., Wilmette, Ill., 1974-78; corp. contr. Johnson Controls Inc., Milw., 1984-85; v.p., contr. Stokely Van Camp Inc., Indpls., 1978-87; exec. v.p., CFO Bindley Western Industries Inc., Indpls., 1987—2001, also bd. dirs.; ptnr. Bindley Capital Ptnrs., LLC, 2001—. Bd. dirs. Priority Healthcare Corp., Nat. Refrigeration Svcs. Inc. Chmn. com. United Way, Indpls., 1989-90. Lt. USN, 1962-65. Mem. AICPA, Fin. Execs. Inst. Republican. Roman Catholic. Home: 3991 Gulf Shore Blvd Naples FL 34103 Office Phone: 317-704-4154.

**SALERNO, CHERIE ANN (C. S. MAU),** artist; b. Chgo., Nov. 21, 1948; d. Henry Jasper and Helen (Polyak) Mau; m. Kenneth Daniel Salerno; children: Nick Anthony, Brittney Ann. AAS in Advt., Triton Coll., River Grove, Ill., 1985; BFA, Art Inst. Chgo., 1999. Freelance comml. artist, Chgo., 1986—90, 2000—; artist Chgo. Fine Arts Exch., 1994—98; artist, owner C.S. Mau Studio, River Grove, Ill., 1992—; art dir., bd. dirs. Harrison St. Coop. Gallery, Oak Park, Ill., 1999—2002; art tchr. grades 3-7, 2000—03, Bethlehem Luth. Sch., River Grove, 2002—. Designer Centennial Quilt, River Grove Libr., 1988; logo designer, River Grove Sch., 1984. Designer stained glass window Bethlehem Luth. Ch., River Grove, Ill., 1999, Celebrating Diversity art exhibit, Chgo., 2002; cover designer Louie Records, Corvallis, Oreg., 1998-99, MSS Pub., Jefferson, Oreg., 2002, A440 Music Group, Chgo., for Henry Johnson and Nancy Wilson, 2003; cover artist Aim Mag., 2003-04, Chicagoland Tails, 2005, Indy Tails, 2005. Vol. tchr. art Bethlehem Luth. Sch., River Grove, Ill., 1996-2002; vol. ElderCare, 1990-94. Fellow: West Suburban Art League (Excellences honor award 1990—2005, excellences awards 1990—), Glenview Art League (Excellence award 1996), Chgo. Artist Coalition; mem.: Oak Park Art League (bd. dirs. 1989—, arts and stds. judge 1991—93, sch. bd. 1993—94, active fundraising 1994, stds. judge 2000—), juror of artist stds., Excellences merit 1990—94). Lutheran. Avocations: gardening, reading, weightlifting, sewing, gourmet cooking. Personal E-mail: cheriesart@salerno.com.

**SALERNO, F. ROBERT,** car rental company executive; b. Springfield, Mass. married; 2 children. D., Marquette U., 1972. Vice pres. eastern region Avis, 1982—87, v.p. field ops., 1987—90, sr. v.p., gen. mgr. 1990—95, exec. v.p., 1995—96, pres., COO, 1996—2002; CEO Cendant Car Rental Group, 2003—. Office: Cendant Car Group Rental 9 W 57th St New York NY 10019

**SALERNO, FREDERIC V.,** retired telecommunications company executive; b. NYC, June 28, 1943; m. Patricia Van Arsdale; 3 children. BSEE, Manhattan Coll., 1965; MBA, Adelphi U.; postgrad. in mgmt., Pace U. With N.Y. Telephone (NYNEX Co.), N.Y.C., 1965—, various positions including staff asst. corp. hdqrs., installation and repair foreman, mgmt. positions, 1965-78, gen. mgr., 1978-93, v.p. transition, 1983-84, v.p. customer service, 1984-85, exec. v.p. chief operating officer New Eng. Telephone and Telegraph Co. (NYNEX Co.), 1985-87, pres., chief exec. officer, 1987-91, vice chmn., pres. worldwide svcs., 1991-94, vice chmn. fin. and bus. devel., 1994-97; now sr. exec. v.p., CFO Verizon Communications, Inc.(formerly Bell Atlantic), 1997—2000; vice chmn., CFO Verizon Communications, Inc., 2000—02. Bd. dirs. Akamai Technologies, Inc., The Bear Stearns Companies, Inc., Consolidated Edison, Inc., Gabelli Asset Mgmt., Popular, Inc., Viacom, Inc.

**SALERNO, SISTER MARIA,** nursing educator, advanced practice nurse; b. Syracuse, N.Y. d. Joseph and Josephine (Ostrowski) S. Diploma in nursing, St. Joseph's Hosp., Syracuse, 1962; BSN summa cum laude, Cath. U. Am., 1974, MS in Nursing, 1976, PhD in Nursing, 1981; cert. nurse practitioner, U. Rochester, 1984. RN, N.Y., Md., Washington; cert. adult, geriatric nurse practitioner ANCC; joined Sisters of Third Franciscan Order, Roman Cath. Ch., 1963. Staff nurse St. Joseph Hosp. Health Ctr., Syracuse, 1962-63; sr. charge nurse ICU, gen. med. surg. units St. Elizabeth Hosp., Utica, NY, 1965-66, head nurse pediat. unit, 1966-69; head nurse ECF Loretto Geriatric Ctr., Syracuse, 1969-72; lectr. Cath. U. Am., Washington, 1977—78, 1980—81, asst. prof. nursing, 1978-79, 81-92, assoc. prof., 1992—, dir. primary care adult/geriatric nurse practitioner programs, 1984—, co-dir. FNP program, 1994-97; dir. Adult CNS Nurse Educator Program, 2004—. Contbr. chpts. to books; contbr. articles to profl. jours. Vol. nurse practitioner Cmty. of Hope, Washington; instl. animal care and use com. George Washington U., 1996—, Cath. U. Am., 2000—. Veteran's Adminstrn. Med. Ctr., 2004—; scholarship com. Franciscan Found. for the Holy Land, 1996—. Grantee NIH, 1984-89, Cath. U. Am., 1989-90. Mem.: AAUP, ANA, D.C. League for Nursing (bd. dirs. 1995—97, 1999—2002), D.C. Nurse Practitioners Assn. (nom. com. 2006), N.Y. Acad. Scis., Nat. League for Nursing, Nat. Orgn. Nurse Practitioner Facilities, Nat. Gerontol. Nurses Assn., Am. Coll. Nurse Practitioners, Am. Acad. Nurse Practitioners, Am. Assn. for History of Nursing, Cath. U. Am. Nursing Alumni Assn. (pres. 1986—87, chpt. exec. bd. 1992—2003, treas. 1998—2003), Nat. Italian Am. Found. (assoc.), Sigma Theta Tau (grad. counselor Kappa chpt. 1985—87, awards com. 1987—89, grad. counselor Kappa chpt. 1991—97, eligibility com. 1991—97, 2002—03). Office Phone: 202-319-6545. Office Fax: 202-319-6485. Business E-Mail: salerno@cua.edu.

**SALERNO-SONNENBERG, NADJA,** violinist; b. Rome, Jan. 10, 1961; arrived in U.S., 1969; d. Josephine Salerno-Sonnenberg. Grad., Curtis Inst. Music, 1975, Juilliard Sch., 1982; D (hon.), N.Mex. State U., 1999. Profl. debut Phila. Orch., 1971; appeared with Am. Symphony Orch., Balt. Symphony, Chgo. Symphony, Colo. Symphony, Cin. Symphony, Detroit Symphony, Houston Symphony, Indpls. Symphony, Milw. Symphony, Montreal Symphony, N.J. Symphony, Pitts. Symphony, San Diego Symphony, Seattle Symphony, St. Louis Symphony, Utah Symphony, Boston Symphony, Dallas Symphony, Minn. Orch., Phila. Orch., L.A. Philharm.; appeared Cabrillo Festival, Ravinia Festival, Blossom Festival, Meadow Brook Festival, Gt. Woods Festival, Caramoor Festival, Hollywood Bowl Festival; internat. appearances Vienna, Munich, Stuttgart, Franfurt, Liverpool, England, Geneva, Rotterdam, Netherlands, Lisbon, Portugal, Tokyo. Founder, recording artist Capital Classics and Jazz Records, 1987—, Nonesuch, 1996—, NSS Music, 2005—. Performer: (recitals) with Anne Marie McDermott, with Regina Carter, with Eileen Ivers, with The Assads; appearances: TV 60 Minutes, CBS Sunday Morning, NBC Nat. News, PBS Live from Lincoln Ctr., CNN Newsstand, Charlie Rose Show, Sesame Street; appearances (TV) The Tonight Show with Johnny Carson, subject (documentaries) Speaking in Strings, 1999 (Oscar nomination, 2000). Recipient 1st prize, Naumburg Violin Competition, N.Y.C., 1981, Avery Fisher prize, 1999; Avery Fisher Career grantee, 1983. Mem.: SAG, AFTRA. Office: care M L Falcone Pub Rels 155 W 68th St Ste 114 New York NY 10023-5808

**SALES, JAMES BOHUS,** lawyer; b. Weimar, Tex., Aug. 24, 1934; s. Henry B. and Agnes Mary (Pesek) Sales; m. Beuna M. Vornsand, June 3, 1956; children: Mark Keith, Debra Lynn, Travis James. BS, U. Tex., 1956, LLB with honors, 1960. Bar: Tex. 1960. Practiced in, Houston, 1960—; head litig. dept. Fulbright & Jaworski, 1979—99, sr. ptnr., 1960—2000, of counsel, 2000—. Author: Products Liability in Texas, 1985; co-author: Texas Torts and Remedies, 6 vols., 1986; assoc. editor: Tex. Law Rev., 1960; contbr. articles to profl. jours. Trustee South Tex. Coll. Law, 1982—88, 1990—2005, A.A. White Dispute Resolution Ctr., 1991—94; cir. chair membership Supreme Ct. Hist. Soc., 1998—2001; trustee Tex. Supreme Ct. Hist. Soc., 2003—; chair commrs. Tex. Access Justice Commn., 2004—; bd. dirs. Tex. Resource Ctr., 1990—97, Tex. Bar Hist. Found., 1990—2001. Named among Best Lawyers in Am., 1989—; recipient Lifetime Achievement award, U. Tex. Law Sch. Alumni, 2005. Fellow: Houston Bar Found. (chmn. bd. 1982—83, sustaining life), Tex. Bar Found. (trustee 1991—95, vice-chmn. 1992—93, chmn. 1993—94, chair adv. bd. planned giving 1994—2004, sustaining mem.), Am. Bd. Trial Advocates, Am. Bar Found. (state chmn. 1993—98, sustaining life), Internat. Acad. Trial Lawyers, Am. Coll. Trial Lawyers (state chmn. 1993—96); mem.: FBA, ABA (bd. of dels. 1984—2003, mem. Commn. on IOLTA 1995—97), Bar Assn. 5th Fed. Cir., Gulf Coast Legal Found. (bd. dirs. 1982—85), Houston Bar Assn. (bd. dirs. 1970—79, pres.-elect 1979—80, pres. 1980—81), Tex. Law Rev. Assn. (bd. dirs. 1996—2002, pres. 1999—2000), Tex. Assn. Def. Counsel (v.p. 1977—79), State Bar Tex. (bd. dirs. 1983—88, chmn. bd. 1985—86, pres. 1988—89), So. Tex. Coll. Trial Advocacy (dir. 1983—87), So. Conf. Bar, Nat. Conf. Bar Pres. (coun. 1989—92), Internat. Assn. Def. Counsel, The Forum, Order of Coif, Inns of Ct. (bd. dirs. 1981—84), Westlake Club (bd. govs. 1980—85). Roman Catholic. Home: 10803 Oak Creek St Houston TX 77024-3016 Office: Fulbright & Jaworski 1301 McKinney St Houston TX 77010-3095 E-mail: jsales@fulbright.com.

**SALETTA, MARY ELIZABETH (BETTY SALETTA),** sculptor; b. Miami, Fla., Sept. 30, 1941; d. Earl Robert and Alta Florence Cotner; m. Albert Michael Saletta, July 1, 1959; children: Tia Suzanne, Kamber Ann. Graphic artist Moore Bus. Forms Inc., Modesto, Calif., 1960-67, Live Oak Pub. Co., Oakdale, Calif., 1977-80; freelance artist U.S. Forest Svc., Modesto Irrigation Dist., Stanislaus Schs., New Don Pedro Dam Project, Calif., 1967-77; sculptor Saletta Sculpture, Oakdale, 1980—. Mem. adv. bd. Calif. State U. Coll. Arts, Letters and Sci., Turlock, 1999-2002; charter mem., dir. Downtown Arts Project, Modesto, 1992-96. One-woman shows City of Oakdale Redevel. Agy., 1990, Modesto C. of C., 1996; group shows include Calif. State U. Stanislaus, Turlock, 1986, Cowboy Artist Am. Mus., Kerrville, Tex., 1988, Benson Park Sculpture Garden, Loveland, Colo., 1989, 90, 93, Danada Sculpture Garden, Chgo., 1991, 93, Tucson Mus. Art, 1995; represented in permanent collections Tucson Mus. Art, Buckaroo Hall of Fame, cities of Modesto, Oakdale, Ripon, Calif., Stockton, Los Banos, Monterey, San Leandro, Calif.; sculptures include life-size pub. sculptures Yesterday Is Tomorrow, 1991, Paperbohy, 1995, Am. Graffiti, 1997, Stockton Firefighters Meml., 1998, World War II Meml., 1999, Nursing, the Finest Art, 2001, Chief Estanislao, 2001, Firefighter Sculpture produced at Laguna Beach Pageant of the Masters, 2002. Recipient Excellence in Fine Art award Bank Am., Stockton, Calif., 1959, Best of Show award Western Art Roundup, Winnamucca, Nev., 1987, 88, Excellence in Visual Arts award Stanislaus Arts Coun., Modesto, 1999. Mem. Nat. League Am. Pen Women, Calif. Art League (advisor 1991, Best of Show award 1987), Rotary (bd. dirs. Oakdale 1997-99). Democrat. Avocations: horses, skiing, mountain climbing, fishing. Home: 4255 Wellsford Rd Oakdale CA 95361-7930 Fax: 209-572-4089. E-mail: salettasculpture@aol.com.

**SALGADO, MARIA ANTONIA,** education educator; b. Puerto de la Cruz, Tenerife, Canary Island, Spain, Jan. 15, 1933; came to U.S., 1951; d. Felipe Antonio Lopez-González and Juliana Rafaela (Garcia) de Lopez; m. Daniel E. Salgado, June 12, 1954; children: M. Liane, Danny. BA cum laude, Fla. State U., 1958; MA, U.N.C., 1960; PhD, U.Ala. 1966. Asst. prof. U.N.C., Chapel Hill, 1967-72, assoc. prof., 1972-77, prof., 1977—. Author: Las caricaturas de J.R.J., 1969, Hablemos!, 1976, Rafael Arevalo Martinez, 1979; contbr. articles to profl. publs. Democrat. Roman Catholic. Office: U NC Rom Langs Clb # 3170 Chapel Hill NC 27599-3170 Business E-Mail: masal@email.umc.edu.

**SALGADO, SUSANA,** musicologist, researcher, consultant; b. Montevideo, Uruguay, June 14, 1927; d. Juan Andres Salgado, Amelia Gomez-Eirin; m. Roberto O. Morassi. Musicologist, Sch. of Humanities, Montevideo, 1965. Chair Uruguayan music rsch., dept. musicology Sch. of Humanities, Montevideo, 1965—71; cons., music divsn. Libr. of Congress, Washington, 1994—. Mem. bd. advisors Garland Pub. for Opera Performances, N.Y.C., 1992—; lectr. in field. Author: (Scholarly Book) The Teatro Solis, 150 Years of Opera, Concert and Ballet in Montevideo, 2003, Breve Historia de la Musica Culta en el Uruguay, Montevideo, 1971, 1980, Cluzeau-Mortet Montevideo, 1983; contbr. 5 Grove Dictionaries including Opera; Music and Musicians; Women Composers, American Music; Encyclopedia of Latin-American History and Culture and many others., articles to profl. publs. Mem.: Authors Guild, Am. Musicological Soc., Women Nat. Book Assn. Avocations: travel, swimming, walking. Office Phone: 703-412-4882. E-mail: saisalgado@aol.com.

**SALGO, PETER LLOYD,** internist, writer, anesthesiologist, journalist, commentator; b. N.Y.C., Nov. 9, 1949; s. Michael Nicholas and Ruth F. Salgo. BA, Columbia U., 1971, MD, 1975. Diplomate Am. Bd. Internal Medicine, Am. Bd. Anesthesiology; lic. physician, N.Y., Calif., Mass.; instrument rated comml. pilot. Internal medicine intern Columbia Presbyn. Med. Ctr., N.Y.C., 1975-76, resident in internal medicine, 1976-78; vis. faculty fellow intensive care medicine and anesthesiology, dept. anesthesiology Columbia U., N.Y.C., 1979-81; lectr. Harvard Med. Sch., Boston; clin. prof. medicine and anesthesiology Columbia P&S; mem. staff in anesthesia and medicine Mass. Gen. Hosp., Boston; attending in anesthesia and internal medicine Presbyn. Hosp., N.Y.C., assoc. dir. surg. ICU. Host syndicated TV broadcast Healthcare 2000; aviation med. examiner FAA; comml. pilot. instrument Rated; host nat. radio med. program Sta. PRN, 1979—81; writer, producer, host med. info. broadcast Sta. WCBS-TV, N.Y.C., 1980—; med. corr. Sta. WCBS News, 1981—; corr. CBS Network Radio News, 1982—92; host Healthtalk, 1982—88; med. corr. CNBC, 1989—, CNBC TV Network, 1989—93; host The Doctor Is In, Eyada.com, 2000—01; cons. to networks on med. content of TV programs; corr. Patient Info. Network, 1989—; anchor Americas Vital Signs, CNBC TV Network, Med. Crossfire, 2001—; lectr. in field.; expert guest on John F.

Kennedy, Jr., crash NTSB Report Discovery Network, 2002; expert guest, med. cons. Fox News, 2001—02; host Second Opinion PBS, 2002—. Author: The Heart of the Matter, 2004. Recipient Leonard Pullman award Columbia U., 1971, Blakesley award Am. Heart Assn., Journalism award Medic-alert Found., Honorable Mention in Journalism, UPI, Alumni Assn. medal Columbia U. P&S, 1975, Emmy award for excellence in broadcast journalism, Journalism award Lions Eye Found. Fellow ACP; mem. AAAS, AMA, AFTRA, N.Y. State Med. Soc., N.Y. County Med. Soc., Am. Soc. Anesthesiologists. Office: Presbyn Hosp Dept Anesthesiology New York NY 10032 Office Phone: 212-305-6494. E-mail: pls1@columbia.edu.

**SALHANY, LUCILLE S. (LUCY SALHANY),** broadcast executive; b. 1946; married; 2 children. LHD (hon.), Emerson Coll., 1992. Program dir. WKBF-TV, Cleve., 1967; program mgr. WLVI-TV, Boston, 1975—79; v.p. television & cable programming Taft Broadcasting Co., 1979—85; pres. Paramount Domestic TV, 1985—91; chmn. 20th Century Television, 1991—93, Fox Broadcasting Co., 1993—94; pres. United Paramount Network (UPN), 1994-97; pres., CEO JH Media, Boston, 1998—2004, HJ Media, LifeFX Networks Inc., 2002—04; co-founder, mng. ptnr. Echo Bridge Entertainment, Needham, Mass., 2004—. Bd. dirs. Hewlett-Packard Co., Am. Media Co., Inc., ION Media Networks, Inc., 2006—. Bd. trustees Emerson Coll.; profl. adv. bd. ALSAC/St. Jude Children's Rsch. Hosp. Named Exec. of Yr., Caucus for Prodrs., Writers & Dirs.; recipient Sherrill C. Corwin Human Rels award, Am. Jewish Com., 1995, Silver Satellite award, Am. Women in Radio and TV, 1995, HELP Humanitarian award, 1997, Avatar award, Cable Fin. Mgmt. Orgn., Silver Circle award, Nat. Acad TV Arts and Sci. Achievements include becoming the first woman to manage an American broadcast television network, 1993. Office: Echo Bridge Entertainment Ste 500 75 Second Ave Needham Heights MA 02494 Office Phone: 781-444-9680.

**SALIB, PHILIP I.,** orthopedic surgeon; b. Belbeis, Egypt, Oct. 3, 1917; s. Salib Ibrahin Khalil and Sadika Ibrahim Habib; m. Maria Asuncion Noain Pernas, Dec. 6, 1953; children: Jean-Philippe, Carlos Blas. MB, Faculty of Medicine, Egypt, 1941, DS, 1944; postgrad., Cairo U., 1948. Cert. Am. Bd. Orthop. Surgeons, 1970. Rotating house officer Kasr El-Ainy Univ. Hosp., Cairo, 1941—42, Ch. Missionary Hosp., Old Cairo, Egypt, 1942; orthop. resident, chief resident Red Crescent Hosp. for Orthop. Surgery & Trauma, Cairo, 1944—49; maj., acting chief orthop. surgeon Mil. Hosp., Cairo, 1949—50; orthop. surgeon Dar El-Shifa Hosp., Cairo, 1951—60; fellow orthop. Boston City Hosp., 1961; orthop. resident Mass. Gen. Hosp., Boston, 1961—64, chief orthop. resident, 1964, sr. fracture resident, 1964, fellow orthop., 1964. Author: (publ. article) Gazette of Faculty of Medicine, 1942, Jour. of Bone and Joint Surgery, 1962, Am. Jour. Orthop., 1964. Fellow: Am. Coll. Surgeons; mem.: Ind. Orthop. Examiner, Arthroscopy Assn. N.Am., Am. Acad. Orthop. Surgeons, Eastern Orthop. Assn., Pan-Am. Med. Assn., Am. Med. Assn., Mass. Med. Soc., New Eng. Orthop. Soc., Internat. Soc. Orthop. Surgery and Traumatology, New England Orthop. Soc. Avocations: music, photography, movies, drawing. Home: 206 Allandale Rd 2-C Chestnut Hill MA 02467

**SALIBA, ANIS KHALIL,** surgeon; b. Karaoun, Bekaa, Lebanon, Jan. 14, 1933; s. Khalil and Rosa (Sallum) S.; m. Siham Saliba, Nov. 8, 1959; children: Khalil Saliba, Nada Saliba. BA, Am. U. Lebanon, 1952; MD with Distinction, Damascus U., 1960. Diplomate Am. Bd. Surgery, Am. Bd. Thoracic and Cardiovascular Surgery, Am. Bd. Surg. Critical Care. Resident Coney Island, Bklyn., 1960-65, St. Vincent Charity, Cleve., 1965-67; cardiovascular surgeon Beebe Med. Ctr., Lewes, Del., 1980—. Trustee Beebe Med. Ctr., 1989—. Fellow Am. Coll. Surgeons; mem. AMA. Home: 30729 Sassafras Dr Lewes DE 19958 Office: 431 Savannah Rd Lewes DE 19958-1460 E-mail: as.saliba@comcast.net.

**SALIBA, JACOB,** manufacturing executive; b. East Broughton, Que., Can., June 10, 1913; s. Said and Nazira (David) S.; m. Adla Mudarri, May 31, 1942; children: John, Thomas, Barbara. BS, Boston U., 1941. Sr. supervising engr. Thompson and Lichtner Co., Boston, 1944-49; pres. Kingston Dress Co., Boston, 1949-51, Indsl. & Mgmt. Assocs., Inc., Boston, 1951-54, Maine Dress Co., Cornish, 1948-61; exec. v.p., mem. exec. com. Cortland Corp., Inc. (formerly Brockway Motor Co., Inc.), N.Y.C., 1954-59; exec. v.p. Sawyer-Tower, Inc., Boston, 1955-56, pres., 1956-59; v.p. Farrington Mfg. Co.; exec. v.p. Farrington Packaging Corp., 1959-61, Farrington Instruments Corp.; pres. N.E. Industries, Inc., from 1961, also bd. dirs.; pres. Fanny Farmer Candy Shops, Inc., 1963-66, W.F. Schrafft & Sons Corp., 1967-68; pres. frozen foods divsn. W.R. Grace & Co., 1966-68; pres. Katy Industries, Inc., Elgin, Ill., 1969-88, chmn., CEO, 1988-94. Chmn. bd. dirs. Schon & Cie; bd. dirs. Dresdner RCM Europe Fund NYSE, Katy Industries, NYSE; spl. cons. Air Material Commmand, USAF, Dayton, Ohio, 1942-43; cons. to chief air staff USAF, 1952-54; co-chmn. Air Force Spare Study Group, 1953. Mem. corp. Mass. Gen. Hosp., Mus. Sci. Mem. Union League Club, Bridgton Club, Highlands Country Club, Palm Beach Yacht Club. Methodist. E-mail: salibagido@earthlink.com.

**SALIBA, PHILIP E.,** archbishop; b. Abou-Mizan, Lebanon, 1931; came to U.S., 1956, naturalized, 1961; s. Elias Abdallah and Salema (Saliba) S. BA, Wayne State U., 1959; MDiv, DD, St. Vladimir's Sem., N.Y., 1964; DHL, Wayne State U., 1986. Became sub-deacon, deacon Antiochian Orthodox Christian Ch., 1945-49, ordained deacon Lebanon, 1949-59, priest, 1959-66, consecrated archbishop, 1966, now met. and primate. Chmn. Standing Conf. Am.-Middle Eastern Christian and Moslem Leaders; chmn. Orthodox Christian Edn. Commn.; vice chmn. Standing Conf. Canonical Orthodox Bishops in Ams. Vice-chmn. St. Vladimir's Orthodox Theol. Sem. Mem. Antiochian Orthodox Christian Ch. Address: 358 Mountain Rd Englewood NJ 07631-3727 Office Phone: 201-871-1355. E-mail: archdiocese@antiochian.org.

**SALICK, ANNE,** sales executive; BFA in Info. Systems cum laude, U. North Tex., 1982, MBA in Fin., 1985. Programmer to bus. systems analyst Mobil Oil Corp., Dallas, 1982—88, tech. project mgr., 1989—92, CRM program mgr., 1993—95; sr. sales cons. Oracle Corp., Irving, Tex., 1996—99; sales solution architect Cygent, Inc., Flower Mound, Tex., 2000—02; jitl. solutions devel. Convergys Corp., Flower Mound, 2003—05; fin. adv., coach Future Primerica Fin. Svcs., 2005—. Bd. dirs. Rose Technologies, Inc., Denton, Tex. Mem.: Assn. of Proposal Mgmt. Profls., Convergys Global Women's Network, U. N. Tex. Alumni Assn., Denton County Women's Bus. Owners, Beta Gamma Sigma. Home: 3405 Emerald Cove Dr Flower Mound TX 75022 Office Phone: 972-874-8180.

**SALIERS, EMILY,** singer, musician; b. New Haven, Conn., July 22, 1963; d. Don Saliers; life ptnr. Leslie Zweben. Student, Vanderbilt U.; BA, Emory U., 1985. Mem. folk rock duo Indigo Girls, 1983—; represented by Epic Records, 1988—2006, Hollywood Records, 2006—. Co-owner Watershed Restaurant, Decatur, Ga.; co-founder Flying Biscuit Cafe, Atlanta. Singer (with Amy Ray): (albums) Early 45, 1985, Strange Fire, 1987, Indigo Girls, 1989 (Grammy award for Best Contemporary Folk Album, 1990), Nomads Indians Saints, 1990, Rites of Passage, 1992, Swamp Ophelia, 1994, Touch Me Fall, 1995, 1200 Curfews, 1995, Shaming of the Sun, 1997, Come on Now Social, 1999, Retrospective, 2000, Become You, 2002, All That We Let In, 2004, Rarities, 2005, Despite Our Differences, 2006, (songs) Closer to Fine, 1989, Hammer and Nail, 1990, Galileo, 1992, Least Complicated, 1994, Shame on You, 1997; composer: (films) One Weekend a Month, 2004; co-author (with Don Saliers): A Song to Sing, A Life to Live: Reflections on Music as Spiritual Practice, 2004; appearances include (films) Boys on the Side, 1995, (documentaries) Wordplay, 2006. Mem.: Phi Beta Kappa. Office: c/o Russell Carter Artist Mgmt Ste 755 315 W Ponce de Leon Ave Decatur GA 30030 Office Phone: 404-377-9900. E-mail: igfan@rcam.com.*

**SALIGMAN, HARVEY,** retired consumer products and services company executive; b. Phila., July 18, 1938; s. Martin and Lillian (Zitin) S.; m. Linda Powell, Nov. 25, 1979; children: Martin, Lilli Ann, Todd Michael, Adam Andrew, Brian Matthew BS, Phila. Coll. Textiles and Sci., 1960. With Queen

Casuals, Inc., Phila., 1960-88, v.p., 1966-68, pres., chief exec. officer, 1968-81, chmn., 1981-88; pres., chief operating officer Interco Inc., St. Louis, 1981-83, chief exec. officer, 1983-85, 1985-89, chmn., 1989-90; ret. Bd. dirs. Ameren Corp. (formerly Union Electric). Trustee Washington U., St. Louis, Nantucket Hist. Assn. Mem. St. Louis Club, Masons.

**SALINAS, BARUJ,** artist, architect; b. Havana, Cuba, July 6, 1935; came to U.S., 1959; s. Moises and Regina (Algazi) S.; 1 child, Shari Regina. BArch, Kent State U., 1958. Chief draftsman Calif. Exploration Co., Coral Gables, Fla., 1961-64; draftsman Stresscon, Miami, Fla., 1964-66; chief draftsman Pillsbury Co., Miami, Fla., 1966-70; artist Miami and Barcelona, Spain, 1970—. Instr. Winchester Sch. Art, Barcelona, 1992, 93, N.Y. Sch. Visual Arts, Barcelona, 1993; instr. art. Miami Dade Coll. interam. campus, 1998—. Vol. Amnesty Internat., Paris, 1989-90; art coord. Internat. Com. for Human Rights, Miami, 1993-94, 95-96, 97, 98, 2000, 02, 03. Fellow Cintas Found., 1969, 70, Internat. Com. Human Rights, 2000, 02; Recipient 1st prize Ft. Lauderdale Mus. Art, 1969, 1st prize Cultura P.R., 1983. Democrat. Jewish. Avocations: travel, reading, music, sports. Studio: 2740 SW 92nd Ave Miami FL 33165-3119 Home: 721 Minorca Ave Coral Gables FL 33134 Personal E-mail: barujs@hotmail.com.

**SALINAS, CELENA IRIS,** reading specialist; b. San Antonio, Dec. 10, 1969; d. Arnoldo C. and Vilma Gloria Salinas. B of Journalism, U. Tex., 1991; MEd, Tex. State U., 2002. Cert. reading tchr. Customer svc. rep. Dun & Bradstreet, Austin, Tex., 1992—95; morning news anchor K99 KRYS, Corpus Christi, Tex., 1991—92; workforce devel. specialist Alamo Area Coun. of Cts., New Braunfels, Tex., 1995—2000; reading specialist U. Tex., Austin, 2000—. Mem. New Braunfels C. of C., Tex., 2002—06, Lion's Club, New Braunfels, Tex., 2004—06; grad. Leadership New Braunfels, Tex., 2005. Mem.: Kappa Delta Pi. Avocations: yoga, gardening. Home: 920 W Bridge St New Braunfels TX 78130 Office: Univ Tex/Univ Charter Sch PO Box 7667 Austin TX 78713 E-mail: celenairis@yahoo.com.

**SALINAS, ELISEO,** research and development company executive, researcher, psychiatrist; Gained initial medical qualifications, U. Buenos Aires, Argentina, 1980; M in Pharmacology, France. US Ednl. Commn. for Foreign Med. Graduates cert. 1981. Resident in Psychiatry les Hôpitaux Psychiatriques de Paris, France; staff psychiatrist Hôpital de Gonesse, France; cons. psychiatrist Hôpital Sainte-Anne, Clinque des Maladies Mentales et de l'Encéphale, Paris; internat. project leader (CNS) Synthelabo Récherche, 1991—93; with Wyeth Rsch., 1993—2004, head of global Central Nervous Systems, v.p. for regional clin. R & D, 1997—2004; chief scientific officer, exec. v.p., global R&D Shire Pharm., Wayne, Pa., 2004—. Lectr. Université René Descartes, Paris. Mem.: Am. Coll. Neuropsychopharmacology, Collegium Internat. Neuro-Psychopharamacologicum, Assn. European Psychiatrists. Office: Shire Pharm 725 Chesterbrook Blvd Wayne PA 19087-5637 Office Phone: 484-595-8800, 484-595-8276. Office Fax: 484-595-8900.

**SALINAS, MARÍA ELENA,** newscaster, columnist; b. LA, 1956; d. Jose Luis Cordero Salinas and Luz Tiznado; m. Eliott Rodriguez, Mar. 1993; children: Julia Alexandra, Gabriela Maria stepchildren: Erica, Bianca. Reporter KMEX-34 TV, LA, 1981—87; co-anchor Noticiero Univisión, Miami, Fla., 1987—; columnist King Features Syndicates. Co-anchor (TV series) Noticiero Univisión, 1987—, co-host Aquí y Ahora, 2002—; author: I Am My Father's Daughter: Living a Life Without Secrets, 2006. Founding mem. Nat. Assn. Hispanic Journalists; active in Nat. Assn. Latino Elected & Apptd. Officials; established Maria Elena Salinas Scholarship for Excellence in Spanish-Language News, 2002—. Named Journalist of Yr., Hispanic Media 100, 2002; named one of 100 Most Influential Hispanics, Hispanic Mag., 1999; named to Nat. Assn. Hispanic Journalists' Hall of Fame, 2006; recipient Edward R. Murrow award, 1997, 2 Nat. News Emmy awards, Nat. Acad. TV Arts & Sciences, 1999, LA Area Emmy award, 2002, Pride award, Hispanic Fedn., 2006, President's award, Nat. Assn. Latino Elected & Apptd. Officials, 2006. Mem.: Nat. Assn. Hispanic Journalists (former v.p.). Office: Univision Communications Inc 9405 NW 41st St Miami FL 33178 also: King Features 15th Fl 300 W 57th St New York NY 10019 Office Phone: 305-471-3900. Office Fax: 305-471-4346.*

**SALINAS, RODNEY JAY C.,** media company executive; b. Philippines; s. Dannie and Trinidad; m. Taryn Costanzo. BA in Internat. Affairs, MA in Polit. Mgmt., George Washington U. Former nat. fin. dir. Jon Amores for Congress Campaign, W.Va.; former comm. coord. Assoc. of Fundraising Professionals; former exec. dir. Asian Pacific Am. Inst. for Congressional Studies; founder, pres. Rainmaker Polit. Group LLC, 2001—; founder, publisher PoliticalCircus.com, 2001—. Contr. editor NetPulse; correspondent Balitang Am.; mem. Human Rights Commn., Alexandria, Va., 2001—. Named Rising Star of Polit., Campaigns & Elections Mag., 2002. Office: Rainmaker Polit Group LLC 2101-B Mount Vernon Ave Alexandria VA 22301

**SALINAS, TRACIE MCLEMORE,** mathematics professor; d. George Scott and Sharon Ford McLemore; m. Rene' Armando Salinas, June 8, 2002; 1 child, Tristan James. BS, William Carey Coll., 1996; MS, U. Tenn., 1999, PhD, 2004. Lectr. U. Tenn., Knoxville, 2000—04; asst. prof. Appalachian State U., Boone, NC, 2004—. Contbr. articles to profl. jours. Mem.: N.C. Coun. Tchrs. Math., Math. Assn. Am. Office Phone: 828-262-3050.

**SALINGER, FRANK MAX,** lawyer; b. Landau, Isar, Germany, Dec. 4, 1951; s. Karl and Ingeborg F. (Herold) S.; m. Susan Ann Wagner, May 20, 1978. Student, Columbia Union Coll., Takoma Park, Md., 1969-72; JD, U. Balt., 1975. Bar: Md. 1975, U.S. Dist. Ct. Md. 1975, U.S. Ct. Appeals (4th cir.) 1978, U.S. Tax Ct. 1978, U.S. Ct. Mil. Appeals 1978, U.S. Ct. Appeals (5th cir.) 1982, U.S. Supreme Ct. 1983, U.S. Ct. Appeals (11th cir.) 1984, U.S. Ct. Appeals (9th cir.) 1986, D.C. 1986, U.S. Ct. Appeals (3d cir.) 1989. Pvt. practice, Balt., 1975-77; counsel Md. State Senate, Annapolis, 1975-76; assoc. counsel Am. Fin. Corp., Silver Spring, Md., 1977-78; govt. rels. counsel Truck Trailer Mfrs. Assn., Washington, 1978-80; v.p., gen. counsel, dir. govt. affairs Am. Fin. Svcs. Assocs., Washington, 1980-92; v.p. govt. rels. Advanta Corp., Wilmington, Del., 1992—. Co-author: (with Alvin O. Wiese and Robert E. McKew) A Guide to the Consumer Bankruptcy Code, 1989; (with Robert W. Green) State Regulations and Statutes on Consumer Credit, 1989, Federal Consumer Credit Regulations and Statutes, 1989. City councilman, Laurel, Md., 1976-78, zoning commr., 1976-78; chmn. Md. State Young Reps., 1977-78; bd. dirs. Am. Bankruptcy Inst., Washington, 1986-88. Mem. ABA (mem. com. on consumer fin. svcs., subcoms. on interest rate regulation and state regulation), Am. League Lobbyists (chair fin. svcs. sect. 1995-97), Federalist Soc. Law and Pub. Policy, Capitol Hill Club, Ford's Theatre Soc. Republican. Office: Advanta Corp One Righter Pkwy Wilmington DE 19803 Business E-Mail: fsalinger@advanta.com.

**SALINGER, J(EROME) D(AVID),** author; b. N.Y.C., Jan. 1, 1919; s. Sol and Miriam (Jillich) S.; m. Claire Douglas, 1953 (div. 1967); children: Margaret Ann, Matthew; m. Colleen. Student, Valley Forge Mil. Acad., Columbia U., Ursinus Coll. Author: Catcher in the Rye, 1951, Nine Stories, 1953, Franny and Zooey, 1961, Raise High the Roof Beam, Carpenters; and Seymour: An Introduction, 1963; contbr. stories to New Yorker mag. Sgt. AUS, 1942-46. Address: care Harold Ober Assocs 425 Madison Ave New York NY 10017-1110*

**SALINGER, MICHAEL ALVIN,** economist, educator; b. Cin., Aug. 24, 1956; s. James Alvin and Joyce (Joslin) S.; m. Julie Landsman, July 6, 1985; children: Philip Landsman, David Herbert, Nicholas Andrew. BA, Yale U., 1978; PhD, MIT, 1982. Asst. prof. Grad. Sch. Bus. Columbia U., N.Y.C., 1982-87, assoc. prof., 1987-90, Boston U., 1990—, faculty dir. undergrad. program, 1999-2000, chmn. dept. fin. and econs., 2000—04, prof., 2001—. Economist FTC, Washington, 1985—86; acad. advisor Princeton Econs. Group, 1989—94; spl. cons. Nat. Econ. Rsch. Assocs., 1994—. vis. assoc. prof. MIT, 1997—98. Contbr. articles to profl. publs.; assoc. editor: Jour. Indsl. Econs., 1996—2002, mem. editl. bd.; 2002—, Rev. of Ind. Orgn.,

2002—. Vol. The Alumni Fund, New Haven, 1978—2004. NSF fellow, 1979-82. Mem. Am. Econ. Assn. Jewish. Avocations: tennis, skiing. Office: Boston U Sch Mgmt 595 Commonwealth Ave Boston MA 02215-1704 E-mail: salinger@bu.edu.

**SALINS, PETER D.,** academic administrator; b. Berlin, June 15, 1938; came to U.S., 1939; s. Irwin and Ilse Daisy (Lessler) S.; m. Rochelle Chensky, Apr. 4, 1971; children: Jessica Elizabeth, Jonathan Andrew. BArch, Syracuse U., 1961, M in Regional Planning, 1968, PhD, 1969. Registered architect. Mass. Chmn. dept. urban affairs and planning Hunter Coll., CUNY, N.Y.C., 1973-93, 96-97, prof. dept. urban affairs and planning, 1980-97, dir. grad. program in urban planning, 1993-95, dir. urban rsch. ctr., 1995-97; provost, vice chancellor acad. affairs SUNY Sys. Adminstrn., Albany, 1997—. Sr. fellow Manhattan Inst. Policy Rsch., N.Y.C., 1985—; mem. Planning Accreditation Bd., Chgo., 1990—; Catherine Bauer Wurster lectr. U. Calif., Berkeley, 1993; dir. SUNY Rsch. Found., 1997—; prof. dept. polit. sci. U. Stony Brook, 1998. Author: The Ecology of Housing Destruction, 1980, Assimilation, American Style, 1997; co-author: Scarcity by Design, 1992; editor: Housing America's Poor, 1987, New York Unbound, 1988; co-editor Jour. of Am. Planning Assn., 1988-93 (Excellence award 1992, Journalism award 1994). Mem. planning com. Am. Acad. Sci., Washington, 1971-72; mem. adv. panel White House Domestic Policy Unit, Washington, 1977; dir. Citizens Housing and Planning Coun., N.Y.C., 1988—; trustee Lavanburg Found., N.Y.C., 1987—; Village of Baxter Estates, Nassau County, N.Y., 1992-99; mem. mayor's adv. commn. N.Y.C. Health and Hosps. Corp., 1995-96. Fellow: Am. Inst. Cert. Planners; mem.: ASPA (v.p. 1982—84, Luther Gulick award for outstanding acad. 1994), Am. Planning Assn. (v.p. 1986—88, policy bd. mem. 1986—, N.Y. met. chpt.), Lambda Alpha, Avocations: golf, reading, hiking. Office: SUNY Suny Plz Albany NY 12246-0001 Office Phone: 518-443-5152. Business E-Mail: peter.salins@suny.edu.

**SALIS, ARI,** radiologist; m. Elaine Salis, Mar. 29, 1997. MD, U. Medicine and Dentistry N.J., Newark, 1995. Lic. N.J., 1995. Prin. Am. Radiology, Balt., 2003—05; chief of radiology Sinai Hosp., Balt., 2004—.

**SALISBURY, ALAN BLANCHARD,** information technology officer; b. Newark, Jan. 21, 1937; s. Lloyd Wade and Elizabeth Barry (Blanchard) S.; m. Florence Dorothy Conrad, May 21, 1971; children: Katherine Anne, Barbara Lynn. BS with distinction, U.S. Mil. Acad., 1958; MSEE, Stanford U., 1964, PhD, 1973; postgrad., Indsl. Coll. of Armed Forces, Washington, 1978. Commd. 2d lt. Signal Corps U.S. Army, 1958, advanced through grades to Maj. Gen., ret., 1987; asst. prof. U.S. Mil. Acad., West Point, N.Y., 1964-67; chief of data communications 1st Signal Brigade, Republic of Vietnam, 1968-69; tech. adv. Directorate of Mgmt. Info., Washington, 1970-71; dir. U.S. Army Ctr. for Tactical Computer Sci., Ft. Monmouth, N.J., 1975-77; project mgr. Operations Tactical Data Systems, Ft. Monmouth, N.J., 1978-82; program mgr. Joint Tactical Fusion Program, Washington, 1982-84; comdr. U.S. Army Info. Systems Engring., Ft. Belvoir, Va., 1984-87; pres. Contel Technology Ctr., Fairfax, Va., 1987-91; exec. v.p. Microelectronics & Computer Tech. Corp., Austin, Tex., 1991-93; pres. Learning Tree Internat. USA, Inc., Reston, Va., 1993-99; ind. cons., 1999—. Bd. dirs. Sybase, Dublin, Calif., Challenger Ctr. for Space Sci. Edn., Alexandria, Va.; dir. Mitretek Systems, Inc., McLean, Va., Assn. Grads. U.S. Mil. Acad.; chmn. Ctr. for Nat. Software Studies; bd. visitors Software Engring. Inst. Carnegie Mellon U., 1988-2002, Coll. of Engring. U. Md., 1993-2001. Author: Microprogrammable Computer Architectures 1976, numerous articles in profl. jours.; founding editor Journal of Systems & Software, 1979-85. Decorated Bronze Star (2), 1969, D.S.M., 1987. Mem. Inst. for Elec. & Electronic Engrs. (sr.), Assn. for Computing Machinery, Armed Forces Communications & Electronics Assn. (chpt. pres. 1981-82), Phi Kappa Phi, Soc. of the Sigma Xi. Office: PO Box 2910 Reston VA 20195-2910 Office Phone: 703-319-2187. E-mail: abslsbry@aol.com.

**SALISBURY, DALLAS L.,** researcher, director; BA, U. Wash., 1970; MPA in Pub. Policy and Adminstrn., Syracuse U., 1973. Employee benefit security adminstrn. U.S. Dept. Labor, 1975—78; with U.S. Dept. Justice, 1974, Wash. State Legislature, 1971-72, Employee Benefit Rsch. Inst., Washington, 1978—, pres., CEO, mem. bd. trustees. Bd. dirs. The Health Project; mem. adv. bd. Nat. Acad. on Aging; lectr. in field; cons. in field. Mem. editl. adv. bd. Benefits Quar., Employee Benefits Jour., Healthplan; contbr. articles to profl. jours. Mem. ERISA adv. coun. Sec. of Labor; pres.'s adv. coun. PBGC. Fellow Nat. Acad. Human Resources. Office: Employee Benefit Research Inst 2121 K St NW Ste 600 Washington DC 20037-1800

**SALISBURY, EUGENE W.,** lawyer, judge; b. Blasdell, N.Y., Mar. 20, 1933; s. W. Dean and Mary I. (Burns) S.; m. Joanne M. Salisbury, July 14, 1950; children: Mark, Ellen, Susan, David, Scott. BA in History and Govt. cum laude, U. Buffalo, 1959, JD cum laude, 1968. Bar: N.Y. 1960, D.C. 1973, U.S. Dist. Ct. (we. and no. dists.) 1961, U.S. Ct. Appeals (2d cir.) 1970, U.S. Ct. Appeals (D.C. cir.) 1973, U.S. Supreme Ct. 1973. Ptnr. Lipsitz, Green, Fahringer, Roll, Salisbury and Cambria, Buffalo, 1960—. Justice Village of Blasdell, 1961-2001; lectr. N.Y. Office Ct. Adminstrn., N.Y.C., 1961—; mem. N.Y. State Commn. on Jud. Conduct, 1989-2001, chmn., 2000-2001. Author: Manual for N.Y. Courts, 1973, Forms for N.Y. Courts, 1977. Capt. U.S. Army, 1949-54, Korea. Decorated Bronze Star, Purple Heart; recipient Citizen of Yr. award Indsl. Rels. Rsch. Assn., 2000; named Jurist of Yr., Erie County Judges and Police Conf., 2001, Magistrate of Yr., Erie County Magistrates Assn., 2001. Mem. ABA (del. spl. ct. sect. 1988-2001), D.C. Bar Assn., Erie County Bar Assn., N.Y. State Bar Assn., World Judges Assn., N.Y. State Magistrates Assn. (pres. 1973, Man of Yr. 1974), N.Y. State Jud. Conf., Upstate N.Y. Labor Adv. Coun., 1995—. Office: Lipsitz Green Fahringer Roll Salisbury and Cambria 42 Delaware Ave Ste 300 Buffalo NY 14202-3857 Office Phone: 716-849-1333. Business E-Mail: esalisbury@1glaw.com.

**SALISBURY, FRANK BOYER,** botanist, educator, writer; b. Provo, Utah, Aug. 3, 1926; s. Frank M. and Catherine (Boyer) S.; m. Lois Marilyn Olson, Sept. 1, 1949; children: Frank Clark, Steven Scott, Michael James, Cynthia Kay, Phillip Boyer (dec.), Rebecca Lynn, Blake Charles; m. Mary Thorpe Robinson, June 28, 1991. BS, U. Utah, 1951, MA, 1952; PhD, Calif. Inst. Tech., 1955. Asst. prof. botany Pomona Coll., Claremont, Calif., 1954-55; faculty Colo. State U., Ft. Collins, 1955-66, prof. plant physiology, 1961-66; plant physiologist Expt. Sta., 1961-66; prof. plant physiology Utah State U., Logan, 1966-97, disting. prof. Agr., 1987-97, prof. emeritus, 1997—; head dept. plant sci., 1966-70; tech. rep. plant physiology AEC, Germantown, Md., 1973-74. Vis. prof. U. Innsbruck, Austria; Lady Davis fellow Hebrew U. Jerusalem, 1983; mem. aerospace medicine adv. com. NASA, 1988-93, life scis. adv. com., 1986-88, chmn. NASA Controlled Ecol. Life Support System Discipline Working Group, 1989-94; leader of project to grow wheat through a life cycle in Russian space station, Mir, 1990-97. Author: The Flowering Process, 1963, Truth by Reason and by Revelation, 1965, The Biology of Flowering, 1971, The Utah UFO Display, 1974, The Creation, 1976, The Case for Divine Design, 2006; co-author: (with R.V. Parke) Vascular Plants, Form and Function, 2d edit., 1970, (with C. Ross) Plant Physiology, 1969, 4th edit., 1992; (with W. Jensen) Botany: An Ecological Approach, 1972, Botany, 2d edit., 1984, (with others) Biology, 1977; editor Jour. Plant Physiology, Ams. and the Pacific Rim, 1989-96; editor, contbr.: Units, Symbols, and Terminology for Plant Physiology, 1996; editor: Geochemistry and The Biosphere, 2006. Trustee Colo. State U. Rsch. Found., 1959-62; leader People to People bot. del. to South Africa, 1984, to China, 1988, Soviet Union, 1990; fin. sec. Ohio Columbus Mission LDS Ch., 1997-99. NSF sr. postdoctoral fellow Germany and Austria, 1962-63. Fellow AAAS; mem. Am. Soc. for Gravitational and Space Biology (Founders award 1994), Am. Soc. Plant Physiologists (editorial bd. 1967-92), Am. Inst. Biol. Scis. (governing bd. 1976-79), Bot. Soc. Am. (merit award 1982), Sigma Xi, Phi Kappa Phi. Mem. Lds Ch. Home: 2250 Bryan Cir Salt Lake City UT 84108-2711 Office Phone: 801-281-1575. *This is an extremely exciting time to live! Science has provided marvelous insight into the cosmos, the earth, and the nature of life. The fact that mankind exists and can contemplate it all cries out that it has purpose and direction. My life is full to overflowing because God's revelation of Himself adds the final capstone to this beautiful structure.*

**SALISBURY, MARIE JOYCE (MARIE JOYCE ALBERTI),** musician, educator; b. Windsor, N.Y., June 13, 1936; d. Raymond Brian and Lillian Elizabeth (Parsons) Salisbury; m. Thomas Edwid Alberti, Nov. 27, 1959 (dec. June 1992); children: Donna Marie, Linda Renée; m. Wm. C. Thompson, June 10, 2004. Student, Zion Bible Coll., Providence, 1954-56, Cen. Bible Coll., Springfield, Mo., 1956-57, U. of Mo. Conservatory, Kansas City, 1962-63. Technician, arranger Gospel Pub. House, Springfield, 1957-59; educator, salesperson Midwest Music, Springfield, 1963-64; pvt. tchr. Springfield, 1957-97; educator, salesperson Sims Kimball Music Ctr., Springfield, 1964-82; entertainer Lakeland Hosp., Springfield, 1975-97; weddings, receptions, and convs. cons., musician, 1963—. Theater organist Radio City Rockettes, N.Y.C., 1995-96; organist Nat. Fox Trotters Shows, Ava, Mo., 1970-78, Springfield Charity Horse Shows, 1978-93; ch. musician Hillcrest Presbyn., 1963-68, 70-72, Antioch United Meth., Springfield, 1992—98. Composer themes, songs, and arrangements; rec. artist, 2004—. Musician Rep. Rally for Pres. Ford, Springfield, Dem. Fund Raiser for Richard Gephardt, Springfield, Gov. John and Janet Ashcroft receptions, Springfield, also numerous fund raisers Springfield Symphony; chairperson Cancer Dr., 1965-97. Ann. Marie Alberti Day named in her honor Antioch United Meth., 1997. Republican. Avocations: entertaining, swimming. Address: 3135 W Edgewood St Springfield MO 65807-3174

**SALISBURY, MICHEAL WAYNE,** education educator; b. Pecos, Tex., Sept. 9, 1971; s. Pat and Jerry Salisbury; m. Tara Katina Collins, July 11, 1992; children: Matthew Wayne, Kimberly D'Ann, Kelly D'Lynn. BS, Angelo State U., San Angelo, Tex., 1994, MS, 1996; PhD, N.Mex State U., Las Cruces, 1996—99. Prof. U. Tenn., Knoxville, 2000—01, Angelo State U., 2001—. Contbr. over 50 papers to profl. jours. and pubs. Mem.: Am. Soc. Animal Scientists. Office Phone: 325-942-2027.

**SALISBURY, ROBERT HOLT,** political science professor; b. Elmhurst, Ill., Apr. 29, 1930; s. Robert Holt and Beulah (Hammer) S.; m. Rose Marie Cipriani, June 19, 1953; children: Susan Marie, Robert Holt, Matthew Gary. AB, Washington and Lee U., 1951; MA, U. Ill., 1952, PhD, 1955. Mem. faculty Washington U., St. Louis, 1955-65, prof., 1965-97, prof. emeritus, 1997—, chmn. dept. polit. sci., 1966-73, 86-92, dir. Center for Study Pub. Affairs, 1974-77, Sidney W. Souers prof. govt., 1982-97. Vis. prof. SUNY, Buffalo, 1965, So. Ill. U., Edwardsville, 1975; affiliated scholar Am. Bar Found., 1981-95; cons. U.S. Conf. Mayors, 1965, Hartford (Conn.) C. of C., 1964, NSF, 1973. Author: Interest Groups Politics in America, 1970, Governing America, 1973, Citizen Participation in the Public Schools, 1980, Interests and Institutions, 1992, The Hollow Core, 1993; contbr. articles to profl. jours. Mem. St. Louis County Charter Commn., 1967, Gov.'s Commn. on Local Govt., 1968-69. Guggenheim fellow, 1990; Rockefeller Ctr. scholar, 1990. Mem. Mo. Polit. Sci. Assn. (pres. 1964-65), Am. Polit. Sci. Assn. (exec. council 1969-71, v.p. 1980-81), Midwest Polit. Sci. Assn. (pres. 1977-78), Pi Sigma Alpha. Democrat. Methodist. Home: 709 S Skinker Blvd Saint Louis MO 63105-3225 Office: Washington U Dept Polit Sci Saint Louis MO 63130

**SALISBURY, TAMARA PAULA,** foundation executive; b. N.Y.C., Dec. 14, 1927; d. Paul Terrance and Nadine (Korolkova) Voloshin; m. Franklin Cary Salisbury, Jan. 22, 1955; children: Franklin Jr., John, Elizabeth, Elaine, Claire. BA, Coll. Notre Dame, 1948; postgrad., Am. U., George Washington U. Chemist depts. pathology and chemotherapy NIH Cancer Inst., Bethesda, Md., 1946-52; asst. to chief of Chemistry Br. Office of Naval Rsch., Bethesda, 1953-55; v.p., COO Nat. Found. Cancer Rsch., Bethesda, 1973—. Mem. Assn. Internat. Cancer Rsch., 1995. Decorated d'Officier De L'Ordre De Leopold II; outstanding contbns. award Internat. Soc. Quantum Biology, 1983, award of appreciation Beth Israel Hosp., Harvard Med. Sch., Brigham & Women's Hosp., 1993. Mem. AAAS, Am. Chem. Soc., N.Y. Acad. Scis., Inst. Phys. and Chem. Biology (fgn.), Krebforschung Internat., Nat. Liberal Club. Home: 10811 Alloway Dr Potomac MD 20854-1504 Office: Nat Found Cancer Rsch 4600 E West Hwy Ste 525 Bethesda MD 20814-6900

**SALITERMAN, RICHARD ARLEN,** lawyer; b. Aug. 3, 1946; s. Leonard Slitz and Dorothy (Sloan) S.; m. Laura Shrager, June 15, 1979; 1 child, Robert Warren. BA summa cum laude, U. Minn., 1968; JD, Columbia U., 1971; LLM, NYU, 1974. Bar: Minn. 1972, DC 1974. Legal staff subcom. on antitrust and monopoly U.S. Senate, Washington, 1971-72; acting dir., dep. dir. compliance and enforcement divsn. Fed. Energy Office, N.Y.C., 1974; mil. atty. Presdl. Clemency Bd., White House, Washington, 1975; pres. Saliterman & Siefferman, PC, Mpls., 1975—. Adj. prof. law Hamline U., 1976-81. Author: Advising Minnesota Corporations and Other Business Organizations, 4 vols., 1975; chmn. Hennepin County Bar Jour., 1985-87. Trustee, sec. Hopkins Edn. Found.; trustee W. Harry Davis Found., 1990-96; pres. Twin Cities Coun.; mem. nat. bd. dirs Navy League U.S., Washington, 1997—, nat. judge adv., 2001-02; bd. dirs., sec. The Pavek Mus., 1992—. lt. USN, 1972-75, res., 1975—. Office Phone: 612-339-1400. Business E-Mail: rsaliterman@saliterman-law.com.

**SALKIND, ALVIN J.,** engineering educator, dean, consultant; b. NYC; s. Samuel M. and Florence (Zins) S.; m. Marion Ruth Koenig, Nov. 7, 1965; children: Susanne, James. B.Ch.E., Poly. Inst. N.Y., 1949, M.Ch.E., 1952, D.Ch.E., 1958; postgrad. and mgmt. courses, Pa. State U., 1965, Harvard U., 1976. Registered profl. engr., N.Y., N.J. Sr. scientist Sonotone Corp., Elmsford, NY, 1954—57; rsch. assoc. Poly. Inst. N.Y., 1956-58, adj. prof. chem. engring., 1960-70; with ESB-Ray OVAC Co., Yardley, Pa., 1958-79, dir. tech., 1971-72, v.p. tech., 1972-79; pres. ESB Tech. Co., 1972—79; prof., chief bioengring. divsn., dept. surgery UMDNJ-Robert Wood Johnson Med. Sch., Piscataway, NJ, 1970—2001, prof. emeritus, 2004—, prof. biomed. engring. and materials sci. and engring. Rutgers U., Piscataway, NJ, 1985—2002, assoc. dean Coll. Engring., 1989—2001, prof. emeritus, 2004—; pvt. engring. practice, 1979—. Vis. prof., exec. officer Case Ctr. Electrochem. Sci., 1981—82; vis. prof. U. Miami, 2003—; bd. dirs., cons. various cos., rsch. instns. and govt. orgns.; mem. rev. panels Nat. Rsch. Coun., NIH. Author (with S.U. Falk): Alkaline Storage Batteries, 1969; author: (with Herbert T. Silverman and Irving F. Miller) Electrochemical Bioscience and Bioengineering, 1973; editor (with E. Yeager): Techniques of Electrochemistry, 1971, Russian edits., 1977, vol. 2, 1973, vol. 3, 1978, History of Battery Technology, 1987; editor: (with F. McLarnon and V. Bogatzky) Rechargeable Zinc Electrodes, 1996; editor: (with A. Landgrebe) Power Sources for Transportation Applications, 2003; contbr. over 200 articles to profl. jours. With USNR, 1945—46. Recipient Alumnus citation Poly. Inst. N.Y., 1975, award Internat. Tech. Exch. Soc., 1992, Frank Booth award Internat. Power Sources Symposium Eng., 1999; Case Centennial scholar Case-Western Res. U., 1980. Fellow Acad. Medicine of NJ, Am. Coll. Cardiology, AAAS, Am. Inst. Med. and Biomed. Engrs.; mem. Electrochem. Soc. (past chmn. new tech. com., past chmn. battery div.), Indsl. Rsch. Inst. (emeritus 1979), NY Acad. Scis., Sigma Xi, Phi Lambda Upsilon. Home: 51 Adams Dr Princeton NJ 08540-5401 Office: Rutgers U Sch Engring 607 Taylor Rd Piscataway NJ 08854 Office Phone: 732-445-6858. Personal E-mail: ajsalkind@verizon.net. Business E-Mail: salkind@rci.rutgers.edu, asalkind@miami.edu.

**SALKIND, MICHAEL JAY,** science administrator, metallurgical engineer; s. Milton and Esther (Jaffe) S.; m. Miriam E. Schwartz, Aug. 16, 1959 (div. 1979); children: Michael Jay, Elizabeth Jane, Jonathan Hillson, Joshua Isaac; m. Carol T. Gill, Dec. 23, 1990. B in Metall. Engring., Rensselaer Polytech. Inst., 1959, PhD, 1962. Chief advanced metallurgy United Techs. Rsch. Labs., East Hartford, 1964-68; chief structures and materials Sikorsky Aircraft div. United Techs. Corp., 1968-75; dir. product devel. Avco Systems div., 1975-76; mgr. structures NASA, 1976-80; dir. aerospace scis. Air Force Office of Sci. Rsch., 1980-89; pres. Ohio Aerospace Inst., 1990—2003, Business Tech Network, 2003—; prin. Indus Internat., 2003—. Adj. faculty metallurgy Trinity Coll., Hartford; adj. faculty aerospace U.S. Mil. Acad., 1982-85; adj. faculty materials Johns Hopkins U., 1985-89; chair Ohio Math. and Sci. Coalition. Cons. editor Internat. Jour. Fibre Sci. and Tech.; editor Applications Composite Materials, 1973; contbr. to profl. jours. and textbooks. Evaluator Accreditation Bd. Engring. and Tech., 1989—1995; mem. Daniel Guggenheim Medal Bd. Awards, 1984-90; mem. Spirit of St. Louis Medal Bd., 1984-89; bd. dirs. Citizens' Acad. Charter Sch., Cleve. Internat. Program, NCCJ, Sustainable Cleve.; co-chair Buckeye H.S. F.I.R.S.T. Robotics Competition; mem. industry adv. com. Kent State U., Coll. Tech. Capt. ord. U.S. Army, 1962-64. Recipient Disting. Leadership award, Cleve. Tech. Socs. Coun., 2002. Fellow AAAS, AIAA (assoc.), ASM Internat.; mem. ASME (Disting. lectr. 1989-93), ASTM (chmn. com. D-30 on high modulous fibers and their composites 1968-74), Am. Helicopter Soc., AIME, Brit. Inst. Metals, Rsch. Soc. Am., Plansee Soc., India Ohio C. of C., Cosmos Club, Union Club, 50 Club, Leadership Cleve., Sigma Xi, Alpha Sigma Mu. E-mail: michaelsalkind@adelphia.net.

**SALKY, BARRY A.,** surgeon; b. Memphis, Nov. 10, 1944; s. Jake and Mary Salky; m. Alma Halski; children: Jonathan, Adam. MD, U. Tenn., Memphis, 1970. Diplomate Am. Bd. Surgery. Intern Mt. Sinai Hosp., NYC, 1971—73, resident in internal medicine, 1975—78, clin. prof. surgery, 1996—2004, prof. surgery, 2004—, chief divsn. laparoscopic surgery, 1992—96, 2004—. Author: Laparscopy for Surgeons, 1990, Advanced Laparoscopy for Surgeons, 1994. Maj. U.S. Army, 1973—75. Recipient Ambassador's award, Am. Friends of Rambom Med. Ctr., 1995. Fellow: ACS, Am. Coll. of Gastroenterology; mem.: Soc. Surgery Alimentary Tract, Soc. Am. Gastrointestinal Endoscopic Surgeons (v.p. 1997—98). Jewish. Avocations: golf, travel. Office: Mt Sinai Hosp 5 E 98th St 14th Fl New York NY 10029 Office Phone: 212-241-5339. Business E-Mail: barry.salky@mountsinai.com.

**SALL, JOHN,** information technology executive; married; 4 children. BS, Beloit Coll.; MS, No. Ill. U. Co-founder, exec. v.p. SAS Inst., Cary, NC; leader JMP Bus. Divsn. Named one of Forbes' Richest Americans, 2006. Office: SAS Inst 100 SAS Campus Dr Cary NC 27513-2414*

**SALL, LARRY DAVID,** library director; b. Portland, Oreg., July 10, 1941; s. David Elmer and Lillian Elisabeth Sall; m. Louise Kuhn, Dec. 13, 1967 (div. Aug. 6, 1978); m. Judy Claire McQuade, Nov. 24, 1979; 1 child, Karl Fredrick. BA, U. Idaho, 1964; exch. fellow, U. Munich, Germany, 1967—68; PhD, Wayne State U., 1971. Assoc. dir. spl. collections U. Tex.-Dallas, Richardson, 1982—99, dir. librs., 1999—2004, dean of librs., 2004—. Translator: (memoir) Pioneer Aviator in China, 1998; contbr.: (biography of Lamar Muse) Encyclopedia of American Business History: The Airline Industry. Friends adv. bd. Dallas Pub. Libr., 2004; libr. adv. bd. So. Meth. U., Dallas, 2003; bd. dirs. Frontiers of Flight Mus., Dallas, 1999. Mem.: Audubon Tex. (bd. dirs. 2004, bd. dirs. Dallas chpt. 2001), Am. Birding Assn. (assoc.), Dallas Com. Fgn. Rels. (assoc.), Tex. Philatelic Assn. (assoc.; pres. 1991—95), Richardson Ctrl. Rotary Club (assoc.; pres. 1989—90), Richardson Rotary Club (assoc.). Achievements include development of History of Aviation collection and others, U. Tex.-Dallas. Avocations: bird watching, mountain hiking, scuba diving, travel, reading. Office: Univ Texas at Dallas PO Box 830643 Richardson TX 75083-0643 Office Phone: 972-883-2960. Office Fax: 972-883-2473. E-mail: sall@utdallas.edu.

**SALLAH, MAJEED (JIM SALLAH),** retired real estate developer; b. Boston, Aug. 5, 1920; s. Herbert K. and Rose (Karem) Sallah; m. Aline C. Powers, Apr. 10, 1970; children: Christopher M., Melissa Rose. Pres., dir. Glo-Bit Fish Co., Gloucester, Mass., 1947—48, Live-Pak of Ohio, Inc., 1947—51, Cape Ann Glass Co., Gloucester, 1950—72, Marias Restaurant, 1960—, Cape Ann Realty Co., 1961—. Pres., treas., dir. Gloucester Hot-Top Constrn. Co., Goucester, 1967—75; pres., bd. dir SGF Corp., 1983—85, SALFAD, Inc., Rossford, Ohio; pres., treas. Points East, Inc.; trustee Christopher Investment Trust; bd. dir. Lustal, Inc.; bd. dir., ptnr. Barsal, Inc., Toledo, Hamsal, Inc. Pres. Lebanese-Am. Bus. Men's Club; treas. Lebanese-Maronite Soc. With U.S. Army, 1942—45. Decorated Bronze Star. Mem.: Gloucester Assoc., Cape Ann Investment Corp., Gloucester Fraternity Assn., Lions, Am. Legion, Amvets, Loyal Order of Moose, Elks, Ky. Cols. (hon.). Roman Catholic. Home and Office: 56 Hilltop Rd Gloucester MA 01931-0078

**SALLAH, MICHAEL D.,** journalist; Grad., U. Toledo. Joined The Blade, Toledo, 1989; nat. affairs writer Block News Alliance (The Blade and The Pitts. Post-Gazette). Named Best Reporter, Ohio Soc. Profl. Journalists, 2002; recipient Touchstone Newsie award, Press Club Toledo, 2002, 2 Crystal awards, Toledo Profl. Chptr., Women Comm., 2002, Medal winner, Investigative Reporters and Editors, Inc., 2004, Pulitzer Prize for investigative reporting, 2004. Office: The Blade 541 N Superior St Toledo OH 43660

**SALLAN, STEPHEN E.,** pediatrician; b. Detroit; MD, Wayne State U., 1967. Cert. pediat. Intern Boston Floating Hosp., 1967-68; resident in pediatrics Children's Hosp., Phila., 1968-69, Hosp. Sick Children, London, 1969-70; fellow in pediatric oncology Children's Hosp. Med. Ctr./Harvard U., Boston, 1973-75; mem. med. staff Dana Farber Cancer Inst., Boston, 1975—, chief of staff, 1995—; prof. pediatrics Harvard Med. Sch., Boston. Mem. AMA, AACR, ASCO, ASH, SPR. Office: Dana Farber Cancer Inst 44 Binney St Boston MA 02115-6084

**SALLEE, WANDA JEAN,** music educator; b. Seminole, Okla., Nov. 30, 1929; d. John Mordecai Cooper and Mary Blanche Jenkins-Cooper; m. William J. Sallee, Jan. 6, 1951; children: Susan Dwan, Martha Jean. MusB in Piano Theory, Okla. State U., 1950; student in Edn. and Pedagogy, Levine Sch. Music, 1990. Cert. tchr. music Am. Coll. Musicians; Tchr. music Itolml (Okla.) Elem. Schs., 1950—51, Mangum (Okla.) Elem. Schs., 1951—52; dir. ch. music First Bapt. Ch., Mangum, 1952—57, Westover Bapt. Ch., Arlington, Va., 1959—72; pvt. piano tchr. Mangum, 1952—58; tchr. Sallee Music Studio, Arlington, Va., 1959—94, Dallas, 1994—. Dir. music Bapt. Ch., Arlington, 1959—72; bd. trustees Oak Hill Acad., Va., 1965—68; presenter in field. Vol. Reagan-Bush Campaign, Arlington, 1980. Mem.: Music Tchrs. Nat. Assn., Am. Coll. Musicians (adjudicator, nat. guild judge), Richardson (Tex.) Music Tchrs. Assn. (pres., v.p., corr.sec.), Tex. State Music Tchrs. Assn. (chmn. practice student affiliate 2003—, named Piano Tchr. of Yr. 2002), Sigma Alpha Iota (life). Avocations: poetry, writing, reading, painting, eggery. Home and Office: Sallee Music Studio 7615 Cliffbrook Dr Dallas TX 75254-8101 Personal E-mail: wjs6214@airmail.net.

**SALLER, RICHARD PAUL,** classics educator; b. Ft. Bragg, N.C., Oct. 18, 1952; s. George E. and Arthea E. (North) S.; m. Carol Joann Fisher, Jan. 12, 1974 (div. Apr. 18, 2002); children: John E., Benjamin T.; m. Tanya M. Luhrmann, Jan. 4, 2003. BA in Greek and History, U. Ill., 1974; PhD in Classics, U. Cambridge, Eng., 1978. Asst. prof. Swarthmore (Pa.) Coll., 1979-84; assoc. prof. U. Chgo., 1984-89, prof., 1990—, dean of social scis., 1994—2001, provost, 2002—. Author: Personal Patronage, 1982, Patriarchy, Property and Death in the Roman Family, 1994; co-editor: Economy and Society in Ancient Greece, 1981; co-author: Roman Empire, 1987; editor Classical Philology, 1991-93. Rsch. fellow Jesus Coll., U. Cambridge, 1978-79; Ctr. for Adv. Study fellow, Stanford U., 1986-87; Trinity Coll. Cambridge fellow commoner, 1991. Mem. Am. Philol. Assn., Am. Hist. Assn., Am. Acad. Arts and Scis. Office: U Chgo Dept History 1126 E 59th St Chicago IL 60637-1580 Office Phone: 773-702-8810.

**SALLES, FELIPE WEISZ,** musician; s. Edmar Salles and Telma Weisz; m. Laura Silva Arpiainen, May 11, 2002. MusM, New Eng. Conservatory, Boston, 1997, degree, 1998; PhD in Musical Arts, Manhattan Sch. Music, NYC, 2005. Musician: (composition comission) South American Suite; composer, performer (recording) Further South, Mind Motions; performer: weddings, restaurants, art galleries, librs. & town events. Recipient First Prize in Composition, Bienal SGAE Jazz Tete Montoliu, 2001; scholar, New Eng. Conservatory, 1996—98, Boston Jazz Soc., 1997, Manhattan Sch. Music, 2003—05. Mem.: Am. Fedn. Musicians. Office Phone: 917-892-8156.

**SALLEY, JOHN JONES,** retired academic administrator, oral pathologist; b. Richmond, Va., Oct. 29, 1926; s. Thomas Raysor and Kathryn (Josey) S.; m. Jean Gordon Cunningham, Dec. 21, 1950; children: Katharine Gordon, John Jones, Martha Cunningham. DDS, Med. Coll. Va., 1951; PhD, U. Rochester, 1954; DSc, Boston U., 1975. Research fellow U. Rochester, 1951-54; from instr. to prof., chmn. dept. oral pathology Med. Coll. Va., 1954-63, prof. emeritus, 1991—; prof. pathology, dean Sch. Dentistry U. Md., 1963-74, dean emeritus Sch. Dentistry, 1977—, ret., 1991; v.p. research and grad. affairs Va. Commonwealth U., Richmond, 1974-85; acting pres. Va. Ctr. for Innovative Tech., 1985, v.p., 1985-87. Cons. divsn. rsch. grants NIH, 1962—66; cons. US Naval Hosp., Portsmouth, Va., USPHS Hosp., Balt., 1963—74, VA Hosp., Balt., 1964—74, US Naval Dental Sch., Bethesda, Md., 1966—75, WHO, 1969—75; cons. Sch. Dentistry, San Marcos U., Lima, Peru, 1965—69; spl. cons. Nat. Inst. Dental Rsch., NIH, 1957—64; dental health divsn. USPHS; mem. Md. Adv. Coun. Comprehensive Health Planning, 1968—74, Nat. Health Coun., 1970—71; pres. Am. Assn. Dental Schs., 1971—72, Conf. So. Grad. Schs., 1983—84; sr. program cons. Robert Wood Johnson Found., 1978—84; mem. career devel. rev. com. VA, 1974—78; mem. com. health care resources in VA, NRC, 1974—77; mem. Va. Gov.'s Task Force Sci. and Tech., 1982—83; sci. advisor to Gov. of Va., 1984—86; mem. rsch. cons. Va. State Coun. Higher Edn., 1974—84; chmn. task force Coun. Grad. Schs. in US, 1979—82. Conbtr. articles in field; editorial rev. bd.: Jour. Dental Edn, 1974-78. Bd. dirs. Md. divsn. Am. Cancer Soc., 1963-70, Am. Fund Dental Health, Rappahannock C.C. Found., 1999—; bd. dirs. Nat. Found. Dentistry for the Handicapped, 1986, pres., 1992-94; mem. adv. bd. Va. Inst. for Devel. Disabilities, 1987-91; bd. trustees Middlesex County Pub. Libr., 1994-98, pres., 1995-97. With USAAF, 1944-46. Recipient Outstanding Civilian Service medal Dept. Army, 1961, Disting. Citizenship award State Md., 1974. Fellow AAAS, Am. Coll. Dentists; mem. ADA, Nat. Conf. Univ. Research Adminstrs., Am. Acad. Oral Pathology, Internat. Assn. Dental Research (Novice award 1953), Internat. Med. Informatics Assn. (chmn. working group 1989-92), Sigma Xi, Sigma Zeta, Omicron Kappa Upsilon. Episcopalian (vestryman). Home and Office: 1500 Westbrook Ct Apt 2140 Richmond VA 23227

**SALLIS, JAMES,** writer; b. Helena, Ark., Dec. 21, 1944; s. Chappelle Horace and Mildred Clodine (Liming) S. Student, Tulane U., 1961-63, U. Tex., 1985-87. Tchr. intensive writing workshops Clarion (Pa.) Coll., U. Wash., Tulane U., Loyola U., Phoenix Coll., Otis Coll., L.A.; guest lectr. modern poetry, European lit., art; writer short stories, essays, poetry and trans. Editor New Worlds 1966-68; editor: (anthologies) The War Book, 1972, The Shores Beneath, 1973; features writer, reviewer, columnist Tex. Jazz, 1980-83, lead book reviewer Dallas Morning News, 1981-83; book reviewer Washington Post Book World, L.A. Times, 1993—; columnist Mag. of Fantasy and Sci. Fiction, Web Del Sol, Boston Globe, 2000--; author: A Few Last Words, 1972, The Guitar Players, 1982, 94, Jazz Guitars, 1984, The Long-Legged Fly, 1992, Saint Glinglin (translator), 1993, Difficult Lives, 1993, Moth, 1993, Black Hornet, 1994, Limits of the Sensible World, 1994, Renderings, 1995, The Guitar in Jazz, 1996, Ash of Stars: On the Writings of Samuel R. Delany, 1996, Death Will Have Your Eyes, 1997, Eye of the Cricket, 1997, Bluebottle, 1999, Gently into the Land of the Meateaters, 2000, Chester Himes: A Life, 2000, Time's Hammers, 2000, Sorrow's Kitchen, 2000, Ghost of a Flea, 2001, Cypress Grove, 2002, A City Equal To My Desire, 2004, A James Sallis Reader, 2005, Drive, 2005, Cripple Creek, 2006.

**SALLQUIST, GARY ARDIN,** minister, non-profit executive; b. Sioux City, Iowa, July 7, 1938; s. Hal Thurston and Rosemary (Daggett) S.; m. Joyce Darleen Casey, June 10, 1960; children: Susan L. Rail, Steven P. BA, U. Nebr., Omaha, 1960; MDiv, Princeton Theol. Sem., 1993; D of Ministry, La. Bapt. U., 1997; D, Am. Coll. ChFC, CLU. Ptnr. Sallquist-Wilkinson Inc., Omaha; pres. Planned Giving Sys., Cin., 1987—90; min. adult edn. Coll. Hill Presbyn. Ch., Cin., 1993—95; dir. planned giving Promise Keepers, Denver, 1995—98; v.p., divsn. higher edn. PhilanthroCorp, Woodland Park, Colo., 1998—2000; headmaster Miami Valley Christian Acad., Cin., 2001—06. Author: A Seminary Journey, 1995, The Counsel of Many, 1999, Classroom Classics, 2003, For the Love of God, 2004. Pres. Omaha Jaycees, 1966-67; dirs. Creighton-St. Joseph Hosp., Omaha, 1975-81, Leadership Cin. Alumni Assn., 1987-89. Recipient Golden Key award Nebr. Jaycees, 1975. Mem. U. Nebr. Omaha Alumni Assn. (pres. 1968-70, Outstanding Alumnus award 1977), Pi Kappa Alpha (nat. pres. 1970-72). Avocations: basketball, running, tennis, reading, public speaking. Home: 5300 Barony Pl Cincinnati OH 45241 Office: Miami Valley Christian Acad 6830 School Rd Cincinnati OH 45244 E-mail: gsallquist@miamivalleychristianacademy.org.

**SALMASSI, SADEGH,** physician; b. Baghdad, Iraq, Aug. 14, 1946; s. Jafar and Kobra (Alavi) S.; m. Tahereh Ali Nazari, Jan. 17, 1970; children: Ali (dec.), Nahal. BS, Pahlavi U., 1966, MD, 1973. Diplomate Am. Bd. Pathology, Am. Bd. Gen. Practice in Medicine and Surgery. Instr. pathology U. Ill. Sch. Medicine, Chgo., 1975-80; asst. prof. pathology, assoc. chmn. dept., dir. blood bank U. Mo., Kansas City, 1980-84; chmn. family practice Delano (Calif.) Regional Med. Ctr., 1984-86; pres. Delano Regional Med. Group, 1989-96. Chief of staff Delano Regional Med. Ctr., 1989. Fellow Am. Coll. Internat. Physicians, Coll. Am. Pathologists, Am. Acad. Family Physicians; mem. AMA, Am. Acad. Gen. Physicians, Calif. Med. Assn. Office: Sadegh Salmassi MD & Assocs Urgent Care Ctr 719 Main St Delano CA 93215-2935 also: Salmassi Cosmetic and Med Inst 719 Main St Delano CA 93215-2935     Office     Phone:     661-725-7060.     E-mail: salmassi@salmassimd.com.

**SALMELA, DAVID DANIEL,** architect; b. Wadena, Minn., Mar. 28, 1945; s. Laurie Fredrick and Lempi Christine (Matti) S.; m. Gladys Elaine Hanka, June 23, 1967; children: Cory, Chad, Tia, Kai, Brit. Grad. high sch., Sebeka, Minn. Registered profl. architect, Minn., Wis. Draftsman McKenzie Hague & Gilles, Mpls., 1965-66, A.G. McKee, Hibbing, Minn., 1966, ABI Contracting, Virginia, Minn., 1966-69, Archtl. Resources, Hibbing, 1969-70; designer, arch. Damberg Scott Peck & Booker, Virginia, 1970-89; arch. Mulfinger Susanka, Duluth, Minn., 1989-90; prin. Salmela Fospick Ltd., Duluth, 1990-94, Salmela, Arch., Duluth, 1994—. Recipient Design award, N.Am. Wood, 1994, 1998, 2 Design awards, 2002, Design award, 2003. Fellow: AIA (17 Minn. Honor awards 1985—2005, WRCL/AIA award 1994, Red Cedar Lumber Hon. award 1994, Record Houses award 1998, Nat. Honor award 1998, AIA/PIA award 2000, Louise Bethune award 2000, ASLA award 2001, 2 Nat. Honor awards 2005); mem.: Nat. Soc. Landscape Artists (Mayo Woodlands award 2004, Jackson Meadow award 2001). Home and Office: Salmelaarchitect 630 W 4th St Duluth MN 55806 Office Phone: 218-724-7517. E-mail: ddsalmela@charter.net.

**SALMI, MIKA,** information technology executive; b. Finland; Student, U. Wis.; MBA, INSEAD, France. Founder AtomFilms, San Francisco, 1998—2001; CEO Atom Entertainment, Inc., San Francisco, 2001. Office: Atomshockware ShockwareCom 114 Sansome St #FL10 San Francisco CA 94104-3803

**SALMOIRAGHI, GIAN CARLO,** physiologist, educator; b. Gorla Minore, Italy, Sept. 19, 1924; came to U.S., 1952, naturalized, 1958; s. Giuseppe Carlo and Dina (Rinetti) S.; m. Eva Tchoukourlieva, Dec. 5, 1970; 1 child, George Charles MD, U. Rome, 1948; PhD, McGill U., 1959; DSc (hon.), Hahnemann U., 1995. Sr. med. officer Internat. Refugee Orgn., Naples, Italy, 1949-52; research fellow Cleve. Clinic Found., 1952-55; lectr. dept. physiology McGill U., Montreal, Que., Canada, 1956-58; from neurophysiologist to dir. sch. spl. mental health research NIMH, Washington, 1959-73; assoc. commr. research N.Y. State Dept. Mental Hygiene, Albany, 1973-77; assoc. dir. for research Nat. Inst. Alcohol Abuse, HHS, Bethesda, Md., 1977-84; prof. neurology and physiology Hahnemann U., Phila., 1984—94, vice provost for research affairs, 1984-85, chmn. dept. physiology, asst. v.p sci. affairs 1986-94; clin. prof. psychiatry George Washington U., 1995. Conbtr. articles to profl. jours. Recipient Superior Service award HEW, 1970 Fellow Am. Coll. Neuropsychopharmacology; mem. AAAS, Am. Physiol. Soc., Am. Soc. Pharmacology and Exptl. Therapeutics, Internat. Brain Research Orgn., Internat. Soc. Psychoneuroendocrinology, Am. Psychiat. Assn., Soc. Neuro-

sci., Royal Soc. Medicine, Soc. Biol. Psychiat., Assn. Research Neurol. and Mental Disease, Research Soc. Alcoholism, Assn. Chmn. Dept. Physiology, Sci. Research Soc., Sigma Xi. Clubs: Cosmos (Washington). Home: 8216 Hamilton Spring Ct Bethesda MD 20817-2714 E-mail: gsalmoiraghi@pol.net.

**SALMON, CATHERINE ANNE,** education educator; b. Kitchener, Ont., Canada, Feb. 28, 1969; d. Ross and Lillian Salmon. PhD, McMaster U., Hamilton, Ont., Canada, 1997. Postdoctoral rschr. Simon Fraser U., Burnaby, B.C., Canada, 1999—2003; asst. prof. U. Redlands, Calif., 2003—. Author: (book) Warrior Lovers. Mem.: Soc. for the Sci. Study of Sexuality, Human Behavior and Evolution Soc. Office: Univ Redlands 1200 E Colton Ave Redlands CA 92373 Office Phone: 909-748-8672. Office Fax: 909-335-5305. Business E-Mail: catherine_salmon@relands.edu.

**SALMON, DENIS R.,** lawyer; b. St. Paul, Sept. 20, 1951; BA magna cum laude, Hamline U., 1973; JD magna cum laude, U. Minn., 1976. Bar: Calif. 1976. Assoc. Brobeck, Phleger & Harrison, Palo Alto, Calif., 1976—83, ptnr., 1983—95; ptnr., co-chair intellectual property group Gibson Dunn & Crutcher LLP, Palo Alto, Calif., 1995—, and ptnr.-in-charge Palo Alto office. Mem.: ABA (litig. section), Fed. Cir. Bar Assn., State Bar of Calif. (intellectual property section), Am. Intellectual Property Law Assn. Office: Gibson Dunn & Crutcher LLP 1881 Page Mill Rd Palo Alto CA 94304 Office Phone: 650-849-5301. Office Fax: 650-849-5001. Business E-Mail: dsalmon@gibsondunn.com.

**SALMON, EDWARD DICKINSON,** cell biologist, educator; BS, Brown U., 1967; PhD, U. Pa., 1973. Mem. faculty to James Larkin and Iona Mae Ballou disting. prof. cell biology U. NC, Chapel Hill, 1976—. Mem. sci. adv. bd. U. Wash. Ctr. Cell Dynamics. Conbtr. articles to profl. jours.; assoc. editor: Molecular Biology of the Cell. Fellow: Am. Acad. Arts & Scis. Office: Dept Biology U NC CB 3280 Coker Hall Chapel Hill NC 27599-3280 E-mail: tsalmon@email.unc.edu.*

**SALMON, EDWARD LLOYD, JR.,** bishop; b. Jan. 30, 1934; s. Edward Lloyd Sr. and Helen Bernice (Burley) S.; m. Louise Hack, 1972; children: Catherine, Edward III. BA, U. of the South, 1956; BD, Va. Theol. Seminary, 1960. Ordained to deaconate Episc. Ch., 1960, to priesthood, 1961. Vicar St. Andrew's Ch., Rogers, Ark., rector, 1963-68; vicar St. James Ch., Eureka Springs, Ark., St. Thomas Ch., Springdale, Grace Ch., Siloam Springs; assoc. St. Paul's Ch., Fayetteville, 1968, rector, 1968-78, Ch. St. Michael and St. George, St. Louis, 1978-90; elected bishop Diocese S.C., 1990—. Pres. province IV Episcopal Ch.; chmn. bd. dirs. Speak, Inc., The Anglican Digest, Voorhees Coll., Denmark, S.C.; trustee, regent Univ. of South; pres. Nashotah House Seminary; pres. Kanuga Confs., Inc.; chmn. Anglican Inst. Chmn. bd. trustees Voorhees Coll. Episcopalian. Office: PO Box 20127 Charleston SC 29413-0127     Office     Phone:     843-722-4075.     E-mail: elsalmon@dioceseofsc.org.

**SALMON, JERRY DERR,** federal air marshall; b. Lawton, Okla., Dec. 4, 1968; s. Jerry and Lauretta Salmon; m. Yunsil C. Salmon; 1 child, Kyri Alana. AAS in Emergency Med. Tech., Okla. City CC, 1995; BS in Criminal Justice, Am. Intercontinental U., Chgo., 2006. Border patrol agt. US Border Patrol, San Diego, 1995—97; immigration detention enforcement officer US Immigration and Naturalization Svc., San Diego, 1997—99, immigration insp. San Diego, 2001—02; fed. air marshal US Dept. Homeland Security, Detroit, 2002—. E4 specialist U.S. Army, 1987—91, Vicenza, Italy. Decorated Basic Parachutist Wings US Army Airborne Sch. R-Consevative. Baptist. Avocations: hunting, reading, computers, travel. Office     Phone:     734-955-8600.     Personal     E-mail: jerrysalmon@gmail.com. Business E-Mail: jerry.d.salmon@secureskies.net.

**SALMON, JOSEPH THADDEUS,** lawyer; b. Auburn, Ala., Nov. 13, 1927; s. William Davis and Helen (Bowman) S.; m. Mabel Marie Groves, July 7, 1951; children: Joseph Thaddeus Jr., Bruce Groves. BS, Auburn U.; 1949; JD, U. Ala., 1951. Bar: Ala. 1951. Practice in, Montgomery, 1953-93; sec., gen. counsel Alfa Mut. Ins. Co., Alfa Mut. Fire Ins. Co., Alfa Mut. Gen. Ins. Co., Alfa Corp., Alfa Ins. Corp., Alfa Gen. Ins. Corp., Alfa Life Ins. Co.; ret., 1993. Served with USNR, 1946-47; to 1st lt. USAF, 1951-53. Mem. Internat. Assn. Def. Counsel, Ala. Def. Lawyers Assn., Montgomery County Bar Assn., Phi Alpha Delta, Kappa Sigma. Episcopalian. Home: 2731 Lansdowne Dr Montgomery AL 36111-1741

**SALMON, MARLA E.,** nursing educator, dean; b. Vermillion, SD, May 2, 1949; d. Everett Lloyd and Marceline Louise (Adamson) Salmon; m. Jerry Steven Anderson, Aug. 1, 1984; children: Jessica Louise White, Matthew Lawrence White. BA cum laude, U. Portland, 1971, BSN cum laude, 1972; MSN, 1999; ScD, Johns Hopkins U., 1977; DSc (hon.), UNMC, 2003. Dir. patient advocacy program Johns Hopkins U., Balt., 1974-75, instr., 1975-78; asst. prof. U. Minn., Mpls., 1978-82, asst. dir. PRONA, 1978-79, acting dir. PRONA, 1978-80, dir. pub. health nursing programs, 1980-85, assoc. prof., 1982-86; prof. pub. health nursing, chmn. dept. U. N.C., Chapel Hill, 1986-92; dir. nursing div., Bureau Health Professions HHS, Rockville, 1991-97; prof., dean Grad. Sch. Nursing U. Pa., Phila., 1997-99, dir. grad. studies; dean, prof. Nell Hodgson Woodruff Sch. Nursing Emory U., Atlanta, 1999—. Cons. in field. Co-editor: News Outlook, 1989—91; conbtr. articles to profl. jours. Trustee Robert Wood Johnson Found., 2002—; mem. Presdl. Task Force Health Care Reform, Washington, 1993; U.S. del. WHO, Geneva, 1995. Recipient Recognition award, Assn. State Territorial Dirs. Nursing, 1993, Achievement award, Nat. Black Nurses Found., 1994, Presdl. award for Meritorious Exec., The White House, 1995; Fulbright scholar, 1972—73, W. K. Kellogg fellow, 1984—87, Reflective Leadership fellow, 1985—86, Rsch. grantee, 1975—78. Mem.: APHA, ANA (v.p. coun. cmty. health nursing 1988—, mem. task froce credentialing 1989), Women's Health Leadership Trust, Assn. Cmty. Healgh Nurses Educators, N.C. Nurses Assn., N.C. Pub. Health Assn., N.C. League Nursing, Nat. League Nursing, Am. Tae Kwon Do Assn., Am. Acad. Nursing, Sigma Xi, Delta Omega, Sigma Theta Tau. Avocations: athletics, gardening. Office: Emory U Nell Hodgson Woodruff Sch 1520 Clifton Rd Ste 402 Atlanta GA 30322-4207 Office Phone: 404-727-7976. Business E-Mail: msalmon@emory.edu.

**SALMON, MATT,** former congressman, communications company executive; b. Salt Lake City, Jan. 21, 1958; s. Robert James and Gloria (Aagard) S.; m. Nancy Huish, June, 1979; children: Lara, Jacob, Katie, Matthew. BA in English Lit., Ariz. State U., 1981; MA in Pub. Adminstrn., Brigham Young U., 1986. Mgr. pub. affairs U.S. West, Phoenix, 1988-94; mem. Ariz. State Senate, Mesa, 1990-94, U.S. Congress from 1st Ariz. dist., Washington, 1995-2001; mem. internat. rels. and sci. coms., asst. major whip; exec. v.p. APCO Worldwide, Scottsdale, Ariz., 2001—. Bd. dirs. Mesa United Way, 1990—, Ariz. Sci. Mus., 1992—. Recipient Outstanding Svc. award Ariz. Citizens with Disabilities, 1991, Excellence in Govt. award Tempe Ctr. for Handicapped, 1992; named Outstanding Young Phoenician, Phelps Dodge/Phoenix Jaycees, 1990, Outstanding Legislator, Mesa United Way, 1991. Republican. Mem. Lds Ch. Avocations: tennis, racquetball, bicycling. Office: 5800 N Kiva LN Paradise Valley AZ 85253-5944

**SALMON, WILLIAM COOPER,** mechanical engineer, engineering company executive; b. NYC, Sept. 3, 1935; s. Chenery and Mary (Cooper) S.; m. Josephine Stone, Sept. 16, 1967; children: William Cooper Jr., Mary Bradford, Pauline Alexandra. SB in Mech. Engring., MIT, 1957, SM in Mech. Engring., 1958, Mech. Engr., 1959, SM in Mgmt. Sci., 1969. Registered profl. engr., Mass. Research and teaching asst. MIT, Cambridge, 1957-59; sr. engr. Microtech, Cambridge, 1959-60; 1st lt. U.S. Army Ord. C., Aberdeen, Md., 1960; asst. sci. advisor U.S. Dept. State, Washington, 1961-74, sr. advisor for sci. and tech., 1978-86; counselor for sci. and tech. Am. embassy, Paris, 1974-78; exec. officer Nat. Acad. Engring., Washington, 1986-99, exec. officer emeritus, advisor to pres., 1999—2001; sec., treas. Internat. Coun. Acad. Engring. and Technol. Scis., Inc., 2000—. Interim exec. dir. Am. Assn. Engring. Soc., 2005—. Recipient Superior Honor award Dept. State, 1984,

Meritorious Svc. award Pres. U.S., 1968, Kenneth A. Roe award Am. Assn. Engring. Socs., 1996, Chair's award Am. Assn. Engring. Socs., 2005; Sloan fellow MIT, 1969. Fellow: ASME; mem.: NSPE, Nat. Soc. Sons Colonial New Eng., Jr. Engring. Tech. Soc. (pres. 1998—2001), Mil. Order Loyal Legion of US, Soc. Colonial Wars, Cosmos Club, Masons. Episcopalian. Home and Office: 3601 N Peary St Arlington VA 22207-5345 E-mail: wsalmon@nae.edu, caets@nae.edu.

**SALNY, ABBIE FEINSTEIN,** psychologist; b. N.Y.C., July 3, 1926; d. Carl and Edith (Cooperman) Feinstein; m. Jerome E. Salny, July 12, 1973. BA, NYU, 1949; MA, Montclair State U., 1953; EdD, Rutgers U., 1966. Lic. psychologist, N.J.; diplomate Am. bd. Profl. Psychology. Sch. psychologist Bd. of Edn., Parsippany, N.J., 1959-66; prof., dep. chair, acting chair psychology dept. Montclair State U., 1966-79; supervisory psychologist Am. and Internat. Mensa, 1979—; trustee Mensa Edn. and Rsch. Found., 1971-96. Chmn. scholarship com. Mensa Edn. and Rsch. Found., 1973-82, dir. sci. and edn. Am. Mensa com., 1983-87, dir. rsch. rev. com., 1984-88. Co-author: Mensa Genius Quiz Book, 1981, Mensa Genius Quiz Book II, 1983, Mensa Think Smart Book, 1985; author: Quiz-A-Day Book, 1986, Book of Literary Quizzes, 1988, Page-A-Day Puzzle Calendar, 1995—, others; conbtr. articles to profl. jours. Fellow Am. Acad. of Sch. Psychologists; mem. Am. Psychol. Assn., N.J. Psychol. Assn., British Psychol. Soc., Am. Soc. of Journalists and Authors, Am. Mensa Ltd. Avocations: travel, cooking. Home and Office: 407 Breckenridge Wayne NJ 07470-4072

**SALO, TOMMY,** retired professional hockey player; b. Surahammar, Sweden, Feb. 1, 1971; Goaltender New York Islanders, 1993-99, Edmonton Oilers, 1999—2004, Colorado Avalanche, 2004. Goaltender Swedish Nat. Team, World Cup, 1995-96, Olympics, 1994, 1998, 2002; led Sweden to 1st ever Olympic gold medal in Lillehammer, 1994. Named Internat. Hockey League Rookie of the Yr., 1994-95, Goaltender of the Yr., 1994-95, Player of the Yr., 1994-95.

**SALOM, ROBERTO,** financial executive; b. Bogota, Colombia, July 12, 1944; arrived in US, 1966; m. Estell Kathleen Millard; children: David Andres, Robert W.A. Student, U. Andes, Bogota, 1965; BS, San Francisco State U., 1969, MBA, 1972; postgrad., U. Calif., Berkeley, 1973; PhD in Econs., NYU, 1977. Rsch. assoc. Fed. Res. Bank San Francisco, 1968-70, fin. analyst, 1970-73; mem. staff UN Devel. Program/Fund for Population Activities, N.Y.C., 1973-82, dep. chief program planning, 1982-83, dep. chief fin. br., 1983-87, chief fin. br., 1987-94; sr. officer UN Adv. Com. on Adminstrv. and Budgetary Questions, 1995—2005. Presenter in field. Home: 5 Elmwood Ave Rye NY 10580-3401 Office: United Nations UN Plaza New York NY 10017 E-mail: salom@un.org.

**SALOMAO, CHERYL MAY LABRIE,** elementary school educator; d. Robert Armand and Dolores Claire Labrie; m. Claudinor Cerveira Salomao, June 29, 1996; children: Lauren, Jocelyn, Brianne. B, Coll. St. Joseph, Rutland, Vt., 1994; M, Lesley U., 2000. Tchr. 1st grade William E. Norris Elem. Sch., Southampton, Mass., 1994—; site coord. Lesley U., Cambridge, 1998—2000. Mem. Lit. Com., Southampton, 1998—2002. Recipient Outstanding Student Tchr. award, Coll. St. Joseph, Vt., 1994. Avocation: reading. Office: William E Norris Elem Sch 34 Pomeroy Meadow Rd Southampton MA 01073

**SALOMON, RICHARD E.,** investment company executive; s. Richard and Edna (Barnes) Salomon; m. Laura Landro. BA, Yale Univ., 1964; MBA, Columbia Univ., 1967. Pres. & mng. dir. Spears Beznak Salomon & Farrell, 1982—2000; pres. Mecox Ventures, N.Y.C., 2000—. Sr. adv. to David Rockefeller; chmn. adv. bd. Blackstone Alternative Asset Mgmt.; dir. Boston Properties. Vice chmn. Mus. Modern Art., N.Y.C.; trustee & chmn. invest-ment com. Rockefeller Univ., N.Y.C.; trustee N.Y. Public Libr., Alfred P. Sloan Found. Mem.: Council on Fgn. Rels. (dir. & mem. investment com.). Office: Mecox Ventures 610 5th Ave New York NY 10020*

**SALOMON, ROGER BLAINE,** retired language educator; b. Providence, Feb. 26, 1928; s. Henry and Lucia Angell (Capwell) S.; m. Elizabeth Helen Lowenstein, June 14, 1950; children— Pamela, Wendy. BA, Harvard, 1950; MA, U. Calif. at Berkeley, 1951, PhD, 1957. Instr. Mills Coll., Oakland, Calif., 1955-57; instr., then asst. prof. Yale U., New Haven, 1957-66; mem. faculty Case Western Res. U., Cleve., 1966—; prof. English, 1969—, Oviatt prof. English, 1990, chmn. dept., 1974-80, part-time prof. English, 1994-99; Oviatt prof. English emeritus, 1990—. Mem. adv. screening com. Am. Lit. Sr. Fulbright-Hayes Program, 1973-76, chmn., 1975; mem. grants-in-aid selection com. Am. Council Learned Socs., 1976-78 Author: Twain and the Image of History, 1961, Desperate Storytelling: Post-Romantic Elaborations of the Mock-Heroic Mode, 1987, Mazes of the Serpent: An Anatomy of Horror Narrative, 2002. Served to 1st lt. USAF, 1952-53. Morse fellow, 1960-61; Guggenheim fellow, 1972-73 Mem. AAUP, MLA. Home: 2830 Coventry Rd Cleveland OH 44120-2231 Office Phone: 216-368-2340.

**SALOMONSON, VINCENT VICTOR,** meteorologist, educator; b. Long-mont, Colo., July 19, 1937; s. Victor Philip and Eunice Cole Salomonson; m. Peggy Lucille Swanner, Feb. 11, 1944; children: Scott Houston, Aaron Phillip, Sarah McBride, Karla Canning, Carol Marie. BS in Agrl. Engring., Colo. State U., Ft. Collins, Colo., 1959; BS in Meteorology, U. Utah, Salt Lake City, Utah, 1960, MS in Agrl. Engring., Cornell U., Ithaca, N.Y., 1964; PhD, Colo. State U., Ft. Collins, Colo., 1968. Weather officer USAF, Washington, 1959—62; from rsch. meteorologist Goddard Space Flight Ctr. to sr. scientist NASA, Greenbelt, Md., 1962—2001, sr. scientist earth scis. directorate Goddard Space Flight Ctr., 2001—05; rsch. prof. U. Utah, Salt Lake City, 2005—. Conbtr. over 130 articles to profl. jours. Bishop LDS Ch., Bowie, Md. 1st lt. USAF, 1959—62. Named Meritorious Exec., Sr. Exec. Svc., U.S. Govt., 1993, Disting. Exec. Sr. Exec. Svc., 1998; recipient Exceptional Sci. Achievement medal, NASA, 1976, 1983, William T. Pecora award, NASA and U.S. Geol. Survey, 1987, Honor Alumnus award, Colo. State U., 1987, William Nordberg award, NASA Goddard Space Flight Ctr., 2002; Goddard Sr. fellow, 2002. Fellow: IEEE (mem. 1980—87, Disting. Achievement award 1998), Am. Soc. Photogrammetry and Remote Sensing (pres. 1991—92). Mem. Lds Ch. Office: University of Utah 135 S 1460 E Rm 809 Salt Lake City UT 84112-0110 Office Phone: 801-585-9492. Office Fax: 801-585-3681. Personal E-mail: vincesalomonson@msn.com. Business E-Mail: vince.salomonson@met.utah.edu.

**SALONEN, ESA-PEKKA,** conductor, music director; b. Helsinki, Finland, June 30, 1958; married; 3 children. Student, Sibelius Acad., Helsinki; studied Composition, Rautavaara; studied Conducting, Panula. Prin. guest condr. Oslo Philharm. Orch., 1985—90, Philharmonia Orch., London, 1985—94; prin. condr. Swedish Radio Symphony Orch., 1985—95; artistic advisor Stockholm Chamber Orch., 1984—; music director L.A. Philharm. Orch., 1992—, Walt and Lilly Disney chair, 1992—; artistic dir. Helsinki Festival, 1995—96. Guest condr. London Orch., Berlin Orch., Paris Orch., LA Orch., Phila. Orch. Named Musician of Yr., Musical Am., 2006; recipient Opera award, Royal Philharm. Soc., 1995, Conductor award, 1997, Litteris et Artibus medal, Sweden, 1996, Officier Ordre des Arts et des Lettres, France. also: Los Angeles Philharm Orch 151 S Grand Ave Los Angeles CA 90012-3013 Office: Columbia Artists Management Llc 1790 Broadway # 6 New York NY 10019-1412*

**SALONGA, LEA,** actress, singer; b. Manila, Feb. 22, 1971; d. Feliciano Genuino and Maria Ligaya (Imutan) Salonga; m. Robert Charles Chien, Jan. 10, 2004. Attended, Ateneo De Manila U., 1988-89. Actress, singer The King and I, Manila, 1978, Annie, Manila, 1980, The Rose Tattoo, Manila, 1980, The Bad Seed, Manila, 1981, The Goodbye Girl, Manila, 1982, Paper Moon, Manila, 1983, The Fantasticks, Manila, 1988, Miss Saigon, London, 1989-90 (Outstanding Performance by Actress in Musical Olivier award 1990), Broadway, 1991-92 (Best Actress in Musical Tony award 1991, Best Actress in Musical Drama Desk award 1991, Best Actress in Musical Outer Critics Circle award 1991, Outstanding Debut Theatre World award 1991), Les

Miserables, Broadway, 1993, My Fair Lady, Manila, 1994, Into the Woods, Singapore, 1994, Les Miserables, London, 1996, 3rd nat. tour, 1996, also The Sound of Music, Manila, Fiddler on the Roof, Manila, Cat on a Hot Tin Roof; Philippine films include Bakit Labis Kitang Mahal?, Dear Diary, Pik Pak Boom, Captain Barbell, Ninja Kids, Like Father, Like Son, Tropang Bulilit; Philippine TV: (host) Kulit Bulilit, Love Lea, Naku, Ha!, Sunday Special, Iba Ito!, That's Entertainment!, This is It!, (co-host) Patok Na Patok!; opening act for Stevie Wonder, Menudo; concerts: The Filipinos of Miss Saigon, A Miss Called Lea, Lea Salonga in Concert, L.A., San Francisco, Les Miserables 10th Anniversary Concert, London, 1995; recs. include Small Voice, 1981 (gold record), Lea, Happy Children's Club, Christmas Album, We are the World, (debut album) Lea Salonga, 1993, Miss Saigon original London cast rec. (gold record), The King and I, Aladdin, 1992 (singing voice Princess Jasmine, motion picture soundtrack), Les Miserables 10th Anniversary Concert Album, 1996, Royal Couyabyab: The Silver Album, 1996, The Little Tramp, (singing voice) Mulan, 1998, (Broadway) Flower Drum Song, 2002; TV films include: Redwood Curtain, 1998, (TV series) As the World Turns, 2001, 03; concert, Carnegie Hall, 2005. Recipient AWIT award outstanding svc. Philippings Recording Industry, 1993, ASEAN Industry award performing arts, 1992, Ten Outstanding Young Men award outstanding debut, 1991, AWIT award outstanding performer, 1990, Presdl. Award of Merit Pres. Aquino, 1990, Laurence Olivier award best actress musical, 1990, Cecil award best recording by a child, 1984, Tinig award one of 10 outstanding singers, 1983, 94, 92, ALIW award best child performer, 1980, 81, 82; named Outstanding Manilan by Govt. City of Manila, 1990. Mem.: Screen Actors' Guild, Actors' Equity Assn., AFTRA. Roman Catholic. Avocations: music, reading, collecting raised-trunk elephants, collecting swatches, working on computers. Office: c/o Jeff Hunter 1325 Avenue Of The Americas New York NY 10019-6026 Home: 1926 Caminito Del Pilar Glendale CA 91208-3051

**SALOOM, KALISTE JOSEPH, JR.,** lawyer, retired judge; b. Lafayette, La., May 15, 1918; s. Kaliste and Asma Ann (Boustany) S.; m. Yvonne Adelle Nassar, Oct. 19, 1958; children: Kaliste III, Douglas James, Leanne Isabelle, Gregory John. BA with high distinction, U. La., 1939; JD, Tulane U., 1942. Bar: La. 1942. Atty. City of Lafayette, 1948—52; judge City and Juvenile Ct., Lafayette, 1952—93; ret., 1993; of counsel Saloom & Saloom, Lafayette, 1993—; Eminent Scholar endowed chair in polit. sci. U. La., Lafayette, 2001. Mem. jud. coun. La. Supreme Ct., 1960-64; bd. dirs. Nat. Ctr. for State Cts., Williamsburg, Va., 1978-84, adv. coun., 1984—, mem. assocs. com., 1986—; judge pro tempore La. Ct. Appeal 3d Cir., 1992; tech. adviser Jud. Adminstrn. of Traffic Cts. mem. adv. com. Nat. Hwy. Traffic Safety Adminstrn., U.S. Dept. Transp., 1977-80, Nat. Com. on Uniform Traffic Laws, 1986; mem. expert panel Drunk Driving Protection Act U.S. Congress, 1989-91. Mem. editl. bd. Tulane Law Rev., 1941; contbr. articles to profl. jours. Active Boy Scouts Am., Evangeline Area coun. With U.S. Army, 1942-45. Recipient Civic Cup, City of Lafayette, 1965, Pub. Svc. award U.S. Dept. Transp., 1980, Disting. Jurist award Miss. State U. Pre-Law Soc., 1987, Disting. Svc. award Nat. Ctr. State Cts., 1988, Disting. La. Jurist award La. State Bar Found., 1992, U.S. Supreme Ct. Chief Justice Warren E. Burger Soc. award, 1999. Mem. ABA (Benjamin Flaschner award 1981, vice chair JAD com. on traffic ct. program 1989-2002), Am. Judges Assn. (William H. Burnett award 1982), Nat. Coun. Juvenile Ct. Judges, La. City Judges Assn. (past pres., panel drafting La. children's code 1989-91), La. Juvenile Ct. Judges Assn. (past pres.), Order of Coif, Equestrian Order of Holy Sepulchre (knight comdr.), Oakbourne Country Club, Rotary (Paul Harris fellow), KC. Democrat. Roman Catholic. Home: 502 Marguerite Blvd Lafayette LA 70503-3138 Office: 211 W Main St Lafayette LA 70501-6843

**SALOTTI, KATHRYN E.,** marriage and family therapist; d. Peter Arthur Floros and Henrietta Judith Albers; m. Richard Vincent Salotti, June 28, 1969; 1 child, Cara Dominique; m. Thomas Lee Moreland (div.); 1 child, Thomas Michael. AA, Pierce Jr. Coll., Calif., 1980; BA in Sociology summa cum laude, Calif. State U., Northridge, 1983, M in Ednl. Psychology, 1986. Lic. marriage and family therapist Calif. Bd. Behavioral Sci., 1989. Marriage and family therapist internship Exceptional Children's Found., Van Nuys, Calif., 1986—87, Tarzana Treatment Ctr., Calif., 1988—89; rschr., writer, editor, tchr. Gerry Grossman Seminars, Santa Monica, Calif., 1989—90; family therapist Crestwood Manor, San Jose, 1990—93; family therapist, treatment coord. Oakview Youth, Santa Barbara, 1993—94; program dir. Sanctuary Psychiatric of Santa Barbara, 1994—98, County of Santa Barbara Children's Svcs., 1998—. Recipient Academic Excellence award, Phi Kappa Phi, 1983. Mem.: Calif. Assn. of Marriage and Family Therapists. Republican. Avocations: writing, genealogy, dance, reading. Home: 1102 Bel Air Dr Santa Barbara CA 93105 Personal E-mail: katcardi_8@msn.com.

**SALPETER, ALAN N.,** lawyer; b. Phila., Oct. 7, 1947; BA with honors, Am. U., 1969; JD, Villanova U., 1972. Bar: Ill. 1972, U.S. Dist. Ct. No. Ill. 1972, U.S. Ct. Appeals 5th cir. 1977, U.S. Ct. Appeals 7th cir. 1974, U.S. Ct. Appeals 8th cir. 1981, U.S. Ct. Appeals 11th cir. 1985, U.S. Ct. Appeals D.C. cir. 1991, U.S. Ct. Appeals 10th cir. 1998. Assoc. Mayer, Brown & Platt, Chgo., 1972—79; ptnr. Mayer Brown Rowe & Maw, Chgo., 1979—. Lectr. and author in field. Mng. editor Law Rev., Villanova U. Mem. ABA, Chgo. Bar Assn., Chgo. Coun. Lawyers, 7th Cir. Bar Assn. (bd. gov.). Office: Mayer Brown Rowe Maw Llp 230 S La Salle St Ste 400 Chicago IL 60604-1407

**SALPETER, EDWIN ERNEST,** physical sciences educator; b. Vienna, Dec. 3, 1924; came to U.S., 1949, naturalized, 1953; s. Jakob L. and Frieder (Horn) S.; m. Miriam Mark, June 11, 1950 (dec. 2001); children: Judy Gail, Shelley Ruth; m. Antonia L. Shouse, 2004. MS, Sydney U., 1946; PhD, Birmingham U., Eng., 1948; DSc, U. Chgo., 1969, Case-Western Reserve U., 1970, U. Sydney, 1994, U. New South Wales, Sydney, 1996. Research fellow Birmingham U., 1948-49; faculty Cornell U., Ithaca, N.Y., 1949-97, now J.G. White prof. phys. scis. emeritus. Mem. U.S. Nat. Sci. Bd., 1979-85 Author: Quantum Mechanics, 1957, 77; mem. editorial bd. Astrophys. Jour, 1966-69; assoc. editor Modern Physics, 1971-92; contbr. articles to profl. jours. Mem. AURA 60, 1970-72. Recipient Gold medal Royal Astron. Soc., 1973, J.R. Oppenheimer Meml. prize U. Miami, 1974, C. Bruce medal Astron. Soc. Pacific, 1987, A. Devaucouleurs medal, 1992, Dirac Meml. medal U. New South Wales, 1996, Crafoord laureate Royal Swedish Acad. Scis., 1997, H. A. Bethe Prize, Am. Phys. Soc., 1999. Mem. NAS, Am. Astron. Soc. (v.p. 1971-73), Am. Philos. Soc., Am. Acad. Arts and Scis., The Royal Soc. (fgn.), Australian Acad. Sci., Deutsche Akademie Leopoldina. Home: 116 Westbourne Ln Ithaca NY 14850-2414 Office: Cornell U 614 Space Science Bldg Ithaca NY 14853-6801 E-mail: ees12@cornell.edu.

**SALSBERG, ARTHUR PHILIP,** publishing executive; b. Bklyn., Aug. 28, 1929; s. Solomon William and Rae (Miller) S.; m. Rhoda Gelb, Sept. 11, 1960; children: Charles Martin, Solomon William. BBA, CCNY, 1951. Mng. editor Ojibway Press, N.Y.C., 1957-64; advt. and promotion mgr. RCA Corp., Harrison, NJ, 1965-67; editor N.Am. Pub. Co., Phila., 1967-70; v.p., gen. mgr. Lawyers World, Inc., Phila., 1970-72; editorial dir. Ziff-Davis Pub. Co., N.Y.C., 1973-83; editor, assoc. pub. CQ Communications, Inc., Hicksville, NY, 1984—. Mag. and newspaper pub. cons.; electronics instr.; local campaign publicist, speech writer for town mayor, town coun., libr. bd., sch. bd. Author: Complete Book of Video Games, 1977, Collier's Ency. Yearbook, 1977, 78, 79, 80, 81, 82, First Book of Modern Electronics Fun Projects, 1986, Second Book of Modern Electronics Fun Projects, 1986; editor: Audio Mag, 1967-70, Lawyers World, 1970-72, Popular Electronics, 1973-83, Comm. Handbook, 1973-83, Stereo Directory, 1973-83, Tape Recorder Directory, 1973-83, Citizens Band Handbook, 1976-83, Invitation to Electronics, 1972-83, Modern Electronics, 1984-91, Computer Craft, 1992-93, MicroComputer Jour., 1994-96; assoc. pub.: Amateur Radio Equipment Buyers Guide, 1988, 89, 90, 91, 92, Amateur Radio Antenna Buyers Guide, 1989, 90, 91-92. Publicity chmn. Nassau coun. Boy Scouts Am., 1975; mem. adv. com. Bramson OR Tech. Inst., 1975. With AUS, 1951-53, Korea. Recipient Indsl. Mktg. Mag. award, 1959 Home: 7844 Lexington Club Blvd Apt A Delray Beach FL 33446-3426

**SALSBURY, FREDDIE R., JR.,** physics professor, educator; b. Berlin, Feb. 18, 1974; s. Freddie and Margaret Salsbury; m. Rebecca Jane Free, July 7, 2006. BS, U. Chgo., 1991—95; PhD, U. Calif., Berkeley, 1995—99. Rsch. assoc. Scripps Rsch. Inst., La Jolla, Calif., 1999—2002; asst. prof. Wake Forest U., Winston-Salem, NC, 2002—. Fulbright Nat. Svc. Rsch. award, NIH, Inst. Gen. Med. Scis., 1999—2002. Mem.: Protein Soc., Biophysical Soc., Am. Chem. Soc., Am. Phys. Soc. Libertarian. Achievements include research in method development in density functional theory and molecular dynamics; application of computational methods to biomedical research, especially relating to cancer biology. Office: Wake Forest Univ Dept Physics PO Box 7507 Winston Salem NC 27109 Business E-Mail: salsbufr@wfu.edu.

**SALSBURY, MICHAEL H.,** lawyer; b. Stamford, Conn., Dec. 12, 1949; AB, Dartmouth Coll., 1971; MBA, JD, U. Va., 1975. Bar: D.C. 1975. Mng.ptnr. Jenner & Block, Bat.; exec. v.p. & gen. coun. MCI, 1995—2003; ptnr. Chadbourne & Parke LLP, Washington, 2004—. Office: Chadbourne & Parke LLP 1200 New Hampshire Ave NW Washington DC 20036 E-mail: msalsbury@chadbourne.com.

**SALSBURY, TIMOTHY IAN,** research scientist; b. Nottingham, England, Aug. 8, 1970; s. Ian Ernest Salsbury and Janet Margaret Heathcote; m. Susanna Tellervo Malin, July 7, 1997; children: Inga Astrid, Freya Edith. PhD, Loughborough U., Eng., 1996; B of Engring. with honors, Loughborough U. Tech., 1992. Rsch. scientist Tech. Rsch. Ctr. Finland, Espoo, 1996—98; rsch. fellow Lawrence Berkeley Nat. Lab., Calif., 1998—2000; prin. rschr. Johnson Controls, Inc, Milw., 2000—. Pres. Analytic Minds, Inc. Whitefish Bay, Wis., 2005—. Contbr. papers to profl. jours. and pubs. Recipient Honorarium, U.S. Dept. Energy, 2006. Mem.: IEEE, ASHRAE. Achievements include patents in field. Home: 163 E Henry Clay St Whitefish Bay WI 53217 Office: Johnson Controls Inc 507 E Michigan St Milwaukee WI 53202 Office Phone: 414-524-4660. Personal E-mail: ti_salsbury@yahoo.com. Business E-Mail: timothy.i.salsbury@jci.com.

**SALSER, SCOTT A.,** music educator; b. Oil City, Pa., June 9, 1962; m. Karen Kreiner, July 11, 1992. BS in Music Edn., Indiana U. of Pa., 1984; MEd in Music Edn., Pa. State U., University Park, 1992. Vocal music tchr. State College (Pa.) Area Sch. Dist., 1984—87; choral dir. East Stroudsburg (Pa.) HS, 1987—91, Indiana (Pa.) HS, 1991—. Mem., soloist Bach Choir of Pitts., 2004—06, asst. dir., 2005—06; guest condr. various county chorus festivals, Pa. Mem.: Am. Choral Dir.'s Assn. (chmn. repertoire and stds. com. 2000—01), Pa. Music Educator's Assn. (chmn. choral policy 2005—). Methodist. Avocations: travel, piano, gardening, church activities. Office: Indiana Sr HS 450 N 5th St Indiana PA 15701

**SALT, ALFRED LEWIS,** priest; b. Hackensack, N.J., Apr. 30, 1927; s. Alfred John and Lily (Tittle) S.; m. Elizabeth May Loveland, June 18, 1949; children: Richard John, Michael Rob, Christopher William, Katharine Anne. BA with honors, Bishop's U., Lennoxville, Can., 1949, MA in History, 1951, BD, 1960; grad. advanced mgmt. program, Harvard U., 1970; D Ministry, Grad. Theol. Found., 1988. Ordained to ministry Episcopal Ch. as deacon, 1951, as priest, 1952. Incumbent St. Philip's, Sawyerville, Que., Canada, 1951—52, St. John the Evangelist, Portneuf, Que., 1952—54; rector Christ Ch., Stanstead, Que., 1954—62, St. Michael's Ch., Sillery, Que., 1962—72, All Saints Ch., Millington, NJ, 1972—93; hon. asst. Grace Ch., Port Huron, Mich., 1993—98, Trinity Ch., Lexington, Mich., 1998—2001, St. Monica's Ch., Naples, Fla., 2002—03, St. John's Ch., Naples, 2004—. Bishop's chaplain Diocese of Que., 1962, hon. canon, 1970; pres. Morris Convocation Morris County, N.J., 1974-78, retreat condr., 1979—; with Victorious Ministry Through Christ, Orlando, Fla., 1981-92, dir., 1986-92, v.p., 1989-92; dir. VMTC Can., 1995-2002. Author: Compass Book on Healing, 1996; contbr. articles to religious jour. Mem. Superior Coun. Edn., Que., 1964-70; commr. Que. Protestant Sch. Bd., 1970-72; trustee Heath Village, Hackettstown, N.J., 1974-76; mem. Passaic Twp. Welfare Bd., Millington, 1977-78, 82. With USAAC Res., 1944-45; with USN, 1945-46. Mem. Naples Deanery Clericus, Order St. Luke (chaplain), Harvard Club of Naples. Home (Summer): 190 Chemin Du Lac North Hatley QE J0B 2C0 Canada Personal E-mail: alemsalt@comcast.net. *The more I come to know Jesus, the more I come to know myself. The more I submit myself to Him, the less I depend upon myself.*

**SALTARELLI, MICHAEL A.,** priest; b. Jersey City, Jan. 17, 1933; s. Angelo Michael and Caroline (Marzitelli) Saltarelli. BA, Seton Hall U., 1956; MA, Manhattan Coll., 1975. Ordained to ministry Cath. Ch., 1960. Assoc. pastor Holy Family Ch., Nutley, NJ, 1960—77; pastor Our Lady of Assumption, Bayonne, 1977—82; exec. dir. Archdiocesan Pastoral Svcs., Newark, 1982—85; pastor St. Catherine Of Siena Ch., Cedar Grove, 1985—90; aux. bishop Archdiocese of Newark, 1990—96; bishop Diocese of Wilmington, Del., 1996—. Vicar for priests Archdiocese of Newark, 1987—96. Office: 1925 Delaware Ave Ste 1-a Wilmington DE 19806-2301

**SALTEN, DAVID GEORGE,** academic administrator; b. NYC, Aug. 23, 1913; s. Max Elias and Gertrude (Brauer) S.; m. Frances Claire Brown (div. 1983); children: Phoebe, Cynthia, Melissa; m. Adrienne O'Brien, 1989. ScB, Washington Sq. Coll., N.Y.C., 1933; AM, Columbia U., 1939; PhD, NYU, 1944; LLD (hon.), Lynn U., 1976; L.H.D., Nova U., Ft. Lauderdale, Fla., 1983; Sc.D. (hon.), N.Y. Inst. Tech., 1984; LHD (hon.), Hofstra U., 1996. Registered psychologist, N.Y. Chemist Almay Cosmetics, 1934-35, City of New York, 1938-40; instr., dept. chair, high sch. prin. N.Y.C. Bd. Edn., 1940-50; assoc. prof. Hunter Coll. Grad. Program, 1947-63; supt. of schs. City of Long Beach, NY, 1950-62, City of New Rochelle, NY, 1962-65; exec. v.p. Fedn. of Jewish Philanthropies, N.Y.C., 1965-69; exec. v.p., provost N.Y. Inst. Tech., Old Westbury, 1969-90; chmn. Nassau County Indsl. Devel. Agy., Mineola, NY, 1985—2002; exec. dir. Nassau County Tax Relief Commn., 1990-93. Mem. White House Conf. on Edn., 1955, White House Conf. on Youth, 1960; U.S. resource person on edn. World Mental Health Congress, Paris, 1961; mem. Bd. Edn., Hawthorne, Cedar Knolls, N.Y., 1963-65; mem. adv. council Columbia U. Sch. of Social Work, 1967-69; chmn. adv. council NYU Sch. Edn., 1963-65; chmn. adv. council to Select Com. on Higher Edn. N.Y. Legislature, 1971-73. Author: Mathematics: A Basic Course, 1957. Editor instructional software. Contbr. articles on edn. and ednl. adminstrn. to profl. publs. Vice chmn. N.Y. State Mental Health Council, Albany, 1965-72; pres. N.Y. State Citizens Council, 1957; pres. Nat. Council on Aging, Washington, 1975-77; chmn. Nassau County Local Devel. Agy., 1982—; Nassau County Local Devel. Corp., N.Y., 1982—, pres., 1992—; chmn. Nassau County Cultural Devel. Bd., 1980—94; bd. dirs. NAACP Legal Def. Fund, 1964-74; chmn. bd. trustees The Hewlett Sch., 1991—. Recipient citation U.S. Navy, 1947, Mental Health Assn., Nassau County, N.Y., 1955, Long Beach Edn. Assn., N.Y., 1962, Council of City of New Rochelle, N.Y., 1965, Council of Town of Islip, N.Y., 1982. Fellow AAAS, Am. Orthopsychiat. Assn.; mem. Princeton Club (N.Y.C.). Avocations: opera, ballet, international travel, photography. Office: Office of the President Hofstra Univ 243D Business Devel Ctr Hempstead NY 11549-1450 Office Phone: 516-463-3930. Personal E-mail: aobrien@optonline.net. Business E-Mail: dsalten@mac.com.

**SALTER, CLAUDIA JOE,** psychologist; BA, Johns Hopkins U., 1998; MA, U. Md., 2000; PhD, George Mason U., 2005. Intern psychology Ctr. Multicultural Human Svcs., Falls Church, Va., 2004—05. Mem.: APA.

**SALTER, EDWIN CARROLL,** retired pediatrician; b. Oklahoma City, Jan. 19, 1927; s. Leslie Ernest and Maud (Carroll) S.; m. Ellen Gertrude Malone, June 30, 1962; children: Mary Susanna, David Patrick BA, DePauw U., 1947; MD, Northwestern U., 1951. Intern Cook County Hosp., Chgo., 1951-53; resident in pediatrics Children's Meml. Hosp., Chgo., 1956-58, Cook County Hosp., Chgo., 1956-58; practice medicine specializing in pediatrics Lake Forest, Ill., 1958-97; attending physician Lake Forest Hosp., 1958—97, pres. med. staff, 1981-87. Attending physician Children's Meml. Hosp., Chgo.; clin. faculty mem. dept. pediatrics Northwestern U. Med. Sch.

Served to capt. M.C., U.S. Army, 1954-56 Mem. AMA, Ill. State Med. Soc., Lake County Med. Soc. (pres. 1984), Phi Beta Kappa Republican. Methodist. Home: 19 N Maywood Rd Lake Forest IL 60045-3233

**SALTER, JAMES,** writer; b. Passaic, N.J., June 10, 1925; m. Ann Altemus, June 6, 1951 (div. 1976); children: Allan Conard, Nina Tobe, Claude Cray, James Owen; m. Kay Eldredge; 1 child, Theo Shaw. BS, USMA, 1945; M in Internat. Affairs, Georgetown U., 1950. Author: The Hunters, 1957, The Arm of Flesh, 1961, A Sport and a Pastime, 1967, Light Years, 1976, Solo Faces, 1981, Dusk and Other Stories, 1989 (Pen, Faulkner prize 1989), Burning the Days, 1997, Cassada, 2001, Last Night, 2005, There and Then: The Travel Writing of James Salter, 2006; Co-Author (with Jessica Benton, William Benton) Gods of Tin: The Flying Years, 2004. Lt. Col. USAF, 1960. Recipient, Edith Wharton Prize, NY State Author, 1998—, English Speaking Union Prize, Pen/West Prize, John Steinbeck Prize. Office: ICM Literary 40 W 57th St New York NY 10019

**SALTER, KEVIN THORNTON,** lawyer; b. NYC, Oct. 21, 1947; s. Hershel Fletcher and Elizabeth (Thornton) S.; m. Eleanor Raftery, Aug. 28, 1982. BA, Iona Coll., 1973; JD, St. John's U., 1977. Bar: N.Y. 1978, U.S. Dist. Ct. (so. and ea. dists.) N.Y., 1978. Atty. Nat. Coun. on Compensation Ins., N.Y.C., 1978-80; coun. James G. Barron, N.Y.C., 1980-81; assoc. St. Regis Paper Co./Champion Internat., N.Y.C. and Stamford, Conn., 1981-88; sr. ptnr. Kroll & Tract, N.Y.C., 1988-94; ptnr. Peterson & Ross, N.Y.C., 1994-98, Querrey & Harrow, 1998—. With U.S. Army, 1967-69. Mem.: N.Y. State Bar Assn. Office: Bolan Jahnsen Salter & Sachs 1 Liberty Plz New York NY 10006 Office Phone: 212-201-6825 E-mail: ksalter@bjaolaw.com.

**SALTER, LESTER HERBERT,** lawyer; b. Waterbury, Conn., Apr. 26, 1918; s. Nathan M. and Eva G. (Levy) S.; m. Nina P. Scheftel, Sept. 15, 1951; 1 child, Ellen Lee. BS in Econs, U. Pa., 1940, LLB, 1948. Bar: R.I. 1948. Trial atty. Office of Chief Counsel, IRS, Newark and Boston, 1949-53; pvt. practice Providence, 1953-57; partner Salter & McGowan, Providence, 1957-70, Salter, McGowan, Arcaro & Swartz, Providence, 1970-74; pres. Salter, McGowan, Swartz & Holden, Inc., Providence, 1974-95, Salter, McGowan & Swartz, Inc., Providence, 1995-97, Salter, McGowan, Swartz & Sylvia, Inc., Providence, 1997-99, Salter, McGowan, Sylvia & Leonard, Inc., Providence, 2000—. Lectr. Northeastern U., 1955-56; chmn. U. R.I. Fed. Tax Inst., 1972-77; chmn. disciplinary bd. Supreme Ct., R.I., 1975-81; mem. R.I. Adv. Commn. Jud. Appts., 1978-82, ethics adv. panel Supreme Ct., R.I., 1987-92. Assoc. editor: R.I. Bar Jour, 1961-68. Served with F.A. AUS, 1941-46. Decorated Bronze Star. Fellow: ABA, Am. Bar Found; mem.: Am. Judicature Soc., New Eng. Bar Assn. (pres. 1996—97), Am. Law Inst. (life), R.I. Bar Assn. (pres. 1986—87), ABA (ho. of dels. 1987—2000, bd. govs. 1999—2000). Home: Apt 220 355 Blackstone Blvd Providence RI 02906-5413 Office: 321 S Main St Providence RI 02903-7108 Office Phone: 401-274-0300.

**SALTER, MARY JO,** poet; b. Grand Rapids, Mich., Aug. 15, 1954; d. Albert Gregory and Lormina (Paradise) S.; m. Brad Leithauser, 1980; children: Emily Salter, Hilary Garner. BA cum laude, Harvard U., 1976; MA, Cambridge U., 1978. Instr. Harvard U., 1978-79; instr. English conversation Japan, 1980-83; lectr. English Mt. Holyoke Coll., South Hadley, Mass., 1984—, Emily Dickinson sr. lectr. in humanities, 1995—. Staff editor Atlantic Monthly, 1978-80; poet-in-residence Robert Frost Place, 1981; poetry editor The New Republic, 1992-95. Author: Henry Purcell in Japan, 1985, Unfinished Painting, 1989 (Lamont prize in poetry 1988), The Moon Comes Home, 1989, Sunday Skaters: Poems, 1994 (Nat. Book Critics Circle award nomination 1994), A Kiss in Space: Poems, 1999, Open Shutters: Poems, 2003; co-editor: Norton Anthology of Poetry, 5th edit., 2005; contbr. to periodicals including New Yorker, New Republic, Kenyon Rev. Amy Lowell scholar, 1995; recipient Discovery prize Nation, 1983; Nat. Endowment for Arts fellow, 1983-84, Guggenheim fellow, 1993. Mem. Internat. P.E.N. Office: care Alfred A Knopf Inc 1745 Broadway New York NY 10019

**SALTIEL, ALAN ROBERT,** biochemist; b. New Brunswick, N.J., Nov. 29, 1953; s. Samuel Albert and Betty (Berg) S.; m. Swanna Elizabeth Cameron, May 30, 1981; children: Jason Ariel, Aren David, Jared Robert. AB, Duke U., 1975; PhD, U. N.C., 1980. Rsch. scientist Burroughs-Wellcome Co., Rsch. Triangle Pk., NY, 1980-84; asst. prof. Rockefeller U., N.Y.C., 1984-90; dir. dept. signal transp. Parke-Davis/Warner-Lambert Co., Ann Arbor, 1990—2000; assoc. prof. U. Mich., Ann Arbor, 1990—94, adj. prof., 1994—2001, prof. medicine & physiology, 2001—, John Jacob Abel collegiate prof. life sciences, 2002—, dir. Life Sciences Inst., 2002—. Mem. sci. rev. Juvenile Diabetes Found., N.Y.C., 1988-91, Am. Diabetes Assn., Alexandria, Va., 1990—; diabetes adv. bd. N.Y. State Health Rsch. Coun., Albany, N.Y., 1986-90; scientific adv. bd. Quatrx; editorial bd. Molecular Medicine, Jour. Biological Chemistry, Jour. Clin. Investigation. Contbr. over 100 papers to profl. jours. Recipient New Investigator award NIH, 1984, Rsch. & Devel. award Am. Diabetes Assn., 1984, John Jacob Abel award Am. Soc. Pharm. & Exptl. Therapy, 1990; named Irma T. Hirschl scholar, 1986, Established Investigator, Am. Heart Assn., 1989. Mem. Am. Soc. Biochem. Molecular Biology, Am. Soc. Pharm. & Exptl. Therapy, Endocrine Soc., Harvey Soc., Am. Soc. Clin. Investigation (hon.), Inst. Medicine. Achievements include discovery of the structure of the second messenger of insulin action; rsch. in role of protein phosphorylation in Nerve Growth Factor action; biology of protein-lipid interactions; biology of lipoproteins; protein synthesis. Office: Life Sciences Inst U Mich 210 Washtenaw Ave Ann Arbor MI 48109-2216 Office Phone: 734-615-9787. Office Fax: 734-763-6492. E-mail: saltiel@umich.edu.*

**SALTMAN, ROBERT ION,** physician, medical educator; b. Holyoke, Mass., Jan. 15, 1954; s. Zariike and Adelaide Saltman; m. Linda Carolynn Eichler; children: Julie, Jane, Zachary. BA, Yale U., 1976; MD, Washington U., 1980. Diplomate internal medicine Am. Bd. Internal Medicine, endocrinology and metabolism Am. Bd. Internal Medicine. Chief resident, instr. medicine Barnes Hosp./Washington U., St. Louis, 1985—86; physician Barnes Jewish Christian Med. Group, St. Louis, 1986—2001; co-ptnr. West County Med. Specialists, St. Louis, 2001—; assoc. prof. clin. medicine Washington U. Sch. Medicine, St. Louis, 2001—. Co-editor: Washington University School of Medicine Manual of Medical Therapeutics, 1986. Mem.: ACP, Internat. Soc. Clin. Densitometry, Endocrine Soc., Am. Diabetes Assn. Avocations: tennis, skiing, wine collecting. Office: West County Med Specialists Ste 145 969 Mason Rd Saint Louis MO 63141 Office Phone: 314-878-6008. Personal E-mail: rlsalt@aol.com.

**SALTYKOV, BORIS GEORGIEVICH,** economist, politician; b. Moscow, Dec. 27, 1940; s. Georgy N. and Evdokia M. (Pukaleva) Saltykov; m. Lubov N. Clochkova; 2 children. Student Moscow Inst. Physics & Tech. Rschr., chief engr. Ctrl. Econ. Math. Inst. USSR Acad. Scis., Moscow, 1967—73; sr. rschr., 1973—86, head dept. Inst. Econ. Forecasting, 1986—91, vice dir. Analytical Rsch. Ctr. on Problems Social, Econ. and Sci. Tech. Devel., 1991—96; min. for sci. and tech. policy, pub. affairs chmn. commn. to UNESCO, vice premier of Russian govt. Russian Fedn., 1992—93; mem. Russian Parliament, 1993—95. Pres. Russian House for Internat. S & T Coop., 1996—. Contbr. over 70 articles to profl. jours. Trustee Oxford Russia Fund, England, 2004—. Mem.: Am. Acad. Arts and Scis. (fgn.). Avocation: yachting. Office: Russian House for Interna S&T Coop Brusov per 11 125009 Moscow Russia Office Phone: 7(495)629-58-40. Business E-Mail: bsaltykov@rd-mnts.ru.

**SALTZ, HOWARD JOEL,** newspaper editor; b. Bronx, NY, Apr. 11, 1960; s. Fred Raymond and Sheila Lois (Goldberg) S. BA in Liberal Arts, SUNY, Stony Brook, 1983. Reporter Greenwich Time, So. Conn. Newspapers divsn. Times Mirror, 1983-85; with MediaNews Group, 1985—; NJ Advance, Dover, 1985-87, editor, 1987-88, Hamilton (Ohio) Jour.-News, 1988-89, Fremont (Calif.) Argus, 1989-91, Johnstown Tribune-Democrat, 1991; dep. bus. editor Denver Post, 1996-98, dep. mng. editor features, 1998-2000, multimedia editor, 2000—02, assoc. editor/new media & strategic devel.

2002—06; v.p. content develop. Media News Group Interactive, 2006—. Adv. com. dept. journalism Ohlone Coll., Fremont, Calif., 1990-91. Bd. dirs. YMCA, Fremont-Newark, Calif., 1990-91, Johnstown Area Heritage Assn., 1991-93. Mem. Greater Johnstown C. of C. (bd. dirs. 1991-96), Soc. Profl. Journalists (bd. dirs. Northern Calif. chpt. 1990-91). Avocations: skiing, travel, scuba. Address: 535 Garfield St Denver CO 80206-4513 Office: Media News Group Interactive 1560 Broadway Ste 2100 Denver CO 80202-5177 Business E-Mail: hsaltz@medianewsgroup.com.

**SALTZBERG, EUGENE ERNEST,** emergency physician, educator; b. Chgo., Feb. 2, 1947; s. Samuel and Florence (Weiner) S.; m. Roberta Rice, Apr. 28, 1984; children: Noah Edward, Evan Hale, Paige Erica. BA in Psychology cum laude, U. Ill., 1968; MD, Chgo. Med. Sch. U. Health Scis., 1972. Diplomate Am. Bd. Emergency Medicine, Am. Bd. Med. Examiners. Resident Children's Meml. Hosp., Chgo., 1974; health officer Pitkin County, Aspen, Colo., 1975-79; clin. instr. dept. medicine Northwestern U., Chgo., 1981—; chief of staff Condell Med. Ctr., Libertyville, Ill., 1996-97; med. dir. The Lambs Farm, Libertyville, 1986—. Asst. clin. prof. U. Health Sci., Chgo. Med. Sch., 1988—; chmn. instnl. rev. bd. Cornell Med. Ctr., 2002—; expert witness in field. Fellow: Am. Acad. Emergency Medicine; mem.: ACP, Coalition and Ctr. for Ethical Med. Testimony (charter), Am. Coll. Forensic Medicine, Physicians for Social Responsibility, Soc. for Critical Care Medicine, Univ. Assn. for Emergency Medicine. Jewish. Avocation: golf. Home: 265 Ravine Dr Highland Park IL 60035 Office Phone: 847-432-2856. Personal E-Mail: genodoc@aol.com.

**SALTZBURG, STEPHEN ALLAN,** law educator, consultant; b. Phila., Sept. 10, 1945; s. Jack Leonard and Mildred (Osgood) Adelman; m. Susan Lee, March 10, 1990; children: Mark Winston, Lisa Marie, Diane Elizabeth, David Lee Mussehl. AB, Dickinson Coll., 1967; JD, U. Pa., 1970. Bar: Calif. 1971, D.C. 1972, Va. 1976. Law clk. U.S. Dist. Ct. (no. dist.) Calif., San Francisco, 1970-71, U.S. Supreme Ct., 1971-72; asst. prof. law sch. U. Va., Charlottesville, 1972-74, assoc. prof., 1974-77, prof., 1977-87, Class of 1962 prof., 1987-90; Howrey prof. trial advocacy, litigation and profl. responsibility George Washington U. Law Sch., Washington, 1990—2004, Wallace and Beverley Woodbury univ. prof., 2004—. Reporter Alaska Rules of Evidence, 1976-77, Alaska Civil Jury Instrns., 1979-81, Adv. Com. on Rules of Criminal Procedure, 1984-89, Va. Rules on Evidence, 1984-85, Civil Justice Act Adv. Group, U.S. Dist. Ct. D.C., 1992-93, chmn., 1994-99, assoc. independant councel, 1987-88; dep. asst. atty. gen. criminal divsn. U.S. Dept. Justice, 1988-89; ex officio mem. U.S. Sentencing Commn., 1989-90; mem. adv. com. on Fed. Rules of Criminal Procedure, 1989-95, on Fed. Rules of Evidence, 1992-95; mediator dispute resolution program U.S. Ct. Appeals, 1993—. Author: Evidence in America, 1987, American Criminal Procedure, 7th edit., 2004, Criminal Law: Cases and Materials, 1994, 2d edit., 2000, Evidence: The Objection Method, 1997, 2d edit., 2000, Federal Rules of Evidence Manual, 1975, 9th edit., 2006, Federal Rules of Evidence Trial Book, 1998, A Modern Approach to Evidence, 2d edit., 1982, Military Rules of Evidence Manual, 5th edit., 2004, Basic Criminal Procedure, 1994, 4th edit., 2005, Military Evidentiary Foundations, 1994, 2d edit., 2000, Trying Cases to Win: Anatomy of a Trial, 1999, Trying Cases to Win: Evidence: Weapons for Winning, Vol. 1, 2000, Vol. 2, 2002, Vol. 3, 2004, California Federal Evidence Trial Book, 1999, Ohio Rules of Evidence Trial Book, 1999, Washington Evidence Trial Book, 1999. Mem.: ABA (chmn. com. on trial advocacy criminal justice sect. 1992—96, co-chmn. task force on civil trial stds. litig. sect. 1996—97, task force on Ind. Counsel Act litig. sect. 1997—99, mem. criminal justice sect. coun. 2000—, task force on terrorism and the law 2001—02, litigation sect. coun. 2001—04, ho. of dels. 2001—05, task force on gatekeeper regulation and the profession 2002—, task force on enemy combatants 2002—, chair ABA Justice Kennedy Commn. 2003—04, co-chair commns. effective criminal sanctions 2005—), Am. Law Inst. (George Washington U Law Sch 2000 H St NW Washington DC 20052 Office Phone: 202-994-7089. Business E-Mail: ssaltz@law.gwu.edu.

**SALTZMAN, IRENE CAMERON,** consumer products company executive; b. Cocoa, Fla., Mar. 23, 1927; d. Argyle Bruce and Marie T. (Neel) Cameron; m. Herman Saltzman, Mar. 23, 1946 (dec. May 1986); children: Martin Howard (dec.), Arlene Norma Hanly. Owner Irene Perfume and Cosmetics Lab., Jacksonville, Fla., 1972—. Mem. Cummer Mus. Art, Jacksonville, 1972-. Mem. NAFE, Nat. Judge Advocates Assn. of USAF (hon.), Mil. Officers Assn. Am., Aircraft Owners and Pilots Assn., Trade, Cosmetic, Toiletry and Fragrance Assn., Ret. Officers Assn., Soc. Cosmetic Chemists (affiliate), Ponte Vedra Club. Democrat. Episcopalian. Avocations: aviation, painting, travel, swimming, golf. Home: 2701 Ocean Dr S Jacksonville Beach FL 32250 Office Phone: 904-641-5171. Business E-Mail: irene@ireneparfums.com.

**SALTZMAN, JARED,** performing arts educator, lighting designer; b. NYC, Apr. 14, 1950; s. Perle and David Saltzman; m. Marjorie Harris, May 28, 1972; children: Aimee Perle, Arielle Jessica. MA, NYU, 1976. Prof. Bergen CC, Paramus, NJ, 1973—; head electrician IATSE Local 632, NJ, 1978—. Mem.: NEA, Internat. Alliance of Theatrical Stage Employees, US Inst. for Theatre Tech. Office: Bergen Cmty Coll 400 Paramus Rd Paramus NJ 07652 Office Phone: 201-447-7197.

**SALTZMAN, JOSEPH,** journalist, educator, television producer; b. LA, Oct. 28, 1939; s. Morris and Ruth (Weiss) S.; m. Barbara Dale Epstein, July 1, 1962; children: Michael Stephen Ulysses, David Charles Laertes. BA, U. So. Calif., 1961; MS, Columbia U., 1962. Freelance writer, reporter, prodr., 1960—; reporter Valley Times Today, LA, 1962-64; editor Pacific Palisades Palisadian Post, 1964; sr. writer, prodr. CBS-TV, LA, 1964-74; freelance broadcast cons. LA, 1974—; prof. journalism U. So. Calif., LA, 1974—, acting dir. Sch. Journalism, 1999, assoc. dean, 1999—2003; assoc. dean Sch. Journalism U. So. Calif. Annenberg, 1996-99; assoc. dean Annenberg Sch. Comm., 1999—2003; sr. prodr. investigative unit Entertainment Tonight, 1983; dir. Image of the Journalist in Popular Culture project Norman Lear Ctr., Annenberg Sch. Comm., U. So. Calif., 2001—. CFO The Jester & Pharley Phund. Author: Frank Capra and the Image of the Journalist in American Film, 2002; prodr.(writer): (documentaries) Black on Black, 1968, The Unhappy Hunting Ground, 1971, The Junior High School, 1971, The Very Personal: Death of Elizabeth Schell-Holt-Hartford, 1972, Rape, 1972, Why Me?, 1974, Entertainment Tonight, 1983; editor (columnist): USA Today, 1983—; King Features Syndicate, 1983—92; contbg. editor: Emmy Mag., 1986—90, Roberts Reviewing Svc., 1964—95, others. Recipient AP cert. of excellence and merit, 1968, 72, 73, 74, 75, Edward R. Murrow awards for disting. achievements in broadcast journalism, 1969, 72, Alfred I. duPont-Columbia U. award in broadcast journalism, 1973-74, Silver Gavel award ABA, 1973, Ohio State award Am. Exhbn. Ednl. Radio-TV Programs and Inst. for Edn. by Radio-TV Telecom. Ctr., 1974, Broadcast Media awards San Francisco State U., 1974, 75, Media award for excellence in comm. Am. Cancer Soc., 1976, Disting. Alumni award U. So. Calif., 1992, Alumni award Columbia U. Grad. Sch. Journalism, 2005, Seymour Berkson fellow, 1961; Robert E. Sherwood fellow, 1962; alt. Pulitzer traveling fellow, 1962-63. Mem. NATAS (regional Emmy awards 1965, 68, 74, 75), Radio-TV News Assn. (Golden Mike awards 1969, 71, 73, 75), Writers Guild Am., Greater LA Press Club (awards 1968, 74, 75), Columbia U. Alumni Assn., U. So. Calif. Alumni Assn., Skull and Dagger, Blue Key, Phi Beta Kappa, Sigma Delta Chi, Pi Sigma Alpha, Alpha Epsilon Rho. Home: 2116 Via Estudillo Palos Verdes Peninsula CA 90274-1931 Office: U So Calif Annenberg Sch Journalism Univ Park Los Angeles CA 90089-0001 Office Phone: 310-377-8883. Business E-Mail: saltzman@usc.edu.

**SALTZMAN, PHILIP,** television producer, writer; b. Sonora, Mexico, Sept. 19, 1928; came to U.S., 1929, naturalized, 1948; s. Louis and Vanya (Liberman) S.; m. Caroline Veiller, Jan. 24, 1960; children: Jennifer, Daniel, Tony. BA, UCLA, 1951, MA, 1953. Free lance writer, 1958-68. Pres. Woodruff Prodns., Inc. Writer: (TV shows) Alcoa Goodyear Theater, 1959, Richard Diamond, 1959, Rifleman, 1961, Perry Mason, 1964, Dr. Kildare, 1964, Fugitive, 1964, Twelve O'Clock High, 1966; producer, writer: (TV shows) Felony Squad, 1966-69, F.B.I, 1969-73, Barnaby Jones, 1973-77;

producer, writer, creator Intertect, 1973; producer: (TV movie) The FBI vs. Alvin Karpis, 1974, Attack on Terror: The FBI vs. the KKK in Mississippi, 1975, Brinks: The Great Robbery, 1976; co-writer: (feature film) The Swiss Conspiracy, 1975; creator, writer, producer: (TV movie) Crossfire, 1975; exec. producer: (TV series) Barnaby Jones, 1978-80, Escapade, 1978, Colorado C-I, 1978, A Man Called Sloane, 1979, The Aliens Are Coming, 1979, Freebie and the Bean, 1980; producer: (TV shows) Bare Essence, 1982; supervising producer-writer Partners in Crime, 1984; producer, writer Crazy Like a Fox, 1985; producer, co-writer (TV movie) That Secret Sunday, 1986; exec. supervising producer The New Perry Mason movies, 1987-88; exec. supervising producer, writer Jake and The Fatman, 1987-88; supervising producer Columbo, 1989-90; creator, writer The Caller, 1991. Mem. dean's coun. Coll. Letters and Sci., UCLA, Friends of English, UCLA. Mem. Writers Guild Am., West, Caucus for Writers, Producers, Dirs., Acad. TV Arts and Scis., PEN Ctr. USA West. Personal E-Mail: cpsaltzman@aol.com.

**SALTZMAN, W. MARK,** engineering educator; BS in Chem. Engring., Iowa State U., 1981; MS in Chem. Engring., MIT, 1984, PhD in Med. Engring., 1987. Asst. prof. chem. engring. The Johns Hopkins U., 1987—92, joint appt. dept. biomedical engring., 1990—96, assoc. prof., 1992—96, prof., 1995—96, Cornell U., 1996—2002, BP Amoco/H. Laurance Fuller Chair in Chem. Engring., 2001—02; Goizueta Found. Prof. Chem. and Biomedical Engring. Yale U., 2002—, chair dept. biomedical engring. Mem. surgery & bioengineering study sect. NIH, 1999—; Britton Chance Disting. Lectr. in Engring. and Medicine U. Pa., 2000. Author: Drug Delivery: Engineering Principles for Drug Therapy, 2001, Tissue Engineering: Engineering principles for the design of replacement organs and tissues, 2004. Named Disting. Lectr., Biomedical Engring. Soc., 2004; recipient Camille and Henry Dreyfus Found. Tchr-Scholar Award, 1990, Allan C. Davis Medal, 1995, Controlled Release Soc. Young Investigator Award, 1996, Profl. Progress in Engring. Award, Iowa State U., 2000. Fellow: Am. Inst. Biol. and Med. Engineers. Office: Yale U Dept Biomedical Engring PO Box 208284 New Haven CT 06511-8284 Office Phone: 203-432-4262. Office Fax: 203-432-0030. Business E-Mail: mark.saltzman@yale.edu.

**SALTZSTEIN, SUSAN L.,** lawyer; b. N.Y., 1965; BA, U. Pa., 1987; JD magna cum laude, Columbia U., 1991. Bar: N.Y. 1992. Atty. Skadden, Arps, Slate, Meagher & Flom LLP, N.Y., 1992—. Office: Skadden Arps Slate Meagher & Flom LLP Four Times Sq New York NY 10036

**SALVANESCHI, LUIGI,** real estate developer, management consultant, educator; b. Casale, Italy, 1929; came to U.S., 1959; s. Ernesto and Carolina (Bassignana) S.; m. Lenore M. Rickels, Aug. 20, 1958; 1 child, Margherita Lina. Classical Maturity, Valsalice, Torino, Italy, 1950; PhD, Vatican U., Rome, 1958; cert. in real estate, UCLA, 1965. Restaurant mgr. McDonalds Co., Chgo., 1959-61, restaurant mgr. and supr. Los Angeles, 1961-63, real estate mgr., 1964-68, v.p. real estate Oakbrook, Ill., 1969-83; sr. v.p. real estate and constrn. Kentucky Fried Chicken, Louisville, 1983-88; pres., COO, dir. Blockbuster Entertainment, Ft. Lauderdale, Fla., 1988-91; disting. adj. prof. Barry Univ., 1991—. Adj. prof. Sch. Bus. U. Louisville, 1987; dir. Fla. Fun-Train subs. First Am. Rwys., Hollywood, Fla. Author: Location, Location, Location, 1997, Renaissance 2000: Liberal Arts Essentials for Tomorrow's Leaders, 1998. Dir. Ft. Lauderdale Internat. Movie Festival. Served as 2d lt. in Italian Infantry, 1945-46. Recipient Outstanding Italo-Am. award Italian Am. Fedn., 1991; named Colonel of the Commonwealth of Ky., 1984. Mem. Nat. Assn. Real Estate Execs. (co-founder, bd. dirs.). Roman Catholic. Avocations: mountain hiking, reading. Office: Barry Univ Sch of Bus 11300 NE 2nd Ave Miami FL 33161-6695

**SALVANTO, MARIA,** counselor; b. Newark, N.J., Apr. 14, 1971; d. Andrew Martin and Virginia Vyniski; m. Richard Salvanto, Aug. 11, 2000. BS, Rutgers U., 1993; MS in Behavioral Sci., Kean U., 1997; MA in Clin. Psychology, U. Calif., San Diego, Calif., 2000, PhD, 2005. Lic. profl. counselor Bd. Marriage & Family Counselors, N.J., 2003. Clinician Children's Aid & Family Svcs., Ridgewood, NJ, 2003—. Mem.: APA (assoc.). Office Phone: 201-445-7015.

**SALVATIERRA, OSCAR, JR.,** transplant surgeon, urologist, educator; b. Phoenix, Apr. 15, 1935; s. Oscar and Josefine S.; m. Pamela Moss; children: Mark, Lisa Marie. BS, Georgetown U., 1957; MD, U. So. Calif., 1961. Intern, resident in surgery and urology U. So. Calif.-Los Angeles County Med. Ctr., 1961-66; practice medicine Pomona, Calif., 1968-72; chief staff Casa Colina Hosp., 1972; post doctoral fellow in transplantation U. Calif.-San Francisco, 1972-73, asst. prof. surgery and urology, 1973-75, assoc. prof., 1975-81, prof., 1981-91, chmn. transplant service, 1974-91; attending surgeon and urologist Moffitt Hosp., 1973—; exec. dir. Pacific Transplant Inst., 1991-94; prof. surgery/pediatrics, dir. pediat. renal transplantation Stanford U. Med. Ctr., 1994—, attending surgeon, urologist and pediat.; advising dean Sch. Medicine Stanford U., 2005—. Chair faculty senate Stanford U. Sch. Medicine, 2002—04; study sect. NIH, 1981-85, nat. adv. bd., 1986-92, chmn. nat. adv. bd. 1990-92, chmn. spl. study sect., 1997, 99 Mem. editl. bd. Transplantation and Immunology, 1984—, Transplantation, 1987—, Transplantation Procs., 1990—, Pediat. Transplantation, 1998—; assoc. editor Am. Jour. Kidney Diseases, 1987-89; contbr. over 280 articles and chpts. to med. lit. Nat. bd. advisors Agent Orange Class Assistance Program, 1988-96. With M.C., U.S. Army, Vietnam, 1966-68. Decorated Army Commendation medal, Grand Ufficiale of Italian Rep. with title His Excellency award; named Oscar Salvatierra lectureship in his honor, 2001; recipient Chancellor's award for pub. svc., U. Calif., 1986, Commendation resolution, Calif. State Legislature, 1990, Presdl. medal and Diploma of Honor, Argentina, 1999, Rambar-Mark award, Stanford U., 1999, Franklin Ebaugh award, 2003; grantee, NIH, 1974—76, 1980—83, 1988—90, 2003—, USPHS, 1986—89; Oscar Salvatierra Am. Lectureship in Transplantation. established in his honor, Stanford U., 2005. Fellow ACS (bd. govs. 1986-92); mem. Am. Surg. Assn., Am. Soc. Transplant Surgeons (bd. dirs. 1977-85, pres. 1983-84, chmn. adv. com. on issues 1984-87), Soc. Univ. Surgeons, Soc. Univ. Urologists, N.Y. Acad. Scis., Am. Soc. Nephrology, Internat. Transplantation Soc. (bd. dirs. 1984—, pres.-elect 1996-98, pres., 1998-2000, Contbns. to Soc. medallion 2006), Soc. Pediatric Urology, Am. Urol. Assn., Nat. Kidney Found. (Pioneer award 2004), Renal Physicians Assn. (bd. dirs. 1984-87), Pacific Coast Surg. Assn., San Francisco Surg. Soc., United Network Organ Sharing (bd. dirs. 1984-88, pres. 1985-86), Internat. Soc. for Organ Sharing (bd. dirs. 1991—, pres. 1993-95), Am. Soc. for Multicultural Health and Transplant Profls. (pres. 1992-94, Lifetime Achievement award, 2005), Nafziger Surg. Soc. Achievements include being the principle lay figure in passage and enactment of National Organ Transplant Act, 1984; introduction of Pope John Paul II to the 18th International Transplantation Congress for Encyclical on Organ Transplantation, 2000. Office: Stanford U Med Ctr 703 Welch Rd Ste H2 Palo Alto CA 94304-1708

**SALVATO, SCOTT VINCENT,** minister; b. Rockville Center, N.Y. s. John Paul Salvato and Jean Marie Downey; m. Catherine Ann Andrews, July 11, 1998; children: Brigid Mary, Anna Therese. BA, St. Bonaventure Univ., Bonaventure, N.Y., 1995; MA, St. John's Univ., Queens, NY, 2000, PhD, 2004—. Tchr. Holy Trinity Diocesan H.S., Hicksville, NY, 1994—97; campus minister St. John's Univ., Queen, NY, 1997—2004, Molloy Coll., Rockville Ctr., NY, 2004—. Sec. Rockville Ctr. Rugby Club, Rockville Ctr., NY, 1995—99; pres. St. Bonaventure Rugby Club, 1992—93; capt. L.I. Rugby Club, L.I., NY, 2000—03; mem. Right to Life. Republican. Roman Catholic. Avocations: rugby, politics, reading. Office: Molley Coll 100 Hempstead Ave PO Box 5002 Rockville Centre NY 11571 Office Phone: 516-678-5000 ext. 6715.

**SALVATORE, DIANE J.,** editor-in-chief; BA in Journalism, Pa. State U.; MA in English and Creative Writing, NYU. Rschr., reporter The Soho News, NYC; editl. asst. Met. Home, NYC, Cosmopolitan, NYC; sr. assoc. editor Ladies' Home Jour., NYC, 1985—88; articles assoc. editor Glamour, NYC, 1988—89; sr. editor Redbook, NYC, 1989—94; dep. editor Good Housekeeping, NYC, exec. editor, 1994—99; editor in chief YM, NYC, 1998—2002; exec. dir. Marie Claire, 2001; editor in chief Ladies Home Jour.,

NYC, 2002—; dir. editl. ops. Hearst Mag., 2002. Contbr. articles and short stories in various nat. periodicals. Mem.: Am. Soc. Mag. Editors. Office Phone: 212-455-1025. Office Fax: 212-455-1313. E-mail: diane.salvatore@meredith.com.*

**SALVATY, BENJAMIN BENEDICT,** lawyer; b. Chgo., Dec. 22, 1940; s. Benjamin Benedict and Marion Therese (Ryan) S.; m. Patircia Louise Recor, Aug. 29, 1964; children: Paul Benedict, Kathleen Anne. BBA, U. Notre Dame, 1962; JD, U. So. Calif., 1965. Bar: Calif. 1966, U.S. Dist. Ct. (no., cen., ea. and so. dists.) Calif., U.S. Ct. Appeals (9th cir.), 1975, U.S. Tax Ct., U.S. Supreme Ct. Sr. trial atty. Calif. Dept. Transp., 1966-79; gen. atty. The Atchison, Topeka and Santa Fe Railway Co., 1980-89; sr. ptnr. Hill, Farrer & Burrill, Los Angeles, 1990—. Chmn. traffic commn. City of San Marino. Mem. ABA (litigation sect. urban, state and local govt. law com. on condemnation, zoning and planning com.), Am. Bd. Trial Advs., Am. Judicature Soc., Internat. Right Way Assn., Irish Am. Bar Assn. (bd. dirs. 1985—, treas. 1991, sec. 1992, v.p. 1992-93, pres. 1993-94), Italian Am. Lawyers Assn., State Trial Attys. Assn. (pres. 1975-79), Calif. State Bar (chmn. condemnation com. 1987-88, vice chmn. 1986-87), Pasadena Bar Assn., L.A. County Bar Assn. (condemnation and land valuation com.). Office: Hill Farrer & Burrill LLP One California Plz 37th Fl 300 S Grand Ave Los Angeles CA 90071-3109 Fax: 213-624-4840. Office Phone: 213-621-0865. Business E-Mail: bsalvaty@hillfarrer.com.

**SALVENDY, GAVRIEL,** industrial engineer, educator; b. Budapest, Hungary, Sept. 30, 1938; came to U.S., 1968; s. Paul and Katarina (Brown) S.; m. Catherine Vivien Dees, Apr. 1, 1966; children: Laura Dorit, Kevin David. MSc in Engring. Prodn., U. Birmingham, Eng., 1966, PhD, 1968; Doctorate (hon.), Academia Sinica, 1995, Chinese Acad. Scis., 1995. Asst. prof. indsl. engring. SUNY, Buffalo, 1968-71; mem. faculty Purdue U., 1971—, prof. indsl. engring., chmn. human factors program, 1977, Fulbright distinguished prof., 1979-80, 81-82, NEC prof. indsl. engring., 1984-99; chair, prof., head dept. indsl. engring. Tsinghua U., China, 2001—. Chmn. Internat. Comm. on Human Aspects in Computing, Switzerland, 1986-91. Co-author: Prediction and Development of Industrial Work Performance, 1973, Human Aspects of Computer Aided Design, 1987; sr. editor: Machine-Pacing and Occupational Stress, 1981, Social, Ergonomic and Stress Aspects of Work with Computers, 1987, Designing and Using Human-Computer Interfaces and Knowledge Based Systems, 1989; editor: Handbook of Industrial Engineering, 1982, 3d edit., 2001, Human Computer Interaction, 1984, Handbook of Human Factors, 1987, 2d edit., 1997, Cognitive Engineering in the Design of Human Computer Interaction and Expert Systems, 1987; founding editor: Internat. Jour. on Human-Computer Interaction, Internat. Jour. Human Factors in Mfg.; co-editor: Work with Computers: Organizational Management, Stress and Health Aspects, 1989, Human Computer Interaction: Software and Hardware Interfaces, 1993, Human-Computer Interaction: Applications and Case Studies, 1993, Design of Work and Development of Personnel in Advanced Manufacturing, 1994, Organization and Management of Advanced Manufacturing, 1994, Advances in Applied Ergonomics, 1996, Handbook of Human Factors and Ergonomics, 2d edit., 1997, Design of Computing Systems (2 vols.), 1997, Ergonomics in Manufacturing, 1998, Handbook of Industrial Engineering, 3d edit., 2001; contbr. articles to profl. jours., chpts. to books. Pres. Lafayette Jewish Sunday Sch., 1980-81. Fellow APA, Inst. Indsl. Engrs. (sr., Phil Carroll award 1973), Human Factors and Ergonomics Soc. (past officer), Ergonomics Soc. (hon., life mem.); mem. NAE. Office: Purdue U Sch Indsl Engring West Lafayette IN 47907 Office Phone: 765-494-5426. Business E-Mail: salvendy@purdue.edu.

**SALVESEN, MAGDA ABERCROMBY,** art and garden historian; b. Edinburgh, Scotland, June 20, 1944; came to US, 1976; d. Harold Keith and Marion Eleanora (Cameron) S.; m. Jon R. Schueler, July 29, 1976 (dec. Aug. 1992). MA, U. St. Andrews (Scotland), 1966, U. London, 1968; Cert. in Secondary Edn., Moray House Coll. Edn., Edinburgh, 1976. Asst. Richard Demarco Gallery, Edinburgh, 1968; exhibn. officer Scottish Arts Coun., Edinburgh, 1969-71; tchr. middle sch. The Day Sch., N.Y.C., 1976-81; ESL tchr. Berlitz Sch. Langs., N.Y.C., 1983-85; exec. adminstr. Archs./Designers/Planners for Social Responsibility, N.Y.C., 1985-88; lectr. art history New Sch. U., N.Y.C., 1988—; lectr. garden history and theory N.Y. Botanical Garden, Bronx, 1990—. Lectr. in field. Editor: (manuscript by Jon Schueler) The Sound of Sleat: A Painter's Life, 1999; co-editor: Artists' Estates: Reputations in Trust, 2005; dir. and exec. prodr.: (video) Jon Schueler: A Life in Painting, 1999. Bd. mem. Queens (N.Y.) Bot. Garden. Democrat. Avocations: museuming, reading, travel, gardening. Address: 40 W 22nd St New York NY 10010 Office Phone: 212-929-7614. E-mail: msalvesen@earthlink.net.

**SALVESON, MELVIN ERWIN,** management sciences company executive, educator; b. Brea, Calif., Jan. 16, 1919; s. John T. and Elizabeth (Green) S.; m. Joan Y. Stipek, Aug. 22, 1944; children: Eric C, Kent Erwin. BS, U. Calif. Berkeley, 1941; MS, MIT, Boston, 1947; PhD, U. Chgo., 1952. Cons. McKinsey & Co., N.Y.C., 1947—48; asst. prof. mgmt. sci. rsch. U. Calif., L.A, 1948—54; mgr. advanced data sys., cons. strategic planning GE, Louisville and N.Y.C., 1954—57; pres. Mgmt. Scis. Corp., L.A., 1957—67; group v.p. Control Data/CEIR, Inc., 1967—68; pres. Electronic Currency Corp., 1964—; chmn. OneCard Internat., Inc., 1983—92, UniCard Sys. Inc., 1992—; founder and pres. So. Calif. Econ. Alliance, 1992—96, also bd. dirs.; founding chair Am. Soc. for Edn. and Econ. Devel., 1996—98, also bd dirs.; exec. dir. Am. Found. for Edn. and Econ. Devel. Bd. dirs. Diversified Earth Scis., Inc., Eco Rx Inc., Excel Enterprise Inc., Veritas et Justus Inc., Algeran, Inc., Electronic Currency Corp.; founder MasterCard Sys., L.A., 1964; chmn. Corp. Strategies Internat.; prof. bus. Pepperdine U. 1972-85; adj. prof. U. So. Calif., Webster U., U. Phoenix, 1972—; adviser data processing City of L.A., 1962-64; futures forecasting IBM, 1957-61; adviser strategic sys. planning USAF, 1961-67; info. sys. Calif. Dept. Human Resources, 1972-73, City L.A. Automated Urban Data Base, 1962-67; tech. transfer NASA, 1965-70; mem. bd. trustees, Long Beach City Coll., 1990-95. Contbr. articles to profl. jours. Served to lt. comdr. USNR, 1941—46. Named to Long Beach City Coll. Hall of Fame; recipient Dist. Alumnus 1992 award Calif. Coll. Sys., 1992. Fellow: AAAS, Inst. Mgmt. Sci. (founder, past pres.), Inst. for Ops. Rsch. and Mgmt. Scis.; mem.: CSSP Alumnus, Calif. Yacht Club, Founders Club (L.A. Philharm. Orch.). Republican. Office: 515 Ocean Ave # 405 S Santa Monica CA 90402-2623 Office Phone: 310-917-1911. Personal E-mail: mesalveson@aol.com.

**SALVINI, EMIL ROBERT,** publishing executive, writer, historian; b. Jersey City, June 8, 1949; s. Armando and Marie Salvini; m. Nancy Ann Levenstein, Dec. 12, 1971; children: Amy Cara, Beth Lauren. BA, William Paterson U., 1971; degree, Harvard Bus. Sch., 2001. Pres. Wheal-Grace Corp., Belleville, NJ, 1975—. Author: The Summer City by the Sea, 1995, Boardwalk Memories, Tales of the Jersey Shore, 2005, Hobey Baker American Legend, 2005, Jersey Memories, Vintage Images of the Jersey Shore, 2006. Commr. Cape May Hist. Preservation Commn., Cape May, NJ, 2004—06. Mem.: North Jersey Country Club, Harvard Bus. Sch. NY, Harvard Club Boston, Harvard Club NY. Achievements include invention of GreenPrint program. Avocations: writing, golf, travel. Office: Wheal-Grace Corp 300 Ralph St Belleville NJ 07109 Office Phone: 973-450-8100 11. Home Fax: 973-839-1403; Office Fax: 973-450-5950. E-mail: esalvini@wheal-grace.com.

**SALVO, J. C.,** lawyer; b. Council Bluffs, Iowa, Dec. 10, 1947; JD, Creighton U. Sch. of Law, Omaha, Neb., 1972. Ptnr. Salvo, Deren, Schenck & Lauterbach, PC, Harlan, Iowa, 1972—. Shelby County atty., 1977—82. Mem.: Iowa Supreme Ct. Nominating Commn., Iowa Supreme Ct. Grievance Commn., Assn. of Trial Lawyers of Am., Am. Bar Assn., Neb. State Bar Assn., Iowa State Bar Assn. (bd. gov. 1999—2003, v.p. 2003, pres.-elect 2004), Iowa Acad. of Trial Lawyers (pres. 1998), Phi Alpha Delta. Office: Salvo, Deren, Schenck & Lauterbach PC 711 Court St PO Box 509 Harlan IA 51537-0509

**SALVUCCI, LINDA,** history professor; b. Pittston, Pa., Mar. 28, 1951; d. Joseph A. and Helen Shegelski Kerrigan; m. Richard Salvucci, Aug. 25, 1973; children: Martin J., Rosemary C. AB in History, Villanova U., 1973; AM in History, Princeton U., 1979, PhD in History, 1985. Asst. prof. history Trinity U., San Antonio, 1985—91, assoc. prof. history, 1991—. Chmn., mem. coms. various confs. in field. Co-author: (textbook) Call to Freedom, various edits., 2000—05; contbr. articles to profl. publs. Trustee St. Luke's Episc. Sch., 1998—2005, vice chmn. 2002—04; bd. editors The Americas, 2002—06; bd. dirs. Youth Orchs. San Antonio, 2005—. Recipient Hubert Herring award for best article, Pacific Coast Coun. on L.Am. Studies, 1985, Coll. Tchrs. award, NEH, 1988—89, prize, Conf. on L.Am. History, 2001. Mem.: Hist. Soc. (bd. govs. 2006—), Nat. Coun. History Edn. (trustee 2005—), Omohundro Inst. Early Am. History and Culture, Am. Hist. Assn. Office: Trinity U Dept History 1 Trinity Pl San Antonio TX 78212 Office Phone: 210-999-7628.

**SALYER, KENNETH E.,** surgeon; b. Kansas City, Kans., Aug. 18, 1936; s. Everett A. and Laurene S.; m. Luci Lara-Salyer; children: Kenneth E. Jr., Leigh Green-Salyer. BS, U. Mo., 1958; MD, U. Kans., 1962. Intern Parkland Meml. Hosp., Dallas, 1962-63, resident in gen. surgery, 1963-67; fellow in surgery U. Tex. SW Sch. Med., Dallas, 1965-67, founder, dir. residency tng. program, 1969-78; prof. surgery, chair plastic surgery, 1969-78; resident in plastic surgery U. Kans. Sch. Med., Kansas City, 1967-69; founder, dir. Internat. Craniofacial Inst., Dallas, 1986—. Editl. bd. mem. Annals of Plastic Surgery, 1977-79, Jour. of Speech and Hearing Disorders (editl. cons.) 1982, Tex. Medicine (cons.) 1981-85, Jour. of Craniofacial Surgery, 1990—, Italian Jour. Craniomaxillofacial Surgery, 1990—, Argentinian Jour. Plastic Surgery (internat. consultative coun. 1995—). Author: Techniques in Aesthetic Craniofacial Surgery, 1989, Cleft Lip and Palate Treatment Center: A Booklet for Parents, 1994, (with J. Bardach) Surgical Techniques in Cleft Lip and Palate, 1987, 2d edit. 1991, (with others) The Atlas of Craniomaxillofacial Surgery, 1982; editor: Symposium on Plastic Surgery in the Orbital Region, 1976; author various book chpts. Recipient Nat. Inst. Health award public health svc., sr. clin. traineeship Cancer Control Program 1967-69, Plastic Surgery Resident Program Participation award 2nd place 1967-69, scholar. competition (hon. mention) Edn. Found. Am. Soc. Plastic and Reconstructive Surgeons, 1972, Rsch. Grant award Edn. Found. Am. Soc. Plastic and Reconstructive Surgeons 1975-76, Hektoen Gold medal for original investigation "Spectrum of Rsch. and Clin. Mgmt. of Craniofacial Anomalies" exhibit at AMA, San Francisco 1977, selected hon. mem. Japanese Soc. Craniofacial Surgery 1993, selected chmn. med. adv. bd. Children's Craniofacial Assn. 1993; grantee Internat. NIH Microvascular Surg. Rsch. 1969, Vets. Admin. Hosp. Maxillofacial Rsch. 1972-78, Sid Richardson Found. med. rsch. 1975-76, Gen. Electric Found. for Craniofacial Deformities 1985-87; recipient various awards for videos. Mem. AMA (mem. various coms.), Am. Acad. Pediat. (exec. com. section on plastic surgery, founding mem., sec.-treas. 1987-90, chmn. 1991—), Am. Assn. of Pediat. Plastic Surgery (founding mem., chmn. 1991—), Am. Assn. Plastic Surgery (mem. various coms.), Am. Burn Assn., Am. Cleft Palate Assn. (mem. various coms.), Am. Coll. Surgeons, Am. Soc. for Aesthetic Plastic Surgery, Am. Soc. Maxiofacial Surgery (mem. various coms.), Am. Soc. Plastic and Reconstructive Surgery (mem. various coms.), Am. Soc. for Reconstructive Microsurgery, Argentine Soc. of Plastic Surgery, Children's Craniofacial Assn. (chmn. med. adv. bd.), Chirugio Soc., Craniofacial Biology Group, Dallas County Med. Soc., Dallas Soc. Plastic Surgery, Euro. Assn. for Craniomaxillofacial Surgery, Internat. Coll. Surgeons, Internat. Confederation for Plastic Reconstructive Surgery (founding mem.), Internat. Craniofacial Club, Internat. Craniofacial Travel Club, Internat. Soc. Clin. Plastic Surgery, Internat. Soc. Cranofacial Surgery (hon. mem.), Lipoplasty Soc. of N.A., Inc., McKorkle Soc., Pan-Pacific Surg. Assn., Physicians Art Assn., Plastic Surgery Rsch. Coun., Soc. for Biomaterials, Soc. Craniofacial Genetics, Soc. Head and Neck Surgery, So. Med. Assn., Southwestern Med. Found., Tex. Soc. Plastic Surgery (mem. various coms., pres.-elect 1982-83, pres. 1983-84), Tex. State Med. Assn., Wound Healing Soc. Avocations: skiing, running, travel. Office: Internat Cranio Inst 7777 Forest Ln Ste C717 Dallas TX 75230-2550

**SALYER, STEPHEN LEE,** educational program administrator; b. Lexington, Ky., July 20, 1950; s. Ralph Conley Salyer and Margaret Miles; m. Susan D. Moeller; children: Samuel Wilmot, Duncan Davis, Clara Josephine stepchildren: Walden Jeffrey Davis, Sethly Martin Davis. BA, Davidson Coll., 1972; MPA, Harvard U., 1975. Pres. Citizens' Com. on Population and the Am. Future, Washington, 1972-73; cons. Rockefeller Family Assocs., NYC, 1973-75; assoc. pub. issues program Population Coun., NYC, 1977-79; asst. to the pres. Ednl. Broadcasting Corp., Sta. WNET TV, NYC, 1975-76, v.p. corp. affairs, 1979-80, v.p. program devel. and mktg., 1981-82, sr. v.p. edn. divsn., 1982-86, sr. v.p. mktg. and comm., 1986-88, pres., CEO Pub. Radio Internat., Mpls., 1988—2005, Salzurb Sem., Washington, 2005—, also bd. dirs., 2005—. Chmn. bd. dirs. Pub. Interactive, LLC, 1999—2005. Co-author: (with James J. Bausch) Toward Safe, Convenient and Effective Contraceptives, 1978. Mem. Nat. Commn. on Population Growth and the Am. Future, Washington, 1970—72; bd. dirs. Philanthropic Rsch., Inc. Guidestar, 2001—, Davidson Coll., 2004—; fellow Japan Soc. US-Japan Leadership, 1996. Root-Tilden scholar, NYU Sch. Law, 1976—79, Salzburg Seminar fellow, 1974, Brit.-Am. Program fellow, 1990. Mem. Harvard Club (N.Y.C.). Home: 9510 Midwood Rd Silver Spring MD 20910 Office: 1828 L St NW Washington DC 20036

**SALYERS, HOLLY AMBER,** social studies educator; b. Dayton, Ohio, July 9, 1979; d. John and Joyce Salyers. Degree in secondary edn. social studies, Morehead (Ky.) State U., 2001. Social studies tchr. Manassas (Va.) City Pub. Schools, 2001—. Named Recognized Tchr., Va. Gov.'s Sch., 2004; recipient Disting. Educator, lst prize for H.S. Scholars, 2005. Mem.: Nat. Coun. Social Studies. Independent. Presbyterian. Avocations: reading, travel. Office Phone: 703-257-8500. Personal E-mail: hasalyers@hotmail.com.

**SALZBERG, BARRY,** finance company executive. Degree in acctg., Bkln. Coll.; JD, Bkln. Law Sch.; LLM in taxation, NYU. Joined Deloitte & Touche USA LLP, 1977, named ptnr., 1985, tri-state group mng. ptnr., 1996—99, nat. tax dep. mng. ptnr., 1999—2000, nat. tax mng. ptnr., 2000—03, US mng. ptnr., 2003—, also mem. bd. dirs., chmn. exec. com. Chmn. bd YMCA of Greater NY, 2004—; bd. mem. Jackie Robinson Found. Mem.: AICPA, NY County Lawyers Assn., NY State Soc. CPAs, NY State Bar Assn. Office: Deloitte & Touche USA LLP 1633 Broadway New York NY 10019-6754

**SALZBERG, RUSS,** sportscaster; b. N.Y. m. Vikki Salzberg; 2 children. Sports radio personality Sta. WFAN, Astoria, N.Y., 1993—; sportscaster Sta. WWOR-TV UPN 9 News, Secaucus, N.J. Sports anchor Sta. WOR-TV; former real estate salesman Sta. WFAN-AM Infinity Broadcasting Kaufman Astoria Studios 34-12 36th St Astoria NY 11106 also: Care Sta Wwor-Tv Upn 9 News 9 Broadcast Plz Secaucus NJ 07094-2913

**SALZMAN, ARTHUR GEORGE,** architect; b. Chgo., June 20, 1929; s. Russell Harvey Salzman and Mildred Olive (Olsen) Erickson; m. Joan Marie Larson, Aug. 16, 1952; children: Lisa Jo Salzman Braucher, David Ralph. BS in Archtl. Engring., U. Ill., 1952; MArch, Ill. Inst. Tech., 1960. Registered architect, Ill., Mich., Nat. Coun. Archtl. Registration Bds. Architect Skidmore, Owings & Merrill, Chgo., 1960, Mies van der Rohe, Arch., Chgo., 1960-69; assoc. The Office of Mies Van Der Rohe, Chgo., 1969-81; v.p. FCL Assocs., Chgo., 1981-86; exec. v.p. Lohan Assocs., Chgo., 1986-91; pvt. practice Evanston, Ill., 1992—. Bldg. code restructuring com. City of Chgo., 1994-96, bldg. code electronic version com., 1997, bldg. code rev. com., 1998-2004; adj. prof. arch. Ill. Inst. Tech., Chgo., 2005—. V.p Chgo. area Unitarian-Universalist Coun., Chgo., 1974—76; bd. dirs. Savoy-aires, Evanston, Ill., 1985—88, 1990—93, pres., 1992—93; active Chgo. Com. on High Rise Bldgs. Cpl. U.S. Army, 1952—54. Mem. AIA (bd. dirs. Chgo. chpt. 1992-96, sec. 1994-96, Ill. region bd., alt. del. 1997-98, del. 1999-2000, Disting. Svc. award for profl. excellence 2003), Am. Soc. Testing and Materials Internat., Constrn. Specifications Inst., Internat. Code Coun. (profl.), Precast-Prestressed Concrete Inst., Cliff Dwellers Club, North Shore Musicians Club. Avocations: acting, singing. Office Phone: 847-332-2440.

**SALZMAN, DAVID ELLIOT,** entertainment industry executive; b. Bklyn., Dec. 1, 1943; s. Benjamin and Rose Harriet (Touby) S.; m. Sonia Camelia Gonsalves, Oct. 19, 1968; children: Daniel Mark, Andrea Jessica, Adam Gabriel. BA, Bklyn. Coll., 1965; MA, Wayne State U., 1967. Dir. TV ops. Wayne State U., 1966-67; producer Lou Gordon Program, 1967-70; program mgr. Sta. WKBD-TV, Detroit, 1970-71, Sta. KDKA-TV, Pitts., 1971-72, gen. mgr., 1973-75; program mgr. Sta. KYW-TV, Phila., 1972-73; chmn. bd. Group W Prodns., N.Y.C and Los Angeles, 1975—; founder, pres. United Software Assocs., 1980-81; creator News Info. Weekly Service, 1981; exec. v.p. Telepictures Corp., 1980-84, vice chmn., 1984; pres. Lorimar Telepictures Corp. (merger Telepictures and Lorimar, Inc.), 1985-90, Lorimar TV, 1986-90; creator Newscope: Nat. TV News Cooperative, 1983; pres., CEO David Salzman Entertainment, Burbank, Calif., 1990-93; co-CEO Quincy Jones-David Salzman Entertainment (QDE), 1993—; exec. prodr. Jenny Jones Show, 1991—2003. Exec. prodr. Mad-TV, The Rerun Show, Jumble, In the House, 68th Ann. Acad. awards, Concert of the Americas, 1995, Vibe-TV, 1997-98, Steel, 1997, Their Eyes Were Watching God, 2005; CEO David Salzman Enterprises, 1998—; co-owner Vibe Mag., 1995—, Spin Mag., 1995—, Sta. WNOL-TV, 1995, Sta. WATL-TV, 1995, Sta. KCWE-TV, 1995, Sta. WGRB-TV, 1998; guest lectr. at schs.; bd. govs. Films of Coll. and Univ. Students; co-prodr. (Broadway shows) Urinetown, The Dinner Party, 2001, Into the Woods, 2002. Contbr. articles to Variety and numerous comms. trade publs. Bd. dirs. Pitts. Civic Light Opera, Am. Blood Bank, Pitts., Hebrew Inst., Jewish Community Ctr., Harrison, NY, Temple Etz Chaim, USC Sch. Cinema-TV, Emory U. Ctr. Leadership, Emory Bus. Sch., Bklyn. Coll. Found.; HELP group; co-founding bd. mem. Tour Calif. Cycling Race, 2006. Recipient award Detroit chpt. Am. Women in Radio and TV, 1969, award Golden Quill, 1971, award Golden Gavel, 1971, local Emmy award, 1972, award AP, 1974, Gold medal Broadcast Promotion Assn., 1983, Lifetime Achievement award Bklyn. Coll., 1990, Disting. Alumnus award, Golden Plate award Am. Acad. Achievement, 1995; BPME Gold medal San Francisco Film Festival, 1984, N.Y., 1985, Chgo., 1986, Tree of Life award Jewish Nat. Fund, 1988. Mem. Acad. TV Arts and Scis., Nat. Assn. TV Program Execs., Radio-TV News Dirs. Assn., Am. Mgmt. Assn., Am. Film Inst., Brooklyn Coll. Found. Office: Mad TV Hollywood Ctr Studios 2d Fl 1040 N Las Palmas Bldg 2 Hollywood CA 90038 E-mail: Davids@madtv.com. *"We know what we are but not what we may be."*.

**SALZMAN, MICHELE RENEE,** historian, educator; b. Bklyn., Aug. 2, 1952; d. Aron and Sylvia Salzman; m. Steven Gregory Brint, 1985; children: Juliana, Benjamin. BA, Bklyn. Coll. CUNY, 1973; MA, Bryn Mawr Coll., 1975, PhD, 1981. Classics lectr. Swarthmore (Pa.) Coll., 1980; vis. asst. prof. classics Columbia U., N.Y.C., 1980-82; asst. prof. classics Boston U., 1982-90, assoc. prof. classics, 1990-95; assoc. prof. history U. Calif., Riverside, 1995—2000, prof., 2000—, chair history dept., 1999—2000, mem. steering com. multi-campus rsch. group, 1999—. Project dir. Inst. for Antiquity and Christianity, Claremont Grad. U., 1999—, prof. in charge of Intercollegiate Ctr. for Classified Studies in Rome, 2003-04. Author: (book) On Roman Time: The Codex-Calendar of 354 and the Rhythms of Urban Life in Late Antiquity, 1990, The Making of a Christian Aristocracy: Social and Religious Change in the Western Roman Empire, 2002; contbr. articles to profl. jours. Mem. Dem. Club, 1999. Grantee Am. Philol. Soc., 1983; fellow Ctr. for Ideas and Soc., U. Calif., Riverside, 1996, Am. Coun. Learned Socs., 1983; Mellon Fellow in Classical Studies Am. Acad. Rome, 1986-87. Mem. Am. Philol. Assn. (chair Colloquium on Late Antiquity 1993-97), Classical Assn. So. Calif., N.Am. Patristics Soc., Assn. for Ancient History, Phi Beta Kappa, Sierra Club. Avocations: tennis, aerobics; reading. Office: U Calif-Riverside Dept History Riverside CA 92521-0001 Office Phone: 951-827-1991. Business E-Mail: michele.salzman@ucr.edu.

**SALZMAN, ROBERT JAY,** accountant; b. Bklyn., Dec. 7, 1941; s. Irving and Sydelle (Feingold) S.; m. Constance A. Freeman, Sept. 16, 1990. BA, Allegheny Coll., Meadville, Pa., 1962; MBA, U. Pa., 1965; JD, N.Y. Law Sch., 1972. Bar: N.Y. 1973; CPA, N.Y. Acct., N.Y.C., 1965—; pvt. practice Robert J. Salzman, CPA, P.C., N.Y.C., 1971—. Office: 10 E End Ave New York NY 10021-1106 also: 82 Sycamore Dr East Hampton NY 11937-1482 also: 2801 NE 183rd St Miami FL 33160-2100 Office Phone: 212-744-2860. Business E-Mail: rsalzman@rjspc.com.

**SAM, DAVID,** federal judge; b. Hobart, Ind., Aug. 12, 1933; s. Andrew and Flora (Toma) S.; m. Betty Jean Brennan, Feb. 1, 1957 (dec. Aug. 2000); children: Betty Jean, David Dwight, Daniel Scott, Tamara Lynn, Pamela Rae, Daryl Paul, Angie, Sheyla; m. Bennie Lynn Malnar, Jan. 5, 2005. BS, Brigham Young U., 1957; JD, Utah U., 1960. Bar: Utah 1960, U.S. Dist. Ct. Utah 1966. Sole practice and ptnr., Duchesne, Utah, 1963-76; dist. judge State of Utah, 1976-85; judge U.S. Dist. Ct. Utah, Salt Lake City, 1985-97; chief judge U.S. Dist. Ct., Salt Lake City, 1997—99, sr. judge, 1999—. Atty. City of Duchesne, 1963-72; Duchesne County atty., 1966-72; commr. Duchesne, 1972-74; adv. com. Codes of Conduct of Jud. Conf. US, 1987-91, Jud. Coun. of 10th Cir., 1991-93; mem. US Del. to Romania, Aug. 1991. Chmn. Jud. Nomination Com. for Cir. Ct. Judge, Provo, Utah, 1983; bd. dirs. Water Resources, Salt Lake City, 1973-76. Served to capt. JAGC, USAF, 1961-63. Named Judge of Yr., Utah State Bar, 2004. Mem. Lds Ch. Avocations: beekeeping, reading, sports. Office: US Dist Ct US Courthouse 350 S Main St Ste 441 Salt Lake City UT 84101-2180 Office Phone: 801-524-6190. Business E-Mail: david_sam@utd.uscourts.gov.

**SAMAHA, ELIE,** producer, film company executive, business owner; b. Beirut; came to U.S., 1981; Bouncer Studio 54; owner Celebrity Cleaners, Los Angeles, 1982—; ptnr. club Roxbury, 1990—; CEO, chmn. Franchise Pictures, Burbank, Calif. Producer, exec. producer over 40 films. With Lebanese Christian army. Office: Elie Samaha 6630 W Sunset Blvd Los Angeles CA 90028-7104

**SAMAL, ABANI RANJAN,** geologist; b. Jajpur, Orissa, India, May 21, 1970; s. Jugal Kishore and Janaki Lata Samal; m. Namita Nayak, Sept. 0, 2001. BS with honors, Ravenshaw Coll., Cuttack, Orissa, India, 1988—91; MS, Berhampur U., Orissa, India, 1991—93; M in Tech., Indian Sch. Mines, Dhanbad, India, 1994—95; MSc/DIS, Imperial Coll., London, 2000. Geologist FACOR, Orissa, 1996—98; sr. tech. mem. WGDSI, Bhubaneswar, Orissa, 1998—99, cons., 2000—01; geologist/geostatistician Pincock, Allen & Holt, Lakewood, Colo., 2006—. Vol. Internat. Students & Scholars, Carbondale, 2002—05. Scholar UGCPC Fellowship, Govt. India, 1994—95. Mem.: Soc. Mining Metallurgy & Exploration, Soc. Econ. Geologists, Soc. Geology Applied Mineral Deposits, Mineral. Assn. Can., Mining Engineers' Assn. India, Internat. Assn. Math. Geology (mem. student affairs com. 2005—), Geol. Soc. Am., Can. Inst. Mining & Metallurgy, Am. Geophys. Union. Home: 11183 West 17th Ave Bldg 4 APT 201; Lakewood CO 80215 Office: Pincock Allen & Holt 165 S Union Blvd Ste 950 Lakewood CO Office Fax: 303-987-8907. Personal E-mail: arsamal@yahoo.com.

**SAMANT, VIJAY B.,** biotechnology company executive; BS Chem. Engring., U. Bombay, 1975; MS Chem. Engring., Columbia U., 1977; MBA, MIT, 1983. Numerous pos., including CEO vaccine divsn. Merck & Co., Inc., 1977—2000; pres., CEO dir. Vical Inc., San Diego, 2000—. Adv. coun. Ctr. Advanced Study of India U. Pa.; dean's adv. engring. coun. sch. engring. & applied sci. Columbia U., vis. com. chem. engring. Office: Vical Inc 10390 Pacific Center Ct San Diego CA 92121-4340

**SAMARAS, LUCAS,** artist, photographer; b. Kastoria, Greece, Sept. 14, 1936; came to U.S. 1948, naturalized, 1955; BA, Rutgers U., 1959; postgrad., Columbia U., 1959-62. Instr. advanced sculpture seminar Yale U., 1969; instr. Bklyn. Coll., 1971-72 Exhibited assemblages and sculptures, 1960s; produced: polaroid series Autopolaroids, 1970-71, Phototransformations, 1973-74; exhbns. include, Whitney Mus., N.Y.C., 1966, Pace Gallery, N.Y.C., 1966, Art Inst. Chgo., 1967, 74, The Obsessive Image, Inst. Contemporary Art, London, 1968, Dada, Surrealism and Their Heritage, Mus. Modern Art, N.Y.C., 1968, Documenta, Kassel, W. Ger., 1968, 72, Retrospective Mus. Contemporary Art, Chgo., 1971, Whitney Mus. Am. Art Ann., 1972, Whitney Mus. Am. Art, 1974, Art Inst. Chgo., 1974, Mus. Contemporary Art, Chgo.,

1975, 81, Art Club Chgo., 1980, Bklyn. Mus., 1981, Pace Gallery, 1981, Denver Art Mus., 1981, Lowe Art Mus., Coral Gables, 1982, Mayor Gallery, London, 1982, Walker Art Ctr., Mpls., 1982; one-man exhibitions. Internat. Ctr. Photography, N.Y.C., 1984, Pace Gallery, 1984; represented in permanent collections. Met. Mus. Art, Whitney Mus. Am. Art, Mus. Modern Art, N.Y.C., Albright-Knox Gallery, Buffalo, Los Angeles County Mus. Art, Walker Art Center, Mpls., City Art Mus., St. Louis. Woodrow Wilson fellow Columbia Sch. Art, 1959-62 Office: care Pace Gallery 32 E 57th St New York NY 10022-2513

**SAMARTINI, JAMES ROGERS,** retired appliance company executive; b. Cleve., Apr. 13, 1935; s. Leonard Henry and Grace Rogers (Tully) S.; m. Irene Ann Kurnava, Sept. 16, 1961 (dec. June 1994); m. Julia S. Rubin, Sept. 8, 1996; children: David L., James F., Patrick R. AB, Dartmouth Coll., 1957; MBA, Harvard U., 1961. Fin. supr. Ford Motor Co., Dearborn, Mich., 1966-72; v.p. fin. and adminstrn. Thomet Industries Inc., Pa., 1972-74; from asst. controller to v.p., CFO Mead Corp., Dayton, 1974-86; CFO Whirlpool Corp., 1986-91, exec. v.p., chief adminstrv. officer Benton Harbor, Mich., 1991-95; ret., 1995. Bd. dirs. Peoples State Bank, St. Joseph, Mich., 1987-95. Trustee, treas. Marvelwood Sch., 2004—; mem. adv. bd. Salvation Army; chmn. bd. trustees Whirlpool Found., 1993—95; trustee Dayton Opera Assn., 1977—86, pres., 1985—86; bd. dirs. Epilepsy Assn. We. Ohio, 1986, S.W. Mich. Symphony Orch., 1991—93; mem. bd. fin. Town of Kent (Conn.), 1999—2005, mem. zoning bd. appeals, 2001—. Mem.: Kent. Libr. Assn. (bd. dirs., treas. 2002—05), Fin. Execs. Inst. (bd. dirs. 1983—86). Home: PO Box 129 South Kent CT 06785-0129

**SAMARTZIS, DINO,** medical researcher, writer; s. Steve and Joanna Samartzis. Vis. student, Charles U., 1997—98; BS, Post-baccalaureate med., Northwestern U., 2000; Neuro-oncology Cert., Nat. Hosp. for Neurology and Neurosurgery, Queen Sq., 2003; ALM (C), Harvard U., 2003; PGC EBHC, U. Oxford, 2003, Dip. EBHC, 2004, MSc EBHC, 2005; Dip. Int. Rel. (C), London Sch. Econs. & Polit. Sci., 2004; DSc, Erasmus U., 2006. Clin. orthop. surgery Advanced Orthop. Assoc., Chgo., 1996—99; surgeon divsn. spine surgery, dept. orthop. surgery Rush-Presbyn. St. Luke's Med. Ctr., Chgo., 1999—; surgeon divsn. spine surgery, dept. orthop. surgery Shriners Hosp. for Children, Chgo., 2003—; numerous additional med. and sci. involvement. Pres. & dir. Spondylo Found., Chgo., 2001—; guest speaker in field. Prodr.(writer/editor): (multimedia/films/ednl.) over 30 spine surgery technique ednl. multimedia (Recipient of numerous awards, scholarships, grants); musician accomplished saxophonist and pianist; editor-in-chief: Pediat. Bone: Devel. and Clin. Applications, mem. editl. bd.: New Eng. Jour. Medicine, SPINE, European Spine Jour., So. Med. Jour., Clin. Orthopaedics & Related Rsch., Am. Jour. Orthopaedics, Cochrane Back Rev. Group, Cochrane Musculoskeletal Group, Minimally Invasive Spine Surgery, Jour. Bone and Joint Surgery, Arthritis Care and Rsch. Jour., assoc. editor: Core Knowledge Sports Medicine Orthop. Surgeons, World Fedn. Neurosurgical Socs., contributing author: numerous medical textbooks; contbr. articles to numerous profl. jours. Devel., editing, prodn., and ednl. activities Spondylo Found., Chgo., 2001—. Recipient Honorariums, Am. Assn. of Neurol. Surgeons and the Congress of Neurol. Surgeons, Various rsch.-based awards, Am. Soc. of Aesthetic Plastic Surgery, Depuy/Acromed, SpineUniverse, Nat. Aeronautics & Space Adminstrn., NSF; grantee Rsch.-Based, Sofamor Danek, Spinal Concepts, Coun. of State Neurosurgical Societies; scholar Otto S. Lehman, Northwestern U. Mem.: Soc. Pediatric and Perinatal Epidemiology, N.Y. Acad. Scis., Am. Soc. Biomechanics, Royal Inst. Pub. Health, Am. Coll. Epidemiology, World Spine Soc. (mem. com. bd.), AANS/CNS Joint Sect. on Disorders of Spine & Peripheral Nerves, Congress of Neurol. Surgeons (mem. com. bd.), N.Am. Spine Soc., Sigma Xi. Achievements include first to edn. and awareness of cutting edge spine surgery techniques and procedures; research in bone biology, biomechanics, minimally-invasive spine techniques, operative procedures, outcomes, radiographometry, degenerative, tumors, deformities, instrumentation; development of numerous spine-related surgical techniques; first to digital spine surgery; elected to membership by several orthopaedic and neurosurgical, public health, and epidemiological societies/organizations; collaborated in the design and execution of numerous medical studies and projects with institutes around the world; first to clin. outcome protocols; spinal degenerative databases; biodynamics of various bone graft substitutes, instrumentation and surgical techniques in spine surgery; research in factors affecting surgical outcomes. Office Phone: 877-897-3919. Personal E-mail: dsamartzis@msn.com.

**SAMBERG, ANDY,** actor; b. Berkeley, Calif., Aug. 18, 1978; Grad., U. Calif., Santa Cruz, NYU Film School. Co-founder, mem. The Lonely Island, NYC, 2001—. Writer G-Phoria, 2004, MTV Movie Awards, 2004, 2005; actor: (TV special) Comedy Central Laughs for Life Telethon, 2004; (TV series) Saturday Night Live, 2005—; guest appearances (TV series) 40 Most Awesomely Bad Dirrty Songs...Ever, 2004, Arrested Development, 2005, Premium Blend, 2005, The Late Show with David Letterman, 2006, Conan O'Brien, 2006. Recipient WIRED Rave Award - TV, 2006. Office: United Talent Agency Inc 9560 Wilshire Blvd Ste 500 Beverly Hills CA 90212 Office Phone: 310-273-6700. Office Fax: 310-247-1111.*

**SAMBERG, ARTHUR J. (ART SAMBERG),** investment company executive; BS, MIT; MS, Stanford U.; MBA, Columbia U. Established first Pequot investment fund, 1986; ptnr. Weiss, Peck & Greer, Inc.; CEO Pequot Capital Mgmt. Bd. mem. Coll. Summit's Nat. Bd. Dirs. Mem.: MIT Corp. Office: Pequot Capital Mgmt 500 Nyala Farm Rd Westport CT 06880

**SAMBERY, ANDY,** actor; b. Berkeley, Calif., Aug. 18, 1978; Grad., UCSC, NYU. Mem. The Lonely Island, 2001—. Actor: (TV series) Saturday Night Live, 2005— (WIRED Rave Award for TV, 2006) (guest appearances) 40 Most Awesomely Bad Dirrty Songs...Ever, 2004, Premium Blend, 2005, Arrested Development, 2005—, The Late Show with David Letterman, 2006, Late Night with Conan O'Brien, 2006; writer, guest appearances (TV Specials) G-Phoria, 2004, 2004—; actor: (TV Specials) Comedy Central Laughs for Life Telethon, 2004; writer (TV Specials) 2004 MTV Movie Awards, 2004, 2005 MTV Movie Awards, 2005—. Office: United Talent Agency Inc 9560 Wilshire Blvd Ste 500 Beverly Hills CA 90212 Office Phone: 310-273-6700. Office Fax: 310-247-1111.*

**SAMBLIS, KELLEY C.,** educator, researcher; b. Joseph and Barbara Faye Chaplauske; children: Colton, Maggie, Mary. Bachelor's degree, U. So. Miss., 1987; Master's degree, Nova U., 1990; EdS, U. West Fla., 2003, Doctorate, 2004. Elem. tchr. Brevard Sch. Dist., Melbourne, Fla., 1987—97; asst. prof. U. So. MIss., Long Beach, 2003—. Mem.: ASCD.

**SAMBOL, DAVID E.,** diversified financial services company executive; b. 1959; m. Ellie M. Sambol. BBA in Acctg., Calif. State U., Northridge, 1982. CPA. Acct. Ernst & Whinney; with Countrywide Fin. Corp., Calabasas, Calif., 1985—94, mng. dir. capital markets, 1994—2000, sr. mng. dir., chief prodn., 2000—02, exec. mng. dir. loans & capital markets, 2003, exec. mng. dir. bus. segment operations, pres., COO Countrywide Home Loans, 2004—, pres., COO, 2006—. Bd. dirs. Countrywide Home Loans, Inc., Balboa Life & Casualty, Countrywide Fin. Holding Co., Inc. Office: Countrywide Fin Corp 4500 Park Granada Calabasas CA 91302-1613*

**SAMBORA, RICHIE (RICHARD STEPHEN SAMBORA),** musician, singer, songwriter; b. Perth Amboy, NJ, July 11, 1959; s. Adam and Joan Sambora; m. Heather Locklear, Dec. 15, 1994 (separated 2006); 1 child, Ava Elizabeth. LHD, Kean U., 2004. Musician of various bands including Screaming Mimis, Mercy, The Next, Message, and Duke Williams & The Extremes; guitarist, vocalist, songwriter Bon Jovi, 1983—. Musician: (solo albums) Stranger In This Town, 1991, Undiscovered Soul, 1994; musician, vocalist (albums) Bon Jovi, 1984, 7800 Fahrenheit, 1985, Slippery When Wet, 1986, Bon Jovi Live, 1987, New Jersey, 1988, Keep the Faith, 1992, Crossroad, 1994, These Days, 1995, Bon Jovi, 1999, Crush, 2000, Bounce, 2002, Distance, 2003, This Left Feels Right, 2003, 100,000,000 Bon Jovi Fans Can't Be Wrong, 2004, Have a Nice Day, 2005, cameo appearances (films) Staying Alive, 1983, On The Line, 2001, guest appearances American Dreams, 2003. Avocations: watching sporting events, including football, basketball, and boxing, jet-skiing, fishing, golf.*

**SAMBURG, A. GENE,** security company executive; b. Indpls., Apr. 25, 1941; s. A. George and Hermine (Wittgenstein) S.; m. Lorrie Silverman, June 26, 1966; children: Kimberly Jill, Thomas Blair. BEE, Cornell U., 1964; OPM, Harvard U., 1985. Engr. Westinghouse Corp., 1964-72; founder, pres. and CEO Kastle Systems, Inc., 1972—. Adv. on bus. programs Cornell U.; lectr. on entrepreneurship Georgetown U.; spl. lectr. for numerous profl. and ednl. courses in field. Patentee in field. Named E&Y Master Entrepreneur of Yr., Washington, 1999. Mem. IEEE, ASME, CPP, Am. Soc. Indsl. Security, Woodmont Country Club, City Club (Washington), Tower Club (McLean, Va.). Home: 1401 N Oak St Arlington VA 22209 Office: Kastle Systems Inc 1501 Wilson Blvd Arlington VA 22209-2403 Office Phone: 703-528-8800. Business E-Mail: gene@kastle.com.

**SAMEC, DIANE PATRICIA,** retired elementary school educator; b. Oak Pk., Ill., Mar. 17, 1942; d. Albert Vincent Samec and Helen Hrubec. BA, Hope Coll., Holland, Mich., 1964; MSc in edn., No. Ill. U., DeKalb, 1988. Tchr. Interboro Schools, Glenolden, Pa., 1964-65, Sch. Dist. u-46, Elgin, Ill., 1966—2004; ret., 2004. Vol. and mem. Willow Creek Cmty. Ch., South Barrington, 1986—, Sherman Hosp. Aux. Ch., Elgin, 2004—. Mem.: Nat. Audubon Soc., Elgin Ret. Teachers Assn., Elgin Edn. Assn., Ill. Edn. Assn., Nat. Edn. Assn., Willow Creek Comm. Ch., Nat. Wildlife Assn., Environ. Def., Sierra Club, Fox Valley Beaux Arts Women's Club. Avocations: travel, reading, photography.

**SAMEK, EDWARD LASKER,** medical transcription executive; b. N.Y.C., Oct. 26, 1936; s. Richard E. and Jane L. Samek; m. Marthann Lauver, June 26, 1960; children: Anne, Margaret, Elizabeth. BS in Commerce and Fin., Bucknell U., 1958; MBA, Columbia U., 1960. Brand mgr. Procter & Gamble Co., Cin., 1960-62; dir. new products Johnson & Johnson, New Brunswick, NJ, 1962-67; v.p., gen. mgr. Avon Products Inc., N.Y.C., 1967-75; pres., CEO Childcraft Edn. Corp., Edison, NJ, 1975-78, also dir.; pres. Hudson Pharm. Corp., West Caldwell, 1978-82; CEO, chmn. bd., pres. Secrephone Ltd., Ft. Washington, Pa., 1982-94, exec. v.p., 1994-95; chmn., pres., CEO Medifax SecrePhone, Atlanta, 1995-96; chmn., CEO The MRC Group, Cleve., 1996-98; vice chmn. Medquist Inc., Marlton, NJ, 1998—2000. Bd. dir. A. Gary Shilling & Co., MedPlus, Inc., Cin., VeriText LLC, Alliance Imaging, Inc., Anaheim, Calif., Third Millenniam Healthcare, Atlanta, N.Am. Mgmt. Corp., Boston, Caremedic Healthcare, St. Petersburg, Fla., WaterJel Products, Inc., Carlstadt, NJ; corp. mem. Jackson Labs., 2004—. Pres. bd. trustees Hartridge Sch., Plainfield, NJ, 1969-76; v.p. bd. trustees Wardlaw-Hartridge Sch., Plainfield and Edison, 1975—; trustee, v.p. bd. Plainfield Symphony, 1976-86; trustee and treas. Friends of Acadia, 2003—; trustee The Jackson Lab., 2004—; corp. mem. The Jackson Labs., 2005—. Served with Ordnance Corps, U.S. Army, 1958-59. Mem. Young Pres. Orgn., Princeton Club, World Pres. Orgn, NYC Univ. Club. Home and Office: 1717 Woodland Ave Edison NJ 08820-1039 Personal E-Mail: ed@samek.net.

**SAMELSON, LAWRENCE ELLIOT,** medical researcher; b. Chgo., Apr. 18, 1951; s. Charles F. and Natalie (Rudeis) S.; m. Elizabeth Trosman, June 8, 1980; children: Seth Aaron, Rebecca Ellen. BA, U. Rochester, 1972; MD, Yale U., 1977. Resident in internal medicine U. Chgo. Hospitals, 1977-80; rsch. assoc. Lab. Immunology Nat. Inst. Allergy and Infectious Diseases, NIH, Bethesda, Md., 1980-85; sr. staff fellow Cell Biology and Metabolism Br., Nat. Inst. Child Health and Human Devel., NIH, Bethesda, 1985-87, named sr. investigator, 1988, chief Sect. Lymphocyte Signaling, 1995, dep. branch chief, 1995; chief Lab. Cellular and Molecular Biology Ctr. Cancer Rsch., Nat. Cancer Inst. NIH, Bethesda, 1999—, dep. dir. Ctr. Cancer Rsch., Nat. Cancer Inst., 2006—. Contbr. articles to profl. publs. Achievements include research in T cell structure and function, T cell activation, and biochemistry of signal transduction. Office: Ctr Cancer Rsch Lab Cellular and Molecular Biology 37 Convent Dr Bldg 37 Rm 2066 Bethesda MD 20892-4256 Office Phone: 301-496-9683. Office Fax: 301-496-8479. E-mail: samelson@helix.nih.gov.

**SAMENUK, GEORGE,** software security company executive; married; 4 children. B in Polit. Sci., Brown U. Various sr. mgmt. positions in the Americas and ASEAN/South Asia regions IBM Corp., 1977—99; pres., CEO Tradeout, 2000—01; chmn., CEO McAfee, Inc. (formerly Network Associates, Inc.), Santa Clara, Calif., 2001—. Mem. listed co. advisory com. NY Stock Exchange; bd. dir. Symbol Technologies, Inc.; spkr. in field. Office: McAfee Inc 3965 Freedom Circle Santa Clara CA 95054*

**SAMER, BILL FRED CARL,** writer, cartoonist; b. Elizabeth, NJ, Sept. 2, 1953; s. Fred Carl and Myrtle Edith (Levey) Samer. BA, Concordia Coll., Bronxville, N.Y., 1994; MA, Kean U. NJ, Union, 1980; AA in Film, Union Coll., Cranford, N.J., 2005. Author: Moongate, 2003, UK, for Mother, 2003. Walker CROP, Clifton, NJ, 1978; vol. I Found It TV campaign, NY, 1976; active Interfaith Hospitality Network, 2003, William Samer Activist Orgn., 1987; mem. choir Grace Luth. Ch. Mem.: Creative and Performing Arts Club, TV and Film Prodn. Club (NJ.) Avocations: hiking, volleyball. Office Phone: 908-577-7733. E-mail: jeff604austin@hotmail.com, billesky9@aol.com.

**SAMEROFF, ARNOLD JOSHUA,** developmental psychologist, educator, research scientist; b. N.Y.C., Apr. 20, 1937; s. Stanley and Zeena (Shapiro) S.; m. Susan C. McDonough, Jan. 2, 1982; children: Shira, Rebecca, Crista. BS, U. Mich., 1961; PhD, Yale U., 1965; MA (hon.), Brown U., 1987. Asst. prof. psychology, pediat. and psychiatry U. Rochester, 1967—70, assoc. prof., 1970—73, prof., 1973—78, dir. developmental psychology tng. program, 1975—78; prof. psychology U. Ill., Chgo., 1978—86, assoc. dir. Inst. for Study Devel. Disabilities, 1978—86; assoc. dir., rsch. Ill. Inst. for Devel. Disabilities, Ill. Dept. Mental Health and Deve. Disabilities, 1978—86; prof. psychiatry and human behavior Brown U., Providence, 1986—92; dir. Bradley Hosp., Devel. Psychopathology Rsch. Ctr., East Providence, 1986—92; prof. psychology, rsch. prof. U. Mich., Ctr. for Human Growth and Devel., Ann Arbor, 1992—; dir. devel. and mental health Rsch. U. Mich., Ann Arbor, 2000—05. Vis. prof. psychology Birkbeck Coll., U. London, 1974-75; vis. scientist Ctr. for Interdisciplinary Rsch., U. Bielefeld, Fed. Republic Germany, 1977; dir. Summer Inst. on Human Devel. and Psychopathology, Ctr. for Advanced Study in Behavioral Scis., Stanford, Calif., 1989; mem. small grants adv. com. NIH, 1977-81, behavioral scis. assessment panel, 1987-88; mem. orgnl. planning com. Internat. Conf. for Infant Studies, 1980-84 Editor: (with R.N. Emde) Relationship Disturbances in Early Childhood: A Developmental Approach, 1989, (with F. Kessel and M. Bornstein) Contemporary Constructions of the Child: Essays in Honor of William Kessen, 1991, (with M. Haith) The Five to Seven Year Shift, 1996 (with F.F. Furstenberg et. al.) Managing to Make It: Urban Families and Adolescent Success, 1999, (with M. Lewis and S. Miller) Handbook of Developmental Psychopathology, 2000, (with S.C. McDonough and K.L. Rosenblum) Treating Early Relationship Problems: Infant, Parent, and Interaction Therapies, 2004; also monographs; mem. editl. bds. Devel. and Psychopathology, 1988-94, Jour. Devel. and Behavioral Pediatrics, 1989-93, Jour. Family Psychology, 1990-91, Parenting: Science and Practice, 2001, others. Mem. social and behavioral scis. rsch. adv. com. March of Dimes Birth Defects Found., 1977-94, rsch. adv. Little City Found., 1986-88; bd. dirs. Zero to Three: Nat. Ctr. for Infants Toddlers and Families, exec. com., 1998-2002; mem. program on successful adolescent devel. among youth in high-risk settings John D. and Catherine T. MacArthur Found., 1986-95, network on early childhood transitions, 1989-92; mem. gov. coun. Soc. Rsch. in Child Devel., 1998-. Recipient rsch. scientist award NIMH, 1994-99; GE fellow Yale U., 1961; NIMH predoctoral rsch. fellow Yale U., 1962, NIMH postdoctoral rsch. fellow, 1965-67, Ctr. for Advanced Study in Behavioral Scis. fellow Stanford U., 1984-85. Fellow AAAS, Am. Acad. Mental Retardation, Am. Psychol. Soc., APA (recipient com. devel. psychology divsn 1978-90, chair 1979, coun. 1980-83, mem.-at-large award). Soc. Rsch. in Child Devel. (governing

coun. 1999-2005, pre.-elect 2005—, Dist. Scientist award, 2005), World Assn. Infant Mental Health, Internat. Soc. for Infant Studies (pres. 2002-2004), Soc. for Rsch. on Adolescence E-mail: sameroff@umich.edu.

**SAMET, DEE-DEE,** lawyer; b. Greensboro, NC, Sept. 18, 1940; BA, U. Ariz., 1962, JD, 1963. Bar: Ariz. 1964. Pvt. practice, Tucson, 1974—; ptnr. Samet & Gage, P.C., Tucson, 2001. Arbitrator U.S. Dist. Ct. Ariz., Gender Equality Task Force, 1993; judge pro tem Pima County Superior Ct., 1985—; Ninth Cir. Lawyer rep., 1990-93; mem. Jud. Performance Rev. Commn., 1996-99; pres. Casa de los Ninos, 2003-05. Mem. Fed. Bar Assn. (pres. Tucson chpt. 2004—), State Bar Ariz. (family law sect., workers compensation sect., trial law sect., co-chair workers compensation sect. 1988-89, gender bias task force, bd. govs. 1994-97, pres. 1999-2000, chmn. elect worker's compensation sect. 2004, chair alternative dispute resolution sect. 2005-), Am. Arbitration Assn. (nat. panel arbitrators, com. on exams., supreme ct. state Ariz. 1984-91), Pima County Bar Assn. (bd. dirs. 1994—), Nat. Assn. Counsel for Children, Ariz. Assn. Counsel for Children, So. Ariz. Women Lawyers Assn. (bd. dirs. 1990, pres. 1994-95, treas. alt. dispute resolution sect. 2003-04, chmn. 2005—), Nat. Orgn. Social Security Claimants' Reps. Office: Dee-Dee Samet PC 717 N 6th Ave Tucson AZ 85705-8304 Office Phone: 520-624-8595. Business E-Mail: dee-dee@samet.psemoil.com.

**SAMET, JACK I.,** lawyer; b. NYC, Aug. 6, 1940; s. William and Tillie (Katz) Samet; m. Helen Ray, Feb. 12, 1967; 1 child, Peter Lawrence. BA, Columbia U., 1961; JD, Harvard U., 1964. Bar: N.Y. 1964, Calif. 1973. Assoc. Whitman & Ransom, N.Y.C., 1966-69, Hall, Casey, Dickler & Howley, N.Y.C., 1969-73; ptnr. Ball, Hunt, Hart, Brown & Baerwitz, LA, 1973-81, Buchalter, Nemer, Fields & Younger, LA, 1981-94, Baker & Hostetler, LA, 1994—, mem. policy com., 1997-98, ptnr.-in-charge, 1997-98. Arbitrator Nat. Assn. Securities Dealers, LA, 1976—; spkr., panelist Calif. Continuing Edn. Bar, 1988. Actor: Playhouse W., 2005—. Named a So. Calif. Superlawyer, 2004—05. Mem.: ABA, Am. Bd. Trial Advs., Million Dollar Advs. Forum, Sport Club/LA. Avocations: exercise, reading, acting. Home: 2741 Aqua Verde Cir Los Angeles CA 90077-1502 Office: 333 S Grand Ave Los Angeles CA 90071-1504 E-mail: jsamet@bakerlaw.com, jsamet@belairmail.com.

**SAMET, JONATHAN MICHAEL,** epidemiologist, educator; b. Va., Mar. 26, 1946; AB in Chemistry and Physics, Harvard Coll., 1966; MD, U. Rochester, 1970; MS in Epidemiology, Harvard Sch. Pub Health, 1977. Diplomate Am. Bd. Internal Medicine, Nat. Bd. Med. Examiners. Intern in medicine U. Ky. Med. Ctr., Lexington, 1970-71; asst. resident in medicine U. N.Mex. Affiliated Hosps., Albuquerque, 1973-74, sr. resident, 1974-75; rsch. fellow in clin. epidemiology Channing lab. Harvard Med. Sch., Boston, 1975-78, rsch. assoc. in medicine, 1978-83; epidemiologist Cancer Rsch. and Treatment Ctr. U. N.Mex., Albuquerque, 1980-87, asst. prof. medicine, 1978-82, assoc. prof. medicine, 1982-88, assoc. prof. family, cmty., and emergency medicine, 1985-88, prof. family, cmty., and emergency medicine, 1986-94, prof. medicine, 1988-94, clin. prof. medicine, 1994—; prof., chmn. dept. epidemiology The Johns Hopkins U., Balt., 1994—, co-dir. risk scis. and pub. policy inst., 1995—. Chief pulmonary divsn. U. N.Mex. Hosp., Albuquerque, 1985-94, chief pulmonary and critical care divsn. dept. medicine, 1986-94; mem. indoor air quality and total human exposure com., sci. adv. bd. U.S. EPA, 1987-95; chmn. biol. effects of ionizing radiation VI com. NRC, 1994-98, mem. bd environ. studies and toxicology, 2002, chmn., 2003; Inst. Medicine, 1997; chmn. com. on rsch. priorities for airborne particulate matter, NRC, 1998-2004; dir. Inst. Global Tobacco Control, 1998-; chmn. epidemiology and disease control study sect. 2 NIH, 2002, Com. Asbestos, Inst. Medicine, 2004—. Editor pro tem Am. Jour. of Epidemiology, 1991—92; editor: Am. Jour. of Epidemiology, 1992—98; assoc. editor Tobacco Control: An Internat. Jour., 1991—; editor: Epidemiologic Revs., 1994—2002, Epidemiology, 2002—. With U.S. Army, 1971-73. Recipient Clinton P. Anderson award Am. Lung Assn. N.Mex., 1988, Surgeon Gen.'s medallion, 1990, Excellence in Environ. Health Rsch. award Lovelace Inst., 1996, Inst. of Medicine NAS, 1997, Prince Mahidol Found. award, 2005 Fellow: AAAS, Am. Coll. Epidemiology (pres. 2000—01); mem.: Md. Thoracic Soc., Internat. Soc. of Indoor Air Quality and Climate, Internat. Epidemiol. Assn., N.Mex. Thoracic Soc. (sec.-treas. 1982—83, v.p. 1983—84, pres. 1984—85), Am. Thoracic Soc. (long range planning com. environ. and occupational health assembly 1992—, program com. behavioral scis. sect. 1994—95), Soc. for Epidemiol. Rsch. (pres.-elect 1988—89, pres. 1989—90, exec. com. 1988—91), Delta Omega Alpha, Alpha Omega Alpha. Office: Dept Epidemiology The Johns Hopkins U 615 N Wolfe St Ste W6041 Baltimore MD 21205-2103 Office Phone: 410-955-3286. Personal E-mail: jsamet@aol.com. Business E-Mail: jsamet@jhsph.edu.

**SAMFORD, YETTA GLENN, JR.,** lawyer, director; b. Opelika, Ala., June 8, 1923; s. Yetta Glenn and Mary Elizabeth (Denson) S.; m. Mary Austill, Sept. 6, 1949; children: Mary Austill Lott, Katherine Park Alford, Yetta Glenn III (dec.). BA, Auburn U., Ala., 1947; LLB, U. Ala., Tuscaloosa, 1949, LLD (hon.), 1995; DHL (hon.), U. Mobile, Ala., 2001. Bar: Ala. 1949, U.S. Dist. Ct. (mid. dist.) Ala. 1950, U.S. Ct. Appeals (5th Cir.) 1961, U.S. Ct. Appeals (11th cir.) 1981. Pvt. practice, Opelika, Ala.; ptnr. Samford & Denson LLP and Predessors, 1949—. Mem. Ala. Senate from Lee and Russell counties, 1958-62; mem. State of Ala. Bd. of Corrections, 1969-75; mem. adv. bd. State Docks, 1987-2000. Trustee U. Mobile, 1963-92, life trustee, 1992—, trustee U. Ala., 1972-93, trustee emeritus, 1993—. Mem. Ala. Law Inst. (exec. com.), Ala. Acad. of Honor, Masons, Phi Delta Phi, Omicron Delta Kappa, Alpha Tau Omega. Republican. Baptist. Home: 615 Terracewood Dr Opelika AL 36801-3850 Office: Samford & Denson LLP PO Box 2345 Opelika AL 36803-2345 Office Phone: 334-745-3504. Personal E-mail: sdhpb@mindspring.com.

**SAMIOS, NICHOLAS PETER,** physicist; b. NYC, Mar. 15, 1932; s. Peter and Niki (Vatick) S.; m. Mary Linakis, Jan. 12, 1958; children: Peter, Gregory, Alexandra. AB, Columbia U., 1953, PhD, 1957. Instr. physics Columbia U., N.Y.C., 1956-59, adj. prof., 1970—; asst. physicist Brookhaven Nat. Lab., Upton, NY, 1959-62, assoc. physicist, 1962-64, physicist, 1964-68, sr. physicist, 1968—75, group leader, 1965-75, chmn. dept. physics, 1975-81, dep. dir. for high energy and nuclear physics, 1981, dir., 1982-97, disting. sr. scientist, 1997—; dep. dir. RIKEN/BNL Rsch. Ctr., 1998—. Adj. prof. Stevens Inst. Tech., 1969-75 Contbr. articles in field to profl. jours. Bd. dirs. Stony Brook Found., 1989, L.I. Assn., 1989. Recipient E.O. Lawrence Meml. award, 1980, award in physics and math. scis. N.Y. Acad. Scis., 1980, Bruno Pontecorvo prize, Joint Inst. for Nuclear Rsch., 2001; named AUI Disting. Scientist, 1992, W.K.H. Panofsky prize, 1993. Fellow Am. Phys. Soc. (chmn. divsn. of particles and fields 1975-76, chmn. PEP exptl. program com. 1976-78); mem. Internat. Ctr. Future Acceleration, Akademia Athenon (corr.) Achievements include being an expert in field of high energy particle and nuclear physics. Office: RIKEN/BNL Rsch Ctr Bldg 510A, Physics Dept Brookhaven Natl Lab Upton NY 11973-5000 E-mail: samios@bnl.gov.

**SAMIS, CHARLES MAURICE,** language educator, mathematics educator; b. Paris, Apr. 1, 1946; arrived in U.S., 1963; s. Jankiel Samis and Frymeta Rozenblat; m. Sylvia Rozenzweig Samis, June 26, 1971; 1 child, Michael. AS, Hartford State Coll., Conn., 1967; BA, U. Cin., 1973, MA, 1975. Cert. French and math. tchr. Ohio, 1985. Instr., lectr. U. Cin., 1977—80; tchr. French and math. Cin. Pub. Schs., 1985—. Adj. instr. U. Cin., 1995—. Treas., mem. exec. bd. Combined Generations of the Holocaust, Cin., 1976—2002. Fellow, NEH, 1985; Charles Phelps Taft fellow, U. Cin., 1974, 1980. Office: Sch for Creative and Performing Arts 1310 Sycamore Cincinnati OH 45202

**SAMMARCO, PAUL W.,** marine science researcher and educator; Prof. La. U. Marine Consortium. Address: 8124 Highway 56 Chauvin LA 70344-2110 Office Phone: 985-851-2876. Business E-Mail: psammarco@lumcon.edu.

**SAMMARCO, PAUL WILLIAM,** ecologist, researcher; b. Hackensack, N.J., Oct. 18, 1948; s. Giacomo and Esther (Galanti) S.; m. Jean Sogioka, May 29, 1971 (div. 1996); children: Mimi Cecile, Dustin Paul, Jack Isao; m.

Donna M. Melancon, Aug. 12, 1998; stepchildren: Lindsay Claire, Ben Charles. BA, Syracuse U., 1970, postgrad., 1970—71; cert., Marine Biology Lab., Woods Hole, Mass., 1971, Fairleigh Dickinson U., 1972; PhD, SUNY Stony Brook, 1977. Tchg. asst. Syracuse U., NY, 1970—71; tchg. asst. Discovery Bay Marine Lab. SUNY-Stony Brook Overseas Acad. Program, Jamaica, 1974; tchg. asst. SUNY, Stony Brook, 1971—77; asst. prof. Clarkson U., Potsdam, NY, 1977—79; vis. asst. prof. tropical ecology SUNY Potsdam, St. Croix, V.I., 1979; sr. rsch. scientist Australian Inst. Marine Sci., Townsville, Queensland, 1979—89; coord. Shelf Seas Rsch. Program, 1985—86; dir. environ. rsch. Resource Assessment Commn. Prime Minister's commn. on natural resources, Canberra, Australia, 1989—91; exec. dir. La. Univs. Marine Consortium, Chauvin, 1991—95, prof., 1995—. Adj. prof. La. State U., U. La. at Lafayette, U. New Orleans, Nicholls State U., U. Campinas-Brazil, 1997-99, Ctrl. Queensland U., Australia, 1997-2002, U. Maine at Orono, 2001—03; pres. Endless Shores Music Pubs.; pres. P&J Records, LLC. Composer, arranger, prodr. popular and sacred music; former mem. Australian Chamber Choir, Wesley Choir, Canberra; editor (with M.L. Heron) The Bio-Physics of Marine Larval Dispersal, 1994, Marine Biology (Berlin), 2000—; contbr. numerous articles to profl. jours.; editl. advisor Marine Ecology Progress Series, 1985-93; co-editor Procs. 6th Internat. Coral Reef Symposium, 1988, Procs. 8th Internat. Coral Reef Symposium. Mem. La. State Gov.'s Platform for Mariculture Task Force, 2004-05; mem. chancel choir First United Meth. Ch., Houma, La. Recipient Internat. Sci. Exch. award, 1988-89. Mem. ASCAP, Australian Marine Scis. Assn. (keynote spkr. 1981, counselor 1984-89, chmn., organizer nat. conf. 1987, chmn. Australia Acad. Sci. Boden Conf. 1990), Internat. Soc. Reef Studies (counselor 1997-2000), Australian Coral Reef Soc., Sigma Xi. Home: 200 Greenwood St Houma LA 70364-4542 Office: La Univs Marine Consortium 8124 Highway 56 Chauvin LA 70344-2110 Office Phone: 985-851-2876. Business E-Mail: psammarco@lumcon.edu.

**SAMMET, JEAN E.,** computer scientist; b. NYC; d. Harry and Ruth S. BA, Mt. Holyoke Coll., Sc.D. (hon.), 1978; MA, U. Ill. Group leader programming Sperry Gyroscope, Great Neck, NY, 1955-58; sect. head, staff cons. programming Sylvania Electric Products, Needham, Mass., 1958-61; with IBM, 1961-88; adv. program mgr. Boston, 1961-65; program lang. tech. mgr. IBM, 1965-68; programming tech. planning mgr. Fed. Systems div., 1968-74, programming lang. tech. mgr., 1974-79, software tech. mgr., 1979-81, div. software tech. mgr., 1981-82, programming lang. tech. mgr., 1983-88; programming lang. cons. Bethesda, Md., 1989—. Chmn. history of computing com. Am. Fedn. Info. Processing Socs., 1977-79; mem. exec. com. Software Patent Inst., 1991—, com. 1992—, chair edn. com., 1992-93; bd. dirs. Computer Mus., 1983-93. Author: Programming Languages: History and Fundamentals, 1969; editor-in-chief: Assn. Computing Machinery Computing Revs, 1979-87; contbr. articles to profl. jours. Recipient Fellow award, Computer History Mus., 2001. Fellow Assn. for Computing Machinery, 1994, (charter; pres. 1974-76, Disting. Svc. award 1985), Computer History Mus.; mem. NAE, Upsilon Pi Epsilon. Home and Office: 3124 Gracefield Rd Apt 311 Silver Spring MD 20904-5818

**SAMMONS, ELAINE D.,** manufacturing executive; m. Charles A. Sammons (dec. 1988). Chmn. Sammons Enterprises, Inc., Dallas, 1988—. Chmn. bd. Sammons Ctr. for the Arts, Dallas, 1988—. Office: Sammons Enterprises Inc 5949 Sherry Ln Ste 1900 Dallas TX 75225-8015

**SAMMONS, MARY F.,** retail executive; b. Portland, Oreg., Oct. 12, 1946; d. Lee W. and Ann (Cherry) Jackson; m. Nickolas F. Sammons, Sept. 12, 1967; 1 child, Peter. BA, Marylhurst Coll., 1970. Buyer Fred Meyer Inc., Portland, 1975-80, v.p., merchandiser, 1980-85, sr. v.p., softgoods div. mgr., from 1986, sr. v.p., apparel & home electronics group, 1996, exec. v.p., apparel, home & home electronics group, 1997—98; pres. Fred Meyer Stores, Portland, 1998, pres., CEO, 1999; pres., COO Rite Aid Corp., Camp Hill, Pa., 1999—2003, pres., CEO, 2003—. Bd. dirs. First Horizon Nat. Corp., Rite Aid Found., Rite Aid Corp., 1999—; chmn. Nat. Assoc. Chain Drug Stores. Named Woman of Achievement, YWCA, Portland, 1987; named one of 100 Most Powerful Women, Forbes mag., 2005—06. Mem. Am. Mgmt. Assn. Office: Rite Aid Corp 30 Hunter Ln Camp Hill PA 17011*

**SAMMONS, MORGAN TAYLOR,** psychologist; b. Waldport, Oreg., Feb. 17, 1954; s. William Marland and Peggy Ann Sammons. BS in fgn. svc., Georgetown U., 1975; M in counseling, Ariz. State U., 1983, PhD, 1989. Bd. dir. Nat. Register of Health Svc. Providers in Psychology, Washington; psychopharmacology curriculum cons. Nova Southeastern U., Ft Lauderdale, Fla., 2001—, Fairleigh Dickinson U., Teaneck, NJ, 2000—, Alliant Internat. U., San Francisco, 1999—; adj. asst. prof. Uniformed Svcs. U. Health Sci. 2002; assoc. editor Psychol. Svcs. Editor: (book) Combined Treatments for Mental Disorders: A Guide to Psychological and Pharmacological Interventions, 2001, Prescriptive Authority for Psychologists: A History and Guide, 2003; contbr. articles to profl. jours. Capt. USN. Fellow: APA (rep. to APA coun. divsn. 55 2002—, mem. divsns. 19, 31, 42, 55, presdl. citation 1994, 1996, 2000, Karl Heiser award 2004, disting. contrbn.in pub. sector award 2005), Md. Psychol. Assn. (pres. 2001—02, Tchr. of Yr. 1998), Nat. Acads. Practice. Avocations: conservation, skiing, backpacking. Home: 7840 Oracle Pl Potomac MD 20854 Personal E-mail: msammons@mindspring.com.

**SAMO, AMANDO,** bishop; b. Moch Island, Federated States of Micronesia, Aug. 16, 1948; s. Benito and Esiper Samo. BA in Psychology, Chaminade U., 1973; diploma in religious edn., EAPI, Manila, Philippines, 1982. Ordained priest Roman Cath. Ch. Parish priest Cath. Ch., Truk, Micronesia, Afghanistan, 1977—87; aux. bishop Diocese of the Carolines and Marshalls, Truk, 1987—95, bishop, 1995—. Founder, bd. dirs. Marriage Encounter-Carolines-Marshalls, Truk, 1982—88, dir. ch. leadership tng. programs, 1986—; mem. Bishop's Conf. Oceania; 1988; pontificial commn. Cor Unum, Rome, Rome, 1995. Chmn. Chmn. Bishop's commn. justice and devel., 1995. Roman Catholic. Home: PO Box 939 Chuuk FM 96942-0939 Office: Diocese Caroline Is PO Box 250 Chuuk FM 96942-0250

**SAMOJLIK, EUGENIUSZ,** medical educator, health facility administrator; b. Kuchmy-Bialystok, Poland, Aug. 20, 1933; s. Michael and Anastazia S.; m. Anna Morozewicz, Apr. 10, 1965; children: Dorothy, Michael. BS in Biomedicine, U. Warsaw, 1958, PhD in Reproductive Endocrinology, 1964. Rsch. asst. Maternity Inst. Dept. Pharmacology, Warsaw, 1958-62, sr. asst., 1962-66; asst. prof., chief reproductive pharmacology & toxicology Inst. Pharmacy Dept. Pharmacology, Warsaw, 1966-70; assoc. prof., chief hormone rsch. lab. Med. Acad. Dept. Clin. Endocrinology, Warsaw, 1970-73; staff rschr. II Syntex, Inc. Rsch. Divsn., Palo Alto, Calif., 1974-75; asst. prof. physiology, dir. radioimmunoassay lab. Milton S. Hershey (Pa.) Med. Ctr., Divsn. Endocrinology, 1975-80; staff endocrinologist VA Med. Ctr. Dept. Medicine, Sect. Endocrinology, East Orange, NJ, 1980-82; dir. endocrine lab. Newark Beth Israel Med. Ctr., Dept. Medicine, 1982-92; assoc. prof. medicine divsn. endocrinology U. Medicine & Dentistry-N.J. Med. Sch., Newark, 1982—; chief endocrine lab. dept. Labs. NBIMC, 1994-96. Vis. researcher UCLA Sch. Medicine, Torrance, Calif., 1973; vis. scientist Nat. Inst. Child Health Human Devel., Reproductive Br., Bethesda, Md., 1973-74; lectr. in field. Internat. adv. bd. Jour. Assisted Reproductive Tech. and Andrology, mem. editorial bd., 1996; contbr. articles to profl. jours. Grantee WHO, 1973-74, Ciba-Geigy, 1982-83, Nat. Cancer Inst., 1983-86, 85-88; tng. program fellow Worcester Found. Experimental Biology, Shrewsbury, Mass., 1967-69. Mem. AAAS, Am. Soc. Andrology, Am. Assn. Clin. Chemistry, Nat. Acad. Clin. Biochemistry, Acad. Medicine NJ, Endocrine Soc. Home: 73 Sykes Ave Livingston NJ 07039-1318 Fax: 973-972-5185. E-mail: samojleu@yahoo.com.

**SAMOLE, MYRON MICHAEL,** lawyer, management consultant; b. Nov. 29, 1943; s. Harry Lionel and Bess Miriam (Siegel) Samole; m. Sandra Rita Port, Feb. 2, 1967; children: Stacey Ann, Karen Lynn, Rena Marie, David Aaron. Student, U. Ill., 1962—65; JD, DePaul U., 1967. Bar: Ill. 1967, U.S. Dist. Ct. (no. dist.) 1968, U.S. Ct. Appeals (7th cir.) 1968, Fla. 1981, U.S. Dist. Ct. (so. dist.) 1989, U.S. Ct. Appeals (11th cir.) 2001. Sole practice, Chgo., 1967—79, Miami, 1981—. Bd. dirs. The Sports Collection, Inc., pres.

Samole Enterprises, Inc. 1986-, Carcand, Inc. 1986-. Pres. Young Israel Kendall. Mem.: Trial Lawyers Assn., Fla. Bar Assn., Ill. State Bar Assn., Chgo. Bar Assn., ABA, Phi Alpha Delta. Office: Samole & Berger PA 9700 S Dixie Hwy Ste 1030 Miami FL 33156-2865 Office Phone: 305-670-5070. Business E-Mail: msamole@samoleberger.com.

**SAMOLYK, KEITH ANDREW,** cardiovascular perfusionist, director; s. Edward and Margret Samolyk; 1 child, Tyler Andrew. BS, Northeastern U., Boston MA, 1989. Cert. perfusion tech. Northeastern U., Boston, 1989, lic. Cardiovascular Perfusionist Commonwealth of Mass., 2001. Cardiovasc. perfusionist Johns Hopkins Hosp., Balt., 1990—95; pediatric specialist perfusion Hartford (Conn.) Hosp., 1996; supr. QA, staff perfusionist Winthrop U. Hosp., Mineola, NY, 1997—2000; staff perfusionist Boston Med. Ctr., 2001—, St Elizabeths Med. Ctr., Boston, 2001—; staff perfusionist (per diem) Maine Med. Ctr., Portland, 2003—. Pres., CEO Global Blood Resources LLC, Somers, Conn., 2001—. Author journal papers. Recipient Alumni award profl. promise, Northeastern U., 1989, Gold award co. global blood resources, Conn. Quality Innovation award, 2006. Mem.: Windsor Marksmen Assn., Soc. for Advancement of Blood Mgmt. (assoc.), Windsor Club. Achievements include invention of Hemobag Whole Blood Salvaging device for Surgery; 3 patents. Avocations: golf, skiing, hunting, fishing. Office Phone: 800-942-9243. Personal E-Mail: ksamolyk@comcast.net.

**SAMONDS, JASON MICHAEL,** biomedical engineer; b. Green Bay, Wis., July 18, 1977; s. Terry Lee Samonds and Shari Marie Murphy. PhD, Vanderbilt U., Nashville, 2004. Postdoctoral fellow Vanderbilt U., Nashville, 2004—05; rsch. assoc. Carnegie Mellon U., Pitts., 2005—. Contbr. articles to profl. jours. Mem.: IEEE, Assn. Rsch. in Vision and Ophthalmology, Biomedical Engring. Soc., Engring. in Medicine and Biology Soc., Am. Physiol. Soc., Visual Scis. Soc. Office: Carnegie Mellon University 4400 Fifth Ave 115 Mellon Institute Pittsburgh PA 15213 Office Phone: 412-268-3922. Business E-Mail: samondjm@cnbc.cmu.edu.

**SAMORS, NEAL,** publishing executive, writer; b. Chgo., July 10, 1943; s. Joseph and Bernette (Schulman) S.; m. Frieda Anschel, May 25, 1969; 1 child, Jennifer Laura. BS, U. Wis., 1965; MA, No. Ill. U., 1967; PhD, Northwestern U., 1979, MA, 2000. Lectr. polit. sci. Loyola U., Chgo., 1967-69; instr. polit. sci. Barat Coll., Lake Forest, Ill., 1969-74; profl. assoc. Ednl. Testing Svc., Evanston, Ill., 1974-80, asst. dir., 1980-84, sr. field mktg. rep., 1984-88, asst. dir. field mktg., 1989-93, exec. dir. field mktg., 1993-95, exec. dir. market devel., 1995-97, exec. dir. client acquisition and retention, 1997-99; pres. Samors & Assocs., Inc. Buffalo Grove, Ill., 1999—2003, Chgo.'s Neighborhoods, Inc. Buffalo Grove, Ill., 2003—. Cons. and evaluator Alverno Coll., Milw., 1978-81, Madonna Coll., Livonia, Mich., 1978-81, Coll. St. Scholastica, Duluth, Minn., 1980-81; cons. Ednl. Testing Svc., Chauncey Group Internat., 1999-2002; cons. U. Ga., 2004-05. Co-author: Chicago's Far North Side: Illustrated History of Rogers Park and West Ridge, 2000, Neighborhoods Within Neighborhoods: Twentieth Century Life on Chicago's Far North Side, 2002, The Old Chicago Neighborhood, Remembering Life in the 1940s, 2003, Real Chicago: Photographs From the Files of the Chicago Sun-Times, 2004, Chicago in the Fifties, 2005, Real Chicago Sports: Photographs From The Files of The Chicago Sun-Times, 2005, Chicago in the Sixties, 2006. Dir. resource devel. Rogers Pk./West Ridge Hist. Soc., 2001—03; rschr. Stevenson for Senator, Chgo., 1970. Ford Found. fellow, 1967. Mem. Am. Assn. Higher Edn., Am. Hist. Assn., Orgn. Am. Historians, Chgo. Hist. Soc., Phi Delta Kappa (rsch. v.p. Northwestern chpt. 1980). Avocations: photography, sketching portraits, american history. Home: 282 Stanton Dr Buffalo Grove IL 60089-6841 Office: Chgo's Neighborhoods Inc 282 Stanton Dr Buffalo Grove IL 60089-6841 Office Phone: 847-913-8322. E-mail: nsamors@comcast.net.

**SAMOSHIN, VYACHESLAV VLADIMIROVICH,** chemistry professor, science educator, researcher; PhD, Moscow State U., 1982, D of Chem. Scis., 1991. Prof., head dept. organic chemistry Moscow State Acad. Fine Chem. Tech., 1992—97; prof. U. of the Pacific, Stockton, Calif., 1997—. Contbr. articles to chem. jours. Mem.: Russian Mendeleev Chem. Soc., Am. Chem. Soc. Achievements include research in organic synthesis and stereochemistry. Office: U of the Pacific 3601 Pacific Ave Stockton CA 95211 Office Phone: 209-946-2921. Office Fax: 209-946-2607. Business E-Mail: vsamoshin@pacific.edu.

**SAMPLE, FREDERICK PALMER,** former college president; b. Columbia, Pa., May 22, 1930; s. William Walter and Erna Rebecca (Roye) S.; m. Mary Jane Drager, Aug. 19, 1951; children: Jeffrey Lynn, Roger Lee. AB, Lebanon Valley Coll., 1952; MEd, Western Md. Coll., 1956; DEd, Pa. State U., 1968; D in Pedagogy, Albright Coll., 1968. Tchr. Annville (Pa.) High Sch., 1952-53; tchr. Red Lion Area (Pa.) High Sch., 1953-57, prin., 1957-59, supervising prin., 1959-64; supt. Manheim Twp. Sch. Dist., Neffsville, Pa., 1964-68; pres. Lebanon Valley Coll., Annville, Pa., 1968-83; supt. Bellefonte (Pa.) Area Sch. Dist., 1987-92. Ednl. cons.; administr. Bucknell U., 1985-87. Mem. Phi Delta Kappa. Republican. Home: 401 Ford Dr Elizabethtown PA 17022-3194 E-mail: fps0522@dejazzd.com. *Despite failures, difficulties, and disappointments I have tried to find the honorable, responsible, productive, true, and humane solutions to problems and make decisions for progress.*

**SAMPLE, JOSEPH SCANLON,** foundation executive; b. Chgo., Mar. 15, 1923; s. John Glen and Helen (Scanlon) S.; m. Patricia M. Law, Dec. 22, 1942 (div.); children: Michael Scanlon, David Forrest, Patrick Glen; m. Miriam Tyler Willing, Nov. 19, 1965. BA, Yale U., 1947. Trainee, media analyst, media dir. Dancer-Fitzgerald-Sample, Inc., advt. agy., Chgo., 1947-50, v.p., media dir., 1952-53; pres. Mont. Television Network KTVQ, Billings, KXLF-AM-TV, Butte, Mont., KRTV, Great Falls, Mont., KPAX-TV, Missoula, Mont., 1955-84; dir., prodr. Yellowstone Pub. Radio KEMC, Billings, 1993—. Chmn. Wheeler Ctr. Mont State U., 1988—. Served with AUS, 1943-46 With U.S. Army, 1950-52. Mem. Rotary, Yellowstone Country Club, Port Royal Club, Hole in The Wall Golf Club, Hilands Golf Club, Naples Yacht Club. Home: 606 Highland Park Dr Billings MT 59102-1909 Office: 14 N 24th St Billings MT 59101-2422 Office Phone: 406-256-5667. Personal E-mail: scatman01@msn.com.

**SAMPLE, STEVEN BROWNING,** academic administrator; b. St. Louis, Nov. 29, 1940; s. Howard and Dorothy (Cunningham) Sample; m. Kathryn Brunkow, Jan. 28, 1961; children: Michelle Sample Smith, Elizabeth Ann. BS, U. Ill., 1962, MS, 1963, PhD, 1965; DHL (hon.), Canisius Coll., 1989; LLD (hon.), U. Sheffield, Eng., 1991; EdD (hon.), Purdue U., 1994; DHL (hon.), Hebrew Union Coll., 1994; DL (hon.), U. Nebr., 1995; EdD, Northwestern U., 2004; DHL (hon.), Northeastern U., 2004; DSc, U. Notre Dame, 2005; DSc (hon.), SUNY, 2006. Sr. scientist Melpar Inc., Falls Ch., Va., 1965—66; assoc. prof. elec. engring. Purdue U., Lafayette, Ind., 1966—73; dep. dir. Ill. Bd. Higher Edn., Springfield, 1971—74; exec. v.p. acad. affairs, dean Grad. Coll., prof. elec. engring. U. Nebr., Lincoln, 1974—82; prof. elec. and computer engring. SUNY, Buffalo, 1982—91; pres. U. So. Calif., LA, 1991—, prof. elec. engring., 1991—, Robert C. Packard pres.'s chair, 1995—. Bd. dirs. Santa Catalina Id. Co., Intermec, William Wrigley Jr. Co., Advanced Bionics, AMCAP/Am. Mut. Fund, Inc., Keck Sch. Medicine; vice-chmn. Western NY Tech. Devel. Ctr., Buffalo, 1982—91; chmn. bd. dirs. Calspan-UB Rsch. Ctr., Inc., Buffalo, 1983—91; mem. Calif. Coun. Sci. and Tech., Irvine, Calif., 1998—2003, L.A. Bus. Advisors, Nat. Acad. of Engring., 1998—; cons. in field; chmn. Pacific-10 Conf., 1997—. Author: Contrarian's Guide to Leadership, 2001, (ref. book) New Dictionary of the History of Ideas, 2004; contbr. articles to profl. jour. Timpanist St. Louis Philharm. Orch., 1958-63; chmn. Western NY Regional Econ. Devel. Coun., 1984—91; trustee U. at Buffalo Found., 1982—91, Studio Arena Theatre, Buffalo, 1983—91, Western NY Pub. Broadcasting Assn., 1991—91; chmn. Gov.'s Conf. on Sci. and Engring. Edn., Rsch. and Devel. 1989—91; sr. warden Ch. of Our Savior, 1996—98; mem. Calif. Bus.-Higher Edn. Forum (CBHEF), 1995—97; trustee LEARN, 1991—96; mem. bd. dir. 1st Interstate Bancorp, 1991—96, Galaxy Inst. Edn., 1991—94, Niagara Mohawk Power Corp., 1988—91; vestry Ch. of Our Savior, 1996—2001; mem. bd. gov. LA Annenberg Met. Project (LAAMP), 1994—2000; mem. bd. dir.

Western Atlas, Inc., 1994—97, The Presley Co., 1991—; bd. dir. Buffalo Philharm. Orch., 1982—91, Regenstrief Med. Found., Indpls., 1982—, Rsch. Found. SUNY, 1987—91; bd. dir. LA chpt. World Affairs Coun.; bd. dir. Rebuild LA Com., Coalition of 100 Club, L.A.; mem. bd. dir. Dunlop Tire Corp., 1987—91, Greater Buffalo C. of C., 1985—91, United Way Buffalo and Erie County, 1985—91; bd. dir. U. So. Calif. Keck Sch. Medicine; bd. trustees J. Paul Getty Trust, 2004—06; mem. leadership coun. Literacy Network of Greater L.A., 2004—; mem. Calif. Commn. for Jobs and Econ. Growth, 2004—. Named Engr. of Yr, NY State Soc. Profl. Engrs., 1985; recipient Disting. Alumnus award, U. Ill., 1980, Alumni Honor award, U. Ill. Coll. Engring., 1985, citation award, Buffalo Coun. on World Affairs, 1986, Outstanding Elec. Engr. award, Purdue U., 1993, Humanitarian award, Nat. Conf. Christians and Jews, 1994, Hollzer Meml. award, Jewish Fedn. Coun. Greater L.A., 1994, Eddy award, LA County Econ. Devel. Corp., 2000, Norton medal, SUNY, 2004, Humanitarian award, Alfred Mann Found., 2004, Heart of City award, Ctrl. City Assn. LA, 2005, KCET Visionary award, 2005, Disting. Bus. Leader award, LA Area C. of C., 2006; fellow, Sloan Found., 1962—63, Grad. fellow, NSF, 1963—65, Am. Coun. Edn. fellow, Purdue U., 1970—71. Mem.: NAE, IEEE (Outstanding Paper award 1976), Am. Acad. Arts and Sci., Assn. Pacific Rim Univ. (co-founder, chmn. 1997—2002), Coun. on Fgn. Rels., Nat. Assn. State Univ. and Land-Grant Coll. (ednl. telecomms. com. 1982—83, chmn. coun. of pres. 1985—86, edn. and tech. com. 1986—87, exec. com. 1987—89), Assn. Am. Univ. (exec. com. 1995—2000, vice-chmn. 1997—98, tenure com. 1997—2001, chmn. 1998—99, assessing quality of univ. edn. and rsch. com. 2000—05, co-chair task force on rsch. accountability 2001—02, internationalization com. 2002—). Episcopalian. Achievements include patents in field. Office: U So Calif Office of Pres University Park Adm 110 Los Angeles CA 90089-0012 Office Phone: 213-740-2111.

**SAMPLE, STEVEN DALE,** secondary school educator; b. Indpls., Aug. 7, 1948; s. Keith Adrian and Elsa Jean (Neilgh) Sample; m. Joy Ann Sample, Sept. 13, 1969; children: Saundra Hope, Susannah Joy. BS, Ill. Coll., Jacksonville, 1970; MS, We. Ill. U., 1971; CAS, Nat. Coll. Edn., Chgo. Grad. tchg. asst. We. Ill. U., Macomb, 1970—72; tchr. biology Morton East H.S., Cicero, Ill., 1973—74; tchr. sci. River Grove Sch. Dist., Ill., 1974—78; tchr. sci., dept. chmn. Elmhurst Cmty. Sch. Dist., Ill., 1978—94, York Cmty. H.S., Elmhurst, 1994—. Author Rock and Mineral Identification software. Recipient Cert. of Merit, 1989, Presdl. award for excellence in sci. and math. teaching, Ill. math. and Sci. Consortium, Those Who Excel award of merit Ill. Bd. Edn., 1990-91, Spl. Svc. award Argonne Nat. Lab. Cmty. of Tchrs., 1991-92, 92-93, 93-94, Pacesetter award Argonne Nat. Lab., 2005; named Tchr. of Yr. Air Force Assn., 1994 Mem. NSTA, ASCD, Ill. Sci. Tchrs. Assn. Office: York Cmty HS 355 W St Charles Rd Elmhurst IL 60126-3271 Home: 401 Willow St Elburn IL 60119-8999 Office Phone: 630-617-7114. E-mail: ssample@gmail.com.

**SAMPLES, JERRY WAYNE,** military officer, educator; b. July 18, 1947; s. Wilmer Clark and Nellie Virginia (Price) Samples; m. Kathleen Miller, Nov. 2, 1969; children: Christopher John, Steven Wayne. BS, Clarkson Coll., 1969; MS, Okla. State U., 1979, PhD, 1983. Registered profl. engr., Va. Lab. asst. Columbia Ribbon & Carbon, Glenn Cove, NY, 1969—70; asst. prof. mech. engring. US Mil. Acad., West Point, NY, 1979—82, assoc. prof. mech. engring., 1985—87; assoc. prof. dept. civil and mech. engrs. U. Pitts., Johnstown, Pa., 1989—96, prof. engring. dir. engring. tech., 1996—; commd. 2d lt. US Army, 1969; with Air Command and Staff Coll. Maxwell AFB, Ala., 1983; exec. officer 10th Engr. Bn., 1983—85; bn. comdr. 10th engr. bn. 3d inf. divsn. Fed. Rep. Germany, 1987—89; advanced through grades to col., 1991. Pres. Tchg. the Tchrs., Inc. Author (with others): (book) Fundamentals of Engrineering Examination, 1991, The Best EIT Review for the Fundamentals of Engrineering Exam, 1995, GRE Engineering, 1996. Decorated Legion of Merit, Meritorious Svc. Medal, Army Commendation Medal. Mem.: SAE (Ralph R. Teetor award 1994), ASEE, ASME (bd. dirs. ASME Found.), AIAA, Phi Kappa Phi. Home: 108 Laurlis Ln Johnstown PA 15904-1742 Office: Univ Pitts at Johnstown Dept Engineering Technology Johnstown PA 15904 E-mail: samps2@twd.net.

**SAMPRAS, PETE,** retired professional tennis player; b. Washington, Aug. 12, 1971; s. Sam and Georgia Sampras; m. Bridgette Wilson, Sept. 30, 2000, 2 children, Christian Charles, Ryan Nikolaos. Mem. U.S. Davis Cup team., named to Olympic Team Atlanta, 1996 Chmn. ATP Tour Charities program, 1992. Winner tournaments including Phila., 1990, Manchester, 1990, US Open, 1990, 1993, Grand Slam Cup, 1990, L.A., 1991, Indpls., 1991, Lyon, 1991, IBM/ATP Tour World Championship-Frankfurt, 1991, 94, US Pro Indoor, 1992, Lipton Internat., 1993, Wimbledon, 1993, 94, 95, 97, 98, 99, 2000; Australian Open, 1994, 97, Italian Open, 1994, US Open, 1990, 93, 95, 96, 2002, San Jose Open, 1996, Memphis Open, 1996, ATP Tour World Championship/Hannover, Germany, 1996, Australian Open Wimbledon, 1997, Advanta Championships, 1998; ranked # 1 during 1993, 94 season, finalist Australian Open, 1995; ret., 2003. Achievements include 1st male to win the US Open, Wimbledon, and Australian Open in succession, mem. US Davis Cup Team, 1991, became only the fourth player to finish as No. 1 three (or more) consecutive years, 1st player to surpass $5 million in a season, all-time leader in career earnings, named ATP Tour Player of the Year, 1993-94, Jim Thorpe Tennis Player, 1993. Office: ATP Tour 420 W 45th St New York NY 10036-3503

**SAMPSON, CLINTON J.,** director; s. Malvin and Ruby Lee Sampson; m. Barbara Sampson, May 26, 1979; children: Candice, Sean, Kimberly, Cameron. BA, La. Tech. U., Ruston, 1981; Masters Degree, So. U., Baton Rouge, 2004. Asst. basketball coach, head softball coach Ruston H.S.; asst. basketball and football coach East Ascension H.S., Gonzales, head basketball coach, Abbeville H.S., La., Bastrop H.S., La.; mem basketball coach Northwestern State U., Natchitoches, La., discipline administr. Prairieville Middle Sch., La. Mem.: La. Assn. Edn., Nat. Collegiate Athletic Assn. Democrat. Baptist. Avocations: chess, fishing, hunting, sports.

**SAMPSON, DAVID ALLAN,** federal agency administrator; b. Washington, Ind., July 2, 1957; s. Beryl Harrel and Laura Evelyn (King) S.; m. Karen Ann Nichols, Dec. 10, 1978. BA, David Lipscomb Coll., Nashville, 1978; MDiv, New Orleans Bapt. Theol. Sem., 1982. Minister Westchurch Ch. of Christ, Hammond, Ind., 1978-82; sr. minister Park Row Ch. of Christ, Arlington, Tex., 1982—; pres., CEO Arlington (Tex.) C. of C.; chmn. Tex. Coun. on Workforce and Econ. Competitiveness; asst. sec. for econ. devel. US Dept Commerce, Washington, 2001—05, acting dep. sec., 2005, dep. sec., 2005—. Bd. dirs. emergency chaplain program Arlington Community Hosp., 1985—, Overseas Private Investment Corp., 2005-; adv. bd. Arlington Meml. Hosp., 1985—; bd. dirs. Neo-natal Bioethics Review Bd., 1986— Contbr. articles to profl. jours. Mem. United Way; bd. dirs. Arlington Ind. Sch. Dists, Communications Bd., 1985—. Named Arlington's Minister of Yr, Kiwanis, 1985. Mem. Arlington C. of C. (bd. dirs. 1985—), chmn. emergency preparedness com. 1985—), Arlington Ministerial Assn. (pres. 1985-86), Soc. Biblical Lit., Internat. Ch. Soc. (chmn. North Tex. chpt.), Phi Alpha Theta. Lodges: Rotary. Republican. Avocations: travel, tennis. Office: US Dept Commerce 14th & Constitution Ave NW Rm 5838 Washington DC 20230

**SAMPSON, DAVID SYNNOTT,** lawyer; b. New York, N.Y., Oct. 2, 1942; s. Stephen Hastings and Ruth (Hall) S.; m. Arlene Mernit, July 1, 1967; children: Christopher Hastings, Jamie Everett. BA, St. Lawrence U., 1965; JD, Albany Law Sch., 1973. Bar: N.Y. 1975, D.C. 1977, U.S. Ct. Appeals (D.C. cir.) 1977. Reporter Troy Record, 1965-67; newsman AP, 1967-70; spl. asst. N.Y. State Dept. Environ. Cons., Albany, 1972-74; panel dir. Com. on Critical Choices for Ams., N.Y.C., 1974-75; chief legis. asst. U.S. Rep. H.J. Heinz, Washington, 1975-77; assoc. Boasberg, Hewes, Finkelstein & Klores, Washington, 1977-79; exec. asst. Am. Land Forum, Washington, 1978-79; ptnr. Pattison, Sampson, Ginsberg & Griffin, Troy, NY, 1979-87; exec. dir. Hudson River Valley Assn., Troy and Cold Spring, NY, 1987-89, Hudson River Valley Greenway Coun., Albany, 1989-2000; of counsel Martin, Shudt, Wallace, DiLorenzo & Johnson, Troy, 2001—; postgrad. in geology and planning U. Albany, 2001—. Adj. prof. Columbia U. Grad. Sch. Arch.,

Planning and Preservation, 2000—. Contbr. book revs., articles to profl. jours. Pres. Samaritan Hosp. Found., 1985-87; bd. dirs. Samaritan Hosp., Troy, 1985-88, St. Gregorys Sch., Loudonville, N.Y., 1982-87, Troy Pub. Libr. Found., 1991—, Scenic Hudson, Poughkeepsie, N.Y., 1982-92, 93-99; mem. Scenic Hudson Land Trust, 1996-01, Husdon River Found., 1999—, Hudsonia, 2001—; mem. adv. bd. Preservation League N.Y., Albany, 1989; mem. N.Y. State Freshwater Wetlands Appeals Bd., 1980-94, chmn., 1984-94; active U.S./UK Countryside Stewardship Exch., Eng., 1989; founder Czech-Hudson Greenway Project, 1992; bd. dirs. Hudson River Found., 1997—. Recipient Greenway award DuPont Corp., 1994, Environ. Alumni award Albany Law Sch., 1997. Mem. Am. Conservation Assn. (bd. dirs. 1987—), N.Y. Pks. and Conservation Assn. (founding dir. 1986-94), N.Y. State Bar Assn. (chmn. hist. preservation com. 1980-85, exec. com. 1985—, chmn. environ. law sect. 1990-91, Bar Assn. City of N.Y. Avocation: bicycling. E-mail: dvsampson@aol.com.

**SAMPSON, EARLDINE ROBISON,** education educator; b. Russell, Iowa, June 18, 1923; d. Lawrence Earl and Mildred Mona (Judy) Robison; m. Wesley Claude Sampson, Nov. 25, 1953; children: Ann Elizabeth, Lisa Ellen. Diploma, Iowa State Tchrs. Coll., 1943, BA, 1950; MS in Edn., Drake U., 1954; postgrad., No. Ill. U., Iowa State U., 1965-66, 74. Cert. tchr., guidance counselor, Iowa. Tchr. elem. sch. various pub. sch. sys., 1943-48; cons. speech and hearing Iowa Dept. Pub. Instrn., Des Moines, 1950-52; speech therapist Des Moines Pub. Schs., 1952-54, 55; lectr. spl. edn. No. Ill. U., DeKalb, 1964-65; tchr. of homebound Cedar Falls (Iowa) Pub. Schs., 1965-68; asst. prof. edn. U. No. Iowa, Cedar Falls, 1968; asst. prof., counselor Wartburg Coll., Waverly, Iowa, 1968-70; instr. elem. edn., then head of advising elem. edn. Iowa State U., Ames, 1972-82; field supr. elem. edn. U. Toledo, 1988, 89; ind. cons. Sylvania, Ohio, 1989—. Cons. Des Moines Speech and Hearing Ctr., 1958-59; cons. Sartori Hosp., Cedar Falls, 1967-69. Fellow, NDEA, 1965. Methodist. Avocations: public speaking on preservation of prose and poetry, reading, music, photography. Home: 4047 Newcastle Dr Sylvania OH 43560-3450 *My creed is based on the words of Edwin Markham: "There is a destiny that makes us brothers; none goes his way alone. All that we send into the lives of others comes back into our own." Just reward came from a former student who stated "I have never known you to compromise your principles".*

**SAMPSON, HUGH ALBERT, JR.,** medical educator; b. Winnipeg, Man., Can., 1948; BA, Hamilton Coll., 1971; MD, SUNY, Buffalo, 1975. Diplomate Am. Bd. Pediats., Am. Bd. Allergy and Immunology. Resident Children's Meml. Hosp.-Northwestern U., Chgo., 1975—78; fellow in allergy and immunology-pulmonary medicine Duke U. Med. Ctr., Durham, NC, 1978—80, mem. staff, 1980—86; prof. pediat. Johns Hopkins U., Balt., 1986—97; prof., pediat. Mt. Sinai Sch. of Medicine, N.Y.C., 1997—. Co-author: Intestinal immunology and Food Allergy, 1995, Food Allergy: Adverse Reactions to Foods and Food Additives, 1991, Pediatric Allergy: Principles and Practice, 2003 Fellow Am. Acad. Allergy and Immunology; mem. Am. Assn. Immunologists, Soc. Pediat. Rsch., Sigma Xi. Office: Mt Sinai Sch Medicine One Gustave L Levy Pl Box 1198 New York NY 10029 Office Phone: 212-241-5548. Business E-Mail: hugh.sampson@mssm.edu.

**SAMPSON, JOHN EUGENE,** food products executive, consultant; b. Feb. 25, 1941; s. Delbert John and Mary Etta (Dodrill) S.; m. Mary Margaret Treanor, Aug. 14, 1965; children: J. Mark, Sharon. AB with distinction, Nebr. Wesleyan U., 1963; MBA, Ind. U., 1964. Mgmt. asst., exec. trainee Office Sec. Def., Washington, 1963—64; mem. staff Econ. Devel., Washington, 1964—69; coord. environ. planning Gen. Mills Inc., Mpls., 1969—72, mgr. devel. planning, 1972—74; dir. corp. planning Cen. Soya Co. Inc., Ft. Wayne, Ind., 1974—76, v.p. corp. planning, 1976—80, v.p. corp. planning and devel., 1980—82, v.p. corp. devel., corp. sec., 1982—84; v.p. corp. planning and devel. Internat. Multifoods, Inc., 1984—96; pres. Sampson Assocs., Edina, Minn., 1996—. Author: How to Sell Your Business and Get the Best Price For It, 2003. Mem. bd. govs. Nebr. Wesleyan U., 1974-80; chmn. bd. trustees St. Joseph United Meth. Ch., Ft. Wayne, 1984; bd. dirs., treas. North Ind. United Meth. Found., 1981-84; lay mem. North Ind. Ann. Conf. United Meth. Ch., 1980-84; bd. dirs. Anthony Wayne coun. Boy Scouts Am., 1984; lay mem. Minn. Ann. Conf. United Meth. Ch., 1985-91, 97-00; chmn. conf. bd. devel. Minn. United Meth. Ch., 1986-91; chmn. bd. trustees Hennepin Ave. United Meth. Ch., Mpls., 1990-92, chair adminstrv. coun., 1993-95, lay leader, 1995-98; chair exec. com. North Naples (Fla.) United Meth. Ch., 2002-05, co-chmn. bldg. com., 2002-05, chair bd. trustees, 2005-. Mem. Ind. U. Sch. Bus. Alumni Assn. (pres. 1984-85), Interlachen Country Club, Country Club of Naples (bd. dirs. 2004—). Home: Unit 1701 4451 Gulf Shore Blvd N Naples FL 34103 Office Phone: 952-928-0800.

**SAMPSON, JOHN J.,** law educator; b. St. Paul, Sept. 30, 1935; s. J.E. and Margaret A. Sampson; m. Joyce C., Aug. 6, 1940; children: Margaret J., Eleanor H. LLB magna cum laude, U. Minn., 1966. Bar: Calif. 1967, Tex. 1980. Assoc. Morriston-Foerster, San Francisco, 1966-69; asst. gen. counsel U.S. Commn. on Obscenity and Pornography, 1969-70; asst. prof. U. Tex. Sch. Law, Austin, 1970-73, prof., 1973-82, Ben Gardner Sewell prof. law, 1982-86, William Benjamin Wynne prof., 1986—. Bd. dirs. Legal Aid Soc. Central Tex.; lectr., legis. draftsman; reporter Nat. Conf. Commrs. Uniform St. Laws, 1990—. Pres. Nat. 1945-66; contbr. numerous articles to legal publs. Mem. State Bar Tex. (editor family law sect. report 1976—). Office: U Tex Sch Law 727 E Dean Keeton St Austin TX 78705-3299 Office Phone: 512-232-1267. E-mail: jsampson@mail.law.utexas.edu.*

**SAMPSON, KELVIN DALE,** college basketball coach; b. Laurinburg, N.C., Oct. 5, 1955; s. John W. and Eva (Brewington) S.; m. Karen Sue Lowry, June 16, 1979; children: Lauren Elizabeth, Kellen Matthew. BS, Pembroke State U., 1978; MS, Mich. State U., 1980. Pres. NABC, 2003; head basketball coach Wash. State U., 1990—94, Univ. of Okla., Norman, Okla., 1994—2006, Ind. Univ., 2006—. Contbr. articles to profl. jours. Mem. Nat. Assn. Basketball Coaches (Dist. Coach of Yr. 1991, PAC 10 Coach of Yr. 1991), AAHPERD. Avocations: golf, reading, exercise. Office: Univ Ind Athletics Dept Assembly Hall 1001 E Seventeenth St Bloomington IN 47408-1590*

**SAMPSON, ROBERT J.,** sociologist, educator; BA, SUNY, Buffalo, 1977; MA, SUNY, Albany, 1979, PhD, 1983. Sr. staff assoc. Columbia U., 1981—83; postdoctoral fellow sch. urban and pub. affairs Carnegie-Mellon U., 1983—84; asst. prof. dept. sociology U. Ill., 1984—88, assoc. prof., 1988—91; prof. sociology U. Chgo., 1991—99, Lucy Flower Prof. Urban Sociology, 1997—2001, Fairfax M. Cone Disting. Svc. Prof., 2001—02; Henry Ford II Prof. Social Scis. Harvard U., 2003—. Vis. summer scholar Nat. Ctr. Juvenile Justice, Pitts., 1988; sci. dir. Project on Human Devel. in Chgo. Neighborhoods, 1994—; rsch. fellow Am. Bar Found., 1994—99, sr. rsch. fellow, 1999—2002; mem. steering com. Carnegie-Mellon U. Consortium on Violence Rsch., 1996—98, Harvard U. Ctr. Geog. Analysis, 2005—; fellow Ctr. Advanced Study in Behavioral Scis., Stanford, Calif., 1994—95, 2002—03; mem. sci. adv. bd. NSF Ctr. Spatially Integrated Social Sci., 2000—03; chair dept. sociology Harvard U., 2005—. Contbr. articles to profl. jours., chapters to books; asst. editor Jour. Rsch. in Crime and Delinquency, 1981—84; co-author: Juvenile Criminal Behavior and Its Relation to Neighborhood Characteristics, 1981, Crime in the Making: Pathways and Turning Points Through Life, 1993 (Michael J. Hindelang Book award for Disting. Scholarly Publ., Am. Soc. Criminology, 1994, Disting. Scholar award, Am. Sociol. Assn. Crime, Law and Deviance sect., 1995, Outstanding Book award, Acad. Criminal Justice Scis., 1995), How Neighborhoods Matter: The Value of Investing at the Local Level, 2001, Shared Beginnings, Divergent Lives: Delinquent Boys to Age 70, 2003 (Michael J. Hindelang Book award for Disting. Scholarly Publ., Am. Soc. Criminology, 2004, Albert J. Reiss, Jr. Disting. Book award, Am. Sociol. Assn. Crime, Law and Deviance sect., 2005, named an Outstanding Academic Title: The Best of the Best in Published Scholarship, 2005, Outstanding Book award, Acad. Criminal Justice Scis., 2005); co-editor: Social Ecology of Crime, 1986, Integrating Individual and Ecol. Aspects on Crime, 1993, Explanation of Crime: Context, Mechanisms, and Devel., 2006; mem. editl. adv. bd.: Criminology, 1988—90; Jour. Quantitative Criminology, 1988—90, Am. Sociol. Rev., 1990—92, consulting editor: Am. Jour. Sociology, 1989—91, mem. editl. bd.; 1991—2003, Law and Soc. Rev., 1997—2000, Social Forces, 1997—2000, Criminology, 2000—, Jour. Rsch. in Crime and Delinquency, 2000—, Theoretical Criminology, 2000—, Contexts, 2000—04, assoc. editor Am. Jour. Sociology, 1993—96, Law and Soc. Rev., 2000—03. Recipient Investigator award, Robert Wood Johnson Found. Prog. on Health Policy Rsch., 2005—. Fellow: Am. Soc. Criminology (exec. counselor 1991—94, Edwin H. Sutherland award 2001), Am. Acad. Arts and Scis., NAS (Communities and Crime panel mem. 1988—89); mem.: Am. Sociol. Assn. (chair Crime, Law and Deviance sect. 2000—03, coun. mem. Cmty. and Urban sect. 2000—03, mem. exec. coun. Crime, Law and Deviance sect. 1995—98, Robert Park award 2000), Sociol. Rsch. Assn. Office: Harvard U Dept Sociology William James Hall 33 Kirkland St Cambridge MA 02138 E-mail: rsampson@wjh.harvard.edu.*

SAMPSON, ROBERT NEIL, professional society administrator, consultant; b. Spokane, Wash., Nov. 29, 1938; s. Robert Jay and Juanita Cleone (Hickman) S.; m. Jeanne Louise Stokes, June 7, 1960; children— Robert W., Eric S., Christopher B., Heidi L. BS in Agr, U. Idaho, 1960; M.Public Adminstrn., Harvard U., 1974. Soil conservationist Soil Conservation Service, Burley, Idaho, 1960-61, work unit conservationist Orofino, Idaho, 1962-65, agronomist Idaho Falls, Idaho, 1967-68, info. specialist Boise, 1968-70, area conservationist, 1970-72, land use specialist Washington, 1974-77, dir. environ. services div., 1977; land use program mgr. Idaho Planning and Community Affairs Agy., Boise, 1972-73; exec. v.p. Nat. Assn. Conservation Dists., Washington, 1978-84, Am. Forestry Assn., Washington, 1984-95; sr. fellow Am. Forests, Washington, 1995-2000; affiliate prof. Dept. Forest Resources U. Idaho, 1997—. Instr. soils and land use Boise State U., 1972; F.K. Weyerhaeuser vis. fellow in comml. forestry Yale Sch. Forestry and Environ. Studies, 2001; pres., The Sampson Group, Inc., 1996—, Vision Forestry LLC, 2000—; rsch. scientist, Yale Sch. Forestry and Environ. Studies, 2001—; land use and forestry cons. Author: Farmland or Wasteland: A Time To Choose, 1981, For Love of the Land, 1985; contbr. articles to profl. and popular publs. Pres. Orofino Golf Assn., 1966, Clearwater County Search and Rescue Unit, 1966-67; chmn. Nat. Commn. on Wildfire Disasters, 1992-94. Recipient President's citation Soil Conservation Soc. Am., 1978; named Boise Fed. Civil Servant of Year Boise Fed. Bus. Assn., 1972 Fellow Soil and Water Conservation Soc. (Hugh Hammond Bennett award 1992); mem. Soc. Am. Foresters. Presbyterian. Office Phone: 703-924-0773. Personal E-mail: rneilsampson@cs.com.

SAMPSON, ROGER, school system administrator; Prin., sch. adminstr. Annette Island Sch. Dist., Metlakatia, Alaska, 1979—84; prin. Kenai Peninsula Borough Sch. Dist., Alaska, 1984—94; supt. Chugach Sch. Dist., Alaska, 1994—99; commr. edn. and early devel. State of Alaska, 2003—. Mem. standards based edn. com. State of Alaska. Named Alaska Prin. of Yr., 1987, Nat. Rural Supt. of Yr., 1997. Office: Dept Edn & Early Devel 801 W 10th St Ste 200 Juneau AK 99801 Office Phone: 907-465-2802. Business E-Mail: roger_sampson@eed.state.ak.us.

SAMPSON, SAMUEL FRANKLIN, sociology educator; b. Malden, Mass., Sept. 22, 1934; s. Samuel Daniel and Margaret Louise (Grimes) S.; m. Patricia Katherine Driscoll, Apr. 8, 1972. BA, U. Okla., 1960, MA, 1961; PhD, Cornell U., 1968. Asst. prof. dept. sociology SUNY, Binghamton, 1965-66; research assoc. dept. sociology Cornell U., Ithaca, NY, 1966-67; lectr., chmn. bd. tutors and advs. Harvard U., Cambridge, Mass., 1967-72; assoc. prof. dept. urban studies and planning MIT, Cambridge, 1971-72; prof. sociology U. Vt., Burlington, 1972-2000, chmn. dept. sociology, 1972-76, 90-96, prof. emeritus, 2000—. Research and policy cons. Public & Community Agys. and Orgns., 1969— Gen. editor: Bobbs-Merrill Studies in Sociology, 1970-77; contbr. articles to profl. jours. Served with USAF, 1954-58. Mem. AAAS, Internat. Sociol. Assn., Am. Sociol. Assn., Am. Acad. Arts and Scis., Ea. Sociol. Soc., Soc. Study Social Problems, New Eng. Sociol. Assn., Soc. Sci. Study Religion. Office: Univ Vt Dept Sociology 31 S Prospect St Burlington VT 05405-1704 Office Phone: 802-864-6751.

SAMPSON, WILLIAM ROTH, lawyer; b. Teaneck, NJ, Dec. 11, 1946; s. James and Amelia (Roth) S.; 1 child, Lara; m. Drucilla Jean Mort, Apr. 23, 1988; stepchildren: Andy, Seth. BA in History with honors, U. Kans., 1968, JD, 1971. Bar: Kans. 1971, Mo. 2004, U.S. Dist. Ct. Kans. 1971, U.S. Dist. Ct. (we. dist.) Mo. 2004, U.S. Ct. Appeals (10th cir.) 1982, U.S. Ct. Claims 1985, U.S. Ct. Appeals (8th cir.) 1992. Assoc. Turner & Balloun, Great Bend, Kans., 1971; ptnr. Foulston & Siefkin, Wichita, Kans., 1975-86, Shook, Hardy & Bacon LLP, Kans. City, 1987. Adj. prof. advanced litig. U. Kans., 1994; mem. faculty trial tactics inst. Emory U. Sch. Law, 1994-97; mem. merit selection panel US Dist. Ct. Kans., 1999; lectr., presenter in field. Author: Kansas Trial Handbook, 1997; mem. Kans. Law Rev., 1969—71, editor, 1970—71; contbr. articles to profl. jours. Chmn. stewardship com. Univ. Friends Ch., Wichita, 1984-86; bd. dir. Friends U. Retirement Corp., Wichita, 1985-87, Lied Ctr. Kans., 1994-97, Nat. Found. Jud. Excellence, 2004—, program chmn., 2004, 05, 06; chmn. capital fund drives Trinity Luth. Ch., Lawrence, Kans., 1990-93, mem. ch. coun., 1990-92, stewardship com. Trinity Episcopal Ch., 2002—. Lt. USNR, 1971-75. Named one of The Best Lawyers in Am., Mo./Kans. Super Lawyers, 2006. Fellow: Nahs. Bar Found., Am. Bar Found.; mem.: ABA, Lawyers for Civil Justice (bd. dirs. 2003—05), Am. Inn Ct. (Judge Hugh Means chpt. Master of Bench), Kans. U. Law Soc. (bd. govs. 1993—96), Kans. Assn. Def. Counsel (pres. 1989—90, legis. coun. 1991, 1993, William H. Kahrs Disting. Achievement award 1994), Def. Rsch. Inst. (Kans. state rep. 1990—98, nat. bd. dirs. 1998—2000, nat. pres. 2003—04, Exceptional Performance citation 1990), Internat. Assn. Def. Coun. (faculty mem. trial acad. 1994), Am. Bd. Trial Advs. (pres. Kans. chpt. 1990—91, nat. bd. dir. 1990—91), Wichita Bar Assn. (bd. dirs. 1985—86), Johnson County Bar Assn. (bench-bar com. 1989—, Boss of Yr. award 1990), Douglas County Bar Assn., Kans. Bar Assn. (chmn. Kans. coll. advocacy 1986, CLE com. 1987—88, long-range planning), Assn. Def. Trial Attys., Club at Porto Cima, Order of Coif, Omicron Delta Kappa, Phi Alpha Theta, Delta Sigma Rho. Republican. Episcopalian. Avocations: jogging, golf, skiing, travel, reading. Office: Shook Hardy & Bacon LLP 2555 Grand Ave Kansas City MO 64108-2613 Office Phone: 816-474-6550. Office Fax: 816-421-5547. Business E-Mail: wsampson@shb.com.

SAMRA, NICHOLAS JAMES, bishop; b. Paterson, N.J., Aug. 15, 1944; s. George H. and Elizabeth L. (Balady) S. BA, St. Anselm Coll., 1966; BD, St. John Sem., Brighton, Mass., 1970. Ordained priest Melkite-Greek Cath. Ch., 1970, bishop Melkite-Greek Cath. Ch., 1989. Assoc. pastor St. Anne Ch., North Hollywood, Calif., 1970—78; pastor Holy Cross Ch., Anaheim, Calif., 1973—78, St. John The Bapt. Ch., Northlake, Ill., 1978—81, St. Michael Ch., Hammond, Ind., 1978—81, St. Anne Ch., West Paterson, NJ, 1981—89; aux. bishop Diocese of Newton, Mass., 1989—. Chaplain Police Athletic League Supporters, North Hollywood, 1970; vicar gen., corp. v.p., and regional bishop of Midwest region Diocese of Newton; transl. articles on Melkite subjects; mem. Ecumenical Commn., L.A., 1974—78. Mem.: US Conf. Catholic Bishops, Christian Churches Together in the USA, Cath. Archives Assn.

SAMS, RONALD F., career military officer; BA, Mich. State U., 1972; grad., Squadron Officer Sch., 1977; MA in Ednl. Systems Mgmt., Chapman U., 1978; student, Air Command and Staff Coll., Maxwell AFB, Ala., 1984, Air War Coll., 1993. Commd. 2d lt. USAF, 1972, advanced through grades to maj. gen., 2002; squadron co-pilot, aircraft comdr., instr. pilot 9th Air Refueling Squadron USAF, Beale AFB, Calif., 1974-79; from instr. pilot to faculty instr. pilot 93d Air Refueling Squadron, SAC Ctrl. Flight Instr. Course, Castle AFB, Calif., 1979-83; faculty instr. Air Command and Staff Coll. USAF, Maxwell AFB, Ala., 1984-86; chief tanker crew tng. br., Directorate of Tng. Hdqs. Strategic Air Command, Offutt AFB, Nebr., 1986-89; comdr. 70th air refueling squadron USAF, Grissom AFB, Ind., 1989-90; asst. dep. comdr. ops. 305th Air Refueling Wing USAF and chief air refueling ops. 1703rd Wing, Grissom AFB, Ind. King, Khalid, Airport, Riyadh, Saudi Arabia, 1990-91; dir. ops. mgmt. Tanker Airlift Control Ctr., USAF, Scott AFB, Ill., 1993-94; comdr. 4409th ops.

group (provisional) USAF, Ridyah AFB, Saudi Arabia, 1994-95; mil. asst. to dir. Defense Tech. Security Adminstrn. Defense Threat Reduction Agy. The Pentagon, Washington, 1995-98; comdr. 55th Wing USAF, Offutt AFB, Nebr., 1998—2000; inspector gen. Air Combat Command, Langley AFB, Va., 2000—02; dir. intelligence, surveillance & reconnaissance, dep. chief of staff, Air & Space Ops. USAF, Washington, 2002—. Decorated Bronze Star medal, Defense Superior Svc. medal, Air medal, Aerial Achievement medal with 2 oak leaf clusters,, Meritorious Svc. medal with 6 oak leaf clusters, Air Force Organizational Excellence award, Combat Readiness medal, Nat. Defense Svc. medal, Armed Fores Expeditionary medal, S.W. Asia Svc. medal with 2 service stars, Kuwait Liberation medal Kingdom of Kuwait, Kuwait Liberation medal Kingdom of Saudi Arabia. Office: USAF 1480 Air Force Pentagon Washington DC 20330

SAMSON, ALVIN, former distributing company executive, consultant; b. NYC, May 2, 1917; s. Morris and Jennie (Buitekant) S.; m. Ann Carol Furmansky, Aug. 15, 1942; children: Leslie Joan, Marla Adriane. Br. mgr. U.S. Hardware and Paper Co., 1947-51; mdse. mgr. U.S. Servateria, 1951-57; dir. purchasing U.S. Consumer Products, Los Angeles, 1959-64, v.p. ops., 1964-66, pres., 1966-72, San Diego, Bakersfield, Las Vegas, Phoenix, 1966-72, Zelman Co., Los Angeles, San Francisco and Las Vegas, 1968-72, Triple A Corp., Los Angeles, 1966-72, U.S. Consumer Products-Wesco Mdse., Los Angeles, 1972-74; v.p. APL Corp., N.Y.C., 1967-74; pres. USCP-WESCO, 1974-85; cons. A. Samson Cons., Beverly Hills, 1985-92; retired, 1992. Active USCG Aux., 1981-02, divsn. capt., 1992—. With USAAC, 1942-45. Named Man of Year Housewares Club So. Calif., 1965 Mem. Nat. Assn. Service Merchandisers (dir. 1982-85)

SAMSON, CHARLES HAROLD, JR., (CAR SAMSON), retired engineering educator, consultant; b. Portsmouth, Ohio, July 12, 1924; s. Charles Harold and Gertrude (Morris) S.; m. Ruth Aileen Baumbach, Sept. 12, 1947; children: Peggy Aileen, Charles Harold III. BS, U. Notre Dame, 1947, MS, 1948; PhD, U. Mo., 1953. Registered profl. engr., Tex., Ind. Asst. field rep. Loebl, Schlossman and Bennett (archs. and engrs.), Chgo., 1948-49; structures engr. Convair Aircraft, Ft. Worth, 1951-52, sr. structures engr., 1952-53, project aerodynamics engr., 1956-58, project structures engr., 1958-60; asst. prof. civil engring. U. Notre Dame, 1953-56; office engr. Wilbur H. Gartner & Assocs., South Bend, Ind., 1954; grad. lectr. civil engring. So. Meth. U., Dallas, 1952-53, 56-60; prof. structural engring. and mechanics, depts. aerospace and civil engring. Tex. A&M U., College Station, 1960-64, prof. civil engring., 1964-94, prof. emeritus 1994—, head dept., 1964-79, assoc. head dept., 1989-92, constrn. area engring. head dir. ctr. constrn. edn., 1992-93; rsch. engr. Tex. Transp. Inst., Tex. A&M U., 1960-62, head structural rsch. dept., 1962-65, acting pres., 1980-81, v.p. planning, 1981-82. Pres. S.W. Athletic Conf., 1979-81; v.p. NCAA, 1981-83, mem. coun., 1983-85; cons. systems engring. and quality mgmt.; Tex. Quality Award examiner, 1998-99; sr. examiner, 2000. Contbr. articles to profl. jours. Served to ensign USNR, 1943-46. Recipient Gen. Dynamics-Ft. Worth Excellence in Tchg. award, 1962, Engring. hon. award U. Notre Dame, 1982, Mo. Honor award for Disting. Svc. in Engring., 2006. Fellow ASCE (life), Nat. Inst. Engring. Mgmt. and Svs. (pres. 1989-90), NSPE (past v.p., chmn. profl. engrs. in edn., pres. 1987-88, award 2000); mem. Am. Soc. Engring. Mgmt., Am. Soc. Engring. Edn., Tex. Soc. Profl. Engrs. (past nat. dir., pres. 1973-74, Tex. Engring. Dream Team 2000), Nat. Assn. Parliamentarians, Internat. Soc. Sys. Sci., Order of Engr. (chmn., bd. govs. 1989-91), Am. Soc. Quality, Internat. Coun. Sys. Engring., Nat. Eagle Scout Assn., Sigma Xi, Sigma Gamma Tau, Tau Beta Pi, Phi Kappa Phi, Chi Epsilon. Home: 810 Dogwood Ln Bryan TX 77802-1144 Office Phone: 979-779-0424. Personal E-mail: charleshsamson@msn.com.

SAMSON, DAVID, lawyer; BA, Rutgers U., 1961; LLB, U. Pa. Law Sch., 1965. Law sec. Hon. Nathan L. Jacobs, NJ Supreme Court, 1965—66; founding prin. Wolff & Samson, 1972; gen. counsel NJ Turnpike Authority, 1982—90; atty. gen. State of NJ, 2002—03; sr. ptnr. Wolff & Samson, 2003—. Mem. Gov. Commn., 1990—91; chmn. Gov. Task Force, 1987—89; legal cons. Ethics Com., 1981—85, NJ Supreme Court Com., 1973—77; legal cons. to atty. gen. Adv. com. on Governmental Immunity, 1967—68. Mem.: U.S. Supreme Court, N.Y. Bar Assn., Am. Bar Found., Am. Bar Assn., N.J. State Bar Assn., Essex County Bar Assn. Office: Wolff & Samson One Boland Dr West Orange NJ 07052

SAMSON, HARVEY GILBERT, lawyer; b. Milw., July 14, 1947; s. Oscar and Pearl (Waitsman) S.; m. Nancy L. Heinze, June 9, 1970; children: Benjamin J., William E. BA, U. Wis., 1970, JD, 1973. Bar: Wis. 1973, U.S. Dist. Ct. (we. dist.) Wis. 1973, U.S. Dist. Ct. (ea. dist.) Wis. 1978, U.S. Ct. Appeals (7th cir.) 1988, U.S. Supreme Ct. 1990. Assoc. Callahan Law Office, Watertown, Wis., 1974-75; ptnr. Block, Seymour, Chudacoff, Samson and Liebzeit S.C., Appleton, Wis., 1975—. Sec. Appleton Police and Fire Commn.; asst. chmn. Appleton Parade Com.; former troop com. chmn. Troop 8 Boy Scouts Am., Appleton. Mem. State Bar of Wis., Outagamie County Bar. Office: Block Seymour Chudacoff Samson & Liebzeit SC 512 W College Ave Appleton WI 54911-5834 Office Phone: 920-731-9101. Business E-Mail: harvey@blocklegalservice.com.

SAMSON, LEONA D., biological engineering educator, research center director; BSc in Biochemistry, Aberdeen U., Scotland, 1974; PhD, London U., 1978. Postdoctoral rschr. U. Calif., San Francisco, Berkeley; from asst. prof. to full prof. dept. molecular and cellular toxicology Harvard Sch. Pub. Health, 1983—2001; prof. biol. engring. and toxicology MIT, 2001—, dir. MIT Ctr. for Environ. Health Scis., MIT Toxicogenomics Rsch. Program, 2001—. Mem. exec. com. Computational and Systems Biology Initiative MIT; mem. bd. sci. counselors NIEHS; mem. coun. for extramural grants ACS. Named Am. Cancer Soc. Rsch. Prof., 2001; recipient Burroughs Wellcome Toxicology Scholar award, 1993, Charlotte Friend Women in Cancer Rsch. award, 2000. Mem.: Inst. Medicine. Office: Ctr for Environ Health Scis MIT Bldg 56-235 Cambridge MA 02139 Business E-Mail: lsamson@mit.edu.*

SAMSON, MICHEL CHARLES, plastic surgeon; b. Sydney, Nova Scotia, Canada, Feb. 14, 1969; arrived in U.S., 2000; s. Nazaire Joseph Samson and Norma Anna Shaw. BS, Mt. Allison U., 1991; MD, Dalhousie U., 1995. Cert. specialist in plastic surgery Royal Coll. Physicians & Surgeons Can., 2000. Resident Dalhousie U., 1995—2000; asst. prof. surgery Dept. Plastic Surgery Cleve. Clinic Fla., Weston, 2001—; dir. residency program Cleve. Clinic, Fla. Plastic Surgery, 2005—. Fellow, Cleve. Clinic, Fla., 2000—01. Fellow: ACS, Royal Coll. Physicians & Surgeons Can.; mem.: AMA, Can. Med. Assn., Fla. Soc. Plastic Surgeons, Can. Soc. Plastic Surgeons, Am. Soc. Plastic Surgeons. Office: Cleve Clinic Florida 2950 Cleveland Clinic Blvd Weston FL 33331 Office Phone: 954-659-5220. Business E-Mail: samsonm1@ccf.org.

SAMSON, RICHARD MAX, theater director, investment company executive; b. Milw., June 13, 1946; s. Harry E. and Rose (Landau) Samson; m. Nancy K. Pinter; children: Gina Shoshana, Alayna Tamar 1 stepchild; Christopher P. BA, U. Wis., 1968. Dir., owner Puppet Co., Jerusalem, 1972-73; pres. Century Hall, Inc., Milw., 1974-75; dir. purchasing Am. Med. Svcs., Inc., Milw., 1975-74; v.p. 1974-82, exec. v.p. 1982-86, pres., 1986-90, Samson Investments, Milw., 1990—2002. Bd. dirs. Liberty Bank, Milw.; sec. Super Sitters, Mequon, Wis., 1987—2004. Dir.(co-prodr.): (plays) Loss of Breath: The Unfinished Life and Death of Edgar Allan Poe, 1999, Stones of Wisdom, 2003, (co-creator) Einstein: Hero of the Mind, 2002, The Apollo of Bellac, 2004, The Trial Adapted from Franz Kafka, 2005, Smoldering Fires, 2006; designer: (mask and puppet design), 2006. Pres. bd. dirs. Theatre X, Milw., 1982, Holton Youth Ctr., Milw., 1994, Children's Outing Assn., 1996, Jewish Found. Econ. Opportunity, 1996—2004; v.p. bd. dirs. ArtReach, Milw., 1987; mem. funding bd. Wis. Cmty. Fund, 1992—93; dir. Mask and Puppet Co. Milw., 1992—; treas. nat. bd. dirs. Am. for Peace Now, 2002—04; bd. dirs. Bnai Or Religious Fellowship, 1988—93, Milw. Jewish Coun., 1992—94. Recipient Humanitarian Peace award, Ecumenical Refugee Coun., 1989, Social Justice award, Wis. Cmty. Fund, 1997, Human Rels. award, Wis.

region NCCJ, 1998, Cmty. Svc. Human Rels. award, Wis. chpt. Am. Jewish Com., 2000. Avocations: chess, comic book collecting, puppetry. Office: Samson Investments 100A E Pleasant St Milwaukee WI 53212-3975

SAMSOT, ROBERT LOUIS, editor, consultant; b. New Orleans, July 20, 1943; s. Robert Desposito and Mary Helen (Dohan) S.; m. Michael Newton, June 9, 1965; children: Kathleen Anderson Samsot English, Robert Dohan Samsot. BA in Journalism, U. N.C., Chapel Hill, 1965; cert. in Bus. Adminstrn., Rockhurst Coll., 1982. Reporter Rocky Mountain News, Denver, 1965-67, The Comml. Appeal, Memphis, 1967-72; reporter, editor Newsday, L.I., N.Y., 1972-80; Gannett profl.-in-residence U. Kans., Lawrence, 1980-81; met. editor The Kansas City (Mo.) Times, 1981-84; city editor The Plain Dealer, Cleve., 1984-87; lifestyle editor, dep. editor N.J., dep. editor nat. The Phila. Inquirer, 1987-97; regional editor Balt. Sun, 1997-98; nat. editor USA Today, 1998-2000; asst. city editor The Washington Post, 2000—. Cons. W.K. Kellogg Nat. Fellowship, Battle Creek, Mich., 1984-93; freelance writer, 1965—. Youth soccer coach Northport, N.Y., 1976-80, dir., 1979-80, Shaker Heights, Ohio, 1984-87, Swarthmore (Pa.) Recreation Assn., 1987-88; coach Johnson County (Kans.) Soccer League, 1983-84, U. Kans. Women's Soccer Club, 1980-81; bd. dirs. Suffolk County Heart Assn., L.I., 1974-75. Mem. Nat. Assn. Hispanic Journalists, Investigative Reporters and Editors. Democrat. Roman Catholic. Avocations: travel, fishing, outdoor sports, cooking. Home: 10413 Breckinridge Ln Fairfax VA 22030-3417 Office: The Washington Post 1150 15th St NW Washington DC 20071-0002

SAMSTEIN, BENJAMIN, transplant surgeon; b. NYC, Nov. 30, 1970; s. Julius and Nancy Samstein; m. TieMei Lee, May 30, 1999; 1 child, Emma Kaylee. MD, SUNY, Stony Brook, 1997. Cert. Am. Bd. Surgery, 2005. Chief resident Columbia U., NYC, 2003—04, transplant fellow, 2004—06, asst. prof. surgery, 2006—. Grantee Nat. Rsch. Svc. award, NIH, 2000—01. Office: Columbia U 622 West 168th St PH 14 Center Room New York NY 10032 Office Phone: 212-305-0914. Personal E-mail: bs212@columbia.edu.

SAMTEN, LOSANG, spiritual leader, artist; b. Ribuce Chang, Tibet, 1953; arrived in Nepal, 1959, arrived in India, 1961, arrived in US, 1988; Studied, Tibetan Inst. Performing Arts, Dharamsala, India; ordained as Buddhist monk, Namgyal Monastery, Dharamsala, India, 1967, M of Sutra and Tantra, 1985, completed intensive three and a half year training program in sand mandala painting; gave back monastic vows and entered lay practitioner's life, 1995; DD (hon.), Trinity Coll., Hartford, Conn., 1994; ArtD (hon.), Maine Coll. Art, Portland, 1995. Ritual dance master Namgyal Monastery, Dharamsala, India; personal attendant to the Dalai Lama, 1985—88; founder, spiritual dir. Tibetan Buddhist Ctr. of Phila., 1989—, Cenrezig Himalayan Cultural Ctr., El Paso, Tex., 1990—, Chenrezig Tibetan Buddhist Center, Middletown, Conn., 1994—, Lake Tahoe Chenrezig Ctr., Nev. Has created sand mandalas at, Am. Mus. Natural History, NYC, 1988, 1996, 2001, U. Pa. Mus. Archaeology and Anthropology, Phila., 1989, Natural History Mus., LA, 1989, 1999, Asian Mus. Art, San Francisco, 1991, Met. Mus. Art, NYC, 1994, Phila. Mus. Art, 1996, 1997, 2001, Temple Gallery, Phila., 2003, Phillips Mus. Franklin and Marshall Coll., Lancaster, Pa., 2003, Helena Art Mus., Mont., Nev. Art Mus., Reno; actor, religious advisor (films) Kundun, 1997. Nat. Heritage Fellowship, Nat. Endowment for the Arts, 2002, Pew Fellowship in the Arts, 2004. Office: Tibetan Buddhist Ctr of Phila 134 Heather Rd Upper Darby PA 19082

SAMUEL, CARREN C., hospital administrator; b. Jan. 7, 1959; arrived in U.S., 1977; d. George A. and Ira P. Dundas; m. Boysing Samuel, Sept. 17, 1984; children: Boysing Jr., Michael C. AS, N.Y.C. Tech. Coll., Bklyn., 1981; BS, L.I. U., Bklyn., 1984, MPA, 1991. Registered respiratory therapist Nat. Bd. Respiratory Care, 1984. Respiratory therapist Kingsbrook Jewish Med. Ctr., Bklyn., 1983—86, asst. dir. respiratory care, 1986—94, dir., respiratory care, 1994—2006, adminstrv. dir., cardiopulmonary svcs., 2001—. Mem.: Am. Assn. for Respiratory Care. Office: Kingsbrook Jewish Med Ctr 585 Schenectady Ave Brooklyn NY 11203

SAMUEL, GREG R., lawyer; b. Oklahoma City, June 24, 1960; s. James H. and Jan Margaret (Allen) S.; children: Emily Grace, Margaret Anne, Sara Katherine. BBA, Abilene Christian U., 1982; JD, Vanderbilt U., 1985. Assoc. Haynes and Boone, LLP, Dallas, 1985-92; ptnr., 1993—. Articles editor: Vanderbilt Law Rev. Mem. State Bar Tex. (chmn. corp. com. of bus. law section, 2003-2005). Office: Haynes and Boone LLP 901 Main St Ste 3100 Dallas TX 75202-3789 Office Phone: 214-651-5645. Business E-Mail: greg.samuel@haynesboone.com.

SAMUEL, MAY LINDA, environmental scientist; d. Joe and Elvira Dixon; m. Earl Samuel; children: Annette Heyward, April Heyward. BS in Biology and Chemistry magna cum laude, Benedict Coll., 1977; MPH in Environ. Health Sci., U. SC, 1982; DD, Inst. Christian Works Coll. and Sem., 1996, PhD, ThD, 1999. Broadcaster Radio Sta. WGCV, Columbia, SC, 1984—86; asst. dir. environ. health scis. Benedict Coll., Columbia, 1990—; exec. dir. SC Environ Econ. Justice Network, Columbia, 2003—. Prof. biology Allen U., Columbia, 1984—86; cons. Inst. for Energy and Environ. Rsch., Tacoma Park, Md., 1999—2004. Contbr. articles to profl. jours. Founder, pastor Light of the World Ch., Winnsboro, SC, 1995—. Recipient SC Dept. Health and Environ. Control award, 1990, SC Dept. Corrections award, 1990; grantee, Dept. of Energy, 1995—97, EPA, 1996—99, Assn. Environ. Health, 2002—03, Sierra Club, 2003. Avocations: travel, reading. Office: Benedict Coll 1600 Harden St Columbia SC 29204-1058 Business E-Mail: samuelm@benedict.edu.

SAMUEL, PAUL, retired cardiologist; b. Janoshaza, Hungary, Feb. 17, 1927; arrived in U.S., 1954, naturalized, 1960; s. Adolf and Magda (Zoliner) Samuel; m. Gabriella R. Zeichner, Mar. 27, 1954; children: Robert Mark, Adrianne Jill. Baccalaureat, Kemeny Zsigmond Gymnasium, Budapest, Hungary, 1945; MD, U. Paris, 1953. Intern Queens Hosp. Ctr., NYC, 1954-55; resident LI Jewish Med. Ctr., New Hyde Park, NY, 1959-61; pvt. practice Forest Hills, NY, 1961—2000; adj. prof. Rockefeller U., NYC, 1971-81; adj. prof. medicine Cornell U., NYC, 1979—; ret., 2000. Dir. Arteriosclerosis Rsch. Lab. LI Jewish-Hillside Med. Ctr., New Hyde Park, 1961—2001; chmn. NY Lipid Rsch. Club Rockefeller U., 1977—78; clin. prof. medicine Albert Einstein Coll. Medicine, Bronx, NY, 1981—. Contbr. articles to profl. jours. Fellow: Am. Coll. Cardiology; mem.: ACP, Am. Fedn. Clin. Rsch., Am. Heart Assn. (fellow coun. arteriosclerosis, Disting. Achievement award), Harvey Soc. Home: 25 Nassau Dr Great Neck NY 11021-2163

SAMUEL, RALPH DAVID, lawyer; b. Augusta, Ga., May 8, 1945; s. Ralph and Louise Elizabeth (Wurreschke) S.; m. Lynn Christel Malmgren, June 12, 1971; children: Lynn Britt, Ralph Erik. AB, Dartmouth Coll., 1967; JD, Dickinson Sch. of Law, 1972. Bar: Pa. 1972, U.S. Dist. Ct. (ea. dist.) Pa. 1972, U.S. Ct. Appeals (3d cir.) 1973, U.S. Supreme Ct. 1976. Law clk. to hon. judge John P. Fullam U.S. Dist. Ct. (ea. dist.) Pa., Phila., 1972-74; assoc. MacCoy, Evans & Lewis., Phila., 1974-76; ptnr. Samuel and Ballard, P.C., Phila., 1976-98; pres., CEO Ralph D. Samuel & Co., P.C., Phila., 1998—. Established Samuel Poetry Fellow Dartmouth Coll., Hanover, N.H., 1994. *For over 30 years Ralph Samuel has fought for the rights of individual Americans to enjoy their civil rights, live and work free from discrimination, and to be fairly and adequately compensated for physical and economic injury. In 1977 he represented the appellants in taking on the nation's chief prosecutor, Hon. Richard Thornburgh, in argument to the U.S. Supreme Court in the landmark Fifth Amendment case by which Ralph Samuel secured the right of an accused to immediate appeal when threatened with double jeopardy. Abney, et al. v. United States, 431 U.S. 651, unanimous opinion by Chief Justice Burger. Additionally, Ralph Samuel has successfully represented clients at all levels of the Pennsylvania state and federal courts. The law office of Ralph D. Samuel & Co., P.C. currently provides consultations and accepts selected representation of individuals, at all levels of compensation, to achieve their optimal results in employment conflicts, injury and other civil cases.* Contbr. articles to profl. jours., poetry to publs. Trustee The George Sch., Newtown, Pa., 1983-90; chmn. bd. dirs. Stapeley in Germantown,

1985-90; mem. Chase Fund Com., 2000; chmn. budget com. Phila. Yearly Meeting of Friends, 1991-93; bd. dirs., mem. fin. com. Phila. Ranger Corps., 1992-94; pres. Cedar Park Neighbors, Phila., 1975-78, West Mt. Airy Neighbors, Phila., 1981-82. Mem. Pa. Soc. Athenaeum of Phila., Sunday Breakfast Club. Mem. Soc. Of Friends. Avocations: music, writing, squash, tennis. Office: PO Box 35185 Philadelphia PA 19128-0185 Fax: (215) 701-1085. Office Phone: 215-893-9992. E-mail: RalphSamuel@RalphSamuel.com.

**SAMUEL, ROBERT THOMPSON,** optometrist; b. Kansas City, Mo., June 27, 1944; s. Manlius Thompson and Helen Evelyn (Syverson) S. BA, William Jewell Coll., 1966; postgrad., U. Mo., Kansas City, 1967; MS, U. Mo., 1968; DOptometry, U. Tenn., Memphis, 1971; postgrad., U. Mo., St. Louis, 1995, Northeastern State U., 1998. Cert. optometrist Mo. Buyer Recco Inc., Kansas City, Mo., 1963-67; histology lab. instr. William Jewell Coll., Liberty, Mo., 1965-66; pvt. practice optometry Gladstone, Mo., 1972—; staff doctor O.H. Gerry Optical Clinics, 1996—. Panel doctor Ford Motor Co., Claycomo, Mo., 1985—, Union Pacific R.R., Kansas City, 1985—, TWA Airlines, 1990, Union Carbide, 1990. Publicity coord. Rep. Party, Kansas City, Mo., 1975-76; chmn. Save Your Vision Week, Kansas City, 1977; mem. Theatre League of Kansas City, 1976—, Kansas City Mus., 1986—, Friends of Art, 1985, Friends of Mo. Town 1955, 1980—. Recipient Outstanding Young Men of Am. award Jaycees, 1978, Good Citizens award DAR, 1962. Mem. Am. Optometric Assn., Mo. Optometric Assn., Optometric Soc. Greater Kansas City, Heart of Am. Contact Lens Congress, Am. Acad. Sports Vision, Vol. Optometric Svcs. for Humanity, Smithsonian Assocs., Lions (exec. bd. dir. Lions Eye Clinic 1974-84, bd. dirs. 1982—, Outstanding Svc. award 1973, 74, editor Lions Optometric Ctr. Quar. 1974-84), Kappa Alpha Order (treas. 1966). Republican. Lutheran. Avocations: photography, music, piano, swimming, travel. Home: 6325 N Monroe Ave Kansas City MO 64119-1923 Office: 1170 W 152 Hwy Liberty MO 64068-2035 also: 5601 NE Antioch Rd Kansas City MO 64119-2302 Office Phone: 816-453-7290.

**SAMUELI, HENRY,** electrical engineer, educator, entrepreneur; b. Buffalo, Sept. 20, 1954; s. Aron and Sala (Traubman) S.; m. Susan Faye Eisenberg, Aug. 22, 1982; children: Leslie Pamela, Jillian Meryl, Erin Sydney. BSEE, UCLA, 1975, MSEE, 1976, PhD in Elec. Engring., 1980. Staff engr. TRW Inc., Redondo Beach, Calif., 1980-83, section mgr., 1983-85; asst. prof. UCLA, 1985-90, assoc. prof., 1990-94, prof., 1994—95, disting. adj. prof., elec. engring. and computer sci., 2003—. Cons. TRW, Inc., Redondo Beach, 1985-89; co-founder, chief scientist PairGain Techs., Inc., Tustin, Calif., 1988-94; co-founder, chief tech. officer Broadcom Corp., Irvine, Calif., 1991-, v.p. rsch. & devel. & co-chmn., 1991-2003, chmn., 2003-; purchased Mighty Ducks of Anaheim NHL, 2005-. Named one of Top 20 Entrepreneurs of 1997, The Red Herring Mag., 1997, one of Top 50 Cyber Elite, Time Digital Mag., 1997; Schs. Engring. at both U. Calif. Irvine and UCLA named in honor of; recipient Presdl. award, U. Calif., 2000, Irvine medal, 2000, Alumnus of Yr. award, UCLA Sch. of Engring. and Applied Sci., 2000. Fellow: IEEE (Circuits and Systems Soc. Indsl. Pioneer award 2000), Am. Acad. Arts & Sci.; mem.: NAE. Republican. Jewish. Named inventor in 22 U.S. patents. Office: Broadcom Corp 16215 Alton Pkwy Irvine CA 92618 Address: U Calif Irvine Henry Samueli Sch Engring Elec Engring and Computer Sci 325 Engineering Tower Irvine CA 92697-2625

**SAMUELL, TIECHERA DAWN,** language educator; d. Alvin Enis and Betty Jeanette House; m. Christopher Michael Samuell, May 26, 2001. BA, Western Ill. U., Macomb, 1997—2001; MA, SE Mo. State U., Cape Girardeau, 2001—03. Edn. and career devel. coord. Boys & Girls Club, Cape Girardeau, 2001—04; writing ctr. assoc., adj. faculty SE Mo. State U. 2003—04; faculty Three Rivers CC, Poplar Bluff, Mo., 2004—. Mem. Mo. Assn. Tchrs. English, Nat. Coun. Tchrs. English. Office: Three Rivers CC 2080 Three Rivers Blvd Poplar Bluff MO 63901 Business E-Mail: tsamuell@trcc.edu.

**SAMUELS, DONALD L.,** lawyer; b. Washington, May 8, 1961; s. Jack Donald Samuels and Francis Diane (Katcher) Yeoman; m. Sherri Tobin Samuels. BA, Brown U., 1983; JD, Columbia U., 1986. Bar: Calif. 1986, Calif. 1988, Tex. 1998, U.S. Dist. Ct. (cen., no., ea. and so. dists.), U.S. Dist. Ct. Colo. 1997, U.S. Ct. Appeals (9th cir.) 1989, Colo. 1996, U.S. Ct. Appeals (7th cir.) 1996, U.S. Ct. Appeals (10th cir.) 1997, U.S. Supreme Ct. 2004. Law clk. Hon. William D. Keller, L.A., 1986-87; assoc. Sidley & Austin, L.A., 1987-94, ptnr., 1994-95, Samuels & Samuels, L.A. 1995-97; officer, dir., shareholder Ireland & Stapleton, Denver, 1997—2002; ptnr. Holme, Roberts & Owen, LLP, Denver, 2002—. Mem. ABA, Calif. Bar Assn., Colo. Bar Assn., Tex. Bar Assn., Phi Beta Kappa. Home: 5692 S Florence St Greenwood Village CO 80111-3713 Office: Holme Roberts & Owen LLP Ste 4100 1700 Lincoln St Denver CO 80203-4541 Office Phone: 303-866-0548. Business E-Mail: donald.samuels@hro.com.

**SAMUELS, DOROTHY J.,** journalist, writer; b. NYC, May 15, 1951; d. Herman and Roz Silver; m. Peter G. Samuels, Dec. 26, 1971; children: Laurah, Tom, Jenny. AB, Bryn Mawr Coll., 1972; JD, Northeastern U., 1975. Bar: NY. Atty. Brown & Wood, NYC, 1975—76; exec. dir. Com. for Pub. Justice, NYC, 1976—79, N.Y. Civil Liberties Union, NYC, 1979—81; cons. Ford Found., NYC, 1981—83. Mem. editl. bd. NY Times, NYC, 1985—. Author: (novels) Filthy Rich, 2001; contbr. book Then and Now, 2000, articles to mags. Office: NY Times 229 W 43d St New York NY 10036 E-mail: dosamu@aol.com.

**SAMUELS, FERN JACQUELINE,** artist, educator; b. Chgo., Feb. 16, 1931; d. Noah S. and Ann (Zager) Andrews; m. Howard Stanley Samuels, Sept. 17, 1950 (dec.); children: Mitchell, Paul, David. BFA, Loyola U., 1973; MFA, Sch. Art Inst. Chgo., 1983. Instr.-coord. Mundelein Coll., Chgo. 1976-83; faculty Columbia Coll., Chgo., 1978-2000. Instr. workshops Field Mus., Chgo., 1976, Lake Forest Coll., Chgo., 1976 Lincoln Park Cultural Ctr. Chgo., 1973, Ill. inst. Tech., Chgo., 1980— Latin Sch., Chgo., 1976; juror St. Louis Arts Guild, 1998. One-women shows include Northwestern U., 1988, Ea. Ill. U., Chgo., 1989, Countryside Gallery, 1988, Upstart Gallery, 1990, Soho 20, N.Y.C., 1993, Loyola U., 1995, Morraine Valley Coll., 1995, McDonough Mus. Art, 1997, Fyr Place Gallery, 2000, Gallery on Azeele, 2000, Mos Art Gallery, Lake Park, Fla., 2004, Cornell Mus., Del Ray, Fla., 2004 (1st award), City Hall, Palm Beach Gardens, 2007; exhibited in group shows including Smithsonian Air and Space Mus., 1983, Freeport Mus., 1995, Rockford Mus., 1996, Butler Inst. Am. Art, 1998, Lafayette Mus., 1999, Columbus Mus. Art, 2000, So. Ohio Mus., 2000, South Bend Regional Mus., 2000, Univ. Mus. S.D., 2001, Gallery 228, N.Y.C., 2003. Mem. LWV, Chgo., 1969—; founding mem. Alternative Fibers, Chgo., 1982; chairperson, coord. Seven Ethnic Museums, Chgo., 1986; membership chmn. ARC Gallery, Chgo., 1983-86, pres. 1988-90; bd. dirs. Artist Book Works, Chgo., 1992-93. Recipient Best of Show award Women in the Visual Arts, Boca Raton, Fla., 2001, Judges Recognition award, Boca Raton, 2001, 2nd award Boca Mus. Artists Guild, 2001, 1st award 2002, 1st prize Women in Visual Arts, Del Ray, Fla., 2002, Mus. Exhibits, 2002, Jewish Mus., Miami, Norton Mus., West Palm Beach, Fla., 2002, 2004, Cornell Mus. of Art and Sci., Del Ray, 2002, Art Club Chgo., 2003, Permanent Collection, Rutgers U., 2003, 1st award Northwood U., West Palm Beach, Fla., 2003, 1st award Boca Mus. Artist Guild, 2003; grantee Columbia Coll., 1981; Fern Samuels Scholarship Fund est. Columbia Coll., Chgo., 1st award Milagro Art Ctr., Del Ray, Fla., 2003, 1st award Boca Mus. Artist Guild, 2003, Artist Guild Inc 1st award 2005, Women in the Visual Arts 1st award, 2005, Fla. Artist's Group, 2nd award, 2005. Mem. Nat. Mus. Women Artists, Internat. Soc. Exptl. Artists, Nat. Collage Soc., Arts Club Chgo., Chgo. Soc. Arts, City of Hope (Bobby Blechman chpt. founding mem.), Sch. Art Inst. Chgo. Alumni (2d prize 2002). Democrat. Avocations: reading, music, theater, exercise. Home: 114A Palm Bay Dr S Palm Beach Gardens FL 33418 E-mail: ucars1@aol.com.

**SAMUELS, JOHN M., JR.,** industrial engineer; B in Indsl. Engring., GM Inst.; M in Indsl. Engring., PhD in Indsl. Engring., Penn. State U. Assoc. prof. indsl. engring. Penn. State U.; numerous positions GM; with Conrail, 1978—96, Norfolk (Va.) So. Corp., 1998—, sr. v.p. ops. planning and

support, 1998—. Mem. exec. com. Transp. Rsch. Bd., 1998-2003, past chmn. exec. com., 2001. Chmn. Accreditation Bd. Engring. and Tech., 2004; chmn. adv. bd. Old Dominion U. Coll. Engring., 2004. Fellow Inst. Indsl. Engrs. (sr. mem.), World Acad. Productivity Sci.; mem. NAE, Am. Rlwy. Engring. Assn. (sr. mem.), Alpha Pi Mu, Tau Beta Pi, Sigma Xi. Office: Norfolk So Corp 3 Commercial Pl Norfolk VA 23510-9237

**SAMUELS, LESLIE B.,** lawyer; b. St. Louis, Nov. 10, 1942; s. Joseph E. and Dorothy J. (Bernstein) S.; m. Judith B. Thorn, June 19, 1966 (div. Aug. 1976); children: Colin T., Polly B.; m. Augusta H. Gross, Nov. 6, 1980. BS in Econs., U. Pa., 1963; LLB magna cum laude, Harvard U., 1966; postgrad., London Sch. Econs., 1966-67. Bar: N.Y., 1969, U.S. Dist. Ct. (so. dist.) N.Y. 1973, U.S. Tax Ct., 1980, U.S. Supreme Ct. 1994; CPA. Tax analyst Gulf Oil Co., London, 1967-68; assoc. Cleary Gottlieb Steen & Hamilton LLP, NYC, 1968-75, ptnr., 1975-93, 96—; asst. sec. for tax policy U.S. Dept. Treasury, Washington, 1993-96; vice-chair com. fiscal affairs OECD, 1994-96. Mem. Pres.'s Com. on the Arts and the Humanities, Washington, 1994-96. Editor Law Rev.; contbr. articles to profl. jours. Dir. Lower Manhattan Cultural Coun., N.Y.C., 1981-93, Roy Lichtenstein Found., N.Y.C., 1999—; active Carter-Mondale Transition Planning Group, Washington, 1976-77. Fulbright fellow London Sch. Econs., 1966-67. Mem. N.Y. State Bar Assn., Assn. of Bar of City of N.Y., Harvard Club (N.Y.C.). Democrat. Office: Cleary Gottlieb Steen & Hamilton LLP One Liberty Plaza New York NY 10006 Office Phone: 212-225-2250. Business E-Mail: lsamuels@cgsh.com.

**SAMUELS, LESLIE EUGENE,** marketing consultant, management consultant; b. St. Croix, V.I., Nov. 12, 1929; s. Henry Francis and Annamartha Venetia (Ford) S.; m. Reather James, Oct. 24, 1959; children: Leslie Jr., Venetia, Yvette, Philip. MusB, NYU, 1956; JD, Blackstone Sch. Law, 1975; MBA, Columbia Pacific U., 1984, PhD, 1985. Concert soloist Van Dyke Studios, N.Y.C., 1956-65; dir. Housing, Preservation and Devel., N.Y.C., 1966—; bandmaster N.Y. State Dept. Rehab. and Recreation, N.Y.C., 1967-76; pres., CEO Samuels and Co., Inc., N.Y.C., 1986—, Coll. Philosophy and Edn., 1998—; exec. dir., CEO Samuels Inst. Hist. Rsch. of Christian Prins., 1991—. Cons. in field., 1984—; mem. N.Y., N.J. Minority Bus. Purchasing Coun., Inc., Nat. Minority Bus. Coun., Inc., Internat. Trade divsn.; evangelist, lectr. Principles of the Christian Faith; adj. prof. St. Martin's Coll. and Sem., 1995; dir. pvt. sch. state edn. dept., 1996. TV apperances include: Bill Silbert's Rev., 1953, Ladies Day, 1953; Author: Redemption, 2000. Mem. chmn. congrl. coun. of the Virgin Island, 1960-64, Bronx County Com., 1969; dist. leader Bronx 86th Assembly Dist., 1969; advisor Astor Home for Children, Bronx, 1973, Bronxville Cl. of C., Bklyn., 1975; charter mem. Rep. Presdl. Task Force, 1989; exec. dir. Samuels Inst. Hist. Rsch. Christian Principles, 1991—; mem. Nat. Rep. Senatorial Com., 1992. With U.S. Army, 1951-53. Mem. Maison Internationale des Intellectuels, Am. Mgmt. Assn., Nat. Black MBA Assn., Harvard Bus. Rev., Sloan Mgmt. Rev., Calif. Mgmt. Rev., Columbia Pacific U. Alumni Assn., Internat. Platform Assn., Smithsonian Assocs., Ind. Citizen's Club (pres. Bronx 1967-77). Republican. Avocation: sports. Home: 2814 Bruner Ave Bronx NY 10469-3403 E-mail: samuelsinstitut@webtv.net.

**SAMUELS, LOUIS EDWARD,** cardiothoracic surgeon; b. Mineola, N.Y., Mar. 20, 1961; s. Nathan Lester and Beverly Ann Samuels; m. Fania Leiderman, June 10, 1984; children: Rosa Dora, Sara Paula, Marissa Raya. Med. degree, Hahnemann U., Phila., 1987. Lic. Am. Bd. Thoracic Surgery. Surg. dir. of cardiac transplantation, dir. artificial heart program Hahnemann Hosp., Phila., 1997—2003; surg. dir. cardiac transplantation Lankenau Hosp., Wynnewood, Pa., 2003—. Mem.: Am. Assn. for Thoracic Surgery, Soc. of Thoracic Surgeons, Alpha Omega Alpha. Achievements include research in Totally Implantable Electric Artificial Heart. Office: Lankenau Hosp MSB Ste 280 100 Lancaster Ave Wynnewood PA 19096 Office Phone: 610-896-9255. Office Fax: 610-896-1947. E-mail: samuelsl@mlhs.org.

**SAMUELS, MARC,** healthcare consultant; b. Bethesda, Md., Feb. 8, 1968; s. Monica (Leiter) Samuels; 1 child, Jeb. BA cum laude, U. Mich., 1989; MPH in Policy and Adminstrn., Yale U., 1992; JD, U. Tex., 1996. Staff asst. McManis Assocs., Health Care Consultants, Washington, Law Offices of Deborah L. Steelman, Washington, Office of Policy Devel., The White House, Washington, V.P.'s Domestic Policy Office, Washington; health care cons. legis. asst., health law sect. Jenkens & Gilchrist PC, Austin, Tex.; asst. to Gov. for Health Policy, Office of Gov. George W. Bush, Austin, Tex.; personal asst. to commr. Tex. Health and Human Svcs. Commn., Austin, Tex.; prin. Samuels Health Strategies, Austin, Tex. Mem. adv. bd. U. Houston Health Law and Policy Inst.; advisor Tex. Lifescience Found., Austin. Co-author: The Managed Care Answer Book, 1996, 4th edit., 1999, Risk Contracting and Capitation Answer Book, 1998, 2d edit., 1999; contbr. articles to profl. jours. Dep. rsch. dir. Kay Bailey Hutchison for U.S. Senate, 1993; health care policy advisor George W. Bush for Gov., 1994, Jeb Bush for Gov., 1998, Bush for Pres. Campaign Exploratory Com., 1999; chmn. A Policy Forum for Young Am., 1996. Spencer Scholar Risk & Ins. Mgmt. Soc., 1996; recipient Baker and Botts prize, 1996. Business E-Mail: msamuels@hillcopartners.com.

**SAMUELS, MARK A.,** lawyer; b. LA, 1957; BA, U. Calif., Berkeley, 1979; JD, U. Calif., LA, 1982. Bar: Calif. 1982, US Dist. Ct., Ctrl. Dist. Calif. 1982, US Ct. Appeals, 9th Cir. 1983, US Dist. Ct., So. and No. Districts of Calif. 1984, US Dist. Ct., Ea. Dist. Calif. 1987, US Ct. Appeals, Fed. Cir. 1991. Ptnr. O'Melveny & Myers LLP, LA, chair, intellectual property & technology dept. Mem. LA Superior Ct. Arbitration Panel. Mem. U. Calif LA Law Review, 1980—81, chief mng. editor, 1981—82. Bd. dir. U. Calif. LA Sch. Law Alumni Assn. Named one of Top 25 Intellectual Property Lawyers, LA Daily Jour. Mem.: Calif. State Bar Assn (mem. intellectual property sect.), Assn. of Bus. Trial Lawyers, Fed. Cir. Bar Assn., Am. Intellectual Property Law Assn., LA County Bar Assn., ABA (liaison, lawyers conf. task force on reduction of litig. cost & delay 1993), Order of the Coif, Thunderbird Racing Club (bd. dir., treas.), Phi Beta Kappa. Office: O'Melveny & Myers LLP 400 S Hope St Los Angeles CA 90071-2899 Office Phone: 213-430-6340. Office Fax: 213-430-6407. Business E-Mail: msamuels@omm.com.

**SAMUELS, MAURICE ANTHONY,** French literature educator; b. Chgo., Aug. 9, 1968; s. Richard Arthur and Virginia Corbisella Samuels. BA, Harvard U., Cambridge, Mass., 1990; PhD, Harvard U., 2000. Asst. prof. of French U. of Pa., Phila., 2000—06; prof. of French Yale U., New Haven, 2006—. Author: (book academic) The Spectacular Past: Popular History and the Novel in Nineteenth-Century France. Office Phone: 203-432-4900.

**SAMUELS, SANDOR ELI,** diversified financial services company executive, lawyer; b. LA, Aug. 22, 1952; m. Claudia Wallack; 3 children. AB summa cum laude, Princeton, 1974; JD, UCLA, 1977. Bar: Calif. 1977, US Dist. Ct. Ctrl. Dist. Calif. 1977. Law clk. Hon. Irving Hill, US Dist. Ct. Ctrl. Dist. Calif., 1977—79; atty. Munger, Tolles and Olson, 1979—83, First Interstate Bancorp, 1984—88, sr. v.p., gen. counsel, sec. 1988; sr. v.p., gen. counsel Fox Inc., 1989—90; sr. v.p., gen. counsel, sec. Countrywide Fin. Corp., Calabasas, Calif., 1990—91, mng. dir., legal, gen. counsel. sec., 1991—2000, sr. mng. dir., legal, gen. counsel, sec., 2001—03 sr. mng. dir., chief legal advisor, sec., 2003—. Bd. dirs. U. Judaism, Ziegler Sch. Rabbinic Studies, Shalhevet Sch., Bet Tzedek Legal Services, Adat Ari El Synagogue. Mem.: Mortgage Bankers Assn. Am. (chmn. legal services com. 1995—96), State Bar Calif., LA County Bar Assn., ABA, Order of the Coif. Office: Countrywide Fin Corp 4500 Park Granada Calabasas CA 91302-1613

**SAMUELS, WILLIAM MASON,** physiology association executive; b. Dover, Ohio, Jan. 17, 1929; s. William Mason and Hernia (Fankhauser) S.; m. Joanne Gorenflo, Oct. 2, 1971; children: Robert Lee, Ann Frances. AB, U. Ky., 1951; postgrad., Georgetown U., 1952. Mng. editor for Ind., Courier-Jour. & Times, Louisville, 1955-65; dir. office of v.p. U. Ky. Med. Center, Lexington, 1965-70; exec. dir. Am. Soc. Allied Health Professions, Washington, 1973—78; assoc. Schs. Allied Health Professions, 1970—73; exec. dir. Am. Assn. Blood Banks, Washington, 1978-80, Nat. Soc. Med. Research Washington 1980-84, Am. Physiol. Soc., Bethesda, Md., 1984-92;

retired, 1992—. Contbr. articles to profl. jours. Mem. secretariat Nat. Commn. Health Certifying Agys.; v.p. Coalition Health Funding; cons. to fed. agys.; vol. Habitat for Humanity, Boca Raton; elder Presbyn. Ch., corp. dir. With USAF, 1951-53, USAFR, 1954-76, lt. col. ret. Named Ky. Man of Yr. Sigma Phi Epsilon, 1968 Mem.: AMA (coun. on allied health edn. accreditation), Washington Soc. Assn. Execs., Health Staff Soc., Am. Hosp. Assn. (coun. on edn.), Am. Optometric Assn. (coun. on edn., coun. on optimetric clin. care, nat. commn. on paraoptometric cert.), Am. Soc. Assn. Execs., Pinehurst (NC) Country Club, Lions. Presbyterian. Home: 6055 S Verde Trail H-120 Boca Raton FL 33433-4406

**SAMUELSON, CECIL O., JR.,** academic administrator; b. 1942; m. Sharon Giauque; 5 children. BS, MS, MD, U. Utah. V.p. health scis. U. Utah, Salt Lake City, 1970-90; sr. v.p. Intermountain Health Care, Inc., Salt Lake City, 1990—94; dean IHC Hosps. Inc., Salt Lake City, 1990—; pres. BYU, Provo, Utah, 2003—. Pres. LDS Ch. No. Area, Utah; Pres. LDS Ch. Europe No. Area; mem. First Quorum of the Seventy, Ch. of LDS, 1994—2003. Office: Office of the Pres Brigham Young U Provo UT 84602*

**SAMUELSON, DONALD B.,** former state legislator; b. Brainerd, Minn., Aug. 23, 1932; s. Walter H. and Ellen (Gallagher) S.; m. Nancy O'Brien, 1952; children: Stephen, Laura, Paula, Christine. Chmn. 6th Dist. Com. on Polit. Edn. State of Minn., 1960-66; mem. Minn. Ho. of Reps., St. Paul, 1969-76, 1981-82, Minn. Senate from 12th dist., St. Paul, 1982—; pres. Minn. Senate, St. Paul, 2000—02. Chmn. Health & Human Svc. Fin. Div. Com., mem. Commerce and Consumer Protection, mem. Family Svc. Com., mem. Fin. and Health Care Com.; former foreman Bor-Son Construct Co.; union bus. mgr. Chmn. 6th Dist. Com. on Polit. Edn., Minn., 1960-66; mem. State Cmt. Com. Dem-Farmer-Labor Party, 1964-66, former chmn. Crow Wing County. Mem. Housing and Redevel. Authority, Minn. AFL-CIO, Bricklayers Union, Am. Legion, Eagles. Democrat. Home: 1018 Portland Ave Brainerd MN 56401-4133

**SAMUELSON, DOUGLAS ALAN,** information technology executive; b. Reno, Nev., July 27, 1948; s. Norman Harold and Shirley (Leder) Samuelson; m. Francine Ruth Kimel, Jan. 7, 1979 (div. Aug. 7, 2003); children: Andrew, Diane. BA, U. Calif., Berkeley, 1969; MS, George Washington U., 1981, DSc, 1990. Computer systems analyst Bank Am., San Francisco, 1972-73; cons. San Rafael, Calif., 1973-75; ops. rsch. analyst U.S. Govt., Washington, 1975-82; analyst, v.p. Micro-Zeit/Internat. Telesystems Corp., Reston, Va., 1983-88; asst. prof. Memphis State U., 1990-92; pres. InfoLogix, Inc., Annandale, Va., 1988—; prin. scientist Puma Sys., Inc., Falls Church, Va., 1997-98; chief statistician FMAS Dyncorp., Columbia, Md., 2000; sr. analyst Synergia LLC, 2004, Homeland Security Inst., 2005—. Vis. rsch. scholar George Washington U., 1993—95, mem. nat. adv. coun. Sch. Engring. and Applied Sci., 1996—2000, adj. prof. lectr., 1997—; adj. assoc. prof. George Mason U., Fairfax, Va., 1994—96, external rsch. prof. Krasnow Inst. Advanced Study, 2001—03; adj. assoc. prof. U. Pa., Phila., 2001—. Co-editor, author (with others): Human Rights and Statistics: Getting the Record Straight, 1992, Health Information and Ethics: Protecting Fundamental Human Rights, 1997, columnist: The Oracle, 1986—; contbr. articles to profl. jours. Mem.: AAAS, Inst. Ops. Rsch. and Mgmt. Sci. (bd. dirs. 1998—2000), Am. Statis. Assn. (chair com. sci. freedom and human rights 1985—88), Washington OR/MS Coun. (pres. 1989—90, 1996—97), George Washington U. Engr. Alumni Assn. (bd. dirs. 1994—, v.p. 1996—98, pres. 1998—2000). Democrat. Jewish. Achievements include patent for systems for regulating arrivals of customers to servers. Office: InfoLogix Inc 8711 Chippendale Ct Annandale VA 22003-3807 Office Phone: 703-978-5030. Personal E-mail: samuelsondoug@yahoo.com.

**SAMUELSON, FRED BINDER,** artist, educator; b. Harvey, Ill., Nov. 29, 1925; s. Frederick Gustav and Theresa Marie (Binder) S.; children: Fredric Michael, Lisa Maria. BFA, Art Inst. Chgo., 1951, MFA, 1953. Head lithography dept. Instituto Allende, San Miguel Allende, Gauanajuanto, Mex., 1955-63, head grad. studies, 1964—; faculty clmn. San Antonio Art Inst., 1963-64. Condr. seminars Laredo Art Assn., 1964, 71, 78, Hill County Art Found., Ingram Tex., 1967—; Brownsville, Beaumont, Lamesa art leagues, Lubbock Art Assn., San Antonio Watercolor Soc., Carrizo Lodge, Ruidoso, N.Mex., Houston Water Color Soc., Laguna Gloria Mus., Austin, Tex. Represented in permanent collections Galeria Moderna, Banjaluka, Yugoslavia; executed mural for Conv. Ctr., Hemisfair, 1968. Served with USAAF, 1943-45. Recipient numerous hon. mentions, 1953—, purchase prizes, including Denver Art Mus., Joslyn Art Mus., Omaha, Mulvane Art Mus., Topeka, Okla. Art Ctr., Hertzberg Gallery, San Antonio, Witte Mus., San Antonio, Ohio U., Athens. Home: 221 Brasswood Ct Daytona Beach FL 32117-7127

**SAMUELSON, KENNETH LEE,** lawyer; b. Natrona Heights, Pa., Aug. 22, 1946; s. Sam and Frances Bernice (Robbins) Samuelson; m. Marlene Ina Rabinowitz, Jan. 1, 1980; children: Heather, Cheryl. BA magna cum laude, U. Pitts., 1968; JD, U. Mich., 1971. Bar: Md. 1972, DC 1980, U.S. Dist. Ct. (trial bar) Md. 1984. Assoc. Weinberg & Green, Balt., 1971-73, Dickerson, Nice, Sokol & Horn, Balt., 1973; asst. atty. gen. State of Md., 1973-77; pvt. practice Balt., 1978; ptnr. Linowes and Blocher, Silver Spring, Md., 1979-93, Semmes, Bowen & Semmes, Balt. and Washington, 1993—95, Wilkes Artis, Chartered, Washington, 1995—2001, Deckelbaum Ogens & Raftery, Washington, 2001—, Bethesda, Md., 2001—. Spkr. in field. Bd. govs. Washington Bldg. Congress, 1990—2002; bd. dirs. DC Assn. Retarded Citizens, Inc., 1986—2001; speaker Harvard Bus. Sch. Club of Washington, 2006. Mem.: ABA (co-chair tech. com. 1999—, coun. mem. sect. real property, probate and trust law 2000—), moderator various programs), Internat. Assn. Attys. and Exec. in Corp. Real Estate, Am. Inns of Ct. (speaker at bankruptcy programs), Montgomery County Bar Assn. (mem. jud. selections com 1988— 90), Internat. Shopping Ctrs. (organized co-faculty program "univ." 1988, NAFTA 1992, condemnations 1994, leasing 1997, high tech. effects 1998, pub./pvt. partnerships 1999), E. Coast Builders Conf., Apt. and Office Bldg. Assn. Met. Washington, Civil Code Drafting Com. Russian Legis., Nat. Assn. Corp. Real Estate Execs., Washington Assn. Realtors, Inc., DC Bldg. Industry Assn., Am. Arbitration Assn. (arbitrator, mediator 1995—2003), Md. Inst. Continuing Profl. Edn. Lawyers, Md. Bar Assn. (litig. sect. 1982—84, real property, planning and zoning sect., chmn. comml. trans. com.), DC Bar (mem. comml. real estate com., chmn. legal opinions project), Am. Coll. Real Estate Lawyers (moderator, speaker various programs), Lambda Alpha, Phi Beta Kappa. Office: Deckelbaum Ogens & Raftery Chartered # 165 2020 Pennsylvania Ave NW Washington DC 20006 Office Phone: 301-347-3469. Personal E-mail: ksamuelson@deckelbaum.com.

**SAMUELSON, KRISTIN WEAVER,** clinical psychologist, educator; b. Fairfax, Va., Feb. 11, 1971; d. Kelly Edward and Cheryl Lynn Weaver; m. Eric John Samuelson, May 28, 2006. PhD, U. Va., 1999. Lic. psychologist Calif. Asst. prof. Calif. Sch. of Profl. Psychology at Alliant Internat. U., San Francisco; rsch. psychologist San Francisco VA Med. Ctr., 2001—. Contbr. articles to profl. jours. (Mensa Award for Excellence, Gifted Rsch. New Investigator of Yr. 1998). Mem.: APA. Office: Alliant Internat U Ste 100 1 Beach St San Francisco CA 94133 Office Phone: 415-955-2119. Office Fax: 415-955-2178. Business E-Mail: krfranklin@alliant.edu.

**SAMUELSON, PAUL ANTHONY,** economist, educator; b. Gary, Ind., May 15, 1915; s. Frank and Ella (Lipton) Samuelson; m. Marion E. Crawford, July 2, 1938 (dec.); children: Jane Kendall, Margaret Wray, William Frank, Robert James, John Crawford, Paul Reid; m. Risha Eckaus, 1981; 1 stepchild, Susan Miller. BA, U. Chgo., 1935; MA, Harvard U., 1936, PhD (David A. Wells prize 1941) 1941; LLD (hon.), U. Chgo., Oberlin Coll., 1961, Boston Coll., 1964, Ind. U., 1966, U. Mich., 1967, Claremont Grad. Sch., 1967, Seton Hall U., 1971, U. N.H., 1971, Keio U., 1971, Widener Coll., 1982, Cath. U. at Riva Aguero U., Lima, Peru, 1980, Harvard, 1972, Gustavus Adolphus Coll., 1974, U. So. Calif., 1975, U. Pa., 1976, U. Rochester, 1976, Emmanuel Coll., 1977, Stonehill Coll., 1978, Indiana U. of Pa., 1993; DLitt (hon.), Ripon Coll., 1962, No. Mich. U., 1973, Valparaiso U., 1987, Columbia U., 1988; LHD (hon.), Williams Coll., 1971; DSc (hon.), U. Mass., 1972, U. R.I., 1972, Tufts

U., 1988, East Anglia U., Norwich, Eng., 1966, Rennselaer Poly. Inst., 1998; D (hon.), U. Catholique de Louvain, Belgium, 1976, City U., London, 1980, New U. Lisbon, 1985, Univ. Nat. de Educacion a Distancia, Madrid, 1989, Univ. Politecnica de Valencia, Spain, 1991; D in Social Scis. (hon.), Yale U., 2005. Prof. econs. MIT, 1940—65, inst. prof., 1966, prof. emeritus, 1986; mem. staff Radiation Lab., 1944—45; prof. internat. econ. relations Fletcher Sch. Law and Diplomacy, 1945; cons. Nat. Resources Planning Bd., 1941—43, WPB, 1945, U.S. Treasury, 1945—52, 1961—74, Bur. Budget, 1952, RAND Corp., 1948—75, Fed. Res. Bd., 1965—; council Econ. Advisers, 1960—68; econ. adviser to Pres. Kennedy; sr. adviser Brookings Panel on Econ. Activity; mem. spl. commn. on social scis. NSF, 1967—68; cons. Congl. Budget Office, Federal Reserve Bd., 1965—; Gordon Y Billard Fellow MIT, Boston, 1986—; vis. prof of polit. econ. Ctr. Japan-U.S. Bus. and Econ. Studies, NYU, 1987—2005. Mem. nat. adv. com. Inst. for Rsch. on Poverty; lectr. in field. Author: Foundations of Economic Analysis, 1947, enlarged edit., 1983, Readings in Economics, 1955; author: (with R. Dorfman and R.M. Solow) Linear Programming and Economic Analysis, 1958; author: Collected Scientific Papers, 5 vols., 1966, 1972, 1978, 1986, Economics 1948-1980, 2005; co-author (with William Nordhaus): Economics 1985-2005, 2005; author: numerous other books; columnist Newsweek, 1966—81; assoc. editor: Jour. Pub. Econs., Jour. Internat. Econs., Jour. Fin. Econs., Jour. Nonlinear Analysis, adv. bd.: Challenge Mag.; contbr. articles to profl. jours. Chmn. Pres.'s Task Force Maintaining Am. Prosperity, 1964; mem. Nat. Task Force on Econ. Edn., 1960—61; econ. adviser to Pres. John F. Kennedy, 1959—63; mem. adv. bd. Nat. Commn. Money and Credit, 1958—60. Recipient David A. Wells prize, Harvard U., 1941, John Bates Clark medal, Am. Econ. Assn., 1947, Alfred Nobel Meml. prize, 1970, medal of Honor, U. Evansville, Ill., 1970, Albert Einstein Commemorative award, 1971, Alumni medal, U. Chgo., 1983, Britannica award, 1989, Gold Scanno prize, Naples, Italy, 1990, Paul A. Samuelson Professorship established in his name, MIT, 1991, Nat. Medal of Sci., Washington, 1996; fellow hon. fellow, London Sch. Econs. and Polit. Sci., Guggenheim, 1948—49, rsch. fellow, Ford Found., 1958—59. Fellow: Econometric Soc. (v.p. 1950, pres. 1951), Am. Philos. Soc., Am. Econ. Assn. (hon.; pres. 1961), Brit. Acad. (corr.); mem.: NAS, AAAS, Nat. Assn. Investment Clubs (Disting. Svc. award in Investment Edn. 1974), Leibniz-Akademie der Wissenschaften und der Literatur (corr.), Internat. Econ. Assn. (pres. 1966—68, hon. pres.), Com. Econ. Devel. (commn. on nat. goals, rsch. adv. bd. 1959—60), Club of Econ. and Mgmt. (medal, hon. Valencia, Spain 1990), Omicron Delta Epsilon (trustee), Phi Beta Kappa. Office: MIT E52 # 383C Dept Econs 50 Memorial Dr Cambridge MA 02142 Office Phone: 617-253-3368.

**SAMUELSON, ROBERT JACOB,** journalist; b. NYC, Dec. 23, 1945; s. Abraham and Joan (Kahn) S.; m. Judith Herr, July 10, 1983; children: Ruth, Michael, John. AB in Govt., Harvard U., 1967. Reporter Washington Post, 1969-73; free-lance writer Washington, 1973-76; reporter, columnist National Jour. mag., Washington, 1976-84; columnist Newsweek, Washington, 1984—. Columnist Washington Post, 1977—. Author: The Good Life and Its Discontents: The American Dream in the Age of Entitlement 1945-1995, 1996, Untruth: Why the Conventional Wisdom is (Almost Always) Wrong, 2001.

**SAMUELSSON, MARCUS (KASSHUN TSEGIE),** food service executive; b. Ethiopia; Degree, Culinary Inst. Göteborg, Switzerland. Chef Aquavit, NYC, 1991, worked under Jan Sendel, exec. chef & co-owner, 1995—, opened Mpls.; chef Georges Blanc, Lyon, France; exec. chef & co-owner AQ Café at Scandinavia House, NYC. Chosen to cook for Sweden's royal family; chosen to cook at gala dinner honoring the late Patrick Clark at Tavern on the Green; launched new line of traditional Swedish prepared foods; chef's coun. Chefs for Humanity. Featured Gourmet, USA Today, Food and Wine, NY Times, Australian Vogue Entertaining, appeared CNN, Discovery Channel, ABC's Good Morning Am., (numerous local N.Y. TV programs); author: Aquavit: And the New Scandinavian Cuisine, 2003, The Soul of a New Cuisine: A Discovery of the Foods & Flavors of Africa, 2006 (Libr. Jour. Fall Editor's Pick, 2006). Named Best Rising Star Chef, James Beard Found., 1999; named one of Great Chefs Am., Culinary Inst. Am.; recipient three-star restaurant rev. for Aquavit, NY Times, four-star rating, Forbes, three and a half-star rating, Crain's. Avocations: museums, art galleries. Office: Aquavit Inc 424 Madison Ave Rm 1410 New York NY 10017-1160*

**SANABRIA, ENRIQUE A.,** history professor; b. L.A., May 9, 1969; s. Enrique E. Sanabria and Delia Margarita Sanabria De La Cruz. BA in Spanish and History, Santa Clara U., Calif., 1991; MA, U. Wis., Madison Wis., 1993; PhD, U. Calif., La Jolla, Calif., 2001. Fellow U. Calif., La Jolla, Calif., 2001—02; asst. prof. Dept. History U. N.Mex., Albuquerque, 2002—. Fellow, Fulbright Found., 1996—97. Mem.: Am. Hist. Assn., Soc. Spanish and Portuguese Hist. Studies (Best Dissertation award 2001), Phi Alpha Theta (hon.; faculty mentor 2003—06). Office: Department of History MSC 06 3760 1 University of New Mexico Albuquerque NM 87131 Office Phone: 505-277-2267. Office Fax: 505-277-6023. Business E-Mail: sanabria@unm.edu.

**SANANMAN, MICHAEL LAWRENCE,** neurologist; b. Bklyn., Oct. 11, 1939; s. Jack and Sarey (Bykofsky) S.; m. Elisa Joan Freeman, Apr. 12, 1964; children: Amy, Peter. AB, Swarthmore Coll., 1960; MD, Columbia U., 1964. Diplomate Am. Bd. Psychiatry and Neurology. Intern U. Hosp., San Francisco, 1964-65; resident in neurology N.Y. Neurol. Inst., N.Y.C., 1966-69; practice medicine specializing in neurology Elizabeth, N.J., 1972—. Cons. neurologist Rahway (N.J.) Hosp., Trinitas Hosp., N.J., Union Hosp., N.J.; instr. neurology Columbia U., N.Y.C., 1971-75; assoc. clin. prof. neurology U. Medicine and Dentistry N.J., Newark, 1975—. Lt. comdr. M.C., USNR, 1969-71. Mem. AMA, Am. Acad. Neurology, Am. Epilepsy Soc., N.J. Acad. Medicine, Am. Eastern EEG Socs., Am. Assn. EMG and Electrodiagnosis. Office: 700 N Broad St Elizabeth NJ 07208-2310 Office Phone: 908-354-3994. Personal E-mail: Mikesan48@aol.com.

**SANBERG, PAUL RONALD,** medical educator; b. Coral Gables, Fla., Jan. 4, 1955; s. Bernard and Molly (Spector) Sanberg BS with honors, York U., 1976; MS, U. B.C., 1979; PhD, Australian Nat. U., 1981, DSc, 1998; grad. diploma sci. edn., We. Australia Inst. Tech., 1986. Postdoctoral fellow Johns Hopkins Med. Sch., Balt., 1981—83; asst. prof. Ohio U., Athens, 1983—86; assoc. prof. U. Cin., 1986—89; prof. Brown U., Providence, 1990—92, U. South Fla., Tampa, 1992—2003, disting. prof., assoc. dean, assoc. v.p., 2003—, assoc. dean, assoc. v.p., 2003—06, chair neurosci., 1997—2005, dir. Ctr. of Excellence for Aging and Brain Repair, 2000—. Co-founder Saneron Therapeutics, Inc., 2000—. Recipient award Am. Coll. Neuropsychopharmacology, Tourette Syndrome Assn., Sir J.G. Crawford medal, Ove Ferno prize Coll. Internat. Neuropsychopharmacology; grantee NIH, Am. Heart Assn., Childrens Med. Rsch. Found., Hereditary Disease Found., Huntington's Disease Found., Outstanding Rschr. award Sigma Xi Mem. APA, Soc. for Neurosci., Psychonomic Soc., Internat. Brain Rsch. Orgn., Internat. Behavioral Neurosci. Soc. (pres. 1994, Outstanding Rschr. award), Am. Soc. for Neural Transplant (pres. 1995), Cell Transplant Soc. (pres. 1996, editor). Home: 11751 Pilot Country Dr Spring Hill FL 34610-7912 Office: U South Fla Coll Medicine Dept NeuroSurgery MDC 78 12901 Bruce B Downs Blvd Tampa FL 33612-4742 Business E-Mail: psanberg@hsc.usf.edu.

**SANBORN, ANNA LUCILLE,** pension fund administrator, consultant; b. Bklyn., Mar. 29, 1924; d. Peter Francis and Matilda M. (Stumpp) Galligen; 1 son, Dean Sanborn. BA, Bklyn. Coll., 1945. Head dept. benefit and estate planning Union Ctrl. Life Ins. Co., N.Y.C., 1949—51; adminstr. employee benefits Seaboard Oil Co., N.Y.C., 1952—56; with Frank J. Walters Assocs., Inc., N.Y.C., 1957—, pres., 1982—. Mem. Am. Acad. Actuaries. Republican. Roman Catholic. Office: Frank J Walters Assocs 58-13 Seabury St Flushing NY 11373-4825 E-mail: fjwainc@aol.com.

**SANBORN, DOROTHY CHAPPELL,** retired librarian; b. Apr. 26, 1920; d. William S. and Sammie Maude (Drake) Chappell; m. Richard Donald Sanborn, Dec. 1, 1943; children: Richard Donald, William Chappell. Asst. cataloger El Paso (Tex.) Pub. Libr. 1954-55, 57-59, Stanford Rsch. Inst.,

Menlo Park, Calif., 1955-57; libr. Auburn (Calif.) Pub. Libr., 1959-62; cataloger Sierra Coll., Rocklin, 1962-64; reference libr. Sacramento (Calif.) City Libr., 1964-66; county libr. Placer County (Calif.), Auburn, 1966-89, ret., 1989. Chmn. Mountain Valley Libr. Sys., 1970-71, 75-76, 1984-85; cons. county libr. Alpine County Libr., Markleeville, Calif., 1973-80. Mem. Auburn Friends of Libr., 2005—, pres., 1995-97; vol. Peace Corps., Thailand, 1991-93. With WAVES, 1944-46. Mem. AAUW (pres. chpt. 1982-84), Calif. Libr. Assn., Auburn Friends of Libr., Soroptimists. Democrat. Mem. United Ch. Christ. Home: 135 Midway Ave Auburn CA 95603-5415 *Personal philosophy: To strive to make a continuing contribution.*

**SANBORN, GEORGE FREEMAN, JR.,** genealogist; b. Laconia, N.H., Jan. 18, 1944; s. George Freeman and Charlotte (Dearborn) S.; m. Melinde Laura Lutz, Mar. 30, 1984 (div.); children: Ruth Alice, Lowell Freeman. AB, Boston U., 1967; AM, U. Ill., 1968; MEd, U. N.H., 1981. French tchr. Souris (P.E.I., Can.) Regional H.S., 1968-69; French and occupational studies tchr. Massey-Vanier H.S., Cowansville, Que., Canada, 1969-70; French and English tchr. Kings Coll. Sch., Windsor, N.S., Canada, 1970-71; translator, revisor Province of N.B., Fredericton, 1971-73; sr. govt. revisor Province of Ont., Toronto, 1973-75; French and Spanish tchr. Tilton (N.H.) Sch., 1978-80; living unit coord. Laconia (N.H.) State Sch., 1982-83; ref. libr. New Eng. Hist. Geneal. Soc., Boston, 1983-85, acquisitions libr., dir. libr. ops., 1985-95, publs. asst., 1996-2000, ref. libr., 2000—05. Editor The N.H. Geneal. Record, 1990-93; co-compiler Vital Records of Hampton, N.H., 1992, 98; compiler: Deaths of Prince Edward Islanders in Massachusetts, 1891-1900, 5 vols., 2005; contbr. articles to profl. jours. Fellow Am. Soc. Genealogists; mem. Soc. of the Cin. in the State of N.H., Soc. Mayflower Descs. in the State of N.H., New Eng. Hist. Geneal. Soc., P.E.I. Geneal. Soc., N.H. Soc. Genealogists (pres. 1988-95), Geneal. Soc. Vt. (chair publs. com. 1992-96), N.B. Geneal. Soc., Cape Breton Genealogy and Hist. Assn. Democrat. Presbyterian. Avocations: gardening, bantam raising, Scottish Gaelic language, antique glass and china. Home: Unit 79 5 Tsienneto Rd Derry NH 03038-1573

**SANBORN, KATHY,** career planning administrator, consultant; BA in Psychology, Calif. State U., Sacramento, 1989. Founder Life and Career Coaching, Sacramento, 2001. Keynote spkr., trainer, workshop presenter in field. Author: (book) Grow Your Own Love, 2001, The Seasons of Your Career, 2003; singer (composer): (CD) Critical Mass, 1996; contbr. articles to profl. jours.; columnist: various web sites. Mem.: Golden Key Honor Soc. (life). Office: Life and Career Coaching PO Box 215664 Sacramento CA 95821 Business E-Mail: Kathy@lifeandcareercoaching.com.

**SANBORN, STEPHEN D.,** systems engineer; m. Constance R. Lopez, June 1997. BS in Engring., Widener U., Chester, Pa., 1978; MS in Systems Engring., U. Pa., 1981; PhD in Decision Sci. Engring. Sys., Rensselaer Poly. Inst., Troy, NY, 1990—95. Sys. & software engr. Lockheed Martin Def. Sys., Pittsfield, Mass., 1983—96; sys. engr. GE Global Rsch., Niskayuna, NY, 1996—. Producing dir. Two of Us Productions, Copake, NY, 2000—. Stage and musical dir.: theater productions; orchestra condr. (musical theatre and jazz orchestras); tech. dir.: (musical theater); contbr. scientific papers. Bd. mem. Upstage Prodns., Hudson, NY, 2000—01; affiliate bd. mem. Pub. Arts Resource Ctr., Pittsfield, Mass., 2004—; pres. Roving Actors' Repertory Ensemble, Copake, NY, 2006. Achievements include 5 patents in field. Avocations: vintage cars, water-skiing, theater, music, power boating. Office: GE Global Rsch 1 Research Cir Niskayuna NY 12309 Business E-Mail: sanborn@research.ge.com.

**SANCAR, AZIZ,** research biochemist; MD, Istanbul Med. Sch., 1969; PhD in Molecular Biology, U. Tex., Dallas, 1977. Assoc. prof. biochemistry U. N.C., Chapel Hill, 1982—, Sarah Graham Kenan prof., 2001—. Recipient Presidential Young Investigator award, NSF, 1984—89, Am. Soc. for Photobiology award, 1990, Basic Sci. award, Turkish Scientific Rsch. Council, 1995, Merit award, NIH, 1966. Fellow: Am. Acad. Arts & Sci.; mem.: NAS, Third World Acad. of Sci. Office: U NC Sch Medicine Dept Biochem and Biophysics Box 7260 Chapel Hill NC 27599-7260 Office Phone: 919-962-0115. Office Fax: 919-966-2852. E-mail: aziz_sancar@med.unc.edu.*

**SANCHEZ, ADALIO T.,** data processing executive; BS in Elec. Engring., Univ. Miami; MBA, Fla. Internat. Univ., 1987. Engr. IBM Corp., Boca Raton, Fla., 1982, gen. mgr., mobile computing, gen. mgr., personal computing divsn., mfg. ops. & bus. transformation unit, gen. mgr., storage networking divsn., v.p. ops., server group, gen. mgr., eServer pSeries. Adv. coun. Fla. Internat. Univ. Sch. Engring. Named one of 50 Most Important Hispanics in Tech., Bus., Hispanic Engineer and Info. Tech. mag., 2005; recipient Disting. Alumni Svc. Medallion, Fla. Internat. Univ., 2004. Office: IBM Corp 1 New Orchard Rd Armonk NY 10504 Office Phone: 914-499-1900.*

**SANCHEZ, ANTONIO RODOLFO, JR.,** oil industry executive; b. Laredo, Tex., Feb. 3, 1943; s. Antonio Rodolfo and Alicia M. Sanchez; m. Maria Josefina Guajardo, 1972; children: Antonio III, Ana Lee, Eduardo, Patricio. BBA, St. Mary's U., San Antonio, 1965, JD, 1969. Aide to lt. gov., Tex.; co-founder, chmn., CEO Sanchez Oil and Gas Corp. (formerly Sanchez-O'Brien Oil & Gas), Laredo, Tex., 1973—; majority owner Internat. Bancshares Corp., Laredo, Tex. Mem. Tex. Parks and Wildlife Commn., 1985—91; mem. bd. regents U. Tex., 1997—2003. Dem. candidate for gov., Tex., 2002.*

**SANCHEZ, DANMARY,** research scientist; b. Havana, Cuba, Dec. 23, 1977; arrived in US, 1991; d. Daniel Sanchez and Mara Haydee Ramirez; m. Roberto Perez Albertini, May 31, 2003. BS in Computer Engring., Fla. Internat. U., Miami, 1999, MS in Computer Engring., 2001, PhD in Elec. Engring., 2006. Software engr. IBM, Research Triangle Park, NC, 1998, Motorola, Plantation, Fla., 1999—; rsch. sci. Fla. Internat. U., Miami Children's Hosp., Miami, 2003—. Catequist St. Cecilia Cath. Ch., Miami, 1999—. Recipient Grad. Rsch. fellowship, NSF, 1999—2004, Motorola scholarship, 1999, IBM scholarship, 1998—99, Fla. Acad. scholarship, State of Fla., 1995—99, Fla.-Ga. Alliance for Minority Participation scholarship, 1997—99, Noel Betancourt scholarship, Assn. of Cuban Am. Engrs., 2006. Mem.: IEEE, Assn. of Cuban Am. Engrs. (sec. 1998—99), Eta Kappa Nu (pres. 1997—98), Tau Beta Pi (pres. 1998—99). Republican. Roman Catholic. Achievements include research in Three Dimensional Brain Fiber Tracking Modeling in Diffusion Tensor Imaging; EEG Analysis for Automatic Detection of Interictal Spikes in Epilepsy. Avocations: travel, photography, dancing. Office: Florida Internat U EAS 2220 10555 W Flagler St Miami FL 33175 Office Phone: 305-348-4106.

**SANCHEZ, FAUSTO H.,** advertising executive; b. Camaguey, Cuba, Oct. 21, 1953; came to US, 1966. s. Fausto Rene and Eloisa (Aparicio) S. AA, Miami (Fla.) Dade Community Coll., 1976; BA, U. Miami, 1979; postgrad., UCLA, 1980-82. Dir., newswriter, anchor Sta. KMEX-TV, Hollywood, Calif., 1980-82; producer, dir. Brighton Comm., Hollywood, 1982-84; dir. mktg. Edward J. DeBartolo Corp., Miami, Fla., 1984-86; chmn., pres., creative dir. Sanchez & Levitan Advt., Miami, 1986—2000; co-chmn., pres. Publicis, Sanchez & Levitan, Miami, 2000—04. Author: Hispanic Market, 1982; prodr. (documentary): Cachao...There's Nothing Like His Rhythm, 1994. Recipient Media award Calif. N.G., 1983, 2 Nat. Addy awards, 2 Radio Mercury awards, TV Campaign of Yr. award CLIO, The Telly, and Se Habla Español. Mem. Advt. Fedn. of Greater Miami. Avocations: films, tennis, sailing.

**SANCHEZ, HELIODORO TORRES, JR.,** education educator; b. San Angelo, Tex., Aug. 15, 1974; s. Heliodoro Torres Sánchez Sr. and Sylvia Torres Sánchez; m. Mary Ann Perez, Mar. 19, 1975. BA in English, Angelo State U., San Angelo, 1997; MEd, Sul Ross State U., Alpine, Tex., 2002. Cert. sch. adminstr. Tex. Edn. Assn., Tex., 2002, tchr. Tex. Edn. Agy., 1998. English tchr. San Angelo Ind. Sch. Dist., San Angelo, Tex., 1998—99, Ector County Ind. Sch. Dist., Odessa, Tex., 1999—2001; prin. St. Mary's Ctrl. Cath. Sch., Odessa, Tex., 2001—03; campus adminstr. Lewisville Ind. Sch. Dist., Flower Mound, Tex., 2003—05; prin. Dogan Middle Sch., Tyler, Tex., 2005—. Presenter in field. Contbr. articles to profl. jours. Mem. John Ben Shepperd

Leadership Inst., Odessa, Tex., 2003—04. Recipient Top Rsch. award, Tex. A&M U. Sys. Ann. Rsch. Symposium, 2004, Doctoral Student of Yr. for ednl. adminstrn., Tex. A&M U., 2004; Carr Acad. scholar, Angelo State U., 1997, Grad. Acad. scholar, Tex. A&M U. Commerce, 2004. Mem.: Am. Acad. Disting. Students, Am. Ednl. Rsch. Assn. (assoc.), K.C. (3d degree), Alpha Lambda Delta, Sigma Tau Delta, Kappa Delta Pi, Alpha Chi. D-Conservative. Roman Catholic. Avocations: writing, running, weight training, team sports. Office: Tyler Intermediate Sch Dist 2621 N Border St Tyler TX 75702 Office Phone: 903-262-1450. Home Fax: 903-279-1821; Office Fax: 903-262-1451. Personal E-mail: sanchezht@cs.com. Business E-Mail: heliodoro.sanchez@tylerisd.org.

**SANCHEZ, ISAAC CORNELIUS,** chemical engineer, educator; b. San Antonio, Aug. 11, 1941; s. Isaac Jr. and Marce (Aguilar) S.; m. Patty Praytor; children: Matthew, Timothy, Treb, Kamron. BS with honors, St. Mary's U., 1963; PhD, U. Del., 1969. Postdoctoral Nat. Bureau Standards, Gaithersburg, Md., 1969-71; assoc. scientist Xerox Corp., Webster, NY, 1971-72; asst. prof. U. Mass., Amherst, 1972-77; rsch. chemist Nat. Bureau Standards, Gaithersburg, 1977-86; fellow Alcoa, Pitts., 1986-88; prof. U. Tex., Austin, 1988—. H.A. disting vis. prof. U. Akron (Ohio), 1995. Mem. editorial bd. Jour. Polymer Sci., 1986-92, Polymer, 1987—; contbr. over 100 articles to profl. jours. Lt. USN, 1963-67. Recipient William J. Murray Endowed Chair in engring U. Tex., 1997, Bronze medal U.S. Dept. Commerce, 1980, Silver medal, 1983, E.U. Condon award Nat. Bur. Standards, 1983. Fellow Am. Phys. Soc.; mem. AAAS, AIChE, Am. Chem. Soc., Nat. Acad. Engring., Materials Rsch. Soc., Soc. Plastics Engrs. (Internat. Rsch. award 1996) Avocations: golf, lay ministry, birdwatching. Office: Univ Tex Chem Engring Dept Austin TX 78712 Office Phone: 512-471-1020. E-mail: sanchez@che.utexas.edu.

**SANCHEZ, LAURA ANN,** music educator; b. Jamaica, NY, Sept. 26, 1959; d. Arthur F. and Audrey M. Crowe; m. David T. Sanchez, Aug. 4, 1990. AAS, Nassau C.C., 1979; BA, Molloy Coll., 1981; MS, LI U. C.W. Post Coll., 1984. Music tchr. Uniondale Pub. Schools, NY, 1985—. Dir.: (performance) Calif. Ave. School Ensemble (First Pl., Dr. Martin Luther King Nassau County award, 2000). Corr. sec. Uniondale Cmty. Coun., NY. Mem.: Nassau Music Educators Assn., Music Educators Nat. Conf., Tech. in Music Edn., N.Y. State Sch. Music Assn. Office: Calif Ave Sch 236 California Ave Uniondale NY 11553 Office Phone: 516-918-1886. E-mail: lsanchez@uniondaleschools.org.

**SANCHEZ, LEONEDES MONARRIZE WORTHINGTON (HIS ROYAL HIGHNESS DUKE DE LEONEDES OF SPAIN SICILY GREECE),** fashion designer; b. Flagstaff, Ariz., Mar. 15, 1951; s. Rafael Leonedes and Margaret (Monarrize) S. BS, No. Ariz. U., 1974; studied, Fashion Inst. Tech., N.Y.C, 1974-75; AA, Fashion Inst. D&M, L.A., 1975; lic., La Ecole de la Chambre Syndical de la Couture Parisian, Paris, 1976-78; certificate, La Mason de Couture, Paris, 2000. Lic. in designing. Contract designer/asst. to head designer House of Bonnet, Paris, 1976—; dress designer-in-residence Flagstaff, 1978—; mem. faculty No. Ariz. U., Flagstaff, 1978-80; designer Ambiance, Inc., L.A., 1985—; designer Interiors by Leonedes subs. Studio of Leonedes Couturier, Ariz., 1977, Calif., 1978, London, Paris, 1978, Rome, 1987, Milan, Spain, 1989, Palazzo de Leonedes, 1998, designer Liturgical Vesture subs.; CEO Leonedes Internat., Design Consortium, Leonedes Internat. Ltd., 1999—; designer El Castillo de Nuevo Espana, Santa Fe, La Maison de Couture, Paris, 2000, La Maison de Couture DeLeonedes Internat., Paris, 2001, His Royal Highness Duke DeLeonedes Leonedes XIV Global Subs., His Royal Highness Duke DeLeonedes Leonedes XIV Royal Consortium Cartel, London, Mobiliare Europa, 2002, Mobiliare Pan Americano Atlantico, South Am., Caribbean, 2005, Mobiliare Asia Pacifico, Taipei, Hong Kong, Beijing, China, 2005; chamber syndicate De Mobiliare Estidio De Leonedes Internat. South Am., El Caribe, Spain, Studio Leonedes, 2005, Studio of Leonedes Consortium Cartel, 2006, Mobiliare Consortium Cartel, 2006, Imperial Consortium Cartel, 2006, Isla De Leonedes, 2006. Owner, CEO, designer Leonedes Internat., Ltd., London, Milan, Paris, Spain, Ambian Ariz, Calif., Appolonian Costuming, Ariz., London, Milan, Paris, El Castillo de Leonedes, Sevilla, Spain, Villa Apollonian de Leonedes, Mykonos, Greece, Palazzo de Leonedes Internat., Sicily; cons. House of Bonnet, Paris, 1976—, Bob Mackie, Studio City, Calif., 1974-75; CEO, designer artistical dir., Leonedes internat.; appointee commn. on religious antiquities Congregation on the Arts, The Vatican, Italy, 1998. Bd. dirs. Roman Cath. Social Svcs., 1985-86, Northland Crisis Nursery, 1985—; bd. dirs., chmn. Pine Country Transit, 1986-88; pres. Chicanos for Edn.; active master's swim program ARC, Ariz., 1979—; eucharistic min., mem. art and environ. com., designer liturgical vesture St. Pius X Cath. Ch.; vol. art tchr., instr. St. Mary's Regional Sch., Flagstaff, 1987-90, vol. art dir.; mem. Flagstaff Parks and Recreation Commn., 1994-96, citizens' adv. com. master plan, 1994-96; mem. cmty. bd. adv. com. Flagstaff Unified Sch. Dist., 1995; active Duke de Leonedes Found. de Nuevo Espana, Santa Fe, Duke de Leonedes Found. de Neuvo Espana, Santa Fe; prin. chair Duke de Leonedes Found., The Netherlands, 1995; de neuvo espana Duke de Leuedes Found., Santa Fe, N.Mex., 1996. Decorated Duke de Leonedes (Spain), 1994, His Royal Highness (Spain, Greece, Sicily), 1998; recipient Camellian Design award 1988, Atlanta, De Nuevo award Duke DeLeonedes Found., Santa Fe, Barcelona, Ireland, 2004, Spain, Greece, Sicily. Mem. AAU (life, chairperson swimming Ariz. 1995, vice chairperson physique, mem. citizen adv. bd. parks and recreation, chairperson state of Ariz. physique, swimming, adv. to Olympic inquiry com., advisor to internat. Olympic com. on physique), Am. Film Inst., Am. Assn. Hist. Preservation, Costume Mem., Am. Nat. Physique Com., Internat. Consortium Fashion Designers, Nat. Cath. Ednl. Assn., La Legion de Honour de la Mode Parisienne, Social Register Assn., Phi Alpha Theta (historian 1972-73, pres. 1973-74), Pi Kappa Delta (pres. 1972-73, historian 1973-74). Republican. Avocations: bodybuilding, swimming. Office: El Castillo de Leonedes Seville Spain also: El Castillo de nuevo Espana Santa Fe NM 87501 also: Villa de Apollonian de Leonedes Mykonos Greece Mailing: PO Box 61623 Phoenix AZ 85082-1623 Address: PO Box 14 14 Dover St Mayfair London W1S 4LW England

**SANCHEZ, LINDA T.,** congresswoman; b. Orange, Calif. m. Mark Sanchez. BA in Spanish Lit., U. Calif., Berkeley; JD, UCLA, 1995. Bar: Calif. 1995. Clk. to Hon. Chief Justice Terry Hatter, Jr. Ctrl. Dist. Ct., Calif.; compliance officer Nat. Elec. Contractors Assn. and Internat. Brotherhood Elec. Workers, 1998—2002; mem. US Congress from 39th Calif. dist., 2003—; mem. judiciary com.; mem. govt. reform com., small bus. com. Lectr. Nat. Assn. Elected and Apptd. Ofcls., 1998—. Exec. sec.-treas. Orange County ctrl. labor coun. AFL-CIO; campaign worker Loretta Sanchez for U.S. Congress, 1996, 1998. Mem.: Internat. Brotherhood Elec. Workers (Local 441). Democrat. Office: US Ho Reps 1007 Longworth Office Bldg Washington DC 20515-0539 also: Dist Office Ste 106 4007 Paramount Lakewood CA 90712

**SANCHEZ, LORETTA,** congresswoman; b. Lynnwood, Calif., Jan. 7, 1960; BA, Chapman U., 1982; MBA, Am. U., 1984. With Orange County Transp. Authority, 1984-87, Fieldman Rolapp & Assocs., 1987-90; strategic mgmt. cons. Booz Allen & Hamilton; owner, operator AMIGA Advisors Inc.; mem. U.S. Congress from 47th Calif. dist., 1997—; former mem. edn. and the workforce com., mem. armed svcs. com.; mem. House Select Com. on Homeland Security, House Blue Dogs. mem. Anaheim Rotary Club. Democrat. Office: US Ho Reps 1230 Longworth Ho Office Bldg Washington DC 20515-0547 also: Dist Office Ste 101 12397 Lewis St Garden Grove CA 92840 Office Phone: 202-225-2965. E-mail: loretta@mail.house.gov.

**SANCHEZ, MANUEL,** retired social services administrator, writer; b. Los Palacios, Cuba, June 6, 1932; s. Emilio and Elena (Lopez) Sanchez. JD, Havana U., Cuba, 1959. Bar: N.J. 1975. Supt. Dept. Social Svcs., N.Y.C., 1964—90; ret., 1990. Author: The Daring Mysteries, 1991, Stories for a Rainy Afternoon, 2005. Avocation: reading. Home: 220W 98th St Apt 12N New York NY 10025

**SANCHEZ, MARY ANNE,** retired secondary school educator; b. Galesburg, Ill., Aug. 4, 1939; d. Stephen Mingare and M. Margaret Kennedy; m. J. Manuel Sanchez, Dec. 26, 1980. BS in Edn., Western Ill. U., 1961; MA, Ill.

State U., 1970. Tchr., Stanford, Ill., 1962-64, Titusville, Fla., 1964-66, Montgomery County Bd. Edn., Chevy Chase, Md., 1969-72, Hillsborough County Bd. Edn., Tampa, Fla., 1972-96; ret., 1996. Mary Anne Sanchez Young Woman scholarship named in her honor by Social Studies Dept. Leto Comprehensive H.S., 1999. Mem. Nat. Coun. for Social Studies, Fla. Coun. for Social Studies, Adult Edn. Assn. Home: 2715 W Ivy St Tampa FL 33607-1922

**SANCHEZ, RAFAEL CAMILO,** physician, educator; b. Tampa, Fla., July 18, 1919; s. Francisco and Catalina (Mateo) S.; children: Stephen Francis, John Thomas, David Lear. BS, Loyola U., New Orleans, 1940; MD, La. State U., 1950. Diplomate: Am. Bd. Family Practice (bd. dirs. 1976-79, assoc. exec. dir. 1979-84). Intern U.S. Marine Hosp., New Orleans, 1950-51; gen. practice medicine New Orleans, 1951-72; med. educator, dir. continuing med. edn. La. State U., 1963-77, prof. family medicine, 1979-84, East Carolina U. Sch. Medicine, Greenville, 1984-90, prof. emeritus, 1990—; dir. family practice residency program Charity Hosp. of Bogalusa, La., 1977-79. Dir. Continuing Med. Edn.; med. dir. Nat. Med. Info. Network, pres. RCS-CME Svcs. Mem. bd. curators Archives for Family Practice, 1993-99. Served with AUS, 1940-46. Recipient Recognition award Soc. Tchrs. Family Medicine, 1987, Willard M. Duff award Accreditation Coun. for Continuing Med. Edn. Fellow AMA, Am. Acad. Family Physicians (Thomas W. Johnson award 1978, Presdl. award 1983, Pres.'s award 1989); mem. Network for Continuing Med. Edn. (past med. dir., chair archives com. alliance), Nat. Med. Info. Network of Lippincott-Raven Healthcare (sr. med. adv.), Alpha Omega Alpha. Democrat. Roman Catholic. E-mail: rsanchezmd@amsouth.net.

**SANCHEZ, RAYMOND G.,** former state legislator; b. Albuquerque, Sept. 22, 1941; s. Gillie and Priscilla S.; 1 child, Raymond Michael. BA, U. N.Mex., 1964, JD, 1967. Bar: N. Mex. 1967. Ptnr. Sanchez, Mowrer & Desiderio, P.C., Albuquerque; mem. N.Mex. Ho. of Reps., 1970—; speaker N. Mex. Ho. of Reps., 1983—84, 1987—88, 1992—2000; mem. judiciary com., rules and order of bus. com., voters and elections com.; interim mem. workers compensation, legis. reform study coms., legis. coun.; pres. Nalep Educational Fund, Albuquerque, 2001. Bd. dirs. New Mex. Amigos, N.Mex. Diamond Jubilee/U.S. Constl. Bicentennial Commn., New Mex. First, Albuquerque Com. Fgn. Rels., N. Valley Neighborhood Assn.; bd. regents U. N. Mex. Mem. Nat. Assn. Latino Elected and Apptd. Ofcls. (bd. dirs.), Alameda Optimist Club (bd. dirs., charter mem.), U. N.Mex. Sch. Law Alumni Assn. (bd. dirs.), Elks Club, Sigma Xi. Democrat. Avocations: handball, scuba diving, swimming, sports. also: PO Box 1966 Albuquerque NM 87103-1966 Office Phone: 505-247-4321.

**SANCHEZ, RICARDO,** broadcast executive; b. Boise, Idaho, Oct. 20, 1970; s. Ricardo Garcia and Barbara Jo Sanchez. BA in English, Boise State U., 1992; MA in Film, Am. U., Washington, 1995. Prodr. Freedom Forum Newseum, Washington, 1995—96, Imagine Media, Brisbane, Calif., 1996—99; v.p. pub. IGN Entertainment, Brisbane, 1999—2005; v.p. programming GameTap, Turner Broadcasting Inc., Atlanta, 2005—. Dir.(writer): (films) Popularity (Best of Show, Best Short Film); contbr. articles to popular mags. Mem.: Sigma Tau Delta, MENSA, Sigma Phi Epsilon (pres. 1989—90). Office: GameTap Turner Broadcasting Inc 1050 Techwood Dr Atlanta GA 30318 Office Phone: 404-885-0205. Personal E-mail: rick@bugeyedmonster.com. Business E-mail: ricardo.sanchez@turner.com.

**SANCHEZ, RICARDO S.,** career military officer; b. Rio Grande City, Tex. B in Math. and History, Tex. A&I U.; M in Ops. Rsch. and Sys. Analysis Engring., Naval Postgrad. Sch. Commd. officer U.S. Army, 1973, advanced through ranks to lt. gen., 2003, platoon leader 4th Bn., 68th Armor, 82nd Airborne Divsn., aide-de-camp to the asst. divsn. comdr. 82nd Airborne Divsn., action control officer Office of the Sec. of the Joint Staff, U.S. Forces Korea/Eighth U.S. Army, ops. officer and exec. officer 3rd Bn., 8th Cavalry, 3rd Armored Divsn. Gelnhausen, Germany, dep. ops. officer 3rd Armored Divsn. Frankfurt, Germany, comdr. 2nd Bn., 69th Armor, 197th (separate) Inf. Brigade Ft. Benning, Ga., investigator Office U.S. Army Insp. Gen. Agy. Washington, comdr. 2nd Brigade, 1st Inf. Divsn. Ft. Riley, Kans., dep. chief staff U.S. So. Command Miami, Fla., dir. ops. U.S. So. Command, asst. divsn. comdr. for support 1st Inf. Divsn., dep. chief staff ops. U.S. Army Europe Heidelburg, Germany, commdg. gen. V Corps 1st Armored Divsn., 2001—03, commdg. gen. Coalition Ground Forces (Combined Joint Task Force 7) Iraq, 2003—04, commdg. gen. V Corps, 2003—04, 2004—, commdr. Multi-Nat. Force Iraq, 2004, commanding gen. V Corps, 2004—. Decorated Def. Superior Svc. medal, Legion of Merit, Bronze Star with V device and oak leaf cluster, Joint Svc. Commendation medal, Army Commendation medal, Meritorious Svc. medal with four oak leaf clusters, Army Achievement medal with oak leaf cluster, Liberation of Kuwait medals, S.W. Asia Campaign medal.

**SANCHEZ, SUSIE RIOJAS,** elementary school educator; b. San Antonio, Dec. 25, 1937; d. Lorenzo and Juanita (Cisneros) Riojas; m. Edward R. Sanchez, Aug. 28, 1960; six children. BA, St. Mary's U., San Antonio, 1984; cert., Our Lady of the Lake, 1985; MS, A&I U., 1990. Tchr. San Antonio Ind. Sch. Dist.; ret. Mem. PTC bd. Ursuline Acad. Mem. NEA, ASCD, San Antonio Tchrs. Coun., Tex. Tchrs. Assn. Home: 1326 Stetson Grn San Antonio TX 78258-7288 Office Phone: 210-977-9301.

**SANCHEZ, VICTOR HUGO,** retired military non-commissioned officer; b. Guayaquil, Ecuador, Mar. 27, 1928; arrived in U.S., 1956, naturalized, 1961; s. Angel Maria Sanchez and Maria Esther Guevara; m. Estel Maria Rivera, Oct. 18, 1963; 1 child, Raphael Albert Sanchez Rivera (dec.); children: Victor Manuel Sanchez Ordonez, Orietta Sanchez Yepez. Student, NYU, 1980—82, Borough of Manhattan CC, 1982—84, Baruch Coll., 1985. Commd. lt. U.S. Army, 1958, acting commdr. Vietnam, 1970, advanced through grades to sgt. first class, 1975, ret., 1978; acctg. tech Dept. War Affairs, Manhattan, NY, 1983—2003. Decorated Air medal U.S. Army, Good Conduct medal, Nat. Def. Svc. medal, U.S. Vietnam Svc. medal, Vietnam Campaign medal, RVN Gallantry Cross with Palm, U.S. Meritorious Unit citation; recipient Silver Cup award, Pres. Ecuador, 1950, Golden medal, Gov. Chimborazo Province, Ecuador, 1950. Republican. Roman Catholic. Avocations: poetry, writing, reading, languages. Home: 66-04 Grand Ctrl Pky Apt 1A Forest Hills NY 11375-1979 Personal E-mail: sancz2537hv@aol.com.

**SANCHEZ, VINCENT A.,** lawyer; b. Bronx, NY, Dec. 12, 1968; BA, Univ. Notre Dame, 1991, JD, 1994; MBA, Northwestern Univ., 2003. Bar: Ill. 1994. Ptnr., co-chmn. Tech. & Sourcing Group DLA Piper Rudnick Gray Cary, Chgo. Adj. prof. Loyola Univ. Sch. Law, 2002—; mem. adv. bd. West Suburban Tech. Enterprise Ctr. Editor (in chief): Notre Dame Jour. of Legislation. Bd. dir. i.c. stars. 1st Lt. USMC Reserve, 1991—95. Named one of 40 Ill. Attorneys Under 40 to Watch, Chgo. Lawyer mag., 2004, Leading Lawyers in Ill. for Tech. & IT Outsourcing, Chambers USA. Mem.: ABA. Office: DLA Piper Rudnick Gray Cary Ste 1900 203 N LaSalle St Chicago IL 60601-1293 Office Phone: 312-368-3420. Business E-mail: vincent.sanchez@dlapiper.com.

**SANCHEZ-BARNETT, SUSAN LYNN,** historian, educator; b. Hollywood, Calif., Aug. 20, 1954; d. James Edwin and Terah May Johnson; m. David Novell Barnett, Dec. 20, 2000; children: Angel Phillip Sanchez, Angela Victoria Sanchez, Alexandra Querida Sanchez, David Matthew Sanchez. BA, Calif. State U. Pomona, 1991; MA, Calif. State U., Fullerton, 1997; PhD, U. Calif., 2003. Cert. tchr. Md., 2000. Secondary tchr. Balt. County Pub. Schs., Balt., 2000—; adj. prof. Strayer U., Millersville, Md., 2005—. Music dir. Marley Pk. Ch. of the Nazarene, Glen Burnie, Md., 2005—. Named hist. Soc. for Ethnohistory, Am. Hist. Assn. Home: 711 Marley Ave Glen Burnie MD 21060 Personal E-mail: sbarnett@bcps.org.

**SANCHEZ KORROL, VIRGINIA,** historian, educator; b. N.Y.C., Aug. 27, 1936; d. Antonio Sanchez Feliciano and Elisa Santiago Rodriguez; m. Charles R. Korrol, May 12, 1934; children: Pamela J. Marshall, Lauren R. Korrol. PhD, SUNY, Stony Brook, 1981. Prof. Bklyn Coll., 1978—. Author: (history

monograph) From Colonia to Community: The History of Puerto Ricans in New York City; co-author: Women in Latin America and the Caribbean, Mujeres en America Latina y el Caribe; co-editor: Latinas in the United States: A Historical Encyclopedia, Latina Legacies: Biography, Identity and Community. Named Woman of Yr., Latina Mag., 2000, El Diario-La Prensa, 2001; 2005; recipient 21 Leaders for the 21st Century award, Women's E News, 2005; Latina History in the U.S. grant, Ford Found., 1999-2001; 2005-2007, Latina Ency. Project grant, NEH, 2001-2003. Office: Bklyn Coll CUNY 2900 Bedford Ave Brooklyn NY 11210-2889 Office Phone: 718-951-5000. Office Fax: 718-951-5561.

**SANCHEZ MILLS, PEGGY,** women's association executive; b. Roswell, N.Mex., Aug. 1, 1953; d. Myron and Gloria Carson; children: Jennifer, Jason. BA in Sociology and Psychology, U. South Fla.; MPA, Golden Gate U. Reading specialist Girl's Clubs Pinellas County, Clearwater, Fla., 1979-80, ctr. supr. St. Petersburg, Fla., 1980-81; project adminstr. YWCA St. Petersburg, 1981-84; exec. dir. YWCA Tampa Bay, St. Petersburg, 1984—2004; CEO YWCA USA, Washington, 2004—. Mem. adv. com. Riviera Mid. Sch., Lealman Discovery. Chair edn. com. Community Alliance, 1989-91; chair Dist. Task Force on Child Abuse Prevention, 1988-91; pres. Leadership St. Pete Assn., mem. planning coun., United Way; pres. Coun. of Exec. Dirs.; sec., bd. dirs. Suncoast Tiger Bay Club; mem. steering com. Teen Parent Self Sufficiency Task Force for Pinellas County; mem. Abuse, Neglect, and Dependency Com., Coalition for Homeless/Affordable Housing, Fla. Ctr. for Children and Youth, Human Svc. Coalition; mem. adv. com. Jr. League of St. Petersburg; apptd. to state coord. coun. early childhood svcs. Recipient Up and Comers award Price-Waterhouse, 1990. Office: YWCA USA 1015 18th St NW Ste 1100 Washington DC 20036 Business E-mail: jsanchezmills@ywca.org.

**SANCHEZ-RAMOS, ROBERTO J.,** attorney general; b. 1968; BS in Computer Sci. and Engring., MIT, 1989; JD summa cum laude, U. PR, 1998; LLM, Yale U., 1993. Admitted to practice: PR, Washington, DC, Supreme Ct. US, US Ct. Appeals for the First Cir. Law clk. to Hon. Federico Hernandez Denton Supreme Ct. PR, 1993—94; assoc. Arnold & Porter LLP, Washington, 1994—96; law clk. to Hon. A. Wallace Tashima US Ct. Appeals (9th cir.), Pasadena, Calif., 1996—97; trial atty., civil divsn., fed. programs branch US Dept. Justice, Washington, 1999—2000; solicitor gen. PR, San Juan, 2001—04, atty. gen., 2004—. Recipient West Publishing award for Excellence in the Study of Anglo-Am. Law, Acad. Excellence award, PR Atty. Bar Assn. Mem.: Eta Kappa Nu Assn., Sigma Xi. Office: Office of Atty General GPO Box 902192 San Juan PR 00902-0192*

**SANCHEZ-SOTELO, JOAQUIN,** surgery consultant; b. Madrid, Mar. 12, 1968; s. Joaquin Sanchez Cota and Adoracion Sotelo Laredo; children: Pablo Sanchez, Marta Sanchez. MD, Univ. Autonoma de Madrid, Spain, 1989, PhD, 1992. Cons. orthop. surgery Hosp. La Paz, Madrid, 2001—04, Dept. Orthop. Surgery Mayo Clinic, Rochester, Minn., 2004—. Spl. fellow adult reconstruction Mayo Clinic, Rochester, Minn., 2001, asst. prof., 2004—. Author scientific papers. Named Tchr. of Yr. in Orthopedics, Mayo Clinic, 2005; recipient Jesus Galan award, Spanish Bd. Medicine, 1992, Coventry Rsch. award, Mayo Clinic, 2001. Mem.: Madrid Orthop. Assn., Spanish Assn. Shoulder and Elbow Surgeons, Am. Acad. Orthop. Surgeons, Spanish Orthop. Assn., Mayo Fellows Assn. Achievements include research in orthopedic surgery. Office: Dept Orthop Surgery Mayo Clinic 200 First St SW Rochester MN 55905 Office Phone: 507-538-1953. Office Fax: 507-284-5539.

**SANCHEZ-WAY, RUTH DOLORES,** public health administrator; b. NYC, Aug. 8, 1940; d. Manuel and Cruz Maria (Rivera) Sanchez; m. Harley Milton Dirks, Feb. 9, 1974 (dec. Aug. 1986); stepchildren: Timothy, Darcy Kimmel, Marcine Thomas, James, David, Dale; m. David Vincent Way, Apr. 16, 1988. BS, St. John's U., 1962; MSW, Fordham U., 1965; PhD, NYU, 1978; postgrad., Emory U., Geroge Washington U. Cert. social worker, Md.; cert. prevention profl. Spl. asst. to dir. Nat. Inst. Alcohol Abuse and Alcoholism, U.S. Dept Health, Edn. and Welfare, Rockville, Md., 1971-79; assoc. dep. adminstr. Equal Employment Opportunity Office Asst. Sec. Health, U.S. Dept. HEW, 1979-83; dep. dir. Office Adolescent Pregnancy Programs Health and Human Svcs., Washington, 1983-91; assoc. adminstr. minority health concerns Substance Abuse & Mental Health Svcs. Adminstrn., Health and Human Svcs., Rockville, 1993-96, divsn. dir. Ctr. for Substance Abuse Prevention, 1991-96, acting dep. dir. Ctr. for Substance Abuse Prevention, 1997, acting dir., 1997—2000, dir., 2000—02; assoc. dir. Ctr. for Faith-Based and Cmty. Initiatives, HHS, 2002—03; v.p. health and cmty. initiatives Mgmt. Scis. for Devel., 2003—. Bd. dirs. Nat. Health Coun., Washington, 1987-94, Nat. Coun. on Alcoholism and Drug Dependence, N.Y.C., 1979-91, Nat. Orgn. Adolescent Pregnancy Parenting and Prevention, Washington, 1991-93. Vol. Girl Scouts U.S.A., N.Y.C., 1996—. Recipient Excellence in Govt. Svc. award Mex.-Am. Legal Def. and Ednl. Fund, 2000, Presdl. Meritorious Exec. Rank award SES, 1998, Sec.'s award for disting. svc. HHS, 2001; primary care policy fellow USPHS. Mem. NASW, APHA, Chesapeake Crusing Multihull Assn. (past commodore, Kilmon award 1996). Roman Catholic. Avocations: sailing, skiing, jazzercise. Office: Mgmt Scis for Devel 4455 Connecticut Ave NW Ste A100 Washington DC 20008 Office Phone: 202-537-7410. Personal E-mail: rsanchez@msdglobal.com.

**SANCHIRICO, CHRIS WILLIAM,** law educator; AB, Princeton U., 1984; JD, Yale U., 1994, PhD in Econs., 1994. Vis. lectr. U. Calif., Berkeley, 1994; acting asst. prof. Dept. Econs. Stanford U., 1995; assoc. prof. Dept. Econs. Columbia U., 1995—99; assoc. prof. U.S.C. Sch. Law, 1999—2002, prof., 2002—03; vis. prof. U. Pa. Law Sch., Phila., 2002, prof. law, bus. and pub. policy, 2003—. Vis. prof. U. Chgo. Law Sch., 2004. Contbr. articles to law jours. Office: U Pa Law Sch 3400 Chestnut St Philadelphia PA 19104 Office Phone: 215-898-4220. E mail: sanchiri@law.upenn.edu.

**SAND, LEONARD B.,** federal judge; b. NYC, May 24, 1928; BS, NYU, 1947; LL.B., Harvard, 1951. Bar: N.Y. 1953, U.S. Supreme Ct. 1956, D.C. 1969. Clk. to dist. ct. judge, N.Y., 1952-53; asst. U.S. atty. So. Dist. N.Y., 1953-54; asst. to U.S. Solicitor Gen., 1956-59; mem. firm Robinson, Silverman, Pearce, Aronsohn Sand and Berman, N.Y.C., 1960-78; judge U.S. Dist. Ct. (So. Dist.), NY, 1978—, now sr. judge N.Y. Adj. prof. law NYU. Note editor: Harvard Law Rev, 1950-51. Del. N.Y. State Constl. Conv., 1967; v.p., treas. Legal Aid Soc. Fellow Am. Coll. Trial Lawyers; mem. ABA, Assn. Bar City N.Y. (v.p.), N.Y. State Bar Assn., Fed. Bar Coun. Office: US Dist Ct US Courthouse 500 Pearl St New York NY 10007-1316

**SAND, SEAWARD ALWYN,** geneticist, researcher; b. Lockport, NY, Sept. 20, 1922; s. Seaward Alwyn Sr. and Gertrude Morris Sand; m. Mavis Hawthorne Gillette, Aug. 15, 1948; children: Beverly Neil, Valerie Waite, Kimberly Warner, Natalie Waugh, Kevin Gillette, Bryan Morris. Student, Kans. State Coll., 1943—44, Cornell U., 1941—43, student, 1946—47, AB in Physics, 1947, MS in Sci. Edn., 1948, PhD in Genetics, 1955. H.S. tchr. physics, chemistry and biology, Honeoye Falls, NY, 1948—50; grad. asst. Dept. Plant Breeding N.Y. State Coll. Agr. Cornell U., Ithaca, 1950—54; from asst. to assoc. geneticist Conn. Agrl. Expt. Sta., New Haven, Windsor and Mt. Carmel, 1954—84; assoc. cancer rsch. scientist N.Y. State Dept. Health, Orchard Park and Buffalo, 1964—84; ret., 1984. Vis. assoc. prof. biology SUNY, Stony Brook, 1962—63; Fulbright lectr. Dept. Genetics Trinity Coll., Dublin, 1963. Rsch. collaborator, guest assoc. geneticist biology dept. Brookhaven Nat. Lab., Upton, NY, 1962—69. Life mem. Rep. Nat. Com., Washington, 2004—; spkr. Niagara County N.Y. Genealogical Soc. Program (Sand Lineage & Father's Photog. Career), Lockport, 2004; platinum mem. Rep. Presdl. Task Force, Washington, 2001—. With U.S. Army, 1943—46. Recipient Eisenhower Commn. award, Rep. Nat. Com., 2005; grantee, Cornell U., 1941—43, 1946—43, Employers' State Budgets, Conn. and NY, 1954—84; scholar, NY State U. Bd. Regents, 1941—43, 1946—47. Fellow: AAAS; mem.: Am. Genetic Assn., Genetics Soc. Am. (jour. referee). Methodist. Avocations: travel, equity investing, national and international policy, science, university relations. Home: 420 Fillmore Ave East Aurora NY 14052-1707

**SAND, THOMAS CHARLES,** lawyer; b. Portland, Oreg., June 4, 1952; s. Harold Eugene and Marian Anette (Thomas) S.; children: Kendall, Taylor, Justin. Student, Centro des Artes y Lenguas, Cuernavaca, Mex., 1972; BA in English, U. Oreg., 1974; JD, Lewis and Clark Coll., 1977. Bar: Oreg. 1977, U.S. Dist. Ct. Oreg. 1977, U.S. Ct. Appeals (9th cir.) 1984. Assoc. Miller, Nash, LLP, Portland, 1977-84, ptnr., 1984—, mng. ptnr., 1999—. Mem. Oreg. State Bar Com. on Professionalism, 1989, chmn., 1989; dir. young lawyers divsn. Multnomah County Bar Assn., 1980; spl. asst. atty. gen. Wasco County 1983 Gen. Election; spkr. in field. Contbr. articles to legal jours. Mem. U.S. Dist. Ct. of Oreg. Hist. Soc., 1990—; bd. dirs. Portland Area coun. Camp Fire, Inc., 1978-90, pres., 1984-86; bd. dirs. Oreg. Indoor Invitational Track Meet, Inc., 1982-84. Disting. Grad. award Lewis and Clark Law Sch., 2004. Mem. ABA (securities litig. com., subcom. on broker-dealer litig.), Oreg. Bar Assn., Multnomah Bar Assn. (bd. dirs. task force on structure and orgn. 1989, chmn. com. on professionalism 1988, nominating com. 1986, participating atty. in N.E. legal clin. Vol Lawyers project, award of merit for svc. to profession 1988), Securities Industry Assn. (compliance and legal divsn.), Northwestern Sch. of Law, Lewis and Clark Coll. Alumni Assn. (bd. dirs. 1992, pres. 1997, law sch. bd. visitors 2004-), Valley Comm. Presbyterian Ch., Multnomah Athletic Club, Portland Golf Club. Avocations: golf, guitar, camping, river rafting, children's sports. Office: Miller Nash LLP 111 SW 5th Ave Ste 3500 Portland OR 97204-3699 Office Phone: 503-224-5858. Business E-Mail: tom.sand@millernash.com.

**SANDAGE, ALLAN REX,** astronomer; b. Iowa City, June 18, 1926; s. Charles Harold and Dorothy (Briggs) S.; m. Mary Lois Connelley, June 8, 1959; children: David Allan, John Howard. AB, U. Ill., 1948, DSc (hon.), 1967; PhD, Calif. Inst. Tech., 1953; DSc (hon.), Yale U., 1966, U. Chgo., 1967, Miami U., Oxford, Ohio, 1974, Graceland Coll., Iowa, 1985; LLD (hon.), U. So. Calif., 1971; D (hon.), U. Chile, 1992. Astronomer Mt. Wilson Obs., Palomar Obs., Carnegie Instn., Washington, 1952—; Peyton fellow Princeton U., 1952; asst. astronomer Hale Obs., Pasadena, Calif., 1952-56; astronomer Obs. Carnegie Instn., Pasadena, Calif., 1956—; sr. rsch. astronomer Space Telescope Sci. Inst. NASA, Balt., 1986—; Homewood Prof. of physics Johns Hopkins U., Balt., 1987-89. Vis. lectr. Harvard U., 1957; mem. astron. expdn. to South Africa, 58; cons. NSF, 1961—64; Sigma Xi nat. astronomer U. Basel, 1985, 92, vis. prof., 94; vis. rsch. astronomer U. Calif. San Diego, 1985—86; vis. astronomer U. Hawaii, 1986; Lindsey lectr. NASA Goddard Space, Durham, England, 1992; Grubb-Parsons lectr. U. Durham, England, 1992. Assoc. editor: Ann. Rev. Astronomy and Astrophysics, 1990—2005. Recipient Helen Warner prize, Am. Astron. Soc., 1960, Pope Pius XI Gold medal, Pontifical Acad. Sci., 1966, Rittenhouse medal, 1968, Russell prize, 1973, Adon medal, Obs. Nice, 1988, Crafford prize, Swedish Royal Acad. Scis., 1991, Tomalla Gravity prize, Swiss Phys. Soc., 1993, Peter Gruber Found. prize for cosmology, 2000; scholar Fulbright-Hays scholar, 1972. Mem.: Astron. Soc. Pacific (Gold medal 1975), Royal Soc. London (fgn.), Am. Philos. Soc., Franklin Inst. (Elliott Cresson medal 1973, Gruber Cosmology prize 2000), Royal Astron. Soc. Can., Royal Astron. Soc. (Eddington medal 1963, Gold medal 1967), Lincei Nat. Acad. (Rome), Phi Beta Kappa. Home: 8319 Josard Rd San Gabriel CA 91775-1003 Office: 813 Santa Barbara St Pasadena CA 91101-1232

**SANDAGE-MUSSEY, ELIZABETH ANTHEA,** retired market research executive; b. Larned, Kans., Oct. 13, 1930; d. Curtis Carl and Beulah Pauline (Knupp) Smith; m. H.I. Danner, 1948 (div. 1956); children: Dianna Louise Danner Wilson, David Alan Danner; m. Charles Harold Sandage, July 18, 1971; m. Robert D. Mussey, Oct. 21, 2000. BS, U. Colo., 1967, MA, 1970; PhD in Comms., U. Ill., 1973. Pub. rels. rep. editor Martin News Martin Marietta Corp., Denver, 1960-63, 65-67; retail advt. salesperson Denver Post, 1967-70; instr. advt. U. Ill., 1970-71, vis. lectr. advt., 1977-84; v.p., corp. sec., dir. Farm Rsch. Inst., Urbana, Ill., 1984-95; ret., 1995. Editor: Advertising as a Social Force: Selected Speeches and Essays by Charles H. Sandage, 1998, Occasional Papers in Advertising, 1971, The Sandage Family Cookbook, 1976, 3d edit., 2002, The Inkling (Carle Hosp. Aux. Newsletter), 1975-76. Bd. dirs. U. Ill. Libr. Friends, 1991-95; exec. dir. Sandage Charitable Trust, 1986—. Mem. U. Ill. Alumni Assn. (pres.'s coun.), Champaign Social Sci. Club, The Book Club, Moneymakers Investment Club, Kappa Tau Alpha.

**SANDALOW, TERRANCE,** law educator; b. Chgo., Sept. 8, 1934; s. Nathan and Evelyn (Hoffing) Sandalow; m. Ina Davis, Sept. 4, 1955; children: David Blake, Marc Alan, Judith Ann. AB, U. Chgo., 1954, JD, 1957. Bar: Ill. 1958, Mich. 1978. Law clk. to judge Sterry R. Waterman U.S. Ct. Appeals (2d cir.), 1957-58; law clk. to justice Potter Stewart U.S. Supreme Ct., Washington, 1958-59; assoc. Ross, McGowan & O'Keefe, Chgo., 1959-61; assoc. prof. law U. Minn., Mpls., 1961-64, prof., 1964-66; prof. law U. Mich., Ann Arbor, 1966-2000, dean Law Sch., 1978-87, Edson R. Sunderland prof. law, 1987-2000, dean emeritus and Edson R. Sunderland prof. law emeritus, 2000—. Author (with F. I. Michelman): (book) Government in Urban Areas, 1970; author: (with E. Stein) Courts and Free Markets, 1982; contbr. articles to legal jours. and periodicals. Mem. Mpls. Commn. Human Rels., 1965—66. Recipient Profl. Achievement award, U. Chgo. Alumni; fellow, Ctr. Advanced Study in Behavioral Scis., 1972—73. Fellow: Am. Acad. Arts Scis.; mem.: Order of Coif (nat. pres. 2001—04), Phi Beta Kappa (hon.). Office: U Mich Law Sch Hutchins Hall Ann Arbor MI 48109-1215 Personal E-mail: terrysan@comcast.net. Business E-mail: sandalow@umich.edu.

**SANDBERG, CRAIG M.,** lawyer; b. Ill., Oct. 25, 1971; BA, Mich. State U., East Lansing, Mich., 1994; JD, Chgo., 1998. Bar: Ill. 1999. Jud. extern to Hon. Allen A. Freeman Cir. Ct. Cook County, Chgo., 1996; jud. extern to Hon. Ronald A. Guzman U.S. Dist. Ct. (no. dist.) Ill., Chgo., 1997; pvt. practice Chgo., 1999—2004; asst. state's atty. Cook County State's Atty.'s Office, Chgo., 2004— Mem. young profls. bd. Chgo. Bar Found. Annual. Ad. mem. Gilda's Club Chgo., 2003—05. Recipient Excellence in Pro Bono and Pub. Interest Svc. award, U.S. Dist. Ct. (no dist.) Ill. and Chgo. Chpt. FBA, 2004. Mem.: Chgo. Bar Assn. (mem. exec. coun. young lawyer's sect. 2005, Rising Star award 2005), Fed. Bar Assn. (bd. dir. young lawyer's 1965—99. 2003). Office: Cook County State's Attorney's Office 50 W Washington Street Room 301 Chicago IL 60602 Office Phone: 312-603-7954. Office Fax: 312-603-3600. Business E-mail: csandberg@cookcountygov.com.

**SANDBERG, IRWIN WALTER,** retired electrical and computer engineering educator; b. N.Y.C., Jan. 23, 1934; s. Ben and Estelle S.; m. Barbara A. Zimmerman, June 15, 1958; 1 dau. Heidi L. B.E.E., Poly. Inst. Bklyn., 1955, M.E.E., 1956, D.E.E., 1958. Tech. aid Bell Telephone Labs., Inc., Murray Hill, NJ, summer 1954, mem. tech. staff, 1958-67, head systems theory research dept., 1967-72, mem. math. and statis. research ctr., 1972-86; prof. elec. and computer engring. U. Tex., Austin, 1986—, Cockrell Family Regents chair in engring. emeritus; engr. Wheeler Labs., Great Neck, NY, summer 1955. Vis. prof. U. Calif.-Berkeley, 1965; U.S. del. Union Radio Scientifique Internationale, Munich, Germany, 1966; U.S. nat. inst. rep. Advanced Study Inst. on Network and Signal Theory, NATO, Bournemouth, Eng., 1972; lectr. study inst. NATO (Knokke), Belgium, 1966, Copenhagen, 1970; disting. invited spkr. Asilomar Conf., 1973-74; main lectr. European Conf. on Circuit Theory and Design, The Hague, 1981; advisor Inst. Electronics, Info. and Comm. Engrs., Tokyo; advisor Am. Men and Women of Sci., 1993. Patentee (in field). Recipient Best Paper award Asilomar Conf., 1970, Achievement award IEEE Circuits and Systems Soc., 1986, Classic Paper citation ISI press, 1984, Outstanding Alumnus award Poly. U., 1993. Fellow IEEE (life, adminstrv. com. group circuit theory 1969-70, vice chmn. group circuit theory 1971-72, Centennial medal, Millennial medal, Cirs. and Sys. Soc. Golden Jubilee medal, Cirs. and Sys. Soc. disting. lectr.), AAAS; mem. NAE, Soc. for Indsl. and Applied Math., Acad. Medicine, Engring. and Sci. Tex., Eta Kappa Nu, Sigma Xi, Tau Beta Pi Home: 8505 Hickory Creek Dr Austin TX 78735-1527 Office: Univ Tex Dept Elec Comp Engr Austin TX 78712 Office Phone: 512-471-6899. E-mail: sandberg@ece.utexas.edu.

**SANDBERG, SHERYL,** information technology executive; BA summa cum laude, Harvard U., MBA. Economist World Bank; mgmt consul. McKinsey & Co.; chief of staff to sec. of treasury US Dept. Treasury, 1999—2001; joined

Google Inc., Mountain View, Calif., 2001, v.p. global online sales and ops. Bd. mem. Ad Coun., Leadership Pub. Schs. Office: Google Inc 1600 Amphitheatre Pkwy Mountain View CA 94043 Office Phone: 650-253-0000. Office Fax: 650-253-0001.*

**SANDBERG, STEVE JASON,** music educator; b. Rochester, Minn., Oct. 15, 1958; s. Warren Sanfridd Sandberg and Mary Maxine Peterson; m. Sandra Lee Bourassa, Aug. 9, 1980; children: Käta Lee, Erik Adam. BA, St. Olaf Coll., Northfield, Minn., 1981; MusM, U. Minn., Mpls., 1996. Choir dir. Mountain Iron Pub. Schs., Minn., 1981—86, St. Peter H.S., Minn., 1986—89; voice instr. Hastings H.S., Minn., 1989—92; part-time voice instr. Bethel U., St. Paul, 1992—95, Northwestern Coll., St. Paul, 1993—95; voice instr. St. Olaf Coll., Northfield, 1995—99; elem. music specialist South Washington County Schs., Cottage Grove, Minn., 1999—. Profl. singer The Dale Warland Singers, 1988—96, Minn. Opera, 1996—. Composer: (choral composition) This Is My Commandment, 2006. Sgt. Minn. Army Nat. Guard, 1988—95. Mem.: Music Educators Nat. Conf., Scottish Rite Freemasonry, Ancient Free and Accepted Masons, Phi Kappa Phi, Pi Kappa Lambda, Phi Beta Kappa. Avocations: music composition, birdwatching, golf, camping. Home: 20951 India Ave Lakeville MN 55044 Office: Red Rock Elem Sch 3311 Commonwealth Ave Woodbury MN 55125 Office Phone: 651-768-5600. E-mail: stevesandberg@charter.net.

**SANDBURG, HELGA,** author; b. Maywood, Ill., Nov. 24, 1918; d. Carl and Lilian (Steichen) S.; m. George Crile, Jr., Nov. 9, 1963; children by previous marriage: John Carl Steichen, Paula Steichen Polega. Student, Mich. State Coll., 1939-40, U. Chgo., 1940. Dairy goat breeder, also personal sec. to father, 1944-51; sec. manuscripts div., also for keeper of collections Library of Congress, 1952-56; adminstrv. asst. for papers of Woodrow Wilson, 1958-59; writer, lectr., 1957—. Author: (novels) The Wheel of Earth, 1958, Measure My Love, 1959, The Owl's Roost, 1962, The Wizard's Child, 1967; (non-fiction) Sweet Music, A Book of Family Reminiscence and Song, 1963; (with George Crile, Jr.) Above and Below, 1969; (poetry) The Unicorns, 1965; To A New Husband, 1970, The Age of the Flower, 1994; (young adult novels) Blueberry, 1963; Gingerbread, 1964; (juveniles) Joel and the Wild Goose, 1963; Bo and the Old Donkey, 1965, Anna and the Baby Buzzard, 1970; Children and Lovers: 15 Stories by Helga Sandburg, 1976; (biography) A Great and Glorious Romance: The Story of Carl Sandburg and Lilian Steichen, 1978; "...Where Love Begins", 1989, (recorded poems) From in the Dream: Helga Sandburg Reads her Poems, 2001; also numerous short stories; rep. in collections.; contbr.short stories, poems, articles to popular mags. including Seventeen. Recipient Va. Quar. Rev. prize for best short story, 1959, Borestone Mountain poetry award, 1962, Poetry award Chgo. Tribune, 1970, 2d prize 7th Ann. Kans. Poetry Contest, Florence Roberts Head Ohioana Book award, 1990; grantee Finnish Am. Soc. and Svenska Inst., 1961 Mem. Authors Guild, Poetry Soc., Am. Milk Goat Record Assn., Am.-Scandinavian Found., Nat. Nubian Club, Coun. Save the Dunes, Am. Luxembourg Soc., Acad. Am. Poets. Address: 2060 Kent Rd Cleveland Heights OH 44106-3339 E-mail: helgacrile@steichen.ws.

**SANDDAL, NELS DODGE,** foundation executive, consultant; b. Salt Lake City, Feb. 17, 1949; s. James Wesley and Charlotte Jean (Ewer) S.; m. Brenda Kay Lille Griffin, Sept. 27, 1970 (div. June 1990); m. Theresa Louise Knipe, Oct. 10, 1992; 1 child, Jami. BA in English, Carroll Coll., 1966-70; MS in Psychology, Mont. State U., 1996; student, Walden U. In-svc. trainer Boulder (Mont.) River Sch. and Hosp., 1974-75; group home mgr. REACH, Inc., Bozeman, Mont., 1975-76; community home trainer Devel. Disabilities Tng. Inst., Helena, Mont., 1976-77; tng. coord. emergency med. svcs. bureau State Dept. Health and Environ. Scis., Helena, 1977-82; cons., lead staff Nat. Coun. State Emergency Med. Svcs. Tng. Coords., Inc., Lexington, Ky., 1981-86; account exec., lead staff Nat. Assn. Emergency Med. Techs., Clinton, Miss., 1986-87; pres., CEO Assn. Mgmt. and Cons., Inc., Boulder, 1983-89; writer, prodr., dir. North Country Media Group, Great Falls, Mont., 1990-91; chief conf. planner S.O.S. Conf. Planning Consortium, Great Falls, 1991-92; exec. dir. Critical Illness & Trauma Found., Bozeman, Mont., 1986-91, pres., CEO, 1991—. Season course leader Nat. Outdoor Leadership Sch., Lander, Wyo., 1966—74; mem. exec. com. Nat. Coun. State EMS Tng. Coords., 1977—82, chmn., Ky., 1979—81; mem. adv. com. pediatric emergency med. svcs. tng. project Children's Hosp. Nat. Med. Ctr., Wash., 1985—88, pediatrics emergency instr., 1986—90; mem. grant peer rev. com. divsn. injury epidemiology Ctrs. for Disease Control, Atlanta, 1986—87; mem. injury prevention profls. New Eng. Network to Prevent Childhood Injuries, Newton, Mass., 1988—95; mem. core faculty devel. trauma sys. tng. program U.S. Dept. Transp., Wash., 1989—; tech. assistance team mem. EMS, 1991—93; EMS instr. and program coord. Great Falls Vocat. Tng. Ctr., 1991—93; rsch. asst. inst. for cmty. studies U. Mo., Kansas city, 1983—95; assoc. rsch. prof. psychology Mont. State U., 1999—2003; asst. clin. prof. surgery U. Nev. Sch. Medicine, 1999—2003; exec. com. Intermountain Regional EMS Children Coord. Coun., Bozeman, Mont., 1994—2002; site reviewer Comm. for Accreditation of Ambulance Svcs., Glenview, Ill., 1997—; firefighter/EMS trainer Gallatin Gateway Vol. Fire Dept., Gallatin Gateway, Mont., 1998—2001; asst. chief Gallatin Gateway Fire Dept., 2001—; med. officer Gallatin River Ranch, 2001—; dir. Rural EMS and Trauma Tech. Assistance Ctr., Bozewick, Mont., 2003; tech. adv. trauma sys. and evaluation com. Am. Coll.; mem. various coms. Inst. Medicine, 2003—; assoc. rsch. prof. Health Scis. Mont. State U., 2003—; cons. in field. Editor and tech. cons.: Workbook for Prehospital Care and Crisis Intervention, 4th edit., 1992, 5th edit., 1993, Instructor Resource Manual for Prehospital Care and Crisis Intervention, 4th edit., 1992, Workbook for First Responder, 1990; contbg. editor Jour. of Prehospital Care, 1984-85, The EMT Jour., 1980-81; editl. cons. Am. Acad. Orthopaedic Surgeons, 1980-81; contbr. numerous articles to profl. jours.; video prodr. and presenter in field. Mem. Park County DUI Task Force, Livingson, 1993-96; inaugural coord. Mont. Safe Kids Coalition, Big Timber, 1988-90; adv. com. Nat. Significance Project for Respite Care, 1977-78; mem. basic life support com. of Mont., Mont. Heart Assn., 1977-82. Recipient Golden award for humanity ARC, 1976, 500 Hour award, 1976, Outstanding Svc. award Nat. Coun. State EMS Tng. Coords., 1979, Leadership award, 1981, Charter Membership award, 1984, J.D. Farrington award for excellence Nat. Assn. Emergency Med. Technicians, 1981, Jeffrey S. Harris award, 1985, Outstanding Svc. award Am. Heart Assn., 1982, Appreciation cert. for paramedic emergency care U.S. Dept. Transp., 1984, Appreciation award Colo. Trauma Inst., 1993, Healthy Mothers/Healthy Babies, Helena, Mont., 1997, Kans. Id of EMS, Topeka, 1996, 98, 2003, Intermountain Regional EMS for Children Coordinating Coun., Inc., 1998; named Provider of Yr., EMS for Children, 2005. Mem. Nat. Registry EMTs (20 yr. recognition), Mont. Bd. Med. Examiners. Democrat. Avocations: mountain climbing, hiking, sailing, golf, skiing. Home: 115 Lay Pass Manhattan MT 59741 Office: 115 Lay Pass Rd Manhattan MT 59741-8032 E-mail: nsanddal@citmt.org.

**SANDE, THEODORE ANTON,** architect, educator, foundation executive; b. New London, Conn., Nov. 21, 1933; s. Lars Anton and Viola (Edgcomb) S.; m. Solveig Inga-Maj Imselius, Aug. 6, 1960; children: Susanne Ingrid, Lars Michael. BSc in Architecture, RI Sch. Design, 1956; MArch, Yale U., 1961; PhD, U. Pa., 1972; grad. Cultural Instns. Mgmt. Program, Mus. Collaborative, 1983; postgrad., Attingham (Eng.) Summer Sch., 1980. Vis. prof. history of architecture Rensselaer Poly. Inst., fall 1973-74, U. Pa., 1976-77; adj. prof. Am. studies and history Case-Western Res. U., 1981—92. Vis. lectr. in historic preservation Cleve. State U., summer 1994, spring 1998; lectr. art Williams Coll., 1972-75; attended teleconfs. non-profit orgn. mgmt. Drucker Found., 1992. Designer, Arkitekt, Hakon Ahlberg, SAR, Arkitekt, Stockholm, 1960, designer, Arkitekt, Skanhem, Luther & Rowley, Architects, Attleboro, Mass., 1961-62, Barker & Turoff, Architects, Providence, 1962-63, jr. partner, Turoff Assocs., Architects, 1964-67, partner, Turoff & Sande, Architects, Providence, 1968-70, prin. Ted Sande, Architect, Cranston, R.I., 1970, Cleve., 1993—; emeritus architect, R.I., 2004— author: Industrial Archaeology: A New Look at the American Heritage, 2d edit, 1978; contbg. author: Guidebook to Philadelphia Architecture, 1974; editor: New England Textile Mill Survey, 1971; co-editor: Historic Preservation of Engineering Works, 1981; contbr. articles to profl. jours.; two-man show drawings, Providence Art Club, 1970. Dir. profl. svcs. office hist. properties Nat. Trust Hist. Preservation, Washington, 1975—77, dir. planning and devel., 1977—78, acting v.p. office hist. properties, 1978—79, v.p., 1979—80; mem. Old Georgetown Bd. Nat. Commn. Fine Arts, 1979—81; co-chmn. Conf. Indsl. Archeology Smithsonian Instn., 1971; active Shaker Heights Landmark Commn., 1982—84, Cleve. Landmarks Commn., 1985—2004; mem. archtl. bd. rev. Village of Hunting Valley, Ohio, 2000—. Recipient Leadership Cleve. Class 86/87, Ohio Gov.'s Commn. on Bicentennials the NW Ordinance and U.S. Const., 1986—89, Cleve. Bicentennial Commn., 1992—94, Stan Hywet Hall and Gardens, Akron, Ohio, trustee, 1997—2005; chmn. Schweinfurth Trust, 1999—; mem. vis. com. Mandel Sch. Scis., Case We. Res. U., 1993—2003; trustee U. Circl Inc., 1991—93, Nat. Rock and Roll Mus. and Hall of Fame, mem. exec. bdlg. com., 1993—95; instnl. rep. Cleve. Arts Consortium, 1987—93. Fellow: We. Res. Hist. Soc. (life; exec. dir. 1981—93, exec. dir. emeritus 1993—); mem.: SAR, AIA (com. hist. resources 1972—74), Cleve. Restoration Soc. (pres. 1994—97, trustee, hon., life trustee), Ohio Mus. Assn. (trustee 1982—87), Am. Assn. Mus., Internat. Com. for Conservation of Indsl. Heritage (chmn. bd. dirs 1978—81), Soc. Archtl. Historians (preservation com. 1972—74), Soc. Indsl. Archeology (co-founder, 1st pres. 1971—72, dir. 1973—76, project supr. handbook on adaptive use of indsl. bldgs., gen. chmn. 15th ann. conf.), Philos. Club Cleve. (past pres.), Rowfant Club (past pres. 2002—03, coun. of fellows). Episcopalian. Home: 13415 Shaker Blvd Ste 11-H-4 Cleveland OH 44120-1586

**SANDEEN, ERIC JOHN,** history professor; b. Kansas City, Mo., June 23, 1948; s. Ernest Emanuel and Eileen Evelyn Sandeen; m. Susan Margaret Strittmatter, June 19, 1971. BA, U. Notre Dame, Ind., 1970; PhD in Am. Studies, U. Iowa, Iowa City, 1977. Master Portsmouth Abbey Sch., RI, 1970—73; asst. prof. English and Am. studies Idaho State U., Pocatello, 1978—82; prof., dir. Am. studies program U. Wyo., Laramie, 1982—. Author: (book) Picturing an Exhibition. Dir. Peace Corps Fellows Program, 2002—06; bd. mem. AmeriCorps Program, Laramie, Wyo., 2004—06; u. rep. Main St. Program, 2005—06. Recipient Mary C. Turpie award, Am. Studies Assn., 2002, Faculty Internationalization award, U. Wyo., 2002, Disting. Alumnus, Coll. Arts and Scis., U. Iowa, 2003. Mem.: Am. Studies Assn. (life; nat. coun. mem. 1975—77, founding mem. Am. studies programs com. 1981—91, nat. coun. mem. 1984—87, internat. com. 1994—97, mem. task force pub. practice 2001—04). Home: 4705 Sunset Drive Laramie WY 82070 Office: University of Wyoming American Studies Program Laramie WY 82071 Office Phone: 307-766-3898. Office Fax: 307-766-3700. Business E-Mail: esandeen@uwyo.edu.

**SANDEFER, G(EORGE) LARRY,** lawyer; b. Washington, Mar. 2, 1950; s. George Hall and Mary Gray (Babers) S. BS, Auburn U., 1972; JD, U. Fla., 1978. Bar: Fla. 1978, U.S. Dist. Ct. (mid. dist.) Fla. 1978, U.S. Ct. Appeals (5th and 11th cirs.) 1981, U.S. Supreme Ct. 1982; cert. in criminal trial law Fla. Bar. Asst. state atty., criminal divsn., lead trial atty. State of Fla., Clearwater, 1977-86; sole practice Clearwater, 1986-88; assoc. Kimpton, Burke and White, P.A., Clearwater, 1988-90; pvt. practice, Clearwater, 1991—. Mem. Indian Rocks Civic Assn., 1994-2000, Leadership Pinellas; city commr. Indian Rocks Beach, 1994-00. 1st lt. USAF, 1973-75. Mem. ATLA, Pinellas County Trial Lawyers Assn., Am. Criminal Def. Attys., Colo. Bar Assn., Fla. Bar Assn., Clearwater Bar Assn., St. Petersburg Bar Assn., Kiwanis. Avocations: tennis, skiing, boating. Address: 111 N Belcher Rd Ste 202 Clearwater FL 33765-3259

**SANDEFUR, DENICE LEE,** science educator; b. Denver, Nov. 24, 1953; d. Lee and Alice Cary; m. Rodney Andrew Sandefur, June 10, 1973; children: Scott Andrew, Ryan Lee. BA, Adams State U., Alamosa, Colo., 1975; MA, Adams State U., 1977. Tchr. sci., biology Nucla (Colo.) H.S., 1977—. Vol. River Watch Colo. Dam; firefighter Nucla Fire Dept. Recipient Gov.'s Environ. award, Gov. Colo., 1993. Avocations: hiking, rafting, animals. Home: 5035 Grape St PO Box 601 Nucla CO 81424 Office: Nucla High School PO Box 570 Nucla CO 81424-0570

**SANDELMAN, JONATHAN E. (JON),** investment banker; Bachelor's Degree, Adelphia U.; JD, Cardozo Sch. Law. Dep. head global equities, mng. dir. equity derivatives Salomon Bros.; head equity fin. products NationsBank (now Bank Am. Securities), N.Y.C., 1998—2002; head equities Banc Am. Securities LLC, N.Y.C., 2002—04, pres., 2004—, head debt and equities, 2004—. Trustee Whitney Mus. Am. Art. Office: Bank of Am Securities LLC 9 W 57th St New York NY 10019

**SANDER, FRANK ERNEST ARNOLD,** law educator; b. Stuttgart, Germany, July 22, 1927; came to U.S., 1940, naturalized, 1946; s. Rudolf and Alice (Epstein) S.; m. Emily Bishop Jones, Apr. 26, 1958; children: Alison Bishop, Thomas Harvey, Ernest Ridgway Sander. AB in Math. magna cum laude, Harvard U., 1949, LLB magna cum laude, 1952. Bar: Mass. 1952, US Supreme Ct. 1952. Law clk. to Chief Judge Magruder U.S. Ct. Appeals, 1st Cir., 1952-53; law clk. to Justice Frankfurter, U.S. Supreme Ct., 1953-54; atty. tax divsn. Dept. Justice, 1954-56; with Hill & Barlow, Boston, 1956-59; mem. faculty Harvard Law Sch., 1959—, prof. law, 1962—, Bussey prof., 1981—, assoc. dean, 1987-2000, emeritus, 2006—. Spl. fields fed. taxation, family law, welfare law, dispute resolution; chmn. Coun. on Role of Cts.; mem. panels Am. Arbitration Assn., Fed. Mediation and Conciliation Svc.; chmn. Coun. on Legal Edn. Opportunity, 1968—70; cons. Dept. Treasury, 1968; treas. Harvard Law Rev., 1951—52; mem. dispute resolution standing com. Mass. Supreme Jud. Ct., 1994—2002; drafting com. Uniform Mediation Act, 1998—2001. Author: (with Westfall and McIntyre) Readings in Federal Taxation, 2d edit., 1983, (with Foote and Levy) Cases and Materials on Family Law, 3d edit., 1985, (with Gutman) Tax Aspects of Divorce and Separation, 4th edit., 1985, (with Goldberg, Rogers and Cole) Dispute Resolution, 4th edit., 2003. Mem. tax mission Internat. Program Taxation to Republic of Colombia, 1959; mem. com. on civil and polit. rights President's Commn. on Status of Women, 1962-63; trustee Buckingham Browne and Nichols Sch., 1969-75; chmn. Mass. Welfare Adv. Bd., 1975-79. With AUS, 1946-47. Recipient Whitney North Seymour medal Am. Arbitration Assn., 1988, spl. award for disting. svc. to dispute resolution Ctr. for Pub. Resources Inst. for Dispute Resolution, 1990, Lifetime Achievement award Internat. Acad. Mediators, 2006. Mem. ABA (chmn. standing com. dispute resolution 1986-89, Kutak medal 1993, D'Alemberte-Raven award 1999), Boston Bar Assn., Phi Beta Kappa. Home: 74 Buckingham St Cambridge MA 02138-2229 Office: Harvard U Sch of Law Cambridge MA 02138 Office Phone: 617-495-3184.

**SANDERCOX, ROBERT ALLEN,** academic administrator, minister; b. Akron, Ohio, May 20, 1932; s. Monroe J. and Elverda (Arnold) S.; m. Nancy Lee Wertz, Sept. 13, 1958; children: Alison Grace, Megan Louise, Robert Philip BA, Bethany Coll., W. Va., 1954; M.Div., Yale U., 1957; postgrad., U. Buffalo, W.Va. U.; LittD, Bethany Coll., 1989. Ordained to ministry Christian Ch. (Disciples of Christ). Asst. minister Park Ave Christian Ch., N.Y.C., 1954-57; asst. provost Bethany Coll., 1957-60, v.p., dean students, 1960-75, v.p., dir. devel., 1975-79, interim pres., 1979-80, v.p., provost for coll. advancement, 1980-89, sr. v.p., 1989-95, cons. to the pres., 1995-97, sr. v.p. emeritus, 1997—. Trustee Bethany Coll., 2004—. Trustee Christian Ch. Disciples of Christ in W.Va., Parkersburg, 1984-88; chmn. Brooke County Landmarks Commn., 1988-98, Brooke County Mus. Bd., 1995-98. Recipient Alumni Disting. Service award Bethany Coll., 1982 Mem. Coun. for Advancement and Support Edn., Duquesne Club (Pitts.), Univ. Club of Jacksonville, Order of Symposiarch, Rotary, Kiwanis (pres. 1967), Alpha Sigma Phi (nat. treas. 1982-84, v.p. 1984-86, grad. sr. pres. 1986-88, bd. dirs., trustee Ednl. Found. 1982-95, chmn. Ednl. Found. 1994-95, Delta Beta Xi svc. award 1960). Republican. Home: 4557 Middleton Park Cir E Jacksonville FL 32224-6609 Address: 715 Buckwood Ln Lititz PA 17543 Personal E-mail: r.sandercox@prodigy.net.

**SANDERS, AARON PERRY,** radiation biophysics educator; b. Phoenix, Jan. 12, 1924; s. DeWitt and Ruth (Perry) S.; m. Betty Mae Gelein, Aug. 11, 1944 (div.); children: Merle Sanders Ireland, Julie Sanders Mitchel, James DeWitt; m. Georgia Anne Bullock, Nov. 26, 1972 (div.); 1 child, Kai Marie; m. Vallie E. Flint. BS, U. Tex., El Paso, 1950; MS (AEC fellow), U. Rochester, 1952; PhD, U. N.C., 1964. Diplomate: Am. Bd. Health Physics. Baggage clk., ticket agt. Greyhound Bus Lines, Phoenix, 1942, dispatcher, ticket agt. El Paso, Tex., 1946-50; asso. health physicist Brookhaven Nat. Lab., Upton, NY, 1951-53; instr. physics, radiol. safety officer N.C. State Coll., 1953; instr. radiology Duke Med. Center, Durham, NC, 1953-56, dir. radioisotope lab., 1953-65; asso. in radiology Duke Med. Ctr., 1956-57, asst. prof., 1957-64, assoc. prof., 1964-65, assoc. prof., dir. div. radiobiology, 1965-70, prof., dir. div. radiobiology, 1970-83, prof. emeritus, 1983—; chmn. Biomed. Physics Dept. King Faisal Specialist Hosp., Riyadh, Saudi Arabia, 1984-86. Fulbright sr. lectr. radiol. physics, Argentina, 1958-59; cons. N.C. Bd. Health, 1961-76; mem. N.C. Radiation Protection Commn., 1976-83, chmn., 1978-79 Contbr. articles to profl. jours. Served with USNR, 1942-45. Mem. AAAS, Am. Assn. Physicists in Medicine, AAUP, Soc. Exptl. Biology and Medicine, Health Physics Soc., Soc. Nuclear Medicine, Biophys. Soc., Radiation Research Soc., Undersea Med Soc., Sigma Xi, Sigma Pi Sigma. *Each individual has an obligation to himself and society to pursue an education to his maximum capability. This capability should then be used in his career in an effort to contribute to society as much, or more, than he receives. In work and personal relations you must never deny a man the dignity of his work by ridicule or denigration, and you must never use people.*

**SANDERS, ADRIAN LIONEL,** retired educational consultant; b. Paragould, Ark., Aug. 3, 1938; s. Herbert Charles and Florence Theresa (Becherer) S.; m. Molly Jean Zecher, Dec. 20, 1961. AA, Bakersfield Coll., 1959; BA, San Francisco State U., 1961; MA, San Jose State U., 1967. 7th grade tchr. Sharp Park Schs., Pacifica, Calif., 1961-62; 5th grade tchr. Mowry Sch., Fremont, Calif., 1962-64; sci. tchr. Blacow Sch., Fremont, Calif., 1964-76; 5th grade tchr. Warm Springs Sch., Fremont, 1977-87, 5th grade gifted and talented edn. tchr., 1987-94; ret., 2006; edn. cons., 1994—2006. Mem. San Diego Hist. Soc., 1999, Mingei Internat. Mus., Balboa Park-San Diego; vol. 7 km. Race for Alzheimer's Disease Willow Glen Founders Day, San Jose, 1988-92. Named Outstanding Young Educator, Jr. C. of C., Fremont, Calif., 1965. Mem. Zoolog. Soc. San Diego, Calif. Ctr. for the Arts (Escondido). Avocations: photography, travel, collecting license plates. Home and Office: 1437 Stoneridge Cir Escondido CA 92029-5514

**SANDERS, BARRY,** retired professional football player; b. Wichita, July 16, 1968; s. William and Shirley Sanders. Student, Okla. State U., 1986—89. Running back Detroit Lions, 1989—99. Co-author (with Mark E. McCormick): Now You See Him: The Barry Sanders Story, 2003. Named NFL Rookie of Yr., 1990, NFL Offensive Player of the Yr., 1991, 1997, NFL Player of the Yr., 1991, 1997; named to Sporting News Coll. All-Am. team, 1987, 1988, Pro Bowl 1989—98; recipient Heisman Trophy award, 1988. Achievements include holds NCAA single season record in rushing yards (2,628); led NFL in rushing, 1990, 94, 96, 97; #3 all-time on NFL rushing list (15,269); inducted into NFL Hall of Fame, 2004.

**SANDERS, BARRY R.,** lawyer; b. Oak Park, Ill., July 21, 1957; s. Eugene Haze and Muriel Efty Sanders; m. Diane Gaffney Sanders, Dec. 28, 1985; 1 child, Mattie Maria Murielle. BA, U. Va., 1979, Cambridge U., 1981; LLM, U. Tex., 1983; MA, Cambridge U., 1986. Bar: Calif. 1984, Ariz. 1985, U.S. Dist. Ct. (no. dist.) Calif. 1984, U.S. Dist. Ct. (ea. dist.) Calif. 1985, U.S. Dist. Ct. Ariz. 1987, U.S. Ct. Appeals (9th cir.) 1989, U.S. Supreme Ct. 1996, U.S. Ct. Appeals (8th cir.) 2001. Shareholder Pohlman & Sanders, PA, Phoenix, 1989—91, Ryley, Carlock & Applewhite, PA, Phoenix, 1991—99, Allen, Price, Padden & Sanders PC, Phoenix, 1999—2005, Mariscal Weeks McIntyre & Friedlander, P.A., 2005—. Recipient Henry prize in Moral Philosophy, U. of Aberdeen, Scotland, 1978. Mem.: State Bar Ariz. (chair antitrust sect. 1998—99, 2002—03). Avocation: golf. Office: Mariscal Weeks McIntyre & Friedlander P A 2901 N Ctrl Ave Ste 200 Phoenix AZ 85012 Business E-Mail: barry.sanders@mwmf.com.

**SANDERS, BERNARD (BERNIE SANDERS),** congressman; b. Bklyn., Sept. 8, 1941; s. Eli and Dorothy (Glassberg) Sanders; m. Jane O'Meara, 1988; children: Levi, Heather, Carina, David. Student, Bklyn. Coll.; BA, U. Chgo., 1964. Freelance writer, carpenter, youth counselor, 1964-76; dir. Am. People's Hist. Soc., Burlington, Vt., 1976-81; mayor Burlington, 1981-89; mem. faculty Harvard U., Cambridge, Mass., 1989, Hamilton Coll., Clinton, NY, 1990; mem. US Congress from Vt. at-large, 1991—. Mem. Progressive Caucus, US Congress, mem. fin. svcs. com., ranking minority mem. fin. instns. and consumer credit subsommittee, mem. govt. reform com. Co-author: Outsider in the House, 1997. Chmn. Vt. Liberty Union Party, 1975-76, candidate for Vt. gov., 1972, 76, 86, US Senate, 1971, 74. Independent. Jewish. Office: US Ho Reps 2233 Rayburn Ho Office Bldg Washington DC 20515-4501 Office Phone: 202-225-4115.*

**SANDERS, BILL,** medical educator; b. Santa Barbara, Calif., June 23, 1972; s. Bill and Elizabeth Sanders. MPhil, Cambridge U., Eng., 1995; PhD, U. of London, 2003. Rsch. assoc. Childrens Hosp. L.A., Hollywood, Calif., 2003—06; asst. prof. U. of So. Calif., L.A., 2006—. Editor: (book) Drugs, Clubs and Young People: Sociological and Public Health Perspectives; author: Youth Crime and Youth Culture in the Inner City, (book chpt.) A Public Health Model for Studying Youth Gangs. Recipient grant for rsch. on negative health outcomes related to substance use, violence, and sexual behaiovrs among gang-identified youth in L.A., Nat. Inst. Drug Abuse, 2005—07. Mem.: APHA, Soc. for the Study of Social Problems, Am. Sociol. Assn., Am. Soc. of Criminology. Avocations: surfing, reading, travel. Office: U So Calif/CHLA Ste 1500 6430 W Sunset Blvd Hollywood CA 90028 Office Phone: 310-429-4085. E-mail: bsanders@chla.usc.edu.

**SANDERS, CARL E.,** lawyer, former governor; b. Augusta, Ga., May 15, 1925; s. Carl T. and Roberta (Ailey) S.; m. Betty Bird Foy, 1947; children: Betty Foy, Carl E. Jr. LLB, Univ. Ga., 1947. Bar: Ga. 1947. Mem. Hammond, Kennedy & Sanders, Augusta, Ga., 1948—52; sr. mem. Sanders, Thurmond, Hester & Jolles, Augusta, Ga., Sanders, Hester, Holley, Ashmore & Boozer; chmn., mem. exec. com. Troutman Sanders LLP (formerly Troutman, Sanders, Lockerman & Ashmore), Atlanta, 1967—; Ga. State Rep., 1954—56; Ga. State Senator, 1957—62; pres. pro tem Ga. State Senate, 1960—62; Gov. State of Ga., 1963—67. Chmn., rules com. Dem. Nat. Conv., 1964; mem., exec. com. Nat. Gov. Conf., 1964—65; chmn. Appalachian Gov. Conf., 1964—65; vice chmn. Southern Gov. Conf., 1965—66; mem. Nat. Commn. on Urban Affairs, 1967; bd. dir. Pub. Broadcasting Corp., 1968—70; chmn., fin. com. Dem. Party, Ga., 1974—83; bd. dir. Healthdyne, 1986—96, Matria Healthcare, 1996—; Wachovia Atlanta Adv. Bank Bd.; mem. Atlanta Com., Olympic Games, 1996. Served to 1st lt. (first pilot of B-17 heavy bomber) USAF, WWII. Named a Super Lawyer, Atlanta Mag., 2004; recipient Order of Sacred Treasure Gold and Silver award, Emperor and Govt. of Japan, 1989. Mem.: ABA, Lawyers Club of Atlanta, Atlanta Bar Assn., Phi Delta Phi. Democrat. Achievements include being inducted into Athletic Hall of Fame, 1968, Aviation Hall of Fame, 1997. Office: Troutman Sanders LLP One Logan Sq 600 Peachtree St NE Atlanta GA 30308-2216 Office Phone: 404-885-3100. Office Fax: 404-962-6674. Business E-Mail: carl.sanders@troutmansanders.com.

**SANDERS, CHARLES FRANKLIN,** energy executive, consultant; b. Louisville, Dec. 22, 1931; s. Charles Franklin and Maragret Rhea (Timmons) S.; m. Marie Audrey Galuppo, Dec. 29, 1956; children: Karen Lynn, Craig Joseph, Keith Franklin. B.Chem. Engring., U. Louisville, 1954, M.Chem. Engring., 1958; PhD, U. So. Calif., 1970. Rsch. engr. Exxon Rsch. and Engring. Co., Linden, NJ, 1955-62; assoc. prof., 1968-71, prof., 1971-82, chmn. dept., 1969-72, dean Coll. Engring. and Computer Sci., 1971-82; pres., chief exec. officer, dir. Rusco Industries, Los Angeles, 1981-82; exec. v.p. Energy Systems Assocs., Tustin, Calif., 1982-89, Energeo, San Francisco, 1989-95, also bd. dirs.; v.p. tech. Smith-Bellingham Capital, San Francisco, 1989-91. Bd. dirs. Catalyst Air Tech., Inc. Bd. dirs. San Fernando Valley Child Guidance Clinic, 1979-81. Served to 1st lt. US Army, 1956-57. NSF fellow, 1965-67 Mem. AIChE, NSPE, Calif. Soc. Profl. Engrs., Am. Soc. for Engring. Edn., Combustion Inst. Republican. Personal E-mail: cfs@cox.net.

**SANDERS, CURTIS ARRA,** music educator; b. Tifton, Ga., Aug. 2, 1967; s. Curtis Lamar Sanders, Jr. and Pat Sanders Berger. BA Cum Laude in Music Edn., Valdosta State U., 1990, M in Music Edn., 1992. Assoc. band dir. Valdosta (Ga.) City Schs., 1990—94, Sandy Creek HS, Tyrone, Ga., 1994—2002, Stockbridge HS, Stockbridge, Ga., 2002—. Mem.: Percussive Arts Soc., Nat. Band Assn., Ga. Music Educators Assn. Office: Stockbridge HS Band 1151 Old Conyers Rd Stockbridge GA 30281

**SANDERS, DALE R.,** lawyer; b. N.Y.C., Feb. 1, 1946; m. Jo-Ann Sanders, Dec. 25, 1967; 1 child. Bar: Fla. 1970, Wyo. 1991, U.S. Dist. Ct. (so. dist.) Fla. 1971, U.S. Tax Ct. 1972. Atty. Kirsch & Druck, P.A., Ft. Lauderdale, Fla., 1970-71, Kirsch, Digiulian, Druck et al, Ft. Lauderdale, Fla., 1971-72, Digiulian, Spellacy, Lyons, Ft. Lauderdale, Fla., 1972-77, Lyons & Sanders, Chartered, Ft. Lauderdale, Fla., 1977—. With USAR, 1969-75. Mem.: Broward County Trial Lawyers Assn. (pres. 1980), Broward County Bar Assn. (pres. 1990), Fla. Bar (bd. govs. 1991—95, mem. 17th cir. jud. nominating commn. 1992—96, vice chair 1996—2002, mem. State of Fla. jud. qualifications commn.). Office: Lyons and Sanders Chartered 600 NE 3rd Ave Fort Lauderdale FL 33304-2618

**SANDERS, DEION LUWYNN,** professional football player; b. Ft. Myers, Fla., Aug. 9, 1967; Student, Fla. State U. Baseball player N.Y. Yankees, 1988—90, Atlanta Braves, 1991—94, Cin. Reds, 1994—95, 1997, 2001; football player Atlanta Falcons, 1989—94, San Francisco 49ers, 1994, Dallas Cowboys, 1995—99, Washington Redskins, 2000, Baltimore Ravens, 2004—; TV Analyst CBS NFL Today, 2001—04. Mem. Championship team Super Bowl XXIX, 1994, Championship team Super Bowl XXX, 1995. Named to Sporting News Coll. All-Am. football team, 1986—88, Sporting News NFL All-Pro football team, 1991, 1992, 1994, Pro Bowl team, 1991—94, 1996—99; recipient Jim Thorpe award, 1988. Office: c/o Baltimore Ravens 1101 Russel st Baltimore MD 21230*

**SANDERS, DONALD BENJAMIN,** neurologist, educator; b. Sumter, S.C., Aug. 3, 1938; s. Colclough E. and Frances Ann Sanders; m. Lynda Louise Frank, July 19, 1976; children: Colclough Allison, Kathleen Chatterton. BS, Univ. of the South, 1959; MD, Harvard Med. Sch., 1964. Diplomate Am. Bd. Neurology, Am. Bd. Electrodiagnostic Medicine. Asst. prof. neurology U. Va. Med. Sch., Charlottesville, 1973-77, assoc. prof. neurology, 1978-80; prof. medicine Duke U. Med. Sch., Durham, N.C., 1980—. Contbr. articles to profl. jours. Maj. USAF, 1969-72. Fellow Am. Acad. Neurology; mem. Am. Neurol. Assn., Am. Assn. Electrodiagnostic Medicine (bd. dirs. 1993-95, pres. 1996-97). Office: Duke U Med Ctr PO Box 3403 Durham NC 27710

**SANDERS, DOUGLAS CHARLES,** horticulturist, researcher, educator; b. Lansing, Mich., May 21, 1942; s. Charles S. and Dorthy Sanders; m. Ellen Joyce, Apr. 26, 1965. BS, Mich. State U., 1965; MS, U. Minn., 1969, PhD, 1970. From rsch. asst. to rsch. assoc. U. Minn., St. Paul, 1965-70; from asst. prof. N.C. State U., Raleigh, 1970-75, assoc. prof., 1975-82, prof., 1982—. Cons. Orgn. of Am. States, others. Contbr. over 185 articles to profl. jours. Recipient Outstanding Ext. award N.C. State U., 1993, Outstanding Ext. Specialist award Epsilon Sigma Phi, 1993; named Covington Outstanding Ext. Educator, 1999. Fellow Am. Soc. Hort. Sci. (Outstanding Extension Educator award, 1993); mem. Am. Soc. Agronomy, Crop Sci. Soc. Am. Achievements include development of drip fertigation systems for vegetables, of cultural systems for vegetables; investigation of integrated aquaculture and vegetable production system, and of nutrient cycling in vegetables; development of new cropping systems for asparagus, carrots, lettuce and onions. Office: NC State U Dept Horticultural Sci PO Box 7609 Raleigh NC 27695-0001 E-mail: Doug_Sanders@ncsa.edu.

**SANDERS, DOUGLAS WARNER, JR.,** lawyer, judge; b. Oklahoma City, Jan. 13, 1958; s. Douglas Warner Sr. and Jane (Livermore) S.; m. Brenda Gail Cox, Apr. 20, 1990; children: Douglas Warner III, Noel Layne, Jonathan Scott, Stephanie Marie. BS, Okla. State U., 1980; JD, Oklahoma City U., 1983. Bar: Okla., U.S. Dist. Ct. (ea., no. and we. dists.) Okla., U.S. Dist. Ct. (we. dist.) Ark. Assoc. Stipe Law Firm, Oklahoma City, 1983-85; ptnr. Sanders, Sanders & Sullivan, Poteau, Okla., 1985—. Mcpl. judge City of Poteau, 1994—, City of Spiro, Okla., 1994—, Town of Shady Point, Okla., 1994—; mem. Okla. Bd. Bar Examiners, 2000—. Recipient Outstanding Alumnus award Oklahoma City U. Law Sch., 1999. Fellow ABA; mem. Okla. Bar Assn. (bd. govs. 1992-94, v.p. 1997, pres. 1999, Pres.'s award 1997, Disting. Svc. award 1999), LeFlore County Bar Assn. (Pres.'s award 1997). Democrat. Presbyterian. Avocation: golf. Home: 900 N Witte St Poteau OK 74953-3636 Office: Sanders Sanders & Sullivan 104 S Church St Poteau OK 74953-3344 E-mail: dougal@clnk.com.

**SANDERS, ELIZABETH ANNE WEAVER (BETSY SANDERS),** management consultant, writer; b. Gettysburg, Pa., July 25, 1945; Student, Gettysburg Coll., 1963—65; BA in German Lang. and Linguistics, Wayne State U., 1967; MEd, Boston U., 1970; postgrad., U. Wash., 1976—78. With Nordstrom, 1971—90, v.p., gen. mgr., 1978—90; prin. The Sanders Partnership, Sutter Creek, Calif., 1971-90, prin., owner, 1990—; founder, dir. Nat. Bank So. Calif., 1971-90. Bd. dirs. Wal Mart Stores, Inc., Washington Mut., Wellpoint Health Sys., Inc., Wolverine Worldwide, Inc., Denny's Inc., H.F. Ahmanson Co., Carl Karcher Enterprises, Sport Chalet, St. Joseph Health Sys., spkr. in field. Author: Fabled Service, 1995. Trustee Gettysburg Coll.; coach; mentor. Recipient Woman of Achievement in Bus. award YWCA South Orange County, Director's Choice award, 1997; named Woman of Yr. Bus. and Industry YWCA North Orange County, Humanitarian of Yr. NCCJ, Author of Yr., 1996, Dir. of Yr., Corp. Gov. Forum for Corp. Dirs., 2002. Mem. Internat. Women's Forum. Office: The Sanders Partnership PO Box 14 Sutter Creek CA 95685-0014 Office Phone: 209-267-5400. E-mail: betsanders@aol.com.

**SANDERS, FRANKLIN D.,** retired insurance company executive; b. Newton, Mass., Apr. 24, 1935; s. Franklin and Ethel Shriner (Dulaney) S.; m. Jane Gray Collier, June 18, 1960; children— Cynthia, Franklin D., Nancy, Carolyn. AB, Amherst Coll., 1957; MBA, Harvard U., 1959. With 1st Boston Corp., N.Y.C., 1960-86, mng. dir., 1976-86; pres. Aegis Ins. Services Inc., Jersey City; ret. Treas., bd. dirs. Assoc. Electric & Gas Ins. Services Ltd., Hamilton, Bermuda, 1986-97. Chmn. Republican Exec. Com., Bernardsville, N.J., 1965-72, Bernardsville Zoning Bd. of Adjustment, 1966-99. Mem. Harvard Club (N.Y.C.). Episcopalian. Avocations: sailing, skiing, golf.

**SANDERS, GERALD HOLLIE,** communications educator; b. Mt. Vernon, Tex., Dec. 10, 1924; s. Elmer Hugh and Velma Mae (Hollowell) S.; m. Mary Dean Crew, July 18, 1947; children: Michael Dwaine, Rose Ann, Susan Kathleen, Randall Wayne. BA, Southeastern Okla. U., 1947; MA, Tex. Tech U., 1969; PhD, U. Minn., 1974. Program dir. Sta. WEWO, Laurenburg, NC, 1947—49; sports dir. Sta. KFYO, Lubbock, Tex., 1949—50; gen. mgr. Sta. KLVT, Levelland, Tex., 1950—51, 1953—54; sports dir. Sta. KCUL, Ft. Worth, 1954—55; asst. mgr. Sta. KDAV, Lubbock, 1955—57; mgr. Sta. KCBD, Lubbock, 1957—58; owner Sta. KSEL, Lubbock, 1958—67, Sta. KBUY, Amarillo, Tex., Sta. KERB, Kermit, Tex., Sta. KBEK, Elk City, Okla., Sta. KZZN, Littlefield, Tex.; lectr. comm. Coll. of Wooster, 1967—68, asst. prof, 1968—75, assoc. prof., 1975—91, chmn. dept. commn., 1974—81, Miami U., Oxford, Ohio, 1981—92, prof. emeritus commn., 1992—. Disting. lectr. Jinan U., Zhong Shan U., Fudan U., Nanjing U., Beijing U., China, 1989; cons. in field, Oxford, 1982—; polit. and trial cons., 1996—. Author: Introduction to Contemporary Academic Debate, 1983; contbr. articles. to profl. jours. Active Political Campaigns. Served in to col. USMC, 1943-46, PTO, 1951-53, Korea. Recipient Disting. Svc. award Delta Sigma Rho-Tau Kappa Alpha, 1991, Am. Forensic Assn., 1991. Mem. Am. Forensic Assn. (pres. 1978-82), Speech Comm. Assn., Speech Comm. Assn. of Ohio (Pres. 1976-77), Disting. award 1978), Am. Inst. Parliamentarians, Soc. Trial Cons. Presbyterian. Avocations: sports, political campaigns. Home: 200 Country Club Dr Oxford OH 45056-9050 Office: Advocacy Unltd PO Box 457 Oxford OH 45056-0457 Office Phone: 513-523-0227. E-mail: gsanders@one.net.

**SANDERS, GINA SUSAN,** publishing executive; d. Arnold R. and Joyce S.; m. Steven Oliver Newhouse, Feb. 28, 1993; 2 children. BA magna cum laude, Tufts Univ. Account mgr. House & Garden Condé Nast, 1988, advt. dir. Details mag., 1993—94, pub. Details mag., 1994—97, pub. Gourmet mag., 1997—2002, v.p. Gourmet mag., 2000—02; founding pub. & v.p. Teen Vogue, 2003—. Named Pub. of Yr., Condé Nast, 2005. Office: Teen Vogue Condé Nast 4 Times Sq New York NY 10036 Office Phone: 212-286-4316.*

**SANDERS, HAROLD BAREFOOT, JR.,** judge; b. Dallas, Feb. 5, 1925; s. Harold Barefoot and May Elizabeth (Forrester) S.; m. Jan Scurlock, June 6, 1952; children— Janet Lea, Martha Kay, Mary Frances, Harold Barefoot III. BA, U. Tex., 1949, LLB, 1950. Bar: Tex. bar 1950. U.S. atty. No. Dist. Tex., 1961-65; asst. dep. atty. gen. U.S., 1965-66; asst. atty. gen., 1966-67; legis. counsel to President U.S., 1967-69; partner firm Clark, West, Keller, Sanders & Butler, Dallas, 1969-79; U.S. dist. judge for No. Dist. Tex., Dallas, 1979—, chief judge, 1989-95. Mem. Tex. Ho. of Reps., 1952-58; Dem. nominee U.S. Senate, 1972. Lt. (j.g.) USNR, World War II. Mem. ABA (chmn. nat. conf. fed. trial judges 1988-89), Fed. Bar Assn. (Disting. Svc. award Dallas 1964), Dallas Bar Assn., State Bar Tex. (jud. conf. U.S. 1989-92, jud. panel on multidistrict litigation 1992-2000, jud. conf. com. to rev. cir. coun. conduct and disability orders 2001—), Blue Key, Phi Delta Phi, Phi Delta Theta. Methodist. Office: US Courthouse 1100 Commerce St Dallas TX 75242-1016 Business E-Mail: barefoot_sanders@txnd.uscourts.gov.

**SANDERS, HOWARD,** investment company executive; b. Phila., June 30, 1941; s. Louis and Freda (Liss) S.; m. Dale Rosenberg, Dec. 15, 1963; children: Lee Michael, Kimberly Joy. BS in Acctg., Temple U., 1962; M in Acctg., Ohio State U., 1963. CPA. Acct., Price, Waterhouse & Co., Phila., 1962-65; asst. prof. acctg. Temple U., 1965-72, v.p. Revere Fund, Inc., Phila., 1966-76; pres. Revere Mgmt. Co., Inc., Phila., 1966-72; chmn. bd. Ladies Center of Nebr., Inc., 1976—, Volk Footwear and Findings Co., 1977-78, Mister Plywood Enterprises, Inc., 1970-82; pres. Sanders Fin. Mgmt., Inc., Fort Lauderdale, 1972—. Chmn. bd. Am. Carpet Backing Distbg. Inc., 1978-80, Polis-Sanders Real Estate Corp., 1981—; exec. chmn. Humedco Corp., 1995—. Contbg. author: How to Start a Mutual Fund, 1970. Mem. adv. bd. Phila. Assn. for Retarded Children, 1970-72; chmn. bd. Women's Med. Center of Providence, Inc., 1977—, Women's Med. Center of North Jersey, Inc., 1977-82, Women's Med. Center of Atlanta, Inc., 1977—, Cherry Hill Women's Center, Inc., 1978—, Metairie Women's Center of New Orleans, Inc., 1980-84, Hartford Gynecol. Center, 1980—. Kaiser Aluminum and Chem. Co. fellow, 1962-63. Mem. Am. Inst. CPAs, Pa. Inst. CPAs (award for paper 1961), Phila. Jaycees (dir. 1966), Nat. Assn. Accts., B'rith Shalom Assn., Beta Gamma Sigma, Beta Alpha Psi, Tau Epsilon Phi. Home and Office: 1666 Victoria Pointe Cir Fort Lauderdale FL 33327-1301 E-mail: howardsanders@hotmail.com. *My life has been guided by careful attention to words which are rapidly disappearing from the "Dictionary of American Life". I have concentrated on integrity, prudence, brevity, clarity, ego control and true friendship. In all dealings I insist upon mutual benefit, taking great effort to assure that the opposite party receives a slightly larger gain. My goal is total value received for all. I attempt to mix my love for life and humor in all my relationships.*

**SANDERS, JACK THOMAS,** religious studies educator; b. Grand Prairie, Tex., Feb. 28, 1935; s. Eula Thomas and Mildred Madge (Parish) S.; m. M. Patricia Chism, Aug. 9, 1959 (dec. Oct. 1973); 1 son, Collin Thomas; m. Susan Elizabeth Plass, Mar. 3, 1979. BA, Tex. Wesleyan Coll., 1956; M.Div., Emory U., 1960; PhD, Claremont Grad. Sch., 1963; postgrad., Eberhard-Karls U., Tuebingen, Germany, 1963-64. Asst. prof. Emory U., Atlanta, 1964-67, Garrett Theol Sem., Evanston, Ill., 1967-68, McCormick Theol. Sem., Chgo., 1968-69; assoc. prof. U. Oreg., Eugene, 1969-75, prof., 1975-97, head dept. religious studies, 1973-80, 85-90, prof. emeritus, 1997—. Author: The New Testament Christological Hymns, 1971, Ethics in the New Testament, 1975, 2d edit., 1986, Ben Sira and Demotic Wisdom, 1983, The Jews in Luke-Acts, 1987, Schismatics, Sectarians, Dissidents, Deviants: The First One Hundred Years of Jewish-Christian Relations, 1993, Charisma, Converts, Competitors: Societal and Sociological Factors in the Success of Early Christianity, 2000; editor: Gospel Origins and Christian Beginnings, 1990, Gnosticism and the Early Christian World, 1990; mem. edit. bd. Jour. Bibl. Lit., 1977-83. Mem. policy bd. Dept. Higher Edn. Nat. Council Chs., N.Y.C., 1971-73. NDEA grad. study fellow, 1960-63; Fulbright Commn. fellow, 1963-64; Am. Coun. Learned Socs. travel grantee, 1981; NEH fellow, 1983-84. Mem. Studiorum Novi Testamenti Soc., Assn. for Jewish Studies, Soc. Bibl. Lit. (regional sec. 1969-76, sabbatical rsch. award 1976-77), Soc. for Sci. Study of Religion, Assn. for Sociology Religion. Democrat. Home: 704 NW 3d Dr Pendleton OR 97801-1411 Office: U Oregon Dept Religious Studies Eugene OR 97403 E-mail: jsands@oregontrail.net.

**SANDERS, JACKIE WOLCOTT,** ambassador; married. BA, Bowling Green State U., 1976. Spl. asst. Congl. affairs Bur. Near Eastern and South Asian Affairs US Dept. State, Washington, 1984—85, White House liaison, 1985—87, dep. asst. sec. for polit. affairs, 1987—89, dep. asst. sec. state Bur. Internat. Orgn. Affairs, 2001—03; assoc. dir. NSC, Washington, 1987—89; US rep. to Conf. on Disarmament, spl. rep. of Pres. of the US for Non-proliferation of Nuclear Weapons Geneva, 2003—; spl. rep. of Pres. for Non-Proliferation of Nuclear Weapons The White House, Washington, 2003—; alt. US rep. spl. polit. affairs, US Mission to UN US Dept. State, NYC, 2006—. Office: US Dept State 2201 C St NW Washington DC 20520*

**SANDERS, JACQUELYN SEEVAK,** psychologist, educator; b. Boston, Apr. 26, 1931; d. Edward Ezral and Dora (Zoken) Seevak; 1 child, Seth. BA, Radcliffe Coll., 1952; MA, U. Chgo., 1964; PhD, UCLA, 1972. Counselor, asst. prin. Orthogenic Sch., Chgo., 1952—65; rsch. assoc. UCLA, 1965—68; asst. prof. tchr. for Early Edn., LA, 1969—72; assoc. dir. Sonia Shankman Orthogenic Sch., U. Chgo. 1977—73 dir., 1973—93 dir., psychol., curriculum cons. day care ctrs. LA Dept. Social Welfare, 1970—72; instr. Calif. State Coll. LA, 1972; lectr. dept. edn. U. Chgo., 1972—80, sr. lectr., 1980—93, clin. assoc. prof. dept. psychiatry, 1990—93, emeritus, 1993—; instr. edn. program Inst. Psychoanalysis, Chgo., 1979—82. Cons. Osawatomie State Hosp., Kans., 1965—68; reading cons. Foreman HS, Chgo.; treas. Chgo. Inst. Psychoanalysis, 2003—. Author: Greenhouse for the Mind, 1989; editor (with Barry L. Childress): Psychoanalytic Approaches to the Very Troubled Child: Therapeutic Practice Innovations in Residential & Educational Settings, 1989; editor: Severely Disturbed Children and the Parental Alliance, 1992; editor: (with Jerome M. Goldsmith) Milieu Therapy: Significant Issues and Innovative Applications, 1993; editor: The Seevak Family, The Zoken Family; contbr. articles to profl. jours. Mem. vis. com. univ. sch. rels. U. Chgo.; bd. dirs. KAM Isaiah Israel Congregation, 1997—2001; bd. dirs., treas. Chgo. Inst. for Psychoanalysis. Recipient Alumna award, Girls' Latin Sch., Boston, Bettelheim award, Am. Assn. Children's Residential Ctrs., Disting. Svc. award, Radcliffe Assn., 2002; scholar Radcliffe Coll. scholar, 1948—52; Univ. fellow, UCLA, 1966—68. Mem.: Chgo. Inst. for Psychoanalysis, Assn. Children's Residential Ctrs. (past pres.), Harvard Club (bd. dirs. 1986—2001, Chgo.), Radcliffe Club (sec.-treas. 1986—87, pres. 1987—89, Chgo.). Home: 5842 S Stony Island Ave Apt 2G Chicago IL 60637-2033

**SANDERS, JAMES ALVIN,** retired minister, retired religious studies educator; b. Memphis, Nov. 28, 1927; s. Robert E. and Sue (Black) S.; m. Dora Cargille, June 30, 1951; 1 son, Robin David. BA magna cum laude, Vanderbilt U., 1948, BD with honors, 1951; student, U. Paris, 1950-51; PhD, Hebrew Union Coll., 1955; DLitt, Acadia U., 1973; STD, U. Glasgow, 1975; DHL, Coe Coll., 1988, Hebrew Union Coll., 1988, Hastings Coll., 1996, Calif. Luth. U., 2000. Ordained teacher Presbyn. Ch., 1955; instr. French Vanderbilt U., 1948-49; faculty Colgate Rochester Div. Sch., 1954-65, assoc. prof., 1957-60, Joseph B. Hoyt prof. O.T. interpretation, 1960-65; prof. O.T. Union Theol. Sem., N.Y.C., 1965-70, Auburn prof. Bibl. studies, 1970-77; adj. prof. Columbia, N.Y.C., 1966-77; prof. Bibl. studies Sch. Theology and Grad. Sch., Claremont, Calif., 1977-97, ret., 1997; vis. prof. Union Theol. Seminary and Columbia U., 1997-98. Ann. prof. Jerusalem Sch. of Am. Schs. Oriental Rsch., 1961-62; fellow Ecumenical Isnt., Jerusalem, 1972-73, 85;

vis. prof. U. N.Mex., 1992, Southwestern U., 1992, Calif. Luth. U., 1992, 94, Willamette U., 1993, U. So. Ariz., 1993, Jewish Theol. Sem., 2001—; session chair, Internat. Congress for Fiftieth Anniversary of Dead Sea Scrolls, Jerusalem, 1997; mem. internat. O.T. text critical com. United Bible Socs., 1969—; mem. nat. adv. acad. bd. Hebrew Union Coll., 1997—; co-founder, exec. officer Ancient Bibl. Manuscript Ctr. for Preservation and Rsch., 1977-80, pres., 1980-2003, pres. emeritus, 2003—; chmn. bd. Shepherd U., L.A., 2002—, bd. mem. Early Manuscripts Electronic Literacy, 2005-, bd. adv. Mus. of Archeology and the Bible, 2006-,; vis. prof. Yale Divinity Sch., 1998, Jewish Theol. Seminary, 2001; lectr. in field Author: Suffering as Divine Discipline in the Old Testament and Post-Biblical Judaism, 1955, The Old Testament in the Cross, 1961, The Psalms Scroll of Qumran Cave 11, 1965, The Dead Sea Psalms Scroll, 1967, Near Eastern Archaeology in the Twentieth Century, 1970, Torah and Canon, 1972, 1974, 2d edit., 2005, Identité de la Bible, 1975, God Has a Story Too, 1979, Canon and Community, 1984, From Sacred Story to Sacred Text, 1987, Luke and Scripture, 1993; editor: Paul and the Scriptures of Israel, 1993, Early Christian Interpretation of the Scriptures of Israel, 1993, The Function of Scripture in Early Jewish and Christian Tradition, 1998, The Canon Debate, 2002; contbr. over 280 articles to profl. jours.; mem. editl. bd. Jour. Bibl. Lit., 1970—76, Jour. for Study Judaism, Bibl. Theology Bull., Interpretation, 1973—78, New Rev. Std. Version Bible Com., 2 vols. of essays: A Gift of God in Due Season, 1996, The Quest for Context and Meaning, 1997. Trustee Am. Schs. Oriental Research. Fulbright grantee, 1950-51, Lilly Endowment grantee, 1980, 1988, 91-92; Lefkowitz and Rabinowitz interfaith fellow, 1951-53, Rockefeller fellow, 1953-54, 85, Guggenheim fellow, 1961-62, 72-73, Human Scis. Rsch. fellow, 1989. Mem. Soc. Bibl. Lit. and Exegesis (pres. 1977-78), Phi Beta Kappa, Phi Sigma Iota, Theta Chi Beta. Home: PO Box 593 Claremont CA 91711-0593 Personal E-mail: sandersja@aol.com.

**SANDERS, JAMES GRADY,** biogeochemist; b. Norfolk, Va., June 10, 1951; s. Allen Buford and Maple Seretha (Myers) S.; m. Dorothea L. Palmer, 2001. BS in Zoology, Duke U., 1973; MS in Marine Scis., U. N.C., 1975, PhD in Marine Scis., 1978. Postdoctoral investigator Woods Hole (Mass.) Oceanog. Instn., 1978-80; vis. scientist Chesapeake Biol. Lab. U. Md., Solomons, 1980-81; asst. curator Estuarine Rsch. Ctr., Md. Acad. Natural Scis., 1981-85, assoc. curator, 1985-89, curator, 1989-99, dir., 1983-99, v.p., 1999; chair dept. ocean, earth and atmospheric scis. Old Dominion U., Norfolk, 1999-2001; dir. Skidaway Inst. Oceanography, Savannah, Ga., 2001—. Cons. EPA Sweden, Stockholm, 1985-90; mem. Md. Sea Grant Adv. Com., College Park, 1983-90, Environ. Commn., Calvert County, Md., 1981-88; mem. environ. biology panel Office R&D EPA, Washington, 1986-95, sci. adv. bd., ecol. processes and effects com., 2003—; regional rep. Coastal Resources Adv. Commn., Md., 1983-86; bd. dirs. Am. Chestnut Land Trust; mem. bd. govs. Consortium for Oceanog. Rsch. and Edn., 1999—, exec. com., 2003—; mem. adv. bd. SC Sea Grant Program, 2005—; mem. Savannah Innovation Coun., 2005—. Assoc. editor Estuaries, 1996-99; mem. editl. bd. Environ. Toxicology and Chemistry, 2000-03; contbr. more than 70 articles to sci. jours. Grantee NOAA, EPA, NSF. Mem. AAAS, Am. Geophys. Union, Am. Soc. Limnology and Oceanography, Estuarine Rsch. Fedn. (treas. 1993-97), So. Assn. Marine Labs. (pres. 2004-05), Nat. Assn. Marine Labs. (pres.-elect 2006-), Oceanography Soc. Achievements include first identification of relationships between algal growth and chemical transformations of arsenic in aquatic systems. Office: Skidaway Inst Oceanography 10 Ocean Science Cir Savannah GA 31411 Home: 11 Wesley Crossing Savannah GA 31411 Office Phone: 912-598-2400. Business E-Mail: jim.sanders@skio.usg.edu.

**SANDERS, JAY OLCUTT,** actor; b. Austin, Tex., Apr. 16, 1953; s. James Olcutt and Phyllis Rae (Abel) Sanders; m. Maryann Plunkett, Oct. 1, 1991; 1 child. BFA in Theatre, SUNY, Purchase, 1976. Actor: (films) Starting Over, 1979, Hanky Panky, 1982, Eddie Macon's Run, 1983, Cross Creek, 1983, The Misfit Brigade, 1987, Tuck: The Man and His Dream, 1988, The Prince of Pennsylvania, 1988, Woman in the Wind, 1990, Just Like in the Movies, 1990, Mr. Destiny, 1990, V.I. Warshawski, 1991, Defenseless, 1991, Meeting Venus, 1991, JFK, 1991, My Boyfriend's Back, 1993, Angels in the Outfield, 1994, The Big Green, 1995, Three Wishes, 1995, Daylight, 1996, Kiss the Girls, 1997, The Matchmaker, 1997, For Richer or Poorer, 1997, Wrestling with Alligators, 1998, The Odd Couple II, 1998, The Confession, 1999, Tumbleweeds, 1999, The Secret Life of Girls, 1999, Music of the Heart, 1999, Endsville, 2000, Dead Dog, 2000, Along Came a Spider, 2001, Second Born, 2003, Abby Singer, 2003, The Day After Tomorrow, 2004, Shooting Livien, 2005, Half Nelson, 2006; (TV films) The Day Christ Died, 1980, Starstruck, 1981, Living Proof: The Hank Williams Jr. Story, 1983, The Doctor's Story, 1984, The Revolt of Mother, 1986, Rage of Angels: The Story Continues, 1986, Private Eye, 1987, Cold Sassy Tree, 1989, Revealing Evidence: Stalking the Honolulu Strangler, 1990, Hostages, 1993, Rio Shannon, 1993, State of Emergency, 1994, Nobody's Children, 1994, Silver Strand, 1995, Down Came a Blackbird, 1995, The Prosecutors, 1996, Earthly Possessions, 1999, The Jack Bull, 1999, A.T.F., 1999, Picnic, 2000, The Familiar Stranger, 2001, Boss of Bosses, 2001, The Last Brickmaker in America, 2001, Salem Witch Trials, 2002, DC Sniper: 23 Days of Fear, 2003; appeared in (TV series) After MASH, 1983, Miami Vice, 1985, Spenser: For Hire, 1985, Crime Story, 1987, A Man Called Hawk, 1989, Kate & Allie, 1989, The Young Riders, 1989, Booker, 1989, LA Law, 1990, Rosanne, 1990, The Outer Limits, 1995, Lonesome Dove: The Outlaw Years, 1995, Northern Exposure, 1996, Nothing Sacred, 1997, Law & Order: Criminal Intent, 2002, Law & Order, 1999, 2002, Hack, 2004; actor: (plays) Buried Child, 1978, Henry V, Measure for Measure, Twelfth Night, King John, 1988, Stuff Happens, 2006; (Broadway plays) Loose Ends, 1979, The Caine Mutiny Court-Martial, 1983, Saint Joan, 1993.*

**SANDERS, JERRY,** mayor, former social services executive; b. San Pedro, Calif., July 14, 1950; m. Rana Sampson; children: Jamie, Lisa. AA, Long Beach City Coll., 1970; BA in Pub. Administrn., Nat. U., 1988; student, San Diego State U. Cert. P.O.S.T. mgmt. Police officer San Diego Police Dept., 1973-93, chief of police, 1993-99; pres. United Way San Diego, 1999—2005; mayor City of San Diego, 2005—. Bd. dirs. The Nat. Conf., San Diego State U. Cmty. Adv. Bd., Children's Initiative, Youth Econ. Enterprise Zones; mem. cmty. leaders adv. bd. ElderHelp of San Diego. Recipient Headliner of Yr. award San Diego Press Club, 1984, 93, Exceptional Performance citation for SWAT leadership, 1986. Office: Office of Mayor 202 C St 11th Fl San Diego CA 92101*

**SANDERS, JOEL STEVEN,** lawyer; b. Mpls., Mar. 25, 1955; s. David M. and Miriam (Gelfand) S.; m. Carol G. Bieri, May 25, 1984; children: Daniel, Elizabeth. BA, Antioch Coll., 1976; JD, U. Calif., Berkeley, 1982. Bar: Calif. 1982, US Dist. Ct. (no. dist.) Calif. 1982, US Dist. Ct. (cen. dist.) Calif. 1984, US Ct. Appeals (9th cir.) 1983. Law clk. to Hon Procter R. Hug Jr. US Ct. Appeals (9th cir.), 1982-83; atty. antitrust div. US Dept. Justice, San Francisco, 1983-87; assoc. Gibson, Dunn & Crutcher, San Francisco, 1987-91; ptnr. Gibson, Dunn & Crutcher LLP, San Francisco, 1992—, ptnr.-in-charge, Bay Area offices, 1995—2000. Former adj. prof. law Univ. Calif. Hastings Coll. of Law; mem. exec. com. Gibson Dunn & Crutcher. Assoc. editor Calif. Law Rev., 1980-82. Mem. ABA, State Bar of Calif., Bar Assn. of San Francisco, Order of Coif. Office: Gibson & Crutcher Ste 3100 1 Montgomery St San Francisco CA 94104 Office Phone: 415-393-8200. Office Fax: 415-374-8439. Business E-Mail: jsanders@gibsondunn.com.

**SANDERS, JOHN LASSITER,** retired academic administrator; b. Four Oaks, NC, June 30, 1927; s. David Hardy and Louie Jane (Lassiter) S.; m. Ann Beal, Aug. 14, 1954; children— Tracy Elizabeth Sanders Justus, Jane Nesbit, William Hardy. AB, U. N.C., 1950, JD, 1954. Bar: NC 1955. Law clk. to judge U.S. Ct. Appeals, 1954-55; pvt. practice Raleigh, NC, 1955-56; mem. faculty Inst. Govt., UNC, Chapel Hill, 1956-94, dir., 1962-73, 79-92, v.p. planning at Univ., 1973-78. Served with USNR, 1945-46. Recipient NC award State of NC, 1996. Democrat. Baptist. Home: 750 Weaver Dairy Rd Apt 102 Chapel Hill NC 27514 Office: U NC CB 3330 Knapp Sanders Bldg Chapel Hill NC 27599-3330 Office Phone: 919-843-3287. E-mail: sandersj@email.unc.edu.

**SANDERS, JULIUS RAY,** music company executive; b. Williamston, Md., Jan. 5, 1956; s. Sanders and Wright. AA, Martin C.C., 1980, MS in Bus., 1999. Engineering Of Computer WILLIAMSTON, 1999. Prin., owner Musical And Lyric. Co., Balt., 2000—; promoter sale rep. Ind. Contractor Joint Venture, Balt., 2001—. Gen. ptnr. Am. Majority Trustees Ltd, Balt., 1995—. Singer (producer): (songs) Song Lyric. Home and Office: Musical And Lyric Co Post Office Box 2024 Mailstop Baltimore MD 21203 Office Phone: 410-710-2050. Business E-Mail: musicalandlyric@netscape.net.

**SANDERS, KATHRYN A.,** lawyer; b. Fresno, Calif., 1958; BA in Bus. and Econs., U. Calif., Los Angeles, 1980; JD, U. So. Calif., 1985. Bar: Calif. 1985. Ptnr. O'Melveny & Myers LLP, LA, co-chair private equity fund practice, mem. policy com. Mem. So. Calif. Law Review, 1983—85. Past pres. Nat. Women's Political Caucus, LA Metro Chpt. Mem.: Inst. for Corp. Counsel, Bd. of Govenors, Calif. State Bar Assn., LA Bar Assn., ABA, Order of the Coif. Office: O'Melveny & Myers LLP 400 S Hope St Los Angeles CA 90071-2899 Office Phone: 213-430-6376. Office Fax: 213-430-6407. Business E-Mail: ksanders@omm.com.

**SANDERS, KEITH PAGE,** journalism educator; b. Ashland, Ohio, Sept. 25, 1938; s. Merwin Morse and Phyllis Pearl (Snyder) S.; m. Jane Carmel Adams, June 11, 1966; children: Paige Ann, Kevin Scott. BS in Journalism, Bowling Green State U., 1960; MS in Journalism, Ohio U., 1964; PhD in Mass Comm., U. Iowa, 1967. Sports editor Ashland (Ohio) Times Gazette, 1960-61, Dover (Ohio) Daily Reporter, 1961-62; instr. journalism Bowling Green (Ohio) State U., 1963-64, U. Iowa, Iowa City, 1965-67; prof. journalism U. Mo., Columbia, 1967—2001, assoc. dean grad. studies Sch. Journalism, 1986-87, 90-91, O.O. McIntyre disting. prof., 1993, prof. emeritus, 2002—. Cons. in field. Contbr. articles to profl. jours. including Journalism Quar., Mass Media Rev., Jour. Broadcasting, Electronic Jour. of Comm.; assoc. editor Mass Comm. Rev., 1981-92, mem. editl. bd., 1972-98; mem. editl. bd. Journalism Monographs, 1973-80, Mass Comm. and Soc., 1998—. Recipient Award for Outstanding Achievement U. Mo. Alumni Assn., 1986; Joyce Swan Disting. Faculty award U. Mo., 1973; inducted into Columbia Bowling Hall of Fame, 1999. Mem.: Soc. Profl. Journalists, Assn. for Edn. in Journalism/Mass Comm. (Trayes Prof. of Yr. 1987), Internat. Soc. for Sci. Study of Subjectivity (treas. 1990—95), U.S. Bowling Congress, Mo. State Bowling Assn. (bd. dirs. 2000—06, Dir. of Yr. 2005), Mo. State-US Bowling Congress (2d v.p. 2006—), Omicron Delta Kappa, Kappa Tau Alpha (exec. dir. 1991—). Avocations: bowling, golf, fishing. Home: 6551 N Creasy Springs Rd Columbia MO 65202-8093 Office: Univ of Missouri Sch Journalism Columbia MO 65211-1200

**SANDERS, LARRY DALE,** funeral director, coroner; b. Batesville, Ark., Dec. 2, 1961; s. Noel Chester and Hazel Laverne Sanders; m. Anna Geraldine Young (div.); 1 child, Whitney JacNichole; m. Carol June Williams, Jan. 18, 1986; 1 child, Cody Dale. Mortuary Sci. Cert., N.W. Miss. Coll., Southaven, 1992. Heavy equipment operator Ark. Hwy. Dept., Salem, 1980—89; mortician Madden Enterprises, Salem, 1989—92, Nelson Funeral Svc., Berryville, Ark., 1992—; dep. coroner Carroll County, Berryville, 1993—2002, coroner, 2003—. Reserve police officer City of Berryville, 1994—2000; dep. sheriff Carroll County, 1993—; vol. fireman Salem Fire Dept., 1986—91. Mem.: Masons. Democrat. Baptist. Avocations: hunting, fishing, camping, golf, scuba diving. Home: 602 Cedarvale Rd Berryville AR 72616 Office: Carroll County Coroner 202 E Madison Berryville AR 72616

**SANDERS, MARLENE,** news correspondent, journalism educator; b. Cleve., Jan. 10, 1931; d. Mac and Evelyn (Menitoff) Sanders; m. Jerome Toobin, May 27, 1958 (dec. Jan. 1984); children: Jeff, Mark. Student, Ohio State U., 1948—49. Writer, prodr. Sta. WNEW-TV, N.Y.C., 1955-60, P.M. program Westinghouse Broadcasting Co., WNEW-TV, N.Y.C., 1961-62; asst. dir. news and pub. affairs Sta. WNEW, N.Y.C., 1962-64; anchor, news program ABC News, N.Y.C., 1964-68, corr., 1968-72, documentary prodr., writer, anchor, 1972-76, v.p., dir. TV documentaries, 1976-78; corr. CBS News, N.Y.C., 1978-87; host Currents Sta. WNET-TV, N.Y.C., 1987-88; host Met. Week in Rev., 1988-90; host Thirteen Live Sta. WNET-TV, 1990-91; prof. dept. journalism NYU, N.Y.C., 1991-93, adj. prof. journalism, 1996—; adj. prof. journalism, adminstr. Columbia U. Grad. Sch. Journalism, N.Y.C., 1994-95. Profl.-in-residence Freedom Forum Media Studies Ctr., 1997-2000; freelance broadcaster, narrator; bd. dirs. womensnews.org.; chair RSVP, Inc., 1997-. Co-author: Waiting for Prime Time: The Women of Television News, 1988. Mem. N.Y.C. Commn. on Women's Issues, 2003—. Recipient award N.Y. State Broadcasters Assn., 1976, award Nat. Press Club, 1976, Emmy awards, 1980, 81, others. Mem. Am. Women in Radio and TV (Woman of Yr. award 1975, Silver Satellite award 1977), Women in Comm. (past pres.), Coun. Fgn. Rels. Office Phone: 212-877-1250. Personal E-Mail: sanders110@aol.com.

**SANDERS, MARY ELIZABETH,** writer, historian; b. Baton Rouge, May 25, 1923; d. Jared Young and Mary (Briggs) S. BA, La. State U., 1944, MA, 1955. Adminstrv. asst. Congressman J.Y. Sanders, Washington, 1942-43, Sanders, Miller, Downing, Rubin & Kean, Baton Rouge, 1946-48; librarian, archivist New Orleans Pub. Libr., 1955-57. Appeared on Restore Am.-La. program Home & Garden TV, 1999. Author: Avoca Plantation Receipts and Other Family Favorites, 1995; editor: Letters of a Southern Family, 1816-1941, 2001, Diary in Gray: Civil War Journal of J.Y. Sanders, 1994; compiler Records of Attakapas District, La., 1739-1811, 1962, Records of Attakapas District, La., Vol II: St. Mary Parish, 1811-1860, 1963, Records of Attakapas District, La., Vol. III: St. Martin Parish, 1808-1860, 1974, St. Mary Parish, Louisana, Heirship Series: Vol. I—Annotated Abstracts of the Successions, 1811-1834, 1972, Vol. II—Selected Annotated Abstracts of Marriage Book 1, 1811-1829, 1973, Vol. III—Selected Annotated Abstracts of Court Records, 1811-1839, 1978. Mem. La. Hist. Records Adv. Commn., Baton Rouge, 1981-85; charter mem., pres. La. Genealogy and Hist. Soc., 1954-56, editor, 1957-58; hon. mem. Morgan City (La.) Arch. Commn., 1985—; co-trustee J. Y. Sanders Found., Baton Rouge, 1988—; pres. La. Archives Found., Baton Rouge, 1988-96, Young-Sanders Ctr. Found., Morgan City, 1998—; mem. La. State U. Found., Baton Rouge, 1988-92; mem. nat. bd. Coun. Conservative Citizens, St. Louis, 1997—; hon. chmn. La. Sovereignty Party, Baton Rouge, 1999. Named Hon. Citizen Morgan City, La., 1985; recipient award of commendation La. State Dept. Archives, Records Mgmt. and History, 1988, cert. of appreciation Coun. Conservative Citizens, 1996, cert. of honor Jud. Watch, 1999. Mem. DAR (registrar La. soc. 1983-86, nat. vice chmn. flag com. 1986-89, corr. soc. 1992-95), United Daus. of the Confederacy (divsn. corr. sec. 1989-91, divsn. pres. 2000-2002, Gen. Grave Markers com. 2002-), Jefferson Davis medal 1989, cert. of merit 1998), Huguenot soc. of Founders of Mamakin in Colony of Va. (nat. registrar 1979-85), Colonial Dames of America Republican. Christian Scientist. Avocations: genealogy, preservationist, cooking. Home: 2332 Wisteria St Baton Rouge LA 70806-5352

**SANDERS, PEGGY JEAN,** artist; b. San Francisco, July 4, 1928; d. Robert and Margaret (Bailey) Canby; m. Joseph P. Marino, July 27, 1947 (div. 1960); children: John P., Joseph P., James P.; m. Meryl Guptill Sanders, Mar. 18, 1962; children: Matthew Lesley, Katherine April; stepchildren: Wayne, Neal, Brian. Student, Santa Rosa (Calif.) Jr. Coll., 1946-47. One-woman shows include Flamingo Galleries, Santa Rosa, 1961, Gilberts Creative Arts, Santa Rosa, 1965-66, New Beginnings Gallery, Santa Rosa, 1961, Marshall House Gallery, Santa Rosa, 1964, Bruner's Fine Arts, Santa Rosa, 1965, Artrium, Santa Rosa, 1966-68, Brotmans, Sausalito, Calif., 1967, Bodega (Calif.) Art Gallery, 1967-69; exhibited in group shows at De Saisset Mus., Santa Clara, Calif., 1967, De Young Mus., San Francisco, 1968-69, 71, Gallerie de tours, Carmel, Calif., 1967, Christopher Queen Galleries, Duncan Mills, Calif. 1994, Martinelli Ranch Art Gallery, Windsor, Calif., 1994, Cody Country Art League, Wyo., 2006. Home: Prairie Art 1065 Lane 8 Powell WY 82435-9124

**SANDERS, PHYLLIS MAY,** musician; b. Cleve., Aug. 7, 1922; d. Charles Lester and Marjorie (Roof) Flick; m. Roger Fred Sanders, Aug. 3, 1946 (div. 1986); children: William Paul, Richard Allen, Bruce Edward, Patricia Ann. MusB in Edn., Drake U., Des Moines, 1944. Music tchr. Jefferson (Iowa) jr. high schs., 1944-45, Des Moines jr. high schs., 1945-46; organist, choir dir. Columbia U. Meth. Ch., Columbia Station, Ohio, 1963-83; organist Magyar United Ch. of Christ, Elyria, Ohio, 1984—. Dir. Lorain County Community Messiah Chorus, Elyria, 1981, 88-91; dir., founder Choraliers, Columbia Station, 1975-80. Mem. Southwest Chorus, Berea, Ohio, 1988-90, Berea Sr. Ctr. Chorus, 1978—; pres. Columbia Rep. Women, Columbia Station; mem. Columbia Mothersingers, Cleve. Messiah Chorus, 1991—. Mem. Sigma Alpha Iota, Beta Gamma Kappa. Republican. Mem. Christian Ch. (Disciples Of Christ). Avocations: ceramics, needlecrafts. Home: Apt 528 55 Barrett Rd Berea OH 44017-1699

**SANDERS, RHEA,** artist; b. Charleston, SC, Nov. 6, 1923; d. Archibald Campbell and Sue (Tarpley) S.; m. Joseph Rabinovich, Apr. 20, 1951; children: Nathaniel, Joshua, Alexander. Studied with Maurice Sterne, N.Y.C., 1941-45, with Philip Pearlstein, 1971-73. Artist in residence Gibbes Art Mus., Charleston, 1982. Featured The Owl and the Rainbow, Paragon Cable Program, N.Y.C., 1990; vis. artist Cooper Union, N.Y.C., 2006. One-woman shows include Gibbes Art Mus., Charleston, SC, 1979, Donnell Libr. Ctr., N.Y.C., 1982, Capricorn Galleries, Bethesda, Md., 1982, Princeton U. League Gallery, N.J., 1986, Ctrl. Pk. Conservancy, N.Y.C., 1986—87, Soho 20 Gallery, 1987, 2000, Art/Network Cultural Ctr., S.I., N.Y., 1987, Charleston County Libr., S.C., 1988, 1st St. Gallery, N.Y.C., 1991, 1994, 1996, Moravian Coll., Bethlehem, Pa., 1991, NY. Tech. Coll., Bklyn., 1993, N.Y.C. Pub. Libr., 1996—98, Coll. at Charleston Libr., 2001, N.Y. Pub. Libr., St. Agnes br., 2002, Prince St. Gallery, 2004, exhibited in group shows at Marymount Manhattan Coll., N.Y.C., 1983, Fordham/Lincoln Ctr., 1983, Leonardo di Mauro Gallery, 1984, Benson Gallery, Bridgehampton, N.Y., 1986, Butler Inst., Youngstown, Ohio, 1987, Atlanta U. Ctr., 1987, 1st St. Gallery, N.Y.C., Marymount Manhattan, 1990, Libr. Nat. Mus. Women in the Arts, Washington, 1991, Cortland Jessup Gallery, Provincetown, Mass., 1991, NGO Forum on Women, Beijing, 1995, Jacques Marchais Mus. Tibetan Arts, S.I., 1995, Orgn. Ind. Artists Gallery, N.Y.C., 2000, Flushing Town Hall, 2001, Prince St. Gallery, 2002, Blue Mountain Gallery, 2002, Queens C.C., 2002, Snug Harbor Cultural Ctr., N.Y., 2002, Berlin Kunst Project, Berlin, 2002, Artist Equity Gallery, N.Y.C., 2004, Gibbes Art Mus., Charleston, S.C., 2005, Prince St. Gallery, N.Y.C., 2005, Artist Equity Gallery, 2005, Represented in permanent collections Libr. of Nat. Mus. Women in the Arts, High Mus., Atlanta, Gibbes Art Mus., Charleston, Brit. Mus. Libr., London, U. N.C. Libr., Chapel Hill, Monistiraki Iera Moni Evagelistrias, Levadia, Greece, others. NEA fellow, 1985, Karolyi Found. resident fellow, 1989, Mishkenet Sha'ananim, Jerusalem resident fellow, 1993; grantee Artists Space, 1980, 83. Mem. Orgn. Ind. Artists (exhbn. com. 1981, 82, grantee 1980), Women's Caucus for Art. Democrat. Home: 617 W End Ave New York NY 10024-1607 Personal E-Mail: rheasanders1@att.net.

**SANDERS, RICHARD BROWNING,** state supreme court justice; b. Tacoma; 1 child: Laura. BA, U. Wash., 1966, JD, 1969. Assoc. Murray, Scott, McGavick & Graves, Tacoma, Wash., 1969, Caplinger & Munn, Seattle, 1971; hearing examiner State Wash., Olympia, 1970; pvt. practice Wash., 1971-95; justice Wash. Supreme Ct., Olympia, 1995—. Adj. prof. U. Wash. Sch. Law; lectr. in field. Contbr. articles to profl. jours. Office: Supreme Court of Washington Temple of Justice PO Box 40929 Olympia WA 98504-0929 Fax: (360) 357-2092. E-mail: j_r.sanders@courts.wa.gov.*

**SANDERS, RICHARD HENRY,** lawyer; b. Chgo., Apr. 10, 1944; s. Walter J. and Marian (Snyder) Sikorski; m. Sharon A. Marciniak, July 8, 1967 (dec.); child, Douglas Bennett; m. Susan Gerhardt Nalepa, Feb. 19, 2005. BS, Loyola U., Chgo., 1967; JD, Northwestern U., 1969. Bar: Ill. 1969, Ind. 1990, D.C. 1990, U.S. Dist. Ct. (no. dist.) Ill. 1970, U.S. Dist. Ct. (no. and so. dists.) Ind. 1990, U.S. Ct. Appeals (7th cir.) 1990, U.S. Supreme Ct. 1990. Assoc. Vedder, Price, Kaufman & Kammholz, Chgo., 1969-76, ptnr., 1976—2003, mem. exec. com., 1991-93, health law area leader, 1989—95, 2001—04, 2006—, shareholder, 2003—, chmn. tech. com., 2003—. Adj. prof. Sch. of Law Northwestern U., 1994—; mem. svc. dispute resolver panel Am. Health Lawyers Assn. Alt. Dispute Resolution, 2000—. Fellow Am. Bar Found.; mem. ABA, Ill. Bar Assn. (chmn. health sect. 1989-90), Chgo. Bar Assn., Ind. Bar Assn., D.C. Bar Assn., Am. Health Lawyers Assn., Ill. Assn. Health Attys., Univ. Club, Evanston Golf Club (Skokie). Avocations: skiing, diving, photography, golf. Office: Vedder Price Kaufman & Kammholz 222 N La Salle St Ste 2600 Chicago IL 60601-1100 Office Phone: 312-609-7644. Business E-Mail: rsanders@vedderprice.com.

**SANDERS, RICHARD KINARD,** actor; b. Harrisburg, Pa., Aug. 23, 1940; s. Henry Irvine and Thelma S. BFA, Carnegie Inst. Tech., 1962; postgrad. (Fulbright scholar), London Acad. Music and Dramatic Art, 1962-63. Pres. Blood Star, Inc. Mem. various acting cos., Front St., Memphis, Champlain Shakespeare Festival, Vt., Center Stage, Balt., N.Y. Shakespeare Festival, N.Y.C., Chelsea Theater Center, N.Y., Mark Taper Forum, Los Angeles, Arena Stage, Washington; appeared on: (Broadway) Raisin; (TV series) Les Nessman on WKRP in Cincinnati and The New WKRP in Cincinnati, Paul Sycamore in You Can't Take It With You, Mr. Beanley in Spenser; writer of many episodes of WKRP and other situation comedies; writer NBC movie Max and Sam; numerous TV and film appearances. Vol. Peace Corps, Northeastern Brazil, 1966-69. Recipient Buckeye Newshawk award, 1974-79, Silver Sow award, 1979 Mem. Writers Guild Am., Screen Actors Guild, AFTRA, Actors Equity Assn. Office: PO Box 1644 Woodinville WA 98072-1644

**SANDERS, RICHARD L.,** academic administrator; b. Clintonville, Wis., Jan. 2, 1937; s. Claude H. and Lucille B. (Wedde) S.; m. Janice Miles, Aug. 30, 1958; children: Scott, Jennifer, Todd, Zachary, Nicolle. BS, U. Wis., Eau Claire, 1959; MS, U. Wis., Milw., 1966; EdD, Marquette U., 1971. Tchr. music Milw. Pub. Schs., 1959-62, rsch. assoc., 1966-67; tchr. music West Allis (Wis.) Pub. Schs., 1962-66; registrar, asst. prof. Lakeland Coll., Sheboygan, Wis., 1967-71; dean Lakewood St. Paul, 1971-81; pres. Lincoln Trail Coll., Robinson, Ill., 1981-84, Mattatuck CC, Waterbury, Conn., 1984-92, Naugatuck Valley CC, Waterbury, Conn., 1992—; sec. Naugatuck Valley CC Founds., Inc., Waterbury. Mem. United Way Bd. of Greater Waterbury. Disting. Svc. award Charter Oak State U., 1993. Mem. Am. Assn. C.C. (mem. rsch. coun.), Conn. Coun. Higher Edn., New Eng.Cmty.-Tech. Coun. (editor The Collegian 1992-94), Alliance C.C. Innovation, Am. Assn. Higher Edn., Am. Assn. Univ. adminstrs., Am. Coun. Edn., C.C. Humanities Assn., Nat. Coun. Occupl. Edn., Nat. Coun. Instrl. Adminstrs., New Eng. Assn. Schs. and Colls., New Eng. Coll. Coun., Conn. Cmty.-Tech. Coll. Coun. Pres., Conn. Assn. Latin Am. in Higher Edn., Greater Danbury C. of C., Greater Valley C. of C., Greater Waterbury C. C., Conn. Cmty. Found., Waterbury Exec. Educators Roundtable, Waterbury Hosp. Health Network, Inc., N.W. Region Workforce Investment Bd., Phi Delta Kappa (cert. outstanding membership 1990). Avocations: music, tennis, public speaking. Office: Naugatuck Valley CC 750 Chase Pkwy Waterbury CT 06708-3011 Office Phone: 203-575-8044. Office Fax: 203-596-8709. Business E-Mail: rsanders@nvcc.commnet.edu.

**SANDERS, ROBIN RENEE,** ambassador; b. Hampton, Va., July 5; d. Robert M. and Geneva (Machoney) Sanders. B.A., Hampton Inst.; M.A., Ohio U., 1979, M.S., 1979. Broadcast lic. FCC 3d class. Editorial assts. Essence Mag., N.Y.C., 1974-76, Fgn. Broadcast Info. Service, Washington, 1976-77; intern account exec. Burson-Marsteller Co., N.Y.C., 1977-78; pub. relations assoc. Seventeen mag., N.Y.C., 1979-80; polit. and counselor officer Am. embassy, Dominican Republic, 1980-83, consular officer Am. consulate, Oporto, Portugal, 1983-86, dep. polit. sect. chief Am. Embassy Khartoum, Sudan, 1986-88; spl. asst. AF Bur., 1989; dir. for pub. diplomacy for Africa, State Dept.; dir. for Africa, Nat. Security Coun. at the White House, 1988-89, 97-99; spl. asst. for L.Am., Africa and internat. crime for the under sec. for polit. affairs Dept. State, Washington; chief of staff, sr. fgn. policy Mem. Ho. Internat. Rels. Com.; U.S. amb. to Republic of Congo, 2002—; cons. Profl.

Women's Seminar, 1983, 84; speaker U. Oporto, 1983; researcher dept. internat. relations Ohio U., 1978; TV producer dept. gerontology Hampton Inst., 1976-77. Recipient 1st place award for painting Two Faces, Scholastic Art Bd., 1981, Dept of State Meritorious award, 1989, three State Dept. Superior Honor awards, three State Dept. Meritorious Honor awards; journalism scholar Syracuse U., 1970. Dir. Nat. Security Coun., 1989; political Econ. Officer Namibia, 1989. Mem. Women in Communications, Pub. Relations Soc. Am., Am. Fgn. Service Assn., Nat. Council Negro Women, Black Caucus, Mus. African Art, Coun. on Fgn. Rels., D.C.C. of C.; Alpha Kappa Alpha, Alpha Kappa Mu. Consular Corps (Oporto); Diplomatic (Santo Domingo), Thursday Luncheon Group, Capital Press (Washington). Address: Embassy Republic of the Congo 310 Avenue des Aviateurs Kinshasa Gombe Republic of the Congo

**SANDERS, SUMMER,** Olympic athlete, news correspondent, newscaster; b. Oct. 13, 1972; d. Bob and Barbara Sanders; m. Mark Henderson, July 1997. Student, Stanford U. Olympic swimmer, Barcelona, 1992; ret. from profl. swimming, 1993; returned but did not qualify for Olympics, 1995—96; hostess, Sandblast MTV, 1994—95; host game show for children Figure It Out Nickelodeon, 1997—99; broadcaster WNBA Lifetime TV, 1997—98; co-host NBA Inside Stuff, 1997—; host Beg, Borrow or Deal ESPN 2, 2002—. Co-author (with Melinda Marshall): Champions are Raised, Not Born: How my Parents made me a Success, 1999. Achievements include gold medal 200-meter butterfly, 400-meter medley relay preliminaries; silver medal, 200-meter individual medley and bronze medal 400-meter individual medley, 1992 Olympic Games, Barcelona, Spain. Office: NBA Inside Stuff care NBA Entertainment Inc 450 Harmon Meadow Blvd Secaucus NJ 07094-3618

**SANDERS, WALLACE WOLFRED, JR.,** civil engineer; b. Louisville, June 24, 1933; s. Wallace Wolfred and Mary Jane (Brownfield) S.; m. Julia B. Howard, June 9, 1956; children— Linda, David. B.C.E., U. Louisville, 1955; MS, U. Ill., Urbana, 1957, PhD, 1960; M.Engring., U. Louisville, 1973. Research asst., then research assoc. U. Ill., 1955-60, asst. prof., 1960-64; mem. faculty Iowa State U., Ames, 1964-98, prof. civil engring., 1970-98, assoc. dir. engring. research, 1980-91, assoc. dean research, 1988-91, interim asst. vice provost for research and advanced studies, 1991-92. Cons. to govt. and industry. Contbr. numerous papers to profl. jours. Bd. dirs. Northcrest Cmty., Ames, 1976-82, 92-98, pres., 1987-91, 96-2003; bd. dirs. Am. Bapt. Homes of the Midwest, Mpls., 1998—. Mem. ASCE (R.C. Reese research prize 1978), Am. Welding Soc. (Adams Meml. membership award 1971), Am. Ry. Engring. Assn., Am. Soc. Engring. Edn. Baptist. Home and Office: 1924 Northcrest Cir Ames IA 50010-5113 Business E-Mail: wsanders@iastate.edu.

**SANDERS, WALTER JEREMIAH,** computer company executive; BSEE, U. Ill., 1958. From sales mgr. to group dir. mktg. Semiconductor divsn. Fairchild Camera and Instrument Corp., 1967—69; sales and mktg. mgr. Motorola Semiconductor; engr. Douglas Aircraft Co.; co-founder Advanced Micro Devices, Inc., Sunnyvale, Calif., 1969, CEO, 1969—2002, chmn., 1969—. Office: Advanced Micro Devices Inc 1 AMD Pl Sunnyvale CA 94086

**SANDERS, WILLIAM EUGENE,** marketing executive; b. Asheboro, N.C., Nov. 16, 1933; s. Arthur Ira and Picola (Loftin) S.; m. Velna Elizabeth Sumner, June 8, 1957; children: William Eugene Jr., George Herbert Sumner. AB in Polit. Sci., U. N.C., 1956, postgrad. in Law, 1956-57. Marketing rep. Encyclopaedia Britannica, Greensboro, N.C., 1957-60, Am. Pubs., Chgo., 1960-66; pres. S&W Distbrs., Inc., Greensboro, 1966—. Little league coach Civitans, Greensboro, 1967—68. With USAR, 1957—63. Named Hon. Amb. Dept. of Labor, Ky., 1976, Ky. Col., 1976, Hon. Mem. La. Lt. Gov. Staff, 1984; recipient Cert. Appreciation Jefferson Davis Parish Libr., Jennings, La., 1986, Top Sales award Am. Media. Corp., 1996, Marshall Cavendish Top Prodn. award, 1990-91, Mktg. award Am. Media, 1995, Gold Cir. award Penworthy Books, 1999, 2000, 01, Marshall Cavendish quota Prodn. award, 1999, 2000, Rosen Prodn. award, 2002. Mem.: Gen. Alumni Assn. (co-chmn. Greensboro chpt. 1979—80, Rosen Prodn. award 2001—02), State Libr. Assn. S.C., State Libr. Assn. N.C., State Libr. Assn. La., State Libr. Assn. W.Va., State Libr. Assn. Va. Democrat. Methodist. Office: S&W Distbrs Inc 1600 E Wendover Ave # H Greensboro NC 27405-6854 Office Phone: 336-272-7394. Personal E-mail: swncbooks1@aol.com, S_W_Distributors@bellsouth.net.

**SANDERS, W(ILLIAM) EUGENE, JR.,** retired internist; b. Frederick, Md., June 25, 1934; s. W(illiam) Eugene and E. Gertrude (Wilburn) Sanders; m. Christine Culp, Feb. 22, 1974. AB, Cornell U., 1956, MD, 1960. Diplomate Am. Bd. Internal Medicine. Intern Johns Hopkins Hosp., Balt., 1960-61, resident, 1961-62; instr. medicine Emory U. Sch. Medicine, Atlanta, 1962-64; chief med. resident, instr. U. Fla. Coll. Medicine, Gainesville, 1964-65, asst. prof. medicine and microbiology, 1965-69, assoc. prof., 1969-72; prof., chmn. dept. med. microbiology, prof. medicine Creighton U. Sch. Medicine, Omaha, 1972-95, prof. emeritus, 1995—. Cons-in-rsch. Fla. Dept. Health and Rehab. Svcs., 1966—. Editor: Am. Jour. Epidemiology, 1974—95; contbr. scientific papers to profl. jours. Med. officer USPHS, 1962—64. Recipient Rsch. Career Devel. award, NIH, 1968—72; John and Mary R. Markle scholar in acad. medicine, 1968—73. Mem.: N.Y. Acad. Scis., Thoracic Soc., Am. Lung Assn., Soc. Epidemiol. Rsch., Infectious Diseases Soc. Am., Am. Soc. Microbiology, Sigma Xi, Phi Beta Kappa, Phi Kappa Phi. Achievements include patents for enocin antibiotic and RBE limonene and perrilyl alcohol. Home: 1901 Pennsylvania Ave Englewood FL 34224-5530 E-mail: ecsanders@gls3c.com. *Each day provides more challenges and more opportunities than the preceding. No individual can possibly cope with each of these in any given day. Success depends upon establishing priorities and maintaining them. Fight only those battles and pursue with fervor only those opportunities that improve both one's self and one's fellow man.*

**SANDERS, WILLIAM JOHN,** research scientist; b. Detroit, July 10, 1940; s. John William and Charlotte Barbara (Linsday) Steele; m. Gary Roberts, Sept. 12, 1961; children: Scott David, Susan Deborah. BS, U. Mich., 1962; MSEE, U. Calif., Berkeley, 1964. Sr. rsch. scientist Stanford (Calif.) U., 1967-97; pres. Sanders Data Systems, 1991—. Pres. Computers in Cardiology, 1990-93, dir., 2000—, info. svcs., 2001—. Inventor cardiac probe; contbr. articles to profl. jours. Mem. IEEE Computer Soc., Assn. Computing Machinery. Avocations: bicycling, wind surfing. Office: Sanders Data Sys 3980 Bibbits Dr Palo Alto CA 94303-4531 Business E-Mail: bill@sandersdata.com

**SANDERS-HALL, PATRICIA E.,** health facility administrator; d. Lloyd M. and Marguerite E. Sanders; m. Steven W. Hall, Dec. 6, 1986; children: Kahliah Aisha-Brown Hall, Rashaad Zahkee-Lloyd Hall. BA, U. Mo., Kansas City, 1972; MA, U. Denver, 1974. Cert. health scis. adminstrn. U. Colo. Health Scis. Ctr., 1988. Dir. speech therapy Hope Ctr., Denver, 1974—76; dir.speech pathology Easter Seal Rehab. Ctr., Lakewood, Colo., 1976—80; mgr. speech and audiology Mercy Med. Ctr., Denver, 1980—88; dir. rehab. medicine U. Colo. Health Scis. Ctr., Denver, 1988—99; v.p. Kans. U. Med. Ctr., Kansas City, 1999—. Pvt. practice mgmt. trainer, Overland Park, Kans., 1990—. Author (performing artist): (poetry & storytelling) A Women's Inalienable Writes (Mayor Award of Excellence in the Arts, 1997). Pres. PTO, Aurora, Colo., 1987—89; v.p. Jack & Jill of Am., Inc., Denver, 1994—96; bd. mem. Denver Black Arts Festival, 1988—98, Colo. Donor Alliance, Denver, 1997—99. Recipient Golden Poet award, World of Poetry, 1988, 1991, 1994; fellow, U. Denver, 1972—74; Curator's Academic scholar, U. Mo., 1968—72. Mem.: NAFE, Assn. Healthcare Execs., Am. Hosp. Assn., Nat. Storytellers Assn., Alpha Kappa Alpha. Democrat. Methodist. Avocations: party/event planning, desktop publishing, cooking. Office: Univ Kans Med Ctr 3901 Rainbow Blvd Kansas City KS 66160 E-mail: psanders@kumc.edu.

**SANDERSON, ARTHUR CLARK,** engineering educator; b. Providence, Oct. 23, 1946; s. Robert Leroy and Julia Ayer (Oldham) S.; m. Susan Rita Walsh, Aug. 14, 1971; children: Angeline Mirada, Andrew McWain. BS,

Brown U., 1968; MS, Carnegie-Mellon U., 1970, PhD, 1972. Rsch. engr. Westinghouse Electric Corp., Pitts., 1968-70; vis. rsch. scientist Delft (The Netherlands) U. Tech., 1972-73; prof. Carnegie-Mellon U., Pitts., 1973-87, co-dir. robotics inst., 1981-87; rsch. dir. Philips Rsch. Labs., Briarcliff Manor, NY, 1985-87; prof., dept. chmn. Rensselaer Poly. Inst., Troy, NY, 1987—; divsn. dir. elec. & comm. systems NSF, Arlington, Va., 1998-2000; v.p. rsch. Rensselaer Poly. Inst., 2000—. Vis. prof. Univ. Iberoamericana, Mexico City, 1975-77, Instn. Sci. & Elecs., U. Tsukuba, Japan, 1996-97. Contbr. 3 books, over 250 articles to profl. jours. Fellow AAAS, IEEE (pres. robotics and automation soc. 1989, 90); mem. AIAA (mem. space automation and robotics tech. com.). Achievements: research in Artificial Intelligence, Soc. Mfg. Engrs. Office: Rensselaer Poly Inst 110 8th St Troy NY 12180-3522 Home: 18 Barberry Coast Rd Newmarket NH 03857 E-mail: sandea@rpi.edu.

**SANDERSON, DAVID R.,** physician; b. South Bend, Ind., Dec. 26, 1933; s. Robert Burns and Alpha (Rodenberger) S.; divorced, 1978; children: David, Kathryn, Robert, Lisa; m. Evelyn Louise Klunder, Sept. 20, 1980. BA, Northwestern U., 1955, MD, 1958. Cons. in medicine Mayo Clinic, Rochester, Minn., 1965—87, chmn. dept. thoracic disease, 1977—87, cons. in medicine Scottsdale, Ariz., 1987—2000, chmn. dept. internal medicine, 1988—96, vice chmn. bd. govs., 1987—94. Assoc. dir. Mayo Lung Project, Nat. Cancer Inst., Rochester. Contbr. articles to profl. jours. Recipient Noble award Mayo Found., Rochester, Chevalier Jackson award Am. Bronchoesophagologic Assn., 1990. Fellow ACP, Am. Coll. Chest Physicians (gov. for Minn. 1981-87); mem. Am. Bronchoesophagologic Assn., World Assn. for Bronchology, Internat. Bronchoesophagologic Soc., Internat. Assn. Study of Lung Cancer, AMA, Sigma Xi, Sigma Chi (Significant Sig award 1989). Presbyterian. Home: 10676 E Bella Vista Dr Scottsdale AZ 85258-6086 Office: Mayo Clinic Scottsdale 13400 E Shea Blvd Scottsdale AZ 85259-5499 Personal E-mail: dsanderson958@cox.net.

**SANDERSON, DEVON LEE,** elementary school educator; b. St Elizabeth, Jamaica; s. George Sanderson and Josephine M. Scarlett-Vaccianna; m. Pauline Vinette Harvey. Cert., Bethlehem Moravian Coll. Cert. nursing asst., 2005. Tchr. Goshen and Belle Plain Basic Schools, Clarendon, Jamaica, 1988—91, Ashton All Age Sch., Westmoreland, Jamaica, 1994—2000, Eber Preparatory and Kindergarten Sch., Jamaica, 2001—03; tchr. Caribbean exam. coun. Bethel Town All Age Evening Inst., 2002—04. Freelance writer-elect Inst. Children's Lit., Conn. Former mem. Montego Bay Writer's Club; former writer, contr. Western Mirror Newspaper; student elect Long Ridge Writers Group, West Redding, Conn. Recipient 1st Place Esteem award, Poetry Jamaica, 2003, Merit award cert. for poetry writing, World of Poetry, 1990. Avocations: reading, gardening, writing, singing. Home: 105 Memorial Dr New Castle DE 19720

**SANDERSON, DOUGLAS JAY,** lawyer; b. Boston, Apr. 21, 1953; s. Warren and Edith S. Sanderson; m. Audrey S. Goldstein, June 6, 1982; children: Scott M.G., Phoebe H.G. BA, Trinity Coll., Hartford, Conn., 1974; JD, George Washington U., 1977. Bar: Va. 1977, D.C. 1978, U.S. Dist. Ct. (ea. dist.) Va. 1978, U.S. Ct. Appeals (4th cir.) 1978. Assoc. Bettius, Rosenberger & Carter, P.C., Fairfax, Va., 1977-82; ptnr. Bettius & Sanderson, P.C. and predecessor firms, Fairfax, 1982-86; prin. Miles & Stockbridge P.C., Fairfax, 1986-95; br. head Miles & Stockbridge, Fairfax, 1989-91; co-owner McCandlish & Lillard, P.C., Fairfax, 1995—. Trustee Cambridge Ctr. Behavioral Studies, Cambridge, 1981-90. Editor: Consumer Protection Reporting Svc., 1976-77. Bd. dirs. Legal Svcs. No. Va., Inc., 1991-97, pres., 1993-95; vol. counsel Arts Coun. of Fairfax County, Inc., 1991--. Mem. ABA, Va. Bar Assn., Fairfax Bar Assn., Ctrl. Fairfax C. of C. (bd. dirs. 1988-93). Avocations: sports, reading. Office: McCandlish & Lillard 11350 Random Hills Rd Ste 500 Fairfax VA 22030-6044 Office Phone: 703-273-2288.

**SANDERSON, GEOFF,** professional hockey player; b. Hay River, N.W.T., Can., Feb. 1, 1972; m. Ellen Sanderson; children: Benjamin, Jake. Left wing Hartford Whalers, Hartford, 1990—97, Carolina Hurricanes, 1997—98, Vancouver Canucks, 1998, 2004, Buffalo Sabres, 1998—2000, Columbus Blue Jackets, 2000—04, 2005, Phoenix Coyotes, 2005—06, Phila. Flyers, 2006—. Player NHL All-Star Game, 1994, 97. Office: Phila Flyers 3601 S Broad St Philadelphia PA 19148*

**SANDERSON, JAMES RICHARD,** retired naval officer, financial consultant; b. Selma, Calif., Dec. 27, 1925; s. Charles Maxwell and Edith (Wente) S.; m. Betty Lee Bradley, Sept. 19, 1947. Student, U. Calif.-Berkeley, 1943-44, U. Wash., 1944, U. Willamette, 1944-45; grad., USNR Midshipman Sch. at Columbia U., 1945, Nat. War Coll., 1966; student, Gen. Line Sch., Monterey, Calif., 1953, Sr. Officers Ship Material Mgmt. Course, Idaho Falls, Idaho, 1979; BA in Internat. Affairs, George Washington U., 1968. Served as enlisted man U.S. Naval Res., 1943-45; commd. ensign USN, 1946, advanced through grades to vice adm., 1980; gunnery officer U.S.S. Mansfield, 1946-47, U.S.S. Bausell, 1947-48; flight trainee Naval Air Sta., Pensacola, Fla., 1949, Corpus Christi, Tex., 1950; served in Attack Squadron 195, Alameda, Calif., 1950-52; flight instr. Naval Air Sta., Pensacola, 1953-55; served in Attack Squadron 16, 1955-57; air ops. officer on staff Comdr. Carrier Div. Four, U.S.S. Forrestal, 1957-60; ops. officer Attack Squadron 43, Naval Air Sta., Oceana, Va., 1960-62; comdg. officer Attack Squadron 76, 1962-63; comdr. Attack Carrier Air Wing Three in U.S.S. Saratoga, 1963-65; spl. support plans officer, Pacific Area Strategic Plans and Policy Div., Office of Chief of Naval Ops., Washington, 1966-67; exec. asst. and sr. aide to dep. chief. naval ops., 1967-69; comdg. officer U.S.S. Ranier, 1969-70; dep. chief of staff for ops. and plans U.S. Sixth Fleet, 1970-71; comdg. officer U.S.S. Saratoga, 1971-73; dep. comdr. Naval Striking and Support Forces, So. Europe, Naples, Italy, 1973-76; vice dir. ops. Joint Chiefs of Staff, Washington, 1976-77; asst. dep. chief naval ops. for plans, policy and ops., 1977-79; comdr. Task Force Sixty, U.S. 6th Fleet, 1979-80, Carrier Group Two, 1979-80, Battle Force Sixth Fleet, 1979-80, Carrier Striking Force So. Region, 1979-80; dep. and chief staff, comdr. in chief Atlantic/U.S. Atlantic Fleet, Norfolk, Va., 1980 93; ret., 1993; pres. Enca. Planning & Investment Co., Inc., Virginia Beach, Va., 1983-85; sr. v.p. for corp. ops. Computer Dynamics, Inc., 1984-86; asst. to pres. Eastern Computers, Inc., 1986—; cons., prin. Exec. Planning and Investment Co., Inc., 1986-94; sr. fellow joint and combined warfare course Armed Forces Staff Coll., 1994—. Decorated 21 campaign medals, including D.S.M., Legion of Merit with 3 gold stars, D.F.C., Meritorious Service medal, Air medal with 4 gold stars, Navy Commendation medal with combat distinguishing device. Mem.: NRA, KT, U. Calif. Alumni Assn., George Washington U. Alumni Assn., Tailhook Assn., Smithsonian Assn., KT Eye Found., Nat. Wildlife Assn., Order of Daedalians, Nat. Assn. Individual Investors, Nat. Eagle Scout Assn. (regent, Disting. Eagle Scout award 1994), The Golden Eagles, Assn. Naval Aviation, Naval Acad. Athletic Assn., Nat. War Coll. Alumni Assn, Nat. Skeet Shooting Assn., Army Navy Country Club (Arlington, Va.), Mystic Shrine, Royal Order of Scotland, Royal Arch, Masons (33 degree), Shriners, Knights Templar, Sojourners.

**SANDERSON, JANET A.,** former ambassador; b. Tucson, Ariz., Apr. 1955; Diploma, Coll. of William and Mary, 1977; MA in Nat. Security Studies, Naval War Coll., 1993. Econ. officer U.S. Fgn. Svc., 1978; various govt. positions, including energy and petroleum advisor Bur. of European Affairs (OECD), 1986—88; various state dept. positions to dept. econ. counselor to min./counselor for econ. affairs U.S. Embassy, Cairo, dept. chief of mission Amman, Jordan, 1997—2000; U.S. amb. to Algeria US Dept. State, Algiers, 2000—03. Recipient Herbert A. Salzman award for Internat. Econ. Performance, U.S. Dept. of State, 1996, numerous honor awards.

**SANDERSON, KENNETH JEROME,** school system administrator, consultant; b. Sandwich, Ill., June 23, 1962; s. Kenneth Lavern and Teresa Ann Sanderson; m. Lisa Marie Buoy, Aug. 5, 1989; children: John Kenneth, Annelise Marie, Katherine Joy, Mary Therese. BA in Polit. Sci., U. Ill., 1984, EdM in Elem. Edn., 1987, Advanced Cert. in Ednl. Adminstrn., 1993. Cert. ednl. adminstrn. Ill., 1993, elem. edn. Ill., 1987. Athletic dir. St. Matthew Sch., Champaign, Ill., 1989—94; prin. St. Anne Sch., East Moline, Ill., 1994—2001; assoc. supt. Office Cath. Schs., Diocese of Peoria, Ill., 2001—. Site coord. Project Lifeline, Champaign, Ill., 1993—94; facilitator Rainbows

for God's Children, East Moline, Ill., 1994—99; pastoral coun. Diocese of Peoria, 1997—97; sec. Black Hawk Fedn., Christian Family Movement, Moline, Ill., 2000—01. Recipient Best-Mannered Tchr. award, Champaign County Chpt., Nat. League of Jr. Cotillions, 2002. Mem.: Nat. Cath. Ednl. Assn. (assoc.) Roman Catholic. Avocations: hiking, travel, camping. Home: 2305 W Wagner Ln Peoria IL 61615 Office: Office of Catholic Schools 412 NE Madison Ave Peoria IL 61603 Office Phone: 309-671-1550. Business E-Mail: jsanderson@cdop.org.

**SANDERSON, MARY LOUISE,** medical association administrator; b. Fairmont, W. Va., Oct. 29, 1942; d. Lawrence Oliver and Frances Evelyn (Shuttleworth) Shingleton; m. William W. Olmstead III, Dec. 1966 (div. June 1974); children: William W. IV, Happy; m. Lester F. Davis, III, Oct. 1979 (div. Dec. 1986); m. David S. Sanderson, Sept. 1992. Student, Vassar Coll., 1960-62, Carnegie Mellon, 1962-63. Real estate broker, N.C. Exec. sec. Creative Dining, Raleigh, NC, 1980-83, Sea Pines Plantation Co., Hilton Head, SC, 1973-79; adminstr. Am. Bd. Neurological Surgery, Houston, 1983—. Vol. Interact, Raleigh, 1984-86, M.D. Anderson Cancer Ctr./Camp Star Trails, 1994-96; docent Mordecai House Hist. Preservation, Raleigh, 1981-83; mem./vol. Reach to Recovery, 1995-2001, Houston Symphony, 2002-. Mus. of Fine Arts, Houston, 1999-. Recipient Vol. award N.C. State Gov., 1986. Mem. Am. Soc. Assn. Execs. Democrat. Episcopalian. Office: Am Bd Neurol Surgery 6550 Fannin St Ste 2139 Houston TX 77030-2718*

**SANDERSON, RITA MARYE,** history educator; b. West Palm Beach, Fla., Dec. 16, 1935; d. Joseph Nicholas and Marie Emma (Dore) Lavan; m. Glenn Smith Sanderson, Nov. 18, 1954; children: Patricia, Shannon, Siena, Keith. BA, Fla. Atlantic U., 1973, MA. Tchr. Northeast High Sch., Oakland Park, Fla., 1967-84; tchr., dept. head Ft. Lauderdale (Fla.) H.S., 1984-99; ret.; instr. Broward C.C. Life mem. Ctr. Study Presidency, Washington, 1983—; patron Met. Opera. Mem.: Ret. Educators Assn., The Heritage Found., Opera Soc. Republican. Roman Catholic. Home: 1629 NE 1st Ave Fort Lauderdale FL 33305-2923

**SANDFORD, MARY ANN,** Spanish language educator; b. Lackawanna, N.Y., May 2, 1947; d. Raymond George and Irene Emma (Beebe) Hubbs; m. Paul B. Sandford, Dec. 20, 1975; children: Paul Nathan, Sarah Kathryn, Daniel Raymond. BA, Am. U., 1969; MEd, SUNY, Buffalo, 1973. Cert. secondary edn. fgn. lang. Tchr. Spanish West Seneca (N.Y.) Schs., 1969-75; instr. Spanish N.Mex. State U., Carlsbad, 1976—; tchr. Spanish Carlsbad Mcpl. Schs., 1988—2003. Dept. chair West Seneca Schs., 1970-75, Carlsbad Mcpl. Schs., 1989-1999. Pres. Child Conservation, Carlsbad, 1987-88. Recipient James D. Allen Dept. award N.Y. State, 1974. Mem. AAUW (v.p. 1983, 2001-03, 05—), pres. 1998-2000, academic coord. 2004—, state outreach coord. 2006—), Am. Assn. Tchrs. Spanish and Portuguese, Delta Kappa Gamma (v.p. 1993-94). Democrat. Methodist. Avocations: collecting antiques, china, glassware, furniture. Home: 1724 Sandy Ln Carlsbad NM 88220-8821 E-mail: m_sandford47@hotmail.com.

**SANDHAAS, JILL T.,** lawyer; b. Manhasset, NY, July 13, 1961; BA, SUNY, Albany, 1988; JD, St. John's U., 1990. Bar: NY 1991. Ptnr. Wilson, Elser, Moskowitz, Edelman & Dicker LLP, Albany, NYC. Past counsel to chmn. NY State Senate Health Com. Mem.: NY State Bar Assn., Nassau County Bar Assn. Office: Wilson Elser Moskowitz Edelman Dicker Ll 677 Broadway Ste 901 Albany NY 12207-2989 Office Phone: 518-449-8893. Office Fax: 518-449-8927. Business E-Mail: sandhaasj@wemed.com.

**SANDHU, HARVINDER SINGH,** spinal surgeon, educator; b. Jalandhar, Punjab, India, Mar. 18, 1962; s. Jagtar singh and Shivtej Kaur Sandhu; m. Sonia Kaur Chattha, May 25, 1997; 1 child, alexi. BS, Northwestern U., 1982, MD, 1987; MBA, Columbia U., 2001. Diplomate Am. Bd. Orthopedic Surgery, Nat. Bd. Med. Examiners. Attending surgeon UCLA, 1994-97, Hosp. for Spl. Surgery, N.Y.C., 1997—. Pres. Sandhu Cons., Scarsdale, N.Y., 1999—. Recipient Outstanding Sci. Exhibit award Internat. Soc. for Study of the Lumbar spine, 1999, Volvo award for Lumbar Spine Rsch., 2002. Mem. Am. Acad. Orthopedic Surgery (biologic implants com. 2000—), Orthopedic Rsch. Soc., N.Am. Spine Soc. (Outstanding Sci. Exhibit award 1996), Scoliosis Rsch. Soc., Beta Gamma Sigma. Office: Hosp for Spl Surgery 535 E 70th St New York NY 10021 Fax: (212) 774-2600. E-mail: sandhuh@hss.edu.

**SAN DIEGO, ARMANDO GONDA,** retired military officer, pathologist, consultant; b. Manila, Philippines, June 17, 1934; arrived in U.S., 1959; s. Amado Robles San Diego and Vicenta Sanvectores Gonda; m. Lolita Aves Tan, Apr. 20, 1959; children: Eric, Eileen, Jerry. AA, U. Santo Tomas, 1954, MD, 1959. Diplomate Am. Bd. Pathology, Forensic Examiners, and Forensic Medicine, cert. in anatomical and clinical pathology Am. Bd. Pathology, 1969, lic. physician Philippine Republic, 1959, Ill., 1969, NY, 1969, Calif., 1975, cert. forensic examiner Am. Bd. Forensic Examiners, 1995, in forensic medicine Am. Bd. Forensic Medicine, 1996. Intern Du Page County Hosp., Elmhurst, Ill., 1960; pathology resident Ravenswood Med. Ctr., Chgo., 1961, Columbus-Cuneo Med. Ctr., Chgo., 1962—65; pathologist Keesler USAF Med. Ctr., Biloxi, Miss., 1967—70; capt. USAF, 1967—74, advanced through grades to col., 1974—96, ret., 1996; chmn. Dept. Pathology USAF Regional Hosp., Clark AFB, Philippines, 1970—74, USAF Regional Hosp., March AFB, Riverside, Calif., 1974—79, David Grant USAF Med. Ctr., Fairfield, Calif., 1979—85; chief pathology and lab. medicine Sheppard AF, Wichita Falls, Tex., 1985—87; assoc. chief hosp. svcs. Sheppard Hosp., Wichita Falls, 1987—88, comdr. and chief med. staff, 1993—96; ret., 1996. Adv. Solano County Regional Occupl. Program, Calif., 1984—85; assoc. med. examiner U.S. Med. Examiners Armed Forces Inst. Pathology; med. dir. med. lab. tng. program Sch. Healthcare Scis. USAF; flight surgeon augmentee Aerospace Medicine Dept. Sheppard AFB; cons. in forensic pathology Contbr. articles to profl. journ. Dir. med. mission Wichita County Med. Alliance, Wichita Falls, 2001, Filipino Am. Club North Tex., Wichita Falls, 2005; vol. physician Annual Hotter "N" Hell Bike Race, Wichita Falls, 1988—2005; mem. appraisal rev. bd. Wichita County, 2000—05. Decorated Nat. Def. Svc. medal USAF, Meritorious Svc. medal, Legion of Merit medal. Fellow: Coll. Am. Pathologists (life; del. 1987—90, inspector lab. accreditation program), Am. Coll. Forensic Examiners (life), Am. Soc. Clin. Pathology (life; adv. coun. 1987—90); mem.: Soc. Med. Cons. to Armed Forces, Soc. Armed Forces Med. Lab. Scientists, Ret. Officers Assn. (life), Assn. Mil. Surgeons U.S. (life), Filipino-Am. Club (pres. 1999—). Avocations: car collecting, painting, bicycling, hunting.

**SANDIFER, KEVIN WAYNE,** archival services executive; b. Shreveport, La., Sept. 5, 1956; s. Glenn Eugene and Beverly Sue (Mauritzen) S. BS in Libr. Sci., La. State U., Shreveport, 1985, BA in History, 1987; M in Spl. Libr. Instrn., U. Arlington, 1989. Pub. Red River Press, Blanchard, La., 1985-87; pres., CEO Archival Svcs., Inc., Blanchard, La., 1988—. Author: Layman's Look at Starting a Religious Archive, 1982 (Disting. Writing award 1983), Complete Document Restoration Manual, 1986, Introduction to Religious Archival Science, 1988. 2d edit., 1998, Public Relations are an Asset for the Museum and Archives, 1986, 2d edit., 1998, Photography Simplified for the Archivist, 1990, 2d edit., 1998, Christianityn and the Ark of the Covenant, 1998, others; editor: (textbook) Oral History, 1985. Archivist Grandstone Bluff Mus., 1985-90. Named Outstanding Historian Northwest La., Shreveport Jour., 1982, Expert Archivist Shreveport Times, 1983. Fellow Soc. Am. Archivists; mem. Am. Assn. State and Local History, La. Hist. Soc., North La. Hist. Assn. Southern Baptist. Avocations: reading, writing, running track. Home and Office: 3900 Roy Rd Apt 37 Shreveport LA 71107-9631

**SANDKUHLER, KEVIN M.,** military officer; b. Queens, NY, Aug. 28, 1953; BA in History, Coll. Holy Cross; JD, Calif. West. Sch. Law, 1981; LLM, George Washington U., 1991; grad., U.S. Army War Coll., 1994. Bar: Calif. 1981. Commd. 2nd lt. NROTC, 1975; advanced through grades to gen. USMC; fire protection officer, platoon comdr., adjutant, 3rd battalion 11th Marines, 1st Marine divsn. Marine Corps, Camp Pendleton, Calif., with office staff judge advocate, head rev. sect., 3rd Force Service Support Group

Okinawa, Japan, 1984, staff judge advocate, 35th Marine Amphibious Unit Republic of Korea, 1984, sr. def. counsel Camp Pendleton, Calif., 1985—86, dir. contracting divsn., contracting officer, 1986—89, assoc. counsel systems command, non-proliferation planner, joint staff directorate strategic plans and policy, 1993—97, staff judge advocate III Marine Expeditionary Force, 3rd Marine divsn. Okinawa, Japan, 1997—2000, dir. appellate govt. divsn.Navy-Marine Corps Appellate Activity Washington, chief def. counsel, 2000, staff judge advocate to commandant, 2001—; advanced through ranks to Brigadier General. Decorated Def. Superior Svc. Medal, Legion of Merit Medal, Meritorious Svc. Medal with Gold Star, Joint Achievement Medal, Navy and Marine Corps Achievement Medal. Office: 3000 Marine Corps Pentagon Washington DC 20350

**SANDLER, ADAM,** actor; b. Bklyn., Sept. 9, 1966; m. Jackie Titone, June 22, 2003; 1 child, Sadie Madison. Grad., NYU. Actor: (films) Remote Control, 1987, Shakes the Clown, 1992, Coneheads, 1993, Mixed Nuts, 1994, Airheads, 1994, Bullet Proof, 1996, The Wedding Singer, 1998, Punch Drunk Love, 2002, 50 First Dates, 2004, Spanglish, 2004; actor, writer: Billy Madison, 1995, Happy Gilmore, 1996; actor, exec. prodr.: The Animal, 2001, Joe Dirt, 2001, Mr. Deeds, 2002, The Master of Disguise, 2002, Anger Management, 2003, The Longest Yard, 2005; actor, exec. prodr., writer: The Water Boy, 1998, Big Daddy, 1999, Little Nicky, 2000; actor, prodr., writer: Eight Crazy Nights, 2002; actor, prodr.: Dickie Roberts: Former Child Star, 2003, Deuce Bigalow: European Gigolo, 2005, Click, 2006; prodr.: Grandma's Boy, 2006, Benchwarmers, 2006; TV appearances include Saturday Night Live: The Best of Chris Farley, 1998, Saturday Night Live: The Best of Mike Myers, 1998, Saturday Night Live: The Best of Phil Hartman, 1998; actor, writer Saturday Night Live (Emmy award nomination for writing 1991, 92); appeared on TV programs ABC Afterschool Special, 1990, Saturday Night Live Mother's Day Special, 1992, MTV Music Video Awards, 1994, Saturday Night Live Presents President Bill Clinton's All-Time Favorites, 1994, The 37th Annual Grammy Awards, 1995, The ESPY Awards, 1996; rec. artist (albums) They're All Gonna Laught at You!, 1993, What the Hell Happened to Me?, 1996, What's Your Name, 1997, Stan and Judy's Kid, 1999 (set record for most comedy albums sold in first week released), Shhh...Don't Tell, 2004. Recipient People's Choice award, 2000, Funny Male Star, People's Choice award, 2006, Choice Comedian, Teen Choice Awards, 2006; named one of 50 Most Powerful People in Hollywood, 2004-06.*

**SANDLER, BERNICE RESNICK,** women's rights specialist; b. N.Y.C., Mar. 3, 1928; d. Abraham Hyman and Ivy (Ernst) Resnick; children: Deborah Jo, Emily Maud. BA cum laude, Bklyn. Coll., 1948; MA, CCNY, 1950; EdD, U. Md., 1969; LLD (hon.), Bloomfield Coll., 1973, Hood Coll., 1974, R.I. Coll., 1980, Colby-Sawyer Coll., 1984; LHD (hon.), Grand Valley State Coll., 1974; Dr. Pub. Svc. (hon.), North Adams State Coll., 1985; LLD (hon.), Goucher Coll., 1991; LHD (hon.), Plymouth State Coll., 1992, Wittenberg U., 1993, Ripon Coll., 1998; LLD (hon.), U. St. Thomas, 2006. Rsch. asst., tchr. nursery sch., employment counselor, adult edn. instr., sec.; psychologist HEW, 1970; tchr. psychology Mt. Vernon Coll., 1970; head Action Com. for Fed. Contract Compliance, Women's Equity Action League, 1970—71; edn. specialist U.S. Ho. Reps., Washington, 1970; dep. dir. Womens Action program, HEW, Washington, 1971; dir. project on status and edn. of women Assn. Am. Colls., Washington, 1971—91; sr. assoc. Ctr. for Women Policy Studies, 1991—94; sr. scholar in residence Nat. Assn. Women in Edn., Washington, 1994—2000; sr. scholar Women's Rsch. and Edn. Inst., 2000—. Cons., 1991—; expert witness, 1990—; writer, 1971—; vis. lectr. U. Md., 1968-69; adv. bd. Women's Equity Action League Ednl. and Legal Def. Fund, 1980—, trustee, 1974-80, Women's Equity Action League, 1971-78; adv. com. Math./Sci. Network, 1979, Wider Opportunities for Women, 1978-85, Women's Legal Def. Fund, 1978-84; Nat. Coun. for Alternative Work Patterns Inc., 1978-85, Women's Hdqs. State Nat. Bank for Women's Appointments, 1977-78, and others. Mem. adv. bd. Jour. Reprints Documents Affecting Women, 1976-78, Women's Rights Law Reporter, 1970-80; editor: (newsletters) On Campus With Women, 1971-91, About Women on Campus, 1991-99; contbr. articles. Mem. bd. overseers Wellesley Coll. Ctr. for Rsch. on Women, 1975-87; bd. dirs. Ctr. for Women's Policy Studies, 1972-75; mem. exec. com. Inst. for Ednl. Leadership, 1982-87, mem. program adv. com., 1987-88, chair bd. dirs., 1981, chair adv. com., 1975-81; mem. affirmative action com., task force on family, nat. affairs comm. Am. Jewish Com., 1978, bd. dirs. D.C. chpt.; tech. adv. com. Nat. Jewish Family Ctr., 1980-89; adv. coun. Ednl. Devel. Ctr., 1980-85; adv. bd. Urban Inst., 1981-85, Women Employed Inst., 1981-84, Ex-New Yorkers for N.Y., 1978-79; mem. adv. com. Arthur and Elizabeth Schlesinger Libr. History of Women in Am., 1981-85; nat. adv. com. Shelter Rsch. Inst., Calif., 1980-82; chair adv. panel project on self-evaluation Am. Insts. for Rsch., 1980-82; bd. dirs. Equality Ctr., 1983, Evaluation and Tng. Inst., Calif., 1980, Inst. for Studies in Equality, 1975-77; exec. v.p. Bd. Women for Women, 1997—. Recipient Athena award Intercollegiate Assn. Women Students, 1974, Elizabeth Boyer award Women's Equity Action League, 1976, Rockefeller Pub. Svc. award Princeton U., 1976, Women Educators award for activism, 1987, Anna Roe award Harvard U., 1988, Readers Choice honors Washington Woman Mag., 1987, Woman of Distinction award Nat. Assn. Women in Edn., 1991, Georgina Smith award AAUP, 1992, Woman of Achievement Turner Broadcasting System, 1994; named one of 100 Most Powerful Women Washingtonian Mag., 1982, one of the nation's 100 Most Important Women, Ladies Home Jour., 1988, Leadership Matters award Inst. Ednl. Leadership, 1997, Medal of Honor, Vet. Feminists, 2001, Donna Shavlik award Am. Coun. Edn., 2003, Mary Keetz award Women's Consortium Pa. State Sys., 2004, Am. Fedn. Tchrs. Women's Rights award Mem. Assn. for Women in Sci. Found. (bd. dirs. 1977—), Am. Soc. Profl. and Exec. Women (adv. bd. 1980). Avocations: birding, music, swimming, hiking. Office: Women's Rsch and Edn Inst 1350 Connecticut Ave NW Ste 850 Washington DC 20036-1740

**SANDLER, GERALD HOWARD,** computer scientist, educator, information technology executive; b. NYC, Sept. 17, 1934; s. Irving and Sally S.; m. Ann Sandler; children: Eric, Steven. BS, CUNY, 1956, MS, 1957. With Grumman Aerospace, 1963-83; past pres. Grumman Data Systems & Svcs., Bethpage, NY, 1983-95; pres. GHS Enterprises, 1995—; prof. computer sci. Poly. U., Farmingdale, NY, 1995—. Author: System Engineering, 1963. Home: 46 Bonnie Dr Westbury NY 11590-2804

**SANDLER, HERBERT M.,** bank executive; b. NYC, Nov. 16, 1931; s. William B. and Hilda (Schattan) S.; m. Marion Osher, Mar. 26, 1961. BSS, CCNY, 1951; JD, Columbia U., 1954. Bar: NY 1956. Asst. counsel Waterfront Comm. NY Harbor, 1956-59; ptnr. Sandler & Sandler, NYC, 1960-62; pres., dir., mem. exec. com. Golden West Savs. & Loan Assn. and Golden West Fin. Corp., Oakland, Calif., 1963-75; co-chmn. bd., co-CEO, dir., mem. exec. com. World Savings Bank and Golden West Fin. Corp., Oakland, 1975—. Charter mem. Thrift Instns. Adv. Coun., to Fed. Res. Bd., 1980-81; former chmn. Legis. and Regulation Com. Calif. Savs. and Loan League; former mem. bd. dirs. Fed. Home Loan Bank, San Francisco. Pres., trustee Calif. Neighborhood Services Found.; chmn. Urban Housing Inst.; mem. policy adv. bd. Ctr. for Real Estate and Urban Econs. U. Calif., Berkeley. With U.S. Army, 1954-56. Named Morningstar's CEO of Yr., 2004. Office: Golden West Fin Corp 1901 Harrison St Oakland CA 94612-3588*

**SANDLER, HOWARD,** medical educator; Prof. U. Mich., Ann Arbor 1989—. Office: University of Michigan 1500 E Medical Center Dr Ann Arbor MI 48109-0010 Office Phone: 734-936-9338. E-mail: hsandler@umich.edu.

**SANDLER, IRVING HARRY,** art critic, art historian; b. N.Y.C., July 22, 1925; s. Harry and Anna (Robin) S.; m. Lucy Freeman, Sept. 4, 1958; 1 child, Catherine Harriet. BA, Temple U., 1948; MA, U. Pa., 1950; PhD, NYU, 1976. Instr. in art history NYU, 1960-71; prof. emeritus art history SUNY, Purchase; art critic N.Y. Post, N.Y.C., 1960-65. Author: The Triumph of American Painting: A History of Abstract Expressionism, 1970, The New York School: Painters and Sculptors of the Fifties, 1978, Alex Katz, 1979, Al Held, 1984, American Art of the 1960s, 1988; editor (with Amy Newman) Defining Modern Art: Selected Writings of Alfred H. Barr Jr., 1986, Mark di Suvero at Storm King Art Ctr., 1996, Art of Postmodern Era: From Late 1960s to Early

1990s, 1996, Natvar Bhavsar, 1998, Stephen Antonakos, 1999, A Sweeper-Up After Artists: A Memoir, 2003, From Avant-Garde to Pluralism: An On-The-Spot History, 2006. John Simon Guggenheim fellow, 1965; Nat. Endowment for Arts fellow, 1977. Mem. Coll. Art Assn., Internat. Assn Art Critics. Home: 60 E 8th St Apt 19E New York NY 10003 Office Phone: 212-533-7447.

**SANDLER, LUCY FREEMAN,** art history educator; b. NYC, June 7, 1930; d. Otto and Frances (Glass) Freeman; m. Irving Sandler, Sept. 4, 1958; 1 child, Catherine Harriet. BA, Queens Coll., 1951; MA, Columbia U., 1957; PhD, NYU, 1964. Asst. prof. NYU, 1964-70, assoc. prof., 1970-75, prof. fine arts, 1975-86, Helen Gould Sheppard prof. art history, 1986—2003, chmn. dept., 1975-89; editorial cons. Viator, UCLA, 1983-97; Helen Gould Sheppard prof. art history emerita, 2003—. Author: The Peterborough Psalter in Brussels, 1974, The Psalter of Robert De Lisle in the British Library, 1983, new edit., 1999, Gothic Manuscripts 1285-1385, 1986, 'Omne Bonum': A Fourteenth-Century Encyclopedia of Universal Knowledge, 1996, The Ramsey Psalter, 1999, Der Ramsey-Psalter (Glanzlichter der Buchkunst 12), 2003, Der Bestiarium aus Peterbourgh/The Peterborough Bestiary, 2003, The Lichtenthal Psalter and the Patronage of the Bohun Family, 2004, (with Jonathan J.G. Alexander and James H. Marrow) The Splendor of the Word, Medieval and Renaissance Illuminated Manuscripts, NY Pub. Libr., 2005; editor: Essays in Memory of Karl Lehmann, 1964, Art the Ape of Nature: Studies in Honor of H.W. Janson, 1981, Coll. Art Assn. Monograph Series, 1970-75, 86-89, Gesta, 1991-94; asst. editor Art Bull., 1964-67, mem. editl. bd., 1994; mem. editl. bd. Jour. Jewish Art, 1978, Speculum, 1994. Trustee Godwin-Ternbach Mus., Queens Coll., 1982-94; chair dels. exec. com. Am. Coun. Learned Socs., 2002-04. NEH fellow, 1967-68, 77; fellow Pierpont Morgan Library; Guggenheim fellow, 1988-89. Fellow: Medieval Acad. Am. (councillor 2002—05), Soc. Antiquaries (London); mem.: AAUP, Coll. Art Assn. (pres. 1981—84), Internat. Ctr. Medieval Art (adv. bd., bd. dirs. 1976—80, 1984—87, 1989—92, 1995—2001). Home: 60 E 8th St Apt 19E New York NY 10012 Office: NYU Dept Fine Arts New York NY 10003 Office Phone: 212-998-8181.

**SANDLER, MARION OSHER,** bank executive; b. Biddeford, Maine, Oct. 17, 1930; d. Samuel and Leah (Lowe) Osher; m. Herbert M. Sandler, Mar. 26, 1961. BA, Wellesley Coll., 1952; postgrad., Harvard U.-Radcliffe Coll., 1953; MBA, NYU, 1958; LLD (hon.), Golden Gate U., 1987. Asst. buyer Bloomingdale's (dept. store, NYC, 1953-55; security analyst Dominick & Dominick, NYC, 1955-61; sr. fin. analyst Oppenheimer & Co., NYC, 1961-63; sr. v.p., dir. Golden West Fin. Corp. and World Savings Bank, Oakland, Calif., 1963-75, vice chmn. bd. dirs., CEO, mem. exec. com., dir., 1975-80, pres., co- chief exec. officer, dir., mem. exec. com., 1980-93, chmn. bd. dirs., CEO, mem. exec. com., 1993—; pres., chmn. bd. dirs., CEO Atlas Assets, Inc., Oakland, 1987—, Atlas Advisers, Inc., Oakland, 1987—, Atlas Securities, Inc., Oakland, 1987—. Mem. adv. com. Fed. Nat. Mortgage Assn., 1983-84. Mem. Pres.'s Mgmt. Improvement Coun., 1980, Thrift Insts. Adv. Coun. to Fed. Res. Bd., 1989-91, v.p., 1990, pres., 1991; mem. policy adv. bd. Ctr. for Real Estate and Urban Econs. U. Calif., Berkeley, 1981—, mem. exec. com. policy adv. bd., 1985—; mem. ad hoc com. to rev. Schs. Bus. Adminstrn. U. Calif., 1984-85; vice chmn. industry adv. com. Fed. Savs. and Loan Ins. Corp., 1987-88, Ins. Corp., 1987-88; bd. overseers NYU Schs. Bus., 1987-89; mem. Glass Ceiling Commn., 1992-93; bd. dirs. Success for All Found., 1997-2005, Manpower Demonstration Rsch. Corp., 1998-2004, Ctr. Am. Progress, 2003-. Named Morningstar's CEO of Yr., 2004; named one of 50 Women to Watch, Wall St. Jour., 2005; recipient Com. Inventor award, Com. 200 Found., 2005, Lifetime Achievement award, US Banker, 2005. Mem. Phi Beta Kappa, Beta Gamma Sigma. Office: Golden W Fin Corp 1901 Harrison St Fl 6 Oakland CA 94612-3588*

**SANDLER, NORMAN,** communications executive; Formerly dir. pub. rels. Motorola, Inc., Schaumburg, Ill., now dir. global strategic issues.

**SANDLER, RICHARD H.,** pediatric gastroenterologist; MD, Mich. State U. Coll. Human Medicine. Resident, pediatrics Mich. State U., Lansing; fellow, pediatric gastroenterology, hepatology, and nutrition Harvard Med. Sch., Boston Children's Hosp.; fellow, human metabolism and nutrition Mass. Gen. Hosp., Boston; asst. in medicine, instr., divsn. of gastroenterology and nutrition The Children's Hosp., Harvard Med. Sch., Boston, 1989—90; dir. Biomed. Acoustics Rsch. Group, Evanston, Ill., 1990—; pres., CEO, 1997—; assoc. prof., pediatrics Rush Med. Coll., Chgo., 1990—; adj. assoc. prof., biomed. engring. U. Ill., Chgo., 2002—. Office: Rush Univ Med Ctr 1725 W Harrison St Chicago IL 60612 Address: 1725 W Harrison St Ste 946 Chicago IL 60612 Office Phone: 312-942-2889.

**SANDLER, RICHARD JAY,** lawyer; b. NYC, Aug. 26, 1947; s. Albert and Ruth (Marcus) S.; children: Elizabeth, Russell, Victoria. BA summa cum laude, Princeton U., 1969; JD cum laude, Harvard U., 1972. Assoc. Davis, Polk & Wardwell, NYC, 1972-79, ptnr., 1979—, Paris, 1982-85, head capital markets practice group. Mem.: ABA. Avocation: winemaking. Office: Davis Polk & Wardwell 450 Lexington Ave Fl 19 New York NY 10017-3982 Office Phone: 212-450-4224. Office Fax: 212-450-3224. Business E-Mail: sandler@dpw.com.

**SANDLER, ROBERT MICHAEL,** insurance company executive; b. NYC, Apr. 20, 1942; s. Albert and Ruth (Marcus) S.; m. Annette L. Marchese, Aug. 18, 1963; children— David, Glenn BA in Math., Hofstra U., 1963. Various actuarial positions Met. Life, N.Y.C., 1963-68; various actuarial positions Am. Internat., N.Y.C., 1968-80; v.p., casualty actuary American Internat. Group, Inc., N.Y.C., 1980-84, sr. v.p., sr. actuary, sr. claims officer, 1984-95, exec. v.p., 1995—, dir. various subs. Mem. Casualty Actuarial Soc. (assoc.), Am. Acad. Actuaries, Internat. Actuarial Assn. Republican. Office: Am Internat Group 70 Pine St New York NY 10270-0002

**SANDLER, ROSS,** law educator; b. Milw., Jan. 31, 1939; s. Theodore T. and Laurette (Simons) S.; m. Alice R. Mintzer, Sept. 15, 1968; children: Josephine, Jenny, Dorothy. AB, Dartmouth Coll., 1961; LLB, NYU, 1965. Bar: N.Y. 1965, Fla. 1965. Assoc. atty. Cahill Gordon Reindel & Ohl, N.Y.C., 1965-68; asst. U.S. atty. So. Dist. N.Y., 1968-72; assoc. atty. Trubin Sillcocks Edelman & Knapp, N.Y.C., 1972-75; sr. staff atty. Natural Resources Def. Coun., N.Y.C., 1975-81, 83-86; spl. advisor to mayor City of N.Y., 1981-82; exec. dir. Hudson River Found., N.Y.C., 1983-86; commr. N.Y.C. Dept. Transp., 1986-90; ptnr. Jones Day Reavis & Pogue, N.Y.C., 1991-93; law prof. N.Y. Law Sch., 1993—, dir. Ctr. for N.Y.C. law, 1993—; mem. N.Y. Legis. Svc., 1998—. Mem. N.Y.C. Procurement Policy Bd., 1994—; vis. lectr. Yale Law Sch., New Haven, 1977; adj. prof. law NYU Law Sch., 1976-94; chair, mem. N.Y.C. Taxi and Limousine Commn., 1980-90. Co-author: A New Direction in Transit, 1978, Democracy by Decree, 2003; columnist Environ. Mag., 1976—80; editor: (jour.) City Law, City Land; contbr. chapters to books, articles. Trustee Woods Hole (Mass.) Rsch. Ctr., 1983—; mem. exec. com. Hudson River Found., 1986-96; mem. adv. coun. Ctr. Biodiversity and Conservation Am. Mus. Nat. History, 1996—. Recipient Pub. Interest award NYU Law Alumni, 1987, Louis J. Lefkowitz award Fordham Law Sch. Urban Law Jour., 1989, Lifetime Achievement award N.Y. State Bar Assn., 1998. Mem. City Club of N.Y. (chair 1992-93, trustee). Office: NY Law Sch 57 Worth St New York NY 10013-2959

**SANDLER, STANLEY IRVING,** chemical engineering educator; b. N.Y.C., June 10, 1940; s. Murray C. and Celia M. (Kamenetsky) S.; m. Judith Katherine Ungar, June 17, 1962; children: Catherine Julietta, Joel Abraham, Michael Howard. BChemE, CCNY, 1962; PhD, U. Minn., 1966. Chartered engr., European Union. NSF postdoctoral fellow Inst. Molecular Physics, U. Md., College Park, 1966-67; successively asst. prof., assoc. prof., prof. dept. chem. engring. U. Del., Newark, 1967-82, H.B. du Pont Prof., 1982-2000, chmn. dept., 1982-86, dir. Ctr. for Molecular and Engring. Thermodynamics, 1992—, interim dean Coll. of Engring., 1992, H.B. duPont chair, 2000—. Vis. prof. Imperial Coll., London, 1973—74, U. Nat. del Sur, Bahia Blanca, Argentina, 1985, Tech. U., Berlin, 1981, Berlin, 1988—89, U. Queensland, Brisbane, Australia, 1989, Brisbane, 96, U. Calif., Berkeley, 1995, U.

Melbourne, Australia, 2003; cons. maj. oil and chem. cos. Author: Chemical and Engineering Thermodynamics, 1977, 3d edit., 1998, Modeling Vapor-Liquid Equilibrium, 1998, Chemical, Biochemical and Engineering Thermodynamics, 2006; editor: Fluid Properties and Phase Equilibria, 1977, Chemical Engineering Education in a Changing Environment, 1989, Kinetic and Thermodynamic Lumping of Multicomponent Mixtures, 1991, Models for Thermodynamic and Phase Equilibria Calculations, 1993, AI Chem E. Jour., 2000—; mem. adv. bd. Jour. Chem. Engring. Data, Chem. Engring. Edn., Indsl. Engring. Chem. Rsch., Indian Chem. Engr., Engring. Sci. and Tech. (Malaysia); also numerous articles. Mem. adv. bd. chem. engring. La. State U., Carnegie-Mellon U., Princeton U. Recipient U. S. Scientist award Alexander von Humboldt Found., 1988, Francis Alison award U. Del., 1993, Ashton Cary award Ga. Tech. U., 1994, Phillips Lecture award Okla. State U., 1993, Rossini Lectureship award Internat. Union Pure Applied Chemistry, 1998; Miegunyah fellow U. Melbourne, Australia, 2003, hon. professorial fellow, 2004—; Hikal Chemcon Dist. Spkr. award, Indian Inst. Chem. Engrs., 2004. Fellow Inst. Chem. Engrs. (Britain), AIChE (jour. adv. bd., editor 2000—, Profl. Progress award 1984, Warren K. Lewis award 1996, Del. Soc. award 1998, Founders award, 2004), U.S. Nat. Acad. Engring., Am. Chem. Soc. (award Del. sect. 1989, E.V. Murphree award 1997), Am. Soc. Engring. Edn. (lectr. chem. engring. div. 1988), Cosmos Club (Washington). Jewish. Avocations: jogging, stamp collecting/philately. Home: 202 Sypherd Dr Newark DE 19711-3627 Office: U Del Dept Chem Engring Newark DE 19716 Office Phone: 302-831-2945. Business E-Mail: sandler@udel.edu.

**SANDLER, THOMAS R.,** accountant, director; b. Mt. Kisco, NY, Dec. 16, 1946; s. Louis and Susan (Rosen) S.; m. Alison G. Corneau, Aug. 26, 1972; children— Justin C., Shawn A. BS summa cum laude, Ithaca Coll., 1968; MS, SUNY-Binghamton, 1972. C.P.A., N.Y., Colo. 1982. Asst. acct. KPMG Peat Marwick, White Plains, N.Y., 1972, mgr. Phoenix, 1975, sr. mgr. N.Y.C., 1978, ptnr. Denver, 1981-92, ptnr. in-charge corp. recovery svcs. N.Y.C., 1993-94; mng. ptnr. BDO Seidman, Denver, 1994-95; CFO, treas., sec. Samsonite Corp., Denver, 1995-98; pres. Samsonite Am., 1998—2004; CEO Case Logic, Inc., Longmont, Colo., 2004—. Contbr. articles to profl. jours. Past trustee, past pres. Colo. Children's Chorale; treas., past pres., gov., mem. exec. com., committeeman Colo. Golf Assn.; committeeman U.S. Golf Assn. bd. dirs. Pacific Coast GOlf Assn.; chmn. Travel Goods Assn. Mem. AICPA, Colo. Soc. CPAs (chmn. real estate and govt. acctg. com.), Bear Creek Golf Club, Country Club at Castle Pines. Home: 896 Anaconda Ct Castle Rock CO 80108-9044 Office: Case Logic Inc 6303 Dry Creek Pkwy Longmont CO 80503

**SANDLER, TODD MICHAEL,** economist, political scientist, educator; b. Mt. Kisco, N.Y., Dec. 16, 1946; s. Louis and Susie Sandler; m. Jean Marie Murdock, June 28, 1985; 1 child, Tristan Jon. BA, SUNY, Binghamton, 1968, MA, 1969, PhD, 1971. Asst. prof. Ariz. State U., Tempe, 1971-76; assoc. prof. U. Wyo., Laramie, 1976-79, prof., 1979-85, U. S. C., Columbia, 1985-86; prof. econs. and polit. sci. Iowa State U., Ames, 1986-2000, Disting. prof., 1995—2001; Dockson prof. U. So. Calif., L.A., 2000—. Author: Collective Action: Theory and Applications, 1992, Global Challenges, 1997, Economic Concepts for the Social Sciences, 2001, Global Collective Action, 2004; co-author: The Theory of Externalities, Public Goods and Club Goods, 1986, The Economics of Defense, 1995, (book) The Theory of Externalities, Public Goods and Club Goods, 2d edit., 1996, International Terrorism in 1980s, 1989, The Political Economy of NATO, 1999, The Future of Development Assistance: Common Pools and International Public Goods, 1999, Regional Public Goods: Typologies, Provision, Financing, and Development Assistance, 2002, The Political Economy of Terrorism, 2006; co-editor: Defense Economics, 1989—94, Handbook of Defense Economics, 1995, Economics of Defense, 2001, Economics of Conflict, 2003; assoc. editor: Jour. Environ. Econs. and Mgmt., 1988—89, Jour. Pub. Econ. Theory, 1999—2005, mem. editl. bd.: Social Sci. Quar., Pub. Fin. Rev., Fiscal Studies, Bull. Econ. Rsch., Internat. Studies Quar., Terrorism and Political Violence; mem. editl. bd. Am. Jour. Polit. Sci., chmn. editl. bd. Jour. Conflict Resolution, 2004—; spl. adv. editor: Def. and Peace Econs., 2000—, reviewer: numerous internat. orgns. Co-recipient Rsch. Related to Prevention of Nuc. War award, Nat. Acad. of Scis., 2003; fellow NATO postdoctoral, 1977, 1998—2000, Australian Nat. U., 1981, 1994, Sr. Inst. Policy Reform, 1990—91, 1992—94, Hon., U. Wis.-Madison, 1990; grantee NSF, 1989, 1993. Mem.: Pub. Choice Soc., So. Econ. Assn., Assn. Environ. and Resource Econs., Royal Econ. Soc., Am. Econ. Assn., Internat. Def. Econs. Assn. (exec. bd.). Office: U Tex Dallas Sch Econ Polit and Policy Scis 2601 N Floyd Rd Richardson TX 75083 Office Phone: 213-740-9695. Business E-Mail: tsandler@usc.edu. E-mail: tsandler@utdallas.edu.

**SANDLIN, JENNIFER APRIL,** education educator; life ptnr. Rodolfo Espino. BA in English, Millsaps Coll., 1992; MA in Anthropology, U. N. Mex, 1995; PhD in Adult Edn., The U. Ga., 2001. Asst. prof. adult edn. Tex. A&M U., College Station, 2002—. Contbr. articles to profl. jours. Recipient Grad. Student Rsch. award, Adult Edn. Rsch. Conf., 2001, Outstanding New Faculty award, Tex. A&M U., Coll. of Edn. and Human Devel., 2003-2004, Early Career award, Commn. of Profs. of Adult Edn., 2005. Home: 1203 Haines Dr College Station TX 77843 Office: Tex A&M Univ 4226 Tamu College Station TX 77843-4226 Business E-Mail: jsandlin@coe.tamu.edu.

**SANDLIN, MAX ALLEN, JR.,** former congressman; b. Texarkana, Ark., Sept. 29, 1952; s. Max Allen and Margie Beth (Barnett) S.; children: Hillary, Max III, Emily, Christian. BA, Baylor U., 1975, JD, 1978. Bar: Tex. Assoc. Huffman & Palmer, Inc., Marshall, Tex., 1978-82; ptnr. Sandlin & Buckner, Marshall, 1982-96; judge County of Harrison, Marshall, 1986-89, county ct. judge, 1989-96; v.p., gen. counsel Howell & Sandlin, Inc., 1990-96; mem. Congress from 1st Tex. dist., 1997—2005; mem. ways & means com. Mem. exec. com. Tex. Supreme Ct. Jud. Edn. Com., Austin, 1987—; bd. dirs. Security State Bank, Elysian Fields, Tex., East Tex. Legal Svcs., Nacogdoches; bd. dirs., treas. East Tex. Housing & Fin. Corp., Marshall, 1990—. Chairman Harrison County Dem. Party, Marshall, 1982-88; mem. exec. com. Marshall-Harrison County Industries, Marshall, 1986-89; founder, sponsor, mem. Michelson-Reves Mus. Art; post supr. Boy Scouts Am., 1982-86; mgr. Marshall Youth Baseball, 1980. Recipient Appreciation award Tex. Dept. Human Resourcs, 1985. Mem. Harrison County Bar Assn. (pres. 1982-84), Baylor U. Alumni Assn. (bd. dirs.), Marshall Symphony Soc. (bd. dirs. 1988-90), Marshall Rotary. Democrat. Baptist. Avocations: politics, hunting, fishing, baseball, classical cars.

**SANDLOW, LESLIE JORDAN,** gastroenterologist, educator; b. Chgo., Jan. 7, 1934; s. Harry H. and Rose (Ehrlich) S.; m. Joanne J. Fleischer, June 16, 1957; children: Jay, Bruce, Lisa. BS, U. Ill., 1956; MD, Chgo. Med. Sch., 1960. Intern Michael Reese Hosp. and Med. Ctr., Chgo., 1961, med. resident, rsch. fellow gastrointestinal rsch., 1961-64; physician-in-charge clin. gastroenterology lab., 1963-74, asst. attending physician, 1964-67, assoc. attending physician, 1967-72, vice chmn. divsn. gastroenterology, dir. ambulatory medicine, 1968, dir. ambulatory care, 1969-76, attending physician, 1972—, assoc. med. dir., 1972-73; clin. asst. Chgo. Med. Sch., 1963-68, clin. instr., 1966; asst. prof. dept. medicine Pritzker Sch. Medicine, U. Chgo., 1973-76, assoc. prof., 1976-85, prof., 1985-90; prof. clin. medicine and med. edn., U. Ill. Coll. Medicine, Chgo., 1990-91, prof. medicine and med. edn., 1992—, sr. assoc. dean for grad. and continuing med. edn., 1993—, head dept. med. edn., 1993—, sr. assoc. dean for med. edn. affairs, 1994—. Dep. v.p. profl. affairs Michael Reese Hosp. and Med. Ctr., 1973-78, dir. Office Ednl. Affairs, 1976-81, assoc. v.p. acad. affairs, 1978-82, dir. quality assurance program, 1981-91, v.p. planning, 1982-83, v.p. profl. affairs and planning, 1983-88, dir. divsn. internal medicine, 1986-93, v.p. profl. and acad. affairs, 1988-91, med. dirs. acad. and med. affairs, 1992-94; med. dir. Michael Reese Health Plan, Inc., 1972-74, interim exec. dir., 1976-77; cons. gastroenterologist Ill. Ctrl. Hosp., 1978-80; vis. prof. Pontifica U. Catolica Rio Grande do Sul, Brazil, 1978, U. Fed. Espirito Santo, Brazil, 1978, Nordic Fedn. for Med. Understanding, Akureyri, Iceland, 1978, Seoul Nat. Sch. Medicine, 1981, Coll. Physicians and Surgeons, Karachi, Pakistan, 1994, U. Tex., Ft. Worth, 1977, U. Ariz., Tucson, 1977, Loyola U. Med. Sch., Maywood, Ill., 1979; cons. in field; coord. Health Scis. Librs. in Ill.; mem. Midwest Med. Libr. Network;

mem. subcom. on delivery of ambulatory med. care Inst. Medicine Chgo.; mem. cmty. resources task force Interinstnl. Cardiovascular Ctr.; chmn. steering group Ill. Regional Med. Program; past chmn. curriculum com. U. Chgo. Reviewer Rsch. in Med. Edn./Assn. Am. Med. Colls., 1985—, Acad. Medicine/Assn. Am. Med. Colls., 1989; contbr. numerous articles to profl. publs. Mem. Skokie (Ill.) Bd. Health, 1973-85, chmn., 1976-85; bd. dirs. Group Health Assn. Am., 1976-78, Portes Ctr., 1980—; bd. dirs. Good Health Program Skokie Valley Hosp., 1978-80; bd. dirs., exec. com. Rsch. and Edn. Found. of Michael Reese Hosp. Med. Staff, 1992—; pres.-elect Inst. Medicine Chgo., 2002-. Recipient numerous grants, including NIH, 1988, Michael Reese Hosp. Found., 1994-95, Chgo. Cmty. Trust, 1994-95. Fellow Am. Coll. Gastroenterology; mem. N.Y. Acad. Scis., Inst. Medicine, Assn. Am. Med. Colls., Am. Coll. Physician Execs. (co-chair resource mgmt. com. of quality assurance forum), Soc. Dirs. Med. Coll. Continuing Med. Edn., Soc. Dir. Rsch. in Med. Edn. Home: 2314 N Lincoln Park W Chicago IL 60614-3455 Office: U Ill Coll Medicine Med Edn MC 784 1819 W Polk St Chicago IL 60612-7331

**SANDMAN, BRADFORD AARON,** coach, educator; b. Omaha, Dec. 11, 1957; s. Darrel Alfred and Alice Sandman; m. Beth Marie Bokorney; children: Keegan Gregary, Colton Bradford. BS, Stephen F. Austin State U., Tex., 1980; Med, Prairie View A&M U. of Tex., 2004. Tchr., coach Sealy HS, Tex., 1985—90, Langham Creek HS, Houston, 1990—. Master: Sr. Men (sponsor), Fellowship of Christian Athletes (sponsor), Unity Club (sponsor), mem.: Honor Soc. Com., Gang Task Com. Home: 303 Briar Ridge Bellville TX 77418 Office: Langham Creek HS 17610 Fm 529 Houston TX 77095 Office Phone: 281-463-5480. Personal E-mail: bradford.sandman@cfisd.net.

**SANDMAN, JAMES JOSEPH,** lawyer; b. Albany, NY, June 16, 1951; s. Edgar A. and Margaret M. (Dugan) S.; m. Elizabeth D. Mullin, June 2, 1985; children: Joseph M., Elizabeth D. AB summa cum laude, Boston Coll., 1973; JD cum laude, U. Pa., 1976. Bar: Pa. 1976, D.C. 1977, U.S. Supreme Ct. 1980, Colo. 1982. Law clk. to judge U.S. Ct. Appeals (3d cir.), Wilkes-Barre, Pa., 1976-77; assoc. Arnold & Porter, Washington, 1977-82, Denver, 1982-83, ptnr., 1984-91, 1991—, mng. ptnr., 1995—2005. Pres. D.C. Bar, 2006—, mem. bd. gov., chmn. com. multijurisdictional practice. Exec. editor U. Pa. Law Rev., 1975-76. Mem. bd. overseers U. Pa. Law Sch.; trustee Wilkes U., NALP Found.; bd. dirs. Washington Performing Arts Soc., Whitman-Walker Clinic. Fellow Am. Bar Found.; mem. ABA (ho. of dels.), Econ. Club of Washington, Federal City Club (trustee), Order of Coif, Phi Beta Kappa. Democrat. Office: Arnold & Porter 555 12th St NW Washington DC 20004-1206 Office Phone: 202-942-5758. Office Fax: 202-942-5999. Business E-Mail: james.sandman@aporter.com.

**SANDMAN, PAUL WILLIAM,** lawyer; b. Albany, NY, June 21, 1947; s. Edgar Augustus and Margaret Mary (Dugan) Sandman; m. Mary Elizabeth O'Brien, Aug. 28, 1971; children: Katherine M., Margaret M., William A. AB, Boston Coll., 1969; JD, Harvard U., 1973. Bar: Mass. 1973, US Dist. Ct. Mass. 1974, US Ct. Appeals 1st cir. 1974. Assoc., Goodwin, Procter & Hoar, Boston, 1973-81; corp. counsel Wang Laboratories, Inc., Lowell, Mass., 1981-84, v.p., corp. counsel, 1984—92, sr. v.p., gen. counsel, sec., 1992-93, Boston Sci. Corp. 1993-. Bd. dirs. AMC of Mass. Bay, Boston, 1987—. Mem. Am. Corp. Counsel Assn. (bd. dirs. 1987—). Office: Boston Sci Corp One Boston Sci Pl Natick MA 01760-1537

**SANDMAN, PETER M.,** risk management consultant; b. N.Y.C., Apr. 18, 1945; s. Howard Edwin and Gertrude Leah (Orgel) S.; m. Susan Marie Goertzel, June 18, 1967 (div. 1975); m. Jody Sue Lanard, June 10, 1990; children: Alison, Jennifer, 1 stepchild, James Sachs. BA in Psychology, Princeton U., 1967; MA in Comm., Stanford U., 1968, PhD, 1971. Reporter Toronto (Ont.) Star, Canada, 1966; stringer Time, 1966-67; instr. comm. Stanford (Calif.) U., 1968-70; instr. journalism Calif. State Coll., Hayward, 1970; sr. editor The Magazine, 1970; asst. prof. Ohio State U., Columbus, 1971-72; asst. prof. natural resources, journalism U. Mich., Ann Arbor, 1972-75, assoc. prof. natural resources, 1975-77; assoc. prof. comm., coord. Cook Coll. comm. program Rutgers U., New Brunswick, NJ, 1977-83, prof. journalism, 1983-94, prof. dept. human ecology, 1992-94; adj. prof., 1994—. Adj. prof. TV, radio Ithaca (NY) Coll., 1976, grad. program in pub. health Rutgers U., 1986—, dept. environ. and cmty. medicine Robert Wood Johnson Med. Sch., Rutgers U., 1987—; adv. com. environ./occupl. health info. program 1984-89; founder, dir. environ. comm. rsch. program NJ Agrl. Exptl. Sta., Rutgers U., 1986-92; vis. scholar urban and environ. policy Tufts U., Medford, Mass., 1990-91; rsch. prof. George Perkins Marsh Inst., Clark U.; comm. coun. Environ. Def. Fund, 1985—; bd. advisors grad. program in tech. and sci. comm. Drexel U., Phila., 1988—; cons. on comm. ACP, 1976-79, Cousteau Soc., 1977-79, Pres. Com. on the Accident at Three Mile Island; specialist in comm. coop. ext. svc. U.S. Dept. Agr., 1977-86; cons. risk commn. office policy analysis EPA, 1986-88; exec. com. Sci. Writing Educators Group, 1978-81; cons. ARCO Chem., Boise Cascade, Chevron, Ciba-Geigy, Consumers Power, Dow, Du Pont, Johnson and Johnson, Johnson Wax, Procter and Gamble, Union Carbide, others. Cons. editor Random House, 1982-89, McGraw-Hill, 1989-94, Holt, Rinehart and Winston, 1978-81; contbg. editor Apt. Life, 1971-75; freelance writer, 1966—; editl. bd. Pub. Rels. Rsch. Ann., 1981-91, Jour. Pub. Rels. Rsch., 1991-94; editl. ad. bd. Environ. and Behavior, 1976-86; contbr. articles to profl. jours. Bd. dirs. N.J. Environ. Lobby, 1984-90, Nuclear Dialogue Project, 1985-90, pres. 1986-90; pub. info. com. N.J. chpt., Am. Cancer Soc., 1981-86, vice-chmn., 1983-86; comm. coord. N.J. Campaign for a Nuclear Weapons Freeze, 1982-85; socioeconomic subcom., com. on biotechnology agr. divsn. Nat. Assn. State Univs. and Land Grant Colls., 1988-90; bd. advisors Environ. Scientists for Global Survival, 1988-91; sci. review panel, radium/radon adv. bd. N.J. Dept. Environ. Protection, 1987-88; com. to survey the health effects mustard gas and lewisite Inst. Medicine, NAS, 1992. Mem. AAUP, ACLU (bd. dirs. N.J. chpt. 1984-87), Environ. Def. Fund, Nat. Assn. Profl. Environ. Communicators, Sci. Writing Educators Group, Soc. for Risk Analysis, Soc. Environ. Journalists, Internat. Assn. Pub. Participation Practitioners, Sigma Delta Chi. Home: 59 Ridgeview Rd Princeton NJ 08540-7601 Fax: 609-683-0566. Office Phone: 609-683-4073. Personal E-mail: peter@psandman.com.

**SANDMEL, DAVID FOX,** rabbi, educator; b. Cin., Aug. 19, 1956; s. Samuel and Frances Fox Sandmel; m. Janet Elise Raffel, Mar. 16, 1980; children: Samuel Jacob Raffel, Sara Michal Raffel. BA, Ohio State U., Columbus, OH, 1974—77; MA in Hebrew Letters, Hebrew Union Coll. - Jewish Inst. of Religion, Cin., 1982; PhD, U. of Pa., 2001. Ordained rabbi Hebrew Union Coll. - Jewish Inst. of Religion, 1983. Rabbi The Temple - Tifereth Israel, Cleve., 1983—85, Congregation Bet Ha'am, Portland, Maine, 1985—90; Jewish scholar Inst. for Christian and Jewish Studies, Balt., 1998—2001; scholar in residence Beth Tphiloh H.S., Balt., 2001—02; rabbi KAM Isaiah Israel Congregation, Chgo., 2002—; Crown Ryan prof. Jewish studies Cath. Theol. Union, Chgo., 2003—. Editor: (book) Christianity in Jewish Terms, Irreconcilable Differences? A Learning Resource for Jews and Christians. Mem.: Soc. of Bibl. Lit., Cen. Conf. of Am. Rabbis (chair interfaith activities com. 2002). Office: KAM Isaiah Israel Congregation 1100 E Hyde Park Blvd Chicago IL 60615 Office Phone: 773-924-1234. Office Fax: 773-924-1238. Personal E-mail: dsandmel@amertiech.net. E-mail: rabbisandmel@kamii.

**SANDMEYER, E. E.,** toxicologist, consultant; b. Winterthur, Zurich, Switzerland, Aug. 9, 1929; came to U.S., 1955; BSChemE, Technikum, Winterthur, 1951; MS in Organic Chemistry, Ohio State U., 1960, PhD in Biochemistry, 1965. Cert. civil svc. chemist II, Nev., biochemist II, Pa., clin. lab. dir. Ctrs. for Disease Control. Asst. prof. sci., gen. chemistry, organic chemistry Friends U., Wichita, 1965-66; asst. prof. biochemistry, labs., and rsch. U. Nev. Reno, 1966-71; head corp. toxicology Gulf Oil Corp., Pitts., 1971-76; divsn. head organic analysis Barringer Labs., Denver, 1987-88; pres., toxicologist, owner Transcontec, Inc., Kelseyville, Calif., 1976—. Div. head organic analysis Barringer Labs., Denver, 1986-88. Contbg. author: Patty's Industrial Hygiene and Toxicology, 1981, A Guide to General Toxicology, 1983. Mem. AAAS, Am. Chem. Soc. Soc. Environ. Health, Sigma Xi, Sigma Delta Epsilon. Office: Transcontec Inc 7305 Live Oak Dr Kelseyville CA 95451-7862

**SANDORSEN, CASSIOPEIA,** public health service officer; b. East Chicago, Ind., July 30, 1958; Health info. mgmt. cons. Wash. U. Sch. Medicine, St. Louis, 2001—; clin. analyst cons. Sisters Saint Mary DePaul Health Ctr., Bridgeton, Mo., 2002—; special corr. Pulitzer, Inc., St. Louis, 2004—. Clin. analyst cons. Gateway Health Info. Mgmt. Project, St. Louis, 2002—. Audio tape and cd series, Sound of Poetry, poetry, Half-Dimension, anthology, Essence of a Dream, Diamonds and Pearls, The Fourth Dimension, New Dawnings, Dreams Gone By, Theatre of The Mind, 2003, Autumn Necklace, Best Poems and Poets of 2003, 2004. Founder Nat. Law Enforcement Mus., Washington, 2003—03; mem. Republican Presdl. Task Force, 2003—04. Recipient Poetic Achievement award, Creative Arts and Sci. Enterprises, 1997, Amherst Soc., 1998, Malcolm Baldrige Nat. Quality award, Bush Adminstrn., 2002, award, Robert Wood Johnson Found., 2003; scholar, Esperanto League of N.Am., 2003. Mem.: Am. Acad. Poets, Internat. Soc. Poets, Mo. Bot. Garden, St. Louis Art Mus., Mo. Hist. Soc., Am. Mus. Natural History, St. Louis Symphony Orch. Vivaldi Soc. Republican. Avocations: nature walks, gardening, fiber arts, travel.

**SANDOVAL, ARTURO ALONZO,** artist, educator; b. Espanola/Cordova, N.Mex., Feb. 1, 1942; s. Lorenzo Sandoval and Cecilia Eulalia (Archuleta) Harrison; (div. Sept. 1982); 1 child, Avalon Valentine Galaglorial. Student, U. Portland, 1959; BA, Calif. State Coll., L.A., 1964, MA, 1969; MFA, Cranbrook Acad. Art, Bloomfield Hills, Mich., 1971. Designer, illustrator Western Lighting Corp., L.A., 1964-66; advt. designer, adult edn. instr. spl. svcs. USN, Yokosuka, Japan, 1966; interior design asst. Walter B. Broderick & Assocs., La Mesa, Calif., 1967; asst. prof. art dept. U. Ky., Lexington, 1974-76, assoc. prof., 1976-86, full prof., 1986—, dir. art dept. Barnhart Gallery, 1976—, curator, 1979—. Teaching asst. Calif. State Coll., L.A., 1969, Cranbrook Acad. Art, Bloomfield Hills, 1969-71; fiber art demonstrator Mus. Art, Grand Rapids, Mich., 1970; batik and tie-dye demonstrator Gwynn's Fabric Shop, Birmingham, Mich., 1970; instr. Calif. State Coll., L.A., 1970, So. Ill. U., Carbondale, 1971, Edwardsville, 1971, 72, 73, asst. prof., 1971-73; presenter various lectures and workshops throughout the U.S., 1973—; juror Mo. Women Festival Arts, St. Louis, So. Ill. U., East St. Louis, 1974, Paramount Arts Assn., Ashland, Ky., 1975, Ind. Weavers Guild, Indpls., 1979, Fed. Corrections Inst., Lexington, 1979, Hawaii Craftsman Hui and Art Dept. U. Hawaii, Manoa, Honolulu, 1982, art dept. Va. Intermont Coll., Bristol, 1982, Arrowmont Sch. Arts and Crafts, Gatlinburg, Tenn., 1984, Ctr. Contemporary Art, U. Ky., Lexington, 1984, Guild Greater Cin., Carnegie Art Ctr., Covington, Ky., 1989, S.C. Arts Commn., Charleston, 1990, Adams Art Gallery, Dunkirk, N.Y., 1994; visual arts cons. Ky. Arts Commn., Frankfort, 1977; curator Visual Arts Ctr. Alaska, Anchorage, 1982, Ky. Art and Crafts Found., Inc., Louisville, 1985; mem. artist adv. panel Ky. Art and Crafts Found., Louisville, 1986, 87, 92-2000; visual arts cons. Arts Midwest, 1987; artistic advisor Ky. Guild Mktg. Bd., Berea, 1988, 91, 92, 93; bd. trustees Ky. Guild 1995-98, Am. Craft Coun., N.Y.C., 1996—; vis. artist/critic Allen R. Hite Inst., U. Louisville, 1992; vis. artist Coll. Human Environ. Scis., U. Ky., Lexington, 1993; vis. artist/ lectr. fiber dept. Cranbrook Acad. Art, Bloomfield Hills, Mich., 1994, Art. Dept. St. Louis Comm. Coll.-Florissant Valley, 2001, U. Ariz., 2001; curator Art Quilts 2001, River Oaks Square Art Ctr., Louisiana, 2001. Exhibited in group shows at Yeiser Art Ctr., Paducah/Paramount Arts Ctr., Ashland/S.E. Cmty. Coll., Cumberland, 1994, Textile Arts Centre, Chgo., 1994, Winnipeg (Man., Can.) Art Gallery, 1994, Riffe Gallery, Ohio Arts Coun., Columbus, 1994, Royal Hiberian Acad., Gallagher Gallery, Dublin, Ireland, Cooper Gallery, Barnsley, South Yorks, Gt. Britain, Shipley Art Gallery, Gateshead, Gt. Britain, 1994, Grand Rapids (Mich.) Art Mus., 1994, Whatcom Mus. History and Art, Bellingham, Wash., The Rockwell Mus., Corning, N.Y., Mus. Art, Washington State U., Pullman, The Hyde Collection, Glen Falls, N.Y., 1994, U. Art Galleries, U. S.D., Vermillion, 1994, Barnhart Gallery, U. Ky., Lexington, 1994, Sawtooth Ctr. Visual Art, 1994, Santa Fe Gallery, Santa Fe Cmty. Coll., Gainesville, Fla., 1994, Liberty Gallery, Louisville, 1994, Asahi Shimbun Gallery, Tokyo, Takashimaya Gallery, Osaka, 1994, Minn. Mus. Art, Landmark Ctr., St. Paul, 1994, S.C. State Mus., Columbia, 1994, Galbreath Gallery, Lexington, 1994, U.K. Art Mus., 1998, Giles Gallery, Richmond, Ky., 2004, Ky. Mus. of Art and Design, 2004, Ronald Barr Gallery, New Albany, Ind., 2004, City Gallery, S.C., 2004, Tuska Gallery, Ky., 2004, Pres. Room. Ky., 2004, numerous others; represented in permanent collections at Wabash Coll., Crawfordsville, Ind., Greenville County Mus. Art, Greenville, S.C., Mus. Modern Art, N.Y.C., St. Mary's Coll., Notre Dame, Ind.; Coll. St. Rose, Albany, N.Y., Bowling Green (Ohio) StateU., U. Notre Dame, Transylvania U., Lexington, U. Ky. Mus. Art, Lexington, Mid-Am. Rare Coin Auction Galleries, Lexington, Henry Luce Found., N.Y.C., Lexington Ctrl. Libr., UK Art Mus., Nat. Mus. Am. Art, Renwick Gallery, J.B. Speed Art Mus., Louisville, Linda Schwartz Gallery, Tuska Gallery, Pres.'s Room, KY, Shands Gallery, Friedman Gallery, KGAG Offices, Actor's Theater, Ronald Barr Gallery, Opera House Gallery, Waltron Ltd., Whitehouse, N.J., Nat. Hispanic Cultural Arts Ctr., Albuquerque, N.Mex., Rocky Mt. Quilt Mus., Golden, Colo., Mus. Art and Design, N.Y. Recipient Alexandra Korsakoff Galston Meml. prize St. Louis Artist's Guild, 1971, Mus. Merit award Mus. Arts and Scis., Evansville, 1972, Creative Rsch. Grant So. Ill. U.-Edwardsville Rsch. Found., 1972, Craftsman fellowship Nat. Endowment for Arts, Washington, 1973, Friend of Mus. award Mus. Arts and Scis., Evansville, 1973, Clay Eugene Jordan ann. bequest prize for crafts St. Louis Artist's Guild, 1973, Teaching Improvement grant U. Ky. Rsch. Found., 1974, Travel grant U. Ky. Rsch. Found., 1977, Judges Choice award Berea (Ky.) Coll., 1978, Handweaver's Guild Am. award, 1978, Fiber award LeMoyne Art Found., Tallahassee, 1981, Elise Strout Merit award Mus. Arts and Scis., Evansville, 1981, Handweavers Guild Am. award, 1983, Martha Ryan Merit award Mus. Arts and Scis., Evansville, 1984, Best of Show award Gayle Willson Galleries, Southampton, 1984, Juror's merit award Brenau Coll., Gainesville, Ga., 1985, Installation Grant Ind. Arts Commn., Ft. Wayne, 1985, All Smith fellowship Ky. Arts Coun., Frankfort, 1987, Merit award Spotlight '88 Am. Craft Coun. Southeast Conf., Tuscaloosa, Ala., 1988, Merit award Mus. Arts and Scis., Evansville, 1989, Design Grant, Arts and Cultural Coun. for O.A. Singletary Ctr for Arts, Lexington, 1990, Visual Arts fellowship Nat. Endowment for Arts, Washington, 1992, Hon. award Ky. Crafts Mktg. Bd., Frankfort, 1994, Rude Osolnik Craftsman award Ky. Crafts Mktg. & KAC Fund, 1998, 1st pl. Lexington Art League, Reverse Raffle, Lexington, 1999, Art-in-Arch. Program commn. Gen. Svcs. Adminstrn., London, Ky., 2002; grantee NEA, Pyramid Atlantic Press, Riverdale, Md., 1996; Gen. Svcs. Adminstrn., Art-in-Architecture, London, Ky., 2002, Artist award Ky. Gov.'s award in the arts, 2003, Merit award ACCSE, 2006; Al Smith fellow Ky. Arts Coun., 1987, 2006. Mem. Lexington Fiber Guild Inc., Louisville Visual Arts Assn., Ky. Art and Craft Found., Inc., Ky. Guild Artists and Crafstmen, Am. Craft Coun., Friends of U. Ky. Mus. Art, Friends of Fiber Art, Surface Design Assn. Home: PO Box 25153 Lexington KY 40524-5153 Office: U Ky Dept Art 207 Fine Arts Bldg Lexington KY 40506-0022 Office Phone: 859-257-8149, 859-230-9635. Personal E-mail: a.sandoval@insightbb.com.

**SANDOVAL, BRIAN EDWARD,** federal judge, former state attorney general; b. Redding, Calif., Aug. 5, 1963; s. Ronald L. and Gloria Sandoval; m. Kathleen T. Sandoval; children: James, Madeline, Marisa. B in English & Econ., U. Nev., 1986; JD, Ohio State U., 1989. Bar: Nev., Calif., DC. Mem. Nev. State Assembly, 1995—97; atty. McDonald, Carano, Wilson, McCune Bergin, Frankovich & Hicks, Reno, 1989—91, Robinson, Belaustegui, Robb & Sharp, Reno, 1991—95, Gamboa, Sandoval & Stovall, Reno, 1995—99, Sandoval Law Office, Reno, 1999—2003; atty. gen. State of Nev., Carson City, 2003—05; judge US Dist. Ct. Dist. Nev., Reno, 2005—. Mem. Nev. Gaming Commn., 1998—2001, chmn., 1999—2001; mem. State and Local Officials' Adv. Com. US Dept. Homeland Security. Bd. trustees Children's Cabinet, Reno, St. Jude's Ranch for Children, Washoe County Law Libr., Nev. Named Public Lawyer of the Yr., Nevada St. Bar Assoc., 2004; recipient Torch of Liberty, Anti-Defamation League, 2003. Republican. Office: US Dist Ct 400 S Virginia St Reno NV 89501*

**SANDOVAL, ISABELLE MEDINA,** education educator; b. Laramie, Wyo., Sept. 30, 1948; d. John Ben and Ida Medina Sandoval; 1 child, Tomas Andres Duran. BA, U. N.Mex., 1970; MA, U. Mo., 1976; EdD, U. Wyo., 1982. Cert. Spanish, reading, English, adminstrn. Tchr. Spanish and English Menaul Sch.,

Albuquerque, 1971-73; tchr. bilingual edn. and reading Kansas City, Mo., 1973-78; tchr. title I Sch. Dist. #60, Pueblo, Colo., 1978-83, administr., 1983-88, Acad. Dist. 20, Colorado Springs, Colo., 1988-95; human resources coord. Harrison Dist. 2, Colorado Springs, 1995-98; prof. edn. Coll. of Santa Fe, N.Mex.; dir. bilingual edn. Santa Fe Pub. Schs. V.p. Hispano Crypto Jewish Resource Ctr., Denver. Author numerous poems. Pres. South Holman Domestic Water Assn. Mem. Geneal. Soc. Hispanic Am., Hispanic Geneal. Rsch. Ctr. N.Mex., Mana del Norte, Olibama Lopez Tushar Hispanic Legacy Rsch. Ctr., N.M. Jewish Hist. Soc. (bd. dirs.), N.Mex. Acequia Assn., N.Mex. Land Grant Forum, Soc. for Crypto Judaic Studies, Nat. Assn. Sephardic Artists, Writers and Intellectuals, LaSallian Leadership (bd. dirs.), Phi Kappa Phi, Kappa Delta Phi, Phi Delta Kappa. Jewish. Avocations: poetry, researching family history and hispano jewish materials. Home: 4358 Lost Feather Santa Fe NM 87507-2580 Office: Santa Fe Pub Schs 1300 Camino Sierra Vista Santa Fe NM 87505 Business E-mail: isandoval@sfps.info.

**SANDOZ, GEORGE ELLIS, JR.,** political science educator; b. New Orleans, Feb. 10, 1931; s. George Ellis and Ruby (Odom) S.; m. Therese Alverne Hubley, May 31, 1957; children: Ellis III, Lisa, Erica, Jonathan. BA in History, La. State U., 1951, MA in Polit. Sci., 1953; D in Polit. Sci., U. Munich, Germany, 1965. Capitol Hill policeman U.S. Ho. of Reps., Washington, 1952-53; instr. to prof. La. Poly. Inst., Ruston, 1959-68; prof., head dept. polit. sci. East Tex. State U., Commerce, 1968-78; prof. polit. sci., chmn. La. State U., Baton Rouge, 1978—, dir. Eric Voegelin Inst., 1987—, Hermann Moyce Jr. disting. prof. polit. sci., 2006—. Mem. Nat. Coun. on the Humanities, Washington, 1982-88; lectr. in field. Author: Political Apocalypse, 1971, 2d edit., 2000, Conceived in Liberty, 1978, The Voegelinian Revolution, 1981, 2nd edit., 2000, A Government of Laws, 1990, 2d edit., 2000; editor: The Collected Works of Eric Voegelin, 1986—; intro introduction, editor. Political Sermons of the American Founding Era, 1730-1805, 1991, Roots of Liberty, 1993, Politics of Truth, 1999, Republicanism, Religion and the Soul of America, 2006. Nat. co-chair Reagan-Bush Presidency, Washington, 1984. Pvt. 1st lt. USMC, 1953-56. Fulbright scholar Bd. Fgn. Scholarships, Washington, 1964-65, Fulbright 40th Anniversary Disting. Am. scholar USIA, Italy, 1987. Mem. Am. Polit. Sci. Assn., So. Polit. Sci. Assn. (coun. 1982-85), Southwestern Polit. and Social Sci. Assn. (pres. 1987-88). Republican. Baptist. Avocations: hunting, fishing, tennis. Home: 2843 Valcour Aime Ave Baton Rouge LA 70820-4424 Office: La State U Eric Voegelin Inst 240 Stubbs Hall Baton Rouge LA 70803-0001 E-mail: esandoz@lsu.edu.

**SANDQUIST, GARY MARLIN,** engineering educator, researcher, consultant, writer, military officer; b. Salt Lake City, Apr. 19, 1936; s. Donald August Sandquist and Lillian (Evaline) Dunn; m. Kristine Powell, Jan. 17, 1992; children from previous marriage: Titia, Julia, Taunia, Cynthia, Carl; stepchildren: David, Michael, Scott, Diane, Jeff. BSME in Mech. Engring., U. Utah, 1956—60; MS in Engring. Sci., U. Calif., Berkeley, 1960—61; PhD in Mech. Nuclear Engring., U. Utah, 1961—64, MBA Exec. MS, 1993—95. Registered profl. engr., Utah, N.Y., Minn., Calif.; cert health physicist, quality auditor; diplomate Am. Acad. Environ. Engring. Staff mem. Los Alamos (N.Mex.) Sci. Lab., 1966; postdoctoral fellow MIT, 1969-70; rsch. prof. surgery Med. Sch., U. Utah, Salt Lake City, 1974—85, prof., nuc. engring. dept. mech. engring., 1975—, acting chmn. dept., 1984-85, adj. prof. civil engring., 1996—; expert in nuc. sci. Internat. Atomic Energy Agy., UN, 1980—; chief scientist Rogers and Assocs. Engring. Corp., Salt Lake City, 1980—90, sr. nuclear engr., 1998—; sr. health physicist URS Corp., 1990—; mgr., owner Applied Sci. Profls., LLC, Salt Lake City, 1998—. Vis. scientist MIT, Cambridge, Mass., 1969-70; advisor rocket design Hercules, Inc., Bachus, Utah, 1962; sr. nuc. engr. Idaho Nat. Engring. Lab., Idaho Falls, 1963-65; cons. nuc. sci. State of Utah, 1982—; vis. prof. Ben Gurion U., Beer Sheva, Israel, 1985, disting. vis. prof. U.S. Mil. Acad., West Point, N.Y., 2003-05; affiliate faculty Idaho State U., 1998-; cons. various cos.; spkr. Nuc. Energy Inst., 1990—; mem. radiation adv com., EPA. Author: Geothermal Energy, 1973, Introduction to System Science, 1985, over 650 pub. presentations, reports in sci. and tech. Comdr. USNR, 1954-56, Korea; ret. Comdr. USNR, 1954—56, Intel officer USNR. Recipient Glen Murphy award in nuc. engring. Am. Soc. Engring. Edn., 1984. Fellow ASME, Am. Nuc. Soc.; mem. Am. Soc. Quality (sr.), Am. Health Physics Soc., Am. Soc. Engring. Edn., Alpha Nu Sigma, Sigma Xi, Tau Beta Pi, Pi Tau Sigma. Republican. Mem. Lds Ch. Achievements include development of 17 major computer codes; participated in 192 tech. meetings, confs., govt. hearings. Home: 2564 E Neffs Cir Salt Lake City UT 84109 Office: U Utah 2232 Merrill Engring Bldg Salt Lake City UT 84112 Office Phone: 801-904-4125. Personal E-mail: gms@asp-llc.com.

**SANDRICH, JAY H.,** television director; b. LA, Feb. 24, 1932; s. Mark R. and Freda (Wirtschafter) S.; m. Nina Kramer, Feb. 11, 1952 (div.); children: Eric, Tony, Wendy; m. Linda Green Silverstein, Oct. 4, 1984. BA, UCLA, 1953. Prodr. (TV show) Get Smart, 1965; dir. (TV shows) He and She, 1967, Mary Tyler Moore Show, 1970-88, Soap, 1977-79, Cosby Show, 1984-92; dir. (films) Seems Like Old Times, 1980, For Richer, For Poorer (HBO), 1992, Neil Simon's London Suite (NBC), 1996. Served to 1st lt. Signal Corps U.S. Army, 1952-55. Mem. Dirs. Guild Am. (award 1975, 85, 86), TV Acad. Arts and Scis. (Emmy award 1971, 73, 85, 86). Office: care Andy Elkin Creative Artists Agy 9830 Wilshire Blvd Beverly Hills CA 90212

**SANDRIDGE, DONALD OTIS,** music educator; b. Waynesboro, Va., Aug. 31, 1950; s. Otis Chester and Lucille Spitler Sandridge. Mus EdB, James Madison U., Harrisonburg, Va., 1973; MS in Edn., Old Dominion U., Norfolk, Va., 1983; Advanced Cert., Westminster Choir Coll., Princeton, N.J., 1986. Cert. Nat. Registered Music Educator 1985. Min. of music Bethany United Meth. Ch., Gloucester Point, Va., 1975—82, Orcutt Bapt. Ch., Newport News, Va., 1983—85, First Presbyn. Ch., Newport News, Va., 1988—94; dir. of choral activities Gloucester County High. Schs. Va. 1973—2001; ret. Chmn. fine arts dept. Gloucester H.S., Va., 1975—2004; chairperson Gloucester County Parks and Recreation Commn., 1999—; bd. dir. Hampton Rds. Educators Credit Union. Concert chmn. Mid. Peninsula Cmty. Concert Assn., Gloucester, Va., 1975—2001; state sponsor Nat. Beta Club (Va. chpt.). Recipient Freedom Goode award, Gloucester County, Youth Adv. award, 30 Yr. Sponsor award, Nat. Beta Club. Mem.: Abingdon Ruritan Club (bd. dir. 2001—). Presbyn. Home: PO Box 1271 7736 Points Pl Gloucester Point VA 23062 Personal E-mail: dotissinger@aol.com.

**SANDRIDGE, WILLIAM PENDLETON, JR.,** lawyer; b. Winston-Salem, N.C., Jan. 27, 1934; m. Jane Carolyn Yeager, Dec. 10, 1966; children: Jane, William. AB, U. N.C., 1956; LLB, U. Va., 1961. Bar: N.C. 1961. Mem. Womble Carlyle Sandridge & Rice, PLLC, Winston-Salem, 1962—. Chmn., bd. dirs. Horizons Residential Care Ctr., 1980, Food Bank N.W. N.C., Inc., 1988-89, Data Max Corp., 1996. Office: Womble Carlyle Et Al One W Fourth St Winston Salem NC 27101 Office Phone: 336-721-3503.

**SANDROK, RICHARD WILLIAM,** lawyer; b. Evergreen Park, Ill., July 8, 1943; s. Edward George and Gertrude Jeanette (Van Stright) Sandrok; m. Rebecca Fittz, June 19, 1973; children: Richard William, Jr., Alexander Edward, Philip Robert, Erika Joy. BA, Wheaton (Ill.) Coll., 1965; JD, U. Ill., 1968. Bar: Ill. 1968, U.S. Dist. Ct. (no. dist.) Ill. 1971, ct. apptd. arbitrator: Cook, DuPage, Kane and Will counties. Assoc. Hinshaw Culbertson Moelmann Hoban & Fuller, Chgo. and Wheaton, 1971-75, ptnr. Wheaton, 1976-89, Lisle, Ill., 1989—2001; sole practice Glen Ellyn, Ill., 2001—. Arbitrator Ill. State Mandatory Arbitration. Reviewer: Legal Checklists. Capt. U.S. Army, 1969—71. Mem.: Ill. U. Sys. Arbitrator, Assn. Def. Trial Attys., DuPage County Bar Assn. (chmn. med./legal com. 1978—79), Am. Arbitration Assn. (arbitrator). Home: 818 Revere Rd Glen Ellyn IL 60137-5537 Office: Richard W Sandrok Atty at Law 818 Revere Rd Glen Ellyn IL 60137 Office Phone: 630-790-1583. E-mail: RWS283@yahoo.com.

**SANDS, CHRISTINE LOUISE,** retired English educator; b. Johnstown, Pa., Oct. 13, 1947; d. Joseph and Margaret (Kocsis) Mayr; m. Angelo Joseph Sands, Dec. 28, 1968 (div. Nov. 1989); children: Vincent, Linda. BS in German, Indiana U. Pa., 1969, BS in English, 1975; postgrad., Slippery Rock

U., 1971-76. Tchg. cert. Pa. Tchr. New Castle (Pa.) Schs., 1969—2004. Student advisor, judge Forensics, New Castle, 1981-96, Youngstown (Ohio) Reading Festival, 1981-95. Pres. New Castle City Coun., 1996, 2004-05; mem. parish coun. St. Vitus Ch., New Castle, 1986-92; basketball referee PIAA, Mechanicsburg, Pa., 1972-91; coach New Castle H.S. Bowling, 1986-97, cheerleading adv., 1993-94, adv. sch. tv studio, NC-TV, 1991-96. Democrat. Roman Catholic. Avocations: reading, travel, sports, cooking, politics. Home: 819 E Hillcrest Ave New Castle PA 16105-2256

**SANDS, DOLORES S.,** dean; BSN, MSN, Wayne State U.; PhD, Ariz. State U. Prof., dir. Ctr. Health Care Rsch. and Evaluation U. Tex., Austin, 1984-89, dir. grad. program nursing adminstrn., 1989—, former acting dean, asst. dean rsch. and resources, asst. dean baccalaureate program, now dean, Laura Lee Blanton chair in nursing, also now Joseph H. Blades Centennial Meml. prof. in nursing. Mem. nursing sci. rev. com. Exploratory Rsch. Ctr. Grants; mem. adv. coun. on nurses edn. and practice divsn. nursing Health Resources and Svcs. Adminstrn. U.S. Dept. Health and Human Svcs., 1991-93, co-chair adv. coun., 1993-95, mem. adv. group nat. task force for workforce projections of nurse practitioners and nurse-midwives, 1993, now mem. joint coun. primary care workforce workgroup; active Nat. Ctr. for Nursing Rsch., NIH. Contbr. articles to profl. jours. Grantee USPHS, 1986-89; recipient Alumni Achievement award Ariz. State U., 1987. Mem. ANA, Coun. Nurse Rschrs., Soc. Rsch. in Nursing Edn., Phi Kappa Phi, Sigma Theta Tau. Office: U Tex Austin Sch Nursing Office Dean 1700 Red River St Austin TX 78701-1412

**SANDS, HAROLD WINTHROP,** banker, financial planner; b. N.Y.C., Aug. 25, 1926; s. Harold Aymar and Muriel Winthrop Sands; m. Joan Hodges Baker, Sept 6, 1961; children: Harold, Serena. Grad., St. George's Sch., 1946; student, CBS-NBS Tellers' Acad., 1950—52, Am. Inst. Banking, 1967—69; postgrad., Miami Dade U., 1968—71. V.p., devel. officer, regional mgr. S.E. Banks, Miami, London, Europe, Caribbean, 1967-79; v.p. Marine Midland Bank N.V., London, 1979-85; sr. cons. fin. adviser Sun Life Assurance Soc., London, 1985-87; U.K. rep. Wright Investment Svc., London, 1987-92; v.p. Kreditbank Global Mgmt., Miami, 1993-94; dir., trustee Kapok Bermuda Ltd., London, 1994-96; gen. ptnr. The Winthrop Group L.P., Newport, RI, 1996-2001; assoc. v.p. Pre-paid Legal Svcs., Inc., Newport, RI, 2001—; gen. mgr. Peace Mgmt. Group LLC, Newport, RI, 2002—. Founder Lorimex Internat., N.Y.C., 1952-60; CEO acctg., sales Paramount Pictures Corp., N.Y.C., 1950-52; founder, CEO Distbrs. for Mexico Rex Chain Belt, Ampudia A.S. Mex., 1960-67. Chair N.Am. com. London C. of C., 1985-88, chmn. Caribbean com., 1988-91; hon. treas. European Atlantic Group, 1980—; mem. Rep. Com.; mem. Woolnoth Soc. Coun., City of London, 1980-93; trustee La Farge Restoration Fund of Newport, 1996—; trustee Preservation Soc. Newport, mem. fin. and edn. coms., 1994-2000; com. mem. Tall Ships Salute, 1995; bd. dirs. Newport Hist. Soc., 2001—. Master sgt. U.S. Army, 101st Armed Cav., 1949-54. Decorated Imperial House of David, 1995, Comdr. of Most Revered Order of the Star of Ethiopia, Freeman of the City of London. Mem.: SAR (Newport chpt.), Order of Founders and Patriots R.I. (gov.), The Guild of Internat. Bankers London, Order of 1st Families of R.I., Soc. Colonial Wars (Providence and Boston chpts.), RAC Club London, Ida Lewis Club (Newport, R.I.), Clambake Club (gov. reading club), Reading Rm. Club, Ends of the Earth Club London, Broad St. Ward Club London, Rotary Internat., Pilgrim's London. Avocations: sailing, tennis, skiing, boating, chess. Home: 10 Cherry Creek Rd Newport RI 02840 Office Phone: 401-846-6143. Fax: 401-846-1066. Personal E-mail: hss6518@aol.com.

**SANDS, HARRY,** psychologist, health administrator, researcher; b. N.Y.C., Jan. 6, 1917; s. Morris and Lena Sandrowitz; m. Helene Purl, June 24, 1945; children: Jeffrey, Richard. AB, NYU, 1941, PhD in Psychology, 1952. Diplomate Am. Bd. Profl. Psychology; lic. psychologist, N.Y. Rsch. fellow dept neurology Neurol. Inst./Columbia U. Phys. and Surg., N.Y.C., 1941-42, rsch. chief psychophysiologist Head Injury Project, 1942-44; assoc. dir., chief psychologist Baird Found. Clinic for Children with Epilepsy/Beth David Hosp., N.Y.C., 1944-46; instr. Washington Sq. Coll./NYU, 1947-50, Bklyn. Coll., 1950-52; exec. dir. Com. Pub. Understanding of Epilepsy, N.Y.C., 1952-53, United Epilepsy Assn. Am., N.Y.C., 1953-56; dir. and clin. psychologist Psychol. Lab., Inc., N.Y.C., 1955-61; dir. Epilesy Asn. N.Y. Epilepsy Found. Am., N.Y.C., 1956-68; dir. program planning and evaluation Epilepsy Found. Am., Washington, 1972-74; assoc. staff adult therapy clinic Postgrad. Ctr. for Mental Health, N.Y.C., 1962-66, assoc. staff supervision therapeutic process, 1971-73, assoc. supr., sr. supr. psychoanalysis, psychotherapy, 1974—85, tng. analyst, pyschoanalysis, psychotherapy, 1993-98, exec. v.p., CEO, 1979—87, exec. dir., CEO, 1987—88. Pvt. practice pyschoanalysis and psychotherapy, N.Y.C., 1952-98; cons. divsn. resource devel. Nat. Inst. on Drug Abuse, Rockville, Md., 1978-79, Commn. for Control of Epilepsy and its Consequences, HEW, Washington, 1977, legal and protective svcs. project, Harvard U. Sch. of Pub. Health, Boston, 1974, cons. classification exceptional children, adequacy of classification for physically and sensorially handicapped, Vanderbilt U., Knoxville, 1974, bd. trustees, exec. com., 1988—; bd. dirs. Postgrad. Ctr. Residences, I, II, and III, N.Y.C., 1991-96, sec., 1991-2000, 2002—, pres. Editor: (book) Epilepsy: A Handbook for the Mental Health Professional, 1982 (Book of Yr. award ANA, 1982); co-author: (books) Epilepsy Fact Book, 1979, Education and Training Beyond the Doctoral Degree, 1995, Impact of Managed Care on Psychodynamic Treatment, 1996, The Guide to Pastoral Counseling and Care, 2000; contbr. chpts. in books, articles to profl. jours. Mem. tech. adv. com. on epilepsy N.Y. State Dept. Health, N.Y.C., 1945, planning com. advisory com. on State of N.Y. on program of pub. health, medicaid and compulsory health and hosp. ins., Albany, 1953; mem com. on Neurol. Disorders in Industry and com. on Emergency Med. Identification, AMA, Chgo., 1953, com. of info. svcs. and employment com., handicapped sect., Comty. Coun. of Greater N.Y. NYC, 1951, joint legis. com. on mental retardation and physical handicaps, State of N.Y., Albany, 1956. Recipient fellowship Internat. Rehab. Rsch. Program of Social and Rehab. Svcs., HEW, Washington, 1972, Gold medal award for lifetime achievement in practice of psychology, Am. Psychol. Found., Washington, 1995; grantee Social Rehab. Svcs, HEW, Washington, 1968, 78. Fellow APA (bd. govs. coll. profl. practice 1994-99, co-chair nat. conf. on postdoctoral edn. and tng., Washington, 1992-94, bd. govs. coll. profl. practice, 1994-99, coun. reps. 1988-91, 1994, treas. com. for advancement profl. practice, practice directorate, 1992-94, cons. 1995, Karl F. Heiser Presdl. award 1993, Disting. Psychologist award Divsn. Psychotherapy 1995); mem. Am. Psychol. Assn., N.Y. State Psychol. Assn. (pres. 1978-79, 1985-86, coun. of reps. 1957-60, 1986-91, Allen J. Williams Jr. Meml. award 1993), Postgrad. Psychoanalytic Soc., Nat. Acad. of Practices (Disting. Practitioner in Psychology 1995), Psi Chi, Sigma Xi. Democrat. Jewish. Avocations: travel, theater, music, ballet. Home and Office: 219 E 69th St Apt 7 D New York NY 10021-5455

**SANDS, JEFF MICHAEL,** medical educator; s. Joseph and Jean Lillian Sands; m. Abbe Maureen Zorn. Mar 23, 1986; children: Jared Samuel, Jenna Shari. BA summa cum laude, Harvard Coll., Cambridge, 1977; MD, Boston U., Mass., 1981. Diplomate internal medicine Am. Bd. Internal Medicine, 1984, nephrology Am. Bd. Internal Medicine, 1992. Asst. prof. medicine Emory U., Atlanta, 1989—93, assoc. prof. medicine, 1993—98, prof. medicine and physiology, 1998—. Renal divsn. dir. Emory U., 2002—06; editor-in-chief Am. Jour. of Physiology - Renal, Bethesda, Md., 2001—. Rsch. grants, Nat. Inst. Health, 1989-2006. Mem.: Am. Physiol. Soc. (councillor 2003—06), Am. Soc. Nephrology (program com. chmn. 2003—04), Am. Soc. Clin. Investigation, Am. Assn. Physicians. Achievements include research in renal physiology. Office: Emory U Renal Divsn WMB Rm 338 1639 Pierce Drive Atlanta GA 30322 Business E-mail: jeff.sands@emory.edu.

**SANDS, KEVIN B.,** dentist; Grad., U. Southern Calif. Sch. Dentistry; grad. Advanced Anterior Aesthetic Dentistry, Las Vegas Institute for Advanced Dental Studies. Mem. Acad. of C.E., Beverly Hills, Calif. Mem.: Acad. Cosmetic Dentistry, Calif. State Dental Assn., ADA. Office: 414 N Camden Dr Ste 940 Beverly Hills CA 90210 Office Phone: 310-273-0111.

**SANDS, MARK D.,** musician, educator; b. Ainsworth, Nebr., Apr. 5, 1953; s. Joel M. and Jean Sands; m. Kathryn L. Long, Apr. 11, 1981; children: Rebecca Ann, Debra Michelle. AA, Suffolk County CC, Selden, N.Y., 1974; MusB in Edn., Crane Sch. Music, Potsdam, N.Y., 1976; postgrad., Crane Sch. Music, Coll. of St. Rose, Albany, N.Y. Permanent tchg. cert. N.Y. Orchestral string tchr. South County Ctrl. Schs., East Patchogue, NY, 1976; band and orch. tchr. Sachem Ctrl. Schs., Holbrook, NY, 1977—78; orch., string tchr. Schenectady (N.Y.) City Schs., 1978—82; sales Nasco Inc., Springfield, Tenn., 1982; restaurant mgr. Midon Restaurant Corp., Latham, NY, 1983—84, Ka-Lo Enterprises, Watertown, NY, 1984; restaurant proprietor Maricliff Inc., Schenectady, 1985—90; orch. tchr. Monticello (N.Y.) Ctrl. Schs., 1990—91, Norwich (N.Y.) City Schs., 1991—. Orch. dir., musical artistic dir. Norwich HS, 1994—; artistic dir. Chenango Cmty. Players, Norwich, 2001—02. Musician (violin, vocal, drums): Utica Symphony, Catskill Symphony, 2000—03. Dir. Norwich City Band, 1994—2001. Mem.: Am. Fedn. Musicians, Nat. Assn. Music Edn., N.Y. State Sch. Music Assn. Avocations: music, theater, sports.

**SANDS, MATTHEW LINZEE,** physicist, researcher; b. Oxford, Mass., Oct. 20, 1919; m. Freya Kidner, 1978; children: Michael, Richard, Michelle. BA, Clark U., 1940; MA, Rice U., 1941; PhD, MIT, 1948. Physicist U.S. Naval Ordnance Lab., 1941-43, Los Alamos Sci. Lab., 1943-46; research asso., then asst. prof. physics Calif. Inst. Tech., 1946-50; sr. research fellow, asso. prof., prof. physics Calif. Inst. Tech., 1950-63; prof., dep. dir. Linear Accelerator Center, Stanford, 1963-69; prof. physics U. Calif.-Santa Cruz, 1969-85, prof. emeritus, 1985—, fellow Kresge Coll.; vice chancellor for sci., 1969-72; pres. Sands-Kidner Assocs., Inc., 1986-90. Vis. prof. U. Paris-Sud, spring 1976; mem. Commn. Coll. Physics, 1960-66, chmn., 1964-66; cons. Office Sci. and Tech., ACDA, Inst. Def. Analyses, 1962-67; mem. Pugwash Conf. Sci. and World Affairs, 1960-63; cons. on accelerator physics, 1975-93. Author: (with W.C. Elmore) Electronics-Experimental Techniques, 1948, (with R.P. Feynman and R.B. Leighton) The Feynman Lectures on Physics, 3 vols, 1965, (with others) Physical Science Today, 1973; also articles. Mem. editorial bd.: Il Nuovo Cimento, 1972-85. Fulbright scholar Italy, 1952-53. Fellow Am. Phys. Soc. (Robert R. Wilson prize 1998); mem. Am. Assn. Physics Tchrs. (Disting. Service award 1972), Fedn. Am. Scientists, AAAS. Achievements include research in electronic instrumentation for nuclear physics; electron storage rings; science and public affairs; science education; high-energy physics; accelerators; cosmic rays. Home: 160 Michael Ln Santa Cruz CA 95060-1704

**SANDS, RICHARD E.,** food products executive; b. Canandaigua, N.Y., Mar. 3, 1951; s. Marvin Sands and Marilyn Alpert; m. Sharon Gillick, Apr. 1991. BA, Univ. Vt., 1974; MA, Univ. NC, 1978, PhD, 1979. Teaching rsch. asst. psychology dept. U. N.C., Chapel Hill, 1974-79; exec. trainee Canandaigua Wine Co. Inc., 1979; exec. v.p. Constellation Brands Inc., Fairport, NY, 1982-86, pres., COO, 1986—93, pres., CEO, 1993—2002, chmn. and CEO, 2002—. Office: Constellation Brands Inc 370 Woodcliff Dr Fairport NY 14450*

**SANDS, RICK (RICHARD SANDS),** film company executive; BA with honors in Economics and Film, Syracuse U. From regional sales to head domestic distbn. divsn. Columbia Pictures; exec. v.p., CFO Miramax Films, 1990—93, RHI Entertainment (sold to Hallmark Entertainment), 1993—95; pres. internat. Miramax Films, 1995—97, chmn. worldwide distbn., 1997—2002, COO, 2002—04; pres., COO DreamWorks SKG, 2005—06; COO MGM (Metro-Goldwyn-Mayer Inc.), LA, 2006—. Recipient Humanitarian award, Variety Boys and Girls Club of Queens, 2003. Office: Metro-Goldwyn-Mayer Inc 10250 Constellation Blvd Los Angeles CA 90067-6241 Office Phone: 310-449-3000. Office Fax: 310-449-8750.*

**SANDS, ROBERT,** food products executive; b. Canandaigua, NY, June 10, 1958; B., Skidmore Coll., 1981; JD, Pace U. Sch. Law, 1984. Assoc. Harter, Secrest & Emery; gen. counsel Constellation Brands, Inc., Fairport, NY, 1986—90, v.p., gen. counsel, 1990—93, exec. v.p., gen. counsel, 1993—2000, CEO, internat., 1998—2000, group pres., 2000—02, pres., COO, 2002—. Pres. bd. trustees Harley Sch.; bd. trustees F.F. Thompson Health Sys.; chmn. bd. trustees ViaHealth Sys. Office: Constellation Brands Inc 370 Woodcliff Dr Ste 300 Fairport NY 14450*

**SANDS, SHARON LOUISE,** art director, publishing executive, artist; b. Jacksonville, Fla., July 4, 1944; d. Clifford Harding Sands and Ruby May MacDonald; m. Jonathan Michael Langford, Feb. 14, 1988. BFA, Ctrl. Washington U., 1968; postgrad, UCLA, 1968. Art dir. East West Network, Inc., L.A., 1973-78, Daisy Pub., L.A., 1978; prodn. dir. L.A. mag., 1979-80; owner, creative dir. Carmel Graphic Design, Carmel Valley, Calif., 1981-85; creative dir., v.p. The Video Sch. House, Monterey, Calif., 1985-88; graphic designer ConAgra, Omaha, 1988; owner, creative dir. Esprit de Fleurs, Ltd., Carmel, Calif., 1988-99; owner Sweden by the Sea, Carmel, Calif., 1999—2001; owner, dir. Sands Art Studios, 1999—. Lectr. Pub. Expo, LA, 1979; panelist Women in Mgmt., LA, 1979; designer corp. ID Carmel Valley CC, 1981, 90; redesign of local newspaper, Carmel, Calif., 82. Contbr. articles to profl. mags.; one-woman shows include Ananda Retreat Ctr., Nevada City, Calif., 2004, Nevada City Winery, 2004. Recipient 7 design awards, Soc. Pub. Designers, 1977, 1978, Maggie award, LA, 1977, 5 Design awards, Ad Club Monterey Peninsula, 1983, 1985, 1987, Design awards, Print Mag. N.Y., 1986, Desi awards, N.Y., 1986, 1988, Oil Painting awards, Monterey Jazz Festival, 1999. Mem.: Sierra Club. Democrat. Avocations: oil painting, interior decorating, hiking, kayaking. Home and Studio: Lake Wildwood 18807 Chaparral Dr Penn Valley CA 95946-9688

**SANDSTEAD, AURIEL J.,** retired secondary school educator, researcher, historian; d. Charles Ford and E. Fae (Stanley) Oram; m. Willard W. Sandstead, Mar. 16, 1946; children: Vicki Jo, Margo Dale, Shauna Gae. BA, Colo. State Coll. (now U. Northern Colo.), 1957, MA, 1961. Emergency tchg. certificate WWII Colo. Tchr. Weld County Dist. #93, New Raymer, Colo., 1942—44; tchr. classroom/gymnasium Logan County Jr. HS, Sterling, Colo., 1956—60; instr. English & Sports Northeastern Jr. Coll., Sterling, 1960—68; social worker, family & children svcs. Logan County Social Svcs., Sterling, 1969—77; ret., 1977. Local historian Keota, Along the Burlington R.R. Sterling to Cheyenne, Homesteaders, Schs., etc., Mary Stanley (1869-1955), quilt collection embodying three generations. Author: (poem) Fifty-one Syllables of Spring, in Best Poems of the 90s, 1995, Boundless, in Best Poems of the 90s, 1996; publisher A Cartouche Collection, 2000, A Cartouche Collection, 6th edit., 2004. Charter mem. Nat. Mus. Women in the Arts, 1987; charter pres. Colo. Quilting Coun., 1979. Named to Hall of Fame (1st inductee), Colo. Quilting Coun., 1988; recipient Heritage award, Colo. Coun. on the Arts, Denver, 2000. Mem.: Am. Quilt Study Group, High Plains Heritage Quilters (life), Alpha Delta Kappa. Avocations: reading, writing, quilting.

**SANDSTEAD, HAROLD HILTON,** physician, researcher, educator, director; b. Omaha, May 25, 1932; s. Harold Russel and Lula Florence (Hilton) S.; m. Kathryn Gordon Brownlee, June 6, 1959 (dec. May 13, 1989); m. Victoria Regan Liddle, Feb. 14, 1990 (div. Oct. 1993); children: Eleanor McDonald, James Brownlee, William Harold; m. Wilma Helen Carter Streaker, Sept. 25, 2004. BA in Pre-Medicine, Ohio Wesleyan U., 1954; MD, Vanderbilt U., 1958. Diplomate Am. Bd. Internal Medicine, 1967, Am. Bd. Nutrition, 1967, Am. Bd. Physician Nutrition Specialists, 2001; lic. physician Tex. Intern, internal medicine Barnes Hosp. Washington U., St. Louis, 1958—59, asst. resident, internal medicine, 1959—60; asst. resident, pathology Vanderbilt Hosp., Nashville, 1960-61; asst. surgeon USPHS U.S. NAMRU 3, Cairo, 1961-63; rsch. resident, internal medicine Thayer VA Hosp., Vanderbilt U., Nashville, 1963-64; chief med. resident, internal medicine Vanderbilt U. Hosp., Nashville, 1964-65; instr. internal medicine, asst. prof. biochemistry Med. Sch. Vanderbilt U., Nashville, 1965-70, asst. prof. internal medicine, assoc. prof. biochemistry in nutrition, 1970-71; dir. USDA-ARS Human Nutrition Rsch. Ctr., Grand Forks, ND, 1971-84; adj. prof. biochemistry and internal medicine U. N.D., Grand Forks, 1971-84; dir. USDA-ARS Human Nutrition Rsch. Ctr. on Aging at Tufts U., Boston,

1984-85; prof. nutrition Tufts U., Medford, Mass., 1984-85; prof. preventive medicine and community health U. Tex. Med. Br., Galveston, 1985—; chmn. preventive medicine and community health Med. Br. U. Tex., Galveston, 1985-90, prof. internal medicine, biochem. and molecular biology, 1986—. Cons. WHO, NIH, USDA, NAS; Joseph Goldberger vis. prof. AMA, 1976, Ellen Swallow Richards Meml. lectr., 1984; W.O. Atwater lectr. USDA, 1984; Sam E. and Mary F. Roberts lectr., 1985, Raymond Ewell Meml. lectr., 1985; Welcome prof. in basic sci. Fedn. Am. Socs. Exptl. Biology, 1988; mem. Permanent Commn. on Occupl. Health, 2004—. Mem. editl. bd. Jour. Nutrition, 1972-76, 81-85, Am. Jour. Clin. Nutrition, 1975-78, Annual Rev. Nutritional Rsch., 1975-1991, Jour. Lab. Clin. Medicine, 1978-1983, Biol. Trace Element Rsch., 1979—, Nutrition Rsch., 1981-85, Nutritional Reports Internat., 1981-88, Trace Elements Medicine Biology, 1983-98, Jour. Trace Elements Exptl. Medicine, 1982-2004, Jour. Am. Coll. Nutrition, 1987-88, Nutrition Rsch. Newsletter, 1989-98, Cancer Prevention, 1990-1994; contbr. 8 chpts. to books, some 270 articles to jours. Asst. surgeon USPHS, 1961—63. Recipient Future Leader award Nutrition Found., 1968-70, Hull Gold medal AMA, 1970, Mead Johnson award, Am. Inst. Nutrition, 1972, Spl. Recognition award USDA, 2003. Fellow ACP, Am. Soc. Nutrition (Mead Johnson award 1972, fellow 1998); mem. Am. Soc. Clin. Nutrition (pres. 1982-83), Internat. Soc. for Trace Element Rsch. in Humans (pres. 2002-04), Sigma Xi, Alpha Omega Alpha. Achievements include research in description of some adverse effects of lead poisoning on endocrine system including supression of renin-aldoserone response to sodium deprivation; of pituitary and adrenal function; of pituitary-thyroid function; zinc deficiency in Egyptian adolescents and their response to zinc treatment; early demonstration in rat of effects of zinc deficiency on nucleic acid and protein synthesis; confirmation in rats of the essentiality of zinc for wound healing; acute effects of developmental zinc deficiency in rats on brain composition and cerebellum histology, and on later long-term behaviors, and hippocampus histology; zinc treatment given with other limiting micronutrients improved neuropsychological functions of children at risk of zinc deficiency; the use of zinc kinetics to show a close relationship between dietary zinc and iron status; the efficacy of zinc and iron given with other limiting micronutrients for neuropsychological function of women. Avocations: gardening, travel, art, music, reading. Office: U Tex Med Br Ewing Bldg Galveston TX 77555-1109 Home: 5100 San Felipe Rd 351E Houston TX 77056 Office Phone: 409-772-4661. Business E-Mail: hsandste@utmb.edu.

**SANDSTEDT, J. ERIK,** lawyer; b. New Brunswick, NJ, Nov. 6, 1970; BA with distinction, Univ. NC, Chapel Hill, 1992; JD, Columbia Univ., 1995. Bar: NJ 1995, NY 1996, US Dist. Ct. (NJ 1995, so. & ea. dist. NY 1996), US Ct. Appeals (3d cir. 1998, 1st cir. 2004). Assoc. Latham & Watkins, 1995—98; asst. U.S. atty. U.S. Dept. Justice, NJ Dist., 1998—2001; dep. chief of staff U.S. Dept. Justice, criminal div., 2001—02; ptnr., securities litigation Bernstein Litowitz Berger & Grossmann LLP, NYC & NJ, 2002—, mng. ptnr. NJ office. Assoc. Edward Bennett Williams Inn of Ct.; instr. Columbia Univ. Law Sch.; adj. prof. Seton Hall Univ. Law Sch. Editor: Columbia Law Jour. Law & Social Problems. Harlan Fiske Stone scholar. Mem.: ABA, NJ State Bar Assn. Office: Bernstein Litowitz Berger & Grossmann 1285 Ave of the Americas New York NY 10019 also: Bernstein Litowitz Berger & Grossmann 220 St Paul St Westfield NJ 07090 Office Phone: 212-554-1495, 908-928-1700. Office Fax: 212-554-1444. Business E-Mail: erik@blbglaw.com.

**SANDSTROM, DALE VERNON,** state supreme court justice; b. Grand Forks, ND, Mar. 9, 1950; s. Ellis Vernon and Hilde Geneva (Williams) S.; m. Gail Hagerty, Mar. 27, 1993; children: Jack, Carrie, Anne. BA, N.D. State U., 1972; JD, U. N.D., 1975. Bar: ND 1975, US. Dist. Ct. ND 1975, US Ct. Appeals (8th cir.) 1976. Asst. atty., chief consumer fraud and antitrust div. State of ND, Bismarck, 1975-81, securities commr., 1981-83, pub. svc. commr., 1983-92, pres. public svc. commn., 1987-91; justice ND Supreme Ct., Bismarck, 1992—. Chair ND Commn. on Cameras in the Courtroom, 1993—, Joint Procedure Com., 1996—, mem. adminstrv. coun., 2005—; mem. exec. com. ND Jud. Conf., 1995—, chair-elect, 1997-99, chair, 1999-2001; mem. Gov.'s Com. on Security and Privacy, Bismarck, 1975-76, Gov.'s Com. on Refugees, Bismarck, 1976; chmn. Gov.'s Com. on Comml. Air Transp., Bismarck, 1983-84. Mem. platform com. ND Reps., 1972, 76, exec. com., 1972-73, 85-88, dist. chmn., 1981-82; former chmn. bd. deacons Luth. Ch.; mem. ch. coun., exec. com., chmn. legal and constl. rev. com. Evang. Luth Ch. Am., 1993—; mem. exec. bd. dirs., No. Lights Coun., dist. chair Boy Scouts Am., 1998-2000. Named Disting. Eagle Scout, Boy Scouts Am., 1997, Master of the Coll. Arts, Humanities, and Social Scis., N.D. State U., 2002; recipient Cmty. Svc. award, N.D. State Bar Assn., 2002. Mem. ABA, ND Bar Assn., Big Muddy Bar Assn., Nat. Assn. Regulatory Utility Commrs. (electricity com.), N.A. Assn. Securities Adminstrs., Order of De Molay (grand master 1994-95, mem. Internat. Supreme coun., Legion of Honor award), Nat. Eagle Scouts Assn. (regent for life), Shriners, Elks, Eagles, Masons (33d degree, chmn. grand youth com. 1979-87, Youth Leadership award 1986), Bruce M. VanSickle Am. Inn of Court (pres. 1999-2001), ND Judges Assn. (v.p. 2005-). Office: State ND Supreme Ct Judicial Wing 1st Fl 600 E Boulevard Ave Bismarck ND 58505 Office Phone: 701-328-2221.*

**SANDUSKY, BILLY RAY,** art educator, artist; b. Bowling Green, Ky., Oct. 23, 1945; s. Wilroe Sandusky and Estelle Ware; m. Giovanna Lenzi, June 28, 1980; children: Marco G., Matteo G. BFA, Herron Sch. of Art, Indpls., 1968; MFA, Tulane U., 1970. Printer, instr. Santa Reparata Graphic Arts, Florence, Italy, 1973—80; instr. Rome program St. Mary's Coll., 1977—80, assoc. prof. Notre Dame, Ind., 1980—2000, prof., chair art dept., 2000—; instr. grad. program Loyola U., Florence, 1979—80. Bd. dirs. Mid-Am. Coll. Art Assn., Indpls., 1990—98; founding mem., exec. bd. Mid-Am. Print Coun., South Bend, Ind., 1991—94; evaluator Ind. Arts Commn., South Bend, 1990, grant rev. panelist, 99; mem. Nat. Scholastic Arts Adv. Panel, South Bend, 1983—86. Named to Who's Who in Am. Art, 1984—; fellow, Eli Lilly Found., 1992; grantee, St. Mary's Coll., 1998, 2003, 2005. Mem.: Coll. Art Assn. Avocations: painting, printmaking, book art, gardening, cooking. Office: Art Dept St Mary's Coll Notre Dame IN 46556 Office Phone: 574-284-4651. E-mail: sandusky@saintmarys.edu.

**SANDVIG, CHRISTIAN EDWARD,** communications educator, researcher; b. Santa Clara, Calif., June 3, 1975; s. James and Diane Sandvig; m. Lisa Nakamura, June 25, 2006. BA, U. of Calif., Davis, 1997; MA, Stanford U., 1999, PhD, 2002. Markle Found. info. policy fellow Oxford U., England, 2001—02, assoc. fellow, 2002—; asst. prof. U. of Ill., Urbana-Champaign, 2001—. Recipient Faculty Early Career Devel. award, U.S. NSF, 2002, 1st Prize for Grad. Student Rsch., Telecom. Policy Rsch. Conf., 2000. Avocation: coffee tasting. Office: U Ill 244 Lincoln Hall 702 S Wright St Urbana IL 61801 Office Phone: 217-333-0141. Office Fax: 217-244-1598. Business E-Mail: csandvig@uiuc.edu.

**SANDWEISS, JACK,** physicist, researcher; b. Chgo., Aug. 19, 1930; s. Charles Ray and Florence (Hymovitz) S.; m. Letha Ann Boeck, Jan. 16, 1956; children: Daniel Howard, Anne Florence, Benjamin Lewis. Student, UCLA, 1948-50; BS, U. Calif., Berkeley, 1952, PhD, 1957. Research assoc. Radiation Lab., U. Calif., Berkeley, 1957; instr. Yale U., New Haven, 1957-59, asst. prof., 1959-62, assoc. prof., 1962-64, prof. physics, 1964—, Donner prof. physics, 1980—, former chmn. dept. physics. Cons. Brookhaven Nat. Lab., Fermi Nat. Accelerator Lab.; chmn. high energy physics adv. panel Dept. Energy-NSF, 1982-86. Editor Phys. Rev. Letters, 1988—; contbr. articles to profl. jours. Fellow Am. Phys. Soc. (chmn. div. particles and fields 1980); mem. NAS, AAAS. Home: 248 Ogden St New Haven CT 06511-1221 Office: Yale Univ Physics Dept Sloane Physics Lab PO Box 2081-21 New Haven CT 06520-8121 E-Mail: sandweiss@hepmail.physics.yale.edu.

**SANDWEISS, MARTHA ANN,** writer, history professor; b. St. Louis, Mar. 29, 1954; d. Jerome Wesley and Marilyn Joy (Gilk) S. BA magna cum laude, Radcliffe Coll., 1975; MA in History, Yale U., 1977, MPhil in History, 1981, PhD, 1985. Smithsonian-Nat. Endowment Humanities fellow Nat. Portrait Gallery, Washington, 1975-76; curator photographs Amon Carter Mus., Ft.

Worth, 1979-86; adj. curator photographs, 1987-89; dir. Mead Art Mus. Amherst Coll., 1989-97, adj. assoc. prof. of fine arts and Am. studies, 1989-94, assoc. prof. Am. studies, 1994-97, assoc. prof. Am. studies and history, 1997-2000, prof. Am. studies and history, 2000—. Author: Carlotta Corpron: Designer with Light, 1980, Masterworks of American Photography, 1982, Laura Gilpin: An Enduring Grace, 1986, (catalogue) Pictures from an Expedition: Early Views of the American West, 1979, Print the Legend: Photography and the American West, 2002; co-author: Eyewitness to War: Prints and Daguerreotypes of the Mexican War, 1989; editor: Historic Texas: A Photographic Portrait, 1986, Contemporary Texas: A Photographic Portrait, 1986, Denizens of the Desert, 1988, Photography in Nineteenth Century America, 1991; co-editor: Oxford History of the American West, 1994. Fellow Ctr. for Am. Art and Material Cultures, Yale U., 1977-79, NEH, 1988, 2000-01, Am. Coun. Learned Socs., 1996-97, Weatherhead, 2000-01; Beinecke fellow Yale U., 2004-05. Office: Amherst Coll Am Studies Dept Box 2225 Amherst MA 01002-5000

**SANDY, LEWIS GORDON,** physician, healthcare executive; b. Detroit, July 18, 1958; s. William Haskell and Marjorie Mindel (Mazor) S.; m. Kathleen Anne Morgan, June 17, 1984; children: Matthew, Natalie, Jonah. BS, U. Mich., 1979, MD, 1982; MBA, Stanford U., 1988. Diplomate Am. Bd. Internal Medicine, Nat. Bd. Med. Examiners. Intern Beth Israel Hosp., Boston, 1982-83, resident, 1983-85; Robert Wood Johnson clin. scholar U. Calif., San Francisco, 1985-86, clin. fellow in medicine, 1986-88; instr. Harvard Med. Sch., 1988-91; assoc. chief internal medicine Harvard Community Health Plan, Boston, 1988-89, dir. Health Ctr., 1989-91; v.p. Robert Wood Johnson Found., Princeton, NJ, 1991—96, exec. v.p., 1997—2003, United Healthcare, Edina, Minn., 2003—; sr. fellow U. Minn. Sch. Pub. Health, 2004—. Cons. Kaiser Found. Health Plan, Oakland, Calif., 1987-88. Fellow ACP; mem. AMA, Soc. Gen. Internal Medicine, Alpha Omega Alpha. Office: 5901 Lincoln Dr Edina MN 55436 Home: 4800 Sunnyslope Rd E Edina MN 55424

**SANDY, SANDRA V.,** psychologist; d. Eugene Leon and Ruby Elizabeth Sandy. BA, W.Va. U., 1967; MA, New Sch. U., 1974; MPhil, Columbia U., 1983, PhD, 1985. Evaluation assoc. NYC Bd. Edn., Bklyn., 1985—87; sr. rsch. assoc. Cornell U. Med. Coll., NYC, 1987—94; dir. rsch. Internat. Ctr. Coop. & Conflict Resolution Columbia U., NYC, 1995—2001; dir. rsch. Ctr. Social & Emotional Edn., NYC, 2001—06; dir. Educating Com. Social Emotional Learning Inst., New York, NY. Cons. NY Acad. Medicine, NYC, 1995—2000, NJ Health Decisions, Verona, NJ, 2000—02; presentations, workshops in field. Author: (curriculum manual) Peaceful Kids Educating Communities in Social Emotional Learning, 2000; contbr. chapters to books. Grantee Homeless Children co-grant, Willliam T. Grant Found., 1988—91, Parent Child Conflict Resolution grant, William & Flora Hewlett Found., 1996—99, Peaceful Kids ECSEL grant, 1999—2002. Mem.: APA, Internat. Assn. Conflict Resolution, Assn. Conflict Resolution (editl. bd. 2001—). Office: Ctr Social & Emotional Edn 1841 Broadway New York NY 10023 Personal E-mail: sandrasandy@earthlink.net.

**SANDY, WILLIAM HASKELL,** training and communication systems executive; b. NYC, Apr. 28, 1929; s. Fred and Rose S.; m. Marjorie Mazor, June 15, 1952; children: Alan, Lewis, Barbara. AB, U. Md., 1950, JD, 1953; postgrad. Advanced Mgmt. program, Harvard Bus. Sch., 1970—71. Bar: Md. 1953. From planner-writer to acct. supr. Jam-Handy Orgn., Detroit, 1953—64, v.p., 1964—69, sr. v.p., 1969—71; pres. Sandy Corp., Troy, Mich., 1971—88, chmn., 1988—96; pres. Rudgate Corp., Bloomfield Hills, Mich. 1996—. Bd. dirs. U. Mich. Press, Asolo Theatre. Author: Forging the Productivity Partnership, 1990. Bd. govs. Northwood Inst., 1976-80; bd. dirs. Cranbrook Sci. Inst., Met. Ctr. High Tech., 1993, Birmingham (Mich.) Cmty. House, 1997-2003, Mich. Opera Theatre; pres. Graphic Arts Coun., 1992-93; trustee Detroit Inst. Arts, 1992-93; v.p. nat. exec. coun. Harvard Bus. Sch., 1985-89; mem. Bloomfield Hills Zoning Bd., Walsh Coll. Leader in Residence, Pres.'s Adv. Coun.; mayor City of Bloomfield Hills, 1996-97; mem. Troy Downtown Devel. Authority, 1996-99; Inst. for Humanities trustee U. Mich Mem. ASTD, Am. Mktg. Assn. (pres. Detroit chpt. 1975), Nat. Found. Am. Mktg. Assn (bd. dirs. 1998), S.E. Mich. BBB (bd. dirs. 1990), Adcraft Club, Nat. Assn. Ednl. Broadcasters, Harvard Bus. Sch. Club (pres. Detroit chpt. 1983-85). Home (Summer): 596 Rudgate Rd Bloomfield Hills MI 48304 Home (Winter): 535 Sanctuary Dr B404 Longboat Key FL 34228-3852 Personal E-mail: sandyfamily@aol.com.

**SANETO, RUSSELL PATRICK,** pediatric neurologist, epileptologist, neurobiologist; b. Burbank, Calif., Oct. 10, 1950; s. Arthur and Mitzi (Seddon) S.; m. Kathleen D. Saneto. BS with honors, San Diego State U., 1972, MS, 1975; PhD, U. Tex. Med. Br., 1981; DO, U. Osteo. Medicine and Surgery, 1994. Tchg. asst. San Diego State U., 1969-75; substitute tchr. Salt Lake City Sch. Dist., 1975; tchg. and rsch. asst. U. Tex. Med. Br., 1976-77, NIH predoctoral fellow, 1977-81, postdoctoral fellow, 1981; Jeanne B. Kempner postdoctoral fellow UCLA, 1981-82, NIH postdoctoral fellow, 1982-87; asst. prof. divsn. neurosci. Oreg. Regional Primate Rsch. Ctr., Beaverton, 1987-89; asst. prof. dept. cell biology and anatomy Oreg. Health Scis. U., Portland, 1988-90, U. Osteo. Medicine and Surgery, 1991-94, Cleve. Clinic, 1994-2001; assoc. prof. neurology and pediat. U. Wash. Children's Hosp. and Regional Med. Ctr., Seattle, 2001—. Lectr. rsch. methods Grad. Sch., 1982; vis. scholar in ethics So. Bapt. Theol. Sem., Louisville, 1981; sci. advisor United Mitochondrial Disease Found. Mem. editl. bd. Epilepsy.com, Pediat. Neurology; contbr. articles to profl. jours. Mem. scientific adv. bd. United Mitochondrial Disease Found., Northwest Epilepsy Found. Recipient Merit award Nat. March of Dimes, 1978; named one of Outstanding Young Men in Am., 1979, 81, one of Men of Significance, 1985. Mem. AAAS, Am. Acad. Pediats., Am. Acad. Neurology, Am. Epilepsy Soc., Bread for World, Winter Confs. Brain Rsch., Neurosci. Study Program, N.Y. Acad. Scis., Am. Soc. Neurochemistry, Soc. Neurosci., Sigma Sigma Phi. Democrat. Mem. Evangelical Free Ch. Office: Childrens Hosp and Regional Med Ctr Neurology B-5552 4800 Sand Point Way NE Seattle WA 98105 Business E-Mail: russ.saneto@seattlechildrens.org.

**SANFELICI, ARTHUR H(UGO),** editor, writer; b. Haledon, N.J., May 23, 1934; s. Hugo and Anna (Schilder) S.; m. Betty Louise Van Riper, Aug. 10, 1957; children: Brian Arthur, Mary Elizabeth, Gary Hugh, Bruce Richard. Attended, Lehigh U., 1952-55. Assoc. editor Flying Mag., N.Y.C., 1961-64; mng. editor Am. Aviation Mag., Washington, 1964-68; dist. sales mgr. Gates Learjet Co., N.Y.C., 1969-71; exec. editor Airport World Mag., Westport, Conn., 1971-74; spl. project editor Aircraft Owners & Pilots Assn., Washington, 1974-75, mng. editor Pilot mag., 1975-79, editor AOPA Newsletter, AOPAirport Report, Gen. Aviation Nat. Report, 1979-88; pub. cons., 1989-90; sr. editor Flight Safety Found., Washington, 1989-92; editor S-Cubed divsn. Maxwell Labs., Alexandria, Va., 1992-95; comms. dir. Helicopter Assn. Internat., Alexandria, 1996-97; editor Shooting Sports USA, 1997-98. Editor, compiler: Yesterday's Wings; Editor Aviation History Mag., Leesburg, Va., 1990—; author: 135 Ways to Get Even With Your Kids, 2003. Pilot USAF, 1955—60. Mem. Nat. Aeronautic Assn., Aero Club of Washington, Soc. Aerospace Comms. Home: 44476 Oakmont Manor Sq Ashburn VA 20147

**SANFELIPPO, PETER MICHAEL,** thoracic surgeon; b. Milw., Nov. 1, 1938; s. Michael L. and Genevieve M. (Gagliano) S.; m. Cecelia Monica Reuss, May 25, 1968. MD, Marquette U., Milw., 1965; MS in Surgery, U. Minn., 1976. Diplomate Am. Bd. Surgery, Am. Bd. Thoracic Surgery, Am. Bd. Gen. Vascular Surgery. Intern Sacred Heart Hosp., Spokane, Wash., 1965-66; gen. surgery fellow Mayo Grad. Sch. Medicine, Rochester, Minn., 1966, 69-73; residency in thoracic surgery USAF Med. Ctr., Lackland AFB, Tex., 1966-75; thoracic surgeon USAF Med. Corps, various locations, 1966-78; pvt. practice cardiac, thoracic and vascular surgery Ohio Heart & Thoracic Surgery Ctr., Columbus, 1978-91; prof. cardiothoacic and vascular surgery U. Tex. Health Ctr., Tyler, Tex., 1991—2004; med. dir. Occupl. Medicine Ctr., Tyler, 2005—. Contbr. articles to profl. jours.; mem. editl. bd. various profl. jours. Lt. col. USAF, 1966-78. Decorated Air Force Commendation medal. Fellow ACS, Am. Coll. Cardiology, Am. Soc. Angiology, Am. Coll. Chest Physicians. Avocations: scouting, camping, photography, gardening. Office Phone: 903-509-1551. Personal E-mail: petersanfelippo@cox.net.

**SANFILIPPO, ALFRED PAUL,** dean, medical educator, pathologist; b. Racine, Wis., Aug. 30, 1949; s. Paul Joseph and Therese (Rhode) Sanfilippo; m. Janet Lee Thompson, 1973; children: Lisa, Joseph. Student, Max Planck Inst. Exptl. Medicine, Gottingen, Germany, 1966—68; BA in Physics, MS in Physics, U. Pa., 1970; PhD in immunology, Duke U., 1975, MD, 1976. Diplomate Am. Bd. Pathology, lic. physician NC, Md. Intern in anatomic pathology Duke U. Hosp., 1976—77, resident in anatomic and clin. pathology, 1977—79, postdoctoral rschr. divsn. tumor virology dept. surgery, 1976—79; asst. prof. pathology and exptl. surgery, lectr. immunology Duke U., 1979—84, from assoc. prof. to prof. pathology, 1984—93, from assoc. prof. to prof. exptl. surgery, 1985—93, prof. immunology, 1990—93; attending pathologist Duke U. and Durham VA Hosps., 1979—93; staff mem. Duke Surg. Pvt. Diagnostic Clinic, 1979—93; dir. Transplantation Lab Durham VA Hosp., 1979—93; dir. immunopathology Duke U. Med. Ctr., 1982—93, exec. com. dept. pathology, 1989—91; Baxley Prof. and chair pathology dept. John's Hopkins U., Balt., 1993—2000; pathologist-in-chief Johns Hopkins Hosp., Balt., 1993—2000; sr. v.p. health scis. Ohio State U., Columbus, 2000—, exec. dean health scis., 2004—, dean. coll. medicine; CEO Ohio State U. Med. Ctr. Mem. Duke Comprehensive Cancer Ctr., 1979—93; dir. rsch. Johns Hopkins Comprehensive Transplant Ctr.; mem. Third Frontier Commn. Adv. Bd., Ohio, 2004—; cons. Battelle Human Affairs Rsch. Ctrs., Seattle, 1985—93, NSF of Switzerland, 1992—93, numerous US govt. adv. coms.; mem. editl. bd. Transplantation, 1985—, Pathobiology, 1989—, Transplantation Now, Japan 1989—, Pathology, Rsch. and Practice, 1990—, Human Immunology, 1992—, Lab. Investigation, 1993— Xeno, 1994—, Virchows Archiv, 1998—, Transplant Immunology; reviewer Am. Jour. Kidney Diseases, Am. Jour. Ophthalmology, Am. Jour. Pathology, New Eng. Jour. Medicine, Jour. of AMA, Jour. Am. Soc. Nephrology, Jour. Clin. Investigation, Jour. Leukocyte Biology, Kidney Internat., others; contbr. numerous articles to prof. jours.; speaker and presenter in field. Bd. trustees Omeris, Columbus, Ohio, 2004—. Recipient Kermit G. Osserman Award, Myasthenia Gravis Found., 1976, Wiley D. Forbus Award, NC Soc. Pathologists, 1979, Reach for Sight Physician Investigator Award, 1990; grantee numerous, NIH. Fellow: Am. Soc. Clin. Pathologists (coun. on edn. and rsch. 1994—96); mem.: Southeastern Organ Procurement Found. (exec. com 1992—97, sec. 1992—93, treas. 1993—94, v.p. 1994—95, pres. 1995—96), Assn. for Rsch. in Vision and Ophthalmology, Am. Soc. Nephrology, Am. Soc. Transplant Physicians (pres. 1985—86), Am. Soc. Histocompatibility and Immunogenetics, Transplantation Soc., US-Can. Acad. Pathology, Am. Assn. Med. Colls., Am. Assn. Immunologists, AMA, Am. Soc. Investigative Pathology (pres. 2002—03), Intersociety Pathology Coun., Assn. Pathology Chairs (sr. fellow), Am. Soc. Transplantation (past pres.), Alpha Omega Alpha. Office: Office Dean Ohio State U Coll Medicine 370 W 9th Ave 200 A Meiling Columbus OH 43210*

**SANFILIPPO, JOSEPH SALVATORE,** gynecologic endocrinologist, educator; b. Bklyn., Feb. 21, 1948; s. Joseph Philip and Elena Teresa (Canepa) S.; m. Patricia M. Cantwell, June 21, 1974; children: Angela, Andrea, Luke. BS, St. John's U., NYC, 1969; MD, Chgo. Med. Sch., 1973. Diplomate Am. Bd. Ob-Gyn., spl. qualification in reproductive endocrinology. Intern Mil. County Gen. Hosp.; resident in ob-gyn. SUNY Upstate Med. Ctr., Syracuse; instr. dept. ob-gyn. U. Louisville Sch. Medicine, 1977—79, asst. prof., 1979—83, assoc. prof., 1983—89, prof., 1989—97, dir. divsn. reproductive endocrinology, 1993—97; James and Marilyn Gilmore prof. ob-gyn. MCP Hahnemann Sch. Medicine, 1998—2001; vice chmn. reproductive sci. Magee-Women's Hosp., Pitts., 2001—, dir. reproductive endorcrinology and infertility, 2003—, dir. residency program, 2004—05; chmn. ob-gyn. Allegheny Gen. Hosp., 1998—2001; prof. ob-gyn. and reproductive sci. U. Pitts. Sch. Medicine, 2001—. Pres. med. staff Alliant Health System/Norton Hosp. and Alliant Med. Pavilion, Louisville, 1994—; dir. gynecology Kosair-Children's Hosp., Louisville, 1979—. Editor: Risk Management for Healthcare Professionals, 2001, MBA Handbook for Healthcare Professionals, 2002, Clinical Gynecology, 2026; editor-in-chief: Jour. Pediat. Adolescent Gynecology, 1989—. Named Disting. Alumnus, Chgo. Med. Sch., 1990. Fellow: N.Am. Soc. for Pediat. Adolescent Gynecology (exec. dir.), Am. Soc. for Reproductive Medicine (pres.); mem.: ACOG (chair sci. program com. 2006, chair gynecol. prolog fifth edit.). Avocations: jogging, boating, fishing, amateur radio. Office: Univ Pitts Sch Medicine Dept Ob-gyn and Reproductive Scis 300 Halket St Pittsburgh PA 15213-3180 Office Phone: 412-641-1204. Business E-Mail: jsanfilippo@mail.magee.edu.

**SANFORD, BRUCE WILLIAM,** lawyer; b. Massena, N.Y., Aug. 5, 1945; s. Doris (Suhrland) Sanford; m. Marilou Green, May 17, 1980; children: Ashley Anne, Barrett William. BA cum laude, Hamilton Coll., 1967; JD, NYU, 1970. Bar: N.Y. 1970, Ohio 1971, D.C. 1981, Md. 1985. Staff reporter Wall St. Jour., 1966-67; assoc. Baker & Hostetler, Washington, 1971-79, ptnr., media law, mem. policy com., 1979—. Mem. adv. bd. Media Law Reporter; former assoc. editor, mem. editorial bd. Litigation Mag. Author: Sanford's Synopsis Law of Libel and Privacy, rev. edit., 1991, Libel and Privacy, 2nd edit., 1991, Don't Shoot the Messenger: How Our Growing Hatred of the Media Threatens Free Speech for All of Us, 1999. Trustee Nat. Symphony Orch. Assn.; bd. dirs. Thomas Jefferson 1st Amendment Ctr., U. Va., Charlottesville; pres. Washington Nat. Cathedral Assn., 2002-05. Named one of 100 Most Influential Lawyers in Am., Nat. Law Jour., 1991, 50 Best Lawyers in Wash., The Washingtonian, 1997; named to Freedom of Information Hall of Fame, 1996. Mem. ABA (governing bd., forum com. on communication law, chmn. defamation torts com. 1985-86). Office: Baker & Hostetler LLP 1050 Connecticut Ave NW Washington DC 20036-5304 Office Phone: 202-861-1500. Office Fax: 212-861-1783. Business E-Mail: bsanford@bakerlaw.com.

**SANFORD, DAVID BOYER,** journalist, editor; b. Denver, Mar. 4, 1943; s. Filmore Bowyer and Alice Irene (Peterson) S. BA with honors, U. Denver, 1964; MS in Journalism with honors, Columbia U., 1965. With New Republic mag., Washington, 1965-76, mng. editor, 1970-76, Politics Today (formerly Skeptic), Santa Barbara, Calif., 1976-78, contbg. editor, 1978-79; editorial writer Los Angeles Herald Examiner, 1978-79; mng. editor Harper's mag., N.Y.C., 1979-80; editor Wall St. Jour. mag., 1980-81; sr. spl. writer Wall Street Jour., 1981—. Syndicated columnist, 1970-71; commentator Can. Broadcasting Corp., 1967-76; judge Heywood Broun award Newspaper Guild, 1971; mem. print screening com. Champion-Tuck award, 1985, 86, Judge Wuxtry award, 1990. Author: Who Put the Con in Consumer?, 1972, Me and Ralph, 1976; editor, co-author: Hot War on the Consumer, 1970. Recipient Sackett Law prize, Columbia, 1965, Eckenberg prize, 1965, Gold award, N.Y. Art Dirs. Club, 1977, Wuxtry award for disting. achievement in headline writing, Internat. Soc. for Gen. Semantics, 1989, Pulitzer prize, 1997, Sci.-in-Soc. award, Nat. Assn. Sci. Writers, 1997; Centennial scholar, 1960—64, N.Y. Newspaper Guild fellow, 1964—65. Mem. Phi Beta Kappa, Omicron Delta Kappa. Democrat. Home: 118 Prospect Park W Brooklyn NY 11215-4270 Office Phone: 212-416-2597. Personal E-mail: david.sanford@wsj.com.

**SANFORD, JAMES KENNETH,** public relations executive; b. Clyde, NC, Jan. 23, 1932; s. James Edward S. and Bernice (Crawford) Peebles; m. Judith Bullard Longshore, 2001; children: Timothy, Scott, Jeannette. AA, Mars Hill (N.C.) Coll., 1952; AB, U. N.C., 1954, MA, 1958. Pub. rels. officer Asheville (N.C.) United Appeal, 1954; reporter, copy editor Winston-Salem (N.C.) Jour., 1957-59, asst. state editor, 1959-61, news editor, 1961-63, editorial writer, 1963-64; dir. pub. info. and publs. U. N.C., Charlotte, 1964-94; pub. rels. cons. Charlotte, N.C., 1994—. Cons. Commn. on Future of Mars Hill Coll., 1990-91, City of Charlotte, 1991. Author: Charlotte and UNC Charlotte: Growing Up Together, 1996, Building Future From the Past: The History of Gaston College 1964-99, 1999; co-author: Fifty Favored Years, 1972; contbg. author: The North Carolina Century: Tar Heels Who Made a Difference, 1900-2000, 2002; contbr. numerous articles to mag. and newspapers. Attractions com. Charlotte Conv. and Visitors Bur., 1994; pres. elect

Internat. House, 2001-2002, adv. com. Sta. WTVI Pub. TV, Charlotte, 1986-94; chmn. bd. deacons local ch., 1994-95; gen. bd. Bapt. State Conv. NC, 2000-2003; active Coun. on Christian Higher Edn., 2000-2003; pres. Mars Hill Coll. Nat. Alumni Bd., 2001; bd. trustees Mars Hill Coll., 2005; bd. dirs. Lions Club Cmty. Found. Named to NC Pub. Rels. Hall of Fame, 1995; recipient Alumnus by Choice award U. NC, Charlotte, 1996. Fellow Pub. Rels. Soc. Am. (chmn. S.E. dist. 1991); mem. Coll. News Assn. Carolinas (Lewis Gaston award 1982), Charlotte Pub. Rels. Soc. (pres. 1974, Infinity award 1986), Coun. for Advancement and Support Edn. (asst. dist. chmn. 1975-76), Phi Kappa Phi. Baptist. Avocations: writing, hiking, photography. Home and Office: 74 Fairway Rdg Lake Wylie SC 29710-9209 Office Phone: 803-831-2999. E-mail: sanf2058@bellsouth.net.

**SANFORD, JAMES L.,** science administrator; BA in Indsl. Mgmt., Mich. State U.; MBA, Utah State U. Mgr. contracts and pricing B-2 divsn. Northrop Grumman Corp, LA, 1985—88, asst. corp. dir. banking and internat. fin., 1988—96, v.p. contracts and pricing, 1996—2003, corp. v.p., treas., 2003—. Bd. vis. Def. Acquisition U. Mem.: Treasury Mgmt. Assn. (cert. cash mgr.), Aerospace Industries Assn. (chmn. procurement and fin. com.). Office: Northrop Grumman Corp 1840 Century Park E Los Angeles CA 90067-2199

**SANFORD, JO ANNE,** state agency administrator; b. Laurinburg, N.C., Oct. 18, 1950; m. William E. Brewer, Jr.; 1 child, Charlotte Brewer. BA Polit. Sci., N.C. State U., 1972; JD, U. N.C. Sch. Law, 1975. Spl. deputy atty. gen. N.C. Atty. Gen.'s Office, 1975—95; chair N.C. Utilities Commn., Raleigh, 1995—2006; bd. dirs. Universal Svc. Administrv. Co., 2001—. Apptd. to N.Am. Numbering Coun. FCC; bd. dirs. Nat. Regulatory Rsch. Inst. Mastr. N.C. Bar Assn.; mem.: Women Execs. in State Govt., Wake County Bar Assn. Office: 4325 Mail Svc Ctr Raleigh NC 27699-4325

**SANFORD, JOHN (JOHN CAMP),** writer, journalist; b. Cedar Rapids, Iowa, Feb. 23, 1944; BA in American studies, U. Iowa, 1966, MA in Journalism, 1971. Journalist Cape Girardeau S.E. Missourian, Miami Herald, 1971—78, St. Paul Pioneer Press, 1978—90; freelance book reviewer Fort Worth Star Telegram. Author: (as John Camp) The Fool's Run, 1989, The Empress File, 1991, (as John Sanford) Rules of Prey, 1989, Shadow Prey, 1990, Eyes of Prey, 1991, Silent Prey, 1992, Winter Prey, 1993, Night Prey, 1994, Mind Prey, 1995, Sudden Prey, 1996, The Night Crew, 1997, Secret Prey, 1998, Certain Prey, 1999, The Devil's Code, 2000, Easy Prey, 2000, Chosen Prey, 2001, Mortal Prey, 2002, The Hanged Man's Song, 2003, Naked Prey, 2003, Hidden Prey, 2004. Pulitzer prize for feature writing for Life on the Land: An American Farm Family, 1986. Office: c/o Putnam Books 375 Hudson St New York NY 10014

**SANFORD, LINDA S.,** information technology executive; b. Jan. 21, 1953; d. William J. and Catherine A. Sanford; 2 children. BA, St. John's U.; MS in Ops. Rsch., Rensselaer Poly. Inst. From mem. staff to gen. mgr. IBM, Westchester, NY, 1975—98, gen. mgr., global industries, 1998—2000, sr. v.p., group exec., storage systems group, 2000—03, sr. v.p. enterprise on demand transformation and info. tech. Somers, 2003—. Mem. bd. dirs. ITT Industries, 1998—. Bd. dirs. St. John's U., Rensselaer Poly. Inst., The Bus. Coun. of N.Y. State. Named one of 50 Most Influential Women in Bus., Fortune Mag., Top 10 Innovators in Tech. Industry, Info. Week Mag., 10 Most Influential Women in Tech., Working Woman Mag.; named to Women in Tech. Internat. Hall of Fame. Mem.: NAE. Office: IBM Corp Rte 100 Somers NY 10589

**SANFORD, MARSHALL (MARK SANFORD),** governor, former congressman; b. Ft. Lauderdale, Fla., May 28, 1960; m. Jenny Sullivan; children: Marshall, Landon, Bolton, Blake. BA, Furman U., 1983; MBA, U. Va., 1988. With Goldman Sachs, 1988, CRC Realty, 1988-89; prin. Southeastern Ptnrs., 1989—, Norton & Sanford, 1993—95, 2001—02; mem. U.S. Congress from 1st Dist. S.C., 1995-2001; mem. govt. reform and oversight com., internat. rels. com., sci. com., joint econ. com.; gov. State of SC, 2003—. Republican. Episcopalian. Office: Office of the Governor PO Box 12267 Columbia SC 29211 Office Fax: 803-734-5167.*

**SANGER, CAROL,** law educator; BA, Wellesley Coll., 1970; JD, U. Mich., 1976. Atty., San Francisco; tchr. U. Oreg., 1979—81, Santa Clara U. Law Sch., 1985—94; vis. prof. Columbia Law Sch., NYC, 1994—96, faculty mem., 1996—, Barbara Aronstein Black prof. law. Vis. scholar, Inst. Rsch. on Women and Gender Stanford U., 1990—91, vis. prof. law, 1991—92; mem. exec. bd. Inst. Rsch. on Women and Gender. Co-editor: Cases and Materials on Contracts, 2001. Fellow, Program on Law and Public Affairs, Princeton U., 2003—04. Office: Columbia Law Sch Jerome Greene Hall, Rm 818 Mailbox D-13 New York NY 10027 Office Phone: 212-854-5478. E-mail: csanger@law.columbia.edu.

**SANGER, FREDERICK,** retired molecular biologist; b. Rendcomb, Gloucestershire, Eng., Aug. 13, 1918; s. Frederick and Cicely Sanger; m. Margaret Joan Howe, 1940; children: Robin, Peter Frederick, Sally Joan. BA, St. John's Coll., Cambridge U., 1940, PhD, 1943; D.Sc. (hon.), Leicester U., 1968, Oxford U., 1970, Strasbourg U., 1970, Cambridge U. Beit Meml. Med. Research fellow U. Cambridge, 1944-51, sci. scientist dept. biochemistry, 1944-61, rsch. scientist, div. head Med. Rsch. Coun. Lab. of Molecular Biology, 1962-83. Contbr. articles in field to sci. jours. Fellow King's Coll., Cambridge U., 1954; recipient Corday-Morgan Medal and Prize, Chem. Soc., 1951, Nobel prize for chemistry, 1958, 80; Gairdner Found. award, 1971, 79, William Bate Hardy prize Cambridge Philos. Soc., 1976, Copley medal Royal Soc., 1977, Hon. Fellow, Royal Coll. Pathologists, 1993, Commander, Order Brit. Empire, 1963, Order of Merit, 1971, Companion of Honour, 1981, Millennium Fellow Royal Soc. Chemistry, 2000. Mem. Am. Acad. Arts and Scls. (hon. fgn. mem.), Am. Soc. Biol. Chemists (hon.), Fgn. Assn., Acad. Sci. Argentina, Acad. Sci. Brazil, Japanese Biochemical Soc. (hon.) Assn. Qulmica Argentina (corr.), NAS. Two time Nobel Prize winner in chemistry for work on amino acids and gene sequencing.*

**SANGER, ROBERT MARSHALL,** lawyer; b. Arlington, Va., Jan. 7, 1949; s. Ned and Julia Sanger; m. Catherine Jeanne Swysen; children: Charles Andrew, Jeffrey Scott, Paul Michael, Sarah Swysen. BA, U. Calif., Santa Barbara, 1970; JD, U. Calif., L.A., 1973. Bar: Calif. 1973, U.S. Supreme Ct. 1979, U.S. Ct. Appeals (9th cir.) 1981, U.S. Ct. Appeals 10th cir. 1998, U.S. Tax Ct. 1975, U.S. Dist. Ct. No. Cen. Ea. & So. Dist. Calif. 1974, U.S. Dist. Ct. Ariz. 1997, U.S. Dist Ct. We. Okla. 1998; cert. criminal law specialist, Calif. Ptnr. Sanger & Swysen, Santa Barbara, Calif., 1973—. Adj. prof. Santa Barbara Coll. Law, 1975-76. Contbr. articles to profl. jours. Chair legal com. Santa Barbara ACLU, 1985-87, 89-91, pres. 1987-89, 1991-93; bd. mem. Death Penalty Focus Calif. 1999-. Recipient Gov.'s award for pro bono legal svcs. Calif. State Bar, 1987, ACLU Civil Liberties award, 1994. Mem. ABA, FBA, Calif. Attys. for Criminal Justice, State Bar Calif., Calif. Pub. Defender's Assn., Santa Barbara Criminal Def. Lawyers Assn. (co-chair 1994-95, Defender of Double Bread), Santa Barbara County Bar Assn. (bd. dir. 1977), Nat. Assn. Criminal Def. Lawyers, Criminal Cts. Bar Assn., William L. Gordon Inn Ct. (Master 2000-). Avocation: golf. Office: Sanger & Swysen 233 E Carrillo St Ste C Santa Barbara CA 93101-7163 Business E-Mail: rsanger@sangerswysen.com.

**SANGER, STEPHEN W.,** consumer products company executive; b. 1945; BA in History, DePauw U., 1986; MBA, U. Mich., 1970. Marketing and sales positions Procter & Gamble, 1970—73; with Gen. Mills, Inc., Mpls., 1974—, v.p., gen. mgr. Northstar Divsn., 1983—86, v.p., gen. mgr. new bus. devel., 1986, pres. Yoplait USA, 1986—88, pres. Big G Divsn., 1988, sr. v.p., 1989—92, vice chmn. bd., 1992-96, pres., 1993-95, CEO, chmn. bd., 1995—. Bd. dirs. Donaldson Co., Inc., Mpls., Target Corp., Wells Fargo & Co., Grocery Manufacturers of Am.; mem. Bus. Council, Bus. Roundtable; bd. adv. Retail Food Industry Ctr. Treas. Guthrie Theatre Found., Mpls., bd. mem. Catalyst, Minnesota Bus. Partnership. Office: Gen Mills Inc One General Mills Blvd Minneapolis MN 55426*

**SAN GIACOMO, LAURA,** actress; b. Hoboken, NJ, Nov. 14, 1962; Appeared in films Vital Signs, 1990, Pretty Woman, 1990, Quigley Down Under, 1990, Once Around, 1991, The Other Woman, 1993, Nina Takes A Lover, 1993, The Stand, 1994, Stuart Saves His Family, 1995, Right to Remain Silent, 1996, Suicide Kings, 1997, Apocalypse, 1997, With Friends Like These..., 1998, Eat Your Heart Out, 1997, Apocalypse, 1997, A House on a Hill, 2003, Checking Out, 2005, Havoc, 2005,; appeared in TV series Gargoyles, 1994, Gargoyles: The Goliath Chronicles, 1996-97, Just Shoot Me, 1997-2003.; guest appearances include: The Equalizer, 1985, Crime Story, 1986, Spenser: For Hire, 1985. Office: More Medavoy Mgmt 7920 W Sunset Blvd Ste 401 Los Angeles CA 90046-3300*

**SANGIOVANNI, MARY ELIZABETH,** writer, freelance manager; b. Orange, NJ, Jan. 28, 1976; d. Michael Louis and Suzanne Kathleen SanGiovanni; 1 child, Adam Joseph. BA in English, Fairleigh Dickinson U., 1998. Asst. editor Marquis Who's Who, New Providence, NJ, 1998—99, from freelance coord. to freelance supr., 1999—2001, freelance mgr., 2002—. Author: (short stories) Under Cover of Night, 2002; contbr. short stories to various periodicals, articles to various periodicals. Mem.: Garden State Horror Writers (v.p. 2001, pres. 2002—03), Horror Writers Assn. (internet mailer editor 2003—), Mid Atlantic Horror Profls., Nat. Assn. Women Writers. Roman Catholic. Avocations: reading, movies, model building, video games, computer art. Office: Marquis Whos Who 630 Central Ave New Providence NJ 07974

**SANGIULIANO, BARBARA ANN,** tax consultant; b. Bronx, N.Y., Dec. 28, 1959; d. Patrick John and Mildred (Soell) Gallo; m. John Warren Sangiuliano, Aug. 28, 1982. BA, Muhlenberg Coll., 1982; MST, Seton Hall U., 1989, JD, 1997. Bar: N.J. 1997, N.Y. 2006; CPA, N.J., 1987; CMA. Sr. tax mgr. KPMG Peat Marwick, Short Hills, N.J., 1988-92; sr. tax analyst Allied Signal, Morristown, N.J., 1992-93; tax mgr. AT&T, Morristown, 1993-96, Lucent Techs., Morristown, 1996-97; tax atty. Witman, Stadtmauer & Michaels, Florham Park, NJ, 1997-98; tax cons. Ernst & Young LLP, Iselin, NJ, 1998—2003, Deloitte Tax LLP, Parsippany, NJ, 2003—06, Smolin, Lupin & Co. PA, Fairfield, NJ, 2006—. Mem. AICPA, ABA, N.J. Soc. CPAs (past pres. Union County chpt.), N.J. Bar Assn., Inst. Mgmt. Accts., Mensa, Omicron Delta Epsilon, Phi Sigma Iota. Republican. Roman Catholic. Avocations: reading, bicycling, fencing. Home: 340 William St Scotch Plains NJ 07076-1430 Office: Smolin Lupin and Co PA 165 Passaic Ave Fairfield NJ 07004 Office Phone: 973-439-7200.

**SANGKIL, MOON,** finance educator; b. Kyungsan, Kyungpook, Repbulic of Korea, June 10, 1965; s. Myung-Sool Moon and Okhae Keum; m. Yunjung Kim, May 15, 1994; 1 child, Noel Moon. PhD, U. Iowa, Iowa City, 2003. Asst. prof. mktg. NC State U., Raleigh, 2003—. Contbr. articles to profl. jours. Mem.: INFORMS. Home: Cary NC 27513-1617 Office: NC State University College of Management Raleigh NC 27695-7229 Personal E-mail: smoon0610@hotmail.com.

**SANGMEISTER, GEORGE EDWARD,** lawyer, consultant, congressman; b. Joliet, Ill., Feb. 16, 1931; s. George Conrad and Rose Engaborg (Johnson) S.; m. Doris Marie Hinspeter, Dec. 1, 1951; children: George Kurt, Kimberley Ann. BA, Elmhurst Coll., 1957; LLB, John Marshall Law Sch., 1960, JD, 1970. Bar: Ill. 1960. Ptnr. McKeown, Fitzgerald, Zollner, Buck, Sangmeister & Hutchison, 1969-89; justice of peace, 1961-63; states atty. Will County, 1964-68; mem. Ill. Ho. of Reps., 1972-76, Ill. Senate, 1977-87, 101st-103rd Congresses from 4th (now 11th) Dist. Ill., 1989-95; ret., 1995; cons. McKeown, Fitzgerald, Zollner, Buck, Hutchison, Ruttle and Assocs., 1990—. Chmn. Frankfort Twp. unit Am. Cancer Soc., Will County Emergency Housing Devel. Corp.; past trustee Will County Family Svc. Agy.; past bd. dirs. Joliet Jr. Coll. Found., Joliet Will County Ctr. for Econ. Devel., Silver Cross Found., Silver Cross Hosp. With inf. AUS, 1951-53. Mem. ABA, Ill. Bar Assn., Assn. Trial Lawyers Am., Am. Legion, Frankfort (past pres.), Frankfort C. of C., Old Timers Baseball Assn., Lions. Achievements include As an Illinois Congressman, established Abraham Lincoln National Cemetery for Veterans in 1992. Home: 20735 Wolf Rd Mokena IL 60448-8927 Office Phone: 815-469-2176.

**SANGREE, WALTER HINCHMAN,** social anthropologist, educator; b. N.Y.C., June 15, 1926; s. Carl Michael and Constance (LaBoiteaux) S.; m. Mary Lucinda Shaw, June 14, 1952 (div. Jan. 1986); children: Margaretta Elizabeth, Mary Cora; m. Ilse Michaelis, Dec. 31, 1988. AB, Haverford Coll., 1950; MA, Wesleyan U., 1952; PhD, U. Chgo., 1959. Asst. prof. anthropology U. Rochester, NY, 1957-64, assoc. prof., 1964-73, prof., 1973-95, prof. emeritus, 1995—, chmn. dept. anthropology, 1974-77, acting chmn. dept., 1990; vis. scholar dept. anthropology Harvard U., 1979-80. Vis. scholar Ctr. for Population Studies, Harvard U., 1986-87; rsch. fellow Ctr. for African Studies, Boston U., 1998—. Author: Age, Prayer & Politics in Tiriki, Kenya, 1966; contbr. articles to profl. jours. Co-clk. Rochester Friends Meeting, 1977-79. Fulbright scholar U.K. and Kenya, 1954-56; NSF research fellow Nigeria, 1963-65 Mem. Am. Anthrop. Assn., African Studies Assn., Sigma Xi. Democrat. Mem. Soc. Of Friends. Home and Office: PO Box 1290 65 Meadow View Dr Nantucket MA 02554-2717 Office Phone: 508-228-4195. Personal E-mail: sangree@comcast.net.

**SANI, ROBERT LEROY,** chemical engineering professor; b. Antioch, Calif., Apr. 20, 1935; m. Martha Jo Marr, May 28, 1966; children: Cynthia Kay, Elizabeth Ann, Jeffrey Paul. BS, U. Calif.-Berkeley, 1958, MS, 1960; PhD, U. Minn., 1963. Postdoctoral researcher dept. math Rensselaer Poly. Inst., Troy, NY, 1963-64: asst prof U. Ill, Urbana, 1964-70, prof., 1970-76, prof. chem. engrng. U. Colo., Boulder, 1976—; co-dir. Ctr. for Low-g Fluid Mechanics and Transport Phenomena, U. Colo., Boulder, 1986-89, dir., 1989—. Assoc. prof. French Ministry Edn., 1982, 84, 86, 92, 94, 95, 96, 97; cons. Lawrence Livermore Nat. Lab., Calif., 1974-84. Contbr. numerous chpts. to profl. publs.; co-author three books; mem. editorial bd. Internat. Jour. Numerical Methods in Fluids, 1981—, Revue Européenne des Éléments Finis, 1990—, Internat. Jour. Computational Engring. Sci., 1998—, Internat. Jour. Computational & Numerical Analysis & Applications, 2000-. Guggenheim fellow, 1970 Mem. AICE, Soc. for Applied and Indsl. Math., World User Assn. in Applied Computational Fluid Dynamics (bd. dirs.). Democrat. Office: U Colo Dept Chem & Biol Engring UCB 424 Boulder CO 80309-0424 Office Phone: 303-492-5517. Business E-Mail: robert.sani@colorado.edu.

**SAN JOSE, ANGEL MOLINA,** surgeon; b. Manila, Dec. 9, 1939; came to U.S., 1966; MD, Far Ea. U., Manila, 1965. Diplomate Am. Bd. Surgery. Intern to resident in gen. surgery Mt. Sinai Hosp., Cleve., 1966-67, 67-71; pvt. med. practice, 1973—. Attending physician Ingalls Meml. Hosp., Harvey, Ill., South Suburban Hosp., Hazel Crest, Ill., Miller County Hosp., Colquitt, Ga., 2003—. Fellow ACS; mem. Ill. Surg. Soc., Am. Soc. Gen. Surgeons.

**SANKAR, HARI,** communications engineer; b. Trivandrum, India; s. Sankaranarayan Iyer and Ramalekshmi Krishnaiyer. B in Tech., Indian Inst. of Tech., India, 2000; PhD, Tex. A&M U., College Station, 2006. Rsch. asst. Tex. A&M U., College Station, 2000—06; engring. intern Qualcomm Inc., San Diego, 2005; sr. commn. sys. engr. Nextwave Wireless, San Diego, 2006—. Co-author (with N. Sindhushayana and K.R. Narayanan): (rsch. article) IEEE Globecomm, 2004; co-author: (with K.R. Narayanan) IEEE Transactions on Communications, 2004, IEEE Transactions on Wireless Communications, 2005. V.p. Elec. Engring. Grad. Students Assn., College Station, Tex., 2003—04. Fellowship, TxTEC Consortium, Tex., 2000—01. Mem.: IEEE. Achievements include research in Design of IRA Codes for OFDM with partial CSI, WCNG Conf., Univ. of Texas at Austin; patents pending for Power Control in UMTS TDD Systems - UMTS TDD is the third generation wireless standard now being deployed widely across the globe. Home: 8155 Cargill Ave #36 San Diego TX 92122 Office Phone: 858-480-3239. Personal E-mail: harisankar@gmail.com.

**SANKARAN, MAHESH,** ecologist; b. India; s. Sankaran; m. Jayashree Ratnam; 1 child, Sidharth Mahesh. PhD, Syracuse U., N.Y., 1993—2001. Post-doctoral rsch. assoc. Centre for Population Biology, Imperial Coll., Silwood Park, London, 2001—02; rsch. scientist, NREL Colo. State U., Fort Collins, Colo., 2002—. Office: NREL Colo State Univ 1231 East Dr Fort Collins CO 80523 Office Phone: 970-491-1964. Office Fax: 970-491-1965. Business E-Mail: mahesh@nrel.colostate.edu.

**SANKARAN, VINOD,** financial analyst; b. Chennai, Tamil Nadu, India, July 7, 1979; s. Sankaran Sivaswamy and Shyamala Sankaran. M in Quantitative Fin., Okla. State U., 2003. Analyst II Sprint, Overland Park, Kans., 2004—.

**SANKOVITZ, JAMES LEO,** retired development director, lobbyist; b. St. Paul, July 3, 1934; s. John L. and Mabel A. (Hanrahan) S.; m. Margaret E. Mathews, Aug. 3, 1957; children: Richard, Therese, Patrick, Margaret, Katherine. BS in Journalism, Marquette U., 1956; MA in Speech, U. Denver, 1963. Dir. pub. rels. Coll. of St. Mary of the Wasatch, Salt Lake City, 1956-57; dir. pub. info. Colo. Sch. of Mines, Golden, 1957-63; assoc. dir. devel. Marquette U., Milw., 1963-66; dir. alumni fund, 1966-67, dir. alumni rels., 1967-69, asst. v.p. univ. rels., 1969-70, v.p. univ. rels., 1970-78, v.p. govtl. rels., 1978-86, v.p. govtl. and community affairs, 1986-97; ret., 1997. Contbr. articles to profl. jours. Founding dir. Univ. Nat. Bank, Milw., 1971-74; bd. dirs. St. Coletta Sch., Jefferson, Wis., 1970-76, 86-93, chair, 1974-76. Mem. Nat. Assn. for Ind. Colls. and Univs. (bd. dirs. Washington 1986-90), Disting. Svc. award 1986), Assn. Jesuit Colls. and Univs. (fed. affairs cons. Washington 1974-90), Assn. Cath. Colls. and Univs. (fed. affairs cons. Washington 1974-85, Blue Key, Alpha Sigma Nu. Roman Catholic. Avocations: woodworking, reading. Home: 4057 N Prospect Ave Milwaukee WI 53211-2121 E-mail: jsankovitz@wi.rr.com.

**SANKS, JOHN CLEMENT,** music educator; b. Salt Lake City, Oct. 31, 1953; s. Robert Leland and Mary Clement Sanks; m. Christine Sanks, Nov. 22, 1997; children: Dawn Mills, Lucas Crane, Gina Payne, Mary. B in Music Edn., Mont. State U., 1980. Music tchr. Three Forks (Mont.) Pub. Sch., 1984—85; dir. bands Rio Grande H.S., Albuquerque, 1985—87, Highland H.S., Albuquerque, 1987—93, 1994—95, Santa Fe H.S., 1993—94, Eldorado H.S., Albuquerque, 1995—. Music dir. Albuquerque Jazz Orch., 1987—; dir. Albuquerque Jazz Festival, 1990—; music dir. Albuquerque Concert Band, 1999—. With U.S. Army, 1972—75. Named Music Educator of Yr., Albuquerque Public Sch., 1991, 1997, 1999, 2001, 2002, 2004, Music Tchr. of Yr., Nat. Fedn. Interscholastic Music Assn., 1999, 2004, Tchr. of Yr., KOAT Channel 7, 1997, 2002, Music Educator of Yr. N.Mex. Music Educators, 2004. Mem.: Musicians Union 618, Music Educators Nat. Conf., N.Mex Music Educators, Internat. Assn. Jazz Educators, Midwest Music Conf. Home: 4817 Basin NE Albuquerque NM 87111 Office: Eldorado High Sch 11300 Montgomery Blvd NE Albuquerque NM 87111 Office Phone: 505-296-4871. Personal E-mail: trbnman1@aol.com.

**SANKS, ROBERT LELAND,** environmental engineer, retired educator; b. Pomona, Calif., Feb. 19, 1916; s. John B. and Nellie G. (Church) S.; m. Mary Louise Clement, May 16, 1946 (dec. Oct. 1994); children: Margaret Sanks Russell, John Clement; m. Edith Millen Harrington, Dec. 2, 1999. AA, Fullerton Jr. Coll., 1936; BS, U. Calif., Berkeley, 1940; MS, Iowa State Coll., Ames, 1949; PhD, U. Calif., Berkeley, 1965. Registered profl. engr., Mont. Draftsman City of La Habra Calif., 1940; asst. engr. Alex Morrison cons. engr., Fullerton, Calif., 1941; jr. engr. U.S. Army Engrs., L.A., 1941-42; asst. research engr. dept. civil engring. U. Calif.-Berkeley, 1942-45; structural engr. The Austin Co., Oakland, Calif., 1945-46; instr. dept. civil engring. U. Utah, Salt Lake City, 1946-49, asst. prof., 1949-55, assoc. prof., 1955-58; structural engr. The Lang Co., Salt Lake City, 1950; instrument man Patti McDonald Co., Anchorage, 1951; checker Western Steel Co., Salt Lake City, 1952; structural engr. Moran, Proctor, Meuser and Rutledge, N.Y.C., 1953, F.C. Torkelson Co., Salt Lake City, 1955; soils engr. R.L. Sloane & Assocs., Salt Lake City, 1956; prof., chmn. dept. civil engring. Gonzaga U., Spokane, Wash., 1958-61; prof. dept. civil engring. Mont. State U., Bozeman, 1966-82, prof. emeritus, 1982—; vis. prof. U. Tex.-Austin, 1974-75; part-time sr. engr. Christian, Spring, Sielbach & Assoc., Billings, Mont., 1974-82. Cons. engr., 1945—; lectr. at pumping sta. design workshops, 1988—; assoc. specialist San. Engring. Research Lab., 1963-65, research engr., 1966. Author: Statically Indeterminate Structural Analysis, 1961; co-author: (with Takashi Assano) Land Treatment and Disposal of Municipal and Industrial Wastewaters, 1976, Water Treatment Plant Design for the Practicing Engineer, 1978; editor-in-chief: Pumping Station Design, 1989 (award Excellence profl. & scholarly pub. div. Assn. Am. Pubs. 1989), 2d edit., 1998, co-editor 3d edit., 2005; contbr. articles on civil engring. to profl. publs. Mem. Wall of Fame, Fullerton High Sch., 1987, Hall of Fame, Mont. Profl. Engrs., 2005; NSF fellow, 1961-63 Mem. ASCE (life, chmn. local qualifications com. intermountain sect. 1950-56, pres. intermountain sect. 1957-58), Am. Water Works Assn. (pres. Mont. sect. 1981-82, George Warren Fuller award), Mont. Water Environ. Fedn., Assn. Environ. Engring. Profs., Rotary, Sigma Xi, Chi Epsilon. Home: 411 W Dickerson St Bozeman MT 59715-4538 Office Phone: 406-587-8220. Personal E-mail: bsanks@mcn.net.

**SAN MIGUEL, LOLITA,** artistic director; Student, Sch. Am. Ballet. Performer Robert Joffrey Co., Benjamin Harkarvy Co., Slavenska-Franklin Ballet; soloist Met. Opera Ballet; founder Puerto Rican Dance Theatre, N.Y., 1970; artistic dir., founder Ballet Concierto de P.R., Santurce, 1978—. Tchr., ballet mistress Ballet Hispánico, N.Y.; tchr. Dance Theatre Harlem, Performing Arts H.S., Adelphi Coll., Hofstra U., L.I. U., Clark Ctr., Met. Opera.

**SAN MIGUEL, MANUEL,** painter, writer; b. Guayama, P.R., Sept. 29, 1930; s. Manuel and Luisa (Griffo) San M.; m. Sandra Bonilla, July 12, 1969; children: Manuel, Ana. Student, U. P.R., 1947-51, U. Pa., 1966-68, Arts Students League, N.Y.C., 1968-69. Historian San Juan Nat. Historic Site, Nat. Park Svc., 1953-63; exec. sec. Acad. Arts and Scis., San Juan, 1963-64. Founder of mus. and study collection El Morro Castle San Juan Nat. Hist. Site; painter, writer, musician, 1964—; co-founder Caribbean Art Gallery, San Juan, PR, Galeria Campeche, N.Y.C.; cons. in field. Exhibited in U. P.R., 1958, 62, Ateneo de P.R., 1962, Pan-Am. Union, Washington, 1963, Bienal Mex., 1972, Bienal Rio de Janeiro, 1976, Orange County Schs. Mus. Art, Orlando, Fla., 1992, Mus. Modern Art, Paris, 1994, Expo of the Americas, Orlando, 1996, 98, Galería Santiago, San Juan, P.R., 2000, Galeria Campeche, San Juan, P.R., 2001, Símon Bolivar Gallery, Caracas, 2001, Galerie Santiago, 2003, Galeriá Colibri, Santo Domingo, numerous other nat. and internat. exhbns.; contbr. monographs on historical work in San Juan Nat. Historic Site to U.S. Nat. Archives, Washington; contbr. poetry to anthologies including Anthology of Latin American Poets, vol. III, 1987; rec. artist popular music of P.R.; soloist U. P.R. choir, Carnegie Hall, N.Y.C., 1949. Capt. U.S. Army, 1951-53, Korea. Decorated Bronze Star with valor clasp and oak leaf cluster, Purple Heart, Combat Infantryman Badge, others; named One of Ten Outstanding Hispanic Men, Orlando, Fla., 1991; recipient Recognition award for contbns. to Hispanic Am. Culture, Govt. P.R., 1996, Hispanic Heritage Found., medal Painters & Designers 20th Century, Cambridge, Eng., 2000; Coqui de Oro award for contbns. to Puerto Rican arts Casa de P.R., Inc., 1999. Mem. AAAS, VFW (life), Disabled Am. Vets. (life), Am. Legion, Ateneo de P.R. (bd. govs. 1959-60), Am. Biog. Inst. (bd. advisors, life mem. bd. govs.), Am Philatelic Soc. (postal commemorative soc.), Inst. P.R. Culture (cons.), P.R. Philatelic Assn. (charter), Internat. Platform Assn., Lions (Lion of Yr. 1962-63). Achievements include documentary research in the restoration of Castillo San Marcos, St. Augustine, Fla., Castillo San Felipe de Barajas, Colombia, South Am., and restoration of San Juan fortifications and city walls. Home: 1214 Howell Creek Dr Winter Springs FL 32708

**SANNER, GEORGE BRADLEY,** bank executive; b. Balt., Sept. 20, 1953; s. George E. and Marjorie (Hohman) S.; m. Ann Margaret Tehan, Aug. 31, 1991 (div.); children: Anne, Meredith, Kimberly. BA, U. Va., 1974; MBA, Loyola Coll., Balt., 1978. Asst. v.p. Union Trust Co., Balt., 1974-82; v.p. Am. Security Bank, Washington, 1982-86; sr. v.p. Bank of Md., Towson, 1986-87; mng. dir. Provident Bank of Md., Balt., 1987-94; sr. v.p. FCNB Bank,

Frederick, Md., 1994-95; pres./CEO Regal Bancorp, Owings Mills, Md., 1995—; also bd. dirs. Bd. dir. Md. Bank Svcs., Inc., Chesapeake Bus. Fin. Corp., Atlantic Ctrl. Bankers Bank; pres., CEO, bd. dir. Regal Bank and Trust. Airman USAF, 1973-75. Mem. Md. Bankers Assn., Alpha Sigma Nu. Republican. Presbyterian. Avocations: golf, tennis, amateur radio. Office: Regal Bancorp 10123 Reisterstown Rd Owings Mills MD 21117-3814 E-mail: bsanner@regalbank.com.

**SANNER, JOHN HARPER,** retired pharmacologist; b. Anamosa, Iowa, Apr. 29, 1931; s. Lee Michael and Helen (Grace) S.; m. Marilyn Joan Eichorst, Dec. 28, 1958; children: Linda Leigh, Steven Bradley. BS, U. Iowa, 1954, MS, 1961, PhD, 1964. Rsch. investigator G.D. Searle & Co., Skokie, Ill., 1963-69, sr. rsch. investigator, 1969-75, rsch. fellow, 1975-86, ret., 1986—. Contbr. articles to profl. jours. Mem. Deerfield (Ill.) Cable and Telecomm. Commn. 1st lt. USAFR, 1955-57. Mem.: Ill. Videographers Assn. Democrat. Achievements include pioneering research in prostaglandin antagonists. Avocation: video photography and production. Office: Sanner Video Svc PO Box 199 Deerfield IL 60015-0199 Personal E-mail: johnsanner@comcast.net.

**SANNER, MYRNA JOYCE,** elementary school educator; d. Harold William Bockbrader and Alta Regina Emch; m. Richard Dean Sanner, Sept. 1, 1963; children: Michelle, Richard, Elizabeth. BS in Edn., Capital U., 1961; M in Edn. Counseling, Toledo U., 1966; postgrad. Ashland U., 1996—. Cert. Nat. Bd. Profl. Tchg. Stds. Tchr. Columbus (Ohio) City Sch., 1961—63, Washington Local Sch., Toledo, 1963—65, Toledo Pub. Sch., 1966—67; learning disability tutor Sylvania (Ohio) City Sch., 1976—78, tchr., 1985—91, Am. Sch., Chofu, Japan, 1979—81, Dublin (Ohio) City Sch., 1995—2005. Mem. Stephan's minister Christ Luth Ch., Columbus, 1996—; docent Toledo Mus. Art, 1982—91. Recipient Golden Shamrock award, Dublin City Sch., 2003, Excellence in Edn. award, 2003, 2005. Mem.: Assn. Supr. and Curriculum Devel. Avocations: golf, tennis, skiing, art, travel. Home: 8518 Stonechat Loop Dublin OH 43017

**SANO, EMILY JOY,** museum director; b. Santa Ana, Calif., Feb. 17, 1942; d. Masao and Lois Kikue (Inokuchi) S. BA, Ind. U., 1967; MA, Columbia U., 1970, MPhil, 1976, PhD, 1983. Lectr. Oriental Art Vassar Coll., Poughkeepsie, NY, 1974-79; curator Asian Art, asst. dir. programs Kimbell Art Mus., Ft. Worth, 1979-89; dep. dir. collections and exhbns. Dallas Mus. Art, 1989-92; dep. dir., chief curator Asian Art Mus., San Francisco, 1993-95, dir., 1995—. Author: Great Age of Japanese Buddhist Sculpture, 1982; editor: The Blood of Kings, 1986, Weavers, Merchants and Kings, 1984, Painters of the Great Ming, 1993. Active Assn. Art Mus. Dirs.; vis. com. Harvard U. Art Mus. Woodrow Wilson Fellow, 1966-67; grantee Carnegie, 1963-64, Fulbright-Hays, 1977-78. Office: Asian Art Museum 200 Larkin St San Francisco CA 94102-4734

**SANOFF, ALVIN PAUL,** writer, educational consultant; b. NYC, July 1, 1941; s. Harry and Sema (Kravitz) m. Jane O. Blakely, Aug. 25, 1968; children: Geoffrey L., Scott L., Michael B. AB cum laude in Sociology, Harvard Coll., 1963; MS in Journalism, Columbia U., 1964. Reporter Washington Star, 1965; editor Newhouse Newspapers Washington Bur., 1965-66; pub. info. editor St. Bus. Administrn., Washington, 1966-67; reporter Balt. Sun, 1967-71; editorial page editor Dayton (Ohio) Jour. Herald, 1971-77; from assoc. editor to asst. mng. editor U.S. News & World Report Mag., Washington, 1977-98, mng. editor Guides to Am.'s Best Colls. and Grad Schs., 1992-98. Sr. v.p. Maguire Assocs., Bedford, Mass., 1998-2000; dir. Edn. Schs.Project, Tchrs. Coll., Columbia U., 2000—04, cons. to project, 2005—; dir. Mo. Schs. of Edn. Rsch. Project, 2003-04, Creator, series editor: Authors' America TV Series, 1992-95; contbg. editor Prism Mag., 2000—, Washingtonian Mag., 2004—. Recipient Best Editl. Writing award Ohio AP, 1974; NEH Fellow, 1974-75. Avocations: reading, music, walking, travel. Office: 5510 Johnson Ave Bethesda MD 20817-3518 Personal E-mail: apsanoff@erols.com.

**SANQUIST, NANCY JOHNSON,** real estate consultant, educator; b. Muncie, Ind., Aug. 31, 1947; d. Charles Elof and Pauline Lydia (Murphy) S.; m. James M. Johnson, Dec. 1988. BA, UCLA, 1970; MA, Bryn Mawr Coll., 1973; MS, Columbia U., 1978. Cert. facilities mgr. Instr. Lafayette Coll., Easton, Pa., 1973—74, Muhlenberg Coll., Bethlehem, Pa., 1974—75, Northampton Area CC, Bethlehem, 1974—75; dir. Preservation Office City of Easton, 1977—78; cons. El Pueblo de Los Angeles State Hist. Pk., 1978—79; dir. restoration Bixby Ranch Co., Long Beach, Calif., 1979—82; mgr. computer applications Cannel-Heumann & Assoc., L.A., 1982—84; dir. Computer-Aided Design Group, Marina del Rey, Calif., 1984—93; v.p. PAE Facility Mgmt. Svcs., L.A., 1993—97, Vanderweil Facility Advisors, Boston, 1997—99; dir. strategic initiatives Peregrine Sys., San Diego, 1999—2002; strategic asset mgmt. adv. Autodesk, San Rafael, Calif., 2003; dir. strategy Manhattan Software, 2004—; adj. prof. U. San Diego Grad. Sch. Bus., 2004—05. Adj. instr. UCLA, 1979-86, Grad Sch. Calif. State U., Dominguez Hills, 1981. Author numerous tech. articles and manuals. Bd. dir. Historic Easton, Inc., 1977-78, Simon Rodia's Towers in Watts, L.A, 1979-81, L.A. Conservancy, 1982-86, Friends of Schindler House, West Hollywood, Calif., 1978-98, pres., 1982-85; mem. Del Mar Libr. Bd., 2005—; v.p. Del Mar Village Assn., 2005—. Recipient Outstanding Contbn. award Nat. Computer Graphics Assn., 1987. Fellow Internat. Facility Mgmt. Assn. (seminar leader, lectr. N.Am., Asia, Australia, Europe and Mid. East 1987—); mem. AIA (assoc.), Friends of Del Mar Libr. Avocations: travel, art, photography, architecture. Office Phone: 858-699-0827. E-mail: nsanquist@phasesix.com.

**SANSALONE, WILLIAM ROBERT,** biochemist, educator, biomedical researcher; b. Vineland, N.J., Feb. 16, 1931; s. Fortunato and Rosa (Pelle) Sansalone; m. Alice E. Koury, June 25, 1960; 1 child, Catherine. BS, Rutgers U., 1953, PhD, 1961; MS, U. N.H., 1955. Biochemistry rsch. asst. U. Conn., Storrs, 1955-56; instr. biochemistry SUNY Downstate Med. Ctr., Bklyn., 1961-64, asst. prof. biochemistry, 1964-70, assoc. prof., 1970-71; project scientist NIH, Bethesda, Md., 1971-72, sr. project scientist, 1972-73, exec. sec. biochemistry study sect., 1973-74, program dir. rev., 1974-83, assoc. dir. sci. program ops., 1983-87, dir. office of program planning and evaluation, 1987-96; sr. fellow Georgetown U., Washington, 1999—2002, adj. prof. biochemistry, 2002—. Vis. assoc. prof. physiology and biophysics Med. Coll. Pa., Phila., 1970. Contbr. articles to profl. jours. Served to 1st lt. USAF, 1956—58. Mem.: AAAS, Soc. Exptl. Biology and Medicine, Am. Soc. Nutritional Scis., Biophys. Soc., Harvey Soc., Sigma Xi, Alpha Gamma Rho (chpt. treas. 1968—70). Roman Catholic. Home: 6835 Old Stage Rd Rockville MD 20852-4359 Office Phone: 202-687-2891. Personal E-mail: ws31@prodigy.net. Business E-Mail: ws23@georgetown.edu.

**SANSBURY, OLIN BENNETT JR.,** retired university and orchestra administrator; b. Florence, S.C., Dec. 10, 1937; s. Olin Bennett and Gladys Ruth (Snipes) S.; m. Helen Cecile Hyman, Aug. 24, 1963; 1 child, Olin Bennett, III. BA in History, Wofford Coll., 1959; PhD in Internat. Studies, U. S.C., 1972. Reporter, editorial writer WBTW-TV, Florence, 1963-64, 1966-67; asst. dir. student affairs U. S.C., Florence, 1969-70, dean students, Francis Marion Coll. Columbia, 1970-71, asst. vice provost, asst. prof. govt. and internat. studies, 1971-73, chancellor, assoc. prof. govt. and internat. studies Spartanburg, 1973-93, chancellor emeritus, 1993—; exec. dir. Greenville Symphony Assn., 1994-99; ret. Bd. dirs. S.C. Coun. Econ. Edn., 1977-94, S.C. Coun. for the Humanities, 1986-96, Am. Coun. Edn. Commn. Govtl. Rels., 1991-93, S.C. Arts Alliance, 1996-99; rep. Pres.' Commn. Divsn. II NCAA, 1991-93; founding com. bd. regents Leadership, Spartanburg, 1980-85. With U.S. Army, 1960-63. H.B. Earhart fellow, 1965-66, 69 Mem. Am. Assn. State Colls. and Univs. (bd. dirs. 1989-92).

**SANSEVERINO, RAYMOND ANTHONY,** lawyer; b. Bklyn., Feb. 16, 1947; s. Raphael and Alice Ann (Camerano) S.; m. Karen Marie Mooney, Aug. 24, 1968 (dec. 1980); children: Deirdre Ann, Stacy Lee; m. Victoria Vent, June 6, 1982 (div. 1995); m. Kimberley Frank, May 11, 2002. AB in English Lit., Franklin & Marshall Coll., 1968; JD cum laude, Fordham U.,

1972. Bar: N.Y. 1973, U.S. Dist. Ct. (so. and ea. dists.) N.Y. 1973, U.S. Ct. Appeals (2d cir.) 1974, U.S. Supreme Ct. 1986. Assoc. Rogers & Wells, N.Y.C., 1972—75, Corbin & Gordon, N.Y.C., 1975—77; ptnr. Corbin Silverman & Sanseverino LLP, N.Y.C., 1978—2001, mng. ptnr., 1985—2001; ptnr. Brown Raysman Millstein Felder & Steiner LLP, N.Y.C., 2001—06, chair comml. real estate leasing group, 2001—06, mem. exec. com., 2003—06; ptnr., chair comml. real estate leasing group Loeb & Loeb LLP, N.Y.C., 2006—. Chmn. comml. real estate leasing group Loeb & Loeb LLP, 2006—. Contbr. articles to profl. jours.; articles editor Fordham Law Rev., 1971-72. Recipient West Pub. Co. prize, 1972. Mem. ABA, Assn. Bar City of N.Y., N.Y. State Bar Assn., Twin Oaks Swim and Tennis Club (bd. dirs. 1981-2002, pres. 1993-2001), Alumni Assn. Franklin and Marshall Coll. (bd. dirs., chair devel. and philanthopy com. 2003-04, treas. 2004-05, exec. com. 2004-, v.p. 2005-06, pres. 2006—). Republican. Roman Catholic. Office: Loeb & Loeb LLP 345 Park Ave New York NY 10154 Office Phone: 212-895-2910, 212-407-4008.

**SANSOM, WILLIAM B.,** consumer products executive; BS in Civil Engring., The Citadel. Commr. transp., commr. fin. and adminstrn. Tenn. State Govt., 1979—83; CEO H.T. Hackney Co., Knoxville, Tenn., 1983—, also chmn. bd. dirs. Mem. bd. dir. Martin Marietta Materials, NC, 1994—, First Tenn. Nat. Corp. Address: PO Box 238 Knoxville TN 37901-0238 Fax: 423-456-1291.

**SANSONE, VICTOR,** broadcast executive; Pres., gen. mgr. Sta. WKHX-FM, WYAY-FM, and WDWD-AM, Atlanta. Bd. mem. Country Music Assn., Board member, Country Music Association (CMA), Nashville, 2004. Office: Fl 6 210 Interstate North Pky SE Atlanta GA 30303

**SANSONETTI, THOMAS L.,** lawyer, former federal agency administrator; b. Hinsdale, IL, May 18, 1949; BA in Fgn. Affairs, with distinction, U. Va., 1971, MBA, 1973; JD, Washington and Lee U., 1976. Chief of staff, legis. dir. to Congressman Craig Thomas US Ho. Reps; assoc. solicitor on energy and natural resources US Dept. Interior, 1987—89, solicitor, 1990—93; ptnr. Holland & Hart LLP, Cheyenne, Wyo., 1993—2001, 2005—; asst. atty. gen. Environment and Natural Resources Divsn. U.S. Dept. Justice, Washington, 2001—05. Founder Wyo. Tennis Assn., 1978; mem. Wyo. Rep. Nat. Com., 1996—2002; chmn. Wyo. Rep. Party, 1983—87; gen. counsel Rep. Nat. Com., 2001; leader Bush-Cheney transition team Interior Dept., 2001. Republican. Office: Holland & Hart LLP 2515 Warren Ave Cheyenne WY 82001-3162 Office Phone: 307-778-4200. Office Fax: 307-778-8175. E-mail: tlsansonetti@hollandhart.com.

**SANSTEAD, WAYNE GODFREY,** school system administrator; b. Hot Springs, Ark., Apr. 16, 1935; s. Godfrey A. and Clara (Buen) S.; m. Mary Jane Bober, June 16, 1957; children: Timothy, Jonathan. BA in Speech and Polit. Sci. St. Olaf Coll., 1957; MA in Pub. Address, Northwestern U., 1966; Ed.D., U. N.D., 1974. Tchr. Luverne, Minn., 1959-60; dir. forensics Minot High Sch., ND, 1960-71, tchr. social sci. ND, 1960-78; mem. ND Ho. of Reps., 1965-70, 83-85, ND Senate, 1971-73; lt. gov. N.D. Bismarck, 1973-81; supt. pub. instrn. State of ND, Bismarck, 1985—. Served with AUS, 1957-59. Recipient Disting. Alumnus award St. Olaf Coll., 1991; named Outstanding Freshman Senator A.P., 1971, Outstanding Young Educator, N.D. Jr. C. of C., 1967, Outstanding Young Man, Minot Jr. C. of C., 1964; Coe Family Found. scholar, 1963, Eagleton scholar Rutgers U., 1969. Mem. N.D. Edn. Assn., NEA (legis. com. 1969—), Central States Speech Assn., Am. Forensic Assn., Jr. C. of C., Sons of Norway, Elks, Toastmasters. Democrat. Lutheran. Home: 1120 Columbia Dr Bismarck ND 58504-6514 Office: State Supt ND Dept Pub Instrn 600 E Boulevard Ave Dept 201 Fl 9-10-11 Bismarck ND 58505-0660 Office Phone: 701-328-4570.

**SANSWEET, STEPHEN JAY,** journalist, writer, marketing executive; b. Phila., June 14, 1945; s. Jack Morris and Fannie (Axelrod) S. BS, Temple U., 1966. Reporter Phila. Inquirer, 1966-69; reporter Wall Street Jour., Phila., 1969-71, Montreal, Que., Canada, 1971-73, L.A., 1973-84, dep. bur. chief, 1984-87, bur. chief, 1987-96; dir. specialty mktg. Lucasfilm Ltd., San Francisco, 1996—97, dir. content mgmt. and fan rels., 1997—; sr. editor Star Wars Galaxy Mag., 1996-2000; columnist Star Wars Insider, 1994—. Lectr. bus. journalism U. So. Calif., L.A., 1984-87. Author: The Punishment Cure, 1976, Science Fiction Toys and Models, 1981, Star Wars: From Concept to Screen to Collectible, 1992, Tomart's Price Guide to Worldwide Star Wars Collectibles, 1994, 2d edit., 1997, The Quotable Star Wars, 1996, Star Wars Scrapbook: The Essential Collection, 1998, Star Wars Encyclopedia, 1998, Star Wars Collectibles: A Pocket Manual, 1998, Anakin Skywalker: The Story of Darth Vader, 1998, Star Wars: The Action Figure Archive, 1999; co-author: The Star Wars Poster Book, 2005, Star Wars Chronicles: The Prequels, 2005; cons. editor: Star Wars Galaxy card sets, 1993, 2d series, 1994, 3d series, 1995; editor: Star Wars Trilogy Spl. Edn. card sets, 1997. Recipient award for best fire story Phila. Fire Dept., 1968, Pub. Svc.-Team Mem. award Sigma Delta Chi, 1977; finalist Loeb award, 1990. Mem. Soc. Profl. Journalists. Avocation: collecting toys and movie memorabilia. Office: Lucasfilm Ltd PO Box 29901 San Francisco CA 94129

**SANT, ROGER W.,** retired energy executive; Masters, Harvard U. Instr. corp. fin. Stanford U. Grad. Sch. Bus.; founder several businesses; asst. adminstr. energy conservation & environ. U.S. Fed. Energy Adminstrn., Washington; dir. Mellon Inst.'s Energy Productivity Ctr.; co-founder AES Corp., Washington, 1981, CEO, 1981—93, chmn. bd., 1981—2003, chmn. emeritus, 2003—06. Bd. dir. Marriott Internat. Inc. Author: The Least-Cost Energy Strategy; co-author: Creating Abundance-America's Least-Cost Energy Strategy; contbr. articles to profl. jours. Chmn. Summit Found., Summit Fund, Washington; bd. dir. World Wildlife Fund, chmn., 1994—2000; regent, chmn. exec. com. Smithsonian Institution; bd. dir. Anacostia Waterfront Corp., Nat. Symphony Orch., DC Coll. Access Prog., Tudor Place. Mailing: Summit Foundation Ste 525 2100 Pennsylvania Ave NW Washington DC 20037*

**SANT, VICTORIA P.,** museum administrator; BA, Stanford U. Docent Nat. Gallery Art, Washington, DC, 1983—85, chmn. trustees coun., 2001—02, immediate past chmn., The Phillips Collection, pres., 2003—. Co-founder, pres. The Summit Found., The Summit Fund of Washington. Bd. mem. Stanford U., Cmty. Found. for Nat. Capitol Region, Nat. Campaign to Prevent Teen Pregnancy, DC Campaign to Prevent Teen Pregnancy, Population Action Internat., Vital Voices for Global Partnership. Office: The Summit Found Ste 525 2100 Pennsylvania Ave, NW, Washington DC 20037 Office Phone: 202-912-2900.

**SANTA-COLOMA, BERNARDO,** secondary school educator, consultant; b. NYC, May 31, 1934; s. Bernardo Santa-Coloma Sr. and Belma Remotti; m. Sofia A. Santa-Coloma, Dec. 22, 1981; children: Ananda, Anita. BA in Humanistic Psychology, U. Calif., Santa Cruz, 1973; MA in Integral Counseling Psychology, Calif. Inst. Integral Studies, San Francisco, 1976; MEd in Secondary Edn., U. Nev., Las Vegas, 1979; 3 level cert. Feuerstein's Instrumental, Enrichment Program; postgrad., U. Sarasota and U. Houston. Cert. secondary edn. tchr. ESL, history, English Tex., guidance counselor Tex. Edn. Agy., nat. bd. counselor, lic. marriage and family therapist Tex., profl. counselor Tex., bd. approved supr., Medicaid provider, CHIPS, CPS. Mem. tchr. corps., vol. VISTA, Las Vegas, Nev., 1976-79; family counselor, English tutor Diocese of Matamoros and Valle Hermoso Tamps, Mexico, Cath. Family Svcs. and Vol. Ednl. and Social Svcs., Amarillo, Tex., 1980-82; grad. asst. Pan Am. U., Brownsville, Tex., 1983-84; at-risk program, low-level reading instr. Brownsville Ind. Sch. Dist., 1984-94; basic skills instr. James Pace High Sch., Brownsville; pres. Alternative Edn. Ctr/Brownsville Ind. Sch. Dist., 1994—2005; ESL/inclusion tchr. Dr. Juliet V. Garcia Middle Sch., 2005—. Counselor and psychotherapist Family Effectiveness and Devel. Program, Kids in Crisis, Teenage Crisis Hotline, La Casa Esperanza Home for Boys; basic adult reading instr. Southmost Coll.; ESL, lang. arts tchr. Alternative Ctr.; at-risk tchr., pvt. practice counselor, Brownsville Ind. Sch. Dist. Family Ctrs., 1994—1998; part-time counselor Holistic Mind and Health Inst.,

Brownsville, 1998; counselor, psychotherapist, contract worker, counselor supr., chem. dependency counselor Recovery Ctr., Cameron County Housing Authority, 1999-2001, Citadel Group, 2000-03; Medicaid provider, approved supr. LPC interns, LMFT assocs.; supr. Weslaco, Deer Oaks Mental Health Assocs., 2002-04, Fed. Bur. Prisons, Tex. Commn. Alcohol/Drug Prevention prog. counselor, supr. recovery ctr., 2003-06. Contbr. articles to profl. jours. in U.S. and Mex. including Integracion Integral, Journey in Matamoros. Vol. VISTA, 1976-79, VISTA Tchr. Corps, Las Vegas, Peace Corps, Thailand, 1979, Vol. Adin./Soc. Svc., Tex., Mex., 1980-82. With USN, 1952-56, medic neuropsychiatric wards San Diego and Guam. Recipient scholarship U. Calif.-Santa Cruz, 1971-73, U. Nev. tchr. corps scholar, 1977-79; named grad. asst. Calif. Inst. Integral Studies, 1974-76. Home: PO Box 3941 Brownsville TX 78523-3941 also: Country Club 2009 Madero Dr Brownsville TX 78526-1734 Office Phone: 956-548-0028 ext. 112. E-mail: berniesanta@sbcglobal.net. *Waking up is really the seed of perfection, of personal and transpersonal realization - involution precedes evolution! to remain asleep, 'waking-sleep' (inconscience) leads to complacency, dry rot, and moral decay. To be is to do and to do IS. In the final analysis, last judgment, what shall we - yes, you and I contribute to our fellowman, to posterity? - we often die before giving birth to ourselves - truly to be reborn is not easy; we create, instead, an intense paradox, toward life, toward our destiny (i.e., a paradoxical process of self denial instead of one of genuine self interest, self-realization,-actualization, ad infinitum, in tune with spirit, the cosmos...'Like trees', we begin with a seed. Some do not develop at all. Some die young. And some grow into towering heights with many flourishing branches).*

**SANTANA, CARLOS,** guitarist; b. Autlan de Navarro, Mexico, July 20, 1947; Guitarist Santana Mgmt., San Rafael, Calif., 1987—. Prin. Guts and Grace Records, 1993. Played guitar in Tijuana nightclubs, recorded with Mike Bloomfield and Al Kooper's Super Session, founder, guitarist rock band Santana, 1966—, appeared at Woodstock Festival, 1969, rec. artist Columbia Records, 1969—97, albums include Santana, 1968, Abraxas, 1970, Santana III, Caravanserai, 1972, Welcome, 1973, Greatest Hits, 1974, Barboletta, 1974, Lotus, 1975, Amigos, 1976, Festival, Moonflower, 1977, Inner Secrets, 1979, Marathon, 1979, Swing of Delight, 1980, Zebop, 1981, Shango, 1982, Havana Moon, 1983, Beyond Appearances, 1985, Freedom, 1987, Viva Santana!, 1988, Doin' It, 1990, Spirits Dancing In the Flesh, 1990, Milagro, 1992, Brothers, 1994, Sacred Fire: Live in South America, 1995, Dance of the Rainbow Serpent, 1995, Supernatural, 1999 (Grammy award for Song of Yr., 2000, Grammy award for Record of Yr., 2000, Grammy award for Album of Yr., 2000), Shaman, 2002, All That I Am, 2005, solo albums include Devadip Carlos-Oneness: Silver Dreams, Golden Reality, 1979, Blues for Salvador, 1987 (Grammy award for Best Instrumental Rock Performance, 1989), appeared in film Soul to Soul, 1971, Love and Music, 1971, Fillmore, 1972, Dominoes: An Uncensored Journey Through the 60s, The All-Star Reggae Session, 1988, Santana: Viva Santana (A Conversation with Carlos), 1989, Carlos Santana: Sacred Fire: Live in Mexico, 1993, History of Rock 'N' Roll, Vol. 6, History of Rock 'N' Roll, Vol. 7, 1995, Blue Note-A Story of Modern Jazz, 1996, Ricky Martin: One Night Only, 1999, 1999, world-wide concert tours with Santana Band, performed and recorded with Buddy Miles, Herbie Hancock, McCoy Tyner, John McLaughlin, Jose Feliciano, Wayne Shorter and Alice Coltrane, Aretha Franklin, Olatunji; rec. artist: Arista Records. Named to Hall of Fame, NAACP Image award, 2006, Rock and Roll Hall of Fame, 1998; recipient Gold Medal award, 1977, Century award Billboard Mag., 1996, Spl. Achievement award ALMA, 1999, Legend Award, World Music Awards, 2005. Office: Santana Mgmt PO Box 10348 San Rafael CA 94912-0348 *Keep an open heart, focus on the positive, be true to your innermost feelings, but most of all make time to visit the Lord within.*\*

**SANTANA, JOHAN ALEXANDER,** professional baseball player; b. Tovar Merida, Venezuela, Mar. 13, 1979; Pitcher Minnesota Twins, 2000—. Recipient Cy Young Award, Am. League, 2004. Achievements include led Am. League in strikeouts (265), ERA (2.61), 2004. Office: c/o Minnesota Twins Metrodome 34 Kirby Puckett Place Minneapolis MN 55415\*

**SANTANELLA, RICHARD CHARLES, JR.,** music educator; b. Rockville, Conn., Mar. 11, 1981; s. Richard Charles and Lynn Ann Santanella. BS in Music Edn., BA in Music, U. Conn., 2004. Cert. tchr. Conn. Instrumental music tchr. Met. Learning Ctr., Bloomfield, Conn., 2004—. Mem.: Kappa Kappa Psi (fundraising coord. 2001—02). Avocations: music, fishing, skiing, boating. Office: Met Learning Ctr 1551 Blue Hills Ave Bloomfield CT 06002 Home: 174 Candlewood Dr Enfield CT 06082 Personal E-mail: richsantanella@yahoo.com.

**SANTANELLO, PATRICIA JANE,** theater educator; b. Teaneck, N.J., July 3, 1953; d. Peter Angelo and Norma Marie Santanello; m. Theodore Paul Shannon, Mar. 23, 2004; stepchildren: Jody Lynn Shannon, Theodore Philip Shannon, Alida Theodora Shannon, Trevor Paul Shannon; children: John Edward Spiker, Stephanie Grace Spiker. BA, Ohio State U., Columbus, 1975, BS in Edn., 1979, MA, 1995. Lang. arts tchr. St. Mary Magdalene Sch., Columbus, Ohio, 1979—80; English, speech tchr. Lancaster H.S., Ohio, 1987—90; dir., theatre Groveport Madison H.S., Ohio, 1990—95, Dublin Scioto H.S., Ohio, 1995—. Trustee Ednl. Theatre Assn., 2002—05, leadership coach, 2005—; bd. dirs. Ohio Edn. Theatre Assn., 1991—, Contemp. Am. Theatre Co., Columbus, Ohio. Duplicating chmn. Theil Meml. Tournament, Dublin, Ohio; com. mem. Festival of Trees, Columbus, Ohio; venue mgr. First Night Columbus, Ohio, 2001. Fulbright Meml. Fund Scholar, 2003. Mem.: Sr. Theatre League Am., Order of the Ea. Star. Episcopalian. Avocations: theater, piano, antiques, writing. Home: 5600 Maleka Ct Columbus OH 43235 Office: Dublin Scioto HS 4000 Hard Rd Dublin OH 43016 E-mail: santanello_patricia@mail.dublin.k12.oh.us.

**SANTANGELO, GASPARE CHARLES,** education educator, retired principal; b. N.Y.C., June 1, 1937; s. Joseph and Rose Santangelo; m. Josephine A. Ciaulli, June 30, 1960; children: Christina, Robert De Lia Jr. children: Steven, Robert, Joseph, Philip. BS, St. Francis Coll., N.Y.C., 1958; MS, SUNY, New Paltz, 1966; PhD, Pacific Western U., L.A., 1990. Cert. tchr. N.Y., supt. schs. Calif., sch. dist. administr. N.Y. Tchr. and asst. prin. South Huntington (N.Y.) Schs., 1959—68; administrv. asst. to the supt. of schs. San Diego City Schs., 1968—71; tchr. and prin. South Country Schools, Bellport, NY, 1971—92; assoc. prof. adn. Dowling Coll., Oakdale, NY, 1972—2003. Dir. Ctr. for Human Interaction, East Patchogue, NY, 1982—99. Author: (training manual) A Rational Approach to Stress Management, 1984, (instructional manual) A Nation in Crisis AIDS: Identifying the Risks, 1988. Achievement in Sci. fellow, Nat. Inst. Sci., 1966. Personal E-mail: gcsant@aol.com.

**SANTANGELO, MARIO VINCENT,** retired dentist; b. Youngstown, Ohio, Oct. 5, 1931; s. Anthony and Maria (Zarlenga) S. Student, U. Pitts., 1949-51; DDS, Loyola U. Chgo., 1955, MS, 1960. Instr. Loyola U., 1957-60, asst. prof., 1960-66, assoc. prof., 1966-70, chmn. dept. radiology, 1962-70, dir. dental aux. utilization program, 1963-70, chmn. dept. oral diagnosis, 1967-70, asst. dean, 1969-70; pvt. practice Chgo., 1960-70; ret., 1970. Conn. Cert. Bd. Am. Dental Assts. Assn., 1967-75, VA Rsch. Hosp., 1969-75; counselor Chgo. Dental Assts. Assn., 1966-69; mem. dental student tng. adv. com. divsn. dental health USPHS, HEW, 1969-71; cons. dental edn. rev. com. NIH, 1971-72; cons. region IV, USPHS, HEW, Atlanta, 1973-76, region V, Chgo., 1973-77; mem. Commn. on Dental Edn. and Practice, Fedn. Dentaire Internat., 1984-92; mem. bd. visitors Washington U. Sch. Dental Medicine, St. Louis, 1974-76; mem. project staff Dental Edn. in the U.S., 1976. Contbr. articles to dental jours. 1st Lt. USAF, 1955—56, Capt. USAF, 1956—57. Recipient Dr. Harry Strusser Meml. award NYU Coll. Dentistry, 1985. Fellow Am. Coll. Dentists (life); mem. ADA (sec. coun. dental edn. 1971-81, acting sec. 1981-82, sec. 1982-90, dir. 1990-91, asst. sec. commn. on dental accreditation 1975-81, acting sec. 1981-82, sec. 1982-90, dir. 1990-92, acting sec. commn. continuing dental edn. 1981-82, sec. 1982-90, dir. 1990-92), Ill. State Dental Assn. (life), Chgo. Dental Assn. (life), AMA (edn. work group 1982-86), Assembly Specialized Accrediting Bodies (coun. on postsecondary accreditation 1981-92, award of merit 1992), Am. Assn.

Dental Schs., Odontographic Soc. Chgo. (life), Am. Acad. Oral Pathology, Am. Acad. Dental Radiology, Can. Dental Assn. (commn. on dental accreditation award of merit 1992), Am. Acad. Oral Medicine, Am. Assn. Dental Examiners (hon.), Blue Key, Omicron Kappa Upsilon, Xi Psi Phi. Home: 1440 N Lake Shore Dr Chicago IL 60610-1626

**SANTAOLALLA, GUSTAVO,** musician, composer, record producer; b. Buenos Aires; Founder Surco Records, LA, 1997. Recordings: Santaolla, 1982, GAS, 1995, Roncoco, 1998; composer of movie soundtracks of Amores perros, 2000, 21 Grams, 2003, Diarios de motociclata (Motorcycle Diaries), 2004, Brokeback Mountain, 2005 (Oscar award for best original score, Acad. Motion Pictures Arts & Sciences, 2006); producer for Carnabailito (Gary Kerpel), Nuevo (Kronos Quartet). Named one of 25 Most Influential Hispanics, Time Mag., 2005. Mailing: Surco Records 1501 Baxter St Los Angeles CA 90026

**SANTEE, DALE WILLIAM,** lawyer, air force officer; b. Washington, Pa., Mar. 28, 1953; s. Robert Erwin and Elsbeth Emma (Bantleon) S.; married; 1 child, Enri De'Von; m. Junko Mori, June 2, 1992. BA, Washington & Jefferson Coll., 1975; MA, U. No. Ariz., 1982; JD, U. Pitts., 1978. Bar: Pa. 1978, US Ct. Mil. Appeals 1979, Calif. 1989. Floor mgr., commn. salesman J.C. Penney Co., Washington, Pa., 1971-76; asst. mgr. Rach Enterprises, Charleroi, Pa., 1977-78; legal intern Washington County Pub. Defender; commd. 2d lt. USAF, 1979, advanced through grades to col., 2001; from asst. staff judge advocate to area def. counsel Luke Air Force Base, Ariz., 1979-81; claims officer 343 Combat Support Group/Judge Advocate, Eielson AFB, Alaska, 1981-83; sr. staff legal adviser Dept. Vet. Affairs, Washington, 1983-89; asst. staff judge advocate Mil. Justice div. Air Force Judge Advocate Gen.'s Office, Washington, 1986-89, 63CSG/Judge Advocate, Norton Air Force Base, Calif., 1989-90; dep. pub. defender Juvenile div. San Diego County, 1990-93, dep. alt. pub. defender, 1993-98; asst. staff judge advocate 452 AMW, March Air Res. Base, Calif., 1991-99, staff judge advocate, 1999-2001; supervising dep., alt. pub. defender Conflict Parent-Child Office, 1998-2001, dep. alt. pub. defender, 2001—; sr. IMA 21 AF/JA, Mc Guire AFB, NJ, 2001—03, HQ Air Res. Pers. Ctr., Denver, 2003—04, HQ PACAF/JA, Hickam AFB, 2004—. V.p. Neuer Enterprises, Nanjemoy, Md., 1983-89; participant Mgmt. Devel. Seminar, 1988. Mem. San Diego County Rep. Party; pres., co-chmn. legis. com. PTA Zamorano Elem. Sch., San Diego, chmn. SITE com.; mem. San Diego County Child Abuse Coord. Coun., San Diego County Commn. on Children and Youth, San Diego County Juvenile Ct. Mental Health Task Force, San Diego County Unified Sch. Dist. Parent Adv. Coun.; bd. dirs. San Diego County Youth Ct. Program, Pub. Defenders Assn., Train Ct. Apptd. Spl. Advocates for Voices for Children, McGill Ctr. Creative Problem Solving Youth Curriculum Com. Decorated Air Force Commendation medal, 1981, 89, Air Force Meritorious Svc. medal, 1991, 96, 99, 2001, 2003, Air Force Achievement medal, 2000; named Outstanding Young Man of Am., U.S. Jaycees, Montgomery, Ala., 1981; acad. scholar Washington & Jefferson Coll., 1971-75, Beta scholar Washington & Jefferson Coll., 1974, Pa. Senatorial scholar Pa. Senate, 1975-78; named Juvenile Justice Commn. Atty of Yr., 1997; recipient Clara Shortridge Foltz award ABA/Nat. Legal Aid and Defender Assn., 1999, Judge Advocates Assn. Outstanding Career Armed Svcs. Atty. award, 2000. Mem. Pa. Bar Assn., Calif. Bar Assn., San Diego County Bar Assn., San Diego County Psych-Law Soc. Avocations: swimming, softball, stamp and coin collecting, foreign travel. Office: 8525 Gibbs Dr Ste 201 San Diego CA 92123 Office Phone: 858-974-5819. E-mail: Dale.Santee@sdcounty.ca.gov.

**SANTELLE, JAMES LEWIS,** prosecutor; b. Milw., Sept. 10, 1958; s. James Nathaniel and Carol Jean (Hasley) S. BA, Marquette Univ., 1980; JD, Univ. Chgo., 1983. Bar: Wis. 1983, U.S. Dist. Ct. (ea. and we. dist.) 1983, U.S. Ct. Appeals (7th cir.) 1983. Clerk Hon. Judge Robert W. Warren, Milw., 1983-85; asst. U.S. atty. Ea. Dist. Wis., Milw., 1985—, civil divsn. chief, 1993—99, interim U.S. atty., 2001—01; prin. dep. dir. Exec. Office U.S. Attys., U.S. Dept. Justice, Washington, 1999—2001, exec. asst. U.S. atty., 2002—03; civil divsn. chief We. Dist. Mich., Grand Rapids, 2003—04. Mem. profl. responsibility com., investigator Wis. Bd. of Attys., 1993-99. Editor: The Milw. Lawyer, 1986-92. Bd. dirs. Waukesha County Coun. Alcoholism and Other Drug Abuse, 1993-99; citizen counselor Badger Boys State, 1986—; coach Wis. Bar Found. High Sch. Mock Trial Tournament, 1986-99. Mem.: Milw. Bar Assn., 7th Cir. Bar Assn. (liaison 2001—), Ea. Dist. Wis. Bar Assn. (sec. 2001—02). Avocations: running, swimming. Office: US Atty Office 517 E Wisconsin Ave Rm 530 Milwaukee WI 53202-4580 Office Phone: 414-297-1700. Business E-Mail: james.santelle@usdoj.gov.

**SANTER, BENJAMIN DAVID,** atmospheric scientist; b. Washington D.C., June 3, 1955; BS Environ. Scis. with 1st class honors, U. East Anglia, Norwich, Eng., 1976; NATO Rsch. Studentship, U. East Anglia, 1977, PhD in Climatology, 1987. Sr. rsch. assoc. Sch. Environ. Scis. U. East Anglia, Norwich, Eng., 1978-79, rsch. assoc. climatic rsch. unit, 1983-87; project engr. dept. new techs., air pollution and Dornier Sys. GmbH, Friedrichshafen, Germany, 1980-83; postdoct., rsch. scientist Max-Planck Inst. Meteorologie, Hamburg, Germany, 1987-92; physicist earth and environ. scis. directorate Lawrence Livermore Nat. Lab., Livermore, Calif., 1992—. Expert witness German Bundestag Enquete Commn. Hearings on Greenhouse-Gas-Induced Climate Change, Bonn, Germany, 1992; cons. Battelle Pacific Northwest Lab., 1992-93, mem. sci. adv. panel climate change, data and detection program NOAA, 1995—; mem. Climate Variability and Predictability Numerical Experimentation Group, 1995—; participant numerous confs., workshops; lectr. in field. Co-author: Proceedings of NATO Advanced Study Institute on Physically-Based Modelling and Simulation of Climate and Climatic Change, 1988, Science and Engineering on Supercomputers, 1990, Supercomputer '90, Greenhouse-Gas-Induced Climate Change: A Critical Appraisal of Simulations and Observations, 1991 Global Warming Concern for Tomorrow, 1993, Agricultural Dimensions of Global Climate Change, 1993, Dahlem Workshop on Global Changes in the Perspective of the Past, 1993, Climate Change int the Intra-American Sea, 1993, Communicating About Climate: the Story of the Model Evaluation Consortium for Climate Assessment, 1997; mem. editl. bd. Climatic Change, 1996—; contbr. numerous articles to profl. jours., chpts. to books. MacArthur fellow John D. and Catherine T. MacArthur Found., 1998; Ford Travel scholar, 1974; recipient Outstanding Scientific Paper award U.S. Dept. Commerce Environ. Rsch. Lab. Nat. Oceanic and Atmospheric Adminstrn., 1997, Norbert Gerbier-MUMM Internat. award World Meteorol. Orgn., 1998, E.O. Lawrence award U.S. Dept. Energy, 2002. Mem. Am. Geophys. Union. Achievements include research in climate modeling and greenhouse-gas effects supporting the hypothesis that human activity contributes to global warming. Office: Lawrence Livermore Nat Lab PCMDI PO Box 808 L-264 Livermore CA 94551-0808 Home: 2160 Goldenrod Ln San Ramon CA 94583-5555 Fax: (925) 422-7675. E-mail: santer1@llnl.gov.

**SANTIAGO, JOSE E.,** film producer, writer, director, educator; s. Diego Santiago and Angela Falcon; m. Louise Colon, Jan. 12, 1960; children: Angela Rebecca, Margaret Linda. BA, Holy Names U., Oakland, Calif., 2001. Tchr. MIT Acad., Vallejo, Calif., 1999—; writer, prodr., dir. Image 8 Films, Vallejo, Calif., 2004—. Prodr.: (film) Nemesis. Vol. Wheel Chair Found., Danville, Calif., 2004—04. Sgt. U.S. Army, 1977—83. Mem.: Amateur Radio Relay League (licentiate). Office Phone: 707-334-0793. E-mail: josesantiago@image8films.com.

**SANTIAGO, MELISSA,** neuroscientist; d. Thomas John and Nancy Paige Caracuzzo; m. Santiago Robert, May 4, 1991; children: Bobby, Michael. BA, SUNY, New Paltz, 1984—88; PhD, U. Miami Sch. Medicine, Fla., 1992—99. Lead scientist post doctoral assoc. AstraZeneca Pharmaceuticals, Wilmington, Del., 1999—2001, sr. sci. mgr., 2001—. Contbr. articles and papers to profl. jours. and pubs. Recipient Faculty Assn. award, U. Miami Sch. Medicine, 1997—98, Symposia Honoree, Subtypes of Muscarinic Receptors Internat. Symposia Series, 1998, Performance award, AstraZeneca Pharmaceuticals, 2002—06; grantee, NIH, 1992—95, Grad. Sch. Tuition scholarship, U. Miami Sch. Medicine, 1992—99. Mem.: Soc. Neurosci., Internat. Soc.

Bipolar Disorders, Soc. Biol. Psychiatry. Achievements include research in Biotinylated m4 receptor ligand. Office: AstraZeneca Pharmaceuticals 1800 Concord Pike Wilmington DE 19850 Office Phone: 800-456-3669. Personal E-mail: mebo91@yahoo.com.

**SANTIAGO, RAYMOND,** library director, educator; b. NYC, July 13, 1949; s. Raymond and Livia Santiago; m. Crystal C. Capelis, May 15, 1979; 1 child, Jason Esrael. BFA, Rochester (N.Y.) Inst. Tech., 1974; MLS, SUNY, Buffalo, 1975. Co-chair, head non-print svcs. World U., San Juan, PR, 1978-84; libr. Tampa-Hillsborough Pub. Libr. Sys., Fla., 1984-88, section mgr. Fla., 1988-90; supr. libr. svcs. Miami-Dade Pub. Libr. Sys., Fla., 1990-91, asst. dir. Fla., 1991—98, dir. Fla., 1998—. Adj. faculty Sch. of Libr. and Info. Sci., U. South Fla., 1994—. Named Libr. of Yr., Libr. Jour., 2003. Mem. ALA, Pub. Libr. Assn., Fla. Libr. Assn. Home: 1300 El Rado St Coral Gables FL 33134-2222 Office: Miami-Dade Pub Libr Sys 101 W Flagler St Miami FL 33130-1504 Office Phone: 305-375-5184. E-mail: SANTIAGOR@miamidade.gov.\*

**SANTIAGO-HUDSON, RUBEN,** actor; b. Lackawanna, NY, Nov. 24, 1956; m. Jeannie Santiago; 2 children. BA in Theatre, Wayne State U. Appeared in Broadway play Jelly's Last Jam; appeared in off-Broadway plays including East Texas Hot Links, Measure for Measure, Ceremonies in Dark Old Men; appeared in plays including Seven Guitars (Tony award winner 1996); dir. Seven Guitars, 2006; solo show nat. tour and TV movie (writer, prodr., actor) Lackawanna Blues; appeared in films including Coming to America, 1988, Blown Away, 1994, Bleeding Hearts, 1994, The Devil's Advocate, 1997, A Gut Feeling, 1999, Shaft, 2000, White Man's Burden, Domestic Disturbance, 2001, Winning Girls Through Psychic Mind Control, 2002, Brother's Shadow, 2006; TV series Spawn 1997, Michael Hayes, 1997; TV films include Which Way Home, 1991, Solomon & Shea, 1995, The Return of Hunter, 1995, Daddy's Girl, 1996, Rear Window, 1998, The Hunt for the Unicorn Killer, 1999, The Inspector General, 2000, American Tragedy, 2000, The Red Sneakers, 2002, Little John, 2002, Their Eyes Were Watching God, 2005; TV guest appearances on Life Goes On, 1990, Another World, 1990-93, The Cosby Mystries, 1994, NYPD Blue, 1995, 99, NY Undercover, 1994, 96, Touched By An Angel, 1999, The West Wing, 1999, Third Watch, 1999, All My Children, 2001, 2002, Law & Order, 1990, 94, 99, 2001, 2003, Wild Card, 2004, Law & Order: Special Victims Unit, 2005. Office: Hardin & Curtis 850 7th Ave Ste 405 New York NY 10019-5230\*

**SANTILLANO, MARK RAMON,** dancer, educator; b. Saint Louis, Sept. 26, 1963; s. Antonio B. and Barbara Jean Santillano; m. Solveig Ruth Olsen, Nov. 25, 1997; 1 child, Ella Ray. BFA in Dance, BS in Comm., SW Mo. State U., Springfield, 1986; MALS, Wesleyan U., Middletown, Conn., 2005. Dancer Dance Kaleidoscope, Indpls., 1986—89; actor West Side Story (nat. tour), 1990, A Chorus Line (nat. tour), 1991—93; dancer Pilobolus Dance Theatre, Washington Depot, Conn., 1995—98; dancer, choreographer Beef and Boards Dinner Theatre, Indpls., 1995—98; artist-in-residence SW Mo. State U., Springfield, Mo., 1998—2000; co-artistic dir., choreographer SoMar Dance Works, Erie, Pa., 1999—; asst. prof. Mercyhurst Coll., Erie, 2000—; actor, dance capt. The King and I (internat. tour). Bd. dirs. Erie Dance Consortium, 2003—. Mem.: Am. Coll. Dance Festival Assn. (bd. dirs. 2005—06), Actors Equity Assn. Office: Mercyhurst Coll 501 E 38th St Erie PA 16546 Office Phone: 814-824-2176.

**SANTIN, ANTONIO,** plastic surgeon; b. Mexico City, Mex., Mar. 1, 1957; s. Guillermo Eduardo Santin and Lorna Ann Hodges; m. Bernadette Schnippenkoetter, Sept. 14, 1985; children: Daniel, Oliver, Thomas, Jacqueline. MD, U. Nacional Autonomo Mex., Mexico City, 1984. Diplomate Am. Bd. Plastic Surgery, 1997. Craniofacial surgery U. Mo., Kansas City, 1994—95; pres. Mont. Plastic Surgery Ctr., Great Falls, 1996—. Legis. com. Mont. Med. Assn., Great Falls, 2005—06. Mem.: Am. Soc. Plastic Surgery (state liason legis. com. 2000—06). Achievements include first to craniofacial surgery and microsurgery. Office: Montana Plastic Surgery Ctr 1600 9th St S Great Falls MT 59405 Office Phone: 406-727-6363. Office Fax: 406-727-6372. E-mail: asantn@mtpsc.com.

**SANTINA, DALIA,** nutritionist, writer, skin care specialist; b. Amman, Jordan, Sept. 24, 1954; d. Mahmoud Dauod Abbasi, Widad Abbasi; m. Mohammed Shafiq Santina. BA in English Lit., U. Riyadh, Saudi Arabia, 1977; diploma in computer programming, Western Bus. Coll., 1980; diploma in Skin Aesthetics, Career Acad. Beauty, 1989; PhD in Holistic Nutrition, Clayton Coll. Natural Health, 1994. Cert. paramedical acne 1990, glycolic acid services 1991, mgmt. aging and sun-damaged skin 1992, natural pharmacology 1992, aesthetic peeling 1992, oxygenation of the skin 1993, lymphatic drainage massage techniques 1994, homeopathic estheticology 1994, iridology diploma 1995, cert. chem. peels 1996, hydrotherapy 1997, glycolic treatments 1998, diploma in iridology 2003, cert. in herbology 2003. Exec. asst. to v.p. Am. Health Ctr., Newport Beach, Calif., 1988—89; skin care co. Skinclub, Huntington Beach, Calif., 1991—96; lectr. holistic nutrition/skin health issues, 1999—. Translator computer sys. tng. manuals, Dallas, 1983—84; tech. translator England and No. Ireland, 1984. Author: Holistic Skin Is...In, 2001, Super Supplements for Skin, Body & Mind, 2004; contbr. articles to profl. jours. Recipient Gold medal in Table Tennis, Sports Bd., Kuwait, 1972. Avocations: horseback riding, reading, antiques. Personal E-mail: dalia4skin@msn.com.

**SANTINI, DEBRAH ANN,** art educator, artist; BFA in Painting, U. Mass., 1983, MFA in Printmaking, 1994; postgrad., Pratt Inst., 1983-84; MEd in Printmaking, U. Hartford, 1988. Cert. tchr. 5-12, Mass., K-12 (provisional), Conn. Art tchr. Granby (Conn.) M nl. H.S., 1989-90, Bulfield (Conn.) H.S., 1990-91; tchr. U. Mass, Amherst, 1991-93; asst. prof. State U. West Ga., Carrollton, 1994—. Artist-in-residence Bridgeport Mus. Art, Sci. and Industry, 1988, Lit. Showcase, Bristol, R.I., 1990, Connecticut Loves to Read, Windsor, Conn., 1991, Internat. Reading Assn., San Antonio, 1993, Am. Book Sellers Assn., Chgo., 1995, 96, Southeastern Book Sellers Assn., Nashville, 1996, So. Festival Books: Tenn. Humanities Coun., 1996, Westside Magnet Sch., LaGrange, Ga., 1997, 5th Annual Children's Storytelling Festival, Mableton, Ga., 1997; adj. prof. U. Hartford, Conn., 1991-92; lectr. in field. One-woman shows include Josoloff Gallery, U. Hartford, 1987, Springfield (Mass.) Ctrl. Gallery, 1988, Western New England Coll., Springfield, 1989, Fitchburg (Mass.) Mus. Fine Arts, 1993, Am. Internat. Coll., Springfield, 1993; group shows include Taipei Mus. Arts, 1988, 90, New Britain (Conn.) Mus. Art, 1989, U. Wis., Kenosha, 1991, Okla. State U., Stillwater, 1991, Associated Artists, Winston-Salem, N.C., 1992, San Jacinto Coll., Houston, 1993, Print Club Albany, Schenectady, N.Y., 1995, Arno Maris Gallery, Westfield, Mass., 1995, Artlink, Fort Wayne, Ind., 1996, Rolling Stone Press, Atlanta, 1996, 97, Appalachian State U., Boone, N.C., 1997, Rutgers U., New Brunswick, N.J., 1997, Cultural Ctr. Recoleta, Buenos Aires, 1997, Cultural Ctr. Trapalanda, Rio Cuarto, Cordoba, 1997, Contemporary Art Ctr., Mendoza, 1997, U. Minn., Mpls., 1998, Woman Made Gallery, Chgo., 1998, Visual Arts Alliance Nashville Am. Pop Culture Gallery, 1998, Museao Emilio Caraffa, Cordoba, 1998, Nat. U. Chaco, 1998, Columbus (Ga.) Mus., 1998; represented in permanent collections Gardiner Art Gallery, Okla. State U., Agawam (Mass.) Pub. Libr., Smith Coll. Rare Book Room, Neilson Libr., Northampton, Mass., Cultural Arts Ctr., Douglasville, Ga., Ga. Coll., Milledgeville, Chattahoochee Valley Art Mus., LaGrange; illustrator: The Baby Who Would Not Come Down, 1989, Santa's Secret Helper, 1990, Tulips, 1992, 96, Cinderella, 1994, The Last Dance, 1996, Wishing, 1996, When Young Melissa Sweeps, 1998, Oh, Georgia, Too!, 1998, (mags.) US KIDS, 1991, CRICKET, 1991, READ, 1993, POCKETS, 1998, 99. Recipient Purchase award Cimarron Nat. Works on Paper, 1991, Douglas County Regional Juried Fine Arts Show, 1994, Pressed & Pulled IV, 1995, XIX LaGrange Nat. Biennial Exhbn., 1996, Merit award Springfield Art League 76th Nat. Exhbn., 1995, Overall Excellence award Southeastern Libr. Assn., 1996; Don Freeman Meml. grantee Soc. Children's Book Writers Illustrators, 1987, Mass. Arts Lottery grantee, 1988, Nat. Endowment Arts/Southern Artists Fedn. grantee, 1996.

**SANTINI, JORGE,** mayor; b. San Juan, P.R., 1960; BA, U. P.R.; law degree cum laude, Interam. U. Ptnr. Miranda Cardenas & Córdova, 1986; legal advisor Gov. of P.R., 1994—96; mem. Sen. of P.R.; mayor City of San Juan, 2001—. Chmn. Sen. Jud. Com.; vice-chmn. Govt. and Fed. Affairs Com., Banking, Consumer Affairs, and Pub. Corps. Com. Lt. col. Puerto Rico Nat. Guard. New Progressive Party. Office: PO Box 9024100 San Juan PR 00902-4100

**SANTISTEBAN, JOSEPH HENRY,** human resources specialist; b. N.Y.C., July 15, 1946; s. Mario Santisteban and Antonia (dec.) Rivera; m. Evangelista Pilapil, Oct. 26, 1969 (dec. Dec. 1998); children: Jason, Damien. BA, Chapman U., 1972—74; BS, U. of Nebr., 1982—84; MA, Embry-Riddle Aero. U., 1986—90; PhD, U. of the Philippines, 1988—90. Cert. tchr. Ariz. State Bd. Edn., 1993. Chief master sgt. USAF, 1963—94; sr. staff recruiter Swift Transp. Co., Phoenix, Ariz., 1993—99; recruiting and tng. mgr. ATC Leasing Co. Inc., Phoenix, Ariz., 1999—2000; human resources dir. Ill. Auto Truck Co. Inc., Des Plaines, 2000—. Chief enlisted mgr. U.S. Air Force, Phoenix, 1963—93; coll. instr. Embry-Riddle Aero. U., Phoenix, 1990—93. Translator. Leader Boy Scouts of Am., 1979—2003, CAP, 1986—92, 2003—. Maj. Civil Air Patrol. Decorated Bronze Star Medal w/V Dept. of Def.; recipient Outstanding Cmty. Svc. Award, Ariz. C. of C., 1992, Outstanding Svc. Award, Mayor of Mayaguez, PR, 1998, Presdl. Humanitarian Award, Republic of the Philippines, 1970, Outstanding Leader of the Yr., CAP, 1992, Cert. of Recognition, U.S. Sec. of Def., 1994. Mem.: VFW, York Rite Coll., Philalethes Soc., Air Force Security Police Assn., Smithsonian Inst. (assoc.), Air Force Assn., Shriners, Masons. Home: 2465 Forest View Rd Lindenhurst IL 60046-8720 Office: Illinois Auto Truck Co Inc 1669 Marshall Dr Des Plaines IL 60018-1840 Office Phone: 847-299-1100. Personal E-mail: joe_sandy2000@yahoo.com

**SANTMAN, LEON DUANE,** lawyer, former federal government executive; b. Phila., July 29, 1930; s. Elmer William and Anna Mary (Moffitt) S.; m. Juliet Gloria Peacock, June 16, 1952; 1 dau., Lorri Leigh Santman Myers. BS, U. S., COAST Guard Acad., 1952; LLB, U. Houston, 1953; LLM, George Washington U., 1968. Bar: Tex. 1963, Md. 1974. Commd. ensign U.S. Coast Guard, 1952, advanced through grades to comdr., 1967, ret., 1972; assoc. gen. counsel Cost of Living Council, Washington, 1972-74; asst. gen. counsel U.S. Dept. Transp., Washington, 1974-77; dir. Materials Transp. Bur., 1977-85; dir. ship ops. Maritime Adminstrn., 1985-88. Episcopalian.

**SANTO, FRED M.,** lawyer; b. Bronx, NY, Oct. 24, 1947; BA, SUNY, Binghamton, 1969; JD, Washington Coll. Law, 1973; LLM, Gerogetown U., 1978. Bar: DC 1973, NY 1979. Law clerk to Chief Judge DC Ct. Appeals, 1973; sr. atty. Div. Corp. Fin., SEC, 1974—76; asst. gen. counsel Commodity Futures Trading Commn., 1976—78; with Katten Muchin Zavis Rosenman, NYC, 1979—, ptnr. Mem.: ABA, Managed Futures Assn., Assn. Bar of City NY. Office: Katten Muchin Zavis Rosenman 575 Madison Ave New York NY 10022 Office Phone: 212-940-8720. Office Fax: 212-940-5663. E-mail: fred.santo@kmzr.com.

**SANTOMERO, ANTHONY M.,** retired bank executive, former public policymaker; b. NYC, Sept. 29, 1946; s. Camillo and Jean (Oddo) Santomero; m. Marlena Belviso, Aug. 21, 1971; children: Jill Renee, Marc Anthony. AB, Fordham U., 1968; PhD, Brown U., 1971; EDhe (hon.), Stockholm Sch. Econs., 1992; LHC, U. Rome, 2003. Asst. prof., then assoc. prof., then prof. fin. Wharton Sch., U. Pa., Phila., 1972-84, R.K. Mellon prof. fin. 1984—2002, R.K. Mellon prof. fin. emeritus, 2002—, vice dean, dir. grad. div., 1984-87, dep. dean, 1990-94; dir. Wharton Fin. Instns. Ctr., 1995-2000; pres. Fed. Res. Bank Phila., 2000—06; sr. advisor McKinsey & Co., 2006—. Asst. prof. econs. Baruch Coll., CUNY, 1971—72; vis. prof. European Inst. Advanced Studies Mgmt., Brussels, 1977—78, Stockholm Sch. Econs., 1989—90, U. Rome, Tor Vergata, 1994—97, Ecole Superieure des Scis. Economiques and Commerciales, France, 1977—78; trustee Drexel U.; mem. adv. bd. Penn Inst. Econ. Rsch. Author: Financial Markets, Instruments and Institutions, 1997, 2001, Challenges for Modern Central Banking, 2001; adv. editor Jour. Banking and Fin., 1978—, assoc. editor Jour. Money, Credit and Banking, 1980—2002, Jour. Fin. Svc. Rsch., 2000—, bd. editors Jour. Econs. and Bus., 1979—, European Fin. Mgmt., 1996—, Advances in Internat. Banking and Fin., 1993—, founding co-editor Brookings-Wharton Papers on Fin. Svcs., 1997—2000, adv. bd. European Banking Report, 1994—, Jour. Internat. Econ. Law, 1997—, editl. bd. Open Econs. Rev., 1990—, mem. faculty adv. bd. Jour. Internat. Econ. Law, 1997—, mem. bd. advisory editors Advances in Fin., Investment and Banking, 1992, editl. adv. bd. Jour. Fin. Stability, 2003—; contbr. articles to profl. jours. Bd. dirs. Gr. Phila. C. of C., 2000—06, Mann. Ctr. Performing Arts; chmn. mayor's coun. econ. advisors Phila., 2000—03. Mem.: Am. Econs. Assn., Am. Fin. Assn. Roman Catholic.

**SANTONA, GLORIA,** lawyer; b. Gary, Ind., June 10, 1950; d. Ray and Elvira (Cambeses) S.; m. Douglas Lee Frazier, Apr. 12, 1980. BS in Biochemistry, Mich. State U., 1971; JD, U. Mich., 1977. Bar: Ill. 1977. Atty. McDonald's Corp., Oak Brook, Ill., 1977-82, dir., 1982-86, assoc. gen. counsel, 1986-92, asst. v.p., 1989-93, v.p., sec., dep. gen. counsel, 1996-99, v.p., U.S. gen. counsel, sec., 1999-2001, sr. v.p., gen. counsel, sec., 2001—03, exec. v.p., gen. counsel, sec., 2003—. Mem. ABA, Chgo. Assn., Am. Corp. Counsel Assn., Am. Soc. Corp. Secs. Office: McDonalds Corp 1 McDonalds Plz Oak Brook IL 60523-1911

**SANTONI, RONALD ERNEST,** philosophy educator; b. Arvida, Que., Can., Dec. 19, 1931; s. Fred Albert and Phyllis (Tremaine) S.; m. Marguerite Ada Kiene, June 25, 1955; children: Christina, Marcia, Andrea, Juanita, Jonathan, Sondra. BA, Bishop's U., Lennoxville, Que., 1952; MA, Brown U., 1954; PhD, Boston U., 1961; postgrad., U. Paris-Sorbonne, 1956-57. Asst. prof. philosophy U. Pacific, Stockton, Calif., 1958-61; postdoctoral rsch. fellow Yale U., New Haven, 1961-62; asst. prof. philosophy Wabash Coll., Crawfordsville, Ind., 1962-64; faculty Denison U., Granville, Ohio, 1964—, prof. philosophy, 1968—2002, chmn. dept., 1971-73, 82-84, 92, Maria Theresa Barney chair in philosophy, 1978—, prof. emeritus, 2002—. Peace lectr. Bethel Coll., 1985; vis. scholar in philosophy Cambridge U., Eng., 1986, 90, 94, 97, 99, 2001, vis. lectr. in philosophy, 1990; vis. fellow Clare Hall, Cambridge U., 1986, lit. mem., vis. scholar, 1990, 94, 97, 99, 2001, 2003, 2004, 2006; vis. fellow in philosophy Yale U., 1975, 81, 93-94, 97; keynote speaker 2d Internat. Conf. on Nuclear Free Zones, Cordoba, Spain, 1985; Internat. Studies Assn., London, 1989, speaker and U.S.A. co-chair Internat. conf. Internat. Philosophers for Prevention of Nuclear Omnicide, Moscow, 1990; del. and rapporteur UN meeting of Peace Messenger Orgns., Dagomys, Sochi, USSR, 1991; invited participant Colloquium on Technological Risks to Environment, Montreal, 1993; invited spkr. U. Paris (Sorbonne), 2004, Internat. Conf. Honoring Centenary of J.P. Sarte, Univ. Amiens, France, 2005; spkr. in field. Contbg. author: Current Philosophical Issues: Essays in Honor of C.J. Ducasse, 1966, Towards an Understanding and Prevention of Genocide, 1984, Nuclear War: Philosophical Perspectives, 1985, Genocide: A Critical Bibliographic Review, 1988, Just War, Nonviolence and Nuclear Deterrence: Philosophers on War and Peace, 1992, The Institution of War, 1991, Violence and Human Co-Existence, 1994, Hiroshima's Shadows, 1998, The Encyclopedia of Genocide, 1999, Human Coexistence and Sustainable Development, 2001, Das Sein und das Nichts, 2003, Global Studies Encyclopedia, 2003, Dictionnaire Sartre, 2004, Sartre Today: A Centenary Celebration, 2006, Pourquoi Sartre? 2006, Uber Sartre: Perspektiven und Kritiken, 2005; author: Bad Faith, Good Faith and Authenticity in Sartre's Early Philosophy, 1995, Sartre on Violence: Curiously Ambivalent, 2003; editor, contbr. Religious Language and the Problem of Religious Knowledge, 1968; co-editor Social and Political Philosophy, 1963; contbg. editor Internat on the Holocaust and Genocide; mem. editl. bd. Jour. Peace and Justice Studies; contbr. over 135 publ. in profl. jours. V.p. NAACP, Licking County, 1967; co-organizer Crawfordsville (Ind.) Human Rights Coun., 1962-64; nat. exec. com. Episcopal Peace Fellowship, 1968-78; internat. coun. Internat. Inst. on the Holocaust and Genocide, 1985—; nat. coun. Fellowship of Reconciliation, 1988-89; trustee Margaret Hall Sch., Versailles, Ky., 1972-74; nat. bd. dirs. Promoting Enduring Peace, 1982-2002. Canadian Govt. Overseas fellow Royal Soc. Can., 1956-57; Church Soc. for

Coll. Work faculty fellow, 1961-62; Yale postdoctoral rsch. fellow, 1961-62; Danforth assoc., 1963-64; Soc. for Religion in Higher Edn. postdoctoral fellow, 1972—; Yale rsch. fellow, 1975; guest fellow Berkeley Coll., Yale U., 1975, 81, 93-94, 97, elected assoc. fellow, 1994—; vis. fellow in philosophy Yale U., 1981, 93-94, 97; Robert C. Good faculty fellow Denison U., 1985-86, 2000-01, Robert C. Good faculty fellow, 1993-94; elected life mem. Clare Hall, Cambridge (Eng.) U., 1986; elected mem. High Table, King's Coll., Cambridge U., 1999; recipient Mellon award for disting. faculty Denison U., 1972, Crossed Keys Faculty of Yr. award Denison U., 1986-87; Philosophy, Freedom and Action Conf. held in his honor, 2002. Mem. Am. Philos. Assn., Ch. Soc. for Coll. Work, Soc. for Phenomenology and Existential Philosophy, Internat. Philosophers for Peace (v.p. 1983-85, v.p. cen. div. 1990-91, internat. pres. 1991-96, internat. exec. com. 1996—), Sartre Soc. of N.Am. (exec. com. 1994—), Sartre Circle (coord. 1997—), le groupe d'Etudes Sartriennes, Gandhi-King Soc., Union of Bi-Nat. Profls. Against Omnicide (v.p. 1978—), Concerned Philosophers for Peace (founding 1980—, pres. 1996-97), Fellowship of Reconciliation, Amnesty Internat., OxFam Am., ACLU. Episcopalian. Home: 500 Burg St Granville OH 43023-1005 Office Phone: 740-587-6318. Business E-Mail: santoni@denison.edu. *Gratitude for what one has been given, commitment to personal growth and integrity, some "gracious gall", listening to the world's humiliated, and a recognition that any genuine success is a gift of grace, never fully deserved.*

**SANTOPIETRO, ALBERT ROBERT,** lawyer; b. Providence, Oct. 18, 1948; s. Alfred and Marie (Epifanio) Santopietro; children: Hope, Spencer, Anna. BA, Brown U., 1969; JD, U. Va., 1972. Bar: R.I. 1973, Conn. 1983, Mass. 1997, U.S. Dist. Ct. R.I. 1973, Ill. 1974, U.S. Dist. Ct. Mass. 1997. Atty. Met. Life Ins. Co., Oak Brook, Ill., 1974—75, Seligman Group, N.Y.C., 1975—76, Mut. Benefit Life Ins. Co., Newark, 1976—78, asst. counsel, 1978—81; counsel Aetna Ins. Co., Newark, 1982—91; assoc. counsel Conn. Mutual Life Ins. Co., Hartford, 1991—95; 2d v.p. and assoc. gen. counsel Mass. Mutual, 1995—. Home: 142 Pond Brook Rd Huntington MA 01050-9620 Office: 1500 Main St Ste 2800 Springfield MA 01115 Office Phone: 413-226-1068. Office Fax: 413-226-2068. E-mail: asantopietro@massmutual.com.

**SANTORA, ELLEN DURRIGAN,** education educator; b. Utica, NY, July 20, 1945; d. John Francis and Maude Henrietta Durrigan; m. John Anthony Santora, Apr. 1, 1967. BA in Polit. Sci., LeMoyne Coll., 1966; MS in Edn., SUNY, Oswego, N.Y., 1982; PhD, Pa. State U., 1997. Cert. secondary social studies tchr. NY. Am. studies and world history tchr. Liverpool (NY) Ctrl. Sch. Dist., 1974—75; mid. sch. social studies and reading tchr. Altmar Parish (NY) Williamstown Ctrl. Sch. Dist., Parish NY, 1975—76, Baldwinsville (NY) Academy and Ctrl. Sch. Dist., 1976—85; mid. sch. social studies and English tchr. Whisman Elem. Sch. Dist., Mountain View, Calif., 1985—91, Winston (Oreg.) Dillard Sch. Dist., 1991—93; grad. rsch. and tchg. asst. Pa. State U., State College, 1993—96; asst. prof. U. Ala., Tuscaloosa, 1997—2000; asst. prof. Warner Sch. Edn. and Human Devel. U. Rochester, NY, 2000—05. Contbr. articles to profl. publs. Advisor Marshall H.S., Law, Govt. and Justice Acad., Rochester, 2001—05. Named Tchr. of the Yr., Crittenden Mid. Sch., 1989—90; recipient Dean Betty Poole Svc. Jr. Faculty Svc. award, Warner Grad. Sch. Edn., U. Rochester, 2002; fellow, Pa. State U., 1993—96; grantee, US Dept. Edn., 2001—05, Susan B. Anthony Inst. for Gender and Womn's Studies, 2001; Regents scholar, NY State, 1962, Instrnl. Tech. grantee, U. Ala., 1999, Fulbright-Hays Seminars Abroad fellow, U.S. Dept. Edn., 1990. Mem.: AAUW, Coll. and U. Faculty Assembly (bd. dirs. 2002—05), Am. Ednl. Rsch. Assn. (Outstanding Dissertation award 1999, Outstanding Paper award 1999, 2005), Nat. Coun. Social Studies, Pi Lambda Theta, Phi Gamma Mu, Phi Delta Kappa. Roman Catholic. Avocations: travel, gardening, showing and breeding St. Bernards and briards. Office Phone: 585-275-5053. Office Fax: 585-473-7598. Business E-Mail: esantora@its.rochester.edu.

**SANTORE, JOSEPH,** painter; BFA, Phila. Coll. Art; MFA, Yale Univ. Faculty NY Studio Sch., NYC. One-man shows include Phila. Art Alliance, NY Studio Sch., exhibited in group shows at 170th Ann. Exhbn., NAD, Whitney Biennial, 1991, Represented in permanent collections Met. Mus. Art, Cin. Art Mus., Phoenix Art Mus. Recipient Am. Acad. Arts and Letters award, Ingram Merrill award; grantee NY Found. of Arts fellowship, Guggenheim fellowship. Office: NY Studio Sch 8 W 8th St New York NY 10011 Office Phone: 212-673-6466. Office Fax: 212-777-0996.

**SANTORO, ANTHONY RICHARD,** history professor; b. Feb. 2, 1939; m. Carol Lynne; 1 child, Melissa. AB, Coll. of the Holy Cross, 1960; MA, U. Calif., 1962; PhD, Rutgers U., 1978. Instr. history Monmouth Coll., West Long Branch, N.J., 1963-67; v.p. for adminstrn., chair depts history and philosophy, registrar Briarcliff Coll., Briarcliff Manor, N.Y., 1967-77; v.p. Devel. and Coll. Rels. Ladycliff Coll., Highland Falls, NY, 1977—78; pres. St. Joseph's Coll., Standish, Maine, 1979-87, Christopher Newport U., Newport News, Va., 1987-96, pres. emeritus, disting. prof. history, 1996—. Author: Theophanes Chronograhia: A Chronicle of 8th Century Byzantium, 1982; co-author: An Eyewitness to History: The Short History of Nikephoros the Patriarch of Constantinople, 1991, (4-track DVD) Triumph of the Will (Leni Riefenstahl), 2001. Office: Christopher Newport U McMurran Hall 217 1 University Pl Newport News VA 23606-2998 Office Phone: 757-594-7709. Office Fax: 757-594-7718. Business E-Mail: santoro@cnu.edu.

**SANTORO, FRANK ANTHONY,** lawyer; b. Plainfield, N.J., Dec. 14, 1941; s. Frank V. and Nancy M. (Scavuzzo) S.; m. Patricia Ferrante, Oct. 10, 1964; children—Frank, Jennifer. B.S. in Chemistry, Seton Hall U., 1963, J.D., 1970. Patent atty. Exxon Corp., Linden, N.J., 1970-73; sole practice, South Plainfield, N.J., 1973—; atty. Planning Bd. Borough South Plainfield, 1971-73; mcpl. prosecutor Borough South Plainfield, 1972. Councilman Borough South Plainfield, 1977-79, mcpl. atty., 1985-93; mcpl. prosecutor South Plainfield Republican Orgn., 1981-84. Mem. Middlesex County Bar Assn., UNICO Nat. Roman Catholic. Office: 304 Maple Ave South Plainfield NJ 07080-0272 Office Phone: 908-561-6868.

**SANTORUM, RICK (RICHARD JOHN SANTORUM),** senator; b. Winchester, Va., May 10, 1958; s. Aldo and Catherine (Dughi) S.; m. Karen Garver, June 2, 1990; children: Elizabeth Anne, Richard John Jr., Daniel James, Sarah Maria, Peter Kenneth. BA in Polit. Sci., Pa. State U., 1980; MBA, U. Pitts., 1981; JD, Dickinson Sch. Law, 1986. Bar: Pa. 1986. Adminstrv. asst. to Sen. Doyle Corman Pa. State Senate, Harrisburg, 1981-86, exec. dir. local govt. com., 1981-84, exec. dir. transp. com., 1984-86; assoc. Kirkpatrick & Lockhart LLP, Pitts., 1986-90; mem. US Congress from 18th Pa. dist., Washington, 1991-95; US Senator from Pa., 1995—. Mem. com. agr., nutrition, and forestry US Senate, com. banking, housing, and urban affairs, com. fin., com. rules and adminstrn., spl. com. aging. Author: It Takes A Family: Conservatism and the Common Good, 2005. Bd. dirs. Mt. Lebanon Extended Day Program, 1987-91; mem. Child Advocacy Project, 1987-91. Recipient Award for Legis. Excellence, Am. Soc. Consultant Pharmacists, 1997, Award for Manufacturing Legis. Excellence, Nat. Assn. Manufacturers, 1999, Disting. Svc. award, Brent Soc. of Arlington, VA Diocese, 1999, Medical Miracle award, Healthcare Leadership Coun., 2000, John Paul II award, Inst. Psychological Sciences, 2003, Legis. of the Yr., Nat. Multiple Sclerosis Soc., 2003, Friend of Seniors award, Bucks County, PA Area Agy. on Aging, 2004, Higher Edn. Leadership award, Washington Ctr. Internships and Academic Studies, 2005. Mem. KC, Italian Sons and Daus. Assn., Allegheny County Bar Assn. Child Advocacy Program. Republican. Roman Catholic. Avocations: golf, racquetball. Office: US Senate 511 Dirksen Senate Bldg Washington DC 20510-0001 also: Widener Bldg One South Penn Sq Ste 960 Philadelphia PA 19107 also: The Ritz Bldg 222 Wyoming Ave Scranton PA 18503 Office Phone: 202-224-6324. Office Fax: 202-228-0604, 570-344-8799, 570-344-8906.*

**SANTOS, ADÈLE NAUDÉ,** architect, educator; b. Cape Town, South Africa, Oct. 14, 1938; came to U.S., 1973; d. David Francis Hugo and Aletta Adèle Naudé. Student, U. Cape Town, South Africa, 1956-58; diploma,

Archtl. Assn., London, 1961; MArch in Urban Design, Harvard U., 1963; MArch, M in City Planning, U., Pa., 1968. Registered arch., Pa., Mass. Pvt. practice architecture with Antonio de Souza Santos, 1966-73; ptnr. Interstudio, Houston, 1973-79; assoc. prof. architecture Rice U., Houston, 1973-78, prof., 1979; prof. architecture, grad sch. design Harvard U., Cambridge, Mass., 1979—81; prof. architecture and urban design, dept. architecture U. Pa., Phila., 1981-90; founding dean Sch. Architecture U. Calif., San Diego, 1990-94; pvt. practice architecture and urban design Adele Naude Santos, Arch., Phila., 1979-90, Adele Naude Santos and Assocs., San Diego and Phila., 1991—2002; prof. architecture Coll. Environ. Design U. Calif., Berkeley, 1994—2003; dean Sch. Architecture and Planning, MIT, Cambridge, 2004—. Project dir., co-filmmaker for 5 part series, 1979-80; works include Albright Coll. Ctr. for the Arts, Reading, Pa., 1991, Franklin-LaBrea Housing, Hollywood, Calif., 1995, Inst. of Contemporary Art, Phila., 1991, Yerba Buena Gardens, San Francisco, 1998. Wheelwright Travelling fellow, Harvard U., 1968; NEA grantee, 1976, Tex. Com. for Humanities grantee, 1979; recipient (with Hugo Naudé) Bronze medal for House Naudé Capt. Inst. South African Architects, 1967, award for public TV program So. Ednl. Communications Assn., 1980, 3d place award Inner city Infill Competition, 1986; winner Internat. Design Competition, Hawaii Loa Coll., hon. mention Cin. Hillside Housing Competition and City Visions, Phila., 1986; winner competition for Franklin/La Brea Affordable Housing Project Mus. Contemporary Art and Community Redevel. Agy. City L.A., 1988, Pa. Soc. Architects design award for Franklin/La Brea Multi-Family Housing, 1988; winning entry collaborative competition for amphitheater, restaurant and natural history mus., Arts Pk., La., 1989; winner competition for 24-unit residential devel., City of Camden, N.J., 1989, for New Civic Ctr., City of Perris, Calif., 1991, children's mus. The Zeum, 1998, child care facility Yerba Buena Gardens, San Francisco, 1998, Please Touch Mus., Phila., 1998, winner design competition ChildCare Ctr. U. Pa., 1999. Fellow Am. Inst. Archs.; mem. Pa. Soc. Archs., Archs. Registration Coun. (U.K.). Office: Dean Sch Architecture 77 Massachusetts Ave Cambridge MA 02139-4307

**SANTOS, ARTHUR MAGNO,** thoracic cardiovascular surgeon; b. Pasay City, Philippines, May 15, 1946; BS in Pre-medicine, Far Eastern U., Manila, Philippines, 1967; MD, U. of the East, 1972. Diplomate Am. Bd. Surgery, Am. Bd. Thoracic Surgery. Intern St. Francis Gen. Hosp., Pitts., 1973-74, resident in gen. surgery, 1974-77; resident McKeesport (Pa.) Hosp., 1977-79; resident in thoracic and cardiovascular surgery Shadyside Hosp., Pitts., 1979-81; pvt. practice Assn. of Thoracic Surgeons, Pitts., 1981—. Fellow ACS. Office Phone: 412-590-0252, 724-612-0959. Personal E-mail: artmagsan@hotmail.com.

**SANTOS, CHARLES DANIEL,** cultural organization administrator; b. San Antonio, July 17, 1960; s. John Joseph and Lucille (Lopez) Santos. BS in Sociology, U. Tex. Prin. dancer, tour mgr. Sharir Dance Co., 1981—92; info. systems administr. Tex. Gen. Land Office/Vets. Land Bd., 1987—95; assoc. prodr. The Juliet Hollister Awards/UN, 1996, 1998; prodr., founder, artistic dir. Austin Festival of Dance, NY, 1991—2001; mng./devel. dir. Eos Music, Inc., N.Y.C., 1995—98; producing dir. Dancers Responding to AIDS, N.Y.C., 1997—2000; prodr., mng. dir. Lower Manhattan Cultural Coun., N.Y.C., 2000—01; exec. dir. TITAS, Dallas, 2001—. Steering com. Human Rights Campaign Austin, 1994—96; chmn. Triangle On Stage, Austin Lyric Opera, 1995; project coord. BodyCount, Day Without Art/World AIDS Day, 1993—95; cultural arts panelist City of San Antonio, 2002; dance panelist Nat. Endowment for the Arts, 2003; numerous others; nat. adv. bd. African Am. Dance Ensemble, 2000—, Estate Project, 1999—, Eos Orch., 2001—; bd. dirs. Sharir Dance Co., 1995—97, Christopher House, 1994—95, AIDS Svcs. Austin, 1992—94, Ronald K. Brown/Evidence Dance Co., 2001, Dance Coun., 2001—, TITAS, 2001—. Named Master of Ceremonies, Christopher House for outstanding achievement in Austin cmty., 1994; recipient Outstanding Cmty. Event/Cmty. Svc. award, Tex. Human Rights Found., 1994, Leadership Austin, 1995, J. Blanton Belk Founders award of Outstanding Achievement, UWP Internat. Alumni Assn., 2000. Home: 5567 Ledgestone Dr Dallas TX 75214-2025 Office Phone: 214-775-1232.

**SANTOS, HERBERT JOSEPH, JR.,** lawyer; b. Reno, Feb. 17, 1963; s. Herbert Joseph Sr. and Jeanette Dorothy (Olivera) S.; m. Kimberly Ellen Saylors, Mar. 8, 1986; children: Herbert Joseph III, Jarred Adam, Hannah McKenzie. BA in Sociology, U. Nev., Las Vegas, 1985; JD, U. of the Pacific, 1991. Bar: Nev. 1991, Calif. 1992, U.S. Dist. Ct. Nev. 1992, U.S. Supreme Ct. 1999. Head social worker Cmty. Welfare, Inc., Reno, 1986-87; inspector Nev. Athletic Commn., Reno, 1986-87; sr. legal rsch. asst. County Sacramento, Calif., 1987-91; assoc. Law Offices of Terry A. Friedman, Ltd., Reno, 1991-98; owner The Law Firm of Herb Santos Jr., 1999—. Mem. State Bar Law Office Mgmt. and Procedures Com., 1996-98; chair election canvassing com. Nev. Bd. Govs, access to justice com., 1998, temp. apptd. jud. selection com. Author (instrn. manual) ORR, County of Sacramento Bankruptcy Forms and Procedures Manual with Practice Pointers, 1990; editor: The Writ, 1997-98; appeared in: (films) Kingpin, Father's Day, (TV miniseries) The Last Don, The Cheater's Partner in Mafia!, Body and Soul, Diamonds. Mem. Cmty. Coalition, Reno, 1986-87; mentor U. Nev., Reno, 1993—. Recipient Am. Jurisprudence award, 1991, Mem. ABA (young lawyers divsn., del. for State of Nev. 1996, 97, 98, 99), ATLA, Nev. Trial Lawyers Assn., State Bar Nev. (exec. coun. mem. young lawyers sect. 1993—, pres. young lawyers sect. 1996-97, com. chair Ask-a-Lawyer young lawyers sect. 1994—. chair pub. com. 1996-97, Pro-Bono award 1997, apptd. alternate dispute resolution sect.-long range planning 1998), Washoe County Bar Assn. (exec. coun., sgt.-at-arms 1997-98, treas. 1998-99, sec. 1999—, Bar Leader award 1998), Am. Inns of Ct. (Hon. Bruce Thompson chpt. 1995-97). Republican. Roman Catholic. Avocations: boxing, basketball, golf. Office: The Law Firm of Herb Santos Jr Liberty Ctr 350 S Center St Ste 350 Reno NV 89501-2113 Home: 14205 Prairie Flower Ct Reno NV 89511-6710

**SANTOS, LEONARD ERNEST,** lawyer; b. Caracas, Venezuela, Aug. 5, 1946; s. Paul Souza and Frieda (Epstein) S.; m. Jeannie Bernadette Niedermeyer, Oct. 28, 1978; children: Jonathan, Matthew, Andrew. BA cum laude, Tufts U., 1967; JD, NYU, 1971. Bar: Ariz. 1972, D.C. 1972, U.S. Dist. Ct. D.C. 1972, U.S. Ct. Appeals (9th and 5th circs.) 1972, U.S. Supreme Ct. 1972. Law clk. to cir. judge U.S. Ct. Appeals (9th cir.), San Francisco, 1971-72; assoc. Hogan & Hartson, Washington, 1972-76; sr. atty. internat. affairs U.S. Dept. Treasury, Washington, 1976-83; internat. trade counsel U.S. Senate Fin. Com., Washington, 1983-87; ptnr. Verner, Liipfert, Bernhard, McPherson & Hand, Washington, 1987-89, Perkins Coie, Washington, 1989-98, World Mae, Washington, 1998-99, Santos Family Found., Washington, 2000—; pres. Martin Santos Properties, LLC, 2001—, JMA Properties, LLC, 2003—. Note and comment editor NYU Law Jour., 1970; contbr. legal publs.; editor ABA Compendium of Foreign Trade Remedy Laws, 1998. Exec. dir. Dole for Pres. campaign, Washington, 1988, 96. Mem. NAFTA (chpt. 19 dispute settlement panels) Republican. Roman Catholic. Avocations: architecture, economics. Office: Martin Santos Prop LLC 900 Seventeeth St NW Ste 900 Washington DC 20006 Office Phone: 202-833-2559. Personal E-mail: santlen@aol.com.

**SANTOS, NICOLE MARIE,** elementary school educator; b. Mayfield Hts., Ohio, Apr. 27, 1978; d. Charles Nipros and Carol Ann Amos; m. Ron Santos (div.). BA, Purdue U., W. Lafayette, Ind., 2000. Lic. standard elem. edn. Ariz. 1st grade tchr. M.C. Cash Elem., Phoenix, 2002—. Mem. sch. improvement team, team leader M.C. Cash Elem., 2002—. Mem.: Purdue Alumni Assn., Kappa Delta Pi.

**SANTOS, SHARON LEE,** parochial school educator; b. Perth Amboy, N.J., June 23, 1955; d. John Anthony Santos and Dolores Estelle Barrett. BA in History, Kean U., 1978, MA in Guidance and Counseling, 1985; MA in Systematic Theology, Seton Hall U., 1998. Religious sr. Franciscan of Our Lady of Guadalupe; cert. tchr. K-12, guidance counelor N.J., religion tchr. Diocese of Metuchen, N.J. Tchr. Archdiocese of Newark, Diocese of Metuchen, Perth Amboy, Fords, NJ, Woodbridge, NJ; dir. religious edn. Vicariate of Perth Amboy, St. Mary Parish, New Monmouth, NJ. Guest spkr. on biblical and doctrinal topics various cities in NJ, 1993—; adv. bd. on evangelization Diocese of Meetuchen, 1999. Mem.: Fellowship of Cath. Scholars, St. Edith Stein Guild (life), Kappa Delta Phi. Avocations: astronomy, gardening. Office: St Mary Cath Ch 26 Leonardville Rd New Monmouth NJ 07748 Home: 355 Carr Ave Keansburg NJ 07734-1419 Office Phone: 732-671-8550.

**SANTOS GOMES, MARIA DA CONCEICAO FIALHO,** financial services executive; b. Viana de Alentejo, Portugal, July 13, 1950; d. Fortunato Tomás and Maria Inês (Fialho) Fernandes; m. Manuel dos Santos Gomes, Oct. 23, 1971; children: Sónia Alexandra Fernandes Gomes, Pedro Filipe Fernandes Gomes. Acctg. mgr. Comundo, Lisbon, 1973-75; fin. mgr. Docapesca, Lisbon, 1975-79; fin. and pers. mgr. Marblarte, Lisbon, 1979-80; gen. mgr., 1980-82; adminstrv. mgr. Mármores do Condado, Lisbon, 1982-83; mem. bd. dirs., 1983-85; fin. and pers. mgr. Datinfor, Lisbon, 1985-90; adminstrv. mgr. Brisa Auto-Estradas de Portugal S.A., Lisbon, 1990—. Fellow Paula Frassineti Assn.; mem. Assn. Portuguese Economists. Avocations: cinema, music, swimming, reading, theater. Home: Rua dos Soeiros 336-80 Esq Lisbon Portugal 1500-585 Office Phone: 00 351 274448722. Business E-Mail: mgomes@beiso.pt.

**SANTOSO, IRENE,** art director, graphics designer; b. Surabaya, Indonesia, Mar. 13, 1974; d. Bing Santoso and Soezana Djohan-Lie. AAS, Fashion Inst. Tech., 1994; BFA, Parsons Sch. Design, 1996. Sr. art dir. Tribal DDB, N.Y.C., 2001—02; creative dir. Hooloo.com, N.Y.C., 2001, USWeb/CKS Cornerstone, N.Y.C., 1997—2000; graphic artist Polo Ralph Lauren, N.Y.C., 1996—97. Design book, Shift Japan Website, 2000 (IMS SRC 100); author: (poetry) Am. Poetry Soc., 1999; website, Pixel Surgeon, 2001 (Outstanding Female Designer, 2001). Recipient Student award, Typographic Dir.'s Club, 1996, Am. Graphic Design award, Mag Graphic Design: USA, 2000. Avocation: fluent in spoken and written Mandarin, Cantonese, Japanese, Bahasa Indonesia. Personal E-mail: irene@irenesantoso.com.

**SANTRY, BARBARA LEA,** venture capitalist; b. Key West, Fla., Jan. 20, 1948; d. Jere Joseph and Frances Victoria (Appel) S. BS in Nursing, Georgetown U., 1969; MBA, Stanford U., 1978. Program analyst, br. chief U.S. Dept. HEW, Washington, 1973-76; mgr. cons. div. Arthur Andersen and Co., San Francisco, 1978-80; asst. v.p. Am. Med. Internat., Washington, 1980-83; v.p. Alex Brown and Sons, Inc., Balt., 1983-86; ptnr. Wessels, Arnold and Henderson, Mpls., 1986-88; v.p. Dain Bosworth Inc., Mpls., 1988-90, sr. v.p., 1990-91; ptnr. Pathfinder Venture Capital Funds, Menlo Park, Calif., 1991—2005, Capstone Ventures, Menlo Park, Calif., 1996—. Sr. cons. Quorum Consulting, San Francisco. Trustee Stanford Bus. Sch. Trust, 1996-2002. Served to lt. USNR, 1967-72.

**SANTULLI, RICHARD T.,** air transportation executive; b. Aug. 14, 1944; m. Peggy Santulli; 4 children. BS in Applied Math, MS in Applied Math, Bklyn. Polytechnic Inst., MS in Operations Rsch. Joined Shell Oil Co.; investment banker Goldman Sachs & Co., 1969—80; founder RTS Capital Services Inc.; chmn., CEO NetJets (name changed from Exec. Jet Aviation, Inc. in 2002), Columbus, Ohio and Woodbridge, NJ, 1984—. Co-founder Jayeff Stables, 1982—. Chmn. Intrepid Fallen Heroes Fund, 2001—. Recipient Vision award, Bus. & Comml. Aviation, 2003. Avocations: golf, horseracing. Office: NetJets Inc 581 Main St Woodbridge NJ 07095*

**SANYOUR, MICHAEL LOUIS, JR.,** diversified financial services company executive; b. Richmond, Va., Aug. 24, 1930; s. Michael Louis, Sr. and Betty (Toobert) Sanyour; m. Therese Marie McCarthy, June 1, 1951 (dec. Sept. 25, 2002); children: Jeffrey, Mark, Jennifer, Florence, Norman, Ned. AA, Union Coll., 1952; SB, Rutgers U., 1954, postgrad., 1978-82; MBA, Harvard U., 1956; postgrad., Am. Coll., 1987-92. CLU; ChFC. V.p. Harbridge Ho., Inc., Boston, 1956-63, also dir.; corp. v.p. mktg. Volkswagen Am., Inc., Englewood Cliffs, NJ, 1963-70; pres., CEO Subaru Am., Pennsauken, NJ, 1970-75, also dir., Wofac Co., Bridgewater, NJ, 1975-82; exec. v.p., dir. Sci. Mgmt. Corp., 1975-82; pres., CEO, dir. Metrologic Instruments Inc., Blackwood, NJ, 1982-85; pres., COO, dir. Avant-Garde Computing, Inc., Mt. Laurel, NJ, 1985-86; ptnr., dir. CMS Cos., Phila., 1986—. Bd. dirs. Phila. Film Soc., Phila. Shakespeare Festival, 1995—2006. Co-author: (book) Chief Executive's Handbook, 1975, Am. Mgmt. Assn.'s Publs., 1990. Trustee West Jersey Chamber Music Soc., 1983—, pres., 1987—88; councilman Moorestown, NJ, 1988—98; dep. mayor, 1999—2002; mayor, 2003—04; bd. dirs. Meml. Health Alliance, 1992—97, ARC Burlington County, 1989—94, Coriell Inst. Med. Rsch., 1992—, v.p., 2002—; bd. dirs. World Affairs Coun., Phila., 1992—98, Moorestown Cmty. House, 2000—06. Phila. Pres.'s Orgn., 1994—97, vice chmn., 1992—93, chmn., 1993—94; class sec. HBS Class of '56, 1986—96. With USNG, 1948—56. Decorated knight of St. John's of Jerusalem; recipient Alumni award, Rutgers U., 1954, award, Am. Cancer Soc., 1978—79. Mem.: World Affairs Coun. Phila., Automotive Orgn. Team, World Pres.'s Orgn., South Jersey C. of C. (v.p., dir.), Am. Mensa Ltd., Harvard Club (N.Y.C.), Union League (Phila.) (bd. dirs. 1993—97), Harvard Bus. Sch. Club (Phila.) (pres. 1980—81, chmn. 1983—84, dir. 1984—), Rotary (pres. Moorestown 1987—88, bd. dirs.), Legatus, Delta Sigma Pi, Beta Gamma Sigma. Home: 201 E Maple Ave Moorestown NJ 08057-2011 Office: 1926 Arch St Philadelphia PA 19103-1444 Office Phone: 215-246-3000. Business E-Mail: mls@cmsco.com. E-mail: mlsanyour@aol.com.

**SANZ, LUIS E.,** gynecologist, educator; b. Camaguey, Cuba; m. Miriam D. Sanz; 1 child, Monica G. MD, Georgetown U., 1976. Uro-gynecology and vaginal reconstruction surgery dept. ob-gyn. Georgetown U. Sch. Medicine, Washington, 1980, prof. dept. ob-gyn., 1980—. Author: Gynecologic Surgery, 1995; contbr. over 40 articles to profl. jours., chapters to books. With U.S. Army, 1966—68, Vietnam. Decorated Vietnam Campaign medal U.S. Army. Fellow: ACOG (assoc.; memberr). Roman Catholic. Avocations: biking, reading, travel, weightlifting. Office: 1625 N George Mason Dr #475 Arlington VA 22101 Office Phone: 703-717-4000 E-mail: lnanz@virginiahospitalcenter.com.

**SANZONE, DONNA S.,** publishing executive; b. Bklyn., Apr. 4, 1949; d. Joseph J. Seitz and Faye (Brooks) Ronson; m. Charles F. Sanzone, Jan. 2, 1972; children: Danielle, Gregory. BA magna cum laude, Boston U., 1970; MA, Northeastern U., 1979. Grad. placement specialist Inst. Internat. Edn., NYC, 1970-72; adminstr. AFS Internat. Scholarships, Brussels, 1972-74; editor Internat. Ency. Higher Edn., Boston, 1974-76, G.K. Hall & Co., Boston, 1977-81, exec. editor, 1981-91, editor-in-chief, 1991-96; v.p. Oryx Press, Boston, 1996-2000; editor-in-chief Greenwood Acad. Reference, Danbury, Conn., 2000—04; exec. editor Collins Reference, Harper Collins, NYC, 2004—. Contbg. author: Access to Power, 1981. Mem.: ALA, Libr. and Info. Tech. Assn's., Assn. Coll. and Rsch. Librs., Soc. for Scholarly and Profl. Pub., Assn. Am. Pubs. Office: Collins Reference 18 Pine St Weston MA 02493-1116

**SAON, GEORGE A.,** computer scientist, researcher; b. Brasov, Romania, Oct. 6, 1970; s. Elena Florina Tripsa and Stelian Saon. PhD in Computer Sci., Henri Poincare U., Nancy, France, 1997. Asst. lectr. Academie de Nancy-Metz, Nancy, Meurthe-et-Moselle, 1997—98; rschr. IBM, Yorktown Heights, NY, 1998—. Contbr. articles to profl. jours. Recipient 1st prize at regional final Alsace-Lorraine, Internat. French Math Problem Solving Championship, 1998. Mem.: AAAS. Avocations: reading, skiing. Office: IBM TJ Watson Rsch Ctr Rt 134 Yorktown Heights NY 10598 Home: 1465 E Putnam Ave 331 Old Greenwich CT 06870-1332 Business E-Mail: saon@watson.ibm.com.

**SAPARETO, FRANK VINCENT, II,** investment advisor, state legislator; b. Haverhill, Mass., Jan. 12, 1960; s. Frank Vincent and Alice Lambert S.; children: Frank V. III, Justin John. BS, U. Mass., 1982. Cert. IAFP; registered investment adviser; lic. ins. profl., Mass., N.H. securities regulation profl., Mass., N.H.; cert. fund specialist. Fin. planner Eastcorp., Inc., Springfield, Mass., 1989-93; pres. FVS Fin., Inc., Derry, N.H., 1993—; state rep. dist. 13, mem. gen. ct. N.H. Ho. of Reps., Concord, 1997—2002; state senator N.H. Sen., Concord, 2003. Vice-chmn. Derry Taxpayers Assn., 1994-96, chmn.,

1995-96; mem. zoning bd. Town of Derry, 1994-96. Mem. several profl. orgns. Avocations: kayaking, scuba diving, skydiving, chess. Home: 14 Oxbow Ln Derry NH 03038-4533 Office: FVS Financial Inc 14 Oxbow Ln Derry NH 03038-4533

**SAPER, CLIFFORD BAIRD,** neurology educator; b. Chgo., Feb. 20, 1952; s. Julian and Susan Menkin S.; m. Barbara Susan Farby, Aug. 26, 1973; children: Rebecca Michelle, Leah Danielle, Sean Zachary. BS, MS, U. Ill., 1972; MD, PhD, Washington U., 1977. Diplomate Am. Bd. Psychiatry and Neurology. Intern Jewish Hosp., St. Louis, 1977-78; resident New York Hosp., N.Y.C., 1978-81; asst. prof. Washington U., St. Louis, 1981-84, assoc. prof., 1984-85, U. Chgo., 1985-88, prof., 1988-92, chmn. com. on neurobiology, 1987-92; James Jackson Putnam prof. neurology and neurosci. Harvard Med. Sch., 1992—; chmn. dept. neurology Beth Israel Deaconess Med. Ctr., Boston, 1992—. Editor-in-chief Jour. of Comparative Neurology, 1994—; contbr. articles to profl. jours. Fellow: Royal Coll. of Physicians (London); mem.: Soc. for Neurosci., Am. Physiol. Soc., Am. Acad. Neurology, Am. Neurol. Assn. Office: 330 Brookline Ave Boston MA 02215-5400

**SAPER, JEFFREY D.,** lawyer; b. Bklyn., Apr. 21, 1948; BA summa cum laude, NYU, 1968, JD, 1971. Bar: N.Y. 1972, Calif. 1979. Ptnr. Wilson, Sonsini, Goodrich & Rosati, PC, Palo Alto, Calif., 1980—, vice chmn., mng. ptnr., Strategy & bus. Devel., mem. exec. mgmt. com. & policy com. Mem. ABA (sect. corp. banking & bus. law), N.Y. State Bar Assn., State Bar Calif. Office: Wilson Sonsini Goodrich& Rosati 650 Page Mill Rd Palo Alto CA 94304-1050 Office Phone: 650-493-9300. Office Fax: 650-493-6811. Business E-Mail: jsaper@wsgr.com.*

**SAPERS, CARL MARTIN,** lawyer, educator; b. Boston, July 16, 1932; s. Abraham E. and Anne (Herwitz) Sapers; m. Judith H. Thompson, Nov. 29, 1959; children: Jonathan Simonds, Rachel Elizabeth, Benjamin Lovell. AB, Harvard U., 1953, JD, 1958. Bar: Mass. 1958. Assoc. Hill, Barlow, Goodale & Adams, Boston, 1958-65; ptnr. Hill & Barlow, 1965—96, of counsel, 1997—2002. Spl. asst. atty. gen. criminal divsn. Commonwealth of Mass., 1963—65; spl. cons. Mass. Ethics Commn., 1978—79; adj. prof. Harvard Grad. Sch. Design, 1983—; mem. Mass. Bd. Registration Medicine, 1995—98, vice chair, 1997—98. Moderator Town of Brookline, 1982—91. With U.S. Army, 1953—55. Mem.: AIA (hon. Allied Professions medal 1975), Am. Coll. Constrn. Lawyers (bd. dirs. 1989—, pres. 1993), Am. Arbitration Assn. (bd. dirs. 1987—2000, Whitney North Seymour medal 1991), Boston Bar Assn. (coun. 1970—73, 1991—94). Home: 26C Bradbury St Cambridge MA 02138 E-mail: csapers@gsd.harvard.edu.

**SAPERSTEIN, DAVID,** writer, film director, television personality; b. Bklyn. s. Louis and Celia S.; m. Ellen Mae Bernard; children: Ivan, Ilena. Student, CCNY Film Inst., CCNY. With CBS-TV Ed Murrow Show-Person To Person; writer, prodr., dir. Skyline Films, Inc., 1963-83. Asst. prof. film NYU Grad. Sch., Tisch Sch. Arts, 1992-93; instr. screenwriting Manhattan Marymount Coll., 1996-99, N.Y. Film Acad., 1997. Lyricist 90 pub. songs; theatrical prodns. include musicals Blue Planet Blue, Clowntown; author: Cocoon, 1985 (bestseller), Fatal Reunion, 1987 (Book of the Month selection), Metamorphosis: The Cocoon Story Continues, 1988, Red Devil: The Book of Satan, 1989, Funerama, 1994, Dark Again, 1999, Retribution, 2003, A Christmas Visitor, 2004, Butterfly: Tomorrow's Children; movies include Cocoon (Best Original Story for Screen 1985, 2 Acad. awards); writer, dir. My Sister's Keeper, Personal Choice (Beyond the Stars), Hearts & Diamonds; writer Torch, Sara Deri, Queen of America, Italian Ices, Joshua's Golden Band, Roamers, Vets, Do Not Disturb, Snatched, Jack in the Box, (with Joe Cacaci) SchoolHouse, Point of Honor, Roberto!, The John Gill Story: In Defense of Ivan the Terrible, Joshua's Golden Band, Fighting Back, Babs' Labs, Silyan, (nonfiction) Woman in the Year 2000, 1975; writer, prodr. Hallmark channel (with George Samerjan) A Christmas Visitor, 2002; co-author (with James Rush) Magi Magic, (with George Samerjan) Christmas Passage, 2006; writer, dir. music videos Dr. Bill, Teenage Mutant Ninja Turtles, Fallow Angel, Wowii; segment prodr. for Northstar Ent./PBS Reppies; dir. over 300 TV commls.; writer dir. over 200 documentaries, corp. and indsl. films, videos including Dance of the Athletes (Emmy nomination), Explorers in Aqua-Space, Radio: A Matter of Style; creator first interactive internet publishing at www.darkagain.com. Recipient Cine Golden Eagle award, N.Y. Film Festival award, San Francisco Film Festival award, Venice Film Festival award, Melbourne Film Festival award, N.Y. Art Dirs. award, Chgo. Film Festival award, Townsend Harris medal CCNY, 1998. Mem. Writer Guild, Dirs. Guild of Am., BMI, Nat. Honor Soc. Office: Ebbets Field Prodns Ltd Wykagyl Station PO Box 42 New Rochelle NY 10804-0042

**SAPERSTEIN, IVAN A.,** lawyer; s. David A. and Ellen Mae Saperstein; m. C. Elizabeth Saperstein. BS, Emerson Coll., 1986; JD, Whittier Coll. Sch. Law, 1991. Pvt. practice law, N.Y.C. Office: Ste 2010 40 Exchange Pl New York NY 10005

**SAPERSTEIN, LEE WALDO,** mining engineering educator; b. N.Y.C., July 14, 1943; s. Charles Levy and Freda Phyllis (Dornbush) S.; m. Priscilla Frances Hickson, Sept. 16, 1967; children: Adam Geoffrey, Clare Freda. BS in Mining Engring., Mont. Sch. Mines, 1964; DPhil in Engring. Sci., Oxford U., 1967. Registered profl. engr., Ky., Mo., Pa. Laborer, miner, engr. The Anaconda Co., Butte, Mont., and N.Y.C., 1963-64; prof. mining engring. Pa. State U., University Park, 1967-71, assoc. prof., 1971-78, prof., 1978-87, sect. chmn., 1974-87; prof., chmn. dept. mine engring. U. Ky., Lexington, 1987-93; dean Sch. Mines and Metallurgy U. Mo., Rolla, 1993—2004, prof. mining engring., 1993—, dean emeritus Sch. Mines and Metallurgy 2004—, chmn. engring. accreditation commn., 1989-90, bd. dirs. Accreditation Bd. for Engring. and Tech., 1992-2001, sec. of bd., 1995-98, pres.-elect, 1998-99, pres. 1999-2000, ABET fellow. Contbr. articles to refereed jours. Rhodes scholar Oxford U., 1964-67; recipient Linton E. Grinter Disting. Svc. award, 2004. Mem. NSPE, ASEE, Soc. Mining, metallurgy and Exploration, Inc. (disting. mem. AIME-Soc. Mining Engrs.), Am. Assn. Rhodes Scholars. Home: 801 Laurel Dr Rolla MO 65401-3841 Office: U Mo 326 V H Mc Nutt Hl Rolla MO 65409-0450 Office Phone: 573-341-4846. Business E-Mail: saperste@umr.edu, saperste@rollanet.org.

**SAPERSTEIN, MARC ELI,** religious studies educator, rabbi; b. NYC, Sept. 5, 1944; s. Harold Irving and Marcia Belle (Rosenblum) S.; m. Roberta Shapiro, June 17, 1970; children: Sara Michal, Adina Ruth. AB, Harvard U., 1966, PhD, 1977; student, Pembroke Coll., U. Cambridge, Eng., 1966-67; MA, Hebrew U., Jerusalem, 1971, Hebrew Union Coll., N.Y.C., 1972. Ordained rabbi, 1972. Lectr. in Hebrew lit. Harvard U., Cambridge, Mass., 1977-79; lectr. in Jewish studies Harvard U. Divinity Sch., 1979-81, asst. prof. Jewish studies, 1981-83, assoc. prof., 1983-86; Gloria M. Goldstein prof. Jewish history and thought Washington U., St. Louis, 1986-97, chmn. program Jewish and Near Eastern Studies, 1989-97; rabbi Temple Beth David, Canton, Mass., 1973-86; Charles E. Smith prof. of Jewish history George Washington U., Washington, 1997—, dir. Judaic studies, 1997—. Mem. exec. bd. Cen. Conf. Am. Rabbis, 1985-87. Author: Decoding the Rabbis, 1980, Jewish Preaching, 1200-1800, 1989, Moments of Crisis in Jewish-Christian Relations, 1989, Your Voice Like a Ram's Horn, 1996, Exile in Amsterdam, 2005, also articles; editor: Essential Papers on Messianic Movements and Personalities in Jewish History, 1992, Witness from the Pulpit, 2000. Fellow Charles and Julia Henry Fund, 1966-67, Am. Coun. Learned Socs., 1983-84, Inst. Advanced Studies Hebrew U. Jerusalem, 1989, Am. Acad. for Jewish Rsch., 1994—, Ctr. for Judaic Studies, U. Pa., 1995-96, Ctr. Jewish Studies, Harvard U., 2005; Danforth Found. Kent fellow, 1973-77. Mem. Assn. Jewish Studies (bd. dirs. 1983-89, book rev. editor 1997-2002), Am. Acad. Jewish Rsch. (exec. bd. 2000—, v.p. 2004—), Phi Beta Kappa. Jewish. Office: George Washington U Dept History 2142 G St NW Washington DC 20037-2721 Office Phone: 202-994-4780. Business E-Mail: msaper@gwu.edu.

**SAPHIR, RICHARD LOUIS,** pediatrician; b. N.Y.C., May 1, 1933; s. Samuel and Grace (Greenberg) Saphir; m. Judith Schwartz, Dec. 6, 1958; 1 child, Steven. BA, NYU, 1954; MD, SUNY, NYC, 1958. Diplomate Nat. Bd. Med. Examiners. Am. Bd. Pediat. Asst. attending pediatrician Mt. Sinai Hosp., NYC, 1965—71, asst dr., pediat. acute care clinic, 1970—78, 1971—82, assoc. clin. prof. pediat., 1982—88, attending pediatrician, 1982—; chief, pediatric svcs. U.S. Naval Hosp., Newport, RI, 1967—69; clin. prof. pediat. Mt. Sinai Sch. Medicine, NYC, 1988—. Bd. dirs. Mt. Sinai Children's Ctr. Found., N.Y.C., 1987—. Contbr. articles to profl. jours. Chmn. cmty. and adv. com. N.Y.C. Info. and Counseling Program for Sudden Infant Death Syndrome, 1979—81; med. bd. YMHA, N.Y.C., 1982—86. Comdr. USNR, 1967—69. Fellow: NY County Med. Soc. (vice chmn. com. child welfare 1974—85), NY Pediat. Soc. (pres. 1978—79), Am. Acad. Pediats. (com. sci. meetings 1985—97, chmn. prep course 1991—96, editl. adv. bd. Continuing Med. Edn. audiotapes 1991—2001, ednl. program rep. ambulatory care quality improvement program 1992—2002, ednl. advisor proficiency testing program 1996—99, editl. bd. Pediat. in Rev. 1997—2003, ednl. adv. Uniformed Svcs. pediat. seminar 1997—, mem. super cont. med. edn. planning com. 2000—06, chmn. super cont. med. edn. planning com. 2002—06, Com. on Continuing Med. Edn. 2002—), NY Acad. Medicine (treas. 1987—89). Office: BSM Pediatrics PC 55 E 87th St New York NY 10128-1043 Office Phone: 212-722-4950. E-mail: richard.saphir@verizon.net.

**SAPIENZA, DAVID VICTOR,** social studies educator; s. Rebecca Sue Bacon; m. Stephanie Ann Varga, June 23, 2001; 1 child, Joshua Stephen. BA, St. Louis U., 1996; FdM, U. Mo., Columbia, 2001. Provisional tchg. lic. Colo., 2005. Tchr. U. Denver H.S., 2002—. Chpt. pres. St. Louis U. Alumni Assn., Denver, 2004—06; past pres. Karis Cmty., Denver, 2002—06; asst. coord. Alum Svc. Corps, St. Louis, 1998—2004. Independent. Roman Catholic. Avocations: travel, cooking, skiing, hiking, snowshoeing. Office Phone: 303-871-2636.

**SAPIENZA, TONY,** public relations executive; With Hewlett-Packard; sr. counsel Miller/Shandwick, Boston, pres. Office: Miller/Shandwick Technologies 101 Main St Cambridge MA 02142-1519

**SAPINSKY, JOSEPH CHARLES,** publishing executive, photographer; b. N.Y.C., Dec. 13, 1923; s. Simon Moses and Janet (Charles) S.; m. Jane Tomney, Oct. 21, 1970; children— Michael Joseph, Jane Anne, Laura Alexandra. Certificate illustration, Pratt Inst., 1943; certificate advt. design, 1947; postgrad., Colgate U., 1943, Cornell U., N.C. U. Art dir. Today's Living, N.Y. Herald Tribune, N.Y.C., 1960-63; art dir. N.Y. Mag., N.Y.C., 1963-65; asso. art dir., dir. photography Sat. Evening Post, N.Y.C., 1965-67; dir. publs. I.O.S., Geneva, 1967-69; art dir. This Week, N.Y.C., 1969, Jock N.Y. mag., N.Y.C., 1970; dir. publs. I.I.G., London, 1970; art dir. Woman's Day mag., N.Y.C., 1971-83; exec. art dir. Woman's Day Spls., N.Y.C., 1983-92; comml. photographer, 1992—. Cons. art dir. Infinity mag., N.Y.C., 1971-73; instr. dept. photography Sch. Visual Arts, N.Y.C., New Sch., N.Y.C. Served with USNR, 1943-46; capt. Res. ret. Recipient numerous art dir. awards. Mem. Am. Soc. Mag. Photographers, Soc. Illustrators, Am. Soc. Mag. Editors, Am. Inst. Graphic Arts, Soc. Publ. Designers, Mil. Officers Assn. Home: 242 Campbell Rd Box 207 Cherry Valley NY 13320-0207 Office Phone: 607-264-3080. E-mail: snipas@telenet.net.

**SAPIR, TAMIR,** entrepreneur; b. Russia, 1948; arrived in USA, 1973; Former owner New York City Electronics Store; supt. 2 Broadway Bldg. Office: Two Broadway New York NY 10011*

**SAPIRO, VIRGINIA,** academic administrator, political science professor; b. East Orange, N.J., Feb. 28, 1951; m. Graham K. Wilson; 1 child, Adam. AB, Clark U., 1972; MA in Polit. Sci., PhD in Polit. Sci., U. Mich., 1976. Asst. prof. polit. sci. and women's studies program U. Wis., Madison, 1976-81, assoc. prof., 1981-86, prof., 1986—; Sophonisba P. Breckinridge prof., 1995—, assoc. vice chancellor teaching and learning, 2002—, interim provost, vice chancellor academic affairs, 2005—06. Vis. lectr. dept. govt. U. Essex, 1979-80, lectr., 1981, 82-83, vis. prof., 1989. Author: Women in American Society: An Introduction to Women's Studies, 1986, 3d edit., 1994, Women, Biology and Public Policy, 1985, The Political Integration of Women: Roles, Socialization and Politics, 1983, A Vindication of Political Virtue: The Political Theory of Mary Wollstonecraft, 1992; contbr. articles to profl. jours. Mem. bd. trustees Clark U., Worcester, Mass., 2001—. CIC Academic Leadership fellowship, 2003-04. Mem. Am. Acad. Arts and Scis., Am. Polit. Sci. Assn. (v.p. 1999-2000, pres. sect. elections, pub. opinion, voting behavior), Midwest Polit. Sci. Assn. (exec. coun. 1984-86), Internat. Soc. Polit. Psychology (governing coun. 1988-90, 2000-03), Phi Beta Kappa. Office: Univ Wisconsin 117 Bascom Mall 500 Lincoln Dr Madison WI 53706-1380 Office Phone: 608-262-5246. Office Fax: 608-265-3353. E-mail: vsapiro@wisc.edu.

**SAPOFF, MEYER,** retired electronics executive; b. NYC, June 2, 1927; s. Benjamin and Mary (Charney) Sapoff. Student, Mohawk Coll., 1946—48; BSEE magna cum laude, Poly. Inst. Bklyn., 1950, postgrad., 1952-53, MIT, 1951, U. Pa., 1951—52; MSEE, Drexel Inst. Tech., 1952. Rsch. engr. Franklin Inst. Labs., Phila., 1950-52; rsch fellow sr. grade Poly. Inst. Bklyn., 1952-53; dir. rsch. Victory Engring. Corp., Springfield, NJ, 1953-57, dir. engring., 1957-63, v.p., 1963-69; cons., sr. staff scientist Keystone Carbon Co., St. Mary's, Pa., 1969-70; pres. Thermometrics, Inc., Edison, NJ, 1970-86, chmn. bd. dirs., 1986-93, sr. staff cons. 1993-96; pres. MS Cons. Princeton, NJ, 1993—96, ret., 1996. Chmn. E20 temperature com. 6th Symposium Temperature, Measurement and Control in Sci. and Industry; U.S. del. to tech. com. 65th Internat. Electrotech. Commn.; cons. in field. Contbr. articles to profl. jours.; patentee in field. Active West Orange (NJ) PTA, 1960—76, Citizens League West Orange, 1962—75; trustee George St. Playhouse, New Brunswick, NJ, 1993—2001; bd. dirs. Jewish Ctr., Princeton, 1995—98, fin. chmn., 1995—96, v.p. fin., 1996—98; bd. dirs. United Jewish Fedn. Princeton Mercer Bucks, 1998—, treas., 2001—03. Recipient Indsl. Rsch. IR-100 award, 1974; fellow, Poly. Inst. Bklyn., 1953; scholar, NYU, 1948—50. Mem.: AAAS, ASTM (1st vice-chmn. E20 com. temperature measurement 2000—, award of merit 1998), IEEE, Am. Ceramic Soc., Poly. Inst. Bklyn. Alumni Assn., Tau Beta Pi, Eta Kappa Nu.

**SAPOLSKY, HARVEY MORTON,** political scientist, educator; b. Haverhill, Mass., Feb. 21, 1939; s. Abraham and Anne Betty (Selig) S.; m. Karen P. Stenbo, Aug. 27, 1966. BA, Boston U., 1961; MPA, Harvard U., 1963, PhD, 1967. Mem. faculty MIT, 1966—, prof. polit. sci., 1977—, dir. comm. forum, 1987-95, dir. security studies program, 1989—; dep. dir. Univ. Health Policy Consortium, 1978-83, assoc. chmn. faculty, 1981-83. Vis. prof. U. Mich., 1971—72; cons. Artificial Heart Assessment Panel Nat. Heart and Lung Inst., Washington, 1972—73; mem. Ethics and Health Policy Panel Hastings (N.Y.) Ctr., 1977-80; mem. com. on Fed. Rsch. on Effect of Ionizing Radiation NRC, Washington, 1980—81, mem. com. on Risk Perception and Comm., 1987—88; mem. com. on tech. alternatives to anti-pers. mines, 1999—2001; mem. Sec. of Energy's Task Force on Alternative Futures for Dept. of Energy Labs, 1994—95; mem. adv. com. U.S. Army Command and Gen. Staff Coll., 2005—. Author: The Polaris System Development, 1972, (with D. Altman and Richard Greene) Health Planning and Regulation, 1981, (with A. Drake, S. Finkelstein) The American Blood Supply, 1982, Science and the Navy, 1990; editor: Consuming Fears: The Politics of Product Risks, 1986; co-editor: Federal Health Programs, 1981, (with S. Altman), 1981, (with R. Crane, W.R. Newman and E. Noam) The Telecommunications Revolution, 1992; also sci. articles. Mem.: AAAS (sec. sect. social and econ. scis. 1968-73), Am. Polit. Sci. Assn., Nat. Acad. Social Ins., Coun. on Fgn. Rels. Home: 37 Edgemoor Rd Belmont MA 02478-3916 Office: MIT Security Studies Program E38-600 Cambridge MA 02139 Office Phone: 617-253-5265. Business E-Mail: sapolsky@mit.edu.

**SAPORTA, JACK,** psychologist, educator; b. NYC, Oct. 21, 1927; s. David and Victoria (Fils) S.; m. Judith Hammond, May 28, 1967 (div. 1979); children: David J., Victoria Johnson. AB cum laude, Adelphi U., 1951; PhD, U. Chgo., 1962. Diplomate Am. Bd. Profl. Psychology; lic. clin. psychologist. Pvt. practice, 1962-99; supt. Tinley Park (Ill.) Mental Health Ctr., 1975-78; chief manpower tng. and devel. Ill. Dept. Mental Health, Chgo., 1978-82; dean, prof. Forest Inst. Profl. Psychology, Des Plaines, Ill., 1982-85; mem. faculty Fielding Grad. U., Santa Barbara, Calif., 1984—2005, Ill. Sch. Profl. Psychology, Chgo., 1985-97. Mem. adj. faculty psychology Lake Forest Grad. Sch. Mgmt., 1987-97; mem. Ill. State Clin. Psychology Lic. and Disciplinary Com., Springfield, 1984-93; profl. staff Forest Hosp., Des Plaines, 1977-96; mem. attending doctoral ment. staff Luth. Gen. Hosp., Park Ridge, Ill., 1986-2000, emeritus, 2000—. Served with U.S. Army, 1946-47, Germany. Named Educator of Yr., Forest Inst., 1982, Outstanding Faculty Mem. Lake Forest Grad. Sch. Mgmt. Fellow Acad. Clin. Psychology, NTL-Inst. (faculty); mem. APA (accreditation site vis. team), Ill. Psychol. Assn., Chgo. Psychol. Assn. (cert. recognition 1999, mem. exec. bd.). Avocations: tennis, computers, do-it-yourself home projects. Home: 13077 Stone Creek Court Huntley IL 60142

**SAPP, JOHN RAYMOND,** lawyer; b. Lawrence, Kans., June 18, 1944; s. Raymond Olen and Amy (Kerr) S.; m. Linda Lee Tebbe, July 3, 1965; children: Jeffrey, Jennifer, John. BA, U. Kans., 1966; JD, Duke U., 1969. Bar: Wis. 1969, U.S. Dist. Ct. (ea. dist.) Wis. 1969, U.S. Ct. Appeals (7th cir.) 1974, U.S. Ct. Appeals (4th cir.) 1984, U.S. Supreme Ct. 1974. Assoc. Michael, Best & Friedrich, Milw., 1969-76, ptnr., 1976-90, mng. ptnr., 1990—2004, sr. ptnr., 2004—. Dir. Roadrunner Freight Sys., Milw., 1992-2004, J.J. Keller Co., 2003-. Bd. dirs. Milw. Symphony, 1981-95, mem. exec. com., 1993-95; bd. dirs. Boy Scouts Am., Milw., 1986—, pres. 1990-92; mem. Milw. Arts Bd., 1990, Greater Milw. Com.; bd. dirs. Zool. Soc., 1995-, v.p., 2000-05, chmn., 2005-; bd. dirs. Lex Mundi, 1997-2000, mem. exec. com., 1997-2001; bd. dirs. Jr. Achievement Greater Milw., 2001—04. Avocations: golf, curling, print collecting. Office Phone: 414-271-6563, 414-271-6560. Business E-Mail: jrsapp@michaelbest.com.

**SAPP, PEGGY G.,** pastor, editor, writer, speech professional; d. Arthur Charles and Mae Belle (Graves) Gibby; m. Roger W. Sapp, Sr., Sept. 4, 1965 (dec.); children: Roger Warren II, LaDonna Hope Sapp Ranke, Jonathan T., Angela Faith Sapp Little. Degree in Bus. Adminstrn., Marsh Bus. Coll., Atlanta, 1963; degree in Theology/Missions, Pentecostal Bible Inst., Jackson, Miss., 1966; degree in Bus. Adminstrn., Mid. Ga. Coll., Cochran, 1968; degree in Theology, Moody Bible Inst., Chgo., 1985. Dean students Inst. Biblical Studies, Dublin, Ga., 1978-85; radio bible tchr. Voice of Truth Ministries, Dublin, 1985—; Bible instr.-tchr., 1985—; adminstr. Ch. Jesus Christ Christian Sch., Dublin, 1986—94; editor Ch. Jesus Christ Orgn., Kingsport, Tenn., 1991—; ordained minister, 1971—; motivational spkr., 1991—; sr. pastor Ch. Jesus Christ Full Gospel, Dublin, 1994—; cert. correctional assoc. Johnson State Prison, Wrightsville, Ga., 2000—, spkr., counselor, 2000—. Author: (books) Anointed Leadership Series, 1985, Institute of Biblical Studies, 1994, (periodical) The Broken Vessel, 2001; editor: (mag. periodicals) The Messenger, 1991. Mem.: Assn. Christian Counselors. Achievements include assisted in providing curriculum for founding of Inst. Biblical Studies, Cebu, Philippines. Office: Ch Jesus Christ Full Gospel 759 Vernon Woodard Rd Dublin GA 31027

**SAPP, R. LACHANZE See LACHANZE**

**SAPP, WALTER WILLIAM,** lawyer, gas industry executive; b. Linton, Ind., Apr. 21, 1930; s. Walter J. and Nona (Stalcup) S.; m. Eva Kaschner, July 10, 1957 (dec.); children: Karen Elisabeth, Christoph Walter. AB magna cum laude, Harvard, 1951; JD summa cum laude, Ind. U., 1957. Bar: Ind. 1957, N.Y. 1959, Colo. 1959, U.S. Supreme Ct. 1972, Tex. 1977. Pvt. practice, N.Y.C., 1957-60, 63-66; practice in Paris, 1960—63; assoc. atty. Cahill, Gordon, Reindel & Ohl, Paris, 1960-63, N.Y.C., 1957-60, 63-65, ptnr., 1966; gen. counsel Colo. Interstate Corp., 1966-76, v.p., 1968-76, sec., 1971-76, sr. v.p., dir., exec. com., 1973-75, exec. v.p., 1975-76; v.p. Coastal States Gas Corp., 1973-76; sr. v.p., gen. counsel Tenneco, Inc., Houston, 1976-92, sec., 1984-86; pvt. practice Houston, 1992—. Editor-in-chief Ind. U. Law Jour., 1956-57. Trustee Houston Ballet, 1982-85, Awty Internat. Sch., 1989-98, 99—, vice-chmn., 1994-97, pres. 1997-98, chmn., 1999-2002, pres., 2002-03; bd. dirs. Harris County Met. Transit Authority, 1982-84, Houston Internat. Protocol Alliance, 1992-94, Houston Symphony, 1989—, v.p., 1991-94, 2001-03; adv. bd. Inst. for Internat. Edn. S.W. region, 1987-2003, chmn., 1992-94; mem. adv. bd. Comparative Law Ctr. Southwestern Legal Found., 1976-92; mem. adv. bd., treas. Texan-French Alliance for the Arts, 2005—. Lt. USNR, 1951-54. Decorated chevalier Ordre Nat. du Mérit (France). Mem.: ABA, Houston Bar Assn., Assn. Bar City of N.Y., Tex. Bar Assn., N.Y. State Bar Assn., Alliance Française Houston (bd. dirs. 1989—2001, v.p. 1991—94, 1998—2001), French-Am. C. of C. Houston (bd. dirs. 1987—92), Order of Coif. Mem. United Ch. of Christ. Office: 1111 Hermann Dr Unit 8B Houston TX 77004-6928

**SAPP, WARREN CARLOS,** professional football player; b. Orlando, Fla., Dec. 19, 1972; m. Jamiko Sapp, Jan. 29, 1998; children: Mercedes, Warren Carlos II. Student, U. Miami. Defensive tackle Tampa Bay Buccaneers, 1994—2003, Oakland Raiders, 2004—. Named NFL Defensive Player of the Yr., 1999; named to Pro-Bowl, 1997—2003. Achievements include being a member of Super Bowl XXXVII Champion Tampa Bay Buccaneers, 2002. Avocation: swimming. Office: c/o Oakland Raiders 1220 Harbor Bay Pkwy Alameda CA 94502*

**SAPPENFIELD, CHARLES MADISON,** architect, educator; b. Columbia, S.C., Mar. 17, 1930; s. Charles Madison and Elizabeth Olive (Moss) S.; m. Mary Frances McGowan Dec. 14, 1963 (div. June 1990); children— Charles Ross, Sarah Kathleen B.Arch., N.C. State U., 1956; Cert., Denmark's Royal Acad., Copenhagen, 1961. Registered arch., Ind. Asst. prof. N.C. State U., Raleigh, 1956-57, asst. prof., 1961-63; head archtl. firm C.M. Sappenfield, Asheville, N.C. and Muncie, Ind., 1961—; assoc. prof. Clemson U., SC, 1963-65; prof. architecture Ball State U., Muncie, Ind., 1965-94, prof. emeritus, 1994—, dean, 1965-81, dean emeritus, 1994—, dir. Design Indiana, 1983-88. Awards juror Interfaith Forum on Religious Art and Architecture, 1981, Am. Cons. Engrs. Council, 1982; mem. accreditation teams Nat. Archtl. Accrediting Bd., 1967-82. Archtl. works include: Dormitories, U. N.C., Gumpert residence, Dave residence. Pres. Asheville Art Mus., N.C., 1964-65; chmn. Ind. Commn. on Aging, Indpls., 1983-85; pres. Alpha Day Care Ctr. for Elderly, Muncie, 1985; mem. State Planning Adv. Commn., Indpls., 1974-82. Served with U.S. Army. Recipient Gold medal for svc. Ball State U., 1983; named Sagamore of the Wabash, Gov. of Ind., 1982 Fellow AIA (dir. nat. bd. dirs. 1989-92); mem. Ind. Soc. Archs. (pres. 1976), Ind. Archtl. Found. (chmn. 1975), Am. Soc. Landscape Archs. (awards juror 1983), Danish Fedn. Archs. (hon., Aeresmedallion 1987), Fulbright Alumni Assn., Alpha Rho Chi. Lodges: Rotary, Civitan. Republican. Episcopalian. Avocations: bicycling, boating, photography. Home and Office: 11607 Oakmont Ct Fort Myers FL 33908

**SAPPINGTON, SHARON ANNE,** retired school librarian; b. West Palm Beach, Fla., Sept. 15, 1944; d. A.D. and Laura G. (Jackson) Chambless; m. Andrew Arnold Sappington III, June 11, 1966; children: Andrew Arnold IV, Kevin Sean. Student, Fla. So. Coll., 1962—64; BA in Edn., U. Fla., 1966; postgrad., U. Ala., 1980. Tchr. 5th grade Tates Creek Elem., Lexington, Ky., 1966—68; tchr. 4th grade Sadieville Elem., Ky., 1968—69; libr. media specialist A.H. Watwood Elem., Childersburg, Ala., 1980—98, ret., 1998. Guest storyteller Young Author's Conf., Winterboro, Lincoln, Sylacauga, and Fayetteville, Ala., 1982-94; vis. com. Southeastern Accreditation Assn.; program presenter Internat. Reading Assn., Birmingham, Ala., 1983; guest spkr. rare children's books By the Way TV talk show, 1983; pres. Tale Tellers of St. Augustine, 2003—05; chmn. RSVP Read Aloud Program, 2002-04. Creator, presenter: (slide presentation) Tellers of Tales and Sketchers of Dreams, 1983, (multimedia programs) Dinosaurs, Teddy Bears, and Wild Things, 1990, Shanghaied in the Beijing Airport, 1994. Circle chmn., Sunday

tchr. Grace United Meth. Ch., Birmingham, 1973, 92-95; delivery mem. Meals on Wheels, Birmingham, 1975-76; radio reader for the blind WBHM Pub. Broadcasting, Birmingham, 1980; guest spkr., program presenter Jaycees, Kiwanis, and C. of C., Childersburg, 1993-94. Grantee Title I grantee, 1991, Stutz Bearcat grantee, 1992. Mem. AAUW (lit. chmn. St. Augustine chpt., 2005-), ALA, Internat. Platform Assn., Am. Assn. Sch. Librs., Ala. Libr. Assn. (children's and sch. divsn. publicity chmn. 1991-93, chmn. Nat. Libr. Week in Ala. 1993-94, Outstanding Youth Svcs. award 1989); People to People Internat. (libr. del. to China 1993), Kappa Delta Pi. Democrat. Methodist. Avocation: book collecting. Home: 5131 Shore Dr Saint Augustine FL 32086-6473

**SAPSOWITZ, SIDNEY H.,** entertainment and media company executive; b. NYC, June 29, 1936; s. Max and Annette (Rothstein) Sapsowitz; m. Phyllis Skopp, Nov. 27, 1957; children: Donna Dawn Chazen, Gloria Lynn Aaron, Marsha Helene Gleit. BBA summa cum laude, Paterson State U., NJ, 1980. Various fin. and oper. systems positions Metro Goldwyn Mayer, Inc., N.Y.C., 1957-68; exec. v.p., dir. Penta Computer Assoc. Inc., N.Y.C., 1968-70, Cons. Actuaries Inc., Clifton, NJ, 1970-73; exec. v.p., CFO Am. Film. Theatre, N.Y.C., 1973-76, Cinema Shares Internat Dristb. Corp., N.Y.C., 1976-79; sr. cons. Solomon, Finger & Newman, N.Y.C., 1979-80; exec. v.p., CFO Metro Goldwyn Mayer, L.A., 1980-82; various positions leading to sr. exec. v.p. fin. and adminstrn., chief fin. operating and adminstrv. officer MGM/UA Entertainment Co., Culver City, Calif., 1982-86, mem. bd. dirs., exec. com., 1982—89; fin. v.p.; chief adminstrv. and ops. officer, Office of Pres., dir. United Artists Corp., Beverly Hills, Calif., 1986-87; chmn. bd., CEO MGA/UA Telecommunications Corp., Beverly Hills, 1986-89; sr. exec. v.p., bd. dirs., mem. exec. com. MGA/UA Communications Co., 1986-89; chmn., CEO Sid Sapsowitz & Assocs., Inc., 1989—. Pres., Wayne Conservative Congregation, N.J., 1970-77; mem. bd. govs. exec. com. City of Hope, 1990-. Mem. Am. Mgmt. Assn., Am. Film Inst., Acad. Motion Picture Arts and Scis., Fin. Exec. Inst., TV Acad. Arts and Scis., KP (chancellor comdr.).

**SARACEVIC, TEFKO,** information science educator; married; 2 children. MS in Libr. Sci., Case Western Reserve U., 1962, PhD in Info. Sci., 1970. Assoc. dean, prof. comm., info. and libr. studies Rutgers U., New Brunswick, NJ. Editor-in-chief: Info. Processing and Mgmt., 1985—. Avocations: reading, skiing. Office: Rutgers U Sch Comm Info & Libr Studies 4 Huntington St New Brunswick NJ 08901-1071 Office Phone: 732-932-7500 Ext. 8222. E-mail: tefko@scils.rutgers.edu.

**SARACHIK, MYRIAM PAULA MORGENSTEIN,** physics professor, condensed matter physicist; b. Antwerp, Belgium, Aug. 8, 1933; arrived in US, 1947; d. Solomon and Sarah (Segal) Morgenstein; m. Philip Sarachik, Sept. 6, 1954; 1 child, Karen Beth. AB, Barnard Coll., 1954; MS, Columbia U., 1957, PhD, 1960. Rsch. assoc. IBM Watson Labs., Columbia U., N.Y.C., 1960-61; mem. tech. staff Bell Telephone Labs., Murray Hill, NJ, 1962-64; asst. prof. physics CCNY (CUNY), 1964-67, assoc. prof., 1967-70, prof., 1971—, Disting. prof. physics, 1995—. Advisor NSF, NRC. Contbr. articles to profl. jours. Recipient NYC Mayor's award for excellence in sci. and tech., 1995, Sloan Pub. Svc. award, 2004, Oliver E. Buckley prize in Condensed Matter Physics, 2005, L'Oreal/UNESCO for Women in Sci. (N.Am.) Laureate, 2005. Fellow AAAS, Am. Phys. Soc. (pres. 2003), N.Y. Acad. Scis.; mem. NAS, Am. Acad. Arts and Scis. Office: CCNY (CUNY) Divsn Sci MR429 Physics Dept Convent Ave and 138 St New York NY 10031 Office Phone: 212-650-5618. Business E-Mail: sarachik@sci.ccny.cuny.edu.

**SARACINO, DAWN M.,** physical therapist, educator; b. N.Y.C., Sept. 9, 1965; d. Joseph John and Eileen C. Saracino; m. Steve Robert Hannan, Oct. 12, 2001; children: Jade, Bryce. MS, U. Fla., 1994. Cert. neurological specialist. Physical therapy instr. U. North Fla., Jacksonville, Fla., 1994—2005. Physical therapist Beacko Rehab. Hosp., Jacksonville, Fla., 1994—2005. E-mail: dsaracino@unf.edu.

**SARAF, SANJEEV R.,** safety and risk management consultant, researcher; b. Nagpur, India, Feb. 6, 1977; s. Raghunath T. and Jyoti R. Saraf. PhD in Chem. Engring., Tex. A&M U., College Station, 2003. Ptnr. ioMosaic, Houston, 2003—. Recipient Best Presentation award, Tex. A&M, 2000. Mem.: NA-TAS, ACS, DIERS, AIChE (assoc.). Achievements include research in application of molecular modeling for predicting chemical hazards. Office: ioMosaic 2650 Fountain View Dr # 410 Houston TX 77057 Office Phone: 713-490-5220. E-mail: saraf@iomosaic.com.

**SARAFPOUR, BEHNAZ,** apparel designer; b. Iran; Grad., Parsons Sch. of Design. Former designer Anne Klein, Isaac Mizrahi, Barney's NY Collection; launched clothing line Behnaz Sarafpour, 2001—. Work featured in Vogue, Elle, Towne & Country, Marie Claire & Vanity Fair. Recipient Golden Thimble award, Perry Ellis award nominee, Council of Fashion Designers of Am., 2002, 2003, 2005. Mem.: Council of Fashion Designers of Am. Office: Behnaz Sarafpour 136 W 21st St 6 Fl New York NY 10011*

**SARAIDARIDIS, SUSAN BRIDGET,** taxonomist; MS, Case Western Res. U., 1978. Cert. mgmt. Harvard Ext. Sch., 2001. Mgr., rsch. libr. Hewlett-Packard Co., Waltham/Andover, Mass., 1978—2000; it project mgr. Philips Electronics, Andover, 2000—03; mgr., taxonomist Harvard Bus. Sch. Pub., Watertown, Mass., 2003—. Office: Harvard Bus Sch Publishing 300 North Beacon St Watertown MA 02472 Office Phone: 617-783-7647.

**SARAKATSANNIS, LEONIDAS NICHOLAS,** musician, concert pianist, music educator, composer, conductor; b. Newport, Ky., May 30, 1929; s. Nicholas Demetrius Sarakatsannis and Melanthia Leonidas Kazangi; m. Frances Charles Nicholas, Jan. 22, 1956; children: Demetrius Leonidas, Nicholas Leonidas, Melanie Leonidas. MusB, Coll. Music, 1951; MusM, Coll.-Conservatory of Music, 1956; D in Musical Arts, U. Cin., 1968; postgrad., U. Mich., 1964. Cert. piano Ohio, 1949. Chmn. piano dept. U. Fla., 1959—63; dir. piano program So. Ill. U., Edwardsville, 1964—65; tchg. asst. U. Cin. Coll. Conservatory Music, 1965—68; chmn. dept. music U. Ctrl. Fla., Orlando, 1968—72; dir. applied music No. Ky. U., Highland Heights, Ky., 1972—77; pianist in residence Bloomsburg (Pa.) U., 1979—80; pianist, prof. music, chmn. music dept. U. Guam, Mangilao, Guam, 1981—93; adj. prof. music Manatee C.C., Bradenton, Fla., 1994—. Coll. recital chmn. Fla. State Music Tchrs. Assn., 1962; adjudicator. World Piano Competition, Cin., 1981—88; condr. Guam Symphony Orch., Mangilao, GM, 1981—85. Composer: (musical composition) Twelve Excursions For The Young Pianist, (voice and piano composition) A Communion Hymn; One Is Holy, (piano composition) Six Guam Sketches for Piano, (various compositions) Sonata for Piano, (musical composition) Hymns for Voice and Piano Entitled Praise the Lord, One is Holy, Yia Tin Photini; musician: (solo) Fla. Symphony, (piano soloist) Three performances with the Cincinnati Symphony Orchestra under Eric Kunzel and Thor Johnson, North Port (Fla.) Orchestra, Delius Festival in Jacksonville, Asolo Theater, Sarasota, Fla., Taft Mus., Cin., Manatee C.C., Saipan, Guam, Hawaii, and 5 Concerts in Japan, Carnegie Libr. Recitals, Xavier U., Coll. Mount Joseph, others, North Port Orchestra. Bd. dirs. Guam Symphony Orch., Mangialo, 1982—86, Ctrl. Fla. Civic Music Assn., Orlando, 1968—72; v.p. Ctrl. Fla. Music Tchrs. Assn., Orlando, 1970—72. Acting sgt. U.S. Army, 1951—53. Recipient Composition award, Fla. Composers League, 1962, Musical Contbn. to the Cultural Life of our Cmty. award, U. Guam, 1983, Concerto Competition, Coll. Conservatory Symphony Orch. Guam; Mem.: Coll. Music Soc., Pi Kappa Lambda (hon.), Phi Mu Alpha Sinfonia (recital chmn. 1950—56). Home: 4539 Hamlets Grove Dr Sarasota FL 34235

**SARALEGUI, CRISTINA MARIA,** Spanish language television personality, journalist; b. Havana, Cuba, Jan. 29, 1948; came to U.S., 1960; d. Francisco and Cristina (Santamarina) Saralegui; m. Marcos Avila, June 19, 1984; 3 children. Student mass comm., U. Miami. Features editor Vanidades Continental, Miami, Fla., 1970-73; editor Cosmopolitan Spanish, Miami, 1973-76, editor-in-chief, 1979-89; dir. enterntainment Miami Herald, 1976-77; editor-in-chief Intimidades mag., Miami, 1977-79, TV y Novelas mag.,

1986-89; hostess The Cristina Show Univision Network, 1989—; publisher Cristina the Magazine; hostess Cristina Opina, ABC radio program. Keynote spkr. Union Am. Women, P.R., 1981, Legendary Women of Miami. Featured in bestseller Latin Beauty, 1982; author autobiography My Life as a Blonde, 1998. Mem. internat. jury Miss Venezuela Pagent, 1982, Miss Columbia Pagent, 1987; bd. dir. Nat. Council of La Raza, Mus. TV & Radio; mem Nat. Council, AmFar. Recipient 10 Emmy awards; Keys to City Cartagena, Colombia, 1987; award of Distinction for Leadership, AmFar, 1995; Outstanding Communicator of the Year award, Nat. Org. for Women in Comm., 1996; Star on the Walk of Fame, 1999; Cmty. Svc. award, Nat. Council La Raza, 2000; Corp. Leader award, Nat. Network of Hispanic Women; VIP Honoree of the Year, Am. Cancer Soc., 2000; Gracie Allen Tribute award, Found. of Am. Women in radio & TV, 2001; Lifetime Achievement award, Imagen Found., 2002. Named one of the 25 Most Influential Hispanics, Time Mag., 2005. Mem. NAFE, Women in Comm. (key note spkr. 1986), Am. Soc. Profl. and Exec. Women, Am. Mgmt. Assn., Nat. Network Hispanic Women (Corp. Leader award), Latin Bus. and Profl. Women's Club. Republican. Roman Catholic. Office: The Christina Show 9405 NW 41st St Miami FL 33178-2301

**SARANDON, SUSAN ABIGAIL,** actress; b. NYC, Oct. 4, 1946; d. Phillip Leslie and Lenora Marie (Criscione) Tomalin; m. Chris Sarandon, Sept. 16, 1967 (div. 1979); children: Eva Maria Livia Amurri, Jack Henry Robbins, Miles Guthrie Robbins. BA in Drama and English, Cath. U. Am., 1968. Actress: (plays) include An Evening with Richard Nixon, 1972, A Coupla White Chicks Sittin' Around Talkin', 1980-81, A Stroll in the Air, Albert's Bridge, Private Ear, Public Eye, Extremities, 1982, (films) Joe, 1970, Lady Liberty, 1972, The Rocky Horror Picture Show, 1975, Lovin' Molly, 1974, The Front Page, 1974, The Great Waldo Pepper, 1975, Dragon Fly, 1976, Crash, 1976, The Other Side of Midnight, 1977, The Last of the Cowboys, 1978, Checkered Flag or Crash, 1978, Pretty Baby, 1978, King of the Gypsies, 1978, Something Short of Paradise, 1979, Loving Couples, 1980, Atlantic City, 1980 (Prix Genie Best Fgn. Actress award 1981, Acad. award nominee 1981), Tempest, 1982 (Best Actress award Venice Film Festival 1982), The Hunger, 1983, Buddy System, 1984, Compromising Positions, 1985, The Witches of Eastwick, 1987, Bull Durham, 1988, Sweet Hearts Dance, 1988, A Dry White Season, 1989, The January Man, 1989, White Palace, 1990, Thelma and Louise, 1991 (Acad. award nominee for best actress 1992, Golden Globe award nominee 1992), The Player, 1992, Light Sleeper, 1992, Bob Roberts, 1992, Lorenzo's Oil, 1992 (Acad. award nominee 1993), The Client, 1994 (Acad. award nominee for best actress), Little Women, 1994, Safe Passage, 1994, Dead Man Walking, 1995 (Golden Globe award nominee for best actress 1996, Acad. award for best actress 1996), James and the Giant Peach (voice), 1996, 187 (voice), 1997, Illuminata, 1998, Twilight, 1998, Stepmom (also producer), 1998, Joe Gould's Secret, 1999, Baby's in Black, 1999, Cradle Will Rock, 1999, Anywhere But Here, 1999, (voice) Rugrats in Paris: The Movie - Rugrats II, 2000, Moonlight Mile, 2002 (also exec. prodr.), The Banger Sisters, 2002, Igby Goes Down, 2002, Noel, 2004, Shall We Dance?, 2004, Alfie, 2004, Jiminy Glick in La La Wood, 2004, Elizabethtown, 2005; TV appearances: The Haunting of Rosalind, 1973, F. Scott Fitzgerald and The Last of the Belles, 1974, Who Am I This Time, 1982, A.D., 1985. Mussolini: The Decline and Fall of Il Duce, 1985, Earthly Possessions, 1999, Friends, 2001 (Emmy nominee), Malcolm in the Middle, 2002 (Emmy nominee), Ice Bound, 2003., The Exonerated, 2005; (TV series) A World Apart, 1970-71, Search for Tomorrow, 1972-73; TV miniseries: Children of Dune, 2003. Mem. AFTRA, Screen Actors Guild, Actors Equity, Acad. Motion Picture Arts and Scis., NOW, MADRE, Amnesty Internat., ACLU Office: Internat Creative Mgmt care Samuel Cohen 40 W 57th St New York NY 10019-4001

**SARAPH, PRASAD VAMAN,** research scientist, industrial engineer; arrived in U., 1998; BSME, Govt. Engring. Coll., Aurangabad, India, 1992; MS, Indian Inst. Tech., 1995; MS Engring., U. Calif., Berkeley, 1999. Prodn. supr. Universal Luggage Mfg. Co., Aurangabad, Maharashtra, India, 1992—93, rsch. assoc. Inst. Devel. Studies U. Sussex, Brighton, England, 1995—96; cons. A.F. Ferguson & Co, Mumbai, Maharashtra, India, 1996—97; grad. rsch. asst. U. Calif., Berkeley, 1998—99; sr. engr. Bayer Corp., Berkeley, 2000—01, project mgr., 2001—02; head Dept. Long Term Planning Bayer Biol. Products, Berkeley, 2003—05, supply chain excellence lead, 2006—. Track coord. healthcare and biotechnology Winter Simulation Conf., 2004—05. Author: Corporate Restructuring: Crompton Greaves and the Challenge of Globalization, 1998; contbr. articles to profl. jours. Recipient First Pl. award, Indian Inst. Tech., 1993, Inst. Indsl. Engrs., 1999. Mem.: YWCA, Capoeira Narahari (capoeirista 2000—). Achievements include first to introduce and successfully implement of discrete event simulation techniques in the biopharmaceuticals industry; research in use of dynamic simulation for risk analysis in biopharmaceuticals industry; development of hierarchical strategic capacity analysis methodology for biopharmaceutical manufacturing; and implementation of organizational decision support structure for biopharmaceutical industry; first to analysis methodology for impact of regulatory strategy on biopharmaceutical product and process life cycle management; successfully introduce optimization tools in supply chain planning for biopharmaceuticals. Avocations: martial arts, classical music, stamp collecting/philately, reading. Office: Bayer HealthCare LLC Biological Products 800 Dwight Way Berkeley CA 94710 Office Phone: 510-705-4703. Personal E-mail: psaraph@yahoo.com. Business E-Mail: prasad.saraph.b@bayer.com.

**SARASON, IRWIN G.,** psychology professor; b. Newark, Sept. 15, 1929; s. Max and Anna Sarason; m. Barbara June Ryrholm, Sept. 19, 1953; children: Suzanne, Jane, Donald. BA, Rutgers U., Newark, 1951; MS, U. Iowa, 1953; PhD, Ind. U., 1955. Intern clin. psychology VA Hosp., West Haven, Conn., 1955-56; from asst. prof. psychology to prof. emeritus U. Wash., Seattle, 1956—2003, prof. emeritus 2003—. Co-author: Abnormal Psychology, 1972, 11th edit., 2005; editor: Jour. Personality and Social Psychology, 1985-91; author over 275 articles. The Netherlands Inst. for Advanced Study fellow, Wassenaar, 1975, 85. Fellow APA, Japan Soc. for Promotion of Sci., AAAS, Western Psychol. Assn. (pres. 1978-79), Wash. State Psychol. Assn. (pres. 1965). Avocations: travel, music, reading. Home: 13516 42nd Ave NE Seattle WA 98125-3826 Office: U Wash Dept Psychology Box 351525 Seattle WA 98195-0001

**SARATH, CAROL ANN,** library and media coordinator; b. Ossining, N.Y., Apr. 2, 1952; d. Edward Noah and Florence Louise (Cafarelli) S.; m. Karl Burton Lohmann, July 9, 1986; children: Maria Estella, Patrick Noah. BS in Early Childhood Edn., So. Conn. State U., 1974; MLS, U. Ariz., 1980. Tchr. Gallup (N.Mex.) McKinley County Schs., 1975-79, libr./media coord., 1982—; rschr. Fenn Galleries, Santa Fe, N.Mex., 1980-82. Chair libr. br. Octavia Fellin Pub. Libr., Gallup, 1990—; mem. libr. adv. coun. State of N.Mex., Santa Fe, 1992-2000; co-chair N.Mex. Task Force on Sch. Librs., 1999—. Contbr.: Exploring the Southwest Through Childrens Literature, 1994. Bd. mem. Red Rock Balloon Rally Assocs., Gallup, 1983—. Mem. ALA, Am. Assn. Sch. Librs., N.Mex. Libr. Assn. Avocations: hot air ballooning, gardening. Office: Gallup McKinley County Schs PO Box 1318 Gallup NM 87305 E-mail: csarath@gmcs.k12.nm.us.

**SARAVOLATZ, LOUIS DONALD,** epidemiologist, medical educator; b. Detroit, Feb. 15, 1950; s. Samuel and Saya Betty (Chonich) S.; m. Yvette Susanne Braymer, Oct. 6, 1990; children: Samuel Francis, Louis Donald II, Stephanie Nicole. BS, U. Mich., 1972, MD, 1974. Fellow Am. Coll. Epidemiology. Intern Henry Ford Hosp., Detroit, 1974-75, 1975-77, fellow, 1977-79, dir. hosp. epidemiology, 1979-82, divsn. head infectious diseases, 1982-96, dir. infectious diseases rsch. lab., 1982-96; prof. medicine Case-Western Res. U., 1993-96, Wayne State U. Sch. Medicine, Detroit, 1996—. Clin. prof. medicine U. Mich. Med. Sch., Ann Arbor, 1986-96; mem. AIDS clin. drug devel. com. NIH, 1990-95; chmn. dept. internal medicine St. John Hosp. and Med. Ctr., 1996—. Contbr. over 170 articles to profl. pubs. Active Blue Ribbon Com. on AIDS State of Mich., Detroit, 1990; chmn. physician com. on AIDS Greater Detroit Health Coun., 1989. Master: ACP, Am. Coll.

Physicians; fellow: Royal Soc. Medicine (London), Infectious Diseases Soc. Am. (chmn. antimicrobial use and clin. trials com. 2000—03). Office Phone: 313-343-3362. Business E-Mail: louis.saravolatz@stjohn.org.

**SARAZIN, CRAIG LEIGH,** astronomer; b. Milw., Aug. 11, 1950; s. Valley V. and Martha V. (Gustafson) Sarazin; children: Stephen N., Andrew T. BS in Physics, Calif. Inst. Tech., 1972; MA in Physics, Princeton U., 1973, PhD in Physics, 1975. Millikan fellow Calif. Inst. Tech., Pasadena, 1975; mem. Inst. Advanced Study, Princeton, NJ, 1975-77; asst. prof. U. Va., Charlottesville, 1977-79, assoc. prof. dept. astronomy, 1979-86, prof., 1986-96, W.H. Vanderbilt prof. astronomy, 1996—, chmn. dept., 1992-95. Vis. asst. prof. U. Calif., Berkeley, 1979; vis. scientist Nat. Radio Astronomy Obs., Charlottesville, 1977-82; vis. prof. physics Inst. Advanced Study, 1981-82, Joint Inst. Lab. Astrophysics vis. fellow U. Colo., Boulder, 1985-86; mem. com. on Space Astronomy Astrophysics, Washington, 1984-86, mem. x-ray astronomy working group, 1989-99, chmn. Heineman prize com., 1995-98; chmn. Chandra users com., 1993-01, Advanced Satellite for Cosmology and Astrophysics users com., 1995-2000; mem. High Energy Astrophysics from Space Panel, 1999-2000; chmn. USRA Sci. Coun., 2000—. Author: X-ray Emission from Clusters of Galaxies; contbr. numerous articles to profl. jours. NSF grantee, 1981-86, NASA grantee, 1979-82, 86—; recipient Haren Fischer Physics prize Calif. Inst. Tech., 1971. Mem. Am. Astron. Soc., Internat. Astron. Union. Home: 664 Courtyard Ct Charlottesville VA 22903-7876 Office: U Va Dept Astronomy PO Box 400325 Charlottesville VA 22904-4325 Office Phone: 434-924-4903. Business E-Mail: sarazin@virginia.edu.

**SARBANES, PAUL SPYROS,** senator; b. Salisbury, Md., Feb. 3, 1933; s. Spyros P. and Matina (Tsigounis) S.; m. Christine Dunbar, June 11, 1960; children— John Peter, Michael Anthony, Janet Matina. AB in Public and Internat. Affairs, magna cum laude, Princeton, 1954; BA in Philosophy, Politics and Economics, Rhodes Scholar, Oxford U., Eng., 1957; LLB, Harvard, 1960. Bar: Md. 1960. Law clk. to Hon. Morris A. Soper US Ct. Appeals (4th Cir.), 1960-61; assoc. Piper & Marbury, Balt., 1961-62; adminstrv. asst. to chmn. Walter W. Heller Coun. Econ. Advisors, Exec. Office of the Pres., Washington, 1962—63; exec. dir. Charter Revision Commn., Balt., 1963-64; assoc. Venable, Baetjer & Howard, Balt., 1965-70; mem. Md. Ho. of Dels., 1967-71, US Congress from 3rd Dist. Md., 1971—77; US Senator from Md., 1977—. Mem. banking com. U.S. Senate, 1977—, mem. fgn. rels. com., 1977—, mem. joint econ. com., 1979—, mem. budget com., 1993—. Co-author (with David R. Obey): The Changing American Economy: Papers from the Fortieth Anniversary Symposium of the Joint Economic Committee of the US Congress, 1986. Recipient Nat. Disting. Svc. award, Am. Pub. Transit Assn., 1999, Paul H. Douglas Ethics in Govt. award, Inst. Govt. & Pub. Affairs, U. Ill., 2003, Restore Am. Hero award, Nat. Trust for Historic Preservation and HGTV, 2005. Fellow: Am. Acad. Arts & Sci. Democrat. Greek Orthodox. Office: US Senate 309 Hart Senate Bldg Washington DC 20510-0001 also: Tower 1 Ste 1710 100 S Charles St Baltimore MD 21201-2725 Office Phone: 202-224-4524, 410-962-4436. Office Fax: 410-962-4156, 202-224-1651.*

**SARBIN, HERSHEL BENJAMIN,** management consultant, lawyer, publishing executive; b. Massillon, Ohio, Dec. 30, 1924; s. Joseph I. and Sarah Charlotte (Reich) S.; m. Susan Challman, July 24, 1973; children by previous marriage: Penelope Sarbin Rische, Richard, Barbara; 1 stepdau., Caroline Cooley. AB, Western Res. U., 1946; JD, Harvard U., 1950. Bar: Ill. 1950, N.Y. 1953. Assoc. firm Lewis and MacDonald, N.Y.C., 1953-58; with Ziff-Davis Pub. Co., 1950-81; pub. Popular Photography mag., 1965-66, sr. v.p. co., 1967-74; assoc. pub. Travel Weekly, 1967-68, pub., 1969-74, pres., pub. dir., chief exec. officer photog. div., 1968-69, pres. Pub. Transp. and Travel div., 1970-74; pres. Ziff-Davis Pub. Co., 1974-78; exec. v.p Ziff Corp., 1978-81, also dir.; chmn., pres. Hershel Sarbin Assocs., Inc., 1981—. Vis. assoc. prof. Fla. Internat. U., 1980; mem. exec. com., nat. photography coordinator Pres.'s Council Youth Opportunity, 1968; fed. commr. Nat. Commn. on New Technol. Uses of Copyrighted Works, 1975-78; mem. policy rev. bd. Public Agenda Found.; pres., CEO Cowles Bus. Media, Inc., 1991-95; Sr. Advisor Cowles Media, 1995; sr. dir. Peppers & Rogers Group, Stamford, Ct., 1998-2001. Author (with George Chernoff): Photography and the Law, 1958, rev. edit., 1977; author: A Different Game: After 50, 2001. Mem. exec. com. Westchester County (N.Y.) Sch. Bd., 1964-66; mem. ethical practices com. N.Y. Sch. Bd. Assn., 1965-68; pres. Hastings-on-Hudson Bd. Edn., 1966-67; bd. dirs. Children's Rights, Inc, 2003. Served with AUS, 1946-47. Mem. Harvard Club, Bedford (N.Y.) Golf and Tennis Club, Phi Beta Kappa. Home: 47 Chestnut Ave Larchmont NY 10538 Office: Herschel Sarbin Associates 525 Park Ave # 3a New York NY 10021-8141

**SARD, SUSANNAH ELLEN,** non-profit executive; b. Boston, May 10, 1944; d. Russell Ellis and Miriam Clark Sard. AB, Bryn Mawr Coll., 1966. Devel. adminstr. Ky. Ednl. TV, Lexington, 1978—88; dir. found. and corp. rels. Sarah Lawrence Coll., Bronxville, NY, 1991—96; dir. devel. The Town Hall, NYC, 1998—2002; exec. dir. Women's City Club NY, NYC, 2002—04; edn. liaison R.J. & S.H. Kaplan Family Found., NYC, 2004—. Alumni bd. Rippowam Cisqua Sch. Mem.: Blue Hill Troupe. Office: Kaplan Family Found 866 UN Plz Ste 306 New York NY 10017 Business E-Mail: owlkap@aol.com.

**SARDISCO, KAREN ANN,** artist, educator; b. Rochester, N.Y., July 18, 1955; d. Samuel Peter and Florence Rose (Montrose) Sardisco; m. Norman A. Williams, Oct. 28, 1990; 1 child, Ian Andrew Williams. BS in Art Edn., SUNY, Buffalo, 1977, MFA in Painting, Rochester Inst. Tech., 1985. Tchr. art, chari dept. art Bishop Kearney High Sch., Rochester, 1979-82; vis. asst. prof. Sch. of Art and Design Rochester Inst. Tech., 2003—05; asst. prof. Monroe C.C., 2005—. Curator Main Gallery, Rochester, N.Y., 1994, Mercer Gallery, Rochester, N.Y. One-woman shows include ARC Gallery, Chgo., 1995, Artemesia Gallery, Chgo., 1996, Gallery 34, Canandaigua, N.Y., 1997, Aljira Newark N Y 1999, Houghton House Gallery, Geneva, N.Y., 2000, many others; group shows include Meml. Art Gallery, Rochester, N.Y., 2004, The Gallery at One Bausch And Lomb Pl., Rochester, N.Y., 2004; permanent collections include Westinghouse Corp., Pitts., Chase Lincoln Bank, Buffalo, Westwood Pharms., Buffalo, others. Recipient Merit award Cheekwood Nat. Contemporary Painting Competition, 1992, Purchase award Three Rivers Arts Festival '87, Pitts. by Westinghouse Corp., Light Impressions award for excellence in two-dimensional artwork Rochester Finger Lakes Exhbn., 1984; artist grantee Constance Salt on Stall Found. Arts. Avocations: reading, cross country skiing, travel.

**SARDO, SANFORD,** music educator; b. New York, NY, Aug. 29, 1969; s. Joan Marie and Joseph James Smith (Stepfather); m. Jennifer Lynn McKenna, July 3, 1999. BA, SUNY, Stony Brook, NY, 1992; MSc in Edn., CUNY-Queens Coll., 1998. Cert. Tchr. N.Y., 1993, Music Edn. Orff-Shulwerk, 1995. Tech. dir. Broadhollow Theaters, Lindenhurst, NY, 1989—93; dir. choral activities Calhoun High School Choral Pgm., 1993—. Music counselor MapleWood Sch. Day Camp, Wantagh, NY, 1991—94. Singer: (performance) Back-up Choir @ Kenny Rogers Christmas Show, 1998; dir., dir.: Choir Performance @ Disney's Magic Music Days, 1998, 2000. Recipient Choral Soc. Award in Music Edn., CUNY- Queens Coll., 1993, Music Educator of the Yr., Long Island Musicians Assn., 1995, Tchr. Recognition Award, Kiwanis Club of Merrick, 1998, Legis. Ciitation, Nassau County Legis., 1998, 2003, Cert. of Recognition, Merrick C. of C., 2002, Nassau County Legis, 2002. Mem.: Nassau Music Educators Assn., NY State Sch. Music Assn., Music Educators Nat. Conf., Am. Fedn. Tchrs., NY Congress of PTAs (life). R-Consevative. Roman Catholic. Home: 89 Charles St Lindenhurst NY 11757 Office: Calhoun HS Choral Program 1786 State St Merrick NY 11566 Personal E-Mail: sardomus@aol.com, chschoir@aol.com.

**SAREMBOCK, IAN JOSEPH,** internist, cardiologist; b. Cape Town, South Africa, June 9, 1951; arrived in US, 1982, naturalized, 1986; m. Ghita Marueen Sarembock; children: Craig Murray, Keri Lauren. MD, U. Cape Town, 1975, PhD, 1988. Diplomate Am. Bd. Internal Medicine, Am. Bd. Cardiovasc. Medicine, Am. Bd. Interventional Cardiology. Sr. house officer

dept. internal medicine U. Cape Town and Groote Schuur Hosp., Cape Town, 1979-80, resident in internal medicine, 1980-83, sr. registrar Cardiac Clinic, 1985-86; Velva Schrire meml. rsch. fellow Cardiac Clinic Groote Schur Hosp., 1983-85; postdoctoral rsch. assoc. divsn. cardiology Yale U., New Haven, 1986-88; attending cardiologist divsn. cardiology VA Ctr., West Haven, Conn., 1987-88; asst. prof. internal medicine cardiovasc. divsn. U. Va. Health Scis. Ctr., Charlottesville, 1988-93, assoc. prof. internal medicine cardiovasc. divsn., 1993-99, dir. coronary care unit, 1988—, prof. internal medicine cardiovasc. divsn., 1999—; interventional cardiologist, 1988—; cardiology cons. Salem (Va.) VA Med. Ctr., 1988—; dir. Ctr. Interventional Cardiology, U. Va. Health System, 2005—. Lectr., presenter in field; invited prof. Heart-Lung Inst., Utrecht, Netherlands, 1992; mem. faculty restenosis summits, Cleve. Clinic, 1992, 93, 97. Contbr. articles to profl. pubs. Mem. policy working com., house staff supervision Commonwealth of Va., 1990—. With South African Def. Force, Med. Corps, 1977—78. Grantee U. Va. Sch. Medicine, 1989, Beecham Labs., 1989-90, Am. Heart Assn., 1989-91, 91-92, 95-98, NIH, 1991-94, 2000-05. Fellow ACP, Coll. Physicians South Africa, Am. Coll. Cardiology (allied health profls. com. 1993—), Coun. Thrombosis Atherosclerosis and Vascular Biology; mem. AAAS, Am. Heart Assn. (bd. dirs. Charlottesville/Albermarle divsn. 1991—, mem. Va. affiliate rsch. peer rev. subcom. 1992—, thrombosis coun. 1987, fellow coun. on clin. cardiology 1989), South African Med. and Dental Coun. Jewish. Office: U Va Health Sys Cardiovasc Div Box 800158 Charlottesville VA 22908-0158 Fax: 434-982-0901. E-mail: ijs4s@virginia.edu.

**SAREYAN, ANDY,** publishing executive; m. Nancy Marshall; children: Alex, Eliza. Graduated summa cum laude in Econ., Middlebury Coll.; MBA, Stanford U. Various consumer mktg. positions Time Inc., 1987—91; consumer mktg. dir., Can. and Latin Am. Time Internat., 1991—93; v.p., consumer mktg. and develop. Entertainment Weekly, 1993—97; v.p., assoc. pub. In Style, 1997—99; founding pub. Real Simple, 1999; pres. Parenting Group, 2001—02, Entertainment Weekly, NY, 2002—05; pub. Better Homes & Gardens Mag., NYC, 2006—; and exec. v.p. Meredith Pub. Group, NYC, 2006—. Office: Meredith Publishing 125 Park Ave New York NY 10017*

**SARFATY, WAYNE ALLEN,** insurance agent, financial planner; b. Rochester, NY, Apr. 18, 1951; s. Benjamin and Grace (Rowan) S.; m. Karen Nugent, July 12, 1957 (div. Apr. 2004); children: Melissa A., Gabrielle M. Student, Parsons Coll., 1971-74. Cert. ins. agt. Sales rep. Met. Life, Rochester, N.Y., 1979-81; register rep. Prudential Fin. Svcs., Rochester, 1981-92; owner, broker Wayne A. Sarfaty & Assocs., Rochester, 1992—. Dir. tng. films. Mem. Eagle Club. Recipient Nat. Quality award Nat. Assn. Life Underwriters, 1982-90; named to Million Dollar Round Table, NALU, 1987. Mem.: Eagle Club, Am. Legion. Avocations: camping, auto racing, darts. Home: 8 Rosencrans St Cohocton NY 14826-0182 E-mail: was2@frontiernet.net.

**SARGEANT, ERNEST JAMES,** lawyer, educator; b. Spokane, Wash., Sept. 26, 1918; s. Ernest Edward and Louise (McWhinnie) S.; m. Helene Sophie Kazanjian, Jan. 29, 1944 BA cum laude, Harvard U., 1940, LL.B. magna cum laude, 1947. Bar: Mass. 1947. Assoc. Ropes & Gray, Boston, 1947, 52-56, ptnr., 1956-90, of counsel, 1991—. Lectr. law Harvard U. Law Sch., Cambridge, Mass., 1961-62, 65-92; adj. prof. Boston Coll. Law Sch., 1990-98. Grad. treas. Harvard Law Rev., Cambridge, 1971-98. Capt. U.S. Army, 1942-46, 51-52. Mem. Am. Law Inst. (council), ABA, Boston Bar Assn. Clubs: Union (Boston); Country (Brookline, Mass.). Home: 24 Highgate Wellesley Hills MA 02481-1420 Office: Ropes & Gray 1 International Pl Boston MA 02110-2624

**SARGENT, ANNEILA ISABEL,** astrophysicist; b. Kirkcaldy, Fife, Scotland; came to US, 1964; d. Richard Anthony and Annie (Blaney) Cassells; m. Wallace Leslie William Sargent, Aug. 5, 1964; children: Lindsay Eleanor, Alison Clare. BSc with honors in Physics, U. Edinburgh, 1963; MS, Calif. Inst. Tech., 1967, PhD in Astronomy, 1977. Postdoctoral rsch. fellow Calif. Inst. Tech., Pasadena, 1977-80, mem. profl. staff, 1980-88, sr. rsch. fellow, 1988-90, sr. rsch. assoc., 1990—98; assoc. dir. Owens Valley Radio Obs., 1992—96, exec. dir., 1996—98, dir., 1998—; prof., assoc. dir. 1998—, Benjamin M. Rosen prof. astronomy, 2004—. Dir. Michelson Interferometry Sci Ctr., 2000—03, dir. combined array for rsch. in millimeter wave astronomy, 2003—. Contbr. articles to profl. jours. Recipient NASA Pub. Svc. medal, 1998, Alumna of Yr., U. Edinburgh, 2002; grantee, NASA, NSF. Fellow Am. Acad. Arts & Scis.; Mem. Royal Astron. Soc. (assoc.), Am. Astron. Soc. (pres. 2000-02), Internat. Astron. Union Roman Catholic. Office: Dept Astronomy Calif Inst Tech MC 105-24 1200 E Calif Blvd Pasadena CA 91125 E-mail: afs@astro.caltech.edu.*

**SARGENT, CHARLES LEE,** manufacturing executive; b. Flint, Mich., Mar. 22, 1937; s. Frank T. and Evelyn M. (Martinson) S.; m. Nancy Cook, June 9, 1962; children: Wendy L., Joy A., Candace L. B ME, GM Inst., 1960; MBA, Harvard U., 1962; D in Engring. (hon.), Kettering U., 2004. Reliability engr. AC Spark Plug div. GM, Flint, 1962-63; with Thetford Corp., Ann Arbor, Mich., 1962-95, pres., chmn. bd. dirs., 1974-95, Thermassan Corp., 1969-72; pres., owner Quality Boat Lifts, Inc., Fort Myers, Fla., 1996—. Trustee Lincoln Cons. Schs., 1973-77, Ketterine U., 1989-2004, chmn. 1995-97. Patentee in field. Elder Presbyn. Ch. Recipient Entrepreneurial Achievement award GMI, 1989; named Entrepreneur of the Yr., Harvard Bus. Sch. Club of Detroit, 1981, Engring. Achievement award Kettering U., 1999. Mem. Barton Hills Country Club (bd. dirs. 1985-87, pres. 1987), Harvard Bus. Sch. Club of Detroit (bd. dirs. 1983-93). Avocations: travel, golf. Home: 3310 Village Harbor Dr Bay Harbor MI 49770

**SARGENT, JOHN,** psychiatrist; MD, U. Rochester, 1973. Diplomate in psychiatry, child and adolescent psychiatry Am. Bd. Psychiatry and Neurology; diplomate Am. Bd. Pediats.; approved clin supr Am Assn. Marriage and Family Therapy. Intern and resident pediat. U. Wis., Madison, 1973—77; resident child and adolescent psychiatry Phila. Child Guidance Ctr., 1978—80; resident gen. psychiatry Hosp. U. Pa., Phila., 1984—87; dir. child and adolescent psychiatry U. Pa. Med. Sch., 1989—97, dir. adult residency program, 1989—97; mem. staff Children's Hosp. Phila., Phila. Child Guidance Ctr., 1980—97; dir. edn. and rsch., dean Karl Menninger Sch. Psychiatry & Mental Health Svcs., Topeka, 1997—2001; prof. psychiatry Baylor Coll. Medicine, Houston, 2001—; dir. child and adolescent psychiatry Ben Taub Hosp., Houston, 2001—. Assoc. prof. psychiatry and pediat. U. Pa. Med. Sch., 1987-97; Pfeiffer/Adams prof. psychiatry Karl Menninger Sch. Psychiatry. Mem. editl. bd. Jour. Am. Acad. Child and Adolescent Psychiatry, Family Process, Bull. of Menninger Clinic; co-author: Madness, Chaos and Violence: Therapy with Families at the Brink; co-editor: Primary Care Pediatrics; contbr. over 60 articles to profl. jours. Dep. dir. Ea. European Child Abuse and Child Mental Health Program, Soros Found. and Children's Mental Health Alliance, 1997-2003. Office: Baylor Coll Medicine One Baylor Plaza BCM 350 Houston TX 77030 Office Phone: 713-798-7889. Business E-Mail: asargent@bcm.edu.

**SARGENT, JOSEPH DANIEL,** motion picture and television director; b. Jersey City, July 22, 1925; s. Domenico and Maria (Noviello) Sargente; m. Carolyn Nelson, Nov. 22, 1970; children: Athena, Lia. Student in Theatre Arts, New Sch. for Social Rsch., 1946—49. Pres. Joseph Sargent Prodns. Inc. Dir.: (films) Street-Fighter, 1959, The Spy in the Green Hat, 1966, One Spy Too Many, 1966, The Hell with Heroes, 1968, Colossus: The Forbin Project, 1970, The Man, 1972, White Lightning, 1973, The Taking of Pelham One Two Three, 1974 (Best Dir. award San Sebastian Film Festival) MacArthur, 1977, Goldengirl, 1979, Coast to Coast, 1980, Nightmares, 1983, Jaws: The Revenge, 1987; (TV films) The Sunshine Patriot, 1968, The Immortal, 1969, Tribes, 1970 (Outstanding Dirctorial Achievement award Dirs. Guild Am.), Maybe I'll Come Home in the Spring, 1971, Longstreet, 1971, Man on a String, 1972, The Marcus-Nelson Murders, 1973 (Emmy award, Dirs. Guild Am. award), The Man Who Died Twice, 1973, Wheeler and Murdoch, 1973, Sunshine, 1973, Hustling, 1975, Friendly Persuasion, 1975, The Night That Panicked America, 1975, Amber Waves, 1980, Freedom, 1981, Tomorrow's Child, 1982, Memorial Day, 1983, Choices of the Heart, 1983, Terrible Joe

Moran, 1984, Sunday Night Live, 1984, Love Is Never Silent, 1985 (Emmy award), Passion Flower, 1986, The Must Be A Pony, 1986, Of Pure Blood, 1986, The Karen Carpenter Story, 1989, Day One, 1989, The Incident, 1990, Miss Rose White, 1992, Somebody's Daughter, 1992, Skylark, 1993, Abraham, 1994, World War II: When Lions Roared, 1994, My Antonia, 1995, Mandela and de Klerk, 1997, Miss Evers' Boys, 1997, The Long Island Incident, 1998, The Wall, 1998, Crime and Punishment, 1998, A Lesson Before Dying, 1999, Vola Sciusciu, 2000, For Love or Country, 2000, Bojangles, 2001, Out of the Ashes, 2003, Something the Lord Made, 2004, Warm Springs, 2005 (Outstanding Dirctorial Achievement in Movies for TV Dirs. Guild Am., 2005); (TV series) Gunsmoke, 1962—65, The Man From UNCLE, 1964, The Girl From UNCLE, 1966, Star Trek, 1966, Gallegher Goes West, 1966, The Invaders, 1967, Garrison's Gorillas, 1967, It Takes A Thief, 1968, The Manions of America, 1981, Space, 1985, Streets of Laredo, 1995, Salem Witch Trials, 2002; dir. & actor (TV films) Caroline?, 1990, Ivory Hunters, 1990, The Love She Sought, 1990. With U.S. Army, 1943—46. Mem.: Actors Equity Assn., AFTRA, Screen Actors Guild, Dirs. Guild Am. Office: c/o Shapiro Lichtman 8827 Beverly Blvd Los Angeles CA 90048-2405*

**SARGENT, JOSEPH DENNY,** insurance executive; b. West Hartford, Conn., Sept. 11, 1929; s. Thomas Denny and Elizabeth (Owen) S.; m. Mary A. Tennant, June 25, 1955; children: Robert Tennant, Thomas Denny II, Mary Diane, Suzanne Davis. BA, Yale U., 1952. Ptnr. Conning & Co., Inc., Hartford, Conn., 1957-86, mng. ptnr., 1986-92; chmn., CEO Conning & Co., Hartford, Conn., 1986-91, chmn., 1992, vice-chmn., 1993-95; chmn. Conning Internat., London, 1986-92; vice chmn. Conning & Co., 1993-95; chmn. Bradley, Foster & Sargent, 1995—. Bd. dirs Beekley Corp., Bristol, Conn., Tenwick Reins., Stamford, Conn.; past trustee MMI Co., Chgo., Mut. Risk, Bermuda, Policy Mgmt. Sys., Columbia, S.C.; chmn. Conn. Surety Corp., Hartford, 1993-97, Bradley, Foster & Sargent, Hartford, Beazley Furlonge Holdings, Ltd., London; trustee McLean Fund; chmn., treas. SKI Ltd, 1956-96. Past trustee Wadsworth Atheneum, Children's Svcs. of Conn.; trustee Hartford Hosp. Mem.: Yale Club (Hartford), Hartford Club, Hartford Golf Club. Home: 25 Colony Rd West Hartford CT 06117-2215 Office: City Place II 185 Asylum St Hartford CT 06103-3408

**SARGENT, MARK A.,** dean, law educator; b. New London, Conn., 1951; m. Joan Taranto; 1 child, Alexander. BA magna cum laude, Wesleyan U., 1973; MA Medieval & Renaissance Hist., Cornell U., 1975, JD, 1978. Bar: Mass. 1978. Atty. Csaplar & Bok, Boston, 1978—80; asst. prof. law U. Baltimore Sch. Law, 1980—83, assoc. prof., 1983—87, prof., 1987—89, U. Maryland Sch. Law, 1989—97, dir. Law and Entrepreneurship prog., 1989—97, Piper & Marbury Prof. Law, 1993—97, assoc. dean, 1994—97; dean, prof. law Villanova U. Sch. Law, 1997—. Vis. prof. law Washington Coll. Law, Am. U., 1987; vis. assoc. prof. law So. Methodist U. Sch. Law, 1988; arbitrator Am. Arbitration Assn., 1998—. Editor: The Business Lawyer, 1991—97; mem. editl. bd. The Business Lawyer, 1997—99, co-editor-in-chief Villanova Jour. Law and Investment Mgmt., 1998—; contbr. articles to profl. law jours. Mem. bd. trustees Wilmington Trust Mutual Funds, 2002—; mem. bd. dirs Saint Thomas More Soc. of Pa., 1998—; independent gen. ptnr. Fiduciary Capital Ptnrs. SBIC, 1998—2002. Office: Villanova U Sch Law 113 Garey Hall 800 Lancaster Ave Villanova PA 19085-1603 Office Phone: 610-519-7007. Office Fax: 610-519-6472. E-mail: sargent@law.villanova.edu.*

**SARGENT, PAMELA,** writer; b. Ithaca, N.Y., Mar. 20, 1948; BA, SUNY, Binghamton, 1968, MA, 1970. Mng. editor, Binghamton, 1970-73; asst. editor, 1973-75; Am. editor Bull. Sci. Fiction Writers Am., Johnson City, NY, 1983-91. Author: Cloned Lives, 1976, Starshadows, 1977, The Sudden Star, 1979, Watchstar, 1980, The Golden Space, 1982, The Alien Upstairs, 1983, Earthseed, 1983, Eye of the Comet, 1984, Homesmind, 1984, Venus of Dreams, 1986, The Shore of Women, 1986, The Best of Pamela Sargent, 1987, Alien Child, 1988, Venus of Shadows, 1988, Ruler of the Sky, 1993 (Nebula best novelette award 1992, Locus best novelette award 1993, Electric Sci. Fiction award 1993), Climb the Wind: A Novel of Another America, 1999, (with Ron Miller) Firebrands: The Heroines of Science Fiction and Fantasy, 1998, Child of Venus, 2001, Behind the Eyes of Dreamers and Other Short Novels, 2002, The Mountain Cage and Other Stories, 2002, Eye of Flame: Fantasies, 2003, Thumbprints, 2004; editor: (anthology) Women of Wonder, 1975, Bio-Futures, 1976, More Women of Wonder, 1976, The New Women of Wonder, 1978, (with Ian Watson) Afterlives, 1986, Women of Wonder, The Classic Years, 1996, Women of Wonder, The Contemporary Years, 1995, Nebula Awards 29, 1995, Nebula Awards 30, 1996, Nebula Awards 31, 1997, Conqueror Fantastic, 2004. Office: care Richard Curtis Assocs Inc 171 E 74th St New York NY 10021-3221 Personal E-Mail: psdel2003@yahoo.com.

**SARGENT, ROBERT GEORGE,** engineering educator; b. Port Huron, Mich., June 14, 1937; s. George O. and Marie L. (Roome) S.; m. Dorothy Baum, 1970; 1 dau., Tiffany. BSE, U. Mich., 1959, MS, 1963, PhD, 1966. Elec. engr. Hughes Aircraft Co., Culver City, Calif., 1959-61; faculty mem. Syracuse U., 1966—, asst. prof., 1966-70, assoc. prof., 1970-81, prof. indsl. engring. and ops. research, 1982-96, chmn. dept., 1982-85, prof. elec. and computer engring., 1994-96, prof. elec. engring. and computer sci., 1996—. Vis. faculty Cornell U., 1981-82, Ctr. Econ. Rsch. Tilburg U., 1996; bd. dirs. Winter Simulation Conf., 1974-84, chmn. bd., 1979-81, gen. chmn., 1977, TIMS Coll. on Simulation and Gaming, 1978-80; pres. WSC Found., 2003-. Dept. editor Comms. of Assn. Computing Machinery, 1980-85; mem. editl. adv. bd. ACM Transactions on Modeling and Simulations, 1998-98; mem. adv. bd. Jour. of Simulation, 2005—; contbr. articles to profl. jours. Recipient Svc. award Winter Simulation Conf., 1984. Fellow Inst. Ops. Rsch. and Mgmt. Scis. (Disting. Svc. award for Simulation 1988 Lifetime Profl. Achievement award 2002)); mem. Assn. Computing Machinery (nat. lectr 1985-89, Svc. award 1985), Inst. Indsl. Engrs. (Svc. award 1985), Soc. Computer Simulation (bd. dirs. 1984-87), Computer Soc. IEEE (mem. exec. com. simulation 1985-99). Office: Syracuse U Dept Elec Engring and Computer Sci Syracuse NY 13244-0001

**SARGENT, RONALD L.,** retail office and business products executive; m. Jill Sargent; 2 children. BS, Harvard U., MBA, 1979. Various mgmt. and planning positions with Kroger Co., 1974-89; regional v.p. ops. Staples Inc., 1989—92, v.p. Staples Direct, 1992—94, pres. Staples Contract and Comml., 1994—98, COO, 1998—2002, pres., 1998—2005, CEO, 2002—, chmn. bd. dir., 2005—. Bd. dir. Aramark Corp., Yankee Candle Corp., Mattel Inc. Office: Staples Inc PO Box 9265 Framingham MA 01701-9265*

**SARGENT, THOMAS ANDREW,** retired political science professor; b. Indpls., Apr. 24, 1933; s. Thomas Edward and Inez (Secrest) S.; m. Cecily Constance Fox-Williams, 1965 (dec.); children: Sarah Beatrice, Andrew Fox; m. 2d Frances Petty, 1967. BA, DePauw U., Greencastle, Ind., 1955; MA, Fletcher Sch. Law and Diplomacy, Tufts U., 1959, MA in Law and Diplomacy, 1968, PhD, 1969. With First Nat. City Bank, N.Y.C., 1959-64, asst. accountant, 1963-64; asst. sec. Irving Trust Co., N.Y.C., 1964-66; mem. faculty Ball State U., Muncie, Ind., 1969-89, dir. London Ctr., 1973-74, chmn. polit. sci. dept., 1977-80, prof. polit. sci., 1979-89, prof. emeritus, 1989—, acting assoc. to dean Coll. Scis. and Humanities, 1981-82, assoc. dean Coll. Scis. and Humanities 1982-85, dir. spl. programs Minnetrista Ctr., 1985-87; dir. E.B. Ball Ctr., Muncie, 1987-89, dir. emeritus, 1989—. Contbg. editor Ripon Forum, 1973-78. Bd. dirs., exec. v.p. Ea. Ind. Cmty. TV, Muncie, 1974-76, pres., 1976-77; mem. nat. bd. govs. Ripon Soc., Washington, 1976-84; mem. Indpls. Com. Fgn. Rels., 1977-2004, com. fgn. rels. Ctrl. Ind., 2004—, bd. dirs., 2005—; bd. dirs. Hist. Muncie, Inc., 1979-85, pres., 1980; bd. dirs. Muncie Civic Theatre Assn., 1978-81, 90-96, 1st v.p., 1992-96; exec. dir. Ind. Consortium for Internat. Programs, 1982-88; mem. Ind. Real Estate Commn., 1983-91; trustee DePauw U., 1983—; bd. dirs. Muncie Symphony Orch., 1985-95, pres., 1991-93; mem. bd. govs. Minnetrista Cultural Ctr., 1988-94, pres. 1994-96; 2d v.p., 1993-94; trustee Malpas Trust, 1990—, pres., 1997—; bd. dirs. Arts Ind., Inc., 1992-99, Muncie Children's Mus., 1994-2000, v.p. 1996-97, pres. 1997; trustee Ind. Colls. Ind., 1996—, United Meth.

Meml. Home, Warren, Ind., 1997—; mem. strategy coun. North Ind. Conf. United Meth. Ch., 2000—. 1st lt. USAF, 1955-58. Named Sagamore of Wabash, 1988. Mem. Am. Polit. Sci. Assn., Delaware County Hist. Alliance (bd. dirs. 1980-86, 87-95, pres., 1987-91), Soc. Profl. Journalists, Delaware Country Club, Columbia Club (Indpls.), Maxinkuckee Yacht Club (Culver, Ind.), Rotary, Phi Delta Theta. Republican. United Methodist. E-mail: tsarg123@aol.com.

**SARGENT, WALLACE LESLIE WILLIAM,** astronomer, educator; b. Elsham, Eng., Feb. 15, 1935; naturalized, 2004; s. Leslie William and Eleanor (Denniss) S.; m. Anneila Isabel Cassells, Aug. 5, 1966; children: Lindsay Eleanor, Alison Clare. B.Sc., Manchester U., 1956, M.Sc., 1957, PhD, 1959. Research fellow Calif. Inst. Tech., Pasadena, 1959-62; sr. research fellow Royal Greenwich Obs., 1962-64; asst. prof. physics U. Calif., San Diego, 1964-66; mem. faculty dept. astronomy Calif. Inst. Tech., 1966—, prof., 1971-81, Ira S. Bowen prof. astronomy, 1981—, dir. Palomar Obs., 1997-2000. Miller prof. U. Calif., Berkeley, 1993; Thomas Gold lectr. Cornell U., Ithaca, NY, 1995; Sackler lectr. Harvard U., Cambridge, Mass., 1995, U. Calif., Berkeley, 1996; Icko Iben lectr. U. Ill., 2002. Contbr. articles to profl. jours. Alfred P. Sloan fellow, 1968-70. Fellow Am. Acad. Arts and Scis., NAS, Royal Soc. (London); mem Am. Astron. Soc. (v.p. 2004—), Helen B. Warner prize 1969, Dannie Heineman prize 1991, Henry Norris Russell Lectureship, 2001), Royal Astron. Soc. (George Darwin lectr. 1987, assoc. 1998), Astron. Soc. Pacific (Bruce Gold medal 1994), Internat. Astron. Union. Clubs: Athenaeum (Pasadena). Home: 400 S Berkeley Ave Pasadena CA 91107-5062 Office: Calif Inst Tech Astronomy Dept 105-24 Pasadena CA 91125-0001 Office Phone: 626-395-4055.

**SARGENT, WALTER HARRIMAN, II,** lawyer; b. Norfolk, Va., Aug. 26, 1958; s. Richard E. and Martha F. (Bassett) S. BS in Philosophy, MIT, 1980, BS in Computer Sci. and Engring., 1980; JD, Harvard U., 1987. Bar: Colo. 1987, U.S. Dist. Ct. Colo. 1988, U.S. Ct. Appeals (3d, 6th, 9th and 10 cirs.), U.S. Supreme Ct. 1992. Assoc. Holme Roberts & Owen, Colorado Springs, 1987-95; pvt. practice Colorado Springs, 1995—; bd. trustees Colorado Legal Aid Found., 1998—2004. Bd. dirs. ARC of the Pikes Peak Region, 1991-97, Coalition for Adult Literacy, Colorado Springs, 1989-93. Recipient John M. Olin prize in law and econs. Harvard Law Sch., 1987, John M. Olin fellow, 1987, fellow Am. Acad. Appellate Lawyers, 2004—. Mem. ABA (appellate practice com.), Colo. Bar Assn. (appellate subcom.), Am. Acad. Appellate Lawyers. Avocation: distance running. Home: 1632 N Cascade Ave Colorado Springs CO 80907-7409 Office: Walter H Sargent A Profl Corp 1632 N Cascade Ave Colorado Springs CO 80907-7409 Office Phone: 719-577-4510. Personal E-mail: wsargent@wsargent.com.

**SARGENT, WILLIAM WINSTON,** retired anesthesiologist; b. Oshkosh, Wis., Feb. 28, 1933; s. Sprague Spencer and Lila Jane (Gjermundson) S. BS in Medicine, U. Ill., Chicago, 1955, MD, 1957; MS in Anesthesiology, U. Minn., 1967. Diplomate Am. Bd. Anesthesiology. Staff anesthesiologist St. Anthony Hosp., Rockford, Ill., 1960-61, Swedish Am. Hosp., Rockford, 1960-61; instr. anesthesiology U. Minn., Mpls., 1967-74, asst. prof. anesthesiology, 1974-80; staff anesthesiologist St. Luke's Hosp., Duluth, Minn., 1980-95, ret., 1995. Contbr. articles to profl. jours. Capt. USAF, 1961-64, France. Fellow Am. Coll. Anesthesiologists; mem. AMA, Am. Soc. Anesthesiologists, Minn. Soc. Anesthesiologists, Minn. State Med. Assn., St. Louis County Med. Soc. Presbyterian.

**SARGENTICH, LEWIS D.,** law educator; b. Feb. 1944. AB, Occidental Coll., 1965; BA, U. Sussex, Eng., 1967; JD, Harvard U., 1970. Bar: DC 1972. Law clk. to Assoc. Justice Thurgood Marshall, US Supreme Ct., 1970-71; staff counsel Washington Residential Project, 1971-72; assoc. gen counsel, United Mine Workers, Washington, 1973-74; lectr. law, Harvard Law Sch., Cambridge, Mass., 1973, asst. prof., 1945-79, prof., 1979—. Co-author: Tort and Accident Law, 2004. Office: Harvard Law Sch 1563 Massachusetts Ave Cambridge MA 02138 Office Phone: 617-495-3165. Office Fax: 617-495-1082. Business E-Mail: lsargent@law.harvard.edu.

**SARGSYAN, DAVID,** library director; b. Yerevan, Armenia, Oct. 6, 1957; s. Mkrtich Sargsian and Elena Davidian; m. Valentina Alaverdian, Apr. 19, 1956. Diploma, Yerevan State U., 1979. Philologist, jr. editor Sovetakan Grogh pub. House, 1980-82, sr. editor, 1982-90; officer CC of CP of Armenia, 1990-91; dir. Hayastan Pub. House, 1991-98; head of apparatus Min. of Culture, Republic of Armenia, 1998; dir. Nat. Libr. of Armenia, 1998—. Mem. Union Armenian Writers, Union Armenian Journalists, Libr. Assn. Armenia (pres. 2005). Mem. Armenian Rev. Con. Party. Mem. Apostolic Ch. Avocations: reading, hunting. Office: Nat Libr Armenia Terian 72 Yerevan 375009 Armenia Office Phone: 584259. Personal E-mail: nla@arm.r.am, dsargsyan@mail.ru.

**SARHAN, MANSOOR MOHAMED,** library director; b. Nuwidrat, Bahrain, Jan. 1, 1945; s. Mohamed Abdulla and Sukainah Ahmed (Ismail) S.; m. Zahra Abul Kassim Dashti, Aug. 22, 1971; children: Nazha, May, Mohamed. BA in History, Beirut (Lebanon) Arab U., 1972; B in Libr. Sci., U. Bombay, India, 1980; MA in Librarianship, Leeds (Eng.) Poly., 1985; diploma exec. mgmt., U. Bahrain, Isa Town, 1990; PhD in Hist. Documentary Studies, Universal Acad., London, 2003. Tchr. for English lab. Ministry of Edn., Manama, Bahrain, 1963-73, libr. Manama (Bahrain) Pub. Libr., 1973-82, head pub. librs. Manama, 1982-88, dir. pub. librs., 1989—. Gen. organizer Bahrain Internat. Book Fair, Manama. Author: The Book and the Libraries, 1983, Cultural Movement in Bahrain 1940-90, 1993, Bahrain National Bibliography, 1995, Libraries in Islamic Dynasties, 1997, Survey of Cultural Movement in Bahrain during Twentieth Century, 2000, Pioneers of Bookshops in Bahrain, 2000, Libraries in Bahrain, 2001, in Memory of Ebrahim Al-arrayed, 2002, Selections from Ebrahim Al-arrayed's Poetry, 2002, The Education in Bahrain Kingdom, 2003, Shaikh Ahmed Mohamed Al-khalifa: The Poet of Nature and Beauty, 2003, Bahrain Journalism 1939-2003, 2004, Children and Mothers Welfare Society in its 50th Anniversary, 2004, Hassan Jawad Al-Jishi: A Pioneer in Enlightenment, 2005, History of Cinema in Bahrain, 2005, Ali Sayar The Doyenn of Bahrain Journalism, 2005. Lectr. schs., clubs and assns., Bahrain, 1975—; gen. organizer yearly piano concert Ministry of Edn., Bahrain, 1988—. Mem. Bahrain Libr. Assn. (pres. 1994—), Arab Fedn. for Librs. and Info., Nuwidrat Club (pres. 1966—). Avocations: reading, music, tennis, chess. Home: House 46 Rd 4301 Nuwidrat 643 Bahrain Office: Ministry of Edn PO Box 43 Manama Bahrain Office Phone: (973) 17231105. E-mail: mansoorsarhan@hotmail.com.

**SARI, DITA,** labor union administrator; b. Medan, Indonesia, 1972; Attended, Univ. Indonesia. Former youth labor organizer, Indonesia; formerly with Indonesian Ctr. for Labor Struggle; with People's Dem. Union (later the People's Democratic Party, PRD), Indonesia, 1996—; founder Indonesian National Front for Labor Struggle. Recipient Ramon Magsaysay award for Emergent Leadership, 2001.*

**SARI, ROBERT B.,** lawyer, retail executive; b. 1956; BA, U. Mich.; JD, Cleve.-Marshall Coll. Law. Bar: Calif. 1981. V.p., legal affairs Thrifty PayLess, 1994—2000; assoc. counsel Rite Aid Corp., Camp Hill, Pa., 1997—2000, v.p. legal affairs, 2000, sr. v.p., dep. gen. counsel, sec., 2000—02.sr. v.p., gen. counsel, sec., 2002—05, exec. v.p., gen. counsel, sec., 2005—, Office: Rite Aid Corp 30 Hunter Lane Camp Hill PA 17011 Business E-Mail: rsari@riteaid.com.

**SARJEANT, WALTER JAMES,** electrical and computer engineering educator; b. Strathroy, Can., Apr. 7, 1944; s. Walter Burns and Margaret (Laurie) S.; m. Ann Richards, June 30, 1972; children: Eric, Cheryl. BSc in Math, Physics, U. Western Ont., Can., 1966, MSc in Physics, 1967, PhD in Physics, 1971. Asst. dir. R&D Gen-Tec Inc., Quebec City, Que., Canada, 1971-73; program mgr. Lumonics Rsch. Ltd., Ottawa, Ont., Canada, 1973-75; staff scientist Nat. Rsch. Coun., Ottawa, Ont., Canada, 1975-78; project leader Los Alamos (N.Mex.) Nat. Lab., 1978-81; James Clerk Maxwell prof. elec. engring. SUNY, Buffalo, 1981—. Dir. High Power Electronics Inst. Author:

High Power Electronics, 1989. Fellow IEEE; mem. Electromagnetics Acad., Electrostatics Soc., N.Y. Acad. Scis., Rotary, Eta Kappa Nu. Office: SUNY Elec Engring Dept PO Box 601900 312 Bonner Hall Buffalo NY 14260-1900 Home: 5854 Main St Apt 305 Williamsville NY 14221-5745

**SARKA, GEORGE,** medical educator; BA in French and Biology, Boston U., 1976; MD, McGill U., Montreal, Can., 1976; MPH, U. Calif., L.A., 2003. Diplomate in internal medicine Am. Bd. Internal Medicine, 1984, in rheumatology Am. Bd. Internal Medicine, 1988, in geriatrics Am. Bd. Internal Medicine, 1996, in sports medicine Am. Bd. Internal Medicine, 2005, in neurology Am. Bd. Psychology and Neurology, 1991. Asst. med. dir. emergency health svcs. Med. Sch. U. So. Calif., L.A., 1993—2005; staff physician, headache specialist Klotz Student Health Ctr. Calif. State U., Northridge, Calif., 2005—. Lectr. in field. Named Physician of Yr., U. Calif. L.A. Student Health Svc., 2001. Fellow: ACP (life), Am. Coll. Rheumatology (life); mem.: L.A. County Med. Assn. (pres. 2006—), L.A. Neurol. Soc. (bd. dirs. 2003—05, pres. 2006—), Delta Omega Soc., Phi Sigma Iota, Phi Beta Kappa. Roman Cath. Avocations: travel, reading. Office: Cal State Univ Northridge Klotz SHC 18111 Nordhoff Street Northridge CA 91330-8270 Office Phone: 818-677-3666. Home Fax: 818-677-2304; Office Fax: 818-677-2304. Personal E-mail: georgesarka@aol.com.

**SARKAR, KAUSIK,** acoustical engineer, educator; MS, Johns Hopkins U., PhD, 1994. Postdoctoral rsch. assoc. U. Ill., Urbana-Champaign, 1997—2001; asst. prof. U. Del., Newark, 2001—. Fellow, Johns Hopkins U., 1988—94; grantee, U. Del. Rsch. Found., 2003, NSF, 2004. Mem.: Am. Soc. Acoustics, Am. Phys. Soc. Office: U Del 126 Spencer Lab Newark DE 19716 Office Phone: 302-831-0149. Business E-Mail: sarkar@me.udel.edu.

**SARKAR, MALANCHA,** research scientist, educator; d. Dhirendranath and Chobbi Sarkar; m. Subbarayan Ramalingam Pochi; children: ShuvamBharathy Subbarayan Pochi, Bhargavi Subbarayan Pochi. BSc, Ranchi U., India, 1989; MSc, Banaras Hindu U., India, 1991, PhD, 1995. Rsch. assoc. U. Miami Miller Sch. of Medicine, 2002—. Author research papers. Recipient Indian Scientist, Internat. Union of Biochemistry and Molecular Biology, 1994; Postdoctoral Fellowship, Sci. and Tech. Agy., Japan, 1995. Office: Univ Miami Miller Sch of Med 1540 NW 10th Ave PAP Bldg Miami FL 33101 Office Phone: 305-243-6553, 305-243-7722.

**SARKAR, SANDIP,** telecommunications industry executive, researcher; b. Calcutta, India, Feb. 23, 1969; arrived in U.S., 1992; s. Pradip and Purabi Sarkar; m. Mahasweta Ghosh, July 22, 1996; 1 child, Aarjish Neil. B Mus, Calcutta, India, 1985; B Tech, Indian Inst. of Tech., Kanpur, India, 1992; MA, Princeton U., Princeton, N.J., 1994, PhD, 1996. Sr engr. to staff engr., mgr. Qualcomm Inc., San Diego, Calif., 1996—2004, mgr., sr. staff engr., 2004—. Reviewer IEEE, Piscataway, NJ, 1996—; mem., rev. bd. Signal Processing, Lausanne, Switzerland, 1998—; organizing com. ICPWC, New Delhi, 2001—02; chair 3GPP2 Text Group. Editor: (cdma2000 wireless standard) Rev C, Rev D, Band Class Standard, (tia standards) Tia-1030, Is-2000; contbr. articles pub. to profl. jour. Recipient Merit Award, Indian Inst. of Tech., Kanpur, 1990, 1991, Outstanding Achievement award, Qualcomm, Inc., 2000, Qualstar award; fellow, Indian Statis. Inst., 1988; grantee Sci. Talent Search, NSTS, 1986; scholar, Princeton U., 1992-1996. Mem.: IEEE. Achievements include patents for Over 10 US patents, many worldwide patents; patents pending for Over 20 patents pending (USA and worldwide); design of Reverse Link Design of cdma2000; first to Development of 1xEV-DV; development of Globalstar System. Office: Qualcomm Incorp 5775 Morehouse Dr San Diego CA 92131 Office Phone: 858-651-2357. Home Fax: 858-658-5006; Office Fax: 858-658-5006. Personal E-mail: ssarkar@qualcomm.com.

**SARKIS, ZIAD JOSEPH,** private equity executive; b. Beirut, July 8, 1968; arrived in France, 1975; s. Nicolas and Claude (Moussalli) Sarkis; m. Elisabeth Kalman, June 21, 1997; 3 children. BAS in Anthropology, Econs. and Math. with distinction and honors, Stanford U., 1990, MS in Engring. and Mgmt., 1990; PhD in Econs., Oxford U., Eng., 1998. Cons. McKinsey & Co., San Francisco, 1990, N.Y.C., 1991—92, Paris, 1992; ptnr. AT Kearney, N.Y.C., London, Paris, 1992—94; co-founder, sr. ptnr., bd. dirs. Mitchell Madison Group, N.Y.C., London, Paris, 1992—2000; ptnr. PAI Ptnrs. (formerly Paribas Affaires Industrielles), London, Paris, 2001—. Bd. dirs. Yoplait, JBB Santé. Greek Catholic. Office: PAI Ptnrs Clarebell House 5/6 Cork St London W1S 3NX England Office Phone: +44 20 7355 0890. E-mail: ziad.sarkis@paipartners.co.uk.

**SARKISIAN, CHERILYN See CHER**

**SARKISIAN, EDWARD,** dermatologist; b. Detroit, Nov. 19, 1962; s. Edward and Elizabeth Sarkisian; m. Darlene Teel, June 0, 1989; children: Katherine, Andrew. BA, BS, Miami U., Oxford, Ohio, 1985; MD, U. Cin., 1989. Bd. cert. Am. Bd. Dermatology, 1993. Intern U. Cin., 1989—90, resident in dermatology, 1990—93; dermatologist Caylor-Nickel Clinic, Bluffton, Ind., 1997—2000, Ft. Wayne (Ind.) Dermatology Consultants, 2000—. Maj. USAF, 1993—97. Office: Fort Wayne Dermatology Consultants 5750 Falls Dr Fort Wayne IN 46804 Office Phone: 260-436-8000.

**SARKISIAN, PAMELA OUTLAW,** artist; b. Spokane, Sept. 26, 1941; d. Willard Clinton and Frances (Montieth) Outlaw; m. Ronald Edward Sarkisian, Nov. 11, 1960; children: Ronald Abraham, Michelle Suzanne. Grad. h.s., Stockton, Calif. Art student, Oceanside, Calif., 1972-80; founder Palette 'N Easel Studio, Oceanside, 1980—2005, operator, mgr., 1980—2005, art tchr. in residence, 1985—; ret., 2004. Publisher greeting cards Polytint, Ltd., Eng., 1995, 96; fine art prints pub. by Bentley House, Ltd., Walnut Creek, Calif. 1994-97. Designer collector plate series Danbury Mint/MBI, Inc., gift items Enesco Internat. Gift Co.; represented by Casay Gallery, Kailau, Kona, Hawaii, 1991, Galeria Jean Lammelin, Paris, 1991, 2d St. Gallery, Encinitas, Calif., 1991, Blondes Gallery, San Diego, 1992, Valentine-Owens Gallery, Santa Monica, Calif., 1992, Sodarco Gallery, Montreal, 1993, Surtex, 1993, Jacob G. Javity Conv. Ctr., NYC, 1993, Laura Larkin Gallery, Del Mar, Calif., 1993-94, Charles Hecht Galleries, Tarzana and Palm Desert, Calif., 1993-96, Lou Martin Gallery, Laguna Beach, Calif., 1994, Charles Hecht Gallery, La Jolla, Calif., 1995-96, Calif. Art Gallery, Laguna Beach, 1996, Hunter Gallery, Tucson, 1996, Cottage Gallery at Carmel, Calif., 1996, Dy'ans-Branham Gallery, Laguna Beach, 1997-99, Aka'mai Gallery, Del Mar, 1998-99, Gallery Adrienne, La Jolla, 1998, Cosmopolitan Gallery, La Jolla, 1998-99, The Lillian Berkley Collection, Escondido, Calif., 1999-2003, Waters Edge Gallery, Rancho Mirage, Calif., 2003; one-woman shows include AKA Mai Gallery, 1999, Lillian Berkley Collection, 2001, Four Seasons-Aviara. La Costa, Calif., 2001, Waters Edge Gallery, Rancho Mirage, 2003, Calix Gallery, 2005. Pres. Corona Internat., Oceanside, 1980-81; mem. Emblem Club #177, Oceanside, 1971-2003; princess Daughters of the Nile, San Diego, 1974; bd. dirs. Oceanside Girls Club, 1980. Recipient 1st Pl. award San Dieguito Art Guild, 1978, 85, 2nd Pl. award, 1983, 89, 3rd Pl. award, 1983, 1990; winner People's Choice award Internat. Show of Women Artists of the West, Las Vegas, 1992. Mem. North County Art Assn. (founder), Carlsbad Oceanside Art League, 1978, San Dieguito Art Guild, Fallbrook Art Assn., San Diego Art Inst., Assn. pour Promotion Artiste Français, Artisphere. Avocations: ceramics, sculpture, swimming. E-mail: pamiwigle@msn.com.

**SARKISOV, SERGEY SERGEYEVICH,** engineering educator; b. Kiev, Ukraine, May 16, 1958; arrived in U.S., 1993; s. Sergey Karpovich Sarkisov and Galina Antonovna Sarkisova; m. Nina Viktorovna Serdjukova, Oct. 13, 1984; 1 child, Sergey. MS in Physics, Kiev U., 1979, PhD in Physics, 1984. Engr. Kiev U., Ukraine, 1979—84, rschr., 1984—91, sr. rschr., 1991—92; rsch. assoc. prof. Ala. A&M U., Normal, 1993—. Owner SSS Optical Techs., Huntsville, Ala., 2002. Contbr. articles to profl. jours. Recipient Best Student Rsch. medal, USSR Min. Higher Edn., 1980; fellow, Fulbright Found., 1993. Mem.: AIA (mem. tech. com. 2004—05), Optical Soc. Am., Internat. Soc.

Photo. Engring. (mem. tech. com. 1991—2005). Achievements include invention of bimorph polymeric actuator. Office Phone: 256-489-0081. Personal E-mail: mazillo@hotmail.com.

**SARLE, CHARLES RICHARD,** health facility executive; b. Saratoga Springs, NY, Sept. 21, 1944; s. John Robert and Marjorie Elizabeth (Swick) S.; m. Marion D. Wallace, June 21, 1968; children: Richard Charles, Robert Edmond. BBA cum laude, Northea. U., 1968; MBA, Babson Coll., 1973. CPA, Mass., Vt. Staff acct. Price Waterhouse & Co., Boston, 1968-70, George Kanavich, CPA, Wellesley, Mass., 1970-72; controller Human Resource Inst., Boston, 1972-73, adminstr., 1977-87; controller Brattleboro (Vt.) Retreat, 1977-78, dir. adminstrn., 1978-85, v.p., 1985-88, chief exec. officer, 1988-97; pres., CEO Carrier Clinic, Belle Mead, NJ, 1997—. Speaker in field. Mem. commn. Vt. Health Bldg. Fin. Agy., 1978—90; trustee Austine Sch. for Deaf and Hard of Hearing, 1990—97, pres., 1994—97; trustee Winston Prouty Ctr. for Child Devel., 1982—97, treas., 1983—90, sec., 1991—97; trustee Health Rsch. and Edn. Trust NJ, 1998—99, NJ Hosp. Assn., 2000—06, policy devel. com., 1998—2001, fin. com., 2000—; bd. govs. NCCJ, 1998—2003, exec. com., 1999—2003. Recipient recognition award Brattleboro C. of C., 1985. Fellow AICPA, Mass. Soc. CPA, Am. Coll. Healthcare Execs. (regent Va. br. 1991-95); mem. Am. Hosp. Assn. (del.-at-large 1988-92, del.-at-large to regional policy bd.), Nat. Assn. Pvt. Psychiat. Hosps. (bd. dirs. polit. action com. 1983-93, trustee 1998-2000), Nat. Psychiat. Alliance (trustee 1989-96, pres. 1994-96), Vt. Soc. CPA (Cmty. Svc. award 1984), Hosp. Fin. Mgmt. Assn. (hosp. cost com. 1985-96), Rescue, Inc. (trustee 1982-83), New Eng. Healthcare Assembly (trustee 1995-97). Avocations: skiing, fishing, tennis, photography. Home: PO Box 840 Belle Mead NJ 08502-0840 Office: Carrier Clinic Rt 601 Belle Mead NJ 08502 E-mail: rsarle@carrierclinic.com.

**SARMA, PALLAV,** research scientist; arrived in US, 2001; s. Bhubaneswar Sarma and Rajeswari Devi; m. Nidhi Gupta, Dec. 27, 2003. BTech in Petroleum Engring., Indian Sch. Mines, Dhanbad, 2000; MS in Petroleum Engring., Stanford U., Calif., 2003, PhD in Petroleum Engring., 2006. Internship Oil & Natural Gas Corp., Ahmedabad, Gujrat, India, 1998, Enron Oil & Gas India Ltd., Mumbai, Maharashtra, India, 1999, Schlumberger Abingdon Tech. Ctr., Abingdon, Oxford, 2002, ExxonMobil Upstream Rsch. Co., Houston, 2003—03, Chevron Energy Tech. Co., San Ramon, Calif., 2005; reservoir engr. Schlumberger GeoQuest, Mumbai, 2000—01; rsch. scientist Chevron Energy Tech. Co., San Ramon, Calif., 2006—. Tech. editor SPE Jour., Stanford, 2005, Sci. Tech. and Future, Stanford, 2005; reviewer Jour. Computational Physics, Stanford, 2005, Computational Geoscis., Stanford, 2005. Contbr. articles to profl. jours. Recipient Ann. Rsch. Excellence award, Soc. Indsl. & Applied Math., 2005; grantee Chevron scholarship, Chevron Corp., 2004—05; Miller Fellowship, Stanford U., 2002, Ramey Fellowship, 2006. Mem.: European Assn. Geologists & Engrs., Can. Petroleum Soc., Soc. Petroleum Engrs. Achievements include development of an optimal control software ResOpt in use by many oil companies; research in the application of Kernel PCA to reservoir engineering problems; development of new mathematical models for dual porosity reservoir simulation; new and efficient algorithms for closed-loop control of petroleum reservoirs for maximixing oil and gas recovery.

**SARMA, RADHA J.,** cardiologist, educator; arrived in U.S., 1968; m. Jonnalagedda S.M Sarma; 1 child, Srinivas J. MBBS, Andhra Med. Coll., Visakhapatnam, India, 1966. Diplomate Am. Bd. of Internal Medicine, 1977, Am. Bd. of Internal Medicine, 1977, Cardiovascular Diseases Am. Bd. of Internal Medicine, 1979. Asst. prof. of medicine USC Sch. of Medicine, Los Angeles, Calif., 1975—77; dir., noninvasive cardiolgy Rancho Los Amigos Med. Ctr., Downey, Calif., 1978—81; dir. noninvasive cardiology King-Drew Med. Center-UCLA, Los Angeles, Calif., 1981—87; chief of cardiology USC Rancho Los Amigos Med. Ctr., Downey, Calif., 1987—96; med. dir. of cardiology & critical care Northridge Hosp. Med. Ctr., Northridge, Calif., 1996—98; assoc. prof. of medicine USC Keck Sch. of Medicine, Los Angeles, Calif., 1998—; dir. cardiac exercise lab. LACUSC Med. Ctr; assoc. dir. echocardiography lab. LACUSC Med. Ctr. Contbr. articles to profl. jour. V.p. Fedn. of Indo-American Assn., L.A., Calif., 1996—97; v.p., planning Fedn. of IndoAmerican Assn. (F.I.A.), L.A., Calif., 1996—97; vice-chair Vedic Edn. and Social Cultural Orgn. (VESCO), L.A., Calif., 2000; coord. 11th tana conf. Telugu Assn. of N.Am. (TANA), Anaheim, Calif., 1995—96; web master Calif. Chpt. of Am. Coll. of Cardiology, Anaheim, Calif., 2001; mem. & regional faculty Am. Heart Assn., L.A., Calif., 1998; pres. Telugu Assn. of So. Calif., L.A., Calif., 1994—95; regional faculty, task force mem. Am. Heart Assn., L.A., Calif., 1998. Grantee Grant in Aid, Am. Heart Assn., 1980-1982. Fellow: ACP, Am. Heart Assn., Am. Coll. of Cardiology. Avocations: computers and electronics, music, dance. Office: USC Keck Sch of Medicine LACUSC Medc 1200 N State St Rm 7440 Los Angeles CA 90033 E-mail: sarma@usc.edu.

**SARMA, SANJAY E.,** electronics engineer, educator; b. M'Nagar, India, May 15, 1968; s. Emani Anantha and Lakshmi Rani Sarma; m. Gitanjali Meher Swamy, June 2, 1991; 1 child, Tara Swamy. B Tech., Indian Inst. Tech., Kanpur, 1989; MS, Carnegie Mellon U., Pitts., 1992; PhD, U. Calif. Berkeley, 1995. Jr. field engr. Schlumberger, Aberdeen, Scotland, 1989—90; asst. prof. MIT, Cambridge, 1996—2000, assoc. prof., 2000—. Chief tech. officer OAT Sys., Waltham, Mass., 2004—; bd. govs. EPCglobal, Brussels, 2003—; bd. dirs. OAT Sys., Waltham; bd. trustees Mass. Software Coop., Boston, 2005—. Recipient Don Hartog award, MIT, 2000, E-BIZ 25, Bus. Week, 2003, FAST 50, Fast Co. Mag., 2004. Achievements include research in revolutionizing the supply industry. Home: 67 Hurd Rd Belmont MA 02478 Office: MIT 77 Massachusetts Ave 35-206 Cambridge MA 02139

**SARMIENTO-FERNANDEZ, JORGE,** mathematics professor, consultant; b. Salas, Asturias, Spain, May 30, 1950; s. Angel Juan Sarmiento and Rosalia Lila Fernandez; m. Maria del Carmen Queipo, Feb. 8, 1975; children: Miguel Angel Sarmiento, Jorge Antonio Sarmiento, Maria Jose Sarmiento, Francisco Javier Sarmiento. Diploma in elec. engring., U. Gijon, Asturias, Spain, 1970; BS, World U., San Juan, PR, 1975; MA, U. PR, Rio Piedras, 1979; D of Arts in Math., U. Miami, Fla., 1982; Assoc. in Computer Sci., County Coll. Morris, Randolph, NJ, 1995. Math. prof. World U.-IIA, San Juan, PR, 1975—80, chmn. natural sci. divsn., 1982—84; math. prof. U. El Turabo, Caguas, PR, 1990—94, County Coll. Morris, 1990—. Rschr. Lawrence Berkeley Lab.-UC/AGMEF, Berkeley, Calif., 1986—89; cons., online prof. Poly. U. PR, San Juan, 1990—; cons. METEM Corp., Morris Plains, NJ, 1995—2005, Lipton-Airtron NJ, Boonton, 1998—99, Agilent Techs., Morristown, NJ, 0200—2001, Coll. Bd. Entrance Exam, San Juan, 1982—94. Contbr. articles to profl. jours. Judge Math Counts Nat. Competition, San Juan; mentor, advisor County Coll. Morris, 1990—2005. Grantee, County Coll. Morris, 1995—97; scholar, FIPSE, 1980—82; Mid-Career fellow, Princeton U., 1996—97. Mem.: MAMA, Math. Assn. Am. (assoc.), Am. Math. Assn. Two Yr. Colls. (assoc.). Office: County Coll Morris 214 Center Grove Rd Randolph NJ 07869 Office Phone: 973-328-5719. E-mail: jsarmiento@ccm.edu.

**SARNAT, BERNARD GEORGE,** plastic surgeon, educator, researcher; b. Chgo., Sept. 1, 1912; s. Isadore M. and Fanny (Silverman) S.; m. Rhoda Elaine Gerard, Dec. 25, 1941; children: Gerard, Joan. SB, U. Chgo., 1933, MD, 1937; MS, DDS, U. Ill., 1940. Diplomate Am. Bd. Plastic Surgery, 1947. Intern Los Angeles County Gen. Hosp., Chgo., 1940-41; asst. to Dr. Marshall Davison (gen. surgery) Univ. Hosp., Chgo., 1942-43; asst. to Drs. Vilray P. Blair and Louis T. Byars (plastic and reconstructive surgery), St. Louis, 1943-46; practice medicine specializing in plastic surgery Chgo., 1946-56, Beverly Hills, Calif., 1956-91; asst. histology U. Ill. Coll. Dentistry, 1937-40, prof., head dept. oral and maxillofacial surgery, 1946-56; asst. dept. surgery, divsn. plastic surgery Washington U. Sch. Medicine, St. Louis, 1944-46; prof., dir. dept. oral and plastic surgery St. Louis U. Coll. Dentistry, 1945-46; clin. asst. prof. surgery (plastic surgery) U. Ill. Coll. Medicine, 1949-56; adj. prof. oral biology Sch Dentistry UCLA, 1969—, mem. Dental Rsch. Inst., 1974-95, adj. prof. plastic surgery Sch. Medicine, 1974—; attending staff Cedars-Sinai Med. Ctr., L.A., 1956-91, emeritus, 1991—, mem. staff, sr. rsch. scientist, chief plastic surgery, 1961-81. Cons. in gen., plastic and maxillofacial surgery VA Regional Office, Chgo., 1956; lectr. in field. Sr. author: (with Isaac Schour) Oral and Facial Cancer, 2d edit., 1957, (with Daniel Laskin) Surgery of the Temporomandibular Joint, 1964; editor: (with Daniel Laskin) The Temporomandibular Joint A Biological Basis for Clinical Practice, 4th edit., 1991, (with Andrew D. Dixon) Factors and Mechanisms Affecting Growth of Bone, 1982, Normal and Abnormal Bone Growth: Basic and Clinical Research, 1985, Fundamentals of Bone Growth: Methodology and Applications, 1991; contbr. chpts. to books, articles to profl. jours. Co-winner Joseph A. Capps prize for med. rsch. Inst. Medicine, Chgo., 1940, Frederick B. Noyes prize, 1940; recipient Kerbs award for rsch. plastic and reconstructive surgery, 1950, 1st prize, sr. award Found. Am. Soc. Plastic and Reconstructive surgeons, 1957, Beverly Hills Acad. of Medicine award, 1959, Nat. Achievement award medicine Phi Epsilon Pi, 1964, 1st prize Am. Rhinologic Soc., 1980, medal Hebrew U., Jerusalem, 1985, medal Tel Aviv U., 1985, Disting. Svc. Alumni award U. Chgo. Pritzker Sch. Medicine, 1987, hon. award Am. Soc. Maxillofiacial Surgeons, 1990, Dallas B. Phemister Profl. Achievement award Dept. Surgery U. Chgo., 1993, Disting. Alumnus award U. Ill. Coll. Dentistry, 1994, Craniofacial Biology Rsch. award Internat. Assn. for Dental Rsch., 1995, Disting. Scientist award, Pioneer in Medicine award Cedars-Sinai Med. Ctr., L.A., 1999, Profl. Achievement citation U. Chgo. Alumni Assn., 2003, citatioon of excellence in rsch. Plastic Surgery Ednl. Found., 2003, Profl. Achievement award U. Ill. Alumni Assn., 2004. Fellow ACS, AAAS, Am. Assn. Plastic Surgeons (hon. award 1993); mem. Calif. Med. Soc., L.A. Med. Soc., Am. Soc. Plastic and Reconstructive Surgeons, Plastic Surgery Rsch. Coun. (founding mem., chmn. 1957), Am. Soc. Maxillofacial Surgeons (hon.), Calif. Soc. Plastic Surgeons, Beverly Hills Acad. Medicine (pres. 1962-63), Internat. Assn. Craniofacial Biology, Am. Assn. Pediat. Plastic Surgeons (hon.), Am. Assn Phys. Anthropologists, Internat. Assn. Study Dento-Facial Abnormalities (hon.), Sigma Xi, Omicron Kappa Upsilon, Zeta Beta Tau, Phi Delta Epsilon, Alpha Omega (Internat. Achievement medal 1988). Home: 1875 Kelton Ave Apt 301 Los Angeles CA 90025-8505 Personal E-mail: bsarnat@verizon.net.

**SARNELLE, JOSEPH R.,** publishing executive; b. Bklyn., Aug. 24, 1951; s. Alphonse Louis and Julie Lena (Mingarelli) S.; m. Ruth Patricia Cullen, Aug. 5, 1982 (dec.); children: Cullen Joseph, D'Arcy Emilie. BA, Cornell U., 1973; postgrad., Sch. Visual Arts, N.Y.C., 1976—77, The New Sch., 1979—80. Graphic artist Lewahl KC Graphics, N.Y.C., 1974-76; editor United Bus. Publs., N.Y.C., 1976-79; mng. editor Lebhar-Friedman Inc., N.Y.C., 1979-88; assoc. mng. editor HomeOwner Mag., N.Y.C., 1988-90; mgr. online sys. devel. Info. Builders Inc., N.Y.C., 1990—. Cons. video Markham-Novelle Pub. Rels., N.Y.C., 1988—89; cons. Best info. Family Media, N.Y.C., 1990—91. Author: dir. (videos) J. Roland Pepe's Guide to New York City, 1980, Underground Roundup, 1981. McMullen scholar, Cornell U., Regents scholar, State of N.Y., 1969; recipient Best Headline of Yr. award Lebhar-Friedman Inc., 1982. Office: Info Builders Inc 2 Penn Plz New York NY 10121 E-mail: joe_sarnelle@ibi.com.

**SARNO, PATRICIA ANN,** biology educator; b. Ashland, Pa.; d. John Thomas and Anna (Harvest) S. BS, Pa. State U., 1966, MEd, 1971; postgrad. Bucknell U., 1967, Bloomsburg U., 1970. Programmer planetarium, tchr. sci. Pottsville (Pa.) High Sch., 1967; tchr. biology Schuylkill Haven (Pa.) Area High Sch., 1967-91, sci. chmn., coord. dist., 1973-91; lead tchr. sci. Pa. Acad. Suprs. and Curriculum Devel. Dist. Pa. Sch., 1991—; cons. Contbr. to profl. jours. Pa. Edn. Dept., career program Pottsville Hosp. Dow Chem. Co. grantee, 1971. Mem. AAAS, AAUW, NEA, Pa. Edn. Assn. (exec. bd.), Nat. Assn. Biology Tchrs., Nat. Tchrs. Assn., Pa. Assn. Supervision and Curriculum Devel., N.Y. Acad. Scis., Pa. Tchrs. Assn., Internat. Biol. Scis., Pa. Acad. Scis., Pa. State U. Alumni Assn., Schuylkill Haven Edn. Assn., Phi Sigma, Delta Kappa Gamma. Discoverer spider species Atypus snetzingeri, 1973. Home: 49 S Ballet St Frackville PA 17931-1703 Office: Schuylkill Haven HS Schuylkill Haven PA 17972

**SARNOFF, ANN M.,** publishing executive, former sports association executive; b. Nov. 2, 1961; m. Richard I. Sarnoff; 2 children. BS in Mktg., Georgetown Univ., 1983; MBA, Harvard Bus. Sch., 1987. Strategic consul. Marakon Assocs., Stamford, Conn., 1987—93; v.p. bus. develop. Nickelodeon, 1994, exec. v.p. consumer products, bus. develop.; dir. corp. devel. Viacom, 1993—94, COO, VH1, Country Music Television, 2001—04; COO WNBA, 2004—05; pres. Dow Jones Ventures, NYC, 2006—. Mem. bd. trustees Georgetown Univ. McDonough Sch. Bus. Office: Dow Jones & Co 1 World Fin Ctr 200 Liberty St New York NY 10281*

**SARNOFF, LILI-CHARLOTTE (LOLO SARNOFF),** artist; b. Frankfurt, Germany (as Swiss citizen), Jan. 9, 1916; arrived in U.S., 1940; d. Willy and Martha (Koch von Hirsch) Dreyfus; m. Stanley Jay Sarnoff, 1948; children: Daniela Martha Bargezi, Robert L. Grad., Reimann Art Sch., Germany, 1936, U. Berlin, 1938; student, U. Florence, Italy, 1936—38; DFA (hon.), Corcoran Coll. Art & Design, 2003. With Red Cross Swiss Motor Corps, 1939—40; Red Cross nurse Bellevue Hosp., N.Y.C., 1942—47; rsch. asst. Harvard Sch. Pub. Health, 1950—54; rsch. assoc. cardiac physiology Nat. Heart Inst., Bethesda, Md., 1954—59; pres. Rodana Rsch. Corp., Bethesda, 1959—61; v.p. Catrix Corp., Bethesda, 1959—61; prin., owner Dara's Sr. Pets for Srs., 2003. Inventor Flolite light sculptures under name Lolo Sarnoff, 1968—; one-woman shows include Agra Gallery, Washington, 1969, Corning (N.Y.) Glass Ctr. Mus., 1970, Gallery Two, Woodstock, Vt., 1970, Gallery Marc, Washington, 1971, 1972, Franz Bader Gallery, 1976, Gallery K, 1978, 1981, 1985, 1987, 1991, Retrospective Show, 1995, Alwin Gallery, London, 1981, Galerie von Bartha, Basel, Switzerland, 1982, La Galerie L'Hotel de Ville, Geneva, 1982, Pfalzgalerie, Kaiserslautern, Germany, 1985, Galerie Les Hirondelles, Geneva, 1988, Represented in permanent collections. Founder, pres., chmn. bd. Arts for Aging, Inc., Bethesda, 1988—; chmn. bd. Dara's Canine Found., Inc., 1999— Recipient Golda Meir award 1991, UN Commitment to Arts award, Swiss Am. Cultural Exch., 1999, Path of Achievement award for Arts and Humanities, Montgomery County, Md., 2000, Outstanding Citizen award, Iona Sr. Citizen Svcs., Washington, 2002. Home: 7507 Hampden Ln Bethesda MD 20814-1331 Personal E-mail: lolos@erols.com.

**SARNOFF, RICHARD,** digital publishing executive; m. Ann Sarnoff; 2 children. BA (summa cum laude), Harvard Univ.; MBA, Harvard Bus. Sch., 1987. Exec. v.p., CFO Bantam Doubleday Dell, Inc., 1996—98, Random House, Inc., 1998—2000, pres., new media, corp. develop. group, 2000—; and pres. Random House Ventures, LLC, 1999—. Supervisory bd. Bertelsmann AG, 2002—; bd. dir. Princeton Review, 1998—, Audible, Inc., 2001—, Oak Hill Capital Fund II. Bd. mem. Ctr. Comm., Children's Mus. Manhattan, Bronx Lab Sch. Mem.: Assn. Am. Pub. (mem. bd. dir.). Office: Random House Publishing 1745 Broadway New York NY 10019*

**SARNOFF, THOMAS WARREN,** television executive; b. NYC, Feb. 23, 1927; s. David and Lizette (Hermant) S.; m. Janyce Lundon, May 21, 1955; children: Daniel, Timothy, Cynthia. Grad., Phillips Acad., 1943-49; student, Princeton, 1943-45; BS in Elec. Engring., Stanford U., 1948, postgrad. Sch. Bus. Adminstrn., 1948-49; D.H.L., Columbia Coll. Engaged in prodn. and sales with ABC, Inc., 1949-51; prodn. Metro-Goldwyn-Mayer, 1951-52; with NBC, 1952-77; v.p. prodn. and bus. affairs NBC (Pacific div.), 1956-60, v.p. adminstrn. West Coast, 1960-62, v.p. charge West Coast, 1962-65, staff exec. v.p. West Coast, 1965-77; pres. NBC Entertainment Corp., 1972-77, Sarnoff Internat. Enterprises, 1977-81, Sarnoff Entertainment Corp., 1981—; exec. v.p. Venturetainment Corp., 1981-87, pres., 1987—. Bd. dirs. Multimedia Games, Inc., 1998—, chmn. bd., 2004—06. Exec. producer Bonanza: The Next Generation, 1987, Bonanza: The Return, 1993, Back to Bonanza Retrospective, 1993, Bonanza: Under Attack, 1995. Mem. Calif. Commn. for Reform Intermediate and Secondary Edn. Pres., Research Found., St. Joseph Hosp., Burbank, 1965-73, Permanent Charities Com. of Entertainment Industries, 1971-72; nat. trustee Nat. Conf. Christians and Jews. Served with Signal Corps AUS, World War II. Mem. Acad. TV Arts and Scis. (chmn. bd. trustees 1972-74, chmn. past pres.'s coun. 1989-92), Acad. TV Arts and Scis.

Found. (pres. 1990-99, chmn., CEO 1999—2005, chmn. emeritus 2005-), The Caucus for Prodrs., Writers and Dirs. Office: 2451 Century Hl Los Angeles CA 90067-3510 Office Phone: 310-203-9234. Personal E-mail: tsarnoff@aol.com.

**SAROFIM, FAYEZ SHALABY,** finance company executive; b. Nov. 19, 1928; m. Louisa Stude (div. 1990); m. Linda Hicks (div. 1996); 5 children. BS in Food Technology, U. Calif., Berkley, 1949; MBA, Harvard, 1951. Founder, chmn., pres. Fayez Sarofim & Co., 1958—. Bd. mgr. Meml. Sloan-Kettering Cancer Ctr.; coun. mem. Rockefeller Univ.; bd. dir. Alley Theatre, Houston Ballet Found., Mus. Fine Arts, Houston; dir. Tex. Heart Inst. Named one of Top 200 Collectors, ARTnews, 2004—, 400 Richest Americans, Forbes, 2006. Mem.: Houston Symphony Soc. (former vice chmn. bd. dirs.). Avocation: collector of Coptic sculpture, Old Masters, 19th century art, Am. Impressionism, modern & contemporary art. Office: Fayez Sarofim & Co Ste 2907 Two Houston Ctr Houston TX 77010*

**SAROFIM, LOUISA STUDE,** art patron, philanthropist; m. Fayez S. Sarofim (div. 1990); 1 child, Allison. Co-author (with Matthew Drutt and Anna Gaskell): Anna Gaskell: Half Life, 2003. Chair Houston Grand Opera Studio; pres. bd. trustees Menil Collection; trustee adv. Rice U.; hon. chair The Drawing Ctr., NYC. Named one of top 200 collectors, ARTnews mag., 2006. Avocation: collecting American and European paintings.*

**SARRAF, SHIRLEY A.,** secondary school educator; BA in polit. sci., U. Calif., Davis, 1968; MEd, Idaho State U., 1976, postgrad., 1976—. Cert. Educator Nat. Bd. Edn., 2001. Asst. psychometrist U. Wash., 1969-72; asst. prof. dept. fgn. lang. Farah Pahlavi U., Teheran-Vanek, Iran, 1978-79; tchr. presch. program T.L.C. Child Care Ctr., Pocatello, Idaho, 1980-82; dir. of curriculum for English as a second lang. Idaho State U., Pocatello, Idaho, 1982-85; tchr. English, Math, History, Computers Highland High Sch. Sch. Dist. 25, Pocatello, Idaho, 1986—2001; tchr. English Folsom H.S., Folsom, Calif., 2001—. Recipient Tchr. of the Year award State of Idaho, 1994-95. Home: PO Box 6001 Folsom CA 95763-6001

**SARREALS, SONIA,** data processing executive, consultant; b. NYC, Sept. 17, 1938; d. Espriela and Sadie Beatrice (Scales) Sarreals; m. Waldro Lynch, Sept. 18, 1981 (div. Oct. 1983). BA in Langs. summa cum laude, CCNY, 1960; cert. in French, Sorbonne, Paris, 1961. Systems engr. IBM, N.Y.C., 1963-69; cons. Babbage Systems, N.Y.C., 1969-70; project leader Touche Ross, N.Y.C., 1970-73; sr. programmer McGraw-Hill, Inc., Hightstown, NJ, 1973-78; staff data processing cons. Cin. Bell Info. Systems, 1978-89; sr. analyst AT&T, 1989-92; lead tech. analyst Automated Concepts Inc., Arlington, Va., 1992-96; tech. cons. Teksystems, Reston, Va., 1996—. Elder St. Andrew Luth. Ch., Silver Spring, 1992-96. Downer scholar CUNY, 1960; Dickman Inst. fellow Columbia U., 1960-61. Mem.: Assn. for Computing Machinery, Phi Beta Kappa. Democrat. Avocations: needlecrafts, sewing. Home: 13705 Beret Pl Silver Spring MD 20906-3030 Office: Teksystems 12343 Sunrise Valley Dr Reston VA 20191 Business E-mail: ssarreals@teksystems.com.

**SARRIS, ANDREW GEORGE,** film critic; b. Bklyn., Oct. 31, 1928; s. George Andrew and Themis (Katavolos) S.; m. Molly Clark Haskell, May 31, 1969. AB, Columbia, 1951. Film critic Village Voice, N.Y.C., 1960-89, N.Y. Observer, 1989—. Editor-in-chief Cahiers du Cinema in English; instr. Sch. Visual Arts, 1965-67; asst. prof. N.Y. U., 1967-69; assoc. prof. films Columbia Sch. Arts, N.Y.C., 1969-81, prof., 1981— Author: The Films of Josef Von Sternberg, 1966, Interviews with Film Directors, 1967, The Film, 1968 The American Cinema, 1968, Confessions of a Cultist, 1970, The Primal Screen, 1973, The John Ford Movie Mystery, 1976, Politics and Cinema, 1978. Served with Signal Corps AUS, 1952-54. Guggenheim fellow, 1969 Mem. Am. Film Inst. (dir.), Soc. Cinema Studies, Nat. Soc. Film Critics, N.Y. Film Critics. I keep on working toward that last deadline.

**SARRY, CHRISTINE,** ballerina; b. Long Beach, Calif., May 25, 1946; d. John and Beatrice (Thomas) S.; 1 child, Maximilian Sarry Varriale. With Joffrey Ballet, 1963—64, Am. Ballet Theatre, 1964—68, prin. dancer, 1971—74; leading dancer Am. Ballet Co., 1969—71; ballerina Eliot Feld Ballet, 1974—81. Dir. faculty Ballet Tech., N.Y.C.; also freelance guest tchr. Performed ballets for Agnes DeMille, Antony Tudor, Jerome Robbins, Twyla Tharp, Eliot Feld; appeared at White House, 1963, 67; U.S. Dept. State tours include, Russia, 1963, 66, S.Am., 1964, 76, various tours of N.Am., Orient, Europe, various appearances U.S. nat. TV; partnered by Mikhail Baryshnikov. Office Phone: 212-777-7710 x 307. E-mail: csarry@ballettech.org

**SARSGAARD, PETER,** actor; b. Scott AFB, IL, Mar. 7, 1971; Grad., Washington U. Actor: (off-Broadway plays) Kingdom of Earth, Laura Dennis; (films) Dead Man Walking, 1995, Minor Details, 1998, The Man in the Iron Mask, 1998, Desert Blue, 1998, Another Day in Paradise, 1998, Boys Don't Cry, 1999, The Cell, 2000, Housebound, 2000, The Center of the World, 2001, Bacon Wagon: The Movie, 2001, Empire, 2002, The Salton Sea, 2002, K-19: The Widowmaker, 2002, Unconditional Love, 2002, Death of a Dynasty, 2003, Shattered Glass, 2003, Garden State, 2004, Kinsey, 2004, The Dying Gaul, 2005, The Skeleton Key, 2005, Flightplan, 2005, Jarhead, 2005; (TV films) Freak City, 1999. Office: Creative Artists Agy 9830 Wilshire Blvd Beverly Hills CA 90212*

**SARSON, JOHN CHRISTOPHER,** television producer, director, writer; b. London, Jan. 19, 1935; s. Arnold Wilfred and Annie Elizabeth (Wright) S.; m. Evelyn Patricia Kaye, Mar. 25, 1963 (div. 2005); children: Katrina May, David Arnold BA with honors. Trinity Coll., Cambridge, Eng., 1960, MA, 1963. Dir. Granada TV, Manchester, Eng., 1960-63; producer, dir. Sta. WGBH-TV, Boston, 1963-73; pres. Blue Penguin, Inc., Boulder, Colo., 1974—; v.p. TV programming Sta. WYNC-TV, N.Y.C., 1989-90. Dir. Pub. Broadcasting Assocs., Newton, Mass.; cons. to numerous pub. TV stations Creator, producer MAsterpiece Theatre, PBS, 1970-73, Zoom, PBS, 1971-73; producer Live From the Met, PBS, 1977-79, Kid's Writes, Nickelodeon, 1982-83, American Treasure, a Smithsonian Journey, 1986, Spotlight Colorado, 1991, Parenting Works, 1993, 95-97, Club 303, 1994, Videographer Roots of Empathy, 1999—, Coo, 2004-2005. Served with Royal Navy, 1956-57 Recipient Emmy award, 1973, 74, Peabody award Ohio State U., 1978, Internat. Emmy award, 1983, Nat. Acad. TV Arts and Scis. Gov.'s award, 1991. Mem. Dirs. Guild Am., Nat. acad. TV Arts and Scis. (gov. Heartland chpt.), Windows on the Rockies User Group (pres.). Avocations: music, cooking, gardening, travel, computers. Home and Office: 2515 7th St Boulder CO 80304 Office Phone: 303-352-1959, 303-447-6457.

**SARTAIN, JAMES EDWARD,** lawyer; b. Ft. Worth, Feb. 9, 1941; s. James F. and May Belle (Boaz) S.; m. Barbara Hardy, Aug. 17, 1962; 1 child, Bethany Sartain Hughes. BA, Tex. A&M U., 1963; LLB, Baylor U., 1966. Bar: Tex. 1966, U.S. Ct. Mil. Appeals, 1971, U.S. Dist. Ct. (no. dist.) Tex. 1974. Staff atty. Dept. Justice, Washington, 1970-72; staff atty. to U.S. Sen. William L. Scott Fairfax, Va., 1972; pvt. practice Ft. Worth, 1973—2001, Abilene, Tex., 2001—. Bd. dirs. Ft. Worth Boys Club, 1980-89, Oakwood Cemetery, Ft. Worth, 1979-84; adv. dir. Grady McWhinney Rsch. Found., Abilene, Tex., 12th Armored Divsn. Meml. Mus., Abilene. Capt. adv. U.S. Army, Vietnam. Fellow Coll. State Bar Tex.; mem. ABA, NRA, VFW, Abilene Bar Assn., Baylor Law Alumni Assn., Masons, Phi Delta Phi. Republican. Presbyterian. Home: PO Box 450 Abilene TX 79604-0450 Office Phone: 325-676-2492.

**SARTAIN, LIBBY,** human resources specialist; BA, So. Methodist U., MBA, U. North Tex. Various positions Southwest Airlines, 1988—98, v.p. people, 1998—2001; sr. v.p. human resources, chief Yahoo!, Inc., Sunnyvale, Calif., 2001—. Fellow: Nat. Acad. Human Resources; mem. Soc. Human Resource Mgmt. (former chmn.). Office: Yahoo Inc 701 1st Ave Sunnyvale CA 94089 Office Phone: 408-349-3300. Office Fax: 408-349-3301.

**SARTOR, DANIEL RYAN, JR.,** lawyer; b. Vicksburg, Miss., June 2, 1932; s. Daniel Ryan and Lucy Leigh (Hubbs) S.; m. Olive Guthrie Moss, Oct. 12, 1957; children— Clara M., Daniel Ryan, Walter M. BA, Tulane U., 1952, LL.B., 1955. Bar: La. 1955. Instr. Tulane U., New Orleans, 1955-56, asst. prof., 1956-57; ptnr. Snellings, Breard, Sartor, Inabnett & Trascher, Monroe, La., 1957—2001, of coun., 2002—. Contbr. articles to profl. jours. Fellow Am. Coll. Trust and Estate Counsel, Am. Bar Found., La. Bar Found.; mem. La. State Law Inst. (mem. council 1969—, sec. civil law sect. 1969-97, sr. officer 1997—), La. State Bar Assn. (chmn. sect. on trust estate, probate and immovable property 1973-74, bd. govs. 1974-75), Lotus Club, Bayou DeSiard Country Club. Democrat. Methodist. Home: 2405 Pargoud Blvd Monroe LA 71201-2326 Office: Snellings Breard Sartor 1503 N 19th St Monroe LA 71201-4960 Office Phone: 318-387-8000. Business E-Mail: rsartor@snellingslawfirm.com.

**SARTOR, DAVID P.,** composer; b. Nashville, May 25, 1956; s. Grayl Bruce and Kathleen Lipscomb Sartor; m. Nancy White Sartor, Oct. 6, 1984; children: John Russell Laws, Sharon Rebecca Farrell. BMus with highest honors, U. Tenn., 1978. Composer: Veni Emmanuel-Fantasy of Abstractions, 1976, Medieval Manifesto for Unaccompanied Contrabass, 1977, Affectations for Brass Quintet, 1977, Variants For Solo Trombone, 1977, Open Door for Organ, 1977, Thrice Told Tales of the Pomegranate Forest for Trumpet, Violin and Bass Clarinet, 1978 (winner U Tenn.Chamber Music Composition, 1978, Contest award New Music For Young Ensembles, 1978), Illusions for Percussion Ensemble, 1981, O Worship the King for Orchestra, 1982, Synergistic Parable for Concert Band, 1985 (Ostwald award Am. Bandmasters Assn., 1987, Composition Contest award Appalachian State U., 87), Polygon for Brass Quintet, 1987 (Nat. Fine Arts award Ill., 1993), We Will be Glad for Chorus, Brass, Timpani and Organ, 1994, Prelude on William Billings' "When Jesus Wept" for Organ, 1996, Postlude on William Billings' "Paris" for Organ, 1996, Thy Light Is Come for Chorus, Brass, Timpani and Organ, 1997, Psalm 67 for Chorus, Organ and Trumpet, 1998, Metamorphic Fanfare for Orchestra, 2000, Concerto For Orchestra, 2001, Simple Blessing for Organ, 2002, Welcome, Christmas Day! for Chorus and Instruments, 2002, Diplomatic Solution for 4 Violoncellos, 2003, Cat's Eye for Brass Ensemble, 2003, Black Ball Counts Double for Strings, 2003, Commendation, Oare Internat. Composing Contest, 2003, Fanfare A4 for Brass Quartet, 2003, Crown Him! for Chorus, Orchestra and Organ, 2004, Ascension for Brass and Timpani, 2005, Search Your Heart for Christmas for Chorus and Violoncello, 2005. Mem. Woodmont Christian Ch., Nashville, Tenn. Recipient various nat. and internat. commns., performances and residencies, Various; Meet The Composer grantee, Creative Connections, NY, 2004. Mem.: ASCAP (17 consecutive panel awards 1989—2005), World Assn. Symphonic Bands and Ensembles, Am. Composers Forum, Ctr. for Promotion of Contemporary Composers, Nat. Assn. Composers USA, Am. Fedn. Musicians, Am. Music Ctr., Soc. Composers, Inc., Pi Kappa Lambda, Phi Kappa Phi. Office: PO Box 190308 Nashville TN 37219-0308 E-mail: mail@davidsartor.com.

**SARTOR, VIVIAN JUANITA,** nursing administrator; b. Mount Enterprise, Tex., Apr. 13, 1937; d. Rochelle Williams and Verline Chambers; children: Renita Starr Yvette Cleary, La Dorsia Parks-Jones. AA, L.A. S.W. Coll., 1971; BA, Calif. State U., L.A., 1973; cert. in pub. health, Long Beach State Coll., 1975; M Health Adminstrn., Chapman Coll., 1994. RN Calif., cert. diabetic educator. Med./surg. staff nurse Martin Luther King Med. Ctr., L.A., 1972—74; emergency traige nurse Cedars Sinai Med. Ctr., L.A., 1975—80; pub. health nurse L.A. County Health Svc., L.A., 1981—91; pvt. duty nurse L.A. Nurses Assn., 1992—95; health care mgr. L.A., 1995—98; asst. adminstr. Oak Car Med. Group, Oakland, Calif., 2001—02; asst. dir. nurses Oakridge Care Ctr., Oakland, 2003—. Med./legal cons. Lancaster (Calif.) Legal, 1990—99; founder WASP Home Health Mgmt. Student recruiter LA Sch. Nursing, 1992—; mem., minister spl. tutoring Allen Temple Missionary Baptist Ch. Fellow: Prince Hall Ea. Star (doorkeeper 1997); mem.: LA Nurses Alumni Assn. (sec. 1975). Avocations: reading, travel, sailing, fishing. Office: Oakridge Care Ctr 2919 Fruitvale Avew Oakland CA 94602 Home: PO Box 27531 Oakland CA 94602-0531 E-mail: taddy07@earthlink.net.

**SARTORELLI, ALAN CLAYTON,** pharmacologist, educator; b. Chelsea, Mass., Dec. 18, 1931; m. Alice C. Anderson, July 7, 1969. BS, New Eng. Coll. Pharmacy Northeastern U., 1953; MS, Middlebury Coll., Vt., 1955; PhD, U. Wis., 1958; MA (hon.), Yale U., 1967. Rsch. chemist Samuel Roberts Noble Found., Ardmore, Okla., 1958—60, sr. rsch. chemist, 1960—61; mem. faculty dept. pharmacology Yale Sch. Medicine, New Haven, 1961—, prof., 1967—, head devel. therapeutics program Comprehensive Cancer Ctr., 1974—90, chmn. dept. pharmacology, 1977—84, 1998—2000, dir. Comprehensive Cancer Ctr., 1984—93, Alfred Gilman prof. pharmacology, 1987—; prof. epidemiology, 1991—97. Head devel. therapeutics program Comprehensive Cancer Ctr., 1974—90, chmn. dept. pharmacology, 1977—84, 1998—2000, dep. dir., 1982—84, dir., 1984—93, Alfred Gilman prof. pharmacology, 1987—; Charles B. Smith vis. prof. Meml. Sloan-Kettering Ctr., 1979; William N. Creasy vis. prof. clin. pharmacology Wayne State U., 1983; Mayo Found. vis. prof. oncology Mayo Clinic, 1983; Walter Hubert lectr. Brit. Assn. Cancer Rsch., 1985; Pfizer lectr. in clin. pharmacology U. Conn. Health Ctr., 1985; William N. Creasy vis. prof. clin. pharmacology Bowman Gray Sch. Medicine, 1987; Wellcome vis. prof. basic sci. U. Pitts. Sch. Medicine, 1990; sci. adv. bd. ImmunoGen, Inc., 1881—90, U. Ind. Cancer Ctr., 1992, Cancer Inst. N.J., 1993—, Cell Pathways, Inc., 1993—2003; chmn. cancer sci. adv. bd. ViraChem., Inc., 1986—93, The Liposome Co., 1986—2001, Vion Pharms., 1993—; bd. dirs. various bd.; chmn. vis. sci. adv. com. Columbia U. Comprehensive Cancer Ctr., 1986—99; chmn. pres.'s cancer adv. bd. Fox Chase Cancer Ctr., 1992—; clin. investigation rev. com. Nat. Cancer Inst., 1968—72; mgmt. cons. to dir. divsn cancer treatment, 1975—77, 1st vol. counselors, divsn. cancer treatment, 1978—81, chmn. com. to establish nat. coop. drug discovery groups, 1982—83, chmn. spl. rev. com. Outstanding Investigator grant applications, 1992, chmn. ad hoc contracts tech. rev. group, 93; instnl. rsch. grants com. Am. Cancer Soc., 1971—76, coun. analysis and projection, 1978—79; cons. in biochemistry U. Tex. M.D. Anderson Hosp. and Tumor Clinic, Houston, 1970—76; cons. Sandoz Forschungs-Institut, Vienna, 1977—80; mem. exptl. therapeutics study sect. NIH, 1973—77, working cadre nat. large bowel cancer project, 1973—76; adv. com. Cancer Rsch. Ctr., Washington U. Sch. Medicine, 1971—75, SLSB Ptnrs., L.P., 1992—96; sci. adv. com. U. Iowa Cancer Ctr., 1979—83; external adv. com. Wis. Clin. Cancer Ctr., 1978—79, Duke Comprehensive Cancer Ctr., 1983—94; external adv. bd. U. Ariz. Cancer Ctr., 1982—92, U. So. Calif. Cancer Ctr., 1983—93, Clin. Cancer Rsch. Ctr., Brown U., 1980—86; nat. program com. 13th Internat. Cancer Congress, 1979—81; cons. Bristol-Myers Co., 1982—93, selection com. prize in cancer rsch., 1977—85, chmn., 1979—81, chmn. selection com. award for disting. achievement in cancer rsch., 1989—92; bd. advisors Drug and Vaccine Devel. Corp. (Ctr. for Pub. Resources), 1980—81, Specialized Cancer Ctr., Mt. Sinai Med. Ctr., 1981—90, Grace Cancer Drug Ctr., Roswell Park Meml. Inst., 1986—89; med. and sci. adv. com. grants rev. subcom. Leukemia Soc. Am., 1983—88; program planning com. Mary Lasker-Am. Cancer Soc. Conf., 1986; external sci. rev. com. Massey Cancer Ctr., 1989—94; bd. visitors Moffit Cancer Ctr. U. South Fla., 1989—92; dep. dir. Cancer Prevention Rsch. Ctr. for Conn., 1989—93, acting dir., 1991—93; nat. bd. Look Good...Feel Better program Cosmetic Toiletry and Fragrance Assn., 1989—91; organizing com. Conf. on Bioreductive Drug Activation, 1993—94; chmn. bd. spl. cons. Inst. for Cancer Therapeutics, 1993; scientific adv. bd. U. Ill. Cancer Ctr., 2001; chmn. sci. adv. bd. Celator Technologies Inc., 2002—. Regional editor Am. Continent Biochem. Pharmacology, 1968—2003, exec. editor, 1993—2003, editor-in-chief Cancer Comm., 1969—93, Oncology Rsch., 1993—; editor: Handbuch der experimentellen Pharmakologie vols. on antineoplastic and immunosuppressive agts., series on cancer chemotherapy Am. Chem. Soc. Symposium, 1976; founder, exec. editor Pharmacology and Therapeutics, 1975—2003, editl. bd. Internat. Ency. Pharmacology and Therapeutics, 1972—94, Seminars in Oncology, 1973—83, Chemico-Biol. Interactions, 1975—78, Jour. Medicinal Chemistry, 1977—82, Cancer Drug Delivery, 1982—85, Jour. Enzyme Inhibition, 1984—2002, Jour. Liposome Rsch., 1986—92, In Vivo, 1990—2002, Cancer

Biotherapy, 1992—97, Cancer Rsch., Therapy and Control, 1993—97, Oncology Reports, 1995—, Molecular and Cellular Differentiation, 1996—, mem. adv. bd. Advances in Chemistry Series, ACS Symposium Series, 1977—80, editl. adv. bd. Cancer Rsch., 1970—71, assoc. editor, 1971—78, Current Awareness in Biol. Scis., Current Advances in Pharmacology and Toxicology, 1983—88, Cancer Cells, 1989—91, Jour. Exptl. Therapeutics and Oncology, 1995—, exec. adv. bd. Ency. of Human Biology, 1987—90, Dictionary of Sci. and Tech., 1989—91, editl. cons. Biol. Abstracts, 1984—88; contbr. articles to profl. jours. Bd. dirs. Schubert Performing Arts Ctr., 1992—2001, Schubert Opera Bd., 1991—2000, chmn., 1993—. Recipient Outstanding Alumni award, Northeastern U., 1987, Mike Hogg award, M.D. Anderson Cancer Ctr., U. Tex., 1989, Alumni Achievement award, Middlebury Coll., 1990, AACR-Bruce F. Cain Meml. award, 2001, Drug Discovery and Devel. award, Glaxo SmithKline, 2002. Fellow: AAAS, N.Y. Acad. Scis.; mem.: Coun. Biology Editors, Conn. Acad. Sci. and Engring., Inst. Medicine NAS (com. on govt. industry collaboration in biomed. rsch. and edn. 1989, mem. Forum on Drug Devel. and Regulation 1989—93), Assn. Am. Cancer Insts. (v.p. 1986, liaison rep. to Nat. Cancer Inst. 1988, bd. dirs. 1986—89, pres. 1987—88, chmn. bd. dirs. 1989), Am. Soc. Pharmacology and Exptl. Therapeutics (award com. 1988, chmn. 1992, award in exptl. therapeutics 1986, Otto Krayer award 2002), Am. Soc. Cell Biology, Am. Soc. Biochemistry and Molecular Biology, Am. Soc. Microbiology, Am. Chem. Soc., Am. Assn. Cancer Rsch. (dir. 1975—78, chmn. publs. com. 1981—88, dir. 1984—87, v.p. 1985—86, fin. com. 1985—88, exec. com. 1985—89, pres. 1986—87, chmn. exec. com. 1987, chmn. awards com. 1987, chmn. nominating com. 1993—95, mem. devel. com. 1995—97). Home: 4 Perkins Rd Woodbridge CT 06525-1616 Office: Yale U Dept Pharmacology 333 Cedar St New Haven CT 06520-8066 Office Phone: 203-785-4533. E-mail: alan.sartorelli@yale.edu.

**SARTORI, MICHAEL A.,** lawyer; b. St. Louis; BSEE, Univ. Notre Dame, 1987, MSEE, 1989, PhD, 1991; JD cum laude, Georgetown Univ., 1998. Bar: Va. 1998, DC 1999, US Patent & Trademark Office, US Ct. Appeals (4th, Fed. cir.). Sr. project mgr. USN Naval Surface Warfare Ctr., 1991—94; patent examiner US Patent & Trademark Office, 1994—96; ptnr., Patent Prosecution, Intellectual Property Litigation Venable LLP, Washington, 2003—. Lectr. Catholic Univ. Am, 1991. Contbr. articles to profl. jours. Mem.: ABA, Am. Intellectual Property Law Assn. Achievements include patents in field of of naval warfare systems. Office: Venable LLP 575 7th St NW Washington DC 20004 Office Phone: 202-344-4004. Office Fax: 202-344-8300. Business E-Mail: masartori@venable.com.

**SARTORY, THOMAS J.,** lawyer; b. Pitts., Apr. 7, 1944; BA magna cum laude, Loyola U., 1966; JD cum laude, Harvard U., 1969. Bar: Mass. 1969, Fla. 1975. Dir. civil litig. Goulston & Storrs, P.C., Boston. Mem. com human studies Harvard Med. Sch., 1980-92; spl. counsel to Mass. Jud. Conduct Commn. Fellow: Am. Coll. Trial Lawyers; mem.: Mass. Bar Assn. (mem. com. profl. ethics, past chmn. bus. litig. com.), Boston Bar Assn. (chmn. professionalism & civility com.). Address: Goulston & Storrs 400 Atlantic Ave Boston MA 02110-3333 Office Phone: 617-574-6411. Office Fax: 617-574-7632. Business E-Mail: tsartory@goulstonstorrs.com.

**SARWER-FONER, GERALD JACOB,** psychiatrist, educator; b. Volkovsk, Grodno, Poland, Dec. 6, 1924; arrived in Can., 1932, naturalized, 1935; s. Michael and Ronia Sarwer-F.; m. Ethel Sheinfeld, May 28, 1950; children: Michael, Gladys, Janice, Henry, Brian. BA, Loyola Coll. U., Montreal, 1945, MD magna cum laude, 1951; DPsychiatry, McGill U., 1955. Diplomate Am. Bd. Psychiatry and Neurology. Intern. Univ. Hosps. U. Montreal Sch. Medicine, 1950-51; resident Butler Hosp., Providence, 1951-52, Hosps. Western Res. U., Cleve., 1952-53, Queen Mary Vets. Hosp., Montreal, 1953-55; cons. psychiatry, dir. psychiatric rsch., 1955-61; lectr. psychiatry U. Montreal, 1953-55; lectr., asst. prof., assoc. prof. McGill U., 1955—70; dir. dept psychiatry Queen Elizabeth's Hosp, Montreal, 1964-71; prof. psychiatry U. Ottawa, Ont., 1971-89, prof., chmn. psychiatry Ont., 1974-86, prof., 1989—; dir. dept. psychiatry Ottawa Gen. Hosp., 1971-87; dir. Lafayette Clinic, Detroit, 1989-92; prof. psychiatry and behavioral Neurosciences Wayne State U., Detroit, 1989—. Cons. in psychiatry Ottawa Gen. Hosp., Royal Ottawa Hosp., Children's Hosp. of Eastern Ont., Ottawa, Windsor (Ont.) Western Hosp. Ctr., Ottawa Sch. Bd.; Z. Lebensohn lectr. Silbey Meml. Hosp. Cosmos Club, Washington, 1991; disting. lectr. XI World Congress Psychiatry, Hamburg, 1999, XII World Congress Psychiatry, Yokohama, Japan, 2002; mem. test com. Nat. Bd. Med. Examiners, 1975-81; pres. Que. Psychiat. Assn., 1966-68; mem. adv. panel on psychiatry Def. Rsch. Bd. Can., Dept. Nat. Def., 1958-62. Editor: Dynamics of Psychiatric Drug Therapy, 1960, Research Conference on the Depressive Group of Illnesses, 1966, Psychiatric Crossroads-the Seventies, Research Aspects, 1972, Social Psychiatry in the Late 20th Century, 1993; founder, editor in chief Psychiat. Jour. U. Ottawa, 1976-90, emeritus editor in chief, 1990—; mem. editorial bds. of numerous internat. and nat. profl. jours.; editor numerous audio-video series; contbr. to more than 200 articles to profl. jours. Bd. govs. Queen Elizabeth Hosp., Montreal, 1966-71; life gov. Queen Elizabeth Hosp. Found.; cons. Protestant Sch. Bd., Westmount, Que., 1966-71; advisor Com. on Health, City of Westmount, 1969-71. Served to lt. col. Royal Can. A Med. Corps, 1949-62. Fulbright fellow, 1951-53; recipient Sigmund Freud award Am. Assn. Psychoanalytic Physicians, 1982, William V. Silverberg Meml. award Am. Acad. Psychoanalysis, 1990, Poca award Assn. Psychiat. Out Patient Ctrs. Am., 1990; Simon Bolivar lectr. Am. Psychiat. Assn., New Orleans, 1981; Can. Forces Decoration: Knight of Malta. Fellow: AAAS, Am. Assn. Social Psychiatry (v.p. 1987—89, pres.-elect 1990, pres. 1992—94), World Psychiat. Assn. (v.p. sect. on edn. 1989—, mem. internat. adv. com. 9th World Congress Rio de Janeiro 1993, lectr., organizing com. sci. com. X World Congress in Madrid, mem. nominating com.), Benjamin Rush Soc. (founding mem., councillor), Am. Coll. Psychiatrists (bd. regents 1978—80, pres. com. long range planning and policy 1986—89, emeritus), Am. Psychopath. Assn., Collegium Internat. Neuropsychopharmacology, Internat. Psychoanalytical Assn. (mem. program com. 31st congress NY 1979), Royal Coll. Psychiatry (Found. fellow), Can. Psychiat. Assn. (life; bd. dirs. 1958—62, founder, chair com., sect. psychotherapy 1962—64), Am. Acad. Psychiatry and the Law (sr.; pres. 1977, Silver Apple award), Am. Coll. Neuropsychopharmacology (life; charter founding fellow), Am. Coll. Neuropsychopharmacology (life; hon. found. 1958—), Am. Psychiat. Assn. (life; chair sci. program com., VI World Congress of Psychiatry, Honolulu 1974—77, v.p., chmn. sci. program com. 1974—77, chair com. psychiatry, law 1975—77, chair task force model commitment code 1976—80, VI World Congress of Psychiatry Honolulu 1974—77), Am. Coll. Psychoanalysts (life; pres.-elect 1983, pres. 1984—85, chair by-laws and constn. com. 1994—2001, Henry Laughlin award 1986), Am. Coll. Mental Health Adminstrn. (life) Royal Coll. Physicians and Surgeons (exec. sec. test psychiat. com. 1987—89), Internat. Coll. Psychosomatic Medicine (sec.-gen. 1979—83); mem.: Am. Psychoanalytic Assn. mem. program com. 1972—76), Alliance for Mental Health Svcs. (pres. 1999—2000), Mich. Psychoanalytic Soc., Soc. Biol. Psychiatry (sr.; pres. 1983—84, H. Azima Meml. lectr. 1963, George M. Thompson award 1997), Can. Assn. Profs. Psychiatry (pres. 1976—77, 1982—86), Can. Psychoanalytic Soc. (pres. 1979—81), Royal Can. Mil. Inst. Club, Cosmos Club. Home and Office: 3220 Bloomfield Shr Dr West Bloomfield MI 48323-3300 Office Phone: 248-855-9080. Office Fax: 248-855-8321. Personal E-mail: sarwfon@aol.com.

**SASAHARA, ARTHUR ASAO,** cardiologist, educator, researcher; b. Del Rey, Calif., May 11, 1927; s. Harold Hango and Blanche (Takayama) S.; m. Alice Ann Guenther, Apr. 2, 1955; children: Ann Mariko, Claire Michiko, Ellen Reiko, Karen Hideko, Mark Tadao. AB, Oberlin Coll., 1951; MD, Case Western Res. U., 1955; AM (hon.), Harvard U., 1987. Diplomate Am. Bd. Internal Medicine. Intern Boston City Hosp., 1955-56; jr. asst. med. resident Mass. Gen. Hosp., Boston, 1956-57; fellow in cardiology West Roxbury VA Med. Ctr., Mass., 1957-58, Children's Hosp. Med. Ctr., Boston, 1958-59; sr. resident in medicine Yale-New Haven Med. Ctr., 1959-60; asst. chief med. svc., dir. cardiopulmonary lab., deps. Gen. Rsch. and edn. com. VA Hosp. West Roxbury, 1960-70, chief cardiopulmonary sect., 1971-74, assoc. chief staff for rsch. and edn., 1970-76, chief med. svc., 1974-82, West Roxbury-

Brockton VA Hosp., 1982-87; prof. medicine Harvard Med. Sch., Boston, 1974-93, prof. emeritus, 1993—; cons. cardiovascular-pulmonary diseases Boston, 1965-87; cons. pediatric cardiology Children's Hosp. Med. Ctr., Boston, 1976-86; physician Brigham and Women's Hosp., Boston, 1979-82, sr. physician, 1982—. Dir. thrombolytics rsch. pharm. products divsn. Abbott Labs., Abbott Park, Ill., 1987—95, sr. med. dir., 1995—97; sr. physician cardiovascular divsn. Brigham and Women's Hosp., 1998—. Author-editor: Pulmonary Embolic Disease, 1965, Pulmonary Emboli, 1975, New Therapeutic Agents in Thrombosis and Thrombolysis, 1997, 2d edit., 2002; contbr. articles to profl. jours.; designer custom infusion med. pump, Harvard Apparatus Co., 1973; mem. editl. bd. New Eng. Jour. Medicine, 1971-73, Jour. Nuclear Medicine, 1981-83, Am. Jour. Medicine, 1971-72, Circulation, 1973-78, VASA, 1978-85, Jour. Cardiovasc. Medicine, 1980-86, Primary Cardiology, 1986-89. With U.S. Army, 1945-47. NIH grantee, 1963-82; VA grantee, 1961-87. Fellow ACP, Am. Coll. Chest Physicians, Am. Coll. Cardiology; mem. AAAS, Internat. Soc. Fibrinolysis and Thrombolysis, Am. Fedn. Clin. Rsch., Internat. Soc. Thrombosis and Hemostasis, Am. Heart Assn., Alpha Omega Alpha. Democrat. Episcopalian. Home: 1115 Beacon St # 12 Newton MA 02461-1154 Personal E-mail: aasasahara@comcast.net.

**SASAKI, CLARENCE TAKASHI,** surgeon, educator; b. Honolulu, Jan. 24, 1941; s. Tsutomu and Carla Harumi (Mirikitani) S.; m. Carolyn Elizabeth Lindahl, June 26, 1967; children: Peter Gordon, John Eric. BA, Pomona Coll., 1962; MD, Yale U., 1966. Diplomate: Am. Bd. Otolaryngology. Intern San Francisco Hosp., U. Calif., 1966-67; resident in surgery Dartmouth Med. Sch., 1967-68; resident in otolaryngology Yale U. Med. Sch. Hosps., New Haven, 1970-73, faculty mem., 1973—, assoc. prof., 1977-82, prof. surgery, 1982—, chief sect. otolaryngology, 1981—, Charles Ohse prof. surgery, 1988—, vice chmn. dept. surgery, 1996. Author: Surgery of the Skull Base, Head and Neck Surgery, Vol. 1 Atlas Otolaryngology, Vocal Fold Physiology, Laryngeal Function in Phonation and Respiration, Neurological Diseases of the Larynx; mem. editl. bd. profl. jours. Served to maj. M.C. U.S. Army, 1968-70. Recipient award Fowler Triological Soc., 1979. Mem. Am. Acad. Otolaryngology (1st prize clin. rsch.), Am. Soc. Head and Neck Surgery (coun.), Assn. Rsch. Otolaryngology, Am. Laryngol. Rhinol. and Otol. Soc. (coun., sec. ea. sect. 1990, v.p. 1998), New Eng. Otolaryngology Soc. (pres. 1987, coun.), Assn. Acad. Depts. Otolaryngology (coun.), Am. Laryngol. Assn. (Casselberry award 1999), Pan Pacific Surg. Assn., Soc. for Neurosci., Soc. Neurovascular Surgery, Soc. for Head and Neck Surgeons, Am. Neurotology. Soc., Pan Am. Assn. Oto-rhino-laryngology and Bronchoesophagology, Conn. Med. Soc., N.Y. Acad. Scis., Soc. Univ. Otolaryngologists, Collegium ORLAS, Cartesian Soc. (co-dir.), Am. Bronchoesophagological Assn. (mem. coun., treas. 2003, Broyles-Maloney award 2004), N.Am. Skull Base Soc., Laryngeal. Cancer Assn. (Padua), Am. Otol. Soc., Dysphagia Rsch. Soc. (treas., pres.), Lawn Club, Mory's Assoc., Yale Club, Phi Beta Kappa, Sigma Xi. Office: Yale U Med Sch Dept Surgery PO Box 208041 333 Cedar St New Haven CT 06520-8041 Office Phone: 203-785-2592.

**SASAKI, JUN,** steel company researcher; b. Tokyo, Aug. 1960; BS, Keio U., 1983, MS, 1986; Dr., Tohoku U., 1995. Sr. rscher. Nippon Steel Corp., Kanagawa, Japan, 1986—2005, Nippon Steel USA, Inc., 2006—. Office: Nippon Steel USA Inc 780 Third Ave 34th Fl New York NY 10017 Business E-Mail: sasaki@nipponsteelusa.com.

**SASAKI, ROBERT J.,** financial services executive; b. Oakland, Calif., May 7, 1962; s. Joseph and Kimiko (Sakanashi) S.; m. Momoe Shimabukuro; children: Lisa, Lynn. BA, U. Calif., Berkeley, 1984; MA, Harvard U., 1988. Arbitrageur L.F. Rothschild, Unterberg, Towbin, Inc., N.Y.C., 1986-88, Merrill Lynch & Co., Inc., N.Y.C., 1988-89, JP Morgan, Tokyo, 1989-2001, Bear Stearns Co., Inc., Tokyo, 2001—04; mng. mem. Pacific Property Capital, LLC, San Francisco, 2004—; chmn., CEO K and S Co., Inc., 2005—. Co-founder Free Merchant.Com, Inc., Emeryville, Calif.; stock market commentator Reuters, CNN, CNBC, Bloomberg Business News, N.Y. Times Wall St. Jour.; mem. Tokyo (Japan) adv. bd. U.S. Japan Bridging Found. Mem. Nat. Eagle Scout Assn. (life), Japan Soc. Investment Profls. (bd. dirs. Tokyo AIMR chpt.), Harvard Club of NYC, Tokyo Am. Club, Faculty Club Berkeley, Peninsula Golf and Country Club. Republican. Buddhist. Avocations: skiing, tennis, japanese art. Home: 881 Vista Rd Hillsborough CA 94010 Office: 50 California St Ste 1500 San Francisco CA 94111

**SASAKI, TSUTOMU (TOM SASAKI),** real estate company executive, trade association administrator, consultant; b. Tokyo, July 28, 1945; came to U.S., 1979; s. Tsuneshiro and Kimiko (Fujiwara) S.; m. Yoko Katsura, Feb. 21, 1971; children: Mari, Tomoko. BA, Sophia U., Tokyo, 1969. Export admnstrn. Ataka & Co., Ltd., Osaka, Japan, 1969-76; officer Seattle-First Nat. Bank, Tokyo, 1976-79, AVP bus. mgr., 1982-84, AVP Japan mgr. Seattle, 1979-82, v.p. Japan mgr., 1984-90; owner, pres. BBS Internat., Inc., Seattle, 1990—. Bd. dir. InterPac Devel. Inc., BBS Bus. Svc., Inc., Japanese Cmty. Svcs. Seattle. Bd. dirs. Adopt-a-Stream Found., Everett, Wash., 1987-2002; bd. trustees N.W. Sch., Seattle, 1987-2002, internat. adv. to bd. trustees, 2002-. Am. Field Svc. scholar, 1963-64. Mem. Japan Am. Soc. Wash. (chmn. membership com. 1988, bd. dir. 1997—, chmn. bd. 2006—), British Am. Bus. Coun., Fairwood Golf & Country Club, Wash. Athletic Club. Avocations: golf, gardening, music, photography. Home: 4625 136th Ave SE Bellevue WA 98006-3007 Office: BBS Internat Inc 2819 Elliot Ave #201 Seattle WA 98121 Business E-Mail: sasaki@bbsint.com.

**SASAKI, Y(ASUNAGA) TITO,** engineering executive; b. Tokyo, Feb. 6, 1938; arrived in U.S., 1967; s. Yoshinaga and Chiyoko Sasaki; m. Janet L. Cline; 1 child, Heather N. Diploma in indsl. design, Royal Coll. Art, London, 1962; MS in Ekistics, Athens (Greece) Tech. Inst., 1965. Cert. planner, Am. Inst. Cert. Planners. Tech. officer London County Coun., 1962-63; sr. rschr. Inst. Battelle, Geneva, Switzerland, 1965-67; planning dir. Golden Gate Bridge, San Francisco, 1970-74; pres. Visio Internat., Inc., San Francisco, 1974-85, Quantum Mechanics Corp., Sonoma, Calif., 1981—. Mem.: AIAA, ASME, Am. Welding Soc., Am. Vacuum Soc. Achievements include co-developer of sensitive helium leak detector; co-developer of the lowest out-gasing stainless steel. Home: PO Box 200 Vineburg CA 95487-0200 Office: Quantum Mechanics Corp 21885 8th St E Sonoma CA 95476-9797

**SASENICK, JOSEPH ANTHONY,** consumer products company executive; b. Chgo., May 18, 1940; s. Anthony E. and Caroline E. (Smicklas) S.; m. Barbara Ellen Barr, Aug. 18, 1962; children: Richard Allen, Susan Marie, Michael Joseph. BA, DePaul U., 1962; MA, U. Okla., 1966. With Miles Labs., Inc., Elkhart, Ind., 1963-70; product mgr. Alka-Seltzer, 1966-68, dir. mktg. grocery products divsn., 1968-70; with Gillette Corp., Boston, 1970-79, dir. new products/new ventures, personal care divsn., 1977; v.p. diversified cos. and pres. Jafra Cosmetics Worldwide, 1977-79; mktg. dir. Braun AG, Kronberg, W. Ger., 1970-73; chmn. mng. dir. Braun U.K. Ltd., 1973-77; with Abbott Labs., North Chicago, 1979-84, corp. v.p., pres. consumer products divsn., 1979-84; pres., CEO Moxie Industries, 1984-87; pres., CEO Personal Monitoring Technologies, Rochester, N.Y., 1987-89; pres. Bioline Labs., Ft. Lauderdale, Fla., 1988; mng. dir., ptnr. Vista Resource Group, Newport Beach, Calif., 1989-90; pres., CEO, Alcide Corp., Redmond, Wash., 1991-92, chmn., CEO, 1992—2004; founder Board Romm Ltd., 2004. Mem. Columbia Tower Club, El Niguel Club, Wash. Athletic Club, Tech. Alliance, Rainier Club. Home and Office: Board Room Ltd 1301 Spring St # 24J Seattle WA 98104

**SASLEKOVA, LILIA EMILIANOVA,** financial analyst; d. Emilian T. Saslekov and Yonka R. Saslekova. AA in Asian studies, Shanghai Acad. Arts, China, 1994—96; degree in bus. & politics, Pace U., NYC, 1997—2000. Econ./polit. rsch. analyst Wasserstein Perella Emerging Markets & Co, Inc., NYC, 1997—98; bus. devel./corp. affairs analyst UN Assn. USA, NYC, 1998—99; bus. devel. & mgmt. market rsch. analyst Harris Interactive Inc., Louis Harris & Assoc., NYC, 1999—2000; fin. rsch. analyst Thomson Fin. Inc., NYC, 2000—01; fin. risk mgmt. analyst Goldman Sachs & Co., NYC, 2001—05, inv. banking mergers deal conflicts mgmt. assoc., 2005—. Contbr. articles to profl. jours. Organizer, adv. First Asia Pacific Spl. Olympics, Shanghai, 1996, Project Hope, Shanghai, 1995—97; organizer, promoter

Internat. Aid & Trade Exhibit UN; organizer, adv. in landmine clearance in Africa initiative UN Assn. of USA, NYC, 1998—99. Recipient U. Trustee Recognition award for outstanding performance & achievements, Pace U., 1997—99. Mem.: Goldman Sachs Bus. Women Network Steering Com. (assoc.), Bond Market Assn. (assoc.). Avocations: skiing, tennis, golf, travel, bicycling.

**SASMAN, IRENE DEAK HANDBERG,** publishing executive; b. Jamaica, N.Y. d. Paul and Irene (Dyroff) Deak; children: Roger B. Handberg III, Ryan Paul Handberg; m. Timothy Carl Sasman. BS, Fla. State U., MEd, U. N.C., 1970. Cert. tchr. in reading and math., N.C. Lead tchr., reading specialist Chapel Hill (N.C.) City Schs., 1966-69; dir. learning lab. Seminole Community Coll., Sanford, Fla., 1974-78; basic skills cons. EDL/McGraw-Hill Book Co., Orlando, Fla., 1978-82; regional dir. EDL/Arista Pub., Orlando, 1982-84; mktg. mgr., product mgr. Arista/Regents/EDL-Hachette, N.Y.C., 1984-85; v.p. mktg. and sales Raintree Pubs., Milw., 1985, gen. mgr., pub., 1985-87; dir. spl. projects Simon & Schuster, Englewood Cliffs, NJ, 1987-88, v.p. corp. devel. N.Y.C., 1988-90, sr. v.p., 1990-91; chmn. Irene Handberg Internat., N.Y.C., 1991—; pres. The Learning Connection, New York, NY, 1991—. Co-author: EDL/McGraw-Hill Teacher's Guide. Elected precinct woman com. Dem. County Com., Fla.; capt. Nat. Cancer So., Fla., chmn. Sch. Adv. Com., Fla. NSF fellow U. N.C., 1969; recipient Svc. award Jr. Achievement. Mem. Chief Exec. Officers Group (coun. small bus. execs.), Sales and Mktg. Execs., Profl. Dimensions, Chief Exec. Officers Club. Lutheran. Avocations: spectator sports, art, music, skiing. Office: The Learning Connection 300 E 93rd St Apt 29C New York NY 10128-6109

**SASMOR, JAMES CECIL,** publishing representative, educator; b. N.Y.C., July 29, 1920; s. Louis and Cecilia (Mockler) S.; 1 child from previous marriage, Elizabeth Lynn; m. Jeannette L. Fuchs, May 30, 1965. BS, Columbia U., 1942; MBA, Calif. Western U., 1977, PhD, 1979. Fellow, Diplomate Am. Bd. Med. Psychotherapists, Am. Assn. Sex Educators, Counselors and Therapists; lic. healthcare risk mgr., Am. Inst. Med. Law; diplomate Am. Bd. Sexology, Am. Bd. Disability Analysts (sr. analyst); cert. tchr. health scis. Registered rep. Nat. Assn. Security Dealers, 1956—57; founder, owner J.C. Sasmor Assocs., Pub.'s Reps., N.Y.C., 1959—89; co-founder, pres., dir. adminstrn. Continuing Edn. Cons., Inc., 1976—. Pub. cons., 1959—; clin. assoc. U. So. Fla. Coll. Medicine, 1987-89, mem. adj. faculty Coll. Nursing, 1980-89; dir. Ednl. Counseling Comprehensive Breast Cancer Ctr., U. So. Fla. Med. Ctr., 1984-89, client life. mental health inst., 1979-89; lectr. divsn. allied health nursing and pub. svc. Yavapi Coll.; co-leader study tours to fgn. countries. Author: Economics of Structured Continuing Education in Selected Professional Journals, Perception May Be Reality Vols. I and II; contbr. chpts. to Childbirth Education: A Nursing Perspective; contbr. articles to profl. jours. Team tchr. childbirth edn. Am. Soc. Childbirth Educators; bd. dirs. Tampa chpt. ARC; pres. Sedona (Ariz.) unit Am. Cancer Soc., 1995—2000, co-chmn. adult edn. com., Founder Am. Cancer Soc. edn. dept. Sedona Med. Ctr., 1995-2005; bd. dirs. Ariz. divsn., mem. pub. edn. com.; county nursing ednl. cons. ARC, chmn. instrnl. com. on nursing and health, 1979-85; founding mem. coun. trustees Ariz. Nurses Found., 1998; co-leader study tours Russia Profl. Seminar Cons., 1986, China People to People Citizen Ambassador Program, 1996, Spain, Morocco Yaupai Coll. Health Inst., 1999, France and Eng. U. Tours Comparative Nursing, 2001. With USN, 1942-58, PTO; lt. USNR ret. Recipient cert. of appreciation ARC, 1979, Am. Fgn. Svc. Assn., 1988, Dept. Health and Rehab. Svcs. award for Fla. Mental Health Inst. Svc., 1980; Internat. Coun. Sex Edn. and Parenthood fellow Am. U., 1981, Accomplished Elder award Ariz. Coun. of Govts. Mem. NAACOG (bd. dirs. Tampa chpt.), Nat. Assn. Pubs. Reps. (pres. 1965-66), Am. Soc. Psychoprophylaxis in Obstetrics (dir. 1970-71), Am. Soc. Childbirth Educators (co-founder, dir. 1972—), Internat. Coun. Women's Health Issues (chmn. resources com.), Health Edn. Media Assn., Nursing Educators Assn. Tampa, Lions (bd. dirs. Found. Ariz. 1991-2000, past pres. Sedona club, bd. dirs., chair sight, hearing, and scholarship coms.), Phi Theta Kappa (Honors scholar 2000-04, hon. advisor chpt. 1996-2002). Home: 235 Arrowhead Dr Sedona AZ 86351-8900 Office: PO Box 2282 Sedona AZ 86339-2282 Office Phone: 928-284-9897. E-mail: jsasmor@iglide.net.

**SASS, GREGORY GEORGE,** ecologist, researcher; b. Sheboygan, Wis., Oct. 16, 1976; s. George Edward and Linda Lee Sass. BS with honors magna cum laude, U. of South Fla., 1995—99; MS in zoology, U. of Wis. - Madison, 1999—2001, PhD in zoology, 2001—04. Project asst. Ctr. for Limnology, Madison, Wis., 1999, NSF IGERT trainee, 1999—2003, rsch. asst. 1999—2004, postdoc. rsch. assoc., 2004—06; tchg. asst. U. Wis., Madison, 2002—03; dir. Illinois River Biol. Sta., Ill. Natural History Survey, Havana, 2006—. Vol. biologist Grand Canyon Monitoring and Rsch. Ctr., Flagstaff, Ariz., 2001; presenter in field. Contbr. oral presentation, articles to profl. jours. Chair Madison Ecology Group Grad. Student Activities Com., Wis., 2001—03; instr. U. of Wis. - Madison Coll. for Kids Program, 1999—2004, U. of Wis. - Madison Saturday Enrichment Program, 1999—2004, Wis. Dept. of Natural Resources Lake Leaders, 2004; mentor Ecol. Soc. of Am. Undergraduate Minority Student Mentoring (SEEDS), Snowbird, Utah, 2000. Recipient Anna Grant Birge Meml. award, U. Wis. Madison, 2001—03, John Jefferson Davis Travel award, 2001—03, Best Student Paper award, 2003; fellow NSF, 1999—2003. Mem.: Internat. Assn. Great Lakes Rsch., Am. Fisheries Soc. (walleye tech. com. of North Ctrl. divsn.), Ecol. Soc. Am., U. Wis.-Madison Limnology and Fisheries Soc. (v.p. 2002—03), Phi Kappa Phi, Golden Key. Cath. Avocations: fishing, hunting, travel, sports. Office: Illinois River Biol Sta Ill Natural History Survey 704 N Schrader Havana IL 62644 Office Phone: 608-262-3088. Office Fax: 309-543-6000. E-mail: ggsass@wisc.edu.

**SASS, JOSHUA LEE,** music educator; b. Atlanta, Oct. 10, 1979; s. Lee E. and Jean J. Sass; m. Kelly L. Doster, July 12, 2003. MusB in Edn., Furman U., Greenville, S.C., 2002. Cert. tchr. Ga., 2002. Tchr. chorus Lanier Mid. Sch., Buford, Ga., 2003—06, Dacula Mid. Sch., Ga., 2006—. Dir. student choir Hebron Bapt. Ch., Dacula, Ga., 2005—06. Mem.: Nat. Assn. Music Edn. Republican. Bapt. Avocations: singing, reading, travel. Home: 570 Duke Rd Bethlehem GA 30620 Office Phone: 770-271-5128, 770-963-1110. Personal E-mail: joshua_sass@gwinnett.k12.ga.us.

**SASS, MARY MARTHA,** freelance writer, artist; b. Chgo. d. George James and Arbutus Laraine (Schwartz) Harles; m. Roger Edward Sass, June 29, 1968. BS in Edn., U. Ill., 1965; MA in Guidance and Counseling, Northeastern Ill. U., 1977. Cert. secondary educator, guidance counselor, Ill. Tchr. English Kelvyn Park High Sch., Chgo., 1965-83; freelance writer, Skokie, Ill., 1983—. Lectr. North Suburban Libr. Sys., Chgo., 1992; author radio scripts Chgo. Pub. Libr. Broadcasting Sys.; author short stories, essays and articles; illustrator short stories and essays. Author (and illustrator): (novels) The Katy Ornament, 2002; exhibitions include Oakton C.C., 1993, All Chgo. Juried Art Show Skokie Pub. Libr., 1993, 1994, 1995, 1996, 1997 (hon. mention), 1998, 1999, 2000, 2001, Woman's Club Evanston Ann. Art Exhibit, 1994, 1995, 1996, 1997, 1998, 1999, 2000, Skokie Hist. Soc., 1993, 1994 (hon. mention), 1995, 1996, 1997, 1998, 1999, 2000 (First prize, 2000), 2001, 2002, 2003 (First prize), Allstate Ins., 1995, 1996, 1997, Blue Moon Art Gallery, 1999, Devonshire Cultural Ctr., 2002, Morton Grove Pub. Libr., 2002, 2004, Lincolnwood Village Hall Gallery, 2005, Emily Oaks Nature Ctr, 2006, South Shore Cultural Ctr., 2006, Represented in permanent collections Artists Archives, Chgo. Pub. Libr. Vol. Emily Oaks Nature Ctr. Skokie Park Dist., Ill. Recipient Radio Script hon. mention award Take One Nat. Radio Theatre Competition, 1994, Women in Cable award for cable TV documentary; Nat. Pub. Radio scholar, 1984. Mem. Mystery Writers Am., Mystery Writers Am. Spkr.'s Bur., Chgo. Artist's Coalition, Nat. Parks & Conservation Assn., Greenpeace, Nature Conservancy, Park Activist Network, Sr. Artists' Network, Ocean Conservancy, World Wildlife Fund Avocations: classical guitar, sculpting, cable television writing and production, gardening. Office Phone: 847-674-7118. Personal E-mail: maryhsass@aol.com.

**SASS, NEIL LESLIE,** toxicologist; b. Balt., Oct. 24, 1944; s. Samuel and Blanche (Radoon) S.; m. Anita Paige Hoswell, June 29, 1984. BS, Wake Forest Coll., 1966; MS, W.Va. U., 1969, PhD, 1971; MS, Johns Hopkins U.,

1984. Commd. officer USPHS, 1966, advanced through grades to capt., 1988, comdr. Preventive Medicine unit, 1989; served as rsch. toxicologist med. labs. U.S. Army, Edgewood Arsenal, Md., 1971-74; chief clin. investigations William Beaumont Army Med. Ctr., El Paso, Tex., 1974-77; toxicologist Bur. of Foods FDA, Washington, 1977-82; spl. asst. to dir. Ctr. for Food Safety and Applied Nutrition, FDA, Washington, 1982-99; dir. divsn. toxicological rsch. Ctr. for Food Safety and Applied Nutrition, Washington, 1996-99; chief toxicologist, chem. lab. dir., state counterterrorism coord., chem. lab. dir. Ala. Dept. Pub. Health, Montgomery, 1999—. Jewish. Office: Ala Dept Pub Health The RSA Tower 201 Monroe St Ste 1450 Montgomery AL 36104-3735 Home: 2160 Woodley Rd Montgomery AL 36111-1013 Office Phone: 334-206-5973. Business E-Mail: nsass@adph.state.al.us.

**SASSA, SCOTT M.,** former internet company executive; b. Feb. 1959; m. Ellen M. Sassa. Formerly with Rogers & Cowan Pub. Rels. Agy.; past v.p. new bus. devel. Ohlmeyer Comm. Co.; past v.p. network mgmt. Fox Broadcasting Co.; dir. sales promotion, then v.p./gen. mgr. Cable Music Channel Turner Broadcasting Sys., exec. v.p. Turner Network TV, then pres. Turner Entertainment Group, bd. dirs., mem. exec. com., 1988—97; past pres. Andrews Group; past CEO Marvel Entertainment; pres. TV Stations divsn. NBC, 1997—98, pres. Entertainment divsn., 1998—99, pres. West Coast Burbank, Inc., 1999—2002, cons. strategic projects, 2002; CEO Friendster, Inc., 2004—05.

**SASSEN, SASKIA,** urban planner, educator; b. The Hague, The Netherlands, Jan. 5, 1949; came to U.S., 1970; d. Willem S. and Mara (Van de Voort) Van Elsloo; m. Daniel J. Koob, Aug. 30, 1973 (div. 1982); 1 child, Hilary Koob-Sassen; m. Richard Sennett, Oct. 23, 1987. Maitrise, U. Poitiers, France, 1973; PhD in Econs. and Sociology, U. Notre Dame, 1974. Postdoctoral fellow Ctr. Internat. Affairs Harvard U., Cambridge, Mass., 1974-75; from asst. to full prof. Queens Coll. CUNY, 1976-85; prof. dept. urban planning Columbia U., N.Y.C., 1985—, chair divsn. planning, preservation and real estate, 1988-91, chair PhD program in urban planning, 1989—92, 1994—98, U. Chgo., 1998—. Mem. faculty Sch. Internat. and Pub. Affairs Columbia U.; past mem. non-govtl. internat. planning com. on yr. of shelter for homeless UN; former mem. Queens Borough Pres. Claire Shulman's Blue Ribbon Panel on Govt., N.Y. State Indsl. Corp. Coun.; mem. Social Sci. Rsch. Coun. working group on N.Y.C. Russell Sage Found., 1985-90, mem. immigration and econ. sociology project; mem. Social Sci. Rsch. Coun. com. Hispanic pub. policy Ford Found., 1987-91; mem. econ. restructuring in U.S. and Japan UN Ctr. on Regional Devel. and MIT, 1988-90; mem. N.Y.-London comparative study Econ. Social Rsch. Coun. of U.K.; mem. comparative urban studies project Woodrow Wilson Ctr., Washington; mem. group of Lisbon Sci. Program of EC and Gulbenkian Found., Portugal; advisor Intl. European U.; disting. lectr. Inst. Advanced Studies, Vienna, Austria; Henry Luce lectr. Clark U., 1995-2000, Theodore Hesbaugh lectures on politics and ethics, Yale Law Sch. Sherril Lecture, 2005; co-curator Trade Rts. exhbn. New Mus. Contemporary Arts, N.Y.C., 1993; cons. UN, PBS, Ford Found., Nat. Urban League N.Y.C. Office Econ. Devel.; Ralph Lewis prof. sociology, mem. faculty law sch., com. internat. affairs; centennial visl prof. London Sch. Econs., 2000-, others; lectr. in field. Author: The Mobility of Labor and Capital, 1988, The Global City: New York, London, Tokyo, 1991, 2d edit. 2001, Cities in a World Economy, 1994, 2d edit., 2000, Losing Control, 1996, Globalization and its Discontent, 1998, Guests and Aliens, 1999, Global Nations/Limited Cities, 2002, Territory: Authority and Rights, 2005; mem. editl. bd. Urban Affairs Rev., Competition and Change, Internat. Planning Studies, others; reviewer Times Lit. Supplement, several acad. jours.; contbr. articles to profl. jours; comments published in N.Y. Times, Fin. Times, The Guardian, Internat. Herald Tribune, others. Rsch. grantee Chgo. Inst. Architecture and Urbanism, 1988-89, Twentieth Century Fund, 1994—, others; fellow Robert F. Kennedy Found., 1970-71, Ford Found., 1972-73, Social Sci. Rsch. Coun., 1977-78, Ford and Tinker Founds., 1980-81, N.Y. Inst. Humanities, 1982-90, Tinker Found., 1982-83, Wissenshaftszentrum, Berlin, 1991-92; scholar Russell Sage Found., 1992-93, Woodrow Wilson Internat. Ctr. Scholars, Ctr. for Advanced Study, summer 1993; fellow World Econ. Forum, 1997-. Office Phone: 773-702-7279. Business E-Mail: s-sassen@uchicago.edu.

**SASSER, BOB,** retail company executive; With Roses Stores, Inc., store mgr., sr. v.p. mdse. and mktg.; v.p. gen. mdse. mgr. Michaels Stores, Inc.; COO Dollar Tree Stores, Inc., Chesapeake, Va., 1999—. Office: Dollar Tree Stores Inc 500 Volvo Pkwy Chesapeake VA 23320

**SASSER, CHARLES WAYNE,** journalist, educator, writer; b. Sallisaw, Okla., Jan. 3, 1942; s. Ben Garland and Mary Louise Sasser; m. Dianne Carol Reilly, Oct. 8, 1965 (div. 1978); children: David, Michael; m. Katherine Renee, Feb. 2, 1979 (div. Oct. 1986); 1 adopted child, Joshua Dale; m. Donna Sue Baker, Oct. 7, 1995; stepchildren: DeAnn, Darren, Michael. AA, Miami (Fla.)-Dade Jr. Coll., 1968; BA, Fla. State U., 1969; postgrad., Okla. State U., 1977-78. Police officer Miami Police Dept., 1965-68; detective Tulsa Police Dept., 1970-79; coll. instr. Tulsa Jr. Coll., 1976—; freelance journalist, 1979—. Horse rancher, trainer, Mannford, Okla., 1971-78, Chouteau, Okla., 1996—; dir. criminal justice program Am. Christian Coll. Tulsa, 1974-78; profl. rodeo clown Profl. Rodeo Cowboy Assn., Okla., 1984-86; pres., CEO Fly High Inc., 2000—; instr. creative writing Tulsa (Okla.) C.C., 1996— Author: No Gentle Streets, 1984, The Girl Scout Murders, 1989, The Walking Dead, 1989, One Shot-One Kill, 1990, Homicide!, 1990, The 100th Kill, 1992, Always a Warrior, 1994, Shoot to Kill, 1994, Last American Heroes, 1994, In Cold Blood: Oklahoma's Most Notorious Murders, 1994, Smoke Jumpers, 1996, First Seal, 1997, Doc: Platoon Medic, 1998, Fire Cops, 1998, At Large, 1998, Arctic Homestead, 2000, Liberty City, 2000, Operation No Man's Land, 2000, Taking Fire, 2001, The War Chaser, 2001, The Return, 2001, Detachment Delta: Punitive Strike, 2002, Raider, 2002, The Encyclopedia of Navy Seals, 2002, Detachment Delta: Iron Weed, 2003, Magic Steps to Writing Success, 2003, Hill 488, 2003, Going Bonkers: The Wacky World of Cultural Madness 2004, Detachment Delta Operation Deep Steel, 2004, Crosshairs on The Kill Zone, 2004, Detachment DELTA: Operation Aces Wild, 2005, Patton's Panthers, 2005, Dark Planet, 2005, OSS Commando: Final Option, 2006; editor Keystone Sportsman Mag., 1975-78; contbr. articles to periodicals; actor Wagoner (Okla.) Playhouse Dinner Theater, 1997— Pres. Keystone Crossroads Hist. Assn., Mannford, 1977; del. Creek County Reps., Sapulpa, Okla., 1977-78, Sequoyah County Reps., Sallisaw, Okla., 1984-85. With U.S. Army Spl. Forces, 1966-67, 72-83; 1st sgt. USAR, 1991-97, ret.; with USN, 1960-64. Recipient Tulsa Author's award, City of Tulsa, 1992. Mem. Okla. Writers Fedn., Tulsa Nightwriters (Nightwriter of the Yr. 1990, 96, 2002, pres. 2003-06). Avocations: martial arts, steer roping, scuba diving, parachuting, horses. Home and Office: 30934 E 660 Rd Chouteau OK 74337-9617 Office Phone: 918-476-6189. Personal E-mail: charlessas@msn.com.

**SASSER, ROBERT,** retail executive; From various positions to sr. v.p. Roses Stores, Inc., sr. v.p. merchandise and mktg., 1997—99; v.p., gen. merchandise mgr. Michaels Stores, Inc., 1994—96; sr. v.p., COO Dollar Tree Stores, Inc., Chesapeake, Va., 1999—2004, pres., COO, 2001—04, pres., CEO, 2004—. Office: Dollar Tree Stores Inc 500 Volvo Pkwy Chesapeake VA 23320*

**SASSO, GARY L.,** lawyer; b. Miami, 1952; BS, U. Pa., 1974, JD, 1977. Bar: Fla., DC, Pa., U.S. Dist. Ct. Fla. (middle and so. districts), U.S. Ct. Appeals (3d, 4th, 6th, 9th and 11th cir.), U.S. Supreme Ct. Law clk. to Hon. Spottswood W. Robinson,III U.S. Ct. Appeals, 1977—78; law clk. to Justice Byron R. White U.S. Supreme Ct., 1978—79; litigator Bredhoff & Kaiser, Washington; various positions including mem. exec. com. and bd. dirs. Carlton Fields, Pa., Tampa, Fla., 1987—, pres., CEO, 2006—. Co-chair civil sect. Fed. Bar Assn. Tampa Bay Chpt.; editor-in-chief U. Pa. Law Rev., 1976—77, Litigation Jour. ABA Sect. Litigation, 2000—02. Contbr. articles to profl. jours. V.p., dir. H.B. Plant Mus., Tampa, Fla.; chmn. bd. dirs. Creative Kids Count, Inc. Fellow: Am. Bar Found., Am. Acad. Appellate Lawyers, Internat. Acad. Trial Lawyers; mem.: Am. Law Inst. Office: Carlton Fields PA 4221 W Boy Scout Blvd Ste 1000 Tampa FL 33607-5736 Office Phone: 813-229-4256. Office Fax: 813-229-4133. E-mail: gsasso@carltonfields.com.

**SASSO, JOHN,** advertising and public strategies executive; BA, Boston U. Chief of staff Gov. Michael Dukakis, Mass., 1983—87; sr. v.p. Hill, Holliday, Connors, Cosmopulos, Inc., Advt., Boston, 1988—90; pres. Advanced Strategies, 1990—. Mgr. Geraldine Ferarro v.p. campaign, 1984; advisor Dukakis pres. campaign, 1988; bd. dirs. Fannie Mae Found., 1993—; gen. election mgr. of the DNC then sr. advisor Kerry-Edwards pres. campaign, 2004—. Bd. dirs. Heller Sch. Social Policy at Brandeis U. Office: Kerry Edwards 2004 Inc PO Box 34640 Washington DC 20043

**SASSOON, ANDRE GABRIEL,** lawyer; b. Cairo, Apr. 13, 1936; arrived in U.S., 1959; s. Gabriel and Sarine (Tawil) S.; m. Barbara Dee Freedman, Aug. 15, 1965 (div. 2001); children: Daniel, Gabriel, Sarina, Nathaniel Andre. GCE, Oxford U., Cambridge U., Eng., 1953; JD, Villanova U., 1969; LLM, Harvard U., 1970. Bar: Pa. 1969, NY 1970. Product mgr. Rohm & Haas Co., Phila., 1960-66; law clk. Dist. Atty.'s Office, Phila., 1968; assoc. Weil, Gotshal & Manges, NYC, 1970-73; pvt. practice NYC, 1973—; pres., CEO Sterimed Internat., Inc., 1999—. Dir. elem. Youth in Distress, NYC, 1982—; v.p., dir. internat. Anti-Drug Abuse Found., NYC, 1987—; v.p., dir., mem. exec. com. Hebrew Immigrant Aid Soc., NYC, 1977—; internat. sec., gov. bd. internat. govs. World Sephardi Fedn., NYC, 1988—; co-pres., chmn., U.S com., dir. internat. Jewish Com. for Sephardi '92, NYC, 1989—; mem. NY State Christopher Columbus Quincetenary Commn., Statewide Outreach Com., 1991—. Editor Villanova Law Rev.; contbr. articles to profl. jours. Chmn. bd. Sloan's Auctioneers & Appraisers, 2001—03, chmn., 1953—, Sloans and Kenyon, 2003—. With USAR, 1960—66. Recipient Israel Trade award Govt. of Israel, 1985. Mem. ABA, Am. Arbitration Assn. (panel mem. 1971—), Am. Soc. Internat. Law, Order of Coif, 0840 Internat. Pvt., 0860 Internat. Pub. Home: 641 Fifth Ave Apt 37D New York NY 10022 Office: 600 Madison Ave New York NY 10022-1615 E-mail: AndreSassoon@aol.com.

**SASTROWARDOYO, TERESITA MANEJAR,** nurse; b. Iloilo, Philippines; came to U.S., 1960; d. Timoteo and Monica (Casianan) Manejar; m. Sumarsongko H. Sastrowardoyo, June 8, 1962; children: Timoteo, Daniel (dec.), Benjamin. BSN, Ctrl. Philippine U., Iloilo, 1957; cert. operating rm. and surgical nursing, St. Luke's Hosp Ctr., N.Y.C., 1960-61. Head nurse med. unit Emmanuel Hosp., Roxas City, Philippines, 1957-58; supr. oper. rm. Brent Hosp., Zamboanga City, Philippines, 1958-60; staff nurse oper. rm. Jewish Meml. Hosp., N.Y.C., 1961-62; evening staff nurse oper. rm. Flower and Fifth Ave Hosp., N.Y.C., 1963-65; staff nurse oper. rm., charge nurse night shift St. Lukes Hosp. Ctr., N.Y.C., 1966-76; staff nurse oper. rm. South Side Hosp., Bayshore, NY, 1976—; asst. head nurse operating room, 2003—. Mem.: N.Y. State Nurses Assn., Ctrl. Philippine U. Alumni Assn. N.Y., N.J. and Conn. (bd. dirs. 1994—95, 1995—97). Baptist. Avocations: gardening, reading.

**SASTRY, SHIVASHANKAR KUDUR,** retired entomologist; b. Kudur, Karnataka State, India, Mar. 2, 1927; s. Seetharama Kudur and Narasamma Begur Sastry; m. Saroja Kudur Udayagiri, June 8, 1948; children: Mahesh Kudur, Bhavani Murthy, Anuradha Murali, Uma Sastry Kher, Jyothi Kudur Rao, Anil Kudur. BS in chemistry/Botany/Zoology, Ctrl. Coll. Mysore U., Bangalore, India, 1947; MS in Agrl. Entomology-Plant Pathology, Indian Agrl. Rsch. Inst. (P.G. Sch.), New Delhi, India, 1962; PhD Biology-Entomology, Wayne State U., Detriot, MI, 1975. Pesticide Applicator Mich., Wash. D.C. & Md., 1995. Sr. entomologist U. of Agrl. Sciences, Bangalore, Karnataka State, India, 1948—66; entomologist U.S. EPA & Office of Pesticide Program, Crystal City, Md., 1995—96, Eradico Exterminators Inc., Ferndale, Mich., 1971—78; chief of pest control sect.- entomologist St. Elizabeths Hosp. NIMH, U.S. DHHS, Washington, 1978—81; dir., tech. ops. Nat. Pest Contol Assn. (current: Nat. Pest Mgmt. Assn.), Dunloring, Va., 1981—82; entomologist (gen. mgr.) Allied Exterminating Services, Sliver Spring, Md., 1982—87; pest mgmt. course coord. Montgomery Coll., Takoma Park, Md., 1981—84; pres. SAI Pest Control Trainers and Consultants Inc., Gaithersburg, 1985—89; instr.- entomologist USDA & UDC Coop. Ext. Svc., Washington, 1992—94; extractor, label use info. vol. AARP, U.S. EPA & Office of Pesticide Program, Arlington, Va., 1994—95; ret., 1996. Listed as forensic entomologist Def. Pest Mgmt. Info. Analysis Ctr., Washington, 1986—87. Contbr. articles to profl. jours. Recipient A New Parasitoid named for me, Recommending Ingenious Ways of Using 'Maxforce' Contest 2d prize, Am. Cyanamid Co., 1982. Mem.: Staff Club, U. of Agrl. Sciences Bangalore, India (exec. sec. 1963—64), Entomol. Soc. of India, Bangalore Br. (exec. sec. 1962—63), Orthopterists Soc. (mem. 1990—96), Institiute of Gerontology (mem.; elder advisor to rsch. (mem.) 2000—04, Appreciation Award 2000-2004), Entomol. Soc. of Am. (hon.; emeritus mem. 1989—2004). D-Liberal. Hindu. Achievements include discovery of a natural enemy (insect) -named Lymaenon Shasthryi- after me. Avocations: travel, gardening, volunteering in cultural & gerontological activities. Home: 1832 Eldridge Dr Troy MI 48083 Personal E-mail: sarojamadh@aol.com.

**SASTRY, SOSALE SHANKARA,** electrical engineer, computer scientist, educator; PhD, U. Calif., Berkeley, 1981. Asst. prof. MIT, 1980—82; Gordon McKay prof. Harvard U., 1994; dir. electronics rsch. lab. U. Calif., Berkeley, 1996—99; dir. info. tech. DARPA, 2000; disting. prof. dept. electrical engring., computer sci., bioengring. U. Calif., Berkeley, chair dept. electrical engring., computer sci., bioengring., 2001—04. Co-author: (books) A Mathematical Introduction to Robotic Manipulation, 1994, An Invitation to 3-D Vision From Images to Models; co-editor: Hybrid Systems II: Lecture Notes in Computer Science, 1995, Hybrid Systems IV: Lecture Notes in Computer Science, 1997, Hybrid Systems: Computation and Control, 1998, Essays in Mathematical Robotics, 1998; author: Nonlinear Systems: Analysis, Stability, and Control, 1999; co-author: over 250 technical papers. Recipient David Marr prize, Internat. Conference in Computer Vision, 1999, Presidential Young Investigator award, NSF, 1994, IBM Faculty Devel. award, 1983—85. Fellow: IEEE, Am. Acad. Arts & Sciences; mem.: Nat. Acad. of Engring. Office: U Calif EECS 253 Cory Hall Berkeley CA 94720-1770

**SATCHER, DAVID,** public health service officer, former Surgeon General of the United States; b. Anniston, Ala., Mar. 2, 1941; s. Wilmer and Anna Satcher; m. Nola Satcher; children: Gretchen, David, Daraka, Daryl. BS, Morehouse Coll., 1963; MD, PhD, Case Western Reserve U., 1970; recipient of many honorary degrees and numerous disting. honors. Resident and fellow Strong Mem. Hosp., U. Rochester, UCLA, and King Drew; former faculty UCLA Sch. Medicine and Pub. Health; faculty, chair dept. family medicine King-Drew Med. Ctr., LA, interim dean, 1977—79; dir. King-Drew Sickle Cell Rsch. Ctr.; prof., chmn. dept. cmty. and family medicine Morehouse Sch. Medicine, Atlanta, 1979—82; pres. Meharry Med. Coll., Nashville, 1982—93; dir. Ctrs. for Disease Control and Prevention, Atlanta, 1993—98; adminstr. Agy. for Toxic Substances and Disease Registry, 1993—98; surgeon gen. US Dept. Health & Human Services, Washington, 1998—2002, asst. sec. health, 1998—2001; sr. vis. fellow Kaiser Family Found., Washington, 2002—; dir. Nat. Ctr. for Primary Care at Morehouse Sch. Medicine, Atlanta, 2002—, also interim pres., 2005—. Apptd. mem. Coun. of Grad. Med. Edn., 1986, chmn.; former Robert Wood Johnson Clin. Scholar; former Macy Faculty Fellow. Named Nashvillian of Yr., 1992; recipient Watts Grassroots award for cmty. leadership, 1979, Nat. Conf. Christians and Jews awards, 1985, Black Achievement award, Ebony Mag., 1994, Brewslow award in pub. health, 1995, Dr. Nathan B. Davis award, AMA, 1996, Lifetime Achievement award, NY Acad. Medicine, 1997, Bennie Mays Trailblazer award, Nat. Found. for Infectious Diseases, Jimmy and Roslyn Carter award, Discovery Health Channel Med. Honors, 2004. Fellow: Am. Acad. of Family Physicians; mem.: Inst. Medicine NAS, Alpha Omega Alpha, Phi Beta Kappa. Focuses on promoting healthy lifestyles and ending disparities in healthcare; has raised childhood immunization rates to 78% in 1996 from 55% in 1992. Office: Kaiser Family Foundation Ste 250 1450 G St NW Washington DC 20005 also: Nat Ctr for Primary Care at Morehouse Sch Medicine 720 Westview Dr SW Atlanta GA 30310 Office Phone: 404-756-5740. Office Fax: 404-756-5767. Business E-Mail: ncpc@msm.edu.*

**SATCHI-FAINARO, RONIT,** medical educator; b. Tel Aviv, Oct. 22, 1971; m. Oded Fainaro; 1 child, Tom Fainaro. BPharm, The Hebrew U. Jerusalem, 1995; PhD, U. London, 1999. Postdoctoral rsch. fellow Dept. Cell Rsch. and Immunology Tel Aviv (Israel) U., 1999—2001, sr. lectr., 2005—; postdoctoral

rsch. fellow Dept. Surgery Children's Hosp. Boston, 2001—02; postdoctoral rsch. fellow Dept. Surgery Med. Sch. Harvard U., Boston, 2001—02; instr. Dept. Surgery Children's Hosp. Boston, 2002—05; instr. Dept. Surgery Med. Sch. Harvard U., 2002—05. Vis. assoc. prof. Children's Hosp. Boston, 2005—, Harvard U., 2005—; cons. in field. Contbr. chapters to books, articles to profl. jours. Recipient Chevening award, Brit. Coun., 1996, A.M. Cook prize, 1998; grantee, Breast Cancer Rsch. Found., 2001—05, Dept. Def., 2004—05; scholar, Fulbright Found., 2001, Rothschild Found., 2001; Wingate scholarship, 1998. Mem.: Am. Assn. Cancer Rsch., The Brit. Pharm. Scis. Group (assoc.), European Assn. Cancer Rsch. (assoc. Young Cancer Rschr. award 2005), Controlled Release Soc. (assoc. Ethypharm Outstanding Pharmaceutical Paper award 2003, Grad. Student award 2000). Achievements include patents in field. Office: Children's Hospital Boston/Harvard Med 1 Blackfan Circle VBP Karp Bldg 12007D Boston MA 02115 Office Phone: 617-919-2410. Office Fax: 617-730-0231. Business E-Mail: ronit.satchi-fainaro@childrens.harvard.edu.

**SATERNOW, TIM,** set designer, lighting designer, theater educator, painter; b. Oswego, NY, Nov. 10, 1960; s. Robert J. and Jo Saternow; life ptnr. Craig Harwood. BFA in Theatrical Design, SUNY, Purchase, 1983; MFA in Set & Lighting Design, Yale U., New Haven, 1987. Design assoc. Seattle Repertory Theatre, 1990—91; asst. prof. dept. drama Carnegie Mellon U., Pitts., 1992—96; prof. dept. dramatic arts U. Conn., Storrs, 1996—; freelance set and lighting designer, 1983—. Lighting designer: (plays) SQUONK on Broadway; set and lighting designer Confessions of a Mormon Boy; set designer The Trojan Woman (Prague Quadrennial - US Exhibit, 2003); art dir. (films) The Piano Lesson (Emmy award for Outstanding Art Direction, 1996). Donald M. Oenslager scholar, Yale U., 1984—87. Mem.: NATAS, Internat. Theatre Scenographer and Technician Orgn., US Inst. Theatre Tech. (chair young designers' forum 1994—2006), United Scenic Artist. Office: U Conn Dramatic Arts 802 Bolton Rd U-1127 Storrs Mansfield CT 06269-1127 Office Phone: 860-486-4185. Business E-Mail: tim.saternow@uconn.edu.

**SATHER, GLEN CAMERON,** professional hockey team executive, coach; b. High River, Alta., Canada, Sept. 2, 1943; m. Ann Sather; 2 children. Former professional hockey player; coach Edmonton Oilers, Nat. Hockey League, Alta., Can., 1977-89, gen. mgr., 1981—2000, pres. Alta., 1982—2000, alt. gov., 1990—2000; pres., gen. mgr NY Rangers, 2000—, head coach, 2003—04. Head coach, Stanley Cup Champions, 1984, 1985, 1987, 1988. Recipient Jack Adams Award for NHL Coach of the Yr., 1986. Office: c/o New York Rangers 2 Pennsylvania Plaza New York NY 10121

**SATHYAMOORTHY, MUTHUKRISHNAN,** engineering educator, dean; b. Sathanur, Tamil Nadu, India, Feb. 21, 1946; s. Kuppusamy and Visalakshi Muthukrishnan; m. Chitra Subbiah, May 26, 1971; children: Mohanakrishnan, Kumaran. B in Civil Engring., U. Madras, India, 1967; M in Engring. Mechanics, Indian Inst. of Tech., Madras, India, 1969, PhD in Aero. Engring., 1973. Lectr. Indian Inst. of Tech., Madras, India, 1969-74; rsch. fellow U. Birmingham, Eng., 1974-76; asst. prof. Clarkson U., Potsdam, NY, 1979-82, assoc. prof., 1982-92, assoc. prof., exec. officer, 1992-94, prof., exec. officer, 1994-97, prof., chair, 1997-2001; dean engring. W.Va. Univ. Inst. Tech., 2001—06; assoc. provost The U. Tex. at Tyler, 2006—. Vis. rsch. faculty U. Calgary, Can., 1977-79. Contbr. author: Handbook of Civil Engineering Practice, 1988; editor: Material Nonlinearity in Vibrations, 1985; author: Nonlinear Analysis of Structures, 1998. Recipient Appreciation cert. U.S. Army, 1990, Outstanding Advisor award Clarkson U., 1993, Tau Beta Pi Faculty award, 1997, Disting. Tchg. award Clarkson Univ., 2001. Fellow ASME (mem. nat. student sect. com. 1992-94, mem. gen. awards com. 1994-99, Nat. Faculty Advisor award 1993, Dedicated Svc. award 1999); AIAA (assoc.), Aero. Soc. India. Avocations: overseas travel, camping, photography, fishing. Office: Office Assoc Provost The U Tex at Tyler 3900 University Blvd Tyler TX 75799 Home: 13325 White Tail Dr Tyler TX 75707 Office Phone: 304-442-3161. Business E-Mail: msathy@wvutech.edu.

**SATIN, CLAIRE JEANINE,** sculptor, artist; b. Bklyn., Jan. 9, 1942; BA, Sarah Lawrence Coll., 1956; MFA, Pratt Inst., 1968. Instr. art edn. dept. edn. Bklyn. Mus., 1958-59; instr. dept. edn. and dept. Fine Arts Broward Cmty. Coll., Ft. Lauderdale, Fla., 1971-83; dir. Broward Cmty. Coll. Gallery, Ft. Lauderdale, 1975-76. Artist rep. Gabriela Herrera, N.Y.C., Art Vitam, Wynwood, Miami, Priscilla Juvelis, Maine, Vamps and Tramps, Birmingham, Ala. Collections include Libr. Congress, Rare Books Collection, Victoria and Albert Mus., London, Getty Ctr. Hist. Art and Humanities, L.A., Mus. Modern Art, N.Y.C., Mus. Art, Ft. Lauderdale, King Stephen Mus., Szekesfeherdt, Hungary, Ruth and Marvin Sackner Archive of Concrete and Visual Poetry, others; commd. works include: Chapman Chronicles, State of Alaska, U. Alaska, Fairbanks, 1992, Alphawalk, New Tampa Regional Libr., Hillsborough County, Tampa, Fla., 1997 (catalog); Alphastory, Pembroke Pines Libr., Pembroke Pines, Fla., Broward County Art in Pub. Places Program (brochure), Am. Ctrs., New Delhi, Bombay, India. Hon. chair Broward County Cultural Affairs Coun., Ft. Lauderdale, 1981-, bd. dirs., 1975-83, Meml. Found. Jewish Culture, N.Y.C. Recipient S. Fla. Cult Consortium award Miami Art Mus., Fla., 1997-98; So. Arts Fedn./NEA Regional Visual Arts fellow, 1996; Fla. State Individual Artist fellow Statewide Exhbn., 1978, 97-98; Cult Consortium fellow Miami Art Mus., 1997-98; Tiffany Found. grantee, 1968-69, Meml. Found. for Jewish Culture, 2001-02. Mem. Internat. Sculpture Ctr., Am. Craft. Coun., Ctr. Book Arts, Fonteneda Soc. (bd. dirs. 1997—). Office: c/o Artworks/Artspace 101 SW 1st St Dania Beach FL 33004-3628 Office Phone: 954-923-9117.

**SATIN, JOSEPH,** language educator, retired dean; b. Phila., Dec. 16, 1920; s. Reuben Philip and Harriet (Price) Satin; m. Selma Rosen (dec. 1978); children: Mark, Diane; m. Barbara Jeanne Dodson (dec. 1987); m. Terrye Sagan, 1992. BA, Temple U., 1946; AM, Columbia U., 1949, PhD, 1954. Instr. Integrated studies W.Va. U., Morgantown, 1952-54; prof. English and Comparative Lit. Moorhead (Minn.) State U., 1954-63; chmn. dept. English and Humanism Midwestern U., Wichita Falls, Tex., 1963-73; dean Sch. Arts and Humanities Calif. State U., Fresno, 1973-89. Mgr.concert series Moorhead State U., 1956—61; mem. nat. bd. con. NEH, Washington, 1979—; dir. London semester Calif. State U., Fresno, 1982—92; dir. Frank Lloyd Wright Auditorium Project. Author: (book) Ideas in Context, 1958, The 1950's: America's "Placid" Decade, 1960, Reading Non-Fiction Prose, 1964, Reading Prose Fiction, 1964, Shakespeare and His Sources, 1966, Reading Literature, 1968, The Humanities Handbook (2 vols), 1969, (poems) The Journey Upward, 1999, Poems on the Internet (www.Poetry.com), 2000; editor: (book) Frank Lloyd Wright-Letters to Apprentices, 1982, Letters to Architects, 1984, Letters to Clients, 1986, Treasures of Taliesin, 1985, The Guggenheim Correspondence, 1986, Frank Lloyd Wright: His Living Voice, 1987, Frank Lloyd Wright, The Crowning Decade, 1989; translator: Federico Fellini, Comments on Film, 1987; contbr. Encyclopedia Int Educ, 1978; dir: Univ Press, Calif State Univ, 1982—94. With USN army, 1943—46, ETO. Named Nat Grand Prize Winner, Nat Library Poetry N Am Ann Poetry Contest, 1998. Jewish. Avocations: creative writing, music. Home: 65 Maywood Dr San Francisco CA 94127-2007 Office Phone: 415-661-3121. E-mail: tewilder@juno.com.

**SATINE, BARRY ROY,** lawyer; b. NYC, July 25, 1951; s. Norman S. and Fay (Mekles) S.; m. Janice Bea Halfond, Aug. 4, 1974; children: David, Leah. BA, CCNY, 1972; JD, George Washington U., 1975. Bar: N.Y. 1976, D.C. 1977, U.S. Dist. Ct. (so. dist.) N.Y. 1978, U.S. Supreme Ct. 1979, U.S. Dist. Ct. (ea. dist.) N.Y. 1982, U.S. Ct. Appeals (2d cir.) 1989. Trial atty. U.S. Civil Svc. Commn., Washington, 1975—78; atty. AT&T, N.Y.C., 1978—81, N.Y. Tel. Co., N.Y.C., 1981—82; mem. assoc. Surrey & Morse, N.Y.C., 1982—84, ptnr., 1985, Jones Day, 1986—. Mem. assoc. of Bar of City of N.Y. Office: Jones Day 222 East 41st St New York NY 10017 Office Phone: 212-326-3904. Business E-Mail: barryrsatine@jonesday.com.

**SATINOVER, JEFFREY B.,** physicist, psychiatrist, writer; b. Chgo., Sept. 4, 1947; s. Joseph and Sena (Rotman) Satinover; m. Julie Rachel Leff, June 10, 1982; children: Sarah Katherine, Anne-Rebecca, Jenny Leigh. BS, MIT, 1971; EdM, Harvard U., 1973; MD, U. Tex., 1982; Diplomate, C.G Jung Inst.,

Zurich, Switzerland, 1976; MS, Yale U., 2002; student in Physics, U. Nice, 2004—. Diplomate Am. Bd. Psychiatry and Neurology, Am. Bd. Geriat. Psychiatry. Fellow dept. psychiatry and child psychiatry Yale U., New Haven, 1982-86; founder, exec. dir. Sterling Inst., Stamford, Conn., 1985-92; med. dir. Temenos Inst., Westport, Conn., 1984—; pvt. practice Westport, Conn.- William James lectr. psychology and and religion Harvard U., 1975; mem. catchment area coun. S. W. Regional Mental Health Bd., 1988—92; mem. Lower Fairfield County Regional Action Coun. Against Substance Abuse, 1990—92; with relativistic heavy ion group dept. physics Yale U., New Haven, 1999—2001, with condensed matter theory group, 2001—03, with theoretical condensed matter physics group, 2002—03; dir. rsch. VKRA Quantitative Fin., 2003—; mem. condensed matter physics group U. Nice, France, 2003—; vis. lectr. Dept. Politics Princeton U., 2004—05. Co-author: Jungian Psychotherapy, 1984, Science and the Fragile Self, 1990, Jungian Analysis, 1993; author: Homesexuality and the Politics of Truth, 1994, The Empty Self: Gnostic Foundations of Modern Identity, 1994, Feathers of the Skylark, 1996, Cracking the Bible Code, 1997, The Quantum Brain, 2001; contbr. articles to profl. jours. Active nat. physician's resource coun. Focus on Family, 1994—97; pres. C. G. Jung Found., NY, 1988—92; founder, mem. exec. bd. com. Save Our Schs., 1994—; bd. dirs. Toward Tradition; bd. advisors Family Inst. Conn., 1996—; bd. dirs. Klingberg Family Ctrs., 1994—96. Capt. N.G. USAR, 1989—94, maj. USAR, 1995—. Recipient Seymour Lustman Residency Rsch. 2d pl. award, Yale U. Psychiatry Dept., 1983, 1985. Mem.: Internat. Assn. Analytical Psychology, Am. Psychiat. Assn. (Burroughs-Wellcome fellow 1983—85), Aspetuck Valley Country Club, Alpha Omega Alpha. Republican. Jewish. Avocations: tennis, harpsichord, jazz keyboard. Business E-Mail: jsatinov@princeton.edu.

**SATINSKY, BARNETT,** lawyer; b. Phila., June 17, 1947; s. Alex and Florence (Talsky) S.; m. Fredda Andrea Wagner, June 17, 1973; children: Meagen, Sara Beth, Jonathan. AB, Brown U., 1969; JD, Villanova U., 1972. Bar: Pa. 1972, U.S. Dist. Ct. (ea. dist) Pa. 1975, U.S. Dist. Ct. (mid. dist.) Pa. 1975, U.S. Ct. Appeals (3d cir.) 1981. Law clk. Phila. U. Common Pleas, 1972-73; dep. atty. gen. Pa. Dept. Justice, Harrisburg, 1973-75; 1st asst. counsel Pa. Pub. Utility Commn., Harrisburg, 1975-77, chief counsel, 1977; assoc. Fox, Rothschild, O'Brien & Frankel, LLP, Phila., 1978-81; ptnr. Fox Rothschild LLP, Phila., 1981—. Children Svcs. Rev. com., United Way Southeast Pa., 1984-86; bd. dirs. ACLU, Harrisburg, 1973-74, Voyage House, Inc., 1994-96. Mem. ABA (pub. utility, labor and employment law sects., employee benefits com. 1984—), Pa. Bar Assn. (labor rels., pub. utility law sects. 1980—, pub. utility law com., governing coun. 1991-93), Phila. Bar Assn. (labor law com. 1980—, chmn. pub. utility law com. 1988-91), Nat. Assn. Coll. and Univ. Attys., Nat. Assn. Regulatory Commrs. (staff subcom. law 1977), Soc. for Human Resource Mgmt., Louis D. Brandeis Law Soc. Democrat. Jewish. Office: Fox Rothschild LLP 2000 Market St Philadelphia PA 19103-3291 Office Phone: 215-299-2088. Business E-Mail: bsatinsky@foxrothschild.com.

**SATIR, BIRGIT H.,** medical educator, researcher; b. Copenhagen, Mar. 22, 1934; Magistra in Biochemistry, U. Copenhagen, 1961. Rsch. assoc. dept. zoology U. Chgo., 1962-66; asst. rsch. physiologist U. Calif. Dept. Physiology-Anatomy, Berkeley, 1967-74, assoc. rsch. physiologist, 1974-76, adj. assoc. prof., 1976-77; sci. dir. Analytical Ultrastructure Ctr., Cancer Rsch. Inst. Albert Einstein Coll. of Medicine, Bronx, NY, 1977-84, prof. dept. anatomy and structural biology, 1977—. Rschr. Phys.- Chem. Inst. Copenhagen, 1956-57, Biol. Inst., Copenhagen, 1958-61; mem. Cellular and Molecular Basis of Disease Rev. Com., Nat. Inst. Gen. Med. Scis., 1977-79; vis. prof. divsn. biology Calif. Inst. Tech., 1984-85. Mem. editl. bd. Jour. Ultrastructural Rsch., 1975-80, Jour. Cell Biology, 1979-81, Modern Cell Biology, 1980-90, Jour. Eukaryotic Microbiology, 1989-95. Rsch. fellow U. Geneva, 1965-66, Spl. fellow USPHS, 1972-73; recipient Outstanding Women Scientist award N.Y. chpt. Assn. Women in Sci., 1990, Rsch. award Am. Diabetes Assn., 1995. Fellow AAAS, Royal Danish Acad. Sci. and Letters; mem. Am. Soc. Cell Biology (coun. 1975-78, minority affairs com. 1987-90, fin. com. 1993—), Am. Assn. Anatomists, Am. Soc. Biochemistry and Molecular Biology, Electron Microscopy Soc. Am. (program vice-chairperson 38th Meeting 1980, program chairperson 39th Meeting 1981), NYSEM (pres. 1979-80), N.Y. Acad. Sci., Biophys. Soc. Office: Albert Einstein Coll of Medicine Jack and Pearl Resnick Campus 1300 Morris Park Ave Bronx NY 10461-1926 E-mail: bsatir@aecom.yu.edu.

**SATLOFF, ROBERT B.,** think-tank executive; BS, Duke U.; MS, Harvard U.; PhD in Oriental Studies, Oxford U. Exec. dir. Washington Inst. for Near East Policy, 1993—2002, 2003—. Author, editor: Troubles on the East Bank: Challenges to the Domestic Stability of Jordan, 1986, Army and Politics in Mubarak's Egypt, 1988, The Politics of Change in the Middle East, 1993, From Abdullah to Hussein: Jordan in Transition, 1994, U.S. Policy toward Islamism, 2000, After Arafat? Succession in Palestinian Politics, 2002, The War on Terror: The Middle East Dimension, 2002; frequent commentator on the Middle East in major Am. newspapers including the Washington Post, N.Y. Times, Wall St. Jour. and L.A. Times; has appeared on various TV and radio programs to offer his analysis of events in the Middle East. Office: The Washington Inst for Near East Policy 1828 L St NW Ste 1050 Washington DC 20036-5128

**SATO, EUNICE NODA,** former mayor, consultant; b. Livingston, Calif., June 8, 1921; d. Bunsaku and Sawa (Maeda) Noda; m. Thomas Takashi Sato, Dec. 9, 1950; children: Charlotte Patricia, Daniel Ryuichi and Douglas Ryuji (twins). AA, Modesto Jr. Coll., 1941; BA, U. No. Colo., 1944; MA, Columbia U., 1948. Pub. sch. tchr. Mastodon Twp. Schs., Alpha, Mich., 1944-47; ednl. missionary Reformed Ch. Am., Yokohama, Japan, 1948-51; coun. mem. City of Long Beach, Calif., 1975-86; mayor, 1980-82. Sec. corp. bd. Los Angeles County Health Systems Agy., 1978-79 Monthly contbr. articles to 2 neighborhood papers, 1975-86. Bd. dirs. Long Beach chpt. ARC, 1975-2000, mem. exec. com., 1978-91, 93-99, pres. and v.p., mem. Calif. state svc. coun., A.R.C., 1995-2001; bd. dirs. Goodwill Industries, 1978-82; trustee St. Mary's Bauer Med. Ctr., 1977—; pres. Industry Edn. Coun., Long Beach, 1984-86, mem. exec. bd., 1984—; bd. dirs. Industry Edn. Coun. of Calif.; treas. So. Calif. Consortium of I.E.C., 1984-86, pres., 1988-89; mem. State Adv. Group on Juvenile Justice and Delinquency Prevention, 1983-91, Calif. Coun. Criminal Justice, 1983-92, legis. com. Girl Scout coun. Calif., 1986-92, chair 1991-92; bd. dirs. Long Beach coun. Girl Scouts U.S., 1986-92, Region III United Way, 1974-88; mem. Asian Pacific adv. com. Calif. Dept. Rehab., 1985-87, recreation commn. City of Long Beach, 1985-86, pub. safety policy com. League Calif. Cities, 1981-86, cmty. econ. and housing devel. com. So. Calif. Assn. Govts., 1976-86, Calif. Task Force to Promote Self-Esteem and Personal and Social Responsibility, 1987-90; Long Beach chpt. pres. NCCJ, 1987-88; pres. Internat. Cmty. Coun., 1986-87, bd. dir. 1986-2001, pres. Japanese Am. Reps., 1987, 88, exec. bd. mem. 1987-2003, 2004—; presdl. appointee Nat. Adv. Coun. Ednl. Rsch. and Improvement, 1991-94; pres. Aux. to Sch. Theology, Claremont, 1990-91, exec. bd. 1989-91, nat. selective svc. sys. local bd. 138, 1990-2001, SCA Edison Co. Equal Opportunity adv. coun., 1990-94; chair selection com. Leadership Long Beach, 1990-91, sec. exec. bd., 1991-92, bd. govs. 2003—; chair adv. bd. AIESEC, 1990-92; chmn. Long Beach Area Rep. Party, 1990-92; asst. sec. cen. com., L.A. 1990-92; sec.-gen. coun. on fin. and administrn. United Meth. Ch., 1992-2000; appointed by Gov. to commn. on tchr. credentialing State Calif., 1994, L.A. coun. svc. coun. A.R.C., 1995-99; chair adminstrv. bd. Leisure World Cmty. Ch., 1996-2002; rep. to South Coast Ecumenical Coun., 1993-2002, chair pastor parish rels. com., 2000; chair Parents Day Festival com. greater L.A. county, 1996-2000, Blue Ribbon Com. for Effective Parenting in Long Beach, 1997-99; mem. adult and elder care adv. com. Long Beach (Calif.) City Coll., 2004—; caregiver Grace First Presbyn. Ch., 2005—. Recipient Outstanding Svc. award Long Beach Coord. Coun., 1969, Mother of Yr. award Silverado United Meth. Ch., 1973, Hon. Svc. award Calif. PTA, 1963, Continuing Svc. award, 1974, hon. life life membership award Nat. PTA, 1974, Outstanding Laywoman of Yr. award Long Beach Area Coun. Chs., 1976, Woman of Yr. award State Women's Coun.-C of C, 1979, Long Beach Internat. Bus. and Profl. Women's Club, Nat. Merit award DAR, 1982, Citizen of Yr. award Los Altos YMCA, 1982, Calif. Cmty. Pool for Handicapped, 1982, Outstanding

Citizen award Torch Club of Long Beach, 1983, W. Odie Wright award Industry Edn. Coun., 1990, Humanitarian award NCCJ, 1992, Vol. of Yr. award ARC, 1995, 1st Life Membership award Long Beach chpt. UN Assn., Kunsho award of Order of the Sacred Treasure, Gold Rays with rosette from Japanese Govt., 1996, Sr. Vol. of Yr. Long Beach C.C., 1999, Al Taucher Rep. of Yr. award, 2001, Excellence in Leadership award Leadership Long Beach, 2004, Am. Hall of Fame honoree Long Beach Century Club, 2006. Mem. Industry Edn. Coun. Long Beach (hon. life), Long Beach C. of C. (Dewey Smith cmty. svc. award), Lions Club (hon. life), Soroptimist Internat. (Woman of Distinction in Econ. and Social Devel. 2001), Alpha Iota. Republican. Presbyterian. Home: Bixby Village 551 Pittsfield Ct Unit 101 Long Beach CA 90803-6355

**SATO, GLENN KENJI,** lawyer; b. Honolulu, Jan. 6, 1952; s. Nihei and Katherine (Miwa) S.; m. Donna Mae Shiroma, Apr. 4, 1980 (dec. Aug. 1985); m. Nan Sun Oh, Mar. 27, 1987 (dec. Nov. 1997); children: Gavan, Allison, Garrett; m. Sandra K. Kumagai, Nov. 21, 1999. BBA, U. Hawaii, 1975; JD, U. Calif., San Francisco 1977. Bar: Hawaii 1978, U.S. Dist. Ct. Hawaii, 1978, U.S. Ct. Claims 1990. Assoc. Fujiyama, Duffy & Fujiyama, Honolulu, 1978-80, 83-87, ptnr., 1987-95; stockholder Law Offices of Glenn K. Sato, Honolulu, 1980-82; pres. ISL Svcs., Inc., Honolulu, 1983; ptnr. Sato & Thomas, Honolulu, 1995-98; pvt. practice Honolulu, 1998—. Vice chmn. Pattern Jury Instrn. Com., State of Hawaii, Honolulu, 1993. Treas. Polit. Action Com., Honolulu, 1993. Mem. Platform Assn., Beta Gamma Sigma. Avocations: golf, hunting, target shooting, surfing. Office: 220 S King St Ste 600 Honolulu HI 96813-4585

**SATO, KAZUYOSHI,** pathologist; b. Shibata, Niigata, Japan, Apr. 3, 1930; came to U.S., 1968; s. Katsueita and Kyo (Sakagawa) S.; m. Ann Marie Farrenkopf, July 5, 1964 (dec. Aug. 1983); children: P.T. Sachiko, P. Miyoko, Michael T., Phillip K. Student, Niigata U., Japan, 1954, MD, 1958. Diplomate Am. Bd. Pathology, Anatomic and Clin. Pathology. Intern USAF Hosp., Tachikawa, Japan, 1958-59, Ellis Hosp., Schenectady, NY, 1959-60, asst. resident in pathology, 1960-61; resident in pathology Free Hosp. for Women, Brookline, Mass., 1961-62, The Children's Hosp. Med. Ctr., Boston, 1962-63, resident in neuropathology, 1963-64; resident fellow in pathology Mayo Grad. Sch. Medicine, Rochester, Minn., 1968-70; dir. labs. Falmouth (Mass.) Hosp., 1972-96; dir. Falmouth Hosp. Service Lab., Sandwich, Mass., 1986-93. Pathologist and rsch. assoc. Atomic Bomb Casualty Commn., Nagasaki, Japan, 1964-68; pathologist, chief of pathology USPHS Hosp., Norfolk Va., 1970-72, Falmouth (Mass.) Hosp., 1972-97. Recipient Fulbright scholarship, 1959. Fellow Coll. Am. Pathologists, Am. Soc. Clin. Pathologists; mem. Assn. Mil. Surgeons U.S. Home: 88 Two Ponds Rd Falmouth MA 02540-2225

**SATO, NORIE,** artist; b. Sendai, Japan, July 19, 1949; came to U.S. 1954; d. Hiroshi and Kyoko (Amemiya) Sato; m. Ralph Moore Berry, July 25, 1980; 1 child, Tomohiro Branik. BFA, U. Mich., 1971; MFA, U. Wash., 1974. Media/visual arts dir. And/Or Arts Center Seattle, 1976-81; instr. Cornish Coll. of the Arts, Seattle, 1978-81, 86-88, Western Wash. U., Bellingham, 1989. Panelist Nat. Endowment for the Arts, Washington, 1977-83. One person shows include Vancouver (B.C.) Art Gallery, 1984, Seattle Art Mus., 1984, Elizabeth Leach Gallery, Portland, Oreg., 1989, 91, 94, Reed Coll., Portland, 1989, Linda Farris Gallery, Seattle, 1990, 1993; group shows include Guggenheim Mus., Bklyn. Mus., Modern Art Mus.; represented in permanent collections at Guggenheim Mus., Seattle Art Mus., Bklyn. Mus., City of Seattle; pub. art projects include Dallas Conv. Ctr. Expansion, Westside Light Rail Project, Portland, Seattle Tacoma Internat. Airport, Seattle Justice Ctr., Salt Lake City Light Rail, Phoenix/Tempe Light Rail, Sound Transit, U. Wash., Cascadia Cmty. Coll., Miami Internat. Airport, City Hall, Federal Way, Wash., Iowa State Labs, Ankeny, U. Wis., Madison, Wallace Chapel Chapman U., Orange, Calif., Iowa State U. Palmer Bldg. Commr. Seattle Arts Commn., 1975-79; trustee Western States Arts Fedn., Santa Fe, N.Mex., 1988-92; commr., v.p. Seattle Planning Commn., 1984-90; trustee Coll. Art Assn., N.Y., 1995—99; bd. dirs. On the Boards, Seattle 2003—; mem. coun. Pub. Art Network, Ams. for the Arts, 2006—. Recipient Gov.'s award, 1990; Wash. State Arts Commn. artist's fellow, 1990, Nat. Endowment for Arts fellow, 1981, Betty Bowen Meml. awardee, Seattle Art Mus., 1983, others. Mem. Ctr. on Contemporary Art, 9-1-1 Media Arts Ctr., Coll. Art Assoc. Office: 619 Western Ave # 14 Seattle WA 98104-1440 Office Phone: 206-467-0734. E-mail: satoservice@satoservice.seanet.com.

**SATOH, YUKO,** music educator; b. Ichinomiya, Aichi, Feb. 8, 1967; s. Naohiro Nakata and Kimiko Satoh. BA, Tokyo Nat. U. of Fine Arts and Music, 1990, MA, 1993, Washington U., St. Louis, 2001. Editor, translator Shogakukan, Tokyo, 1990—91; asst. editor Musicol. Soc. Japan, Tokyo, 1993—94; rsch. assoc. Washington U., St. Louis, 2000—01; asst. dir. JUST Inst., Columbus, Ohio, 2001—. Mem.: Am. Translators Assn. Office: JUST Inst 5295 Olentangy River Rd Columbus OH 43235 E-mail: yukosatoh777@hotmail.com.

**SATRE, DEREK DAVIES,** psychologist, researcher; s. Neal and Jeanne Satre. BA, U. Calif., Berkeley, 1989; MPhil, U. Cambridge, 1990; PhD, U. So. Calif., L.A., 2001. Lic. clin. psychologist Calif., 2001. Rschr. Kaiser Permanente Divsn. Rsch., Oakland, 2001—; asst. adj. prof. psychiatry U. Calif., San Francisco 2004—. Clin. psychologist U. Calif., 2003—. Contbr. scientific papers, chapters to books. Fellow, Nat. Inst. Aging, 1997—2001, Nat. Inst. Drug Abuse, 2001—04, U. Calif., San Francisco, 2001—04; grantee, NIH, 2005. Mem.: APA, Gerontol. Soc. Am. Episcopalian. Avocations: travel, rowing, tennis. Office: U Calif 401 Parnassus Ave Box 0984 San Francisco CA 94143 E-mail: dereks@lppi.ucsf.edu.

**SATRE, PHILIP GLEN,** casino entertainment executive, lawyer; b. Palo Alto, Calif., Apr. 30, 1949; s. Selmer Kenneth and Georgia June (Sterling) S.; m. Jennifer Patricia Arnold, June 30, 1973; children: Malena Anne, Allison Neal, Jessica Lilly, Peter Sterling. BA, Stanford U., 1971; JD, U. Calif.-Davis, 1975; postgrad. sr. exec. program, MIT, 1982. Bar: Nev. 1975, Calif. 1976. Assoc. Vargas & Bartlett, Reno, 1975-79; v.p., gen. counsel, sec. Harrah's, Reno, 1980-83, sr. v.p., 1983-84; pres. Harrah's East, Atlantic City, 1984; pres., CEO Harrah's Hotels and Casinos, Reno, 1984-91, sr. v.p. Gaming Group The Promus Cos., Inc., Memphis, 1988-91, dir., pres., COO, 1991-94, dir., pres. CEO, 1994-95; pres., CEO Harrah's Entertainment, Inc., Memphis, 1995—, chmn., pres., CEO, 1997—; dir. JDN Realty Co., Memphis, 1999—. Dir., treas. Nat. Jud. Coll., Reno. Active The Stanford Athletic Bd., 1996—. Mem. ABA, Nev. Bar Assn., Calif. Bar Assn., Order of Coif, Phi Kappa Phi, Stanford Alumni Assn. (pres. Reno chpt. 1976-77), Young Pres. Orgn., The Bus. Roundtable. Office: PO Box 29526 Las Vegas NV 89126-9526

**SATTEN, WAYNE RICHARD,** psychologist; s. Mortimer and Alyce Moffitt Satten; m. Ana Maria Lopez, 1985; children: Elena Satten-Lopez, David Satten-Lopez. BA magna cum laude, Haverford Coll., 1981; PsyD, Hahnemann U., 1988. Lic. psychologist Ariz. Psychologist So. Ariz. Mental Health Ctr., Tucson, 1988—95, Palo Verde Hosp., Tucson, 1995—98, Palo Verde Behavioral Health Assn., Tucson, 1998—2003; pvt. practice Tucson, 2003—. Rschr. U. Med. Ctr., Tucson, 1995—2000. Bd. dirs. Amphi Dist. Little League, Tucson, 1997—2000. Mem.: APA, Ariz. Psychol. Assn., So. Ariz. Psychol. Assn., Phi Betta Kappa. Avocations: skiing, golf, travel. Office: 5240 E Knight Dr Ste 120 Tucson AZ 85712 Office Phone: 520-795-0309.

**SATTER, RAYMOND NATHAN,** judge; b. Denver, Oct. 19, 1948; s. Charles Herbert and Muriel Vera (Tuller); m. Suzanne Elizabeth Ehlers, May 28, 1977. BA, U. Denver, 1970; JD, Cath. U., 1973. Bar: Colo. 1973, U.S. Dist. Ct. Colo. 1973, U.S. Ct. Appeals (10th cir.) 1973, U.S. Supreme Ct. 1976, U.S. Tax Ct. 1981. Assoc. Wallace, Armatas & Hahn, Denver, 1973-75; ptnr. Tallmadge, Wallace & Hahn, Denver, 1975-77; pvt. practice Denver, 1978-87; Denver County judge, 1987—; presiding judge Denver County Ct., 2001—04. Gen. counsel Satter Dist., Denver, 1977-78; assoc. mcpl. judge City of Englewood, Colo., 1985-86; com. on civil rules Colo. Supreme Ct., 1988-2003. Pres. Young Artists Orch. Denver, 1985-87; sec. Denver Sym-

phony Assn., 1985-86. Mem. Colo. Bar Assn. (ethics com.), Denver Bar Assn. (bd. trustees 1998-2001, Jud. Excellence award 1992, 95). Avocations: sailing, bicycling, classical music, fishing, bridge. Office: Denver County Ct 108 City & County Bldg 1437 Bannock St Denver CO 80202-5337 Office Phone: 303-640-4718. Business E-Mail: rsatter@ci.denver.co.us.

**SATTERTHWAITE, GEORGE, II,** security firm executive; b. San Jose, Costa Rica, Apr. 18, 1935; s. Livingston Lord andAdelaide (Bristol) S.; m. Helen Marie McCann, June 28, 1958 (div. July 1982); children: Patricia Ann, Livingston Lord, Frank Lord; m. Deanna Marie Kelliher, Apr. 30, 1983; 1 child, Kelley Elizabeth. BA in Internat. Rels., U., Pa., 1957; MA in History, Johns Hopkins U., 1965. Commd. 2d lt. U.S. Army, 1957, advanced through grades to col., 1979, retired, 1987; chief indsl. security PRC Inc., McLean, Va., 1987-89; corp. dir. security PRC Inc., McLean, 1989-96; cons., 1996-98; cons., contracts officer SSI Inc., McLean, Va., 1998—2000, photography and security cons., 2000—. Mem. County Bd. Elections, Prince George County, 2003—; mem. admissions coun. U. Pa., 2002—. Mem.: SAR, Mil. Officers Assn. (life), Piscataway Citizens Assn. (bd. dirs. 2003—). Republican. Roman Cath. Avocations: photography, music, volks marching, travel. Home and Office: 513 Holly Rd Fort Washington MD 20744-6606 Personal E-mail: GS2nd@aol.com.

**SATTERTHWAITE, HELEN FOSTER,** retired state legislator; b. Blawnox, Pa., July 8, 1928; d. Samuel J. and Lillian (Schreiber) Foster; m. Cameron B. Satterthwaite, Dec. 23, 1950 (div. July 1979); children: Mark Cameron, Tod Foster, Tracy Lynn, Keith Alan, Craig Evan (dec.). BS in Chemistry, Duquesne U., 1949. Rsch. asst. Gulf R & D, Harmarville, Pa., 1950; rsch. chemist E.I. duPont de Nemours & Co., Wilmington, Del., 1951-53; biol. technician USDA, 1967-68; lab. technician U. Ill. Coll. Agr., 1968-70; rsch. asst. Iowa State U. Coll. Agr., 1971; technician Nat. Sci. Lab., U. Ill. Coll. Vet. Medicine, 1971-74; rep. Ill. Ho. of Reps., Springfield, 1974-92, majority leader, 1991-92, mem. sch. fin. task force, 1990-92, chmn. com. on higher edn., 1983-91, vice chmn. elem. and secondary edn., 1983-91; ret., 1993. Mem. Commn. on Mental Health and Devel. Disabilities, 1975-85, mem. exec. com., 1977-85, vice chmn., 1979-85; mem. Commn. to Visit and Examine State Instns., 1977-85; mem. Task Force on Global Climate Change, 1991-96; treas. LWV, 1995-98, sec., 1998-2001; treas. Bus. and Profl. Women's Club, 1993-94, sec., 1994-95; bd. dirs. East Ctrl. Ill. Health Sys. Agy., 1977-79, Champaign County Mental Health Ctr., 1993-2002, Univ. YWCA, U. Ill., 1987—, Girls Inc., 1992-96; bd. dirs. Champaign County United Way, 1970-74, mem. budget com., 1973-74, mem. joint rev. com. on funding Champaign County mental health programs, 1973; co-chmn. task force on mental retardation Champaign County Mental Health Bd., 1973; mem. Ill. Devel. Disability Advocacy Authority, 1977-85, vice chmn., 1979-80; chmn. Ill. House Dem. Study Group, 1979-81; mem. Edn. Commn. on States, 1985-92, Nat. Conf. State Legis. Commn. on Labor and Edn., 1985-92; bd. govs. U. YMCA, 1995-2003. Recipient Freshman Legislator of Yr. award Ill. Edn. Assn., 1975, commndation Ill. State's Attys. Assn., 1975, Best Legislator award Ind. Voters Ill., 1976, 78, 80, 82, 84, 86, 88, 90, cert. of honor Assn. Student Govts., 1977, Disting. Svc. cert. AMVETS, 1977, Environ. Legislator of Yr. award Ill. Environ. Coun., 1977, 79, 81, 83, Meritorious Svc. award Champaign County Coun. on Alcoholism, 1978, Ill. C.C. Trustees ASsn., 1986, Perfect Voting Record award Ill. Credit Union League, 1979, Ill. Wildlife Fedn., 1979, cert., of spl. recognition Ill. Women's Polit. Caucus, 1979, 80, Pub. Svc. award Izaak Walton League, 1980, Friend of Edn. award Ill. Bd. Edn., 1985, cert. of appreciation Champaign County Urban League, 1987, Resolution of Honor, Ill. Libr. Assn., 1987, 100 Percent award Ill. Coun. Sr. Citizens Orgns., 1989, Dare To Be Great award Ill. Women Adminstrs., 1989; named Person of Yr., Champaign County Mental Health Assn., 1981, Pub. Citizen of Yr., Illino Dist. and Ill. chpt. NASW, 1981, Legislator of Yr., Ill. Assn. Sch. Social Workers, 1989. Mem. Ill. Conf. Women Legislators (co-convenor 1981-83), Nat. Order Women Legislators (bd. dirs. region IV 1982, treas. 1983-84), State Univs. Annuitants Assn. (exec. com. U. Ill. Urbana Champaign chpt. 2003—), Champaign County League Women Voters, Delta Kappa Gamma. Mem. Soc. Of Friends.

**SATTERTHWAITE, JANET F.,** lawyer; b. Washington, Apr. 29, 1960; BA, Yale Univ., 1982; attended, Christ's Coll., Cambridge Univ.; JD, Univ. Va., 1986. Bar: Va. 1988. Ptnr., trademark & domain Name practice Venable LLP, Washington, 2001—. U.S. corr. Marques newsletter, Assn. European Trademark Owners. Contbr. articles to profl. jours. Office: Venable LLP 575 7th St NW Washington DC 20004 Office Fax: 202-344-4974, 202-344-8300. Business E-Mail: jfsatterthwaite@venable.com.

**SATTERTHWAITE, MARK A.,** economics professor; BS, Calif. Inst. Tech., 1967; MS, Univ. Wis., Madison, 1969, PhD, 1973. Asst. prof. Kellogg Sch. Mgmt., Northwestern Univ., 1972—78, prof., 1978—83, Earl Dean Howard prof., 1983—2003, IBM rsch. prof., 1979—81, Herman Smith rsch. prof., 1981—83, prof. mgmt. strategy, 1985—, dir. Gen. Motors Rsch. Ctr. for Strategy in Mgmt., 1987—, chmn., dept. Mgmt. & Strategy, 1990—92, assoc. dean, 1992—96, A.C. Buehler prof. hosp. & health svc. mgmt., 2003—. Vis. prof. Calif. Inst. Tech., 1989. Editor (assoc.): Journal of Economic Theory, 1987—; contbr. articles to profl. jour. Fellow: Econometric Soc., Am. Acad. Arts & Sci.; mem.: Game Theory Soc. Office: Kellogg School of Management Northwestern University Evanston IL 60208 Business E-Mail: m-satterthwaite@northwestern.edu.

**SATTERTHWAITE, SHAWN BRISCOE,** musician, educator; s. Duane V. and Alicia Price Satterthwaite; m. Jill Wendy Watts, June 13, 1987; children: Angela Jill, Heather Alicia, Julia Rose, Mari Annette, Shawn Andrew, Christopher Duane. BA, Weber State U., 1991; MusM, No. Ariz. U., 1993. Secondary tchg. cert. Utah. Pvt. music tchr., Roy, Utah, 1986—2002; coll. grad. asst. No. Ariz. U., Flagstaff, 1992—93; music tchr. N. Summit Sch. Dist., Coalville, Utah, 1993—95; band tchr. North Layton (Utah) Jr. HS, 1995—2003, West Point (Utah) Jr. HS, 2003—, dept. chair, 2005—. Musician (vocal percussionist): (acapella vocal band) T Minus 5; musician: (vocal jazz group) Cold Fusion, Lars Yorgason Singers. Ward music dir. various local LDS wards, Roy, Utah, 1987—2005; stake music dir. Roy Utah West Stake, 2002—05. Theodor Presser Music scholar, Weber State U., 1987-88. Mem.: Jazz Arts Mountainwest, Utah Music Educators Assn., Internat. Assn. Jazz Educators, Music Educators Nat. Conf., Am. Choral Dirs. Assn. (life). Mem. Lds Ch. Home: 5932 S 3260 W Roy UT 84067 Office: West Point Jr HS 2775 W 550 N Clearfield UT 84015 Office Phone: 801-402-8169. Personal E-mail: ssatterthwaite@dsdmail.net.

**SATTLER, BRUCE WEIMER,** lawyer; b. South Gate, Calif., July 30, 1944; s. LeRoy Edward and Mary Beth (Weimer) S.; m. Earle Martha Ross, July 22, 1972. BA, Stanford U., 1966, JD, 1969. Bar: Colo. 1969, U.S. Dist. Ct. Colo. 1969, U.S. Dist. Ct. Mont. 1982, U.S. Dist. Ct. (no. dist.) Tex. 1989, U.S. Ct. Appeals (10th cir.) 1969, U.S. Ct. Appeals (9th cir.) 1984. Assoc. Holland & Hart, Denver, 1969-75, ptnr., 1975-87; supervising trial atty. Equal Employment Opportunity Commn., Denver, 1973; ptnr. Morris, Lower & Sattler, Denver, 1987-90, Faegre & Benson, Denver, 1990—2004. Bd. dirs. ACLU of Colo., Denver, 1975-80, 88-94, 2003-, Colo. Legal Svcs., Legal Aid Soc. of Metro Denver, 1976—, Colo. Lawyers Com., Denver, 1990-94, Children's Legal Clinic, Denver, 1989-91, Colo. Women's Employment and Edn., Denver, 1986-89. Fellow Am. Coll. Trial Lawyers, Coll. Labor and Employment Lawyers; mem. ABA, Denver Bar Assn., Colo. Bar Assn. Office Phone: 303-321-5837. Business E-Mail: bruce@mesattler.com.

**SATTLER, JOAN LINDA,** education educator, dean; b. Adrian, Mich., Oct. 21, 1947; s. Allen Henry and Ruth Alice (Beyer) M.; m. Edward Lee Sattler, June 7, 1969; children: Linda Grace, Allen Edward, Michael Edward. BS, Western Mich. U., 1969; EdM, U. Ill., 1974, EdD, 1977. Cert. elem. and spl. edn. tchr., Nebr., Miss., Ill. Tchr. pub. schs., Springfield, Wis.. 1969-70; spl. edn. tchr. Lindoln (Nebr.) Pub. Schs., 1970-71, Jackson (Mich.) Pub. Schs., 1971-72; assoc. prof., then chmn. spl. edn. Bradley U., Peoria, Ill., 1977-85, prof., 1985—, assoc. dean Coll. Edn. and Health scis., 1985, dean, 1985—. Mem. higher edn. adv. com. Ill. Bd. of Edn., 1979—; mem. sch. bd.

Montessori Sch., Peoria, Ill., 1980-81. Assoc. editor Tchr. Edn. and Spl. Edn. jour., 1983—; contbg. editor Ill. Coun. for Exceptional Children Quar. jour., 1981—. Bd. dirs. Allied Agys., Peoria, 1981-82, Easter Seal Soc., Peoria, 1985. Fellow U.S. Office Edn., 1972-76, U. Ill., 1974-76, Coll. Medicine Peoria Cmty. Assocs. Bd., 1994—. Mem. AAUP, Coun. for Exceptional Children (faculty adviser 1969—), Am. Coun. for Learning Disabilities, Nat. Coun. for Accreditation Tchr. Edn. (team evaluator 1978—, bd. examiners, unit accreditation bd. 1978—, specialty area studies bd., 2000—), Am. Ednl. Rsch. Assn., Am. Assn. Coll. for Tchr. Edn. (bd. 1994—), Phi Delta Kappa (del. 1983—, rsch. com. 1984). Unitarian Universalist. Home: 228 N Whispering Oaks Dr Metamora IL 61548-9123 Office: Bradley U 219 Westlake Hall Peoria IL 61625-0001 Business E-Mail: jls@bradley.edu.

**SATTLER, ROLF,** retired plant morphologist, educator; b. Göppingen, Germany, Mar. 8, 1936; arrived in Can., 1962; s. Otto and Emma Sattler; m. Liv Hamann, May 1, 1963 (div. 1985). PhD, U. Munich, 1961; DSc (hon.), Colombo U. Asst. prof. McGill U., Montreal, Que., Canada, 1964-69, assoc. prof., 1969-77, prof., 1977-97, emeritus prof., 1997—. Author: Organogenesis of Flowers, 1973 (Lawson medal 1974), Biophilosophy, 1986; editor: Theoretical Plant Morphology, 1978, Axioms and Principles of Plant Construction, 1981; contbr. articles to profl. jours. NATO fellow, 1962-64. Fellow Royal Soc. Can., Linnean Soc. London; mem. Can. Bot. Assn., Sci. and Med. Network.

**SATULOFF, BARTH,** accountant, dispute resolution professional, investment strategist, publishing executive, rancher; b. Buffalo, Dec. 13, 1945; s. Bernard and Annette (Lurie) S.; m. Gail Lois Seid Jaffe, Aug. 23, 1992. BBA in Acctg., U. Miami, 1967, MBA, 1969. CPA, Fla., N.Y., Ill., La.; registered securities arbitrator, NYSE, AMEX, NASD; cert. state ct. arbitrator, Fla.; Am. Arbitration Assn., 1992-2005; Spl. Master, Fla. pvt. property and land use cases; cert. comml. arbitrator Am. Arbitration Assn., 1992-2005. Staff acct. Price Waterhouse, Miami, Fla., 1969-71; tax specialist Laventhol & Horwath, Miami, 1973-74; mng. dir. Barth Satuloff, CPA, Miami, 1974-99; chief investment officer, pres., chmn. bd. dirs. Caddis & Co., Reno, 1998—. Pres., bd. dirs. Satuloff Bros., Inc., Buffalo, 1974-94, Miami, 1994-97. Satuloff Bros. Nev., Inc., Reno, 1997—; CEO, dir. Papillon Press, Inc., Miami, 1998-2001, Vero Beach, 2001—. Mem. Ctr. for the Arts, Vero Beach, Fla., Met. Mus. Art, N.Y.C., Pagoda Springs Art Coun.; mem. Fla. state com. Nat. Mus. Women in the Arts, Washington. With Fla. N.G., 1970—76. Mem.: AICPA (mem. small bus. taxation com. of tax divsn. 1993—96, mem. fed. tax forms com. of tax divsn. 1997—99), Fla. Inst. CPAs, Idaho Rivers United, Audubon Soc., Nature Conservancy, Miami Country Day Sch. Alumni Assn. (sec. 1987—93), Ducks Unltd. (sr. v.p. 2001, treas. 1994—2001), Rocky Mountain Elk Found. (life; founder Indian River chpt., Fla. state chmn. Habitat coun.), Trout Unltd. (life), Nat. Wild Turkey Fedn., Safari Club Internat., Antique Automobile Club Am., Cadillac-LaSalle Club, Am. Rivers. Avocations: hunting, fishing, photography, antique automobiles. Home and Office: 23 Seagull Pl Vero Beach FL 32960

**SATZ, JEFFREY S.,** telecommunications industry executive, consultant; b. Jackson Heights, NY, Feb. 10, 1973; s. Robert L. and Linda J. Satz; m. Elizabeth Stacy Panzer, Dec. 27, 1997; children: Zachary C., Madeline R. BS/ME, Rensselaer Poly. Inst., 1995. Engr. Nortel Networks, Richardson, Tex., 1995—98, sr. engr., 1998—2000, mgr., 2000—. Recognition from Am. Registry of Outstanding Profls. Mem.: IEEE, NY Acad. Scis., Mensa. Avocations: home repair, reading, walking. Home: 4456 Big Sky Dr Plano TX 75024

**SATZ, LOUIS K.,** publishing executive; b. Chgo., Ill., Apr. 28, 1927; s. Harry Addison and Faye Satz; m. Janet Maas, Jan. 2, 1952 children: Jay, Jonathan BS in Mktg, U. Ill., 1949. Circulation dir. Pubs. Devel. Corp., Chgo., 1953, Guns mag., Jr. Arts and Activities, 1961; wholesaler sales mgr., then v.p., dir. sales Bantam Books, Inc., N.Y.C., 1962-80, sr. v.p., dir. diversified markets, 1980-84; pub. Passport Books, Lincolnwood, Ill., 1985-88; pres. Louis K. Satz Assocs., Pub. Cons., N.Y.C., 1988-91; ptnr. Scott/Satz Group, Pub. Cons., Walnut Creek, Calif., 1991—. Guest lectr. Sarah Lawrence Coll.Pub. Sch., Pace U.; faculty Hofstra U., Denver Pub. Inst.; cons. World Book Encyclopedia; bd. dirs. NY is Book Country, Brandeis U. Pub. Scholarship Fund, Oscar Dystel Fellowship NYU. Served with AUS, World War II, ETO. Mem. Am. Assn. Pubs. (chmn. small books mktg. div. 1975) Home and Office: Scott Satz Group 1949 Highridge Ct Walnut Creek CA 94597 Office Phone: 925-934-2919. Business E-Mail: louksatz@astound.net.

**SAUBEL, KATHERINE SIVA,** Indian culture consultant, educator; b. Los Coyotes Indian Reservation, Calif., Mar. 7, 1920; d. Juan C. and Melana Sewaill; m. Mariano Saubel, Oct. 2, 1940 (dec.); 1 child, Allen. Grad. high sch., Palm Springs, Calif. Tchr.'s asst. dept. anthropology UCLA, 1959-60; cons. to Dr. Hansjakob Seiler, U. Cologne, Banning, Calif., Germany, 1964-74; on Cahuilla Indian culture throughout U.S., 1960—; pres., editor press Malki Mus., Banning, 1964—. Lectr. U. Cologne, 1971; vis. lectr. U. Calif., Riverside, 1990; lectr. to sch. classes, Indian gatherings, 1958—. Author: Kunvachmal: A Cahuilla Tale, 1969; co-author: Temelpakh: Cahuilla Knowledge and Use of Plants, 1972, Chem'villu' (Lets Speak Cahuilla), 1981. Mem. Native Am. Heritage Commn., Calif.; speaker to various orgns. fighting nuclear and hazardous waste dumps in areas significant to Native Ams.; keynote spkr. Symposium on Am. Indian Religious Freedom, UCLA, 1992. Named County Historian of Yr., Riverside County Hist. Soc., 1986; named to Nat. Women's Hall of Fame, 1993. Home: PO Box 373 Banning CA 92220-0003 Office: Malki Mus Morongo Indian Reservation PO Box 578 Banning CA 92220-0017

**SAUBERT, NICOLE J.,** communications educator, social studies educator; b. Chgo., Nov. 9, 1977; d. Howard Martin and Lynn Carol Saubert. BS in Comm., Ill. State U., Normal, 2000; MAT, Nat. Louis U., Chgo. 2006 Account exec. Grand Harsh Internat., Chgo., 2000—02; substitute tchr. Sch. Dist. 230, Orland Park, 2002—04; tchr. social studies and speech South Wilmington H.S., Gardner, 2004—. Mem. Nat. Sci. Coun., 2003—05; student improvement sponsor Pro Bono, Gardner, Ill., 2006. Home: 14011 Creek Crossing Dr Orland Park IL 60467

**SAUCERMAN, ALVERA ADELINE,** elementary school educator; b. Colorado Springs, Nov. 29, 1932; d. Alva Arthur and Delpha Adeline (Cole) Gieck; m. James Ray Saucerman; 1 child, James Randall. Student, Stephens Bus. Sch., Denver, 1950-51; AA, Scottsbluff Coll., 1961; BEd, NW Mo. State U., 1965, MEd, 1971. Cert. French, reading specialization and learning disabilities tchr. Tchr. Lake Alice (Nebr.) Sch., 1961-62, West Nodaway Sch., Clearmont, Mo., 1965-67; remedial reading tchr. Maryville (Mo.) R II, 1968-74, dir. learning lab., 1975-88, tchr. learning disabilities, 1974-97; ret. Lectr. spl. edn. N.W. Mo. State U., Maryville, 1978—97. Mem. Maryville State Tchrs. Assn. (sec. 1978-79), AAUW (life, pres. 1981-83 Maryville Br.), Mo. State Tchrs. Assn. (life), Delta Kappa Gamma, Kappa Delta Pi (life). Avocations: travel, photography, reading, dance. Home: 1331 NW 107th Ter Gainesville FL 32606-5489

**SAUCIER, GENE DUANE,** retired state legislator, retired import/export company executive; b. Dallas, Sept. 25, 1931; s. Albert L. and Myrtle Irene (West) S.; m. Marilyn Emmy Cox, Dec. 27, 1952 (div. Sept. 1980); children: Alan, Steve, Renee; m. Giulia Riga LaCagnina, Nov. 28, 1981. BS in Agronomy Soils, Miss. State U., 1953; MS in Counseling, U. So. Miss., 1970, EdD in Adult Edn., 1978. Builder, developer Saucier Co., Hattiesburg, Miss., 1957-70; dir. admissions U. So. Miss., Hattiesburg, 1970-74; dean spl. acad. svcs., 1974-84, asst. v.p. bus. and fin., 1984-93; mem. Miss. Ho. of Reps. Jackson, 1993-99; ret., 1999. Mem. conservation and devel. com. S.E. Mo., 2005. Mem. Fed. Land Coun., 1997—2003; scoutmaster Boy Scouts Am., 1960—70, chmn. camping and activities Pine Burr area, 1970; bd. dirs., founder Hub Coop., 1981. Lt. bd. dirs. Wild Turkey Fedn., Pine Burr chpt., 2000. 1st lt. pilot USAF, 1953—56. Named Forrest County Tree Farmer of Yr., 1996, Miss. Tree Farmer Yr., 1996; recipient Forestry award Miss. Wildlife Fedn., 1997, Legislator of Yr. Coastal Conservation Assn., 1997.

**SAUCIER, GUYLAINE,** corporate financial executive; b. Noranda, Que., Can., June 10, 1946; d. Gérard and Yvette (Thiffault) S. Chartered acct., École Hautes Etudes Commls., Montreal, Can., 1971. Formerly chair Joint Com. on Corp. Governance. Bd. dirs. Petro-Can., Axa Assurances Inc., Bank Montreal, Altran Techs., CHC Helicopter Corp., Areva Group. Fellow Inst. Chartered Accts., Inst. Corp. Dirs.; mem. Order Can. Avocation: tennis. Office Phone: 514-397-5494. Business E-Mail: gsaucier@gsaucier.com.

**SAUDEK, CHRISTOPHER D.,** medical educator; b. Bronxville, N.Y., Oct. 8, 1941; s. Robert and Elizabeth (Koch) S.; m. Susan Saudek; children: Mark S., Deborah M., Christina A., Anthony C. AB, Harvard U., 1963; MD, Cornell U., 1967. Resident in medicine Presbyn. St. Luke's Hosp., Chgo., 1967-69, Boston City Hosp., 1969-70; fellow in metabolism Thorndike Lab, Harvard U., Cambridge, Mass., 1970-72; asst prof. Cornell U., Ithaca, N.Y., 1973-80; assoc. prof. Johns Hopkins U., Balt., 1981-91, prof., 1991—; former pres. American Diabetes Assoc. Author Johns Hopkins Guide to Diabetes, 1997; co-author (with Sandra Woodruff) The Complete Diabetes Prevention Plan, 2004. Named Outstanding Clinician in Diabetes, Am. Diabetes Assn., 1991. Office: Johns Hopkins U Med Sch Osler 576 600 N Wolfe St Baltimore MD 21287-0005

**SAUER, DAVID ANDREW,** librarian, writer; b. Urbana, Ill., Feb. 25, 1948; s. Elmer Louis and Frances (Hill) S. BA, Northwestern U., 1970; MS, Simmons Coll., 1975. Reference libr. Boston U., 1976-78, bibliographer, 1978-84, sci. bibliographer, 1984-88, founder and head libr. Stone Sci. Libr., 1988-94; v.p. info. svcs. CyberHelp, Inc., 1995-98; sr. tech. editor Qualcomm, Inc., 1997-2000, 2003—04, sr. tech. writer, 2004—06; staff tech. writer Quaalcomm, Inc., 2006—; tech. pubs. supr. QCP Inc., 2000—01, staff tech. writer/libr., 2001—02; librarian San Diego Maritime Mus., 2002—03. Co-author of 12 books including: Access for Windows 95: The Visual Learning Guide, 1995, Windows NT 4.0 Visual Desk Reference, 1997, Discover Netscape Communicator, 1997. Mem. S.W. Corridor Project, Boston, 1977-87, Forest Hills Neighborhood Improvement Assn., Boston, 1977-90, Forest Hills/Woodbourne Neighborhood Group, 1991-94. Mem. ALA, IEEE, Spl. Librs. Assoc., Soc. Tech. Comm. Democrat. Home: 2340 29th St San Diego CA 92104 Personal E-mail: dasauer@cox.net.

**SAUER, ELISSA SWISHER,** nursing educator; b. Williamsport, Pa., Jan. 9, 1935; d. Oliver S. and Emily Louisa (Gehron) Swisher; m. Raymond James Sauer, Nov. 27, 1964. Diploma, Reading (Pa.) Hosp. Sch. Nursing, 1957; BS, Albright Coll., Reading, 1958; MSN, U. Pa., 1964. Instr. Reading Hosp. Sch. Nursing, 1957—60, 1964—66, 1969—70, Abington Meml. Hosp. Sch. Nursing, 1960—63; nurse Cmty. Health and Civic Assn., Ardmore, Pa., 1966-67; pub. health nurse, 1968-73; clin. faculty Schuylkill County AVTS, 1973-74; pvt. duty nurse Reading Area CC, 1975-80, dir. nursing programs, asst. dean health svcs., 1989-2000, asst. dean emerita, 2001—, adj. instr. nursing, 2003—; oncology nurse adminstr.-educator Comprehensive Cmty. Cancer Ctr., Allentown, Pa., 1981-85; exec. dir. Holy Family Home Health Care, Orwigsburg, Pa., 1985-89. Cons. nursing edn. and continuing edn.; evaluator for nat. nurse aide cert. assessment program, 2000—; adj. instr. nursing Reading Area C.C., 2003—. Author: Procedure Manual to accompany Fundamentals of Nursing: Human Health and Function, 3d edit., 2003. Mem.: Sigma Theta Tau. Home: 1114 Pepper Ridge Dr Reading PA 19606-3803 E-mail: esauer@ptd.net.

**SAUER, HARRY JOHN, JR.,** mechanical engineer, educator, academic administrator; b. St. Joseph, Mo., Jan. 27, 1935; s. Harry John and Marie Margaret (Witt) S.; m. Patricia Ann Zbierski, June 9, 1956; children: Harry John, Elizabeth Ann, Carl Andrew, Robert Mark, Katherine Anne, Deborah Elaine, Victoria Lynn, Valerie Joan, Joseph Gerard. BS, U. Mo., Rolla, 1956, MS, 1958; PhD, Kans. State U., 1963. Instr. mech. engring. Kans. State U., Manhattan, 1960-62; sr. engr., cons. Midwest Rsch. Inst., Kansas City, Mo., 1963-70; mem. faculty dept. mech. and aerospace engring. U. Mo., Rolla, 1957—, prof., 1966—, assoc. chmn., 1980-84, dean grad. study, 1984-92. Cons. in field; mem. Gov.'s Commn. on Energy Conservation, 1977; mem. Mo. Solar Energy Resource Panel, 1979-83; mem. Accreditation Bd. for Engring. and Tech. Co-author: Environmental Control Principles, 1975, 4th edit., 1985, Thermodynamics, 1981, Heat Pump Systems, 1983, Engineering Thermodynamics, 1985, Principles of Heating, Ventilating and Air Conditioning, 1991, 5th edit., 2006; contbr. articles to profl. jours. Pres. St. Patrick's Sch. Bd., 1970-72, St. Patrick's Parish Council, 1975-76. Recipient Ralph R. Teetor award Soc. Automotive Engrs., 1968; Hermann F. Spoehrer Meml. award St. Louis chpt. ASHRAE, 1979; also E. K. Campbell award of merit, 1983; Louise and Bill Holladay disting. fellow, 1999. Mem. ASME, ASHRAE (disting. svc. award 1981, exceptional svc. award 2001), NSPE, Soc. Automotive Engrs., Am. Soc. Engring. Edn., Mo. Soc. Profl. Engrs., Mo. Acad. Sci. (Most Disting. Scientist award 2003), Sigma Xi. Roman Catholic. Home: 10355 College Hills Dr Rolla MO 65401-7726 Office: Dept of Mech Engring U Mo Rolla MO 65401 Office Phone: 573-341-4143. Business E-Mail: sauer@umr.edu.

**SAUER, JAMES LESLIE,** librarian, educator; b. Buffalo, Aug. 7, 1953; s. Edwin C. and Margaret M. (Denne) S.; m. Paula J. Westerling, Aug. 20, 1977; children: Jacob, Adam, Joseph, Ariel, Abigail, Isaac, Mary Denise, Martha. BA, SUNY, Buffalo, 1975, MLS, 1977; MA, Villanova U. 1985. Libr. Buffalo and Erie County Pub. Librs., 1977-78, Masten Park Rehab. Ctr., 1979; dir. libr. Eastern U., St. Davids, Pa., 1980—. Pres. Tri-State Coll. Libr. Coop., 1999—2003. Coun. Biblical Manhood and Womanhood, 1996—. Mem. ALA, Pa. Libr. Assn., Assn. Christian Librs., Evang. Theol. Soc., Timothy Bitterman Soc. Republican. Presbyterian. Avocations: painting, parenting, book collecting. Home: 1207 Stirling St Coatesville PA 19320-3526 Office Phone: 610-341-5957. E-mail: jsauer@eastern.edu.

**SAUER, JEFF,** university hockey coach; b. St. Paul, Minn. m. Jamie Sauer Adler; children: Chip, Beth. BA in Sociology, Colo. Coll., 1965. Asst. hockey, baseball coach Colo. Coll., Colo. Springs, 1966-68, head coach hockey, 1971-82; asst.coach hockey U. Wis., Madison, 1968-71, head coach hockey, 1980—. Mem. U.S. Olympic Hockey Com., 1984; coach Olympic Festival, 1987, USA Select Team, Pravda Cup, Leningrad, Russia, 1989, Team USA, Goodwill Games, 1990, U.S. Nat. Team World Championships, 1995, U.S. Select Team, Tampere Cup, Finland, 1997, coach, organizer youth hockey camps in summer; asst. coach USA World Jr. Team, 2003—; head coach USA Team TUI Cup, Manheim, Germany. Counselor Stan Mikita's Hockey Camp for Hearing Impaired, Chgo. Named We. Coll. Hockey Assn. Coach of Yr. 1972-73, 74-75 (Colo. Coll.); NCAA championship (Wis.) 1983, 90, WCHA championship 1987-88, 97-98, WCHA Playoff Championship, 1982-83, 87-88, 94-95. Office: Western Collegiate Hockey Assn 559 D'onofrio Dr Ste 103 Madison WI 53719 Personal E-mail: coachjsauer@juno.com.

**SAUER, MARY JULIA,** special education educator; b. Pitts., Oct. 10, 1949; d. Edward Henry and Julia Ann (Kobkla) Sauer; 1 child, Jason Michael Sauer; m. John Harold Moore, Oct. 27, 1990 (div.); 1 adopted child, Jocelyn Quan. BS in Art Edn., Edinboro State Coll., 1971; MS in Spl. Edn., Clarion State Coll., 1980; postgrad, U. Pitts., 1988—. Cert. art tchr., spl. edn. tchr. for mentally retarded. Tchr. Polk (Pa.) State Sch. & Hosp., 1971-72; vol. VISTA, Bath, NY, 1972-73; tchr. Polk Ctr., 1973-80, program specialist, 1980-92; residential svc. supr., qualified mental retardation profl. Polk (Pa.) Ctr., 1992—. Lectr., speaker, video on TV on history of Polk Ctr., 1987. Patentee beer bottle shaped cake pan; cakes displayed in TV videos and in various mags.; creator history video Polk Ctr., Some Leaky Boot Statues, Polk Center-100 Years; creator video A Century of Care-The History of the

Evolution of Institional Care of the Devlopment Disabled. Past vol. Big Bros./Big Sisters. Democrat. Roman Catholic. Avocations: cake decorating, reading. Home: PO Box 97 Franklin PA 16323

**SAUER, PAUL FREDERICK,** plastic surgeon; b. Kitchener, Ont., Canada, Feb. 12, 1954; s. Walter Herman and Hilda Sauer; m. Carol L. Scannell, July 28, 1984; children: Paul Jr., John Philip. BA, Emory U., 1976; MD, Tufts U., 1980. Diplomate Am. Bd. Plastic Surgery with qualification surgery of the hand. Assoc. U. Ala., Birmingham, 1985—88; assoc. prof. Med. Ctr. Va., Richmond, 1988—89; pvt. practice plastic surgery Birmingham, 1989—. Fellow: ACS; mem. AMA. Avocation: gardening. Office: 840 Montclair Rd # 707 Birmingham AL 35213

**SAUERBREY, ELLEN ELAINE RICHMOND,** federal agency administrator, former ambassador; b. Balt., Sept. 9, 1937; d. Edgar Arthur and Ethel Frederika (Landgraf) Richmond; m. Wilmer John Emil Sauerbrey, June 27, 1959. AB summa cum laude in Biology and English, Western Md. Coll., 1959. Biology instr., chmn. sci. dept. Baltimore County Sch. System, 1959-64; dist. mgr. Baltimore County U.S. Census, 1970; mem. Md. Ho. of Dels., Annapolis, 1978-94, minority leader, 1986-94; radio talk show host Sta. WBAL, Balt., 1996; US amb. to Commn. on the Status of Women UN, 2002—05; asst. sec. Bur. Population, Refugees & Migration US Dept. State, Washington, 2006—. Rep. nominee for Gov., 1994, 98; U.S. del. commn. human rights UN, 2001, 03; head U.S. del. Baltic states conf., 03; U.S. del econ. commn. Latin Am. and Caribbean, 04; mem. adv. com. women in svcs. US Dept. Def., 2004—06. Nat. chmn. Am. Legis. Exec. Coun., 1990—91; trustee Md. Coun. Econ. Edn., Franklin Sq. Hosp.; founder United Citizen's for Md.'s Future; bd. advisors Yorktown University; Rep. Nat. Com. Women Md., 1996—2003; Rules com., 1996; del. Rep. Nat. Convs., 1968, 1976, 1984, 1988, 1992, 1996, 2000, platform com., chmn. subcom. on economy, 1977; nat. adv. bd. Nat. Conservative Campaign Fund; mem. credentials com. Rep. Nat. Convs., 1984; vice chmn. Rep. State Ctrl. Com. of Balt. County, 1966—71; state chmn. Md. chpt. George W. Bush for Pres., 1999—2000. Recipient Pvt. Property award Greater Balt. Bd. Realtors, 1984; named Legislator of Yr., Md. Assn. Builders and Contractors, 1982, Am. Legis. Exec. Coun., 1986, Western Md. Coll. Alum of Yr., 1988, Outstanding Legis. Leader, Am. Legis. Exec. Coun., 1992, Rep. Woman of Yr., Md. Rep. Party, 1995, Nat. Fedn. Ind. Bus., Guardian of Small Bus. award, 1989, Lifetime Svc. award Baltimore County Rep. Party, 2003, Md. State of Mind award, 2004; named one of top 100 Md. Women, The Daily Record, 1998. Mem. DAR, Nat. Fedn. Rep. Women (Margaret Chase Smith award 1995, Md. State of Mind award 2004), Md. Fedn. Rep. Women, Am. Legis. exch. Coun. (chmn. emeritus), Md. Farm Bur., Md. Conservative Union, Beta Beta, Beta, Phi Beta Kappa. Presbyterian. Avocations: gardening, travel. Office: US Dept State Harry S Truman Bldg 2201 C St NW Rm 5824 Washington DC 20520 Personal E-mail: Ellen99@erols.com.

**SAUERBRUNN, MARK AARON,** music educator; b. Metropolis, Ill., Apr. 30, 1976; s. Charles Woodrow Sauerbrunn and Angela Darlene Woodney. MusB in Edn., Murray State U., Ky., 2001. Lic. tchr. Ky., 2002. Dir. band Logan County H.S., Russellville, Ky., 2002—. Asst. chmn. bd. prodrs. Campus Lights Orgn., Murray, 1999—2000. Mem.: Logan County Educators Assn., Third Dist. and Dir.'s Assn., Music Educators Nat. Conf., Ky. Educator's Assn., Ky. Music Educators' Assn., Phi Mu Alpha (pres. 2000—01, sec. 1999—2000). Home: 109 Forrest Park Drive Russellville KY 42276 Office: Logan County High School 2200 Bowling Green Road Russellville KY 42276 Office Phone: 270-726-8454. Personal E-mail: msauerbrunn@logan.k12.ky.us.

**SAUERHAFT, STAN,** retired public relations executive, retired consultant; b. NYC; s. Al and Rae S.; m. Rosalie Cynthia Tolkin; children: Richard Craig, Douglas Clark, Robert James. BA, U. Mich., 1948, MA, 1949. Editor, scriptwriter Paramount News, 1950-51; scriptwriter Hearst Metrotone News, N.Y.C., 1951-52; editor Food Bus. Mag., N.Y.C., 1952-53; acct. supr. Selvage, Lee & Chase, N.Y.C., 1953-55; v.p., mem. creative plans bd. Comm. Counselors, Inc. McCann-Erickson, N.Y.C., 1955-59; pres. Chase and Sauerhaft Assocs., N.Y.C., 1959-65; exec. v.p., dir., mem. mgmt. com. Hill & Knowlton, Inc., N.Y.C., 1965-86; vice chmn. bd., dir. Burson-Marsteller U.S., 1987-88; vice chmn., dir. Burson-Marsteller Internat., 1988—2003; ret., 2003. Instr., lectr. Columbia U. Grad. Sch., 1962-65, Wharton Grad. Sch., 1968, U. Mich. Bus. Sch., 1969, NYU Grad. Bus. Sch., 1984-87; initiated pub. rels. course NYU Grad. Bus. Sch. Author: The Merger Game, 1971, (novels) End Game, 2004, Dead Cat Bounce, 2005; co-author: Image Wars, 1989; contbr. numerous bus. articles and chpts. to anthologies. Chmn. West Point Civilian Pub. Affairs Adv. Com., 1986-2003; mem. exec. com. of bd. Inst. for Pub. Rels. Rsch. and Edn., 1984-87; mem. bd. visitors LS&A Coll. of U. Mich., 1990-95. Staff sgt. AUS, 1945-46. Mem. Pub. Rels. Soc. Am. (Coll. of Fellows); nat. accreditation bd. 1981-83), Pub. Rels. Soc. N.Y. (pres. 1983-85), Soc. Profl. Journalists, Authors Guild Inc., Pub. Affairs Coun. (bd. dirs.), Am. Platform Tennis Assn. (v.p.), U. Mich. Alumni Club, Union League Club N.Y. (chmn. pub. affairs com. 1980-84), Burning Tree Country Club (Greenwich, Conn.), Windmill Club (Armonk, N.Y.), Seabrook Island Club (S.C.), Sigma Delta Chi. Republican. Avocations: golf, platform tennis, bridge, writing. Personal E-mail: rsoauerh@aol.com. *A father's advice to his sons: If you can't outthink them, outwork them. But better yet, try to do both. Also, the best luck seems to befall the hardest workers.*

**SAUERS, WILLIAM DALE,** lawyer, playwright; b. Santa Cruz, Calif., June 18, 1926; s. Myrl Melvin and Helen (Fightmaster) S.; m. Barbara Gean Cole, May 9, 1945. JD, Stanford U., 1952. Bar: Calif. 1953, U.S. Dist. Ct. (no. dist.) Calif. 1953, U.S. Ct. Appeals (9th cir.) 1953, U.S. Supreme Ct. 1964. Asst. sec. State Bar of Calif., San Francisco, 1952-55; dep. dist. atty. County of Santa Clara, San Jose, Calif., 1955-58; ptnr. Finch, Sauers et al., Palo Alto, Calif., 1958-88; pvt. practice law Palo Alto and San Jose, Calif., 1988—. Playwright: A Rainbow on Mt. Olympus and San Jose, 1993, Did Not I Dance with You?, 1994, A Fork in the Road, 1995, What'll We Do With Mama, 1996, Reluctant Strangers, 1997, Lynch Mob Hunt, 1998. Sec. Human Coaliton of Palo Alto, 1969-72; chmn. ARC chpt. Palo Alto, 1973-76, Family Svc. Assn., 1973-76, Sr. Corp. Affiliates, Palo Alto, 1981-85, Oreg. Stage Works, Ashland, 2002-; chmn. bd. trustees Menlo Coll., Atherton, Calif., 1984-88; dir. Oreg. Shakespeare Festival, Ashland, 1989-95; pres. San Jose Repertory Theatre, 1989-91; chmn. San Francisco Shakespeare Festival, 1994-98. Mem. ABA, Calif. State Bar Assn., Phi Delta Phi. Republican. Episcopalian. Avocations: skiing, tennis, golf, fly fishing, back packing. Office: Mount Stoelker Pc 333 W San Carlos St Ste 1700 San Jose CA 95110-2740 E-mail: wsauers@mount.com.

**SAUFLEY, LEIGH INGALLS,** state supreme court chief justice; b. Portland, Maine, June 21, 1954; m. William Saufley; 2 children. BA, U. Maine, Orono, 1976; JD, U. Maine Sch. of Law, 1980. Pvt. practice, Ellsworth; asst. counsel U.S. VA; asst., then dep. atty. gen. Maine, 1981-90; judge Maine Dist. Ct., 1990—93; justice Maine Superior Ct., 1993—97; assoc. justice Maine Supreme Judicial Ct., 1997—2001, chief justice, 2001—. Mem.: ABA. Maine's first female chief justice. Office: Cumberland County Courthouse PO Box 368 142 Federal St Portland ME 04112-0368 E-mail: amanda.j.martin@maine.gov.

**SAUL, ANDREW M.,** investment company executive; b. NYC, 1946; m. Denise Saul; 2 children. BS, Wharton Sch. Fin., Univ. Pa., 1968. Exec. v.p. Brooks Fashion Stores, 1968—80, pres., 1980—85, BR Investors, 1985—86; gen. ptnr. Saul Partners, 1986—; dir. Caché Inc., 1986—, chmn., 1993—2000. Chmn. Fed. Retirement Thrift Investment Bd.; trustee Federation of Jewish Philanthropies, United Jewish Appeal; commr. Met. Transp. Authority, NY, 1996—; mem. exec. com. Mt. Sinai Med. Ctr., chmn. audit com.; trustee Sarah Neuman Nursing Home, Wharton Sch., Univ. Pa., Manhattan Inst.; trustee & mem. Chmn. Council Met. Mus. Art, N.Y.C.

Named one of Top 200 Collectors, ARTnews Mag., 2004, 2005, 2006. Avocation: Collector of Chinese Bronzes, Modern & Contemporary Art, especially Postwar American. Office: Caché Inc 1440 Broadway New York NY 10018*

**SAUL, B. FRANCIS, II,** bank executive, director; b. Washington, Apr. 15, 1932; s. Andrew Maguire and Ruth Clark (Sheehan) S.; m. Elizabeth Patricia English, Apr. 30, 1960; children: Sharon Elizabeth, B. Francis III, Elizabeth Willoughby, Andrew Maguire II, Patricia English Grad., Georgetown Prep. Sch., 1950; BS, Villanova U., 1954, DCS (hon.), 1989; LLB, U. Va., 1957; LLD (hon.), Nat. U. Ireland, 1998. Bar: D.C. 1959. Chmn., pres. B.F. Saul Co., Chevy Chase, Md., 1957—; chmn., trustee B.F. Saul Real Estate Investment Trust Co., Chevy Chase, 1964—; with Chevy Chase Bank, F.S.B., 1969—, chmn., CEO, founder; chmn. Fin. Gen. Bankshares, Inc., 1978-82; chmn., CEO, trustee Saul Ctrs., Inc., 1993—. Chmn. bd. dirs. 1st Am. Bankshares, Inc., Washington, 1978—85; dir. Colonial Williamsburg Hotel Properties, Inc., 1983—96. Honors com. John F. Kennedy Ctr. Performing Arts, 1995—; trustees coun. Nat. Gallery of Arts, 1995—; bd. visitors and govs. Washington Coll., 1995—; hon. trustee Brookings Inst., 1993—; dir. Nat. Sporting Libr., 1998—; trustee Fed. City Coun., Nat. Geog. Soc., 1985—, Suburban Hosp., 1972—76, Johns Hopkins Med. Bd., 2000—01, Corcoran Gallery ARt, Washington, 1972—90; bd. dirs. Wadsworth Preservation Trust, 1983—91; vis. com. Sch. Arch. U. Va., Greenway, 1985—90, Portsmouth (R.I.) Abbey Sch., 1979—84, United World Coll. of Am. West, Montezuma, N.Mex., 1982—85, D.C. Fund for Creative Space, 1980—82, D.C. chpt. ARC, 1964—86, Cork U. Found., 1997—; mem. Ea. Shore Land Conservancy, 2002—; James Madison Coun., 1997—; trust fund bd. Libr. of Congress, 2003; archdiocese fin. coun. for Archbishop of Washington, 1990—. Mem. Mortgage Bankers Assn. Met. Washington (pres. 1968), Nat. Assn. Real Estate Investment Truste (pres. 1973-74), Internat. Coll. Auditors Prefecture Econ. Affairs Holy See, Alfalfa Club, Alibi Club, Met. Club, Knights of Malta, Chevy Chase Club, Burning Tree Club, Friendly Sons of St. Patrick (pres. 1992), Wianno Club, The Brook Club, Bohemian Club, Md. Club, White's Club (London) Roman Catholic. Home: 1 Quincy St Chevy Chase MD 20815-4226 Office: BF Saul Co 7501 Wisconsin Ave Bethesda MD 20814

**SAUL, CONNIE CLINE,** secondary school educator; b. Portsmouth, Va., Aug. 26, 1954; d. Barry Armstrong and Alice Grayson (Henderson) Cline; m. Robin Alan Saul, Apr. 28, 1979; 1 child, Bryan Geoffrey. BS in Edn., Old Dominion U., 1976, MS in Edn., 1982; EdS, Coll. William and Mary, 1990, postgrad., 1991. Tchr. Chesapeake Pub. Schs., Va., 1976—85, instrnl. specialist, 1985—93; adj. prof. We. Md. Coll., 1995—2002; coord. profl. devel. specialist Villa Julie Coll., 2002—. Presenter, cons. workshops in field; mem. Supt.'s Planning Coun., Chesapeake; chair Region II Profl. Devel. Coun.; v.p., treas. Balt. Area Coun. Student Tchg., 2000-2002. Mem., v.p. Polit. Action Com., Chesapeake Edn. Assn., 1983-85; mem. Jr. Woman's Club; rec. sec. Greensboro Symphony Guild; chair bd. dirs. YMCA, Carroll County, 1998-2000; bd. dirs. Ctrl. Md. YMCA, ARC Recipient Disting. Svc. award Norfolk Highlands PTA, Chesapeake, 1983, Leadership Effectiveness award Va. Commonwealth Leadership, 1988; Hampton Rhoads Inst. for Advanced Study fellow, 1989. Mem. ASCD, Salem Woods Civic Assn., Bishopsgate Civic League Assn., Jr. Women's Club Westminster, Kappa Delta Pi, Phi Delta Kappa, Alpha Delta Kappa (historian 1986-88, rec. sec. 1988-90, v.p. 1990—), Sigma Sigma Sigma. Republican. Avocations: sports, music, crafts. Home: 8 Sunfish Pt Greensboro NC 27455

**SAUL, IRVING ISAAC,** lawyer; b. July 9, 1929; s. Israel Jacob and Jennie (Green) S.; m. Lita Brown, Dec. 29, 1950; children: Joanne Ilene, Sandra Lynn. BA, Washington and Jefferson Coll., 1949; postgrad., Georgetown U., 1949, Ohio State U., 1951; LLB, U. Pitts., 1952. Bar: Ohio 1952, U.S. Dist. Ct. (so. dist.) Ohio 1954, U.S. Supreme Ct. 1961, U.S. Ct. Appeals (6th cir.) 1966, U.S. Dist. Ct. (no. dist.) Ohio 1967, U.S. Dist. Ct. (ea. dist.) Ohio 1973, U.S. Ct. Appeals (7th cir.) 1978, U.S. Ct. Appeals (4th cir.) 1978, U.S. Ct. Appeals (fed. cir.) 1991. Pvt. practice, Dayton, Ohio, 1952—. Cons. in antitrust litigation; bd. advs. Fed. Civil Practice Abstracts, 1986-88, Ohio Dist. Ct. Rev., 1988-2002; adj. prof. complex litigation Sch. of Law U. Dayton, 1996-98; lectr. in field. Contbr. articles to profl. jours. James Gillespie Blaine scholar, 1948. Mem. Ohio Bar Assn. (chmn. fed. cts. and practice com. 1977-79, chmn. pvt. enforcement com. 1979-92, bd. govs. antitrust sect. 1982-94), Dayton Bar Assn. (chmn. fed. ct. practice com. 1976-77, 78-80, chmn. com. on judiciary 1987-88), Am. Judicature Soc., Masons (Shriner), Phi Beta Kappa. Jewish. Office: 113 Bethpolamy Ct Dayton OH 45415-2512 Office Phone: 937-278-4858.

**SAUL, JOHN WOODRUFF, III,** writer; b. Pasadena, Calif., Feb. 25, 1942; s. John Woodruff and Adeline Elizabeth (Lee) S. Student, Antioch Coll., 1959-60, Cerritos Coll., 1960-61, Mont. State U., Missoula, 1961-62, San Francisco State Coll., 1963-65. In various positions, primarily in L.A. and San Francisco, 1965-76. Author: Suffer The Children, 1977, Punish the Sinners, 1978, Cry for the Strangers, 1979, Comes the Blind Fury, 1980, When the Wind Blows, 1981, The God Project, 1982, Nathaniel, 1984, Brainchild, 1985, Hellfire, 1986, The Unwanted, 1987, The Unloved, 1988, Creature, 1989, Second Child, 1990, Sleep Walk, 1990, Darkness, 1991, Shadows, 1992, Guardian, 1993, The Homing, 1994, Black Lightning, 1995, The Blackstone Chronicles, 1997, The Presence, 1997, The Right Hand of Evil, 1999, Nightshade, 2000, The Manhattan Hunt Club, 2001, Midnight Voices, 2002, Black Creek Crossing, 2004, Perfect Nightmare, 2005; also other novels under pseudonyms; creator computer game "John Saul's Blackstone Chronicles," 1998. Bd. dirs. Seattle Theatre Arts, 1978-80; bd. govs. Tellurian Communities, inc., Madison, Wis.; v.p. Chester Woodruff Found., N.Y.C. Mem. Authors Guild. Democrat. Swedenborgian. Office: care Jane Rotrosen 318 E 51st St New York NY 10022-7803 *For a writer, the education of experience is without doubt the best education.*

**SAUL, MARK E.,** secondary school educator, consultant; b. NYC, June 17, 1948; s. Sidney and Shura Saul; m. Carol Portnoy, June 26, 1968; children: Susanna, Michael, Peter. BA, Columbia U., 1969; MS, Courant Inst. Math. Scis., NYU, 1975; PhD, NYU, 1987. Tchr. math. and computer sci. Bronx High Sch. Sci., NY, 1969—85; tchg. fellow Adm. Hyman N. Rickover Found., 1985; tchr. Bronxville Schs., NY, 1985—2003; project dir. NSF, 2003—05; dir. for curriculum rsch. and innovation Gateway Project, CUNY Rsch. Found., 2003—05. Dir. Rsch. Sci. Inst. Ctr. Excellence in Edn., McLean, Va., 1987, San Diego, 90, Cambridge, Mass., 1992—99, Shanghai, 2006; cons. computer graphics 1984 Olympics ABC-TV, N.Y.C., 1983—84; pres. N.Y.C. Interscholastic Math. League, N.Y.C., 1979—89, Am. Regions Math. League, 1989—2000; dir. ARML-Soviet Student Exch., 1991—96; cons. Ednl. Testing Svc., Princeton, NJ, 1980—82; panelist/cons. LaGuardia HS Performing Art, N.Y.C., 1977—86; tchr. trainer N.Y.C. Bd. Edn., 1981; tchr.-coord. computer sci. Hollingworth Ctr. for Gifted, Tchrs. Coll., Columbia U., 1984; instr. Lehman Coll., 1984—92, Johns Hopkins U. Ctr. Talented Youth, 1986, Sophie Davis Biomed. Ctr. CCNY, 1986—94, Sarah Lawrence Coll., 1987—94; mem. U.S. del. to Internat. Congress Math. Educators, Budapest, 1988, Quebec, 92, Seville, 96, Tokyo, 2000, Copenhagen, 04; cons. John Templeton Found., 2005—, Math. Scis. Rsch. Inst., Berkeley, Calif., 2005—, Ednl. Devel. Ctr., Newton, Mass., 2005—. Co-author: Science/Mathematics Research Programs in the High School, 1982, The New York City Problem Book, 1986, Read the Question: A Thinking Student's Guide to the SAT's, 1992; co-author: (with I.M. Gelfand) Trigonometry, 2001; author: Enrichment Problems in Leadership Manual for High School Supervisors in Mathematics, 1982; assoc. editor edn. Notices of Am. Math. Soc., 1996—, math. field editor Quantum, 1991—2001, mem. editl. bd. Mathematics and Informatics Jour., 1991—, Math. Horizons Jour., 1992—96, mem. editl. panel MAA Anneli Lax New Math. Libr., 1996—2004. Judge Internat. Math. Olympiad, Washington, 1981, chief guide, 2001; author contest questions Mass. Math. League Ann. Contest, 1981; mem. authors' com. Educating Teachers of Science, Mathematics, and Technology: New Practices for the New Millennium, 1998—2000. Recipient Presdl. award for Excellence in Teaching Math., NSF, 1984, Paul Erdos award, World Fedn. Nat. Math. Competitions, 1998; Tandy Tech. scholar, 1994, Gabriela and Paul

Rosenbaum Found. fellow, 1995. Mem.: Nat. Coun. Tchrs. Math. (bd. dirs. 2001—04), Am. Math. Soc., Math. Assn. Am. (mem. com. on high sch. contests 1981—92), Assn. Tchrs. Math. (exec. bd. mem. 1980—85). Avocation: chamber music. Office Phone: 917-796-8697. Personal E-mail: marksaul@earthlink.net, marksaul@edc.com.

**SAUL, NORMAN EUGENE,** historian, educator; b. LaFontaine, Ind., Nov. 26, 1932; s. Ralph Odis and Jessie (Neff) S.; m. Mary Ann Culwell, June 27, 1959; children: Alyssa, Kevin, Julia. BA, Ind. U.- Bloomington, 1954; MA, Columbia U., 1959, PhD, 1965; postgrad., Leningrad State U., 1960-61. Asst. prof. Brown U., 1965-68; vis. assoc. prof. Northwestern U., 1969-70; assoc. prof. U. Kans., Lawrence, 1970-75, prof. history, 1975—, chmn. dept. history, 1981-89. Inst. Advanced Study, Princeton U., 2000. Author: Russia and the Mediterranean 1797-1807, 1970, Sailors in Revolt, 1978, Distant Friends: The United States and Russia, 1763-1867, 1991, Concord and Conflict: The United States and Russia, 1867-1914, 1996, War and Revolution: The United States and Russia, 1914-1921, 2001, Friends or Foes: The United States and Soviet Russia, 1921-1941, 2006; editor: Russian-American Dialogue on Cultural Relations, 1776-1914, 1997. Fulbright scholar, London, 1954-55, Helsinki, 1968-69, Soviet Am. Exch. scholar Internat. Rsch. and Exch. Bd., Moscow, 1973-74, 91-92; fellow Ford Found., 1957-59, Hall Ctr. for Humanities, 1989, 95; recipient Byron Caldwell Smith Book award for Distant Friends, 1993, Robert H. Ferrell book award for Concert and Conflict, Soc. Historians Am. Fgn. Rels., 1997, Pub. Scholar award Kans. Humanities Coun., 1997, Higuchi Rsch. award U. Kans., 1997, Steeples award for Svc. to Kans., 2000, Herbert Hoover Libr. Assn. award, 2001, Franklin and Eleanor Roosevelt Inst. award, 2002. Mem. Am. Assn. Advancement of Slavic Studies, Kans. State Hist. Soc. Home: 1002 Crestline Dr Lawrence KS 66049-2607 Business E-mail: nsaul@ku.edu.

**SAUL, RALPH SOUTHEY,** diversified financial services company executive; b. Philadelphia, Pa., May 21, 1922; s. Walter Emerson and Helen Douglas (Coutts) S.; m. Bette Jane Bertschinger, June 16, 1956; children: Robert Southey, Jane Adams. BA, U. Chgo., 1947; LL.B., Yale U., 1951. Bar: D.C. 1951, N.Y. 1952. With Am. Embassy, Prague, Czechoslovakia, 1947-48; assoc. Lyeth & Voorhees, N.Y.C., 1951-52; asst. counsel to gov. State of N.Y., 1952-54; staff atty. RCA, 1954-58; with SEC, 1958-65, dir. divsn. trading and markets, 1963-65; v.p. corporate devel. Investors Diversified Services, Inc., Mpls., 1965-66; pres. Am. Stock Exch., N.Y.C., 1966-71; co-chief exec., chmn. mgmt. com. 1st Boston Corp., 1971-74; chmn., CEO. INA Corp., Phila., 1975-82, CIGNA Corp., Phila., 1982-84. Trustee Com. for Econ. Devel., Brookings Inst.; mem. adv. coun. Pub. Co. Acctg. Oversight Bd. With USNR, 1943-46, PTO. Mem. ABA, Union League, Merion Golf Club, Links Club. Office: Cigna Corp One Logan Square PO Box 7716 18th and Cherry Sts Philadelphia PA 19192 Office Phone: 215-523-5051. Personal E-mail: yobigdad@aol.com.

**SAUL, WILLIAM EDWARD,** engineering educator; b. NYC, May 15, 1934; s. George James and Fanny Ruth (Murokh) S.; m. J. Muriel Held Eagleburger, May 11, 1976. BSCE, Mich. Tech. U., 1955, MSCE, 1961; PhD in Civil Engring., Northwestern U., 1964. Registered profl. engr., Wis., Idaho, Mich., profl. structural engr., Idaho. Mech. engr. Shell Oil Co., New Orleans, 1955-59; instr. engring. mechanics Mich. Tech. U., Houghton, 1960-62; asst. prof. civil engring. U. Wis., Madison, 1964-67, assoc. prof., 1967-72, prof., 1972-84; dean, prof. civil engring. U. Idaho Coll. Engring., Moscow, 1984-90; prof. civil engring. Mich. State U., East Lansing, 1990—2000, chmn. dept. civil and environ. engring., 1990-91, chmn. emeritus, prof. emeritus, 2000. Cons. engr., 1961—; vis. prof. U. Stuttgart, Germany, 1970-71. Co-editor Conf. of Methods of Structural Analysis, 1976. Bd. dirs. Idaho Rsch. Found., 1984-90. Fulbright fellow 1970-71; vo Humboldt scholar, 1970-71. Fellow ASCE (pres. Wis. sect. 1983-84), NSPE (bd. dirs.), Mich. Soc. Profl. Engrs. (Steinman award 2003); mem. Internat. Assn. Bridge and Structural Engrs., Am. Concrete Inst., Am. Soc. Engring. Edn., Sigma Xi, Phi Kappa Phi, Tau Beta Pi, Chi Epsilon Avocations: hiking, reading, travel, gadgets. Home: 1971 Cimarron Dr Okemos MI 48864-3905 Office: Mich State U 3546 Engring Bldg E East Lansing MI 48824 Business E-Mail: saul@egr.msu.edu.

**SAULINO, MICHAEL FRANCIS,** physiatrist; b. Philadelphia, Pa., Mar. 16, 1961; MD, PhD, Hershey Med. Ctr., 1986—93. Cert. Phys. Medicine and Rehab. Am. Bd. PM&R, 1998, Spinal Cord Injury Am. Bd. PM&R, 2000. Attending physician Magee Rehab. Hosp., Phila., 1998—; residency program dir. Thomas Jefferson U. Hosp., Phila., 2001—. Consulting physician Thomas Jefferson U., Phila., 1998—. Recipient AMA Physician Recognition Award, AMA, 2001-2004. Mem.: Assn. Am. Colls., Nat. Stroke Assn., Physiatric Assn. Sports, Spine, and Orthop. Rehab., Am. Coll. Sports Medicine, Internat. Soc. Phys. and Rehab. Medicine, Am. Coll. Physician Execs., Am. Acad. Phys. Medicine and Rehab., Am. Assn. Neurol. Surgeons (assoc.). Office: Magee Rehab Hosp 1513 Race St Philadelphia PA 19102 Business E-Mail: msaulino@mageerehab.org.

**SAULS, DON,** clergyman; b. Eureka, N.C. m. Marie Brown; children: Donna, Dale. B in Sacred Lit., Holmes Sch. of the Bible, Greenville, S.C., 1967; MA in Adult Edn., N.C. State U., 1984; postgrad., N.C. Wesleyan Coll. Ordained to ministry Pentecostal Free Will Bapt. Ch., 1966. Pastor Pentecostal Free Will Bapt. Ch., Benson, N.C., 1967-84; gen. dir. Christian Edn. dept., 1971-84, gen. supt., 1984-96; pastor Pikeville Pentecostal Free Well Bapt. Ch., Goldsboro, N.C., 1996—. Tchr. Heritage Bible Coll., Dunn, N.C., 1971—, also trustee; chmn. bd. dirs., sec., mem. bd. adminstrn. Pentecostal Fellowship N.Am., 1988-91, Pentecostal and Charismatic Chs. of N.Am.; lectr. U.S. and abroad; host, preacher weekly TV program; frequent radio spkr. Columnist Messenger, 1984—; contbr. articles to jours. in field. Former chmn. bd. dirs. Cape Fear Christian Acad.; pres. Harnett County Helpnet. Mem. Kiwanis (former pres. Dunn club, bd. dirs., dir. children's programs dist. 11). Office: Pikeville Pentecostal Free Will Bapt Ch 401 W Main St Pikeville NC 27863

**SAUNDERS, ALAN KEITH,** professional football coach; b. London, Feb. 1, 1947; m. Karen Saunders; children: Korrin Elizabeth, William Joseph, Robert Charles. Grad., San Jose State U., 1969; MA, Stanford U., 1970; postgrad., U. So. Calif., 1983-85. Football coach U. Mo., 1972, Utah State U., 1973-75; asst. head coach U. Calif., 1976-81; offensive coordinator, quarterback coach U. Tenn., 1982; coach San Diego Chargers, NFL, 1983—, asst. head coach, 1985-86, head coach, 1986-88; offensive coord. Kans. City Chiefs, 2001—06, Wash. Redskins 2006—. Mem. ad-hoc com. state lic. and designated sports Calif. State Legis.; hon. chmn. S.D. chpt. Arthritis Found.; bd. dirs. Easter Seal Soc., San Diego; bd. govs. Athletes for a Stronger America; mem. S.D. Chem. Dependency Adv. Bd. Office: Wash Redskins 2400 E Capitol St Washington DC 20003

**SAUNDERS, AUDREY J.,** tax specialist, writer; b. Cin. d. Robert James and Margaret Ann (Philpot) Saunders. BA, U. Cin., 1971; MS, Xavier U., Cin., 1975; postgrad., Lehman Coll., Bronx, 1990—92. Tchr. N.Y.C. Bd. Edn., 1985—94; with IRS, Cin., 1995—2003, tax examining asst. Holtsville, NY, 2003—05. Adult basic edn. tchr. Gen. Edn. Devel. Program Math, 1974—77. Author short stories, Going From Just A Boxer To A Super Bowler, 2005, The Evolutionary War, 2006. With U.S. Army, 1977—81. Methodist. Home: 646 West End Dr Medford NY 11763

**SAUNDERS, BARRY WAYNE,** state official; b. Roxboro, N.C., June 9, 1944; s. Charlie Clifton and Mary Louise (Mooney) S.; m. Brenda Kaye Bell, Oct. 18, 1987; children: Dara Louise Saunders Lockamy, Erin Elissa (dec.). BA, Campbell u., 1971; MEd, U N.C. 1974; EdD, N.C. State U., 1990. Tchr. Granville County Sch. System, Oxford, NC, 1966-69; mental health counselor Vocat. Rehab., Henderson, NC, 1971-75; staff devel. specialist John Umstead Hosp., Butner, NC, 1975-82; trainer, asst. mgr., mgr. tng. N.C. Dept. Transp., Raleigh, 1982—; mgr. tng. (on loan from N.C. Dept. Transp.) Gov.'s Office of Quality Improvement, 1995-96; mgr. tng. N.C. Dept. Transp., Raleigh, 1996-2000; ret., 2000. Pres. Omicron Cons., Mill Spring, NC,

1982—. Contbr. articles to profl. jours., poems to N.C. Poetry Soc., 1981. Sec. Dem. Party, Person County, N.C., 1980-84. Mem. Nat. Mgmt. Assn. (bd. dirs. state govt. chpt. 1992-95, v.p. 1997-98), Triangle Quality Coun. (bd. dirs. 1995-96), Nat. Transp. Tng. Dirs. Assn. (v.p. 1997-2000). Methodist. Home: 121 Canoe Dr Mill Spring ND 28756

**SAUNDERS, CHARLES ALBERT,** lawyer; b. Boulder, Colo., Jan. 18, 1922; s. Charles and Anna (Crouse) S.; m. Betti Friedel, Oct. 18, 1946; children—Melanie, Stephen, Cynthia, Shelley. BA, U. Houston, 1942; LLB, U. Tex., 1945. Bar: Tex. 1945. Ptnr. firm Fulbright & Jaworski, L.L.P., 1959—. Editor: How To Live-and Die-With Texas Probate, 8 vols., 1968, Texas Estate Administration, 1975. Bd. dirs. Houston Symphony Soc., 1964—; bd. dirs. Am. Lung Assn., San Jacinto, 1965—, pres., 1972-73; past mem. bd. govs. U. Houston. Recipient Leon Jaworski award for cmty. svc., Houston Bar Assn., 1997, U. Tex. Law Sch. Disting. Alumnus award in Cmty. Svc., 1999. Mem. ABA, State Bar Assn., Houston Bar Assn., Am. Coll. Trust and Estate Coun. (regent 1972-80, pres. 1978-79), Internat. Acad. of Estate and Trust Law, Assn. Cmty. TV (bd. dirs. 1970—). Republican. Presbyterian. Home: 19 Willowron Dr Houston TX 77024-7618 Office: Fulbright & Jaworski 1301 Mckinney Ste 5100 Houston TX 77010-3031 Office Phone: 713-651-5374. Business E-Mail: csaunders@fulbright.com.

**SAUNDERS, CHARLES BASKERVILLE, JR.,** retired association executive; b. Boston, Dec. 26, 1928; s. Charles Baskerville and Lucy (Carmichael) S.; m. Margaret MacIntire Shafer, Sept. 9, 1950; children— Charles Baskerville III, George Carlton, Margaret Keyser, Lucy C., John R. Grad., St. Mark's Sch., 1946; AB, Princeton, 1950. News reporter, polit. columnist Ogdensburg (N.Y.) Jour., 1950-51; edn. reporter Hartford (Conn.) Times, 1951-53; asst. dir. pub. relations Trinity Coll., Hartford, 1953-55; asst. dir. pub. info. Princeton, 1955-57; legis. asst. Sen. H. Alexander Smith, 85th Congress, 1957-58; asst. to asst. sec. for legislation HEW, 1958-59; asst. to sec. Arthur S. Flemming, 1959-61, dep. asst. sec. for legislation, 1969-71; asst. to pres. Brookings Instn., 1961-69; dep. commr. of edn. for external affairs U.S. Office Edn., 1971-72; dep. asst. sec. for edn. HEW, 1973-74; dir. govt. relations Am. Council on Edn., 1975-78, v.p. for govt. relations, 1978-87, sr. v.p., 1987-92. Author: Brookings Institution: A Fifty-Year History, 1966, Upgrading the American Police, 1970, Four Centuries in America, 2000, rev. edit., 2006. Mem. Montgomery County Bd. Edn., 1966-70, Md. Higher Edn. Commn., 1989-2002 (chmn. 1994-95, vice chmn. 1995-2002); chmn. bd. dirs. Md. Higher Edn. Loan Corp., 1994-95. Mem. Jamestowne Soc. Democrat. Presbyterian. Home: 7622 Winterberry Pl Bethesda MD 20817-4848 Personal E-mail: saunders3@earthlink.net.

**SAUNDERS, DONALD LESLIE,** hotel executive, real estate developer; b. Brookline, Mass., Jan. 28, 1935; s. Irving M. Saunders and Shirley Brown; m. Liv. Ullmann, 1985; children: Lisa M., Pamela R. AB in Econs., Brown U., 1957; grad., Inst. Real Estate Mgmt., 1963; LLB, 1989. Cert. property mgr. Inst. Real Estate Mgmt., Ill. Chmn., pres., CEO D.L. Saunders Real Estate Corp., Boston, 1957—; CEO, chmn. D.L. Saunders Cos., Boston; co-owner Boston (Mass.) Pk. Plz. Hotel & Towers, 1976—, chmn., 1976—, CEO, 1976—; gen. ptnr. SaunStar Land Co.; ptnr. 20 & 50 Park Plaza Complex, LLC. Bd. dirs. Park Sch. Corp., Brookline, Mass.; with Brown U. Comml. Real Estate Devel. Co.; mem. real estate subcom. Brown U.; pres. Farview Inc., 1976—; trustee emeritus Brown U., 1972—. Mem. Nat. Assn. Realtors, Ea. Point Residents Assn., Ocean Reef Club, Ocean Reef Yacht Club, Racquet Club, Brown U. Club, Lotos Club, The Players, Union League Club, Hope Club, Boston Tennis and Racquet Club, Ea. Point Yacht Club, Belmont Country Club, Univ. Club, Providence, Union Club, Charles River Yacht Club, The Worcester (Mass.) Club, Harvard Club, Confrerie Chaine des Rotisseurs, N.Y.C. Office: DL Saunders Cos 20 Park Plz Boston MA 02116-4399

**SAUNDERS, FLIP (PHILIP D. SAUNDERS),** professional basketball coach; b. Cleve., Feb. 23, 1955; m. Debbie Saunders; children: Ryan, Mindy, Rachel and Kimberly (twins). Student, U. Minn. Asst. coach U. Minn Golden Golphers, 1982-86, U. Tulsa, 1986-88; head coach Continental Basketball Assn. Rapid City (S.D.) Thrillers, 1988-89, La Crosse (Wis.) Catbirds, 1989-94, gen. mgr., 1991-93, team pres., 1991-94; head coach Continental Basketball Assn. Sioux Falls (S.D.) Skyforce; gen. mgr., head coach Minn. Timberwolves, 1995—2005; head coach Detroit Pistons, 2005—. Named CBA Coach of the Yr., 1989, 92. Office: The Detroit Pistons Four Championship Dr Auburn Hills MI 48326*

**SAUNDERS, GEORGE LAWTON, JR.,** lawyer; b. Mulga, Ala., Nov. 8, 1931; s. George Lawton and Ethel Estell (York) S.; children: Kenneth, Ralph, Victoria; m. Terry M. Rose. BA, U. Ala., 1956; JD, U. Chgo., 1959. Bar: Ill. 1960. Law clk. to chief judge U.S. Ct. Appeals (5th cir.), Montgomery, Ala., 1959-60; law clk. to Justice Hugo L. Black U.S. Supreme Ct., Washington, 1960-62; assoc. Sidley & Austin, Chgo., 1962-67, ptnr., 1967-90; founding ptnr. Saunders & Monroe, Chgo., 1990—. With USAF, 1951-54. Fellow: Am. Coll. Trial Lawyers; mem.: Law Club, Quadrangle Club, Point-O-Woods Club, Chgo. Club, Order of the Coif, Phi Beta Kappa. Democrat. Baptist. Home: 179 E Lake Shore Dr Chicago IL 60611-1306 Office: Saunders Monroe Law Offices 20 S Clark St Ste 1720 Chicago IL 60603-1847

**SAUNDERS, GEORGE WENDELL,** management consultant, retired government official; b. Hubbard, Ohio, Oct. 17, 1917; s. Phillip and Mary (Shafer) S.; m. Audrey Edna Bogue (dec. Nov. 1979); children: Wayne George, Wendy Jean; m. Virginia Hutson Baker, June 25, 1987; stepchildren: John Milton Jr., Kathee Eloise. B in Acctg., Rider Coll., 1937; postgrad., Harvard U., 1943; grad., Indsl. Coll. Armed Forces, 1955. Fgn. Service Inst., Naval War Coll.; student, Grad. Sch. Dept. Agr., Dept. Def. Computer Inst. Auditor, acct. U.S. Rubber Co., N.Y.C., 1937-39; acct., office mgr. S. King Fulton, Inc., Washington, 1939-40; with War Dept. and Civil Aero. Adminstrn., Washington, 1940-41; adminstrv. asst., sr. investigator Bur. Fed. Supply Treas. Dept., Washington, 1941-47; ops. planning analyst, orgn. and methods examiner, supply specialist Fed. Supply Services GSA, Washington, 1957-55, dep. dir. stores mgmt. div., 1955-61, dir. supply distbn. div., acting asst. dir. nat. buying div., 1956-61, dir. distbn. programs div., 1961-64, asst. commr. supply distbn., 1964-71, asst. commr. trans. and pub. utilities 1971-73, dep. commr., 1973-75; v.p. Washington Mgmt. Group, Washington Mktg. Group, 1975-79; pvt. practice cons., 1979—. Mem. Fed. Safety Council, Fed. Fire Council and Nat. Def. Trans. Bd., 1970-75 Contbr. to govt. pubs. Chmn. bd. dirs., past pres. North Chevy Chase Swimming Pool Assn., 1960; vestryman, treas. Episc. Ch., Silver Spring, Md., 1950. Served with USN World War II, PTO, ATO, comdr. Res. ret., 1975. Recipient Adminstrs. Exceptional Service award GSA, 1975. Mem. Ret. Officers Assn., Am. Legion (exec. bd. Thad Dulin chpt. 1986-87, adj. 1988, vice comdr. 1989-91, comdr. 1994-95), Leisure World Golf Club, Kenwood Country Club, Montgomery Village Golf Club, Lions (pres. Rossmoor Club Silver Spring, 1988-89), Fireside Forum (v.p., bd. dirs.), Leisure World Republican Club. Republican. Avocations: golf, travel, aviation, swimming. Home and Office: Apt 318 333 Russell Ave Gaithersburg MD 20877-2879

**SAUNDERS, HAROLD HENRY,** foundation administrator; b. Phila., Dec. 27, 1930; s. Harold Manuel Saunders and Marian Elizabeth Weihenmayer; m. Barbara Mc Garrigle, May 4, 1963 (dec. Oct. 1973); children: Catherine Elizabeth, Mark Harril; m. Carol Eleanor Jones Cruse, June 2, 1990. AB, Princeton U., 1952; PhD, Yale U., 1956; LittD, New Eng. Coll., 1999; D of Internat. Rels., Dickinson Coll., 2004. With CIA, Washington 1959—61; sr. staff Nat. Security Coun., Washington, 1961—74; dir. intelligence and rsch., asst. sec. Near East and South Asian affairs Dept. of State, Washington, 1974—81; fellow Am. Enterprise Inst. Brookings Inst., Washington, 1981—91; profl. lectr. Johns Hopkins U., SAIS, George Mason U., 1984—91; dir. internat. affairs Kettering Found., Washington, 1991—. Author: The Other Walls: Arab-Israeli Peace Process in Global Perspective, 1985, 91, A Public Peace Process: Sustained Dialogue to Transform Racial and Ethnic Conflicts, 1999, Politics Is About Relationship: Blueprint for the Citizens' Century, 2005. Trustee Princeton U., 1996—2000; pres. Class of '52, 2002—; ruling elder Lewinsville Presbyn. Ch., McLean, Va., 1971—; bd. dirs. East-West Inst., N.Y.C., 1981—89, Ptnrs. Dem. Change, San Francisco, 1995—2005, InterNews, Arcata, Calif., 1999—2001. Lt. USAF, 1957—59. Recipient Disting. Fed. Civilian Svc. award Pres. U.S., 1978, Disting. Honor award Dept. of State, 1981, First Disting. Achievement award Germantown Acad., Phila., Lifetime Achievement award Search for Common Ground, 2004. Mem. Internat. Soc. Polit. Psychology (gov. coun. 1991-94), Coun. Fgn. Rels., Princeton Club N.Y., Phi Beta Kappa. Avocation: writing. Home: 2101 Lorraine Ave Mc Lean VA 22101 Office: Kettering Found 444 N Capitol St NW Washington DC 20001

**SAUNDERS, JOSEPH W.,** bank executive; BS, U. Denver, 1967, MBA, 1968. V.p., credit card ops. Bank of Am., 1984—85; with Household Fin. Corp., 1985—97; chmn., CEO Fleet Credit Card Services L.P., 1997—2001; chmn. bd, CEO & pres. Providian Fin. Corp., 2001—05; pres. card services divsn. Washington Mutual, Inc., Seattle, 2005—. Office: Washington Mutual Inc Washington Mutual Tower 1201 Third Ave Seattle WA 98101

**SAUNDERS, LONNA JEANNE,** lawyer, newscaster; b. Cleve. d. Jack Glenn and Lillian Frances (Newman) Slaby. Student, Dartmouth Coll.; AB in Polit. Sci. with honors, Vassar Coll.; JD, Northwestern U., 1981; cert. advanced study in Mass Media, Stanford U., 1992. Bar: Ill. 1981. News dir., morning news anchor Sta. WKBK-AM, Keene, NH, 1974-75; reporter Sta. KDKA-AM, Pitts., 1975; pub. affairs dir., news anchor Sta. WJW-AM, Cleve., 1975-76; helicopter traffic reporter WERE-AM Radio, Cleve., 1976-77; morning news anchor Sta. WBBG-AM, Cleve., 1978; talk host, news anchor Sta. WIND-AM, Chgo., 1978-82; atty. Arvey, Hodes, Costello & Burman, Chgo., 1981-82; host, "The Stock Market Observer", news anchor WCIU-TV, Chgo., 1982-85; staff atty. Better Govt. Assn., Chgo., 1983-84; news anchor, reporter Sta. WBMX-FM, Chgo., 1984-86; pvt. practice law Chgo., 1985—; news anchor Sta. WKQX-FM, Chgo., 1987; arbitrator Cir. Ct. 17th Jud. Dist., Ill., 2005—; tchr. Rockford Pub. Schs., Ill., 2005—; Allen County Pub. Schs., Ohio, 2005—. Instr. Columbia Coll., Chgo., 1987-90; guest talk host Sta. WMCA, N.Y.C., 1983, Sta. WMAQ, Chgo., 1988, Sta. WLS, Chgo., 1989, Sta. WWWE, Cleve., 1989, Sta. KVI, Seattle, 1994, WCBM-AM, Balt., 1996, WRC-AM, Wash., D.C., 1997; host, prodr. The Lively Arts, Cablevision Chgo., 1986; talk show host The Lonna Saunders Show, Sta. KIRO-AM, Seattle, 1995-96; news anchor, WTOP-AM Radio, Washington, D.C., 1996-97; talk host, "Today and Tomorrow show", WMAL-AM radio, Washington, D.C., 1997, freelance reporter, CBS Radio Network, N.Y.C., 1975—; atty. Lawyers for Creative Arts, Chgo., 1985-91; guardian Ad litem and child rep., 2005—. Mem. editl. bd. Jour. Criminal Law and Criminology, 1979-81; creator pub. affairs program WBBM-AM, Chgo., 1985; law columnist Chgo. Life Mag., 1986-99; sports columnist (Cleve.) Indians Ink mag., 1998-2000; writer Rock River Times newspaper, 2004; guest columnist Gainesville Sun, Fla., 1998-99, Rockford Register Star newspaper, 1998-2006; contbr. articles to profl. jours.; contbr. columns to mags. and newspapers. Atty., county counsel voter protection project Kerry-Edwards 2004, Inc.; mem. women's action coun. Amnesty Internat., 2000—. Recipient Akron Press Club award for best pub. affairs presentation, 1978; grantee Scripps Howard Found., 1978-81; AFTRA George Heller Meml. scholar, 1980-81. Fellow Am. Bar Found.; mem. ABA (mem. exec. coms. Lawyers and the Arts, Law and Media 1986-92, chmn. exec. com. Law and Media 1990-91, 91-92, Young Lawyers divsn. liaison to Forum Com. on Comm. Law 1991-93, Commn. for Partnership Programs 1993-94, regional divsn. chair Forum on Comm. Law 1995-96). Roman Catholic. Avocations: theater, piano, baseball. Office Phone: 815-218-9773. Personal E-mail: lonnasaunders@yahoo.com.

**SAUNDERS, MARTHA DUNAGIN,** academic administrator; m. Joseph Bailey; 7 children. BA, U. So. Miss., 1969; MA, U. Ga.; PhD in comm. theory, Fla. State U. Asst. prof. comm. U. West Fla., dir. Univ. Honors Prog., dean Coll. Arts and Scis., 1999; v.p. Academic Affairs Columbus State U.; chancellor U. Wis., Whitewater, 2005—. Author: Eastern's Armageddon: Labor Conflict and the Destruction of Eastern Airlines, 1992. Mem.: Pub. Relations Soc. Am. (Silver Anvil award). Avocations: fishing, gardening. Office: U Wis 800 W Main St Whitewater WI 53190 Office Phone: 262-472-1918. Office Fax: 262-472-1518.

**SAUNDERS, MARTIN,** chemistry educator, researcher; b. 1931; BS, CCNY; PhD, Harvard U., 1956. Prof. Chemistry Yale U., New Haven, 1955—; Kharasch prof. U. Chgo., 1983. Contbr. articles to profl. jours. including Science, Nature, J. Am. Chem. Soc. Recipient Sr. U.S. Scientist award Alexander von Humboldt Found. 1977-78, 85, Arthur C. Cope Scholar award Am. Chem. Soc., 1998-99, James Flack Norris award in Physical Organic Chemistry, 2005. Fellow: Japanese Soc. Promotion of Nat. Sci.; mem.: NAS, Am. Acad. Arts and Scis. Achievements include creation of new methods for studying carbocations, one of the three main species of reactive intermediates in organic reactions; discovery of detailed mechanisms and rates of very rapid rearrangement reactions of cation intermediates. Office: Yale U Dept Chemistry 225 Prospect St New Haven CT 06520-8107 Office Phone: 203-432-3974. Business E-Mail: ms@gaus90.chem.yale.edu.

**SAUNDERS, MARY JANE,** lawyer; b. Waltham, Mass., Oct. 15, 1956; BA, Va. Polytech. Inst., 1978; JD, Mercer Univ., 1981. Bar: Va. 1982, DC 1993, US Supreme Ct. 1992. Ptnr., Copyright & Unfair Trade, Nonprofit Org. practices Venable LLP, Washington. Mem.: DC Computer Law Forum (past pres.). Office: Venable LLP 575 &th St NW Washington DC 20004 also: Venable LLP Suite 300 8010 Towers Crescent Dr Vienna VA 22182 Office Phone: 202-344-8108, 703-760-1950. Office Fax: 202-344-8300. Business E-Mail: mjsaunders@venable.com.

**SAUNDERS, PATRICIA GENE KNIGHT,** freelance writer, editor; b. Tulsa, Okla., Nov. 20, 1946; d. Eugene Merritt and Patricia May (Hough) Knight; m. Joseph Eugene Saunders, June 24, l989. BA, Baylor U., 1969. Nat advt. svc. KTVT-TV, Ft. Worth 1969-71; tchr. Arlington (Tex.) Ind. Sch. Dist., 1971-77, Garland (Tex.) Ind. Sch. Dist., 1977-79; payroll, spl. projects assoc. Electronic Data Systems, Dallas, 1979-81; adminstrv. asst. Diversified Innovators, Dallas, 1981-82; system ops. mgr. Span Instruments, Plano, Tex., 1982-86; data processing mgr. Claire Mfg., Addison, Ill., 1986-87, Everpure, Inc., Westmont, Ill., 1987-88; software cons. Software Alternatives, Inc., Downers Grove, Ill., 1988-89; sys. ops. asst., cons. J&J Maintenance, Inc., Austin, Tex., 1989-90; pres., computer cons. Cardinal Software Solutions, Inc., Austin, 1990-93; editor Holt, Rinehart & Winston, Austin, 1993-99. Mem.: Writers' League of Tex., Soc. of Children's Book Writers and Illustrators, N.Y. Met. Mus. Fine Art, Smithsonian Instn., Nat. Mus. Women in the Arts, Nat. Arbor Day Found., Nat. Wildlife Fedn. Republican. Baptist. Avocations: cats, gardening, travel, movies, reading. Home: 410 Teal Ln Kyle TX 78640-8888 Office Phone: 512-262-2062. Office Fax: 512-268-1625.

**SAUNDERS, PAUL CHRISTOPHER,** lawyer; b. NYC, May 21, 1941; s. John Richard and Agnes Grace (Kelly) Saunders; m. Patricia Newman, Sept. 14, 1968; children: Dr. Paul Christopher, Michael Eagan. AB, Fordham Coll., 1963; JD, Georgetown U., 1966; certificat, Institut d'Etudes Politiques, Paris, 1962. Bar: NY 1966, DC 1967, US Supreme Ct 1969. Assoc. Cravath, Swaine & Moore LLP, N.Y.C., 1971-77, ptnr., litig., 1977—; disting. visitor from practice Georgetown U. Law Ctr., 2003—. Mem ed bd: Georgetown Law Jour, 1965—66; editor (editor-in-chief): The Advocate, 1969—70. Trustee Fordham U., 1991—96, 2004—; bd. regents Georgetown U., 1991—96, bd. visitors Law Ctr., 1996—; trustee, vice-chmn Fordham Prep. Sch., 1986—94; v.p., bd. dirs. Legal Aid Soc., 1983—88; bd. dirs., trustee Lawyers Com. Civil Rights Under Law, 1985—, co-chair 1995—97; v.p., trustee Vols. Legal Svc., Inc., 1999—; bd. dirs. Office of the Appellate Defender 1999—; mem. N.Y. State Judicial Inst. on Professionalism in the Law, 2000—; chmn. bd. dirs. Constitution Project, 2000—. Capt JAGC U.S. Army, 1967—71. Decorated Meritorious Svc. medal; recipient John Carroll medal, Georgetown U., 1995, Whitney N. Seymour award, Lawyers Com. Civil Rights Under Law, 2000, Paul R. Dean award, Georgetown U. Law Ctr., 2006. Fellow: Am. Bar Found., Am. Coll. Trial Lawyers; mem.: ABA, London Ct. Internat. Arbitration, Assn. Bar City N.Y., NY State Bar Assn., Westchester Country Club (Rye, NY),

Apawamis Club (Rye, NY), Phi Beta Kappa, Pi Sigma Alpha. Democrat. Roman Catholic. Address: 455 Polly Pk Rd Rye NY 10580-1960 Office: Cravath Swaine & Moore LLP Worldwide Plz 825 8th Ave Fl 39 New York NY 10019-7475 Office Phone: 212-474-1404. Office Fax: 212-474-3700. Business E-Mail: psaunders@cravath.com.

**SAUNDERS, PETER PAUL,** investor; b. Budapest, Hungary, July 21, 1928; emigrated to Can., 1941, naturalized, 1946; s. Peter Paul and Elizabeth (Halom) Szende; m. Nancy Louise McDonald, Feb. 11, 1956; children: Christine Elizabeth McBride, Paula Marie McMullen. Student, Vancouver Coll., 1941-44; B.Com., U. B.C. 1948. Acct. Canadian Pacific Rly. Co., 1948-50; founder, pres. Laurentide Fin. Corp. Ltd., 1950-66, vice chmn., 1966-67; chmn., pres. Coronation Credit Corp. Ltd., Vancouver, B.C., Canada, 1968-78, Versatile Corp. (formerly Coronation Credit Corp. and Cornat Industries Ltd.), Vancouver, B.C., Canada, 1978-87; prin., pres. Saunders Investment Ltd., Vancouver, 1987—. Past pres. Vancouver Symphony Soc., 1968-70, Can. Cancer Soc., B.C. and Yukon Region, 1975-77, Vancouver Art Gallery Assn., 1981-83; chmn. Vancouver Opera Round Table, 1984-92; chmn. Arthritis Rsch. Ctr. of Can. Mem. Vancouver Club, Shaughnessy Golf and Country Club, Royal Vancouver Yacht Club, Thunderbird Country Club (Rancho Mirage, Calif.). Avocations: golf, skiing, hunting, boating. Home: 3620 Alexandra St Vancouver BC Canada V6J 4B9 Office: Saunders Investment Ltd PO Box 49352 Bentall Ctr Vancouver BC Canada V7X 1L4

**SAUNDERS, RAYMOND JENNINGS,** artist, educator; b. Pitts., Oct. 28, 1934; Student (Nat. Scholastic scholar), Pa. Acad. Fine Arts, U. Pa., Barnes Found.; B.F.A., Carnegie Inst. Tech., 1960; M.F.A., Calif. Coll. Arts and Crafts. Teaching asst. Calif. Coll. Arts and Crafts, 1960-61; resident Am. Acad. in Rome, 1964-66; art and urban affairs cons. N.Y.C. Bd. Edn. and Human Resources Adminstrn., 1967; art faculty Calif. State Univ., Hayward, 1968—88; prof. painting, drawing Calif. Coll. Arts and Crafts, Oakland, 1988—. Vis. artist, R.I. Sch. Design, 1968, artist-in-residence, vis. artist and critic at various art schs., univs., 1968—; subject of profl. articles.; one-man shows include San Francisco Mus. Modern Art, 1971, Seattle Art Mus., 1981, Pa. Acad. Fine Arts, 1990, Tampa Mus. Art, 1992, Stephen Wirtz Gallery, San Francisco, 1979, 1980, 1982, 1989, 1993, 1996, 1999, 2001, 2003, Galerie Resche, Paris, 1993, Oakland Mus., 1994, M.H. de Young Meml. Mus., San Francisco, 1995, Carnegie Mus. of Art, 1996, Galerie Resche, Paris, 1998, Hunsaker/Schlesinger Fine Art, 2001, Centre Jerome Cuzin, France, 2002, Schneider Mus. Art, So. Ore. Univ., 2004; represented in permanent collections, Mus. Modern Art, N.Y.C., Whitney Mus. Am. Art, N.Y.C., Phila. Mus. Art, Chrysler Mus., Va.; author: Black is a Color, 1968. Served with U.S. Army, 1957-59. Recipient Cresson European traveling scholar, 1956, Thomas Eakins prize, Schwabacher-Frey award San Francisco Mus. Art Ann., 1961, award Nat. Inst. Arts and Letters, 1963, Prix de Rome Am. Acad. in Rome, 1964-66, Ford Found. Purchase award, 1964, award City of Phila., Atwater Kent award Soc. Four Arts, 1970, Granger Meml. award Pa. Acad. Fine Arts, 1972, Art award KQED, 1975, Guggenheim Fellow, 1976, Nat. Endowment for Arts award, 1977, 84, Visual Arts award So. Ea. Ctr. for Contemporary Art, 1989. Office: Painting & Drawing Dept Calif Coll Arts & Crafts 5212 Broadway Oakland CA 94618-1426 Office Phone: 510-594-3600.

**SAUNDERS, RICHARD HENRY, III,** museum director; b. Rochester, N.Y., Aug. 13, 1949; s. Richard Henry and Betsy (Macmillan) S.; m. Barbara Fox Williams, June 12, 1971; children: Elizabeth, Christopher, Katherine. BA, Bowdoin Coll., 1970; MA, Del. U., 1973; MPhil, Yale U., 1976, PhD, 1979. Curator Wadsworth Atheneum, Hartford, Conn., 1978-81; asst. prof. U. Tex., Austin, 1981-85; dir. Middlebury Coll. Mus. Art, Vt., 1985—; Walter Cerf Disting. Coll. Prof. Middlebury Coll., 1985—. Lectr. Yale U., New Haven, Conn., 1979. Author: Collecting the West, 1988, John Smibert, 1995, Horatio Greenough, 1999, The Brook Collection, 2005; co-author: American Colonial Portraits, 1987. Trustee Williamstown Regional Art Conservation Lab., 1990, The Shelbourne Mus., 1997-, Preservation Trust of Vt., 2003-; bd. dirs. Vt. Mus. and Gallery Alliance, Shelburne, 1988—, Vt. State Craft Ctr., Middlebury, 1985-88; adv. panel New Eng. Found. for the Arts, Cambridge, Mass., 1987-88. Named Lamont Dupont Copeland fellow, Winterthur Mus., Del., 1971-73, Deerfield fellow, Historic Deerfield, Mass., 1969, Kress fellow, Courtauld Inst., Samuel Kress Found., N.Y., 1976-77, Andrew Wyeth fellow, Yale U., New Haven, Conn., 1975-76. Mem. Coll. Art Assn., Nat. Trust, Yale Club. Office: Middlebury Coll Ctr for Arts Rt 30 S Middlebury VT 05753 E-mail: rsaunder@middlebury.edu.

**SAUNDERS, ROBERT SAMUEL,** venture capitalist; b. Akron, Ohio, Dec. 3, 1951; s. Samuel Robert and Rose Saunders; m. Heidi Ruth Fulkerson, Mar. 18, 1978. AB with distinction, Stanford U., 1973; MSc with distinction, London Sch. Econs., 1974; diploma, U. Stockholm, 1976; MA, Harvard U., 1978. Cons. World Bank, Washington, 1975—77; sr. cons. Boston Cons. Group, 1978—82; dir. competitive strategy analysis Bain and Co., Boston, 1982—86; sr. v.p., chief planning officer Krupp Cos., Boston, 1986—88. Chmn. Saunders Capital Group, Boston, 1988—94, Internat. Mktg. Concepts, Louisville, 1998—2005, Venture Club, Louisville, 2001—05, Compliance & Ethics Learning Solutions, Chgo., 2004—; mng. dir. Providian Capital Mgmt., Louisville, 1993—97; sr. mng. dir. Chrysalis Ventures, Louisville, 1997—; vice chmn. Telemics, Inc., Louisville; fin. com. chmn. Pub. Radio Partnership, Louisville, 1996—2003; investment com. chmn. African Am. Venture Capital Fund, 1993—; chmn. adv. bd. dept. computer engring. and computer sci. U. Louisville, 2001—05; bd. dirs. Metacyte, Inc., Louisville, Constrn. Software Tech., Inc., Cin., Ygnition, Inc., Seattle, RAD Electronics, Inc., LA, Tech Skills LLC, Austin, Actor's Theater, Louisville; dev. com. chmn. Walden Theater, Louisville, 2003—06. Editor: Stanford Quar. Rev., 1973. Co-founder Weston Conservation Trust, Mass., 1988; del. Mass. Dem. Nat. Conv., San Francisco, 1984. Named Entrepreneur of the Yr. award for Ky. and U. S. Ohio, Ersnt and Young, 2004; Marshall scholar, 1973—75, NIH fellow, 1978. Swedish Govt. Fulbright grantee, 1975. U.S. Congress Profl. Devel. grantee, 1976. Mem.: Internat. Union Sci. Study Population, Am. Econ. Assn. Unitarian Universalist. Home: PO Box 99252 Louisville KY 40269-0252 Office: Chrysalis Ventures Ste 1650 National City Tower, 5th St Louisville KY 40202

**SAUNDERS, SALLY LOVE,** poet, educator; b. Bryn Mawr, Pa., Jan. 15, 1940; d. Lawrence and Dorothy (Love) S. Student, Sophia U., Tokyo, Japan, 1963, U. Pa., Columbia; BS, George Williams Coll., 1965. Tchr. Shipley Sch., Bryn Mawr, 1962-65. Agnes Irwin Sch., Wynnewood, Pa., 1964-65, Montgomery County Day Sch., Wynnewood, 1962, Miquon (Pa.) Sch., Waldron Acad., Merion, Pa., 1965-66, Phelps Sch., Malvern, Pa., 1965-70, Frankford Friends Sch. Phila., 1965-66, Haverford (Pa.) Sch., 1965-66, Friends Sem. Sch., N.Y.C., 1966-68, Ballard Sch., N.Y.C., 1966-67, Lower Merion Sch., Ardmore, Pa., nights 1967-71, Univ. Settlement House, Phila., 1961-63, Navajo Indian Reservation, Fort Defiance, Ariz., 1963, Young Men's Jewish Youth Center, Chgo., 1964-65, Margaret Fuller Settlement House, Cambridge, Mass., 1963; poetry therapist Pa. Hosp. Inst., 1969-74, also drug rehab. house Phila.; poet in residence Tyrone Guthrie Ctr., Newbliss, Ireland, Aug. 1988; poetry workshop leader Pendle Hill Quaker Ctr., Wallingford, Pa., Apr. 1988; poetry week leader Ferry Beach, Saco, Maine, summer 1988. Pioneer in poetry therapy. Poet, 1946—; poems pub. in periodicals including others; author: Past the Near Meadows, 1961, Pauses, 1978, Fresh Bread, 1982, Random Thoughts, 1992, Patchwork Quilt, 1993, Quiet Thoughts and Gentle Feelings, 1996, Word Pictures, 1998, Bits of Thought, 2006; contbr. poems to newspapers. Mem. Acad. Am. Poets, Nat. Fedn. State Poetry Socs., Am. Poetry League, Nat. League Am. Pen Women, Poetry Therapy Assn. (v.p.), Avalon Orgn., Authors Guild, Nat. Writers Club, Pen and Brush Club, N.H.Poetry Soc., Pa. Poetry Soc., Cath. Poetry Soc. (asso.), Fla. State Poetry Soc. (asso.) Episcopalian. Home: 2030 Vallejo St Apt 501 San Francisco CA 94123-4854 Office: 609 Rose Hill Rd Broomall PA 19008-2254 Office Phone: 610-356-0849. E-mail: slovesndrs@aol.com. *So often during my life I have found great comfort and strength in writing and reading poetry. With my poetry I want to help others to get in touch with their own powers. Poetry, to me, is a rare and beautiful freedom and this is what I want to share with others.*

**SAUNDERS, STACY DAWN,** secondary school educator, music educator, singer; b. West Union, Ohio, Dec. 8, 1975; d. Russell Caskey and Linda Darlene Glasgow; m. Russell Edwin Saunders, Jr., Aug. 30, 1996; 1 child, Catherine Joy. AA in Arts and Scis., So. State S.C., Hillsboro, Ohio, 1995; BA in English and Humanities summa cum laude, Shawnee State U., 1996. Cert. tchr. Ohio Dept. Edn., profl. educator Assn. Christian Schs. Internat. Tchr. Adams County Christian Sch., West Union, Ohio, 1996—97; min. music Farmersville (Ohio) United Meth., 1997—2000; tchr. Ridgeville Christian Schs., Springboro, Ohio, 1998—2003, Christian Cmty. H.S., White House, Tenn., 2003—05; accompanist The Ch. at Grace Pk., White House, 2004—05; accompanist, song leader Hendersonville (Tenn.) Cumberland Presbytn., 2003—06; pianist White House 1st United Meth. Ch. Pvt. music instr. Stacy's Studio, White House, 1998—2006; youth music dir. St. Timothy Luth. Ch., Hendersonville, 2005—06; sponsor music/drama club Christian Cmty. H.S., White House, Tenn., 2003—04; del. Assn. Christian Schs. Internat., Birmingham, Ala., 2004, Birmingham, 05. Author: (novels) Dark Knight, 2000; author/artist: record Come With Me, 2005. Sponsor/ptnr. Compassion Internat., Colorado Springs, Colo., 1996—; Capitol Hill ptnr. Concerned Women for Am., Washington, 2004—; active Am. Conservative Union, Alexandria, Va., 2004—; Bible-A-Month Club mem. Am. Bible Soc., N.Y.C., 2005—; choir mem. Solid Rock Ch., Monroe, Ohio, 2003. Recipient Outstanding Grad. award, Shawnee State U., 1996. Republican. Avocations: writing, hiking, aerobics, yoga.

**SAUNDERS, SYLVIA CHRISTIE,** biologist, educator; arrived in U.S.A., 1958; d. Zachariah and Cleodine Christie; m. Hermon Saunders, June 24, 1971; children: Reeka, Eric. BSc, NYU, 1962, MSc, 1965, PhD, 1969. From asst. prof. to prof. CUNY, N.Y.C., 1966—75, prof., 1975—, asst. dean, 1966—75. Founder and coord. Cleo & Zack Project CUNY, 2000—. Nominee Chase Nat. Prof. of Yr.; grantee, NIH, 1970—, NSF, 1970—. Mem.: AAAS, N.Y. Acad. Scis. Avocations: gardening, writing, reading, mentoring. Office: Borough of Manhattan Cmty Coll 199 Chambers St New York NY 10007

**SAUNDERS, TERRY ROSE,** lawyer; b. Phila., July 13, 1942; s. Morton M. and Esther (Hauptman) Rose; m. George Lawton Saunders Jr., Sept. 21, 1975. BA, Barnard Coll., 1964; JD, NYU, 1973. Bar: D.C. 1973, Ill. 1976, U.S. Dist. Ct. (no. dist.) Ill. 1976, U.S. Ct. Appeals (7th cir.) 1976, U.S. Supreme Ct. 1983. Assoc. Williams & Connolly, Washington, 1973-75, Jenner & Block, Chgo., 1975-80, ptnr., 1981-86, Susman, Saunders & Buehler, Chgo., 1987-94; pvt. practice Law Offices of Terry Rose Saunders, Chgo., 1995—2002; ptnr. Saunders & Doyle, Chgo., 2002—. Author: (with others) Securities Fraud: Litigating Under Rule 10b-5, 1989. Recipient Robert B. McKay award NYU Sch. Law. Mem. ABA (co-chair class actions and derivative suits com. sect. litig. 1992-95, task force on merit selection of judges, co-chair consumer and personal rights litig. com. sect. litigation 2000-02), Chgo. Bar Assn., Order of Coif, Union League Club.

**SAUNDERS, THOMAS A., III,** investment banker; BS, Va. Mil. Inst., 1958; MBA, U. Va. Darden Sch., 1967. Mng. dir. Morgan Stanley & Co. Inc., NYC, 1974—89; founding ptnr. Saunders, Karp & Megrue. Bd. dirs. Dollar Tree Stores, Hibbett Sports, Targus Group Internat. Chmn. bd. trustees Thomas Jefferson Found. Office: 445 Park Ave 45th Fl New York NY 10022*

**SAUNDERS, WILLIAM ARTHUR,** management consultant; b. Ottawa, Ont., Can., Oct. 13, 1930; BS with honors, McGill U., 1954; MBA in Econs. and Fin., U. Western Ont., 1956; M Commerce in Econs. and Mktg., U. Toronto, 1960. Econ. analyst Imperial Oil Ltd., Toronto, Ont., 1956-63; supr. distbrn. Polysar Ltd., Sarnia, Ont., 1963-69; venture mgr. Polysar Plastics, Inc., Westport, Conn., 1969-77; adv. strategy devel. Gulf Oil Chems. Co., Houston, 1977-82; mgmt. cons. Houston, 1982—; pres. William A. Saunders Co., 1987—. Methodist. Home and Office: 8585 Woodway Dr Apt 112 Houston TX 77063-2438

**SAUNDERS, WILLIAM HUNDLEY, JR.,** retired chemist, educator; b. Pulaski, Va., Jan. 12, 1926; s. William Hundley and Vivian (Watts) S.; m. Nina Velta Plesums, June 25, 1960 (dec. June 1982); children: Anne Michele, Claude William; m. Barbara Andrews, Apr. 27, 2002 (dec. May 2005) BS in Chemistry, Coll. William and Mary, 1948; PhD in Organic Chemistry, Northwestern U., 1952. Rsch. assoc. MIT, 1951-53; instr. U. Rochester, 1953-56, from. asst. to assoc. prof., 1956-64, prof. chemistry, 1964-91, faculty sr. assoc., 1991-95, chmn. dept., 1966-70, prof. emeritus, 1996—. Author: Ionic Aliphatic Reactions, 1965; (with A.F. Cockerill) Mechanisms of Elimination Reactions, 1973; (with L. Melander) Reaction Rates of Isotopic Molecules, 1980; contbr. numerous articles to profl. jours. With U.S. Army, 1944—45, ETO. Guggenheim fellow, 1960—61, Sloan Found. fellow, 1961—64, NSF sr. postdoctoral fellow, 1970—71. Mem. Am. Chem. Soc., Royal Soc. Chemistry, Phi Beta Kappa, Sigma Xi, Phi Lambda Upsilon. Democrat. Unitarian Universalist. Avocations: bicycling, cross country skiing, travel. Home: 15 Parkwood Ave Rochester NY 14620-3401 Office: U Rochester Dept Chemistry River Sta Rochester NY 14627 Office Phone: 585-275-4235. Business E-Mail: saunders@chem.rochester.edu.

**SAUNDERS FURDA, DENISE ELIZABETH,** music educator; b. Red Bank, N.J., June 22, 1979; d. David John and Pamela Joan Saunders; m. Steven William Furda, June 12, 2004. MusB in Music Edn. magna cum laude, Crane Sch. Music, 2001. Cert. music tchr. N.J. State Bd. Edn. Tchr. music Highlands Elem. Sch., NJ, 2000—. Collaborative music dir. Bayshore Jointure Mid. Sch. Honor Band, Keansburg, NJ, 2004—06; mem. youth music Ch. Worship Com., Oakhurst, 2003—05. Composer sheet music for children marching band, for youth choir and bell choir. Dir. youth choir First United Meth. Ch., Oakhurst, 2003—, dir. youth handbell, 2003—. Mem.: Nat. Assn. Music Edn. Avocations: northern harmony/shape note singing, digital videotaping. Office: Highlands Elem Sch 360 Navesink Ave Highlands NJ 07732

**SAUSMAN, KAREN,** zoological park administrator; b. Chgo., Nov. 26, 1945; d. William and Annabell (Lofaso) S. BS, Loyola U., 1966; student, Redlands U., 1968. Keeper Lincoln Park Zoo, Chgo., 1966-68; tchr. Palm Springs (Calif.) Unified Sch., 1968-70; ranger Nat. Park Svc., Joshua Tree, Calif., 1968-70; zoo dir. The Living Desert, Palm Desert, Calif., 1970—. Natural history study tour leader internat., 1974—; part-time instr. Coll. Desert Natural History Calif. Desert, 1975-78; field reviewer conservation grants Inst. Mus. Svcs., 1987—, MAP cons., 1987—, panelist, 1992—; internat. studbook keeper for Sand Cats, 1988-2001, for Cuvier's Gazelle, Mhorr Gazelle, 1990-2000; co-chair Arabian Oryx species survival plan propagation group, 1986-95; spkr. in field. Author Survival Captive Bighorn Sheep, 1982, Small Facilities- Opportunities and Obligations, 1983; wildlife illustrator books, mags, 1970—; editor Fox Paws newsletter Living Desert, 1970—, ann. reports, 1976—; natural sci. editor Desert Mag., 1979-82; compiler Conservation and Management Plan for Antelope, 1992; contbr. articles to profl. jours. Past bd. dirs., sec. Desert Protective Coun.; adv. coun. Desert Bighorn Rsch. Inst., 1981-85; bd. dirs. Palm Springs Desert Resorts Convention and Visitors Bur., 1988-94; bd. dirs., treas. Coachella Valley Mountain Trust, 1989-92. Named Woman Making a Difference Soroptomist Internat., 1989, 93, 97, Woman of Distinction, Riverside Bus. Press, 2000. Fellow Am. Assn. Zool. Parks and Aquariums (bd. dirs., accreditation field reviewer, desert antelope taxon adv. group, caprid taxon adv. group, felid taxon adv. group, small population mgmt. adv. group, wildlife conservation and mgmt. com., chmn. ethics com. 1987, mem. com., internat. rels. com., ethics task force, pres.' award 1972-77, outstanding svc. award 1983, 88, editor newsletter, Zool. Parks and Aquarium Fundamentals 1982); mem. Internat. Species Inventory System (mgmt. com., policy adv. group 1980-96, bd. trustees 1997-2004), Calif. Assn. Mus. (v.p. 1992-96), Calif. Assn. Zoos and Aquariums, World Assn. Zoos and Aquariums (coun. 2002-, governing coun. 2002-, pres. 2005), Western Interpretive Assn. (so. Calif. chpt.), Am. Assn. Mus., Arboreta and Botanical Gardens So. Calif. (coun. dirs.), Soc. Conservation Biology, Nat. Audubon. Soc., Jersey Wildlife Preservation Trust Internat., Nature Conservancy, East African Wildlife Soc., African Wildlife Found., Kennel Club Palm Springs (past bd. dirs., treas. 1978-80), Scottish

Deerhound Club Am. (editor Scottish Deerhounds in N.A., 1983, life mem. U.K. chpt.), Internat. Bengal Cat Soc. (pres. 1994-96). Avocations: pure bred dogs, cats, dressage, painting, photography. Office: The Living Desert 47 900 Portola Ave Palm Desert CA 92260 E-mail: kastld@aol.com.

**SAUTER, JOHNNY,** race car driver; Race car driver Richard Childress Racing, Welcome, NC. Named Champion, Rookie of Yr., Am. Speed Assn., 2001, 10 Time winner. Office: c/o Richard Childress Racing PO Box 1189 236 Industrial Dr Welcome NC 27347

**SAUTER, MICHAEL JOSEPH,** real estate company executive; b. Cleve., Oct. 10, 1957; s. Harry Albert and Carmel Ann Sauter; m. Carol Ann Sauter, Sept. 6, 1988; children: Ryan, Rory, Mary Colleen. BA, Seattle U., 1981. Cert. real property administr. Bldg. Owners & Mgmt. Inst., lic. real estae broker Wash., Ariz. With asset mgmt. divsn. Corp. Cath. Archdiocese, Seattle, 1979—89; asst. mgr. Portland, Oreg., 1989—92; v.p. Jones & Murphy, Inc., Seattle, 1992—2001; CEO S-J Mgmt. LLC (formerly Jones & Murphy, Inc.), Seattle, 2001—. Mem.: Comml. Brokers Assn., Rental Housing Assn. Puget Sound, Master Builders Assn., Wash. Multi-Housing Assn., Nat. Multi Housing Coun. Avocations: sports, coaching, running, travel. Office: S J Mgmt LLC 2150 N 107th Ste 440 Seattle WA 98133 Office Phone: 206-365-7900. Office Fax: 206-361-2105. Business E-Mail: msauter@sjm.biz.

**SAUVAGEAU, YVON,** application developer; b. Montreal, Que., Can., Dec. 10, 1961; arrived in US, 1998; s. Yvon Sauvageau and Huguette Bergeron. BSc in Computer sci., McGill U., Montreal, 1986. Cert. Java developer Sun Microsystems. Software engr. NSK Technologies, Paris, 1997—99, Merrimac Interactive Media, Cocoa, Fla., 1999—2000, Cisco Sys., Inc., San Jose, Calif., 2000—. Mem.: IEEE. Achievements include patents for method and apparatus for drawing line graphs; development of compression algorithm for the Java language binaries; software tool for the evaluation of binary compatibility between Java language binaries; graphical user interface of network topology maps. Office: Cisco Sys Inc 3550 Cisco Way SJC19/3/3 San Jose CA 95134 Personal E-mail: ysauv@ieee.org.

**SAVA, VASYL,** education educator; b. Zelene, Ukraine, May 16, 1951; arrived in U.S., 2002; s. Mykhail and Galyna Sava; m. Alla Krivich, Aug. 25, 1973; children: Yuri, Dmytro. BS, Odessa State U. Ecology, Ukraine, 1973; PhD, Inst. of Bioorganic Chemistry, Minsk, USSR, 1985. Cert. Sr. Scientist Higher Certifying Bd. of Ukraine, 1993. Investigator Internat. Rsch. Program INTAS, Parma, Italy, 1995—97; assoc. prof. Odessa State U. Ecology, 1997—99; sr. scientist and group leader Bogatsky Physico-Chemical Inst. NAS of Ukraine, Odessa, Ukraine, 1989—99; rsch. assoc. Pig Rsch. Inst., Miaoli, Taiwan, 1999—2000, China Med. Coll., Taichung, Taiwan, 2000—01; vis. asst. prof. Inst. of Botany, Academia Sinica, Taipei, Taiwan, 2001—02; rsch. assoc. U. South Fla., Tampa, 2002—04, asst. prof., 2004—. Head of soc. of inventors and rationalizers Bogatsky Physico-Chemical Inst. NAS of Ukraine, Odessa, Ukraine, 1984—89. Recipient Rank of Sr. Scientist, Higher Certifying Bd. of Ukraine, 1993, Zelinsky Prize, Bd. of Odessa Br. of Mendeleev Chem. Soc., 1978, 1983; grantee Intas 94-0839, Consiglio Nazionale dele Richerche, Italy, 1995-1997. Mem.: AAAS (assoc.), Am. Soc. for Neurochemistry (assoc.), Am. Soc. for Neuronal Transplantation and Repair (assoc.), Soc. for Neuroscience (USA) (assoc.), Internat. Soc. for Free radical Biology and Medicine (assoc.). Achievements include patents for Holder of 21. Business E-Mail: vsava@hsc.usf.edu.

**SAVAGE, CLARE LEAVY,** school psychologist; b. NYC, Mar. 20, 1953; d. Charles Joseph Leavy and Catherine Theresa Frary; m. Paul Jonathan Savage; children: Stephanie, Matthew. BA, Marymount Manhattan Coll., 1975; MSc, Hunter Coll., 1977; Advt. Cert. in Sch. Psychology, CUNY, 1986; PhD, Kennedy Western U., 2003. Cert. sch. psychologist NY, tchr. K-6 NY. Sch. psychologist, spl. edn. tchr. Western Suffolk Bd. Coop. Ednl. Svcs., 1986—99; sch. psychologist Babylon Union Free Sch. Dist., 1999—. Extraordinary min. Eucharist Ch. St. Mary, Manhasset, 1999—; extraordinary min. of Eucharist North Shore Univ. Hosp., Manhasset, 1999—2001; catechist religious edn. program Ch. St. Mary, 1999—2005. Mem.: NY State United Fedn. Tchrs., Nat. Assn. Sch. Psychologists. Roman Cath. Avocations: calligraphy, reading, theater, writing. Home: 24 Stuart Pl Manhasset NY 11030 Personal E-mail: clsavage@optonline.net.

**SAVAGE, DANIEL KEENAN,** columnist, editor-in-chief; b. Chgo., Oct. 7, 1964; life ptnr. Terry Miller; 1 adopted child, Daryl Jude Pierce. Founder Greek Active Theater, Seattle; syndicated columnist The Stranger, Seattle, 1991—, assoc. editor, 1995—2001, editor-in-chief, 2001—. Author: (columns) Savage Love, 1991—, Dear Dan, 1998—2000, (books) Savage Love: Straight Answers from America's Most Popular Sex Columnist, 1998, The Kid: What Happened After My Boyfriend and I Decided to Go Get Pregnant, 2000, Skipping Towards Gomorrah: The Seven Deadly Sins & the Pursuit of Happiness in America, 2003, The Commitment: Love, Sex, Marriage, and My Family, 2005; host (radio programs) Savage Love Live, KEXP FM 90.3, Seattle, 1994—97, contbr. This American Life; actor: (films) Crocodile Tears, 1998, 20 Gay Stereotypes Confirmed, 2004; author & dir. (plays) Greek Active Theater, Seattle, 1995, Egguss, 2001. Co-founder Gay City Health Project, Seattle, 1995. Office: The Stranger 3rd Fl 1535 11th Ave Seattle WA 98122 Office Phone: 206-323-7101. Office Fax: 206-323-7203. E-mail: editor@thestranger.com.*

**SAVAGE, DAVID WILLIAM,** lawyer; b. Seattle, Nov. 14, 1944; s. Kenneth and Mary Savage; m. Sally Savage, Aug. 1, 1982; children: Jesse, Erin, Kathryn. BA in Polit. Sci., Wash. State U.; JD, U. Idaho. Bar: Wash. 1973, U.S. Dist. Ct. (ea. dist.) Wash. 1977, Idaho 1991, U.S. Dist. Ct. Idaho 1991, Mont. 1996, U.S. Ct. Appeals (9th cir.) 1997, U.S. Supreme Ct. 1999. Shareholder, pres. Irwin, Myklebust, Savage & Brown, P.S., Pullman, Wash., 1973—. Mem.: ABA, Wash. State Bar Assn. (pres.-elect 2002—03, pres. 2003—04), Idaho State Bar Assn. Office: Irwin Myklebust Savage & Brown PS 1230 SE Bishop Blvd Pullman WA 99163 Office Phone: 509-332-3502. Business E-Mail: savage@imsblaw.com.

**SAVAGE, ELDON PAUL,** retired environmental health educator; b. Bedford, Iowa, Apr. 4, 1926; s. Paul and Nora (Arthur) S.; m. Ella May, June 5, 1948; children: Steven P., Michael D. BS, U. Kans., 1950; MPH, Tulane U., 1958; PhD, Okla. U., 1968. Coord. environ. sanitation demonstration projects USPHS, Kans., Iowa and Pa., 1950-64; chief state aids sect. pesticide ctr. Ctr. for Disease Control, Atlanta, 1964-70; chief chem. epidemiology sect. Inst. Rural Environ. Health, Colo. State U., Ft. Collins, 1970-84, prof., dir. environ. health divsn., 1984-85, head dept. environ. health, 1985-90, dir. environ. health svcs., 1987-93, prof. emeritus, 1993—. Contbr. articles to profl. jours. Mem. Am. Acad. Sanitarians (sec., treas., diplomate), Nat. Environ. Health Assn., Sigma Xi, Gamma Sigma Delta. Home: Savage EE Arabian Horses 5220 Apple Dr Fort Collins CO 80526-4302 Office: Colo State U Inst Rural Envrion Health Fort Collins CO 80523-0001

**SAVAGE, FRANK,** investment executive; b. Rocky Mount, N.C., July 10, 1938; s. Frank and Grace Vivian (Pitt) S.; B.A., Howard U., 1961; M.A., Sch. Advanced Internat. Studies, Johns Hopkins U., 1964; m. Lolita Valderrama, Apr. 19, 1980; children— Eric, Brett, Mark, Antoine, Grace, Frank Jr. Officer overseas div. Citibank, N.Y.C., 1964-70; v.p., then pres. Equico Capital Corp., N.Y.C., 1970-73; exec. v.p. TAW Internat. Leasing, N.Y.C., 1973-75; mem. staff of chmn. bd., v.p. Equitable Life Assurance Soc. U.S., N.Y.C., 1975-76, then v.p., investment officer, then exec. v.p., dep. to chief exec. officer; now chmn. Equitable Life Assurance Corp. subs. Equitable Life Assurance Soc. U.S., sr. v.p. Equitable Life Assurance Soc. U.S.; bd. dirs. Lockheed, Essence Communications, Equico Capital Corp., United Mut. Life Ins. Co.; former chmn. bd. Freedom Nat. Bank of N.Y. Chmn. bd. Ops. Crossroads Africa, 1980; mem. task force White House Conf. on Small Bus., 1978—; trustee Johns Hopkins U., 1977—; bd. dirs. Essence Communications, N.Y. Philharm. Mem. Coun. Fgn. Rels., N.Y.C. Pvt. Industry Coun. (former chmn.).

Recipient Blackafrica award, 1977, Harlem Commonwealth Coun. Banking award, 1979, Outstanding Alumni award Howard U., 1982. Presbyterian. Office: Equitable Capital Mgmt 19th Fl 1285 Avenue Of The Americas fl 19 New York NY 10019-6028

**SAVAGE, JAMES FRANCIS,** editor; b. Boston, July 23, 1939; s. James and Hanora (Enright) S.; m. Sharon Kaye Base, May 29, 1965; 1 son, Sean. AA, Boston U., 1959, BS, 1961. Reporter Quincy (Mass.) Patriot Ledger, 1961-63; reporter Miami (Fla.) Herald, 1963-67, investigative reporter, 1967-78, investigations editor, 1978-84, assoc. editor investigations, 1984—. Investigative reporter Boston Herald Traveler, 1967 Served with AUS, 1962. Recipient Nat. Headliners award, 1969, Fla. Press Assn. award, 1972, George Polk Meml. award for investigative reporting, 1973, 80, Pub. Service award Nat. A.P. Mng. Editors, 1974, 80, award Fla. Soc. Newspaper Editors, 1974, 75, Nat. Disting. Service award Sigma Delta Chi, 1979, 87, Pulitzer Prize Staff award for Nat. Reporting, 1987, Outstanding Investigative Reporting award Investigative Reporters and Editors, 1988, Disting. Alumni award Boston U. Coll. Communications, 1990, Pulitzer Prize Staff Pub. Svc. award, 1993; Profl. Journalism fellow Stanford, 1974-75 Home: 1004 Orange Is Fort Lauderdale FL 33315-1651 Office: 1 Herald Plz Miami FL 33132-1609

**SAVAGE, JOHN EDMUND,** computer science educator, researcher; b. Lynn, Mass., Sept. 19, 1939; s. Edmund J. and Eldora A. (Guay) S.; m. Patricia Joan Landers, Jan. 29, 1966; children: Elizabeth, Kevin, Christopher, Timothy ScB, ScM, MIT, 1962, PhD, 1965. Mem. tech. staff Bell Telephone Labs., Holmdel, NJ, 1965-67; prof. computer sci. Brown U., Providence, 1967—, chmn. dept. computer sci., 1985-91. Vis. prof. U. Paris, 1980—81, Warwick (Eng.) U., 1991—92; cons. in field. Author: The Complexity of Computing, 1977; author: (with others) The Mystical Machine, 1986; author: Models of Computation: Exploring the Power of Computing, 1996; editor (with Thomas Knight): Advanced Research in VLSI and Parallel Systems, 1992; chmn. editl. bd. Computing Rsch. News, 1990—96, mem. editl. bd. Jour. Computer and Sys. Scis., 1993—, patentee data scrambler, 1970, means and methods for generating permutation of a square, 1976, stochastic assembly of sublithographic interfaces, 2005, sublithographic nanoscale memory architecture, 2005. Mem. MIT Corp. vis. com. dept. elec. engring. and computer sci., 1991-2002. Fulbright-Hays grantee, 1973; NSF fellow, 1961, Guggenheim fellow, 1973 Fellow AAAS, IEEE, Assn. Computing Machinery; mem. Computing Rsch. Assn. (bd. dirs. 1990-96), Sigma Xi, Tau Beta Pi. Avocations: reading, bicycling, walking. Office: Brown U Dept Computer Sci 115 Waterman St Providence RI 02912-9016 Office Phone: 401-863-7642. Business E-Mail: john_savage@brown.edu.

**SAVAGE, JOSEPH GEORGE,** academic administrator; b. Bklyn. s. Joseph George Jr. and Eileen (Schnell) S.; m. Lynn Ann Campbell; children: Kimberly, Patricia, Joseph IV. BA, Oswego Coll., 1977; postgrad., Seton Hall U., 1985. Pub. affairs dir. L.I. chpt. Nat. Multiple Sclerosis Soc., N.Y.C., 1977-79, exec. dir. Conn. chpt., 1979-80; dir. devel., mktg. Clara Mass Meml. Med. Ctr., Belleville, N.J., 1980-81; exec. dir. Found. of St. Joseph's Hosp. Med. Ctr., Paterson, N.J. 1981-89; sr. v.p. St. Francis Hosp. Heart Ctr., Roslyn, N.Y., 1989-92; v.p. St. Vincents Hosp. and Med. Ctr., N.Y.C., 1992-98; exec. v.p. Cathedral Health Care Sys., Newark, 1998—2001, Caldwell (NJ) Coll., 2001—. Commr. health City of Clifton, 1990-94; bd. dirs. N.Y. Heart Coun., 1989-93, Cath. Family and Cmty. Svcs., 1992-2006, Osweo Coll. Alumni, 1992—, St. Mary's Hosp., Passiac, N.J. 1993-99, v.p., 1998—; v.p. Caldwell Coll. Fellow Nat. Assn. Hosp. Devel. (communication chair 1982-85, edn. chair 1985-86, bd. dirs., regional dir. 1988-89), Friendly Sons of St. Patrick (N.Y.), Ancient Order of Hibernians, Rotary (past pres. Clifton Club, Paul Harris fellow, Walter Head fellow), Caldwell Club. Roman Catholic. Avocations: swimming, golf. Office: Caldwell Coll 9 Ryerson Ave Caldwell NJ 07006-1558 Home: 300 Alexandria Dr Hackettstown NJ 07840-3804 Office Phone: 973-618-3242. E-mail: jsavage@caldwell.edu.

**SAVAGE, KIM I.,** academic administrator; d. William T. and Sylvia V. Savage; 1 child, Nicholas. BA, North Ctrl. Coll., 1977; MEd, Oreg. State U., 1980. Asst. dir., Hermann Hall Ill. Inst. Tech., Chgo., 1977—78; program advisor Oreg. State U., Corvallis, 1978—80; asst. program dir. Ohio State U. Columbus, 1980—81; various positions in student centers adminstrn. U. Ill., Chgo., 1981—2001, campus aux. svcs., 2001—05, asst. to vice chancellor student affairs, 2005—. Contbr. articles to profl. jours. Vice chmn. Downers Grove Twp. Dem. Orgn., Ill., 2004—06, precinct committeeman, 2000—06; mem. Ill. Dem. Women, Springfield; dir. Alford Am. Family Assn., Florrissant, Mo., 2001—04. Mem.: AAUW, LWV, Assn. Coll. Unions Internat. (various regional and nat. leadership positions 1980—2003, pub. policy liaison 2005—), Woodridge Toastmasters (v.p. 2005—).

**SAVAGE, MARK RANDALL,** lawyer; b. Chicopee, Mass., Mar. 10, 1959; m. Lucia Clara Savage; children: David, Ryan. BA, U. Calif., Berkeley, 1982; JD, Stanford U., 1988. Bar: Calif. Jud. law clk. to Judge James Holden, North Bennington, Vt., 1988-89; mng. atty. Pub. Advs., Inc., San Francisco, 1989—2003; sr. atty. Consumers Union of U.S., Inc., San Francisco, 2003—. Gen. counsel Cmty. Tech. Found. Calif., San Francisco, 1998—; bd. dirs. Family Bridges, Inc., Oakland, Calif. Contbr. articles to profl. jours. Bd. dirs. Unitarian Ch., Oakland, Calif., 2006—, Inst. for Civic Arts and Pub. Spaces, Inc., Albuquerque, 1996—2001. Recipient Drum Maj. award So. Christian Leadership Conf., 1998, Diversity, Innovation and Reform in Edn. award, 1995, El Fuego Nuevo award Assn. Mex. Am. Educators, 1999, Leadership Recognition award Calif. Primary Care Assn., 1999, Screaming Eagle award Calif. Reinvestment Coalition, 2004; Officer Consumers Union 1535 Mission St San Francisco CA 94103-2566 Office Phone: 415-431-6747. Business E-Mail: MarkSavage@igc.org.

**SAVAGE, MAUREEN WALLS,** retired history professor; b. Paterson, NJ, Nov. 16, 1930; d. George A. and Mary Duffy Walls; m. Harry Michael Savage, Nov. 27, 1948; children: Terry, Aileen, Kathleen, Timothy, Russell. BA, Rutgers U., Newark, 1963; MA, Rutgers U., New Brunswick, NJ, 1974. Tchr. social studies, English grades 7-8 pub. schs., Orange, NJ, 1963—66, tchr. social studies, English world history grades 7-12 Cranford, NJ, 1966—88; prof. polit. sci. Coll. St. Elizabeth, Convent Station, NJ, 1998; prof. Irish history and culture Stockton Coll., Pomona, NJ, 1993—2003. Historian Ctr. for Cmty. Arts, Cape May, NJ, 1996—2006; curator Historic Colonial Ho., Cape May, 2003, African Am. history exhibits, 1996—; pres., v.p., moderator LWV, Cape May County, 1990—, nominating com. state bd., 2002—; leader NJ del. 75th anniversary women's suffrage re-enactment, Washington, 1995. Grantee NJ Hist. Soc., Historic Commn. Cape May County. Mem.: Greater Cape May Hist. Soc. (v.p. 2001—), Irish Am. Cultural Soc. Roman Catholic. Avocations: piano, history, Irish dancing, travel, theater. Home: 916 Columbia Ave Cape May NJ 08204 Home Fax: 609-898-8107. Personal E-mail: hmsavage@webtv.net.

**SAVAGE, MICHAEL PAUL,** medicine educator, interventional cardiologist; b. Wilkes-Barre, Pa., Jan. 25, 1955; s. Peter J. and Olga J. (Sekerchak) S.; m. Kathleen A. Gallagher, June 1989; children: Katherine, Andrew. BA, Wesleyan U., Middletown, Conn., 1976; MD, Jefferson Med. Coll., 1980. Diplomate Am. Bd. Internal Medicine, Am. Bd. Cardiovascular Disease Interventional Cardiology, Nat. Bd. Med. Examiners. Intern, then resident New Eng. Deaconess Hosp.-Harvard U. Med. Sch., Boston, 1980—83; fellow Jefferson Med. Coll., Phila., 1983—86, asst. prof. medicine, 1986—91, assoc. prof., 1991—, dir. cardiac catheterization, 1990—, dir. interventional cardiology sect., 1996—. Cons. Johnson & Johnson Interventional Sys. Co., Warren, N.J., Scimed/Boston Scientific, Maple Grove, Minn., GlaxoSmith-Kline, Phila.; lectr. coronary angioplasty and cardiac catheterization. Contbr. articles to profl. jours. including New Eng. Jour. Medicine, Circulation, Am. Jour. Cardiology, Jour. Am. Coll. Cardiology, JAMA, Lancet, chpts. to books. Fellow Am. Coll. Cardiology, Soc. Cardiac Angiography and Interventions, Pa. Med. Soc., Am. Heart Assn., Am. Fedn. for Clin. Rsch. Roman Catholic. Achievements include rsch. in interventional cardiology concerning new techniques in treatment of coronary artery disease, culminating in international, prospective trials demonstrating superiority of implantable coronary

stents over conventional balloon angioplasty. Office: Jefferson Heart Inst 925 Chestnut St Philadelphia PA 19107-5001 Office Phone: 215-955-6478. Business E-Mail: michael.savage@jefferson.edu.

**SAVAGE, NORA F.,** environmental engineer; BS in Chem. Engring., Prairie View A&M U., Tex., 1992; MS in Environ. Engring. & Sci., U. Wis., Madison, 1992—95, PhD, 1995—2000. Internship Wis. Dept. Natural Resources, Madison, 1993—2000; postdoctoral rsch. fellow Howard U., 2000—01; environ. engr. US EPA, 2001—. Team leader nanotechnology US EPA, 2001—06. Contbr. articles to profl. jours. Asst. Homeless Women's Shelter, 2004—05. Mem.: Am. Chem. Soc. (assoc.), Air & Waste Mgmt. (assoc.; vice-chair tech. coordinating com. 2004—06), Tau Beta Pi Engring. Honor Soc. Democrat-Npl. Avocations: skydiving, writing, travel, reading. Home: 1200 Pennsylvania Ave NW MC8722F Washington DC 20460 Office: US EPA 1025 F St Washington DC 20004 Home Fax: 202-233-0679; Office Fax: 202-233-0678. Business E-Mail: savage.nora@epa.gov.

**SAVAGE, SUSAN M.,** state official, former mayor; b. Tulsa, Okla., 1936; married; 2 children. Student, U. Aix-Marseilles, Aix-en-Provence, France, 1969, City of London Poly., Eng., 1972; BA in Sociology with honors, Beaver Coll., 1974. Pre-trial rep. Phila. Ct. Common Pleas, 1974-75; criminal justice planner Montgomery County Criminal Justice Unit, 1975-77; exec. dir. Met. Tulsa Citizens Crime Com., 1977-87; vol. coord. Vote Yes For Tulsa, 1987; chief of staff to mayor City of Tulsa, 1988-92, mayor, 1992—2002; sec. of state State of Okla., Oklahoma City, 2003—. Active Lee Elementary Sch. PTA; bd. dirs., treas. Okla. Crime Prevention Assn.; bd. dirs. Youth Svcs. of Tulsa County, 1984-88, pres., 1986-87; co-chair Street/Enhanced 911 Steering Com., 1987; mem. C. of C. Task Force/Community Edn. Network, 1983. Mem. U.S. Conf. Mayors (chmn. com. energy and environment). Democrat. Office: Office Sec of State State Capitol Rm 101 Oklahoma City OK 73105 Home: 224 NW 33rd St Oklahoma City OK 73118-8614 Office Phone: 405-521-3911. Office Fax: 405-521-3771. Business E-Mail: susan.savage@sos.state.ok.us.*

**SAVAGE, TERRY,** television personality, journalist, stockbroker; Grad., U. Mich. Registered investment advisor stocks and commodity futures. Founding mem., 1st woman trader Chgo. Bd. Options Exch.; mem. Internat. Monetary Market; columnist Chgo. Sun Times, Chgo.; personal fin. columnist Barron's Online; featured columnist MSN Money website; columnist pvt. website www.TerrySavage.com. Bd. dirs. Devon Energy, Broadway Stores, Chicago Mercantile Exchange; former bd. mem. McDonald's Corp., Pennzoil-Quaker State Corp.; former co-editor Options Trading Strategies newsletter; spkr. in field. Host Money Talks; author: Terry Savage's New Money Strategies for the 90s, 1993, Terry Savage Talks Money: The Common-Sense Guide to Money Matters, 1999, The Savage Truth on Money, 1999; columnist Chgo. Sun-Times. Dir. Chgo. Mus. Sci. and Industry, Northwestern Meml. Hosp. Found., Econ. Club Chgo., Execs. Club Chgo., Jr. Achievement Ill., Ill. Coun. on Econ. Edn., Women's Bus. Devel. Ctr. Recipient Outstanding Consumer Journalism award Nat. Press Club, 1987, Dir.'s Choice award, 1994, 2 Emmy awards, Outstanding Personal Finance Columnist award, Northwestern U.; Woodrow Wilson fellow in Am. history and econs. Mem. Phi Beta Kappa. Office: Terry Savage Productions 676 N Michigan Ave Ste 3610 Chicago IL 60611 also: Chicago Sun Times 350 N Orleans St Ste 1270 Chicago IL 60654-2148 E-mail: savage@suntimes.com.

**SAVAGE, THOMAS RYAN,** lawyer; b. Milw., Dec. 1, 1947; s. John F. and Dorothy R. (Ryan) S.; m. Patricia C. Savage: children: Ryan, Patrick, Molly. BA, Quincy Coll., 1969; JD, Marquette U., 1973. Bar: Wis. 1973, U.S. Dist. Ct. (ea. and we. dists.) Wis. Sr. atty. Clark Oil & Refining Corp., Milw., 1973-82; assoc. Mulcahy & Wherry, Milw., 1982-84; v.p., sec., gen. counsel Sta-Rite Industries, Milw., 1984-92; v.p. adminstrn., gen. counsel Briggs & Stratton Corps., Wauwatosa, Wis., 1992—97, sr. v.p. adminstrn., 1992—. Mem. Dist. Export Coun., Milw., 1983-88, Gov.'s Adv. Coun. on Internat. Trade, Madison, Wis., 1982-85; solicitor United Way, Milw., 1990; bd. dirs. Goodwill Industries Wis., 1995—. Mem. Am. Counsel Assn. (bd. govs. Wis. chpt. 1988-94, pres. 1993-94), Engine Mfrs. Assn. (pres. 2001-02). Office: Briggs & Stratton Corp 12301 W Wirth St Wauwatosa WI 53222-2110 Office Phone: 414-259-5333.

**SAVAGE, WILLIAM WOODROW, JR.,** historian, consultant, social sciences educator; b. Richmond, Va., Oct. 13, 1943; s. William Woodrow and Margaret (Clarke) Savage; m. Sheila Bobalik, July 30, 1983; 1 child, William Woodrow III. BA in Journalism, U. S.C., 1964, MA in History, 1966; PhD in History, U. Okla., 1972. Instr. Coll. Gen. Studies U. S.C., Columbia, 1966; vis. lectr. history Iowa State U., Ames, 1970; asst. editor U. Okla. Press, Norman, 1972-75; from asst. prof. to assoc. prof. history U. Okla., Norman, 1974—89, prof., 1989—. Tech. adviser Korine-Dunlap Prodns., Nashville, 1982—83; adviser Am. Frontier Project, N.Y.C., 1982—85; bd. cons. editors Popular Culture Librs., Binghamton, NY, 1991—99. Author: The Cherokee Strip Live Stock Association, 1973, The Cowboy Hero, 1979, Singing Cowboys and All That Jazz, 1983, Comic Books and America, 1945-54, 1990; editor: Indian Life, 1977, Cowboy Life, 1993; co-editor: The Frontier, 1979; editor (newsletter): Comparative Frontier Studies, 1975—86, Norman and Cleve. County Hist. Mus., 1975; co-prodr., host (TV series) Norman Cable TV, 1986—88; columnist: Okla. Gazette, 1993—95, Jour. Scholarly Publ., 2004—; contbr. articles to profl. jours. Recipient Spl. Recognition award, Okla. Jazz Hall of Fame, 1993. Mem.: Western History Assn., So. Hist. Assn., Okla. Hist. Soc., Phi Alpha Theta, Omicron Delta Kappa, Sigma Delta Chi. Avocations: panelology, mixed media and collage. Office: Univ Okla Dept History 455 W Lindsey Rm 424 Norman OK 73019-6304 Office Phone: 405-325-6001.

**SAVAIANO, DENNIS ALAN,** education educator, dean; PhD, U. Calif., Davis, 1980. Asst. prof. U. Minn., St. Paul, 1980—86, assoc. prof., 1986—92, prof. and assoc. dean, 1992—95; prof. and dean Purdue U., West Lafayette, Ind., 1995—. Office: Purdue Univ CFS Stone Hall Rm 110 700 W State Street West Lafayette IN 47907-2059 Office Phone: 765-494-8210. Business E-Mail: savaiano@purdue.edu.

**SAVANT, DOUG,** actor; b. Burbank, Calif., June 21, 1964; m. Dawn Savant, 1983 (div. 1997); 2 children; m. Laura Leighton, 1998; children: Jack Douglas, Lucy Jane. Actor: (films) Swing Shift, 1984, Secret Admirer, 1985, Teen Wolf, 1985, Trick or Treat, 1986, The Hanoi Hilton, 1987, Masquerade, 1988, Paint It Black, 1989, Red Surf, 1990, Shaking the Tree, 1992, Maniac Cop 3: Badge of Silence, 1993, Godzilla, 1998, Dropping Out, 2000, The One, 2001, First Shot, 2002; (TV series, guest appearance) Cagney & Lacey, 1985, Hotel, 1986, Alfred Hitchcock Presents, 1986, The Facts of Life, 1987, Stingray, 1987, In the Heat of the Night, 1988, China Beach, 1990, Jake and the Fatman, 1990, Burke's Law, 1995, The Love Boat: The Next Wave, 2001, The District, 2001, Family Law, 2001, Firefly, 2002, JAG, 2002, According to Jim, 2002, The Guardian, 2004, 24, 2004, Navy NCIS: Naval Criminal Investigative Service, 2004, Nip/Tuck, 2004, CSI: Crime Scene Investigation, 2004; (TV films) The Knife and Gun Club, 1990, Aftermath: A Test of Love, 1991, Columbo: No Time to Die, 1992, Bonnie & Clyde: The True Story, 1992, Fight for Justice: The Nancy Conn Story, 1995, Terminal, 1996, A Face to Kill for, 1999, First Daughter, 1999, First Shot, 2002, Faultline, 2004; (TV series) Melrose Place, 1992—97, Desperate Housewives, 2004— (Screen Actors Guild Award for outstanding performance by an ensemble in a comedy series, 2006); Office: Desperate Housewives Touchtone Television 100 Universal City Plaza Universal City CA 91608*

**SAVARI, SERAP AYSE,** engineering educator, researcher; b. Astoria, N.Y., Nov. 4, 1968; d. Aykut and Sirin Savari. MS, MIT, Boston, 1991, PhD, 1996. Mem. tech. staff Bell Labs., Lucent Techs., Murray Hill, 1996—2003; acad. guest faculty computer sci. and comm. sys. Swiss Fed. Inst. Tech. 2003; assoc. prof. dept. elec. engring. and computer sci. U. Mich., Ann Arbor, 2003—. Contbr. articles to profl. jours. Team leader info. processing Internat. Symposium on Info. Theory, 2005; mem program. com. Info. Theory

Workshop, 2004, 2006; mem. program com. Internat. Symposium in Info. Theory, 2001, 2002, 2004. Mem.: IEEE (program com. Data Compression Conf. 2000—06, assoc. editor Source Coding IEEE Transactions on Info. Theory 2002—05, team leader program com. info. processing 2005, program com. symposium 2001, 2002, 2004), Toastmasters, Tau Beta Pi, Phi Beta Kappa. Home: 3070 Whisperwood Dr Apt 431 Ann Arbor MI 48105 Office: 4225 EECS Bldg 1301 Beal Ave Ann Arbor MI 48109 Business E-Mail: savari@eecs.umich.edu.

**SAVAS, EMANUEL S.,** finance educator, public official; b. NYC, June 8, 1931; s. John and Olga (Limbos) S.; m. Helen Andrew, Dec. 25, 1955; children: Jonathan, Stephen. BA, U. Chgo., 1951, BS, 1953; MA, Columbia U., 1956, PhD, 1960; PhD (hon.), U. Piraeus, Greece, 2000. Control systems cons. IBM, Yorktown Heights and White Plains, NY, 1959-65; urban systems mgr. N.Y.C., 1966-67; 1st dep. city adminstr. Office of Mayor of N.Y.C., 1967-72; chmn. Mayor's Urban Action Task Force, 1969-72; prof. pub. mgmt. Columbia U., N.Y.C., 1972-83, dir. Center for Govt. Studies, 1973-83, assoc. dir. Center for Policy Rsch., 1973-81; asst. sec. for policy devel. and rsch. HUD, Washington, 1981-83; prof. mgmt. Baruch Coll., CUNY, 1981-94, prof. public affairs, 1994—, dir. public policy program, 1994-97, chm. dept. mgmt., 1986-93; dir. Privatization Rsch. Orgn., 1986—. Cons. NSF, HUD, Dept. Transp., Dept. Energy, World Bank, AID, U.S. Dept. State, Pres.'s Commn. on Privatization, UN, UN Devel. Program, ILO, UNIDO, USIA, also others; mem. Pres-Elect's Urban Affairs Task Force, 1980, N.Y. State Senate Adv. Commn. on Privatization, 1990-95; mem. Gov. Pataki privatization coun., N.Y., 1995-2000; dir. U.S.-USSR Joint Project on Mgmt. of Large Cities, 1973-81; advisor on privatization Govt. Poland, 1990-92, Govt. Lesotho, 1992, Govt. Ukraine, 1993, N.Y.C. Mayor Giuliani, 1994-98, Govt. South Africa, 1996, Govt. Botswana, 1996, Govt. Philippines, 1997, others. Author: Computer Control of Industrial Processes, 1965, Organization and Efficiency of Solid Waste Collection, 1977, Privatizing the Public Sector, 1982, Moscow's City Government, 1985, Privatization, 1987, Privatization and Public-Private Partnerships, 2000, 21 fgn. edits., Privatization in the City, 2005, others; editor: Alternatives for Delivering Public Services, 1977, Privatization for New York, 1992, Managing Welfare Reform in New York City, 2005; co-author The New Public Management, 2002; mem. editl. bd. Urban Affairs Quar., Privatization Report, Privatization Watch, State and Local Govt. Rev.; contbr. 115 articles to profl. jours. Mem. NYC Mayor-elect Giuliani transition team, 1993, NY Gov.-elect Pataki transition team, 1994; mem. Tenafly (NJ) Borough Coun., 1996. With US Army, 1953-55, Korea. Recipient Systems Sci. and Cybernetics award IEEE, 1968, Louis Brownlow award Am. Soc. Public Adminstrn., 1970, Honor award Templeton Found., 1989, Leadership award Nat. Coun. Pub.-Private Partnerships, 1993, Outstanding Acad. award Am. Soc. Pub. Adminstrn., 1996, Presidential Excellence award for Disting. Scholarship, 2006. Mem. Sigma Xi, Psi Upsilon. Clubs: City of N.Y. (trustee 1974-77, Richard Childs award 1979). Greek Orthodox. Office: CUNY Baruch Coll Box D 901 17 Lexington Ave New York NY 10010-5518 Office Phone: 646-660-6780. Personal E-mail: prisect@aol.com.

**SAVEDGE, ANNE CREERY,** artist, educator; b. Richmond, Va., Jan. 29, 1947; d. Leslie Roy Jr. and Dorothy (Rakes) C.; m. Edwin Clement Savedge Jr., Aug. 11, 1967; 1 child, Ross Alan. BS, James Madison U., 1969; M in Art Edn., Va. Commonwealth U., 1977. Art instr. Colonial Heights HS, Va., 1969-78; instr. Va. Mus. Robinson House, Richmond, Va., 1983-86; vis. artist Office of Youth and Cmty. Svc., Dinwiddie, Va., 1986-87; artist-in-residence Richmond Children's Mus., 1987-88; instr. Shenandoah Photographic Workshops, 1988; adj. faculty Va. Mus. of Fine Arts, 2000—. Adj. faculty U. Richmond, 1978-2000—; artist-in-residence Va. Mus. of Fine Arts, Richmond, 1984-86, Richmond Children's Mus., 1987-88; curator Bedford Gallery Photoshow Longwood Coll., Farmville, Va., 1985, Light Images Gallery Photoshow James Madison U., Harrisonburg, Va., 1985, 1708 East Main Gallery Photoshow, Richmond, 1987, 90, New Realities/Digital Transformations show, 1997; artist Fay Gold Gallery, Atlanta, 1985-87; artist-in-edn. gifted program Dinwiddie, Va., 1988; instr. Chesterfield Tech. Ctr., 1989—; presenter in field. One-woman shows include Marsh Gallery, U. Richmond, 1986, 1708 Gallery, 1994, Baton Rouge, 1991, 1912 Gallery, 2000, Bishop Gallery, Longwood Ctr. for the Visual Arts, Farmville, 2003, Cultural Arts Ctr. at Glen Allen, 2002, E3 Gallery, NYC, 2004; artist, photographer (one-woman shows) Capital One Gallery, 2005, Va. Mus. Architecture, 2005; one-woman shows include Agora Gallery, NYC, 2006, Riverside Gallery, Lynchburg, 2006, Quirk Gallery, Richmond, 2006; artist, photographer (one-woman shows) Va. Ctr. Architecture, 2005—; Exhibited in group shows at Pleiades Gallery, NYC, 1989, Martin Gallery, Washington, 1989, Midwest Invitational, 1993—94, Mars Gallery, Ariz., 1994, Bloom Gallery, Milan, 1995, Longwood Ctr. for Visual Arts, 1997, Chrysler Mus., 1999, Art Mus. Western Va., 2002, Cultural Arts Ctr. Glen Allen, 2002, Daegu Culture and Arts Ctr., Daegu, Korea, 2004; artist, photographer (group shows) 1708 Gallery, 2004—05, George Mason U., 2005; Exhibited in group shows at A.I.R. Gallery, N.Y.C., 2005, C3 Gallery, 2005, at Bishop Gallery, 2006; artist, photographer (group shows) Agora Gallery, NYC, 2006—; Represented in permanent collections Polaroid Internat. Collection, Fed. Res. Bank, Chrysler Mus., Valentine Mus., Longwood Ctr.for Visual Arts, Va., Art Mus. Western Va., Capital One; artist, photographer (permanent collections) Agora Gallery, NYC; pub. in, Magic Wand, 1st and 2nd edits., 1998, Exploring Color Photography, 4th edit., 2005; artist, photographer Intro to Digital Photography 2nd edit., 2005. Adv. coun. Richmond Arts Coun.; evaluation com. Partners-in-Arts; master tchr. Va. State T&I Skills USA Nat. Conf.; chmn. 1708 Gallery Exhbns., 1995-96, sec. bd. dirs., 2004-2006. Named Art Tchr. of Yr., Chesterfield County, 1997-98, Art Educator of Yr., Va. Art Edn. Assn., 1999, hon. mention Excellence in Photographic Tchg. award Santa Fi Ctr. for the Visual Arts; individual artist fellow Va. Commn. for Arts, 1999, profl. fellow Va. Mus. Fine Arts. Mem. Nat. Art Edn. Assn. (presenter Chgo. chpt. Nat. Conf. 1998, Chgo. chpt. Washington Nat. Conf. 1999, Southeastern Art Educator of Yr. 2000), Richmond Artists Assn. (pres. 1978-80, cert. distinction 1980), Soc. for Photographic Edn., Va. Soc. for Photographic Arts (steering com. 1976—, fundraising chmn. 1978—, mem. chmn. 1980-86). Methodist. Home: 5318 Verlinda Dr Richmond VA 23237-3307 E-mail: asavedge@savedge.com.

**SAVEDRA, JEANNINE EVANGELINE,** artist, educator; b. Montebello, Calif., Dec. 21, 1965; d. Robert Anthony Savedra and April Baroth Student, Pasadena C.C., Calif., 1985—87, Parsons Sch. Design, 1987—88, BA Studio Art, Calif. State U., L.A., 1991; MA Humanities and Art, Calif. State U., Dominguez Hills, 2000; postgrad. IMMEX Inst., UCLA, 1999; postgrad., Otis Sch. Art and Design, 2001—02. Cert. art tchr., Calif. Children's counselor Salvation Army, Pasadena, 1987—88; graphic artist Calif. State U., L.A., 1989; pvt. investigator Larry J. Larsen Investigations and Trial Preparations, L.A., 1990—93; instr. studio art Visual Arts and Design Acad., Pasadena, 1995—2001; tchg. supr. Dept. Edn. Mount St. Mary's Coll., 2002—; restoration artist, painter St. Gaudens Fine Art Restoration and Conservation, Pasadena, 1999—; visual arts edn. specialist Calif. Living History, Pasadena, Calif., 2005—. Supr. mural Pasadena Playhouse Improvement Assn., 1995-96; mentor Puente program U. Calif., Berkeley, 1995-2000; educator Nat. Conf. Human Rels., Temescal Canyon, Calif., 1996, Annenberg Inst. Sch. Reform, Brown U., 1998-2000; apptd. to ednl. adv. com. Jack Scott, Cultural Master Plan, Sierra Madre; mem. Assembly, Calif. State Legislature, 1997-99; apptd. to Sierra Madre Arts Commn., 1999-2006, chairperson, 2002-06; ofcl. assessor tchg. performance Calif. Commn. on Tchr. Credentials Author: (art curriculum) Me, Myself and Eye, 2006; author, illustrator Art Heals, 2003 Bd. dirs. Calif. Living Histories, Pasadena; mem. Nat. Campaign for Tolerance, Montgomery, Ala. Calif. Partnership Acad. grantee, 1996—, NEH, 2004; recipient Excellence in Visual Arts award Calif. State U., 1990, VIP award Pntrs. Edn. Pasadena Unified Sch. Dist., 2004 Mem. L.A. County Mus. Art, Arboretum and Botanic Garden E-mail: jeanninesavedra@yahoo.com.

**SAVELA, JUDITH GHELDOF,** librarian; b. Ferndale, Mich., June 27, 1942; d. Ernest Joseph and Dorothy Margaret (Smith) Gheldof; m. Alan Walter, Apr. 24, 1965; children: Scott Alan, Shannon Mary. BA, Marygrove Coll., 1964; MSLS, Wayne State U., 1981. Cert. secondary tchr., Mich., Libr., Mich. Tchr. English, journalism Warren Woods Schs., Mich., 1964—68, Utica Cmty. Schs., Sterling Heights, Mich., 1968—69; columnist Advisor Newspaper, Utica, Mich., 1974—79; libr., programs coord. Sterling Heights Pub. Libr., 1978—95; ret., 1995. Editor: Michigan Municipalities, 1989; editor, publisher: St. Lawrence parish 125th Anniversary History, 1991; developer computer, video tng. program Shelvers of Lost Books, 1987; editor libr. newsletters, 1980-95. Tchr./mentor Evart Mid. Sch., 1997—, Elem. Sch. Diocese of Venice, Arcadia, Fla., 2001—05; sec. treas. Golden Eye Valley Homeowners Assn., 1997—; Bldg. coord. St. Ephrem Catechism Program, Sterling Heights, 1973—74; pres. St. Lawrence Sch. Bd., Utica, Mich., 1977; condr. Bible studies St. Philip Neri Ch., Reed City, Mich., 2003—, tchr. faith formation classes, 2005—. Grantee LSCA mktg., 1992, Allied Signal Target for parenting programs, 1995. Fellow Newspaper Fund; mem. Mich. Libr. Assn. (Loleta D. Fyan award 1990), Wayne State U. Libr. Sci. Alumni Assn., Marygrove Coll. Alumnae Assn., Librs. Using Computers (bd. dirs., treas. 1986-92). Roman Catholic. Avocations: reading, computer graphics, theater, classical music, knitting.

**SAVELL, EDWARD LUPO,** lawyer; b. Atlanta, Apr. 29, 1921; s. Leon M. and Lillian (Lupo) S.; m. Bettie Patterson Hoyt, Oct. 11, 1944; 1 dau., Mary Lillian Savell Clarke. BBA, Emory U., 1947, LL.B., 1949. Bar: Ga. 1948, U.S. Dist. Ct. (mid. and no. dist.) Ga. Assoc. A.C. Latimer, Atlanta, 1948-53; ptnr. Carter, Latimer & Savell, Atlanta, 1953-56, Woodruff, Latimer & Savell (and successor firms), Atlanta, 1956-87; of counsel Savell & Williams, Atlanta, 1987—. Instr. John Marshall Law Sch., 1951—55; dir. Legal Aid Soc., 1955—58; investigator Fulton county Judges Grievance Com. Contbr. articles to legal jours. With USAF, 1942-45, CBI. Fellow Internat. Acad. Trial Lawyers (pres. 1978-79, Dean of Acad. 1976); mem. Atlanta Bar Assn. (sec.-treas. 1953-54), ABA, State Bar Ga., Ga. Def. Lawyers Assn. (founder, v.p.), Internat. Assn. Ins. Counsel, Atlanta Claims Assn., Lawyers Club Atlanta, Cherokee Town and Country Club, Commerce Club, Univ. Yacht Club (past commodore), Chi Phi, Phi Delta Phi (past pres.). Presbyterian. Office: Savell and Williams 1500 Equitable Bldg 100 Peachtree Atlanta GA 30303

**SAVERCOOL, SUSAN ELISABETH,** elementary school educator; b. La Grande, Oreg., Aug. 1, 1947; d. Edwin Gilbert and Francis Gwynne Kirby; m. Niles Seymour Duncan, June 21, 1971 (div. Sept. 1976); m. Lawrence Yeldham Savercool, Aug. 6, 1983; 1 child, David R. BA in Theater/English, Calif. State U., Northridge, 1969; MA in Elem. Edn., No. Ariz. U., 1988. Cert. elem. tchr. Calif., Ariz. Elem. tchr. St. Catherine of Siena Sch., Reseda, Calif., 1969—71; presch. tchr. La Palma E. Preschool, Anaheim, Calif., 1973—74; elem. tchr. Egremont Sch., Encino, Calif., 1977—80, Ganado Intermediate, Ariz., 1980—84, Blue Ridge Elem., Lakeside, Ariz., 1986—98; freelance writer Penn Yan, NY, 2000—03. Presenter poetry for tchrs. workshop Blue Ridge Elem., Lakeside, 1991—96; instr. elem. lang. arts No. Ariz. U., Flagstaff, 1992. Editor: Mountains of Time, vols. 1-5, 1992—97, Saint Sobo and Other Contemporary Short Stories, 1994. Actress, make-up head Theater Mountain, Lakeside, 1993—97; compile. author Oliver House Mus., Penn Yan, 2000—03; contbr. Internat. Libr. Poetry, Famous Poets Soc., Noble House, 2005. Scholar, Arts Coun., 1968. Mem.: Nat. Acad. Songwriters, Nat. Homer Poet Famous Poets Soc. (outstanding poet/contbr., internat. libr. poetry editions 2004, 2005, 2006), Phi Kappa Phi. Democratic. Unitarian Universalist. Achievements include development of PhotoLit Posters gift lines; freelance writing (as Glenna MacCauley). Avocations: reading, fishing, community chorus, community theater, writing.

**SAVETH, EDWARD NORMAN,** historian, educator; b. NYC, Feb. 16, 1915; s. Isidor and Eva (Vasa) S.; m. Harriet Obstler, June 22, 1975; 1 child by previous marriage, Henry. BSS., CCNY, 1935; MA, Columbia U., 1937, PhD, 1946. Prof. history Grad. Faculty New Sch. for Social Research, N.Y.C., 1960-63; Fulbright prof. Kyoto U., Kyoto, Japan, 1964-65; prof. Dartmouth Coll., 1965-66; Disting. vis. prof. Tex. Lutheran U., Seguin, 1966-67; Disting. prof. SUNY-Fredonia, 1967-85; adj. prof. SUNY, Buffalo, 1987—; lectr. USIA, Nepal, 1965, Morocco, 1977; Fulbright prof. Hebrew U., Jerusalem, 1981. Vis. prof. U. Rochester, 1972; lectr. Beijing Tchrs. Coll., 1989. Author: American historians and European immigrants, 1947; author, editor: Understanding the American Past, 1954, Henry Adams, 1963, American History and the Social Sciences, 1964; editorsin writer: Ency. Americana, 1962; contbr. numerous articles to mags. Mem. Am. Hist. Assn., Orgn. Am. Historians Home: 50 Stahl Rd Apt 201 Getzville NY 14068-1552

**SAVIANO, JEFFREY D.,** criminologist, consultant; b. Chgo., Dec. 3, 1956; s. Ruth Demicell; m. Jeri Kay Lapp, June 14, 1993; children: Steffan Anthony, Rachel Suzanne. AAS in Criminalistics, Pikes Peak CC, Colorado Springs, 1985. Criminalist Metro Forensic Lab., Colorado Springs, 1985—. Instr. Pikes Peak C.C., Colorado Springs, 2004—. Contbr. articles to profl. jours. Mem.: Assn. Crime Scene Reconstruction, Internat. Crime Scene Investigators Assn., Internat. Assn. Bloodstain Pattern Analists, Internat. Assn. Identification. Avocations: writing, poetry, philosophy. Office: JDS Criminalistics PO Box 75070 Colorado Springs CO 80970 Office Phone: 719-337-0869. Business E-Mail: jsaviano@jdscriminalistics.com.

**SAVIC, JELENA,** technologist, educator; d. Johanna Gertrude and Vid Spacoje Savic. BS (hon.), N.E. Ill. U., 1973, M in Math. Edn., 1989. Edn. K-9 Ill., 1973, edn. 9-12 Ill., 1979, bilingual edn. Ill., 1993, ESL edn. Ill., 1993. H.s. math tchr. Ctrl. Jr. H.S., Evergreen Park, Ill., 1973—79, Proviso East H.S., Maywood, Ill., 1979—99; instrnl. technologist Proviso West H.S., Hillside, Ill., 1999—. Workshop presenter - tchr. topics Proviso Twp. 209, Maywood, Ill., 1999—; writer ednl. curriculum Proviso Twp. H.S., Hillside, Ill., 1999—; web. photographer Proviso West H.S., Hillside, Ill., 2000—; home schooling instr. U. Nebr.-Lincoln, 2002—. Filmmaker (animated short film) The Insect Reaction (Best Film, 1992). Walk animals mem. Humane Farming Assn., Chicago, 2003; humanitarian Serbia orphanages and refugee camps, 2006. Named 1 of Top 10 Tchrs. in US nat. TV documentary, Arnold Shapiro Prodns., 1984, featured spkr. Channel 5 More You Know Ore., Channel 5 Nat. TV, 1984; recipient Larry Stilgebauer Tech. award, West 40 Ednl. Ctr., 1988, 2001. Mem.: Ill. Fedn. Tchrs. Avocations: photography, filmmaking, dance, designing costumes. Home: 3228 N Newland Chicago IL 60634 Office: Proviso W HS 4701 W Harrison St Hillside IL 60162 Office Phone: 708-202-6220. Home Fax: 708-449-3636. Personal E-Mail: jxm73@hotmail.com.

**SAVICKIS, RODNEY FREDRICK,** theater educator, theater director; b. Pequannock, N.J., June 10, 1965; s. Ivar Savicku and Gerda Savickis. BA in History, William Paterson U., Wayne, N.J., 1988; MEd in Theatre Edn., U. S.Fla., 1994. Tutor, lang. lab. Passaic County CC, 1987—89; theatre & dance companies mgr., booking agent Inner City Ensemble, Paterson, NJ, 1988—89; tchr. Kennedy HS, Paterson, 1988—89; substitute tchr. Osceola Bd. Edn., 1989—90, hosp.-homebound coord., 1990—93; tchr. world geography, world history, Am. history, drama & stagecraft Poinciana HS, 1993—96; instr. drama, TV prodns., world history, hosp.-homebound, theatre mgr. Melbourne HS, 1996—. Mem. Fla. Theatre Conf., 1998—99; mem. sch. adv. com. Melbourne HS, 2001—; mem. global study exch. Rotary Internat., 2004—05. Actor: (profl. theatre) A Midsummer's Night Tale, Fenda Maria, Oklahoma, Remember When, Grand Hotel, (cmty. theatre) The Pajama Game, Romeo and Juliet, Evita. Recipient Student Govt. scholarship, 1983, Tchr. of Yr. award, Poinciana HS, 1996, Melbourne HS, 1999, 2005, Brevard County Area I Secondary Tchr. of Yr. award, 2005; grantee Alumni scholarship, 1987. Mem.: Fla. Soc. Theatre Educations, Internat. Thespian Soc. (treas. dist. XI 1999—). Office: Melbourne HS 74 Bulldog Blvd Melbourne FL 32901-3198

**SAVILLE, DERRIC JAMES,** lawyer; b. Ft. Madison, Iowa, Oct. 2, 1964; s. Jacob Abraham and Brenda K. (Lawrence) S.; m. Jeannene Irene Abbott, Mar. 21, 1987. BS, U. Iowa, 1987; M of Studies in Law, JD cum laude, Vt. Law

Sch., 1991. Bar: Minn. 1991, U.S. Dist. Ct. Minn. 1995, Upper Sioux Comty. Tribal Ct. 1996. Atty. Saville Law Office, Mpls., 1991—98; with Saville Title Svcs., Inc., Plymouth, Minn. Chair subcom. Dist. Planning Adv. Commn. #279, Maple Grove, Minn., 1994-96. Articles editor Ferae Naturae, 1991. State del. Reform Party, Maple Grove, 1996; chair mental health adv. bd. Hennepin County Commitment Def. Project, 1998-2002. Mem.: Brain Injury Assn. Minn. (bd. dirs. 1996—2000, chair 1998—99), Minn. Head Injury Assn. (bd. dirs. 1995—96). Avocations: fishing, hiking, golf. Office: Saville Title Svcs Inc 505 Hwy 169 N Ste 230 Plymouth MN 55441 Office Phone: 763-398-0377. E-mail: dsaville@savilletitleservices.com.

**SAVILLE, DUDLEY ALBERT,** chemical engineering educator; b. Lincoln, Nebr., Feb. 25, 1933; s. George A. and Alta (Goddard) S.; m. Joy Wagner, Mar. 7, 1959; children: Alexander, Andrea. BS, U. Nebr., 1954, MS, 1959; PhD, U. Mich., 1966. Engr. Carbide & Carbon Chem. Co. (Institute), W. Va., 1954-55; research engr. Chevron Research Corp. (Richmond), Calif., 1959-61, Shell Devl. Co., Emeryville, Calif., 1966-68; asst. prof. Princeton U. (N.J.), 1968-71, assoc. prof., 1971-77, prof. dept. chem. engring., 1977, Stephen C. Mocaleer prof. Engring. and Applied Sci., 2001. Assoc. editor Jour. Physico-Chem. Hydrodynamics, 1980-87; mem. adv. bd. Jour. Colloid Interface Sci., 1992-94; contbr. articles to profl. jours. Served to 1st lt. USAF, 1955-58. Recipient Alpha Chi Sigma award for chem. engring. rsch. AIChE, 1997. Mem. NAE, AIChE, Am. Chem. Soc., Am. Phys. Soc. Office: Princeton U Dept Chem Engring Princeton NJ 08544-0001

**SAVILLE, PAT,** state senate official; b. Marysville, Kans., Sept. 10, 1943; Sec. Kans. Senate, Topeka, 1991—. Mem.: Nat. Conf. State Legis. Exec Com., Am. Soc. Legis. Clks. and Secs. (past pres.). Office: Kans Senate State House 374 E Topeka KS 66612 Office Phone: 785-296-2456. E-mail: pats@senate.state.ks.us.

**SAVILLE, PAUL C.,** construction executive; Sr. v.p. fin., CFO, treas. NVR Inc., McLean, Va., 1993—2002, exec. v.p., CFO, 2002—05, CEO, 2005—. Office: Nvr Homes 11700 Plaza America Dr Ste 500 Reston VA 20190-4792*

**SAVILLE, ROYCE BLAIR,** lawyer; b. Cumberland, Md., Aug. 5, 1948; s. E. Blair and Audrey (Cosner) S.; m. Sharon Ann Brinkman, Apr. 3, 1981; children: Melissa Anne, Lauren Ashley, Meagan Elizabeth, Philip Clarke. BA, W.Va. U., 1970, JD, 1974. Bar: W.Va. 1974, U.S. Dist. Ct. (so. and no. dists.) W.Va. 1974. Assoc. William J. Oates, Jr. Atty. at Law, Romney, W.Va., 1974—75; ptnr. Oates & Saville Attys. at Law, Romney, 1975—78; pvt. practice Romney, 1978—99; mng. ptnr. Saville and Davis, PLLC, 1999—2001, Saville and Stewart, PLLC, 2001—05; pvt. practice, 2006—. Pres. Potomac Land Co., 1975—; mental hygiene commr. Hampshire County, Romney, 1976—2006; mcpl. judge City of Romney, 1980-90. Mem. W.Va. Jud. Hearing Bd., Charleston, Hampshire County Devel. Authority, Romney, Hampshire County Farm Bur., Nat. Trust for Hist. Preservation; dir. Potomac Highlands Travel Coun., Elkins, W.Va., 1984-88; mem. adv. bd. Peterkin Conf. Ctr. of Renewal, Romney, 1988-90; W.Va. Dem. Conv., Charleston, 1984; vestryman St. Stephen's Episcopal Ch., Romney, 1984-86, Bd. of Trustees, Indian Mound Cemetery 2003-. Mem. ABA, ATLA, NRA (life), W.Va. Bar Assn., South Branch Valley Bar Assn. (pres. 1996-97), W.Va. Trial Lawyers Assn., Waterfowl U.S.A. (life), N.Am. Hunting Club (life), Hampshire Camp 284 SCV (judge adv.), Civil War Preservation Trust, W.Va. Law Sch. Assn. (life), W.Va. U. Alumni Assn. (life), Am. Legion, Masons, Shriners, Scottish Rite, Order Eastern Star, Rotary (Paul Harris fellow), Phi Alpha Delta (life). Episcopal. Avocations: gun collecting, antiques, history. Home: Liberty Hall 276 E Main St Romney WV 26757-1821 also: Mill Island Moorefield WV 26836 Office: 95 W Main St PO Box 2000 Romney WV 26757-2000 Office Phone: 304-822-3875.

**SAVILLE, THORNDIKE, JR.,** coastal engineer; b. Balt., 1925; s. Thorndike and Edith Saville; m. Janet Foster, Aug. 28, 1950; children: Sarah, Jennifer, Gordon. AB, Harvard U., Cambridge, Mass., 1947; MS, U. Calif., Berkeley, 1949. Registered profl. engr., D.C. Rsch. asst. U. Calif., Berkeley, 1947-49; hydraulic engr. Beach Erosion Bd. and Coastal Enging. Rsch. Ctr., Washington, D.C. and Ft. Belvoir, Va., 1949-81, chief rsch. divsn., 1964-71, tech. dir., 1971-81; cons., 1981—. Mem. coun. wave rsch. Enging. Found., 1954—64; adv. bd. Nat. Oceanographic Datat Ctr., 1964—72, chmn. bd., 1968; mem. ad hoc adv. group spacecraft oceanography NASA, 1966—69; bd. cons. Ins.t Hydraulic Rsch. U. Iowa, 1968—70. Contbr. more than 85 articles to engring. and sci. pubs. With air corps. U.S. Army, 1943—46, with engring. corps. U.S. Army, 1955-68. Recipient Meritorious Civilian Svc. award, Dept. Army, 1981, Comdr.'s award, 1998, Annual Nat. Cap. award, D.C. Coun. Engrs. and Archs., 1964, Annual Sci. Achievement in Enging. Scis. award, 1964. Fellow: ASCE (mem. coastal engring. rsch. coun. 1964—94, com. engring., edn. and rsch. policy 1985—87, mem. exec. com. tech. coun. ocean engring., chmn. exec. com. tech. coun. ocean engring., tech. coun. rsch., mem. mgmt. group, Huber award 1963, Moffatt-Nichol award 1979, Internat. Coastal Engring. award 1991), AAAS (mem. coun. 1971—74), Wash. Acad. Scis. (bd. mgrs. 1962—69); mem.: Am. Shore and Beach Preservation Assn. (bd. dirs. 1976—97, v.p. 1988—95, M. P. O'Brien award 1997), Permanent Internat. Assn., Navigation Congresses (hon.) U.S. commr. 1971—78, U.S. commr. emeritus 1987—, U.S. rep. PTC II 1991—97, Nat. Acad. Engring. (mem. nat. com. engring. and oceanic resources 1971—77), Am. Geophys. Union, Cosmos Club (Washington). Home and Office: 5601 Albia Rd Bethesda MD 20816-3304 Office Phone: 301-320-4751.

**SAVIN, RONALD RICHARD,** chemicals executive; b. Cleve., Oct. 16, 1926; s. Samuel and Ada (Silver) Savin; m. Gloria Ann Hopkins, Apr. 21, 1962; children: Danielle Elizabeth, Andrea Lianne. BA in Chemistry and Lit., U. Cin., 1944 46, In Chemistry and Literature, U. Mich., 1948; postgrad., Columbia U., 1948-49, Sorbonne, Paris, 1949-50; grad., Air War Coll., 1975, Indsl. Coll. Armed Forces, 1976. Pres., owner Premium Finishes, Inc., Cin., 1957-91. Cons. aerospace and anti-corrosive coatings; inventor, owner Hyperseal, Inc. Contbr. articles to profl. jours. With USAF, 1948—55, World War II, Korea, col. USAFR, 1979—96. Mem.: Fedn. Coatings Tech., Fedn. Paint Techs., Nat. Assn. Corrosion Engrs., Steel Structures Painting Coun., Res. Officers Assn., Air Force Assn., Army Navy Club. Achievements include patents in field. Avocations: scientific development, photography, tennis.

**SAVINELL, ROBERT FRANCIS,** engineering educator; b. Cleve., May 26, 1950; s. Robert D. and Lotte R. Savinell; m. Coletta A. Savinell, Aug. 23, 1974; children: Teresa, Robert, Mark. BSChemE, Cleve. State U., 1973; MS, U. Pitts., 1974, PhD, 1977. Registered profl. engr., Ohio. Rsch. engr. Diamond Shamrock Corp., Painesville, Ohio, 1977-79; assoc. prof. U. Akron, Ohio, 1979-86; prof. Case Western Reserve U., Cleve., 1986—; dir. Ernest B. Yeager Ctr. for Electrochem. Scis., 1991—; assoc. dean engring., 1998—, interim dean of engring., 2000, dean engring., 2001. Divsn. editor Jour. Electrochem. Soc., 1988-91; N.Am. editor Jour. Applied Electrochemistry, 1991-97; contbr. articles to profl. jours. Named Presdl. Young Investigator, NSF, Washington, 1984-89, Outstanding Engring. Alumnus, Cleve. State U., 1984. Fellow Electrochem. Soc., AIChE (program chmn. 1986-92), Am. Inst. Chem. Engrs.; mem. Electrochem. Soc. (divsn. officer 1992—), Internat. Soc. Electrochemistry (v.p. 1995-98). Avocations: sailing, skiing. Office: Case Sch Engring CRWU-500 Nord Hall Cleveland OH 44106-7220 Office Phone: 216-368-4436. Business E-Mail: rfs2@case.edu.

**SAVING, JASON,** economist; BA, Rice U., Houston, 1991; PhD, Caltech, Pasadena, Calif., 1995. Postdoctoral fellow George Mason U., Fairfax, Va., 1995—96; sr. economist Fed. Res. Bank, Dallas, 1996—. Sr. fellow Nat. Ctr. for Policy Analysis, Dallas, 2005—. Office: Federal Reserve Bank of Dallas 2200 N Pearl Dallas TX 75201 Office Phone: 214-922-5167.

**SAVIO, FRANCES MARGARET CAMMAROTTA,** music educator; b. Phila., Oct. 2, 1936; d. Frank Cammarotta and Margaret Eleanor Cammarotta Parilla; m. Savio, Sept. 12, 1959; 1 child, Margaret Mary. B Music Edn., Immaculata Coll., 1958; M Music Edn., Trenton State U., 1976. Music and

English tchr. East Lansdowne (Pa.) schs., 1958—59; music tchr. Mary Calcott Elem. Sch., Norfolk, Va., 1959—61; music and English tchr. Northside Jr. High, Va., 1961—63; kindergarten tchr. Bar H. Crocker Country Day Sch., Oceanside, NY, 1965—68; gen. music tchr. K-8, drama dir. St. Bartholomew Sch., NJ, 1968—. Leader Girl Scouts U.S.A.; music dir., counselor, music coord. summer camps, Pa., N.J., Va.; organist, pastoral musician St. Bartholomew Ch., East Brunswick, 1968—90; mem. curriculum com. Diocese of Trenton, 1977; organist adult choir, dir. folk group St. Bartholomew Ch., East Brunswick, NJ; mem. profl. day com., mem. com. for outstanding Cath. educator Metuchen Diocese; mem. Altar Rosary Soc. Named Tchr. of Excellence, Diocese of Metuchen, 1995. Mem.: Nat. Music Honor Soc., Pi Kappa Lambda. Home: 14 Hershey Rd East Brunswick NJ 08816 Office Phone: 732-390-9691.

**SAVIOLA, BEATRICE JEANEANE,** microbiologist; d. Kevin Saviola and Barbara Krahn; m. Thomas Wheeler, Sept. 16, 1995; children: Parker Wheeler, Patrick Wheeler. PhD, Johns Hopkins U., Balt., 1997. Cert. fluorescence activated cell sorting Becton Dickinson, 2000. Postdoctoral fellow Johns Hopkins U., Balt., 1997—2001; asst. prof. Western U. of Health Sci., Pomona, Calif., 2002—. Contbr. articles to profl. jours. Fellow Postdoctoral fellow, Heiser Found., 1998—2000; grantee Biomedical Rsch. grantee, Am. Lung Assn., 2005—, RO3 grantee, Nat. Inst. of Allergy and Infectious Disease, 2003-2005, Rsch. grantee, Potts Found., 2002, 2004. Office: Western University of Health Sciences 309 E Second St Pomona CA 91766 Office Phone: 909-469-5595.

**SAVIT, ROBERT STEVEN,** physics professor, consultant; b. Chgo., Aug. 21, 1947; BA with honors, U. Chgo., 1969; MS in Physics, Stanford U., 1970, PhD in Physics, 1973. Vis. scientist CERN, Geneva, 1974-75; physicist Fermi Nat. Accelerator Lab., Batavia, Ill., 1975-78; asst. rsch. scientist U. Mich., Ann Arbor, 1978-83, assoc. prof. physics, 1983-90, prof., 1990—, dir. program for study complex sys., 1994—2000; dir. Alaska Summer Inst. in Complex Sys., 2000—. Vis. rsch. scientist Inst. Theoretical Physics, Santa Barbara, Calif., 1981-82; vis. prof. Racah Inst. Physics, Hebrew U., Jerusalem, 1986; rsch. fellow Columbia Futures Ctr., Columbia U., N.Y.C., 1988; cons. Powers Rsch., Jersey City, 1987-88, various fin. instns., non-profit instns.; govt. agys., 1988—; mem. fin. strategies group Merrill-Lynch, N.Y.C., 1988. NDEA grad. fellow Stanford U., 1969-71, postdoctoral fellow NATO, Geneva, 1974-75, fellow Am. Swiss Found., 1974-75, rsch. fellow A.P. Sloan Found., 1981-85. Office: U Mich Physics Dept Ann Arbor MI 48109 Office Phone: 734-764-3426. Business E-Mail: savit@umich.edu.

**SAVITS, BARRY SORREL,** surgeon; b. Phila., Feb. 14, 1934; s. Frank and Sophia (Cohen) S.; children: George, Frank, Alexander. BA, Princeton U., 1955; MD, U. Pa., 1959; cert. surg. residency, Mt. Sinai Hosp., N.Y.C., 1965. Prof. surgery Project Hope, Ecuador, 1965-66; instr. surgery Albert Einstein Med. Coll., Bronx, NY, 1966-67; surgeon LaGuardia Med. Group, Queens, NY, 1970-72; dir. surgery St. Mary's Hosp., Bklyn., 1973-91, Kingsbrook Jewish Med. Ctr., Bklyn., 1991-2000; attending N.Y. Meth. Hosp. 2000—, N.Y. Cmty. Hosp., 2001—. Vis. surgeon Hope-Ecuador, 1965-66, Care-Medico, Afghanistan, 1976. Comdr. USN, 1967-69. Fellow ACS (gov. 1991-97); mem. Soc. Am. Gastrointestinal Endoscopic Surgeons, Assn. Acad. Surgery, Assn. Surg. Program Dirs., Bklyn. Surg. Soc. (pres. 1992-93). Jewish. Avocations: reading. Office: 263 7th Ave Ste 4E Brooklyn NY 11215 Fax: 718-369-8121. Office Phone: 718-832-4992. Personal E-mail: bsavits@aol.com.

**SAVITSKY, DANIEL,** retired structural engineer, retired educator; b. NYC, Sept. 26, 1921; s. Maxim and Anna (Oleksiw) S.; m. Mary Wysocki; children: Jean, James, Anne. BCE, CCNY, 1942; MSc, Stevens Inst. Tech., 1952; PhD, NYU, 1971. Registered profl. engr. N.Y. Structural engr. EDO Corp., College Point, NY, 1942-44; aero. rsch. scientist Nat. Adv. Com. for Aero., Langley Field, Va., 1944-47; prof. emeritus Stevens Inst. Tech., Hoboken, NJ, 1947—. Chmn. high speed vehicle com. Internat. Towing Tank Conf., 1978-88; cons. Naval Studies Bd., Nat. Rsch. Coun. Author: (with others) Yearbook of Science and Technology, 1987; patentee hydrofoil controls. Fellow Soc. Naval Architects and Marine Engrs. (hon. mem., Adm. Cochrane award 1967, Davidson medal 1996), Am. Soc. Naval Engrs., Niantic Bay Yacht Club (Conn.), Sigma Xi. Roman Catholic. Avocations: sailing, skiing, tennis. Home: 597 Delcina Dr Westwood NJ 07675-6111 Office: Davidson Lab 711 Hudson St Hoboken NJ 07030-5953 Office Phone: 201-216-5307. Business E-Mail: dsavitsk@stevens.edu.

**SAVITT, STEVEN LEE,** computer scientist; b. Mpls., May 25, 1949; s. Leonard Robert and Claire (Hurwitz) S.; m. Gloria Lynn Kumagai; children: Mariko, Leilani, Joshua. BSEE, U. Minn., 1971, PhD in Computer Sci., 1992. Founder, CEO Compmark I Corp., Mpls., 1972-83; rsch. sect. head Honeywell, Inc., Mpls., 1983-89; rsch. staff scientist Alliant Techsystems, Inc., Mpls., 1989-96, engring. sect. head, 1996—. Co-chair database com. Automatic Target Recognizer Working Group, 1985-87. Mem. IEEE, Japanese-Am. Citizens League. Avocations: piano, classic car collecting, canoeing, tennis, swimming. Home: 332 Westwood Dr N Golden Valley MN 55422-5263 Personal E-mail: stevesn.savitt@aik.com.

**SAVITZ, MAXINE LAZARUS,** aerospace transportation executive; b. Balt., Feb. 13, 1937; d. Samuel and Harriette (Miller) Lazarus; m. Sumner Alan Savitz, Jan. 1, 1961; children: Adam Jonathan, Alison Carrie. BA in Chemistry magna cum laude, Bryn Mawr Coll., 1958; PhD in Organic Chemistry, MIT, 1961. Instr. chemistry Hunter Coll., N.Y.C., 1962-63; sr. electrochemist Mobility Equipment Rsch. and devel. Ctr., Ft. Belvoir, Va., 1963-68; prof. chemistry Federal City Coll., Washington, 1968-72; program mgr. NSF, Washington, 1972-74; dir. FEA Office Bldgs. Policy Rshc. U.S. Dept. Energy, Washington, 1974-75, dir. div. indsl. conservation, 1975-76, from dir. div. bldgs. and community systems to dep.asst sec., 1975-83; pres. Lighting Rsch. Inst., 1983-85; asst. to v.p. engring. Ceramic Components div. The Garrett Corp., 1985-87; gen. mgr. ceramic components divsn. AlliedSignal Inc., Torrance, Calif., 1987-99; gen. mgr. tech. partnerships Honeywell, Torrance, Calif., 1999—2001, ret., 2001; prin. Washington Adv. Group. Bd. dirs. Am. Coun. for Energy Efficient Economy, Draper Corp.; bd. dirs. divsn. engring. and phys. sci. NRC; cons. State Mich. Dept. Commerce, 1983, N.C. Alternative Energy Corp., 1983, Garrett Corp., 1983, Energy Engring. Bd., Nat. Rsch. Bd., 1986—93, Office Tech. Assessment, U.S. Congress Energy Demand Panel, 1987—91; nat. materials adv. bd. NRC, 1989—94, adv. bd. on energy and environ. systems, divsn. of engring. and physical sci., 2002—; chmn. U.S. Advanced Ceramic Assn., 1992; adv. com. divsn. ceramics/materials ORNL, 1989—92, adv. com. dir., 1992—96; mem. lab. adv. com. Pacific N.W. Nat. Lab., 2000—; adv. bd. Sec. Energy, 1992—2002; mem. Def. Sci. Bd., 1993—96; vis. com. adv. tech. Nat. Inst. Stds. and Tech., 1993—98, Nat. Mat. Sci. Bd., 1999—2004; mem. bd. on energy and environ. sci. NRC, 2002—, mem. divsn. on engring. and phys. sci., 2003—; bd. dir. Fedn. Am. Scientists, Am. Coun. for an Energy Efficient Economy; mem. adv. bd. Sandia Sci., 2006—. Editor Energy and Bldgs.; contbr. articles to profl. jours. Mem. policy com. NAE, 1994—98. NSF postdoctoral fellow, 1961, 62, NIH predoctoral fellow, 1960, 61. Mem. NAE (v.p. 2006—), AAAS. Office Phone: 310-271-0874. E-mail: maxinesavitz@aol.com.

**SAVITZ, SAMUEL J.,** actuarial consulting firm executive; b. Phila., Dec. 23, 1936; s. Paul and Ann (Gechman) S.; m. Selma Goldberg, June 15, 1958; children: Jacqueline Beverly, Steven Leslie, Michelle Lynn. BS in Adminstrn., Temple U., 1958; postgrad., 1965, U. Pa., 1960-62. Pension analyst provident Mut. Life Ins. Co., Phila., 1958-61; v.p. The Wirkman Co., Phila. 1961-64; pres. Samuel J. Savitz & Assoc., Inc., Phila., 1964-86; sr. prin. Laventhol & Horwath, Phila., 1986-90; chmn. Savitz Orgn., Inc., Phila. 1990—. Vis. lectr. U. Pa., Phila., 1960, La. State U., 1972-74; faculty Villanova U., 1971-75; cons. in field. Contbr. articles to profl. jours. Mem. pension com. Fedn. Jewish Agys., Phila., 1960; bd. dirs. Am. com. Weizmann Inst. Sci., 1984-85, Phila. All-Star Forum, 1987-95; vice chmn. Mann Music Assn., 1992—2005; vice chmn., trustee Fgn. Policy Rsch. Inst., 1996—, Pa. Acad. Fine Arts, 1998—, Nat. Liberty Mus. and Edn. Ctr., 1999—, Am. Interfaith Inst., 1999—, Abraham Lincoln Found., 2005—; chmn. Encore

Series, Inc., 1999—; Philly Pops, 1999—, Florentine Festivals USA, Inc., 2000-02, Regional Performing Arts Ctr., 2002—, Kimmel Ctr. for the Performing Arts, 2002—, Nat. Mus. Am. Jewish History, 2002—, Abraham Lincoln Found.; vice chmn. Phila. Orch., 2005—. With USAR, 1954-62 Mem. Am. soc. Pension Actuaries (dir. 1969-75), Union League Phila. Jewish. Home: 470 Conshohocken State Rd Bala Cynwyd PA 19004-2639 Office: 1845 Walnut St Philadelphia PA 19103-4708 Business E-Mail: samsavitz@savitz.com. E-mail: samuel-savitz@comcast.net.

**SAVNER, DAVID A.,** lawyer; b. Chgo., Mar. 15, 1944; m. Libby Savner; children: Jennifer, Michael. BA, Northwestern U., 1965, JD magna cum laude, 1968. Bar: Ill. 1968. Ptnr. Jenner & Block, Chgo., 1987—98; sr. v.p., gen. counsel, sec. Gen. Dynamics Corp., Falls Church, Va., 1998—. Editor Northwestern U. Law Review, 1967-68. Mem. ABA, Chgo. Bar Assn., Chgo. Coun. Lawyers, Order of Coif. Office: General Dynamics Corp 2941 Fairview Park Dr Ste 100 Falls Church VA 22042-4541

**SAVOIA, MARIA CHRISTINA,** vice dean; BA with highest honors, Wellesley Coll., 1972; MD, Harvard U., 1976. Diplomate Am. Bd. Internal Medicine. Med. intern U. Calif., San Diego, 1976-77, med. resident, 1977-79, fellow divsn. infectious diseases, 1980-84, clin. instr. medicine, 1980-84, asst. adj. prof. medicine, 1984-90, acting vice-chair dept. medicine, 1987-89, assoc. prof. clin. medicine, 1990-96, assoc. dean curriculum and student affairs sch. medicine, 1990—2003, vice dean med. edn., 2003—, acting dir. office learning resources sch. medicine, 1991-95, acting assoc. dean admissions sch. medicine, 1991, chief acad. officer sch. medicine, 1994—, prof. clin. medicine, 1996—; sr. fellow in med. edn. Harvard Macy Inst., Boston, 1996-97; assoc. investigator VA Med. Ctr., San Diego 1981-84, asst. chief to acting chief med. svc., 1984-90, 87-89. Author: (with others) Medical Microbiology and Infectious Diseases, 1986, Infectious Disease, 1986, Principles and Practice of Infectious Diseases, 1989, Infections in Urology, 1990, Medical Complications During Pregnancy, 1995, and others; contbr. numerous articles and abstracts to profl. jours. Recipient Calif. Women in Govt. award, 1987; NSF grantee, 1972; Durant scholar Wellesley (Mass.) Coll., 1968-72. Fellow Infectious Diseases Soc. Am.; mem. Am. Soc. Microbiology. Office: Univ Calif Sch Medicine Vice Dean for Med Edn 9500 Gilman Dr La Jolla CA 92093-0602

**SAVOIE, BRIETTA DOLORES,** librarian; b. Milw., Aug. 28, 1933; d. Walter and Vera Margaret (Rueger) Giger; m. Edmond Albert Savoie, Oct. 11, 1959; children: Philip Edmond, Raymond Walter, Anne-Marie Margaret. BA, Ohio State U., 1955; MSLS, Columbia U., NYC, 1957. Profl. librarian's cert., NY, NJ Libr. Bklyn. Pub. Libr., 1957-59; cataloger, reference librr. New Sch. Social Rsch., NYC, 1959-60; children's librr. Teaneck Pub. Libr., NJ, 1981-86; asst. reference and circulation libr. River Edge Pub. Libr., NJ, 1986-92, libr. adult svcs., 1992-2002, ret., 2002. Substitute reference librr. Glen Rock Pub. Libr., NJ, 2005-; V.p. United Way of Ridgewood, Glen Rock, Hohokus and Midland Park, NJ, 1980-81; pres. Ridgewood chpt. UN Assn., 1981-85; mem. Fair Housing Coun. Northern NJ. Mem. LWV (chmn. voter registration Glen Rock chpt. 1978-81, chmn. membership Glen Rock chpt. 2004—, co-pres. Glen Rock chpt. 2005—), Am. Libr. Assn., Nat. Arbor Day Soc., So. Poverty Law Ctr. Klanwatch Project, UN Assn., LWV, Native Am. Rights Fund, Sierra Club. Democrat. Unitarian. Avocations: international relations, social justice, environmental protection, bicycling, gardening. Home: 654 Doremus Ave Glen Rock NJ 07452-2033

**SAVOIE, LEONARD NORMAN,** transportation company executive; b. Manchester, N.H., Aug. 8, 1928; s. Joseph Peter and Angelina (Desmarais) S.; m. Elsie Anne Berscht, June 9, 1951; children: Deborah Anne, Judith Lynn, Andrew Peter. BS, Queen's U., 1952; MBA, U. Detroit, 1955. Indsl. engr. Kelsey-Hayes Can. Ltd., Windsor, Ont., Can., 1952-60; mgmt. cons. P.S. Ross & Partners, Toronto, Ont., 1960-64; pres., gen. mgr. Kelsey-Hayes Can. Ltd., 1964-70; pres., chief exec. officer Algoma Central Ry., Sault Ste. Marie, Ont., 1970-93, vice-chmn., 1993-96. Bd. dirs. Can. Gen. Ins. Co., E-L Fin. Corp. Ltd., Empire Life Ins. Co., Newaygo Forest Products Ltd., Gt. Lakes Power Ltd. Bd. dirs. United Appeal. Mem. Profl. Engrs. Ont., Engring. Inst. Can., Canadian, Sault Ste. Marie chambers commerce. Clubs: Rotary, Toronto, Toronto Ry, Sault Ste. Marie Golf. Office: 517 Conservation Dr Brampton ON Canada L6T 3S1 Personal E-mail: lens@sprint.ca. Business E-Mail: len.sav@shapiro.ca.

**SAVONENKO, ALENA,** neuroscientist, educator; d. Valerji and Elizabeth Savonenko; life ptnr. Amy Huberman. MD, Tomsk U., Russia, 1989; PhD, Lomonosov's Moscow State U., Moscow, Russia, 1994. Post-doctoral fellow Johns Hopkins U., Balt., 1999—2001, asst. prof. Sch. Medicine, 2006—. Grantee, Alzheimer's Assn., 2005—, Adler Found., 2005—. Mem.: Internat. Behavioral Neuroscience Soc., European Brain and Behaviour Soc., Soc. Neuroscience. Achievements include research in different experimental treatments to prevent aging-related effects on cognition in rodent models of human diseases. Office: Johns Hopkins University Med School 720 Rutland Ave Ross 558 Baltimore MD 21205 Office Phone: 410-502-5859. Business E-Mail: asavone1@jhmi.edu.

**SAVOY, DOUGLAS EUGENE,** bishop, writer, religious studies educator; b. Bellingham, Wash., May 11, 1927; s. Lewis Dell and Maymie (Janett) S.; m. Elvira Clarke, Dec. 5, 1957 (div.); 1 son, Jamil Sean (dec.); m. Sylvia Ontaneda, July 7, 1971; children: Douglas Eugene, Christopher Sean, Sylvia Jamila. Student, U. Portland, 1947-8; DST, D Canon and Sacred Law, Jamilian U. of the Ordained, 1980. Ordained to ministry Internat. Community of Christ Ch., 1962, bishop, 1971. Head bishop Internat. Community of Christ Ch., 1971—; lectr. in ministerial tng. studies, 1972—; pastor Univ. Chapel, Reno, 1979—; founder Jamilian Parochial Sch., 1976; chancellor, founder Sacred Coll. of Jamilian Theology; pres., founder Jamilian U. of the Ordained, 1980; pres. Advs. for Religious Rights and Freedoms; chmn. World Coun. for Human Spiritual Rights, 1984—; head Jamilian Order of Patriarchs, 1990—; engaged in newspaper pub. West Coast, 1949-56; began explorations in jungles east of Andes in Peru to prove his theory that high civilizations of Peru may have had their origin in jungles, 1957; pres., founder Andean Explorers Found & Ocean Sailing Club, Reno. Expedition dir. Grand Ophir Sea Expedition; capt. Feathered Serpent III-Ophir, 1997-98. Author: Anti-suyo, The Search for Lost Cities of the High Amazon, 1970, Vilcabamba, Last City of the Incas, 1970, The Cosolary Papers, vol. 1, 1970, vol. 2-3, 1972, The Child Christ, 1973, Arabic edit., 1976, Japanese edit., 1981, The Decoded New Testament, 1974, Arabic edit., 1981, Millenium Edition, 1983, On The Trail of the Feathered Serpent, 1974, Code Book and Community Manual for Overseers, 1975, Prophecies of Jamil, First Prophecy to the Americas, vol. 1, 1976, Second Prophecy to the Americas, 1976, The Secret Sayings of Jamil, The Image and the Word, vol. 1, 1976, vol. 2, 1977, Project X— The Search For the Secrets of Immortality, 1977, Prophecy to the Races of Man, Vol. 2, 1977, Solar Cultures of The Americas, 1977, Dream Analysis, 1977, Vision Analysis, 1977, Christoanalysis, 1978, The Essaei Document: Secrets of an Eternal Race, 1978, Millennium edit., 1983, The Lost Gospel of Jesus: Hidden Teachings of Christ, 1978, Millennium edit., 1983, Secret Sayings of Jamil, vol. 3, 1978, vol. 4, 1979, Prophecy to The Christian Churches, vol. 3, 1978, The Sayings, vol. 4, 1979, Solar Cultures of Oceania, 1979, Prophecy of The End Times, vol. 4, 1980, Solar Cultures of Israel, vols. 1 and 2, 1980, Solar Cultures of China, 1980, Christotherapy, 1980, Christophysics, 1980, Christodynamics, 1980, Code Book of Prophecy, 1980, The Sayings, vol. 5, 1980, vol. 6, 1981, Solar Cultures of India, 1981, Prophecy on the Golden Age of Light and the Nation of Nations, Vol. 5, 1981, Solar Cultures of Israel, vol. 3, 1981, The Counsels, 1982, Prophecy of the Universal Theocracy, vol. 6, 1982, Prophecy of the New Covenant, vol. 7, 1982, The Book of God's Revelation, 1983, Miracle of the Second Advent, 1984, Clerical Studies in Theology, Book I, Book II, Book III, Book IV, Transformative Theology: The School of Revelation, Transformative Theology: The School of Prophecy, Liturgical Studies: Preparation for Advanced Degrees, 1993; over 400 audio tape rec. lectures, 1974—, numerous others.; dir. documentary film Adventure: Trail of the Feathered Serpent, 1970, Lost City of the Andes, 1987; wrote, dir. videos Royal Roads to Discovery, Mystery of the Essenes of Old Israel, Secrets From the High Andes of Peru, 1993, The Gran Vilaya

Expeditions, 1996; contbr. articles on Peruvian cultures to mags., also articles on philosophy and religion; discoverer lost city of Incas at Vilcabamba Cuzco, numerous ancient cities in Amazonia including Gran Pajaten, Gran Vilaya, Monte Peruvia, Twelve Cities of the Condor, Gran Saposoa. Trustee in Trust Head Bishop Internat. Community of Christ. Served with AS USNR, 1944-46. Decorated Order of the Grand Cross Senate of Peru, 1989; recipient Participant's medallion Seawanhaka Yacht Club, 1977; Gold medal Ministry Industry and Tourism Peru, Silver Hummingbird, 1987; Silver medal and scroll City of Ica, Peru; honored with Gene Savoy Day by City of Reno, 1996, numerous exploring awards. Mem. Geog. Soc. Lima, Andean Explorers Found., Ocean Sailing Club (Explorer of the Century 1989, Flag awards), World Coun. for Human Spiritual Rights, Advs. for Religious Rights and Freedoms, Authors Guild, Explorers Club (N.Y.C., Flag awards), L.A. Yacht Club. Home: 2025 La Fond Dr Reno NV 89509-3025 Office: 643 Ralston St Reno NV 89503-4436 E-mail: gene@savoy.reno.nv.us. *One who makes dreams come true is that person who gets an idea, figures out how to make it work and then throws all of his energy into the project, stopping at nothing.*

**SAVRIN, LOUIS,** lawyer; b. Phila., Jan. 20, 1927; s. William Philip and Anna (Sass) S.; m. Barbara J. Schwimmer, Jan. 16, 1954; children: Jonathan Eric, Philip Wade, Daniel Scott. BS, NYU, 1948; JD, U. Pa., 1951. Bar: N.Y. 1952. Atty. tax dept. Arthur Young & Co., N.Y.C., 1951-55; pvt. practice N.Y.C., 1955—2005. Gen. counsel, sec. Pickwick Internat., Inc., N.Y.C., 1965-77 Assoc. editor: U. Pa. Law Rev, 1949-51. Mem. sch. bd. Dist. 21, Bklyn., 1962-68; docent Whitney Mus. Am. Art. With U.S. Army, 1945—46. Mem. B'nai B'rith (pres. lodge 1957-59, named to lodge Hall of Fame 1967, Torch of Freedom award Anti-Defamation League 1982). Home: 50 Park Ave Apt 17H New York NY 10016-3082

**SAVVIDES, MARIOS,** electrical engineer, computer engineer, research scientist; b. Nicosia, Cyprus, Nov. 11, 1975; arrived in US, 1998; s. Loucas Savvides and Anastasia Savvidou. BE in MicroElectronics Sys. Engring., U. Manchester, 1997; MSc in Robotics, Carnegie Mellon U., 2000, PhD in Elec. and Computer Engring., 2004. Rsch. assoc. Carnegie Mellon U., Pitts., 1998—2004, rsch. faculty in sys. sci., 2004—. Lectr. in field. Contbr. articles to profl. jours. Recipient Best Lectr. award, Carnegie Mellon U., 2004; fellow, 1998—2004. Mem.: IEEE, Soc. of Photo Optical Instrumentation Engrs. Achievements include patents pending for reducing complexity correlation filters for biometric recognition. Office: Carnegie Mellon University 5000 Forbes Ave Pittsburgh PA 15213 Office Phone: 412-268-1142. Office Fax: 412-268-6345. Personal E-mail: marios.savvides@ri.cmu.edu.

**SAWADA, STEPHEN GEORGE,** cardiologist, researcher; b. Milw., Nov. 14, 1955; s. Fred and Susanne Sawada; m. Mary Vandermar, Oct. 28, 1995; children: Hayley, Samuel. BS, Houghton Coll., NY, 1977; MD, U. Rochester, 1982. Diplomate Am. Bd. of Internal Medicine, 1985, cert. in cardiovascular diseases Am. Bd. of Internal Medicine, 1987. Internal medicine resident U. Rochester, 1982—85; cardiology fellow St. Mary Med. Ctr., 1985—87, Ind. U., 1987—88; rsch. assoc. Krannert Inst. of Cardiology, Indpls., 1991—; prof. Sch. Medicine Ind. U., Indpls., 1996—. Assoc. editor: Jour. of Am. Soc. of Echocardiography, 2000—; contbr. articles to profl. jours. Mem. Ctrl. Ind. Youth for Christ, Indpls., 1993—99. Fellow: Am. Coll. Cardiology; mem.: Am. Heart Assn. (assoc.; coun. clin. cardiology), Am. Soc. Echocardiography (assoc.). Evang. Achievements include patents for method for raising the hypoxic threshold; method for determining viability of a myocardial segment. Office: Krannert Inst Cardiology 1801 North Senate Blvd MPC II Indianapolis IN 46202 Office Phone: 317-962-0533. E-mail: ssawada@iupui.edu.

**SAWAI, DAHLEEN EMI,** language educator; b. Honolulu, Mar. 13, 1954; d. Kiyoto and Aiko Sawai. BA, U. Hawaii, Manoa, 1975, diploma in elem. edn., 1977, diploma in secondary edn., 1981, MEd, 1984. Cert. tchr. Hawaii. English tchr. Tokyo Family Court, 1977—78; Japanese tchr. Kailua H.S., Honolulu, 1978—80; English tchr. Family Ct. Probation Officer Tng. Sch., Tokyo, 1983—84; Japanese tchr. W. R. Farrington H.S., Honolulu, 1985—; educator Consortium for Tchg. Asia and the Pacific in the Schs., Honolulu, 1989—95; mentor tchr., 1995—. Instr. Sch. Cmty. Based Mgmt., Honolulu, 2000—04; interpreter Star Tanjo, 1976; chmn. dept. world langs. W.R. Farrington H.S., Honolulu, 2001—. Dir. Moanalua Gardens Cmty. Assn., Honolulu, 1976—77, sec., 1978—80; ad hoc com. mem. Sch. Cmty. Coun., 2005. Scholar, Keio Gijuku Daigaku, 1982—84. Mem.: Hawaii Assn. Tchrs. Japanese, Nat. Coun. Japanese Lang. Tchrs., Farrington Alumni and Cmty. Found., Japanese Cultural Ctr. Hawaii, Alliance Drama Edn., Temari Ctr. for Asian and Pacific Arts, Pi Lambda Theta.

**SAWALLISCH, WOLFGANG,** conductor; b. Munich, Aug. 26, 1923; s. Wilhelm and Maria (Obermeier) Sawallisch; m. S. Mechthild. Student, Wittelsbacher Gymnasium, Munich, Musikalische Ausbildung; pvt. music studies; D (hon.), Curtis Inst. of Music, Westminister Choir Coll. of Rider U., Villanova U. Condr., Augsburg, Germany, 1947-53; musical dir. Aachen, Germany, 1953-58, Wiesbaden, Germany, 1958-60, Cologne Opera, 1960-63; condr. Hamburg Philharm. Orch., 1960-73, hon. mem., 1973—; music dir. Phila. Orch., 1993—2003. Prin. condr. Vienna Symphony Orch., 1960—70, hon. mem.; prof. Staatliche Hochschule fur Musik, Cologne, 1960—63; musical dir. Bayerische Staatsoper Munich, 1971—92; dir. Staatsoper Munich, 1982—92, hon. mem., 1992—; permanent condr. Teatro alla Scala, Milan. Rec. artist U.S. and Britain, hon. condr. NHK Symphony Orch., Tokyo, 1967, artistic dir. Suisse Romande Orch., Geneva, 1973—80, music dir. Phila. Orch., 1993—. Decorated Osterreichisches Ehrenkreuz fur Kunst und Wissenschaft, Bundesverdienstkrenz, Bayerischer Verdienstorden, Grosses Bundesverdienstkreuz mit Stern Fed. Republic Germany, Order of Rising Sun Japan; recipient Accademico Onorario Santa Cecilia, 1975, Toscanini Gold Baton, La Scala, 1993, Bruckner-Ring, Vienna Symphony Orch., 1980, Bayerisches Maximilians-order fur Wissenschaft and Kunst, 1984, Chevalier dans L'ordre Nat. de la Legion d'Honneur de France, 1991, Pa. Gov. Disting. Artist award, Avatar award for artistic excellence, Arts and Bus. Coun., Phila. Mem.: Richard Strauss Gesellschaft Munich (pres. 1976). Office: Phila Orch 260 S Broad St Fl 16 Philadelphia PA 19102-5002*

**SAWCH, WILLIAM B.,** lawyer; b. 1954; BS, Princeton U., 1976; JD, Georgetown U., 1980. Bar: 1980. Atty. Cummings & Lockwood, Conn.; corp. atty. Applera Corp., Norwalk, Conn., 1982—85, sr. corp. atty., 1985—92, v.p. bus. devel., 1992—93, sr. v.p., gen. counsel, 1993—, mem. exec. com. Former mgmt. cons. Andersen Consulting. Office: Applera Corp 301 Merritt 7 Norwalk CT 06851-1070 Office Phone: 203-840-2900. E-mail: sawch@applera.com.

**SAWCZUK, IHOR S.,** urologist; b. NYC, Oct. 5, 1952; s. Stefan and Stefania (Mruczkewycz) S. BA, NYU, 1974; MD, Med. Coll. of Pa., 1979. Diplomate Am. Bd. Urology. Chief Allen Pavilion Urology Columbia-Presbyn. Med. Ctr., N.Y.C., 1988—99; prof. urology Columbia U., N.Y.C., 1993—, vice chmn. Dept. of Urology, 1990—2001; chmn. urology Hackensack (NJ) U. Med. Ctr., 2001—, chief urologic oncology Cancer Ctr.; prof. surgery U. Medicine and Dentistry NJ, Newark, 2003—. Adv. bd. Kidney Cancer Assn., 1994—, Kidney and Urology Found. 2002—; dep. dir. Internat. Coop. Urological Edn. Project, 1994-96. Co-editor: (book) Urologic Clinics of North America, 1993. Bd. dirs. Children of Chernobyl, Short Hills, N.J., 1992-98. Recipient Young Investigator award Nat. Kidney Found., 1987, Alpha Omega Alpha Vol. Clin. Faculty award N.J. Med. Sch., 2003. Mem. ACS, Am. Urol. Assn. (scholar 1986), N.Y. Acad. Scis., Soc. Internat. de Urologie, Soc. Urologic Oncology, European Acad. Scis., Internat. Minimally Invasive Robotics Assn. Office Phone: 201-336-8090.

**SAWH, RAVI-PERSAD,** lab administrator, researcher; s. Sire Persad and Joyce Eileen Sawh; m. Tashi Chetty, Sept. 25, 2004. BS in Physics, U. Houston, 1994. Lab supr. I U. Houston, 1994—98, lab supr. II, 1998—. Mem.: Houston Alumni Orgn., Sigma Pi Sigma, Nat. Physics Honor Soc. Achievements include discovery of a class of double perovskite pinning ceners in high temperature superconductors. Office: U Houston 632 Sci & Rsch Bldg 1 Houston TX 77204 Office Phone: 713-743-3600. Office Fax: 713-747-4526. Business E-Mail: rsawh@uh.edu.

**SAWHILL, ISABEL VAN DEVANTER,** economist; b. Washington, Apr. 2, 1937; d. Winslow B. and Isabel E. Van Devanter; m. John C. Sawhill, Sept. 13, 1958; 1 son, James W. BA, NYU, 1962, PhD, 1968. Asst. prof. econs. Goucher Coll., Balt., 1969—73; sr. rsch. assoc. Urban Inst., 1973—77, program dir., sr. fellow, 1980—93; dir. Nat. Commn. Employment Policy, Washington, 1977—79; program assoc. dir. Office Mgmt. and Budget, 1993—95; sr. fellow and Arjay Miller chair in pub. policy Urban Inst., 1995—97; sr. fellow Brookings Instn., Washington, 1997—, v.p., dir. econ. studies, 2003—06. Vis. prof. Georgetown U. Law Ctr., 1990-91; chairperson rsch. adv. bd. Com. for Econ. Devel., 1995-98; bd. dirs. Greenhill & Co., Inc. Author: Getting Ahead, 1998, One Percent for the Kids, 2003, Restoring Fiscal Sanity, 2004, 05. Bd. dirs. Manpower Demonstration Res. Corp.; pres. Nat. Campaign Prevent Teen Pregnancy, 1996—. Mem. Am. Econ. Assn., Assn. Pub. Policy Analysis and Mgmt. (pres. 1988), Phi Beta Kappa. Office: Brookings Inst 1775 Massachusetts Ave NW Washington DC 20036-2103

**SAWHNEY, MOHANBIR S.,** finance educator; BSEE, Indian Inst. of Tech., Delhi, India, 1985; MS in Mktg., Indian Inst. Mgmt., Calcutta, India, 1987; MA in Mktg., PhD in Mktg., U. Penn., Wharton Sch., 1993. Asst. prof., mktg. Kellogg Sch. of Mgmt., Northwestern U., 1993—99, McCormick Tribune prof. of tech., 1999—, dir., ctr. for rsch. in tech. and innovation. Former adv. Govt. of Oman, U.S. Jordan Bus. Alliance; bd. dirs. Edmunds.com, Intelli-Seek, MarketRx, Confluent Surgical, Autodaq, ConvergeLabs, Instill Corp.; fellow World Economic Forum. Co-author: (books) The Seven Steps to Nirvana: Strategic Insights into eBusiness Transformation, Techventure: New Rules for Value and Profit from Silicon Valley, Kellogg on Technology & Innovation, author numerous jour. articles. Named one of 25 most influential people in e-business, Bus. Week, 40 under 40 bus. leaders, Crain's Chicago Bus. Office: Northwestern U Kellogg Sch of Mgmt Jacobs Ctr Rm 5245B 2001 Sheridan Rd Evanston IL 60208

**SAWICKI, ZBIGNIEW PETER,** lawyer; b. Hohenfels, Germany, Apr. 13, 1949; came to U.S., 1951; s. Witold and Marianna (Tukiendorf) S.; m. Katheryn Marie Loman, Aug. 19, 1972; children: James, Jeffrey, Jessica, Jason. BSChemE, Purdue U., 1972; MBA, Coll. St. Thomas, St. Paul, 1977; JD, Hamline U., 1980. Bar: Minn. 1980, U.S. Dist. Ct. Minn. 1981, U.S. Ct. Appeals (8th cir.) 1981, U.S. Patent and Trademark Office 1981, U.S. Ct. Appeals (fed. cir.) 1982, Can. Patent Office 1994, Can. Trademark Office 1995. Process engr. 3-M Co., St. Paul, 1973-75; process engring. supr. Conwed Corp., St. Paul, 1975-77; shareholder, bd. dirs. Kinney & Lange, Mpls., 1980—2003, Westman, Champlin & Kelley, 2003—. Bd. dirs. Orono (Minn.) Hockey Boosters, 1992—2000. With USAF, 1970-76. Mem. Am. Intellectual Property Assn., Internat. Trademark Assn., Minn. Intellectual Property Assn. (past treas.), Licensing Exec. Soc., The Federalist Soc., Am. Legion. Home: 4510 N Shore Dr Orono MN 55364-9602 Office: Westman Champlin & Kelly 900 2d Ave S Ste 1400 Minneapolis MN 55402-1624 Office Phone: 612-330-0581. Business E-Mail: psawicki@wck.com.

**SAWIN, NANCY CHURCHMAN,** educational consultant; b. Wilmington, Del., June 21, 1917; d. Sanford W. and Ellen (Quigley) S. BA, Principia Coll., 1938; MA, U. Del., 1940; EdD, U. Pa., 1962; PhD (hon.), Golden Beacom Coll., 1987. With Sanford Sch., Hockessin, Del., 1938-74, dean girls, 1945-62, head sch., 1962-74; coordinator student services U. Del. Div. Continuing Edn., Newark, 1974-77; ednl. cons. DuPont Co., ICI Ams., 1976-80. Chmn. Del. State Sci. Fair com., 1962; mem. com. Jr. Sci. and Humanities Symposium, 1962-76; mem. English, lang. arts adv. com. State Del., 1965-68; sec., dir. Recreation, Promotion and Service, Inc., 1963-74; mem. All-Am. Hockey Team, 1948-59. One-person shows include Ctr. for Creative Arts, 1993—, others; editor: The Eagle, 1961-62; co-pub., illustrator: Between the Bays, 1997, Delaware Sketchbook, 1976, Backroading Through Cecil County, 1977, Brick and Ballast, Canal Town Historic Chesapeake City, 1985; author, illustrator: Man-O-War My Island Home, 1978, Up the Spine and Down the Creek, 1982, Locks Traps and Corners, 1984, China Sketchbook, 1985, A Hockessin Diary, 1987, Privy to the Council, 1987, The Oulde King's Roade, 1989, North from Wilmington by Oulde Roads and Turnpikes, 1992, Once Upon a Time in the Country, 1994, Sketches of Early Delaware Main Streets, 1997, The Vanishing Countryside-Ghosts on the Landscape, 1998, Delaware USA - My hometown, 1999, Delaware Lacrosse Hall of Fame, 1999. Trustee Goldey Beacom Coll., pres., 1974-81, 97-98, mem. safety coun., 1964-74, trustee emeritus, 1999—; pres. Del. Sports Hall of Fame, 1982—; pres. bd. dirs. Del. Soc. for Preservation of Antiquities, 1986-88, chair, 1990—; chair fundraising com. Hockessin County Libr., 1989-94, chair fundraising com. for creative arts, 1997—; bd. dirs. Preservation Del., 1996—; trustee emeritus Sanford Sch., Hockessin, 1997—. 2d lt. CAP, 1942-45. Named to U.S. Field Hockey Hall of Fame (charter mem.), 1988, Del. Sports Hall of Fame, 1977, Hall of Fame of Del. Women, 1991, Wall of Fame, U. Del., 1991, Del. Lacrosse Hall of Fame, 1999, Nat. Mus. Women in the Arts (elected), 2001; recipient medal of merit, U. Del., 1989, History medal, DAR, Hist. Preservation award, New Castle County, 1996, Gold medal, Del. Sr. Olympic Swimming, 1994, 1995, 1996, 2 Gold medals, U.S. Sr. Olympics, 1997, 2000, Disting. Svc. award, Ctr. for Creative Arts, 1997, Pathfinder award, State of Del., Nat. Assn. Girls' and Women's Sports, 1998, She Knows Where She Is Going award, Girls Inc. of Del. and Wilmington Women in Bus., 1998, Sanford Sch. Alumni award, 2000. Mem. AARP, Headmistress Assn. East, Del. Art Mus., Rehoboth Art League, Middle Atlantic States Assn. Colls. and Secondary Schs. (past pres.), Commn. on Secondary Schs., Red Clay Creek Assn., Internat. Fedn. Women's Hockey Assns. (past pres.), U.S. Field Hockey Assn. (past pres., named to Sports Hall of Fame 1997), Int. Field Hockey Assn. (past pres.), Nat. League Am. Pen Women, DAR (History medal), Daus. of Founders and Patriots, Nat. Soc. New Eng. Women, Daus. Colonial Wars, Del. Greenbank Questars (pres. 1993-94), Hockessin Cmty. Club, Delta Kappa Gamma (past pres.), Pi Lambda Theta. Republican. Presbyterian (elder). Club: Quota (pres. Wilmington 1971-73, gov. 10th Dist. 1979-80). Home: PO Box 1228 Hockessin DE 19707-5228 Office Phone: 302-239-2416.

**SAWOROTNOW, PARFENY PAVLOVICH,** mathematician, educator; b. Ust Medveditskaya, Russia, Feb. 20, 1924; came to U.S., 1949, naturalized, 1965; s. Pavel Ivanovich and Anna Davidovna (Soloview) S.; student U. Graz (Austria), 1946-49; MA (Peirce scholar), Harvard U., 1951, PhD (Shattuck fellow), 1955. Teaching fellow Harvard U., 1953-54; instr. math. Cath. U. Am., Washington, 1954-57, asst. prof., 1957-62, assoc. prof., 1962-67, prof., 1967-96, prof. math. emeritus, 1997—. NSF grantee, 1967, 70; with Georgetown U. and George Washington U., 1971-77. Mem. Am. Math. Soc., Math. Assn. Am., Calcutta Math. Soc., N.Y. Acad. Scis., Sigma Xi. Mem. Eastern Orthodox Ch. Contbr. articles to and referred papers for math. rsch. jours. Home: 6 Avon Pl Hyattsville MD 20782-3328 Office: Cath U Am Dept Math 4th And Michigan Ave NE Washington DC 20064-0001

**SAWTELLE, CARL S.,** psychiatric social worker; b. Boston, July 14, 1927; s. Carl Salvador and Martha (Bellamacina) S.; BA, Suffolk U., Boston, 1951; MSW, Simmons Sch. Social Work, 1953; m. Thelma Florence Ramsay, Aug. 20, 1950; children: Tracy Lynn, Lisa June. Social worker Tewksbury (Mass.) State Hosp., 1952; psychiat. social worker, head psychiat. social worker, dir. clin. social work Taunton (Mass.) State Hosp., 1953-74; 1st dir. clin. social work Plymouth, Mass., 1974-78; co-founder, v.p. 1st legally established War On Poverty program Triumph, Inc., Taunton; co-founder 1st Greater Taunton Coun. on Alcoholism, 1972. With USCG, 1944-46. 1st lic. social worker in Mass., 1980. Mem. Nat. Assn. Social Workers co-founder Southeast Mass. chpt. 1957, pres. 1957, Spl. Mass. Chpt. award 1978), Acad. Cert. Social Workers (chmn. 1962-72), Am. Legion, Mass. Mental Health Social Workers Assn. (co-founder, pres. 1972-74, other offices). Created innovated programs, resources, opportunities, svcs. to state mental hosp. patients and their

families; mentor to young social workers; contbr. advancement of knowledge, practice quality and standards of psychiat. social work; father of licensing and registration of Social Workers in Mass. Home: 9 Tracywood Rd Canton MA 02021-3501

**SAWYER, CHARLES F.,** lawyer; b. 1956; Student, Northwestern Univ. Sch. Music, 1974—76; AB in Econ. with honors and high distinction, Univ. Mich., 1978; JD, Univ. Chgo., 1981. Bar: Minn. 1982. Law clerk, Hon. Charles L. Levin, 1981—82; assoc. Dorsey & Whitney LLP, Mpls., 1982—88, ptnr., corp. dept., 1989—, and co-chair, securitization group. Exec. editor Univ. Chgo. Law Rev., 1980—81. Office: Dorsey & Whitney LLP Ste 1500 50 S Sixth St Minneapolis MN 55402-1498 Office Phone: 612-343-7986. Office Fax: 612-340-8738. Business E-Mail: sawyer.charles@dorsey.com.

**SAWYER, DIANE (L. DIANE SAWYER),** newscaster, journalist; b. Glasgow, Ky., Dec. 22, 1945; d. E. P. and Jean W. (Dunagan) Sawyer; m. Mike Nichols, Apr. 29, 1988. BA, Wellesley Coll., 1967. Reporter Sta. WLKY-TV, Louisville, 1967—70; adminstr. press office White House, 1970—74; rschr. Richard Nixon's memoirs, 1974—78; gen. assignment reporter, then Dept. State corr. CBS News, 1978—81; co-anchor Morning News CBS, 1981—, co-anchor Early Morning News, 1982—84; corr., co-editor 60 Minutes CBS-TV, 1984—89; co-anchor PrimeTime Live (now known as PrimeTime Thursday) ABC News, 1989—; co-anchor Day One, 1995, Turning Point, 1996, Good Morning Am. ABC News, N.Y.C., 1999—. Co-recipient George B. Polk award for TV reporting, 2005; named one of 100 most powerful women, Forbes mag., 2005; named to TV Hall of Fame, 1997; recipient 2 Peabody awards for pub. svc., 1988, Robert F. Kennedy award, 13 Emmy awards, 2 Dupont awards (one Spl.), IRTS Lifetime Achievement award. Office: Good Morning America Fl 10 147 Columbus Ave New York NY 10023-5900*

**SAWYER, DOLORES,** motel chain executive; b. Shreveport, La., Oct. 16, 1938; d. Orlan B. Greer and Doris Lucile (Sanders) Eckman; m. Raymond Lee Sawyer Jr., June 11, 1960; children: Lisa Kay, Linda Faye. BSN, Northwestern State Coll., 1960; MSN, Tex. Woman's U., 1975. Supr. obstetrics dept. Highland Hosp., Shreveport, La., 1962-64; head nurse (3-11 shift) Scott and White Meml. Hosp., Temple, Tex., 1966-71, dir. of nursing edn., 1975-76; sch. nurse Temple Ind. Sch. Dist., 1971-72; instr. Mary-Hardin Baylor Coll., Belton, Tex., 1972-74; asst. prof., clin. specialist U. Tex. Arlington, 1976-86; v.p. Budget Host Internat., Arlington, Tex., 1986-96, sr. v.p., 1996—, also bd. dirs. Recipient Amoco Outstanding Tchg. award, 1981. Mem. Sigma Theta Tau. Republican. Methodist. Avocations: reading, tole painting, gardening, crafts, piano. Office: Budget Host Internat Ste B 2307 Roosevelt Dr Arlington TX 76016-5865 Office Phone: 817-861-6088. Personal E-mail: rsawyerl@airmail.net. Business E-Mail: dsawyer@budgethost.com.

**SAWYER, HARRIET BEHNER,** retired secondary school educator; b. Monroe, Mich., Feb. 21, 1942; d. Frederick G. Jr. and Wilma Eloise (Wymer) Behner; m. Robert Nute Sawyer, Jr., Feb. 6, 1965; children: Catherine Ann, Robert Frederick. ABA, Stephens Coll., Columbia, Mo., 1962; BA, Mich. State U., East Lansing, 1964; MAT in Reading, Oakland U., Rochester, Mich., 1981; Edn. Specialist, Wayne State U., Detroit, 1991, EdD, 2000. Cert. secondary tchr.; cert. adminstrv. bldg. and cen. office. Tchr. English and reading Jefferson Sch. Dist., Monroe, Mich., 1964-65; tchr. English and social studies Clarenceville Sch. Dist., Livonia, Mich., 1965-66; coord. statewide petition drive, scheduler Levin for Gov. Campaign, Detroit, 1978; tchr. English, social sci., reading Adult and Community Edn., Wayne-Westland Community Schs., Westland, Mich., 1979-85; instr. English Schoolcraft Community Coll., Livonia, 1983-85; tchr. English St. Mary's of Redford High Sch., Detroit, 1985-87; learning specialist Livonia Pub. Schs., 1987-89; tchr. mid. sch. English and social studies Holmes Middle Sch., Livonia, 1989-91; tchr., dept. chair social studies Franklin High Sch., Livonia, 1992—2005; ret. Mem. suicide crisis prevention teams Livonia Schs., 1988-2005; mem. secondary content list. com., conf. com. State Bd. Edn., 1989-94; bd. dirs. Found. for Ednl. Opportunities Wayne County Regional Ednl. Svc. Agy.; mem. edn. legis. adv. com. State Bd. Edn., Lansing, Mich., 1986-88, Mich. Edn. Forum, Lansing, 1983-85. Precinct del. Dem. party, Northville, Mich., 1986-90; pres., sec. Berkley Bd. Edn., Mich., 1973-79; mem., treas. Oakland Sch. Bd. Assn., Oakland County, Mich., 1975-78; candidate selection com. U.S. Mil. Acads., Royal Oak, Mich., 1977; state chair Mich. ERAmerica, 1988-92; selection com. Mich. Women's Hall of Fame, 1983, 90. Mem. AAUW (state pres. 1983-85, regional conf. com. 1984, nat. bylaws com. 1981-83, grantee 1982, Outstanding Woman Mich. 1979, Liz Kummer award 1993), ASCD, Internat. Reading Assn., Mich. Reading Assn. (secondary rep., region 8 rep., MRA/IRA coord., conf. presenter), Wayne County Reading Coun. (pres., pres.-elect), Mich. Secondary Reading Interest Coun. (sec., membership chmn., bylaws chmn., v.p., pres.). Democrat. Presbyterian. Home: 39679 Dun Rovin Dr Northville MI 48168-4302

**SAWYER, HOWARD JEROME,** physician; s. Howard C. and Dorothy M. (Risley) S.; m. Janet Carol Hausen, July 24, 1954; children: Daniel William, Teresa Louise BA in Philosophy, Wayne State U., Detroit, 1952, MD, 1962, postdoctoral, 1969-72. Diplomate Am. Bd. Preventive Medicine in Occupational and Environ. Medicine. Intern William Beaumont Hosp., Royal Oak, Mich., 1962-63, resident in surgery, 1963-64; chief physician gen. parts div. Ford Motor Co., 1964-66; med. dir. metall. products dept. Gen. Electric Co., Detroit, 1966-73, chem. and metal div., 1972-73; staff physician Detroit Indsl. Clinic, Inc., 1973-74; pres., med. dir. OccuMed Assocs., Inc., Farmington Hills, Mich., 1974-84; dir. OccuMed div. Med. Service Corp. Am., Southfield, Mich., 1984-86; dir. occupational, environ. and preventive medicine Henry Ford Hosp., 1987-91; pres. Sawyer Med. Cons., P.C., 1991— Adj. asst. prof. occupational and environ. health sci. Wayne State U., 1974—, lectr. occpl. and environ. medicine Sch. of Medicine, 1998—; lectr. Sch. Pub. Health, U. Mich., Ann Arbor, 1977-88; cons. med. dir. St. Joe Minerals Corp., 1976-87, Chesbrough Pond's Inc., 1979-83; cons. Anaconda, Bendix, Borg Warner Chems., Fed. Mogul, Gen. Electric, Gt. Lakes Chems., other corps. Contbr. articles to profl. jours., chpts. to textbooks. Fellow Am. Coll. Preventive Medicine, Am. Occupational and Environ. Med. Assn., Mich. Occupational and Environ. Med. Assn. (pres. 1986), Am. Acad. Occupational Medicine; mem. AMA, Detroit Occupational Physicians Assn. (pres. 1984), Mich. State Med. Soc., Oakland County Med. Soc., Am. Indsl. Hygiene Assn., Mich. Indsl. Hygiene Soc. Office: Sawyer Med Cons PC 7072 Edinborough Dr West Bloomfield MI 48322-4025 Office Phone: 248-626-8061. Personal E-Mail: buzsaw@comcast.net.

**SAWYER, JAMES S.,** manufacturing executive; BS in Geology, Wesleyan U.; MBA, MIT. V.p. Praxair, treasurer, 1992—2000, CFO, 2000—. Office: Praxair 39 Old Ridgebury Rd Danbury CT 06810-5113

**SAWYER, JAY M.,** theater educator; s. Even Jones and Eula Van Sawyer; m. Liana Burch, May 23, 1998; children: Katherine Burch, Jayson, Noah. AA, Coll. of the Mainland, Texas City, Tex., 1979; MusB, East Tex. Bapt. Coll., Marshall, 1982; M of Arts in Comm, Southwestern Bapt. Theol. Sem., Ft. Worth, 1988; MFA, Tex. Tech., Lubbock, 1999. Assoc. prof. theatre Wayland Bapt. U., Plainview, Tex., 1990—2002, Sul Ross State U., Alpine, Tex., 2002—. Mem.: SW Tex. Theatre and Film Assn., Tex. Ednl. Theatre Assn., US Inst. Theatre Tech., Alpha Psi Omega. Home: 302 E June Ave Alpine TX 79830 Office: Sul Ross State Univ East Hwy 90 Alpine TX 79832 Office Phone: 432-837-8376. Business E-Mail: jsawyer@sulross.edu.

**SAWYER, JOHN EDWARD,** management educator; b. Florence, Ariz., July 26, 1954; s. Almus Wilmore and Betty (Mossman) S.; m. Dana Lee Strandberg, Aug. 5, 1989; children: Adrian John, Alexander Lyn, Jordan Estelle. BA in Psychology, Calif. State U., Long Beach, 1977; MA in Counseling Edn., Calif. State U., Fresno, 1979; AM in Indsl./Orgnl. Psychology, U. Ill., 1985, PhD of Indsl./Orgnl. Psychology, 1987. Project dir. Youth Svc. Bur., Modesto, Calif., 1979-81; counselor Horizons Youth Svc. Bur.,

Livermore, Calif., 1981-82; lectr., tchg. asst. U. Ill., Urbana, 1982-87; asst. prof. Tex. A&M U., College Station, 1987-91; asst. prof. mgmt. U. Del., Newark, 1991-95, assoc. prof., 1995—2003, mgmt. area head, 1998—2001, chair dept. bus. adminstrn., 2001—, prof., 2003—. Human resources rschr. Xerox Corp., Rochester, N.Y., 1985-86; orgnl. cons. Mercy Hosp., Urbana, 1983, Tex. Dept. Mental Health, San Antonio, 1989-90; trainer, cons. DuPont Merck Pharm. Co., Wilmington, 1994, Hercules, Wilmington, 1996. Mem. editl. bd. Jour. Mgmt., Jour. Behavioral Decision Making; contbr. chpt. in book and articles to profl. jours. Grantee Tex. Engring. Experiment Sta., 1989, Tex. Higher Edn. Coordinating Bd., 1990, Gen. Univ. Rsch. Program, 1993, Ctr. for Info. Sys. Mgmt. Edn. and Rsch., 1994, NSF-IOC, 2004. Mem. APA, Acad. Mgmt. (invited guest editl. bd.), Judgment and Decision Making Soc., Soc. Indsl. and Orgnl. Psychology. Home: 214 Cullen Way Newark DE 19711-6112 Office: Univ Delaware Dept Bus Adm Newark DE 19716 Office Phone: 302-831-1787. Business E-Mail: sawyerj@lerner.udel.edu.

**SAWYER, JOHN WESLEY,** retired mathematics and computer science educator, consultant; b. Nov. 2, 1917; s. Joseph Edmond and Inez Avent Sawyer; m. Edna Matthews, Aug. 31, 1939 (dec. Jan. 31, 2002); 1 child, John Wesley Jr. BA, Wake Forest Coll., 1938, MA, 1941, U. Mo., 1948, PhD, 1951. Instr. math. U. Mo., Columbia, 1946—51; assoc. prof. math. Ga. State U., Atlanta, 1951—53, U. Richmond, Va., 1953—56; prof. computer sci. Wake Forest U., Winston-Salem, NC, 1956—88, emeritus prof. computer sci., 1988—. In-house cons. R. J. Reynolds Tobacco Co., Winston-Salem, 1958—86. Contbr. (book) Operations Research Tools for Systems Engineering, articles to profl. jours. Wake Forest Bapt. Ch., Winston-Salem, 1964—89; bd. dirs. Salemtowne Retirement Cmty., Winston-Salem, 1999—2004; pres. (4 terms) Atlantic Coast Conf., Greensboro, NC, 1964—86; v.p. NCAA, Kansas City, Mo., 1980—84. Named Tar Heel of Week, Raleigh (N.C.) News & Observer, 1977; grantee NSF, 1960. Fellow: AAAS (life); mem.: Math. Assn. Am., Ops. Rsch. Soc. Am. Achievements include development of computer simulations for business and manufacturing operations; creation and development of computer science department at Wake Forest University. Home: 6113 Salemtowne Dr Winston Salem NC 27106-3497

**SAWYER, LINDA,** advertising executive; married; 2 children. Avrett, Free & Ginsberg; SSC& B; Ted Bates Worldwide NYC; Goldberg Marchesano Washington; exec. v.p., group acct. dir. Deutsch, Inc., NYC, gen. mgr., 1997—2001; mng. ptnr., COO Interpublic Group Deutsch, Inc., NYC, 2001—. Bd. dir. Advt. Ednl. Found. Named one of Women to Watch, Advt. Age Mag., 2002. Office: Deutsch Inc 111 Eighth Ave New York NY 10011

**SAWYER, MALCOLM JAMES, JR.,** religious studies educator; b. Farmington, Maine, Oct. 31, 1951; s. Malcolm James and Bertha Brindley Sawyer; m. Kay Lynn Fuqua, Dec. 15, 1973; children: James Daniel, Jonathan David, Joel Nathaniel, Joshua William. BA, Biola U., 1973; ThM, Dallas Theol. Sem., 1978, PhD, 1987. Asst. prof. Simpson Coll., San Francisco, 1984—89; prof. Western Sem., Los Gatos, Calif., 1989—. Bd. mem. Bay Cities Bible Inst., Oakland, Calif., 1995—97; mem. adv. bd. Christian Counseling Internat., Scott's Valley, Calif., 1999—2002. Author: Charles Augusts Briggs and Tensions in Late Nineteenth Century America Theology, 1994, Taxonomic Charts on Biblical and Theological Studies, 1999; contbr. articles to profl. jours.; co-editor Who's Afraid of the Holy Spirit?, 2005. Fellow, Christus Nexus, 2005—. Mem.: Am. Acad. Religion, Soc. for Bibl. Lit., Evang. Theol. Soc. (far west pres. 2001—02). Home: 16485 Severn Rd San Leandro CA 94578 Office: Western Seminary 16330 Los Gatos Blvd Los Gatos CA 95032 Office Phone: 510-329-5643.

**SAWYER, MARGO LUCY,** artist, educator; b. Washington, May 6, 1958; d. Eugene Douglas and Joan Imogen (Alford) S. BA hons., Chelsea Sch. Art, London, 1980; MFA, Yale U., 1982. Prof. U. Tex., Austin, 1988—. Vis. artist Chelsea Sch. Art, London, 1982—. One-person shows include Brit. Coun., Bombay, India, 1983, Barbara Toll Fine Arts, N.Y.C., 1989, 91, Sagacho Exhibit Space, Tokyo, 1996, Gallery Gallery, Kyoto, Japan, 1996, Internat. House of Japan, Tokyo, 1996, Austin (Tex.) Mus. Art, 1998, Artplace, 2000, Mattress Factory, Pitts., 2003, Blatter Gallery, Houston, 2004, others; group shows include Whitechapel Gallery, London, 1979, ICA, London, 1979, 80, Leo Castelli Gallery, N.Y.C., 1986, Portland (Maine) Mus. Art, 1987, U. Md. Art Gallery, Balt., 1988, Meyers/Bloom Gallery, Santa Monica, Calif., 1989, Archer M. Huntington Art Gallery, Austin, Tex., 1990, 91, 92, 93, 94, Harn Mus. Art, Gainesville, Fla., 1992, Laguna Gloria Art Mus., Austin, 1994, Abilene (Tex.) Outdoor Sculpture exhbn., 1995-96, Artspace A Found. for Contemporary Art, 2000, Finesilver Gallery, San Antonio, 2002; permanent collections include Hyde Park, London, Cityarts Workshop, Portland Mus. Art, Samuel O. Harn Mus. Art, U. Fla., Prudential Ins., Chem. Bank, Champion Paper, and various pvt. collections. Recipient Louis Comfort Tiffany Found. award, 2001; Am. Acad. Rome fellow, 1986-87, Japan Found. visual arts fellow, 1996; Travel grantee Ford Found., 1981, Fulbright rsch. grantee, India, 1982-83, Japan, 1995-96, N.Y. State Coun. on Arts grantee, 1987, Travel grantee NEA, 1994. Office: U Tex Dept Art and Art History Austin TX 78712-1104

**SAWYER, MELVIN WAYNE,** psychologist; b. Rock Springs, Wyo., Sept. 24, 1933; m. Sylvia Sawyer. BA, Brigham Young U., 1959, PhD, 1975. Lic. psychologist Utah, 1986. Probation officer Orange County, Calif., 1960—66; med. adminstr., acting supr. mobile counseling, sr. counselor Thiokol Chem., Clearfield (Utah) Job Corps, 1966—68; psychologist Utah State Hosp., Provo, 1968—. Psychol. examiner, instr. Brigham Young U., Provo, 1969—72; dist. dir. State of Utah Juvenile Ct., Provo, 1972—81; program dir., coord. adolescent unit, assessment therapist Charter Canyon Hosp., Provo Charter Canyon Sch, 1981—88; psychologist State of Utah, Edwin Rollins, svc., Salt Lake City, 1989. Bishop Brigham Young U. student ward LDS Ch., Provo, 2003—05. With USAR, 1954. Mem.: APA (assoc.). R-Consevative. Mem. Lds Chj. Avocations: fishing, basketball, travel. Home: 709 E 60 N Orem UT 84097 Office: Utah State Hosp 1300 E Center St Provo UT 84603 Office Phone: 801-344-4415.

**SAWYER, MILDRED CLEMENTINA,** retired real estate agent; b. Boston, Nov. 19, 1928; d. Joseph Felix and Assunta (Malone) Volpe; m. Frederick Myles Sawyer, June 15, 1957 (dec. Jan. 1995); children: Frederick G., Bernard G. Grad. h.s., Brockton, Mass. Clk. Prudential Ins. Co., Brockton, Mass., 1947-57, Clark Bros., Brockton, 1957-58; typist NJ, 1958-87, RI, 1958—87; real estate sales rep. JLC & Home Realty, Chepachet, No. Scituate, 1984-97; ins. sales agt. Mass. Indemnity Life Ins. Co., Cranston, RI, 1984-89; security sales rep. First Am. Nat. Securities, Cranston, 1986-89; ret., 1995. Author: A Lifetime of Hints for Everyday Living, 1996, The Path Into Vietnam: An Historical Reflection, 2002; author numerous poems. Sec. Cold Springs Harbor Heights Civic Assn., Huntington, LI, NY, 1961-63; Save All Foster's Environ., Foster, RI, 1969-83; Students for a Dem. Soc., Warwick, 1970-72; mem. RI Coun. for the Humanities. Mem. Soc. Children's Book Writers and Illustrators, Union Concerned Scientists, Noetic Sci. Avocations: reading, exercising, gardening, cooking, sewing. Home: 49A Mount Hygeia Rd Foster RI 02825-1923

**SAWYER, NELSON BALDWIN, JR.,** credit union executive; b. Jacksonville, Fla., Nov. 11, 1948; s. Nelson Baldwin and Nancy (Watson) S.; m. Carla Lee Dowden, Aug. 9, 1986. BA, U. North Fla., 1974. Program cons. State of Fla., Jacksonville, 1974-81; product mgr. Qualified Plan Designs, Inc., Jacksonville, 1981-83, Associated Gen. Contractors, Jacksonville, 1983-86; membership mgr. Calif. Credit Union League, Pomona, 1986-87, comm. mgr., 1987-90; sr. v.p., COO Calif. League Svcs. Corp., Pomona, 1990-93; sr. v.p. Wescorp, San Dimas, Calif., 1994-97; v.p. Travis Fed. Credit Union, Vacaville, Calif., 1997-2000; pres., CEO Chevron Valley Credit Union, Bakersfield, Calif., 2000—. Chmn. bd. dirs. Calif. Credit Union, 1996-97, Product Rsch. Orgn. for Credit Unions. Bd. dirs. Jacksonville. of C., 1983-84, Taft Coll. Found., 2001—; bd. dirs. Am. Heart Assn., Bakersfield, 2002—, chmn., 2005-06; mem. assembly of dels. Calif. Credit Union League, 2002-04. Mem. U.S. Jaycees (pres. Jacksonville 1983-84, chmn. bd. 1984-85,

U.S. senator 1984—, internat. senator 1984—, Outstanding Young Man of Am. 1983), Rotary Club of Bakersfield, Fla. Yacht Club. Republican. Episcopalian. Office: Chevron Valley Credit Union 8200 Granite Falls Dr Bakersfield CA 93312-5592

**SAWYER, RAYMOND TERRY,** lawyer, consultant, theater producer; b. Cleve., Oct. 1, 1943; s. R. Terry and Fanny Katherine (Young) S.; m. Katherine Margaret Schneider, Aug. 5, 1972; children: Margaret Young, John Terry. BA, Yale U., 1965; LLB, Harvard U., 1968. Bar: Ohio 1969, U.S. Dist. Ct. (no. dist.) Ohio 1970, prin., Sawyer LLC, 2002-. Assoc. Thompson Hine LLP, Cleve., 1968-76, ptnr., 1976—83, 1986—2001, chmn. bus. transactions and org. dept., 1998—2001; exec. dir. Ohio Housing Fin. Agy., Columbus, 1983-84; counsel to gov. State of Ohio, Columbus, 1984, chief of staff, 1985-86, chmn. Gov.'s commn. on housing, 1989-90; prin. Sawyer LLC, Cleve., 2002—. Bd. dirs. Premix, Inc., North Kingsville, Ohio. Assoc. prodr.: Frankie and Johnny in the Clair de Lune, 2002—03 (Tony award nomination for best revival of a play); Match, 2004. Vol. VISTA, East Palo Alto, Calif., 1968—69; mem. Tech. Leadership Coun., 1987—95, Leadership Cleve., 1986—87, Cleve. Found. Study Commn. on Med. Rsch. Edn., 1991—92, George W. Codrington Charitable Found., 1989—, chmn., 1989—2003; mem. Ohio Bd. Regents, Columbus, 1987—96, chmn., 1992—93; trustee Cleve. Ballet, 1987—2000, Cleve. Orch., 1993—, sec., exec. com., 1997—; mem. exec. com. MetroHealth Sys., 1998—; mem. Juilliard Coun. Juilliard Sch.; mem. pres.'s adv. coun. Case Western Res. U. Named Man of Yr. Womanspace, 1982. Mem. Ohio State Bar Assn. (chair corp. law com. 1993-95), Yale U. Alumni Assn. (pres. Cleve. chpt. 1980-81), Yale Alumni (del. 1996-99). Democrat. Presbyterian. Office: Sawyer LLC 3900 Key Ctr Cleveland OH 44114-1291 Office Phone: 216-566-5837.

**SAWYER, ROBERT MCLARAN,** historian, educator; b. St. Louis, Nov. 12, 1929; s. Lee McLaran and Harrie (Alcock) S.; m. Patricia Ann Covert, Nov. 23, 1955; children— Ann Marie, Lee McLaran, Gail Louise. BS, S.E. Mo. State Coll., 1952; MA, U. Ill., 1953; PhD, U. Mo., 1966. Tchr. Rolla (Mo.) Public Schs., 1955; asst. prof., then asso. prof. history U. Mo., Rolla., 1956-67; mem. faculty U. Nebr., Lincoln, 1967—, prof. history of edn., 1969—, chmn. dept. history and philosophy of edn., 1975-81; mem. council U. Nebr. (Coll. Arts and Scis.), 1979—. Vis. prof. Ark. State U., Jonesboro, 1966; proposal reviewer Nat. Endowment Humanities, 1979 Author: The History of the University of Nebraska, 1929-1969, 1973, The Many Faces of Teaching, 1987, The Art and Politics of College Teaching, 1992, The Black Student's Guide to College Success, 1993, The Handbook of College Teaching, 1994; contbr. articles to profl. jours. With AUS, 1953—55. Mem. Orgn. Am. Historians, History Edn. Soc., Am. Ednl. Studies Assn., Soc. Profs. Edn., Phi Alpha Theta, Phi Delta Kappa. Home: 2640 S 35th St Lincoln NE 68506-6623 Office: Univ Nebr 29 Henzlik Hall Lincoln NE 68588 Business E-Mail: rsawyer1@unl.edu.

**SAWYER, THOMAS EDGAR,** management consultant; b. Homer, La., July 7, 1932; s. Sidney Edgar and Ruth (Bickham) S.; m. Joyce Mezzanatto, Aug. 22, 1954; children: Jeffrey T., Scott A., Robert J., Julie Anne. BS, UCLA, 1959; MA, Occidental Coll., 1969; PhD, Walden U., 1990. Project engr. Garrett Corp., LA, 1954-60; mgr. devel. ops. TRW Systems, Redondo Beach, Calif., 1960-66; spl. asst. to gov. State of Calif., Sacramento, 1967-69; prin., gen. mgr. Planning Rsch. Corp., McLean, Va., 1969-72; dep. dir. OEO, Washington, 1972-74; assoc. prof. bus. mgmt. Brigham Young U., 1974-78; pres., chmn. bd. Mesa Corp., Provo, Utah, 1978-82; pres., dir. Sage Inst. Internat., Inc., Provo, 1982-88; chmn. bd., CEO Pvt. Telecom. Networks, Inc. (name changed to Nat. Applied Computer Techs, Inc.), Orem, Utah, 1988-98; chief tech. officer GST Telecom. (formerly Greenstar Telecom., Inc.), San Francisco, 1993-98, also bd. dirs. Vancouver, Wash., 1995-98; chmn. bd. NeTrue Comm., Inc., Fullerton, Calif., 1998—2002; chmn. bd., CEO Telecom, Inc., Salt Lake City, 2002—; sr. dir. Econ. Rsch. Inst., MMG Holdings, Tokyo, 2003—; consul gen. for Republic of Liberia Monrovia, 2004—; dir. ops. First European Investment Found., Fruitland Park, Fla., 2004—. Bd. dirs. Intechna Corp., HighTech Corp., Indian Affiliates, Inc., Greenstar USA, Inc., San Francisco, 1994-98, GST Global Comm., Inc., Vancouver, Can., 1998-2002, Highpoint Telecom., Inc., Vancouver, 1998-01, World Wide Wireless Comm., Inc., Salt Lake City, 1998-2000, Columbia Hosp., Orem, 1998-05; sr. dir. Econ. Rsch. Inst., AIM Holdings, Ltd., Tokyo, 2003-; consul gen. for Republic of Liberia, Monrovia, 2004—. Author: Assimilation Versus Self-Identity: A Modern Native American Perspective, 1976, The Promise of Funding a New Educational Initiative Using the Microcomputer, 1988, Computer Assisted Instruction: An Inevitable Breakthrough, Current Challenges of Welfare: A Review of Public Assistance as Distributive Justice, 1989, New Software Models for Training and Education Delivery, 1989, New Organizations: How They Deviate from Classical Models, 1989, Increasing Productivity in Organizations: The Paradox, 1989, An Introduction and Assessment of Strategic Decision Making Paradigms in Complex Organizations, 1989, The Future of Technology in Education, 1989, Impact of Failure by Senior Executives to Receive Accurate Critical Feedback on Pervasive Change, 1990, The Influence of Critical Feedback and Organizational Climate on Managerial Decision Making, 1990. Chmn. Nat. Adv. Coun. Indian Affairs, Utah State Bd. Indian Affairs, So. Paiute Restoration Com., Utah Cmty. Mediation Ctrs., 2002-05; trustee Utah Valley State Coll., Orem, 2000-05, Coll. Ea. Utah, Price, 2001—; mem. Utah Dist. Export Coun., Utah dist. SBA Coun.; mem. adv. coun. Nat. Bus. Assn.; mem. Utah Job Tng. Coordinating Coun. Served with USMC, 1950-53. Mem. ASPA, Am. Mgmt. Assn., Utah Coun. Small Bus. (dir.), Utah State Hist. Soc. (bd. dirs. 1993-99), Masons. Republican. Mem. Lds Ch. Home: 548 W 630 S Orem UT 84058-6154 Office Phone: 801-944-4090. Business E-Mail: tesawyer@tesawyer.com.

**SAWYER, TONI,** actress; d. Howard White and Alice Prince (Woodruff) Smith; m. Arleigh Curtis Sawyer, Aug. 9, 1952 (dec.); children: A. Curtis, Roland Woodruff. Degree, Vermont Coll., 1949, Coll. of Marin, 1969, Am. Conservatory Theatre, 1974. Tchr. Springfield Day Nursery, Mass., 1949—52; publicist Actors' Enterprise Theatre, San Francisco, 1972—73, LA Actors' Theatre, 1977—79. Prodr. LA Actor's Theatre, 1977; prodr., dir. Ensemble Studio Theatre, 1987; casting com. SAG, 1987—91. Actor: (films) Goodbye, Norma Jean, 1976, Hughes & Harlow, 1977, (film, with Cher) Mask, 1985, (film with Jessica Lange) Sweet Dreams, 1985, (film with George Burns) 18 Again!, 1988, (film with Jim Carey) High Strung, 1991, (film with Nicole Kidman) My Life, 1993; (films) The Thirteenth Floor, 1999, Wildly Available, 1999, The Sky is Falling, 2000, numerous TV appearances, numerous stage prodns. Founder, pres. Zero Population Growth, Marin County, Calif., 1970—71; mem. Eco Earth Commn., LA, 1984—90, Women in Film, LA, 1985—95; Ovation Awards voter LA Stage Alliance, 2004—07. Recipient Outstanding Cooperation award, Coll. of Marin, Drama Dept., 1967—68, Outstanding Achievement in Theatre award, Drama-Logue Critics, 1991. Mem.: Film Ind., Colony Theatre. Office: c/o Schiowitz Connorz Ankrum Wolf 1680 N Vine St Ste 1016 Los Angeles CA 90028

**SAWYER, WILLIAM C.,** lawyer; b. Bangor, Maine, Aug. 26, 1929; s. Frank S. and Linda M. (Makanna) S.; m. Mary A. Eaton (div.); m. Joan N. Gardner; children: William D., Constance, Faith. AB cum laude, Harvard Coll., 1951, JD, 1954. Bar: Mass., U.S. Dist. Ct. Mass., U.S. Ct. Mil. Appeals, U.S. Supreme Ct. Assoc. Palmer & Dodge, Boston, 1958-61; ptnr. Sawyer, Burlingham, Tucker & Salloway, Boston, 1961-85, Dicara, Selig, Sawyer & Holt, Boston, 1985-90, Clarkin, Sawyer & Phillips, P.C., Boston, 1990—. Bd. dirs. Jones & Vining, Inc., Ayer Sales, Inc., others. Contbr. articles to profl. jours. Bd. trustees Mass. Conv. Ctr. Authority, 1991-97; pres., treas., chmn. Metro. Area Planning Coun., 1975-87; pres. Mass. Regional Planning Agys., 1980, 87; bd. dirs. Nat. Assn. Regional Couns., 1980-86; mem. Mass. Selectman's Assn., 1975—; bd. selectman Town of Action, 1967-75, chmn., 1969, 75; Rep. candidate Mass. Atty. Gen., 1990; pres. New Eng. Rep. Coun.; mem. Rep. State Com.; Rep. candidate Congress, 5th Congl. Dist., Mass., 1980. 1st lt. U.S. Army, 1955. Recipient Regional Leadership award Planning

Commns. and Couns. New Eng., 1987, and others. Mem. ABA, Mass. Bar Assn., Boston Bar Assn. Avocations: golf, painting, reading. Office: Clarkin Sawyer & Phillips PC 1 Center Plz Ste 240 Boston MA 02108-1801 Office Phone: 617-742-2525.

**SAWYER, WILLIAM DALE,** internist, educator, dean, foundation administrator; b. Roodhouse, Ill., Dec. 28, 1929; s. Cloyd Howard and Eva Collier (Dale) S.; m. Jane Ann Stewart, Aug. 25, 1951; children: Dale Stewart, Carole Ann. Student, U. Ill., 1947-50; MD cum laude, Washington U., St. Louis, 1954; ScD (hon.), Mahidol U., Bangkok, 1988; DPH (hon.), Chiang Mai U., Thailand, 1993, Chulalongkorn U., 1998. Intern Washington U.-Barnes Hosp., 1954-55, resident, 1957-58, fellow, 1958-60; asst. prof. microbiology Johns Hopkins U., Balt., 1964-67; prof., chmn. dept. microbiology Rockefeller Found.-Mahidol U., Bangkok, 1967-73, Ind. U. Sch. Medicine, Indpls., 1973-80; prof. depts. medicine, microbiology and immunology Wright State U., Dayton, Ohio, 1981-87, dean Sch. Medicine, 1981-87; pres. China Med. Bd. N.Y., Inc., 1987-97. Adj. prof. biology Ball State U., Muncie, Ind., 1978-80; hon. prof. microbiology Sun Yat Sen U. Med. Sci., 1987; hon. prof. Peking Union Med. Coll., 1989; hon. advisor Beijing Med. U.; cons. U.S. Army Med. R & D Command, WHO Immunology Ctr., Singapore, 1969-73; mem. bd. sci. advisers Armed Forces Inst. Pathology, 1975-80, chmn., 1979-80; adj. prof. medicine and microbiology and immunology N.Y. Med. Coll., Valhalla, 1990-96; hon. prof. China Med. U., 1995, West China U. Med. Sci., 1995, Zhejiang Med. U., 1995, Jiujang Med. Coll., 1995, Hunan Med. U., 1996, Xian Med. U., 1996, Shanghai Med. U., 1996. Contbr. numerous articles to profl. jours. Mem. Lobund adv. bd. U. Notre Dame; dir. Georgetown Area Cmty. Found., 1998-2002, pres. 1999; mem. exec. com. Georgetown Cmty. Resource Ctr., 2000-03. Served to maj. M.C., USA, 1955-64. Recipient Gold medal of merit Airlangga U., Indonesia, 1992, Pub. Health Recognition award Asia-Pacific Acad. Consortium Pub. Health, 1993, China Health medal, 1996, White Magnolia award, 1996. Fellow ACP; mem. AAAS, Am. Soc. Microbiology (br. pres. 1976), Sci. Rsch. Soc. Am., Am. Fedn. Clin. Rsch., Ctrl. Soc. Clin. Rsch., Infectious Diseases Soc. Am., Soc. Exptl. Biology and Medicine, Am. Acad. Microbiology, Am. Assn. Pathologists, Assn. Am. Med. Colls. (coun. deans 1980-87), Phi Beta Kappa, Sigma Xi, Alpha Omega Alpha. Home: The Summit #313 1034 Liberty Pk Dr Austin TX 78746 E-mail: wllmsawyer@aol.com.

**SAWYERS, AL BAKER,** lawyer; b. Nashville, Sept. 10, 1960; s. John Lazelle and Julia (Edwards) S.; m. Ikee Iekyung Junn, June 17, 1989. BA magna cum laude, Vanderbilt U., 1982; JD, MBA, U. Chgo., 1986. Bar: Ariz. 1986, U.S. Dist. Ct. Dist. Ariz. 1986, Tenn 1987, Ill. 1987, N.Y. 1995. Atty. Snell & Wilner, Phoenix, 1986—87, Chapman & Cutler, Phoenix, 1987—94; ptnr. Orrick Herrington & Sutcliffe LLP, N.Y.C., 1994—. Mem.: N.Y. State Bar Assn., Ariz. Bar Assn., Ill. Bar Assn., Tenn. Bar Assn. Office: Orrick Herrington & Sutcliffe LLP 666 Fifth Ave New York NY 10103 Office Phone: 212-506-5041. Business E-Mail: absawyers@orrick.com.

**SAWYERS, ELIZABETH JOAN,** librarian, director; b. San Diego, Dec. 2, 1936; d. William Henry and Elizabeth Georgiana (Price) S. AA, Glendale Jr. Coll., 1957; BA in Bacteriology, UCLA, 1959, M.L.S., 1961. Asst. head acquisition sect. Nat. Library Medicine, Bethesda, Md., 1962-63, head acquisition sect., 1963-66, spl. asst. to chief tech. services div., 1966-69, spl. asst. to assoc. dir. for library ops., 1969-73; asst. dir. libraries for tech. services SUNY-Stony Brook, 1973-75; dir. Health Scis. Library Ohio State U., Columbus, 1975-90, spl. asst. to dir. Univ. librs., 1990—. Mem. Assn. Acad. Health Scis. Library Dirs. (sec./treas. 1981-83, pres. 1983-84), Med. Library Assn., Am. Soc. for Info. Sci., Spl. Libraries Assn., ALA Office: Ohio State Univ Librs 1858 Neil Ave Columbus OH 43210-1225 Office Phone: 614-292-4491. E-mail: sawyers.l@osu.edu.

**SAWYIER, MICHAEL TOD,** lawyer; b. Boston, Jan. 6, 1948; s. Calvin Parker and Fay (Horton) S.; m. Judith Puistonen, June 6, 1968; children: Julianne Patricia, Justine Fay, Alexandra Lee, Sydney Anne Helena. BA, Harvard U., 1969; JD, U. Chgo., 1972; LLM, Yale U., 1973, LLM (Tax) John Marshall Law Sch., 2001. Bar: Ill. 1972, D.C. 1974, Calif. 1976, Ind. 1983, Tex. 1989, U.S. Dist. Ct. (no. dist.) Ill. 1979, U.S. Ct. Appeals (7th cir.) 1981, U.S. Dist. Ct. (no. and so. dists.) Ind. 1983, U.S. Supreme Ct. 1984. Atty.-adviser Office of Legal Adviser U.S. Dept. State, Washington, 1974-75; assoc. Pillsbury, Madison and Sutro, San Francisco, 1975-77, Baker and McKenzie, Chgo., 1977-79, Foss, Schuman, Drake & Barnard, Chgo., 1979-87; ptnr. Mathewson, Hamblet & Casey, Chgo., 1987-89; ptnr. Sawyier and Stewart, Chgo., 1989-93, Watt and Sawyier, Chgo., 1993-2002; prin. Law Offices Michael T. Sawyier, 2002-2005. Dir. Ct. Theatre, Chgo., 1989-. Recipient Paul Cornell prize Hyde Park Hist. Soc., Chgo., 1982. Mem. ABA, Ill. Bar Assn., Chgo. Bar Assn., Ind. Bar Assn., Tex. Bar Assn., Am. Soc. Internat. Law., Chgo. Rotary Club, Saddle and Cycle Club, Chgo. Club. Home: 424 W Melrose St Apt 15A Chicago IL 60657-3862 Office: 150 N Michigan Ste 2700 Chicago IL 60601-3713 Office Phone: 312-856-9741. Business E-Mail: mtsawyier@estateplanningattorneychicago.com.

**SAX, DANIEL SAUL,** neurologist, educator; b. Balt., Jan. 27, 1935; s. Benjamin and Miriam (Helfgott) S.; m. Joan Atherton Bond, Mar. 25, 1962; children: Karen Bond, John Derek, Diana Atherton. AB, Johns Hopkins U., 1955; MD, U. Md., 1959. Diplomate Am. Bd. Psychiatry and Neurology. Intern Boston City Hosp., 1959—60, resident in neurology and neuropathology neurologic unit, 1961—64; resident in neurology N.E. Med. Ctr., Boston, 1961; asst. prof. neurology Northwestern U., Chgo., 1966-67; assoc. prof. neurology Albert Einstein Med. Sch., N.Y.C., 1967-69, Boston U. Sch. Med., 1969-76, prof. neurology, 1976-2000, prof. emeritus neurology, 2000—. Chief neurology svcs. Boston VA Outpatient Clinic, 1974-90; EEG lab. dir., cons. Gifford Med. Ctr., Randolph, Vt., 1977-2003, neurologist, 1977-2003; cons. neurology Boston VA Med. Ctr., 1991-2000, hon. staff, 2002. Mem. clin. adv. com. V. divsn. Nat. MS Soc., 2001, clin. adv. com. ctrl. N.E. chpt., 1977-03; bd. dirs. Ctrl. Vt.-Upper Valley N.H. chpt. ARC, 2003—. Lt. comdr. USNR, 1964-66. Lt. comdr. USNR, 1964—66. Fellow: Am. Acad. Neurology; mem. AMA, Internat. Soc. Women Health and Sexuality, Huntington's Study Group, Huntington's Dx Soc. (mem. adv. bd. Mass. chpt. 1980—2000, clin. adv. bd. 2001—03), Multiple Sclerosis Soc. (clin. adv. bd. 1977—2003), Boston Soc. Neurology and Psychiatry (pres. 1982—83), exec. com. 1985—2003, Vt. bd. med. practice 2002—03), Mass. Med. Soc., Am. Soc. Neuroimaging, Am. Assn. for Study of Headache, Am. Neurol. Assn. Avocations: tree farmer, oenology, music. Office: 4142 VT Rte 66 # 185 Randolph Center VT 05061 Personal E-mail: dssax@adelphia.net.

**SAX, JOSEPH LAWRENCE,** lawyer, educator; b. Chgo., Feb. 3, 1936; s. Benjamin Harry and Mary (Silverman) S.; m. Eleanor Charlotte Gettes, June 17, 1958; children: Katherine Elaine Dennett, Valerie Beth Sax, Amber Sax Rosen. AB, Harvard U., 1957; JD, U. Chgo., 1959; LLD (hon.), Ill. Inst. Tech., 1992. Bar: D.C. 1960, Mich., 1966, U.S. Supreme Ct. 1969. Atty. U.S. Dept. Justice, Washington, 1959-60; pvt. practice law Washington, 1960-62; prof. U. Colo., 1962-65, U. Mich., Ann Arbor, 1966-86; dep. asst. sec. and counselor U.S. Sec. Interior, Washington, 1994-96; prof. U. Calif. Law Sch., Berkeley, 1986—. Fellow Ctr. Advanced Study in Behavioral Scis., 1977-78, Order of the Coif Disting. Visitor, 2004. Author: Waters and Water Rights, 1967, Water Law, Planning and Policy, 1968, Defending the Environment, 1971, Mountains Without Handrails, 1980, Legal Control of Water Resources, 4th edit., 2006, Playing Darts with a Rembrandt, 1999. Fellow: AAAS. Office Phone: 510-642-1831. Business E-Mail: saxj@law.berkeley.edu.

**SAX, MARY RANDOLPH,** speech and language pathologist; b. July 13, 1925; d. Bernard Angus and Ada Lucile (Thurman) TePoorten; m. William Martin Sax, Feb. 7, 1948. BA magna cum laude, Mich. State U., 1947; MA, U. Mich., 1949. Cert. clin. competence in speech and lang. pathology. Supr. speech correction dept. Waterford Twp. Schs., Pontiac, 1949—69; lectr. Marygrove Coll., Detroit, 1971-72; pvt. practice in speech and lang. pathology Wayne and Oakland Counties, Mich., 1973—. Co-investigator Support Pers. Profl. Practice of Speech-Lang. Pathology; counselor to divsn. stroke liaisons Am. Heart Assn. Mich.; liaison between Am. Heart Assn. of Mich. and Am. Heart Assn., Dallas, 1996—98; adj. speech pathologist, Southfield,

Mich.; lectr. on stroke Mich. Spkrs. Bur., Am. Heart Assn., 1990—; pub. spkg. coach, 1989—; mem. adj. faculty SS Cyril and Methodius Sem., Orchard Lake, Mich., 1989—90; adj. St. Mary's Prep. Sch., Orchard Lake, 1990—; mem. Met. Detroit Operation Stroke com. Am. Stroke Assn., 1999—2004, mem. med. subcom. to move area hosps. to become primary stroke ctrs. with active stroke teams, 2001—; founder, mem. Stroke Project Task Force for Detroit, 1993—98; com. mem. Charette, study Arch. and Design for phys. restructuring Franklin, Mich., 1993; invited speech pathology del. Internat. Health Programs People to People Citizen Amb. Program, 1996; mem. sci. coun. on stroke Am. Heart Assn., 1980—2002; invited U.S. rep. speech and lang. pathology (cancelled because of 9/11) Med. People to People Amb. Program, neurol. sci., Czech Republic, Hungary and Austria; mem. quality improvement and med. edn. subcom. Am. Heart Assn. New Heart and Stroke Network Metro Detroit, 2005—; mem. stroke adv. com./stroke advocacy com. Midwest affiliate Am. Heart Assn., 1995—2005; mem. stroke adv. com./stroke advocacy com. Greater Midwest Affiliate Mich., Ind., Ill., Wis., ND, SD, Minn. Am. Heart Assn., 2005—. Contbr. articles to profl. jours. including Lang. and Lang. Behavior Abstracts, Lang. Speech and Hearing Svcs., Speech Lang. Hearing Jour. Active Franklinites for Responsible Svc.; mem. stroke com. Mich. Heart Assn., 1982—99. Recipient Svc. Recognition award Coll. Edn. Mich. State U.; grantee Inst. Articulation and Learning, 1969, others; Christian svc. commn. St. Owen, Birmingham co-chmn. blood dr. Red Cross, Franklin, Mich., 1991—. Mem. Founders Soc. of Detroit Inst. Arts, Franklin Found. (mem. natural resources adv. coun. 1991—99, bd. dirs. 1994—98), Pvt. Practitioners Speech-Lang. Pathology (co-founder), Internat. Assn. Logopedics and Phoniatrics (Switzerland), Am. Heart Assn. Mich. (mem. stroke awareness seminars, continuing edn. for physicians and other profls., planning and operation edn.), Mich. Speech-Lang.-Hearing Assn. (pvt. practitioner liaison 1991—, developer structural parameters for State Clin. Svc. award 1999—, com. comty. and hosp. svcs., mem. state award selection com.), Am. Speech-Lang.-Hearing Assn. (clin. competence cert.), Mich. Humane Soc., Gamma Phi Beta, Kappa Delta Pi, Phi Kappa Phi, Theta Alpha Phi. Achievements include research in language and speech acquisition in children in reference to the development of and prediction of biological speech change; research interests in developmental phonatory voice disorders, and in adult acquisition of language and speech relative to central and autonomic nervous systems. Office: 31320 Woodside Dr Franklin MI 48025-2027

**SAX, PAUL J.,** lawyer; b. Sacramento, 1944; AB, Calif. State U., Sacramento, 1965; JD, U. Calif., San Francisco, 1968; LLM in Taxation, NYU, 1969. Bar: Calif. 1969. Mem. Orrick, Herrington & Sutcliffe, San Francisco, ptnr., chmn. tax group. Vice chair pubs. sect. of taxation ABA, 1990—, chair, vice chair standards tax practice com., 1984-88, coun. dir., 1988-90, dept. editor Jour. Taxation, 1990—. Grad. editor Tax Law Rev., 1968-69. Fellow Am. Bar Found.; Am. Coll. Tax Counsel, Am. Tax Policy Inst.; mem. Order of Coif, Thurston Honor Soc., ABA- Sect. Taxation (chmn. 1999-2000, House Delegates 2001-), ABA-Standard Tax Practice Com. (vice chmn./chmn. 1984-1988, coun. dir. 1988-1990), ABA (vice chmn. publ.), Calif. Bd. Legal Specialization (cert. specialist taxation 1975-), Am. Law Inst. (tax adv. group), Office: Orrick Herrington & Sutcliffe LLP The Orrick Building 405 Howard St San Francisco CA 94105 Office Phone: 415-773-5949. Office Fax: 415-773-5759. Business E-Mail: pjsax@orrick.com.

**SAXBE, WILLIAM BART,** lawyer, former United States attorney general; b. Mechanicsburg, Ohio, June 24, 1916; s. Bart Rockwell and Faye Henry (Carey) S.; m. Ardath Louise Kleinhans, Sept. 14, 1940; children: William Bart, Juliet Louise Saxbe Blackburn, Charles Rockwell. AB, Ohio State U., 1940; LLB, 1948; degree (hon.), Central State U., Findlay Coll., Ohio Wesleyan U., Walsh Coll., Capital U., Wilmington Coll., Ohio State U., Bowling Green State U. Bar: Ohio 1948. DC. Practiced in, Mechanicsburg, Ohio, 1948-55; ptnr. Saxbe, Boyd & Prine, 1955-58; mem. Ohio Ho. Reps., 1947—54, majority leader, 1951-52, speaker, 1953-54; atty. gen. State of Ohio, 1957-58, 63-68; ptnr. Dargusch, Saxbe & Dargusch, 1960-63; mem. US Senate from Ohio, 1969-74; atty. gen. US, 1974—75; US amb. to India, 1975-77; ptnr. Chester, Saxbe, Hoffman & Wilcox, Columbus, Ohio, 1977-81; of counsel Jones, Day, Reavis & Pogue, Cleve., 1981-84, Pearson, Ball & Dowd (merger Pearson, Ball & Dowd and Reed, Smith & McClay), Washington, 1984-93, Chester Willcox & Saxbe, Columbus, Ohio, 1994—; ind. spl. counsel Central States Teamsters Pension Fund, 1982—. Served with 107th Cav. AUS, 1940-42, 107th Cav. USAAF, 1942-45; col. Res. Mem. ABA, Ohio Bar Assn., Am. Judicature Soc., Chi Phi, Phi Delta Phi. Clubs: Mason (Rufus Putnam Disting. Svc. Award), University, Columbus Athletic, Scioto Country, Urbana Country, Burning Tree Country, Bethesda, Md., Country of Fla., Boynton Beach. Republican. Episcopalian. Office: Chester Wilcox & Saxbe LLP 65 E State St Ste 1000 Columbus OH 43215

**SAXE, DEBORAH CRANDALL,** lawyer; b. Lima, Ohio, July 23, 1949; d. Robert Gordon and Lois Barker (Taylor) Crandall; m. Robert Saxe, June 3, 1989; children: Elizabeth Sara, Emily Jane. BA, Pa. State U., 1971; MA, UCLA, 1973, JD, 1978. Bar: Calif. 1978, D.C. 1979, U.S. Dist. Ct. D.C. 1979, U.S. Dist. Ct. (ea. dist.) Calif. 1981, U.S. Dist. Ct. (ctrl. dist.) Calif. 1982, U.S. Dist. Ct. (so. and no. dists.) Calif. 1987, U.S. Ct. Appeals (4th and D.C. cirs.) 1979, U.S. Ct. Appeals (6th cir.) 1985, U.S. Ct. Appeals (8th and 9th cirs.) 1987, U.S. Ct. Appeals (2nd cir.) 1990, U.S. Supreme Ct. 1982, U.S. Dist. Ct. (no. dist.) Ill. 2001, U.S. Ct. Appeals (7th cir.) 2001. Assoc. Seyfarth, Shaw, Fairweather & Geraldson, Washington, 1978-83, Jones, Day, Reavis & Pogue, Washington, 1983-85, L.A., 1985-87, ptnr., 1988-97; shareholder Heller Ehrman LLP, 1997—2005; ptnr. Jones Day, L.A., 2006—. Judge pro tem, Small Claims Ct., L.A., 1985-88. Co-author: Advising California Employers, 1990, 3d edit., 2005; contbg. editor Employment Discrimination Law, 1989. Bd. dirs. Constitutional Rights Found., 1997—2002; chair Eisner Pediatric and Family Med. Ctr., L.A., 1996—98, bd. dirs., 1990—2003, Los Angeles County Bar Found., 1997—99. Fellow: Coll. Labor and Employment Lawyers; mem.: ABA (labor law sect. 1978—), L.A. County Bar Assn. (labor and employment law sect. 1985—, mem. exec. com. 1988—, chair 2002—03, trustee 2005—), Calif. Bar Assn. (labor law sect. 1985—), Phi Beta Kappa, Pi Lambda Theta. Office: Jones Day 555 S Flower St 50th Fl Los Angeles CA 90071 Office Phone: 213-689-3939. Office Fax: 213-243-2539. Business E-Mail: dsaxe@jonesday.com.

**SAXE, GLENN N.,** child psychiatrist, researcher; s. Kenneth and Roslyn Saxe; m. Joanna Bures, Oct. 3, 1993; children: Ryan, Benjamin. BSc, McGill U., Montreal, 1984; MD, McMaster U., Hamilton, Ont., Can., 1988. Lic. psychiatry Harvard Med. Sch., trauma psychiatry Harvard Med. Sch., child and adolescent psychiatry Harvard Med. Sch. Rsch. psychiatrist Nat. Ctr. for Posttraumatic Stress Disorder, Boston, 1995—98; chmn. dept. of child and adolescent psychiatry Boston U. Sch. of Medicine, 1998—; dir. Ctr. for Med. and Refugee Trauma Nat. Child Traumatic Stress Network, Boston, 2001—. Contbr. articles to profl. jours. Recipient Harry and Maida Solomon award for best rsch. by a psychiat. trainee, Harvard Med. Sch., 1994, APA/Dista Products award for best rsch. by a psychiat. resident, APA, 1992, rsch. grant to study risk factors for PTSD in children with burns, NIMH, 1998—2003, Developing interventions for traumatized children and refugee trauma grant, Substance Abuse and Mental Health Svcs. Adminstrn., 2001—05, Adolescent Suicide Prevention grant, 2005—07; grantee rsch. grant to study risk factors for PTSD in children with injuries, NIMH, 2002—08. Achievements include research in Nature And Treatment Of Posttraumatic Stress Disorder In Children. Office: Boston Univ Sch Medicine 1 Boston Medical Center Place Boston MA 02118 Office Phone: 617-414-7504. E-mail: glenn.saxe@bmc.org.

**SAXE, LEONARD,** social psychologist, educator; b. N.Y.C., June 12, 1947; s. Theodore and Majorie (Mayers) S.; m. Marion Gardner, Aug. 9, 1970; 1 child, Daniel. BS in Psychology, U. Pitts., 1969, MS in Psychology, 1972, PhD in Social Psychology, 1976. Asst. instr. U. Pitts., 1973-75; asst. then assoc. prof. psychology Boston U., 1976-88, assoc. dir. Ctr. Applied Social Sci., 1982-84, dir., 1984-87; rsch. prof. Heller Sch. Social Welfare Brandeis U., Waltham, Mass., 1988-90, adj. prof. psychology, adj. rsch. prof., 1990—; prof. psychology Grad. Ctr. CUNY, 1991—; head social-personality psychology, 1993-95; prof. social policy and mgmt. Brandeis U., dir. Cohen Ctr. Modern Jewish Studies. Fulbright sr. lectr. U. Haifa, Israel, 1981—82; mem. task force Children's Mental Health Rsch. Inst. of Medicine-NAS, 1988—89; mem. rev. coms. HHS-Healthcare Fin. Adminstrn. NIMH, Nat. Inst. Drug Abuse, Dept. Edn.; cons., contractor Office Tech. Assessment, US Congress, 1980—88; bd. govs. U. Haifa, 1993—. Author: (with others) Children's Mental Health: Problems and Treatment, 1987,)with A. Sales) How Goodly Are Thy Tents, (with M. Fine) Social Experiments: Methods for Design and Evaluation, 1981; editor: (with M.J. Saks) Advances in Applied Social Psychology, Vol. 3, 1986, (with D. Koretz) New Directions for Program Evaluation, 1982, (with D. Bar-Tal) The Social Psychology of Education: Theory and Research, 1978; contbr. chpts. to books, articles to profl. jours.; assoc. and mng. editor Personality and Social Psychology Bull., 1978-81; ad hoc reviewer various jours.; book reviewer various pubs. Congl. fellow Office Tech. Assessment, 1979. Fellow APA (bd. dirs. sect. social and ethical responsibility 1985-88, Disting. Contbn. award 1989), AAAS, Soc. Psychol. Study Social Issues (coun. 1982-84, 87-89). Office: Cohen Ctr M5014 Brandeis U Waltham MA 02454 Office Phone: 212-642-2501. E-mail: saxe@brandeis.edu.

**SAXENA, ARJUN NATH,** physicist; b. Lucknow, India, Apr. 1, 1932; came to U.S., 1956, naturalized, 1976; s. Sheo and Mohan (Piyari) Shanker; m. Veera Saxena, Feb. 9, 1956; children: Rashmi, Amol, Varsha, Ashvin. BSc, Lucknow U., 1950, MSc, 1952, profl. cert. in German, 1954; post MS diploma, Inst. Nuc. Physics, Calcutta, India, 1955; PhD, Stanford U., 1963. Rsch. asst. Stanford U., 1956-60; mem. tech. staff Fairchild Semicondr. Co., Palo Alto, Calif., 1960-65; dept. head Sprague Electric Co., North Adams, Mass., 1965-69; mem. tech. staff RCA Labs., Princeton, NJ, 1969-71; pres., chmn. bd. Astro-Optics, Phila., 1972; pres. Internat. Sci. Co. Princeton Junction, NJ, 1973—. Disting. vis. scientist Centre de Rcherches Nucléaires, Strasbourg, France, 1973, 77; sr. staff scientist, mgr. engring. Data Gen. Corp., Sunnyvale, Calif., 1975-80; mgr. process tech. Signetics Corp., Sunnyvale, 1980-81; Gould AMI scientist, dir. advanced process devel. Gould AMI Semicondr., Santa Clara, Calif., 1981-87; dir. Ctr. for Integrated Electronics, prof. dept. elec. and computer system engring. Rensselaer Poly. Inst., Troy, N.Y., 1987-96, emeritus prof., 1996—; disting. vis. scientist Inst. Microelectronics, Stuttgart, Germany, 1993-94. Contbr. articles to semicondr. tech., optics, nuc. and high-energy physics to sci. jours.; patentee in field. Treas. pack 66 Boy Scouts Am., West Windsor, N.J., 1970-74. Recipient Disting. Citizen award State of N.J., 1975. Mem. IEEE (life, sr.), Stanford U. Alumni Assn. (life). Home: 4217 Pomona Ave Palo Alto CA 94306-4312

**SAXENA, BRIJ B.,** endocrinologist, biochemist, educator; PhD, India; DSc, U. Muenster, W.Ger.; PhD, U. Wis., 1961; DSc (hon.), Bundelkhand U., India, 2002. Asst. prof. biochemistry and endocrinology N.J. Coll. Medicine., 1966-74; assoc. prof. biochemistry Cornell U. Med. Coll., N.Y.C., 1974—; prof. biochemistry, 1974—, prof. endocrinology, 1981—, dir. div. reproductive endocrinology, Harold and Percy Uris endowed prof. reproductive biology, 2000—. Contbr. articles to profl. jours. Recipient Career Scientist award N.Y.C Health Research Council; Upjohn research award; Campoz da Paz award. Fellow Royal Soc. Medicine (London); mem. Am. Soc. Biol. Chemists, AAAS, Endocrine Soc., Harvey Soc., Am. Physiol. Soc., Am. Chem. Soc. Office: Cornell U Med Coll 515 E 71st St Ste 412 New York NY 10021-4805 Office Phone: 212-746-3067. Business E-Mail: brs2003@med.cornell.edu.

**SAXER, RICHARD KARL,** metallurgical engineer, retired military officer; b. Toledo, Aug. 31, 1928; s. Alexander Albert and Gertrude Minnie (Kuebeler) S.; m. Marilyn Doris Mersereau, July 19, 1952; children: Jane Lynette, Robert Karl, Kris Renee, Ann Luette. Student, Bowling Green State U., 1946-48; BS, U. S. Naval Acad., 1952; MS in Aero. Mechanics Engring., Air Force Inst. Tech., 1957; PhD in Metall. Engring., Ohio State U., 1962; grad., Armed Forces Staff Coll., 1966, Indsl. Coll. Armed Forces, 1971; disting. grad., Air Force Inst. Tech., 2003. Commd. 2d lt. U.S. Air Force, 1952, advanced through grades to lt. gen., 1976; electronics officer, mech. officer (4th Tactical Support Sqadron, Tactical Air Command), Sandia Base, N.Mex., 1953-54; electronics and mech. officer, spl. weapons assembly sect. supr. (SAC 6th Aviation Depot Squadron), French Morocco, 1954-55; project engr. mech. equipment br. Air Force Spl. Weapon's Center, Kirtland AFB, N.Mex., 1957-59; project officer Nuclear Safety div., 1959-60; assoc. prof. dept. engring. mechanics Air Force Inst. Tech., 1962-66; asso. prof., dep. dept. head USAF Acad., 1966-70; comdr., dir. Air Force Materials Lab., Wright-Patterson AFB, Ohio, 1971-74; dep. for Reentry System Space and Missile Systems Orgn., 1974-77; dep. for aero equipment Aero. Systems Div., 1977-80, dep. for tactical systems, 1980, vice comdr., 1981-83; aero. systems div. dir. Def. Nuclear Agy., 1983-85, ret., 1985; pres. R.K. Saxer & Assocs., 1985-91; CEO Universal Tech. Corp., Dayton, Ohio, 1991—96. Research and tech. com. materials and structures NASA, 1973-74; chmn. planning group aerospace materials Interagy. Council Materials, 1973-74; mem. Nat. Mil. Adv. Bd., 1971-74, NATO adv. group for research and devel., 1973-74 Contbr. articles to profl. jours. Decorated Def. Disting. Svc. medal, Legion of Merit, Meritorious Service medal USAF, D.S.M., Joint Svc. Commendation medal, Air Force Commendation medal with 3 oak leaf clusters, Army Commendation medal U.S., Def. Superior Service medal, Cross of Gallantry with palm Vietnam, Def. Meritorious Service medal; recipient Disting. award for systems mgmt. Air Force Assn., 1979; Disting. Alumnus award Ohio State U., 1986, Disting. Alumni award Air Force Inst. Tech., 2003. Mem. Air Force Assn., Am. Def. Preparedness Assn. (pres. Dayton 1977-78), Sigma Xi, Phi Lambda Epsilon, Alpha Sigma Mu, Masons, Shriners. Home: 215 Dalfaber Ln Springboro OH 45066-1571

**SAXMAN, ANNA ESTHER,** lawyer; b. Latrobe, Pa., May 14, 1949; d. Harry Suydam and Eleanor Ruth S.; m. Robert Halpert, Feb. 18, 1989. BS magna cum laude, U. Vt., 1978, JD magna cum laude, 1985. Clk. to presiding justice Vt. Supreme Ct., Montpelier, 1985-86; assoc. Langrock, Sperry, Parker & Wool, Burlington, Vt., 1986—; atty. Vt. Defender Gen., dep. defender gen., 2000—. Mem. Task Force on Gender Bias in the Legal System, Montpelier, 1988—. Editor U. Vt. Law Rev. Pres., bd. trustees Vt. Assn. for Mental Health, Montpelier, 1989—. Mem. ABA, ATLA, Vt. Bar Assn. (chmn. women's sect. 1989—, chmn. com. on rights of the mentally and physically handicapped, 1988-89, pres. 2003-04). Office: Vermont Def Gen Office 120 State St Montpelier VT 05620-3301

**SAXON, JOHN DAVID,** lawyer, policy analyst, educator; b. Anniston, Ala., July 21, 1950; s. J.Z. and Sarah Elizabeth (Steadham) S.; m. Elizabeth Ford, Mar. 10, 1973. BA with honors, U. Ala., 1972, JD, 1977; grad. Exec. Program Stanford U., 1986; MA, U. N.C., 1973. Bar: Ala. 1977, U.S. Dist. Ct. (no. dist.) Ala. 1977, U.S. Supreme Ct. 1983, U.S. Dist. Ct. (mid. dist.) Ala. 1989, U.S. Dist. Ct. (so. dist.) Ala. 1990, U.S. Ct. Appeals (11th cir.) 1990, U.S. Ct. Appeals (5th cir.) 1992. Adminstrv. asst. to acting chief exec. officer U. Ala.-University, 1976-77; assoc. Sirote, Permutt, Friend, Friedman, Held & Apolinsky, P.A., Birmingham, Ala., 1977-78; spl. asst. to Vice Pres. U.S., Washington, 1978-79; counsel subcom. on jurisprudence and govt. rels. Com. on Judiciary, U.S. Senate, Washington, 1979-80, counsel Select Com. on Ethics, 1980-83; dir. corp. issues RCA, Washington, 1983-86; Washington rep., Gen. Electric Co., 1986-87; assoc. counsel U.S. Senate Select com. on secret mil. assistance to Iran and the Nicaraguan Opposition, 1987-88; spl. counsel U.S. Senate Armed Svcs. com., 1988; counsel, Johnston, Barton, Proctor, Swedlaw & Naff, Birmingham, 1988-90; atty. Gathings & Davis, Birmingham, 1990-92; ptnr. Cooper, Mitch, Crawford, Kuykendall & Whatley, 1992-95; pres. and dir. John D. Saxon, P.C., 1995—; adj. instr. polit. communication U. Md., 1982-83; instr. speech communication U. Ala.-University, 1973; instr. speech communication and mgmt. Brewer Jr. Coll., Tuscaloosa, 1975-77; adj. prof. instr. civil litigation Samford U., Birmingham, 1977-78; adj. prof. Washington Coll. Law The Am. U., 1988; adj. prof. adminstrn. law U. Ala., Birmingham, 1998; vis. scholar The Hastings Ctr., 1983; mem. Am. Observer Delegation, Kettering Found., 1975.-China Task Force, 1986; bd. dirs. White House Fellows Found., 1981-84, pres., 1983-84; mem. bd. advisers Center for Publ. Law and Service, U. Ala. Sch. Law, 1976-83; bd. trustees Farrah Law Soc., 1988-94, vice-chmn., 1990-92, chmn.,

1992-94; bd. dirs., exec. com. U. Ala. Law Found., vice chmn., 1996-98, chmn. 1998—; mem. Pres.'s Commn. White House Fellowships, 1983-84, 93—; mem. Washington Local Devel. Corp, 1986-88; chmn. Ala. Clinton for Pres. Campaign, 1992, 96; mem. platform com. Dem. Nat. Conv., 1992, del., 1996; treas. Ala. Dem. Party, 1995-99; mem. Fed. Appointments Patronage Com., 1997—; mem. policy adv. com. The Coalition for Excellence in Edn., chmn., 1991-92; dir. The A+ Rsch. Found.; mem. bd. advisors N.E. Ala. Devel. Forum, 1992—, Nat. Governing Bd. Common Cause, 1997; treas Common Cause Ala., 1998—, Leadership Birmingham Class of 1993-94; mem. pres. adv. coun. Birmingham So. Coll., 1993—; mem. adminstrv. bd. First United Meth. Ch., 1994-97; co-pres. Birmingham Boys Choir Found., 1994-96; asst. scoutmaster Troop 57 Boy Scouts of Am.; pres. Southside Baseball, 1995-97; adv. com. The Blackburn Inst., U. Ala.; bd. dir. Miles Coll. Ctr. for Cmty. Econ. Devel., 1995—. Served to 2d lt. U.S. Army, 1974, capt. Res. White House Fellow, 1978-79; named Disting. Mil. Grad., U. Ala., 1972, Outstanding Alumnus in Speech Communication, 1988. Mem. ABA (spl. com. litigation sect.), Ala. Bar Assn., Birmingham Bar Assn. (chmn. profl. ethics com. 1991-92, mem. grievance com. 1992-98, co-chmn. 1995-96, chmn. 1997-98, bd. dirs., solo practitioner small firm sect. 1997—, chmn. budget com. 1999, co-chmn. long range planning com. 2000), Ala. Trial Lawyers Assn. (bd. govs. 1990-94, exec. com. 1994—), White House Fellows Assn. (pres. 1983-84), Kiwanis Club (Birmingham), Scabbard and Blade, The Order of Barristers, Bench and Bar (Outstanding Sr. award 1977), Downtown Dem. Club (pres. 1992-93), Jasons, Omicron Delta Kappa, Omicron Delta Epsilon, Phi Alpha Theta, Pi Sigma Alpha. Methodist. Contbr. articles to newspapers and legal publs., chpts. to books.

**SAXON, RANDALL LEE,** pastor, author, educator; b. Waverly, N.Y., Oct. 28, 1947; s. Sherman Kenyon and Velma Marie (Dunning) S.; m. Diane Louise Kennedy, June 23, 1973 (div. Feb. 1985); children: Heather Marie, David Arthur; m. Anna Louise Clock, Mar. 15, 1986; children: Jennifer Elizabeth, Austin Todd. BA, Mansfield U., 1969; MDiv, Princeton Sem., 1973; certificate, Mansfield Coll., Oxford, Eng., 1980, Wadham Coll., Oxford, 2003; D of Ministry, Drew U., 1992. Ordained to ministry Presbyn. Ch. U.S.A., 1973. Asst. pastor United Meth. Ch., Flemington, 1970—71, Fewsmith Presbyn. Ch., Bellville, 1972—73; intern pastor Wattsburg (Pa.) Presbyn. Ch., 1971—72, East Greene Presbyn. Ch., Erie, Pa., 1971—72; asst. chaplain Bayberry State Hosp., Phila., 1973; assoc. pastor Presbyn. Ch., Gettysburg, Pa., 1973—78; sr. pastor 1st Presbyn. Ch., Southampton, 1978—86, Presbyn. Ch. of the Covenant, Port Arthur, Tex., 1986—91, 1st Presbyn. Ch., Wilmette, Ill., 1991—94, Peoria, Ill., 1994—2004; pastor United Presbyn. Ch., Peoria, 2004—; instr. parish nursing program OSF St. Francis Med. Ctr., Peoria, Ill., 1995—99; instr. Inst. Learning in Retirement Bradley U., Peoria, Ill., 1995—; instr. social scis. Ill. Ctrl. Coll., East Peoria, Ill., 1999—. Nat. chaplain Sigma Theta Epsilon, Mansfield, Pa., 1968-72; permanent clk. Presbytery of Carlisle, Camp Hill, Pa., 1975-77, Synod of the Trinity, Camp Hill, 1977-78; jour. clk. Presbytery of L.I., Commack, N.Y., 1980-84; mem. Presbytery of Great Rivers; guest lectr. in field. Author: Voices in the Wilderness, 1985, At the Ffeete of Christe and His Church, 1981, Developing A Ministry of Evangelism With Baby Boomers in A Suburban Setting, 1992, America's Debt to the Native American, 1999, Watch Your Mouth! A Brief History of Everyday Words and Phrases, 2003, Good Grief, Gravestones!, 2005; editor: Special Prayers and Prose for Special People of God, 1998; author articles, poetry, hymns. Program dir. Camp Brule, Boy Scouts Am., Forksville, Pa., 1972; dir. Youth in Govt. Seminar, Harrisburg, Pa., 1977; v.p. Internat. Seamen's Ctr., Houston, 1987-89; chairperson City Task Force on Edn. Summit, Port Arthur, 1990-91; active Presbyn. Hist. Soc.; camp commr. Boy Scouts Am., Forksville, Pa., 1971, dist. commr., Peoria, Ill., 1999 Recipient cert. Shinnecock Indian Tribe, 1981; named an Outstanding Young Man of Am., Jaycees, 1971; Susquehanna Collegiate Inst. grantee, 1972. Mem. Acad. Parish Clergy, Am. Soc. Ch. History, Presbyn. Hist. Soc., Presbyn. Writers Guild, Ctr. Theology and Natural Scis., Presbyn. Assn. Sci, Tech., and Christian Faith, Surrat Soc., Am. Forestry Assn., Presbyns. Renewal Creation, Scottish Soc. S.E. Tex. (pres. 1990-91), Ill. State Hist. Soc., The Co. of Pastors, The Lincoln Party, The Lincoln Project, Abraham Lincoln Assn., Nat. Eagle Scout Assn., Rotary (pres. 1977-78). Democrat. Avocations: coin collecting/numismatics, canoeing, white-water rafting, skydiving, gardening. Home: 3628 N Breckenridge Ct Peoria IL 61614-8034 Office: United Presbyn Ch 2400 W Northmoor Rd Peoria IL 61614-3343 Office Phone: 309-693-2002. E-mail: rls@unitedpc.org.

**SAXON, WOLFGANG ERIK GEORG,** journalist; b. Leipzig, Germany, Sept. 5, 1930; arrived in US, 1952; s. Erich Otto and Klare (Wochatz) Richter; m. Anna Forti, 1967. BS, Columbia U., 1954; postgrad., Columbia U. (Russian Inst.), 1960. Newspaper reporter, obituarist New York Times, NYC, 1956—2006; freelance writer, 2006—. Draftee U.S. Army, 1954—56. Mem.: Phi Beta Kappa, The Silurians. Avocations: reading, walking, travel. Office: NY Times 229 W 43rd St New York NY 10036-3959 Business E-Mail: saxon@nytimes.com.

**SAXTON, CATHERINE PATRICIA,** public relations executive; b. Sheffield, Eng., July 5, 1944; d. Clifford and Kate Ann Saxton. BA cum laude, Fordham U., 1978. Mgr. corp. comms. Westinghouse Broadcasting & Cable Co., N.Y.C., 1981-82; prin., pres. Saxton & Assocs., N.Y.C., 1983—; CEO Potter/Saxton Assocs., Inc., N.Y.C., 1985-90; The Saxton Group Ltd., 1990—, co-founder, co-chair A-List Strategic affiliate, 2003—. Prof. pub. speaking Katharine Gibbs Coll., N.Y.C., 1977—. Mem. exec. com. Mayor's Commn. for a Vietnam Vets. Meml., 1982-90. Roman Catholic. Home: 325 E 90th St New York NY 10128-5260 Office Phone: 212-672-0509. Business E-Mail: cpsaxton@hotmail.com.

**SAXTON, CELESTE DAWN,** social studies educator, consultant; b. Balt., Feb. 27, 1958; d. Harvey Lewis and Angela Alice-Attardo Saxton; children: Sara Megan Sciarretta, Natalie Allison-Bianca Sciarretta. AA in Arts & Sci. Transfer, Villa Julie Coll., Stevenson, Md., 1978; BS in History & Secondary Edn., Hood Coll., Frederick, Md., 1980; MS in Sch. Adminstrn. & Supervision, The Johns Hopkins U., Balt., 1993; EdD in Ednl. Leadership & Adminstrn., Nova Southeastern U., Ft. Lauderdale, Fla., 2002. Tchr. social studies Balt. County Pub. Schs., Towson, 1980—86; mid. sch. interdisciplinary team leader Balt. County Pub. Schs., 1986—90; social studies dept., 1990—96, mentor tchr. county level, 1996—97, h.s. adminstr., 1997—2002, social studies supr. & educator, 2002—. Sat adminstrv. coord. Balt. County Pub. Schs., 1997—2002, sch.-based minority achievement coord., 1989—93. Advisor for 1st mid. sch. key club Kwanis, Reisterstown, Md., 1987—89; team leader-highway clean-up Md. State Dept. Transp., Westminster, 1998—2001; student govt. advisor Balt. County Pub. Schs., 1989—93. Scholar, Balt. County Pub. Schs., 1999—2001. Mem.: Md. Coun. Social Studies, Nat. Coun. Social Studies. Roman Catholic. Avocations: reading, gardening, swimming, boating, travel. Home: 548 Old Bachmans Valley Road Westminster MD 21157 Office: Carroll County Public Schools 125 N Court Street Westminster MD 21157 Office Fax: 410-751-3000. Home Fax: 410-751-3159; Office Fax: 410-751-3159. Business E-Mail: cdsaxto@k12.carr.org

**SAXTON, JIM (HUGH JAMES SAXTON),** congressman; b. Nicholson, Pa., Jan. 22, 1943; s. Hugh R. and Helen M. (Billings) Saxton; m. Helen Jean Gadomski, June 9, 1965; children: Jennifer, James Martin. BA in Edn., East Stroudsburg State U., Pa., 1965; grad. student in elem. edn., Temple U., 1967-68. Tchr. Bordentown Pub. Schs., NJ, 1965-68; owner, realtor Jim Saxton Realty Co., Bordentown, NJ, 1968-80; mem. NJ Gen. Assembly, 1976—81, NJ State Senate, 1981-84, US Congress from 3rd NJ dist., 1984—. Asst. minority whip NJ Gen. Assembly, 1980, NJ State Senate, 1981—84; mem. armed svcs. com. US Congress, mem. resources com., chair joint econ. com. Chair Am. Cancer Com.; mem. Burlington Coun. Boy Scouts Am.; mem. Bordentown C. of C., NJ. Named Outstanding Fed. Legislator of Yr., NJ Vets. of Fgn. Wars, 2000; recipient Henry M. Jackson Disting. Svc. award, Jewish Inst. Nat. Security Affairs, 2003, Leadership award, Nat. Marine

Sanctuary Found., 2003. Mem.: USAF Assn., Leadership Found. NJ, Rotary, Elks. Republican. Office: US Ho Reps 2217 Rayburn Ho Office Bldg Washington DC 20515-3003 Office Phone: 202-225-4765.*

**SAXTON, LLOYD,** psychologist, writer; b. Loveland, Colo., Sept. 28, 1929; s. Oliver George and Alice Augusta (Andersen) S.; m. Nancy Alison Roberts, Dec. 17, 1955; children: Perry Brent, Jay Ronald, Barbara Jean. AB in English, U. Calif., Berkeley, 1950, BS in Psychology, 1954; MS in Psychology, San Francisco State U., 1955; PhD in Psychology, U. of the Pacific, Stockton, Calif., 1957. Diplomate Am. Bd. Forensic Examiners, lic. psychologist Calif. Intern in clin. psychology Childlren's Hosp., San Francisco, 1955-56; teaching fellow U. Pacific, San Francisco, 1955-57, instr. psychology, 1957-58, asst. prof. psychology, 1958-60; assoc. prof. psychology Am. Acad. of Asian Studies, San Francisco, 1960-62, prof. psychology, 1962-65; chmn. dept. psychology Coll. of San Mateo, Calif., 1965-75, prof. psychology Calif., 1975-92; pvt. practice San Francisco/Larkspur, 1958—; emeritus, 1995. Author: Individual, Marriage and the Family, 1968, Individual, 9th edit., 1996; author/editor: A Marriage Reader, 1970, The American Scene, 1970. Mem. APA, AAAS, AAUP, Am. Assn. Marriage and Family Therapists, Western Psychol. Assn., Am. Coll. Forensic Examiners, Mensa, Am. Chess Fedn. Democrat. Avocations: chess, sailing, music, ballet, opera. Home and Office: 57 Hatzic Ct Larkspur CA 94939-1992 Office Phone: 415-924-5840.

**SAXTON, MARTHA,** history educator, writer; m. Enrico Ferorelli; children: Francesco, Josephine. BA, U. Chgo., 1967; PhD, Columbia U., 1989. Editorial asst. Mass. Hist. Soc., Boston, 1967-68; editor Doubleday Works in Progress, N.Y.C., 1969-71; writer pvt. practice, 1972—; lectr. and Mellon fellow Columbia U., N.Y.C., 1988-90, adj. asst. prof., 1991, 93, asst. prof. colonial history, 1993—97; assoc. prof. history and women's and gender studies Amherst Coll., Mass., 1997—. Editor, free lance Book of Month Club, 1976-85; adj. asst. prof. NYU, 1992; translator On the Glass Boxes of Chiara Briganti (from Italian), 1980, Through an Artist's Eye (from French), 1989; steering com. Early Am. History Seminr Columbia U., Writing Women's Lives Seminar N.Y. Inst. for the Humanities. Author: Jayne Mansfield and the American Fifties, 1975, Louisa May Alcott, 1977 (Boston Globe Annual award 1977), Being Good: Women's Moral Values in Early America, 2003; contbr. articles and essays to lit. mags. and newspaper book sects., also chpts. to books. Presdl. fellow Columbia U., 1985-88, Mellon fellow Soc. Fellows in the Humanities, Columbia, 1988-90; Bunting fellow Radcliffe Coll., 1995-96; recipient Mary Ellen Shimke award, Wellesley Coll., 1986-87, Lane-Cooper award Columbia U., 1987-88. Mem. PEN (sec. exec. bd. 1986-89, judge Martha Albrand award 1992), Authors' League, Authors' Guild, Nat. Book Critics' Circle, Orgn. Am. Historians, Am. Hist. ASsn., So. Assn. Women's Historians. Home: 50 W 29th St New York NY 10001-4227 E-mail: msaxton@amherst.edu.

**SAXTON, WILLIAM MARVIN,** lawyer; b. Joplin, Mo., Feb. 14, 1927; s. Clyde Marvin and Lena Ann (Farnan) S.; m. Helen Grace Klinefelter, June 1, 1974; children: Sherry Lynn, Patricia Ann Painter, William Daniel, Michael Lawrence. AB, U. Mich., 1949, JD, 1952. Bar: Mich. Mem. firm Love, Snyder & Lewis, Detroit, 1952-53, Butzel, Long, Detroit, 1953—, dir., chmn., CEO, 1989-96, dir. emeritus, 1997—. Lectr. Inst. Continuing Legal Edn.; sec., bd. dirs. Fritz Broadcasting, Inc., 1983-97; mem. mediation tribunal hearing panel for 3d Jud. Dist. Mich., 1989—, 6th Jud. Dist., 1994—. Trustee Detroit Music Hall Ctr. Soc. for the Performing Arts, 1984-99; trustee Hist. Soc. U.S. Dist. Ct. (ea. dist.) Mich., 1992-95, pres., 1993-95. Recipient Disting. award Mich. Road Builders Assn., 1987. Master of Bench Emeritus Am. Inn of Court; fellow Am. Coll. Trial Lawyers, Am. Bar Found., Am. Coll. Labor and Employment Lawyers, Mich. Bar Found.; mem. ABA, FBA, Detroit Bar Assn. (dir. 1974-79, Goodnow Pres.'s award 1996), Mich. Bar Assn. (atty. discipline panel, Disting. Svc. award 1998, Champion of Justice award, 2003), Detroit Indsl. Rels. Rsch. Assn. 1980—, v.p. 1982, pres. 1984-85), Mich. Young Lawyers (pres. 1954-55), Am. Law Inst., Indsl. Rels. Rsch. Assn. Am. Arbitration Assn., U.S. 6th Cir. Ct. Appeals (life, mem. jud. conf., mem. bicentennial com.), Am. Inn Ct., Cooley Club, Renaissance Club, Detroit Golf Club (dir. 1983-89), Detroit Athletic Club. Office: Butzel Long 150 W Jefferson Ave Ste 100 Detroit MI 48226-4416 Office Phone: 313-225-7001. Personal E-mail: saxton214@aol.com.

**SAY, ALLEN,** writer, illustrator; b. Yokohama, Japan, Aug. 28, 1937; arrived in U.S., 1953; s. Masako Moriwaki; m. Deirdre Myles, Apr. 18, 1974; 1 child, Yuriko. Weekend arts program, Chouinard Art Inst., L.A.; classes, Art Ctr. Coll. Design, L.A.; studied arch., U. Calif., Berkeley. Pub. EIZO Pr., Berkeley, 1968. Author, illustrator: Dr. Smith's Safari, 1972, Once Under the Cherry Blossom Tree: An Old Japanese Tale, 1974, The Feast of Lanterns, 1976, The Bicycle Man, 1982, A River Dream, 1988, The Lost Lake, 1989, Tree of Cranes, 1991, Grandfather's Journey, 1993 (Caldecott medal 1994, Boston Globe/Horn Book award 1994), The Stranger in the Mirror, 1995, Emma's Rug, 1996; author: The Innkeeper's Apprentice, 1989, El Chino, 1990, Home of the Brave, 2002; illustrator: A Canticle to the Waterbirds, 1968, Two Ways of Seeing, 1971, Magic and Night River, 1978, The Lucky Yak, 1980, The Secret Cross of Lorraine, 1981, How My Parents Learned to Eat, 1984 (Horn Book honor list 1984, Christopher award 1985), The Boy of the Three Year Nap, 1988 (Boston Globe/Horn Book award 1988, Caldecott honor book 1989), Allison, 1997; retrospective Japanese Am. Nat. Mus., L.A., 2000. Office: care Houghton Mifflin Children's Book Dept 222 Berkeley St Boston MA 02116-3748

**SAY, BURHAN,** retired physician; b. Istanbul, Turkey, Feb. 26, 1923; came to U.S. 1951; s. Ethem Serif and Ayse Say; m. Elizabeth E. Jackson, Nov. 5, 1955; children: Tony, Daniel Demir. MD, U. Istanbul, 1946. Diplomate Am. Bd. Pediatrics, Am. Bd. Med. Genetics Asst. prof. pediatrics Hacettepe U., Ankara, Turkey, 1960-64, prof. pediatrics, 1964-73; clin. prof. of pediatrics U. of Okla./Tulsa Med. Coll., 1975—; ret. Dir. H.A. Chapman Inst., Tulsa, 1982—; v.p. Children's Med. Ctr., Tulsa, 1988—. Contbr. articles to profl. jours. Pres. Am. Cancer Soc., Tulsa, 1980-90, Great Plains Genetics Soc., Tulsa, 1993. Lt. Turkish Army, 1946-48, Turkey., Fulbright scholar, Boston, 1966—68. Avocation: sports. Home: 6216 E 99th St Tulsa OK 74137-5503 Office Phone: 918-299-5891. Personal E-Mail: mbsay@cox.net.

**SAYER, RONALD J.,** composer, educator; b. Rochester, NY, Oct. 12, 1961; s. Barbara Sayer. B Music Edn., U. Mo., Kansas City, 1985; MEd, Tex. Wesleyan U., 2002. Instr. vocal music Lansing Unified Sch. Dist., Kans., 1985—97; artistic dir. Marshall (Mo.) Cmty. Chorus, 2000—; instr. vocal music Marshall (Mo.) H.S., 1997—, chmn. fine arts dept., 2000—. V.p. Mid-Mo. Fine Arts Coun., Marshall, 2002—. Mem. music com. St. Peter's Cath. Ch., Marshall, 1999—2003. Recipient Tchr. award, Mo. Fine Arts Acad., 2000, 2002—04, 2006, Sharon Murphey award, Kans. NEA, 1996, Tchr. of the Yr., Marshall HS, 2006;, U. Mo.-Kansas City school, 1994. Mem.: Nat. Assn. Tchrs. Singing, Nat. Choral Dirs. Assn. (chmn. cmty. choirs 2002—04), Music Educators Nat. Conf., Am. Choral Dirs. Assn. (chmn. cmty. choirs southwest divsn. 2004—), Pope John Paul II Cultural Ctr., Omicron Delta Kappa, Pi Kappa Lambda, Phi Mu Alpha Sinfonia. Home: 1017 S Ann Drive Marshall MO 65340 Office: Marshall Public Schs 805 S Miami Ave Marshall MO 65340 Office Phone: 660-886-2244.

**SAYERS, GALE,** computer company executive, retired professional football player; b. Wichita, Kans., May 30, 1943; s. Roger Earl and Bernice (Ross) S.; m. Ardythe Elaine Bullard, Dec. 1, 1973; children: Gale Lynne, Scott Aaron, Timothy Gale, Gaylon, Guy, Gary. Student phys. edn., Kans. U., N.Y. Inst. Finance. Running back Chgo. Bears Profl. Football Team, 1965—72; then asst. to athletic dir. Kans. U.; athletic dir. So. Ill. U., to 1981; v.p. mktg. Computer Suppy by Sayers, Northfield, Ill., 1984—86; pres. Crest Computer Supply Co., Skokie, Ill., 1986—; pres., CEO Sayers Computer Source, Mt. Prospect, Ill., 1983—2006, chmn.; pres., CEO Sayers40, Inc., Mt. Prospect, Ill., 2006—. Columnist Chgo. Daily News; bd. dir. Global Healthcare Exchange, 2003. Author: (with Al Silverman) I Am Third, 1970. Co-chmn. legal def. fund sports com. NAACP; co-ordinator Reach-Out program, Chgo.; hon. chmn. Am. Cancer Soc.; commr. Chgo. Park Dist. Recipient numerous awards for playing, also holder numerous Nat. Football League records; named to Pro Football Hall of Fame, 1977 Mem. Kappa Alpha Psi. Office: Sayers Computer Source 1150 Feehanville Dr Mount Prospect IL 60056-6007

**SAYERS, MARTIN PETER,** pediatric neurosurgeon; b. Big Stone Gap, Va., Jan. 2, 1922; s. Delbert Bancroft and Loula (Thompson) S.; m. Marjorie W. Garvin, May 8, 1943; children: Daniel Garvin Sayers, Stephen Putnam Sayers, Julia Hathaway Sayers Bolton, Elaine King Sayers Buck. BA, Ohio State U., 1943, MD, 1945; postgrad., U. Pa., 1948-51. Intern Phila. Gen. Hosp., 1945-46; resident in neurosurgery U. Pa. Hosps., Phila., 1948-51; practice medicine specializing in neurosurgery Columbus, Ohio, 1951—; mem. faculty Ohio State U., Columbus, 1951-87, clin. prof. neurosurgery, 1968-87, emeritus, chief dept. pediatric neurosurgery, 1960-87. Cons. Bur. Crippled Children Services Ohio.; Neurosurgeon Project Hope, Ecuador, 1964, Ceylon, 1968, Cracow, Poland, 1979. Served as lt. jr. grade M.C. USN, 1946—48. Mem. Am. Assn. Neurol. Surgeons (chmn. pediatric sect.), Congress Neurol. Surgeons (pres.), Neurosurg. Soc. Am. (pres.), Am. Soc. Pediatric Neurosurgery, Soc. Neurol. Surgeons. Office: 931 Chatham Ln Columbus OH 43221-2417

**SAYKIEWICZ-SAJKIEWICZ, JAN NAPOLEON,** marketing educator; b. Lublin, Poland, June 10, 1939; arrived in U.S., 1987; s. Jan Sajkiewicz and Ewa Komorowska; m. Elzbieta Katarzyna Przetacznik, Aug. 27, 1966; children: Jan Rafal, Olaf Xawery, Mateusz Konstanty. MS in Econs., Ctrl. Sch. Planning & Stats., Warsaw, Poland, 1962, PhD, 1969; diploma in African studies, U. Warsaw, 1968; diploma, U. Calif., Berkeley, 1972. Cert. internat. tourism profl. Rsch. assoc. U. Calif., Berkeley, 1972-73; asst., assoc. prof. Ctrl. Sch. Planning & Stats., Warsaw, 1962-75; lectr. in mktg. Exec. Tng. Ctrs., Warsaw, 1969-88; assoc. prof. U. Warsaw, 1974-88; lectr., prof. Warsaw Acad. Arts, 1980-87; prof. Duquesne U. Sch. Bus. Adminstrn., Pitts., 1987—, L. Kozminski Acad. Entrepreneurial and Mgmt., Warsaw, 1998—. Vis. prof. Fordham U., N.Y.C., 1978, Duquesne U., Pitts., 1981, No. Jiaotong U., Beijing, 1997, Rome Campus, Italy, 2005. Duquesne U. Rome Campus Italy, 2005; Fulbright prof., 2000-2001; expert Internat. Labor Orgn., Geneva, 1982; vice-chmn., bd. dirs Consumer Cooperative Enterprises, Warsaw, 1982-88; mem. Inter-Polcom, Chamber of Industry, Commerce, Warsaw, 1984-86; sec. gen., chief treas. Polish Mktg. Assn., 1974-81, exec. bd., 1985-88 Author: Concentration of Commercial Activities, 1972, Marketing Concept in Business Management, 1975, 2nd edit., 1976, 3rd edit., 1977, Management Systems in Integrated Capitalist Business, 1975; contbr. articles to profl. jours.; transl. profl. lit. Active Solidarity Movement, Poland, 1980-81; social and econ. coun., The Capital City of Warsaw, Poland, 1987-88. Recipient Silver and Gold Crosses of Merit, Coun. of State, Poland, 1980, 1982, Individual award for pedagogical performance, Min. Edn., Poland, 1981, Golden Mermaid Hon. Decoration for svc., Capital City of Warsaw, 1985, Akdeniz Univ. award, Turkey, 2002, award, Fulbright Fgn. Scholarship Bd. and U.S. Dept. State, 2002, Spl. award, Lansbridge U. and Kingston Coll., Can., 2003, Recognition award, Maastricht Sch. Mgmt., The Netherlands, 2004, Fourteenth World Bus. Congress Spl. Svc. award, Internat. Mgmt. Devel. Assn., Fundacion Euroarabe, and Euroarab Mgmt. Sch., Granada Spain, 2005; vis. scholar, U. Calif., Berkeley, 1972—73, Fordham U., N.Y., 1978, No. Jiaotong U., Beijing, 1997, fellow, Ford Found., 1972—73, rsch. grantee, U.S. Dept. Edn., 1993, 1994. Fellow: Am. Acad. Mktg. Sci.; mem.: Polish Inst. Arts and Scis. in Am. (bd. dirs. 1995—97, adv. coun. 2003—, chmn. 2004—), Am. Mktg. Assn. (profl. and exec. mem.), Acad. Internat. Bus., Internat. Mgmt. Devel. Assn. (exec. v.p. 1997, pres. 2002, chmn. bd. regional dirs. 2005, chair bd. retional dirs. 2005, award 2001, Spl. Svc. award 2005). Roman Catholic. Avocations: social studies, books, travel, cognac. Home: 5853 Douglas St Pittsburgh PA 15217-2101 E-mail: saykiewicz@duq.edu.

**SAYLER, ROBERT NELSON,** lawyer, educator; b. Kansas City, Mo., June 1, 1940; s. John William and Roberta (Nelson) S.; m. Martha Leith, Aug. 1962; children: Christina, Bentley. BA, Stanford U., 1962; JD, Harvard U., 1965. Bar: U.S. Dist. Ct. D.C. 1966, U.S. Ct. Appeals (D.C. cir.) 1966, U.S. Supreme Ct. 1971, D.C. 1972, U.S. Ct. Appeals (2d cir.) 1977. From assoc. to ptnr. Covington & Burling, Washington, 1965—; prof. U. Va., 2003—. Vis. prof. U. Va., 1995, 2002. V.p Neighborhood Legal Services, Washington, 1980-82; pres. Legal Aid Soc., Washington, 1983-84. Fellow Am. Bar Found.; Am. Coll. Trial Lawyers; mem. ABA (dir. programs, program chmn. 1981, 85, coun., chmn. litigation sect., mem. standing com. on fed. judiciary). Democrat. Office: Covington & Burling PO Box 7566 1201 Pennsylvania Ave NW Washington DC 20004-2401 also: U Va Sch Law 580 Massie Rd Charlottesville VA 22903-1789 Office Phone: 434-924-4741. E-mail: rns5b@virginia.edu.

**SAYLES, JOHN THOMAS,** film director, writer, actor; b. Schenectady, NY, Sept. 28, 1950; s. Donald John and Mary (Rausch) S. BS, Williams Coll., 1972. Film dir., writer, actor Paradigm, L.A., 1994—. Author: Pride of the Bimbos, 1975, Union Dues, 1979, Thinking in Pictures: The Making of the Movie "Matewan," 1987, The Anarchists Convention, 1979, Los Gusanos, 1991; short stories I-80 Nebraska, M.490 - M.205, 1975 (O Henry award); Breed, Golden State, 1977 (O Henry award); Hoop; writer, dir. plays: New Hope for the Dead, 1981, Turnbuckle; screenwriter (films) Piranha, 1978, The Lady in Red, 1979, Battle Beyond the Stars, 1980, Alligator, 1981, The Challenge, 1982, Enormous Changes at the Last Minute, 1985, Wild Thing, 1987, The Clan of the Cave Bear, 1988, Breaking In, 1989; actor, screenwriter (films) The Howling, 1981; dir., screenwriter (films) Baby, It's You, 1983, Passion Fish, 1992; dir., screenwriter, actor (films) Return of the Secaucus Seven, 1980 (Los Angeles Film Critcs award, 1980), Lianna, 1983, The Brother From Another Planet, 1984, Matewan, 1987, Eight Men Out, 1988, City of Hope, 1991; dir., screenwriter; dir., writer (film) Lone Star, 1996, Limbo, 1999, Sunshine State, 2002, Casa de los babys, 2003, Silver City, 2004; actor(films) Hard Choices, 1986, Something Wild, 1986, Little Vegas, 1990, Straight Talk, 1992, Malcolm X, 1992, Matinee, 1993, My Life's in Turnaround, 1994; dir. Bruce Springsteen music videos Born in the U.S.A., I'm on Fire, Glory Days; TV work includes A Perfect Match, Unnatural Causes, Shannon's Deal, spl. Mountain View. MacArthur Found. grantee. Office: Paradigm c/o Lucy Stille 360 N Crescent Dr Beverly Hills CA 90210

**SAYLES, LETORY BRUNO,** retired priest, monk; b. New Orleans, La., Apr. 24, 1918; s. George Rene and Evangeline (Letory) Sayles. BA, Xavier U. of La., 1939; MA, U. of Minn., Mpls., 1959. Vows to become Benedictine monk 1944, ordained Roman Cath. priest, 1948. Benedictine monk St. John's Abbey, Collegeville, Minn., 1944—; music instr. St. John's U., Collegeville, 1947—57; Roman Cath. priest St. John's Abbey, Collegeville, 1948—2002; faculty instr. St. Augustine's Coll., Nassau, Bahamas, West Indies, 1957—70; co-pastor St. Anselm's Ch., N.Y.C., 1970—71, part-time asst., 1971—75; chaplain Convent of St. Benedict's, St. Joseph, Minn., 1980—86. Dir. Gregorian chant choir St. John's U., Collegeville, 1947—57; cons. Gregorian chant parish chs. in various locations, Collegeville, 1948—50; dir. Lucayan Chorale, Nassau, 1964—70. Mem.: Nat. Assn. Teachers of Singing (life; founding mem., emeritus mem.), Nassau Music Soc. Democrat. Roman Catholic. Office: St John's Abbey PO Box 2015 Collegeville MN 56321-2015 Office Phone: 320-363-3858.

**SAYLES, WAYNE GERALD,** numismatist, writer; b. Waukesha, Wis., Mar. 8, 1943; s. Wayne F. Sayles and Betty Joy Harris; m. Sharon L. Greshay, 1962 (div. 1982); m. Janet M. Foth Olson, 1984 (div. 1993); m. M. Doris Jean Ivey, 1997; children from previous marriage: Scott Allen, Steven Andrew, Stephanie Anne Sayles Bloedorn. B of Gen. Studies, U. Nebr., 1972; MA, U. Wis., 1986. Enlisted USAF, 1961, advanced through grades to capt., 1976, comdr. 2081st comms. squadron Goodfellow AFB, Tex., 1973, comdr. detachment 15, 2140 comm. group Athens, Greece, 1975, AF advisor to air res. forces and Air Nat. Guard, 1976—80, ret., 1982; pres. Celator, Inc., Lodi, Wis., 1986—; exec. dir. Ancient Coin Collectors Guild, Gainesville, Mo., 2004—. Pub. Clio's Cabinet, Lodi, Wis., 1986—. Author: (6 vol. survey) Ancient Coin Collecting, (monograph) Classical Deception, (reference) Turkoman Figural Bronze Coins and Their Iconography; editor: (jour.) The Celator; contbr. Encyclopedia Britannica. Sec. Ancient Coin Collectors Guild,

Gainesville, Mo., 2004—04; bd. edn. Am. Cmty. Schs., Athens, 1974—75; v.p. bd. edn. Lodi Sch. Dist., Wis., 1988—93. Decorated Small Arms Expert Marksmanship medal USAF, Meritorious Svc. medal, Commendation medal, Expeditionary Svc. medal, Nat. Def. Svc. medal, Good Conduct medal; recipient Numismatic Ambassador award, Krause Publs., 2006, award for exceptional contbns. to ancient numismatics, Ancient Coin Collectors Guild, 2006. Fellow: Royal Numis. Soc. (London), Am. Numis. Soc. (life); mem.: Numis. Lit. Guild, Oriental Numis. Soc., Classical and Medieval Numis. Soc., Am. Israel Numis. Assn. (life), Hellenic Numis. Soc. (life). Achievements include founder of The Celator, numismatic journal; founder of the Ancient Coin Collectors Guild. Avocations: coin collecting/numismatics, travel, genealogy. Home and Office: Ancient Coin Collectors Guild PO Box 911 Gainesville MO 65655 Office Phone: 417-679-2142. Personal E-mail: wayne@ancientcoins.ac. Business E-mail: director@accg.us.

**SAYLOR, CAROL HANNAH,** school system administrator, educator; b. Sunbury, Pa., May 10, 1950; d. Earl William and Ruth Eleanor Ferry; children: Matthew William, Christopher Eric. BA, Susquehanna U., 1972; MS, Bucknell U., 1984; EdD, Nova U., 1987. Cert. home and sch. visitor Dept. of Edn., Pa.; supt. Dept. of Edn., Pa., elem. prin. Dept. of Edn., Pa., secondary prin. Dept. of Edn., Pa., supr. curriculum and instrn. Dept. of Edn., Pa., comprehensive English Dept. of Edn., Pa. Tchr. English Shikellamy Sch. Dist., Sunbury, 1972—82, prin., 1982—87; supt. of schs. Fairfield (Pa.) Area Sch. Dist., 1987—96, Manheim (Pa.) Cen. Sch. Dist., Manheim, 1996—. Adj. prof. Millersville (Pa.) U., 2005—06. Account exec. Lancaster (Pa.) County United Way, 2003—06. Named Friend to Art Edn., Pa. Art Edn. Assn., 1995, Pa. Supt. of Yr.; recipient Outstanding Ednl. Improvement Project award, Nova U., 1987. Mem.: Am. Assn. of Sch. Adminstrs. (governing bd. 2004—06), Manheim Area C of C. (bd. dirs. 1998—2001), Pa. Assn. of Sch. Adminstrs. (pres. 2002—03), Manheim Lions Club (bd. dirs. 1996—2006), Delta Kappa Gamma. Lutheran. Avocations: travel, cooking, golf, reading. Office: Manheim Cen Sch Dist 71 N Hazel St Manheim PA 17545 Office Phone: 717-665-3422. Home Fax: 717-665-7631; Office Fax: 717-665-7631. Personal E-mail: saylorc@manheimcentral.org. E-mail: saylorc@manheimcentral. org.

**SAYLOR, CHARLOTTE VERNELLE,** biology professor; m. James Michael Rittner, Oct. 29, 2005. BA in Biology, Western Md. Coll., Westminster, 1998; MS in Biology, Towson U., Md., 2001. Rsch. coord. The Ingenuity Project, Balt., 2001—05; part time faculty Towson U., 2005—. Cons. The Ingenuity Project, Balt. 2005—06; adj. faculty Howard C.C., Columbia, Md., 2005—06, C.C. Balt. County, 2005—. Recipient Ceres Connection award, MIT Lincoln Lab., 2005. Mem.: Nat. Assn. Biology Tchrs., Nat. Sci. Tchrs. Assn., AAAS, Phi Mu. Office: Towson University 8000 York Rd Towson MD 21252 Business E-Mail: csaylor@towson.edu.

**SAYLOR, PETER M.,** architect; b. Phila., July 26, 1941; s. Harry T. and Dorothy (Johnson) S.; m. Caroline Metcalf, Apr. 4, 1970; children: Thomas S., Elizabeth B. BArch, U. Pa., 1963, MArch, 1965. Registered arch., Iowa, Pa., N.J., Ind., Wis., Conn., Ohio, Minn. Architect Mitchell-Giurgola, Phila., 1967-70; ptnr. Dagit-Saylor Architects, Phila., 1970—. Design critic, juror U. Pa., 1975—; bd. dirs. Found. for Architecture, Phila., 1980-90. Bd. dirs. Chestnut Hill Cmty. Assn., Phila., 1976—79, v.p., 1979; bd. dirs. All Saints Hosp., Wyndmoor, Pa., 1981—86, Cathedral Village Retirement Cmty., 1998—2001. Recipient various bldg. design award Fellow AIA (bd. dirs. Phila. chpt. 1973-82, chpt. pres. 1981-82); mem. Pa. Soc. Archs., Chestnut Hill Hist. Soc. (bd. dirs. 1988-95, pres. 1989-92), Phila. Soc. Preservation of Landmarks (bd. dirs. 1989-96, pres. 1993-94), Phila. Mus. Art (friends bd. dirs. 1990-93), Phila. Cricket Club (bd. dirs. 1985-91), Mask and Wig Club (pres. 1980-81, bd. dirs. 1970-84). Republican. Episcopalian. Office: Dagit-Saylor Archs 100 S Broad St Philadelphia PA 19110-1023 Office Phone: 215-972-0500. E-mail: psaylor@dagitsaylor.com.

**SAYLOR, THOMAS G.,** state supreme court justice; b. Meyersdale, Pa., Dec. 14, 1946; BA in Govt., U. Va., 1969; JD, Columbia U., 1972; LLM, U. Va., 2004. Atty. pvt. practice, 1972—82; 1st asst. dist. atty. Somerset County, 1973-76; dir. Pa. Bur. Consumer Protection, 1982-83; 1st dep. atty. gen. Commonwealth of Pa., 1983-87; atty. pvt. practice, 1987—93; judge Pa. Superior Ct., 1993—97; justice Pa. Supreme Ct., 1997—. Contbr. articles to legal publications. Bd. overseers Widener U. Sch. Law. Mem. ABA, Am. Law Inst., Pa. Bar Assn., Cumberland County Bar Assn., Dauphin County Bar Assn., Appellate Judges Conf. Office: Fulton Bldg 16th Fl 200 N 3d St Harrisburg PA 17101

**SAYRE, DAVID,** physicist; b. N.Y.C., Mar. 2, 1924; s. Ralph E. and Sylvia (Rosenbaum) S.; m. Anne Bowns, Dec. 26, 1947. BS, Yale U., 1944; MS, Auburn U., 1948; PhD, Oxford (Eng.) U., 1951. Staff mem. radiation lab. MIT, Cambridge, 1943-46; rsch. assoc. U. Pa., Phila., 1951-55; mathematician IBM Corp., N.Y.C., 1955-59, corp. dir. programming, 1959-62; mem. rsch. staff IBM T.J. Watson Rsch. Ctr., Yorktown Heights, NY, 1962-90, ret., 1990. Cons. U.S. Office Naval Rsch., London, 1951; mem. U.S.A. Nat. Com. for Crystallography, 1952-55, 81-84, vice chmn., 1984-86; vis. fellow All Souls Coll., Oxford U., 1972-73; guest scientist dept. physics SUNY, Stony Brook, 1980-2004, adj. prof., 2004—; guest rschr. Brookhaven Nat. Lab., Upton, N.Y., 1993—; disting. guest prof. dept. chemistry Rutgers U., 1996-98. Co-author: Waveforms, 1947; editor: Computational Crystallography, 1983; co-editor: Structural Studies on Molecules of Biological Interest, 1983, X-Ray Microscopy II, 1988; contbr. numerous articles to profl. jours. Trustee Village of Head-of-the-Harbor, L.I., N.Y., 1975-95. Named one of Most Notable 20th Century Crystallographers, Hist. Atlas Crystallography. Mem. Am. Crystallographic Assn. (treas. 1952-55, pres. 1983, Fankuchen award 1989) Episcopalian. Achievements include development of atomicity-based direct phasing method for x-ray crystallography; development(with others) of first FORTRAN compiler and first virtual computer system; research in x-ray microscopy; measurement of (with others) x-ray diffraction pattern from single biol. cell; research in extension of x-ray crystallographic methods into field of non-crystals; obtaining with others of first diffraction microscopy images of yeast cell.

**SAYRE, DONNA,** elementary school educator; b. Goshen, NY; d. Wesley and Dorothea Sayre. BS in Edn. summa cum laude, Bloomsburg U., 1995, MEd in Reading, 1997. Reading tchr. Port Jervis (NY) City Sch. Dist., 1998—. Participant Relay for Life Am. Cancer Soc.; Sunday sch. tchr. Craigville Bible Ch., Chester, NY, 2005, nursery provider, 2005. Mem.: NY State Reading Assn., Internat. Reading Assn., Amy Bull Crist Reading Coun. (v.p. 2005—06).

**SAYRE, EDWARD VALE,** chemist; b. Des Moines, Sept. 8, 1919; s. Edward Agnew and Audrey (Vale) S.; m. Virginia Nelle Rogers, Oct. 20, 1943. BS, Iowa State U., 1941; AM, Columbia U., 1943, PhD, 1949. Mgr. rsch. sect. Manhattan Dist. project Columbia U., 1942-45; rsch. chemist Eastman Kodak Rsch. Labs., Rochester, N.Y., 1949-52; sr. chemist Brookhaven Nat. Lab., Upton, N.Y., 1952-84; Dir. rsch. Museum Fine Arts, Boston, 1975-80, sr. scientist, 1980-84; sr. scientist Alexander von Humboldt Found., 1980; vis. lectr. Stevens Inst. Tech., 1955-61; adj. prof. fine arts Inst. Fine Arts, N.Y. U., 1960-74; disting. vis. prof. Am. U. Cairo, 1970; Regents prof. U. Calif., Irvine, 1972; mem. sci. adv. coun. Winterthur Mus. Contbr. numerous rsch. articles to profl. jours.; assoc. editor Archaeometry, 1969-93, Art and Archaeology Tech. Abstracts, 1970-87, Jour. Archaeol. Sci., 1971-77. Guggenheim fellow, 1969; recipient U.S. sr. scientist award Alexander von Humboldt Found., 1980-81, George von Hevesy medal, 1984, Alumni Disting. Achievement citation Iowa State U., 1996, Pomerance award Archaeol. Inst. Am., 1999. Fellow: Inst. for Conservation of Hist. and Artistic Works, Am. Inst. for Conservation of Hist. and Artistic Works; mem. Am. Chem. Soc. Clubs: Cosmos. Home: Apt 616 1330 Massachusetts Ave NW Washington DC 20005-4152 E-mail: EVSayre@aol.com.

**SAYRE, JOHN MARSHALL,** lawyer, former government official; b. Boulder, Colo., Nov. 9, 1921; s. Henry Marshall and Lulu M. (Cooper) S.; m. Jean Miller, Aug. 22, 1943; children: Henry M., Charles Franklin, John Marshall Jr., Ann Elizabeth Sayre Taggart (dec.). BA, U. Colo., 1943, JD, 1948. Bar: Colo. 1948, U.S. Dist. Ct. Colo. 1952, U.S. Ct. Appeals (10th cir.) 1964. Law clk. trust dept. Denver Nat. Bank, 1948-49; asst. cashier, trust officer Nat. State Bank of Boulder, 1949-50; ptnr. Ryan, Sayre, Martin, Brotzman, Boulder, 1950-66, Davis, Graham & Stubbs, Denver, 1966-89, of counsel, 1993—; asst. sec. of the Interior for Water and Sci., 1989-93. Bd. dirs. Boulder Sch. Dist. 3, 1951-57; city atty. City of Boulder, 1952-55; gen. counsel Colo. Mcpl. League, 1959-63; prin. counsel No. Colo. Water Conservancy Dist. and mcpl. subdist., 1964-87, spl. counsel, 1987, bd. dirs dist., 1960-64; former legal counsel Colo. Assn. Commerce and Industry. Lt. (j.g.) USNR, 1943-46, ret. Decorated Purple Heart; recipient William Lee Knous award U. Colo. Law Sch., 1999. Fellow Am. Bar Found. (life), Colo. Bar Found. (life); mem. ABA, Colo. Bar Assn., Boulder County Bar Assn. (pres. 1959), Denver Bar Assn., Nat. Water Resources Assn. (Colo. dir. 1980-89, 93-95, pres. 1984-86), Denver Country Club, Phi Beta Kappa, Phi Gamma Delta, Phi Delta Phi. Home: Park Place 111 Emerson St Apt 1462 Denver CO 80218 Office: Davis Graham & Stubbs 1550-17th St Ste 500 Denver CO 80202 E-mail: john.sayre@dgslaw.com.

**SAYRE, LINDA DAMARIS,** human resources professional; b. Washington, Nov. 26, 1945; d. Wallace Stanley and Kathryn Louise (McKnight) S. BA in English, Wells Coll., 1967; MA in Sociology, U. Sussex, Brighton, Eng., 1969; EdD in Adult and Continuing Edn., Rutgers U., 2002. Human resources specialist N.Y.C. Human Resources Adminstrn., 1967-68; rsch. assoc. Presdl. Campaign Gov. Nelson Rockefeller, N.Y.C., 1968; ednl. coord. Isabella Geriat. Ctr., N.Y.C., 1970-72; rsch. assoc. N.Y.C. Mayor's Commn. on City Fins., 1973-75; project mgr. Urban Acad. for Mgmt., N.Y.C., 1976-80; internal and external tng. cons. Boston and N.Y.C., 1980-83; tng. cons. N.Y.S. Bd. of Edn., 1983-84; tng. and edn. dir. Gen. Hosp. Ctr., Passaic, NJ, 1984-87; dir. human rels. Bronx Lebanon Hosp., NY, 1987-90; external cons. Atlanta, N.Y.C., 1990-95; tng. & devel. mgr. BOC Gases, Murray Hill, NJ, 1995-99. Mem. steering com. Broadway Dems., N.Y.C., 1974-80, 93-96, 2006, pres., 1975, 77; coord. Carter Presdl. Campaign, N.Y. 20th Congl. Dist., 1976; bd. Westside Cares Food Voucher, N.Y.C., 1993-95. Mem.: ASTD (no. N.J. programs 1985—86, Atlanta chmn. nat. affairs 1991, nat. leadership design team), Am. assn. for Adult and Continuing Edn. (co-chair commn. for workplace and profl. devel. 2004—06), N.Y. ASTD (v.p. prof. edn. 1993, pres. 1994, past pres. 1995, co-chair adv. coun. 1996, nominating com. 1997—98, chair succession planning com. 1998, cmty. action team 1999). Democrat. Avocations: writing, community service. Home: 448 Riverside Dr New York NY 10027-6801

**SAYRE, PHIL,** editor; BA, DePauw Univ., 1971; MA, Boston Univ. Reporter, editor Messenger-Inquirer, Owensboro, Ky., Argus Leader, Sioux Falls, SD, Trenton Times, NJ, The Record, Hackensack, NJ, New York Times, 1989—2002, asst. nat. editor, 2002, dep. political editor, 2003, currently night editor, nat. desk. Office: New York Times 229 W 43d St New York NY 10036 Office Phone: 212-556-7356. Office Fax: 212-556-7614.*

**SAYRE, ROBERT FREEMAN,** language educator; b. Columbus, Ohio, Nov. 6, 1933; s. Harrison M. and Mary (White) S.; (divorced); children: Gordon, Nathan, Laura; m. Hutha Refle, May 7, 1988. BA, Wesleyan U., Middletown, Conn., 1955; PhD, Yale U., 1962. Instr. English U. Ill., Urbana, 1961-63; Fulbright lectr. Lund (Sweden) U., 1963-65; faculty U. Iowa, 1965-72, prof. English, 1972-98, prof. emeritus, 1998—. Dir. inter-prof. seminars NEH, 1978, 79; Fulbright lectr. Montpellier, France, 1984; exch. prof. U. Copenhagen, 1988-89; mem. adv. bd. Leopold Ctr. for Sustainable Agr., 1994-2004, chair, 1996; pres. Johnson County Heritage Trust, 2000-04. Author: The Examined Self: Benjamin Franklin, Henry Adams and Henry James, 1964, Adventures, Rhymes and Designs of Vachel Lindsay, 1968; Thoreau and the American Indians, 1977; editor: A Week on the Concord and Merrimac Rivers, Walden, The Maine Woods, Cape Cod (H.D. Thoreau), 1985, Take This Exit: Rediscovering the Iowa Landscape, 1989, New Essays on Walden, 1992, American Lives: An Anthology of Autobiographical Writing, 1994, Recovering the Prairie, 1999, Take the Next Exit, 2000; contbr. articles to profl. jours. Guggenheim fellow, 1973-74.

**SAYRE, ROBERT MARION,** ambassador; b. Hillsboro, Oreg., Aug. 18, 1924; s. William Octavius and Mary Sayre; m. Elora Amanda Moyhihan, Dec. 29, 1951; children: Marian Amanda, Robert Marion, Daniel Humphrey. BA summa cum laude, Willamette U., 1949; JD cum laude (Alexander Welborn Weddell Peace prize 1956), George Washington U., 1956; MA, Stanford U., 1960; LLD, Willamette U., 1965. Bar: D.C. 1956, U.S. Ct. Appeals 1956, U.S. Supreme Ct. 1962. Joined U.S. Fgn. Service, 1949; econ. adviser on Latin Am., dir. Truman Point 4 Program, 1950-52; mil. adviser, 1952-57; officer charge inter-Am. security affairs, 1955-57; polit. counselor embassy Lima, Peru, 1957-59; fin. attache embassy Havana, Cuba, 1960; exec. sec. Task Force Latin Am., State Dept., Kennedy's Alliance for Progress, 1961; officer charge Mexican affairs Task Force Latin Am., State Dept., 1961-63; dep. dir. Office Caribbean and Mexican Affairs, 1963-64; dir. Office Mexican Affairs, 1964; sr. advisor White House, 1964-65; sr. dep. asst. sec. Bur. Inter-Am. Affairs, Dept. State, 1965-68; acting asst. sec. Dept. State, 1968—; Am. ambassador to Uruguay, 1968-69, to Panama, 1969-74; sr. insp. Dept. State, 1974-75, insp. gen., 1975-78; ambassador to Brazil, 1978-81; chmn. U.S. Interdepartmental group on Terrorism, dir. Counter-terrorism and Emergency Planning Dept. State, 1981-84, sr. insp., 1985; ptnr. IRC Group, Inc., 1986-87; from adv. to U.S. rep. to under sec. for mgmt. Orgn. of Am. States, 1987-94; sr. assoc. Global Bus. Access, Ltd., Washington, 1995—; chair Open Forum Working Group on Internat. Econs. U.S. Dept. State, 1995-96. Sr. councilor Atlantic Coun. Washington Inst. Fgn. Affairs. Capt. AUS, WWII; col. Res., ret. Decorated Soc. Cross (Brazil); Cross of Balboa (Panama); recipient Outstanding Employee award Dept. State, 1952, Superior Honor awards, 1964, 75, Disting. Honor award, 1978, Outstanding Performance award, 1982-85, Presdl. Meritorious award, 1986, Fgn. Svc. Cup award, 1990, Sec.'s Cert. of Appreciation, U.S. Dept. State, 1996. Mem. Am. Acad. Diplomacy, Inter Am. Bar Assn., Inter Am. Dialogue, Atlantic Coun. Washington Inst. Fgn. Affairs, Cosmos Club, Dacor House, Blue Key, Phi Delta Theta, Phi Eta Sigma, Tau Kappa Alpha. Episcopalian. Home: 3714 Bent Branch Rd Falls Church VA 22041-1028 Office: Global Business Access Ltd 1825 I St NW Ste 400 Washington DC 20006-5415

**SAYRES, EDWIN J., JR.,** animal welfare organization administrator; b. White Plains, N.Y., Nov. 25, 1948; s. Edwin J. and Catherine Marie (Phelan) S.; m. Michelle Diane Dimino, May 21, 1978; children: Christopher, Alexander. BA, Calif. State U., Sonoma, 1970, MA, 1972. Dir. Marin Found., San Rafael, Calif., 1970-74; dir. edn. St. Hubert's Giralda, Madison, N.J., 1974-79, v.p., 1978-81, pres., 1982—95; dir. animal protection divsn. Am. Humane Assn., 1995—97; pres. San Francisco SPCA, 1998—2003; pres., CEO ASPCA, NYC, 2003—. Mem. Humane Soc. U.S., Delta Soc. Lodges: Rotary. Office: ASPCA 424 E 92nd St New York NY 10128

**SAYWELL, EDWARD,** curator; Lynn and Philip A. Straus Intern Dept. Drawing, Fogg Art Mus., Harvard U., Cambridge, Mass., 1996—97, John S. Newberry Rsch. Asst., assoc. curator, Charles S. Cunningham Sr. Curatorial Assoc. Curator (exhibitions) Christopher Wilmarth: Drawing into Sculpture, 2003, The Privilege of Solitude: Alfred Jensen and Forest Bess, 2004 (Award for Best Show in a Comml. Gallery Nationally, Internat. Assn. Art Critics/USA, 2005). Office: Fogg Art Mus Harvard U 32 Quincy St Cambridge MA 02138

**SAYWELL, WILLIAM GEORGE GABRIEL,** business development and management consultant; b. Regina, Sask., Can., Dec. 1, 1936; s. John Ferdinand Tupper and Vera Marguerite S.; m. Helen Jane Larmer; children: Shelley Jayne, William James Tupper, Patricia Lynn. BA, U. Toronto, 1960, MA, 1961, PhD, 1968; LLD (hon.), U. BC, 1994, Simon Fraser U., 1997. Asst. prof. dept. East Asian studies U. Toronto, 1963-69; assoc. prof., 1969-71; assoc. prof. RDt., 1971-82, prof., 1982-83, chmn. dept., 1971-76; prof. dept.

history, pres., vice chancellor Simon Fraser U., Burnaby, B.C., Can., 1983-93; pres., chief exec. officer Asia Pacific Found. of Can., Vancouver, B.C., 1993-99; vice chmn. Intercedent Ltd., 1999—; pres. William Saywell & Assocs., Vancouver, 1999—. Cons. in higher edn.; sinologist and 1st sec. Can. Embassy, Beijing, 1972-73; dir. U. Toronto-York U. Ctr. Modern East Asia, 1974-75; prin. Innis Coll., 1976-79; vice provost U. Toronto, 1979-83; dir. Tokyo-Mitsubishi Bank (Can.), VLinx Ltd. Author articles and revs. on Chinese affairs to profl. jours. Decorated Order of Can., Order of B.C. Office: 701 2095 Beach Ave Vancouver BC Canada V6G 1Z3

**SAZAMA, KATHLEEN,** pathologist, lawyer; b. Sutherland, Nebr., May 8, 1941; d. Roger William and Esther Mary (Reitz) Paulman; m. Franklin Jed Sazama, Aug. 26, 1962; children: Clare Ann, Jill Patrice. BS, U. Nebr., 1962; MS, Am. U., 1969; MD, Georgetown U., 1976; JD, Cath. U. Am., 1990. Diplomate Am. Bd. Pathology; lic. pathologist Mich., Va., Md., D.C., Calif., Pa., Tex.; bar: Md. Intern and resident Georgetown U. Med. Ctr., Washington, 1976-78; resident NIH, Bethesda, Md., 1978-79; clin. asst. prof. pathology Uniformed Svcs. U. Health Scis., Bethesda, 1981-89; clin. affiliate Ferris State Coll., Big Rapids, 1985-86; chief lab. of blood bank practices FDA Ctr. for Biologics Evaluation and Rsch., Bethesda, 1986-89; cons. Ober, Kaler, Grimes & Shriver, Balt., 1989-90; assoc. med. dir. Sacramento (Calif.) Med. Found. Blood Ctr., 1990-92; asst. clin. prof. pathology U. Calif., Davis, 1990-92, assoc. prof., dir. clin. pathology, 1992-93; prof. pathology and lab. medicine Allegheny U. of the Health Scis., Phila., 1994—99; v.p. for faculty acad. affairs U. Tex./M.D. Anderson Cancer Ctr., Houston, 2000—02, prof. lab. medicine, 2000—. V.p. bd. Met. Washington Blood Banks, Inc., 1981-84; pres. bd. Am. Assn. Blood Banks, 2003-04; spkr. in field. Author: (with others) Stat: The Laboratory's Role, 1986; contbr. numerous articles to profl. jours. Comdr. USPHS, 1986-89. Fellow Coll. Am. Pathologists, Am. Soc. Clin. Pathologists; mem. ABA, Am. Health Lawyers Assn. (bd. dirs.), Health Lawyers Assn., Soc. Advancement Blood Mgmt. (bd. dirs.), Phi Kappa Phi, Beta Beta Beta. Avocations: tennis, playing bridge. Address: Univ of Texas MD Anderson Cancer Center 1515 Holcombe Blvd # 800 Houston TX 77030-4009 Office Phone: 713-792-7791. Business E-Mail: ksazama@mdanderson.org.

**SAZEGAR, MORTEZA,** artist; b. Tehran, Iran, Nov. 11, 1933; s. Hassan Ali and Zahra (Frootan) S.; m. Patricia Jean Kaurich, July 13, 1959. BA, U. Tex., El Paso, 1955, BS, 1956; postgrad., Baylor U. Coll. Medicine, 1956-57, Cornell U., 1958-59. One man exhibitions include, Poindexter Gallery, N.Y.C., 1964, 67, 69, 71, 73, 75, 77, group exhibitions include, Detroit Inst. Arts, 1965, Chgo. Art Inst., 1965, Univ. Art Mus., U. Tex., Austin, 1965, 72, Whitney Mus. Am. Art, 1970, Cleve. Mus. Art, 1972, Corcoran Gallery Art, Washington, 1973, Tyler Sch. Art, Temple U., Phila., 1979; represented in permanent collections, Whitney Mus. Am. Art, N.Y.C., San Francisco Mus. Modern Art, Riverside Mus., N.Y.C., U. Mass., Amherst, Corcoran Gallery Art, Prudential Ins. Corp. Am., Mus. Contemporary Art, Tehran, Iran. Mem. Artists Equity Assn. Democrat. Address: 1223 Homeville Rd Cochranville PA 19330-1712

**SBRAMANIAM, CHITRA P.,** educational consultant; b. Chennai, Tamil Nadu, India, May 12, 1968; d. Pathiavadi and Lalitha Subramaniam; 1 child, Arvind Mallikarjunan. Ednl. cons. Internat. Acad. Design and Tech., Tampa, Fla. Office: Internat Acad Design and Tech 18229 Collridge Dr Tampa FL 33647

**SCACCHI, GRETA,** actress; b. Milan, Feb. 18, 1960; m. Vincent D'Onofrio, 1991 (div. 1993); 2 children. Films include Das Zweite Gesicht, 1982, Heat and Dust, 1982, Defence of the Realm, 1985, The Coca-Cola Kid, 1985, White Mischief, 1987, Un Homme Amoureux, 1987, Good Morning, Babylon, 1987, Paura e Amore, 1988, La Donna della Luna, 1988, Presumed Innocent, 1990, Turtle Beach, 1991, Fires Within, 1991, The Player, 1992, Desire, 1993, Country Life, 1994, The Browning Version, 1994, Jefferson in Paris, 1995, Emma, 1996, Bravo Randy, 1996, The Serpent's Kiss, 1997, Tom's Midnight Garden, 1998, The Red Violin, 1998, Ladies Room, 1999, The Manor, 1999, Looking for Alibrandi, 2000, Festival in Cannes, 2001, Baltic Storm, 2003, Beyond the Sea, 2004, Syriana, 2005, The Book of Revelation, 2005; TV movies include The Ebony Tower, 1984, Camille, 1984, Dr. Fischer of Geneva, 1985, Rasputin, 1996 (Emmy award), The Odyssey, 1997, Macbeth, 1998; (TV mini series) Waterfront, 1984, The Farm, 2001, Daniel Deronda, 2002. Office: c/o Susan Smith & Assocs 121 N San Vicente Blvd Beverly Hills CA 90211-2303

**SCAFFIDI, JUDITH ANN,** academic administrator; b. Bklyn., Aug. 2, 1950; d. Anthony William and Rose Virginia (Nocera) S. BA, SUNY, Plattsburg, 1972, MS, 1973; postgrad., Einstein Coll. Medicine, 1983; PhD (hon.), Internat. U. Bombay, 1993; HHD (hon.), London Inst. Applied Rsch., 1993. Cert. secondary edn. English. VISTA mem. ACTION, N.Y.C., 1976-77; coord. cultural resources Learning Leaders, N.Y.C., 1977-80, tng. splst. in Bklyn., 1980—. Field supr., adj. faculty Coll. for Human Svcs., N.Y.C., 1984-86; adv. coun. chair Ret. Sr. Vol. Program in Bklyn., 1983-86; adv. bd. Ret. Sr. Vol. Program in N.Y.C., 1983-86. Acvive Am. Friends Svc. Com., 1994—. Recipient award for svcs. in promotion literacy Internat. Reading Assn. and Bklyn. Reading Coun., 1986, award for outstanding leadership Ret. Sr. Vol. Program, 1986, cert. of appreciation Mayor City of N.Y., 1991, cert. of appreciation for exceptional support and encouragement of volunteerism, 1998. Mem. NAFE, Cath. Tchrs. Assn. Bklyn. (del. sch. dist. 18, 1982-91), Internat. Platform Assn., World Found. Successful Women, Am. Biog. Inst. (rsch. bd. advisors 1992-93), Am. Biog. Inst. Rsch. Assn. (bd. govs. 1992—), Internat. Parliament for Safety and Peace (dep. mem. and diplomatic passport), Maisson Internat. de Intellectuals (Acad. MIDI), Cath. Alumni Club N.Y., Amnesty Internat. Roman Catholic. Avocations: travel, reading, walking. Address: 2330 Ocean Ave Apt 3H Brooklyn NY 11229-3036 Office: Learning Leaders Inc 80 Maiden Ln New York NY 10038-4811

**SCAGLIONE, LOUIS, III,** music educator, conductor; b. Berwyn, Ill., June 7, 1969; s. Louis F. and Sharon L. Scaglione. BS Music Edn., U. Ill., 1992; M Music, Temple U., 1996. Cert. K - 12 Instnl. I in Music Pa., 1998, Spl. K - 12 Tchg. in Music Ill., 1992. Artistic dir. Arts at Andalusia, Andalusia, Pa., 1995—; conductor Phila. Young Artists Orch., 1997—; assoc. conductor Phila. Youth Orch., 1998—2005, pres., 2001—; mem. faculty Temple U. Music Preparatory Divsn., Phila., 1998—2003, Montgomery County C.C., 2002—; artistic dir. Choral Soc. of Montgomery Coll., 2002—; music dir., condr. Phila. Youth Orch., 2005—, pres., 2001—. Trustee Andalusia Found., Andalusia, Pa., 2000—; bd. trustees Youth Work Found., Union League Phila., 2002—. Mem.: Music Educators Nat. Conf., Am. Choral Dirs. Assn., Coll. Music Soc., Am. Symphony Orch. League (sec. youth orch. divsn. 2000—, vice-chmn. 2000—), Union League of Phila. (mem. house com. 2000—), Pi Kappa Lambda, Phi Eta Sigma, Kappa Delta Pi, Golden Key Soc. Office: Phila Youth Orch PO Box 41810 Philadelphia PA 19101 Personal E-mail: louiscag@aol.com.

**SCAIFE, RICHARD MELLON,** philanthropist; married; 2 children. Mgr. Scaife Newspapers. Chmn., trustee Sarah Scaife Found., Inc.; donor, chmn., trustee Carthage Found., Allegheny Found. Named one of Forbes' Richest Americans, 2006. Office: Scaife Family Found 3 Mellon Bank Ctr Pittsburgh PA 15259-0001*

**SCALA, JAMES,** health facility administrator, consultant, writer; b. Ramsey, NJ, Sept. 16, 1934; s. Edvigi and Lorene (Hendricksen) Scala; m. Nancy Peters, June 15, 1957; children: James, Gregory, Nancy, Kimberly. BA, Columbia U., 1960; PhD, Cornell U., 1964; postgrad., Harvard U., 1968; LHD (hon.), Hofstra U., 1998. Cert. nutrition specialist. Staff scientist Miami Valley Labs., Procter and Gamble Co., 1964-66; head life scis., dir. fundamental rsch. Owens Ill. Corp., 1966-71; dir. nutrition T.J. Lipton Inc., 1971-75; dir. health scis. Gen. Foods Corp., 1975-78; v.p. sci. and tech. Shaklee Corp., San Francisco, 1978-85, sr. v.p. sci. affairs, 1986-87. Lectr. Georgetown U. Med. Sch.; instr. U. Calif., Berkeley; nutritionist U.S. Olympic Ski Team, 1981—87. Author: Making the Vitamin Connection,

---

1985, The Arthritis Relief Diet, 1987, 2d edit., 1989, Eating Right for a Bad Gut, 1990, 2d edit., 1992, Eating Right for a Bad Gut, new edit., 1999, The High Blood Pressure Relief Diet, 1988, 2d edit., 1990, Look 10 Years Younger, Feel 10 Years Better, 1991, 2d edit., 1993, Prescription for Longevity, 1992, 2d edit., 1994, If You Can't/Won't Stop Smoking, 1993, The New Arthritis Relief Diet, 1998, 25 Natural Ways to Manage Stress and Avoid Burnout, 2000, 25 Natural Ways to Relieve Irritable Bowel Syndrome, 2000, 20 Natural Ways to Reduce the Risk of Prostate Cancer, 2001, 25 Natural Ways to Lower Blood Pressure, 2002; editor: Nutritional Determinants in Athletic Performance, 1981, New Protective Roles for Selected Nutrients, 1989; columnist: Dance mag.; contbr. articles to profl. jours. With USAF, 1953—56. Disting. scholar, U. Miami, Fla., 1977, Atlantic U., 1977. Fellow: Am. Coll. Nutrition; mem.: AAAS, Am. Diabetic Assn., Mt. Diablo Astron. Soc., Eastbay Astron. Soc., Astron. Soc. Pacific (bd. dirs., chmn. devel. coun.), Inst. Food Technologists, Am. Soc. Cell Biology, Sports Medicine Coun., Brit. Nutrition Soc., Am. Inst. Nutrition, Oakland Yacht Club, Olympic Club (San Francisco), Sigma Xi. Libertarian. Avocations: astronomy, photography. Office Phone: 925-283-2753. Personal E-mail: jscala2@comcast.net. *I am in awe of the incredible resiliency of living things, but most of all the human spirit.*

**SCALES, JAMES LEONARD, JR.,** orthopedic surgeon; b. Sacramento, May 15, 1952; s. James Leonard and Ruth Marie S.; m. Donna Marie Coppola, Oct. 11, 1983; children: James, Steven, Kevin. AB cum laude, Harvard U., 1974; MS, Rutgers U., 1978; MD, U. Medicine & Dentistry N.J., 1979; attended, Rutgers U., 1980—82. Diplomate Am. Bd. Orthopedic Surgery, 1988. Resident in surgery U. Medicine and Dentistry N.J., Rutgers Med. Sch., Piscataway, 1979—80; resident in orthop. surgery U. Medicine and Dentistry N.J., N.J. Med. Sch., Newark, 1982—86; staff physician med. unit Meadowlands Sports Complex, East Rutherford, NJ, 1980—88; orthop. surgeon D'Ascoli Orthop. Surgery, Sparta, NJ, 1986—88; pres. Andover Orthop. Surgery & Sports Medicine Group, PA, Newton, NJ, 1988—. Cons. orthop. N.J. Cardinals, Augusta, 1997—; chief surgery Newton Meml. Hosp., 1994—96; med. dir. N. Jersey Surgery Ctr., Newton, 1998—. Vol. physician U.S. Olympic Com., U.S. Olympic Tng. Ctr., Lake Placid, NY, 1997; Interviewer Harvard Club N.J., 1975—98. Fellow: Am. Acad. Orthop. Surgeons; mem.: AMA, Am. Coll. Sports Medicine, Am. Med. Soc., Pa. Med. Soc., N.J. Med. Soc., Pa. Orthop. Soc., N.J. Orthop. Soc. Avocations: running, music. Office: Andover Orthop Surgery 280 Newton-Sparta Rd Newton NJ 07860 Office Phone: 973-579-7443.

**SCALES, MAURICEO LAMONT,** history educator; s. Thomas Donnell and Geraldine Millner Scales; m. Cynthia Watson, Nov. 22, 1996; children: Brittany Ariana, Lauryn Ashley, Sara Kathryn. BA, Wake Forest U., Winston-Salem, 1993. Sales Jefferson-Pilot Ins., Winston-Salem, NC, 1994—98; tchr. Winston-Salem/Forsyth County Schs., 1998—2006. Dir., founder STAR Football Camp, Winston-Salem, 2002—. Office Phone: 336-817-3950.

**SCALES, RICHARD LEWIS,** retired sales representative; b. Indpls., Nov. 16, 1928; s. Ortho Lorton and Nina L. (Julian) S.; m. E Jean Rankin, Dec. 21, 1951; children: Richard, Allan, Anne. BSME, Purdue U., 1952. Rsch. and devel. engr. Bell Labs./Western Electric, Chgo., also Whippany, N.J., 1955-58; sales engr. Bodine Electric Co., Chgo., 1958-61; dist. sales mgr. Wabash (Ind.) Magnetics, 1961-66; foreman chm. bd. (emeritus) Richard Scales Assocs., Wabash, 1966—, RSA Inc., Wabash, 1985—. Contbr. articles to mag. Elder, Presbyn. Ch. Lt. USNR, 1952-55, Korea; past pres. Wabash Rotary Club. Recipient Paul Harris award Rotary Internat. Republican. Avocations: computers, photography. Home: 550 Sommers Ave Wabash IN 46992-2021 Personal E-mail: rscales@netusa1.net.

**SCALES, ROBERT H., JR.,** former academic administrator, retired army officer; b. Gainesville, Fla., Aug. 5, 1944; m. Diana Weiss; children: Maria, Monica. BS, U.S. Mil. Acad., 1966; MS, Duke U., PhD in History. Commd. 2d lt. U.S. Army, 1966, advanced through grades to maj. gen.; dep. chief staff for base ops./dep. chief staff for doctrine Tng. and Doctrine Command, Ft. Monroe, Va., 60 1997; comdr. U.S. Army War Coll., Carlisle Barracks, Pa., 1997—2000; pres., CEO Walden Univ., 2000—02; sr. v.p. Sylvan Learning Sys., 2002—. Prin. author: Certain Victory: The U.S. Army in the Gulf War, 1993, Firepower in Limited War, 1995, Yellow Smoke: The Future of Land Warfare for America's Military, 2003. Decorated DSM, Silver Star, Legion of Merit with 4 oakleaf clusters, Bronze Star medl, Air medal, others. Office: Sylvan Learning Sys 1001 Fleet St Baltimore MD 21202

**SCALES, WILLIAM CLINTON, SR.,** minister, small business owner; b. Charleston, W.Va., July 2, 1915; s. Edward F. and Zephyr Ivory Scales; m. Myra Elizabeth Wills, Mar. 7, 1934; 1 child, William Clinton Jr. Co-owner M. and S. Shoe Repair Co., Charleston, W.Va., 1936; pres. Scales Delicious Potato Chip Co., Cleve., 1938—41, Hal'Le-Lu'Jah Records Co., Cleve., 1941—45; min. Allegheny Conf. Seventh Day Adventist Ch., Pine Forge, Pa., 1945—81; founder, owner Real Truth Assoc. Inc., 1981—. Author: (book) Born to Win Souls, 1996, co-author various religious tracts, Bible lessons, manuals. Recipient Soulwinning Super Star award, Gen. Conf. Ministerial Assoc., 2001. Home: 3625 Shandwick Pl Birmingham AL 35242 Office: Real Truth Assoc Inc PO Box 381824 Birmingham AL 35242 E-mail: R.L.Truth@aol.com.

**SCALET, J. CHRIS (JAMES CHRISTOPHER SCALET),** pharmaceutical executive; BS in Mgmt. Sci. and Computer Systems, Okla. State U.; student Exec. Development Prog. Kellogg Sch. Mgmt., Northwestern U. V.p., info. tech., CIO MAPCO Inc., 1993—97; sr. v.p., info. tech., CIO Internat. Paper, 1998—2003; sr. v.p., info. services, CIO Merck & Co., Inc., 2003—05, sr. v.p. global process and services, CIO, 2006—. Office: Merck PO Box 100 Whitehouse Station NJ 08889-0100*

**SCALETTA, PHILLIP RALPH, III,** lawyer; b. Iowa City, Dec. 18, 1949; s. Phillip Jasper and Helen M. (Beedle) S.; m. Karen Lynn Scaletta, May 13, 1973; children: Phillip, Anthony, Alexander. BSIM, MS, Purdue U., 1972; JD, Ind. U., 1975. Bar: Ind. 1975, U.S. Dist. Ct. Ind. 1975, Ill. 1993. Assoc. Ice Miller, Indpls., 1975-81, ptnr., 1981—. Contbr. articles to profl. jours. Chmn. Ind. Continuing Legal Edn. Found., Indpls., 1989; mem. Environ. Quality Control Water Com., 1988-98. Mem. Ind. Bar Assn., Indpls. Bar Assn., Def. Rsch. Inst., Internat. Assn. Def. Counsel, Gyro Club Indpls. (v.p. 1992-93, pres. 1993-94, bd. dirs. 1990—). Avocations: golf, skiing, tennis. Home: 7256 Tuliptree Trl Indianapolis IN 46256-2136 Office: Ice Miller 1 American Sq Indianapolis IN 46282-0020 Office Phone: 317-236-2330. Business E-Mail: scaletta@icemiller.com.

**SCALIA, ANTONIN,** United States Supreme Court Justice; b. Trenton, NJ, Mar. 11, 1936; s. S. Eugene and Catherine Louise (Panaro) Scalia; m. Maureen McCarthy, Sept. 10, 1960; children: Ann Forrest, Eugene, John Francis, Catherine Elisabeth, Mary Clare, Paul David, Matthew, Christopher James, Margaret Jane. AB, Georgetown U., 1957; student, U. Fribourg, Switzerland, 1955—56; LLB, Harvard U., 1960. Bar: Ohio 1962, Va. 1970. Assoc. Jones Day Cockley & Reavis, Cleve., 1961—67; assoc. prof. U. Va. Law Sch., 1967—70, prof., 1970—74; gen. counsel Office Telecomm. Policy, Exec. Office of Pres., 1971—72; chmn. Administv. Conf. U.S., Washington, 1972—74; asst. atty. gen. Office Legal Counsel US Dept. Justice, Washington, 1974—77; prof. law U. Chgo., 1977—82; judge U.S. Ct. Appeals (D.C. cir.), 1982—86; assoc. justice U.S. Supreme Ct., Washington, 1986—. Vis. prof. Georgetown Law Ctr., 1977, Stanford Law Sch., 1980—81; resident scholar Am. Enterprise Inst., 1977. Editor: Regulation mag., 1979—82; author: A Matter of Interpretation, 1998. Sheldon fellow, Harvard U., 1960—61. Republican. Office: US Supreme Ct One First St NE Washington DC 20543-0001*

**SCALIA, FRANK R.,** neuroscientist; b. Bklyn., Mar. 18, 1939; s. Frank and Isabelle Scalia; m. Marilyn J. Turano, Jan. 2, 1993; children: Jason, Russell, Katherine C. Scalia/Hutson. BA, NYU, N.Y., 1959; PhD, SUNY, Bklyn.,

---

1964. Prof. Downstate Med. Ctr. SUNY, Bklyn., 1977—. Office: SUNY Downstate Medical Center 450 Clarkson Avenue Brooklyn NY 11203 Office Phone: 718-270-1018. Business E-Mail: fscalia@downstate.edu.

**SCALLEN, THOMAS KAINE,** broadcast executive; b. Mpls., Aug. 14, 1925; s. Raymond A. and Lenore (Kaine) S.; m. Bille Jo Brice; children by previous marriage: Thomas, Sheila, Patrick, Eileen, Timothy and Maureen (twins). BA, St. Thomas Coll., 1949; JD, U. Denver, 1950. Bar: Minn. Asst. atty. gen. State of Minn., Mpls., 1950-55; sole practice Mpls., 1955-57; pres. Med. Investment Corp., Mpls., 1957—, Internat. Broadcasting Corp., Mpls., 1977—; owner Harlem Globetrotters. Pres., exec. producer Ice Capades; chmn. bd. dirs. Century Park Pictures Corp., Los Angeles, chmn. bd. dirs. Blaine-Thompson Co., Inc., N.Y.C.; chmn. Apache Plastics, Inc., Stockton, Calif. Served with AUS. Mem. World Pres. Orgn., Minn. Club, Calhoun Beach Club, L.A. Athletic Club. Clubs: University (St. Paul, Mpls.), Rochester (Minn.) Golf and Country, Edina (Minn.) Country, Athletic (Mpls.). Home: Heron Cove Windham NH 03087 Office: Internat Broadcasting Corp 80 S 8th St Ste 4701 Minneapolis MN 55402-2207

**SCALZA, MARGARET T.,** publishing executive; b. Jersey City, May 27, 1936; d. Louis Patrick and Josephine M. (Cleary) Scalza; m. David Jenkins, Sept. 30, 1951 (div. 1962); children: Alison Brittain, Cynthia Higgins, Ann Jenkins Tunis Owner Towne House Restaurant, Hackettstown, N.J., 1963-65; pres. Kinsley Assocs., Inc., Hackettstown, N.J., 1966—. Pub. purchasing guides, sch. directories, N.J., N.Y., Calif., Ill. Co-chmn. Northwestern N.J. divsn. U.S. Postal Customer Coun., 1978—; trustee Tranquility United Meth. Ch. Mem. NAFE, Nat. Assn. Sch. Bus. Ofcls., North Ctrl. Jersy Assn. Realtors, Hackettstown Trade Assn. (sec.-treas., bd. dirs. 1963). Republican. Avocations: cooking, sewing, reading, flower arranging, crabbing. Home: 9 House Wren Hackettstown NJ 07840-2815 Office: 4 Woodward Terr Hackettstown NJ 07840-4602 Office Phone: 908-850-6555. E-mail: marge9@optonline.net.

**SCANDARY, E. JANE,** special education educator, consultant; b. Saginaw, Mich., Sept. 12, 1923; d. Leonard William and Reva Charlotte (Smith) Leipprandt; m. Theodore John Scandary; children: John S., Robert G. BA, Mich. State U., East Lansing, 1945, EdS, 1963, PhD, 1968, MEd, Wayne State U., 1951. Cert. secondary and spl. edn. tchr., Mich. Therapist speech and lang. Ann J. Kellogg Sch., Battle Creek, Mich., 1945-47; supr. speech therapy programs Wayne County Schs., Detroit, 1948-52; supr. programs for phys., hearing and visually impaired Ingham Intermediate Schs., Mason, Mich., 1960-78; spl. edn. cons. Mich. Dept. of Edn., Lansing, 1978-87, Livingston Intermediate Schs., Howell, Mich., 1987—. Rsch. assoc. Mich. State U., East Lansing, 1965-66, adj. prof., 1969-75, 81-82; mem. adv. com. China-U.S. Sci. Exchange Program Spl. Edn.; guest lectr. seminars spl. edn. Australia, Eng., Iran, Israel, Aruba, Germany, Scotland. Editor Chronicles newsletter, 1987—; contbr. articles to profl. jours. Vol. Mich. Hist. Mus., 1995—, Meals-on-Wheels, 1998-2001, Salvation Army, 2000—; chair futures com. Mich. Dept. Edn., 1992, editor, chair Task Force Futuresin Spl. Edn. 2000 AD and Beyond, 1992; bd. dirs. Delta Dist. Libr. 1998—. 1st Chance Early Childhood grantee, 1972-78; recipient Resolution of Tribute Mich. State Senate, 1986, 3d Pl. award Mid-Mich. Spring Art Show, 1998; Scandary award for outstanding contbrs. early childhood edn. established in her name, 1990. Mem. Nat. Coun. Exceptional Children (field editor 1976-86, pres. div. physically handicapped 1982-83), Mid-Mich. Art Guild, World Future Soc., Capitol Area Quilt Guild. Avocations: painting, writing, reading, creative sewing.

**SCANDURA, JOSEPH MICHAEL,** neuroscientist, application developer; b. Bay Shore, N.Y., Apr. 29, 1932; s. Joseph and Lucy S.; m. Alice Baker, Aug. 13, 1960; children: Jeanne, Janette, Joseph, Julie. AB, U. Mich., 1953, MA, 1955; PhD, Syracuse U., 1962; postdoctoral, Stanford U., summer 1964, 68-69, U. Calif.-Berkeley, summer 1968, MIT, summer 1972; postgrad., U. Kiel, W.Ger., 1975, Inst. Ednl. Tech., Italy, summer 1978. Tchr. math., sci. White Plains, Bay Shore, 1953-56; instr. math., head wrestling coach Syracuse U., NY, 1956-63; asst. prof. edn., math. SUNY-Buffalo, 1963-64; research asst. prof. math. edn. Fla. State U., Tallahassee, 1964-66; dir. instructional systems, structural learning U. Pa., Phila., 1966-96; Fulbright prof. U. Koblenz & Dresden, 1998-99. Vis. rsch. prof. Drexel U., 2005; founder, chmn. Intelligent Micro Systems, Narberth, Pa., 1978-2002; chmn. bd. sci. advisors MERGE Rsch. Inst., 1973-2002; prin. investigator NIST Advanced Tech. Program Project on Automating Supply Chain, 1977—; cons. U.S. Office Edn., NSF, NAS, Tex. Instruments, Borg-Warner, U.S. Army; organizer, lectr., participant profl. confs., 1963—; dir. NATO Advanced Study Inst. on Structural Process Theories of Complex Human Behavior, 1977; coach undefeated Ea. Intercollegiate Wrestling Championship Team, 1963. Author: Mathematics - Concrete Behavioral Foundations, 1971, (with others) An Algorithmic Approach to Mathematics - Concrete Behavioral Foundations, 1971, Structural Learning I - Theory and Research, 1973, Problem Solving - A Structural Process Approach with Instructional Implications, 1977, (with A.B. Scandura) Structural Learning and Concrete Operations - An Approach to Piagetian Conservation, 1980, Cognitive Approach to Software Development, 1988, Prodoc (comprehensive suite of software devel. and maintenance tools), 1989, Cognitive Approach to Software Engineering and Re-engineering, 1991, ongoing projects; Flexys-customizable reengineering automation, Autobuilder-automated specification and implementation component based software while guaranteeing correctness, intelligent tutor authoring of devel. sys. model IT and tutor IT, 1992—, NATO Advanced Study Inst., 1993, Automated Software Conversions and Re-engineering, 1993; contbr. 200 articles to profl. jours.; editor: Research in Mathematics Education, 1967, Structural Learning II - Issues and Approaches, 1976, (with C.J. Brainerd) Structural Process Models of Complex Human Behavior, 1978, developer, producer numerous computer-based instructional systems and software devel. systems; multiple software patents. Recipient Rensselaer award, 1949, Bausch and Lomb award, 1949, Nat. AAU Wrestling Champion and Outstanding Wrestler award, 1955; Fulbright scholar, 1975-76, 1998-99; U.S. Office Edn. fellow, 1978-79. Fellow: APA (chmn. E.L. Thorndike award com. 1974—79), Structural Learning Soc. (sr.; chmn. 1969—80, editor in chief Jour. Structural Learning 1976—90, chmn. 1985—88, Jour. Structural Learning and Intelligent Systems 1990—2001, chmn. 1995—, founder, sci. advisor Tech., Instr., Cognition & Learning 2002—); mem.: IEEE, AAUP, Univ. Profs. for Acad. Order, Psychonomic Soc., Math. Assn. Am., Nat. Coun. Tchrs. Math. (past fed. funds com. chmn.), Am. Ednl. Rsch. Assn. (chmn. tech., instrn., cognition and learning), Assn. Computing Machinery, Phi Delta Kappa, Phi Eta Sigma, Phi Kappa Phi. Home: 1249 Greentree Ln Narberth PA 19072-1219 Office: U Pa Instructional Systems Philadelphia PA 19104 Personal E-mail: scandura@scandura.com. *Accomodation to -- as well as leadership of -- groups, institutions and/or societies is an essential ingredient of success in most walks of life. There are circumstances, however, which require inner direction, whether developing a new scientific paradigm or standing firm against political pressures. Although vindication is rarely complete and often delayed, following one's best instincts yields its own rewards— perhaps the satisfaction of ultimately being proven right but more often simply knowing one did what had to be done.*

**SCANLAN, JAMES PATRICK,** philosophy and Slavic studies educator; b. Chgo., Feb. 22, 1927; s. Gilbert Francis and Helen (Meyers) S.; m. Marilyn A. Morrison, June 12, 1948. BA, U. Chgo., 1948, MA, 1950, PhD, 1956. Research fellow Inst. Philos. Research, San Francisco, 1953-55; instr. Case Inst. Tech., Cleve., 1955-56; from instr. to assoc. prof. Goucher Coll., Balt., 1956-68; prof., dir. Slavic Ctr. U. Kans., Lawrence, 1968-70; prof. Ohio State U., Columbus, 1971-91, dir. Slavic Ctr., 1988-91, prof. emeritus, 1992—. Vis. rsch. scholar Moscow State U., 1964-65, 69, 98, Acad. Scis. USSR, Moscow, 1978, 93, Russian State U. for the Humanities, 1995; fgn. vis. fellow Slavic Rsch. Ctr., Hokkaido U., Sapporo, Japan, 1987-88. Author: Marxism in the USSR, 1985, Dostoevsky the Thinker, 2002, Russian trans., 2006; editor: Historical Letters by Peter Lavrov, 1967, Soviet Studies in Philosophy, 1987—92, Russian Studies in Philosophy, 1992—97, Technology, Culture and Development: The Experience of the Soviet Model, 1992, Russian Thought After Communism, 1994; co-editor: Russian Philosophy, 1965,

Marxism and Religion in Eastern Europe, 1976. Served with USMC, 1945-46. Woodrow Wilson Internat. Ctr. fellow, 1982; recipient Translation award Nat. Translation Ctr., 1967, Faculty Rsch. award Fulbright-Hays, 1982-83. Mem. Am. Philos. Assn., Am. Assn. Advancement Slavic Studies, Phi Beta Kappa. Home: 1000 Urlin Ave Apt 206 Columbus OH 43212-3324 Personal E-mail: scanlan.1@osu.edu.

**SCANLAN, JOHN DOUGLAS,** retired ambassador; b. Thief River Falls, Minn., Dec. 20, 1927; s. Paul Douglas and Ruby (Bennes) S.; m. Margaret Anne Calvi; children: Kathleen, Michael, Malia, John. BA, U. Minn., 1952, MA in Russian Studies, 1955. Instr. U. Minn., 1955; Soviet research analyst U.S. Dept. State, Washington, 1956-58; third sec. Am. Embassy, Moscow, 1958-60, cultural attache Warsaw, 1961-65, second sec. Montevideo, 1966-67; prin. officer Am. Consulate, Poznan, Poland, 1967-69; sr. rep. to U.S. Dept. Defense, Washington, 1969-71; desk officer U.S.-Soviet bilateral relations, 1971-73; polit. counselor Am. Embassy, Warsaw, 1973-75; mem. state exec. seminar Washington, 1975-76; spl. asst. to Dir. Gen. of Fgn. Service, 1976-77; dep. dir. for Europe, USIA, 1977-79; dep. chief Mission in Belgrade, Yugoslavia, 1979-81; dep. asst. sec. of state for European affairs, 1981-82; fgn. affairs fellow Fletcher Sch. Law and Diplomacy, Tufts U., 1983-84; chmn. U.S. del. to Conf. on Security and Coop. in Europe, Cultural Forum Preparatory Conf., Budapest, 1984; amb. to Yugoslavia, Am. Embassy, Belgrade, 1985-89; dep. comdt. U.S. Army War Coll., Carlisle Barracks, Pa., 1989-91. Mem. exec. bd. Project on Ethnic Rels.; mem. Ctr. Strategic and Internat. Studies U.S.-European-Poland Action Commn. Mem. Planning Commn., Falls Church, Va., 1972-73, City Council, 1975-79. Recipient Presdl. Meritorious Service award for Diplomacy, 1984. Office Phone: 239-263-1903. E-mail: ambscan@earthlink.net.

**SCANLAN, MICHAEL,** priest, academic administrator; b. Far Rockaway, N.Y., Dec. 1, 1931; s. Vincent Michael and Marjorie (O'Keefe) Scanlan. BA, Williams Coll., 1953; JD, Harvard U., 1956; MDiv, St. Francis Sem., Loretto, Pa., 1975; LittD (hon.), Coll. Steubenville, 1972; LLD (hon.), Williams Coll., Williamstown, Mass., 1978; PdD (hon.), St. Francis Coll., Loretto, Pa., 1987; STM, 3d Order Regular of St Francis, 1996. Ordained priest Roman Catholic Ch., 1964; Cross Pro Ecclesia et Pontifice, 1990. Acting dean Coll. Steubenville, Ohio, 1964-66, dean Ohio, 1966-69; rector pres. St. Francis Major Sem., Loretto, Pa., 1969-74; pres. Franciscan U. Steubenville, 1974-2000, chancellor, 2000—. Pres. (FIRE) Cath. Alliance for Faith, Intercession, Repentence and Evangelism, 1984—. Author: The Power in Penance, 1972, Inner Healing, 1974, A Portion of My Spirit, 1979, The San Damiano Cross, 1983, Turn to the Lord-A Call to Repentance, 1989, The Truth About Trouble, 1989, rev. edit. 2005, What Does God Want: A Practical Guide to Making Decisions, 1996, (with James Manney) Let the Fire Fall, 1997, The Holy Spirit: Holy Desire, 1998, Rosary Companion with Luminous Mysteries, 2002; chmn. editl. bd. New Covenant mag., 1985-92. Mem. Diocese of Steubenville Ecumenical Commn., 1964-69; bd. dirs. Rumor Control Ctr., Steubenville, 1968-69, C. of C., Steubenville, 1976-79; bd. trustees St. Francis Prep. Sch., Spring Grove, Pa., 1969-74; vice-chmn. bd. trustees St. Francis Coll., Loretto, Pa., 1969-74; trustee United Way, Steubenville, 1975-80; chmn. nat. svc. com. Cath. Charismatic Renewal, 1975-78. Staff judge adv. USAF, 1956-57. Named Sacrae Theologiae Magister Third Order Regular St Francis, 1996. Roman Catholic. Avocations: tennis, golf, skiing. Office: Franciscan U Office of Chancellor 1235 University Blvd Steubenville OH 43952-1796 Office Phone: 740-283-6466. *If you are going to change something, you've got to live on vision, before you live on reality. You have to be so inspired by the vision, that you keep telling everybody until it gets in them, and they start living it with you.*

**SCANLAN, THOMAS CLEARY,** publishing executive, editor; b. Birmingham, Mich., May 18, 1957; s. Thomas Matthew and Emily (Cleary) S.; m. Sally Sachs, June 20, 1981; children: Bridget C., Thomas M., Patrick J. BS, St. Louis U., 1979. Salesman Walter Heller Co., Chgo., 1979-82; pub., editor Surplus Record, Inc., Chgo., 1982—. Office: Surplus Record Inc 20 N Wacker Dr Chicago IL 60606-2806

**SCANLAN, THOMAS JOSEPH,** college president, educator; b. NYC, Mar. 5, 1945; s. Thomas Joseph and Anna Marie (Schmitt) S. BA in Physics, Cath. U. Am., 1967; MA in Math., NYU, 1972; PhD in Bus. Adminstrn., Columbia U., 1978; LLD (hon.), Coll. Mt. St. Vincent. Prin. Queen of Peace HS, North Arlington, NJ, 1972-75; dir. fin., ednl. NY Province, Bros. of Christian Sch., Lincroft, NJ, 1978-81; vice chancellor Bethlehem U., Israel, 1981-87; pres. Manhattan Coll., Bronx, NY, 1987—. Bd. dirs. Am. Coun. on Edn. Trustee Commn. on Ind. Colls. and Univs., 2002, Assn. Cath. Colls. and Univs., 1994—. Recipient Pro Ecclesia et Pontifice medal, Pope John Paul II, Vatican City, 1986. Mem. Bros. of Christian Schs., Am. Coun. Edn., Assn. Cath. Colls. and Univs. (trustee 1994—), Assn. Am. Colls., Nat. Cath. Edn. Assn., Nat. Asns. Ind. Colls. and Univs., Nat. Collegiate Athletic Assn. (exec. com. and divsn. 1), Metro Atlantic Athletic Assn., Equestrian Order of the Holy Sepulchre of Jerusalem, Phi Beta Kappa, Beta Gamma Sigma, Phi Beta Kappa Fellows. Avocations: golf, reading, movies. Office: Manhattan Coll Office of Pres Manhattan Coll Pky Bronx NY 10471-3913 Office Phone: 718-862-7301. Business E-mail: thomas.scanlan@manhattan.edu.

**SCANLON, ANDREW,** structural engineering educator; b. Bridge of Allan, Scotland, Apr. 16, 1944; BSc with honors, U. Glasgow, Scotland, 1966; PhD, U. Alta., Can., 1972. Civil engr. Pub. Works Can., St. John, N.B., Canada, 1966-67; project engr. N.B. Devel. Corp., Fredericton, Canada, 1967-68; teaching asst. U. Alta., Edmonton, Canada, 1968-71; structural design engr. Duthie Newby and Assocs., Edmonton, 1971-73; structural divsn. head Reid, Crowther and Ptnrs. Ltd., Edmonton, 1973-78; sr. structural engr. structural evaluation sect. Constrn. Tech. Labs., Inc., 1978-80, mgr. analytical design sect., 1980-82; assoc. prof. civil engring. U. Alta., 1982-83, prof., 1983-87, Pa. State U., University Park, 1987—, dir. transp. structures program Pa. Transp. Inst., 1993—2002, assoc. dir. of Inst., 1999—2002, head dept., 2002—. Recipient Le Prix P.L. Pratley award Can. Soc. Civil Engring., 1990. Fellow Am. Concrete Inst., Am. Soc. of Civil Engrs. Office: Pa State U 212 Sackett Bldg University Park PA 16802-1408 Office Phone: 814-863-3084. Business E-mail: axs21@psu.edu.

**SCANLON, CHARLES FRANCIS,** retired military officer, writer; b. Nashville, Jan. 31, 1935; s. Francis James Gordon and Dorothy Rose (Compton) S.; m. Barbara Coddington Wall Scanlon, June 18, 2005; children: Teri, Brett, Ashlyn, Kellie. BA in Polit. Sci., U. Fla., 1960; grad., Command and Gen. Staff Coll., Ft. Leavenworth, Kans., 1970, Naval War Coll., Newport, R.I., 1977; MA in Am. Studies, U. Hawaii, 1974; postgrad., Pa. State U., 1982, Harvard U., 1984, 92. Commd. 2d lt. U.S. Army, 1960, advanced through grades to maj. gen., 1988; chief collection U.S. Army Europe, Heidelberg, Germany, 1977-78; comdg. officer 66th Mil. Intelligence Brigade, Munich, 1978-80; chief ops. U.S. Army Intelligence and Security Command, Arlington, Va., 1980-82; exec. officer Dept. Army Asst. Chief Staff Intelligence, Washington, 1982-83; dep. commdr. gen. U.S. Army Intelligence and Security Command, Arlington, 1983-85; dir. estimates Def. Intelligence Agy., Washington, 1985-86, dir. attaches, 1986-90; comdg. gen. U.S. Army Intelligence and Security Command, Ft. Belvoir, Va., 1990-93; ret., 1993; pres. Internat. Security, Counterintelligence Cons. Svcs., Fairfax Station, Va., 1993—, Satellite Beach, Fla., 1993—99, Melbourne Beach, Fla., 1999—2004, Indian Harbour Beach, Fla., 2004—. Decorated Def. D.S.M., Army D.S.M., Nat. Intelligence D.S.M., Legion of Merit with 3 oak leaf clusters, Bronze Star with 2 oak leaf clusters; elected to U.S. Mil. Intelligence Hall of Fame, 1995. Mem. Assn. U.S. Army, Nat. Mil. Intelligence Assn. (pres. 1974-76), 101st Airborne Divsn. Assn., Berlin US Military Vets. Assn., Def. Intelligence Alumni Assn., Sigma Nu. Baptist. Avocations: boating, scuba diving, racquetball, soaring, reading. Home and Office: 16F Marina Isles Blvd Indian Harbor Beach FL 32937 Personal E-mail: chuckscanlon@aol.com.

**SCANLON, GAIL GRETCHEN,** librarian, nurse; b. Holyoke, Mass., Aug. 2, 1955; d. Rudy John and Josephine Sophia (Burek) Wojnarowski; m. Michael John Scanlon, June 5, 1976; children: Jonathan Spencer Scanlon, Douglas Todd, Abigail Jillian. Diploma in Nursing, Framingham Union Hosp.

Sch. Nursing, Mass., 1976; BA, Mount Holyoke Coll., So. Hadley, Mass., 1995; MLS, U. Albany, 1999; grad. student, Frye Institute, Emory Univ., 2002. RN; lic. real estate agent. Real estate sales agt. Chestnut Hill Real Estate, South Hadley, Mass., 1987—; owner The Elegant Basket, 1988-91; libr. circulation asst. Mt. Holyoke Coll., 1993—96; dir. access svcs. Mt. Holyoke Coll. Libr., 1996—2003, dir. access, tech. svcs., 2003—. Creator: (mus. exhibit) Past, Present and Future: Women Making a Difference in South Hadley, 1995. Trustee South Hadley Pub. Libr., 1989—; mem. town mtg. Town South Hadley, 1990—2000; dir. South Hadley Youth Ctr., 1994; bd. dirs. South Hadley Swim Club, Mass., 1988—94. Mem. ALA, ACRL, Libr. Adminstrn. and Mgmt. Assn., Mass. Libr. Trustees Assn., Mass. Friends of Libraries Assn., Know Your Town, Mass. State Adv. Coun. for Librs Home: 20 Mary Lyon Dr South Hadley MA 01075 Office: Mount Holyoke Library South Hadley MA 01075 Office Phone: 413-538-2434. Business E-Mail: gscanlon@mtholyoke.edu.

**SCANLON, JANE CRONIN,** mathematics professor; b. NYC, July 17, 1922; d. John Timothy and Janet Smiley (Murphy) Cronin; m. Joseph C. Scanlon, Mar. 5, 1953 (div.); children: Justin, Mary, Anne, Edmund. Student, Highland Park Jr. Coll., 1939-41; BS, Wayne State U., 1943; MA, U. Mich., 1945, PhD, 1949. Mathematician Air Force Cambridge Research Center, 1951-54; instr. Wheaton Coll., Norton, Mass., 1954-55; asst. prof. Poly. Inst. Bklyn., 1957-58, assoc. prof., 1958-60, prof., 1960-65; prof. math. Rutgers U., New Brunswick, N.J., 1965-91, prof. emerita, 1991—. Cons. Singer-Kearfott Div., Naval Research Lab. Office Naval Research Fellow Princeton, 1948-49; Horace H. Rockham Postdoctoral fellow U. Mich., 1950-51, Rutgers Research Council fellow, 1968-69, 72-73; NSF vis. professorship for women Courant Inst., NYU, 1984-85. Author: Fixed Points and Topological Degree in Nonlinear Analysis, 1964, Advanced Calculus, 1967, Differential Equations: Introduction and Qualitative Theory, 1980, 2d edit., 1994, Mathematics of Cell Electrophysiology, 1980, Mathematical Aspects of Hodgkin-Huxley Neural Theory, 1987; editor: Analyzing Multiscale Phenomena using Singular Perturbation Methods, 1999. Mem. Am. Math. Soc., Soc. for Indsl. and Applied Math., Internat. Soc. Chronobiology. Home: 110 Valentine St Highland Park NJ 08904-2106 Office: Rutgers U Dept Math New Brunswick NJ 08903 Personal E-mail: croninscanlon@optonline.net.

**SCANLON, JANICE LYNN,** retired gifted and talented educator; b. Goodland, Kans., July 28, 1940; d. Milton Parish Jr. and Bertha May Adams Parish. BS, Ft. Hays State U., 1962; MA, U. Denver, 1980. Tchr. kindergarten, music Brewster Pub. Schs., Kans., 1962—63; tchr. kindergarten Jefferson County Pub. Schs., Lakewood, Colo., 1963—81; tchr. gifted Washington Twp. Pub. Schs., Sewell, NJ, 1983—98; ret., 1998. Del. gifted tchrs. to visit China with People to People, 1990; sec. N.J. Tchrs. Gifted, 1990—92; pres. Jefferson County Kindergarten Tchrs. Assn., Lakewood, Colo., 1964—65. Author: Jefferson County Kindergarten Curriculum, 1974; actor: (films) Teaching Children in Remote Areas, 1968; contbg. author (lessons in book) Teaching Children in Remote Areas, 1968; author: Guides for Washington Twp. Schs., 1983—98; co-author: Ruleton and Its School, 2005, Adams and Parrish Family, 2005. Fund raiser Palm Aire Women's Club, Sarasota, Fla., 1999—; pres. Palm Aire Nine Hole Golf, 2000—03, assoc., 2002—03; presenter Indian hist. Ch. of Incarnation Sch., 2001—; active Clare's Sewing Angel; mem Dem. Party, S.E. Manatee County, Sarasota, Fla., 2003—. Nominee N.J. Sci. Tchr. of Yr.; scholar, Kiwanis Club, Goodland, Kans., 1958, Tuition grant, U.S. Edn. Office, U. Denver, 1977-80. Mem.: N.J. Ret. Tchrs. Assn., Alpha Delta Kappa (treas.). Democrat. Roman Catholic. Avocations: travel, painting, quilting, genealogy, golf. Home: 7222 Coachlight St Sarasota FL 34243 Personal E-mail: josescan@aol.com.

**SCANLON, KERRY ALAN,** lawyer; AB cum laude, Harvard U., 1973; JD, Antioch Law Sch., 1977. Bar: DC 1977, US Ct. Appeals, 4th Cir. and DC Cir., US Supreme Ct. Ptnr. litig., chair Equal Rights Litig. and Compliance Group Kaye Scholer LLP, Washington, DC. Mem.: ABA, DC Bar Assn. Office: Kaye Scholer LLP McPherson Bldg 901 Fifteenth St NW Ste 1100 Washington DC 20005 Office Phone: 202-628-3660. E-mail: kscanlon@kayescholer.com.

**SCANLON, LAWRENCE EUGENE,** language educator; b. Montclair, N.J., Sept. 12, 1927; s. Leo Dudley and Margaret Gertrude (Kennedy) S.; m. Anne Maxwell Sherrerd, Aug. 23, 1952; children: Lawrence Francis, Neal Patrick, Heidi Anne. BA, Wesleyan U., 1951; MA, Rutgers U., 1952; PhD, Syracuse U., 1958. Asst. prof. English Mount Holyoke Coll., South Hadley, Mass., 1958-63; prof. Hartford (Conn.). Coll. for Women, 1963-92. Author: First Came Commodore Perry, 1969, A Memorial of Ebensee, 1994, The Story He Left Behind Him Paddy the Cope, 1994. Justice of the peace Town of East Granby, Conn., 1970-72; v.p. Capital Region Libr. Coun., Hartford, 1970-74. With U.S. Army, 1945-46. Fulbright grantee, Austria, 1952-53, Japan, 1964-65, West Germany, 1980-81, summer grantee NEH, 1974. Avocations: writing, travel, gardening, investing. Home: 101 Holcomb St East Granby CT 06026-9531

**SCANLON, PAT H.,** lawyer; b. Houma, La., Aug. 4, 1936; s. Leo Joseph and Mary (Ezell) S.; m. Carlene Myers, June 10, 1961; children: Margaret, Pat, Jr., Cissy, John. BS in Geology, La. State U., 1957; LLB with distinction, U. Miss., 1960. Assoc. Satterfield, Shell, Williams & Buford, Jackson, Miss., 1960-62; ptnr. Young, Scanlon & Sessums, Jackson, 1962—95; with Scanlon, Sessums Parker & Dallas PLLC, 1995-2002; with Watkins & Eager PLLC, 2003—; chmn., commnr. Miss. Jud. Performance Commn., Jackson, 1980-83; instr. Jackson Sch. Law, 1963-66; chmn. Miss. Law Inst., Jackson, 1970. Mem. editorial bd. Miss. Law Jour., 1959-60; contbr. articles to profl. jours. Mem. vestry St. James Episcopal Ch., Jackson, 1972-75, 79-82). Served to capt. USAR. Fellow Am. Coll. Trial Lawyers, Internat. Soc. Barristers, Am. Bar Found., Miss. Bar Found. (pres. 1986-87, trustee 1980-83); mem. Miss. Bankruptcy Conf. (pres. 1984-85), Miss. Young Lawyers Assn. (pres. 1969-70), Miss. State Bar Assn. (2d v.p. 1970-71, pres. 1988-89), Hinds County Bar Assn. (pres. 1974-75), Fed. Bar Assn. (pres. Miss. chpt. 1972-73), Am. Arbitration Assn. (panel mem.), Nat. Arbitration Forum (panel mem.). Office: 1650 Mirror Lake Plaza 2829 Lakeland Dr Jackson MS 39232

**SCANLON, PETER REDMOND,** retired accountant; b. NYC, Feb. 18, 1931; s. John Thomas and Loretta Dolores (Ryan) S.; m. Mary Jane E. Condon, Mar. 7, 1953; children: Peter, Barbara, Mark (dec.), Brian, Janet. BBA in Acctg., Iona Coll., 1952, LLD (hon.), 1992. CPA, N.Y. Mem. profl. staff Coopers & Lybrand, NYC, 1956-66, ptnr., 1966-91, vice chmn., 1976-82, chmn., CEO, 1982-91, ret. chmn., 1991—. Hon. ptnr. N.Y.C. Partnership, 1991. Mem. fin. coun. Diocese of Palm Beach, 1995-2002. Lt. USN, 1952-56. Decorated Knight of Malta, Knight Holy Sepulchre; recipient Arthur A. Loftus award Iona Coll., 1973, Trustee award, 1990, Crain's N.Y. All Star award, 1990, Best in Class award Conf. Bd. Youth Edn., 1991. Mem.: AICPA, NY State Soc. CPAs, Jupiter Inlet Beach Club, NY Athletic Club. Roman Catholic. Personal E-mail: prsmjes3179@aol.com. E-mail: prsmjes.3179@aol.com.

**SCANLON, ROSEMARY,** economist; b. Dec. 25, 1939; d. Donald Angus and Mary Agnes (MacDonald) MacLellan; m. Michael Scanlon, Apr. 24, 1965 (div. 1979); children: Sean Donald, Jennifer. AB, St. Francis Xavier U., N.S., 1959; MA (Ford Found. scholar), U. New Brunswick, 1960; PMD, Harvard Bus. Sch., 1981. Instr. econs. Coll. of William and Mary, Williamsburg, Va., 1960—63; asst. prof. Old Dominion U., Norfolk, Va., 1963—65; econ. analyst Port Authority N.Y. and N.J., 1969—93, sr. economist for regional rsch., 1977—80, mgr. econ. devel. planning, 1980—83, chief economist, 1983—. Asst. dir. Planning and Devel. Dept., 1985; apptd. dep. state contr. N.Y.C., 1993—97; vis. rsch. fellow London Sch. Econ., 1997—2000; cons. urban and regional econs., 2000—; assoc. prof. econs. Real Estate Inst. NYU, 2001—. Author (with others): Cities in a Global Society, 1989; author: The Arts as an Industry, 1993, The Regional Economy, 1993; editor: The London-NY Study, 2000; author: Bldg. for Growth, A development strategy, 2002. Bd. dirs. Transit Ctr. Inc., Accion, NY, 2005—. Recipient Outstanding Achievement award, Exec. Dirs. award, 1987, de Luca award for lifetime achievement in econ. devel., 1999, Disting. Alumnus award, St. Francis

Xavier U., 2001. Mem.: Transit Ctr., Inc. Home: 10 Clinton St Apt 9T Brooklyn NY 11201-2710 Office: 11 W 42nd St New York NY 10036 Office Phone: 917-922-8268. Personal E-mail: rosemaryscanlon@msn.com.

**SCANLON, TERRENCE MAURICE,** foundation administrator; b. Milw., May 1, 1939; s. Maurice John and Anne (Hayes) S.; m. Judy Ball, June 14, 1969; children: Michael Mansfield, Justin Ball, Brendan Hayes. BS, Villanova U., 1961. Staff asst. The White House, Washington, 1963-67; with SBA, Washington, 1967-69, Dept. of Commerce, Washington, 1969-83, mem. office Minority Bus. Enterprise, 1969-80, with Internat. Trade Adminstrn., 1980-81, with Minority Bus. Devel. Agy., 1981-83; mem. Consumer Product Safety Commn., Washington, 1983-89, vice chmn., 1983-84, chmn., 1985, 86-89; v.p., treas. The Heritage Found., Washington, 1989-91, v.p. corp. rels., 1991-94; chmn., pres. Capital Rsch. Ctr., Washington, 1994—. Am. Polit. Sci. Assn. Congl. fellow, 1967-68 Mem. Sovereign Mil. Order of Malta, University Club. Home: 4510 Dexter St NW Washington DC 20007-1115 Office: Capital Rsch Ctr 1513 16th St NW Washington DC 20036-1401 Office Phone: 202-483-6900. Business E-Mail: tscanlon@capitalresearch.org.

**SCANNELL, HERB,** broadcast executive; m. Sarah Scannell; 1 child, Caroline. BA in English and History, Boston Coll. Dir. program promotion Showtime/The Movie Channel; dir. programming Nickelodeon, NYC, 1988—89, v.p. programming, 1989—90, sr. v.p. programming; exec. v.p. Nickelodeon Networks, pres., 1996—2006; group pres. MTV Networks, NYC, 2003—06.

**SCANNELL, WILLIAM EDWARD,** aerospace transportation executive, consultant, psychologist; b. Muscatine, Iowa, Nov. 11, 1934; s. Mark Edward and Catharine Pearson (Fowler) S.; m. Barbara Ann Hoemann, Nov. 23, 1957; children: Cynthia Kay, Mark Edward, David Jerome, Terri Lynn, Stephen Patrick. BA in Gen. Edn., U. Nebr., 1961; BS in Engring., Ariz. State U., 1966; MS in Systems Engring., So. Meth. U., 1969; postgrad. in law, Western State U., 1977, 81-82; PhD, U.S. Internat. U., 1991. Commd. 2d lt. USAF, 1956, advanced through grades to lt. col., 1972; B-47 navigator-bombardier 98th Bomb Wing, Lincoln Air Force Base, Nebr., 1956-63; with Air Force Inst. of Tech., 1963-65, 68-69; chief mgmt. engring. team RAF Bentwaters, England, 1965-68; forward air contr. 20th Tactical Air Support Squadron, Danang, Vietnam, 1970-71; program mgr. Hdqrs. USAF, Washington, 1971-74, staff asst. Office of Sec. Def., 1974-75, ret., 1975; account exec. Merrill Lynch, San Diego, 1975-77; program engring. chief Gen. Dynamics, San Diego, 1977-79, engring. chief, 1979-80, program mgr., 1980-83; mgr. integrated logistics support Northrop Corp., Hawthorne, Calif., 1984-88, mgr. B-2 program planning and scheduling Pico Rivera, Calif., 1988-91; pres. Scannell and Assocs., Fredericksburg, Tex., 1991—. Author: The Nature of Motivation in Aerospace Executives, 1991. Cpl. USNG, 1952-54. Decorated DFC with three oak leaf clusters, Air medal with 11 oak leaf clusters, Vietnamese Cross Gallantry with palm, Meritorious Svc. medal. Mem. APA, Psi Chi. Republican. Roman Catholic. Home: 6130 Center Point Rd Fredericksburg TX 78624 Office Phone: 830-990-6670. E-mail: william@scannell.net.

**SCANTLEBURY, VELMA PATRICIA,** surgeon; b. Barbados, West Indies, Oct. 6, 1955; came to U.S., 1970; d. Delacey Whitstanley and Kathleen (Jordan) S.; 2 children. BS, LI U., 1977; MD, Columbia U., 1981; DrPA, LI U., 1998, Seton Hall Coll. PA. Intern in surgery Harlem Hosp. Ctr., N.Y.C., 1981-82, resident in surgery, 1982-86; fellow in transplantation U. Pitts., 1988, assoc. prof. surgery, 1998—2002; prof. surgery, dir. transplantation U. South Ala. Med. Ctr., Mobile, 2002—. Mem. med. advisory bd. Nat. Kidney Found. Vol. King County Hosp., Bklyn., 1972. Recipient Martin Luther King Sch. award, 1973-74, Am. Fedn. Tchrs. Sch. award, 1973-75, Nat. Med. Found. award 1977-78, Joseph Collins Found. Sch. award 1978, Gift of Life award Nat. Kidney Found., OMNI Life Models award, Women of Spirit award Carlow Coll.; named Outstanding Young Women of Am. 1988. Fellow, ACS; mem. AMA (listed by AMA as nation's first African-Am. female transplant surgeon), P&S Alumni Assn., Black and Latin Students Orgn. (treas. N.Y.C. 1979-80), Sigma Epsilon Delta, Phi Sigma Soc. (sec. Bklyn. chpt. 1976-77), Am. Soc. Transplantation, Am. Soc. Transplant Surgeons, Soc. Black Academic Surgeons, Am. Soc. Minority Health and Transplant Professionals (bd. dirs.), Internat. Women's Forum We. Pa., Nat. Assn. Negro Bus. and Profl. Women. Democrat. Office: Univ S Ala Med Ctr 2451 Fillingim St Mobile AL 36617-2293*

**SCAPARROTTI, CURTIS M.,** career military officer; m. Cindy Bateman; children: Michael, Stephanie. BS, U.S. Military Acad., West Point, 1978; M Ed, Univ. S.C. Commd. 2d lt. U.S. Army, advanced through grades to brig. gen.; platoon leader, ops. officer, co. comdr. 82nd Airborne Div., 1978—84; tactical officer, supt. aide-de-camp U.S. Mil. Acad., West Point, 1985—88; battalion ops. officer, chief of ops. branch 10th Mountain Div., Fort Drum, NY, 1989—92; with Army Personnel command & Army chief of staff office Washington, 1992—94; comdr. 3d battalion, 325th airborne combat team So. European Task Force, Vicenza, Italy, 1994—96; ops. officer 10th Mountain Div., Fort Drum, NY, 1996—98; chief of Army Initiatives group dep. chief of staff for ops. & plans, Washington, 1998—99; comdr. 2d brigade 82nd Airborne Div., Fort Bragg, NC, 1999—2001; asst. dep. dir. joint ops. Joint Staff, Washington, 2001—03; asst. div. comdr. 1st Armored Div., Operation Iraqi Freedom, 2003—04; comdt. Corps of Cadets U.S. Mil. Acad., West Point, 2004—. Decorated Def. Superior Svc. medal, Legion of Merit, 3 oak leaf clusters, Bronze Star with oak leaf cluster, Meritorious Svc. medal with 4 oak leaf clusters, Army Commendation medal with 4 oak leaf clusters, Army Achievement medal, Global War on Terrorism Expeditionary medal, Global War on Terrorism Svc. medal, Expert Infantryman badge, Master Parachutist badge, Ranger tab, Army Staff Identification badge. Office: USMA Office of the Commandant Washington Hall Bldg 745 West Point NY 10996

**SCARBOROUGH, ANN BARLOW,** secondary school educator; Tchr. sci. Farmville (N.C.) Mid. Sch., South Ctrl. HS, Winterville, NC. Recipient Outstanding Earth Sci. Tchr. award, 1992. Mem.: N.C. Sci. Tchrs. Assn. (pres. 2003).

**SCARBOROUGH, CHARLES BISHOP, III,** broadcast journalist, writer; b. Pitts., Nov. 4, 1943; s. Charles Bishop and Esther Francis (Campbell) S.; m. Linda Anne Gross, Dec. 14, 1972; children: Charles Bishop IV, Elizabeth Anne; m. Anne Ford Uzielli, Oct. 2, 1982; m. Ellen Carol Ward, Sept. 25, 1994. BS, U. So. Miss., 1969. Prodn. mgr. Sta.-WLOX-TV, Biloxi, Miss., 1966-68; reporter, anchorman Sta.-WDAM-TV, Hattiesburg, Miss., 1968-69; reporter, anchorman, mng. editor Sta.-WAGA-TV, Atlanta, 1969-72; reporter, anchorman Sta.-WNAC-TV, Boston, 1972-74, NBC News, N.Y.C., 1974—. Author: (novels) Stryker, 1978, The Myrmidon Project, 1981, Aftershock, 1991. Served with USAF, 1961-65. Recipient awards for journalism AP (9), 1969-72, Emmy awards (29), 1974-2005, award Aviation/Space Writers Assn., 1977, 78, 88, UPI award for journalism N.Y. Press Club award, 1988, 89, Sigma Delta Chi award, Deadline Club award, Terry Anderson Journalism award Working Press Assn. N.J., 1992 Mem.: Phi Kappa Phi. Office: NBC News 30 Rockefeller Plz Rm 723 New York NY 10112-0036

**SCARBOROUGH, CHUCK,** newscaster, writer; b. Pitts. married; 2 children. BS, U. So. Miss.; LittD (hon.), U. Mercy Coll., Dobbs Ferry, N.Y. Anchor, ops. mgr. WLOX-TV, Biloxi, Miss.; reporter, anchor WDAM-TV, Hattiesburg, Miss., 1968—69; anchor, reporter, mng. editor news WAGA-TV, Atlanta, 1969—72; anchor, reporter WNAC-TV, Bost; co-anchor, reporter NewsChannel 4 NBC, NYC, 1974—. Author: (novels) Stryker, 1978, The Myrmidon Project, 1980, Aftershock, 1991; contbr. articles mags. in N.Y., Boston, Am. Home. Hon. mem. Nat. Soc. to Prevent Blindness; bd. trustees Silver Shield Found., Juvenile Diabetes Found. Named NYC's Best Anchor Team (with Sue Simmons), NY Daily News, 2003; recipient 30 Emmys, award, UPI, N.Y. Press Club, N.Y. State Broadcasters Assn., Best in Bus.

award, Washington Rev. of Journalism, 1994, Terry Andersen award, Working Press Assn., 1992, Humanitarian award, Juvenile Diabetes Found., Nat. Headliner award, 2005. Office: NBC 30 Rockefeller Ctr New York NY 10112

**SCARBOROUGH, MARION NICHOLS,** nutritionist, recreational facility executive; b. Enosburg Falls, Vt., July 26, 1915; d. George Leonard and Clara May (Woodward) Nichols; m. Mat. Scarborough, Aug. 30, 1950 (dec. Mar., 1960); 1 child Mary Anne Scarborough O'Donnell Adams. ASS, Green Mountain Coll., Poultney, Vt., 1935; BS, Kans. State U., 1937; MPH, Harvard U., 1947. Chief dietitian Newton (Mass.) Wellesley Sch., 1938-43, 182d Gen. Hosp., U.S. Army, 1943-45; nutritionist, author food exch. list U.S. Pub. Health Diabetes Sect., Boston, 1947-50; nutritionist Fla. Bd. Health, Jacksonville, 1950-52; owner Happy Acres Ranch, Inc., Jacksonville, 1953—. Sec. Fla. Assn. Children Under Six ECA, 1965, pres., 1966, 67. Commd. officer USPHS, 1948-50. Mem. APHA, Am. Dietetic Assn., Am. Camping Assn., Nat. Assn. Edn. of Young Children. Episcopalian. Avocations: childrens' day care, summer camp. Home and Office: Happy Acres Ranch Inc 7117 Crane Ave Jacksonville FL 32216-9012 Office Phone: 904-725-1410.

**SCARBOROUGH, ROBERT HENRY, JR.,** entrepreneur; b. Hawkinsville, Ga., Mar. 12, 1923; s. Robert Henry and Janet Augusta (Burton) S.; m. Walterene Brant, July 1, 1946; children— Robert Henry, James Burton BS, U.S. Mcht. Marine Acad., 1944; BBA, U. Hawaii, 1969, MBA, 1971; MS, George Washington U., 1971, Armed Forces Staff Coll., 1963, Nat. War Coll., 1971. Commd. lt. (j.g.) USCG, 1949; advanced through grades to vice adm., 1978; chief Office of Ops. USCG, 1974-75, chief of staff, 1975-77, comdr. 9th Coast Guard Dist., 1977-78, vice comdt. Washington, 1978-82, ret., 1982; exec. dir. Navy League U.S., 1982-84; pres. Polaris Potomac Corp., 1985-96. Entrepreneur, 1996—. With USNR, 1942-49 Decorated DSM, Legion of Merit. Mem. Beta Gamma Sigma Office: 5357 37th St N Arlington VA 22207-1312 Personal E-mail: rhswbs46@verizon.net, jbsrun@aol.com.

**SCARBOROUGH, STEPHEN J.,** construction executive; Pres. Orange County div. Std. Pacific Corp., Irvine, Calif., 1181—96, exec. v.p., 1996, pres., 1996—2000, pres., CEO, 2000—01, chmn., CEO, 2001—. Named Builder of the Yr., Bldg. Ind. Assn. So. Calif., 2004. Office: Standard Pacific Corp 15326 Alton Pkwy Irvine CA 92618*

**SCARBOROUGH, VERNON LEE,** archaeologist, anthropologist; s. James and Lucille Scarborough; m. Pat Mora, May 25, 1984. PhD, So. Meth. U., 1981. Prof. anthropology U. Khartoum, Sudan, 1981—82; Fulbright resch. lectr. U. Peshawar, Pakistan, 1986; prof. U. Cin., 1988—. Author: The Flow of Power: Ancient Water Systems and Landscapes (Rieveschl All-Faculty award for scholarly and creative work, 2005). Recipient Rieveschl All-Faculty award for scholarly and creative work, 2005; fellow Sch. Am. Rsch., 1994—95. Mem.: Sigma Xi (assoc.; pres. U. Cin. chpt. 2000—01). Achievements include archaeological fieldwork in Belize, Guatemala, Indonesia, Greece, US Southwest, Sudan, Pakistan. Home: 1871 Calle de Sebastian Santa Fe NM 87505 Office: U Cin Clifton Ave Cincinnati OH 45221-0312 Fax: 513-556-2778. Office Phone: 513-556-2772. E-mail: vernon.scarborough@uc.edu.

**SCARBOROUGH, WILLIAM KAUFFMAN,** historian, educator; b. Balt., Jan. 17, 1933; s. James Blaine and Julia Irene (Kauffman) Scarborough; m. Patricia Estelle Carruthers, Jan. 16, 1954; children: Catherine Krohn, William Bradley. AB, U. N.C., 1954; MA, Cornell U., 1957; PhD, U. N.C., 1962. Asst. prof. history Millsaps Coll., Jackson, Miss., 1961—63, N.E. La. U., Monroe, 1963—64; assoc. prof. history U. So. Miss., Hattiesburg, 1964—76, prof. history, 1976—, chair and prof. history, 1980—90, Charles W. Moorman Disting. Alumni Prof. in the Humanities, 1996—98. Author: (book) The Overseer: Plantation Management in The Old South, 1966, Masters of the Big House, 2003 (Landry award, 2003); editor: The Diary of Edmund Ruffin, 3 vols., 1972—89 (Landry award, 1989). Lt. (j.g.) USNR, 1954—56. Recipient Grand Marshal award, 2003, Wright Lit. Excellence award, 2004. Fellow: St. George Tucker Soc. (pres. 2002—03); mem.: AAUP (chpt. pres. 2002—03), The Hist. Soc., S.C. Hist. Soc., Agr. History Soc., Miss. Hist. Soc. (pres. 1979, Willie D. Halsell prize 1993, B.L.C. Wailes award 2005), So. Hist. Assn., Phi Beta Kappa. Avocations: golf, gardening, football, basketball. Home: 1120 Estelle St Hattiesburg MS 39402 Office: Univ So Miss Dept History 118 College Dr # 5047 Hattiesburg MS 39406 Office Phone: 601-266-4336. Business E-Mail: william.scarborough@usm.edu.

**SCARCHUK, LYNN NETTLETON,** music educator; b. Hartford, Conn., July 25, 1950; d. Russell Chaffee Nettleton and Katharine Risley Chaffee; 1 child, James Paul. BS, Western Conn. State U., 1968—72; MS, Ctrl. Conn. State U., 1978. Tchr. Meriden Bd. Edn., Meriden, Conn., 1972—, Jefferson Mid. Sch., Meriden, 1972—84, Washington Mid. Sch., Meriden, 1984—87; choral dir., tchr. Maloney H.S., Meriden, 1988—. Dir.(and prodr.): (sch. prodn.) Oklahoma, 1990, My Fair Lady, 1992, Anything Goes, 1994, South Pacific, 1996, 42d St, 1998, Hello Dolly, 2000, Crazy for You, 2002, Footloose, 2004 (hon. mention for set building, Mag.). Music dir. Kiwanis Club Kapers, Meriden, Conn., 2000—01. Mem.: Conn. Music Educators Assn. (25 Yrs. Svc. award). Avocations: travel, bicycling.

**SCARDINO, DAME MARJORIE MORRIS,** publishing executive; b. Flagstaff, Ariz., Jan. 25, 1947; d. Robert Weldon and Beth (Lamb) Morris; m. Albert James Scardino, Apr. 19, 1974; children: Adelaide Katherine Morris, William Brown, Albert Henry Hugh. BA, Baylor U.; JD, U. San Francisco. Ptnr. Brannen Wessels & Searcy, Savannah, Ga., 1976-85; pub. Ga. Gazette Pub. Co., Savannah, 1978-85; pres. The Economist Newspaper Group, Inc., NYC, 1985-93; chief exec. The Economist Group, London, 1993-97, Pearson P.L.C., London, 1997—. Non-exec. dir. Nokia Corp. Trustee Carter Ctr.; bd. dir. The Bus. Coun., MacArthur Found., Atlantic Council of U.S.; trustee Victoria and Albert Mus. Named Dame Comdr. British Empire 2002, named one of Most Powerful Women, Forbes mag., 2005, 50 Women to Watch, Wall St Journal, 2005, 50 Most Powerful Women in Global Bus., Fortune mag., 2005. Office: Pearson PLC 80 Strand London WC2R 0RL England

**SCARDINO, PETER T.,** urologic oncologic surgeon; b. Portsmouth, Va., Sept. 28, 1945; m. Alice Barrow ("Barrie") Myrick, 1965; children: Allison Kelly, Peter Daniel Robinson, Elizabeth Barrow. BA, Yale U., 1967; MD, Duke U., 1971. Diplomate Am. Bd. Urology. Resident in surgery Mass. Gen. Hosp., Boston, 1971-73; clin. assoc. surgery br. Nat. Cancer inst., NIH, 1973-76; resident in urology UCLA Sch. Medicine, 1976-79, instr., 1978-79; asst. prof., then assoc. prof. Baylor U. Coll. Medicine, Houston, 1979-86, prof. urology, 1986-98, Russell and Mary Hugh Scott prof., chmn. dept. urology, 1989-98; chmn. dept. urology Alfred P. Sloan chair, head prostate cancer program Meml. Sloan-Kettering Cancer Ctr., N.Y.C., 1999—, mem. Inst. for Cancer Rsch. prostate cancer program, 1999—; prof. Weill Med. Coll. Cornell U., N.Y.C., 1998—. Co-author (with Judith Kelman): Dr. Peter Scardino's Prostate Book, 2005. Recipient Eugene Fuller Triennial Prostate award 1995, Pres.'s award Am. Found. Urolog. Disease, 1996, Alumnus award Duke U. Med. Ctr., 1999, Gordon Wilson lectr. Am. Clin. and Climatological Assn., 1999. Fellow ACS, Am. Surg. Assn.; mem. Am. Urology Assn. (Gold Cytoscope award 1989), Clin. Soc. Genitourinary Surgeons, Am. Assn. Genitourinary Surgeons, Am. Soc. Clin. Oncology, Am. Assn. Cancer Rsch., Inst. Medicine Nat. Acad. Sci., N.Y. Acad. Sci.

**SCARF, MARGARET (MAGGIE SCARF),** author; b. Phila., May 13, 1932; d. Benjamin and Helen (Rotbin) Klein; m. Herbert Eli Scarf, Jan. 1953; children: Martha Samuelson, Elizabeth Stone, Susan Merrell. BA, South Conn. State U., 1989. Contbg. editor New Republic, Washington, 1978—, Self Mag., N.Y.C., 1991—; writer-in-residence Jonathan Edwards Coll., 1995—. Assoc. fellow Jonathan Edwards Coll. Yale U., New Haven, 1979—; sr. fellow Bush Ctr. in Child Devel. and Social Policy, Yale U., 1991—; mem. adv. bd. Am. Psychiat. Press, Poynter Fellowship Journalism Yale U., 1995-96. Author: Meet Benjamin Franklin, 1968, Antarctica: Exploring the Frozen Continent, 1970, Body, Mind, Behavior, 1976 (Nat. Media award Am. Psychological Assn. 1977), Unfinished Business: Pressure

Points in the Lives of Women, 1981, Intimate Partners: Patterns in Love and Marriage, 1987, Intimate Worlds: Life Inside the Family, 1996, Secrets, Lies, Betrayals: The Body/Mind Connection, 2005; contbr. numerous articles to jours. including N.Y. Times mag. and book rev., Psychology Today; TV appearances include: David Letterman Show, Oprah Winfrey Show, CBS News, Good Morning Am., Today Show, Phil Donahue, numerous others. Recipient Nat. Media award Am. Psychol. Found., 1971, 74, 77, Conn. UN award Outstanding Conn. Women, 1987, cert. commendation Robert T. Morse Writers Competition Am. Psychiat. Assn., 1997, Disting. Svc. award Am. Psychiat. Assn., 1999, cert. of recognition N.Y. State Soc. Clin. and Social Work, 1998; grantee Smith Richardson Found., 1991-94; Ford Found. fellow, 1973-74, Neiman fellow Harvard U., 1975-76, Ctr. Advanced Study in Behavioral Scis. fellow, 1977-78, 85-86, Alicia Patterson Found. fellow, 1978-79. Mem. Conn. Soc. Psychoanalytic Psychologists, Am. Psychiat. Press (mem. adv. bd. 1992), Lawn Club, Elizabethans, PEN Writer's Assn. Avocations: reading, hiking, swimming. Office: Jonathan Edwards Coll Yale U 68 High St New Haven CT 06511-6643 Business E-Mail: maggie.scarf@yale.edu.

**SCARINGI, MELANIE WALZ,** lawyer; b. Harrisburg, Pa., July 14, 1976; d. Shaubut C. Walz III and Judith T. Walz; m. Marc A. Scaringi, July 1, 2000. BA, Dickinson Coll., 1998; JD, Pa. State U., 2001. Bar: Pa. 2001, U.S. Dist. (mid. dist.) Pa. 2001. Ptnr. Walz, Walz, Scaringi and Scaringi, Newport, Pa., 2001—05; shareholder Scaringi & Scaringi, P.C., Harrisburg, Pa., 2005—. Active Highland United Presbyn. Ch. Mem.: Venture Club of Harrisburg, Newport Lions Club. Office: Scaringi & Scaringi PC Ste 103 2000 Linglestown Rd Harrisburg PA 17110 Office Phone: 717-657-7770. E-mail: melanie@scaringilaw.com

**SCARLATA, PAUL ANTHONY,** oral surgeon; b. McKeesport, Pa., Apr. 3, 1935; s. Joseph Mario and Josephine Gloria (Battaglia) S.; m. Mary Jane Parks, June 15, 1963 (dec. 1982); children: Stephanie, Anthony, Christopher, Matthew, Sarah; m. Darla K. Hosler, May 27, 1988 (div. 1994); m. Helen Walterick Meyers, Jan. 3, 2006. BS, U. Pitts., 1957, DDS, DMD, U. Pitts., 1961. Resident in oral surgery Western Pa. Hosp., Pitts., 1962-63, St. Luke's Hosp., NYC, 1963-64; practice gen. dentistry and oral surgery Chambersburg, Pa., 1967—; chief dental svc. Chambersburg Hosp., 1974-76, 82-84. Treas. Franklin County (Pa.) Heritage, 1971—, pres., 1977-78; fgn. student exch. host Youth for Understanding, appointed regional field dir. Capt., oral surgeon AUS, 1964—67, Mannheim, Germany. Recipient Buhl Planetarium Sci. award 1st prize Astronomy 6" Newtonian Reflector, 1952. Mem. ADA (life), Pa. Dental Assn., We. Pa. Assn. Oral Surgeons, Gt. Lakes Soc. Oral Surgeons, N.Y. Soc. Clin. Oral Pathologists, Am. Soc. of Anesthetists, Cumberland Valley Dental Soc. (pres. 1982-83), Am. Legion (life), Chambersburg Club, Antique Studebakers Club, Antique Auto Assn. (life), K.C., Pitts. Athletic Club. Office: 421 Phoenix Dr Chambersburg PA 17201-2328 Home: 6703 Congressional Terr Fayetteville PA 17222-9403 Personal E-Mail: poppars@comcast.net.

**SCARLETT, JOSEPH H., JR.,** agricultural products executive; Various mgmt. positions Two Guys Discount Stores (subs. Vornado Inc.), 1963—79; various exec. positions to exec. v.p. Tractor Supply Co., Brentwood, Tenn., 1979—87, pres., COO, 1987—93, CEO, 1993—2004, chmn., 1993—. Bd. dir. O'Charley's Inc., 2005—. Mem.: Retail Industry Leaders Assn. (pres.). Office: Tractor Supply Co 200 Powell Pl Brentwood TN 37027

**SCARLETT, LYNN (PATRICIA LYNN SCARLETT),** federal agency administrator; b. Pitts., Dec. 8, 1949; d. James Miles and Virginia (Young) S.; m. James R. Trotter, May 6, 1978; 1 child, Rachel Scarlett Trotter. BA, U. Calif., Santa Barbara, 1970, MA, 1972. Vis. lectr. U. Calif., Santa Barbara, 1980-81; book rev. editor Reason Mag., Santa Barbara, 1982-85; dir. rsch. Reason Found., Santa Monica, Calif., 1985-89, v.p. rsch., 1990—2001, pres., CEO, 2001; asst. sec. policy, mgmt. & budget US Dept. Interior, Washington, 2001—05, dep. sec., 2005—, acting sec. 2006. Mem. task force Calif. Joint Legis. Com. on Surrogate Parenting, Calif., 1989-90; panel reviewer Project 88 Phase II, 1989; chmn. issues com. Citizens for Balanced Community, Santa Barbara, 1989—; chmn. "How Clean Is Clean" Working Group, Nat. Environmental Policy Inst., 1993-98; bd. dirs. Laguna Blanca Sch., Santa Barbara. Author: (chpt.) Food Politics, 1982; contbr. articles to profl. jours. Chmn. Jim Trotter for City Coun., Carpinteria, Calif., 1990—; mem. parents aux. Laguna Blanca, 1986-88. Geneva Inst. of Internat. Studies fellow, 1974-75. Mem. Friends of Girls Club Corp. (2d v.p. 1986-87). Republican. Avocations: birdwatching, drawing, swimming. Office: US Dept Interior 1849 C St NW Rm 5110 Washington DC 20240

**SCARNE, JOHN,** game company executive; b. Steubenville, Ohio, Mar. 4, 1903; s. Fiorangelo and Maria (Tamburro) S.; m. Steffi Kearney, 1956; 1 son, John Teeko. Student pub. schs., Guttenberg, N.J. Pres. John Scarne Games, Inc., North Bergen, NJ, 1950—. Gaming cons. Hilton Hotels Internat. Magician stage, screen and television; Author: Scarne on Dice, 1945, Scarne on Cards, 1950, Scarne on Card Tricks, 1950, Scarne on Magic Tricks, 1952, Scarne's New Complete Guide to Gambling, 1962, The Odds Against Me, 1967, Scarne's Encyclopedia of Games, 1973, The Mafia Conspiracy, 1976, Scarne's Guide to Casino Gambling, Scarne's Guide to Modern Poker; Contbr. to: World Book Ency, 1970, Ency. Brit, 1975. Cons. to U.S. Armed Forces, 1941-45. Named Man of Year for Police Chiefs of U.S., 1960 Achievements include creating the board games Teeko, Scarney, plus dice, card and solitaire games. Office: Unit 312 2581 Countryside Blvd Clearwater FL 33761-3521 Office Phone: 727-791-7180. Personal E-mail: sscarne@tampabay.rr.com.

**SCARNECCHIA, SUELLYN,** dean, law educator; BA, Northwestern U., 1978; JD, U. Mich., 1981. Bar: Mich. Ptnr. McCroskey, Feldman, Cochrane & Brock, Battle Creek, Mich.; clin asst. prof. U. Mich. Sch Law, 1987, clin. prof. law, 1993, clin. coord., 1994—96, assoc. dean clin. affairs, 1996—2002, assoc. dean administr., 1999—2001, asst. provost academic and faculty affairs, 2002; dean, prof. law U. N.Mex., 2003—; chair Jud. Nominating Commn. Govt. N.Mex. Atty. U. Mich. Child Advocacy Law Clinic, 1987; bd. dirs. Clin. Legal Edn. Assn.; panelist Mich. Atty. Disciplinary Bd.; tech. adv. Mich. Supreme Ct. Task Force on Gender and Race Bias. Mem.: Women Lawyers Assn. Mich. (past pres.), Battle Creek Area Orgn. Against Domestic Violence (past bd. pres.). Office: U NMex Sch Law 1117 Stanford NE Albuquerque NM 87131-1431 Office Phone: 505-277-4700. Home Fax: 505-277-0068. E-mail: scarnecchia@law.unm.edu.

**SCAROLA, JOHN MICHAEL,** dentist, educator; b. NYC, Nov. 18, 1934; s. Michael Fidelis and Filomena Mary (Turso) S.; m. Theodora Mary Marty, June 15, 1963; children: Michael A., John P., Stephen A., Robert M., Mary E. BS, Fordham Coll., 1956; DDS, Columbia U., 1960. Instr. Columbia Dental Sch., N.Y.C., 1962-68, 1969-72, 1969-72, assoc. clin. prof., 1973-86, course dir. prosthodontic elective, 1977-91, clin. prof., 1986—; ethics facilitator Columbia U., Sch. Dental and Oral Surgery, 1992—. Lectr., clin. prof. postgrad. prostodontics Columbia U., N.Y.C., 1986—, AEGD-Columbia N.Y.C., 1990-92, Luth. Med. Ctr., Bklyn., 1993—; cons. in prosthodontics Northport VA Hosp., East Northport, N.Y., 1970-91. Scoutmaster Boy Scouts Am., Port Washington, NY, 1976-78; chmn. spl. gifts Bishop's Annual Appeal, St. Peter's-Port Washington, 1977-78; KC (4th degree) sports coach St. Paul the Apostles Coun., Brookville, NY, 1980-83; fundraising com. The Yard, Martha's Vineyard, Mass., 1990; concert com. Musician's Emergency Fund, NYC, 1992. Lt. USNR, 1960-62. Fellow Am. Coll. Dentists (chmn. NY sect. 1994, v.p. 2005-06, Regent of Regency 1998-2002, pres.-elect 2006—), NY Acad. Dentistry (pres. 1989-90), Greater NY Acad. Prosthodontics (dir. 1993-97); mem. Greater NY Acad. Prosthodontics Found. (dir., pres. 1989-97), NY Acad. Dentistry Endowment Fund (dir., pres. 1992-93). Republican. Roman Catholic. Avocations: golf, opera, classical music, gardening. Home: 83 Fruitledge Rd Glen Head NY 11545-3317 Office: 501 Madison Ave New York NY 10022-5602 Office Phone: 212-758-9690. Personal E-Mail: jscaroladds@aol.com.

**SCARPA, A. MICHAEL,** apparel executive, corporate financial executive; Degree in acctg., 1982. CPA 1982. Fin. analyst Krementz & Co.; from budget mgr. to CFO Liz Claiborne, N.Y., 1983—2000, CFO, 2000—, sr. v.p., 2002—. Office: Liz Claiborne 1441 Broadway New York NY 10018-1805

**SCARPA, ANTONIO,** medical educator, researcher, director, physiologist; b. Padua, Italy, July 3, 1942; s. Angelo and Elena (DeRossi) S. MD cum laude, U. Padua, 1966, PhD in Pathology, 1970; MA (hon.), U. Pa., 1978. Asst. prof. biochemistry, biophysics U. Pa., Phila., 1973-76, assoc. prof., 1976-80, prof., 1980-86, dir. biomed. instrumentation group, 1983-86; prof., chmn. dept. physiology and biophysics Case Western Res. U., Cleve., 1986—2005, dir. tng. ctr., program project, 1983—, prof. medicine, 1989—, D. and I. Myers prof., 1998—2005; dir. Ctr. Sci. Rev., NIH, Bethesda, Md., 2005—. Cons. study sect. NIH, Bethesda, 1984—, Am. Heart Assn., Dallas, 1986-91; pres., assoc. chair dept. physiology, 1993-94; vice chair Nat. Caucus Basic Sci. Presidents, Washington. Editor (books): Frontiers of Biological Energetics, Calcium Transport and Cell Function, Transport ATPases, Membrane Pathology, Membrane and Cancer Cells; editor (jours.) Archives Biochemistry and Biophysics, Cell Calcium, Biochemistry Internat., The Scientific Jour.; mem. editl. bd. Circulation Rsch., 1978-81, Biophys. Jour., 1979-82, Jour. Muscle Rsch., 1979—, Magnesium, 1982—, Physiol. Revs., 1982-90, FASEB Jour., 1987-92, Molecular Cellular Biochemistry, 1988—; contbr. numerous articles to profl. jours. Mem. Am. Soc. Physiologists, Am. Soc. Biol. Chemistry, Biophys. Soc. (exec. coun. 1980-83, 85-89, 94-97), U.S. Bioenergetics Group (program chmn. 1974-75, 82, 83, exec officer 1985-90, assoc. chmn. dept. physiology, pres. 1993-95), Biophys. Soc. (treas. 1998—), Assn. Am. Med. Colls. (adminstrv. bd., exec. coun.), Federated Am. Soc. Exptl. Biologists (bd. dirs.). Avocations: farming, sailing, painting. Office: NIH Ctr Sci Rev 6701 Rockledge Dr Rm 3016 Bethesda MD 20892-7776 Office Phone: 301-435-1114. Business E-Mail: scarpat@csr.nih.gov.

**SCARPELLI, BOB,** advertising executive; Copywriter Needham Harper, Chgo., 1977—80, named creative dir., 1980; chief creative officer DDB Chgo., 1994, vice chmn., 1995, chmn., 2001; chief creative officer DDB Worldwide (U.S), 2000; elected bd. dirs. DDB Worldwide, 1994, chief creative officer, 2005—, chmn., 2006—. Mem. bd. Chgo. Internat. Film Festival, The Va. Commonwealth Univ. AdCenter, The Chgo. Creative Club, The Off the Street Club, Partnership for a Drug-Free Am.; chmn. Internat. ANDY Awards, 2000, Radio Mercury Awards, 2001, Irish Internat. Advt. Festival, 2001, Clio Festival, 2003. Office: DDB Worldwide 437 Madison Ave New York NY 10022 Office Phone: 212-415-2000.*

**SCARPELLI, VITO,** retired adult education educator, small business owner; b. Passaic, N.J., July 17, 1946; s. Peter and Celia (Pignataro) S.; m. JoAnn Motti, Aug. 23, 1970; children: Anthony, Michele. BA in Acctg. and Edn., Montclair State Coll., 1968; MA, Kean Coll., 1984; postgrad., St. Peters, Jersey City State U., Seton Hall U., Kans. State U. Prin. Roselle Park Mid. Sch., 1996—2004; supr. P. Scarpelli & Sons, Nutley, N.J., 1968-84; bus. adminstr. John J. Baum, Inc., Wayne, N.J.; salesman Realty World-Monaco Realty, Nutley, 1980—; asst. track coach, tchr. jr. H.S. Belleville Bd. Edn., 1968-69; dir. adult edn. and summer programs Roselle Park (N.J.) Bd. Edn., 1984-96; interim prin. Roselle Park Academy, 2005, ret., 2005; prin., owner Aiskai Instrnl. Drawing Sch., Nutley, NJ, 2003—. Dir. Union County Summer Youth Employment and Tng., Roselle Park, 1986, asst. curriculum coord., 1992-96, dir. tech., 1993-96; adj. prof. Jersey City State Coll., 1993-96. Pres. Nutley Am. Little League, 1987-97; v.p. Nutley Basketball Assn.; past pres. Lincoln Sch. PTA. Mem. N.J. Prins. and Supr. Assn., Nas. Assn. Secondary Sch. Prins., N.J. Bus. Edn. Assn., N.J. Edn. Assn., Roselle Park Edn. Assn., LERN, KC (grand knight 1976). Independent. Roman Catholic. Avocation: fishing. Home: 81 Milton Ave Nutley NJ 07110-3017 Office: Roselle Park Bd Edn 510 Chestnut St Roselle Park NJ 07204-1928 E-mail: vscarpelli@optonline.com.

**SCARR, SANDRA WOOD,** retired psychology educator, researcher; b. Washington, Aug. 8, 1936; d. John Ruxton and Jane (Powell) Wood; m. Harry Alan Scarr, Dec. 26, 1961 (div. 1970); children: Phillip, Karen, Rebbecca, Stephanie; m. James Callan Walker, Aug. 9, 1982 (div. 1994). AB, Vassar Coll., 1958; AM, Harvard U., 1963, PhD, 1965. Asst. prof. psychology U. Md., College Park, 1964-67; assoc. prof. U. Pa., Phila., 1967-71; prof. U. Minn., Mpls., 1971-77, Yale U., New Haven, 1977-83; Commonwealth prof. U. Va., Charlottesville, 1983-95, chmn. dept. psychology, 1984-90; CEO, chmn. bd. dirs. KinderCare Learning Ctr., Inc., 1995-97; ret., 1997. Mem. nat. adv. bd. Robert Wood Johnson Found., Princeton, N.J., 1985-91; coord. coun. psychology SUNY Bd. Regents, N.Y.C., 1984-92; prof. Kerstin Hesselgren, Sweden, 1993-94. Author: Race, Social Class and Individual Differences in IQ, 1981, Mother Care/Other Care, 1984 (Nat. Book award APA 1985), Caring for Children, 1989; editor Jour. Devel. Psychology, 1980-86, Current Directions in Psychol. Sci., 1991-95. Fellow Ctr. for Advanced Studies, Stanford U., Calif., 1976-77; grantee NIH, NSF, others, 1967-95. Fellow AAAS, APA (chmn. com. on human rsch. 1980-83, coun. of reps. 1984-89, bd. dirs. 1988-90, Award for Disting. Contbn. to Rsch. on Pub. Policy 1988), Am. Psychol. Soc. (bd. dirs. 1992—, pres. 1996-97, James McKeen Cattell award 1993); mem. Am. Acad. Arts and Scis. (coun. mem. 1995-2000), Behavior Genetics Assn. (pres. 1985-86, exec. coun. 1975-79, 84-87, Dobzhansky award 2004), Soc. for Rsch. in Child Devel. (governing coun. 1974-76, 87-93, chmn. fin. com. 1987-89, pres. 1989-91), Internat. Soc. for Study of Behavioral Devel. (exec. bd. 1987-94). Avocations: dogs, gardening. Home: 77-6222 Kaumalumalu Dr Holualoa HI 96725-9757 Office Phone: 808-322-9445. Personal E-mail: sandrascar@aol.com.

**SCARRITT, THOMAS VARNON,** newspaper editor; b. Tuscaloosa, Ala., Jan. 28, 1953; s. Charles Wesley and Valerie (Varnon) S.; m. Kathryn Ruan Hubbard, Dec. 28, 1973; children: Sara Kathryn, Thomas Varnon Jr. BA in Journalism, U. N.C., 1974; MBA, Samford U., 1995. Reporter The Birmingham (Ala.) News, 1975-79, Washington corr., 1979-83, news editor, 1983-85, editl. page editor, 1986-89, exec. editor, 1989-97, editor, 1997—. Bd. dirs. Workshops Inc. Mem. Am. Soc. Newspaper Editors, Soc. Profl. Journalists, Kiwanis (Birmingham), Phi Beta Kappa. Episcopal. Home: 4240 Clairmont Ave S Birmingham AL 35222-3724 Office: The Birmingham News 2200 4th Ave N Birmingham AL 35203-3840 Office Phone: 205-325-2205. E-mail: tscarritt@bhamnews.com.

**SCARWID, DIANA ELIZABETH,** actress; b. Savannah, Ga. d. Anthony and Elizabeth Scarwid. Grad., Am. Acad. Dramatic Arts, 1975; degree in Theater Arts, Acting, Pace U., 1975. Appeared in films including Pretty Baby, Honeysuckle Rose, Inside Moves, (Oscar award nomination Best Supporting Actress), Mommie Dearest, Rumble Fish, Strange Invaders, Silkwood, Psycho III, Extremities, Heat, Neon Bible, The Cure, Gold Diggers: The Secret of Bear Mountain, What Lies Beneath, The Angel Doll, A Guy Thing, Party Monster, The Clearing; TV films include Thou Shalt Not Kill, Studs Lonigan, Guyana Tragedy: The Story of Jim Jones, Desperate Lives, A Bunny's Tale, After the Promise, Night of The Hunter, Critical Choices, Bastard Out of Carolina, Angel of Pennsylvania Avenue, Truman (Emmy nomination), If These Walls Could Talk, Ruby Bridges Story, also mini-series From the Earth to the Moon, Before He Wakes; theater prodns. include Key Exchange, Toronto, Can., A Thousand Clowns, Jupiter, Fla., Camelshine Springs, Mark Taper Forum, LA, Spoon River Anthology, Ring 'round the Moon, NYC, Nat. Shakespeare Conservatory, NY; (TV films) Down Will Come Baby, Dirty Pictures, Path to War, (series) WonderFalls. Avocations: reading, bicycling, crabbing, walking.

**SCATENA, LORRAINE BORBA,** retired rancher, women's rights advocate, researcher; b. San Rafael, Calif., Feb. 18, 1924; d. Joseph and Eugenia (Simas) de Borba; m. Louis G. Scatena, Feb. 14, 1960, dec. Nov. 1995; children: Louis Vincent, Eugenia Gayle. BA, Dominican Coll., San Rafael, 1945; postgrad., Calif. Sch. Fine Arts, 1948, U. Calif., Berkeley, 1956—59. Cert. elem. tchr. Calif. Tchr. Dominican Coll., 1946; tchr. of mentally handicapped San Anselmo (Calif.) Sch. Dist., 1946; tchr. Fairfax (Calif.) Pub. Elem. Sch., 1946—53; asst. to mayor Fairfax (Calif.) City Recreation,

1948—53; tchr., libr. U.S. Dependent Schs., Mainz am Rhine, Germany, 1953—56; translator Portugal Travel Tours, Lisbon, 1954; bonding sec. Am. Fore Ins. Group, San Francisco, 1958—60; rancher, farmer Yerington, Nev., 1960—98. Hostess com. Caldecott and Newbury Authors' Awards, San Francisco, 1959; mem. Nev. State Legis. Commn., 1975; coord. Nevadans for Equal Rights Amendment, 1975-78, rural areas rep., 1976-78; testifier Nev. State Senate and Assembly, 1975, 77; mem. adv. com. Fleischmann Coll. Agr. U. Nev., 1977-80, 81-84; speaker Grants and Rsch. Projects, Bishop, Calif., 1977, Choices for Tomorrow's Women, Fallon, Nev., 1989. Poetry presenter World Congress on Arts and Comm., Lisbon, Portugal, 1999, Washington, 2000, St. John's Coll.-Cambridge U., 2001, Vancouver, B.C., Can., 2002. Trustee Wassuk Coll., Hawthorne, Nev., 1984-87; mem. Lyon County Friends of Libr., Yerington, 1971—, Lyon County Mus. Soc., 1978—; sec., pub. info. chmn. Lyon County Rep. Women, 1968-73, program v.p., 1973-75; mem. Lyon County Rep. Ctrl. Com, 1973-74, Marin County Soc. Artists, San Anselmo, Calif., 1948-53; charter mem. Eleanor Roosevelt Edn. Fund for Women and Girls, 1990, sustaining mem., 1992—; Nev. rep. 1st White House Conf. Rural Am. Women, Washington, 1980; participant internat. reception, Washington, 1980; mem. pub. panel individual presentation Shakespeare's Treatment of Women Characters, Nev. Theatre for the Arts, Ashland, Oreg., Shakespearean Actors local performance, 1977; mem. Nev. Women's History Project, U. Nev., 1996—; mem. pres.'s circle Dominican U. Calif., 1997-; mem. Bancroft Libr.'s coun. U. Calif., Berkeley, 2002-. Recipient Outstanding Conservation Farmer award Mason Valley Conservation Dist., 1992, Soroptimist Internat. Women Helping women award 1983, invitation to first all-women delegation to U.S.A. from People's Republic China, U.S. House Reps., 1979; Public Forum Grant grantee Edn. Title IX, Oakland, Calif., 1977; Internat. Biog. Ctr. (Cambridge) fellow World Lit. Acad., 1993. Mem. AAUW (life mem. nat. br. 1975—, Leaders Circle 1998-), Lyon County Ret. Tchrs. Assn. (unit pres. 1979-80, 84-86, v.p. 1986-88, Nev. State Outstanding Svc. award 1981, state conv. gen. chmn. 1985), Rural Am. Women Inc., AAUW (br. pres. 1972-74, 74-76, chair edn. found. programs 1983—, state conv. gen. chmn. 1976, 87, state sec. 1970-72, state legis. program chmn. 1976-77, state chmn. internat. rels. 1979-81, state pres. 1981-83, br. travelship, discovering women in U.S. history Radcliffe Coll. 1981, State Humanities award 1975, Future Fund Nat. award 1983, Lorraine Scatena endowment gift named in her honor for significant contbns. to AAUW Edn. Found. 1997), Mason Valley Country Club, Italian Cath. Fedn. (pres. 1986-88), Uniao Portuguesa Estado da Calif., Nat. Mus. of Women in the Arts (charter mem., 1987, assoc., mem. mus. coun. 2000—). Roman Catholic. Avocations: writing, photography, travel, history. Home: PO Box 247 Yerington NV 89447-0247

**SCATES, ALICE YEOMANS,** retired federal official; b. Pitts., Jan. 21, 1915; d. William E. and Georgiana L. (Lloyd) Yeomans. BS, State Tchrs. Coll., Glassboro, N.J., 1936; MEd, Duke U., 1949; EdD, George Washington U., 1963. Tchr. elem. sch., Haddon Heights, N.J., 1937-43; civilian personnel officer Sedalia Army Airfield, Mo., Greenfield Army Airfield, S.C., 1944-46; pers. tng. officer VA Ctr., Dayton, Ohio, 1947—48; rsch. assoc., dir. Am. Coun. on Edn. Staff for Office Naval Rsch. Projects, 1949-53; asst. dir. Nat. Home Study Coun., 1954; editor, rsch. asst. Office of Edn. HEW, 1955, rsch. analyst, coord. coop. rsch. program, 1956-64, program planning officer occupl. rsch. program, 1965-66, dir. basic rsch. br. secondary edn., 1967-69; program planning and eval. officer Nat. Ctr. Ednl. R & D, 1969-71; eval. specialist Office Program Eval., 1971-80; eval. officer Office of Mgmt. U.S. Dept. Edn., 1980-82, cons., 1982-91; mem. continuing care adv. com. Md. State Office on Aging, 1994-99. Contbr. articles to profl. jours.; editor: Life Line, 1998—. Mem. Nat. Continuing Care Residents Assn.; bd. dirs. Town Ctr. Cmty. Assn., Columbia, Md., 1997-2001. Capt. U.S. Army, 1943-46. Fellow AAAS; mem. LWV, Am. Sociol. Assn., Am. Ednl. Rsch. Assn., Adult Edn. Assn., Kappa Delta Pi, Phi Delta Gamma. Home and Office: Vantage House # 1006 5400 Vantage Point Rd Columbia MD 21044-2667 Personal E-mail: ayscates@msn.com.

**SCATES, ALLEN EDWARD,** coach; BA, UCLA, 1961, MS, 1962. Coach volleyball UCLA, 1970—. Coached UCLA to 18 NCAA championships. Recipient All Time Great Coach awrd USA Volleyball, 1995, Alumnas of Yr. in Profl. Devel., UCLA, 2003; inducted Volleyball Hall of Fame, 1993, Calif. Beach Volleyball Hall of Fame, 1998, UCLA Hall of Fame, 2003; named Coach of Yr., 5 times, U.S. Olympic Com. Coach Yr., 1998. Office: UCLA Morgan Ctr PO Box 24044 Los Angeles CA 90024-0044 E-mail: ascates@athletics.ucla.edu.

**SCATURRO, PHILIP DAVID,** investment banker, academic administrator; b. Newark, Dec. 8, 1938; s. Charles and Rose (Montino) Scaturro. BA, Williams Coll., 1960; JD, MBA, Columbia U., 1963. Analyst Ladenburg, Thalmann & Co., Inc., N.Y.C., 1964-67; v.p. Sellin, Forbes & Smith, N.Y.C., 1967, Allen & Co. Inc., N.Y.C., 1967-71; mng. dir., exec. v.p., 1977—; gen. ptnr. R&S Assocs., N.Y.C., 1972-76; pvt. investor, N.Y.C., 1976-77; chmn. bd. trustees New Sch U, N.Y.C., 1999—. Bd. dirs. Wilmorite, Inc., Rochester, NY, 2000—05, Mass. Mus. Contemporary Art Found., Inc., North Adams, 1997—, NYC Opera, 2005—2005, mem. exec. com., 1985—2005, chmn. fin. com., 1985—2005, treas., 1985—2005, trustee, 1985—, mem. exec. com., 1985—; trustee New Sch. U., 1989—. Mem.: Century Assn., Univ. Club (N.Y.C.). Avocations: opera, music, theater, wine, fly fishing. Office: Allen & Co 711 Fifth Ave 9th Fl New York NY 10022-3111

**SCAVARDA, DONALD ROBERT,** composer, artist; b. Iron Mountain, Mich., June 18, 1928; m. Barbara Janet Regner, Nov. 13, 1965. MMus, U. Mich., 1953. Co-founder, organizer Once Festival Musical Premieres, Ann Arbor, Mich., 1960-65. Composer: Groups For Piano, 1959, Sounds for Eleven, 1961, (Haiku song cycle) In the Autumn Mountains, 1961, Matrix for Clarinetist (widely recognized as the pioneering work in discovery and development of clarinet multiphonics), 1962, (piano, clarinet, 8mm film) Landscape Journey, 1963, (film score for electronic realization) Greys, 1963, (multiple film projection and tape) Caterpillar, 1965; paintings include Chamber Music, 1997, Portrait of Helen P., 1998; video films: Cinamatrix, 2002; composed recs. named to Top 10 List, Art Forum Mag., 2003; boxed CD-set, Music From the Once Festival-1961-1966, 2003. Fulbright schol., 1953; recipient 1st prize for Fantasy For Violin And Orchestra BMI Inc., 1954. Mem.: World Wildlife Fund, Humane Soc. U.S. Home: PO Box 1908 Ann Arbor MI 48106-1908

**SCEARSE, PATRICIA DOTSON,** nursing educator, dean; b. Wabash, Ind., Sept. 4, 1931; d. Claude Richard and Lilly Etta (Colvill) D.; m. Vernon Quinton Scearse, June 26, 1955 (dec. Mar. 1990); 1 child, Victoria Lynn Lenderman. BS, Earlham Coll., 1955; MS, U. Colo., 1968; D in Nursing Sci., U. Calif., San Francisco, 1974. RN Staff nurse Reid Meml. Hosp., Richmond, Ind., 1954-55; head nurse, instr. Hillcrest Bapt. Hosp., Waco, Tex., 1955-56; instr. Sch. Nursing Candler Hosp., Savannah, Ga., 1956-60; adminstrv. asst., edn. cons. Wyo. State Bd. Nursing, Cheyenne, 1964-68; asst. prof. San Diego State U., 1969, Ball State U., Muncie, Ind., 1969-71; assoc. prof., area chairperson U. Mich., Ann Arbor, 1974-80; prof., dean Coll. Nursing Tex. Christian U., Ft. Worth, 1980-95, emeritus dean, prof., 1995—. Pub. policy editor Jour. Profl. Nursing, Phila., 1986-89; editorial cons. Jour. Pub. Health Nursing, New Haven, 1984-89; contbr. articles to profl. jours. Recipient Outstanding Nurse award Sigma Theat Tau, Beta Alpha, Ft. Worth, 1986; Kennedy Inst. Ethics postdoctoral fellow, Georgetown U., 1978. Mem. ANA, APHA (bd. govs. 1976), Am. Assn. Colls. of Nursing (bd. dirs. 1982-84, 85-87), Nat. League for Nursing, Coun. Baccalaureate and Higher Degree Programs (bd. rev.), Assn. Community Health Nurse Educators (named Great 100 Nurses 1992). Home: 3301 Quail Run Dr High Point NC 27265-2589

**SCELFO, CHRIS,** university football coach; b. Abbeville, La., Sept. 30, 1963; m. Nancy Caldwell; children: Sarah Beth, Joseph II. BS, N.E. La. U., 1986, MEd, 1988. Asst. coach River Oaks H.S., Monroe, La., 1986; asst. offensive line and tight ends coach N.E. La. U., 1986-87; offensive line grad. asst. coach U. Okla., Norman, 1988, receiver coach, 1989; offensive line coach Marshall U., 1990-95, offensive coord., 1993-95; asst. head coach, offensive line coach U. Ga., Augusta, 1996-98; head football coach Tulane U., New Orleans, 1998—. Office: Tulane U Dept Athletics 6823 Saint Charles Ave New Orleans LA 70118-5665

**SCELSA, JOSEPH VINCENT,** sociologist, educator, dean; b. NYC, Dec. 7, 1945; s. Albert John and Katherine Mary S.; m. Joyce Ann Tisi, Nov. 13, 1981; 1 child, Jonathan. AA, LIU, 1966, BA, 1968; MA, CUNY, 1973, MSEd, 1978; MA, Columbia U., 1983, EdD, 1984. Lic. mental health counselor, NY, 2006; cert. sch. counselor, NY. Counselor, tchr. NYC Bd. Edn., 1970-78, coord. career and occupational edn., 1979; coord. specialized counseling CUNY, 1979-81; pvt. practice counseling, NYC, 1975—; lectr. grad. faculty Herbert H. Lehman Coll., CUNY, 1980—; dean Calandra Inst., CUNY, 1994—; prof. student pers. Queens Coll., CUNY, 1999, v.p., 2000. Consul gen. of Italy in NY; pres. Italian Am. Mus., 2001—. Active Coun. of 1000 nat. Italian-Am. Found.; past cive chair multi cultural adv. bd. NYC Bd. Edn., 1990-91; NY State Mentoring Program Adv. Bd., 1990—; bd. dirs. Nat. Ethnic Coalition Orgns., 1990—, Coalition Italo-Am. Assn., 2000—; Italian Apostalate, NY, 1993. Decorated cavaliere Order of Merit Republic of Italy; recipient Disting. Alumni award LIU, 1985, Organizational Leadership award Coalition Italo-Am. Assns., Inc., 1988, Americus award Bronx Community Coll., 1989, Role Model award Club DaVinci, 1990, Inte I-A Student Assn. award, CUNY, 1991, Intergroup Rels. Chancellor's award, 1994, FIERI Leadership award, 1993, Philip Mazzei award, 1993, Ellis Island medal of honor, 1997, N.Y. State Govs. award for Excellence, 1999, Medal for 3d Millennium, 2000, Good Shapers Award, Woman & Work Program, 2005; named House of Savoy, 1997; Italian fellow John Jay Coll., 1993; inductee St. Lucy's Hall of Fame, 1996. Mem. Am. Counseling Assn., Am. Mental Health Counselors Assn. (cert. of recognition 1979, counselor of yr. 1983-84), Nat. Acad. Cert. Clin. Mental Health Counselors, Nat. Bd. for Cert. Counselors, Am.-Italian Hist. Assn., NY State Mental Health Counselors Assn. (past pres., Outstanding Work award 1980), Ill. Club. Home: 41 Carwall Ave Mount Vernon NY 10552-1211 Office: CUNY 555 W 57th St Ste 1137 New York NY 10019 Office Phone: 718-931-6935.

**SCEUSA, NICHOLAS A.,** pharmacologist; b. Bklyn., July 22, 1948; s. Nicolo Sceusa and Maria Rita Anastasi; m. Donna Lynn Klein, Feb. 23, 1973; children: Amanda, Nicholas. BS in Biology, Syracuse U., 1971; BS in Pharmacy, L.I. U., 1977; PharmD, U. Ill., Chgo., 1996. Registered pharmacist, N.Y. Sr. staff pharmacist King Khalid Univ. Hosp., Riyadh, Saudi Arabia, 1984-86, Tawam Hosp., Al Ain, United Arab Emirates, 1986-87; staff pharmacist II St. Luke's - Roosevelt Hosp., N.Y.C., 1987—90; staff pharmacist St. Clare's Hosp., 1990—95; pres., CEO Gelsus Rsch. and Consulting, Inc., 1997—. Author (with others): The Secret History of Italian-American Evacuation and Internment during World War II; contbr. articles to profl. jours. Advisor to Sch. Bd. Dist. 3, N.Y.C., 1996-98. Mem.: Am. Assn. Pharm. Scientists, Aurora Upata Day Star Lodge (treas.). Episcopalian. Achievements include patents for biofiltration and (Teorell-Meyer) dosage forms; invention of RAPID drug delivery system; rechargeable cardiac stent; new forms of surgical bandages and novel nutraceutical products. Avocations: hunting, fishing, outdoors, science, invention. Home and Office: 145 W 96th St Ste 1A New York NY 10025-6449 Fax: 212-280-1255. Office Phone: 212-663-7905. Personal E-mail: gelsus@aol.com.

**SCHAAB, ARNOLD J.,** lawyer; b. Newark, 1939; s. Robert George and Pauline Schaab; m. Marcia Stecker, 1964 (div. 1978); children: Emily Diana, Genevieve; m. Patricia Caesar, 1981 (div. 1996); m. Susan McGlamery, 2000; one child: Robert George II. BA, New Sch. U., 1962; LLB, Harvard U., 1965. Bar: NY 1967, US Dist. Ct. (so. and ea. dists.) NY 1967. Assoc. Chadbourne & Parke, NYC, 1966-69; ptnr. Anderson, Kill & Olick, NYC, 1969-78; sr. ptnr. Pryor, Cashman, Sherman & Flynn LLP, NYC, 1978—. Chmn. Literacy Ptnrs., Inc. Fulbright scholar Law Faculty U. Paris. Fellow NY Bar Found.; Am. Bar Found.; mem. ABA (vice chair internat. fin. transactions com., sections bus. law, sci. tech law, intellectual property law internat. law practice), NY State Bar Assn. (chmn. internat. law practice sect., chmn. spl. com. free trade Ams., ho. dels., fin. com., long range planning com., by-laws com.), Assn. Bar City NY (com. pvt. investment funds, com. internat. trade, com. fgn. comparative law), Computer Law Assn., Univ. Club (treas., chmn. fin. com., chmn. audit com., mem. coun.), Doubles, Archaeol. Inst. Am., Bibl. Archaeology Soc. Office: Pryor Cashman Sherman & Flynn 410 Park Ave New York NY 10022-4441

**SCHAAF, DOUGLAS ALLAN,** lawyer; b. Green Bay, Wis., Nov. 18, 1955; s. Carlton Otto and Fern (Brunette) S.; m. Kathlyn T. Bielke, Feb. 23, 1988. BBA magna cum laude in Internat. Bus., St. Norbert Coll., DePere, Wis., 1978; JD, U. Notre Dame, 1981. Bar: Ill. 1981, Calif. 1987. Assoc. McDermott, Will & Emery, Chgo., 1981-84; Skadden, Arps, Slate, Meagher & Flom, 1984-89; ptnr. Paul Hastings, Janofsky & Walker, L.A., 1989—, vice chmn. tax dept. Adj. faculty mem. John Marshall Law Sch., 1984-87. Atty. Chgo. Vol. Legal Services, 1984-87; bd. dirs. Orange County Alzheimer's Assn. Mem. Orange County Bar Assn. (chair tax sect. 1994-96). Office: Paul Hastings Janofsky & Walker 695 Town Center Dr Ste 1700 Costa Mesa CA 92626-7191 Office Phone: 714-668-6221. Office Fax: 714-668-6441. Business E-Mail: dougschaaf@paulhastings.com.

**SCHAAL, BARBARA ANNA,** evolutionary biologist, educator; BS in Biology with honors, U. Ill., Chgo., 1969; MPhil in Population Biology, Yale U., 1971, PhD in Population Biology, 1974. spkr. in field. Assoc. prof. biology Washington U., St. Louis, 1980-86, prof., 1986—; prof. genetics Wash. U. Sch. Medicine, Spencer T. Olin prof. biology in arts and scis., chair dept. biology, 1993-97, mem. various coms. Assoc. editor Molecular Biology and Evolution, Am. Jour. Botany, Molecular Ecology, Conservation Genetics. Trustee St. Louis Acad. Scis. Fellow AAAS, Am. Acad. Arts & Sciences; mem. NAS (v.p. 2005-), Bot. Soc. Am. (pres. 1995-96, Merit award 1999), Nature Conservancy (trustee Mo. chpt.). Achievements include research on the evolutionary process within plant populations. Office: Washington U Sch Medicine 660 S Euclid Ave Saint Louis MO 63110*

**SCHABACKER, BETTY BARCHET,** artist; b. Balt., Aug. 14, 1925; d. Stephen George and Louise (Lankford) Barchet; m. Robert Bailey Schabacker, June 8, 1945; 1 child, Elizabeth M Student, Conn. Coll. Women, 1946. Freelance artist, Santa Fe, 1950—. Mem. Soc. Animal Artists, Nat. Water Color Soc., Audubon Artists, Inc., Coll. Artists Am.

**SCHABACKER, ELIZABETH M.,** literature educator; d. Robert Bailey and Betty Barchet Schabacker; 1 child, Susan. BA, Wilson Coll., 1964—68; MS, Rensselaer Poly. Inst., 1968—69. Cert. tchr. N.Mex, NY, Mass., 1972, painting instr. Priscilla Hauser; Roses, Basic I and Basic II, 2004, tchr. decorative art, traditions tchr. Tchr. Emma Willard, Troy, NY, 1969—70, Troy Pub. Schools, Troy, NY, 1970—72, Mt. Ida Coll., Newton Ctr., Mass., 1977—85; dir. Inst. of Decorative Art Studies, Lexington, Mass., 1985—92; asst. prof. N.Mex Mil. Inst., Roswell, N.Mex., 1992—98; dir. of the writing ctr. Winston-Salem State U., NC, 1998—. Tchr. decorative art., author Soc. of Decorative Painters, Wichita, Kans., 1985—2005; tv show: make it spl. NMMI-Productions, Roswell, N.Mex., 1996—97; columnist Roswell Daily Record, N.Mex.; traditions tchr. Jansen Art Traditions. Author: (children's book) Huckleberry Robin; painted ornament, Patinated Angel, Rosemaled tambourine; contbr. articles to jours.; Represented in permanent collections Smithsonian Inst., painted ornament, White House Ofcl. Christmas Tree, 2004. Edn. dir. Roswell Guild of the Santa Fe Opera, N.Mex., 1996—98. Recipient Wilma Lassiter Master Tchr. award, Winston-Salem State U., 1993; Bogle Professorship, N.Mex Mil. Inst., 1996. Mem.: Triad Decorative Painters (v.p., seminar dir. 2001—03), Soc. of Decorative Painters (life). Avocations: painting, writing. Office: Winston-Salem State Univ 601 Martin Luther King Jr Dr Winston Salem NC 27110 E-mail: prieste@wssu.edu

**SCHACHT, HENRY MEVIS,** writer, consultant; b. Pasadena, Calif., Feb. 28, 1916; s. Henry and Amelia (Claussen) S.; m. Mary Joan Turnbull, Dec. 30, 1937; children: Henry John, Linda Joan. BA, U. Calif., Berkeley, 1936.

Info. specialist U. Calif., Berkeley, 1936-42; dir. agr. NBC, San Francisco, 1942-59, ABC, San Francisco, 1959-60; agrl. columnist San Francisco Chronicle, 1959-93. Dir. agrl. info. U. Calif., 1961-65; v.p. corp. relations, corp. sec. Calif. Canners & Growers, San Francisco, 1965-81; freelance writer, 1936—; cons. radio-TV to FAO of UN, Cairo, 1963, Mexico City, 1965, Tokyo, 1966; dir. Calif. Co. for Internat. Trade; dir. Agrl. Issues Ctr., U. Calif. Author: (books) To the 21st Century - Study of Agribusiness to the Year 2000, 1983, History of the San Francisco Engineers Club, 1987, The Long and Winding Trail (History of the California Cattlemen's Association), 1991, Vision Solo - California Agriculture Report to State Dept. of Food and Agriculture, 1999, The California Cowboy, 2000. Pres. U.S. Fruit Export Coun., 1972-75; exec. sec. Commn. Calif. Agr. and Higher Edn., 1993-95; adv. bd. Agrl. Issues Ctr. U. Calif., 1990—2002. Mem. Pub. Rels. Soc. Am., Pub. Rels. Roundtable San Francisco, Nat. Assn. Farm Broadcasters, Agrl. Rels. Coun., Nat. Canners Assn. (dir. 1966-81) Home: 60 Hiller Dr Oakland CA 94618-2351

**SCHACHT, JOCHEN HEINRICH,** biochemistry educator; b. Königsberg, Fed. Republic Germany, July 2, 1939; arrived in U.S., 1969; s. Heinz and Else (Sprenger) S.; m. Helga Hildegard Seidel, Jan.27, 1967; children: Miriam Helga, Daniel Jochen. BS, U. Bonn, Fed. Republic Germany, 1962; MS in Chemistry, U. Heidelberg, Fed. Republic Germany, 1965, PhD in Biochemistry, 1968. Asst. research chemist, Mental Health Research Inst. U. Mich., Ann Arbor, 1969-72, from asst. prof. to assoc. prof. biochemistry, Dept. Biol. Chemistry & Otolaryngology, 1973-84, prof., 1984—, chmn. grad. program in physiol. acoustics, 1981—; hon. prof. Med. Acad. of the Chinese PLA, Beijing, 1998. Vis. prof. Karolinska Inst., Stockholm, 1979-80; acting dir. Kresge Hearing Rsch. Inst., U. Mich., 1983-84, assoc. dir., 1989-99, dir., 2000—; mem. hearing rsch. study sect. USPHS, NIH, Nat. Inst. Neurol. and Communicative Disorders and Stroke, 1986-89, Task Force Nat. Strategic Rsch. Plan, Nat. Insts. Deafness and Communication Disorders, USPHS, NIH; hon. prof. Hunan Med. U., Changsha, China, 1999—, Tonghi Med. U., Wuhan, China, 1999—; guest prof. Fourth Mil. Med. U., Xian, China, 1999—. Mem. editl. bd. Hearing Rsch., 1990—; assoc. editor Audiology & Neuro-Otol., 1995—; contbr. more than 200 articles to profl. jours., book chpts., revs.; co-editor Neurochemistry of Cholinergic Receptors, 1974. Fogarty Sr. Internat. fellow NIH, 1979, Sen. J. Javitz Neurosci. investigator, 1984; recipient Chercheur Etranger rsch. award INSERM, Paris, 1986, 94, Animal Welfare award Erna-Graff Found., Berlin, 1987, Disting. Faculty Achievement award U. Mich., 1989, Employer of Yr. award Nat. Tech. Assist Assoc. Coop. Edn. and Gallaudet U., Washington. Mem. Am. Soc. Neurochemistry, Internat. Soc. Neurochemistry, Soc. for Neurosci., Assn. for Rsch. in Otolaryngology, Am. Soc. Biol. Chemists, Assn. Espanola de Audiologia Exptl. Avocations: photography, travel, birding. Office: U Mich Kresge Hearing Rsch Inst Ann Arbor MI 48109-0506 Office Phone: 734-763-3572. Business E-Mail: schacht@umich.edu.

**SCHACHTE, MARGARET PRINGLE,** director; b. Charleston, SC, Jan. 29, 1948; d. Ashmead Forrester and Helen Johansen Pringle; m. Hal Sevier Currey, Jan. 15, 1983; children: Christopher Charles, Anna Pringle, Nancy McDonald Currey, Kathleen O'Neill Currey, Elizabeth Currey McCaleb. BA, Duke U., Durham, NC, 1968; MBA, Emory U., Atlanta, 1981. Exec. v.p. Drug Sci. Found., Charleston, 1981—88; dir. rsch. adminstrv. svcs. and planning Med. U. SC, Charleston, 1989—93, dir. office rsch. devel., 1993—, asst. prof. libr. sci. and informatics, 2004—. Exec. v.p. Joanna Found., Sullivans Island, SC, 1989—, trustee, 1989. Recipient Gordon A. Siefkin award, Emory U. Sch. Bus., 1981, Wall St. Jour. award, 1981, Disting. Faculty Svc. award Med. U. SC., 2005; scholar, Atlanta Mktg. Club, 1979—80. Mem.: Phi Beta Kappa. Office: Med U SC PO Box 250501 171 Ashley Ave Charleston SC 29425 Office Phone: 843-792-0868. Office Fax: 843-792-1657. E-mail: schachte@musc.edu.

**SCHACHTER, JAMES ROBERT,** editor; b. Glendale, Calif., July 20, 1959; s. Stanley Herman and Margot (Lipiner) S.; m. Pamela Haag, May 19, 1985; children: Ariel Shira, Miriam Rachel, Naomi Tikvah, Benjamin Lev. BA, Columbia U., 1980. Reporter Jacksonville Jour., Fla., 1980-82, Kansas City Star, Mo., 1982-84, labor writer, 1984-85; reporter LA Times, San Diego, 1985-87, bus. writer LA, 1987-90, asst. bus. editor, 1990-93, Sunday bus. editor, 1993-94, sr. asst. bus. editor, 1994-95; enterprise editor Bus. Day NY Times, NYC, 1995, editor Sunday Money and Bus., dep. editor Bus. Day Desk, 2000—04, dep. culture editor, 2004-06, dep. editor, 2006—. Recipient award of Distinction, Soc. Newspaper Design, 1992, Cert. of Merit, Greater L.A. Press Club, 1989, 90, Bus. and Fin. Journalism award John Hancock Ins. Co., 1988, Best News Article award San Diego Press Club, 1987, Best Local News Reporting award Inland Daily Press Assn., Chgo., 1984. Mem. Investigative Reporters and Editors. Office: NY Times 229 W 43rd St New York NY 10036-3959 Office Phone: 212-556-1144. Business E-Mail: jims@nytimes.com.

**SCHACHTMAN, NATHAN A.,** lawyer; b. 1953; AB, Rutgers U., 1975, JD magna cum laude, 1982. Bar: NJ 1984, Pa. 1984, US Ct. of Appeals, Third Circuit, US Dist. Ct., NJ, US Dist. Ct., Pa (Ea. Dist.). Law clerk to Judge H. Emory Widener, Jr. US Ct. of Appeals, Fourth Circuit, NJ, 1982—83; ptnr., litigation, products liability & toxic torts McCarter & English, Phila. Mem. Defense Rsch. Inst.; peer reviewer Federal Judicial Ctr. Mem.: ABA, Pa. State Bar Assn., NJ State Bar Assn. Office: McCarter & English Mellon Bank Ctr 1735 Market St Ste 700 Philadelphia PA 19103 Office Phone: 215-979-3876. Office Fax: 215-988-4323. Business E-Mail: nschachtman@mccarter.com.

**SCHACTER, BRENT ALLAN,** oncologist, health facility administrator; b. Winnipeg, Man., Can., June 1, 1942; s. Irvin C. and Claire (Easton) S.; m. Sora Ludwig, Dec. 20, 1981; children: Isanne, Jennifer, Miriam. BSc, U. Man., 1965, MD with honors, 1965. Intern Winnipeg Gen. Hosp., 1965-66, jr. asst. resident, 1967-68; asst. resident in internal medicine Barnes Hosp., St. Louis, 1968-69; clin. fellow hematology Barnes Hosp. and Washington U., St. Louis, 1969-70; rsch. fellow, asst. in medicine U. Tex. Southwestern Med. Sch., Dallas, 1970-72; asst. prof. internal medicine U. Man., Winnipeg, 1972-77, assoc. prof. medicine, 1977-87, prof., 1987—; pres., CEO Cancer-Care Manitoba, Winnipeg, 1993—2003; CEO Can. Assn. Provincial Cancer Agys., 2003—. Lectr. in field; sci. officer grant panel C, Nat. Cancer Inst. Can., 1978, mem., 1979-82; mem. Man. Health Rsch. Coun. grant panel, 1982-84, 89-91, Coun. for Canadian Strategy for Cancer Contro, 2002-; adv. bd. Can. Porphyria Found., 1988—; mem. steering com. Can. Strategy For Cancer Control, 1999-2002, co-chair steering com., 2000-02, mem. coun., 2002—; mem. steering com. Can. Cancer Stats., 2000-03; adv. task force Coun. for Can. Strategy for Cancer Control, 2002-. Contbr. numerous articles and abstracts to profl. jours. Bd. dirs. Nat. Cancer Inst. Can., 2000—. Recipient Med. Rsch. Coun. Can. Vis. Scientist award, 1986; fellow Muscular Dystrophy Assn., 1964, John S. McEachern Meml. fellow Can. Cancer Soc., 1969-70, Med. Rsch. Coun. Can. fellow, 1970-72, Med. Rsch. Coun. Can. rsch. fellow, 1966-67; Isbister scholar, 1962, 63, Med. Rsch. Coun. Can. scholar, 1975-80. Fellow Royal Coll. Physicians; mem. AAAS, Royal Coll. Physicians and Surgeons of Can. (specialty com. in med. oncology 1985-94, bd. med. examiners in med. oncology 1987-90, specialty com. in hematology 1989-93, core com. mem. 1990-96, chmn. bd. examiners med. oncology 1990-93, mem. regional adv. com. Sask./Man. dist. 1992-97), Am. Fedn. for Clin. Rsch., Can. Soc. for Clin. Investigation (awards com. 1980-82, chmn. 1981-82), Am. Soc. Hematology, Can. Soc. Hematology, Am. Soc. Clin. Oncology, Can. Bone Marrow Transplant Group, Can. Assn. Provincial Cancer Agys., Can. Hemophilia Soc. (mem. clinic dirs. group 1990-93, sec-treas. 1991-93, Golden Jubilee medal Queen Elizabeth II 2002). Avocations: cross country skiing, scuba diving, model railroading. Home: 224 Lamont Blvd Winnipeg MB Canada R3P 0E9 Office: CancerCare Manitoba 675 McDermot Ave Winnipeg MB Canada R3E 0V9 E-mail: brent.schacter@cancercare.mb.ca.

**SCHADOW, KAREN E.,** public speaking trainer, educator; b. Mar. 1949; 1 child, Kelby. BA in com. and humanities magna cum laude, Fla. State U., 1971, MA in theatre magna cum laude, 1973. Previous cameraperson numerous programs, ABC TV, previous prodn. staff mem.; pres. The Voice of

Success!, NYC. Adj. asst. prof. NYU, 1990—; instr. Bergen Cmty. Coll., NJ; creator, presenter various lectures and seminars for sch. and orgn. including Nat. Acad. TV Arts & Scis., NY Coalition Women in Arts and Media, Ctr. Arts Edn., The Learning Annex, nationwide; prodr. student career conf. NY Women in Comm., 2002—05; nominating judge Drama League. Mem.: Nat. Acad. TV Arts & Scis. (past mem. bd. govs., Emmy award 1984), Fla. State U. Theatre Project, New England Soc., Univ. Film & Video Assn., Screen Actors Guild, Actors' Equity, NY Women in Comm. (v.p. student affairs). Office Phone: 212-563-2615. Business E-Mail: karen@thevoiceofsuccess.com.

**SCHADT, JAMES PHILLIP,** investment and software executive; b. Saginaw, Mich., Aug. 7, 1938; s. Phillip Jr. and Jean D. (Cardy) S.; m. Barbara L. Soldmann, Aug. 16, 1959; children: Lauren C., Andrew F. BA, Northwestern U., 1960. With Procter & Gamble USA, 1960-65, Glendinning Cos., 1965-70, Squibb Corp., 1971-73, Pepsi Co., 1973-77, Sara Lee, 1977-80; pres., CEO Cadbury Schweppes Inc., 1981-91; dir., pres., COO Reader's Digest Assoc. Inc., Pleasantville, NY, 1991-94, pres., CEO 1994—97, chmn., pres., CEO 1995-97; chair Dailey Capital Mgmt., L.P., Southport, Conn., 1997—; chmn. Mercator Software, Inc., Wilton, Conn., 2000—03. Trustee Northwestern U. Mem. Blind Brook Club (Purchase, N.Y.), Chgo. Club, Am. Enterprise Inst. (trustee), Country Club of Fairfield, Conn., John's Island Club, Lotos Club N.YC.

**SCHAECHTER, MOSELIO,** microbiology educator; b. Apr. 26, 1928; children: Judy, John. Student, Cen. U., Ecuador, 1947-49; MA, U. Kans., 1952; PhD, U. Pa., 1954. Postdoctoral fellow State Serum Inst., Copenhagen, 1956-58; from instr. to asst. prof. to assoc. prof. U. Ill., Champaigne, 1958-62; from assoc. to disting. prof. dept. microbiology Tufts U., Boston, 1962-95, prof. emeritus, 1995—. Adj. prof. San Diego State U., 1995—, U. Calif., San Diego, 2004—. Editor: Molecular Biology Bacterial Growth, 1985, Escherichia coli and Salmonella Typhimurium, 1987, 95, Mechanisms of Microbiol. Disease, 1989, 92; author: In the Company of Mushrooms, 1997, Microbe, 2005. Mem. Am. Soc. Microbiology (pres. 1985-86, chmn. internat. activities), Am. Soc. Med. Sch. Microbiology (mem. pres. 1984-85), Soc. Gen. Microbiology, Boston Mycol. Club, Sigma Xi. Avocations: field mycology, hiking. Business E-Mail: mschaech@sunstroke.sdsu.edu.

**SCHAEDE, RICHARD EDWIN,** retired family practice physician; b. Thomasboro, Ill., Aug. 28, 1927; s. Mayo William and Opal Mae (Hutchison) S.; m. Ila Marlene Coffey, June 13, 1949; children: Pamela, Janet, Mark. BS in chemistry, U. Ill., 1949; BS in Medicine, U. Ill., Chgo., 1951, MD, 1953. Diplomate Am. Bd. Family Practice. Chief dept. internal medicine, cardiology, Shilling AFB, 1955-57; physician Chanute AFB, Rantoul, Ill., 1954-55; founder, pvt. practice Rantoul Clinic, 1957-80; assoc. dean medicine U. Ill., Champaign, 1972-78, assoc. prof. clin. medicine, 1978-86; dir. Christie Clinic Satellite, Champaign, 1980-85; pvt. practice Marion, Ill., 1986—2003; ret. Mem. faculty Parkland Coll., Champaign, 1970-72. Bd. dirs. Rantoul Elem. Sch. Bd., 1959-70; pres. Outlook T.B. Sanitorium Bd., 1959-69. Seaman first class USNR, 1945-46; capt. USAF, 1955-57. Fellow Am. Acad. Family Practice; mem. Rotary. Republican. Lutheran. Avocations: hunting, fishing. Home: 10242 Limb Branch Ln Marion IL 62959-6020

**SCHAEFER, BONNIE (E. BONNIE SCHAEFER),** retail executive; b. Chgo., Mar. 16, 1963; d. Rowland Schaefer. From sales assoc. to store mgr. Claire's Stores, Inc., 1987—90, v.p. real estate, 1994—2002, co-vice chmn., 1999—2002, co-chmn., 2002—, co-CEO, 2002—. Bd. dirs. Claire's Stores, Inc., 1998—, Claire's Nippon. Office: Claires Stores Inc 3 SW 129th Ave Pembroke Pines FL 33027 Office Phone: 954-433-3900. Office Fax: 954-433-3999.*

**SCHAEFER, C. BARRY,** rail transportation executive, investment company executive; b. Elizabeth, N.J., Feb. 23, 1939; s. Carl H. and Evelyn G. (Conk) S.; m. Carol Ann Craft, July 11, 1970; children: Sara Elizabeth, Susan Craft. BS in Engring., Princeton U., 1961; MS in Engring., U. Pa., 1962; LLB, Columbia U., 1965; MBA, NYU, 1970. Bar: N.Y. 1966, Nebr. 1972. With Kelley, Drye, Warren, N.Y.C., 1966-69; asst. gen. counsel Union Pacific Corp., N.Y.C., 1969-72; western gen. counsel Union Pacific R.R. Co., Omaha, 1972-74, v.p., western gen. counsel, 1974-77, v.p. law, 1977-82; sr. v.p. planning and corp. devel. Union Pacific Corp., N.Y.C., 1984-88, exec. v.p. Bethlehem, Pa., 1988; sr. advisor Dillon Read & Co. Inc., 1989-91; mng. dir. The Bridgeford Group, 1992-97, 2001—06, Beacon Group 1997-01. Nat. bd. dirs. Jr. Achievement, Colorado Springs, Colo., 1986-2004. Mem. Racquet and Tennis Club (N.Y.C.), Round Hill Club (Greenwich, Conn.), Desert Mountain Club (Scottsdale, Ariz.). Office Phone: 212-705-0886.

**SCHAEFER, CHARLES JAMES, III,** advertising executive, consultant; b. Orange, NJ, Dec. 17, 1926; m. Eleanor Anne Montville, Apr. 8, 1961; 1 child, Charles James IV. AB, Dartmouth Coll., 1948, M in Comml. Sci., 1949. Mgr. foods promotion Beech-Nut, 1949—52; v.p. Dickie-Raymond, 1952-67; sr. v.p. Metromedia, 1968-69; exec. v.p., treas. The DR Group, Boston and NYC, 1969-76, pres. 1976-87; exec. v.p., dir. Needham Harper Worldwide Inc., NYC, 1984-87; chmn. bd. Marcoa DR Group, Inc., NYC, 1987-88; cons. Rapp Collins Marcoa, NYC, 1989-92; advt. cons., 1992—. Pres. Dartmouth Class of 1948, 1998-2000; trustee, mem. exec. com. Direct Mktg. Edn. Found., 1983-89; campaign chairperson United Way Millburn-Short Hills, 1994, 95, trustee, 1991-98, 2000—, v.p., 2004—. With USN, 1945—46. Mem. Direct Mktg. Assn. (chmn. awards com. 1971-76, Hall of Fame com. 1978-81, ethics com. 1981-86), Assn. Direct Mktg. Agys. (pres. 1980-82, gen. chmn. Caples awards 1985, chmn. Direct Mktg. Days NY 1988, NY Direct Marketer of Yr. award 1987, Silver Apple award 1989, contbr. to jour.), Dartmouth Club of NY (pres. 1968-70), Lotos Club (bd. dirs. 1985-88, treas. 1987-88), Canoe Brook Country Club (Summit, NJ). Home and Office. 307 Hobart Ave Short Hills NJ 07078-2207

**SCHAEFER, DAVID ARNOLD,** lawyer; b. Cleve., May 3, 1948; s. Leonard and Maxine V. (Bassett) S.; m. Riki C. Freeman, Aug. 8, 1971; children: Kevin, Lindsey, Traci. BS, Miami U., Oxford, Ohio, 1970; MA, Northwestern U., 1971; JD, Case Western Res. U., 1974. Bar: Ohio 1974, U.S. Dist. Ct. (no. dist.) Ohio 1974, U.S. Ct. Appeals (6th cir.) 1978, U.S. Supreme Ct. 1978. Ptnr. Guren, Merritt et al, 1980-84, Menexch. Friedlander et al, Cleve., 1984-93, McCarthy, Lebit, Crystal & Haiman, Cleve., 1993—. Author: Deposition Strategy, 1981, 2d edit., 1984; contbr. articles to profl. publs. Mem. ABA, Internat. Assn. Def. Counsel, Fed. Bar Assn. (pres. 1992-93), Nat. Inst. Trial Advocacy (faculty), 8th Cir. Jud. Conf. (life). Office: McCarthy Lebit Crystal & Haiman 1800 Midland Bldg 101 W Prospect Ave Ste 1800 Cleveland OH 44115-1027

**SCHAEFER, ELEANOR MONTVILLE,** retired publishing executive; b. Worcester, Mass., June 27, 1926; d. Joseph Samuel and Monica Savage Montville; m. Charles James Schaefer; 1 child, Charles James IV. AB, Trinity U., 1949. Radio/tv dept. Sullivan Staufer Colwell & Bayles, Inc., NYC, 1949—50; promotion dept. staff Life Mag., NYC, 1951—52; asst. promotion mgr. Sports Illustrated, NYC, 1953—59; promotion mgr. Glamour mag., NYC, 1960. V.p. League Women Voters, 1971—77; found. dir. Summit Coll. Club; vol. auxilliary mem. Assn. U. Women, Summit, NJ, 1998—99. Mem.: Trinity U. Alumni Assn. (past pres. 1959—60), Summit Coll. Club, Canoe Brook Country Club. Achievements include being first woman staffer on "Project X" which eventually became Sports Illustrated. Avocations: golf, interior decorating. Home: 307 Hobart Ave Short Hills NJ 07078 E-mail: montvilles@aol.com.

**SCHAEFER, FRANK WILLIAM, III,** microbiologist, researcher; b. Dayton, Ohio, Sept. 1, 1942; s. Frank William Jr. and Irene Josephine (Krouse) S. BA, Miami U., Oxford, Ohio, 1964; MS, U. Cin., 1970, PhD, 1973. Rsch. assoc. parasitologist U. Notre Dame, South Bend, Ind., 1973-78; U.S. EPA EPA, Cin., 1978—. Mem. ASTM, AAAS, Am. Soc. Parasitology, Am. Soc. Microbiology, Am. Water Works Assn., Soc. Protozoologists, Sigma Xi.

Home: 9948 McCauley Woods Dr Sharonville OH 45241-1489 Office: US EPA 26 Martin Luther King Dr Cincinnati OH 45268 Office Phone: 513-569-7222. Personal E-mail: f.schaeferiii@att.net. Business E-Mail: schaefer.frank@epa.gov.

**SCHAEFER, GEORGE A., JR.,** bank executive; b. Cincinnati, Ohio, 1945; BS Engineering, U.S. Mil. Acad., West Point, 1967; MBA, Xavier U., 1974. Joined as mgmt. trainee Fifth Third Bancorp, Cin., 1971, pres., CEO, 1990—. Bd. dirs. Fifth Third Bancorp, Fifth Third Bank, Anthem, Inc, Ashland, Inc, Greater Cin./N. Ky. Internat. Airport, Cin. Bus. Com. Chmn., bd. trustees U. Cin.; bd. dirs. Children's Hosp. Med. Ctr., Greater Cin. C. of C., Health Alliance Greater Cin. Served U.S. Army, 1967—70, Europe and Vietnam. Recipient Bronze Star. Office: Fifth Third Bancorp Fifth Third Center 38 Fountain Square Plz Cincinnati OH 45263-0001*

**SCHAEFER, GORDON EMORY,** food products executive; b. 1932; married. BS, Marquette U., 1956. CPA Wis. With Peat, Marwick, Mitchell & Co., 1955-59; contr., sec. Wells Badger, Badger Carton Co., 1960—64; treas. Pabst Brewing Co., Milw., 1965-72, v.p. adminstrn., 1972-75, v.p. ops., 1975—80, exec. v.p. ops, 1980—85, dir.; pres., dir. Krier Foods Inc., Belgium, Wis., 1981-85, Corrs Beverages, Chgo., 1985-86; dir. bus. devel. Lakeside Packing Co., Manitowoc, Wis., 1989-92; mng. dir. Robertson Assocs., Mfg. Europe Ltd.; Cardiff, Wales, 1993-94. Bd. dirs. Fox Fin. Co., Berg Industries, Inc.; fin. and ops. cons.; owner, operator Schaefer's Orchards. Home: N27 W6567 Alyce St Cedarburg WI 53012

**SCHAEFER, GREGORY LAUREN,** music professor; b. Phoenix, Apr. 5, 1953; s. Albert Joseph and Dorothy M. Schaefer; m. Brenda Sue Sheesley, Sept. 20, 1975; children: Christopher Lauren, Kirsten Ann, John David. MA in Ch. Music, Southwestern Bapt. Theol. Sem., Ft. Worth, Tex., 1978; MusM, Northwestern U., Evanston, Ill., 1994. Music adj. prof. Trinity Internat. U., Deerfield, Ill.; pastor music and worship North Suburban Evang. Free Ch., Deerfield, Ill., 1988—96, Bethany Bible Ch., Phoenix, 1996—2003; music adj. prof. Southwestern Coll., Phoenix, 1999—2000; music prof. Grand Canyon U., Phoenix, 2000—; pastor music and worship Apollo Bapt. Ch., Glendale, Ariz., 2003—. Pastoral rep. Christian Heritage Acad., Northbrook, Ill., 1991—92. Michael Rabin Meml. Scholarship, U. Ariz., 1972. Mem.: Am. Choral Dirs. Assn., Nat. Hymn Soc. (assoc.). Avocations: travel, antiquarian book collecting, antique furniture restoration, hiking. Home: 508 West Villa Rita Dr Phoenix AZ 85023 Office: Grand Canyon Univ 3300 West Camelback Rd Phoenix AZ 85017-1097 Office Phone: 623-842-1281. Personal E-mail: schaeferclan1@quest.net.

**SCHAEFER, HENRY FREDERICK, III,** chemistry professor; b. Grand Rapids, Mich., June 8, 1944; s. Henry Frederick Jr. and Janice Christine (Trost) S.; m. Karen Regine Rasmussen, Sept. 2, 1966; children: Charlotte, Pierre, Theodore, Rebecca, Caleb. BS in Chem. Physics, MIT, 1966; PhD in Chem. Physics, Stanford U., 1969; D (hon.), U. Plovdiv, 1998, U. Sofia, 1999, Beijing Inst. Tech., 1999, Huntington Coll., 2002. From asst. prof. to prof. chemistry U. Calif., Berkeley, 1969—87; Graham Perdue prof., dir. Ctr. for Computational Chemistry U. Ga., Athens, 1987—. Apptd. Professuur d'Echange U. Paris, 1977, Gastprofessor Eidgenossische Technische Hochshule, Zurich, 1994, 95, 97, 2000, 02, 04, 06; Wilfred T. Doherty prof., dir. Inst. Theoretical Chemistry, U. Tex., Austin, 1979-80; lectr. in field. Author: Science and Christianity: Conflict or Coherence? 2003; contbr. articles to profl. jours. including Electronic Structure of Atoms and Molecules: A Survey of Rigorous Quantum Mechanical Results, 1972, Modern Theoretical Chemistry, 1977, Quantum Chemistry, 1983, A New Dimension to Quantum Chemistry, 1994; editor Molecular Physics, 1991-94, editor in chief, 1995-2005. Recipient Pure Chemistry award Am. Chem. Soc., 1979, Leo Hendrik Baekeland award, 1983, Schrödinger Medal, 1990, Centenary medal Royal Soc. Chemistry, London, 1992, Gold medal Comenius U., Bratislava, Slovakia, 2000; Sloan fellow, 1972, Guggenheim fellow, 1976-77; named one of 100 Outstanding Young Scientists in Am., Sci. Digest, 1984, named 3d Most Highly cited chemist in world Science Watch, 1992. Fellow AAAS, Am. Phys. Soc., Am. Sci. Affiliation, Am. Acad. Arts and Scis., Royal Soc. Chemistry (London); mem. Internat. Acad. Quantum Molecular Sci., Am. Chem. Soc. (chmn. divsn. phys. chemistry 1992, award in theoretical chemistry 2003, Ira M. Remsen award 2003), World Assn. Theoretical and Computational Chemists (pres. 1996-2005, Joseph O. Hirschfelder prize, 2005). Presbyterian. Office: U Ga Ctr Computational Chemistry Athens GA 30602 Office Phone: 706-542-2067. Business E-Mail: hfs@uga.edu.

**SCHAEFER, JOHN H.,** finance company executive, security firm executive; b. 1952; BS in Chemistry, Polytechnic Inst. of Brooklyn, 1955; PhD, U. Ill., 1958. Chief strategic and adminstrv. officer, exec. v.p. Morgan Stanley & Co., Inc., NYC, 1998—2000, pres., COO, individual investor group, 2000—. Office: Morgan Stanley & Co Inc 1585 Broadway New York NY 10036 Office Phone: 212-761-4000.

**SCHAEFER, KELLY MARIE,** theater educator, costume designer; b. Berwyn, Ill., May 10, 1974; Studied dance, Lou Conte Dance Studio, 1992—96; studied with Louise Parkin opera and vocal tng., 1992—96, studied with Charlotte Megginson opera and vocal tng., 1996—97; BFA in Musical Theatre Performance, Roosevelt U., Chgo., Ill., 1996; MFA in Theatre, Western Ill. U., Macomb, Ill., 2001; studied with Matt Bean vocal tng., 2001. Surp. costume shop Bard Coll., Annandale, NY, 2001—02; asst. prof. Ark. State U., Jonesboro, Ark., 2002—. Supr. costume shop, designer costumes Summer Repertory Theatre, New Paltz, NY, 2002. Actor(kate): Dancing at Lughnasa, (mary): On the Verge, (the gypsy acid queen): The Who's TOMMY, (adrianna) The Comedy of Errors; costume designer (various plays), 2001—. Office: Arkansas State University Jonesboro AR 72401 Office Phone: 870-972-2037. Business E-Mail: kschaefer@astate.edu.

**SCHAEFER, M. ELAINE,** music educator, conductor; b. Frederick, Okla., Apr. 13, 1945; d. Arthur Lloyd and Mary Ellen Bush; m. Edward T. Vrable, July 28, 2001; children: Joel, Anne Marie, Scott Patrick Gillespie. Student, Diablo Valley Coll., Pleasant Hill, Calif., 1961—63, Chico State Coll., Calif., 1963—64; BA, Calif. State U. Hayward, 1967; MA, U. Regina, Sask., Can., 1988. Tchrs. cert. Calif., 1967. Instrumental music tchr. Kenilworth Jr. HS, Petaluma, Calif., 1967—72; music tchr. Incline Village HS, Nev., 1972—78; instrumental and choral tchr. Humboldt HS, Sask., Canada, 1978—86; music tchr. Balgonie HS, Sask., Canada, 1988—96; music instr., condr. Coll. Siskiyous, Weed, Calif., 1996—. Adjudicator Sask. Music Festivals, 1985—96; condr. Holy Rosary Cathedral Choir, Regina, Sask., 1987—96, Royal Can. Mounted Police Choir, 1987—89; pres. Sask. Choral Dirs., 1989—90. Bd. mem. Sask. Coun. Cultural Orgns., 1990—96. Sgt. U.S. Army, 1974—78. Named Tchr. of Yr., Col. of the Siskiyans, 2006, Faculty Mem. of Yr., 2006; recipient award of Appreciation, Sask. Music Educators, 1982. Fellow: Nat. Assn. Jazz Educators, Calif. Music Educators Assn., Am. Choral Dirs.; mem.: Internat. Fedn. Choral Music, Assn. Can. Choral Dirs. (bd. mem.), Nat. Assn. Jazz Educators, Calif. Music Educators Assn., Am. Choral Dirs. Roman Catholic. Home: 5925 Mule Deer Ct Weed CA 96094 Office: College Siskiyous 800 College Ave Weed CA 96094 Office Phone: 530-938-5315. Business E-Mail: schaefer@siskiyous.edu.

**SCHAEFER, MARILYN LOUISE,** artist, writer, educator; b. Cedar Rapids, Iowa, Apr. 22, 1933; d. Henry Richard and Maria Augusta (Dickel) S. AA, Monticello Coll. for Women, 1953; BFA, Cranbrook Acad. Art, 1956, MFA, 1960; MA cum laude, U. Chgo., 1958; MA, St. John's Coll., Santa Fe, 1979. Rsch. asst. editor Encyclopaedia Britannica, Chgo., 1960-63; humanities editor Encyclopedia Americana, NY, 1964-68; acquisitions editor Litton Ednl. Pub., NY, 1968-70; from instr. to prof. emeritus art and advt. design dept. N.Y.C. Tech. Coll. CUNY, 1970—. Contbg. editor Encyclopedia Americana, 1979—, Coll. Teaching jour., 1979. Contbr. articles to profl. jours. including Art and Auction mag., Art and Antiques mag., Am. Artist mag., Encyclopedia Americana, 1970—. Luce Found. postgrad. study fellow St. John's Coll.,

1976-79; Ingram Merrill Found. grantee, 1983-84. Mem. AAUW, CUNY Acad. Arts and Scis. Home: 306 W 76th St New York NY 10023-8065 Office: NYC Tech Coll CUNY 300 Jay St Brooklyn NY 11201-1909

**SCHAEFER, MARLA L.,** retail executive; b. Chgo., May 19, 1949; d. Rowland Schaefer; 2 children. BA, Fla. Internat. U., 1973; MA in Orgnl. Psychology, Columbia U., 2003. Resident buyer NY Office Claire's Boutiques, 1986, v.p. fashion merchandising, 1990—98, sr. v.p., 1998—, sec., 2002—; vice chmn. bd. dirs. Claire's Stores Inc., Pembroke Pines, Fla., 1998—99, co-vice chmn., 1999—2003, acting co-chmn., co-CEO, 2002—03, co-chmn., co-CEO, 2003—. Office: Claire's Stores, Inc 3 SW 129th Ave Pembroke Pines FL 33027 Office Phone: 954-433-3900. Office Fax: 954-433-3999. E-mail: marla.schaefer@claires.com.*

**SCHAEFER, PATRICIA,** retired librarian; b. Ft. Wayne, Ind., Apr. 23, 1930; d. Edward John and Hildegarde Hartman (Hormel) S. MusB, Northwestern U., 1951; MusM, U. Ill. 1958; AMLS, U. Mich., 1963; DLS (hon.), Ind. Inst. of Tech., 2003. With U.S. Rubber Co., Ft. Wayne, 1951-52; sec. to promotion mgr. Sta. WOWO, Ft. Wayne, Ind., 1952, sec. to program mgr., 1953-55; coord. publicity and promotion Home Telephone Co., Ft. Wayne, 1955-56; sec. Fine Arts Found., Ft. Wayne, 1956-57; libr. asst. Columbus (Ohio) Pub. Libr., 1958-59; audio-visual libr. Muncie (Ind.) Pub. Libr., 1959-86, asst. libr. dir., 1981-86, libr. dir., 1986-95; ret. Chmn. Ind. Libr. Film Cir., 1962-63; treas. Ind. Libr. Film Svc., 1969-70, 83-85; mem. trustee adv. coun. Milton S. Eisenhower Libr., Johns Hopkins U.; mem. presdl. counsellors Johns Hopkins U., 1994—; cons. Franklin Electric Co., 2004—. Weekly columnist Libr. Lines, Muncie Evening Press, 1981-83; program annotator Muncie Symphony Orch., 1963-2003, Masterworks Chorale, 1982-2003; contbr. articles to profl. jours. Bd. dirs. Muncie Symphony Assn., 1964-74, 85-91, Ctrl. City Bus. Assn., 1984-92; mem. Ind. Inst., Ind. Humanities Coun., 1996-2002, 05—, Sta. WIPB-TV, 1996-2002, Muncie Ctr. for the Arts, 1999-2001; mem. adv. coun. Coll. Fine Arts, Ball State U., found. bd. dirs.; adv. com., bookshop dir. Midwest Writers Workshop, 1976-77; sec. Del. County Coun. for the Arts, 1978-79, pres., 1979-81, bd. dirs., 1985-86; pres.'s coun. Berea Coll., 1990-2001; bd. dirs. Muncie YWCA, 1977-82, 85-89, 95-2001, treas. 1981-82, 88-89; bd. govs. Minnetrista Cultural Ctr., 1998-2001; gen. chmn. Ind. Renaissance Fair, 1978-79; pres. Muncie Matinee Musicale, 1965-67; mem. adv. bd. Cornerstone Ctr. for the Arts; past pres. Ind. Film and Video Coun.; adv. bd. Cmty. Found. Muncie and Delaware County; bd. dirs. Wapehani coun. Girl Scouts U.S., 1989-96, Hoosier Heartland chpt. ARC, 1997-2003, Ball State U. Found., 2006—. Named Woman Achievement Pub. Svc., 1986; recipient Sagamore of the Wabash award Gov. State of Ind., Outstanding Libr. award Ind. Libr. Fedn., 1995, Cert. of Congrl. Recognition, 1995, Cert. of Achievement, Women's Coalition, 1996, Cert. of Appreciation, Masterworks Chorale, 1998. Mem. ALA, Ind. Libr. Assn. (pres. 1987-88), Nat. League Am. Pen Women (pres. Muncie br. 1974-78), Altrusa (pres. 1986-87, cmty. svc. award 2000), Art Students League, Del. Country Club, Delta Zeta, Mu Phi Epsilon. Republican. Roman Catholic. Home: 5400 W Deer Run Ct Muncie IN 47304-5775

**SCHAEFER, PATRICIA ANN,** retired librarian; b. Lebanon, Ohio, Jan. 22, 1933; d. Riley Ray and Louise Collette (Fraher) Freeze; m. William H. Schaefer, Aug. 11, 1956; children: Susan P., Nancy A., William H. III(dec.). BS, Miami U., Oxford, Ohio, 1954. Med. technologist Mercy Hosp., Hamilton, Ohio, 1954-58, Middletown (Ohio) Hosp., 1958-62; libr. Middletown City Schs., 1979-93; intermediate libr. McKinley Sch., 1982-93; ret., 1993. Hon. bd. dirs. Am. Cancer Soc., 1961—; cons. legis. City Charter Rev. Com., 1970, charter revision com., 1989; active YMCA, 1977—79; bd. dirs. Middletown Symphony, 1974—78, Arts in Middletown, 1983—, Middletown Symphony Women, 1992—; exec. bd., 1995—; residential chmn. United Way, 1976, residential-retiree chmn., 1990; chmn. Sch. Tax Levy, 1978; co-chmn. Luncheon Style Show, 1998—2003; exec. com. Ohio-Ky.-Ind. Regional Coun., 1986—88; mem. Bicentennial Com., Middletown; pres. Middletown Needy Youth Bd.; adv. bd. Manchester Tech. Ctr., Middletown Schs.; bd. dirs. Citizens Adv. Bd. Manchester Tech., Middletown Fine Arts, 1993—, Dental Emergency Fund Area Children, 1994—; exec. bd. Leadership Middletown; pres. Care View Home Health, 2000, 2003—; co-chmn. Mary Alice Mack City Golf Tournament, 1998; mem. Middletown City Commn., 1983—88; adminstrv. bd. Meth. Ch.; mem. fin. com., sec. bd. trustees 1st United Meth. Ch., 1999—; exec. bd. United Meth. Women; mem. citizen's adv. com. Miami U., Middletown, co-chair major capital campaign, 2003—. Named Outstanding Woman of Butler County, 1997, hon. chmn., Charity Ball, 1998, Woman of Distinction, Soroptomists Internat., 2000; recipient Stuart Ives Svc. to Youth award, 1980. Mem.: PEO (pres. 1995—, co-chair state conv. 1997), LWV (pres. 1962—63), Am. Bus. Women's Assn. (pres. 1961—62), Registry Med. Technologists, Am. Soc. Clin. Pathologists, Miami U. Hughes Soc., Middletown C. of C., Miami U. Pres. Club, Browns Run Country Club, Sigma Sigma Sigma. Methodist. Home: 1909 Antrim Ct Middletown OH 45042-2901

**SCHAEFER, PAUL ROBERT,** religious studies educator; b. Buffalo, Oct. 24, 1959; s. Paul Robert and Elizabeth Anne Salada Schaefer; m. Bonnie Lou Maclay, Aug. 14, 1982; children: Andrew Noel, Stephanie Renae. BA, U. Pa., Phila., 1981; MS, Emory U., Atlanta, Ga., 1988; DPhil, Oxford U., England, 1992. Asst. pastor Tenth Presbyn. Ch., Phila., 1982—85; tchg. asst. Emory U., Atlanta, 1986—88; assoc. prof. Ref. Episcopal Sem., Phila., 1992—94, Northwestern Coll., Orange City, Iowa, 1994—97; prof., chair dept. religion Grove City Coll., Pa., 1997—. Pastor East Unity Presbyn. Ch., Cherry Valley, Pa., 1996—. Mem.: 16th Century Studies Soc. (life), Conf. Faith and History (life), Calvin Studies Soc. (life), Evang. Theol. Soc. (life), Official Grove City College 100 Campus Drive Grove City PA 16127 Office Phone: 724-458-2000. Business E-Mail: prschaefer@gcc.edu.

**SCHAEFER, PAUL WILLIAM,** retired entomologist; b. Hartford, Conn., Mar. 10, 1940; s. Reinhold August and Mabel Churchill Schaefer; m. Jane C. Rushforth, Apr. 1, 1967; children: Barbara, William, Heidi. BS, U. Maine, 1966, PhD, 1975; MS, U. Hawaii, 1969. Rsch. technician (summers) Conn. Agrl. Exptl. Sta., New Haven, 1964—70; rsch. entomologist, location leader Asian Parasite Lab., USDA, Sapporo, Japan, 1975—79; rsch. entomologist USDA, Agrl. Rsch. Svc. Beneficial Insects Introduction Lab., Newark, Del., 1979—2006; ret. 2006. Contbr. articles to profl. jours., chapters to books. Served with USCG, 1958—62. Mem.: The Lepidopterists' Soc., Hawaiian Entomol. Soc., Am. Entomol. Soc. (rec. sec. 1992—94). Avocations: birdwatching, travel, basketball. Home: 4 Dare Dr Elkton MD 21921 Office: USDA ARS Beneficial Insects Introduction Lab 501 S Chapel St Newark DE 19713 Office Phone: 302-731-7330. Office Fax: 302-737-6780. E-mail: paulschaefer60@hotmail.com.

**SCHAEFER, ROBERT WAYNE,** banker; b. Balt., Feb. 28, 1934; s. Roland Elmer and Lillian (Reid) S.; m. Elaine Lennon, May 18, 1963; children: Linda, Karen. Student, Balt. City Coll., 1949-51; BS in Acctg., U. Balt., 1955; MBA in Fin., Loyola Coll., 1971. C.P.A., Md. With First Nat. Bank of Md., Balt., 1951-55, 59—, comptroller, 1961—, v.p., 1965-69, sr. v.p., 1969-73, exec. v.p. 1973-96; exec. dir. France-Merrick Founds., Balt., 1996—. Instr. accounting N.C. State Coll., 1956-58; instr. accounting, econs., taxes, credit Balt. chpt. Am. Inst. Banking, 1960-66, Investment Com. State of Md. Retirement System and Baltimore Fire, Police Retirement System. Mem. Balt. City Sch. Bd., 1973-75, Balt. City Bd. Fire Bd., dirs., treas. Balt. Area United Fund, 1964-79; past bd. dirs. Balt. coun. Boy Scouts Am., Balt. chpt. ARC, Boys Latin Sch.; trustee, pres. Wesley Home for Aged; bd. dirs. Balt. City Aquarium, Roland Park Country Club. Md. Gen. Hosp., Western Md. Coll., 1981-92, Lyric Theatre, 1985—, Enoch Pratt Libr., 1986-93, Ind. Coll. Fund Md., 1991—. Cons. on Econ. Edn., YMCA Ctrl. Md. Council; past lt. USMCR, 1956-58. Mem.: Fin. Execs. Inst., Md. CPA Assn., Bank Adminstrn. Inst. (past bd. dirs. Balt. chpt.), U. Balt. Found., U. Balt. Alumni Assn. (bd. dirs. 1972—), L'Hirondelle Club, Valley Country Club. Republican. Methodist (bd. dirs., mem. finance com.). Home: 5903 Meadowood Rd Baltimore MD 21212-2436 Office: France-Merrick Foundations 1122 Kenilworth Dr Ste 118 Baltimore MD 21204-2142 Office Phone: 410-832-5700. Personal E-mail: rwsels@aol.com. Business E-Mail: rschaefer@france-merrickfdn.org.

**SCHAEFER, RONALD DEAN,** secondary school educator; s. Russell Earl and Jewell Dean Schaefer; m. Jeanette Rozanne Bradshaw, Sept. 1, 1962; children: Ronald David, Christian Ann. BA, So. Ill. U., Edwardsville, 1963; MS, So. Ill. U., Carbondale, 1965, PhD, 1969. Analytic chemist Dow Chemical Co., Midland, Mich., 1969—72; mgr. quality control Dow Diagnostics, Indpls., 1972—77; dir. quality assurance/quality control HYCEL Corp., Houston, 1977—79; rsch. scientist Boehringer-Hennheim Corp., Tustin, Calif., 1979—81; dir. quality assurance/quality control Ciba Corning Diagnostics, Irvine, Calif., 1981—99; educator Santa Ana HS, 1999—. Home: 5 Fulton Irvine CA 92620 Personal E-mail: ronald_schaefer@yahoo.com.

**SCHAEFER, THEODORE PETER,** retired chemistry professor; b. Gnadenthal, Man., Can., July 22, 1933; s. Paul Jacob and Margarethe (Wiebe) S.; m. Nicola Caroline Sewell, Dec. 26, 1960; children: Catherine, Dominic, Benjamin. BS with Honors, U. Man., 1954, MS, 1955; D.Phil. (Shell scholar), Oxford U., Eng., 1958; D.Sc. (hon. causa), U. Winnipeg, 1982. Prof. chemistry U. Manitoba, Winnipeg, Can., 1958—, Univ. Disting. prof., 1982-97, emeritus, 2000—; researcher NRC, Ottawa, Can., 1959, 62, Nat. Phys. Lab., Teddington, U.K., 1960, 65, Argonne Nat. Lab., Chgo., 1967, 68; sr. fellow, mem. grants com. NRC, Ottawa.; mem. council Nat. Scis. and Engring. Research Council, Ottawa., 1980-85. Contbr. articles on nuclear magnetic resonance to sci. jours. Recipient Herzberg award Spectroscopy Soc. Can., 1975. Fellow Chem. Inst. Can. (Noranda award 1973), Royal Soc. Can.; mem. Order of Can. Home: 210 Oak St Winnipeg MB Canada R3M 3R4 *Persistence can sometimes emulate perspicacity.*

**SCHAEFER, WILLIAM DAVID,** language educator; b. Dighton, Mass., May 11, 1928; s. Louis and Elsie K. (Otterbein) S.; m. Josephine R. Lamprecht, Aug. 8, 1958; 1 dau., Kimberly. BA, NYU, 1957; MS, U. Wis., 1958, PhD, 1962. Mem. faculty UCLA, 1962-90, prof. English, 1970-90, chmn. dept., 1969-71, exec. vice chancellor, 1978-87. Author: James (BV) Thomson: Beyond the City, 1965, Speedy Extinction of Evil and Misery, 1967, Education Without Compromise: From Chaos to Coherence in Higher Education, 1990; contbr. articles to profl. jours., short stories to literary mags. Served with AUS, 1954-56. Fulbright fellow Eng., 1961-62 Mem. MLA (exec. dir. 1971-78). Home: 164 Stagecoach Rd Bell Canyon CA 91307-1044 Office: UCLA 405 Hilgard Ave Los Angeles CA 90095-9000 Personal E-mail: wschae444@aol.com.

**SCHAEFER, WILLIAM DONALD,** state official, former governor; b. Balt., Nov. 2, 1921; s. William Henry and Tululu (Skipper) S. LLB, U. Balt., 1942, LLM, 1951, LLD (hon.), 1976; JD (hon.), Loyola Coll., 1976; D of Pub. Svc. (hon.), U. Md., 1979, LLD (hon.), 1981; JD, Goucher Coll., 1980; DHL (hon.), Towson State U., 1982; LLD (hon.), Morgan State U., 1983; D Pub. Svc. (hon), Gettysburg Coll., 1986; DHL (hon.), Villa Julie Coll., 1990; LLD (hon.), Coll. Notre Dame, 1991. Bar: Md. 1943. Practiced in Balt., 1943—; mem. Balt. City Coun., 1955-67, pres., 1967-71; mayor City of Balt., 1971-87; gov. State of Md., Annapolis, 1987—95; of counsel Gordon, Feinblatt, Rothman, Hoffberger & Hollander, LLC, Baltimore, 1995—99; comptroller State of Md., Annapolis, 1999—. Chmn. Chesapeake Bay Exec. Coun.; mem. Mayors Adv. Com., Nat. Coun. for Urban and Econ. Devel., U.S. Conf. Mayors. Served with AUS, 1942-45; col. Res. (ret.). Recipient numerous awards, including Alumni of Yr. award U. Balt., 1971, Man of Yr. award Jewish Nat. Fund, 1972, 1st ann. Civic Statesmanship award Citizens Planning and Housing Assn., Jefferson award for outstanding pub. svc., 1979, William Fell Pub. Svc. award Johns Hopkins U., 1980, Disting. Svc. award Nat. Coun. for Urban Econ. Devel., 1980, award of excellence Urban Land Inst., 1980, Michael A. DiNunzio award U.S. Conf. Mayors, 1981, Man of Decade award Athletic Club Balt., 1982, Nat. award Urban Energy Mgmt. Energy Task Force of Urban Consortium, 1982, Disting. Mayor award Nat. Urban Coalition, 1982, commendation for Exemplary Achievement Sister Cities Internat., 1985, Congl. cert. Merit for Outstanding Citizenship, 1986, Man. of Yr. award Md. Soc. Acctg., 1987, award for Exec. Acg. Policy on Smoking Am. Heart Assn., 1987, Disting. Pub. Svc. award Brandeis U., The Doctor Henry P. and Page Laughlin award, 1988, commendation Pres'. Coun. Phys. Fitness and Sport, 1988, Gov. of Yr. Nat. Multiple Sclerosis Soc., 1989, Gov.'s award Nat. Assn. State Outdoor Recreation Liaison Officers, 1987, cert. Appreciation for Outstanding Record in Appointment of Women to State Cabinet Positions Nat. Women's Polit. Caucus, 1991, Making Marylanders Safe award Marylanders Against Handgun Abuse, 1991, Ann. Svc. award Outstanding Contrbn. to Growth and Progress of Retail Industry Md. Retail Merchants Assn., 1991, award Outstanding Visionary Support of Arts in Md. Md. Citizens for Arts, 1991, Preservation award Hist. Annapolis Found., 1991, various others. Mem. AIA (hon.), Nat. League Cities (bd. dirs.), Md. Assn. Counties, Chesapeake Bay Exec. Coun. (chmn.), U.S. Conf. Mayors (Outstanding Leadership award 1979, Michael A. DiNunzio award 1981), Md. Mcpl. League, Balt. Bar Assn., Citizens Planning and Housing Assn. Balt., Nat. Hist. Soc., Balt. Ecol. Soc., Md. Ret. Officers Assn., Balt. Assn. Retarded Citizens, Md. Acad. Scis., VFW, Navy League U.S., Am. Inst. Banking (hon.), Am. Pub. Works Assn., Md. Law Enforcement Officers, Md. 4H Club., Md. Jaycees, Edgar Allen Poe Soc., Exchange Club Md., Pres'. Club U. Md. (hon.), Md. Enlisted Assn. Nat. Guard Honorees (hon.), U. Balt. Alumni Assn., Rotary, Phi Delta Phi, Sigma Delta Kappa. Democrat. Office: Office of Comptroller 80 Calvert St Annapolis MD 21401*

**SCHAEFER, WILLIAM GOERMAN,** lawyer; b. Kansas City, Mo., June 16, 1941; m. Sharon Saylor, Dec. 21, 1963; children: James, Kristen. BA, U. Kans., 1963; JD, Harvard U., 1966. Bar: Ill. 1966, D.C. 1978, Md. 1984. Ptnr. Sidley & Austin, Chgo. and Washington, 1966-74, 78-93; v.p., gen. counsel DeKalb Genetics Corp., Ill., 1974-77; spl. counsel Bechel Corp., Gaithersburg, Md., 1993-96; sr. v.p. corporate affairs Vertis, Inc., Balt., 1996-2000; cons., 2000—.

**SCHAEFFER, CHARLES PERRY,** writer, editor; b. Cumberland, Md., Mar. 20, 1926; s. Charles Perry and Dorothy Frances Schaeffer; m. Eliza Ann Riggins, June 16, 1950; children: Sally Ann Canepa, John, Jennifer Bartell. BA, U. Md., 1950. Writer U.S. Info. Agy., Washington, 1950—53; news picture writer UPI, N.Y.C., 1953—54; reporter Balt. Evening Sun, 1954—55, Am. Aviation Publs., Md., 1955—61; sci. writer Newhouse Newspapers, Washington, 1961—65; writer, exec. editor Kiplinger Personal Fin. Mag. (formerly Changing Times) Kiplinger Washington Editors, Inc, 1966—89. Mem. profit sharing bd. Kiplinger Washington Editors. Contbg. author: anthology Esquire's World of Humor, 1964, Saturday Review's Phoenix Nest, 1965; author: short mystery fiction, 2002; contbr. articles to mags. Chmn. scout troop Walter Reed Army Med. Ctr., Silver Spring, Md., 1971—72; pres Neighborhood Civic Assn., Silver Spring, 1963—64; bd. dirs. Woodlin Elem. Sch., Silver Spring, 1963—64. EM 3/C USN, 1943—46, PTO. Decorated Phillippine Liberation Ribbon, 2 Stars USN, Pacific Theater Ribbon, Six Stars, Victory medal, Am. Theater ribbon; recipient Blakeslee Nat. Sci. Writing award, Am. Heart Assn., 1965. Mem.: Soc. Profl. Journalists, Nat. Assn. Sci. Writers (life), Nat. Press Club (1st pl. consumer journalism 1987). Home: 6036 Chatsworth Ln Bethesda MD 20814 E-mail: schaeffer528@cs.com.

**SCHAEFFER, GLENN WILLIAM,** casino corporate financial executive; b. Pomona, Calif., Oct. 11, 1953; s. William Donald and Mary Louise (Miller) S.; m. Deborah Lynn Helfer, Sept. 6, 1974 (div. Apr. 1981); m. Renee Sue Riebel, May 25, 1985 AB summa cum laude, U. Calif., Irvine, 1974, MA, 1975; MFA, U. Iowa, 1977. Fin. cons. Dean Witter, Los Angeles, 1977-78; assoc. Hill and Knowlton, Inc., Los Angeles, 1978-81; v.p. Ramada Inns, Inc., Phoenix, 1981-84; exec. v.p., chief fin. officer Circus Circus Enterprises, Inc., Las Vegas, Nev., 1984-91, pres., 1991-93, also bd. dirs. Las Vegas; pntr. Gold Strike Resorts, Jean, Nev., 1993-95; pres. Mandalay Resort Group, 1995—. Wine grower and estate bottler, N.Z. Founder and patron Internat. Inst.

Modern Letters. Pres. Hitch fellow U. Calif.-Irvine, 1973-74 Mem. Phi Beta Kappa. Avocations: reading, bicycling. Office: Mandalay Resort Group 3950 Las Vegas Blvd S Las Vegas NV 89119

**SCHAEFFER, LEONARD DAVID,** health insurance company executive; b. Chgo., July 28, 1945; s. David and Sarah (Levin) Schaeffer; m. Pamela Lee Sidford, Aug. 11, 1968; children: David, Jacqueline. BA, Princeton U., 1969. Mgmt. cons. Arthur Andersen & Co., 1969—73; dep. dir. mgmt. Ill. Mental Health/Devel. Disability, Springfield, 1973—75; dir. Ill. Bur. of Budget, Springfield, 1975—76; v.p. Citibank, N.A., NYC, 1976—78; asst. sec. mgmt. and budget HHS, Washington, 1978, adminstr. HCFA, 1978—80; exec. v.p., COO Student Loan Mktg. Assn., Washington, 1980—82; pres., CEO Group Health, Inc., Mpls., 1983—86; chmn., CEO Blue Cross of Calif., Woodland Hills, 1986—96, WellPoint Health Networks Inc., Thousand Oaks, Calif., 1992—2004; chmn. WellPoint Inc., 2004—05. Bd. dirs. Allergan, Inc., Irvine, Calif., Amgen, Inc., Thousand Oaks; bd. councilors U. So. Calif. Sch. Policy, Planning & Devel., 1988—; bd. dirs., exec. com. Blue Cross-Blue Shield Assn., Chgo., 2004—; mem. Congl. Prospective Payment Assessment Commn., 1987—93, Pew Health Professions Com., Phila., 1990—93; chmn. bd. trustees Nat. Health Found., LA, 1992—2001; chmn. bd. dirs. Nat. Inst. Health Care Mgmt., 1993—2006; mem. Coun. on the Econ. Impact of Health Sys. Change, 1996—; co-chair adv. coun. dept. of health care policy Harvard Med. Sch., 1998—; founding chmn. Coalition for Affordable and Quality Healthcare, 2000; regents lectr. U. Calif., Berkeley, Calif., 2005—06; sr. advisor Tex. Pacific Group, 2006—. Bd. govs. Town Hall, L.A., 1989—2006; trustee The Brookings Inst., Nat. Health Mus., 2000—; adv. coun. Dept. Econs. Princeton U., NJ; adv. group Coun. on Health Care Econs. and Policy. Recipient Citation for Outstanding Svc., Am. Acad. Pediat., 1981, Disting. Pub. Svc. award, HEW, Washington, 1980; fellow, Kellogg Found., 1981—89; Internat. fellow, King's Fund Coll., London, 1990—. Mem.: Am. Assn. Health Plans (bd. dirs. 2001—04), Health Ins. Assn. Am. (chmn. 1999), Inst. Medicine of NAS, Regency Club, Princeton Club, Cosmos Club. Office: 1733 Ocean Ave Ste 325 Santa Monica CA 90404

**SCHAEFFER, MARY L.,** geneticist; d. Oliver A. and Viola A. Long Schaeffer; children: Laura C Polacco, Joseph M Polacco, Benjamin J Polacco. PhD, Duke U., Durham, N.C. Adj. prof. U. Mo., Columbia, 1979—; rsch. geneticist, curator maizegdb USDA ARS, Columbia, Mo., 1995—. Office: USDA ARS Univ Mo 203 Curtis Hall Columbia MO 65211 Office Phone: 573-884-7873.

**SCHAEFFER, RICHARD,** mercantile exchange executive; Grad., U. Md. Exec. dir. global energy futures ABN Amro Inc.; treas. NY Mercantile Exch. Inc., 1993—2004, vice chmn., 2004—06, chmn., 2006—, NYMEX Holdings Inc., 2006—. Mem. bd. dirs. NY Mercantile Exch. Inc., 1990—, exec. com., 1992—. Office: NY Mercantile Exch World Fin Ctr One N End Ave New York NY 10282 Office Phone: 212-299-2000.*

**SCHAEFFER-YOUNG, JUDITH,** library director; b. York, Pa., Aug. 26, 1944; d. Robert Jackson and Helen Josephine (Chiappy) Schatz; m. Karl Schaeffer, Jan. 28, 1967 (div. Sept. 1981); children: Stephen Matthew, Elizabeth Chatten; m. Harrison H. Young Jr., Dec. 29, 1990. BA, Barnard Coll., 1966; MLS, Columbia U., 1968. part-time reference libr. Hewlett-Woodmere Pub. Libr., Hewlett, 1971-78; part-time reference libr. Chestnut Hill Hosp. Sch. Nursing, Phila., 1981-85; interim reference libr. Pa. State U., Abington, 1986. Editor std. catalog dept. H.W. Wilson Co., Bronx, N.Y., 1968-69; cataloger Hewlett-Woodmere (N.Y.) Pub. Libr., 1970-71, Merrick (N.Y.) Pub. Libr., 1972-78; sr. sch. libr. Chestnut Hill Acad., Phila., 1978-81; mgr. tech. svcs. Med. Coll. of Pa., Phila., 1981-83; libr. Sch. Nursing Albert Einstein Med. Ctr., Phila., 1983-86; coord. rsch. alerts Inst. for Sci. Info., Phila., 1986-89, mgr. editorial svcs., 1989-91; dir. med. libr. Wills Eye Hosp., Phila., 1991—. Cataloger St. Paul's Episcopal Ch., Phila., 1985—. Author: Index to Song Collections in the Hewlett-Woodmere Pub. Libr., 1974; contbr. articles to profl. jours. Bd. dirs. Friends of Glenside (Pa.) Libr., 1992—; mem. libr. com. St. Paul's Ch., Chestnut Hill, Pa., 1985—. Mem. Med. Libr. Assn., Acad. Health Info. Profls., Assn. Vision Sci. Librs. (sec.1996-97, chmn. 1998-99, treas. 2000—). Home: 529 Custis Rd Glenside PA 19038-2011 Office: Wills Eye Hosp 840 Walnut St Philadelphia PA 19107-5599 Office Phone: 215-928-3288. E-mail: jyoung@willseye.org.

**SCHAEFFLER, GEORG,** lawyer, manufacturing executive; b. Oct. 19, 1964; BA in Bus. Admin., U. of St. Gallen, Switzerland, 1990; JD cum laude, Duke U., LL.M. in International and Comparative Law, 1999. Bar: Texas 2000. Owner INA Schaeffler Group, Herzogenaurach, Germany, 1996—; assoc. fin. and internat. groups Haynes and Boone LLP, Dallas. 1st Lt. German Air Force, 1984—86. Mem.: ABA. Office: Haynes and Boone LLP Ste 3100 901 Main St Dallas TX 75202-3789

**SCHAFER, ALICE TURNER,** retired mathematics professor; b. Richmond, Va., June 18, 1915; d. John H. and Cleon (Dermott) Turner; m. Richard Donald Schafer, Sept. 8, 1942; children: John Dickerson, Richard Stone. AB, U. Richmond, 1936, DSc, 1964; MS, U. Chgo., 1940, PhD (fellow), 1942. Tchr. Glen Allen (Va.) High Sch., 1936-39; instr. math. Conn. Coll., New London, 1942-44, asst. prof., 1954-57, asso. prof., 1957-61, prof., 1961-62; prof. math. Wellesley Coll., 1962-80, Helen Day Gould prof. math., 1969-80, Helen Day Gould prof. math. emerita, 1980—; affirmative action officer, 1980-82; prof. math. Marymount U., Arlington, Va., 1989-96; ret., 1996. Instr. U. Mich., Ann Arbor, 1945-46; lectr. Douglass Coll., New Brunswick, N.J., 1946-48; asst. prof. Swarthmore (Pa.) Coll., 1948-51, Drexel Inst. Tech., Phila., 1951-53; mathematician Johns Hopkins Applied Physics Lab., Silver Spring, Md., 1945; lectr. Simmons Coll., Boston, 1980-88, Radcliffe Coll. Seminars, Cambridge, Mass., 1985; U.S. chair postsecondary math. edn. U.S./China Joint Conf. on Edn., 1992, co-chair Citizen Amb. program People to People U.S. and China Joint Conf. on Women's Issues, 1995, session women in sci. and math. Contbr. articles on women in math. and other articles to math. jours. Recipient Disting. Alumna award Westhampton Coll., U. Richmond, 1977; NSF sci. faculty fellow Inst. for Advanced Study, Princeton, N.J., 1958-59. Fellow AAAS (math. sect. A nominating com. 1979-83, mem.-at-large 1983-86, chair-elect sect. A 1991, chair 1992, retiring chair 1993, Assn. for Women in Math. rep., 1993—), AAUP (chmn. nat. com. W 1980-83, mem. nat. coun. 1984-87), Am. Math. Soc. (chmn. postdoctoral fellowship com. 1973-76, affirmative action procedures com. 1980-82, chair com. on Human Rights of Mathematicians 1988-94), Soc. Indsl. and Applied Math., Am. Statis. Assn., Inst. Math. Stats., Nat. Coun. Tchrs. of Math. (chair com. on women 1976-81), Math Assn. Am. (adv. com. for Women and Math. program 1987-89, dir. fund raising 1989-92, lectr. 1982—, chair devel. com. 1988-92, Yueh-Gin Gung and Charles Y. Hu disting. svc. to math. award 1998), Internat. Congress Mathematicians (mem. fund raising com. 1986), Assn. for Women in Math. (pres. 1973-75, Alice T. Schafer Prize established 1989, chair fund raising com. 1992-94, leader math. del. women mathematicians to China 1990, Disting. Svc. award 1990), Emily's List (mem. majority coun.), Cosmos Club, Phi Beta Kappa, Sigma Xi, Sigma Delta Epsilon. Achievements include first study of singularities of space curves in projective differential geometry; research on undulation point of a space curve. Home: 1010 Waltham St Apt A404 Lexington MA 02421-8064

**SCHAFER, ELIZABETH DIANE,** historian, writer; b. Opelika, Ala., Sept. 26, 1965; d. Robert Louis and Carolyn Louise (Henn) S. BA in History cum laude, Auburn U., 1986, MA in History of Sci., 1988, PhD in History of Tech. magna cum laude, 1993; MA magna cum laude, Hollins Coll., 2003; MFA, Hollins U. Archivist Lee County Hist. Soc. Mus., 1988—. Ind. scholar, 1993—; presenter in field. Author: Exploring Harry Potter, 2000, Lake Martin: Alabama's Crown Jewel, 2002, Auburn: Plainsmen, Tigers and War Eagles, 2003, Auburn Football, 2004; co-author: Women Who Made A Difference in Alabama, 1995; cons. editor Ency. of Sci., 1998; freelance editor various tech. docs.; editl. asst. Proceedings of the We. Soc. for French History, 1988-91, Nat. Forum: The Phi Kappa Phi Jour., 1990-91; contbr. History News Svc.; reviewer Children's Lit. database; contbr. articles to profl. jours., encys., mags., chpts. to books. Recipient hon. mention poetry Writer's Digest, 1994 hon. mention children's non-fiction, 1997, children's non-fiction and

fiction, 1998, Writer's Digest, Shirley Henn Meml. award Critical scholar, Hollins Coll., 1998. Mem. AAAS, AAUW, Am. Hist. Assn., Orgn. Am. Historians, Soc. History Tech., History Sci. Soc., Women's History Network, N.Y. Acad. Scis., So. Hist. Assn., Soc. Children's Book Writers and Illustrators, Children's Lit. Network, Ala. Poetry Soc., Children's Lit. Assn., Ala. Writer's Forum, Authors Guild, Lancaster Mennonite Hist. Soc., Lee County Hist. Soc. (life mem.), Auburn U. Alumni Assn. (life), Descs. Mex. War Vets., DAR (chpt. historian), Phi Alpha Theta. Home and Office: PO Box 57 Loachapoka AL 36865-0057 Personal E-mail: Elizabeth_D_Schafer@yahoo.com.

**SCHAFER, GERALD LEWIS (JAY SCHAFER),** library director; b. El Paso, Tex., Apr. 20, 1949; s. Norman Oscar and Clarice S. BA, U. Tex., El Paso, 1971; MLS, U. Denver, 1973. Info. specialist Denver Rsch. Inst., 1973-75; area mgr. Denver Pub. Libr., 1975-80; dir. profl. communications Skidmore, Owings & Merrill, Denver, 1981-84; coord. collection devel. svcs. to asst. dir. for rsch. svcs. Auraria Libr., Denver, 1984—97; dir. libr. and info. svcs. Hatch Library, Bay Path Coll., Longmeadow, 1997—2000; coord. collection devel. U. Mass., Amherst, 2000—04, interim dir. librs., 2004—05, dir. librs., 2005—. V.p., pres. elect Mgmt. Consortium. Boston Libr. Consortium, 2006—. Editor: Master Plan-U.S. Air Force Academy, 1984. Chair collections task force Colo. State Libr., Denver, 1993-94, Access Colo. Libr. and Info. Network Collection Devel. Com., 1996—. Mem. ALA, Colo. Libr. Assn. Avocation: landscape architecture and library space planning. Office: Dir Librs U Mass Amherst Amherst MA 01003-9275*

**SCHAFER, JACQUELINE ELLEN,** federal agency administrator; b. Greenport, NY; AB, Middlebury Coll., 1967. Analyst, rsch. asst. Fed. Reserve Bank NY, 1967—70; legis. asst. to Sen. James L. Buckley U.S. Senate, 1971—76; asst. sec. installations and environ. U.S. Navy; regional adminstr. region 2 U.S. Environ. Protection Agy., 1982—93; dir. Calif. Dept. Fish and Game, 1993—99, Ariz. Dept. Environ. Quality, 1999—2002; dep. asst. adminstr. bur. econ. growth USAID, 2002—, asst. adminstr. for econ. growth agrl. & trade, 2005—. Office: US Agy Internat Devel 1300 Pennsylvania Ave NW Washington DC 20523*

**SCHAFER, JAMES ARTHUR,** physiologist; b. Buffalo, Oct. 10, 1941; s. Joseph James and Gladys Lita (Lighty) S.; m. Margaret Anne Schiefer, Aug. 16, 1964; children: James Arthur Jr., Kirsten Ann. BS, U. Mich., 1963, PhD, 1968. Postdoctoral fellow Gustav-Embden Ctr., Frankfurt, Germany, 1968-69, Duke U., Durham, NC, 1969-70; asst. prof. U. Ala., Birmingham, 1970-72, assoc. prof., 1972-76, prof., 1976—2004, prof. emeritus, 2004—, sr. scientist Nephrology Rsch. and Tng. Ctr. Birmingham, 1980—. Author: (with H. Valtin) Renal Function. Mechanisms Preserving Fluid and Solute Balance in Health, 3d edit., 1994; editor Am. Jour. Physiology: Renal, 1983-89, mem. editl. bd., 2001—; assoc. editor News in Physiol. Scis., 1997-03; cons. editor Jour. Clin. Investigation, 1998-03; mem. editl bd. Jour. Gen. Physiology, 1979-97, adv. editor, 1998—; mem. editl. bd. Kidney Internat., 1990-95; author textbooks on physiology; editor sci. monographs in Membrane Transport in Biology, 1992, Methods in Membrane and Transporter Research, 1994; contbr. articles to profl. jours. Chmn. rsch. com. Nat. Kidney and Urol. Diseases Adv. Bd. U.S. Dept. HHS, 1987-90. Fellow Jane Coffin Childs Meml., 1968-69; recipient Robert F. Pitts. Meml. award Internat. Union Physiol. Scis., Sydney, Australia, 1983, Homer W. Smith award Am. Soc. Nephrology and NY Heart Assn., 1993, Max Planck-Von Humboldt Rsch. award, Govt. of Germany, 1994. Mem. Am. Physiol. Soc. (councilor 1992-95, pres.-elect 1995-96, pres. 1996-97, past pres. 1997-98, Carl W. Gottschalk award 2001, Robert W. Berliner award 2004), Am. Soc. Nephrology (sec.-treas. 1989-92, councilor 1992-95), Am. Soc. Clin. Investigation (hon.), Fedn. Am. Socs. Exptl. Biology (bd. dirs. 1995-99, exec. com. 1996-97, pub. affairs exec. com. 1997-99), Am. Heart Assn. (Established Investigator award, 1971-76), Biophys. Soc., Int. Soc. Nephrol., Soc. Gen. Physiol. Avocations: classical music, mountain hiking, skiing. Office: U Ala Dept Phys & Biophysics 834 MCLM Bldg 1918 University Blvd Birmingham AL 35294-0005 Office Phone: 205-934-7106. Business E-Mail: jschafer@uab.edu.

**SCHAFER, JOHN FRANCIS,** plant pathologist, researcher; b. Pullman, Wash., Feb. 17, 1921; s. Edwin George and Ella Frances (Miles) S.; m. Joyce A. Marcks, Aug. 16, 1947; children— Patricia, Janice, James BS, Wash. State U., 1942; PhD, U. Wis., 1950. Asst. prof. to prof. plant pathology Purdue U., 1949-68; head dept. plant pathology Kans. State U. 1968-72; chmn. dept. plant pathology Wash. State U., Pullman, 1972-80; integrated pest mgmt. coordinator sci. and edn. USDA, 1980-81, acting nat. research program leader plant pathology Agrl. Research Service, 1981-82, dir. cereal rust lab. St. Paul, 1982-87, biol. sci. collaborator, 1987-95; ret., 1995. Vis. rsch. prof. Duquesne U., 1965-66; adj. prof. plant pathology U. Minn., 1982-92. Contbr. chapters to books, articles to profl. jours. With AUS, 1942-46. Phi Sigma scholar, 1942. Fellow AAAS, Ind. Acad. Sci., Am. Phytopathol. Soc. (past pres.); mem. Am. Soc. Agronomy, Crop Sci. Soc. Am., Coun. for Agrl. Sci. and Tech. Achievements include identification of increased resistance to wheat leaf rust by genetic recombination; demonstration of probabilities of virulence to genetic resistance combinations, of tolerance as a mechanism of disease control, and of use of cultivaral diversity for disease protection; bred (with others) over 30 disease resistant cultivars of cereal crops, including Arthur wheat. Home: 3585 Round Barn Blvd Apt 121 Santa Rosa CA 95403 Personal E-mail: jacjoy@sbcglobal.net.

**SCHAFER, JOHN STEPHEN,** poet; b. N.Y.C., Sept. 5, 1934; s. Stephen James and Siiri (Halmi) S.; m. Gertrud Rosa Fleischmann, June 14, 1958; children: Sylvia F., John Stephen, Karen D., Kristen H. BA, Rutgers U., 1956, MBA, 1963. Advt. research mgr. Union Carbide Corp., N.Y.C., 1959—65; rsch. mgr. Bus. Week, N.Y.C., 1965—66; v.p. Opinion Rsch. Corp., Princeton, NJ, 1966—80; pres. Am. Econ. Found., Cleve., 1981—2002, trustee, 1975—2002; v.p., dir. Ams. for Competitive Enterprise System, Phila., 1970-82. Editor Linde Electric Welding Progress, 1959-62, ORC Pub. Opinion Index, 1968-72, AEF Straight Talk, 1981-82, Bellcore Exch., 1993-94; works pub. in Famous Poems of the Twentieth Century, 1996, Perceptions in Harmony, 1998, The Communicator, 2000-05, Best Poems and Poets of 2003, 2004, others. Polit. pollster Ed Clark for U.S. Pres., 1980; chmn. N.J. Libertarian party, 1983; nat. dir. U.S. Jaycees, 1965-66, v.p. N.J., 1964-65. Served to 1st It. U.S. Army, 1957-59. Mem. Jr. Chamber Internat. (hon. life), Philosophean Soc., Scabbard and Blade, Delta Phi Alpha Presbyterian. Home: 114 Walton Palm Rd Panama City FL 32413-7311

**SCHAFER, MARIE,** nurse, educator; b. Eric Martelly and Jacqueline Gabriel; m. Raymond Schafer, July 19, 1997. BA, Fla. Internat. U., Miami, 1994; BSN, Barry U., Miami Shores, Fla., 1997, MSN, 2003. Acting nurse mgr. Miami VA Healthcare Sys., 1998—2001, staff nurse, 2001—03, 2003—04, nurse educator, 2003—. Cons. William Sterns & Assoc., Miami, 2003—04; case mgr. Home Health Agy., Miami, 2003—04. Editor (editor-in-chief): (newsletter) Nightingale News; contbr. articles to profl. jours. Named Excellence Award in Tchg. finalist, Nursing Spectrum, 2006. Mem.: Am. Soc. Parenteral Enteral Nutrition, Am. Holistic Nurses' Assn., Fla. Nurses Assn., Sierra Club. Office: Miami VA Healthcare Sys 1201 NW 16th St Miami FL 33125 Office Phone: 305-575-7000 ext. 4239. Home Fax: 18772160328. Personal E-mail: mariem@gate.net. E-mail: marie.schafer@med.va.gov.

**SCHAFER, MICHAEL FREDERICK,** orthopedic surgeon; b. Peoria, Ill., Aug. 17, 1942; s. Harold Martin and Frances May (Ward) S.; m. Eileen M. Briggs, Jan. 8, 1966; children: Steven, Brian, Kathy, David, Daniel. BA, U. Iowa, 1964, MD, 1967. Diplomate Am. Bd. Orthopedic Surgery. Intern Chgo. Wesley Meml. Hosp., 1967-68; resident in orthop. surgery Cook County Program, Northwestern U., Chgo., 1968-72; asst. prof. orthop. surgery Northwestern U.—; Reyerson prof. and chmn. dept. orthopedic surgery; asso. attending orthopedic surgeon Northwestern Meml. Hosp., 1974—. Adj. staff Children's Meml. Hosp., Chgo., 1974—; cons. VA Lakeside Hosp., 1974—; panelist Bur. Health Manpower, HEW, 1976; sec.-treas. Orthop. Rsch. and Edn. Found.; attending orthop. surgeon Northwestern Meml. Hosp., 1980—, exec. dir. Back and Neck Inst. Contbr. articles to profl. jours. Maj.

U.S. Army, 1973-74. Fellow Am. Orthopaedic Assn., Am. Acad. Orthopaedic Surgeons; mem. AMA, Am. Orthopedic Soc. Sports Medicine, Ill. Med. Soc., Chgo. Med. Soc., Scoliosis Rsch. Soc. Roman Catholic. Home: 1815 Ridgewood Ln W Glenview IL 60025-2205 Office: Northwestern U Med School Ste 910 645 N Michigan Ave Chicago IL 60611-2876 Business E-Mail: m-schafer@northwestern.edu.

**SCHAFER, MILTON,** composer, pianist, educator; b. N.Y.C., Sept. 24, 1920; s. Abraham and May (Meyerson) S.; div. 1974; 1 child, Nina Kathryn. Cert., Paris Conservatory, 1950; student. Am Conservatory, Fontainbleu, France; pvt. study, Nadia Boulanger, Paris, 1949-50; BS, Juilliard Sch. Music, N.Y.C., 1952; MA, CCNY, N.Y.C., 1967; studied with, Alfred Mirovitch, Irwin Freundlich, Lonnie Epstein. Lectr. music CCNY, N.Y.C., 1954—56, prof. music John Jay Coll., 1976—96; asst. to Frank Loesser Frank Music Pub., N.Y.C., 1956—58; music. dir. Am. Theatre Wing, N.Y.C., 1962. Mem. So. Hampton Poetry Workshop, 1997—. Piano recitals at Am. Embassy, Paris, 1949, Quaker Ctr. Internat., Paris, 1949, Town Hall, N.Y.C., 1950, 54; composer, lyricist: (children's song cycle) Mommy Gimme a Drinka Water, 1957 (recorded by Danny Kaye and televised by Nathan Lane with Boston Pops 1999), (Broadway musicals) Bravo Giovanni, 1962 (reading revival, Cleve. 2005), Lyrics: Ronny Graham, (Tony award nomination for score), Drat! The Cat!, 1965 (staged revival "Musicals Tonight", N.Y.C. 2005, voted Best Score of Yr. by Walter Kerr, book, lyrics by Ira Levin), (three revivals) He Touched Me, 1965 (recorded by Barbara Streisand), The No-Color Time of the Day (recorded by Frank Pourcel), I'm Five (recorded by The Muppets), I Like Old People, Don't You? (recorded by Michael Feinstein); songs recorded by Peggy Lee, Sarah Vaughn, Jerry Vale, Eddie Fisher, Ah!Camminare, Frank Pourcel.; author: Practical Technique for Popular Piano Playing, 1947; author, composer adaptation Kate Simon's Bronx Primitive 1990 (staged reading at ASCAP 1998, Hell's Kitchen 2005, Jewish Ctr. of Hamptons, 2006); music critic High Fidelity, 1975, Music Jour., 1976-78; author: (children's book) Crazy Barbara, 2003, I'm Big, 2006, also numerous poems. Staff sgt. USAAF, 1942-46. Co-winner Nat. Guild Piano Tchrs. Competition, N.Y.C., 1948. Mem. ASCAP, Dramatists Guild, The Bohemians. Avocations: reading, yoga, swimming, travel, poetry. Home: 33 Riverside Dr New York NY 10023-8012 Office Phone: 212-769-8720.

**SCHAFER, OSCAR S.,** investment company executive; Bachelor's Degree, Harvard Coll.; MBA, Harvard U. Portfolio mgr. Steinhardt Partners, gen. ptnr., Cumberland Associates, 1982—2001; mng. ptnr. OSS Capital Mgmt. Bd. mem. Parker Vision Inc.; dir. Global Healthcare Ptnrs. Office: OSS Capital Mgmt 605 3rd Ave Lobby New York NY 10158

**SCHAFER, ROBERT LOUIS,** agricultural engineer, researcher; b. Burlington, Iowa, Aug. 1, 1937; s. Marion Louis and Pansy (Head) S.; m. Carolyn Louise Henn, Aug. 1, 1959; 1 child, Elizabeth Diane. BS, Iowa State U., 1959, MS, 1961, PhD, 1965. Agrl. engr. Agrl. Rsch. Svc., USDA, Ames, Iowa, 1959-64, Auburn, Ala., 1964-95. Co-author: Advances in Soil Dynamics, 1994; contbr. articles to profl. jours. Fellow Am. Soc. Agrl. Engrs. (McCormick Case Gold medal 1997). Home: PO Box 189 Loachapoka AL 36865-0189 E-mail: rls@laltek.com.

**SCHAFER, RONALD WILLIAM,** electrical engineering educator; b. Tecumseh, Nebr., Feb. 17, 1938; s. William Henry and Esther Sophia Schafer; m. Dorothy Margaret Hall, June 2, 1960; children: William R., John C. (dec.), Katherine L., Barbara student, Doane Coll., Crete, Nebr., 1956-59; BEE, U. Nebr., 1961, MEE, 1962; PhD in Elec. Engring., MIT, 1968. Tech. staff Bell Labs., Murray Hill, NJ, 1968-74; John and Marilu McCarty prof. elec. engring. Ga. Inst. Tech., Atlanta, 1974—2004, Inst. prof., 1991—2004, emeritus prof., 2004—; HP fellow Hewlett-Packard Labs., Palo Alto, Calif., 2004—. Chmn. bd. Atlanta Signal Processors Inc., 1983-2001. Co-author: Digital Signal Processing, 1974, Digital Processing of Speech Signals, 1979, Speech Analysis, 1979, Discrete-Time Signal Processing, 1989, 2d edit., 1999, Computer-Based Exercises for Signal Processing Using Matlab, 1995, DSP First: A Multimedia Approach, 1998, Signal Processing First, 2003. Recipient Class of 34 Disting. Prof. award Ga. Inst. Tech., 1985. Fellow IEEE (Emanuel R. Piore award 1980, Edn. medal 1992, 3d millennium award 2000), Acoustical Soc. Am.; mem. IEEE Processing Soc. (soc. award 1982, edn. award 2000), Nat. Acad. Engring. Democrat. Office: Hewlett-Packard Labs 1501 Page Mill Rd Palo Alto CA 94304 Office Phone: 650-857-4142.

**SCHAFER, SHARON MARIE,** anesthesiologist; b. Detroit, Mar. 23, 1948; d. Charles Anthony and Dorothy Emma (Schweizer) Pokriefka; m. Timothy John Schafer, Nov. 12, 1977; children: Patrick Christopher, Steven Michael. BS in Biology, Wayne State U., 1971, MD, 1975; MBA in Practice Mgmt., Madonna U., 2000. Diplomate Am. Bd. Anesthesiology. Intern, resident Sinai Hosp. Detroit, 1975-78; pvt. practice anesthesiology Troy, Mich., 1988—. Mem. AMA, Am. Soc. Anesthesiologists. Roman Catholic. Home and Office: 5741 Folkstone Dr Troy MI 48085-3154 Office Phone: 248-879-6246.

**SCHAFERMEYER, ROBERT WILLIAM,** emergency physician, educator, health policy consultant; b. St. Louis, Jan. 9, 1948; s. William Jacob and Virginia Rose (Cumming) S.; m. An-ping Yuan, May 12, 1973; children: Christina, David, Matthew, Joseph. Student, St. Louis U., 1966-69; MD, U. Mo., 1973. Diplomate Am. Bd. Emergency Medicine, Am. Bd. Pediats., sub-bd. pediat. emergency medicine. Mem. dept. emergency medicine East Tenn. Children's Hosp., Knoxville, 1979-81, Carolinas Med. Ctr., Charlotte, NC, 1981—; clin. assoc. prof. pediats. U. N.C. Sch. Medicine, Chapel Hill, 1981-85, clin. prof. emergency medicine and pediats., 1994—; assoc. chair dept. emergency medicine Carolinas Med. Ctr., Charlotte, 1982—. Dir. E.D. Cons. and Lectrs., Charlotte, 90—. Assoc. editor: Pediatric Emergency Medicine Concepts and Clinical Practice, 1997, editor: Pediatric Emergency Medicine. A Comprehensive Study Guide, 1995, 2d edit. 2002; contbr. articles and revs. to profl. jours. including Annals Emergency Medicine Jour.; reviewer Pediat. Emergency Medicine, Acad. Emergency Medicine; past mem. editl. bd. Pediat. Emergency Med. Jour. Com. mem. MEMAC Adv., Mecklenberg County, 1991-93; mem. task force Drug Abuse for County Commrs., Mecklenberg, 1989-90. Lt. commdr. USPHS, 1974—76. EMS-C grantee Maternal and Child Health, 1992-94. Fellow Am. Coll. Emergency Physicians (bd. dirs. 1994-2002, pres.-elect 1999-2000, pres. 2000-01, past pres. 2001-02, Nightingale Outstanding Leadership award 2004); mem. Am. Acad. Pediats., NC chpt. Am. Coll. Emergency Physicians (councillor 1984-94, bd. dirs. 1983-89, pres. 1986-88, Leadership/Svc. award 1988, George Podgorny Emergency Medicine Svc. award 1996), Soc. Acad. Emergency Medicine (bd. dirs. 2004-). Roman Catholic. Avocations: tae kwan do, photography, skiing. Office: Carolinas Med Ctr 1000 Blythe Blvd Charlotte NC 28203-5812 Office Phone: 704-355-3181.

**SCHAFF, MANYA,** foundation administrator; b. Chgo., Mar. 12, 1931; d. Louis Lipkin and Allene Ewing; m. Jay Barash Schaff, Mar. 25, 1951 (div. Jan. 20, 1971); children: Pamela Beth, William Franz Kim, Elizabeth Aline; m. Dimitri Polonsky, PhD, June 27, 1971 (div. Dec. 14, 2000). MusB, Northwestern U., 1953. Tchr. Carnegie-Mellon U., Pitts., 1961—65, Chatham Coll., Pitts., 1964—71, Immaculate Heart Coll., LA, 1972—79; instr. UCLA, 1973—79; program dir. Performing Tree, Inc., LA, 1982—88; program officer The Ahmanson Found., Beverly Hills, Calif., 1988—; tchr., performer Shady Side Acad., Pitts., 1968—71. Panelist L.A. Cultural Affairs Dept., 1983—85, L.A. Ednl. Partnership, Small Grants to Teachers, 1988—98; sr. facilitator Inst. for the Arts. Pitts. Pub. Schs., Pitts., 1985; bd. dir. Vista Del Mar Child Care, LA, 1979—82. Editor: Piano for Two Directory. Bd. dirs. Chamber Music Soc. of L.A., 1990—95. Recipient Drawing prize, Assoc. Artists Pitts., 1963, Pennational Artists Annual, 1964, Fiber Art prize, Annual Ehrman Mansion Show, 1977. Mem.: Pi Kappa Lambda (life), Sigma Alpha Iota (life). Democrat. Home: 2139 Roscomare Rd Los Angeles CA 90077 Office: The Ahmanson Found 9215 Wilshire Blvd Beverly Hills CA 90210 Personal E-mail: mschaff@mindspring.com.

**SCHAFFER, AKIVA,** writer, director; b. Berkeley, Calif., Dec. 1, 1977; Grad., U. Calif., Santa Cruz. Co-founder, mem. The Lonely Island, 2001—. Writer MTV Movie Awards, 2004, 2005, G-Phoria, 2004, Saturday Night Live, 2005—, guest appearances (TV specials) 40 Most Awesomely Bad Dirrty Songs...Ever, 2004. Recipient WIRED Rave Award - TV, 2006. Office: United Talent Agency Inc 9560 Wilshire Blvd Ste 500 Beverly Hills CA 90212 Office Phone: 310-273-6700. Office Fax: 310-247-1111.*

**SCHAFFER, ARCHIE, III,** food products executive; b. Ft. Smith, Ark., 1948; B in Natural Scis., U. Ark., 1970. Adminstrv. asst. Gov. Dale Bumpers, 1971—75, Senator Bumpers, 1975—77; adminstr. Greenhurst Nursing Home, Charleston, Ark.; owner Schaffer & Assocs., Little Rock; exec. dir. Ark. Bus. Coun., 1987—91; dir. media, pub. and govtl. affairs Tyson Foods Inc., Springdale, Ark., 1991—99, sr. v.p. external rels., 1999—. Mem. Ark. Leadership Acad.; mem. agrl. devel. coun. U. Ark.; mem. adv. bd. Ark. LWV. Mem.: Ark. Nature Conservancy (bd. mem.). Office: Tyson Foods Inc 2210 W Oakland Dr Springdale AR 72762-6999

**SCHAFFER, DAVID EDWIN,** retired systems administrator; b. Nov. 3, 1929; s. Karl and Jeanette (Gotthelf) S.; m. Ariel Williams Sullivan, May 3, 1951 (dec. Dec. 2004) stepchildren: Adrienne Sullivan Smith, James W. Sullivan; m. Patricia Owen, Feb. 25, 2006; stepchildren: Christopher Owen, Patricia Taylor. Student, Wharton Sch. of U. Pa., 1948-49; BA, New Sch. for Social Rsch., 1959. Spl. edn. tchr. of emotionally disturbed children various schs. and hosps., 1954-65; br. mgr. 1st Westchester Nat. Bank, New Rochelle, NY, 1965-66; v.p. Longines-Symphonette Inc.; spl. asst. to chmn. bd. Longines Wittnauer Inc., Larchmont, NY, 1966-72; pvt. practice mgmt. cons. Franconia, NH, 1973-77; v.p./dir. ops. Carroll Reed Ski Shops, Inc., 1978-80; ret. Instr. econs. Am. Inst. Banking, 1965-66. Moderator, Town of Franconia, 1973-2005; founding trustee emeritus Frost Pl., 1975—; bd. dirs. White Mountain Community Svcs., 1973-77; bd. dirs., past pres. No. N.H. Mental Health Services, 1975-77. Prodr.: numerous record albums. Vol., bd. dirs. Hospice of the Littleton Area, Jansen Hospice; mem. com. St. Mathews Chapel, Sugar Hill, N.H. With Signal Corps, AUS, 1951-53. Mem. Direct Mail Credit Assn. Am. (founding mem.), Asso. Retail Credit Men of N.Y.C., Direct Mail Assn. Am. (past chmn. subcom. on consumer affairs and regulatory agys.), Profile Club (pres., dir.). Democrat. Episcopalian. Home: 21 River Rd Franconia NH 03580

**SCHAFFER, DAVID IRVING,** lawyer; b. NYC, Oct. 17, 1935; s. Frank and Edith (Montlack) S.; m. Lois Ann Warshauer, June 16, 1957; children: Susan Edith, Eric Michael. BA, U. Pa., 1956; LL.B., Harvard U., 1959. Bar: N.Y. 1960. Assoc. Shearman & Sterling, N.Y.C., 1960-65; sec., counsel Yale Express System, Inc., N.Y.C., 1965-66; sr. v.p., gen. counsel Avis, Inc., Garden City, NY, 1966-83; v.p., gen. counsel U.S. Surgical Corp., Norwalk, Conn., 1983-86; of counsel Meltzer, Lippe, Goldstein & Schlissel, LLP, Mineola, NY, 1986-89; ptnr. Meltzer, Lippe, Goldstein & Breitstone, LLP, Mineola, 1989—. Past pres. Nassau County Legal Aid Soc., 1984-86. Bd. dirs. United Cmty. Fund, Great Neck, NY, 1980, Great Neck Estates Civic Assn., 1998—, L.I. Venture Group, 1988-2003. With USAR, 1960. Mem. ABA, N.Y. State Bar Assn., Nassau County Bar Assn., L.I. Software Assn., Harvard Club. Democrat. Home: 31 Amherst Rd Great Neck NY 11021-2910 Office: Meltzer Lippe Et Al 190 Willis Ave Mineola NY 11501-2693 Office Phone: 516-747-0300. Personal E-mail: dlefty35@optonline.net. Business E-Mail: dschaffer@meltzerlippe.com.

**SCHAFFER, HENRY M.,** lawyer; b. Bklyn., Aug. 22, 1943; AB, Columbia U., 1964; MA, Wash. U., St. Louis, 1964; JD, U. Calif., Berkeley, 1973. Bar: Ill. 1973, Ohio (inactive) 1980, US Dist. Ct. No. Dist. Ill. 1974, US Dist. Ct. No. Dist. Ohio 1980, US Supreme Ct. 1980, US Ct. Appeals 8th Cir. 1985. Atty. Jenner & Block LLP, Chgo., 1973—77, Rothschild, Barry & Myers, Chgo., 1977—78, Cooper, Straub, Walinski & Cramer, Toledo, 1983—87; co-dir. civil law clinic U. Toledo, Ohio, 1979—83, Ohio, 1987—89; ptnr. Howe & Hutton, Ltd., Chgo., 1989—2003; of counsel Jenner & Block LLP, Chgo., 2003—. Office: Jenner & Block LLP 1 IBM Plz Chicago IL 60611-7603 Office Phone: 312-840-7673. Office Fax: 312-840-7773. Business E-Mail: hschaffer@jenner.com.

**SCHAFFER, KENNETH B.,** communications executive, mechanical engineer, consultant; b. N.Y.C., Oct. 19, 1947; s. Louis and Rose Schaffer; m. Alla Fyodorovna Kliouka, Aug. 26, 1993; 1 child, Kibo. BA, CCNY, 1969. Pres., founder Sound Images, Inc., N.Y.C., 1969-72; exec. v.p. Douglas Internat., N.Y.C., 1972-75; pres., founder Ken Schaffer Group, Inc., N.Y.C., 1975-82, Orbita Techs. Corp., N.Y.C., 1981-86; v.p., founder Belka Internat. Inc., N.Y.C. and Moscow, 1986-91; pres., founder Belcom, Inc., N.Y.C., Moscow, and Almaty, 1991-96, also bd. dirs.; CEO K2B, Inc., N.Y.C. Cons. wireless, satellite, internetworking, Russia. Profiled in The New Yorker, 1991. Recipient Golden Ace award Cable TV Assn., 1989. Mem. Am. Radio Relay League, Aircraft Owners and Pilots Assn., Internet Soc. Achievements include invention of wireless guitar; satellite system to intercept internal Soviet television; TV2Me, a system that enables global access to any cable television system. Avocations: flying, amateur radio. Home: 21 W 58th St New York NY 10019-1604

**SCHAFFER, ROBERT (BOB SCHAFFER),** former congressman; b. Cin., July 24, 1962; s. Robert James and Florence Ann (Bednar) S.; m. Maureen Elizabeth Menke, Feb. 8, 1986; children: Jennifer and Emily (twins), Justin, Sarah Mary. BA in Polit. Sci., U. Dayton, 1984; doctorate (hon.), Colo. Tech. U. Speechwriter republican caucus Ohio Gen. Assembly, 1984-85; legis. asst. State of Ohio, Columbus, 1985; majority adminstrv. asst. Colo. State Senate, Denver, 1985-87, mem., 1987-96, U.S. Congress from 4th Colo. dist., Washington, 1997—2003, mem. agr. com. agr. and workforce com., resources com. Mem. Rep. Policy Com., GOP Theme Team; commr. Colo. Advanced Tech. Inst. 1988—; propri'n for Mo., Front Range Mktg. and Distbn., Inc. Mem. Mental Health Bd. Larimer County, 1986-87; mem. com. on human svcs. Nat. Conf. State Legislatures; campain co-chmn. Arnold for Lt. Gov.; Republican candidate for Lt. Gov. of Colo., 1994. Named Nat. Legislator of Yr., Rep. Nat. Legislators Assn., 1995, Taxpayer Champion, Colo. Union of Taxpayers, 1995, Bus. Legislator of the Yr. Colo. Assn. Commerce and Industry, Named Guardina Small Bus. Nat. Fedn. Ind. Bus.; recipient Spirit of Enterprise award U.S. C. of C. Mem. Jaycees (Mover and Shaker award 1989). KC. Republican. Roman Catholic. Avocations: backpacking, skiing, baseball, painting, reading. Home: 5027 Alder Ct Fort Collins CO 80525-5588

**SCHAFFER, SANDRA SUE,** artist, educator; b. Kansas City, Mo., Jan. 12, 1947; d. Robert William and Marian Frances Effertz; m. Larry Alan Schaffer, Nov. 10, 1972; children: Kristen Noelle, Scott David. BA in Psychology, U. Mo., 1969; MSEd in Learning Disabilities, Ctrl. Mo. State U., 1974. Diagnostician and learning disabilities specialist Cenl. Mo. State U., Kansas City, Mo., 1997—. Diagnostician, spl. educ. coord. The Plaza Acad., Mercier, Mo., 2003—. One-woman shows include Corridor Gallery, 2005, Park Ctrl. Gallery, 2006, exhibitions include Finding the Extraordinary in the Ordinary: Works from Peru, Nepal and other Travels, Nepali Matron (MKEC Engring. award Kans. Watercolor Soc. Regional Show, 2004), Ledgemates (Excellence award Red River Watercolor Soc. Nat. Show, 2004), Rooftop Perspective (Past Pres.'s award Western Colo. Watercolor Soc. Nat. Show, 2001), Village Life (Friends Cash award Miss. Watercolor Soc. Nat. Show, 2001). Newsletter editor Watercolor Honor Soc., Springfield, Mo., 2004—05; bd. dirs. Mattie Rhodes Arts Ctr., Kansas City, Mo., 1994—95. Recipient First Pl. award, Wyo. Watercolor Soc. Nat. Exhbn., 2001, New Orleans Sch. of Fine Art and Daler-Rowney award, La. Watercolor Soc. Internat. Show, 2002, Nielsen-Bainbridge award, Western Colo. Watercolor Soc. Nat. Show, 2001, Pacific Gallery Artists' award, Pensicola Art League Nat. Show, 2004, Colvin Cash award, Baker Arts Ctr. Nat. Show, 2003, Catherine M. Mulkare Cash award, RI Watercolor Soc., 2005, George Latta Cash award, Mo. Watercolor Soc., 2005, Merit award, Watercolor Art Soc. Houston, 2005, Juror's Art award, Ctr. Nat. Show, 2005, Honorable Mention, Watercolor Art Soc. Houston, 2006, numerous others; grantee Merit award, Rod River Watercolor Soc., 2005. Mem.: Watercolor West Watercolor Soc., N.W. Watercolor Soc.

(signature mem.), Tex. Watercolor Soc. (Purple Sage award, signature mem.), Watercolor Honor Soc. (assoc.; bd. dirs. 2004—05, Winsor-Newton award 2004, signature mem.). Democrat. Unitarian-Universalist. Avocations: international travel, bicycling, reading. Home: 12700 E 64th Ct Kansas City MO 64133 Office: The Plaza Acad 4232 Mercier Kansas City MO 64111 Office Phone: 816-561-0770. Home Fax: 816-373-2112; Office Fax: NA. Personal E-mail: lschaffer@kc.rr.com. E-mail: na.

**SCHAFFER, SCOTT R.,** lawyer; b. Bronx, NY, Dec. 17, 1959; BS, U. Fla., 1981; JD, Bklyn. Law Sch., 1984. Bar: NJ 1985, NY 1986, US Dist. Ct. So. Dist. NY, US Dist. Ct. Ea. Dist. NY, US Dist. Ct. Dist. NJ. Ptnr. Wilson, Elser, Moskowitz, Edelman & Dicker LLP, NYC, coord. nat. D&O (directors & officers) practice team. Mem.: ABA (tort & ins. practice sect., labor & employment sect.), Assn. of the Bar of City of NY (chmn. D&O ins. com.), NY State Bar Assn. (tort, ins. & compensation law sect.). Office: Wilson Elser Moskowitz Edelman & Dicker LLP 150 E 42nd St 23rd Fl New York NY 10017-5639 Office Phone: 212-490-3000 ext. 2771. Office Fax: 212-490-3038. Business E-Mail: schaffers@wemed.com.

**SCHAFFER, SETH ANDREW,** lawyer; b. Bklyn., Jan. 7, 1942; m. Karen (Kiki) Cohn, Dec. 1, 1968; children: Amanda, Julia, James. BA in Econs. magna cum laude, Harvard U., 1963, LLB cum laude, 1967; postgrad., Cambridge (Eng.) U., 1964. Bar: N.Y. 1970, U.S. Dist. Ct. (so. dist.) N.Y. 1973, U.S. Ct. Appeals (2nd cir.) 1973, U.S. Supreme Ct. 1980. Tchr. math. and econs. York (Pa.) Country Day Sch., 1967-68; assoc. dir. Vera Inst. Justice, 1969-72; asst. U.S. atty. U.S. Dist. Ct. (so. dist.) N.Y., 1972-75; chief counsel Moreland Act Commn. on Nursing Homes, NYC, 1975-76; of counsel Stanley S. Arkin, P.C., Attys. at Law, 1976-77; v.p., gen. counsel, sec. of univ. NYU, NYC, 1977-93, sr. v.p., gen. counsel, sec., 1993—2005; deputy commnr. for legal matters NYPD, 2005—. Adj. prof. law NYU Sch. Law. Dir. Nat. Ctr. Philanthropy and the Law, N.Y.C. Henry fellow Cambridge U., 1964. Mem. Nat. Assn. Coll. and Univ. Attys. (past pres.), Assn. of Bar of City of N.Y., Phi Beta Kappa. Home: 3 Washington Mews New York NY 10003-6608 Office: Deputy Commnr for Legal Matters NYPD One Police Plaza New York NY 10038 Office Phone: 646-610-8423. Business E-Mail: andrew.schaffer@nyu.edu.

**SCHAFFER, STUART F.,** lawyer; b. N.Y.C., Sept. 14, 1957; BS with high honors, Univ. Fla., 1979; JD with distinction, Duke Univ., 1982. Bar: Tex. 1982. Ptnr. & chmn. global projects dept. Baker Botts LLP, Houston. Mem. editl. bd. Duke Law Jour. Named a Texas Super Lawyer, Texas Monthly mag. & Law & Politics mag., 2003—04. Mem.: ABA, Houston Bar Assn., Internat. Tax Forum of Houston, Order of the Coif. Office: Baker Botts LLP One Shell Plz 910 Louisiana St Houston TX 77002-4995 Office Phone: 713-229-1780. Office Fax: 713-229-7780. Business E-Mail: stuart.schaffer@bakerbotts.com.

**SCHAFFER, WILLIAM D.,** music educator, alderman; b. Norfolk, Va., Mar. 21, 1964; s. Ula Edward and Elizabeth J. Schaffer; m. Jennifer Charissa Smotherman, June 11, 1986; children: Douglas J., Conner Lee. B in Music Edn., S.E. Miss. State U., 1993; MusM in Performance, Ark. State U., 1997. Dir. bands Portageville (Mo.) Schs., 1993—96, Elsberry (Mo.) Schs., 1996—97; ednl. cons. Brook Mays Music, O'Fallon, Mo., 1997—2000; dir. bands Wright City (Mo.) Schs., 2000—. Drill designer Drills Concepts, Elsberry, 1996—; dir. Cotton Bowl Grand Champion Band, 2005. City alderman City of Wright City, 2003—. Staff sgt. U.S. Army, 1986—90. Mem.: Mo. Music Educators, Mo. Bandmasters Assn. Republican. Baptist. Avocations: golf, computers, music. Home: 582 Indian Lake Est Wright City MO 63390 Office: Wright City Sch 520 Westwoods Wright City MO 63390

**SCHAFFNER, ADAM DAVID,** plastic surgeon; b. Chgo., Sept. 26, 1971; s. Dorann Cohn, Robert Marc and Marjorie Schaffner (Stepmother). BS in Biology summa cum laude, Emory U., 1993; MD, Rush U., Chgo., 1998. Diplomate Am. Bd. Otolaryngology. Clin. asst. instr., resident SUNY at Stony Brook, 1998—2003; fellow facial plastic surgery Stanford Hosp., 2003—04, mem. med. staff, 2005. Summer rsch. fellow NCI, Bethesda, Md., 1994; rsch. assoc. CDC, Atlanta, 1992—93; clin. assoc. prof. Joan and Sanford I. Weill Med. Coll., Cornell U., 2005—; mem. med. staff Greenwich (Conn.) Hosp., 2004—; mem. staff Sound Shore Med. Ctr. of Westchester, New Rochelle, NY, 2004—; trainer, cons., mem. spkrs. bur. Sanofi-Aventis, 2005—; vol. cons. in field ABC News, 2004—; cons. Pfizer Upper Respiratory New Products N.Am. Market Coun., 2005. Contbr. articles to profl. jours. Participant Face to Face, 2004—; mem. exec. com. Rush Cmty. Svc. Initiatives Program, Chgo., 1996—98; steering com. co-chmn. St. Basil's Free People's Clinic, Chgo., 1996—98; vol. Egleston Children's Hosp. at Emory U., Atlanta, 1991—93. Recipient The Jack Boozer, Ph.D., award for Social and Religious Ethics, Emory U., 1992, CibaGeneva award for outstanding svc., 1996; Messing Meml. Merit scholar, Zeta Beta Tau Found., 1993, Humanitarian Effects Travel grantee, Am. Acad. Otolaryngology-Head and Neck Surgery Found., 2002. Fellow: ACS (assoc.); mem.: AMA, Am. Acad. Otolaryngology-Head and Neck Surgery, Am. Acad. Head and Neck Surgeons, NY State Soc. Otolaryngology, NY Facial Plastic Surgery Soc., Westchester County Med. Soc., Med. Soc. State of N.Y., Am. Acad. Facial Plastic and Reconstructive Surgery. Avocations: piano, swimming, theater, travel, skiing. Home: 25 LeRoy Pl Apt 311 New Rochelle NY 10805-2863 Office Phone: 914-309-8300. Personal E-mail: adamdavidschaffner@yahoo.com.

**SCHAFFNER, BERTRAM HENRY,** psychiatrist; b. Erie, Pa., Nov. 12, 1912; s. Milton and Gerta (Herzog) S. Student, Harvard U., 1928-29, 32-33; AB, Swarthmore Coll., 1932; MD, Johns Hopkins U., 1937; diploma, William Alanson White Inst., 1953, Diplomate Am. Bd. Psychiatry, Am. Bd. Neurology, Johns Hopkins Hosp., Balt., 1937-38; resident in neurology Mt. Sinai Hosp., N.Y.C., 1938-39; resident in psychiatry Bellevue Hosp., N.Y.C., 1939-40, N.Y. State Psychiat. Inst., N.Y.C., 1946-47; pvt. practice psychiatry and psychoanalysis N.Y.C., 1947—. Lectr. Sch. Nursing Cornell U., N.Y.C., 1950-60; mem. faculty, clin. supr. in psychotherapy William Alanson White Inst. Psychoanalysis, 1960—, med. dir. HIV svc., clin. supr. psychoanalysis, 1993—; cons., editor contrb. Josiah Macy Jr. Found., 1949, 50, 51; cons. U.S. Children's Bur., 1946-47, Bur. Mental Health, V.I., 1954-60, World Fedn. Mental Health, 1958-68, others; mem. N.Y. County dist. bd. Com. on Gay and Lesbian Issues; cons. WHO, 1960-67; founder, exec. dir. U.S.-Caribbean Aid to Mental Health, Inc., 1960-68; organizer Biennial Caribbean Confs. for Mental Health, 1959-65; organizer, cons. Caribbean Fedn. for Mental Health, 1959-65; mem. rsch. study Pre-Soviet Russian Family in the Research in Contemporary Cultures, Columbia U., 1949-51. Mem. editl. bd. Jour. of Gay and Lesbian Psychotherapy, 1987—; author: Father Land: A Study of Authoritarianism in the German Family, 1948; contbr. numerous articles to profl. publs. Mem. acquisitions com. The Bklyn. Mus. of Art, 1995—; trustee Bklyn. Mus. of Art. Recipient Adolf Meyer award for Disting. Svc. on Behalf of Improved Care and Treatment of the Mentally Ill in the Caribbean, 1961. Fellow AMA (life), Am. Psychiat. Assn. (chmn. 1983-86, mem. com. on AIDS N.Y. County dist. br. 1989-99, life), Am. Acad. Psychoanalysis (life), Caribbean Psychiat. Assn.; mem. Group for Advancement of Psychiatry (chair internat. rels. com. 1960-65, chair com. on human sexuality 1967-88), Internat. Acad. Sex Rsch. Avocation: collecting asian and indian art. Home and Office: 220 Central Park S New York NY 10019-1417 Office Phone: 212-265-5539. Personal E-mail: bertschmd@aol.com.

**SCHAFFNER, CAROLYN MARIE,** research administrator, biologist; b. Clarkson, N.Y., Oct. 20, 1960; d. Michael Frank and Carolyn Gertrude Skill; m. Kurt Charles Klotzbeucher, Oct. 23, 1987 (div. May 1996); m. Paul Lawrence Schaffner, Sept. 23, 2000; children: William Elliott, Josephine Marte. AS, Alfred State Coll., 1980; BS, Delaware Valley Coll., 1983; Master's degree, Villanova U., 1993. Rsch. technologist Wyeth Labs., Great Valley, Pa., 1984-86; sr. rsch. technician Arbus Rsch. Labs., Horsham, Pa., 1986; biologist Merck & Co. Inc., West Point, Pa., 1986-88, staff biologist, 1988-90, assoc. med. program coord., 1990-94, med. program coord., 1994-95, sr. med. edn. specialist, 1995-96, mgr. outcomes rsch. and mgmt., 1996—. Rschr., presenter in field. Author, rsch., presenter: Guidelines for

Diagnosis and Treatment of Osteoporosis, 1998. Mem. APHA, Nat. Osteoporosis Found., Ea. Pa. Osteoporosis Soc. (founding mem.), Older Womens League. Office: Merck & Co Inc Broad St and Sumneytown Pk West Point PA 19486

**SCHAFFNER, HOWARD SHELDON,** lawyer; b. Chgo., Nov. 2, 1943; s. Irving and Frieda Schaffner; m. Gail Schaffner, July 14, 1970; children: Paula, Stacy. JD, John Marshall Law Sch., 1970. Bar: Ill. 1970. Asst. state's atty. Cook County States Atty.'s Office, Chgo., 1970-78; ptnr. Hofeld & Schaffner, Chgo., 1978—. Mem. ABA, Ill. State Bar Assn., Ill. Trial Lawyers Assn. (bd. mgrs. 1980—; author Cont. Legal Edn. 1980—), Ill. Inst. Cont. Legal Edn. 1980, 83, 86), Ill. State Bar Assn., Internat. Soc. Barristers Office: Hofeld & Schaffner 30 N Lasalle St Ste 3120 Chicago IL 60602-2576 Office Phone: 312-372-4250.

**SCHAFFNER, KAREN ANN See FIELD, KAREN**

**SCHAFFZIN, JONATHAN A.,** lawyer; b. NYC, Aug. 4, 1960; BA, Northwestern U., 1982; JD, Columbia Law Sch., 1985. Bar: NY 1986. Assoc. Finley, Kumble, Wagner, Weine, Underberg, Manley, Myerson & Casey, 1985—86, Cahill Gordon & Reindel LLP, 1986—94, ptnr., 1994—. Named Dealmaker of Yr., Am. Lawyer, 2001; named one of Am. Lawyer 45 Under Forty-Five, 2003, Chambers U.S.A. and Global Leading Lawyers, 2004, 2005, 2006; scholar Harlan Fiske Stone scholar, Columbia Law Sch. Office: Cahill Gordon & Reindel LLP 80 Pine St New York NY 10005-1702 Office Phone: 212-701-3000. Business E-Mail: jschaffzin@cahill.com.

**SCHAIE, K. WARNER (KLAUS WARNER SCHAIE),** human development and psychology educator; b. Stettin, Germany (now Poland), Feb. 1, 1928; came to U.S., 1947, naturalized, 1953; s. Sally and Lottie Luise (Gabriel) S.; m. Coloma J. Patmore, Aug. 9, 1953 (div. 1973); 1 child, Stephan; m. Sherry L. Willis, Nov. 20, 1981. AA, City Coll., San Francisco, 1951; BA, U. Calif., Berkeley, 1952; MS, U. Wash., 1953, PhD, 1956; DPhil (hon.), Friedrich-Schiller U., Jena, Germany, 1997; ScD (hon.), W.Va. U., 2002. Lic. psychologist, Calif., Pa. Fellow Washington U., St. Louis, 1956-57; asst. prof. psychology U. Nebr., Lincoln, Nebr., 1957-64, assoc. prof., 1964-68; prof. chmn. dept. psychology W.Va. U., Morgantown, W.Va., 1964-73; prof. psychology, dir. Gerontology Rsch. Inst., U. So. Calif., 1973-81; Evan Pugh prof. human devel. and psychology Pa. State U., University Park, 1981—, dir. Gerontology Ctr., 1985—2003; affiliate prof. psychiatry and behavioral scis. U. Wash., 1991—. Devel. behavior study sect. NIH, Bethesda, Md., 1970-72, chmn., 1972-74, chmn. human devel. and aging study sect., 1979-84, expert panel in comml. airline pilot retirement, 1981, data and safety bd. ship project, 1984-91. Author: Developmental Psychology; A Life Span Approach, 1981, Adult Development and Aging, 1982, 5th rev. edit., 2002, Japanese, Chinese and Spanish edits., 2003, Intellectual Development in Adulthood: The Seattle Longitudinal Study, 1996, Developmental Influences on Adult Intelligence, 2005; editor: Handbook of Psychology of Aging, 1977, 6th rev. edit., 2006, Longitudinal Studies of Adult Development, 1983, Cognitive Functioning and Social Structure over the Life Course, 1987, Methodological Issues in Research on Aging, 1988, Social Structure and Aging: Psychological Processes, 1989, Age Structuring in Comparative Perspective, 1989, The Course of Later Life, 1989, Self-Directedness: Cause and Effects Throughout the Life Course, 1990, Aging, Health Behaviors and Health Outcomes, 1992, Caregiving Systems: Formal and Informal Helpers, 1993, Societal Impact on Aging: Historical Perspectives, 1993, Adult Intergenerational Relations: Effects of Societal Change, 1995, Older Adults Decision Making and the Law, 1996, Impact of Social Structures on Decision Making in the Elderly, 1997, Impact of the Workplace on Older Persons, 1998, Handbook of Theories of Aging, 1999, Mobility and Aging, 2000, Evolution of the Aging Self, 2000, Effective Health Behavior in the Elderly, 2002, Mastery and Control in the Elderly, 2003, Influence of Technology on Successful Aging, 2003; Independent Aging: Living Arrangements and Mobility, 2003, Religious Influences on Health and Wellbeing in the Elderly, 2004, Historical Influences on Lives and Aging, 2005, Social Structures, Self-Regulation and Aging, 2006; editor Ann. Rev. Gerontology and Geriat., vol. 7, 1987, vol. 11, 1991, vol. 17, 1997, series editor, 1996—; contbr. articles to profl. jours. Fellow APA (coun. reps. 1976-79, 83-86, Disting. Contbn. award, 1992), Am. Psychol. Soc., Gerontol. Soc. (Kleemeier award 1987, Disting. Mentorship award 1996); mem. Psychometric Soc., Internat. Soc. Study Behavioral Devel., Mensa (Lifetime Achievement award, 2000). Unitarian Universalist. Avocations: hiking, stamps. Home: 425 Windmere Dr apt 3A State College PA 16801-7670 Office: Pa State Univ Gerontology Ctr 135 E Nittany Ave Ste 405 State College PA 16801 Office Phone: 814-863-9735. Business E-Mail: kws@psu.edu.

**SCHAIN, RICHARD,** neurologist, consultant; s. Maurice and Beatrice Gaier Schain; m. Melanie Dreisbach, Aug. 15, 1980; children: Eliot, Randy. BA in philosophy, NYU, 1950, MD, 1954. Cert. neurologist Am. Bd. of Psychiatry and Neurology, 1965. Assoc. prof. U. Nebr., Coll. of Medicine, Omaha, 1962—66; prof. UCLA, 1967—80; cons. neurology Sonoma Devel. Ctr., Eldridge, Calif., 1980—. Author: Neurology of Childhood Learning Disorders, 1975, Legend of Nietzsche's Syphilis, 2001, Reverence for the Soul, 2001, Radical Metaphysics, 2002. Cpt. USAF, 1955—57, Maine. Mem.: Phi Beta Kappa. Home: PO Box 7508 Cotati CA 94931 Office: PO Box 1493 Eldridge CA 95431 Office Fax: 707-793-7519. E-mail: rjschain@lycos.com.

**SCHAIR, ROBIN A.,** lawyer; b. Bronx, NY, Sept. 30, 1961; BA, SUNY, Binghamton, 1982; JD, Albany Law Sch., Union Coll., 1985. Bar: NY 1986, US Dist. Ct. Ea. Dist. NY, US Dist. Ct. So. Dist. NY. Asst. dist. atty. Bronx Dist. Atty.'s Office, NY, 1985—93; ptnr. Wilson, Elser, Moskowitz, Edelman & Dicker LLP, NYC. Office: Wilson Elser Moskowitz Edelman & Dicker LLP 150 E 42nd St 23rd Fl New York NY 10017-5639 Office Phone: 212-490-3000 ext. 2209. Office Fax: 212-490-3038. Business E-Mail: schairr@wemed.com.

**SCHAITBERGER, HAROLD,** protective services official, labor union administrator; From firefighter to lt. Fairfax County, Va., 1966, lt.; from head legis. programs to gen. pres. Internat. Assn. Fire Fighters, Washington, 1976—2000, gen. pres., 2000—. Chmn. bd. trustees Internat. Assn. Fire Fighters Burn Found.; bd. dir. Internat. Assn. Fire Fighter Meml., Nat. Fallen Fire Fighter Meml. Mem.: AFL-CIO (exec. coun., v.p. transp. trade dept., v.p maritime trade dept.), Muscular Dystrophy Assn. (v.p.). Office: Federal Firefighters Assn 1750 New York Ave NW 3rd Fl Washington DC 20006

**SCHAKE, LOWELL MARTIN,** zoology educator, writer; b. Marthasville, Mo., June 6, 1938; s. Martin Charles and Flora Olinda (Rocklage) S.; m. Wendy Anne Walkinshaw, Sept. 11, 1959; children: Sheryl Anne, Lowell Scott. BS, U. Mo., 1960, MS, 1962. Tex. A&M U., 1967. Asst. prof. Tex. A&M U., College Station, 1965-67, assoc. prof., 1969-72, prof., 1972-84, asst. prof. animal sci., 1969; prof., head animal sci. dept. U. Conn., Storrs, 1984-92; prof., chmn. animal sci. dept. Tex. Tech. U., Lubbock, 1992—95. Developer applied animal ethology program Tex. A&M U., 1970, New Eng. Biotech Conf. series, 1990, S.W. Beef Forum, 1993; chmn. Am. Registry of Profl. Animal Scientist from on Profl. Stds., 1988; chmn. Nat. Com. Exec. Officers of Animal Vet., Dairy and Poultry Sci. Depts., 1992; cons. Alpart, Kingston, Jamaica, 1975, U.S. Feeds Grain Coun., 1970-73, A.O. Smith Products Inc., 1968-92, Humphrey Land & Cattle Co., Dallas, 1980-86; lectr. in field. Author: Growth and Finishing of Beef Cattle, A Class Handbook, 1982, La Charette: Village Gateway to the American West, 2003; contbr. articles to profl. jours. Recipient Innovative Teaching award Tex. A&M U., 1978. Mem. Am. Soc. Animal Sci., Plains Nutrition Coun. (adv. bd. 1967-80, sec.-treas. 1994-95, founder), Nat. Assn. Colls. and Tchrs. Agr., Am. Registry Profl. Animal Scientists (dir. for Northeast 1987-89), Coun. for Agr. Sci. and Tech. World Conf. on Animal Prodn., Am. Soc. Dairy Sci., Tiger Club (College Station) (pres.), Gamma Sigma Delta. Republican. Avocations: genealogy, fishing, gardening. Home: 142 Five Dove Cir Port Aransas TX 78373 E-mail: wschake1@centurytel.net.

**SCHAKOWSKY, JANICE,** congresswoman; b. Chgo., May 26, 1944; d. Irwin and Tillie (Cosnow) Danoff; m. Harvey E. Schakowsky, Feb. 17, 1965 (div. 1980); children: Ian, Mary; m. Robert B. Creamer, Dec. 6, 1980; 1 stepchild, Lauren. BS, U. Ill., 1965. Cert. elem. tchr., Ill. Tchr. Chgo. Bd. Edn., 1965-67; organizer Ill. Pub. Action Coun., Chgo., 1976-85; exec. dir. Ill. State Coun. Sr. Citizens, Chgo., 1985-90; mem. Ill. Ho. Reps., 1990-98, US Congress from 9th Ill. dist., 1999—; mem. banking and fin. svcs. com., 1999—2000; mem. govt. reform com., 1999—2000; Ho. Dem. leadership team-deputy whip; mem. energy and commerce Com. Bd. dirs. Ill. Pub. Action, 4 C's Day Care Coun., Evanston, Ill.; steering com. mem. Cook County Dem. Women, 1986-90; del. Nat. Dem. Conv., 1988; governing coun. Am. Jewish Congress, 1990—. Named Outstanding Legislator Interfaith Coun. for Homeless, 1993, Legislator of Yr. Ill. Nurses Assn., 1992, Ill. Assn. Cmty. Mental Health Agys., 1994, Coalition of Citizens with Disabilities and Ill. Coun. Sr. Citizens, 1993, Cmty. Action Assn., 1991, Champaign County Health Care Assn., 1992, Rookie of Yr. Ill. Environ. Coun., 1991. Mem. ACLU, NOW, Nat. Coun. Jewish Women, Ill. Pro-Choice Alliance, Evanston Mental Health Assn., Evanston Hist. Soc., Evanston Friends of Libr., Rogers Park Hist. Soc. Democrat. Jewish. Avocations: travel, horsebackriding, reading. Office: US Ho Reps 1027 Longworth Ho Office Bldg Washington DC 20515-1309 also: Dist Office 5533 Broadway St Chicago IL 60640 Office Phone: 202-225-2111.

**SCHALIT, ROBERT EDWARD,** advertising executive; b. Albany, N.Y., Nov. 19, 1954; s. Samuel and Ann Ethal S.; m. Margaret Foye, Aug. 26, 1989. BA in English Lit., SUNY, Binghamton, 1976. Sr. writer Fairbrother & Co. Advt., Valatie, NY, 1999—2000; sr. copywriter Rueckert Advt. Pub. Rels., Albany, NY, 2000—. Freelance advt. copywriter Robert Schalit Freelance Copywriter, Schenectady, NY, 1990—. Author: (numerous ads, tv and radio commls.) CDPHP (HMO) Advertising Campaign. Bd. mem. Ind. Living in the Capital Dist., Schenectady, NY, 1983—84; support group facilitator The Samaritans Suicide Prevention, Albany, NY, 1990—93; pres. Creative Club, Albany, NY, 1988—89. Recipient awards, NORI. Mem.: Am. Mktg. Assn. (Capital region chpt.), The Ad Club, Phi Beta Kappa (bd. dirs. Upper Hudson Assn.). Democrat. Jewish. Avocations: reading, poetry, blues harmonica, fitness activities, ship model building. Home: 1133 Van Curler Ave Schenectady NY 12308 Office: Rueckert Advtsg Pub Rels 638 Albany-Shaker Rd Albany NY 12211

**SCHALK, GERWIN,** research scientist, software engineer; b. Fuerstenfeld, Styria, Austria, July 6, 1971; s. Dieter Erwin and Rosina Schalk; m. Renate Eva Brunner, Dec. 19, 1973; children: Erik Christopher, Alexander Tristan. MS, Graz U. of Tech., Austria, 1999, Rensselaer Poly. Inst., Troy, N.Y., 2001, PhD, 2006. Rsch. scientist Wadsworth Ctr., N.Y. State Dept. of Health, Albany, 1999—. Contbr. articles to sci. jours. Recipient Frontiers of Engring. award, NAE, 2004, Kurt Goedel stipend, Graz U. of Tech., 1997, Altran Tech. Innovation award (mem. of winning group), Altran Corp., 2005, Pirelli Internetional award (mem. of winning group), Pirelli Corp., 2005. Mem.: IEEE Medicine and Biology, Soc. for Neurosci., Sigma Xi. Achievements include patents for Brain computer interface. Office: Wadsworth Ctr NY State DOH E1001 Empire State Plz Albany NY 12201 Office Phone: 518-486-2559. Office Fax: 518-486-4910. E-mail: schalk@wadsworth.org.

**SCHALL, ALVIN ANTHONY,** federal judge; b. NYC, 1944; s. Gordon William and Helen Schall; m. Sharon Frances LeBlanc, Apr. 25, 1970; children: Amanda Anthony Davis. BA, Princeton U., 1966; JD, Tulane U., 1969. Bar: N.Y. 1970, U.S. Dist. Ct. (so. and ea. dists.) N.Y. 1973, U.S. Ct. Appeals (2d crct.) 1974, D.C. 1980, U.S. Dist. Ct. D.C. 1991, U.S. Ct. Appeals (D.C. crct.) 1991, U.S. Ct. Fed. Claims 1982, U.S. Ct. Appeals (fed. crct.) 1987, U.S. Supreme Ct. 1989. Assoc. Shearman & Sterling, N.Y.C., 1969—73; asst. U.S. atty. ea. dist. N.Y. Borough of Bklyn., 1973—78, chief appeals divsn., 1977—78; trial atty. civil divsn. U.S. Dept. Justice, Washington, 1978—87, sr. trial counsel, 1986—87, asst. to atty. gen., 1988—92; ptnr. Perlman & Ptnrs., Washington, 1987—88; judge U.S. Ct. Appeals (fed. cir.), Washington, 1992—. Office: 717 Madison Pl NW Washington DC 20439-0002

**SCHALL, DEBRA JEAN,** secondary school educator; b. Hartford, Wis., Oct. 2, 1952; d. Eugene Ernst and Elva Lydia (Baerenwald) S. BS, U. Wis., Oshkosh, 1974; MA, Marian Coll., 1992. Lic. secondary educator English, history, reading. Tchr. Oshkosh Area Pub. Schs., Wis., 1974—; coach volleyball, 1974—98, coach track, 1974-88, coach basketball, 1982-84. Mem. Sch. Improvement and Effectiveness Com., Oshkosh, 1984-91, 93-2001. Mem. Sch. Partnership Com., 1995-2001. Named Mid. Sch. Tchr. of Yr., Oshkosh Area Sch. Dist., 1996—97. Mem.: Wis. Edn. Assn. (del., rep. assembly 2004—06), Oshkosh Edn. Assn. (v.p. 2004—), Wis. Assn. Mid. Level Edn., NEA. Avocations: gardening, reading, crochet work.

**SCHALLER, ANTHONY JOSEF,** technology management executive; b. Pitts., Nov. 17, 1957; s. Josef and Ruth Bridgette (Petschick) S.; m. Anna Marie Johnson (div. Nov. 1997); children: Kristofer, Derek. BS in Computer Sci. and Bus. Mgmt., U. Pitts., 1982; grad. degree computer sci., Carnegie-Mellon U., 1987. Mgr. sys. devel. Carnegie-Mellon U., Pitts., 1980-87; sr. mgr. applications engring. Ingres Corp., Alameda, Calif., 1988-91; dir. tech. mktg. MTI/SF2 Corp., Sunnyvale, Calif., 1991-92; dir. multidatabase sys. devel. MDL Info. Sys., Inc., San Leandro, Calif., 1992-93, dir. intersect project, 1993-94; pres., founder Intersect Software, Inc., Alameda, 1994-97; v.p. engring., chief tech. officer Open Object/Electric Classifieds, Inc., San Francisco, 1997-98; v.p. tech. Ticketmaster Online-CitySearch, Inc., Pasadena, Calif., 1998-99; sr. v.p. tech., chief tech. officer, COO RioPort.com, San Jose, Calif., 1999—2003; sr. v.p. tech. strategy Yahoo, Sunnyvale, Calif., 2003—. Bd. dirs. Altenheim Assn., Oakland, Calif., ZealMedia, Inc., L.A.; tech./mgmt. cons. Turnaround Mgmt. Assn., Alameda, 1998-2004. Mem. Assn. for Computing Machinery (program devel. and spkr. liason/coord. Pitts. chpt. 1983-84, vice-chmn. Pitts. chpt. 1984-85, chmn. Pitts. chpt. 1985-86, Svc. Recognition award 1985, 86). Achievements include patent for system and methods for performing multi-source searches over heterogeneous databases. Home: 211 Encounter Bay Alameda CA 94502-7909 Office: RioPort com 2895 Zanker Rd San Jose CA 95134-2101 Office Phone: 510-541-5480. Fax: 707-221-1598. E-mail: tony@schaller.net.

**SCHALLER, BARRY R.,** judge; BA, Yale U., 1960, JD, 1963. Bar: Conn. 1963, US Dist. Ct. Conn. 1963, US Ct. Appeals (2nd cir.) 1964, US Supreme Ct. 1966. Ptnr. Bronson & Rice, Atty., New Haven, 1963-74; judge Ct. of Common Pleas, Cir., Conn., 1974-78, Superior Ct., Conn., 1978-92, Appellate Ct., Conn., 1992—. Counsel to Ho. of Reps., 1969; bd. pardons State of Conn., 1971-74, chair, 1973-74; exec. com. Conn. Planning Com. on Criminal Adminstrn., 1972-74; chair Superior Ct. Benchbook Com., 1985-92; vis. lectr. Yale Coll., 1986, 88, Trinity Coll., 2003—, Wesleyan (Conn.) U., 2003-, Vt. Law Sch., 2003-04, U. Conn. Sch. Pub. Health, 2005—; clin. instr. evidence and trial practice Yale Law Sch., 1989—; adj. prof., Quinnipiac Law Sch., 2002; lectr. W.Va. Magistrates Conf., 1990, Vt. Jud. Coll., 1992, Fla. Jud. Coll., 1993-94, 96, 99, 2002, 04, Ohio Jud. Coll., 1999, 2002, Mo. Jud. Coll., 2002, hosp. ethics com., others; faculty Nat. Jud. Coll. Conn. Judges Inst., 1997-99; mem. Superior Ct. Jury Instrn. Com., 1993-97; exec. com. Conn. Ctr. for Jud. Edn., 1989-92; active Superior Ct. Civil Case Mgmt. Task Force; jud. evidence code drafting com.; mem. biochem. com. Middlesex Hosp., 2004—. Author: A Vision of American Law: Judging Law, Literature, and the Stories We Tell, 1997, A Legal Prescription for Bioethical Ills, Quinnipiac Law Review, 2002; contbr. articles to profl. jours. Assoc. fellow Branford Coll., 1990-2005, adminstrv. co-sec. Yale Class of 1960; mem. adv. com. Fair Haven Mediation Bd., 1980-82; bd. dirs. Russian-Am. Rule of Law Project, 2001-04; mem. working groups Yale Bioethics Project, adv. com. Donghahue Found. Yale; vestry mem., tchr. Trinity Ch., Branford, St. Andrew's Ch., Madison; mem. bioethics com. Middlesex Hosp.; mem. instnl. review bd. (IRB) St. Francis Hosp. and Health Ctr. Recipient book award Quinnipic Law Sch., 1997; Guggenheim fellow Yale Law Sch., 1975-76, 84, 85-86. Fellow Conn. Bar Found. (charter life, fellows adv. com.); mem. Conn. Bar Assn., Hartford County Bar Assn., New Haven County Bar Assn., Conn. Judges Assn. (dir. 1990-92), Am. Law Inst., Yale Law Sch. Assn. (exec. com.

**SCHALLER, GEORGE BEALS,** zoologist; b. Berlin, May 26, 1933; s. Georg Ludwig S. and Bettina (Byrd) Iwersen; m. Kay Suzanne Morgan, Aug. 26, 1957; children: Eric, Mark. BS in Zoology, U. Alaska, 1955, BA in Anthropology, 1955; PhD in Zoology, U. Wis., 1962. Rsch. assoc. Johns Hopkins U., Balt., 1963—66; rsch. zoologist Wildlife Conservation Soc., Bronx, NY, 1966—. Rsch. assoc. Am. Mus. Natural History. Author: The Mountain Gorilla, 1963 (Wildlife Soc. award 1965), The Year of the Gorilla, 1964, The Deer and the Tiger, 1967, The Serengeti Lion, 1972 (Nat. Book award 1973), Golden Shadows, Flying Hooves, 1973, Mountain Monarchs, 1977, Stones of Silence, 1980, The Giant Pandas of Wolong, 1985, The Last Panda, 1993, Tibet's Hidden Wilderness, 1997, Wildlife of the Tibetan Steppe, 1998; co-editor (with E.Vrba) Antelopes, Deer and Relatives, 2000. Decorated Order of Golden Ark, Netherlands, 1978; recipient Gold medal World Wildlife Fund, 1980, Explorers medal Explorers Club, 1990, Cosmos prize Japan, 1996, Tyler Environ. prize, 1997; Ctr. Advanced Study in Behavorial Scis. fellow Stanford U., 1962, fellow Guggenheim Found., 1971. Office: Wildlife Conservation Soc Bronx Park Bronx NY 10460 Business E-Mail: asiaprogram@wcs.org.

**SCHALLER, JANE GREEN,** pediatrician; b. Cleve., June 26, 1934; d. George and May Alice (Wing) Green; children: Robert Thomas, George Charles, Margaret May. AB, Hiram Coll., Ohio, 1956; MD cum laude, Harvard U., 1960. Diplomate Am. Bd. Pediat., Am. Bd. Med. Examiners. Resident in pediat. Children's Hosp.-U. Wash., Seattle, 1960-63; fellow immunology Children's Hosp. U. Wash., 1963-65; faculty U. Wash. Med. Sch., 1965-83, prof. pediat., 1975-83; head divsn. rheumatic diseases Children's Hosp., Seattle, 1968-83; prof. chmn. dept. pediat., pediatrician-in-chief Tufts U. Sch. Medicine/New Eng. Med. Ctr., 1983-98; Karp prof. pediat. Tufts U. Sch. Medicine, Boston, 1983—, disting. prof., 1995—. Vis. physician Med. Rsch. Coun., Taplow, Eng., 1971-72; adj. prof. diplomacy The Fletcher Sch. Law and Diplomacy, Tufts U., 1998-2000. Contbr. articles to profl. jours. Bd. dirs. Seattle Chamber Music Festival, 1982-85; trustee Boston Chamber Music Soc., 1985—; mem. Boston adv. coun. UNICEF, tech. advisor UN Study on the Impact of Armed Conflict on Children, 1995-97; chmn. adv. com. children's rights divsn. Human Rights Watch, 1995—; mem. adv. com. Middle East divsn., 1998—; exec. com. Women's Commn. for Refugee Women and Children Internat. Rescue com., 1989-94, adv. coun. 1994—. Mem.: AAAS, Royal Coll. Pediats. U.K., Internat. Women's Forum, Mass. Women's Forum, Harvard U. Med. Sch. Alumni Coun. (v.p. 1977—80, pres. 1982—83), Physicians for Human Rights (founding pres. 1986—89, exec. com. 1986—), Com. Health in So. Africa (exec. com. 1986—92), Assn. Med. Sch. Pediat. Chmn. (exec. com. 1986—89, rep. to coun. on govt. affairs and coun. acad. socs.), New Eng. Pediat. Soc. (pres. 1991—93), Am. Coll. Rheumatology, Internat. Pediat. Assn. (pres.-elect 1998—2001, pres. 2001—04, exec. dir. 2004—), Am. Acad. Pediat. (exec. com. sect. on internat. child health, head children's rights program, rep. to UNICEF), Am. Pediat. Soc., Soc. Pediat. Rsch., Inst. Medicine of NAS, Saturday Club, Tavern Club, Aesculapian Club (pres. 1988—89). Office: Floating Hosp for Children 750 Washington St # 8683 Boston MA 02111-1526 Business E-Mail: jschaller@tufts-nemc.org.

**SCHALLER-DEMERS, DEBRA SUSAN,** education coordinator; b. Bronx, N.Y., Feb. 12, 1956; d. Emanuel and Gloria (Rosenberg) Schaller; m. Richard Raymond Demers, Sept. 11, 1977; children: Jaeson Demers, Alexander Demers. BA cum laude, Queens Coll., N.Y., 1977; MS, Capella Univ., 2004—. Graphic artist Reproducta, Inc., N.Y., 1979—83; calligraphy instr. Forest Hills Adult Ctr., N.Y., 1989—95; program assoc., parent coord. Educators for Social Responsibility, N.Y., 1992—2002; edn. coord., rsch. integrity Weill Med. Coll. Cornell Univ., N.Y., 2002—. Cons. in field. Mem. PTA, Forest Hills, 2003—; vol. Forest Hills Youth Athletic Assn., 1990—2002; founding. mem. Grand Ctrl. Pkwy. Players, 1993—99. Mem.: Responsible Conduct of Rsch. Edn. Consortium, Soc. Rsch. Adminstrt. Internat. Avocations: art, parent/student education advocacy. Office: Weill Med Coll Cornell Univ 425 E 61 St Ste 301 New York NY 10021

**SCHALLERT, EDWIN GLENN,** lawyer; b. LA, Aug. 7, 1952; s. William Joseph and Rosemarie Diane (Waggner) S. AB, Stanford U., 1974; JD, MPP, Harvard U., 1981. Bar: N.Y. 1974, U.S. Ct. Appeals (7th cir.) 1986, U.S. Ct. Appeals (2d cir.) 1989, U.S. Dist. Ct. (so. dist.) N.Y. 1975. Legis. aid to U.S. rep. Les Aspin, Washington, 1975-78; law clk. to Hon. J. Skelly Wright, 1981-82; law clk. to Hon. Thurgood Marshall, 1982-83; assoc. Debevoise & Plimpton LLP, NYC, 1983-89, ptnr., 1989—, mem. litig. dept., 1983—90. Mem. Internat. Inst. for Strategic Studies, Coun. Fgn. Rels. (term mem. 1983-88), Phi Beta Kappa. Democrat. Avocation: tennis. Office: Debevoise & Plimpton LLP 919 Third Ave New York NY 10022 Office Phone: 212-909-6295. Office Fax: 212-909-6836. E-mail: egschallert@debevoise.com.

**SCHALLERT, WILLIAM JOSEPH,** actor; b. Los Angeles, July 6, 1922; s. Edwin Francis and Elza Emily (Baumgarten) S.; m. Rosemarie Diann Waggner, Feb. 26, 1949; children: William Joseph, Edwin G., Mark M., Brendan C. BA, UCLA, 1946. Co-founder, owner Circle Theatre, Hollywood, Calif., 1947-50. Appeared in motion pictures, TV, stage, radio, 1947—; movies include Lonely Are the Brave, Heat of the Night, Charley Varrick, Red Badge of Courage, Teachers; starred in TV series Patty Duke Show, 1963-66, Nancy Drew Mysteries, 1977-78, Little Women, 1979, The New Gidget, 1986-88, The Torkelson's, 1991-92; starred as judge in stage play and film The Trial of the Catonsville Nine, N.Y.C., Los Angeles, 1971 (Obie award 1971); starred as Dr. Pangloss in Candide, L.A., 1995; recorded voice of Abraham Lincoln for permanent installation at Lincoln Mus., Springfield, Ill., 2004. Trustee Motion Picture and TV Fund, 1977—. With AUS, 1942-44; with USAAC, 1944-45. Fulbright fellow Brit. Repertory Theatre, 1952-53. Mem. ASCAP, SAG (pres. 1979-81, trustee pension and health plan 1983—, founder Com. for Performers with Disabilities 1981—, Ralph Morgan award 1993). Personal E-Mail: schlat80@yahoo.com.

**SCHALLY, ANDREW VICTOR,** endocrine oncologist, researcher; b. Poland, Nov. 30, 1926; arrived in U.S., 1957; s. Casimir Peter and Maria (Lacka) Schally; m. Ana Maria Comaru, Aug. 1976 (dec. Sept. 2004). BSc, McGill U., Can., 1955, PhD in Biochemistry, 1957; 29 hon. doctorates. Research asst. biochemistry Nat. Inst. Med. Research, London, 1949—52; dept. psychiatry McGill U., Montreal, Que., 1952—57; rsch. assoc., asst. prof. physiology and biochemistry Coll. Medicine, Baylor U., Houston, 1957—62; assoc. prof. Tulane U. Sch. Medicine, New Orleans, 1962—67, prof., 1967—2006; chief Endocrine Polypeptide and Cancer Inst. VA Med. Ctr., New Orleans, 1962—2006, with Miami, Fla., 2006—. Sr. med. investigator VA Med. Ctr., 1973—99, disting. med. rsch. scientist, 1999—; prof. Miller Sch. Medicine U. Miami, 2006—. Author: The Hypothalamus and Pituitary in Health and Disease, 1972; contbr. articles to profl. jours. Co-recipient Nobel prize for medicine, 1977; recipient Van Meter prize, Am. Thyroid Assn., 1969, Ayerst-Squibb award, Endocrine Soc., 1970, William S. Middletown award, VA, 1970, Ch. Mickle award, U. Toronto, 1974, Gairdner Internat. award, 1974, Borden award, Assn. Am. Med. Colls. and Borden Co. Found., 1975, Lasker Basic Rsch. award, 1975; fellow sr. rsch. fellow, USPHS, 1961—62. Mem.: AAAS, NAS, Royal Acad. Medicine Spain, Acad. Sci. Mex., Acad. Sci. Russia, Acad. Sci. Hungary, Acad. Med. Poland, Acad. Medicine Venezuela, Nat. Acad. Medicine Brazil, Mexican Acad. Medicine, Soc. Internat. Brain Rsch. Orgn., Soc. Exptl. Biol. Medicine, Soc. Biol. Chemists, Am. Physiol. Soc., Endocrine Soc. Home: Apt 1405 8440 S Dixie Hwy Miami FL 33143 Office: VA Hosp Research 151 1201 NW 16 St Miami FL 33125 Office Phone: 305-575-3477. Office Fax: 305-575-3126. Business E-Mail: andrew.schally@va.gov.

**SCHALOW, FRANK HICKEY,** philosopher, educator; b. Denver, Feb. 23, 1956; s. Berthold Erich and Frances Schalow. BA summa cum laude, U. Denver, 1978; MA, Tulane U., 1980, PhD, 1984. Vis. asst. prof. Loyola U.,

New Orleans, 1984-86, asst. prof., 1986-90, assoc. prof., 1990-92; lectr. Dillard U., New Orleans, 1993—; vis. assoc. prof. Xavier U., New Orleans, 1994-97, U. New Orleans, 1995—. Mem. editl. adv. bd. Auslegung U. Kans., Lawrence, 1983-97, Heidegger Studies U. Wis., LaCrosse, 2000—; mem. dissertation adv. bd. Union Inst., Cin., 1999—. Author: Imagination and Existence, 1986, Renewal of the Heidegger-Kant Dialogue, 1992, Language and Deed, 1998, Heidegger and the Quest for the Sacred, 2001, Incarnality of Being, 2006; co-author: Traces of Understanding, 1990. Mem. Am. Philos. Assn., N.Am. Heidegger Conf. (sec. convenor 1992), S.W. Philosophy Soc. (exec. com. 1993), Phi Beta Kappa. Avocation: golf. Home: 7310 Freret St New Orleans LA 70118 Office: U New Orleans Lakefront Campus New Orleans LA 70148 Business E-Mail: fschalow@uno.edu.

**SCHAMA, SIMON,** historian, educator, author; b. London, Feb. 13, 1945; married; 2 children. BA, Cambridge (Eng.) U., 1966, MA in History, 1969. Fellow Christ's Coll. Cambridge U., England, 1966—76; fellow and tutor in modern history Brasenose Coll., Oxford, England, 1976—80; prof. history, Mellon prof. social sciences, and William Kenan prof. humanities Harvard U., Cambridge, Mass., 1980—93, sr. assoc. Ctr. European Studies; prof. Ecole des Hautes Etudes en Sciences Sociales; Trevelyan lectr. Cambridge U.; Tanner lectr. on Rubens and Rembrandt Oxford U.; Tanner lectr. Harvard U. 2002; University prof. Columbia U., NYC. Author: Patriots and Liberators: Revolution in the Netherlands, 1780-1813, 1977 (Wolfson prize for history 1977, Leo Gershoy Meml. prize Am. Hist. Assn. 1978), Two Rothschilds and the Land of Israel, 1979, The Embarrassment of Riches: An Interpretation of Dutch Culture in the Golden Age, 1987, Citizens: A Chronicle of the French Revolution, 1989 (NCR prize for non-fiction), Dead Certainties, 1991, Landscape and Memory, 1995, Rembrandt's Eyes, 1999, A History of Britain: At the Edge of the World, 3500 BC - 1603 AD, 2000, A History of Britain: The Wars of the British, 1603-1776, 2001, A History of Britain: The Fate of Empire, 1776-2000, 2002, Rough Crossings: Britain, the Slaves and the American Revolution, 2006; TV series for BBC: Art of the Western World, Rembrandt: The Public Gaze, Landscape and Memory, A History of Britain, The Power of Art, 2004. Office: Columbia U Dept History 522 Fayerweather Hall 1180 Amsterdam Ave New York NY 10027-7039 E-mail: sms53@columbia.edu.*

**SCHAMUS, JAMES ALLAN,** film company executive, film producer, screenwriter; b. Detroit, Sept. 7, 1959; s. Julian John Schamus and Clarita (Gershowitz) Karlin; m. Nancy Jean Kricorian; children: Nona Esther, Djuna Mariam. AB, U. Calif., Berkeley, 1982, MA, 1984. Asst. prof. Columbia U. N.Y.C., 1991-97, assoc. prof., 1997—; co-pres., co-chmn. GOOD Machine (bought by Universal Pictures and merged into new studio, Focus), N.Y.C., 1991—2002; co-pres. Focus Features, N.Y.C., 2002—06, pres., 2006; CEO specialty film divsn. NBC Universal, Inc., 2006—. Assisted in the finding of Independent TV Series, 1988; involved with Apparatus. Actor Keep It for Yourself, 1991; prodr: (films) The Golden Boat, 1991, Chicken Delight, 1991, Roy Cohn/Jack Smith, 1994, Walking and Talking, 1996, She's the One, 1996, Assault on Precinct 13, 2005; assoc. prodr., co-writer (films): Eat Drink Man Woman, 1994; assoc. prodr. In the Soup, 1992; exec. prodr.: (films) Warrior: Poison, 1991, The Life of Leonard Peltier, 1992, Swoon, 1992, What Happened Was..., 1994, Safe, 1995, The Brothers McMullen, 1995, Greetings From Africa, 1996, Arresting Gena, 1997, Office Killer, 1997, The Myth of Fingerprints, 1997, Wonderland, 1997, Happiness, 1998, Lola and Billy the Kid, 1999, Love God, 1999, The Lifestyle: Group Sex in the Suburbs, 2000, Crouching Tiger Hidden Dragon, 2000 (also writer), Buffalo Soldiers, 2001, Auto Focus, 2002; co-prodr. Thank You and Good Night, 1991, Sense and Sensibility, 1995; writer (films) Tortilla Soup, 2001; writer, prodr.: (films) The Wedding Banquet, 1993, Pushing Hands, 1995, The Ice Storm, 1997 (Best Screenplay, Cannes Film Festival 1997), Ride with the Devil, 1999, Hulk, 2003, Brokeback Mountain, 2005 (Best Theatrical Motion Picture, Producer Guild Am., 2006, Best Feature, Spirit Independent award, 2006, Outstanding Film, British Acad. Film and TV Arts, 2006) Recipient Brian Greenbaum award, 1994, NBC Screenwriter's Tribute, Natucket Film Festival, 2002; named one of 50 Most Powerful People in Hollywood, 2006. Mem. Assn. for Ind. Video and Film (bd. dirs.). Office: NBC Universal Rm 30 Rockefeller Plz New York NY 10112*

**SCHANFIELD, FANNIE SCHWARTZ,** community volunteer; b. Mpls., Dec. 25, 1916; d. Simon Zouberman and Mary (Schmilovitz) Schwartz; m. Melvin M. Stock, Oct. 27, 1943 (dec. Apr. 1944); 1 child, Moses Samuel Schanfield; m. Abraham Schanfield, Aug. 28, 1947; children: David Colman, Miriam Schanfield Kieffer. Student, U. Minn., 1962-75. Author: My Thoughts, 1996, Son, I Have Something to Tell You, 1997, Ma, I Wrote It Down, 1997, 20 April 44 WWII, 2001, The Other Family's Kids, 2004, The Duplex: Fran and Dan Lived Upstairs, 2004. Bd. dirs. Jewish Cmty. Ctr., Mpls., 1975-96, chairperson older adult needs, 1982-88; past pres. Bnai Emet Women's League, Mpls., 1988-90; rschr., advocate Hunger Hennepin County, Mpls., 1969-75; sec. Joint Religious Legis. Coalition (v.p., bd. dirs. Cmty. Housing Svc., Mpls., 1971-85. Recipient Citation of Honor, Hennepin County Commn., 1989, Lifetime Achievement award Jewish Comty. Ctr. Greater Mpls., 1995. Mem. NOW, Lupus Found. Minn., Internat. Soc. Poets, Hadassah (pres. 1967-69, Citation 1969, Nat. Leadershio award 2006). Jewish. Avocations: needlepoint, rug hooking, writing.

**SCHANNEP, JOHN DWIGHT,** brokerage house executive; b. Newport News, Va., May 23, 1934; s. Dwight Bahney and Harriet Louise (Quinn) S.; m. Helen Ann Harris, June 21, 1958; children: John Barton, Dwight David, Timothy Michael, Marie Louise. BS, U.S. Mil. Acad., 1956. Commd. 1st lst. U.S. Air Force, 1956, resigned, 1960; acct. exec. Dean Witter Reynolds, Phoenix, 1960-68, v.p., resident mgr. Tucson, 1968-83, sr. v.p., 1983-89; ret. Pres. Tucson Stock/Bond Club, 1971-72; bd. dirs. SNEDCO. Author, pub. Schannep Timing Indicator and the Dow Theory Investment Timing Newsletter (available on Internet), 1980—. Pres. Big Bros. Tucson, 1972-74. Mem. Nat. Assn. Security Dealers (Ariz. committeeman and chmn 1971 73), Tucson C. of C (v.p. 1971), Pinetop Lakes Golf and Country Club (mem. 1990-91, pres. 1991-93), West Point Soc. (pres. 1967), Lions (pres. Phoenix chpt. 1966.) Republican. Home: 5191 E Hill Place Dr Tucson AZ 85712-1346 E-mail: jackschannep@theriver.com, editor@thedowtheory.com.

**SCHAPIRO, DONALD,** lawyer; b. N.Y.C., Aug. 8, 1925; s. John Max and Lydia (Chaitkin) S.; m. Ruth Ellen Goldman, June 29, 1952 (dec. Aug. 1991); m. Linda N. Solomon, Oct. 10, 1993; children: Jane G., Robert A. AB, Yale U., 1944, LL.B., 1949. Bar: N.Y. 1949. Assoc. Paul, Weiss, Rifkind, Wharton & Garrison, N.Y.C., 1949-51; asst. chief counsel subcom. ways and means com. on adminstrn. revenue laws U.S. Ho. of Reps., Washington, 1951-52; assoc. Barrett, Smith, Schapiro, Simon & Armstrong, N.Y.C., 1952-55, partner, 1955-88; ptnr. Chadbourne & Parke, 1988—. Vis. lectr. law Yale U. Law Sch., 1949-78, 94-95, instr. law and econs., 1945-49. Mem. Order of Coif, Phi Beta Kappa, Phi Delta Phi. Home: 1035 5th Ave New York NY 10028-0135 Office: Chadbourne & Parke 30 Rockefeller Plz Fl 32 New York NY 11112-0129 E-mail: dschapiro@chadbourne.com.

**SCHAPIRO, JEROME BENTLEY,** chemicals executive; b. NYC, Feb. 7, 1930; s. Sol and Claire (Rose) Schapiro; m. Edith Irene Kravet, Dec. 27, 1953; children: Lois, Robert, Kenneth. B.Chem. Engring., Syracuse U., 1951; postgrad., Columbia U., 1951-52. Project engr. propellants Jr. US Naval Air Rocket Test Sta., Lake Denmark, NJ, 1954—; pres., Hwe.—. Lectr. detergent stds., drycleaning, care labeling, consumers stds., orgns., U.S., 1968—; U.S. del. spokesman on drycleaning Internat. Stds. Orgn.,Newton, Mass., 1971, Burssels, 1972, U.S. del. spokesman on dimensional stability of textiles, Paris, 1974, Ottawa, Can., 1977, Copenhagen, 1981; chmn. U.S. del. com. on consumer affairs, Geneva, 1974, 75, 76, spokesman U.S. del. on textiles, Pairs, 1974, mem. U.S. del. on care labeling of textiles, The Hague, Holland, 1974, U.S. del., chmn. del. coun. com. on consumer policy, Geneva, 1978, 79, 82, Israel, 1980, Paris, 1981, observer Internat. Std. Orgn./Consumer Com. on Policy meeting, Kyoto, Japan, 2000, Oslo, 2001; leader U.S. del. com. on dimensional stability of textiles, Manchester, Eng., 1984; fed. govtl. appointee to Industry Functional Adv. Com. on Stds., 1980-81; legal expert drycleaning techniques

and procedures. Mem. Montclair (N.J.) Sch. Study Com., 1968-69; co-founder Jewish Focus, Inc., 1991, pub. Catskill/Hudson Jewish Star, 1991-98; v.p., treas. synagogue. 1st lt. USAF, 1952-53. Fellow ASTM (chmn. com. D-12 Soaps and Detergents 1974-79, mem. standing com. on internat. stds. 1980-84, hon. mem. award com. D-13 textiles); mem. AIChE, Am. Nat. Stds. Inst. (vice-chmn. bd. dirs. 1983-85, exec. com. 1979-81, 83-85, bd. dirs. 1979-85, fin. com. 1982-85, chmn. consumer coun. 1976, 79, 80, 81, mem. steering com. to advise Dept. Comerce on implementation GATT agreements 1976-77, mem. exec. stds. coun. 1977-79, internat. stds. coun., chmn. internat. consumer policy adv. com. 1978-86), Am. Assn. Textile Chemists and Colorists (mem. exec. com. on rsch. 1974-77, chmn. com. on dry cleaning 1976-88, vice-chmn. internat. test methods com. 1982-86), Am. Chem. Soc. (emeritus), Stds. Engring. Soc. (cert.), Internat. Stds. Orgn. (mem. internat. stds. steering com. for consumer affairs 1978-81), Nat. Small Bus. Assn. (assoc. trustee 1983-85), Masons. Jewish. Home: PO Box 42 Gardiner NY 12525 Office: 158 Central Ave PO Box 7038 Rochelle Park NJ 07662-7038

**SCHAPIRO, MARY L.,** financial regulatory service executive; b. NYC, June 19, 1955; d. Robert D. and Susan (Hall) S.; m. Charles A. Cadwell, Dec. 13, 1980, 2 children BA, Franklin and Marshall Coll., 1977; JD, George Washington U., 1980. Bar: D.C. 1980. Trial atty., 1980-81; counsel to chmn. Commodity Futures Trading Comm., 1981-84; sr. v.p. Futures Industry Assn., 1984, gen. counsel, 1984-88; commr. SEC, Washington, 1988-94, acting chmn., 1993—94; chmn. Commodity Futures Trading Comm. (CFTC), Washington, 1994-96; pres. Nat. Assn. Securities Regulation, Inc., Washington, 1996—2002; vice chmn., pres., regulatory policy oversight divsn. Nat. Assn. Securities Dealers, Washington, 2002—06, chmn., CEO, 2006—. Mem. Tech. Com, and the Develop. Markets Com. of the Internat. Org. of Securities (IOSCO); chmn IOSCO Cons. Com., 2001—. Mem. bd. trustees, vice chmn. audit com. Franklin and Marshall Coll.; bd. dirs. Cinergy Corp., 1999—, Kraft Foods. Named Fin. Women's Assn. Pub. Sector Woman of the Yr., 2000. Office: Nat Assn Securities Dealers 1735 K St NW Washington DC 20006-1516*

**SCHAPIRO, MIRIAM,** artist; b. Toronto, Ont., Can., Nov. 15, 1923; d. Theodore and Fannie (Cohen) S. BA, State U. Iowa, 1945, MA, 1946, MFA, 1949; doctorate (hon.), Wooster Coll., 1983, Calif. Coll. Arts Crafts, 1989, Mpls. Coll. Art Design, 1994, Miami U., 1995, Moore Coll. Art, Phila., 1995. Co-orignator Womanhouse, Los Angeles, 1972, Heresies mag., N.Y.C., 1975; co-originator feminist art program Calif. Inst. Arts, Valencia, 1971; founding mem. Feminist Art Inst., N.Y.C.; mem. adv. bd. Women's Caucus for Art; assoc. mem. Heresies Collective; lectr. dept. art history U. Mich., 1987. Works in numerous books and catalogues; numerous one-woman shows including, Galerie Liatowitsch, Basel, Switzerland, 1979, Lerner Heller Gallery, N.Y.C., 1979, Barbara Gladstone Gallery, N.Y.C., 1980, Spencer Mus. Art, Lawrence, Kans., 1981, Everson Mus., Syracuse, N.Y., 1981, Galerie Rudolf Zwirner, Cologne, Fed. Republic Germany, 1981, Staatagalerie, Stuttgart, Fed. Republic Germany, 1983, Dart Gallery, Chgo, 1984, Bernice Steinbaum Gallery/Steinbaum Krauss Gallery, N.Y.C., 1986, 88, 90, 91, 94, 97, Brevard Art Ctr. and Mus., Melbourne, Fla., 1991, Guild Hall Mus., East Hampton, N.Y., 1992, ARC Gallery, Chgo., 1993, James Madison U., Harrisburg, Va., 1996, Nat. Mus. Am. Art Smithsonian Inst., Washington, 1997. others; retrospective exhbn., Wooster (Ohio) Coll. Art Mus., 1980; exhibited in numerous group shows, including, Palais de Beaux Arts, Brussels, 1979, Inst. Contemporary Art, Phila., 1979, Delahunty Gallery, Dallas, 1980, Indpls. Mus., 1980, Va. Mus., Richmond, 1980, Laguna Gloria Mus., Austin, Tex., 1980, R.O.S.C., Dublin, Ireland, 1980, Biennale of Sydney, Australia, 1982, Zurich, Switzerland, 1983, Sidney Janis Gallery, N.Y.C., 1984, Am. Acad. Arts and Letters, N.Y.C., 1985, Mus. Modern Art, N.Y.C., 1988, Whyte Mus. Can. Rockies, Banff, Alta., 1991, Nat. Mus. Women in Arts., Wash., 1993, Jane Voorhees Zimmerli art mus. Rutger's U., New Brunswick, N.J., 1994, Mus. of F.A. Boston, 1994, Santa Barbara Mus. of Art, 1994, Hudson River Mus. of Westchester, Yonkers, N.Y., 1995, Mus. of Contemporary Arts, Los Angeles, Calif. Bronx Mus. of the Arts, N.Y., 1995, Columbus (Ga.) Mus., 1996, Parrish Mus., Southampton, N.Y., 1997, Austin (Tex.) Mus., 1997, Whitney Mus., 2000; represented in permanent collections, Hirshhorn Mus., Washington, Bklyn. Mus., Met. Mus. Art, N.Y.C., Mus. Contemporary Art, San Diego, Mpls. Inst. Art, Mulvane Art Center, Topeka, Nat. Gallery Art, Washington, N.Y.U., Peter Ludwig Collection, Aachen, Germany, Stanford U., Palo Alto, Calif., Univ. Art Mus., Berkeley, Calif., Whitney Mus., N.Y.C., Worcester (Mass.) Art Mus., Santa Barbara (Calif.) Mus. Art, Nat. Mus. Am. Art Smithsonian Inst., Washington, also others; author: (books) Women and the Creative Process, 1974, Rondo: An Artists Book, 1988; sculpture Anna and David, Rosslyn, Va., 1987. Guggenheim fellow, 1987, Nat. Endowment for Arts fellow; grantee Ford Found.; recipient numerous other grants and fellowships. Mem. Coll. Art Assn. (past dir.). Office: Elly Flomenhaft Gallery 547 W 27th St Ste 308 New York NY 10001 *Process and ideology in an opulent, multilayered, eccentric and hopeful abstract art: 1. The need for order and stability. 2. The need to destroy order and stability in order to find something else. 3. Finding something else. Pattern, itself an architectural species, reflects order and stability. Then a need to create chaos as though life itself were taking place. Finally the binding layer by layer, the interpenetration of paint, fabric, photograph, tea towel, ribbon, lace, and glue. A collage: a simultaneity; a visual dazzlement, a multi-layering, a final message for the senses. And the ideology which inspires the work itself? That is feminism, the wish to have the art speak as a woman speaks. To be sensitive to the material used as though there were a responsibility to history to repair the sense of omission and to have each substance in the collage be a reminder of a woman's dreams. All of my works are auto-biographical. They are about the yearnings of a woman who decided a long time ago to become a painter.*

**SCHAPIRO, MORTON OWEN,** academic administrator; m. Mimi ? s pirro; children Matt Alissa, Rachel. BA in economics, Hofstra U., 1975; PhD, U. Pa., 1979. Prof. economics, asst. provost Williams Coll., 1980—91; chair, dept. economics U. So. Calif., 1991—94, dean, Coll. Letters, Arts and Sciences, 1994—2000, v.p. planning, 1998—2000; prof. economics Williams Coll., 2000—, pres., 2000—. Commentator Pub. Radio Internat; expert witness on econ. issues in higher edn. U.S. Congress; bd. dirs. Marsh & McLennan Cos. Inc., 2002—. Co-author (with Michael S. McPherson): Keeping College Affordable, 1991, Paying the Piper, 1993, The Student Aid Game, 1998; contbr. articles to profl. jours. Office: Office of the President Williams Coll PO Box 687 Williamstown MA 01267*

**SCHAPPELL, ABIGAIL SUSAN,** retired speech, language and hearing specialist, massage therapist, Reiki master; b. Pa., May 25, 1952; d. Felix and Ann (Getty) DeMoise; m. Gery Mylan Schappell, Oct. 20, 1979; 1 child, Jonathan Michael. BS with Master's equivalency, Longwood Coll., 1974; postgrad., Bloomsburg U., 1975—77; cert., Lehmann Sch. Massage and Muscle, 1991, East-West Sch. Massage Therapy, 1995—. Lic. speech-lang. pathologist, Pa. Speech-lang.-hearing specialist dept. pub. welfare Hamburg (Pa.) Ctr., 1975—2004; ret., 2004. Judge deaf posters and essays Virginville (Pa.) Grange, 1990—, judge Pa. State Grange Conv., 1997, tchr. emergency pers. on communicating with deaf and hard of hearing, 1991, 92; leader demonstrations and workshops on sign lang. and dysphagia, non-verbal comm., active listening to various orgns., 1978—; instr. ARC, 1999-2002; bd. dirs. Berks Deaf and Hard of Hearing Svcs., 2000—; sec., 2005—; presenter in field. Pub: (Boy Scouts Coun. manual), Scouting for the Handicapped, Hawk Mountain, 1981-82. Sign/del. to conf. Bible Sch. dir., mem. Zion's United Ch. of Christ, Windsor Castle, Pa., 1985—; rep. nat. triann. conv. Penn Laurel coun. Girl Scouts U.S., 1975; vol. residential monitoring project Berks County ARC, 1998-99. Named Virginville Grange Cmty. Citizen of Yr., 1994—95; named co-chair of outstanding Young Women of Am., 1984. Mem.: AAUW, Schuykill Haven Bus. and Profl. Women (Young Careerist local, dist. and state honors 1980—81, pres. 1983—84, asst. dir. dist. 9 1997—99, dist. 9 dir. 1999—2001, state mentoring com. 2001—03, dist. 9 parliamentarian 2002—04, state edn. and svc. funds com. 2003—05, state chair edn. and svc. funds 2005—06, individual devel. leadership program facilitator 2005—, state PAC com. 2006—; involvement on dist. and state level, presenter local, dist. and state level workshops, Eleanor Briner award as dist. 9 dir. 2000), Pa.

**SPEECH** and Hearing Assn., Yorktown chpt. DAR, Young Careerist Alumni Assn. (life), Hamburg Area Soccer Assn. (sec. 1989—94), Order Ea. Star (chaplain Blue Mountain chpt. 1981, 1982, assoc. conductress 2005—06, conductress 2006—). Republican. Avocations: massage, signing, music. Home: 531 S 4th St Hamburg PA 19526-1307

**SCHAR, DWIGHT C.,** construction executive; b. 1942; With Ryan Homes, Washington, 1986-77, NVLand, 1977—, NVR Inc., 1980-86, pres., CEO, 1986—2005, chmn., 2005—. Bd. dirs. NVCompanies Inc. Office: Dwight Schar 11700 Plaza America Dr Ste 500 Reston VA 20190-4792*

**SCHARF, CHARLES W.,** bank executive; married; two children. B, Johns Hopkins U., 1987; MBA, N.Y. U. With Comml. Credit Corp., 1987-95; various sr. positions to CFO Smith Barney, 1995-98; CFO global corp. & investment bank Citibank, 1998-2000; exec. v.p., CFO Bank One Corp., Chgo., 2000—. Office: Bank One Corp 1 Bank One Plaza Chicago IL 60670

**SCHARF, MICHAEL PAUL,** law educator; b. Pitts., Apr. 25, 1963; s. Harry and Joan (Seder) S.; m. Trina Elizabeth Smith, May 9, 1988; 1 child, Garrett Michael. AB, Duke U., 1985, JD, 1988. Bar: D.C. 1989. Jud. clk. U.S. Ct. Appeals (11th cir.), Jacksonville, Fla., 1988-89; atty.-adviser Office Legal Adviser, U.S. Dept. State, Washington, 1989-93; asst. prof. law New England Sch. of Law, Boston, 1993—96, assoc. prof. law, 1996—98; prof. law New England Sch. Law, Boston, 1998—2002, Case Western U., 2002—; founder, ptnr. Publ. Internat. Law Policy Group, 1995—. Mem. U.S. Del. to 46th and 47th Sessions of UN Gen. Assembly, U.S. Del. to 49th Session of UN Human Rights Commn.; adj. prof. Georgetown U. Law Ctr., Washington, 1992; chmn. bd. dirs. Internat. Model UN Assn. Inc. N.Y.C., 1984-88; dir. New Eng. Ctr. for Internat. Law and Policy, 1996—; expert commentator Ct. TV, 1996. Author: An Insider's Guide to the International Criminal Tribunal for the Former Yugoslavia, 1995, International Criminal Law: Cases and Materials, 1996, Balkan Justice: The Story Behind the First International War Crimes Trial Since Nuremberg, 1997, The Internat. Criminal Tribunal For Rwanda (with Morris), 1998. Nominee Nobel Peace Prize, 2005. Mem. ABA (U.S. Govt. rep. blue ribbon task force on internat. criminal ct. 1991-93), D.C. Bar (chmn. steering com. internat. law sect. 1991-93), Internat. Law Assn. (exec. com. Am. br. 1996—), Order of Coif, U.N. Assn. Greater Boston (bd. dirs. 1993—); Pub. Internat. Law Group (bd. dir., 1996-); Internat. Law Students Assn. Avocations: skiing, sailing, tennis, softball. E-mail: mps17@case.edu.*

**SCHARF, STEPHANIE A.,** lawyer; m. Jeffry Mandell; children: Meredith, Jonathan. BA, Rutgers U.; MA, Stanford U.; PhD, U. Chgo., 1978, JD, 1985. Bar: Ill. 1985, US Dist. Ct. (no. ctrl. and so. dists.) Ill., US Dist. Ct. (no. dist.) Ind., US Dist. Ct. (we. dist.) Mich., US Ct. Appeals (first cir.). Sr. study dir. Nat. Opinion Rsch. Ctr., Chgo.; ptnr. Jenner & Block, Chgo. Author: Consumer Fraud Litigation: Law and Defenses in Illinois, 2004, The Business of Drug Development, 2004, Direct-to-Consumer Advertising of Prescription Pharmaceuticals and Medical Devices, 2004, Through the Glass Ceiling: Best Practices for Women Lawyers and Their Firms, 2004, Benchmarking for Success: Introducing NAWL Assessment Questionnaire, 2004, A Business Approach to Minimizing Product Liability Litigation, 2005; co-author: The Media and Products Litigation, 1996, Communications Specialists Help With Damage Control, 1997, Marketing Pharmaceutical Products on the Internet: Managing Risks and Limiting Liabilities in the World of E-Commerce, 2001, Post-Sale Duties to Warn, Recall, and Retrofit Defective Products in Illinois, 2003, The Evidentiary Impact of Regulatory Action on Product Litigation in the United States, 2004, FDA's Comments Herald New Strength for Preemption Defense in Drug Product Litigation, 2006, Immigration Reform and the Federal Law of Employment Discrimination; editor: The Use of Epidemiology in Tort Litigation: A Survey of Federal and State Jurisdictions, 2003; co-editor: The Use of Toxicology in Tort Litigation, 2005; contbr. articles in prof. jour. Bd. mem. The Youth Campus, Chgo.; chair, Best Interest of the Child Subcommittee Cir. Ct. Cook County, mem. Chief judge's Pub. Guardian Com. Harper Fellow, Univ. Chgo. Mem.: ABA (co-editor Product Liability newsletter 1997—2000, editor Mass Torts newsletter 2001, co-chair sect. litig. products liability com. 2005—, mem. mass torts com., bd. dirs. mem. spl. com. bioethics), Pub. Guardian Com., Best Interest of Child Subcom. of Child Protection Com. (chair 1995—96), Circuit Ct. Cook County, Def. Rsch. Inst., Ill. Bar Found. (bd. mem. 2005—), Univ. Chgo. Women's Bus. Group, Products Liability Adv. Coun. (mem. case selection com.), Nat. Assn. Women Lawyers (exec. bd. 2000—, bd. dir. 2002—, pres. 2004—05, founding chair NAWL com. evaluation Supreme Ct. nominees, Outstanding Mem. award 2002). Office: Jenner & Block One IBM Plz Chicago IL 60611 Office Phone: 312-923-2884. Business E-Mail: sscharf@jenner.com.

**SCHARF, WILLIAM,** artist; b. Media, Pa., Feb. 22, 1927; s. Lester William and Ebba (Anderson) S.; m. Diana Denny, Mar. 11, 1947 (div. 1951); 1 child, William Denny; m. Sally Kravitch, Mar. 25, 1956; 1 child, Aaron Anderson. Student, Barnes Found., 1946-47; cert. in painting, Pa. Acad. of Fine Arts, 1947. Instr. Mus. Modern Art, N.Y.C., 1964, Sch. Visual Arts, N.Y.C., 1965-73, San Francisco Inst. Fine Arts, 1963, 66, 69, 74, 89. One-man shows include David Herbert Gallery, NYC, 1960, 62, San Francisco Inst. Fine Arts, 1969, Neuberger Mus., Purchase, NY, 1976, High Mus., Atlanta, 1978, Armstrong Gallery, NYC, 1987, U. Mich. Mus. Art, Ann Arbor, 1993, Phillips Collection, Washington, 2000-01, Frederick R. Weisman Mus., Malibu, Calif., 2001, P.S.I., MOMA, Queens, 2002, Richard York Gallery, NYC, 2004, Meredith Ward Fine Art, NYC, 2005; exhibited in group shows at Guggenheim Mus., NYC, 1982, Hirschl-Adler Gallery, NYC, 1980, Smith-Anderson Gallery, Palo Alto, Calif., Nat. Mus. Am. Art, Washington, 1987, 91-92, Am. Acad. and Inst. Arts and Letters, NYC, 1989, 91, Richard York Gallery, NYC, 2002, Nat. Acad. Design Mus. NYC, 2003, 05; represented in permanent collections Phila. Mus., Boston Inst. Contemporary Art, Bklyn. Mus., Solomon R. Guggenheim Mus., NYC, Newark Mus., Nat. Mus. Am. Art, Smith Coll. Mus., Northampton, Mass., Zimmerli Mus., Rutgers U., New Brunswick, NJ, U. Mich. Mus. art, Phillips Collection, Washington, The Neuroscience Inst., San Diego, The High Mus., Atlanta, Colgate U., Telfair Mus. of Art, Savannah, Ga., Rose Art Mus., Brandeis U., Montgomery (Ala.) Mus. Art, Cath. U., Washington, Fogg Art Mus. Harvard U., Cambridge, Mass., Yale U. Mus., New Haven. Trustee Rothko Found., N.Y.C., 1979—87; instr. Art Students League, NY, 1987—2006. With USAF, 1945—46. Emmlen Cresson fellow Pa. Acad. Fine Arts. 1948. Mem.: Nat. Acad. Design, Soc. of Illustrators, Artist Equity Assn.

**SCHARF, Y. DAVID,** lawyer; b. N.Y.C., Apr. 10, 1968; BS in Mktg., NYU, 1988; JD, Bklyn. Law Sch., 1991. Assoc. Graubard Mollen & Miller, 1992—96, McDermott, Will & Emery, N.Y.C., 1996—98, ptnr., 1998—2000, Morrison Cohen Singer & Weinstein, N.Y.C., 2000—. Contbr. articles to profl. jours. Founder, trustee, bd. dirs., pro bono counsel Lifetime Care for the Jewish Disabled, Inc.; exec. Jewish Orgns. of the West Side, N.Y.C. Named to, Crain's N.Y. Bus. "40 under 40", 2004; recipient Founder's award, Lifetime Care Found., 1998. Mem.: ABA, N.Y. State Bar. Office: Morrison Cohen Singer & Weinstein 750 Lexington Ave New York NY 10022

**SCHARFENBERG, MARGARET ELLAN,** retired elementary school educator; b. Lansing, Mich., Mar. 22, 1924; d. John Milton and Florence Lucille (Craig) Amiss; m. Howard Edward Scharfenberg, June 29, 1946; children: Ann Derr Scharfenberg White, Joan Carol Scharfenberg Andrea, John Howard. Student, Oberlin Coll., 1942-44; BA, Mich. State U., 1946; MA in Teaching, Rollins Coll., 1966. Cert. tchr., elem. supr., Fla. Tchr. Hill Elem. Sch., Maitland, Fla., 1964-65, Cheney Elem. Sch., Orlando, Fla., 1965-66; reading lab. tchr. Richmond Heights Elem. Sch., Orlando, Fla., 1966-68; supr. perceptual planning, oral clinician Orange County Schs., Orlando, Fla., 1968-69; reading lab. tchr. Winter Park HS, Fla., 1969-72; from perceptual trainer to exptl. reading lab. tchr. Gateway Sch., Orlando, Fla., 1972-74; tchr. of highest clinician Zellwood Elem. Sch., Fla., 1974-93; ret., 1993. Pioneer white/black sch. staffing Richmond Heights Elem. Sch., 1966-68; dir. Learning Skills Profl. Ctr., Orlando, 1971-74; speaker, cons. in field. Author, editor (newsletter) Paper Meeting, 1968-69; (perception package) Patterns for a Purpose, 1968-69; producer films on perceptual tng.,

1968-69. Vol. Women of Hospice, Hospice Hope Chest, Sun. sch. tchr; choir mem., chmn. prayer chain Congl. Ch. Mt. Dora. Named Tchr. of Yr., Zellwood Elem. Sch., 1993. Mem.: NEA, AAUW, Internat. Reading Assn. (sec. Orange County coun. 1965, pres. 1969), Lakes & Hills Garden Club (Oleander Garden Cir. chaplain, past sec.), Rosicrucian Order (A.M.O.R.C.), Humane Soc., Lions (staff mem. seminars on perception, recipient various certs. and plaques), Gamma Phi Beta (past pres. alumna group). Republican. Avocations: reading, boating, gardening, choir. Home: 6492 Dora Dr Mount Dora FL 32757-7064

**SCHARFF, JOSEPH LAURENT,** lawyer; b. New Orleans, Oct. 2, 1935; s. Joseph Roy and Celia Ray S.; m. Mary Susan Greulach, June 29, 1963; children: Catherine Elizabeth, Robert Laurent, Anne Victoria. BS in Journalism, Northwestern U., 1957; JD, Harvard U., 1964. Bar: D.C. 1965, U.S. Supreme Ct. 1970, U.S. Ct. Appeals (D.C. cir.) 1965, U.S. Ct. Appeals (2nd cir.) 1980, U.S. Ct. Appeals (5th cir.) 1973, U.S. Ct. Appeals (10th cir.); U.S. Ct. Claims 1965. From assoc. to ptnr. Pierson, Ball & Dowd, Washington, 1964-89; ptnr. Reed Smith Shaw & McClay, Washington, 1989-95, counsel, 1996. Mem. ABA (fair trial-free press com. 1973-76, com. reps. media 1985-95, co-chmn. 1989-92), Fed. Comm. Bar Assn., Soc. Profl. Journalists, Radio-TV News Dirs. Assn. (counsel 1965-95, Disting. Svc. award 1987, J. Laurent Scharff Legal Internship established 1996), Media Inst. (First Amendment Adv. Coun. 1993-2003). Home and Office: 12000 Turf Ln Reston VA 20191-2123

**SCHARFF, MATTHEW DANIEL,** immunologist, cell biologist, educator; b. NYC, Aug. 28, 1932; s. Harry and Constance S.; m. Carol Held, Dec. 19, 1954; children: Karen, Thomas, David. AB, Brown U., 1954, DrMedSci (hon.), 1994; MD, NYU, 1959. House officer II and IV med. service Boston City Hosp., 1959—61; rsch. assoc. NIH, 1961—63; asst. prof. Albert Einstein Coll. Medicine, Yeshiva U., Bronx, NY, 1963—67, assoc. prof., 1967—71, prof. dept. cell biology, 1971—, chmn. dept., 1972—83, dir. div. biol. scis., 1975—81; assoc. dir. Cancer Ctr., 1975—86, dir., 1986—95, dep. dir., 1995—2002. Served with USPHS, 1961-63. Recipient Alumni Achievement award NYU Sch. Medicine, 1980, N.Y. Acad. Medicine medal, 1990, Commemorative award Albert Einstein Coll. Medicine, 1993, Mayor of NY Lifetime Achievement award in sci. and tech., 2003. Mem. Am. Assn. Immunologists (Mentoring Excellence award 1998), Am. Soc. Clin. Investigation, Nat. Acad. Scis., Am. Acad. Arts and Sci., Phi Beta Kappa, Sigma Xi, Alpha Omega Alpha. Office: Albert Einstein Coll Med Dept Cell Biology 1300 Morris Pk Ave Bronx NY 10461-1926

**SCHARFFE, WILLIAM GRANVILLE,** academic administrator, educator; b. Saginaw, Mich., Mar. 12, 1942; s. William Edward and Marion Kittie (Granville) S.; m. Mary Jo Whitfield, Sept. 4, 1965; children: Sue L., William W. BA, Mich. State U., 1965, MA, Mich. State U., 1969, PhD, 1977. Tchr. English Webber Jr. High Sch., Saginaw, 1965-66; tchr. speech Arthur Hill High Sch., Saginaw, 1966-68; staff asst. for pers. Saginaw City Schs., 1968-73, dir. pers., 1977-94, dir. employee devel. and media ops., 1994-99; prin. Zilwaukee Jr. High Sch., Saginaw, 1973-74; asst. prin. North Intermediate Sch., Saginaw, 1974-75, 1975-77; dir. policy svcs. Mich. Assn. Sch. Bds., Lansing, 1999—. Adj. asst. prof. Mich. State U., East Lansing, 1977; adj. lectr. Ctrl. Mich. U., Mt. Pleasant, 1987, Mich. State U., 1977, Saginaw Valley State U., 1991; cons. in field. Author: Elfred Alanzo & Santa's Surprise, 1987. Bd. dirs. Japanese Cultural Ctr. and Tea House, Saginaw, 1986-97, pres., 1993-95. Recipient Key Man award United Way Saginaw County, 1978, Outstanding Svc. award, 1978. Mem.: Am. Assn. State Policy Svcs. (pres. 2004—05), Soc. For Human Resource Mgmt., Mich. Mid. Cities Pers. and Labor Rels. Task Force (pres. 1980—82), Mich. Assn. Sch. Pers. Assn. (sec., bd. dirs. 1988—90, pres., bd. dirs. 1992—93), Mich. State U. Alumni Club (pres. Saginaw County chpt. 2002—04), Saginaw Club (pres. 1996—97), Exch. Club (Saginaw chpt. pres. 1981), Phi Delta Kappa. Republican. Episcopalian. Avocations: writing, golf, photography, public speaking. Home: 2812 Adams Blvd Saginaw MI 48602-3103 Office Phone: 517-327-5928. Business E-Mail: bscharffe@masb.org.

**SCHARLAU, CHARLES EDWARD, III,** natural gas company executive; b. Chgo., Apr. 24, 1927; s. Charles Edward II and Esther (Powell) S.; m. Clydene Yvonne Sloop, Aug. 13, 1960; children: Caryn, Robin, Greg, Charles, Marti. LLB, U. Ark., 1951. Bar: Ark. 1951, U.S. Dist. Ct. (western dist.) Ark. 1951, U.S. Supreme Ct. 1958. Atty. Ark. Western Gas Co., Fayetteville, 1951-61, v.p., 1961-68, pres., 1968-78; pres., chmn. S.W. Energy Co., Fayetteville, 1978—98. Bd. dirs. Ablest, Inc., Clearwater, Fla., Arvest Bank, S.W. Energy Co., Fayetteville. Chmn. U. Ark. Devel. Coun., 1989-97; trustee U. Ark., 1997—, chmn. bd. trustees, 2005. With USMC, 1945-46. Mem. ABA, Ark. Bar Assn., So. Gas Assn., Nat. Assn. Mfrs. (bd. dirs. 1986-89), Am. Gas Assn. (bd. dirs. 1987-90), U. Ark. Alumni Assn. (pres. 1972-73), Ark. C. of C. (pres. 1977-79), Beta Gamma Sigma. Methodist. Avocations: reading, tennis, canoeing, sports. Home: 1506 Sunset Pl Fayetteville AR 72701-1627 Office: Southwestern Energy Co 1083 Sain St Fayetteville AR 72703-6206 Office Phone: 479-521-0472. E-mail: ccsharlau@aol.com.

**SCHARLEMANN, ROBERT PAUL,** theology studies educator, minister; b. Lake City, Minn., Apr. 4, 1929; s. Ernst Karl and Johanna Meta (Harre) S. Student, Northwestern U., Watertown, Wis., 1946-49; BA, Concordia Coll. and Sem., St. Louis, 1952; BD, MDiv, Concordia Coll. and Sem., 1955; Dr. theol., U. Heidelberg, Germany, 1957. Ordained to ministry, Lutheran Ch., 1960. Tchr. Luth. parochial sch., Mobridge, SD, 1949—50; instr. philosophy Valparaiso U., 1957-59; postdoctoral fellow Yale U., 1959-60; pastor Bethlehem Luth. Ch., Carlyle, Ill., 1960-62, Grace Luth. Ch., Durham, NC, 1962-63; asst. prof. religion U. So. Calif., 1963-64, assoc. prof., 1964-66; assoc. prof. religion U. Iowa, Iowa City, 1966-68, prof., 1968-81; Commonwealth prof. religious studies U. Va., Charlottesville, 1981-97, prof. emeritus, 1997—. Fulbright-Hays prof. U. Heidelberg, 1975-76. Author: Thomas Aquinas and John Gerhard, 1964, Reflection and Doubt in the Thought of Paul Tillich, 1969, The Being of God, 1981, Inscriptions and Reflections, 1989, The Reason of Following, 1991, L'intemporel et l'eternel, 1993, Can Religion be Understood Philosophically?, 1995, The Mystical Correlate of Symbolic Appearing, 2001, Religion and Reflection, 2004; editor Jour. of Am. Acad. Religion, 1980-85; contbr. articles to profl. jours. Fulbright scholar U. Heidelberg, 1955-57. Mem. Am. Acad. Religion, Am. Theol. Soc., Deutsche Paul-Tillich Gesellschaft, European Soc. Culture, Soc. for Philosophy of Religion. Lutheran.

**SCHAROLD, MARY LOUISE,** psychoanalyst, psychiatrist, educator; b. Wichita Falls, Tex., Mar. 3, 1943; d. Walter John and Louise Helen (Hartmann) Baumgartner; m. William Ballew McCollum, Aug. 23, 1964 (div. 1981); m. Harry Karl Scharold, June 19, 1982; children: Margaret Louise, Walter Ballew. BA with highest distinction, U. Kans., 1964; attended, U. Kans. Sch. Medicine 1964—66; MD, Baylor Coll. Medicine 1968; attended, Houston-Galveston Psychoanalytic Inst., 1974—76; postgrad., Topeka Inst. Psychoanalysis, 1981. Diplomate Am. Bd. Psychiatry and Neurology, 1975, cert. adult psychoanalysis Am. Psychoanalytic Assn., 1982. Intern Meml. Bapt. Hosp., Houston, 1968-69; resident in psychiatry Baylor Coll. Medicine, Houston, 1969—72, chief resident, 1971-72; psychoanalyst Houston, 1972—. Asst. prof. Baylor Coll. Medicine, Houston, 1973-76, asst. clin. prof., 1981-84, assoc. clin. prof., 1984—; dir. Baylor Psychiat. Clinic, Houston, 1973-76; co-dir. Rice U. Psychiat. Svc., Houston, 1981-82; asst. clin. prof. U. Kans. Sch. Medicine, Kansas City, 1977-81; tchg. assoc. Topeka Psychoanalytic Inst., 1984-86; tchg. analyst, Houston-Galveston Psychoanalytic Inst., 1986-90, tng. and supervising analyst, 1990—, v.p., 1994-96, pres., 1996-01, bd. dirs., 2001-04; pres. bd. trustees Child Devel. Ctr., 2005. Adv. bd. Leavenworth (Kans.) Mental Health Assn., 1977-81; sec. bd. trustees, Child Devel. Ctr., 2005. Watkins scholar U. Kans., 1961-64; Grad. Fellowship award, Pi Beta Phi, 1965; recipient Hilltopper, Ten Outstanding Sr. Women, U. Kans., 1963, Greater U. Fund award, 1964, U. Kans., Eugen Kahn award, Outstanding Baylor Psychiatry Resident, 1972, 1st Disting. Svc. award, Houston-Galveston Psychoanalytic Soc., 2004; named Outstanding Woman Med. Student, AMWA, Houston Branch, 1968; named to Best Doctors in Am., 1998-. Mem. Am. Psychiat. Assn. (disting. life fellow, mem. com.

quality assurance 1986-87, chair Tex. peer rev. 1984-88), Am. Coll. Psychoanalysts, Am. Psychoanalytic Assn. (cert. 1982, peer rev. com. 1985-90, prof. ins. commn. 1986-93, bd. profl. stds. 1994-2001, CME com. 1994-96, exec. coun. 1994-96, cert. com. 1995-98, preparedness and progress com. 1998-06, chair preparedness and progress com. 2000-06, coordinating com. bd. profl. stds. 2000-06, bylaws com. 2001—, fin. com. 2003—, councilor-at-large 2005—, hon. membership com. 2005-, election oversight com. 2005—, com. on coun., 2006—), Am. Group Psychotherapy Assn., Ctr. Advanced Psychoanalytic Studies, Houston Psychiat. Soc. (v.p. 1984-85, pres.-elect 1985-86, pres. 1986-87), Houston-Galveston Psychoanalytic Soc. (sec.-treas. 1984-86, pres.-elect 1986-88, pres. 1988-90, alt. councillor 1994-96), Houston Group Psychotherapy Soc. (adv. bd. 1984-85), Mortar Bd., Phi Beta Kappa, Delta Phi Alpha, Alpha Omega Alpha, Pi Beta Phi Alumni Assn. Republican. Lutheran. Office: 2301 Westheimer Rd Houston TX 77098-1317 Office Phone: 713-590-2302. Personal E-mail: mlscharold@mindspring.com.

**SCHARTZ, ELIZABETH A.,** lawyer; b. Boulder, Colo., Mar. 22, 1963; d. Russell and Sandra Schartz. BA in History and Econs., St. Mary of the Plains, 1985; JD, U. Kans., 1988. Bd. cert. labor and employment law: Tex. Bd. Legal Specialization 1996. Clk. Hon. James K. Logan, Olathe, Kans., 1988—89; assoc. Thompson & Knight LLP, Dallas, 1989—94, ptnr., 1995—2001, sr. ptnr., 2002—. Mem. bd. govs. U. Kans. Sch. Law, Lawrence, 2001—04. Mem.: ABA, Dallas Bar Assn., Tex. Bar Assn. Office: Thompson & Knight LLP Ste 3300 1700 Pacific Ave Dallas TX 75201 Office Phone: 214-969-1737.

**SCHATKEN, NANCY LEAH,** medical editor; b. NYC, Jan. 7, 1938; d. Robert V. and Lillian Belle (Neff) S. BS, U.N.C., 1959; cert. med. tech., Albany Sch. Med. Tech., 1960. Med. tech., instr. various orgns., 1960-66; acting emp. editor med. jours. Harper & Row, N.Y.C., 1966-69; assoc. editor Med. World News-McGraw-Hill, N.Y.C., 1969-70; owner, founder Mostly Med., N.Y.C., 1970—, St. James, Barbados, 1978-98. Avocations: travel, reading, swimming, entertaining. Address: 2677 Parkview Dr Hallandale FL 33009 Office Phone: 954-455-0039. E-mail: schatken@bellsouth.net.

**SCHATTEN, GERALD PHILLIP,** stem cell biologist, reproductive biologist, educator; b. NYC, Nov. 1, 1949; s. Frank and Sylvia Schatten; m. Heather Aronson, July 4, 1994; children: Daniel, Madeline, Samantha. BS, U. Calif., Berkeley, 1971, PhD, 1975. Instr. U. Calif., Berkeley, 1975; postdoctoral fellow Rockefeller Found., 1976-77; from asst. prof. to prof. Fla. State U., Tallahassee, 1979-86; prof. molecular biology, zoology and obstetrics gynecology U. Wis., Madison, 1986-97, rsch. dir. women's health rsch., 1997—, dir. integrated microscopy resource for biomed. rsch., 1986-92, dir. gamete and embryo biol. tng. program, 1989-97; program dir. Mellon Ctr. of Excellence in Reproductive Biology, 1996-97, 99—; prof. ob-gyn. and cell-devel. biology, sr. scientist Oreg. Regional Primate Rsch. Ctr. Oreg. Health Scis. U., Portland, 1997-2001; dir. Pitts. Devel. Ctr., dep. dir. Magee-Women's Rsch. Inst., Pitts., 2001—, vice chair, prof. dept. ob/gyn./reproductive scis., prof. cell biology and physiology, 2001—. Dir. gamete and embryo biol. tng. program U. Wis., Madison 1989-97; exec. bd. UNESCO Internat. Cell Rsch. Orgn., 1995—; co-dir. frontiers in reprodn. course Marine Biol. Lab., Woods Hole, Mass., 1998-2001. Editor Current Topics in Devel. Biology, 1996—. Recipient Rsch. Career Devel. award NIH, 1981-86, Merit award, 1997, Sadler award, 1998; Purkinje medal of sci. Czech Acad. Scis., 2000. Office: Pitts Devel Ctr Magee Womens Rsch Inst 204 Craft Ave Pittsburgh PA 15213

**SCHATTENBURG, MARK L.,** physicist, educator; BS in Physics, U. Hawaii, 1978; PhD in Physics, MIT, 1984. Rsch. scientist Soft X-ray & Electron Spectroscopy Lab., U. Hawaii; postdoctoral assoc. MIT, 1984—96; principal rsch. scientist MIT Ctr. for Space Rsch., 1996—; dir. MIT Space Nanotechnology Lab.; assoc. dir. MIT NanoStructures Lab.; senior rsch. staff MIT Microsystems Tech. Lab. Mem. NASA Chandra Sci. & Instrument Devel. Teams. Author: over 150 scientific papers. Mem.: Ame. Soc. for Precision Engring., IEEE, Internat. Soc. for Optical Engring. (BACUS prize 2003), Am. Vacuum Soc., Optical Soc. of Am. Co-inventor of attenuated phase-shift mask for patterning advanced computer chips. Holds six patents. Office: MIT Room 37-487 70 Vassar St Cambridge MA 02139

**SCHATTSCHNEIDER, DORIS JEAN,** retired mathematics professor; b. NYC, Oct. 19, 1939; d. Robert W. Jr. and Charlotte Lucile (Ingalls) Wood; m. David A. Schattschneider, June 2, 1962; 1 child, Laura E. AB, U. Rochester, 1961; MA, Yale U., 1963; PhD, 1966. Instr. in math. Northwestern U., Evanston, Ill., 1964—65; asst. prof. U. Ill., Chgo., 1965—68; prof. Moravian Coll., Bethlehem, Pa., 1968—2002, prof. emerita, 2003—. Project dir. Fund for the Improvement of Post-Secondary Edn. U.S. Dept. Edn., 1991—93, 1995—97; vis. scholar U. V.I., 2004. Author (with W. Walker): (books and models) M.C. Escher Kaleidocycles, 1977, 1987; co-author: (videos and activities) Visual Geometry Project, 1986—91; author: M.C. Escher: Visions of Symmetry, 1990, 2d edit., 2004; co-author: A Companion to Calculus, 1995, 2d edit., 2005; editor: Geometry Turned On, 1997, M.C. Escher's Legacy, 2003. Exhbn. curator Allentown Art Mus., 1979, Payne Gallery, 1987. Grantee NEH rsch. grantee, 1988—90. Mem.: Assn. for Women in Math., Am. Math. Soc., Math. Assn. Am. (editor 1980—85, gov. 1980—89, 1st v.p. 1994—96, Allendoerfer award 1979, Meritorious Svc. award 1991, Dist. Math. Tchg. award 1993), Pi Mu Epsilon (councillor 1990—96). Mem. Moravian Ch. Office: Moravian Coll Math Dept PPHAC 1200 Main St Bethlehem PA 18018-6650 E-mail: schattdo@moravian.edu.

**SCHATZ, BARBARA A.,** law educator; b. 1948; BA, U. Pa., 1969; JD, Harvard U., 1973. Bar: N.Y. 1974. Asst. gem. counsel Health Svcs. Adminstrn., NYC, 1973-74; assoc. Rosenman, Colin, Freund, Lewis & Cohen, NYC, 1974-77; exec. dir. Coun. NY Law Assocs., NYC, 1977-85; lectr. Columbia U., NYC, 1985, clin. prof., 1986—. Bd. dirs. Spl. Advis. Mem. Lawyers Com. Human Rights, Phi Beta Kappa (vice chmn.). Office: Columbia U Sch Law 435 W 116th St New York NY 10027-7297 E-mail: bschatz@law.columbia.edu.

**SCHATZ, GARY STEWART,** marketing professional; b. N.Y., 1951; s. Irving and Esther Schatz; m. Rita Schatz. BA, Syracuse U., NY, 1973; MBA, Canadian Sch. Mgmt., 1994. With Century 21, Inc., Montvale, NJ, 1975—82; mktg. rep. Centrac Rsch., Bergenfield, NJ, 1982—84; regional field rep. Certified Mktg., Inc., Kinderhock, NY, 1984—99. Mem. consumer panel NPD Group, Fort Washington, NY, 1990—93. Vol. U.S. Army Corps. Engrs., 1996—98. Mem.: Am. Inst. Computer Scis. Home: 353 W 57t St New York NY 10019 Office Phone: 888-240-6089.

**SCHATZ, IRWIN JACOB,** cardiologist, educator; b. St. Boniface, Man., Can., Oct. 16, 1931; came to US, 1956, naturalized, 1966; s. Jacob and Reva S.; m. Barbara Jane Binder, Nov. 12, 1967; children: Jacob, Edward, Stephen and Brian (twins). Student, U. Man., Winnipeg, 1951, MD with honors, 1956. Diplomate: Am. Bd. Internal Medicine. Intern Vancouver (B.C.) Gen. Hosp., 1955-56; resident Hammersmith Hosp., U. London, 1957, Mayo Clinic, Rochester, Minn., 1958-61; head sec. peripheral vascular disease Henry Ford Hosp., Detroit, 1961-68; assoc. prof. medicine Wayne State U., 1968-71, chief sect. cardiovascular disease, 1969-71; assoc. prof., assoc. prof. sect. cardiology U. Mich., 1972-73, prof. internal medicine, 1973-75; prof. medicine John A. Burns Sch. Medicine, U. Hawaii, 1975—, chmn. dept. medicine, 1975-90, interim chmn. dept. medicine, 2003—05. Author: Orthostatic Hypotension, 1986; contbr. numerous articles to med. jour. Mem. jud. coun. State of Hawaii Supreme Ct., 2000—. Rockefeller Found. scholar, 1991. Master ACP (bd. gov. 1984-89, Laureate award Hawaii chpt. 1992); fellow Am. Coll. Cardiology (bd. gov. 1980-84); mem. Am. Heart Assn. (fellow coun. cardiology), Am. Fedn. Clin. Rsch., Asian-Pacific Soc. Cardiology (v.p. 1987-91), Accreditation Coun. for Grad. Med. Edn. (chmn. residence rev. com. internal medicine 1989-95), Hawaii Heart Assn. (pres.), Western Assn. Physicians, Am. Autonomic Soc. (med. bd. gov., pres. 1996-98), Pacific Interurban Club. Jewish. Home: 4983 Kolohala St Honolulu HI 96816-5126 Office: 1356 Lusitana St Honolulu HI 96813-2421

**SCHATZ, WAYNE ARDALE,** district technology coordinator, educator; b. Cody, Wyo., July 27, 1947; s. Albert R. and Leona Mildred (Johnston) S.; m. Roanne Longwith, Dec. 16, 1966; children: Edith, Heidi, Robert, Leon, Dale, Anne. BS, Ea. Mont. Coll., 1969; MEd, Lesley Coll., 1987. Cert. Elem. tchr., Wyo. Tchr. Coffeen Elem. Sch., Sheridan, Wyo., 1969-78, Woodland Park Elem., Sheridan, 1978-87; computer tchr. Cen. Mid. Sch., Sheridan, 1987-94; in-svc. instr. Sch. Dist. #2, Sheridan, 1987—, dist. tech. coord., 1994-97; computer tchr. Sheridan Jr. H.S., Sheridan, 1997—2001, elem. technology tchr., 2001—. Extension instr. U. Wyo., Laramie, 1989—. Bd. dirs. Bighorn Audobon Soc., Sheridan, 1966-77, pres., 1977-80; active Sheridan County Red Cross, Sheridan. Mem. Sheridan Cen. Edn. Assn. (pres. 1979-80, Tchr. of the Month 1988, 92, Tchr. of Yr. 1992), Wyo. Edn. Assn. (bd. dirs. 1980-82, treas. 1982-84), Wyo. Ednl. Computing Coun. (pres. 1989-92), Wyo. Bus. Edn. Assn. (pres. 2002-03), Wyo. Assn. Career & Tech. Edn. (bd. dirs. 2001-03). Republican. Mem. Lds Ch.

**SCHATZBERG, ALAN FREDERIC,** psychiatrist, researcher; b. N.Y.C., Oct. 17, 1944; s. Emanuel and Cila (Diamand) S.; m. Nancy R. Silverman, Aug. 27, 1972; children: Melissa Ann, Lindsey Diamand. BS, NYU, 1965, MD, 1968; MA (hon.), Harvard U., 1989. Diplomate Nat. Bd. Med. Examiners, Am. Bd. Psychiatry and Neurology. Intern Lenox Hill Hosp., NYC, 1968-69; resident in psychiatry Mass. Mental Health Ctr., Boston, 1969-72; clin. fellow in psychiatry Harvard Med. Sch., Boston, 1969-72, asst. prof. psychiatry, 1977-82, assoc. prof., 1982-88, prof., 1988-91; interim psychiatrist-in-chief McLean Hosp., Belmont, Mass., 1984-86, dir. depression rsch. facility, 1985—, svc. chief, 1982-84, 86-88; psychiatrist adv. panel Eli Lilly & Co., Indpls., 1986-93; clin. dir. Mass. Mental Health Ctr., Boston, 1988-91; Kenneth T. Norris, Jr. prof. psychiatry and behavioral scis. Stanford (Calif.) U., 1991—, chmn. dept. psychiatry and behavioral scis. Sch. Medicine, 1991—. Cons. AMA Videoclinics, Chgo., 1979-83; mem. AMA/FAA panel on health regulations, Chgo., 1984-86; mem. NIH Biol. Psychopathology and Clin. Neuroscis. Intitial Rev. Group, 1991-95, chmn., 1993-94. Co-author: Manual of Clinical Psychopharmacology, 1986, 5th edit., 2005; co-editor: Depression: Biology, Psychodynamics and Treatment, 1978, Hypothalamic-Pituitary-Adrenal Axis, 1988, Textbook of Psychopharmacology, 1996, 2d edit., 1998, 3d edit., 2004; mem. editl. bd. McLean Hosp. Jour., 1975—88, Jour. Psychiat. Rsch., 1988—, co-editor-in-chief, 2000—, mem. editl. bd. Harvard Rev. Psychiatry, 1992—, Anxiety, 1993, Jour. Clin. Psychopharmacology, 1993—, Archives of Gen. Psychiatry, 1995—, Psychoneuroendocrinology, 1995—, Am. Jour. Psychiatry, 2002—05, assoc. editor-in-chief Depression and Anxiety, 1992—, traslational field editor Neuropsychopharmacology, 2002—; contbr. more than 300 articles to profl. publs., chapters to books. Maj. USAF, 1972-74. Rsch. grantee NIMH, 1984-87, 94—, Poitras Charitable Found., 1985-93, Pritzker Found., 1997—; recipient Mood Disorders Rsch. award Am. Coll. Psychiatrists, 2002, Klerman Lifetime Rsch. award Nat. Depressive and Manic Depressive Assn., 1998, Strecker award U. Pa., 2002, Falcone award Nat. Alliance Rsch. in Schizophrenia and Affective Diseases, 2005. Fellow: APA (Rsch. award 2002), Am. Coll. Psychiatrists (Disting. Svc. award in psychiatry 2005), Am. Coll. Neuropsychopharmacology (coun. 1994—97, pres. 2000—01), Am. Psychopathol. Assn.; mem.: NAS, Inst. Medicine, No. Calif. Psychiat. Soc. (v.p. 1997—99), Psychiat. Soc. (coun. 1987—90). Avocations: travel, swimming, fine arts, theater, golf. Office: Stanford U Sch Medicine 401 Quarry Rd Rm 300 Stanford CA 94305-5717 Office Phone: 650-723-6811. Business E-Mail: afschatz@stanford.edu.

**SCHAUB, MARILYN MCNAMARA,** theology studies educator; b. Chgo., Mar. 24, 1928; d. Bernard Francis and Helen Katherine (Skehan) McNamara; m. Thomas Schaub, Oct. 25, 1969; 1 child, Helen Ann. BA, Rosary Coll., 1953; PhD, U. Fribourg, Switzerland, 1957; diploma, Ecole Biblique, Jerusalem, 1967. Asst. prof. classics and Bibl. studies Rosary Coll., River Forest, Ill., 1957-69; prof. Bibl. studies Duquesne U., Pitts., 1969-70, 73-01. Participant 8 archeological excavations, Middle East; hon assoc Am Schs Oriental Research, 1966—67, trustee, 1986—89; Danforth assoc 1972—80; admin dir expedition to the Southeast Dead Sea Plains, Jordan, 1989—. Author: (book) Friends and Friendship for St. Augustine, 1964; translator (with H Richter): Agape in the New Testament, 3 vols, 1963—65. Mem.: Am Acad Religion, Cath Biblical Assn, Soc Biblical Literature. Democrat. Home: 25 Mckelvey Ave Pittsburgh PA 15218-1452

**SCHAUB, ROBERT GEORGE,** pharmaceutical executive; b. Bellevue, Pa., Dec. 16, 1947; s. Edward Clarence Schaub and Barbara Marie Zuratovitch; m. Kathy Anne Gates, Apr. 3, 1983; 1 child, Caitlin Elizabeth. BS, U. Nev., Las Vegas, 1970; PhD, Wash. State U., 1973. Postdoctoral fellow Wash. Heart Assn., Pullman, Wash., 1973—75, Temple U. Med. Sch., Philadelphia, 1975—77; asst. to assoc. prof. U.Tenn., Knoxville, 1977—81; rsch. scientist Upjohn Co., Kalamazoo, 1981—90; sr lab. head to dir. Genetics Inst., Cambridge, Mass., 1990—97; sr. dir. to asst. v.p. Wyeth Pharmaceuticals, Cambridge, 1997—2006; v.p. Archemix Corp., Cambridge, 2006—. Adj. prof. Boston U. Sch. Medicine, 2006—. Recipient Outstanding Educator of Yr., U. Tenn., 1978. Mem.: AAAS, NY Acad. Sci., Internat. Soc. Thrombosis and Haemostasis, Am. Soc. Hematology, Soc. Leukocyte Biology, Am. Soc. Investigative Pathology, Am. Assn. Investigative Pathology, Am. Physiol. Soc., Sigma Xi. Achievements include patents in field. Office: Archemix Corp 300 Third St Cambridge MA 02142 Office Phone: 617-621-7700. Office Fax: 617-621-9300. Business E-Mail: bschaub@archemix.com.

**SCHAUBLE, JOHN EUGENE,** physical education educator; b. Paterson, N.J., Aug. 14, 1949; s. Charles Eugene and Rosemary (White) S.; children: Sarah, Angela. BA, Bemidji State U., 1973, BS, 1974; MA, U. Ala., 1984. Cert. tchr. health, phys. edn., K-12; cert. swimming coach/level 4; cert. aquatic mgr.; cert. pool operator, ARC water safety instr., lifeguard instr., waterfront lifeguard instr., lifeguard mgmt. instr., first aid instr., CPR instr., water safety instr. trainer, AED essentials instr., disease prevention instr., oxygen adminstrn. instr., safety tng. for swim coaches instr.; cert. U.S.A. Track & Field level II. Northeast dir. Phys. Fitness Inst. of Am., Albany, N.Y., 1974-75; head swim coach Lake Forest (Ill.) Swim Club, 1975-78; asst. swim coach/grad. asst. U. Ala., Tuscaloosa, 1978-79; head swim coach Palm Springs (Calif.) Swim Team, 1979-80; asst. swim coach Ft. Lauderdale (Fla.) Swim Team, 1980-82; aquatic dir., head swim coach Briarwood of Richmond Aquatic Club, Richmond, Va., 1982-83; head swimming coach, intramural coord. William Rainey Harper Coll., Palatine, Ill., 1983-85; boys/girls asst. swim coach Sch. Dist. 211, Palatine, 1985-90; nat. coach Palatine Swim Team, 1983-92; head boys and girls swim coach Adlai E. Stevenson High Sch., Lincolnshire, Ill., 1990-96, aquatic coord., 1990—, asst. girls track and field coach, 1992-99, varsity cross-country coach, 1999—, boys distance track and field coach, 1999—. Head coach Patriot Aquatic Club, 1992-94, head coach sr. team, 1994-99; fund raising com. U.S. Swimming, Inc., Colorado Springs, Colo., 1990-94; coaches rep. Ill. Swimming, Inc., Aurora, 1990-94, bd. dirs., tech. planning com., others. Nominated Coach of Yr., Nat. Jr. Coll. Athletic Assn., Ft. Pierce, Fla., 1984; named Boys Sectional Coach of Yr., Ill. High Sch. Assn., 1992. Mem. Ill. Swimming Assn. (nominated Coach of Yr. coll. divsn. boys 1984), Nat. Interscholastic Swimming Coaches Assn., Am. Swimming Coaches Assn., Am. Coll. Sports Medicine, Nat. Strength and Conditioning Assn., Ill. Track and Cross Country Coaches Assn (Dave Pasquini award, 2006), AAPHERD, NEA. Republican. Roman Catholic. Avocations: computer, running, swimming, tennis, weight tng. Home: 608 Applegate Ln Lake Zurich IL 60047-2363 Office: 1 Stevenson Dr Lincolnshire IL 60069-2824 Office Phone: 847-634-4000 ext 1226. Personal E-Mail: coachswim@aol.com.

**SCHAUER, FRANZ PETER,** civil and nuclear engineer, educator; b. Mankato, Minn., Nov. 29, 1932; s. Albert Franz and Marie Petrich (Nielsson) S.; m. Joan Malacne; children: Marie, Barbara, Franz, Jr. Lisa, Jill. BS, U.S. Mil. Acad., 1955; MSCE, Iowa State U., 1961, MS in Nuc. Engring., 1961, PhD, 1969. Cert. civil engr. Commd. 2d lt. U.S. Army, 1955, advanced through grades to col., 1980, ret., 1989; engr. U.S. AEC, Germantown, Md., 1964-75; exec. U.S. Nuc. Regulatory Commn., Bethesda, Md., 1975-82; prof. Minn. State U., 1982-93; chief. ADU Engring. Assn., Bethesda, 1994—. Engring. cons. Tex-La Power, Stone and Webster, Boston, 1987, Burns and

Roe, NYC, 1986, U.S. Army, Washington, 1984, Todd Shipbuilding, Washington, 1983. Author: Advances in Structural Dynamics, 1981. Trustee Christ Luth. Ch. Fellow ASCE (com. mem.); mem. IEEE Computer Soc., ASME (com.mem.), Phi Kappa Phi, Sigma Xi. Lutheran. Avocations: tennis, computers. Home: Unit 261 6860 Gulfport Blvd S Saint Petersburg FL 33707-2108 Office: PO Box 1423 Mc Lean VA 22101-1423 Office Phone: 703-401-5454. Personal E-mail: franzschauer1000@hotmail.com.

**SCHAUER, FREDERICK FRANKLIN,** law educator; b. Newark, Jan. 15, 1946; s. John Adolph and Clara (Balayti) S.; m. Margery Clare Stone, Aug. 25, 1968 (div. June, 1982); m. Virginia Jo Wise, May 25, 1985. AB, Dartmouth Coll., 1967, MBA, 1968; JD, Harvard U., 1972. Bar: Mass. 1972, U.S. Supreme Ct. 1976. Assoc. Fine & Ambrogne, Boston, 1972-74; asst. prof. law W.Va. U., Morgantown, 1974-76, assoc. prof., 1976-78, Coll. William and Mary, Williamsburg, Va., 1978-80, Cutler prof., 1980-83; prof. of law U. Mich., Ann Arbor, 1983-90; Frank Stanton prof. of 1st Amendment Kennedy Sch. of Govt., Harvard U., Cambridge, Mass., 1990—, acad. dean, 1997—2002, acting dean, 2001. Vis. scholar, mem. faculty law Wolfson Coll. Cambridge (Eng.) U., 1977-78; vis. prof. Law Sch., U. Chgo., 1990, 05; vis. fellow Australian Nat. U., 1993, 98; William Morton Disting. sr. fellow in humanities Dartmouth Coll., 1991; vis. prof. law Harvard Law Sch., 1996, 97, 00, 04, 05, 06; Ewald Disting. vis. prof. law U. Va., 1996, vis. prof. govt. Dartmouth Coll., 1997; disting. vis. prof. law U. Toronto, 2000; Fischel-Neil Disting. vis. prof. law, 2005. Author: The Law of Obscenity, 1976, Free Speech: A Philosophical Enquiry, 1982 (ABA cert. merit 1983), Supplements to Gunther Constitutional Law, 1983-96, Playing by the Rules: A Philosophical Examination of Rule Based Decision-Making in Law and Life, 1991, The First Amendment: A Reader, 1992, 2d edit., 1995, The Philosophy of Law, 1995, Profiles, Probabilities and Stereotypes, 2003; editor Legal Theory, 1995-2000; contbr. articles to profl. jours. Mem. Atty. Gen.'s Commn. on Pornography, 1985-86. Served with Mass. Army N.G., 1970-71. NEH fellow, summer 1980, Guggenheim fellow, 2001-02. Fellow Am. Acad. Arts and Scis., Radcliffe Inst. Adv. Studies; mem. Am. Philos. Assn. (chair com. philosophy and law 2006—), Am. Soc. Polit. and Legal Philosophy (v.p. 1996-99), Assn. Am. Law Schs. (chmn. sect. constl. law 1984-86). Office: Kennedy Sch of Govt Harvard U Cambridge MA 02138 Office Phone: 617-495-8737. Business E-Mail: fred_schauer@harvard.edu.

**SCHAUER, THOMAS ALFRED,** insurance company executive; b. Canton, Ohio, Dec. 24, 1927; s. Alfred T. and Marie A. (Luthi) S.; m. Joanne Alice Fay, Oct. 30, 1954; children: Alan, John, David, Susan, William. BSc, Ohio State U., 1950. With Ind. Ins. Svc. Corp., 1964—, Ind. Benefit Svc. Corp., 1984—2003. Dir. Bank One, Akron, N.A., Ohio, 1991-97, mem. adv. bd., 1997-2000. Chmn. Joint Hosp. Blood Com., 1974; bd. dirs. McKinley Life Ins. Co., 1991-95; bd. dirs. Better Bus. Bur., Canton, 1970-81, chmn., 1979-80; bd. dirs. area YMCA, 1974-92, v.p., 1975-82, pres., 1982-84; trustee Canton Cemetery Assn., 1988-91, Stark County Blue Coats, 1987-, Plain Local Schs. Found., 2004-; bd. dirs. Hosp. Bur. Ctrl. Stark County, 1972-78; vice chmn. bd. Aultman Hosp., 1981-84, chmn., 1984-87; chmn. Aultman Health Svcs. Assn., 1990-93; pres. Aultman Hosp. Found., 1987-90, trustee, 1971-98, trustee emeritus, 1998—; chmn. bd. JMS Found., 1968—; bd. dirs. United Way, 1974-84, pres., 1976-78; mem. distbn. com. Stark County Found., 1977-87, chmn. distbn. com., 1984-87, dir. Dime Bank, Canton, 1965-72, First Nat. Bank of Canton/Ctrl. Trust Co. NE Ohio, N.A., 1972-91; adv. bd. Malone Coll., 1979-92; trustee Kent State U., 1980-88, trustee emeritus, 1988—, N.E. Ohio Univs. Coll. Medicine, 1983-88; past trustee Canton Urban League, Boys Village, Smithville, Ohio, Canton Art Inst., Buckeye Coun. Boy Scouts Am. With USN, 1946-48. Recipient gold key award United Way Stark County, 1981, award of merit Canton C. of C., 1984, red triangle award Canton Area YMCA, 1985. Mem. Chartered Ins. Inst. London, Nat. Assn. Mfg., Am. Soc. CPCUs, Am. Soc. CLUs, Assn. Advanced Life Underwriters, Am. Risk and Ins. Assn., Am. Soc. Pension Actuaries, Stark County Accident and Health Underwriters (past pres.), Canton Club (past pres.), Brookside Country Club, Atwood Yacht Club. Home: 1756 Dunbarton Ave NW Canton OH 44708-1807 Office: Millennium Ctr 200 Market Ave N Ste 100 Canton OH 44702 E-mail: tomschauer@att.net.

**SCHAUER, VICTORIA YOUNG,** elementary school educator, writer; b. L.A., Dec. 24, 1959; d. Willard Clark Young and Anne Kathryn Masters-Young; children: Kenneth Charles, Ardan Nathaneil, William Christopher, Sarah Jane Rose. A magna cum laude in Arts and Scis., Tacoma C.C., Wash. 1993; BA magna cum laude in Pub. and Print Arts, Pacific Luth. U., Tacoma, Wash., 1996, MA magna cum laude in Anthrop., 1996, MA magna cum laude in Edn., 2002. Cert. tchr. Wash. Coord. printing Virginia Mason Hosp., Seattle, 1984—88; prin., owner Peninsula Childbirth Edn., Vaughn, Wash., 1989—92; reporter Ariz. State Press, Tempe, Ariz., 1995—96; mgr. comm. Multi Care Health Sys., Tacoma, 1996—2001; grad. asst. Sch. Edn. Pacific Luth. U., 2001—02; tchr. Mid. Sch. Peninsula Sch. Dist., Gig Harbor, Wash., 2002—. Judges pubs. contests Nat. Electric Power Cos., 2000; trainer Safe and Curl Schs., Gig Harbor, 2004—05. Author: Why Adults Should Listen, 2002; editor: N.W. Reading Jour., 1996, Multicare Health Sys., 2001, Pierce County Transit, 2004. Named Student of Yr., Tacoma C.C., 1993; recipient Freddie award, Nat. Hosp. and Health Care Advertisers, 1999; Scripps Howard Journalism scholar, 1992—95. Mem.: ACLU, Wash. Edn. Assn. (conf. del. 2006), Internat. Reading Assn., Nat. Coun. Tchrs. English, Women in Black (peace activist 2001—), Pierce County Dems. (precinct capt. 1992, 1996, 2000). Democrat. Avocations: travel, running, jewelry design, journalism. Office: Key Peninsula Mid Sch 5510 Key Peninsula Hwy N Lakebay WA 98349

**SCHAUF, VICTORIA,** pediatrician, educator; b. NYC, Feb. 17, 1943; d. Maurice J. and Ruth H. (Baker) Bisson; m. Michael Delaney; 2 children. BS in Microbiology with honors, U. Chgo., 1965, MD with honors, 1969. Intern in pediat. U. Chgo. Hosp., 1969—70, resident in pediat. 3hnal Hosp. of Balt., 1970—71; chief resident pediat. Children's Hosp. Nat. Med. Ctr., Washington, 1971—72; rsch. trainee NIH, Bethesda, Md., 1972; adj. asst. prof. microbiology Rush Med. Coll., Chgo., 1972—74; prof. pediat., head pediatric infectious diseases U. Ill., Chgo., 1974—84; med. officer FDA, Rockville, Md., 1984—86; chmn. dept. pediat. Nassau County Med. Ctr., East Meadow, NY, 1986—90; prof. pediat. SUNY, Stony Brook, 1987—94; pvt. practice, 1995—; chief pediatric svcs. Ridgecrest Regional Hosp., 2005—. Vis. prof. Rockefeller U., 1990-92; mem. vis. faculty Shang-Hai (Thailand) U., 1978; mem. ad hoc com. study sects. NIH, Bethesda, 1981-82; bd. dirs. Pearl Stetler Rsch. Found., Chgo., 1982-84; cons. FDA, 1987-88, 93-95, Can. Bur. Human Prescription Drugs, Ottawa, 1990-2004, Biotech. Investors, 1993-95, Calif. Children's Svcs., 2005—; course dir. pediat. infectious diseases rev. course Cornell U. Med. Coll., N.Y.C., 1994, faculty, 1995. Co-author: Pediatric Infectious Diseases: A Comprehensive Guide to the Subspecialty, 1997; prodr. radio and TV programs in field; contbr. articles to profl. jours., chpts. to books. Vol. physician Cook County Hosp., Chgo., 1974-84; mem. adv. com. Nat. Hansen's Disease Ctr., La., 1986, Nassau County Day Care Coun., N.Y., 1988-90; mem. adv. bd. Surg. Aid to Children of World, N.Y., 1986-90; commr., sec. Kern County Children and Families Commn., 1999-2002; sec., bd. dirs. Indian Wells Valley Cmty. Found., 2001-. Am. Lung Assn. grantee U. Ill., 1977; recipient contract NIH, U. Ill., 1978-81, grantee, 1979-84. Fellow Infectious Diseases Soc. Am.; mem. Pediatric Infectious Diseases Soc. (exec. bd.), Soc. Pediatric Rsch., Am. Pediatric Soc., AAAS, Am. Soc. Microbiology, Am. Acad. Pediat., Phi Beta Kappa, Alpha Omega Alpha. Avocation: walking. Office Phone: 760-371-2128. Business E-Mail: vschauf@pol.net.

**SCHAUMBER, PETER CAREY,** federal agency administrator; b. NYC, May 29, 1942; m. Kathleen Charbonnet; children: Kathleen, Drew, Alexandra. BA, Georgetown U., 1964; JD, Georgetown U. Law Ctr., 1968. Asst. corp. counsel Dist. of Columbia; asst. US Dept. Justice; tax trial atty., assoc. dir. law dept. divsn., Office Comptr. of the Currency US Dept. Treasury; ptnr., dir. litigation dept. Colton & Boykin P.C., 1980—87; of counsel Wickwire Gavin, 1987—93; adj. prof. law Law Ctr George Washington U.; mem. NLRB, 2002—. Adj. prof. Georgetown U. Sch. Bus. Office: NLRB 1099 14th St NW Washington DC 20570-0001*

---

**SCHAUMBURG, HERBERT HOWARD,** neurology educator; b. Houston, Nov. 6, 1932; m. Joanna Jane Austin; children: Barnabas Paul, Kristin Elizabeth. AB cum laude, Harvard Coll., 1956; MD, Washington U., 1960. Instr. in neurology Albert Einstein Coll. of Medicine, N.Y.C., 1964-67, asst. prof. neurology, 1967-69, assoc. prof. neurology, 1972-76, prof., 1976—, vice chmn., 1977-84, acting chmn., 1984-86, chmn., 1986—; instr. pathology Harvard Med. Sch., Boston, 1969-71. Mem. Am. Acad. Neurology, Am. Assn. Neuropathologists, Am. Neurol. Assn., Soc. Toxicology, Soc. Neurosci. Home: 616 King Ave City Island Bronx NY 10464 Office: Albert Einstein Coll Medicine 1300 Morris Park Ave Bronx NY 10461-1926 Office Phone: 718-430-2002. Business E-Mail: schaumb@aecom.yu.edu.

**SCHAUPP, JOAN POMPROWITZ,** trucking executive, writer; b. Green Bay, Wis., Sept. 29, 1932; d. Joseph and Helen Elizabeth (VanderLinden) Pomprowitz; m. Robert James Schaupp, Sept. 4, 1956; children: Margaret Schaupp Siebert, Frederick, John Robert, Elizabeth Schaupp Sidles. BS cum laude, U. Wis., 1954; cert. in theology, St. Norbert Coll. Theol. Inst., 1979; MA, U. Wis., Green Bay, 1982; DMin, Grad. Theol. Found., 1996. Woman's editor Green Bay Press-Gazette, 1955-56; freelance writer Green Bay, 1957-75; sec.-treas., dir. L.C.L. Transit Co., Green Bay, 1962-70; chmn., dir. P & S Investment Co., Green Bay, 1982—; mgmt. cons., 1984-89, dir. strategic planning, 1992, vice chmn., 1994—. Pres. The Manna Co., Green Bay, 1992—; adv. com. Women's Ctr. St. Norbert Coll., 1999—; chmn. P&S Investment Co., 2004. Author: Jesus Was a Teenager, 1972, Woman Image of Holy Spirit, 1975 (Thomas More Book award), Elohim: A Search for a Symbol for Human Fulfillment, 1995. Master gardener De Pere (Wis.) Beautification Com., 1991-92; design cons. Nat. Fedn. Grden Clubs, 2004; lector St. Francis Xavier Cathedral, Green Bay, 1991-92. Recipient Ambassador award, St. Norbert Coll., 1997, Disting. Svc. award, 2004, Disting. Citizenship award, St. Norbert Coll. Alumni Assn., 2004. Mem.: Nat. Press Club, Nat. Fedn. Press Women, Am. Acad. Religion, Franciscan Internat., Secular Franciscan Order (vice min. Assumption Province 1991—92), Equestrian Order of the Holy Sepulchre Jerusalem (lady grand cross), Soc. Bibl. Lit. Avocations: gardening, walking, swimming.

**SCHAUT, JOSEPH WILLIAM,** retired bank executive; b. Cleve., May 30, 1928; s. Francis Xavier and Emma Gertrude (Urmann) S.; m. Susan Stiver, Apr. 23, 1955; children: Deborah Anne Schaut Payne, Gregory F., Mary Theresa Schaut Bentley, Michael J. B in Social Sci. in Econs., Georgetown U., 1950, JD, 1953. Bar: D.C. 1953, U.S. Mil. Ct. Appeals 1953, U.S. Dist. Ct. D.C. 1953, U.S. Ct. Appeals (D.C. cir.) 1953, Ohio 1954. Tax analyst Republic Steel Corp., Cleve., 1953-60, asst. to sec., 1960-67, asst. sec., 1967-81, dir. corp. properties, 1976-84, corp. sec. Cleve., 1981-84; bus. cons., 1984-85; sr. trust officer AmeriTrust Co., Cleve. N.A., 1986-92; sr. trust officer Soc. Nat. Bank, Cleve., 1992-93, v.p., 1993-96, Mellon Bank F.S.B., 1996-98; ret., 1998. Col. ret. USAR, 1950—78. Recipient award Silver Beaver Greater Cleve. Coun., Boy Scouts Am., 1975. Mem. Am. Soc. Corp. Secs. (dir 1976-79), Ohio State Bar Assn., Greater Cleve. Growth Assn., Delta Theta Phi, Pi Gamma Mu Roman Catholic.

**SCHEAR, BETTY Z.,** engineering executive, consultant; b. Dayton, Ohio, Dec. 17, 1925; d. Jacob Zukerman and Esther (Groban) Litwack; m. Burt E. Schear, July 4, 1948; children: Abe, Martin, Edith, Jesse. BS in Engring., U. Cin., 1948; MBA, U. Dayton, 1968. Assoc. editor Gardner Pubs., Cin., 1948-50; adminstrv. mgr. Schear Family Practice, Dayton, 1952-85; cons. Dayton, 1985—. Cons. Health Power, Inc., Columbus, Ohio, 1984-2000. One-woman shows include U. Dayton, 1972. Mem. NSPE, NAFE, Nat. Mus. Women in the Arts (charter), Soc. Women Engrs., Am. Mgmt. Assn. Avocations: reading, art, travel, theater, music.

**SCHECHNER, RICHARD,** theater director, educator; b. Newark, Aug. 23, 1934; s. Sheridan and Selma Sophia (Schwarz) S.; m. Carol Martin; children: Samuel MacIntosh, Sophia Martin. BA, Cornell U., 1956; postgrad., Johns Hopkins U., 1957; MA, State U. Iowa, 1958; PhD, Tulane U., 1962. Asst. prof. theatre Tulane U., 1962-66, assoc. prof., 1966-67; prof. performance studies NYU, 1967-91, Univ. prof., 1991—; co-founder, co-dir. New Orleans Group, 1965-67; founder, dir. Performance Group, N.Y.C., 1967-80; founder, artistic dir. East Coast Artists, 1991—; Andrew H. White prof.-at-large Cornell U., 1999—2005; sr. fellow Ctr. for Cultural Sociology, Yale U., 2004—. Hon. prof. Shanghai Theatre Acad., 1995—; prof. titular agl. Instituto Superior de Arte, Havana, Cuba; bd. dirs. Theatre Comms. Group, 1977-78; advisor Internat. Theatre Inst., 1975-77, Ctr. Performance Rsch., Aberwrystwich, Wales, 1993-97; pres. Bunch of Exptl. Theatres, 1975, 77, Fulbright Theatre Discipline Com., 1988-91. Author: Public Domain, 1968, Environmental Theater, 1973 (with others) Theatres, Spaces, Environments, 1975, Essays on Performance Theory, 1977, 2d edit. 1988, 3d edit., 2003, (with others) Makbeth, 1977, The End of Humanism, 1982, Performative Circumstances, 1983, Between Theater and Anthropology, 1985, (with Samuel MacIntosh-Schechner) The Engleburt Stories: North to the Tropics, 1987, The Future of Ritual, 1993, Performance Studies-An Introduction, 2002, 2d edit., 2006, Over, Under and Around, 2004, (with others) Yokastas, 2003; editor: Dionysus in 69, 1970; adv. editor: Asian Theatre Jour., 1985-; co-editor: Free Southern Theater, 1968, Ritual, Play, and Performance, 1976, By Means of Performance, 1990; gen. editor: (series) Worlds of Performance, 1993—, (with Lisa Wolford) Grotowski Sourcebook, 1997, (with Carol Martin) Enactments, 2006; editor: The Drama Rev., 1962-69, 85—, contbg. editor, 1971-85; adv. editor Jour. Ritual Studies, 1987—; dir. Dionysus in 69, 1968, Macbeth, 1969, Commune, 1970, The Tooth of Crime, 1972, Mother Courage, 1975, The Marilyn Project, 1975, Oedipus, 1977, Cops, 1978, The Balcony, 1979, The Red Snake, 1981, Richard's Lear, 1981, The Cherry Orchard, 1983, Prometheus Project, 1985, Don Juan, 1987, Tomorrow He'll Be Out of the Mountains, 1989, Ma Rainey's Black Bottom, 1992, Faust/Gastronome, 1993, The Oresteia, 1995 Three Sisters, 1997, Hamlet, 1999, Waiting for Godot, 2002, Yokastas, 2003, Yokastas Redux, 2005. Served with AUS, 1958-60. Recipient Modello prize, 1985, Contbns. to Theatre Spl. award New England Theatre Conf., 1991, Work in Theatre award Towson State U., 1991, Lifetime Achievement award Performance Studies Internat., 2002; grantee John D. Rockefeller 3d Fund, 1971-72, 76, Asian Cultural Coun., 1988, 95; Guggenheim fellow, 1976, Fulbright fellow, 1976, 83, N.Y. Inst. Humanities fellow, 1987-94, NEH sr. rsch. fellow, 1988, Humanities fellow Princeton U., 1992, Am. Inst. Indian Studies fellow, 1997, Montgomery fellow Dartmouth Coll., 1998, Am. Coun. Learned Socs. fellow, 2005, Ctrl. Sch. Speech and Drama fellow, London, 2005. Office: NYU 721 Broadway 6th Fl Washington Sq New York NY 10003 Office Phone: 212-998-1638. Business E-Mail: rs4@nyu.edu.

**SCHECHTER, ARTHUR LOUIS,** lawyer; b. Rosenberg, Tex., Dec. 6, 1939; s. Morris and Helen (Brilling) S.; m. Joyce Proler, Aug. 26, 1965; children: Leslie Schechter Karpas, Jennifer Schechter Rosen. BA, U. Tex., 1962, JD, 1964; postgrad., U. Houston, 1964-65. Bar: Tex. 1964, U.S. Dist. Ct. (ea. and so. dists.) Tex. 1966, U.S. Ct. Appeals (5th cir.), U.S. Supreme Ct. 1976; cert. Tex. Bd. Legal Specialization to Personal Injury Trial Law, 1964-. Pres. Arthur L. Schechter P.C., Houston, 1992-94, Schechter & Marshall, Houston, 1994-96; amb. U.S. to Commonwealth Bahamas, 1998-2000; atty. Schechter, McElwee & Shaffer, LLP, Houston, 2001—05; shareholder Greenberg Traurig, LLP, Houston, 2005—06; sr. counsel Schechter McElure Shaffer & Harris LLP, Houston, 2006—. Spkr. Marine Law Sem., 1983; spkr. in field. Contbr. articles to profl. jours. Bd. dirs. Theatre Under the Stars, Houston, 1972—78, Congregation Beth Israel, Houston, 1972—84, pres., 1982—84; bd. dirs. Inst. Internat. Edn., 1996—98, S.E.A.R.C.H., 1996—98; pres. Am. Jewish Com., Houston, 1982—84, chmn. fgn. rels. com., chmn. United Jewish Campaign exec. com., chmn., 1993—94; pres. Jewish Fedn. Ctr. Houston, 1994—96; mem. Deans Coun. U. Tex. Law Sch.; chmn. bd. Harris County Met. Transit Authority, 2002—04; chmn. internat. travelor task force Mayor of Houston, 2005; mng. trustee mem. fin. com. Dem. Nat. Com., 1992, fin. chmn. Tex. Clinton/Gore '96; vice chmn. Clinton/Gore Jewish Leadership Coun., 1996; v.p. exec. com. Nat. Jewish Dem. Coun., 1992, chmn., 2004—; mem. Leadership Ctr. Dem. Senatorial Campaign Com.; trustee mem. Kerry/Edwards and Dem. Nat. Com.; fin. coun. Nat. Dem. Orgn., 1979; chmn. bd. Met. Transit Authority of Harris County, 2002—04;

---

bd. dirs. U. Tex. Med. Sch. Named one of Houston's Most Fascinating Mems. of the Med. Cmty., 2003; recipient Career and Recovery Resources Barrier Breaker award, United Way Agy., 2003, Search's Outstanding Leadership award, 2003, Israel Bonds Nat. Leradership award, 2004. Home: 19A West Ln Houston TX 77019-1007 Office Phone: 713-757-7811. Personal E-mail: aschechter@qzip.net. Business E-Mail: aschechter@smslegal.com.

**SCHECHTER, DANIEL SCOTT,** child and adolescent psychiatrist, researcher; b. Miami Beach, Fla., Aug. 15, 1962; s. Harold and Evelyn Iris (Miller) Schechter; m. Christine Breede, June 25, 1996; 1 child, Jan Nikolai Breede-Schechter. BA summa cum laude, Columbia Coll., 1983; MA in Music Theory, Composition, Columbia Grad. Sch. Arts and Sci., 1987; MD, Columbia Coll., 1991. Diplomate Am. Bd. Psychiatry. Med. intern NY Presbyn. Hosp., NYC, 1992—93, clin. fellow child psychiatry, 1996—99, NY State Psychiat. Inst., resident in psychiatry, 1993—96; NIMH T-32 rsch. fellow Columbia U., NYC, Psychol. U., NYC, 1999—2002; med. dir. Infant-Family Svc., NY Pub. Health, NYC, 1998—; asst. prof. clin. psychiatry in pediat. Columbia Coll. P & S, NYC, 2003—. Mem. bd. dirs. NY Zero to Three Network, NYC, 2004—; mem. adv. bd. Columbia Head Start Program, NYC, 2004—. Editor, contbr. September 11: Trauma and Human Bonds, 2003, revised edit., 2004. Mem. NYC Dept. Health and Mental Hygiene Strategic Working Group on Early Childhood Mental Devel., 2003—; early childhood mental health adv. NYC Dept. Health and Early Childhood Mental Hygiene Strategic Working Group, 2003—. Recipient K-23 award, NIMH, Washington, 2003, Significant Contbr. award, Internat. Psychoanalytical Assn., 2005; grantee, 2000, 2002, 2005; Solnit fellow, Zero to Three Nat. Ctr., Washington, 2001, Ruane scholar, Columbia U., 2003. Mem.: APA, Am. Acad. Child Adolescent Psychiatry (mem. infancy com., co-chair subcom. on practice parameters 2003—, Presdl. scholar 1999, Pilot Rsch. award 2001). Avocations: cello, languages. Office: Columbia U NY State Psychiat Inst Unit 40 Rm 6407 1051 Riverside Dr New York NY 10032 also: 1 Milligan Pl 1F New York NY 10011

**SCHECHTER, LYNN RENEE,** psychologist; b. NYC, July 7, 1969; d. Joel David and Sandra Bauman Schechter; m. Issam E. El-Zahr, July 8, 2001; children: Leah Joy El-Zahr, Leo Harris El-Zahr. BS, Cornell U., 1991; MA, Columbia U., 1992, EdM, 1997, PhD, 2001. Lic. psychologist N.Y. Sch. psychologist Reece Sch., N.Y.C., 1997—2000; psychologist Albert Einstein Coll. Medicine, Bronx, NY, 1997—2002; neurodevelopmentalist Jacobi Med. Ctr., Bronx, 2000—02; pvt. practice Baton Rouge, 2003—. Creator, dir. tutoring and mentoring program for children with HIV Jacobi Med. Ctr., Bronx, 2001—02. Mem.: APA (divsn. 16 sch. psychology), Golden Key, Kappa Delta Pi, Omicron Nu. Avocations: reading, music, sports. Office: Bluebonnet Psychol Svc 2356 Drusilla Ln Baton Rouge LA 70809 Office Phone: 225-926-7500. E-mail: lynnschechter@aol.com.

**SCHECHTER, ROBERT SAMUEL,** chemical engineer, educator; b. Houston, Feb. 26, 1929; s. Morris S. and Helen Ruth Schechter; m. Mary Ethel Rosenberg, Feb. 15, 1953; children: Richard Martin, Alan Lawrence (dec.), Geoffrey Louis. BS in Chem. Engring, Tex. A&M U., 1950; PhD in Chem. Engring. U. Minn., 1956. Registered profl. engr., Tex. Asst. prof. chem. engring. U. Tex. at Austin, 1956-60, assoc. prof., 1960-63, prof., 1963—; adminstrv. dir. Ctr. Statis. Mechs. and Thermodynamics, 1968-72, chmn. dept. chem. engring., 1970-73, chmn. petroleum engring., 1975-78, E.J. Cockrell, Jr. prof. chem. and petroleum engring., 1975-81, Dula and Ernie Cockrell prof. engring., 1981-83, Getty prof. engring., 1984-85, Getty Oil Centennial chair in Petroleum Engring., 1985-89, W.A. (Monty) Moncrief Centennial Endowed chair in Petroleum Engring., 1989-97; prof. emeritus U. Tex., 1997. Vis. prof. U. Edinburgh, Scotland, 1965-66; Disting. vis. prof. U. Kans., spring 1968; vis. prof. U. Brussels, 1969; Disting. Lindsay lectr. Tex. A&M U., 1993; cons. in field. Author: Variational Method in Engineering, 1967, (with G.S.G. Beveridge) Optimization: Theory and Practice, 1970, Adventures in Fortran Programming, 1975, (with B.B. Williams and J.L. Gidley) Acidizing Monograph, 1979, (with D.D. Shah) Enhanced Oil Recovery by Surfactants and Polymers, 1979 (with Maurice Bourrel) Microemulsions and Related Systems, 1988, Oil Well Stimulation, 1991; contbr. (with D.D. Shah) numerous articles to profl. jours. Served to 1st lt., Chem. Corps AUS, 1951-53. Decorated Chevalier Order Palmes Academique, 1978; recipient Outstanding Teaching award U. Tex., 1969, Outstanding Paper award, 1973, Gen. Dynamics award for Excellence in Engring. Teaching, Gen. Dynamics Corp., 1987, Sr. Rsch. award Engring. Rsch. Coun. of Am. Soc. Engring. Educators, 1991. Mem. AIME (Industry Edn. award 1998), AIChE (Founders award 1998), Am. Chem. Soc., Soc. Petroleum Engrs. (John Franklin Carll award 1994, Improved Oil Recovery Pioneer 1996), Nat. Acad. Engrs., Sigma Xi, Tau Beta Pi. Achievements include developing methods of measuring surface viscosity and ultra low inter-facial tensions; discovering instability of thermal diffusion. Home: 4700 Ridge Oak Dr Austin TX 78731-4724 Office: U Tex Dept Petroleum & Geosystems Austin TX 78712 Office Phone: 512-471-3245. Business E-Mail: rsschechter@mail.utexas.edu.

**SCHECHTERMAN, LAWRENCE,** chef, business consultant; b. Elizabeth, N.J., June 23, 1943; s. Josef and Sylvia (Berger) S.; children: Jill Laura, Danielle Sara, Gregory Jared. BA, U. Miami, Fla., 1966; JD, Suffolk U., 1969; LLM, NYU, 1973; AS in Culinary Arts, Art Inst. Ft. Lauderdale, 2001. Tax assoc. Coopers & Lybrand, N.Y.C., 1969-70; assoc. Bendit, Weinstock & Sharbaugh, Newark, 1970-72; pvt. practice East Brunswick, NJ, 1972-81; gen. counsel Equinox Solar, Inc., Miami, 1981-83; mem. Lawrence Schechterman, P.A., Boca Raton, Fla., 1983-93; pres. Ocean Cons. Group divsn. Securities Arbitration Recovery, Inc., Boca Raton, 1993-97; pvt. chef, 2000—; bridgetenor Boca Raton, Fla., 2006—. Author: (books) In the Mood with Food, A Bachelor's Guide to Wooing Her with Food, 1998, 2000, 01; (poetry) New Dimensions; An Anthology of American Poetry, 1967, The Harmony of Silence, 2000, Touched by Grace, 1999, Touched by Love, 1999, Surrounded By Dreams, 1998, A Trusting Heart, 2000; contbr. articles to profl. jours. Mem. coun. Twp. of East Brunswick, NJ, 1976—80; pres. B'nai Torah Congregation of Boca Raton Inc., 1987—89, trustee, 1989—91. Mem.: B'nai B'rith Men's Lodge (co-founder Lodge 2935, charter pres. 1973—74). Office: 20889 Saint Andrews Blvd Apt 4 Boca Raton FL 33433-1710

**SCHECHTMAN, SAUL,** conductor; b. Winchester, Conn., Sept. 4, 1924; s. Isidore Schechtman and Clara Goodman; m. Carolyn Raney, July 31, 1952; children: Carol, Julia. BA, Bklyn. Coll., 1947; post grad., Juilliard Sch. of Music, N.Y.C., 1949. Music dir. Bronx Symphony Orch., N.Y.C., 1953—56; conductor, music dir. Omnibus Program (CBS), N.Y.C., 1954—57; music dir. Bergen Philharmonic, Teaneck, NJ, 1956—60, Carnival (Broadway show), N.Y.C., 1961—63, Hello Dolly, N.Y.C., 1966—70, Orch. Piccola, Balt., 1976—80; kapellmeister Theatre Oberhausen, Oberhausen, Germany, 1981—84. Composer: Auntie Mame, 1956, Diaspora variations, 1989, German Radio Orchs., 1990—94; dir.: (plays) Kiss Me Kate, 1958, How To Succeed in Business, 1963-64, My Fair Lady, 1960. Pvt. 1st class U.S. Army, 1943—46. Europe. Fellowship in orch. conducting, Juilliard Sch. of Music, 1949—51. Mem. Am. Soc. Composers, Authors and Publishers. Avocation: tennis. Home: 134 Cathedral Ave Hempstead NY 11550

**SCHECK, BARRY C.,** legal association administrator, educator; b. Queens, NY, 1949; BS, Yale U., 1971; JD, U. Calif., Berkeley, 1974. Bar: N.Y. 1974. Staff atty. Legal Aid Soc, NYC, 1974—77; prof. Law, dir. Clin. Legal Edn., Trial Advocacy Programs Benjamin N. Cardozo Sch. Law, Yeshiva U., NYC, 1977—, dir. Jacob Burns Ctr. for Study of Law and Ethics, 1977—, lawyer, dir. Innocence Project, 1992—. Former faculty mem. Nat. Inst. Trial Advocacy and Def. Coun.; tchr., organizer trial advocacy programs numerous pub. defender offices, bass assns. and law firms; commn. mem. NY State Commn. on Forensic Sci.; lectr. in field. Co-author: Raising and Litigating Claims of Electronic Surveillance, Actual Innocence: Five Days to Execution and Other Dispatches from the Wrongly Convicted; contbr. articles to profl. jours. Commr. NY Forensic Sci. Rev. Bd.; co-founder, co-dir. Innocence Project, 1992—; bd. dir. Nat. Inst. of Justice's Commn. on the Future of DNA Evidence, 1999. Mem.: Nat. Assn. Bar NYC (com. on criminal cts.), Nat. Assn. of Criminal Defense Lawyers (life; bd. dirs., co-chair, DNA Task Force, Most Outstanding Criminal Def. Lawyer in Am., Robert C. Heeney award

1996). Office: Innocence Project Benjamin N Cardozo Sch Law 55 5th Ave New York NY 10003-4301 Address: Nat Assn of Criminal Defense Lawyers 1150 18th St NW Ste 950 Washington DC 20036 Fax: 202-872-8690. E-mail: barry@nacdl.org.

**SCHECK, FRANK FOETISCH,** retired lawyer; b. Albuquerque, Apr. 9, 1923; s. Frank Henry and Ethel Jane (Garrett) S.; m. Jane Leonore Rembowski, Aug. 17, 1946; children: Christopher J, Jennifer J., Carl F. BS, Calif. Inst. Tech., 1948; LLB, Columbia U., 1951. Bar: N.Y. 1951, U.S. Dist. Ct. (so. dist.) N.Y. 1953, U.S. Ct. Appeals (2d cir.) 1959, U.S. Supreme Ct. 1959, U.S. Ct. Appeals (7th cir.) 1966, U.S. Ct. Appeals (D.C. and Fed. cirs.) 1983. Assoc. Pennie, Edmonds, Morton, Barrows & Taylor, N.Y.C., 1951-60; ptnr., Pennie, Edmonds, Morton, Taylor & Adams, N.Y.C., 1961-69; sr. ptnr. Pennie & Edmonds, 1970-91; retired, Pennie & Edmonds, 1991. With U.S. Army, 1942-45. Decorated Purple Heart. Mem. N.Y. Patent Law Assn. (dir. 1982-85, v.p. 1987-89, pres. elect 1989-90, pres. 1990-91). Conservative. Presbyterian. Home: 5 Linden Gate Ln Newport RI 02840-3334

**SCHECTER, ARNOLD JOEL,** public health physician, researcher; b. Chgo., Dec. 1, 1934; s. Benjamin and Leonore Natalie (Lyon) S.; m. Martha-Jean Berenson, Feb. 14, 1964; children: Benjamin, David, Anna. BA in Liberal Arts, U. Chgo., 1954, BS in Physiology-Neurophysiology, 1957; MD, Howard U., 1962; MPH, Columbia U., 1975. Diplomate Am. Coll. Preventive Medicine; med. lic., Ky., N.Y., N.J., N.C. Postdoc. dept. anatomy Harvard Med. Sch., Boston, 1962—64; instr. dept. medicine Mass. Gen. Hosp., Harvard Med. Sch., Boston, 1964-65; intern Beth Israel Hosp., Boston, 1966; gen. practitioner, sr. aviation med. examiner West Point, Ky., 1969-70; dir. inpatient rehab. ctr., drug and alcohol rehab. program Region Eight Mental Health and Mental Retardation Bd., Inc., Louisville, 1971-72; asst. prof. dept. psychiatry, divisional drug and alcohol abuse SUNY Downstate Med. Ctr., Bklyn., 1973-75; clin. assoc. prof. dept. preventive medicine N.J. Med. Sch., Newark, 1975-79; prof. dept. preventive medicine SUNY, Binghamton, 1979—98; prof. environ. scis. U. Tex. Sch. Pub. Health, Dallas, 1999—; pres. Zumwalt Inst. for Environ. Health Inc., 1996—. Spl. expert Nat. Inst. Environ. Health Scis. NIH, 1997—98; cons. U.S. EPA, Washington, 1985—86, Washington, 1999—2000, WHO, 1986—90; sci. peer reviewer dioxin U.S. EPA, 1995, 2000; peer reviewer A.T.S.D.R. of C.D.C., 1995—2005; dir. clin. rsch. in drug abuse, coord., faculty mem. Career Tchr. Tng. Ctr., SUNY Downstate, 1972—75; assoc. dir. office primary health care edn., office of the dean NJ Med. Sch., 1976—79; advisor Environ. Def. Fund, 1991—92, Nat. Vets. Legal Svcs. Project, 1991—92; co-founder assoc. editor Am. Jour. Drug and Alcohol Abuse, N.Y.C., 1973—78, editl. bd., 1978—86; editl. adv. bd. Substance and Alcohol Actions/Misuse, Elmsford, NY, 1979—85; adj. prof. epidemiology U. N.C. Sch. Pub. Health, 1998—2004; adj. prof. occupl. medicine Duke Med. Ctr., 1998—99. Editor: Rehabilitation Aspects of Drug Dependence, 1977, Treatment Aspects of Drug Dependence, 1978, Biomedical Issues in Drug Abuse, 1981, Sociological Issues in Drug Abuse, 1981, Dioxins and Health, 1994, 2003, Maxcy Rosenau Last Public Health and Preventive Medicine, 14th edit., 1998; sr. editor: 2d edit., 2003; co-editor (with H. Alksne, E. Kaufman): Drug Abuse: Modern Trends, Issues and Perspectives, 1978, Critical Concerns in the Field of Drug Abuse, 1978; contbr. over 300 articles to profl. jours. Maj. M.C., U.S. Army, 1967-69. Recipient Pacesetter award Commonwealth Mass., 1990. Fellow: ACP, Am. Coll. Occupl. and Environ. Medicine, Am. Coll. Preventive Medicine; mem.: AAAS, APHA (chair Vietnam caucus), Soc. Epidemiology Rsch., Tex. Pub. Health Assn., Soc. for Epidemiologic Rsch., Am. Occupl. and Environ. Medicine Assn., Am. Coll. Epidemiology, Am. Statis. Tchrs. Preventive Medicine. Achievements include discovery of PBDE brominated flame retardant contamination in breast milk of all US mothers tested, and that these levels as well as blood and food are highest in the world; PCB transformer fires can lead to contamination of buildings by dioxins and elevated dioxin body burden from Agent Orange in Vietnamese and in American Vietnam Veterans; dioxin contamination of body tissues of general population of the US; dioxin hot spots in Vietnam with current contamination of Vietnamese by contaminated food; development of congener specific tissue dioxin analysis as biomarker for dioxin exposure; developed naltrexone, a narcotic antagonist in rehabilitation of opiate addicts. Home: 16606 Loch Maree Ln Dallas TX 75248-1711 Office: U Tex Sch Pub Health 6011 Harry Hines Blvd Dallas TX 75248 Personal E-mail: ajschecter@aol.com. Business E-Mail: arnold.schecter@utsouthwestern.edu.

**SCHECTMAN, STEPHEN BARRY,** pharmaceutical executive; b. Washington, Oct. 20, 1947; s. Samuel and Rae (Tarnef) S.; m. Barbara L. Butcher, Sept. 10, 1969 (div. May 1994); children: Christopher, Matthew. BS, Randolph Macon Coll., 1970; postgrad., U. Tenn., 1974. Pres., CEO Medvac Corp., N.Y.C., 1993-94; spl. cons. Medco Containment Svcs., Montvale, NJ, 1991-93; ptnr. Hudson BioCapital Corp., N.Y.C., 1993-96; sr. dir. Schering-Plough Pharms., Kenilworth, NJ, 1996—2003; v.p. strategy CRI, L.A., 2003—; pres. NewHealth Solutions Group, N.J. and Calif., 2003; pres., COO Impact Med. Solutions, Inc., Tustin, Calif., 2004—; mng. ptnr. New Health Solutions Group, LLC. Author (with others) Biomedical Innovation, 1980. Fellowship NIMH, NIH, 1969-73, postgrad. fellowship dept. physiology Georgetown U. Sch. of Medicine, 1975-76. Mem. AAAS, N.Y. Acad. Sci., Beta Beta Beta. Jewish. Home and Office: Ste 4D 609 S Orange Ave South Orange NJ 07079-1063 Personal E-mail: cydney102047@yahoo.com. E-mail: medicine55@hotmail.com.

**SCHEEDER, LOUIS,** theater producer, director, educator; b. N.Y.C., Dec. 26, 1946; s. Louis W. and Julia H. (Callery) S. BA in English Lit., Georgetown U., 1968; postgrad., Sch. of Arts, Columbia U., 1968-69; MA in Performance Studies, NYU, 1995, PhD in Performance Studies, 2004. Founder, dir. The Classical Studio Tisch Sch. of the Arts, NYU, 1991—; Master Tchr., 1995—2004, assoc. arts prof., 2004—06, arts prof., 2006—; assoc. dean of faculty and interdisciplinary studies, 2006—. Dir. NYU Tisch Sch. of the Arts, Shakespeare Ensemble, 1989-90; mem. adv. council Nat. Com. on Arts and Edu., 1977-82; mem. D.C. Commn. on Arts and Humanities, 1976-80; bd. advs. New Playwrights' Theatre of Washington, 1975-82; asst. stage mgr. Arena Stage, Washington, 1969-70; assoc. artistic dir., dir., Folger Theatre Group, Washington, 1971-73, dir. producer, 1973-81; cons. Ctr. for Renaissance and Baroque Studies U. Md., 1984-91; asst. dir. Royal Shakespeare Co. Stratford-Upon-Avon, Eng., 1988. Dir., prodr. plays including Creeps (Am. premiere), 1973, The Farm (Am. premiere), 1974, The Collected Works of Billy the Kid (Am. premiere), 1975, Henry V, 1976, The Fool (Am. premiere), 1976, Mummer's End (world premiere), 1977, Teeth 'n' Smiles (Am. premiere), 1977, Two Gentlemen of Verona, 1977, Mackerel (world premiere), 1978, Black Elk Speaks (tour), 1978, Richard III, 1978, Whose Life Is It Anyway? (Am. premiere), 1978, Richard II, 1978, As You Like It, 1979, Custer (Kennedy Ctr.), 1979, Charlie and Algernon (Kennedy Ctr.), 1980, Crossing Niagara (Am. premiere), 1981, Love's Labour's Lost, 1981; also dir. Broadway, Off Broadway, regional prodns. including Charlie and Algernon, 1980, (Off Broadway) Creeps, 1973, Passover, 1986, (Off-Off-Broadway) The Gettysburg Sound Bite, 1989, Brunch at Trudy and Paul's, 1990, The Christmas Rules, 1991, The Monkey Business, 1992, Mankynde, N.Y Fringe Festival, 2005; dir. All's Well That Ends Well, 1990; dance: dir. Near Ruins, Ruby, 1996, Let's Go Thundering, 1997, Give Us a Kiss, Johnny, 1998, Keeper, 1999; prodr. How I Got That Story (Off Broadway), 1982, Diamonds (Off Broadway), 1984, Today, I Am a Fountain Pen (Off Broadway), 1986; dir. Man. Theatre Ctr., 1982, 83, 84, Nat. Arts Ctr., Ottawa, Ont., Can., 1984, Hedda Gabler, Ctr. Stage, Toronto, 1985, Reg: Life in the Trees, GeVa Theatre, 1991; asst. dir. Broadway prodn. Carrie, 1988, Pacific Rep. prodn. Merchant of Venice, 2002, Much About Nothing, Santa Monica Shakespeare Project, 2004, All's Well that Ends Well, Shakespeare Santa Monica, 2005, King Lear, Shakespeare Santa Monica, 2006; author: (with Shane Ann Younts) All the Words on Stage: A Complete Pronunciation Dictionary for the Plays of William Shakespeare, 2002. Bd. advisors Women's Project, 2006—. Recipient Dixon award Georgetown U., 1968, Alumni Achievement award Georgetown U. Alumni Club Met. Washington, 1981, Mayor's Arts award, D.C., 1982, Acad. Excellence award NYU, 1995, Hall of Fame, Georgetown Theatre Alumni, 2005. Mem.: Soc. Stage Dirs. and Choreographers, Episc. Actors' Guild (life; coun. 1990—96, 2002—04, 2006—). Home: 7 Stuyvesant Oval New York NY 10009-1901 E-mail: louis.scheeder@nyu.edu, ls36@nyu.edu.

**SCHEEL, NELS EARL,** corporate financial executive, accountant; b. Spencer, Wis., Sept. 25, 1925; s. Roland Edward and Louise Ernestine Scheel; m. Elaine Marie Carlisle, Aug. 28, 1949; children: Thomas W., John E., Martha L., Mark A., Mary E. BA, Youngstown Coll., 1949; MBA, U. Pa., 1950. CPA, Ohio. Staff acct. Lybrand Ross Bros., Cleve., 1950-54; asst. controller Century Foods, Youngstown, Ohio, 1954-62; treas., controller The Bailey Co., Cleve., 1962-63, Golden Dawn Foods, Sharon, Pa., 1963-82; v.p.; chief fin. officer Peter J. Schmitt Co., Sharon, 1982-89; cons. to industry Columbiana, 1989—. Part-time faculty Youngstown (Ohio) State U., 1954—94; bd. mem. Sovereign Cirs., Inc., North Jackson, Ohio, 1992—2001, bd. chmn., 1995—99, sec.-treas., 1999—2001. Pres. Crestview Bd. Edn., Columbiana, Ohio, 1970-81; trustee Columbiana Cmty. Found., 2002—. Staff sgt. AUS, 1943-46, PTO, hon. discharge. Mem. Am. Inst. CPA's, Ohio Soc. CPA's.

**SCHEELE, JENNIFER JOY,** music educator; b. Dallas, Mar. 2, 1981; d. Jes and Joy Rene Tarp; m. Adam Wallace Scheele, June 11, 2004; children: Annastasia Pearl, Seth Gordon. BS in Music summa cum laude, U. of Wis. Platteville, 2004. Cosmetology practitioner Wis. Cosmetologist The Hair Studio, Platteville, 2000; accompanist Platteville Sch. Dist., 2001—05; choir accompanist U. of Wis., Platteville, 2002—05; accompanist Cuba City (Wis.) Sch. Dist., 2003—05, Southwestern Sch. Dist., Hazel Green, Wis., 2004; piano tchr. Platteville, 2002—05; asst. music dir. Montello Sch. Dist., Montello, Wis., 2005—; piano tchr. Montello, 2005—; pianist Marquette Cmty. Ch., 2006—. Vice pres., treas. Univ. Singers, Platteville, 2002—04; sec. Symphony Band, Platteville, 2001—03. Ch. pianist Comty. Evang. Free Ch., Platteville, 2004—05; worship team mem. Intervarsity Christian Fellowship, Platteville, 2000—03. Recipient Valerie Beighley scholarship, U. of Wis. - Platteville, 2003, William Dennis scholarship, 2001, 2002. Mem.: Nat. Guild of Piano Tchrs., Music Tchrs. Nat. Assn., Nat. Vocat.-Tech. Honor Soc., Sigma Alpha Iota (life; v.p. membership 2003—04, Rose of Honor 2004, Most Valuable Mem. 2004). Avocations: reading, scrapbooks.

**SCHEELE, NICHOLAS V.,** automotive executive; b. Jan. 3, 1944; married; 3 children. With Ford British and European Ops., 1978; pres. Ford of Mex., 1988; chmn., CEO Jaguar Cars Ltd., 1992—99; chmn. Ford Europe, 2000—01; group v.p. Ford N.Am., 2001—02; COO Ford Motor Co., 2001—04, pres., 2001—; also bd. dirs. Chancellor U. Warwick, 2002—; adv. bd. Coventry U., Fulbright Commn., Durham U.; Midland coun. mem. Inst. Dirs. Active Save the Children, St. Basil's Appeal for Homeless Children; adv. bd. British Am. C. of C.; chmn. Foresight 2020. Decorated knight British Queen, Order of St. Michael and St. George. Master: Nat. Soc. for the Prevention Cruelty to Children (life); mem.: Soc. Motor Mfrs. and Traders (exec. com.). Avocations: reading, music. Office: Ford Motor Co One American Rd Dearborn MI 48126-1899

**SCHEELER, JAMES ARTHUR,** architect; b. Pontiac, Ill., Dec. 20, 1927; s. Aman B. and Jane (Steele) S.; m. Barbara Jean Lloyd, Sept. 2, 1950; children: James Erich, Carl Aman, Orissa Jane Elizabeth. BS with highest honors, U. Ill., 1951, MS, 1952; postgrad., U. Liverpool, 1952-53. Grad. asst. U. Ill., Urbana, 1950-52; draftsman-designer Lundeen & Hilfinger, Bloomington, Ill., 1952-53; designer Skidmore, Owings & Merrill, Chgo., 1955-59; partner Richardson, Severns, Scheeler & Assos., Inc., Champaign, Ill., 1959-65, v.p., treas., 1965-71; vice chmn. bd., dir. Prodn. Systems for Architects and Engrs., Inc., 1973-81. Vis. critic U. Ill., 1959-60. Mem. Plan Commn., Champaign, 1966—71, chmn., 1966—71; mem. Champaign County Regional Planning Commn., 1967-71; bd. dirs. Nat. Center for a Barrier-Free Environment, 1978—81, pres., 1981. Served with USN, 1946-47. Recipient various archtl. awards.; Francis J. Plym fellow, 1953-54; Fulbright fellow, 1953. Fellow AIA (treas. Ctrl. Ill. chpt. 1967-68, nat. dep. exec. v.p. 1970-71, nat. dep. exec. v.p. 1971-76, press. coun. 1974-78, exec. v.p. 1977-78, program devel. group exec. 1976-85, sr. exec. 1985-88, v.p. design practice group 1989, resident fellow 1990—, Edward D. Kemper award 2000), Internat. Union of Archs. (Profl. Practice Commn. (sec., co-dir. 1994-2003, internat. union archs. coun. 2005—), Fedn. Colls. Archs. Republic Mex. (hon.), Royal Australian Inst. Architects (hon.); mem. Ill. Arts Coun. (archtl. adv. bd. 1966-71), Japan Inst. Architect (hon.), Montessori Soc. Champaign-Urbana (dir. 1964-66), Gargoyle, Scarab, Phi Kappa Phi, Lambda Chi Alpha, Lambda Alpha, Cosmos Club. Episcopalian. Address: 11179 Saffold Way Reston VA 20190-3824

**SCHEER, JANET KATHY,** mathematics professor; b. Bklyn., Apr. 22, 1947; d. Seymour and Hilda (Shoer) S. BA, Bklyn. Coll., 1968; MS, Syracuse U., NY, 1969; PhD, Ariz. State U., 1977. Cert. tchr., N.Y., Ariz.; cert. prin., Ariz. Math. tchr. Jamesville (N.Y.) DeWitt Middle Sch., 1969-72; math. tchr., middle sch. coordinator Am. Internat. Sch., Kfar Shmaryahu, Israel, 1972-74; from asst. prof. to assoc. prof. So. Ill. U., Carbondale, 1977—86; sr. nat. math. cons. Holt, Rinehart & Winston, 1986—89; nat. product devel. specialist Scott, Foresman and Co., Glenview, Ill., 1989-90, dir. field svcs. for math., 1991—; exec. dir. Create A Vision, Foster City, Calif. Sr. nat. math. cons. Holt, Rinehart & Winston, N.Y.C., 1986-89, Harcourt Brace-Jovanovich/Holt, 1989. Editor Ill. Math. Tchr. jour., 1980-83; author: Manipulatives in Mathematics Unlimited, 1987, Harcourt Math, 2002, 04, Holt Middle School Math, 2004; columnist Learning Mag., 1996-97; contbr. to textbooks and profl. jours. Named one of Outstanding Young Women Am., 1978, 81-85, Outstanding Tchr. Yr. So. Ill. U., 1978-79; recipient numerous grants. Mem. Nat. Council Tchrs. Math., Research Council for Diagnostic and Prescriptive Math. (charter mem., v.p. 1984-86), Ill. Council Tchrs. Math. (various offices), Phi Delta Kappa, Kappa Delta Pi. Avocations: swimming, golf, tennis. Office: Create A Vision 1175 Chess Dr Ste 206 Foster City CA 94404-1108 Office Phone: 650-357-8004. E-mail: scheervision@sbcglobal.net.

**SCHEER, JOEL MARTIN,** lawyer; b. Bklyn., Dec. 6, 1950; s. Jack H. and Sheila (Gams) S.; m. Linda M. Miller, Aug. 3, 1975; children: Jennie Shayne, Rachel Jayne, Zachary Judd. BA cum laude, Bklyn. Coll., 1972; JD with distinction, Hofstra U., 1975. Bar: Pa. 1975, U.S. Dist. Ct. (ea. dist.) Pa. 1976, U.S. Ct. Appeals (3d cir.) 1986, U.S. Supreme Ct. 1985. Law clk. to judge, Easton, Pa., 1975-76; sole practice, 1976-77; assoc. Fishbone and Refowich, Easton, 1977-80; pres., atty. Fishbone & Scheer, Easton, 1980—; asst. city solicitor Easton, 2002—. Bd. dirs. Lehigh Valley Legal Svcs., Allentown, Pa., 1979-83, Easton Heritage Alliance, 1995-2001; treas. Easton Area Neighborhood Ctr., 1980-81; pres. Historic Easton, Inc., 1983-85; v.p. B'nai Abraham Synagogue, Easton, 1983-85, pres., 1986-88; mem. exec. bd. Easton Area Econ. Devel. Corp., 1991-92. Mem. Pa. Bar Assn. (ho. of dels. 1999-2000, 02—), Northampton County Bar Assn. (bd. govs. 1990-2000, v.p. 1997, pres. 1999), Two Rivers Area C. of C. (v.p. Easton 1989-91, bd. dirs. 1989-). Democrat. Home: 179 Pennsylvania Ave Easton PA 18042 Office: Fishbone & Scheer 940 W Lafayette St Easton PA 18042 Office Phone: 610-258-5306. Personal E-mail: joel.scheer@verizon.net. Business E-Mail: joel@hfjslaw.com.

**SCHEER, JOHN C.,** librarian; b. Jeffersonville, Ind., Mar. 28, 1961; s. John H. and Marilyn B. Scheer. BA in History and Geography, U. Louisville, 1984; MLS, Ind. U., 1986. Asst. librarian, archivist Willard Libr., Evansville, Ind., 1988—91, tech. svcs. librarian, 1991—. Author: Patchwork Central: An Urban Ministry, 2005. Mem.: ALA, Evansville Astron. Soc., Soc. Am. Archivists. Mem. United Ch. Of Christ. Avocation: history. Office: Willard Library 21 First Ave Evansville IN 47710 Office Phone: 812-425-4309.

**SCHEER, JOSEPH H.,** artist, education educator; b. Heildeberg, Germany, Sept. 6, 1958; arrived in U.S., 1960; s. James H. and Kathleen M. Scheer. BFA, Alfred Univ., Alfred, NY, 1984; MA, Univ. New Mex., Albuquerque, New Mex., 1986, MFA, 1987. Artist ind., Los Nutrius, N.Mex., 1986—89; prof. print media Sch. Art Design Alfred Univ., Alfred, NY, 1989—; co-dir. Inst. Electronic Art Alfred Univ., Alfred, NY, 1997—. Author: Night Visions: Secret Designs of Moths, 2003, Night Flyers, 2003; one-man shows include over 30; contbr. articles pub. in over 50 profl. jour. Recipient Silver award, 16th Gold Internat., Chgo., 2003, Stiftung Bockkunst Best Book Design award, Frankfurt, Germany, 2003; grantee Project grant, NYSCA, 2001. Mem.: Entomol. Soc. Am., Lepidoptersit Soc., Phi Kappa Phi. Office: Sch of Art & Design Alfred Univ 2 Pine St Alfred NY 14802

**SCHEER, TEVA SCHEER,** human resources specialist; d. Hubert D. and Sally Ruler Waldo; m. Jon F. Scheer, Jan. 30, 1982; children: Catherine Lepay, Charles Frederick. Student, Monmouth Coll., 1970; diploma in Estudios Hispanicos, U. Madrid, 1971; BA, U. No. Colo., 1972; MPA, U. So. Calif., 1980; PhD, U. Colo., 2000. Resources mgmt. divsn. chief IRS, Richmond, Va., pers. dir. Denver, 1994—96, tng. curriculum mgr. Washington, 1996—2003; human resources cons. Dept. of Treasury, Washington, 2003—05. Cons., Denver, 2005—06. Author: (biography) Governor Lady: The Life and Times of Nellie Tayloe Ross, Bd. sec. S.W. Improvement Coun., Denver, 2001—06. Recipient Millstein award, Grad. Sch. Pub. Affairs, U. Colo., 2000. Avocations: travel, gardening.

**SCHEET, ETHEL LOUISE,** rental company executive, consultant; b. Helena, Mont., Apr. 27, 1942; d. Benjamin and Maxine Fleury; m. Gerald A. Scheet, Sept. 13, 1958; children: Bradly, Barbara Scheet Anez, Breck. Student, Carroll Coll., 1985, Western Mont. Coll., 1980. Owner, operator Northwest Computer Supply, Helena, Mont., 1985—95; owner Antique Restoration, East Helena, Mont., 1990; CEO Home Mgmt. Cons., East Helena, 1970—; mgr. Rental Properties Mgmt., East Helena, 1970—. Author: Mama Cat's Family, 2002. Lobbyist Sch. Bd. Legis., Helena; adv. Mont. Dept. Transp., Helena; active Helena C. of C.; chair Helena Crimestoppers, 1986, Sch. Bd. Trustee, East Helena, 1976; trustee Mont. Sch. Bd. Assn. Named one of 50 Who Make a Difference, Ind. Record, Helena, 1987; recipient Marvin Heintz award, Mont. Sch. Bd. Assn., 1982. Mem.: Mont. Little Shell Tribe Chippewa Indians, Helena Rep. Womens Club (pres., v.p.), Last Chance Pachyderm Club (pres., bd. dirs., award 1993). Republican. Avocations: tennis, fishing, woodworking, writing. Home: 3510 Keir Ln Helena MT 59602

**SCHEETZ, MARC HOWARD,** pharmacist; s. Howard E. and Joann S. Scheetz; m. Megan J. Huisingh, Aug. 5, 2006. PharmD, Butler U., Indpls., 2003. Infectious diseases pharmacist Northwestern Meml. Hosp., Chgo., 2003. Office: Northwestern Meml Hosp 251 E Huron St Feinberg Pavilion Chicago IL 60611 Business E-Mail: mscheetz@nmh.org.

**SCHEETZ, SISTER MARY JOELLEN,** English language educator; b. Lafayette, Ind., May 20, 1926; d. Joseph Albert and Eileen Isabelle (Fitzgerald) S. AB, St. Francis Coll., 1956; MA, U. Notre Dame, 1964; PhD, U. Mich., 1970. Tchr. English, Bishop Luers High Sch., Fort Wayne, Ind., 1965-67; acad. dean St. Francis Coll. (now U. St. Francis), Fort Wayne, 1967-68, pres. Ft. Wayne, Ind., 1970-93, pres. emeritus, English lang. prof. Ft. Wayne, Ind., 1993—. Mem.: Delta Epsilon Sigma. Office: U St Francis 2701 Spring St Fort Wayne IN 46808-3939 Office Phone: 260-434-3229. Business E-Mail: jscheetz@sf.edu.

**SCHEFDORE, RONALD L.,** dentist; BS in Biology with honors, Southern Ill. U., 1979, DMD, 1983; Implant Cert., Northwestern U., 1985. Author & lectr. Dentist Worldwide, 2001—. Author: Better Service Better Dentistry, 2003. Mem.: ADA, Am. Acad. Cosmetic Dentistry, Ill. Dental Assn., Chgo. Dental Soc. Office: 345 West Ogden Ave Westmont IL 60559 Office Phone: 630-971-0682. Office Fax: 630-971-0072. Business E-Mail: celebritysmiles@aol.com.

**SCHEFFEL, DONNA JEAN,** elementary school educator; b. Balt., Sept. 20, 1953; d. G. Donald Scheffel and Mary LaVerne (Perry) Jones; 1 child, Amanda Lynne. BS, Salisbury (Md.) State Coll.; Cert., Baldwin-Wallace Coll., Berea, Ohio, 1983. Tchr. Wadsworth (Ohio) city schs., 1984-85, Parma (Ohio) city schs., 1984-85; elem. tchr. St. Leo the Great Sch., Cleve., 1985-91. 1st aux. svcs. computer sci. tchr. Bethel Christian Acad., Parma. Named one of Outstanding Young Women of Am., 1986. Mem.: ASCD, PEA, NEA, NAFE, Ohio Edn. Assn., N.E. Ohio Edn. Assn. Office: Bethel Christian Acad 12901 W Pleasant Valley Rd Parma OH 44130-5702

**SCHEFFEL, KENNETH PAUL,** retired archivist; b. Cin., Aug. 18, 1937; s. Edwin Reuben and Ivy Catherine (Happel) Scheffel. AB, Columbia U., N.Y.C., 1959; MS, U. Wis., 1963. Archivist U. Mich., Ann Arbor, 1967—2003, archivist emeritus, 2003—. Mem.: So. Hist. Assn., Orgn. of Am. Historians. Methodist. Home: 7857 Harrison Ave Apt 4 Mount Healthy OH 45231-3151 Personal E-Mail: kenschef@umich.edu.

**SCHEFFING, DIANNE ELIZABETH,** special education educator; b. St. Louis, Mar. 17, 1963; d. Eugene Shibley Scheffing Jr. and Sarah Ann (Lukens) Scheffing. BS, Mo. Bapt. Univ., 1988; MA, Fontbonne U., St. Louis, 1999, A in Computer Edn., 2005; postgrad., Webster U., St. Louis, 2002. Cert. elem. edn. grades 1-8 Mo., mild/moderate cross-category grades K-12 Mo., severely developmentally delayed 2002. Kindergarden tchr. asst. Andrews Acad., St. Louis, 1989—91; sci. tchr. edn. dept. St. Louis Sci. Ctr., 1994—96; tchr. asst. multi-handicapped Kehrs Mill Elem./Rockwood Sch. Dist., St. Louis, 1996—2000; tchr. spl. edn. Gateway/Hubert Wheeler State Sch. for Severely Handicapped, St. Louis, 2000—. Mem., sec. St. Louis Young Reps. Club, 1988—94; majority mem. Bethel #44 Internat. Order of Job's Daughters, Ballwin, 1978—84. Named Woman of Yr., St. Louis Young Reps. Club, 1992, 1994. Mem.: Am. Cancer Soc. Methodist. Avocations: Olympic supporter, bowling, travel. Office: Gateway/Hubert Wheeler State Sch 100 S Garrison Saint Louis MO 63103 Personal E-Mail: applecore@prodigy.net.

**SCHEFFLER, ECKART ARTHUR,** publisher; b. Glauchau, Germany, June 8, 1941; arrived in U.S., 1963; s. Arthur Ernst and Marianne (Baltzer) S.; m. Hannelore Baustian, July 29, 1966; children: Thomas, Daniel. Bookseller Buchhändlerschule, Leipzig, Germany, 1955-58; bookstore mgr. Bücher-Binder, Stuttgart, Germany, 1959-62; v.p. Adler's Fgn. Books Inc., N.Y.C., 1963-72; v.p., gen. mgr. Walter de Gruyter, Inc., Ossining, NY, 1972—. Served with USAR, 1964-69. Mem. Am. Assn. Pubs., Internat. Group of Sci., Tech. and Med. Pubs., Scholarly Pubs. Assn., Rotary. Lutheran. Office: Walter de Gruyter Inc Ste 306 500 Executive Blvd Ossining NY 10562

**SCHEFFLER, ISRAEL,** philosopher, educator; b. N.Y.C., Nov. 25, 1923; s. Leon and Ethel (Grünberg) S.; m. Rosalind Zuckerbrod, June 26, 1949; children: Samuel, Laurie. BA, Bklyn. Coll., 1945, MA, 1948; M.H.L., Jewish Theol. Sem., 1949; PhD (Ford fellow 1951), U. Pa., 1952; A.M. (hon.), Harvard U., 1959; D.H.L. (hon.), Jewish Theol. Sem., 1993. Mem. faculty Harvard U., 1952-92, prof. edn., 1961-62, prof. edn. and philosophy, 1962-64, Victor S. Thomas prof. edn. and philosophy, 1964-92, professor emeritus, 1992—, hon. research fellow in cognitive studies, 1965-66, co-dir. Philosophy Edn. Rsch. Ctr., 1983-98, dir. Philosophy Edn. Rsch. Ctr., 1998—2003; scholar-in-residence The Mandel Ctr., Brandeis U., 2003—. Fellow Center for Advanced Study in Behavioral Scis., 1972-73 Author: The Language of Education, 1960, The Anatomy of Inquiry, 1963, Conditions of Knowledge, 1965, Science and Subjectivity, 1967, Reason and Teaching, 1973, Four Pragmatists, 1974, Beyond the Letter, 1979, Of Human Potential, 1985, Inquiries, 1986, In Praise of the Cognitive Emotions, 1991, Teachers of My Youth, 1995, Symbolic Worlds, 1997, Gallery of Scholars, 2004; co-author: Work, Education and Leadership, 1995; editor: Philosophy and Education, 1958, 66; co-editor: Logic and Art, 1972, Visions of Jewish Education, 2003; contbr. articles to profl. jours. Recipient Alumni Award of Merit Bklyn. Coll., 1967, Disting. Svc. medal Tchrs. Coll., Columbia, 1980, Benjamin Shevach award Boston Hebrew Coll., 1995; Guggenheim fellow, 1958-59, 72-73; NSF grantee, 1962, 65. Mem. Am. Acad. Arts and Scis., Am. Philos. Assn.,

Philosophy Edn. Soc., Nat. Acad. Edn. (charter), Philosophy of Sci. Assn. (prs. 1973-75), Charles S. Peirce Soc. (pres. 1998). Address: Apt 328 125 B Seminary Ave Auburndale MA 02466 Office: Brandeis Univ Mandel Ctr Waltham MA 02454

**SCHEFFLER, LEWIS FRANCIS,** pastor, educator, research scientist; b. Springfield, Ohio, Oct. 13, 1928; s. Lewis Francis and Emily Louise (Kloker) S.; m. Willa Pauline Cole, Aug. 9, 1949 (div. 1978); children: Lewis F. Fischer, Richard Thomas, Gary Arlen, Tonni Kay; m. Mary Lee Smith, Apr. 18, 1978; stepchildren: Kimberly McCollum, Jeffrey McIlroy, Kerry Buell. BA in Liberal Arts, Cin. Bible Seminary, 1950; AA in Bus., Jefferson Coll., 1989; MAT, Webster U., 1989. Quality assurance Tectum Corp., Newark, 1954-57; rsch. group leader Owens-Corning Fiberglas, Granville, Ohio, 1957-64; tech. asst. to v.p. R&D and Engring., 1960-63; pres. Ohio Glass Fibers Cons., 1962-68; rsch. administr. Modiglas Fibers Corp., Bremen, Ohio, 1965-68; dir. R & D Flex-O-Lite Corp., St. Louis, 1968-71; pastor Christian Ch., St. Louis, 1972-75; police commns. Brentwood (Mo.) Police Dept., 1975-87; pastor Christian Ch., Potosi, Mo., 1988-89, Slater (Mo.) Christian Ch., 1989-93, Clark (Mo.) Christian Ch., 1996-99; asst. prof. English lang. and lit. Mo. Valley Coll., Marshall, 1989-94; adj. prof. theology Mo. Sch. Religion, 1993-97; adj. prof. English Moberly Area C.C., 1996-98; min. Ctrl. Union Cmty. Ch., Vaudalia, Mo., 1998—. Organizing co-chmn. aerospace composite materials com. ASTM, 1961; mem. exec. bd. Northwest Area Christian Ch., 1989-93; mem. Coun. of Areas of Mid-Am. Region Christian Ch., 1990-93; cons. and lectr. in field. Contbr. articles to profl. jours. Patentee in field. Money raiser United Appeal, chaplaincy Blessing Hosp., Quincy, Ill., 1974; vol. Ill. Divsn. Children and Family Svcs., 1972-75; sec. exec. com. N.W. Area Christian Ch. (Disciples of Christ), 1992-94. Mem. Medieval Acad. Am., Mo. Philol. Assn. Avocation: philosophy and pomology. Home: PO Box 15 Rush Hill MO 65280 *Now and then, God has so touched people in such a way that, recognizing it, we think "So that's what God must be like!" and our ethical and moral sensitivities are heightened.*

**SCHEFFLER, SAMUEL,** philosophy educator; b. NYC, Oct. 20, 1951; s. Israel and Rosalind (Zuckerbrod) S.; m. Kathryn Granzow, Jan. 16, 1983; children: Adam Nathaniel, Gabriel Alexander. BA, Harvard U., 1973; PhD, Princeton U., 1977. Asst. prof. philosophy U. Calif., Berkeley, 1977-79, assoc. prof., 1979-85, prof., 1985-89, Class of 1941 World War II Meml. prof. Vis. fellow All Souls Coll., Oxford, 1990; chmn. adv. bd. Kadish Ctr for Morality Law & Public Affairs. Author: The Rejection of Consequentialism, 1982 (Franklin J. Machette prize Am. Philos. Assn. 1983), Human Morality, 1992, Boundaries and Allegiances; editor: Consequentialism and Its Critics, 1988; adv. editor Philosophy and Public Affairs; contbr. articles to profl. jours. U. Calif. Humanities Research fellow, 1982, Guggenheim Found. fellow, 1984, Pres.'s fellow U. Calif, 1989, NEH fellow, 1989. Fellow Am. Acad. Arts & Sci.; mem. Am. Philos. Assn. Office: Department of Philosophy 314 Moses Hall 2390 University of California Berkeley CA 94720-2390 Business E-mail: scheffler@berkeley.edu.

**SCHEFFLER, STUART JAY,** lawyer; b. Phila., Oct. 9, 1950; s. Walter and Fritzy (Salkoff) S.; m. Barbara Jane Green, July 3, 1975. BA cum laude, Pa. State U., 1972, MPA, 1973; JD, Temple U., 1980. Bar: Pa. 1980, U.S. Dist. Ct. (ea. dist.) Pa. 1981, U.S. Ct. Appeals (3d cir.) 1983, U.S. Supreme Ct. 1986. Tchr. Sch. Dist. of Phila., 1974-75; claims authorizer Social Security Adminstrn., HEW, Phila., 1975-76, equal opportunity specialist Office of Civil Rights, 1976-77; paraprofessional Law Offices of Ronald A. Bell., Bala Cynwyd, Pa., 1977-80; assoc. Law Office of Robert B. Mozenter, Phila., 1980-81, Gekoski & Bogdanoff, Phila., 1981-82; ptnr. Rubin & Scheffler, Phila., 1982-94; sole practice, Phila., 1994-2004; of counsel Solomon, Berschler, Warren & Schatz, P.C., Norristown, Pa., 1998—. Councilman Bakers Bay Condominium Assn., Phila., 1982; bd. dirs. Key West Coun. on the Arts, 1999—2003. Fellow Acad. of Advocacy, mem. ATLA, ABA (tort and ins. practice, sports and entertainment, civil litigation sects.), Pa. Bar Assn. (legis. liaison, medico-legal coms.), Phila. Bar Assn., Phila. Trial Lawyers Assn., Pa. Trial Lawyers Assn., Drug Info. Assn., Internat. Platform Assn., Phi Beta Kappa, Delta Sigma Rho, Tau Kappa Alpha, Zeta Beta Tau. Democrat. Club: Hartikvah Basketball Assn. (Phila.) (v.p. 1974—). Home: 540 Chandler Ln Villanova PA 19085-1204 Personal E-mail: stukw@bellsouth.net.

**SCHEFFMAN, DAVID THEODORE,** economist, management educator, consultant; b. Milaca, Minn., Dec. 1, 1943; s. David Theodore and Fern Virginia (Maas) Scheffman; 1 child, Christopher. BA magna cum laude, U. Minn., 1967; PhD, MIT, 1971. Lectr. Boston Coll., 1970-71; from asst. prof. to assoc. prof. Univ. Western Ont., London, Canada, 1971-81; sr. economist FTC, Washington, 1979-82, dep. dir., 1983-86; prof., dir. Inst. Applied Econs. Concordia U., Montreal, Que., Canada, 1982-83; dir., bur. econs. FTC, Washington, 1985-88; Justin Potter prof., adj. prof. bus. strategy and mktg. Vanderbilt U., Nashville, 1989-99, prof. of bus. strategy and mktg., 1999—; dir. LECG, N.Y.C., 1993-2001, 2003—; Bur. Econs., FTC, Washington, 2001—03; adj. prof., dir. bus. strategy Cornell U., 2001—02. Adj. prof. Georgetown U. Law Ctr., Washington, 1986; cons. Ont. Econ. Coun., Toronto, 1973-81, GM, 1977, Ctrl. Oil Inquiry, Ottawa, Ont., 1982-84, Ctrl. Govt., Ottawa, 1973-81, Can. Competition Tribunal, 1987-89, Can. Bur. Competition Policy, 1988-91, U.S. Sentencing Commn., 1988-89, PepsiCo, 1989-2000, Kraft Gen. Food, 1989-2001, PacifiCorp, 1989-93, NERA, 1991-93, Boeing, 1992-96, Berwind Industries, Inc., 1993-95, Comm. Ctrl., Inc., Applied Innovation, Inc., TEC, 1995-98, Nortel, 1995, Coca Cola, 1996-98. Author: Speculation and Monopoly in Urban Development: Analytical Foundations, 1977, An Economic Analysis of Provincial Land Use Policies in Ontario, 1980, Social Regulation in Markets for Consumer Goods and Services, 1982, An Economic Analysis of the Impact of Rising Oil Prices on Urban Structure, 1983, Strategy, Structure, and Antitrust in the Carbonated Soft Drink Industry, 1992. Dissertation fellow NSF, 1967-68; vis. scholar U. Minn., 1978. Office: LECG 1725 I St NW #800 Washington DC 20005 Office Phone: 202-466-4422 Business E-Mail: dscheffman@lecg.com.

**SCHEHR, KEVIN JOHN,** art gallery owner; b. Tulsa, Mar. 23, 1966; s. Louis Valentine Schehr, Jr. and Bonnie Louise Sadle; m. Melissa Aileen Boeckl, Feb. 4, 1995; m. Melissa Diane Bell, June 1, 1985 (dec. Feb. 22, 1992); children: Kevin John Schehr, Jr., Alicia Katelyn. AS, Fla. C.C. at Jacksonville, 1990; B of Vocat. Edn., So. Ill. U., 1990; MBA, U of Phoenix, 1999. Ops. mgr. New Orleans Windustrial, New Orleans, 1992—95; gen. mgr. Source Prodn. & Equipment Co, Inc., St. Rose, La., 1995; pres. Galerie Rouge, Inc, New Orleans, 2002—. Nat. alerting officer Am. Disaster Res., 2003; vol. USA Freedom Corps, Washington, 2003. With USN, 1985-92. Recipient Pres.'s Vol. Svc. award Silver, USA Freedom Corps, 2004, Pres.'s Vol. Svc. award Gold, 2005. Mem.: Am. Soc. for Non-Destructive Testing (assoc.; New Orleans sect. chmn. 1996—2002), Naval Order of the U.S., State Guard Assn. of the U.S. (assoc.), Am. Legion, VFW (life). Roman Catholic. Home: 2658 Hudson Pl New Orleans LA 70131 Office: Galerie Rouge Inc 623 Royal St New Orleans LA 70130 Office Phone: 504-586-0061. Personal E-mail: kschehr826@aol.com.

**SCHEIB, GERALD PAUL,** art educator; b. LA, Dec. 26, 1937; s. Harry William and Olive Bauer (Cartwright) S.; m. Elizabeth Ann Galligan, Dec. 27, 1965 (div. 1978); children: Gregory Paul, m. Dedra Lynn True, Oct. 1, 1983; 1 child, Adam True. AA, East L.A. Jr. Coll., 1959; BA, Calif. State U., L.A., 1962, MFA, 1968. Cert. life teaching credential in fine arts, secondary and coll. tchr., Calif. Secondary tchr. art L.A. Unified Sch. Dist., 1963-77; profl. fine art L.A. Community Coll. Dist., 1977-2001; rel., 2001; pres. faculty senate L.A. Mission Coll., San Fernando, Calif., 1983-84. Bargaining unit rep., AFT Coll. Guild Local 1521; elected Arts and Letters chair L.A. Mission Coll., 1993; owner, mgr. Artificers Bench, Sylmar, Calif., 1976—; cons. to Edward H. Bohlin Co. Custom Silver Works, 1998. Mem. policy bd. The Calif. Arts Project, 1995-97; chair Los Angeles County Art Edn. Coun., 1997-98; plank owner U.S. Naval Meml., Washington; trustee L.A. Artcore, 2001. LA Judge for Coca Cola's June. of Art Harmony Student Art Scholarship Compeition. With USNR, 1955-97, ret. Recipient of tribute City of L.A., 1983, Citizen of Month award, Los Angeles County, 1983, Cold

War Cert. of Recognition, Sec. of Def., 2000. Mem. Calif. Art Edn. Assn. (membership chmn. 1985-87, pres.-elect 1989-91, pres. 1991-93, Calif.'s Outstanding Art Educator in Higher Edn. 1994-95), San Fernando Active 20-30 Club (pres. 1981-82), Nat. Assn. Scholars, Sons of Union Vets of Civil War, U.S. Naval Cryptologic Vets. Assn., L.A. Artcore (bd. dirs. 2001--). Republican. Avocations: collecting antiques, Civil War reenacting, creating custom jewelry. Office: 13356 Eldridge Ave Sylmar CA 91342-3200 Office Phone: 818-364-7678. Personal E-mail: geraldart@aol.com.

**SCHEIBE, KARL EDWARD,** psychology professor; b. Belleville, Ill., Mar. 5, 1937; s. John Henry and Esther Julia (Friesen) S.; m. Elizabeth Wentworth Mixter, Sept. 14, 1965 (dec. Jan. 1977); m. Marian Diamond, Sept. 1982. BA, Columbia U., 1944, MD, 1946; MS, U. Ill., 1952. Intern Mt. Sinai Hosp., N.Y.C., 1946-47; resident in psychiatry Barnes and McMillan Hosp., St. Louis, 1947-48, Ill. Neuropsychiat. Inst., Chgo., 1950-52; asst. prof. psychiatry and anatomy U. Tenn. Med. Sch., 1952-53, assoc. prof., 1953-55, UCLA Med. Ctr., 1955-67, prof., 1967—; mem. Brain Rsch. Inst., 1960—, acting dir. Brain Rsch. Inst., 1987-90, dir., 1990-95. Cons. in field. Contbr. numerous articles to tech. jours, chpts. to books.; mem. editl. bd. Brain Rsch., 1967-77, Developmental Psychobiology, 1968—, Internat. Jour. Neurosci., 1969—; Jour. Biol. Psychiatry, 1968—, Jour. Theoretical Biology, 1980—; assoc. editor News Report, 1989—. Mem. Pres.'s Commn. on Aging, Nat. Inst. Aging, 1980—. Served with AUS, 1943-46; from lt. to capt. M.C. AUS, 1948-50. Guggenheim fellow (with wife), 1953-54, 59; recipient Disting. Svc. award Calif. Soc. Biomed. Rsch., 1998. Fellow Am. Acad. Arts and Scis., Norwegian Acad. Scis., Am. Psychiat. Assn. (life, Harriet and Charles Luckman Disting. Tchg. award 1997) AAAS; mem. Am. Neurol. Assn., Soc. Neuorosci., Pyschiat. Rsch. Assn., Soc. Biol. Psychiatry, So. Calif. Psychiat. Assn. Home: 16231 Morrison St Encino CA 91436-1331 Office: UCLA Dept Neurobiology Los Angeles CA 90024 Business E-Mail: scheibel@mednet.ucla.edu. *Intense personal tragedy can embitter life and choke off further personal creativity. It may also offer the opportunity to open new doors in the discovery of self. I am more aware than ever of my good fortune in having the opportunity to teach, to continue investigative work in the structure and function of the brain, and to give love and care to those who need it. I am more than ever convinced that loving and being loved is the greatest good that we can know, the state in which we most nearly fulfill our roles as human beings.*

**SCHEIBEL, ARNOLD BERNARD,** psychiatrist, educator, research director; b. NYC, Jan. 18, 1923; s. William and Ethel (Greenberg) S.; m. Madge Mila Ragland, Mar. 3, 1950 (dec. Jan. 1977); m. Marian Diamond, Sept. 1982. BA, Columbia U., 1944, MD, 1946; MS, U. Ill., 1952. Intern Mt. Sinai Hosp., N.Y.C., 1946-47; resident in psychiatry Barnes and McMillan Hosp., St. Louis, 1947-48, Ill. Neuropsychiat. Inst., Chgo., 1950-52; asst. prof. psychiatry and anatomy U. Tenn. Med. Sch., 1952-53, assoc. prof., 1953-55, UCLA Med. Ctr., 1955-67, prof., 1967—; mem. Brain Rsch. Inst., 1960—, acting dir. Brain Rsch. Inst., 1987-90, dir., 1990-95. Cons. in field. Contbr. numerous articles to tech. jours, chpts. to books.; mem. editl. bd. Brain Rsch., 1967-77, Developmental Psychobiology, 1968—, Internat. Jour. Neurosci., 1969—; Jour. Biol. Psychiatry, 1968—, Jour. Theoretical Biology, 1980—; assoc. editor News Report, 1989—. Mem. Pres.'s Commn. on Aging, Nat. Inst. Aging, 1980—. Served with AUS, 1943-46; from lt. to capt. M.C. AUS, 1948-50. Guggenheim fellow (with wife), 1953-54, 59; recipient Disting. Svc. award Calif. Soc. Biomed. Rsch., 1998. Fellow Am. Acad. Arts and Scis., Norwegian Acad. Scis., Am. Psychiat. Assn. (life, Harriet and Charles Luckman Disting. Tchg. award 1997) AAAS; mem. Am. Neurol. Assn., Soc. Neuorosci., Pyschiat. Rsch. Assn., Soc. Biol. Psychiatry, So. Calif. Psychiat. Assn. Home: 16231 Morrison St Encino CA 91436-1331 Office: UCLA Dept Neurobiology Los Angeles CA 90024 Business E-Mail: scheibel@mednet.ucla.edu.

**SCHEIBEL, KENNETH MAYNARD,** journalist; b. Campbell, Nebr., May 17, 1920; s. G. Alfred and Rachel Christine (Koch) S.; m. Helen Schmitt, May 14, 1955 (div. Sept. 1977); children: Victor Warren Schmitt, William Becker Schmitt, Kenneth Jr., Sally. Student, George Washington U., 1938—41; BA, U. Va., 1947, MA, 1949. Mag. salesman Periodical Pubs. Svc. Bur., Inc., 1935-38; reporter Internat. News Svc., Washington, 1940-41, Wall St. Jour., Washington, 1949-51; Washington corr. Gannett Newspapers, 1951-63; syndicated columnist N.Am. Newspaper Alliance, 1963-64; chief Washington bur. Donrey Media Group, 1964-67; founder, bur. chief Washington Bur. News, 1967—; founder nat. syndicated column Washington Farm Beat, 1970-85. Washington corr. Wis. State Jour., 1963-66, LaCrosse (Wis.) Tribune, 1963-66, Billings (Mont.) Gazette, 1964-71, V.I. Network, 1966-67, Moline (Ill.) Daily Dispatch, 1967-68, Drovers' Jour., 1967-68, Newport News (Va.) Daily Press & Times Herald, 1969-71, Packer Pub. Co., 1964-74, Gasoline Retailer, 1966-67, Okla., Farmer Stockman; congl. corr. F-D-C Reports, 1975-77; Washington columnist Farm Jour., 1960-75; dir. Nat. Press Bldg. Corp., 1973, v.p. pres. club and bldg corp., 1974; covered nat. polit. convs., campaigns; v.p. Fraser Assocs. (pub. rels.), Washington, 1976-79; Congl. broadcast interviewer; founder Wash. Broadcast News, Ft. Smith, Ark., Miami, Las Vegas. Contbr. nat. mags., newspaper syndicates. Incorporator War Meml. of Korea, Washington, 1981; editor Nat. Ctr. Fin. and Econ. Info., U.S.-Saudi Arabian Joint Econ. Commn., Riyadh, 1985-86; mem. Nat. Com. Korean War Meml., 1981. Capt. AUS, 1941-46, 755th Tank Bn., 1942-45, Europe, N. Africa, Italy. Decorated Bronze star, U.S. Army Occupation medal, Combat Infantryman badge; co-recipient Croix De Guerre (France), Thoth award for excellence in pub. rels., 1980. Mem. Izaak Walton League Am., White House Corrs. Assn., Overseas Press Club of Am., Am. Radio Relay League, Nat. Press Club (Washington; fin. sec., gov. 1969-73, vice chmn. bd. 1971, v.p., pres., 1974), Sigma Chi. Presbyterian. Avocation: amateur radio. Home: 1325 18th St NW Apt 302 Washington DC 20036-6505 Personal E-mail: kenscheib@earthlink.net. *The greatest sins are timidity and self indulgence, the greatest virtue is to love. Live each day, don't fret about yesterday or tomorrow. Enjoy the senses, learn from others, and never forget that both love and hate are returned.*

**SCHEIBER, HARRY N.,** law educator; b. 1935; BA, Columbia U., 1955; MA, Cornell U., 1957, PhD, 1961; MA (hon.), Dartmouth Coll., 1965; D.Jur.Hon., Uppsala U., Sweden, 1998. Instr. to assoc. prof. history Dartmouth Coll., 1960-68, prof., 1968-71; prof. Am. history U. Calif., San Diego, 1971-80; prof. law Boalt Hall, U. Calif., Berkeley, 1980—. Chmn. jurisprudence and social policy program, 1982-84, 90-93, assoc. dean, 1990-93, 96-99; The Stefan Riesenfeld prof., 1991—; vice chair Univ. Academic Senate, 1993-94, chair 1994-95; dir. Earl Warren Legal Inst., 2002-05, Inst. for Legal Rsch., 2005—, Sho Sato Program, 1993—; Fulbright disting. sr. lectr., Australia, 1983, marine affairs coord. Calif. Sea Grant Coll. Program, 1989-2000; vis. rsch. prof. Law Inst. U. Uppsala, Sweden, 1995, hon. prof. DiTella U., Buenos Aires, 1999; cons. Calif. Jud. Coun., 1992-93; acting dir. Ctr. for Study of Law and Soc., 1999-2001; co-dir. Law of the Sea Inst., 2002—; Cassel lectr., Stockholm U., 2003. Author: The Wilson Administration and Civil Liberties, 1960, Ohio Canal Era, 1970, Inter-Allied Conflicts and Ocean Law (1945-1953), 2001; co-author: American Law and the Constitutional Order, 1988, The State and Freedom of Contract, 1998, American Law and the Constitutional Order, 1978, Law of the Sea: The Common Heritage and Emerging Challenges, 2000, Bringing New Law to Ocean Waters, 2004, Earl Warren and the Warren Court, 2006; editor: Yearbook of the California Supreme Court Historical Society, 1994—2006; contbr. articles to law revs. and social sci. jours. Chmn. Littleton Griswold Prize Legal History, 1985-88; pres. N.H. Civil Liberties Union, 1969-70; chmn. Project '87 Task Force on Pub. Programs, Washington, 1982-85; dir. Berkeley Seminar on Federalism, 1986-95; cons. judiciary study U.S. Adv. Commn. Intergovernmental Rels., 1985-88, Pew Oceans Commn., 2002-03, Nat. Rsch. Coun., 2002-03, Joint Ocean Commn. Initiative, 2006—; dir. NEH Inst. on Constitutionalism, U. Calif., Berkeley, 1986-87, 88-91. Recipient Sea Grant Colls. award 1981-83, 84-85, 86-2002; fellow Ctr. Advanced Study in Behavioral Scis., Stanford Calif., 1967, 71; Guggenheim fellow, 1971, 88; Rockefeller Found. humanities fellow, 1979, NEH fellow, 1985-86; NSF grantee 1979, 80, 88-89. Fellow AAAS, Am. Acad. Arts and Scis., U. Calif. Humanities Rsch. Inst., Am. Soc. for Legal History (hon., pres. 2003—), Japan Soc. for Promotion of Sci. (invitational fellow); mem. Am. Hist. Assn., Orgn. Am. Historians, Agrl. History Soc. (pres. 1978), Econ. History Assn. (trustee 1978-80), Law and Soc. Assn. (trustee 1979-81, 96-99), Nat. Assessment History and Citizenship Edn. (chmn. nat. acad. bd. 1986-87), Marine Affairs and Policy Assn. (bd. dir. 1991-96), Ocean Governance Study

Group (steering com. 1991-2004), Internat. Coun. Environ. Law, Calif. Supreme Ct. Hist. Soc. (bd. dir. 1993—, v.p. 1997-98). Office: U Calif Berkeley Law Sch Boalt Hall Berkeley CA 94720-2150 Office Phone: 510-643-9788. E-mail: scheiber@law.berkeley.edu.

**SCHEIBER, STEPHEN CARL,** psychiatrist, director; b. NYC, May 2, 1938; s. Irving Martin and Frieda Olga (Schor) S.; m. Mary Ann McDonnell, Sept. 14, 1965; children: Lisa Susan, Martin Irving, Laura Ann. BA, Columbia Coll., 1960; MD, SUNY, Buffalo, 1964. Diplomate Am. Bd. Psychiatry and Neurology. Intern Mary Fletcher Hosp., Burlington, Vt., 1964-65; resident in psychiatry Strong Meml. Hosp., Rochester, NY, 1967-70; asst. prof. U. Ariz., Tucson, 1970-76, assoc. prof., 1976-81, prof., 1981-86; exec. sec. Am. Bd. Psychiatry and Neurology, Inc., Deerfield, Ill., 1986-89, exec. v.p., 1989—2006. Adj. prof. psychiatry Northwestern U., Chgo. and Evanston, 1986—, Med. Coll. Wis., Milw., 1986—. Co-editor: The Impaired Physician, 1983, Certification, Recertification and Lifetime Learning in Psychiatry, 1994, Core Competencies for Psychiatric Practice, 2003, Core Competencies for Neurologists, 2003; contbr. articles to profl. jours. Mem. med. adv. com. Casas de los Ninos, Tucson, 1974-85; mem. mental health adv. com. Tucson Health Planning Coun., 1974-75; med. student interviewer Office of Med. Edn., 1975; mem. Glenbrook (Ill.) North H.S. Boosters Club, 1988-91; treas. Robert E. Jones Found., 1988-96. Surgeon USPHS, 1965-67. Recipient Outstanding Tchr. award, U. Ariz., 1986, Lifetime Achievement award, SUNY, Buffalo, 1998; grantee Group Therapy Outcome Studies on Inpatient Svc., 1980, Dialysis and Schizophrenia Pilot Project, NIH, 1978, Fellow: Group for Advancement of Psychiatry (invited mem., chmn. mem. edn. com. 1987—91, bd. dirs., sec. 1993—97, pres.-elect 1997—99, pres. 1999—2001), Assn. Acad. Psychiatry (parliamentary sec. 1979—84, treas. 1984—88, pres.-elect 1988—89, pres. 1989—90, Lifetime Educator award 2002), Am. Assn. Dirs. Psychiat. Residency Tng. (pres. 1981—82), Am. Coll. Psychiatrists (bd. regents 1992—2001, treas. 1995—2001), Am. Psychiat. Assn. (life; chmn. impaired physician com. 1985—88, cons. 1988—92, Disting. Life Fellow 2002); mem.: Oracle Heights Club (pres. 1983—84). Democrat. Jewish.

**SCHEIBERG, SUSAN L.,** librarian; b. Chgo., Dec. 19, 1962; d. Steven M. Scheiberg, Margo Scheiberg. BA (hon.), Ind. U., 1984; MA, UCLA, 1986; MS in Libr. Sci., U. Ky., 1997. Grad. rsch. libr. U. So. Calif., 1997—98, team leader, serials acquisitions, 1998—2001; head acquisitions and serials, coord. outreach and cost-ctr. svcs. RAND Corp., Santa Monica, Calif., 2001—02, assoc. dir., 2002—. Editor: (book) NASIG 2001: A Serials Odyssey, 2002, Transforming Serials: The Revolution Continues, 2003; contbr. articles to profl. jours. Fellow Univ., UCLA, 1984-1987; grantee Bardin Endowment Rsch., U. So. Calif., 1998, 1999, 2000. Mem.: ALA (Tony B. Leisner grantee 1996), Reference and User Svcs. Assn., Assn. Coll. & Rsch. Librs., N.Am. Serials Interest Group (proceedings editor 2000—), Libr. Adminstrn. and Mgmt. Assn., Assn. Libr. Collections and Tech. Svcs., Spl. Librs. Assn., Beta Phi Mu, Phi Beta Kappa. Office Phone: 310-393-0411. Personal E-mail: susanls@rand.org.

**SCHEICH, JOHN F.,** lawyer; b. Bklyn., Aug. 6, 1942; s. Frank A. and Dorothy (O'Hara) Scheich. BA, St. John's U., N.Y.C., 1963, JD, 1966; postgrad., John Marshall Law Sch., Chgo., 1968. Bar: N.Y. 1967, U.S. Ct. Internat. Trade Admission 1969, U.S. Dist. Ct. (ea. and so. dists.) N.Y. 1971, U.S. Ct. Appeals (2d cir.) 1971, U.S. Supreme Ct. 1989. Spl. agt. FBI, U.S. Dept. Justice, Washington, 1966-69; asst. dist. atty. Queens County, Kew Gardens, N.Y., 1969-72; pvt. practice Richmond Hill, N.Y., 1970—76, 1979—91; ptnr. Raia & Scheich, P.C., Richmond Hill, 1976-79; sr. ptnr. Scheich & Goldsmith, PC, Richmond Hill, 1991—95, 2003—, Scheich, Goldsmith & Dreishpoon, PC, Richmond Hill, 1996—2003; mortgage settlement atty. GMAC, N.Y., 1996—. Mem. assigned counsel panel for indigent defendants in major felony and murder cases 9th and 11th jud. dists. N.Y. State Supreme Ct., Queens County, 1972—94; v.p. Ra-Li Brokerage Corp., 1975—, bd. dirs.; lectr. Lawyers in Classroom, 1979—91; chmn. arbitration panel Civil Ct. City of N.Y., 1981—90; trial judge St. John's U. Sch. Law Civil Trial Inst. Student Competition, 1992—; lectr. estate planning Nat. Bus. Inst., 1994; mem. adv. bd. 1st Am. Title Ins. Co. Am., 1995—2004; mortgage settlement atty. Gen. Motors Acceptance Corp. N.Y. State, 1996—. Editor: Conashaugh Courier, 1989-92; mem. editorial bd., 1988-92; contbg. columnist, 1981-89. Active Performing Arts Ctr. Pinellas County, St. Petersburg, 1995—2003; mem. Com. for Beautification of East Norwich, Nassau County, L.I., NY, 1983—, bd. dirs., 1993—96, pres., 1996—; mem. Friends of the Arts, Locust Valley, L.I., NY, 1985—; chmn. tri-centennial celebration com. Village of East Norwich, 1996—97; mem. St. Edward the Confessor Sch. Bd., Syosset, NY, 1986—90; nat. trust and estate assoc. Meml. Sloane Kettering Cancer Ctr., NYC, 1994—; active Internat. Wine Ctr., 1985—96; mem. Fransiscan Ctr. Guild, Tampa, Fla., 1996—, Tilles Ctr. Performing Arts, Inc., Long Island U., Brookville, NY, 1997—, Lincoln Ctr. Performing Arts, Inc., 1985—, Bravo Soc., 1994—, Concern for Dying, 1984—2002, Sea Cliff Chamber Players, 1992—99; active Pact, Inc. Ruth Eckerd Hall-Richard B. Baumgardner Ctr. for Performing Arts, Clearwater, Fla., 1995—2001, Rep. Nat. Senate Adv. Coun., 1997—2002, Rep. Nat. Com. Chmn.'s Honor Roll (cert. Achievement 1998), 1997; appointed to Bus. Advisory Coun. by Nat. Repub. Congressional Comm.; mem. East Norwich Rep. Club, 1982—, bd. dirs., 1984—87, 1993—, v.p., 1987—89, pres., 1989—93; mem. Nat. Rep. Senatorial Com., 1988—2004, Nassau County Rep. Com., Town of Oyster Bay, 1993—, Holy Name Soc. of Our Lady of Perpetual Help Ch., 1963—, sec., 1965—67, v.p., 1969—71, pres., 1971—73; parish coun. Our Lady of Perpetual Help Roman Cath. Ch., 1976—82, pres., 1978—80, fin. com., adv. to pastor, 1970—82, chmn. fin. com., 1979—82; active St. Edward the Confessor Ch., Syosset, 1982—90, St. Vincent Ch, Dingman Hills, Pa., 1977—2004, St. Dominic's Ch., Oyster Bay, NY, 1982—, apptd. pastor's adv. coun. on estate planning, 1998—2003, mem. St. Dominic's Legacy Soc., 1998—; mem. St. John Vianney Roman Cath. Ch., St. Petersburg Beach, Fla., 1994—; bd. dirs. Northslope II Homeowners Assn., Shawnee-on-Delaware, Pa., 1988—90, Shawnee-on-Del., Pa., 1992—94, 2000—02, East Norwich Civic Assn., 2002—04, Conashaugh Lakes Cmty. Assn., Milford, Pa., 1981—90; organizing mem. Conashaugh Lakes Lot Owners interim com., 1977—81, sec., 1981—82, v.p., 1982—84, pres., 1984—86, past pres., 1986—88; Non-Resident Fellow, James Beard Found., NYC, 1995—. Recipient J. Edgar Hoover award, 1967, award of appreciation, Civil Trial Inst., St. John's U. Sch. of Law, 1991, 95, Disting. Svc. award, 1992, cert. of appreciaiton Conashaugh Lakes Cmty. Assn., 1990, Dist. Svc. award Kiwanis Club, 1992, Cert. of Merit for Disting. Svc. award Nassau County Exec. Hon. Thomas Gulotta, 1989, Presdl. Order of Merit award Pres. George Bush, 1991, Order of Merit award Nat. Rep. Senatorial Com., 1994, Cert. Achievement, Rep. Nat. Com. 1998; named one of Best Trial Lawyers in the U.S., Town and Country Mag., 1986; non-resident fellow James Beard Found., N.Y.C., 1995—, Blue Ribbon Survey Commn. cert. of recognition, 2002. Mem. ABA (cert. of appreciation Am. Bar Endowment 1992), ATLA, Pa. State Bar Assn., NY State Bar Assn., Queens County Bar Assn., Nassau County Bar Assn., NY State Trial Lawyers Assn., Ciminal Cts. Bar Assn., John Marshall Lawyers Assn. (bd. dirs. 1992—, pres. 1992-97, treas. 1997—), Soc. Former Spl. Agts. of Nat. chpt., L.I. chpt., chmn. L.I. chpt. 2003—, charter chmn. 2003-06), NY State Assn. Criminal Def. Lawyers, Legal Lawyers Assn. (bd. dirs. 2001—, bd. dirs. found. 1995-98, 2001—, sec. 2003-05), St. John's Coll. Alumni Assn., Asst. Dist. Attys. Assn. Queens County, St. John's U. Sch. of Law Alumni Assn., St. John's Prep. Sch. Alumni Assn., Friends of the Arts of Nassau County, Inc., Cath. Lawyers Guild of Queens County, NY, KC, Brookhaven Wine Lovers Soc., East Norwich Civic Assn., San Island Assn. (bd. dirs. 2001-02), St. John's U. McCallen Soc., Business Advisory Coun., Phi Alpha Delta. Avocation: fine wines. Home: 170 Sugar Toms Ln East Norwich NY 11732-1153 Office: Scheich & Goldsmith PC 103-42 Lefferts Blvd South Richmond Hill NY 11419-2012 also: 109 Newbridge Rd Hicksville NY 11801-3908 Office Phone: 718-843-7200. Personal E-mail: jacksesq@aol.com.

**SCHEID, STEVEN L.,** investment company executive; 3 children. BS in acctg., Michigan St. U. CFO The Charles Schwab & Co. Inc., 1996—99, vice-chmn. San Francisco, 1999—2002; CEO Charles Schwab Investment

Mgmt., 1999—2002; pres. Schwab Retail Group, 2000—02; chmn. Janus Capital Group, Denver, 2004—, CEO, 2004—06. Fed. Reserve Bank of San Francisco's representative Fed. Advisory Coun., 2001—02; bd. dirs. The PMI Group Inc., Auto Desk Inc. Avocations: piano, clarinet, running, wine collecting. Office: Janus Capital Group Inc 151 Detroit St Denver CO 80206-4923*

**SCHEIDT, W. ROBERT,** chemistry educator, researcher; b. Richmond Heights, Mo., Nov. 13, 1942; s. Walter Martin and Martha (Videtich) S.; m. Kathryn Sue Barnes, Aug. 9, 1964; children: Karl Andrew, David Martin. BS, U. Mo., 1964; MS, U. Mich., 1965, PhD, 1968; postdoctoral studies, Cornell U., 1970. Asst. prof. U. Notre Dame, Ind., 1970-76, assoc. prof. Ind., 1976-80, prof. Ind., 1980—, William K. Warren prof. Ind., 1999—. Vis. prof. U. Wash., Seattle, 1980, U. Paris (Orsay), Paris, 1991, U. René Descartes, 2005, 06, U. Strasbourg, France, 1998; mem. rev. sec. Metallobiochemistry NIH, Bethesda, 1991—96. Contbr. articles to profl. jours. Fellow AAAS; mem. Am. Chem. Soc. (assoc. editor Chem. Revs. jour. 1980-85), Am. Crystallographic Assn., Biophys. Soc., Sigma X. Democrat. Office: U Notre Dame Dept Chemistry Notre Dame IN 46556 Business E-Mail: scheidt.1@nd.edu

**SCHEIMAN, EUGENE R.,** lawyer; b. Bklyn., July 15, 1943; BA, L.I. U., 1966; JD cum laude, Bklyn. Law Sch., 1969. Bar: N.Y. 1970, U.S. Dist. Ct. (so. and ea. dists.) N.Y. 1971, U.S. Ct. Appeals (1st cir.) 1972, U.S. Ct. Appeals (5th cir.) 1973, U.S. Ct. Appeals (4th cir.) 1974, U.S. Supreme Ct. 1976, U.S. Ct. Appeals (2nd cir.) 1977, U.S. Ct. Appeals (fed. cir.), U.S. Ct. Appeals (11th cir.) 1989, U.S. Ct. Appeals (3rd cir.) 1990. Formerly shareholder Buchanan Ingersoll, N.Y.C.; now ptnr. McCarter & English LLP, N.Y.C. Rsch. editor Bklyn. Law Rev., 1968, editor-in-chief, 1969. Mem. ABA (sect. on individual rights and responsibilities, franchise forum constrn.), ATLA, N.Y. State Bar Assn., Assn. Bar City of N.Y., Philonomic Honor Soc., County Bar Assn. (constrn. law forum), Am. Assn. Trial Lawyers. Office: McCarter & English LLP 245 Park Ave New York NY 10167 Office Phone: 212-605-6832. Business E-Mail: escheiman@mccarter.com.

**SCHEIN, EDGAR HENRY,** management educator; b. Zurich, Mar. 5, 1928; came to U.S., 1939, naturalized, 1944; s. Marcel and Hilde (Schoenbeck) S.; m. Mary Louise Lodmell, July 28, 1956; children: Louisa, Elizabeth, Peter. PhB, U. Chgo., 1946, BA, 1947, Stanford U., 1948, MA, 1949; PhD, Harvard U., 1953. Teaching asst. statistics Stanford U., 1947-49; teaching asst. social psychology Harvard U., 1949-52; research psychologist, neuropsychiatry div. Walter Reed Army Inst. Research, also chief social psychology sect., 1952-56; mem. faculty MIT, 1956—, prof. orgnl. psychology and mgmt., 1964—, chmn. orgn. studies group Sloan Sch. Mgmt., 1972-81, Sloan Fellows prof. mgmt., 1978-97, prof. emeritus, sr. lectr., 1995—; mem. bd., exec. com. Nat. Tng. Labs., 1962-64; cons. to govt. and industry, 1956—. Author books and articles in field. Capt. AUS, 1950-56. Recipient Aux. Rsch. award Social Sci. Rsch. Coun., 1958. Fellow APA; mem. Am. Sociol. Assn., Acad. Mgmt. Business E-Mail: scheine@mit.edu.

**SCHEIN, VIRGINIA ELLEN,** psychologist, editor; b. June 23, 1943; d. Jacob Charles and Anne Schein; m. Rupert F. Chisholm (dec. 2004); 1 child, Alexander Nikos. BA cum laude, Cornell U., 1965; PhD, NYU, 1969. Lic. psychologist, Pa. Sr. rsch. assoc. Am. Mgmt. Assn., N.Y.C., 1969-70; mgr. personnel rsch. Life Office Mgmt. Assn., N.Y.C., 1970-72; dir. personnel rsch. Met. Life Ins. Co., N.Y.C., 1972-75; assoc. prof. Sch. Mgmt. Case Western Res. U., Cleve., 1975-76; vis. assoc. prof. Sch. Orgn. and Mgmt. Yale U., New Haven, 1977-80; mgmt. cons. Va. E. Schein, PhD, P.C., 1975—; assoc. prof. psychology Bernard M. Baruch Coll. CUNY, 1982-85; prof. mgmt. and psychology Gettysburg Coll., Pa., 1986—, chair mgmt. dept., 1993-95. Co-author: Power and Organization Development, 1988; author: Working from the Margins, 1995; mem. editl. rev. bds. Women Mgmt. Rev., Acad. Mgmt. Execs.; contbr. articles to profl. jours. Bd. dirs. Family Planning Ctr., 1988-91, Pvt. Industry Coun., 1990-93, Keystone Rsch. Ctr., 1996-98, Women Cmty. Svc., 1997-2003; bd. dirs. Survivors, Inc., pres. bd. dirs., 1991-92, Adams County Children and Youth Adv. Bd., 2003-04. Mem.: APA (coun.rep. 1978—80, com. women 1980—83), Internat. Assn. Applied Psychology (divsn. orgnl. psychology chair sci. program com. 1995—98, pres.-elect 1998—2002, pres. 2002—06), Acad. Mgmt. (rep. orgn.devel. divsn. 1979—81, exec. com. women mgmt. divsn.), Met. Assn. Applied Psychology (pres. 1973—74), Psi Chi. Office: Gettysburg Coll Dept Mgmt Gettysburg PA 17325

**SCHEINBERG, PHYLLIS F.,** federal agency administrator; BA, Simmons Coll.; MS, U. Calif. Sr. budget examiner trasp. and natural resources, office mgmt. and budget Exec. Office Pres., Washington, 1981—90; dir. transp. issues U.S. Gen. Acctg. Office, Washington; acting asst. sec. budget and programs, CFO US Dept. Transp., Washington, dep. asst. sec. budget & programs, 2001—05, asst. sec. budget & programs, CFO, 2005—. Office: US Dept Transp 400 Seventh St SW Rm 10101 Washington DC 20590 Office Phone: 202-366-9191. Office Fax: 202-366-6031.

**SCHEINDLIN, RAYMOND PAUL,** literature educator, religious organization administrator; b. Phila., May 13, 1940; s. Irving and Betty (Bernstein) S.; m. Shira Ann Joffe, 1969 (div. 1981); children: Dov Baer, Dahlia Rachel; m. Janice C. Meyerson, 1986. BA, U. Pa., 1961; M.H.L., Jewish Theol. Sem., N.Y.C., 1963; PhD, Columbia U., N.Y.C., 1971. Ordained rabbi, 1965. Asst. prof. McGill U., Montreal, Que., Canada, 1969-72; asst. prof. Cornell U., Ithaca, NY, 1972-74; assoc. prof. Jewish Theol. Sem. of Am., NYC, 1974-85, prof. Hebrew lit., 1985—, provost, 1984-90; dir. Shalom Spiegel Inst. of Medieval Hebrew Lit., 1996—; rabbi Congregation Baith Israel Anshei Emes, Bklyn., 1979-82; fellow Cullman Ctr. Scholars and Writers, NY Pub. Libr., 2005—06. Mem. publ. com. Jewish Publ. Soc., Phila., 1985-90; mem. internat. adv. com. Ctr. for Judaic Studies U. Pa., 1995—; mem. bd. acad. advisors Catalan Mus. Jewish Culture, Gerona, Spain, 1993—; mem. editl. com. Jewish Quar. Rev., 1995—. Translator: (novella) Of Bygone Days by Mendele Mokher Seforim, 1973, Jewish Liturgy: A Comprehensive History by Ismar Elbogen, 1993; author: Form & Structure in the Poetry of Al-Mu'tamid Ibn 'Abbad, 1974, 201 Arabic Verbs, 1978, Wine, Women, and Death: Medieval Hebrew Poems on the Good Life, 1986, The Gazelle: Medieval Hebrew Poems on God, Israel and the Soul, 1991, Chronicles of the Jewish People, 1996, The Book of Job, 1998, A Short History of the Jewish People, 1998, (libretto) Miriam and the Angel of Death, 1984; mem. editl. com. Prooftexts, 1988—2004, Edebiyat, 1992—, Studies in Muslim-Jewish Rels., 1992—; mem. editl. bd. Arabic and Mid. Ea. Lits., Medieval Iberia; co-editor The Literature of Al-Andalus, 2000. Fellow Cullman Ctr. Scholar and Writers, N.Y Publ. Libr., 2005—. Recipient Jewish Cultural Achievement award Nat. Found. for Jewish Culture, 2004; Guggenheim fellow, 1988, Annenberg Inst. fellow, 1993; sr. assoc. fellow Oxford Centre for Postgrad. Hebrew Studies. Fellow: Am. Acad. Jewish Rsch. (mem. exec. com. 2003—); mem.: PEN Am. Ctr., Jewish Publ. Soc. (bd. dirs. 1987—93), Assn. Jewish Studies, World Union Jewish Studies, Soc. Judeo-Arabic Studies. Home: 420 Riverside Dr New York NY 10025-7773 Office: Jewish Theol Sem Am 3080 Broadway New York NY 10027-4650 E-mail: ibngabirol@aol.com.

**SCHEINESON, IRWIN BRUCE,** insurance and investment company executive; b. Cin., Aug. 8, 1955; s. Julian and Joan (Klein) Scheineson; married; children: Kate Marie, John Philip. BBA, U. Cin., 1978. Pres., prin. Lang-Kruke Fin. Group, Cin., 1978—97; agt. adv. liaison Community Mut. Ins. Co. (Blue Cross), Cin., 1978—80, Cen. Benefits Mut., Columbus, Ohio, 1986—88; pres. Gt. Am. Filter Co., Norwood, Ohio, 1990—98; pres., CEO Planning Works, Ltd., 1997. Lectr. in field. Contbr. articles to profl. jours. Fund raiser Guilford Sch., Cin., 1985—. Mem. Internat. Assn. Fin. Planning, Nat. Assn. Health Underwriters, Nat. Assn. Life Underwriters (Nat. Sales Achievement award 1979), Cin. Assn. Health Underwriters (bd. dirs. 1984-87), Nat. Soc. CLUs and Chartered Fin. Cons., 2002 Top of the Table Million Dollar Roundtable, Crest Hills Country Club (bd. dirs. 1988-93). Republican. Jewish. Avocations: tennis, skiing, travel, golf, marathon running. Office:

Planning Works Ltd Ste 250 11111 Montgomery Rd Cincinnati OH 45249-3305 Office Phone: 513-489-7526. Personal E-mail: runner@cinci.rr.com. Business E-Mail: planningworks@cinci.rr.com.

**SCHEINFELD, JAMES DAVID,** retired travel company executive; b. Milw., Wis., Nov. 11, 1926; s. Aaron and Sylvia (Rosenberg) S.; children from previous marriage: John Stephen, Shaina, Robert Alan; m. Elna Magnusson, 1994. BA in Econs. magna cum laude, U. Wis., 1949. With Manpower, Inc., 1948-78, salesman, Chgo., 1949-51, br. mgr., 1951-53, nat. sales mgr., Milw., 1953-56, dir. sales, corp. sec., 1956-59, v.p. sales, 1959-62, exec. v.p. mktg., 1962-65, exec. v.p. (sr.), chief ops. officer, 1965-76, v.p. spl. projects, 1976-78, mem. exec. com., bd. dirs., 1959-76, cons., 1978-84; exec. v.p., chief exec. officer, bd. dirs. Transpersonal, Inc., Any Task Inc., Manpower Argentina, Manpower Europe, Manpower Ltd. (U.K.), Manpower Australia, Manpower Japan, Manpower Germany GmbH, Manpower Norway, Manpower Denmark, Manpower Venezuela, 1966-76; pres. Travway Internat. Inc.- Funway Holidays, Funjet, 1976-81, Aide Svcs., Inc., Tampa, Fla., 1976-81; pres., chief exec. officer Travelpower Inc., 1976-84; sr. v.p. Carlson Travel Network, 1984—2004. Mem. Travway Travel Systems Inc., 1977-85, bd. dirs., 1978-85, pres., 1980-82, pres. emeritus, 1982—. Contbr. articles to profl. jours. Chmn. Cancer Crusade Milwaukee County, 1970; bd. dirs. Sinai-Samaritan Med. Ctr., Better Bus. Bur. Milw., 1979-90, Found. for Santa Barbara City Coll., 1989—, pres., 1996-2000; trustee U. Wis. Milw. Found., 1981-91, emeritus trustee, 1991—; mem. bus. adv. bd. U. Wis.-Milw., 1987—; chmn. bus. adv. bd. Santa Barbara City Coll., 1988-92; dir. Santa Barbara Trust for Hist. Preservation, 1995—, v.p. 1998-2004, pres. 2004-06; mem. Greater Milw. Comm., 1984-97; bd. dirs. Sansum Santa Barbara Med. Found. Clinic, 1989—, chmn., 2005—. With USNR, 1944-46. Mem. Nat. Assn. Temporary Svcs. (pres. 1975-76, bd. dirs. 1969-77), La Cumbre Country Club (Santa Barbara), Rotary Club of Montecito Calif. Home and Office: 129 Rametto Rd Santa Barbara CA 93108-2317 Office Phone: 805-969-5671. Personal E-mail: jimscheinfeld1@cox.net. *I do not often walk or look back where my footprints are. I prefer to walk that part of the beach I have never walked before. I am a person who thinks more about tomorrow than yesterday...more about what can be done than what has been done...more about challenges than accomplishments. Looking back is helpful only if I can find a sign to help me in my future.*

**SCHEINHOLTZ, LEONARD LOUIS,** lawyer; b. Pitts., June 2, 1927; s. Bernard A. and Marie (Getzel) Scheinholtz; m. Joan R. Libenson, Aug. 16, 1953; children: Stuart, Nancy, Barry. BA, U. Pa., 1948, MA, 1949; LLB, Columbia U., 1953. Bar: Pa. 1954, U.S. Ct. Appeals (3d cir.) 1959, U.S. Ct. Appeals (6th cir.) 1968, U.S. Supreme Ct. 1972, U.S. Ct. Appeals (4th cir.) 1973, U.S. Ct. Appeals (5th cir.) 1981, U.S. Ct. Appeals (11th cir.) 1991, U.S. Ct. Appeals (2d cir.) 1993. Assoc. Reed, Smith, LLP, Pitts., 1953—62, spl. ptnr., 1962—64, gen. ptnr., 1964—97, head labor dept., 1980—86, of counsel, 1997—. Dir. Am. Arbitration Assn., N.Y.C., 1980—96. Author: Exemption Under the Anti-Trust Laws for Joint Employer Activity, 1982, The Arbitrator as Judge and Jury: Another Look at Statutory Law in Arbitration, 1985. Vice-chmn. Pa. AAA Fedn., Harrisburg, 1982—85; chmn. W. Pa. AAA Motor Club, 1979—82; trustee Jewish Healthcare Found., 2004—; bd. dirs. Nat. Aviary, 1999—, Jewish Chronicle, Pitts., 1997—2003, United Jewish Fedn., Pitts., 1997—2000; trustee Montefiore Hosp., Pitts., 1976—79. With USN, 1945—46. Mem.: ABA, Allegheny County Bar Assn., Pa. Bar Assn. Republican. Jewish. Home: 746 Pinoak Rd Pittsburgh PA 15243-1153 Office: Reed Smith LLP Mellon Sq 435 6th Ave Pittsburgh PA 15219-1886 Office Phone: 412-288-3178. Personal E-mail: leolen@adelphia.net. Business E-Mail: lscheinholtz@reedsmith.com.

**SCHEINMAN, A. DANIEL,** computer system networks executive; b. 1963; BA, Brandeis U.; JD, Duke U. Bar: Calif. 1990. Atty. Gray, Carey, Ware & Freidenrich, Palo Alto, Calif.; with Cisco Sys. Inc., San Jose, Calif., 1992—97, v.p., legal and govtl. affairs, 1997—2002, sr. v.p., corp. devel. 2002—. Bd. visitors Duke U. Law Sch. Office: Cisco Sys Inc 170 W Tasman Dr San Jose CA 95134

**SCHEINMAN, STANLEY BRUCE,** corporate financial executive; b. NYC, Nov. 13, 1933; s. Samuel and Sadie (Seiffer) S.; m. Susan L. Eisten (dec.); m. Janet L. Donnely, Dec. 30, 1975 (dec.); children: Catherine Amy, Anthony Paul, Sarah Jean, Norah Jane; m. Maria Shea Burke, Nov. 17, 2000. AB, Cornell U., 1954; MBA, CCNY, 1957; JD (Harlan Fisk Stone scholar), Columbia U., 1960. Bar: N.Y. 1960. Assoc. firm Cravath, Swaine & Moore, N.Y.C., 1960-62; capital projects officer, legis. programs staff coord. AID, Washington, 1962-64; sr. exec. officer Bur. Pvt. Enterprise, AID, 1982-83; v.p. fin. and adminstrn. svcs. industries div., also v.p., counsel internat. div. PepsiCo. Inc., 1965-70; v.p. fin. and adminstrn. pharm. divsn. Revlon, Inc., 1970-72; sr. v.p. MCI Comm., 1972-76; pres., COO FSC Corp., Pitts., 1976-81; pres. New Venture Capital Corp., Washington, 1984-85; prin. Re Venture Assocs., Salisbury, Conn., 1985-86; chmn., CEO Internat. 800 Telcom Corp., Geneva, 1987-88; pres., CEO Zurich Depository Corp., Manhasset, NY, 1988-89; exec. v.p AMIF&S Ltd., N.Y.C., 1989-91; pres. IT Svc. Corp., Westport, Conn., 1991-92; v.p. ops. and bus. devel. EQ Corp., Westport, 1992-95; exec. v.p., CFO, Computer Products and Svcs. Inc., Wilton, Conn., 1995-96; pres., mng. dir. TTC Internat. Ltd., London, 1996—. Mem.: ABA, Internat. Execs. Assn., Fin. Execs. Inst., Inst. for Dirs. (U.K.), Assn. Bar City N.Y., Brit.-Am. Club, Cornell Club, Eng. Svc. Club, Paris-Am. Club. Home: PO Box 2398 Westport CT 06880 Office: 50 Wash St Ste 1211 Norwalk CT 06854 E-mail: stanbsch@aol.com, stanbsch@btinternet.com.

**SCHEINMAN, STEVEN JAY,** dean, medical educator; b. Monticello, NY, Oct. 22, 1951; 2 children. AB summa cum laude, Amherst Coll., 1973; MD cum laude, Yale U., 1977. Diplomate Am. Bd. Internal Medicine in Nephrology, lic. physician N.Y., Conn. Resident internal medicine Yale-New Haven Hosp., 1977-80; chief resident internal medicine Upstate Med. Ctr., Syracuse, NY, 1980-81, fellow nephrology, 1981-83, Yale-New Haven Hosp., 1983-84; asst. prof. medicine SUNY Upstate Med. U., Syracuse, 1984-90, asst. prof. pharmacology, 1988-90, assoc. prof. medicine and pharmacology, 1990-94, prof. medicine and pharmacology, 1994—, chief nephrology divsn. dept. medicine, 1994—2004, exec. v.p., dean Coll. Medicine, 2004—, officer-in-charge, 2006. Vis. scientist MRC Molecular Medicine Group, Royal Postgrad. Med. Sch. Hammersmith Hosp., London, 1992, London, 95; vis. scholar dept. biochemistry U. Oxford, 1985; attending physician U. Hosp., Syracuse, Crouse-Irving Meml. Hosp., Syracuse, VA Med. Ctr., Syracuse; dir. Nephrology Fellowship Program, 1993—; spkr. seminars, confs., orgns. Assoc. editor: Neph SAP, 2002—; mem. editl. bd. Yale Jour. Biology and Medicine, 1975—77, Jour. Am. Soc. Nephrology, 2000—02, mem. NIDDK Spl. Rev. Group, 1998—; contbr. Recipient Lange award, Yale U. Sch. Medicine, 1976, Resident Merit award, ACP (Conn. chpt.), 1980, Nat. Rsch. Svc. award, NIH, 1981—83, Clin. Investigator award, 1985, Charles R. Ross Rsch. award, SUNY-Health Sci. Ctr., 1992, Pres.'s award for Excellence and Leadership in Rsch., SUNY Upstate Med. U., 2001, Chancellor's Rsch. Recognition award, SUNY, 2002; grantee, Nat. Inst. Arthritis Diabetes Digestive and Kidney Diseases, 1981—83, 1985—90, 1995—2002, 2000—04, 2003—, Am. Heart Assn., 1985, 1988—90, 1990—91, 1992—95, 1995—97, NATO, 1995—98. Mem.: Assn. Am. Med. Colls. Coun. Deans, Assn. Subspecialty Profs., Nat. Kidney Found., Am. Heart Assn. Coun. on Kidney, Am. Soc. Bone and Mineral Rsch., Am. Physiol. Soc., Internat. Soc. Nephrology, Am. Soc. Nephrology (mem. editl. bd. Jour. 2000—02), Am. Fedn. Med. Rsch., Am. Soc. Clin. Investigation, Alpha Omega Alpha, Phi Beta Kappa. Office: Office of Dean SUNY Upstate Med Univ 1257 Weiskotten Hall Syracuse NY 13210 Office Phone: 315-464-9720. Business E-Mail: scheinms@upstate.edu.

**SCHEIRER, WILLIAM KENNETH,** economist, consultant; b. Bethlehem, Pa., Oct. 17, 1937; s. Kenneth Raymond Scheirer and Pansy Elinor Ruch; m. Rita Gertrud Aase Simmersbach (div.); children: Nicola, Erik, Peter, Karl. AB, Princeton U., 1959; student, London Sch. Econs., 1959—60, MIT, 1960—63. Sr. economist U.S. Small Bus. Adminstrn., Wash., 1980—95. Cons. Lehigh Valley Techonomics, Bethlehem, Pa., 1995—2006. Mem. editl. bd. Jour. Small Bus. Econs., 1988—93; contbr. chapters to books. Life mem., past pres. Kalorama Citizens Assn., 1968—; life mem. Com. 100 on Fed. City,

Wash., 1999—, Citizens for a Better Bethlehem. Mem.: Am. Econ. Assn., Torch Club. Avocation: reading. Home and Office: Lehigh Valley Techonomics 1890 Eaton Ave Bethlehem PA 18018 Office Phone: 610-954-9997. Personal E-mail: bethlehembill@hotmail.com.

**SCHEIRING, MICHAEL JAMES,** college official; b. Canton, Ohio, Oct. 11, 1949; s. Robert J. and Madonna L. (Geisigi) S.; m. Marcia L. Young, May 13, 1972; children: Kristy L., Lauren M. BA, Kent State U., 1971, MPA, 1972. Sect. supr. N.J. Dept. Treasury, Trenton, 1974-78; policy analyst to gov. Trenton, 1978-80; dir. adminstrn. N.J. Dept. Community Affairs, Trenton, 1980-82; dir. corp. budgeting N.J. Transit Corp., Newark, 1982-83; v.p. adminstrn. and fin. Thomas A. Edison Coll., Trenton, 1983—; exec. dir. Gov. Mgmt. Rev. Com., Gov.'s Office, Trenton, N.J., 1990-93. Trustee N.J. Ednl. Computer Corp., 1984-90; trustee, comptroller Edison Found., Trenton, 1984—; mem. adv. bd. National Ctr. Productivity; past pres. U.D. Dollars for Scholars Found.; pres. Cerebral Palsy of NJ; chmn. Trenton Audit Commn.; mem. citizen's delegation to China; trustee Robert Wood Johnson U. Hosp. Hamilton. Contbg. author: N.J. Zero-Based Budgeting, 1979. Named Vol. of Yr. N.J. United Cerebral Palsy; recipient Libr. Champion award. Mem. ASPA (nat. coun., v.p. programs 1984, v.p. membership 1985, pres. 1987-89), Old Barracks Assn. (trustee, past pres.), Rotary (pres.). Roman Catholic. Home: 2 Lotus Ln Trenton NJ 08648-3211 Office: Thomas Edison State Coll Trenton NJ 08625 Office Phone: 609-984-1110 x 2300. E-mail: mscheiring@tesl.edu.

**SCHEITHE, JEANNE MARIE,** language educator, mathematician, educator; b. Waterbury, Conn., Apr. 9, 1952; d. Robert Ernest and Jane (Smith) Crosby; m. Frederick Raymond Scheithe, Oct. 7, 1983. BS in Elem. Edn. cum laude, So. Conn. State Coll., 1974, MS in Reading cum laude, 1981. Substitute tchr. Naugatuck (Conn.) Bd. Edn., 1976-77, tchr., 1977-79, mid. sch. tchr., 1979—2003, Hop Brook Intermediate Sch., 2003—. Advisor, chaperone acad., cultural and social activities Hillside Mid. Sch. and Hop Brook Intermediate Sch., 1977—2003; vol. tutor to athletes in need Hillside Mid. Sch., 1985—; creator math. remediation program, 1987—94, report card revision com., 1988—89, organizer student fair, 1990—95, report card revision com., 1994—95, Conn. Thinking Cap Quiz Bowl advisor, 1995—2005. Contbg. writer Math. Curriculum, 1986-87. Treas., bldg. rep. Naugatuck Tchrs. League, 1981-84; treas. CARE, 1988, 89. Named Co-Educator of Yr., Naugatuck Exch. Club, 2004; named to Naugatuck Hall of Fame, 2006; recipient award, Naugatuck H.S. Alumni Assn., 1998. Mem. Conn. Edn. Assn., NEA, Nat. Honor Soc. Avocations: aerobics, swimming, attending student events, golf. Home: 243 Millville Ave Naugatuck CT 06770-3848 Office: Hop Brook Intermediate Sch 75 Crown St Naugatuck CT 06770-4018 Office Phone: 203-720-5231.

**SCHEJBAL, NANCY KAY,** secondary school educator; b. St. Louis, Mar. 5, 1949; d. Casper A. and Melba M. Borgmeyer; children: Annette, Debra, Sherry, Chip. AA in Arts and Sci., Meramec Community Coll., St. Louis, 1983; BS in Elem. Edn., U. Mo., St. Louis, 1985, MA in Secondary Edn. 1991. Cert. elem., sci. and social studies tchr. Mo., tchr. gifted Mo. Elem. tchr. St. Francis of Assisi Sch., St. Louis, 1985-87; tchr. sci. Mehlville Sch. Dist., St. Louis, 1987—98, tchr. gifted, 1998—. Presenter in field. Mem.: NEA. Roman Catholic. Avocations: volleyball, reading, gardening. Office: Mehlville Sch Dist Washington Mid Sch 5165 Ambs Rd Saint Louis MO 63128 Business E-Mail: schejbaln@mehlville.k12.mo.us.

**SCHEKMAN, RANDY W.,** molecular biology administrator, biochemist; b. St. Paul, Dec. 30, 1948; married, 1973; 1 child. BA, UCLA, 1970; PhD in Biochemistry, Stanford U., 1975; PhD (hon.), U. Geneva, 1997. Fellow U. Calif., San Diego, 1974-76, from asst. to assoc. prof. Berkeley, 1976-83, prof., 1983—, head divsn. biochemistry and molecular biology, 1990-97, co-chair dept. molecular and cellular biology, 1997—. Fellow Woodrow Wilson Found., 1970, Cystic Fibrosis Found., 1974, John S. Guggenheim Found., 1982-83; recipient Research award in microbiology & immunology, Eli Lilly, 1987, Lewis S. Rosenstiel award in basic biomedical sci., 1994, Gairdner Found. Internat. award, 1996, Albert Lasker award for basic med. rsch., Albert and Mary Lasker Found., 2002, Louisa Gross Horwtiz prize, Columbia U., 2002; named Amgen award lecturer, Protein Soc., 1999, Berkeley Faculty Rsch. lecturer, U. Calif., 1999. Mem. Am. Soc. Microbiology, Am. Soc. Biochemists & Molecular Biologists, Am. Acad. of Arts & Sciences (elected 2000), NAS (elected 1992); hon. mem. Japanese Biochemical Soc.; foreign assoc. EMBO. Achievements include research on molecular mechanism of secretion and membrane assembly in eucaryotic cells. Office: U Calif Dept Molecular Cell Bio 401 Barker Hall Spc 3202 Berkeley CA 94720-3202 Office Phone: 510-642-5686. E-mail: schekman@uclink4.berkeley.edu.*

**SCHELBERT, HEINRICH RUEDIGER,** nuclear medicine physician; b. Wuerzburg, Germany, Nov. 5, 1939; MD. U. Würzburg, Germany, 1964. Diplomate Am. Bd. Nuclear Medicine. Intern Mercy Med. Ctr., Phila., 1966-67, resident, 1967-68, 70-71; resident in cardiology U. Dusseldorf, Germany, 1971-72; fellow in cardiology, resident in nuclear medicine U. Calif., San Diego, 1968-69, asst. rsch. cardiologist, 1972-75, assoc. rsch. radiologist, 1975-76; hosp. assoc. UCLA Med. Ctr., 1977—; prof. radiol. scis. UCLA Sch. Medicine, 1980-90, prof. pharmacol. and radiol. scis., 1993—. Editor-in-chief: Jour. Nuc. Medicine, 2004. Recipient Georg von Hevesy prize 2d Internat. Congress World Fedn. Nuclear Medicine and Radiation Biology, 1978, 3d Internat. Congress World Fedn. Nuclear Medicine and Radiation Biology, 1982. Fellow Am. Coll. Cardiology; mem. Am. Heart Assn. (disting. scientific achievement award 1989), Soc. Nuclear Medicine (Herrman L. Blumgart pioneer lectr. award 1989, George De Hevesy Nuclear Medicine Pioneer award 1998), German Soc. Nuc. Med. (hon.), Swiss Soc. Nuc. Medicine (hon.)(editor-in-chief). Office: UCLA Sch Medicine Dept Molecular Med B2 085J Box 956948 Los Angeles CA 90095-6948 Office Phone: 310-825-3076. Business E-Mail: hschelbert@mednet.ucla.edu.

**SCHELD, WILLIAM MICHAEL,** internist, educator; b. Middletown, Conn., Aug. 15, 1947; s. William Herman and Lucille Laverne (Houchens) S.; m. Susan Ella Vaughan, June 14, 1969; 1 child, Sarah Walker. BS, Cornell U., 1969, MD, 1973. Diplomate Am. Bd. Internal Medicine. Intern, then resident U. Va. Sch. Medicine, Charlottesville, 1973-76, fellow in infectious diseases, 1976-79, asst. prof., 1979-82, assoc. prof., 1982-88, prof., assoc. chair dept. infectious diseases, 1988—. Chair Inter-sci. Conf. on Antimicrobial Agents and Chemotherapy. Editor: Infections of the Central Nervous System, 1991, 97, 2004; contbr. sci. articles to profl. publs., chpts. to books. Fellow ACP, Infectious Diseases Soc. Am. (pres. 2002-2003); mem. Am. Soc. Clin. Investigation, Nat. Found. Infectious Diseases (pres.), Alpha Omega Alpha. Achievements include research on meningitis and other central nervous system infections, bacterial endocarditis, sepsis, anthrax, etc. Home: 2075 Earlysville Rd Earlysville VA 22936-9634 Office: U Va Health Systems Box 801392 Charlottesville VA 22908

**SCHELER, BRAD ERIC,** lawyer; b. Bklyn., Oct. 11, 1953; s. Bernard and Rita Regina (Miller) S.; m. Amy Ruth Frolick, Mar. 30, 1980; children: Ali M., Maddie H., Zoey B. BA with high honors, Lehigh U., 1974; JD, Hofstra U., 1977. Bar: N.Y. 1978, U.S. Dist. Ct. (so. and ea. dists.) N.Y. 1978. Assoc. Weil, Gotshal & Manges, NYC, 1977-81; sr. ptnr., chmn. bankruptcy and restructuring practice Fried, Frank, Harris, Shriver & Jacobson, LLP, NYC, 1981—. Contbg. author: Collier on Bankruptcy, 15th edit. revised, Norton Annual Survey of Bankruptcy Law; rsch. editor Hofstra U. Law Rev., 1975-77. Treas.; bus. mgr. Trustees of Gramercy Park, N.Y.C., 1979-87; bd. trustees Lehigh U.; mem. bd. advisors Leadership Coun., Linderman Libr. Project, Wall St. Coun. Coll. Bus. and Econs.; adv. bd. K&A Register of Restructuring Profls.; bd. dirs. Vol. Lawyers for Arts, inMotion Justice All Women, Am. Friends of Sheba Med. Ctr. at Tel Hashomer. Fellow Am. Coll. Bankruptcy; mem. ABA (bus. bankruptcy com. bus. reorg. and bus. law sect., creditors' rights com. litig. sect.), N.Y. State Bar Assn., Assn. Bar City of N.Y. (com. on bankruptcy and corp. reorgn. 1991-94), Sigma Alpha Mu (v.p. 1973). Jewish. Home: 94 Larchmont Ave Larchmont NY 10538-3723 Office: Fried Frank Harris Shriver & Jacobson LLP 1 New York Plz Fl 23 New York NY 10004-1980 Office Phone: 212-859-8019. Business E-Mail: Schelbr@ffhsj.com.

**SCHELL, ALLAN CARTER,** retired electrical engineer; b. New Bedford, Mass., Apr. 14, 1934; s. Charles Carter and Elizabeth Schell; m. Shirley T. Sardineer; children: Alice Rosalind, Cynthia Anne. BS, MS.E.E., MIT, 1956, Sc.D., 1961; student, Tech. U. Delft, Netherlands, 1956-57. Research physicist Air Force Cambridge Research Labs., Bedford, Mass., 1956-76, Guenter Loeser Meml. lectr., 1965; dir. electromagnetics directorate Rome Air Devel. Ctr., Bedford, 1976-87; chief scientist Hdqrs. USAF Systems Command, 1987-92; chief scientist, dep. dir. sci. and tech. Hdqrs. USAF Materiel Command, 1992-94. Dir. Electro; vis. assoc. prof. MIT, 1974; chair dept. of elec. engring. adv. coun. U. Pa., 1992-94. Contbr. articles to profl. jours.; patentee in field (9). Lt. USAF, 1958—60. Recipient Fulbright award, 1956-57, Meritorious Exec. award U.S. Govt., 1989, IEEE APS Disting. Achievement award; NSF fellow, 1955-56, 60-61. Fellow IEEE (bd. dirs. 1981-82, editor IEEE Press 1976-79, Procs. of IEEE 1990-92), Antennas and Propagation Soc. of IEEE (pres. 1978, editor tran. 1969-71, chair awards and fellows com., 2000-05, John T. Bolljahn award 1966, Disting. Achievement award 2006), Internat. Sci. Radio Union, MIT Alumni Assn. (bd. dirs. 2003-05), Sigma Xi, Tau Beta Pi. Business E-Mail: a.schell@ieee.org.

**SCHELL, BRAXTON,** lawyer; b. Raleigh, NC, Feb. 24, 1924; s. Marshall H. and Margaret (Newsom) S.; m. Ann Cooper Knight, Mar. 30, 1951 (div. 1982); children: Braxton, Richard Knight, James Gray (dec.); m. Mary Rehill, Apr. 16, 1983. Student, N.C. State Coll., 1942-43; BS, U. N.C. 1948, JD with honors, 1951. Bar: NC 1931. Since practiced in, Greensboro; assoc. Smith, Moore, Smith & Pope, Greensboro, 1951-56; ptnr. Smith Moore Smith Schell & Hunter, Greensboro, 1956-85, Smith, Helms, Mullis, and Moore, 1986-87, Schell, Bray, Aycock, Abel & Livingston, 1987—. Gen. counsel, dir. Flagler Sys. and The Breakers Palm Beach, Inc. Assoc. editor N.C. Law Rev., 1950—51. Chmn. Special Liaison Tax Com. Southeastern Region, 1960-61; bd. dirs. N.C. Outward Bound Sch., 1975-88, chmn., 1977-80; trustee Outward Bound, Inc., 1978-81; bd. dirs. William R. Kenan Funds for Pvt. Enterprise, Arts and Engring., Tech. and Sci. and Ethics. Pilot USAAF, 1943-45. Fellow Am. Bar Found.; mem. ABA, N.C. Bar Assn., Greensboro Bar Assn., Order of Coif, Figure Eight Island Yacht Club, Greensboro City Club (dir. 1980-2003), Phi Beta Kappa. Presbyterian. Home: 422B Fisher Park Cir Greensboro NC 27401-1615 Office: Schell Bray Aycock Abel & Living 1500 Renaissance Pla Greensboro NC 27420 Business E-Mail: bschell@sbaal.com.

**SCHELL, FARREL LOY,** transportation engineer; b. Amarillo, Tex., Dec. 14, 1931; s. Thomas Phillip and Lillian Agnes (McKee) S.; m. Shirley Anne Samuelson, Feb. 6, 1955; children: James Christopher, Maria Leslyn Schell Peter. BS, U. Kans., 1954; postgrad., Carnegie-Mellon U., 1974. Registered profl. engr., Calif., Colo. Resident engr. Sverdrup & Parcel, Denver, 1957-61; project engr. Bechtel Corp., San Francisco, 1961-62, Parsons, Brinckerhoff-Tudor-Bechtel, San Francisco, 1962-67; mgr. urban transp. dept. Kaiser Engrs., Oakland, Calif., 1967-78; program dir. San Francisco Mcpl. Rwy I.C., 1978-80; project mgr. Houston Transit Cons., 1980-83, Kaiser Transit Group, Miami, 1983-85; mgr. program devel. Kaiser Engrs., Oakland, 1985-87; project mgr. O'Brien-Kreitzberg & Assocs., San Francisco, 1987-89; sr. project mgr. Bay Area Rapid Transit Dist., Oakland, Calif., 1989—96. Dir./CEO Schelter Devel. Corp., Piedmont, Calif., 1982—. Contbr. articles to profl. jours. Chmn., bd. dirs Achenbach Graphic Arts Coun., 1996-2002. Lt. (j.g.) USN, 1954-57, PTO. Mem. ASCE, ASME, Nat. Soc. Profl. Engrs., Nat. Coun. Engring. Examiners, Am. Planners Assn., Am. Pub. Transit Assn., Lakeview Club, Scarab Club, Pachacamac Club, Sigma Tau, Tau Beta Pi. Avocations: fly fishing, camping. Home: 100 Bay Pl #1517 Oakland CA 94610 Personal E-Mail: fschell2@mac.com.

**SCHELL, JAMES MUNSON,** finance company executive; b. Kalamazoo, Mich., Mar. 25, 1944; s. Frank John and Shirley I. S.; m. Susan O'Laughlin, Aug. 6, 1966; children: Karen, Michael, Ryan. BA, Vanderbilt U., 1966; MBA, Washington U., 1968. Dir. term and internat. financing Chrysler Fin. Corp., Troy, Mich., 1976-79, v.p., treas., 1980-81; v.p. domestic treasury Am. Express Co., N.Y.C., 1981-82; v.p. fin. resources Hertz Corp., N.Y.C., 1982-83; v.p., chief fin. officer Clabir Corp., Greenwich, Conn., 1983-84; v.p., treas. Fairchild Industries, 1985-87; ind. fin. cons., 1987—. Bd. dirs. Jackson-Jordan Corp., CTI Industries, Country Home Bakers. Republican. Roman Catholic. Home: 40 Stony Brook Rd Darien CT 06820-4326 E-mail: jmsschell@aol.com.

**SCHELL, MELVIN FRANK, JR.,** real estate agent; b. Binghamton, NY, Feb. 3, 1938; s. Melvin Frank and Irene Schell; m. Dollie Sedot Knowles, May 31, 1958; children: Mark Stephen, Jeremy Joel. BA, Tenn. Temple U., 1971; MBA, Ga. State U., 1987. Ordained Minister of the Gospel Brightlarlake Bapt. Ch., Atlanta GA, 1976; lic. Real Estate Agent Ga. Real Estate Commn., 2002, Fla. Real Estate Commn., 2004. Mktg. rep. Internat. Bus. Machines, Inc., Chattanooga, 1960—73; asst. min. First Alliance Ch., Atlanta, 1973—74; exec. dir. Evangelism Explosion Atlanta, Atlanta, 1974—75; pres. Ch. Growth Ministries, Atlanta, 1976—81, Omega Info. Systems, Inc., Atlanta, 1981—2003; regional mgr., AT&T computers MicroAge, Tempe, Ariz., 1990—91; pres. Aarist Internat., Inc, Atlanta, 1993—2003; real estate agt. Prudential Ga. Realty, Gainesville, Ga., 2002—, Century 21 Prestige Realty, Key West, Fla., 2005—06. Cons. to churches and non-profit organizations Fuller Evangelistic Assn., Pasadena, Calif., 1980—83. Author: (training materials) The Total Church Growth Model. Electronics technician second class USN, 1956—59, Key West, Fla. Decorated Good Conduct medal USN; recipient Class Pres., Internat. Bus. Machines, Inc., 1972. Dedicated Follower Of Jesus Christ.

**SCHELL, NORMAN BARNETT,** preventive medicine physician, consultant; b. N.Y.C., May 25, 1925; s. Jack and Ada Sylvia (Rosen) S.; m. Lila Barbara Mendelsohn, Aug. 27, 1950; children: Martin, Judith, Steven. AB cum laude, NYU, 1946, MD, 1950; MPH, Harvard U., 1971. Diplomate Am. Bd. Pediats., Am. Bd. Preventive Medicine, Nat. Bd. Med. Examiners; lic. physician, N.Y. Rotating intern Beth Israel Hosp., N.Y.C., 1950-51; asst. resident in pediats. Mt. Sinai Hosp., N.Y.C., 1951-52; clin. fellow in pediats. N.Y.-Cornell Med. Ctr., N.Y.C., 1952-53; pvt. practice Jericho and Hicksville, NY, 1956-69; pub. health physician Nassau County Health Dept., Mineola, NY, 1969-76, dep. commr., 1976-90. Prof. preventive medicine SUNY, Stony Brook, 1974-90; pediat. cons. N.Y. State Health Dept., 1956-69, HEW Project Head Start, N.Y.C., 1968-75; emeritus pediat. staff Nassau County Med. Ctr. Author: Keys to Childhood Illnesses, 1992; contbr. articles to profl. jours. Lt. M.C., USN, 1953-55, capt. M.C., USNR, 1981-85. Recipient Physician Recognition award AMA, 1970, Grade 1A Health Officer N.Y. State Health Dept., 1973. Fellow Am. Acad. Pediats. (com. on sch. health 1971-77, citation com. on med. edn. 1977), Am. Coll. Preventive Medicine, N.Y. Acad. Medicine; mem. Am. Coll. Legal Medicine (assoc.), Nassau County Med. Soc. (chmn. sch. health com.), Harvard Club (N.Y.C.), West Point Club, Phi Beta Kappa. Avocations: photography, music, computer technology. Home and Office: 63 Birchwood Park Dr Jericho NY 11753-2238

**SCHELL, RICHARD A.,** federal judge; b. 1950; BA, So. Meth. U., 1972, JD, 1975. Bar: Tex. 1975. Asst. dist. atty. Collin County, Tex., 1976; atty. pvt. practice, 1977—81; judge County Ct. Law Collin County, 1982—86, 219th Jud. Dist. Ct. Tex., 1986—88, U.S. Dist Ct. (ea. dist.) Tex., Beaumont, 1988—2003, U.S. Dist. Ct., Sherman, Tex., 2003—. Instr. rsch. methods and legal writing So. Meth. U., 1975—76. Mem.: State Bar Tex. Office: US Dist Ct 200 N Travis Sherman TX 75090

**SCHELLENBERGER, ROBERT EARL,** retired management educator, department chairman; b. Janesville, Wis., July 25, 1932; s. Ervin William and Adelaide Louise (Keller) S.; m. Linda Eula Todd, Dec. 30, 1961; children: Brian T., Keith W., Heidi L. BSBA, U. Wis., 1958, MBA, 1959; PhD, U. N.C.,

1963. Personnel supr. Libby McNeill and Libby, Janesville, Wis., 1957-58; from asst. prof. to assoc. prof. chmn. div. stats. dept. bus U. Md., College Park, 1963-68; chair dept. mgmt. So. Ill. U., Carbondale, Ill., 1968-70, dir. planning Sch. Human Resources Devel., 1970-71, prof. mgmt., 1968-71; vis. prof., dir. program evaluation Babcock Grad. Sch. Mgmt., Wake Forest U., Winston-Salem, NC, 1971-73; prof. dept. mgmt. Temple U., Phila., 1973-81, from chmn. dept. mgmt. to asst. to acad. vice chancellor, 1975-77; prof. decision scis. dept. East Carolina U., Greenville, NC, 1981-2000, chmn. decision scis. dept., 1989-95; ret., 2001. Pres. Md. Rsch. and Cons., Hyattsville, 1964-67; v.p. Ea. Acad. Mgmt., 1967; cons. Comml. Credit Corp., Balt., 1966. Author: Managerial Analysis, 1967, Policy Formulation, 1978, 2d edit., 1982; co-editor Jour. of Econs. and Bus., 1976; developer (software package) MANYSYM, 1965, 68, 78, 82, 86. Chmn. Utilities Com., Carbondale, 1970-72. Title IV NDEA fellow U. N.C., 1960-62, Earhart Jr. fellow U. Wis. Mem. Assn. for Bus. Simulation, SE Decision Scis. Inst., Decision Scis. Inst. (bd. dirs. 1974-77), Beta Gamma Sigma. E-mail: dcschell@cox.net.

**SCHELLER, RICHARD H.,** physiologist, science educator; b. Milw., Oct. 30, 1953; BA in Biochemistry with honors, U. Wis., Madison, 1975; PhD in Chemistry, Calif. Inst. Tech., 1980. Postdoctoral fellow divsn. biology Calif. Inst. Tech., 1980—81; postdoctoral fellow in molecular neurobiology Columbia U. Coll. Physicians and Surgeons, 1981—82; asst. prof. dept. biol. scis. Stanford (Calif.) U., 1982—87, assoc. prof. dept. biol. scis., 1987—90, assoc. prof. dept. molecular and cellular physiology, 1990—93, assoc. prof. dept. biol. scis. by courtesy, 1990—93, prof. dept. molecular and cellular physiology, 1993—, prof. dept. biol. scis., 1993; assoc. investigator Howard Hughes Med. Inst., Stanford U. Med. Ctr., 1990—94, investigator, 1994—2001; sr. v.p., research Genentech, Inc., South San Francisco, 2001—03, exec. v.p., research, 2003—. Mem. molecular, cellular and devel. neurobiology rev. com. NIMH, 1993—96; mem. sci. adv. bd. Hereditary Disease Found., 1995—96; mem. neurobiology adv. bd. Cold Spring Harbor Lab., 1995; mem. sr. rev. com. McKnight Endowment Fund, 1995; mem. adv. bd. Nat. Adv. Mental Health Coun., NIH, 1996. Mem. editl. bd. Jour. Neurosci., 1984—90, DNA, 1984—, Ann. Rev. Neurosci., 1985—90, Molecular Brain Rsch., 1985, Cellular and Molecular Neurobiology, 1986, Synapse, 1989—91, Neuron, 1990, Current Opinion in Neurobiology, 1990, sect. editor Jour. Neurosci., 1991—95, monitoring editor Jour. Cell Biology, 1991, assoc. editor Genes to Cells, 1995; contbr. articles to profl. jours. Recipient Basil O'Connor award, March of Dimes Found., 1983, Presdl. Young Investigator award, 1985, Alan T. Waterman award, NSF, 1989, Merit award, NIMH, 1992, W. Alden Spencer award, Columbia U., 1993; fellow, NIH, 1976—80, 1981—82, Alfred P. Sloan Found., 1984, Klingstein fellow in Neuroscis., 1985; scholar, McKnight Found., 1983, Pew scholar in biomed. scis., 1986, Camile and Henry Dreyfus Tchr. scholar, 1986. Mem.: Acad. of Arts and Sciences, NAS (award in Molecular Biology 1997), Soc. for Neurosci. (young investigator award selection com. 1994). Office: Genentech Inc 1 DNA Way South San Francisco CA 94080 Office Phone: 650-225-1000.

**SCHELLHASE, KENNETH GEORGE,** medical educator, researcher; s. Beva Mae and William Lester Richards (Stepfather); m. Janet Schellhase. BS in Internat.l Affairs, Georgetown U., Washington, 1985, MA, 1990, MA in Ethics, 1990; MD, U. Pa., Phila., 1994; MPH, U. Wash., Seattle, 1999. Diplomate Am. Bd. Family Medicine. Resident in family medicine U. Wash., 1994—97, fellow Robert Wood Johnson clin. scholars program, 1997—99, instr. family medicine, 1997—99; asst. prof. U. Ill. Coll. Medicine, Rockford, 1999—2001; asst. prof. family medicine Med. Coll. Wis., Milw., 2001—, dir. rsch. family medicine dept., 2005—; asst. dir. Waukehsa (Wis.) Family Practice Residency, 2001—. 1st lt. U.S. Army, 1985—87. Roman Catholic. Office: Med Coll Wis 8701 Watertown Plank Rd Milwaukee WI 53226 Office Phone: 414-456-4723.

**SCHELLING, DONALD LAWRENCE,** lawyer; b. Clearwater, Fla., June 5, 1959; s. Dorothy Ann Allen and Donald Anthony Schelling; m. Myrna Ytis Marca, Aug. 11, 1996. BSc, U. Manchester, England, 1985; PhD, Dundee U., Scotland, 1991; JD, No. Ill. U., 2001. USPTO Registration: US Patent Office 2002. Patent atty. Polsinelli Shalton Welte Seulthaus, Kans. City, Mo., 2004—, Townsend and Townsend and Crew, San Francisco, 2001—04. Author: (book) Regulation of Hepatic Phosphatases, Patent Law Primer. Mem.: AIPLA, Calif. Bar Assn., Brit. Biochemical Soc., San Francisco Intellectual Law Assn., ABA, Veterans Rugby Club, Carnoustie Golf Club, PAD. Achievements include research in regulation of phosphatases by ancillary proteins. Office: Polsinelli Shalton Welte Suelthaus 700W 47th St Kansas City MO 64112-1802 Office Phone: 816-753-1000. Office Fax: 816-753-1536. E-mail: dschelling@pswslaw.com.

**SCHELLING, THOMAS CROMBIE,** economist; b. Oakland, Calif., Apr. 14, 1921; s. John M. and Zelda M. (Ayres) S.; m. Corinne T. Saposs, Sept. 13, 1947 (div. 1991); children: Andrew, Thomas, Daniel, Robert; m. Alice M. Coleman, Nov. 8, 1991. AB in Econ., U. Calif., Berkeley, 1944; PhD in Econ., Harvard U., 1951; Doctorate (hon.), The RAND Grad. Sch. of Policy Analysis; Doctorate Honoris Causa, Erasmus U. Rotterdam. Economist US Bur. of the Budget, Washington, 1945—46, The Marshall Plan, Copenhagen and Paris, 1948—50; economist, Exec. Office of Pres. The White House, Washington, 1951—53; assoc. prof. and prof. econs. Yale U., 1953-58; prof. economics Harvard U., Cambridge, Mass., 1958-90, mem., John F. Kennedy Sch. Govt., 1969—90, Lucius N. Littauer prof. polit. economy emeritus; prof. econs. and pub. affairs U. Md., College Park, 1990—2003, disting. prof., 1990—2003, disting. prof. emeritus. Sr. staff mem. RAND Corp., 1958-59; chmn. rsch. adv. bd. Com. Econ. Devel., 1978-81, 84-85; mem. sci. adv. bd. USAF, 1960-64, def. sci. bd., 1966-70; mem. mil. econ. adv. panel CIA, 1980-85; dir. Inst. for Study of Smoking Behavior and Policy, Harvard U., 1984-90; trustee Aerospace Corp, 1984-93; trustee Ctr. for Advancement of Health, Co author (with Morton H. Halperin): Strategy and Arms Control, 1961; author: Nat. Income Behavior, 1951, Internat. Economics, 1958, The Strategy of Conflict, 1960, Arms and Influence, 1966, Micromotives and Macrobehavior, 1978, Thinking Through the Energy Problem, 1979, Choice and Consequence, 1984, Strategies of Commitment, 2006. Trustee Ctr. for Advancement of Health. Recipient Frank E. Seidman Disting. award in polit. economy, 1977; Nobel Prize in Econ. Sci., 2005. Fellow AAAS, Assn. for Pub. Policy Analysis and Mgmt., Am. Econ. Assn. (pres. 1991, Disting. Fellow award); mem. NAS (Award Behavioral Rsch. Relevant to the Prevention of Nuclear War, 1983). Inst. Medicine, Ea. Econ. Assn. (pres. 1996). Office: Univ Md Sch Pub Policy College Park MD 20742-0001 Mailing: 4506 Wetherill Rd Bethesda MD 20816 Office Phone: 301-405-3494. E-mail: tschelli@umd.edu.

**SCHELLMAN, JOHN A.,** chemistry professor; b. Phila., Oct. 24, 1924; s. John and Mary (Mason) S.; m. Charlotte Green, Feb. 10, 1954; children: Heidi M., Lise C. AB, Temple U., 1948; MS, Princeton U., 1949, PhD, 1951; PhD (hon.), Chalmers U., Sweden, 1983. USPHS postdoctoral fellow U. Utah, 1951-52, Carlsberg Lab., Copenhagen, 1953-55; DuPont fellow U. Minn., Mpls., 1955-56, asst. prof. chemistry, 1956-58; assoc. prof. chemistry Inst. Molecular Biology, U. Oreg., Eugene, 1958-63, prof. chemistry, rsch. assoc., 1963—. Vis. Lab. Chem. Physics, Nat. Inst Arthritis and Metabolic Diseases, NIH, Bethesda, Md., 1980; vis. prof. Chalmers U., 1986, U. Padua, 1987. Contbr. articles to profl. jours. Served with U.S. Army, 1943-46. Fellow Rask-Oersted Found., 1954, Sloan Found., 1959-63, Guggenheim Found., 1969-70. Fellow Am. Phys. Soc., Biophys. Soc.; mem. NAS, Am. Chem. Soc., Am. Soc. Biochemistry and Molecular Biology, Am. Acad. Arts and Scis., Phi Beta Kappa, Sigma Xi. Democrat. Business E-Mail: john@molbio.uoregon.edu.

**SCHELM, ROGER LEONARD,** information systems specialist; b. Kingston, N.Y., July 29, 1936; s. Frederick G. and Elizabeth M. (Wojciechowski) S.; m. Gloria Mae Dutterer, June 13, 1958; children: Sandra Lee Kern, Theresa Jean Sollito, Ginger Lisa Shah. BA in Polit. Sci., Western Md. Coll., 1958; MA in Pub. Adminstrn., Am. U., 1970; postgrad., U. Md., 1960-62. Analytic equipment programmer Nat. Security Agy., Ft. Meade, Md., 1958-60; computer cons. various cons. firms Balt., 1960-68, Washington,

1960—68; mgr. army plans and programs Informatics Inc., Bethesda, Md., 1968; mgr. def. programs Automation Tech. Inc., Wheaton, 1968-69; dir. advanced planning Genasys Corp., Washington, 1969-71; mgr. info. systems Ins. Co. North Am., Phila., 1971-72, sect. mgr. computing ops., 1972-74; mgr. tech. services INA Corp., 1974-75; mem. spl. tech. projects INA Corp. merger with Conn. Gen. Ins. Co. to form CIGNA Corp. 1982, 1975-76, asst. dir. tech. services, 1977, asst. dir. spl. tech. projects, 1977-78, asst. dir. adminstrn., 1978-79, asst. dir. resource mgmt., data ctr. design, contingency planning, 1979-80; dir. corp. info. tech. now CIGNA Corp., 1981-82, dir. planning and control ops. div., 1982-83, v.p. strategic planning, systems div., 1983-84, v.p. applied research/expert systems, systems div., 1984-92; co-founder, pres. Schelm Internat., Inc., Cherry Hill, NJ, 1992—2002. Mem. adj. faculty Camden Coll., N.J., 1978-82; mem. Camden County EDP Adv. Com., 1980-82; mem. faculty Drexel U., Phila., 1983-95. Author: Edni. Computer mag., 1982; mem. editl. adv. bd., author Small Sys. World mag., 1982-84; mem. editl. adv. bd. Magna-Sobinson Report, 1986-87, Machine Intelligence News, 1987-93, AI Expert mag., 1985-88; cons. editor Expert Sys. Jour., 1987-91. Tech. advisor various sch. bds., colls., univs. and non-profit orgns. Served to capt. U.S. Army, 1959. Mem. Am. Assn. Artificial Intelligence, Assn. Computing Machinery (founder Delaware Valley chpt. vice. chmn., program chmn. 1983-84, chmn. 1984-85, founder Del. Valley Spl. Interest Group in Artificial Intelligence, 1985, vice chmn. 1985-87), World Future Soc. Home and Office: 506 Balsam Rd Cherry Hill NJ 08003-3202

**SCHEMSKE, DOUGLAS WILLIAM,** science educator; b. Chgo., Sept. 8, 1948; PhD, U. Ill., Champaign-Urbana, 1977. Postdoctoral rsch. assoc. Smithsonian Instn., Panama City, Panama, 1977—78; asst. prof. Amherst Coll., Mass., 1978—79, U. of Chgo., 1979—85, assoc. prof., 1985—89, U. of Wash., Seattle, 1989—92, prof., 1992—2001, Mich. State U., East Lansing, 2001—. Hannah chair of biology Mich. State U., East Lansing, 2001—. Contbr. articles to sci. publs. (Mercer award Ecol. Soc. of Am., 1986, E. O. Wilson Naturalist award Am. Soc. of Naturalists, 2002). Named Highly Cited Rschr., Thomson Sci., 2002; recipient Evolutionary Signficance of Selfing and Outcrossing in Impatiens pallida grant, NSF, 1981—83, Using Demographic Analysis to Assess Biocontrol of an Invasive Plant grant, USDA, 2004—06, Genetics of Adaptation in Wild Oryza Species grant, NSF, 2005—08, Gradients in Biodiversity and Speciation grant, 2005—07, Demographic Consequences of Stage-Specific Plant-Animal Interactions in a Neotropical Herb grant, 1982—84, Temporal and Spatial Variation in Plant-Animal Interactions grant, 1985—88, Evolutionary Dynamics of a Flower-Color Polymorphism grant, 1990—93, Evolution of the Mating Sys. in Neotropical Begonia grant, Mellon Found., 1992—94, Molecular Genetics of Reproductive Isolation in Mimulus grant, NSF, 1997—2000, Evolution of Floral Characters in Neotropical Costus grant, Mellon Found., 1997—2001, Genetic Basis of Adaptive Differentiation in Mimulus grant, NSF, 2000—04, Integrated Ecol. and Genomic Analysis of Speciation in Mimulus grant, 2003—08. Fellow: Am. Acad. Arts and Scis. Achievements include research in adaptation, speciation and the origins of biodiversity in temperate and tropical communities. Office: Mich State Univ 166 Plant Biology Bldg East Lansing MI 48824 Office Phone: 517-432-5289. Business E-Mail: schem@msu.edu.

**SCHENARTS, PAUL JOSEPH,** surgeon, educator; b. Garden City, N.Y., Jan. 1, 1965; s. Elizabeth Ann Schenarts; m. Kimberly Dean, Nov. 5, 2005; 1 child, Spencer Dean. BS, Fordham U., Bronx, 1987; MD, U. Conn., Farmington, 1992. Cert. gen. surgery Am. Bd. Surgery, 2001, surg. critical care Am. Bd. Surgery, 2002. Resident gen. surgery Maine Med. Ctr., Portland, 1992—99; asst. prof. surgery East Carolina U. Sch. Medicine, Greenville, NC, 2001—, surg. residency dir., 2002, dir. undergrad. surg. edn. Maj. M.C. U.S. Army, 1994, Iraq, Afghanistan. Decorated Bronze Star; recipient Outstanding Tchg. award, Assn. Surg. Educators, Tchg. award, U. N.C. Bd. Govs., Master Educator award, Robert Jones Tchg. award. Fellow: Am. Coll. Physicians. Office: East Carolina Univ Sch Medicine 600 Moye Blvd Greenville NC 27858 Office Phone: 252-847-4299. Business E-Mail: pschenar@pcmh.com.

**SCHENCK, JACK LEE,** retired electric utility executive; b. Morgantown, W.Va., Aug. 2, 1938; s. Ernest Jacob and Virginia Belle (Kelley) S.; m. Rita Elizabeth Pietschmann, June 7, 1979; 1 son, Erik. BSE.E., BA in Social Sci., Mich. State U., 1961; MBA, NYU, 1975. Engr. AID, Tunis, Tunisia, 1961, Detroit Edison Co., 1962-63; engr., economist OECD, Paris, 1963-70; v.p. econ. policy analysis Edison Electric Inst., N.Y.C. and Washington, 1970-81; v.p., treas. Gulf States Utilities Co., Beaumont, Tex., 1981-92, sr. v.p., CFO, 1992-94. Cons. on electric utility restructuring and privatization in the former Soviet Union, 1994—. Mem. Internat. Assn. Energy Econs., Triangle Club, Eta Kappa Nu. Republican. Office Phone: 281-360-3960. E-mail: schenck1@aol.com.

**SCHENCK, JOHN FREDERIC,** physician; b. Decatur, Ind., June 7, 1939; s. John C. Schenck and Mildred Blosser; m. Jane Stark, Oct. 12, 1962 (div. 1982); children: Brooke, Kimberly, David; m. Susan J. Kalia, Oct. 8, 1994; 1 stepchild, Tania. BS in Physics, Rensselaer Poly. Inst., 1961, PhD in Physics, 1965; MD, Albany (NY) Med. Coll., 1977. Staff scientist electronics lab. GE, Syracuse, NY, 1965-73; assoc. prof. elec. engring. Syracuse (NY) U., 1970-73; intern Albany Med. Ctr. Hosp., 1977-78; staff mem., sr. scientist GE Global Rsch., Schenectady, NY, 1973—; mem. med. staff Ellis Hosp., Schenectady, 1981—98. Adj. prof. dept. radiology U. Pa., 1983-2000; adj. prof. neurology Albany Med. Coll., 2003-; chmn. Workshop on Advances in Magnetic Resonance Imaging Safety and Compatibility, McLean, Va., 1996; dir. Magnetic Resonance Imaging rsch. Neuroscis. Rsch. Ctr., Albany Med. Ctr., 2001-. Contbr. articles pub. to profl. jours. Recipient S S Greenfield award Am. Assn. Phys. in Medicine, 1993, Nat. Merit scholar, 1957-61; NSF fellow, 1962-63, Coolidge fellow GE, 2003. Fellow Am. Phys. Soc.; mem. IEEE, AAAS, Internat. Soc. Magnetic Resonance in Medicine, NY Acad. Scis., Sigma Xi. Achievements include 19 patents for magnetic resonance imaging. Home: 22 E Claremont Dr Voorheesville NY 12186-9104 Office: GE Global Rsch Bldg K1 NMR Schenectady NY 12309 Office Phone: 518-387-6543. Business E-Mail: schenck@research.ge.com.

**SCHENCK, ROBERT ROY,** hand surgeon; s. Isaac Barrett Schenck and Pearl Irene Murnan; m. Ruth Helm (div.); children: Rebecca VanNydeggen, Karen Schmidt, Heidi McCluskey, Robert Paul; m. Marcia Anne Whitney, June 13, 1982. B cum laude, Taylor U., 1952; MD, U. Ill., Chgo., 1955. Diplomate Am. Bd. Plastic Surgery. Asst. attending plastic and orthop. surgery Rush U., Chgo., 1972—80, dir. sect. hand surgery, 1972—, assoc. attending plastic and orthop. surgery, 1980—85, sr. attending plastic and orthop. surgery, 1985—. Cons. orthop. and gen. surgery West Suburban Hosp., Oak Park, Ill., 1973—; pres. Hand Therapy Ltd., Chgo., 1985—95. Bd. dirs. Bishop Anderson House, Chgo., 2004—; founding pres. The Hand Surgery Endowment, 1996—2001. Sr. surgeon USPHS, 1957—59. Mem.: Am. Assn. Hand Surgery. Episcopalian. Achievements include invention of dynamic traction for finger fracture. Avocations: photography, art, sculpting. Home: 1100 N Lake Shore Dr Apt 33-A Chicago IL 60611 Office: Hand Surgery Ltd 1725 W Harrison St #319 Chicago IL 60612 Office Phone: 312-738-3426. Personal E-mail: rschenckmd@aol.com.

**SCHENDEL, DAN ELDON,** management consultant, finance educator; b. Norwalk, Wis., Mar. 29, 1934; s. Leonard A. and Marian T. (Koch) S.; m. Mary Lou Sigler, Sept. 1, 1956; children: Suzanne, Pamela, Sharon. BS in Metall. Engring., U. Wis., 1956; MBA, Ohio State U., 1959; PhD (Ford Found. fellow), Stanford U., 1963. With ALCOA, 1956, U.S. Civil Svc., 1959-60, SRI, 1963-65; prof. mgmt., dir. exec. edn. programs Purdue U., Lafayette, Ind., 1965-85, Blake Family endowed chair emeritus in strategic mgmt.; vis. prof. U. Mich., 1988-89, U. Chgo., 1990-91, 1999—2004. Former dean German Grad. Internat. Sch. Mgmt. and Adminstrn., Hannover, Germany, 1999-2005; pres. Strategic Mgmt. Assocs., Inc. Author: (with others) Strategy Formulation: Analytical Concepts, 1978, Divided Loyalties, 1980, Fundamental Issues in Strategy, 1994; editor: (with others) Strategic Management: A New View of Business Policy and Planning, 1979; founding editor Strategic Mgmt. Jour., 1980—. With USAF, 1956—59. Fellow Acad.

Mgmt., Strategic Mgmt. Soc. (founding pres., exec. dir.); mem. Lafayette Country Club, Univ. Club Chgo. Home: 1327 N Grant St West Lafayette IN 47906-2463 Office: Krannert Grad Sch Mgmt Purdue U West Lafayette IN 47907 Office Phone: 765-494-4386. Business E-Mail: schendel@purdue.edu.

**SCHENDEL, STEPHEN ALFRED,** surgeon, educator; b. Mpls., Oct. 10, 1947; s. Alfred Reck and Jeanne Shirley (Hagquist) S.; children: Elliott, Mélisande. BA, St. Olaf Coll., Northfield, Minn., 1969; BS with high distinction, U. Minn., 1971, DDS, 1973; diplome asst. etranger with high honors, U. Nantes, France, 1980; MD, U. Hawaii, 1983. Diplomate Am. Bd. Plastic Surgery, Nat. Bd. Med. Examiners, Nat. Bd. Dental Examiners, Am. Bd. Oral and Maxillofacial Surgery (adv. com., bd. examiner 1991-95). Intern, then resident in oral and maxillofacial surgery Parkland Meml. Hosp., Dallas, 1973-74; resident in gen. surgery Baylor U. Med. Ctr., Dallas, 1983-84, Stanford (Calif.) U. Med. Ctr., 1984-86, resident in plastic surgery, 1986-89, acting assoc. prof. surgery, 1989-91, assoc. prof., 1991-95, head divsn. plastic and reconstructive surgery, 1992—2002, dir. residency tng., 1992-98, chmn. dept. functional restoration, 1994—2001, prof. surgery, 1995—2002; head plastic surgery, dir. Craniofacial Ctr. Lucile Salter Packard Children's Hosp., Stanford, chief pediat. surgery, 1997—2002. Asst. to Dr. Paul Tessier, Paris, 1987-88; asst. dept. stomatology and maxillofacial surgery Centre Hospitalier Regional Nantes, 1979-80; med. bd. Lucile Salter Packard Children's Hosp. at Stanford, 1991—. Assoc. editor Selected Readings in Oral and Maxillofacial Surgery, 1989—; mem. editl. bd. Jour. Cranio-Maxillofacial Surgery; contbr. articles to profl. jours., chpts. to books. Recipient Disting. Alumnus award St. Olaf Coll., 1993; Fulbright fellow, Nantes, 1979-80, Chateaubriand fellow Govt. of France, 1987-88. Fellow ACS, Am. Acad. Pediat.; mem. Internat. Soc. Craniofacial Surgeons, European Assn. Cranio-Maxillofacial Surgeons, Am. Soc. Pediat. Plastic Surgeons, Am. Assn. Plastic Surgery, Soc. Baylor Surgeons (founding), Am. Cleft Palate-Craniofacial Assn., Am. Soc. Plastic Surgeons (sec. 1996—), Am. Soc. Maxillofacial Surgeons (sec., pres. 2000-01), Assn. Acad. Chairmen Plastic Surgery, Zedplast (bd. dirs. 1993—), Omicron Kappa Upsilon. Avocations: fly fishing, painting and sculpture. Office: Stanford U Med Ctr Divsn Plastic Reconstr Surg 770 Welch Rd Ste 400 Palo Alto CA 94304 Office Phone: 650-723-5824. Business E-Mail: sschendel@stanford.edu.

**SCHENDEL, WINFRIED GEORGE,** insurance company executive; b. June 19, 1931; came to U.S., 1952, naturalized, 1956; s. Willi Rudolf Max and Anna Margarete (Sassen) S.; m. Joanne Wiiest, Aug. 24, 1953; children: Victor Winfried, Bruce Lawrence, Rachelle Laureen. BS in Elec. and Indsl. Engring., Hannover-Stadthagen U., Hannover, Fed. Republic of Germany, 1952. Elec. draftsman Houston Lighting & Power Co., 1954-57; elec. draftsman, corrosion technician Transcontinental Gas Pipeline Co., Houston, 1957-59; elec. engr. Ken R. White Cons. Engrs., Denver, 1959-61; sales engr. Weco divsn. Food Machinery & Chem. Corp., various locations, 1961-64; ins. field underwriter N.Y. Life Ins. Co., Denver, 1964-66, asst. mgr., 1966-70, mgmt. asst., 1970-71, gen. mgr., 1971-77, mgr., 1979-85, field underwriter, 1985—; gen. agt. Woodmen Accident and Life Ins. Co., Ft. Collins, Colo., 1998—, Assurity Life, Inc., 2001—. Ind. gen. agt., Denver, 1978-79; ins. broker and adviser, 1979—; gen. agent Assurity Life Ins., Lincoln, Nebr.; spkr. in field. Instnl. rep., advancement chmn. Denver Area coun. Boy Scouts Am., Lakewood, Colo., 1968-72; precinct chmn. Rep. party, Jefferson County, Colo., 1976, 78; founder, life mem. Sister City Program, Lakewood, Colo.; chmn. adv. bd. ARC, Jefferson County, 1987-89; elder Presbyn. Ch.; lay min. First United Meth. Ch., Ft. Collins, Colo., 1999—; bd. of character City Fort Collins, 2003-. Recipient Centurion award, 1966, Salesman of Yr. award Jefferson County Salesman with a Purpose Club, 1983, Top awards ARC, 1988-89. Mem. Nat. Assn. Life Underwriters, Gen. Agts. and Mgrs. Assn. (Conf. Nat. Mgmt. award 1975), Colo. Life Underwriters (reg. v.p. Denver met. area 1989-90), Mile High Assn. Life Underwriters (pres. 1986-87, nat. com. 1988, 91), Lakewood C. of C. (pres. people-to-people, Trailblazer of Yr. award 1982-83, Trail Boss of Yr. 1983), Lions, Edelweiss Club, Internat. Order Rocky Mountain Goats, N.Y. Life Star, Masons, Rotary (bd. dirs. Foothills chpt. 2002—, Ft. Collins bd. dirs. 1999-2005, Paul Harris award 1995), Shriners. Home and Office: 925 Deerhurst Cir Fort Collins CO 80525-6919 Home Fax: 970-206-9082.

**SCHENDLER, AUDEN,** recreational facility executive; b. NYC, July 25, 1970; s. Mary Jo Schendler; m. Ellen Beth Freedman, Sept. 13, 1997; 1 child, Willa Echo. BA in Biology and Environ. Studies, Bowdoin Coll., 1992. LEED accreditation, US Green Bldg. Coun. Math. and English tchr. Colo. Rocky Mountain Sch., Carbondale, 1993—96; instr. Colo. Outward Bound Sch., Denver, 1993—96; rsch. assoc. Rocky Mountain Inst., Snowmass, Colo., 1996—99; dir. environ. affairs Aspen (Colo.) Skiing Co., 2001—. Exec. dir. Environment Found., Aspen, 2001—; spkr. in field. Contbr. articles to profl. jours. EMT Carbondale and Rural Fire Protection Dist., 1995—2000; bd. dirs. Gen. Svc. Found., Aspen, 2005—; mem. steering com. Rocky Mountain Climate Orgn., Denver, 2004—06. Avocations: kayaking, mountaineering, writing, backpacking, skiing. Home: PO Box 3509 Basalt CO 81621 Office: Aspen Skiing Co PO Box 1248 Aspen CO 81612 Personal E-mail: aschendler@aspensnowmass.com.

**SCHENK, DEBORAH HUFFMAN,** law educator; b. 1947; BA, Cornell U., 1969; JD, Columbia U., 1972; LLM in Taxation, NYU, 1976. Bar: NY 1973. Asst. prof. Bklyn. Law Sch., 1974—77, assoc. prof., 1977—80, prof., 1980—85, NYU Sch. Law, 1985—, AAA-CPA Olincey prof. law, 1995—96, Ronald and Marilyn Grossman prof. taxation, 1996—, editor-in-chief Tax Law Rev. Vis. prof. Harvard U., spring 1982, NYU, 1983-85, Yale U., 1989. Author: Federal Taxation of S Corporations, 1985, 2000; co-author: (with M. Graetz) Federal Income Taxation, Principles and Policies, 1995; (with B. Wolfman & J. Holden) Ethical Problems in Federal Tax Practice, 1995. Mem. ABA (tax sect.), Am. Law Inst., Am. Coll. Tax Counsel, NY State Bar Assn. Office: NYU Sch Law Vanderbilt Hall Rm 430H 40 Washington Sq S New York NY 10012-1099 Office Phone: 212-998-6163. E-mail: deborah.schenk@nyu.edu.

**SCHENK, QUENTIN FREDERICK,** retired social work educator, psychologist, mayor; b. Fort Madison, Iowa, Aug. 25, 1922; s. Fred Edward John and Ida (Sabrowsky) S.; m. Patricia J. Kelley, Aug. 6, 1946 (div. Apr. 1970); children: Fred W. (dec. 1972), Patricia, Karl, Martha; m. Emmy Lou Willson, May 23, 1970. BA, Willamette U., 1948; MS, U. Wis., 1950, MS in Social Work, 1953, PhD, 1953. Lic. ind. clin. social worker, Wis.; cert. longterm care, Ariz. Asst. prof. social work U. Wis.-Madison, 1953-55, prof., chmn. extension social work, 1961-63; prof., former dean Sch. Social Welfare, Milw., 1962-68, prof. emeritus, 1990—; assoc. prof. U. Mo., 1955-61; project specialist Ford Found., 1968-71. Spl. cons. on urban mission in Africa United Presbyn. Ch., 1971-, World Council Chs., 1971-; advisor to Haile Sellassie I U., Addis Ababa, Ethiopia, 1968-71; Alderman City of Cedarburg (Wis.), 1974-82, mayor, 1982-86. Author: (with Emmy Lou Schenk) Pulling Up Roots, 1978, Welfare Society and the Helping Professions, 1981; author sect. on Ethiopia, Welfare in Africa, 1987; contbr. articles, bulls., reports to profl. lit. Mem. Nat. Trust for Hist. Preservation Wis. Hist. Preservation Negotiating Bd., 1975-76; chmn. bd. Guest House, Milw., 1987-89; mem. Sierra Club, Planned Parenthood, Unitarian Ch. S.E. Ariz. (v.p. 1999), ACLU, Dem. Party of Wis. With USNR, 1942—46, carrier pilot WWII, ret. lt. Decorated Air medal with four gold stars, Disting. Flying Cross; recipient Presdl. citation Pres. Harry Truman, 1948; scholar Fulbright Found., 1959-60. Mem. DAV (life), Am. Assn. Ret. Persons, Aircraft Owners and Pilots Assn., Nat. Audubon Soc., Nature Conservancy. Democrat. Unitarian Universalist. Avocations: hiking, boating, travel. Home: 3443 E Wild Rabbit Rd Hereford AZ 85615-9653 Personal E-mail: schenk@myvine.com.

**SCHENK, SUSAN KIRKPATRICK,** nursing educator, consultant, small business owner; b. New Richmond, Ind., Nov. 29, 1938; d. William Marcius and Frances (Kirkpatrick) Gaither; m. Richard Dee Brown, Aug. 13, 1960 (div. Feb. 1972); children: Christopher Lee, David Michael, Lisa Catherine; m. John Francis Schenk, July 24, 1975 (widowed Apr. 1995). BSN, Ind. U., 1962; postgrad., U. Del., 1973-75. RN, PHN, BCLS; cert. community coll. tchr., Calif.; cert. vocat. edn. tchr., Calif. Staff nurse, then asst. dir. nursing

Bloomington (Ind.) Hosp., 1962-66; charge nurse Newark (Del.) Manor, 1967-69; charge nurse GU Union Hosp., Terre Haute, Ind., 1971-72; clin. instr. nursing Ind. State U., Terre Haute, 1972-73; clin. instr. psychiatric nursing U. Del., Newark, 1974-75; psychiatric nursing care coord. VA Med. Ctr., Perry Point, Md., 1975-78; from nurse educator to cmty. rels. coord. Grossmont Hosp., La Mesa, Calif., 1978—91; dir. psychiat. svcs. Scripps Hosp. East County, El Cajon, Calif., 1991-97; nursing instr., adult edn. Grossmont Union H.S. Dist., La Mesa, 1996—. Tech. advisor San Diego County Bd. Supervisors, 1987; tech. cons. Remedy Home and Health Care, San Diego, 1988; expert panelist Srs. Speak Out, KPBS-TV, San Diego, 1988; guest lectr. San Diego State U., 1987. Editor: Teaching Basic Caregiver Skills, 1988; author, performer tng. videotape Basic Caregiver Skills, 1988. Mem. patient svcs. com. Nat. Multiple Sclerosis Soc., San Diego, 1986-89; bd. dirs. Assn. for Quality and Participation, 1989. Adminstrn. on Aging/DHHS grantee, 1988. Mem. Ind. U. Alumni Assn. (life), Calif. Coun. Adult Edn., Mensa, Sigma Theta Tau. Avocations: piano, gardening, reading. Home and Office: 9435D Carlton Oaks Dr Santee CA 92071-2582 Personal E-mail: susansks@aol.com.

**SCHENK, WILLIAM EARL, III,** senior special agent, criminal investigator; b. Fort Worth, July 25, 1952; s. William Earl Schenk II and Hildreth Howells Schenk; m. Carol Jean Kortzendorf, Oct. 17, 1993; children: Wesley Elliot, Amanda Nicole, Amanda Leigh Byers, Mark Christopher O'Neill, William Earl Schenk IV. BA, Auburn U., 1977. Lic. Chemical Agents Instructor FBI, Va., 1991, Criminal Investigator Fed. Law Enforcement Tng. Ctr., Ga., 1981, cert. Self Defense Instructor Kans. City Police Dept., 1985, lic. White Collar Crime Investigator Fed. Law Enforcement Tng. Ctr., Ga., 1985. Grad. criminal justice tchg. asst. U. of Ill., Chgo., 1977—79; police officer, detective U. S. Vets. Adminstrn., Hines, Ill., 1978—80; spl. agt. Insp. Gen., Investigations, U.S. Dept. of Agr., Chgo., 1980—97, sr. spl. agt. Indianapolis, Ind., 1997—. Chpt. pres. Lambda Alpha Epsilon Criminal Justice Honor Soc., Mobile, Ala., 1973—74; spl. investigator Grant County Prosecutor, Marion, Ind., 1983—84; self def. instr. Insp. Gen., Investigations, U.S. Dept. of Agr., 1985—96; chem. agents instr. Insp. Gen., Investigations, US Dept. of Agr., 1991—95; group leader Joint Task Force on Illegal Grain Handling Practices, Indpls., 1994—99. Editor: (book) Songs From the Shelf of Retirement; co-author (federal legislation, US criminal code) Title 7, United States Code, Section 87, Penalties (Superior Svc. Award from U.S. Sec. of Agr., 1988). Recipient Outstanding Prosecutive Achievement, U.S. Justice Dept., 1998, Investigative Excellence, Fed. Law Enforcement Officers Assn., 1999, Group Honor award for Excellence, U.S. Sec. of Agr., 1998, Superior Performance, U.S. Vets. Adminstrn., 1980. Mem.: Fed. Law Enforcement Officers Assn. Avocations: travel, reading, running, cooking, soccer. Office: Inspector Genl Investigations USDA 6039 Lakeside Blvd Indianapolis IN 46278 Office Phone: 317-290-3000 305.

**SCHENKEL, BARBARA ANN,** minister, nurse, social worker; b. Albuquerque, Mar. 17, 1951; d. Richard Henry and Mildred (Voth) S. BSN, U. N.Mex., 1972; MDiv, Iliff Sch. Theology, 1978; MSW, Ariz. State U., 1988. RN, N.Mex.; ordained to ministry Meth. Ch., 1979. Minister intern Christ Ch. U. Meth. Ch., Denver, 1975-77; parish minister Herman (Nebr.) Federated and Riverside Bapt. Ch., 1978-82, Cambridge (Nebr.) Bartley U. Meth. Ch., 1982-85; family minister Red Mountain U.M.C., Mesa, Ariz., 1988-94; nurse Ariz. Health Cost Containment Sys., Phoenix, 1994—; minister Life in the Spirit Ministry, Crossroads, Ariz., 1999—2003; prayer coord., life in spirit leader Sunrise United Meth. Ch., Phoenix, 2005—. Christ Ch. Caring Community Coordinator, Denver, 1975-77; advisor alcohol treatment program Immanuel Hosp., Washington County, Nebr., 1980-82; mem. task group to study Ministry Effectiveness in Nebr., 1981; vis. del. to World Meth. Conf., Honolulu, 1981; registrar for candidacy Bd. or Ordained Ministry, 1980-84, strategy com., 1984-85; drug and alcohol cons. Salvation Army Adult Rehab. Ctr., Phoenix, 1987-88, Adult Protective Svcs., 1988—. Chaplain Jackson-Peck Am. Legion Post, Herman, 1980—82; prayer coord., spiritual life min. Sunrise United Meth. Ch., Phoenix, 2005—. Served to 1st lt. USAF Nurse Corps, 1973—75. Mem. Nebr. Ann. Conf. United Meth. Chs., Cambridge Ministerial Assn. (pres. 1984), Tekamah-Herman Ministerial Assn. (pres. 1981), S.W. Dist. Coun. Ministries (past com. memberships). Avocations: horseback riding, bowling, crochet, needlepoint, crewel. Office: Ariz Health Cost Containment Sys 2830 W Glendale Ave Phoenix AZ 85051-8400 Home: Unit 1134 2150 E Bell Rd Phoenix AZ 85022

**SCHENKEL, SUZANNE CHANCE,** retired natural resource specialist; b. Phila., Mar. 12, 1940; d. Henry Martyn Chance II and Suzanne (Sharpless) Jameson; m. John Lackland Hardinge Schenkel, June 15, 1963 (div. 2002); children: John Jr., Andrew Chance. BS in Edn., Tufts U., 1962. Tchr. Roland Pk. Country Sch., Balt., 1962-65; exec. dir. Mass. Citizens' Com. for Dental Health, Springfield, 1981-83; pub., editor Women's Investment Newsletter, Longmeadow, Mass., 1985-89; pub. affairs officer USDA's Soil Conservation Svc., Amherst, Mass., 1990-93; resource conservationist conservation & ecosys. assistance divsn. USDA's Natural Resources Conservation Svc., Washington, 1993-97; ops. partnership liaison East Regional Office, Beltsville, Md., 1997—2002; ret. 2002. Staff Merchant Marine and Fisheries com. U.S. Ho. of Reps., Washington, 1993. Author Wetlands Protection and Management Act. Chmn. Longmeadow (Mass.) Conservation Commn., 1984-90; supr. Hampden County (Mass.) Conservation Dist., 1985-90; bd. dirs., v.p. League of Women Voters of Mass., Boston, 1974-85; exec. com. Water Supply Citizens' Adv. Com.; adv. bd. Water Resources Authority, Mass., 1979-90; bd. dirs. Alliance for Chesapeake Bay, 2001. Mem. Soil and Water Conservation Soc., Nat. Assn. Conservation Dists. Episcopalian. Avocations: golf, tennis, sailing. Home: 304 W Coral Trace Cl Delray Beach FL 33445

**SCHENKER, CECIL,** lawyer; b. San Antonio, Tex. BBA, Univ. Okla., 1964; JD, Univ. Tex., 1966. Bar: Tex. 1966. Ptnr.-in-charge San Antonio office, mem. mgmt. com. Akin Gump Strauss Hauer & Feld LLP, San Antonio. Mem.: ABA, San Antonio Bar Assn., Phi Eta Sigma. Office: Akin Gump Strauss Hauer & Feld LLP Ste 1500 300 Convent St San Antonio TX 78205-3732 Office Phone: 210-281-7007. Office Fax: 210-224-2035. Business E-Mail: cschenker@akingump.com.

**SCHENKER, ERIC,** university dean, economist; b. Vienna, Feb. 24, 1931; came to U.S., 1939, naturalized, 1945; s. Adolph and Olga (Strauss) S.; m. Virginia Martha Wick, Apr. 14, 1963; children: David, Richard, Robert. BBA, CCNY, 1952; MS, U. Tenn., 1955; PhD, U. Fla., 1957. Asst. prof. Mich. State U., 1957-59; mem. faculty U. Wis.-Milw., 1959—, prof. econs., 1965—; dean U. Wis.-Milw. (Sch. Bus. Adminstrn.), 1976—, dean, prof. emeritus, 1997—; dir. Urban Research Center, 1974-76; asso. dir. Center Great Lakes Studies, 1967-74, sr. scientist, 1974—; asso. dean Coll. Letters and Scis., 1963-69. Bd. dirs. Am. Med. Bldgs., Ampco Metal, Pressed Steel; cons. in field. Author: The Port of Milwaukee: An Economic Review, 1967; co-author: Port Planning and Development as Related to Problems of U.S. Ports and the U.S. Coastal Environment, 1974, The Great Lakes Transportation System, 1976, Port Development in the United States, 1976, Maritime Labor Organizations on the Great Lakes-St. Lawrence Seaway System, 1978, Great Lakes Transportation System in the 80s, 1986; also monographs and articles. Sr. mem. Milw. Bd. Harbor Commrs., 1960-72, chmn., 1965-68; chmn. panel on future port requirements of U.S., Maritime Transp. Research Bd., Nat. Acad. Scis., 1973-76, chmn. panel on reducing tankbarge pollution, 1980-81; mem. pilotage adv. bd. to U.S. sec. transp., 1972-75; trustee Mt. Sinai Med. Ctr., 1984-88; mem. Econ. Progress Authority of Milw. Met. Sewerage Dist., 1983-88, Marine Bd., NAS, 1982-83, Gov.'s Coun. on Econ. Issues, 1983—. Served with AUS, 1952-54. Mem. Am. Econs. Assn., So. Econs. Assn., Phi Kappa Phi, Alpha Kappa Psi, Beta Gamma Sigma, Beta Alpha Psi. Home: 6792 N Melissa Ct Glendale WI 53209-3473 E-mail: esconinc@aol.com, Schenker@uwm.edu.

**SCHENKER, LEO,** retired utilities executive; b. Vienna, Jan. 3, 1922; came to U.S., 1952, naturalized, 1959; s. Max and Selda Lea (Podhorcer) S.; m. Alda R. Tinson, Jan. 20, 1949; children: Michael Gregory, Deborah Anne. BS with first class honors, U. London, 1942; MA in Sci. (Can. Inst. Steel Constrn.

fellow), U. Toronto, 1950; PhD, U. Mich., 1954. Mng. dir. METAG Ltd., London, 1945-48; asst. rsch. engr. Hydro-Electric Power Commn. of Ont. (Can.), Toronto, 1948-52; rsch. assoc. U. Mich., Ann Arbor, 1952-54; with Bell Telephone Labs., 1954-87, various positions, dir. mil. electronic tech., 1968-71; dir. Loop Maintenance Systems Lab., 1971-80, exec. dir. Central Office Ops. div., 1980-83, exec. dir. network system planning div., 1983-84, exec. dir. tech. info. div., 1984-87. Adj. prof. elec. engring. Cooper Union, N.Y.C., 1989-97. Patentee communications tech. field. Served with RAF, 1942-45. Recipient Duggan medal Can. Inst. Steel Constrn., 1950 Fellow IEEE, Sigma Xi, Phi Kappa Phi. Personal E-mail: leoschenker@msn.com.

**SCHENKER, MARC BENET,** preventive medicine physician, medical educator, department chairman; b. LA, Aug. 25, 1947; s. Steve and Dosella Schenker; m. Heath Massey; children: Yael, Phoebe, Hilary. BA, U. Calif., Berkeley, 1969; MD, U. Calif., San Francisco, 1973; MPH, Harvard U., Boston, 1980. Instr. medicine Harvard U., Boston, 1980-82; asst. prof. medicine U. Calif., Davis, 1982-86, assoc. prof., 1986-92, prof., 1992—, chmn. dept. pub. health scis., 1995—. Fellow ACP; mem. Am. Thoracic Soc., Am. Pub. Health Assn., Soc. Epidemiologic Rsch., Am. Coll. Epidemiology, Soc. Occupl. Environ. Health, Internat. Commn. Occupl. Health, Assn. Tchrs. Preventive Medicine, Phi Beta Kappa, Alpha Omega Alpha.

**SCHENKER, STEVEN,** internist, educator; b. Poland, Oct. 5, 1929; came to U.S., 1943, naturalized, 1946; s. Alfred and Ernestyna S.; m. Sally Ann Wood, May 11, 1956; children: Julie C. Schenker Burn, Steven A., David S., Andrew G., Jennifer E. Schenker Campeggi; m. Jo Ann Neumann, Nov. 24, 1985. BA, Cornell U., 1951, MD, 1955. Intern Harvard Service-Boston City Hosp., 1955-56, resident in medicine, 1956-58; asst. prof. medicine U. Cin. Sch. Medicine, 1961-63; asst. prof. U. Tex., Southwestern Sch. Medicine, 1963-67, assoc. prof. medicine, 1967-70; prof. medicine, biochemistry, dir. div. gastroenterology Vanderbilt U. Sch. Medicine, Nashville VA Hosp., 1970-82; prof. medicine and pharmacology U. Tex. Sch. Medicine, San Antonio, 1982—, dir. divsn. gastroenterology, 1982—2001. Chmn. study sect. Nat. Inst. on Alcohol Abuse and Addiction, 1980-83; chmn. study sects. VA, 1985-88. Editor: Hepatology, 1985-90; contbr. numerous articles in field to profl. jours. Recipient Markle award, 1963; Career Devel. award NIH, 1968; Jurzykowski Found. for Research in Medicine award, 1979, Alcoholism Research Soc. award 1987. Mem. Am. Assn. for Study of Liver Diseases (pres. 1980, Disting. Svc. award 1997), Am. Soc. Clin. Investigation, Assn. Am. Physicians, Am. Gastroent. Soc., Am. Soc. Pharm. and Exptl. Therapeutics, Am. Soc. Clin. Nutrition, Internat. Soc. for Study of Liver Diseases, Alpha Omega Alpha. Home: 26025 Mesa Oak Dr San Antonio TX 78255-3533 Office: U Tex Med Sch San Antonio TX 78284 E-mail: stvschenker@aol.com.

**SCHENKKAN, ROBERT FREDERIC,** playwright, scriptwriter; b. Chapel Hill, Mar. 19, 1953; s. Robert Frederic Sr. and Jean (McKenzie) Schenkkan; m. Maria Dahvana Headley; children: Sarah Victoria, Joshua McHenry. BA in Theatre Arts, U. Tex., 1975; MFA in Acting, Cornell U., 1977. Author: (plays) Final Passages, 1981, The Survivalist, 1982 (best of the fringe award Edinburgh Festival, 1984), Tachinoki, 1987, Tall Tales, 1988 (Playwrights Forum award, 1988, Best One Act Plays, 1993), Heaven on Earth, 1989 (Julie Harris Playwright award Beverly Hills Theatre Guild, 1989), The Kentucky Cycle, 1991 (Pulitzer prize for drama, 1992, L.A. Drama Critics Circle Best Play award, 1992, Penn Ctr. West award, 1993, Best Play Tony award nominee, 1993, Best Play Drama Desk award nominee, 1993), Conversations with the Spanish Lady and Other One-Act Plays, 1993, The Dream Thief, 1998, Handler, 1996, The Marriage of Miss Hollywood and King Neptune,The Devil and Daniel Webster, 2002, By the Waters of Babylon, 2004, Lewis and Clark Reach the Euphrates, 2005, (TV films) Crazy Horse, (TV miniseries) Spartacus, (films) The Quiet American, 2002. Grantee Vogelstein Found., 1982, Arthur Found., 1988, Fund for New Am. Plays, 1990, Calif. Arts Coun., 1991. Mem.: SAG, Actors Equity, Writers Guild, Ensemble Studio Theatre, Dramatists Guild.

**SCHENKMAN, JOHN BORIS,** pharmacologist, educator; b. NYC, Feb. 10, 1936; s. Abraham and Theresa (Moses) S.; m. Deanna Owen, June 5, 1960; children: Jeffrey Alan, Laura Ruth. BA in Chemistry, Bklyn. Coll., 1960; PhD in Biochemistry, SUNY Upstate Med. Ctr., Syracuse, 1964. Postdoctoral fellow U. Pa. Johnson Found., Phila., 1964-67, Inst. Protein Research Osaka U., Japan, 1967-68, Inst. Toxicology Tübingen U., Germany, 1968; asst. prof. Yale U. Sch. Medicine, New Haven, 1968-71, assoc. prof., 1971-78; prof. pharmacology U. Conn. Health Ctr., Farmington, 1978-2000, head dept., 1978-87; dir. grad. program cellular and molecular pharmacology U. Conn., Farmington, 1995-99, prof. emeritus, 2000—. Assoc. editor Drug Metabolism and Drug Interactions, 1988—, Xenobiotica, 1990—; mem. editl. bds.; contbr. articles to profl. jours. Served as sgt. U.S. Army, 1953-55. Research grantee NIH, NSF; recipient Research Career Devel award NIH, 1971-76. Mem. Am. Soc. Biochemists and Molecular Biologists, AM. Soc. Pharmacology Exptl. Therapeutics, Am. Med. Sch. Pharmacologists (councilor 1987-88), Jewish. Avocations: fishing, botany, winemaking, acting. Office: U Conn Sch Medicine Dept Pharm Farmington CT 06030-0001

**SCHENTAG, JEROME JOHN,** pharmacy educator; b. St. Clair, Mich., Jan. 25, 1950; s. John and Rose Schentag; m. Rita R. Sloan, June 26, 1976; 1 child, Annie. BS in Pharmacy, U. Nebr., 1973; D. Pharmacy, Phila. Coll. Pharmacy, 1975. Postdoctoral fellow SUNY, Buffalo, 1975-76, asst. prof. of pharmacy, 1976-81, assoc. prof., 1981-86, prof., 1986—; CEO CPL assoc., LLC, 2001—. Dir. Clin. Pharmacokinetics Lab., Millard Fillmore Hosp., Buffalo, 1981-2000. Editor: Applied Pharmacokinetics, 1981, 4th edit., 2004; contbr. articles to profl. jours. Am. Coll. Clin. Pharmacy fellow, 1985; recipient Disting. Young Alumni award Phila. Coll. of Pharmacy, 1989. Fellow Am. Assn. Pharm. Scientists; mem. Am. Soc. Microbiology. Office: U Buffalo Sch Pharms 543 Hochstetter Hall Buffalo NY 14260 Office Phone: 716-839-4931. Business E-Mail: Schentag@Buffalo.edu.

**SCHEPARTZ, ALANNA,** biochemist, educator; b. NYC, Jan. 9, 1962; m. Thomas E. Schrader; 1 child, Abigail BS, SUNY, Albany, 1982; PhD in Chemistry, Columbia U., 1987. NIH fellow Calif. Inst. Tech., 1988; asst. prof. Yale U., New Haven, Conn., 1988-92, assoc. prof. chemistry 1992-94, Milton Harris assoc. prof. chemistry, 1994-95, prof., 1995—. And prof. Howard Hughes Med. Inst., 2002—. Contbr. numerous articles to profl. jours. Recipient Presdl. Young Investigator award NSF, 1991, Camille and Henry Dreyfus Teacher-Scholar award, 1993; David and Lucille Packard Found. fellow, 1991, Eli Lilly Biochemistry fellow, 1991, Alfred P. Sloan Rsch. fellow, 1994, Howard Hughes Med. Inst. grantee for chemistry, 2002. Mem. Am. Chem. Soc. (A. Cope Scholar award 1995, Eli Lilly award 1997). Achievements include rsch. in bioorganic chemistry. Office: Dept Chemistry Yale Univ PO Box 208107 New Haven CT 06520-8107 Office Phone: 203-432-5094. Office Fax: 203-432-3486.

**SCHEPIS, ANTHONY JOSEPH,** artist, educator; b. Cleve., Mar. 6, 1927; s. Andrew Peter Schepis and Sarah Antonette Miraglia; children: Andrea, Pamela, Roman. Diploma, Cooper Sch. Art, Cleve., 1951; cert. painting, Cleve. Inst. Art, 1955; MA, Kent State U., Ohio, 1977. Instr. drawing and painting Cooper Sch. Art, Cleve., 1957—74; instr. drawing Cuyahoga C.C., Cleve., 1974—75, Lakeland C.C., Kirtland, Ohio, 1975—76; instr. drawing and painting Cleve. Inst. Art, 1976—78, prof. drawing and painting, 1979—96, prof. emeritus, 1999. Chair found. art dept. Cooper Sch. Art, Cleve., 1965—70. Represented in permanent collections Massillon Mus., Butler Inst. Am. Art, Canton Mus. Art, Richmond Art Mus. Recipient Individual Fellowship award, Ohio Arts Counc., 1980, Major Painting award, Cleve. Mus. Art, 1988, Thomas J. Ruddy Meml. award, Associated Artists Pitts.-Carnegie Mus. Art, 1999. Mem.: Cleve. Artists Found. Avocation: collecting recordings early 20th century Italian folk singers. Home: 125 Osprey Heights Dr N Winter Haven FL 33880 also: 14709 Lenox St Strongsville OH 44136 Personal E-mail: ajschepis@yahoo.com.

**SCHEPP, RICHARD D.**, lawyer, retail executive; b. July 1960; m. Beth Schepp. BBA, U. Wis., Eau Claire; JD, U. Wis. Atty. Quarles & Brady, Milw.; dir. legal affairs, asst. corp. sec. Shopko Stores, Inc., 1992—96, v.p. legal affairs, corp. sec., 1996—98, sr. v.p., gen. counsel, 1998—2000; sr. v.p. Kohl's Corp., 2000—01, gen. counsel, sec., 2000—, exec. v.p., 2001—. Office: Kohl's Corp N56 W17000 Ridgewood Dr Menomonee Falls WI 53051-5660

**SCHEPPELE, KIM LANE**, law educator; AB, Barnard Coll., 1975; MA, U. Chgo., 1977, PhD in Sociology, 1985. Asst. prof. sociology Bucknell U., 1980—84; rsch. assoc. Ctr. for Social Scis. Columbia U., 1980; asst. prof. sociology U. Mich., 1985—86, assoc. prof. polit. sci., 1990—96, Arthur F. Thurnau assoc. prof. polit. sci. and pub. policy, 1993—96; co-dir. Program on Gender and Culture Ctrl. European U., Budapest, 1996—98; prof. law and sociology U. Pa. Law Sch., Phila., 1996—2004, John J. O'Brien prof. of comparative law and sociology, 2004—. Contbr. articles to profl. jours. Mem.: Am. Polit. Sci. Assn., Nat. Constitution Ctr., Am. Sociological Assn., Assn. Am. Law Schs., Law and Soc. Assn. Office: U Pa Law Sch 3400 Chestnut St Philadelphia PA 19104 Office Phone: 215-898-7674. Office Fax: 215-573-2025. E-mail: kimlane@law.upenn.edu.

**SCHER, ERIK**, physical chemist; BS in Chemistry, Rice U.; PhD in Phys. Chemistry, U. Calif., Berkeley, 2002. Rsch. & devel. scientist Nanosys Inc., 2002—. Contbr. articles to profl.jours. Named one of Top 100 Young Innovators, MIT Tech. Review, 2004. Office: Nanosys Inc 2625 Hanover St Palo Alto CA 94304

**SCHER, HOWARD DENNIS**, lawyer; b. Ft. Monmouth, NJ, Apr. 23, 1945; s. George Scher and Rita (Eitches) Zar; m. Linda J. Scher; children: Seth Micah, Eli David, Nicholas Earl, Sara Catherine. BA, Brandeis U., 1967; JD, Rutgers U., 1971. Bar: Pa. 1971, U.S. Dist. Ct. (ea. dist.) Pa. 1971, U.S. Ct. Appeals (3rd cir.) 1971, U.S. Supreme Ct. 1975. Asst. city solicitor City of Phila., 1971-73; assoc. Goodis, Greenfield, Henry & Edelstein, Phila., 1973-77, Montgomery, McCracken, Walker & Rhoads, Phila., 1977-80, ptnr., 1980-2001; shareholder Buchanan Ingersoll P.C., Phila., 2001—, mng. ptnr., Phila. office, mem. exec. com. Trustee Fedn. of Jewish Agys. of Greater Phila., 1994—; dir. Akiba Hebrew Acad., Merion, Pa., 1996-98; mem. pres.'s coun. Brandeis U.; chair Jewish Employment and Vocat. Svcs., 1998-02; chmn. Com. of Seventy, 2002. Fellow Am. Coll. Trial Lawyers, Internat. Acad. Trial Lawyers; mem. ABA, Pa. Bar Assn. (ho. of dels.), Phila. Bar Assn. (chmn. fed. cts. com. 2001-02), Brandeis U. Alumni Assn. (v.p. 1983-87). Home: 2222 Locust St Philadelphia PA 19103-5511 Office: Buchanan Ingersoll & RooneyPC 1835 Market St 14th Fl Philadelphia PA 19103 Office Phone: 215-665-3920. Office Fax: 215-665-8760. Business E-Mail: howeard-scher@bipc.com.

**SCHER, HOWARD S.**, oncologist; b. Indpls., June 20, 1951; MD, NYU, 1976. Diplomate Am. Bd. Internal Medicine, Am. Bd. Med. Oncology. Intern Bellevue Hosp. Ctr-NYU Sch. Medicine, N.Y.C., 1976—77, resident, 1977—80; fellow Meml. Sloan-Kettering Cancer Ctr., 1980—83, genitourinary oncology; assoc. prof. medicine Cornell U., 1992—. Office: Memorial Sloan Kettering Cancer Ctr 1275 York Ave New York NY 10021-6007

**SCHER, ROBERT SANDER**, instrument design company executive; b. Cin., May 24, 1934; m. Audrey Erna Gordon, Oct. 21, 1961; children: Sarahh, Alexander, Aaron. SB, MIT, 1956, SM, 1958, Diploma in Mech. Engring., 1960, ScD, 1963. Rsch. and teaching asst. MIT, Cambridge, Mass., 1957-62; control system engr. RCA, Hightstown, NJ, 1963-65; engring. mgr. Sequential Info. System, Elmsford, NY, 1965-71; tech. dir. Teledyne Gurley, Troy, NY, 1971-78, v.p. engring., 1978-86, pres., Encoder Design Assocs., Clifton Park, NY, 1993—. Co-author patent Linear Digital Readout, 1975. Mem. ASME, Optical Soc. Am. Jewish. Avocation: chamber music. Home: 2 Laurel Oak Ln Clifton Park NY 12065-4712 Office Phone: 518-383-4910. E-mail: bobscher@nycap.rr.com.

**SCHER, STEVEN PAUL**, literature educator; b. Budapest, Hungary, Mar. 2, 1936; came to U.S., 1957, naturalized, 1963; Diploma in piano, Bela Bartok Conservatory of Music, Budapest, 1955; BA cum laude, Yale U., 1960, MA, 1963, PhD, 1966. Instr. German, Columbia U., N.Y.C., 1965-67; asst. prof. German, Yale U., New Haven, 1967-70, assoc. prof., 1970-74; prof. German and comparative lit. Dartmouth Coll., Hanover, N.H., 1974—, chmn. dept., 1974-80, 93-96, acting chmn. dept., 1982-83, Ted and Helen Geisel 3d Century prof. humanities, 1984-89, Daniel Webster prof. German and comparative lit., 2000—. Vis. prof. U. Paderborn, Fed. Republic Germany, summer 1980, Karl-Franzens-U. Graz, Austria, summer 1984; grant reviewer Guggenheim Found., NEH, Am. Council Learned Socs., others; cons. univ. presses and scholarly jours.; lectr. throughout world Author: Verbal Music in German Literature, 1968; editor: (with Charles McClelland) Postwar German Culture: An Anthology, 1974, 2d edit., 1980, Interpretationen: Zu E.T.A. Hoffmann, 1981, (with Ulrich Weisstein) Literature and the Other Arts. Proc. of IXth Congress of Internat. Comparative Lit. Assn., Innsbruck, vol. 3, 1981, Literatur und Musik. Ein Handbuch zur Theorie und Praxis eines komparatistischen Grenzgebietes, 1984, Music and Text: Critical Inquiries, 1992 (with Walter Bernhart and Werner Wolf) Word and Music Studies: Defining the Field, 1999; contbr. articles and essays to scholarly jours. Morse fellow, 1969-70; Humboldt fellow, 1972-73; Yale Coll. scholar, 1957-60, grad. fellow, 1960-62; DAAD grantee U. Munich, 1964-65 Mem. MLA (chmn. bibliography com. of div. lit. 1972-86), Am. Comparative Lit. Assn., Internat. Comparative Lit. Assn., Internat. P.E.N. Club Home: 6084 Dartmouth Hall Hanover NH 03755-3511 Office: Dartmouth College Dept German Studies 6084 Dartmouth Hall Hanover NH 03755-3511 E-mail: steven.p.scher@dartmouth.edu.

**SCHERAGA, HAROLD ABRAHAM**, physical chemistry professor; b. Bklyn., Oct. 18, 1921; s. Samuel and Etta (Goldberg) S.; m. Miriam Kurnow, June 20, 1943; children: Judith Anne, Deborah Ruth, Daniel Michael. BS, CCNY, 1941; A.M., Duke U., 1942, PhD, 1946, Sc.D. (hon.), 1961, U. Rochester, 1988, U. San Luis, 1992, Technion, 1993, U. Gdansk, 2005. Teaching, research asst. Duke U., 1941-46; fellow Harvard Med. Sch., 1946-47; instr. chemistry Cornell U., 1947-50, asst. prof., 1950-53, assoc. prof., 1953-58, prof., 1958-65, Todd prof. chemistry, 1965-92, Todd prof. chemistry emeritus, 1992—, chmn. dept., 1960-67. Vis. assoc. biochemist Brookhaven Nat. Lab., summers 1950, 51, cons. biology dept., 1950-56; vis. lectr. div. protein chemistry Wool Rsch. Labs., Melbourne, Australia, 1959; vis. prof. Weizmann Inst., Israel, 1970-80, Soc. for Promotion Sci., Japan, Aug. 1977; Ramachandran prof., India, 2002; mem. tech. adv. panel Xerox Corp., 1969-71, 74-79; mem. biochemistry com. NIH, 1963-65, reviewers res., 1995-98; mem. rsch. career award com. NIGMS, 1967-71, NIH BBCA study sect. mem., 1998-2002; commn. molecular biophysics Internat. Union for Pure and Applied Biophysics, 1965-69, mem. commn. macromolecular biophysics, 1969-75, pres., 1972-75, mem. commn. subcellular and macromolecular biophysics, 1975-81; adv. panel molecular biology NSF, 1960-62; Welch Found. lectr., 1962, Harvey lectr., 1968, Gallagher lectr., 1968, Lemieux lectr., 1973, Hill lectr., 1976, Venable lectr., 1981; co-chmn. Gordon Conf. on Proteins, 1963; mem. coun. Gordon Rsch. Confs., 1969-71. Author: Protein Structure, 1961, Theory of Helix-Coil Transitions in Biopolymers, 1970; co-editor Molecular Biology, 1961-86; mem. editl. bd. Physical Chemistry and Physics, 1969-75, Mechanochemistry and Motility, 1970-71, Thrombosis Rsch., 1972-76, Biophys. Jour., 1973-75, Macromolecules, 1973-84, Computers and Chemistry, 1974-84, Internat. Jour. Peptide and Protein Chemistry, 1982-96, Jour. Peptide Rsch., 1997—; corr. PAABS Revista, 1971-73; mem. editl. adv. bd. Biopolymers, 1963—, Biochemistry, 1969-74, 85—, Structural Chemistry, 1989-93, Jour. Computational Polymer Sci., 1991-95, Jour. Biomolecular NMR, 1991—, Computational and Theoretical Polymer Sci., 1996-2000, Jour. Biomed. Sci., 1994—, Jour. Am. Chem. Soc., 1995-2000. Mem. Ithaca Bd. Edn., 1958-59; Bd. govs. Weizmann Inst., Israel, 1970-97; mem. staff Naval Research Lab. Project, Air Force OSRD Project, World War II. Fulbright, Guggenheim fellow Carlsberg Lab., Copenhagen, 1956-57, Weizmann Inst., Israel, 1963; NIH Spl. fellow Weizmann Inst., 1970; Fogarty scholar NIH, 1984, 86, 88-91; recipient

Townsend Harris medal CCNY, 1970, Chemistry Alumni Sci. Achievements award, 1977, Kowalski medal Internat. Soc. Thrombosis and Haemostasis, 1983, Linderstrøm-Lang medal Carlsberg Lab., 1983, Internat. Soc. of Quantum Chemistry and Quantum Pharmacology award in Theoretical Biology, 1993, Stein & Moore award Protein Soc., 1995; named Hon. mem. Soc. Polymer Sci. Japan, 1995. Fellow AAAS, Biophys. Soc. (coun. 1967-70); mem. NAS, Am. Peptide Soc. (hon.), Am. Chem. Soc. (chmn. Cornell sect. 1955-56, mem. exec. com. div. biol. chemistry 1966-69, vice chmn. divsn. biol. chemistry 1970, chmn. divsn. biol. chemistry 1971, Eli Lilly award 1957, Nichols medal 1974, Kendall award 1978, Pauling award 1985, Mobil award 1990, Repligen award 1990, IBM award for computers in chem. and pharm. rsch. 1997, Hirschmann award in peptide chem., 1999), Am. Soc. Biol. Chemists, Am. Acad. Arts and Scis., N.Y. Acad. Scis. (hon. life), Hungarian Biophys. Soc. (hon.), Phi Beta Kappa, Sigma Xi, Phi Lambda Upsilon. Home: 212 Homestead Ter Ithaca NY 14850-6220 Business E-Mail: has5@cornell.edu.

**SCHERDIN, MARY JANE LISKOVEC**, retired librarian, researcher; b. LaCrosse, Wis., Sept. 29, 1940; d. Ambrose John and Martha Marie (Borgmeier) Liskovec; m. Arthur William Scherdin, Apr. 15, 1961 (div. 1976); children: James William, Laurette Therese (dec.), Amy Lynn; m. William A. Wera, July 11, 1998. BS in Elem. Edn., U. Wis., LaCrosse, 1961; MS in Libr. Sci., U. Wis., Madison, 1972, PhD in Edn. Adminstrn., 1989; MEd Profl. Devel. in Audiovisual Media, U. Wis., Whitewater, 1980. Children's libr. LaCrosse Pub. Libr., 1961; sch. libr. LaCrosse Pub. Schs., 1961-64; media dir. Whitewater Pub. Schs., 1971-75; head learning matter ctr. U. Wis., Whitewater, 1979-86, supr. arts media ctr., 1975-79, instr., 1976-78, asst. dean Milw., 1986-88, collection access coord. Madison, 1988-92; libr. dir. Edgewood Coll., Madison, 1992—2004, doctoral advisor, 2004—. Rschr. The Highsmith Co., Ft. Atkinson, Wis., 1983, ALA, Chgo., 1991—96; cons. Psychologists Press, Palo Alto, Calif., 1991—96, Myers-Briggs Type Indicator, 1992—; vis. prof. U. Wis., Madison, 1992—2005. Co-author: K-12 Library Curriculum, 1974; author of bio-bibliographies of Wis. authors, 1981-83; designer; instructional computer programs 1983, 87, 89; author,editor: Discovering Librarians: Profiles of a Profession, 1994; contbr. articles to profl. jours. Pres. Jefferson (Wis.) Jaycettes, 1968-69; state and internal exec. v.p. Wis. Jaycettes, 1969-71; edn. chair Nat. Found. March of Dimes, Jefferson, 1970-74; vol. Nat. Found. Sudden Infant Death, Wis., 1975-83. Mem. AAUW (vis. prof. Ft. Atkinson 1974-75), Assn. Coll. and Rsch. Librs. (task force chair 1991-93, coll. libr. sect. nominating com., 1996, chair appts. com. 1997-98), Libr. Adminstrv. and Mgmt. Assn. (pubs. and bibliography com. 1989-91), Wis. Health Sci. Libr. Assn. (long range planning com. 1990-92, bd. dirs. 1992-93), Wis. Libr. Assn. (lit. awards com. 1980-84, chair lit. awards com. 1983, bd. dirs. 1987-88, chair edn. sect. 1993), Wis. Acad. Librs. (chair conf. planning 1985, 96, chair pubs. 1993, chair 1988, info. literacy com. 1996-2001, chair info. lit. nat. immersion conf. 2000-01, ACRL liaison 1997), U. Wis. Sch. Libr. and Info. Studies Alumni Assn. (sec. 1993-95, v.p. 1999-2001, pres. 2002, past pres. 2003), Wis. Fedn. Ind. Colls. (tech planning team 1997-2002), Coun. Wis. Librs. (del. 1994-96), Czechoslovak Geneal. Soc. Internat. (conf. planning co-chair 2006—). Avocation: violin. Home: 6111 Winnequah Rd Madison WI 53716-3459

**SCHERE, JEAN**, researcher; b. Paris, Dec. 5, 1947; s. Robert Eugene Schere and Marie Rose Graillat; m. Danielle A. Cosson, Dec. 31, 1986; children: Constance, Elizabeth. BA, U. Pa., 1969, MBA in MIS, 1972, PhD in Mgmt., 1981; MA in Internat. Law, Fletcher Sch., 1995. Lectr. mgmt. Wharton Bus. Sch., Phila., 1974—82; asst. prof. mgmt. Phila. Coll. Textiles, 1982—84; venture capitalist Inter Hotel, Montreal, Que., Canada, 1987—91; asst. prof. econs. Tufts U., Medford, Mass., 1995—97; rsch. assoc. Fletcher Sch., Medford, 1997—2001. Dir. Sage, Phila., 1995—. U.S. del. Dem. Liberale, Paris, 2000—. Recipient Heizer award for best dissertation, Heizer Corp., 1982, Chevalier de L'Ordre, Nat. du Merite, 1998. Mem.: Aleps, Gesellschaft der Freunde von Bayreuth. Dl. Roman Catholic. Avocations: opera, swimming, skiing. Home: Apt 2 11 Edison Ave Medford MA 02155-5829 Office: Can Lodge 2 Grange Ter GY1 2BQ Guernsey Channel Islands E-mail: jschere@wanadoo.fr.

**SCHERER, FREDERIC MICHAEL**, economics professor; b. Ottawa, Ill., Aug. 1, 1932; s. Walter King and Margaret (Lucey) Scherer; m. Barbara A. Silbermann, Aug. 17, 1957; children: Thomas, Karen, Christina. AB with honors, U. Mich., 1954; MBA with high distinction, Harvard U., 1958, PhD, 1963; D (hon.), Univ. Hohenheim, 1996. Asst. prof. Princeton (N.J.) U., 1963-66; prof. econs. U. Mich., Ann Arbor, 1966-72; chief economist FTC, Washington, 1974-76; prof. econs. Northwestern U., Evanston, Ill., 1976-82; Joseph Wharton prof. polit. economy Swarthmore (Pa.) Coll., 1982-89; Aetna prof. pub. policy and mgmt. Harvard U., Cambridge, Mass., 1989-2000, emeritus prof., 2000—. Vis. prof. Ctrl. European U., Prague, 1993—94; Arthur Andersen disting. visitor U. Cambridge, 1997; lectr. Princeton U., 2000—05; Ludwig Erhard vis. prof. U. Bayreuth, 2000; vis. prof. Haverford Coll., 2004—06. Author: The Weapons Acquisition Process, 1964, Industrial Market Structure and Economic Performance, 1990, The Economics of Multi-Plant Operation, 1975, Innovation and Growth, 1984, International High-Technology Competition, 1992, Competition Policies for an Integrated World Economy, 1994, Industry Structure, Strategy and Public Policy, 1996, New Perspectives on Economic Growth and Technological Innovation, 1999, Quarter Notes and Bank Notes, 2004; co-author: Mergers, Sell-Offs and Economic Efficiency, 1987. Mem. adv. panel NSF, Washington, 1980—83, U.S. Office Tech. Assessment, 1989—93, U.S. Bur. of Census, 1997—2000. Recipient Lifetime Achievement award, Am. Antitrust Inst., 2002; grantee, NSF, 1970, 1979, 1982, Sloan Found., 1996; sr. rsch. fellow, Internat. Inst. Mgmt., 1972—74, Census fellow, Am. Stats. Assn., 1989—90, Baker scholar, Harvard U., 1957, Centennial Rsch. grantee, O'Melveny & Myers, 1989. Mem.: Indsl. Orgn. Soc. (p.s 1991), Am. Econ. Assn. (v.p. 1988), European Assn. for Rsch. in Indsl. Econs. (co-founder 1974). Roman Catholic. Avocations: listening to music, musicology. Home: 53 Standish St Cambridge MA 02138 Office: CBG: John F Kennedy Sch Govt Harvard U Cambridge MA 02138 Office Phone: 617-495-1100. Business E-Mail: mike_scherer@harvard.edu.

**SCHERER, HAROLD NICHOLAS, JR.**, electric power industry executive; b. Plainfield, NJ, Apr. 5, 1929; s. Harold Nicholas and Nora (McDonough) S.; m. Jane Neely, Sept. 6, 1952 (div.); children: Anne Scherer McConnell, Peter; m. Patricia Condon, May 4, 1974; stepchildren: James, John, Joseph, Jeffery Ludwig, Jean Ludwig Ransdell. BE, Yale U., 1951; MBA, Rutgers U., 1955. Registered profl. engr., N.J. Mass. Various engring. positions Pub. Svc. Electric and Gas Co., Newark, 1951-63, Am. Electric Power Svc. Corp., N.Y.C., 1963-68, asst. chief. elec. engr., 1968-69, chief elec. engr., 1969-73, v.p. elec. engr., 1973-82, sr. v.p. elec. engring. Columbus, Ohio, 1982-90, also dir. until 1990; pres. Commonwealth Electric Co., Wareham, Mass., 1990-93, Cambridge (Mass.) Electric Light Co., Canal Electric Co., Com/Steam Co., 1990-93. Bd. dirs. Commonwealth Electric Co., Cambridge Electric Light Co., Com/Steam Co., Commonwealth Svcs. Co., Canal Electric Co.; joint U.S.-USSR working group on power transmission, 1975-81, joint U.S.-Italy working group on power transmission, 1979-88; vice-chmn. Am. Nat. Stds., 1975-82, v.p. U.S. Nat. Com., 1985-93, pres., 1993-99, chmn. U.S. tech. com. Internat. Conf. on Large High Voltage Electric Sys., 1985-91, internat. adminstrv. coun., 1988-99, internat. exec. com., 1993-99; engring. rev. bd. Bonneville Power Adminstrn., 1984-94; chmn. elec. sys. and equipment com. Edison Electric Inst., 1989-90, press. power engring. edn. found., 1992-96; chmn. blue-ribbon panel Pacific Coast Blackouts, Bonneville-Power Adminstrn., 1996-97; bd. dirs. NY State Ind. Sys. Operator, chmn. audit and compliance com., 1998—; cons. in field Contbr. articles to profl. jours. Press N.J. Jr. C. of C., 1960-61; councilman City of Plainfield, 1963-65; mem. Watchung (N.J.) Hills Regional H.S. Bd. Edn., 1970-72; pres. Woods at Josephinum Civic Assn., Worthington, Ohio, 1983-84; trustee, treas. Beech Leaf Landing Trust, 2001-. Recipient Clayton Frost award U.S. Jaycees, 1961, Young Man of Yr. award Plainfield Jaycees, 1963, Lifetime Achievement award T&D Mag., 1990. Fellow IEEE (v.p. power engring. soc. 1988-89, pres. 1990-91, William Habirshaw award for transmission and distbn. engring. 1986, Disting. Mem. award Internat. Conf.

on Large High Voltage Electric Systems 1996, Hon. Mem. award Internat. Conf. on Large High Voltage Electric Systems 2000, Philip Sporn award U.S. nat. com. Internat. Conf. on Large High Voltage Electric Systems 2002); mem. NAE, Yale Club N.Y.C., Tau Beta Pi, Beta Gamma Sigma. Home and Office: 467 Bay Ln Centerville MA 02632-3352 Personal E-mail: scherehn@aol.com.

**SCHERER, KARLA**, foundation executive, venture capitalist; b. Detroit, Jan. 13, 1937; d. Robert Pauli and Margaret (Lindsey) S.; m. Peter R. Fink, Sept. 14, 1957 (div. July 1989); children: Christina Lammert, Hadley McKenzie Tolliver, Allison Augusta Thomas; m. Theodore Souris, Sept. 5, 1992. Student, Wellesley Coll., 1954-55; BA, U. Mich., 1957; MA, U. Chgo., 1999. Chmn. Karla Scherer Found., Chgo., 1989—. Advisor on shareholders' rights; speaker on corp. governance to various univs. and profl. assns.; condr. workshops in field; leader only successful proxy contest of maj. U.S. publicly held corp., 1988; bd. dirs. J. Stephen Scherer, Inc., Ct. Theatre of U. Chgo. Mem. vis. com. U. Chgo., Sch. for Humanities; former mem. bd. dirs Cottage Hosp., Univ. Liggett Sch., Music Hall, Detroit League for Handicapped, Eton Acad.; former mem. adv. bd. Wellesley Coll; former mem. Rep. Dennis M. Hertel's Candidate Selection Com. for Armed Svcs. Acads.; former mem. U. Mich. Ctr. for Edn. of Women Leadership Coun.; bd. dirs. Chgo. Humanities Festival, The Cradle. Named Outstanding Woman Leader of Yr. Oakland U., 1990, one of Metro Detroit's Dynamic Women Women's Econ. Club, 1992; recipient Most Influential Women award Crain's Detroit Bus., 1997, Northwood Univ. 1997 Disting. Women award, Women of Achievements Courage award Mich. Women's Found., 1997. Mem. Internat. Women's Forum, Chgo. Network, Arts Club of Chgo., Chgo. Club, Casino Club. Office: 737 N Michigan Ave Ste 2330 Chicago IL 60611-2680

**SCHERER, RONALD CALLAWAY**, voice scientist, educator; b. Akron, Ohio, Sept. 11, 1945; s. Belden Davis and Lois Ramona (Callaway) S.; children: Christopher, Maria. BS, Kent State U., 1968; MA, Ind. U., 1972; PhD, U. Iowa, 1981. Research asst. U. Iowa, Iowa City, 1979-81, asst. research scientist, 1981-83, adj. asst. prof., 1983-88, adj. assoc. prof., 1988—; adj. asst. prof. U. Denver, 1984-86; asst. adj. prof. U. Colo., Boulder, 1984-93, adj. assoc. prof., 1993-96; research scientist The Denver Ctr. for the Performing Arts, 1983-88, sr. scientist, 1988-96; lectr. voice and speech sci. Nat. Theatre Conservatory, Denver, 1990-94; asst. clin. prof. Sch. Medicine U. Colo., Denver, 1988-96; assoc. prof. Bowling Green State U., Ohio, 1996—2001, prof. Ohio, 2001—05, Ohio, 2006—; rsch. prof. U. Cin., 2005—. Adj. assoc. prof. U. Okla., 1992-96; affiliate clin. prof. U. No. Colo., 1993-96; Oberlin Coll. affiliate schol. 1996—; mem. exec. and legis. bd. Nat. Ctr. for Voice and Speech, 1990-96; G. Paul Moore lectr., The Voice Found., 2002. Author: (with Dr. I. Titze) Vocal Fold Physiology: Biomechanics, Acoustics and Phonatory Control, 1983; contbr. articles to profl. jours. Nat. Inst. Dental Research fellow, 1972-76. Fellow: Internat. Soc. Phonetic Scis. (auditor 1988—91); mem.: Am. Assn. Phonetic Scis. (nominating com. 1985—87, counselor 2000—03, councelor 2000—03), Internat. Assn. Logopedics and Phoniatrics, Acoustical Soc. Am., Am. Speech-Lang.-Hearing Assn., Internat. Arts Medicine Assn., Collegium Medicorum Theatri, Sigma Xi, Pi Mu Epsilon (G. Paul Moore lectr.). Office: U Cin Dept Otolaryngology/Surgery Cincinnati OH Office Phone: 419-372-2515.

**SCHERER, VICTOR RICHARD**, physicist, computer scientist, consultant, musician; b. Poland, Feb. 7, 1940; came to U.S., 1941; s. Emanuel and Florence B. Scherer; m. Gail R. Dobrofsky, Aug. 11, 1963; children: Helena Cecile, Markus David. BS magna cum laude, CCNY, 1960; MA, Columbia U., 1962; PhD, U. Wis., 1974. Health physics asst. Columbia U., N.Y.C., 1961-63; rsch asst. physics. dep. U. Wis., Madison, 1967-74; project assoc., project mgr. Inst. for Environ. Studies, World Climate-Food Rsch. Group, 1974-78; specialist computer systems U. Wis. Acad. Computing Ctr., 1978—; coord., sr. cons. Divsn. Info. Tech. U. Wis., Madison; concert pianist; tchr.; promoter contemporary composers. Researcher in particle physics, agroclimatology, soil-yield relationships and computer graphics; cons. on computer sys., electronic mail, geographic analysis, help desk and supercomputing applications. Fellow AEC, 1960-61. Mem. AAAS, Am. Phys. Soc., Am. Meteorol. Soc., Am. Soc. Agronomy, Assn. Computing Machinery, Nat. Computer Graphics Assn., Phi Beta Kappa, Sigma Xi. Office: U Wis-Madison Divsn Info Tech 1210 W Dayton St Madison WI 53706-1613 Office Phone: 608-262-3570. Business E-mail: scherer@doit.wisc.edu.

**SCHERF, DIETMAR**, publishing executive, artist, minister; b. Graz, Austria, June 12, 1961; came to US, 1990; s. Friedrich and Maria S.; m. Patricia Michaela Rech, Apr. 9, 1987; children: Alexander, Deborah, Daniel, David. Diploma, trade sch., Graz, 1979. CEO Handelshaus D. Scherf, Vienna, 1987-90; CEO, pres. Scherf, Inc., Las Vegas, Nev., 1990-2000, creative dir., 2001—03; pastor, founder Megagrace Christian Ctr., Las Vegas, 2003—05; chief designer Cascada Design Studios, Creative Consultant, Cascada Resorts, 2005; CEO, pres. Cascada Corp., 2006—. Author: Short Term Trading, 1990, (booklet) Ross Perot, 1992, I Love Me: Avoiding and Overcoming Depressions, 1998, (as Alec Donzi) The Consultant, 2000; composer, producer, performer (CD) Nice to Meet Ya!, 1994. Avocations: movies, reading, contemporary architecture, bible studies, music. Office: Cascada Corp PO Box 80180 Las Vegas NV 89180-0180 Business E-Mail: ds@scherf.com.

**SCHERF, UWE**, research scientist; b. Minden, Northrhine Westfalia, Germany, Apr. 22, 1963; arrived in U.S., 1994; s. Horst Karl and Renalin Scherf; m. Lee Hong Pai, Mar. 28, 1998; children: Ana Renalin, Karl Luis. MSc, U.Marburg, 1990; PhD, U. Marburg, 1993. Dir. genomics R&D Gene Logic Inc., Gaithersburg, Md., 2000—03, sr. dir., head R&D, 2003—04; sci. reviewer CDRH/FDA, Rockville, Md., 2004—. Mem. editl. adv. bd. Current Cancer Drug Targets, Bentham Sci. Publishers Ltd., Karachi, Pakistan, 2001—05; mem. adv. bd. Sch. Computational Scis., George Mason U., Fairfax, Va., 2004—. Contbr. articles to profl. jours. Grantee, German Sci. Found., 1994—96; scholar DFG-Spl. Rsch. Program, 1991—93; Grad. fellow, U. Marburg, 1990—93, Fogarty vis. fellow, Nat. Cancer Inst., 1996—99. Mem.: AAAS, German Soc. Microbiology, German Soc. Biochemistry and Molecular Biology, Am. Soc. Human Genetics, Am. Assn. Cancer Rsch. (assoc.), Cosmos Club (life), Corps Teutonia Marburg (life; pres. 1985—86). Achievements include patents pending for Method for Gene Expression Profiling from Whole Blood; development of cDNA microarray gene expression database for the molecular pharmacology of cancer. Office: CDRH/FDA 2098 Gaither Rd Rockville MD 20850 Business E-Mail: uwe.scherf@fda.hhs.gov.

**SCHERGER, JOSEPH EDWARD**, family physician, educator; b. Delphos, Ohio, Aug. 29, 1950; m. Carol M. Scherger, Aug. 7, 1973; children: Adrian, Gabriel. BS summa cum laude, U. Dayton, 1971; MD, UCLA, 1975. Family practice residency U. Wash., Seattle, 1975-78; clin. instr. U. Calif. Sch. Medicine, Davis, 1978-80, asst. clin. prof., 1980-84, assoc. clin. prof., 1984-90, clin. prof., 1990—, dir. predoctoral program, 1991-92; med. dir. family practice and community medicine Sharp Healthcare, San Diego, 1992-96; assoc. dean primary care, chair dept. family medicine U. Calif., Irvine, 1996—2001, prof. dept. family medicine, 1996—2001; dean Fla. State U., Coll. Medicine, Tallahassee, 2001—03; prof. family and preventive medicine U. Calif., San Diego, 2003—. Editor (in chief): (med. jour.) Hippocrates. Recipient Hippocratic Oath award UCLA, Calif. Physician of Yr. award Am. Acad. Family Physicians. Mem. NAS (mem. Inst. Medicine), Am. Acad. Family Physicians, Soc. Tchrs. Family Medicine. Home: 2658 Del Mar Heights Rd # 604 Del Mar CA 92014 Office Phone: 858-232-8858. Business E-Mail: jscherger@ucsd.edu.

**SCHERICH, ERWIN THOMAS**, civil engineer, consultant; b. Inland, Nebr., Dec. 6, 1918; s. Harry Erwin and Ella (Peterson) Scherich; m. Jessie Mae Funk, Jan. 1, 1947; children: Janna Rae Scherich Thornton, Jerilyn Mae Scherich Dobson, Mark Thomas. Student, Hastings Coll., 1937—39, N.C. State Coll., 1943—44; BS, U. Nebr., 1948; MS, U. Colo., 1951. Registered profl. engr., Colo. Civil and design engr. U.S. Bur. Reclamation, Denver, 1948—84, chief spillways and outlets sect., 1974—75; chief dams br. divsn. design, 1975—78, chief tech. rev. staff, 1978—79; chief divsn. tech. rev.

Office Asst. Commr. Engring. and Rsch. Ctr., 1980—84; cons., 1984—. Mem. U.S. Com. Internat. Commn. Large Dams. With U.S. Army, 1941—45. Fellow: NSPE (nat. dir. 1981—87, v.p. southwestern region 1991—93), ASCE; mem.: Profl. Engrs. Colo. (pres. 1977—78), Jefferson County West C. of C. Roman Catholic. Methodist. Home and Office: 3915 Balsam St Wheat Ridge CO 80033-4449

**SCHERKENBACH, FRANK EVERETT,** lawyer; b. Milw., July 17, 1963; s. Frank Anthony and Donna Mae (Fohr) S. BS with distinction, BA with distinction, Stanford U., 1986; JD, Harvard U., 1989. Bar: Calif. 1989, U.S. Ct. Appeals (fed. cir.) 1990, Mass. Law clk. to judge H. Robert Mayer U.S. Ct. Appeals (fed. cir.), Washington, 1989—91; assoc. Brown & Bain, PA, Fish and Richardson, PC, 1992—2002, prin. Boston, 2002—. Notes and comments editor Harvard Jour. Law & Tech., 1987-88, editor-in-chief, 1988-89. Mem. ABA, State Bar Calif., Fed. Cir. Bar Assn., Am. Intellectual Property Law Assn., Phi Beta Kappa, Tau Beta Pi. Avocations: sports, hiking, history. Office: Fish & Richardson PC 225 Franklin St Boston MA 02110-2804 Office Phone: 617-521-7883. E-mail: scherkenbach@fr.com.

**SCHERLER, KATHY LOUISE,** music educator, researcher; b. Okla. City, Aug. 17, 1958; d. Jimmie Mack Cosby and Avis Norvell Cosby (Bailey); m. David Kent Scherler, Jr., Aug. 5, 1978; children: David Kent III, Kale Cosby. BA, Cameron U., 1980; MusM, Tex. A & M, 1982; PhD in Music Edn., U. No. Tex., 2005. Mid. sch. choral dir. Hugo Jr. HS, Okla., 1980—81; choral dir. Valliant HS, Okla., 1981—83; music tchr. Wilson Elem. Sch., Bartlesville, Okla., 1988—90; choral dir. North Lamar HS, Paris, Tex., 1990—94; adj. prof. music Dallas Bapt. U., 1995—2000; tchg. fellow U. North Tex., Denton, 1996—98; music tchr. Walnut Hill Elem. Sch., Dallas, 1998—99; mid. sch. choral dir. Sam Houston Mid. Sch., Irving, Tex., 1999—2001; HS choral dir. Grapevine HS, Grapevine, Tex., 2001—02; asst. prof. music Midwestern State U., Wichita Falls, Tex., 2004—. Author: (jour. article) Southwestern Musician; dir.: (conducted chorus and orch.) Messiah by Handel; musician: (voice recital) Les Filles de Cadix by Leo Delibes, (soprano soloist) Gloria by Vivaldi, Merry Wives of Windsor by Otto Nicolai, Trial by Jury by Gilbert and Sullivan, Help, Help the Globolinks by Menotti, The Prodigal Son by Debussy; author: (paper presentation) 19th Ann. Conf. on Interdisciplinary Qualitative Studies; musician (and lectr.): (recital) Coll. Music Soc., So. Ctrl. chpt., Midwestern State U. Faculty Forum; dir.(co-dir.): (opera) Die Fledermaus; musician: (voice recital) U. North Tex., Dallas Bapt. U., Der Hirt auf dem Felsen, by Schumann. Accompanist Meml. Bapt. Ch., Grapevine, Tex., 2000—06. Finalist, Nat. Assn. Tchrs. of Singing, 1987; recipient Okla. All State Choir, 1974—76, winner Sweepstakes Choral Competition, U. Interscholastic League, 1994, Superior Ratings: Grapevine High Choir, 2001—02, music scholarship, Cameron U., Lawton, Okla., 1976—79, Best Actress award, Okla. Theater Ctr., 1976, Best in Class for Superior Ratings, Blue Bonnet Choral Festival, 2002; grantee, Midwestern State U. Fine Arts Dept., 2005. Mem.: Tex. Assn. Coll. Tchrs., Coll. Music Soc., Am. Choral Dirs. Assn., Phi Delta Kappa, Tex. Music Educators Assn., Nat. Assn. Tchrs. of Singing, Music Educators Nat. Conf. Home: 204 Mineral Springs Keller TX 76248 Office: Midwestern State Univ 3410 Taft Blvd Wichita Falls TX 76308-2099 Office Phone: 940-397-4624. Business E-Mail: kathy.scherler@mwsu.edu.

**SCHERLING, BRUCE A.,** civil engineer; b. San Jose, Calif., Apr. 19, 1957; s. Henry George and Virginia Pauline Scherling; m. Bonita Green, Apr. 26, 1980; children: Elizabeth, Charles, Michael, Laurie, Stephen. A, N. Idaho Coll., 1990; BS, U. Idaho, 1994—2004. EIT Idaho Bd. Registration, 1994, aggregate testing technician, Western Alliance for Quality Transp. Constrn., 1999, field testing technician, Am. Concrete Inst., 1999, lic. on-site waste water designer/inspector, Wash. Dept. Lic., 2001, qualified sanitary surveyor State of Wash., Office of Drinking Water, 2001, cert. pool and spa operator Nat. Swimming Pool Found., 2001, registered sanitarian Nat. Environ. Health Assn., 2002. Quality control engr. DeAtley Corp., Lewiston, Idaho, 1994—96; project mgr. Poe Ashpalt and Paving, Clarkston, Wash., 1996—98; staff civil engr. Prog. Engring., Lewiston, Idaho, 1998—2000; environ. health dir. Asotin County Health Dept., Clarkston, Wash., 2000—01; environ. health specialist Skamania County Health Dept., Stevenson, Wash., 2001—. Com. mem. WRIA 29 Watershed Planning, Wash. State, Stevenson, 2001—05, Wind River Watershed Coun., Stevenson, 2001—06, Skamania County Solid Waste Adv. Coun., Stevenson, 2001—06; county pub. health bioterrorism emergency response coord. Skamania County, Stevenson, 2001—06; well driller insp. Wash. State Dept. Ecology Delegated Authority, Stevenson, 2001—06. Mem.: Nat. Environ. Health Assn. (licentiate; registered sanitarian, rs 2002—06). Office: Skamania County Health Dept 683 SW Rock Creek Dr PO Box 162 Stevenson WA 98648 Office Phone: 509-427-3870.

**SCHERR, ALLAN LEE,** computer scientist, software executive; b. Balt., Nov. 18, 1940; s. Morris and Sarah (Kratzmar) S.; m. Marsha Kahn, Sept. 2, 1962 (div. 1974); children: Elise A., Stephanie L.; m. Linda Martin, June 8, 1980; 1 child, Katherine M. B.E.E., M.E.E., MIT, 1962, PhD.E.E., 1965. Mgr. time sharing option (TSO) design System Devel. div. IBM, Poughkeepsie, NY, 1967-70, mgr. multiple virtual storage (MVS) project, 1971-74, mgr. distributed systems programming System Communications div. Kingston, NY, 1977-80, dir. communications programming, 1980-81, dir. communications and applications systems corp. staff Armonk, NY, 1981-83, dir. engring. and programming systems products div. White Plains, NY, 1983-86, dir. integrated applications info. systems div. Milford, Conn., 1986-88, v.p. devel. and integration application systems div., 1988-89, application solutions dir. architecture and devel., Application Solutions Line Bus., 1990-91; v.p. tech. World Wide Cons. Practices IBM Cons. Group, Milford, Conn., 1991-93; ind. cons. bus. process engring., info. tech., tech. mgmt. Weston, Conn., 1993-94; sr. v.p. software engring. EMC Corp., Hopkinton, Mass., 1994-2000, sr. v.p. tech., new bus. devel., 2000—01; ind. cons., 2001—; chief tech. officer Mission Control Productivity, Inc., 2000—03. Seminar leader Werner Erhard & Assocs., NYC, 1982-90; co-creator, co-tchr. new course leadership Simon Sch. Bus. U. Rochester, NY, 2005-. Author: An Analysis of Time-Shared Computer Systems, 1966 (Grace Murray Hopper award Assn. Computing Machinery 1975); patentee in field. Mem. The Hunger Project, San Francisco, 1977. IBM fellow, 1984 Fellow IEEE; mem. Sigma Xi, Tau Beta Pi, Eta Kappa Nu Democrat. Home and Office: 18 Wyndclyffe Ct Rhinebeck NY 12572 Office Phone: 845-876-0785. E-mail: scherr@alum.mit.edu.

**SCHERR, BARRY PAUL,** foreign language educator; b. Hartford, Conn., May 20, 1945; s. Joseph and Helen Lillian (Shapiro) S.; m. Sylvia Egelman, Sept. 8, 1974; children: Sonia, David. AB magna cum laude, Harvard U., 1966; AM, U. Chgo., 1967, PhD, 1973. From acting asst. prof. to asst. prof. U. Washington, Seattle, 1970-74; from asst. prof. to prof. Russian, Dartmouth Coll., Hanover, NH, 1974—, chmn. dept. Russian, 1981-90, 96-97, chmn. program linguistics and cognitive sci., 1998-96, assoc. dean for humanities, 1997—2001, assoc. provost, 2001, provost, 2001—. Co-organizer Internat. Conf. Russian Verse Theory, 1987, Internat. Conf. Anna Akhmatova and the Poets of Tsarskoe Selo, 1989, Internat. Conf. Eisenstein at 100: A Reconsideration, 1998. Author: Russian Poetry: Meter, Rhythm and Rhyme, 1986, Maxim Gorky, 1988; co-trans. The Seeker of Adventure, Alexander Grin, 1989; mem. editorial bd. Slavic and East European Jour., 1978-88; co-editor: Russian Verse Theory: Procs. of the 1987 Conference at UCLA, 1987, O RUS! Studia litteraria Slavica in honorem Hugh McLean, 1995, A Sense of Place: Tsarskoe Selo and Its Poets, 1993, Twentieth-Century Russian Literature, 2000, Eisenstein at 100: A Reconsideration, 2001; co-translator, co-editor Maksim Gorky: Selected Letters, 1997; contbr. articles to profl. jours. Scholar Harvard Coll., 1963-66; fellow NDEA, 1966-69; grantee Internat. Rsch. and Exch. Bd., 1969-70, NEH, 1987, 89, U.S. Dept. Edn., 1987-89, Dartmouth Coll. Sr. Faculty, 1988; summer rsch. grantee Grad. Sch. Comparative and Fgn. Area Studies U. Wash., 1973. Mem. MLA (mem. exec. com. assoc. dept. fgn. langs. 1983-85, del. assembly 1986-88), Am. Assn. Advancement Slavic Studies, Am. Assn. Tchrs. Slavic and East European Langs. (pres. 1987-88, founder, past pres. No. New Eng. chpt., numerous coms.). Office: Dartmouth Coll Russian Dept Reed Hall Hanover NH 037553-3506 Office Phone: 603-646-2070. Business E-Mail: Barry.scherr@Dartmouth.edu.

**SCHERR, LAWRENCE,** internist, educator; b. NYC, Nov. 6, 1928; s. Harry and Sophia (Schwartz) S.; m. Peggy L. Binenkorb, June 13, 1954; children: Cynthia E., Robert W. AB, Cornell U., 1950, MD, 1957. Diplomate Am. Bd. Internal Medicine (bd. dirs., sec.-treas. 1979-86). Intern Cornell Med. divsn. Bellevue Hosp. and Meml. Ctr., NY, 1957-58, asst. resident, 1958-59, rsch. fellow cardiorenal lab., 1959-60, chief resident, 1960-61, co-dir. cardiorenal lab., 1961-62, asst. vis. physician, 1961-63, assoc. vis. physician, 1963-65, dir. cardiology and renal unit, 1963-67, assoc. dir., 1964-67, vis. physician, 1966-68; physician to out-patients NY Hosp., 1961-63, asst. attending physician, 1963-66, assoc. attending physician, 1966-71, attending physician, 1971-2000; asst. attending physician, cons. Sloan-Kettering Cancer Ctr., 1962—2000. Chmn. dept. medicine North Shore Univ. Hosp., 1967-01, chmn. emeritus, 2001—; dir. acad. affairs, 1969-93, sr. v.p. med. affairs, 1993-00; exec v.p. for med. and acad. affairs North Shore-LI Jewish Health Sys., 1998-00, trustee, 2000—; chief acad. officer, sr. v.p. acad. affairs, 2000-05, Betsey Cushing Whitney acad. dean emeritus, chmn. bd. regents 1985-86, chmn. bd. regents emeritus, nat. pres.-elect 1986-87, pres. 1987-88, pres. emeritus, Alfred Stengel Meml. medal); mem. AMA, Am. Fedn. Clin. Rsch., Harvey Soc., NY Med. Soc., Nassau County Med. Soc., Assn. Am. Med. Colls., Am. Clin. and Climatologic Assn. Office: N Shore LIJ Health Sys 125 Community Dr Great Neck NY 11021-5502 Office Phone: 516-465-2536. Business E-Mail: scherr@nshs.edu.

**SCHERRER, HELENE CHALIFOUR,** Canadian government official; b. Que., Can., July 6, 1950; 2 children. Grad., Sillery's Jesus-Marie Coll.; BA in Social Work, Laval U. Councillor for Sillery, 1990—94; mem. Can. Parliament, 2000—; min. Can. heritage Govt. Can., Gatineau, Que., 2003—. Office: House of Commons Ottawa ON Canada K1A 0A6 also: Can Heritage Les Terrasses de la Chaudiere 12th Fl 15 Gatineau PQ Canada K1A 0M5

**SCHERY, STEPHEN DALE,** physicist; b. Jan. 1, 1945; (parents Am. citizens); s. Robert Walter and Lois (Keller) S.; m. Patricia Cooksey, Nov. 1986. BS cum laude, Ohio State U., 1967; MS, U. Ark., 1970; PhD, U. Colo., 1973. Tchr. Cassville (Mo.) H.S., 1968-70; vis. asst. prof. Kenyon Coll., Gambier, Ohio, 1973-74; asst. prof. Tex. A&M U., Galveston, 1974-79; asst. prof., rsch. physicist N.Mex. Inst. of Mining and Tech., Socorro, 1979-84, assoc. prof., rsch. physicist, 1984-90, prof., rsch. physicist, 1990—. Cons. Mich. State U., East Lansing, 1975-78, Kerr McGee Corp., Chgo., 1983; vis. sr. scientist Australian Atomic Energy Commn., Sydney, 1986; vis. scientist dept. geology, Yale U., 1987; vis. scholar Australian Nuclear Sci. and Tech. Orgn., Sidney, 1990; investigator U.S. Dept. Energy Rsch. Contract in Natural Radioactivity, 1979—. Contbr. articles to profl. jours. NDEA fellow, 1968; NSF grantee, 1977-79. Mem. Am. Phys. Soc., Am. Geophys. Union, Health Physics Soc., Sierra Club, Phi Beta Kappa, Sigma Chi, Soaring Soc. Am. Office: Dept Physics New Mex Inst Mining Tech Socorro NM 87801 Home: 746 Bounty Dr Apt 4608 Foster City CA 94404-2674

**SCHETKY, DIANE HEISKELL,** psychiatrist; b. NYC, Feb. 8, 1940; d. Andrew Heiskell and Cornelia (Scott) Chapin; m. Charles H. Browning, Aug. 3, 1963 (div. June 1977); children: James Andrew, Scott Hamilton; m. L. McDonald Schetky, Nov. 26, 1977 (div. Jan. 1986). BA, Sarah Lawrence Coll., 1961; MD, Case Western Reserve U., 1966. Diplomate in adult psychiatry, child psychiatry and forensic psychiatry Am. Bd. Psychiatry and Neurology. Intern Babies and Children's Hosp., Cleve., 1966-67; resident dept. psychiatry Univ. Hosp., Cleve., 1967-69, fellow in child psychiatry, 1969-73; dir. child psychiat. clinic U. Oreg. Health Scis. Ctr., Portland, Oreg., 1974-77; pvt. practice Wilton, Conn., 1978-86, Rockport, Maine, 1986—2005; assoc. clin. prof. psychiatry U. Vt. Coll. Medicine, 1986—2000, clin. prof. psychiatry, 2000—. Assoc. univ. clin. prof. psychiatry Yale Child Study Ctr., New Haven, 1978-86; examiner Maine State Forensic Svc., 1998—. Co-author: Child Sexual Abuse: A Guide for Health Care and Legal Professionals, 1988; co-editor Child Psychiatry and The Law, 1980, Emerging Issues in Child Psychiatry and The Law, 1985, Clinical Handbook of Child Psychiatry and the Law, 1991, Principles and Practice of Child and Adolescent Forensic Psychiatry, 2002 (winner Guttmacher award); contbr. articles to profl. jours. Vol. bd. dirs. Coastal Family Hospice Vols., Coastal Family Vols. Fellow Am. Acad. Child and Adolescent Psychiatry (councillor 1995-98), Am. Psychiat. Assn. (coun. on psychiatry and law 2001-05); mem. Am. Acad. Psychiatry and Law, Maine Assn. Psychiat. Physicians. Democrat. Avocations: singing, kayaking, cross country skiing. Office Phone: 207-236-6588.

**SCHETLIN, ELEANOR M.,** retired associate dean; b. NYC, July 15, 1920; d. Henry Frank and Elsie (Chew) Schetlin. BA, Hunter Coll., 1940; MA, Tchrs. Coll., Columbia U., 1942, EdD, 1967. Playground dir. Dept. Parks, N.Y.C., 1940-42; libr. Met. Hosp. Sch. Nursing, N.Y.C., 1943-44, dir. recreation and guidance, 1945-58, historian Alumnae Assn., 2004—06; coord. student activities SUNY, Plattsburgh, 1959-63, asst. dean students, 1963-64; asst. prof., coord. student personnel svcs. CUNY, Hunter Coll., 1967-68; asst. dir. student personnel Columbia U., Coll. Pharm. Scis., N.Y.C., 1968-69, dir. student personnel, 1969-71; assoc. dean students Health Scis. Ctr. SUNY, Stony Brook, 1971-73, asst. v.p. student svcs., 1973-74, assoc. dean students, dir. student svcs., 1974-85. Founding mem. Sea Cliff unit 300 Nassau County Aux. Police; founding mem. Nassau NOW Women of Color Task Force. Author: Myths of the Student Personnel Point of View, The Peter Principle and Student Personnel Work; contbr. articles to profl. jours. Recipient NOW Alliance PAC award, 1991, 1999, Lifetime Achievement award, Nassau NOW, 1992, Task Force Women of Color award, NOW, 1994. Mem.: So. Poverty Law Ctr., Wellesley Ctrs. Rsch. Women, Nat. Women's History Project, Women's Environment and Devel. Orgn., Nat. Mus. Women in the Arts. Home: 60 Hildreth Pl East Hampton NY 11937

**SCHETZ, JOSEPH ALFRED,** aerospace engineer, educator; b. Orange, NJ, Oct. 19, 1936; s. Alfred John and Teresa (Zanga) S.; m. Katherine Frances Giorgianni, Jan. 31, 1959; children: Holly, Joseph, Katherine, John. BS, Webb Inst. Naval Architecture, 1958; MS, MA, PhD, Princeton U. Sr. scientist Gen. Applied Sci. Lab., Westbury, NY, 1961-64; assoc. prof. aerospace engring. U. Md., 1964-69; Fred D. Durham chair aerospace and aerospace engring. Va. Poly. Inst. and State U., Blacksburg, 1999—, chmn. dept., 1969-93. Cons. Applied Physics Lab., Johns Hopkins, 1964-96, Atlantic Rsch. Corp., Alexandria, Va., 1966-72, Du Pont Corp., Richmond, Va., 1980-85; guest prof. Inst. for Theoretical Gas Dynamics, Aachen, Germany, summer 1970; religious ordn. tchr. St. John's Roman Cath. Ch., Colesville, Md., 1965-69; prin. H.S. religion St. Mary's Roman Cath. Ch., Blacksburg, 1970-71; vis. scholar Beijing Rsch. Lab., 1985; vis. scientist Wright Labs., Dayton, Ohio, 1993. Author books; contbr. chpts. to books; contbr. articles to profl. jours. Republican precinct chmn., Montgomery County, Md., 1965-69; mem. Rep. Exec. Com., 1973-86; faculty adviser Va. Poly. Inst. Rep. Club, 1973-76. Fellow AIAA (assoc. editor jour. 1975-77, editor-in-chief edn. book series, publs. com. 1978-84, edn. com. 1978-81, air breathing propulsion tech. com. 1994-97, Pendray Aerospace Lit. award 1997, Air Breathing Propulsion Tech. award 1998, Aerospace Contbn. to. Svc. award 1999, J. Leland Atwood award 2004), ASME (life); mem. Soc. Naval Architects and Marine Engrs., Sigma Gamma Tau, Tau Beta Pi, Sigma Xi. Home: 607 Rainbow Ridge Dr Blacksburg VA 24060-5535 Office Phone: 540-231-9056. E-mail: ptiger@vt.edu.

**SCHEUERELL, MARK DAVID,** biologist, researcher; b. Milw., Jan. 17, 1969; s. Robert Joseph and Judy Judd Scheuerell; m. Jennifer Marie Anson, Sept. 6, 2003; 1 child, Liv Kira. BS, U. Wis., Madison, 1987—91; MS,

Cornell U., Ithaca, NY, 1993—95; PhD, U. Wash., Seattle, 1997—2002. Rsch. assoc. U. Wash., 1997—2003; rsch. biologist Nat. Marine Fisheries Svc., Seattle, 2003—. Fellow Grad. Rsch. Tng. grant, NSF, 1999, Fellowship in Environ. Sci., Ford Found., 2002, Rsch. Associateship, NRC, 2003. Fellow: Conservation Sci. Inst.; mem.: Am. Soc. Limnology & Oceanography, Am. Fisheries Soc., Ecol. Soc. Am. Avocations: skiing, hiking, bicycling. Office: Nat Marine Fisheries Svc 2725 Montlake Blvd E Seattle WA 98112

**SCHEUNEMAN, CHRISTINE A.,** lawyer; b. Kansas City, Mo., Dec. 30, 1950; BA, Univ. Kansas, 1972; JD, DePaul Univ., 1981. Bar: Ill. 1981, Calif. 1984. Ptnr., chmn. Orange County Litigation group Pillsbury Winthrop Shaw Pittman, Costa Mesa, Calif. Mem. nat. panel of arbitrators Am. Arbitration Assn. Pres. bd. dir. Orange County Chamber Orch. Mem.: Order of the Barristers. Office: Pillsbury Winthrop Shaw Pittman 7th Fl 650 Town Ctr Dr Costa Mesa CA 92626 Office Phone: 714-436-6814. Office Fax: 714-436-2800. Business E-Mail: christine.scheuneman@pillsburylaw.com.

**SCHEUSNER, RONALD L.,** music educator; b. Watertown, S.D., Aug. 12, 1950; s. William H. and Edna Scheusner; m. Marsha Kay Herther, May 26, 1973; children: Heidi, Geoffrey. BS in Edn., No. State U., 1972; MusM, Wichita State U., 1976. Dir. bands Milbank (S.D.) H.S., 1978—80; asst. prof. Trevecca Nazarene U., Nashville, 1980—82; instr. music Va. Intermont Coll., Bristol, Va., 1982—84; dir. bands Douglas Middle Sch., Rapid City, SD, 1986—97, S.D. Sch. Mines and Tech., Rapid City, 1994—97, Battle Ground Acad., Franklin, Tenn., 1999—. Recipient Wolf Trap Acad. award, Nat. Fedn. Music Clubs, Washington, 1972. Mem.: Middle Tenn. Band and Orch. Assn., Internat. Trumpet Guild. Avocations: driving, model trains. Home: 1502 Jewell Dr Columbia TN 38401-5212 E-mail: RonS@bgacademy.com

**SCHEVILL, JAMES ERWIN,** poet, playwright; b. Berkeley, Calif., June 10, 1920; s. Rudolph and Margaret (Erwin) S.; m. Margot Helmuth Blum, Aug. 2, 1966; children (by previous marriage): Deborah, Susanna. BS, Harvard U., 1942; MA (ad eundem), Brown U.; LHD (hon.), R.I. Coll., 1986. Mem. faculty San Francisco State Coll., 1959-68, prof. English, 1968, dir. Poetry Center, 1961-68; prof. Brown U., 1969-85, prof. emeritus, 1985—. Reader various univs., insts., and orgns. Author: New and Selected Poems, 2000. Served to capt. AUS, 1942-46. Ford Found. grantee, 1954, 60-61, R.I. Com. on Humanities grantee, 1975; Fund Advancement Edn., 1953-54, Office for Advanced Drama Rsch. fellow, 1957, Rockefeller fellow, 1964, Guggenheim fellow, 1981, McKnight fellow, 1984; recipient Performance prize Nat. Theatre Competition, 1945, 2d prize Phelan Biography Competition, 1954, 2d prize Phelan Drama Competition, 1958, William Carlos Williams award, 1965, Roadsted Found. award, 1966, Gov.'s award R.I., 1975, Best Story of Yr. award Ariz. Quart., 1977; story selected for O. Henry Awards Prize Stories, 1978; award in lit. Am. Acad. Arts and Letters, 1991; work commd. by Nat. Coun. Chs., 1956-61, Fromm Found., 1959, Trinity Repertory Co., R.I. State Coun. on the Humanities, 1986, Providence Coll., 1986, Magdalena Group, 1992. Home: 1309 Oxford St Berkeley CA 94709-1424 Office: Brown U Dept English Providence RI 02912-0001 Personal E-mail: mschevill@aol.com.

**SCHEWE, DONALD BRUCE,** archivist, library director; b. Cleve., Oct. 28, 1943; s. Norman Edward and Theodora (Robinson) S.; m. Charlene R. Wenz, June 10, 1965; children: Amanda Marie, Ann Elizabeth. BA, U. Nebr., 1964, MA, 1968; PhD, Ohio State U., 1971. Archivist Franklin D. Roosevelt Library, Hyde Park, N.Y., 1972-77, supervisory archivist, 1977-79, asst. dir.; 1979-81; dir. Carter Presdl. Materials Project, Atlanta, 1981-86, Jimmy Carter Library, Atlanta, 1986-99, Ga. Dept. Archives and History, 2000; pres. Pawnee Creek Enterprises, 1999—. Editor: Franklin D. Roosevelt and Foreign Affairs, 1981. With U.S. Army, 1964-66, Vietnam, lt. lt. col. Mem. Assn. Records Mgrs. and Adminstrs., Soc. Ga. Archivists, Orgn. Am. Historians, Inst. of Cert. Records Mgrs. (pres. 1996-2000), Rotary. Episcopalian. E-mail: dschewe@mindspring.com.

**SCHEXNAYDER, BRIAN EDWARD,** vocalist, educator; b. Port Arthur, Tex., Sept. 18, 1953; s. Leonard and Dorothy (Carrier) S.; m. Sherri Scallan, Oct. 2, 1976. BA in Music, U. Southwestern La., 1976; postgrad., Juilliard Sch. Music, 1976-80. Vocal instr. Brian Schexnayder Vocal Studio, N.Y.C., 1995-97, Plano, Tex., 1997—. Performances with Met. Opera, N.Y.C., Paris Opera Co., Edmonton (Alta., Can.) Opera Co., New Orleans Opera Co., Santiago (Chile) Opera, Winnipeg (Man., Can.), St. Petersburg (Fla.) Opera, Jackson (Miss.) Opera Co., San Francisco Opera, Frankfurt Opera, Hamburg Staatsoper Opera, Oper der Studt Bonn, Spoleto (Italy) Festival of Two Worlds, Cin. Opera, Fla. Grand Opera. Mem. Am. Guild Musicians. Avocations: computers, billiards, remote control airplanes.

**SCHEXNAYDER, CHARLOTTE TILLAR,** state legislator; b. Tillar, Ark., Dec. 25, 1923; d. Jewell Stephen and Bertha (Terry) Tillar; m. Melvin John Schexnayder Sr., Aug. 18, 1946; children: M. John Jr., Sarah Holden, Stephen. BA, La. State U., 1944, postgrad., 1947-48. Asst. editor La. Agrl. Extension, Baton Rouge, 1944; editor The McGehee (Ark.) Times, 1945-46, 48-53; editor, co-publisher The Dumas (Ark.) Clarion, 1954-85, pub., 1985-99; mem. Ark. Ho. of Reps., Little Rock, 1985-99, asst. speaker pro tem, 1995—. Pres. Ark. Assn. Women, 1955, Nat. Newspaper Assn., Washington, 1991-92, Ark. Press. Assn., Little Rock, 1982, Nat. Fedn. Press Women, Blue Springs, Mo., 1977-78, Little Rock chpt. Soc. Profl. Journalists, 1973; mem. pres.'s coun. Winrock Internat., 1990—; chmn. Dumas Area Cmty. Found., 2000-02; pres. Main Street Dumas. Editor: Images of the Past, 1991. 1st woman mem. Ark. Bd. Pardons and Parole, 1975-80; mem. Ark. Legis. Coun., 1985-92; bd. dirs. Women's Found. Ark., sec. 1999—; bd. dirs. Chicot-Desha Port Indsl. Com.; v.p. Desha County Mus., 1989—; dir. Dumas Indsl. Found., 1986—; exec. com. Ark. Ctrl. Radiation Therapy Inst., 1991-92; mem. adv. bd. Ark. Profl. Women Achievement, 1992—; vice chair Ark. Rural Devel. Commn., 1991-96, chair 1996-97; mem. Winrock Internat. Adv. Coun., 1991—; founding incorporator Ark. Waterways Commn., 1996—, bd. dirs.; bd. visitors Manship Sch. Comm., La. State U., 1998—; bd. dirs. Main Street Ark., Hist. Preservation Alliance Ark.; active Ark. Transitional Employment Coun., 1999—, Ark. Transitional Employment Assistance Bd., 2000; sec. Dumas Area Cmty. Fund, 2000—; bd. dirs. Enterprise Corp. for the Delta, 1999-2002, Dumas Main St., v.p.; bd. dirs. Historic Preservation Alliance Ark, 2000—; outstanding bd. mem. Ark. Main St., 2002; outstanding bd. chair Ark. Cmty. Found., 2003. Named Disting. Alumnus Ark. A&M Coll., 1971, Woman of Achievement Nat. Fedn. Press Women, 1970, Outstanding Arkansan C. of C., 1986; recipient Ark. Profl. Women of Distinction award No. Bank, Little Rock, 1990, Emma McKinney award Nation's Top Cmty. Newspaper Woman, 1980, Journalist award Nat. Conf. of Christians and Jews, 1989, Lifetime Achievement award Nat. Fedn. Press Women, 1992, Outstanding Svc. award Ark. Assn. Elem. Prins., Disting. Svc. award Ark. Press Assn., 1993, Disting. Svc. award Internat. Soc. Weekly Newspaper Editors, 1996, Golden Svc. award Ark. Press Assn., 1996, State Leadership award Ark. Waterways Commn., 1996, Horizon award League Women Voters Ark., 1998 Ernie Deane award U. Ark., 2005, Chilcote award Ark. Cmty. Found., 2006; named to La. State U. Alumni Hall of Distinction, 1994, Journalism Hall of Fame La. State U., 1998; named one Top 100 Ark. Women, Ark. Bus., 1995-98; named Outstanding Bd. Mem. of Yr., Main Street Ark., 2002, Outstanding Bd. Mem., Ptnrs. of Ark. Cmty. Found., 2003, Extraordinary Svc. award Ark. Cmty. Found., 2006; honored Outstanding Svc. Women's Found. Ark., 2003. Mem.: Main St. Dumas (pres. 2005), Ark. Delta Coun. (chmn., pres. Dumas Main St., mem. Main St. Ark. adv. bd.), Pi Beta Phi (Crest award 1992). Democrat. Roman Catholic. Home: 322 Court St Dumas AR 71639-2718 Office: PO Box 160 Dumas AR 71639-0160 E-mail: cts@seark.net.

**SCHIAFFINO, S(ILVIO) STEPHEN,** retired medical association administrator; b. Bklyn., Nov. 1, 1927; s. Stephen Anthony and Jane (DiDonato) S.; m. Josephine Rose Bovello, Apr. 25, 1954; children: Susan, Stephen. BS, Georgetown U., 1946, MS, 1948, PhD in Biochemistry, 1956. Rsch. biochemist divsn. nutrition FDA, Washington, 1948-50, asst. br. chief divsn., 1954-60; mgr. chemistry dept. Hazelton Labs., Vienna, Va., 1960-61; with NIH, 1961—; scientist adminstr. NIH (Nat. Cancer Inst.), 1961-64, asst. chief rsch.

grants rev. br., 1964-69, chief., 1969-72, assoc. dir. for sci. rev., 1972-78, dep. dir. divsn. rsch. grants, 1978-86; sr. sci. advisor office of extramural rsch. and tng., office of dir. NIH, 1986-87; exec. officer, sci. officer Am. Soc. for Clin. Nutrition, Bethesda, Md., 1987-93; cons., 1993—. Cons. with U.S. Army, 1950—53. Recipient Superior Svc. award FDA, 1960, Superior Svc. award NIH, 1969. Mem. Am. Soc. for Clin. Nutrition., Am. Soc. for Nutritional Scis.

**SCHIANO, CHARLES,** transportation executive; Mgr. systems devel. Met. Transp. Authority/LI R.R. Named one of Premier 100 IT Leaders, Computerworld, 2005. Office: Met Transp Authority 347 Madison Ave New York NY 10017-3739 Office Phone: 212-878-7000. Office Fax: 212-878-0186.*

**SCHIAVONE, JOHN,** state agency administrator; b. Phila., Aug. 8, 1924; s. Louis and Sadie Ferrara Schiavone; m. Judith Ann Helm. Grad. h.s., Bangor, Pa. From employment intern to mgr. office Bur. Employment Security, Easton, Pa., 1955—87. Mgr. Bangor Little League, 1958; coach Cath. Youth Orgn. Basketball Team Our Lady Good Coun., 1961; founder, 1st pres. Bangor Booster, 1959; pres. 4th Ward Citizens Club, Bangor, 1965. Sgt. Amphibian Engrs. U.S. Army, 1943—46. Decorated Bronze star (2), Medal of the Jubilee of Liberty French Govt. Avocation: horse breeding and racing. Home: 2530 Delabole Rd Bangor PA 18013-9402

**SCHIAZZA, GUIDO DOMENIC (GUY SCHIAZZA),** educational association administrator; b. Phila., May 17, 1930; s. Guido and Claudina (DiPrinzio) S.; m. Irmgard Heidi Reissmueller, May 15, 1954. BA, Pa. State U., 1952; postgrad., St. Joseph's U., 1954-55, Villanova U., 1954-55, Temple U., 1955-58. Cert. tchr., Pa.; cert. clinician, ednl. specialist, instructional specialist, sch. psychologist, guidance counselor, reading specialist. Speech therapist, lang. arts instr. Commonwealth of Pa., Dept. Edn., 1956-59; founder, clinician, instr., dir., bd. pres. Communicative Arts Ctr., Inc., Drexel Hill, Pa., 1958, Comm. Skills, Cmty. Resources Ctr., Inc., Drexel Hill, Pa., 1958, 1964—; charter mem. exec. bd., bd. pres. United Pvt. Acad. Schs., Assn. of Pa., Drexel Hill, 1966—; exec. bd. govs., bd. chmn. The Accrediting Commn., Drexel Hill, 1971—. Charter mem. Pa. State Univ. Radio and TV Guild, University Park, Pa., 1951—; mem. legis. action com., Pa. State U., Univ. Park, 1988—; cons. communications skills, The Accrediting Commn., 1971—, United Pvt. Acad. Schs. Assn., Pa., 1966—. Founder, chmn., CEO Am. Ednl. Group, 1991—; chmn. CEO Internat. Ednl. Group, 1991—; CEO Cmty. Resources Ctr., Drexel Hill, 1991—, project coord. Energy Quest, 1992—; active Nat. Com. to Preserve Social Security and Medicare, Washington, 1986—, Am. Immigration Control Found., Monterey, Va., 1987—, English First, Springfield, Va., 1988—; mem. pres.'s coun. Rep. Nat. Com., 1989—, Nat. Rep. Senatorial Com., 1989—, Rep. Presdl. Task Force, 1989—; mem. Congrl. Legis. Agenda steering com. Empower Am., 1999. 1st Lt. Signal Corps, U.S. Army, 1952-54. Recipient Svc. award United Pvt. Acad. Sch. Assn. Pa., Monroeville, Pa., 1978, Disting. Achievement and Svc. award Bd. Govs. of the Accrediting Commn., Downington, Pa., 1980, Dr. Charles Boehm Edn. of Yr. award University Park, Pa., 1990, Loyal and Dedicated Svc. award The Accrediting Commn., 1974. Mem. NEA, Libr. Congress (chartered), Internat. Platform Assn., Pa. Edn. Assn., Jefferson Ednl. Found., World Affairs Coun. Phila., Heritage Found., Nat. Trust for Hist. Preservation, Nat. Congl. Club, Pa. State U. Nittany Lions Club, Pa. State U. Alumni Assn., Pa. State U. Football Lettermen's Club, Pa. State U. Varsity "S" Club. Republican. Roman Catholic. Avocations: music, home and garden design, automotive design, reading, golf. Office: The Accrediting Commn 436 Burmont Rd Drexel Hill PA 19026-3630 Office Phone: 610-623-7890.

**SCHICK, EDGAR BREHOB,** language educator; b. Phila., June 28, 1934; s. Claude Ernest and Martha Henrietta (Brehob) S.; m. Margaret Barbara Buehl, Feb. 12, 1938; children: Susanne, Christina. AB magna cum laude, Muhlenberg Coll., 1955; MA, Rutgers U., 1962, PhD, 1965. Asst. prof. German SUNY, Binghamton, 1963-68, asst. to pres. Albany, 1968-72, asst. prof., 1968-72; v.p. acad. affairs St. John Fisher Coll., Rochester, NY, 1972-78, exec. v.p. 1978-80, assoc. prof., 1972-80; pres. Nasson Coll. Springvale, Maine, 1980-83; provost, v.p. acad. affairs, prof. Eastern Ill. U., Charleston, 1984-87; exec. dir. Bd. Trustees, Md. State Univs. & Colls., Annapolis, 1987-88; vice chancellor for policy and planning U. Md. System, Adelphi, 1988-91; sr. fellow Am. Assn. State Colls. and Univs., 1991-94; cons. Assn. Governing Bds., 1993-95; interim v.p., dean St. Mary Coll. Lawrence, Kans., 1997-98; pres. Luther Inst., Washington, 1998—2003, pres. emeritus, 2003—. Chmn. visitation team Mid. States Assn. Colls. and Schs., Phila., 1975-79; cons. IBM, Yorkville, N.Y., 1968, Nat. Luth. Campus Ministry, 1968-85, USAID, 1992-95. Author: Metaphorical Organicism in the Early Herder, 1971, Shared Visions of Public Higher Education Governance: Structures and Leadership Styles That Work, 1992, The "Local Board" in Multi-Campus Public Universities, 1994; contbr. articles on German lit. and higher edn. to profl. jours. Bd. dirs. United Way, 1981-82, Maine Ind. Colls. Assn., 1981-93, Deaton Hosp., Balt.; v.p. Christ Luth. Ch. Found., Balt.; mem. Accreditation Bd. for Engring. Tech.; pres. Oakleigh Forest Civic Assn. Fellow Univ. fellow, Rutgers U., New Brunswick, N.Y., 1962—63; grantee, Carnegie Found. Mem. Am. Assn. Higher Edn., Am. Assn. Univ. Admninstrs., Am. Assn. Tchrs. German, Assn. for Instl. Rsch., Soc. for Coll. and Univ. Planning, Thomas Mann Soc., Nat. Soc. Fund-Raising Execs. Lutheran. Home: 106 Quinn Rd Severna Park MD 21146-3015 E-mail: ebschick@erols.com.

**SCHICK, HARRY LEON,** investment company executive; b. NYC, Oct. 24, 1927; s. Martin and Sadie (Spitz) S.; m. Eleanor Alter, Oct. 17, 1982; m. Inge Nussbaum, Oct. 12, 1964 (div. Nov. 1971); 1 child, Susan. AB magna cum laude, Bklyn. Coll., 1947; MS, Columbia U., N.Y.C., 1948; postgrad. NYU, 1948-52. Securities analyst Sutro Bros., N.Y.C., 1948-52; asst. to pres. Claindalu Enterprises, Inc., N.Y.C., 1953-66; mgr. arbitrage dept. First Manhattan Co., N.Y.C., 1966-69; gen. ptnr., 1969-91, mng. dir., 1992—. Lectr. Donaldson Sch. Orgn. and Mgmt., Yale U., New Haven, 1978-88, NYU Grad. Sch. Bus. Adminstrn., N.Y.C., 1977; lectr. in field. Bd. overseers Libr. of Jewish Theol. Sem.; trustee Washington Inst. for Near East Rsch. Mem. Inst. Chartered Fin. Analysts, Am. Fin. Assn., Am. Econ. Assn., N.Y. Soc. Security Analysts (bd. dirs. 1975-76), Beta Gamma Sigma. Jewish. Home: 215 E 68th St Apt 15Y New York NY 10021-5726 Office: First Manhattan Co 437 Madison Ave New York NY 10022-7001 Business E-Mail: hschick@firstmanhattan.com.

**SCHICK, MICHAEL WILLIAM,** public relations executive; b. San Antonio, July 17, 1956; s. Lawrence Martin and Jeanne Frances (McCuen) S.; m. Diana Lynn McGinty, Mar. 14, 1988; children: Tiffany Michele, Jessica Diane. B in Media Arts with honors, U. S.C., 1979. Dir. prodns., asst. v.p. S.C. Savs. & Loan League, Columbia, 1978-81; dep. press sec. to U.S. Sen. Strom Thurmond Washington, 1981-85; sr. exec. Civic Svc. Inc., Washington, 1985-2000; COO Justice Fellowship, Washington, 2000—01; dir. comm. U.S. Chamber of Commerce Inst. for Legal Reform, 2001—03; sr. v.p. Porter Novelli, 2003—. Co-founder, chmn. First Monday Night, McLean, Va., 1981-94; Fourth Presbyn. Ch., Bethesda, Md., 1988—; Creative Living Internat., Reston, 1988—. C.S. Lewis fellow C.S. Lewis Inst., 1999-2000. Republican. Avocations: golf, tennis, soccer, guitar. Home: 11560 Brass Lantern Ct Reston VA 20194-1221 Office Phone: 202-419-3246. Business E-Mail: michael.schick@porternovelli.com.

**SCHICK, ROBERT MICHAEL,** lawyer; b. Elizabeth, N.J., Oct. 3, 1954; s. Donald E. and Virginia (Dotterweich) S.; m. Shelley Woodward, May 26, 1979; children: Cameron, Catherine. AB, Princeton U., 1976; JD, U. Houston, 1981. Bar: Tex. 1981, U.S. Ct. Appeals (5th cir. ea. and ea. dists.) Tex. Mem. Assn. State Vinson & Elkins LLP, Houston, 1981-88, ptnr., 1988—, co-head Litig. Sect. Fellow Tex. Bar Found.; mem. Product Liability Adv. Coun. Office: Vinsons & Elkins LLP First City Tower 1001 Fannin St Ste 2300 Houston TX 77002-6706 Office Phone: 713-654-4582. Business E-Mail: rschick@velaw.com.

**SCHICK, THOMAS,** diversified financial services company executive; Sr. exec. v.p. Shearson Lehman Brothers, 1986—92; exec. v.p.b. pub. affairs and comms. Travel Related Svcs. sub. Am. Express, 1992—93, Am. Express Co., 1993—. Office: Am Express Co World Fin Ctr 200 Vesey St New York NY 10285

**SCHIEBLER, GEROLD LUDWIG,** pediatrician, educator; b. Hamburg, Pa., June 20, 1928; s. Alwin Robert and Charlotte Elizabeth (Schmoele) Schiebler; m. Audrey Jean Lincourt, Jan. 8, 1954; children: Mark, Marcella, Kristen, Bettina, Wanda, Michele. BS, Franklin and Marshall Coll., 1950; MD, Harvard U., 1954. Intern pediat. and internal medicine Mass. Gen. Hosp., Boston, 1954—55, resident, 1955—56; resident pediat. U. Minn. Hosp., Mpls., 1956—57, fellow pediatric cardiology, 1957—58, rsch. fellow, 1958—59; rsch. fellow sect. physiology Mayo Clinic and Mayo Found., 1959—60; from asst. prof. pediatric cardiology to prof. emeritus U. Fla., 1960—2001, prof. emeritus, 2001—. Dir. divsn. Children's Med. Svcs. State of Fla., 1973—74, area med. dir., 1974—2000, cons., 2001—. Author (with L.P. Elliott): The X-ray Diagnosis of Congenital Cardiac Disease in Infants, Children and Adults, 1968, 1979; author: (with L.J. Krovetz and I.H. Gessner) Pediatric Cardiology, 1979. Named Children's Med. Svcs. Pediatrician of Decade, Gov. Jeb Bush, 1999; recipient Lifetime Achievement award, Coll. Medicine, 2004. Mem.: AMA (Benjamin Rush award 1993), AAAS, Fla. Med. Assn. (past v.p., bd. govs., pres. 1991—92), Fla. Heart Assn. (past pres.), Fla. Pediat. Soc. (exec. com.), Soc. Pediatric Rsch. (emeritus), Am. Coll. Cardiology, Am. Acad. Pediat. (Abraham Jacobi award 1993), Inst. Medicine NAS, Alpha Omega Alpha, Phi Beta Kappa. Home: 408 Beachside Villas Amelia Island Plantation Amelia Island FL 32034-6551 Home Fax: 904-277-7211. Business E-Mail: gls@vpha.ufl.edu.

**SCHIECK, FREDERICK W.,** federal agency administrator; m. Sara Schieck; 1 child, Sara. B Fgn. Svc., Georgetown U.; MBA, Harvard U. With USAID, 1965—90, dep. adminstr. Washington, 2002—, acting adminstr., 2005—06; with Inter-Am. Devel. Bank, Washington, 1990—2000. With USAR. Office: USAID 1300 Pennsylvania Ave NW Washington DC 20523

**SCHIEFFER, BOB,** newscaster; b. Austin, Tex., Feb. 25, 1937; m. Patricia Penrose; children: Susan, Sharon. BA in Journalism, Tex. Christian U., 1959. Reporter Ft. Worth Star-Telegram; news anchorman Sta. WBAP-TV, Dallas-Ft. Worth; with CBS News, 1969—, Pentagon corr., 1970-74, White House corr., 1974-79, chief Washington corr., 1982—85; anchorman CBS Sunday Night News, 1973-74, CBS Evening News (Saturday edit.), 1976—96, CBS Morning News, 1979-80, 1985; anchor, Face the Nation CBS News, 1991—; interim anchor CBS Evening News, NYC, 2005—06, weekly commentator, polit. analyst, 2006—; participant CBS news spls. and spl. reports, including Peace and the Pentagon, 1974, Watergate-The White House Transcripts, 1974, The Mysterious Alert, 1974, 1976, Ground Zero, 1981; mem. Emmy award-winning team CBS Evening News with Walter Cronkite, 1971; chief Washington corr. CBS News, 1975; co-author (with Gary Paul Gates): The Acting President, 1989; author: This Just In: What I Couldn't Tell You On TV, 2003 (NY Times Bestseller). Named Broadcaster of Yr., Nat. Press Found., 2002; named to Broadcasting/Cable Hall of Fame; recipient 2 Sigma Delta Chi awards, 6 Emmy awards, Paul White award, Radio-TV News Directors Assn., 2003, Internat. Radio & TV Soc. Found. award, 2004, Helen Thomas award excellence in journalism, Am. News Women's Club, 2004. Office: Face the Nation with Bob Schieffer 2020 M St NW Washington DC 20036-3304*

**SCHIEFFER, JOHN THOMAS,** ambassador, former professional baseball team executive; b. Ft. Worth, Oct. 4, 1947; m. Susanne Silber, Sept. 22, 1979; 1 child, Paul Robert. BA in Govt., minor in History, U. Tex., 1970, MA in Internat. Relations, 1972, JD. Bar: Tex. 1979. Mem. Tex. Ho. Reps., 1972—76; ptnr.-in-charge of ballpark devel. Texas Rangers Baseball Club, 1990—91, pres., 1991—94, gen. ptnr., 1994—99; pres. J. Thomas Schieffer Mgmt. Co. & Pablo Operating Co., 2000—01; real estate devel. cons. Dallas, 1999—2000; US amb. to Australia US Dept. State, Sydney, 2001—05, US amb. to Japan Tokyo, 2005—. Office: 9800 Tokyo Pl Washington DC 20521*

**SCHIEKEN, RICHARD MERRILL,** physician; b. Phila., May 6, 1939; s. Benjamin B. and Edythe (Lesser) S.; m. Barbara Lynn Newman, Aug. 23, 1964; children: Julia, William, Shira. AB, LaSalle U., 1961; MD, U. Pa., 1965, MSHA, Va. Commonwealth U., 1998. Diplomate Am. Bd. Pediatrics. Intern, then resident in pediatrics Children's Hosp. of Pa., Phila., 1965-68, fellow in pediatric cardiology, 1968-70; asst. instr. pediatrics U. Pa., Phila., 1966-67; clin. asst. prof. Sch. Medicine Georgetown U., Washington, 1971-73; with U. Iowa, Iowa City, 1973-82, prof. pediatrics Sch. Medicine, 1980-82, prof. preventive medicine Sch. Medicine, 1981-82; prof. Med. Coll. of Va., Richmond, Va., 1982—, chmn. Dept. Pediatric Cardiology, 1982—2002, clin. prof. pediat., 2002—. Mem. exec. com. Nat. Cholesterol Edn. Program, Bethesda, 1986-96. Contbr. articles to profl. jours. Chmn. epidemiology disease control study sect. NIH, Bethesda, Md. Maj. U.S. Army, 1970-73. Fellow Am. Coll. Cardiology (chmn. preventive cardiovascular disease com. 1984-86), Am. Acad. Pediatrics, Am. Heart Assn. (epidemiology coun.); mem. Nat. Acad. Sci. (diet and health coun.). Jewish. Home: 422 September Dr Richmond VA 23229-7318 Personal E-mail: rschieken@verizon.net.

**SCHIELE, JAMES LEO,** museum director; b. Devils Lake, ND, May 23, 1944; s. Philip George and Emelia Marie (Tuchscherer) Schiele; m. Louise Ann Metzgar, Sept. 23, 1967; children: Tara Louise, Jamie Lynn, Lanny Jon, Carli Nicole, Perry Philip. Student, Lake Region Cmty. Coll., 1963. Grain and livestock farmer Self-Employed, Webster, ND, 1963—84; salesman Siegs Office Supply, Devils Lake, ND, 1984—94; mus. dir. Lake Region Heritage Ctr., Inc., Devils Lake, 1991—, v.p. ND Art Gallery Assn., Minot, 2004—. County dir. ND Farmers Union, Jamestown, 1978—84; bd. dirs. Ramsey County Hist. Soc., 1992—94; co-founder Dakota Postal History Soc., 1983. Recipient Unsung Hero award for cmty. svc., Ramsey Nat. Bank, 1998. Mem.: Philatelic Soc, Eagles Club, K. of C. Democrat. Roman Cath. Avocations: history, hunting, stamp collecting/philately. Home: 413 13th St NW Devils Lake ND 58301 Office: Lake Regiona Heritage Ctr 502 4th St NE Devils Lake ND 58301

**SCHIELE, PAUL ELLSWORTH, JR.,** retired academic administrator, writer; b. Phila., Nov. 20, 1924; s. Paul Ellsworth Sr. and Maud (Barclay) S.; m. Sarah Irene Knauss, Aug. 20, 1946; children: Patricia Schiele Sommers, Sandra Schiele Kicklighter, Deborah Schiele Hartigan. AT, Temple U., Phila., 1949; BA, LaVerne U., 1955; MA, Claremont Grad. U., Calif., 1961; PhD, U.S. Internat. U., San Diego, 1970. Cert. sec. tchr., Calif. 1961. Tchr. sci. and math. Lincoln High Sch., Phila., 1956-57, Ontario (Calif.) Sch. Dist., 1957-65; math. and sci. cons. Hacienda La Puente U. Sch. Dist., Calif., 1965-75; asst. prof. Calif. State U., Fullerton, 1975-83; pres., owner Creative Learning Environments and Resources, Glendora, Calif., 1983—, cons. sci. curriculum, 1985—. Dir. title III project ESEA, 1974-75, cons. for project, 1975-77; cons. in field. Author: (student workbook) Beyond the Earth, 1969, Primary Science, 1972, 2d edit., 1976, (novel) Under Cover of Night, 1995, Chasing the Wild Geese, 1996, Deceptive Appearances, 1997; editor: A Living World, 1974, 2d edit., 1986; writer 9 sound filmstrips, model units for sci. and math. activity books, 10 sci. activities for L.A. Outdoor Edn. Program, 1980; editor 21 sci. and math. activity books, 1975-76; writer, co-dir. (TV) Marine Biology Series, 1970-71; contbr. numerous articles to profl. mags., 1962-89; writer and designer of 2 sci. ednl. games; designer in field. Apptd. adv. com. Sci. and Humanities Symposium Calif. Mus. Sci. and Industry, 1974; mem. State Sci. Permit Com., Tide Pools of Calif. Coast, 1974-75; mem. Friends of Libr., Friends Libr. Found. Mem. Internat. Platform Assn., Internat. Soc. Photographers, Glendora Hist. Soc., ABI Rsch. Assn. (bd. govs.), Calif. Elem. Edn. Assn. (hon.), Nat. PTA (hon.), Calif. Inter-Sci. Coun. (pres., chmn. 1971, 72), Elem Sch. Scis. Assn. (past pres., bd. dirs.), Paddlewheel Steamboating Soc. of Am., Phi Delta Kappa (chartered). Republican. Lutheran. Avocations: travel, etchings, art collecting, fencing. Home: 231 Catherine Park Dr Glendora CA 91741-3018

**SCHIER, DONALD STEPHEN,** language educator; b. Ft. Madison, Iowa, Sept. 10, 1914; s. Francis and Marcella (Kenny) S. BA, State U. Iowa, 1936; MA, Columbia U., 1937, PhD, 1941. Mem. faculty State Tchrs. Coll., Bemidji, Minn., 1939-41, 41-42, Ill. Inst. Tech., 1946; mem. faculty Carleton Coll., Northfield, Minn., 1946-80, prof. French, 1953-80. Vis. prof. U. Wis., 1964-65; Brown tutor in French U. of South, Sewanee, Tenn., 1980-81 Author: Louis-Bertrand Castel, 1942; editor: (with Scott Elledge) The Continental Model, 1960, 2d edit., 1970; (Bertrand de Fontenelle), Nouveaux Dialogues des morts, 1965, rev. edit., 1974; translator: Letter on Italian Music (Charles de Brosses), 1978. Mem. selection com. Young Scholar Program, Nat. Found. Arts and Humanities, 1966-67. Served to capt. AUS, 1942-46. Mem. MLA, Am. Assn. Tchrs. French, Am. Soc. Eighteenth-Century Studies Home: 750 Weaver Dairy Rd Apt 1106 Chapel Hill NC 27514-1441

**SCHIERINGA, PAUL KENNETH,** special education educator, entertainer; b. Holland, Mich., Mar. 28, 1934; s. Peter and Mary (Van Kampen) Schieringa; m. Patti Ann Poling, Dec. 27, 1987. BA in Bus. Administrn., Hope Coll., 1957; MDiv, Founding Ch., Washington, 1963. Cert. nursing home adminstr., Ill. Quality control officer U.S. R.R. Retirement Bd., Chgo., 1957—61; entertainer, 1961—; med. mgr. hosps., nursing homes, mental health agencies, Chgo. and Ionia, Mich., 1971—87; theater adminstr. Croswell Opera House, Adrian, Mich., 1987—88; tchr. music/spl. edn./career edn. Guam Dept. Edn., Hagatna, 1991—2001. Cons. various nursing homes, Chgo., 1977—83, Betty's Learning Ctr., Upper Tumon, Guam, 1997—2001; mem. diabetes policy adv. bd. Mich. Dept. Pub. Health, Lansing, 1983—88; chairperson Citizens' Adv. Coun. for Southgate (Mich.) Mental Health Ctr., 1984—88. Composer: (songs) Free As A Gull, 1964, 23rd Psalm, 1972, He Cared So Much For Me, 1991, Lo, He Comes, 1992, It Still Took Calvary, 1997, (Chaplains Verse for Navy Hymn) Eternal Father Strong to Save, 1992. Co-chair restoration adv. bd. Naval Air Sta., Hagatna, 1993—2001; bd. dirs. Friends of Guam Pub. Libr., Hagatna, 1996—2001. Named to Ancient Order of the Chamorri, Gov. of Guam, 2001. Avocations: writing childrens' books, World War II historian, organ, fishing. Home: 879 W 32d St Holland MI 49423

**SCHIESEL, SETH,** reporter; Grad. Yale Univ., 1994, JD, 1997. Tech., gaming reporter NY Times, NYC, 1996—. Office: Bus Day Desk NY Times 229 W 43rd St New York NY 10036 Office Phone: 212-556-7135. Office Fax: 212-556-1448. Business E-Mail: thegamer@nytimes.com.*

**SCHIESER, HANS ALOIS,** education educator; b. Ulm, Germany, July 15, 1931; arrived in U.S., 1965; s. Alois and Anna (Stegmann) S.; m. Margret H. Schröer, June 6, 1962; children: Peter, Elisabeth. BA, Kepler Gymnasium, Ulm, 1952; MA in Philosophy, U. Passau, Fed. Republic Germany, 1959; EdM, Pedagogic Acad., Weingarten, Fed. Republic Germany, 1962; PhD, Loyola U., Chgo., 1970. Head tchr. Pestalozzischule, Ulm, 1964-65; learning disabilities tchr. Jeanine Schultz Meml. Sch., Skokie, Ill., 1966-67; co-dir. Oak Therapeutic Sch., Evanston, Ill., 1967-70; from assoc. prof. to prof. edn. DePaul U., Chgo., 1969-91, prof. emeritus, 1991—; cons. in field; program cons. Delphian Soc., L.A., 1977-90; rschr., tchr. in Germany, 1991—; active in tchrs. edn. Midwest Montessori Tchr. Tng. Ctr., Evanston, Ill.; guest prof. State U. Chelyabinsk, State Linguistic U., Irkutsk, Russia, 1998-2005; ord. prof., dean of studies Gustav-Siewerth-Akademie, Germany, 1995-2003. Author chpts. in books; contbr. articles to profl. jours.; adv. bd. Ann. Edits. Sociology, Dushkin Pub. Group, 1985-91. Pres. N.Am. Family Svc. Found., Oak Lawn, Ill., 1974-91; bd. dirs. S.O.S. Children's Villages USA, Washington, 1986-94; pres. emeritus S.O.S. Children's Village Ill., Inc., Chgo.; bd. govs. Invest-in-Am. Nat. Found., Phila., 1988-90. Rsch. grant DePaul U., 1985-86, Rsch. sabbatical, 1989. Mem. Am. Ednl. Studies Assn., Nat. Soc. for Study of Edn., Philosophy of Edn. Soc. U.S.A., Soc. Educators and Scholars (bd. dirs. 1984-90), Am. Montessori Soc., Thomas More Gesellschaft/Amici Mori Europe, Phi Delta Kappa (pres. Zeta chpt., Chgo. 1973-75). Home: Veilchenweg 9 D-89134 Bermaringen Germany also: 400 E Main/6B/DJURI Evanston IL 60202 Office: DePaul U 2320 N Kenmore Ave Chicago IL 60614-3210 Personal E-mail: prof_schieser@aol.com, prof_schieser@hotmail.com.

**SCHIEVELBEIN, THOMAS CLAYTON,** shipyard executive, sales executive; b. Ft. Lewis, Wash., July 4, 1953; s. Clayton Glenn and Helen Faye (Jensen) S.; m. Betty Jo DeMent, Aug. 22, 1976; children: Stacy Jo, Lisa Jeanne. BS in Marine Engring., U.S. Naval Acad., 1975; ME in Nuclear Engring., U. Va., 1976. Regional sales mgr. GE, Schenectady, N.Y., 1976-82, mgr. advanced tech. Washington, 1982-87; dir. field sales Newport News Shipbuilding, Arlington, Va., 1987-92, dir. naval mktg., 1992-93, v.p. strategy and naval prog. devel., 1993-94, v.p. human resources and adminstr., 1994-95, exec. v.p., 1995—2001; corp. v.p. Northrop Grumman Corp, 2001—; pres. Northrop Grumman Newport News, 2001—. Founding mem. Virginia Career Education Foundation. Mem. assn. Naval Aviators, Naval Submarine League, NSIA (bd. trustees). Office: Northrop Grumman Newport News Shipbuilding 4101 Washington Ave Bldg 86 Newport News VA 23607-9700

**SCHIFANO, KATH M.,** artist, educator; b. N.Y.C. d. John A. Theiss and Mary Connolly; m. Carl M. Schifano, Oct. 7, 1972; children: Robin, Charles. BA, SUNY, Fredonia, 1971; MA, U. Buffalo, 1975. Cert. art tchr. K-12 permanent cert. N.Y. State. Art instr. Niagara Falls (N.Y.) Bd. Edn. 1974—2005, chair art and music, 1993—2003. Workshop presenter, adviser Niagara Falls Tchr. Resource Ctr., 2000—. Exhibited in group shows at N.Y. State Art Tchrs Juried Shows, 1987, 1989, 1991, 1992, 1994, Kenan Ctr., Niagara County Art Tchrs. Shows, 1991, 1993, 1995, 2001, Williger Society Gallery - Fine Arts League, 1997, Grand Island Art Soc., 1999, 2002, Locus Media Gallery, N.Y.C., 2004, Albright Knox Regional Artist Exhibit, 2004, 2006, SUNY Fredonia Alumni Invitational, 2004, one-woman shows include Earl Brydges Libr., Niagara Falls, 1996, Ransomville Libr., 1997, Barnes and Noble Bookstore, 1997. Contbg. artist Castellani Mus., Niagara Arts Coun., Buffalo Philharmonic, 1998—2004; asst. curator Am. Niagara Falls City Sch. Dist. Art Shows, 1985—2005. Recipient partial fellowship, Global Arts Village, 2006, Corp. Award for Art, Albright Knox Art Gallery, 2004. Mem.: Niagra Frontier Plein Air Painters, Internat. Plein Air Painters, N.Y. State United Tchrs., N.Y. State Art Tchrs. Assn., Coll. Club Niagara Falls. Avocations: reading, travel, gardening. Office: Niagara Falls H S 4455 Porter Rd Niagara Falls NY 14305

**SCHIFF, ADAM BENNETT,** congressman, lawyer; b. Framingham, Mass., June 22, 1960; s. Edward Maurice and Sherrill Ann (Glovsky) S.; m. Eve Schiff; 2 children; Alexa Marion, Elijah Harris. BA, Stanford U., 1982; JD cum laude, Harvard U., 1985. Bar: Calif. 1986. Assoc. Gibson, Dunn & Crutcher, LA, 1986; asst. U.S. atty. U.S. Atty.'s Office, LA, 1987—95; mem. Calif. Senate, 1997—2001; chmn. Senate Judiciary Com.; mem. U.S. Congress from 29th Calif. dist., Washington, 2001—; mem. judiciary com., internat. rels. com. Spl. assignment to Czechoslovakia, Justice Dept., Bratislava, 1992. Democrat. Associate: creative writing. Office: 326 Cannon HOB Washington DC 20515-0529 Business E-Mail: congressman.schiff@mail.house.gov.

**SCHIFF, CHARLENE,** adult education educator; b. Horochow, Wolyn, Poland, Dec. 16, 1929; arrived in U.S., 1948; d. Simcha and Fruma Perlmutter; m. Erwin H. Schiff; 1 child, Stephen Frank. Student, Ohio State U., 1949—50. Cert. Ikebana Internat., Yokohama, Japan, 1959, Art of Chinese Cooking Benedictine Sisters of Peking, 1958, Le Cordon Bleu, 1972. Lectr. on the Holocaust, various locations/orgns., 1985—. Contbg. author: Echoes of Memory, vol. 1, 2003, Echoes of Memory, vol. 2, 2004. Mem. Va. Planning Com. for Holocaust Days of Remembrance, 1985; past coord. Holocaust Child Survivors Group, Washington; gray lady U.S. Army Hosp., Munich, 1952—54; past mem. adv. bd., vol. U.S. Holocaust Meml. Mus. Named One of Alexandria's Outstanding Citizens, 1993; recipient 2d Century award, Jewish Theol. Sem., 1997. Mem.: Survivors of the Holocaust and Friends of

Greater Washington, McCosh Infirmary Aux. Princeton U. (life), U.S. Army Quartermaster Wives Club, Hadassah (life). Avocations: reading, foreign films, gourmet cooking. Home: 309 Yoakum Pkwy #815 Alexandria VA 22304

**SCHIFF, DAVID TEVELE,** investment banker; b. N.Y.C., Sept. 3, 1936; s. John Mortimer and Edith Brevoort (Baker) S.; m. Martha Elisabeth Lawler, May 11, 1963; children: Andrew Newman, David Baker, Kathryn Reynolds. B.Engring., Yale U., 1958. Trainee Chem. Bank N.Y. Trust, N.Y.C., 1959-62; analyst Madison Fund, N.Y.C., 1962; assoc., then partner Kuhn, Loeb & Co., N.Y.C., 1963-77; vice chmn. Kuhn Loeb & Co. Inc., 1977; mng. dir. Lehman Bros. Kuhn Loeb Inc., N.Y.C., 1977-83, also dir.; mng. ptnr. Kuhn, Loeb & Co. (formerly KLS Enterprises), 1984—. Dir., vice chmn. Am. Crown Life Ins. Co., N.Y.C., 1981-95; bd. dirs. Crown Life Ins. Co. Toronto, 1971-92; mem. lower Manhattan adv. bd. Chem. Bank, 1977-85; bd. advisors Venture Capital Fund of Am., 1998—; mem. leadership coun. Yale Sch. Forestry and Environ. Studies, 2000—. Trustee, chmn. bd. Wildlife Conservation Soc.; trustee Met. Mus. Art, Citizens Budget Commn., NYC, Greater NY coun. Boy Scouts Am., 1965—91, Beekman Downtown Hosp., 1966—82, chmn., 1975—79; trustee Brooks Sch., North Andover, Mass., 1972—90, treas., 1987—90; bd. govs. Yale U. Art Gallery, 1973—97, Fed. Hall Meml. Assn.; mem. adv. bd. dirs. Outward Bound, Inc., 1983—99; mem. Provident Loan Soc. NY; bd. dirs. Am. Hosp. of Paris Found., NYC, 1987—2006. With U.S. Army, 1959. Mem. Econ. Club N.Y.C., Pilgrims U.S., Brook Club, Century Assn., The Pilgrims of U.S. (mem. exec. com.), River Club, Maroon Creek Club (Aspen, Colo.), Mill Reef Club (Antigua), Yale Club N.Y.C. Episcopalian. Home: 770 Park Ave New York NY 10021-4153 Office: 50 Rockefeller Plz 15th Fl New York NY 10020-1622 Office Phone: 212-655-7044. Personal E-mail: gorilla@kuhnloebco.com.

**SCHIFF, DONALD WILFRED,** pediatrician, educator; b. Detroit, Sept. 11, 1925; s. Henry and Kate (Boesky) S.; m. Rosalie Pergament; children: Stephen, Jeffrey, Susan, Douglas. Student, Wayne State U., 1943-44, Oberlin Coll., 1944-45; MD, Wayne State U., 1949. Diplomate Am. Bd. Pediatrics. Intern Detroit Receiving Hosp., 1949-50; resident in pediatrics U. Colo., 1954-55, chief resident in pediatrics, 1955-56; instr. U. Colo. Health Scis. Ctr., Denver, 1956-59, asst. clin. prof., 1959-69, assoc. clin. prof., 1969-78, clin. prof., 1978-87, prof., 1987—; pvt. practice Littleton (Colo.) Clinic, 1956-86, chmn. bd., 1973-79; med. dir. HMO Colo., Denver, 1980-86; med. dir. Child Health Clinic The Children's Hosp., Denver. Contbr. articles to profl. jours. Bd. dirs. Bd. Trust. SW Colo., Colo., 1962; pres. Arapahoe Mental Health Clinic, Denver, 1968-70, bd. dirs., 1964-70; adv. coun. State of Colo. Medicaid, Denver, 1981—. With USN, 1944-46, USPHS, 1952-54, Turtle Mountain Indian Reservation, N.D. Recipient 25 Yrs. Teaching award U. Colo. Sch. Medicine, 1981. Mem. Am. Acad. Pediatrics (chmn. Colo. chpt. 1973-79, alternate dist. chmn. 1977-81, chmn. dist. 8 1981-86, nat. pres. 1988-89), Rocky Mountain Pediatric Soc., Colo. Med. Soc. Home: 600 Front Range Rd Littleton CO 80120-4052 Office: The Childrens Hosp Child Health Clinic Box BO32 1056 E 19th Ave Denver CO 80218-1088

**SCHIFF, ERIC ALLAN,** physics professor; b. LA, Aug. 29, 1950; s. Gunther Hans and Katharine Shepard (MacMillan) S.; m. Nancy Ruth Mudrick, Aug. 12, 1973; children: Nathan, Evan. BS, Calif. Inst. Tech., 1971; PhD, Cornell U., 1979. Rsch. assoc. U. Chgo., 1978-81; asst. prof. Syracuse (N.Y.) U., 1981-87, assoc. prof., 1987-95, prof., 1995—, dept. chair, 1997—2003, assoc. dean sci. and math., 2003—. Vis. Brown U., Providence, 1988-90, Xerox Palo Alto Rsch. Ctr., 1995. Contbr. articles to profl. jours. Rsch. grant NSF, 1983-86, 2002—. Mem. Am. Phys. Soc. (exec. com. NY state chpt. 1991-94), Materials Rsch. Soc. (symposium organizing com. 1992-97, 2003-04), Internat. Conf. Amorphous and Nanocrystalline Semicondrs. (organizing com. 1999—). Office: Syracuse U Dept Physics Syracuse NY 13244-1130

**SCHIFF, FRANK,** investment company executive; BS magna cum laude, U. Colo.; JD cum laude, Cornell Law Sch. Ptnr. White & Case LLP, head corp. dept.; mng. dir. DB Capital Ptnrs.; ptnr. MidOcean Ptnrs. Mem.: NY State Bar. Office: MidOcean Ptnrs 320 Park Ave Ste 1700 New York NY 10022 Office Phone: 212-497-1390. Business E-mail: fschiff@midoceanpartners.com.

**SCHIFF, GILBERT MARTIN,** virologist, microbiologist, medical educator; b. Cin., Oct. 21, 1931; married, 1955; 2 children. BS, U. Cin., 1953, MD, 1957. Intern U. Hosp., Iowa City, 1957-58, resident internal medicine, 1958-59; med. officer lab br. Communicable Diseases Ctr., Ga., 1959-61; head tissue culture investigation unit, perinatal rsch. br. Nat. Inst. Neurol. Diseases and Blindness, 1961-64; dir. clin. virology lab. U. Cin., 1964-78, asst. prof. medicine and microbiology, 1964-67, asst. prof. microbiology, 1967-71, prof. medicine Coll. Medicine, 1971—; pres. James N. Gamble Inst. Medical Rsch., 1984—. Attending physician dept. medicine Emory U., Atlanta, 1959-61; cons. com. maternal health Ohio State Med. Assn., 1964-70, Hamilton County Neuromuscular Diagnostic Clinic, 1966, 75, Contract Immunization Status in U.S., 1975-77; mem. com. viral hepatitis among dental pers. VA; mem. immunization practice adv. com. Surgeon Gen., 1971-75; dir. Christ Hosp Inst. Med. Rsch., Cin., 1974-83, chairperson libr. com., 1974—, mem. com. cancer programs, 1979—, mem. com. human rsch., 1980—, chairperson search com., dir. radiotherapy, 1980-82; mem. com. infection control, 1981—, mem. com. univ. liaisons, 1982—; mem. subcom. antimicrobial agents U.S. Pharmacopeia, 1977-80; mem. study sect., adv. com., review com. NIH; mem. com. Rubella immunization Ohio Dept. Health; com. Rubella control Cin. Dept. Health. Trustee Children's Hosp. Med. Ctr., rsch. com., 1985—; community adv. com. Hoxworth Blood Ctr., 1991—. Recipient career rsch. devel. award Nat. Inst. Child Health and Human Devel., 1970-74; grantee USPHS, 1964-67, Nat. found., 1965-67. Fellow ACP; mem. AAAS, Am. Soc. Microbiology, Am. Fedn. Clin. Rsch. (sec.-treas. 1967-70), Am. Pub. Health Assn., Sci. Rsch. Soc. Am., Ctrl. Soc. Clin. Rsch. (sec.-treas. 1977-81, v.p. 1983, pres. 1984), Infectious Disease Soc. Am. Am. Soc. Clin. Investigation, Sigma Xi. Office: Dept Pediatrics U Cincinnati Coll Med 3333 Burnet Ave Cincinnati OH 45229-3026 E-mail: gilbert.schiff@cchmc.org.

**SCHIFF, GUNTHER HANS,** lawyer; b. Cologne, Germany, Aug. 19, 1927; came to U.S., 1936; s. Hans and Alice (Goldstein) S.; m. Katharine MacMillan, Jan. 27, 1950 (div. 1957); children: Eric Alan, Mary Alice; m. JoAnn R. Schiff; children: Jage, Hans Judson. BSFS., Georgetown U., 1949, JD, 1952. Bar: D.C. 1952, Calif. 1953. Assoc., ptnr., of counsel various firms, Beverly Hills, Calif., 1954-94; pvt. practice Beverly Hills, Calif., 1994—. Sec. Los Angeles Copyright Soc., Beverly Hills, 1975-76 Contbr. articles to profl. jours. Pres. Beverly Hills Civil Svc. Commn., 1984-85, 88-89; pres. Free Arts for Abused Children, 1993-94, dir.; chmn. Rent Control Rev. Bd., Beverly Hills, 1980-84; trustee Young Musicians Found. With USNR, 1945-46. Mem. Alameda Beverly Hills Bar Assn. (chmn. Resolutions Com. 1977-78), Los Angeles County Bar Assn., Los Angeles Copyright Soc., USCG Aux., Calif. Yacht Club. Avocations: sailing, skiing, golf. Office: 9430 W Olympic Blvd Beverly Hills CA 90212-4552 Office Phone: 310-557-9081. Personal E-mail: hgschiff@pacbell.net.

**SCHIFF, HOWARD IRWIN,** urologist; b. Bklyn., May 15, 1948; s. Frank and Mildred Schiff; m. Debbie Mathews Schiff, Aug. 29, 1970; children: Jonathan, Richard, Robin, Meredith, Amanda. BA, Hofstra U., 1970; MS, W.Va. U., 1973, MD, 1975. Diplomate Am. Bd. Urology, lic. physician N.Y. Intern dept. surgery Montefiore Hosp., Bronx, 1975—77; intern dept. urology Mt. Sinai Med. Ctr. N.Y., 1977—80; asst. attending physician Mt. Sinai Med. Ctr., N.Y.C., 1980—; consulting urologist City Hosp. Ctr., Elmhurst, NY, 1980—2004; attending urologist Beth Israel Med. Ctr., N.Y.C., 1983—2003; asst. attending physician Weill-Cornell Med. Ctr., N.Y.C., 1984—; clin. instr. urology Mt Sinai Sch. Medicine, N.Y.C., 1982—; adj. asst. clin. prof. urology Weill-Cornell Sch. Medicine, N.Y.C., 2001—. Contbr. articles to profl. jours. Named one of Best Drs. in N.Y., N.Y. Mag., 1998, 2000, 2001, Best Drs. in N.Y. Metro Region, Castle Connelly Guide, 1997—2004; recipient Ferdinand Valentine Residents Essay award, N.Y. Acad. Mag., 1979,

Physicians Recognition award, AMA, 1980—. Fellow: ACS; mem.: Med. Soc. State of N.Y., Am. Urol. Assn. Office: 1120 Park Ave New York NY 10128 Office Phone: 212-996-6660. Personal E-mail: hschiffmd@gmail.com.

**SCHIFF, JANIS BOYARSKY,** lawyer; b. Bridgeport, Conn., July 6, 1958; BA cum laude, Brandesi U., 1980; JD, Suffolk U. Law Sch., 1983. Bar: Md. 1983, DC 1984, US Dist. Ct. (DC and Md.) 1985. Law clerk to Hon. Alan Wilner Md. Ct. of Appeals, 1983—1984; ptnr. Holland & Knight LLP, Washington, dir. on dir. com., dep. sect. leader, real estate sect., runs Rising Star mentoring and leadership program. State dir., gov. affairs chair, state ops. chair for Md., DC, No. Va. Internat. Coun. Shopping Ctrs., 1996—99; past pres. Suburban Md. Chpt. of Comml. Real Estate Women; active mem. Women in Real Estate; mem. Nat. Network Comml. Real Estata; serves on Washington, DC Dist. Coun. of Urban Land Inst.; instr. Allan Berman Inst., John Hopkins U.; bd. dir. Georgetown U. Law Sch. Advanced Comml. Leasing Inst.; lectr. in field. Comment editor Suffolk Transnational Law Jour., 1982—83; contbr. articles to profl. jours. Named one of Top Women in Comml. Real Estate, Real Estate Forum Mag. Mem.: Women's Bar Assn., DC Bar, ABA, Md. Bar Assn., Montgomery County Bar Assn. Office: Holland & Knight LLP 2099 Pennsylvania Ave NW Ste 100 Washington DC 20006 Office Phone: 202-862-5994. Business E-Mail: jschiff@hklaw.com.

**SCHIFF, JAYNE NEMEROW,** underwriter; b. NYC, Aug. 8, 1945; d. Milton E. Nemerow and Shirley (Kaplan) Wachtel; m. Albert John Schiff, Mar. 7, 1971; children: Matthew Evan, Kara Anne. BS in Bus., Marymount Coll., 1981; M.Profl. Studies in Elem. and Spl. Edn., Manhattanville Coll., 1995. Corp. sec., treas. Albert J. Schiff Assocs., Inc., NYC, 1970—78; field underwriter Mut. NY Fin. Svcs., Greenwich, Conn., 1973—90; freelance employee benefit cons. Greenwich, 1990—99; sr. account exec., contr. Nylex Benefits, Stamford, Conn., 1999—2005; dir. exec. benefits The NIA Group. LLC, 2005—. Regional dir. mktg., MONY Fin. Svcs., NYC, 1978-79; tutor HELP program Manhattanville Coll., 1996-2000. Bd. dirs. NY League Bus. Profl. Women, 1976-78, Temple Sinai, Stamford, Conn., 1979-84; leader Webelos Cub Scouts, 1977-78; treas. Ann. Mothers Bd. Benefit Greenwich Acad., 1988, upper sch. acquisitions chmn., 1989, chmn. spl. acquisitions Greenwich Acad. Benefit, 1990-91, chmn. advt., 1992; ESL tutor Lit. Vols. Am., ESL tutor, trainer, 1993; co-chair U. Rochester Parents Coun., 1993-96. Named Conn.'s Outstanding Young Woman, 1979. Mem. LWV, Am. Soc. Chartered Life Underwriters, NY Ctr. Fin. Studies (bd. dirs.), NYC Life Underwriters Assn. (bd. dirs. 1977-78). Jewish. Avocations: sailing, knitting, playing piano, reading. Office: Nylex Benefits 301 Tresser Blvd Stamford CT 06901-3284

**SCHIFF, JOHN JEFFERSON, JR.,** finance company executive; BS, Ohio State U., 1965. Chmn., CEO John J. & Thomas R. Schiff & Co., Inc., 1983-96; COO Cin. Fin. Corp., 1999—99, pres., CEO, 1999—, also chmn. bd. dirs. Trustee Am. Inst. Chartered Property Casualty Underwriters; dir. Cinergy Corp., Fifth Third Bancorp, Cin. Bengals Inc., John J. & Thomas R. Schiff & Co. Inc., Std. Register Co. Office: Cin Fin Group PO Box 145496 Cincinnati OH 45250-5496*

**SCHIFF, LAURIE,** lawyer; b. Newark, Apr. 24, 1960; d. Norman Nathan and Claire Jane (Schott) Schiff. BS in Law, Western State U., Fullerton, Calif., 1987, JD, 1988. Bar: Calif. 1989. Ptnr. Schiff Mgmt., Newport Beach, Calif., 1983-89; pvt. practice Schiff & Assocs., Irvine, Calif., 1989-91; ptnr. Schiff & Shelton, Newport Beach, 1991—, Attys. Equity Law Group, LLP, 2001—. Probation monitor State Bar Ct. Calif., 1991—97, spl. prosecutor, 1997—. Prodr.: (Albums) Boys Just Want to Have Sex, 1984; author: Genetics of Pointed Mink and Sepia, 2006. Bd. dirs. Jewish Family Svcs. Orange County, 1994—99. Mem.: Nat. Bus. Women Orgn., Assn. Trial Lawyers Am., Nat. Assn. Women Bus. Owners, Orange County Bar Assn. (arbitrator 1995—), Am. Mensa, Online Feline Fanciers (v.p. 1995—97, bd. dirs. 1997—), Tonkinese Breed Assn., Tonks West (v.p. 1994—96, pres. 1996—97), Internat. Cat Assn. (chair legis. com. 1995—97, 1998—99, legal counsel 1999—, lic. splty. judge 2001—04, chair Tonkinese breed com. 2002—, lic. allbreed judge 2004—), Internat. Politically Correct Cat Club (v.p. 1996—). Democrat. Jewish. Office: Schiff & Shelton 3700 Campus Dr Ste 202 Newport Beach CA 92660-2603 Office Phone: 949-417-2211.

**SCHIFF, MARLENE SANDLER,** entrepreneur; b. Great Barrington, Mass. d. Jack and Lena Yetta (Klein) Sandler; m. Haskel Schiff (dec. Feb. 1967), 1 child, Melissa Robin. BA, U. Mass., 1970; OPM, Harvard U., 1985. Founder, chief exec. officer, chmn. Transceiver East Inc., N.Y.C., 1971-88; founder, CEO, pres. MSS Assoc., Inc., N.Y.C., 1995—. Founder, CEO, pres. MSS Assocs., Inc. Pub. Best of American Lifestyles mag./catalog, 1995-97. Eye adv. com. N.Y. Hosp./Cornell Med. Ctr., 1988—; adv. bd. dirs. Sol C. Schneider Entrepreneurial Ctr. of the Wharton Bus. Sch. U. Pa., 1989, chair, 1991-95; adv. bd. nutrition and fitness project Harvard U. Sch. Pub. Health. Mem. Com. of 200 (bd. dirs. 1989-91, N.E. regional chair 1989-91, C200 Found. bd, 1991-93), Am. Fedn. Arts (membership and adv. com. mem. 1990). Home: 950 5th Ave New York NY 10021-1741 Fax: 212-737-0100. E-mail: mssnyny@aol.com.

**SCHIFF, MARTIN,** physician, surgeon; b. Phila., July 16, 1922; s. Isidore and Cecelia (Miller) S.; m. Mildred Tepley, Jan. 5, 1946; children: Denise Schiff Simon, Michael, David BS, Pa. State U., 1943; MD, U. Calif.-Irvine, 1951. Intern L.A. County Gen. Hosp., 1950-51; gen. practice medicine specializing in bariatrics L.A., 1951—. Lectr. L.A. area community colls. Author: Eat & Stay Slim, 1972, Miracle Weight-Loss Guide, 1976, One-Day-At-A-Time Weight Loss Plan, 1980, (5 tapes) Weight Loss Plan for Health, Happiness & A Longer Life Span, 1982, The Thin Connection, 1986, Lose Unwanted Pounds Permanently Without Dieting/Trying/Playing Games, 1998, Weight Control-Fact or Fiction?, 1999, The Power of Your Will, 1999, Connections: Feelings and Emotions, 2000, YOU: A Guide to Yourself and a Mental Roadmap to Your Inner Being, 2002, Mental Conditions and Situations-Fact or Fiction?, 2006, An Overview and Understanding of Mental Activity and Action, Conditions and Situations, 2006, Weight Thinkers, 2006. Lt. USN, 1943-45, PTO Mem. AMA, Calif. Med. Assn., L.A. Med. Assn., Am. Soc. Weight Control Specialists.

**SCHIFF, MOLLY JEANETTE,** artist, researcher; b. Chgo., Oct. 19, 1927; d. David Nathan and Beatrice (Aisenberg) Rice; m. Haskell Schiff, June 12, 1946; children: Darryll Nat, Lesley Nan, Brad Scott, Rae Ellyce Student, U. Chgo., 1958—63, student, 1968—69; BFA, Art Inst., Chgo., 1962, MFA, 1963, MA Edn., 1969. Cert. art tchr. Ill. Instr. art Chgo. Bd. Edn. and Park Dist., 1962—66, Jewish Cmty. Ctrs., Chgo., 1962—65; pvt. practice Chgo., 1962—; instr. art New Trier Extensions, Winnetka, Ill., 1965—78, Evanston Art Ctr., Ill., 1965, St. Tarsissus Sch., Chgo., 1968, Young Artists Studio Art Inst., Chgo., 1968—69, Ill. Visually Handicapped Inst., Chgo., 1968—73, Govs. State U., Monee, Ill., 1975—76. Cons. Markal Corp., Chgo., 1968-94; cons., presenter, regional rep. Shiva Corp., Chgo., 1984-87 Prin. works include Facades, 1971 (Honors award 1971), Drawn Paintings, 1976 (Honors award 1976), Acapulco Balcony, 1978 (Honors award 1980), Mexican Scenics, 1980 (Honors award 1980), Figures on Paper, 1988-89 (Honors award 1989), Low Seam, 1988 (Honors award), Later Impressions, 1989 (Honors award), Acapulco Nite View, 1989 (Honors award), Impressions, 1990 (Honors award), Mannequin Cut Outs, 1990 (Honors award), Union League, 1993 (Honors award), Jarvis Still Life, 1993 (Honors award), Blue Moon, 1997 (Honors award), Triplets, 1997 (Honors award 1998), Sunset at Pushkar, 1998 (Honors award 1999), Mannequis Soiree 1992 (Honors award 2000), Rain Forest, Brazil, 2003 (Honors award 2003), I'm Not Square, 2003 (Honors award 2003-2004), I Forgot My Sketch Book, 2003 (Honors award 2004), V is For Vashti, 2003 (Honors award 2003-2004), I Remember Purim-A Visual Narrative, 2006 (Honors award 2006); exhibs. include Biennale Internat., Florence, Italy, 2003 Pres. I.G.C.C. chpt. Am. Jewish Congress, Chgo., 1955 Recipient Cash award Foremost Corp., 1963, Ill. Dept. Energy and Natural Resources, 1988, Purchase award Rotarian Mag., 1978, Ill. State Mus., 1978, Nite View, 1989, Honors award U.S. State Dept., 1996 Mem. Archives, Figurative Art League, Nat. Mus. Women in Arts, Chgo. Artists Coalition, Chgo. Soc. Artists, Am. Jewish Artists Assn. (program dir. 1970-74,

89-93, pres. 2004-2005, exhbn. com. 2006), Dutch Folk Art Assn. (cons., juror 1979), Alumni Assn. Art Inst. Chgo., Am. Jewish Artists Club, Scan Chgo. (bd. dir. 1988-91) Avocations: tour directing, travel. Home and Office: 744 Sheridan Rd Evanston IL 60202-2502 Office Phone: 312-274-0930. E-mail: mollyjart@msn.com.

**SCHIFF, RICHARD,** actor; b. Bethesda, Md., May 27, 1955; s. Edward and Charlotte Schiff; m. Sheila Kelley, 1996; children: Gus, Ruby Christine. Grad., CCNY, 1983. With Actors Gang; founder, artistic dir. Manhattan Repertory Theatre. Dir.: (plays, off-Broadway) Antigone; actor: (films) Arena Brains, 1988, Medium Straight, 1989, Young Guns II, 1990, Stop! Or My Mom Will Shoot, 1992, Rapid Fire, 1992, The Public Eye, 1992, Malcolm X, 1992, The Bodyguard, 1992, Hoffa, 1992, My Life, 1993, Ghost in the Machine, 1993, The Hudsucker Proxy, 1993, Major League II, 1994, Speed, 1994, Tank Girl, 1995, Skinner, 1995, Rough Magic, 1995, Se7en, 1995, City Hall, 1996, The Arrival, 1996, The Trigger Effect, 1996, Grace of My Heart, 1996, Michael, 1996, Santa Fe, 1997, Touch, 1997, Volcano, 1997, Loved, 1997, The Lost World: Jurassic Park, 1997, Deep Impact, 1998, Doctor DoLittle, 1998, Heaven, 1998, Living Out Loud, 1998, Crazy in Alabama, 1999, Forces of Nature, 1999, Gun Shy, 2000, Whatever It Takes, 2000, Forever Lulu, 2000, Lucky Numbers, 2000, What's the Worst That Could Happen?, 2001, I Am Sam, 2001, People I Know, 2002, With It, 2004, Ray, 2004; (TV films) Trenchcoat in Paradise, 1989, Till Death Us Do Part, 1992, Cruel Doubt, 1992, The Positively True Adventures of the Alleged Texas Cheerleader-Murdering Mom, 1993, Amelia Earhart: The Final Flight, 1994, Saved by the Bell: Wedding in Las Vegas, 1994, Special Report: Journey to Mars, 1996, The Taking of Pelham One Two Three, 1998, The Pentagon Wars, 1998; (TV series) Relativity, 1996—97, The West Wing, 1999—2006 (Emmy award, best supporting actor in drama series, 2000); (plays) Goose and Tom Tom (Dramalogue award, best actor), Urban Folktales (Ovation award), Underneath the Lintel, 2006. Recipient Townsend Harris medal, CCNY, 2000. Mailing: NBC Universal 3000 W Alameda Ave Burbank CA 91523-0001*

**SCHIFF, ROBERT,** healthcare consulting company executive; b. N.Y.C., Jan. 7, 1942; s. Henry and Jeanette (Levine) S.; m. Adrianne Bendich, Aug. 16, 1964 (div. July 1979); children: Jorden, Debra; m. Joann McTaggart, Aug. 24, 1986. BS, CCNY, 1964, MS, Iowa State U., 1966; PhD, U. Calif., Davis, 1968. Asst. prof. anatomy Tufts U. Sch. Medicine, Boston, 1969-72; mgr. serology rsch. Hyland divsn. Baxter Labs., Costa Mesa, Calif., 1972-74; dir. R & D J.T. Baker Diagnostics, Bethlehem, Pa., 1974-77; dir. diagnostic R & D Hoffmann-LaRoche, Nutley, N.J., 1977-80; group v.p. Warner Lambert Co., Morris Plains, N.J., 1980-82; pres., CEO Schiff & Co., Inc., West Caldwell, N.J., 1982—. Del. Nat. Commn. for Clin. Lab. Stds., 1979-80; vice chmn. R & D Coun. N.J., 1980-82; bd. dirs. E.P.I. subs. E-Z-EM, Westbury, N.Y., 1991-98. Contbr. numerous articles to profl. jours.; patentee in field. Bd. dirs. Pharm. Tng. Inst., 2002. Post Doctoral fellow U. Calif., Davis, 1969; Aid to Cancer Rsch. grantee, Mass., 1970. Mem. N.Y. Acad. Sci., Regulatory Affairs Profl. Soc. (cert., bd. editors Focus 2006), Am. Soc. Quality Control (cert. quality auditor), Am. Assn. Clin. Chemistry, Brit. Inst. Regulatory Affairs, Parenteral Drug Assn., Sigma Xi. Avocation: flying. Office: Schiff & Co 1129 Bloomfield Ave West Caldwell NJ 07006-7123 Office Phone: 973-227-1830. Personal E-mail: rschiff13@aol.com. Business E-Mail: schiffandcompany@aol.com.

**SCHIFF, STACY,** writer; b. Adams, Mass., Oct. 26, 1960; married. BA, Williams Coll. Sr. editor Simon and Schuster. Author: Saint-Exupery: A Biography, 1994 (Pulitzer prize finallist for Biography, 1995), Véra (Mrs. Vladimir Nabokov): Portrait of a Marriage, 1999 (Pulitzer prize for Biography, 2000), A Great Improvisation: Franklin, France, and the Birth of America, 2005 (George Washington Book prize, 2006); contbr. The New Yorker, The N.Y. Times Book Rev., The Times Literary Supplement, others. Fellow, Guggenheim Found., 1996, Nat. Endowment for the Humanities.*

**SCHIFFER, CLAUDIA,** model; b. Rheinberg, Germany, Aug. 25, 1970; m. Matthew Vaughn, May 25, 2002; 2 children. Model Guess? jeans, 1989, Revlon cosmetics, Chanel; amb. internat. spokesperson L'Oréal; co-owner Fashion Cafe restaurants. Ptnr. Fashion Cafe, N.Y.C., London, New Orleans, Barcelona, Jakarta, Manila, others; host World Music Awards with Luke Perry, Monte Carlo, 1995. Runway debut in Chanel fashion show, 1990; appeared on covers of Mademoiselle, Cosmopolitan, Vogue, and over 100 others; creator series of exercise videos (with Kathy Kaehler) Claudia Schiffer's Perfectly Fit, 1996; pub.: (pictorial book) Memories. Hon. bd. dirs. Dishes AIDS; spokesperson Nat. Breast Cancer Coalition.

**SCHIFFER, LOIS JANE,** lawyer; b. Washington, Feb. 22, 1945; d. Benjamin and Clara (Goldberg) S. BA, Radcliffe Coll., 1966; JD, Harvard U., 1969. Bar: Mass. 1969, D.C. 1971, U.S. Supreme Ct. 1973. Legal svcs. lawyer Boston Legal Assistance Project, 1969-70; ct. law clk. D.C. Circuit Ct., Washington, 1970-71; assoc. Leva, Hawes, Symington, Martin, Oppenheimer, Washington, 1971-74; lawyer Ctr. for Law and Social Policy, Washington, 1974-78; chief gen. litig. sect. Land and Natural Resources divsn. U.S. Dept. Justice, Washington, 1978-81, spl. litig. counsel, 1981-84; gen. counsel Nat. Pub. Radio, Washington, 1984-89; ptnr. Nussbaum & Wald, Washington, 1989-93; acting asst. atty. gen. environ. and natural resources divsn. U.S. Dept. Justice, Washington, 1993-94, asst. atty. gen. environ. and natural resources divsn., 1994-2001; sr. v.p. for pub. policy Nat. Audubon Soc., 2001—02; ptnr. Baach Robinson & Lewis, Washington, 2002—05; gen. counsel Nat. Capital Planning Commn., Washington, 2005—. Adj. prof. environ. law Georgetown U. Law Ctr., Washington, 1986—; lectr. Harvard Law Sch., 2004; bd. dirs. DC Appleseed, Keystone Ctr., Internat. Sr. Project. Bd. dirs. Women's Legal Def. Fund, 1975-86, Am. Rivers, 1989-93; bd. dirs. ACLU/NCA, 1982-95, pres., 1988-90. Fellow Am. Bar Found.; mem. ABA (del.), Am. Law Inst., Phi Beta Kappa Democrat. Jewish. Avocations: reading, movies, hiking. Home: 4640 Brandywine St NW Washington DC 20016-4449 Office Phone: 202-482-7223. Business E-Mail: lois.schiffer@ncpc.gov.

**SCHIFFMAN, DANIEL,** lawyer, admin. advocate; b. N.Y.C., Nov. 7, 1932; s. Jacob and Eva (Katzin) Schiffman; m. P.G. Galex, June 26, 1955 (div.); m. Nancy A. Ozelli, Apr. 7, 1990. BBA, CCNY, 1959; JD, NYU, 1962. Bar: N.Y. 1962, U.S. Dist. Ct. (so. dist.) N.Y. 1966, U.S. Ct. Appeals (3d cir.) 1966, U.S. Dist. Ct. (ea. dist.) N.Y. 1979, U.S. Supreme Ct. 1975, U.S. Ct. Appeals (2d cir.) 1980, U.S. Ct. Appeals (1st cir.) 1998, U.S. Ct. Appeals (4th cir.). Musician, 1950—55; pub. acct. Meyerson and Levine, CPA, N.Y.C., 1959—61; legal sec. to chief city magistrate City of N.Y., 1961—62; assoc. Maxwell and Diamond, N.Y.C., 1962—66; mem. Schiffman and Ellenbogen, N.Y.C., 1975—78, Schiffman and Frank, N.Y.C., 1996—2004; pvt. practice, N.Y.C., 1966—74, 1978—96, 2004—. Cons., lectr. Practising Law Inst., N.Y.C., 1963—68, N.Y.C., 1982; counsel, migration div. Commonwealth of P.R. Labor Dept., 1970—72; counsel to adminstr. Commonwealth of P.R. Econ. Devel. Adminstrn., 1971—73; advisor U.S. GSA, 1979; lectr., moderator, panelist World Gaming Congress, 1987—99; moderator and panelist ABA, 1988, 2001; referee, special master, mental hygiene evaluator, guardian ad litem, receiver Supreme and Surrogate's Cts., N.Y., 1991—; adv. com. Little Hoover Com. (CA), 1997; co-chair, moderator and planning com. mem. ALI-ABA CLE courses, 1998, 2000, 01; panelist Global Gaming Expo., 2006. Contbg. author: Casino Credit and Collection Law, 1989, Internat. Casino Law, 1991, 1993, 1999, columnist and contbg. author: The Gaming Lawyer, 1998—, Global Gaming Bus. Mag., 2003—, mem. ed. bd.: Gaming Law Rev., 1997—, mem. staff: NYU Law Rev., 1961—62. Bd. dirs. Am. Symphony Orch., 1989—2005, treas., 1990—93, sec., 1997—2004; bd. dirs. MAESTRO Found., London, 1985—87; treas. Citizens for a Responsive Congress, 1978—80; co-founder, exec. prodr., pres. (hon.) Cala Records, Inc., 1991—. Mem.: Am. Fedn. Musicians, NYC. Jr. C. of C. (legal advisor 1980—90), Internat. Masters of Gaming Law (membership com., publications com.), Internat. Assn. Gaming Attys., Assn. Bar City NY, Nat. Arts Club (bd. dirs. 1986—, chmn. music com. 1994—, Pres.'s medal 1989). Home: 903 Park Ave New York NY 10021-0362 Office Phone: 212-628-6433.

**SCHIFFMAN, GERALD,** microbiologist, educator; b. NYC, May 22, 1926; s. Samuel and Mollie (Brookner) S.; m. Lillian Ebert, July 12, 1951; children: Stewart, Howard. BA cum laude, NYU, 1948, PhD, 1954. Asst. prof. microbiology Coll. Physicians and Surgeons, Columbia U., NYC, 1960—63; asso. prof. dept. research medicine and microbiology U. Pa., Phila., 1963-70; prof. SUNY Health Sci. Ctr., Bklyn., 1970-97, disting. svc. prof., 1995-97, prof. emeritus, 1997. Cons. Contbr. articles to profl. jours. Served in U.S. Army, 1943-45, ETO. Decorated Bronze Star; recipient Nichols award, 1947; Atomic Energy fellow, 1948-52; NIH grantee, 1974-94. Mem. Am. Assn. Immunologists, Am. Chem. Soc., Am. Soc. Microbiology, AAAS, Harvey Soc., Soc. Complex Carbohydrates, Sigma Xi, Phi Beta Kappa, Mu Chi Sigma, Pi Mu Epsilon. Jewish. Office: 450 Clarkson Ave Brooklyn NY 11203-2056 Personal E-mail: gs1246@verizon.net.

**SCHIFFMAN, HAROLD FOSDICK,** Asian language educator; b. Buffalo, Feb. 19, 1938; s. Merl and Mathilda (Keller) S.; m. Marilyn Gail Hornberg, June 10, 1978; 1 son, Timothy Marc Rajendran. BA, Antioch Coll., 1960; MA, U. Chgo., 1966, PhD, 1969. Lectr. anthropology U. Calif.-Davis, 1966-67; asst. prof. U. Wash., Seattle, 1967-73, assoc. prof., 1973-78, prof., 1978-95, chmn. dept. Asian langs., 1982-87; prof. South Asian studies U. Pa., Phila., 1995-2000, acad. dir. Penn Lang. Ctr., Luce prof. lang. learning, 1995-2000, rsch. dir. Penn. Lang. Ctr., 2000—; dir. Consortium for Lang. Policy and Planning, 2001—, Pedagogical Materials Project South Asia Lang. Resource Ctr., 2002—05. Trustee Am. Inst. Indian Studies, Chgo., 1979-82; lang. dir. Southeast Asian Summer Studies Inst., 1992-93, mem. lang. adv. com., 1993-94. Author: A Grammar of Spoken Tamil, 1979, A Reference Grammar of Spoken Kannada, 1983, Linguistic Culture and Language Policy, 1996, A Reference Grammar of Spoken Tamil, 1999; co-editor: Dravidian Phonological Systems, 1975; co-author: Language and Society in South Asia, 1981. Pres. bd. dirs. Seattle Pro Musica (choral group), 1976-78; mem. Pacific Northwest Chamber Chorus, Seattle, 1983-87. Sr. fellow Am. Inst. Indian Studies, 1976, 78; grantee U.S. Office Edn., 1971, 74, 78, NEH, 1984-87, Smithsonian Inst., 1984-87, Fulbright Rsch., 1993-94. Mem. Assn. Asian Studies (S. Asia council 1982-85), Am. Inst. Indian Studies (trustee 1979-82), Soc. S. Indian Studies (sec.-treas. 1973-75), Internat. Assn. Tamil Research (v.p. 1987-89). Mem. Soc. Of Friends. Office: U Pa Dept South Asia Studies 820 Williams Hall Philadelphia PA 19104-6305 Office Phone: 215-898-5825. Business E-Mail: haroldfs@ccat.sas.upenn.edu.

**SCHIFFMAN, LOUIS F.,** management consultant; b. Poland, July 15, 1927; s. Harry and Bertha (Fleder) S.; m. Mina R. Hankin, Dec. 28, 1963; children: Howard Laurence, Laura Lea. BChemE, NYU, 1948, MS, 1952, PhD, 1955. Rsch. engr. Pa. Grade Crude Oil Assn., Bradford, 1948-50; tchg. fellow dept. chemistry NYU, 1950-54; rsch. chemist E.I. DuPont de Nemours & Co., Wilmington, Del., 1954-56, Atlantic Refining Co., Phila., 1956-59; project leader, group leader, head corrosion sect. Amchem Products Inc., Ambler, Pa., 1959-70; pres. Techni Rsch. Assocs. Inc., Willow Grove, Pa., 1970—. Bd. dirs. Techno Ventures, Inc., Tecxchange.com; real estate developer: ptnr. Bay Properties Co., Bay Club Marina, Margate, N.J., Willow Grove U. Assocs.; pub.: editor Patent Licensing Gazette, 1968—, World Tech., 1975—; panelist on forum patents and inventions Delaware Valley Industry, 1973; mem. adv. oversight com. NSF, 1975, moderator energy conf. ERDA, Washington, 1976, Las Vegas, 1977; mem. adv. group in small bus. R&D programs Dept. Def., 1980. Editor: (with others) Guide to Available Technologies, 1985; contbr. to Encyclopedia of Chemical Technology, 1967; contbr. articles to profl. jours.; patentee in field. Recipient Founders Day award NYU, 1956. Fellow Am. Inst. Chemists; mem. Am. Chem. Soc., N.Y. Acad. Scis., Lic. Exec.s Soc., Tech. Transfer Soc., Assn. Univ. Tech. Mgrs., Assn. Small Rsch. Cos. (editl. contbr. newsletter); Sigma Xi, Phi Lambda Upsilon. Home: 1001 Easton Rd 206M Willow Grove PA 19090 Office: Techni Rsch Assocs Inc PO Box 1036 Willow Grove PA 19090-0922 E-mail: techniresearch@yahoo.com.

**SCHIFFNER, CHARLES ROBERT,** architect; b. Reno, Sept. 2, 1948; Robert Charles and Evelyn (Keck) S.; m. Iovanna Lloyd Wright, Nov. 1971 (div. Sept. 1981); m. Adrienne Anita McAndrews, Jan. 22, 1983. Student, Sacramento Jr. Coll., 1967-68, Frank Lloyd Wright Sch. Architecture, 1968-77. Registered architect, Ariz., Nev., Wis. Architect Taliesin Associated Architects, Scottsdale, Ariz., 1977-83; pvt. practice architecture Phoenix, 1983—. Lectr. The Frank Lloyd Wright Sch. of Architecture, 1994, 95. Named one of 25 Most Promising Young Americans Under 35, U.S. mag., 1979; recipient AIA Honor award Western Mountain Region, 1993, Western Home awards Sunset Mag., 1989, 91, AIA Ariz. Merit award, 1993 and numerous others. Home: 5202 E Osborn Rd Phoenix AZ 85018-6137 Office: 2944 N 44th St Ste 101 Phoenix AZ 85018

**SCHIFFRIN, MILTON JULIUS,** physiologist; b. Rochester, NY, Mar. 23, 1914; s. William and Lillian (Harris) S.; m. Dorothy Euphemia Wharry, Oct. 10, 1942; children: David Wharry, Hilary Ann. AB, U. Rochester, 1937, MS, 1939; PhD cum laude, McGill U., 1941. Instr. physiology Northwestern U. Med. Sch., Chgo., 1941—45; lectr. pharmacology U. Ill. Med. Sch., 1947—57, clin. asst. prof. anesthesiology, 1957—61; with Hoffmann-La Roche, Inc., Nutley, NJ, 1946—79; dir. drug regulatory affairs, 1964—71, asst. v.p., 1971—79; pres. Wharry Rsch. Assn., Seattle, 1979—. Chmn. Everglades Health Edn. Ctr., 1986—87. Author: (with E.G. Gross) Clinical Analgesics, 1955; editor: Management of Pain in Cancer, 1957. Bd. dirs. Univ. Adult Day Ctr., 1993—; mem. adv. bd. Regional Ombudsman Program, 1998—, Residents Coun. Washington, 1998—. Capt. USAAF, 1942-46. Mem. Am. Med. Writers Assn. (bd. dirs. 1967-70, pres. N.Y. chpt. 1967-68, nat. pres. 1972-73), Am. Physiol. Soc., Internat. Coll. Surgeons, Am. Therapeutic Soc., Coll. Clin. Pharmacology and Therapeutics, Am. Chem. Soc. Home and Office: Unit 308 4400 Stone Way N Seattle WA 98103-7486 Office Phone: 206-284-8809. Personal E-mail: grampa@highstream.net.

**SCHIFTER, RICHARD,** lawyer; b. Vienna, July 31, 1923; came to U S 1938; s. Paul and Balbina (Blass) S.; m. Lilo (Couqour, July 12, 1948; children: Judith, Deborah, Richard P., Barbara, Karen BS in Social Sci. summa cum laude, CCNY, 1943; LLB, Yale U., 1951; DHL (hon.), Hebrew Union Coll., 1992. Bar: Conn. 1951, D.C. 1952, U.S. Supreme Ct. 1954, Md., 1958. Assoc. Fried, Frank, Harris, Shriver & Jacobson, Washington, 1951-57, ptnr., 1957-84; dep. U.S. rep. with rank of ambassador UN Security Council, N.Y.C., 1984-85; asst. sec. of state for human rights and humanitarian affairs Dept. State, Washington, 1985-92; U.S. rep. UN Human Rights Commn., Geneva, 1983-86, 93; spl. asst. to pres., counselor Nat. Security Coun., Washington, 1993-97, spl. adviser to Sec. of State, 1997-2001. Head U.S. del. Conf. on Security and Cooperation in Europe Experts Meeting on Human Rights, Ottawa, Ont., Can., 1985, Dem. Insts., Oslo, 1991; bd. dirs. U.S. Inst. Peace, 1986-92; mem. Congl. Commn. on Security and Cooperation in Europe, 1986-92. V.p., pres. Md. Bd. Edn., Balt., 1959-79; chmn. Md. Gov.'s Commn. on Funding Edn. of Handicapped Children, 1975-77, Md. Values Edn. Commn., 1979-83; Montgomery County Dem. Cen. Commn., Md., 1966-70; del. Dem. Nat. Conv., 1968; bd. govs. Am. Jewish Commn., 1992-93, 2001-04, mem. exec. com., 2001-04; chmn. Internat. Rels. Commn., 2001-04; chmn. bd. dirs. Ctr. for Democracy and Reconciliation in Southeastern Europe, 2002—, Am. Jewish Internat. Rels. Inst., 2005—; bd. trustees Inst. for Christian and Jewish Studies, 2002—. With U.S. Army, 1943-46, ETO. Decorated Austrian Gt. Golden Decoration with star, comdr. Order of the Romanian Star, Bulgarian Stara Planina Order 1st class; recipient Disting. Svc. award, Sec. of State, 1992. Mem. Phi Beta Kappa. Democrat. Jewish. Home: 6907 Crail Dr Bethesda MD 20817-4723 Personal E-mail: rschifter@aol.com.

**SCHILD, A. FREDERICK,** surgeon; b. Conway, S.C., May 19, 1932; s. Samuel and Lillian Schild; m. Judy Schild; children: Lisa Henschel, Bill. Degree, U. N.C., Chapel Hill, 1953; MD, Med. U. S.C., Charleston, 1957. Cert. in surgery. Intern I.A. County Hosp., 1957—58; resident gen. surgery Med. U. S.C., 1958—59, Jackson Meml. Hosp., U. Miami, 1959—62, chief resident gen. surgery, 1962—63; attending physician Jackson Meml. Hosp., 1962—, VA Med. Ctr., 1962—, U. Miami Hosp. and Clinics, 1962—; pvt. practice, 1962—92; from. clin. instr. to assoc. prof. surgery Sch. Medicine U. Miami, 1966—86, clin. prof. surgery Sch. Medicine 1986—92, prof. clin.

surgery div. transplantation DeWitt Daughtry Family dept. surgery Sch. Medicine, 1992—; chief surgery Coral Reef Gen. Hosp., 1974; med. dir. Group Health, Inc., 1977—78; chief surgery Highland Pk. Gen. Hosp., 1978—79. Prof. surgery U. Miami, 1992—. Contbr. articles to profl. jours. Apptd. mem. Miami Retreat on Generalist Edn. State U. Sys. Fla., 1993; facilitator/resource person issues forum on health care delivery Fla. Ho. of Reps., 1992—. With U.S. Army, 1963-65. Named Dr. of Yr., S. Fla. Mag., 1991, Disting. Alumni, Med. U. S.C., 1992; recipient Duane G. Hutson Lifetime Achievement in Edn. award, Chief Residents, The DeWitt Daughtry Family Dept. Surgery, U. Miami, 2004, Physician Polit. Leadership award, Med. Bus., 1993, Award of Appreciation, AMA med. student chpt. U. Miami Sch. Medicine, 2001; grantee, Ethicon, Inc., Ark Therapeutics, Closure Med., Vectra Graft, Applied Med., Atrium, Hancock, Coalescent. Fellow ACS; mem. AMA, Fla. Med. Assn., Dade County Med. Assn. Home: 6801 SW 112 St Miami FL 33156 Office: U Miami Sch Medicine Dept Surgery Div Transplantation PO Box 012440 (R-440) Miami FL 33101 Office Phone: 305-585-5286.

**SCHILD, NANCY LOIS,** realtor, music educator; b. Hartford, Conn., May 31, 1947; d. William and Elsie Lena Brusick; m. William Adrian Schild, Mar. 19, 1947. B in Music Edn., Fla. State U., 1967; MS, Portland State U., 1976; MusM in Conducting, U. Wis., Milw., 2001. Music tchr. Orlando (Fla.) Luther H.S. and Middle Sch., 1996—99, Hales Corner (Wis.) Luth. Sch., 1996—99, choir dir., 1997—2002; music tchr. St. Joan Antida H.S., Milw., 1999—2002; accompanist, part-time organist Christ Our Redeemer Luth. Ch., Temple Terrace, Fla., 2002—; music tchr. Christ Our Redeemer Luth. Sch., Temple Terrace, 2004—; realtor Century 21, Tampa, Fla., 2004—05, Exit Realty Advisors, Tampa, 2005—. Founder, condr. Hales Corners Children's Choir, 1997—2001; singer Master Singers Milw., 1997—99, Milw. Choral Artists, 1999—2002. Mem.: Temple Terrace C. of C. (amb. 2005—), Greater Tampa Assn. Realtors, Nat. Assn. Realtors, Temple Terrace Svc. League. Republican. Lutheran. Avocations: golf, oil painting. Office: Exit Realty Advisors 11502 N 56th St Tampa FL 33617

**SCHILL, CHARLES F.,** lawyer; BS in Chemistry, Le Moyne Coll., 1968; JD, Capital Univ. Coll. of Law, 1973. Bar: Ohio 1973, DC 1985, US Supreme Ct. 1985, US Ct. Internat. Trade 1985, US Ct. Appeals, Fed., DC circuits 1985; registered: to practice before US Patent and Trademark Office 1975. Sr. staff atty., Office Legal Svcs. and Office of Gen. Counsel US Internat. Trade Commn.; ptnr., internat. trade & investment tech. dept Steptoe & Johnson LLP, Washington. Frequent lectr. on internat. trade regulation, WTO, intellectual property and litig. Mem.: Fed. Cir. Bar Assn. (pres. 2004—05), Internat. Trade Commn. Trial Lawyers Assn., Am. Intellectual Property Law Assn., Order of the Curia. Office: Steptoe & Johnson LLP 1330 Connecticut Ave NW Washington DC 20036 Office Phone: 202-429-8162. Office Fax: 202-429-3902. Business E-Mail: cschill@steptoe.com.

**SCHILL, MICHAEL H.,** dean, law educator; b. Schenectady, N.Y., 1958; AB, Princeton U., 1980; JD, Yale Law Sch., 1984. Law clerk Hon. Marvin Katz fed. Dist. Pa., 1984—85; assoc. Fried, Frank, Harris, Shriver & Jacobson, 1985—87; vis. lectr. Yale Law Sch., 1987; asst. prof. law U. Pa. Law Sch., 1987—91; assoc. prof., 1991—92; prof. law and real estate U. Pa. Law Sch. and Wharton Sch., 1993—95; vis. prof. Harvard Law Sch., 1999; dir. Furman Ctr. for Real Estate and Urban Policy, NYU, 1994—2004; prof. law and urban planning NYU Sch. Law and Robert F. Wagner Grad. Sch. Pub. Svc., 1995—2003, Wilf Family Prof. in property law and prof. urban planning, 2003—04; dean, prof. law UCLA Sch. Law, 2004—. Asst. counsel N.Y. State Assembly, Com. Housing, 1979; dir. Study of Neighborhood Reinvestment Princeton Urban and Regional Rsch. Ctr., 1980—81; vis. faculty U. Miami Law Sch., Grad. Prog. in Real Estate, 1994. Co-author: Revitalizing America's Cities: Neighborhood Reinvestment and Displacement, 1983, Reducing the Cost of New Housing Construction in New York City, 1999, The State of New York City's Housing and Neighborhoods, 2001; author: Housing and Community Development in New York City: Facing the Future, 1999; contbr. articles to law jours. Office: UCLA Sch Law Box 951476 Los Angeles CA 90095-1476 E-mail: schill@law.ucla.edu.

**SCHILLE, JOHN R.,** insurance company executive; b. Iowa; BS in math., U. Iowa. Programmer trainee Am. Fidelity Assurance Co., 1968, now sr. v.p., chief info. officer. Named one of Premier 100 IT Leaders, Computerworld, 2005. Office: Am Fidelity Assurance Co PO Box 25523 Oklahoma City OK 73125-0523*

**SCHILLER, ARTHUR A.,** architect, educator; b. N.Y.C., July 23, 1910; s. Valentine and Rose (Bayer) Schiller; m. Anne O'Donnell, June 12, 1937; children: Valerie Schiller Schaefer, Virginia Schiller Waicul, Eileen Schiller Toomey. BArch, NYU, 1933; diploma, Beaux Arts Inst. Design, N.Y.C., 1935; MArch, MIT, 1939. Registered profl. architect, N.Y. Architect U.S. Govt., Washington, 1936-38, N.Y.C. Dept. Parks, 1938-47; chief architect Bd. Higher Edn., N.Y.C., 1947-51, dir. architecture and engring., 1951-67; coord. campus planning Queens Coll., N.Y.C., 1967-73; adj. prof. N.Y. Inst. Technology, Old Westbury, 1973-91. Cons. Triboro Bridge Authority, N.Y.C., 1946; lectr. CCNY, 1957-67. Mayor Village of Plandome Manor, N.Y., 1965-87, trustee, 1960-65; trustee Nassau Mus. L.I. 1986—; conductor defensive driving courses for older citizens. Named Man of Yr. AARP, 1990, Sr. Citizen of Yr. Nassau County, State of N.Y., 1992. Fellow AIA (pres. Queens chpt. 1957-58); mem. N.Y. State Assn. Architects (dir. 1959-60), Assn. Univ. Architects (emeritus), U.S. Power Squadron (comdr. 1961-62, budget dir. 1988-91), Elks (life). Avocations: boating, gardening. Home: 15 Luquer Rd Manhasset NY 11030-1015

**SCHILLER, BARBARA,** retired special education educator; b. N.Y.C., Jan 1, 1943; d. Harry M. and Lee C. Browner; m. Charles Philip Schiller, July 16, 1967; children: Andrew Barry, Zachary Alan. BS in Edn., SUNY, Cortland, 1964; MS in Edn. of Visually Impaired, Hunter Coll., 1971. Tchr. children with limited vision NYC Bd. Edn., 1964—95. Sculpture exhbns., SUNY, Purchase, 1980—2005, sculpture in two-person show, Gallery at Marmara, N.Y.C., 2003, Cirque d'Art, N.Y., 2003, sculpture juried show, Katonah Mus., N.Y., 2003, sculpture in one-woman shows, John C. Hart Libr., Shrub Oak, N.Y., 2003, sculpture in permanent collections, Amsterdam Whitney Gallery, N.Y.C., 2004. Mem. bd. gov. Temple Beth Shalom, Mahopac, NY, 1995—2004. Named Woman of Yr., Temple Beth Shalom, Mahopac, NY, 2004; recipient NY award for sculpture, Knickerbocker Artists, multiple awards 4 first place, Quilts Along the Bay, Barnegat, NJ, 2003—04. Mem.: Katonah Mus., Nat. Women in Arts, Hadassah (life), State Quilter Guild NJ, No. Star Quilters Guild (3d pl. 2004, 2d pl. 2006, 2006). Hadassah. Avocations: reading, interior decorating, music, doll making. Home: 3600 Curry St Yorktown Heights NY 10598

**SCHILLER, DONALD CHARLES,** lawyer; b. Chgo., Dec. 8, 1942; s. Sidney S. and Beatrice (Lastick) S.; m. Eileen Fagin, June 14, 1964; children—Eric, Jonathan Student, Lake Forest Coll., 1960-63; JD, DePaul U., 1966. Bar: Ill. 1966, U.S. Dist. Ct. (no. dist.) Ill. 1966, U.S. Supreme Ct. 1972. Ptnr. Schiller, DuCanto & Fleck (formerly Schiller & Schiller and Schiller & DuCanto), Chgo., 1966—; lectr. in law U. Chgo. Law Sch., 2001—. Chair domestic rels. adv. com. Cir. Ct. Cook County, 1993—2001, co-chmn. rules revision com., 2003—; spkr. profl. confs. Contbr. chpts. and articles to profl. publs. Mem. steering com. on juvenile ct. watching, LWV, 1980-81. Recipient Maurice Weigle award Chgo. Bar Found., 1978, Disting. Alumni award, DePaul U., 1988, various certs. of appreciation profl. groups: named One of Am.'s Best Divorce Lawyers, Town and Country, 1985, 98, The Nat. Law Jour., 1987, The Best Lawyers in Am., 1987—, One of Chgo's Best Div. Lawyers, Crain's Chgo. Bus., 1981, Today Chgo. Woman, 1985, Inside Chgo. mag., 1988, Chgo. Sun Times, 2000, Worth Mag., 2002, Nat. Top 500 Lawyers, Law Dragon Mag., 2005, Ill. 10 Top Lawyers, Super Lawyer Mag., 2006. Fellow Am. Bar Found., mem. Am. Acad. Matrimonial Lawyers (nat. chair continuing legal edn. 1993-94); mem. ABA (bd. govs. 1994-97, chmn. family law sect. 1985-86, Ill. State del. 1980-84, mem. Ho. of Dels. 1984-2003, editor-in-chief Family Law Newsletter 1977-79; mem. editorial bd., assoc. editor Family Adv. Mag. 1979-84, speaker at confs. and meetings), Am. Bar

Retiredment Funds (pres. 2005—), Ill. Bar Assn. (pres. 1987-88, chmn. family law sect. 1976-77, editor Family Law Bull. 1976-77, bd. govs. 1977-83, treas. 1981-84, v.p. 1984-86, chmn. various coms., lectr., incorporator and pres. Ill. State Bar Assn. Mutual Ins. Co., Inc. 1988-89), Chgo. Bar Assn., Am. Coll. Family Law Trial Lawyers (diplomate). Office: Schiller DuCanto & Fleck 200 N La Salle St 30th Fl Chicago IL 60601-1098 Office Phone: 312-609-5560. Business E-Mail: dschiller@sdflaw.com.

**SCHILLER, HARVEY W.,** risk management company executive; m. Marcia Schiller. BS in chemistry, The Citadel; MS in chemistry, PhD in chemistry, U. Mich.; PhD (hon.), The Citadel, No. Mich. U. V.p. sports programming Tuner Broadcasting Sys., Inc., 1994—99; chmn. YankeeNets, 2000—02, Assante US, 2002—03; chmn. bd. GlobalOptions, Inc., Washington, 2003—. Chmn. mgmt. com. NYC2012 Olympic Bid Com.; exec. dir., sec. gen. US Olympic Com., 1990—94. With USAF, 1962—86. Office: GlobalOptions Inc 1615 L St NW Ste 300 Washington DC 20036 Office Phone: 202-293-2490.

**SCHILLER, JONATHAN DAVID,** lawyer; b. Washington, Sept. 25, 1946; s. Irving and Patricia Schiller; m. Margaret I. Miller, July 24, 1976; children: Zachary, Joshua, Aaron. BA, Columbia U., 1969, JD, 1973. Bar: U.S. Dist. Ct. D.C. 1973, U.S. Ct.Appeals (7th cir.) 1975, U.S. Dist. Ct. (ea. dist.) Ky. 1985, U.S. Dist. Ct. (ea. dist.) Mich. 1988, U.S. Ct. Appeals (6th cir.) 1988, U.S. Ct. Appeals (2d and 3d cirs.) 1990, U.S. Supreme Ct. 1991. Law clk. U.S. Dist. Ct. D.C., Washington, 1973-74; assoc. Arnold & Porter, Washington, 1974-76; ptnr. Rogovin, Huge & Schiller, Washington, 1976-90, Donovan, Leisure, Rogovin, Huge & Schiller, Washington, 1991—94, Kaye Scholer Fierman Hays & Handler, Washington, 1994—97; mng. ptnr. Boies Schiller & Flexner, Washington, 1997—. Pres. Washington Tennis & Edn. Found., 1993—; dir. Irwin Sweeney Miller Found., Washington, 1976—. Life Fellow, Am. Bar Found.; bd. mem. Washington Council of Lawyers; mem. Jud. Conf. D.C. Cir. (standing com. pro se and pro bono matters); Milan Chamber Nat. & Internat. Arbitration; Club of Arbitrators. Avocations: tennis, golf. Office: Boies Schiller & Flexner LLP Suite 800 5301 Wisconsin Ave NW Washington DC 20015 Business E-Mail: jschiller@bsfllp.com.

**SCHILLER, JUSTIN GALLAND,** antiquarian bookseller, researcher, editor; b. Bklyn., Sept. 10, 1943; s. S. Gary and Constance Audrey (Galland) S. BA in English Renaissance Lit., Ithaca Coll., 1965; postgrad., SUNY, Binghamton, 1965—66. Prin. Justin G. Schiller, Bklyn., 1960-69; pres. Justin G. Schiller, Ltd., N.Y.C., 1969—. Instr. hist. children's literature Rare Books Sch., Columbia U., 1984-89, U. Va., Charlottesville, 1996—; lectr. in field. Editor: (with A. Lurie) Garland's Classics in Children's Literature, 73 vols.; contbr. articles to Horn Book mag., Am. Book Collector, The Book Collector, others. Mem. coun. Bibliog. Soc., Am., 2001—. Mem Antiquarian Booksellers Assn. Am., assn. Internat. de Bibliophilie, Am. Antiquarian Soc., Grolier Club. Home: 77 W Chestnut St Kingston NY 12401-5929 Office: Justin G Schiller Ltd Antiquarian Booksellers Ste 302 Rockefeller Ctr 1270 Ave of the Americas New York NY 10020-1702 Office Phone: 212-332-7070. E-mail: justin.schiller@usa.net.

**SCHILLER, PHILIP W.,** information technology executive; BS in biology, Boston Coll., 1982. Former programmer and systems analyst Mass. Gen. Hosp.; former IT mgr. Nolan, Norton & Co., Lexington, Mass.; mktg. positions Apple Computer Inc., 1986—93, sr. v.p. worldwide product mktg. Cupertino, Calif., 1997—, interim v.p. mktg. Japan, 2006—; dir. product mktg. FirePower Systems, Menlo Park, Calif., 1993—95; v.p. product mktg. Macromedia, Inc., San Francisco, 1995—97. Office: Apple Computer Inc 1 Infinite Loop Cupertino CA 95014 Office Phone: 408-996-1010.*

**SCHILLER, PIETER JON,** retired venture capital executive; b. Orange, N.J., Jan. 14, 1938; s. John Fasel and Helen Roff (Roberts) S.; m. Elizabeth Ann Williams, Nov. 20, 1965; children— Cathryn Ann, Suzanne Elizabeth. BA in Econs. with honors, Middlebury Coll., 1960; MBA, NYU, 1966. Fin. analyst Merck & Co., N.Y.C., 1960—61; fin. analyst, asst. divsn. contr., dir. auditing, then asst. contr. Allied Chem. Corp., N.Y.C. and Morristown, NJ, 1961—75, treas., 1975—79, v.p. planning and devel., 1979—83; exec. v.p. diagnostic ops. Allied Health & Sci. Products Co., 1983—86; pres. subs. Instrumentation Lab., Lexington, Mass., 1983—86; gen. ptnr. Advanced Tech. Ventures, Waltham, Mass., 1986—2005, ptnr. emeritus, 2006—. Bd. dirs. CytoLogix Corp., Waltham, Mass.; bd. advisors Fresh Tracks Capital, LLC, Middlebury, Vt. Chmn. bd. trustees Newark Boys Chorus Sch., 1976—78, pres. bd., 1974—76; trustee Colonial Symphony Soc., 1978—85, v.p.: 1980—82, pres., 1982—83; active Morris Mus., Morristown, Concord (Mass.) Mus.: 1994—96, v.p., 1996—2000, chmn. bd. trustees, 2002—; pres. Middlebury Coll. Alumni Assn., 1994—96; chmn. allocations com. United Way of Morris County, 1974—79, v.p. bd. dirs., mem. exec. com., 1979—80; trustee Morris Mus. Arts and Scis., 1980—83; bd. dirs. New Eng. Coun., Boston, 1983—86; v.p. Middlebury Coll. Alumni Assn., 1992—94; bd. dirs. John Adams Innovation Inst., Westborough, Mass., 2005—. Mem. Fin. Execs. Inst. Republican. Episcopalian. Avocations: skiing, photography. Home: 18 S Meadow Rdg Concord MA 01742-3051 Business E-Mail: pschiller@atvcapital.com.

**SCHILLER, ROBERT E.,** former school system administrator; PhD, U. Pa. Supt. local sch. districts, NJ, 1984—87; state dep. supt. edn. La., 1988—89; state dep. supt. pub. instrn. Del., 1989—91; supt. pub. instrn. Mich. State Dept. Edn., Lansing, 1992—95; interim CEO Balt. Pub. Schs. 1997—98; supt. Caddo Parish Pub. Sch. Dist., Shreveport, La., 1999—2002; state supt. edn. Ill. Dept. Edn., 2002—04.

**SCHILLER, WILLIAM RICHARD,** surgeon; b. Bennett, Colo., Jan. 14, 1937; s. Francis T. and Frances M. (Finks) S.; m. Beverlee Schiller; children from previous marriage: Julie, Lisa. BS, Drury Coll., Springfield, Mo., 1958; MD, Northwestern U., 1962; MA in Liberal Arts, St. John's Coll., 2005. Diplomate Am. Bd. Surgery; cert. of added qualifications in surg. critical care, 1987, recertified in surg. critical care, 1994. Intern Passavant Meml. Hosp., Chgo., 1962-63; resident Northwestern U. Clin. Tng. Program, Chgo., 1963-68; assoc. prof. surgery Med. Coll Ohio, Toledo, 1970-78; prof. surgery U. N.Mex, Albuquerque, 1978-83; dir. Trauma Ctr. St. Joseph's Hosp., Phoenix, 1983-89; dir. burn and trauma ctr. Maricopa Med. Ctr., Phoenix, 1989-98; prof. surgery So. Ill. U., Springfield, 1998—2002; ret., 2002. Clin. prof. surgery U. Ariz. Health Sci. Ctr.; prof. surgery Mayo Grad. Sch. Medicine, Rochester, Minn. Contbr. chpts. to books, articles to profl. jours. Served as maj. M.C. U.S. Army, 1968-70, Vietnam. Recipient Disting. Alumnus award for career achievement, Drury Coll., 2004. Fellow ACS; mem. Am. Assn. Surgery of Trauma, Cen. Surg. Assn., Western Surg. Assn., Soc. Surgery of Alimentary Tract, Am. Burn Assn., Internat. Soc. of Surgery. Republican. Home: 784 Aspen Compound Santa Fe NM 87501 E-mail: wrschiller@hughes.net.

**SCHILLING, ARLEEN MARIE,** social studies educator; d. Phil and Colleen Schilling. AA, Aims C.C., Greeley, Colorado, 1990; BS, U. No. Colo., 1992. Cert. tchr. Colo. Social studies tchr. Walt Clark Mid. Sch., Loveland, Colo., 1994—95, Thompson Valley H.S., Loveland, 1995—96; lang. arts tchr. Conrad Ball Mid. Sch., Loveland, 1998—2000, Mountain View H.S., Loveland, 2000—02, social studies tchr., 2000—. Grantee, Project TEACH, 2003—05. Mem.: Thompson Edn. Assn., Colo. Geog. Assn., Golden Key Nat. Honor Soc. Roman Catholic. Avocations: landscaping, fashion design, hiking, woodworking, scrapbooks. Office: Mountain View HS 3500 Mountain Lion Dr Loveland CO 80357 E-mail: schillinga@thompson.k12.co.us.

**SCHILLING, CURTIS MONTAGUE,** professional baseball player; b. Anchorage, Alaska, Nov. 14, 1966; m. Shonda Schilling; children: Gehrig, Grant, Gabriella, Garrison. Student, Yavapai Coll., Ariz. Selected by Boston Red Sox, 1986—88; pitcher Balt. Orioles, 1988—91, Houston Astros, 1991—92, Phila. Phillies, 1992—2000, Ariz. Diamondbacks, 2000—03, Boston Red Sox, 2004—. Named to MLB All-Star game, 1997—99, 2001,

2002, 2004; recipient Lou Gehrig award, Phi Delta Theta, 1996, Nat. League Championship Series Most Valuable Player, 1993, co-World Series Most Valuable Player, 2001, Best Championship Performance, ESPY awards. Achievements include led Nat. League in strikeouts (319), 1997, (300), 1998; led Nat. League in wins (22), 2001, Am. League (21), 2004; being a member of World Series Champion Arizona Diamondbacks, 2004; being a member of World Series Champion Boston Red Sox, 2004; has had over 200 career wins, over 3,000 career srikeouts. Office: c/o Boston Red Sox 4 Yawkey Way Boston MA 02215-3496

**SCHILLING, FRANKLIN CHARLES, JR.,** retail management professional; b. Balt., Apr. 17, 1958; s. Franklin Charles and Shirley Jean (Whitehurst) S.; m. Dana E. Schilling, Apr. 21, 2005; children: Franklin Charles III, Tyler Kyle, Brittany Alexandra Stainbrook. Student, Dundalk C.C., 1975—77. Dept. mgr. Santonis Market, Inc., Balt., 1976-80; store mgr. A&P Plus Food Stores, Balt., 1980-82; area supr. Southland Corp/7-Eleven, Suitland, Md., 1982-85; mgr. retail ops. Moore Oil Co./Makin' Tracks Stores, Washington, NC, 1986, Besche Oil Co./Quik Shop Stores, Waldorf, Md., 1987-89; dist. mgr. Cloverland Greenspring Dairy/Royal Farm Stores, Balt., 1989-97, dir. ops., 1997-98, dir. mktg. and merchandising, 1999—. Lutheran. Avocations: reading, sports, music. Office: Cloverland Dairies/Royal Farm Stores 3611 Roland Ave Baltimore MD 21211-2408 Home: 649 Budleigh Cir Lutherville MD 21093 Office Phone: 410-889-0200. Business E-Mail: fschilling@royalfarms.com.

**SCHILLING, FREDERICK AUGUSTUS, JR.,** geologist, consultant; b. Phila., Apr. 12, 1931; s. Frederick Augustus and Emma Hope (Christoffer) S.; m. Ardis Ione Dovre, June 12, 1957 (div. 1987); children: Frederick Christopher, Jennifer Dovre. BS in Geology, Wash. State U., 1953; PhD in Geology, Stanford U., 1962. Registered geologist, Calif.; cert. engring. geologist, Calif.; registered environ. assessor, Calif. Computer geophysicist United Geophys. Corp., Pasadena, Calif., 1955-56; geologist various orgns., 1956-61, U.S. Geol. Survey, 1961-64; underground engr. Climax (Colo.) Molybdenum Co., 1966-68; geologist Keradamex Inc., Anaconda Co., M.P. Grace, Ranchers Exploration & Devel. Corp., Albuquerque and Grants, N.Mex., 1968-84, Hecla Mining Co., Coeur d'Alene, Idaho, 1984-86, various engring. and environ. firms, Calif., 1986-91; prin. F. Schilling Cons., Canyon Lake, Calif., 1991—. Author: Bibliography of Uranium, 1976. Del. citizen amb. program People to People Internat., USSR, 1990-91. With U.S. Army, 1953-55. Fellow The Explorers Club; mem. Geol. Soc. Am., Am. Assn. Petroleum Geologists, Soc. Mining Engrs., Internat. Platform Assn., Adventurers' Club L.A., Masons, Kiwanis, Sigma Xi, Sigma Gamma Epsilon. Republican. Presbyterian. Avocation: track and field. Office: F Schilling Cons 30037 Steel Head Dr Canyon Lake CA 92587-7460 also: 14661 Myford Rd Ste C Tustin CA 92780-7205 Office Phone: 714-731-8438. E-mail: faschill@pacbell.net.

**SCHILLINGER, RANDI,** lawyer; b. Bklyn., Sept. 25, 1958; d. Lester and Blance Schillinger; m. Marshall Bennett Fleer, June 2, 1984; 1 child, Alexander Fleer. BA, Boston Univ., Boston, Mass., 1980; JD, St. John's Univ. Sch. of Law, Queens, N.Y., 1983. Bar: N.Y. 1984, N.J. 1986, Pa. 2004. Assoc. atty. Fisher & Fisher, Bklyn., 1983, Clapp & Eisenberg, Newark, 1985—94; atty., firm mem. Saiber Schlesinger Satz & Goldstein, LLC, 1996—. Lectr. in field. Contbr. articles pub. to profl. jour. Recipient Top Ten Women in Real Estate, Women's Fund of N.J., 2003. Mem.: ABA (Real Property, Probate & Trust Section, Environ., Energy and resource Section), Indsl. Comml. Real Estate Women (co-programming dir., mem. bd.), Mortgage Bankers Assn. (comml. property divsn.), Pa. State Bar Assn. (environ., Mineral & Natural Resources Law Section), N.J. State Bar Asssn. (Environ. Law Section). Avocations: Broadway shows, ballet, opera, cultural events, tennis. Office: Saiber Schesinger Satz & Goldstein LLC one Gateway Ctr 13th flr Newark NJ 07102

**SCHILLINGS, DENNY LYNN,** retired history professor, educational and grants consultant; b. Mt. Carmel, Ill., June 28, 1947; s. Grady Lynn and Mary Lucille (Walters) S.; m. Karen Krek; children: Denise, Corinne. AA, Wabash Valley Coll., 1967; BEd, Ea. Ill. U., 1969, MA in History, 1972; MA in Adminstrn., Govs. State U., 1996; postgrad., Ill. State U. Grad. asst. dept. history Ea. Ill. U., Charleston, 1969; tchr. Edwards County High Sch., Albion, Ill., 1969-70, Sheldon (Ill.) High Sch., 1971-73, Homewood-Flossmoor (Ill.) High Sch., 1973—2003, tchr. history, grants and devel. mgr., 1994—2003; supr. history dept. Coll. Liberal Arts and Scis, No. Ill. U., Dekalb, 2003—; ret., 2003; adj. prof. Trinity Christian Coll., 2003—. Participant, con. Atlantic Coun. U.S. and NATO, Washington, 1986, Internat. Soviet-U.S. Textbook Project Conf., Racine, Wis., 1987; moderator Soviet-U.S. Textbook Study: Final Report, Dallas, 1987; chair history content adv. com. Ill. Tchr. Certification Requirements Com. 1986; mem. Ill. State Bd. Edn., Com. to Establish Learner Outcomes, 1984, Joint Task Force on Admission Requirements Ill. State Bd. on Higher Edn., 1986—; mem. adv. com. for Jefferson Found. Sch. Programs, 1987-90, Ill. State Bd. Edn.'s Goals Assessment Adv. Com., 1987-90; chair Ill. Learning Standards Project, 1996-97; pres. Corinne Jeannine Schillings Found., 2004—. Author: (with others) Economics, 1986, The Examination in Social Studies, 1989, Links Across Time and Place: A World History, 1990, Illinois Government Text, 1990, 99, 2003, Challenge of Freedom, 1990; author: The Living Constitution, 1991, 3d edit., 2002; co-editor: Teaching the Constition, 1987; reviewer, cons. for ednl. instns. and organizations; chair editorial bd. Social Edn., 1983; contbg. editor Social Studies Tchr., 1987-88. Mem. steering com. Homewood-Flossmoor High Sch. Found., 1983-84; elected bd. edn. Homewood Elem. Dist. 153, 1999—, found. pres., 2005—. Mem. NEA, Am. Hist. Assn. (James Harvey Robinson prize com. 1990-91), Ill. Coun. Social Studies (v.p. 1981, editor newsletter 1979-84, pres. 1983), Ill. Edn. Assn. (Gt. Lakes coord. com. 1982-83), Nat. Coun. Social Studies (publs. bd. 1983-86, bd. dirs. 1987-90, 94-96, exec. com. 1989-90, chair conf. com. 1989-90, pres. 1993-94, program planning com. 1989, 91), Phi Alpha Theta. Avocations: computers, reading. Home and Office: 18447 Aberdeen St Homewood IL 60430-3525 Office Phone: 630-886-0507. Personal E-mail: dschillings1@comcast.net.

**SCHILLINGS, KAREN MARIE,** elementary school educator; d. August and Joanna Krek; m. Denny L. Schillings, June 6, 1970; children: Denise M., Corinne J. BS in Edn., Ea. Ill. U., 1969; MS in Edn., So. Ill. U., Edwardsville, IL, 1971. Cert. tchr. Ill., 1969. Tchr. Oblong Jr. H.S., Oblong, Ill., 1970—71; substitute tchr. Sheldon Dist. #5, 1971—72, tchr. 6th grade, 1972—73; tchr. Pk. Forest Sch. Dist., 1973—74; dir., tchr. Cookie Jar Coop. Nursery Sch., Homewood, Ill., 1978—84; tchr., dir. pre-school St. Andrew's Ch., Homewood, 1989—90; tchr. St. Kieran's Sch., Chcgo. Heights, Ill., 1991—94, Homewood Dist. #153, Homewood, Ill., 1994—. Chmn. profl. devel. com. Homewood (Ill.) Sch. Dist. #153, 2002—04. Mem. Homewood (Ill.) Heritage Com., 2002—; founder, bd. dirs. Corinne Jeannine Schillings Found., 2004—; chmn. Willow Sch. Wellness Com., 2004—. Recipient St. Anne award, Archdiocese Chgo., 2001, Heart of Sch. award, St. Kieran Sch., 1994, St. Elizabeth Seton award, 1990. Mem.: NEA, Nat. Art Edn. Assn., Ill. Edn. Assn., Girl Scout USA (life Daisy pin Sycamore chpt. 1985, named Outstanding Leader of Yr. Sycamore chpt. 1990, named Vol. of Yr. Sycamore chpt. 1998), Girl Scouts South Cook County (life; pres. 1999—2005, bd. dirs. 2005—, Honor pin 1991, Thanks badge 1996, Thanks badge II 2003). Roman Catholic. Personal E-mail: kschillings@comcast.net.

**SCHILLOW, NED WILLIAM,** mathematics professor; b. Skippack, Pa., Aug. 3, 1950; s. William James and Doris Elizabeth (Shaffer) S. BS, Ursinus Coll., Collegeville, Pa., 1972; MS, Rutgers U., 1974; MEd, Temple U., Phila. 1976. Sec. tchr. Cherry Hill (N.J.) Sch. Dist., 1974-76; prof. math. Lehigh Carbon C.C., Schnecksville, Pa., 1976—. Assoc. editor the UMAP Jour., 1986—2005; asst. newsletter editor Pa. State Math. Assn. Two Yr. Colls. 1982-90; columnist Mo. Coun. Tchrs. Math. newsletter, 1985-90; contbr. articles to profl. jours. and chpts. to books. Recipient Faculty Appreciation award Student Govt. of Lehigh Carbon C.C., 1987, George Elison Faculty Svc. award, 1988, Employee Recognition award, 1989, Pa. Outstanding Teaching award State Commn. for C.C., 1992, Faculty Excellence award,

Lehigh Carbon C.C., 2003; NSF-MSP grantee, 2003—. Mem. Math Assn. Am., Am. Math. Assn. of 2-Yr. Colls., Nat. Coun. Tchrs. Math. (rep. 1988—), Pa. State Math. Assn. of 2-Yr. Colls. (exec. bd. 1982—), Pa. Coun. Tchrs. Math (exec. bd. 1979-84, conv. publicity com. 1991-92), Ea. Pa. Coun. Tchrs. Math. (exec. bd. 1979—, pres. 1980-82). Republican. United Ch. of Christ. Avocations: reading, travel, crystal. Home: PO Box 539 Skippack PA 19474 Office Office Phone: 610-799-1752. Business E-Mail: nschillow@lccc.edu.

**SCHILSKY, RICHARD LEWIS,** oncologist, researcher; b. N.Y.C., June 6, 1950; s. Murray and Shirley (Cohen) S.; m. Cynthia Schum, Sept. 24, 1977; children: Allison, Meredith. BA cum laude, U. Pa., Phila., 1971; MD with honors, U. Chgo., 1975. Diplomate Nat. Bd. Med. Examiners, Am. Bd. Internal Medicine (subspecialty med. oncology); lic. physician, Mo., Ill. Intern, resident medicine Parkland Meml. Hosp., Southwestern Med. Sch., Dallas, 1975-77; clin. assoc. medicine br. and clin. pharmacology br. Divsn. Cancer Treatment, Nat. Cancer Inst., Bethesda, Md., 1977-80, cancer expert clin. pharmacology br., 1980-81; asst. prof. dept. internal medicine U. Mo. Sch. Medicine, Columbia, 1981-84; asst. prof. dept. medicine U. Chgo. Pritzker Sch. Medicine and Michael Reese Med. Ctrs., 1984-86, assoc. prof. dept. medicine, 1986-89; assoc. dir. joint sect. hematology and med. oncology U. Chgo. and Michael Reese Med. Ctrs., 1986-89; assoc. prof. dept. medicine, assoc. dir. sect. U. Chgo. Pritzker Sch. Medicine, 1989-91, prof. dept. medicine sect. hematology-oncology, 1991—; dir. U. Chgo. Cancer Rsch. Ctr., 1991-99; chmn. Cancer and Leukemia Group B, Chgo., 1995—; assoc. dean clin. rsch. biol. scis. divsn. U. Chgo., 1999—. Vivian Saykaly vis. prof. oncology McGill U., 1992; sci. com. Internat. Congress on Anti-Cancer Chemotherapy, 2002; adv. panel on hematologic and neoplastic disease U.S. Pharmacopeial Conv., 1991-95; cancer ctr. support grant rev. com. Nat. Cancer Inst., NIH, 1992-95; expert panel on advances in cancer treatment, 1992-93; mem. Cancer Ctrs. Working Group, 1996-97; oncologic drugs adv. com. FDA, 1996-2000, chmn., 1999-2000; mem. NCI Clin. Trials Implementation com., 1997-98; bd. scientific advisors Nat. Cancer Inst., 1999—, mem. clin. trials working group, 2004-05, mem. translational rsch. working group, 2005-. Mem. editl. bd. Investigational New Drugs, 1988-95, Jour. Clin. Oncology, 1990-93, Contemporary Oncology, 1995-99, Jour. Cancer Rsch. and Clin. Oncology, 1991—, Seminars in Oncology, 1997—; assoc. editor Clin. Cancer Rsch., 1994—, Cancer Therapeutics, 1997-99, Cancer, 1999—; contbr. articles to profl. jours., chpts. to books. With USPHS, 1977-80. Recipient Spl. Advancement for Performance award VA, 1983, Fletcher Scholar award Cancer Rsch. Found., 1989; grantee VA, 1981-87, Am. Cancer Soc., 1983-86, 92-95, Ill. Cancer Coun., 1985-86, Michael Reese Inst. Coun. 1985-86, Nat. Cancer Inst., 1987, 88-90, Burroughs-Wellcome Co., 1987-88, NIH/Nat. Cancer Inst., 1988— Fellow ACP; mem. AAAS, Am. Soc. Clin. Oncology (bd. dirs. 2002-05), Am. Assn. Cancer Rsch. (chmn. Ill. state legis. com. 1992—), Am. Fedn. Clin. Rsch. (senator Midwest sect. 1983-84, councilor 1983-86, chmn. 1988-89), Am. Cancer Soc. (bd. dirs. Ill. divsn. 1997—), Am. Assn. Cancer Edn., Am. Soc. Clin. Pharmacology and Therapeutics, Ctrl. Soc. Clin. Rsch., N.Y. Acad. Scis., Assn. Am. Cancer Insts. (bd. dirs. 1995-99), Chgo. Soc. Internal Medicine, Sigma Xi, Alpha Epsilon Delta, Alpha Omega Alpha. Office: U Chgo Biol Scis Divsn 5841 S Maryland Ave Chicago IL 60637-1463 Office Phone: 773-834-3914. Business E-Mail: rschilsk@medicine.bsd.uchicago.edu.

**SCHIMEK, DIANNA RUTH REBMAN,** state legislator; b. Holdrege, Nebr., Mar. 21, 1940; d. Ralph William and Elizabeth Julia (Wilmot) Rebman; m. Herbert Henry Schimek, 1963; children: Samuel Wolfgang, Saul William. AA, Colo. Women's Coll., 1960; student, U. Nebr., Lincoln, 1960-61; BA magna cum laude, U. Nebr., Kearney, 1963. Former tchr. and realtor; mem. Nebr. Legislature from 27th dist., Lincoln, 1989—; chmn. govt., mil. and vets. affairs com. Nebr. Legislature, Lincoln, 1993-94, 99—, vice chair urban affairs com., 1995-98. Dem. Nat. committeewoman, 1984-88; chmn. Nebr. Dem. Com., 1980-84; mem. exec. com. Dem. Nat. Com., 1987-88; past pres., sec. bd. dirs. Downtown Sr. Ctr. Found., 1990-96; mem. exec. bd. Midwestern Legis. Conf., 1995—, co-chair health and human svcs. com., 1995-96; exec. dir. Nebr. Civil Liberties Union, 1985; former bd. dirs. Nebr. Repertory Theater, Exon Found., 1997-2000; mem. adv. bd. Martin Luther Home, 1997-2003; chair Midwestern Legis. Conf. Coun. of State Govts., 2000-01, co-chair com. intergovtl. affairs; mem. Midwest Interstate passenger Rail Commn., 2001-05; mem. exec. bd. Coun. State Govts., 2000-05; chair NCSL Task Force on Initiative and Referendum, 2001-02; bd. dirs. Midwest Humanity, 2006—. Toll fellow, 1999; recipient Outstanding Alumni award U. Nebr., 1989, Tribute award YWCA, 1992, Friend of Psychology award N.E. Psychol. Assn., 1998, Woman of Yr. award Nova Chpt. Bus. & Profl. Women, 1999, Disting. Svc. award Nat. Guard Assn., 2000, Woman of Distinction award Soroptimists, 1999, Legis. of Yr. award N.E. Dental Hygienists Assn., 2001, Disting. Svc. award N.E. League of Municipalities, 2002, Lincoln Interfaith Leadership award, 2003, Harold Steck award ARC of N.E., 2004, Alice Paul award Lancaster Status of Women Commn., 2006, Civil Libertarian of Yr. award ACLU Nebr., 2006, others. Mem. Nat. Conf. State Legislators Women's Network (bd. dirs. 1993-96, 1st vice chmn.), PEO, Soroptimists, Delta Kappa Gamma (hon.), Mortar Bd. (cmty. advisor 1998, hon.), Rotary Internat. Democrat. Unitarian Universalist. Home: 2321 Camelot Ct Lincoln NE 68512-1457 Office: Dist # 27 State Capital Lincoln NE 68509 Office Phone: 402-471-2632. Business E-Mail: dschimek@unicam.state.ne.us.

**SCHIMEK, JOHN BRADLEY,** music educator, musician; b. Houston, Tex., July 21, 1955; m. Pamela J. Schimek; 1 child, Joel. MusB in Edn., U. Wis., 1979; MusM in Double Bass Performance, Rice U., 1981; EdD, La Salle U., 1996; student, U. North Tex. Instr. music Sam Houston State U., 1979—82; dir. orch. Oshkosh Pub. Schs., 1982—86; dir. youth symphony U. Wis., Oshkosh, Wis., 1982—86; instr. music U. North Tex., 1986—92; from asst. prof. music to prof. Okla. City U., 1993—95, prof., 1999—. Adv. bd. Classen H.S. Arts, 1993—, De Vinci Inst., 2003—; lectr. in field. Contbr. articles to profl. jours.; musician: Okla. City Philharmonic. Named Outstanding Music Faculty, Okla. City U., 1997. Mem.: AAUP, Coll. Music Soc., Am. Fedn. Musicians, Okla. Music Educators Assn., Music Educators Nat. Conf., Internat. Soc. Bassists, Am. String Tchrs. Assn. Office: Okla City Univ 2501 N Blackwelder Ave Oklahoma City OK 73106

**SCHIMKE, DENNIS J.,** former state legislator; m. Olive Young, Dec. 1964 (dec. 1998); 3 children. BS in Ed., U. N.D., 1968, MS, 1972. Bison rancher, Coteau Hills, ND, 1987—; tchr. h.s. math. and physics LaMoure, N.D., 1975-2000; lectr. math. N.D. State U., 2001—; rep. Dist. 28 N.D. Ho. of Reps., 1991-93, rep. dist. 26, 1995-97, mem. edn. and agr. com., 1991—93, 1995—97. Founding bd. dirs. N.D. Buffalo Assn., 1991—95. Home: PO Box 525 Edgeley ND 58433-0525

**SCHIMMEL, PAUL REINHARD,** biochemist, biophysicist, educator; b. Hartford, Conn., Aug. 4, 1940; s. Alfred E. and Doris (Hudson) S.; m. Judith F. Ritz, Dec. 30, 1961; children: Kirsten, Katherine. AB, Ohio Wesleyan U., 1962; postgrad., Tufts U. Sch. Medicine, 1962-63, Mass. Inst. Tech., 1963-65, Cornell U., 1965-66, Stanford U., 1966-67, U. Calif., Santa Barbara, 1975-76; PhD, Mass. Inst. Tech., 1966; DSc (hon.), Ohio Wesleyan U., 1996. Asst. prof. biology and chemistry MIT, 1967-71, assoc. prof., 1971-76, prof. biochemistry and biophysics, 1976-92, John D. and Catherine T. MacArthur prof. biochemistry and biophysics, 1992-97; prof. Scripps Rsch. Inst. and The Skaggs Inst. for Chem. Biology, 1997-2001, Ernest and Jean Hahn prof. molecular biology and chemistry, 2001—. Mem. study sect. on physiol. chemistry NIH, 1975-79; indsl. cons. on enzymes and recombinant DNA; bd. dirs. Cubist Pharms., 1993-2002, Repligen Corp., Alkermes, Inc., Alaylam, Inc. Author: (with C. Cantor) Biophysical Chemistry, 3 vols., 1980; mem. editl. bd. Archives Biochemistry, Biophysics, 1976-80, Nucleic Acids Rsch., 1976-80, Jour. Biol. Chemistry, 1977-82, Biopolymers, 1979-88, Internat. Jour. Biol. Macromolecules, 1983-89, Trends in Biochem. Scis., 1984—, Biochemistry, 1989—, Accounts of Chem. Rsch., 1989-94, European Jour. Biochemistry, 1991-96, Protein Sci., 1991-94, Proc. Nat. Acad. Scis., 1993-99. Alfred P. Sloan fellow, 1970-72; recipient Emily M. Gray award Biophys.

Soc., 2000. Fellow AAAS, Am. Acad. Arts and Scis. (chmn. Amory prize com. 1995-96); mem. NAS (class II biochemistry sect. rep. 1995-96), Am. Philos. Soc., Am. Chem. Soc. (Pfizer award 1978, chmn. divsn. biol. chemistry 1984-85) Am. Soc. for Biochemistry and Molecular Biology (chmn. nominating com. 1990, awards com. 1995-97), Inst. Medicine, Ribonucleic Acid Soc. Office: The Scripps Rsch Inst 10550 N Torrey Pines Rd La Jolla CA 92037-1000

**SCHINDEL, DONALD MARVIN,** retired lawyer; b. Chgo., Jan. 5, 1932; s. Harry L. and Ann (Schiff) S.; m. Alice Martha Andrews, Apr. 24, 1960; children: Susan Yost, Judith Harris, Andrea Glickman. BS in Acctg., U. Ill., 1953; JD, U. Chgo., 1956. Ptnr. Sonnenschein, Nath & Rosenthal, Chgo., 1956-2000, ret., 2000. Author: Estate Administration and Tax Planning for Survivors, 1987, supplements, 1988-1996. Pres. United Way Highland Park-Highwood, Ill., 2000—03; v.p. campaign United Way of the North Shore, 2004—05; pres. Congregation Beth Or, Deerfield, Ill., 1983—85. Fellow Am. Coll. Trust and Estate Counsel; mem. Chgo. Estate Planning Coun. (Austin Fleming Disting. Svc. award 1999), ABA, Ill. Bar Assn., Chgo. Bar Assn. (chmn. probate practice com. 1981-82). Clubs: East Bank (Chgo.). Avocations: tennis, travel, bridge, golf, running. Home: 636 Rice St Highland Park IL 60035-5012

**SCHINDERLE, ROBERT FRANK,** retired hospital administrator; b. Mayville, Wis., Aug. 3, 1921; m. Elizabeth, June 23, 1949; children— David, Gary, Mary, Brian. BS, Marquette U., 1949; MS, Northwestern U., 1959. Asst. office mgr. Western Leather Co., Milw., 1949-51; mgr. bus. office St. Francis Hosp., Peoria, Ill., 1951-55; credit mgr. Mercy Hosp., Chgo., 1955-59, asst. to adminstr., 1957-58, controller, 1958-59, asst. adminstr., 1959-65, St. Joseph Hosp., Joliet, Ill., 1965-70, assoc. adminstr., 1970-71, adminstr., 1971-76, exec. dir. 1976-86; dir. corp. legis. affairs and devel. Franciscan Sisters Health Care Corp., Mokena, Ill., 1986-89, ret. Chmn. Areawide Hosp. Emergency Services Council. Bd. dirs. Region IX Health Systems Agy., Our Lady of Angels Retirement Home, Joliet, Joliet YMCA, St. Joseph Coll. Nursing, Joliet. Fellow Am. Coll. Health Care Execs. (life); mem. Am. Hosp. Assn., Ill. Hosp. Assn. (chmn. 1975-76), Ill. Hosp. Licensing Bd. (chmn. 1982-97, vice chmn. 1997-), Catholic Hosp. Assn. (dir.), Ill. Cath. Hosp. Assn. (chmn. 1972-73) Lodges: Rotary, Elks, KC. Roman Catholic. Home: 408 W Newkirk Dr Plainfield IL 60544-1838

**SCHINDLER, ALBERT ISADORE,** physicist, researcher; b. Pitts., June 24, 1927; s. Jonas and Esther (Nass) S.; m. Phyllis Irene Liberman, June 17, 1951; children— Janet Mae, Jerald Scott, Ellen Susan. BS, Carnegie Inst. Tech., 1947, MS, 1948, DSc, 1950. Research asst. Carnegie Inst. Tech., Pitts., 1947-50, research physicist, 1950-51; supervisory rsch. physicist Naval Rsch. Lab., Washington, 1951-75; assoc. dir. research for material sci. and component tech. Naval Research Lab., 1975-85; prof. materials engring. and physics Purdue U., West Lafayette, Ind., 1985-92, cons., 1992-97, dir. Ind. Ctr. for Innovative Superconductor Tech., 1988-91, dir. Midwest Superconductivity Consortium, 1990-91; dir. div. materials rsch. NSF, Washington, 1988-90; chief scientist Office Naval Rsch., Arlington, Va., 1997-99; cons., 1999—. Cons. in field. Recipient E.O. Hulburt award Naval Research Lab., 1956, Nat. Capitol award for applied sci., 1962, Pure Sci. award Naval Research Lab.-Sci. Research Soc. Am., 1965, award Washington Acad. Scis., 1965, USN Disting. Achievement in Sci. award, 1975, Alumni Merit award Carnegie Mellon U., 1976, Sr. Exec. Service award Dept. Navy, 1983, Superior Pub. Svc. award Dept. Navy, 1999. Fellow Am. Phys. Soc., Washington Acad. Scis.; mem. Sigma Xi. (dir.) Home: 6615 Sulky Ln Rockville MD 20852-4344 Personal E-mail: al.schindler@verizon.net.

**SCHINDLER, JO ANN,** librarian, director; b. A. U. Hawaii, Manoa; MLS, U. Calif., Berkeley. With San Francisco Pub. Libr. Sys., LA County Libr. Sys.; head Bus., Sci., and Tech. Sect. Hawaii State Pub. Libr. Sys., dir., state libr. Named Hawaii State Pub. Libr. Sys. Employee of Yr., 1999, MCI Cybrarian of Yr. for State of Hawaii. Mem.: ALA, Hawaii Libr. Assn. Office: Hawaii State Pub Libr Sys 235 S Beretania St Honolulu HI 96813*

**SCHINDLER, LAURA ANN,** piano teacher, accompanist; b. St. Louis, Aug. 17, 1943; d. Francis Joseph and Alice Binkley (Hurtgen) Schindler; m. John Charles Noto, Dec. 27, 1986. BM cum laude, Fontbonne Coll., St. Louis, 1970; MAT, Washington U., St. Louis, 1972; student, Ecole Normale de Musique, Paris, 1973-74. Nat. cert. tchr. of music; cert. Orff Schulwerk, Mozarteum Acad., Salzburg, Austria. Organist, choir dir. St. John's Basilica, St. Louis, 1971-73; piano tchr. Cmty. Music Schs., St. Louis, 1971-73, St. Louis Inst. Music, 1972-73; accompanist Robert McFerrin, Jr., N.Y.C., Chgo.,Springfield, St. Louis, 1974-77; piano tchr., Orff instr. St. Louis Conservatory, 1974-82; pvt. piano tchr. and accompanist St. Louis, 1982—. Vocal accompanist Affiliate Artist Program, St. Louis, 1977; accompanist MTNA West. Ctr. Divsn. Auditions, St. Louis, 1979, Forest Park C.C. Chorus, 1980-82, Ethical Soc. Chorus, 1980-83, Washington U. Music Sch., 1970-72; adjudicator piano competitions, Mo. and Ill., 1978—; clinician Piano Tchr. Workshops, Mo./Ill., 1979—. Contbr. articles to profl. jours.; performer Today Show, NBC, 1976, Capella Soloists Sunset concerts, 1976, Bicentennial Horizons of Am. Music, 1976, Rubinstein Music Club Meetings, 1997—, Benefit for Mo. Com. for Firearms Safety, 1982; performer, composer Am. Composers Concert, 1976. Recipient Mid-Am. Disting. Ind. Piano Tchr. award N.W., 1997, Disting. Piano Tchr. award Cedarhurst Chamber Music and Beethoven Soc., 1992; Acad. fellow Washington U., 1970-72. Mem.: Piano Tchrs. Round Table (pres. 1999—2001, exec. bd. 2001—05), Musical Diversions Soc. (bd. dirs. 1995—2005), St. Louis Area Music Tchrs. Assn. (v.p. for programs 1986—88, pres. 1988—92, chair nominating com. 1996—2000), Rubinstein Music Club. Democrat. Mem. Ethical Soc. Avocations: travel, walking, reading, eastern european folk dancing, ballroom dancing. Home: 7567 Lindbergh Dr Saint Louis MO 63117-2173

**SCHINDLER, TERI,** sports association executive; m. Mike Gorman, 1988. Grad. summa cum laude, U. Notre Dame, Ind., 1983. News/sports desk runner 1984 Summer Olympic Games, 1984; exec. prodr. women's basketball Conn. Pub. TV; mgr. Big East TV Network; dir. broadcasting NBA Entertainment, 1997—2004; v.p. programming, mktg. Nat. Basketball Assn. Entertainment, N.Y.C., 2004—. Freelance writer specializing in women's and environ. issues. Contbr. articles to newspapers including the Boston Globe. Nominee 8 Emmy awards for basketball, football; recipient Emmy award (New Eng. region), 1993, Emmy award, NBC Sports, Olympics Sydney, 2000; scholar, Rotary scholar, 1983. Mem.: Phi Beta Kappa. Home: 5 Truesdale Lake Dr South Salem NY 10590-1317

**SCHINDLER, WILLIAM STANLEY,** retired public relations executive; b. Detroit, Jan. 4, 1933; s. William Henry and Katherine (Schilling) S. Student, Wayne State U., 1950-53. Sr. v.p. Campbell-Ewald Co., Warren, Mich., 1968-85; v.p. pub. rels. Detroit Med. Ctr., 1985-92; interim v.p. Wayne State U., Detroit, 1993. Cons. to bus., univs., and founds.; v.p. Sandusky Pub. Co., Mich. Editor: Progress Report-New Detroit, Inc, 1969. Past mem. Detroit Hist. Commn., Detroit Fire Commn.; chmn. Detroit CSC; mem. Gov.'s Sesquicentennial Commn., Peoria, Ariz. Fire Pension Bd., Pers. Bd., Hist. Preservation Com.; mem. trans. needs assessment com.; bd. dirs. Adult Well-Being Svcs., Sacred Heart Rehab. Ctr., Brush Park Devel. Authority, Harper Hosp. Aux. With U.S. Army, 1954—56. Decorated Commendation Medal with pendant. Mem. Pub. Rels. Soc. Am., Adcraft Club Detroit, Detroit Press Club, Sons Whiskey Rebellion, Recess Club, Univ. Club, Detroit Athletic Club, Prismatic Club, Box 12 Club, Heard Mus. Coun. Home: 8741 W Wescott Dr Peoria AZ 85382-8773

**SCHINK, JAMES HARVEY,** lawyer; b. Oak Park, Ill., Oct. 2, 1943; s. Norbert F. and Gwendolyn H. (Hummel) S.; m. Lisa Wilder Haskell, Jan. 1, 1972 (div. 1990); children— David, Caroline, Elizabeth; m. April Townley, Aug. 14, 1982. BA, Yale U., 1965; JD, 1968. Bar: Ill. 1968, Colo. 1982. Assoc. Sidley & Austin, Chgo. 1968; law clk. to judge U.S. Ct. Appeals, Chgo., 1968-69; assoc. Kirkland & Ellis, Chgo., 1969-72, ptnr., 1972—. Sustaining fellow Art Inst. Chgo. Mem. ABA, Ill. Bar Assn., Chgo. Bar Assn.,

Chgo. Club, Saddle and Cycle Club, Mid-Am. Club, Econ. Club of Chgo., Sonnenalp Golf Club, Vail Racquet Club, Yale Club of Chgo., Racquet Club Chgo., Game Creek Club. Republican. Presbyterian. Home: 1530 N State Pkwy Chicago IL 60610-1614 Office: Kirkland & Ellis 200 E Randolph St Ste 6100 Chicago IL 60601-6436 Office Phone: 312-861-2258. Business E-Mail: jschink@kirkland.com.

**SCHINK, ROBERT KELLY,** sales executive; b. Joplin, Mo., Aug. 16, 1921; s. Domonic Charles and Cleo Kelly Schink; life ptnr. James B. Battle. A. Joplin Jr. Coll., 1942; BBA, Western Res. U., Cleve., 1948. Stock contr. RCA TV Svc. Co., Cleve., 1948—57, office mgr., 1957—58; salesman Fullber Brush Co., Plantation, Fla., 1958—. Sgt. USAF, 1942—45, ETO. Named to Honor Roll of Vets., World War II Meml., Washington, D-Day Meml., New Orleans. Mem.: Hollywood Stamp Club. Democrat. Avocations: stamp collecting/philately, travel, theater. Home and Office: 921 W County Club Cir Plantation FL 33317

**SCHIRG, BRANDON MICHAEL,** lawyer; s. Glenn Richard and Carolyn Jeanne Schirg; m. Lori Leigh Sweeney, June 5, 2004. Student, U.S. Naval Acad., Annapolis, Md., 1993—95; BS in Fin., U. Tenn., Knoxville, 1998; JD, U. Tenn. Coll. Law, 2001. Lic.: Tenn. 2001, US Dist. Ct.: (mid. dist.) Tenn. 2001. Atty. Sherrard & Roe, PLC, Nashville, 2001—03, Waller, Lansden, Dortch & Davis PLLC 2003—. Mem. Number One Vol. Fire Dept., Gallatin, Tenn., 1993—2004. Mem.: Am. Health Lawyers Assn. (assoc.), ABA (assoc.), Nashville Bar Assn. (assoc.), Tenn. Bar Assn. (assoc.). Office: Waller Lansden Dortch & Davis PLLC 511 Union St Ste 2700 Nashville TN 37219

**SCHIRMEISTER, CHARLES F.,** retired lawyer; b. Jersey City, June 18, 1929; s. Charles F. and Louise P. (Schneider) Schirmeister; m. Barbara Jean Fredericks, Feb. 9, 1952; children: Pamela, Charles Bradford. BA, U. Mich., 1951; LLB, Fordham U., 1956. Bar: N.Y. 1956, U.S. Dist. Ct. (so. dist.) N.Y. 1961, U.S. Ct. Appeals (2d cir.) 1961, U.S. Supreme Ct. 1961. Asst. dist. atty. New York County, N.Y., 1956-61; assoc. Thelen, Reid & Priest, N.Y.C., 1961-71, ptnr., 1971-94; ret., 1994. Trustee Ocean Grove (N.J.) Camp Meeting Assn.; deacon Cmty. Congl. Ch., Short Hills, N.J. Capt. USMC, 1951—53. Mem.: Canoe Brook Country Club (Summit, NJ), Univ. Club (NYC), Sigma Alpha Epsilon. Republican. Avocations: tennis, oenology, golf. Home: 15 Beechcroft Rd Short Hills NJ 07078-1648

**SCHIRMER, ANDREW L.,** application developer; b. Independence, Mo., Mar. 1, 1950; BA, Carleton Coll., 1972. Sys. analyst Sperry Univac, UNISYS, Wellesley, Mass., 1980—84; sr. software engr. Computer Corp. Am., Cambridge, Mass., 1984—87; sys. arch. Lotus Devel. Corp., Cambridge, Mass., 1987—90, product design arch., 1990—98; sr. software designer and strategist IBM, Westford, Mass., 1998—. Composer: (instrumental music cd) One Score, (piano score) Day of Joy, (baritone solo with piano accompaniment) The Emperor of Ice Cream; musician: (Tanglewood Festival Chorus) Mahler's 8th Symphony, 1981—82, 9 Below O degrees, 1973—79. Bd. dirs. Unitarian Universalist Congregation, Andover, Mass., 2003—05, Chorus pro Musica, Boston, 1981—89. Mem.: Assn. for Computing Machinery. Liberal. Achievements include patents pending in field; patents in field. Avocations: music composition and performance, photography, graphic arts, model railroading. E-mail: aschirme@us.ibm.com.

**SCHIRRA, WALTER MARTY, JR., (WALLY SCHIRRA),** business consultant, retired astronaut; b. Hackensack, NJ, Mar. 12, 1923; s. Walter Marty and Florence (Leach) S.; m. Josephine Cook Fraser, Feb. 23, 1946; children: Walter Marty III, Suzanne Karen. Student, Newark Coll. Engring., 1940-42; BS, U.S. Naval Acad., 1945; D. Astronautics (hon.), Lafayette Coll., U. So. Calif., N.J. Inst. Tech. Commd. ensign US Navy, 1945, advanced through grades to capt., 1965; designated naval aviator, 1948; service aboard battle cruiser Alaska, 1945-46; service with 7th Fleet, 1946; assigned Fighter Squadron 71, 1948-51; exchange pilot 154th USAF Fighter Bomber Squadron, 1951; engaged in devel. Sidewinder missile China Lake, Calif., 1952-54; project pilot F7U-3 Cutlass; also instr. pilot F7U-3 Cutlass and FJ3 Fury, 1954-56; ops. officer Fighter Squadron 124, U.S.S. Lexington, 1956-57; assigned Naval Air Safety Officer Sch., 1957, Naval Air Test Ctr., 1958-59; engaged in suitability devel. work F4H, 1958-59; joined Project Mercury, man-in-space, NASA, 1959; pilot spacecraft Sigma 7 in 6 orbital flight, Oct. 1962; in charge operations and tng. Astronaut Office, 1964-69; command pilot Gemini 6 which made rendezvous with target, Gemini 7, Dec. 1965; comdr. 11 day flight Apollo 7, 1968; ret., 1969; pres. Regency Investors, Inc., Denver, 1969-70; chmn., chief exec. officer ECCO Corp., Englewood, Colo., 1970-73; chmn. Sernco, Inc., 1973-74; with Johns-Manville Corp., Denver, 1974-77; v.p. devel. Goodwin Cos., Inc., Littleton, Colo., 1978-79; ind. cons., 1979-80. Dir. Kimberly Clark, 1983-91. Decorated D.F.C.(3), Air medal (2), Navy D.S.M.; recipient Distinguished Service medal (2) NASA, Exceptional Service medal. Fellow Am. Astronautical Soc., Soc. Exptl. Test Pilots. Home and Office: PO Box 73 Rancho Santa Fe CA 92067-0073*

**SCHISGAL, MURRAY,** playwright; b. NYC, Nov. 25, 1926; s. Abraham and Irene (Sperling) S.; m. Reene Schapiro, June 29, 1958; children: Jane, Zachary. Student, Bklyn. Conservatory of Music, 1948, L.I. U., 1950; LLB, Bklyn. Law Sch., 1953; BA, New Sch. Social Research, 1959. Playwright, screenwriter and prodr. movies, TV and theatre. Author: The Typists and The Tiger, London, 1960, N.Y.C., 1963, Ducks and Lovers, London, 1961, Knit One, Purl Two, Boston, 1963, Luv (One of the Best Plays of 1964-65), London, 1963, N.Y.C., 1964, Fragments, Windows and other plays, 1965, Best Short Plays, 1981, 83, 85; contbr. to Best Short American Plays 1994-1995; original TV plays The Love Song of Barney Kempinski, 1966, Natasha Kovolina Pipishinski, 1976; off-Broadway Fragments, 1967, The Basement, 1967; Jimmy Shine, 1968, 69, Shooting Towards the Millinneum, 1997, Playtime, 1997; Broadway The Chinese, N.Y.C., 1970 (pub. in Best Short Plays of the World Theatre 1973), Dr. Fish, 1970, An American Millionaire, 1974, All Over Town, 1974 (pub. Best Plays 1974-75); screenplay The Tiger Makes Out, 1967, The Pushcart Peddlers, prod. off-off-Broadway, 1979 (pub. as The Pushcart Peddlers, The Flatulist and other plays); novel Days and Nights of a French Horn Player, 1980, Walter and the Flatulist; prod. off-Broadway The Downstairs Boys, 1980, The Songs of War, 1989; prod. regional theatre A Need for Brussels Sprouts, 1981, Play Time, Denver Ctr. Theatre, 1991, The Japanese Foreign Trade Minister, Cleve. Playhouse, 1992, 74 Georgia Ave., 1992, Circus Life, 1992; prod. Broadway Twice Around the Park, 1982; Other Plays, 1983, Closet Madness and Other Plays, 1984, Popkins, Paris, 1990, Play Time, 1991, The Songs of War, 1989; prod. Off Broadway The New Yorkers, 1984, Circus Life, 1995; prodr. Extensions, 1994; co-author: screenplay Tootsie (Winner Los Angeles Film Critics, N.Y. Film Critics, Nat. Soc. Film Critics, Writers Guild Am. award for best comedy); author Luv and Other Plays, 1983, The Rabbi and the Toyota Dealer, 1985, Jealousy, There are No Sacher Tortes in Our Society, 1985, Old Wine in a New Bottle, 1987, Road Show, 1987, Man Dangling, 1988, Oatmeal and Kisses, 1990, (with others) Best Short American Plays of 1991, 92-93, Sexaholics and Other Plays, 1995, Extensions, 1994, Circus Life, 1995, The Artist and The Model (Best Am. Short Play), 1994-95, Play Time (Published by Dramatists Play Svc., 1997), The Man Who Couldn't Stop Crying (Best Am. Short Plays, 1997-98); We Are Family, 2002, produced regional theaters and Berlin undertitle Warum Nicht and Prague, 2003; produced in Rome Regret Undertitle Tutto in Famiglia, 2004; produced in Paris under title La Regard, 2002; 74 Georgia Ave. produced in regional theater, 2002; First Love (Best Am. Short Plays 1991-2000); prodr. feature films A Walk on the Moon, 1999, cable TV) The Devil's Arithmetic, 1999, Boys and Girls, 2000, Clubland, 2000 (also exec. prodr.); exec. prodr. (cable TV) A Separate Peace, 2003. Recipient Vernon Rice award outstanding achievement off-Broadway Theatre, 1963; Outer Circle award Outstanding Theatre, 1963; recipient Outstanding Playwright, 1963. Office: care Arthur B Greene 101 Park Ave 26th Fl New York NY 10178-0002

**SCHISSEL, DAVID PAUL,** physicist, director; s. Paul O. and Freda K. Schissel. BS, U. Wis., 1979; MS, MIT, 1982. Rsch. scientist DIII-D Nat. Fusion Facility, San Diego, 1982—97, mgr. data analysis applications group, 1997—; dir. advanced imagery lab. Gen. Atomics, San Diego, 2001—. Vis.

scientist Centre D'Etudes Nucleaires de Cadarache, France, 1993—94, Culham Lab., Abingdon, England, 1993—94. Contbr. articles to profl. jours. Tech. com. La Jolla (Calif.) Country Day Sch., 1995—2005. Recipient Excellence in Sci. Edn. award, NSTA, 1994. Fellow: Am. Phys. Soc. (life; mem. nomination com. 2004—). Achievements include design of mobile high-resolution military command and control system; research in energy confinement scalings for the international thermonuclear experimental reactor; design of ultra-high resolution optical camera; research in advanced collaborative environments for magnetic fusion research. Office: General Atomics 3550 General Atomics Court San Diego CA 92121 Office Phone: 858-455-3387. Personal E-mail: schissel@alum.mit.edu.

**SCHIZER, DAVID MICHAEL,** dean, law educator; b. Bklyn. s. Zevie Baruch and Hazel Gerber Schizer; 2 children. BA, Yale U., 1990, MA in hist., 1990, JD, 1993. Law clerk for Judge Alex Kozinski US Ct. Appeals, 1993—94; for Justice Ruth Bader Ginsburg US Supreme Ct., 1994—95; tax law atty. Davis Polk & Wardwell, NYC, 1995—98; prof. Columbia U., NYC, 1998—, Wilbur H. Friedman prof. tax law, 1998—2004, dean and Lucy G. Moses prof. law, chair Columbia appointment com., 2002—04. Chair Columbia U. Clerkship Com., 2000—02. Exec. editor Yale Law Jour.; contbr. articles to law jours. Named one of Top 40 Lawyers Under 40, Nat. Law Jour., 2005; recipient Willis L.M. Reese Prize for Excellence in Tchg., 2002. Mem.: Tax Forum, Tax Club, N.Y. State Bar Assn. Tax Sec. (exec. com., co-chair Com. on Fin. Insts.). Office: Columbia U Sch Law Dean's Office 8th Fl Jerome L Greene Hall 435 W 116th St New York NY 10027 Office Phone: 212-854-2675. Office Fax: 212-854-9740. E-mail: dschiz@law.columbia.edu.

**SCHIZER, ZEVIE BARUCH,** lawyer; b. Bklyn., Dec. 19, 1928; s. David and Bertha (Rudavsky) S.; m. Hazel Gerber, Aug. 23, 1962; children: Deborah Gail, Miriam Anne, David Michael. BA magna cum laude, NYU, 1950; JD, Yale U., 1953. Bar: N.Y. 1954, U.S. Dist. Ct. (so. and ea. dist.) N.Y. 1959, U.S. Ct. Appeals (2d cir.) 1959, U.S. Supreme Ct. 1959. Assoc. Guzik & Boukstein, N.Y.C., 1953-54; teaching fellow NYU Sch. Law, 1954-55; assoc. Philips, Nizer, Benjamin & Krim, N.Y.C., 1955-56, Aranow, Brodsky, Einhorn & Dann, N.Y.C., 1956-57; asst. counsel iqn. inquiry Appellate Divsn. 2nd Dept., Bklyn., 1957-62; assoc. Hays, Porter, Spanier & Curtis, N.Y.C., 1963-68, ptnr., 1968-85; sec. United Aircraft Products, Inc., Dayton, Ohio, 1970-83; ptnr. Schizer & Schizer, N.Y.C., 1985—. Trustee Bklyn. Pub. Libr., 1966—2003, pres., 1985—88, N.Y. Young Dem. Club, N.Y.C., 1960—61; trustee East Midwood Jewish Ctr., Bklyn., 1991—, pres., 2003—06; dir. N.Y. met. region United Synagogue Conservative Judaism, N.Y.C., 2004—. Mem. N.Y. County Lawyers Assn. (mem. profl. ethics com., mem. com. on profl. discipline), Phi Beta Kappa. Democrat. Jewish. Home: 1134 E 23rd St Brooklyn NY 11210-4519 Office: Schizer & Schizer 3 New York Plz New York NY 10004-2442 Office Phone: 212-943-3340.

**SCHJELDAHL, PETER,** poet, critic; b. Fargo, N.D., 1942; Student, Carleton Coll., The New Sch. Art critic New York Sunday Times, N.Y.C., 1970-75; with The Village Voice, N.Y.C., 1966, art critic, 1981-82, 1990—98, Vanity Fair, N.Y.C., 1983-84, Seven Days, The New Yorker, 1998—. Lectr. in field; curator in field. Author: (poetry collections) White Country, 1968, An Adventure of the Thought Police, 1971, Dreams, 1973, Since 1964: New and Selected Poems, 1978, Sun, (books) Hydrogen Jukebox: Selected Writings of Peter Schjeldahl, 1978-1990, 1991, The Seven Days Art Columns, 1991, Columns and Catalogues, 1994; co-founder poetry mag. Mother; contbg. editor Art in America; contbr. articles to art jours. including Artforum, Art News, Art Internat., Art & Antiques, Camera Arts, Am. Craft and others Recipient Frank Jewett Mather award Coll. Art Assn., 1980, grant, John Simon Guggenheim Meml. Found. Office: The New Yorker 4 Times Sq New York NY 10036-6592

**SCHJERVEN, ROBERT E.,** manufacturing executive; With McQuay-Perfex Inc., Trane Co.; v.p. mktg. and engring. Heatcraft Inc. (subs. Lennox Internat. Inc.), 1986—88, v.p., gen. mgr., 1988—91; pres., COO Armstrong Air Conditioning Inc., 1991—95, Lennox Industries Inc. (subs. Lennox Internat. Inc.), 1995—2000; COO Lennox Internat. Inc., 2000—01, CEO, 2001—. Office: 2140 Lake Park Blvd Richardson TX 75080*

**SCHLACKS, STEPHEN MARK,** lawyer; b. Pitts., Kans., Oct. 13, 1955; BA, Austin Coll., Sherman, Tex., 1978; MBA, U. Dallas, 1982; JD, Baylor U., 1986. Bar: Tex. 1987, U.S. Dist. Ct. (so. dist.) Tex. 1987, (no., ea. and we. dists.) Tex. 1988, U.S. Ct. Appeals (5th cir.) 1987, (8th cir.) 1989, U.S. Supreme Ct. 1990; bd. cert. personal injury trial law Tex. Bd. Legal Specialization. In mgmt. Johnson & Johnson Products, Inc., Sherman, 1978-84; assoc. atty. Wetzel & Assocs., The Woodlands, Tex., 1986-92; ptnr. Hope, Causey & Schlacks, P.C., Conroe, Tex., 1992-96, Law Office of Stephen M. Schlacks, The Woodlands, Tex., 1996-99, Schlacks, Harrison & Cox PLLC, The Woodlands, 1999—2003; prin. The Schlacks Law Firm, PLLC, The Woodlands, Tex., 2003—. Leon Jaworski scholar, 1984, Harcourt Brace Jovanovich scholar, 1986. Mem. Montgomery County Bar Assn., Sigma Iota Epsilon, Pi Gamma Mu. Republican. Presbyterian. Home: 66 Racing Cloud Ct The Woodlands TX 77381-5203 Office: 2202 Timberloch Pl Ste 107 The Woodlands TX 77380-1163 Office Phone: 281-363-3977. E-mail: schlacks@shcpllc.com.

**SCHLAFER, DONALD HUGHES,** veterinary pathologist; b. Sidney, N.Y., July 15, 1948; s. Donald Hughes and Mildred (Gamewell) S.; Jr.; m. Judith Ann Appleton, Aug. 2, 1980; children: Nathan James, Russell Matthew. BS, Cornell U., 1971, MS, 1975; DVM, N.Y. State Coll. Vet. Medicine, Ithaca, 1974; PhD, Coll. Vet. Medicine, Athens, Ga., 1982. Diplomate Am. Coll. Vet. Pathologists, Am. Coll. Theriogenologists (exam. com 1991-95), Am. Coll. Vet. Microbiologists. Gen. practice vet. medicine Guilderland Animal Hosp., Altamont, NY, 1975-77; resident dept. vet. pathology U. Ga., Athens, 1977-79; rsch. pathologist USDA Plum Island Animal Disease Ctr., Greenport, NY, 1975-82; asst. prof. dept. vet. pathology Cornell U., Ithaca, 1982-88, assoc. prof., 1988-97, prof. comparative reproductive pathology, 1997—, dir. Bovine Rsch. Ctr., 1982-91. Vis. fellow Oxford (Eng.) U., 1990—91; vis. pathologist San Diego Zoo, 2003; vis. prof. U. Padua, Italy, 2004; cons. in field. Contbr. articles to profl. publs. Named Theriogenologist of Yr., 2004. Mem. AVMA, Soc. for Theriogenology (exec. com. 1993-96). Office: T6020 Coll Vet Medicine Cornell U Ithaca NY 14853 Office Phone: 607-253-3352. Business E-Mail: dhs2@cornell.edu.

**SCHLAFF, BARBARA E.,** lawyer; b. Detroit, Mar. 21, 1950; BA, Brandeis U., 1971; attended. U. Mich. Law Sch.; JD, Boston Coll., 1974. Bar: D.C. 1979, Md. 1980. Ptnr., Employee Benefits, Taxation practices Venable LLP, Balt. Mem. adv. com. Univ. Balt. Law Sch. Officer Ctr. for Jewish Edn.; trustee, past v.p. Har Sinai Congregation. Mem. ABA, Md. State Bar Assn., D.C. Bar, Bar Assn. Balt. City. Office: Venable LLP 1800 Mercantile Bank & Trust Bldg 2 Hopkins Plz Baltimore MD 21201 Office Phone: 410-244-7494. Office Fax: 410-244-7742. Business E-Mail: beschlaff@venable.com.

**SCHLAFLY, HUBERT JOSEPH, JR.,** communications executive; b. St. Louis, Aug. 14, 1919; s. Hubert J. and Mary Ross (Parker) S.; m. Leona Martin, June 12, 1944. BSEE, U. Notre Dame, 1941; postgrad., Syracuse U., 1946—47; DHL (hon.), Sacred Heart U., 2003; LHD (hon.). Electronics engr. Gen. Electric Co., Schenectady, 1941-44, Syracuse, 1946-47; project engr. radiation lab. MIT, 1944-45; dir. TV rsch. 20th Century-Fox Film Corp., N.Y.C., 1947-51; founder, v.p. Teleprompter Corp., N.Y.C., 1951-74, pres., 1971-72, exec. v.p. tech. devel., 1972-74; pres. Transponder Corp., Greenwich, 1977-86; chmn., CEO Portel Services Corp., 1984-86; chmn., pres. Portel Services Network, Inc., 1987-91, chmn. bd., 1991-97, ret., 1998. Cons. in field; industry coord., chmn. exec. com., cable tech. adv. com. FCC, 1972—75; adviser com. telecommt. Nat. Acad. Engring.; adviser Sloan Comm. Cable Comms.; mem. engring. adv. coun. U. Notre Dame, 1977, vice chmn., 83, chmn., 84; bd. dirs., sec. Milbrook Corp., 1994—2001; lectr. in field. Author: Computer in the Living Room, 1977. Bd. govs. Milbrook Club, 1993-98. Recipient Engring. Honor award, U. Notre Dame, 1976,

Emmy award, NATAS, 1992, 1999, Sci. Initiative award, Sacred Heart U., 1997, Discovery award, 2001, David Sarnoff citation award, Radio Club Am., 2004. Fellow Soc. Motion Picture and TV Engrs.; mem. IEEE (life, Delmer Ports award 1979), Nat. Cable TV Assn. (chmn. standards com. 1965-69, chmn. domestic satellite com. 1971-73, chmn. future svcs. com. 1972, assns. com. 1981, Outstanding Tech. Achievements award 1974), Electronic Industries Assn. (chmn. broadband cable sect. 1971-73, founding chmn. broadband comm. com.), Soc. Cable TV Engrs. (sr.), Fairfield Found. (hon.); named Notre Dame alumni Man of Yr., 1992, Rotary (pres. Greenwich club 1991-92), Knights of Malta, Knight St. Gregory the Great. Roman Catholic. Achievements include patents in field. Home and Office: 27 Orchard Dr Greenwich CT 06830-6711 E-mail: hschlafly@aol.com.

**SCHLAFLY, PHYLLIS STEWART,** writer; b. St. Louis, Aug. 15, 1924; d. John Bruce and Odile (Dodge) Stewart; m. Fred Schlafly, Oct. 20, 1949; children: John F., Bruce S., Roger S., Phyllis Liza Forshaw, Andrew L., Anne V. BA, Washington U., St. Louis, 1944, JD, 1978; MA, Harvard U., 1945; LLD, Niagara U., 1976. Bar: Ill. 1979, DC 1984. Mo. 1985, U.S. Supreme Ct. 1987. Syndicated columnist Copley News Svc., 1976—. Broadcaster Spectrum, CBS Radio Network, 1973—78; commentator Matters of Opinion sta. WBBM-AM, Chgo., 1973—75, Cable TV News Network, 1980—83; pres. Eagle Forum, 1975—. Author, pub.: Phyllis Schlafly Report, 1967—; author: A Choice Not an Echo, 1964, The Gravediggers, 1964, Strike From Space, 1965, Safe Not Sorry, 1967, The Betrayers, 1968, Mindszenty The Man, 1972, Kissinger on the Couch, 1975, Ambush at Vladivostok, 1976, The Power of the Positive Woman, 1977, First Reader, 1994, Turbo Reader, 2001, Feminist Fantasies, 2003, The Supremacists: The Tyranny of Judges and How to Stop It, 2004; editor: (book) Child Abuse in the Classroom, 1984, Pornography's Victims, 1987, Equal Pay for Unequal Work, 1984, Who Will Rock the Cradle, 1989, Stronger Families or Bigger Government, 1990, Meddlesome Mandate: Rethinking Family Leave, 1991. Del. Rep. Nat. Conv., 1956, 1964, 1968, 1984, 1988, 1992, 1996, 2004, alt., 1960, 1980, 2000; 1st v.p. Nat. Fedn. Rep. Women, 1964—67; nat. chmn. Stop ERA, 1972—; mem. Ronald Reagan's Def. Policy Adv. Group, 1980, Commn. on Bicentennial of U.S. Constn., 1985—91, Adminstrv. Conf. U.S., 1983—86; pres. Ill. Fedn. Rep. Women, 1960—64; mem. Ill. Commn. on Status of Women, 1975—85. Named Woman of Achievement in Pub. Affairs, St. Louis Globe-Democrat, 1963; named one of 10 Most Admired Women in World, Good Housekeeping poll, 1977—90, 100 Most Important Women of 20th Century, Ladies Home Jour., 1998; recipient 10 Honor awards, Freedom Found., Brotherhood award, NCCJ, 1975. Mem.: DAR (nat. chmn. Am. history 1965—68, nat. chmn. bicentennial com. 1967—70, nat. chmn. nat. def. 1977—80, 1983—95), ABA, Ill. Bar Assn., Phi Beta Kappa, Pi Sigma Alpha. Office: Eagle Forum 7800 Bonhomme Ave Saint Louis MO 63105-1906 Office Phone: 314-721-1213. E-mail: phyllis@eagleforum.org.

**SCHLAGEL, DEBORAH "DEVO" LYNN,** chemist, materials scientist; b. Sante Fe, N.Mex., Feb. 18, 1970; d. Paul and Mary Ann Gray; m. Donald Henry Schlagel; children: Jordan Corrina, Taylor Rose. BS with honors, No. Ariz. U., 1993; MSc in Inorganic and Analytical Chemistry, Iowa State U., 1997. Asst. scientist II Ames Lab., Ames, Iowa, 1997—. Contbr. articles to profl. jours. Ch. Of Christ, Christian. Avocations: cooking, sewing, gardening, hiking, travel. Office: Ames Lab 110 Metals Develop Ames IA 50011 Office Phone: 515-294-3924. E-mail: schlagel@iastate.edu.

**SCHLAGEL, RICHARD H.,** retired philosophy educator; b. Springfield, Mass., Nov. 22, 1925; BS in Pre-Med cum laude, Springfield Coll., 1949; MA in Philosophy, Boston U., 1952, PhD, 1955. Instr. philosophy Coll. of Wooster, 1954-55; instr. Clark U., 1955-56; asst. prof. George Washington U., 1956-62, assoc. prof., 1962-68, prof., 1968—, chmn. dept., 1965-69, 70-71, 77-83, named Elton prof. philosophy, 1986, Elton prof. emeritus, 2001—. Sabbatical, Paris, with travel throughout Europe, 1962-63, 69-70, 76-77, 83-84, 90-91. Author: The Vanquished Gods: Science, Religion, and the Nature of Belief, 2001, From Myth to Modern Mind: A Study of the Origins and Growth of Scientific Thought, vol. 1, Theogomy through Ptolemy, 1995, vol. 2, Copernicus through Quantum Mechanics, 1996; Contextual Realism: A Metaphysical Framework for Modern Science, 1986; contbr. articles and reviews to profl. jours. Borden Parker Browne fellow, 1953-54. Mem. AAUP, Am. Philos. Assn., Washington Philosophy Club (v.p. 1964-65, pres. 1965-66). Personal E-mail: richschlagel@aol.com.

**SCHLAGENHAUF, SHERRY DENISE,** music educator; b. Spruce Pine, N.C., Oct. 9, 1961; d. Billy J and Glenna P Buchanan; m. Claude Schlagenhauf, June 9, 1984; children: Lauren Nicole, Brittany Ann. MusB, Mars Hill Coll., 1983. Tchr. music Burnsville Elem. Sch., NC, 1983—84, Tuttle Mid. Sch., Maiden, NC, 1984—88; dir. choir Trinity United Ch. of Christ, Conover, NC, 1984—89; tchr. Blackburn Mid. Sch., Newton, NC, 1988—95, Fred T. Ford H.S., Newton, 1988—95; tchr. music Blackburn Elem. Sch., Newton, 1995—. Recipient Tchr. of the Yr., Tuttle Mid. Sch., 1987—88. Mem.: Music Edn. Assn. Home: 1132 Brookstone Dr Hickory NC 28602 Office Phone: 704-462-1344.

**SCHLAGETER, ROBERT WILLIAM,** museum administrator; b. Streator, Ill., May 10, 1925; s. Herman Pete and Ida (Ladtkow) S.; divorced; children— David Michael, Robert William Diploma, Karl Ruprecht Univ., Heidelberg, Fed. Republic Germany, 1950; BA, U. Ill., 1950, MFA, 1957. Asst. prof. U. Tenn., Knoxville, 1952-58; dir. Mint Mus. Art, Charlotte, N.C., 1958-66; assoc. dir. Downtown Gallery, N.Y.C. 1966, Ackland Art Ctr., N.C., Chapel Hill, 1967-76, dir. Cummer Gallery Art, Jacksonville, Fla., 1976-92, dir. emeritus, 1992—. Fine arts cons. corp. and pvt. collecting, 1993—. Author: (exhbn. catalogue) Winslow Homer's Florida, George Inness' Florida, Martin Johnson Heade Florida, Robert Henri-George Bellows. Served with U.S. Army, 1943-45, ETO Home: 45 Katherine Blvd Apt 406 Palm Harbor FL 34684-3649

**SCHLAIN, BARBARA ELLEN,** lawyer; b. NYC, May 28, 1948; d. William and Evelyn (Youdelman) S. BA, Wellesley Coll., 1969; MA, Columbia U., 1970; JD, Yale U., 1973. Bar: N.Y. 1974, U.S. Dist. Ct. (so. dist.) N.Y. 1974, U.S. Ct. Appeals (2d cir.) 1975, U.S. Dist. Ct. (ea. dist.) N.Y. 1977. Assoc. firm Donovan Leisure Newton & Irvine, N.Y.C., 1973-76, Graubard Moskovitz McGoldrick Dannett & Horowitz, N.Y.C., 1976-79; atty. McGraw-Hill, Inc., N.Y.C., 1979-80, asst. gen. counsel, 1980-86, v.p., assoc. gen. counsel, asst. sec., 1986—. Sec. proprietary rights com. Info. Industry Assn., 1982-83. Author: outlines Practicing Law Inst., 1983, 84, 85, 86, 88; contbr. numerous articles to profl. jours. Bd. dirs., v.p., sec. Dance Rsch. Found., N.Y.C., 1983-86, chmn., 1986-98. Phi Beta Kappa scholar, Durant scholar Wellesley Coll., 1967-69. Mem. ABA, Assn. Am. Pubs. (lawyers com. 1979—), Assn. Bar City N.Y. (comm. law com. 1985-88). Office: The McGraw-Hill Companies Inc 1221 Avenue Of The Americas New York NY 10020-1095

**SCHLECHTE, DEBORAH WHITLEY,** music educator; d. Norwood and Shirley Whitley; m. Gene Schlechte, Sept. 6, 1980; children: Jennifer, Christopher. BS in Music Edn., U. N.C., Greensboro, 1978. Dir. choral music Wilson County Pub. Sch., NC, 1978—80, Brunswick County Pub. Sch., Leland, NC, 1981—84; dir. music Naval Postgrad. Sch., Monterey, Calif., 1985—86, Seaville UMC, Seaville, NJ, 1987—90, NATO Base Chapel, Keflavik, Iceland, 1990—92; dir. mid. sch. choral music Prince William County Sch., Dale City, Va., 1994—2004; dir. music Woodbridge Youth Chorale, Manassas, 1995—98; judge All-State Chorus, Va., 1995—; mem. Gifted Edn. Adv. Bd., Prince Williams County, Va., 1992—97. Vice-chmn. Wilson County Dem. Party, NC, 1978—80; basketball rep. Osbourn Pk. Booster Club, Manassas, Va., 2003—; mem. youth salute exec. bd. Prince William County, 2003—. Mem.: Am. Choral Dir. Assn., Music Educators Nat. Conf. Republican. Baptist. Avocations: cooking, basketball, gardening, decorating. Office: Parkside Mid Sch 8602 Mathis Ave Manassas VA 20110

**SCHLEGEL, FRED EUGENE,** lawyer; b. Indpls., July 24, 1941; s. Fred George and Dorothy (Bruce) S.; m. Jane Wessels, Aug. 14, 1965; children: Julia, Charles, Alexandra. BA, Northwestern U., 1963; JD with distinction, U. Mich., 1966. Bar: Ind. 1966. Assoc. lawyer Baker & Daniels, Indpls., 1966-72, ptnr., 1972—; vice chmn. Meridian St. Preservation Commn., Indpls., 1975-90. Contbr. articles to profl. jours. Chmn. Pub. Schs. Edn. Found., Indpls., 1988—90; pres. Festival Music Soc., 1974—75, 1979, 1986—87; bd. dirs. Indpls. Symphony Orch., chmn., 2002—04; bd. dir. Arts Coun., Indpls, 1996—2002. Mem. ABA, Ind. Bar Assn., Energy Bar Assn., Northwestern U. Alumni Club Indpls. (pres. 1992-94), Northwestern U. Alumni Assn. (bd. dirs. 2002-). Republican. Episcopalian. Office: Baker and Daniels 300 N Meridian St Ste 2700 Indianapolis IN 46204-1782 Office Phone: 317-237-1410. Business E-Mail: fred.schlegel@bakerd.com.

**SCHLEGEL, JOHN FREDERICK,** management consultant, personal trainer; b. Ogden, Utah, Dec. 18, 1944; s. Max Joseph and Mary Georgia (Whittaker) S.; m. Priscilla Mary Hecht, Sept. 8, 1967. BS in Pharmacy, U. Pacific, 1967; D of Pharmacy, U. So. Calif., 1972, MS in Edn., 1980; ScD in Pharmacy (hon.), Mass. Coll. Pharmacy, 1984, L.I. U., 1985. Lic. pharmacist, Calif., Nev.; cert. assoc. exec. Chief pharmacist U. So. Calif. Sch. Pharmacy, LA, 1967-73, postdoctoral fellow, 1972—73, dir. pharmacy admissions, 1973-75; dir. office student affairs Am. Assn. Colls. Pharmacy, Alexandria, Va., 1975-77, asst. exec. dir., 1977-81, exec. dir., 1981-84; CEO Am. Pharm. Assn., Washington, 1984-89; exec. v.p., CEO Am. Acad. Facial Plastic and Reconstructive Surgery, Washington, 1989-92; pres. Schlegel & Assocs., 1992—. Cons. in field. Contbr. over 100 articles on pharmacy, health care and assn. mgmt.; presenter in field. Nat. del. White House Coun. on Aging, Washington, 1981. Disting. alumnus U. So. Calif. Sch. Pharmacy, 1985, U. the Pacific Sch. Pharmacy, 1987. Fellow Am. Soc. Assn. Execs.; mem. Fla. Soc. Assn. Execs., The Meadows Country Club (bd. govs), Phi Delta Chi (charter, bd. counsellors). Avocations: tennis, classical music, gardening, bridge. Office: 3390 Highlands Bridge Rd Sarasota FL 34235-6859 Office Phone: 941-341-0434. Business E-Mail: jschlegel@comcast.net.

**SCHLEGEL, JOHN P.,** academic administrator; b. Dubuque, Iowa, July 31, 1943; s. Aaron Joseph and Irma Joan (Hingtgen) S. BA, St. Louis U., 1969, MA, 1970; BDiv, U. London, 1973; DPhil, Oxford U., 1977. Joined Soc. of Jesus, 1963, ordained priest Roman Cath. Ch., 1973. From asst. prof. to assoc. prof. Creighton U., Omaha, 1976—79, asst. acad. v.p., 1979—82; dean Coll. Arts and Scis. Rockhurst Coll., Kansas City, Mo., 1982—84, Marquette U., Milw., 1984—88; exec. and acad. v.p. John Carroll U., Cleve., 1988—91; pres. U. San Francisco, 1991—2000, Creighton U., Omaha, 2000—. Cons. Orgn. for Econ. Devel. and Cooperation, Paris, 1975-76. Author: Bilingualism and Canadian Policy in Africa, 1979; editor: Towards a Redefinition of Development, 1976; contbr. articles to profl. jours. Mem. Milwaukee County Arts Coun., 1986—88, Mo. Coun. on Humanities, Kansas City, 1984; trustee St. Louis U., 1985—91, Loyola U., Chgo., 1988—2004, Loyola U. New Orleans, 1995—98, St. Ignatius H.S. Cleve., 1990—91, Loyola Coll. in Md., 1992—98, Xavier U., 1998—2003. Oxford U. grantee, 1974-76; Govt. of Can. grantee, 1977-78. Mem.: Am. Coun. Edn., Omaha Country Club, Bohemian Club. Avocations: racquet sports, classical music, cooking, hiking.

**SCHLEGEL, PETER NILES,** urologist, educator; b. Malden, Mass., Feb. 17, 1958; s. Niles Matthew and Mary Patricia (McIntyre) S.; m. Suzanne Marie Bozzo, Sept. 14, 1991; children: Andrew Peter, Lucy Filice, Nicholas Halloran. AB, Hamilton Coll., 1979; MD, U. Mass., 1983. Diplomate Am. Bd. Urology, Nat. Bd. Med. Examiners; lic. physician, N.Y. Intern in gen. surgery and resident Johns Hopkins Hosp., Balt., 1983-85, resident, chief resident in urology, 1985-89, instr. urology, 1989; fellow-in-residence The Population Coun., N.Y.C., 1989-91, staff scientist, 1991—; asst. attending surgeon New York Hosp., N.Y.C., 1991-96; assoc. attending surgeon N.Y. Hosp., N.Y.C., 1996—; assoc. vis. physician Rockefeller U., N.Y.C., 1991—; asst. prof. urology Cornell Med. Coll., N.Y.C., 1991-96, assoc. prof. urology, 1996—2004, prof., 2004—, vice chmn. urology, 1999-2001, acting chmn., 2001—03, chmn., 2003—. Vis. prof. Austria, Israel, Indonesia, Saudi Arabia, Brazil, others; vis. fellow Royal Coll. Surgeons, 1993; co-dir. Ctr. for Male Reproduction and Microsurgery, Cornell Inst. for Reproductive Medicine, 2000—03; lectr. in field. Co-editor Jour. of Audiology; mem. numerous editl. bds.; contbr. numerous articles, abstracts to profl. jours., chpts. to books. Recipient Edwin Beer Program award N.Y. Acad. Medicine, 1996-98, New Investigator award Am. Found. for Urol. Disease, 1993-95, fellow, 1989-91; fellow Am. Cancer Soc., 1986-87, NIH, 1989-91; established Clinician award ESHRE, 1996; named one of Medical Marvels, New York Mag., 2006 Mem.: Soc. for Male Reprodn. /Urology (pres.), Soc. for Study of Male Reprodn. (pres.), Am. Urol. Assn., Soc. for Basic Urol. Rsch., Soc. for Study of Reprodn., Am. Soc. Andrology, Am. Soc. Reproductive Medicine (bd. dirs.), Alpha Omega Alpha. Roman catholic. Avocation: sailing. Office: New York Hosp Dept Urology 525 E 68th St New York NY 10021-4885 Office Phone: 212-746-5491. E-mail: pnschleg@med.cornell.edu.

**SCHLEGELMILCH, MARGARET ANN,** elementary school educator; b. Rome, N.Y., June 2, 1957; d. Reuben Orville and Margaret Elizabeth (Roberts) S. BA in Edn., Va. Poly. Inst. and State U., 1979; MEd, U. Va., 1986, EdS, 1992. Tchr. Chambliss Elem. Sch., Wakefield, Va., 1979—81, Spotswood Elem. Sch., Fredericksburg, Va., 1981—91; adminstrv. asst. intern Lee Hill Elem. Sch., Fredericksburg, 1991—92; tchr. Salem Elem. Sch., Fredericksburg, 1992—2000; asst. prin. Lee Hill Elem. Sch., Fredericksburg, 2000—. Mem. Spotsylvania (Va.) County Sch. Adv. Coun., 1981-83, sch. vol. program com., 1985-86, 88, supt.'s tchr. adv. coun., 1989-90; workshop presenter Rappahannock Regional Assn. Tchrs. Math., Fredericksburg, 1989. Mem. choir United Meth. Ch., Fredericksburg, 1982-91, tchr. Sunday sch., 1984-89, cir. mem., 1982—; past com. mem. coun. on ministries, adminstrv. bd., young adults, nominations com. Mem.: ASCD, AAUW, NEA, Rappahannock Reading Assn., Internat. Reading Assn., Va. Assn. Elem. Sch. Prins., Spotsylvania Edn. Assn., Va. Edn. Assn., Mary Ball WC (1st v.p. 2006—), Phi Delta Kappa, Alpha Delta Kappa (pres. Nu chpt. 1994—96, v.p. Nu chpt. 2006—, scholar). Avocations: reading, needlecrafts, travel. Home: 3712 Fountain Bridge Ct Fredericksburg VA 22408-9208 Office: Lee Hill Elem Sch 3600 Lee Hill School Dr Fredericksburg VA 22408 Business E-Mail: mschlege@s.spotsylvania.k12.va.us. E-mail: pschlege@adelphia.net.

**SCHLEICHER, NORA ELIZABETH,** bank executive, treasurer, accountant; b. Balt., Aug. 10, 1952; d. Irvin William and Eleanor Edna S.; m. Ray Leonard Settle Jr., July 27, 1985. AA cum laude, Anne Arundel Community Coll., 1972; BS summa cum laude, U. Balt., 1975. CPA, Md. Staff auditor Md. Nat. Bank, Balt., 1975-76, sr. staff auditor, 1976-77, supt. auditing dept., 1977-78; full charge acct. Wooden & Benson, CPA's, Balt., 1978-81; asst. to treas. First Fed. Savs. & Loan Assn., Annapolis, Md., 1981, asst. treas., 1982-83, v.p., 1984; v.p., treas. First Fed. Savs. & Loan Assn. (now First Annapolis Bank), 1984—. Bd. dirs., treas. Coll. Manor Community Assn. Mem. AICPA, Md. Assn. CPA's, Fin. Mgrs. Soc., Coll. Manor Community Assn. (bd. dirs., treas.). Methodist. Office: First Annapolis Savs Bank 1832 George Ave Annapolis MD 21401-4103

**SCHLEIFER, ALISON PEDICORD,** educational consultant; b. Norristown, Pa., Nov. 6, 1942; d. Harry William and Adah (Alison) Pedicord; A.B., Mt. Holyoke Coll., 1964; certs. U. Paris, 1962, 63; M.S., So. Conn. State Coll., 1975; m. James Thomas Schleifer, Aug. 15, 1964; children: Katharine Alison, Margaret Elizabeth. Tchr. Amity Regional Sch. Dist., Woodbridge, Conn., 1964-71, dept. chmn. fgn. langs., 1968-71, tchr. French, part-time, 1976-77; ednl. cons., New Haven, 1976—; dept. chmn. fgn. lang. Hopkins Sch., New Haven, 1992-2001. Bd. dirs. YWCA, 1971-76, v.p. 1976; bd. dirs. Downtown Cooperative Ministry, 1971—, pres., 1973-75, v.p., 1976-82; del. gen. synod United Ch. of Christ, 1975, 77; bd. dirs. United Way Greater New Haven, 1986-92. Named Chevalier de l'Ordre des Palmes Academique, 2003. Mem. Ind. Ednl. Cons. Assn. (bd. dirs. 1987-91). Mem. United Ch. of Christ. Mem. Am. Assn. Tchrs. French (Conn. chpt. exec. com. 1990—, pres. 2002—), Alliance Francaise, Mt. Holyoke Club. Contbr. articles to profl. jours. Address: 220 Alston Ave New Haven CT 06515-2038

**SCHLEIFER, STEVEN J.,** psychiatrist, educator; b. N.Y.C., Mar. 10, 1950; s. Jack and Caroline (Rapps) S.; m. Sarah L. Rosenberg, Dec. 1971; children: Jonathan, Jason, Justin, Tara. MD, Mt. Sinai Sch. of Medicine, 1975; BA, Columbia Coll., 1971. Diplomate Nat. Bd. Med. Examiners, Am. Bd. Psychiatry and Neurology. Asst. prof. of psychiatry Mt. Sinai Sch. of Medicine, New York, NY, 1982—87; assoc. prof. of psychiatry UMDNJ-New Jersey Med. Sch., Newark, 1987—92, prof. of psychiatry NJ, 1992—, chair, dept. of psychiatry NJ, 1992—2001. Cons. NIH, Bethesda, Md., 1984—, Hackensack U. Med. Ctr., NJ, 1988—, Veterans Adminstrn. Med. Ctr., East Orange, NJ, 1988—2002; chief of svc., dept of psychiatry UMDNJ-Univ. Hosp., Newark; chief of svc. UMDNJ-Univ. Behavioral Healthcare, Newark, 1992—2002. Contbr. articles to profl. jours. Grantee NIMH, 1982, Chernow Found., N.Y.C., 1983, Upjohn Co., Kalamazoo, 1989, NIAAA, 1990. Fellow Am. Psychiat. Assn. (disting.); mem. N.J. Psychiat. Assn., Soc. Biol. Psychiatry, Internat. Soc. Psychoendocrinology, Am. Psychosomatic Soc., Psychoneuroimmunology Rsch. Soc., Acad. Psychosomatic Medicine. Avocations: opera, skiing. Office: UMDNJ-New Jersey Med Sch 183 South Orange Ave Newark NJ 07103 E-mail: schleife@umdnj.edu.

**SCHLEIN, DOV C.,** banker; BA, Baruch Coll., 1970, MBA, 1975. Former chmn. Republic N.Y. Corp., N.Y.C.; now sr. advis. group chmn. on Israel HSBC, N.Y.C. Vice-pres. Baruch Coll. Found.

**SCHLEIN, MICHAEL EDWARD,** diversified financial services company executive; m. Lisa Jordan Tamagni. BS in Econs., MIT, 1984, MS in Polit. Sci., 1984. Assoc., pub. fin. investment banking divsn. Smith Barney; chief of staff N.Y.C. dep. mayor for fin. and econ. devel., U.S. SEC, 1994—97; sr. v.p., global corp. affairs, human resources, and bus. practices Citigroup, Inc., N.Y.C., 1997—. Mem.: Phi Beta Kappa. Office: Citigroup Inc 399 Park Ave New York NY 10043

**SCHLEINER, ANNE-MARIE,** computer graphics designer; b. Providence, 1970; Attended. U. Michoacan, Mex., U. Kiel, U. Calif., Santa Cruz; MFA, San Jose State U. Asst. prof. interactive arts Tech. U., BC, Canada, 1999—2000; adj. faculty of digital art U. Calif., Irvine, 2001; fellow Akademie Schloss Solitude, 2003; asst. prof. U. Colo., Boulder, 2003—. Madame Polly Game Patch, 1998, Epilepsy Virus Patch, 1999, Cracking the Maze, 1999, mutation.fem, 2000, Luckykiss xxx, 2000, Skool, 2001, Snow Blossom House, 2001, Anime Noir, 2002, Velvet Strike, 2002, Parangari Cutiri, 1999—, PS2 Diaries, 2004—, OUT: Operation Urban Terrain, 2004—, Whitney Biennial, Whitney Mus. Am. Art, NY, 2004. Office: University Art & Art History University Colorado at Boulder 318 UCB Boulder CO 80309

**SCHLEIS, THOMAS HENRY,** music educator, organist; b. Green Bay, Wis., Dec. 13, 1949; s. Samuel Henry and Jeanette Mary (Hall) Schleis. MusB, Lawarence U., 1968—72; MusM, U. Wis., 1972—74. Organist St. John's Cath. Chapel, Champaign, Ill., 1975—; prin. coach Opera Program, U. Ill., Urbana 1987—, mgr., prin. coach, 1999—; lectr., vocal music lit. U. Ill., Urbana, 1981—. Dir. music, dance divsn. Nat. Acad. Arts, Champaign, 1982—87. Author classical music program annotator. Recipient Fulbright scholar, Georg-August U., Gottingen, Germany, 1977—78. Mem.: Am. Guild Organists (dean-east ctrl. Ill. chpt. 1994—2004). Roman Catholic. Avocations: reading, travel, working out. Home: 807 W Illinois Apt 9 Urbana IL 61801 Office: Sch Music Univ Ill 1114 W Nevada Urbana IL 61801 Office Phone: 217-333-3206. E-mail: tschleis@uiuc.edu.

**SCHLENDER, WILLIAM ELMER,** management sciences educator; b. Sawyer, Mich., Oct. 28, 1920; s. Gustav A. and Marie (Zindler) S.; m. Lela R. Pullen, June 9, 1956 (dec. June 1983); m. Margaret C. Krahn, Mar. 3, 1987. AB, Valparaiso U., 1941; MBA, U. Denver, 1947; PhD, Ohio State U., 1955. With U.S. Rubber Co., 1941-43, 46; asst. prof., assoc. prof. bus. adminstrn. Bowling Green State U., 1947-53; asst. prof. bus. orgn., prof. Ohio State U., 1954-65, asst. dean, 1959-62; assoc. dean Ohio State U. (Coll. Commerce and Adminstrn.), 1962-63; prof. mgmt. U. Tex., 1965-68, chmn. dept., 1966-68; dean Cleve. State U. Coll. Bus. Adminstrn., 1968-75, prof. mgmt., 1975-76; Internat. Luth. Laymen's League prof. bus. ethics Valparaiso (Ind.) U., 1976-79, Richard E. Meier prof. mgmt., 1983-86, Richard E. Meier prof. emeritus, 1986—. Vis. assoc. prof. mgmt. Columbia U., 1957-58; vis. prof. mgmt. U. Tex., Arlington, 1981-82; cons. in field; bd. govs. Internat. Ins. Soc., 1972-90. Author: (with M.J. Jucius) Elements of Managerial Action, 3d edit, 1973; (with others) Management in Perspective: Selected Readings, 1965; editor: (with others) Management in a Dynamic Society, 1965; Contbr. articles to profl. jours. Served with AUS, 1943-45. Decorated Bronze Star. Recipient Exec. Order Ohio Comodr. for outstanding contbn. to growth and devel. of state. Fellow Acad. Mgmt.; mem. Indsl. Rels. Rsch. Assn. (pres. N.E. Ohio chpt. 1971-72), Am. Legion, Tau Kappa Epsilon, Rotary, Beta Gamma Sigma, Sigma Iota Epsilon, Pi Sigma Epsilon, Alpha Kappa Psi, Phi Kappa Phi. Home: PO Box 446 Sawyer MI 49125-0446 Office: Coll Bus Adminstrn Valparaiso U Valparaiso IN 46383 Personal E-mail: bschlend@aol.com. *I resolved long ago that where I worked and what I did would be guided not by prestige considerations, but by the answers to three questions: (1) Will my work allow me to grow by discovering and developing my capabilities? (2) Will it make a significant contribution to my profession and to the community? (3) Will I enjoy doing it? My career, and my personal philosophy, have these underlying guidelines.*

**SCHLENOFF, CRAIG,** mechanical engineer; b. Balt., May 1, 1971; s. Marvin and Harriet Schlenoff; m. Rani Einziger, June 19, 1994; children: Jake, Alec, Tali. BS in Engring., U. Md., Coll. Park, Md., 1993; MS in Engring., Rensselaer Poly. Inst, Troy, N.Y., 1996. Mgr. process engring. program NIST, Gaithersburg, Md., 1996—2000, rschr., project leader, 2002—; dir. ontologies and domain knowledge VerticalNet, Inc., Horsham, Pa., 2000—02. Chmn. rsch. adv. com. NIST, 2006; mem. organizing com. PerMIS Conf., Gaithersburg, 2002—06; spkr. in field. Editor: (Operas) Robotics and Autonomous Sys. Jour.; contbr. over 80 articles to profl. jours. Recipient Retention award, NIST, 1997, Spl. Act or Svc. Recognition award, 1999, 2002, 2005, 2006, Letter of Recognition, Def. Advanced Rsch. Projects Agy., 2006;, Rensselaer Poly Inst. scholar, 1994, U. Md. scholar, 1992. Mem.: IEEE (assoc.), ASME (assoc.), Am. Assn. for Artificial Intelligence (chmn. workshop 2004, spkr.). Achievements include research in a novel approach for the moving object prediction in dynamic environments for the purpose of autonomous vehicle path planning and collision avoidance; development of the process specification language which serves as a neutral representation to integrate manufacturing software applications; an approach to measure the performance of intelligent systems; a suite of knowledge representations to enhance the performance of intelligent systems. Home: 12305 Milestone Manor Lane Germantown MD 20876 Office: National Institute of Standards and Tech 100 Bureau Drive Stop 8230 Gaithersburg MD 20899 Office Phone: 301-975-3456. Office Fax: 301-990-9688. Personal E-mail: craig.schlenoff@nist.gov. Business E-Mail: craig.schlenoff@nist.gov.

**SCHLENSKER, GARY CHRIS,** landscape company executive; b. Indpls., Nov. 12, 1950; s. Christian Frederick and Doris Jean (Shannon) S.; m. Ann Marie Tobin, Oct. 27, 1979; children: Laura Patricia, Christian Frederick II. Student, Purdue U., 1969-71, 73; A Bus. Adminstrn., Clark Coll., 1979; cert. emergency med. technician, Ind. Vocat. Tech. Inst., Lafayette, 1974. Salesman Modern Keraceramic Redpaths, Indpls., 1971; orthopaedic technician St. Elizabeth Hosp., Lafayette, 1973-75, asst. mgr. ambulance service, 1975; sales asst. Merck, Sharpe & Dohme, Oakbrook, Ill., 1975-77; v.p. Turfco, Inc., Zionsville, Ind., 1977-84; pres. Turfscape, Inc. Zionsville, 1984—. Speaker Midwest Turf Conf., 1991; del. erosion and sediment control eco. summit Internat. Erosion Control Assn., New Orleans, 2000. With U.S. Army, 1971-73. Mem. ASTM (erosion control subcom.), BBB, Nat. Fedn. Ind. Bus., Midwest Turf Found., Ohio Turf Found., Internat. Erosion Control Assn. (bd. dirs. Gt. Lakes chpt. 1998-2002), U.S. C. of C., Zionsville C. of C., Phi Kappa Psi. Presbyterian. Avocations: woodworking, golf. Business E-Mail: gary@turfscapeinc.com.

**SCHLESINGER, ARTHUR, JR., (ARTHUR MEIER SCHLESINGER),** writer, educator, historian; b. Columbus, Ohio, Oct. 15, 1917; s. Arthur M. and Elizabeth (Bancroft) S.; m. Marian Cannon, 1940 (div. 1970); children: Stephen Cannon, Katharine Kinderman, Christina, Andrew Bancroft; m. Alexandra Emmet, July 9, 1971; 1 son, Robert Emmet Kennedy. AB summa cum laude, Harvard U., 1938; postgrad. (hon.), Cambridge U., 1938—39; degree (hon.), Muhlenberg Coll., 1950, Bethany Coll., 1956, U. NB, 1966, New Sch. Social Rsch., 1966, Tusculum Coll., 1966, RI Coll., 1969, Aquinas Coll., 1971, Western New Eng. Coll., 1974, Ripon Coll., 1976, Iona Coll., 1977, Utah State U., 1978, U. Louisville, 1978, Northeastern U., 1981, Rutgers U., 1982, SUNY, 1984, U. NH, 1985, U. Oxford, 1987, Akron U., 1987, Brandeis U., 1988, U. Mass., Boston, 1990, Hofstra U., 1991, Adelphi U., 1992, Dominican Coll., 1992, Mt. Ida Coll., 1993, Middlebury Coll., 1994, Roosevelt U., 1995, Lynn U., 1996, No. Ill. U., 1996, City U. NY, 1999, Harvard U., 2001, U. SC, 2001, Miami U., 2001, Pa. State U., 2002, Ohio State U., 2003, U. South, 2003, Whitman Coll., 2003. With OWI, 1942-43, OSS, 1943-45; assoc. prof. history Harvard U., 1946-54, prof., 1954-62; vis. fellow Inst. Advanced Study, Princeton, NJ, 1966; Schweitzer prof. humanities CUNY, 1966-95. Cons. Econ. Cooperation Adminstrn., 1948, Mutual Security Adminstrn., 1951-52; spl. asst. to Pres. of U.S., 1961-64; mem. jury Cannes Film Festival, 1964; mem. Adlai E. Stevenson campaign staff, 1952, 56; chmn. Franklin Delano Roosevelt Four Freedoms Found., 1983—; trustee Robert F. Kennedy Meml., Twentieth Century Fund.; adv. Arthur and Elizabeth Schlesinger Library. Author: Orestes A. Brownson, 1939, The Age of Jackson, 1945 (Pulitzer prize for history 1946), The Vital Center, 1949, (with R.H. Rovere) The General and the President, 1951, The Age of Roosevelt Vol. I: The Crisis of the Old Order 1919-1933, 1957 (Francis Parkman prize Soc. Am. Historians 1957, Frederic Bancroft prize Columbia U. 1958), The Age of Roosevelt Vol. II: The Coming of the New Deal, 1958, The Age of Roosevelt III: The Politics of Upheaval, 1960, Kennedy or Nixon: Does It Make Any Difference?, 1960, The Politics of Hope, 1963, (with John Blum) The National Experience, 1963, A Thousand Days, 1965 (Pulitzer prize for biography 1966, Nat. Book award 1966), The Bitter Heritage, 1967, The Crisis of Confidence, 1969, The Imperial Presidency, 1973 (Sidney Hillman Found. award 1973), Robert Kennedy and His Times, 1978 (Nat. Book award 1979), The Cycles of American History, 1986, The Disuniting of America, 1991, A Life in The 20th Century: I, Innocent Beginnings, 2000, War and the American Presidency, 2004; contbr. articles to mags. and newspapers; film reviewer: Show mag, 1962-64, Vogue, 1967-72, Saturday Rev., 1977-80, Am. Heritage, 1981-82; editor: Harvard Guide to American History, 1954, Guide to Politics, 1954, Paths to American Thought, 1963, The Promise of American Life, 1967, The Best and the Last of Edwin O'Connor, 1970, History of American Presidential Elections 1789-1972, 1971, 1972-1984, 1986, The Coming to Power, 1972, The Dynamics of World Power: A Documentary History of United States Foreign Policy 1945-1973, 1973, History of U.S. Political Parties, 1973, Congress Investigates, 1975, Running for President, 1994; screenwriter: (teleplay) The Journey of Robert F. Kennedy. Served with AUS, 1943-45. Decorated comdr. Order of Orange-Nassau, The Netherlands, Ordem del Libertador, Venezuela, Order of St. Michael and St George, Gt. Britain; recipient gold medal in history and biography, Am. Acad. Arts and Letters, 1967, award for history, Ohio Gov., 1973, award in edn., Eugene V. Debs, 1974, Fregen Prize for Lit., Italy, 1983, award for internat. understanding, U. Thant, 1998, medal, Nat. Humanities1998, 1998; fellow, Guggenheim, 1946; grantee, Am. Acad. Arts and Letters, 1946. Mem. Am. Hist. Assn., Orgn. Am. Historians, Soc. Am. Historians (pres. 1989-92), Am. Acad. Arts and Letters (pres. 1981-84, chancellor 1984-87), Am. Philos. Soc., Mass. Hist. Soc., Colonial Soc. Mass., Russian Acad. Scis., Franklin and Eleanor Roosevelt Inst. (co-chmn. 1983—), ACLU, Coun. Fgn. Rels., Ams. for Dem. Action (nat. chmn. 1952-54), Century Assn., Knickerbocker Club, Phi Beta Kappa. Democrat. Unitarian. Home: 455 E 51st St New York NY 10022-6474

**SCHLESINGER, B. FRANK,** architect, educator; b. N.Y.C., Sept. 17, 1925; s. Augustus and Ethel (Brower) S.; m. Draga A. Christy; children: Jeff, Nike, Katherine, Daniel, Christy Anna; 1 stepson, Frances L. Haley Jr. Student, Middlebury Coll., 1946—48; BS, U. Ill., 1950; MArch, Harvard U., 1954. Draftsman Hugh Stubbins Assocs., 1953-55, Marcel Breuer, 1955-56; pvt. practice architecture Princeton, NJ, 1956-59, Doylestown, Pa., 1959-69, Phila., 1969-71, Washington, 1971—. Instr. archtl. design U. Pa., 1957-60; vis. critic Columbia Sch. Architecture, 1962-63, U. Pa., 1965; prof. emeritus Sch. Architecture, U. Md., 1971, prof. architecture, 1971-2001. With USNR, 1943-46. Wheelwright fellow Harvard U., 1963; AIA fellow, 1970; Disting. Designer fellow Nat. Endowment for the Arts, 1984; recipient Design awards Pa. Soc. Archs., 1960-65, 69, 84, Bronze medal, 1965, Silver medal, 1973; Design awards Progressive Arch., 1966-67, 69, 72, 74; Design awards Interfaith Forum on Religion, Art and Arch., 1987, 92; Design awards Philia. chpt. 1960-61, 1963-65, 1968-69; Design awards No. Va. chpt. 1975, 2001; Design awards Wash. chpt. 1990, 92, 95, 2002, 05; Centennial medal Wash. chpt. 2001. Mem.: Associated Harvard Alumni (dir. 1972), Harvard Grad. Sch. Design Alumni Assn. (pres. 1971—73). Address: 1015 33rd St NW Apt 806 Washington DC 20007-3538 E-mail: schlesingerfaia@msn.com.

**SCHLESINGER, DEBORAH LEE,** retired librarian; b. Cambridge, Mass., Sept. 13, 1937; d. Edward M. and Edith D. (Schneider) Hershoff; divorced; children: Suzanne, Richard. BA, U. Mass., 1961; MS, Simmons Coll., 1974; postgrad., U. Pitts., 1983. Reference librarian Bently Coll., Waltham, Mass. 1964-65; dir. Carnegie Library, Swissvale, Pa., 1973-77, South Park Twp. Library, Library, Pa., 1977-81, Monessen (Pa.) Library, 1981-82, Lewis & Clark Library, Helena, Mont., 1983—88, 1989—2004, ret., 2004; state librarian Mont. State Library, Helena, Mont., 1988-89. Vis. scholar Pitts. Regional Library Ctr., 1982-83. Editor Pa. Union List, 1982-83. Mem. exec. bd. Mont. Cultural Advocacy, 1983-2004. Mem. Mont. Libr. Assn. (chmn. legis. com. 1984-92, lobbyist 1992-2001), AAUW (exec. mem. 1985-86). Clubs: Montana (Helena). Democrat. Avocations: flying, painting, reading, rafting, travel. Personal E-mail: dbooks@aol.com.

**SCHLESINGER, HARVEY ERWIN,** judge; b. June 4, 1940; BA, The Citadel, 1962; JD, U. Richmond, 1965. Bar: Va. 1965, Fla. 1965, U.S. Supreme Ct. 1968. Corp. counsel Seaboard Coast Line R.R. Co., Jacksonville, Fla., 1968-70; chief asst. U.S. atty. Mid. Dist. Fla., Jacksonville, 1970-75, U.S. magistrate judge, 1975-91, U.S. Dist. judge, 1991—. Adj. prof. U. North Fla., 1984-91; mem. adv. com. on Fed. Rules of Criminal Procedure to U.S. Supreme Ct., 1986-93; mem. Jud. Conf. Adv. Com. on Adminstrn. of Magistrate Judges Sys., 1996-2003, chmn., 1998-2003; chmn. U.S. Dist. Ct. Forms Working Group, Washington, 1983—, Jud. Ct. Ad hoc Com. on Long Range Planning, 1998-2003; Jud. Conf. Jud. Officers Resources Working Group, 1998-99; 11th Cir. Dist. Judges Assn., 1991—, sec., treas. 1996- 97, v.p. 1997-98, pres.-elect., 1999-2001, pres., 2001-02. Bd. dir. Pine Castle Ctr. for Mentally Retarded, Jacksonville, 1970-87, pres., 1972-74, mem. bd. dirs., 1973-74; trustee Pine Castle Found., 1972-76, Congregation Ahavath Chesed, Jacksonville, 1970—, v.p., 1975-80, pres., 1980-82; v.p. S.E. Coun. Union Am. Hebrew Congregations, 1984-88; asst. commr. for exploring North Fla. Coun. Boy Scouts Am., 1983-86, exec. com., 1986-98, adv. bd., 1998—; active Boy Scouts Am. Nat. Jewish Com. on Scouting, Irving, Tex., 1986-93, Fla. Sesquicentennial Commn., 1995-96; trustee River Garden Home for Aged, 1982—, sec., 1985-1990; co-chmn. bd. gov. Jacksonville chpt. NCCJ, 1983-1993, presiding co-chmn. 1984-89; nat. bd. trustees, NYC, 1986-93; trustee Jacksonville Cmty. Found., 2000—, vice-chair, 2003-05, chmn. 2006—. Capt. JAGC, U.S. Army, 1965-68. Recipient Silver Beaver award Boy Scouts Am., 1986; George Washington Medal of Honor, Freedoms Found., Valley Forge, Pa., 1987, Silver Medallion Humanitarian award NCCJ, 1992, Founders award, Fed. Magistrate Judges Assn., 1999, William Green award for profl. excellence U. Richmond Law Sch., 2000, Jurist of Yr. award Am. Bd. Trial Adv., 2001. Mem. ABA (fed. rules of evidence and criminal procedure com. 1979-98, Nat. Conf. Spl. Ct. Judges, 1975-90, conf. newsletter editor, 1988-90, Nat. Conf. Fed. Trial Judges, 1990—, chmn. legis. com., 1996-97, Flascher award 1989), Va. Bar Assn., Fla. Bar Assn., Fed. Judges Assn., Jacksonville Bar Assn.; Fed. Bar Assn. (pres. Jacksonville chpt. 1974, 75, 81-82), Am. Judicature Soc., Chester Bedell Am. Inns of Ct. (pres. 1992-96), Rotary (Paul Harris fellow, pres. S. Jacksonville club), Masons (past master, past venerable master, knights comdr. of Ct. Honour, 33 degree Scottish Rite bodies), Shriners. Office: 300 N Hogan St Ste 11-150 Jacksonville FL 32202-4246 Office Phone: 904-549-1990.

**SCHLESINGER, IRWIN D.**, neurologist; b. Bklyn., Sept. 13, 1935; s. Edward Schlesinger and Eva Parkoff; m. Marcia Rubinstein; 1 child, Lisa. BS, Bklyn. Coll., 1956; MD, SUNY, Med. U., Syracuse, 1961. Diplomate Am. Bd. Psychiatry and Neurology, Am. Bd. Clin. Neurophysiology. Intern then resident medicine Cornell med. divsn. Bellevue Hosp., N.Y.C., 1961—63; resident neurology Albert Einstein Coll. Medicine Bronx Mcpl. Hosp., 1965—68; neurologist Neurol. Specialities L.I., Manhasset, NY, 1968—. Attending neurologist N. Shore Univ. Hosp., Manhasset, 1968—; staff neurologist L.I. Jewish Med. Ctr., Glen Oaks, NY, 1969—; cons. neurologist St. Francis Hosp., Roslyn, NY, 1975—; clin. assoc. prof. neurology Cornell U. Med. Coll., N.Y.C., 1971—95, NYU Med. Sch., N.Y.C., 1995—. Capt. USAF, 1963—65. Fellow: ACP, Am. Acad. Neurology; mem.: AMA, Am. Clin. Neurophysiology Soc., Am. Assn. Electrodiagnostic Medicine, Alpha Omega Alpha. Office: Neurological Specialties Long Island 170 Great Neck Rd Great Neck NY 11021 Office Phone: 516-487-4464.

**SCHLESINGER, LEONARD ARTHUR**, retail executive; b. NYC, July 31, 1952; s. Joe and Edith (Smukler) S.; m. Phyllis Barbara Fineman, Dec. 23, 1972; children: Rebecca, Emily, Katharine. BA, Brown U., 1972; MBA, Columbia U., 1973; DBA, Harvard U., 1979. Mgr. Procter & Gamble, Green Bay, Wis., 1973-75; asst. prof., assoc. prof. bus. sch. Harvard U., Boston, 1978-85; exec. v.p., COO Au Bon Pain, Inc., Boston, 1985-88; prof. bus. adminstrn. Harvard U., Boston, 1988-98; sr. v.p. Brown U., 1998-99; exec. v.p., COO Limited Brands, 1999—2003, vice chmn., 2003—. Bd. dirs. Limited Brands, Columbus, Ohio Editor: Human Resources Mgmt. Jour., Jour. Mgmt. Inquiry; contbr. articles to profl. jours. Jewish. Avocations: travel, music, bicycling. Home: 3900 Kitzmiller Rd New Albany OH 43054 Office: Limited Brands 3 Limited Pkwy Columbus OH 43230-1467 Business E-Mail: lschlesinger@limitedbrands.com.

**SCHLESINGER, SANFORD JOEL**, lawyer; b. NYC, Feb. 8, 1943; s. Irving and Ruth (Rubin) Schlesinger; m. Lianne Lazetera; children: Merideth, Jarrod, Alexandra. BS in Govt. with hons., Columbia U., 1963; JD, Fordham U., 1966. Bar: N.Y. 1966, U.S. Dist. Ct. (so. and ea. dists.) N.Y. 1967, U.S. Ct. Appeals (2d cir.) 1968, U.S. Ct. Internat. Trade 1969, U.S. Tax Ct. 1993, U.S. Supreme Ct. 1978. Assoc. Frankenthaler & Kohn, N.Y.C., 1966—67; asst. atty. gen. trusts and estates bur. charitable found. div. State of N.Y., N.Y.C., 1967—69; prtnr. Rose & Schlesinger, N.Y.C., 1969—81, Goldshmidt, Oshatz, Powsner & Saft, N.Y.C., 1981—85; ptnr., head trusts and estates dept. Shea & Gould, N.Y.C., 1985—93; ptnr., head wills and estates dept. Kaye Scholer LLP, N.Y.C., 1993—2004, ptnr. co-chair family owned bus. practice group, 1993—2004; founding ptnr. Schlesinger Gannon & Lazetera LLP, N.Y.C., 2004—. Adj. faculty Columbia U. Sch. Law, 1989-94; adj. prof. N.Y. Law Sch., 1978-2003; adj. prof. grad. program in estate planning U. Miami Grad. Sch. Law, 1995-2003, N.Y. State Bar Jour., 1995-2005, emeritus, 2005—; dir. N.Y. State Bar Found.; mem. estate planning adv. com. Practising Law Inst., 1990—; bd. advisors and contbrs. Jour. of S Corp. Taxation, 1989-96; lectr. in field; condr. workshops in field. Author: Estate Planning for the Elderly Client, 1984, Planning for the Elderly or Incapacitated Client, 1993; columnist, mem. editl. bd. Estate Planning mag., 1995—; contbr. articles to profl. jours. Mem. adv. bd. Inst. Fed. Taxation NYU, 1988-96, chmn., 1993-94; mem. legis adv. com. Scarsdale (N.Y.) Sch. Bd., 1981-83, mem. nominating com., 1979-82; pres. dist. 17 N.Y.C. Cmty. Sch. Bd., 1970-71; mem. fin. and estate planning adv. bd. Commerce Clearing House, 1988—; mem. adv. bd. Tax Hotline, 1997—. Fellow Am. Coll. Trust and Estate Counsel (chmn. Downstate N.Y. 2001-06); mem. ABA (chmn. social security and other govt. entitlements com. 1990-91, chmn. probate and trust com.-estate planning, drafting charitable giving coms., 1992-94), Internat. Acad. Estate & Trust Law (Academician 1992—), Nat. Acad. Elder Law Attys., Bklyn. Bar Assn., Assn. of Bar of City of N.Y., N.Y. State Bar Assn. (treas. trusts and estates sect. 1991-92, sec. trusts and estates sect. 1992-93, chmn. trusts and estates sect. 1994-95, chmn. exec. com. 1st jud. dist. 1987-91, jour. bd. editors 1995-2006, emeritus 2006—), N.Y. State Bar Found. Avocations: baseball, writing. Office: Schlesinger Gannon & Lazetera LLP 499 Park Ave New York NY 10022 Office Phone: 212-652-3777. Business E-Mail: sschlesinger@sglllp.com.

**SCHLESINGER, STEPHEN CANNON**, think-tank executive; b. Boston, Aug. 17, 1942; s. Arthur Meier and Marian (Cannon) S.; m. Judith Barbara Elster, Mar. 18, 1984; 1 child, Sarah Elizabeth. BA in Am. History and Lit. cum laude, Harvard U., 1964, JD, 1968; cert. study in European History, Cambridge U., 1965. Legal asst. to pres. N.Y. State Urban Devel. Corp., 1968; founder, editor The New Dem., 1969-72; speechwriter Dem. Presdl. Candidate George McGovern, 1972; staff writer TIME Mag., 1974-78; editorial writer, chief polit. corr. N.Y. Post, 1978; spl. asst. to Gov. Mario Cuomo, 1983-90; dir. for internat. orgns. N.Y. State Dept. Econ. Devel., 1990—94; vis. scholar Taub Urban Rsch. Ctr. NYU, 1995-97; spl. advisor UN Ctr. for Human Settlements, 1995-97; dir. World Policy Inst. at New Sch., N.Y.C., 1997—. With Gore Presdl. Campaign, 2000, Kerry Presdl. Campaign, 2004; mem. internat. election observer teams Nat. Dem. Inst., 1993, 90; tchg. fellow in English composition Harvard U., 1968; adj. prof. Am. politics New Sch. U., 1976-77; lectr. Royce Carlton Agy., 1984-88. Author: The New Reformers, 1975, Bitter Fruit: The Untold Story of the U.S. Coup in Guatemala, 1982, Act of Creation: The Founding of the United Nations, 2003 (Harry Truman Book award 2004); contbr. numerous articles and book revs. to profl. jours., mags. and newspapers; columnist Boston Globe, 1973-74. Mem. Coun. Fgn. Rels., Roosevelt Inst., PEN, Author's Guild, Overseas Press Club. Unitarian Universalist. Avocations: bicycling, jogging, skiing, swimming, tennis. Home: 500 W 111th St Apt 4A New York NY 10025-1905 Office: World Policy Inst 66 5th Ave Fl 9 New York NY 10011 Office Phone: 212-229-5808 4266. E-mail: schlesis@newschool.edu

**SCHLESS, PHYLLIS ROSS**, investment banker; d. Lewis H. and Doris G. Ross; m. Aaron Backer Schless, July 7, 1970; 1 son, Daniel Lewis Ross. Cert., Neighborhood Playhouse Sch. of Theatre, 1962, N.Y. Sch. Interior Design, 1964; BA in Econs., Wellesley Coll., 1964; MBA, Stanford U., 1966. Cert. theater prodns. Am. League Theater Owners and Prodrs. Assoc. internat. fin. Kuhn Loeb & Co., N.Y.C., 1966—70; fin. cons., 1971—73; sr. fin. analyst Trans World Airlines, N.Y.C., 1974—75; corp. fin., mergers and acquisitions Lazard Freres & Co., 1976—79; dir. mergers and acquisitions Am. Can Co., Greenwich, Conn., 1979—82; v.p. mergers and acquisitions Bear, Stearns & Co., N.Y.C., 1982—84; sr. v.p. corp. acquisitions Integrated Resources, 1984—85; chmn., CEO Ross Fin. Svcs. Group Inc., 1995—; supervisory dir. Merrill Lynch HYTS Funds, 1991—96. Bd. dirs. Calvary Hosp. Fund Bd., 1990-2000, chair investment com., 1995-99; trustee A.R. Tinker Fund, 1993-2004, hon. trustee, 2004—; trustee Nat. Child Labor Com., 1981-95, chmn., 1992-94; trustee New World Found., 1986-92, chair fin. com., treas. 1988-92; bd. dirs. Stanford Bus. Sch. Assn., N.Y., 1990-2003; bd. advt. asst. prof. NYU, 1996—; Columbia U. Sch. Bus., 2001—; bd. dirs. Nat. Found. Tchg. Entrepreneurship, metro. N.Y. chair, 2000-05. Pres. Greater Bridgeport Nat. Coun. Jewish Women, 1971-73; bd. dirs., 1974-75; bd. dirs. Girls Clubs Am., 1975-89, mem. exec. com., 1982-89, pres., 1984-86; bd. dirs. Pauline Koner Dance Co., 1979-81, So. Conn. Child Guidance Clinic, 1981-83, New Canaan United Way, 1981-83; treas. Wellesley Class '64, 1984-89. Mem. Univ. Club. Office Phone: 212-223-1781.

**SCHLESSINGER, JOSEPH**, pharmacology educator; BSc in Chemistry/Physics magna cum laude, The Hebrew U., Jerusalem, 1968, MSC in Chemistry magna cum laude, 1969; PhD, The Weizmann Inst. Sci., Rehovot, Israel, 1974. Postdoctoral assoc. dept. chemistry Sch. Applied Physics, Cornell U., 1974-76; vis. scientist immunology br. Nat. Cancer Inst., NIH, Bethesda, Md., 1977-78; sr. scientist dept. chem. immunology The Weizmann Inst. Sci., Rehovot, 1978-80, assoc. prof. dept. chem. immunology, 1980-84, prof. dept. chem. immunology, Ruth & Leonard Simon prof., 1984-91; dir. div. molecular biology Biotech. Rsch. Ctr. Meloy Labs., Inc., Rockville, Md., 1985-86, dir. Biotech. Rsch. Ctr., 1986-88; rsch. dir. Rorer

Biotech., Inc., King of Prussia, Pa., 1988-90; prof., chmn. dept. pharmcology NYU Med. Ctr., N.Y.C., 1990—2001; prof., chmn. pharmcology Yale U. Sch. of Medicine, New Haven, 2001—. Mem. editorial bds. European Molecular Biology Orgn. Jour., Jour. Cell Biology, Cell Regulation, Cancer Rsch. Receptors, Growth Factors, Cell Crowth & Differentiation, Protein Engineering, Oncogenes and Growth Factor Abstracts; contbr. articles to profl. jours. Recipient Sara Leedy prize, Weizmann Inst. Sci., 1980, Hestrin prize, Biochem. Soc. Israel, 1983, Levinson prize, 1984, The Drew-Ciba prize (with G. Blobel and A. Levine), 1995, Antoine Lacassagne prize, 1995, Disting. Service award, Miami Nature Biotechnology, 1999, Taylor prize (with T. Hunter and T. Pawson), 2000. Mem. European Molecular Biology Orgn., NAS, Am. Academy of Arts and Sciences, Inst. Medicine. Office: Yale U Sch Medicine Dept Pharmacology PO Box 208066 New Haven CT 06520-8066 Office Phone: 203-785-7395. Office Fax: 203-785-3879. E-mail: joseph.schlessinger@yale.edu.*

**SCHLESSINGER, LAURA**, radio talk show host; b. Brooklyn, Jan. 16, 1947; d. Monroe and Yolanda Schlessinger; m. Lewis G. Bishop, 1982; 1 child, Deryk. BS in Biological Sciences, SUNY, Stonybrook; MS in Physiology, M Phil in Physiology, PhD in Physiology, Columbia U. Lic. in marriage and family therapy; cert. marriage, family and child counseling, U. So. Calif. Psychotherapist in private practice, Los Angeles, Calif., 1980—90; nat. syndicated radio talk show host The Dr. Laura Schlessinger Program, 1990—. Past mem. faculty U. So. Calif., Pepperdine U, instr. UCLA, UC Irvine; pres. Dr. Laura Schlessinger Foundation. Author: Ten Stupid Things Women Do to Mess Up Their Lives, 1994, How Could You Do That?! The Abdication of Character, Courage and Conscience, 1996, Ten Stupid Things Men Do To Mess Up Their Lives, 1997, The Ten Commandments: The Significance of God's Law in Everyday Life, 1998, Damsels, Dragons, and Regular Guys, 2000, Parenthood by Proxy; Don't Have Them If You Won't Raise Them, 2000, Ten Stupid Things Couples Do To Mess Up Their Relationships, 2002 The Proper Care & Feeding Of Husbands, 2004; books for children Why Do You Love Me?, 1999, But I Waaannt It!, 2000, Dr. Laura Schlessinger's Growing Up is Hard, 2001, I Hate My Life!, 2001, Dr. Laura Schlessinger's Where is God?, 2003; featured on The Oprah Winfrey Show, A&E Biography, Larry King Live, Lifetime's Intimate Portrait, 20/20, The Today Show, PBS, Hannity & Colmes, CBS This Morning, 48 Hours, Meet the Press with Tim Russert, Crier Today, Eye to Eye with Connie Chung, ABC This Week, Dateline; featured in Time, U.S. News and World Report, People, USA Today, The New York Times Magazine, The Los Angeles Times, The Wall Street Journal and others; featured spkr. Nat. Congressional Prayer Breakfast, Mus. Radio and Television, Claremont Inst., PBS, Nat. Religious Broadcasters, Country Radio Seminar. Recipient Marconi Award for Network/Syndicated Personality of the Yr., 1997, Genii Award, American Women in Radio & Television, 1998, Israel 50th Anniversary Tribute award, 1998, Crystal Cathedral Academy award, 1998, Love of a Child award, Childhelp USA, 1998, Chairman's award, Nat. Religious Broadcasters, 2000, Nat. Heritage award, Nat. Council of Young Israel, 2001, Conservative Leadership award, Clare Booth Luce Institute, 2001, Woman of the Yr. award, 2002. Mem.: AFTRA, SAG, Nat. Assn. At-Home Mothers (bd. adv.). Achievements include being broadcast on approximately 300 stations with 12 million listeners; the second most popular talk show host in the country; show syndicated since June 1994; on nat. radio career for more than 25 years. Office: Premiere Radio Networks 15260 Ventura Blvd Ste 300 Sherman Oaks CA 91403-5337

**SCHLEUSE, WILLIAM**, retired psychiatrist, psychoanalyst; b. Austin, Oct. 18, 1932; s. Louis W. and Oleta Vivian (Hedgpeth) S.; m. Virginia Walker, 1965 (div. 1977); children: Martin, Stuart, Paul; m. Doris Laird, Apr. 20, 1985 (div. 2004). BA, U. Tex., 1953; MD, U. Tex. Med. Br., Galveston, 1957. Diplomate Am. Bd. Psychiatry and Neurology. Pvt. practice psychiatry and psychoanalysis, Houston, 1962-81, Austin, 1981—2000; mem. med. staff Hedgecroft Hosp., Houston, 1966; ret., 2000. Photography exhibited in numerous shows, 1993—. Pres. Houston Psychiat. Soc., 1967, Austin chpt. Am. Assn. Individual Investors, 1992. Fellow Am. Psychiat. Assn. (life); mem. San Antonio/Austin Psychoanalytic Soc. (pres. 1996-98), Austin Fine Art Photography Group (founding mem.), Houston Yacht Club, Phi Beta Kappa. Avocations: sailing, boating, fine-art photography. Home: 2301 S Mopac # 315 Austin TX 78746-7957

**SCHLEUSENER, RICHARD AUGUST**, college president; b. Oxford, Nebr., May 6, 1926; s. August William and Katherine Charlotte (Albrecht) S.; m. Elaine Emma Wilhelm, June 12, 1949; children: Kathryn Jeanne Schleusener Miller, Richard Dennis, Rand Lee, Debra Sue, Jeffrey Thomas. BS, U. Nebr., 1949, DSc (hon.), 1984; MS, Kans. State U., 1956; PhD, Colo. State U., 1958; postgrad., NIT, 1951-52. Rsch. engr. Colo. State U., 1958-64, dir. Inst. Atmospheric Sci.; prof., head dept. meteorology S.D. Sch. Mines and Tech., Rapid City, 1965-74, v.p., dean engring., 1974-75, acting pres., 1975-76, pres., 1976-86, Black Hills Regional Eye Inst. Found., 1987-96, ret., 1996. Cons. weather modification U.S. Dept. Interior, 1964—, U.S. Forest Svc., 1966—, UNESCO, 1971—, also pvt. firms. Contbr. articles to tech. jours. With USAF, 1950-55. Inductee S.D. Hall of Fame, 2000. Mem. Am. Meteorol. Soc., Am. Geophys. Union, Rotary, Sigma Xi, Beta Sigma Psi. Lutheran. Home: Unit 104 4120 Villa Ridge Ct Rapid City SD 57701 E-mail: dickelaine@rushmore.com

**SCHLEY, REEVE, III**, artist; b. NYC, Mar. 11, 1936; s. Reeve and Elizabeth (Boies) S.; m. Georgia Terry, Oct. 5, 1968; children: Marie B., Reeve T. BA, Yale U., 1959; M.F.A., U. Pa., 1962; studied with Josef Buchty, Munich, 1954-55. Instr. watercolor NAD, N.Y.C., 1981—. Exhibited in group shows including Spook Farm Gallery, Farm Hills, N.J., 1958, Hunterdon County Art Ctr. Ann., 1959, Pa. Acad., 1966, NJ State Mus., Trenton, 1967, Tenn. Fine Arts Ctr., Nashville, 1973, Okla. Art Ctr., Oklahoma City, 1974, Butler Inst. Am. Art, Youngstown, Ohio, 1974, Drew U., 1975, fillwminn Guild Artists, 1975, NAD, 1977-78, Bklyn. Mus., 1984; one-man shows Vendo Nubes Gallery, Chestnut Hill, Pa., 1967, 71, Phila. Art Alliance, 1969, Spook Farm Gallery, 1970, Saratoga (N.Y.) Gallery, 1972-75, James Graham Gallery, N.Y., 1973-05, N.J. State Mus., 1978, Hull Gallery, Washington, 1978, 80, Byck Gallery, Louisville, 1979, Peale House Gallery, Pa. Acad. Fine Arts, 1980, Gallerie Arnoldi-Livie, Munich, 1985, New Orleans Acad. Fine Arts, 1985, 96; represented in permanent collections NJ State Mus., Trenton, NAD, Newark Mus., Bklyn. Mus., Yale U. Art Gallery, Met. Mus., Heublein Collection, Somerset County Coll., Tenneco Chems. Recipient Best in Show award Hunterdon County Art Ctr., 1974, Laura M. Gross Meml. award Silvermine Guild Artists, 1975, Purchase prize Somerset County Coll. Tri-State Exhbn., 1975, 2d prize for watercolor Somerset Art Assn., 1975, Ranger Fund Purchase prize NAD, 1981, 85, Cert. of Merit, 1978, Schweitzer prize NAD, 1999; Cresson travel scholar Pa. Acad. Fine Arts, 1962; fellow NJ Coun. Arts, 1979.

**SCHLEY, WAYNE ARTHUR**, political scientist, consultant; b. Hamilton, Mont., May 22; AA, Shasta Coll., 1960; BS, Sacramento State U., 1963; MS, Am. U., 1974; postgrad., U. Alaska, 1970, Harvard U. Cert. high sch. tchr. (lifetime), Calif. Dept. Edn. Tchr., admin. Placer H.S., Auburn, Calif., 1963-70; spl. asst. to Sen. Ted Stevens, Washington, 1971-77; staff dir. minority and majority subcom. civil svc. Post Office and Gen. Svcs., Washington, 1977-86; minority staff dir. Senate Com. on Rules and Adminstrn., Washington, 1987-92; commr. U.S. Postal Rate Commn., Washington, 1992-95; cons. on legis. and postal issues Washington, 1995—. Elected bd. dirs. Assn. Postal Commerce, 2003—; chmn. Calif. Teenage Reps., 1963-64; regional v.p. Calif. Young Reps., 1964-66, state sgt. at arms, 1965-67; mem. Placer County Rep. Ctrl. Com., 1965-70. Recipient Cert. of Achievement, JFK Sch. Govt. Harvard U., 1982. Home and Office: 614 Massachusetts Ave NE Washington DC 20002-6006 Office Phone: 202-547-9476. E-mail: was2nate@hotmail.com.

**SCHLEY, WILLIAM SHAIN**, otolaryngologist; b. Columbus, Ga., Sept. 21, 1940; s. Frances Brooking Schley and Susie (Smith) Mathews. BA, Emory U., 1962, MD, 1966. Intern mixed surg. The Roosevelt Hosp., N.Y.C., 1966-67, resident in surgery, 1967-68; resident in otorhinolaryngology N.Y.

Hosp.-Cornell Med. Ctr., N.Y.C., 1970-73; clin. instr. otorhinolaryngology Cornell U. Med. Coll., 1972-75, clin. asst. prof., 1975-81, assoc. prof., 1982—, acting chmn. dept. otorhinolaryngology, 1988-94, chmn. dept. otorhinolaryngology, 1994—2005. Otorhinolaryngologist to outpatients with pvt. patient privileges N.Y. Hosp., 1973-75, asst. attending otorhinolaryngologist with pvt. patient privileges, 1975-81, assoc. attending, 1992—, acting otorhinolaryngologist-in-chief, 1988-94, otorhinolaryngologist-in-chief, 1994-2005; assoc. asst. surgeon otolaryngology Manhattan Eye, Ear, Nose and Throat Hosp., 1988-99; v.p. and sec. med. bd. N.Y. Hosp., 1994-97, pres., 1998-99; pres., v.p. med. bd. The N.Y. and Presbyn. Hosp., 1998, pres., 1998-99, mem. ex officio bd. trustees, 1998-99; mem. co-chmn. vis. day com. The N.Y. Hosp.-Cornell Med. Ctr., 1995-98; pres. N.Y. Hosp.-Cornell Med. Coll. Alumni Coun., 1996-98; course dir. Salzburg Cornell Med. Seminars, 1996—, steering com., 1999—. Author: (with others) Pulmonary Diseases of the Fetus Newborn and Child, 1999; contbr. numerous articles to profl. publs. Vestry St. James Ch., N.Y.C., 1994-97; mem. ad hoc bd. visitors Emory U., 1994-95; bd. dirs. Health Ministries Bd. of Older People, 1997—; mem. adv. bd. Sch. Medicine Emory U., 2000—, chmn. adv. bd., 2002—. Lt. comdr. USNR. Recipient The Emery medal, 2001. Fellow ACS (Manhattan dist. #2 com. on applicants 1991-97, Manhattan Credentials Com. 1991-99); mem. Am. Acad. Otolaryngology-Head and Neck Surgery, Med. Soc. State of N.Y. N.Y. State Soc. Otolaryngology-Head and Neck Surgery (exec. coun. 1974-80, dist. dir. 1980), County Med. Soc. N.Y., N.Y. Laryngol. Soc. (sec.-treas. 1981-84, v.p. 1984-85, pres. 1985-86), N.Y. Bronchoscopic Soc. (v.p. 1986-94, pres. 1994-97), N.Y. Clin. Soc. (v.p. 1998-99, pres. 1999-2000, sec.-treas, 2005—), Assn. Emory Alumni (bd. govs. 1990-97, pres.-elect 1993-94, pres. 1994-95), Omicron Delta Kappa. Episcopalian. Avocations: astronomy, ornithology. Home: 430 E 63d St Apt 5E New York NY 10021-7927 Office: DS10 449 E 68th St New York NY 10021-6310 Office Phone: 212-746-2223. E-mail: schley@med.cornell.edu.

**SCHLEYER, WILLIAM T.**, cable company executive; b. Phila. BS in Mech. Engring., Drexel U.; MBA, Harvard Bus. Sch. Mgr. IBM, Abbott Labs.; from sys. mgr. to pres., COO US West Media Group Continental Cablevision, 1977-97; pres., COO MediaOne, Boston, 1997—2000; prin. Pilot House Ventures, LLC, 2001; pres., CEO, broadband services unit AT&T Corp., 2001—03; chmn., CEO Adelphia Communications Corp., Greenwood Village, Colo., 2003—. Office: Tele Communications Inc 183 Inverness Dr W Englewood CO 80112-5203

**SCHLICHER, RONALD LEWIS**, ambassador; With Fgn. Svc., 1982—; min.-counselor sr. fgn. svc.; vice-consul Dhahran, 1982—84; consul Damascus, Syria, 1984—86; staff asst. Bur. Near Ea. Affairs US Dept. State; dep. prin. officer Am. Embassy, Alexandria, Egypt, 1987—89, first sec. Cairo, 1989—91; chief civilian officer Multinational Force and Observers, Israel, 1991—92; dep. dir. regional affairs Office of Coord. Counter Terrorism, 1994—97; dep. chief of mission Am. Embassy, Beirut, 1994—97; dir. office Egyptian and N. African affairs, Bur. Near Eastern Affairs US Dept. State, Washington, 1997—2000; chief of mission, counsul-gen. Am. Embassy, Jerusalem, 2000—02; dir. Iraqi Task Force, 2003; dep. asst. sec. US Dept. State, Washington, US amb. to Cyprus Nicosia, 2005—. Recipient Disting. Honor award, Superior Honor award (3), Meritorious Honor award (2), Nat. Human Intelligence Collector award, Christian A. Herter award. Office: Am Embassy 5450 Nicosia Pl Washington DC 20521*

**SCHLICHTING, CATHERINE FLETCHER NICHOLSON**, librarian, educator; b. Huntsville, Ala., Nov. 18, 1923; d. William Parsons and Ethel Loise (Breitling) Nicholson; m. Harry Fredrick Schlichting, July 1, 1950 (dec. Aug. 1964); children: James Dean, Richard Dale, Barbara Lynn. BS, U. Ala., 1944; MLS, U. Chgo., 1950. Asst. libr. U. Ala. Edn. Libr., Tuscaloosa, summers 1944-45; libr. Sylacauga (Ala.) H.S., 1944-45, Hinsdale (Ill.) H.S., 1945-49; asst. libr. Centre for Children's Books, U. Chgo., 1950-52; instr. reference dept. libr. Ohio Wesleyan U., Delaware, 1965-69, asst. prof., 1969-79, assoc. prof., 1979-85, prof., 1985—, curator Ohio Wesleyan Hist. Collection, 1986—, student pers. libr., 1966-72. Author: Introduction to Bibliographic Research: Basic Sources, 4th edit., 1983, Checklist of Biographical Reference Sources, 1977, Audio-Visual Aids in Bibliographic Instruction, 1976, Introduction to Bibliographic Research: Slide Catalog and Script, 1980; info. cons. (documentary) Noble Achievements: The History of Ohio Wesleyan 1942-1992, 1992, 150 Years of Excellence: A Pictorial View of Ohio Wesleyan University, 1992. Mem. adminstrv. bd. Meth. Ch., 1973-81, chmn. adminstrv. bd., 1985—, mem. coun. on ministries, 1975-81, chmn., 1975-77, trustee, 1999—2003. Recipient Algernon Sidney Sullivan award U. Ala., 1944, Hon. Alumna award Ohio Wesleyan U., 1997; Ohio Wesleyan U.-Mellon Found. grantee, 1972-73, 84-85; GLCA Tchg. fellow, 1976-77. Mem. ALA, Ohio Libr. Assn., Midwest Acad. Libr. Conf., Acad. Librs. Assn. Ohio (dir. 1984-86), AAUP (chpt. sec. 1967-68), United Meth. Women (pres. Mt. Vernon dist. 1994-97, newsletter editor 1998-2002), Ohio Wesleyan Woman's Club (exec. bd. 1969-72, 77-79, 81-84, pres. 1969-70, sec. 1977-78), History Club (pres. 1971-72, v.p. 1978-79, 2003-04) Fortnightly Club (pres. 1975-76, 87-88, 2003-04), Am. Field Svc. (pres. Delaware chpt. 1975-76), Kappa Delta Pi, Alpha Lambda Delta. Democrat. Home: 57 Willow Brook Way S Delaware OH 43015 Office: Ohio Wesleyan U La Beeghly Library Delaware OH 43015

**SCHLICHTING, NANCY MARGARET**, hospital administrator; b. N.Y.C., Nov. 21, 1954; BA, Duke U., 1976; MBA, Cornell U., 1979. Adminstrv. resident Meml. Hosp. Cancer, N.Y.C., 1978; fellow Blue Cross-Blue Shield Assn., Chgo., 1979-80; asst. dirs. ops. Akron (Ohio) City Hosp., 1980-81, assoc. dir. planning, 1981-83, exec. v.p., 1983-88, Riverside Meth. Hosps., Columbus, Ohio, 1988-92, pres., COO, 1992-93, pres., CEO, 1993-96; pres. Ea. region Cath. Health Initiatives, Aston, Pa., 1996-97; exec. v.p., COO Summa Health Sys., Akron, Ohio, 1997—98; pres., CEO Henry Ford Health Sys. 1998—. Bd. dirs. Third Bank Corp., First Nat. Bank of Ohio, Mich. Health and Hosp. Assn., Greater Detroit Area Health Council. Trustee Kresge Found. Home: 15 Turnberry Ln Dearborn MI 48120-1167 Office: Henry Ford Health Sys 1 Ford Pl Detroit MI 48202*

**SCHLICHTING, WILLIAM HENRY**, lawyer, writer; b. Austin, Minn., Jan. 24, 1944; s. John Frederick and Frances Amelia (Garbisch) Schlichting. BA, St. Olaf Coll., 1966; MS, U. Chgo., 1970; JD, Columbia U., 1973; LLM in Taxation, NYU, 1979. Bar: NY 1974, Minn. 1981, US Tax Ct. 1982. Assoc. Shea & Gould, NYC, 1973—76; editor Law Jour. Pub. Co., NYC, 1976—79, Matthew Bender & Co., Inc., NYC, 1979—81; assoc. Peterson, Hanson, Schlichting & Davies, albert Lea, Minn., 1981—83; gen. counsel, sec. Med. Venture, Inc., Mpls., 1983—89; writer Matthew Bender & Co., Inc., NYC, 1989—91; acquisitions editor, classifier West Group, Eagan, Minn., 1991—2002; bd. dirs. The Aliveness Project, Inc., 2004—, pres., chmn., 2005—. Writer Butterworth Legal Pub., Mason divsn., St. Paul, 1983—84. Author, editor Banking Law, 1993, Clark's Digest-Annotator, 1976—79; contbr. articles to profl. jours. Mem. investments and fin. com. Philanthrofund Found., 2005—. Fellow, NSF, 1966—70; Erik Hetle scholar, 1966—67. Mem.: Minn. Bar Assn., Phi Beta Kappa, Sigma Pi Sigma. Lutheran. Home: 5901 Laurel Ave #325 Golden Valley MN 55416-1075 Personal E-mail: wmhenrys@comcast.net.

**SCHLICK, AUSTIN C.**, lawyer; JD, Yale Law Sch., 1990. Bar: DC, Pa. Law clk. to Chief Judge Abner Mikva US Ct. Appeals (DC Cir.); law clk. to Justice Sandra Day O'Connor US Supreme Ct.; assoc. Klein, Farr, Smith & Taranto, Washington, 1992—93; assoc. to ptnr. Kellogg, Huber, Hansen, Todd & Evans, Phila. & Washington DC, 1993—2000; asst. solicitor gen. Office of Solicitor Gen., US Dept. Justice, Washington, 2000—04; dep. gen. counsel Fed. Communications Commn., Washington, 2004—05, acting gen. counsel, 2005—.

**SCHLICKEISEN, RODGER OSCAR**, non-profit environmental organization executive; b. Houston, Jan. 24, 1941; s. Oscar and Elvene Alice (Rennemo) S.; m. Susan Jane Culver, May 23, 1970; 1 child, Derek. BA, U. Wash., 1963; MBA, Harvard U., 1965; DBA, George Washington U., 1978. Loan officer Export-Import Bank of U.S., Washington, 1968-70; pres.

Gryphon, Inc., Washington, 1970-74; group dir. com. on budget U.S. Senate, Washington, 1974-79; assoc. dir. econs. and govt. U.S. Office of Mgmt. and Budget, Washington, 1979-80; v.p. Craver, Mathews, Smith & Co., Falls Church, Va., 1980-81, CEO, 1981-87; chief of staff Office of U.S. Senator Max Baucus, Washington, 1987-91; pres.. CEO Defenders of Wildlife, Washington, 1991—, Defenders of Wildlife Action Fund, Washington, 2001—. Bd. dirs. Partnership Project, Inc., Washington, League Conservative Voters, Washington, Keystone Ctr., Colo.; bd. advisors Environ. Comms. Orgn., L.A., 1992—; Environ. Media Assn., L.A., 1992—. Contbr. articles to profl. publs. Va. state chmn. Common Cause, 1971-74. Office: Defenders of Wildlife 1130 17th St NW Washington DC 20036

**SCHLIEKER, JANICE ELAINE JONES,** campus minister; b. Omaha, Jan. 10, 1957; d. Robert W. and Greta Jane (Young) Jones; m. John F. Schlieker, III, Sept. 12, 1981. BTh in New Testament, Ozark Bible Coll., 1980. Cashier, bookkeeper Northampton 4 Theaters, Omaha, 1973-75; florist Higdon's Florist, Joplin, Mo., 1978-80; assoc. campus min. Koinonia Campus Ministry, Joplin, Mo., 1978-80; campus min. Colo. Christian Campus Ministries, Ft. Collins, 1980—2000; florist Bath Nursery, 1997—99, Rocky Mountain Floral Supply, 1999—2003; cons. Longaberger Basket Co., 2003—; office mgr. Alicia's Attic & Poudre Aviation, 2004—. Mem. local planning com. N.Am. Christian Conv., Cin., 1990—91. Mem.: Aircraft Owners and Pilots Assn., Univ. Religious Dirs. Assn. (v.p. Ft. Collins chpt. 1986—87), Nat. Assn. Christian Campus Ministries (sec.-treas. 1987—93), No. Colo. Running Club, Ft. Collins Running Club. Avocations: running, crocheting, flying, photography, reading.

**SCHLIEVE, HY C. J.,** school administrator; b. Mandan, N.D., Apr. 4, 1952; s. Calvin L. and Loretta L. (Johnson) S.; m. Terri Ann Hansen, Dec. 30, 1977; children: Derek, Aaron, Jessica. BA, N.D. State U., 1974, MS, 1984; EdD, Calif. Coast U., 1994. Tchr., coach Halliday (N.D.) Pub. Sch., 1974-75, Drake (N.D.) Pub. Sch., 1975-76, Montpelier (N.D.) Pub. Sch., 1976-81; prin. Unity Pub. Sch., Petersburg, N.D., 1981-83, Page (N.D.) Pub. Sch., 1983-85; supt. Wolford (N.D.) Pub. Sch., 1985-87, Garrison (N.D.) Pub. Schs., 1987-93; prin. Buhl Joint Sch. Dist. 412, Idaho, 1993-95, Oconto Falls Area Sch. Dist., Wis., 1995-99; supt. Ellendale (N.D.) Pub. Schs. #40, 1999—. Com. mem. NDASA Rsch. and Evaluation, Garrison, 1988-93; fiscal agt. Mo. Hills Consortium, McLean County, N.D., 1989-93; cons. asbestos Garrison Pub. Sch. Dist., 1987-93. Sec. Govtl. Affairs Com., Garrison, 1987-93; mem. Tourism Com., Garrison, 1988-92, Econ. Devel. Com., 1988-89. Recipient Nat. Superintendent of the Yr. awd., North Dakota, Am. Assn. of School Administrators, 1992. Mem. Nat. Assn. Secondary Sch. Prins. (prin. assessor tng. 1990), NSBA Fed. Policy Coords. Network. Avocations: golf, hunting, fishing, bowling, outdoor activities. Office: Ellendale Pub Schs PO Box 400 321 N 1st St Ellendale ND 58436 Home: 1330 12th St N Apt 18 Wahpeton ND 58075-5028

**SCHLOERB, PAUL RICHARD,** surgeon, educator; b. Buffalo, Oct. 12, 1919; s. Herman George and Vera (Gross) S.; m. Louise M. Grimmer, Feb. 25, 1950; children: Ronald G., Patricia S. Johnson, Marilyn A. Hock, Dorothy S. Hoban, P. Richard. AB, Harvard U., 1941; MD, U. Rochester, 1944. Intern U. Rochester Med. Sch., 1944—45, asst. resident, 1947—48, instr. surgery, 1952; rsch. fellow, resident Peter Bent Brigham Hosp., Boston, 1948—52; faculty U. Kans. Med. Ctr., Kansas City, 1952—79, prof. surgery, 1964—79, 1988—2006, prof. surgery emeritus, 2006—, dean for rsch., 1972—79, dir. nutritional support svc., 1993—2002; dir. surgery U. Rochester (NY) Med Ctr., 1979—88, adj. prof. surgery, 1988—90; surgeon Strong Meml. Hosp., 1979—88, dir. Surg. ICU, 1979—85, dir. surg. nutritional support service. Contbr. over 100 articles to profl. jours. Lt. (j.g.), M.C. USNR, 1944-45; to lt. 1953-55. Mem. AMA, ACS, AAAS, Am. Surg. Assn., Soc. U. Surgeons, Am. Physiol. Soc., Internat. Soc. Surgery, Ctrl. Surg. Assn., Am. Assn. for Surgery of Trauma, Am. Assn. Cancer Rsch., Biomed. Engring. Soc., Am. Inst. Nutrition, Am. Soc. Clin. Nutrition, Sigma Xi. Achievements include first to measure total body water in humans. Office: Dept Surgery U Kansas Med Ctr Kansas City KS 66160-0001 Office Phone: 913-588-7565. Business E-Mail: pschloer@kumc.edu.

**SCHLOM, JEFFREY BERT,** research scientist; b. NYC, June 22, 1942; s. David and Anna Schlom; m. Karlene; children: Amy Melissa, Steven Michael. BS (Pres.'s scholar), Ohio State U., 1964; MS, Adelphi U., 1966; PhD, Rutgers U., 1969. Instr. Columbia Coll. Phys. and Surg., 1969-71, asst. prof., 1971-73; chmn. breast cancer virus segment Nat Cancer Inst., NIH, Bethesda, Md., 1973-76, chief lab. tumor immunology and biology, 1983—, head exptl. oncology sect., 1976-83; prof. George Washington U., Washington, 1975—. Disting. lectr. Can. Cancer Soc., 1985 Contbr. articles to profl. jours. Recipient Dir.'s award NIH, 1977, 89, Tech. Transfer award NIH, 1994, 95, 96, Disting. Scientist award Turin U., 1996, others. Mem. Am. Assn. Cancer Rsch. (Rosenthal award 1989), Am. Soc. Cytology (Basic Rsch. award 1987). Office: Inst Health Bldg 10 Rm 8B09 Bethesda MD 20892 Business E-Mail: js141c@nih.gov.

**SCHLOSBERG, THEODORE K.,** music educator; b. New Brunswick, N.J., Sept. 1, 1936; s. Ralph Schlosberg and Renee Aronson Schlosberg Sosin; m. Kathryn Sell Levine, Sept. 25, 1982; children: Lindsey Levine, Stephanie Levine Harvey; m. Natalie Berkowski, Aug. 14, 1959 (div. Feb. 1982); children: Susan Schlosberg McWilliams, Gail Schlosberg Sokoloff. BA in Music Edn., Trenton State Coll., MusM; EdD in Creative Arts, Rutgers U. Music tchr. Plainfield Pub. Schs., 1960—67, Westfield Pub. Schs., 1967—96; founder, exec. dir. N.J. Workshop for Arts, 1972—. Dir. fine arts Lanark Camp, Maine, 1960—68; dir. Plainfield Sch. Music, 1960—68; dir. Plainfield Summer Music Workshop, 1964—67, Summer Music Workshop, Plainfield, 1964—67, Plainfield, 1997—, Workshop for Arts, Greenbrook, NJ, 1995, Recreation Dept. Music Workshops, Fanwood, NJ, 1995, Saturday Music Workshop, Plainfield, 1999—, Westfield Cmty. Ctr. Sr. Citizens Music Workshop, 2002. Recipient Faith in Westield award, Westfield C. of C., 1991, 2001, numerous grants. Home: 26 Scudder Rd Westfield NJ 07090 Office: NJ Workshop for Arts Inc 150-152 E Broad St Westfield NJ 07090

**SCHLOSS, IRVING STEVEN,** lawyer; b. NYC, Feb. 3, 1945; s. Arthur and Bianca (Steinberger) S.; m. Christine Skeeles, June 28, 1970 (div. Mar. 1999); children: Tracy, David; m. Deborah V. Abildsoe, Nov. 21, 1999. AB magna cum laude, Harvard Coll., 1966; LLB, Yale U., 1970. Bar: Conn. 1972, U.S. Dist. Ct. Conn. 1972, U.S. Ct. Appeals (2d cir.) 1973, U.S. Tax Ct. 1985; cert. mediator, 2003. Law clerk for Judge Spottswood Robinson, III (D.C. cir.) U.S. Ct. Appeals, Washington, 1970-71; ptnr. Tyler, Cooper & Alcorn, LLP, New Haven and Madison, 1976—. Co-author: Understanding TIAA-CREF: Planning for a Secure and Comfortable Retirement, 2000; bd. editors Tax Mgmt. Estates, Gift & Trust Jour.; contbr. articles to profl. jours. Bd. dirs. Guilford (Conn.) Free Libr., 1986-92, Shoreline Found., Guilford, 1984-93, 97—, New Haven Symphony Orch., 1995-2001; vol. CPTV Auction, West Hartford, 1987-88; mem. Rep. Town Commn., Guilford, 1987-91. Recipient Man of Yr. award Guilford YMCA, 1990. Mem. ABA, Conn. Bar Assn. (chmn. sect. corps. and other bus. orgns. 1988-90, mem. exec. com. estates and probate sect. 1996—), Am. Coll. Trust and Estate Counsel (editor ACTEC Studies), New Haven Conn. Bar Assn., Mory's Assn., Quinnipiack Club. Office: Tyler Cooper & Alcorn PO Box 1936 New Haven CT 06509-0906 also: 23 Woodland Rd Madison CT E-mail: ischloss@attglobal.net, schloss@tylercooper.com.

**SCHLOSS, NATHAN,** retired economist; b. Balt., Jan. 14, 1927; s. Howard L. and Louise (Levi) S.; m. Rosa Montalvo, Mar. 1, 1958; children: Nina L., Carolyn D. BS in Bus., Johns Hopkins U., 1950. Buyer Pacific Coast gen. merchandise office Sears Roebuck & Co., Los Angeles, 1955-60; staff econ. rsch. dept. Chevy Corp., 1960-63; sr. market analyst corp. rsch. dept. Montgomery Ward & Co., Chgo., 1963-65; rsch. mgr. real estate dept. Walgreen Co., Chgo., 1970-72; v.p. rsch. and planning Maron Properties Ltd., Montreal, Que., Can., 1972-74; corp. economist, fin. analyst Real Estate Rsch. Corp., Chgo., 1974-88, sr. v.p. 1986-88, treas., chief fin. analyst, 1982-88; economist Office of Ill. Atty. Gen., Chgo., 1988-97. Cons. in field, 1965-97. Contbr. articles on fin. and market analysis of real estate to profl.

jours. Mem. Plan. Commn., village of Wilmette, Ill., 1975-77, tech. adv. com. on employment and tng. data Ill. employment and Tng. Coun., 1979-82, tech. adv. com. Ill. Job Tng. Coordinating Council, 1983-87; mem. com. on price indexes and productivity fgn. labor Bus. Rsch. Adv. Coun. of Bur. Labor Stats, Dept. Labor, 1979-88, chairperson, 1985-86, com. on employment and unemployment. Recipient Commendable Svc. Citation, Bur. Labor Stats., Dept. Labor, 1987. Mem. Am. Mktg. Assn., Nat. Assn. Bus. Economists, Ill. Econ. Assn., Lambda Alpha. Home and Office: 115 Hollywood Ct Wilmette IL 60091-3122 Office Phone: 847-251-9582.

**SCHLOSSER, ANNE GRIFFIN,** librarian; b. NYC, Dec. 28, 1939; d. C. Russell and Gertrude (Taylor) Griffin; m. Gary J. Schlosser, Dec. 28, 1965. BA in History, Wheaton Coll., Norton, Mass., 1962; MLS, Simmons Coll., 1964; cert. archives adminstrn., Am. U., 1970. Head UCLA Theater arts Libr., 1964-69; dir. Louis B. Mayer Libr., Am. Film Inst., L.A., 1969-88, dir. film/TV documentation workshop, 1977-87; head Cinema-TV Libr. and Archives of the Performing Arts, U. So. Calif., L.A., 1988-91; dir. Entertainment Resources Seminar, 1990; dir. rsch. libr. Warner Bros., 1991—2001; part-time libr. Nevada County Libr., 2002—. Project dir. Motion Pictures, Television, Radio: A Union Catalogue of Manuscript and Special Collections in the Wesern U.S., 1977. Recipient numerous grants for script indexing, manuscript cataloging, libr. automation. Mem. Soc. Calif. Archivists (pres. 1982-83), Theater Libr. Assn (exec. bd. 1983-86), Spl. Librs. Assn. Democrat. Episcopalian. Avocations: swimming, reading, dog training.

**SCHLOSSER, ERIC,** writer; Writer, contributor Atlantic Monthly Mag. Author: (books) Fast Food Nation; television appearances 60 Minutes, CNN, NBC Nightly News, Fox News; contbr. articles to numerous profl. jours. Achievements include several months on new york times best-seller list, 2004-2005; film based on first book produced, 2006. Office: c/o Houghton Mifflin 222 Berkeley St Boston MA 02116*

**SCHLOSSER, HERBERT S.,** broadcasting company executive; b. Atlantic City, Apr. 21, 1926; s. Abraham and Anna (Olesker) S.; m. Judith P. Gassner, July 8, 1951; children: Lynn C., Eric M. AB summa cum laude, Princeton, 1948; LL.B., Yale, 1951. Bar: N.Y. 1952. Assoc. firm Wickes, Riddell, Bloomer, Jacobi & McGuire, N.Y.C., 1951-54; Phillips, Nizer, Benjamin, Krim & Ballon, N.Y.C., 1954-57; with NBC, 1957-78; v.p., gen. mgr. Calif. Nat. Prodns., Inc. sub. NBC, 1960-61, dir. talent and program adminstrn., 1961-62, v.p. talent and program adminstrn., 1962-66; v.p. programs West Coast NBC, 1966-72 v.p. NBC-TV Network, 1972-73, pres., 1973-74, mem. bd. dirs., 1973-78; pres. NBC, Inc., 1974-78, CEO, 1977-78; exec. v.p. RCA, 1978-85; sr. advisor broadcasting and entertainment Schroder & Co., Inc., N.Y.C., 1986—2000; sr. advisor, ind. cons. comms. investment banking Citigroup Global Markets Inc., 2000—. Ptnr. Arts and Entertainment Cable Network, RCA/Columbia Home Video. Trustee Internat. Radio and TV Found., 1972-74; former mem. govs. Ford's Theatre Soc.; former trustee Nat. Urban League; chmn. bd. Am. Mus. of the Moving Image; bd. dirs. Chamber Music Soc. of Lincoln Ctr. With USNR, 1944-46. Recipient Humanitarian award NCCJ, 1974, Gold Brotherhood award, 1978 Mem. ABA, Assn. Bar City N.Y., Coun. on Fgn. Rels., Acad. TV Arts and Scis., Advt. Coun. (past dir.), Yale Law Sch. Assn., Internat. Radio and TV Soc. (trustee 1973-74), Hollywood Radio and TV Soc. (trustee 1970-72), Century Assn., Princeton Club (N.Y.), Phi Beta Kappa (pres. alumni assn. So. Calif. 1970-72. Office: Citigroup Global Markets 388 Greenwich St New York NY 10013-2375

**SCHLOSSMAN, HOWARD HARVEY,** psychoanalysis educator; b. Bklyn., Nov. 8, 1915; s. Joseph and Sadie (Kosakofsky) S.; m. Sylvia Simkin, Apr. 14, 1920; children: Doralynn Pines, Paul. MD, St. Louis U., 1939. Diplomate Am. Bd. Psychiatry and Neurology; cert. Am. Psychoanalytical Assn. Assoc. clin. prof. NYU Sch. Medicine, N.Y.C., 1947—, Albert Einstein Coll. Med., N.Y.C., 1961-74; clin. prof. N.J. Coll. Medicine and Dentistry, Newark, 1961—. Contbr. articles to profl. jours. Capt. U.S. Army, 1941-45, ETO. Fellow Am. Psychiat. Assn.(disting. life); mem. Am. Psychoanalytic Assn., N.Y. Psychoanalytic Inst. (treas. 1976-80), Internat. Psychoanalytic Assn. (treas. 1985-91). Democrat. Avocation: egyptian hieroglyphs. Office: 39 Park Pl Englewood NJ 07631-2918 Office Phone: 201-567-2490.

**SCHLOSSMAN, JOHN ISAAC,** architect; b. Chgo., Aug. 21, 1931; s. Norman Joseph and Carol (Rosenfeld) S.; m. Shirley Goulding Rhodes, Feb. 8, 1959; children: Marc N., Gail S. Mewhort, Peter C. Student, Grinnell Coll., 1949-50; BA, U. Minn., 1953, BArch, 1955, MArch, MIT, 1956. Registered architect, Ill. Archtl. designer The Architects Collaborative, Cambridge, Mass., 1956-57; architect Loebl Schlossman & Hackl and predecessors, Chgo., 1959-65, assoc., 1965-70, prin., 1970-98, cons. prin., 1998—. Bd. overseers Coll. Arch. Ill. Inst. Tech., Chgo.; adv. bd. Coll. of Arch. and Landscape Arch. U. Minn., 2003—; founding bd. dirs. Chgo. Archtl. Assistance Ctr., 1974-79 Chmn. Glencoe Plan Commn., Ill., 1977-82; mem. Village of Glencoe Contextual Design Rev. Commn., 2005-0; trustee Com. for Green Bay Trail, Glencoe, 1970-77, Chgo. Arch. Found., 1971-75, Graham Found. for Advanced Studies in Fine Arts, 1995-99, pres. 1999-2001; adv. bd. dirs. Merit Sch. of Music, Chgo., 1983-93, pres., 1988-90, hon. trustee, 1996; governing mem. Chgo. Symphony Orch.; mem. founders coun. Field Mus., Chgo.; mem. zoning and planning com. Greater North Michigan Ave. Assn., Chgo., 2000-01; mem. Nat. Trust Coun., Nat. Trust for Hist. Preservation, Washington. Named dir. for life Young Men's Jewish Coun., Chgo., 1971; Rotch travelling scholar, 1957; sustaining fellow Art Inst. Chgo. Fellow AIA (trustee ins. trust 1971-76, chmn. ins. com. 1974-75, v.p. Chgo. chpt. 1975, chmn. architects liability com. 1976, 80-82, hon. found. trustee 1995—), Tavern Club (gov. 1986-88, v.p. 1990), The Club at Symphony Ctr., The Arts Club, Alpha Rho Chi. Office: Loebl Schlossman & Hackl 232 Mary St Winnetka IL 60093-1522 E-mail: jschloss@worldnet.att.net.

**SCHLOSSMAN, STUART FRANKLIN,** physician, educator, researcher; b. NYC, Apr. 18, 1935; s. Abe and Pearl (Susser) Schlossman; m. Judith Seryl Rubin, May 25, 1958; children: Robert, Peter. BA magna cum laude, NYU, 1955, MD, 1958; MA, Harvard U., 1975. Intern in medicine med. divsn. III Bellevue Hosp., N.Y.C., 1958—59, asst. resident in medicine med. divsn. III, 1959—60; Nat. Found. fellow dept. microbiology Coll. Physicians Columbia U., N.Y.C., 1960—62; asst. physician med. svc. Vanderbilt Clinic, Coll. Physician USPHS, Washington, 1960—62; Ward hematology fellow dept. internal medicine Sch. Washington U., St. Louis, 1962—63; rsch. assoc. lab. biochemistry Nat. Cancer Inst. USPHS, Washington, 1963—65; clin. instr. in medicine Sch. of Medicine George Washington U., 1964—65; assoc. in medicine, dir. blood bank Beth Israel Hosp., Boston, 1965—66; instr. Med. Sch. Harvard U., Boston, 1966—68, asst. physician, 1967—68, chief clin. immunology, 1971—73; physician Beth Israel Hosp., Boston, 1968—; from asst. to assoc. prof. medicine Harvard Med. Sch., Boston, 1968—77, prof., 1977—, Baruj Benacerraf prof. medicine, 1990—, chief divsn. tumor immunology and immunotherapy, 1973—; sr. physician Brigham and Women's Hosp., Boston, 1976—. Mem. editl. bd. Jour. of Immunology, 1969—74, Cellular Immunology, 1970—, Human Immunology, 1979—84, Clin. Immunology and Immunopathology, 1979—, mem. editl. bd.Hybridoma Hybridoma, 1980—, Cancer Investigation, 1981—, Stem Cells, 1981—, Cancer Revs., 1984, Internat. Jour. of Cell Cloning, 1983—86, mem. editl. bd. Cancer Treatment Reports, 1976—80, assoc. editor Human Lymphocyte Differentation, 1980—82; contbr. articles to profl. jours. Recipient Solomon Berson Achievement award, 1984, Robert Koch prize and medal, 1984. Fellow: AAAS; mem.: NAS, Assn. Am. Physicians, Am. Soc. Clin. Investigation, Am. Soc. Immunologists, Am. Soc. Hematology, Inst. of Medicine of NAS, Alpha Omega Alpha. Office: Dana-Farber Cancer Inst Divsn Tumor Immunology 44 Binney St Mayer 557 Boston MA 02115-6084 Office Phone: 617-632-3325. Business E-Mail: stuart_schlossman@dfci.harvard.edu.

**SCHLOSSTEIN, RALPH L.,** diversified financial services company executive; With White House, Washington, Treasury Dept., Washington; mem. staff U.S. Congress, Washington; with Lehman Bros.; co-founder, pres. BlackRock Inc., N.Y., 1988—. Bd. dirs. BlackRock Inc., PNC Asset Mgmt. Group Inc. Office: BlackRock Inc 40 East 52nd St New York NY 10022

**SCHLOTMAN, J. MICHAEL,** food products executive; Joined The Kroger Co., Cin., 1985—, v.p. financial services & control, 1995—2000, CFO, 2000—, sr. v.p., 2003—. Office: Kroger 1014 Vine St Cincinnati OH 45202*

**SCHLOTTERBECK, DAVID L.,** medical products executive; BSEE, GM Inst.; MSEE, Purdue U.; grad., Stanford U. Exec. Inst., 1984. Exec. v.p., COO Nellcor, Inc., 1991—94; pres.. CEO Vitalcom, Inc., 1995—97; pres., COO Pacific Sci. Co., 1997—98, ALARIS Med. Systems, 1999; CEO Clin. Technologies and Svcs. Cardinal Health, CEO Pharm. and Med. Products, 2006—. Office: Cardinal Health 7000 Cardinal Pl Dublin OH 43017*

**SCHLOTTERBECK, WALTER ALBERT,** manufacturing executive, lawyer; b. N.Y.C., Dec. 22, 1926; s. Albert Gottlob and Maria Louise (Fritz) S.; m. Pauline Elizabeth Hoerz, Sept. 2, 1951; children— Susan, Thomas, Paul. AB, Columbia U., 1949, LL.B., 1952. Bar: N.Y. 1953. Counsel Gen. Electric Co. (various locations), 1952-87; v.p., corp. counsel Gen. Electric Co., N.Y.C., 1970-77, sec., 1975-76; gen. counsel Gen. Electric Co. (various locations), 1976-87, sr. v.p., 1977-87. Served with USNR, 1944-46. Home: 201 Overlake Dr E Medina WA 98039-5331

**SCHLOW, MICHAEL,** food service executive; b. Bklyn. Diploma, Acad. Culinary Arts N.J.; trained with Mark Straussman. Chef, owner Radius, Boston; chef Coco Pazzo, Le Madri; exec. chef Sapore di Mare, L.I., 75 Main; owner Ariel & Michael; chef, owner Radius, Boston, 1999—. Author: (cookbooks) It's About Time: Great Recipes for Everyday Life, 2005. Named Best Chef (twice), Boston Mag.; recipient Culinary Award of Excellence, Robert Mondavi Winery, 2000, American Express Best Chef: Northeast award, James Beard Found., 2001. Office: Radius 8 High St Boston MA 02110

**SCHLOZMAN, BRADLEY J,** prosecutor; b. Overland Park, Kans. BA in Hist., U. Pa.; JD, George Washington U. Law Sch. Clk. Chief US Dist. Judge G. Thomas VanBebber, Dist. Kans., US Ct. Appeals, 10th Cir.; atty. Howrey, Simon, & White, LLP, Washington, 1999—2001; counsel to Dep. Atty. Gen. Larry Thompson; dep. asst. atty. gen. US Dept. Justice, 2003, acting asst. atty. gen., Civil Rights divsn., prin. dep. asst. atty. gen., Civil Rights divsn., US atty. (we. dist.) Mo., 2006—. Office: US Attys Office Charles E Whittaker Courthouse 400 E 9th St Kansas City MO 64106*

**SCHLUB, TERESA RAE,** minister; b. Oak Park, Ill., July 11, 1946; d. Robert Carl and Shirley Rae (Listhartke) Grupe. BA, Westmar Teikyo U., 1971; MDiv, Garrett Evangel. Seminary, Evanston, Ill., 1974. Ordained deacon United Meth. Ch., 1973, elder, 1978. Asst. minister First United Meth. Ch., Morris, Ill., 1974-76; minister Leaf River (Ill.) German Valley United Meth. Ch., 1976-82, East Jordan United Meth. Ch., Sterling, Ill., 1982-86, Paw Paw (Ill.) United Meth. Ch., 1986-89, Community United Meth. Ch., LaMoille, Ill., 1989-95, Capron (Ill.) United Meth. Ch., 1995—2000, North Boone Coop. Ministries, Poplar Grove, Ill., 1998—2000. Mem. alumni coun., sec. Garrett Evangel. Theol. Seminary, Evanston, 1974-76; mem. Conf. Bd. of Evangelism, 1974-76, founder, Schlub Ministries Bd. dirs. Green Hills coun. Girls Scouts U.S., Freeport, Ill., 1986-88, Lee County Red Cross, Dixon, Ill., 1986-89, Crossroads Counseling Ctr., Mendota, 1989-91; bd. dirs. Quad County Counseling Ctr., Princeton, 1991—, treas., 1993-94; mem. Ill. Home Extension Assn., Grundy, Ogle, Whiteside and Lee Counties, 1974-89; sec. DeKalb Dist. Com. of Ordained Ministry; mem. Boone County Coun. Aging, 1997-2000, Boone County Planning Commn., 1998-2000; founder Schlub Ministries, Pathways to Paralegal, Kaplan U., 2005. Home: 4027 Albright Ln Rockford IL 61103 *Life becomes meaningful when one is able to become vulnerable and be willing to take risks. This becomes possible when one has faith in God and confidence in the self. It also helps to know and experience the love of others.*

**SCHLUETER, DAVID ARNOLD,** law educator; b. Sioux City, Iowa, Apr. 29, 1946; s. Arnold E. and Helen A. (Dettmann) S.; m. Linda L. Boston, Apr. 22, 1972; children: Jennifer, Jonathan. BA, Tex. A&M U., 1969; JD, Baylor U., 1971; LLM, U. Va., 1981. Bar: Tex. 1971, D.C. 1973, U.S. Ct. Mil. Appeals 1972, U.S. Supreme Ct. 1976. Legal counsel U.S. Supreme Ct., Washington, 1981—83; assoc. dean St. Mary's U., San Antonio, 1984—89, prof. law, 1986—, Hardy prof. trial advocacy, dir. advocacy programs, 2000—; reporter Fed. Adv. Com. on Criminal Rules, 1988—2005. Chmn. JAG adv. coun., 1974-75. Author: Military Criminal Justice: Practice and Procedure, 1982, 6th edit., 2004; (with others) Military Rules of Evidence Manual, 1981, 5th edit., 2003, Texas Rules of Evidence Manual, 1983, 7th edit., 2005, Texas Evidentiary Foundations, 1992, 3d edit., 2005, Military Evidentiary Foundations, 1994, 2d edit., 2000, Military Criminal Procedure Forms, 1997, 2d edit., 2003, Federal Evidence Tactics, 1997, Texas Rules of Evidence Trial Book, 2000; editor-in-chief: Emerging Problems Under the Federal Rules of Evidence, 3d edit., 1998; contbr. articles to legal publs. Maj. JAGC, U.S. Army, 1972-81. Fellow Am. Law Inst., Tex. Bar Found. (life), Am. Bar Found. (life); mem. ABA (vice-chmn. criminal justice sect. coun. 1991-94, vice-chmn. com. on criminal justice and mil. 1983-84, chmn. standing com. on mil. law 1991-92, mem. standing com. on armed forces law, chmn. editl. adv. bd., Criminal Justice Mag., 1989-91, 2000-), Tex. Bar Assn. Republican. Lutheran. Office: St Marys U Sch Law 1 Camino Santa Maria St San Antonio TX 78228-8603

**SCHLUETER, JUNE MAYER,** literature educator, writer; b. Passaic, N.J., Nov. 4, 1942; m. Paul Schlueter. BA in English magna cum laude, Fairleigh Dickinson U., 1970; MA in English, Hunter Coll., CCNY, 1973; PhD in English and Comparative Lit., Columbia U., 1977. Asst. prof. Lafayette Coll., Easton, Pa., 1977-84, assoc. prof., 1984-91, prof., 1991-92, Charles A. Dana prof., 1992—, head English dept., 1992-93; asst. to provost, 1986-90; acting provost., 1993-94; provost Lafayette Coll., Easton, Pa., 1994—. Fulbright prof. Gesamthochschule Kassel Univ., Fed. Republic Germany, 1978-79; chmn. Shakespeare Seminar Columbia U., 1989-91, 2004-06, exec. bd., 1989—; active NEH summer seminar for coll. profs., 1981, lectr. Commonwealth Partnership Summer Lit. Inst., 1985-87, dir. summer seminar for sch. tchrs., 1988, selection panel, 1989, 91, evaluator Instl. Grant Program, 1990. Author: Metafictional Characters in Modern Drama, 1979, The Plays and Novels of Peter Handke, 1981, Dramatic Closure: Reading the End, 1995; (with James K. Flanagan) Arthur Miller, 1987; (with James P. Lusardi) Reading Shakespeare in Performance: King Lear, 1990; editor: Feminist Rereadings of Modern American Drama, 1989, Modern American Drama: The Female Canon, 1990, Critical Essays: The Two Gentlemen of Verona, 1995; (with Paul Schlueter) The English Novel: Twentieth Century Criticism, Vol. 2: Twentieth Century Novelists, 1982, Modern American Literature, Supplement II, 1985, An Encyclopedia of British Women Writers, 1988, Francis A. March: Selected Writings of the First Professor of English, 2005; (with Enoch Brater) Approaches to Teaching Beckett's Waiting for Godot, 1991; (with Paul Nelsen) Acts of Criticism: Performance Matters in Shakespeare and His Contemporaries, 2006; co-editor Shakespeare Bull., 1983-2003; assoc. editor Stages, 1984-90; editl. bd. Studies in Am. Drama, 1945-Present, 1989—2000; editl. cons. Modern Drama, Theatre Jour., PMLA, Studies in Twentieth Century Lit., Shakespeare Quar., others; contbr. revs., essays to profl. jours. Bd. govs. Fairleigh Dickinson U., Rutherford, N.J., 1985-90, bd. dirs., Madison, N.J., 1997-2005; mem. adv. com. Lehigh Valley Ednl. Coop., 1988-90; selection panel German Acad. Exch. Svc., Bonn, 1979. Rsch. grantee Lafayette Coll., 1977-93, NEH summer rsch. grantee, 1990, DAAD summer rsch. grantee, 1991. Mem. MLA (Shakespeare Assn. Am., Internat. Shakespeare Assn., Coll. English Assn., Samuel Beckett Soc., AAUP, Columbia Shakespeare Seminar. Home: 123 High St Easton PA 18042-1609 Office: Lafayette Coll Lafayette College Easton PA 18042

**SCHLUNTZ, ROGER,** architecture educator; BArch, U. Nebr.; MArch, U. Calif., Berkeley. Faculty mem. Calif. Poly. State U., San Luis Obispo, Calif., U. Nebr., 1969—77; dir. arch. program Ariz. State U., 1980—89; prof., dean arch. U. Miami, 1992—99; dean Sch. Arch. and Planning U. N.Mex., Albuquerque, 1999—. Mem. Nat. Register Peer Profls. U.S. Gen. Svcs. Adminstrn.; bd. mem. Nat. Archtl. Accrediting Bd., 2001—04. Co-author (with Tom Laging): The Nebraska Capitol and Environs Plan (First Honor award Progressive Arch. mag.). Fellow: AIA (exec. dir.); mem.: Assn. Collegiate Schs. Arch. Office: Univ NMex Sch Arch and Planning 2414 Central Ave SE Albuquerque NM 87131

**SCHLUTER, PETER MUELLER,** electronics executive; b. May 24, 1933; s. Fredric Edward and Charlotte (Mueller) S.; m. Jaquelin Ambler Lamond, Apr. 18, 1970 (div. June 1990); children: Jane Randolph Amitsis, Charlotte Mueller Bashforth, Anne Ambler; m. Christine Moon Van Ness, Feb. 7, 1998. BME, Cornell U., 1956; postgrad., Harvard U. Grad. Sch. Bus. Adm, 1982. Sr. engr. Thiokol Chem. Corp., Brigham City, Utah, 1958-59; assoc. Porter Internat. Co., Washington, 1960-65, v.p., pres., treas., dir., 1966-70; pres., treas., dir. Zito Co., Derry, NH, 1970-72; internat. bus. cons. Washington, 1972-74; v.p., dir. Buck Engring. Co. Inc. (now Lab-Volt Sys., Inc.), Farmingdale, NJ, 1975, pres., CEO, dir., 1975—. Mem. Rep. Inaugural Book and Program Com., 1969; mem. cmty. adv. bd. Monmouth coun. Girl Scouts US, NJ; mem. adv. coun. Monmouth U. Sch. Bus. Adminstrn.; bd. dirs. United Way of Monmouth County; trustee Monmouth Med. Ctr.; N.Am. rep., mem. presidium WORLDDIDAC, Bern, Switzerland, v.p., 1996—. Recipient Golden Osprey award So. Monmouth County C. of C., 1995. Fellow City and Guilds of London Inst. (hon.); mem. World Assn. Mfrs. and Distbrs. of Ednl. Materials (N.Am. rep.), Met. Club Washington, Rumson Country Club, Pi Tau Sigma. Home: 4 Quaker Ln Little Silver NJ 07739-1806 Office: PO Box 686 Farmingdale NJ 07727-0686

**SCHMALBECK, RICHARD LOUIS,** dean, lawyer; b. Chgo., Dec. 31, 1947; s. George Louis and Betty Jeanne Schmalbeck; m. Linda Michaels; children: Suzanne, Sabine. AB in Econs. with honors, U. Chgo., 1970, JD, 1975. Bar: Ohio 1975, D.C. 1977. Asst. to dir. and economist Ill. Housing Devel. Authority, Chgo., 1971-73; assoc. Vorys, Sater, Seymour & Pease, Columbus, Ohio, 1975-76; spl. asst. to assoc. dir. for econs. and govt. Office of Mgmt. and Budget, Washington, 1976-77; assoc. Caplin & Drysdale, Washington, 1977-80; assoc. prof. law Duke U., Durham, N.C., 1980-84, prof. law, 1984-90, 93—, vice chmn. acad. coun., 1984—85, 2001—02; dean U. Ill. Coll. Law, Champaign, 1990-93. Assoc. editor U. Chgo. Law Rev., 1974-75; contbr. articles to profl. jours. Mem. ABA (articles editor jour. 1977-80), Am. Law Inst., Phi Beta Kappa. Office: Duke University Sch of Law PO Box 90360 Durham NC 27708-0360

**SCHMALE, NEAL E.,** utilites company executive; BS in Petroleum Engring., Colo. Sch. Mines; LLD, Loyola U. With UNOCAL, sr. v.p., pres. petroleum products and chem. divsn., CFO; exec. v.p., CFO Sempra Energy, San Diego, 1997—2005, pres., COO, 2006. Office: Sempra Energy 101 Ash St San Diego CA 92101-3017

**SCHMALENSEE, RICHARD LEE,** dean; b. Belleville, Ill., Feb. 16, 1944; s. Fred and Marjorie June (Veigel) S.; m. Edeth Diane Hawk, Aug. 19, 1967; children: Alexander Clayton, Nicholas Hawk. SB, MIT, 1965, PhD in econs., 1970. Asst. prof. econs. U. Calif., San Diego, 1970—74, assoc. prof. econs., 1974—77; instr. Sloan Sch. Mgmt., MIT, Cambridge, Mass., 1967—69, asst. prof., 1970, assoc. prof. applied econs., 1977-79, prof., 1979—, prof. dept. econs., 1986—, Gordon Y Billard Prof. of Econs. and Mgmt., 1988-99, dep. dean, 1996—98, interim dean, 1998, dean, 1998—2000, John C Head III Dean, 2001—; dir. Ctr. for Energy and Environ. Policy Rsch. MIT, Cambridge, Mass., 1991-99. Vis. prof. Harvard Bus. Sch., 1985—86, U. Louvain, Belgium, 1985, vis. assoc. prof., rsch. fellow, Belgium, 1973—74; vis. scholar dept. econs. Harvard U., 1980—81; editl. bd. Jour. of Econs. and Mgmt. Strategy, 1992—98; assoc. editor Internat. Jour. Indsl. Orgn., 1982—89, Zeitschrift für Nationalökonomie, 1987—89, 1993—, Jour. Econ. Perspectives, 1992—98; bd. editors Am. Econ. Review, 1982—86; assoc. editor Jour. Indsl. Econs., 1977—81, bd. editors, 1981—89; founding editor Regulation of Econ. Activity, 1978—89, co-editor, 1989—; mem. Pres.'s Coun. Econ. Advisers, 1989—91; bd. dirs. Am. Coun. for Capital Formation Ctr. for Policy Rsch., 1991—, environ. policy fellow, 1997—98; rsch. assoc. Nat. Bur. Econ. Rsch., 1992—; Internat. Rsch. Fellow Kiel Inst. World Econs., 2001—; spl. cons. NERA Econ. Cons., 1981—89, 1991—; bd. dirs. Internat. Securities Exch., 2000—, MFS Investment Mgmt., 2002—. Author: The Economics of Advertising, 1972, Applied Microeconomics, 1973, The Control of Natural Monopolies, 1979; co-author: An Introduction to Applied Macroeconomics, 1973, Markets for Power, 1983, Economics, 1988, Paying with Plastic, 1999, Markets for Clean Air, 2000, Did Microsoft Harm Consumers? Two Opposing Views, 2000, Paying With Plastic, 2005; co-editor: The Empirical Renaissance in Industrial Economics, 1987, Handbook of Industrial Organization, 1989, Management: Inventing and Delivering Its Future, 2003. NSF grant, 1975-77, 81-83; Co-recipient Edward A. Hewett Prize, Am. Assn. for the Advancement of Slavic Studies, 1995 Fellow: AAAS, Econometric Soc.; mem.: Internat. Acad. Mgmt., Am. Econ. Assn. (nominating com. 1987, exec. com. 1993—95). Office: MIT Sloan Sch Mgmt 50 Memorial Dr Rm E52-473 Cambridge MA 02142-1347

**SCHMALSTIEG, WILLIAM RIEGEL,** retired Slavic languages educator; b. Sayre, Pa., Oct. 3, 1929; s. John William and Dorothy Augusta (Riegel) S.; m. Emily Lou Botdorf, Mar. 28, 1952; children: Linda, Roxanne. BA, U. Minn., 1950; postgrad., Columbia U., 1952; MA, U. Pa., 1951, PhD, 1956; PhD (hon.), Vilnius U., 1994. Instr. U. Ky., Lexington, 1956-59; assist. prof. Lafayette Coll., Easton, Pa., 1959-63; assoc. prof. U. Minn., Mpls., 1963-64; prof. Pa. State U., University Park, 1964—2002, head dept. Slavic langs., 1969-91. Mem. Internat. Commn. Balto-Slavic Linguistics, 1973—; appointed Edwin Erle Sparks prof. Slavic Lang., 1990. Author: (with L. Dambriunas and A. Klimas) An Introduction to Modern Lithuanian, 1966, 4th edit., 1990, 5th edit., 1993, reprinted as Beginner's Lithuanian, 1999, An Old Prussian Grammar, 1974, Studies in Old Prussian, 1976, Indo-European Linguistics, 1980, An Introduction to Old Church Slavic, 1976, 2d edit., 1983, A Lithuanian Historical Syntax, 1988; (with Warren Held and Janet Gertz) Beginning Hittite, 1988, A Student Guide to the Genitive of Agent in the Indo-European Languages, 1995, An Introduction to Old Russian, 1995, The Historical Morphology of the Baltic Verb, 2000; editor Gen. Linguistics, 1971-82; mem. editl. adv. bd. Jour. Indo-European Studies, Baltistica, Linguistica Baltica, Acta Linguistica Lithuanica, Archivum Lithuanicum, Lietuviu Kalbotyros Klausimai, Baltu Filologija. Served to 1st lt. U.S. Army, 1952-54. NEH grantee, 1978-79, Fulbright grantee and exch. scholar Acad. Scis., Vilnius, USSR, 1986; recipient Humanities medal Pa. State U., 1983, Friend of Lithuania award Knights of Lithuania, 1990, Lithuanian Govt. Mazvydas medal, 1997; named Disting. Alumnus Breck Sch., 1990. Mem.: Lithuanian Acad. Scis. (hon.), Assn. Advancement Baltic Studies (pres. 1982—84). Episcopalian. Home: 814 Cornwall Rd State College PA 16803-1430 Personal E-mail: emily@leanonemily.com.

**SCHMALZ, CARL NELSON, JR.,** artist, educator, art appraiser, printmaker; b. Ann Arbor, Mich., Dec. 26, 1926; s. Carl Nelson and Esther Dorothy (Fowler) S.; m. Dolores Irene Tourangeau, Dec. 2, 1950; children: Stephen Theodore (dec.), Mathew Nelson, Julia Irene. AB, Harvard U., 1948, MA, 1949, PhD, 1958; MA (hon.), Amherst Coll., 1969. Teaching fellow in fine arts Harvard U., Cambridge, Mass., 1950-52; asst. prof. Bowdoin Coll., Brunswick, Maine, 1953-62; curator, asst dir. Walker Art Mus., 1953-62; asst. prof. Harvard U., 1960; prof. Amherst Coll., 1962-95, prof. emeritus, 1995—. Lectr. in field; workshop tchr. in field. Author: Watercolor Lessons from Eliot O'Hara, 1974, Watercolor Your Way, 1978, Finding and Improving Your Painting Style, 1986, paperback, 1992; co-author: Science Education in the United States: Issues, Crises and Priorities, 1990; author numerous essays and reviews; exhibited in one-man shows including Cambridge (Mass.) Art Assn., 1948, Laing Gallery, Portland, Maine, 1955, Amherst (Mass.) Coll., 1963, U. Mass., 1965, W.C. Rawls Mus., Va., 1972, Concord (Mass.) Art Assn., 1974, Govt. House, Hamilton, Bermuda, 1979, Jones Library, Amherst, Mass., 1979, The Arlington, Kennebunkport, Maine, 1980, Harmon-Meek Gallery, Naples, Fla., 1987, 91, 92, 98, Gallery at 6 Deering St., Portland, Maine, 1987, 91, Fretz Gallery, Portland, 1987-88, Marsh Gallery, Amherst Coll., 1995, Kennebunk Free Libr, 2005; exhibited in group shows including Jordan Marsh Co., 1947, 48, 50, 71-73, Colby Coll., 1958, Carnegie Inst., Pitts., 1963, FAR Gallery, N.Y.C., 1964-68, Am. Watercolor Soc., 1966, 68, 70,

Bowdoin Coll. Mus., 1973, Balt. Watercolor Soc., 1976, Boston Atheneum, 1979, Watercolor U.S.A. Honor Soc., 1989, 91, Maine Art Gallery, 1991, Rolly-Michaux Gallery, Boston, 1995; represented in permanent collections: Signet Soc., Cambridge, Mass., Walker Art Mus., Brunswick, Maine, Jones & Laughlin Steel Corp., Diners Club Am., Kalamazoo Art Center, Hampshire Coll., Zanesville Art Inst., Blue Cross/Blue Shield, Philharmonic Ctr. for the Arts, Naples, Fla., Springfield (Mo.) Art Mus., Amherst Coll., Bowdoin Coll., Hampshire Coll., Kalamazoo Art Inst., Springfield (Mo.) Art Mus.; work published in various pubs. including The Artist's Guide for Using Color, 1992, The Artist's Mag., 1994, Splash 3: Ideas and Inspirations, 1994. Mem. exec. bd. Interfaith Housing Corp., Amherst, 1966-76; pres. bd. trustees Amherst Day Sch., 1966-69; mem. Pelham Arts Lottery Coun., 1984-90; v.p. bd. dirs. Portland Mus. Art, 1957-62, Kennebunk, Maine, Libr., 2005. Bacon fellow, 1951; recipient 1st prize watercolor Cambridge Art Assn. Ann., 1947, 1st prize for traditional watercolor Virginia Beach Boardwalk Show, 1965, South Mo. Trust purchase award Watercolor U.S.A., 1970, 1st prize watercolor 30th Ann. Kennebunk River Club Show, 1985, Purchase prize Watercolor U.S.A., 1997. Mem.: Coll. Art Assn., The Signet Soc., Watercolor U.S.A. Honor Soc. Democrat.

**SCHMALZ, DOUGLAS J.,** agricultural company executive; sr. v.p., CFO Archer Daniels Midland Co., Decatur, Ill., 2002—. Bd. dir. Cmty. Found. of Decatur Macon County, Ill. Office: Archer Daniels Midland Co 4666 E Fairies Pkwy PO Box 1470 Decatur IL 62526 Office Phone: 217-424-5200.*

**SCHMALZ, ELIZABETH MOODY,** cosmetics company executive; b. Pittsburgh, Pa., Feb. 18, 1951; d. Norman F. and Mary Edith (Husted) Moody; m. David A. Forsythe, Sept. 16, 1978 (div. 1988); m. Brian F. Schmalz, Dec. 16, 1989; children: Brian Norman, Elizabeth Mary. Studentt, Rumson Fair Haven, 1969; student, Vermont Coll., 1971, U. Arizona, 1973. Mgr. AGI Inc., N.Y.C., 1974-75; mktg. mgr. Germaine Monteil Cosmetics Inc., N.Y.C., 1976-79; product mgr. Estee Lauder Clinique Inc., N.Y.C., 1980-86; v.p. Revlon Inc., N.Y.C.; v.p. corp. product Estee Lauder, N.Y.C., 1986—2006, sr. v.p., 1986—93; prin., owner Elizabeth Forsyth Schmalz & Co., LLC, 1993—98; exec. v.p. Bath & Bodyworks, 1998—, exec. v.p. creative tech. innovations, 1998—; exec. v.p. creative tech. innovation Beauty Avenues, 2006—, exec. v.p. creative, tech., fragrance innovations N.Y.C., 2006—. Mem. Cosmitsi Exec. Women, Fashion Group. Home: 15 Downing Hill Ln Colts Neck NJ 07722-1414 Office Phone: 212-904-8030. Business E-Mail: BSchmalz@beautyavenues.com.

**SCHMALZRIED, MARVIN EUGENE,** financial consultant; b. Dighton, Kans., Nov. 11, 1924; s. Carl D. and Marie M. (Bahm) S.; m. Jean Landino, Nov. 27, 1946 (dec.); children— Darlene, Candace, Cynthia, Derek, Valerie, Rebecca; m. Judith Reichardt Stuart, Oct. 23, 2004. BBA, Northwestern U., 1949; LL.B., U. Conn., 1955. Bar: Conn. bar 1955; C.P.A., Conn. Acct. Webster, Blanchard & Willard, CPA's (named changed to Price Waterhouse & Co.), Hartford, Conn., 1950-55; contr., asst. treas. J.B. Williams Co., Glastonbury, Conn., 1955-57; treas., sec. Curtis 1000, Inc. (name changed to Am Bus. Products, Inc.), Atlanta, 1957-61; asst. to pres. Wyeth Labs., N.Y.C., 1961-63, comptroller, 1964-67, v.p., 1967-72, sr. v.p., 1972-84; pres. Venda Vid, Inc., N.Y.C., 1986-90; sr. v.p. View-Master Ideal Group, Inc., N.Y.C., 1987-90; exec. v.p. Strategics Inc., 1993-95. Recipient Gold medal Conn. Soc. C.P.A.'s, 1953 Mem. AICPA, ABA, Old Greenwich Friday Evening Reading Soc. (pres.) Clubs: Darien Country, Bent Tree Country. Home and Office: 4874 Cherry Laurel Cir Sarasota FL 34241-6442

**SCHMANDT-BESSERAT, DENISE,** archaeologist, educator; b. Ay, France, Aug. 10, 1933; came to U.S., 1965, naturalized, 1970; d. Victor and Jeanne (Crabit) Besserat; m. Jurgen Schmandt, Dec. 27, 1956; children: Alexander, Christopher, Phillip. Ed., Ecole du Louvre, 1965. Rsch. fellow in Near Eastern Archaeology Peabody Mus. Harvard U., Cambridge, Mass., 1969-71; fellow Radcliffe Inst., Cambridge, 1969-71; asst. prof. Middle Eastern studies U. Tex., Austin, 1972-81, assoc. prof., 1981-88, prof., 1988—2004; acting chief curator U. Tex. Art Mus., 1978—79. Vis. assoc. prof. U. Calif., Berkeley, 1987-88; curator Legacy of the Middle East exhbn. Jeddah (Saudi Arabia) Hist. Preservation Dept. Author: Before Writing, 1992, How Writing Came About, 1996, History of Counting, 1999; adv. editor Tech. and Culture, 1978-92; editl. adv. bd. Archaeology Odyssey, 2003-06; mem. editl. bd. Written Communication, 1993-95, Visible Lang., 1985—, Explorations in Media Ecology, 2001-05, Ancient Adminstrn., 2001; mem. editl. bd. Near Eastern Archaology, 2005—; contbr. articles to profl. jours. Recipient Kayden Nat. U. Press Book award, 1992, Robert W. Hamilton Author award, 1998, Walter J. Ong award Media Ecology Assn., 2004; named in Am. Scientist, 1999; Wenner-Gren Found. grant, 1970-71, NEA grant, 1974-75, 77-78, ACLS grant, 1984, Deutscher Akademischer Austauschdienst grant, 1986, NEH grant, 1992; NEH fellow, 1979-80, U. Wis. Inst. for Rsch. in Humanities fellow, 1984-85, USIA, Am. Ctr. Oriental Rsch. fellow, 1994-95, 97, 2001, Malone fellow 1997, 99, 2005, Weeks fellow Humanities Rsch. Ctr. Stanford U., 2003—. Mem. Am. Oriental Soc., Archeol. Inst. Am. (governing bd. 1983-89), Am. Anthropol. Assn., Am. Schs. of Oriental Rsch., Centro Internat. Rsch. Archeologiche Anthropologiche e Storiche (Rome). Business E-Mail: dsb@mail.utexas.edu.

**SCHMARGE, AGAPI GEORGIOU,** social studies educator; b. N.Y.C., June 11, 1974; d. Vassilios N. and Hrisoula Georgiou; m. Kenneth Robert Schmarge, July 7, 2001. BA, Rutgers U., New Brunswick, N.J., 1996; EdM, Rutgers U., 1999. Cert. tchr. N.J. Tchr. social studies Alexander Hamilton H.S., Elizabeth, NJ, 1999—2000, Arthur L. Johnson H.S., Clark, NJ, 2000—03, Palisades Park Jr./Sr. H.S., NJ, 2003—. Camp dir. Meadowlands Area YMCA, North Arlington, NJ, 1999—. Mem.: Nat. Coun. Social Studies, N.J. Edn. Assn. Home: 50 W Oak St Ramsey NJ 07446 Office: Palisades Park Jr/Sr HS 1 Veterans Plz Palisades Park NJ 07650

**SCHMECK, DEBORAH M.,** literature and language educator; d. Edwin Theodore and Gretel Holzschuh Erickson; m. Forrest Allen Schmeck. BS Edn. cum laude, Kutztown State Coll., 1979; MEd magna cum laude, Kutztown U., 1984; EdD, Lehigh U., 1993. Cert. elem. prin. Pa. Dept. of Edn., supr. elem. edn. Pa. Dept. of Edn., supr. reading instrrn. Pa. Dept. of Edn., reading specialist Pa. Dept. of Edn., instr. II elem. Pa. Dept. of Edn. Tchr., reading specialist Schuylkill Valley Sch. Dist., Leesport, Pa., 1979—, acting elem. prin., 1991—92. Conf. presenter Millersville U., Pa., 1996, Northampton Area Sch. Dist., Pa., 1994; edn. cons. to tchrs. Schuylkill Valley Sch. Dist., Leesport, 1985—90, instr. in-svcs., 1990—91; conf. presenter Kutztown U., 1986; asst. dance instr. Kutztown State Coll. Continuing Edn., 1977—78; assoc. faculty Ea. U., St. Davids, Pa., 1995—, Arcadia U., Glenside, Pa., 2000—03. Com. chair Rockland Twp., Fleetwood, Pa. Recipient doctoral residency grants, Lehigh U., 1987—88. Mem.: NEA, ASCD (assoc.), Schuylkill Valley PTO (adminstrv. rep. 1991—92), Schuylkill Valley Edn. Assn. (sch. rep. 2002—), Pa. Edn. Assn., Tri-County Reading Coun., Keystone State Reading Assn., Kutztown U. Grad. Reading Alumni Assn. (v.p. 1986—87), Internat. Reading Assn., Phi Delta Kappa (local historian 1990—91). Avocations: reading, skiing, jogging, gardening. Office: Schuylkill Valley Sch Dist 929 Lakeshore Dr Leesport PA 19533 Office Phone: 610-926-7111. E-mail: dschmeck@schuylkillvalley.org.

**SCHMELING, GARETH,** classics educator; b. Algoma, Wis., May 28, 1940; married. BA, Northwestern Coll., 1963; MA (Knapp fellow), U. Wis., 1964, PhD (Knapp travelling grantee 1965-66, Univ. fellow 1967-68), 1968. Asst. prof. classics U. Va., 1968-70; assoc. prof. U. Fla., 1970-74, prof., 1974-93, chmn. classics, 1974—, chmn. humanities, 1974-76, dir. Center for Studies in Humanities, 1978-87, prin. investigator Humanities Perspectives on Professions, 1975-87, acting chmn. dept. philosophy, 1986-88, disting. prof., 1998—. Vis. prof. U. Colo., Boulder, 1992; panelist, research div. Nat. Endowment for Humanities, also mem. nat. bd. consultants; dir. writing programs, U. Fla., 2003—. Translator and author introduction: Cornelius Nepos: Lives of Famous Men, 1971; author: Petronius' Satyricon, 1971, Ovid's the Art of Love, 1972, Chariton and the Rise of Ancient Fiction, 1974, Homer's the Odyssey, 1974, A Bibliography of Petronius, 1977, Xenophon of Ephesus, 1980, Historia Apollonii Regis Tyri, 1988, The Novel in the Ancient

World, 1996, Qui Miscuit Utile Dulci, 1998; contbr. numerous articles, revs. to profl. jours.; editor Newsletter Petronian Soc. 1970—; editorial com.: U. Fla. Press Humanities Monographs, 1978—, Ancient Narrative. Named 1 of 5 Tchrs. of Yr. for Arts and Scis. U. Fla., 1973; recipient Rome prize Am. Acad., 1977-78; U. Va. faculty fellow, summer 1969, summer 1970; U. Fla. fellow, summer 1971, summer 1974; Nat. Endowment for Humanities fellow, 1973-74; Am. Council Learned Socs. summer fellow, 1974; Am. Philos. Soc. grantee, 1970, 71, 72, 77-78, 84-85; U. Fla. grantee, 1977-78 Fellow Am. Acad. in Rome; mem. Am. Philol. Assn., Am. Classical League, Vergilian Soc., Classical Assn. of Middle West and South (sec.-treas. 1975-82, pres. 1985-86) Home: 320 NW 30th St Gainesville FL 32607-2524 Office: U Fla Dept Classics Gainesville FL 32611 Office Phone: 352-392-2075. Business E-Mail: schmelin@classics.ufl.edu.

**SCHMELTZER, EDWARD,** lawyer; b. NYC, Aug. 22, 1923; s. Harry A. and Julia (Hoffman) S.; m. Elizabeth Ann Cooper, June 19, 1949; children: Henry Cooper, Elizabeth Sabine. BA, Hunter Coll., N.Y.C., 1950; MA, Columbia U., N.Y.C., 1951; JD, George Washington U., Washington, 1954. Bar: D.C. 1954, U.S. Supreme Ct 1958. Economist PHA, 1951-53; econ. cons., 1953-54; trial atty. Fed. Maritime Bd. Maritime Adminstrn., 1955-60; dir. bur. domestic regulation Fed. Maritime Commn., 1961-66, mng. dir., 1966-69; ptnr. Morgan, Lewis & Bockius, 1969-76, Schmeltzer, Aptaker & Shepard, 1976—99, of counsel, 2001—; sr. v.p., gen. counsel Sea Star Line, Jacksonville, 1999—2001. U.S. rep. 12th Diplomatic Conf. on Internat. Maritime Law, Brussels, 1967, 13th Diplomatic Conf., Brussels, 1968 Mem. bd. editors: Jour. Maritime Law and Commerce; Contbr. articles to profl. jours. Served with USAAF, 1943-46. Recipient Fed. Maritime Commn.; Distinguished Service award, 1969 Mem. Maritime Adminstrv. Bar Assn. (pres. 1971-73) Clubs: Cosmos (Washington). Home: 10412 Buckboard Pl Potomac MD 20854-3805 Office: The Watergate Ste 1000 2600 Virginia Ave NW Washington DC 20037-1905 Office Phone: 202-333-8800. E-mail: es@saslaw.com, eals@comcast.net.

**SCHMELZER, JANET L.,** history professor, researcher; b. Milw., Dec. 7, 1950; d. Robert Benjamin and Jessie Mae (Brady) Schmelzer; m. Charles H. Woods III, June 28, 1998. BA, Tex. Christian U., 1973, MA in History, 1975, PhD in Am. History, 1978. Instr. Temple (Tex.) Jr. Coll., Tex., 1978—79; asst. prof. Sam Houston State U., Huntsville, Tex., 1979—80; vis. asst. prof. Tex. Tech. U., Lubbock, 1980—82; asst. prof. U. Nebr., Lincoln, 1982—83; prof. Tarleton State U. Stephenville, 1983—. Author: Where the West Begins, 1985; co-author: Texas USA, 1996. Pres. Southwestern Hist. Assn., 1992—93, Erath County Women's Plit. Caucus, 1987—88. Fellow, Eleanor Roosevelt Inst., 1980; Moody fellow, Lyndon Baines Johnson Found., 1979. Mem.: Tex. Faculty Assn. (pres. 2004—), East Tex. Hist. Assn., So. Hist. Assn., Tex. State Tchrs. Assn. (bd. dirs.), Tex. State Hist. Assn. (Disting. Spkr. 2005, Coral H. Tullis award 1993), Southwestern Social Sci. Assn. (pres. 2001—02), Phi Alpha Theta (internat. adv. bd. 1995—99), Delta Zeta. Democrat. Methodist. Office: Tarleton State Univ Stephenville TX 76402

**SCHMEMANN, SERGE,** journalist; b. Paris, Apr. 12, 1945; arrived in U.S., 1951; s. Rev Alexander and Juliana (Ossorguine) Schmemann; m. Mary Schidlovsky, Sept. 13, 1970; children: Anne, Alexander, Nathalie. BA cum laude, Harvard U., 1967; MA, Columbia U., 1971; LittD (hon.), Middlebury Coll., 1995. Desk editor AP, NYC, 1972—75, UN corr., 1975—77, South Africa corr., 1977—79, Moscow corr., 1979—80; Moscow bur. chief NY Times, 1980—87, 1991—95, Bonn bur. chief, 1987—90, Jerusalem bur. chief, 1995—98, dep. fgn. editor, 1998—2001, UN bur. chief, 2001—02; editor, editl. page Internat. Herald Tribune, Paris, 2003—. Author: Echoes of a Native Land: Two Centuries of a Russian Village, 1997, When the Wall Came Down: The Berlin Wall and the Fall of Communism, 2006; contbr. articles to profl. publs. With U.S. Army, 1968—70, Vietnam. Recipient Hal Boyle award, Overseas Press Club, 1986, Pulitzer Prize for coverage of German reunification, 1991, Emmy award for Outstanding Individual Achievement in a Craft, Nat. TV Acad., 2003. Mem.: Phi Beta Kappa. Avocations: carpentry, piano. Office: NY Times 229 W 43rd St New York NY 10036-3959 also: Internat Herald Tribune, 6 bis, rue des Graviers 92521 Paris France Office Phone: 33 1 4143 52 00. E-mail: serge@nytimes.com.

**SCHMERLING, ERWIN ROBERT,** counselor, retired physicist; b. Vienna, July 28, 1929; came to U.S., 1955, naturalized, 1962; s. Heinrich H. and Lily (Goldsmith) S.; m. Esther M. Schmerling, Apr. 5, 1957; children: Susan D., Elaine M. BA, Cambridge U., 1950, MA, 1954, PhD in Radio Physics, 1958; grad., Advanced Mgmt. Program, Harvard, 1969, Fed. Exec. Inst., 1975. Asst. prof. elec. engring. Pa. State U., University Park, 1955-60, assoc. prof., 1960-62, 63-64; staff scientist NASA-Hdqrs., Washington, 1962-63, program chief ionospheric physics, magnetospheric physics, space plasma physics, 1964-82; asst. dir. space and earth scis. Goddard Space Flight Ctr., NASA, Greenbelt, Md., 1984-86; chief data system scientist Office Space Science and Applications NASA Hdqrs., Washington, 1986-88; SAIS program scientist NASA, Washington, 1988-89; data system scientist solar system exploration div. NASA Hdqrs., Washington, 1989-90, program mgr. astrophysics data systems, 1991-94; counselor Svc. Corps of Retired Execs. (SCORE), 1995—98. Mem. U.S. coms. III and IV Internat. Sci. Radio Union, 1985—, sec. U.S Com. III, 1966-69, chmn., 1969-72; chmn. subcom. C1 Com. Space Rsch. (COSPAR), 1984-88; mem. Adv. Group Aerospace R&D, NATO, 1978-85; vis. scholar Stanford U., 1983; cons. RCA, Gen. Electric, 1959-62. Contbr. papers to profl. jours. Recipient medal for contbns. to internat. geophys. programs, Soviet Geophys. Soc., 1985. Fellow IEEE (mem. wave propagation standards com.); mem. Am. Geophys. Union, AAAS, Sigma Xi. Home: 2101 Wind Ln Wilmington DE 19810 E-mail: erwinschmerling@comcast.net.

**SCHMERTMANN, JOHN HENRY,** civil engineer, educator, consultant; b. N.Y.C., Dec. 2, 1928; s. Johannes Conrad Schmertmann and Margaret Anna-Marie (Carstens) Schmertmann Ottesen; m. Pauline Anne Grange, Aug. 11, 1956; children: Carl, Gary, Neil, Joy. BSC.E., MIT, 1950; MSC.E., Northwestern U., 1954, PhD in Civil Engring., 1962. Registered profl. engr., Fla. Soils engr. Mueser Rutledge Cons. Engrs., N.Y.C., 1951-54; soils engr. C.E., U.S. Army, Wilmette, Ill., 1954-56; asst. prof. civil engring. U. Fla., Gainesville, 1956-62, assoc. prof., 1962-65, prof., 1965-79, adj. prof., prof. emeritus; prin. Schmertmann & Crapps, Inc., Gainesville, 1979-97, LoadTest Inc., Gainesville, 1991—, Office John H. Schmertmann Inc., Gainesville, 1997—. Postdoctoral fellow Norwegian Geotech. Inst., Oslo, 1962-63; vis. scientist div. bldg. research NRC Can., Ottawa Ont., 1971-72 Author numerous profl. papers Fellow ASCE; pres. 1972, Collingwood prize 1956, Norman medal 1971, State of the Art award 1977, Middlebrooks award 1981, Terzaghi lectr. 1989), Fla. Engring. Soc.; mem. Nat. Acad. Engring. Lutheran. Avocation: sport fishing. Office: John H Schmertmann Inc 4509 NW 23rd Ave Ste 19 Gainesville FL 32606-6570 Office Phone: 352-378-2792.

**SCHMERTZ, ERIC JOSEPH,** lawyer, educator, commissioner; b. NYC, Dec. 24, 1925; married; 4 children. AB, Union Coll., 1948, LL.D. (hon.), 1978; cert., Alliance Francaise, Paris, 1948; JD, NYU, 1954. Bar: N.Y. 1955. Internat. rep. Am. Fedn. State, County and Mcpl. Employees, AFL-CIO, N.Y.C., 1950-52; asst. v.p. dir. labor tribunals Am. Arbitration Assn., N.Y.C., 1952-57, 59-60; indsl. relations dir. Metal Textile Corp. subs. Gen. Cable Corp., Roselle, NJ, 1957-59; exec. dir. N.Y. State Bd. Mediation, 1960-62, corp. dir., 1962-68; labor-mgmt. arbitrator, N.Y.C., 1962—; mem. faculty Hofstra U. Sch. Bus., 1962-70; prof. Hofstra U. Sch. Law, 1970—, Edward F. Carlough disting. prof. labor law, 1981-98, dean Sch. Law, 1982-89, disting. prof. emeritus of law, 1998—; of counsel The Dweck Law Firm, N.Y.C., 1999—; commr. labor rels. City of N.Y., 1990-91. Scholar-in-residence Pace U. Sch. Law, 1998-2000, Disting. Practioner in residence, 2005—; 1st Beckley lectr. in bus. U. Vt., 1981; bd. dirs. Wilshire Oil Co.; mem. N.Y. State Pub. Employment Rels. Bd., 1991-97; cons. and lectr. in field. Co-author: (with R.L. Greenman) Personnel Administration and the Law, 1978; contbr. chpts. to books, articles to profl. jours.; co profl. law confs., seminars and workshops. Mem. numerous civic orgns. Served to lt. USN, 1943-46. Recipient Testimonial award Southeast Republican Club, 1969; Alexander

Hamilton award Rep. Law Students Assn.; Eric J. Schmertz Disting. Professorship Pub. Law and Pub. Svc. established Hofstra Law Sch., 1993. Mem. Nat. Acad. Arbitrators, Am. Arbitration Assn. (law com., Whitney North Seymour Sr. medal 1984), Fed. Mediation and Conciliation Svc., N.Y. Mediation Bd., N.J. Mediation Bd., N.J. Pub. Employment Rels. Bd., Hofstra U. Club, Princeton Club. Office: The Dweck Law Firm 230 Park Ave Rm 416 New York NY 10169-0422 Office Phone: 212-687-8200. Business E-Mail: schmertz@dwecklaw.com.

**SCHMERTZ, MILDRED FLOYD,** editor-in-chief, writer; b. Pitts., Mar. 29, 1925; d. Robert Watson and Mildred Patricia (Floyd) S B.Arch., Carnegie Mellon U., 1947; M.F.A., Yale U., 1957. Archtl. designer John Schurko, Architect, Pitts., 1947-55; assoc. editor Archtl. Record, N.Y.C., 1957-65, sr. editor, 1965-80, exec. editor, 1980-85, editor-in-chief, 1985-90. Vis. lectr. Yale Sch. Architecture, 1979— Editor, contbr.: New Life for Old Buildings; contbr. articles to profl. jours.; chpts. to books. Bd. mgrs. Jr. League, City of N.Y., 1964-65; commr. N.Y. Landmarks Preservation Commn., 1988-92 Fellow AIA; mem. Mcpl. Art Soc. N.Y., Century Assn. (N.Y.C.) Home and Office: 310 E 46th St Apt 15E New York NY 10017-3002

**SCHMETTERER, ROBERT ALLEN,** advertising executive; b. NYC, Nov. 23, 1943; s. Robert Mayer and Rosalie (Fernandez) S.; children: Adam, Tyler; m. Stacy Lynn Chiarello, Sept. 26, 1987. BS, Fairleigh Dickinson U., 1967, MBA, 1970. Sales promotion mgr. Brit. Motor Corp., Leonia, NJ, 1963-68; market research dir. Volvo, Rockleigh, NJ, 1968-71; v.p. market rsch. Scali, McCabe, Sloves Inc., NYC, 1971-73, sr. v.p. dir. account service, 1974-79, exec. v.p., chief oper. officer, mng. dir., 1979-84; pres., chief exec. officer/worldwide HCM, NYC and Paris, 1984-87; pres., ptnr. Messner Vetere Berger McNamee Schmetterer, N.Y.C., 1987—97; chmn., CEO Euro RSCG Worldwide, NYC, 1997—2004; pres., COO Havas, 2002—04. Bd. dirs. N.Y.C. Partnership, 1987. Author: Leap: A Revolution in Creative Business Strategy, 2003. Bd. dirs. NYC Partnership, 1985—87, NYC Hist. House Trust, 2005—, J Mandle Performance, Inc., chmn. Mem.: Coral Beach and Tennis Club, Ocean Reef Club, NY Yacht Club. Address: 15 Washington Spring Rd Palisades NY 10964

**SCHMETZER, ALAN DAVID,** psychiatrist; b. Louisville, Sept. 3, 1946; s. Clarence Frederick and Catherine Louise (Wootan) Schmetzer; m. Janet Lynn Royce, Aug. 25, 1968; children: Angela Beth, Jennifer Lorraine. BA, Ind. U., 1968, MD, 1972. Diplomate Am. Bd. Psychiatry and Neurology, subsplty. cert. in addiction psychiatry; diplomate Am. Psychotherapy Assn., Am. Bd. Forensic Med. Examiners, Assn. Convulsive Therapy. Intern Ind. U. Hosps., Indpls., 1972-73, resident, 1972-75; dir. clinics PCI, Inc., Anderson, Beech Grove, Kokomo, Ind., 1975-79; psychiat. cons. Cmty. Addiction Svcs. Agy., Indpls., 1975-80; instr. psychiatry in primary care Family Practice Residency Programs St. Francis Hosp., St. Vincent's Hosp. and Ind. U. Hosps., Indpls., 1975-91; med. dir. Child Guidance Clinic of Marion County, Indpls., 1980-81; chmn. psychiatry dept. St. Francis Hosp., Beech Grove, 1980-82; med. dir. Crisis Intervention Unit Midtown Mental Health Ctr., 1980-90, dir. 1990-96, med. dir., 1996-98; coord. emergency psychiat. svcs. Ind. U. Med. Ctr., Indpls., 1980-90, asst. prof. psychiatry, 1975-94, assoc. prof. psychiatry, 1994—2002, prof. psychiatry, 2002—, coord. psychiat. edn. of med. students, 1989-95, asst. chmn. dept. psychiatry, 1993-96, dir. psychiat. edn., 1995-97, vice chmn. edn. dept. psychiatry, 1997—, dir. psychiatry residency tng., 1998—, dir. addiction psychiatry residency tng., 1999—; chief psychiatry Wishard Meml. Hosp., 1990-98. Primary psychiat. cons. Ind. Dept. Mental Health and Addiction, 1988-89; med. dir. Ind. Divsn. Mental Health, 2001—03; supt. Larue D. Carter Meml. Hosp., 2003-05; examiner Am. Bd. Psychiatry and Neurology. Contbr. articles to profl. jours. Maj. Ind. N.G. 1972-79. Decorated Army Commendation medal; recipient Residents award for outstanding teaching, 1985, 90, 97, 2003, Roeske Excellence in Teaching award, 1992, Med. Student Psychiatry Clin. Tchg. award, 2000, Irma Bland Residency Tchg. award, 2005, Alumnus of the Yr., Silver Creek H.S., 2005, Eugene E. Levitt svc. award in psychology, 2003, Exemplary Psychiatrist award NAMI, 2004. Fellow Am. Psychiat. Assn., Am. Ortho-psychiat. Assn.; mem. AMA (Physicians Recognition award 1978-), Ind. Med. Assn., Indpls. Med. Soc., Ind. Psychiat. Soc. (pres. 1989-90, 97-98), Am. Orthopsychiat. Assn., Am. Acad. Clin. Psychiatry, Univ. Faculty Club Indpls. (v.p. 1999-2000, pres. 2000-01), Athenaeum Turnverein Club, Alpha Phi Omega, Phi Beta Pi, Psi Chi, Alpha Epsilon Delta. Presbyterian. Office: Dept Psychiatry 1111 W 10th St PB-A212 Indianapolis IN 46202-4800 Office Phone: 317-274-1224. E-mail: aschmetz@iupui.edu.

**SCHMID, CHARLES ERNEST,** acoustical engineer, academic administrator; b. Jamaica, N.Y., Oct. 30, 1940; s. Edson Scofield Schmid and Agatha Sofia Zimmermann; m. Linda Dexter, June 18, 1966; children: Andrew, Jenny. BSEE, Cornell U., 1963; MSEE, U. Conn., 1968; PhD, U. Wash. 1977. Systems engr. Gen. Dynamics/Electric Boat, Groton, Conn., 1963-66; fellow Honeywell, Seattle, 1966-90; exec. dir. Acoustical Soc. Am., Woodbury, N.Y., 1990—. With physics vis. com. U. Wash., 1999—. Congl. Sci. Engring. fellow AAAS, Washington, 1985-86. Fellow Acoustical Soc. Am.; mem. Am. Inst. Physics (gov. bd. 1991—, exec. com. 1993-99, 2003-). Achievements include research in simulation and analysis of underwater sound. Office: Acoustical Soc of Am 2 Huntington Quadrangle Melville NY 11747-4501 E-mail: charles@aip.org.

**SCHMID, HARALD HEINRICH OTTO,** biochemistry educator, academic administrator; b. Graz, Styria, Austria, Dec. 10, 1935; Came to U.S., 1962; s. Engelbert and Annemarie (Kletetschka) S.; m. Patricia Caroline Igou, May 21, 1977. MS, U. Graz, 1957, LLD, 1962, PhD, 1964. Rsch. fellow Hormel inst. U. Minn., Austin, 1962-65, rsch. assoc., 1965-66, asst. prof., 1966-70, assoc. prof., 1970-74, prof., 1974—2003, prof. emeritus, 2003—. Cons. NIH, Bethesda, Md., 1977-04; acting dir. Hormel inst. U. Minn., 1985-87, exec. dir., 1987-01; faculty mem. Mayo Med. Sch., Rochester, Minn., 1990-03. Mng. editor Chemistry and Physics of Lipids, Elsevier Sci. Publs., Amsterdam, The Netherlands, 1984-01; contbr. numerous articles to profl. jours. Rsch. grantee NIH, 1967-01. Mem. AAAS, Am. Soc. Biochemistry and Molecular Biology, Am. Chem. Soc., The Oxygen Soc. Avocations: yacht racing, downhill skiing, classical music. Office: U Minn Hormel Inst 801 16th Ave NE Austin MN 55912-3679 Business E-Mail: hoschmid@hi.umn.edu.

**SCHMID, JOHN A.,** musician, voice educator; b. Danville, Ill., Oct. 27, 1944; s. Herman A. and Marjorie E. Schmid; m. Kara Sue Schmid, Sept. 20, 1986; 1 child, Jordan Olivia. MusB, Butler U., 1968; MusM, Jordan Coll., 1969; student of pvt. voice, Indiana U., 1979. Accompanist Butler U., Indpls., 1968—70, voice instr., 1970—87; dir. music and studios Fairview Presbyn., Indpls., 1982—; chorus master Indpls. Opera, 1984—; dir. Indpls. Matinee Musicale Ensemble, 2003—. Voice tchr., coach Butler U., 1970—82; dir. Fairview Studios, 1982—. Mem.: Nat. Assn. Tchrs. of Singing, Nat. Assn. Tchrs. Music, Presbyn. Assn. of Musicians, Nat. Choral Dir. Assn. Presbyn. Avocations: cooking, opera. Office: Fairview Studios 4609 N Capitol Ave Indianapolis IN 46208 Office Phone: 317-253-5982. Business E-Mail: jschmid@fairviewpresbyterian.org.

**SCHMID, PATTI A.,** library director; d. Harold and Anna May Schmid. BA, Drew U., Madison, NJ, 1971, M in Theol. Studies, 1975; MS in Libr. Sci., Cath. U. of Am., Washington, 1980. Libr. ops. cons., procurement analyst Bus. Mgmt. Rsch. Assocs., Arlington, Va., 1980—82, info. and systems mgr., 1983—89; bibliographic and quality assurance profl. Raven Systems and Rsch., Inc., Washington, 1982; dir. rsch. and info. mgmt. ODS Inc., Silver Spring, Md., 1984—92; cost and billings mgr. OAO Corp., Greenbelt, Md., 1989—91; tech. asst. III-libr. Cumberland County Coll., Vineland, NJ, 1992—97, head libr., 1997—. Adj. faculty Cumberland County Coll., Vineland, 1997—; presenter in field. Editor: (glossary) Federal Contracting Handbook. Mem.: NAFE, AAUW, Cumberland Libraries. United Electronic Sys., Virtual Academic Libr. Environment, Coun. NJ Coll. and Univ. Libr. Dirs., NJ Edn. Assn., NJ Libr. Assn. Office: Cumberland County Coll Libr 3322 College Dr Vineland NJ 08360 Office Phone: 856-691-8600. Office Fax: 856-691-1969.

**SCHMID, RUDI (RUDOLF SCHMID),** retired internist, educator, academic administrator; b. Switzerland, May 2, 1922; arrived in U.S., 1947, naturalized, 1954; s. Rudolf and Bertha (Schiesser); m. Sonja D. Wild, Sept. 17, 1949. BS, Gymnasium Zurich, 1941; MD, U. Zurich, 1947; PhD, U. Minn., 1954. Intern U. Calif. Med. Ctr., San Francisco, 1948—49; resident medicine U. Minn., 1949—52, instr., 1952—54; rsch. fellow biochemistry Columbia U., 1954—55; investigator NIH, Bethesda, Md., 1955—57; assoc. medicine Harvard Med. Sch., 1957—59; asst. prof. Harvard U., 1959—62; prof. medicine U. Chgo., 1962—66, U. Calif., San Francisco, 1966—91, recall prof. medicine, 1991—2004, prof. emeritus, 2005, dean Sch. Medicine, 1983—89, assoc. dean internat. rels., 1989—95. Cons. to U.S. Army surgeon gen. NIH; hon. prof. Peking Union Med. Coll., Shanghai Second Med. U., Xian U. of Med. Sci., Jillin U. Medicine. Mem. editl. bd.: Blood, 1962—75, Jour. Clin. Investigation, 1965—70, Gastroenterology, 1965—70, Jour. Investigative Dermatology, 1968—72, Annals Internal Medicine, 1975—79, Procs. Soc. Exptl. Biology and Medicine, 1974—84, Chinese Jour. Clin. Scis., Jour. Lab. Clin. Medicine, 1991—, Hepatology Rsch. (Japan), 1993—, World Jour. Gastroenterology (China), 2002—, cons. editor: Gastroenterology, 1981—86. With Swiss Army, 1943—47. Master: ACP; fellow: Royal Coll. Physicians, N.Y. Acad. Scis., Am. Acad. Arts and Scis.; mem.: NAS, German-Am. Acad. Coun. (exec. com. 1992—99), Leopoldina/German Acad. Sci., Swiss Acad. Med. Scis., Am. Assn. Study Liver Disease (pres. 1965), Am. Gastroenterol. Assn., Am. Soc. Hematology, Am. Soc. Biol. Chemistry and Molecular Biology, Am. Soc. Clin. Investigation, Assn. Am. Physicians (pres. 1986), Internat. Assn. Study Liver (pres. 1980—82), IOM (sr.). Achievements include research in biochemistry, metabolism of hemoglobin, heme, prophyrins, bile pigments, liver and muscle. Home: 211 Woodland Rd Kentfield CA 94904-2631 Personal E-mail: s.d.schmid@comcast.net.

**SCHMID, SIGI,** professional soccer coach; b. Tuebingen, West Germany, Mar. 20, 1953; came to U.S., 1962; children: Erik, Kurt, Kyle. BS in Econs., UCLA, 1976; MA in Bus. Adminstrn., U. So. Calif. CPA, Calif. Coach UCLA Bruins, 1980-99; head coach L.A. Galaxy, 1999—. Office: L A Galaxy 18400 Avalon Blvd 200 Carson CA 90746-2172

**SCHMID, WILFRIED,** mathematician, educator; b. Hamburg, Germany, May 28, 1943; came to U.S., 1960; s. Wolfgang and Kathe (Erling) S. BA, Princeton U., 1964; MA, U. Calif., Berkeley, 1966, PhD, 1967. Asst. prof. math. U. Calif., Berkeley, 1967-70; prof. math. Columbia U., 1970-78, Harvard U., 1978—. Vis. mem. Inst. for Advanced Study, Princeton, 1969-70, 75-76; vis. prof. U. Bonn, 1973-74; hon. prof. U. Cordoba, Argentina, 1989; math. advisor Mass. Dept. Edn., 2000-02. Editor: Letters in Mathematical Physics, Jour. Algebraic Geometry; contbr. articles to profl. jours. Recipient Prix Scientifique de l'UAP, 1986; Sloan fellow, 1968-70, Guggenheim fellow, 1975-76, 88-89. Mem.: Am. Acad. Arts and Scis. Home: Silver Hill Rd Lincoln MA 01773 Office: Harvard U Dept Mathematics Cambridge MA 02138

**SCHMIDHAUSER, JOHN RICHARD,** political science professor; b. N.Y.C., Jan. 3, 1922; s. Richard J. and Gertrude (Grabinger) S.; m. Thelma Lorraine Ficker, June 9, 1952; children: Steven, Paul, Thomas, John C., Martha, Sara, Susan. BA with honors, U. Del., 1949; MA, U. Va., 1952, PhD, 1954. Instr. U. Va., 1952-54; prof. constl. law U. Iowa, 1954-64, prof. polit. sci., 1967-73, U. So. Calif., 1973-92, prof. emeritus, 1993—. Mem. 89th Congress 1st dist. Iowa.; research fellow Research Inst. on Jud. Process, Social Sci. Research Council, 1958; sr. fellow law and behavorial scis. U. Chgo. Law Sch., 1959-60; Talbot vis. prof. govt. U. Va., 1982-83. Author: The Role of Supreme Court as Final Arbiter in Federal-State Relations, 1789-1957, 1958, The Supreme Court; Its Politics, Personalities and Procedures, 1960, Constitutional Law in the Political Process, 1963, (with Berg) The Supreme Court and Congress, 1972, (with Berg and Hahn) American Political Institutions and Corruption, 1976, (with Totten) Whaling in Japan-U.S. Relations, 1978, Judges and Justices, 1979, Constitutional Law in American Politics, 1984, Comparative Judicial Politics, 1987; contbr. chpt. to book; also numerous articles in jours. Chmn. Citizens Action Com. for Fair Representation in Iowa Legislature, 1961; dist. chmn. Operation Support Pres. Kennedy and Johnson, 1961—; chmn. Johnson County Dem. Ctrl. Com., 1961-64; del. Iowa Dem. Convs., 1956, 58, 60, 62; mem. Dem. Nat. Com. Alumni Coun., 1986—; chmn. Santa Barbara, Calif. Dem. Ctrl. Com., 1991-92; mem. exec. com. Los Padres chpt. of the Sierra Club, 1992-96; sec. Santa Barbara Dem. League, 1993-96. With USNR, 1941-45, PTO. Recipient Raubenheimer award U. So. Calif., 1991, Golden Key award for Comparative Rsch, 1991. Mem. Iowa City Mgr. Assn. (bd. reps. 1956-59, chmn. handbook revision 1958), Internat. Polit. Sci. Assn. (chmn. research com. for comparative jud. studies 1980-88), Am. Polit. Sci. Assn., Western Polit. Sci. Assn. (v.p., program chmn. 1980-81, pres.-elect 1981-82), AAUP (sec.-treas. State U. Iowa 1958-59, mem. com. on relationship fed. and state govt. to higher edn., mem. exec. com. U. So. Calif. chpt. 1983-92), Humanities Soc., Raven Soc., Phi Beta Kappa, Phi Kappa Phi. Unitarian (chmn. Iowa City Soc. Men's Club 1960-61). Avocation: French horn. Home: 726 Arbol Verde St Carpinteria CA 93013-2508 E-mail: jschmidhauser@verizon.net. *For the young today the opportunity for a good education puts them at the threshold of great opportunities. I encourage them to enjoy that with the same spirit that my generation experienced.*

**SCHMIDLI, KEITH WILLIAM,** vocational education administrator, educator, researcher; b. Niagara Falls, N.Y., Oct. 11, 1952; s. Duane Irving and Jennie Mary (Schultz) S.; m. Jaquline Barbara Irish, May 27, 1978 (div. Jan. 3, 1982). AA in Liberal Arts and Scis., Niagara County C.C., Sanborn, N.Y., 1972; journeyman cert. auto/diesel mechanics, Trott Vocat. Sch., 1982; BS in Vocat. Tech. Edn. summa cum laude, SUNY, Buffalo, 1992, MS in Edn. summa cum laude, 1993; PhD magna cum laude, U. Buffalo, 1999; MBA, DBA, Cambridge State U., 2000, 01. Cert. tchr., N.Y.; cert. career devel. facilitator; cert. coach. for diversified coop. work-study programs. Maintenance mechanic, operating engr. machinist St. Lakes Carbon Corp., Niagara Falls, NY, 1973-82; owner, mgr. Apt. Rental Units, Niagara Falls, 1975-88; mechanic Tracy-Luckey Co. Inc., Andalusia, Ala., 1984-85; mechanic, operating engr. Niagara Falls Country Club, Lewiston, NY, 1985-86; millwright Custom Maintenance, Buffalo, 1986-87; pipefitter John Martin Plumbing, Niagara Falls, 1987; engring. technician Precious Plate, Niagara Falls, 1987-90; grad. adminstrv. asst. SUNY Coll., Buffalo, 1993-94, asst. prof., 1999—; adminstr. Niagara County C.C., Sanborn, NY, 1995-96. Faculty selection com. Dept. Tech. SUNY, Buffalo, 1992-94; tchg./curriculum com. LaSalle Sr. H.S., Niagara Falls, 1992—; grad. student selection com. U. Buffalo, 1994-95, rsch. symposium com., 1994-95, acad. stds. com., 1995-99. Author: Increasing Enrollment in Secondary Vocational Eduction Programs Through Teacher-Based Promotion, 1993, Career Education: Exploring the Unfinished Agenda of Providing Applied Practical Knowledge and Skills Needed in a Changing Economy, 1999, Career Readiness and Employers' Expectations, 2000; contbr. articles to profl. jours. Vol., donor Red Cross Western N.Y., Buffalo, 1991-95; vol. Am. Heart Assn., Buffalo, 1990, Dept. Comty. Edn./Resource Devel., Niagara Falls, 1992. Mem. ASCD, ASME, Assn. Study of Higher Edn., Coun. Exceptional Children, Am. Soc. Quality, Soc. Mfg. Engrs., Libr. Congress Assoc., Am. Mus. Natural History, Postal Commemorative Soc., Alpha Sigma Lambda (charter mem. 1993-94), Kappa Delta Pi. Avocations: guitar playing, songwriting, camping, hunting, home remodeling. Office: SUNY Coll at Buffalo 109 Bacon Hall Buffalo NY 14222 Home: 5165 Lewiston Rd Lewiston NY 14092-1930 E-mail: schmidkw@buffalostate.edu, schmidkw@juno.com.

**SCHMID-SCHOENBEIN, GEERT WILFRIED,** biomedical engineer, educator; b. Albstadt, Baden-Wurttemberg, Germany, Jan. 1, 1948; came to U.S., 1971; s. Ernst and Ursula Schmid; m. Renate Schmid-Schoenbein, July 3, 1976; children: Philip, Mark, Peter. Vordiplom, Liebig U., Giessen, Germany, 1971; PhD in Bioengring., U. Calif., San Diego, 1976. Staff assoc. dept. physiology Columbia U., N.Y.C., 1976-77, sr. assoc., 1977-79; asst. prof. dept. applied mechs. & engring. scis. U. Calif., San Diego, 1979-84, assoc. prof., 1984-89, prof., 1989-94, prof. dept. bioengring., 1994—. Editor: Frontiers in Biomechanics, 1986, Physiology and Pathophysiology of Leukocyte Adhesion, 1994, Molecular Basis of Microcirculatory Disorders, 2002; author more than 280 rsch. reports. Recipient Melville medal ASME, 1990, Ratschow medal European Soc. Phlebology, 1999. Fellow Am. Inst. for Med. and Biol. Engring.; Am. Heart Assn.; mem. NAE, Biomed. Engring. Soc. (pres. 1991-92), Am. Microcirculatory Soc. (pres. 2003-04), N.Am. Soc. Biorheology (pres. 1989-99), European Microciculatory Soc., Am. Physiol. Soc., Am. Mech. Engring. Soc. Achievements include bioengineering research on cardiovascular disease, microcirulation, bioengineering, and lymphology. Office: U Calif San Diego Dept Bioengineering Gilman Dr 9500 0412 La Jolla CA 92093-0412

**SCHMIDT, ALBERT JOHN,** retired history professor; b. Louisville, Aug. 27, 1925; s. Christian Carl Schmidt and Mary Margaret Jann; m. Kathryn Estelle Jung, Aug. 25, 1951; children: Christine Elise, Elizabeth Suzanne. AB, DePauw U., Ind., 1949; MA, U. Pa., 1950, PhD, 1953. Asst. prof., assoc. prof., prof. history Coe Coll., Cedar Rapids, Iowa, 1953—65; Arnold Bernhard prof. history U. Bridgeport, Conn., 1965—90; dean U. Bridgeport Coll. Arts and Scis., 1972—76, v.p. acad. affairs, 1976—78, prof. of law, 1979—90, Bernhard prof. of history emeritus, 1990—; prof. law emeritus Quinnipiac U., Hamden, Conn., 1992—; rsch. assoc. George Washington U., Washington, 1992—. Supr. electronics US Dept. of State, Washington, 1997, 98, 2000. Editor: The Architecture and Planning of Classical Moscow, 1989; contbr. articles to profl. jours. Sgt. USAF, 1944—46, New Guinea, Philippines. Fulbright scholar, US Dept. State, U. London, 1952—53. Mem.: Am. Hist. Soc. (life). Democrat. Avocations: reading, hiking, bicycling, writing, travel.

**SCHMIDT, BARNET MICHAEL,** communications and electronic engineer; b. New Milford, N.J., June 30, 1958; s. Frank Lowell and Lee (Fishkin) S. BSEE, Stevens Inst. Tech., 1980, BS Computer Sci., 1980, MSEE, 1985, PhD, 2003. Cert. comml. pilot/instrument. Electronic engr. Cessna Aircraft Co., Boonton, N.J., 1980-81; sr. sys. engr. Timeplex Corp., Unisys Co., Woodcliff Lake, N.J., 1981-85; tech. staff, cons. AT&T Bell Labs., Holmdel, N.J., 1985-90; tech. staff Bell Comms. Rsch. (now Telcordia Technologies, Inc.), Piscataway, NJ, 1990—95; tech. staff network transmission sys. lab. Lucent Technologies Bell Labs., Holmdel, N.J., 1995-99; sr. tech. staff data arch. divsn. AT&T Corp. R&D, Middletown, NJ, 1999—2000; mem. tech. staff network ops. sys. engring. lab Lucent Tech., Middletown, 2000—02; project engr., comm. sys. analysis BAE Sys. Inc., Totowa, NJ, 2002—; pres. Schmidt and Assocs., PC, Cons. Comms. Engrs., Oradell, NJ, 1999—. Cons. engr. Computer Scis. Corp., El Segundo, Calif., 1986-90; prin. Schmidt & Assocs., PC Tech. Assocs., LLC Cons. Mem. IEEE (sr.), Sigma Xi (assoc.). Achievements include development of optimal SONET network architectures and routing methods; robust fault tolerant optical transmission system; network surveillance systems; dense wavelength division multiplexing system; invention of novel adaptive filter synthesis techniques, statistical signal identification methods, multiplanar image correlation, parallel image processing systems; neural-network based intelligent systems for isolating hidden troubles in telecommunications networks; performance analysis and tuning of communications networks and operational support systems; spread-spectrum optimal modulation and systems engineering; spread spectrum/secure wireless system; patents in field; research in wireless network modulation error correcting codes. Office: BAE Sys Inc 18A40 150 Parish Dr Wayne NJ 07474-0975 Office Phone: 973-305-2013.

**SCHMIDT, BENNO CHARLES, JR.,** lawyer; b. Washington, Mar. 20, 1942; s. Benno Charles and Martha (Chastain) S.; children by previous marriage— Elizabeth, Benno III, Christina. BA, Yale U., 1963, JD, 1966; LLD (hon.), Princeton U., 1986; LittD (hon.), Johns Hopkins U., 1987; LLD (hon.), Harvard U., 1987. Bar: D.C. 1968. Law clk. Chief Justice Earl Warren, U.S. Supreme Ct, Washington, 1966-67; spl. asst., asst. atty. gen. Office Legal Counsel U.S. Dept. Justice, Washington, 1967-69; Harlan Fiske Stone prof. constl. law Columbia U., N.Y.C., 1969-86, dean Law Sch., 1984-86; pres., prof. law Yale U., New Haven, 1986-92; chmn. Edison Schs., N.Y.C., 1992—. Author: Freedom of the Press versus Public Access, 1976; (with A.M. Bickel) The Judiciary and Responsible Government 1910-1921, 1984. Dir. Nat. Humanities Ctr., Chapel Hill, N.C., 1985—; chmn. bd. trustees CUNY, 2000—. Office: Edison Schools 521 5th Ave Rm 1100 New York NY 10175-1599

**SCHMIDT, BRIAN ARNOLD,** composer, conductor; b. Red Wing, Minn., May 7, 1980; s. Dennis Arnold and JoAnn Caroline Schmidt; m. Andrea Marie Meyer, June 20, 2003. MusB in Edn. and Choral Conducting, SD State U., Brookings, 2003. Artistic dir. Dakota Men's Ensemble, Brookings, 2001—; dir. music ministries Gloria Dei Luth. Ch., Sioux Falls, SD. Guest condr., composer, Sioux Falls. Composer: (choral composition) Lux Aeterna; featured performer: demonstration choir Dakota Men's Ensemble Nat Conv., 2005, 2006. Mem.: Am. Choral Dirs. Assn. (repertoire stds. chairperson 2005—, Raymond W. Brock Student Composition award 2003). Office: Gloria Dei Luth Ch 2800 E 57th St Sioux Falls SD 57106

**SCHMIDT, CHAUNCEY EVERETT,** banker, director; b. Oxford, Iowa, June 7, 1931; s. Walter Frederick and Vilda (Saxton) S.; m. Anne Garrett McWilliams, Mar. 3, 1954; children: Carla, Julia, Chauncey Everett. BS, U.S. Naval Acad., 1953; MBA, Harvard U., 1959. With First Nat. Bank, Chgo., 1959-76, v.p., gen. mgr. br. London, Eng., 1965-68, v.p. for Europe, Middle East, Africa, 1968-69, sr. v.p. Chgo., 1969-72, exec. v.p., 1972, vice chmn. bd., 1973, pres., 1974-76; chmn. bd., chief exec. officer, dir. Bank of Calif. N.A., San Francisco, 1976—; chmn. bd., pres., chief exec. officer, dir. BanCal Tri-State Corp., 1976—. Dir. Amfac, Inc., Honolulu; mem. Adv. Council Japan-U.S. Econ. Relations; adv. bd. Pacific Rim Bankers Program. Exec. bd. and pres. San Francisco Bay Area council Boy Scouts Am.; council SRI Internat.; bd. dirs. Bay Area Council; bd. govs. San Francisco Symphony; trustee U.S. Naval War Coll. Fedn., Newport, R.I. Served with USAF, 1953-56. Mem. Assn. Res. City Bankers, Am. Bankers Assn., Internat. Monetary Conf., Calif. Bankers Clearing House Assn. (dir.), Calif. Roundtable (dir.), Japan-Calif. Assn. Clubs: Comml. (Chgo.); Bankers (San Francisco), Bohemian (San Francisco). Home: 40 Why Worry Farm Woodside CA 94062-3654 Office: Ste 140 525 Middlefield Rd Menlo Park CA 94025

**SCHMIDT, CHRISTINE ALICE,** art gallery owner; b. St. Albans, NY, Sept. 1, 1932; d. Paul Joseph and Alice Patricia (McKane) Schmidt. BA magna cum laude, Adelphi U., 1964; MA, Pratt Inst., 1968. Cert. clothing design McDowell Art Sch., 1952, edn. NY, 1964. Asst. buyer May Co., N.Y.C., NY, 1952—54; asst. and designer Finger & Rabiner, Linker, Grioni, N.Y.C., 1955—59; fashion illustrator, freelance clothing designer NYC, 1959—63; parochial sch. art tchr. St. Brigid's, St. Francis, St. Christopher, 1963—64; art tchr. Cold Spring Harbor (NY) HS, 1964—84; owner, operator Christine's Gallery, Southwest Harbor, Maine, 1972—. Etchings and watercolor paintings in numerous collections in Europe and US, 1972—. Ambulance driver Am. Red Cross, Garden City, NY, 1950—65; bd. mem. Southwest Harbor C. of C., Southwest Harbor, Maine, 1994—99. Achievements include various coat and suit designs for the covers and interior of Vogue, Harper's Bazaar, Mademoiselle. Avocations: sewing, photography, european travel. Home and Office: 19 Artists Way Lamoine ME 04605 Office Phone: 207-664-2667.

**SCHMIDT, CLAUDE HENRI,** retired science administrator; b. Geneva, May 6, 1924; came to U.S., 1935; s. Roger Auguste Schmidt and Lucette (Henriette) Wuhrman; m. Melicent Esther Hane, June 25, 1953; children— Valerie Lynn, Jeffrey Allan AB, Stanford U., 1948, MA, 1950, PhD, Iowa State U., 1956. With Agrl. Rsch. Svc., USDA, 1956-88; rsch. entomologist Orlando, Fla., 1956-62; project leader Fargo, N.D., 1964-67; br. chief Beltsville, Md., 1967-72; area dir. N. Cen. region Fargo, 1972-82; lab. dir., 1982-88; acting dir. Red River Valley Agrl. Rsch. Ctr., 1988; collaborator, 1988-94; with Cass County Vector Control Dist., 1994—2003; ret. Entomologist IEAA, Vienna, Austria, 1962-64; sec. Nat. Mosquito Fish and Wildlife Commn., Washington, 1968-72 Editor Leafy Spurge News, 1994—2005; contbr. articles to profl. jours. mem. state legis. com. AARP, N.D., 2000-03; mem. Fargo Sr. Commn., 2001—, chmn., 2003—; docent Plaines Art Mus., Fargo, 2005—. With AUS, Signal Corps 1942-46, to 1st lt. Med. Service

Corps, 1950-53. Fellow Washington Acad. Sci., AAAS; mem. Am. Mosquito Control Assn. (pres. 1981-82), Am. Chem. Soc., Entomol. Soc. Am., Nat. Assn. Ret. Fed. Employees (pres. N.D. fedn., 1988-89). Republican. Home: 1827 3rd St N Fargo ND 58102-2335

**SCHMIDT, CYRIL JAMES,** librarian; b. Flint, Mich., June 27, 1939; s. Cyril August and Elizabeth Josephine S.; m. Martha Joe Meadows, May 22, 1965; children: Susan, Emily. BA, Cath. U. Am., 1962; MSLS, Columbia U., 1963; PhD, Fla. State U., 1974. Asst. bus. and industry dept. Flint Pub. Library, 1963-65; reference librarian Gen. Motors Inst., Flint, 1965; asso. librarian S.W. Tex. State U., San Marcos, 1965-67; head undergrad. libraries, asst. prof. Ohio State U., 1967-70; dir. libraries SUNY, Albany, 1972-79; also mem. faculty SUNY (Sch. Library and Info. Sci.); univ. librarian Brown U., Providence, 1979-81; exec. v.p. Rsch. Libraries Group, Stanford, Calif., 1981-89; prin. cons. Schmidt & Assocs., Palo Alto, Calif., 1989—; univ. prof. San Jose (Calif.) State U., 1992—. Author papers in field. Libr. Svcs. Act fellow, 1962-63, Higher Edn. Act fellow, 1970-72 Mem. ALA, ACLU, Pi Sigma Alpha, Beta Phi Mu. Home: 244 Forest Ave Palo Alto CA 94301-2510 Office: San Jose State U 1 Washington Sq San Jose CA 95192-0001 Office Phone: 408-924-2465. Business E-Mail: jim_schmidt@sjsu.edu.

**SCHMIDT, DANIEL EDWARD, IV,** lawyer, arbitrator; b. NYC, Dec. 17, 1946; s. Daniel Edward III and Mary (Mannion) S.; m. Gail Kennedy, Sept. 5, 1980; children: Kathryn Kennedy, Michael Kennedy. BA, St. Lawrence U., 1971; postgrad., New Sch., 1972; JD, St. John's U., 1976; cert. arbitrator. From asst. counsel to assoc. counsel Prudential Property & Casualty, Holmdel, NJ, 1978—81, assoc. gen. counsel, divsn. head, 1981—82; v.p., assoc. gen. counsel, asst. sec. Prudential Reins Co., Newark, 1982—84; dir., v.p., gen. counsel, corp. sec. Scor U.S. Group, N.Y.C., 1984—86, dir., sr. v.p., gen. counsel, corp. sec., 1986—89; dir., exec. com., sr. v.p., gen. counsel, corp. sec. Sorema N.A. Group, N.Y.C., 1989—94, dir., exec. com., exec. v.p., group gen. counsel, 1995—99, dir. exec. com., group exec. v.p., chief legal officer, 1999—2000; dep. gen. mgr., gen. counsel, corp. sec. Sorema Internat. Holding, N.V., Netherlands, 1993—96; U.S. counsel Groupama, France, 1996—2000; cons. Sorema NA Group, 2000—03. Pvt. practice counsel, arbitrator, umpire, Little Silver, N.J., 1987—; reins. lectr., 1986—; founding dir., 1994-2003; pres., 1999-2002, chmn. 2002-2003, bd. dirs. ARIAS (U.S.), N.Y.C. Assoc. editor Arias-U.S. Quar. Presiding judge Ecclesiastical Trial Ct., 1999—2000, Episcopal Diocese of N.J., 1997—; bd. dirs., exec. com. ARC, Monmouth County, Shrewsbury, NJ, 1981—84. With U.S. Army, 1967—70. Mem. ABA, Am. Arbitration Assn. (panel comml. arbitrators, roster of umpires, panel internat. arbitrators), N.Y. Bar Assn., Assn. Internat. Droit des Assureurs (U.S. chpt.), Bamm Hollow Country Club, Desert Mountain Club, Sands Beach Club. Episcopalian. Avocations: bicycling, golf, skiing. Home and office: Dispute Resolution Svcs Internat 628 Little Silver Point Rd Little Silver NJ 07739-1737 Office Phone: 732-741-3646. E-mail: dschmidt4@comcast.net.

**SCHMIDT, DEREK,** state legislator; b. Independence, Kans., Jan. 23, 1968; m. Jennifer Shaw, May 23, 1998. Student, Independence C.C.; B, Kans. U., 1990; M in Internat. Politics, U. Leicester, Eng., 1992; JD, Georgetown U., 1996. Bar: Kans. 1996, D.C. 1996, U.S. Supreme Ct. 2003. Mem. legis. staff Senator Nancy Kassebaum, 1992—96; gen. counsel, legis. dir. Senator Chuck Hagel, 1996—98; asst. atty. gen. State of Kans., 1999; legis. liaison, spl. counsel to Kans. Gov. Bill Graves, 2000; pvt. practice Scovel, Emert, Heasty & Chubb, Independence, 2000—; mem. Kans. Senate from 15th dist., Topeka, 2001—, majority leader, 2005—, chmn. agr. com., 2001—05, chmn., post audit com., 2004—05, chmn. confirmation oversight com., 2005—, chmn. spl. com on Medicaid reform, 2005. Bd. dirs. Independence Industries, Inc. Grad. Leadership Kans., 1999; trustee, ea. Kans. br. Nat. Multiple Sclerosis Soc.; active Am. Coun. Young Polit. Leaders. Ralph Kirchner scholar U. Leicester; fellow Bowhay Inst. for Legis. Leadership Devel.; Henry Toll fellow, 2002, Simons Pub. Humanities fellow U. Kans., 2006. Mem.: Kans. State Hist. Soc., Inc. (bd. dirs.), Rotary. Republican. Office: State Capitol Rm 392E Topeka KS 66612 Office Phone: 785-296-2497.

**SCHMIDT, EDWARD CRAIG,** lawyer; b. Pitts., Nov. 26, 1947; s. Harold Robert and Bernice (Williams) Schmidt; m. Elizabeth Lowry Real, Aug. 18, 1973; children: Harodl Robert II, Robert Real. BA, U. Mich., 1969; JD, U. Pitts., 1972. Bar: Pa. 1972, U.S. Dist. Ct. (we. dist.) Pa. 1972, U.S. Ct. Appeals (3d cir.) 1972, U.S. Ct. Appeals (DC cir.) 1975, U.S. Supreme Ct. 1981, U.S. Ct. Appeals (9th and 4th cirs.) 1982, U.S. Ct. Appeals (6th cir.) 1987, U.S. Ct. Appeals (2d cir.) 1992, U.S. Ct. Appeals (D.C. cir.) 2004. Assoc. Rose, Schmidt, Hasley & Di Salle, Pitts., 1972—77, ptnr., 1977—90, Jones, Day, Reavis & Pogue, Pitts., 1990—2001, Thompson Coburn LLP, Washington, 2002—06; counsel Edward C. Schmidt LLC, Washington, 2006—. Mem. adv. com. Superior Ct. Pa., 1978—80; instr. NITA Duquesne U., 1998—99. Asst. editor: Antitrust Discovery Handbook, 1980; co-editor: Antitrust Discovery Handbook-Supplement, 1982; contbr. articles to profl. jours. Bd. dirs. Urban League, Pitts., 1974—77. Mem.: Acad. Trial Lawyers Allegheny County (bd. govs. 1980), Internat. Acad. Trial Lawyers, Allegheny County Bar Assn. (bd. govs., mem. pub. rels. com. civil litig. sect. 1977—80), DC Bar Assn., Pa. Bar Assn., Supreme Ct. Hist. Soc., We. Res. Acad. Alumni Assn. (trustee 1998—2000), Country Club Woodmore (Md.), Longue Vue Club (Pitts.), Duquesne Club (Pitts.), Rolling Rock Club (Ligonier, Pa.). Office: PO Box 1091 20 Hazlett St Chautauqua NY 14722 Office Phone: 716-357-2448. Personal E-mail: edwardcschmidt@adelphia.net.

**SCHMIDT, ERIC EMERSON,** information technology executive; b. Washington, Apr. 27, 1955; BSEE, Princeton U., 1976; MS in Computer Sci., U. Calif., Berkeley, 1979, PhD in Computer Sci., 1982. With Bell Labs., Zilog; research intern Xerox PARC, Palo Alto, Calif., 1979-80, mem. research staff, 1980-83; software mgr. Sun Microsystems, Mountain View, Calif., 1983-84, software dir., 1984-85, v.p., gen. mgr. software products div., 1985-88, v.p. gen. systems group, 1988-91, chief tech. officer, 1994—97, pres. Sun Tech. Enterprises, Inc., Mountain View, Calif., 1991-94; chmn., CEO Novell, Inc., Provo, Utah, 1997—2001; chmn. exec. com., CEO Google, Inc., Mountain View, Calif., 2001—. Bd. dirs. Google, Inc., 2001—, Apple Computer, Inc., 2006—. Bd. trustee Princeton U. Named one of Forbes' Richest Americans, 2006. Mem. IEEE, Assn. Computing Machinery, Sigma Xi. Achievements include patents in field. Office: Google Inc 1600 Amphitheatre Pkwy 41 Mountain View CA 94043-1351 Office Phone: 650-623-4000. Office Fax: 650-618-1499.

**SCHMIDT, GARY DAVID,** language educator; b. Massapequa, N.Y., Apr. 14, 1957; s. Robert H. and Jeanne A. (Smith) S.; m. Anne E. Stickney, Dec. 22, 1979; six children. BA, Gordon Coll., 1979; MA in Lit., U. Ill., 1981, PhD in Lit., 1985. Teaching asst. U. Ill., Urbana, 1979-85; prof. English Calvin Coll., Grand Rapids, Mich., 1985—. Book reviewer, 1987—. Author: Robert McCloskey, 1990, Hugh Lofting, 1992, Anson's Way, 1999, Straw into Gold, 2001, A Passionate Usefulness: The Life and Literary Labors of Hannah Adams, 2004, Lizzie Bright and the Buckminster Boy, 2005, Mara's Stories, 2005, First Boy, 2005; co-editor: Voice of the Narrator, 1989, Sitting at the Feet of the Past, 1992, Communities of Discourse, 1992. Mem. Early English Text Soc. Republican. Avocation: farming. Office: Calvin Coll English Dept Grand Rapids MI 49546 Office Phone: 616-957-6540. E-mail: sdg@calvin.edu.

**SCHMIDT, GARY P.,** lawyer, personal care industry executive; b. Youngstown, Ohio, Mar. 25, 1951; BA, Miami U., 1973; JD, U. Akron, 1976. Gen. counsel Lyphomed, Inc., 1988—90; v.p., assc. sec., gen. counsel Fujisawa USA, Inc., 1990—97; v.p., asst. sec., gen. counsel Alberto-Culver Co., Melrose Park, Ill., 1997—2000; sr. v.p., gen. counsel. Mem.: ABA, Patent Law Assn., Ill. State Bar Assn., Chicago Bar Assn. Office: Alberto-Culver Co 2525 Armitage Ave Melrose Park IL 60160

**SCHMIDT, GEORGE,** physicist, educator; b. Budapest, Hungary, Aug. 1, 1926; s. Laszlo Schmidt and Katalin Wellisch; m. Katalin Varkonyi, June 26, 1955; children: Franklin R., Ronald W. Diploma in Elec. Engring., Tech. U., Budapest, 1950; PhD in Physics, Hungarian Acad. Scis., Budapest, 1956; M

in Engring., Stevens Inst. Tech., 1961. Sr. lectr. Israel Inst. Tech., Haifa, Israel, 1957-58; asst. prof. Stevens Inst. Tech., Hoboken, NJ, 1959-61, assoc. prof., 1961-63, prof. physics, 1963-83, George Meade Bond prof. physics and engring. physics, 1983-92, prof. emeritus, 1992—. Vis. prof. U. Wis., 1965, UCLA, 1972-73; vis. scientist Culham Labs., Culham, Eng., 1965, Ecole Polytechnique, Paris, 1979-80; cons. Sci. Applications Inc., Washington, 1981—, Poly. U. of N.Y., 1984—, Berkeley Assocs., Washington, 1985. Author: Physics of High Temperature Plasmas, 1966, 2nd rev. edit., 1979; contbr. sci. articles to profl. jours. Recipient Research award Stevens Inst. Tech., 1961. Fellow Am. Phys. Soc.; mem. N.Y. Acad. Scis. Office: Stevens Inst of Tech Dept Of Physics Hoboken NJ 07030 E-mail: gschmidt@stevens.edu.

**SCHMIDT, GLENN NORBERT,** special education educator; b. LaCrosse, Wis., Sept. 19, 1949; s. Norbert John and Arlene Louise Schmidt; m. Kristine Kay Hoover, Jan. 15, 1972; 1 child, John Charles. BA, U. Wis., Madison, 1971; MS in Edn., U. Wis., LaCrosse, 1976. Tchr. LaCrosse Home for Children, 1974—77; spl. edn. tchr. Sun Prairie (Wis.) Pub. Schs., 1977—. Mem. adv. panel on spl. edn. State Supt. of Schs., Madison, Wis., 1998—2001; Dem. Nat. Conv. L.A., 2000. Grantee Fulbright Meml. Fund, Japan, 1998. Mem.: NEA (alt. del., Washington 2001—, del. Edn. Internat. Gen. Assembly, Costa Rica, Stockholm and Washingto 1989—98), Wis. Edn. Assn. Coun. (bd. dirs. 1995—), Sun Prairie Edn. Assn. (pres. 1990—). Democrat. Avocations: golf, travel, writing for periodicals. Home: 227 North St Sun Prairie WI 53590 Office: Sun Prairie Pub Schs 230 W Klubertanz Dr Sun Prairie WI 53590

**SCHMIDT, HILDRED DORIS,** music educator; b. Marion County, Kans., Aug. 13, 1932; d. Rudolf B Schmidt and Susie Voth. B of Music Edn., Coll. Emporia, 1954, BA, 1954; M of music edn. with highest distinction, Ind. U., 1958. Cert. Teacher Kans. State Bd. Edn., Service Playing Certificate Am. Guild Organists. Music tchr. Mullinville Grade Sch., Kans., 1954—57, Zenda Grade and H.S., Kans., 1958—60, Inman Grade Sch., 1960—67, Lyons Jr. High, Mid. and H.S., Lyons, Kans., 1967—96; ret., 1996. Founding mem. The Silver Sounds (flute quartet); organizer music festivals Lyons Jr. High Music Dept. Mem. People to People Lifeline et al., Bob Larson Communicator Club. Recipient Master Teacher award, Discipline and Classroom Mgmt., 1984. Mem.: Kans. Assn. of Retired Sch. Personnel, Kans. Bandmasters Assn., Music Educators Nat. Conf. (50 yr. mem.), Am. Guild Organists (sub-dean, Hutchinson chpt. 1988—93, 1996—98, dean Hutchinson chpt. 1998—2001, sub-dean, Hutchinson chpt. 2001—05), Kans. Music Educators Assn. So. Ctrl. Dist. (exec. sec. 1974—2004, 50 yr. mem.), Tabor Mennonite Ch., Coll. Emporia Alumni Assn. (bd. dirs.), Mu Phi Epsilon (pres. chpt. Phi Epsilon 1952—54). Avocations: gardening, needlecrafts, travel, photography.

**SCHMIDT, HOLLIE,** secondary school educator; 1 child. BS in Health Sci., Dance cum laude, Calif. State U., Sacramento, 1991. Cert. fitness instr. Am. Coun. Exercise. Tchr. Napa H.S., 1992—. Dir., head coach and dir. NHS dance dept. NHS Spirit Leader Team, Napa, 1992—; fitness instr. Health Quest, Napa, 1992—. Office: Napa HS 2475 Jefferson St Napa CA 94558

**SCHMIDT, JAMES CRAIG,** retired bank executive, savings and loan association executive; b. Peoria, Ill., Sept. 27, 1927; s. Walter Henry and Clara (Wolfenbarger) S.; m. Jerrie Louise Bond, Dec. 6, 1958; children: Julie, Sandra, Suzanne. Student, Ill. Wesleyan U., 1945, 48-50, Ph.B. in Bus. Adminstrn, 1952; postgrad., U. Ill. Coll. Law, 1950-52; JD, DePaul U., 1953. Spl. agt. Fidelity & Deposit Co., Chgo., 1956-58; with Home Fed. Savs. & Loan Assn., San Diego, 1958-67; asst. sec. bus. and transp. State of Calif., 1967-69; vice-chmn., pres. Gt. Am. Bank, San Diego, 1969-88. Pres. Conf. Fed. Savs. and Loans of Calif., 1974-75; mem. Calif. Toll Bridge Authority, 1969-74; mem. Calif. State Transp. Bd., 1972-78; past chmn. San Diego Bal. Commn. Task Force. Pres. San Diego Holiday Bowl Football Game, 1986; bd. dirs. San Diego Internat. Sports Coun., San Diego Hwy. Devel. Assn.; pub. mem. San Diego County Sunset Adv. Bd.; mem. City-County Re-Investment Task Force. Mem. Calif. Bar Assn., Ill. Bar Assn., Calif. League Savs. Instns. (chmn. 1986-87), Calif. C. of C. (bd. 1987-90), U.S. Savs. Instn. League (exec. com. 1983-86), San Diego East County C. of C. (bd. dirs.), Catfish Club, Sigma Chi, Phi Beta Phi. Office: 8383 Center Dr Ste 2 La Mesa CA 91942-2913 Office Phone: 619-469-4641.

**SCHMIDT, JASON,** professional baseball player; b. Lewiston, Idaho, Jan. 29, 1973; Pitcher Atlanta Braves, 1995—96, Pitts. Pirates, 1996—2001, San Francisco Giants, 2001—. Named NL Starting Pitcher MLB All-Star Game, 2003; recipient NL ERA Leader award, MLB, 2003. Office: SBC Park 24 Willie Mays Plz San Francisco CA 94107*

**SCHMIDT, JEAN,** congresswoman; b. Cin., Nov. 29, 1951; m. Peter W. Schmidt; 1 child, Emilie. BS in Polit. Sci., U. Cin., 1974. Tchg. cert. in secondary edn. U. Cin., 1988. Trustee, Miami, Ohio, 1989—2000; mem. Ohio State Ho. Reps. from Dist. 66, 2001—04, US Congress from 2nd Ohio dist., 2005—. Chmn. Clermont County Rep. Party, 1996—98, Taft for Gov., 1998; mem. agr. com. US Congress, mem. govt. reform com., mem. transp. and infrastructure com. Mem. Milford Miami Twp. C. of C., 1989—, Ohio Twp. Assn., 1990—, Clermont County Twp. Assn., 1990—, Clermont County 20/20 Com., 1990—, Clermont County League of Women Voters, 1990—, Clermont County Agrl. Soc., 1990—, Clermont County C. of C., 1990—, mem. econ. devel. com., 1995—2005; mem. Leukemia Soc. Team in Tng., 1994—, mentor, 1996—; bd. trustees Clermont County Libr., 1980—92, 1994—2000, 2005—; bd. mem. Clermont County Mercy Hosp. Found. 1997—, Phoenix Pl., 2005—; founder, chmn. Sauls Found. 5K Race, 1995—. Named Marriage & Family Therapy Legislator of Yr., 2003, Empowerment Coalition Legislator of Yr., 2004, Am. Liver Found. Legislator of Yr., 2004, Bioscience Legislator of Yr., 2004; recipient Clermont County Cmty. Devel. of the Greater Cin. Found. Appreciation award, 2003, Clermont County Mental Health Svc. Recognition Award, 2003, Children's Hosp. Award of Distinction, 2003, So. Ohio Agrl. and Cmty. Devel. Found. Disting. Svc. Award, 2004. Republican. Roman Catholic. Avocations: long distance running, auto racing. Office: US Ho Reps 238 Cannon Ho Office Bldg Washington DC 20515 Office Phone: 202-225-3164.*

**SCHMIDT, JOHN CHARLES,** music educator; b. Kenedy, Tex., Feb. 19, 1941; s. Bruno Carl and Frances Mae (Schuessler) Schmidt; m. Jacqueline Sue Yetter, June 16, 1973. PhD in Musicology, NYU, N.Y.C., 1978; M. Sacred Music, Union Theol. Sem., N.Y.C., 1963; MusB, Southwestern U., Georgetown, TX, 1961. Instr. NYU, Bronx, 1969—73; prof. Texas State U., San Marcos, 1976—; organist Covenant Presbyn. Ch., Austin, 1998—. Author: The Life and Works of John Knowles Paine; editor: (scholarly edition) John Knowles Paine Complete Piano Music, John Knowles Paine: Three Chamber Works for Piano and Strings, John Knowles Paine: Vocal Chamber Music, John Knowles Paine: The Nativity, Op. 39; contbr. articles to profl. jours. Recipient John G. Tower Disting. Alumnus award, 2005. Fellow: Am. Guild Organists (S. Lewis Elmer award 2002); mem.: Am. Musicological Soc., Soc. for Am. Music, Coll. Music Soc. (life), Phi Mu Alpha (chpt. faculty advisor 1991—, Orpheus Award 1995), Sigma Alpha Iota (nat. arts assoc. 2005), Kappa Sigma Frat. Presbyterian. Home: P O Box 1373 San Marcos TX 78667-1373 Office: Tex State Univ Sch Music 601 University Dr San Marcos TX 78666-4616 Business E-Mail: js26@txstate.edu.

**SCHMIDT, JOHN FREDERICK, III,** government agency administrator, consultant; b. Natchez, Miss., May 13, 1949; s. John Frederick Schmidt, Jr. and Dorothy Eugenia Schmidt Swann; m. Joyce Evelyn Jones, Feb. 14, 1992 (div. Nov. 1994); 1 child, Nicholas Andrew. BS in Fin., La. State U., 1971. Mgmt. trainee La. Nat. Bank, Baton Rouge, 1971—72; profl. golfer Natchez, 1972—74; golf course mgr. Bayou Bend Country Club, Sumner, Miss., 1974—77; sales rep. Healthco, Miss., Jackson, 1977—78; grant mgr. North Delta Planning, Clarksdale, Miss., 1978—81; exec. dir. North Delta Regional Housing Authority, Clarksdale, Miss., 1981—. Bd. mem. Delta Workforce Investment Bd., Clarksdale, Miss., 2000—, vice chmn. Mem.: Garden Club (King Natchez Pilgrimage 1972), Pi Tau Pi, Phi Kappa Phi. Episcopal.

Avocations: golf, reading, hunting. Office: North Delta Regional Housing Auth PO Box 1148 # 4 E Second St Clarksdale MS 38614 Office Phone: 662-627-9627. Business E-Mail: 1ndrha@clarksdale.com.

**SCHMIDT, JOHN R.,** lawyer; b. Chgo., Nov. 24, 1943; s. Edward F. and Josephine (Roggen) S.; m. Janet Gilroy, Apr. 24, 1982; 1 child, Laura. BA, Harvard U., 1964, JD, 1967. Bar: Ill. 1967, U.S. Dist. Ct. (no. dist.) Ill. 1972, U.S. Supreme Ct. 1972. Assoc. Mayer, Brown & Platt, Chgo., 1967-73, ptnr., 1973-84, Skadden, Arps, Slate, Meagher & Flom, Chgo., 1984-93; assoc. atty. gen. U.S. Dept. Justice, Washington, 1994—97; ptnr. Mayer, Brown, Rowe & Maw, LLP, Chgo., 1997—98. Vis. scholar Northwestern U. Sch. Law, 1997—98. Contbr. articles to profl. jours. Chmn. Ill. Guardianship and Advocacy Commn., 1979-82, Met. Pier and Exposition Authority, Chgo., 1989-94; chief of staff City of Chgo., 1989; co-chmn. Citizens for Ct. Reform, Chgo., 1986-92; trustee Ill. Inst. Tech., 1991-93, 1998-, Chgo. Symphony Orch., 1978-93, 1998-; amb. chief U.S negotiator Uruguay Round of World Trade Talks, Geneva, 1993-94. Recipient Judge Learned Hand Human Rels. award Am Jewish Com., 1992. Fellow Am. Bar Found.; mem. ABA, Chgo. Coun. Lawyers (pres. 1974-76). Office: Mayer Brown Rowe Maw Llp 230 S La Salle St Ste 400 Chicago IL 60604-1407 Office Phone: 312-701-8597. Office Fax: 312-706-8397. E-mail: jschmidt@mayerbrown.com.

**SCHMIDT, JOSEPH DAVID,** urologist; b. Chgo., July 29, 1937; s. Louis and Marian (Fleigel) S.; m. Andrea Maxine Herman, Oct. 28, 1962. BS in Medicine, U. Ill., 1960, MD, 1961. Diplomate Am. Bd. Urology. Rotating intern Presbyn. St. Luke's Hosp., Chgo., 1961-62, resident in surgery, 1962-63; resident in urology The Johns Hopkins Hosp., Balt., 1963-67; faculty U. Iowa Coll. Medicine, Iowa City, 1969-76, U. Calif., San Diego, 1976—, prof., head divsn. urology, 1976—2006, vice-chmn. dept. surgery, 1985-97. Cons. U.S. Dept. Navy, San Diego, 1976—; attending urologist Vets. Affairs Dept., San Diego, 1976—; assoc. dir. for clin. rsch. U. Calif. San Diego Cancer Ctr., 1997-98. Author, editor: Gynecological and Obstetric Urology, 1978, 82, 93. Capt. USAF, 1967-69. Recipient Francis Senear award U. Ill., 1961. Fellow ACS; mem. AMA, Am. Urol. Assn. Inc., Alpha Omega Alpha. Avocations: collecting antique medical books, manuscripts. Office: U Calif Med Ctr Divsn Urology 200 W Arbor Dr San Diego CA 92103-8897 Office Phone: 619-543-5904. Office Fax: 619-543-6573. Business E-Mail: jdschmidt@ucsd.edu.

**SCHMIDT, JOSEPH W.,** lawyer; b. Jeffersontown, Ky., July 6, 1946; s. A. W. and Olivia Ann Schmidt; m. Angela Petchara Apiradee, Dec. 20, 1969; children: Narissa Ann, Suriya Christine. BA in Psychology, Bellarmine Coll., 1969; AB in Commerce, U. Md., Far East Divsn., 1972; JD, Columbia U., 1975. Bar: N.Y. 1976. Law clk. to presiding judge U.S. Dist. Ct. (so. dist.) N.Y., 1975-76; assoc. Breed, Abbott & Morgan, N.Y.C., 1976-83, ptnr., 1983-93, Whitman Breed Abbott & Morgan, N.Y.C., 1993-96, Coudert Bros. LLP, N.Y.C., 1996—2002; v.p., gen. counsel, sec. Dover Corp., N.Y.C., 2003—. Adminstrv. editor: Columbia Jour. Law and Social Problems, 1974—75. Woodrow Wilson fellow, 1968, Harlan Fiske Stone scholar, 1975. Mem.: ABA, Assn. Corp. Coun., Soc. Corp. Secs. and Governance Profls., Assn. Bar City N.Y. Avocations: skiing, reading. Office: Dover Corp 280 Park Ave 34W New York NY 10017-1292 Office Phone: 212-922-1640. Business E-Mail: jws@dovercorp.com.

**SCHMIDT, JULIUS,** sculptor; b. Stamford, Conn., June 2, 1923; s. Louis Frank and Susie (Koment) S.; m. Carolyn Marsha Wolf (div.); children: Ania J., Ianos; m. Mary Katherine Powers, 1981 (div.); 1 child, Araan J. Student, Okla. A&M U., 1950-51; BFA, Cranbrook Acad. Art, 1952, MFA, 1955; student, Ossip Zadkine, Paris, 1953, Accademia di Belle Arti, Florence, Italy, 1954. Chmn. sculpture dept. Kansas City Art Inst., 1954-59, R.I. Sch. Design, 1959-60, U. Calif.-Berkeley, 1961-62, Cranbrook Acad. Art, 1962-70, U. Iowa, Iowa City, 1970-93; ret., 1993. Exhibited in 43 one-man shows 1953—; group shows include Allen Meml. Art Mus., Oberlin, Ohio, 1958, Arts Club of Chgo., Mus. Modern Art, N.Y.C., 1960, Whitney Mus., 1960-63, Gallerie Claude Bernard, paris, 1960, Guggenheum Mus., 1962, San Francisco Mus. Art, 1962, Phila. Art Alliance, 1963, Battersea Park, London, 1963, Sai Paolo Bienal, Brazil, 1963, White House Festival of Arts, Washington, 1965, Bienale Middleheim, Belgium, 1971; represented in permanent collections Nelson Gallery-Atkins Mus., Kansas City, Mo., Art Inst., Chgo., Mus. Modern Art, N.Y.C., Mus. U. Nebr., Whitney Mus. Art, N.Y.C., Krannert Art Mus., Urbana, Ill., Washington, U. Walker Art Center, Mpls., Albright-Knox Mus., Buffalo, Detroit Inst. Art, U. Calif. Art Mus., Cranbrook Acad. Art, Mich., Princeton Mus. Art, Hirschhorn Mus., Washington, Numerous others. Served with USNR, World War II. Decorated Air medal (2); recipient Lifetime Achievement award in sculpture edn. Internat. Sculpture Ctr., 1998; Guggenheim fellow, 1963-64. Address: 5 Highview Knl NE Iowa City IA 52240-9149 Office Phone: 319-351-1665. Personal E-mail: jfeschmidt@earthlink.net.

**SCHMIDT, KARL A.,** lawyer; b. Stockton, Calif., Sept. 18, 1947; BS, U. Calif., Berkeley, 1969, JD, 1974. Bar: Calif. 1974. Mem. Parker, Milliken, Clark, O'Hara & Samuelian, L.A. Contbr. Retaliation Matters to L.A. Daily Jour. Ann. Employment Update, 1997, USC TAx Inst. 2003: Exec. Terminations. Mem. ABA. Office: Parker Milliken Clark O Hara & Samuelian 333 S Hope St Ste 2700 Los Angeles CA 90071-1449 Office Phone: 213-683-6518. E-mail: kschmidt@pmcos.com.

**SCHMIDT, KLAUS DIETER,** marketing professional, management consultant, educator; b. Eisenach, Germany, May 8, 1930; came to U.S., 1951; naturalized, 1952; s. Kurt Heinrich and Louise (Kruger) b.; m. Lynda Hollister Wheelwright, June 29, 1950; children: Karen, Claudia. BA in Econs., U. Calif., Berkeley, 1951; MBA, Stanford U., 1953; PhD in Bus. Adminstrn., Golden Gate U., 1978. Buyer, jr. mdse. mgr. Broadway Hale, 1952-54; sales mgr. Ames Harris Neville Co., 1954-56, ops. mgr., 1956-57; gen. mgr. Boise Cascade Corp., 1957-60; pres., chmn. bd. Kimball-Schmidt Inc., San Rafael, Calif., 1960-73, chmn. bd. Kalwall Pacific, 1962-67, chmn. subs. AFGOA, 1966-69; asst. prof. mgmt. and mktg. San Francisco State U., 1970-75, assoc. prof. mgmt., 1975-80, prof. mgmt. and mktg., 1989-85, chmn. dept., 1979-85, prof. emeritus 1989—, assoc. dean emeritus Sch. Bus., 1985-88; chmn. Schmidt Cons. Group, Brooklin, Maine, 1988—. Dir. Ctr. for World Bus., 1976-88; dir. US-Japan Inst., 1981-88, editor-in-chief Sch. Bus. Jours., 1980-88; US negotiator for Pres. Carter White House on Afghanistan issue, 1980-88; mem. Dept. Commerce Dist. Export Council, 1982-88; rsch. cons. SRI Internat. Author: (20 booklet series) Doing Business In..., Stanford Rsch. Inst., 1978-80, A Spy For Life, 2004, Living Your Life, 2005. Mem. Univ. Club (San Francisco), Alpha Delta Phi, Beta Gamma Sigma. Republican. Office: PO Box 269 Brooklin ME 04616-0269 Office Phone: 207-359-4644.

**SCHMIDT, KLAUS FRANZ,** advertising executive; b. Dessau, Germany, May 25, 1928; came to U.S., 1951; naturalized, 1957; s. Franz and Elfriede (Klamroth) S.; m. Gisela Garbrecht, June 19, 1954; children: Dagmar Schmidt Etkin, Ena Schmidt Reynen. Student, Coll. of Journalism, Aachen, Germany, 1947-48. Sch. of Design and Printing, Bochum, Germany, 1948-50; BA, Wayne State U., 1956. Printer, compositor, 1948-56; type dir. Mogul Williams & Saylor, N.Y.C., 1956-59, Doyle, Dane, Bernbach, N.Y.C., 1959-61, Young & Rubicam, N.Y.C., 1961-68, v.p., dir. print ops., 1968-75, v.p., dir. creative support, 1975-85, sr. v.p., mgr. prodn. svcs., 1985-91; advt./graphic arts cons., 1991—. Co-organizer Vision Congress Internat. Ctr. for Communications Arts & Scis., N.Y.C., 1965, 67, 69, 77; chmn., bd. trustees Internat. Ctr. Typographic Arts, N.Y.C. 1969-70 Author: Signs of the Times, 1997; Am. editor Der Druckspiegel, 1957-64; contbg. editor Print Mag., 1968-01; The Dunn Report, 1991-95 Recipient Typomundus award, 1964, Internat. Book Exhbn. award, Leipzig, Germany, 1965 Mem. Print Advt. Assn. N.Y. chpt. 1969-71, nat. sr. v.p. 1971-75), Am. Assn. Advt. Agys. (chmn. subcom. on phototypography 1969-75), Digital Distribn. of Advt. to Publ. Assn. (vice chmn. 1991-95), N.Y. Type Dirs. Club (pres.

1984-86, awards 1962, 64-66, 68, 69), N.Y. Art Dirs. Club (v.p. 1984-86), Advt. Prodn. Club (pres. 1982-84), Gravure Advt. Coun. (chmn. 1970-72) Home and Office: 549 Munroe Ave Sleepy Hollow NY 10591-1333 E-mail: kaschmi@optonline.net.

**SCHMIDT, L. LEE, JR.,** retired university official; b. Mullinville, Kans., Oct. 2, 1937; s. Lester Lee and Mary (Gilliam) S.; m. Sarah Sue Lookingbill, Aug. 12, 1961; children: Suzanne, Jon. BS in Bus. Adminstrn., U. Ark., 1962, PhD, 1971; MBA, Tex. Tech U., 1963. CPA, Colo. Audit sr. Ernst & Young, Fort Worth, 1963-66; mgr. acctg. The Western Co., Fort Worth, 1966-67; asst. prof. U. Tex.-Arlington, 1967-68; instr. U. Ark., Fayetteville, 1968-71; prof. acctg., chmn. dept Colo. State U.; Ft. Collins, 1971-87, assoc. dean Coll. Bus., 1988-92; assoc. dean Coll. Bus. Adminstrn., U. Tex., El Paso, 1992-96; dean Coll. Bus. and Tech. Tex. A&M U., Commerce, 1996-2000; ret., 2000. Speaker in field Contbr. articles to profl. jours. Served with USN, 1955-58. Earhart Found. fellow, 1968-69 Mem. AICPA, Am. Acctg. Assn., Fin. Execs. Inst., Beta Gamma Sigma, Beta Alpha Psi. Office: Tex A&M U-Commerce Office of the Dean PO Box 3011 Commerce TX 75429-3011

**SCHMIDT, LAURA JEAN,** mathematics professor; b. Pittsford, NY, Aug. 12, 1975; d. Arthur William Spencer and Carol Thibault Thomson; m. Dennis Allen Schmidt, Aug. 6, 2000. BS, Bucknell U., 1997; MA, U. Ky., 1999, PhD, 2003. Lab mgr. U. Ky., 1999—2000; instr. Ctr. for Talented Youth, John Hopkins U., 2000—01; tchg. asst. U. Ky., 1997—2002; adj. prof. Transylvania U., Lexington, Ky., 2003; asst. prof. Berea Coll., Berea, Ky., 2003—04, U. Wis., Stoudt, 2004—. Fellow Project NEXT, 2004—05. V.p. Bluegrass Alumnae, Lexington, Ky., 2002—03; team leader Relay for Life Phi Mu, Menomonie, Wis., 2005; proctor, grader State Sci. Olympiad, Menomonie, 2005. Finalist Tchg. award., U. Ky., 2002; grantee, Office Profl. and Instructional Devel., 2005—06; Profl. Develop. grant, U. Wis. Stout, 2006. Mem.: Math. Assn. Am. (grantee 2004—05), Assn. for Women in Math., Am. Math. Soc. Avocations: racquetball, reading. Office: U Wis Stout 202H Harvey Hall Menomonie WI 54751

**SCHMIDT, LYNDA WHEELWRIGHT,** psychotherapist; b. Beijing, July 29, 1931; came to the U.S., 1931; d. Joseph Balch and Jane Byers (Hollister) Wheelwright; m. Klaus Dieter, May 8, 1930; children: Karen Calley, Claudia Lewis. BA, U. Calif., Berkeley, 1965, MSW, 1968. Cert. Jungian analyst; bd. cert. diplomate Am. Bd. Examiners Clin. Social Work. Staff psychiat. social worker Pacific Med. Ctr., San Francisco, 1968-71; pvt. practice psychotherapy and Jungian analysis San Francisco, 1971-87, Brooklin, Maine, 1985—. Tng. analyst CG Jung Inst., San Francisco, 1978—; mem. certifying com. CG Jung Inst., San Francisco, 1980-84; cons. and lectr. in field. Author: Time Out of Mind: Trekking the Hindu Kush, 1978, The Long Shore, A Psychological Experience of the Wilderness, 1991; contbr. articles to profl. jours. Fellow Calif. Soc. Clin. Social Workers; mem. NASW, Acad. Cert. Social Workers, inc., CG Jung Inst. (chair certifying com. 1980-84), Alpha Phi Sorority. Democrat. Avocations: reading, horseback riding, travel, music. Home and Office: PO Box 269 Brooklin ME 04616-0269

**SCHMIDT, NANCY ANNE,** psychotherapist; b. Jersey City, July 18, 1958; d. William John Lawrence and Ruth Martha (Morant) S. BA summa cum laude, Fordham U., 1986; MA summa cum laude, N.J. City State U., 1990; cert. pastoral counselor, World Christianship Ministries, 1994. Cert. social worker, criminal justice specialist, hypnotherapist, addiction counselor, eating disorders specialist; cert. domestic violence counselor, cert. crisis counselor. Adj. prof. N.J. City State U. (formerly Jersey City State Coll.), 1988-91, adj. prof. psychology, 1990-94; pvt. practice West New York, 1990—; counselor Substance Abuse Treatment Ctr., Union City, NJ, 1994-96; substance abuse program dir. Sr. Treatment and Edn. Program, Union City, 1994-96; staff psychotherapist North Hudson Cmty. Action Corp. Mental Health Ctr., West New York, 1996-98, dir. mental health, addictive svcs., social work, psychiatry, 1998—. Bd. dirs. Hudson Health Care Partnership, Jersey City; bd. dirs. Hudson County Healthy Families 2000, mem. Hudson County Task Force on Women & Addiction, co-dir. Union City Police Dept./NHCAC Domestic Violence Outreach Program, Union City Police Dept. stress reduction cons.; presenter in field. Mem. APA, Am. Counseling Assn., Am. Assn. Family Counselors (cert.), Nat. Assn. Alcohol and Drug Abuse Counselors, Am. Assn. Christian Counselors, Am. Psychotherapy Assn., Alpha Sigma Lambda, Phi Kappa Phi, Psi Chi. Avocations: swimming, walking, reading, writing, poetry. Office: North Hudson Cmty Action Corp Mental Health Addictive Svc 5301 Broadway West New York NJ 07093-2622

**SCHMIDT, PAUL WICKHAM,** lawyer; b. Milw., June 25, 1948; s. Edmund Julian and Barbara (Wickham) S.; m. Cathryn Ann Piehl, June 27, 1970; children: Thomas Wickham, William Piehl, Anna Patchin. BA cum laude, Lawrence U., 1970; JD cum laude, U. Wis., 1973. Bar: Wis. 1973, U.S. Dist. Ct. (we. dist.) Wis. 1973, U.S. Supreme Ct. 1982, D.C. 1988. Atty. advisor Bd. Immigration Appeals, Washington, 1973-76; gen. atty. office of gen. counsel Immigration and Naturalization Service, Washington, 1976-78, acting gen. counsel, 1979-81, 86-87, dep. gen. counsel, 1978-87; assoc. Jones, Day, Reavis & Pogue, Washington, 1987-89, ptnr., 1990-92; mng. ptnr. Fragomen, Del Ray & Bernsen, PC, Washington, 1993-95; chmn. Bd. of Immigration Appeals, Falls Church, Va., 1995-2001, mem., 2001—03; judge Arlington (Va.) Immigration Ct., 2003—. Mem. ABA, D.C. Bar Assn., Wis. Bar Assn., Fed. Bar Assn. (immigration sect.). Avocations: crew volunteer, gardening, camping, history. Home: 711 S View Ter Alexandria VA 22314-4923 Office: Arlington Immigration Ct 901 N Stuart St Ste 1300 Arlington VA 22203 Business E-mail: paul.schmidt@usdoj.gov.

**SCHMIDT, PETER GUSTAV,** marine engineer; b. Tumwater, Wash., Dec. 3, 1921; s. Peter G. and Clara Louise (Muench) S.; m. Elva May Ingalls, Dec. 3, 1945; children: Mimi Schmidt Fielding, Jill Schmidt Crowson, Janet Schmidt Mano, Hans. BSME, U. Wash., 1948; MS in Naval Architecture and Marine Engring., U. Mich., 1950. Naval architect Nat. Steel Shipbldg. Corp., San Diego, 1950-52, Carl J. Nordstrom/P. Spaulding, Seattle, 1952-53; pres. Marine Constrn. & Design Co., Seattle, 1953—. Astilleros Marco Chilena Ltd., Santiago, Chile, 1960—, Marco Peruana S.A., Lima, Peru, 1965—, Campbell Industries, San Diego, 1979-99, Campbell Ship Design & Engring., Seattle, 2000—; chmn. Marco Global, Inc., 2005—. Author papers on fishing gear and vessels. Served to lt (j.g.) USN, 1942-45, PTO. Recipient Puget Sound's Maritime Man of Yr. award Puget Sound Press Assn., 1975, Naval Arch. and Marine Engring. Merit award U. Mich., 1996. Mem. Soc. Naval Architects and Marine Engrs., Wash. State Boatbuilders Assn. (pres. 1956-58), Alpha Delta Phi. Avocations: sailing, classical music. Office: Marine Constrn & Design 4259 22d Ave W Seattle WA 98199 Office Phone: 206-285-3200.

**SCHMIDT, RAYMOND PAUL,** military officer, historian, government agency administrator; b. Western, Nebr., Sept. 14, 1937; s. Reuben Edward and Angeline Agnes (Kudlik) Schmidt; m. Roberta Ruth Schrom, June 11, 1961; 1 child, Douglas Craig. B in Edn., History and Social Sci., U. Nebr., 1958; postgrad., U. Md., 1960-62, The Am. U., 1975-81; M in History, U. Wis., 1966. Instr. math. and social sci. Sr. High Sch., Bellevue, Nebr., 1958-59; history instr. James Madison Meml. High Sch., Madison, Wis., 1966-68; ensign USN, 1959, historian, archivist Naval Security Group Command Washington, 1968-81, advanced through grades to capt., 1981, sr. congl. security policy rev. officer, Naval Intelligence Washington, 1981-82, sr. res. forces advisor Dept. Def., 1982-88, head Navy info. security policy, 1988-98, mgr. declassification program, 1998-00; cons., 2000—03; freelance rschr., writer, 2001—. Mem. Nat. Disclosure Policy Com. Team, Japan, 1989, Thailand, 89, Germany, 91, leader, Albania, 95. Author (with others): Naval Officers Guide, 1983, And I Was There, 1985; contbr. articles to profl. jours. Pres. North Ashburton Citizens Assn., Bethesda, Md., 1982—; merit badge counselor Boy Scouts Am., 1974—93; info. officer U.S. Naval Acad., Annapolis, Md., 1978—93; spkr. Pearl Harbor Symposium Adm. Nimitz Found., Tex., 1991, symposium moderator, 1992; active Montgomery County Planning Bd. Citizens Adv. Com., Md., 1989—94; ret. pers. adv. coun. Naval Dist. Washington. Named Hon. Adm. Great Navy, State of Nebr., 1983. Mem.: DAV (life), Nat. Cryptologic Mus. Found., U.S. Naval Cryptologic Vets. Assn., Naval Intelligence Profls., Am. Hist. Assn., Nat. Trust Hist. Preservation, Nat. Classification Mgmt. Soc. (editor Viewpoints 1991—96), Nat. Assn. Active and Ret. Fed. Employees, Naval Res. Assn. (life; sec./treas. 1966—68), Mil. Officers Assn. Am. (life), Res. Officers Assn. (life), Nat. Assn. Uniformed Svcs. (life), U.S. Naval Inst. (life; contbr.), Phoenix Soc., Colonial Williamsburg Found., U. Nebr. Alumni Assn. (life). Unitarian. Home: 6205 Lone Oak Dr Bethesda MD 20817-1743

**SCHMIDT, ROBERT,** retired mechanics and civil engineering educator; b. Reshetylivka, Ukraine, May 18, 1927; arrived in U.S., 1949, naturalized, 1956; s. Alfred and Aquilina (Konotop) S.; m. Irene Hubertine Bongartz, June 10, 1978; 1 child, Ingbert Robert Floyd. Student, UNRRA-Univ., Munich, 1946—47, Technische Hochschule Karlsruhe, Germany, 1947—49, Vorpruefung; BS, U. Colo., Boulder, 1951; MS, U. Colo., 1953; PhD, U. Ill. Champaign-Urbana, 1956. Tech. draftsman, Kalisch, Poland, 1943-45; rsch. asst. U. Ill., Urbana, 1953-56, asst. prof. mechanics, 1956-59; assoc. prof. U. Ariz., Tucson, 1959-63; prof. mechanics and civil engring. U. Detroit, 1963-99, chmn. civil engring. dept., 1978-80; ret., 1999. Lectr. Oakland U., 1997-98; rschr. in linear and nonlinear theory of elasticity, theories of arches, plates, and shells, and approximate methods of analysis. Editor: Indsl. Math., 1969—; book reviewer Applied Mechanics Rev., Indsl. Math. Jour.; contbr. numerous articles to profl. jours. With C.E., U.S. Army, 1951-52. Grantee NSF 1960-78. Mem. AAUP, ASCE, ASME (cert. recognition 1972), Am. Acad. Mechanics (founder), Indsl. Math. Soc. (pres. 1966-67, 81-84, 1st Gold award 1986), Sigma Xi. Avocations: biosophy, walking, bicycling, swimming.

**SCHMIDT, ROBERT CHARLES, JR.,** finance company executive; b. Oklahoma City, Apr. 2, 1942; s. Robert Charles and Francis Laura (Schiele) S.; m. Susan G. Dietz-Felbinger, Nov. 8, 1974; children: Laura Stewart, Elizabeth Berry Saldebar. BA, Westminster Coll., Fulton, Mo., 1964; postgrad., U. Okla., 1972, London Grad. Sch. Bus. Studies, 1974-76. Exec. trainee First Nat. Bank in St. Louis, 1967-68, comml. banker, 1968-74, v.p., mgr. client services div., 1974-76; v.p. treasury ops. Am. Express Co., N.Y.C., 1976-81, dep. treas., 1981-86; chmn. bd. Am. Express Export Credit Corp., 1982-86; group v.p., gen. mgr. Nat. Data Corp., Atlanta, 1986-88, exec. v.p., 1988-89, Capital Guaranty Corp., San Francisco, 1989-91; pres. Tampsco Enterprises, Inc., St. Louis, 1993; ptnr. The Whitelaw Group, St. Louis, 1994-96; pres. SCM Group, Inc., St. Louis, 1996—. Cons. City of N.Y., 1977 Loaned exec. United Fund, St. Louis, 1973; trustee Congl. Summer Assembly Edn. Fund, 1993—; Served with U.S. Army, 1965—67; dir. Crystal Lake Assn., The Endowment for Experimental Arch., Ltd. Decorated Army Commendation medal; recipient cert. of merit USO, 1966, Alumni Achievement award Westminster Coll., 1977 Mem. Treas. Group (chmn. 1982-83), Noonday Club (St. Louis), Crystal Downs Country Club (Frankfort, Mich.), Beta Theta Pi Republican. Episcopalian. Home: 2013 Pilgrim Hwy Frankfort MI 49635-9497

**SCHMIDT, ROBERT MILTON,** preventive medicine physician, educator, medical association administrator; b. Milw., May 7, 1944; s. Milton W. and Edith J. (Martinek) S.; children Eric Whitney, Edward Huntington. AB, Northwestern U., 1966; MD, Columbia U., 1970; MPH, Harvard U., 1975; PhD in Law, Medicine and Pub. Policy, Emory U., 1982; MA, San Francisco State U., 1999. Diplomate Am. Bd. Preventive Medicine, Am. Bd. Internal Medicine, Am. Bd. Hematology. Resident in internal medicine Univ. Hosp. U. Calif.-San Diego, 1970-71; resident in preventive medicine Ctr. Disease Control, Atlanta, 1971-74; commd. med. officer USPHS, 1971; advanced through grades to comdr., 1973; dir. hematology div. Nat. Ctr. for Disease Control, Atlanta, 1971-78, spl. asst. to dir., 1978-79, inactive res., 1979—; clin. asst. prof. pediatrics Tufts U. Med. Sch., 1974-86; clin. asst. prof. medicine Emory U. Med. Sch., 1971-81, clin. assoc. prof. community health, 1976-86; clin. assoc. prof. humanities in medicine Morehouse Med. Sch., 1977-79; attending physician dept. medicine Wilcox Meml. Hosp., Lihue, Hawaii, 1979-82, Calif. Pacific Med. Ctr., San Francisco, 1983—; dir. Ctr. Preventive Medicine and Health Rsch., 1983—, dir. Health Watch, 1983—; sr. scientist Inst. Epidemiol. and Behavioral Medicine, Inst. Cancer Rsch., Calif. Pacific Med. Ctr., San Francisco, 1983-88; prof. hematology and gerontology, dir. Ctr. Preventive Medicine and Health Rsch., chair health professions program San Francisco State U., 1983-99, prof. medicine, 1983—, prof. emeritus, Calif. State U. Sys., 1999—; founding dir. Health Watch Internat., 1994—, CEO, pres. Cons. WHO, FDA, Washington, NIH, Bethesda, Md., Govt. of China, Mayo Clinic, Rochester, Minn., Northwestern U., Evanston, Ill., Chgo., U. R.I., Kingston, Pan Am. Health Orgn., Inst. Pub. Health, Italy, Nat. Inst. Aging Rsch. Ctr., Balt., U. Calif., San Diego, U. Ill., Chgo., Columbia U., NYC, Harvard U., Johns Hopkins U., U. Chgo., UCLA, U. Calif. Berkeley, Brown U., Providence, U. Calif., San Francisco, Stanford U., Boston, Emory U., Atlanta, Duke U., NC, U. Tex., Houston, Ariz. State U., U. Hawaii, Honolulu, U. Paris, U. Geneva, U. Munich, Heidelberg U., U. Frankfurt, U. Berlin, Cambridge U., England, U. Singapore, others; vis. rsch. prof. gerontology Ariz. State U., 1989—90; mem. numerous sci. and profl. adv. bd., panels, com. Mem. editorial bd. Am. Jour. Clin. Pathology, 1976-82, The Advisor, 1988—, Generations, 1989—, Contemporary Gerontology, 1994—, Alternative Therapies in Health and Medicine, 1995—, Aging Today, 1997—; book and film reviewer Sci. Books and Films, 1988—, many other jours.; author: 17 books and manuals including Hematology Laboratory Series, 4 vols., 1979-86, CRC Handbook Series in Clinical Laboratory Science, 1976—; assoc. editor: Contemporary Gerontology, 1993—; contbr. more than 400 articles to sci. jours. Alumni regent Columbia U. Coll. Physicians and Surgeons, 1980—. Northwestern U. scholar, 1964-66; NSF fellow, 1964-66; Health Professions scholar, 1966-70; USPHS fellow, 1967-70; Microbiology, Urology, Upjohn Achievement, Borden Rsch. and Virginia Kneeland Frantz scholar awards Columbia U., 1970; recipient Am. Soc. Pharmacol. and Exptl. Therapy award in pharmacology, 1970, Commendation medal USPHS, 1973, Meritorious Performance and Profl. Promise award, 1989, Student Disting. Teaching and Svc. award Pre-Health Professions Student Alliance, 1992, Leadership Recognition awards San Francisco State U., 1984-89, 91-96, Meritorious Svc. award, 1992. Fellow: ACPM, AAAS (med. scis. sect.), ACP (commentator ACP Jour. Club/Annals of Internal Medicine 1993—), Internat. Soc. Hematology, Am. Soc. Clin. Pathology, Am. Coll. Preventive Medicine (sci. com.), Am. Geriat. Soc., Royal Soc. Medicine (London), Gerontol. Soc. Am.; mem.: APHA, AMA, Emory Sch. Pub. Health, Calif. Coun. Gerontology and Geriat., Nat. Assoc. Adv. for Health Professions, Internat. Health Eval. Assn. (v.p. for Ams. 1992—94, bd. dirs. 1992—, pres. 1994—96), Calif. Med. Assn., San Francisco Med. Soc., NY Acad. Sci., Am. Soc. Aging (editl. bd. 1990—, Dychtwald Pub. Speaking award 1991), Am. Soc. Microbiology, Assn. Tchr. Preventive Medicine (edn. com., rsch. com.), Am. Coll. Occupl. and Environ. Medicine, Calif. Coun. Gerontology and Geriat., Am. Assn. Med. Info., Nat. Assn. Advisors for Health Professions (bd. dirs.), Am. Assoc. Blood Banks, Acad. Clin. Lab. Physicians and Scientists, Internat. Soc. Thrombosis and Hemostasis, Am. Soc. Hematology (hon.; emeritus), Internat. Commn. Standardization in Hematology, Am. Assn. Med. Info. (chair prevention and health evaln. informatics WG), Nat. Gallery of Art (Washington), Columbia U. Club No. Calif., Circle Club (Washington), Army and Navy Club, Golden Key (hon. faculty mem.), Harvard Club (NY and San Francisco), Northwestern U. Club. No. Calif., Cosmos Club (mem. art com. 1997—), Knights of Malta, Sigma Xi, Phi Beta Kappa. Home: Whaleship Plaza 25 Hinckley Walk San Francisco CA 94111-2303 Office: Health Watch Med Ctr Calif Pacific Med Ctr San Francisco CA 94120-7999 Office Phone: 415-956-5670. Personal E-mail: rmschmidtmd@aol.com.

**SCHMIDT, RONALD HANS,** architect; b. Hoboken, N.J., Sept. 9, 1938. BArch., Syracuse U., 1961. Sr. designer Skidmore, Owings & Merrill, N.Y.C., 1963-68; ptnr., dir. archtl. design Grad. Partnership, Newark, 1968-81; pres., chief exec. officer Ronald Schmidt & Assocs., P.A., Englewood, N.J., 1981—. Chmn. Bergen County (N.J.) Econ. Devel. Corp.; mem. bd. regents Felician Coll.; mem. exec. com. Network of Opportunity. Recipient numerous awards. Office: 222 Grand Ave Englewood NJ 07631-4352 E-mail: rschmidt@RSAaia.com.

**SCHMIDT, RUSSEL ALAN, II,** sales executive; b. Stuttgart-Bad Canstatt, Germany, Nov. 18, 1953; arrived in U.S., 1954; s. Russell Allen and Phyllis (Coty) S.; m. Christie Ellen Duncan, Oct. 18 1975; children: Rachel Lea, Russell Alan III. BS, U. Minn., 1984. Lic. FCC gen. radiotelephone operator; cert. Motorola Effective Presentations, Successful Negotiator. Pres. Electronic Engring. Inds. Co., St. Paul, 1971—77, Dis-Com Inc., St. Paul, 1978—81; sales engr. Motorola Inc., Mpls., 1984—85, dist. sales engr., 1985—86, dist. sales mgr., 1987—89, sr. account sales mgr., 1989—93, sr. acct. sales mgr., 1993—95, market devel. mgr., 1995—2001; v.p. Essential Bus. Svcs. Roseville, Minn., 1986—; pres. Forefront Devel. Inc., 2001—; chief mgr. RAC Schmidt Properties LLC, 2001—. Bd. dirs. Dis-Com Inc. 1978-81; chief TV engr. Renewal Internat. Inc., St. Paul, 1984-87; pres. Forefront Devel., Inc., 2001; chief mgr. R&C Schmidt Properties LLC; v.p. Essential Bus. Svcs. Roseville, 2001. Pub. (music CD) Living In Laodicea, 1999. Mem. Nat. SBA, St. Paul C. of C., North Suburban C. of C., Mpls. C. of C., North Oaks Golf Club. Republican. Lutheran. Avocations: small business or real estate ventures, non-fiction reading, computer programming, travel. Office: Motorola Semiconductor Products 5620 Smetana Dr Minnetonka MN 55343-9611 Business E-mail: russ2@spacestar.net.

**SCHMIDT, RUTH ANN,** retired academic administrator; b. Mountain Lake, Minn., Sept. 16, 1930; d. Jacob A. and Anna A. (Ewert) S. BA, Augsburg Coll., Mpls., 1952; MA, U. Mo., 1955; PhD, U. Ill., 1962; LLD, Gordon Coll., 1987. Asst. prof. Spanish Mary Baldwin Coll., Staunton, Va., 1955-58, SUNY-Albany, 1962-67, assoc. prof., 1967-78, dean of humanities, 1971-76; prof. and provost Wheaton Coll., Norton, Mass., 1978-82; pres. Agnes Scott Coll., Decatur, Ga., 1982-94, pres. emerita, 1994—. Interim pres. Lyon Coll., 1998; chair Women's Coll. Coalition, 1986-88. Author: Ortega Munilla y sus novelas, 1973, Cartas entre dos amigos del teatro, 1969. Trustee Gordon Coll., Wenham, Mass., 1980-86, Lyon Coll., 1993-2001; bd. dirs. DeKalb C. of C., 1982-85, Atlanta Coll. Art, 1984-94; mem. exec. com. Women's Coll. Coalition, 1983-88; v.p. So. Univ. Conf., 1993. Named Disting. Alumna Augsburg Coll., 1973 Mem. Assn. Am. Colls. (dir. 1979-82, treas. 1982-83), Soc. Values in Higher Edn., Am. Coun. Edn. (commn. on women in higher edn. 1985-88), AAUW, Assn. Pvt. Colls. and Univs. Ga. (pres. 1987-89), Internat. Women's Forum, Young Women's Christian Assn. Acad. Women Achievers, Women's Action for New Directions. Democrat. Presbyterian. E-mail: ruthschmidt@mindspring.com.

**SCHMIDT, SHERI LYNN,** band director; b. Kalamazoo, Mich., Dec. 21, 1969; d. Robert LaDuke and Judith LaDuke; m. Darin Schmidt, Mar. 29, 1993. B Music Edn., Western Mich. U., 1992; M Music Edn., VanderCook Coll. of Music, 1999. Cert. tchr. Asst. dir. bands Pennfield Schs., Battle Creek, Mich., 1992—98; dir. bands Shakamak Schs., Jasonville, Ind., 1998—2001; band dir. Lakeview Schs., Battle Creek, Mich., 2001—. Flute tchr., Battle Creek, 1985—2001. Mem.: Music Educator's Nat. Conf., Mich. Sch. Band and Orch. Assn. (treas. Dist. 8 1995—98). Presbyterian. Avocations: photography, yoga.

**SCHMIDT, SHERRIE,** library director, dean; BA, Ohio State U., 1970, MLS, 1974. With Ohio State U.; cataloger U. Fla., 1974—75; head user svcs. AMIGOS Bibliographic Coun., 1975—78; assoc. dir. libr. svcs. U. Tex., Dallas, 1979—82; S.W. US sales rep. Faxon Co., 1982—84; asst. info. sys. planning U. Tex., Austin, 1984—86; asst. dir. collections and bibliographic svcs. Tex. A&M U., 1986—90; assoc. dean libr. svcs. Ariz. State U., 1990—91, dean univ. libraries, 1991—. Contbr. articles to profl. jours. Sr. fellow, UCLA, 1989. Mem.: ALA (mem. Office for Info. Tech. Policy Adv. Com. 2002—04). Office: Ariz State U 113 Hayden Libr PO Box 871006 Tempe AZ 85287-1006 Office Phone: 480-965-3417. Office Fax: 480-965-9169.*

**SCHMIDT, STANLEY ALBERT,** editor, writer; b. Cin., Mar. 7, 1944; s. Otto Elliott William and Georgia (Metcalf) S.; m. Joyce Mary Tokarz, June 9, 1979. BS, U. Cin., 1966; MA, Case Western Res. U., 1968, PhD, 1969. Asst. prof. physics Heidelberg Coll., Tiffin, Ohio, 1969-78; freelance writer Lake Peekskill, N.Y., 1968—; editor Analog Sci. Fiction and Fact Dell Mags., N.Y.C., 1978—. Mem. bd. advisors Nat. Space Soc., Washington, 1982—; Sci. Fiction Mus. and Hall of Fame, Seattle, 2003-. Author: Newton and the Quasi-Apple, 1975, The Sins of the Fathers, 1976, Lifeboat Earth, 1978, Analog Yearbook II, 1981, Analog's Golden Anniversary Anthology, 1980, Analog: Readers' Choice, 1981, Analog's Children of the Future, 1982, Analog's Lighter Side, 1982, Analog: Writers' Choice, 1983, War and Peace: Possible Futures from Analog, 1983, Aliens from Analog, 1983, Writer's Choice, Vol. II, 1984, From Mind to Mind, 1984, Analog's Expanding Universe, 1986, Tweedlioop, 1986, Unknown, 1988, Unknown Worlds, 1989, Analog Essays in Science, 1990, Writing Science Fiction and Fantasy, 1991, Aliens and Alien Societies, 1995, Roads Not Taken, 1998, Which Way to the Future?, 2001, Generation Gap and Other Stories, 2002, Argonaut, 2002; contbr. stories to sci. fiction mags., articles to mags., chapters to books. Mem. Sci. Fiction and Fantasy Writers Am., Am. Assn. Physics Tchrs., Am. Fedn. Musicians. Avocations: photography, hiking, linguistics, cooking, flying. Office: Analog Sci Fiction 475 Park Ave S New York NY 10016-6901 Personal E-mail: analog@dellmagazines.com.

**SCHMIDT, STANLEY EUGENE,** retired speech educator; b. Harrington, Wash., Dec. 14, 1927; s. Otto Jacob and Ella Genevieve (Wilson) S.; m. Jayne Brown; children: Randall Lee, Stephen Douglas. BS in Edn., Beta Theta Pi, U. Idaho, 1956; MEd in Adminstrn., U. Oreg., 1958; MA in Speech, Wash. State U., 1975. Supt., tchr. coach Rose Lake (Idaho) Sch. Dist. #35, 1949-55; forensics coach, speech tchr., dir. forensics Jefferson H.S., Portland, Oreg., 1955-65; dir. forensics Portland C.C., 1965-93, lead speech instr., 1979-82, subject area chmn., 1986-90; adj. prof. speech U. Portland, 1987-93; ret., 1993. Parliamentarian faculty senate, 1975-80. Co-author anthology: The Literature of the Oral Tradition, 1963. Chmn., precinct committeeman Rep. Party, Kootenai County, Idaho, 1951-53; pres. Kootenai County Tchrs. Assn., 1953-54, North Idaho Edn. Assn., 1954-55, Oreg. Speech Assn., 1960-61, Oreg. C.C. Speech Assn., 1971-72. Recipient Excellence award U.S. Bank, Portland, 1993, Merit award N.W. Forensic Assn., 1992, Faculty Merit award Portland C.C., 1984. Mem.: N.W. Comm. Assn., Am. Forensic Assn., Oreg. Speech Assn. (pres.), Speech Comm. Assn., Western Speech Comm. Assn., Oreg. Ret. Tchrs. Assn, Am. Rose Soc., Portland Rose Soc. (Best Rose Garden in Portland Grand Sweepstakes award 2003), Allied Masonic Degrees, Scottish Rite (comdr. multnomah coun. kadosh 1990—91, pres. found. 2002—, 33 degree), Benevolent and Protective Order of the Elks, Royal Arch Masons, Shriners (dir. of the work 1990—, pres. Tualtin valley shrine club 1991, group leader of the guides 1998—, mem. Order of Quetzalcoatl), Royal Ark Mariners, Royal Order Scotland, York Rite Sovereign Coll., Red Cross of Constantine (dir. of the work 1989—2001, recorder 1993—97, sovereign 2000—01, St. Laurence Conclave), Order of Ea. Star (Worthy Patron 1953, 1970), Knights Templar (knight comdr. of temple of grand encampment), Cryptic Masons of Oreg. (grand orator 1994—95, illustrious master 1997), Masons (worshipful master 1984—85, dist. dep. 1986—90, jr. grand deacon 1990—91, jr. grand steward 1991—92, grand orator 1992—93, grand lodge edn. com. chmn. 1993—95, chmn. grand lodge programs com. 1996—), Royal Rosarian. Baptist. Avocations: gardening, stamp collecting/philately, coin collecting/numismatics, fishing, sports. Home: 5460 SW Palatine St Portland OR 97219-7259

**SCHMIDT, STEFAN,** mechanical engineer, economist; b. Darmstadt, Hessen, Germany, 1950; s. Josef and Elisabeth (Urnauer) S.; m. Elizabeth Anne Godwin-Schmidt, 1983; children: Rebecca Elizabeth, Benjamin Stefan Godwin. Diploma mech. engring., Fachhochschule Frankfurt, Germany, 1972; diploma indsl. engring. and mgmt., Technische U. Berlin, Germany, 1980. Profl. mech. engr. Engr. Mech. Engring. Lab., Tokyo, 1973, C & P Telephone Co. of Md., Balt., 1978-79; planning engr. Systemtechnik, Darmstadt, Germany, 1980; rsch. assoc. Univ. Dortmund, Germany, 1981-84; logistics, strategy, maintenance, quality assurance, and internat. mfg. engr. BMW AG, Munich, 1984—. Lectr. in field; mgmt. trainer Centre of Technol. Cooperation, Berlin, 1985—; seminar presenter C. of C., Passau and Munich, Germany, 1986—, Sabel Bus. Sch., 2000—, REFA/VDI, 2001, others. Contbr. articles to profl. jours.; pub. bus. books, 1994—. Econ. commentator

Internat. Newspapers and Jours., Frankfurt, Munich, Berlin, 1990—. Recipient 1st prize Precision Instrument Maker, 1969. Fellow Verein Deutscher Wirt. ing. Home: Fritzstrasse 41 D-82140 Olching Bayern Germany Office: BMW AG D-80788 Munich Germany E-mail: stefan.sb.schmidt@bmw.de.

**SCHMIDT, STEPHEN CHRISTOPHER,** agricultural economist, educator; b. Isztimer, Hungary, Dec. 20, 1920; came to U.S., 1949, naturalized, 1965; s. Francis Michael and Anne Marie (Angeli) S.; m. Susan M. Varszegi, Dec. 20, 1945; children— Stephen Peter, David William. Dr.Sc., U. Budapest, Hungary, 1945; PhD, McGill U., Montreal, Que., Can., 1958. Asst. head dept. Hungary Ministry Commerce, Budapest, 1947-48; asst. prof. U. Ky., Lexington, 1955-57, Mont. State U., Bozeman, 1957-59, U. Ill., Urbana-Champaign, 1959-63, assoc. prof., 1963-70, prof. agrl. mktg. and policy, 1970-91, prof. emeritus, 1991—. Fulbright grantee Bulgaria, 1992-93; Ford Found. fellow, 1959; Agrl. Devel. Coun. grantee, 1966, U. Man. Rsch. fellow, 1968-69, Ford Found. rsch. grantee, 1973, 74, Whitehall found. grantee, 1979, Internat. Inst. Applied Systems Analyses (Laxenburg, Austria) rsch. scholar, 1976-77, USDA Intergovtl. Personnel Act grantee, 1983-84. Mem. Am. Agrl. Econs. Assn. (award 1979), Internat. Assn. Agrl. Economists, Am. Assn. Advancement Slavic Studies, Ea. Econ. Assn., Sigma Xi, Gamma Sigma Delta. Office: 1301 W Gregory Dr Urbana IL 61801-9015

**SCHMIDT, STEPHEN R.,** psychology professor; s. Richard and Elizabeth S. Schmidt; m. Constance R. Rojko; children: Theresa L., Kathleen E. BEd, U. Va., Charlottesville, 1975; MS, Purdue U., West Lafayette, Ind., 1977, PhD, 1980. With Dept. Psychology Mid. Tenn. State U., Murfreesboro, Tenn. Contbr. chapters to books, articles to profl. jours. Recipient Outstanding Rschr. award, Mid. Tenn. State U. 2002; grantee, 1989, 1990, 1993, 1994, 2001. Mem.: Midwestern Psychol. Assn., Psychonomic Soc. Office: Psychology Dept Middle Tenn State Univ Murfreesboro TN 37132 Office Phone: 615-898-2556. Personal E-mail: s.r.schmidt@comcast.net. Business E-Mail: sschmidt@mtsu.edu.

**SCHMIDT, SUSAN,** journalist; m. Glen Nishimura; 2 children. BA, Mary Baldwin Coll., 1975. News asst. Washington Star; reporter Herald Examiner, L.A., Patriot Ledger, Quincy, Mass.; metro desk editor to bus. news reporter Washington Post, 1983—92, nat. news desk reporter, 1992—. Co-author: Truth at Any Cost, 2000. Recipient Pulitzer Prize for investigative reporting, 2006, Seldon Ring award, 2006, Worth Bingham prize, 2006. Office: Washington Post Nat News Desk 1150 15th St NW Washington DC 20071-0070 Office Phone: 202-334-6157. Office Fax: 202-496-3883. E-mail: schmidts@washpost.com.

**SCHMIDT, TERRY L.,** healthcare executive; b. Chgo., Nov. 28, 1943; s. LeRoy C. and Eunice L.P. Schmidt; children: Christie Anne, Terry L. II. BS, Bowling Green State U., 1965; MBA in Health Care Adminstrn, George Washington U., 1971; Dr Health Adminstrn., Med. U. S.C., 2001. Resident in hosp. adminstrn. U. Pitts. Med. Center, VA Hosp., Pitts., 1968-69; adminstrv. asst. Mt. Sinai Med. Center, N.Y.C., 1969-70; asst. dir. Health Facilities Planning Council of Met. Washington, 1970-71; asst. dir. dept. govtl. relations A.M.A., Washington, 1971-74; contract lobbyist and govtl. rels. Wash. Reps. in health, Washington, 1974-87; pres. Terry L. Schmidt Inc. Physician Svcs. Group, San Diego, 1987-99, Washington Actions on Health, 1975-79; partner Washington Coun. Medicine and Health, 1979-81; pres. Recreational Enterprises, Inc., Washington, 1977-78; v.p. Crisis Communications Corp. Ltd., 1982-90; pres. Med. Cons. Inc., 1983-84, Ambulance Corp. Am., La Jolla, Calif., 1984-87; exec. dir., chief operating officer Emergency Health Assocs. P.C., Phoenix, 1989-91, Charleston Emergency Physicians, Inc., S.C., 1990-94, Joplin Emergency Physican Assocs., 1991-92, Big Valley Med. Group, 1991-92, Blue Ridge Emergency Physicians, P.C., 1992-94, Berkeley Emergency Physicians, P.C., 1992-94; chmn., pres. Univ. Inst., Inc., 1992—; asst. dir. dept. emergency medicine Med. U.S.C., 1999—2001. Bd. dirs., Univ. Inst., 1997—, lectr., instr. dept. health svcs. adminstrn. George Washington U., 1969-83, preceptor, 1975-84; adj. prof. grad. sch. Pub. Health San Diego State U., 1996—, preceptor, 1989—, guest lectr. health care adminstrn. Nat. U. San Diego, 1992-93; guest lectr. Bus. Adminstrn. U.S. Internat. U., San Diego, 1994—; instr. Naval Sch. Health Care Adminstrn., 1971-73; faculty Civil Svc. Commn. Legis. Insts., 1972-76; fac. Am. Assn. State Colls. and U. Health Tng. Insts., 1975-78; mem. adv. com. ambulatory care standards Joint Commn. Accreditation of Hosps., 1971-72, pres., Recreational Enterprises, Inc., Wash., 1977-78, guest lectr. Med. U.S.C., 1998-99, preceptor, 1999—, assoc. prof. Coll. of Health, Med. U.S.C., 1999—. Author: Congress and Health: An Introduction to the Legislative Process and the Key Participants, 1976, A Directory of Federal Health Resources and Services for the Disadvantaged, 1976, Health Care Reimbursement: A Glossary, 1983; mem. editl. adv. bd. Nation's Health, 1971-73; contbr. articles to profl. jours. Bd. dirs. Nat. Eye Found., 1976-78. Mem. Med. Group Mgmt. Assn., Health Care Fin. Mgmt. Assn., Assn. Venture Capital Groups (bd. dirs. 1984-89), Amer. Coll. of Health Execs., Amer. Coll. of Med. Prac. Exec., Assn. of Univ. Progs. in Health Admin., San Diego Venture Group (chair 1984-87), Univ. Club (life), Natl. Rep. Club (life), Nat. Dem. Club (life), Capitol Hill Club (life), Alpha Phi Omega (pres. Bowling Green alumni chpt. 1967-70, sec.-treas. alumni assn. 1968-71). Office: University Inst Inc Ste 113 611 7770 Regents Rd San Diego CA 92122-1967

**SCHMIDT, THOMAS CHARLES,** biomedical engineer, researcher; b. Jersey City, Feb. 21, 1947; s. Ernest J. and Shirley J. Schmidt; m. Marilyn I. Karcheski, Aug. 3, 1968; 1 child, Thomas M. B in Engring., Stevens Inst. Tech., 1968, M in Engring., 1973. Registered profl. engr., Fla., Calif. Vis. lectr. physiol. psychology Stevens Inst. of Tech., Hoboken, NJ, 1974—76; engr. Perry Techs., Riviera Beach, Fla., 1976—80; sr. rsch. engr., rsch. specialist, staff engr., sr. staff engr. Lockheed-Martin, San Diego, 1980—. Participant NASA Med-Ops. Task Group (Clin. Care Capability Project), Houston, 2000; chair ASME PVHO design sub-com., 2003—. Contbr. The Underwater Handbook: A Guide to Physiology and Performance for the Engineer, 1976, articles to profl. jours.; patentee in field. Dir., pub. safety chair Clairemont Town Coun., San Diego, 1997—; chair Balboa Ave. Citizens Adv. Com., San Diego, 1999—2003; mem. Cmty. Engagement Action Forum County Health and Human Svcs., San Diego, 1999—, participant strategic planning process, 1999—2003; mem. Clairemont-Mesa Planning Com., San Diego, 2000—. Recipient cert. of appreciation, State of Calif. (78th Assembly Dist.), 1999, cert. of recognition, 2000, 2001, State of Calif. (76th Assembly Dist.), 2003, 2004, spl. commendation, City of San Diego (6th Dist. Councilmember), 1998, 1999, cert. of appreciation, County of San Diego (3rd Dist. Supr.), 1999, County of San Diego (Asst Dir. Health and Human Svcs.), 2000, spl. commendation, City of San Diego (6th Dist. Councilmember), 2000, 2001, 2002, 2004, Cmty. Svc. award, City of San Diego (Dir. of Planning), 2001, 2002, commendation, Gov. of Calif., 2003, spl. commendation, City of San Diego (6th Dist. Councilmember), 2004, cert. of recognition, U. S. Congress (Calif. 50th Dist.), 2004, cert. of appreciation, ASME (Codes and Standards), 2004. Mem.: ASME (ANSI/ASME safety code sub-com.—pressure vessels for human occupancy 1987—, chair PVHO design sub-com. 2003—), Calif. Environ. Health Assn. (exec. bd. S.W. chpt. 2000—), Undersea and Hyperbaric Med. Soc. (safety com. 1981—, submarine medicine com. 1984—). Home: 5953 Castleton Dr San Diego CA 92117 Office: Lockheed Martin Services 3853 Calle Fortunada San Diego CA 92123-1824 E-mail: thomas.c.schmidt@lmco.com.

**SCHMIDT, WALDEMAR ADRIAN,** pathologist, educator; b. L.A., Aug. 22, 1941; s. Waldemar Adrian and Mary Charlotte (Parker) S.; m. Karmen LaVer Bingham, Feb. 1, 1963; children: Rebecca, Sarah, Waldemar, Diedrich. BS, Oreg. State U., 1965; PhD, MD, U. Oreg., 1969. Intern U Oreg. Hosps. and Clinics, Portland, 1969-70, resident, 1970-73; pathologist LDS Hosp., Salt Lake City, 1973-77; prof. pathology U. Tex. Med. Sch., Houston, 1977-91, Oreg. Health and Scis. U., Portland, 1991—2003, prof. emeritus, 2003—; chief pathology and lab. medicine svc Oreg. Health and Scis. U. and VA Med. Ctr., Portland, 1991—2001, vice chair pathology, 1997—2001; CEO Cascadia Placenta Registry, 1996—2002, dir., 2002—03; pres. Cascadia Med. Consultants, PC, 2004—. Author: Principles and Techniques of Surgical Pathology, 1982; editor Cytopathology Annual, 1991-94, Revs. in Pathology-

Cytopathology, 1994-99. Asst. scoutmaster Boy Scouts Am., Houston, 1982-91. Maj. U.S. Army, 1970-76. Fellow Am. Soc. Clin. Pathologists, Coll. Am. Pathologists; mem. Internat. Acad. Cytology, Sigma Xi, Alpha Omega Alpha. Avocation: photography. Office: U Oreg Health and Scis U Sch Medicine Dept Pathology 3181 SW Sam Jackson Park Rd Portland OR 97201-3098 E-mail: cme@ccwebster.net.

**SCHMIDT, WILLIAM ARTHUR, JR.,** lawyer; b. Cleve., Oct. 2, 1939; s. William Arthur and Caroline (Jäger) S.; m. Gerilyn Pearl Smith, Sept. 30, 1967; children: Deborah, Dawn, Jennifer. BSBA, Kent State U., 1962; JD, Cleve. State U., 1968. Bar: Ohio 1968, Ill. 1990. Contract specialist NASA-Lewis, Cleve., 1962-66, procurement analyst, 1967-68; atty. Def. Logistics Agy., Alexandria, Va., 1968-73; assoc. counsel Naval Sea Sys. Command, Arlington, Va., 1973-75; procurement policy analyst Energy R & D Adminstrn., Germantown, Md., 1975-76; sr. atty. U.S. Dept. Energy, Germantown, 1976-78, counsel spl. projects Oak Ridge, Tenn., 1978-83; judge Agr. Bd. Contract Appeals, Washington, 1983-87; judge Bd. Contract Appeals HUD, Washington, 1987; chief legal counsel Fermilab, Batavia, Ill., 1987-92; gen. counsel Univ. Rsch. Assn., Inc., Washington, 1992—. Co-author: (NASA handbook) R & D Business Practices, 1968. Founder/dir. DOE Contractor Attys. Assn.; dir. Spotsylvania Crime Solvers. Mem. ABA, Fed. Bar Assn. (past pres. East Tenn. 1978-83, 25 Yr. Svc. award 1994), Ill. Bar Assn., Bd. Contract Appeals Judges Assn. (dir.-sec. 1986-88), Sr. Execs. Assn., Delta Theta Phi (dist. chancellor 1978-83), Sigma Chi. Republican. Lutheran. Avocations: classic cars, m-1 carbines. Home: 10611 King Elder Ct Spotsylvania VA 22553-3666 Office: Univ Rsch Assn Inc 1111 19th St NW Ste 400 Washington DC 20036-3627 Business E-Mail: wschmidt@ura.nw.dc.us.

**SCHMIDT, WILLIAM C.,** retired chemicals executive; b. Niles, Mich., Sept. 27, 1938; s. Felix A. and Anna (Reifschneider) S.; m. Bethany Ann Boyd, Dec. 17, 1966; 1 child, Craig W. BBA, U. Mich., 1960, MBA, 1961. Cert. Mgmt. Acct. Various acctg. positions Dow Chem. Co., Midland, Mich., 1961-73; controller Dow Chem. Pacific Ltd., Hong Kong, 1973-78; area controller Dow Chem. Co., Midland, Mich., 1978-82, asst. corp. controller, 1982-98; v.p., chief fin. officer DowElanco, Indpls., 1989-98; chmn. bd. Wolverine Bank, F.S.B., 2004—. Bd. dirs. Midland Hosp., 1982-89, 98—, chmn. bd., 1986-88, 2004-06; bd. dirs. Mid-Mich. Health Corp., 1983-89, 2001—, chmn. bd., 1986-88; treas., bd. dirs. Indpls. Symphony Orch., 1992-98; dir. West Midland Family Ctr., 2000—06; mem., vice chmn. Midland County Bldg. Authority, 2003—. Cpl. U.S. Army, 1962-64. Mem. Inst. Mgmt. Accts., Inst. Cert. Mgmt. Accts. (regent 1985-89), Am. Indsl. Health Coun. (treas. 1986-87), Ind. C. of C. (bd. dirs. 1992-98). Presbyterian. Home: 5908 Londonberrie Ct Midland MI 48640-6965

**SCHMIDT, WILLIAM E.,** editor; b. Detroit, Mar. 15, 1947; s. E. F. and Irene E Schmidt; m. Margo Jean Doble, Nov. 4, 1972 (div. May 11, 2005); children: Jordan Alison, Lindsay Ella, Peter William. BA, U. Mich., Ann Arbor, 1967. Reporter Detroit Free Press, 1968—73; bur. chief Newsweek, Miami, Fla., 1975—76, Cairo, 1976—79, Moscow, 1979—81, corr. Chgo, 1973—75; bur. chief N.Y. Times, Denver, 1981—83, Atlanta, 1983—87, Chgo., 1987—91, corr. London, 1991—95, dep. nat. editor N.Y.C., 1995—97, assoc. mng. editor, 1997—2005, asst. mng. editor, 2005—. Bd. dirs. Maynard Inst. Journalism Edn., Oakland, Calif., 2005—. With USAR, 1968—74. Recipient George Polk award for Nat. Reporting, L.I. U., 1971, Mag. Reporting award, Overseas Press Club, 1976, Pulitzer Prize in Nat. Reporting, Columbia U., 1988. Mem.: Assn. Am. Correspondents in London (pres. 1993—94). Lutheran. Office: NY Times 229 W 43rd St New York NY 10036 Office Phone: 212-556-1211. Office Fax: 212-556-4401. Business E-Mail: schmidt@nytimes.com.

**SCHMIDT, WILLIAM MAX,** management consultant, marketing executive; b. Danville, Pa., Nov. 23, 1947; s. Frank Wilhelm and Doris Savilla (Maurer) S.; m. Marylea O'Reilly, Sept. 20, 1980. BS, U. Pa., 1969; MBA, Northwestern U., 1971. Mktg. specialist Moody's Investors Svc., Inc., N.Y.C., 1971-72; cons. William E. Hill & Co. Inc., N.Y.C., 1972-74; product supr. Internat. Paper Co., N.Y.C., 1974-79; dir. market analysis U.S. Industries, Inc., Stamford, Conn., 1979-82, mgr. corp. devel., 1982-84; dir. corp. mktg. Combustion Engring., Inc., Stamford, Conn., 1984-86, v.p. mktg., planning Union, NJ, 1986-91; pres. Pragmatics, Basking Ridge, NJ, 1991—2000; dir. global mktg. Gemplus Internat., Montgomeryville, Pa., 2000—. Author (newsletter): Think Again, 1995. Bd. dirs. Curbing Hunger, Inc., Basking Ridge, N.J., 1995—; adv. Jr. Achievement, N.Y.C., 1976-78. Mem. TAPPI, Exec. Forum, Strategic Leadership Forum, Univ. Club, Sons of the Revolution, Wharton Club (N.Y.C.), Sigma Chi. Republican. Mem. United Ch. of Christ. Avocations: tennis, astronomy, canoeing, community service, coin collecting/numismatics. Home: 46 Quincy Rd Basking Ridge NJ 07920-2245 Office: Gemplus Corp 101 Park Dr Montgomeryville PA 18936 Office Phone: 908-580-1259. E-mail: billprag@att.net.

**SCHMIDTBERGER, MICHAEL J.,** lawyer; b. 1959; BA, Columbia Coll., 1982; JD, Columbia Univ., 1985. Bar: NY 1986. Assoc. Sidley Austin Brown & Wood, NYC, 1990—93, ptnr. securities and futures-related funds and corp. transactions, 1993—, and mem. exec com. Editor-in-chief Columbia Human Rights Law Rev., 1985. Mem.: ABA, NYC Bar Assn. (com. on futures regulation 1997—2000), Phi Beta Kappa. Office: Sidley Austin Brown & Wood 787 Seventh Ave New York NY 10019 Office Phone: 212-839-5458. Office Fax: 212-839-5599. Business E-Mail: mschmidtberger@sidley.com.

**SCHMIDT-HOLTZ, ROLF,** music company executive; b. Martinsreuth, Germany, Aug. 31, 1948; 2 children. Degree in Law, Polit. Sci., Psychology, U. Erlangen, U. Kiel, 1973; JD, U. Kiel, 1976. Paralegal, 1973-76; asst. prof. law U. Kiel, 1976; svc. chief Federal Press Office, 1977-80; contbr. West Deutscher Rundfunk 1980-84, editor Tagesschau and Tagesthemen, 1980-84; TV corr. ARD Studio Bonn, WDR, 1981-84; dir. Federal Press Conf., Bonn, 1984-86; mgr. dirs. bur. info. and publicity Bertelsmann AG, Gütersloh, 1985-86; editor in chief TV program listings WDR, 1986-88; editor Der Stern Mag., Gruner & Jahr AG & Co., 1988—; Hamburger Morgenpost, Gruner & Jahr AG & Co., 1989-90; bus. dir. Gruner & Jahr Zeitschriften TV GmbH, 1990—; editor in chief Der Stern Mag., Gruner & Jahr AG & Co., 1990-94; head TV and Film Europe divsn. Bertelsmann AG, 1994—97; CEO, CLT-Ufa Luxemburg, 1997—2000; chief creative officer, mem. exec. bd. Bertelsmann AG, 2000—; chmn., pres., CEO BMG Entertainment, New York, 2001—04; chmn. Sony BMG Music Entertainment, 2004—06, CEO, 2006—; mem. supervisory bd. Gruner & Jahr AG & Co., 2000—, RTL Group, 2002—. Office: Sony BMG Music Entertainment 550 Madison Ave New York NY 10022*

**SCHMIDT-NIELSEN, BODIL MIMI (MRS. ROGER G. CHAGNON),** retired physiologist, retired educator; b. Copenhagen, Nov. 3, 1918; came to U.S., 1946, naturalized, 1952; d. August and Marie Jorgensen Krogh; m. Knut Schmidt-Nielsen, Sept. 20, 1939 (div. Feb. 1966); children: Astrid, Bent, Bodil; m. Roger G. Chagnon, Oct. 1968 (dec. 2003). DDS, U. Copenhagen, 1941, DOdont, 1946, DPhil, 1955; DS (hon.), Bates Coll., 1983; MD (hon.), U. Aarhus, Denmark, 1997. Mem. faculty Duke U., Durham, NC, 1952-64; prof. biology Case Western Res. U., Cleve., 1964-71, chmn. dept., 1970-71, adj. prof., 1971-84; trustee Mt. Desert Island Biol. Lab., Maine, rsch. scientist Maine, 1971-86, exec. com. Maine, 1978-85, v.p. Maine, 1979-81, pres. Maine, 1981-85; prof. dept. physiology U. Fla., Gainesville, 1985—. Adj. prof. Brown U., Providence, 1971-75, dept. physiol. U. Fla., Gainesville, 1986—; mem. tng. grant com. NIGMS, 1965-71. Author: August and Marie Krogh, Lives in Science, 1995, Danish edit., 1997; editor: Urea and the Kidney, 1970; assoc. editor Am. Jour. Physiology: Regulatory, Integrative and Comparative Physiology, 1978-81. Trustee Coll. of Atlantic, Bar Harbor, Maine, 1972-92. Recipient Career award NIH, 1964-69, John Simon Guggenheim Meml. fellow, 1952-53; Bowditch lectr., 1958, Jacobaeus lectr., 1974. Fellow AAAS (del. coun. 1977-79), NY Acad. Scis., Am. Acad. Arts and Scis.; mem. Am. Physiol. Soc. (coun. 1971-77, pres. 1975-76, Ray G. Daggs award 1989, Orr Reynolds award 1994, August Knogh lectr. 1994, Berliner award 1998), Soc. Exptl. Biology and Medicine (coun. 1967-71). Achieve-

ments include research, publications on biochemistry of saliva, water metabolism of desert animals, urea excretion, peristalsis of renal pelvis and concentrating mechanism, comparative kidney physiology, comparative physiology of excretory organs. Office: U Fla Dept Physiology 2015 SW 16th Ave Gainesville FL 32605 Business E-Mail: bodil@gator.net.

**SCHMIDT-NIELSEN, KNUT,** physiologist, educator; b. Norway, Sept. 24, 1915; came to U.S., 1946, naturalized, 1952; s. Sigval and Signe Torborg (Sturzen-Becker) Schmidt-N. Mag. Scient., U. Copenhagen, 1941, Dr. Phil., 1946; Dr. Med. (hon.), U. Lund, Sweden, 1985; D in Philosophy (hon.), U. Tondheim, Norway, 1993. Research fellow Carlsberg Labs., Copenhagen, 1941-44, Carlsberg Labs. (U. Copenhagen) 1944-46; research assoc. zoology Swarthmore (Pa.) Coll., 1946-48; docent U. Oslo, Norway, 1947-49; research assoc. physiology Stanford U., 1948-49; asst. prof. Coll. Medicine, U. Cin., 1949-52; prof. physiology Duke U., Durham, NC, 1952—, James B. Duke prof. physiology, 1963—; Harvey Soc. lectr., 1962; Regents' lectr. U. Calif. at Davis, 1963; Brody Meml. lectr. U. Mo., 1962; Hans Gadow lectr. Cambridge (Eng.) U., 1971; vis. Agassiz prof. Harvard, 1972. Wellcome vis. prof. U. S.D., 1988; mem. panel environmental biology NSF, 1957-61; mem. sci. adv. com. New Eng. Regional Primate Center, 1962-66; mem. nat. adv. bd. physiol. research lab. Scripps Instn. Oceanography, U. Calif. at San Diego, 1963-69, chmn., 1968-69; organizing com. 1st Internat. Conf. on Comparative Physiology, 1972-80; pres. Internat. Union Physiol. Scis., 1980-86, mem. U.S. nat. com. 1966-78, vice chmn. U.S. nat. com., 1969-78; mem. subcom. on environmental physiology U.S. nat. com. Internat. Biol. Programme, 1965-67; mem. com. on research utilization uncommon animals, div. biology and agr. Nat. Acad. Scis., 1966-68; mem. animal resources adv. com. NIH, 1968; mem. adv. bd. Bio-Med. Scis., Inc., 1973-74; chief scientist Scripps Instn. Amazon expdn., 1967. Author: Animal Physiology, 3d. edit., 1970, The Physiology of Desert Animals; Physiological Problems of Heat and Water, 1964, How Animals Work, 1972, Animal Physiology; Adaptation and Environment, 1975, 5th edit., 1997, Scaling: Why is Animal Size So Important?, 1984, The Camel's Nose: Memoirs of a Curious Scientist, 1998; sect. editor Am. Jour. Physiology, 1961-64, 70-76; editor Jour. Applied Physiology, 1961-64, 70-76; mem. editorial bd. Jour. Cellular and Comparative Physiology, 1961-66, Physiol. Zoology, 1959-70, Am. Jour. Physiology, 1971-76, Jour. Applied Physiology, 1971-76, Jour. Exptl. Biology, 1975-79, 83-86; cons. editor: Annals of Arid Zone, 1962—; hon. editorial adv. bd. Comparative Biochemistry and Physiology, 1962-63; chief editor News in Physiol. Scis., 1985-88, cons. editor, 1988—; contbr. articles to sci. publs. Guggenheim fellow, 1953-54; grantee Office Naval Rsch., 1952-54, 58-61, UNESCO, 1953-54, Office Q.M. Gen., 1953-54, Office Surgeon Gen., 1953-54, NIH, 1955-86, NSF, 1957-61, 59-60, 60-61, 61-63; recipient Rsch. Career award USPHS, 1964-85, Internat. prize for biology Japan Soc. for the Promotion of Sci., 1992, Disting. Svc. medal Smithsonian Instn., Nat. Zool. Park, 1998; recipient N.C. award in sci., 1999. Fellow AAAS, N.Y. Acad. Sci., Am. Acad. Arts and Scis.; mem. NAS, N.C. Acad. Sci. (Poteat award 1957), Am. Physiol. Soc., Am. Soc. Zoologists (chmn. div. comparative physiology 1964), Soc. Exptl. Biology, Royal Danish Acad., Acad. Scis. (France) (fgn. assoc.), Royal Norwegian Soc. Arts. and Sci., Norwegian Acad. Scis. and Letters, Physiol. Soc. London (assoc.), Royal Soc. London (fgn.); hon. mem. Soc. Integrative & Comparative Biology, Harvey Soc., Zool. Soc. London, Deutsche Ornitologengesellshaft. Office: Duke U Dept Biology PO Box 90338 Durham NC 27708-0338

**SCHMIT, LUCIEN ANDRÉ, JR.,** retired structural engineer; b. NYC, May 5, 1928; s. Lucien Alexander and Eleanor Jessie (Donley) S.; m. Eleanor Constance Trabish, June 24, 1951; 1 son, Lucien Alexander, III. BS, MIT, 1949, MS, 1950. Structures engr. Grumman Aircraft Co., Bethpage, NY, 1951-53; rsch. engr., aeroelastic and structures lab. MIT, 1954-58; asst. prof. engring. Case Inst. Tech., 1958-60, assoc. prof., 1961-63, prof., 1964-70; prof. engring. and applied sci. UCLA, 1970-91, Rockwell prof. aerospace engring. emeritus, 1991—; ret., 1991. Sci. adv. bd. USAF, 1977-84. Contbr. articles on analysis and synthesis of structural systems, finite elements methods, design of fiber composite components and multidisciplinary design optimization to profl. jours. Fellow AIAA (Design Lecture award 1977, Structures, Structural Dynamics and Materials award 1979, Multidisciplinary Design Optimization award 1994, Walter J. and Angeline H. Crichlow Trust prize 1999), ASCE, Am. Acad. Mechanics; mem. NAE. Home: 545 3rd Ave S Edmonds WA 98020-4103 Personal E-mail: schmit13@comcast.net.

**SCHMIT, TIMOTHY BRUCE,** musician; b. Oakland, Calif., Oct. 30, 1947. Band mem. Tim, Tom & Ron, the Contenders, New Breed, Glad, Poco, 1970—77, The Eagles, 1977—. Performed on albums with various artists including Warren Zevon, Robert Lamm, Dwight Yoakam, Ringo Starr, Tim McGraw, Jeff Larson, Dan Fogelberg, Elton John, The Wilsons, Don Henley, Beach Boys, Vince Gill, Eddie Money, Poison and many others. Musician: (albums) (solo) Playing it Cool, 1984, Timothy B., 1987, Tell Me the Truth, 1990, Feed the Fire, 2001, (with Poco) Poco, 1971, Deliverin', 1971, From the Inside, 1971, Good Feelin' to Know, 1972, Crazy Eyes, 1973, Cantamos, 1974, Seven, 1974, Head Over Heels, 1975, Very Best of Poco, 1975, Rose of Cimarron, 1976, Live, 1976, Indian Summer, 1977, Song of Richie Furay, 1979, Songs of Paul Cotton, 1979, Inamorato, 1984, Crazy Loving: The Best of Poco..., 1989, Forgotten Trail (1969-1974), 1990, (with The Eagles) Long Run, 1979, Eagles Live, 1980, Eagles Greatest Hits, Vol. 2, 1982, Hell Freezes Over, 1994, The Very Best of the Eagles, 1994, Selected Works: 1972-79, 2000, The Very Best of the Eagles, 2001, 2003. Named to with The Eagles, Rock and Roll Hall of Fame, 1998.

**SCHMITT, EDWARD A.,** manufacturing executive; b. July 25, 1946; BS, La. State Univ., 1969. Gen. mgr. ops. Ga. Gulf Corp., Atlanta, v.p. ops., 1993-97, exec. v.p., COO, 1997-98, chmn., CEO, pres., 1998—. Office: Georgia Gulf Corp Ste 460 115 Perimeter Pl Atlanta GA 30346 Mailing: Georgia Gulf Corp PO Box 105197 Atlanta GA 30348*

**SCHMITT, GEORGE FREDERICK, JR.,** materials engineer; b. Louisville, Nov. 3, 1939; s. George Frederick and Jane Limbird (Hurst) S.; m. Ann Cheatham, July 31, 1965; 2 children. BS, U. Louisville, 1962, MS, 1963; MBA, Ohio State U., 1966. Advanced engring devel. mgr. USAF Materials Lab., Wright Patterson AFB, Ohio, 1986-90, chief plans and programs br. Wright AFB, Ohio, 1989-90, asst. chief nonmetallic materials divsn., 1990-96, chief integration and ops. divsn., 1997—2005; dir. internat. programs Air Force Rsch. Lab. USAF Materials Directorate, Wright Patterson AFB, Ohio, 1966—. Guest lectr. U. Dayton, 1970, 95, Cath. U., 1973, U. Mich., 1975. Contbr. articles to profl. jours. Mem. Kettering (Ohio) Civic Band, 1965—, Affiliate Socs. Coun. Dayton, 1972-81; mem. Dayton Philharm Chorus, 1999—, Dayton Letter Carriers Band, 2000—, Windjammers Circus Music Preservation Soc., 2001—. 1st lt. USAF, 1963-66. Named Fed. Profl. Employee of Yr., Dayton, 1972, One of Ten Outstanding Engrs., Engrs. Week, 1975; recipient Air Force Meritorious Civilian Svc. award, 1994, Burton award for svc., Playhouse South Cmty. Theater, 1998, Tech. Transfer award, Fed. Lab. Consortium, 2001, Internat. Program Supr. award, 2002. Fellow Soc. for Advancement Materials and Process Engrs. (Best Paper award 1973, nat. sec. 1975-76, nat. membership chmn. 1977-79, nat. v.p. 1979-81, nat. pres. 1981-82, chmn. long-range planning com. 1983-87, trustee 1991—, chmn. Internat. SAMPE Symposium 1996, chmn. SAMPE Trophy com. 1998-2004, chmn. SAMPE Internat. conf., 2003, adminstr. SAMPE Fellows Program 1997—), AIAA (assoc., materials tech. com.); mem. ASTM (rec. sec. 72-75, chmn. com. on erosion and wear 1976-79, chmn. liaison subcom. 1979-83, award of merit 1981), Am. Chem. Soc., Affiliate Socs. Coun. Dayton (chmn. 1978-79). Republican. Lutheran. Home: 1500 Wardmier Dr Dayton OH 45459-3354 Office: AFRL Materials and Mfg Directorate MLO Wright-Patterson AFB 2977 Hobson Way Bldg 653 Dayton OH 45433-7733 Office Phone: 937-656-9209. Business E-Mail: george.schmitt@wpafb.af.mil.

**SCHMITT, JOHANNA MARIE,** plant population biologist, educator; b. Phila., Mar. 12, 1953; d. William Francis and Laura Belle (Wear) S.; m. Darrell Marion West, Aug. 6, 1983. BA, Swarthmore (Pa.) Coll., 1974; PhD, Stanford U., 1981. Postdoctoral rsch. assoc. Duke U., Durham, N.C., 1981-82; asst. prof. Brown U., Providence, 1982-87, assoc. prof. biology,

1987-94, prof., 1994—. Mem. R.I. Task Force, New Eng. Plant Conservation program, 1991—; mem. regional advisory com. New Eng. Plant Conservation program, 2000-. Assoc. editor Evolution, 1990-92, Am. Naturalist, 2000-2001; contbr. articles to profl. jours. including Evolution, Ecology, Am. Naturalist, Genetics, Nature. Bd. dirs Sojourner House, Providence, 1989-92. NSF grad. fellow, 1974, mid. career fellow, 1992-93; rsch. grantee, 1984—; recipient faculty award for women, 1991—. Mem. Soc. for Study of Evolution (coun. mem. 1990-92, exec. v.p. 1994-95, v.p. 1999), Bot. Soc. Am., Ecol. Soc. Am., Am. Soc. Naturalists (v.p. 1997, pres. 2002). Achievements include research on ecological genetics and genomics of natural plant populations: density-dependent phenomena, gene flow and population structure, inbreeding depression, the evolution of sex, maternal effects, seed ecology, natural selection, evolution of plasticity, adaptive significance of phytochrome, ecological risks of transgenic plants. Office: Brown Univ Dept Ecology & Evolution Providence RI 02912-0001

**SCHMITT, JOHN K.,** army officer; b. Buffalo, July 17, 1949; m. Mee Ja; children: Charlene, Jeffrey. BS in Chemistry, St. Bonaventure U., 1971; MS in Sys. Mgmt., U. So. Calif. Commd. 2d lt. U.S. Army, 1971, advanced through grades to brig. gen.; dep. comdg. gen. Ft. Carson, Colo., to 1998; dep. chief of staff for ops. and plans, dir. Army Digitization Office, Pentagon, Washington, 1998—. Decorated Legion of Merit, Meritorious Svc. medal with 3 oak leaf clusters, Order Nat. Security Merit Samil medal (Korea), Def. Superior Svc. medal, Republic of Korea Order Nat. Security Merit Semil medal, Army Commendation medal, Nat. Def. Svc. medal with Svc. star, Expert Infantryman badge, Master Army Aviator badge, Sr. Parachutist badge, Ranger Tab, Dept. Army Staff Identification badge, Republic of Korea Army Hon. Aviator Wings. Office: Dep Chief Staff Operations and Plans 3A522 400 Army Pentagon Washington DC 20310-0400

**SCHMITT, KARL MICHAEL,** retired political scientist; b. Louisville, Ky., July 22, 1922; s. Edward Peter and Mary Ann (Iula) S.; m. Grace Bernadette Leary, June 18, 1949; children: Karl, Edward, Barbara, William, Michael. BA, Cath. U. Am., 1947, MA, 1949; PhD, U. Pa., 1954. Teaching asst. U. Pa., 1948-50; instr. history Niagara U., 1950-54, asst. prof., 1954-55; research analyst U.S. Dept. State, 1955-58; asst. prof. dept. govt. U. Tex., 1958-63, assoc. prof., 1963-66, prof., 1966-91, prof. emeritus, 1991—, chmn., 1975-80. Vis. prof. U. Calif., LA, New Zealand, 1970-71; vis. sr. fellow U. Manchester, Eng., 1988-89; cons. Dept. of State, 1962-70 Author: Communism in Mexico; A Study in Political Frustration, 1965, Mexico and the United States, 1821-1973: Conflict and Coexistence, 1974, others. Contbr. articles to profl. jours. With U.S. Army, 1943—45. Decorated Purple Heart. Mem. Tex. Cath. Hist. Assn. (pres. 1976-77). Roman Catholic. Home: 2603 Pinewood Ter Austin TX 78757-2136

**SCHMITT, LEE AUBREY,** surgeon; b. Leeds, Ala., Sept. 11, 1964; s. Vernon Neil Schmitt and Jean Beverly Byers; 1 child, Payton. BA, U. Ala., Tuscaloosa, 1986; MD, U. Ala., Birmingham, 1990. Diplomate Am. Bd. Surgery. Pvt. practice, Birmingham, Ala., 1995—. Fellow: ACS; mem.: Sons Confederate Vets., Phi Beta Kappa. Baptist. Avocations: motorcycling, skydiving, drag racing. Office: 52 Medical Pk Dr E Ste 307 Birmingham AL 35235

**SCHMITT, NEAL,** psychology professor, department chairman; b. Decorah, Iowa, June 13, 1944; s. Leo A. and Beatrice M. Schmitt; m. Kara L. Knight, Aug. 24, 1968; 1 child, Krista Megan Loose. PhD, Purdue U., West Lafayette, Ind., 1972. Asst. prof. No. Ky. U., Highland Heights, 1972—74; from asst. prof. to full prof. Mich. State U., East Lansing, 1974—, chair of psychology. Cons. in field, 1975—. Author books in field; contbr. scientific papers to profl. jours. With U.S. Army, 1969—71. Named Univ. Disting. Prof., Mich. State U., 1992; recipient Disting. Faculty award, 1987. Fellow: APA (pres.-elect divsn. 5), Soc. for Indsl. and Orgnl. Psychology (pres. 1987—88, Disting. Sci. Contbn. award 1999), Am. Psychol. Soc.; mem.: Acad. of Mgmt. (Heneman Career Achievement award Human Resources Divsn. 2000). Home: 2956 Dobie Rd Mason MI 48854 Office: Mich State U Dept Psychology East Lansing MI 48824-1116 Office Phone: 517-355-9563. Business E-Mail: schmitt@msu.edu.

**SCHMITT, ROBERT LEE,** computer scientist; b. Astoria, NY, Oct. 1, 1948; s. Edward and Margaret Louise (Gleason) S.; m. Elsy Evagelene Burnett, June 1999; stepchildren: Eric Jason Marin, Alexis Michelle Marin. AAS in Data Processing, SUNY, Farmingdale, 1972; student, Hofstra U., 1972-73; BS in Computer Sci., SUNY, Stony Brook, 1974, MS in Computer Sci., 1975; postgrad., U. Md., 1979-80, 94-96; grad. diploma in strategic sci., U.S. Naval War Coll., 1991. Cert. computer programmer, data processor. Computer programmer U.S. Army Environ. Hygiene Agy., Aberdeen Proving Ground, Md., 1976; data sys. programmer Dept. Def., Ft. George G. Meade, Md., 1976—78, data sys. analyst, 1978—83, computer sys. analyst, 1983—85, sr. computer sys. analyst, 1985—86, computer scientist, 1986—89, mgr. sys. acquisition, 1989—94, dep. dir. for tech. fellow, 1994—95, sr. computer scientist, 1995—96, stds., tng. and verification engr., 1996—97, sys. engr., 1997—99, mgr. sys. 2000 compliance, 1999, sys. arch. implementation engr., 2000—01, sys. engr., 2001—02, dep. chief engring. divsn., 2002—03, acting dep. chief Sys. Engring Office, engr., 2003, lead sys. engr., 2003—. With Va. Summer Inst. for Math. Tchrs., 1995-96, dir. 1996-2000. With USNR, 1968-79. Home: 3002 Viburnum Pl Olney MD 20832-3073 Office: 9800 Savage Rd Fort George G Meade MD 20755-6000 Personal E-Mail: robertleeschmitt@comcast.net.

**SCHMITT, ROLAND WALTER,** retired academic administrator; b. Seguin, Tex., July 24, 1923; s. Walter L. and Myrtle F. (Caldwell) S.; m. Claire Freeman Kunz, Sept. 19, 1957; children: Lorenz Allen, Brian Walter, Alice Elizabeth, Henry Caldwell. BA in Math, U. Tex., 1947, BS in Physics, 1947, MA in Physics, 1948; PhD, Rice U., 1951; DSc (hon.), Worcester Poly. Inst., 1985, U. Pa., 1985; DCL (hon.), Union Coll., 1983; DL (hon.), Lehigh U., 1986; DSc (hon.), U. S.C., 1988, U. Tech. De Compeigne, 1991; DL (hon.), Coll. St. Rose, 1992, Russell Sage, 1993, Hartford Grad. Ctr., 1995, Ill. Inst. Tech., 1996, Rensselaer Polytechnic Inst., 1997. With GE, 1951-88, R & D mgr. phys. sci. and engring. Schenectady, 1967-74, mgr. energy sci. and engring. R & D, 1974-78, v.p. corp. R & D, 1978-82, sr. v.p. corp. R & D, 1982-86, sr. v.p. sci. and tech., 1986-88, ret., 1988; pres. Rensselaer Poly. Inst., Troy, NY, 1988-93; ret., 1993. Bd. dirs. Blasch Precision Ceramics, GlobalSpec, Logical Net, Value Innovations; chair adv. bd. NYSTAR; bd. advisors LearnLinc, 1996-2000; tech. adv. bd. Chrysler Corp., 1990-93; tech. adv. coun. Mobil Corp., 1997-99; mem., past pres. Indsl. Rsch. Inst., 1978-88; energy rsch. adv. bd. U.S. Dept. Energy, 1977-83; mem. Nat. Sci. Bd., 1982-94, chmn., 1984-88; chmn. CORETECH, 1988-93; mem. Comm. on Japan, NRC, 1988-90, Comml. Devel. Ind. Adv. Group, NASA, 1988-90; exec. com. Coun. on Competitiveness, 1988-93; chmn. NRC Panel on Export Controls, 1989-91; mem. Dept. Commerce Adv. Commn. on Patent Law Reform, 1990-92; adv. bd. Oak Ridge Nat. Lab., 1993-98; chair Rev. NATO Sci. program, 1998; mem. NRC panel rev. state dept. use sci. tech. and health, 1999; chmn. rsch. priority panel for NRC Future of Space Sci., 1994-99. chmn. Motorola's Sci. Adv. Bd., 1995-99, ICSU, 1997. Trustee N.E. Savs. Bank, 1978-84; bd. advisors Union Coll., Schenectady, 1981-84, Argonne Univs. Assn., 1979-82, RPI, 1982-88; bd. govs. Albany Med. Ctr. Hosp., 1979-82, 88-90; sec. Sunnyview Hosp. and Rehab. Ctr., 1978-86. Coun. on Superconductivity for Am. Competitiveness, 1987-89; mem. exec. com. N.Y. State Ctr. for Hazardous Waste Mgmt., 1988-89; chmn. Office of Tech. Assessment adv. panel on industry and environment; mem. Nat. Commn. Ill. Inst. Tech., 1993-94; chair NSF Acad. Rsch. Fleet Rev., 1998-99. With USAAF, 1943-46. Recipient RPI Cmty. Svc. award, 1982, award for disting. contbns. Stony Brook Found., 1985, Disting. Alumni award Rice U., 1985, IRI Medalist award, 1989, Royal Swedish Acad. Engring. Sci., 1990, Arthur M. Bueche award Nat. Acad. Engring., 1995, NY State Bus. Coun.'s Corning award, 2001, Tech Mentor award CEG, 2006; named Fgn. Assn. of Engring. Acad. Japan, U. Albany Found. Acad. Laureate, 1997; named to Jr. Achievement Capital Region Bus. Hall of Fame, 1996, RPI Hall of Fame, 1999. Fellow AAAS, IEEE (Centennial medal 1984, Engring. Leadership award 1989, Founders medal 1992, Hoover medal 1993), Am. Phys. Soc. (Pake

award 1993), Am. Acad. Arts and Scis.; mem. NAE (coun. 1983-89), Am. Inst. Physics (chmn. 1993-98), Coun. Sci. Soc. Pres. (chair 1993-97), N.Y. Acad. Scis. (pres. coun. 1993—2001), Dirs. Indsl. Rsch., Rensselaer Alumni Assn. (Disting. alumni award 1993), Eta Kappa Nu (eminent mem.) Office: PO Box 240 Rexford NY 12148-0240 Office Phone: 518-384-0965. E-mail: roland@schmitt.org.

**SCHMITT, WILLIAM ALLEN,** lawyer; b. Louisville, Aug. 29, 1909; s. Michael Joseph and Naoma Katherine Schmitt; m. Dorothy S. Turner, June 12, 1936 (dec. Feb. 1998); 1 child, Selene S. Kaelin. Student, U. Louisville, 1933. Bar: Ky. 1936, U.S. Dist. Ct. (we. dist.) Ky. 1936, NC 1997. Pvt. practice law, Louisville, 1936—; assoc. atty. Schmitt & Schmitt, Louisville, 1936-60; judge Jefferson County Probate Ct., Louisville, 1962-70; alcohol beverage control adminstr. Jefferson County Govt., Louisville, 1962-70; law ptnr. Schmitt & Sandmann, Louisville, 1968-74; pvt. practice law Louisville, 1974—, Jamestown, NC, 1997—. Author: Kentucky Probate, 1980, 2nd edit., 1997; contbr. articles to profl. jours. Election poll judge various gen. elections, Louisville; active Muir Chapel United Meth. Ch.; pres. Wildwood Country Club, 1964, Legal Aid Soc., Louisville, 1968. Lt. USN, 1944-46. Named to, Ky. Tennis Hall of Fame, 1993. Mem. ABA, ATLA, Am. Arbitration Assn. (arbitration panelist 1983-2003, cert. mediator 1985-99), Nat. Assn. Securities Dealers (arbitration panelist 1990-2004, cert. mediator 1994-2004), Am. Coll. Trust and Estate Counsel (state chmn. 1978-83), Ky. Bar Assn. (life, spkr. at seminars and convs. 1960-80, pres. 1970-71, probate com. 1970-86, chmn. 1977-81, trustee 1971-86, chmn. 1978-86, clients indemnity fund), N.C. State Bar Assn., N.C. State Bar, Louisville Bar Assn. (spkr. at seminars 1960-80, pres. 1966, chmn. probate com. 1974-79, various meritorious svc. awards 1966-75). Avocation: tennis. Home: 109 Sagewood Rd Jamestown NC 27282-9489 also: 500 Ky Home Life Bldg 239 S 5th St Louisville KY 40202-3213 Office Phone: 336-887-1135.

**SCHMITT, WOLF RUDOLF,** consumer products executive; b. Koblenz, Germany, Mar. 12, 1944; s. Josef H. and M.H. (Baldus) S.; m. Toni A. Yoder, June 30, 1974. BA, Otterbein Coll., 1966; AMP, Harvard U. Bus. Sch., 1986. With Rubbermaid Inc., Wooster, Ohio, 1966—, pres., gen. mgr. housewares products div., 1984-91, exec. v.p., bd. dirs., 1987-91, pres., chief operating officer, 1991-92; chmn., CEO, 1993-99; ret., 1999. Bd. dirs. Parker Hannifin Corp. Bd. dirs. Otterbein Coll., 1992—, Secrest Arboretum, 2002—. Avocations: horticulture, tennis, sailing. Office: Trends 2 Innovation 105 E Liberty St Wooster OH 44691-4345

**SCHMITZ, ANDREW,** agricultural studies educator; b. Central Butte, Saskatchewan, Canada, Oct. 5, 1940; s. Andreas and Katherine Schmitz; m. Helen Carole Anderson, July 16, 1966; children: Troy Gordon, Katrina Laur-Ayn Funk, Andre Lloyd, Evan Denis, Dean Michael. BSA, MSc, U. of Sask., 1963; PhD, U. Wis., 1968. D. of Letters-D.Lit. U. of Sask., 1999. Prof. U. of Calif. Dept. Agrl. and Resource Econs., Berkeley, Calif., 1968—94; rsch. prof. U. of Calif., 1986—; adj. prof. U. of Sask., Saskatoon, Canada 1986—; chair U. of Calif. Dept. Agrl., Resource Econs., Berkeley, Calif., 1989—93; eminent scholar-ben hill griffin jr. endowed chair U. of Fla. Food and Resource Economics, Gainesville, Fla., 1994—; hon. chair U. Sask. Ctr. Study of Agrl., Law, Environment, Saskatoon, Canada, 2001. Project dir. Econ. Coun. Can., Saskatoon, SK, Canada, 1986—89; fellow Am. Agrl. Economics Assn., 1985—; rsch. dir. Turkish Agrl. Econs. Rsch. Inst., Ankara, Turkey, 1998—98; cons. various govt. agencies, various legal firms. Contbr. articles to prof. jours. Recipient Best Pub. Rsch., Western Agrl. Econs. Assn. 1980, Am. Agrl. Econs. Assn., 1981, Rsch. of Enduring Quality, 1984, 1987, Best Pub. Rsch., 1970, 1978, Quality of Comm., 1979, Lifetime Achievement award, So. Agrl. Econs. Assn., 2003, Enduring Rsch. Quality award, Am. Agrl. Econs. Assn., 2003. Fellow: Am. Agrl. Econs. Assn. Office: U Fla 1130A McCarty Hall Gainesville FL 32611-0240 Office Phone: 352-392-1845. Business E-Mail: aschmitz@ifas.ufl.edu.

**SCHMITZ, BARBARA,** art preservationist; b. Cin., 1936; AM, U. Chgo., 1960; MA, PhD, NYU, 1981. Author: (illustrated catalogs of Islamic paintings) Islamic Manuscripts, N.Y. Pub. Libr., 1992, Islamic and Indian Manuscripts and Paintings, Pierpont Morgan Libr., 1996; co-author (with Z.A. Desai): Mughal and Persian Painting and Illustrated Manuscripts in the Raza Library, Rampur (U.P.), 2006; editor, contbr.: After the Great Mughals: Painting in Delhi and the Regional Courts in the 18th-19th Centuries, 2004. Fulbright grantee, 1992—93, 1997—98, Indira Gandhi Nat. Ctr. for the Arts grantee, New Delhi, 1995, Am. Inst. Indian Studies grantee, 1998—99, Brownlee Grant, Mo. Hist. Soc., 2002. E-mail: barbaraschmitz65016@yahoo.com.

**SCHMITZ, DENNIS MATHEW,** retired language educator; b. Dubuque, Iowa, Aug. 11, 1937; s. Anthony Peter and Roselyn S.; m. Loretta D'Agostino, Aug. 20, 1960; children— Anne, Sara, Martha, Paul, Matthew. BA, Loras Coll., 1959; MA, U. Chgo., 1961. Instr. English Ill. Inst. Tech., Chgo., 1961-62, U. Wis., Milw., 1962-66; asst. prof. Calif. State U., Sacramento, 1966-69, assoc. prof., 1969-74, prof., 1974-99; ret., 1999. Poet-in-residence, 1966-99. Author: We Weep for Our Strangeness, 1969, Double Exposures, 1971, Goodwill, Inc., 1976, String, 1980, Singing, 1985, Eden, 1989, About Night: Selected and New Poems, 1993, The Truth Squad, 2002. Recipient Discovery award Poetry Center, N.Y., 1968; winner First Book Competition Follett Pub. Co., 1969; di Castagnola award Poetry Soc. Am., 1986; Shelley Meml. award Poetry Soc. Am., 1987; NEA fellow, 1976-77, 85-86, 92-93, Guggenheim fellow, 1978-79. Mem. PEN, Assoc. Writing Programs. Roman Catholic.

**SCHMITZ, DOLORES JEAN,** primary school educator; b. River Falls, Wis., Dec. 27, 1931; d. Otto and Helen Olive (Webster) Kreuziger; m. Karl Matthias Schmitz Jr., Aug. 18, 1956; children: Victoria Jane, Karl III. BS, U. Wis., River Falls, 1953; MS, Nat. Coll. Edn., 1982; postgrad., U. Minn., Mankato, 1969, U. Melbourne, Australia, 1989, U. Wis., Milw., 1989, Carroll Coll., 1990, Cardinal Stritch Coll., 1990. Cert. tchr., Wis. Tchr. Manitowoc (Wis.) Pub. Schs., 1953-56, West Allis (Wis.) Pub. Schs., 1956-59, Lowell Sch., Milw., 1960-63, Victory Sch., Milw., 1964, Palmer Sch., Milw., 1966-84, 86-94, unit leader, 1984-86; ret., 1994. Co-organizer Headstart Tchg. Staff Assn., Milw., 1968; insvc. organizer Headstart and Early Childhood, Milw., 1969-92; pilot tchr. for Whole Lang., Hi-Scope and Math Their Way, 1988-93; bd. dirs. Curriculum Devel. Ctr. of Milw. Edn. Ctr., 1993-94. Author: (curriculum) Writing to Read, 1987, Cooperation and Young Children (ERIC award 1982), Kindergarten Curriculum, 1953. Former supporter Milw. Art Mus., Milw. Pub. Mus., Milw. County Zoo, Whitefish Bay Pub. Libr., Riveredge Nature Ctr.; vol. fgn. visitor program Milw. Internat. Inst., 1966-94, holiday folk fair, 1976-94, Earthwatch, 1989; lobbyist Milw. Pub. Sch. Bd. and State of Wis., 1986-93; coord. comty. vols., 1990-94. Grantee, Greater Milw. Ednl. Trust, 1989. Mem. NEA (life), ASCD, Milw. Kindergarten Assn. (rec. sec. 1986-93), Nat. Assn. for Edn. of Young Children, Tchrs. Applying Whole Lang., Wis. Early Childhood Assn., Milw. Tchrs. Ednl. Assn. (co-chmn. com. early childhood 1984-86), Assn. for Childhood Edn. Internat. (charter pres. Manitowoc chpt. 1955-56), Milw. Educating Computer Assn., Alpha Psi Omega. Roman Catholic. Avocations: bicycling, nature, world travel. Home: 9572 Commodore Dr Seminole FL 33776 Personal E-mail: dolintv@aol.com. *Like a very old song said-Accentuate the POSITIVE, eliminate the negative,and don't mess with Mr. In-Between. Life is better for you and everyone around you if these "rules" are followed. Success=If it is to be, it is up to me. I can.*

**SCHMITZ, JOHN,** grain company executive; BS in Acctg., St. Cloud State U. CPA, Minn. With Harvest States (merged with Cenex, now Cenex Harvest States), Inver Grove Heights, Minn., 1974—, v.p., contr., 1986, sr. v.p., CFO, 1999, exec. v.p., CFO. Mem. AICPA, Nat. Soc. Accts. for Transportation, Minn. Soc. CPAs. Office: Cenex Harvest States 5500 Cenex Dr Inver Grove Heights MN 55077*

**SCHMITZ, JOHN J.,** writer, educator; b. Fond du Lac, Wis., Mar. 9, 1937; s. John L. Schmitz and Josephine Knaus; children: David, Rebecca. BA, St. Francis Sem., 1963. CLU Am. Coll. Life Underwriters, 1975. Pres. John Schmitz Agy., Brookfield, Wis., 1992—; instr. Hondros Coll., Columbus, Ohio, 1994—. Cons. Bryant and Stratton Coll., Milw., 2003—04. Author: A Funny Thing Happened On My Way Out of Church, JoAnn: In Search of N.E.D. Bd. mem., officer Elmbrook Sch. Bd., Brookfield, Wis., 1988—92. Mem.: KC (assoc.; grand knight 1996—97). Achievements include development of Insurance Courses for Continuing Education. Avocations: writing, photography, travel. Home: 405 Lynnwood Lane Brookfield WI 53005-6134 Office: John Schmitz Agency 405 Lynnwood Lane Brookfield WI 53005-6134 Personal E-mail: jschmitz13@wi.rr.com.

**SCHMITZ, JOHN PHILLIP,** maxillofacial surgeon, researcher; b. Frankfurt, Germany, Germany, Jan. 3, 1953; s. Dorothy Budzein Schmitz; children: John Andrew, Anne Katherine, Kathleen Elizabeth. DDS, Marquette U., 1978; MS, U. Maryland, 1987; PhD in Biochem., Univ Tex. Health Sci. Ctr., 1996—96. Bd. cert. oral and maxillofacial surgery, diplomate Internat. Congress Oral Implantologists, 2005. Resident Univ. Hosp, San Antonio; prof. dept. orthopaedics UTHSCSA, San Antonio, 2003—. Assoc. prof. UTHSCSA, 1993—2000. Mem. Leadership San Antonio, Tex., 2002—03. Ltc U.S. Army, 1972—2000. Achievements include first to develop endoscopic Approaches For Mandibular Surgery In Children; developed and patented biodegradable bone repair substitutes. Office: San Pedro Facial Surgery 14500 San Pedro Ste 102 San Antonio TX Office Phone: 210-491-0015. Office Fax: 210-491-0352. Personal E-mail: schmitzjp@hotmail.com.

**SCHMITZ, MARIANINA ALICE,** literature and language educator; d. Dominick and Alice Marie Santi; m. Terrence Lee Schmitz, Jan. 20, 1973; children: Lisa, Lyle, Teresa. BA, U. No. Iowa, Cedar Falls, 1973. Tchr. English BGM H.S., Brooklyn, Iowa, 1974—79, Iowa Juvenile Home, Toledo, 1979—85; creative writer Telecross Comm., Waterloo, 1985—87; computer cons. pvt. practice, 1987—88; sch. sec. and vol. coord. Trinity Luth. Ch., 1988—93; tchr. English Aplington-Parkersburg Consol. Sch. Dist., 1993—. Head English dept. Aplington-Parkersburg Consol. Sch. Dist., 1996—, drama dir., 1993—, TAG coord., 1995—, advisor yearbook, 1996—, Nat. Honor Soc. advisor, 1997—. Mem. Am. Legion Women's Aux., Dumont, Iowa, 2001; lector St. Mary's Cath. Ch., Ackley, 2000. Mem.: Assn. Secondary Curriculum Devel., Nat. Coun. Tchrs. English, Profl. Educators Iowa, Parkersburg's Women's Club. Avocations: music, gardening, golf, reading. Home: 15908 Main St PO Box 6 Kesley IA 50649 Office: Aplington-Parkersburg CSD 610 N Johnson Rd Parkersburg IA 50665 Office Phone: 319-346-1571. Office Fax: 319-346-1012. Personal E-mail: nina1@iowatelecom.net. E-mail: nschmitz@apl-park.k12.ia.us.

**SCHMITZ, ROBERT ALLEN,** publishing executive, investor; b. Chgo., Ill., Jan. 19, 1941; s. John and Lee (Zeal) S.; m. Jenny Ann Quest, Aug. 23, 1969 (div.); m. Judith Mair Grey, Oct. 25, 1997; children: Alexander, Nicholas, Lara, Maximilian. BA with distinction, U. Mich., 1963; MBA, MIT, 1965. Asst. to pres. Lima (Peru) Light and Power Co., 1965-67; acquisition analyst W.R. Grace Co., N.Y.C., 1967-69; asst. to chmn. N.W. Industries, N.Y.C., 1969-70; prin. McKinsey & Co., Inc., N.Y.C., 1970-82; v.p. books Dow Jones & Co., N.Y.C., 1982-88; chmn., pres., chief exec. officer Richard D. Irwin, Inc., Homewood, Ill., 1983-89; pres., founder Quest Capital Ltd., 1989—; investment cons. Soros Fund Mgmt., 1990-92; mgn. dir., sr. ptnr. Trust Co. of the West, 1993-97; mng. dir., founder. Quest Turnaround Advisors, 1999—; chmn., founder Headline Media Group, 2001—; COO, PTV Inc., 2003—. Mem. adv. bd. Coll. Commerce De Paul U., Chgo., 1985—; bd. dirs. Two Way Media, London, Premium TV LLC, London, Cablecom GmBH, Zurich, Adams Rite Sabre, Inc., Glendale, Calif., Superior Fireplace Co., Fullerton, Calif., Houston Foods Co., Chgo., Archibald Candy Co., Chgo., US Media Group, Inc., Crystal City, Mo., Ctrl. Valley Publ., Merced, Hobby Products Co., Inc., Penrose, Colo., Automated Bar Controls, Vacaville, Calif., Spectran Techs., Inc., Sturbridge, Mass.; non-exec. chmn. PTV Ltd., London, 2 Way Media Ltd., London. Pres. Cultural Arts Ctr. Found., Homewood, Ill. Mem. Assn. Am. Pubs. (chmn. higher edn. divsn. 1989), Nature Conservancy (trustee N.Y. state chpt.). Office: Quest Turnaround Advisors Ltd 287 Bowman Ave Purchase NY 10577 Office Phone: +44-7968285821. E-mail: bob.schmitz@ptvinc.com.

**SCHMITZ, ROGER ANTHONY,** chemical engineer, educator, academic administrator; b. Carlyle, Ill., Oct. 22, 1934; s. Alfred Bernard and Wilma Afra (Aarns) Schmitz; m. Ruth Mary Kuhl, Aug. 31, 1957; children: Jan, Joy, Joni. BSChemE, U. Ill., 1958; PhD chem. Engring., U. Minn., 1962. Prof. chem. engring. U. Ill., Urbana, 1962-79; Keating-Crawford prof. chem. engring. U. Notre Dame, Ind., 1979—2005, prof. emeritus, 2005—, chmn. dept. chem. engring. Ind., 1979-81, dean engring. Ind., 1981-87, v.p., assoc. provost Ind., 1987-95. Cons. Amoco Chems., Naperville, Ill., 1966—77; vis. prof. Calif. Inst. Tech., L.A., 1968—69. Contbr. articles to profl. jours. With U.S. Army, 1953—55. Fellow, Guggenheim Found., 1968. Mem.: AIChE (A.P. Colburn award 1970, R.H. Wilhelm award 1981), Am. Soc. Engring. Edn. (George Westinghouse award 1977), Nat. Acad. Engring. Roman Catholic. Home: 16865 Londonberry Ln South Bend IN 46635-1444 Office: U Notre Dame 301 Cushing Hall Notre Dame IN 46556 Office Phone: 574-631-7798. Business E-Mail: schmitz.1@nd.edu.

**SCHMOKE, KURT L.,** dean, former mayor; b. Balt., Dec. 1, 1949; m. Patricia Schmoke; children: Katherine, Gregory. BA, Yale U., 1971; JD, Harvard U., 1976. Former assoc. Piper & Marbury; former pvt. practice; asst. U.S. atty Balt.; state's atty. Maryland, 1982-87; mayor City of Baltimore, 1987-99; ptnr. Wilmer Cutler Pickering LLP, Balt., 2000—03; dean Howard U. Sch. Law, Washington, 2003—. Apptd. mem. White House Domestic Policy Staff, 1977-78; former mem. Gov.'s Commn. on Prison Overcrowding; former mem. Md. Criminal justice Coord. Coun. & Task Force to Reform Insanity Def.; founder Balt. Community Devel. Financing Corp., 1988—. Office: Howard Univ Sch Law Office of the Dean 2900 Van Ness St NW Washington DC 20008

**SCHMOLKA, LEO LOUIS,** law educator; b. Paris, Apr. 25, 1939; came to U.S., 1944; s. Francis and Irene S.; m. Lucille J. Schoenbaum, July 29, 1965; children— Andrew, Gregory. AB, Dartmouth Coll., 1960; LL.B., Harvard U., 1963; LL.M., NYU, 1971. Bar: N.Y. 1964. Assoc. Weil, Gotshal and Manges, N.Y.C., 1964-71, ptnr., 1971-81, of counsel, 1981—; adj. asst. prof. law NYU Sch. of Law, 1971-75; adj. assoc. prof. law NYU Law Sch., 1975-76, adj. prof., 1977-80, assoc. prof., 1981-84, prof., 1985—, mem. faculty, dir. IRS/NYU continuing profl. edn. program, 1987—. Cons. U.S. Treasury Dept. Office Tax Policy, Washington, 1994-95, Am. Law Inst., 1979-86, U. Miami (Fla.) Estate Planning Inst., 1976-80; vis. adj. prof. law U. Miami Sch. Law, 1977, 80, U. San Diego Sch. Law, 1999; vis. lectr. continuing legal edn. various univs. and tax insts., 1973—. Contbr. articles to legal jours. Fellow Am. Coll. Trust and Estate Counsel; mem. ABA, N.Y. State Bar Assn. (chmn. com. on income taxation estates and trusts 1973-75, estate and gift tax 1976-77, mem. exec. com. tax sect. 1978), Internat. Acad. Estate and Trust Law (academician). Office: NYU Sch Law 40 Washington Sq S Rm 430 New York NY 10012-1099 Personal E-mail: schmolka@optonline.net.

**SCHMOLL, HANS JOACHIM,** hematology and oncology educator; b. Hannover, Germany, June 21, 1946; s. Johannes and Edeltraut (Schneider) S. MD, Med. U. Hannover, 1970, PhD, 1982. Rsch. assoc. Med. U., Hannover, 1971—84, prof. medicine and hematology-oncology, 1994—95; prof. medicine and hematology, chair hematology/oncology Martin Luther U., Halle-Wittenberg, Germany, 1996—. Author, editor: Kompendium Intern Onkologie, 1986, 4th edit., 2003; assoc. editor Cancer Rsch., 2002—; editor-in-chief Annals of Oncology, 2001—; mem. editl. bd. European Jour. Cancer Annals of Oncology. Recipient German Cancer award, 2001, Sci. award, German Assn. Med. Oncologists, 1998. Mem.: German Assn. Med. Oncology (pres., chmn. 2001—). Home: Ludwig Barnay Strasse 9 D-30175 Hanover Germany Office: Martin Luther Univ Dept Hematol/Oncol Int Med IV D-06120 Halle Germany Office Phone: 0049 345-55572924. Business E-Mail: haematologie@medizin.hin.halle.de. E-mail: hjschmoll@yahoo.de.

**SCHMULTS, EDWARD,** retail executive; BA, Yale U.; MBA, Harvard U. Vaious positions Goldman, Sachs & Co., NY and London; vaious sr. level positions including COO, CIO and mng. dir. Patagonia Japan, 1990—97; pres. Moonstone Mountain Equipment, 1997—2000; pres. global accounts Freeborders, 2000—03; sr. v.p. ops. RedEnvelope, Inc., 2004—05, COO, 2005; CEO FAO Schwarz, 2005—. Office: FAO Schwarz 767 5th Ave New York NY 10153*

**SCHMULTS, EDWARD CHARLES,** lawyer, think-tank executive; b. Paterson, N.J., Feb. 6, 1931; s. Edward M. and Mildred (Moore) S.; m. Diane E. Beers, Apr. 23, 1960; children: Alison C., Edward M., Robert C. BS, Yale U., 1953; JD, Harvard U., 1958. Bar: N.Y. 1959, D.C. 1974. Assoc. White & Case, N.Y.C., 1958-65, ptnr., 1965-73, 77-81; gen. counsel US Dept. Treasury, Washington, 1973-74, under sec., 1974-75; dep. counsel to Pres. The White House, Washington, 1975-76; dep. atty. gen. US Dept. Justice, Washington, 1981-84; sr. v.p. external rels., gen. counsel GTE Corp., Stamford, Conn., 1984-94; sr. advisor Iraqi Ministry of Justice - Coalition Provisional Authority, 2004. Lectr. securities laws. Served to 1st lt. USMC, 1953-55; capt. USMCR. Mem. Am. Bar Assn., Assn. Bar City N.Y., Adminstrv. Conf. U.S. (council 1977-84), Sakonnet Golf Club, Met. Club. Personal E-mail: eschmults@msn.com.

**SCHMUTZ, JOHN FRANCIS,** lawyer; b. Oneida, N.Y., July 24, 1947; s. William L. and Rosemary S. Schmutz; m. H. Marie Roney, June 7, 1969; children: Gretchen, Jonathan, Nathan. BA cum laude, Canisius Coll., 1969; JD cum laude, Notre Dame U., 1972; LLM, George Washington U., 1975. Bar: Ind. 1972, DC 1975, Tex. 1993, U.S. Ct. Mil. Appeals 1972, U.S. Tax Ct. 1973, U.S. Supreme Ct. 1975. Legislation and maj. projects officer Office Judge Adv. Gen., 1972—74; appellate atty. U.S. Army Legal Svcs. Agy., 1974—75; assoc. Ice, Miller, Donadio & Ryan, Indpls., 1976—77; staff atty. Burger Chef Sys., Inc., Indpls., 1977—78, sr. atty., 1979, asst. chief legal counsel, 1978—80, chief legal counsel, 1980, v.p., gen. counsel, sec., 1981—91; v.p.-legal Hardee's Food Sys., Inc., 1983—91; v.p., gen. counsel Sbarro, Inc., 1991—92; v.p., gen. counsel, sec. La Quinta Inns, Inc., 1992—98, gen. counsel, sec., 1998—99; sr. v.p., gen. counsel, sec. Meditrust Cos., Inc., 2000—01, La Quinta Cos., Inc., 2001—02; founding prin. Turtle Creek Group, LLC, 2002—. Dir., v.p. Bursan Credit Union; dir. Food Svc. and Lodging Inst., RIX Sys., Inc., Burger Chef Distributive Corp.; v.p. Hardee's Food Sys., Inc. Exec. editor: Notre Dame Law Rev., 1971—72. Exec. bd. Boy Scouts Am.; bd. dirs. Blessed Sacrament Acad. Found. Mem. ABA (dir. hospitality com., cmty. recreation and common interest devel. com.), Am. Corp. Counsel Assn. (bd. dirs.), Internat. Corp. Sec. Assn., Am. Hotel and Motel Assn. (gen. counsel com.), Nat. Restaurant Assn., Am. Assn. Corp. Counsel, San Antonio Bar Assn., Tex. Bar Assn., Indpls. Bar Assn., DC Bar Assn., Ind. Bar Assn., Fed. Bar Assn. Republican. Roman Catholic. Home: 17122 Eagle Star San Antonio TX 78248-1548 Personal E-mail: johnschmutz@sbcglobal.net.

**SCHMUTZHART, BERTHOLD JOSEF,** sculptor, educator; b. Salzburg, Austria, Aug. 17, 1928; came to U.S., 1958, naturalized, 1963; s. Berthold Josef and Anna (Valaschek) S. Student, Acad. for Applied Art, Vienna, Austria, 1956. Cert. fed. tchr., Austria. Prof. Werkschulheim Felbertal, Salzburg, 1951-58; sculptor Washington, 1959-60; tchr. Longfellow Sch., Bethesda, Md., 1960-63; prof., chmn. dept. sculpture Corcoran Sch. Art, Washington, 1963-94, prof. emeritus, 1994—; lectr. Smithsonian Instn. Washington, 1968-84. One-man shows include Fredericksburg Gallery Fine Art, Va., 1967-73, Franz Bader Gallery, Washington, 1978, 81, 83, 86, 88; group shows include Nat. Collection Fine Arts, Washington, 1961-70, High Mus. Art, Atlanta, 1965, Ark. Art Ctr., Little Rock, 1966, Birmingham Mus. Art, Ala., 1967, Hirschhorn Mus. and Sculpture Garden, Washington, 1981, Nat. Gallery Modern Art, New Delhi, 1990; represented in permanent collections Hirschhorn Collection; designer fountain, Gallery of Modern Art, Fredericksburg, 1967; author: The Handmade Furniture Book, 1981; contrb. articles to profl. jours. Fine arts panelist D.C. Commn. for Arts, 1973-79; chmn. bd. Mather Five Gallery, Washington, 1978-82; bd. dirs. Franz Bader Gallery, Washington, 1981-86; trustee Arts for the Aging Inc., Washington, 1990—98; chmn. Franz and Virginia Bader Fund, 2001-06, bd. dirs., 2006-. Recipient 1st prize Washington Religious Arts Council, 1960, for sculpture, Little Rock, 1966, Louisville, 1968, Silver medal Audubon Soc., Washington, 1971 Mem. Guild for Religious Architects, Artists Equity Assn. (pres. D.C. chpt. 1973-75), AAUP, Am. Austrian Soc. (pres. 1968-70, exec. com.), Soaring Soc. Am. Home: 32 Layline Ln Fredericksburg VA 22406-4061 E-mail: gn15bs@earthlink.net.

**SCHNABEL, JULIAN,** artist; b. 1951; B.F.A., U. Houston, 1972; postgrad., Whitney Mus. Ind. Study Program, N.Y.C., 1973-74. Exhibited one-man shows, Contemporary Art Mus., Houston, 1976, Galerie Dezember, Dusseldorf, West Germany, 1978, Mary Boone, N.Y.C., 1979, Daniel Weinberg Gallery, San Francisco 1979, Bruno Bischofberger, Zurich, Switzerland, Young-Hoffman Gallery, Chgo., 1980, Mary Boone-Leo Castelli, N.Y.C., 1981, Stedelijk Mus., Amsterdam, Holland, 1982, Bruno Bischofberger, Zurich, Switzerland, 1982, Los Angeles County Mus. Art, 1982, U. Art Mus., Berkeley, Calif., 1982, The Tate Gallery, London, 1982, Mary Boone, N.Y.C., 1982, Bruno Bischofberger, Zurich, Switzerland, 1983, Leo Castelli, N.Y.C., 1983, Akron Art Mus., 1983, Leslie Waddington Gallery, London, 1983, Daniel Templon Gallery, Paris, 1983, Galerie Mario Diacono, Rome, 1983, Akira Ikeda Gallery, Tokyo, 1983, Donald Young Gallery, Chgo., 1983, Martine Hamilton Gallery, N.Y.C., Pace Gallery N.Y., 1984, Whitney Mus., 1988, San Francisco Mus. Modern Art, 1988, Mus. Fine Arts, Houston, 1988, Mus. Contemporary Art, Chgo., 1990, numerous others; group shows, Hidden Houston, U. St. Thomas, 1971, La Gallery, Houston, 1972, W.I.S.P. Exhibition, Whitney Mus. Am. Art, N.Y.C., 1974, Holly Solomon Gallery, N.Y.C., 1977, Rennaissance Soc. U. Chgo., 1979, Daniel Templon, Paris, 1980, L'Amerique Aux Independants, Grand Palais, Paris, 1980, Mary Boone, N.Y.C., 1980, La Biennale di Venezia, Venice, Italy, 1980, Indpls. Mus. Art, 1980, The Royal Acad., London, 1981, Whitney Mus. Am. Art, N.Y.C., 1981, Addison Gallery, Andover, Mass., 1981, Basel Kunstmuseum, Switzerland, 1981, Gayden Gallery, MIT, Cambridge, 1981, Kinsthallen, Goteborg, Sweden, 1981, Frankfurter Kunstverein, Frankfurt, West Germany, 1982, Inst. Contemporary Art, Boston, 1982, Whitney Mus. Am. Art, N.Y.C., 1982, Mus. Contemporary Art, LaJolla, Calif, 1982, Stedelijk Mus., Amsterdam, 1982, Art Inst. Chgo., 1982, la Biennale di Venezia, Venice, Italy, 1982, Fort Worth Art Mus., 1982, Milw. Art Mus., 1982, Stifelsen Karlsvik 10, Stockholm, 1983, Whitney Mus. Am. Art, N.Y.C., 1983, The Hirshhorn Mus., Washington, 1983, Nat. Mus. Am. Art, 1983, Bklyn. Mus., 1983, Mary Boone Gallery, N.Y.C., 1983, 64th Whitney Biennial, 1987, Pace Gallery, N.Y.C., 1990, Poche Gallery, Paris, 1991, Gian Ferrari Arte Contemporanea, Milan, 1993-94, Ramis Barquet Gallery, Mexico, 1995, Modern Art Gallery, Bologna, 1996-97, Thaddaeus Ropac, Salzburg, 1998-99, Galerie Forsblom, Helsinki, 2000; author: Nicknames of Maitre D's and Other Excerpts From Life, 1988; dir., screenwriter (film) Basquiat, 1996; writer, prodr. dir. (film) Before Night Falls, 2000. Office: Pace Gallery NY 32 E 57th St Fl 4 New York NY 10022-2530

**SCHNABEL, ROBERT VICTOR,** retired academic administrator; b. Scarsdale, N.Y., Sept. 28, 1922; s. Frederick Victor and Louise Elizabeth (Frick) S.; m. Ellen Edyth Foelber, June 7, 1946; children: Mark F., Philip P. Student, Concordia Sem., St. Louis, 1943-45; AB, Bowdoin Coll., 1944; MS, Fordham U., 1951, PhD, 1955; LLD (hon.), Concordia Coll., 1988. Tchr. St. Paul's Sch., Ft. Wayne, Ind., 1945-49; prin. St. Matthew's Sch., N.Y.C., 1949-52; assoc. supt. edn. Central Dist., Luth. Ch.-Mo. Synod, 1952-56; asst. prof. philosophy Concordia Sr. Coll., Ft. Wayne, 1956-60, assoc. prof., 1960-65, prof., acad. dean, 1966-71; pres. Concordia Coll., Bronxville, NY, 1971-76; acad. v.p., dean Wartburg Coll., Waverly, Iowa, 1976-78; pres. Valparaiso (Ind.) U., 1978-88. Cons. Luth. Edn. Conf. N.Am., 1977-88. Contrb. articles to profl. jours. Mem. AAUP, Luth. Acad. Scholarship, Assoc. Colls. Ind., Nat. Assn. Ind. Colls. and Univs., Rotary, Phi Delta Kappa. Office: Valparaiso Univ 23 Huegli Hall Valparaiso IN 46383

**SCHNABEL, ROCKWELL ANTHONY,** former ambassador; b. Amsterdam, Holland, Dec. 30, 1936; s. Hans and Wilhelmina S.; m. Marna Belle Del Mar, 1964; children: Mary Darrin, Christy Ann, Everton Anthony. BS in Bus. Adminstrn., Trinity Coll., The Netherlands, 1951-56; LLD (hon.), Pepperdine U. Pres. Unilife Assurance Group S.H. Luxembourg, 1974-78, Bateman Eichler Hill Richard Group, Los Angeles, 1981-83; U.S. amb. to Finland U.S. Dept. State, Helsinki, 1986—89; under sec. for travel and tourism U.S. Dept. Commerce, Washington, 1989-91, dep. sec., 1991-92, acting sec., 1992-93; U.S. amb. to the European Union U.S. Dept. State, Brussels, 2001—06; sr. ptnr. Trident Capital LLP, Palo Alto, Calif., 1992—2001, advisory dir., 2006—; chmn. Sage Group LLC, 2006—. Bd. dirs. Internat. Game Tech., CSGystems Inc.; chmn. La.-Inc.; bd. trustees U. Calif. Bus. Sch. Co-author (with Francis X. Rocca): The Next Superpower? The Rise of Europe and its Challenge to the United States, 2005. Past pres. L.A. Pension Bd., Calif., 1982; mem. L.A. Olympic Organizing Com., 1983-84. With Air N.G., 1958-64. Decorated comdr. Order of Good Hope, South Africa, Grand Cross of Lion of Finland; recipient Gold medal Dutch Govt., U.S. Dept. Commerce, medal of honor the Netherlands Olympic Com. Mem. L.A. Beach Club, Calif. Club, L.A. Country Club. Office: Trident Capital Ste 200 505 Hamilton Ave Palo Alto CA 94301*

**SCHNACKENBERG, GJERTRUD CECELIA,** poet; b. Tacoma, Aug. 27, 1953; d. Walter Charles and Doris Ione Schnackenberg; m. Robert Nozick, Oct. 5, 1987. BA summa cum laude, Mount Holyoke Coll., 1975, LittD (hon.), 1985. Fellow The Bunting Inst., Radcliffe and Cambridge, Mass., 1979-80; lectr. in writing MIT, Cambridge, 1980-81; Hurst prof. poetry Washington U., St. Louis, 1987; Conkling writer in residence Smith Coll., Northampton, Mass., fall 1994. Vis. fellow St. Catherine's Coll., Oxford U., 1997, Getty Rsch. Inst. 2000 Author: numerous poems. Recipient Rome prize in lit. Am. Acad. Arts and Letters, 1983, Acad. award in lit. Am. Acad. Arts and Letters, 1998, Brandeis citation in poetry, 1989, Berlin prize, 2004; Nat. Endowment for the Arts fellow in poetry, 1986, Guggenheim fellow, 1987; Book Prize in Poetry, L.A. Times, 2000. Fellow: Am. Acad. Rome, Am. Acad. Arts and Scis., Am. Acad. in Berlin. Democrat.

**SCHNAITMAN, WILLIAM KENNETH,** retired finance company executive; b. Talbot County, Md., May 12, 1926; s. William and Catherine Almeda (Cheezum) S.; m. Beverly June Marshall, July 13, 1963. Student, Strayer Bus. Sch., Balt., 1943. Clk. Comml. Credit Co., Balt., 1946-70, asst. sec., 1970-72, treas., 1972-75, dir. cash mgmt., 1976-87, ret., 1987. With AUS, 1944-46, ETO. Home: 12520 Wye Landing Ln Wye Mills MD 21679-2050

**SCHNAKE, RICHARD LANE,** lawyer; b. Carthage, Mo., Aug. 3, 1957; s. Ivan Eugene and Phyllis Lea (Stewart) S.; m. Kelly Dawn Barfield, Oct. 9, 1999. BA in History, S.W. Mo. State U., 1979; JD, Washington U., St. Louis, 1982. Bar: Mo., 1982, U.S. Dist. Ct. (we. dist.) Mo. 1982, U.S. Ct. Appeals (8th cir.) 1984, U.S. Supreme Ct. 1986, U.S. Ct. Appeals (7th cir.) 1989. Law clk. to Hon. Warren D. Welliver Supreme Ct. of Mo., Jefferson City, 1982-83; assoc. Neale, Newman, Bradshaw & Freeman, Springfield, Mo., 1983-87; ptnr. Neale, Newman, Bradshaw & Freeman, Neale & Newman, L.L.P., Springfield, Mo., 1988—. Mem. Mo. Supreme Ct. Civil Rules Com., Jefferson City, 1994—2002, mem. Appellate Practice Com., 2002—; spl. asst. Atty. Gen. Mo., Jefferson City, 1990-93; chmn. Springfield Metro. Bar Assn. Law Day Com., 1989-91, 2003—, sec., bd. dirs., 1992-95. Author: Civil Rules Practice, Rules 85-88, 17A Missouri Practice, 1999; contbr. articles to profl. jours. Bd. dirs., pres., sec. Ozark Counseling Ctr., Springfield, Mo., 1987-88, 89-91, 92-94, 95—. Recipient Scribes award for legal writing, 1982, David J. Dixon Appellate Advocacy award Mo. Bar Found., Jefferson City, Mo., 1990; nominee for nonpartisan appt. to Mo. Ct. Appeals, 2003. Mem. ABA, Springfield Met. Bar Assn. (seminar lectr.), Mo. Bar Assn. (seminar lectr.), Order of Coif, Phi Kappa Phi. Mem. Ch. of Christ. Avocation: autograph collecting. Home: 1674 S Raford Dr Springfield MO 65809-2336 Office: Neale & Newman LLP 1949 E Sunshine St Ste 1-130 Springfield MO 65804-1682 Address: PO Box 10327 Springfield MO 65808-0327 Office Phone: 417-882-9090. E-mail: rschnake@nnlaw.com.

**SCHNAPP, ROGER HERBERT,** lawyer, consultant; b. NYC, Mar. 17, 1946; s. Michael Jay and Beatrice Joan (Becker) S.; m. Candice Jacqueline Larson, Sept. 15, 1979; 1 child, Monica Alexis. BS, Cornell U., 1966; JD, Harvard U., 1969; postgrad. Pub. Utility Mgmt. Program, U. Mich., 1978. Bar: NY 1970, US Ct. Appeals (2d cir.) 1970, US Supreme, 1974, US Dist. Ct. (so. dist.) NY 1975, US Ct. Appeals (4th and 6th cirs.) 1976, US Ct. Appeals (7th cir.) 1977, US Ct. Appeals (3d cir.) 1980; US Dist. Ct. (no. dist.) Calif. 1980, US Ct. Appeals (8th cir.) 1980, Calif., US Dist. Ct. (cen. dist.) Calif. 1982, US Dist. Ct. (ea. dist.) Calif., 1984. Atty. CAB, Washington, 1969-70; labor atty. Western Electric Co., NYC, 1970-71; mgr. employee rels. Am. Airlines, NYC, 1971-74; labor counsel Am. Electric Power Svc. Corp., NYC, 1974-78; sr. labor counsel, 1978-80; indsl. rels. counsel Trans World Airlines, NYC, 1980-81; sr. assoc. Parker, Milliken, Clark & O'Hara, LA, 1981-82; ptnr. Rutan & Tucker, Costa Mesa, Calif., 1983-84; Memel, Jacobs, Pierno, Gersh & Ellsworth, Newport Beach, Calif., 1985-86, Memel, Jacobs & Ellsworth, Newport Beach, 1986-87; prt. practice Newport Beach, 1987—. Bd. dirs. Dynamic Constrn., Inc., Laguna Hills, Calif., 1986—; commentator labor rels. Fin. News Network; commentator Sta. KOCN Radio, 1990-91; commentator employment law Orange County Register; lectr. Calif. Western Law Sch., Calif. State U.-Fullerton, Calif. State Conf. Small Bus.; lectr. collective bargaining Pace U., NYC; lectr. on labor law Coun. on Edn. in Mgmt.; NE regional coord. Pressler for Pres., 1979-80; adv. bd. manufacturingzone.com; dir. Orange County Bur. Jewish Edn.; Friends of Fertility Found. Author: Arbitration Issues for the 1980s, 1981, A Look at Three Companies, 1982; editor-in-chief Indsl. and Labor Rels. Forum, 1964-66; columnist Orange County Bus. Jour., 1989-91; contbr. articles to profl. publs. Mem. Fin. Rsch. Adv. Coun. US Dept. Labor; trustee Chapman U., 1991-95. Mem. Calif. Bar Assn. (chmn.), Labor Law Consulting Group, Calif. Bd. of Legal Specialization, Balboa Bay Club, The Ctr. Club (chmn. membership com.), Club 33, Jewish Cmty. Ctr. Orange County. Republican. Jewish. Office: PO Box 9049 Newport Beach CA 92658-1049 Office Phone: 949-752-0491. E-mail: rhs@schnapp.com.

**SCHNARRE, THOMAS DALE,** education educator; b. Taylorville, Ill., Dec. 19, 1957; s. Emil Frederick and Anna Eileen Schnarre. BS in Edn., Eastern Ill. U., 1980, MA in Edn., 1996. Spl. edn. tchr. Arcla Elem. Sch., Ill. 1980—82; develop. disabilities tchr. CCAR, Charleston, Fla., 1982—87; infant skill coord., 1987—94; english instr. Eastern Ill. U., 1995—2001; assoc. prof. Parkland Coll., Champaign, Ill., 2001—. Advisor Colours Group, Champaign, Ill., 2001—; dir. Parkland Theatre, Champaign, 2005—06. Actor: Parkland Theatre, 2003—05, CUTC, 2005, Charleston Alley Theatre, 1994—2000. Avocation: theater. Office: Parkland Coll 2400 W Bradley Ave Champaign IL 61821

**SCHNEBERGER, SCOTT L.,** information systems educator; b. Robert Montgomery Schneberger and Shirley Katherine Laurin; m. Cosanne E. Scholet, Aug. 31, 1980; 1 child, Sondra Kealoha. BA in Polit. Sci., Principia Coll., Elsah, Ill., 1970; MS in Info. Sys., Naval Postgraduate Sch., Monterey, Calif., 1981; PhD in Info. Sys., Ga. State U., Atlanta, 1995. Commd. ensign USN, 1970, advanced through grades to comdr., 1985, ret., 1990; assoc. prof. MBA program U. Western Ont., London, Ontario, Canada, 1997—2001; assoc. prof. info. sys. Appalachian State U., Boone, NC, 2005—; mng. dir. Ctr. Applied Rsch. Emerging Techs., 2006—. Author: (academic book) Cases in Electronic Commerce, 1997; mem.: Naval Intelligence Profls. (life). Avocations: flying, cribbage board collecting. Office: Appalachian State University CIS/College of Business Boone NC 28608 Office Phone: 828-262-2035. Business E-Mail: schnebergers@appstate.edu.

**SCHNECK, JEROME M.,** psychiatrist, historian, medical educator; b. NYC, Jan. 2, 1920; s. Maurice and Rose (Weiss) S.; m. Shirley R. Kaufman, July 24, 1943. AB, Cornell U., 1939; MD, SUNY, Bklyn., 1943. Diplomate Am. Bd. Psychiatry and Neurology, Am. Bd. Psychotherapy. Intern Interfaith Med. Ctr., 1943; psychiat. staff Menninger Clinic, Topeka, 1944-45; chief psychiatry and sociology dept. Fort Missoula, Mont., 1946, Camp Cooke,

Calif., 1947; mem. psychiat. staff L.I. Coll. Hosp. 1947-48, Kings County Hosp., 1948-70, SUNY Hosp., Bklyn., 1955-70; assoc. vis. psychiatrist Kings County Hosp., 1949-70; mem. psychiat. staff State U. Hosp., Bklyn., 1955-70; pvt. practice N.Y.C., N.Y.C. 1947—; attending psychiatrist St. Vincent's Hosp. and Med. Ctr. N.Y., 1970—, hon. sr. psychiatrist, 1990—. Psychiat. cons. VA Regional Office, 1947-48, NY State Dept. Social Svcs., 1977-83, NY State Dept. Civil Svc., 1978-84, NY State Office Cit. Adminstrn., 1978-85, NY State Dept. Edn., 1981-83; dir. Mt. Vernon Mental Hygiene Clinic, 1947-52; assoc. chief psychiatrist Westchester County Dept. Health, 1949-50, cons., 1951-52; clin. instr. L.I. Coll. Medicine, 1947-50; clin. assoc. SUNY Coll. Medicine, Bklyn., 1950-53, asst. prof., 1955-58, assoc. prof., 1958-70; supervising psychiatrist Cmty. Guidance Svcs., 1955-70; cons. coun. on mental health AMA, 1956-58; cons. NBC, 1962, Ctr. Rsch. in Hypnotherapy, 1964-70; vis. lectr. N.Y. Med. Coll.-Met. Hosp., 1965; faculty, fellow Am. Inst. Psychotherapy and Psychoanalysis, 1970-85. Author: Hypnosis in Modern Medicine, 1953, 2d edit., 1959, Spanish lang. edit., 1962, 3rd edit., 1963, Studies in Scientific Hypnosis, 1954, A History of Psychiatry, 1960, The Principles and Practice of Hypnoanalysis, 1965 (Best Book award Soc. for Clin. and Exptl. Hypnosis 1965); editor: Hypnotherapy, Hypnosis and Personality, 1951; author over 400 med. and sci. publs., book chpts., articles; mem. bd. editors: Personality: Symposia on Topical Issues, 1960-61, Jour. Integrative and Eclectic Psychotherapy, 1986-89; contbg. editor Psychosomatics, 1961-75; mem. editorial bd. Voices—The Art and Science of Psychotherapy, 1965; features editor The Interne, 1942, co-editor, 1943. Lt. U.S. Army Field Arty. Res., 1939-42; capt. M.C. AUS, 1945-47. Recipient Shirley R. Schneck award to physician making significant contbns. to devel. of med. hypnosis, 1970, Clarence B. Farrar award for history of Am. psychiatry rsch, Clarke Inst. Psychiatry, U. Toronto, 1976, Roy M. Dorcus award for best clin. paper on hypnosis, 1981, Spl. Presdl. award for lifetime contbns. to lit. on sci. hypnosis, 1986. Fellow AAAS, APA (disting. life), Am. Med. Authors, Acad. Psychosomatic Medicine, Am. Psychiat. Assn. (disting. life), Am. Soc. Clin. Hypnosis (life), Soc. for Clin. and Exptl. Hypnosis (life, founder, founding pres. 1949-56, exec. coun. 1949—, assoc. editor Jour. 1953—, Merit award 1955, Gold medal 1958, Bernard B. Raginsky award 1966, Shirley Schneck award 1970, Roy M. Dorcus award 1980, Spl. Presdl. award 1986), Am. Acad. Psychotherapists (co-founder, v.p. 1956-58), Am. Med. Writers Assn., Am. Soc. Psychoanalytic Physicians (hon., bd. dirs. 1958-62), Internat. Soc. Clin. and Exptl. Hypnosis (co-founder, bd. dirs. 1958-68, founding fellow), Internat. Acad. Eclectic Psychotherapists (charter); mem. AMA, NY Acad. Scis., Soc. Acad. Achievement (charter), Soc. Apothecaries London, Inst. Practicing Psychotherapists, Pan Am. Med. Assn. (v.p. sect. clin. hypnosis 1960-65, N.Am. v.p. 1966), NY Soc. Med. History (exec. com. 1956-62), Am. Bd. Med. Hypnosis (life, founder, pres. 1958-60, bd. dirs.), Inst. Rsch. in Hypnosis Inc. (bd. dirs., editor publs. 1957-70), Am. Assn. History Medicine, History of Sci. Soc., Assn. Advancement Psychotherapy (charter) Can. Med. History Assn., NY Soc. for Clin. Psychiatry (chmn. com. on history of psychiatry), Charles F. Menninger Soc., Internat. Soc. Hypnosis (hon. life), Brit. Soc. Med. Hypnosis (hon.), Internat. Soc. Hypnosis (hon. life), Sigma Xi. Address: 26 W 9th St New York NY 10011-8971

**SCHNECK, STUART AUSTIN,** retired neurologist, educator; b. N.Y.C., Apr. 1, 1929; s. Maurice and Sara Ruth (Knapp) S.; m. Ida I. Nakashima, Mar. 2, 1956; children: Lisa, Christopher. BS magna cum laude, Franklin and Marshall Coll., 1949; MD, U. Pa., 1953. Diplomate Am. Bd. Psychiatry and Neurology (bd. dirs., sec. 1990-91, v.p. 1991-92, pres. 1992-93). Intern Hosp. U. Pa., Phila., 1953-54; resident in medicine U. Colo. Med. Center, Denver, 1954-55, 57-58, resident in neurology, 1958-61; instr. neurology U. Colo. Sch. Medicine, 1959-61; instr. neuropathology Columbia U., N.Y.C., 1961-63; vis. fellow in neuropathology Columbia-Presbyn. Med. Ctr., N.Y.C., 1961-63; asst. prof. neurology and pathology U. Colo., 1963-67, assoc. prof., 1967-70, prof., 1970-95, assoc. dean clin. affairs Sch. Medicine, 1984-89, emeritus prof., 1996—. Cons. Fitzsimons Army Hosp., VA, Nat. Jewish Hosp.; pres. med. bd. Univ. Hosp., Denver, 1983-89, bd. dirs., 1989-90; mem. benefits adv. bd. U. Colo., 1999—, v.p. retired faculty assn. health sci. ctr., 1998-99, pres., 1999-2001. Author (with Ida I. Nakashima) The Geezers' Guide to Colo. Hikes, 2002; contbr. articles to profl. jours. Served with USAF, 1955-57. USPHS fellow, 1961-63 Mem. Am. Acad. Neurology, Am. Assn. Neuropathologists, Am. Neurol. Assn., Univ. Srs. Assn. (chmn. bd. dirs. 1997-2002), Rocky Mountain Stroke Assn. (bd. dirs. 1998—), Ctr. for Personalized Edn. Physicians (bd. dirs. 1999—), Alpha Omega Alpha (bd. dirs, 1979-89, treas., pres. 1990 93, edit. bd. 1994—).

**SCHNEE, CARL,** lawyer, former prosecutor; BA, Muhlenberg Coll.; JD, Villanova U.; MA in Liberal Studies, U. Del., 2000. Bar: Del. 1962. Asst. pub. defender, 1965-69; former sr. ptnr. Prickett, Jones, Elliot, Kristol and Schnee; U.S. atty. Del. dist. U.S. Dept. Justice, 1999—2001; ptnr. Duane, Morris & Heckscher, Wilmington, Del., 2001; sr. counsel Bifferato, Gentilotti Biden & Balick, LLC. Mem. advisory com. cultural diplomacy US Dept. State. Mem., bd. dirs. Del. Ctr. Justice. Recipient 18th Ann. Gerald K. Kandler Meml. award, ACLU and Found. Del., 2003. Mem.: Del. Bar Found. (bd. dirs.), Del. Bar. Office: Bifferato Gentilotti Biden & Balick LLC PO Box 2165 Wilmington DE 19806 Business E-Mail: cs@bgbblaw.com.*

**SCHNEEMAN, BARBARA OLDS,** nutritionist, educator; m. Paul Schneeman; 1 child, Eric. BS in Food Sci. and Tech., U. Calif., Davis, 1970; PhD in Nutrition, U. Calif., Berkeley, 1974. NIH postdoctoral fellow gastrointestinal physiology Children's Hosp., Oakland, Calif., 1974-76; faculty mem. nutrition dept. nutrition and food sci. & tech. U. Calif., Davis, 1976—, prof. dept. internal medicine divsn. clin. nutrition, 1986—, assoc. dean Coll. Agrl. and Environ. Scis., 1985-88, chair dept. nutrition, 1988-93, dean Coll. Agrl. and Environ. Scis., 1993-99. Pres., bd. dirs. Dannon Inst., 1996—; vis. scientist Cardiovascular Rsch. Inst., U. Calif. San Francisco, 1991 92; lectr. written in res. sci. series Coll. St. Catherine, St. Paul, 1987; adv. dir. Blue Cross Calif., 1992-95; mem. dietary guidelines for Ams. adv. com. to Secs. of Agr., Health and Human Svcs., 1989-90, 94-95; mem. expert panel on food safety and nutrition Inst. Food Technologists, 1985-91; mem. external adv. bd. Post Ctr. for Nutrition and Health, 1989-90; councilor Soc. for Exptl. Biology and Medicine, 1988-91. Assoc. editor Jour. Nutrition, 1991-94; contbg. editor Nutrition Revs., 1982-90; editl. bd. Jour. Nutrition, 1982-87, Procs. for Soc. Exptl. Biology and Medicine, 1985-91, Acad. Press: Food Sci. and Nutrition, 1988-2001. Fellow NDEA, U. Calif., Berkeley; recipient Outstanding Cmty. Svc. award Tierra Del Oro coun. Girl Scouts U.S., 1995, Future Leaders award for rsch. Nutrition Found., 1978-80, Samuel Cate Prescott award for rsch. Inst. Food Tech., 1985, Farma Food Internat. Fibre prize, Copenhagen, 1989, Ethel Austin Martin disting. lectr. on Human Nutrition, SD State U., 1999. Fellow AAAS; mem. Inst. Food Technologists (sec.-treas. nutrition divsn. 1988-89), Am. Physiol. Soc., Am. Inst. Nutrition (treas. 1989-92), Am. Heart Assn. (atherosclerosis coun.), Food and Nutrition Bd. IOM, 2001—. Office: U Calif Davis Dept Nutrition Davis CA 95616

**SCHNEIDER, ADELE GOLDBERG,** librarian, educator; b. N.Y.C., May 13, 1924; d. Abraham and Anna (Levy) Goldberg; m. Noel Schneider, Jan. 1, 1950; children: Adam Matthew, Tracy Lynn. BA, Bklyn. Coll., 1945; MLS, Pratt Inst., 1965; MA, L.I. Univ. 1971. Field interview Gallup Poll, N.Y.C. 1941-48; social worker N.Y.C. Dept. Social Svcs., 1949-52; editor Bklyn. Coll. Alumni Quar., 1961-65; instr. Kingsborough C.C./CUNY, 1965-70, asst. prof. dept. libr., 1972-88, prof. emeritus, 1988-92, prof. emeritus, 1992—. Contbr. articles to profl. jours. Recipient lifetime achievement award Bklyn. Coll., 2000. Mem. ALA, Libr. Assn. CUNY, N.Y. Tech. Svcs. Librs., Beta Phi Mu. Home: 124 Oxford St Brooklyn NY 11235-2311 Office: 2001 Oriental Blvd Brooklyn NY 11235-2333 Personal E-mail: lordduffy@msn.com.

**SCHNEIDER, ALLAN STANFORD,** biophysics, neuroscience and pharmacology educator, biomedical research scientist; b. N.Y.C., Sept. 26, 1940; s. Harry and Edith (Gonsky) S.; m. Mary-Jane Beekman Tunis, Dec. 14, 1980; children: Henry Seth, Joseph Benjamin B.Chem. Engring., Rensselaer Poly. Inst., 1961; MS, Pa. State U., 1963; PhD, U. Calif.-Berkeley, 1968. Chem. engr. E.I. du Pont de Nemours & Co. Exptl. Sta., Wilmington, Del., 1963-64;

postdoctoral fellow Weizmann Inst. Sci., Rehovot, Israel, 1969-71; staff fellow NIH, Bethesda, Md., 1971-73; assoc. Sloan-Kettering Inst. Cancer Research, N.Y.C., 1974-80, assoc. mem., 1980-85; asst. prof. Cornell U. Grad. Sch. Med. Scis., N.Y.C., 1974-80, assoc. prof. biochemistry, 1981-83, assoc. prof. cell biology and genetic, 1983-85, chmn. biochemistry unit Sloan-Kettering div., 1982-83; assoc. prof. pharmacology and toxicology Albany (N.Y.) Med. Coll., 1985-86, prof. pharmacology and toxicology, 1986-94, prof. pharmacology and neurosci., 1995—, dir. grad. studies, 1987-91. Adjunct prof. Biomedical Sci., Sch. of Public Health, St. U. N.Y., Albany, 1987—; vis. prof. Weizmann Inst. Sci., Rehovot, Israel, 1987; vis. rsch. scholar U. Bergen, Norway, 1989, 95; vis. rsch. scholar, U. of Melbourne, Australia, 1998. Contbr. chpts to books, sci. articles to profl. jours. Rsch. grantee Am. Cancer Soc., 1980-83, Am. Heart Assn., 1977-82, 90-93, NIH, 1982-93, 2001—05, NSF, 1977-79, 1997-2002, Cystic Fibrosis Found., 1980-82; established investigator Am. Heart Assn., 1977-82. Mem. Biophys. Soc., Soc. Neurosci., Soc. of Gen. Physiologist, Am. Heart Assn. (coun. on basic sci. 1977-95), Phi Lambda Upsilon, Tau Beta Pi (internat. com. for chromaffin cell biology 1987-93). Achievements include first isolation and characterization of chromaffin cells of the adrenal gland now widely used as a model neuronal cell culture system; determination of the relation between cytosolic calcium signals and neurohormone (adrenaline) secretion, relevant to cellular mechanism of hormone and neurotransmitter release; spectroscopic characterization of protein structure in situ in biomembranes and cells; theoretical and experimental analysis of optical activity spectra of turbid biological suspensions; research on neurochemistry of adrenal chromaffin cells, regulation of cell calcium and hormone and neurotransmitter release; mechanisms of nicotine dependence and fetal nicotine syndrome and effects of maternal smoking on fetal brain development. Office: Ctr for Neuropharmacology & Neurosci Albany Med Coll MC 136 Albany NY 12208 Office Phone: 518-262-5837. Business E-Mail: schneia@mail.amc.edu.

**SCHNEIDER, ANN IMLAH**, federal agency administrator, education consultant; b. Boston, Jan. 3, 1934; d. Albert Henry and Helen (Woodbridge) Imlah; m. John Hoke Schneider, Mar. 26, 1966 (div. 1978); children: Helen May, James Christopher. BA, Swarthmore Coll., 1955; MA, Fletcher Sch., 1956; PhD, London Sch. Econs., 1963. Asst. dir. Davis House, Am. Friends Service Com., Washington, 1956-57; admnstrv. asst. Nat. Acad. Scis., Washington, 1957-60; fgn. affairs research analyst U.S. Dept. State, Washington, 1964-70; sr. program specialist U.S. Dept. Edn., Washington, 1970—95; internat. edn. cons., 1995—. Author: Britain and Switzerland 1845-60, 1966, Federal Funding for International Studies: Does It Help? Does It Matter?, 1999, Internationalizing Teacher Education: What Can Be Done?, 2003; contbr. articles. Sec. Alumni and Friends of London Sch. Econs., Washington, 1983—91, chair scholarship com., 1990—98, pres., 1999—2003. Mem.: AAAS, Soc. for Hist. in Fed. Govt., Am. Hist. Assn., Soc. Woman Geographers (asst. treas. 1987—90, treas. 1990—96, oral history com. 1996—, chair membership com. 2003—), Internat. Studies Assn. (editl. bd. for Internat. Studies Perspectives 1979—2005, pres. local chpt. 1980—81, nat. exec. coun. 1981—82). Avocations: hiking, theater, concerts, gardening, needlecrafts. Home: 3319 Fessenden St NW Washington DC 20008-2034 Office Phone: 202-363-0109. Personal E-Mail: aimlahs@aol.com.

**SCHNEIDER, ARTHUR PAUL**, retired videotape and film editor, author; b. Rochester, N.Y., Jan. 26, 1930; s. Mendell Phillip and Frieda (Bl) S.; m. Helen Deloise Thompson, June 5, 1954; children: Robert Paul, Lori Ann. Student, U. So. Calif., 1948. With NBC, 1951-68, film and videotape editor, 1953-60, developer double system method of editing video tape, 1958; pres. Burbank (Calif.) Film Editing, Inc., 1968-72, Electronic Video Industries Inc., 1977-79; supr. video tape editing Consol. Film Industries Inc., Hollywood, Calif., 1972-76, editorial supr., 1980-83; pvt. practice editing, 1983-88. Cons., lectr., author. Film and tape editor: all: Bob Hope shows, 1951-67; supr. NBC kinescope and video tape editors (1966-67); video tape editor: Laugh-In Series, 1967-68; video tape editor: Comedy Shop Series, 1977-80; postprodn. cons. to Video Systems and Broadcast Engring. mag.; video tape editor: TV series Sonny & Cher, 1973, Sonny Comedy Revue, 1974, Tony Orlando and Dawn, 1974, Hudson Bros., summer, 1974, Dean Martin Series, 1975-76, Mickey Mouse Club Series, Walt Disney Prodns., 1976, Redd Foxx Series, 1977; (author: Electronic Post Production and Videotape Editing, 1989 (pub. in Chinese 1995), Electronic Post Production Terms and Concepts, 1990; contbg. author: Association of Cinema and Video Laboratores (ACVL) Handbook, 5th edit., 1995, Focal Guide to Electronic Media CDRom Version, 1998, Jump Cut: Memoirs of a Pioneer Television Editor, 1997, (autobiography) My 50 Years of Television History: Been There, Done That, 2005; oral history interview for Acad. TV Arts and Scis. Found. Archive of Am. TV First 50 Yrs., 2001; contbr. articles to publs. in field. Recipient Broadcast Preceptor award San Francisco State U., 1975; named hon. Ky. Col. Mem. Acad. Television Arts and Scis. (Emmy nominations and Emmy award for video tape editing 1966, 68, 73, 84, gov. 1977-80, sec. 1980-81), Am. Cinema Editors (life, Life Achievement award 1999), Soc. Motion Picture and TV Engrs., Delta Kappa Alpha (life). Home: 2586 Neptune Pl Port Hueneme CA 93041 Personal E-Mail: art2586@earthlink.net.

**SCHNEIDER, BENJAMIN**, psychology professor, consultant; b. NYC, Aug. 11, 1938; s. Leo and Rose (Cohen) S.; m. H. Brenda Jacobson, Jan. 29, 1961; children: Lee Andrew, Rhody Eve. BA, Alfred U., 1960; MBA, CUNY, 1962; PhD, U. Md., 1967. Lic. psychologist, Md. asst. prof. adminstrv. scis. and psychology Yale U., New Haven, 1967-71; prof. psychology-mgmt. U. Md., College Park, 1971-79, prof. psychology and mgmt., 1982—2004; sr. rsch. fellow Valtera Corp., 2003—; John A. Hannah prof. orgnl. psychology Mich. State U., East Lansing, 1979-82. Vis. prof. Inst. Adminstrn. and Enterprise, U. Aix-Marseille, 1993, 99, 2001, Peking U., 1989, Tuck Sch. Bus. Adminstrn., Dartmouth Coll., 1999. Author: (with D.T. Hall) Organizational Climates and Careers, 1973, Staffing Organizations, 1976, (with N. Schmitt) 2d edit., 1986, (with F.D. Schoorman) Facilitating Work Effectiveness, 1988, Organizational Climate and Culture, 1990, (with D.E. Bowen) Winning the Service Game, 1995, (with S.S. White) Service Quality: Research Perspectives, 2004, (with D.B. Smith) Personality and Organizations, 2004, (with R.E. Playhart and N. Schmitt) Staffing Organizations, 3d edit., 2006; mem. editl. rev. bd. Jour. Applied Psychology, 1988-98, 02-. Internat. Jour. Svc. Industry Mgmt., 1989—, Jour. Svc. Rsch., 1998—, Orgnl. Behavior and Human Decision Processes, 2002-, Cornell Quar., 2002-. Fulbright grantee, 1973-74 Fellow APA, Am. Psychol. Soc., Soc. for Indsl. and Orgnl. Psychology (pres. 1984-85, Disting. Sci. Contbns. award 2000, Scholarly Contbn. award 2004), Acad. Mgmt. (pres. orgnl. behavior divsn. 1982-83), San Diego Indsl. and Orgnl. Profls. (pres. 2005—). Office: 1363 Caminito Floreo Ste G La Jolla CA 92037 Office Phone: 858-488-7594. Business E-Mail: bschneider@valtera.com.

**SCHNEIDER, CALVIN**, physician; b. NYC, Oct. 23, 1924; s. Harry and Bertha (Green) S.; m. Elizabeth Gayle Thomas, Dec. 27, 1967. AB, U. So. Calif., 1951, MD, 1955; JD, LaVerne Coll., 1973. Intern L.A. County Gen. Hosp., 1955—56, staff physician, 1956—57; pvt. practice medicine West Covina, Calif., 1957—. Staff Inter-Community Med. Ctr., Covina, Calif. With USNR, 1943-47. Republican. Lutheran.

**SCHNEIDER, CARL EDWARD**, law educator; b. Exeter, N.H., Feb. 23, 1948; s. Carl Jacob and Dorothy (Jones) S.; m. Joan L. Wagner, Jan. 6, 1976. BA, Harvard Coll., 1972; JD, U. Mich., 1979. Curriculum specialist Mass. Tchrs. Assn., Boston, 1972-75; law clk. to judge U.S. Ct. Appeals (D.C. cir.), Washington, 1979-80; law clk. Potter Stewart U.S. Supreme Ct., Washington, 1980-81; asst. prof. law U. Mich., Ann Arbor, 1981-84, assoc. prof. law, 1984-86, prof. law, 1986—, prof. internal medicine, 1998—, Chauncey Stillman prof. ethics, morality and practice of law; vis. prof. U. Tokyo, 1998. Author: The Practice of Autonomy: Patients, Doctors and Medical Decisions, 1998, (with Margaret F. Brinig) An Invitation to Family Law, 1996, (with Marsha Garrison) The Law of Bioethics, 2003; editor: (book) The Law and Politics of Abortion, 1980, Family Law in Action: A Reader, 1999 (with Margaret F. Brinig and Lee E. Teitelbaum), Law at the End of Life: The Supreme Court and Assisted Suicide, 2000; contbr. articles to profl. jours.

Fellow Am. Council of Learned Socs., Ford Found., 1985, Hastings Ctr.; life fellow Clare Coll., Cambridge. Mem. Order of Coif. Office: U Mich Law Sch 801 Monroe St Ann Arbor MI 48109-1210 Office Phone: 734-647-4170.

**SCHNEIDER, CARL STANLEY**, physics professor, researcher; b. Balt., Dec. 20, 1942; s. Stanley Samuel and Viola Jeannette Schneider; m. Carole Bottom, Dec. 24, 1971; children: Kathleen Schneider Sollars, James Andrew. BA, Johns Hopkins U., Balt., 1960—63; MS, MIT, Cambridge, 1963—65, PhD, 1963—68. Prof. U.S. Naval Acad., Annapolis, Md., 1968—. Dir. sch. U.S. Naval Acad., 1986—96. Pres. Broadneck Fedn. Communities, Annapolis, 1974—76; cmty. program dir. Annapolis Rotary Club, 1995—96. Recipient Outstanding Young Men in Am., Jaycees, 1975, Meritorius Civilian Svc. award, USN, 1986—96, Frank R. Haig prize, Am. Assn. Physics Tchrs., 1998. Mem.: Mine Warfare Assn. (hon. Charles Rowzee award 1996), Phi Kappa Phi, Sigma Xi, Phi Beta Kappa. R-Liberal. Methodist. Achievements include patents for closed loop degaussing control system. Avocations: singing, photography, travel, hiking, gardening. Office: US Naval Acad 572C Holloway Rd Annapolis MD 21402 Office Phone: 410-293-6663. Office Fax: 410-293-3792. Business E-Mail: schneide@usna.edu.

**SCHNEIDER, CARL WILLIAM**, lawyer; b. Phila., Apr. 27, 1932; s. Nathan J. and Eleanor M. (Milgram) S.; m. Mary Ellen Baylinson; children: Eric, Mark, Adam, Cara BA, Cornell U., 1953; LLB magna cum laude, U. Pa., 1956. Bar: Pa. 1957. Law clk. U.S. Ct. Appeals (3d cir.), Phila., 1956-57; sr. law clk. U.S. Supreme Ct., Washington, 1957-58; assoc. Wolf, Block, Schorr and Solis-Cohen LLP, Phila., 1958-65; ptnr. Wolf, Block, Schorr and Solis-Cohen, Phila., 1965-2000, of counsel, 2000—. Spl. advisor divsn. corp. fin. SEC, Washington, 1964; lectr. securities law U. Pa., 1968-70; vis. assoc. prof., 1978-81, acting dir. Ctr. for Study Fin. Instns.; bd. editors and advisors Rev. Securities and Commodities Regulations. Author: SEC Consequences of Corporate Acquisitions, 1971, Pennsylvania Corporate Practice and Forms: The Wolf, Block, Schorr and Solis-Cohen Manual, 1997; also numerous articles. Bd. dirs. Found. Jewish Families and Children's Svc., Abramson Ctr. Jewish Life; chmn. bd. dirs. Jewish Family and Children's Svc. Greater Phila., 2000—03; trustee Jewish Fedn. Greater Phila. Mem. ABA, Pa. Bar Assn., Phila. Bar Assn. (chmn. sect. corp. banking and bus. law 1972), Am. Law Inst. (life). Home: 1601 Locust St Apt 500 Philadelphia PA 19102-3315

**SCHNEIDER, CAROL GEARY**, educational association administrator; BA in History, magna cum laude, Mount Holyoke Coll.; postgrad., U. London Inst. Historical Rsch.; PhD in Early Modern History, Harvard U. Instr. Chgo. State U., DePaul U., Boston U., U. Chgo., 1978—88, dir. Midwest Faculty Seminar, founding dir. Inst. on Teaching and Learning; exec. v.p. Assn. Am. Colls. and Univs., Washington, 1988—98, pres., 1998—. Contbr. articles to profl. jours. Bd. trustees Mt. Holyoke Coll. Woodrow Wilson fellow, Harvard U., Kent fellow, Harvard Prize fellow, Mina Shaughnessy fellow, U.S. Dept. Edn., 1982. Mem.: Phi Beta Kappa. Office: Am Assn Colls and Univs 1818 R St NW Washington DC 20009

**SCHNEIDER, CAROLYN ALICE BRAUCH**, elementary school educator; b. N.Y.C., Dec. 15, 1946; d. Elliott David and Marie Alice (Giroux) B.; m. Thom J. Schneider, Aug. 3, 1978; children: Logan, Whitney, Brock. BS, U. Bridgeport, 1968. Tchr. phys. edn. Westview (Colo.) Elem. Sch., 1968-72, McElwain (Colo.) Elem. Sch., 1972-75; tchr. phys. edn., health Northglenn (Colo.) Mid. Sch., 1975—, coach gymnastics, 1975-84, coach track, 1975—2000, coach softball, 1998—2000, coach volleyball, 1975—96; coach xtreme competitive soccer, 2007—2003; coach explosion soccer, 1988—97. Coach North Area Soccer Assn., Thornton, Colo., 1995-96, 96-97 Rec. (competitive), 97— U-11B/Explosion White coach traveling competitive team, U-12 O-Colo. XTreme -U/17B competitive soccer team, 1997-2003; instr., bldg. supr. Northglenn Recreation Dept., 1969-84, mem. sch. improvement team, rep. Dist. Sch. Improvement Team. Mem. NEA, AAHPERD (Colo. recipient Nat. Pathfinder award for Outstanding Leadership in Girls and Womens Sports, 2002), Colo. Edn. Assn., Am. Health Assn. Roman Catholic. Avocations: sports, reading, travel.

**SCHNEIDER, CATHERINE CHEMIN**, occupational therapist, consultant; d. Anthony Joseph Chemin and Irma Jena Bizzotto; m. Daniel Patrick Schneider, Sept. 25, 1970; children: David Patrick, Patricia Marie. BS in Occupl. Therapy, Wayne State U., 1970. Staff therapist Henry Ford Hosp., Detroit, 1971; Plymouth Ctr. for Human Devel., 1971—73, Oak Park Devel. Tng. Ctr., Mich., 1973—75; itinerant staff therapist, cons. Ingham Intermediate Sch. Dist., Mich., 1975—76; sch. therapist, cons. Birmingham (Mich.) Pub. Schs., 1978—91; cons., pres. The Positive Difference, LLC, Northville, Mich., 1992—2000; sch. therapist, cons. Bloomfield Hills (Mich.) Sch., 1992—99; presenter in field, 2003—. Author: Sensory Secrets: How to "Jump-Start" Learning in Children, 2001, 2006; co-author (with Carol Poltorak): Your Sensational Brain, 2006. Mem.: Am. Occupl. Therapy Assn. Avocations: reading, music, needlecrafts. Office Phone: 248-344-8188. E-mail: posdiff@aol.com.

**SCHNEIDER, CHARLES IVAN**, newspaper executive; b. Chgo., Apr. 6, 1923; s. Samuel Hiram and Eva (Smith) S.; m. Nancy Barrier-Schneider; children: Susan, Charles I. Jr., Kim, Karen, Traci. BS, Northwestern U., 1944. Indsl. engr., sales mgr., v.p. mktg. and sales Curtis-Electro Lighting Corp., Chgo., 1945-54, pres., 1954-62, Jefferson Electronics, Inc., Santa Barbara, Calif., 1962-64; pres. 3 sub., v.p., asst. to pres. Am. Bldg. Maintenance Industries, Los Angeles, 1964-66; group v.p. Times Mirror Co., Los Angeles, 1966-88, ret.; pvt. investor and cons., 1988—. Bd. dirs. Jeppesen Sanderson, Inc., Denver, Graphic Controls Corp., Buffalo, Regional Airports Improvement Corp. Bd. regents Northwestern U., Evanston, Ill.; trustee, past pres. Reiss-Davis Child Study Center, L.A.; bd. govs., past pres. The Music Ctr.; trustee the Menninger Found.; pres. St. John's Hosp. and Health Ctr. Found., Santa Monica, Calif. Served with AUS, 1942-44. Mem. Chief Execs. Orgn. (past pres., bd. dirs.). Clubs: Standard (Chgo.); Beverly Hills Tennis (Calif.); Big. Ten of So. Calif. Avocations: tennis, squash, music, reading. Home: 522 N Beverly Dr Beverly Hills CA 90210-3318 *An individual's growth and success as a manager are in direct proportion to his or her ability to develop, motivate and lead able, capable people.*

**SCHNEIDER, CHRISTINE LYNN**, customs inspector; b. Staten Island, N.Y., Feb. 3, 1960; d. Howard Thomas and Ina Elise (Beyer) S. BS, SUNY Maritime Coll., Bronx, 1984. Lic. 3d mate, U.S. Mcht. Marine; cert. U.S. customs firearms instr. Chief inspector Customs and Border Protection, San Diego, 1989—. Served to lt. comdr. USNR, 1984-87, 91—. Democrat. Lutheran. Avocations: coin collecting/numismatics, pistol shooting, golf. Home: 3505 Valley Rd Apt 3 Bonita CA 91902 Office: Customs and Border Protection 720 E San Ysidro Blvd San Ysidro CA 92173-3115 Office Phone: 619-690-8800. Personal E-Mail: cschne6548@aol.com.

**SCHNEIDER, CYNTHIA PERRIN**, former ambassador, political science professor; b. Pa., Aug. 16, 1953; m. Thomas J. Schneider; 2 children. BA in Fine Arts magna cum laude, Harvard U., 1977, PhD in Fine Arts, 1984. Asst. curator European paintings Mus. Fine Arts, Boston, unitl 1984; asst. prof. art history Georgetown U., Washington, 1984-90, assoc. prof. art history, 1990—2004; amb. to The Netherlands Am. Embassy, The Hague, 1998-2001; dir., life sciences & society initiative Georgetown U., Washington, 2003—, disting. prof. in practice of diplomacy, Pfizer Med. Humanities Initiative scholar-in-residence. Lectr. on Rembrandt and Dutch art in US and Europe; vice-chair President's Com. on Arts and Humanities. Author: Rembrandt's Landscapes, 1990; organizer, writer (catalog) Rembrandt's Landscape Print and Drawings, Nat. Gallery Art, 1990; contbr. articles to profl. jour. Mem. steering com. Creative Am., chair fed. design subcom.; coord. arts policy Clinton-Gore Campaign, 1992; bd. dir. Nat. Mus. Women in Arts, Australian-Am. Leadership Dialogue; supervisory bd. Royal Ahold, 2001—05; adv. bd. Strawberry Frog, Inc.; bd. dir. Wesley Theological Sem., Coun. Am. Ambassadors; bd. adv. Inst. for Cultural Diplomacy; internat. bd. adv., Inst. for the Study of Europe Columbia U.; Am. bd. Anne Frank House Found. Recipient Exceptional Svc. Order, Office of US Sec. of Def., 2001. Office: Distin-

guished Prof in Practice of Diplomacy Georgetown Univ 3300 Whitehaven St NW Ste 500 Washington DC 20057 Office Phone: 202-687-0703. Office Fax: 301-924-8715. E-mail: schneidc@georgetown.edu.*

**SCHNEIDER, DAN W.**, lawyer, consultant; b. Salem, Oreg., Apr. 28, 1947; s. Harold Otto and Frances Louise (Warner) S.; m. Nancy Merle Schmalzbauer, Mar. 29, 1945; children: Mark Warner, Edward Michael. BA cum laude, St. Olaf Coll., 1969; JD, Willamette U., 1974; LLM, Columbia U., 1975. Bar: Oreg. 1974, D.C. 1978, Ill. 1987. Trial atty. U.S. Dept. Justice Antitrust, Washington, 1975-79; dep. assoc. dir. U.S. SEC, Washington, 1979-86; gen. ptnr. Schiff Hardin & Waite, Chgo., 1986-95; name ptnr. Smith Lodge & Schneider, Chgo., 1995-98; ptnr. Hopkins & Sutter, Chgo., 1998-2000; internat. ptnr. Baker & McKenzie, Chgo., 2000—. Bd. dirs. NygaarArt, Northfield, Minn. Contbr. articles to profl. jours. Trustee, sec. Ill. Acad. Fine Arts, Chgo., 1990-98; mem. adv. bd. Flaten Art Mus., Northfield, 1990—; mem. adv. bd. Hallie Ford Mus. Art, Salem, Oreg., 1999—; pres. adv. group arts in edn. Willamette U., 2004— Recipient 1st prize Nathan Burkan Law Essay Competition ASCAP, N.Y., 1974, Christie award Securities Transfer Assn., 1987. Mem. Met. Club. Chgo., Monroe Club, Plaza Club. Avocations: art collecting, art writing, music composition. Office: Baker & McKenzie 1 Prudential Plz 130 E Randolph St Ste 3700 Chicago IL 60601-6342 Business E-Mail: dan.w.schneider@bakernet.com.

**SCHNEIDER, DANIEL B.**, reporter; bureau asst., UN New York Times. Office: New York Times 229 W 43d St New York NY 10036 Office Phone: 212-556-1510. Office Fax: 212-556-1421.*

**SCHNEIDER, DAVID WALTER**, lawyer; b. Chillicothe, Ohio, Sept. 7, 1942; s. August L. and Ruth M. (Sifferd) S.; m. Virginia Glann, Oct. 28, 1967; children: Tanya, Alina, Toby. BA, Gettysburg Coll., 1964; BD, Yale U., 1967, JD, 1971. Bar: Conn. 1971, U.S. Dist. Ct. Conn. 1973, U.S. Ct. Appeals (2d cir.) 1973, U.S. Supreme Ct. 1975, U.S. Tax Ct. 1992. Clergyman United Ch. of Christ, Stamford, Conn., 1967-68; law clk. to judge U.S. Ct. Appeals (2d cir.), N.Y.C., 1971-73; assoc. Tyler, Cooper & Alcorn, New Haven, 1973-79, ptnr., 1979—, mng. ptnr., 1987-92. Mem.: Conn. Bar Assn. (chmn. liaison with state cts. com. 1985—87). Home: 25 Cassway Rd Woodbridge CT 06525-1214 Office: Tyler Cooper & Alcorn 205 Church St New Haven CT 06510-1805 Office Phone: 203-784-8216. Business E-Mail: dschneider@tylercooper.com.

**SCHNEIDER, DENNIS RAY**, microbiology educator and executive; b. Sinton, Tex., June 10, 1952; 2 children. BA with honors, U. Tex., 1974, PhD, 1978. Post-doctoral fellow Behringwerke AG, Marburg/Lahn, West Germany, 1978-79; postdoctoral fellow U. Mo. Med. Sch., Columbia, 1980-81; rsch. microbiologist New England Nuc., North Billerica, Mass., 1981-82; dir. R & D Austin (Tex.) Biol. Lab., 1982-88; adj. assoc. prof. U. Tex., Austin, 1986—; dir. R & D devel. Micro-Bac Internat., Austin, 1988-94, v.p. Round Rock, Tex., 1994—. Author: Bioremediation: A Desktop Manual for the Environmental Professional; contbr. chpt. to Microorganism Adaptation to Host Defense. Grantee NASA, 1988, 92, 93. Mem. AAAS, Am. Soc. for Microbiology, Mensa, Profl. Assn. Dive Instrs. Avocations: scuba diving, writing. Office: Micro-Bac Internat 3200 N I H 35 Round Rock TX 78681-2430 Office Phone: 512-310-9000. Business E-Mail: drdiver@mail.utexas.edu. E-mail: drdivet2001@yahoo.com.

**SCHNEIDER, DONALD (CHARLES SCHNEIDER)**, communications executive; b. Owosso, Mich., Apr. 15, 1923; s. Gordon Alexander and Kathleen Emily (Skelly) S.; m. Catherine Shuttle, 1944 (dec. 1955); life ptnr. Valerie SoRelle (dec. 1995). Student, Army Air Corps Photo Sch., Denver, 1943, Pasadena Playhouse, 1956-57; cert. in video studio prodn., Valley Cable TV Sta., 1982-83. Developer, negative cutter Technicolor, Hollywood, Calif., 1942-43; printer, timer George W. Colburn Lab., Chgo., 1951-54; ind. producer, editor, writer, 1952—; cameraman, dir. Sancho The Homing Steer, Disney Prodns., Burbank, Calif., 1960; assoc. producer, dir., editor, mixer, dubbing dir. Fairway Internat., Burbank, 1961-65; lab. supr. Telefilm, Hollywood, 1965-70; Erwin Wasey Advt. Agy., 1970-71; post-prodn. supr. Intromedia, Hollywood, 1972; founder, CEO The Movie Mus., Mich., 1979—. V.p. Internat. Puppetry Mus., North Hollywood, Calif., 1984—. Editor Movie Museum newsletter, 1979—; prodr.: (bus. film) Majestic Visitor, 1952, (film) How to Use Tools, 1958, (news documentary) Gay Rights Motorcade, 1966, Magic Hands of Sculptor Rudy Mercado, 1987, (travel film) Cruise to the Falls, 1953, (musical) Broadway Comes Alive, 1999; prodr. Mardi Gras Magic Show, 1999, Haunted Castle Movie Set, 1999; dir.: (film) Eegah, The Prehistoric Giant, 1961, (stage prodn.) The Women, 1967; composer: Sonata to a Rose, 1946; set decorator, lights They're Playing Our Song, 1984; actor Let's Do It Again, 1974, Lepke, 1975, Rocky, 1976; film editor Incredible Creatures, 1962, Sadist, 1963, Spies A-Go-Go, 1964, Weekend of Fear, 1965, Man from Clover Grove, 1972, Our Hispanic Heritage, 1977, Norseman, 1978, Mission to Glory, 1979, Brigham Young, 1984, Forty Days of Musa Dagh, 1987; set designer and cast Waltz Dream, 1939. Recipient Award for Saving Demille Barn (Hollywood Bowl), Historic Preservation Soc., 2000. Achievements include establishing Conflict-Resolution Libr., 1956; National Endowment for the Arts, 1962; perfecting Eastman color positive/negative process, 1966. Avocation: counseling. Office Phone: 989-725-7621. Personal E-Mail: movemuseum@aol.com.

**SCHNEIDER, DONALD J.**, trucking company executive; b. Green Bay, Wis., 1935; married; 5 children. BA, St. Norbert Coll., 1957; MBA, U. Pa. Pres. Schneider Transport Inc., Green Bay, Wis., 1957—; CEO, pres. Schneider National, Inc., 1977—2002, chmn. Office: Schneider National Inc PO Box 2545 Green Bay WI 54306-2545*

**SCHNEIDER, DUANE BERNARD**, English literature educator; b. South Bend, Ind., Nov. 15, 1937; s. William H. and Lillian L. (Pitchford) S.; m. Crystal J. Gips; children: Jeffrey, Eric, Lisa, Emily. BA, Miami U., Oxford, Ohio, 1958; MA, Kent State U., 1960; PhD, U. Colo., 1965. Instr. engring. English U. Colo., 1960-65; asst. prof. English Ohio U., Athens, 1965-70, assoc. prof., 1970-75, prof., 1975-98, chmn. Faculty Senate, 1981-83, chmn. dept. English, 1983-86, prof. emeritus, 1998—; dir. Ohio U. Press, 1986-95; part-time faculty New Sch. U., NYC, 2000—05. Editor, pub. Croissant & Co., 1968-2002. Author: (with others) Anais Nin: An Introduction, 1979. Mem. Thomas Wolfe Soc. (trustee, pres. 1979-81). Home: 102 Baybery Cir Saint Simons Island GA 31522 E-mail: schneide@ohio.edu.

**SCHNEIDER, EDGAR ROLF GOTTFRIED**, retired mathematician, application developer, writer; b. Bklyn., Apr. 9, 1932; s. Richard Bernhard Grunewald and Sylvia Goldberg, adopted s. Nathan Schneider; m. Sally Jane Mitchell, Oct. 3, 1959 (div.); children: Elisabeth Sutter, Christian, Eric; m. Alexandra Khan Kazan, June 26, 1999. BA, City Coll. of N.Y., 1954; MA, The Am. U., Washington, 1970. Mathematician, sci. computer programmer Svc. Bur. Corp., N.Y.C., 1959—63, LA, 1963—66, IBM Corp., Bethesda, Md., 1966—70, Atlantic City, 1970—74, Warminster, Pa., 1974—75, Owego, NY, 1975—82. Spkr. Autism Soc. Fla., Fort Lauderdale, 1994—. Author: Discovering My Autism, 1999, Living the Good Life with Autism, 2003. Singer Fla. Philharmonic Chorus, Fort Lauderdale, 1974—2003. 2nd lt. U.S. Army, 1954—58. Mem.: Phi Beta Kappa, Sigma Xi. Roman Catholic. Avocations: art, music, photography, history, literature. E-mail: hansachsthegreat@juno.com.

**SCHNEIDER, EDWARD LEE**, botanist, researcher; b. Portland, Oreg., Sept. 14, 1947; s. Edward John and Elizabeth (Mathews) S.; m. Sandra Lee Alfarone, Aug. 2, 1968; children: Kenneth L., Cassandra L. BA, Ctrl. Wash. U., 1969, MS, 1971; PhD, U. Calif., Santa Barbara, 1974. From asst. to assoc. prof. botany S.W. Tex. State U., San Marcos, 1974-84, prof., 1984-94, chmn. biology dept., 1984-89, dean sci., 1989-92; pres., CEO Santa Barbara (Calif.) Botanic Garden, 1992—. Author: The Botanical World, CEOs and Trustees—Building Working Partnerships; contbr. articles to profl. jours. Bd. dirs. Ctr. for Plant Conservation; bd. dirs. Coun. Sci. Soc. Presidents, 2005-06. Recipient Presdl. Rsch. award S.W. Tex. State U., 1986, Disting. Alumnus award Ctrl. Wash. U., 1996, Centennial medallion; grantee NSF, 1980, 90. Fellow Tex. Acad. Sci. (pres. 1992-93); mem. Internat. Water Lily Soc. (bd. dirs., sec. 1989-96, inducted into Hall of Fame, Award of Appreciation 1997), Bot. Soc. Am. (bd. dirs., pres.-elect 2004, pres. 2005-06, Award of Merit 1998), Am. Assn. Bot. Gardens and Arboreta (bd. dirs.), Internat. Pollination Congress, Nat. Coun. Deans, Am. Assn. Mus. (assessment program adv. com., nat. program com. Home: 1140 Tunnel Rd Santa Barbara CA 93105-2134 Office: Santa Barbara Botanic Garden 1212 Mission Canyon Rd Santa Barbara CA 93105-2126 Office Phone: 805-682-4726 ext. 123. Business E-Mail: eschneider@sbbg.org.

**SCHNEIDER, EDWARD MARTIN,** retired internist, medical educator; b. Cleve., May 12, 1922; s. Sol S. and Beatrice Hilda (Sicherman) Schneider; m. Jane H. Einstein, June 18, 1950 (dec. Aug. 2001); children: Douglas A., Robert S. 1 stepchild, Donald E. Deutsch. Student, Northwestern U., 1940-43; MD, U. Cin., 1946. Diplomate Am. Bd. Internal Medicine. Intern Mt. Sinai Hosp., Cleve., 1946-47, asst. resident medicine, 1947-48, sr. asst. resident medicine, 1950-51; fellow in medicine Cin. Gen. Hosp., 1951-52; asst. prof. of medicine U. Okla. Sch. Medicine, Oklahoma City, 1952-57; sr. physician gastroenterology Miner's Meml. Hosp. Assn., McDowell, Ky., Beckley, W.Va., 1957-61; chief of medicine Cameron Meml. Hosp., Bryan, Ohio, 1961-62; chief medical rsch. sect. Upjohn Co., Kalamazoo, Mich., 1962-67; pvt. practice Woodland Hills, Calif., 1968-81. Author 17 rsch. papers. Capt. M.C., AUS, 1948-50. Recipient Cert. of Recognition, Dept. Def. Fellow ACP, Am. Coll. Gastroenterologists; mem. Assn. Mil. Surgeons (life), Am. Assn. Study Liver Disease (emeritus), Sigma Xi. Avocations: amateur radio, music appreciation. Home: 1521 Lake Forest Dr Charlottesville VA 22901 E-mail: edwardmd@sprintmail.com.

**SCHNEIDER, EDWIN KAHN,** research scientist; b. Philadelphia, Pa., May 6, 1948; s. Abraham and Edna May Schneider; m. Penelope Lee Ganzel, Aug. 5, 1980; children: Andrew Ganzel, Thomas Schmidt. AB, Harvard U., 1970, PhD, 1975. Postdoctoral rsch. assoc. MIT, Cambridge, Mass., 1974—77, prin. rsch. scientist, 1984—84; NATO postdoctoral fellow Reading U., England, 1977—78; rsch. fellow, assoc. Harvard U., Cambridge, Mass., 1978—83; assoc., sr. rsch. scientist U. Md., College Park, Md., 1984—93; sr. rsch. scientist Ctr. for Ocean-Land-Atmosphere Studies, Calverton, Md., 1993—; prof. climate dynamics George Mason U., Fairfax, Va., 2002—; exec. editor Climate Dynamics, 2004—. Author: (book chapter) Climate Change: An Integrated Perspective; contbr. (articles) Encyclopedia of Global Environmental Change; contbr. articles to profl. jours. Fellow, NSF, 1970—72; grantee, NSF, NOAA, NASA, DOE, EPRI, 1985—2002; Nat. Merit scholar, 1966—70. Fellow: Am. Meteorol. Soc.; mem.: Am. Geophys. Union. Achievements include research in Hadley circulation, El Nino/Southern Oscillation, atmospheric and oceanic dynamics, climate change. Avocations: orchestral violinist, golf. Office: Center for Ocean-Land-Atmosphere Studies 4041 Powder Mill Rd Suite 302 Beltsville MD 20705 Office Phone: 301-595-7000.

**SCHNEIDER, ELAINE CAROL,** lawyer, researcher, writer; b. Mpls., Aug. 28, 1957; d. Allan William and Deborah G. Schneider; m. William Mack Olivé, Oct. 10, 1987 (div. July 1996); 1 child, Vanessa Inez Olivé; m. G.R. Smith, Jan. 2, 2002. BA, U. Minn., 1979; JD, William Mitchell Coll. Law, St. Paul, 1982. Bar: N.Mex. 1984, Minn. 1998, D.C. 1999. Assoc. Settles, Kalamarides & Assocs., Anchorage, 1982, Dickson, Evans & Esch, Anchorage, 1982; legal rschr. John Hanson, Anchorage, 1983; acct. rep. Westlaw Svcs., Inc., Albuquerque, 1984, sales rep. New Orleans, 1985-86; libr. sales rep. West Pub. Co., Spokane, Wash., 1986-87, reference atty. St. Paul, 1988-97, product mgr., 1997-2001; pvt. practice Mpls.; CEO, mem. Coeur à Coeur Fashion Beauty Products, LLC, Minn., 2004. Ethics adv. bd. N.Mex. Bar, Albuquerque, 1984-85; midwest regional conf. com. Am. Immigration Lawyers Assn., 2000. Author: Substantive Judicial Law Outline of Habeas Corpus, 1984, What They Don't Teach You in the Bar Review Course, 1991, Challenging an Incredibility Finding on Appeal, An Incredibility Paradigm, 2001; mem. law rev. staff: William Mitchell Coll. Law, 1980—81. Atty. immigration and naturalization law Minn. Advocates for Human Rights, Refugee and Immigrant Project. Recipient Vol. Pro Bono Atty. award, 15th Ann. Minn. Advocates for Human Rights, 1999. Mem. Phi Beta Kappa. Avocations: ventriloquism, skiing, swimming, travel, languages. Office: 701 4th Ave S Ste 500 Minneapolis MN 55415-1810 Personal E-mail: avocatecs@aol.com.

**SCHNEIDER, ELIZABETH KELLEY,** law librarian; b. Bloomington, Ill., July 10, 1946; d. George Raymond and Lucille Genvieve (Sutter) Kelley; m. John James Schneider, Aug. 21, 1982. BA in History, Wesleyan U., Ill., 1968; MLS, U. Minn., 1969; JD, William Mitchell Coll. of Law, 1973; LLM in Health Law, St. Louis U., 1997. Bar: Minn. 1974, U.S. Dist. Ct. Minn. 1979. Librarian Ramsy County Law Library, St. Paul, 1971-73; asst. law librarian U. of Akron (Ohio) Coll. of Law, 1973-74; prof. law librarian Hamline U. Sch. Law, St. Paul, 1974-81; dir. Maricopa County Law Library, Phoenix, 1981-91; assoc. dir. law libr., asst. prof. Tex. Tech. Sch. Law, 1992-2000. Instr. legal research Ariz. Legal Secs. Assn., 1982, Phoenix Coll., 1982-85, Ariz. State Library Assn., 1984. Mem. ABA, Am. Assn. Law Libraries (chair Legal Info. Svcs. to the Pub. 1988-89), Ariz. Assn. Law Libraries (pres. 1985-86), Ariz. Women Lawyers Assn., Desert Sun Aux., Nat. Assistance League (sec. 1985-86, chmn. 1986-87), Southwestern Assn. of Law Libr. (sec. 1987-90, v.p. 1990-91), Alpha Gamma Delta (pres. 1985-86). Office: Plattner Schneidman & Schneider 4201 North 24th St Ste 100 Phoenix AZ 85016 Office Phone: 602-274-7955. E-mail: eksphx@yahoo.com.

**SCHNEIDER, GERALD L.,** plastic surgeon; b. Mechanicsburg, Pa., Oct. 25, 1945; s. Gordon Henry and Pauline Emma (Rife) S.; 1 child, Ross Roberts. BS, No. Ariz. U., 1968; MD, U. Ariz., 1973. Intern Naval Regional Med. Ctr. San Diego, 1973 74; resid in gen. surgery U.S. Naval Hosp., San Diego, 1974-78, resident in plastic surgery Portsmouth, Va., 1978-80, staff surgeon divsn. plastic surgery San Diego, 1981-83, chief divsn. plastic surgery, 1983-84; pvt. practice Flagstaff, Ariz., 1984-90; staff surgeon La Jolla (Calif.) Cosmetic Surgery Ctr., 1990-91; surgeon Scripps Clinic & Rsch. Found., La Jolla, 1991—. Capt. USNR Fellow ACS; mem. Am. Soc. Plastic Surgeons. Avocation: golf. Office: Scripps Clinic & Rsch Found 10666 N Torrey Pines Rd La Jolla CA 92037-1092 Office Phone: 858-554-9606. Business E-Mail: gschneider@scrippsclinic.com.

**SCHNEIDER, GISELA HELGA,** medical technician; arrived in U.S., 1959; d. Bernhard Richard Hackstein and Martha Maria Bruckhoff-Hackstein; children: Hans, Sigfried, Gisela, Erika, Walter. Cert. histo-technologist ASCP; Bd. Registry Chgo. Histo-technologist Kaiser-Med. Group, Walnut Creek, Calif., 1964—74, C.C. County Hosp., Martinez, Calif., 1974—75, Alta Bates Hosp., Berkeley, Calif., 1975—83, Pathology Svcs., Inc., Berkeley, 1983—90, histo-pathology supr., 1983—90; histo-technologist U. Calif., San Francisco, 1990—2003. Avocations: reading, writing, travel, music, foreign languages. Home: 280 Tono Ln Walnut Creek CA 94597 Office Phone: 415-353-1610.

**SCHNEIDER, HARRY H., JR.,** lawyer; b. San Antonio, Jan. 12, 1954; AB, U. Calif., Berkeley, 1976; JD, U. Chgo., 1979. Bar: Wash. 1979, US Ct. Appeals (9th Cir.), US Dist. Ct. (We. Dist.) Wash., US Dist. Ct. (Ea. Dist.) Wash. Clk. Contra Costa County Dist. Atty. Office, Martinez, Calif., 1972—76; with Kobin & Meyer, Portland, 1977, Cooley, Godward, Castro, Huddleson & Tatum, San Francisco, 1978, ptnr. Perkins Coie LLP, Seattle, mem. mgmt. com. Office: Perkins Coie LLP 1201 Third Ave Ste 4800 Seattle WA 98101-3029 Office Phone: 206-359-8508. Office Fax: 206-359-9000. Business E-Mail: hschneider@perkinscoie.com.

**SCHNEIDER, HILARY A.,** Internet company executive; BA in Econs., Brown U., 1982; MBA, Harvard Bus. Sch., 1986. Dir. devel. The Balt. Sun Co., 1992—94, v.p. new bus. devel., 1994—95, v.p. sales, 1996—97, v.p. sales and mktg., 1997—98, gen. mgr., 1998—99; v.p. corp. fin. Drexel Burnham Lambert Inc., 1986—90; dir. bus. devel. Times Mirror Corp.,

1990—92; pres., CEO Times Mirror Interactive, Balt., 1999—2000; CEO Red Herring Comm., 2000—02; v.p. Knight Ridder Digital, 2002—04, pres., CEO, 2002—04; sr. v.p. Knight Ridder, 2005—06; sr. v.p. marketplaces Yahoo! Inc., Sunnyvale, Calif., 2006—. Bd. dirs. CareerBuilder.com. Office: Yahoo Inc 701 1st Ave Sunnyvale CA 94089*

**SCHNEIDER, HOWARD,** lawyer; b. NYC, Mar. 21, 1935; s. Abraham and Lena (Pincus) S.; m. Anne Evelyn Gorfinkle; children: Andrea Rose, Jeffrey Winston. AB, Cornell U., 1956, JD with distinction, 1959. Bar: N.Y. 1960, D.C. 1976. Assoc., then ptnr. Stroock & Stroock, N.Y.C., 1959—75; gen. counsel Commodity Futures Trading Commn., Washington, 1975—77, Rosenman & Colin (now Katten Muchin Rosenman LLP), NYC, 1977—2005; sr. v.p. regulatory affairs Man Fin. Inc., NYC, 2005—. Contbr. articles to profl. jours. Served to capt. USAR, 1956-66. Mem.: ABA (chmn., com. on regulation of futures and derivative insts. 1997—2001), Assn. Bar City of N.Y. (chmn. com. 1982—86). Republican. Jewish. Home: 20 E 74th St New York NY 10021 Office: Man Fin Inc 717 Fifth Ave New York NY 10022 Office Phone: 212-589-6266. Business E-Mail: hschneider@manfinancial.com.

**SCHNEIDER, HOWARD STEWART,** former newspaper editor; b. Bklyn., Oct. 10, 1945; s. Robert and Helen (Friedman) S.; m. Ilene Roberta Weinstein, July 3, 1967; children—Lara Joy, Scott Michael, Jillian Debra BA cum laude in Journalism and Psychology, Syracuse U., 1966; MS in Journalism, Columbia U., 1967. Co-editor, founder weekly newspaper Syracuse U., NY, 1965-66; editor-pub. Poor Howard's Wednesday Afternoon Post, Wellfleet, Mass., 1966-68; reporter Newsday, Long Island, NY, 1969-76, editor, 1976-85, sr. editor, 1985, mng. editor, 1986—2003, editor, exec. v.p., 2003—04. Adj. prof. journalism SUNY, Stony Brook 1983-87, vis. prof. journalism and media ethics, LI, 2005— Author profiles on Luciano Pavarotti, Tom Seaver, Edward Albee, and Johnny Carson Recipient Nat. Hearst award Syracuse U., 1965; editor George Polk award-winning series, 1979, 1st pl. N.Y. State Pub.'s Assn., 1982, (supr. reporting and editing team) Pulitzer prize for local reporting, 1984 Jewish. Business E-Mail: howardschneider@stonybrook.edu.

**SCHNEIDER, JAMES M.,** computer company executive; b. 1950; B, Carroll Coll, Waukesha, Wis., 1973. Mgmt. to ptnr. Price Waterhouse; sr. v.p. fin. MCI Commns.; corp. planning, controller Dell Computer, now sr. v.p., CFO, 2000—. Bd. dirs. Dell Fin. Svcs., Gen. Commn., Inc., GAP Inc., Lockheed Martin Corp. Mem. Fin. Exec. Inst. Office: Dell Computer 1 Dell Way Round Rock TX 78682*

**SCHNEIDER, JAN,** retired obstetrics and gynecology educator; b. Prague, Czechoslovakia, Dec. 10, 1933; came to U.S., 1963, naturalized, 1967; s. Evzen and Erika S.; m. Sandra Wilson, May 20, 1961; children—Hana, Donald, Kathryn, Jonathan. M.B., U. London, 1957; M.P.H., U. Mich., 1967. Prof. ob-gyn, chief obstetric service dept. ob-gyn U. Mich. Med. Sch., Ann Arbor, 1963-77; prof., chmn. ob-gyn. Med. Coll. Pa. and Hahnemann U. (now Drexel U. Coll. Medicine), Phila., 1978-97, assoc. dean, 1997-99, prof. and chmn. emeritus of ob-gyn., 1999—. Editor: (with R. J. Bolognese and R. H. Schwarz) Perinatal Medicine, 2d edit, 1981. Fellow Am. Coll. Obstetricians and Gynecologists, Soc. Perinatal Obstetricians, Am. Gynecol. and Obstet. Soc., Phila. Obstet. Soc. Presbyterian.

**SCHNEIDER, JANET M.,** arts administrator, curator, painter; b. N.Y.C., June 6, 1950. d. August Arthur and Joan (Battaglia) S.; m. Michael Francis Sperendi, Sept. 21, 1985. BA summa cum laude, Queens Coll., CUNY, 1972; spl. study fine arts Boston U. Tanglewood Inst., 1971. With Queens Mus., Flushing, N.Y.C., 1973-89, curator, 1973-75, program dir., 1975-77, exec. dir., 1977-89. Collections arranged include: Sons and others, Women Artists See Men (author catalog), 1975, Urban Aesthetics (author catalog), 1976, Masters of the Brush, Chinese Painting and Calligraphy from the Sixteenth to the Nineteenth Century (co-author catalog), 1977, Symcho Moszkowicz: Portrait of the Artist in Postwar Europe (author catalog), 1978, Shipwrecked 1622, The Lost Treasure of Philip IV (author catalog) 1981, Michaelangelo: A Sculptor's World (author catalog), 1983, Joseph Cornell: Revisited (author catalog), 1992, Blueprint for Change: The Life and Times of Lewis H. Latimer (co-author catalog), 1995. Chmn. Cultural Instns. Group, N.Y.C. 1986-87; mem. N.Y.C. Commn. for Cultural Affairs 1991-93; bd. dirs. N.Y. State Partnership, 1987-88, Gallery Assn. N.Y. State 1979-81; exec. dir. Cultural Inst. Group, 1995—. Mem. Artists Choice Mus. (trustee 1979-82), Am. Assn. Mus., Phi Beta Kappa.

**SCHNEIDER, JOANNE,** artist; b. Lima, Ohio, Dec. 4, 1919; d. Joseph and Laura (Office) Federman; m. Norman Schneider, May 15, 1941; children—Melanie Schneider Tucker, Lois Schneider Oppenheim. BFA, Syracuse U., 1941. One-man shows John Heller Gallery, N.Y.C., 1954, 55, 57, 58, Tirca Karlis Gallery, Provincetown, Mass., 1963, Frank Rehn Gallery, N.Y.C., 1965, 66, 69, 72, 75, Elaine Benson Gallery, Bridgehamton, N.Y., 1972, 74, 79, 85, St. Mary's Coll., St. Mary's City, Md., 1978, Alonzo Gallery, N.Y.C., 1978, Discovery Art Gallery, Clifton, N.J., 1978; group shows include Whitney Mus., N.Y.C., Pa. Acad. Arts, Corcoran Galleries, Washington, Toledo Mus., U. Nebr., Everson Mus., Syracuse, N.Y.; represented in permanent collections Met. Mus. Art, N.Y.C., Colby Coll., Syracuse U., Butler Inst., St. Mary's Coll., U. Notre Dame, Guild Hall, East Hampton, N.Y. Recipient Audubon Artists Stephen Grumbacher Meml. award, 1972 Address: 35 E 75th St New York NY 10021-2761 *A life spent in pursuit of creative expression is a fuller, more satisfying life*

**SCHNEIDER, JOHN ARNOLD,** investor; b. Chgo., Dec. 4, 1926; s. Arnold George and Anna (Wagner) S.; m. Elizabeth C. Simpson, Oct. 20, 1951; children: Richard Paul, William Arnold, Elizabeth Anne. BS, U. Notre Dame, 1948. Exec. assignments with CBS-TV, in Chgo. and N.Y.C., 1950-58; v.p., gen. mgr. sta. WCAU-TV, Phila., 1958-64; sta. WCBS-TV, N.Y.C., 1964-65; pres. CBS TV Network, 1965-66, CBS/Broadcast Group, 1966-69, 71-77; exec. v.p. CBS, Inc., 1969-71, sr. v.p., from 1977; pres., chief exec. officer MTV Networks, Inc., 1979-84. Trustee, mem. exec. com. U. Notre Dame; trustee Com. for Econ. Devel. Served with USNR, 1943-46. Mem.: Indian Harbor Yacht. Roman Catholic. Home: 155 Clapboard Ridge Rd Greenwich CT 06831-3304

**SCHNEIDER, KATY,** painter, educator; BA, Yale U.; MFA, Ind. U. Lectr. art Smith Coll., Northampton, Mass. Recipient Blanche Coleman Award, Purchase Prize, AAAL; fellow Guggenheim Meml. Found., 2004; grantee Mass. Cultural Coun. Artists Grant, New England Found. for Arts Regional Fellowship. Office: Smith Coll Dept Art Hillyer Hall Brown Fine Arts Ctr Northampton MA 01063 Office Phone: 413-585-3100. E-mail: schneiderkaty@hotmail.com.

**SCHNEIDER, KENNY,** artist, educator; b. Ellenville, N.Y., Jan. 3, 1939; s. Herbert Eli and Ruth Lillian (Star) S.; m. Judith Sara Oliver, 1960 (div. 1980); children: Janice Marion, Lisa Marie; m. Nella Maria Barriga, Oct. 5, 1985; children: Rachel, Gina, Sofia. BA in Art, U. Miami, 1960; MA in art, Adams St. Coll., 2002. With Children & Youth Devel. Svcs., Bklyn.; videotape instr. Western Conn. State Coll., video technician; film lectr. CCNY, Cooper Union, CW Post; art instr. Trinidad State Jr. Coll., 1996—2002. Guest panelist Internat. Continuing Ednl. Inst., SUNY; mem. constrn. staff Flowering of Am. Folk Art, Whitney Mus. Am. Art, Am. Pop Art; artist-in-residence MPO Videotronics; videotape technician, cameraman Rimyth Ednl. Program, Bklyn. One person shows include Gallerie 99, Bay Harbor Island, Fla., 1983, Ground Zero Gallery, Miami Beach, Fla., 1988, Fiona Whitney Gallery, L.A., 1991; exhibited in group shows at 80 Washington Square East Galleries, NYU, N.Y.C., 1979, 84, Zane Gallery, Rochester, N.Y., 1982, 84, Provincetown Art Assn., 1983, Allied Arts Coun., Las Vegas, 1984, Woodstock (N.Y.) Sch. Art, 1984, Temari-Book Art, Honolulu, 1984, Shreveport Art Guild, 1984, Fla. Gulfcoast Art Ctr., Bellaire, Fla., 1985, Francis Wolfson Art Gallery, Miami, 1985, Lowe Art Gallery, U. Miami, Coral Gables, Fla., 1985, Brea Gallery, Fullerton, Calif., 1985, Southeastern Ctr. Contemporary Art,

Winston-Salem, N.C., 1985, Mus. Contemporary Art, Miami, 1986, Gloria Luria Gallery, Bay Harbor Island, Fla., 1986, Helander Gallery, Palm Beach, Fla., 1986, Southwest Tex. State U., San Marcos, 1986, Mus. Art, Ft. Lauderdale, Fla., 1987, Matrix Gallery, Sacramento, 1987, Soc. 4 Arts, Palm Beach, 1987, Orange County Ctr. Contemporary Art, Santa Ana, Calif., 1995, Rocky Mt. Biennial, 2004, Moca Ft. Collin, 2004; commd. by Caribbean Cruise Lines, 1987, Seattle Arts Commn., 1987, Miami-Site/Crandon Gardens, 1987, Palm Beach Internat. Airport Project, 1988, Hollywood Blvd. Project, 1993, NOHO Sculpture Project, 1994, Selma Park Project, 1994, Miami Beach Transp. Mgmt. Assn., 1996; (commissioned) Children's Mus., Pueblo Colo., Homestead Pk. Project, City Ft. Collins, 2003Lincoln Rd. Project City of Miami Beach, Fla.; represented in pvt. collections Senator and Mrs. Howard Metzenbaum, Mel Brooks and Ann Bancroft, Mr. and Mrs. Milton Sidley, Mr. and Mrs. Gerald Robins, Mr. and Mrs. Joel Friedland, Mr. and Mrs. Steven Muss, Ms. Meryle Samuels, Ms. Ann Rachlin, Gloria Luria, Mr. and Mrs. Alan Greenwald, Joy Moos, Dr. Paul Dermer, Mr. and Mrs. Larry Samson, Mr. and Mrs. Ron Seiden, Mr. and Mrs. Eugene Massin, Mr. and Mrs. Neal Amdur, Mr. and Mrs. Barry Sugarman, Tony Goldman, Raymond Zimmerman, Mr. and Mrs. Charles Burson, Mr. and Mrs. Barry Massin, and Mr. and Mrs. Michael Shapiro, Ms. Michelle Isenburg, Ms. Barbara Marcus, (pub. collections) David W. Bernant Found., Santa Barbara, Calif., Cmty. Redevel. Agy., L.A., Seattle Arts Commn., Palm Beach Internat. Airport, The Miami-Dade Arts in Pub. Places Trust, Holiday Inn Corp., AT&T Transtec, The Miami-Dade Pub. Libr. Sys., Walter Annenburg collction, Caribbean Cruise Lines, La Cinematique Francaise, Musee de Cinema, Paris, N.Y. Pub. Libr., Bklyn. Pub. Libr., Bklyn. Coll. Film Libr., Nassau and Suffolk County Librs., L.I., N.Y., Colo. State Libr., Denver, U. Calif., Berkeley, Boston Pub. Libr., Rochester Pub. Libr.; film festivals: Chgo. Internat. Film Festival, 1969, Antioch Film Festival, 1969, Rochester Internat. Film Festival, 1970, Sorrento (Italy) Internat. Film Festival, San Francisco Internat. Film Festival, 1970, Festival de Film Underground, Paris, 1971, Festivale di Popoli, Florence, Italy, 1972, Yale Film Festival, 1968, 70, 72, Ann Arbor Film Festival, 1972-73, Tampere (Finland) Internat. Film Festival, 1973, among others; films shown at Bklyn. Coll., 1968, Millenium Workshop, N.Y.C., 1969, Robert Flaherty Film Seminar, 1970, Whitney Mus. Am. Art, 1971, Temple U., 1973, 74, Art Dirs. Club, N.Y.C., 1975; dir. Adonde Fue Juan Jose, 2002. Art advisor, pub. art Hist. Ark. River Project, Pueblo, Colo., 1996-98; arts commr. Arts Commn. of Ojai, 1994-95; bd. dirs. La Clinica, Inc., Gardner, Colo., 1996—; bd. chmn. Spanish Peaks Regional Health Ctr., Colo. State Vets. Mursing Home, Walsenburg, Colo., 1997. With USAR, 1959-67. Recipient Cert. of Appreciation Cmty. Redevel. Agy. City of LA, City Capital Projects Design awards Seattle Design Commn., 1987-88, 24th Ann. Small Painting Exhibit hon. mention, Art in Cauly Sq. award, NY Film Festival award, award of merit Tampere Film Festival, Chgo. Internat. Film Festival, awards Yale Film Festival, Oskar Kokoschka prize Sommer Akademie fur Bildende Kunst; NY State Coun. on the Arts grant, Visual Arts fellow Colo. Coun. on Arts and NEA, 1999. Home: PO Box 542 La Veta CO 81055 Office Phone: 719-742-3918. Personal E-mail: kenetics@centurytel.net.

**SCHNEIDER, KIRK J.,** psychologist, writer; b. Cleve., July 27, 1956; s. Murray Harold Schneider and Laura Siegal; m. Jurate Elena Raulinaitis, Sept. 17, 1989. BA in Psychology, Ohio State U., 1978; MA in Psychology, West Ga. Coll., 1979; PhD in Psychology, Saybrook Inst., 1984. Lic. psychologist Mass., Calif. Suicide prevention staff Columbus Mental Health Ctr., 1977—78; family therapy trainee Ohio State U., 1978—79; counseling intern West Ga. Coll., 1978—79, grad. tchg. asst., 1978; adv. psychology trainee N.E. Cmty. Mental Health Ctr/Fairhill Psychiat. Hosp., East Cleveland, Ohio, 1979—80; intern, supervisee InterLogue-James F.T. Bugental, PhD, Santa Rosa, Calif., 1980—83; post-doctoral trainee Massillon (Ohio) State Hosp., 1984—85; staff psychologist Human Resources Inst., Norton, Fall River, Mass., 1985—87; pvt. practice, founder Ctr. for Existential Therapy, San Francisco, 1987—. Staff psychologist Ctr. for Nutritional Rsch., Quincy, Mass., 1987—88; mem. crisis counseling team Merrill-Lynch & Co., Boston, 1988; staff psychologist South Shore Coun. on Alcohol, Quincy, 1988—89; instr. Existential-Humanistic Inst., San Francisco, 1997—; adj. faculty Lesley Coll., Cambridge, 1986—90, Bentley Coll., Waltham, Mass., 1989, Union Inst., Cin., 1989—90, Calif. Sch. Profl. Psychology, Berkeley, Alameda, 1990—96, The Profl. Sch. Psychology, San Francisco, 1992, Saybrook Grad. Sch., San Francisco, 1995—, Calif. Inst. Integral Studies, San Francisco, 1996—, clin. supr., 1990—; adj. faculty Ctr. for Humanistic Studies, Detroit, 2001—; spkr. in field. Author, editor: The Paradoxical Self: Toward an Understanding of Our Contradictory Nature, 1990, Horror and the Holy: Wisdom-teachings of the Monster Tale, 1993, The Psychology of Existence: An Integrative, Clinical Perspective, 1995, The Handbook of Humanistic Psychology: Leading Edges in Theory, Research, and Practice, 2001, Rediscovery of Awe: Splendor, Mystery and the Fluid Center of Life, 2004; contbr. chapters to books, articles to profl. jours. Pres. Existential-Humanistic Inst., San Francisco, 1999—. Fellow: APA (Rollo May award 2004); mem.: AAAS, Assn. for Humanistic Psychology.

**SCHNEIDER, LAWRENCE ALAN,** lawyer; b. Richmond, Va., Feb. 4, 1949; m. Susan Ness, Oct. 13, 1974; children: Elisabeth, David. BA cum laude, Yale U., 1971; JD cum laude, Harvard U., 1974. Bar: D.C. 1975, U.S. Ct. Appeals (D.C. cir.) 1975, U.S. Supreme Ct. 1982, U.S. Ct. Internat. Trade 1985. Assoc. Arnold & Porter, Washington, 1974-81, ptnr., Internat. Trade Practice Group, 1982—. Mem. D.C. Bar Com. on Pub. Service Activities, 1979-88, chmn. 1985-87; dir. Washington Council of Lawyers, 1981—, pres. 1984-85. Mem. ABA. Office: Arnold & Porter LLP 555 12th St NW Washington DC 20004-1206 Office Phone: 202-942-5694. Office Fax: 202-942-5999. Business E-Mail: lawrence.schneider@aporter.com.

**SCHNEIDER, MARK,** political science professor; b. NYC, Oct. 28, 1946; s. Irving and Ida Schneider; m. Susan Roth, June 27, 1980; children: Johanna, Elizabeth. BA, Bklyn. Coll., 1967; PhD, U. N.C., 1974. Asst. prof. polit. sci. U. Mich., Ann Arbor, 1973-74, SUNY, Stony Brook, 1974-78, assoc. prof., 1978-85, prof., 1985—2004, chmn. dept., 1986—2004, disting. prof., 2004—. Fulbright sr. lectr., India, 1980—81; dep. commr. Inst. Edn. Scis., 2004—05. Author: The Competitive City, 1989, Public Entrepreneurs, 1995, Choosing Schools, 2000, Charter Schools: Hope or Hype, 2005; contbr. articles to profl. jours. Dep. commr. Inst. Edn. Scis., 2004—05; commr. Nat. Ctr. for Ednl. Stats., 2005—. Mem. Am. Polit. Sci. Assn. (v.p. 2000-01), Midwest Polit. Sci. Assn. Office: Inst of Edn Scis Washington DC 20208

**SCHNEIDER, MARK LEWIS,** foreign policy executive, retired government agency administrator; b. Newark, Dec. 31, 1941; s. Benjamin and Ruth (Kobran) S.; m. Susan Gilbert, June 20, 1965; children: Aaron Mitchell, Miriam Beth. AB in Journalism with honors, U. Calif., Berkeley, 1963; MA in Polit. Sci., San Jose State Coll., 1965; LLD (hon.), Am. U., 2000. Reporter UPI, San Francisco, 1963-64, San Francisco News Call Bull., 1965; vol. Peace Corps, El Salvador, 1966-68; reporter Washington Daily News, 1969-70; mem. staff U.S. Senate Judiciary Subcom., 1970-71; legis. asst. to Sen. Edward M. Kennedy, 1971-77, 80-81; dep. asst. sec. for human rights Dept. State, Washington, 1977-79; mem. del. UN Gen. Assembly, 1978, UN Human Rights Commn., 1979; coordinator policy planning, sr. advisor Pan Am. Health Orgn., 1981-93; adminstr. for Latin Am. and Caribbean U.S. AID, 1993-99; dir. The Peace Corps, 1999-2001; sr. v.p. Internat. Crisis Group, Washington, 2001—. Lectr. Kennedy Inst. Politics, Harvard U., 1976; adj. prof. Georgetown U., 1996. Bd. dirs. Internat. Human Rights Law Group, 1981-92; trustee Am. U. Fulbright fellow, 1976; recipient George W. Eastman medal U. Rochester, 2000, Bernardo O'Higgins medal Govt. Chile, 1993 Mem. Am. Polit. Sci. Assn., Latin Am. Studies Assn. Democrat. Jewish. Home: 3517 Tilden St NW Washington DC 20008-3122 Office Phone: 202-785-1601. E-mail: mschneider@crisisgroup.org.

**SCHNEIDER, MARTIN AARON,** photojournalist, educator, ecologist, engineer, writer, artist, television director, filmmaker, public advocate, medical researcher; b. NYC, Sept. 23, 1926; s. Morris and Florence (Frohlich) S. Student, Stuyvesant Sci., 1941-44; BC, CUNY, 1944-53. Reporter, writer; artist, 1941—; photographer, 1954—. Photojournalist Life, Time, Newsweek, Sports Illustrated, NY Times, NBC-TV, Ency. Britannica, Mpls. Tribune,

Handball Illustrated, Time Annual Year in Review, Grolier Ency., Crowell-Collier Ency., NBC Startime, Variety, Time-Life: Ecology, Saturday Review of Literature, 1960—; ecologist, USPHS, US Senate, US EPA, NYCEPA, NY State Dept. Environ. Conservation, NYC Dept. Air Pollution, 1964—; product safety engineer, designer, builder, crash-safety, pollution and radiation monitoring, multi-alternate fuel, laboratory vehicle, stereotactic radiosurgery: safer therapy delivery collimator, 1967—, univ. faculties NYU, Cornell U., Ithaca, NY, New Sch. Social Rsch., NYC, SUNY, Albany, Cooper Union for Advancement of Sci. and Art, NYC, CUNY, Iowa U., lectr. in field, 1969—; pub. advocate, NYC Health Dept., NY State Health Dept., NY State Dept. Environ. Conservation, Gov. Rockefeller's State Study Commission for NYC (Scott Commission), US District Ct., NY Supreme Ct., People of NYC, NYC Council, NY Atty. Gen., 1970—. TV news guest NBC Today, CBS, ABC, FOX, PBS, 1970—; radio news guest NBC, CBS, NPR, 1970; TV and radio commentator, NBC, CBS, ABC, PBS, Fox, 1970—; author: Breath of Death, 1972, Consumer Genocide: Censored Survival Kit 1992; The Schneider Tapes, 1996, War Against War, ed. 1996, CARnage: 3 Million Killed by Suppressed 100 mph Safety, 1997, The Food You Eat–Eats You: How to Get Safe Food in Same Stores at Same Price, 1998; co-author: NBC Startime, 1963, America-Photographic Statements, 1972, Eye of Conscience, 1974 (chpt. Martin Schneider); dir., prodr., writer, videographer, cinematographer (TV documentaries) Environment Crusade, CBS, 1970, The Poisoned Air, CBS, 1970, Killers of the Environment, NBC, 1971, Censorship of Pollution Solutions by Media and Government, PBS, 1974, No Justice for Victims-Criminals Only, 1992; contbr. NY Times, Ency. Britannica, Macmillan Ency. of Photographic Artists, NY Village Voice "Whole Earth Ranger: Ecology's Batman", New World Or No World (Frank Herbert) 1970—; photography exhibited at Mus. Modern Art, NYC, 1958—, George Eastman House Mus., Rochester, NY, 1963, 64—, Libr. Congress, 1970, Smithsonian Instn., 1972—, Art Inst. Chgo., 1973—, Whitney Mus., NYC, 1978—; permanent exhibit includes NY Mus. of TV and Radio, 1999; painting exhibited at Guggenheim Mus., NYC, 1943; film exhibited at Am. Mus. Natural History, NYC, 1969-72, network TV guest appearances; dir. documentaries, 1969-. Served with US Army Paratroopers, 1944-46, PTO. Fellowship grantee Creative Artists Pub. Svc., 1977, 78; recipient TV Franny Consumer Advocacy award, 1974, for work that was a basis for the first Clean Air Act of 1970. Jewish. Achievements include advocacy for Mayo Clinic non-toxic patient-derived vaccine cancer therapy now offered alternative to chemotherapy uniquely in US for all stages, 2004. Office: 545 8th Ave Ste 401 New York NY 10018 *Where millions are endangered where my work makes a difference–despite gunfire, vehicle sabotage, seizure of home and all possessions, censorship–I cannot compromise public health for private wealth- for there is no dream for me in moving mere mountains, but only in moving man to move himself.*

**SCHNEIDER, MARY EK,** literature and language educator; d. Bruce and Marilyn Krentz; m. Slim Schneider, Dec. 11, 1965; children: Troy J., John Wayne. BA in English, S.D. State U., 1994. Tchr. Armour H.S., SD, 1996—; freelance writer, 2004—. Treas. DU, Armour, SD, 2003—06. Office: Armour HS PO Box 640 Armour SD 57313 Office Phone: 605-724-2153.

**SCHNEIDER, MARY LOUISE,** retired elementary school educator; b. Waterville, Wash., Oct. 17, 1918; d. John Steve and Alice Ray (Jones) S. BA in Edn., Holy Names Coll., 1940. Cert. elem. tchr. Wash., 1940. Tchr. Mud Springs/Douglas County, Mansfield, Wash., 1941-42; elem. tchr. Mansfield Sch. dist., Douglas County, Wash., 1942-43, Waterville (Wash.) Sch. Dist., Douglas County, Wash., 1943-49, Lewis and Clark Elem. Sch., Wenatchee, Wash., 1949-60; spl. reading tchr. H.B. Ellison Jr. High, Wenatchee, 1960-62, Orchard Jr. High, Wenatchee, 1962-67; lang. arts tchr. Pioneer Jr. High, Wenatchee, 1967-77; retired, 1977. Author lang. arts learning packages for students, 1967; co-author: Name on the Schoolhouse, 1989. Vol. Am. Heart Assn., Wenatchee, 1975-90, Am. Cancer Soc., Wenatchee, 1975-88. Recipient Cert. of Recognition, Wash. State Ct. Cath. Daus. of the Ams., 1970, 72, 74. Mem.: AAUW (treas. 1973—75), PEO (pres. 1980—82, 1988—90), Chelan-Douglas County Sch. Retirees Assn. (com. chmn. 1989—90), Cath. Daus. of the Ams. (state pres. 1984—86, nat. evangelization chmn. 1986—88, local ct. pres. 1958—60, 1999—2001, author Wash. State Ct. of Cath. Daus. 1988). Avocation: sewing.

**SCHNEIDER, MATTHEW ROGER,** lawyer; b. NYC, Nov. 7, 1948; s. Theodore David Schneider and Rosalind (Schwartz) Werner; m. Marjorie Ann Friedlander, Mar. 6, 1976; children: Adam Benjamin, Emily Beth. BA, Cornell U., 1970; student, Georgetown U., 1973; JD, Cath. U., Washington, 1974. Bar: D.C. 1976, U.S. Dist. Ct. D.C., 1994. Staff asst. U.S. Senate Jud. Com., Washington, 1973-74; counsel U.S. Senate Govt. Ops. Com., Washington, 1974-77; spl. asst. Office of Sec. Def., Washington, 1977-79; dir. legis. affairs SEC, Washington, 1979-81; sr. counsel, divsn. corp. fin., 1981-82; chief of staff U.S. Senator Jeff Bingaman, Washington, 1983-85; prin. Law Office Matthew Schneider, Washington, 1985-87; ptnr. Willkie, Farr & Gallagher, Washington, 1987-95, Garvey Shubert Barer, Washington, 1996—98, mng. dir. D.C. office, 1998—. Bd. dirs. Nat. Epilepsy Found., 2000—04, mem. exec. com., 2001—04; bd. dirs Capitol Hill Hosp., Washington, 1987—95, chmn. govt. and legal affairs com., 1997—2003. Avocations: physical fitness training, singing, guitar. Office: Garvey Schubert Barer 5th Fl 1000 Potomac St NW Ste 5 Washington DC 20007-3501 Office Phone: 202-965-7880.

**SCHNEIDER, NIKLAS,** educator; Assoc. prof. U. Hawaii, Honolulu, 2002—. Office: Oceanography University of Hawaii 1000 Pope Road Honolulu HI 96822 Office Phone: 808-956-8383. Office Fax: 808-956-9425. E-mail: niklas.schneider@hawaii.edu.

**SCHNEIDER, PAM HORVITZ,** lawyer; b. Cleve., Nov. 29, 1951; m. Milton S. Schneider, June 30, 1973; 1 child, Sarah Anne. BA, U. Pa., 1973; JD, Columbia U., 1976. Bar: N.Y. 1977, Pa. 1979. Assoc. White & Case, N.Y.C., 1976-78, Drinker Biddle & Reath LLP, Phila., 1978-84, ptnr., 1984-2001; founding ptnr. Gadsden Schneider & Woodward LLP, King of Prussia, Pa., 2001—. Contbr. articles to profl. jours. Fellow Am. Coll. Trust and Estate Counsel (past regent); mem. ABA (past chair, real property probate and trust law sect.), Internat. Acad. Estate and Trust Law (academician). Office: Gadsden Schneider & Woodward LLP The Merion Bldg 700 S Henderson Rd Ste 345 King Of Prussia PA 19406 E-mail: pschneider@gsw-llp.com.

**SCHNEIDER, PETER,** theater producer; m. Hope Schneider; 2 children. BA in Theater, Purdue U., 1972. Mng. dir. St. Nicholas Theater, Chgo., 1976-80; gen. mgr. Apollo Theater Prodns., London, 1980-83; dir. Olympic Arts Festival, L.A., 1984; with Walt Disney Studios, 1985—; pres. Walt Disney Theatrical Prodns. Walt Disney Pictures, Burbank, Calif., 1996-2000; chmn. Walt Disney Studios, Burbank, Calif., 2000—01; dir. Hyperion Theatricals, 2002—. Dir. plays The WPA, Playwrights Horizon, Circle Repertory Theater, N.Y.C.

**SCHNEIDER, PETER RAYMOND,** political scientist; b. Muskogee, Okla., Aug. 8, 1939; s. Leo Frederick and Tillie Oleta (Cannon) S.; m. Anne Larason, Jan. 22, 1964 (div. 1983); children: Christopher, Geoffrey; m. Adrienne Armstrong, Dec. 19, 1986; children: Robbie, Samantha. BS, Okla. State U., 1966, MS, 1968; PhD, Ind. U., 1974. News editor No. Va. Sun, Arlington, 1961-62; news writer AP, Balt., 1962, Balt. News-Am., 1962-65; asst. prof. U. Oreg., Eugene, 1974-76; pres. Inst. of Policy Analysis, Eugene, 1976-83; v.p. Am. Justice Inst., Sacramento, 1983; dir. Ctr. for Assessment of The Juvenile Justice Ctr., Sacramento, 1983; v.p. Nat. Partnership, Washington, 1985; sr. rsch. scientist Pacific Inst. for Rsch. and Evaluation, Bethesda, Md., 1984-92, dir. justice div., 1986-89; pres. Inst. of Policy Analysis, McLean, Va., 1992-95; CEO IPA Internat., Inc., Vienna, 1995—. Contbr. numerous articles to profl. jours., chpts. to books. Recipient Julia Lathrop award Am. Criminal Justice Assn., 1985. Mem. Am. Polit. Sci. Assn., Am. Restitution Assn., Pi Sigma Alpha, Sigma Delta Chi, Phi Kappa Phi, Omicron Delta Kappa, Phi Kappa Theta. Avocations: flying, tennis, selling wine. Office: IPA Internat Inc 7291 Jones Branch Dr Ste 501 Mc Lean VA 22102

Home: 1345 Woodside Dr Mc Lean VA 22102-1530 *In a career devoted to the pursuit of knowledge, I have learned that nothing - absolutely nothing - is worth more than lessons learned from painful personal experience. To my regret, I usually learned such lessons after the opportunities to profit from them had already passed. If I could do it over again I would be more daring and venturesome and make my mistakes early, while there was still plenty of time to invest the information.*

**SCHNEIDER, PHYLLIS LEAH,** writer, editor; b. Seattle, Apr. 19, 1947; d. Edward Lee Booth and Harriet Phyllis (Ebbinghaus) Russell; m. Clifford Donald Schneider, June 14, 1969; 1 child, Pearl Brooke. BA, Pacific Luth. U., 1969; MA, U. Wash., 1972. Fiction, features editor Seventeen Mag., N.Y.C., 1975-80; mng. editor Weight Watchers Mag., N.Y.C., 1980-81; editor YM mag., N.Y.C., 1981-86. Author: Parents Book of Infant Colic, 1990, Kids Who Make a Difference, 1993, Straight Talk on Women's Health: How to Get the Health Care You Deserve, 1993, Hot Health Care Careers, 1993, What Kids Like To Do, 1993; contbr. The Parents Answer Book, 1998; The Prose Reader, 2001, 2004. Recipient Centennial Recognition award Pacific Luth. U., 1990. Democrat. Episcopalian.

**SCHNEIDER, RICHARD GRAHAM,** lawyer; b. Bryn Mawr, Pa., Aug. 2, 1930; s. Vincent Bernard and Marion Scott (Graham) S.; m. Margaret Peter Fritz, Feb. 15, 1958; children: Margaret W., Richard Graham Jr., John F. BA, Yale U., 1952; JD, U. Pa., 1957, MLA, 2001. Bar: Pa. 1958. Assoc. Dechert Price & Rhoads, Phila., 1957-66, ptnr., 1966-95; of counsel, 1995—. Case editor U. Pa. Law Rev., 1956-57. Trustee Baldwin Sch., Bryn Mawr, 1971-79, Episcopal Acad., Merion, Pa., 1976-83, Episcopal Cmty. Svcs., Phila., 2003—. 1st lt. USAF, 1952-54, PTO. Mem. ABA, Pa. Bar Assn., Phila. Bar Assn., Order of Coif, Merion Cricket Club, Merion Golf Club (sec. 1997-2002), Yale Club (pres. 1966-68). Republican. Presbyterian. Office: Dechert LLP CIRA Ctr 2929 Arch St Philadelphia PA 19104-2808 Personal E-mail: gladwyne@aol.com.

**SCHNEIDER, RICHARD T. (RICHARD THEODORE SCHNEIDER),** optics scientist, researcher, engineer; b. Munich, July 29, 1927; came to U.S., 1961; s. Wilhelm and Martha E. (Hofmann) S.; m. Lore M. Reinhard, May 16, 1950; children: Ursula M. Schneider Long, Richard W. Diploma in physics, U, Stuttgart, Fed. Republic of Germany, 1958, PhD, 1961. Registered profl. engr. Calif. Teaching asst. U. Stuttgart, 1958-61; sect. chief Allison div. Gen. Motors Corp., Indpls., 1961-65; assoc. prof. U. Fla., Gainesville, 1965-68, prof., 1968-88, prof. emeritus, 1988-90; pres. Eye Rsch. Lab., Inc., Alachua, Fla., 1984-90; chief scientist RTS Labs., Inc., Alachua, 1984-92. Cons. Allison div. Gen. Motors Corp., Indpls., 1965-67; IPA assignment Eglin AFB, Ft. Walton Beach, Fla., 1983; liaison scientist USN Office Naval Rsch., London, 1975. Editor: Uranium Plasmas, 1971; patentee in field; contbr. articles to profl. jours. Recipient Medal for Exceptional Sci. Achievement, NASA, 1975. Outstanding Tech. Achievement award, Fla. Engring. Soc., 1978. Mem. Internat. Soc. for Optical Engring., Sigms Xi, Tau Beta Pi (Eminent Engr. 1970). Home: 12903 NW 112th Ave Alachua FL 32615-6520 Office Phone: 386-462-2666. Personal E-mail: schneider-labs@worldnet.att.net.

**SCHNEIDER, ROB,** actor; b. Pacifica, Calif., Oct. 31, 1963; s. Marvin and Pilar Schneider; m. London King, 1988 (div. 1990); 1 child, Chole Autumn. Co-owner restaurant Eleven, San Francisco. Actor: (films) Martians Go Home, 1990, Necessary Roughness, 1991, Home Alone 2: Lost in New York, 1992, Surf Ninjas, 1993, Demolition Man, 1993, The Beverly Hillbillies, 1993, Judge Dredd, 1995, Down Periscope, 1996, The Adventures of Pinocchio, 1996, Knock Off, 1998, Susan's Plan, 1998, The Waterboy, 1998, Deuce Bigalow: Male Gigolo, 1999, Big Daddy, 1999, Muppets From Space, 1999, Little Nicky, 2000, The Animal, 2001, The Hot Chick, 2002, Mr. Deeds, 2002, (voice) Eight Crazy Nights, 2002, 50 First Dates, 2004, Around the World in 80 Days, 2004, The Longest Yard, 2005, Deuce Bigalow: European Gigolo, 2005, Grandma's Boy, 2006, The Benchwarmers, 2006, (TV series) Saturday Night Live, 1990-94, Men Behaving Badly, 1996-97, (TV films) The Mummy Parody, 2001, (voice) The Electric Piper, 2003, Back to Norm, 2005. Office: United Talent Agy 9560 Wilshire Blvd Fl 5 Beverly Hills CA 90212-2400*

**SCHNEIDER, ROBERT JAY,** oncologist; b. Miami, Fla., May 31, 1949; s. Irving and Ethel (Pack) S.; m. Barbara Cunningham, June 1, 1974; children: Matthew, Kirsten. Student, Washington U., 1967-69; BA cum laude, Boston U., 1971; MD, Albert Einstein Coll. Medicine, N.Y.C., 1975. Diplomate Am. Bd. Internal Medicine, Am. Bd. Oncology; lic. physician, N.Y. Intern., jr. and sr. resident internal medicine Bronx Mcpl. Hosp., N.Y.C., 1975-78; fellow med. oncology Meml. Sloan-Kettering Cancer Ctr., N.Y.C., 1978-80, adj. attending physician/cons. dept. medicine, 1981—; asst. prof. medicine N.Y. Med. Coll., Valhalla, 1980-81. Clin. instr. medicine Cornell U. Med. Coll., 1978-80; jr. clin. faculty fellow Am. Cancer Soc., 1980-81; mem. N.Y. Met. Breast Cancer Group, 1990—; cons. cancer program No. Westchester Hosp. Ctr., Mt. Kisco, N.Y., 1981-82; mem. staff Westchester County Med. Ctr., Valhalla, N.Y., No. Westchester Hosp. Ctr., Mt. Kisco, Meml. Sloan-Kettering Cancer Ctr., N.Y.C. Contbr. articles to profl. jours. mem. adv. bd. Cancer Care, Inc. Conn., 1997-99. Recipient Clin. Fellowship award Am. Cancer Soc., 1978-79. Mem. Am. Soc. Clin. Oncology, Westchester County Med. Soc., Soc. Integrative Oncology, Am. Soc. Breast Disease, N.Y. State Med. Soc., Woodway Country Club. Republican. Presbyterian. Achievements include research in detection and treatment of early breast cancer, the human spirit in the fight against cancer, salvage chemotherapy with etoposide, ifosfamide and cisplatin in refractory germ cell tumors. Office: 101 S Bedford Rd Ste 202A Mount Kisco NY 10549-3456

**SCHNEIDER, ROBERT JEROME,** lawyer; b. Cin., June 22, 1947; s. Jerome William and Agnes (Moehringer) S.; m. Janice Loraine Eckhoff, Dec. 13, 1968; children: Aaron Haisley, Jared Alan, Margot Laraine. BSME, U. Cin., 1970, JD, 1973. Bar: Ill. 1973, U.S. Dist. Ct. (no. dist.) Ill. 1973, U.S. Ct. Appeals (7th cir.) 1973, U.S. Ct. Appeals (fed. cir.) 1973. Ptnr. Mason, Kolehmainen, Rathburn & Wyss, Chgo., 1973-82; ptnr., asst. chmn. patents, chmn. intellect. property dept. McDermott, Will & Emery, Chgo., 1982-94; chmn. intellectual property dept. Chapman & Cutler, Chgo., 1995—. Mem. ABA, ASME, Ill. Bar Assn., Chgo. Bar Assn., Licensing Execs. Soc., Intellectual Property Law Assn. Chgo. (sec. 1981-83), Fedn. Internat. des Conseils en Priorite Industrielle, Assn. Internationale pour la Protection de la Propriètè Industrielle, Internat. Pat-Got Assn. (treas. 2001-05, pres. 2005-), Internat. Trademark Assn., Internat. Trade Commn. Trial Lawyers Assn., Am. Intellectual Property Law Assn., Tower Club (bd. govs. 1988—, v.p. 1994-95, pres. 1995—), Univ. Club Chgo. (bd. dirs. 2003—). Republican. Roman Catholic. Home: 1609 Asbury Ave Winnetka IL 60093-1303 Office: Chapman & Cutler Chicago IL 60601 Office Phone: 312-845-3000. Fax: 312-803-3529. E-mail: iplaw@chapman.com.

**SCHNEIDER, RUDOLPH F.,** education educator; b. Buffalo, June 30, 1925; s. Rudolph Albert and Marguerite Caroline Schneider; m. Grace Ann Kilbert, Sept. 10, 1949; children: Mark, Karen, Rudolph, Mary. BS, U. Buffalo, 1949; MS, Buffalo State Coll., 1963. V.p., plant mgr. Hornell (NY) Brewing Co., 1950—60; instr. tech. electronics Hornell City Sch. Dist., 1960—63; dir. occupational edn. Oswego State Bd. Coop. Edn., Bath, NY, 1960—83; adj. prof. edn. Oswego State Coll., Oswego, NY, 1983—91. State pres. Assn. of Vocational Adminstr., NY, 1981—83. Pres. C. of C., Hornell, 1960; bd. dirs. Conquestador Home Owners, 1998—2000. CPO USN, 1943—46, Samar. Mem.: Knights of Columbus (faithful navigator 1960—63). Republican. Cath. Avocations: reading, golf, fishing. Home: 7728 Lexington Dr Hudson OH 44236-1401

**SCHNEIDER, SHARON M.,** systems administrator, information technologist; b. Detroit, Mar. 15, 1958; d. Peter and Mary S.; m. Wesley A. Comes, May 23, 1987. BS, Kutztown U., 1990; MS, MSIS, Drexel U., 1998. Reference and info. asst. Bucks County Free Libr., Doylestown, Pa., 1988-94;

computer sys. tech. Cedar Crest & Muhlenberg Colls., Allentown, Pa., 1994-95; sys. adminstr., info. technologist Cedar Crest Coll., 1995—. Mem. Assn. Computing Machinery, World Future Soc., Beta Phi Mu.

**SCHNEIDER, STEPHEN HARLEY,** medical educator; b. Neptune, N.J., Apr. 1, 1948; s. Joseph and Edith (Himmelman) S.; m. Carole Robin Lowenstein, Aug. 31, 1981; children: Ari, Rachel. BA, MD, Boston U., 1972. Cert. in internal medicine and endocrinology, N.J. Rsch. assoc. Boston City Hosp., 1975-76, fellow divsn. diabetes and metabolism, 1976-77, asst. dir. diabetes clinic, 1976-77, dir. diabetes clinic, 1977-78, dir. diabetes and metabolism svcs., 1978-79; instr. medicine Boston Univ. Sch. Medicine, 1978-79; asst. prof. medicine U. Medicine and Dentistry N.J.-Robert Wood Johnson Med. Sch., New Brunswick, NJ, 1979-85, assoc. prof. clin. medicine 1985-88, assoc. prof. medicine, 1988-95, prof. medicine, 1995—. Mem. editl. bd. Diabetes Forcast Mag.; contbr. numerous articles to profl. jours. including Jour. Clin. Endo. & Nutr., New Eng. Jour. Medicine, Diabetes Care, Atherosclerosis, Japanese Heart Jour., Diabetologia, Metabolism. Bd. dirs. Juvenile Diabetes Assn., East Brunswick Jewish Ctr. Youth Com.; founding mem. affiliate Internat. Diabetic Athlete's Assn. Recipient McKeen Cattell award Am. Coll. Clin. Pharmacology, 1986; rsch. fellow Am. Heart Assn., 1976. Fellow ACP; mem. Am. Soc. Internal Medicine, Am. Coll. Sports Medicine, Am. Fedn. Clin. Rsch., Begg Soc., Phi Beta Kappa, Alpha Omega Alpha. Jewish. Avocations: football, soccer, history, theology, bicycling. Office: UMDNJ-Robert W Johnson Med Divsn Endocrinology PO Box 19 New Brunswick NJ 08903-0019 Office Phone: 732-235-7749. Business E-Mail: schneide@umdnj.edu.

**SCHNEIDER, THOMAS PAUL,** non-profit agency administrator; b. June 5, 1947; s. Milton and Gloria (Bocaner) S.; m. Susan G. Stein, May 31, 1987; children: Rachel Jenny, Daniel Joshua. BA with honors, U. Wis., 1972, JD, 1972. U.S. dist. U.S. Dist. Dist. Ct. (ea. dist.) Wis., Milw., 1993-2001; exec. dir. youth svcs. COA Youth & Family Ctrs., Milw., 2001—. Mem. Wis. Bar Assn. Democrat. Jewish. Office: COA Youth & Family Ctrs 909 E North Ave Milwaukee WI 53212 Office Phone: 414-263-8383. Business E-Mail: tomschneider@coa-yfc.org.

**SCHNEIDER, VALERIE LOIS,** retired speech educator; b. Chgo., Feb. 12, 1941; d. Ralph Schneider and Gertrude Blanche (Gaffron) S. BA, Carroll Coll., 1963; MA, U. Wis., 1966; PhD, U. Fla., 1969; CAS, Appalachian State U., 1981. Tchr. English and history, dir. forensics and drama Montello (Wis.) H.S., 1963-64; instr. speech U. Fla., Gainesville, 1968-68, asst. prof. speech, 1969-70, Edinboro (Pa.) State Coll., 1970-71; assoc. prof. speech East Tenn. State U., Johnson City, 1971-76, prof. speech, 1976-97. Instr. newspaper course Johnson City Press Chronicle, 1979, Elizabethton Star, Erwin Record, Mountain City Tomahawk, Jonesboro Herald and Tribune, 1980; mem. investor panel USA Today, 1991-92. Editor East Tenn. State U. evening and off-campus newsletter, 1984-91; assoc. editor Homiletic, 1974-76; columnist Video Visions, Kingsport Times-News, 1984-86; book reviewer Pulpit Digest, 1986-90; contbr. articles to profl. jours. Chmn. AAUW Mass Media Study Group Com., Johnson City, 1973-74. Recipient Creative Writing award Va. Highlands Arts Festival, 1973, award Kingsport Times News, 1984, 85, Tri-Cities Met. Advt. Fedn., 1983, 84, hon. life mem. Tenn. Presbyn. Women, 2000; named Danforth assoc., 1977; finalist Money mag. contest, 1994, Writer's Digest contest, 2000. Mem.: AAUW (v.p. chpt. 1974—75, pres. 1975—76), Tenn. Basic Skills Coun. (pres. 1975—76, exec. bd. 1979—80, v.p. 1980—81), Religious Speech Comm. Assn. (Best Article award 1976), Tenn. Speech Comm. Assn. (exec. bd. 1974—77, publs. bd. 1974—78, pres. 1977—78), So. Speech Comm. Assn., Speech Comm. Assn. (Tenn. rep. to states adv. coun. 1974—75), Mensa, Presbyn. Women (hon.: life mem.), Johnson City Book Club (pres. 2001—03), Bus. and Profl. Women's Club (chpt. exec. bd. 1972—73, v.p. 1976—77), Pi Gamma Mu, Phi Delta Kappa, Tau Kappa Alpha, Delta Sigma Rho. Presbyterian.

**SCHNEIDER, VIVIAN I.,** psychologist, researcher; b. Wichita Falls, Tex., Sept. 6, 1949; d. Robert and Vivian H. Davis; m. Robert Jordan Schneider, June 8, 1972 (dec. Mar. 13, 2002); children: Kayt, Amy J. Kim, Jay Robert. BA in Psychology, Met. State Coll. Denver, 1972; MA in Psychology, U. Colo., Boulder, 1988, PhD in Psychology, 1991. Sr. rsch. assoc. U. Colo., Boulder, 1991—. Co-author: (chpts.) Learning and Memory of Knowledge and Skills: Durability and Specificity, Foreign Language Learning: Psycholinguistic Studies on Training and Retention, The Psychology of Learning and Motivation: Advances in Research and Theory; contbr. articles to profl. jours. Ham radio operator Boulder County Amateur Radio Emergency Svcs., 1995—2006; vol. Lamb's Lunch, Boulder, 2004—06; children's leader Bible Study Fellowship, Boulder, 1975—85, 2006; Sunday sch. tchr. Bethany Ch., Boulder, 1976—2006. Mem.: Psychonomic Soc. Avocations: reading, quilting. Home: PO Box 1097 Boulder CO 80306 Office: U Colo Ucb 345 Boulder CO 80309 Office Phone: 303-735-6488. Office Fax: 303-492-8895. Business E-Mail: vivian.schneider@colorado.edu.

**SCHNEIDER, WESLEY CLAIR,** marketing communications company executive; b. Chgo., May 2, 1953; s. Clair A. and Ruth (Jenks) S.; m. Jeanie A. Tomaino, Nov. 23, 1990. BA magna cum laude, Ill. Wesleyan U., 1975. Sales rep. confectionery div. Am. Home Products, Chgo., 1975-77; midwest regional sales mgr. confectionery & snacks div. Beatrice Foods, Denver, 1977-78, mktg. analyst, 1978-80; product mgr. Tootsie Roll Industries, Chgo., 1980-85, mgr. internat. mktg., 1985-88; v.p., gen. mgr. Marden-Kane, inc., Chgo., 1988-91; pres., owner Creative Mktg. Comm., Inc., Chgo., 1991—. Bd. dirs. Wesleyan Co., Inc., Chgo.; speaker Inst. for Internat. Rsch. and Promotion Mktg. Assn. Am., N.Y.C., 1991. Patentee in field. Cubmaster Boy Scouts Am., Chgo., 1991; founder Silver Wicket Charity Event; mem., chair candidates slating subcom. Kenilworth Citizens Adv. Com.; bd. dirs. Kenilworth Assembly Hall Soc., 2001—; chmn. Am. Leadership Fund., 2003; leadership coun. Ill. Wesleyan U.; asst. committeeman New Trier Rep. Orgn., 2003—, fin. chmn., 1998-2002; founder Christ The King Anglican Ch., 2004, warden, 2005. Recipient Best Design award retail food category Nat. Flexible Packaging Assn., 1979, Indian statue Point of Purchase Advt. Inst., 1986, 87, U.S. Senatorial Medal of Freedom, 1999. Mem. Am. Def. Preparedness Assn., Exec. Club Chgo. (comms. com.) Internat. Platform Assn., Masons, Shriners, Sigma Chi. Anglican. Avocations: fishing, reading, politics. Office: Creative Mktg Comm Inc 980 N Mich Ave Ste 1400 Chicago IL 60611

**SCHNEIDER, WILLIAM GEORGE,** chemist, research consultant; b. Wolseley, Sask., Can., June 1, 1915; s. Michael and Phillipina (Krauschaar) S.; m. Jean Purves, Sept. 2, 1940; children: Judith Schneider Saunders, Joanne Schneider Spurrier. B.Sc., U. Sask., 1937, M.Sc., 1939, D.Sc., 1969; PhD, McGill U., 1941, D.Sc. (hon.), York U., 1966, Meml. U., 1968, McMaster U., 1969, Laval U., 1969, Moncton U., 1969, U. N.B., 1970, U. Montreal, 1970, Acadia U., 1976, U. Regina, 1976, Ottawa U., 1978; LL.D., U. Alta., 1968, Laurentian U., 1968. Head phys. chemistry sect., div. chemistry NRC Can., Ottawa, 1946-63, dir. div. pure chemistry, 1963-65, v.p., 1965-67, pres., 1967-80; research cons., 1980—. Author: (with J.A. Pople, H.J. Bernstein) High Resolution Nuclear Magnetic Resonance, 1959; contbr. articles to profl. jours. Decorated Order of Can., 1977 Fellow Royal Soc. Can. (Henry Marshall Tory medal), Royal Soc. London, Chem. Inst. Can. (medal 1969, Montreal medal 1973); mem. Internat. Union Pure and Applied Chemistry (pres. 1983-85) Office: 200 Rideau Terrace Ottawa ON Canada K1M 0Z3

**SCHNEIDER, WILLYS HOPE,** lawyer; b. NYC, Sept. 27, 1952; d. Leon and Lillian (Friedman) S.; m. Stephen Andrew Kass, Jan. 21, 1979; children: Peter, Josefine. AB cum laude, Princeton U., 1974; JD, Columbia U., 1977. Bar: NY 1978, US Tax Ct. 1979, US Tax Ct. 1979. Law clk. to hon. Jack B. Weinstein US Dist. Ct. (ea. dist.) NY, Bklyn., 1977-78; assoc. Paul, Weiss, Rifkind, Wharton & Garrison, NYC, 1978-83, Kaye Scholer LLP, NYC, 1983-87, 1987—. Articles editor Columbia Law Rev., 1976—77; contbr. articles to profl. jours. Mem.: ABA, Internat. Tax

Inst. (pres.), Assn. Bar City of NY, NY State Bar Assn. Home: 320 W End Ave New York NY 10023-8110 Office: Kaye Scholer LLP 425 Park Ave New York NY 10022-3506 Office Phone: 212-836-8693. E-mail: wschneider@kayescholer.com.

**SCHNEIDER-CRIEZIS, SUSAN MARIE,** architect; b. St. Louis, Aug. 1, 1953; d. William Alfred and Rosemary Elizabeth (Fischer) Schneider; m. Demetrios Anthony Criezis, Nov. 24, 1978; children: Anthony, John and Andrew. BArch, U. Notre Dame, 1976; MArch, MIT, 1978. Registered architect, Wis. Project designer Eichstaedt Architects, Roselle, Ill., 1978-80, Solomon, Cordwell, Buenz & Assocs., Chgo., 1980-82; project architect Gelick, Foran Assocs., Chgo., 1982-83; asst. prof. Sch. Architecture U. Ill., Chgo., 1980-86; exec. v.p. Criezis Architects, Inc., Northfield, Ill. 1986—2005; dir. cmty. devel. Village of Kenilworth, 2005—. Graham Found. grantee MIT, 1977, MIT scholar, 1976-78; Prestressed Concrete Inst. rsch. grantee, 1981. Mem. AIA, Chgo. Archtl. Club, Chgo. Women in Architecture, Am. Solar Energy Soc., NAFE, Jr. League Evanston, Evanston C. of C. Roman Catholic. Avocations: tennis, swimming. Office: 419 Richmond Rd Kenilworth IL 60043 Office Phone: 847-251-1666. E-mail: scriezis@villageofkenilworth.org.

**SCHNEIDERMAN, ANNE MERCEDES,** lawyer, neurobiologist; b. Ithaca, NY; d. Howard Allen and Audrey MacLeod Schneiderman. JD, Stanford U., Calif., 1997—2000, BS in Biol. Scis. with distinction, 1977; PhD in Neurobiology, Harvard U., Cambridge, Mass., 1984. Registered: US Patent and Trademark Office (patent atty.) 1998, bar: NY 2001, Calif. 2001, Washington, DC 2003; cert. Kripalu Yoga Tchr. Kripalu Ctr. for Yoga & Health, 2005, Notary Public NY, 2004. Asst. prof. neurobiology Cornell U., Ithaca, 1989—96; law clk. Pennie & Edmonds LLP, NYC, 1996—97, law clk., patent agt.. 1998—2000, assoc. atty., 2000—03; legal counsel Advanced Design Consulting, USA, Lansing, NY, 2003—04; of counsel Wall Marjama & Bilinski LLP, Syracuse, NY, 2005—; atty. at law, patent atty. Law Offices of Anne M. Schneiderman PhD, Ithaca, NY, 2004—. Contbr. articles to profl. jours. Recipient Law Star - Law Stars Hall of Fame, Lawcrossing.com, 2005, Nat. Merit Scholar, Nat. Merit Scholarship Corp., 1973-1977, Influential Educator Citation, Cornell U., Merrill Presdl. Scholars Program, 1994, Capranica Found. Award in Neuroethology, Capranica Found., 1987, Finalist, Donald B. Lindsley Prize for Best Doctoral Dissertation in Behavioral Neuroscience, Soc. for Neuroscience, 1985, Best Paper Award, Am. Soc. of Zoologists, Divsn. of Devel. Biology, 1980, Top Ten Coll. Women Award, Condé Nast Publications / Glamour Mag., 1977; fellow Helen Hay Whitney Found. Postdoctoral Fellowship, Helen Hay Whitney Found., 1984-1987, NSF Grad. Fellowship, NSF, 1977-1980, Undergraduate Rsch. Fellowship, Calif. Heart Assn., 1977; Postdoctoral fellow, Yale U., 1984—88. Mem.: ABA, Kripalu Yoga Tchrs. Assn., Tompkins County NY Bar Assn., Soc. for Neuroscience, NY State Bar Assn., Monroe County NY Bar Assn. Office: Law Offices of Anne M Schneiderman PhD PO Box 422 Ithaca NY 14851-0422 Home: 307 Iradell Rd Ithaca NY 14850-9257 Office Phone: 607-227-7263. Office Fax: 815-361-9050. E-mail: anne@schneidermanlaw.com.

**SCHNEIDERMAN, IRWIN,** lawyer; b. NYC, May 28, 1923; s. Meyer and Bessie (Klein) S.; m. Roberta Haig, Nov. 28, 1966; 1 child, Eric T. BA, Bklyn. Coll., 1943; LLB cum laude, Harvard U., 1948; DHL (hon.), Bklyn. Coll., 1993. Bar: NY 1949, D.C. 1952. Assoc. Cahill Gordon & Reindel, NYC, 1948-59, ptnr., 1959-89, sr. counsel, 1990—. Spl. cons. to chmn. SEC, 1981-82, mem. adv. com. on tender offers, 1983. Trustee Bklyn. Coll. Found., 1983—, N.Y. Ctrl Park Conservancy, 2004; chmn. N.Y.C. Opera, 1993-2004, chmn. emeritus, 2004—; bd. dirs. WNYC Radio, 1989—, NARAL-Pro-Choice, N.Y.C., 1990—, Lincoln Ctr. for Performing Arts, Inc., 1994-2004, dir. emeritus; chmn. NARAL-Pro-Choice N.Y. Found., 1998-. Lt. (j.g.) USNR, 1943-46. Mem. Harvard Club. Home: 203 E 72nd St New York NY 10021-4568 Office: Cahill Gordon & Reindel 80 Pine St Fl 17 New York NY 10005-1790 Office Phone: 212-701-3800. Personal E-mail: irwinschneiderman@yahoo.com.

**SCHNEIDERMAN, JULIUS,** retired orthopedic surgeon; b. N.Y.C., Dec. 3, 1914; s. Michael and Annie Schneiderman; children: Peter, Stephen. BA, Ind. U., 1936. Emeritus N.Y. Hosp., Queens, NY, L.I. Jewish Hosp., Queens. Maj. U.S. Army, 1943—46. Home: 6800 Gulf of Mexico Dr Longboat Key FL

**SCHNEIDERS, RICHARD J.,** food service company executive; b. Remsen, Iowa, 1948; m. Beth Schneiders; 2 children. BA in Maths., U. Iowa, 1970. Dir. supplies and equipment, v.p.; exec. v.p. Sysco Corp., Memphis, 1982-88; pres., CEO, chmn. Hardin's Sysco Food Services, LLC, Memphis, 1988—92; sr. v.p. merchandising svcs. Sysco Corp., Houston, 1992—97, sr. v.p. corp. merchandising svcs. and multi-unit sales, 1997—99, exec. v.p. foodservice ops., 1999-2000, pres., COO, 2000—03, chmn. CEO, 2003—, pres., 2005—. Bd. dirs. Aviall, Inc. Office: Sysco Corp 1390 Enclave Pkwy Houston TX 77077-2099 E-mail: schneiders.rick@corp.sysco.com.

**SCHNEIER, BRUCE,** information technology executive; BS in Physics, U. Rochester; MS in Computer Sci., Am. U. Founder, chief info. officer Counterpane Internet Security, Calif. Adv. bd. Electronic Privacy Info. Ctr.; bd. dir. Internat. Assn. Cryptologic Rsch., Voter's Telcom Watch. Author: Protect Your Macintosh, 1994, E-Mail Security, 1995, Applied Cryptography, 1995, The Twofish Encryption Algorithm, 1996, The Electronic Privacy Papers, 1997, Secrets and Lies, 2000, Practical Cryptography, 2003, Beyond Fear, 2003; contbr. articles to newspapers; author: Crypto-Gram, monthly newsletter. Named one of top 25 CTOs, InfoWorld Media Group. Office: Counterpane Internet Security 1090 LaAvenida Ave Mountain View CA 94043 Office Phone: 612-823-1098. E-mail: schneier@counterpane.com.*

**SCHNEIROV, ALLISON R.,** lawyer; b. Phila., 1966; BA magna cum laude, U. Pa. 1988; JD cum laude, NYU, 1991. Bar: N.Y. 1992. Atty. Skadden, Arps, Slate, Meagher & Flom LLP, N.Y., 1993—. Office: Skadden Arps Slate Meagher & Flom LLP Four Times Sq New York NY 10036

**SCHNEITER, GEORGE MALAN,** professional golfer, real estate developer; b. Ogden, Utah, Aug. 12, 1931; s. George Henery and Bernice Slade (Malan) S.; m. JoAnn Deakin, Jan. 19, 1954; children: George, Gary, Dan, Steve, Elizabeth Ann, Michael. BS in Banking and Fin., U. Utah, 1955. With 5th Army Championship Golf Team, U.S. Army, 1955-56; assoc. golf pro Hidden Valley Golf Club, Salt Lake City, 1957; golf pro Lake Hills Golf Club, Billings, Mont., 1957-90, sec., 1957-61, pres., 1964-90, Schneiter Enterprises, Sandy, Utah, 1974—; developer Schneiter's Golf Course, 1973—, and subdiv., 1961—; player PGA tour, 1958-78, Sr. PGA tour, 1981—. Missionary So. State Mission, LDS Ch., 1951-52. Served with U.S. Army, 1955-56. Named winner, Utah sect. Sr. Championship, Wyo., Open Super Sr. Championship, Salt Lake City Parks Tournament, Vernal Brigham Payson Open, Yuma Open, Utah Sr. PGA Chamption, Utah Super Sr. Championship, World Pro Am., Kona, Hawaii, Ft. Carson Golf Championship; fellow Banking & Fin. fellow, First Security Bank Utah, 1953. Mem. PGA, Salt Lake City C. of C., Intermountain Golf Courst Supertaints Assn. also: 8968 S 1300 E Sandy UT 84094 Office: 2009 Brassy Dr Las Vegas NV 89142-2033 Fax: 801-567-0408. Office Phone: 801-232-5488.

**SCHNELL, CARLTON BRYCE,** lawyer; b. Youngstown, Ohio, Jan. 1, 1932; s. Carlton Wilhelm and Helen Jean (Alexander) S.; m. Dorothy Stewart Apple, Aug. 15, 1953; children— Laura, Margaret, Heidi BA, Yale U., 1953, LL.B., 1956. Bar: Ohio 1956. Assoc. Arter & Hadden, Cleve., 1956-65, 1991, 1966-96, mng. ptnr., 1977-82, Washington, 1982-84. Exec. comm. mem. Greater Cleve. Growth Assn., Cleve., 1983-97; chmn. Build Up Cleve., 1981-89; profl. chmn. United Way, Cleve., 1983; co-chmn. Charter Rev. Commn., Cleve., 1983-84; pres. Citizen's League Rsch. Inst., 1992-95. Named Vol. of Yr., Leadership Cleve., 1985. Mem. Tex. Club Cleve. (pres. 1972-73), Cleve Tax Inst. (chmn. 1978), Ohio C. of C. (trustee 1977-80) Clubs: Tavern, Pepper Pike. Republican. Presbyterian. Avocations: golf, tennis. Home: 31450 Shaker Blvd Pepper Pike OH 44124-5153

**SCHNELL, FREDERICK MARK,** oncologist, hematologist; b. Cleve., Apr. 2, 1948; s. Frederick Raymond and Cora Belle Schnell; m. Kim Diane Taylor, Nov. 17, 1973; children: Frederick Joseph, Elizabeth Anne, David Brandon. MD, Case Western Res. U. Sch. Medicine, Cleve., 1974. Lic. Ohio 1974. Medical oncologist Ctrl. Ga. Cancer Care PC. Pres. Cmty. Oncology Alliance, Washington, 2006—; chair bd. dir. GA-CORE, Atlanta, 2001—. Mem. Mt. de Sales Acad., Inc., Macon, Ga., 2001—06. Mem.: Am. Soc. Clin. Oncology (mem. clin. practice com. 2002—05). Office: Ctrl Ga Cancer Care PC 1062 Forsyth St Macon GA 31201 Office Phone: 478-743-7068. Office Fax: 478-741-1354.

**SCHNELL, GEORGE ADAM,** geographer, educator; b. Phila., July 13, 1931; s. Earl Blackwood and Emily (Bernheimer) S.; m. Mary Lou Williams, June 21, 1958; children: David Adam, Douglas Powell, Thomas Earl. BS, West Chester U., 1958; MS, Pa. State U., 1960, PhD, 1965; postdoctoral study, Ohio State U., 1965. Asst. prof. SUNY, New Paltz, 1962-65, assoc. prof., 1965-68, prof. geography, 1968-99, founding chmn. dept., 1984-94, prof. emeritus, 1999—. Adj. prof. SUNY, 2000—; vis. assoc. prof. U. Hawaii, summer, 1966; cons. cmty. action programming, 1965; manuscript reader, cons. to several pubs., 1967—; founder, founding bd. dirs., investigator Inst. for Devel., Planning and Land Use Studies, 1986-96; cons. Mid-Hudson Pattern for Progress, 1986, Open Space Inst., 1987, Mid-Hudson Regional Econ. Devel. Coun., 1989, Urban Devel. Corp., 1989-90, 93, Tech. Devel. Ctr., 1991, Catskill Ctr., 1991, Ednl. Testing Svc., 1993-94, 96, 97; cons. editor Exams Unltd., Albany, N.Y., 1995-99; ind. contractor and cons. Excelsior U., 2003-; founding mem. exec. bd. dirs Hudson Valley Study Ctr., 1995-98; cons. several depts. geography, 1988—, Pa. Geog. Alliance, 1999; ind. contractor Excelsior U., 2003, cons., 2004; presenter in field. Author. (with others) the Local Community: A Handbook for Teachers, 1971, The World's Population, Problems of Growth, 1972; contbr. Pennsylvania Coal: Resources, Technology, Utilization, 1983, West Virginia and Appalachia: Selected Readings, 1977, Hazardous and Toxic Wastes: Technology, Management and Health Effects, 1984, Environmental Radon: Occurrence, Control and Health Hazards, 1990, Natural and Technological Disasters: Causes, Effects and Preventive Measures, 1992, Conservation and Resource Management, 1993, Medicine and Health Care into the 21st Century, 1995, Forests: A Global Perspective, 1996, (with M.S. Monmonier) Ecology of the Wetlands and Associated Systems, 1998, (with M.S. Monmonier) Renewable Energy: Trends and Prospects, 2002; co-author: (with M.S. Monmonier) The Study of Population: Elements, Patterns, Processes, 1983, Map Appreciation, 1988; editor, contbr.: (with G.J. Demko and H.M. Rose) Population Geography: A Reader, 1970; contbr. articles to profl. jours. Appt. mem. local bds. and coms. Town and Village New Paltz, New Paltz Ctrl. Sch. Dist., 1965-2003; elder Reformed Ch. New Paltz; Rep. committeeman Town of Gardiner, Ulster County, NY, 2000-01; trustee Gardiner (NY) Pub. Libr., 2005-. With AUS, 1952-54. Recipient Excellence award N.Y. State/United Univ. Professions, 1994; Disting. Alumnus award West Chester U., 1994. Mem. Assn. Am. Geographers, Pa. Geog. Soc. (mem. editl. bd. Pa. Geographer, Disting. Geographer award 1994), Pa. Acad. Sci. (assoc. editor jour. 1988-2005), Nat. Coun. for Geog. Edn., Paltz Club. Home: 29 River Park Dr New Paltz NY 12561-2636 Office: SUNY at New Paltz Dept Geography 75 S Manheim Blvd New Paltz NY 12561-2400 Personal E-mail: georgeschnell@msn.com.

**SCHNELL, ROBERT LEE, JR.,** lawyer; b. Mpls., Sept. 20, 1948; s. Robert Lee and Dorothy Mae (Buran) S.; m. Jacqueline Irene Husak, Dec. 19, 1969 (div. Aug. 1988); children: Robert Lee III, Elizabeth Anne, Jennifer Irene; m. Julie Ann Bemlott, Sept. 29, 1989; children: Helen Bridget, Michael Henry. BA cum laude, Princeton U., 1970; JD magna cum laude, Harvard U., 1974. Bar: Minn. 1974, U.S. Dist. Ct. Minn. 1974, U.S. Ct. Appeals (8th cir.) 1975, U.S. Supreme Ct. 1990. Assoc. Faegre & Benson, Mpls., 1974-81, ptnr., 1982—. Bd. dirs. United Way of Mpls., 1992-93. Office: Faegre & Benson 2200 Wells Fargo Ctr 90 S St Ste 2200 Minneapolis MN 55402-1109 Office Phone: 612-766-7225. E-mail: rschnell@faegre.com.

**SCHNELL, ROGER THOMAS,** small business owner, retired state official; b. Wabasha, Minn., Dec. 11, 1936; s. Donald William and Eva Louise (Barton) Schnell; m. Barbara Ann McDonald, Dec. 18, 1959 (div. Mar. 1968); children: Thomas Allen, Scott Douglas. A in Mil. Sci., Command and Gen. Staff Coll., 1975; A in Bus. Administn., Wayland Bapt. U., 1987. Commd. 2d lt. Alaska N.G., 1959, advanced through grades to col., 1975, shop supt. Anchorage, 1965-71, personnel mgr., 1972-74, chief of staff, 1974-87, dir. logistics, 1987; electrician Alaska R.R., Anchorage, 1955-61, elec. foreman, 1962-64; dir. support personnel mgmt. Joint Staff Alaska N.G., 1988-92, ret.; personnel mgr. State of Alaska, 1992, asst. commr. dept. mil. and vets. affairs Ft. Richardson, 1992-95, dep. commr. dept. mil. and vets. affairs, 1995-98, 2002—; owner RTS Enterprises, Anchorage, 1999—. Prin., owner RTS Enterprises, 1999—; adv. bd. state joint armed svc. com. State of Alaska, 2001—; dep. commr. dept. Mil. and Vet. Affairs, 2003—. Chmn. Alaska Nat. Guard Mus. Trust Fund, 2001—02; appointed to Gov.'s State Seismic Hazard Safety Commn., 2005—; chmn. pastor parish rels. com. Meth. 1st Ch., 2001—02; bd. dirs. Meth. Trust Fund, 2002—04. Mem. Fed. Profl. Labor Relations Execs. (sec. 1974-75), Alaska N.G. Officers Assn. (pres. 1976-78, bd. dirs. 1988—), Assn. U.S. Army (corp.), NG Assn. U.S. (life, retiree rep. from Alaska 1993—), Am. Legion, Amvets, Elks. Republican. Methodist. Avocations: travel, photography. Home and Office: Huntwood Park Estates 6817 Queens View Cir Anchorage AK 99504-5203 Personal E-mail: rogertschnell@gci.net, rtschnellenterprises@gci.net.

**SCHNELLDORFER, THOMAS,** surgeon; arrived in US, 2001; MD, U. Ulm, Germany, 2001. Lic. S.C., 2001, Minn., 2006. Resident gen. surgery Med. U. S.C., Charleston, SC, 2001—06; fellow gastrointestinal surgery Mayo Clinic, Rochester, Minn., 2006— Contbr. articles to profl. jours. Named to America's Top Surgeons, Consumers' Rsch. Coun. Am., 2004; recipient Student Abstract prize, Am. Gastroent. Assn., 1999, Young Investigator award, Internat. Electrogastrography Soc., 2006, Poster of Distinction award, Am. Hepato-Pancreato-Biliary Assn., 2006, Gold Medal Forum award, Southeastern Surg. Congress, 2006; grantee, German Academic Exch. Svc., 2000. Mem.: AMA, ACS, Zumbro Valley Med. Soc., Minn. Med. Assn., Assn. Academic Surgery, Am. Hepato-Pancreato-Biliary Assn., Soc. Surgery Alimentary Tract, Mayo Fellows' Assn., Pancreas Club. Achievements include research in defining the role of glutathione for cell growth and radiochemotherapy in pancreatic cancer; describing outcome for operative management of chronic pancreatitis. Office: Mayo Clinic 200 First Street SW Rochester MN 55905 Office Phone: 507-284-2511.

**SCHNELLE, KARL BENJAMIN, JR.,** chemical engineering professor, consultant, researcher; b. Canton, Ohio, Dec. 8, 1930; s. Karl Benjamin and Kathryn Emily (Hollingsworth) S.; m. Mary Margaret Dabney, Sept. 8, 1954; children: Karl Dabney, Kathryn Chappell. BS, Carnegie Mellon U., 1952, MS, 1957, PhD, 1959. Registered profl. engr., Tenn. Chem. engr., shift foreman Organics area Pitts. Plate Glass Co., New Martinsville, W.Va., 1952-54; asst. prof. chem. engring. Vanderbilt U., Nashville, 1958—61, assoc. prof., 1961—64, assoc. prof. environ. and air resources engring., 1967—70, prof., 1970—80, chmn. divsn. socio-tech. sys., 1972—75, chmn. environ. and water resources engring., 1975—76; mgr. edn. svcs. Instrument Soc. Am., Pitts., 1964—67; chmn. environ. engring. and policy mgmt. dept. Vanderbilt U., 1976—80, chmn. chem. engring., 1980—88, prof. chem. and environ. engring., 1980—; Alexander Heard disting. svc. prof., 1995-96. V.p. ECCE, Nashville, 1983-88, pres., 1989—; mem. Air Pollution Control Bd., State Tenn., 1978-82, 82-87; Fulbright prof. U. Liege, Belgium, 1977; invited prof. Universite Catholique de Louvain, Belgium, 1982; vis. prof. chem. engring. Danish Tech. Inst., Lyngby, Denmark, 1988-89. Fellow AICE; mem. Air and Waste Mgmt. Assn. (Lyman A. Ripperton Environ. Educator award 2006), Instrument Soc. Am. (mgr. edn. and rsch. 1964-67), Am. Soc. Engring. Edn., Am. Soc. Environ. Engrs., Sigma Xi, Phi Kappa Phi, Tau Beta Pi. Office: Vanderbilt U VU Station B 351604 Nashville TN 37235-1604 Office Phone: 615-322-3370. Business E-mail: karl.b.schnelle@vanderbilt.edu.

**SCHNELLE, PHILLIP DAVID,** electrical engineer, consultant; b. Orange, Tex., Feb. 29, 1952; s. Philip Davis and Mary (Lyons) Schnelle; m. Janie Lou Wilson, June 17, 1972; children: Brandy Glennon, Elisabeth, Phillip. MSEE, U. Del., Newark, 1975. Registered Profl. Engr., Tex., 1982. Cons. DuPont Engring. Project Group, Wilmington, Del., 1974—80; sr. cons. DuPont Engring. Services Divsn., Beaumont, Tex., 1980—85; prin. cons. DuPont Engring. Tech., Wilmington, Del., 1985—. Lyme disease activist London Britian Twp., Landenberg, Pa., 1990—. Recipient Engring. Excellence Award, DuPont Co., 2001. Mem.: Instrumental Soc. of Am. Achievements include research in dynamic modeling, advanced control applications (regulatory and MPC), data modeling (neural networks MVS and TSA)and interfaces between SPC and APC (Lab Feedback Control and Performance Monitoring). Avocations: fishing, sailing.

**SCHNELLER, EUGENE STEWART,** health administration and policy educator; b. Cornwall, NY, Apr. 9, 1943; s. Michael Nicholas and Anne Ruth (Gruner) Schneller; m. Ellen Stauber, Mar. 24, 1968; children: Andrew Jon, Lee Stauber. AA, SUNY, Buffalo, 1965; BA, LI U., 1967; PhD, NYU, 1973; grad. physician assoc. (hon.), Duke U., 2004. Rsch. asst. dept. sociology NYU, N.Y.C., 1968-70; project dir. Montefiore Hosp. and Med. Ctr., Bronx, NY, 1970-72; asst. prof. Med. Ctr. and sociology Duke U., Durham, NC, 1973-75; assoc. prof., chmn. dept. sociology Union Coll., Schenectady, 1975-79, assoc. prof., dir. Health Studies Ctr., 1979-85; prof., dir. Sch. Health Mgmt. and Policy, Ariz. State U., Tempe, 1985—91, assoc. dean rsch. and adminstrn. Coll. Bus., 1992-94; dir. L. William Seidman Rsch. Ctr., Tempe, 1992-94, counselor to pres. for health profl. edn., 1994-96; clin. prof. cmty. and family medicine U. Ariz., 1995-96, clin. prof. prevention, rsch., 1997—2002; prof., dir. Sch. Health Mgmt. and Policy W.P. Carey Sch. Bus. Ariz. State U., 1996—2002, prof. Sch. Health Mgmt. and Policy, 2003—; prin. Health Care Sector Supply Chain Initiatives, 2002—; prin. Health Care Sector Advances, 2004—. Mem. health rsch. coun. N.Y. State Dept. Health, 1977—85; vis. rsch. scholar Columbia U., N.Y.C., 1983—84; fellow Accrediting Commn. Edn. Health Svcs. Adminstrn., 1983—84; chmn. Western Network Edn. Health Adminstrn., Berkeley, Calif., 1987—92; commr. Calif. Commn. Future Med. Edn., 1996—97; mem. Ariz. Medicaid Adv. Bd., 1990—92, Ariz. Data Adv. Bd., 1989—91, Ariz. Health Care Group Adv. Bd., 1989. Author: The Physician's Assistant, 1980; mem. editl. bd. Work and Occupations, 1975—93, Hosps. and Health Svcs. Adminstrn., 1989—92, Health Adminstrn. Press, 1991—94, Health Mgmt. Rev., 1996, Electronic Hallway, 1999; contbr. articles to profl. jours., chapters to books. Trustee Barrow Neurol. Inst., Phoenix, 1989—95; chair nat. adv. com. Investigator Awards Health Svcs. Rsch. Robert Wood Johnson Found., 1993—96. Mem.: APHA, Pharm. and Therapeutics Soc. (trustee 1999—2005, sec. 1999—2005), Assn. Univ. Health Programs Health Adminstrn. (bd. dirs. 1990—96, chmn. bd. dirs. 1994—95), Am. Sociol. Assn. Home: 4163 N 114th Way Scottsdale AZ 85259-2609 Office: Ariz State U Sch Health Mgmt and Policy WP Carey Sch Bus Tempe AZ 85287 Office Phone: 602-320-1512. Business E-Mail: gene.schneller@asu.edu.

**SCHNELLER, MARINA VELENTGAS,** lawyer; b. Portland, Maine, Feb. 24, 1943; d. Peter Constantine and Katherine Rena (Zolotas) Velentgas; 3 children. AB, Smith Coll., 1965; MS, U. Vt., 1968; JD, Am. U., 1972. Bar: Va. 1972, D.C. 1973, U.S. Patent & Trademark Office, U.S. Ct. Appeals (DC cir.), U.S. Supreme Ct. Atty. Cushman Darby & Cushman, Washington, 1974-80; pvt. practice, 1980-82; tech. asst. Cir. Judge Nies US Ct. Appeals, Washington, 1982-84; counsel Mobil Oil Corp., Fairfax, Va., 1984-98; ptnr., Patent Prosecution, Intellectual Property Group Venable LLP, Washington, 1998—. Lectr. George Mason Univ. Sch. Law. Adv. bd. mem. BNA U.S. Patents Quarterly, Washington; contbr. articles to profl. jours. Coach Alexandria (Va.) Soccer Assn., 1986-89, 91-93. Mem. Am. Chem. Soc. (Am. Chemists Medal 1961), ABA, Am. Intellectual Property Law Assn. (patent law com. 2005-), Patent Lawyers Club, Women Patent Lawyers Club, Hellenic Lawyers Assn. (pres.), Sigma Xi. Office: Venable LLP 575 7th St NW Washington DC 20004 Office Phone: 202-344-4062. Office Fax: 202-344-8300. Business E-Mail: mvschneller@venable.com.

**SCHNEPF, HARRY ERNEST,** microbiologist, consultant; b. Chula Vista, Calif., Feb. 1, 1952; s. Harry Ernest and Jane Voorhees Schnepf; m. Cameron Lee Fosterling, July 8, 1955; children: Sidney Lee, Kai Dale. BA, U. Calif., La Jolla, Calif., 1977; PhD, U. Wash., Seattle, 1984. Post-doctoral fellow, dept. microbiology and immunology U. Wash., Seattle, 1984—90; from rsch. scientist to sci. fellow Mycogen Corp., San Diego, 1990—99, sci. fellow, 1996; rsch. scientist, sci. leader, subject matter expert Dow AgroSciences, LLC, San Diego, 1999—2002; ind. cons. in field San Diego, 2003—. Fellow, Achievement Rewards Coll. Scientists Found., 1984. Mem.: Am. Soc. Microbiology. Achievements include first to clone insecticidal protein genes from Bacillus thuringiensis, leading ultimately to genetically engineered insect resistant plants, such as cotton and corn; 43 patents in field. Avocations: piano, gardening. Personal E-mail: eschnep1@san.rr.com.

**SCHNEPS, JACK,** physics professor, department chairman; b. NYC, Aug. 18, 1929; s. Elias and Rose (Rephen) S.; m. Lucia De Marchi, Mar. 11, 1960; children: Loredana, Melissa, Leila. BA, N.Y. U., 1951; MS, U. Wis., 1953, PhD, 1956. Asst. prof. physics Tufts U., 1956-60, assoc. prof., 1960-63, prof., 1963—, chmn. dept. physics, 1980-89, Vannevar Bush chair, 1995—. Vis. scientist European Orgn. Nuc. Rsch., Geneva, Switzerland, 1965-66; lectr. Internat. Sch. Elementary Particle Physics, Yugoslavia, 1968; vis. rsch. fellow Univ. Coll., London, Eng., 1973-74; vis. prof. Ecole Polytechnique, Palaiseau, France, 1982-83, The Technion, Haifa, Israel, 1989-90, Coll. de France, Paris, 1997; chmn. Internat. Neutrino Com., 2002—; vis. scholar Harvard U., 2005-06. Contbg. author: Methods in Subnuclear Physics, Vol. IV, 1970; editor Proc. of Neutrino 88, 1989; contbr. articles to profl. jours. NSF postdoctoral fellow U. Padua, Italy, 1958-59. Fellow Am. Phys. Soc.; mem. Europe an Phys. Soc., AAUP, Phi Beta Kappa, Sigma Xi. Home: 3 Foxcroft Rd Winchester MA 01890-2407 Office: Dept Physics Tufts U Medford MA 02155 Office Phone: 617-627-3374. E-mail: jacob.schneps@tufts.edu.

**SCHNEIDERS, RICHARD J.,** food products executive; b. Remsen, Iowa; 2 children. BA in Math., U. Iowa 1970. With exec. devel. program SYSCO Corp., Memphis, 1982; dir. supplies and equipment, v.p. merchandising and exec. v.p., promoted to pres., CEO, 1988, chmn., sr. v.p. merchandising svcs. dept. Houston, 1992, responsible multi-unit sales, dir. corp., 1997, exec. v.p. food svc. ops., 1998, pres., COO, 2000—03, chmn., CEO, 2003—. Mem. Aviall Inc. (bd. dirs.). Office: SYSCO Corp 1390 Enclave Pkwy Houston TX 77077-2099*

**SCHNITZLER, STEVEN C.,** lawyer; b. Balt., Apr. 6, 1962; BA, U. Md., 1984; JD cum laude, Touro Coll., 1988. Bar: Conn. 1988, NY 1989, DC 1990. Assoc. corp. fin. dept. Debevoise & Plimpton, NYC, 1988—94; ptnr. corp. group Crowell & Moring LLP, Washington, DC, 1994—2001; ptnr. Katten Muchin Zavis Rosenman, Washington, DC, 2001—. Office: Katten Muchin Zavis Rosenman E Lobby, Ste 700 1025 Thomas Jefferson St, NW Washington DC 20007 Office Phone: 202-625-3605. Office Fax: 202-339-8293. E-mail: steven.schnitzer@kmzr.com.

**SCHNITZLER, ROBERT NEIL,** cardiologist; b. Bklyn., Dec. 12, 1940; BA, N.Y. Heights Coll. Arts & Sci., N.Y.C., 1961; MD, SUNY, Buffalo, 1965. Lic. physician, N.Y., Tex.; diplomate Am. Bd. Cardiovascular Diseases; cert. specialty Bd. Internal Medicine, sub-specialty Bd. Cardiovascular Medicine, Bd. Clin. Cardiac Electrophysiology. Intern Kings-County Downstate Med. Ctr., Bklyn., 1965-66, resident, 1966-67, N.Y. Hosp.-Cornell Med. Ctr., N.Y.C., 1967-68; asst. physician N.Y. Hosp., N.Y.C., 1967-68; trainee, fellow U. Rochester (N.Y.) Med. Ctr., 1968-70; asst. physician Strong Meml. Hosp., Rochester, 1968-69; dir. med. intensive care units Bexar County Hosp. and Audie L. Murphy VA Hosp., San Antonio, 1973-76; dir. cardiac intensive care units, 1976-77; pres. Cardiovascular Inst. for Continuing Med. Edn. and Rsch., San Antonio, 1983—; pvt. practice cardiology San Antonio, 1977—. Asst. instr. U. Rochester Med. Sch., Strong Meml. Hosp., 1968-69, instr., 1969-70; rsch. assoc. USPHS Hosp., S.I., 1970-72; assoc. attending physician

St. Vincent's Hosp., S.I., 1971-72; asst. prof. U. Tex. Health Sci. Ctr., San Antonio, 1972-76, assoc. prof., 1977, clin. assoc. prof., 1977-83, clin. prof., 1983—; cons. electrophysiology USAF Wilford Hall Med. Ctr., San Antonio, 1979—; chief staff S.W. Tex. Meth. Hosp., 1992, chief cardiology Methodist Specialty and Transplant Hosp., Tex., 2001-. Contbr. articles to profl. jours. Mem. adv. bd. health City of San Antonio, 1987—; med. coor. City of San Antonio Internat. Drug Summit, 1992. Surgeon USPHS, 1968-70. Fellow ACP, Am. Coll. Cardiology, Am. Coll. Chest Physicians, Coun. of Clin. Cardiology Am. Heart Assn., Soc. Cardiovascular Angiography and Intervention; mem. N.Y. Acad. Scis., N.Y. Heart Assn., Assn. for Advancement Med. Instrumentation, Am. Fedn. Clin. Rsch., Emergency Med. Soc., Coun., Heart Rhythm Soc., Heart Failure Soc., S.W. Tex. Angioplasty Soc., Am. Coll. Angiology, Internat. Soc. Heart and Lung Transplantation, Soc. Cardiac Angiography and Interventions, Am. Soc. Internal Medicine, Alpha Omega Alpha. Achievements include research in internal medicine, cardiology and vascular diseases and electrophysiology. Home and Office: 4330 Medical Dr Ste 400 San Antonio TX 78229-3324 Office Phone: 210-615-0600.

**SCHNOBRICH, ROGER WILLIAM,** lawyer; b. New Ulm, Minn., Dec. 21, 1929; s. Arthur George and Amanda (Reinhart) Schnobrich; m. Angeline Ann Schmitz, Jan. 21, 1961; children: Julie A. Johnson, Jennifer L. Holmers, Kathryn M. Kubinski, Karen L. Holetz. BBA, U. Minn., 1952, JD, 1954. Bar: Minn. 1954. Assoc. Fredrikson and Byron, Mpls., 1956-58; pvt. practice Mpls., 1958-60; ptnr. Popham Haik, Schnobrich & Kaufman, Mpls., 1960-97, Hinshaw & Culbertson, Mpls., 1997—2004; officer Cooperative Agy., Inc., Richfield, Minn., 2004—. Bd. dirs. numerous corps. With U.S. Army, 1954—56. Mem.: ABA, Hennepin County Bar Assn., Minn. Bar Assn., Order of Coif. Roman Catholic. Avocations: jogging, reading, golf. Home: 530 Waycliff Dr N Wayzata MN 55391-1385 Office: Gramercy Corporation 6640 Lyndale Ave S Ste 100 Minneapolis MN 55423-2385 E-mail: rnapana@aol.com.

**SCHNOEBELEN, ANNE MARY,** musicologist, educator; b. Tomahawk, Wis., Aug. 4, 1933; d. Herman Sabas and Katherine Alma (Yenor) Schnoebelen; m. John Albert Meixner, May 7, 1980. BA, Rosary Coll., 1958; MusM, U. Ill., 1960, PhD, 1966. From chmn. dept. musicology to prof. emerita Shepherd Sch. Music Rice U., Houston, 1974—2004, interim dean, 1981, 2002—03, prof. emerita Shepherd Sch. Music, 2004—. Author: Padre Martini's Collection of Letters in the Civico Museo Bibliografico Musicale: An Annotated Index, 1979; editor: Cantatas by Maurizio Cazzati in the Italian Cantata in the Seventeenth Century, 1985, Solo Motets from the Seventeenth Century, 10 vols., 1987—89, Seventeenth Century Italian Sacred Music, 10 vols., 1995—99; contbr. articles to profl. jours. Fellow, Fulbright, 1964; grantee, NEH, 1969, 1983; Travel grant, Am. Coun. Learned Societies, 1984. Fellow: AAUW; mem.: Am. Musicol. Soc. (coun. sec. 1986—88). Home: 2001 Holcombe Blvd #702 Houston TX 77030-4214 Office Phone: 713-348-4217. Business E-Mail: aschnoeb@rice.edu.

**SCHNOLL, HOWARD MANUEL,** financial consultant, investment company executive; b. Milw., June 6, 1935; s. Nathan P. and Della (Fisher) Schnoll; m. Barbara Ostach, Dec. 3, 1988; children: Jordan, Terry, Jeffrey, Robert, Tammy, Daniel. BBA, U. Wis., 1958. CPA Wis.; cert. mgmt. cons., registered investment advisor. Mng. ptnr. Nankin, Schnoll & Co., S.C., Milw., 1966-86; mng. ptnr., bd. dirs BDO Seidman, 1986-90; pres., COO Universal Med. Bldgs., L.P., Milw., 1990, also bd. dirs.; pres. Howard Schnoll & Assocs., Milw., 1991; mng. dir. Grande, Schnoll & Assocs., Milw., 1992-93; exec. mng. dir., COO Glaisner, Schilffarth, Grande & Schnoll, Ltd., Milw., 1993-98; exec. v.p., treas., bd. dirs. GS2 Securities, Inc., Milw., 1998—2004; sr. v.p. B. C. Ziegler and Co., Milw., 1999—, mng. dir., 2005—. Bd. dirs. Milw. World Festival, Inc., 1968—pres., 2003—, chmn. bd., 2005—; bd. dirs. City of Festivals Parade, Milw., 1983—89, Aurora Health Care Ventures, Milw. Heart Rsch. Found., Milw., Milw. Heart Inst., Arthritis Found.; pres. Impact, 1993—, bd. dirs.; pres., treas. Am. Heart Assn., Milw., 1978—82; capt. United Way, Milw., 1985; mem. greater Milw. com. Nat. Found. Ileitis and Colitis. Served to sgt. U.S. Army, 1956—63. Mem.: AICPA, Acct. Computer Users Tech. Exchange, Wis. Inst. CPAs, B'nai Brith (pres. 1960—62), Boca Grove Golf and Tennis (bd. dirs. 2003—, treas. 2006—, v.p. 2005—), Brynwood Country Club (pres. 1988—2000, bd. dirs., treas.). Jewish. Avocations: golf, tennis. Office: BC Ziegler & Co 250 E Wisconsin Ave Ste 2000 Milwaukee WI 53202-4298 Office Phone: 414-978-6503. Business E-Mail: hschnoll@ziegler.com.

**SCHNOOR, JEFFREY ARNOLD,** lawyer; b. Winnipeg, Man., Can., June 22, 1953; s. Toby and Ray (Kass) S. BA, U. Man., 1974, LLB, 1977. Bar: Man. 1978. Assoc. McJannet Weinberg Rich, Winnipeg, 1977-84, ptnr., 1984-86; exec. dir. Man. Law Reform Commn., Winnipeg, 1986-97; dir. criminal justice policy Man. Dept. Justice, Winnipeg, 1998—2002, exec. dir. policy devel. and analysis, 2003—, asst. dep. min. cts. divsn., 2005—. Pres. Fedn. Law Reform Agys. Can., 1995-98; del. Uniform Law Conf. Can. 1986-2003, exec. com. 1996-2001, chair civil sect., 1996-97, v.p., 1998-99, pres., 1999-2000. Trustee United Way of Winnipeg, 1990-97, 99-2005, exec. com., 1997-99, 2001-05, treas., 1991-92, pres., 1994-95, cmty. rels. com. 1995-98, chmn. 1996-97, chair United Way 2005 com., 1997-98, hon. solicitor, 2001-05, chmn 211 implementation com., 2001—; mem. R&D 2000 steering com., United Way of Can., 1995-98; bd. dirs. Winnipeg Libr. Found., 1997-2001, St. Boniface Gen. Hosp., 2005—; Man. Voluntary Sector Coun., 2001-04, U. Man. Winnipeg area study adv. group, 2001-04. Named Queen's Counsel Govt. of Man., 1992; recipient Chair's award of distinction United Way of Can., 1997. Mem. Law Soc. Man. (lectr. bar admission course 1981-96), Man. Bar Assn. (life, governing coun. 1988-96, recipient Cmty. Svc. award 1999), Can. Bar Assn. (legis. and law reform com. 1994-2000, 01—03, vice-chair 1997-2000, chair 2001-03, nat mag. editl. bd. 2002—). Avocations: travel, languages, performing arts, exercise. Office: 235-405 Broadway Winnipeg MB Canada R3C 3L6 Office Phone: 204-945-3027. E-mail: jschnoor@gov.mb.ca.

**SCHNOOR, JON PETER,** military officer; b. Norfolk, Nebr., Jan. 30, 1959; s. Melvin Irvin and Vera Schnoor; m. Patricia Michelle DuBeau, Mar. 31, 1979; children: Michael Joshua, Peter Irvin. BS, Ferris State U. Registered Sanitarian Nat. Environ. Health Assn. Hosp. corpsman U.S. Coast Guard, Kodiak, Alaska, 1979—91; environ. health officer U.S. Pub. Health Svc., Governers Island, NY, 1991—96, CDC Vessel Sanitation Program, Ft Lauderdale, Fla., 1996—2003, asst. dep. chief, 2003—. Comdr. U.S. Coast Guard, US Pub. Health Svc., 1977—2006, Governers Island, NY; Ft Lauderdale, FL. Decorated CG Commendation USCG, PHS Commendation USPH, PHS Achieve. Mem.: Nat. Environ. Health Assn. (licentiate), Uniformed Svcs. Environ. Health Assn. (assoc.; pres. 2003—05). Home: 16300 SW 101 Ave Miami FL 33157 Office: CDC Vessel Sanitation Program 1850 Eller Dr Ste 101 Fort Lauderdale FL 33316 Office Phone: 954-356-6650.

**SCHNOOR, NEAL HENRY,** music educator; b. Norfolk, Nebr., July 19, 1966; s. Walden Lowell and Ann Magdalene (Zach) Schnoor; m. Teresa Lynn Travis, Sept. 8, 1965; children: Rachel Ann, Graham Ronald. BFA in Edn., Wayne State Coll., Detroit, 1990; MusM, U. Nebr., Lincoln, 1996, PhD, 1999. Cert. tchr. Nebr., 1990. Band dir. Wakefield Pub. Sch., Wakefield, Nebr., 1990—91; dir. of bands Kearney H.S., Kearney, Nebr., 1991—94; dir. bands Lincoln Northeast H.S., Lincoln, Nebr., 1996—97; assoc. prof. music and edn. U. of Nebr., Kearney, Nebr., 1997—. Contbr. articles to profl. jours. Bd. dirs. Nebr. Network for Ednl. Renewal, Kearney, Nebr., 2001—04. Mem.: NEA, Internat. Soc. Music Edn., U. Nebr. Kearney Edn. Assn., Nebr. State Edn. Assn., Coll. Music Soc., Nebr. State Bandmasters Assn. (pres. 2006—), Outstanding Young Band Dir. award 1994), Nebr. Music Educators Assn. (exec. bd. 2002—, chair rsch. 2005—), Music Educators Nat. Conf., Phi Beta Mu, Tau Beta Sigma, Phi Kappa Phi, Pi Kappa Lambda. Roman Catholic. Avocations: golf, private pilot, travel, reading. Office: U Nebr Kearney 905 W 25th Kearney NE 68845-4238 Office Phone: 308-865-8631. Business E-Mail: schnoorn@unk.edu.

**SCHNUCK, CRAIG D.,** grocery store company executive; b. Apr. 20, 1948; s. Donald Schnuck. BS, Cornell U., 1967, MBA, 1971. With Schnuck Markets, Inc., Hazelwood, Mo., 1971—, v.p., 1975-76, exec. v.p., sec., 1976-83, pres., chief exec. officer, 1983-91, also bd. dirs., 1991, chmn., CEO, 1991—. Office: Schnuck Markets Inc 11420 Lackland Rd Saint Louis MO 63146-3559

**SCHNUCKER, ROBERT VICTOR,** historian, educator; b. Waterloo, Iowa, Sept. 30, 1932; s. Felix Victor and Josephine (Maasdam) S.; m. Anna Mae Engelkes, Sept. 18, 1955; children: Sarai Ann, Sar Victor, Christjahn Dietrich. AB, NE Mo. State U., 1953; BD, U. Dubuque, 1956; MA, U. Iowa, 1960, PhD, 1969. Ordained to ministry Presbyn. Ch., 1956. Pastor United Presbyn. Ch. USA, Springville, Iowa, 1956-63, Meth.-Presbyn. Ch., Labelle, Mo., 1976-97; asst. prof. N.E. Mo. State U., Kirksville, 1963-65, assoc. prof., 1963-65, prof., 1969—99; interim pastor Bethany Presbyn. Ch., Grundy Center, Iowa, 1999—2001, First Presbyn. Ch., Aplington, 2002—04, Immanuel Presbyn. Ch., Waterloo, Iowa, 2004—05. Dir. Thomas Jefferson U. Press; supr. Bible exam. Presbyn. Ch. USA, Louisville, 1977-89; bd. dir. Ctr. for Reformation Rsch., St. Louis, 1984-99; pres. Conf. of Hist. Jours., 1993; adj. prof. religion U. No. Iowa, 1999—; vis. prof. religion and humanities, 2001-02. Author: A Glossary of Terms for Western Civilization, 1975, Helping Humanities Journal Survive, 1985, History Assessment Test, 1990; editor: Calviniana, 1989, Historians of Early Modern Europe, 1976-93, 97, Network News Exch., 1978-88; pres. 1st and 2d Editing History, Conf. for Hist. Jour., 1985-97; book rev. editor, mng. editor 16th Century Jour., 1972-97; pub. 16th Century Essays and Studies, 1980-97; contbr. articles to profl. jours. Recipient 16th Studies Conf. medal for Significant Achievement in Early Modern Studies, 1997, Presdl. Citation for Contbns. to the Univ., Truman State U., 1997; fellow Soc. Sci. Study of Religion, 1988, Sixteenth Century Studies conf., 1998; NEH grantee for jour. pubs., 1980. Mem. AAUP, Am. Acad. Religion, Renaissance Soc. Am., Am. History Assn. (chmn. Robinson prize com. 1987), Am. Soc. Ch. History, Soc. History of Edn., Soc. Bibl. Lit., Soc. for Reformation Rsch., Soc. Scholarly Pubs., Soc. for Values in Higher Edn., Conf. for Hist. Jour., Am. Coun. Learned Soc. (exec. bd. conf. adminstr. officers 1993-96, sec. 1994, chmn. 1995-96), Conf. Faith and History, 16th Century Studies Cons. (exec. sec. 1972-97), Humanities Iowa (bd. dirs. 1999-2003, pres. 2002-03). Office: Dept Philosophy and Religion UI No Iowa Cedar Falls IA 50614-0501 E-mail: rvs@cedarnet.org.

**SCHNUELL-RUTH, KAREN D.,** elementary school educator; b. Detroit, July 22; m. William A. Ruth, Jan. 21. M in Edn. Leadership, Madonna U., Mich. Cert. Elem. Edn. Mich. Tchr. South Redford (Mich.) Sch. Dist., 2002—. Home: 10123 Tecumseh Redford MI 48239

**SCHNUR, ROBERT ARNOLD,** lawyer; b. White Plains, NY, Oct. 25, 1938; s. Conrad Edward and Ruth (Mehr) S.; children: Daniel, Jonathan. BA, Cornell U., 1960; JD, Harvard U., 1963. Bar: Wis. 1965, Ill. 1966. Assoc. Michael, Best & Friedrich, Milw., 1966-73, ptnr., 1973—. Chmn. Wis. Tax News, 1983-90; adj. prof. tax law U. Wis. Law Sch., 1988—; vis. prof. tax law Cornell U. Law Sch., 2006-. Capt. U.S. Army, 1963-65. Fellow Am. Coll. Tax Counsel; mem. ABA, Wis. Bar Assn. (chmn. tax sect. 1986-88), Milw. Bar Assn. Home: 3093 Timber Ln Verona WI 53593 Office: Michael Best Friedrich 100 E Wisconsin Ave Ste 3300 Milwaukee WI 53202-4108 Business E-Mail: raschnur@michaelbest.com.

**SCHNURR, BRITTON LEIGH,** psychologist; b. Cortland, N.Y., Sept. 18, 1974; d. Robert Stephen Schnurr, Jr and Jeannine Marie Schnurr. BA, Syracuse U., NY, 1996; MSc, SUNY, Oswego, N.Y., 1999; D in Psychology, U. Albany, 2004. Cert. sch. psychologist Nat. Assn. Sch. Psychologists, 1999, N.Y., 1999. Psychologist Hoosic Valley Ctrl. Sch. Dist., Schaghticoke, NY, 1999—2002, Guilderland (N.Y.) Ctrl. Sch. Dist., 2004—. Presenter in field. Contbr. chapters to books, articles to profl. jours. Recipient Grad. Rsch. award, Dept. Counseling and Psychol. Svcs., SUNY, 1999; grantee, SUNY, Oswego, 1998. Mem.: Nat. Assn. Sch. Psychologist, NY Assn. Sch. Psychologists (del. assembly 2001—), Syracuse U. Alumni Assn., Delta Delta Delta (life; sec. 1995—96). Independent. Roman Catholic. Office Phone: 518-221-7411.

**SCHOCHET, BARRY P.,** health care executive; b. NYC, Mar. 13, 1951; s. George and Freda Schochet. BA in Zoology, U. Maine, 1973; MA in Health Care Adminstrn., George Washington U., 1975. Asst. adminstr. Doctors Hosp., Hollywood, Fla., 1975-76, Cypress Community Hosp., Pompano Beach, Fla., 1976-77, adminstr., 1977-78, exec. dir., 1978-79; asst. regional v.p. Nat. Med. Enterprises, St. Petersburg, Fla., 1979-80, asst. v.p. Los Angeles, 1980-81, v.p. ops. Tampa, Fla., 1981-83, sr. regional v.p., 1984-87, sr. divisional v.p., 1987-89, exec. v.p., 1989-91, sr. exec. v.p. and COO Santa Monica, Calif., 1991-93, pres., COO hosp. group, 1993-95; exec. v.p. operations Tenet Healthcare (formerly Nat. Med. Enterprises), Dallas, 1995—99; vice chmn. Tenet Healthcare, 1999—. Mem. Am. Hosp. Assn., Fedn. Am. Health Care Systems (bd. govs. 1985—, bd. dirs. 1989—, chmn 2000), Am. Coll. Health Care Execs., Fla. League Hosps. (bd. dirs. 1981—, chmn. 1988-89), bd. dir. Healthcare leadership coun., 1999—. Office: Tenet Healthcare 13737 Noel Rd Ste 100 Dallas TX 75240-2017

**SCHOCHOR, JONATHAN,** lawyer, educator; b. Suffern, N.Y., Sept. 9, 1946; s. Abraham and Betty (Hechtor) S.; m. Joan Elaine Brown, May 31, 1970; children: Lauren Aimee, Daniel Ross. BA, Pa. State U., 1968; JD, Am. U., 1971. Bar: D.C. 1971, U.S. Dist. Ct. D.C. 1971, U.S. Ct. Appeals (D.C. cir.) 1971, Md. 1974, U.S. Dist. Ct. Md. 1974, U.S. Supreme Ct. 1986. Assoc. McKenna, Wilkinson & Kittner, Washington, 1970-74, Ellin & Baker, Balt., 1974-84; ptnr. Schochor, Federico & Staton, Balt., 1984—. Lectr. in law; expert witness to state legis. Editor-in-chief: Am. U. Law Rev., 1970—71. Mem. ABA, ATLA (state del. 1991, state gov. 1992-95), Am. Bd. Trial Advs. (membership com. 1994—), Am. Bd. Trial Advs., Am. Judicature Soc., Md. State Bar Assn. (spl. com. on health claims arbitration 1983), Md. Trial Lawyers Assn. (bd. govs. 1986-87, mem. legis. com. 1985-88, chmn. legis. com. 1986-87, sec. 1987-88, exec. com. 1987-92, v.p. 1987-88, pres.-elect 1989, pres. 1990-91), Balt. City Bar Assn. (legis com. 1986-87, spl. com. on tort reform 1986, medicolegal com. 1989-90, cir. ct. for Balt. City task force-civil document mgmt. sys. 1994-95), Bar Assn. D.C., Internat. Platform Assn., Phi Alpha Delta. Office: Schochor Federico & Staton PA 1211 Saint Paul St Baltimore MD 21202-2783 Office Phone: 410-234-1000. Business E-Mail: jschochor@sfspa.com.

**SCHOCK, ROBERT NORMAN,** geophysicist; b. Monticello, NY, May 25, 1939; s. Carl Louis and Norma Elizabeth (Greenfeld) S.; m. Susan Esther Benton. Nov. 28, 1959; children: Pamela Ann, Patricia Elizabeth, Christina Benton. BS, Colo. Coll., 1961; MS, Rensselaer Poly. Inst., 1963, PhD, 1966; postgrad., Northwestern U., 1963-64. Cert. Calif. state wine judge. Jr. geophys. trainee Continental Oil Co., Sheridan, Wyo., 1960; jr. geologist Texaco In., Billings, Mont., 1961; teaching asst. Rensselaer Poly. Inst., Troy, NY, 1961-63, research asst., 1964-66; research assoc. U. Chgo., 1966-68; sr. research scientist Lawrence Livermore Nat. Lab., U. Calif., 1968—2006, group leader high pressure physics, 1972-74, sect. leader geoscis. and engring., 1974-76, div. leader earth scis., 1976-81, head dept. earth scis., 1981-87, energy program leader, 1987-92, dep. assoc. dir. for energy, 1992-98, sr. fellow Ctr. Global Security Rsch., 1998—2006. Pres. Pressure Sys. Rsch. Inc.; mem. faculty Chabot Coll., 1969-71; dir. Alameda County Flood Control and Water Conservation Dist., 1984-86, chair, 1985; mem. adv. panel on geoscis. U.S. Dept. Energy, 1985-87; chair adv. com. U. Calif. Energy Inst., 1992-98; mem. rsch. adv. com. Gas Rsch. Inst., Chgo., 1995-2001; chmn World Energy Coun., London, dir. studies 2005—, Study Group Energy Tech. in 21st Century, 1999-2004; mem. instrumentation and facilities rev. panel NSF, 2001-04. Mem. editl. bd. Rev. Sci. Instruments, 1975-77; assoc. editor Jour. Geophys. Rsch., 1978-80; bd. assoc. editors 11th Lunar and Planetary Sci. Conf., 1980; mem. adv. bd. Physics and Chemistry of Minerals, 1983-97; rsch. and pubs. on high pressure physics, solid state physics, physics of earth interior, rock deformation, energy R&D and energy policy; lead author, intergovernmental panel on climate change, 2004—;

Fulbright sr. fellow U. Bonn, Germany, 1973; vis. research fellow Australian Nat. U. Canberra, 1980-81 Mem. AAAS, Am. Geophys. Union, Sigma Xi, Commonwealth of Calif. Club, Cosmos Club (Washington). Business E-Mail: schock1@llnl.gov.

**SCHOCKET, SANDRA KLAMKIN,** career management consultant, writer; b. Amityville, N.Y., May 5, 1936; d. Harry Isaac and Ruth Lillian Klamkin; children: Barry Schocket (dec.), Andrew. BA, Mount Holyoke Coll., South Hadley, Mass., 1958; EdM, Rutgers U., 1966. Nat. cert. counselor Nat. Bd. for Cert. Counselors, career counselor Nat. Bd. for Cert. Counselors. Asst. dir. placement N.J. Inst. Tech., Newark, 1982—90; dir. placement Simmons Grad. Sch. Mgmt., Boston, 1990—91; pvt. practice career mgmt. cons. Mountain Lakes, NJ, 1991—2002. Author: Summer Jobs, 1985 (NJ Author of Year, 1986), My Life Closed Twice: Surviving a Double Loss, 2003; contbr. articles to newspapers. Active Environ. Commn., Mountain Lakes, 1996—2002; vol. N.Y.C. Ballet, N.Y.C., 1995—2002; docent Toledo Mus. Art, 2002—. Mem.: Authors Guild, Ea. Assn. Colls. and Employers (hon.; pres. 1992—93, Disting. Svc. award 1994), Alumnae Assn. Mount Holyoke Coll. (bd. dirs. 1977), Mount Holyoke Coll. Class of 1958 (pres. 1998—2003), Mount Holyoke Club No. N.J. (pres. 1969—71). Personal E-mail: skschocket@bex.net. Business E-Mail: monroe50@bex.net.

**SCHOECK, RICHARD J.,** English and humanities scholar, poet; b. NYC, Oct. 10, 1920; s. Gustav J. and Frances M. (Kuntz) S.; m. Reta R. Haberer, 1945 (div. 1976); children: Eric R., Christine C., Jennifer A.; m. Megan S. Lloyd, Feb. 19, 1977 (dec. Nov. 17, 2005). MA, PhD, Princeton U., 1949. Instr. English Cornell U., 1949-55; from asst. prof. to assoc. prof. U. Notre Dame, 1955-61; prof. English U. Toronto, 1961-71; head dept. English St. Michael's Coll., 1965-70; prof. vernacular lit. Pontifical Inst. Mediaeval Studies, Toronto, 1964-71; dir. rsch. activities Folger Shakespeare Libr., also dir. Folger Inst. Renaissance and 18th Century Studies, 1970-74; adj. prof. English Cath. U. Am., 1972; prof. English, medieval and renaissance studies U. Md., 1974-75; prof. English and humanities U. Colo., Boulder, 1975-89, prof. emeritus, 1987—, chmn. dept. integrated studies 1976-79; chmn. comparative lit., 1983-84; prof. Anglistik Univ. Trier, 1987-90, head dept. (Geschäftsführer), 1988-89; adj. prof. English U. Kans., Lawrence, 1990—2000. Vincent J. Flynn prof. letters Coll. St. Thomas, 1959; vis. prof. Princeton U., 1964, U. Dallas, 1985; vis. fellow Inst. Advanced Studies in Humanities, Edinburgh, 1984-85; vis. scholar Corpus Christi Coll., Oxford, 1994, Wolfson Coll., Oxford, 1997; fellow Assn. Advancement Edn., 1952-53, Yale U., 1959-60, Can. Coun. 1967-68, Ctr. for the Book, Brit. Libr., 1995-96; cons. NEH: bd. dir. Natural Law Inst. U. Notre Dame; advisor Italian Acad. for Advanced Studies in Am., 1993; presenter in field. Author: The Achievement of Thomas More, 1976, Intertexuality and Renaissance Texts, 1984, Erasmus Grandescens, 1988, (poems) A Raging Against Chaos, 1989, The Eye of a Traveller, 1992, The Knight's Book, 1993, My Hiroshima, 1997, (poems) Laurentian Codicil, 2002, rev. edit., 2004, Prairie Epiphanies, 2003, Childhood and Old Age, 2001, The Wakaruska Wetlands in Word Image, 2005; Erasmus of Europe, Vol. I, The Making of a Humanist, 1467-1500, 1990, Vol. II The Prince of Humanists, 1501-1536, 1993; contbr. numerous articles, papers, revs. on edn. to jours. and mags.; editor: Delehaye's Legends of the Saints, 1961, Editing 16th Century Texts, 1966, Roger Ascham: The Scholemaster, 1966, Shakespeare Quar., 1972-74, Acta Conventus Neo-Latini Bononiensis, 1985; gen. editor: The Confutation of Tyndale, 3 vols., 1973; co-editor: Voices of Literature, 2 vols., 1964, 66, Chaucer Criticism, 2 vols, 1960, 61, Style, Rhetoric and Rhythm: Essays by M.W. Croll, 1966, Acta Conventus Neo-Latini Torontonensis, 1991; past gen. editor: Patterns of Literary Criticism; spl. editor Canada vol. Rev. Nat. Literatures, 1977, Sir Thomas Browne and the Republic of Letters, 1982, A Special Number of English Language Notes, 1982; gen. editor (series) Renaissance Masters, 1992-99; mem. editl. bds. profl. jours. With U.S. Army, 1940—46. Guggenheim Found. fellow, 1968-69, Fulbright fellow, 1983; recipient Centennial medal U. Colo., 1976, Falconer Madan award Bibliographical Soc., London, 1997; co-recipient 1st prize Mellen Poetry Competition, 1997; grantee Can. Coun., UNESCO, Am. Coun. Learned Socs., U. Toronto, U. Colo. Fellow Royal Soc. Can., Royal Hist. Soc.; mem. Internat. Assn. Neo-Latin Studies (pres. 1976-79), MLA, Renaissance Soc. Am., PEN (N.Y.), Internat. Assn. U. Profs. English, HEH. Home: 1516 Fountain Drive Lawrence KS 66047 Personal E-mail: rjschoeck@sunflower.com. *More than a thousand years ago Bede summed up what are for me the principles of my professional career: I have always thought it fitting to learn and to teach and to write.*

**SCHOEING, BENJAMIN SAMUEL,** music educator, conductor; b. Racine, Wis., Nov. 18, 1978; s. Stephen and Susan Schoeing. BA in voice and French horn performance, Luther Coll., Iowa, 2000; MusM in Orchestral Conducting, U. Ill., 2003. Music dir. White Mountain Symphony Orch., Show Low, Ariz., 2004—. Composer: (orchestral work) Elegy, (choral) Choral Wayfaring Stranger, Scarborogh Fair, May You Rest, Requiem. Mem.: Am. Symphony Orch. League. Conservative. Avocation: athletics. Office: Northland Pioneer Coll PO Box 610 Holbrook AZ 86025 Office Fax: 928-536-6212. Personal E-Mail: symphony_conductor78@yahoo.com. Business E-Mail: bschoeining@npc.edu.

**SCHOELEN, MARY JEANETTE,** federal judge; b. Rota, Spain; BA, U. Calif. Irvine, 1990; JD, George Washington U. Law Sch., 1993. Law clk. Nat. Veterans Legal Services Project; staff atty., veteran's benefits program Vietnam Veterans of Am., 1994; intern, com. veterans' affairs US Senate, 1994, minority counsel, com. veterans' affairs, 1997—2001, minority gen. counsel, com. veterans' affairs, 2001, dep. staff dir. benefits programs and gen. counsel, com. veterans' affairs, 2001—04; judge US Ct. Appeals Veterans Claims, 2004—. Office: US Ct Appeals Veterans Claims 625 Indiana Ave NW Ste 900 Washington DC 20004 Office Phone: 202-501-5970.

**SCHOELER, GEORGE BERNARD,** medical entomologist; b. Seattle, Aug. 5, 1961; s. Robert Gene and Inez (Stegman) S.; m. Jaime A. Rabdau, Aug. 31, 1985; children: Robert James, Jessika Ann. BS in Biology, Boise State Univ., 1989; MS in Entomology, Univ. Calif., 1992. Rsch tech. USDA, ARS, ADRU, Caldwell, Idaho, 1986-89; rsch. asst. Univ. Calif., Berkeley, 1989-92; entomologist Navy Disease Vector Ecology and Control Ctr., Alameda, Calif., 1992—. Contbr. articles to profl. jours. Lt. USN, 1992—. Recipient Navy Ach. medal, 1993, grant Sigma Xi, 1991. Mem. Entomological Soc. Am., Sigma Xi (assoc.). Republican. Roman Catholic. Office: Disease Vector Ecology Control Ctr Naval Air Sta Alameda CA 94501-5013

**SCHOEN, ALLEN HARRY,** retired aerospace engineering executive; b. NYC, Mar. 10, 1936; s. Harry Alfred and Dorothy Julia (Browne) S.; m. Patricia Alice O'Madigan, June 1, 1958 (div. 1989); children: Theresa Mary, James Allen, Karen Linda; m. Lauria Juliette Trahan, Feb. 14, 2001. SB in Aero. Engring., MIT, 1958, postgrad., 1989. Aerodynamicist Douglas Aircraft Co., Santa Monica, Calif., 1958-61, United Aircraft Co., Farmington, Conn., 1961-66; with Boeing Helicopters, Phila., 1966-98, tech. mgr., 1980-84, dir. tech., 1984-86, dep. tech. dir. V-22 Osprey joint program, 1986-88, dir. preliminary design, 1988-92, dir. devel. engring., 1992-95, dir. devel. program, 1995-98; ret., 1998. Aero. adv. com. NASA, Washington, 1985-90. Patentee propulsion sys.; contbr. articles to profl. jours. Fellow AIAA (assoc.), Am. Helicopter Soc. (hon., pres. Phila. chpt. 1983-84, v.p. Mideast region 1986-88, dir.-at-large 1988-90, Paul E. Haueter Meml. award 1989), Brewster Assn. Part-time Residents (founder, pres. 2002-04). Republican. Episcopalian. Avocations: photography, gardening, woodworking, woodcarving.

**SCHOEN, CHARLES JUDD,** service executive; b. Owatonna, Minn., Sept. 6, 1943; s. John Nicholas and Dorothy Georgine (Jacobson) S.; m. Birgitta Marianne Haggren, Dec. 15, 1972; 1 child, Vanja Karina. BA, U. Minn., 1965. Stockbroker Harris, Upham and Co., Mpls., 1967-70; with Litton Industries, Sydney, Australia, 1970-71; gen. mgr. Westinghouse Electric, Mpls., 1971-77; pres. Westco Security, Wayzata, Minn., 1977—, Automatic Alarm Corp., Wayzata, Minn., 1986-95; pres., chmn. Westec Security Products, Laguna Beach, Calif., 1993—. Bd. chmn. SpyderNet, Minn.,

1993—. Author: History of Wayzata, 2004. Past pres. Wayzata Hist. Soc. With USN, 1966-67 Named Alumni Notable Achievement, U. Minn., 1999. Mem. Assn. Former Intelligence Officers. Office: Westco Security 401 Lake St E Wayzata MN 55391-1667

SCHOEN, MARC ALAN, pension and employee benefits executive; b. Worcester, Mass., May 30, 1938; s. A. Robert and Ruth D.Schoen; m. Joanne S. Schultz, June 24, 1962; children: Elliott, Aaron, Jennifer, Matthew. BBA, BS, U. Miami, 1965. Asst. buyer Allied Stores, Miami, Fla., 1965-66; agt. Fidelity Mut. Ins., Miami, 1966-67, Prudential Ins. Co., Miami, 1967-68; pvt. practice registered rep., agt. Miami, 1968-73; pres. A Pension Store, Inc., Miami, 1973—2004. Cons. Criterion Funds, Inc., Houston, 1983-1987, TMG Holding LLC, Chgo., 2004—; newspaper columnist, 1969-1976, 1984. Mem. So. Fla. Employee Benefits Coun., Dade Estate Planning Coun.; scoutmaster Boy Scouts Am., Miami, 1966-90; exec. bd. dirs. Crouse Found. to Pub. Arts at CUNY, N.Y.C., 1983—. With USN, 1957-62. Recipient Cmty. Svc. award Prudential Ins., 1967; CFC Designation, Employers Coun. on Flexible Compensation; named Outstanding Young Man Yr., Optimists, 1967; named to Rollins Coll. Sports Hall of Fame, 1987. Mem. (assoc.) Am. Soc. Pension Actuaries, Internat. Assn. Fin. Planners, Million Dollar Round Table (qualifying life), Nat. Assn. Ins. and Fin. Advisors, Employers Coun. on Flexible Compensation, Rotary, Masons. Avocations: stamp collecting/philately, camping, hiking. Home: 838 Blue Heather Ct Lawrenceville GA 30045 Office Phone: 786-514-1933. E-mail: marc@apensionstore.com, maschoen@bellsouth.net.

SCHOEN, RICHARD MELVIN, mathematics professor, researcher; b. Celina, Ohio, Oct. 23, 1950; s. Arnold Peter and Rosemary (Heitkamp) S., m. Doris Helga Fischer-Colbrie, Oct. 29, 1983; children: Alan, Lucy. BS, U. Dayton, 1972; PhD, Stanford U., 1976. Lectr. U. Calif.-Berkeley, 1976-78, prof. math., 1980-85; asst. prof. Courant Inst. NYU, 1978-80; prof. math. U. Calif.-La Jolla, 1985-87, Stanford U., 1987—. Contbr. articles to profl. jours. Recipient Bocher prize, 1989; fellow NSF, 1972, Alfred P. Sloan Found., 1979, MacArthur Found. prize, 1983, Guggenheim Found., 1996. Mem. Am. Acad. Arts and Scis., Am. Math. Soc., Nat. Acad. Sci. Office: Stanford U Mathematics Dept Stanford CA 94305 Business E-Mail: schoen@math.stanford.edu.

SCHOEN, WILLIAM JACK, finance company executive; b. L.A., Aug. 2, 1935; s. Jack Conrad and Kathryn Mabel (Stegmayer) S.; m. Sharon Ann Barto, Oct. 1, 1966; children: Kathryn Lynn, Karen Anne, Kristine Lea, William Jack. BS in Fin. magna cum laude, U. So. Calif., 1960, MBA, 1963. Mktg. mgr. Anchor Hocking Glass Co., 1964-68; v.p. sales and mktg. Obear-Nester Glass Co., 1968-71; pres. Pierce Glass Co., Port Allegheny, Pa., 1971-73; pres., chief exec. officer, dir. F.&M. Schaefer Brewing Co., N.Y.C., 1973-81; now chmn., pres. Wilshar Mgmt. Co. Inc., Naples, Fla., 1981—; chmn. Health Mgmt. Assocs. Inc., Naples, 1983—, also bd. dirs. Contbr. to indsl. publns. Founder Marine Corp. Heritage Found.; mem. Bus. Coun. of 100 of Fla.; bd. dir. Internat. Coll. Found.; chmn. Schoen Found.; mem. bd. advisors U. So. Calif. Bus. Sch.; trustee U. So. Calif. Avocations: food, wine. Served with USMC, 1953-56, Korea. Mem. Naples Yacht Club, Port Royal Club, Quail Creek Country Club, Teton Springs Club, Phi Kappa Phi. Republican. Lutheran. Office Phone: 239-598-3175.

SCHOENBAUM, ALAN, lawyer; b. Washington, June 25, 1957; s. Stanley and Virginia W. Schoenbaum; m. Kathleen Kuper, Mar. 14, 1981; children: Alexander, James. BA, U. Tex., 1982, JD, 1983. Bar: Tex. 1983. Assoc. Akin, Gump, Strauss, Hauer and Field, San Antonio, 1984—91, ptnr. corp. and securities, 1991—, and co-head mergers and acquisitions practice. Office: Akin Gump Strauss Hauer & Field 300 Convent St Ste 1500 San Antonio TX 78205-3732 Office Phone: 210-281-7234. Business E-Mail: aschoenbaum@akingump.com.

SCHOENBERG, MARK GEORGE, government agency administrator; b. Bklyn., Nov. 22, 1947; s. Abraham Arthur and Ruth Millie (Dunn) S. BA, Columbia U., 1971, postgrad., 1972-73, N.C. State U., 1971-72. Research asst. NIMH-sponsored project at N.C. State U., Raleigh, 1971-72; asst. to pres. Key Electric Ltd., Glen Oaks, NY, 1973-76, gen. mgr. Los Angeles, 1976; asst. to pres. Kalsan Electric, Hempstead, NY, 1977; asst. mgr. Lincoln Inn, Rockville Ctr., NY, 1978; expert, cons. EPA, Washington, 1978; assoc. dir. U.S. Regulatory Council, Washington, 1979-82; exec. dir. Regulatory Info. Service Ctr., Washington, 1982-99; sr. advisor to dep. adminstr. Gen. Svcs. Adminstrn., 1999—. Avocations: healthy gourmet cooking, early music, wine collecting, travel, photography.

SCHOENBERGER, JAMES EDWIN, retired federal agency administrator; b. Dayton, Ohio, Sept. 7, 1947; s. Harry Robert and Elizabeth Jane Schoenberger; m. Aura Victoria Montana, June 24, 1977; children: David, Eric. BSCE, Purdue U., 1969; MBA, Harvard U., 1971. V.p. ops. for midwestern housing developer Herman Devel. Group, Indpls., 1971-74; various positions New Communities Adminstrn. and with sec. HUD, Washington, 1974-77, assoc. dep. asst. sec., 1981-83; dir. land utilization Peabody Coal Co., St. Louis, 1977-81; sr. v.p. ops. The Investment Group, Washington, 1983-86; assoc. gen., dep. asst. fed. housing commr. HUD, Washington, 1987-89, assoc. gen., dep. asst. sec., 1990-97, ret., 1997. Roman Catholic. Avocations: computers, philanthropy.

SCHOENBERGER, STEVEN HARRIS, physician, research consultant; b. Cleve., Nov. 26, 1950; s. Stanford L. and Irene (Gold) S. BA, Tulane U., 1972; MD, U. Autonoma Guadalajara, Mex., 1976. Diplomate Am. Bd. of Urology. Asst. prof. Tulane U. Sch. Medicine, New Orleans, 1983—. Rsch. assoc. Delta Regional Primate Rsch. Ctr., Covington, La., 1983-85, chief section of urology Lawrence and Meml. Hosp., New London, Conn.; chmn. laser com., Lawrence and Meml. Hosp., New London, Conn., 1989—, chief sect. urology, 2003—; rsch. cons. Pfizer Med. Group, Groton, Conn., 1989—. Fellow ACS, Am. Soc. Laser Medicine and Surgery; mem. Soc. Univ. Urologists, N.Y. Acad. Scis., New Eng. Escadrille. Office: 3 Shaws Cv Ste 206 New London CT 06320-4968 Office Phone: 860-443-0622.

SCHOENDORFER, DONALD W., engineer; b. Albany, NY, Mar. 1949; m. Laurie Schoendorfer; children: Erika, Heidi, Anna. BA, Baldwin Wallace Coll., Berea, 1972; BS, Columbia U.; MS in Mech. Engring., MIT, PhD in Mech. Engring., 1977. Cofounder, v.p. rsch. and devel. Subdormed, Santa Ana, Calif.; cofounder, CEO Free Wheelchair Mission, 2001—. Recipient Beta Gamma Sigma Medallion for entrepreneurship, 2005, Outstanding Alumni award, Baldwin Wallace Coll., 2006, Mayor's award, Orange County, Calif., Feb., 2006. Achievements include 53 US patents for human blood collection and processing equipment, drug testing and fingerprinting materials and procedures; invention of wheelchair made from $3 lawn chair and other inexpensive materials, costing $41 to manufacture; distributed more than 145,000 free wheelchairs in over 57 countries since 2004. Office: Free Wheelchair Mission 9341 Irvine Blvd Irvine CA 92618*

SCHOENEMANN, DAVID LEROY, real estate broker, small business owner; b. Newport, R.I., Dec. 20, 1954; s. Leroy John and Barbara Christine Schoenemann; m. Jacklynn Anne Storm, Aug. 22, 1993. BS, Tex. A & M U., College Station, 1980. Cert. CCIM Nat. Assn. of Realtors, 1996. Land technician MDG, Inc., Houston, 1981—86; real estate salesperson ERA-Sandlin & Co., Austin, Tex., 1987—90; real estate broker A&M Properties, Inc., College Station, 1990—91; real estate broker/owner El Rey Properties, Bryan, Tex., 1991—94; real estate broker Yancey-Hausman & Assocs., Austin, Tex., 1994—99; real estate broker/owner CRES, Inc., Austin, Tex., 1999—. Mem.: CCIM Inst. (assoc.). Libertarian. Avocations: golf, travel, horses. Office: CRES Inc 1406 Camp Craft Rd #206 Austin TX 78746 Office Phone: 512-828-6542. Office Fax: 512-828-7419. E-mail: cresinc@austin.rr.com.

SCHOENER, THOMAS WILLIAM, zoology educator, researcher; b. Lancaster, Pa., Aug. 9, 1943; BA, Harvard Coll., 1965, PhD, 1969. Asst. prof. Harvard Coll., Cambridge, Mass., 1972-73, assoc. prof., 1973-75, U. Wash., Seattle, 1975-76, prof., 1976-80, U. Calif., Davis, 1980—, chairperson sect. evolution and ecology divsn. biol. scis., 1993-99. Mem. editl. bd. dirs. Oecologia, 1984-93; past mem. editl. bd. Evolution, Am. Naturalist, Sci., Acta Oecologia; contbr. chpts. to books, articles to profl. jours. Recipient MacArthur prize Ecol. Soc. Am., 1987; grantee NSF, 1975—, Nat. Geog. Soc.; jr. fellow Harvard U., 1969-72; Guggenheim fellow, 1992-93. Mem. NAS, Am. Acad. Arts and Scis., Am. Ornithologists Union (elective), Am. Soc. Naturalists, Ecol. Soc. Am., Am. Soc. Ichthyologists and Herpetologists, Cooper Ornithol. Soc., Am. Arachnological Soc., Soc. Study of Amphibians and Reptiles. Avocations: weightlifting, reading. Office: U Calif Sect Evolution Ecology Davis CA 95616 Office Phone: 530-752-8319. E-mail: twschoener@ucdavis.edu.

SCHOENFELD, ALAN HENRY, mathematician, researcher, education educator; b. NYC, July 9, 1947; s. Neil Howard and Natalie (Weinberg) S.; m. Jean Snitzer, June 14, 1970. BS in Math., Queens Coll., 1968; MS in Math., Stanford U., 1969, PhD in Math., 1973. Lectr. U. Calif., Davis, 1973-75; from asst. prof. to assoc. prof. Hamilton Coll., Clinton, NY, 1978-81, U. Rochester, NY, 1981-84; lectr. U. Calif., Berkeley, 1975-78, assoc. prof. edn., math., 1985-86, prof., 1986—, chmn. div. edn. in math., sci. and tech., 1987—98, chmn. Sch. Edn., 1994—98. Chmn. Grad. Group in Sci. and Math. Edn., U. Calif., Berkeley, 1985-87; chief organizer IV Internat. Congress Math. Edn., 1984. Author: Mathematical Problem Solving, 1985, Mathematical Association of AmericaNotes # 1, Problem Solving, 1983; editor: Cognitive Science and Mathematics Education, 1987, A Source Book for College Mathematics Teaching, 1990, Mathematical Thinking and Problem Solving, 1994, Research in Collegiate Mathematics Education, vol. 1, 1994, vol. 2, 1996, vol. 3, 1998, vol. 4, 2000. Mem. State Calif. Math. Framework Com., 1988-90; mem. adv. panel Calif. Assessment Program, 1988—; mem. Supt.'s Math. Task Force, 1995. Grantee NSF, 1979, 85, 87, 90-92, 96-97, 2001-06, Sloan Found., 1984, 87, Spencer Found., 1983, 93. Mem.: Nat. Rsch. Coun. (math. sci. edn. bd. task force on K-12 1986—88, bd. testing/assessment 1993—98), Nat. Bd. for Profl. Tchg. Stds. (math. panel 1990—95), Nat. Coun. Tchrs. Math. (rsch. adv. com. 1990—93, chair 1992—93, leader prins. and stds. 1997—2000), Cognitive Sci. Soc., Am. Math. Soc. (com. on edn. 1992—97), Am. Ednl. Rsch. Assn. (exec. com. Spl. Interest Group Math. Edn. 1984—86, chair publs. com. 1994—, pres. 1998—2000), Math. Assn. Am. (chmn. tchg. undergrad. math. com. 1982—89), Nat. Acad. Edn. (exec. bd. 1995—2006, v.p. 2001—06). Avocations: food, wine. Home: 830 Colusa Ave Berkeley CA 94707-1839 Office: U Calif Dept Edn Berkeley CA 94720-1670

SCHOENFELD, DAVID ALAN, statistician, educator; b. Ft. Monmouth, N.J., Apr. 19, 1945; s. Robert Louis Schoenfeld and Helene Flapan; m. Ellen Maureen Beeks, Dec. 30, 1973; children: Heather, Elizabeth, Jonathan. BA, Reed Coll., 1967; MA, U. Oreg., 1968, PhD, 1974. Postdoctoral fellow Stanford U., Calif., 1974—75; rsch. asst. prof. SUNY, Buffalo, 1975—77; from asst. to assoc. scientist Dana-Farber Cancer Inst., Boston, 1977—86; from asst. prof. to prof. dept. of biostats., Sch. Pub. Health Harvard U., Boston, 1977—, assoc. prof. to prof. dept. medicine, 1985—; dir. Biostatistics Ctr. Mass. Gen. Hosp., Boston, 1985—. Co-editor: (book) Aids Clinical Trials, 1995. Fellow: American Statis. Assn.; mem.: assn. of GCRC Statisticians, Internat. Statis. Inst., Biometric Soc., Inst. of Math. Stats. Avocation: skiing. Home: 41 Rural Rd Sharon MA 02067 Office: Mass Gen Hosp 50 Staniford St Boston MA 02114 Personal E-mail: david@schoenfeld.com. E-mail: dschoenfeld@partners.org.

SCHOENFELD, GERALD, performing company executive; BS, Univ. Ill.; LLB, N.Y. Univ.; postgraduate, Mass. Inst. Tech., Columbia Univ.; DHL (hon.), CUNY, 1999, Emerson Coll., 2001. Faculty Yale Drama Sch.; chmn. Schubert Org., N.Y., 1972—. Adj. prof. Sch. Arts, Columbia Univ.; chmn. League Am. Theatres & Producers; chmn. bd. gov. League of N.Y. Theatres & Producers. Bd. mem. N.Y. Conv. & Vis. Bureau; chmn. Mayor's Midtown Citizens Com., NYC & Company. Recipient Humanitarian award, N.Y. Soc. Assn. Executives. Fellow: Am. Acad. Arts & Sci. Office: League of American Theatres & Producers 226 W 47th St New York NY 10036

SCHOENFELD, HANNS-MARTIN WALTER, finance educator; b. Leipzig, Germany, July 12, 1928; came to U.S., 1962, naturalized, 1968; s. Alwin and Lisbeth (Kirbach) Schoenfeld; m. Margit Frese, Aug. 10, 1956 (dec. Jan. 21, 2005); 1 child, Gabriele. MBA, U. Hamburg, Fed. Republic Germany, 1952, DBA, 1954; PhD, U. Braunschweig, Fed. Republic Germany, 1966. Pvt. practice acctg., Hamburg, 1948-54; bus. cons. Europe, 1958-62; faculty accountancy U. Ill., Champaign/Urbana, 1962—, prof. acctg., bus. adminstrn. Urbana, 1967—, Weldon Powell prof. acctg., 1976, 80-81, H. T. Scovill prof. acctg., 1985-94; prof. emeritus, 1994—; dir. Office of West European Studies, 1982-84. Lectr., cons. in bus. and acctg., Eng., Belgium, Austria, Denmark, Brazil, Mex., Germany, Poland, Indonesia, Korea, Japan, Switzerland, Hungary, Czechoslovakia, 1962—; vis. prof. Econs. U. Vienna, Austria, 1984-2002, Handelshochschule, Leipzig, Germany, 1996-2002. Author: Management Dictionary 2 vols., 4th edit, 1971, Cost Accounting, 8th edit, 1974-95, Management Development, 1967, Cost Terminology and Cost Theory, 1974, (with J. Sheth) Export Marketing: Lessons from Europe, 1981, (with H.P. Holzer) Managerial Accounting and Analysis in Multinational Enterprises, 1986, (with L. Noerreklit) Resources of the Firm, 1996. With German Army, 1944-45. Recipient Dr. Kausch prize for internat. integration of acctg. U. St. Gall, Switzerland, 1996. Mem. Am. Acctg. Assn. (chmn. internat. sect. 1976-77), Acad. Acctg. Historians (v.p. 1976-77, pres. 1978-79, Hour Glass award for best book publs. 1975), Acad. Internat. Bus. German Profs. Dur. Adminstrn., German Assn. Indsl. Engring., European Acctg. Assn., Coun. of European Studies, Internat. Assn. for Acctg. Edn. and Rsch., Beta Gamma Sigma, Beta Alpha Psi. Home: 1014 Devonshire Dr Champaign IL 61821-6620 Office: U Ill Dept Acctg 360 Wohlers Hall 1206 S 6th St Champaign IL 61820-6915 Office Phone: 217-333-4530. Business E-Mail: hschoenf@uiuc.edu.

SCHOENFELD, LAWRENCE STEVEN, psychology educator; b. N.Y.C., Dec. 22, 1941; s. Irving and Muriel (Levy) S.; m. Heidi Ellen Buchbinder, Aug. 19, 1967; children: Jennifer Dawn, Jessica Leah. BA, Ohio Wesleyan U., 1963; MA, U. Fla., 1965, PhD, 1967. Diplomate Am. Bd. Profl. Psychology. Dir. psychology resident tng. U. Tex. Health Sci. Ctr., San Antonio, 1976-81, 97—, chmn. IRB, 1977-78, prof. anesthesiology, 1980—, prof. psychiatry, 1979—. Cons. psychology Audie Murphy VA Hosp., San Antonio, 1975—; ethics chmn. Tex. Psychol. Assn., Austin, 1980-86; cons. City of San Antonio, 1973-89, S.W. Rsch. Inst., San Antonio, 1978-90; vice chmn. Tex. State Bd. Examiners of Psychologists, 1988-94. Contbr. articles to profl. jours. Trustee Planned Parenthood, San Antonio, 1979-85, Julie Jordan Free Clinic, San Antonio, 1978-80; bd. dirs. Alamo chpt. Big Bros./Big Sisters, 1983-92; exec. dir., founder Crisis Ctr. for San Antonio, 1972-79; bd. dirs. Hidden Forest, 1984-87. Fellow: APA. Home: 680 E Basse Rd Apt 320 San Antonio TX 78209-8332 Office: U Tex Health Sci Ctr Dept Psychiatry 7703 Floyd Curl Dr San Antonio TX 78229-3901 Office Phone: 210-567-5494. Business E-Mail: schoenfeldl@uthscsa.edu.

SCHOENFELD, ROBERT LOUIS, biomedical engineer; b. NYC, Apr. 1, 1920; s. Bernard and Mae (Kizelstein) S.; m. Helene Martens, Jan. 22, 1944 (div. 1965); children: David, Joseph, Paul; m. Florence Moskowitz, Dec. 11, 1965 (dec. 1989); children: Nedda, Bethany; m. Shulamith Stechel, July 8, 1990. BA, Washington Square Coll., 1942; BSEE, Columbia U., 1944; MEE, Poly. Inst. Bklyn., 1949, DEE, 1956. Rsch. assoc. Columbia U. Med. Sch., N.Y.C., 1947-51; rsch. fellow Sloan Kettering Cancer Rsch. Inst., N.Y.C., 1951-56; assoc. prof. Poly. Inst. Bklyn., 1957—59; biomed. engr. Rockefeller U., N.Y.C., 1957—59, prof. emeritus, 1990—. Contbr. articles to profl. jours. Lt. Signal Corps, U.S. Army, 1944-46. ETO. Fellow IEEE (mem. editl. bd. 1965-75, Centennial medal 1985), Am. Inst. for Med. and Biol. Engring. Democrat. Jewish. Achievements include

pioneering application of computer automation to biological laboratory experiments. Office: Rockefeller U 1230 York Ave New York NY 10021-6399 Business E-Mail: rls@mail.rockefeller.edu.

SCHOENFELD, WALTER EDWIN, manufacturing executive; b. Seattle, Nov. 6, 1930; s. Max and Edna Lucille (Reinhardt) S.; m. Esther Behar, Nov. 27, 1955; children— Lea Anne, Jeffrey, Gary. BBA, U. Wash., 1952. Dir. Reading Railroad, 1964—68; v.p., dir. Sunshine Mining Co., Kellogg, Idaho, 1964-69, First N.W. Industries, Inc. (Seattle Super Sonics), 1968-79; chmn. bd., pres. Schoenfeld Industries, Inc. (diversified holding co.), 1968-93; vice chmn., acting pres., CEO, Vans, Inc., 1993-97, chmn., bd. dirs., 1997—2004; non-exec. chmn. Found. Bank, 2005—. Ptnr. Seattle Mariners Baseball Club, 1977-81, Seattle Sounders Soccer Club, 1974-79; bd. dirs. Hazel Bishop Cosmetics. Bd. dirs. Wash. China Rels. Coun., 1980—, Sterling Recreation Orgn., 1985-90; chmn. Access Long Distance of Washington; bd. govs. Weizmann Inst. Sci., Rehovot, Israel, 1980—; trustee Barbara Sinatra Children's Ctr., Eisenhower Hosp., Rancho Mirage, Calif., 1990—. With AUS, 1952-55, Korea. Recipient various service awards. Mem. Chief Execs. Orgn. (v.p., bd. dirs. 1987-93), Rainier Club, Tamarisk Country Club (Rancho Mirage, Calif.), Mission Hills Country Club, Alpha Kappa Psi. Office: 999 3rd Ave Ste 3800 Seattle WA 98104-4023

SCHOEN-GIDDINGS, LINDA N., science assessment specialist, science education consultant; d. Judith Henrietta and Morton J. Rosen; m. Daryl W. Giddings, Oct. 19, 2002; m. Roy M. Schoen, Sept. 5, 1964 (div. 1994); children: Aliza J. Schoen, Jonathan A. Schoen, Rachel B. Schoen. BS, CCNY, NYC, 1965; MSc, Hebrew U., Jerusalem, Israel, 1969; MA, Adelphi U., LI, NY, 1989; PhD, Queens Coll., NY, 1993; EdD, Hofstra U., LI, 2005. Cert. biology tchr. NY State/SC, 1965, ednl. adminstr. NY State/SC, 1993. Tchr. Aux. Svcs. for High Schools, NYC, 1983—88, ctr. adminstr., 1988—94; asst. prin. Math., Sci. and Tech. Magnet HS, Cambria Heights, NY, 1994—98; title I sci. cons. SC Dept. Edn., Columbia, 1998—2003, sci. assessment specialist, 2003—. Pres. bd. dirs. Hadassah, Port Washington, NY, 1977—2006; bd. dirs. Beth Shalom Synagogue, Columbia, 2001—06; pres. Sisterhood of Beth Shalom Synagogue, Columbia, 2000—06, treas., 2000—06. Mem.: AERA, ASCD, NSTA, SC Sci. Coun., Coun. State Sci. Supervisors (sec. of bd. 2004—). Avocations: travel, fine dining, theater, hiking. Home: 77 Olde Springs Rd Columbia SC 29223 Office: SC Dept Edn 1429 Senate St Columbia SC 29201 Office Phone: 803-734-6471. Personal E-mail: lns326@aol.com. Business E-Mail: lschoen@sde.state.sc.us.

SCHOENHARD, WILLIAM CHARLES, JR., health facility administrator; b. Kansas City, Mo., Sept. 26, 1949; s. William Charles S. and Joyce Evans (Thornsbery) Bell; m. Kathleen Ann Klosterman, June 3, 1972; children: Sarah Elizabeth, Thomas William. BS in Pub. Adminstrn., U. Mo., 1971; M of Health Adminstrn. with honors, Washington U., St. Louis, 1975. V.p., dir. gen. svcs. Deaconess Hosp., St. Louis, 1975-78; assoc. exec. dir. St. Mary's Health Ctr. St. Louis, 1978-81; exec. dir. Arcadia Valley Hosp., Pilot Knob, Mo., 1981-82, St. Joseph Health Ctr., St. Charles, Mo., St. Joseph Hosp. West, Lake St. Louis, 1982—86; exec. v.p., COO SSM Health Care, St. Louis, 1986—. Adv. bd. dirs. Firstar Bank, 1998-01, Midwest Bank Ctr., 2004, Coll. Bus. Mgmt. U. Mo., Columbia, Mo., 2005-. Contbr. articles to profl. jours. Mem. Mo. Commn. on Patient Safety, 2003—04; mem. adv. bd. St. Louis chpt. Lifeseekers, St. Louis, 1985—94; mem. bd. mgrs. Kirkwood-Webster (Mo.) YMCA, 1990—96, sec., 1996; mem. healthcare adv. bd. Sanford Brown Colls., 1992—94; bd. dirs. St. Andrews Mgmt. Svcs., Inc., 1994—2002, Mid Am. Transplant Svcs., 1995—, sec., 2005—; bd. dirs. Lindenwood U., 1997—, Civic Entrepreneurs Orgn., 1997—2000, Greater St. Louis Boy Scouts Am., 1997—, Benedictine Health Sys., 2002. With USN, 1971—72, Vietnam. Fellow Am. Coll. Health Care Execs. (regent Mo.-Gateway area 1997-01, bd. govs. 2002—, chmn. 2006—); mem. VFW, Am. Hosp. Assn. (del. regional policy bd. 1999-2005), Mo. Hosp. Assn. (bd. trustees 1999-2005, chmn. 2000), Am. Heart Assn. (mem. bd. Greater St. Louis chpt. 2001-03), Cath. Health Assn. U.S. (mem. fin. com. 1999-01), Am. Legion, US Navy League, Westborough Country Club, Phi Eta Sigma, Pi Omicron Sigma, Delta Upsilon, Delta Sigma Pi. Roman Catholic. Avocations: reading, walking. Home: 420 Fairwood Ln Saint Louis MO 63122-4429 Office: SSM Health Care 477 N Lindbergh Blvd Saint Louis MO 63141-7832 Office Phone: 314-994-7810.

SCHOENHERR, JOHN (CARL), artist, illustrator; b. NYC, July 5, 1935; s. John Ferdinand and Frances (Braun) S.; m. Judith Gray; children: Jennifer L., Ian G. BFA, Pratt Inst., 1956. Painter, illustrator Owl Moon, 1987 (Caldecott medal, 1988); exhibitions include Hiram Blauvelt Art Mus., 1997. Recipient World Sic. Fiction award, World Sci. Fiction Conv., London, 1965, Silver medal, Phila. Acad. Natural Sci., 1984, purchase award, Hiram Blauvelt Art Mus., 1997; mem.: Soc. Animal Artists (medal 1979, 1985, 2003), Am. Soc. Mammalogists (emeritus). Home and Office: 135 Upper Creek Rd Stockton NJ 08559-1209

SCHOENHUT, FREDERICK W., stock exchange executive; Prin. owner Copia Trading Co., Ltd, 1980; vice chmn. NY Bd. Trade, 2002—03, chmn., 2003—. Mem.: NY Board of Trade (NYBOT) (bd. mem. 1994—97, 1999—), NY Cotton Exchange (NYCE), Coffee, Sugar, and Cocoa Exchange (CSCE), Commodity Floor Brokers and Traders Assn. (CFBTA) (vice chmn. 2003—). Office: NY Bd Trade One N End Ave 13th Fl New York NY 10282 Office Phone: 212-748-4040. Office Fax: 212-748-4156.*

SCHOENING, RUTH IRENE, retired music educator, musician; b. Moline, Ill., Mar. 23, 1922; d. Karl John and Cora Irene (Reynolds) Wilhelmsen; m. Raymond Edward Schoening, Apr. 28, 1945; children: Stephen Ray, Carol Irene Haertel, John Edward. MusB Bun., U. Wis., 1945, MusM, 1979. Cert. music tchr. Pvt. piano instr., Racine, Wis., 1945—; music instr. Racine Christian Sch., 1960-75; workshop presenter Music Educators Nat. Confs., 1975-82; instr. music U. Wis.-Parkside, Racine, 1985-90, 95, 98. Author, editor: From Sound to Symbol, 1969, Can You Do This?, 1984, Shortcuts for the Older Beginner, 1987. Organist Luth. Ch. Resurrection, Racine, 1960—; accompanist Racine Symphonic Chorus, 1987-98; vol. accompanist Racine Pub. Schs., 1983-93, Park High Sch. Concert Choir, Women's Concert Choir, 1998-2005; active vol. Christian Coalition, Chesapeake, Va., 1990-99, nat. and state Rep. coms., 1993—; tutor Racine Literacy Coun., 2006. Mem. Am. Guild Organists, Music Tchrs. Nat. Assn. Avocations: reading, walking, computers, entertaining, volunteering. Home: 923 Illinois St Racine WI 53405-2223 Personal E-mail: ruth.schoening@sbcglobal.net.

SCHOENL, WILLIAM JAMES, history professor; b. Buffalo, Feb. 15, 1941; s. William and Erma Osborne Schoenl; m. Linda Volker, May 14, 1966; children: Karen Schoenl Carpenter, Lauren Schoenl van Loon, Mark William. BS in Math., Canisius Coll., 1963; MA in History, Columbia U., 1964, PhD in History, 1968. Prof. humanities Mich. State U., East Lansing, 1968-89, prof. history, 1989—. Mem. com. on Am. Soc. Ch. History, Chgo., 1988-93. Author: Intellectual Crisis in English Catholicism, 1982, C.G. Jung, 1998; editor: Major Issues in Jung, 1996, New Perspectives on the Vietnam War, 2002; author of poetry; contbr. articles and revs. to profl. jours. Mem., chair disbursement com. for dire needs overseas St. John Student Parish, East Lansing, Mich., 1991—; founder scholar Meridian Non-Traditional H.S., 2005— Rsch. grantee Nat. Endowment for the Humanities, Washington, 1970, Am. Philos. Soc., Phila., 1975, global competence grantee Mich. State U., East Lansing, 1993. Mem. Am. Hist. Assn., Ctr. for Jung Studies Detroit (trustee 1991-94), Kiwanis Club Okemos (chair internat. iodine deficiency disorders project 1994-98, chair Salvation Army project 1996—, chair human and spiritual values com. 1999-2002, 04-05). Avocations: fishing, walking, travel, reading mysteries, snowshoeing. Home: 2643 Roseland East Lansing MI 48823 Office: Mich State Univ Dept History East Lansing MI 48824 Office Phone: 517-355-7500.

SCHOENRICH, EDYTH HULL, internist, preventive medicine physician; b. Cleve., Sept. 9, 1919; d. Edwin John and Maud Mabel (Kelly) Hull; m. Carlos Schoenrich, Aug. 9, 1942; children: Lola, Olaf. AB, Duke U., Durham,

N.C., 1941; MD, U. Chgo., 1947; MPH, John Hopkins U., Balt., 1971. Diplomate Am. Bd. Internal Medicine, Am. Bd. Preventive Medicine. Intern John Hopkins Hosp., Balt., 1948-49, asst. resident medicine, 1949-50, fellow medicine, 1950-51, chief resident, pvt. wards, 1951-52; asst. chief acting chief dept. chronic and cmty. medicine Balt. City Hosp., Balt., 1963-66; dir. svc. to chronically ill and aging Md. State Dept. Health, Balt., 1966-74; dir. divsn. pub. health adminstrn. Sch. Pub. Health, John Hopkins U., Balt., 1974-77, assoc. dean acad. affairs, 1977-86, dir. part time profl. programs and dep. dir. MPH program, 1986—, prof. dept. health policy and mgmt., 1974—, joint appointment medicine, 1978—. Contbr. articles to profl. jours. Trustee Friends Life Care Cmty., 1984—, Kennedy-Krieger Inst., Balt., 1985—, Vis. Nurses Assn., 1990-95, Md. Home and Cmty. Care Found., 1995—. Recipient Stebbins medal John Hopkins U., 1989, Disting. Med. Alumna award, 1997; named to Md. Women's Hall of Fame, 2000. Fellow ACP, Am. Coll. Preventive Medicine; mem. APHA, Assn. Tchrs. Preventive Medicine, Med. and Chirurg. Soc., Md., Balt. City Med. Soc., Phi Beta Kappa, Alpha Omega Alpha, Delta Omega. Avocations: gardening, music, theater, swimming. Home: 1402 Boyce Ave Baltimore MD 21204-6512 Office: Johns Hopkins Univ Sch Pub Health 615 N Wolfe St Baltimore MD 21205-2103 Office Phone: 410-825-1291. E-mail: eschoenr@jhsph.edu.

**SCHOENWALD, MAURICE LOUIS,** retired lawyer; b. N.Y.C., Mar. 30, 1920; s. Jacob and Gertrude (Maier) S.; m. Susan Zysman, Nov. 24, 1943; children: David, Beth, Robin. BA, NYU, 1943; JD, Case Western Res. U., Cleve., 1947. Bar: N.Y. 1947, Fla. 1978, U.S. Dist. Ct. (so. dist.) N.Y. 1950, U.S. Dist. Ct. (ctrl. dist.) Fla. 1980, U.S. Ct. Appeals (11th dist.) Ga. 1986. Pvt. practice, N.Y.C., 1948-80. Founder New Alternatives Fund, Melville, N.Y; pres. Accrued Equities Inc., fin. advisor, since 1954; prin. broker dealer; mem. faculty Hofstra U., 1968-69. Author: Investment Contracts, 1982, (handbook) Wealth Management, 1974. Bd. dirs. ACLU, Sarasota, Fla., 1984-86. Lt. (j.g.) USN, 1942-45. Decorated Philippine Presidl. Unit citation, Philippine Liberation medal with Bronze star attachment. Fellow Acad. Matrimonial Lawyers, Sarasota Sailing Squadron. Democrat. Achievements include development of first nationally traded mutual fund investing solely in environ. concerned companies and alternative energy.

**SCHOEPF, U. JOSEPH,** radiologist; b. Graefelfing, Bavaria, Germany, Sept. 18, 1969; s. Josef J. and Ursula M. Schoepf. MD, Ludwig Maximilians U., Munich, 1996. Assoc. prof. radiology and medicine Med. U. S.C., Charleston, 2004—. Office: Med Univ SC 169 Ashley Avenue Charleston SC 29425 Office Phone: 843-792-2633.

**SCHOETTGER, THEODORE LEO,** city official; b. Burton, Nebr., Sept. 2, 1920; s. Frederick and Louise Cecelia (Gierau) S.; m. Kathlyn Marguerite Hughey, June 3, 1943; children— Gregory Paul, Julie Anne. BS in Bus. Adminstrn. with Distinction, U. Nebr., 1948. C.P.A., Calif. Sr. acct. Haskins & Sells, Los Angeles, 1948-55; controller Beckman Instruments, Inc., Fullerton, Calif., 1955-58, corp. chief acct., 1958-60; treas. Docummun Inc., Los Angeles, 1960-77; fin. dir. City of Orange, Calif., 1977-93. Mem. fin. com., treas., bd. dirs. Childrens Hosp., 1975-98. Served to lt. USNR, 1942-45. Mem. Calif. Soc. CPA's (nat. dir., v.p., past pres. Los Angeles chpt.), Fin. Execs. Inst., Mcpl. Fin. Officers Assn., Beta Gamma Sigma, Alpha Kappa Psi. Clubs: Jonathan, Town Hall. Methodist. Home: 19331 Wembley Ave Orlando FL 32833-5501

**SCHOETTLE, ENID C.B.,** federal agency administrator; m. Herbert Stuart Okun., Dec. 27, 1990. BA, Radcliffe Coll.; PhD in Polit. Sci., MIT, Cambridge, Mass. Faculty polit. sci. U. Minn., Mpls., Swarthmore Coll.; staff mem. Ford Found., 1976—91, dir. internat. affairs program, 1981—91; sr. fellow Coun. on Fgn. Rels., 1991—93; nat. intelligence officer for global and multilateral issues Nat. Intelligence Coun., 1993—96; chief advocacy and external rels. unit UN Dept. Humanitarian Affairs, 1996—97; spl. advisor Nat. Intelligence Coun., Washington, 1997—. Prof. polit. sci. Univ. Minn., Swarthmore Coll. Office: Central Intelligence Agy Nat Intelligence Coun Washington DC 20505

**SCHOETTLER, GAIL SINTON,** former ambassador; b. LA, Oct. 21, 1943; d. James and Norma (McLellan) Sinton; children: Lee, Thomas, James; m. Donald L. Stevens, June 23, 1990. BA in Econs., Stanford U., 1965; MA in History, U. Calif., Santa Barbara, 1969, PhD in History, 1975. Businesswoman, Denver, 1975-83; exec. dir. Colo. Dept. of Personnel, Denver, 1983-86; treas. State of Colo., Denver, 1987—95, lt. gov., 1995—99; chmn. bd. Fischer Imaging Corp. U.S. amb. World Radio Comm. Conf., Istanbul, 1999-2000; bd. dirs. AspenBio, Inc., CancerVax Corp., A4S Security, Inc. Active Douglas County Bd. Edn., Colo., 1979-87, pres., 1983-87; trustee U. No. Colo., Greeley, 1981-87; pres. Denver Children's Mus., 1975-85; bd. dirs. Gunnison Ranchland Conservation Legacy, Colo. Conservation Trust, Progress Now, Ctr. for Women's Health Rsch. Decorated chevalier French Legion of Honor; recipient Disting. Alumna award U. Calif., Santa Barbara, 1987, Trailblazer award AAUW, 1997, Childrens Advocacy award Colo. Soc. Sch. Psychologists, 1997. Mem. Internat. Women's Forum (mem. bd. dirs. 1981-89, pres. 83-85), Women Execs. in State Govt. (bd. dirs. 1981-87, chmn. 1988), Leadership Denver Assn. (bd. dirs. 1987, named Outstanding Alumna 1985), Nat. Congress Lt. Govs., Stanford Alumni Assn. Democrat.

**SCHOETTLER, JAMES ANTHONY, JR.,** lawyer; b. Balt., Nov. 3, 1956; s. James Anthony and Ellouise (Diggle) S.; m. Monica Gladys Solorzano, Jan. 14, 1984; children: Juliana Kathryn, Alison Louise. BA, Johns Hopkins U., 1978; MS in Fgn. Svc., Georgetown U., 1982, JD magna cum laude, 1982. Bar: D.C. 1982, Mass. 1982, U.S. Army Ct. Mil. Rev. 1983. Assoc. Dewey Ballantine, Washington, 1987—92, 1993—94, Prague, Czech Republic, 1992—93; asst. gen. counsel USEC Inc., Bethesda, Md., 1994—, acting gen. counsel, 2004—05, Capt. U.S. Army, 1983-87; col. USAR, 1987—. Mem. Bar Assn. D.C. Roman Catholic. Office: USEC Inc 6903 Rockledge Dr Bethesda MD 20817 Office Phone: 301-569-3325. Business E-Mail: schoettlerj@usec.com.

**SCHOETZ, DAVID JOHN, JR.,** colon and rectal surgeon, educator; b. Milw., Oct. 29, 1948; s. David John and Beverly (Rogers) S.; m. Ruthanne Brennan, Mar. 25, 1972; children: Elizabeth Anne, David John III. BA, Coll. of Holy Cross, 1970; MD, Med. Coll. Wis., Milw., 1974. Diplomate Am. Bd. Surgery, Am. Bd. Colon and Rectal Surgery (sr. examiner 1996—). Resident in surgery Boston U. Med. Ctr., 1974-81; resident in colon/rectal surgery Lahey Clinic Med. Ctr., Burlington, Mass., 1981-82, staff colon-rectal surgeon, 1982—, chmn. dept. colon-rectal surgery, 1987—2002; prof. surgery Med. Sch. Tufts U., Boston, 1999—, chmn. dept. med. edn., 2000—. Fellow ACS (commn. on cancer 1998-2003, gov., 2004—), Am. Bd. Colon and Rectal Surgery (sr. examiner 1996—, assoc. exec. 2005-), Am. Soc. Colon and Rectal Surgeons (sec. 1999-2002, pres.-elect 2002-03, pres. 2003—04). Office: Lahey Clinic Med Ctr 41 Mall Rd Burlington MA 01803-4521

**SCHOEWE, THOMAS M.,** retail executive; BA, MBA, Loyola U. of Chicago. CFO Beatrice Consumer Durables; v.p. business planning The Black & Decker Corp., 1986—89, v.p. finance, 1989—93, senior v.p., CFO, 1993—99; exec. v.p., CFO Wal-Mart Stores, Bentonville, 2000—. Dir. Centex Corp., 2001—. Office: Wal-Mart Stores 702 SW 8th St Bentonville AR 72716*

**SCHOFER, JOSEPH LANDY,** civil engineer, educator; b. Columbus, Ohio, Feb. 19, 1941; s. August and Rose (Landy) S.; m. Nancy Levy, June 29, 1969; children: Susan Jessica, Daniel Abraham. B in engring., Yale U., 1963; MS in civil engring.-transp., Northwestern U., 1965, PhD in civil engring.-transp., 1968. Asst. instr. Yale U., New Haven, 1963-64; asst. prof. sys. engring. U. Ill., Chgo., 1967-70; assoc. prof. civil engring. Northwestern U., Evanston, Ill., 1970-73, prof., 1974—, dir. rsch. transp. ctr., 1979-97, chmn. civil and environ. engring., 1997—2002, assoc. dean for faculty affairs Robert R. McCormick Sch. of Engring. and Applied Sci., 2003—, interim dean, 2004—05. Chmn. Transp. Commn., Wilmette, 1990-98; bd. advisors Inst. Transp. Studies U. Calif.-Davis, 1998-; adv. com. US Travel Model Improve-

ment Program. Contbr. over 120 articles to profl. jours., chpts. to books on transp. planning, policy analysis, impacts, traveler response and evaluation. Mem. AAAS, ASCE (life), Transp. Rsch. Bd., Inst. Transp. Engrs. (Wilbur Smith Disting. Educator award, 2003), Tau Beta Pi, Sigma Xi, Chi Epsilon Office: Dept Civil Engring Northwestern U 2145 Sheridan Rd Evanston IL 60208-3109

**SCHOFF, DENNIS L.,** lawyer; b. Apr. 17, 1959; m. Nina Schoff. BS in fin., Ind. U., JD cum laude. Bar: Ind., Ohio, Pa. Atty. Taft, Stettinius & Hollister, Cin.; various positions Lincoln National Corp., Phila., 1990—2000, v.p., assoc. gen. counsel, 2000—01, v.p., dep. gen. counsel, 2001—02, sr. v.p., gen. counsel, 2002—, mem. sr. mgmt. com. Mem.: ABA, Am. Corp. Counsel Assn., Exec. Bd. Gen Counsel Roundtable, Ind. Bar Assn., Pa. Bar Assn., Allen County Bar Assn. Office: Lincoln National Corp 1500 Market St Philadelphia PA 19102-2112 Home: 301 Durham Dr Villanova PA 19085-1451 Office Phone: 215-448-1400. Office Fax: 215-448-3215.

**SCHOFIELD, ANTHONY WAYNE,** judge; b. Farmington, N.Mex., Mar. 5, 1949; s. Aldred Edward and Margueriete (Knudsen) S.; m. Rebecca Ann Rosecrans, May 11, 1971; children: Josie, Matthew Paul, Peter Christian, Addie, Joshua James, M. Thomas, Jacob L., Daniel Z. BA, Brigham Young U., 1973, JD, 1976. Bar: Utah 1976, U.S. Dist. Ct. Utah 1976, U.S. Ct. Appeals (7th and 10th cirs.) 1977. Law clk. to hon. judge A. Sherman Christansen U.S. Dist. Ct. Utah, Salt Lake City, 1976-77; assoc. Ferenz, Bramhall, Williams & Gruskin, Agana, Guam, 1977-79; pvt. practice American Fork, Utah, 1979-80; assoc. Jardine, Linebaugh, Brown & Dunn, Salt Lake City, 1980-81; mem., dir. Ray, Quinney & Nebeker, Provo, Utah; judge 4th Jud. Dist. Ct., Provo, 1993—. Bishop Mormon Ch., American Fork, 1985-88; commr. American Fork City Planning Commn., 1980-85; trustee American Fork Hosp., 1984-93. Mem. Ctrl. Utah Bar Assn. (pres. 1987, 91). Office: 125 N 100 W Provo UT 84601-2849 Office Phone: 801-429-1045. E-mail: awschofield@yahoo.com.

**SCHOFIELD, BARBARA CURTRIGHT,** retired principal; b. Paris, Mo., Dec. 24, 1942 (div. 1986); children: Dianna Kay, Nichol LaVaughn, Theresa Alana. BS, U. Mo., Columbia, 1964; MEd, U. Mo., St. Louis, 1978; Cert. Ednl. Specialist, Southeast La. U., 1986. Cert. ednl. adminstr., La. Tchr. phys. sci. Neal Jr. High Sch., North Chicago, Ill., 1964-66, Deerfield (Ill.) High Sch., 1966-67, Holy Child H.S., Waukegan, Ill., 1970-72; dean of girls Antioch (Ill.) High Sch., 1972-74; dean of students, extra-curricular activities Washington (Mo.) High Sch., 1974-78; phys. edn. tchr. Clearwood Jr. High Sch., Slidell, La., 1978-83; asst. prin. Boyet Jr. High Sch., Slidell, 1983-2000; prin. Washington Jr. HS, Mo., 2000—03. Elder 1st Presbyn Ch., Slidell, 1985—90, 1993—95, clk. of session, 1993—95, 1997—99, 2003—05. Mem. Mo. State Tchrs. Assn., Nat. Assn. Secondary Sch. Prins. La./Mo. Ret. Tchrs. Assn, U. Mo. Alumni Assn., Mid. Sch. Assn., La. Assn. Educators (mem. congrl. contact team dist. 1), La. Assn. Sch. Exec., St. Tammany Assn. Educators (legis. chmn. 1980-81, pres. 1981-83), St. Tammany Adminstrs. Assn. (sec. 1991-92), Alpha Delta Kappa (pres. 1990-92), Delta Kappa Gamma Avocations: bridge, reading, golf, bicycling, walking.

**SCHOFIELD, EDMUND ACTON, JR.,** botanist, academic administrator; b. Worcester, Mass., Nov. 26, 1938; s. Edmund Acton Schofield and Phyllis Louise Parslow; m. Eileen Kathryn Carroll (div.). BA in Biology, Clark U., 1962, MA in Biology, 1964; PhD in Botany, Ohio State U., 1972. Postdoc. rsch. fellow Calif. Inst. Tech., 1972—73; ecologist Ohio Dept. Natural Resources, Columbus, 1973—76; dir. rsch. Sierra Club, San Francisco, 1976—77; staff scientist Inst. Ecology, Indpls., 1977—80; assoc. editor Horticulture Mag., Boston, 1982—85; editor Harvard U., Boston, 1986—88; various positions Worcester, Mass., 1989—2002; dir. edn. Tower Hill Botanic Garden, Boylston, Mass., 2002—. Plant ecologist Clark U./NSF, Antarctica, 1963—69, Ohio State U./NSF/Internat. Biol. Program, Barrow and Prudhoe, Alaska, 1963—64, Barrow and Prudhoe, 1967—68, Barrow and Prudhoe, 1968—69, Barrow and Prudhoe, 1973. Editor: Earthcare: Global Protection of Natural Areas, 1978; assoc. editor: Horticulture mag., 1982—85; co-editor: Thoreau's World and Ours, 1993. Mem. Worcester Hist. Commn., Mass., 1999—2003; docent Preservation Worcester, Mass., 1999—. With USNR, 1956—62. Recipient Antarctice Svc. medal, U.S. Congress, 1972, Resident Rsch. associateship, NASA/NAS, 1972—73. Mem.: Thoreau Soc. (pres. 1990—92). Democrat. Avocations: poetry, walking, reading, dining, scholarly research. Home: 707 Main St Boylston MA 01505 Office: Tower Hill Botanic Garden 11 French Dr Boylston MA 01505 Office Phone: 508-869-6111 ext. 21. Office Fax: 508-869-0314. Personal E-mail: edmundschofield@yahoo.com. Business E-Mail: edschofield@towerhillbg.org.

**SCHOFIELD, JAMES ROY,** medical consultant, educator; b. July 12, 1923; s. Arthur Monroe and Grace Pearl (West) S. BS, Baylor U., 1945, MD, 1947; LLD (hon.), Queens U., Kingston, Ont., Can., 1988. Instr. to prof. Baylor U. Coll. Medicine, Houston, 1947-71, asst. dean to acad. dean, 1953-71; sec., liaison com. on med. edn. Assn. Am. Med. Colls. and AMA, Washington, 1972-87; ind. cons. on med. edn. Washington, 1987—. Mem. transitional coun. United Arab Emirates U., 1986-89; external auditor Sultan Qaboos Coll. Medicine, Muscat, Oman, 1987-97; vis. disting. prof. history of medicine, univ. cons. on premed. edn. Baylor U., 1992—; facult Baylor in the British Isles, 1994—; cons. in field. Author: New and Expanded Medical Schools: Effectivity to the 1980's, 1985; contbr. articles to profl. jours. Bd. dirs. Am-Polish Found., 1995; leader Md. Boy Scout Jamborie, 1951. Capt. M.C. U.S. Army, 1954—57. Recipient disting. Achievement award Baylor U., 1992, Disting. Alumnus award Baylor Coll. Medicine, 1996. Mem. Sigma Xi, Alpha Omega Alpha. Republican. Baptist. Avocations: woodcarving, cabinet work, collecting old tools, music, writing. Address: 700 Greenwood Dr Georgetown TX 78628-8371 Fax E-mail: jschof@aol.com.

**SCHOFIELD, JAMES ROY,** computer programmer; b. Reedsburg, Wis., Aug. 16, 1953; s. G. C. Schofield and Margaret (Collies) Tverberg. BA, Carleton Coll., 1976. Programmer Brandon Applied Systems, San Francisco, 1977-78, Rand Info. Systems, San Francisco, 1979-83; systems programmer IBM, San Jose, Calif., 1983-91; programmer Office of Instnl. Rsch./U. Calif., Berkeley, 1991-94, Datis Corp., San Mateo, Calif., 1994-95, Compuware Corp., Los Gatos, Calif., 1995-96, Pacific Bell, San Ramon, Calif., 1996—2001, AT&T, San Ramon, Calif., 2002. Mem. Assn. for Computing Machinery, Commonwealth Club of Calif., Phi Beta Kappa. Avocations: guitar, reading, swimming. Home: PO Box 25143 San Mateo CA 94402-5143 Office: AT&T 2600 Camino Ramon San Ramon CA 94583-5099

**SCHOFIELD, LORNA GAIL,** lawyer; b. New Haven, Ind., Jan. 22, 1956; d. Donald Earl and Priscilla (Tiango) S.; 1 child, Sarah. BA, Ind. U., 1977; JD, NYU, 1981. Bar: N.Y. 1982, U.S. Dist. Ct. (so and ea. dists.) N.Y. 1982, U.S. Ct. Appeals (11th cir.) 1983, U.S. Ct. Appeals (2d cir.) 1985, U.S. Tax Ct. 1991, U.S. Dist. Ct. Fed. Claims 1992, U.S. Ct. Appeals (10th cir.) 1993, U.S. Ct. Appeals (6th cir.) 1995, U.S. Supreme Ct. 1996, U.S. Ct. Appeals (3d cir.) 1997. Assoc. Cleary, Gottlieb, Steen & Hamilton, N.Y.C., 1981-84; assoc. U.S. atty. U.S. Dist. Ct. (so. dist.) N.Y., N.Y.C., 1988-91, ptnr., 1991—. Contbr. articles to profl. jours. Mem. ABA (litig. sect., budget officer 2002-, mem. standing com. Judiciary, co-dir. divisions 2000-01, co-chair task force on discovery 1997—2000, coun. 1997—2000, co-chair class actions and derivative suits com. 1994-97, vice chair accts.' liability subcom. 1993-94, co-chair Woman Advocate Com. 1994, planning com. 1993), Am. Law Inst., Fed. Bar Coun., N.Y. Coun. Def. Lawyers Assn. of Bar of City of N.Y. Office: Debevise & Plimpton LLP 919 Third Ave New York NY 10022-3904 Office Phone: 212-909-6094. Business E-Mail: lgschofield@debevoise.com.

**SCHOFIELD, REGINA BROWN,** federal agency administrator; b. Natchez, Miss., Jan. 14, 1962; d. Elvia John and Velma Marie (Cameron) Brown; m. Stephen Gerard Schofield, Nov. 2, 1996. BSBA, Miss. Coll., 1983; MBA, Jackson (Miss.) State U., 1990. Sales rep. Philip Morris, USA,

Jackson, 1983-91; spl. asst. U.S. Dept. Edn., Washington, 1991-92, White House liaison, 1992-93; mgr. environ. issues Internat. Coun. Shopping Ctrs., Alexandria, Va., 1993—98; mgr. govt rels US Postal Svc., 1998—2002; dir. Office of Intergovernmental Affairs US Dept. HHS, 2002—05, White House liaison, 2002—05; asst. atty. gen. Office of Justice Programs US Dept. Justice, Washington, 2005—. Bd. dirs. Nat. Wetlands Coalition, 1997—99, Va. Dept. Agrl. and Consumer Svcs., Richmond 1995—99, Va. Fedn. Rep. Women, Richmond, 1996-98, 2001-05; bd. visitors Coll. William and Mary, Williamsburg, Va., 1997—2001, The Endowment Assn. of the Coll. of William and Mary, 2004-05; mem. Commonwealth Rep. Women's Club, Alexandria, 1995, Am. Coun. Young Polit. Leaders, 1998-2005. Roman Catholic. Avocation: reading. Office: US Dept Justice 810 7th St NW Rm 6400 Washington DC 20531

**SCHOFIELD, ROBERT E(DWIN),** historian, educator, academic administrator; b. Milford, Nebr., June 1, 1923; s. Charles Edwin and Nora May (Fullerton) S.; m. Mary-Peale Smith, June 20, 1959; 1 son, Charles Stockton Peale. AB, Princeton U., 1944; MS, U. Minn., 1948; PhD, Harvard U., 1955. Research asst. Fercleve Corp. and Clinton Labs., Oak Ridge, 1944-46; research assoc. Knolls Atomic Power Lab., Gen. Electric Co., 1948-51; asst. prof., then assoc. prof. history U. Kans., Lawrence, 1955-60; mem. faculty Case Western Res. U., Cleve., 1960-79, prof. history of sci., 1963-72, Lynn Thorndike prof. history of sci., 1972-79; prof. history Iowa State U., Ames, 1979-93, prof. emeritus, 1993—, dir. grad. program history tech. and sci., 1979-92. Mem. Inst. Advanced Study, 1967-68, 74-75; Sigma Xi nat. lectr., 1978-80 Author: The Lunar Society of Birmingham, 1963, Scientific Autobiography of Joseph Priestley: Selected Scientific Correspondence, 1966, Mechanism and Materialism: British Natural Philosophy in an Age of Reason, 1970, (with D.G.C. Allan) Stephen Hales: Scientist and Philanthropist, 1980, The Enlightenment of Joseph Priestley: A Study of His Life and Work from 1733 to 1773, 1997, The Enlightened Joseph Priestley: A Study of His Life and Work from 1773 to 1804, 2004. Served with AUS, 1945-46. Fulbright fellow, 1953-54; Guggenheim fellow, 1959-60, 67-68 Fellow Am. Phys. Soc., Royal Soc. Arts; mem. History of Sci. Soc., Soc. History Tech., Midwest Junto History of Sci., Am. Soc. 18th Century Studies, Acad. Internat. d'Histoire des Scis. (corr.) Home and Office: 44 Sycamore Rd Princeton NJ 08540-5323

**SCHOGGEN, PHIL H(OWARD),** psychologist, educator; b. Tulsa, Aug. 28, 1923; s. Walter B. and Emma F. (Alexander) S.; m. Maxine F. Spoor, June 28, 1944; children: Leida, Christopher, Ann, Susan. AB in Psychology, Park Coll., 1946; MS, U. Kans., Lawrence, 1951, PhD in Psychology, 1954. Asst. prof. psychology U. Oreg., 1957-62, assoc. prof., 1962-66; prof., chmn. dept. psychology George Peabody Coll., 1966-75; prof. human devel. and family studies N.Y. State Coll. Human Ecology, Cornell U., 1977-90, prof. emeritus, 1990—, chmn. dept., 1977-82. Author: (with R. G. Barker) Qualities of Community Life, 1973; Behavior Settings: A Revision and Extension of Roger G. Barker's Ecological Psychology, 1989. Served with USNR, 1944-46, 50-51. Mem. APA. Home: 121 Vossland Dr Nashville TN 37205-3617 Personal E-mail: schoggph@comcast.net.

**SCHOLEFIELD, PETER GORDON,** health facility administrator; b. Newport, Wales, June 26, 1925; emigrated to Can., 1947, naturalized, 1952; s. Tom and Margaret (Bithell) S.; m. Erna Mary Cooper, Sept. 29, 1951; children— David, John, Paul. B.Sc., U. Wales, 1944, M.Sc., 1946, D.Sc., 1960; PhD, McGill U., Montreal, Que., Can., 1949. From research fellow to prof. biochemistry McGill U., 1949-65, dir. cancer research unit, 1965-69; asst. exec. dir. Nat. Cancer Inst. Can., Toronto, 1969-80, exec. dir., 1980-91, spl. adviser to chief exec. officer, 1991-92; dir. grants and awards Alta. Heritage Found. for Med. Rsch., Edmonton, 1992-94; coord. acad. affairs Samuel Lunenfeld Rsch. Inst. Mt. Sinai Hosp., Toronto, 1994-99. Chair rsch. policy com., bd. dirs. Alzheimer Soc. of Can., 1994-2000; mem. health adv. com. Alta. Heritage Found. Med. Rsch, 1994-99; bd. dirs. Ont. Neurotrauma Found., 1999-2004, sec., 2003-04, chmn. rsch. com., 2003-04; mem. adv. bd. Inst. Neurosci. Mental Health and Addiction, Can. Insts. Health Rsch., 2001-04, mem. committee on grants and awards competitions, 2005—. Home: 2010 Islington Ave # 1503 Etobicoke ON Canada M9P 3S8 Personal E-mail: peter.scholefield@rogers.com.

**SCHOLER, SUE WYANT,** retired state legislator; b. Topeka, Oct. 20, 1936; d. Zint Elwin and Virginia Louise (Achenbach) Wyant; m. Charles Frey Scholer, Jan. 27, 1957; children: Elizabeth Scholer Truelove, Charles W., Virginia M. Scholer McCal. Student, Kans. State U., 1954-56. Draftsman The Farm Clinic, West Lafayette, Ind., 1978—79; assessor Wabash Twp., West Lafayette, 1979-84; commr. Tippecanoe County, Lafayette, Ind., 1984-90; state rep. Dist. 26 Ind. Statehouse, Indpls., 1990—2004, ret., 2004. Asst. minority whip, 1992-94, Rep. whip, 1994-2000, asst. Rep. leader, 2001—04; mem. Tippecanoe County Area Plan Commn., 1984-90; chmn. Midwestern legis. conf. CSG, 1998. Bd. dirs. Crisis Ctr., Lafayette, 1984-89, Tippecanoe Arts Fedn., 1990-99, United Way, Lafayette, 1990-93; mem. Lafayette Conv. and Visitors Bur., 1988-90. Recipient Salute to Women Govt. and Politics award, 1986, United Sr. Action award, Outstanding Legislator award, 1993, Small Bus. Champion award, 1995, Ind. Libr. Fedn. Legislator award, 1995, Disting. Legislator award Nat. Alliance for Mentally Ill, 1997., 2003, West Ctrl. Ind. Advocate award, 2003, Friend of Cmty. Action award, 1999, Disting. Pub. Svc. award Am. Legion, 2004, Family Svcs. Advocacy award Family Svcs., 2004, Sagamore of the Wabash, 2004, Order of the Griffin, Purdue U., 2004. Mem. Ind. Assn. County Commrs. (treas. 1990), Assn. Ind. Counties (legis. com. 1988-90), Greater Lafayette C. of C. (ex-officio bd. 1984-90), LWV, P.E.O., Purdue Women's Club (past treas.), Kappa Kappa Kappa (past pres. Epsilon chpt.)., Delta Delta Delta (past pres. alumnae, house corp. treas.). Republican. Presbyterian. Avocations: golf, needlecrafts, reading. Home: 807 Essex St West Lafayette IN 47906-1534

**SCHOLES, EDISON EARL,** military officer; b. McCaysville, Ga., Aug. 16, 1939; s. Alvin L. and Marie (Plemmons) S.; m. Elva E. Bussey, June 4, 1961; children: Juana Kimberly Scholes, Tracy Michele Scholes Heller, Michael Lee. BS in Physics cum laude, No. Ga. Coll., 1961; MS in Ops. Rsch., Naval Postgrad. Sch., 1970; postgrad., Army War Coll., 1980, Harvard Def. Policy Seminar, 1991. Commd. 2d lt. U.S. Army, 1961, advanced through grades to maj. gen., 1991; comdr. A Detachment, 10th Spl. Forces Group U.S. ArmyEurope, 1963-66; comdr. Co. D, 2d Bn.(Abn.), 8th Cav., 1st Cav. Divsn. U.S. Army, Republic of Vietnam, 1967-68, sr. adv. I Corps. Ranger Commd. Vietnam, 1970—71, comdr. 1st Bn., 23d Inf., 2d Inf. Divsn. Republic of Korea, 1976-77, comdr. 2d Tng. Bn., Sch. Brigade, U.S. Army Inf. Sch. Ft. Benning, Ga., 1978-79, comdr. 1st Inf. Tng. Brigade, U.S. Army Infantry Tng. Ctr., 1983-85, dep. commanding gen. chief of staff 3d U.S. Army/U.S. Army Cen. Command Ft. McPherson, Ga., 1986-88, asst. divsn. comdr. 82d Airborne Divsn. Ft. Bragg, NC, 1988-89, chief of staff XVIII Airborne Corps, 1989-90, chief of staff joint task force-south, Op. Just Cause, 1989-90, dep. commanding gen. XVIII Airborne Corps, Operation Desert Shield/Desert Storm Saudi Arabia, Iraq, 1990-91, dep. commanding gen. XVIII Airborne Corps Ft. Bragg, 1991-93; dep. comdr. Allied Land Forces, S.E. Europe NATO, 1993-95; program gen. mgr. Saudi Arabia N.G. Modernization Program, Vinnell Arabia, 1996—2002; pvt. contractor numerous countries, 2002—. Decorated Dept. Def. Disting. Svc. medal, Army Disting. Svc. medal with oak leaf cluster, Silver Star, Legion of Merit with oak leaf cluster, Bronze Star with V device and 4 oak leaf clusters, Purple Heart with oak leaf cluster, 6 Air medals, Army Commendation medal with V device and oak leaf cluster, Armed Forces Expeditionary medal, Combat Infantryman badge, Expert Infantry badge; Cross of Gallantry with Silver and Bronze Stars and Palm (Republic of Vietnam); numerous other domestic and frgn. decorations. Inducted into North Ga.'s Coll. and State U. Hall of Fame. Mem. 82d Airborne Divsn. Assn., Spl. Forces Assn., U.S. Army Ranger Assn., Spl. Ops. Assn. Baptist. Avocations: reading, camping, fishing. Personal E-mail: escholes@cox.net.

**SCHOLES, MYRON S.,** financier, former law and finance educator; b. Timmins, Ont., Can., July 1, 1941; BA, McMaster U., 1959—62, MBA, 1962—64; PhD in finance, U. Chgo., 1964—69; D (hon.), U. Paris-Dauphine,

1989, McMaster U., 1990, U. Leuven, 1998. Rsch. assoc., Ctr. for Math. Studies in Bus. and Econs. U. Chgo., 1966—67, instr. in fin., grad. sch. bus., 1967—68, assoc. prof., 1973—74, prof., 1975—79, dir., Ctr. for Rsch. in Security Prices, 1975—81, Edward Eagle Brown prof. fin., 1979—82; asst. prof. in fin. MIT Mgmt. Sch., Cambridge, 1968—72, assoc. prof., 1972—73; prof. law Stanford U., Calif., 1983—96. Frank E. Buck prof. Grad. Sch. Bus., 1983—96, sr. rsch. fellow, Hoover Instn., 1988—96, Frank E. Buck prof. emeritus fin., 1996—; mng. dir., sr. advisor Salomon Bros., 1990—93; prin. Long-Term Capital Mgmt., Greenwich, Conn., 1994—98; chmn. Oak Hill Platinum Ptnrs., Rye Brook, NY, 1999—; mng. ptnr. Oak Hill Capital Mgmt., 1999—. Bd. trustees Math. Scis. Rsch. Inst.; bd. dirs. Chgo. Mercantile Exchange, 2000—, chmn. Competitive Markets Adv. Coun., 2004—; bd. dirs. Chgo. Mercantile Exchange Holdings, 2001—, Intelligent Markets, Am Century, FEP/Constellation, UNext Inc., Salomon Swapco Inc. Contbr. articles to profl. jours. Recipient Nobel Prize for econ. scis., 1997. Mem.: Am. Fin. Assn. (v.p. 1989, pres. 1990), Econometrics Soc. Office: Arbor Investors 2775 Sand Hill Rd Ste 220 Menlo Park CA 94025-7019 Address: Oak Hill Platinum Ptnrs Reckson Exec Park 1100 King St Bldg 4 Rye Brook NY 10573 E-mail: mscholes@pacbell.net.

**SCHOLES, ROBERT THORNTON,** allergist, researcher, science administrator; b. Bushnell, Ill., June 24, 1919; s. Harlan Lawrence and Lura Zolene (Camp) S.; m. Kathryn Ada Tew, Sept. 3, 1948; 1 child, Delia. Student, Knox Coll., 1937-38; BS, Mich. State U., 1941; MD, U. Rochester, 1950; postgrad., U. London, 1951-52; U. Chgo., 1953. Intern Gorgas Hosp., Ancon, C.Z., 1950-51; lab. assist. dept. entomology Mich. State U., 1940-41; rsch. asst. Roselake Wildlife Expt. Sta., 1941; rsch. assoc. Harvard U., 1953-57; served to med. dir. USPHS, 1954-71; med. officer, dep. chief health and sanitation divsn. U.S. Ops. Mission, Bolivia, 1954-57, chief health and sanitation divsn., Paraguay, 1957—60; internat. health rep. Office of Surgeon Gen., 1960-62; br. chief, rsch. grants officer, acting assoc. dir. Nat. Inst. Allergy and Infectious Diseases, NIH, Bethesda, Md., 1962-71; co-founder, pres. The Bioresearch Ranch, Inc., Rodeo, N.Mex., 1977—. Cons. Peace Corps, 1961, Hidalgo County Med. Svcs., Inc., 1979-99, N.Mex. Health Sys. Agy., 1980-86, N.Mex. Health Resources, Inc., 1981-93, Luna County Charitable Found., 1993—. Contbr. articles to profl. jours. Capt. USAAF, 1942-45. Commonwealth Fund fellow, 1953. Mem. AAAS, AMA, APHA, Am. Ornithologists Union, N.Y. Acad. Sci., Sembot Hon. Soc. Achievements include research, writing and field test of first health survey indices detailing anthropological parameters; institution of first country wide malaria control project in Paraguay. Home and Office: PO Box 117 Rodeo NM 88056-0117 Personal E-mail: scholes@vtc.net.

**SCHOLLANDER, WENDELL, III,** lawyer; b. East Ridge, Tenn., Oct. 15, 1974; s. Wendell and Jayn Schollander. BA, U. N.C., Chapel Hill, 1997; JD, Wake Forest Law Sch., Winston-Salem, N.C., 2001. Missionary Presbyn. Ch., Guatemala, 1998; pvt. practice Winston-Salem, NC, 2001—. Co-author: (book) Forgotten Elegance, 2001, Small Business Owner's Guide to Bankruptcy, 2002, Forsyth Estate Planning, 2003, Small Business Owner's Guide to Bankruptcy, 2002, Forsyth Water Commissioner, 2004—. Scoutmaster Boy Scouts of Am., Winston-Salem, 2002—04. Recipient Point of Light award, Pres. George Bush, 1992, Chevron Conservation award, Chevron Award Program, 1992, Take Pride in Am. award, Dept. of Interior, 1991, 1992. Mem.: SAR (awards chair 2002—). Office: Schollander 2000 W First St Ste 308 Winston Salem NC 27104 Business E-mail: schollanderlaw@bellsouth.net.

**SCHOLLANDER, WENDELL LESLIE, JR.,** lawyer; b. Ocala, Fla., May 17, 1943; m. Jayn Cochran; 1 child, Wendell Leslie III. BS, U. Pa., 1966, MBA, 1968; postgrad., Stetson U., 1969-70; JD, Duke U., 1972. Bar: N.C. 1977, Tenn. 1972. Fla. 1987. With Container Corp. Am., Fernandina, Fla., 1968-69; assoc. Miller, Martin, Chattanooga, 1972-75; asst. counsel R.J. Reynolds Industries, Inc., 1975-78, assoc. counsel, 1978-79, sr. assoc. counsel, 1979-82, sr. counsel, 1982-85; gen. counsel RJR Archer, Inc., Winston-Salem, NC, 1979-85; of counsel Finger, Parker & Avram, Winston-Salem, 1985-87; ptnr. Schollander, Winston-Salem, 1987—. Gen. counsel Splty. Tobacco Council, 1985-87. Mem. ABA, N.C. Bar Assn., Forsyth County Bar Assn., Mensa, SAR, Phi Delta Phi, Kappa Sigma. Presbyterian. Office: 2000 W 1st St Ste 308 Winston Salem NC 27104-4225 Office Phone: 336-727-0900.

**SCHOLSKY, MARTIN JOSEPH,** retired priest; b. Stafford Spring, Conn., Jan. 16, 1930; s. Sigmund Felix and Mary Magdalen (Wysocki) S. BA, St. John's Sem., 1952, MA in History, 1956; MA in Classical Greek, Cath. U. of Am., 1966. Ordained priest Roman Cath. Ch., 1956. Asst. pastor St. Peter's Ch., Hartford, Conn., 1956-61; prin. St. Peter's Sch., Hartford, 1956-58; instr. St. Thomas Sem., Bloomfield, Conn., 1961-67, admissions dir., 1965-67; vocations dir. Archdiocese of Hartford, 1967-78; chaplain Newington (Conn.) Children's Hosp., 1971-78; weekend asst. St. Mary's Ch., Newington, 1961-78; pastor St. Bartholomew Ch., Manchester, Conn., 1978-90; dean Manchester Deanery, 1989-91; spiritual dir. St. Thomas Aquinas HS, New Britain, Conn., 1991—92; pastor St. Mary's Ch., East Hartford, Conn., 1992—2005. Weekend asst. St. Francis of Assis Ch., South Windsor, Conn., 1991-92; instr. Holy Apostle's Sem. & Coll., Cromwell, Conn., 1988-94. Contbr. articles to profl. jours. Home: 36 Griswold St Manchester CT 06040-3928 Personal E-mail: mjscholsky@aol.com. *Conscience is not our own personal feelings about things; rather, it is our innate awareness of the rightness and wrongness of our deeds as God sees them, an awareness, often denied, that still remains the measure by which God will ultimately judge us all.*

**SCHOLTEN, GARY P.,** finance company executive; Grad., U. No. Iowa, 1980. From asst. planning analyst to v.p. retail info. scs. Prin. Fin. Group, Des Moines, 1980—2002, sr. v.p., CIO, 2002—. Fellow: Life Office Mgmt. Inst. (chmn. ind. product sys. com.). Office: Prin Fin Group 711 High St Des Moines IA 50392

**SCHOLTEN, MENNO NICO,** mortgage banker; b. Assen, Drenthe, Netherlands, June 18, 1943; arrived in U.S., 1949; s. Nico Menno and Hennie (Nienhuis) S.; m. Susan Sumnar, Aug. 11, 1973; 1 child, Paul Menno. BArch., U. Calif., Berkeley, 1967; MBA, DePaul U., 1980. Registered architect. Architect various, including Skidmore, Owings & Merrill, others, Chgo., 1968-78, Knight Architects, Engrs. and Planners, Chgo., 1978-81, 1989-92; asst. v.p. constrn. lending adminstr. First Nat. Bank of Chgo., 1981-85; v.p. real estate group First Tex. Savs., Dallas, 1985-87; mgr. constrn. lending Household Internat. (Household Bank), Prospect Heights, Ill., 1992-94; pres. The Mesu Group, Ltd., Evanston, Ill., 1995—. Bd. dirs. Global Med. Relief Program. Patentee chair design, 1979. Bd. dirs. Global Med. Relief Program. Recipient award of merit Chgo. Assn. of Commerce and Industry and Internat. Trade Club of Chgo., 1979. Mem. AIA (Chgo. chpt.), Am. Guild Organists (bd. dirs., treas. 1991-99), Calif. Scholarship Fedn. (life mem.), Inst. Mgmt. Cons., Rotary Internat., Delta Mu Delta. Avocations: tennis, skiing. Home: 3521 Central St Evanston IL 60201-4915

**SCHOLTEN, ROGER KEITH,** lawyer; b. Jan. 25, 1955; BA, Northwestern U.; JD, U. Iowa. Atty. Maytag Corp., 1981—87, assoc. gen. counsel, 1987—94, asst. gen. counsel, 1994—2001, v.p. strategic planning & corp. devel., 2000—01, sr. v.p. & gen. counsel, 2001—. Office: Maytag Corp Legal Dept 403 W 4th St N Newton IA 50208 Home: 4106 John Lynde Rd Des Moines IA 50312-3040 Office Phone: 641-791-8309. Office Fax: 641-791-8102. Business E-Mail: rschol@maytag.com.

**SCHOLTZ, ROBERT ARNO,** electrical engineering educator; b. Lebanon, Ohio, Jan. 26, 1936; s. William Paul and Erna Johanna (Weigel) Scholtz; m. Laura Elizabeth McKeon, June 16, 1962; children: Michael William, Paul Andrew. BSEE, U. Cin., 1958; MSEE, U. So. Calif., 1960; PhD, Stanford U., 1964. Co-op student Sheffield Corp., Dayton, Ohio, 1953-58; MS and PHD fellow Hughes Aircraft Co., Culver City, Calif., 1958-63, sr. staff engr., 1963-78; prof. U. So. Calif., L.A., 1963—. Vis. prof. U. Hawaii, 1969, 78; cons. LinCom Corp., L.A., 1975-81, Axiomatix Inc., L.A., 1980-86, JPL, Pasadena, 1985, Tech. Group, 1987-89, TRW, 1989, Pulson Comm., 1992-93,

Colley-Godward, Palo Alto, 1994-97, Time Domain Corp., 2000-01. Coauthor: Spread Spectrum Comm., 3 vols., 1984, Spread Spectrum Communications Handbook, 1994, Basic Concepts in Information Theory and Coding, 1994; contbr. articles to profl. jours. (recipient Leonard G. Abraham award 1983, Donald G. Fink award 1984, Sr. Paper award Signal Processing Soc. 1992, Comm. Soc. Fred Ellersick Paper award 1997, Mil. Comms. Conf. award 2001, S.A. Shelkunoff prize Antennas and Propagation Soc., 2003, Eric E. Sumner award 2006). Pres. South Bay Cmty. Concert Orgn., Redondo Beach, Calif., 1975—79. Fellow: IEEE (bd. govs. info. theory group 1981—86, bd. govs. communication soc. 1981—83, chmn. fin. com. NTC 1977, program chmn. ISIT 1981, Eric E. Sumner award 2006). Office: U So Calif Comm Scis Inst Dept Elec Engring Los Angeles CA 90089-2565 E-mail: scholtz@usc.edu.

**SCHOLZ, JOHN KARL,** economist, educator; BA in Econs. and Math.; PhD in Econs., Stanford U., 1988. Asst. prof. econs. dept. LaFollette Inst. Pub. Affairs U. Wis., Madison, 1988—95, prof. dept. econs., 1998—. Sr. staff economist Coun. Econ. Advisers Exec. Office of the Pres., Washington, 1990—91; faculty rsch. assoc. Nat. Bur. Econ. Rsch., 1991—; dep. asst. sec. Office Tax Analysis U.S. Treasury Dept., 1997—98; dir. Inst. for Rsch. on Poverty, 2000—; mem. panel to evaluate the USDA's methodology for estimating eligibility and participation for the WIC program NRC, 2001—03; sr. rsch. affiliate Mich. Nat. Poverty Ctr.; mem. bd. outside scholars Mich. Retirement Rsch. Ctr., 2003—. Contbr. articles to profl. jours.; co-editor: Jour. Human Resources, 1994—; mem. editl. bd.: Nat. Tax Jour., 1998—, The B.E. Jours. in Econ. Analysis and Policy, 2001—. Office: Univ Wis-Madison Dept Econs 1180 Observatory Dr Madison WI 53706-1397

**SCHOLZ, PETER M.,** surgeon, director; MD, U. Basel, Switzerland, 1970. Diplomate Am. Bd. Surgery, 1983, Am. Bd. Thoracic Surgery, 1985. Intern in Surgery Duke U. Med. Ctr., Durham, NC, 1974—75, resident gen. and thoracic surgery, 1975—83; physician divsn. thoracic surgery Robert Wood Johnson U. Med. Group, New Brunswick, NJ, 1983—, chief divsn. cardiovasc. surgery, 2005—. Office: Clin Acad Bldg Ste 4100 125 Paterson St New Brunswick NJ 08901-1977 Office Phone: 732-235-7642.

**SCHONBERG, ALAN ROBERT,** personnel director; b. N.Y.C., Oct. 23, 1928; s. Julius and Evelyn (Guzik) S.; m. Carole May Kreisman, Dec. 27, 1975; children: William, Evelyn, David, Jeffrey. Nat. sales mgr. Majestic Specialties, Inc., Cleve., 1953-63; pres. Internat. Personnel, Inc., Cleve., 1963-65; chmn. Mgmt. Recruiters Internat., Inc., Cleve., 1965-98, 1998—2000, chmn. emeritus, 2001—. Pres., bd. dirs. Jewish Vocat. Service, Cleve., 1983—; trustees Mt. Sinai Hosp. (now Mt. Sinai Found.), Cleve., bd. dirs. Cleve. Jewish News; gen. chmn. Welfare Fund Campaign; trustee Am. Jewish Commn., Mt. Sinai Med. Ctr., Hebrew Immigrant Aid Soc. Named one of Cleve.'s 86 Most Interesting People, Cleve. Mag., 1986, Man of Yr. local chpt. Orgn. through Rehab. and Tng., 1996, Entrepreneur of Yr. Inc. Mag., Merrill Lynch Ernst & Young, 1995; recipient Human Rels. award Cleve. chpt. Am. Jewish Comm., 1998. Mem. Internat. Franchise Assn., Internat. Confederation Pvt. Employment Agys. Assns., Am. Mgmt. Assn., Assn. Human Resource Cons. (chmn. 1980—), Org. for Rehab. and Training (ORT), Assn. Am.-Israel C. of C. (pres.), Ohio Israel C. of C. (co-chmn.), Jewish Family Svcs. Assn. (v.p., pres. 1998-2002). Avocation: travel.

**SCHONBRUN, MICHAEL K.,** senior housing developer and operator; b. N.Y.C., Jan. 26, 1948; s. Arnold Laurance and Madeline (Courland) Schonbrun; m. Michelle I. Fredson, June 6, 1971 (div. Dec. 1998); 1 child, Ethan F.; m. Susan E. Juroe, Feb. 17, 2001; children: Adam J., Theodore C. BA, Yale U., 1969; JD, U. Pa., 1973. Bar: Ohio 1973, Colo. 1975. Asst. to gov. Ohio Gov.'s Office, Columbus, 1973—74, Colo. Gov.'s Office, Denver, 1974—75; asst. dir. Colo. Dept. Health, Denver, 1976—78; pres., CEO Nat. Jewish Hosp., Denver, 1979—91; ex. v.p. Blue Cross/Blue Shield of Colo., Denver, 1991—93; exec. v.p. Vitas Healthcare Corp. Inc., Miami, Fla., 1994—95; pres. Schonbrun & assocs., Boulder, Colo., 1995—97; founder, pres., CEO Balfour Sr. Care, Boulder, 1997—. Chmn. Young Pres.'s Orgn. Healthcare Focus Forum, Dallas, 1999—2001; bd. dirs. Colo. Assn. Housing and Svcs., Denver, United Bank of Denver, 1985—91; mem. leadership coun. Assisted Living Fedn. Am., Washington, 1999—. Contbr. articles to profl. jours. Chmn. bd. dirs. Rocky Mountain Alzheimers Assn., 2002, Denver Met. Air Quality Coun., 1985—89, Internat. Med. Corp., L.A., 1996—2000; mem. Colo. 2002 Winter Olympic Games Com., 1988—90. Democrat. Jewish. Avocation: travel, running, tennis, reading fiction, movies. Home: 10200 Niwot Rd Longmont CO 80504 Office: Balfour Sr Care 1331 Hecla Dr Louisville CO 80027-2325

**SCHÖNEMANN, PETER HANS,** psychologist, educator; b. Pethau, Germany, July 15, 1929; arrived in U.S., 1960, naturalized, 2003; s. Max Paul Franz and Hertha Anna (Kahle) S.; m. Roberta Dianne Federbush, Jan. 29, 1962; children: Raoul Dieter, Nicole Deborah. Vordiplom in Psychologie, U. Munich, 1956; Hauptdiplom in Psychologie, U. Goettingen, 1959; PhD, U. Ill., 1964. Thurstone postdoctoral fellow U. N.C., 1965-66; asst. prof., then assoc. prof. Ohio State U., 1966-69; postdoctoral fellow Ednl. Testing Service, Princeton, NJ, 1967-68; vis. prof. Technische Hochschule, Aachen, Fed. Republic Germany, 1981; mem. faculty Purdue U., 1969—, prof. psychology, 1971-2001, emeritus, 2001—. Vis. prof. Univs. Munich, Bielefeld and Braunschweig, 1984-85, Nat. Taiwan U., 1992, 96, 97. Author papers in field. Recipient Found. for the Advancement of Outstanding Scholarship award, Taiwan, 1996. Office: Dept Psychol Scis Purdue U Lafayette IN 47907 Personal E-mail: phs@psych.purdue.edu.

**SCHONFELD, GUSTAV,** medical educator, researcher, administrator; b. Mukacevo, Ukraine, May 8, 1934; came to U.S., 1946; s. Alexander Schonfeld and Helena Gottermann; m. Miriam Steinberg, May 28, 1961; children: Joshua Lawrence, Julia Elizabeth, Jeremy David. BA, Washington U., St. Louis, 1956, MD, 1960. Diplomate Am. Bd. Internal Medicine. Intern Bellevue Med. Ctr. NYU, 1960—61, resident in internal medicine, 1961—63; chief resident in internal medicine Jewish Hosp., St. Louis, 1963—64; from NIH trainee in endocrinology & metabolism to Kountz prof. medicine Washington U., St. Louis, 1964—96, Busch prof., chair medicine, 1996—99, Samuel E. Schechter prof. medicine, 2002—; rsch. assoc. Cochran VA Hosp., St. Louis, 1965—66, clin. investigator, 1968—70, cons. in internal medicine, 1972—; rsch. flight med. officer USAF Sch. Aerospace Medicine, Brooks AFB, Tex., 1966—68; from asst. physician to physician Barnes Hosp., St. Louis, 1972—96; physician-in-chief Barnes Jewish Hosp., St. Louis, 1996—99; clin. instr. medicine Harvard U. Med. Sch., Boston, 1970—72; assoc. prof. metabolism and human nutrition, asst. dir. Clin. Rsch. Ctr. MIT, Cambridge, 1970—72. Mem. rsch. com. Mo. Heart Assn., 1978-80; expert witness working group on atherosclerosis Nat. Heart, Lung and Blood Inst., 1979, Nat. Diabetes Adv. Bd., 1979; mem. endocrinologic and metabolic drugs adv. com. USPHS, FDA, 1982-86; mem. nutrition study sect. NIH, 1984-88, spl. reviewer metabolism study sect.; mem. adult treatment guidelines panel Nat. Cholesterol Edn. Program, 1986; mem. Consensus Devel. Conf. on Triglyceride, High Density Lipoprotein and Coronary Heart Disease, 1992; cons. Am. Egg Bd., Am. Dairy Bd., Inst. Shortening and Edible Oils, Ciba-Geigy, Sandoz, Fournier, Parke-Davis, Bristol-Meyers Squibb, Monsanto/Searle. Past editor: Atherosclerosis, past mem. editl. bd.: Jour. Clin. Endocrinology and Metabolism, Jour. Clin. Investigation, Jour. Lipid Rsch., past assoc. editor: Circulation. Recipient Berg Prize in Microbiology, 1957, 58, Faculty/Alumni award Washington U., 1995; named Physician honoree Am. Heart Assn. Mo. Affiliate, 1995; grantee MERIT status NIH, Vascular Biology Spl. Merit award, Am. Heart Assn. Fellow ACP, AAAS; mem. Assn. Am. Physicians, Am. Soc. for Clin. Investigation, Am. Physiol. Soc., Am. Soc. Biol. Chemists, Am. Inst. Nutrition, Am. Diabetes Assn., Am. Heart Assn. (program com. coun. on atherosclerosis 1977-80, 86-88, nutrition com. 1980-84, pathology rsch. com. 1980-83, budget com. 1991, awards com. 1992, exec. com. 2001—), Spl. Vascular Biology award 2005, G.L. Duff lecture award, 2006). Endocrine Soc., Alpha Omega Alpha. Office: Washington U Sch Medicine Box 8046 660 S Euclid Ave Saint Louis MO 63110-1010 Office Phone: 314-362-7040. Business E-Mail: gschonfe@wustl.edu.

**SCHONFELD, WILLIAM ROST,** political science professor; b. NYC, Aug. 28, 1942; s. William A. and Louise R. (Rost) S.; m. Elena Beortegui, Jan. 23, 1964; children: Natalie Beortegui, Elizabeth Lynn Beortegui. Student, Cornell U., 1960-61; BA cum laude with honors, NYU, 1964; MA, Princeton U., 1968, PhD, 1970. Research asst. Princeton U., 1966-69, research assoc., 1969-70, vis. lectr., 1970; asst. prof. polit. sci. U. Calif.-Irvine, 1970-75, assoc. prof., 1975-81, prof., 1981—, dean Sch. Social Scis., 1982—2002; sr. lectr. Fond. Nat. de Sci. Politique, Paris, 1973-74; researcher Centre de Sociologie des Organisations, Paris, 1976-78; dir. Ctr. for Study of Democracy, 2004—. Author: Youth and Authority in France, 1971, Obedience and Revolt, 1976, Ethnographie du PS et du RPR, 1985 Recipient Disting. Teaching award U. Calif.-Irvine, 1984, Disting. Faculty Lectureship award for tchg., 1998, Daniel G. Aldrich Disting. Univ. Svc. award, 2000-01; Fulbright fellow Bordeaux, France, 1964-65; Danforth grad. fellow, 1964-69; Fulbright sr. lectr. Paris, 1973-74; NSF-CNRS Exchange of Scientists fellow Paris, 1976-78; Ford Found. grantee France, Spain, 1978-79; finalist Prof. Yr. Council for Advancement and Support of Edn., 1984; Lauds & Laurels Extraordinarious award, U. Calif.-Irvine Alumni Assn., 2002. Mem. Am. Polit. Sci. Assn., Assoc. Francaise de Sci. Pol., Phi Beta Kappa. Office: U Calif Sch Social Scis Irvine CA 92697-0001 Personal E-mail: wrschonf@uci.edu.

**SCHONHORN, HAROLD,** chemist, researcher; b. N.Y.C., Apr. 2, 1928; s. Benjamin and Dorothy (Gitlin) S.; m. Esther Matesky, Jan. 18, 1954; children: Deborah, Jeremy. BS, Bklyn. Coll., 1950; PhD, N.Y. Polytech. U., 1959. Mem. tech. staff Bell Labs., Murray Hill, NJ, 1961-84; v.p. R & D Polyken Tech. div. Kendall Co., Lexington, Mass., 1984-93; pres. Schonhorn Consultants, 1993—. Contbr. over 100 articles to profl. jours. Pres. B'nai B'rith Lodge, Summit, N.J., 1970. With U.S. Army, 1953-55, Korea. Mem. Am. Chem. Soc. Achievements include 15 patents. Office Phone: 617-738-4742. Office Fax: 617-738-4742. Personal E-mail: HaroldSchonhorn@cs.com.

**SCHOOLAR, JOSEPH CLAYTON,** psychiatrist, pharmacologist, educator; b. Marks, Miss., Feb. 28, 1929; s. Adrian Taylor and Leah (Covington) S.; m. Betty Jane Peck, Nov. 2, 1960; children: Jonathan Covington, Cynthia Jane, Geoffrey Michael, Catherine Elizabeth, Adrian Carson AB, U. Tenn., Knoxville, 1950, MS, 1952; PhD, U. Chgo., 1957, MD, 1960. Diplomate Am. Bd. Psychiatry and Neurology. Chief drug abuse research TRIMS, Houston, 1966-72; assoc. prof. U. Tex. Grad. Sch. Biomed. Scis., Houston, 1968—; prof. psychiatry Baylor Coll. Medicine, Houston, 1975—, prof. pharmacology, 1974—2002, prof. emeritus pharmacology and psychiatry, 2003—, chief div. psychopharmacology, 1973-82; dir. Tex. Research Inst. Mental Scis., Houston, 1972-85. Mem. Nat. Bd. Med. Examiners' Task Force on Drug Abuse and Alcoholism, 1982-; mem. Drug Abuse Adv. Com., FDA, Washington, 1983-85, chmn., 1984; chmn. profl. needs planning task force Nat. Inst. Drug Abuse, Washington, 1977- Editor: Current Issues in Adolescent Psychiatry, 1973, Research and the Psychiatric Patient, 1975, The Kinetics of Psychiatric Drugs, 1979, Serotonin in Biological Psychiatry - Advances in Biochemical Psychopharmacology, 1982. Cons. Parents' League Houston, 1972-74; mem. coordinating com. Citizens Mental Health Service, Houston, 1976; mem. acad. com. for study of violence Houston Police Dept., 1979; bd. dirs. Can-Do-It, Houston, 1982-. Served with U.S. Army, 1945-47, to 1st lt. USAR, 1950-62. Recipient Eugen Kahn award Baylor Coll. Medicine, Houston, 1964, Alumni award for Disting. Svc., U. Chgo., 1995, Psychiat. Excellence award Tex. Soc. Psychiat. Physicians, 1995. Fellow Am. Psychiat. Assn. (disting. life), Am. Coll. Psychiatrists, Am. Coll. Neuropsychopharmacology, Collegium Internationale NeuroPsychopharmacologicum, Am. Soc. Pharmacology and Exptl. Therapeutics. Episcopalian. Home: 1111 Hermann Dr Unit 17E Houston TX 77004-6930 Office: Baylor Coll Medicine PO Box 66575 Houston TX 77266-6575 Office Phone: 713-524-9700. E-mail: jschoolar@pol.net.

**SCHOOLAR, LAUREL ANN,** artist, educator; b. Phoenix, Jan. 17, 1950; d. Robert Day and Mary Ellen (Smith) Skelton; m. James Robert Schoolar; children: Tom, Ellen. BFA, Old Dominion U., 1973. Profl. artist, 1973—; drawing and painting instr. enrichent program Millsaps Coll., Jackson, Miss., 1990—; painting instr. cmty. edn. program Rankin County Sch. Dist., Brandon, Miss., 1989-94. Designer cover artwork for enrichment program Millsaps Coll., 1991-96; contbr. art to Unity Canvas, N.Y.C., 2002. Vol. New Stage Theatre, CONTACT Crisis Line, Miss. Symphony, Jackson, 1990—. Mem. Nat. Mus. Women in Arts (assoc.), Miss. Mus. Art (assoc.), Mcpl. Art Gallery (exhibiting mem., bd. dirs.), Miss. Watercolor Soc. (charter mem., signature artist, 2d pl. award Grand Nat. Watercolor Exhbn. 1995), Profl. Artists League of Miss. (rec. sec. 1995—). Home: 175 Summit Ridge Dr Brandon MS 39042-2063 Office Phone: 601-825-8059. Personal E-mail: schoolarart@yahoo.com.

**SCHOOLAR, YIH-CHING WANG,** music educator; arrived in U.S., 1988; d. Kao-Chin Wang and Li-Chin Wu; m. Geoffrey M. Schoolar. MusB, U. North Tex., Denton, 1988—91; MusM in Applied Music, U. Houston, 1991—93. Piano prof. Hsin-Zhu Teachers Coll., Taiwan, 1993—94, Tainan Teachers Coll., 1993—94; piano instr. Tainan Girls First H.S., 1993—94; music instr. Linsly Sch., Wheeling, W.Va., 1996—; piano prof. Bethany Coll., Bethany, 2002—. Guest artist Thursday Music Club, Wheeling, W.Va., 1996—2003, Wheeling Symphony, 1999, 2004; hon. spkr. Assn. Chinese Profls. W.Va., Morgantown, 2004; piano competition judge Plano Piano Tchrs. Assn., 2004. Author: Have a Good Life (Liberty Times Short Novel Contest, 1996). Recipient hon. mention, Pinault Music Assn., 1998, Favorite Mentor, W.Va. Gov. Sch. Arts, 2003, 2005. Mem.: Pi Kappa Lambda.

**SCHOOLER, CHARLES,** music educator; m. Joan Schooler. MusB, U. of Idaho, Moscow; MusM, U. of Ariz. Music tchr. Coeur d'Alene (Idaho) Pub. Schs., 1978—88, North Thurston Pub. Schs., Lacey, Wash., 1988—94, Olympia (Wash.) Sch. Dist., 1994—. Named Tchr. of the Yr., Timberline H.S., 1994, Outstanding String Educator in Wash., Wash. String Tchrs. Assn., 1998, Outstanding Music Educator, Chinook Music Tchrs., 2000. Mem.: ASTA (Wash. state pres. 2006—), Wash. Music Edn. Assn. (orch. officer 2002—04). Office Phone: 360-596-7324.

**SCHOOLS, CHARLES HUGHLETTE,** banker, lawyer; b. Lansing, Mich., May 24, 1929; s. Robert Thomas and Lillian Pearl (Lawson) S.; m. Rosemarie Sanchez, Nov. 22, 1952; children: Charles, Michael. BS, Am. U., 1952, MA, 1958; JD, Washington Coll. of Law, 1973; LLD, Bethune-Cookman U., 1973. Dir. phys. plant Am. U., 1952-66, owner, 1957—, Gen. Security Co., Washington, 1969—. Chmn., pres. Consol. Ventures Ltd.; pres., chmn. bd. McLean Bank (Va.), 1974—, Instl. Environ. Mgmt. Services; chmn. bd. Harper & Co.; chmn., pres. Community Assos. of Va., Associated Real Estate Mgmt. Services; dir. Computer Data Systems Inc., DAC Devel. Ltd., Am. Indsl. Devel. Corp., Intercoastal of Iran; mem. Met. Bd. Trades. Pres. McLean Boys' Club; bd. dirs. D.C. Spl. Olympics, Nat. Kidney Found.; trustee Bethune Cookman Coll., Western Md. Coll., Randolph Macon Acad. With USAAF, 1946-47, USAF, 1947-48. Mem. Va. C. of C., Profl. Businessman's Orgn., Georgetown Club of Washington, Touchdown Club of Washington, Univ. of Washington Club, Washington Golf and Country Club, Pisces Club (Washington), Halifax Club (Daytona Beach, Fla.), Masons, Alpha Tau Omega. Democrat. Office: 1313 Dolley Madison Blvd Mc Lean VA 22101-3926 Home: 458 S Beach St Ormond Beach FL 32174-7034

**SCHOOMAKER, PETER J.,** career military officer; BS in Edn. Adminstrn., U. Wyo., 1969; MA in Mgmt., Cen. Mich. U.; grad., USMC Amphibious War Sch., U.S. Army Command/Gen. Staff, Nat. War Coll.; LLD (hon.), Hampden-Sydney Coll. Commd. 2d lt. U.S. Army, 1969, advanced through grades to gen., 1997; comdr. troop C, 1st Squadron, 2d Armored Cavalry Regiment U.S. Army Europe and 7th Army, Germany, 1974-75; assignment officer Officer Pers. Mgmt. Directorate U.S. Army Mil. Pers. Ctr., Alexandria, Va., 1976-78; comdr. 1st Spl. Forces Operational Detachment Ft. Bragg, N.C., 1978-81; exec. officer 2d Squadron, 2d Armored Cavalry Regiment U.S. Army Europe and 7th Army, Germany, 1982-83; spl. ops. officer J-3 Joint Spl. Ops. Command Ft. Bragg, N.C., 1984-85; comdr. Combat Applications

Group, Ft. Bragg, 1989-92; asst. divsn. comdr. 1st Cavalry Divsn., Ft. Hood, Tex., 1992-93; dep. dir. ops., readiness and mobilization Office of Dep. Chief of Staff Ops. and Plans, U.S. Army, Washington, 1993-94; comdg. gen. Joint Spl. Ops. Command U.S. Spl. Ops. Command, Ft. Bragg, 1994-96, comdg. gen., 1996-97, comdg. in chief, 1997—2000; chief of staff US Army, Washington, 2000—. Decorated Disting. Svc. medal, Def. Superior Svc. medal with 3 oak leaf clusters, Legion of Merit with 2 oak leaf clusters, Bronze Star medal with oak leaf cluster, Def. Meritorious Svc. medal with oak leaf cluster, Meritorious Svc. medal with 2 oak leaf clusters. Office: Pentagon 200 Army Washington DC 20310*

**SCHOON, KENNETH JAMES,** science educator, writer; b. Gary, Ind., Aug. 23, 1946; s. Lester K. and Vivian B. Schoon; m. Margaret Shipley Schoon, Nov. 22, 1969; children: Jacob Kenneth, Robert Kendall. AB in Geology, Ind. U., Bloomington, 1968, MS in Secondary Edn., 1972; PhD in Curriculum and Instrn., Loyola U., Chgo., 1989. Sci. tchr. Sch. City East Chgo., Ind., 1968—90; prof. sci. edn. Ind. U. NW, Gary, 1990—, assoc. dean edn., 1999—. State membership dir. Ind. Sci. Olympiad, 1993—; evaluator for initiative for schools, industries, and scis. Valparaiso (Ind.) U., 2003—; pres. Ind. Dunes Environ. Learning Ctr., Porter, Ind., 2006—. Author: Calumet Beginnings: Ancient Shorelines and Settlements at the South End of Lake Michigan, 2003 (Ind. U. Outstanding Rsch. award, 2004), Portraits of a Ridge Family: The Jacob Schoons. Mem., former dir. Munster (Ind.) Hist. Soc., 1982—2006; mem. and former pres. Munster Bd. Pks. and Recreation, 1994—2006; chair Munster Centennial Com., 2005—06. Mem.: Munster Lions. Presbyterian. Avocations: Calumet area geology and history, genealogy, travel. Office: Ind U NW 3400 Broadway Gary IN 46408 Office Phone: 219-980-7766. Office Fax: 219-981-4208.

**SCHOONHOVEN, RAY JAMES,** retired lawyer; b. Elgin, Ill., May 24, 1921; s. Ray Covey and Rosina Madeline (Schram White) S.; m. Marie Theresa Dunn, Dec. 11, 1943; children: Marie Kathleen (Kamie), Ray James, Jr., Pamela Suzanne, John Philip, Rose Lynn. BSc, U. Notre Dame, 1943; JD, Northwestern U., 1948. Bar: Ill. 1949, U.S. Supreme Ct. 1954, D.C. 1973, U.S. Ct. Mil. Appeals 1954. Assoc. Seyfarth, Shaw Fairweather & Geraldson, Chgo., 1949-57; ptnr. Seyfarth, Shaw Fairweather & Geraldson now Seyfarth Shaw, Chgo., 1957-92; ret. Chief rulings and ops. Sr. Wage Stabilization Bd. Region VII, Chgo., 1951-52. Book rev. editor: Ill. Law Rev., 1948. Served to lt.comdr. USNR, 1942-62. Mem. ABA, Ill. State Bar Assn., Chgo. Bar Assn., D.C. Bar Assn., Chgo. Athletic Assn., Univ. Club. Chgo., Fed. Bar Assn., Order of Coif. Republican. Roman Catholic. Home: 1182 Lynette Dr Lake Forest IL 60045-4601 Office: Seyfarth Shaw 55 E Monroe St Ste 4200 Chicago IL 60603-5863 *I work hard to preserve our free enterprise system and, hopefully, to make such contribution to our society that it is better for my having been a part of it.*

**SCHOONMAKER, GAIL GRAHAM,** voice educator, director; d. Walter Alvin and Betty Griffith Graham; m. Bruce Warder Schoonmaker, Aug. 4, 1973; children: Geoffrey Noel, Richard Graham. MusB, Furman U., 1973; MusM, Northwestern U., Evanston, Ill., 1974. Libr. asst. Northwestern U. Libr., Evanston, 1974—77; prof. voice Furman U., Greenville, SC, 1977—. Coord. chapel music Furman U., Greenville, 2000—, sorority adv., 2002—06. Singer Chgo. Symphony Chorus, 1975—77; pres. Travelers Rest (SC) Elem. PTA, 1989—90, Travelers Rest HS PTA, 1995—96; co-dir. music Luth. Ch. of Our Savior, Greenville, 1987—. Mem.: Nat. Assn. Tchrs. Singing, Music Club (Greenville). Baptist. Avocations: music, bridge, composition. Home: 41 Flatwoods Rd Travelers Rest SC 29690 Office: Furman Univ Poinsett Hwy Greenville SC 29613

**SCHOONMAKER, SAMUEL VAIL, III,** lawyer; b. Newburgh, N.Y., Sept. 1, 1935; s. Samuel V. Jr. and Catherine (Wilson) S.; m. Carolyn Peters, Sept. 18, 1965; children: Samuel V. IV, Frederick P. BA magna cum laude, Yale U., 1958, JD, 1961. Bar: Conn. 1961, U.S. Dist. Ct. Conn. 1961, U.S. Dist. Ct. (so. and ea. dist.) N.Y. 1964, U.S. Ct. Appeals (2d cir.) 1964, U.S. Supreme Ct. 1965. Assoc. Cummings & Lockwood, Stamford, Conn., 1961-70, co-mng. ptnr., 1987-90, mng. ptnr., 1990-94, chmn. exec. com., 1987-96; founder, pres. Schoonmaker George & Colin, P.C., Greenwich, Conn., 1996—. State trial referee Conn. Superior Ct., 1989; pres. Schoonmaker Family Assn., New Paltz, N.Y., 1975-77. Sr. topical editor Conn. Bar Jour., 1977-81; mem. editl. bd. Fairshare and Am. Jour. Family Law, 1992—; contbr. articles to profl. jours. Chmn. Conn. Child Support Commn., 1984-86; mem. Conn. Family Support Com., 1986-90; mem. Darien (Conn.) Rep. Town Com., 1974-76, rep. town meeting, 1990-98; pres. Youth Tennis Found. New Eng., Needham, Mass., 1975-77; pres. New Eng. Lawn Tennis Assn., 1977-79 (Man of Yr. award 1979); pres., trustee Huegenot Hist. Soc., 1999—. Fellow Am. Acad. Matrimonial Lawyers Conn. (bd. mgrs., Disting. Svc. award 1988), Internat. Acad. Matrimonial Lawyers, Am. Bar Found.; mem. ABA (chmn. family law sect. 1982-83), Conn. Bar Assn. (chmn. family law sect. 1971-74), Conn. Bus. and Industry Assn. (bd. dirs. 1993-98), S.W. Conn. Bus. and Industry Assn. (bd. dirs. 1990-97), Pub. Defenders Assn. (bd. dirs.), Wee Burn Country Club (Darien, Conn., asst. sec.), Yale Club (N.Y.C.), Phi Beta Kappa. Avocations: tennis, platform tennis. Home: 231 Old Kings Hwy S Darien CT 06820-5931 Office: Schoonmaker George & Colin PC PO Box 5059 81 Holly Hill Ln Greenwich CT 06831-5059

**SCHOONMAKER POWELL, THELMA,** film editor; b. Jan. 3, 1940; m. Michael Powell, May 19, 1984 (dec. 1990). Editor: (films) Who's That Knocking at My Door, 1968, Woodstock, 1970 (nominee Best Film Editing Acad. award, 1970, Am Cinema Editors award best film editing, 1980), Raging Bull, 1980 (Best Film Editing Acad. award, 1980, Best Film Editing award Am. Cinema Editors, 1980, Best Film Editing award Brit. Acad., 1981, Am. Cinema Editors award best film editing, 1980), The King of Comedy, 1983, After Hours, 1985, The Color of Money, 1986, The Last Temptation of Christ, 1988, New York Stories (Life Lessons segment), 1989, GoodFellas, 1990 (nominee Best Film Editing Acad. award, 1990, Brit. Acad. award best film editing, 1990), Cape Fear, 1992, The Age of Innocence, 1993, A Personal Journey with Martin Scorsese Through American Movies, 1995, Casino, 1995 (Am. Cinema Editors nominee best film editing, 1995), Kundun, 1997, Bringing Out the Dead, 1999, Il Mio Viaggio in Italia, 2000, Gangs of New York, 2002 (Am. Cinema Editors award best dramatic film editing, 2003, Acad. nominee best film editing, 2003), The Aviator, 2004 (Acad. award best film editing, 2005, Am. Cinema Editor award best dramatic film editing, 2005).

**SCHOONOVER, BRENDA B.,** ambassador; BA, Morgan State U., Balt.; postgrad., Howard U. Vol. Peace Corps, Philippines, 1961, adminstr. Office Talent Search Washington, assoc. dir. Tanzania, dir. sch. partnership program Washington; affirmative action officer Govt. of Arlington County, Va.; with Fgn. Svc. U.S. Dept. State, Manila, Colombo, Sri Lanka, Tunis, Tunisia, with Bur. Near East and South Asia Washington, 1978-88, chief pers. Bur. European and Can. Affairs, 1988-91, mem. Sr. Seminar, 1996-97; adminstrv. officer, dept. dir. Office Joint Adminstrv. Svcs. Am. Embassy, Brussels, 1992-96; Capstone fellow Nat. Def. U., Washington, 1997; U.S. amb. to Togo Am. Embassy, Lome, 1998-2000; amb.-in-residence Chapel Hill, NC, 2000—01; chargé d'affaires, ad interim min. counselor Am. Embassy, Brussels, 2001—04. Bd. dirs. Am. Diplomacy On-line Mag. Mem. adv. bd. Carolina for Kibera. Recipient Order of the Mono award, The Togolese Govt., 2000, Presdl. Meritorious award, U.S., 2003, Sec. of State Career Achievement award, 2004. Mem.: LWV. Office: 108 Ironwoods Dr Chapel Hill NC 27516 E-mail: RCSchoon2@aol.com.

**SCHOONOVER, JACK RONALD,** senior judge; b. Winona, Minn., July 23, 1934; s. Richard M. and Elizabeth A. (Hargeisheimer) S.; m. Ann Marie Kroez, June 18, 1965; children: Jack Ronald, Wayne J. Student, Winona State Coll., 1956-58; LLB, U. Fla., 1962. Bar: Fla. 1962. Atty. Wotitzky, Wotitzky & Schoonover, 1962-69, Schoonover, Olmsted & Schwarz, 1969-75; spl. asst. state's atty. State of Fla., 1972-9; city atty. City of Punta Gorda, Fla., city judge, 1973-74; judge 20th Jud. Cir. Ct., Ft. Myers, Fla., 1975-81, 2d Dist. Ct. Appeal, 1981-97, chief judge, 1990-92, ret. 1997. Atty. Charlotte County Sch. Bd., 1969-75, Charlotte County Zoning Bd., Charlotte County Devel.

Authority; mem. unauthorized practice law com. 12th Jud. Cir., mem. grievance com. 20th Jud. Cir.; adj. prof. Edison C.C.; tchr. Charlotte County Adult Edn. Assn. Served with USAF, 1952-56. Home and Office: 14380 Olde Hickory Blvd Fort Myers FL 33912-0816

**SCHOONOVER, JAMES A.,** lab administrator; Divisional l. vice-pres. Olsten Corp.; with Medtox Labs., 1997—2000, vice-pres. sales and mktg., chief mktg. officer, 2000—. Office: Medtox Scientific Inc 402 W County Rd D Saint Paul MN 55112

**SCHOONOVER, PHILIP J.,** retail executive; m. Cindi Schoonover; 2 children. Degree in mktg. and fin., U. N.H.; postgrad., Boston Coll. Former sales and mktg. exec. Sony Corp. Am.; former exec. v.p., gen. merchandise mgr. TOPS Appliances; Sr. v.p. digital tech. Best Buy Co., Inc., 1995—2001, exec. v.p. digital solutions, 2001—02, exec. v.p. bus. devel., 2002—04, exec. v.p. customer segments, 2004; exec. v.p., chief merchandising officer Circuit City Stores Inc., Richmond, Va., 2004—05, pres., 2005—, CEO, 2006—. Active Anti-Defamation League, United Jewish Appeal, Chabad Ho., United Way, Wayzata (Minn.) Yacht Club Youth Sailing Program. Avocation: sailing. Office: Circuit City Stores Inc 9950 Maryland Dr Richmond VA 23233-1464*

**SCHOONOVER, STANLEY R.,** music educator, consultant; b. Bethesda, Md., July 27, 1955; s. William and Martha Schoonover. MusM, West Chester U., 1982. Cert. music edn. K-12 Pa. Dir. of bands Mt. Vernon HS, Alexandria, Va., 1982—92, Robinson Secondary Sch., Fairfax, Va., 1993—98; music specialist Fairfax County Pub. Schs., Fairfax, 1998—. Music cons., Va., 1990—; founding condr. Fairfax Wind Symphony, 1999. Dir.: (internat. band clinic performance) MidWest Band and Orchestra Clinic, 1993 (5 NBA Citations of Excellence). Named to East Stroudsburg Music Hall of Fame, 2004. Mem.: Va. Band and Orch. Dirs. Assn. (pres. 1993—95), Phi Delta Kappa. Office: Alan E Leis Instructional Ctr 7423 Camp Alger Ave Falls Church VA 22042 Office Phone: 703-208-7717. Personal E-mail: stanschoonover@verizon.net. E-mail: stan.schoonover@fcps.edu.

**SCHOPF, JAMES WILLIAM,** paleobiologist, researcher, educator; b. Urbana, Ill., Sept. 27, 1941; s. James Morton and Esther Julie (Nissen) S.; m. Julie Morgan, Aug. 7, 1965 (div. 1979); 1 child, James Christopher; m. Jane Shen, Jan. 16, 1980. AB with high honors, Oberlin Coll., 1963; A.M., Harvard U., 1965, PhD (Harvard fellow, NSF fellow), 1968. Research chemist NASA, Ames Research Center, Calif., 1967; mem. lunar sample preliminary exam. team Manned Spacecraft Center, Tex., 1968-71; asst. prof. dept. earth and space scis. UCLA, 1968-70, assoc. prof., 1970-73, prof., 1973—, mem. Inst. Evolutionary and Environ. Biology, 1970-76, mem. Inst. Geophysics and Planetary Physics, 1973—, dean honors div. Coll. Letters and Sci., 1983-85, dir. Ctr. for Study Evolution and Origin of Life, 1985—, Sigma Xi Disting. lectr., 1976, Rubey lectr., 1976, Golden Yr. Disting. lectr., 1980, Faculty Research lectr., 1984; Sigma Xi Disting. lectr. U. Cin., 1980; Disting. lectr. Buffalo Mus. Sci., 1982; J.A. Bownocker lectr. Ohio State U., 1982. Vis. lectr. Am. Inst. Biol. Scis. Vis. Biologists Program, 1969-72; faculty rsch. learner, UCLA Acad. Senate, 1984, M.W. Haas vis. disting. prof. geology U. Kans., 1979; extraordinary vis. prof. exobiology U. Nijmegen, Netherlands, 1980-81; C. O'Neal lectr. Ohio Wesleyan U., 1982; Sandia disting. lectr. U. N.Mex., 1985; Sigma Xi disting. lectr. U. Oreg., 1985; Du Pont disting. lectr. U. Ill., 1985; R. Stanier disting. lectr. U. Calif.-Berkeley, 1987; H.P. Mangelsdorf disting. lectr. U. N.C., 1987; mem. Bot. Soc. Am. del., People's Republic China, 1978; Academia Sinica vis. research scientist, People's Republic China, 1981, 82; mem. NASA Terrestrial Bodies Sci. Working Group, 1975-76, space program adv. council NASA Life Scis. Com., 1976-78, NASA Working Group on Origins of Life, 1978-79, NASA Space Sci. Adv. Com., 1979-82, mem. NASA Life Scis. Strategic Planning Study Com., 1985—; Alan T. Waterman Award com. NSF, 1978-81; mem. working group on precambrian biostratigraphy Internat. Geol. Correlation Program, UNESCO, 1975—; mem. Working Group on Cambrian-Precambrian Boundary, 1976—; mem. adv. com. USSR and Eastern Europe, Commn. Internat. Relations NRC, 1981-85, mem. bd. earth sci. Commn. Phys. Scis., Math. and Resources, 1982-85, mem. space sci. bd., 1983-86; mem. com. on guidelines for paleontol. collecting, 1984-86, sub.-com. on evolution and diversity Commn. on Life Scis., 1986; mem. Internat. Congress Systematic and Evolutionary Biology, 1990—; mem. com. space research Internat. Council Sci. Unions; chair Gordon Rsch. Conf. Origin of Life, 1999; mem. sci. coun., Geo-bio Ctr., Ludwig-Maximilians U., 2003; lecturer and spkr. in field, 1980—. Mem. editorial bd.: Origins of Life, 1973-87, Precambrian Research, 1973-91, Evolutionary Theory, 1973-85, U. Calif. Press, 1973-82, Paleobiology, 1974-80, Geomicrobiology Jour., 1977—, Evolutionary Monographs, 1977-85, Quarterly Rev. Biology, 1988—, Artificial Life, 1993—, Astrobiology, 2001—, Geokimiya: Internat. Geochemistry, 2005—; contbr. articles to profl. jours. Bd. dirs. Brentwood Glen (Calif.) Assn., 1972-75; trustee UCLA Found., 1983-85; bd. trustees Oberlin Coll., 1992-97. Recipient N.Y. Bot. Garden award Sch. Am., 1966; Group Achievement award NASA, 1969; Outstanding Paper award Jour. Paleontology, 1971; Charles Schuchert award Paleontol. Soc., 1974; Disting. Teaching award UCLA, 1977; Alan T. Waterman award NSF, 1977; G. Hawk award U. Kans., 1979; spl. recognition diploma NASA, 1979, Group Achievement award, 1997; Outstanding Vol. in Phys. Scis. award Am. Assn. Pubs., 1983; Mary Clark Thompson medal Nat. Acad. Scis., 1986, Profl. and Scholarly Pub. award. Am. Pubs., 1983, 1992, Disting Sci. award, IGPP Ctr. for Study of Evoluton & The Origin of Life, 2000; Guggenheim fellow, 1973, John Simon Guggenheim Found. fellow, 1988; U.S. Nat. Acad. Scis. exchange scientist USSR, 1975; named one of So. Calif.'s 50 Leading Scientists of 20th Century, 1999. Fellow Geol. Soc. Am. (vice-chmn. Cordilleran sect. 1983-84, chmn. 1984-85); mem. NAS, AAAS, Bot. Soc. Am. (com. on sci. liaison with People's Republic China 1978—), Paleontol. Soc. (mem. Schuchert Award com. 1978-82), Internat. Soc. Study of Origin of Life (treas. 1977-83, nat. meeting adv. com. 1980, 83, 86, councilor, 1983—), Geochem. Soc. (nominating com. 1980-82), Soc. Study of Evolution (edn. com. 1980-83), Am. Philos. Soc., Linnean Soc. London, Internat. Assn. Plant Taxonomy, Internat. Org. Paleobotany, Psychol. Soc. Am., Am. Assn. Univ. Profs., Am. Inst. Biol. Scis., Internat. Psychol. Soc., Am. Soc. Naturalists, Soc. Econ. Paleontologists and Mineralogists, Paleontological Assn., Am. Soc. Mibrobiology, Soc. Molecular Biology and Evolution, Sigma Xi (treas. UCLA chpt. 1972-74, chpt. v.p. 1984-85, pres. 1984-85). Office: UCLA Dept Earth Space Scis Los Angeles CA 90095-0001 Office Phone: 310-825-1170. Business E-mail: schopf@ess.ucla.edu.

**SCHOPF, WILLIAM GRANT,** lawyer; b. Muskegon, Mich., Sept. 7, 1948; s. William G. and June Marie (Bodine) Schopf; children: Brody A., Alexandra J., Anaïs M.E. AB, Princeton U., 1970; JD, Cornell U., 1973. Bar: Ill. 1973, U.S. Dist. Ct. (no. dist.) Ill. 1973, U.S. Supreme Ct. 1977. Assoc. Keck, Mahin & Cate, Chgo., 1973-79; ptnr. Reuben & Proctor, Chgo., 1979-86, Isham, Lincoln & Beale, Chgo., 1986-87, Schopf & Weiss, Chgo., 1987—. Adj. prof. John Marshall Law Sch., Chgo., 1977-78; owner Music Box Theatre & Schopf Gallery on Lake, Chgo. Author: Money in the Bank, 1988; contbr. articles, chpts. to legal publs. Mem. ABA, Chgo. Bar Assn., Union Internationale des Avocats, Union League Club (Chgo.), Princeton Club (N.Y.C.). Office: Schopf & Weiss 312 W Randolph St Ste 300 Chicago IL 60606-1721 Office Phone: 312-701-9308. Business E-Mail: schopf@sw.com.

**SCHOPP, DAVID L.,** music educator; b. Tyrone, Pa., Oct. 1, 1965; s. David A. and Lee A. Schopp; m. Beth L. Rogers, June 24, 2000; children: Maxwell, Mackenzie. BS in Music Edn., Pa. State U., 1987. Music tchr. Tredyffrin-Easttown, Devon, Pa., 1987—88; band dir. Norristown (Pa.) Area HS, 1988—99, Hatboro-Horsham (Pa.) HS, 1999—. Recipient Gift of Time award, Am. Family Inst., 1990, 1992. Mem.: Music Educators Nat. Conf., Pa. Music Educators Assn. Office: Hatboro Horsham HS 899 Horsham Rd Horsham PA 19044 E-mail: dschopp@hatboro-horsham.org.

**SCHOPPMEYER, MARTIN WILLIAM,** education educator; b. Weehawken, N.J., Sept. 15, 1929; s. William G. and Madeleine M. (Haas) S.; m. Marilyn M. Myers, Aug. 9, 1958; children: Susan Ann, Martin William. BS, Fordham U., 1950; EdM, U. Fla., 1955, EdD, 1962. Tchr. Fla. pub. sch., 1955-59; instr., then asst. prof. U. Fla., 1960-63; assoc. prof., then prof. edn.

Fla. Atlantic U., Boca Raton, Fla., 1963-68, dir. continuing edn., 1965-67; mem. faculty U. Ark., Fayetteville, Ark., 1968—, prof. edn., 1971-93, Univ. prof., 1993—99, Univ. prof. emeritus, 1999—, program coord. for ednl. adminstrn., 1983-90. Mem. Nat. Adv. Coun. Edn. Professions Devel., 1973-76; exec. sec. Ark. Sch. Study Coun., 1976—; evaluator instructional tng. program Nat. Tng. Fund, 1978; bd. dirs. Women's Ednl. and Devel. Inst., 1977-80, Nat. Sch. Devel. Coun., sec., 1989-90, v.p. 1990, pres., 1990-92; mem. oversight com. South Conway (Ark.) County Sch. Dist.; mem. state commn. to study effect of Amendment 59 to Ark. Constn.; cons. Lake View V. Huckabee, 1994-2002. Author books, monographs, articles in field. Mem. president's coun. Subiaco Acad., 1984-90; chmn. Subiaco Sch. Bd., 1990-93, mem., 1993-97. With U.S. Army, 1951-53, Korea. Recipient numerous fed. grants. Mem. VFW, KC (past grand knight), Ark. Edn. Assn. (past chpt. pres.), Ark. Assn. Ednl. Adminstrs., Am. Legion, Rotary, Kappa Delta Pi, Phi Delta Kappa, Delta Tau Kappa. Roman Catholic. Home: 2950 Sheryl Ave Fayetteville AR 72703-3542 E-mail: mschoppmeyer@cox.-internet.com. *The only really sound investment for a family, a community, or a society is that money spent for the education of its youth.*

**SCHOPPMEYER, MARTIN WILLIAM, JR.,** school system administrator; b. Ft. Lauderdale, Fla., Nov. 1, 1966; s. Martin William and Marilyn Myers Schoppmeyer; m. Carin Anne Morales. MEd in Ednl. Tech., U. Ark., Fayetteville, 1996, EdD in Ednl. Leadership and Instrnl. Design, 1999. Dir. corp. rels. Coll. Engring., U. Ark., 1999—2003; founder, supt. schs. Haas Hall Acad., Farmington, Ark., 2003—; founder, CEO Digi-Tell ID Sys., Fayetteville, 2000—, chmn., 2001. Adj. faculty U. Ark., 1995—2003. Contbr. articles to profl. jours., chapters to books. Chmn. The Acad., Inc., Fayetteville, 2003—. Recipient Charles and Nadine Baum Tchg. Excellence award, U. Ark., 1999; grantee Roy B. Allen Doctoral scholarship, 1998; Rsch. grant, Ark. Dept. Edn., 2003—04, 2004—05, Fed., 2004—06, Walton Family Found., 2004—06. Mem.: Am. Ednl. Rsch. Assn. (life), Rotary Internat. (life), Am. Ednl. Rsch. Assn. (life), Phi Delta Kappa (life; bd. mem. 2001—02), Rotary Club Internat. (life), Elk's Lodge (life), Phi Delta Kappa (life; bd. mem. 2000—03), Phi Kappa Phi (life; sec. 2000—03). Achievements include development and patent of iCard technology to link our clients to their digital profile; created the first only open-enrollment charter high school in the state of Arkansas. Home: 1156 East Glenn Ln Fayetteville AR 72703 Office: Haas Hall Acad 13370 Rheas Mill Rd Farmington AR 72703 Business E-Mail: martinschoppmeyer@haashall.org.

**SCHOR, ADAM MATTHEW,** history professor; b. San Francisco, Apr. 29, 1976; s. Robert Alan and Deborah Sue Schor; m. Leah Rose Doberne-Schor, June 9, 2002. BA in History and Classics, Pomona Coll., 1998, MA in History, U. Mich., 2000, PhD in History, 2004. Adj. instr. Borough of Manhattan C.C., NYC, 2001—02; adj. asst. prof. LI U., Bklyn., 2002—03, vis. asst. prof. history CW Post Campus Brookville, NY, 2004—05, asst. prof. history, 2005—. Recipient Kimble prize, Pomona Coll., 1998, Mudge Latin prize, 1998, History Dept. Dissertation award, U. Mich., 2004. Mem.: Am. Hist. Assn., N.Am. Patristics Soc., Byzantine Studies Conf. Jewish. Avocations: cooking, hiking, guitar. Office: LI U CW Post Campus 720 Northern Blvd Greenvale NY 11548 Office Phone: 516-299-2407. E-mail: schora@umich.edu.

**SCHOR, JOSEPH MARTIN,** pharmaceutical executive, biochemist; b. Bklyn., Jan. 10, 1929; s. Aaron Jacob and Rhea Iress (Kay) S.; children: Esther Helen, Joshua David, Gideon Alexander, Eric, Neil; m. Laura Sharon Struminger, June 14, 1992. BS magna cum laude, CCNY, 1951; PhD, Fla. State U., 1957. Sr. rsch. chemist Armour Pharm. Co., Kankakee, Ill., 1957-59, Lederle Labs., Pearl River, N.Y., 1959-64; dir. biochemistry Endo Labs., Garden City, N.Y., 1964-70; head dept. biochemistry DuPont and Endo Labs., 1970-77; v.p. sci. affairs Forest Labs., N.Y.C., 1977-94, sr. v.p. sci. affairs emeritus, 1996—. Editor, contbr.: Chemical Control of Fibrinolysisthrombolysis, 1970. Contbr. articles to profl. jours. Patentee in field. USPHS fellow, 1955-57. Fellow Am. Inst. Chemists (cert. profl. chemist); mem. Am. Chem. soc. (chmn. Nassau County subsect. 1971-72), Internat. Soc. on Thrombosis and Hemostasis, N.Y. Acad. Scis., AAAS, Phi Beta Kappa, Sigma Xi. Home: 28 Meleny Rd Locust Valley NY 11560-1221 E-mail: joseph.m.schor@verizon.net.

**SCHOR, LAURA STRUMINGHER,** historian; b. NYC, June 24, 1945; d. David Charles and Esther Rachel (Pearl) Gross; children: Eric Alain, Neil Remy; m. Joseph Martin Schor, June, 1992. BA, Queens Coll., CUNY, 1967; MA, U. Rochester, 1970, PhD, 1974. Asst. prof. SUNY, Fredonia, 1973-79; assoc. prof., dir. women's studies U. Cin., 1979-85, prof., vice provost, 1985-89; prof., provost, v.p. acad. affairs Hunter Coll., CUNY, N.Y.C., 1989-98; exec. dir. Hadassah, The Women's Zionist Orgn. of Am., Inc., N.Y.C., 1998-2000; dean CUNY Honors Coll., 2001—. Author: Women and the Making of the Working Class, 1979, What Were Little Boys and Girls Made Of?, 1984, The Odyssey of Flora Tristan, 1988, Les Jolies Femmes d'Edouard de Beaumont, 1994, The Life and Legacy of Baroness Betty de Rothschild, 2006. Mem.: Internat. Soc. for Study European Ideas, Am. Hist. Assn., French Hist. Assn., Phi Beta Kappa.

**SCHOR, OLGA SEEMANN,** mental health counselor, real estate broker; b. Havana, Cuba, Mar. 2, 1951; came to U.S., 1961; d. Olga del Carmen (Hernandez) S.; m. David Michael Schor, Apr. 22, 1979; 1 child, Andrew. AA, Miami Dade Community Coll., 1971; BA, U. Fla., Gainesville, 1973; M.Edn., U. Miami, Fla., 1976; Psy.D., Nova U., 1981. Cert. Bert Rodgers Sch. Real Estate, Miami, 1981, Gold Coast Sch. Real Estate, 1988; lic. real estate broker. Teaching asst. U. Fla., Gainesville, 1972-73; counselor U. Miami, 1974-79; assoc. psychotherapist Linda H. Jamrozy & Assocs., Miami, 1976-78, Interactive Systems, Miami, 1978-79; psychometrist Jackson Meml. Hosp., Miami, 1979-85, tony Ciminero & Assocs., Miami, 1985-86; lectr. U. Miami, 1976-78, Jackson Meml. Hosp. Sch. Nursing, Miami, 1976; real estate broker The Keyes Co. Realtor, Coral Gables, 1981-88, Keyes Asset Mgmt., Miami, 1988—; CEO My Co. Realty, Inc., 1997—. Sec./treas. bd. dirs. BODS Inc., Miami. Chmn. creative writing Jr. Orange Bowl competition. Recipient Assoc. of Quarter award Keyes Co. Realtors, 1986. Mem. Am. Psychol. and Guidance Assn., Keyes Comml. Roundtable, Keyes Inner Circle, Coral Gables Bd. Realtors, Guilliver Acad.'s Parents Bd., Dade County Mental Health Assn., Million Dollar Sales Club. Clubs: South Fla. Sailing Assn. (Miami). Avocations: sailing, travel, reading, kayaking, theater, acting, tennis. Office: My Company Realty Inc 2050 Coral Way Ste 505 Miami FL 33145-2682 Home: 15000 Old Cutler Rd Miami FL 33158-2116 Office Phone: 305-856-8574. E-mail: artistme@aol.com

**SCHOR, SUZI,** lawyer, psychologist; b. Chgo., Feb. 1, 1947; d. Samuel S. and Dorothy Helen (Hineline); 1 child, Kate. BSBA, Ind. U., 1964; JD, Northwestern U., 1970, U. Palmer's Green, London, 1971; PhD in Fine Arts (hon.), U. Nev., PhD in Clin. Psychology, 1989, Kensington U., 1989. Bar: Ill., 1971. Pvt. practice, L.A., 1971-80; v.p. legal affairs Little Gypzy Mgmt., Inc., Beverly Hills, Calif., 1980—; trust officer, pvt. fiduciary svcs. Bank of Am., L.A. Mem. Pres.'s Coun. on Alcoholism. Author: 13th Step to Death, 1995; contbg. author Wine and Dine Mag.; contbr. articles to profl. jours. Bd. dirs. Nat. Ctr. for Hyperactive Children, L.A., 1989-91, sec. Rainbow Guild Cancer Charity, L.A., 1985-89, nat. cons. Jewish Legal Aid, L.A., 1988—; campaign special. advisor Dem. Nat. Campaign, L.A., 1990, 94, 2000; donor mem. L.A. Coun. on World Affairs. Recipient Poet of Yr. award Nat. Libr. and Assn. of Poetry, 1995, 98. Mem. ABA (criminal justice com. 1994), AAUW, NAADAC, CAADAC, L.A. Breakfast Club (chmn. entertainment 1988-90), Rotary, Mensa, Beverly Hills Bar Assn., Century City Bar Assn. Jewish. Avocations: singing, skiing, writing. Home: 21530 Califa St Apt 109 Woodland Hills CA 91367-4907

**SCHORER, SUKI,** ballet teacher; b. Boston; d. Mark and Ruth (Page) S.; 1 child, Nicole. Studied with George Balanchine. Dancer San Francisco Ballet, 1955-59, N.Y.C. Ballet, 1959-72; prin. dancer N.Y.C. Ballet Co., 1968-72, artistic assoc. lecture demonstration program, 1972-95; mem. faculty Sch. Am. Ballet, 1972—, Brown Found. Sr. faculty chair, 1990—. Internat. guest tchr. and lectr. specializing in Balanchine tng. and technique; artist dir., tchr.

on Balanchine Essays (videos). Author: Suki Schorer on Balanchine Technique, 1999 (de la Torre Bueno prize 2000), Put Your Best Foot Forward, 2005; created roles in Balanchine's Harlequinade, Don Quixote, Midsummer Night's Dream, Jewels, La Source, Raymonda Variations; repertory included prin. roles in Apollo, Serenade, Concerto Barocco, Symphony in C, La Somnambula, Stars and Stripes, Tarantella, Valse Fantaisie, The Nutcracker, Brahams Schoenberg, La Valse, Western Symphony, Ivesiana, Divertimento # 15, Ballet Imperial, others. Recipient Disting. Tchr. in Arts award Nat. Found. Advancement in Arts, 1997, award Dance mag., 1998. Office: Sch of Am Ballet 70 Lincoln Center Plz New York NY 10023-6548 Office Phone: 212-769-6600. E-mail: suki.schorer@rcn.com.

**SCHORI, KATHARINE JEFFERTS,** bishop; b. Pensacola, Fla., Mar. 26, 1954; m. Richard M. Schori, 1979; 1 child, Katharine. BS in Marine Biology, Stanford U., 1974; MS in Oceanography, Oreg. State U., Corvallis, 1977, PhD in Oceanography, 1983; MDiv, Ch. Div. Sch. of the Pacific, Berkeley, Calif., 1994. Worked in oceanography, including at the Nat. Marine Fisheries Svc. in Seattle; ordained deacon, 1994, priest, 1994; asst. rector Episcopal Ch. of the Good Samaritan, Corvallis, Oreg., 1994–2001; consecrated bishop, 2001; bishop Episcopal Diocese of Nev., Las Vegas, 2001—; chief pastor elect Episcopal Church USA, 2006. Achievements include being first woman to lead a church in the worldwide Anglican Communion. Office: Episcopal Church Ctr Second Ave New York NY 10017 Office Phone: 702-737-9190. Office Fax: 702-737-6488.*

**SCHORLING, WILLIAM HARRISON,** lawyer; b. Ann Arbor, Mich., Jan. 7, 1949; s. Otis William Schorling and Ruthann (Bales) Schorling Moorehead; m. Lynne Ann Newcomb, June 1, 1974; children: Katherine Pearce, Ann Oury, John Roberts. BA cum laude, Denison U., 1971; JD cum laude, U. Mich., 1975. Bar: Pa. 1975, U.S. Ct. Appeals (3d cir.) 1977, N.J. 1998, Del. 2001, U.S. Dist. Ct. (so. and ea. dists.) N.Y. 2005. Ptnr. Eckert, Seamans, Cherin & Mellott, Pitts., 1984-89, Klett Rooney Lieber & Schorling, PC, Phila., 1989—2006, Buchanan Ingersoll & Rooney, P.C., Phila., 2006—. Lectr. Pa. Bar Inst., Harrisburg, 1983—, Comml. Law League, N.Y.C., 1984—, mem. exec. coun. bankruptcy sect., 2003—, Profl. Edn. Systems, Inc., Eau Claire, Wis., 1986—, Southwest Legal Found., Dallas, 1994—; founders' coun. Comml. Fin. Assn. Edn. Found., 1991—; bd. dirs. Consumer Bankruptcy Assistance Project; adj. prof. Temple U. Beasley Sch. Law, 1999-2004. Contbr. articles to profl. jours. Trustee Pa. Acad. Fine Arts. Fellow Am. Coll. Bankruptcy, Am. Bar Found.; mem. ABA (bus. law section coun. 2000-04, chmn. bus. bankruptcy com. 1996-99, lectr. 1988—), Am. Banker Inst. (lectr. 1994—), Phila. Bar Assn. (lectr. 1996—), E. Dist. Bankruptcy Conf., Pa. Bar Assn. (lectr. 1983—), Allegheny County Bar Assn. (chmn. bankruptcy and comml. law sect. 1991), The Com. of Seventy (chmn. 2003-04), Longue Vue Club, Duquesne Club, Pyramid Club, Pa. Soc. Presbyterian. Home: 933 S 2nd St Philadelphia PA 19147 Office: Buchanan Ingersoll & Rooney PC 2 Logan Sq Fl 12 Philadelphia PA 19103-2707 Office Phone: 215-567-7508. Business E-Mail: whschorling@klettrooney.com.

**SCHORNACK, JOHN JAMES,** accountant; b. Chgo., Nov. 22, 1930; s. John Joseph and Helen Patricia (Patrickus) S.; m. Barbara Anne Lelli, June 5, 1965; children: Mark Boyd, Anne Marguerite Schornack Trueman, Erin Keeley Schornack Dickes, Tracy Bevan Schornack Power. BS, Loyola U., 1951; MBA, Northwestern U., 1956; grad., Advanced Mgmt. Program, Harvard Bus. Sch., 1969. With Ernst & Young (formerly Arthur Young & Co.), 1955-91, partner, 1964-91; firm dir. personnel Ernst & Young LLP (formerly Arthur Young & Co.), N.Y.C., 1966-71, asst. mng. ptnr. N.Y.C. office, 1971-72, mng. ptnr., 1972-74, mng. ptnr. Chgo. office, 1976-85, mng. ptnr. Midwest region, vice chmn., 1985-91; mem. mgmt. com. Arthur Young & Co. Mgmt. com. Arthur Young & Co.; vice chmn., mng. ptnr. Midwest region Ernst & Young, 1989-91; bd. dirs., chmn. Ernst & Young Found., 1981-91; chmn., bd. dirs. North Shore Bancorp, Inc., 1992-, Wintrust Fin. Corp., 1996-. Pres. Chgo. Youth Ctrs., 1979-95; bd. govs. Chgo. Symphony, 1979-85, trustee, 1985-2003, life trustee; vol. United Way, 1975-92, dir., 1989-92; vis. adv. com. sch. accountancy DePaul U., 1980-83; mem. Loyola U. Citizens Bd., 1977-94, chmn., 1993-94; mem. adv. com. Northwestern U. Grad. Sch. Mgmt., 1967-91; coun. U. Chgo. Grad. Sch. Bus., 1982-91; bd. dirs. Met. Planning Coun., 1992-95; trustee Kohl Children's Mus., 1994-2005, life trustee, 2005—; trustee Lyric Opera, 1984-92, Cath. Charities Chgo., 2004—, Cath. Theol. Union, 1992-97, Graham Found., 1992-98; trustee Barat Coll., 1983-98, life trustee, 1999-2001, vice chmn., 1985-90, chmn., 1990-97; trustee St. Francis Hosp., 1986-97, vice chmn., 1991-94; trustee Night Ministry, 1998-004 Recipient Order of the Sacred Treasure, Emperor of Japan, 1999. Mem. AICPA, Am. Acctg. Assn., Ill. Soc. CPAs, Midwest-Japan Assn. (chmn. 1983-99), Japan Am. Soc., 410 Club, Chgo. Club, Glen View Club, The Little Club. Home: 314 Regent Wood Rd Northfield IL 60093-2762 Office: Ernst & Young LLP Great Lakes Reg Office 233 S Wacker Dr Chicago IL 60606-6306

**SCHORR, ALAN EDWARD,** librarian, publishing executive; b. NYC, Jan. 7, 1945; s. Herbert and Regina S.; m. Debra Genner, June 11, 1967; 1 son, Zebediah. BA, CUNY, 1966; MA, Syracuse U., 1967; postgrad., U. Iowa, 1967-71; MLS, U. Tex., 1973. Tchr., rsch. asst. dept. history U. Iowa, 1967-70; govt. publs. and map libr. asst. prof. Elmer E. Rasmuson Libr., U. Alaska, 1973-78; assoc. prof., dir. libr. U. Alaska, Juneau, 1978-84; prof., dean univ. libr. Calif. State U., Fullerton, 1984-86; pres. The Denali Press, Juneau, 1986—. Freelance indexer and bibliographer; vis. lectr. Birmingham (Eng.) Poly., 1981; mem. Alaska Ednl. Del. to China, 1975. Author: Alaska Place Names, 1974, 4th edit., 1991, Directory of Special Libraries in Alaska, 1975, Government Reference Books, 1974-75, 1976, 1976-77, 1978, Government Documents in the Library Literature 1909-1974, 1976, ALA RSBRC Manual, 1979, Federal Documents Librarianship 1879-1987, 1988, Hispanic Resource Directory, 1988, 3d edit., 1996, Refugee and Immigrant Resource Directory, 1990, 92, 94; editor: The Sourdough, 1974-75, Directory of Services for Refugees and Immigrants, 1987, 3d edit., 1993, Guide to Smithsonian serial publs., 1987; book reviewer, columnist: S.E. Alaska Empire, 1979-82, L.A. Times; contbr. articles to profl. jours. Mem. Auke Bay (Alaska) Vol. Fire Dept., 1978—81, Juneau Borough Libr. Adv. Com., 1981—82, Juneau Borough Cemetery Adv. Com., 1980—81, Am. Book Awards Com., 1980; chmn. program evaluation com., former chmn. facilities com., former chmn. policy com. to v.p. Juneau Bd. of Edn., 2000—; mem. Juneau Bd. Edn., 1991—94, 1995—97, 1997—2000, 2000—03, 2003—04; mem. citizens adv. coun. Juneau Empire Newspaper, 2003—. Mem. ALA (mem. reference and subscription books rev. com. 1975-86, mem. reference and adult svcs. divsn. publs. com. 1974-75, Nat. Assn. Hispanic Publs., Mudge citation comm. 1977-79, 84-86, Dartmouth Coll. Medal Commn., Governing Coun. 1977-84, mem. Dewey medal com. 1984-85, Denali Press award), Alaska Libr. Assn. (mem. exec. bd. 1974-75, mem. nominating com. 1977-79), Pacific N.W. Libr. Assn. (rep. publs. com. 1973-75), Assn. Coll. and Rsch. Librs. (mem. publ. com. 1976-80), Spl. Librs. Assn. (assoc. editor geography and map divsn. bull. 1975-76), Internat. Assn. Ind. Pubs (bd. dirs. 1990-92), True North Fed. Credit Union (bd. dirs. 1997-, treas. 2001-2002, vice chmn., 2002-04, chmn., 2004-), PEN Ctr. USA West, Explorers Club N.Y., Wash. Athletic Club (Seattle). Office: Denali Press PO Box 1535 Juneau AK 99802

**SCHORR, BRIAN LEWIS,** lawyer, writer; b. NYC, Oct. 5, 1958; s. Philip I. and Hannah Schorr; m. Amy B. Horowitz; 2 children. BA magna cum laude, MA, Wesleyan U., Middletown, Conn., 1979; JD, NYU, 1982. Bar: N.Y. 1983, D.C. 1985, U.S. Supreme Ct. 1988; Assoc. Paul, Weiss, Rifkind, Wharton & Garrison, N.Y.C., 1982-90, ptnr., 1991-94; exec. v.p., gen. counsel Triarc Cos., Inc., N.Y.C., 1994—. Mem. bd. advisors Jour. Lit. Liability Cos., 1994-98. CLE programs. Author: Schorr on New York Limited Liability Companies and Partnerships, 1994; contbr. articles to legal jours. Trustee NYU Sch. Law; bd. dirs. Montefiore Hosp. (N.Y.) HS Sci. Endowment Fund, Inc. Mem. ABA, N.Y. State Bar Assn., Assn. Bar City N.Y. (chmn. com. on corp. law 1993-96, co-chmn. joint drafting com. N.Y. ltd. liability co. law, mem. spl. com. on mergers, acquisitions and corp. control contests 1996—, com. on securities regulation 2004—), Tri Bar Opinion Com. Office: Triarc Cos Inc 280 Park Ave New York NY 10017-1216

**SCHORR, DANIEL LOUIS,** broadcast journalist, author, lecturer; b. NYC, Aug. 31, 1916; s. Louis and Tillie (Godiner) S.; m. Lisbeth Bamberger, 1967; children: Jonathan, Lisa. BSS, CCNY, 1939; doctorate (hon.), Kalamazoo Coll., Columbia Coll., Chgo., Wilkes U., Nebr. Wesleyan U., LI U., Brandeis U., Spartus Coll., Bates Coll., Haverford Coll. Asst. editor Jewish Telegraphic Agy., 1934-41; news editor ANETA (Netherlands) News Agy. in N.Y., 1941-43; freelance corr. N.Y. Times, Christian Sci. Monitor, London Daily Mail, 1948-53; Washington corr. CBS News, also spl. assignments L.Am. and Europe, 1953-55; reopened CBS Moscow Bur., 1955; roving assignments U.S. and Europe, 1958-60; chief CBS News Bur., Germany, 1960-66; Washington corr. CBS, 1966-76; Regents prof. U. Calif., Berkeley, 1977; columnist Des Moines Register-Tribune Syndicate, 1977-80; sr. Washington corr. Cable News Network, 1980-85; sr. analyst Nat. Pub. Radio, 1985—. Author: Don't Get Sick in America!, 1971, Clearing the Air, 1977, Forgive Us Our Press Passes, 1999, Staying Tuned, 2001. With U.S. Army, 1943-46, 47. Decorated officer Orange Nassau (The Netherlands), Grand Cross of Merit (Germany); recipient citations of excellence for radio-TV reporting Soviet Union Overseas Press Club, 1956, Best TV Interpretation of Fgn. News award 1963, ACLU and other awards for pub. suppressed Congsl. intelligence report, Emmy awards for coverage of Watergate, 1972, 73, 74, Peabody award for lifetime of uncompromising reporting of highest integrity, 1992, George Polk award for radio commentary L.I. U., 1994, Disting. Svc. award Am. Soc. Journalism and Mass Comm., 1994, Golden Baton award for lifetime achievement A.I. DuPont Columbia U., 1996; inducted in Hall of Fame Soc. Profl. Journalists, 1991, Comms. Hall of Fame CCNY, 1999. Mem. Am. Acad. Arts and Scis. (elected), Coun. on Fgn. Rels. N.Y.C., Nat. Press Club. Office Phone: 202-513-2277. E-mail: dschorr@npr.org. *Journalism, for more than 60 years, has been both profession and outlook on life. I have always felt myself the observer and nonparticipant, the quintessential outsider. I have pursued the sense of things behind the appearance of things, the meaning behind the manipulation. I have fought, with dubious success, against the blurring of the media line between reality and fantasy.*

**SCHORR, LISBETH BAMBERGER,** sociologist, researcher; b. Munich, Jan. 20, 1931; d. Fred S. and Lotte (Krafft) Bamberger; m. Daniel L. Schorr, Jan. 8, 1967; children: Jonathan, Lisa. BA with highest honors, U. Calif., Berkeley, 1952; LHD (hon.), Wilkes U., 1991, U. Md., 1994, Bank St. Coll. Edn., 1999, Wheelock Coll., 2000, Lewis & Clark Coll., 2001, Whittier Coll., 2003. Med. care cons. U.A.W. and Community Health Assn., Detroit, 1956—58; asst. dir. Dept. Social Security AFL-CIO, Washington, 1958—65; acting chief CAP Health Svcs., OEO, 1965—66; chief program planning Office for Health Affairs, OEO, Washington, 1967. Cons. Children's Def. Fund, Washington, 1973—79; scholar-in-residence Inst. of Medicine NAS, 1979—80; chmn. Select Panel on Promotion Child Health, 1979—80; adj. prof. maternal and child health U. N.C., Chapel Hill, 1981—85; lectr. social medicine Harvard U. Med. Sch., 1984—; dir. project on effective interventions Harvard U., 1988—; founder www.PathwaysToOutcomes.org; nat. coun. Alan Gutmacher Inst., 1974—79, 1982—85; pub. mem. Nat. Bd. Pediat., 1978—84; vice chmn. Found. for Child Devel., 1978—84, bd. dirs., 1976—84, 1986—94; mem. coun. Nat. Ctr. for Children in Poverty, 1987—96; mem. children's program adv. com. Edna McConnell Clark Found., 1987—97; bd. dirs. Pub. Edn. Fund Network, 1991—93; co-chair Roundtable on Cmty. Change Aspen Inst., 1992—; mem. bd. on children and families NAS, 1993—95; mem. Nat. Commn. State and Local Pub. Svcs., 1992—94; mem. task force on young children Carnegie Corp., 1992—94; mem. sec.'s adv. com. Head Start quality and expansion, 1993—94; mem. nat. selection com. Ford Found./Kennedy Sch. Awards for Innovations in Am. Govt., 1998—. Author: Within Our Reach: Breaking the Cycle of Disadvantage, 1988, Common Purpose: Strengthening Families and Neighborhoods to Rebuild America, 1997. Co-chmn. Boundaries task force Harvard Children's Initiative, 1998—2000; mem. Brookings Children's Roundtable, 1999—2002; bd. dirs. Nat. Student Partnerships, 2001—03, Eureka Cmtys., 1995—, Civic Ventures, 1997—99. Recipient Dale Richmond Meml. award, Am. Acad. Pediat., 1977, 9th ann. Robert F. Kennedy Book award, 1989, Nelson Cruikshank award, Nat. Coun. Sr. Citizens, 1990, Porter prize, 1993, PASS award, Nat. Coun. on Crime and Delinquency, 1997, Marian F. Langer award, Am. Orthopsychiat. Assn., 1999, Empatheia award, Vols. of Am., 1999. Mem.: Nat. Acad. on Social Ins., Inst. Medicine NAS, Phi Beta Kappa. Home and Office: 3113 Woodley Rd NW Washington DC 20008-3449 Office Phone: 202-462-3071. Business E-Mail: lisbeth_schorr@hms.harvard.edu.

**SCHORR, PAUL C., III,** electrical contracting executive; Pres., CEO ComCor Holdings Inc., 1988—; chmn. Western Sizzlin Corp. (formerly Austin Steaks & Saloon), Roanoke, Va., 1995—99, 2002—. Trustee Whitney Mus. Am. Art, NYC; bd. dir. Ameritas Life Ins. Corp., Schorr Family Co. Inc., Nat. Rsch. Corp., Western Sizzlin Corp., Roanoke, Va., 1994—. Recipient Univ. Neb. Builder award, 1984. Office: ComCor Holdings Inc Ste 336 6940 O St Lincoln NE 68510 also: Western Sizzlin Corp 317 Kimball Ave NE Roanoke VA 24016 Mailing: Schorr Family Co PO Box 57310 Lincoln NE 68505 Office Phone: 402-464-3456, 540-345-3195.

**SCHORR, S. L.,** lawyer; b. NYC, Feb. 19, 1930; s. Charles and Clara (Lerech) S.; m. Eleanor Daru, Mar. 23, 1956; children: Lewis, Andrew, Emily, Roberta. Student, L.I. U., 1948-50; LLB, Bklyn. Law Sch., 1953. Bar: N.Y. 1955, Ariz. 1962, U.S. Dist. Ct. Ariz. 1962, U.S. Supreme Ct. 1979. Planning commr. Pima County, Tucson, 1959-62; asst. city mgr. Tucson, 1962-63; ptnr. Lewis and Roca, Tucson, 1988—. Co-chair Continuing Legal Edn. Seminar on Ballot Box Zoning, U. Ariz., 1991, Ariz. State Bar Continuing Legal Edn. Seminar on Land Use Regulation and Litigation, 1977, 86, 89, 95. Bd. dirs. Pima Coll., 1966-67, So. Ariz. Leadership Coun., 1997—; mem. Commn. on Improved Govtl. Mgmt., Tucson, 1974-77, Gov.'s Econ. Planning and Devel. Adv. Bd., Phoenix, 1983-85, regional trans. authority; chmn. Gov.'s Task Force on Seriously Mentally Ill, Phoenix, 1989-91, Ariz. State Transp. Bd., 2003, mem. Nat. Bar Assn., Pima County Bar Assn. Democrat. Office: Lewis Roca 1 S Church Ave Ste 700 Tucson AZ 85701-1611 Office Phone: 520-622-2090.

**SCHORR-RIBERA, HILDA KEREN,** psychologist; b. N.Y.C., May 2, 1942; d. Leon and Rosa Schorr-Ribera; m. Ira Eli Wessler, Aug. 6, 1971; children: Mike, Daniel. BA, Hunter Coll., 1963; MEd, U. No. Fla., 1982; PhD, U. Pitts., 1988. Lic. psychologist, Pa.; diplomate Am. Bd. Forensic Examiners; diplomate, fellow Am. Bd. Med. Psychotherapists and Psychodiagnosticians; diplomate Am. Bd. Forensic Medicine, Am. Acad. Experts in Traumatic Stress; cert. in clin. hypnosis. Psychotherapist South Hills Interfaith Ministries, Bethel Park, Pa., 1989-92, Profl. Psychol. Assn. of Greater Pitts., 1992; pvt. practice psychologist Pitts., 1993—. Child therapist Forbes Hospice, 1993—; group facilitator of adult wellness group and children's support groups Burger King Cancer Caring Ctr., Pitts., 1989—, Allegheny Hospice, Pitts., 1994—96; psychol. evaluator Washington (Pa.) County Ct., 1993—2005, Allegheny County Ct., Pitts., 1995—98; cons. psychologist to sch. dists. Allegheny and Washington Counties. Author (with others): Educating the Child With Cancer, 1993. Keynote spkr. on illness and bereavement to profl. assns., hosps., schs. and agys., Pitts., 1989—. Mem. APA, Internat. Soc. Hypnosis, Am. Soc. Clin. Hypnosis, Am. Acad. Experts in Traumatic Stress, Am. Counseling Assn., Am. Coll. Forensic Examiners, Pa. Psychol. Assn., Greater Pitts. Psychol. Assn. Avocations: music, bilingual services, reading, walking, travel. Office: 117 Ridgeway Ct Pittsburgh PA 15228-1729 Office Phone: 412-344-0222. Personal E-Mail: schorrribera@yahoo.com.

**SCHORSCH, ISMAR,** theology studies educator, rabbi; b. Hannover, Germany, Nov. 3, 1935; m. Sally Korn; children: Jonathan, Rebecca, Naomi. BA, Ursinus Coll., 1957; MA, Columbia U., 1961, PhD, 1969; MHL, Jewish Theol. Sem. Am., 1962; LittD (hon.), Wittenberg U., 1989, Ursinus Coll., 1990, Gratz Coll., 1995, Russian State U., 1996, Tufts U., 2000. Ordained rabbi, 1962. Instr. Jewish Theol. Sem. Am., N.Y.C., 1964-68; asst. prof. Jewish Theol. Sem. Am., N.Y.C., 1970-72, assoc. prof., 1972-76, 1976—, dean Grad. Sch., 1975-79, provost, 1980-84; chancellor, 1986—; asst. prof. Jewish history Columbia U., N.Y.C., 1968-70. Bd. dirs. Leo Baeck Inst., 1976, mem. exec. com., 1980, pres., 1985-86, 90—, mem. editorial bd. of yearbook, 1987; participant symposium Spirit and Nature: Religion, Ethics and Environ.

Crisis, Middlebury Coll.; organizer Nat. Religious Partnership for the Environment. Author: From Text to Context: The Turn to History in Modern Judaism, 1994, (monograph) Sacred Cluster: The Core Values of Conservative Judaism, 1995; contbr. articles to profl. publs. Chaplain U.S. Army, 1962—64. Recipient Clark F. Ansley award Columbia U. Press, 1969, Life Achievement award in Jewish history Nat. Found. for Jewish Culture, 2003; NEH fellow, 1979-80 Fellow Am. Acad. Jewish Rsch. Jewish. Office: Jewish Theol Sem 3080 Broadway New York NY 10027-4650 E-mail: Isschorsch@JTSA.edu.

**SCHORSCH, LOUIS L.,** metal products executive; b. Chgo. married; 3 children. BA, Georgetown U., 1971; PhD, Am. U. Analyst U.S. Congl. Budget Office; prin. McKinsey & Co., 1985—2000; pres., CEO Global Steel Exchange, 2000—03; with LNM Group, 2003; pres. CEO Ispat Inland, Inc., 2003—05; CEO Mittal Steel USA, 2005—; economist Am. Iron and Steel Inst., vice chmn. Washington, 2006, chmn., 2006—. Co-author (with Donald F. Barnett): (book) Steel: Upheaval in a Basic History, 1983; contbr. articles to profl. jours. Office: Am Iron and Steel Inst 1140 Connecticut Ave NW Ste 705 Washington DC 20036-4011 Office Phone: 202-452-7100. Office Fax: 202-463-6573.*

**SCHORSKE, CARL EMIL,** historian, educator; b. N.Y.C., Mar. 15, 1915; s. Theodore A. and Gertrude (Goldschmidt) S.; m. Elizabeth Gilbert Rorke, June 14, 1941; children: Carl Theodore, Anne (Mrs. J. L. Edwards), Stephen James, John Simon, Richard Robert. AB, Columbia U., 1936; MA, Harvard U., 1937, PhD, 1950; DLitt (hon.), Wesleyan U., 1967; DLitt (hon.), Bard Coll., 1982, Clark U., 1983, New Sch. Social Rsch., 1986, Miami U., 1987, Monmouth Coll., 1994, Princeton U., 1997; DPhil (hon.), U. Salzburg, 1986, U. Graz, 1996. Prof. history Wesleyan U., Middletown, Conn., 1946-60; prof. history U. Calif.-Berkeley, 1960-69, Princeton U., 1969-80, emeritus, 1980—. Author: (with Hoyt Price) The Problem of Germany, 1947, German Social Democracy 1905-17, 1955, Fin-de-Siècle Vienna, 1980, Thinking with History, 1998. Lt. (j.g.) USNR, 1943-46; with OSS, 1941-46. Recipient Austrian Cross of Honor for arts and scis., 1979, Pulitzer prize for gen. nonfiction, 1981, Grand prize for cultural edn. City of Vienna, 1985, Harvard Centennial medal, 1999, Wittgenstein prize, 2004; named Officer, French Order Arts and Letters, 1987, Great Silver medal of Honor, Austria, 1996, Gold Cross of Honor, City of Vienna, 2000; MacArthur fellow, 1981-86. Fellow Royal Acad. Fine Arts Netherlands (hon.); mem. Am. Acad. Arts and Scis., Austrian Acad. Scis. (corr.), Am. Hist. Assn. (council 1964-68, Disting. Scholar award 1992), Ctr. Advanced Study Behavioral Sci., Inst. Advanced Study, Getty Ctr. Home: 45 Meadow Lakes 01 Hightstown NJ 08520

**SCHOTLAND, DONALD LEWIS,** retired medical educator, neurologist; b. Orange, N.J., Sept. 21, 1930; s. Joseph Henry and Elsie (Block) S.; m. Marilyn Goldfeder, July 6, 1955 (dec. 1974); m. Estherina Shems, Jan. 11, 1976; children: John, Thomas, Peter. AB, Harvard U., 1952, MD, 1957; spl. student, MIT, 1955-56; MA (hon.), U. Pa., 1973. Diplomate Am. Bd. Psychiatry and Neurology 1964. Intern U. Ill. Research and Edn. Hosp., 1957-58; asst. resident in neurology Columbia Presbyn. Med. Center, N.Y.C., 1958-61, asst. neurologist, 1961-65, asst. attending neurologist, 1965-66; asst. in neurology Coll. Physicians and Surgeons, Columbia U., N.Y.C., 1960-61, vis. fellow in neurology, 1961-64, assoc. in neurology, 1964-66, asst. prof. neurology, 1966-67; assoc. prof. Sch. Medicine, U. Pa., Phila., 1967-72, prof., 1972-98, prof. emeritus, 1998—. Speaker profl. confs., U.S., Can., Italy, Japan, China, France, Israel, Finland; dir. Henry M. Watts, Jr. Neuromuscular Disease Rsch. Ctr., 1974-90. Editor: Diseases of the Motor Unit, 1982; contbr. articles, papers to profl. pubs. Served to 1st lt. USAR, 1958-65. NIH postdoctoral fellow, 1961-64; recipient Research Career Devel. award, 1966-67, various grants NIH and Muscular Dystrophy Assn. Fellow Coll. of Physicians of Phila.; mem. Am. Acad. Neurology, Am. Neurol. Assn., Phila. Neurol. Soc., Muscular Dystrophy Assn. (sci. adv. com. 1974-86, chmn. fellowship com. 1974-86, chmn. 6th Internat. Conf. 1980). Home: 1310 Wyngate Rd Wynnewood PA 19096-2455 Office: Hosp of Univ Pa 3400 Spruce St Philadelphia PA 19104-4283 Personal E-mail: dlschotl@mail.med.upenn.edu.

**SCHOTT, DONALD KARL,** lawyer; b. Lynwood, Calif., Sept. 13, 1955; s. Otto H. and Violet M. (Reiman) S.; m. Cynthia A. Cronkrite, Aug. 9, 1980; children: Nathan Daniel, Anna Katherine, Laura Elizabeth BS in History and Polit. Sci., U. Wis., Madison, 1977; JD, Harvard U., 1980. Bar: Wis. 1980, U.S. Dist. Ct. (ea. and we. dists. Wis. 1980, no. dist. Ill. 1991), U.S. Ct. Appeals (7th cir. 1980, 9th cir. 2003), US Supreme Ct. 1995. Assoc. Quarles & Brady LLP, Milw., 1980-82, 85-87, ptnr., litig. practice Milw. & Madison, Wis., 1987—, mem. exec. com., 1999—; legis. asst. to Gov. State of Wis., Madison, 1983-85. Master: James E. Doyle Am. Inn Ct.; fellow: Am. Coll. Trial Lawyers; mem.: ABA, State Bar Wis. (bd. dir., young lawyers div. 1982—83), We. Dist. Bar Assn. (chmn. com. alternative dispute resolution 1992—97), Dane County Bar Assn., Phi Beta Kappa. Office: Quarles & Brady Ste 600 1 S Pinckney St Madison WI 53703-2808 Office Phone: 608-283-2426. Office Fax: 608-294-4923. Business E-Mail: dks@quarles.com.

**SCHOTT, JOHN ROBERT,** international consultant, educator; b. Rochester, NY, Jan. 30, 1936; s. John and Ellen (Waite) S.; m. Diane Elizabeth Dempsey, June 19, 1963; children: Elizabeth Anne (dec.), Jennifer, Jared Reed, George Kermit Alexander. BA magna cum laude, Haverford Coll., 1957; postgrad., Oxford U., 1957-59; PhD, Harvard U., 1964. Resident tutor in govt. Eliot House, Harvard Coll., Cambridge, Mass., 1960-64; inst. polit. sci. Wellesley (Mass.) Coll., 1964-66; policy planning specialist AID, Washington, 1966-67; chief Title IX div. AID, Washington, 1967-68; vis. prof. polit. devel. Fletcher Sch. Law & Diplomacy, Tufts U., Medford, Mass., 1968-70; sr. v.p. Thunderbird Grad. Sch. Internat. Mgmt., Phoenix, 1970-71; cons. internat. affairs Dun Foundtn, NH, 1971-74; pres. Schott & Assocs., Inc., Jaffrey Center, NH, 1974-93. Mem. U.S. Del. World Assembly Internat. Secretariat for Voluntary Service, New Delhi, 1967; advisor Office Prime Minister Royal Thai Govt., Bangkok, 1978-80, Minister Cooperatives Govt. of Indonesia, Jakarta, 1983-84; research asst. spl. appointment The Brookings Inst., Washington, 1960-61 Author: Kenya Tragedy: European Colonization in East Africa, 1964, Frances' Town: History of Francestown, N.H., 1972, 2d edit., 1998, A Five-Year Comprehensive Plan for Development of Agricultural Cooperatives in Thailand, 1979, Recana-Komprehensip Pengembangan Kud, Jakarta, Indonesia, 1985; editor: An Experiment in Integrated Rural Development, 1978; contbr. articles to profl. jours. Mem. Bd. of Selectmen, Francestown, NH, 1975-78; trustee Spaulding Youth Ctr., Tilton, N.H., 1971-82, 85-89, pres. bd. trustees, 1972-75; trustee Internat. Inst. Rural Reconstrn., NYC, 1979-89, exec. com., 1985-89, bd. trustees NH Pub. Radio, 1990-96, chmn., 1992-2000, chmn., 1993-95; spl. study commn. Coop. Extension Svc. State of NH, 1980-81, scenic and cultural by-ways com., 1993-96; forestry rep. County Extension Coun., Hillsboro County, NH, 1979-82; pres. NH Timberland Owner's Assn., 1989-90, bd. dirs., 1988-91; chmn. NH chpt. Nature Conservancy, 1990-3, hon. trustee, 1993—, chmn. NH Timber-Tourism Coalition, 1990-94; vice-chmn. Foresters Lic. Bd. State of NH, 1990-95; bd. trustees Cheshire Med. Ctr., 1992-94, RiverMead Retirement Cmty., Peterborough, NH, 1992-2000, chmn., 1996-2000; bd. overseers cmty. econ. devel. program So. NH U., 1997-2001, chmn., 1997-2000; trustee Sharon Arts Ctr., 2001-03; bd. dirs. Granite State Conservation Voters Alliance, 2004—. Recipient The Haverford award, Haverford Coll., Pa., 1999, Global Alumni Svc. to Humanity award, Rotary Internat. Found., 2005—06; fellow, Rotary Found., 1957—58, Harvard U. Arts and Sci., 1959—60; scholar, Coslett Found., 1957—59, Harvard Found. Found. Assn., 1953-62. Home and Office: Schott & Assocs 15 Upper Troy Rd Fitzwilliam NH 03447

**SCHOTT, JOHN WILLIAM,** psychiatrist, investment advisor; b. LaSalle, Ill., July 2, 1940; s. Joseph William and Anne Marie Schott; m. Sarah Purdy, June 4, 1966; children: Anne Rutherford, Hannah Elizabeth, Lilly Hamilton. AB, Johns Hopkins U., 1962; MD, Harvard U., 1966. Clin. dir. Dorchester Mental Health, Boston, 1970-73, Westboro (Mass.) State Hosp., 1973-75; chmn. dept. psychiatry Leonard Morse Hosp., Natick, Mass., 1975-91, MetroWest Med. Ctr., Framingham & Natick, Mass., 1991—2004; clin. instr. Harvard Med. Sch., Boston, 1991—; portfolio mgr. Steinberg Global Asset

Mgmt., Boston, 1993—. Treas. AEMS Corp., Natick, 1990—2000; pres. Cochituate Enterprises, Natick, 1991—2004. Author: Mind Over Money, 1998, From Behind the Couch, 1999; assoc. editor Jour. of Psychology and Fin. Markets, 2000-2002, Jour. Behavior Finance, 2003—; writer, publisher The Schott Letter, 1983—. Dir. Learning Ctr. Deaf Children, Framingham, 197-2004; chmn. bd. trustees Dover (Mass.) Ch., 1978-80; trustee John Templeton Found., 2006—, First Congrl. Ch., Winter Park, Fla., Templeton World Charities Found. Mem. Am. Psychoanalytic Assn., Am. Psychiat. Assn., Mass. Med. Soc., Boston Psychoanalytic Soc. (treas. 1983-90, 2000-04, chmn. bd. trustees 1986-90), East Chop Tennis Club, East Chop Beach Club, Univ. Club (Winter Park, Fla.) Mem. United Ch. of Christ. Avocations: croquet, chess, gardening. Home: 3968 Lower Pk Rd Orlando FL 32814 Office Phone: 561-750-0800.

**SCHOTT, MICHAEL J.,** library director; b. Atlantic City, Sept. 28, 1950; s. Joseph Louis and Dorothy Theresa Schott; m. Janice Alexander, Aug. 4, 1984; children: Christopher Windsor, Rebecca Katherine. BA in Am. History, LaSalle Coll., Phila., 1972; MA in Libr. Sci., Glassboro State Coll., 1978; MLS, So. Conn. State Coll., 1993. Asst. libr. dir. N.Y. Med. Coll., Valhalla, 1985—86; hosp. libr. dir. Danbury (Conn.) Hosp., 1987—99; med. libr. dir. W.Va. U., Charleston, 2000—. Author: Medical Library Downsizing; contbr. articles to profl. jours. Recipient Pub. Rels. award, Conn. Libr. Assn., 1982, 1984, 1986. Mem.: Beta Phi Mu. Home: 108 Vista Ln Hurricane WV 25526 Office: WVa Univ 3110 MacCorkle Ave SE Charleston WV 25304 Office Phone: 304-347-1219. E-mail: mschott@hsc.wvu.edu.

**SCHOTT, ROBERT W. (BOB SCHOTT),** film producer, actor, film director; b. Feb. 2, 1949; Student, Ill. Ctrl. U. Exec. prodr. Global Media Prodns., Platinum Blues Music. Founder Internat. SeaLand Enterprises, 1975—; former profl. bodybuilder. Actor: (films) Future Hunters, 1989, Head of the Family, 1996, In the Line of Fire, Fear, Force: Five, Million Dollar Mystery, VAMP, Gymkata, Blood Fist III, Aftershock, Out for Blood, Shoot Fighter, (TV episodes) Knightrider, Simon & Simon, Kaz, Eight is Enough; (TV films) Steel Cowboys, Jarret, The Norliss Tapes, Amateur Night at the Dixie Bar & Grill; prodr.: (documentaries) Adventures Beyond, The Women's Secret Weapon for Auto Buying; performer (composer (with Loretta Mears): (songs) Remembrance. Nominee Clio award, 1981; named U.S. Arm Wrestling Champion, 1981, World Arm Wrestling Champion, 1981. Mem.: SAG, Nat. Assn. TV Programming Execs., Broadcast Music Inc. Office: GMP PO Box 36773 Los Angeles CA 90036 Office Phone: 323-960-7700. Business E-Mail: isle@iwlink.com.

**SCHOTT, SALLY MARIA,** music publisher, arts education consultant; b. San Antonio, Feb. 7, 1943; d. Valentine Felix Schott, Jr. and Doris Faye. MusB, Okla. Coll. Women, 1964; MusM Edn., North Tex. State U., 1966. Choral dir. Jackson Intermediate, Pasadena, Tex., 1965—74, South Houston H.S., 1974—2004; founding ptnr. Alliance Music Publs., Houston, 1994—. Ednl. cons. Bay Area Chorus, Houston, 2004—; supr. student tchrs. U. Houston, 2004—; text correlations writer McGraw-Hill, Woodland Hills, Calif., 2005—; minority ptnr. AMC Music, Houston, 1975—2006; pres. Quaid/Schott Media Prodns., LLC, 2005—, Schott Bradshaw Publ., LLC, 2006—. Editor: Something to Sing About, 1981, Howard Swan: Conscience of a Profession, 1987; coord. writing team Sing, 1988. Mem. advt. bd. Am. Classic Festivals, San Antonio, 2006—; ednl. adv. bd. Houston Chamber Choir, 2004—. Named to Hall Fame, U. Sci. & Arts Okla., 1996; recipient Outstanding Young Educator, Pasadena Jaycees, 1974, Tchrs. Make a Difference award, KTRK, 1988. Mem.: Tex. Choral Dirs. Assn. (state v.p. 1976—77), Am. Choral Dirs. Assn. (R&S 1994—98, pres. 2000—02, editor newsletter 2002—04), Tex. Music Educators Assn. (pres., state vocal chair 1981—86), Pasadena Area Ret. Sch. Employees, Delta Kappa Gamma, Sigma Alpha Iota (pres. 1966, Leadership award Svc. to Music in Houston 1987). Republican. Methodist. Avocations: photography, travel, sports. Home: 4403 Regal Pine Trail Houston TX 77059

**SCHOTTENFELD, DAVID,** retired epidemiologist, retired educator; b. N.Y.C., Mar. 25, 1931; m. Rosalie C. Schaeffer; children: Jacqueline, Stephen. AB, Hamilton Coll., 1952; MD, Cornell U., 1956; MS in Pub. Health, Harvard U., 1963. Diplomate Am. Bd. Internal Medicine, Am. Bd. Preventive Medicine. Intern in internal medicine Duke U., Durham, NC, 1956-57; resident in internal medicine Meml. Sloan-Kettering Cancer Ctr., Cornell U. Med. Coll., N.Y.C., 1957-59; Craver fellow med. oncology Meml. Sloan-Kettering Cancer Ctr., 1961-62; clin. instr. dept. pub. health Cornell U., N.Y.C., 1963—65, asst. prof. dept. pub. health, 1965-70, assoc. prof. dept. pub. health, 1970-73, prof. dept. pub. health, 1973-86; John G. Searle prof., chmn. epidemiology sch. pub. health U. Mich., Ann Arbor, 1986—2004, prof. internal medicine, 1986—2004, prof. emeritus internal medicine and epidemiology Sch. Pub. Health, 2004—. Vis. prof. epidemiology U. Minn., Mpls., 1968, 71, 74, 82, 86; W.G. Cosbie lectr. Can. Oncology Soc., 1987. Editor: Cancer Epidemiology and Prevention, 1982, 2d. edit., 1996, 3d edit., 2006; author 10 books; contbr. more than 250 articles to profl. jours. Served with USPHS, 1959-61. Recipient Acad. Career award in Preventive Oncology, Nat. Cancer Inst., 1980-85, Disting. Achievement award Am. Soc. Preventive Oncology, 1992. Fellow AAAS, ACP, Am. Coll. Preventive Medicine, Am. Coll. Epidemiology (Abraham Lilienfeld award 2002), Armed Forces Epidemiology Bd.; mem. Soc. Epidemiologic Rsch. (pres. 1998-99), Phi Beta Kappa. Office: U Mich Sch Pub Health Dept Epidemiology 109 Observatory St Ann Arbor MI 48109-2029 Home: 25 River Birch Ln Dalton MA 01226-2104 Business E-Mail: daschott@umich.edu.

**SCHOTTENFELD, RICHARD STEVEN,** psychiatrist; b. East Orange, N.J., Apr. 27, 1949; s. Alvin Carl and Pearl Natalie (Feller) S.; m. Tanina Rostain. BA, Yale U., 1971, MD, 1976. Diplomate Am. Bd. Psychiatry and Neurology. Intern Mt. Sinai Hosp., N.Y.C., 1976-77; resident Yale U. Sch. Medicine, New Haven, 1979-82, Robert Wood Johnson clin. VA fellow, 1982-84; asst. prof. psychiatry Yale U., New Haven, 1984-90, assoc. prof. psychiatry, 1990—; dir. alcohol treatment Conn. Mental Health Ctr., New Haven, 1984-87, dir. evaluation unit, 1984-87, assoc. dir. substance abuse treatment unit, 1987-89, co-dir. substance abuse treatment unit, 1989-91, dir. substance abuse treatment unit, 1991—; med. dir. APT Found., New Haven, 1987—, acting chief exec. officer, 1989-91, chief exec. officer, 1991—. Mem. Conn. Psychiat. Soc. (co-chair AIDS subcom. 1988-89). Avocations: cross country skiing, backpacking, bicycle riding. Office: Conn Mental Health Ctr 34 Park St Rm S-103 New Haven CT 06519-1187

**SCHOTTENHEIMER, MARTY (MARTIN EDWARD SCHOTTENHEIMER),** professional football coach; b. Canonsburg, Pa., Sept. 23, 1943; m. Patricia Schottenheimer; children— Kristen, Brian BA, U. Pitts., 1964. Football player Buffalo Bills, NFL, 1965-68, Boston Patriots, 1969-70; real estate developer Miami and Denver, 1971-74; asst. coach World Football League, Portland, 1974, N.Y. Giants, 1975-77, Detroit Lions, 1978-79, Cleve. Browns, 1980-84, head coach, 1985-88, Kansas City Chiefs, 1989-99, Wash. Redskins, 2001, San Diego Chargers, 2002—; tv analyst ESPN, 1999—2001. Named Coach of the Year, AP, 2004. Mailing: San Diego Chargers PO Box 609609 San Diego CA 92160-9609 Office: San Diego Chargers 4020 Murphy Canyon Rd San Diego CA 92123*

**SCHOTTENSTEIN, JAY L.,** retail executive; b. 1954; Grad., Ind. U. With Schottenstein Stores, Columbus, Ohio, vice chmn., exec. v.p., CEO, 1992—; chmn. Value City Department Stores, Columbus, Ohio, 1992; CEO Am. Eagle Outfitters, Warrendale, Pa., 1992—2002, chmn., 2002—, Retail Ventures Inc., 2002—. Office: Schottenstein Stores 1800 Moler Rd Columbus OH 43207-1680 Address: Retail Ventures Inc 3241 Westerville Rd Columbus OH 43224 also: American Eagle Outfitters 150 Thorn Hill Dr Warrendale PA 15086-7528

**SCHOTTER, ANDREW ROYE,** economics professor, consultant; b. N.Y.C., June 6, 1947; s. I. Harvey and Sara (Rothstein) S.; m. Anne Howland, June 7, 1970; children: Geoffrey, Elizabeth. BS, Cornell U., 1969; MA, PhD, NYU, 1974. Asst. prof. Syracuse (N.Y.) U., 1974-75, NYU, 1975-81, assoc.

prof., 1981-86, prof., chmn. econs. dept. N.Y.C., 1989-93, 96-99, chmn. C.V. Starr Ctr. for Applied Econs., 1986-89, dir. Ctr. for Experiential Social Sci., 2001—. Vis. asst. prof. Cornell U., Ithaca, 1974-75; vis. prof. U. Venice, 1993, U. Amsterdam; cons. Gulf & Western Corp., N.Y. 1987, Pegalis & Wachsman, Great Neck, N.Y., 1987-88, Nat. Econ. Rsch. Assocs., White Plains, N.Y., 1989—. Author: Economic Theory of Social Institutions, 1981, Free Market Economics: A Critical Appraisal, 1985, 2 edit., 1990, Microeconomics: A Modern Approach, 1993, 3d edit., 2000; mem. editl. bd.: Am. Econ. Rev., 1995—, Exptl. Econs., 1997; assoc. editor: Games and Econ. Behavior; spl. editor: Exptl. Econs. Grantee Office of Naval Rsch., 1980-85, NSF, 1988-90, 97—; recipient Kenan Enterprise award, 1993. Mem. Am. Econ. Assn., Econometric Soc., Econ. Sci. Assn. (pres.-elect 1997), Game Theory Soc. Office: NYU Dept Econs 269 Mercer St New York NY 10003-6633

**SCHOTTLAENDER, BRIAN E.C.,** university librarian; BA in German studies, U. Tex., Austin, 1974; MSLS, Indiana U., 1980. Past various libr. positions at Firma Otto Harrassowitz, Wiesbaden, Germany, Ind. U., U. Ariz.; from asst. head cataloging dept. to asst. univ. libr. tech. svc. UCLA, 1984—93, assoc. univ. libr. for collections and tech. svc., 1993—99; univ. libr. U. Calif., San Diego, 1999—. ALA rep. to internat. Joint Steering Com. for Revision Anglo-Am. Cataloguing Rules, 1995—2001; chair Program Coop. Cataloguing Libr. Congress, 1997—98; chair Pacific Rim Digital Alliance, 1999—2001, San Diego Libr. Circuit, 1999—. Editor: (book) Retrospective Conversion: History, Approaches, Considerations, 1992. Sr. fellow Palmer Sch. Libr. Sci., Long Island U., 1995. Mem.: Assn. Rsch. Libr. (bd. dir. 2001—), ALA (bd. dir. Assoc. Libr. Collections and Tech. Svc. 1996—, pres. Assoc. Libr. Collections and Tech. Svc. 2003—, recipient Margaret Mann Citation award 2001), Beta Phi Mu. Office: Adminstrv Office Geisel Libr Univ Calif 9500 Gilman Dr #0175G La Jolla CA 92093-0175 Office Phone: 858-534-3060. E-mail: becs@ucsd.edu.*

**SCHOULTZ, LARS,** political scientist, educator; b. San Gabriel, Calif., Aug. 23, 1942; s. Ture Wilhelm and Bernice (Bowie) S.; m. Jane Volland, Jan. 18, 1969; children: Nils Gibson, Karina Anne. BA, Stanford U., 1964, MA, 1966; PhD, U. N.C., 1973. Prof. Miami U., Oxford, Ohio, 1973—77, U. Fla., Gainesville, 1977—79; William Rand Kenan Jr. prof. polit. sci. U. N.C., Chapel Hill, 1979—. Author: Human Rights and U.S. Policy Toward Latin America, 1981, National Security and U.S. Policy Toward Latin America, 1987, The Populist Challenge, 1983, Beneath the United States, 1998. Sgt. U.S. Army, 1966-67. MacArthur fellow in internat. peace and security MacArthur Found., 1990-91, Fulbright fellow, Rockefeller Found. fellow, Ford Found. fellow, Social Sci. Rsch. Coun., Woodrow Wilson fellow, 1994-95, Nat. Humanities Ctr. fellow, 1999-00. Mem. Latin Am. Studies Assn. (pres. 1991-92, v.p. 1990-91). Democrat. Home: 250 Glandon Dr Chapel Hill NC 27514-3816 Office: U NC Inst Latin Am Studies Chapel Hill NC 27599-0001 Office Phone: 919-962-0422. E-mail: Schoultz@unc.edu.

**SCHOUMACHER, BRUCE HERBERT,** lawyer; b. Chgo., May 23, 1940; s. Herbert Edward and Mildred Helen (Wagner) S.; m. Alicia Wesley (Sanchez), Nov. 4, 1967; children: Liana Cristina, Janina Maria. BS, Northwestern U., 1961; MBA, U. Chgo., 1963, JD, 1966. Bar: Nebr. 1966, U.S. Dist. Ct. Nebr. 1966, Ill. 1971, U.S. Dist. Ct. (no. dist.) Ill. 1971, U.S. Ct. Appeals (7th cir.) 1979, U.S. Supreme Ct. 1982, U.S. Ct. Fed. Claims 1986. Assoc. Luebs, Tracy, and Huebner, Grand Island, Nebr., 1966-67, McDermott, Will, and Emery, Chgo., 1971-76; ptnr. McDermott, Will,and Emery, Chgo., 1976-89, Querrey and Harrow, Ltd., Chgo., 1989—. Instr. bus. adminstrn., Bellevue Coll., Nebr., 1967-70; lectr., U. Md. Overseas Program, 1970. Author: Engineers and the Law: An Overview, 1986; contbg. author: Construction Law, 1986, Construction Law Handbook, 1999, Construction Business Handbook, 2004; co-author: Successful Business Plans for Architects, 1992; contbr. articles to profl. jour. Capt., USAF, 1967-71, Vietnam. Decorated, Bronze Star, 1971. Fellow Am. Coll. Constrn. Lawyers; mem. ABA, AIA (profl. affiliate), Nebr. Bar Assn., Ill. State Bar Assn. (ad hoc com. large law firms 1992-98), chmn. membership and bar activities com. 1988-89, coun. ins. law sect., 1986-91, mem. spl. com. on computerized legal rsch. 1986-87, Chgo. Bar Assn. (chmn. fed. civil procedure com. 1982-83), Def. Rsch. Inst., Ill. Assn. Def. Trial Counsel, Chgo. Bldg. Congress (bd. dirs. 1985—, sec. 1987-89, 95—, v.p. 1989-91), Soc. Ill. Constrn. Attys. (steering com. 2004-2005, sec. 2005—), Western Soc. Engr. (assoc.), The Lawyers Club of Chgo., Tower Club, Chgo., Univ. Club Chgo., Rolling Green Country Club, Pi Kappa Alpha, Phi Delta Phi. Republican. Methodist. Office: Querrey & Harrow Ltd 175 W Jackson Blvd Ste 1600 Chicago IL 60604-2827 Office Phone: 312-540-7046.

**SCHOUTEN, RONALD,** psychiatrist, educator; b. Paterson, N.J., Sept. 3, 1953; s. Neil and Charlotte Schouten; m. Evan Sue Hoffman, Aug. 21, 1977; children: Schuyler John, Alison Meg. JD, Boston U., 1978; MD, U. Ill., 1985. Lic. psychiatry Am. Bd. of Psychiatry and Neurology, added qualifications in forensic psychiatry Am. Bd. of Psychiatry and Neurology. Dir. law and psychiatry svc. Mass. Gen. Hosp., Boston, 1989—; assoc. prof. of psychiatry Harvard Med. Sch., Boston, 2000—. Pres. KeyPeople Resources, Inc., West Newton, Mass., 2000—. Recipient Jonas Rappeport fellowship, Am. Acad. of Psychiatry and the Law, 1987. Mem.: Am. Coll. of Occupl. and Environ. Medicine, Acad. Orgnl. and Occupl. Psychiatry (pres. 2002—04), Am. Psychiat. Assn., Cambridge Boat Club. Office: Mass Gen Hosp WAC 812 15 Parkman St Boston MA 02114 Office Phone: 617-726-5195. Business E-Mail: rschouten@partners.org.

**SCHOVILLE, DENNIS A(RNOLD),** lawyer; b. Richland Ctr., Wis., May 31, 1945; BS, U. Wis., 1967; JD with Distinction, Ill. Inst. Tech., 1973; LLM, Northwestern U., 1974. Bar: Wis. 1973, Ill. 1973, U.S. Dist. Ct. (no. dist.) Ill. 1973, Calif. 1974, U.S. Dist. Ct. (so. dist.) Calif. 1974, U.S. Ct. Appeals (9th cir.) 1985, U.S. Ct. Claims. Ptnr. Schoville & Arnell, LLP, San Diego. Capt. U.S. Army, 1968-73. Recipient Broderick award for professionalism, integrity and ethics, 1996; named Consumer Attys. San Diego Trial Lawyer of the Yr., 1995, 99. Mem. ABA, ATLA, Am. Coll. Trial Lawyers, Am. Bd. Trial Advocates (nat. bd. dirs., past pres. San Diego chpt.), Consumer Attys. San Diego (past pres., Trial Advocacy award 2005, Consumer Adv. of Yr. award 2005), Ill. State Bar Assn., State Bar Wis., State Bar Calif., San Diego County Bar Assn. (jud. evaluation com. 2006), San Diego Trial Lawyers Assn. (Outstanding Trial Advocacy award-civil 1984, 89, 94), Am. Inns of Ct. (sr. master), DFC Soc. (gen. counsel, nat. sec.). Office: Schoville & Arnell LLP 1230 Columbia St Ste 800 San Diego CA 92101-3571 Office Phone: 619-232-9901.

**SCHOW, THOMAS ALBERT,** music educator, educator, military officer; b. Cleve., Nov. 8, 1954; s. Robert Bouton and Lorna Davies Schow; m. Deniece LaVonne Gugler, Sept. 9, 1980; children: Carl Vaughn, Robert Bouton II. MusB, Peabody Conservatory Music of Hopkins U., Balt., Md., 1979; MusM, Bowling Green State U., Ohio, 1984. Commnd. It. U.S. Army, 1980, advanced through grades to maj.; instr. piano Lee Coll., Cleve., 1982—84; dir. chorale music Red Bank H.S., Chattanooga, 1984—86; dir. instrumental music Baylor Sch., Chattanooga, 1986—. Musician: (albums) Romantic Variations for Flute and Piano. Dir. music St Peters Epsic. Ch., Chattanooga, 2004—06. Recipient Outstanding Tchr. award, Tenn. Gov.'s Sch. Arts, 1993, 1998, 2006. Mem.: East Tenn. Band and Orch. Dirs. Assn. U.S. Army, Res. Officers Assn., Music Tchrs. Nat. Assn. Avocations: swimming, bicycling, travel. Home and Office: Baylor School 171 Baylor School Road Chattanooga TN 37405 Office Phone: 423-267-8506 548. Personal E-mail: taspiano1@comast.net. Business E-mail: tschow@baylor.chattanooga.net.

**SCHOWALTER, JOHN ERWIN,** child and adolescent psychiatry educator; b. Milw., Mar. 15, 1936; s. Raymond Phillip and Martha (Kowalke) S.; m. Ellen Virginia Lefferts, June 11, 1960; children: Jay, Bethany. BS, U. Wis., 1957, MD, 1960. Diplomate Am. Bd. Psychiatry and Neurology (com. on cert. in child psychiatry 1983-85, chmn. 1986-87, bd. dirs. 1993-2000, chmn. com. added qualifications forensic psychiatry 1993-97); cert. in adult and child psychiatry also psychoanalysis. Intern in pediat. Yale-New Haven Hosp., 1960-61; asst. resident in psychiatry Cin. Gen. Hosp., 1961-63; fellow

in child psychiatry Yale U. Child Study Ctr., New Haven, 1963-65; psychiatrist Mental Hygiene Clinic U.S. Army, Ft. Ord, Calif., 1965-67; asst. prof. Yale U. Child Study Ctr., 1967-70, assoc. prof. Sch. Medicine, 1970-75, dir. tng., 1971-96, prof. pediat. and psychiatry, 1975-89, chief child psychiatry, 1982-90, dir. child psychiatry clin. svcs., 1990—2003, Albert J. Solnit prof. child psychiatry and pediat., 1989—2003, interim chmn. 2001—02, prof. emeritus, sr. rsch. scientist, 2003—. Mem. publ. com. Yale U. Press., 1992-97; mem. sci. adv. bd. Sophia Found. Med. Rsch., Rotterdam, The Netherlands, 1984-89; dir. mental health and substance abuse Yale Preferred Health Plan, 1995-99. Co-author: The Family Handbook of Adolescence, 1979; contbr. numerous articles, book revs.; mem. editl. bd. Pediatrics, 1976-81, Children's Health Care, 1977-2003, Jour. Am. Psychoanalytic Assn., 1978, Pediatrics in Rev., 1978-85; asst. editor: Jour. Am. Acad. Child and Adolescent Psychiatry, 1988-97; co-editor: Yearbook Psychiatry and Applied Mental Health, 1988-97. Capt. U.S. Army, 1965-67. Fellow Am. Acad. Child and Adolescent Psychiatry (sec. 1985-87, pres. 1989-91, Simon Wile award 1996, mem. fin. planning com. 2001-04, chair governance com. 2001-04, chmn. presdl. scholars com. 2005—, chmn. policy statements com. 2005—), Am. Coll. Psychiatrists (chair Laughlin fellowship com. 2000-01, chair membership com. 2002—), Am. Acad. Pediat.; mem. AMA (residency rev. com. for psychiatry 1983-87, 89-94), Am. Pediatric Soc., Am. Psychoanalytic Assn. (cert. adult and child), Group Advancement Psychiatry (life fellow, com. on child psychiatry 1981, bd. dirs. 1989-91, pres. 1993-95, chair life fellowship com. 2000—), Assn. Care Children's Health (pres. 1984-86), Am. Psychiat. Assn. (McGavin award 2006), Soc. Profs. Child Psychiatry (pres. 1984-86), Western New Eng. Inst. Psychoanalysis (mem. faculty in child psychoanalysis 1984—, pres. 1986-88), Conn. Med. Soc., New Haven Med. Soc., Conn. Coun. Child Psychiatrists (pres. 1979-81), Benjamin Rush Soc. (sec., treas. 1998-99, v.p. 1999-2000, pres. 2000-02), Sigma Xi. Lutheran. Home: 256 Ives St Hamden CT 06518-2200 Office: Yale U Child Study Ctr PO Box 207900 230 S Frontage Rd New Haven CT 06520-7900

**SCHOWALTER, WILLIAM RAYMOND,** college dean, educator; b. Milw., Dec. 15, 1929; s. Raymond Philip and Martha (Kowalke) S.; m. Jane Ruth Gregg, Aug. 22, 1953; children: Katherine Ruth, Mary Patricia, David Gregg. BS, U. Wis., 1951; postgrad., Inst. Paper Chemistry, 1951-52; MS, U. Ill., 1953, PhD, 1957; PhD (hon.), Inst. Nat. Poly. Lorraine, France, 1996. Asst. prof. dept. chem. engring. Princeton U., 1957-63, assoc. prof., 1963-66, prof., 1966-86, Class of 1950 prof. engring. and applied sci., 1986-89, acting chmn. dept. chem. engring., 1971, chmn. dept. chem. engring., 1978-87, assoc. dean Sch. Engring. and Applied Sci., 1971-77, class of 1950 prof. engring. and applied sci. emeritus, 2000—; dean Coll. Engring. U. Ill., Urbana, 1989-2001, dean, prof. emeritus, 2001—; Mobil prof. chem. engring. Nat. U. Singapore, 1998, sr. advisor to pres., 2001—. Sherman Fairchild disting. scholar Calif. Inst. Tech., 1977-78; vis. fellow U. Salford, Eng., 1974; vis. sr. fellow Sci. Rsch. Coun., U. Cambridge, Eng., 1970; cons. to chem. and petroleum cos.; editl. adv. bd. McGraw-Hill Pub. Co., 1964-92; co-chmn. Internat. Seminar for Heat and Mass Transfer, 1970; vis. com. for chem. engring. MIT, 1979-87, Lehigh U., 1980-87; mem. vis. com. Sch. Engring., Stanford U., 1990-2001; evaluation panelist Ctr. Chem. Engring. Nat. Bur. Standards, 1982-88, chmn., 1986-88; mem. commn. engring. and tech. sys. NRC, 1983-88; engring. rsch. bd., 1984-86; adv. coun. chem. engring. Cornell U., 1983-91; adv. coun. Sch. Engring., Rice U., 1986-92; adv. com. Ill. Inst. Tech., 1992-97; adv. coun. Coll. Engring., U. Calif., Berkeley, 1997-2001, Coll. Engring. U. Mich., 1997-2001, Sch. Engring. and Applied Sci., Princeton U., 1998-2002, Carnegie Inst. Tech., 1999-2001; acad. adv. bd. Sematech Corp., 1992-2001; internat. adv. panel Nat. U. Singapore, 1996, 2002; Reilly lectr. in chem. engring. U. Notre Dame, 1985, Van Winkle lectr. in chem. engring. U. Tex., Austin, 1986, David M. Mason lectr. chem. engring. Stanford U., 1987; Bird Stewart and Lightfoot lectr. chem. engring. U. Wis., 2001; R.H. Wilhelm lectr. in chem. engring. Princeton U., 2002; mem. fellowship program Packard Found. Sci. Adv. Panel, 1988—; mem. sci. adv. bd. Singapore Inst. for Chem. and Engring. Scis., 2003-06; mem. panel for U.K., Rsch. Assessment Exercise 2008, 2006—. Author: Mechanics of Non-Newtonian Fluids, 1978; co-author: Colloidal Dispersions, 1989; mem. editl. com. Ann. Rev. Fluid Mechanics, 1974-80, Internat. Jour. Chem. Engring., 1974-94, Indsl. and Engring. Chemistry Fundamentals, 1975-78, Jour. Non-Newtonian Fluid Mechanics, 1976-2001, AIChE Jour., 1979-83; contbr. articles to profl. jours. Mem. Ill. Gov.'s Sci. Adv. Com., 1989-96. Served with U.S. Army, 1953-55. Decorated officier des Palmes Académiques (France); recipient Disting. Svc. citation Coll. Engring., U. Wis., Madison, 1983; Guggenheim fellow, 1987-88. Fellow AIChE (William H. Walker award 1982, bd. dirs. 1992-94), NAS (class membership com. 2000, 2002, class chmn. 2002-05), Am. Acad. Arts and Scis.; mem. Am. Soc. Engring. Edn. (Lectr. award chem. engring. divsn. 1971, exec. com. engr. deans coun. 1992-95, vice-chair, engring. deans coun. pub. policy com. 1998, chair engring. deans coun. pub. policy com. 1999-2001), NAE (awards com. 1986-88, chmn. 1987, acad. adv. bd. 1991-94, chmn. 1992-94, coun. 1994-2000, Draper Award com. 2001-03), Am. Chem. Soc., Soc. Rheology (exec. com. 1977-79, v.p. 1981-83, pres. 1983-85, Bingham medal 1988), Sigma Xi, Tau Beta Pi, Phi Lambda Upsilon, Phi Eta Sigma.

**SCHOYEN, JEFFREY GERALD,** music educator, conductor; b. Atlanta, Dec. 19, 1960; s. Gerald Hjalmer and Sybil Gabrielle (Carey) Schoyen; m. Sachiho Cynthia Murosugi-Schoyen; children: Miyuki, Teiji. MusB, New Eng. Conservatory, 1983; MFA, Carnegie Mellon U., 1990; DMA, Stony Brook U., 1994. ARCM Royal Coll. Music, London, 1984. Prin. cellist Filarmonica del Bajio, Guanajunto, Mexico, 1984—96; musician La. Philharmonic, New Orleans, 1995—98; asst. prof./conductor U. Nebr., Kearney, 1998—2001; vis. asst. prof. U. Dayton, Ohio, 2001—05; asst. prof. Salisbury U., Md., 2005—. Conductor Salisbury Symphony Orch., 2005—. Active recitalist: cello Tour of Mex., 2005. Recipient Gustav Gulden award, Tanglewood, 1981; grantee Beebe grant for Musicians, 1983, Chamber Music Rural Residency grant, NE Arts, 1994. Mem.: Coll. Music Soc. Office: Salisbury Univ 1101 Camden Ave Salisbury MD 21804

**SCHPOK, TERRY M.,** lawyer; b. Akron, Ohio; BA in Polit. sci., We. Mich. Univ., 1973; JD summa cum laude, Univ. Notre Dame, 1976; student, Univ. Dallas Graduate Sch. Mgmt. Bar: Ind. 1976, Mich. 1976, Tex. 1977. Various mgmt. positions, including assoc. gen. counsel Assoc. Corp. of No. Am., 1973—79; joined Akin Gump Strauss Hauer & Feld LLP, 1979—, now ptnr., tech. practice group Dallas. CEO Roundtable Forum, Dallas Chapter, Am. Electronics Assn.; bd. mem. Entrepreneurs Found. of No. Tex.; pres. Sammons Ctr. for Arts, Dallas, Dallas Arts Devel. Corp. Mem.: State Bar of Mich., Indiana State Bar Assn., Dallas Bar Assn. Office: Akin Gump Strauss Hauer & Feld LLP Ste 4100 1700 Pacific Ave Dallas TX 75201-4675 Office Phone: 214-969-2800. Office Fax: 214-969-4343. Business E-Mail: tschpok@akingump.com.

**SCHRADER, KARA JEAN,** science educator; b. Madison, Wis., Sept. 18, 1973; d. Lawrence Edwin Schrader and Joyce Louise Hawley, Louis George Hawley (Stepfather) and Elfriede Massier (Stepmother). BA, Dartmouth Coll., Hanover, N.H., 1995; MS, Rensselaer Poly. Inst., Troy, N.Y., 2003. Cert. sci. tchr. Ill. Sci. tchr. Buffalo Grove (Ill.) H.S., 1997—. Student coun. sponsor Buffalo Grove H.S., 2001—, cross-country asst. coach, 2003—. Mem.: Nat. Assn. of Biology Tchrs. Home: 225 W Wood St Palatine IL 60067 Office: Buffalo Grove H S 1100 W Dundee Rd Buffalo Grove IL 60089 E-mail: kara.schrader@d214.org.

**SCHRADER, LAWRENCE EDWIN,** plant physiologist; b. Atchison, Kans., Oct. 22, 1941; s. Edwin Carl and Jenna Kathryn (Tobiason) S.; m. Elfriede J. Massier, Mar. 14, 1981 BS, Kans. State U., 1963; PhD, U. Ill., 1967; grad., Inst. Edtl. Mgmt., Harvard U., 1991. Asst. prof. dept. agronomy U. Wis., Madison, 1969-72, assoc. prof., 1972-76, prof., 1976-84; prof., head dept. agronomy U. Ill., Urbana, 1985-89; dean Coll. Agr. and Home Econs. Wash. State U., Pullman, 1989-94, prof. dept. horticulture, 1994—. Chief competitive rsch. grants office Dept. Agr., Washington, 1980-81; trustee, treas. Agrl. Satellite Corp., 1991-94. Contbr. chpts. to books, articles to profl. jours. Active Consortium for Internat. Devel., 1989-94, chair fin. com., vice chair exec. com., 1990-92, trustee 1989-94; mem. exec. com. Coun. Agrl.

Heads of Agr., 1992-94. Capt. U.S. Army, 1967-69. Recipient Soybean Researchers Recognition award 1983, Disting. Service award in Agriculture Kansas State U., 1987; Romnes Faculty fellow U. Wis., 1979 Fellow AAAS (steering group sect. agr. 1991-95, chair-elect sect. on agr., food and renewable resources 1995-96, chmn. 1996-97, past chmn. 1997-98, coun. mem. 1997-98), Am. Soc. Agronomy, Crop Sci. Soc. Am.; mem. Internat. Soc. for Hort. Sci., Am. Soc. for Hort. Sci., Am. Soc. Plant Biologists (sec. 1983-85, pres.-elect 1986, pres. 1987), Am. Chem. Soc., Coun. for Agrl. Sci. and Tech., Blue Key, Sigma Xi, Gamma Sigma Delta (Outstanding Alumnus award, 2003), Phi Kappa Phi, Phi Eta Sigma, Alpha Zeta (named to Centennial Honor Roll 1997). Methodist. Home: 3504 Crestview Rd Wenatchee WA 98801-9668 Office: Wash State U Tree Fruit Rsch & Extension Ctr 1100 N Western Ave Wenatchee WA 98801-1230 Office Phone: 509-663-8181 x265. Business E-mail: schrader@wsu.edu.

**SCHRADER, MICHAEL EUGENE,** columnist, editor; b. Jersey City, Apr. 3, 1938; s. Eugene Charles and Anne Veronica (Kane) S. BA in Latin, NYU, 1961, MA in English, 1963; postgrad., UCLA, 1965—67, postgrad., 1968—69, Trinity Coll. Dublin, 1967—68, U. Copenhagen, 1970. Asst. editor Macmillan Co., N.Y.C., 1962—64; tchg. asst. U. Ill., Urbana, 1964—65; tchg. asst., rsch. asst. UCLA, 1965—67, 1968—69; sr. copy editor Dell Pub. Co., N.Y.C., 1971—72; copy chief Sat. Rev. mag., N.Y.C., 1972—76, Penthouse mag., N.Y.C., 1976—82; assoc. editor Med. Econs. mag., Oradell, NJ, 1982; sr. copy editor Woman's World mag., Englewood, NJ, 1983—84, Nation's Restaurant News, N.Y.C., 1995—2005. Columnist: From the Bookshelf, in Nation's Restaurant News, 1988—, columnist, contributing editor, 2005—. Friend of Bobst Libr., Soc. of Torch, NYU, 1994—; established Anne Kane Schrader Cookbook and Nutrition Collection. Recipient Danish Marshall award U. Copenhagen, 1970; Fulbright scholar, 1967-68. Fellow James Beard Found. (judge food and beverage book awards 1991-94); mem. Soc. of the Torch (charter), Internat. Assn. Culinary Profls. Democrat. Roman Catholic. Avocations: growing house plants, travel, movies, theater, reading. Office: Lebhar-Friedman Inc Nation's Restaurant News 425 Park Ave New York NY 10022-3549 Home: 1281 Somerset Dr #308 Lauderdale Lakes FL 33311 Office Phone: 212-756-5202. E-mail: mschrade@nrn.com.

**SCHRADER, WILLIAM L.,** communications executive; BS, Cornell U. Exec. dir., co-founder Cornell Theory Ctr.; founder, pres., CEO NYSERNet; dir., founder N.E. Paralle Archs. Ctr. Syracuse (N.Y.) U.; chmn., CEO, founder PSINet, Inc., Herndon, Va., 1989—. Participant panel discussions of industry trends CNN, CNBC, MSNBC, FNN, First Bur., TechnoPolitics. Office: PSI Networks 45969 Nokes Blvd Ste 150 Sterling VA 20166-6553

**SCHRADY, DAVID ALAN,** civilian military employee, educator; b. Akron, Ohio, Nov. 11, 1939; s. Marvin G. and Sheila A. (O'Neill) S.; m. Mary E. Hilt, Sept. 1, 1962; children: Peter, Patrick, Matthew. BS, Case Inst. Tech., 1961, MS, 1963, PhD, 1965. Prof., chmn. Naval Postgrad. Sch., Monterey, Calif., 1974-76, dean acad. planning, 1976-80, provost and acad. dean, 1980-87, prof. ops. rsch., 1988—, Disting. prof., ops. rsch. educator, 1995—. Vis. prof. Cranfield Inst. Tech./Royal Mil. Coll. of Sci., Shrivenham, Eng., fall 1987-spring 88. Contbr. articles to profl. jours. Recipient Goodeve medal Ops. Rsch. Soc., U.K., 1992, Navy Disting. Civilian Svc. medal, 2006 Fellow: Inst. for Ops. Rsch. and the Mgmt. Scis., Mil. Ops. Rsch. Soc. (hon. treas. 1988—97), Ops. Rsch. Soc. Am. (pres. 1983—84, Kimball medal 1994). Avocations: guitar, motor sports. Office: Naval Postgrad Sch Dept Ops Rsch Monterey CA 93943-5000 Business E-mail: dschrady@nps.edu.

**SCHRAG, ADELE FRISBIE,** business education educator; b. Cynthiana, Ky., May 7, 1921; d. Shirley Ledyard and Edna Kate (Ford) S.; m. William Albert Schrag, Apr. 6, 1963; 1 stepchild, Marie Carol. BS, Temple U., 1942; MA, N.Y. U., 1944, PhD, 1961. Tchr. Manor Twp. High Sch., Millersville, Pa., 1942-43, Downingtown (Pa.) Sr. High Sch., 1943-50; instr., asst. prof. Temple U. Sch. Bus. and Pub. Administrn., Phila., 1950-60; prof. bus. edn. and vocat. edn. Coll. Edn., 1960-85, sr. prof. edn., 1985-88, prof. emeritus, 1988—. Vis. lectr. N.Y. U.; cons. Phila. Community Coll., 1967-82 Editor: Business Education for the Automated Office, 1964; author: (with Estelle L. Popham and Wanda Blockhus) A Teaching-Learning System for Business Education, 1975, How to Dictate, 1981, Office Procedures Update, 1982, (with Robert Poland) A Teaching System for Business Subjects, 1988; contbr. articles to profl. jours., chpts. to books. Trustee Meth. Hosp., 1981—85, Sun Cities Symphony Assn., 1988—93, Habitat for Humanity West Valley, 1994—2005, co-pres., 1999—2001; trustee Habitat for Humanity Ariz., 1999—2003. Recipient Profl. Panhellenic award, 1963; Kensington High Sch. Alumnae award, 1972 Mem. Soc. Automation in Bus. Edn. (pres. 1969-73, dir. 1974). Nat. Assn. Bus. Tchr. Edn. (pres. 1983-84), Bus. Edn. Certification Council, Phi Gamma Nu (nat. treas. 1952-54, nat. sec. 1954-56), Delta Pi Epsilon (policy commn. for bus. and econ. edn. 1975-78, dir. research found. 1978-83, pres. research found. 1983). Home: 14515 W Granite Valley Dr # 644 Sun City West AZ 85375-6021 E-mail: as107@cox.net.

**SCHRAG, DANIEL P.,** geochemist, educator; BS in Geology/Geophysics and Polit. Sci., Yale U., New Haven, 1988; PhD in Geochemistry, U. Calif., Berkeley, 1993. Asst. prof. dept. geosciences Princeton U., NJ, 1994—97; mem. faculty to prof. geochemistry Harvard U., 1997—, dir. Lab. Geochemical Oceanography. Contbr. articles to sci. jours. Recipient Macelwane medal, grantee MacArthur fellowship, 2000. Fellow: Am. Geophys. Union. Office: Lab Geochemical Oceanography Harvard U Dept Earth and Planetary Scis 20 Oxford St Cambridge MA 02138 E-mail: schrag@eps.harvard.edu.*

**SCHRAG, EDWARD A., JR.,** lawyer; b. Milw., Mar. 27, 1932; s. Edward A. and Mabel Lena (Baumbach) Schrag; m. Leslie Jean Israel, June 19, 1954; children: Amelia Marie Schrag Prack, Katherine Allison Schrag Roberts, Edward A. III(dec.) BS in Econs. U. Pa., 1954 JD, Harvard 1960 Dar Ohio 1961. From assoc. to ptnr. Vorys, Sater, Seymour & Pease, Columbus, Ohio, of counsel, 1960—. Sec. Ranco Inc., 1972—87; trustee Lake of Woods Water Co., 1972—91; mem. Ohio divsn. Securities Adv. Com. Mem. Downtown Area Com., 1970—74. Served to lt. (j.g.) USNR, 1954—57. Mem.: ABA, Columbus Bar Assn., Ohio Bar Assn., Navy League, Columbus Area C. of C., Ohio State U. Pres.'s Club, Capital Club, Crichton Club, Pi Gamma Mu, Phi Sigma Alpha, Beta Gamma Sigma, Alpha Tau Omega. Episcopalian. Home: 9400 White Oak Ln Westerville OH 43082-9606 Office: Vorys Sater Seymour and Pease PO Box 1008 52 E Gay St Columbus OH 43216-1008 Office Phone: 614-464-6400. Business E-mail: easchrag@vssp.com.

**SCHRAG, PETER,** editor, writer; b. Karlsruhe, Germany, July 24, 1931; arrived in U.S., 1941, naturalized, 1953; s. Otto and Judith (Haas) S.; m. Melissa Jane Mowrer, June 9, 1953 (div. 1969); children: Mitzi, Erin Andrew; m. Diane Divoky, May 24, 1969 (div. 1981); children: David Divoky, Benaiah Divoky; m. Patricia Ternahan, Jan. 1, 1988. AB cum laude, Amherst Coll., 1953. Reporter El Paso (Tex.) Herald Post, 1953-55; asst. sec., asst. dir. publs. Amherst Coll., 1955-66, instr. Am. Studies, 1960-64; assoc. editor Sat. Rev., 1966-68, exec. editor, 1968-69; editor Change mag., 1969-70; editor at large Saturday Rev., 1969-72; contbg. editor Saturday Review/Education, 1972-73; editl. adv. bd. The Columbia Forum, 1972-75; editl. bd. Social Policy, 1971—; contbg. editor More, 1974-78, Inquiry, 1977-80, The Am. Prospect, 1995—; editl. page editor Sacramento Bee and McClatchy Newspapers, 1978-96, contbg. editor, 1996—. Vis. lectr. U. Mass. Sch. Edn., 1970-72; fellow in profl. journalism Stanford U., Palo Alto, Calif., 1973-74; lectr. U. Calif., Berkeley, 1974-78, 90—; Pulitzer Prize juror, 1988-89; vis. scholar U. Calif. Inst. Govtl. Studies, Berkeley, 1998—. Author: Voices in the Classroom, 1965, Village School Downtown, 1967, Out of Place in America, 1971, The Decline of the Wasp, 1972, The End of the American Future, 1973, Test of Loyalty, 1974, (with Diane Divoky) The Myth of the Hyperactive Child, 1975, Mind Control, 1978, Paradise Lost: California's Experience, America's Future, 1998, Final Test: The Battle for Adequacy in America's Schools, 2003, California: America's High-Stakes Experiment, 2006; contbr. articles to profl. publs. Adv. com. Student Rights Project, N.Y. Civil Liberties Union, 1970-72; mem. Com. Study History, 1958-72; trustee Emma Willard Sch., 1967-69; bd. dirs. Park Sch., Oakland, Calif., 1976-77, Ctr. for

Investigative Reporting, 1979-81, Ed Source, 1998—; bd. adv. Pub. Policy Inst. Calif. Guggenheim fellow, 1971-72; Nat. Endowment for Arts fellow, 1976-77 Office: 5835 Colton Blvd Oakland CA 94611-2204 Business E-Mail: pschrag@sacbee.com.

**SCHRAGE, ELLIOT,** information technology executive; BA, MPP, JD, Harvard U. Mng. dir. Clark & Weinstock, NYC; sr. v.p. global affairs Gap Inc.; Bernard L. Schwarz sr. fellow in bus. and fgn. policy Coun. on Fgn. Rels., NYC; v.p. global comm. and pub. affairs Google Inc., Mountain View, Calif., 2005—. Mem. adv. com. on internat. child labor enforcement US Dept. Treasury, 1999—2001; adj. prof. Columbia U. Bus. Sch., Columbia U. Law Sch. Contbr. Harvard Bus. Review, Washington Post, Fin. Times. Mem.: AAAS (mem. com. on sci. freedom and human rights 1998—2000). Office: Google Inc 1600 Amphitheatre Pkwy Mountain View CA 94043 Office Phone: 650-253-0000. Office Fax: 650-253-0001.*

**SCHRAGE, ROSE,** retired academic administrator; b. Montelimar, France, Apr. 15, 1942; came to U.S., 1947; d. Abraham and Celia (Silbiger) Levine; m. Samuel Schrage, Dec. 12, 1935 (dec. 1976); children: Abraham, Leon. BRE, Beth Rivkah Tchrs. Sem., Bklyn., 1968; Paralegal, Manpower Career Devel. Agy., Bklyn., 1973; MS, L.I. U., 1975; Advanced Cert. Ednl. Adminstrn., Bklyn. Coll., 1983. Cert. sch. dist. adminstr., guidance counselor, tchr., asst. prin. Sec., N.Y.C., 1964-68; police adminstrv. aide N.Y.C. Police Dept., 1974-75; coord. state reading aid program Sch. Dist. 14, Bklyn., 1977-78, project dir. Title VII, 1978-81, asst. dir. reimbursable fed. and state programs, 1981-85, dist. bus. mgr., 1985-94, asst. prin., 1994—99, spl. edn. instrn. specialist, adminstr., 1999—; ednl. adminstr. Ctrl. Liaison Office for Impartial Hearings divsn. student support svcs. Dept. Edn., NYC, 2001—04; ret., 2004. Chmn. N.Y.C. Bd. Edn. IMPACT Com., Bklyn., 1986—. Author (poem): Never Again, 1983; contbg. editor Chai Today; contbr. articles to profl. jours. Del. Republican. Jud. Conf., 1968; founder, pres Concerned Parents, Bklyn., 1977; radio co-host Israeli War Heroes Fund-Radiothon, Bklyn.; family counselor local social agys., Bklyn.; co-founder cmty. vol. ambulance Hatzalah, 1977. Recipient Cert. of Appreciation as vol. regional coord. N.Y. State Mentoring Program N.Y. Gov. Cuomo, 1991, Proclamation, N.Y. City Coun., 2003, State of N.Y. Legis. Resolution Proclamation N.Y. State Senate, 2003, U.S. Congress Proclamation, 2003, Excellence in Fiscal Mgmt. award IMPACT. Mem. Am. Assn. Sch. Adminstrs., Assn. Orthodox Jewish Tchrs. (v.p. exec. bd., pres. 2004, Orgn. award 2003), N.Y. State Assn. Sch. Bus. Ofcls., N.Y.C. Assn. Sch. Bus. Ofcls., Coun. Suprs. and Adminstrs. Avocations: piano, reading, composing music.

**SCHRAGER, IAN,** hotel executive; b. 1946; m. Rita Narona; children: Sophie, Ava. Co-owner (with Steve Rubell) Studio 54 (discotheque), 1977—80; owner Royalton Hotels, NYC, Hudson Hotels; founder, pres., CEO Ian Schrager Hotels, LLC; owner Morgans Hotel Group, LLC, studio operator, pres. Bd. dirs. Mncpl. Art. Soc., Legal Action Ctr. Office: Ian Schrager Co 818 Greenwich St New York NY 10014*

**SCHRAGER, MINDY RAE,** software company professional; b. Paterson, N.J., Jan. 18, 1958; d. Julius Maxwell and Miriam (May) S.; m. Jim Flannery, 1993. BA, Dickinson Coll., 1979; MBA, Babson Coll., 1981. Cert. NLP Master Practitioner, NLP Coach, Aura-Soma Practitioner, HBDI (Herrmann Brain Dominance Indicator) facilitator. Cons. Nolan Norton & Co., Lexington, Mass., 1981—86; mgr. Logos Corp., Dedham, Mass., 1986—87; resource ctr. supr., customer satisfaction mgr., dir. quality Motorola ISG, Mansfield, Mass., 1987—95; dir. quality, dir. bill payment ops., dir. project mgmt. Fidelity Investments, Boston, 1995—99; sr. program mgr., sr. mgr. collaborative product delivery, dir. program and operational excellence Ascential Software, Westboro, Mass., 1999—2005; mgr. IBM, Westboro, 2005—06, program dir., project ops., 2006—. Mem.: NAFE, Internat. Coach Fedn., Am. Soc. Quality, Assn. Rsch. and Enlightenment, Internat. Assn. Facilitators. Avocations: gardening, coaching. Home: 10 Magnolia Pointe Ashland MA 01721-2529 Office: IBM 50 Washington St Westborough MA 01581-1013 Office Phone: 508-599-7117.

**SCHRAM, LEE J.,** manufacturing executive; married; 2 children. BS, Miami Univ., Ohio; MBA, Univ. Dayton. Corp. contr. NCR Corp., Dayton, Ohio, 1999—2000, CFO retail & fin. group, 2000—02, v.p., gen. mgr. fin. solutions div., 2002—03, sr. v.p. retail solutions div., 2003—06; CEO Deluxe Corp., Saint Paul, Minn., 2006—. Mailing: Deluxe Corp PO Box 64235 Saint Paul MN 55164-0235 Office: Deluxe Corp 3680 Victoria St S Saint Paul MN 55126*

**SCHRAM, MARTIN JAY,** journalist; b. Chgo., Sept. 15, 1942; s. Marlo Joseph and Charleene Janice (Fidler) S.; m. Patricia Stewart Morgan, May 23, 1964; children—Kenneth Marlo, David Morgan. BA, U. Fla., 1964. Reporter The Miami (Fla.) News, 1964-65; reporter Newsday, Garden City, NY, 1965-67, mem. Washington bur., 1967-69, White House corr., 1969-73, chief Washington bur., sr. editor paper, 1973-79; writer on the presidency Washington Post, 1979-81, nat. affairs writer, 1981-86; assoc. editor, editor Sunday edits. Chgo. Sun-Times, 1986-87; asst. mng. editor, editor Sunday edits. Rocky Mountain News, Denver, 1987-88; commentator Cable News Network, 1988-98; nat. editor Washingtonian Mag., 1988-90; polit. columnist United Feature Syndicate, Newspaper Enterprise Assn., 1989-94, Scripps Howard News Svc., Washington, 1994—; news story edit., columnist Fox News, Washington, 1998-2000; mng. editor Avoiding Armageddon, PBS/Ted Turner Documentaries TV Series, 2001—03. Fellow Gannett Ctr. for Media Studies, Columbia U., 1985-86; guest scholar Woodrow Wilson Internat. Ctr., 1990-91 Author: Running for President: 1976, A Journal of the Carter Campaign, 1976, Running for President: 1976, The Carter Campaign, 1977; (with others) The Pursuit of the Presidency, 1980, The Great American Video Game: Presidential Politics in the Television Age, 1987, Speaking Freely, 1995; co-author: Cell Phonex: Invisible Hazards in the Wireless Age, 2001, Avoiding Armaegeddon: Our Future. Our Choice, 2003; co-editor: Mandate for Change, 1993. Recipient James Wright Brown Meml. award Sigma Delta Chi, 1965, Lowell Mellet award Pa. State U., 1988. Office: Scripps Howard News Svc 1090 Vermont Ave NW Ste 1000 Washington DC 20005-4906 Personal E-mail: martin.schram@gmail.com.

**SCHRAM, RONALD BYARD,** lawyer; b. Detroit, Sept. 7, 1942; s. Byron Canby and Mary Louise (Byard) S.; m. Carol Lorraine Anderson, July 19, 1969; children: Laura Mary, Alison Leigh. BA, Dartmouth Coll., 1964; MA in Econs., Cambridge U., England, 1966; JD, U. Mich., 1969, LLM, 1970, SJD, 1971. Bar: Mass. 1970. Assoc. Ropes & Gray, Boston, 1970-78, ptnr., 1978—2002. Author: Non-Billable Hours: A Poetic Journey Through the 1st Year of Retirement, 2005. Trustee Dartmouth Coll., Hanover, NH, 1981-92, Dartmouth-Hitchcock Med. Ctr., Lebanon, NH, 1983-93, New Eng. Sports Mus., Cambridge, Mass., 1984-1999, Derby Acad., Hingham, Mass., 1982-89; trustee Ctrl. New Eng. chpt. Nat. Multiple Sclerosis Soc., Waltham, Mass., 2002—, chair, 2004—; bd. visitors Rockefeller Ctr. of Pub. Policy, Dartmouth Coll., 2003—, chair, 2004—. Keasbey Found. fellow, Cambridge U., 1964-66; George M. Humphrey fellow in law econ. policy, U. Mich. Law Sch., Ann Arbor, 1969-70. Mem.: Phi Beta Kappa. E-mail: cschram1@aol.com.

**SCHRAMEK, TOMAS,** ballet dancer, educator; b. Bratislava, Czechoslovakia, Sept. 11, 1944; emigrated to Can., 1968, naturalized, 1973; s. Hans and Valeria (Neudorfer) S. BFA, Acad. Mus. and Theatre Arts, Bratislava, 1968. Mem. Sluk, Slovakia folk dance ensemble, 1959-68, prin. dancer, 1964-68; dancer Nat. Ballet Can., 1969-71, soloist, 1971-73, prin. dancer, 1973-91, prin. character artist, ballet master, 1991—. Mem. Actors Equity Assn., Assn. Can. TV and Radio Artists. Home: 125 Rose Park Dr Toronto ON Canada M4T 1R6 Office: Nat Ballet Canada 470 Queens Quay West Toronto ON Canada M5V 3K4 Office Phone: 416-345-9686. E-mail: tomaschr@rogers.com.

**SCHRAMM, BERNARD CHARLES, JR.,** retired advertising agency executive; b. Balt., Jan. 23, 1928; s. Bernard C. and Juliet Marie (Barranger) Schramm; m. Florence Mae Fangman, 1950; children: Stephanie Schramm McDaniel, Carol Schramm Molander, Bernard Charles III, Claudia Schramm Smith. Grad., Balt. Poly. Inst., 1946. Prodn. mgr. Van Sant, Dugdale & Co., Balt., 1946-52; media dir. AWL Advt., Balt., 1952-55; dir. prodn. Henry J. Kaufman Assocs., Washington, 1955-58; exec. v.p. Avalon Hill Co., Balt., 1958-64; v.p. Cargill, Wilson & Acree Advt., Richmond, Va., 1964-68; pres. William Cook Advt. Inc. (now William Cook Mktg. Comm.), Jacksonville, Fla., 1968-89, chmn. bd., 1989-97; ret., 1997. Chmn. Otis F. Smith Found., 1991—97. Mem. exec. com., v.p. United Way N.E. Fla., 1982-87, bd. dirs., 1982-93; bd. dirs. N.E. Fla. chpt. ARC, 1976-89, chmn., 1980-81; bd. dirs. Fla. C.C. Found., 1976-89. Mem.: Am. Assn. Advt. Agys. (chmn. Fla. coun. 1984—85, So. Region Bd. of Govs. 1988—92, chmn. 1989, nat. bd. dirs., agy. mgmt. com. 1989—92), Jacksonville Area C. of C., Rotary Club. Republican. Roman Catholic. Avocations: golf, reading, spectator sports, hunting. Home: 12856 Bay Plantation Dr Jacksonville FL 32223-0784

**SCHRAMM, CARL J.,** foundation administrator; BA, LeMoyne Coll., Syracuse; MA, PhD, U. Wis., Madison; JD, Georgetown U. Law Ctr. Former prof., health policy mgmt. Johns Hopkins U.; founder, dir. Johns Hopkins Ctr. for Health Care Fin. and Mgmt., 1980—87; former dir. Health Insurance Assn. of Am.; former exec. v.p. Fortis (now Assurant), 1992—96; founder HCIA, Inc., Patient Choice Health Care, 1999, Greenspring Advisors; pres., CEO Ewing Marion Kauffman Found. Chair Am. Assembly on Health Care Costs, 1987; Robert Wood Johnson Health Policy fellow NAS, Inst. of Medicine; Batten fellow Darden Sch., U. Va.; fellow N.Y. Acad. of Medicine; mem. Council on Foreign Relations; contbg. editor: Inc. mag. Recipient NIH Career Sci. award. Office: Ewing Marion Kauffman Found 4801 Rockhill Rd Kansas City MO 64110*

**SCHRAND, RICHARD HENRY,** broadcast executive, educator; b. Cin., Nov. 1, 1957; s. Edward August and Jane Marie (Scheib) S.; m. Deborah Fortner, 1979 (div. 1985); 1 child, Cynthia Lanette; m. Sharon Lynn Lassandro, Dec. 24, 1986; children: Courtney Lynne, Richard Jr., Brandon Ian. Student, Ohio State U., 1975-76, No. Ky. U., 1976-77. Intern Sta. WCPO-TV, Cin., 1971-75; producer Sta. WKRC-TV, Cin., 1975-79; pub. affairs dir., reporter, anchor Sta. WCSC-TV, Charleston, SC, 1979-83; actor Phila. Experiment, L.A., 1984; asst. promotion dir. Sta. WLWT-TV, Cin., 1983-86; spl. projects coord. Sta. KXAS-TV, Dallas/Ft. Worth, 1986-87; mgr. media svcs. NBC TV Network, Burbank, Calif., 1987-89; pres. Cyn-Court Enterprises, Burbank, 1989-91; mktg. dir. Sta. WPTA-TV, Ft. Wayne, Ind., 1991-92; v.p., gen. mgr. Branson (Mo.) Broadcasting Corp., 1992-95; dir. spl. projects/nat. media, graphics and advt. creator Jim Owens & Assocs., 1995-98; gen. mgr. Jim Owens Radio, Inc., Nashville, 1995-98; pres. GRFX ByDesign, Nashville, 1996—2004, Broadsword Prod., 2002—; v.p. Komodo Studios, L.A., 1999-2000; instr. computer graphics and web design Nossi Coll. Art, Nashville, 2001—, chmn. Dept. Computer Graphics, 2001—, mem. adv. bd., 2001—. Instr., spkr. Graphic Design Tour, 2000—; computer design Nossi Coll. Art, 2001—, edu. bd., 2002—, adv. bd., 2003—, instr. graphic art and design, 2004—; demonstrator 3D software SigGraph, MacWorld, 2001—. Author: Canoma Visual Insight. 2000, 3D Creature Workshop vol. 2, 2000, Macromedia Web Design Handbook, 2000, Adobe Golive 5F/X & Design, 2000, Adobe Live Motion Visual Jumpstart, 2000, Adobe Photoshop 6 Visual Jumpstart, 2000, Poser 4 Pro Pack F/X & Design, 2001, Final Cut Pro 3: The Complete Reference, 2002; contbr.: Pixels: 3D Book, 1999, Mastering Pixels: 3D, 2001; webmaster Crook & Chase Theater, Middle Tenn. LightWave Users Group, Nossi Coll. of Art, Games Plus, Handshak Prodns. Bd. dirs. Project Graduation, Dallas/Ft. Worth, 1986-87; mem. Muscular Dystrophy Assn., Charleston, 1980-83; publicist Housing Now, L.A., 1988. Recipient Regional Emmy award NATAS, 1975, award Broadcast Promotion and Mktg. Exec., Seattle, 1992. Avocations: guitar, writing, singing, golf. Office Phone: 615-812-2705. Business E-Mail: rschrand@broadswordproductions.com.

**SCHREADLEY, RICHARD LEE,** newswriter, retired editor; b. Harrisburg, Pa., Jan. 3, 1931; s. Harry Leroy and Flora Rebecca (McQuilken) S.; m. Doris Arlene Sheaffer, Dec. 18, 1952; 1 child, Rhys Leroy. BA, Dickinson Coll., 1952; MA, Tufts U., 1968, MAL.D., 1969, PhD, 1972. Reporter The News and Courier, Charleston, SC, 1975; asso. editor The Evening Post, Charleston, 1975-76, editorial page editor, 1976-77; editor, 1977-81; exec. editor The Evening Post and The News and Courier, 1981-88; assoc. editor and sr. writer mil. and polit. affairs The News and Courier, 1989. Author: From the Rivers to the Sea, The United States Navy in Vietnam, 1992, Valor and Virtue, The Washington Light Infantry in Peace and in War, 1996. Chmn. Fgn. Affairs Forum of Charleston, 1987-88, mem. steering com., 1989. Served to comdr. USN, 1949-52, 56-73. Mem. Navy League, Ret. Officer Assn., Washington Light Infantry, German Friendly Soc. Charleston, Army-Navy Club of Washington, Country Club of Charleston. Home: 812 Clearview Dr Charleston SC 29412-4511 Personal E-mail: rlschrea@bellsouth.net.

**SCHRECK, RICHARD THOMAS,** accountant; b. Waterloo, N.Y., USA, Apr. 27, 1930; s. George Leonard and Isabella Cowan Schreck; m. Virginia Doris Main Schreck, Aug. 13, 1994; m. Barbara Ann Walsh Schreck, June 25, 1960 (dec. Sept. 1990); children: Michael Joseph, James Edward, Mary Ann. MS Music Edn., Ithaca Coll., Ithaca N.Y., 1948—55; Post Grad. Acctg., Syracuse U., 1956—63. Pub. acct. G.L. Schreck Acctg. Firm, Waterloo, NY, 1955—56; pub. acct. pvt. practice Waterloo, NY, 1956—. Pub. acct. Nat. Soc. Acct., Waterloo, NY, 1961—. Author: Waterloo in 1858, 1969; co-author: The History and Origin of Meml. Day In Waterloo, New York, 1966; author: The Descendants of Michael And Mary Blind Schreck, 1978. Mem. Augusta (GA) Symphony Orch., 1954 7th Army Symphony Orch., 1955. Waterloo Chamber of Commerce, 1956—68, pres., 1967—68; trustee Village of Waterloo, 1964—77; founder, rsch. chmn. Waterloo Meml. Day Centennial Com., 1965—66; trustee Waterloo Libr. and Hist. Soc., 1965—97; ch. historian St. Mary's Ch., Waterloo, NY, 1966—; co-chmn. Waterloo Ctrl. Sch. Centennial Comm., 1985—86. With U.S. Army, 1953—55. Democrat. Catholic. Achievements include Co-Founder: Waterloo Meml. Day Museum; Provided the concept for the artist's design of the official Meml. Day Emblem; Had a major role in obtaining official nat. recognition for Waterloo, N.Y., as the birthplace of Meml. Day through congressional legislation and Presidential Proclamation, 1966. Office: Richard T Schreck Pub Acct 75 Washington St Waterloo NY 13165-1703

**SCHRECK, ROBERT A., JR.,** lawyer; b. Buffalo; BS in Bus. Adminstrn., Georgetown U., 1974; MBA, Northwestern U., 1975, JD, 1978. Bar: Ill. 1978. Ptnr. McDermott, Will & Emery, Chgo., 1978—. Mem. ABA. Office: McDermott Will & Emery 227 W Monroe St Ste 4400 Chicago IL 60606-5096 E-mail: rschreck@mwe.com.

**SCHRECKER, JOHN,** historian, educator; b. Rumburk, Czech Republic, Aug. 22, 1937; s. Karl Steiner and Marian Schrecker-Heller, Franz Schrecker (Stepfather); m. Ellen Wolf, Feb. 18, 1962 (div.); m. Janet Barry, May 11, 1992; children: Michael Franz, Daniel Edwin. BA, U. Pa., 1958; MA, Harvard U., Cambridge, Mass., 1959; PhD, Harvard U., 1968. Asst. prof. of history Princeton U., NJ, 1965—71; prof. of history Brandeis U., Waltham, Mass., 1971—. Assoc. in rsch. Fairbank Ctr. for East Asian Rsch., Harvard U., Cambridge, 1971—. Author: (book) Imperialism and Chinese Nationalism, 1971, The Chinese Revolution in Historical Perspective, 1991, 2nd rev. edit., 2004; author: (with Ellen Schrecker) Mrs. Chiang's Szechwan Cookbook, 1976; editor (with Paul Cohen): Reform in Nineteenth-Century China, 1976. Fellow Fulbright, Social Sci. Rsch. Coun., NAS. Mem.: Am. Hist. Assn., Assn. for Asian Studies, Phi Beta Kappa. Avocation: classical piano. Office: History Dept MS 036 Brandeis Univ Waltham MA 02454 Office Phone: 781-736-2284. Office Fax: 718-736-2273. E-mail: schrecker@brandeis.edu.

**SCHRECKINGER, SY EDWARD,** advertising executive, consultant; b. Bklyn., Jan. 10, 1937; s. Robert and Bessie (Gable) S.; m. Linda Fiarman, Mar. 4, 1962; children: Jamie Fran, Jon Gary. B.F.A., Pratt Inst., 1958. Art dir.

Sudler and Hennesey, N.Y.C., 1958-61; sr. art dir. Marschalk Co., N.Y.C., 1961-63; group supr. Grey Advt., N.Y.C., 1963-66; v.p., assoc. creative dir. Hicks & Greist, N.Y.C., 1966-69; sr. v.p., assoc. creative dir. Young & Rubicam Inc., N.Y.C., 1969-88; advt. and mktg. cons. Oceanside, NY, 1988—2005; advt.-mktg. dir. Magnificent Muffin Corp., 1995—. Recipient Lion Venice Internat. Film Festival, 1972, Andy Ad Club, N.Y., 1965, 86, award Internat. Bus. Assn., Best award Hollywood Radio & TV Soc., 1971, Clio Am. TV Comml. Festival, 1967, 72, 82, 85, Effy, 1985. Jewish.

**SCHREIBER, ALAN HICKMAN**, lawyer; b. Muncie, Ind., Apr. 4, 1944; s. Ephriam and Clarrisa (Hickman) S.; m. Phyllis Jean Chamberlain, Dec. 22, 1972; children: Jennifer Aline, Brett Justin. Student, DePauw U., 1962-64; BS in Bus., Ind. U., 1966, JD, 1969. Bar: Fla. 1971, U.S. Dist. Ct. (so. dist.) Fla. Asst. State Atty.'s Office, Ft. Lauderdale, Fla., 1971-76; pub. defender 17th Jud. Cir., Ft. Lauderdale, 1976—. Cons. Fla. Bar News on Criminal Law, 1982; lobbyist for indigent funding, Fla., 1980—; apptd. to Supreme Ct. Com. on Racial and Ethic Bias; co-chair Chiles-MacKay task force on criminal justice. Contbr. articles to profl. jours. Mem. Dem. Exec. Com., Ft. Lauderdale, 1980; mem. Plantation Dem. Club, 1983; campaign chmn. Goldstein for Atty. Gen. Fla., 1982. Named Young Dem. of Yr., Broward County Young Dems., 1980; Man of Yr., Jewish War Vets., 1982; recipient B'nai B'rith Pub. Servant award, 1990, Dem. of Yr. award 2000, Harry Galkin Meml. award 2002. Mem. Fla. Bar Assn., Broward County Bar Assn., ABA, Nat. Legal Aid Defenders Assn., Phi Alpha Delta. Home: 885 Orchid Dr Fort Lauderdale FL 33317-1221 Office: 201 SE 6th St Fort Lauderdale FL 33301-3303 Office Phone: 954-993-5433. Personal E-mail: alschreiber@direcuay.com.

**SCHREIBER, BERTRAM MANUEL**, mathematics professor; b. Seattle, Nov. 4, 1940; s. Isador and Amy (Hurwitz) S.; m. Rita Ruth Stusser, June 30, 1963; children: Susannah M. Schreiber Bechhofer, Deborah H. Schreiber Shapiro, Abraham D., Elisabeth T. Schreiber Seigel. BA, Yeshiva U., 1962; MS, U. Wash., 1966, PhD, 1968. Asst. prof. Wayne State U., Detroit, 1968-71, assoc. prof., 1971-78, prof., 1978—, chair dept. math., 1987-90. Vis. prof. Hebrew U., Jerusalem, 1975, 2000, Mich. State U., East Lansing, 1982-83, Nat. U. Singapore, 1992, U. New South Wales, Australia, 1992, Indian Statis. Inst., 1993, Tata Inst. Fund Res., Bombay, 1993, Bar Ilan U., 1993, Tel Aviv U., 1993, U. Utrecht, The Netherlands, 1993, U. Wroclaw, Poland, 1993, U. Paris VII, 1999, U. Granada, Spain, 1999-2000, U. Wash., Seattle, 2000. Contbr. articles to profl. jours. NSF grantee, 1968-87; Sci. and Engring. Rsch. Coun. Gt. Britain fellow U. Edinburgh, Scotland, 1976. Mem. Am. Math. Soc., Math. Assn. Am., Israel Math. Union, Edinburgh Math. Soc. Achievements include research in fields of harmonic analysis, topological groups, and probability theory. Office: Wayne State U Dept Math Detroit MI 48202 Office Phone: 313-577-8838. Business E-Mail: berts@math.wayne.edu.

**SCHREIBER, CLARE ADEL**, journalist; b. Chgo., Feb. 22, 1914; d. Otto Herman Mentz and Martha Toll; m. William I. Schreiber, June 18, 1934 (dec. Jan. 1998); children: William M., James L., Ralph W.(dec.), Stephen T. BS in Journalism, U. Ill., 1935; LHD, Coll. of Wooster, 1995. Freelance writer Fairfield Iowa Ledger, 1937, The Daily Record, Wooster, Ohio, 1956; dir. Coll. of Wooster Nursery Sch., 1956—85; family life educator Cmty. Action Wayne Medina, 1985—. Exec. bd. Wayne Assn. of the Edn. of Young Children, Wooster, Ohio, 1983—. Author, editor (book) Green Grow the Children, 1984; contbr. articles. Mem. human rights group Am. Assn. for Univ. Women, Wooster, Ohio; mem. League of Women Voters, Nat. Assn. for Edn. of Young Children, Philos. Edn. Orgn. Internat. Recipient Child Advocate of the Yr., Wayne County Children's Services, 2002; fellow Paul Harris fellow, Rotary Internat., 2004. Mem.: Theta Phi Alpha, Kappa Tau Alpha. Democrat. Presbyn. Home: 1471 Cleveland Rd Wooster OH 44691 Office: Cmty Action Wayne/Medina 2375 Benden Dr Wooster OH 44691

**SCHREIBER, EILEEN SHER**, artist; b. Denver, 1925; d. Michael Herschel and Sarah Deborah (Tannenbaum) Sher; m. Jonas Schreiber, Mar. 27, 1945; children: Jeffrey, Barbara, Michael. Student, U. Utah, 1942-45, NYU, 1966-68, Montclair State Coll., NJ, 1975-79; also pvt. art study. Exhibited Morris Mus. Arts and Scis., Morristown, N.J., 1965-73, N.J. State Mus., 1969, Lever House, N.Y.C., 1971, Paramus (N.J.) Mus., 1973, Newark Mus., 1978, 1991-92, Am. Water Color Soc., Audubon Artists, N.A.D. Gallery, N.Y.C., Pallazzo Vecchio Florence, Italy, Art Expo 1987, 1988, India Mus., 1994, 95, Athens (Greece) Mus., 1996, 97, Gaelin Gallery, Whippany, N.J., 2004, Solstice Gallery, Beach Haven, NJ, Municipal Bldg. of West Orange, NJ; represented in permanent collections Tex. A&M U., Telesoft Inc., Phoenix, State of N.J., Morris Mus., Seton Hall U., Bloomfield (N.J.) Coll., Barclay Bank of Eng., N.J., Somerset Coll., NYU, Morris County State Coll., Broad Nat. Bank, Newark, Ind. Cmty. Bank, Consulting Actuaries, Internat., IBM, Am. Tel. Co., RCA, Johnson & Johnson, Champion Internat. Paper Co., Sony, Mitsubishi, Celanese Co., Squibb Corp., Nabisco, Nat. Bank Phila., Data Control, Ind. Cmty. Bank, Sperry Univac, Ga. Pacific Co., Pub. Svc. Co. N.J., Diane Levine Gallery, Boston, S.W. Gallery, Long Beach Island, N.J., Solstice Gallery, Beach Haven, NJ, Town Hall Libr., West Orange, NJ; others; also pvt. collections. Recipient awards N.J. Watercolor Soc., 1969, 72, 1st award in watercolor Hunterdon Art Ctr., 1972, Best in Show award Short Hills State Show, 1976, Tri-State Purchase award Somerset Coll., 1977, Art Expo, N.Y.C., 1987, 88, numerous others. Mem. Nat. Assn. Women Artists (chmn. watercolor jury, Collage award 1983, Marian Halpren Meml. award 1995), Nat., N.Y. Artists Equity, Printmaker Coun. Visual Artists (1st award in printmaking 1996), Women Visual Artists (Fla.). Home and Office: 10 Jackson Dr Egg Harbor Township NJ 08234 Office Phone: 609-927-0440. Personal E-mail: artess25@aol.com.

**SCHREIBER, GEORGE RICHARD**, publishing executive, writer; b. Ironton, Ohio, July 4, 1922; s. George Joseph and Marie Frances (Heitzman) S.; m. Veva Jeanette Hopkins, May 14, 1945; children— Susan (Mrs. Arlan Shorey), George, Ellen (Mrs. Norman Hodge). AB, St. Joseph's Coll., Rensselaer, Ind., 1943, L.H.D., 1974; MA, U. Chgo., 1944. Exec. editor Billboard mag., 1945-60; editor, pub. Vend mag., 1946-66; editorial dir. Billboard Publs., 1966-70; pres., chief exec. officer Nat. Automatic Mdsg. Assn., Chgo., 1970-88, pres. emeritus, 1988—; pres., chief exec. Sunrise Books, 1994—. Mem. staff and faculty U. Chgo., 1944-60. Author: Verses from the River Country, 1941, What Makes News, 1943, Automatic Selling, 1954, A Concise History of Vending in the U.S.A, 1965, revised 2d edit., 1990, Millenium edit., 1999, The Bobby Baker Affair— How to Make Millions in Washington, 1964, Vending For Investors-How to Spot Phony Deals, 1994, 2d edit., 1996; contbg. author: Handbook of Modern Marketing, 1986. Chmn. Glenview (Ill.) Plan Commn., 1962-64, mayor, 1964-67; chmn. Region 1, Chgo. Area Transp. Study Group, 1962-63; bd. dirs. Rockefeller Meml. Chapel, U. Chgo., 1944-45; trustee St. Joseph's Coll., 1964—, chmn., 1970-76, life trustee, 1978—. Recipient Jesse H. Neal award for editorial achievement, 1964; dedication of St. Joseph's Coll. (Ind.) G. Richard Schreiber Dept. Humanities, 1987. Mem. The Authors Guild Inc., Am. Bus. Press (editorial bd.), Assn. Econs. Council, Am. Soc. Assn. Execs., Tavern Club, Internat. Club, Tower Club. Home: 735 Ravine Ave Lake Bluff IL 60044-2625 E-mail: vevaj@aol.com.

**SCHREIBER, HOWARD E.**, lawyer; b. Balt., May 18, 1959; BA in Polit. Sci., Dickinson Coll., 1981; JD with honors, Duke U., 1984. Bar: Tex. 1984. Shareholder Jenkens & Gilchrist, P.C., Dallas, 1993—, firm leader real estate practice group. Mem.: ABA, Am. Coll. Mortgage Attorneys, Dallas Bar Assn., Tex. State Bar Assn. Office: Jenkens & Gilchrist PC Ste 3200 1445 Ross Ave Dallas TX 75202-2799 Office Phone: 214-855-4370. Office Fax: 214-855-4300. Business E-Mail: hschreiber@jenkens.com.

**SCHREIBER, JAY**, journalist; asst. sports editor The New York Times. Author: (articles) Judges Decision Lifts Ban on Sale of Ephedra in Utah, 2005. Office: The New York Times Sports Desk 229 W 43rd St New York NY 10036 Office Phone: 212-556-7371. Office Fax: 212-556-5048.*

**SCHREIBER, KURT GILBERT**, lawyer; b. Milw., Aug. 22, 1946; s. Raymond R. and Mildred L. (Kleist) S.; m. Nelda Beth Van Buren, May 3, 1974; children— Katharine Anne, Matthew Edward. AB in Econs., Cornell U., 1968; JD, U. Mich., 1971; M in Theol. Studies, Vanderbilt U., 2003. Bar: Wis. 1971, Tex. 1979, Tenn. 1997. Internat. atty. Tenneco Internat. Holdings Co., London, 1974-78; atty. Tenneco Inc., Houston, 1978-80; 2d v.p., asst. gen. counsel Am. Gen. Corp., Houston, 1980-83, v.p., gen. counsel, 1983-84, sr. v.p., gen. counsel, 1984-93, sr. v.p., corp. sec., 1993-94; pvt. practice Houston, 1994-96; exec. v.p., gen. counsel Direct Gen. Corp., Nashville, 1996-98, pres., 1998—2001. Bd. dir. Cumberland Trust and Investment Co., Urban Housing Solutions. Fellow Tex. Bar Found.; mem. ABA, Wis. Bar Assn., Tex. Bar Assn., Tenn. Bar Assn. Home: 4117 Dorman Dr Nashville TN 37215

**SCHREIBER, LIEV (ISAAC LIEV SCHREIBER)**, actor; b. San Francisco, Oct. 4, 1967; s. Tell and Heather Schreiber. Student, Bklyn. Tech., Royal Acad. Dramatic Arts, London; BA, Hampshire Coll., 1988; MFA, Yale Sch. Drama, 1992. Actor: (Broadway plays) In the Summer House, 1993, Betrayal, 2000—01, Glengarry Glen Ross, 2005 (Tony award for best performance by a featured actor in a play, 2005); (TV films) The Sunshine Boys, 1995, Buffalo Girls, 1995, Since You've Been Gone, 1998, Young Dr. Freud, 2002, Hitler: The Rise of Evil, 2003, Lackawanna Blues, 2005, (voice) Oil Storm, 2005,: (films) Mixed Nuts, 1994, Party Girl, 1995, Mad Love, 1995, Denise Calls Up, 1995, The Daytrippers, 1996, Ransom, 1996, Scream, 1996, Scream 2, 1997, Phantoms, 1998, Party Girl, 1995, Jacob the Liar, 1999, The Hurricane, 1999, Scream 3, 2000, Kate & Leopold, 2001, The Manchurian Candidate, 2004, The Omen, 2006; dir.: Everything is Illuminated, 2003. Avocations: basketball, fencing, bicycling.*

**SCHREIBER, MARK TRAUDT**, psychiatrist; b. Denver, Oct. 6, 1947; s. Charles William and Sophie Emily Schreiber; m. Constance Anne Rabe, Nov. 27, 1976; children: Vanessa, Laura, Charles, Anne, John S. U. Nebr., Lincoln, 1970; MD, Washington U., St. Louis, Mo., 1975. Diplomate Am. Bd. Psychiatry and Neurology, 1980, Am. Bd. Addictionology, 1986. Intern, resident Banes Hosp. Washington U., St. Louis; psychiatrist Hearst, Fischer & Schreiber, Va. Beach, Va., 1978—84, Crossroads Clin., Va. Beach, 1984—89, Atlantic Psychiatric, Va. Beach, 1989—. Med. dir. Serenity Lodge, Chesapeake, Va., 1984—91; assoc. med. dir. Va. Beach Psychiat. Ctr., 1991—. Contbr. articles to profl. jours. Elder Bayside Presbyn. Ch., Va. Beach, 1980—, chmn. com., 1980—; vice chmn. internat. partnership com. Presbytery Ea. Va., Portsmouth, 1982—. Named Am.'s Top Psychiatrists, Consumers' Rsch. Coun. Am. Fellow: Am. Soc. Addiction Medicine (regional chmn. 2000—04), Am. Psychiat. Assn. (Disting. fellow 2005). Avocations: ballroom dancing, skiing, reading, camping, travel. Office: Atlantic Psychiatric 780 Lipshua Pkwy Ste 450 Virginia Beach VA 23452

**SCHREIBER, PAUL SOLOMON**, lawyer; b. Krakow, Poland, Mar. 29, 1941; came to U.S., 1949; s. John and Betty (Silber) S.; m. Joan A. Perlmutter, Mar. 20, 1971; children: Douglas Arun, Stacey Lauren. BS, CCNY, 1963; LLB, NYU, 1966, LLM, 1967; postgrad., U. Paris, 1967-68. Bar: N.Y. 1966. Assoc. Marshal, Bratter, Greene, Allison & Tucker, N.Y.C., 1969-76, ptnr., 1976-82, Kramer, Levin, Naftalis, Nessen, Kamin & Frankel, N.Y.C., 1982-94, Shearman & Sterling LLP, N.Y.C., 1994—. Bd. dirs. Harbor Trust Co., Hoboken, N.J., 1985-92. Editor: Annual Survey Am. Law; co-author articles, papers and revs. Trustee Park Ave. Synagogue, N.Y.C., 1985—, pres., 1998-2003, hon. pres., 2003—; bd. dirs. Am. Friends of the Rambam Med. Ctr., N.Y.C., 1989-99, N.Y.C chpt. Nat. Multiple Sclerosis Soc., 1991—, Sch. for Strings, 1994-96, Jr. Achievement of N.Y., 2005—; bd. overseers Rabbinical Sch. Jewish Theol. Sem., 1995-96. Arthur Garfield Hayes fellow; Ford Found. fellow. Democrat. Jewish. Office: Shearman & Sterling LLP 599 Lexington Ave Fl C2 New York NY 10022-6069 Office Phone: 212-848-8920. E-mail: pschreiber@shearman.com.

**SCHREIBER, SALLY ANN**, lawyer; b. El Paso, Tex., July 23, 1951; d. Warren Thomas and Joyce (Honey) S.; children: Amanda Honey, Ryan Thorp Luther. BBA, U. N.Mex., 1973; JD, Stanford U., 1976. Bar: Calif. 1976, Tex. 1977. Assoc. Johnson & Swanson, Dallas, 1976-81, ptnr., 1981-89; mem. firm Johnson & Gibbs, P.C., Dallas, 1989-93; of counsel Cox & Smith, Inc., Dallas, 1993-94; shareholder Munsch Hardt Kopf & Harr, P.C., Dallas, 1994—. Spkr. in field. Editor Stanford U. Law Rev., 1975-76; co-author paper Internat. Bar Assn., 1986. Bd. dirs. The Lyric Opera of Dallas, 1982-86; law sch. bd. vis. Stanford (Calif.) U., 1981-84, 2004—; dir. Tex. Bus. Law Found., 1989—, treas. 1994-96, sec. 1996-98. Mem. ABA, Tex. Bar Assn. (corp. law com. 1981—, vice-chair 1993-97, chair 1997-2001, ptnrship. law com. 1985—, ltd. liability com. 1992—, opinion com. 1989-98, codification com. 1997—, bus. law sect. coun. 1996—, vice chmn. 2004-05, chair 2005-06), Calif. Bar Assn., Dallas Bar Assn. Home: 2737 Purdue Ave Dallas TX 75225-7910 Office: Munsch Hardt Kopf & Harr PC 500 N Akard St Ste 3800 Dallas TX 75201 Office Phone: 214-855-7598. Business E-Mail: sschreiber@munsch.com.

**SCHREIBER-ABSHIRE, WENDY ELLEN**, meteorologist; b. Denver, Aug. 23, 1963; d. Richard and adopted d. Marie Schreiber; m. Allen Abshire, Sept. 3, 1988; children: Lane Alton Abshire, Logan Lee Abshire. BS, Met. State Coll., Denver, 1985; MS, U. Wyo., Laramie, 1989. Assoc. scientist II, III, IV U. Corp. Atmospheric Rsch./ Coop. Program Operational Meteorology, Edn. and Tng., Boulder, Colo., 1992—2005, project mgr., sci. supr., 2005—. Comm. mentor U. Corp. Atmospheric Rsch./Significant Opportunities in Atmospheric Rsch. and Sci., 2002—; lectr. in field. Nominee Outstanding Publ. award, Nat. Ctr. Atmospheric Rsch., 1987; named Vol. of Yr., Colo. Fencing Acad., Arvada, 2005; Colo. scholar, 1984, 1985. Mem.: Nat. Weather Assn., Am. Meteorol. Soc. (annual meeting program co-chair 2004—06, chair bd. outreach and pre-coll. edn. 2002—, chair local chpt. affairs com., officer Denver-Boulder chpt. 1995—98). Achievements include major contributions to first laser disc, CD-ROM, Web-based and Web with audio interactive multimedia training modules produced for professional meteorologists by the Coop. Program Operational Meteorology, Edn. and Tng. program; contribution to atmospheric science research that solved the mystery of microbursts and worked with other scientists to make major strides in forecasting convective storm initiation.

**SCHREIER, BRADLEY**, management executive; b. Aug. 19, 1951; m. Marge St. Pierre; children: Ryan, Kyle. BS in Social Studies and Econs., Minn. State U., Mankato, 1973. Letterpress supr. Carlson Craft, Mankato, Minn., 1973-74, custom svc. supr., 1974-76, office mgr., 1976-79; v.p. sales and mktg. Taylor Corp., Mankato, 1980-85, pres., COO, 1985—2001, CEO, 2001—. Bd. dir. Malto Meal Corp., Mpls. Bd. dirs. Mankato Area United Way, 1975-81, v.p., 1979, 80, pres, bd. dirs., 1981; bd. dirs. YMCA, 1983-92, chmn. fin. com., co-chair spl. gifts divsn. 1 million dollar bldg. expansion capital campaign; bd. dirs. Immanuel-St. Joseph's Hosp., 1984-94, treas., 1988, vice chmn., treas, 1989, chmn. bldg. task force, 1990, vice chmn., 1990, chmn. bd. dirs., 1991, 92, mem. exec., 1993-94; bd. dirs. Mankato Area Cath. Sch. Found., 1988—; pres. parish coun., mem. coun. Holy Rosary Ch., 1988—, chmn. fin. com., mem. com., 1989—; mem. pers. com. Loyola Cath. High Sch., 1989-90, mem. sch. bd., 1989-90; chmn. Mankato Area Cath. Sch. Bd., 1990—; coach Mankato Area Youth Baseball Assn., 1986—, bd. dirs., 1991—; pres. Mankato Royals Baseball, 1989, 90, bd. dirs., 1989-93; Fitzgerald 7th and 8th grade basketball coach, 1988, mem. Loyola Booster Club; bd. dirs. Mankato Basketball Assn., 1989—, traveling team coach, 1989—; basketball team coach Holy Rosary. Recipient Book of Golden Deeds award for Outstanding Cmty. Svc., Mankato Exch. Club, 1994, Disting. Alumni award Minn. State U., Mankato, 1994. Mem. KC. Office: Taylor Corp 1725 Roe Crest Dr Mankato MN 56003-1807 Office Phone: 507-625-2828.*

**SCHREIER, KAREN ELIZABETH**, judge; b. Sioux Falls, SD, 1956; AB, St. Louis U., 1978; JD, St. Louis U. Law Sch., 1981. Law clk. to Hon. Francis Dunn, SD Supreme Ct., 1981—82; pvt. practice Sioux Falls, SD, 1982—93;

US atty. US Dept. Justice, Sioux Falls, SD, 1993-99; judge US Dist. Ct., Rapid City, SD, 1999—. Office: US Dist Ct 515 9th St Rm 318 Rapid City SD 57701-2626 Office Phone: 605-343-3744.

**SCHREIER, PETER**, tenor; b. Meissen, Germany, July 29, 1935; Student, Dresden Hochschule für Musik, Germany. With Dresden State Opera, Germany, 1959-63, Berlin Staatsoper, Germany, 1963. Appearances include Vienna State Opera, Salzburg Festival, La Scala, Milan, Sadler's Wells, London, Met. Opera, N.Y.C., Teatro Colon, Buenos Aires; recital debut London, 1978; debut as conductor, 1969; has conducted recordings of several choral works by J.S. Bach and Mozart. Office: Kammersänger Calberlastr 13 D-01326 Dresden Germany

**SCHREINER, ALBERT WILLIAM**, internist, educator; b. Cin., Feb. 15, 1926; s. Albert William and Ruth Mary (Neuer) S.; m. Jean Tellstrom, Dec. 12, 1953; 1 child, David William. BS, U. Cin., 1947, MD, 1949. Diplomate Am. Bd. Internal Medicine, 1958. Clin. investigator VA Hosp., Cin., 1957-59, chief med. svc., 1959-68, dir. dept. internal medicine, 1968-93; dir. resident program internal medicine Christ Hosp., Cin., 1978-87; mem. faculty U. Cin. Coll. Medicine, 1955—, assoc. prof. medicine, 1962-67, prof. internal medicine, 1967-98, emeritus prof. internal medicine, 1998—; attending physician Cin. Gen. Hosp., 1957—95. Cons. to med. dir. Gen. Electric, 1987-96; med. dirs. United Home Care Hospice, 1993-99, United Home Care Agy.; chair instnl. rev. bd. The Christ Hosp., 1988—; subinvestigator Sterling Rsch. Group, 2003—. Contbr. articles to profl. jours. Bd. dirs., chmn. health com. Cmty. Action Commn., 1968-71; trustee Drake Meml. Hosp., 1975-78, Leukemia Found. Southwest Ohio, Cancer Control, Am. Cancer Soc., bd. dirs. Hamilton County unit, 1990; bd. dirs., chair profl. affairs com. United Home Care Agy., 1998; bd. dirs. Gamble Inst. Med. Rsch., Cin., 1991-96. Fellow: ACP; mem.: Am. Soc. Clin. Rsch. Program Dirs. Internal Medicine, Assn. Program Dirs. Internal Medicine, Clin. Soc. Internal Medicine (pres. 1979—80), Ohio Soc. Internal Medicine (trustee 1978, sec.-treas. 1981—85, v.p. 1982—83, pres. 1984—85), Ohio Med. Assn., Am. Fedn. Clin. Rsch., N.Y. Acad. Scis., Am. Cancer Soc. (bd. dirs. Hamilton County unit 1990—92), Am. Leukemia Soc. (med. adv. exec. bd.), Phi Beta Kappa, Sigma Xi. Roman Catholic. Home: 8040 S Clippinger Dr Cincinnati OH 45243-3248 Office: 2139 Auburn Ave Cincinnati OH 45219-2906 Office Phone: 513-585-2742. Business E-Mail: schreia@healthall.com.

**SCHREINER, JOHN CHRISTIAN**, economics consultant, software publisher; b. Los Angeles, Nov. 2, 1933; s. Alexander and Margaret S.; m. Marie Nielsen, June 19, 1967; children: Christian Alexander, Carl Arthur, Elizabeth, Nathan Alexander. BSM.E., U. Utah, 1958; MBA, Harvard U., 1960; PhD, UCLA, 1970. Chartered fin. analyst. Design engr. Eimco Corp., Salt Lake City and N.Y.C., 1957-59; credit exec. James Talcott, Inc., N.Y.C. and Boston, 1960-65; lectr. mgmt. U. Utah, 1965-66; mem. faculty Grad. Sch. Mgmt., U. Minn., Mpls., 1969-84, chmn. dept. fin. and ins., 1973-74, 76-81; pres. The Sebastian Group, Inc., 1984—. Cons. to corps. and govt. agys. Co-author: Executive Recruiting: How Companies Obtain Management Talent, 1960; contbr. articles to profl. jours. Mem. Fin. Execs. Inst., Fin. Analysts Fedn., Tau Beta Pi, Phi Kappa Phi. Republican. Mem. Ch. Jesus Christ of Latter-day Saints (missionary, Ger. 1953-56). Club: Harvard Bus. Sch. Minn. Office: The Sebastian Group Inc 2040 Douglas Dr Minneapolis MN 55422

**SCHRENK, GARY DALE**, foundation executive; b. San Jose, Calif., Apr. 29, 1949; s. Robert Shepard and Katherine Mildred (Grant) S.; m. Rhonda Lynn King, Oct. 9, 1981 (div. Jan. 1989); children: Stephen, Kristen, James. BA in Comm., Am. U., 1970; M in Nonprofit Mgmt., Regis U., 2002. TV dir. WTOP (now WUSA), Washington, 1971-73, KBTV (now KUSA), Denver, 1973-75; with Denver Area Boy Scouts Am., 1975-80; regional dir. St. Jude Children's Rsch. Hosp., Memphis, 1980-83; dir. devel. Denver Art Mus., 1983-85; asst. dir. devel. The Children's Hosp., Denver, 1985-87; pres. North Colo. Med. Ctr. Found., Greeley, 1987—. Dir. instr. Fast Start Course, 1985—2001; pres. Monfort Children's Clinic, Greeley, Colo., 1994—2001. Pres. Vision Together, Weld County, Colo., 1994—95; chmn., founding dir. Weld Citizen Action Network, 1995—98, 2000—02; founding dir. First Steps Weld County, 1993—99; chmn. Weld Cmty. Health Coalition, 1992—98; bd. dirs. North Colo. Health Alliance, 2002—; chmn. pub. support com. Team Colo. ARC, 1997—2004; regional svc., area 2 public support com. ARC, 2004—06, bd. dirs. Centennial chpt., 2003—. Recipient Disting. Citizen award Highlanders, Denver, 1974 Mem. Assn. Fundraising Profls. (nat. found. bd. 1998-2003, nat. assembly 1994-98, bd. dirs. Colo. chpt. 1979-2000, 03-, pres. 1984, internat. bd. dirs. 2004—, Colo. Outstanding Devel. Profl. 2004), Colo. Assn. Nonprofit Orgns. (founding dir. 1987-92), Rotary, Greeley Country Club, Tahosa Alumni Assn. (past pres., past chair). Methodist. Avocation: golf. Home: 4956 13th St Greeley CO 80634-2215 Office: North Colo Med Ctr Found 1801 16th St Greeley CO 80631-5154 Office Phone: 970-356-9020. Business E-Mail: gary.schrenk@bannerhealth.com.

**SCHREYER, CHARA**, foundation administrator, art collector; Chmn. Kadima Found., Mill Valley, Calif. Trustee Mus. Modern Art, San Francisco, Contemporary Jewish Mus. Named one of Top 200 Collectors, ARTnews Mag., 2004, 2005, 2006. Avocation: Collector of Modern & Contemporary Art & Photography. Mailing: Kadima Foundation PMB 200 38 Miller Ave Mill Valley CA 94941*

**SCHREYER, LESLIE JOHN**, lawyer; b. NYC, Apr. 11, 1946; s. Oscar and Greta (Loebl) S.; m. Judith Camps, Sept. 25, 1994; 1 child, Gabrielle. BA, Columbia U., 1967; LLB, Yale U., 1970; LLM in Taxation, N.Y.U., 1977. Bar: N.Y. 1971. Assoc. Chadbourne & Parke, N.Y.C., 1970-78, ptnr., 1978-81, 83—; dep. internat. tax counsel U.S. Treasury Dept., 1981-83; gen. counsel GLG Ptnrs. Svcs. Ltd., 2000—, also bd. dirs. Adj. assoc. prof. law NYU, 1990-97; cons. Am. Law Inst., Fed. Income Tax Project on Internat. Aspects of U.S. Income Taxation, 1983-91. Author: (with others) Foreign Tax Credit, 1980; contbr. numerous articles to profl. jours. Trustee Am. Friends of the Victoria and Albert Mus., Inc. Mem. ABA, Internat. Bar Assn., Internat. Fiscal Assn., N.Y. State Bar Assn., Assn. of Bar of City of N.Y., Phi Beta Kappa. Republican. Home: 60 E End Ave New York NY 10028-7907 Office: Chadbourne & Parke 30 Rockefeller Plz Fl 31 New York NY 10112-0129 E-mail: lschreyer@chadbourne.com, les@glgpartners.com.

**SCHREYER, WILLIAM ALLEN**, retired finance company executive; b. Williamsport, Pa., Jan. 13, 1928; s. William L. and Elizabeth (Engel) S.; m. Joan Legg, Oct. 17, 1953; 1 child, DrueAnne Frazier. BA, Pa. State U., 1948. With Merrill Lynch, Inc. and predecessors, N.Y.C., 1948-93; CEO Merrill Lynch & Co., N.Y.C., 1984-92, chmn., 1985-93, chmn. emeritus, 1993—. Trustee Ctr. for Strategic and Internat. Studies, Pa. State U., 1986—, chmn. bd. trustees, 1993-96. Mem. USAF, 1955-56. Mem. River Club, Links Club, Saturn Club, Springdale Golf Club, Bedens Brook Club, Eldorado Country Club, Georgetown Club, Met. Club, Nassau Club, Carnegie Club at Skibo Castle, Bond Club NY, Knights of Malta. Roman Catholic. Office: Merrill Lynch & Co Inc 800 Scudders Mill Rd Plainsboro NJ 08536-1606

**SCHRIBMAN, SHELLEY IRIS**, database engineer, consultant; b. Weehawken, N.J., July 29, 1944; d. George and Mildred (Kamen) Shulman; m. Marshall Melvin Schribman, Aug. 26, 1979. BFA cum laude, Art Inst. Chgo., 1966; MBA, Simmon Coll. Grad. Sch. Mgmt., 1982. Asst. dir. Advanced Inst. Devel. Am. Repertory Theatre, N.Y.C., 1970—71; ptnr. Sir Charles Cleaning Co., Boston, 1982—83; owner SIS Internat., Boston, 1984—87; database developer (freelance) Boston, 1995—; sys. analyst Dept. Pub. Health, Boston, 2000—. Cons. Boston Computer Soc., 1995-96, Catchpole Corp., Wellesley, Mass., 1996-97, Ptnrs. In Home Care Inc., Missoula, Mont., 1996-97; designer, developer Shulman Bankruptcy Program, 1998-99 Pres. Orgn. for Rehab. Through Tng., Boston, 1986-88; mem. LWV, Boston (housing specialist 1989-91, pres. 1990-91, nat. credentials chairperson 1991-92). Mem. Belmont Dramatic Club, Alumni Theatre, Lexington Players. Jewish.

Avocations: acting, composing music. Home: 8 Whittier Pl #23D Boston MA 02114-1402 Office: Dept Public Health 250 Washington St Fl 5 Boston MA 02108-4619 Office Phone: 617-624-5595. Personal E-mail: ShelleyISchriman@rcn.com.

**SCHRIEFFER, JOHN ROBERT,** physics professor, science administrator; b. Oak Park, Ill., May 31, 1931; s. John Henry and Louise (Anderson) Schrieffer; m. Anne Grete Thomsen, Dec. 30, 1960; children: Anne Bolette, Paul Karsten, Anne Regina. BS, MIT, 1953; MS, U. Ill., 1954, PhD, 1957, ScD, 1974; ScD (hon.), Tech. U., Munich, 1968, U. Geneva, 1968, U. Pa., 1973, U. Cin., 1977, U. Tel Aviv, 1987, U. Ala., 1990. NSF postdoctoral fellow U. Birmingham, England, Niels Bohr Inst., Copenhagen, 1957—58; asst. prof. U. Chgo., 1958—59; asst. prof., then assoc. prof. U. Ill., 1959—62; prof. U. Pa., Phila., 1962—79, Mary Amanda Wood prof. physics, 1964—79; Andrew D. White prof. at large Cornell U., 1969—75; prof. U. Calif., Santa Barbara, 1980—91, Chancellor's prof., 1984—91, dir. Inst. for Theoretical Physics, 1984—89; Univ. prof. Fla. State U., Tallahassee, 1992—, Univ. Eminent Scholar prof., 1995—, chief scientist Nat. High Magnetic Field Lab., 1992—. Pres.'s com. Nat. Medal of Sci., 1996—98. Author: Theory of Superconductivity, 1964. Recipient Comstock prize, NAS, 1968, Nobel prize for Physics, 1972, John Ericsson medal, Am. Soc. Swedish Engrs., 1976, Alumni Achievement award, U. Ill., 1979, Nat. medal of Sci., 1984; fellow Guggenheim, Copenhagen, 1967, Los Alamos Nat. Lab., Exxon faculty, 1979—89. Fellow: Am. Phys. Soc. (v.p. 1994, pres.-elect 1995, pres. 1996, past pres. 1997, Oliver E. Buckley solid state physics prize 1968); mem.: NAS (coun. 1990—), Acad. Sci. USSR, Royal Danish Acad. Scis. and Letters, Am. Acad. Arts and Scis. Office: Fla State Univ NHMFL 1800 E Paul Dirac Dr Tallahassee FL 32310-3748 Business E-Mail: schrieff@magnet.fsu.edu.*

**SCHRIER, ARNOLD,** historian, educator; b. N.Y.C., May 30, 1925; s. Samuel and Yetta (Levine) S.; m. Sondra Weinshelbaum, June 12, 1949; children— Susan Lynn, Jay Alan, Linda Lee, Paula Kay. Student, Bethany Coll., W.Va., 1943-44, Ohio Wesleyan U., 1944-45; BS, Northwestern U., 1949, MA, 1950, PhD (Social Sci. Research Council fellow, Univ. fellow), 1956. Asst. prof. history U. Cin., 1956-61, assoc. prof., 1961-66, prof., 1966-95, dir. grad. studies history, 1969-78, Walter C. Langsam prof. modern European history, 1972-95; Walter C. Langsam prof. history emeritus, 1995—. Vis. assoc. prof. history Northwestern U., Evanston, Ill., 1960; vis. assoc. prof. history Ind. U., Bloomington, 1965-66; vis. lectr. Russian history Duke U., 1966; disting. vis. prof. U.S. Air Force Acad., 1983-84; dir. NDEA Inst. World History for Secondary Sch. Tchrs., U. Cin., 1965; Am. del. Joint U.S.-USSR Textbook Study Commn., 1989. Author: Ireland and the American Emigration, 1958, reissued, 1970, paperback edit., 1997, The Development of Civilization, 1961-62, Modern European Civilization, 1963, Living World History, 1964, rev., 1993, Twentieth Century World, 1974, History and Life: the World and Its People, 1977, rev., 1993, A Russian Looks at America, 1979, Irish Immigrants in the Land of Canaan, 2003. Pres. Ohio Acad. History, 1973-74, Midwest Slavic Conf., 1980. Served with USNR, 1943-46, 52-54. Recipient Disting. Svc. award Ohio Acad. History, 1992; Am. Council Learned Socs. fgn. area fellow, 1963-64 Mem. World History Assn. (v.p. 1986-88, pres. 1988-90). Home: 10 Diplomat Dr Cincinnati OH 45215-2073 Personal E-mail: arnsond@aol.com.

**SCHRIER, ERIC WOODSIDE W.,** publishing executive; b. San Francisco, Nov. 21, 1951; s. Elliot and Nancy (Gennes) S.; m. Ellen Woodside, Dec. 30, 1978; 3 children. BA in Human Biology, Brown U., 1973; MA in Journalism, U. Calif., Berkeley, 1977. Marine biologist URS Co., San Mateo, Calif., 1973-77; pub., editor Novus mag., San Francisco, 1977-78; co-founder, mng. editor Science mag., Washington, 1979-85; editor-in-chief Hippocrates (now Health mag.), San Francisco, 1985—95, Time Inc. Ventures, 1990—95; pres., CEO Time Inc. Health, 1995—99; editor-in-chief to pres. RD N. Am. Readers Digest, Pleasantville, NY, 2000—05, pres., CEO, 2005—. Co-editor: Newton At the Bat, The Science of Sport, 1984, Esquire (mag.) Register, 1985. Regents fellow U. Calif.-Berkeley, 1975 Mem. Am. Soc. Mag. Editors, Sigma Xi Office: Reader's Digest PO Box 200 Pleasantville NY 10572-0200*

**SCHRIER, ROBERT WILLIAM,** physician, educator; b. Indpls., Feb. 19, 1936; s. Arthur E. and Helen M. Schrier; m. Barbara Lindley, June 14, 1959; children: David, Debbie, Douglas, Derek, Denise. BA, Depauw U., 1957; DSc (hon.), U. Colo., 1996, Silesian Acad. Medicine, Katowice, Poland, 1997; MD, Ind. U., 1962; DSc (hon.), DePauw U., 2004. Intern Marion County (Ind.) Hosp., 1962; resident U. Wash., Seattle, 1963-65; asst. prof. U. Calif. Med. Ctr., San Francisco, 1969—72, assoc. dir. renal divsn., 1971-72, assoc. prof., 1972; prof., head renal disease U. Colo. Sch. Med., Denver, 1972-92, prof., chmn. dept. medicine, 1976—. Editor 45 textbooks in internal medicine, geriat., drug usage, and kidney disease; contbr. over 800 sci. articles to profl. jours. Pres. Western Soc. Clin. Investigation, 1981, Nat. Kidney Found., 1984-86. With U.S. Army, 1966—69. Recipient David Hume award Nat. Kidney Found., 1987, Louis Pasteur medal U. Strasburg, 1987, Mayo Soley award Western Soc. Clin. Investigation, 1989, Robert H. Williams award Assn. Profs. Medicine, 1996, Torchbearer award 1997, Edward N. Gibbs Meml. award NY Acad. Medicine, 2000, Alexander von Humboldt Rsch award 2004, Grand Hamdan Internat. Med. Scis. award 2004. Mem. ACP (master, John Phillips award 1992), Am. Soc. Nephrology (treas. 1979-81, pres. 1983, John Peters award 1997), Internat. Soc. Nephrology (treas. 1980-84, v.p. 1990-95, pres. 1995-97, Jean Hamburger award 2003), Am. Clin. and Climatol. Assn. (v.p. 1986), Assn. Am. Physicians (pres. 1994-95, Francis Blake award 1995), Western Assn. Physicians (pres. 1982), Inst. of Medicine of NAS, Alpha Omega Alpha. Achievements include research contributions centered on the pathogenesis of acute renal failure, genetic renal disorders, mechanisms of cell injury, diabetic nephropathy and renal and hormonal control of body fluid volume; advancement of a unifying hypothesis of sodium and water regulation in health and disease which has stimulated world-wide interest in the medical scince community. Office: U Colo Health Scis Ctr Renal Divsn PO Box B173 Denver CO 80262-0001 Business E-Mail: Robert.Schrier@uchsc.edu.

**SCHRIESHEIM, ALAN,** science administrator; b. NYC, Mar. 8, 1930; s. Morton and Frances (Greenberg) Schriesheim; m. Beatrice D. Brand, June 28, 1953; children: Laura Lynn, Robert Alan. BS in Chemistry, Poly. Inst. Bklyn., 1951; PhD in Phys. Organic Chemistry, Pa. State U., 1954; DSc (hon.), No. Ill. U., 1991; Laureate, Lincoln Acad., 1996; PhD (hon.), Ill. Inst. Tech., Chgo., 1992, Pa. State U., 2001. Chemist Nat. Bur. Standards, 1954—56; with Exxon Rsch. & Engring. Co., 1956—83, dir. corp. rsch., 1975—79; gen. mgr. Exxon Engring., 1979—83; sr. dep. lab. dir., COO Argonne Nat. Lab., 1983—84, lab. dir., CEO, 1984—96, dir. emeritus, 1996—; prof. chemistry dept. U. Chgo., 1984—96, lectr. Bus. Sch., 1996—99; prin. Washington Adv. Group, 1996—. Karcher lectr. U. Okla., 1977; Hurd lectr. Northwestern U., 1980; Rosensteil lectr. Brandeis U., 1982; Welsh Found. lectr., 87; com. svc. NRC, 1980—; vis. com. chemistry dept. MIT, 1977—82; mem. vis. com. mech. engring. and aerospace dept. Princeton (N.J.) U., 1983—87, mem. vis. com. chemistry dept., 1983—87; mem. Pure and Applied Chemistry Com.; del. to People's Republic of China, 1978; mem. Presdl. Nat. Commn. on Superconductivity 1989—91, U.S.-USSR Joint Commn. on Basic Sci. Rsch., 1990—93; mem. U.S. nat. com. Internat. Union Pure and Applied Chemistry, 1982—85; mem. magnetic fusion adv. com. Divsn. Phys. Scis. U. Chgo. Magnetic Fusion adv. com. to U.S. DOE, 1983—86; mem. Dept. Energy Rsch. Adv. Bd., 1983—85, Congl. Adv. Com. on Sci. and Tech., 1985—96; mem. vis. com. Stanford (Calif.) U., U. Utah, Tex. A&M U., Lehigh U.; bd. govs. Argonne Nat. Lab., 1984—96; mem. adv. com. on space sys. and tech. NASA, 1987—93; mem. nat. medal of engring. physics vis. com. U. Wis., Madison; mem. Coun. Gt. Lakes Govs. Regional Econ. Devel. Commn., 1987—, rev. bd. Compact Ignition Tomamak Princeton U., 1988—91; advisor Sears Investment Mgmt. Co., 1988—89; bd. dirs. HEICO, Smart Signal Corp.; adv. bd. Batterson Venture Ptnrs., Influx, UHV Aluminum, Valley Indsl. Assn., Coun. on Superconductivity for Am. Competitiveness; mem. State of Ill. Commn. on the Future of Pub. Svc., 1990—92; co-chair Indsl. Rsch. Inst. Nat. Labs./Industry Panel, 1984—87; mem. Nat. Acad. Engring. Adv. Commn. on Tech. and Sci., 1991—92, Sun Electric Corp. Bd., 1991—92, U.S. House of Reps. subcom. on Sci.-Adv. Group on Renewing

U.S. Sci. Policy, 1992—96, Chgo. Acad. Scis. acad. coun., 1994—; mem. adv. bd. Chemtech; mem. sr. action group on R&D investment strategies Ctr. for strategic and Internat. Studies, 1995; bd. vis. Astronomy and Astrophysics Pa. State U., 1995—; bd. overseers Fermi Nat. Lab., 2003—. Adv. bd.: Chemtech, 1970—85, editl. bd.: Rsch. & Devel., 1988—92, Superconductor Industry, 1988—95; patentee in field. Mem. spl. vis. com. Field Mus. of Natural History, Chgo., 1987—88; trustee The Latin Sch. of Chgo., 1990—92; adv. bd. WBEZ Chicagoland Pub. Radio Cmty., 1990—96; mem. Conservation Found. DuPage County, 1983—96, Econ. Devel. Adv. Commn. of DuPage County, 1984—88, Ill. Gov.'s Commn. on Sci. and Tech., 1986—90, Inst. for Ill. Coun. Advisors, 1988—, Ill. Coalition Bd. Dirs., 1989—, Inst. for Ill. Adv. Rev. Panel, 1986—88, NASA Sci. Tech. Adv. Com. Manpower Requirements Ad Hoc Rev. Team, 1988—91, Ill. Sci. and Tech. Adv. Com., 1989—, chmn., 1997; mem. Ill. Ill. Engring. Vis. com., Urbana-Champaign, 1986—95; trustee Tchrs. Acad. for Math. and Sci. Tchrs. in Chgo., 1990—96; bd. visitors astronomy and astrophysics Pa. State U., 1995—; bd. dirs. LaRabida Children's Hosp. and Rsch. Ctr., 1987—95, Children's Meml. Hosp., Children's Meml. Inst. for Edn. and Rsch. Recipient Outstanding Alumni Fellow award, Pa. State U., 1985, laureate, Lincoln Acad. Ill., 1996, Disting. fellow, Poly. U., 1989, Disting. Alumni award, Pa. State U., 2005. Fellow: AAAS (coun. del. chem. sect. 1986—92, sci. engring. and pub. policy com. 1992, standing com. audit 1992, bd. dirs. 1992—96, selection com. to bring FSU scientists to ann. mtg. 1995—), N.Y. Acad. Scis.; mem.: AIChE (award com. 1992—), NAE (adv. com. tech. and soc. 1991—92, mem. program adv. com. 1992—), chair study fgn. participation in U.S. R&D 1993—96, NRC com. on dual use tech. 1996—97, com. to assess policies and practices of Dept. of Energy to design, ma 1998—99), NASA Com. on Aeronautics Innovation Models (chmn. 2003—), Ctr. Strategic and Internat. Studies (sr. action group 1995—96), Indsl. Rsch. Inst. (co-chmn. Nat. Labs. Indsl. Panel 1984—87, fed. adv. com. to Fed. Sci. and Tech. Com. 1992—96, sr. action group on R&D Investment Strategies), Am. Nuc. Soc., Am. Petroleum Inst. (rsch. coord. coun.), Nat. Conf. Advancement Rsch. (conf. com. 1985—, site selection com. 1994, conf. com. 50th ann. 1996), Am. Mgmt. Assn. (R&D coun. 1988—), Am. Chem. Soc. (joint bd. coun. on sci. 1983—87, chmn. petroleum divsn. 1983—91, councilor, com. on chemistry and pub. affairs 1983—91, petroleum chemistry award 1969, 1995—96), Econ. Club, Comml. Club, Cosmos Club, Carleton Club (bd. govs. 1992—), Phi Lambda Upsilon, Sigma Xi. Home: 1440 N Lake Shore Dr Apt 31ac Chicago IL 60610-5927 Office: Argonne Nat Lab 9700 S Cass Ave Argonne IL 60439-4803 Office Phone: 630-252-3872. E-mail: schriesheim@anl.gov.

**SCHRIEVER, FRED MARTIN,** management consultant, financial investor; b. NYC; s. Samuel and Sara S.; m. Cheri G. Spatt; children: Melissa Ann, Elizabeth Ellen. BME, Poly. U. N.Y., 1956, MME, 1958. Registered profl. engr., N.Y., Wash.; cert. mgmt. cons. Chief engr. divsn. Sperry Corp., N.Y.C., 1956-64; ptnr. Booz, Allen and Hamilton, N.Y.C. and Washington, 1964-71; chmn., pres. RCG Internat. Inc., N.Y.C., 1971—96. Investor and cons. in field; dir. Nat. Exec. Svc. Corps., 1998—, Hagler Bailly Inc., 1996-2000. Fellow Inst. of Dirs., Inst. Mgmt. Consultants U.K.; mem. ASME, Inst. Mgmt. Cons., Chemists Club. Home: PO Box 32 Westport CT 06881-0032

**SCHRIVER, JOHN T., III,** lawyer; b. Evanston, Ill., May 18, 1945; AB, Coll. of Holy Cross, 1967; JD, Georgetown U., 1970. Bar: Ill. 1971, Fla. 1972. Ptnr. Duane Morris LLC, Chgo. Mem. ABA, Chgo. Bar Assn., Fla. Bar. Office: Duane Morris LLC 227 W Monroe St Ste 3400 Chicago IL 60606-5096

**SCHROCK, DONALD E.,** communications executive; BSEE, U. Ill.; MSEE, Ariz. State U., degree in bus. adminstrn. Various positions Motorola Semiconductor; v.p., divsn. gen. mgr. Burr-Brown Corp.; past v.p. ops Applied Micro Circuit Corp.; past group v.p., divsn. mgr. Hughes Aircraft Co.

**SCHROCK, RICHARD ROYCE,** chemistry professor; b. Berne, Ind., Jan. 4, 1945; m. Nancy F. Carlson, 1971; children: Andrew, Eric. AB, U. Calif., Riverside, 1967; PhD, Harvard U., 1971. Rsch. chemist, Ctrl. R&D dept. E.I. du Pont de Nemours & Co., Wilmington, Del., 1972-75; asst. prof. MIT, Cambridge, 1975-78, assoc. prof., 1978-80, prof., 1980-89, Frederick G. Keyes prof. chemistry, 1989—. Assoc. editor: Organometallics; contbr. articles to profl. jours. Co-recipient Nobel Prize in Chemistry, 2005; recipient Bailar medal, U. Ill., 1998, Sir Geoffrey Wilkinson medal, Royal Soc. Chemistry, 2002, Sir Edward Frankland prize, 2004, August Wilhelm von Hofmann medal, German Chem. Soc., 2005; NSF postdoctoral fellow, Cambridge U., 1971—72. Mem.: NAS, AAAS, Am. Chem. Soc. (award organometallic chemistry 1985, Harrison Howe award 1990, Humboldt award 1994, award inorganic chemistry 1996, Arthur C. Cope Scholar award 2001, F. Albert Cotton award in Synthetic Inorganic Chemistry 2006), Am. Acad. Arts and Scis. Office: MIT Dept Chemistry Rm 6 331 77 Massachusetts Ave Cambridge MA 02139 Office Phone: 617-253-1596. Office Fax: 617-253-7670. E-mail: rrs@mit.edu.*

**SCHROCK, SIMON,** retail executive; b. Oakland, Md., Dec. 28, 1936; s. Noah and Cora (Burkholder) S.; m. Eva Lena Yoder, June 7, 1959 (dec. Apr. 1962); m. Pauline Yoder, Sept. 29, 1963; children: Janice Yvonne, Eldon Laverne, Ivan Dale. With Eastern States Farm Supply Co., Oakland, Md., 1957-59, Children's Hosp., Washington, 1959-61, Copp Properties, Vienna, Va., 1961-75; pres. Choice Books of No. Va., Fairfax, Va., 1975—. Chmn. Lighthouse Lit., 1976-2001. Author: Get on With Living, 1976, Price of Missing Life, 1981, One-Anothering, 1986, Vow-Keepers Vow-Breakers, A Smoother Journey, 1994, What Shall The Redeemed Wear, 2001, Where Has Integrity Gone, 2001, Don't Throw In the Towel, 2003; contbr. articles to ch. jours. Bishop Faith Christian Fellowship, Catlett, Va., 1981—. Avocations: travel, writing, biking. Office: 10100 Piper Ln Bristow VA 20136 Business E-Mail: schrock@nva.choicebooks.org.

**SCHROCK, THEODORE R.,** surgeon; b. Berne, Ind., Oct. 21, 1939; s. N.J. and M.A. Schrock; married. AB, U. Calif., San Francisco, 1961, MD, 1964. Diplomate Am. Bd. Surgery. Intern U. Calif. Hosps., San Francisco, 1964-65, resident, 1965-67, 69-71; fellow Mass. Gen. Hosp., Boston, 1967-69; chmn. dept. surgery U. Calif. San Francisco Med. Ctr., 1993-99, J. Englebert Dunphy prof. surgery, 1998—, assoc. dean clin. svcs., chief med. officer, 1999—. Fellow ACS; mem. Am. Gastroenterological Assn., Am. Soc. Colon and Rectal Surgery, Am. Soc. Gastroenterological Endoscopy, Am. Surg. Assn., Soc. Surgery Alimentary Tract. Office: UCSF Campus Box 0296 500 Parnassus Ave San Francisco CA 94143-0296*

**SCHRODER, DIETER KARL,** electrical engineering educator; b. Lübeck, Germany, June 18, 1935; arrived in U.S., 1964; s. Wilhelm and Martha (Werner) S.; m. Beverley Claire (Parchment), Aug. 4, 1961; children: Mark, Derek. BS, McGill U., Montreal, Que., Can., 1962, MS, 1964; PhD, U. Ill., 1968. Sr. engr. rsch. and devel. sect. Westinghouse Electric Corp., Pitts., 1968-73; fellow engr. rsch. and devel. sect. Westinghouse Electric Corp., Pitts., 1973-77, adv. engr., 1977-79, mgr., 1979-81; prof. elec. engring. Ariz. State U., 1981—. Rsch. Inst. Solid State Physics, Freiburg, Fed. Republic Germany, 1978-79. Author: Advanced MOS Devices, 1987, Semiconductor Material and Device Characterization, 2006; patentee in electrical field; contbr. articles to profl. jour. Life Fellow IEEE (life, disting. nat. lectr. 1993-2006); mem. Electrochem. Soc., Sigma Xi, Eta Kappa Nu. Mem. Baha'i Faith. Home: 10572 E Firewheel Dr Scottsdale AZ 85255-1911 Office: Ariz State U Dept Elec Engring Tempe AZ 85287-5706 Office Phone: 480-965-6621. Business E-Mail: schroder@asu.edu.

**SCHRODER, JACK SPALDING, JR.,** lawyer; b. Atlanta, July 10, 1948; s. Jack Spalding Sr. and Van (Spalding) S.; m. Karen Keyworth, Sept. 1, 1973; children: Jack Spalding III, James Edward. BA, Emory U., 1970; JD, U. Ga., 1973. Bar: Ga. 1973, U.S. Dist. Ct. (no. dist) Ga. 1973, U.S. Ct. Appeals (11th cir.) 1982. Assoc. Alston & Bird, Atlanta, 1973-78, ptnr., 1978—2003, sr. counsel, 2004—. Author: Credentialing: Strategies for a Changing Environment/BNA's Health Law and Business Series, 1996; co-editor, contbg. author: Georgia Hospital Law manual, 1979, 84, 92. Bd. dirs. Rsch.

Atlanta, 1996-00, pres., 1999, co-chair bd. advisors, 2003—; participant Leadership Ga., Atlanta, 1986. United Way (chmn. legal divsn.), Atlanta, 1980. Decorated comdr. S.E. Commandery Mil. and Hospitaller Order of St. Lazarus of Jerusalem. Mem. ABA (vice chmn. medicine and law com. 1989-90), Am. Health Lawyers Assn. (bd. dirs. 1994-99, chmn. med. staff and physician rels. com. 1991-94, vice chair hosps. and health systems law inst. 2001-), Ga. Acad. Healthcare Attys. (pres. 1981-82), State Bar Ga. (bd. dirs. 1987-89), Atlanta Coun. Younger Lawyers (pres. 1977-78), Atlanta Bar Assn. (pres. 1982-83), Atlanta Bar Found. (pres. 1991-95), Mil. and Hospitaller Order St. Lazarus Jerusalem (comdr. S.E. commandery 2003—). Office: Alston & Bird One Atlantic Ctr 1201 W Peachtree St NW Atlanta GA 30309-3424 Office Phone: 404-881-7685.

**SCHRODER, RICK,** actor; b. SI, NY, Apr. 13, 1970; s. Richard and Diane Schroder; m. Andrea Bernard, Sept. 1992; children: Holden Richard, Luke William, Cambrey, Faith Anne. Attended and majored in Farm and Ranch Mgmt., Mesa State Coll., Grand Junction, Colo. Actor: (films) The Champ, 1979 (Golden Globe award 1979), The Last Flight of Noah's Ark, 1980, The Earthling, 1981, There Goes My Baby, 1994, Crimson Tide, 1995, I Woke Up Early the Day I Died, 1998, Poolhall Junkies, 2002, Consequence, 2003, Face of Terror, 2003; (TV series) Silver Spoons, 1982-86, NYPD Blue, 1998-2001, Strong Medicine, 2005-; (TV movies) Little Lord Fauntleroy, 1980, Something So Right, 1982, Two Kinds of Love, 1983, A Reason to Live, 1985, Hansel and Gretel, 1982, Too Young the Hero, 1988, Terror on Highway 91, 1989, Out on the Edge, 1989, A Son's Promise, 1990, The Stranger Within, 1990, Blood River, 1991, My Son Johnny, 1991, Across the Tracks, 1991, Miles from Nowhere, 1992, Call of the Wild, 1993, To My Daughter with Love, 1994, Innocent Victims, 1996, Too Close to Home, 1997, Detention: The Siege at Johnson High, 1997, Heart Full of Rain, 1997, Ebenezer, 1997, What We Did That Night, 1999, Lost Battalion, 2001, 14 Hours, 2005; (TV mini series) Lonesome Dove, 1989, Return to Lonesome Dove, 1993; (video) Texas, 1994; (TV spls.) The Jimmy McNichol Special, Doug Henning's World of Magic, An Orchestra is a Team, Too, Walt Disney's Tenth Anniversary Special, Battle of the Network Stars, Circus of the Stars, Missing, Have You Seen this Person?, S.O.S., Secrets of Surviving, Kraft Salutes Walt Disney World's 10th Anniversary; actor, writer, dir. (films) Black Cloud, 2004; dir. (music video) "Whiskey Lullaby" (Music Video of Yr., Country Music Assn., 2004, Video Dir. of Yr., Country Music Television Music award, 2005, Video of Yr., Vocal Event of Yr., Acad. Country Music Awards, 2005); guest appearances (TV) Scrubs, 2003. Office: c/o ICM 8942 Wilshire Blvd Beverly Hills CA 90211

**SCHROEDER, BRIAN S.,** philosopher, educator; b. Quantico, Va., June 15, 1959; s. Gary Stephen and Faye Mary (Monette) Schroeder; m. Silvia Benso, June 5, 1999; 1 child, Erik Aren. MA, PhD, Stony Brook U.; MDiv, Princeton Theol. Sem. Prof. philosophy Rochester Inst. Tech., Rochester, 2001—. Coord. religious studies Rochester Inst. Tech. Author: (book) Altared Ground: Levinas, History, and Violence, 1995, Pensare ambientalista: Tra filosofia e ecologia, 2000; editor: Thinking Through the Death of God, 2004, Contemporary Italian Philosophy: Crossing the Borders of Ethics, Politics, and Religion, 2006; co-editor: SUNY Series Contemproary Italian Philosophy, 2005—; editor: (journal) Studies in Practical Philosophy. Fellow: J. William Fulbright Scholarship Commn., 2000—01; Miller Rsch. Fellowship, Rochester Inst. of Technology, 2003—04, Sr. Fellowship in Religion and Soc., Princeton Theol. Sem., 1984. Mem.: Levinas Rsch. Seminar (co-dir. 2003—04), Wisdom Rendezvous (bd. dirs. 1992—), Found. for the Philosophy of Creativity (exec. bd. 2000—), Internat. Soc. for Universal Dialogue (treas. 2001—03), Soc. for the Philosophy of Creativity (v.p. ea. divsn. 2000—), Nietzsche Soc. (exec. com. 2001—04), Soc. for Phenomenology and Existential Philosophy, Am. Acad. of Religion, Am. Philos. Assn., Internat. Assn. for Environ. Philosophy (chmn. bd. dirs. 2002—). Independent. Office Phone: 585-475-6346.

**SCHROEDER, DAVID J. DEAN,** psychologist; b. Hutchinson, Kans., Mar. 21, 1942; s. D.J.W. and Louise (Wedel) S.; m. Nevonna Joyce Thomas, May 24, 1964; children: Taryn Dee Schroeder Dye, Anita Joy Fitch. BA, Tabor Coll., 1964; MS, Kans. State Tchrs. Coll., 1967; PhD, U. Okla., 1971. Lic. psychologist, Kans. Rsch. psychologist Civil Aerospace Med. Inst., Oklahoma City, 1970-72, clin. rsch. psychologist, 1980-89, supr., 1989-90, mgr. human factors rsch. lab., 1990-91, mgr. aerospace human factors rsch. divsn., 1991—; intern Norfolk (Nebr.) Regional Ctr., 1972-73; clin. psychologist VA Hosp., Murfreesboro, Tenn., 1973-75, Topeka, 1975-80. Co-author: FAA Employee Survey: National Report, 1984, 86, FAA Employee Survey: Regional/Center Reports, 1984, 86, FAA Job Satisfaction Survey National Report, 1988, FAA Job Satisfaction Survey: Regional/Center/Work Group Reports, 1988; mem. adv. editl. bd. Aviation Space and Environ. Medicine, 1993-95, 99-2001. Mem. senate adv. com. Tabor Coll., Hillsboro, Kans., 1987-89; Christian edn. com. conv. So. Dist. Conf. Mennonite Brethren Ch., Hillsboro, 1989; Sunday Sch. tchr. Western Oaks Christian Ch., Oklahoma City, 1990—. Fellow APA, Aerospace Med. Assn. (chmn. sci. program com. 1990-91, mem. coun. 1992-95, v.p 1996-97, v.p. edn. and rsch. 1999-2002, pres.-elect 2002-03, pres. 2003-04, program com. chair APA divsn. applied exptl. and engring. psychology 1996-97, sec.-treas. 1998-2001, pres.-elect 2001-02, pres. 2002-03, chmn. aerospace human factors com. 1999-2002, Raymond F. Longacre award for outstanding accomplishmnts in psychol. and psychiat. aspects of aerospace medicine 1997), Aerospace Human Factors Assn. (pres. 1994-95), Henry L. Taylor Founders award 2001); mem. Okla. Psychol. Assn. (bd. dirs. 1988-89, pres.-elect 1991, pres. 1992), Internat. Acad. Aviation and Space Medicine. Democrat. Achievements include research in assessing the interactive effects of alcohol, age and drugs on dynamic tracking and cognitive performance, personality characteristics and training success of air traffic control students, biofeedback anxiety and humans in government employees, human factors of air traffic control operational errors, fatigue and shiftwork. Home: 2601 NW 23rd St Oklahoma City OK 73107-2209 Office: PO Box 25082 Oklahoma City OK 73125-0082 Personal E-mail: davids20@cox.net.

**SCHROEDER, DOUGLAS FREDRICK,** architect; b. Omaha, June 12, 1935; s. Walter Elmer and Ellen Ruth (Niles) S.; m. Joanne Vlecides, July 5, 1980. B.Arch., U. Mich., 1959. Registered Architect, Ill., N.C., Mich. Designer, draftsman C.F. Murphy Assocs., Chgo., 1959-63; architect, sr. architect Skidmore, Owings & Merrill, Chgo., 1964-67; architect, ptnr. Schroeder, Yamamoto & Schreiber, Chgo., 1968-69; ptnr. Hinds & Schroeder, Ltd., Chgo., 1972-74; propr. Douglas Schroeder Assocs., Chgo., 1974-83, 93—; ptnr. Siegel & Schroeder, P.C., Chgo., 1983-91; dir. SGA Planning and Constrn. Cons. Co. div. Goforth Group, Chgo., 1991-93; v.p. Yacht Harbor Mgmt. Co., South Haven, Mich., 1983-88. Dir. Inland Architect Mag. Contbr. articles to profl. jours. Bd. dirs. Chgo. Archtl. Assistance Ctr., 1982-84; chmn. Mass. Transp. Crisis Com., Chgo., 1973, Ill. Futures Forum, 1976-77; pres. Ill. Planning and Conservation League, Chgo., 1971-74. Named Outstanding Alumnus Lake Superior State U., 1971. Fellow AIA; mem. Arbitration Assn. (arbitrator) Clubs: Cliff Dwellers (dir. 1971-74). Unitarian Universalist. Home: 700 W Irving Park Rd Apt 4A Chicago IL 60613-3133 Office: Douglas Schroeder Assocs Arch & Planners 980 N Michigan Ave Ste 1277 Chicago IL 60611-4523 E-mail: dschroeder@dsa-architects.com

**SCHROEDER, EDMUND R.,** lawyer; b. NYC, Feb. 6, 1933; s. Robert C. and Rose A. (Garramone) S.; m. Elaine P. Diserio, Jan. 21, 1961; children: Edmund Jr., Christopher, Elizabeth. AB cum laude, Harvard U., 1953, LLB, 1958. Assoc. Archibald R. Graustein, N.Y.C., 1958-61, Rovett, Barrett, Cohen, Knapp & Smith, N.Y.C., 1961-67; ptnr. Barrett Knapp Smith & Schapiro, N.Y.C., 1967-88, Lord Day & Lord/Barrett Smith, N.Y.C., 1988-94, Cadwalader, Wickersham & Taft, N.Y.C., 1994-2000, sr. counsel, 2000—. Mem. adv. com. Commodity Futures Trading Commn. on Definition and Regulation of Market Instruments, 1975-76. Contbr. articles to profl. jours. Bd. dirs. Orch. St. Luke's N.Y.C., 1987-2005, chmn. exec. com., 1993-95; trustee The United Way of Scarsdale-Edgemont, 1990-92; mem. Scarsdale Bd. Edn., 1976-79; co-founder, 1st chmn. Edn. Through Music, Inc., N.Y.C., 1991—; trustee Hoff-Barthelson Music Sch., Scarsdale, 1974—, chmn. bd., 1986-90, hon. chmn., 1990—; trustee The Nat. Guild Cmty. Schs. Arts, Englewood,

N.J., 1992-96; bd. advisors Sacred Heart/Mt. Carmel Sch. for Arts, Mt. Vernon, 1995-97; arbitrator Am. Arbitration Assn., Nat. Futures Assn. Mem.: ABA (chmn. com. futures regulation 1981—85), N.Y. State Bar Assn. (com. comty. and futures law and regulation 1996—), Bar Assn. City of N.Y. (founder, 1st chmn. com. futures regulation 1976—). Office: Cadwalader Wickersham & Taft One World Financial Center New York NY 10281 Office Phone: 212-504-6916. Business E-mail: edmund.schroeder@cwt.com.

SCHROEDER, EILEEN ELIZABETH, education educator; b. Allentown, Pa., June 6, 1955; d. Randall Wisser and Betty Mae (Baker) S. BS in Edn., Kutztown State Coll., 1977; MS in Libr. and Info. Sci., Drexel U., 1982; MA in Ednl. Founds., U. N.Mex., 1987; MS, Syracuse U., 1992; PhD in Instructional Systems, Pa. State U., 1993. Cert. sch. libr. media specialist. Libr. Drum Point Elem. Sch., Brick Town, N.J., 1977-82; dir. Tireman Learning Materials Libr., U. N.Mex., Albuquerque, 1983-85; teaching materials reference/bibliographer SUNY, Cortland, 1985-89, 91; asst. prof. ednl. founds. U. Wis., Whitewater, 1990—2000, assoc. prof., 2000—. Mem. ALA, Assn. for Ednl. Comms. and Tech. (Dean and Sybil McCluskey award 1993), Am. Assn. Sch. Librs., Wis. Ednl. Media Assn. Office: U Wis Ednl Founds 1005 Winther Hall Whitewater WI 53190

SCHROEDER, FRED ERICH HARALD, humanities educator; b. Manitowoc, Wis., June 3, 1932; s. Alfred William and Sissel Marie (Lovell) S.; m. Janet June Knope, Aug. 21, 1954; 1 child, Erich Karl. BS, U. Wis., 1960; MA, U. Minn., 1963, PhD, 1968. Elementary sch. tchr. various locations, Wis., 1952-60; asst. prof. English U. Minn., Duluth, 1968-71, assoc. prof. English, 1971-74, prof. behavioral sci., 1977-82, prof. humanities, 1974-96, dir. Ctr. for Am. Studies, 1986-87, dir. Interdisciplinary Studies, 1987-90, dir. dept. humanities and classics, 1989-90, dir. grad. liberal studies, 1992-95, prof. emeritus, 1996—. Author: Joining the Human Race: How To Teach Humanities, 1972, Outlaw Aesthetics: Arts and the Public Mind, 1977, Front Yard America: The Evolution and Meanings of a Domestic Vernacular Landscape, 1993; co-author: Encyclopedia of Modern Everyday Inventions, 2003; editor Interdisciplinary Humanities (formerly Humanities Edn. jour.), 1983-95, assoc. editor, 1995—; editor 5000 Years of Popular Culture, 1980, 20th Century Popular Culture in Museums and Libraries, 1981; lectr., writer Nat. Humanities Series, 1969-71; adv. editor Guide to U.S. Popular Culture, 2001. Mem. Minn. Humanities Commn., 1985-90. Woodrow Wilson Nat. Found. fellow, 1960-61, dissertation fellow 1963; NEH scholar, 1969-70; Inst. for Human Values in Medicine fellow, 1976. Mem. Am. Culture Assn. (pres. 1984-87), Nat. Assn. Humanities Edn. (pres. 1987-89, exec. sec.-treas. 1989-96), Am. Assn. for State and Local History (seminar instr. 1978-82), Popular Culture Assn. Avocations: collecting art, woodworking, gardening. Home: 5756 N Shore Dr Duluth MN 55804-9660 E-mail: fschroed@d.umn.edu.

SCHROEDER, GERALD FRANK, state supreme court chief justice; b. Boise, Idaho, Sept. 13, 1939; s. Frank Frederick and Josephine Ivy (Lucas) S.; children: Karl Casteel, Erich Frank. BA magna cum laude, Coll. of Idaho (now Albertson Coll. of Idaho), 1961; JD, Harvard U., 1964. Bar: Idaho 1965. Assoc. Moffatt, Thomas, Barrett & Blanton, Boise, 1965—66; pvt. practice Boise, 1966—67; asst. U.S. atty. Dept. Justice, Boise, 1967—69; judge Ada County Probate Ct., Boise, 1969—71; magistrate State of Idaho, Boise, 1971—75; dist. judge U.S. Dist. Ct. (4th dist.) Idaho, 1975—95; justice Idaho Supreme Ct., 1995—, chief justice, 2004—. Instr. Boise Bar Rev., 1973—; adj. faculty law Boise State U., 1986—95; former mem. Gov. Coun. on Crime and Delinquency. Author: Idaho Probate Procedure, 1971, (Novel) Triangle of the Sons-Phenomena, 1983; contbr. chpt. to history text. Adminstrv. and dist. judge 4th dist. State of Idaho, 1985—95; Bd. dirs. Boise Philharm. Assn., 1979—81. Football Tod fellow, Nat. Coun. State Govt., 1990. Mem.: Idaho Bar Assn., Boise Racquet and Swim Club (pres. bd. dirs. 1991—93). Office Phone: 208-334-3324. Business E-mail: gschroeder@isc.state.io.us.*

SCHROEDER, HERMAN ELBERT, scientific consultant; b. Bklyn., July 6, 1915; s. Henry W. and Caroline (Schmidt) S.; m. Elizabeth Barnes, June 13, 1938 (dec. July 27, 2002); children: Nancy Schroeder Tarczy (dec.), Edward L., Peter H., Martha L. Schroeder Lewis. AB summa cum laude, Harvard, 1936, A.M., 1937, PhD, 1939. With E.I. du Pont de Nemours & Co., Wilmington, Del., 1938-80, asst. dir. R&D, 1957-63, dir. R&D, 1963-80; pres. Schroeder Sci. Svcs., Inc., 1980—. cons. Met. Mus. Art, N.Y.C., Smithsonian Instn., Winterthur Mus. Mem. Chester County Sch. Bd., Unionville, Pa., 1950-56; pres. Assn. Harvard Chemists, 1955-57; mem. vis. com. Harvard Chemistry Dept., 1960-72; mem. sci. adv. com. Winterthur Mus.; trustee, chmn. research com. U. Del. Research Found., 1976-84, former v.p. Recipient award Internat. Inst. Synthetic Rubber Producers, 1979, Lavoisier medal DuPont, 1992, Disting. Achievment award PolyPrep, N.Y.C., 1997. Mem. AAAS, Am. Chem. Soc. (Charles Goodyear medal 1984), N.Y. Acad. Scis., Phi Beta Kappa, Alpha Chi Sigma. Home and Office: 74 Stonegates 4031 Kennett Pike Greenville DE 19807-2033 Personal E-mail: her2schro@aol.com. *A life in industrial research has been for me both challenging and rewarding. Forces which impel me are largely the compulsion to look for the new, to change for the better, be it by finding better ways to do things or by inventing products to make the world function better. Gratifyingly, these often make the world aesthetically more pleasant and sometimes cleaner. I am concerned by the growing hostility of society to science and to developments that ensure a more comfortable life and safer food and energy than would otherwise be possible.*

SCHROEDER, JAMES EDWARD, minister, consultant; m. Amanda Arn, Jan. 18, 1998; children: David Webb, Robert. BA in Philosophy and Religion, Richard Stockton Coll., Pomona, NJ, 1994; MA, Asbury Theol. Sem., Wilmore, Ky., 1997; MDiv, United Theol. Sem., Dayton, Ohio, 1998. Pastor Decatur and Mt. Olivet United Meth. Ch., Decatur, Ohio, 1995—98; sr. pastor Indian Mills United Meth. Ch., Shamong, NJ, 1998—2001; asst. to the pres. Circleville (Ohio) Bible Coll., 2001—04; pres. The Rison Group, Indian Mills, NJ, 2002—; devel. officer World Gospel Mission, Marion, Ind., 2005; founding pastor Crossroads Ch., Indian Mills, 2005—. Dir. Delanco Holiness Camp Meeting, Tabernacle, NJ, 1998—. Contbg. author: (devotional) Reflections. Recipient Cmty. Svc. award, Richard Stockton Coll. Mem.: Ky. Cols. (hon.). Avocations: rugby, reading. Home and Office: Crossroads Evang Cmty Ch 6A Oakview Rd Indian Mills NJ 08088

SCHROEDER, JAMES WHITE, retired lawyer; b. Elmhurst, Ill., Apr. 19, 1936; s. Paul W. and Thelma C. (White) S.; m. Patricia N. Scott, Aug. 18, 1962; children: Scott W. and Jamie C. BA, Princeton U., 1958; JD, Harvard U., 1964. Bar: Colo. 1964, U.S. Ct. Colo. 1964, U.S. Ct. Appeals (10th cir.) 1965, U.S. Supreme Ct. 1972, U.S. Dist. Ct. D.C. 1973, U.S. Ct. Appeals (D.C. cir.) 1974, U.S. Ct. Appeals (8th cir.) 1977, U.S. Ct. Appeals (3d cir.) 1981, U.S. Claims Ct. 1983, U.S. Ct. Appeals (fed. cir.) 1983. Ptnr. Mosley, Wells & Schroeder, Denver, 1965-72, Kaplan Russin & Vecchi, Washington, 1973-92; counsel Whitman & Ransom, Washington, 1992-93; dep. asst. sec. U.S. Dept. Agr., 1993-2001. Arbitrator Am. Arbitration Assn. Active Ams. for Democratic Action, Smithsonian Instn.; bd. trustees Orlando Opera, 2003—. Lt. USNR, 1958-64. Am. Field Svc. scholar, 1953, NROTC scholar, 1954. Mem. ABA, Fed. Bar Assn., Denver Bar Assn., Colo. Bar Assn., D.C. Bar Assn., Cap and Gown Club, Lincoln's Inn Club, Tennis City Club Denver (pres. 1972), Princeton Club Washington (pres. 1982-84). Democrat. Home: 621 Nadina Pl Celebration FL 34747

SCHROEDER, JOHN A., systems engineering consultant, educator; s. John Bruno and Gertrude Dorothy Schroeder; m. Joanne Louise Galt, Mar. 2, 1985; children: Sarah Louise, Jeanette Lynne. BS, Purdue U., Lafayette, Ind., 1963; MS, U. Calif., Berkeley, 1964. Cert. advanced comms. sys. engring. U. Calif., Irvine. Sr. engr. Rockwell Internat., Anaheim, Calif., 1970—80; sys. engr. Boeing Co., San Beach, Calif., 1980—98, dir. sys. engring. Huntington Beach, Calif., 2000—04; COO Maxsys Tech., Irvine, Calif., 1998—2000; sr. cons. Booz Allen Hamilton, LA, 2004—; part time lectr. U. So. Calif., LA, 2005—; pres. Skill Sessions Seminars, Lake Forest, Calif., 1992—96. Mem. City Redevelopment Coun., Huntington Beach, Calif., 1980, 1981; angel

supporter Fred Jordan Mission, LA, 2005. Mem.: Internat. Coun. on Sys. Engring., Am. Mensa. Avocation: Bible study. Home: 22621 Manalastas Dr Lake Forest CA 92630 Personal E-mail: jschroeder@mail.com.

SCHROEDER, JOHN H., university chancellor; b. Twin Falls, Idaho, Sept. 13, 1943; s. Herman John and Azalia (Kimes) S.; m. Sandra Barrow; children: John Kimes, Andrew Barrow. BA, Lewis and Clark Coll., Portland, Oreg., 1965; MA, U. Va., 1967, PhD, 1971. Instr. history U. Wis., Milw., 1970-71, asst. prof., 1971-76, assoc. prof., 1976-86, prof., 1986—, Am. Coun. on Edn. fellow, 1982-83, assoc. dean, 1976-82, asst. to vice chancellor, 1982-85, acting vice chancellor, 1985-87, vice chancellor, 1987-90, chancellor, 1990-98, U. Wis. sys. prof., 1998—. Louis M. Sears Meml. lectr. Purdue U., 1978. Author: Mr. Polk's War: American Opposition and Dissent, 1973, The Commercial and Diplomatic Role of the American Navy 1829-1861, 1985, Matthew C. Perry: Antebellum Sailor and Diplomat, 2001 (Theodore and Franklin Roosevelt Naval History prize 2002, John Lyman Naval History award 2002). V.p. bd. dir. John Michael Kohler Arts Ctr.; bd. dir. Wis. Hist. Soc., We. Golf Assn. Recipient Edward and Rosa Uhrig award U. Wis.-Milw., 1974, Disting. Teaching award AMOCO/U. Wis.-Milw., 1975. Mem. Orgn. Am. Historians, Soc. for History of Early Republic, Soc. for History Am. Fgn. Rels. Office: U Wis Dept History PO Box 413 2310 E Hartford Ave Milwaukee WI 53211-3165 Office Phone: 414-229-4976. E-mail: jhs@uwm.edu.

SCHROEDER, JOYCE KATHERINE, state agency administrator, research analyst; b. Moline, Ill., Apr. 1, 1951; d. Reinhold J. and Miriam May (Schroeder). BS in Math., U. Ill., Champaign-Urbana, 1973; MA in Ops. rsch., U. Ill., Springfield, 1978. Underwriter, programmer, Springfield, Ill., 1973—76; ops. rsch. analyst Ill. Dept. Transp., Springfield, 1976—78, data analyst, 1978—80, team leader, fatal accident reporting sys., 1980—83, mgr. safety project evaluation, 1983—92, mgr. accident studies and investigation, 1992—. Sys. engring. del. to China, China Assn. Sci. and Tech., 1986; mem. staff Driving While Intoxicated Adv. Coun. and Task Force, State of Ill., 1983-86, 89-92, Gov. Task Force on Occupant Protection, 1988-90; Ill. Traffic Safety Info. Sys. Coun., 1993-95; mem. safety engring. tech. adv. group Ill. Ctr. Transp., 2005—; mem. Ill. Traffic Records Coord. Com., 2004-. Vol. Animal Protective League, Springfield; leader bd., co-chair LPGA Rail Classic, Springfield, 1983-87. Named to Pres.'s Coun., U. Ill., 2004. Mem.: Ill. Traffic Safety Leaders, N. Am. Conf. Lions Found. (ann. conf. steering com. 2001—03, bd. dir., treas. 2005—), Past Dist. Gov. Assn. (sec.-treas. 1993—), Lions of Ill. Endowment Fund (trustee 1998—99, coord. meml. and endowments 1999—), Springfield Lincoln Land Lions Club (charter pres. 1988—90, treas. 1993—95, news editor 1995—, treas. 2002—), Lions Ill. Found. (amb. goodwill 1993, trustee 1995—99, treas. found. bd. 1996—97, v.p. found. bd. 1997—98, chmn. long range planning com. 1997—, pres. found. bd. 1998—99, policy ad hoc com. 1999—, chmn. policy ad hoc com. 2002—, fellow 1995, fellow laureate 2002, Disting. Svc. award 2003), Internat. Assn. Lions Clubs (dist. Gov. Ill. 1992—93, state membership coord. 1994—96, Melvin Jones fellow 1993), Kappa Delta Pi, Phi Kappa Phi. Avocations: travel, dogs, music, sports, humanitarian service. Office: Ill Dept Transp 3215 Exec Pk Dr Springfield IL 62703-4514 Personal E-mail: jksplus3@sbcglobal.net.

SCHROEDER, JULIAN IVAN, biology professor; b. Summit, N.J., June 11, 1958; s. Manfred Robert and Anny (Menschik) S.; m. Marianne G. Spors, Aug. 9, 1991; children: Julia Sofia K., Nicola A.J. Dr. rer. nat., U. Gottingen, Max Planck Inst., 1987. Postdoctoral rsch. dept. physiology UCLA Sch. Medicine, 1988-90; from asst. to prof. dept. biology U. Calif. San Diego, La Jolla, 1990-2000, Novartis Endowed chair in plant scis., 2000—. Dir. U. Calif. San Diego Plant Sys. Biology Grad. Tng. Program, La Jolla, 2005—. Contbr. articles to profl. jours. Named Highly Cited Rschr., Inst. for Sci. Info., 2002; recipient Heinz Meier Leibnitz prize, Deutsche Forschungs Gemeinschaft, 1984, Presdl. Young Investigator award NSF, 1991, Blasker award in environ. sci. and engring., San Diego Found., 2001; vis. scholar guest prof., ETH Zurich, 2005; Alexander von Humboldt fellow, 1988, 1996. Mem. Biophys. Soc., Am. Assn. Plant Biologists (Charles Albert Shull award 1997). Achievements include identification of ion channels in higher plant cells, characterization of their functions and regulation in membrane signal transduction; cloning and functional roles of mineral nutrient and heavy metal transport and detoxifying enzymes in plants. Office: U Calif San Diego Div Biology Ctr Molec Gene 9500 Gilman Dr La Jolla CA 92093-0116 Office Phone: 858-534-7759. Business E-mail: jischroeder@ucsd.edu.

SCHROEDER, KENNETH L., electronics executive; b. 1946; BSEE, U. Wis.; MBA, U. Pa. Gen. mgr. constrn. sys. divsn. Spectra-Physics; ops. mgr. computer group Hewlett-Packard; pres., COO Genus, Inc.; various KLA-Tencor Corp., San Jose, Calif., pres., COO, 1991-99, CEO, 1999—. Bd. dirs. SEMI, GaSonics Internat. Office: KLA Tencor Corp 160 Rio Robles San Jose CA 95134 Fax: 408-875-3030.

SCHROEDER, MARVIS LYNN, accountant, artist; b. Gary, Ind., June 19, 1946; d. William Isaac and Leva Marcella (Pierce) Marlatt; m. Douglas Eugene Testerman (div.); 1 child, Tiffany Lynn Courtois; m. Charles Edward Schroeder, July 19, 1988. BS in Art Edn., Ind. U., 1969, MSBA, 1984; MA in Spl. Edn., U. Wyo., 1975. Cert. in Acctg., 1992; tchr. Wyo., Ind., Calif. Tchr. Glasgow AFB (Mont.) Jr. High, 1967-68; tchr. art and spl. edn. Cheyenne (Wyo.) Pub. Schs., 1969—71; tchr. spl. edn. NW Ind. Spl. Edn. Coop., Crown Point, 1974—80; tchr. learning disabilities Riverside (Calif.) Schs., 1980—81; tchr. art Hobart (Ind.) Schs., 1981—84; group mgr. softlines Zayre, Merrillville, Ind., 1985; fin. aid counselor Ind. U., Northwest Gary, 1986—2001; acct. Harold Sullivan CPA, Portage, Ind., 2001—03. Exhibitions include Portage Sr. Artists Exhibit, 2002, 2003, 2004, 2005, 2006, Art Barn Gallery, Valparaiso, Ind., 2004, Porter County Administrn. Ctr., Valparaiso, 2005, Chesterton Women's Art Ctr., Ind., 2003, 2005, 1st United Meth. Ch., Valparaiso Art Acad. Gallery, 2005. Mem.: Illiana Artists Assn., Chesterton Art Ctr. Home: 2527 Pryor Rd Portage IN 46368

SCHROEDER, MARY MURPHY, federal judge; b. Boulder, Colo., Dec. 4, 1940; d. Richard and Theresa (Kahn) Murphy; m. Milton R. Schroeder, Oct. 15, 1965; children: Caroline Theresa, Katherine Emily. BA, Swarthmore Coll., 1962; JD, U. Chgo., 1965. Bar: Ill. 1966, D.C. 1966, Ariz. 1970. Trial atty. Dept. Justice, Washington, 1965—69; law clk. to Hon. Jesse Udall Ariz. Supreme Ct., 1970; mem. Lewis and Roca, Phoenix, 1971—75; judge Ariz. Ct. Appeals, Phoenix, 1975—79, U.S. Ct. Appeals (9th cir.), Phoenix, 1979—2000, chief judge, 2000—. Vis. instr. Ariz. State U. Coll. Law, 1976—78. Contbr. articles to profl. jours. Recipient Disting. Achievement award, Ariz. State U. Coll. of Public Programs; mem. ABA (Margaret Brent award 2001), Am. Judicature Soc., Am. Law Inst. (coun. mem.), Fed. Bar Assn., Ariz. Bar Assn. (James A. Walsh Outstanding Jurist award 2004), Soroptimists. Office: US Ct Appeals 9th Cir US Courthouse Ste 610 401 W Washington St SPC-54 Phoenix AZ 85003-2156 Fax: 602-322-7320. E-mail: mary_schroeder@ca9.uscourts.gov.*

SCHROEDER, MICHELLE SHAWN, agricultural studies educator; d. Robert Earl and Mary Patricia Schroeder; m. Tomas Bolivar Moreno, Mar. 16, 2002; 1 child, Miguel Sebastian Schroeder Moreno. PhD, U. Miami, Fla., 2003. Tchg. asst. prof. NC State U., Raleigh, 2004—06, asst. prof., 2006—. Master: Sigma Alpha (exec. advisor 2006—); mem.: Ecol. Soc. Am., N.Am. Colls. and Tchrs. of Agr. (assoc.). Democrat. Roman Catholic. Avocations: travel, reading, gardening. Office: NC State U Crop Sci Campus Box 7620 Raleigh NC 27695-7620 Office Phone: 919-513-0085. E-mail: michelle_schroeder@ncsu.edu.

SCHROEDER, PATRICIA SCOTT, trade association administrator, former congresswoman; b. Portland, Oreg., July 30, 1940; d. Lee Combs and Bernice (Lemoin) Scott; m. James White Schroeder, Aug. 18, 1962; children: Scott William, Jamie Christine. BA magna cum laude, U. Minn., 1961; JD, Harvard U., 1964. Bar: Colo. 1964. Field atty. NLRB, Denver, 1964-66; practiced in Denver, 1966-72; mem. faculty U. Denver, 1969-72, C.C. Denver, 1969-70,

Regis Coll., Denver, 1970-72; hearing officer Colo. Dept. Personnel, 1971-72; mem. 93d-104th Congresses from 1st Colo. dist., Washington, 1973-96; co-chmn. Congl. Caucus for Women's Issues, 1976-96; prof. Woodrow Wilson Sch. of Pub. and Internat. Affairs Princeton U., 1997; pres., CEO Assn. Am. Pubs., Washington, 1997—. Mem. Nat. Security Com.; dean Congl. Women; chair Ho. Select Com. Children, Youth and Families, 1991—93. Author: Champion of the Great American Family, 1989, 24 Years of House Work and the Place is Still a Mess: My Life in Politics, 1998. Bd. dirs. Marguerite Casey Found. Named to Nat. Women's Hall of Fame, 1995. Congregationalist. Office: Assn Am Publishers 50 F St NW Fl 4 Washington DC 20001-1530 Office Phone: 202-347-3375. Business E-mail: pschroeder@publishers.org.

SCHROEDER, PAUL J., JR., lawyer; b. Mo., 1947; BA magna cum laude, U. Notre Dame, 1969; JD, Washington U., 1972. Bar: Mo. 1972. Ptnr. Bryan Cave, St. Louis; vice-pres., sec. and gen. counsel Dillard's Inc., Little Rock. Mem. ABA. Office: Dillard's Inc PO Box 486 1600 Cantrell Rd Little Rock AR 72203-0486

SCHROEDER, RAYMOND ERNEST, educational administrator; b. South Bend, Ind., Dec. 8, 1949; s. Marvin Klopsch and Jean (Hirsch) S.; m. Gail Arnsdorf, Mar. 5, 1977; children: Geneva Marie, Mary Lynn. BA in Speech, Augustana Coll., Rock Island, Ill., 1970; MS in Radio-TV, U. Ill., 1972. Reporter Sta. WOWO, Ft. Wayne, Ind., 1969; gen. mgr. Sta. WVIK, Rock Island, 1970; news reporter Sta. WILL-AM-FM, Urbana, Ill., 1971-74; instr. radio-TV U. Ill., Urbana, 1975-77; asst. prof. communication Sangamon State U., Springfield, Ill., 1977-83, assoc. prof. comm., 1983-95, dir. TV Office, 1984-97, faculty assoc. to v.p. for acad. affairs, 1984-94; prof. comm. U. Ill., Springfield, 1995—; interim exec. dir. Inst. for Pub. Affairs, 1992-93; dir. office of technology & advanced learning Sangamon State U., 1997—. Part-time photographer Sta. WAND-TV, Decatur, Ill., 1975-77; coordinator community access Dimension Cable, Springfield, 1984-97. Editor, cons. TV documentary Breadbasket or Dustbowl, 1983; tech. cons. TV documentary Illinois Prairies: Sense of Place, 1986; co-dir. TV documentary Mr. Lincoln of Illinois, 1986 (Spl. Achievement award 1987); creative cons. TV documentary The Lincolns of Springfield, Illinois, 1990 (Spl. Achievement award 1991). V.p. Holy Spirit Frat., 1986-87. Grantee Ill. State Bd. Edn., 1994, Application of Learning Technologies to Higher Edn., 1995; recipient Finalist award Nat. Fedn. Local Cable Programmers, 1987, 88, 93. Mem. Internat. TV Assn., Broadcast Edn. Assn., Sangamon State U. Faculty Union (pres. 1993). Roman Catholic. Avocations: running, bicycling. Office: U Ill at Springfield Shepherd Rd Springfield IL 62794 Office Phone: 217-206-7531. Business E-Mail: schroeder.ray@uis.edu.

SCHROEDER, STEPHANIE LYNN, human resources specialist, director; b. Chgo., Jan. 28, 1962; d. Richard Thomas and Phyllis Mae (Helfers) Zeek; m. Joseph James Schroeder, Aug. 3, 1985; children: Nicholas Scott, Natalie Mae. BA, U. Mo., Columbia, 1984; MEd, U. Fla., Gainesville, 1990. Cert. profl. in human resources. Mgr. tchr. edn. ctr. fiscal system Coll. Edn. U. Fla., Gainesville, 1986-89, asst. dir. extended svcs. Coll. Edn., 1989-90; human resource coord. Carter Presidential Ctr., Atlanta, 1991—95; human resources dir. dept. surgery, neurosurgery, orthop. surgery, transplant and urology U. Mich. Health Sys., 1995—. Vol. VA Hosp., Columbia, 1980-81, March of Dimes, Gainesville, 1986-89, Atlanta Project, 1992-95; bd. dir. Midwest Fin. Credit Union, 2002—. Mem. ASTD, Counselor Edn. Student Assn. (activities dir. Gainesville chpt. 1988-90), German/Slavic Club (v.p. Columbia chpt. 1982-83, pres. 1983-84), Fla. Assn. Staff Devel., Soc. for Human Resource Mgmt., Jaycees, Emory U. Women's Club, Phi Delta Kappa, Kappa Delta Pi, Chi Sigma Iota. Methodist. Avocations: water-skiing, volleyball, reading, walking, travel. Home: 10870 Reynard Rd Brighton MI 48114-9031 Office Phone: 734-615-0867. Business E-Mail: sschroed@umich.edu.

SCHROEDER, STEVEN ALFRED, medical educator; b. NYC, July 26, 1939; s. Arthur Edward and Norma (Scheinberg) Schroeder; m. Sally B. Ross, Oct. 21, 1967; children: David Arthur, Alan Ross. BA, Stanford U., 1960; MD, Harvard U., 1964; LHD (hon.), Rush U., 1994; DSc (hon.), Boston U., 1996, U. Mass. Med. Ctr., 1997, Georgetown U., 2000; DSc, Med. Coll. Wis., 2002; DHL (hon.), U. Medicine Dentistry NJ, 2003. Diplomate Am. Bd. Internal Medicine. Intern and resident in internal medicine Harvard Med. Svc., Boston City Hosp., 1964—66, 1968—70; asst. prof., then assoc. prof. George Washington Med. Ctr., Washington, 1971—76; vis. prof. St. Thomas' Hosp. Med. Sch., London, 1982—83; prof. medicine, chief div. gen. internal medicine, mem. Inst. Health Policy Studies U. Calif., San Francisco, 1976—90; pres., CEO Robert Wood Johnson Found., Princeton, NJ, 1990—2002; clin. prof. medicine U. of Medicine and Dentistry N.J., 1990—2002; disting. prof. health and health care U. Calif., San Francisco, 2003—, dir. smoking cessation leadership ctr., 2003—. Conv. various govtl. and philanthropic health orgns.; chair internat. adv. com. faculty medicine Ben Gurion U., Israel. Sr. editor: Current Med. Diagnosis and Treatment, 1987—93, mem. editl. bd.: New Eng. Jour. Medicine Mag.; contbr. numerous articles to profl. jours. Mem. U.S. Prospective Payment Assessment Commn., 1983—88; bd. overseers Harvard Coll., 2000—06; bd. dirs. Am. Legacy Found., 2000—05, vice chair, 2001—03, chair, 2003—05; bd. dirs. Save Ellis Island, 2002—; dir. James Irvine Found., Charles R. Drew U. Medicine and Sci., 2005—. Named a Nat. Pub. Health Hero, U. Calif. Berkeley, 2004. Master: ACP; mem.: APHA, Albany Med. Ctr. (Medicine prize 2000—), Soc. Gen. Internal Medicine (past pres.), Inst. Medicine, Assn. Am. Physicians, Physicians for Social Responsibility, Harvard Med. Alumni Assn. (pres.), Alpha Omega Alpha, Phi Beta Kappa. Office: U Calif San Francisco 3333 California St Ste 430 San Francisco CA 94143-1211 Office Phone: 415-502-1881. Business E-Mail: schroeder@medicine.ucsf.edu.

SCHROEDER, THOMAS D., lawyer; b. Atlanta, May 26, 1959; Attended, Conservatory of Music, U. Cin., 1977—78; BS, U. Kans., 1981; JD, Notre Dame Law Sch., 1984. Bar: NC 1984. Jud. clerk for Hon. George E. MacKinnon US Ct. Appeals (DC Cir.) 1984—85; practice group leader, product liability practice group Womble Carlyle Sandridge & Rice, PLLC, Winston-Salem, NC, 1994—2002, mem. firm mgmt. com., 1996—, vice chmn. firm mgmt. com., 2005. Lectr. in field; faculty, trial tng. program Womble Carlyle Sandridge & Rice, PLLC, Winston-Salem, NC. Editor-in-chief Notre Dame Law Review, 1983—84. Mem.: Def. Rsch. Inst., Internat. Ass. Def. Counsel, NC Assn. Def. Attys. (bd. dir. 1997—99, sec. 1999—2001), 21st Jud. Dist. Bar Assn., Forsyth County Bar Assn., NC Bar Assn., Assn. of Trial Lawyers of Am. (assoc.), Phi Alpha Delta. Mailing: Womble Carlyle Sandridge & Rice PLLC PO Box 84 Winston Salem NC 27102 Office: Womble Carlyle Sandridge & Rice PLLC One W 4th St Winston Salem NC 27101 Office Phone: 336-721-3691. Office Fax: 336-733-8354.

SCHROEDER, W(ILLIAM) WIDICK, religion educator; b. Newton, Kans., Nov. 12, 1928; s. William Fredric and Irene (Widick) S.; m. Gayle Eadie, Sept. 1, 1956; children: Scott David, Carla Gayle. BA, Bethel Coll., 1949; MA, Mich. State U., East Lansing, 1952; BDiv, Chgo. Theol. Sem., 1955, DD (hon.), 1995; PhD, U. Chgo., 1960. Ordained to ministry Congl. Christian Ch., 1955. Instr. Mich. State U., 1953-54, U. Chgo., 1958-60; from asst. prof. to prof. religion and society Chgo. Theol. Sem., 1960-94, prof. emeritus, 1994—. Vis. fellow Mansfield Coll., Oxford, Eng., 1966; vis. lectr. Yale U., 1970; vis. scholar Ctr. for Process Studies, Claremont, Calif., 1976; vis. lectr. in ethics and soc. Div. Sch. U. Chgo., 1967-71, 76; editor Rev. of Religious Rsch., 1964-69. Author: (with Victor Obenhaus) Religion in American Culture: Unity and Diversity in a Midwestern County, 1964; Cognitive Structures and Religious Research, 1970; (with Victor Obenhaus, Larry A. Jones and Thomas P. Sweetser) Suburban Religion: Churches and Synagogues in the American Experience, 1974; (with Keith A. Davis) Where Do I Stand? Living Theological Options for Contemporary Christians, 1973, rev. edit., 1975, 3d edit., 1978; Flawed Process and Sectarian Substance: Analytic and Critical Perspectives on the United Church of Christ General Synod Pronouncement, Christian Faith: Economic Life and Justice, 1990; Toward Belief: Essays in the Human Sciences, Social Ethics, and Philosophical Theology, 1996; co-editor: (with Philip Hefner) Belonging and Alienation:

Religious Foundations for the Human Future, 1976; (with Gibson Winter) Belief and Ethics: Essays in Ethics, the Human Sciences and Ministry in Honor of W. Alvin Pitcher, 1978; (with John B. Cobb, Jr.) Process Philosophy and Social Thought, 1981; (with Perry LeFevre) Spiritual Nurture and Congregational Development, 1984, Pastoral Care and Liberation Praxis: Essays in Personal and Social Transformation, 1986, Creative Ministries in Contemporary Christianity, 1991; (with Franklin I. Gamwell) Economic Life: Process Interpretations and Critical Responses, 1988; co-editor Studies in Religion, Society and Personality, Center for the Scientific Study of Religion, 1972-2001. Mem. Religious Rsch. Assn., Soc. Christian Ethics. Home: 6315 Longwood Rd Libertyville IL 60048-9447 *The aims of existence are aesthetic satisfaction and intensity of feeling. In facilitating these aims, the Divine Reality is the locus of potentiality, the mediator of experience, the evoker of feeling and the ultimate recipient of all that has become.*

**SCHROEDER-LEIN, GLENNA RUTH,** librarian, historian; b. Pasadena, Calif., Sept. 23, 1951; d. Walter A. Schroeder and Ruth L. Mueller; m. Lonnie Keith Lein, Aug. 4, 1990. BA in History, Calif. State U., Fullerton, 1975, MA in History, 1978; MLS, U. Ariz., 1981; PhD in History, U. Ga., 1991. Archivist Southwest Mus., L.A., 1977—81; photo libr. World Vision, Monrovia, Calif., 1982—84; vis. asst. prof. Washington Coll., Chestertown, Md., 1990; adj. instr. U. Tenn., Knoxville, 1990—2000; vis. asst. prof. Lincoln Meml. U., Harrogate, Tenn., 2000; manuscript libr. Abraham Lincoln Presdl. Libr., Springfield, Ill., 2005—. Asst. editor: Papers of Andrew Johnson, 1990—2000, Papers of Abraham Lincoln, 2001—03; author: Confederate Hospitals on the Move: Samuel H. Stout and the Army of Tennessee, 1994, Andrew Johnson: A Biographical Companion, 2001; contbr. articles to profl. jours. Office: Abraham Lincoln Presdl Libr 112 N 6th St Springfield IL 62701

**SCHROER, GENE ELDON,** lawyer; b. Randolph, Kans., Aug. 29, 1927; s. Harry Edward and Florence Lillian (Schwartz) S.; m. Edith Grace Kintner, Apr. 7, 1956 (div.); children: Kenneth G., Rebecca J., Sonya J., Connie J.; m. Anne Oliver, Dec. 21, 1988; child: Paul R., John O., Andrew M., Edward G. AB, LLB, Washburn U., 1957. Bar: Kans. 1957, U.S. Dist. Ct. Kans. 1957, U.S. Ct. Appeals (10th cir.) 1970, U.S. Supreme Ct. 1983. Pvt. practice, Topeka, 1957-68; ptnr. Schroer, Rice, P.A., Topeka, 1968—2004, pres., 1970—2004, also bd. dirs.; pvt. practice, 2004—. Contbr. articles to profl. jours. and chpts. to books. Supr. Shawnee County Soil Conservation Dist., Topeka, 1968-84. With U.S. Army, 1951-53. Mem. ABA, Kans. Bar Assn., Assn. Trial Lawyers Am. (gov. 1976-79, seminar lectr. 1973—, chmn. tort sect. 1974-75, instr. Nat. Coll. Adv. 1978, 81-88), Kans. Trial Lawyers Assn. (gov. 1972—, seminar lectr. 1974—, pres. 1974-75), Nat. Bd. Trial Advocacy (sustaining founder), Am. Bd. Trial Advs. (sec., treas. Kans. chpt. 1990-91, pres. 1991-92), Civil Justice Found. (founding sponsor), Trial Lawyers for Pub. Justice (bd. dirs. 1982-96). Democrat. Methodist. Office: 115 SE 7th St Topeka KS 66603 Office Phone: 785-357-7300. E-mail: gschroer@schroer.kscoxmail.com

**SCHROPP, TOBIN,** lawyer; b. 1962; BS in Fgn. Svc., Georgetown U., 1984, JD, 1987, LLM in Taxation, 1991. Bar: 1987. Sr. v.p., gen. counsel Peter Kiewit Sons' Inc., Omaha. Office: Peter Kiewit Sons Inc 1000 Kiewit Plaza Omaha NE 68131

**SCHROTH, JOYCE ABLE,** social worker; b. Bloomington, Ill., Apr. 4, 1948; d. Raymond Daniel Able and Lois Martha Vielhak; m. Thomas H. Schroth, July 22, 1972; children: Bradley, Michael. BA, Ill. Wesleyan U., 1971. Dir. City of Westlake, Ohio, 1998—. Mem. cmty. adv. bd. Lakewood Hosp., Ohio, 1998—, St. John West Shore Hosp., Westlake, 1998—, mem. mission & values com., 1998—; pres. adv. coun. Retired Sr. Vol. Program, Brookpark, 1999—; mem. adv. bd. Brighton Gardens by Marriott, Westlake, 2000—, Westlake Healthcare Ctr., 2002—; pres. Cuyahoga County Mcpl. Offices on Aging Assn.; mem. cmty. adv. bd. Fairview Hosp., 2003—; mem. Cuyahoga County Adv. Coun. Dept. Sr. and Comty. Svc. Chmn. citizen's adv. com. Westlake City Schs., 1985—88, chair levy com., 1988; mem. Westlake Bd. Edn., 1987—90, Cuyahoga County Adv. Coun. on Sr. and Adult Svcs., 2003; bd. dirs. Univ. Settlement, 2005. Recipient Cmty. Leadership award, St. John West Shore Hosp., 2002, Cleve. State U., 2005, Luth.'s Maldonado award, 2005. Mem.: Westlake Lions Club, Sigma Kappa. Republican. Mem. Lds Ch. Avocations: travel, reading, genealogy. Home: 1800 Holdens Arbor Run Westlake OH 44145-2040 Office: City Westlake 29694 Ctr Ridge Rd Westlake OH 44145-5114 Office Phone: 440-899-3544. Business E-mail: jschroth@cityofwestlake.org

**SCHROTH, PETER WILLIAM,** lawyer, management and law educator; b. Camden, N.J., July 24, 1946; s. Walter and Patricia Anne (Page) S.; children: Laura Salome Erickson-Schroth, Julia James. AB, Shimer Coll., 1966; JD, U. Chgo., 1969; M in Comparative Law, U.Chgo., 1971; SJD, U. Mich., 1979; postgrad., U. Freiburg, Fed. Republic Germany, Faculté Internationale pour l'Enseignement de Droit Comparé; MBA, Rensselaer Poly. Inst., 1988; DHL, Shimer Coll., 2000; MSc, Sch. Oriental and African Studies, 2000. Bar: Ill. 1969, N.Y. 1979, Conn. 1985, Mass. 1990; solicitor Supreme Ct. England and Wales 1995. Asst. prof. So. Meth. U., 1973-77; fellow in law and humanities Harvard U., 1976-77, vis. scholar, 1980-81; assoc. prof. N.Y. Law Sch., 1977-81; prof. law Hamline U., St. Paul, 1981-83; dep. gen. counsel Equator Bank Ltd., 1984-87; v.p., dep. gen. counsel Equator Holdings Ltd., 1987-94, v.p., gen. counsel, 1994-2000. Adj. prof. law U. Conn., 1985-86, Western New Eng. Coll., 1988—, adj. prof. of mgmt. Rensselaer Poly. Inst., 1998-99, prof., 1999—, dir. Ctr. for Global Bus. Studies, 2000—. Author: Foreign Investment in the United States, 2nd edit., 1977; author: (with Stiefel) Products Liability: European Proposals and American Experience, 1981; author: Doing Business in Sub-Saharan Africa, 1991; bd. editors Am. Jour. Comparative Law 1991—94, 1991—, mem. edit. bd. Conn. Bar Jour., 1988—, sr. editor, 1993—2000, editor-in-chief, 2000—, recent decisions editor N.Y. Internat. Law Rev., —, mem. edit. rev. bd. Jour. Bus. in Developing Nations, 1996—2000, editor-in-chief, 2000—, co-editor-in-chief Jour. Legal Studies in Bus. Treas., mem. bd. trustees Shimer Coll. Mem. ABA (editor in chief ABA Environ. Law Symposium 1980-82), Am. Soc. Comparative Law (bd. dirs. 1978-84, 91—), Am. Fgn. Law Assn., Internat. Bar Assn., Internat. Law Assn. (com. multinat. banking), Acad. Internat. Bus., Conn. Civil Liberties Union (bd. dirs. 1985-92), Environ. Law Inst. (assoc.), Columbia U. Peace Seminar (assoc.), Hartford Club (bd. govs. 1995-98), Am. Corp. Counsel Assn. (com. chpt.1997-2000), Conn. Bar Assn. (chair sect. of internat. law 1997-2000). Office: Rensselaer Poly Inst Lally Sch Mgmt and Tech 275 Windsor St Hartford CT 06120-2910

**SCHROTH, THOMAS NOLAN,** editor; b. Trenton, N.J., Dec. 21, 1920; s. Frank David and Loretta (Nolan) S.; m. Colette Streit, May 1, 1948 (div. 1958); 1 child, Valerie; m. Patricia Wiggins, Sept. 27, 1958; children: Jennifer, Amy, Anne. Student, Tuck Sch. Bus. Adminstrn., 1942; AB, Dartmouth Coll., 1943. Reporter Time, Washington, 1946-47, UPI, Boston, 1947-48; reporter, news editor Bklyn. Eagle, 1948-51, mng. editor, 1951-55; editorial adviser Magnum Photos, Inc., N.Y.C., 1955; exec. editor, pub. Congl. Quar. Inc. and Editorial Research Reports, Washington, 1955-68; founder, editor Nat. Jour. Ctr. Polit. Rsch., Washington, 1969-70; communications adviser Pub. Broadcasting Environment Ctr., Washington, 1970-71; asst. dir. pub. affairs for communications EPA, Washington, 1970-71, com., 1972; exec. editor The Ellsworth (Maine) American, 1972-77; co-pub.-editor (with Patricia Schroth) Maine Life Mag., Ellsworth, 1977-81; editorial cons. U. Maine, Bangor, 1976-90; mng. editor South-North News Svc., Hanover, N.H., 1987-91; co-pub. New Leaf Pubs., Sedgwick, Maine, 1990—. Mem. Am. Press Inst. Seminar for Mng. Editors, 1953, Regional Transp. Adv. Com., 1996-99. Editor: Congress and the Nation, 1946-64–A Review of Government and Politics in the Postwar Years; editor Improving the U. of Maine trustee's pamphlet. Elected selectman Town of Sedgwick, 1989-94, moderator 1995—; bd. dirs. Blue Hill (Maine) Meml. Hosp., 1978-93, Bangor Symphony Orch., 1981-87, Blue Hill Concert Assn., 1991-2003; bd. dirs., v.p. Island Nursing Home, Deer Isle, Maine, 1985—; mem. Maine State Dem. Com., Augusta, 1985-92, 97—; bd. dirs. Downeast Transp., Inc., 1993—; del.

Maine Dem. Nat. Conv., 2000. 1st lt. Army Airways Comm. Sys., USAAF, WWII. Mem. Sigma Delta Chi. Avocations: gardening, walking, music. Home and Office: 16 Reach Rd Sedgwick ME 04676

**SCHROYER, MICHAEL KEVIN,** healthcare consultant, hospital executive; b. Kewanee, Ill., Sept. 14, 1956; s. Jesse Wayne and Shirley Ann (Brown) S.; m. Joy Anne, June 20, 1987; children: Tiffany Marie, Rebecca Ann, Adam Michael. Diploma, Moline Pub. Hosp. Sch. Nursing, 1980; BSN, Loyola U., 1984; MSN, Seton Hall U., 1987; postgrad., Rush U., 1990-91; MBA, Auburn U., 2006. Cert. hosp. adminstr. Nurse mgr., CCU, ICU, PICU, CCFP Jersey Shore Med. Ctr., Neptune, NJ; assoc. dir., critical care nursing Hyde Park Hosp., Chgo.; adminstrv. dir., transplant svcs Rush-Presbyn./St. Lukes Med. Ctr., Chgo.; adminstrv. coord., v.p. cardiovascular and med./surg. svcs. United Med. Ctr., Moline, Ill.; adminstrv. leader, v.p. Regional CardioLife Ctr., Tenet Brookwood Med. Ctr., Birmingham, Ala.; v.p. clin. svcs. MedCath McAllen (Tex.) Heart Hosp., 1996-98, MedCath Dayton (Ohio) Heart Hosp., 1998-2000, interim CEO, 2000, v.p. ops./COO, 2000—01; pres. / CEO Okla. Heart Hosp., Oklahoma City, 2001—03; prin., cons. TRG Cardiovascular, Denver, 2001—; exec. dir. cardiac and vascular svcs. Meml. Heart & Vascular Inst., Springfield, Ill., 2004—. Author: Emergency Nursing, 1989, Nursing Spectrum, 1989, Comprehensive Nursing Care Plans, 1995. Former bd. dirs. Rock Island County chpt. Am. Heart Assn. Mem.: AACN, Am. Heart Assn. (bd. dirs. Oklahoma City chpt., bd. dirs. Springfield chpt.), Am. Assn. Med. Cardiovasc. Adminstrs., Am. Coll. Healthcare Execs., Sigma Theta Tau. Home: 509 Chase Haven Dr Rochester IL 62563-9294 Office: Meml Health System 701 N 1st St Springfield IL 62702 Office Phone: 217-757-7351. Business E-mail: mschroyer@insighthh.com, schroyer.michael@mhsil.com

**SCHRUM, JAKE BENNETT,** academic administrator; b. Greenville, Tex., Feb. 9, 1946; s. Jake M. and Julia (Bennett) S.; m. Jane Woodman, Dec. 28, 1968; children: Julia Elizabeth, Emily Katharine. BA, Southwestern U., 1968; MDiv, Yale U., 1973; postgrad., Harvard U., 1983. Ordained to ministry Meth. Ch., 1969. Devel. officer Yale U., New Haven, 1973-77; dir. devel. Muhlenberg Coll., Allentown, Pa., 1977-78; v.p. Tex. Wesleyan Coll., Ft. Worth, 1978-82; v.p. univ. rels. Southwestern U., Georgetown, Tex., 1982-85; v.p. Emory U., Atlanta, 1985-91; pres. Tex. Wesleyan U., 1991-2000, Southwestern U., Georgetown, Tex., 2000—. Chmn. CASE, 1995—96; chair Associated Colls. of the South, 2005—; mem. Coun. Ind. Colls., Am. Coun. on Edn.; immediate past chair Ind. Colls. & Univs. Tex., 2004—; vice chair higher edn. com. Austin Area Rsch. Orgn.; bd. dirs. First Tex. Bank. Author: Democracy's Last Stand: The Role of the New Urban University, 1999; editor: A Board's Guide to Comprehensive Campaigns, 2000, Justice for All, 2001. Mem. exec. com. Tex. Ind. Coll. Fund; bd. dirs. Georgetown Area Cmty. Found.; chair Georgetown Project. Named Man of Yr., Bnai Brith North Tex., 1995. Mem.: Assn. Governing Bds. (mem. coun. pres.). Avocations: golf, public speaking. Office: Southwestern U PO Box 770 Georgetown TX 78627-0770

**SCHRUMP, DAVID STUART,** medical association administrator, researcher; b. New Haven, Conn., Dec. 21, 1956; s. LeRoy Everett and Myra Ruth Schrump; m. Brenda Ann Willett, Mar. 13, 1984; children: William David, Christopher Eldridge, Nathaniel Stuart. BA, NYU, N.Y.C., 1979; MD, Univ. of Conn., Farmington, 1983. Diplomate Am. Bd. Thoracic Surgeons, 1994. Asst. prof thoracic surgery UT-MD Anderson Cancer Ctr., Houston, 1993—97; head thoracic oncology sect. surgery br. Nat. Cancer Inst., Bethesda, Md., 1997—. Contbr. articles to profl. jours. Hockey coach Montgomery Youth Hockey Assn., Rockville, Md., 1998. Recipient NIH Merit award for the Devel. of an Innovative Translational Rsch. Program in Thoracic Oncology, Nat. Cancer Inst., 2005, Bench to Bedside award for Outstanding Translational Lung Cancer Rsch., 2001. Fellow: ACS.; mem.: John Alexander Soc., Soc. of Clin. Oncology, Internat. Assn. for the Study of Lung Cancer, Am. Assn. for Cancer Rsch., Am. Assn. forThoracic Surgery, Soc. of Thoracic Surgeons. Achievements include fundamental research pertaining to lung cancer; expert in lung cancer surgery; expert in esophageal cancer surgery; expert in pleural mesothelioma surgery. Office: National Cancer Institute Building 10 Rm 4-3942 10 Center Drive Bethesda MD 20892-1201 Office Phone: 301-496-2128. Office Fax: 301-451-6934. E-mail: david_schrump@nih.gov.

**SCHTEINGART, DAVID EDUARDO,** internist; b. Buenos Aires, Oct. 17, 1930; came to U.S., 1957; s. Mario and Flora (Garfunkel) S.; m. Monica Naomi Starkman, July 3, 1960; children: Miriam, Judith, M. Daniel. MD, U. Buenos Aires, 1955. Diplomate Am. Bd. Internal Medicine. Fellow Mt. Sinai Hosp., N.Y.C., 1957-58; Maimonides Hosp., Bklyn., 1958-59, U. Mich., Ann Arbor, 1959-62, instr., 1962-63, asst. prof., 1963-68, assoc. prof., 1968-72, prof., 1972—. Contbr. articles to profl. jours., books. Pres. Beth Israel Congregation, Ann Arbor, 1974-79, Hebrew Day Sch., Ann Arbor, 1984-86, Jewish Fedn. Washtenaw County, Ann Arbor. Recipient rsch. grants NIH, Bethesda, Md., 1985—. Fellow Am. Coll. Physicians; mem. Endocrine Soc., N.Y. Acad. Scis., Am. Soc. Clin. Nutrition, Cen. Soc. Clin. Rsch., Am. Fedn. Clin. Rsch. Jewish. Avocations: tennis, running, community activities. Office: U Mich Med Sch 1150 W Medical Center Dr Ann Arbor MI 48109-0726

**SCHUBEL, JERRY ROBERT,** marine scientist educator, dean; b. Bad Axe, Mich., Jan. 26, 1936; s. Theodore Howard and Laura Alberta (Gobel) S.; m. Margaret Ann Hostetler, June 14, 1958; children: Susan Elizabeth, Kathryn Ann. BS, Alma Coll., 1957; MA in Tchg., Harvard U., 1959; PhD, Johns Hopkins U., 1968; DSc (hon.), Mass. Maritime Acad. 1997. Rsch. assoc. Chesapeake Bay Inst., Johns Hopkins U., Balt., 1968-69, rsch. scientist, 1969-74, adj. rsch. prof., assoc. dir., 1973-74; dir. Marine Sci. Rsch. Ctr. SUNY, Stony Brook, 1974-83, dean, leading prof., 1983-94, acting dir. Waste Mgmt. Inst. 1985-87 provost, 1986-89, dir. COAST Inst., 1989. Dining Svc. prof., 1994-95, prof. emeritus, 1995—; pres. emeritus, CEO New England Aquarium, Boston, 1994—2001; vis. prof. Wash. Coll., Chestertown, Md., 2002—. Alternative Futures Forum, 2002—; pres., CEO Aquarium of Pacific, Long Beach, Calif., 2002—. Hon. prof. East China Normal U., Shanghai, 1985—; sec. exec. com. Commn. on Food, Environ. and Renewable Resources, 1993, chair steering com., 1994; mem. governing bd. Regional Marine Rsch. Program, Greater N.Y. Bight, 1993-94; v.p., founding dir. Gulf of Maine Ocean Observing Sys., 1998-2002; adv. panel Nat. Whale Conservation Fund Found., 2001—; mem. Nat. Sea Grant Adv. Panel, 2002—, chair, 2004-05; bd. dirs. Internat. Resources Group, 2002—, rev. panel Census of Marine Life, U.S. Nat. Com., 2003-, mem. NSF Edn. and Human Resources Adv. Com., 2003-05, South Bay Salt Pond Restoration, Nat. Sci. Panel, 2003-05; nat. assoc. Nat. Acads. Sci. and Engring.; mem. marine bd. NRC, 1989-94, 2002—. Author: The Living Chesapeake, 1981, The Life and Death of the Chesapeake Bay 1 986; (with H.A. Neal) Solid Waste Management and the Environment, 1987, Garbage and Trash: Can We Convert Mountains Into Molehills?, 1992; editor: (with B.C. Marcy Jr.) Power Plant Entrainment, 1978; (with others) The Great South Bay, 1991; sr. editor Coastal Ocean Pollution Assement News, 1981-86; co-editor in chief Estuaries, 1986-88; mem. editl. bd. CRC Revs. in Aquatic Scis.; contbr. articles to profl. jours. Mem. adv. bd. Environ. Sci. Com. Outer Continental Shelf, Minerals Mgmt. Scs., 1984-86, chmn., 1986; bd. dirs. N.E. Area Remote Sensing Sys., 1983-85, L.I. Incubator Corp.; v.p. L.I. Forum for Tech., 1989-92; chair Mass. Outfall Monitoring Task Force, 1995-98; mem. sci. adv. bd. EPA, 1996-99, concurrent. Nat. Rsch. Commn. on Engring. Tech. Sys., 1996-2000; mem. vis. com. dept. ocean engring MIT, 1995-2002; trustee Natural Heritage Insts., 1995-2001; mem. Boston Artery Bus. Bd. Dirs., 1994-2001; mem. Boston Mcpl. Rsch. Bur. Bd. Dirs., 1994-2001; mem. Annenberg Challenge Adv. Com., 1995-2002; hon. trustee Sci. Mus. L.I., 2000-02. Recipient L.I. Sound Am. Environ. Edn. award, 1987, Stony Brook U. medal, 1989, Matthew Fontaine Maury award, 1990, Ben Gurion U. medal, 1993, sci. achievement award Sci. Mus. L.I., 2000; Alfred P. Sloan fellow, 1959; Wheaton Coll. Disting. fellow, 2000. Mem. NAS (mem. exec. com. 1990, vice chair 1991-94, chair 1992-94, com. on Coastal Ocean 1989-93), Nat. Assn. State Univ. and Land Grant Colls. (bd. dirs. marine divsn., chmn. 1986-88), L.I. Environ. Coun., L.I. Marine Resources Adv. Coun. (chair 1990-94), L.I. Rsch. Inst. (bd. dirs. 1992-94), L.I. Environ.-

Econ. Roundtable (co-chair 1991-92), Suffolk County Recycling Commn., (chmn. 1987-88), Estuarine Rsch. Fedn. (v.p. 1982-83, pres. 1985-87), N.Y. Sea Grant Inst. (chmn. governing bd. 1988-90, mem. gov.'s task force on coastal resources 1990-91), Census Marine Life (mem. U.S. nat. com. 2003—), The Nature Conservancy (trustee L.I. chpt. 1991-94), Franklin Electronic Pubs. (bd. dirs. 1991—), Taproot (bd. dirs. 1988-93, vice chair 1990-93), Internat. Resources Group (bd. dirs., 2002—), Sigma Xi, Phi Sigma Pi. Avocation: photography. Office: Aquarium of the Pacific 100 Aquarium Way Long Beach CA 90802 Office Phone: 562-951-1608. Business E-Mail: jschubel@lbaop.org.

**SCHUBERT, BARBARA SCHUELE,** retired performing arts association administrator; b. Cleve., Feb. 21, 1939; d. William Edward and Mildred Marianne (Matousek) Schuele; m. John Dwan Schubert, June 15, 1963; children: William Edward, Christopher John, David Matthew. BS in Social Scis., John Carroll U, 1962, MA in English, 1967; MEd, 1980. Cert. secondary tchr., elem. remedial reading tchr., Ohio. Tchr. Sch. on Magnolia, Cleve., 1980-82, Ruffing Montessori, Cleve., 1982-83; tchr. English U. Sch., Chagrin Falls, Ohio, 1983-86; gen. mgr. Ohio Ballet, Akron, 1987-90, assoc. dir., 1990-99; ret. Bd. trustees Ohio Ballet, 1974-87, 91-99. Bd. dirs. John Carroll U., 1990—; trustee Boys Hope Girls Hope, 2001. Mem.: Cleve. Skating. Roman Catholic. Personal E-mail: matousek04@yahoo.com. E-mail: BJSchubert@earthlink.net.

**SCHUBERT, BLAKE H.,** lawyer; b. Wheeling, W.Va., Apr. 21, 1939; s. John Arnold and Esther Elizabeth (Masters) Schubert; m. Carol Jean Cramp, Jan. 13, 1962; children: Cheryl Lynn, Charles Bradley, Elisabeth Anne. BA, Ohio Wesleyan U., 1961; JD, U. Chgo., 1964. Bar: Ill. 1964, U.S. Dist. Ct. (no. dist.) Ill. 1968, U.S. Tax Ct. 1994. Counsel Brunswick Corp., Chgo., 1964—68; asst. group counsel FMC Corp., Chgo., 1968—73; gen. counsel Dresser Tool Group, Chgo., 1973—79; chmn. Schubert Securities, Oak Park, Ill., 1979—84, Inter-Am. Investments, Inc., Oak Park, 1980—, Midwestern Bus. Devel. Corp., Oak Park, 2005—. Gen. ptnr. Investment Trust Ltd., St. Petersburg, Fla., 1981—91, Inter-Am. Fund, Oak Park, 1982—91, Inter-Am. Fund l, Oak Park, 1982—91, Inter-Am. Fund ll, Oak Park, 1984—89; chmn. Compath Video Corp., Oak Park, 1984—85; lectr. Am. Inst. Banking, 1965, Chgo. Inst. Fin. Studies, 1984—85. Author: The Well-Kept Secrets of Investing, 1982. Chmn. Park Forest Co-op., Ill., 1966—70; mem. Chgo. Bd. Options Exch., 1979—83; chmn. 1st United Ch. Endowment Fund, Oak Park, 1975—80. Home and Office: 522 Linden Ave Oak Park IL 60302-1659

**SCHUBERT, GUENTHER ERICH,** pathologist; b. Mosul, Iraq, Aug. 17, 1930; s. Erich Waldemar and Martha Camilla (Zschitzschmann) Schubert; children: Frank, Marion, Dirk. MD, U. Heidelberg, Germany, 1957; pvt. docent in pathology, U. Tuebingen, Germany, 1966. Asst. med. dir. University Tuebingen, Germany, 1966—76; prof. pathology, 1972; head Inst. Pathology, Wuppertal, Germany, 1976—96; chair of pathology U. Witten-Herdecke, Germany, 1985—96. Co-author: Coloratlas of Cytodiagnosis of the Prostate, 1975, Pathologie, 1984, 1997, Endoscopy of the Urinary Bladder, 1989, Textbook of Pathology, 1981, 1987. Mem. Wissenschaftlicher Beirat, Bundesarztekammer, Bonn, Germany, 1976—85; pres. Medizinisch Naturwissenschaftliche Gesellschaft, Wuppertal, 1984—85, Onkologischer Schwerpunkt, Wuppertal, 1985—93, OSP Bergisch-Land, 1992—95, Bergische Arbeitsgemeinschaft fur Gastroenterologie, Wuppertal, 1987—88, 1990—91, 1994—95. Mem.: NY Acad. Scis., Internat. Acad. Pathology, Deutsche Gesellschaft fur Urologie, Deutsche Gesellschaft fur Nephrologie, Deutsche Gesellschaft fur Pathologie, Lions. Avocations: music, diving, photography. Office: Inst Pathology Am Anschlag 71 42113 Wuppertal Germany

**SCHUBERT, HELEN CELIA,** public relations executive; b. Washington City, Wis. d. Paul H. and Edna (Schmidt) S. BS, U. Wis., Madison. Dir. pub. rels. United Cerebral Palsy, Chgo., 1961; adminstrv. dir. Nat. Design Ctr., Chgo., 1962-67; owner Schubert Pub. Rels., Chgo., 1967—. Bd. dirs. Fashion Group, Chgo., 1988—95; adj. prof. comm. Roosevelt U., 1992—. Mem. women's bd. Am. Cancer Soc., Chgo., 1988—, Art Resources in Tchg., Chgo., 1988-92. Recipient Comm. award Am. Soc. Interior Designers, Chgo., 1979, 83, 88, 94; named to Chgo. Women's Hall of Fame City of Chgo., 1990. Fellow Nat. Home Fashion League; mem. Women's Ad Club Chgo. (pres. 1981-83, Woman of Yr. award 1987), Women in Comm. (pres. 1969-70, Matrix award Lifetime Achievement 1996), Am. Advt. Fedn. (lt. gov. 1983-85). Lutheran. Personal E-mail: schube@mail.com.

**SCHUBERT, JEANNE,** artist; b. Harlan, Ky., June 2, 1932; d. Lewis Marion and Bertha Faye (Paul) Conklin; m. Robert Breckenridge Stroup, Feb. 5, 1953 (dec. May 1954); 1 child, Robert Breckenridge; m. Robert Buxton (div. 1967); 1 child, Beverly Buxton; m. Robert Kenyon Schubert, Apr. 25, 1970 Student, Cumberland Coll., Williamsburg, Ky., 1951, Rollins Coll., Winter Park, Fla., 1974, Art Students' League, N.Y.C., 1984. Mortgage clk. Orlando (Fla.) Fed. Savs., Fla., 1962—76; real estate broker Orlando; co-owner, creator Art Works Orlando, 1993—96. Mem./exhibitor Orlando Mus. Art, 1972—, Dayton Beach Mus., 1972—, Arts on Douglas, New Smyrna Beach, Fla., 1995—, Albertson-Peterson Gallery, Winter Park, 1990-99 One woman shows include Lighthouse Gallery, Tequesta, Fla., Orlando Mus Art Assocs., Valencia C.C., Orlando, LeMoyne Ctr. for Visual Arts, Tallahassee, Melvin Gallery, Lakeland, U. Ctr. Fla., Orlando, Vero Beach (Fla.) Ctr. for the Arts, Osceola Ctr. for Arts, Kissimmee, Fla., Gallery Contemporanea, Hot Springs, Ark., Brevard Art Ctr. and Mus., Melbourne, Fla., Melvin Gallery, Fla. So. Coll., Albertson-Peterson Gallery, First Union Tower, Orlando, Arts on Douglas, New Smyrna Beach, Orlando City Hall, 2006; exhibited in group shows at Orlando Mus. Art, 1984, 87, 88, 92, Barbara Gilman Gallery, Miami, Miami-Dade Coll., 1986, North Miami Mus. Art, Salmagundi Club, N.Y., Fla. Gulf Coast Art Ctr., Belleaire, 1986, U. Ctrl. Fla., 1987, Harmon Gallery Am. Art, Sarasota, Fla., Crealde Art Ctr. Gallery, Winter Park, Mus Arts and Sci, Daytona Beach, Daytona Beach Art Ctr., Epcot Ctr., Lake Buena Vista, 1994-2001, Soc. of Four Arts, West Palm Beach, 1997-2001; works in permanent collections at Maitland Art Ctr., Rollins Coll., Valencia C.C., Mus. Arts and Scis., Walt Disney World, Flagship Banks, Melbourne, Gen. Mills Corp., Orlando, Hyatt Regency Corp., Orlando, Orlando City Hall, Barnett Bank Fla., Jacksonville, Orange County Courthouse, Shands Hosp., Gainesville, Mayo Clinic, Jacksonville, Baker & Hostetler, Orlando, Akerman, Senterfitt & Eidson, Orlando, Holland and Knight, Orlando, City Orlando Collections, Orange County Collection, Suntrust Collection, Orlando. Bd. dirs. Maitland (Fla.) Art Ctr. Art Svcs. Coun. Art grant Mem. Fla. Watercolor Soc., Fla. Artist Group (area rep. 1985-2001) Home: 318 N Riverside Dr Edgewater FL 32132

**SCHUBERT, JOSEPH EDWARD,** music educator; b. L.A., Nov. 21, 1956; s. Lawrence Donald and Zita Catherine Schubert; m. Teri Ellen Kramer, Dec. 27, 1982; children: Anna Teresa, Timothy Wayne. MusB, Calif. State U., Fullerton, 1980, BA, 1985; MusM, Calif. State U., L.A., 2006. Cert. tchr. Calif., 1985. Choral music tchr. Fullerton Sch. Dist., Calif., 1985—96, Western H.S., Anaheim, Calif., 1996—. Ch. organist, choir dir. St. Andrews Presbyn. Ch., Redondo Beach, Calif., 1977—95, First United Meth. Ch., Orange, Calif., 1995—. Composer: (choral music) A Canticle of Praise, 2006. Recipient Los Cancioneros award, Los Cancioneros Choral Soc., 1976, Merit award in keyboard performance, Dept. Music, Calif. State U., Fullerton, 1980, Tchr. of Yr. award, Ladera Vista Jr. H.S., 1993, Merit award, Roger Wagner Ctr. for Choral Studies, 2002. Mem.: The Donald Brinegar Singers (baritone), So. Calif. Vocal Assn., Am. Musicological Soc., Am. Choral Dirs. Assn., Am. Guild of Organists. Roman Catholic. Avocations: musician, hiking, Tae Kwon Do. Home: 108 Harvard Ct Placentia CA 92870 Office: Western HS 501 S Western Ave Anaheim CA 92804 Office Phone: 714-220-4036. Personal E-mail: josephschubert@earthlink.net. Business E-Mail: schubert_j@auhsd.k12.ca.us.

**SCHUBERT, RICHARD FRANCIS,** social services administrator, consultant; b. Trenton, N.J., Nov. 2, 1936; s. Yaro and Frances Mary (Hustak) S.; m. Virginia Thomas Austin, Sept. 15, 2000; children: Robyn, Regina. BA cum laude, Eastern Nazarene Coll., 1958; LLB, Yale U., 1961. Bar: Pa. 1962, U.S. Supreme Ct 1972. Arbitration atty. Bethlehem Steel Corp., Pa., 1961-66, asst.

mgr. labor relations, 1966-70; exec. asst. to undersec. labor Washington, 1970; gen. counsel labor, 1971-73; dep. sec. labor, 1973-75; asst. to v.p. indsl. relations Bethlehem Steel Corp., 1973, asst. v.p. public affairs, 1975-77, v.p. public affairs, 1977-79, pres., 1979-80, vice chmn., 1980-82; pres., CEO ARC, 1982-89, Points of Light Found., 1990-95. Bd. dirs. Internat. Ctr. for Religion and Diplomacy, Mgmt. Tng. Corp. Bd. dirs. Women in Cmty. Svc.; exec. v.p. EXCN; chmn. emeritus Internat. Youth Found., chmn., Nazarene Compassionate Ministries; vice chmn. Leader to Leader Inst.; chmn. Nat. Job Corps Assn. Mem.: Ctr. Excellence in Govt., Coun. on Fgn. Rels., Northampton County Bar Assn., Pa. Bar Assn., Ea. Nazarene Alumni Assn. (pres. 1969—73), Phi Alpha Delta. Mem. Ch. of Nazarene. Home: 6615 Madison McLean Dr Mc Lean VA 22101-2425 Office: 200 12th St S Ste 701 Crystal Gateway 4 Alexandria VA 22202 Office Phone: 703-416-6656. E-mail: rfs@iyfnet.org.

**SCHUBERT, RUTH CAROL HICKOK,** artist, educator; b. Janesville, Wis., Dec. 24, 1927; d. Fay Andrew and Mildred Wilamette (Street) Hickok; m. Robert Francis Schubert, Oct. 20, 1946; children: Stephen Robert, Michelle Carol. Student, DeAnza Coll., 1972—73; AA Scholarship, Monterey Peninsula Coll., Calif., 1974; BA with honors, Calif. State U., San Jose, 1979. Owner, mgr. Casa De Artes Gallery, Monterey, Calif., 1977—86; dir. Monterey Peninsula Art Coun., 1975—76; quick-draw artist So. Oreg. Pub. TV, KSYS; leader painting workshops; demonstrator, lectr., judge in U.S., B.C. Can., New Zealand and Loreto, Baja, Mexico. One-woman shows include Aarhof Gallery, Aarau, Switzerland, 1977, Degli Agostiniani Recolletti, Rome, 1977, Wells Fargo Bank, Monterey, 1975, 1978, 1979, Seaside (Calif.) City Hall Gallery, 1979, 1989, Village Gallery, Lahaina, Hawaii, 1983, 1986, 1989, 1994, Portola Valley Gallery, 1984, 1985, Rose Rock Gallery, Carmel, 1986—84, Taupo (N.Z.) Arts Soc., 1988, Geyserland Art Mus., Rotorua, N.Z., 1988, Wanganui (N.Z.) Art Soc., 1988, Hallei Brown Ford Gallery, Roseburg, Oreg., 1991, 1995, Collection of Ann Cunningham, Carmel, 1993—95, Libr. Found., Medford, Oreg., 2005, catalog nat. group juried shows include, Sierra Nev. Mus. Art, Reno, 1980, Bard Hall Gallery, San Diego, 1980, San Diego Nat. Watercolor Show, Mid-West Nat. Watercolor Show, Rahr-West Mus., Manitowoc, Wis., 1980, Rosicrucian Mus., San Jose, 1981, 1984, Calif. State Agri-Images, Sacramento, 1984, XVII Watercolor West, Brea Civic Cultural Ctr., 1985, Watercolor West XXIII, Grand Art Galleries, Glendale, Calif., 1991, Watercolor West XXV, Riverside (Calif.) Art Mus., 1993, Nat. Pen Women at Marjorie Evans Gallery, Carmel, 1986, Monterey County Juried Expo, Monterey Peninsula Mus. Art, 1986, 1987, Am. Artists Group Exhbn., 1993, 1994, 1995, Gallery Hirose, Tsukuba, Ibaragi, Japan, Internat. Art Show and End of World Hunger, Ashland, Oreg., 1990, biann. art exhbn. Sumner Mus., Washington, D.C., 1992, State of the Art, New Eng. Fine Arts, Boston, 1993, N.W. Wildlife, Nightingale Gallery, Ea. Oreg. Coll., La Grande, 1993, N.W. Visual Arts Ctr. 19th Ann., Panama City, Fla., 1993, NW Watercolor Soc. Waterworks N.W. Juried Show, Mercer Island, Wash., 1994, Represented in permanent collections Rogue Valley Manor Spl. Svcs., Medford, Oreg., Monterey Calif. Peninsula Mus. Art, Nat. Biscuit Co. subs. RJR Nabisco, San Jose, Waikato Mus. Art, Hamilton, N.Z., Muscular Dystrophy Assn., San Francisco, Old Sch. Hous Mus., Qualicum Bay, Vancouver Island, B.C., USS George Washington Aircraft Carrier, Adm. Robert Sprigg, Pres. Bill Clinton, Barbara Bush, George Montgomery, Marilyn Horne, Alison Krauss, also numerous pvt. collections. Recipient 1st prize, Monterey County Fair, 1979, Jade Fon Watercolor award, Hall of Flowers, San Francisco, 1980, 1st Nat. Art Show, NY Am. Artist mag., 1980, Nat. Art Appreciation award, 1984, award, Norcal State Art Fair, 1985, Watercolor award, 25 Ann. Aqueous Media Show, Salem, Oreg., 1990, award, Calif. Watercolor Soc., 2001, Silver award, Oreg. Watercolor Soc. Portland, 2000, numerous other awards for watercolor paintings. Mem.: NW Watercolor Soc. (signature, Watercolor Transparent award, Mercer Island 1994, Waterworks, Seattle 1999), Art Du Jour Gallery (dir. Medford, Oreg.), Watercolor West (signature), Women Artists Registry N.Am., Nat. Mus. Women in Arts, Art Alumni San Jose State U., Nat. League Am. Pen Women (pres. 1983—84, 1986—87), Cen. Coast Art Assn. (pres. 1982—85), Arts Coun. So. Oreg., Watercolor Soc., Rogue Valley Art Gallery (bd. officer 2004—05), LaHaina Arts Soc., Artists Equity Assn., Nat. Watercolor Soc. (assoc. Nat. award 2005, Viva Sherman Oaks (Calif.) award), Am. Watercolor Soc. (assoc.). Achievements include Artwork selected for inclusion in profl. pubs. including "Best of Watercolor" in Rockport Publr. and "The California Art Preview" Les Krantz. Home: 3533 Southvillage Dr Medford OR 97504-9283 Office Phone: 541-772-0136. E-mail: schubert0136@msn.com.

**SCHUBERT, SCOTT E.,** corporate financial executive; BS in Mgmt., Purdue U., 1975, MBA in Fin., 1976. With Amoco Corp., 1976—91, internat. contr. exploration and prodn., 1991—95, v.p. worldwide fin. svcs., 1995—99; CFO WilTel, 1999—2003, NTL, Inc., NYC, 2003—. Office: Ntl 909 3rd Ave Rm 2800 New York NY 10022-4790

**SCHUBERT, WILLIAM HENRY,** curriculum studies educator; b. Garrett, Ind., July 6, 1944; s. Walter William and Mary Madeline (Grube) S.; children by previous marriage: Ellen Elaine, Karen Margaret; m. Ann Lynn Lopez, Dec. 3, 1977; children: Heidi Ann, Henry William. BS, Manchester Coll., 1966; MS, Ind. U., 1967; PhD, U. Ill., 1975. Tchr. Fairmount, El Sierra and Herrick Schs., Downers Grove, Ill., 1967—75; clin. instr. U. Wis., Madison, 1969—73; tchg. asst., fellow U. Ill., Urbana, 1973—75, asst. prof. Chgo., 1975—80, assoc. prof., 1981—85, prof., 1985—, coord. secondary edn., 1979—82, coord. instrnl. leadership, 1979—85, dir. grad. studies Coll. Edn., 1983—85, coord. grad. curriculum studies, 1985—, coord. edn. studies, 1990—94, 1996—, chair area curriculum and instrn., 1990—94, 2002—05, Univ. scholar, 2005—. Vis. assoc. prof. U. Victoria (B.C., Can.), 1981; disting. vis. prof. U. S.C., 1986; presenter in field. Author (with Ann Lopez Schubert): Curriculum Books: The First Eighty Years, 1980; author: Curriculum: Perspective, Paradigm and Possibility, 1986, with Edmund C. Short and George Willis, 1985; author: (with J. Dan Marshall and James T. Sears) Turning Points in Curriculum: A Contemporary American Memoir, 2000; author: (with Ann Lopez Schubert, Thomas P. Thomas, Wayne M. Carroll) Curriculum Books: The First Hundred Years, 2002; editor (with Ann Lopez): Conceptions of Curriculum Knowledge: Focus on Students and Teachers, 1982; editor: (with George Willis) Reflections from the Heart of Educational Inquiry: Understanding Curriculum Teaching Through the Arts, 1991; editor: (with William Ayers) Teacher Lore: Learning From Our Own Experience, 1992, 2001; editor: (with George Willis, R. Bullugh, C. Kridel, J. Holton) The American Curriculum: A Documentary History, 1993; assoc. editor, mem. editl. bd. Ednl. Theory, mem. editl. bd. Catalyst: Voices of Chicago School Reform, Taboo: The Jour. of Culture and Edn., former mem. editl. bd. Ednl. Studies, former cons. editor Phenomenology and Pedagogy, adv. bd. Tchg. Edn., Pi Lamda Pubs., 1995—; editor: (book series) Student Lore, 1990—; cons. editor Jour. Curriculum Discourse and Dialogue, mem. adv. bd. Jour. Critical Issues in Curriculum and Instrn., 2000—, contbr. over 200 articles to profl. jours., chpt. to books. Mem.: ASCD (steering com. curriculum com. 1980—83, publs. com. 1987—90, internat. polling panel 1990—), Am. Assn. for Advancement of Curriculum Studies, Internat. Assn. for Advancement of Curriculum Studies, Soc. Profs. of Edn. (exec. bd. 1988—97, pres.-elect 2000—01, pres. 2001—02), John Dewey Soc. (bd. dirs. 1986—95, chair awards com. 1988—90, co-chair lectures commn. 1989—91, 1989—91, pres.-elect 1990—91, pres. 1992—93), Inst. Dem. in Edn., Nat. Soc. Study Edn., World Coun. Curriculum and Instrn., Am. Ednl. Rsch. Assn. (chmn. creation and utilization of curriculum knowledge 1980—82, program chmn. curriculum studies divsn. 1982—83, sec. divsn. B 1989—91, v.p. 2000—01, Lifetime Achievement award in Curriculum Studies 2004), Am. Assn. Colls. Tchr. Edn., Soc. Study Curriculum History (sec.-treas. 1981—82, pres. 1982—83), Profs. of Curriculum (factotum 1984—85), Internat. Acad. Edn., Scottish Rite, Masons, Phi Kappa Phi (pres. U. Ill. Chgo. chpt. 1981—82), Phi Delta Kappa. Office: U Ill Coll Edn M/C 147 1040 W Harrison St Chicago IL 60607-7129 Business E-Mail: schubert@uic.edu.

**SCHUBERT, WILLIAM KUENNETH,** hospital medical center executive; b. Cin., July 12, 1926; s. Wilfred Schubert and Amanda Kuenneth; m. Mary Jane Pamperin, June 5, 1948; children: Carol, Joanne, Barbara, Nancy. BS, U. Cin., 1949, MD, 1952; LHD (hon.), Coll. Mt. St. Joseph, Cin., 1997. Diplomate Am. Bd. Pediat. Pvt. practice specializing in pediat., Cin., 1956-63; dir. clin. rsch. ctr. Children's Hosp. Med. Ctr., Cin., 1963-76; dir. divsn. gastroenterology Children's Hosp., Cin., 1968-79; prof. pediat. U. Cin., 1969-96, prof. emeritus, 1997—, assoc. sr. v.p. for children's hosp. affairs Coll. Medicine, 1993-96; chief of staff Children's Hosp. Med. Ctr., Cin., 1972-88; chmn. dept. pediat. U. Cin., 1979-93; dir. Children's Hosp. Rsch. Found., Cin., 1979-93; pres., CEO Children's Hosp. Med. Ctr., Cin., 1983-96, trustee, 1983—. V.p. Ohio Solid Organ Transplant Consortium, Columbus, 1986-87, pres., 1987-88, alt. trustee, 1988-96; trustee med. rsch. James N. Gamble Inst., Cin., 1989-95; bd. dirs. Choice Care Found., Health Found. of Greater Cin.; mem. fetal oversight com. Fetal Care Ctr. Cin., 2005—. Contbr. over 100 articles to profl. jours. Trustee Greater Cin. Hosp. Coun., 1986-96, Assn. of Ohio Children's Hosp., Columbus, 1986-96, The Children's Hosp. Found., 1990—, Springer Sch., Cin., 1994-2003, Children's Convalescent Hosp., 1997—, The Children's Hosp., 2001—; chmn. Greater Cin. Hosp. Coun., 1989; co-chmn. Citizen's Com. for Med. Ctr., Cin., 1980-81; chmn. Hosp. Divsn. 1988 Fine Arts Fund, Cin., 1987; hon. trustee Babies' Milk Fund, Children's and Prenatal Clinics, Cin., 1994-2002. Recipient Disting. Alumni award U. Cin., 1992, Donald Newkirk award Ohio Hosp. Assn., 1997, Health Care Heros Lifetime Achievement award Bus. Courier, Cin., 2003, Great Living Cincinnatian award, 2004, Fellow Am. Acad. Pediat. (Murray Davidson award sect. on gastroenterology/nutrition 2003); mem. Am. Pediatric Soc. (councillor 1986-93), Soc. Pediatric Rsch., Assn. Med. Sch. Pediatric Dept. Chmn., Cin. Acad. Medicine, AMA, Midwestern Soc. for Pediatric Rsch., Am. Assn. for Study of Liver Diseases, Cin. Soc. Clin. Rsch., Am. Gastroenterological Assn., N.Am. Soc. Pediatric Gastroenterology, Nat. Reye's Syndrome Found. (med. dir. 1976-87), Internat. Assn. Study Liver Diseases. Clubs: Queen City (Cin.). Office: Children's Hosp Med Ctr Cin ML 5005 3333 Burnet Ave Cincinnati OH 45229-3026 Business E-Mail: william.schubert@cchmc.org.

**SCHUBKEGEL, JOYCE CATHERINE,** music educator, composer; b. New Haven, Ind., Apr. 23, 1937; d. Clarence Frederick Nahrwold and Helen Edith Ross; m. Francis Luther Schubkegel, June 30, 1962; children: Catherine Biedenbender, Timothy, Jean Reiners, David. AA, Condoria Jr. Coll., Ft. Wayne, Ind., 1957; BS in Edn., Concordia U., River Forest, Ill., 1959; MusM, Northwestern U., Evanston, Ill., 1966. Organist Concordia Luth. Ch., Ft. Wayne, Ind., 1956—57; music dir. First Immanuel Luth. Ch., Chgo., 1958—59; tchr., music dir. St. John's Luth. Sch., Wheaton, Ill., 1959—60; music instr. Concordia Tchrs. Coll., River Forest, Ill., 1960—62; music dir. Bethlehem Luth. Ch., Rover Grove, Ill., 1960—62, Good Shepherd Luth. Ch., Palos Heights, Ill., 1963—66; music instr. Wis. Luth. Coll., Milw., 1966—70; music prof. Dr. Martin Luther Coll., New Ulm, Minn., 1970—95, Martin Luther Coll., New Ulm, Minn., 1995—. Mem.: Am. Choral Dir. Assn. Lutheran. Avocation: gardening. Home: 1303 Southridge Rd New Ulm MN 56073

**SCHUCH, BEVERLY,** anchor; Bachelor, Muskingum Coll., New Concord, Ohio; grad. student in comm., Simmons Coll., Boston. Anchor, reporter, Portland, Maine, Providence; corr. N.Y. gen. news unit CNN, N.Y.C., reporter Moneyline, host Pinnacle; co-anchor Biz Buzz, CNN Fin. News, N.Y.C., co-anchor Take It Personally. Recipient George Foster Peabody Broadcasting Award, 1987.

**SCHUCHARD, ROBERT L.,** lawyer; b. LA, Feb. 14, 1952; BA in Polit. Sci., Stanford U., 1974; JD, Santa Clara U., 1977. Bar: Calif. 1977. Ptnr. Sonnenschein Nath & Rosenthal LLP, LA, 1997—. Office: Sonnenschein Nath & Rosenthal 601 S Figueroa St, Ste 1500 Los Angeles CA 90017 Office Phone: 213-892-5075. Office Fax: 213-623-9924. Business E-Mail: rschuchard@sonnenschein.com.

**SCHUCHMAN, PHILIP MELCHOR,** education educator; b. St. Charles, Mo., Feb. 19, 1951; s. Philip Melchor Schuchmann and Pauline Eleanor Schuchman; m. Lynn Christine Stolte, Sept. 2, 1971; children: Cassandra Lynn, Philip Ezekiel. MA, U. of Mo., 1971—80. Grad. rsch. asst. U. of Mo., 1973, grad. tchg. asst., 1973—75; instr. Avila Coll., Kansas City, Mo., 1975—82, Donnelly Coll., Kansas City, Kans., 1976—78; exec. dir. Westport Free Health Clinic, Kansas City, Mo., 1980—86; instr. Johnson County C.C., Overland Park, Kans., 1986—87; sr. prof. DeVry U., Kansas City, Mo., 1987—. Spkr. Kans. City Profl. Devel. Coun., 1996—. Author: Test Bank to Accompany Corley/Reed The Legal Environment of Business: Briefed Case Edition, Test Item File Principles of Economics, PowerPoint Lectures to a Company Macionis Sociology, 9th edit. Adv. bd. Red Bridge YMCA, Kansas City, Mo. Recipient Governor's Award for Excellence in Tchg., Coordinating Bd. for Higher Edn., 1998. Mem.: AAUP, Am. Sociol. Assn. Democrat. Roman Catholic. Office: DeVry University 11224 Holmes Rd Kansas City MO 64131-3626 Office Phone: 816-941-0430 ext. 5253. Business E-Mail: pschuchman@kc.devry.edu.

**SCHUCK, PETER HORNER,** lawyer, educator; b. NYC, Apr. 26, 1940; s. Samuel H. and Lucille (Horner) S.; m. Marcy Cantor, June 26, 1966; children: Christopher, Julie. BA with honors, Cornell U., 1962; JD cum laude, Harvard U., 1965, MA, 1969; LLM, NYU, 1966; MA (hon.), Yale U., 1982. Bar: N.Y. State 1966, D.C. 1972. Practiced law, NYC, 1965-68; teaching fellow in govt. Harvard U., 1969-71; cons. Center for Study of Responsive Law, Washington, 1971-72; dir. Washington office Consumers Union, 1972-77; dep. asst. sec. for planning and evaluation HEW, Washington, 1977-79; vis. scholar Am. Enterprise Inst. for Public Policy Research, Washington, 1979; assoc. prof. law Yale U., 1979-81, prof., 1981-86, Simeon E. Baldwin prof. law, 1986—, dep. dean, 1993-94. Vis. prof. Georgetown U. Law Ctr., 1986-87, NYU Law Sch., fall 1994, N.Y. Law Sch., spring 1997, 98, 99 Author: The Judiciary Committees, 1975, Suing Government, 1983, Citizenship Without Consent, 1985; co-author: Agent Orange on Trial, 1986, enlarged edit., 1987, Citizens, Strangers and In-Betweens: Essays on Immigration and Citizenship, 1998, The Limits of Law: Essays on Democratic Governance, 2000, Diversity in America: Keeping Government at a Safe Distance, 2003, Meditations of a Militant Moderate: Cool Views on Hot Topics, 2006; editor: Tort Law and the Public Interest, 1991, Foundations of Administrative Law, 1994, 2nd edit. 2004; co-editor: Paths to Inclusion, 1998, Immigration Stories, 2005; contbr. articles and revs. to profl. and popular publs. Recipient Silver Gavel award ABA, 1987; Guggenheim fellow, 1984-85; Fulbright scholar, 2004. Jewish. Office: Yale Law Sch PO Box 208215 New Haven CT 06520 Office Phone: 203-432-4967. E-mail: peter.schuck@yale.edu.

**SCHUCK, THOMAS ROBERT,** lawyer, farmer; b. Findlay, Ohio, Feb. 7, 1950; s. Robert Damon and Katherine Margaretta (Beynon) S. BA, DePauw U., 1972; MA, U. Kent, U.K., 1974; JD, Harvard U., 1976. Bar: Ohio 1976, U.S. Dist. Ct. (no. dist.) Ohio 1977, U.S. Dist. Ct. (so. dist.) Ohio 1979, Ariz. 1990, U.S. Ct. Appeals (6th cir.) 1978, U.S. Ct. Appeals (9th cir.) 1991, U.S. Ct. Appeals Armed Forces, 2000, U.S. Supreme Ct. 2001. Law clk. U.S. Dist. Ct., Cleve., 1976-79; assoc. Taft, Stettinius & Hollister, Cin., 1979-87, ptnr., 1987—; owner, operator Rural Hill Farm. Participant Ohio Bench Bar Conf., Columbus, 1990-91, Glenmoor Justice Inst., 2000; barrister Am. Inn of Ct., 1986-87, LEAD Clermont, 1997-98; bar exam com. U.S. Dist. Ct. (so. dist.) Ohio; merit panel for bankruptcy judge selection U.S. Ct. Appeals Sixth Cir. 1998, chair, 2002; life mem. Jud. Conf. of 6th Cir. Author: Federal Employment Litigation Practice Guide, 2006; contbg. author: Aids and the Law, 2d edit. 1992; contbr. articles to profl. jours. Trustee Mental Health Svcs. East, Inc., Cin., 1985-91; sec. bd. trustees Joy Outdoor Edn. Ctr., Inc., 1999-2005; active May Festival Assocs., Cin., 1984-86, WGUC Radio Cmty. Bd., 1984-86, Clermont County Mental Health Bd., Batavia, Ohio, 1992-2000, vice-chmn., 1997-2000; steering com. Clermont County Mental Retardation Developmental Disabilities Levy, 1996, trustee, 2000-02, vice-chmn., 2002; spl. gifts com. Cin. Art Acad., 1987, Ohio Found. Ind. Colls., 1995-, bd. dir., 2003—; pres. Fed. Bar Assn. Found. Cin. Grad. fellow Rotary Internat. Found., 1972-73. Mem. Fed. Bar Assn. (pres. Cin. chpt. 1994-95, v.p. 6th cir.

1996-99, nat. membership chair 1997-99, nat. sec. 2001-2002, nat. treas., nat. v.p. 2002-03, nat. pres.-elect 2003-04, nat. pres. 2004-05, govt. rels. com., pres. Foun. of Cin.), Potter Stewart Am. Inn of Ct. (barrister 1986-87), U.S. Rowing Assn. (asst. referee), Harvard Club Cin. (pres. 1995-96), Ohio Soc. (sec. 2002-03, treas. 2004-05, v.p. 2005—), Soc. Bacchus Ms., Masons (33rd degree, trustee Valley of Cin. 2003-05), Phi Beta Kappa, Delta Chi, Phi Eta Sigma, Sigma Delta Chi. Republican. Methodist. Avocations: reading, photography. Home: PO Box 615 189 State Route 133 Felicity OH 45120 Office: Taft Stettinius & Hollister LLP Ste 1800 425 Walnut St Cincinnati OH 45202-3957 Office Phone: 513-381-2838.

**SCHUCKENBROCK, STEPHEN,** information technology executive; BA in adminstrn., Elon Coll. Sales and tech. mgmt. positions IBM, 1983—93; ptnr. Feld Group, 1993—95, COO, 2000—04; chief info. officer Frito-Lay, 1995—98; sr. v.p. info. tech. PepsiCo. Inc., 1998—2000; exec. v.p. global sales and client solutions EDS, Plano, Tex., 2004—. Office: EDS Corp HQ 5400 Legacy Dr Plano TX 75024 Office Phone: 972-604-6000. Office Fax: 972-605-6033.

**SCHUDER, RAYMOND FRANCIS,** lawyer; b. Wickford, R.I., Dec. 27, 1926; s. Rollie Milton and Selma (Ball) S.; m. Betty Jo Williams, Mar. 14, 1948; children: Gregg Williams, Glen Arva. AB, Emory U., 1949, JD, 1951. Bar: Ga. 1951. With Trust Co. Ga., Atlanta, 1951—54; assoc. firm Wheeler Robinson & Thurmond, Gainesville, Ga., 1954—59; pvt. practice law Gainesville, 1959—70, 1981—96; ptnr. Schuder & Brown, Gainesville, 1971—76, Schuder & Hartness, Gainesville, 1977—80. Mcpl. ct. judge Gainesville, 1956-60, 73-75; magistrate ct. judge, 1985-2000, sr. magistrate, 2001-03. Supr. Upper Chattahoochee Soil and Water Conservation Dist., 1971-74; CEO, bd. dirs. Charles Thompson Estes Found., Inc., Gainesville. Cpl. USMCR, 1944-50; 1st lt. USAR, 1950-56, ret. Mem. State Bar Ga. (gov. 1966-70), Gainesville-Northeastern Bar Assn. (pres. 1969-70), Am. Legion, VFW, Elks. Methodist. Home: 2224 Riverside Dr Gainesville GA 30501-1232 E-mail: xrfs@charter.net.

**SCHUELE, DONALD EDWARD,** retired physics professor, dean; b. Cleve., June 16, 1934; s. Edward and Mildred (Matousek) S.; m. Clare Ann Kirchner, Sept. 5, 1956; children: Donna, Karen, Melanie, Judy, Rachel, Ruth. BS, John Carroll U., Cleve., 1956, MS, 1957; PhD, Case Inst. Tech., 1962. Instr. physics and math. John Carroll U., 1956-59; part-time instr. physics Case Inst. Tech., 1959-62, instr., asst. prof., assoc prof., 1962-70; mem. tech. staff Bell Telephone Labs., 1970-72; assoc. prof. physics Case Western Res. U., 1972-74, prof., 1974—, dean undergrad. coll., 1973-76, chmn. dept. physics, 1976-78; vice dean Case Inst. Tech., 1978-83, v.p. for undergrad. and grad. studies, 1983-84, dean, 1984-86, prof. physics, 1986-88, dean math. and natural sci., 1988-89, Albert A. Michelson prof. physics, 1989—2006, Albert A. Michelson prof. emeritus physics, 2006, acting chmn. elec. engring. and applied physics, 1992-93. Cons. in field. Co-editor: Critical Revs. in Solid State Scis, 1969-84; contbr. articles to profl. jours.; patentee in field. Mem. adv. bd. St. Charles Borromeo Sch., 1970-72; pres. Seed Found., 1986-89; trustee St. Mary's Sem., 1980-93; mem. Olympic Sports Equipment and Tech. Com., 1982-93; trustee Newman Found., 1983—, Northeastern Ohio Sci. Fair, 1983—; mem. Diocesan Pastoral Coun., 1992-94; active Rep. Presdl. task force. Recipient Disting. Physics Alumnus award John Carroll U., 1983; NSF Faculty fellow, 1961-63; Sam Givelber fellow Case Alumni Assn., 2001. Mem.: North Coast Thermal Analysis Soc., Am. Assn. Physics Tchrs., Am. Phys. Soc. (vice chair Ohio sect. 1995—96, chair 1996—97), Newman Apostolate, Case Alumni Coun. (life; 3d v.p. 2001—02, 1st v.p. 2002—03, pres. 2003—04, treas. 1992, chair Case Fund Bd. 2004—), Tau Beta Pi, Sigma Xi, Alpha Sigma Nu. Republican. Roman Catholic. Achievements include patents fluid pressure device, impact wrench torque calibrator, detection of wear particles and other impurities in industrial fluids, electrical oil analysis instrument. Home: 4892 Countryside Rd Cleveland OH 44124-2513 Office: Case Western Res U 10900 Euclid Ave Cleveland OH 44106-1712 Office Phone: 216-368-4013. Business E-Mail: des3@case.edu.

**SCHUELEIN, MARIANNE IDA,** neurologist, educator; b. Stuttgart, Germany, Apr. 16, 1934; d. Curt Charles and Gertrude (Weil) S.; m. Ralph Mack Krause, June 26, 1960; children: Peter C., Steven C. AB, Wellesley Coll., 1955; MD, NYU, 1959. Diplomate Am. Bd. Pediatrics; diplomate in neurology and child neurology Am. Bd. Psychiatry and Neurology. Intern in pediatrics Yale U., New Haven, 1959-60; resident in pediatrics Michael Reese Hosp., Chgo., 1960-62; fellow in neurology Children's Hosp., Washington, 1962-63; resident in neurology Georgetown U., Washington, 1964-67, asst. prof. neurology and pediatrics, 1967—; chair divsn. neurology Sibley Meml. Hosp., Washington, 2001—02. Mem. Bd. Medicine, Washington, 1988—2001, acting chair, 2001; lectr. Georgetown U. Law Sch., 1992; mem. staff Georgetown U. Hosp., Children's Hosp. D.C., Fairfax Hosp., Prince George's Hosp. Ctr., Washington Hosp. Ctr., Sibley Meml. Hosp., Va. Hosp. Ctr.; bd. dirs. St. John's Devel. Svcs.; mem. Folger Poetry Bd.; examiner Am. Bd. Psychiatry and Neurology, 1980—2000; cons. USLME. Contbr. articles to profl. publs. Recipient Cert. of Recognition, MD Assn., 1978, Disting. Svc. award Epilepsy Fedn., 1981, Newmyer award Sidwell Friends, 1985, Vicennial medal Georgetown U. Med. Ctr., 1987, presdl. cert. of Appreciation Med. Soc. of the D.C., 1995; featured physician Nat. Libr. Medicine Exhibit women in medicine. Fellow: Am. Acad. Pediatrics, Am. Acad. Neurology; mem.: Nat. Tuberous Sclerosis Assn. (bd. dirs. 1986—), Med. Soc. D.C. (chmn. neurology sect. 1992—93), Child Neurology Soc., Am. Acad. Devel. Medicine, NYU Med. Sch. Alumni Assn. D.C. (pres. 1993), Cosmos Club (bd. mgmt. 1994—2003, sec. 1998—2000, v.p. 2000-01, pres. 2001—02). Office: Georgetown U Sch Medicine Kober-Cogan #307 3800 Reservoir Rd NW Washington DC 20007 Office Phone: 202-687-4947. E-mail: ms43@georgetown.edu.

**SCHUELER, GERALD JOSEPH,** writer, systems analyst, consultant; b. Darby, Pa., Oct. 29, 1942; s. Charles Carroll and Bertha Julia (Fadgen) S.; m. Betty Jane Sherlin, Aug. 17, 1963; children: Diane Sue, Joseph Carroll, Andrew Tyson, Crystal Ann. BS, U. Md., 1965; MS in Adminstrn., Ctrl. Mich. U., 1991; PhD, Capella U., Minn., 1996, 98. Lic. profl. counselor, D.C. Test dir. U.S. Army Test and Evaluation Command, Aberdeen Proving Ground, Md., 1965-75, ops. rsch. analyst, 1975-94; tech. writer Harford Writers Group, Aberdeen, Md., 1984—; sys. analyst Quantum Rsch. Internat., Bel Air, Md., 1990—2003. Co-owner Shellay, Aberdeen, 1964-99, Creative Sales & Svc., Aberdeen, 1975—; cons. Compucats Computer Store, Aberdeen, 1982-1989. Author: Enochian Magic, 1984, Enochian Physics, 1988; co-author: Coming into the Light, 1989, Angels Message to Humanity, 1996. Leader/com. mem. Boy Scouts Am., Aberdeen, 1974-80; officer Friends of Harford County Libr., Aberdeen, 1975—; county leader Harford County 4-H Club, Aberdeen, 1978-95. Mem.: Am. Counseling Assn., Internat. Assn. Transpersonal Psychology, Noetic Inst. Dem. Avocations: computers, reading, crafts. Personal E-mail: jerry@schuelers.com.

**SCHUELER, JOHN R.,** newspaper executive; b. Grosse Point, MI; m. Linda Schueler; children: Tracie, Lindsey. BA, W. Mich. U. Dir. sales Atlanta Jour. & Constn., 1979—82; with Miami Herald, Miami, Fla., 1984—89; pres. New England Newspapers, 1989—91; v.p. consumer mktg. & circulation The Orange County Register, Santa Ana, Calif., 1991—92, exec. v.p. & gen. mgr., 1992—95, pres., COO, 1995-98; publisher Star Tribune, Mpls., 1998—2001; pub. Los Angeles Daily News, 2001—04; pres., CEO Los Angeles Newspaper Group, 2004—05; pres. Fla. Comm. Group, 2005—. Office: Media General Broadcast Group 200 S Parker St Tampa FL 33606 Office Phone: 813-221-5757.*

**SCHUELKE, JOHN PAUL,** religious organization administrator; b. Benton Harbor, Mich., Nov. 5, 1934; s. Alwin E. and Martha M. (Schoeneberg) S.; m. Noreta H. Petersen, Sept. 9, 1956; children: Alvin, Mary, Sheryl, Brian. BS in Acctg., U. Wyo., 1957; LLD (hon.), Concordia U., Irvine, Calif., 1983. CPA. From acct. to sr. acct. Colo. Interstate Gas Co., Colorado Springs, 1957-63; staff acct. Arthur Anderson & Co., Denver, 1963-64; mgr. fin. control Colo. Interstate Corp., Colorado Springs, 1964-67, dir. fin. control, 1967-71; adminstrv. v.p. mfg. divsn. Marsh Instrument Co. subs. Colo. Mfg. Corp.,

Skokie, Ill., 1971-72; exec. officer bd. dirs., CAO Luth. Ch.-Mo. Synod, St. Louis, 1972-98, ret., 1999. Former chmn. Concordia Asia Ednl. Found.; lectr. in field. Asst. scoutmaster Boy Scouts Am., Colorado Springs; former mem. governing bd., sec. Luth. Svcs. in Am.; former mem. governing bd. Luth. Coun.-USA, com. Luth. Coop.; v.p. Faith Luth Ch., Woodland Park; former mem. bd. human care ministries, sec., mem. lic. deacon com. Rocky Mountain dist. Luth. Ch.-Mo. Synod. Recipient God and Country award Eagle Scout. Mem. Alpha Kappa Psi, Gamma Delta (former pres.). Lutheran. Avocations: travel, fishing, reading.

**SCHUENEMAN, DIANE L.,** diversified financial services company executive; Account exec. instl. sales Merrill Lynch, 1971, head global ops. and infrastructure svcs., 2004—06, sr. v.p., head global infrastructure solutions grp., 2006—. Bd. mgrs. Omgeo; bd. dirs. Depository Trust and Clearing Corpn. Office: Merrill Lynch 4 World Fin Ctr 250 Vesey St New York NY 10080*

**SCHUEPPERT, GEORGE LOUIS,** financial executive; b. Merrill, Wis., July 1, 1938; s. George Henry and Eleanor Natalie (Pautz) S.; m. Kathleen Kay Carpenter, May 6, 1967; children—Steven Andrew, Stephanie Roanne, Stenning Karl BBA, U. Wis., Madison, 1961; MBA, U. Chgo., 1969. Treas., controller Steiger-Rathke Devel. Co., Phoenix, 1964-65; various positions Continental Ill. Nat., Chgo., 1965-76, 1981-86; mng. dir. Continental Ill Ltd., London, 1977-81; sr. v.p. Continental Ill. Nat. Bank, Chgo., 1982-86; ptnr. Coopers & Lybrand, Chgo., 1986-87; exec. v.p. fin. CBI Industries Inc, Oak Brook, Ill., 1987-95, also bd. dirs., 1987-95; exec. v.p., CFO Outboard Marine Corp., Waukegan, Ill., 1996-97. Bd. dirs. Wells Mfg. Co., Barrington Bank & Trust Co. Pres. Gt. Books Found.; chmn., bd. dirs. De Paul U. Gov. Asst. Program. Lt. (j.g.) USN, 1961-64. Recipient Herfurth award U. Wis., 1960 Mem. Econ. Club Chgo. (bd. dirs., chmn. membership com.). Republican. Avocations: history, architecture, travel, golf. Home: 97 Otis Rd Barrington IL 60010-5129 Office: Great Books Found 35 E Wacker Dr Ste 2300 Chicago IL 60601-2298

**SCHUERHOLZ, JOHN BOLAND, JR.,** professional baseball executive; b. Balt., Oct. 1, 1940; s. John Boland and Maryne (Wyatt) Schuerholz; m. Ellen Louise Lawson, June 21, 1963; 1 child, Regina Marie Reagan; m. Karen Louise Wiltse, Sept. 18, 1978; 1 child, Jonathan Lawrence. B.E., Towson State U., 1962; postgrad., Loyola Coll., Md., 1964—66. Tchr. various schs., 1962—66; adminstrv. asst. Balt. Orioles, 1966—68, Kansas City Royals, 1968—70, asst. farm dir., 1970—75, farm dir., 1975, dir. scouting and player devel., 1976—79, v.p. player personnel, 1979—81, exec. v.p., gen. mgr., 1981—90, Atlanta Braves, 1990—. With AUS, 1962-72. Recipient Lifetime Achievement award, Baseball America, 2004. Lutheran. Office: Atlanta Braves PO Box 4064 Atlanta GA 30302-4064

**SCHUESSLER, JOHN T. (JACK SCHUESSLER),** retired food service executive; b. Dec. 21, 1950; m. Patty A. Schuessler. BS, Spring Hill Coll. Mgr. trainee Wendy's franchise, Atlanta, 1974-76; joined Wendy's Internat., 1976, dist. mgr., dir. area ops., regional dir. various zones US, 1976-83, regional v.p.e ea. divsn., 1983-84, zone pres., 1984-86, divsn. v.p., 1986-87, sr. v.p. N.E. region, 1987-95, exec. v.p. US ops., 1995-97, pres., COO US ops., 1997-2000, pres., COO Can., 1999-2000, pres., CEO, 2000—06, chmn., 2001—06. Trustee Wendy's Nat. Advtsg. Program.*

**SCHUESSLER FIORENZA, ELISABETH,** theology studies educator; b. Tschanad, Romania, Apr. 17, 1938; parents German citizens; d. Peter and Magdalena Schuessler; m. Francis Fiorenza, Dec. 17, 1967; 1 child, Chris. MDiv, U. Wuerzburg, Germany, 1962; Lic. Theol., U. Wuerzburg, 1963; DrTheol., U. Muenster, Germany, 1970. Asst. prof. theology U. Notre Dame, South Bend, Ind., 1970-75, assoc. prof., 1975-80, prof., 1980-84; instr. U. Muenster, 1966-67; Talbot prof. N.T., Episcopal Div. Sch., Cambridge, Mass., 1984-88; Krister Stendahl prof. Divsn. Scripture and Interpretation Harvard U., Cambridge, Mass., 1988—. Harry Emerson Fosdick vis. prof. Union Theol. Sem., N.Y.C., 1974-75; guest prof. U. Tuebingen, Federal Republic of Germany, 1987, Cath. Theol. Faculty Luzern, Switzerland, 1990; Stiftungs prof. Humboldt U., Berlin, 1997; Ernst Troeltsch prof. U. Heidelberg, Germany, 1999. Author: Der Vergessene Partner, 1964, Priester für Gott, 1972, The Apocalypse, 1976, Invitation to the Book of Revelation, 1981, In Memory of Her, 1983, Bread not Stone, 1984, Judgement or Justice, 1985, Revelation: Vision of a Just World, 1991, But She Said - Feminist Practices of Biblical Interpretation, 1992, Discipleship of Equals: A Critical Feminist Ekklesialogy of Liberation, 1993, Jesus: Miriam's Child and Sophia's Prophet, Critical Issues in Feminist Christology, 1994, Sharing Her Word, 1998, Rhetoric and Ethic The Politics of Biblical Studies, 1999, Jesus and the Politics of Interpretation, 2000, Wisdom Ways, 2001, Grenzen überschreiten, 2004; editor: Searching the Scriptures, 2 vols, 1993, 94, The Power of Naming, 1996; founding co-editor Jour. Feminist Studies in Religion; also editor other works. Mem.: Am. Acad. Arts and Scis., Soc. Bibl. Lit. (past pres.), Am. Acad. Religion. Office: Harvard Div Sch 45 Francis Ave Cambridge MA 02138-1911 Office Phone: 617-495-5751.

**SCHUETTE, CHARLES A.,** lawyer; b. Columbus, Ind., Feb. 24, 1942; BBA, U. Okla., 1964, JD, 1967. Bar: Okla. 1967, Fla. 1970, U.S. Supreme Ct. 1979, U.S. Dist. Ct. (so. dist.) Fla. 1982, U.S. Dist. Ct. (mid. dist.) Fla. 1982. With Akerman Senterfitt. Fellow Am. Bar Found.; mem. ABA, Fla. Bar, Okla. Bar Assn., Dade County Bar Assn. Office: Akerman Senterfitt 1 SE 3rd Ave Fl Miami FL 33131-1700

**SCHUETTINGER, BRUCE MICHAEL,** conservator; b. Frederick, Md., Apr. 15, 1955; s. Arthur George Schuettinger and Shirlee Price; children: Kathryn, Alison. BS in Fine Arts cum laude, Towson State U., 1978. Conservator Antique Restorations, Frederick, Md., 1983—90, Antique Restorations Ltd, New Market, Md 1990—, personal property appraiser internat. Soc. of Appraisers (Indiana U.), 1985, 1986, U. Md., 1985. Presenter in field. Co-author: (directory) Conservation Resources for Art and Antiques, 2001. Mem. curatorial com. Hist. Soc. of Frederick County, Md., 2002—05. Mem.: Wash. Conservatory Guild, Internat. Soc. Appraisers, Am. Inst. for Conservation of Historic and Artistic Wants (assoc.). Independent. Episc. Avocations: painting, photography. Home: 13724 Pryor Rd Thurmont MD 21788 Office: Antique Restorations Ltd 17 North Alley New Market MD 21774 Office phone: 301-869-3009.

**SCHUETZE-COBURN, MARJE,** university librarian; BA in German and History, Univ. Calif., Berkeley; MLS, UCLA, MA in History. Cataloger, Feuchtwanger Collection USC, 1989—91, Feuchtwanger Libr. and Curator, 1991—2001, dir., Spl. Libraries and Archival Collections, 2001—, also assoc. dean faculty affairs for Univ. Libraries, interim libr. head, 2006—. Office: Dir SLAC Univ So Calif Los Angeles CA 90089 Office Phone: 213-740-7119. Business E-Mail: schuetze@usc.edu.*

**SCHUH, DALE R.,** insurance company executive; Joined Sentry Ins., A Mutal Co., Stevens Point, Wis., 1972, v.p. planning, 1988, pres., COO, 1996, CEO, pres., chmn., 1997—. Office: Sentry Ins A Mutual Co 1800 North Point Dr Stevens Point WI 54481

**SCHUH, FRANK JOSEPH,** oil industry executive, consultant; b. Columbus, Ohio, Feb. 3, 1935; s. Sebastian and Elizabeth (Zorn) S.; m. Alice Virgene Kasler, June 16, 1956; children: Dwain Joseph, Michael James, Barbara Ann. BS in Petroleum Engring., MS in Petroleum Engring., Ohio State U., 1956. Registered profl. engr., Ohio. Drilling and rsch. engr. Atlantic Refining Co., Tex., La., 1956-62; mem. drilling engring. staff, dir. engring. Atlantic Richfield Co., Dallas, 1962-82, mgr. drilling rsch., sr. advisor Plano, Tex., 1982-86; v.p. Enertech Engring. & Tech., Dallas, 1986-87; pres. Drilling Tech., Inc., Plano, 1987—; v.p. Supreme Resources Corp., Dallas, 1988-92. Founder, 1st pres. Drilling Engring. Assn., Dallas, 1983-85; mem. tech. adv. com. Internat. Ocean Drilling Program, 2002—. Author: Drilling Equations, 1975; patentee horizontal drilling, high pressure drilling system, continuous heavy oil production process, 31 other patents. Precinct, region chmn. Rep.

Party, Dallas, 1964-74; vol. bldg. com. Mary Immaculate Ch., Dallas, 1965-66; mem. tech. engring. and devel. com. Ocean Drilling Program, Bryan, Tex., 1980—. Recipient outstanding achievement in field of engring. award Nat. Engrs. Coun., 1980, Robert Earl McConnell award Am. Inst. Mining Engrs., 1994, Ohio State Univ. Coll. of Engring. Benjamin G. Lamme Meritorious Achievement medel, 1995. Mem. NAE, Soc. Petroleum Engrs. (nat. bd. dirs. 1983-86, Drilling Engring. award 1986, Disting. Mem. award 1989), Am. Petroleum Inst. (chmn. com. 6, 1985-88, svc. citation 1986), Am. Assn. Drilling Engrs., Soc. Ind. Profl. Earth Scientists, Petroleum Engrs. Club (pres. 1974-75), Ohio State U. Alumni Club (pres. 1968-69), Dallas-Ft. Worth Oilman's Club (handicapper 1973-86). Avocations: golf, sailing. Office: Drilling Technology Inc 5808 Wavertree Ln Ste 1000 Plano TX 75093-4513 Office Phone: 972-380-2103.

**SCHUH, G(EORGE) EDWARD,** dean, agricultural economist; b. Indpls., Sept. 13, 1930; s. George Edward and Viola (Lentz) S.; m. Maria Ignez, May 23, 1965; children: Audrey, Susan, Tanya. BS in Agrl. Edn, Purdue U., 1952, DAgr, PhD, Purdue U., 1992; MS in Agrl. Econs., Mich. State U., 1954; MA in Econs. U. Chgo., 1958, PhD, 1961; prof. (hon.), Fed. U. Vicosa, Brazil, 1965. From instr. to prof. agrl. econs. Purdue U., 1959-79; dir. Center for Public Policy and Public Affairs, 1977-78; dep. undersec. for internat. affairs and commodity programs Dept. Agr., Washington, 1978-79, chair bd. for internat. food and agrl. devel., 1995—2002; prof. agrl. and applied econs., head dept. U. Minn., Mpls., 1979-84; dir. agr. and rural devel. World Bank, Washington, 1984-87; dean Humphrey Inst. for Pub. Affairs U. Minn., 1987—96; Orville and Jane Freeman Endowed chair Humphrey Inst. for Pub. Affairs, U. Minn., 1996—; regents prof. U. Minn., 1998—. Program advisor Ford Found., 1966-77; sr. staff economist Pres.'s Coun. Econ. Advisors, 1974-75; mem. bd. on agr. and natural resources NRC, 1998—2004; trustee Internat. Food Policy Rsch. Inst., 1997-2003, Internat. Potato Ctr., 2004—. Contbr. articles to profl. jours. Trustee Sasakawa Africa Assn., 1998—. Served with U.S. Army, 1954-56. Recipient 60 at 60 award, Internat. Insts. Cooperation in Agr., Order Sci. Merit, Grand Cruz. Fellow: AAAS, Brazilian Acad. Sci., Brazilian Soc. Rural Econs., Am. Acad. Arts and Scis., Am. Agrl. Econs. Assn. (bd. dirs. 1977—80, pres.-elect 1980—81, pres. 1981—82, Thesis award 1962, Pub. Rsch. award 1971, Article award 1975, Policy award 1979, Publ. of Lasting Value award 1988); mem.: Brazilian Soc. Agrl. Economists, Am. Econ. Assn., Internat. Assn. Agrl. Econs. Office: Humphrey Ctr U Minn 301 19th Ave S Minneapolis MN 55455-0429 Office Phone: 612-625-8388. Business E-Mail: geschuh@hhh.umn.edu.

**SCHUHMANN, PETER W.,** economist, educator; b. Red Bank, N.J., Sept. 24, 1968; m. Lara-Ann Linkfield, May 26, 2006. BS, U. N.C. Wilmington, 1990; PhD, N.C. State U., Raleigh, 1996. Asst. prof. econs. U. Richmond, Va., 1996—99, U. N.C., Wilmington, 1999—2001, assoc. prof. econs. 2001—. Recipient Chancellor's Tchg. award, U. N.C., 2005. Office: Univ NC 601 S College Rd Wilmington NC 28403 Office Phone: 910-962-3417.

**SCHUKER, STEPHEN ALAN,** historian, educator; b. NYC, Feb. 16, 1939; s. Louis A. and Millicent (Milchman) S.; m. Elisabeth Glaser, 1998. AB summa cum laude, Cornell U., 1959; AM, Harvard U., 1962, PhD, 1969; children: Lauren, Daniel. Asst. head hist. rsch. naval history div. Office Chief Naval Ops., 1959-61; instr. history Harvard U., Cambridge, Mass., 1968-69, asst. prof., 1969-74, lectr., 1974-75; vis. assoc. prof. European studies Sch. Advanced Internat. Studies, Johns Hopkins U., Washington, 1977, adj. prof., 1978-83; assoc. prof. history Brandeis U., Waltham, Mass., 1977-82, prof., 1982-91; Commonwealth prof. history U. Va., Charlottesville, 1991-92, William M. Corcoran prof., 1992—; syndic U. Press New Eng., 1979-81; cons. Nat. Commn. Documents and Records Federal Ofcls., 1976, Rockefeller Found., 1981. Author: The End of French Predominance in Europe (George Louis Beer prize, Gilbert Chinard prize), 1976, American "Reparations" to Germany, 1919-1933: Implications for the Third World Debt Crisis, 1988; editor: Deutschland und Frankreich vom Konflikt zur Aussöhnung, 2000; mem. bd. editors Internat. History Rev. 2001-2004; contbr. articles to profl. jours. Lt. USNR, 1959-61. NEH fellow, 1972-73; Am. Council Learned Socs. fellow, 1976-77, 85; sr. fellow USIA-Fulbright Commn., 1984, fellow internat. security John D. and Catherine T. MacArthur Found., 1987-89, fellow Historisches Kolleg, Bayerische Akademie der Wissenschaften, 1996—, fellow German Marshall Fund, 1998-99. Mem. Am. Hist. Assn., Soc. Historians Am. Fgn. Relations, Hist. Soc. Office: U Va Corcoran Dept History University Station Charlottesville VA 22904 Office Phone: 434-924-6405. Business E-Mail: sas4u@virginia.edu.

**SCHULBERG, BUDD,** author; b. N.Y.C., Mar. 27, 1914; s. Benjamin P. and Adeline (Jaffe) S.; m. Virginia Ray, July 23, 1936 (div. 1942); 1 dau., Victoria; m. Victoria Anderson, Feb. 17, 1943 (div. 1964); children: Stephen, David; m. Geraldine Brooks, July 12, 1964 (dec. 1977); m. Betsy Anne Langman, June 9, 1979; children: Benn Stuart, Jessica A. Student, Deerfield Acad., 1931-32; AB cum laude, Dartmouth Coll., 1936, LLD, 1960; LittD, Long Island U., 1983; DHL, Hofstra U., 1987, Five Points Coll., 2001. Boxing editor Sports Illustrated; pres., prodr. Schulberg Prodns. Founder, dir. Watts Writers Workshop, L.A., 1965—; founder, chmn. Frederick Douglass Creative Arts Ctr., N.Y.C., 1971—. Screenwriter, Hollywood, 1936-39; writer "The Schulberg Report", Newsday Syndicate; author: What Makes Sammy Run?, 1941, The Harder They Fall, 1947, The Disenchanted, 1950, Some Faces in the Crowd, 1953, Waterfront, 1955 (Christopher award 1955), Sanctuary V, 1969, The Four Seasons of Success, 1972, Loser and Still Champion: Muhammad Ali, 1972, Swan Watch, 1975, Everything that Moves, 1980, Moving Pictures: Memories of a Hollywood Prince, 1981, Writers in America Love, Action, Laughter and Other Sad Tales, 1990, Sparring with Hemingway: And Other Legends of the Fight Game, 1995. La Foret Interdite, including dialogue in Black and White with James Badwin, 1997; editor: From the Ashes: Voices of Watts, 1967; screenwriter: (film) (with Samuel Orula) Little Orphan Annie, 1938, (with F. Scott Fitzgerald) Winter Carnival, 1939, (with Dorothy Parker) Weekend for Three, 1941, (with Martin Berkeley) City without Men, 1943, (with Dudley Nichols) Government Girl, 1943, On the Waterfront, 1954 (Academy award best original story and screenplay 1954, N.Y. Critics award 1954, Fgn. Corrs. award 1954, Screen Writers Guild award 1954, Venice Festival award 1954), A Face in the Crowd, 1958 (German Film Critics award 1957), Wind Across the Everglades, 1958, (teleplays) The Pharmacist's Mate, 1951, Paso Doble, Memory in White, The Legend That Walks Like a man, A Question of Honor, A Table At Ciro's; playwright: The Disenchanted: A Play in Three Acts, 1958, What Make's Sammy Run?, 1959, (musical) Senor Discretion Himself, 1985, (play in 2 acts) The Disenchanted, 1999, On the Waterfront, 2001; contbr. to Sports Illustrated, Life, N.Y. Times Book Rev., Esquire, Newsday Syndicate, L.A. Times Book Rev., N.Y. Times Sunday Mag., Playboy, The New Yorker, Vanity Fair. Bd. dirs. Westminster Neighborhood Assn., L.A., 1965-68, Inner City Cultural Ctr., L.A., 1965-68; mem. nat. adv. commn. on black participation John F. Kennedy Ctr. for Performing Arts; trustee Humanitas Prize. Lt. (j.g.) USNR, 1943-46, assigned to OSS. Awarded Army Commendation Ribbon for gathering photog. evidence of war crimes for Nuremberg Trial, 1945-46; recipient Susie Humanitarian award B'nai B'rith, Image award NAACP, Journalism award Dartmouth Coll., Merit award Lotos Club., L.A. Community Svc. award, 1966, B'hai Human Rights award, 1968, spl. award for Watts Writers Workshop, New Eng. Theater Conf., 1969, Heritage award Deerfield Acad., 1986, Amistad award, award for work with black writers Howard U., Prix Literaire, Deauville Festival 1989, 2005, Westhampton Writers Lifetime Achievement award, 1989, World Boxing Assn. Living Legend award, 1990, 97, Southampton Cultural Ctr. 1st Annual Literature award, 1992, Lifetime Achievement award Guild Hall, 2003, Lifetime Achievement award L.A. (Calif.) H.S., 2005. Am. Achievement award Congresswoman Maxine Waters, 2005; named to Internat. Boxing Hall of Fame, 2003. Mem. Dramatists Guild, ASCAP, Authors Guild N.Y.C. (mem. council), ACLU, Writers Guild East (mem. coun.), Boxing Writers Am. (A. J. Liebling award 1997), P.E.N., Sphinx (Dartmouth), The Players Club, Yale/Dartmouth Club, Phi Beta Kappa. Address: Mr Mickey Freiberg Acme Literary Agy 4727 Wilshire Blvd Los Angeles CA 90064 also: Ms Miriam Altshuler 53 Old Post Rd N Red Hook NY 12571 Office Phone: 631-288-0514. E-mail: bschul@optonline.net.

**SCHULBERG, HERBERT CHARLES,** psychologist; b. N.Y.C., Feb. 10, 1934; s. Philip and Sarah (Bookin) S.; m. Phyllis Gitelman, June 23, 1957; children: Mark Ira, Michelle Tobi. BA, Yeshiva Coll., 1955; PhD, Columbia U., 1960; MS, Harvard U., 1963. Prof. psychiatry, psychology and medicine Sch. Medicine U. Pitts., 1976-99, prof. emeritus of psychiatry, 1999—; prof. psychology in psychiatry Weill Med. Coll., Cornell U., 2000—. Office Phone: 914-997-5798. Personal E-mail: hcspgs@earthlink.net.

**SCHULDINER, MICHAEL JOSEPH,** language educator, writer; b. Wetzlar, Germany, Jan. 29, 1948; arrived in U.S., 1950; s. Max and Toby Schuldiner; m. Lea Schultz Schuldiner; children: Ruth Faye, Effrat Pasha. BA, Goddard Coll., 1969; PhD, Kent State U., 1979; MPhil, U. Cambridge, Eng., 2000. From lectr. to asst. prof. Rutgers Coll., New Brunswick, NJ, 1979—80; prof. U. Alaska, Fairbanks, 1980—. Chair English U. Alaska, Fairbanks, 2004—. Editor: Gifts and Works: Spiritual Life and Political Controversy in 17th Century New England, 1990, Tayloring Shop: Essays on Edward Taylor, 1997, Selected Writings of Mordecai Noah, 1999. Recipient Sr. lectr., Fulbright, Israel, 1987; fellow, Huntington Libr., 1986;. Meml. Found. for Jewish Culture, 1999. Jewish. Home: 4589 Drake St Fairbanks AK 99709 Office: Univ Alaska 854 Greening Bldg Fairbanks AK 99775 Business E-Mail: ffmgs@uaf.edu.

**SCHULEIT, ANNA,** artist; b. Mainz, Germany, 1974; BFA, RI Sch. Design, 1998; MFA, Dartmouth Coll., Hanover, NH, 2005. Cons. Met. Transit Authority, NYC, 2005; art instr. Nightingale-Bamford Sch., NYC, 2005. Guest lectr. Dept. Sociology, Brown U., 1999, 2002, 05, Smith Coll, 2000, Comm. River Valley Hospital, Middletown, Conn., 2000, Springfield Coll., 2001, Brattleboro Mus. and Art Ctr., 2001, The Delaney House, Holyoke, Mass., 2001, RI Sch. Design, 2005; presenter Forum on Hist. Records, U. Mass. Amherst, 2001, Nat. Conv. State Art Agencies, 2001, Sch. Arch., McGill U., Montréal, 2003; vis. artist Westborough Sate Hospital, Mass., 2001—04; disting. visitor Sch. Art & Design, U. Mich., 2006. Exhibitions include A Translantantic Project, Muhle der schoenen Kunste, Germany, 1995, Off the Wall, 16 S. Main St. Gallery, Providence, 1998, National Prize Show, Cambridge Art Assn., Mus. Fine Art, Boston, 1998, Summer Show, Harvard U., 1999, Medfield State Hospital Closing: Projections, Dept. Mental Health, Westborough, Mass., 2004, Amherst Art Show, 2004, The Matzo Files, NYC, 2004—05, one-woman shows include Nada Mason Gallery, Northfield, Mass., 2000, Northampton Ctr. for Arts, 2000, exhibited in group shows at Kaelin Gallery, Boston, 2002, Pioneers of Public, Revolving Mus., Lowell, Mass., 2002, Inch x Inch, Arlington Ctr. for Arts, 2002, CHi of Ancestry, Gallery Luna, Salem, Mass., 2004, 1939 The Missing Year, New Art Ctr., Newton, Mass., 2005, Goliath, Brooklyn, 2006, installations, Habeas Corpus, Northampton State Hospital, 2000, When At Last, Brattleboro Mus. and Art Ctr., 2001, Bloom, Mass. Mental Health Ctr., 2003. Recipient Grad. Alumni award, Dartmouth Coll., 2005, Thesis Rsch. award, 2005; fellow MacDowell Colony, 2002, 2006, Yaddo, 2005, Radcliffe Inst., Harvard U., 2006—07; Artist Grant, Elizabeth Greenshields Found., 1996, Northampton Arts Coun., 2000, Mass. Found. for Humanities, 2000, Chubb Life Am. Fellow, Mac-Dowell Colony, 2000—01, MacArthur Fellow, John D. and Catherine T. MacArthur Found., 2006. Office: HIstoric Northampton 46 Bridge St Northampton MA 01060 Office Phone: 413-584-6011. Office Fax: 413-584-7956.*

**SCHULER, ALISON KAY,** lawyer; b. West Point, N.Y., Oct. 1, 1948; d. Richard Hamilton and Irma (Sanken) S.; m. Lyman Gage Sandy, Mar. 30, 1974, (dec. Mar. 2002); 1 child, Theodore. AB cum laude, Radcliffe Coll., 1969; JD, Harvard U., 1972. Bar: Va. 1973, D.C. 1974, N.Mex. 1975. Assoc. Hunton & Williams, Richmond, Va., 1972-75; asst. U.S. atty. U.S. Atty.'s Office, Albuquerque, 1975-78; adj. prof. law U. N.Mex., 1983-85, 90, 98—; ptnr. Sutin, Thayer & Browne, Albuquerque, 1978-85, Montgomery & Andrews, P.A., Albuquerque, 1985-88; sole practice Albuquerque, 1988—. Bd. dirs. Intellite, Inc. Bd. dirs. Am. Diabetes Assn., Albuquerque, 1985-85, chmn. bd. dirs., 1984—85; bd. dirs. June Music Festival, 1980—95, pres., 1983—85, 1993—94; bd. dirs. Albuquerque Conservation Trust, 1986—90, N.Mex. Osteo. Found., 1993—96; chairperson Albuquerque Pub. Fgn. Rels., 1984—85; mem. N.Mex. Internat. Trade and Investment Coun., Inc., 1986—; chartered org. rep. troop 444 Boy Scouts Am., 1997—, mem. nominating com., mem.-at-large com. Sandia dist., 1998—, dist. vice chmn., 1999—2002, v.p. Great S.W. coun., 2001—05, pres. Great S.W. coun., 2006—, mem. staff, 2002—04, wood badge course dir., 2005; mem. adv. bd. Care Net Pregnancy Ctr. of Albuquerque, 2003—; mem. coun. St. Lukes Luth. Ch., 1976—80, 1982—84, 1991—96, v.p., 1978—80, 1982—84, pres., 1994—95; bd. dirs. Chamber Music Albuquerque, 2006—. Recipient Award of Merit, Sandia Dist., 2000, Svc. award, Albuquerque Astron. Soc., 2002, Silver Beaver award, Gt. S.W. Coun., 2002. Mem. Fed. Bar Assn. (coord.), ABA, Va. Bar Assn., N.Mex. Bar Assn. (chmn. corp., banking and bus. law 1982-83, bd. dirs. internat. and immigration law sect. 1987-95, chmn. 1993-94), Albuquerque Astron. Soc. (Svc. award 2002), Harvard U. Alumni Assn. (mem. fund campaign, regional dir. 1984-86, v.p. 1986-89, chmn. clubs com. 1985-88, chmn. communications com. 1988-91), Radcliffe Coll. Alumnae Assn. Bd. Mgmt. (regional dir. 1984-87, chmn. comms. com. 1988-91), Harvard-Radcliffe Club (pres. 1980-84). Home: 632 Cougar Loop NE Albuquerque NM 87122-1808 Office: 2155 Louisiana Blvd NE Ste 8500 Albuquerque NM 87110-5483 Office Phone: 505-872-0800. Personal E-mail: akschuler@aol.com.

**SCHULER, DOROTHY R.,** education educator, consultant, retired elementary school educator; b. Tex., May 1, 1947; d. Raymond Lowell and Violet Marie Hayes; m. Robert Dale Schuler, Aug. 17, 1968; children: Christy Anne Bryant, Amy Lynne. BS in Elem. Edn., U. Tex., Austin, Tex., 1968; MS in Edn., So. Ill. U. at Edwardsville, Edswardsville, Ill., 1989. Cert. Nat. Bd. Tchr. Nat. Bd. for Profl. Tchg. Standards, 2001. Third grade tchr. Ashlawn Elem., Arlington, Va., 1968—69; fourth grade tchr. Bret Harte Elem., Cherry Hill, NJ, 1969—70; kindergarten tchr. Dow Elem. Sch., Dow, Ill., 1982—86; second grade tchr. Grafton Elem. Sch., Grafton, Ill., 1986—2004; coll. instr. and cons. Greenville Coll., Greenville, Ill., 2004—. Cons./presenter Schuler's Schoolars Consulting, Elsah, Ill., 1996—; coll. instr. So. Ill. at Edwardsville, Edswardsville, Ill., 1990—2000. Contbr. scientific papers to profl. jours. Recipient Tchr. of the Yr., Wal Mart, 1999. Mem.: Nat. Assn. Edn. of Young Children, Ill. Project Support Group. Methodist. Avocations: golf, writing, reading, gardening. Office: 13610 Schuler Ln Dow IL 62022-9721 Office Phone: 618-466-5345. Business E-Mail: dorothy.schuler@greenville.edu.

**SCHULER, JUANITA LOUISE,** education educator; b. Washington, Mo., May 30, 1959; d. Eugene Vivian and Emma Irene Schuler; m. Robert Thomas Carollo, Aug. 3, 2001; children: Paul David, Ariella Lee Schuler Brumley, Tracy Alan Carollo, Travis Wade Carollo. BS, S.W. Mo. State U., 1981; MA in Tchg., Webster U., 1993. 7-12 art educator Iberia R-V, Mo., 1981—89; k-4 art educator Sullivan Pub. Mo., 1989—94, 9-12 art educator, 1994—; adj. art prof. East Ctrl. Coll., Union, Mo., 1994—. Adv., sponsor Nat. Honor Soc., Sullivan, Mo., 2002—, Class of 2006, Sullivan, Mo., 2002—, Art Club, Sullivan, Mo., 1994—. Team capt., nat. honor soc. Relay for Life, Sullivan, Mo., 2005. Grantee Sullivan Cultural and Tech. Grant, City Coun. 2004. Mem.: Nat. Art Edn. Assn., Mo. State Teachers Assn., Phi Theta Kappa, Kappa Kappa Iota (past state pres. 1999—2001, Iva Duggan Scholarship 1993). Bapt. Home: 383 Vernon St Sullivan MO 63080 Office Phone: 573-468-5181.

**SCHULER, MARY CALLAGHAN,** artist, educational association administrator; b. Upper Darby, Pa., Aug. 15, 1938; d. John J. Callaghan and Catherine Graham Callaghan O'Reilly; m. Richard E. Schuler, May 12, 1962; children: Richard E., Anne E., Judith M. Cert. in Oil Painting, R.I. Sch. Design, 1972; BS, Cornell U., 1979. Dir. activities Ithacare Ctr., Ithaca, NY, 1979—82; exec. staff asst. Einaudi Ctr. Internat. Studies Cornell U., Ithaca, 1983—93. Exhibitions include Logan Ridge Winery, 2002, Clinton Ho. Artspace, 2002, State of the Art Gallery, 2004—06, Upstairs Gallery, 2005, 2006. Bd. dirs. State of the Art Gallery, Ithaca, 2004—06. Mem.: Cornell

Alumni Assn. and Club, Cornell Campus Club, Ithaca (N.Y.) Garden Club, Sigma Alpha Iota (Ithaca Coll. Chpt.). Avocations: painting, reading, walking. Home: 2 Captains Walk Ithaca NY 14850-8502 Personal E-mail: mcs@lightlink.com.

**SCHULER, RANDALL STEVE,** education educator, writer; b. Saginaw, Mich., Apr. 29, 1945; s. Wilson Andrew and Mary Schuler. MBA, Mich. State U., 1968, MLIR, 1972, PhD, 1973. Prof. NY U., 1982—97; rsch. faculty mem. GSBA Zurich, Switzerland, 1986—; prof. ii Rutgers U., Piscataway, NJ, 1997—. Fellow: APA (life), Brit. Acad. of Mgmt. (life), Soc. for Indsl. and Orgnl. Psychology (life), Acad. of Mgmt. (life). Office: Rutgers U 94 Rockafeller Rd Piscataway NJ 08854 Office Phone: 732-445-5827. E-mail: schuler@rci.rutgers.edu.

**SCHULER, ROBERT LEO,** appraiser, consultant; b. Cin., June 15, 1943; s. Del D. and Virginia D. (Heyl) S.; m. Shelagh J. Moritz, Aug. 11, 1962; children: Robert C., Sherry L. Vp. Comprehensive Appraisal Service, Cin., 1977—. Bd. dirs. Hamilton County Regional Planning Commn., Cin., 1987-88; mem. exec. com., past pres. OKI Regional Coun. Govts., Cin., 1981-92. Councilman City of Deer Park, Ohio, 1979-86; trustee Sycamore Twp., 1988-92; Ohio state rep. 36th dist., 1993—2000; senator, 7th Dist., Ohio, 2003-; active Scarlet Oaks Bus. Adv. Coun. Recipient United Conservatives of Ohio Watchdog of the Treasury award, 1994, 1996, 1998, 2005; Coun. of State Govts. Toll fellow, 2004. Mem. Cin. Bd. Realtors, Ohio Assn. Realtors, Jaycees (v.p.). Republican. Roman Catholic. Home: 3648 Jeffrey Ct Cincinnati OH 45236-1544 Office: State House of Ohio Columbus OH 43215 Office Phone: 614-466-9737.

**SCHULER, THEODORE ANTHONY,** retired civil engineer; b. Louisville, July 1, 1934; s. Henry R. and Virginia (Meisner) S.; m. Jane A. Bandy, July 29, 1979; children: Marc, Elizabeth, Eric, Ellen. BCE, U. Louisville, 1957, M Engring., 1973. Registered profl. engr., Tenn. Design constrn. engr. Brighton Engring. Co., Frankfort, Ky., 1960—65; design engr. Hensley-Schmidt Inc., Chattanooga, 1965—68, assoc., 1969—73, sr. assoc., 1973—75, prin., asst. v.p., head Knoxville office, 1975—81; chief planning engr. engring. dept. City Knoxville, 1981—96, ret., 1996. Served to lt. (j.g.) USNR, 1957-60. Fellow ASCE. Home: 5907 Adelia Dr Knoxville TN 37920-5801 Personal E-mail: tschu30447@aol.com.

**SCHULER, WALTER E.,** lawyer; b. Memphis, Tenn., Sept. 8, 1962; s. James D. and Clare A. Schuler. BBA magna cum laude, U. Memphis, 1993; JD cum laude with cert. in health law with hons., St. Louis U., 1996. Bar: Tenn. 1996, U.S. Dist. Ct. (Western Dist.) Tenn. 1996, U.S. Ct. Appeals (6th cir.), 1998. Assoc. The Bogatin Law Firm, PLC, Memphis, Tenn., 1996—. Contbr. articles to profl. jours., chpt. to book. Sgt. (E-5), U.S. Army, 1985-90, staff sgt. (E-6) USAR, 1990-93. Recipient Commendation Medal-1st Oak Leaf Cluster, U.S. Army, 1989, Army Achievement Medal-2nd Oak Leaf Cluster, 1989, Nat. Def. Svc. Med., 1992. Mem. Am. Health Lawyers Assn., ABA, Tenn. Bar Assn., Memphis Bar Assn. Office: Bogatin Law Firm PLC Ste 300 International Place Dr Memphis TN 38120

**SCHULHOF, MICHAEL PETER,** electronics company executive; b. N.Y.C., Nov. 30, 1942; s. Rudolph B. and Hannelore (Buck) Schulhof; m. Paola Nissim, Apr. 17, 1969; children: David Kenneth, Jonathan Nissim. BA, Grinnell Coll., 1964, DSc (hon.), 1990; MS, Cornell U., 1967; PhD, Brandeis U., 1970. Lic. comml. pilot. Am. rsch. fellow Brookhaven Nat. Lab., Uptown, NY, 1969—71; asst. to v.p. mfg. CBS Records, Inc., N.Y.C., NY, 1971—73, exec. com., bd. dirs., 1987—88; from gen. mgr. bus. products divsn. to sr. v.p. Sony Corp., N.Y.C., NY, 1973—86; pres. Sony Industries, N.Y.C., NY, 1978—86; chmn. Digital Audio Disc Corp., Terre Haute, Ind., 1986—96; pres. Sony Software Corp., 1991—96; pres., CEO Sony Corp. Am., 1993—95. Chmn. bd. dirs. Quadriga Art Inc., 1980—, World On Line, 1998—99; bd. dirs. Sony Corp., Japan, Sony Corp. Am., Sony Pictures Entertainment, Materials Rsch. Corp., J2 Global Commn., 1997—, CBS/Sportsline; chmn. Sony Music Entertainment; former chmn. Comml. Electronics, 1998—; chmn., CEO Global Tech. Investments, 2001—; mem., coun. of fgn. rels. and investment; svcs. policy adv. com. U.S. Trade Rep. Contbr. articles to profl. jours. Trustee Brandeis U., 1990—, Lincoln Ctr. for Performing Arts, Inc., N.Y.C., Brookings Instn., Washington; investment and svcs. policy adv. com. U.S. Trade Rep.; active Coun. Fgn. Rels.; bd. dirs. Ctr. on Addiction and Substance Abuse at Columbia U., N.Y.C., Am. Hosp. of Paris Found. Fellow, NSF, 1970. Master: Am. Phys. Soc. (bd. dirs. 1978); mem.: Am. Radio Relay League, Computer and Bus. Equipment Mfrs. Assn. (bd. dirs.), Whitney Mus., Guggenheim Mus., Aircraft Owners and Pilots Assn., Atlantic Golf Club, Fenway Golf Club, Profile Club, East Hampton Tennis Club, Gipsy Trail Club, Harmony Club. Achievements include patents for audio disc apparatus. Office: 375 Park Ave New York NY 10152-0002

**SCHULHOFER, STEPHEN JOSEPH,** law educator; b. N.Y.C, Aug. 20, 1942; s. Joseph and Myrelle S.; m. Laurie Wohl, May 28, 1975; children: Samuel, Jonah. AB, Princeton U., 1964; LLB, Harvard U., 1967. Bar: DC 1968, US Dist. Ct. Ea. Dist. Pa. 1973, US Supreme Ct. 1973. Law clk. to Justice Hugo L. Black, US Supreme Ct., Washington, 1967-69; assoc. Coudert Freres, Paris, 1969-72; asst. prof. law U. Pa., Phila., 1972-77; assoc. prof., 1977-81; prof., 1981-85, Ferdinand Wakeman Hubbell prof., 1985-86; prof. U. Chgo. Law Sch., 1986-2001; dir. Ctr. for Studies Criminal Justice, 1987-2001; prof law NYU Sch. Law, 2001-, Robert B. McKay prof. law, 2002-. Vis. prof. U. Chgo., 1985, NYU Sch. Law, 2001; speedy trial reporter US Dist. Ct. Dist. Del., Wilmington, 1975-80; cons. US EPA, Washington, 1977-78, US Sentencing Commn., Washington, 1987-94. Author: Prosecutorial Discretion and Federal Sentencing Reform, 1979, Unwanted Sex: The Culture of Intimidation and the Failure of Law, 1998, The Enemy Within: Law Enforcement and Civil Liberties in the Wake of September 11, 2002; Editor: Criminal Law and its Processes, 1983, 89, 95, 2001; contbr. articles to profl. journals. Trustee, Cmty. Legal Services, Phila., 1981-86. Walter Meyer grantee Am. Bar Found., 1984. Mem. ACLU (Ill. bd. dirs. 1993-97), Law and Soc. Assn. Office: NYU Sch Law Vanderbilt Hall Rm 319 40 Washington Sq S New York NY 10012-1099 Office Phone: 212-998-6260. E-mail: schulhos@juris.law.nyu.edu.

**SCHULIAN, JOHN (NIELSEN SCHULIAN),** screenwriter, author; b. LA, Jan. 31, 1945; s. John and Estella Katherine (Nielsen) S.; m. Paula Lynn Ellis, Aug. 20, 1977 (div. Oct. 1984). BA, U. Utah, 1967; MS, Northwestern U., 1968. Copy editor Salt Lake City Tribune, 1968; reporter Balt. Evening Sun, 1970-75; sportswriter Washington Post, 1975-77; sports columnist Chgo. Daily News, 1977-78, Chgo. Sun-Times, 1978-84, Phila. Daily News, 1984-86; staff writer Miami Vice, Universal City, Calif., 1986-87, story editor, 1987, The Slap Maxwell Story, North Hollywood, Calif., 1987-88; exec. story editor TV series Wiseguy, Hollywood, 1988-89; co-prodr. TV series Midnight Caller, Burbank, Calif., 1989-90, supervising prodr., 1990-91; co-exec. prodr. TV series Reasonable Doubts, Burbank, 1991-92; creative cons. TV series The Untouchables, LA, 1992-93; co-exec. prodr. TV series Hercules, Universal City, Calif., 1994-96; co-creator Xena: Warrior Princess, Universal City, 1995; assoc. prodr. (documentary) Ben Johnson: Third Cowboy on the Right, 1996; co-exec. prodr. (TV series) Lawless, 1996-97; consulting prodr. (TV series) JAG, 1999-2000; exec. prodr. (TV series) The Outer Limits, Vancouver, Canada, 2000-01; culture columnist MSNBC.com, 2001—02; co-exec prodr. (TV series) Tremors, Universal City, 2002—03. Spl. contbr. Sports Illustrated, 1998—; profl. in residence U. Utah, 2004. Author: Writers' Fighters and Other Sweet Scientists, 1983, Twilight of the Long Ball Gods, 2005; contbg. editor Panorama mag., 1980-81; syndicated columnist UP Syndicate; commentator Nat. Pub. Radio, 1985-86; cons. The Reader's Catalog, 1989; contbr. articles to NY Times, Playboy, Gentlemen's Quar., Oxford Am.Mag., The National, LA Times; included in The Best Am. Sports Writing, 1994. Mem. Pacific Coast League Hist. Soc. With U.S. Army, 1968-70. Recipient Nat. Headliners Club award, 1980, Column Writing award AP Sports Editors, 1979, 82, Best Sports Stories award, 1983, 84, Nat Fleischer Excellence in Boxing Journalism award Boxing Writers Assn. Am.,

1985. Mem. Writers Guild Am., Phi Beta Kappa. Office: Endeavor Talent Agy 9701 Wilshire Blvd 10th Fl Beverly Hills CA 90212 also: Sterling Lord Literistic 35 Bleecker St New York NY 10012 Personal E-mail: jschulian@aol.com.

**SCHULLER, DAVID EDWARD,** cancer center administrator, otolaryngologist; b. Cleve., Oct. 20, 1944; m. Carole Ann Hauss, June 24, 1967; children: Rebecca, Michael. BA, Rutgers U., 1966; MD cum laude, Ohio State U., 1970. Diplomate Am. Bd. Otolaryngology 1975. Intern dept. surgery U. Hosps. Cleve., 1970-71; resident dept. otolaryngology Ohio State U., Columbus, 1971-72; resident dept. surgery U. Hosps. Cleve., 1972-73; fellow head and neck surgery Pack Med. Found. with John Conley, N.Y.C., 1973; resident dept. otolaryngology Ohio State U. Hosps., Columbus, 1973-75; fellow head and neck oncology and facial plastic and reconstructive surgery U. Iowa, Iowa City, 1975-76; trustee Ohio Cancer Found, 1988—; from clin. instr. to prof. and chmn. dept. otolaryngology The Ohio State U., Columbus, 1971—; dir. Am. Bd. Otolaryngology, 1988—2000, Comprehensive Cancer Ctr., Columbus, 1997—; prof. sect. oral biology, Coll. Dentistry The Ohio State U., 1990—; dir. Arthur G. James Cancer Hosp. & Richard J. Solove Rsch. Inst., Columbus, 1988—; chair dept. otolaryngology Ohio State U., Columbus, 1990—; past pres. American Board of Otolaryngology. Mem., chmn. various coms. Ohio State U. Hosps. and Coll. Medicine, 1976—; dir. CCC head and neck oncology program Ohio State U., 1977—, hosps. physician flr. coord. 10th flr., 1977-82, dir. laser-microsurgery teaching and rsch. lab., 1987-88; mem. various coms. Grant Hosp., 1980-84; mem. Accreditation Coun. for the Grad. Med. Edn. Residency Review Com. for Otolaryngology, 1985—, chmn., 1988—; vis. prof., lectr., ACS prof. clin. Oncology, 1989-94. numerous instns. Author: (books) (with others) Otolaryngology-Head and Neck Surgery-4 Vols., 1986, Textbook of Otolaryngology-7th Edit., 1988, Otolaryngology-Head and Neck Surgery-Update I, 1988, Musculocutaneous Flaps in Head and Neck Reconstructive Surgery, 1989, Otolaryngology-Head and Neck Surgery Update II, 1990, Otorinolaringologia-Cirugia de Cabeza y Culleo, 1991, Otolaryngology-Head and Neck Surgery-4 Vols., 1992; contbr. chpts. to books and articles to profl. jours.; mem. editorial bd. New Horizons in Otolaryngology/Head and Neck Surgery, 1982-87, The Laryngoscope, 1986—, Am. Jour. Otolaryngology, 1988—, Facial Plastic Surgery Internat. Quar. Monographs, 1992—; mem. rev. bd. Jour. Head and Neck Surgery, 1985—; mem. editorial rev. bd. Otolaryngology-Head and Neck Surgery, 1990—; reviewer New Eng. Jour Medicine, 1992—. Recipient Cert. of Appreciation, Scioto Meml. Hosp., 1982, Edmund Prince Fowler award Triological Soc., 1984; Henry Rutgers scholar Rutgers U., 1965-66; grantee Nat. Cancer Inst., 1980-88, 90-97, Bremer Found., 1982-83, 87-88, Photomedica Inc., 1986-89, Upjohn Co., 1986-90, others. Mem. AMA (mem. rev. panel Archives of Otolaryngology-Head and Neck Surgery 1984—), Am. Cancer Soc. (mem. instl. grant rev. com. 1980—, chmn. rehab. com. Franklin County unit 1981-82, mem. profl. edn. com. 1981—, chmn. 1982-85, v.p. 1982-83, pres. 1986, 87, trustee Ohio divsn. 1988—), Am. Assn. Cosmetic Surgeons, Am. Acad. Facial Plastic and Reconstructive Surgery (mem. rsch. com. 1977-82, chmn. residency rels. com. 1982-85, mem. program com. 1982-85, v.p. mid. sect. 1983-87, chmn. by-laws com. 1985-90, treas. 1988-90, Honor award 1989), Am. Coll. Surgeons, Am. Cleft Palate Assn., Assn. Am. Cancer Insts., Am. Soc. Head and Neck Injury, Am. Acad. Otolaryngology Head and Neck Surgery (mem. editorial bd. self-instructional package program 1982—, del. bd. govs. 1982-87, Honor award 1983), Am. Soc. Laser Medicine and Surgery, Am. Laryngological, Rhinological, Otological Soc., Inc., Am. Laryngological Assn., Am. Soc. Clin. Oncology (mem. program com. 1989—), Am. Assn. Cancer Researchers, Am. Soc. Head and Neck Surgery (mem. coun. 1983-86, chmn. scholastic and fellowship award com. 1984-86, mem. profl. rels. and pub. edn. com. 1989—), Southwest Oncology Group (chmn. head and neck com. 1983—), Collegium ORLAS, Ohio State Med. Assn. (pres. sect. otolaryngology 1987—), Ohio Soc. Otolaryngology (pres. 1985, 86, 87), Acad. Medicine of Columbus and Franklin County, Columbus E.E.N.T. Soc., Franklin County Acad. Medicine (mem. profl. rels. com. 1982—), Head and Neck Intergroup (vice-chmn. 1984-86, chmn. 1986-89), Assn. Rsch. Otolaryngology, Ohio State U. Med. Alumni Soc. (class rep. 1980—, v.p. 1987-88, pres. 1989-90), Med. Forum, Med. Review Club, Order of Hippocrates (charter), Alpha Omega Alpha. Office: 456 W 10th Ave Columbus OH 43210-1240 also: Ohio State Univ Comp Cancer Ctr 300 W 10th Ave Columbus OH 43210-1240*

**SCHULLER, GUNTHER ALEXANDER,** composer; b. N.Y.C., Nov. 22, 1925; s. Arthur E. and Elsie (Bernartz) Schuller; m. Marjorie Black, June 8, 1948; children: Edwin Gunther, George Alexander. Student, St. Thomas Choir Sch., N.Y.C.; MusD (hon.), Manhattan Sch. Music, 1987, Northeastern U., 1967, U. Ill., 1968, Colby Coll., 1969, Williams Coll., 1975, Cleve. Inst. Music, 1977, New Eng. Conservatory Music, 1978, Rutgers U., 1980, Manhattan Sch. Music, 1987, Oberlin Coll., 1989. Tchr. Manhattan Sch. Music, 1950—63; head composition dept. Tanglewood, 1963—84; pres. New Eng. Conservatory Music, 1967—77; artistic dir. Berkshire Music Ctr., Tanglewood, 1969—84, Festival at Sandpoint, 1985—. Founder, pres. Margun Music Inc., 1975, GM Recs., 1980. French horn player Ballet Theatre, then prin. horn player Cin. Symphony Orch., 1943—45, prin. French horn Met. Opera Orch., 1945—59, Concerto #1 for Horn, 1945; composer: Concerto for Cello and Orchestra, 1945, Six Early Songs, 1945, Quartet for Four Double Basses, 1947, Jumpin' in the Future for jazz ensemble, 1948, Perpetrum Mobile for Four Horns, 1948, Fantasy for Unaccompanied Cello, 1951, Adago for Flund String Trio, 1952, Recitative and Rondo for Violin and Piano, 1953, Music for Violin, Piano and Percussion, 1957, Contours, 1958, Woodwind Quintet, 1958, Seven Studies on Themes of Paul Klee, 1959, Spectra, 1960, Six Renaissance Lyrics, 1962, String Quartet No. 2, 1965, Symphony, 1965, opera The Visitation, 1966, opera Fisherman and His Wife, 1970, Capriccio Stravagante, 1972, The Power Within Us, 1972, Tre Invenzioni, 1972, Three Nocturnes, 1973, Four Soundscapes, 1974, Concerto No. 2 for Orch., 1975, Triplum II, 1975, Horn Concerto No. 2, 1976, Violin Concerto, 1976, Diptych for organ, 1976, Sonata Serenata, 1978, Contrabassoon Concerto, 1978, Deaí for 3 orchs., 1978, Trumpet Concerto, 1979, Octet, 1979, Eine Kleine Posaunemusik, 1980, In Praise of Winds (Symphony for Large Wind Orch.), 1981, Symphony for Organ, 1982, Concerto Quaternio, 1983, Concerto for Bassoon and Orch., 1984, On Light Wings (piano quartet), 1984, Farbenspiel (Concerto No. 3 for Orch.), 1985; author: Horn Technique, 1962, Early Jazz: Its Roots and Development, 1968, Musings: The Musical Worlds of Gunther Schuller, 1985; composer: A Bouquet for Collage for chamber ensemble, 1988; author: The Swing Era, 1989; premier of Symphony for Brass and Percussion, Cin., 1950, Salzburg Festival, 1957; Dramatic Overture, N.Y. Philharm., 1956; String Quartet, Number 1 Contemporary Arts Festival, U. Ill., 1957, Concertino for Jazz Quartet and Orch., Balt. Symphony Orch., 1959, Seven Studies on Themes of Paul Klee, Ford Found., commn., Minn. Symphony, 1959, Spectra, N.Y. Philharm., 1960, Music for Brass Quintet, Coolidge Found., Libr. of Congress, 1961, Concerto No. 1 for Orch., Chgo. Symphony Orch., 1966, Triplum, N.Y. Philharm. commd. Lincoln Ctr., 1967, Aphorisms for Flute and String Trio commd., Carleton Coll. Centennial, 1967, Eine Kleine Posaunenmusik, 1980, In Praise of Winds, 1983, Concerto Quaternio, N.Y. Philharm., 1983, Duologue for Violin and Piano, 1984, Farbenspiel, Berlin Philharm., 1985, Concerto for Viola and Orch., 1985, String Quartet No. 3, 1986, Chimeric Images, 1988, Concerto for String Quartet and Orchestra, 1988, Concerto for Flute and Orchestra, 1988, On Winged Flight: A Divertimento for Band, 1989, Chamber Concerto, 1989, Concerto for Piano Three Hands, 1989, Phantasmata for Violin and Marinba, 1989, 5 Impromptus Eng. Horn and String Quartet, 1989, Impromptus and Cadenzas, 1990, premier of Hommage à Rayechka for 8 cellos/or multiples thereof, 1990, A Trio Setting for clarinet, violin, piano, 1990, Violin Concerto No. 2, 1991, Sonata Fantasia for piano, 1992, Ritmica-Melodia-Armonia for orch., 1992, Of Reminiscences and Reflections for orch., 1993 (Pulitzer prize for music, 1994), Brass Quintet No. 2, 1993, The Past is in the Present for orch., 1994, Sextet for left hand piano and woodwind quintet, 1994, Concerto for organ and orch., 1994, Mondrian's Vision, 1994, Magnificat and Nunc Dimittis (choir), 1994, Headin Out, Movin In (jazz ensemble), 1994, Lament for M (jazz ensemble), 1994, Rush Hour an 23d St., 1994, Blue Dawn into White Heat (concert band), 1995, An Arc Ascending, 1996; composer: Bright and Sassy, 1997, Ohio River Reflections for Piano Trio and Horn, 1998, Sonata for Alto

Saxophone, 1999, Fantasie Impromptu for Flutet Hpschd, 2000, Quodlibet - Vln, Cello, Oboe, Horn, and Harp, 2001, The Birth of the Cool Suite, 2001, String Quartet No. 4, 2002, Concerto da Camera No. 2, 2002, rev. Duo Concertante for Cello and Piano, 2002, Four Preludes for Harp, 2002, Encounters for Jazz Band and Large Symphony Orch., 2003, String Trio, 2003, Grand Concerts for Percussion Ensemble and Three Keyboards, 2005, Nature's Way for Band/Wind Ensemble, 2006. Named Guggenheim fellow, 1962, 1963, MacArthur fellow, 1991, Composer of Yr., Mus. Am., 1995; named to Am. Classical Music Hall of Fame, 1998; recipient Creative Arts award, Brandeis U., 1960, Deems Taylor award, ASCAP, 1970, Alice M. Ditson Conducting award, 1970, Rodgers and Hammerstein award, 1971, Friedheim award, 1988, William Schuman award, Columbia U., 1989, Down Beat Lifetime Achievement award, 1993, BMI Lifetime Achievement award, 1994, Gold medal, Am. Acad. Arts and Letters, 1997, Order of Merit Cross, Fed. Republic of Germany, 1997, Max Rudolf award, 1998. Mem.: Am. Acad. Arts and Scis., Nat. Inst. Arts and Letters. Address: 167 Dudley Rd Newton Center MA 02459-2830 Office Phone: 617-332-6328.

**SCHULLER, IVAN KOHN,** physicist; b. Cluj, Romania, June 8, 1946; came to U.S., 1970, naturalized, 1980; s. Franz Berla and Iolanda Blum (Kohn) S.; m. Jacqueline M. Scheibel, Mar. 2, 1974; children— Daniel, Jonathan. B.Math., U. Chile, 1965, Licenciado, 1970; MS (fellow), Northwestern U., 1972, PhD, 1976; D (hon.), U. Complutense, Madrid. Research asst. Argonne (Ill.) Nat. Lab., 1974-76, sr. physicist, group leader, 1978-87; prof. physics U. Calif., San Diego, 1987—. Adj. prof. UCLA, 1976-78 Contbr. chpts. to books, articles to profl. jours. Named Disting. New Citizen, 1980—81; recipient medal for Disting. Performance, U. Chgo., 1981, Award for Outstanding Accomplishment in Solid State Physics, U.S. Dept. Energy, Materials Rsch. Soc. Medal, 2003, E.O. Lawrence Award, U.S. Dept. Energy, 2004. Fellow: Belgian Acad. Sci., Am. Phys. Soc. (Adler Award 2002, Wheatley Award); mem.: Spanish Acad. Sci. (foreign mem.), Chilean Acad. Sci., Sigma Xi. Patentee. Office: U Calif at San Diego Physics Dept 9500 Gilman Dr La Jolla CA 92093-0319 E-mail: ischuller@ucsd.edu.

**SCHULLER, ROBERT HAROLD,** minister, writer; b. Alton, Iowa, Sept. 16, 1926; s. Anthony and Jennie (Beltman) Schuller; m. Arvella DeHaan, June 15, 1950; children: Sheila, Jeanne, Carol, Gretchen. BA, Hope Coll., 1947; BD, Western Theol. Sem., 1950; DD, Hope Coll., 1973; LLD, Azusa Pacific Coll., 1970, Pepperdine U., 1976; LittD, Barrington Coll., 1977. Ordained to ministry Reformed Ch. Am., 1950. Pastor Ivanhoe Ref. Ch., Chgo., 1950—55; founder, sr. pastor Garden Grove Cmry. Ch., Calif., 1955—; founder, pres. Hour of Power TV Ministry, 1970—; founder, dir. Robert H. Schuller Inst. for Successful Ch. Leadership, 1970—; chmn. nat. religious sponsor program Religion in Am. Life, N.Y.C., 1975—. Bd. dirs. Freedoms Found. Author: God's Way to the Good Life, 1963, Your Future Is Your Friend, 1964, Move Ahead with Possibility Thinking, 1967, Self Love, the Dynamic Force of Success, 1969, Power Ideas for a Happy Family, 1972, The Greatest Possibiloty Thinker That Ever Lived, 1973, Turn Your Scars into Stars, 1973, You Can Become the Person You Want To Be, 1973, Your Church Has Real Possibilities, 1974, Love or Loneliness - You Decide, 1974, Positive Prayers for Power-Filled Living, 1976, Keep on Believing, 1976, Reach Out for A New Life, 1977, Peace of Mind Through Possibility Thinking, 1977, Turning You Stress Into Strength, 1978, Daily Power Thoughts, 1978, The Peak to Peek Principle, 1981, Living Positively One Day at a Time, 1981, Self Esteem: The New Reformation, 1982, Tough Times Never Last, But, Tough People Do!, 1983, Tough Minded Faith for Tender Hearted People, 1984, The Be-Happy Attitudes, 1985, Be Happy You Are Loved, 1986, Success is Never Ending, Failure is Never Final, 1988, Believe in the God Who Believes in You, 1989; co-author: The Courage of Carol, 1978. Founder Robert H. Schuller Corr. Ctr. Possibility Thinkers, 1976; bd. dirs. Religion in Am. Life; pres. bd. dirs. Christian Counseling Svcs. Named Headliner of Yr. in Religion, Orange County, 1977, Clergyman of Yr., Religious Heritage Am., 1977; recipient Ddisting. Alumnus award, Hope Coll., 1970, Prin. award, Freedoms Found., 1974. Mem.: AIA (bd. dirs. 1986—), Religious Guild Architects (hon.), Rotary. Office: Religion Am Life 12141 Lewis St Garden Grove CA 92840-4627

**SCHULLER, STEPHEN ARTHUR,** lawyer; b. Wilmington, N.C., 1951; s. Reinhold S. and Gisela (Krause) S.; m. Linda Joy McIntosh, 1977; 1 child. BA, Northwestern U., Evanston, Ill., 1973; JD, U. Tulsa, Okla., 1976. Bar: Okla. 1976, U.S. Dist. Ct. (no. dist.) Okla. 1976, Ill. 1977, U.S. Ct. Appeals (10th cir.) 1993. Corp. atty. Roper Corp., Kankakee, Ill., 1977; assoc. Prichard, Norman, Reed & Wohlgemuth, Tulsa, 1977-82; ptnr. Prichard, Norman & Wohlgemuth, Tulsa, 1982-83, Barrow, Gaddis, Griffith & Grimm, Tulsa, 1983-91; pvt. practice law Tulsa, 1991-95; ptnr. Schuller & Mills, Tulsa, 1995-98, Boone, Smith, Davis, Hurst & Dickman, Tulsa, 1998—2006; shareholder Gable & Gotwals, Tulsa, 2006—. Trustee Employees' Retirement System Tulsa County, 1990—, co-chairperson Dist. 6 planning team, 1989-92; mem. sales tax overview com. City of Tulsa, 1991-94; trustee Tulsa Authority for Recovery of Energy, 2002—, chmn., 2002—; mem. Citizens' Commn. on City Govt., 2006. Mem. ABA, Okla. Bar Assn. (bd. dirs. real property sect. 1983-93, chmn. 1986), Tulsa County Bar Assn., Tulsa Title and Probate Lawyers Assn. (dir. 1986-89, pres. 1989) Office: 100 W 5th St Ste 1100 Tulsa OK 74103-4217 Office Phone: 918-595-4800.

**SCHULMAN, ALAN,** lawyer; b. Bklyn., Sept. 7, 1949; BA, NYU, 1971; JD, La. State Univ., 1974. Bar: La. 1974, Tex. 1974, Wash. 1982, Calif. 1986, US Dist. Ct. (so. dist. Calif. 1987, no. & ctrl. dist. Calif. 1989), US Ct. Appeals (5th & 11th cir. 1981, 9th cir. 1982), US Supreme Ct. 1995. Ptnr., Complex Class Action Litigation Bernstein Litowitz Berger & Grossmann, San Diego. Adj. prof. Univ. San Diego Sch. Law, 2000—; co-chmn. so. dist. Calif. Lawyer Reps. Ninth Cir. Judicial Conf., 2000—01, mem. exec. com., 2002—04, Conf. co-chmn., 2005. Editor (assoc.): La. Law Rev. Mem.: ABA (co-chmn. Securities Law coun.), Fed. Bar Assn., Wash. State Bar Assn., La. State Bar Assn., State Bar Tex., State Bar Calif., Assn. Bus. Trial Lawyers San Diego (pres. 2001, mem. bd. gov. 1995—2001), Order of the Coif. Office: Bernstein Litowitz Berger & Grossmann Suite 150 12544 High Bluff Dr San Diego CA 92130 Office Phone: 858-720-3185. Office Fax: 858-793-0323. Business E-Mail: alans@blbglaw.com.

**SCHULMAN, ALAN MICHAEL,** small business owner; b. Chgo., Feb. 5, 1946; s. Aaron and Anne Schulman; m. Barbara Picard, May 27, 1984; 1 child, Jeffrey. BS, Roosevelt U., 1968. Salesman Dictaphone Corp., Chgo., 1968-69; sales engr. Boston Gear, Chgo., 1969-70; mgr. Imperial Packaging, Chgo., 1970-71; owner A.M.S. Distbg., Skokie, Ill., 1971-77; owner, pres. Greater Distbn. Svcs., Glenview, Ill., 1977-90, The Battery Bank div. Jalco, Inc., Glenview, 1982-92, Glentronics Inc., Glenview, 1989—. Host TV gardening program. Author (newspaper column) Gardening Information, 1980; host numerous TV fishing programs; contbr. articles on battery to nat. mags.; patentee in field; subject of mag., newspaper articles; appearances in nat. radio program Home Improvement U.S.A.; inventor in field. Named to, Freshwater Fishing Hall of Fame for world record catch, U. Ill. Chgo. Entrepreneurship Hall of Fame, 2003. Mem. Entrepreneurs Network. Clubs: Men's Garden of North Shore (Highland Park) (pres. 1984-85). Achievements include inventing basement watchdog pumps, socklight drawer lights, timely lighting care, plant light. Office: 1150 Willis Ave Wheeling IL 60090-5817

**SCHULMAN, CATHY,** film producer; Prodn. and acquisitions exec. Samuel Goldwyn Co.; founder Artists Production Group, 1999, pres.; ptnr. Bull's Eye Enterntainment. Co-dir. Sundance Film Festival, 1989—91. Assoc. prodr. (films) Isn't She Great?, 2000, Tears of the Sun, 2003; prodr.: (films) Sidewalks of New York, 2001, You Stupid Man, 2002, Employee of the Month, 2004, Godsend, 2004, Crash, 2005 (Best Motin Picture of Yr., Acad. Motion Pictures Arts and Sciences, 2006); exec. prodr.: Thumbsucker, 2005. Office: Bull's Eye Entertainment 4th Floor 10850 Wilshire Blvd Los Angeles CA 90024*

**SCHULMAN, CLIFFORD A.,** lawyer; b. Dec. 6, 1947; s. George and Henrietta Schulman; m. Michele Weissman, June 28, 1969; 1 child, David Michael. B.S. in Journalism and Communications cum laude, U. Fla., 1969,

J.D., 1972. Bar: Fla. 1972, U.S. Supreme Ct. 1981, U.S. Ct. Appeals (5th cir.) 1975. Law clk. to Eugene P. Spellman, Miami, Fla., 1970-71; research aide to Judge Norman Hendry, Miami, 1972-73; asst. county atty. Met. Dade County, Miami, 1973-79; ptnr. Greenberg, Traurig (formerly Greenberg, Traurig, Askew, Hoffman, Lipoff, Rosen & Quentel) Miami, 1979—. Editor-in-chief continuing legal edn. manual Environ. Regulation and Litigation in Fla., 1981 edit. Mem. Gov.'s Task Force on Biscayne Bay Rules, 1978; del. 57th biennial conv. Am. Hebrew Congregations, 1983. Served to capt. USAR, 1969-73. Mem. Fla. Bar (co-editor environ. law sect. newsletter 1977-80; exec. council environ. and land use law sect. 1979-83, sec.-treas. 1981-83, chmn. 1984-85). Office: Greenberg Traurig 1221 Brickell Ave Miami FL 33131-3224 Office Phone: 305-579-0613. Office Fax: 305-961-5613. Business E-Mail: schulmanc@gtlaw.com.

**SCHULMAN, HAROLD**, obstetrician, gynecologist; b. Newark, Oct. 26, 1930; m. Rosemarie Vincenti; children: Stanley H., Sandra C., Gina M. BS, U. Fla., 1951; MD, Emory U., 1955. Diplomate Am. Bd. Ob-Gyn., Am. Bd. Maternal and Fetal Medicine; registered diagnostic med. sonographer. Intern Jackson Meml. Hosp., Miami, Fla., 1955-56, resident, 1958-61; instr. dept. ob-gyn. U. Miami (Fla.) Sch. Medicine, 1961; instr., asst. prof. dept. ob-gyn. Temple U. Sch. Medicine, Phila., 1961-65; asst. prof. dept. ob-gyn. Albert Einstein Coll. Medicine, Bronx, 1965-67, assoc. prof., 1968-71, prof., 1971—, acting dept. chmn., 1972—80, chmn., 1973-80; assoc. dir. dept. ob-gyn Bronx Mcpl. Hosp. Ctr., 1967-70, dir. dept. ob-gyn., 1970-72; chmn. dept. ob-gyn. Winthrop U. Hosp., Mineola, NY, 1984-93; ob-gyn SUNY, Stony Brook, 1984-93; chmn. dept. ob-gyn. Lawnwood Regional Med. Ctr., Ft. Pierce, Fla., 1995-2000. Author: Tipping the Scales, 2005; contbr. articles to profl. publs. Served U.S. Army, 1956-58. Am. Cancer Soc. fellow, 1959-60; USPHS trainee, 1965-66 Fellow ACOG (vice chmn. Dist. II 1972-75); mem. Bronx County Obstet. Soc. (pres. 1974) AAAS, Obstet. Soc. (sec. 1978-80, pres. 1982-83), N.Y. Obstetrical Soc., Soc. Maternal Fetal Medicine, Am. Gynecologic and Obstet. Soc., Am. Gynecol. Obstetrics, N.Y. Obstetrics Soc. (pres. 1982), Phi Beta Kappa, Alpha Omega Alpha; hon. mem. Miami Ob-Gyn. Soc., South Atlantic Obstetricians and Gynecologists Soc., Buffalo Gynecologic and Obstetric Soc. (E.G. Winkler meml. lect.), Croatian Ultrasound Soc. (hon.). Democrat. Jewish. Office Phone: 914-747-4168. Personal E-Mail: hschulman@sprintmail.com.

**SCHULMAN, JOSEPH DANIEL**, physician, health facility administrator, medical geneticist, educator; b. Bklyn., Dec. 20, 1941; s. Max and Miriam (Grossman) S.; m. Dixie A. King; children: Erica N., Julie K. BA, Bklyn. Coll., 1961; MD, Harvard U., 1966. Diplomate Am. Bd. Pediat., Am. Bd. Ob-Gyn., Am. Bd. Med. Genetics. Intern, then resident in pediat. Mass. Gen. Hosp., Boston, 1966-68; clin. assoc. Nat. Inst. Arthritis and Metabolic Diseases, 1968-70; resident in obstetrics and gynecology and fellow in pediatrics N.Y. Hosp.-Cornell Med. Ctr., 1970-73; Gilbert and Nat. Found. fellow Cambridge (Eng.) U., 1973-74; head sect. human biochem. genetics Nat. Inst. Child Health and Human Devel., NIH, Bethesda, Md., 1974-83; dir. med. genetics program NIH, Bethesda, 1979-1983; prof. ob-gyn., pediat., genetics George Washington U., 1983-84; CEO Genetics & IVF Inst., Fairfax, Va., 1984-98, chmn., 1984—2001, 2004—; prof. human genetics, pediat., ob-gyn. Med. Coll. Va. Commonwealth U., 1984—; with dept. ob-gyn. Fairfax Hosp., 1984—. Affiliate prof. ob-gyn. U. Cal., San Diego, 2003—; advisor to numerous govt. and pvt. orgns. Author 3 books; contbr. numerous articles to med. jours.; editorial bd. Molecular Human Reproduction, 1995—, numerous other sci. jours. With USPHS, 1968-70, 74-83. Fellow ACOG; mem. Soc. Pediat. Rsch., Soc. Gynecologic Investigation, Am. Soc. Clin. Investigation, Am. Soc. Human Genetics, Am. Fertility Soc., Harvard Club, Cosmos Club, Calif. Club, Phi Beta Kappa, Sigma Xi. Office: 3015 Williams Dr Fairfax VA 22031

**SCHULMAN, ROBERT S.**, lawyer; b. NYC, July 9, 1941; s. Donald Benedict and Edythe (Smythe) Schulman; m. Susan Jan Von Helbig, Sept. 18, 1974; children: Elizabeth Jane, Jennifer Lynn. BA, Rutgers U., New Brunswick, 1963; JD cum laude, Rutgers U., Newark, 1966. Bar: NJ 1967, US Dist. Ct. NJ 1967, US Supreme Ct. 1970, Calif. 1976, US Dist. Cts. (ctrl., no., so. and ea. dists.) Calif. 1976, US Ct. Appeals (9th cir.) 1976. With Pitney, Hardin & Kipp, Newark, 1966-74; dep. atty. gen. Office of NJ Atty. Gen., Trenton, 1974-75; assoc. Cox, Castle & Nicholson, LA, 1976-80; ptnr. Zobrist, Garner & Garrett, LA, 1980-83, Stephens, Berg, Lasater & Schulman, LA, 1984-91, Crosby, Heafey, Roach & May, LA, 1991—2002, Fulbright & Jaworski, LLP, LA, 2002—. Atty. Bd. Adjustment, Fairview, NJ, 1971—73, Bd. Edn., Fairview, 1972. Contbr. articles to profl. jours. Dir. Deafwest Theater, LA, 1991—97. Mem.: State Bar of Calif., Calif. Club. Congregationalist. Home: 13600 Marina Pointe Dr Unit 710 Marina Del Rey CA 90292-9250

**SCHULMAN, RUTH MERYL ARONSON**, research and development company executive; BA, SUNY at Postdam, Potsdam, NY, 1977—81. Interim regional dir./asst. to the dir./interim edn. coord. Anti-Defamation League, NY State Regional Office, Albany, NY, 1987—96; dir. of ann. giving United Jewish Fedn. of Northeastern NY, Latham, NY, 1996—99; asst. dir. of devel. Equinox, Inc., Albany, NY, 1999—2000; dir. of resource devel. United Way of Schenectady County, Schenectady, NY, 2000—01; dir. of devel. Animal Protective Found., Scotia, NY, 2001—05; dir. devel. U. Albany, NY, 2005—. Bd. dirs. So. Saratoga YMCA, 2004—. Mem.: Women In Devel. of Northeastern NY, Assoc. of Fundraising Professionals, Hudson-Mohawk Chpt. (chapter pres.). Home: 51 Grant Hill Court Clifton Park NY 12065 Office: Univ Albany Sch Edn Rm 246 1400 Washington Ave Albany NY 12222 Office Phone: 518-442-4991. Office Fax: 518-442-4953. Business E-Mail: rschulman@uamail.albany.edu.

**SCHULMAN, SIDNEY**, neurologist, educator; b. Chgo., Mar. 1, 1923; s. Samuel E. and Ethel (Miller) S.; m. Mary Jean Diamond, June 17, 1945; children—Samuel E., Patricia, Daniel. BS, U. Chgo. 1944 MD, 1946. Asst prof in urology U. Chgo., 1952-57, assoc. prof., 1957-65, prof., 1965-75, Ellen C. Manning prof., divsn. biol. scis., 1975-93, Ellen C. Manning prof. emeritus, 1993—. Served with M.C. AUS, 1947-49. Mem. Am. Neurol. Assn., U. Chgo. Med. Alumni Assn. (pres. 1968-69, Norman Maclean award 1997), Chgo. Neurol. Soc. (pres. 1964-65)

**SCHULT, THOMAS P.**, lawyer; b. Great Falls, Mont., Sept. 12, 1954; s. Peter Henry and Louise (de Russy) S.; m. Margo C. Soulé, Sept. 18, 1982. BS in Russian History, U. Va., 1976, JD, 1979. Bar: U.S. Dist. Ct. (we. dist.) Mo. 1979, U.S. Ct. Appeals (10th cir.) 1983, U.S. Ct. Appeals (7th, 8th and 11th cirs.) 1984, U.S. Ct. Appeals (5th cir.) 1985, U.S. Supreme Ct. 1987, U.S. Ct. Appeals (9th cir.) 1988. Ptnr. Lathrop Koontz & Norquist, Kansas City, Mo., 1979-89, Bryan Cave, Kansas City, 1989-94; Stinson, Mag & Fizzell, Kansas City, 1994-2001; ptnr. Berkowitz Feldmiller, 2001—. Committeeman Jackson County Reps., Kansas City, 1984—. Mem. ABA (products liability com.), Products Liability Adv. Coun., Mo. Bar Assn. (editor continuing legal edn.), Fedn. of Ins. and Corporate Counsel, Def. Rsch. Inst. Episcopalian. Office: Stinson Mag & Fizzell 1201 Walnut St Ste 2800 Kansas City MO 64106-2117

**SCHULTE, BRUCE JOHN**, lawyer; b. Burlington, Iowa, June 27, 1953; s. James Andrew and Julia Germaine S.; m. Mary E. Guest, July 1988 (div. Feb. 1995); children: James, John, Julian; m. Catherine Tobben, 2001 BA in Am. Studies, U. Notre Dame, 1975; JD, U. Iowa, 1978. Bar: Iowa 1978, U.S. Dist. Ct. (so. dist.) Iowa 1979, U.S. Ct. Appeals (8th cir.) 1982, Minn. 1988, U.S. Dist. Ct. Minn. 1988, Ill. 1988. Law clk. Justice K. David Harris Supreme Ct. Iowa, Des Moines, 1978-79; ptnr. Dailey, Ruther, Bauer, Schulte & Hahn, Burlington, Iowa, 1979-87; atty. Bennett, Ingvaldson & McInerny, Mpls., 1988; gen. counsel Blackwood Corp., St. Paul, 1988-89; publs. editor Nat. Inst. for Trial Advocacy-U. Notre Dame, Ind., 1989-91; asst. dean pub. affairs Chgo. (Ill.) Kent Coll. Law, 1991-94; dep. dir. assoc. rels. West Pub., Eagan, Minn., 1995-97; dir. mktg., v.p. acad. consulting Performance Comm. Group, Chgo., 1997-2001; cons. BJS Assocs., Evanston, Ill., 2001—; fin. advisor Merrill Lynch, 2005—. Key person com. ATLA, 1984-88; mem. commn. on jud. dists. Supreme Ct. Iowa, 1987-88; cons. Merrill Lynch, 2005—; cons. in field. Author: Persuasive Expert Testimony, 1990, Laser Disc Technology in

the Courtroom, 1990; editor: Cases and Materials on Evidence, 1991, Modern State and Federal Evidence, 1991, Problems and Cases for Legal Writing, 1991. State ctrl. com. Iowa Dem. party, 1984-88; devel. com. Frances Xavier Ward Sch., Chgo., 1993-95; cmty. task force Chgo. (Ill.) Downtown Circulator Project, 1994-96; v.p. pub. affairs U. Notre Dame Alumni Class of 1975; mem. adv. coun. Coleman Ctr. Entrepreneurship DePaul U., 2003-05; publs. com. Nat. Law Firm Mktg. Assn., 1993-94. Notre Dame scholar U. Notre Dame, Ind., 1971-72; recipient Spectra award Internat. Assn. Bus. Communicators, 1993, Silver Trumpet, Publicity Club Chgo., 1994. Mem. ABA (tech. com. lawyers com. jud. adminstrn. divsn. 1995-2000, vice chair task force on image of judiciary 2000-01), Ill. Bar Assn. (standing com. legal edn. and admission to bar 1993-97), Chgo. Bar Assn. (law office tech. com. 1995-97), Assn. Am. Law Schs., Chgo. Pub. Rels. Forum (treas. 1997), Notre Dame Club Chgo. (co-chair Hesburgh Forum com. 1993-98, trustee 1995-98, sec. 1997-98), Nat. Soc. Fundraising Profls. (cert. fundraising prof., Midwest conf. steering com. 1997-99), Execs. Club of Chgo. (co-chair standing com. on edn. and pub. svc.). Avocations: sailing, choir, gardening, skiing. Home: 816 Main St Evanston IL 60202-1706 Personal E-mail: brucejschulte@aol.com.

**SCHULTE, DAVID MICHAEL**, investment banker; b. NYC, Nov. 12, 1946; s. Irving and Ruth (Stein) S.; m. Patricia Gordon, Sept. 5, 1999; children: Michael B., Katherine F. BA, Williams Coll., 1968; postgrad., Exeter Coll., Oxford U., Eng., 1968-69; JD, Yale U., 1972. Bar: DC 1973. Law clk. to Mr. Justice Stewart, US Supreme Ct., 1972-73; spl. asst. to pres. NW Industries, Inc., Chgo., 1973-75, v.p. corp. devel., 1975-79, exec. v.p., 1979-80; sr. v.p. Salomon Bros., Chgo., 1980-84; mng. ptnr. Chilmark Ptnrs., Chgo., 1984—. Editor-in-chief: Yale Law Jour, 1971-72. John E. Moody scholar Exeter Coll., Oxford U., 1968-69 Mem. Washington Bar Assn., Chgo. Club, Racquet Club, Bryn Mawr Country Club, Vineyard Golf Club. Office: Chilmark Ptnrs 875 N Michigan Ave Ste 3460 Chicago IL 60611-1957 Office Phone: 312-984-9711.

**SCHULTE, FRANCIS B.**, retired archbishop; b. Phila., Dec. 23, 1926; Grad., St. Charles Borromeo Sem. Ordained priest Roman Cath. Ch. 1952. Apptd. titular bishop of Afufenia and aux. bishop of Phila., 1981—85; bishop Wheeling-Charleston, W.Va., 1985—88; archbishop Archdiocese of New Orleans, 1989—2002, archbishop emeritus, 2002—. Office: c/o 7887 Walmsley Ave New Orleans LA 70125-3431

**SCHULTE, FREDERICK JAMES**, newpaper editor; b. Mpls., June 6, 1952; s. Philip William and Katherine Schulte. BA, U. Va., 1974. News reporter Internat. Med. News Group, Washington, 1976-78; med. writer, gen. assignment reporter Sun-Sentinel, Ft. Lauderdale, Fla., 1978-83, investigative team leader, 1983-88, asst. regional editor, 1988-90, investigations editor, 1990—. Author: Fleeced! Telemarketing Rip-Offs and How to Avoid Them, 1995. Recipient Excellence in Med. Journalism award Fla. Med. Assn., 1983, 1st Pl. Investigative Reporting award Fla. Press Club, 1983, 1st Pl. Sustained Coverage award Inland Daily Press Assn., 1983, Non-deadlin Reporting prize Sigma Delta Chi, 1983, Green Eyeshade award Sigma Delta Chi, 1983, 1st Pl. Pub. Svc. award Fla. Press Club, 1986, 87, 89, 90, Media Merit award Assn. Trial Lawyers Am., 1986, 1st Pl. award Big Bros./Big Sisters Am., 1987, 1st Pl. Pub. Svc. award Fla. Soc. Newspaper Editors, 1987, Children's Express Jounalism award, 1987, 1st Pl. Investigative Reporting award Unity Awards in Media, 1987, Pulitzer Prize finalist, 1987, Worth Bingham Meml. Final prize, 1989, 96, Freedom of Info. award AP Mng. Editors Assn., 1990, Lowell Thomas award, 1992, John Hancock award, 1992, Silver Gavel award ABA, 1992, Depth Reporting award The Soc. Newspaper Editors, 1993, Pub. Affairs/Social Issues Reporting award Unity Awards in Media, 1993, George Polk award L.I. U., 1993, Gerald Loeb award U. Calif., 1994; Pulitzer prize finalist for beat reporting, 1996, investigative reporting, 1999; Alicia Patterson Found. fellow, 1997. Mem. Investigative Reporters and Editors (S.E. regional coord., Disting. Investigative Reporting award 1985). Office: Sun-Sentinel 200 E Las Olas Blvd Ste 1000 Fort Lauderdale FL 33301-2293

**SCHULTE, GREGORY L.**, ambassador; married; 2 children. Grad. magna cum laude, U. Calif. Berkeley, 1980; MPA, Princeton U., 1983. Presdl. mgmt. intern office of sec. def., Washington, 1983—85; dir. strategic forces policy, asst. theater nuc. forces policy, 1985—92; with internat. staff NATO, Belgium, 1992—98; spl. asst. to Pres. for implementation of Dayton Peace Accords Nat. Security Coun., 1998—99; prin. dir. requirements, plans and counterproliferation policy for sec. of def. The Pentagon, 1999—2000; sr. dir. S.E. European affairs Nat. Security Coun., 2000—02; exec. sec., 2003—05; permanent rep. UN, Vienna, 2005—, IAEA, 2005—. Recipient two Presdl. Rank awards. Address: US Dept State 2201 C Street NW Washington DC 20520

**SCHULTE, JEFFREY LEWIS**, lawyer; b. N.Y.C., July 24, 1949; s. Irving and Ruth (Stein) S.; m. Elizabeth Ewan Kaiser, Aug. 13, 1977; children: Andrew Riggs, Ian Garretson, Elizabeth Alexandra. BA, Williams Coll., 1971; postgrad., Harvard U., 1971-72; JD, Yale U., 1976. Bar: Pa. 1978, Ga. 1993. Law clk. to hon. John J. Gibbons U.S. Ct. Appeals (3d cir.), Newark, 1976-77; assoc. Schnader, Harrison, Segal & Lewis, Phila., 1977-84, ptnr., 1985-92, founding ptnr. Atlanta, 1992-98, exec. com., 1994-98; ptnr. Morris, Manning & Martin, Atlanta, 1998—. Chair securities law com. Ga. State Bar, 2005—; nat. steering com. lawyers com. to end "Pay-to-Play."; bd. adv. Cole Sch. Bus. Kennesaw State U. Contbr. articles to profl. jours. Mem.: ABA, Bus. and Tech. Alliance, Atlanta Venture Forum, Atlanta Bar Assn. (chmn. comm. and media rels. com.), Phila. Bar Assn., State Bar Ga. (chmn. securities com. 2005—), Pa. Bar Assn., Weekapaug Tennis Club, Yale Club of Ga. (bd. dirs. 1996—2002, pres. 2000—01, chmn. of bd. 2001—02), Weekapaug Yacht Club R.I., Williams Club N.Y.C., Williams Club Atlanta, Merion Cricket Club, Phi Beta Kappa. Office: Morris Manning & Martin Atlanta Financial Center 3343 Peachtree Rd NE Ste 1600 Atlanta GA 30326-1044 Office Phone: 404-233-7000. Business E-Mail: jls@mmmlaw.com.

**SCHULTE, STEPHEN JOHN**, lawyer, educator; b. NYC, July 7, 1938; s. John and Marjorie (Fried) S.; m. Patricia Walker, June 6, 1962 (div.); children: Susan Jean, Jeffrey David, Elizabeth Ann; m. Margaret Van Doren Cook, Mar. 12, 1975. BA, Brown U., 1960; JD, Columbia U., 1963. Bar: N.Y. 1964. Assoc. Lowenstein, Pitcher, Hochkiss & Parr, N.Y.C., 1963-66, Fried, Frank, Harris, Shriver & Jacobson, N.Y.C., 1966-69; founding ptnr. Schulte Roth & Zabel LLP, N.Y.C. 1969-2005, of counsel, 2005—. Adj. prof. law Benjamin N. Cardozo Law Sch., 1992—2000, vice chmn. bd. dirs., 1995—2000, bd. dirs.; adj. prof. law Columbia U., 2000—, Fordham U., 1992—97; lectr. securities law field; panelist various forums. Life trustee Choate Rosemary Hall Sch., Wallingford, Conn., 1982—, chmn. investment and fin. com., 1984-85, chmn. devel. com., 1985-86, chmn. nominating com., 1986-89, chmn. bd. trustees, 1990-95; trustee York Sch.; bd. dirs. Innocence Project; trustee Big Sur Band Trust, 2004— Mem. ABA, NY State Bar Assn. (com. on securities regulation), Assn. of Bar of City of NY (chmn. com. on securities regulation 1998-2000) Office: Schulte Roth & Zabel LLP 919 3rd Ave New York NY 10022-4774 Business E-Mail: stephen.schulte@srz.com.

**SCHULTHEIS, ADAM JOHN**, music educator, consultant; b. Quebec City, Que., Canada, Apr. 23, 1962; s. August Thomas and Joan Helen Schultheis; m. Cynthia Anne Forcey, Dec. 14, 1995; children: Johnathon Michael Bohnet, Caroline Emily, Thomas Gabriel, Christopher Addison, Aidan Patrick. MusB in Edn., U. Ariz., Tucson, 1980—86; MS, Nova U., Ft. Lauderdale, Fla., 1987—89. Cert. elem. tchr. Nev. Orch. tchr. McCall Elem. Sch., North Las Vegas, 1986—92, Orr Mid. Sch., Las Vegas, 1992—97, Boulder City H.S., Nev., 1997—. Music leader, cons. Boy Scouts of Am., Boulder City, Nev., 1998—; hon. composer Vincennes U., Ind., 2001—; advisor U.S. Jr. Congl. Leadership Conf., Washington, 2001—. Composer: Prayer, Vincennes U. Bicentennial, 2001, Vegas Fiddle Dance, 2005. Founder, dir. Boulder City Hometown Fiddlers, Nev., 1999—; vol. Make A Difference Day Found., Las Vegas, 1999—; chmn. Nev. Nat. Anthem Project. Named Tchr. of Yr., VFW, Nev., 2006; named to, Clark County Sch. Dist.'s Hall of Fame, Las Vegas, 2001, Wall of Tolerance, San Francisco State U., 2004; recipient Disney Am.

Tchr. Honoree, Disney Corp., 1999, Achievement in Edn award, Rotary Club, Boulder, City, Nev., 2001, Music For 1000 Children Award, U. Hartford, Hart Sch. Music, 2002, Nev. Cmty. award, DAR, 2006, Vol. of Yr. award, Am. Legion, 2005, Cmty. Achievement award, DAR, 2026; grantee Arts in the Cmty., Target Edn. Found., 2002, 2003, 2004; Cuban Music fellow, San Francisco State U., 2001. Mem.: Sons of the Am. Legion, Music Educators Nat. Conf. (life), Am. String Tchr. Assn. (life; advisor, cons. 1986—2003), Music Tchr. Nat. Assn. (life), KC, Pi Lambda Theta, Valley Forge Freedom Found. (hon. Past George Washington Honor Medal Winner 2001). Conservative. Achievements include being Nevada's only participant in the 2001 National Independence Day Parade, Washington, DC; being Nevada's only music participant in National World War Two Memorial Dedication, Washington, 2004; Las Vegas' centennial committee commissioned composition Vegas Fiddle Dance, 2005. Avocations: fiddling, woodworking, gardening, hiking. Home: 1327 Bayleaf Terr Ave Henderson NV 89014 Office: Boulder City HSI 1101 Fifth St Boulder City NV 89005 Office Phone: 702-799-8200. Personal E-mail: adamschultheis@cox.net.

**SCHULTHEIS, EDWIN MILFORD**, dean, business educator; b. NYC, Apr. 15, 1928; s. Milford Theodore and Lillian May (Hill) S.; m. Joan Edna Bruckner, June 23, 1956. BS, Hofstra Coll., 1950; MBA, NYU, 1958, EdD, 1972. Officer mgr., sales rep. Topton Rug Mfg. Co., N.Y.C., 1950-54; area mgr., trainer Mobil Oil Co., N.Y.C., 1954-62; coord. distributive edn. North Babylon (N.Y.) Pub. Schs., 1962-88, chmn. bus. mktg. and indsl. edn. depts., 1988-91; prof. bus. adminstrn. SUNY, Farmingdale, 1970-91; asst. prof. edn. NYU, 1973—; dir. edn. Syracuse (N.Y.) U., 1973-78; chmn. dept. bus. adminstrn. Five Towns Coll., Seaford, N.Y., 1991-92, divsn. chmn. bus. and tech. Dix Hills, N.Y., 1992-98, dean interim, 1993-98, dir. assoc. of faculty, 1993-98, assoc. dean, 1996-97, prof. emeritus, 1998—. Test writer, cons. N.Y. State Dept. Edn., Albany, 1965—; textbook reviewer McGraw-Hill Book Co., N.Y.C., 1967-69; cons. Cornell U., 1975; dist. adviser Distributive Edn. Clubs N.Y., 1970, bd. govs., trustee, 1975-78; mem. curriculum adv. coun. Suffolk County (N.Y.) Distributive Edn. Assn., 1967—. Author: Modern Petroleum Marketing, 1971, Content and Structure of Belief-Disbelief Systems, 1972. Elder Presbyn. Ch., U.S.A. Named N.Y. State Tchr. of Yr., 1976, Outstanding Tchr. in N.Y. State, 1978; recipient Outstanding Svc. award Distributive Edn. Clubs N.Y., Suffolk County Distributive Edn. Assn., Tchr. Excellence award N.Y. State, 1980, Citation for Excellence in Edn. Gov. Mario Cuomo N.Y., 1991, Citation Excellence in Teaching Babylon Twp., 1991. Mem. Acad. Mgmt., Am. Petroleum Inst., Am. Security Coun., Suffolk County Assn. Distributive Edn. Tchrs. (mem. exec. bd. 1962-74), N.Y. State (pres. 1975-78), L.I. Distributive Edn. Assn. (hon. life, exec. bd. 1972-75), N.Y. State Occupl. Edn. Assn. (v.p. 1975-78), L.I. Bus. Edn. Chmns. Assn. (hon. life, exec. bd. 1972-75), N.Y. State Occupl. Edn. Assn. (v.p. 1975-78), L.I. Bus. Edn. Chmns. Assn. (hon. life), Distributive Edn. Clubs Am. (regional leader 1972-75, hon. life 1991), Bellport (N.Y.) Golf Club, Phi Delta Kappa, Kappa Delta Pi, Sigma Alpha Lambda, Phi Sigma Eta. Presbyterian (ordained ruling elder). Home: 14 Thorn Hedge Rd Bellport NY 11713-2616

**SCHULTHEIS, PATRICIA ANN**, writer, editor; b. Bridgeport, Conn., Aug. 11, 1943; d. Ralph and Clare Podufaly; m. William Christian Schultheis, Oct. 15, 1966; children: Kurt Christian, Matthew Christian. BA, Albertus Magnus Coll., 1965; MA in Liberal Arts, Johns Hopkins U., 1973. Prodn. mgr. Balt. Mag., 1976—77; rschr. Med. Pub. TV, Owings Mills, 1977—79; rsch. assoc. Changing Times Mag., DC, 1979—81; editor U. Med. Balt., 1981—85; dir. publs. CC Balt., 1985—89; copy editor The Balt. Sun, 1990; editor Skills Bank Corp., Baltimore County, 1991—95; freelance writer, 1995—; fiction editor Balt. Review, 2001—; Editor Mt. Wash. Newsletter, Balt., 1973—75, U. Md. Sch. Law Alumni Newsletter, Balt.; contbr. Bread Loaf Writer's Conf.; rschr. Ft. McHenry Nat. Monument. Co-author: Personal Mathematics, Media Materials; Soc. Charles Village Improvement Assn., Balt., 1967—69; mentor Dickey Hill Elem. Sch., Balt., 2002—. Mem.: Hamilton St. Club. Avocations: ice skating, folk art painting, embroidery. Home: 2509 Pickwick Rd Baltimore MD 21207 Personal E-Mail: bpschult@yahoo.com.

**SCHULTHEIS, PATRICK JOSEPH**, lawyer; b. Spokane, Wash., Sept. 3, 1964; s. John Arthur and Catherine Christina (McCann) Schultheis. AB in History, Stanford U., 1986; JD, U. Chgo., 1989. Bar: Calif. 1989, Wash. 1998, US Dist. Ct. No. Dist. Calif., US Ct. Appeals, ninth cir. Assoc. Wilson, Sonsini, Goodrich & Rosati, Palo Alto, Calif., 1989-96, mem., 1997—, Seattle, 1997—. Co-author: The Initial Public Offering: A Guidebook for Executives & Boards of Directors, 2004. Mem.: Federalist Soc., ABA-Bus. Law Sect., Inglewood Golf Club, Bellevue Club, Buck Cardinal Club, Mem. Club Aldarra, Kappa Sigma. Republican. Roman Catholic. Office: Wilson Sonsini Goodrich & Rosati 701 Fifth Ave Ste 5100 Seattle WA 98104-7036 Office Phone: 206-883-2500. Office Fax: 206-883-2699. Business E-Mail: pschultehi@wsgr.com.

**SCHULTHEIS, RITA VIRGINIA**, artist; b. Parkersburg, W.Va., Apr. 2, 1954; m. Thomas D. Schultheis, Nov. 16, 1973; 1 child, Theresa L. Grad. Famous Artist Sch., 1973. Vet. asst., 1971-72; framing and store mgr. Marj Teague Art Gallery, Williamstown, W.Va., 1972-80. V.p. Lawrence Elem. PTL, 1992, 93, 94; bd. dirs. Humane Soc. Ohio Valley, 1989-93, chairperson Art for Animals show, 1980-93. Recipient cert. Marietta Area C. of C., 1991; recipient Nat. Nature Art award, 1980, 85, 86, 87. Mem. Marietta Area Arts and Crafts League (past sec., past v.p., past pres.), Ohio Arts and Crafts Guild. Avocations: horseback riding, swimming, reading, photography. Office: RVS Art & Frames 222 Putnam St Marietta OH 45750-3014 Office Phone: 740-374-2062. E-mail: rvsart@sbcglobal.net.

**SCHULTIS, GAIL ANN**, library director; b. Freeport, Ill., May 12, 1951; d. Richard C. and Ida G. Schultis. BA, Cornell Coll., 1973; MLS, U. Mo., 1976; MA, U. Tex., San Antonio, 1989. Reference libr. U. Tex., San Antonio, 1976-79; El Paso, 1979-84, 89, head access svcs., 1984-88; reference libr. Park U., Parkville, Mo., 1989-96, dir. libr. sys., 1996—. Co-author: Best Self-Help & Self-Awareness Books, 1995. Mem. ALA, Am. Hist. Assn., Orgn. Am. Historians. Home: 10307 NW 57th Ter Parkville MO 64152-3396 Office: Park Univ Libr 8700 NW River Park Dr Parkville MO 64152-4358 Office Phone: 816-584-6704. Business E-Mail: ann.schultis@park.edu.

**SCHULTZ, ALBERT BARRY**, engineering educator; b. Phila., Oct. 10, 1933; s. George D. and Belle (Seidman) S.; m. Susan Resnikov, Aug. 25, 1955; children: Carl, Adam, Robin BS, U. Rochester, 1955; M.Engring., Yale U., 1959, PhD, 1962. Asst. prof. U. Del., 1962-65; asst. prof. U. Ill., Chgo., 1965-66, assoc. prof., 1966-71, prof., 1971-83; Vennema prof. U. Mich., Ann Arbor, 1983-99. Contbr. numerous articles to profl. jours. Served to lt. USN, 1955-58 Rsch. Career award NIH, 1975-80; Javits Neurosci. Investigator award NIH, 1985-92 Mem. NAE, Internat. Soc. for Study Lumbar Spine (pres. 1981-82), ASME (chmn. bioengring. div. 1982-83), H.R. Lissner award 1990), Am. Soc. Biomechanics (pres. 1982-83, Borelli award 1996), U.S. Nat. Com. on Biomechanics (chmn. 1982-85), Phi Beta Kappa Business E-Mail: aschultz@umich.edu.

**SCHULTZ, ARTHUR LEROY**, clergyman, educator; b. Johnstown, Pa., June 14, 1928; s. Elmer Albert Robert and Alice Lizetta (Flegal) S.; m. Mildred Louise Stouffer, Nov. 29, 1948; children: Thomas Arthur, Rebecca Louise. BA, Otterbein Coll., 1949; MDiv, United Theol. Sem., 1952; MEd, U. Pitts., 1955, PhD, 1963. Sr. min. Albright United Meth. Ch., Pitts., 1952-56; dir. pub. rels. Otterbein Coll., Westerville, Ohio, 1956-65, adj. prof. religion and philosophy, 1990-98; pres. Albright Coll., Reading, Pa., 1965-77, Ashland (Ohio) Coll., 1977-80; prof. Am. Cen. Ohio Radio Reading Svc., Columbus, 1980-84; parish min. Ch. Master United Meth., Westerville, 1984-89; min. of visitation Ch. Messiah United Meth. Westerville, 1991—2002. Pres. Pa. Assn. Colls. & Univs., Harrisburg, 1974-75. Trustee Reading Hosp., 1967-77, Wyoming Sem., Kingston, Pa., 1971-80; v.p. Found. for Ind. Colls. Pa., Harrisburg, 1972-73; pres. Pa. Coun. on Alcohol Problems, Harrisburg, 1968-76; pres. Westerville (Ohio) Hist. Soc., 1986-89, Westerville Area Ministerial Assn., 1992-93. Named Outstanding Young Man of the Year Jr. C. of C., Westerville, Ohio, 1960. Mem. Brookstone Cmty. Assn. (sec. bd. trustees 1994-99, v.p. 1999-2000), Rotary (charter pres. 1959, dist. gov.

1965-66, dist. sec.-treas. 1982-93), Masons, Shriners, Torch Club. Republican. Methodist. Avocations: collecting post cards, golf, tennis, travel. Home: 151 Sandstone Loop W Westerville OH 43081-4599

**SCHULTZ, ARTHUR WARREN,** retired communications executive; b. NYC, Jan. 13, 1922; s. Milton Warren and Genevieve (Dann) S.; m. Elizabeth Carroll Mahan, 1949 (div. 1987); children: Arthur Warren, John Carroll (dec.), Julia Hollingsworth; m. Susan Keefe, 1988. Grad., U. Chgo.; DLitt (hon.), Rosary Coll. With Foote, Cone & Belding Comms., Chgo., 1948-82, v.p., 1957-63, sr. v.p., dir., 1963-69, exec. v.p., 1969, chmn. bd., CEO, 1970-81, chmn. exec. com., CEO, 1981-82; dir. Chgo. Sun-Times Co.; vice chmn. Chgo. Sun-Times Newspaper Co., 1989-94. Lectr. in field. Author: In Praise of America's Collectors, 1997; co-author: Valley Club of Montecito, 1999; editor Caring for Your Collections, 1992. Pres. Cook County Sch. Nursing, 1963-64, Welfare Coun. Met. Chgo., 1965-67; mem. bus. adv. coun. Urban League Chgo., 1971-82; chmn. Nat. Com. to Save Am.'s Cultural Collections, 1990-94; mem. Pres.'s Com. Arts and Humanities, 1984-93; bd. dirs. Chgo. Crime Commn., 1965-71, Cmty. Fund Chgo., 1966-67, Better Bus. Bur., 1970-78, Lyric Opera Chgo., 1967-77, Chgo. Coun. Fgn. Rels., 1977-86, Chgo. Pub. TV, 1978-82, Chgo. Central Area Com., 1978-82; mem. milennium Com. to Save Am.'s Treasures, 1998; trustee YWCA, 1962-74, Calif. Coll. Arts & Crafts, 1985-87; trustee Art Inst. Chgo., 1975-2002, chmn. bd., 1981-84; trustee U. Chgo., 1977—, Santa Barbara Mus. Art, 1988—, pres., 1989-92. 1st lt. USAF, 1943-45. Recipient Alumni Svc. award U. Chgo., 1986. Mem. Am. Assn. Advt. Agys. (dir. 1968-71, 74-76, chmn. Chgo. coun. 1964-65, chmn. Ctrl. region 1970-71), Comml. Club, Valley Club (Montecito, Calif.), Delta Kappa Epsilon. Roman Catholic. Home and Office: 2072 China Flat Rd Santa Barbara CA 93108-2211

**SCHULTZ, BARBARA MARIE,** investment advisor; b. Chgo., Sept. 9, 1943; d. Edwin and Bernice (Bartsis) Legner; m. Ronald J. Schultz, Sr., May 1, 1965; 1 child, Ronald J. Student, Prairie State Coll. Fin. planner Metlife Fin. Svcs., NYC, 1981–2001; fin. advisor Morgan Stanley Dean Witter, NYC, 2001—02; agt., investment advisor rep. Country Ins. and Fin. Svcs., Hickory Hills, Ill., 2002–04; investment advisor Edward Jones Investments, Palm Harbor, Fla., 2004; mature mktg. specialist AIG/Am. Gen., Tampa, 2005—. Qualifier Met. Life Leaders Conf., 1990. Fellow: South Cook County Assn. Life Underwriters (edn. chmn. 1988—91), Life Underwriters Tng. Coun. (chmn. 1986—88), Nat. Assn. Life Underwriters (edn. chmn. 1988—91, citation 1987, nat. quality award, Robert L. Rose award 1990), Country Club (1st pl. award 2002). Roman Catholic. Avocations: boating, aerobics, golf. Office: 6800 N Dale Mabry Hwy Tampa FL 33614 Office Phone: 813-884-7553.

**SCHULTZ, CARL HERBERT,** real estate developer; b. Chgo., Jan. 9, 1925; s. Herbert V. and Olga (Swanson) S.; m. Helen Ann Stevesson, June 6, 1948; children: Mark Carl, Julia Ann BS Gen. Engring., Iowa State U., 1948. With Schultz Bros. Co., 1948—, mdse. mgr. and store planner Chgo., 1962—70, v.p. Lake Zurich, Ill., 1968—72, pres., 1972—2000, Ill. Schultz Bros. Co., Ind. Schultz Bros. Co., Iowa Schultz Bros. Co., Wis. Schultz Bros. Co.; chmn. Schultz Bros. Co., 2000—. Mem. Lake Bluff Zoning Bd. Appeals, Ill., 1976-85, chmn., 1978-85. Served with U.S. Army, 1944-46 Mem. Lake Zurich Indsl. Coun. (sec. 1976), Assn. Gen. Mdse. Chains (dir. 1975-86, exec. com. 1983-86, chmn. nat. conv. 1982), Ill. Retail Mchts. Assn. (dir. 1984-89), Wis. Retail Fedn. (dir. 1981-89), Bath and Tennis Club Lake Bluff Presbyn. Home: 701 E Center Ave Lake Bluff IL 60044-2607 Office: 815 Oakwood Rd Unit I Lake Zurich IL 60047 Office Phone: 847-438-3900. Personal E-mail: chs701@sbcglobal.net.

**SCHULTZ, CHARLES ROY,** archivist; b. Giddings, Tex., Dec. 6, 1935; s. Walter George and Irma Albers Schultz; m. Frances Elizabeth Harter, Dec. 30, 1959; children: George Edwin, Paul Alvin. BA, Tex. Luth. U., 1958; MA, Bowling Green State U., 1960; PhD, Ohio State U., 1966. Cert. archivist Acad. Cert. Archivists, 1989. Archivist/libr. Mystic Seaport Mus., Conn., 1963—71; archivist/records mgr. Tex. A&M U., College Station, 1971—. Author: (monograph) Forty Niners 'Round the Horn (Best Book in Am. Maritime History, 2000). Chmn. Brazos County Hist. Commn., Bryan, Tex., 1989–2006. Recipient Disting. Librarianship award, Tex. A&M U., 2003. Mem.: Acad. Cert. Archivists (v.p. 1996—97, pres. 1997—98), Soc. Southwest Archivists (v.p. 1976—78, pres. 1978—80). Office: Texas A&M Univ Univ Libraries College Station TX 77843-5000 Office Phone: 979-862-1555. Office Fax: 979-458-1472. Business E-mail: c-schultz@tamu.edu.

**SCHULTZ, CLARENCE JOHN,** minister; b. Morris Twp., Wis., Aug. 4, 1937; s. Clarence John Sr. and Ella Mae (Feavel) S.; m. Doroland Kay King, Aug. 24, 1957 (dec. Jan. 1974); children: Sharon Kay Braun, Susan May Schultz Rogers; m. Martha Ann Aylor, Apr. 5, 1975. BS, Bryan Coll., 1960. Ordained to ministry Conservative Congl. Ch., 1961. Min. 1st Congl. Ch., Herreid, SD, 1961-66, Immanuel Evang. Congl. Ch., Sheboygan, Wis., 1966-77, Hope Congl. Ch., Superior, Wis., 1977-83, Zion Evang. Ch., Scottsbluff, Nebr., 1983-89, 1st Congl. Ch., Buffalo Center, Iowa, 1989-92, Kenosha, Wis., 1992-98, St. Lucas Cmty. Ch., Lake Elmo, Minn., 1998—. Mem. Conservative Congl. Christian Conf. (rec. sec. 1973-82, v.p. 1994-96, pres. 1996-99, Rocky Mountain area rep. 1987-89, endorser of chaplains 1988-2000, mem. credentials com. 1988–), Rotary (ch. chaplain com. 1993-95). Avocations: amateur radio, golf. Home and Office: 1195 Manning Ave N Lake Elmo MN 55042-9607 Office Phone: 651-436-6021. Personal E-mail: clarence.j.schultz@comcast.net.

**SCHULTZ, CONNIE,** reporter; m. Sherrod Brown; 2 children, 2 stepchildren. BA in Journalism, Kent State Univ., 1979. Freelance writer, 1978—93; with Cleve. Plain Dealer, 1993—, now columnist. Contbr. essay to book Best Newspaper Writing, 2002. Finalist ASNE award for commentary, 2002, Pulitzer Prize in featur writing, 2003; recipient third place Nat. Headliner award for commentary, Robert F. Kennedy award for Social Justice, 2003, Nat. Headliner Best of Show award, 2003, Batten Medal, 2004, Pulitzer Prize for commentary, 2005. Office: Cleveland Plain Dealer 1801 Superior Ave E Cleveland OH 44114 Office Phone: 216-999-4800.

**SCHULTZ, DAVID FRANKLIN,** psychologist; b. Pontiac, Ill., June 7, 1952; s. David Franklin Schultz and Bernadine Yvonne Riffey, Marilyn Schultz (Stepmother); m. Lori Dale Edwards, May 15, 2005. PhD, U. Tex., 1991. Master Traumaticalist Internat. Traumatology Inst., 2002. Chief psychologist Polk Youth Devel. Ctr., Polk City, Fla., 1996—2000; clin. psychologist D. Franklin Schultz, Ph.D., Lakeland, Fla., 1994—; adj. prof. Webster U., 2001—. Cons. Lakeland, Fla., 2001—. Author: (self help book) A Language of the Heart: Therapy Stories that Heal; co-author (therapist training manual) Trauma Practice: Tools for Stabilization and Recovery. Bd. mem., trainer, team mem. Polk County Critical Incident Stress Mgmt. Team, Bartow, Fla., 2002—05. Master: Masonic Order. Avocations: skiing, golf, fishing, scuba diving. Home: PO Box 717 Auburndale FL 33823 Office: D Franklin Schultz PhD 930 Alicia Rd Lakeland FL 33801 Office Phone: 863-680-1950. Home Fax: 863-683-4654; Office Fax: 863-683-4654. Personal E-mail: drfrank@aloth.com.

**SCHULTZ, DENNIS BERNARD,** lawyer; b. Detroit, Oct. 15, 1946; s. Bernard George and Madeline Laverne (Riffenberg) Schultz; m. Andi Lynn Leslie, Apr. 18, 1967; 1 child, Karanne Anne. BS, Wayne State U., 1970; JD, Mich. State U., 1977. Bar: Mich. 1977, U.S. Dist. Ct. (ea. and we. dist.) Mich., U.S. Ct. Appeals (6th cir.), U.S. Dist. Ct. (we. dist.) Pa. V.p. Barkay Bldg. Co., Ferndale, Mich., to 1976; law clk. Hon. George N. Bashara, Mich. Ct. Appeals, Detroit, 1977; shareholder Butzel Long, Detroit, 1978—. Editor: Detroit Coll. Law Rev., 1977. Scholar Detroit Coll. Law Assn., 1976, Mich. Consol. Gas Co., 1977. Mem.: Mich. Bar Assn., Detroit Bar Assn. Republican. Roman Catholic. Avocations: boating, bicycling, golf. E-mail: dbs@comcast.net.

**SCHULTZ, E. EUGENE, JR.,** computer engineer; b. Chgo., Sept. 10, 1946; s. Earl Eugene and Elizabeth Claire Schultz; m. Cathy Brown Schultz, Aug. 9, 1975; children: Sarah Ardelle, Rachel Elizabeth, Leah Brown. BA, UCLA, 1968; MS, Purdue U., 1973, PhD, 1977. Cert. info. sys. security prof. Internat. Info. Sys. Security Cert. Consortium, info. security mgr. Info. Sys. Audit and Control Assn. Project leader, engr. Lawrence Livermore (Calif.) Nat. Lab., 1986—92; prin. Eugene Schultz and Assocs., Livermore, 1992—93; prin. security engr. ARCA Sys., San Jose, Calif., 1993—94; sr. cons. SRI Internat., Menlo Park, Calif., 1994—98; rsch. dir. Global Integrity Corp., Reston, Va., 1998—2001; prin. engr. Lawrence Berkeley (Calif.) Nat. Lab., 2001—. Adj. prof. Purdue U., West Lafayette, Ind., 1998—2001; mem. adv. bd. Recourse Techs., Redwood City, Calif., 1999—2002, ArcSight Corp., Sunnyvale, Calif., 2001—. Secure Soft, Carlsbad, Calif., 2003—. Author: Internet Security for Business, 1996, Windows NT/2000 Network Security, 2000, Incident Response, 2001, Intrusion Detection and Prevention, 2004; editor-in-chief: Computers and Security, 2002—(Golden Page award, 2003); contbr. articles to profl. jours. Active Livermore (Calif.) Vision 2000, 2001. Recipient Tech. Innovation award, NASA, 1986. Mem.: Info. Sys. Audit & Control Assn., Computer Security Inst., Info. Sys. Security Assn. (Profl. Contbn. award, Hall of Fame). Achievements include development of decluttering method for visual displays; founding the Department of Energy's Incident Response Team. Avocations: bicycling, travel. Home: 2587 Pienza St Livermore CA 94550 Office: Lawrence Berkeley Nat Lab 1 Cyclotron Rd Berkeley CA 94720

**SCHULTZ, EILEEN HEDY,** art director, advertising executive; b. Yonkers, N.Y. d. Harry Arthur and Hedy Evelyn (Morchel) S. BFA, Sch. Visual Arts, 1955. Staff artist C.A. Parshall Studios, N.Y.C., 1955-57; editorial art dir. Paradise of the Pacific, Honolulu, 1957-58; graphic designer Allied Advt. Agy., N.Y.C., 1958-59; art dir. Good Housekeeping Mag., N.Y.C., 1959-82, creative dir. advt. and sales promotion, 1982—86; creative dir. Hearst Corp., 1986—87; pres. Design Internat., 1987—. Creative dir. The Depository Trust Co., 1987-99. Art dir., editor, designer, 50th Art Directors Club Annual, 1973; columnist: Art Direction, 1969-1994. Dir. Sch. Visual Arts, N.Y.C., 1978—; trustee Sch. Art League, 1978—; advisor Fashion Inst. Tech., 1979—; adv. commn. N.Y.C. Cmty. Colls., 1979—. Named Yonkers Ambassador of Good Will to Netherlands, 1955; recipient Outstanding Achievement Sch. Visual Arts Alumni Soc., 1976, Sch. Art League Youth award, 1976. Mem. Art Dirs. Club (pres. 1975-77), Soc. Illustrators (pres. 1991-93), Joint Ethics Com. (chmn. 1975-78), Am. Inst. Graphic Arts, Soc. Publ. Designers, Type Dirs. Club. Office Phone: 212-371-0121.

**SCHULTZ, FRANKLIN M.,** retired law.educator; b. Cin., June 16, 1917; s. Max and Goldie (Wise) S.; m. Jean Carol Barnett, Apr. 5, 1946 (dec. 1981); children: William B., John M., Katherine, Caroline; m. Virginia B. Henderson, Sept. 4, 1983 BA, Yale U., 1939, LLB, 1942. Bar: Ohio 1947, D.C. 1954, Mass. 1985, U.S. Supreme Ct. 1954. Atty. Fed. Power Commn., 1946-47; assoc. prof. Sch. Law, Ind. U., Bloomington, 1947-53; with firm Purcell & Nelson, Washington, 1953-80, ptnr., 1957-80, Reavis & McGrath, Washington, 1980-85; lawyer-in-residence Sch. Law, Washington and Lee U., 1985, vis. prof., 1991-94, ret., 1994; vis. prof. Sch. Law, U. Iowa, 1986-90. Lectr. Sch. Law, George Washington U., 1958-59; vis. prof. Sch. Law, U. Va., 1975; mem. ednl. appeal bd. U.S. Dept. Edn., 1974-82. Contbr. articles to profl. jours. Trustee Nantucket Land Coun., 1992—. Served to capt. AUS, 1942-46. Decorated Bronze stars. Mem. ABA (mem. council adminstrv. law sect. 1966-69, chmn. 1970-71, del. ho. of dels. 1972-74), D.C. Bar (gen. counsel 1977-79, mem. legal ethics com. 1976-81), Am. Law Inst., Am. Bar Found., Adminstrv. Conf. U.S. (council 1980-82) Home: 1953 Marthas Rd Alexandria VA 22307-1966 E-mail: fschultz3@cox.net.

**SCHULTZ, FREDERICK HENRY,** investor, former government official; b. Jacksonville, Fla., Jan. 16, 1929; s. Clifford G. and Mae (Wangler) S.; m. Nancy Reilly, Aug., 1951; children: Catherine G., Frederick H. Clifford G., John R. BA, Princeton U., 1951; postgrad., U. Fla. Sch. Law, 1954-56. With Barnett Nat. Bank, Jacksonville, 1956-57; owner, operator investment firm, from 1957; mem. Fla. Ho. of Reps., 1963-70, speaker of the house, 1968-70; chmn. bd. Barnett Investment Svcs., Inc.; dir. Barnett Banks Inc., to 1979; vice chmn. bd. govts. Fed. Res. System, Washington, 1979-82. Served to lt. U.S. Army, 1952-54, Korea Decorated Bronze Star Roman Catholic. Office: PO Box 1200 Jacksonville FL 32201-1200

**SCHULTZ, GERALD ALFRED (JERRY SCHULTZ),** retired chemicals executive; b. Lockport, NY, Jan. 22, 1941; s. Alfred Henry and Lucy Vivian (Proctor) S.;m. Barbara Joan Beals, July 13, 1962; 1 child, Amy Lynn Schultz-Kessler. AAS, Erie County Tech. Inst., Buffalo, 1961; BA in Chemistry, SUNY, Buffalo, 1969; postgrad., Harvard U., 1979. Rsch. technician Occidental Chem. Corp., Niagara Falls, NY, 1961—63; rsch. engr. Nat. Gypsum Co. Inc., Buffalo, 1963-66; from chemist, devel. engr., gen. mgr. to v.p. Akzo Chems., Burt, N.Y. and Chgo., 1966-86; CEO VanDeMark Inc. subs. Groupe SNPE, Lockport, NY, 1986—2003; ret., 2003. Cons. in field. Contbr. articles to profl. jours; patentee in field. Fund raiser United Way, Newfane, N.Y., 1982-84; treas., bd. dirs Newfane Intercommunity Meml. Hosp., 1980-84; bd. dirs. ARC, Lockport, N.Y., 1980-84, 97-2000; mem. United Way Ea. Niagara Allocations Com., 1994-97. Mem. Am. Chem. Soc., Soc. Plastic Engrs., Soc. Plastics Industry (bd. dirs. 1974-76), Organic Peroxide Prodn. Safety Divsn. (chmn. 1974-76), Synthetic Organic Chem. Mfrs. Assn. (bd. dirs. 1991-94), Soc. Plastics Engrs., NY State Bus. Coun., NY State Chem. Alliance, Lockport Indsl. Coun. (treas. 1991-98), Ea. Niagara C. of C. (bd. dirs. 1992-95), Lockport Town and Country Club (bd. dirs. 1995-96), Olcott Yacht Club (past commr. 1975) Republican. Avocations: golf, gardening, computers, boating. Home: 6846 Lockhaven Dr Lockport NY 14094 Personal E-mail: schultz_gerald@msn.com.

**SCHULTZ, GREGORY S.,** biochemist; b. Enid, Okla., Sept. 30, 1949; BS, Okla. State U., 1971, PhD, 1976; Medicinae Doctoreum, Linkoping U., Sweden, 1996. Postdoctoral fellow Yale U., New Haven, 1976-79; asst. prof. biochemistry U. Louisville, 1979-85, assoc. prof. biochemistry, 1985-89; prof. ob-gyn U. Fla., Gainesville, 1989—, dir. Inst. for Wound Rsch., 1989—; v.p. lab & clinical rsch. Quick-Med Technologies Inc., Gainesville, 2000—. Scientific cons. Chiron Corp., Emeryville, Calif., 1982-85, Ethicon Corp., Summerville, N.J., 1985-86, Santen, Inc., Sonoma, Calif., 1997-98, U.S Biomaterials, Gainesville, 1998—; bd. dirs. Quick-Med Technologies Inc., 2000—; Everett Kinsey lectr. Contact Lens Assn. Ophthalmologists, 1997. Editor: Exptl. Eye Rsch., 1997—; patentee in field. Named Time Mag. Innovator, 2006. Mem. Wound Healing Soc. (pres.-elect 1997-98, pres. 1999-2001), Am. Soc. Biochemistry and Molecular Biology (Ethicon Endo-Surgery Lectureship 1997), Assn. for Rsch. in Vision and Ophthalmology, Phi Kappa Phi. Avocations: travel, sailing, tennis. Office: U Fla 1600 SW Archer Rd Gainesville FL 32610 also: Quick Med Technologies Inc 3427 42nd Way Gainesville FL 32608 Office Phone: 352-392-4060. E-mail: SchultzG@obgyn.ufl.edu.

**SCHULTZ, HARLEY,** consulting company executive; b. NYC; s. William and Rose Diane Schultz. MBA, NYU, 1981. Pres. Harley Schultz & Assocs., Cons. in Mktg., Mgmt. and Internet Bus. Devel., Scarsdale, NY, 1987—. Mem. various charitable orgns. Avocations: sailing, golf, French literature, 19th-century art, classical music. Office: Harley Schultz & Assocs 130 Garth Rd # 250 Scarsdale NY 10583-3750 Business E-Mail: harleyschultz@consultant.com.

**SCHULTZ, HARRY,** health science organization administrator; Dir. St. Boniface Gen. Hosp. Rsch. Ctr., Winnipeg, MB, Canada; chief innovation officer Winnipeg Regional Health Authority, Winnipeg. Office: Winnipeg Regional Health Authority 1800-155 Carlton St Winnipeg MB Canada R3C 4Y1

**SCHULTZ, HEIDI RENEE,** psychologist; b. Sycamore, Ill., Dec. 6, 1976; d. Keith and Jane Strinmeon; m. Jason Joseph Schultz, June 12, 1999; children: Cora Elizabeth, Lydia Anne, Zachary Joseph. BSc, St. Ambrose U.,

1999; MA, No. Ill. U., 2002. Cert. Sch. Psychologist Ill., 2002. Sch. psychologist Livingston County Spl. Svcs. Unit, Pontiac, Ill., 2002—. Mem.: NASP, Ill. Sch. Psychologist Assn. Home: 1503 Schultz Pl Streator IL 61364 Office: Livingston County Special Services Unit 920 Custer Ave Ste A Pontiac IL 61764

**SCHULTZ, HOWARD,** beverage service executive, professional basketball team owner; b. Bklyn., July 19, 1953; m. Sheri Kersch; 2 children. BS, No. Mich. U., 1975. Joined as saleman Xerox Corp.; v.p., gen. mgr. Hammarplast, USA, (divsn. Perstorp); dir. retail ops. & mktg. Starbucks Coffee Co., 1982—85; founder, chmn. Starbucks Corp., 1987—, CEO, 1987—2000, chief global strategist, 2000—04; chmn. & owner Seattle Supersonics, 2001—06. Bd. govs. Nat. Assn. of Securities Dealers, 1998—2001. Author (with Dori Jones Young): Pour Your Heart Into It: How Starbucks Built a Company One Cup at a Time, 1996. Named Exec. of the Year, Restaurants and Institutions mag., 2000. Office: Seattle Supersonics 351 Elliott Ave W Ste 500 Seattle WA 98119*

**SCHULTZ, JOHN L.,** writer, educator; b. Columbia, Mo., July 28, 1932; s. Gerard Frederick William and Jennie Lee (Brumley) S.; m. Anne Bray, Dec. 10, 1963 (div. Nov. 1975); children: Timothy, Susan; m. Betty E. Shiflett, May 9, 1992. Student, U. Mo., 1950-51, U. Iowa, 1951-53, U. Chgo., 1955-56, 58-59. Direct mail mgr. U. Chgo. Press, 1959-60; dir. mail cons. Free Press, Chgo., 1960-62, Aldine Pub. Co., Chgo., 1962-65, Quadrangle Books, Chgo., 1965-67; story workshop classes Chgo., 1965-70; chair English and writing Columbia Coll., Chgo., 1967-86, chair fiction writing, 1986-95, prof. emeritus, 1995—. Pres. The Story Workshop Inst., Schultz Group, Inc., Chgo., 1997—, F Mag., Inc., Chgo., 1967—; cons. John Schultz Assocs., Chgo., 1986—, Schultz Group, Inc., 2000—; pub. Ga. Rev., Ohio Rev., Chgo. Tribune Law Rev. Author: The Tongues of Men, 1969, No One Was Killed, 1969, The Chicago Conspiracy Trial, 1993, Writing From Start to Finish, 1982, 90, 97; contbg. editor Evergreen Rev., N.Y.C., 1969-73; featured in PBS prodn. Daley: The Last Boss, 1996, A&E prodn. The Chgo. Conspiracy Trial, 1994, BBC radio drama The Chgo. Conspiracy Trial, 1993, Court TV The Chicago Conspiracy Trial, 1999, Jury in Politicized Trials. Cpl., M.C., U.S. Army, 1953-55, Korea. Ill. Arts Coun. fellow, 1983-84. Mem. MLA, Assoc. Writing Programs, Nat. Coun. Tchrs. English, Coll. Composition and Comms. Avocations: running, hunting, archery, rock climbing, travel, theater. Office: Columbia Coll Chicago 600 S Michigan Ave Chicago IL 60605-1900 E-mail: jschu10054@aol.com.

**SCHULTZ, KENNETH CARL,** antiques dealer; b. Hoboken, NJ, July 16, 1938; s. Arthur Edgar and Edna Caroline Schultz. BA, Jersey City State Coll., 1960. Tchr. fifth grade Bd. Edn., Union City, N.J., 1960-61; window display artist B. Altman & Co., N.Y.C., 1962-69; display dir. Fortunoff's, N.Y.C., 1969-73; self employed antiques dealer Hoboken, 1973—. Owner, pub., writer Steamship Catalogues, 1980—. Lutheran. Avocation: collecting motion picture costumes and memorabilia. Office: Box M 753 Hoboken NJ 07030 Office Phone: 201-656-0966.

**SCHULTZ, KURT LEE,** lawyer; b. Chgo., Feb. 13, 1946; s. William Ernst Schultz and Patricia Marie (Chelminski) Facchine; m. Jane Marmet Lerro, Sept. 9, 1972; children: Jane, Melissa, Katherine, Laura. BA, U. Pa., 1967; JD, Ohio State U., 1972. Bar: Ill. 1972, U.S. Dist. Ct. Ill. (no. dist.), U.S Dist Ct. Mich. (ea. dist.) Law clk. to Judge Richard B. Austin U.S. Dist. Ct. (no. dist.) Ill., Chgo., 1972-73; assoc. Winston & Strawn, Chgo., 1972-78, ptnr., 1978—. Arbitration panelist Nat. Assn. Securities Dealers. Trustee Ravinia Festival, Highland Park, Ill., 1989-97; bd. dirs., past pres. Youth Guidance, Chgo. 1st lt. U.S. Army, 1967-69. Mem. Order of Coif. Office: Winston & Strawn LLP 35 W Wacker Dr Ste 4200 Chicago IL 60601-9703 Office Phone: 312-558-5700. E-mail: kschultz@winston.com.

**SCHULTZ, LEANNE,** violinist, performer, music educator; b. Topeka, Jan. 15, 1953; d. Ted Wilder Baehni and Lucille Elizabeth Reuter; m. Larry Wayne Schultz, June 30, 1984. BA in Music, Washburn U., Topeka, Kans., 1988. Pvt. music tchr. Marquardt Music Store, Topeka, 1972—73; sec. Inlet Ins. Agy., Homer, Alaska, 1976—78; pvt. piano and violin tchr. Allegro Music Shop, Homer, 1978—80; permanent emergency substitute music dir., tchr., 6th grade elem. band tchr. Homer Alaska Jr. and Sr. H.S., 1978—79; escrow sec. and recorder deeds Peninsula Title Ins. Co., Homer, 1979—80; clk. typist II Office Pers. Dept. Adminstrn., State of Kans., Topeka, 1980—81; computer/word-processor divsn. water resources State Bd. Agriculture, Topeka, 1981—84; office adminstrv. asst. III SRS Dept., Topeka, 1985; music condr., tchr. Cair-Paravel/Topeka Latin Sch., Topeka, 1986—88; escrow sec. Lawyers Title Topeka, 1988—94; pvt. violin, viola and piano tchr. Topeka, 1994—. Concert, mem., violinist Topeka Civic Symphony, 1971—74, 1981, Topeka Symphony Orch., 1990—; pvt. traditional classical violin music tchr. Marquardt-Manning Music Store, Topeka, 1985—90, Manning Music Store, Topeka, 1991—2000; student-music tchr., adjudicator Washburn U. Collegiate Music Educators Nat. Conf., Topeka, 1986—88; accompanist/pianist pvt. music students solo performances Collegiate Music Educators Nat. Conf., Kans. State HS Activities Assn., Mid. Sch., Regional, Statewide Solo Fest Contests; adjudicator Topeka Youth Symphony, 1992—2000; violist 125th Ann. Mesiah Festival, Bethany Coll., 2006. Violist: 124th Messiah Festival, Bethany Coll., 2005. Mem., sec. Latchkey bd. advisors NE Kans. Music Tchrs. Assn., 1999—2003. Recipient Scholarship winner, Sitka Music Festival Winter Session, Student-Institute Workshop, Univ. of Alaska at Juneau/Juneau, Alaska, 1980. Mem.: Music Tchrs. Nat. Assn., Topeka Symphony League, Am. String Tchrs. Assn., Kans. Music Tchrs. Assn., N.E. Kans. Music Tchr. Assn. (sec. 1998—2003), Topeka Music Tchr. Assn. (chmn. honors recitals 1999—2001), Washburn Univ. Alumni Assn., Topeka HS Alumni Hist. Soc., Woman's Kans. Day Club. Avocations: music, literature. Home and Office: 3618 SW 33d St Topeka KS 66614-2812 Office Phone: 785-271-0402. Personal E-mail: schultzstringstorm@sbcglobal.net.

**SCHULTZ, LOUIS WILLIAM,** retired judge; b. Deep River, Iowa, Mar. 24, 1927; s. M. Louis and Esther Louise (Behrens) S.; m. D. Jean Stephen, Nov. 6, 1949; children: Marcia, Mark, Paul. Student, Central Coll., Pella, Iowa, 1944-45, 46-47; LLB, Drake U., Des Moines, 1949. Bar: Iowa. Claims supr. Iowa Farm Mut. Ins. Co., Des Moines, 1949-55; partner firm Harned, Schultz & McMeen, Marengo, Iowa, 1955-71; judge Iowa Dist. Ct. (6th dist.), 1971-80; justice Iowa Supreme Ct., 1980-93; county atty. Iowa County, 1960-68; ret., 1993. Served with USNR, 1945-46. Mem. Iowa Bar Assn. (bd. govs.), Iowa Judges Assn. (pres.)

**SCHULTZ, MARIAN STARR,** musician, educator; b. Buffalo, Aug. 4, 1956; d. Joseph Starr and Catherine Marian Haroney; m. Paul Howard Schultz, July 29, 1985; 1 child, Alexandra Louise. MusB, Shenandoah Conservatory, 1979, PhD in Music Arts, 2000; MusM, Cath. U. Am., 1988. Music specialist Green Acres Sch., Rockville, Md., 1983—2003, FCPS, Fairfax City, Md., 2003—. Advisory council mem. Assn. Ind. Md. Schs., 1992—94, conf. chair, 2000—. Author: (book) A Study to Determine the Effect..., 2005. Donor St. Louis RC Ch., Buffalo, 2004, St. Anthony's Parish, Buffalo, 2003—04. Mem.: Music Educators Nat. Conf., Sigma Alpha Iota (treas. 1986—88). Avocations: fencing, swimming, gardening, travel.

**SCHULTZ, MARVIN E.,** historian, educator; b. Albuquerque, N.Mex., Oct. 8, 1949; s. Marvin and Elizabeth Schultz; life ptnr. Shelia Kaye Jenkins. BA, Angelo State U., San Angelo, Tex., 1971; MA, Tex. State U., San Marcos, 1984; PhD, Tex. Christian U., Fort Worth, 1994. Asst. instr. history Tex. State U., San Marcos, 1980—84; instr. history, history, 1984—85; fellow Vanderbilt U., Nashville, 1985—87; adj. instr. history Vol. State CC, Gallatin, Tenn., 1987—88; tchg. asst. Tex. Christian U., Fort Worth, Tex., 1990—94; lectr. in Tex. history U. of Tex. at Dallas, Richardson, 1994; dir. Ctr. Am. Culture and History in Edn., Malvern, Ark., 1999—; instr. history Ouachita Tech. Coll., Malvern, Ark., 1994—. Hist. cons., editor Applied Acad. Assocs., Fort Worth, Tex., 1990—92; jr. rsch. fellow Tex. State Hist. Assn., Austin, Tex., 1983—84; prodn. mgr. On With the Show, Austin, Tex., 1972—79; presenter in field. Editor: U. S. History Documents, 1996, Encyclopedia of Arkansas

History and Culture, 2005—; author: Study Guide to Accompany Out of Many, 2005; contbr. chapters to books, articles papers and revs. to profl. jours. Commr., sec. City Parks Commn., Malvern, Ark., 2001—06; mem. Garvan Woodland Garden, Hot Springs, Ark., 2001—; Ouachita River Park Commn., 2003—05, chmn., 2004—05; mem. adv. bd. Ark. Studies Living Curriculum Project, 2003—. Recipient Kent Trinkle Book Collecting award, Friends of the Tex. Christian U. Libr., 1991. Fellow: Grady McWhiney Rsch. Found.; mem.: Ark. Hist. Assn., Friends of the Malvern/Hot Spring County Libr. (life), So. Hist. Assn., Alpha Chi, Phi Alpha Theta. Avocations: gardening, travel, public history, birdwatching. Office: Ouachita Tech Coll One College Circle Malvern AR 72104 Office Phone: 501-337-5000 x1147. Business E-Mail: mschultz@otcweb.edu.

**SCHULTZ, NANCY JANSSON,** artist; b. Kanas City, Mo., Apr. 15, 1933; d. Carl Albert Jansson and Lora Elizabeth Wilson; m. Everett Hoyle Schultz, June 24, 1955; children: Susan, Frank, Janet, Sally. Student, Park Coll. Parkville, Mo., 1951—54. Founder Women on Paper, Augusta, Ga., 1987—; exhibit organizer Art of the Sketchbook, Ga., 2005. Exhibitions include Genema Gallery, Altanta, McCormick Arts Ctr., S.C. (Purchase award, 2004, 2005, 2006), Quinlan Arts Ctr., Gainsville, Ga., Gwinnett Fine Arts Ctr., Duluth, Ga., U. S.C., Aiken, Cotton Exch. Gallery, Augusta, 1998, Clayton St. Gallery, Athens, Ga., 1998, Emory U. Law Sch. Libr., Atlanta, 2000, Barnes & Noble Bookstore, Augusta, 2000, State Capitol Gallery, Ga. Arts Day, Atlanta, 2001, Aiken Ctr. Arts, 2001, State Bot. Gardens, Athens, 2002, Cork Gallery, Avery Fisher Hall, N.Y.C., 2002—05, Birmingham So. Coll. Durbin Gallery, 2006 (Merit award, 2006), Represented in permanent collections Bank Fla., Deloritte & Touche, Charlotte, N.C., Med. Coll. Ga., U. Hosp., Augusta, St. Joseph's Hosp., PAC 2000, N.H., Jud. Ctr., Ocala, Fla., prin. works include Carpenter's Gallery, Augusta, Ann Jacob Gallery, Highlands, NC, The Pheasants Eye, Lynchburg, Va., Suzannes Frame Design, St. Petersburg, Fla., McCormick Arts Coun., S.C., represented by, Broad Strokes Gallery, Augusta, Art on Broad. Named to Archives on Women Artists, Nat. Mus. of Women in the Arts, Washington, 1995; recipient Honorable Mention, Eyes for the Art, Augusta, 1992, Merit award, Images in Art, Ocala, 1992, First Pl., Fine Arts for Watercolor, Blue Crab Festival, N.C., 1989, Merit award, Miss. Watercolor Soc., 1989, 1st pl. Watercolor, Columbia County Renaissance Festival, 2005, Honorable Mention, Art on Main Hendersonville, N.C., 2005, Merit award, Ala. Watercolor Soc., 2006. Mem.: Gertude Herbert Inst. of Art, Nat. League of Am. Pen Women (1st pl. 1994, 3d pl. 1997, Pres. award. 1997, Marel Brown award 1998, 1st pl. in mixed media 2002, 3d pl. 2002, 2d pl. 2005, 2d pl. Watercolor Spring Juried Show 2006), Ga. Watercolor Soc. (newsletter editor 1990—92, signature mem.). Achievements include development of booklet for newcomers to Augusta area 'A Guide For Visual Artists'. Avocations: aerobics, writing, reading, making hand made books. Home and Studio: 608 Aumond Rd Augusta GA 30909

**SCHULTZ, NORBERT J.,** retired music educator; b. Gardner, Ill., Apr. 25, 1937; s. Lewis H. and Vera Schultz; m. Janet A. Schultz, Aug. 19, 1979; children: Sonia, Shelly Luppen 1 stepchild, John Bracamontes. BS in Music Edn., Ill. State U., 1959. Band, vocal and gen. music tchr., grade and H.S. Kempton and Cabrey (Ill.) Schs., 1959—61; vocal tchr. Piper City (Ill.) Grade and H.S., 1961—63; band and vocal dir. Taft Grade Sch. Lockport, Ill., 1963—67; band dir. Lyons (Ill.) Sch. Dist., 1967—70, Edwardsville (Ill.) elem, jr. high and H.S., 1970—85; gen. music tchr. Shenandoah and Woodward Elem. Schs., St. Louis, 1986—99; beginning and intermediate band dir. St. Paul's Luth. Sch., Troy, Ill., 1999—2001; ret., 2001. Profl. entertainer, band dir. Musical dir. chapel Charles Melvin Price Support Ctr. Army Facility, Granite City, Ill., 1995—2000; deacon Holy Cross Luth. Ch., Collinsville, Ill., 1988—96, elder, 1999, St. Paul's Luth. Ch., Troy, 2002—. Named team mem. in citizen ambassador program elementary edn. del. to Vietnam, Eisenhower award, U. Toledo, 1994; recipient numerous 1st pl. band awards at state competitions. Mem.: Music Tchrs. Nat. Assn., Ill. State Music Tchrs. Assn. Republican. Lutheran. Avocations: fishing, travel, private teaching. Home: Holiday Shores 846 Newport Bay Edwardsville IL 62025 Office Phone: 618-659-8736.

**SCHULTZ, PATRICIA BOWERS,** vocal music educator, conductor; b. Gomer, Ohio, Apr. 26, 1941; d. Paul Edward and Blodwen (Watkins) Bowers; m. Charles Albert Schultz; children: Todd Matthew, Vaughn Andrew, Cinnamon Paulette. BS in Edn., French & Music, Miami U., Oxford, Ohio, 1963; MEd in Counseling, U. Ill., 1964; D of Musical Arts in Vocal Performance, U. Mo-Kansas City, 1984. Performer freelance USA and Europe, 1964—; music educator, counselor Northmont Pub. Schs., Dayton, Ohio, 1964-66; French educator Bowling Green (Ohio) H.S., 1967-68; instr. music and French Dickinson (N.D.) State U., 1972-74; instr. voice Ctrl. State U., Wilberforce, Ohio, 1975-76; dir. choral activities Savannah (Mo.) H.S., 1979-80; prof. music N.W. Mo. State U., Maryville, 1981—2002. Dir. music First United Meth. Ch., Maryville, 1977—88; tour mgr. Jenny Lind Ensemble, 1978—; musical dir. N.W. MO. State U., Maryville, 1981—2002; vis. prof. Internat. Enrichment, London, 2000, 02, 06, 2004—06, 2006; adjudicator Nat. Assn. Tchrs. of Singing, Mo. H.S. Activities Assn.; co-dir. Summer in London Program Internat. Enrichment, 2006. Accomplishments in music include author, lead role in music drama Encore for Jenny Lind, 1976—(London Premiere 1992); conductor choral music Welsh Gymanfoedd Ganu, 1989— (Nat. Selection 1992, 1993, 2005); Coloratura soprano recitals and concerts throughout U.S.; soloist European tour Cin. Symphony, 1969; presentator Am. Assn. Higher Edn. Teaching Learning & Tech. Conf., 1997. Pres. Univ. Women, Maryville, 1978-79; first judge of vocal competition Nat. Glenn Miller Scholarship Competition, Clarinda, Iowa, 1992, 94, 2001; pres. Faculty Senate N.W. Mo. State U., 1993-95, Centennial Soc. 2002-; organizer, charter mem. Mo. Assn. Faculty Senates, Springfield, Mo., 1993-94. Named Faculty Fellow Mo. Coordinating Bd. Higher Edn., 1997-98, Outstanding Alumnae Conservatory of Music, U. Mo.-Kansas City, 1990; grantee Mo. State Coun. on Arts, 1991-95. Mem. AAUW, Coll. Music Soc., Nat. Assn. Tchrs. Singing (Teacher of regional state and chpt. winners in Mo., N-W and Ming state region 1986, 88, 90, 92, 97, 98), Am. Choral Dirs. Assn. (hon.) Mortar Bd. (Outstanding advisor, 2003), Sigma Alpha Iota (patroness and advisor 1995-2002), Delta Omicron. Avocations: gardening, reading, travel. Home: 1004 W Cooper St Maryville MO 64468-2005 Office: NW Mo State Univ Dept Music 800 University Dr Maryville MO 64468-6015

**SCHULTZ, RICHARD CARLTON,** plastic surgeon; b. Grosse Pointe, Mich., Nov. 19, 1927; s. Herbert H. and Carmen (Huebner) S.; m. Pauline Zimmermann, Oct. 8, 1955; children: Richard, Lisa, Alexandra, Jennifer. MD, Wayne State U., 1953. Diplomate Am. Bd. Plastic Surgery. Intern Harper Hosp., Detroit, 1953-54, resident in gen. surgery, 1954-55, U.S. Army Hosp., Ft. Carson, Colo., 1955-57; resident in plastic surgery St. Luke's Hosp., Chgo., 1957-58, U. Ill. Hosp., Chgo. 1958-59, VA Hosp., Hines, Ill. 1959-60; practice medicine specializing in plastic surgery Park Ridge, Ill. 1961-96; ret., 1996; clin. asst. prof. surgery U. Ill. Coll. Medicine, 1966-70, assoc. prof. surgery, 1970-76, prof., 1976-96, head divsn. plastic surgery, 1970-87; pres. med. staff Luth. Gen. Hosp., Park Ridge, 1977-79. Vis. prof. U. Pitts., 1972, U. Miss., 1973, U. Pisa, Italy, 1974, Jikei U. Coll. Medicine, Tokyo, 1976, Ind. U., 1977, U. Helsinki, 1977, U. N.Mex., 1978, U. Milan, 1981, So. Ill. Sch. Medicine, 1982, Tulane U. Med. Sch., 1983, Shanghai 2d Med. Coll., 1984, U. Guadalajara (Mex.), 1986, Gazi U., Turkey, 1988, U. Coll. Medicine Tsuksba, Japan, 1996, Taegu (Korea) U., 1996; sr. Fulbright lectr. U. Uppsala, Sweden, 2003; participant, guest surgeon Physicians for Peace, Turkey and Greece, 1988, Israel and Occupied Ters., 1990, Egypt, 1991, Lithuania, Estonia, 1993 (team leader); leader citizen amb. People to People Internat. Del. Plastic Surgeons to Albania & Russia, 1994, del. leader, Tibet and China, 1998. Author: Facial Injuries, 1970, 3d edit., 1988, Maxillo-Facial Injuries from Vehicle Accidents, 1975, Outpatient Surgery, 1979. Mem. sch. bd., Lake Zurich, Ill., 1966-72, pres., 1968-72; pres. Chgo. Found. for Plastic Surgery, 1966-. Served to capt. M.C., AUS, 1955-57. Fulbright Found. scholar, Sweden, 1960-61; recipient Auto Safety award Med. Tribune, 1967, Robert H. Ivy award 1969, Disting. Sci. Achievement award Wayne U. Coll. Medicine Alumni, 1975, Sanvenero-Rosselli award, 1981; McGregor scholar, U. Mich., 1946-49; grantee Ednl. Found. Am. Soc. Plastic and Reconstructive Surgery, 1964-65. Fellow ACS (pres. local

commn. on trauma 1985-87); mem. Am. Assn. Plastic Surgeons (trustee 1990-91), Am. Soc. Plastic and Reconstructive Surgeons, Midwestern Assn. Plastic Surgeons (pres. 1978-79), Chgo. Soc. Plastic Surgeons (pres. 1970-72), Midwestern Assn. Plastic Surgeons (pres. 1978-79), Am. Soc. Maxillofacial Surgeons (pres. 1988-89, award of honor 1986), Am. Assn. Automotive Medicine (pres. 1970-71, A. Merkin award 1982), Am. Cleft Palate Assn., Am. Soc. Aesthetic Plastic Surgery, Tord Skoog Soc. Plastic Surgeons (pres. 1971-75), Can. Soc. Plastic Surgery, Chilean Soc. Plastic Surgery (corr.), Japanese Soc. Plastic Surgery (corr.), Cuban Soc. Maxillofacial Surgery (corr.), Korean Soc. Plastic Surgery (corr.). Office: PO Box 357 Northport MI 49670-0357 Office Phone: 231-386-5950.

**SCHULTZ, RICHARD DALE,** national athletic organization executive; b. Grinnell, Iowa, Sept. 5, 1929; s. August Henry and Marjorie Ruth (Turner) S.; m. Jacquilyn Lu Duistermars, June 26, 1949; children: Robert Dale, William Joel, Kim Marie. BS, Ctrl. Coll., Pella, Iowa, 1950; EdD (hon.), Ctrl. Coll. 1987; LLD (hon.), Wartburg Coll., 1988, Alma Coll., 1989, Luther Coll. 1991; PhD (hon.), U.S. Sports Acad., 1993; LLD (hon.), Daniel Webster Coll., 1997, Gettysburg Coll., 1998. Head basketball coach, athletic dir. Humboldt (Iowa) High Sch., 1950-60; freshman basketball coach U. Iowa, Iowa City, 1960-62, head baseball coach, assoc. basketball coach, 1962-70, head basketball coach, 1970-74, asst. v.p., 1974-76; dir. athletics and phys. edn. Cornell U., Ithaca, NY, 1976-81; dir. athletics U. Va., Charlottesville, 1981-87; exec. dir. NCAA, Mission, Kans., 1987-94; pres. Global Sports Enterprises, 1994-95; exec. dir. U.S. Olympic Com., Colorado Springs, Colo. 1995—2004; chmn. Mktg. Assocs. Internat., 2000—04; chmn., CEO, Internat. Partnerships, 2002—. Mem. honors ct. Nat. Football Found. and Hall of Fame, Nat. Basketball Hall of Fame, 1992; chmn. bd. NCAA Found., 1989; organizer Iowa Steel Mill, Inc.; bd. trustees Gettysburg Coll., 1996—; cons. to the CEO Forum, 2004—; mem. bd. dirs. Hanspree Corp., Tacipe, Twaian. Author: A Course of Study for the Coaching of Baseball, 1964, The Theory and Techniques of Coaching Basketball, 1970; Contbr. articles to mags. Bd. dirs. Fellowship of Christian Athletes, 1986, chmn., 1990; chmn. Multiple Sclerosis, 1974-75; mem. Knight Found. Commn. on Intercollegiate Athletics, 1990—; mem. adv. com. on svc. acad. athletic programs Def. Dept. Recipient Disting. Alumni award Ctrl. Coll., Pella, 1970, 98, Lifetime Svc. award U. Iowa, 1994, Corbett award Nat. Assn. Collegiate Dirs. Athletics, 1994, medal of honor Ellis Island, 1997, Disting. Alumni award Ctrl. Coll. 1998, Casey award, 1999, Pres. and Mrs. Bush Cmty. Impact award 1999; mem. Basketball Hall of Fame Honor Ct., 1992, Sportsman of Yr. award Marine Corp., 1997; inducted into Iowa Baseball Hall of Fame, 1993, Ctrl. Coll. Hall of Honors, 2002, Des Moines Register Hall of Fame, 2003. Mem. Nat. Assn. Coll. Basketball Coaches, Ea. Coll. Athletic Assn. (mem. exec. com. 1980-81), Am. Basketball Coaches Assn. (Award of Honor 1994), Am. Football Coaches Assn. (lifetime membership award 1995). Home: 3670 Twisted Oak Cir Colorado Springs CO 80904-4720 Office Phone: 719-685-3245. Personal E-Mail: dschultzprint2@earthlink.net.

**SCHULTZ, RICHARD H.,** state agency administrator; MS, Ctrl. Wash. Univ. Adminstr. div. health Idaho Dept. Health & Welfare, Boise, 1986—. Office: Div Health 450 W State St Boise ID 83720-0036

**SCHULTZ, RICHARD OTTO,** ophthalmologist, educator; b. Racine, Wis., Mar. 19, 1930; s. Henry Arthur and Josephine (Wagoner) S.; m. Diane Haldane, Sept. 29, 1990; children: Henry Reid, Richard Paul, Karen Jo. BA, U. Wis., 1950, MS, 1954; MD, Albany Med. Coll., 1956; MSc, U. Iowa, 1960. Diplomate Am. Bd. Ophthalmology. Intern, Univ. Hosps., Iowa City, 1956-57, resident in opthalmology, 1957-60; chief ophthalmology sect. div. Indian health USPHS, Phoenix, 1960-63; practice medicine specializing in ophthalmology Phoenix, 1963; NIH spl. fellow in ophthalmic microbiology U. Calif., San Francisco, 1963-64, clin. assoc., 1963-64, research assoc. 1963-64; assoc. prof., chmn. dept. ophthalmology Marquette U. Sch. Medicine (now Med. Coll. Wis.), Milw., 1964-68, prof., chmn., 1968-97, prof. ophthalmology, 1997—2000, prof. emeritus, 2000—. Mem. nat. adv. eye coun. NIH, 1984-88; cons. Froedert Hosp., Milw.; adj. prof. optical scis. U. Ariz., 1995—. Contbr. articles to profl. jours. Served with USPHS, 1960-63. Fellow: ACS (life), Am. Ophthalmol. Soc. (emeritus), Am. Acad. Ophthalmology (life); mem.: Milw. Acad. Medicine, Oxford Ophthalmol. Congress (Eng.), Rsch. to Prevent Blindness, N.Y. Acad. Scis. (emeritus), Pan Am. Assn. Ophthalmology (life), Assn. Rsch. Vision and Ophthalmology (emeritus), Milw. Ophthal. Soc. (sec. emeritus), Univ. Profs. Ophthalmology (past pres., trustee). Home: 7505 S Kangaroo Lake Rd Baileys Harbor WI 54202 Office Phone: 414-456-7915. Personal E-Mail: eyeotto@aol.com.

**SCHULTZ, ROBERT JORDAN,** orthopaedic surgeon, educator; b. Bklyn., June 29, 1930; m. Marcie Schultz. Student, Muhlenberg Coll., 1948-49; BS, Bklyn. Coll., 1952; MD, Chgo. Med. Sch., 1957. Diplomate Am. Bd. Orthopedic Surgery (examiner). Intern Meadowbrook Hosp., Hempstead, NY, 1957-58; resident in surgery Mt. Sinai Hosp., Miami, Fla., 1958-59; resident in orthopaedic surgery Charity Hosp., New Orleans, 1959-62; fellow in hand surgery Columbia Presbyn. Med. Ctr., N.Y.C., 1968; instr. dept. orthopaedic surgery Albert Einstein Coll. Medicine, N.Y.C., 1966-73, asst. prof., 1968-73, assoc. prof., 1973-77; lectr. div. prosthesis and orthotics NYU Postgrad. Med. Sch., 1968—; dir. dept. orthopaedic surgery Albert Einstein Coll. Medicine, N.Y.C., 1969-77; prof. dept. surgery N.Y. Med. Coll., Valhalla, 1988-90, prof. dept. anatomy, 1987-90, dir. sports medicine, dept. orthopaedic surgery, 1980—, dir. Sylvester J. Carter Hand Svc., 1980—, prof., chmn. dept. orthopaedic surgery, 1977—; with U. S. Fal. Med. Ctr., Tampa, 1990—. Dir. attending surgeon dept. orthopaedic surgery Westchester County Med. Ctr., Valhalla, 1977—, dir. sports medicine, 1978—; attending orthopaedic surgeon, Met. Hosp., N.Y.C., 1977—; Lincoln Hosp., Bronx, 1977—, Lenox Hill Hosp., N.Y.C., 1982—; Terence Cardinal Cooke Health Care Ctr., N.Y.C. 1977—; Bronx Mcpl. Hosp. Ctr., 1966-77; dir. and attending orthopaedic surgeon Hosp. of Albert Einstein Coll. Medicine, Bronx, 1969-77; prosthetic papers, exhibits, invited lectr. to numerous nat. and internat. assns., hosps., med. colls., postgrad. courses; spl. orthopaedic del. to People's Republic of China, 1981, chmn. dels., 1983, 86; med. cons. N.Y. State Athletic Commn., chmn. of med. adv. bd.; adv. coun. USN; vis. prof. Haddasah Hosp. and Med. Sch., Jerusalem, 1972, Browley Bristow Orthopaedic Hosp., Surrey, Eng., 1973, U. Colo., 1977, University Cattolica del Sacro Cuore, Rome, 1984, Michael Reese Hosp. & Med. Ctr., Chgo., 1984, Bethesda Naval Hosp., 1986, U. W.Va. Med. Sch., Morgantown, 1988;; adv. com. State of Conn. Higher Edn. Supplemental Loan Authority, 1983—; police surgeon of Westchester County (N.Y.) Police Dept., 1983—, commdg. officer police surgeons, 1984—. Author: The Language of Fractures, 1972; editor Jour. Hand Surgery; mem. editorial bd. Jour. Orthopaedic Surg. Techniques, Surg. Rounds for Orthopaedics; contbr. chpts. to books, articles and abstracts to sci. and med. jours. Mem. grant rev. com. Orthopedic Rsch. and Edn. Found. Career Devel. Awards Com., Fellowship Grant Com., The Mary and David Hoar Fellowship Com. N.Y. Acad. Medicine; sr. investigator N.Y. Med. Coll. for Aging and Adult Devel., 1984—. With USN, 1962-66; flight surgeon, 1963-65, capt. USNR, 1980—. Fellow ACS, Am. Acad. Orthopaedic Surgeons, N.Y. Acad. Medicine (sec. sect. orthopaedic surgery 1979-80, chmn. 1980-81); mem. AMA, Am. Orthopaedic Assn., Am. Soc. for Surgery of the Hand, Societe Internationale de Chirurgie Orthopedique et de Traumatologie, Sociedad de Cirugia de la Mano del Caribe (hon.), Amicale Internationale de Chirurgie de la Main (hon.), Soc. Med. Cons. to Armed Forces, Ea. Orthopaedic Assn., Am. Rheumatism Assn., N.Y. Soc. Orthopaedic Surgeons, Westchester Acad. Medicine (chmn. sect. sports medicine, 1979-81), N.Y. Soc. for Surgery of the Hand (sec. 1981-83, v.p. 1983-84, pres. 1985-86).

**SCHULTZ, ROGER C.,** career military officer; b. LeMars, Iowa, Oct. 13, 1945; s. Harry Willis and Sylvia Dorothy (Aronson) S.; m. Barbara J. Kaiser, Feb. 14, 1969. BS, Upper Iowa U., 1988; MPA, Shippensburg U., 1992. Commd. USNG, advanced through grades to brig. gen., 1996; rifle platoon leader Co. A 2d Bn., 133d Inf., Ft. Carson, Colo., 1968-69; scout leader Hdqs. and Hdqs. Co. 2d Bn., 22d Inf., Vietnam, 1969; logistics, personnel, intelligence officer HHC 2d Bn., 133d Inf., Sioux City, Iowa, 1970-75, rifle co. comdr. Co. B Sheldon, Iowa, 1975-76, ops. and tng. officer HHC Sioux City, Iowa, 1976-78; brigade ops. and tng. officer 34th Brigade, 47th Inf.,

Boone, Iowa, 1978-81, exec. officer, 1981-82; bn. comdr. 1st Bn., 168th Inf., Council Bluffs, Iowa, 1982-84; dir. op. and tng. Iowa Army Nat. Guard, Johnston, Iowa, 1984-88, chief of staff, 1988-95, dep. adjutant gen., 1995—98; dir. Army Nat. Guard, Washington, 1998—. Lobbyist Dept. Pub. Def., Des Moines, 1996. Decorated Silver Star, 1969, Bronze Star, 1969, Purple Heart (2 awards), 1969, Legion of Merit, 1995. Presbyterian. Office: NG Bur 1411 Jefferson Davis Hwy Arlington VA 22202-3231

**SCHULTZ, STANLEY GEORGE,** physiologist, educator, dean; b. Bayonne, NJ, Oct. 26, 1931; s. Aaron and Sylvia (Kaplan) S.; m. Harriet Taran, Dec. 25, 1960; children: Jeffrey, Kenneth. AB summa cum laude, Columbia U., N.Y.C., 1952; MD, NYU, 1956. Intern Bellevue Hosp., NYC, 1956-57, resident, 1957-59; research assoc. in biophysics Harvard U., 1959-62, instr. biophysics, 1964-67; assoc. prof. physiology U. Pitts., 1967-70, prof. physiology, 1970-79; prof., chmn. dept. physiology U. Tex. Med. Sch., Houston, 1979-96, prof. dept. internal medicine, 1979—, prof. dept. integrative biol. pharm. physiology, 1997—, vice chmn., 1999—2003, Fondren chair in cell signalling, 1999—, dean Sch. Medicine, 2003—06, H. Wayne Hightower Dist. prof. biomed. sci., 2005—. Cons. USPHS, NIH, 1970—; mem. physiology test com. Nat. Bd. Med. Examiners, 1974-79, chmn., 1976-79 Editor Am. Jour. Physiology, Jour. Applied Physiology, 1971-75, Physiol. Revs., 1979-85, Handbook of Physiology: The Gastrointestinal Tract, 1989-91—; mem. editl. bd. Jour. Gen. Physiology, 1969-88, Ann. Revs. Physiology, 1974-81, Current Topics in Membranes and Transport, 1975-81, Jour. Membrane Biology, 1977—, Biochim. Biophys. Acta, 1987-89; assoc. editor Ann. Revs. Physiology, 1977-81; assoc. editor News in Physiol. Scis., 1989-94, editor, 1994-2003; contbr. articles to profl. jours. Served to capt. M.C. USAF, 1962-64. Recipient Rsch. Career award NIH, 1969-74, Solomon Berson award NIH, 2004; overseas fellow Churchill Coll., Cambridge U., 1975-76 Mem. AAAS, AMA (coun. on med. edn.), Am. Heart Assn. (estab. investigator 1964-68), Am. Physiol. Soc. (councillor 1989-91, pres.-elect 1991-92, pres. 1992-93, past pres. 1993-94, Guyton award 1997, Orr Reynolds award 1999, Daggs award 2003), European Acad. Sci., Fed. Am. Soc. Exptl. Biology (exec. bd. 1992-95), Biophys. Soc., Soc. Gen. Physiologists, Internat. Cell Rsch. Orgn., Internat. Union Physiol. Scis. (chmn. internat. com. gastrointestinal physiology 1977-80, chmn. U.S. nat. com. 1992-98), Assn. Am. Physicians, Am. Assn. Ob-Gyn. (hon. fellow), Assn. Chmn. Depts. Physiology (pres. 1985-86), Houston Philos. Soc., Phi Beta Kappa, Sigma Xi. Office Phone: 713-500-5012. Business E-Mail: stanley.g.schultz@uth.tmc.edu.

**SCHULTZ, STEPHEN W.,** art educator; s. Robert Walter and Joan Warren Schultz; m. Romey Stuckart, Jan. 7, 1984. Student, R.I. Sch. Design, 1965—67; BFA, San Francisco, 1971; MFA, Stanford U., 1974. Tchg. fellow Stanford (Calif.) U., 1974; prof. U. Iowa, Iowa City, 1975—94. Vis. artist Bellagio Study Ctr., Lake Como, Italy, 1984, Camargo Found., Cassis, France, 1985, Am. Acad., Rome, 1997; vis. prof. U. Fine Arts, Belgrad, Yugoslavia, 1986, U. Washington, Seattle, 2003. Exhibitions include Sid Deutsch Gallery, N.Y.C., 1984, 1986, Lowe Gallery, Santa Monica and Atlanta, 1991—2000, Chac-Mool Gallery, L.A., 1997, Chase Gallery, Spokane Civic Ctr., Wash., 2001, Victoria Boyce Gallery, Scottsdale, Ariz., 2002, Salt Lake Art Ctr., 2003, Mus. Arts and Culture, Spokane, Wash., 2006. Recipient Visual Arts award, NEA, 1981, Faculty Scholar award, U. Iowa, 1986, Visual Arts award, Rockefeller Found., 1981; fellow, Tiffany Found., 1979, Idaho Commn. for Arts, 1994; scholar, U. Iowa, 1984—86; Fulbright fellow, 1986, Westaf fellow, NEA. 1990. Mem.: Coll. Art. Assn. Democrat. Avocations: skiing, motorcycling. Office: ART 915 Poplar St Sandpoint ID 83869 Office Phone: 208-255-7787.

**SCHULTZ, T. PAUL,** economics professor; b. Ames, Iowa, May 24, 1940; s. Theodore W. and Esther (Werth) S.; m. Judith Hoenack, Sept. 16, 1967; children: Lara, Joel, Rebecca. BA, Swarthmore Coll., 1961; PhD, MIT, 1966; MA (hon.), Yale U., 1974. Cons. Joint Econ. Com., Washington, 1964; senior econ. dept. Rand Corp., Santa Monica, Calif., 1965-72, dir. population rsch., 1968-72; prof. econ. U. Minn., Mpls., 1972-75, Yale U., New Haven, 1974—; dir. Econ. Growth Ctr., 1983-96; prof. econ. Malcolm K. Brachman, 1977. Cons. World Bank, Rockefeller Found., InterAm. Devel. Bank; mem. com. on population NAS, Washington, 1987-89, 90-93. Author: Structural Change in a Developing Country, 1971, Economics of Population, 1981; editor: (books) The State of Development Economics, 1988, Investment In Women's Human Capital, 1995, (periodical) Research in Population Economics, 1985, 88, 91, 96; assoc. editor Jour. Population Econs., 1991—, Econ. of Edn. Rev., 1993-2004, China Econ. Rev., 1994—. Mem. commn. on behavioral sci. and edn. Nat. Rsch. Coun., 1997-2002. Fellow: AAAS (population resources environ. com. 1985—89, nomination com. 1987—90); mem.: Econ. Rsch. Forum for Arab Countries (trustee 1993—2001), European Soc. for Population Econs. (bd. dirs., pres. 1997), Soc. for Study Social Biology (bd. dirs. 1986—91), Internat. Union for Sci. Study Population, Population Assn. Am. (bd. dirs. 1979—81), Econometrics Soc., Am. Econ. Assn. Office: Yale U Econ Growth Ctr PO Box 208269 27 Hillhouse Ave New Haven CT 06520-8269 E-mail: paul.schultz@yale.edu.

**SCHULTZ, VICKI L.,** law educator; b. Waltham, Mass., May 22, 1957; d. Jimmy and Virginia (Gaines) S. BA, U. Tex., 1977; JD, Harvard U. 1981. Bar: Mass. 1983, U.S. Dist. Ct. Mass. 1983, Wis. 1990. Law clk. to judges U.S. Dist. Ct. for Mass., Boston, 1981-83; atty. civil rights div. U.S. Dept. Justice, Washington, 1983-86; asst. prof. U. Wis. Law Sch., Madison, 1986—93, assoc. prof., 1992; prof. law Yale U., New Haven, 1993—2002, Ford Found prof., 2002—. Vis. prof. Harvard U., 2001. Contbr. articles to legal jours. Fellow Whitney Humanities Ctr., 1999—2000; Evelyn Green Davis Fellow, Radcliffe Inst. for Advanced Study, 2000—01. Mem. ABA, Law and Society Assn. E-mail: vicki.schultz@yale.edu.

**SCHULTZ, VICTOR H.,** physician; b. Pitts., Aug. 14, 1932; s. Irvin and Rose (Reiss) S. BS, Kent (Ohio) State U., 1953; MD, Ohio State U., Columbus, 1958. Diplomate Am. Bd. Dermatology. Pvt. practice, Santa Monica, Calif., 1965—. Fellow Am. Acad. Dermatology, Pacific Dermatologic Assn.; mem. AMA, Am. Coll. Physicians, Calif. Med. Assn., L.A. County Med. Assn. Avocations: skiing, tennis, golf, music, swimming. Office: 2461 Santa Monica Blvd Santa Monica CA 90404-2049 Office Phone: 310-828-7492.

**SCHULZ, DIANA,** film company executive; Grad. summa cum laude, Claremont McKenna Coll.; MBA, Stanford U. With Bain and Co., Microsoft Corp., McKinsey and Co. Consulting, L.A., 1991—97; mem. corp. devel. and strategic planning roup Vivendi Universal Entertainment, Universal City, Calif., 1997—99, head of group, 1999—2001, sr. v.p. corp. devel. and strategic planning, 2001—. Office: Vivendi Universal Entertainment 100 Universal City Plaza Universal City CA 91608-1002

**SCHULZ, EKKEHARD,** metal products executive; b. 1941; PhD in metallurgy, Clausthal U., 1971. Chmn. exec. bd. Thyssen Krupp AG; mem. sci. staff & chief engr. Clausthal U., 1967—72; with Thyssen Group, 1972, appt. dep. mem., 1985—; appt. regular mem., exec. bd. ThyssenStahl AG, 1986—, head tech. directorate, 1988—, appt. chmn. exec. bd., 1991—, mem. exec. bd., 1991—; chmn. exec. bd. Thyssen Krupp Stahl AG, 1997—, Thyssen AG, 1998—; co-chmn. exec. bd. ThyssenKrupp AG, 1999—2001, chmn exec. bd., 2001—; ThyssenKrupp Steel AG, 1999—2001. Bd. dirs. Budd Co.; mem. supervisory bds. Commerzbank AG, Hapag Lloyd AG, MAN AG, Energie AG, Strabag AG; pres. Eurofer; com. mem., bd. Wirtschaftsvereinigung Stahl, VDEh. Recipient hon. professorship, Clausthal U., 1999. Office: Thyssen Krupp AG August Thyssen Str 1 40211 Düsseldorf Germany

**SCHULZ, JOHN JOSEPH,** communications educator; BA in Journalism, U. Mont., 1962; MPhil, Oxford U., 1979, DPhil, 1981; student, Naval War Coll., Washington, 1985-86. Newswriter, reporter Voice of Am. News, Washington, 1971-72, corr. Hong Kong, 1972-74, bur. chief Tokyo, 1974-77; commentator BBC, London, 1977-79; coverage editor Voice of Am., 1979-

82; dep. dir. Voice of Am. News Divsn., 1982—85; South Asia corr. Voice of Am. News, Islamabad, Pakistan, 1987-89; thinktank analyst Oxford Analytica, 1977-79, 84-88; prof. Nat. War Coll., Washington, 1989-91; sr. corr. Voice of Am. News, 1986—87, 1991—92; assoc. dir. publs. The Arms Control Assn., 1992-95; prof. internat. comm. Coll. Comm. Boston U., 1995—97, 2000—03, chair dept. mass. comm., advt., and pub. rels., 1997—2000, dean. Coll. Comm., 2003—; editor Arms Control Today, 1992-95. Presenter in field. Editor-in-chief Global Beat Syndicate, 2002—; contbr. articles to profl. jours. With USAF, 1963-71. Decorated 3 DFC, silver star, air medals, gallantry crosses; recipient disting. alumni award U. Mont., 1995. Office: Coll Communication 640 Commonwealth Ave Boston MA 02215-2422 Office Phone: 617-353-3488. Business E-mail: jjschulz@bu.edu.

**SCHULZ, JUERGEN,** art historian, educator; b. Kiel, Germany, Aug. 18, 1927; came to U.S., 1938; s. Johannes Martin Askan Schulz and Ilse (Lebenbaum) Hiller; m. Justine Hume, Sept. 1951 (div. 1968); children: Christoph (dec.), Ursula, Catherine; m. Anne Markham, May 19, 1969; 1 child, Jeremy. BA, U. Calif., Berkeley, 1950; PhD in History of Art, U. London, 1958. Reporter San Francisco Chronicle, 1950-51; copy editor UPI, London, 1952-53; from instr. to prof. history of art U. Calif., 1958-68; prof. Brown, Providence, 1968-90, Andrea V. Rosenthal prof. history art and architecture, 1990-95; Samuel H. Kress prof. Nat. Gallery of Art, 2000-2001. Mem. Inst. for Advanced Study, Princeton, N.J., 1971-72. Author: Venetian Painted Ceilings of the Renaissance, 1968, Printed Plans and...Views of Venice, 1971, La cartografia tra scienza e arte, 1990, The New Palaces of Medieval Venice, 2004; also articles. Staff sgt. U.S. Army, 1945-48. Decorated grande ufficiale Ordine della Stella della Solidarieta della Repubblica Italiana; Guggenheim fellow, 1966-67. Mem. Ateneo Veneto, Centro Internaz. di Studi di Architettura A. Palladio. Office: Brown U Dept History Art and Architecture PO Box 1855 Providence RI 02912-1855 Office Phone: 401-863-1174.

**SCHULZ, KEITH DONALD,** corporate lawyer, writer; b. Burlington, Iowa, Dec. 20, 1938; s. Henry Carl and Laura Iral (Bowlin) S.; m. Emily Brook Roane, Apr. 19, 1985; children: Keith Jr., Sarah, Christine, Stefan. BA, U. Iowa, 1960, JD, 1963. Bar: Iowa 1963, Ill. 1966, Wis. 1990. Dep. Sec. of State, State of Iowa, Des Moines, 1965-66; atty. AT&T, Chgo., 1966-67; sec., gen. counsel Borg-Warner Acceptance Corp., Chgo., 1967-74; asst. gen. counsel Borg-Warner Corp., Chgo., 1974-84, v.p., gen. counsel, 1984-88; of counsel Bell, Boyd & Lloyd, Chgo., 1988—. Chmn., CEO Downtown Ptnrs., Inc., 1995-96. Author: (novel) Keepers of the River, 2001; contbr. articles to Harvard Bus. Rev., Jour. for Corp. Growth. Chmn. bd. dirs. Vol. Legal Svcs. Found., Chgo., 1984-91, pres.; bd. dirs. Southeast Iowa Symphony Orch., pres., 1998-2000, 2003—, Heritage Trust Found. Mem.: Assn. Gen. Counsel, Wis. Bar Assn., Econ. Club, Univ. Club. Avocations: tennis, bicycling, skiing. Office: Bell Boyd & Lloyd 70 W Madison St Ste 3300 Chicago IL 60602-4284 Office Phone: 312-372-1121. Personal E-mail: KDons@aol.com.

**SCHULZ, MICHAEL,** physicist; b. Petoskey, Mich., July 14, 1943; s. Helmuth Martin Walter and Annette Elaine Marie (Steimel) Schulz. BS in Physics, Mich. State U., 1964; PhD in Physics, MIT, 1967. Physicist Nat. Bur. Stds., Washington, 1964—65; mem. tech. staff Bell Tel. Labs., Murray Hill, NJ, 1967—69; from staff scientist to sr. scientist The Aerospace Corp., El Segundo, Calif., 1969—93; sr. physicist Lockheed Martin Advanced Tech. Ctr., Palo Alto, Calif., 1993—. Co-author (with L. J. Lanzerotti): (book) Particle Diffusion in the Radiation Belts, 1974; contbr. articles to profl. jours. Recipient Outstanding Alumnus award, Coll. Natural Sci., Mich. State U., 1983; Alumni Disting. scholar, Mich. State U., 1961—64, NSF Grad. fellow, MIT, 1964—67. Fellow: Am. Geophys. Union (sec. for magnetospheric physics 1980—84), Am. Phys. Soc.; mem.: European Geophys. Soc. Home: 1037 Twin Oak Ct Redwood City CA 94061-1818 Office: Lockheed Martin Adv Technology Ctr Dept ADCS Bldg 255 3251 Hanover St Palo Alto CA 94304-1187 Office Phone: 650-424-2659. Business E-mail: mike.schulz@lmco.com.

**SCHULZ, RAYMOND ALEXANDER,** medical marketing professional, consultant; b. Paris, June 2, 1946; s. Helmut W. and Colette (Prieur) S.; m. Dixie Lee Suzanne Specht, Apr. 9, 1977 (div. Dec. 1990); children: Christopher, William; m. Casey Elizabeth Watson, Apr. 10, 1999; 1 child, Francis John. BA in Physics, W.Va. U., Morgantown, 1970; MS in Computer Sci., Columbia U., N.Y.C., 1975. Sr. programmer Meml. Sloan Kettering Cancer Ctr., N.Y.C., 1972-74; program coord. Neurol. Inst. Columbia Presbyn. Hosp., N.Y.C., 1974-76; engring. mgr. EMI Med. Systems, Northbrook, Ill., 1976-78; product mgr. Johnson & Johnson (Technicare), Solon, Ohio, 1978-80; group product mgr. Siemens Corp., Iselin, NJ, 1980-82; mktg. mgr. Toshiba Am. Med. Systems (formerly Diasonics MRI), South San Francisco, Calif., 1983-92; dir. mktg. Voxel, Laguna Hills, Calif., 1992—98; v.p. mktg. and customer support Voxel, Inc., Provo, Utah, 1999—2001; prin. RA Enterprises, San Mateo, Calif., 2001—; v.p. mktg. and sales Scanis, Inc., Foster City, Calif., 2002—03; tech. dir. Accuray, Sunnyvale, Calif. Bd. dirs. Dynecology, Harrison, NY; presenter in field. Editor (publ.): Robtoic Radiosurgery, 2005; contbr. articles to profl. jours. Mem. vestry St. Matthews Episcopal Ch., San Mateo, Calif., 2006—. Recipient first prize Roentgen Centenary Congress, 1995, Best Paper prize Am. Assn. Neurosurgeon/Cong Neurosurg. Brain Tumor Meeting, San Francisco, 2000. Mem. Am. Assn. Physicists in Medicine, N.Y. Acad. Scis., Internat. Soc. Magnetic Resonance in Medicine, Med. Mktg. Assn., Larchmont Yacht Club, Commonwealth Club Calif., Eta Kappa Nu. Avocations: skiing, running, hiking, swimming, mountainbiking. Office Phone: 408-716-4704. Business E-mail: ras257@columbia.edu.

**SCHULZ, RENATE ADELE,** German studies and second language acquisition educator; b. Lohr am Main, Germany, Feb. 24, 1940; came to U.S., 1958; 1 child, Sigrid Diane. BS, Mankato State Coll., 1962; MA, U. Colo., 1967; PhD, Ohio State U., 1974. Edn. officer U.S. Peace Corps, Ife Ezinihitte, Nigeria, 1963-65; asst. prof. Otterbein Coll., Westerville, Ohio, 1974-76, State U. Coll. N.Y., Buffalo, 1976-77; from asst. to assoc. prof. U. Ark., Fayetteville, 1977-81; from assoc. to prof. U. Ariz., Tucson, 1981—, head dept. German, 1984-90, chair PhD program in second lang. acquisition and teaching, 1994-97. Disting. vis. prof. USAF Acad., Colorado Springs, Colo., 1990-91. Recipient Creative Tchg. award, U. Ariz. Found., Tucson, 1984, Stephen A. Freeman award, N.W. Conf. Tchg. Fgn. Langs., 1984, Bundesverdienstkreuz, Fed. Govt. Germany, 1990, Anthony Papalia award for excellence in tchr. edn., Am. Coun. on the Tchg. of Fgn. Langs./N.Y. State Assn. Fgn. Lang. Tchrs., 2002, Henry and Phyllis Köffler prize for outstanding accomplishments in tchg., U. Ariz., 2005. Mem.: MLA (del. 1989—91), Nat. Fedn. Modern Lang. Tchrs. Assns. (v.p. 2004—05, pres. 2006—), Am. Assn. Applied Linguistics, Tchrs. of ESL, Am. Assn. Tchrs. German (v.p. 1988—90, pres. 1990—91), Am. Coun. on the Tchg. of Fgn. Langs. (exec. coun. 1979—81, Florence Steiner award 1993). Office: U Ariz Dept German Studies Tucson AZ 85721-0105 Office Phone: 520-621-7388. Business E-mail: schulzr@u.arizona.edu.

**SCHULZ, SALLY ANN,** pastoral musician, conductor, educator; b. Red Oak, Iowa, Mar. 12, 1951; d. Robert Lionel and Mary Ellen Evans; m. Thomas Richard Schulz, Dec. 29, 1972; children: Matthew Thomas, Joanne Elizabeth. MusB, U. of Iowa, 1969—73. Indepnt piano tchr. Schulz Studio, Bettendorf, Iowa, 1973—77; ind. piano & organ tchr. Freeport, Ill., 1977—88; dir. music St. Thomas Aquinas Ch., Freeport, Ill., 1984—90; elem. vocal music tchr. Freeport Cath. Sch., Freeport, Ill., 1988—90, Trinity Episcopal Day Sch., Baton Rouge, 1991—92; dir. music St. Ann's Ch., Long Grove, Iowa, 1993—95; dir. music & liturgy St. John Vianney Ch., Bettendorf, Iowa, 1995–2005. Mem. Diocesan Liturgical Commn., Davenport, Iowa, 2002—05. Mem.: Am. Guild of English Handbell Ringers, Am. Guild of Organists, Nat. Pastoral Musicians, Nat. Soc. Colonial Dames of Am., Delta Gamma. Achievements include Selected as a member of the MASTER CHORALE of The USA for the 2003 Festival Internazionale di Music e Arte Sacra in Rome; Selected by Paul Wilkes for his book Excellent Catholic Parishes published by Paulist Press. Home: 2993 Greenview Dr Bettendorf IA 52722

**SCHULZ, WALTER KURT,** accountant, information technology consultant; b. Hamburg, Germany, Apr. 9, 1940; came to U.S., 1970; s. Richard and Karla (Halm) S.; m. Beth Ann Edwards, June 21, 1972; children: Alec, Elli, Peter, Andrew, Heidi. MBA, U. Münster, Germany, 1969; M in Acctg., Ohio State U., 1972. Auditor Dr. Kaase, CPA, Bad Oeynhausen, Germany, 1966-71; systems analyst United Airlines, Chgo., 1973-77; v.p. fin. Eickhoff-Nat. Corp., Pitts., 1977-79; div. controller Mobay Corp., Pitts., 1979-86; owner Infotek/Euronet, Inc., Charlotte, N.C., 1986—; cons. Penske Nascar Racing, Charlotte Hornets. Cons. Westinghouse Corp., Mercy Hosp., Pitts, Charlotte Hornets. Lt. German Air Force, 1960-63. Mem. Am. Mgmt. Assn., Assn. MBA Execs. Republican. Avocation: flying. Home: 301 Sardis Rd N Charlotte NC 28270-2245 Office Phone: 704-442-2414. Personal E-mail: walterkurts@hotmail.com.

**SCHULZ, WILLIAM FREDERICK,** human rights scholar and advocate; b. Pitts., Nov. 14, 1949; s. William F. and Jean Smith; m. Beth Graham, 1993. AB, Oberlin Coll., 1971; MA, Meadville/Lombard Theol. Sch., 1973, DMin, 1975, DDiv, 1987; MA, U. Chgo., 1974; DHL (hon.), Nova Southeastern U., 1995, Grinnell Coll., 2004, Willamette U., 2005, Oberlin Coll., 2005, U. Cinn., 2005, Lewis and Clark Coll., 2006. Minister First Parish Unitarian Universalist, Bedford, Mass., 1975-78; dir. social responsibility Unitarian Universalist Assn., Boston, 1978-79, exec. v.p., 1979-85, pres., 1985-93; exec. dir. Amnesty Internat. USA, 1994—2006; fellow Carr Ctr. Hunan Rights Policy, Kennedy Sch. Govt., Harvard U., 2006—; adj. prof. The New Sch., 2006—; sr. fellow Ctr. for Am. Progress, 2006—. Author: Finding Time and Other Delicacies, 1992, In Our Own Best Interest: How Defending Human Rights Benefits Us All, 2001, Making the Manifesto: The Birth of Religious Humanism, 2002, Tainted Legacy: 9/11 and the Ruin of Human Rights, 2003; editor, contbr.: Transforming Words: Six Essays on Preaching, 1984; editor, contbr.: 2d edit., 1996. Named Humanist of Yr., Am. Humanist Assn., 2000. Mem. ACLU, Unitarian Universalist Mins. Assn., Coun. Fgn. Rels. Democrat. Office Phone: 212-807-8400. E-mail: williamfschulz@yahoo.com.

**SCHULZE, CHERYL RANEA,** secondary school educator; b. Nevada, Mo., Dec. 16, 1959; d. Nelson Ray and Ella Mae Brooks; m. Ron Schulze, June 15, 1979; children: Christopher, Kyle. BS in Edn., Pittsburg State U., Kans., 1982, MS in Secondary Edn., 1995. Tchr. 7th grade English, 8th grade reading Nevada Mid. Sch., 1983—85; tchr. 10th grade English Nevada R-5 Schs., 1986—. Coord. R-5 Drug Free Schs., Nevada, 1997—; bldg. rep. Nevada CTA; bd. dirs. Nevada Pks. Bd., 2000—03. Named Educator of Yr., Vernon County C. of C., 1996, Tchr. of Yr., Nevada R-5 Cmty. Tchrs. Assn., 1997—98, Mo. Wal-Mart Tchr. of Yr., 2006. Baptist. Home: Rte 1 Box 23 Nevada MO 64772 Office: Nevada HS 800 W Hickory Nevada MO 64772 Office Phone: 417-448-4020. Office Fax: 417-448-2039. E-mail: crschulze@nevada.k12.mo.us.

**SCHULZE, FRANZ, JR.,** critic, educator; b. Uniontown, Pa., Jan. 30, 1927; s. Franz and Anna E. (Krimmel) Schulze; m. Marianne Gaw, June 24, 1961 (div. 1975); children: F. C. Matthew, Lukas A.; m. Stephanie Mora, 1992 (div. 1996). Student, Northwestern U., 1943; PhB, U. Chgo., 1945; BFA, Sch. Art Inst. Chgo., 1949, MFA, 1950; postgrad., Acad. Fine Arts, Munich, 1956-57. Instr. art Purdue U., 1950-52; chmn. dept. art Lake Forest (Ill.) Coll., 1952-58, artist-in-residence, 1958-61, prof. art, 1961—, Hollender prof. art, 1974-91, Hollender prof. art emeritus, 1991—; art critic Chgo. Daily News, 1962-78, Chgo. Sun-Times, 1978-85. Chgo. corr. art Christian Sci. Monitor, 1958—62; art. and arch. critic Chicagoan, 1973—74; mem. vis. com. dept. art U. Chgo., 1974—87; adj. prof. U. Ill., Chgo., 1996. Co-author: Art, Architecture and Civilization, 1969; co-author: (with Rosemary Cowler and Arthur Miller) Thirty Miles North, 2000, Philip Johnson: Life and Work, 1994; co-author: (with Kevin Harrington) Chicago's Famous Buildings, 2003; co-author: Mariotti II, 2004; author: Fantastic Images: Chicago Art Since 1945, 1972, 100 Years of Chicago Architecture, 1976, Stealing is My Game, 1976, Mies van der Rohe: A Critical Biography, 1985, The University Club of Chicago: A Heritage, 1987, Mariotti, 1988, Illinois Institute of Technology. Campus Guide, 2005; editor: Mies van der Rohe: Critical Essays, 1989, Mies van der Rohe Archive, 1993; editor: (with Kevin Harrington) Chicago's Famous Buildings, 1993; co-editor: A. James Speyer, Architect, Curator, Exhibition Designer, 1997, The Farnsworth House, 1997, Illinois Institute of Technology, Campus Guide, 2005; contbg. editor: Art News, 1973—, Inland Arch., 1975—94, corr. editor: Art in Am., 1975—. Trustee Ragdale Found., Lake Forest, 1981—. Recipient Harbison award for tchg., Danforth Found. St. Louis, 1971, Disting. Svc. award, Chgo. Phi Beta Kappa soc., 1972, Hon. Mention Hitchcock Book award, Soc. Archtl. Historians, 1987, Excellence in Architecture award, Ill. Inst. Tech., 1999; Adenauer fellow, 1956—57, Ford Found. fellow, 1964—65, Graham Found. for Advanced Studies in the Fine Arts fellow, 1971, 1981, 1993, NEH fellow, 1982, 1988, Skidmore Owings & Merrill Found. fellow, 1983. Mem.: AAUP, Soc. Archtl. Historians (Hon. Mention Hitchcock Book award), Archives Am. Art (mem. adv. com.), Coll. Art Assn. (bd. dirs. 1983—86). Office: Lake Forest Coll Dept Art Lake Forest IL 60045 Office Phone: 847-735-5084. Business E-mail: schulze@lakeforest.edu.

**SCHULZE, RICHARD HANS,** evironmental engineering executive; b. Buffalo, May 28, 1933; s. Hans Joachim and Lucy (Kawczynska) S.; m. Jacqueline Van Luppen, Nov. 2, 1967 (div. Aug. 1979); children: Richard Hans Jr., Linda Neale, John; m. Enika Grooters, Aug. 29, 1987. BSME, Princeton U., 1954; MBA, Northwestern U., 1958. Registered profl. engr., Tex. Rsch. analyst U.S. Steel Corp., Pitts., 1958-60; chief engr. G&H Rsch. and Devel., McKeesport, Pa., 1960-62; cons. Mgmt. and Mktg. Inst., N.Y.C. 1962-63, Ill. Inst. Tech. Rsch. Inst. mgmt. consulting divsn., N.Y.C., 1963-64; market analyst Mobil Chem. Co., N.Y.C., 1964-66; market devel. mgr., plastics divsn. Mobil Chem. Co. (now PACTIV), Jacksonville, Ill., 1966-68, dist. sales mgr. Dallas, 1967-71; pres. Ecology Audits, Inc. (Core Labs.), Dallas, 1971-74; pres., CEO Trinity Cons., Inc., Dallas, 1974-97, chmn. bd. dirs., 1997—, CEO, 2001—. Instr. over 200 short courses on dispersion modeling of air pollutants throughout world; vis. lectr. air quality Princeton U., 1998; adv. bd. Dept. of Environ. Civil Engring, So. Meth. U., 2001—. Contbr. articles to Jour. of Air and Waste Mgmt. Assn., Atmospheric Environ., others; presented papers at sci. symposiums, seminars, confs. Mem. Dallas Symphony Assn., Mus. Art; trustee Dallas Opera, 1993—; elder Preston Hollow Presbyn. Ch., 1996-98; commr. to Grace Presbytery, 1996-98. Lt. (j.g.) USNR, 1954-56. Mem. ASME, Am. Acad. Environ. Engrs. (diplomate, trustee 2001-2003), Am. Chem. Soc., Am. Meteorol. Soc., Air and Waste Mgmt. Assn. (bd. dirs. 1986-89, 90-93, v.p. 1988-89, 1st v.p. 1990-91, pres. 1991-92, past pres. 1992-93, chmn. honors and awards com. 1996-97, vice chmn. planning com. 1999-2000), Soc. Petroleum Engrs. (chmn. environ. health and safety award com. 1994-95), Soc. for Risk Analysis, Verein Deutscher Ingenieure, Assn. Francaise des Ingénieurs et Techniciens Environ., Inst. Profl. Environ. Practice (qualified environ. profl., trustee 1993-95), European Assn. for the Sci. of Air Pollution. Home: 7619 Marquette St Dallas TX 75225-4412 Office: Trinity Cons Inc 12770 Merit Dr Ste 900 Dallas TX 75251 Office Phone: 972-419-5606. E-mail: rschulze@trinityconsultants.com.

**SCHULZE, RICHARD M.,** retail executive; b. St. Paul, Minn., 1941; D (hon.), Univ. of St. Thomas, St. Paul, 1998. With No. States Gas Co. 1962-66; founder, chmn. Sound of Music (now Best Buy Co., Inc.), Eden Prairie, Minn., 1966—; CEO Best Buy Co., Inc., Eden Prairie, Minn., 1983—2002, chmn., 2002—. Mem. Minn. Bus. Partnership; bd. dir. Pentair Inc., Nat. Entrepreneur of Yr. Inst., 1992—; bd. of overseers Carlson Sch. of Mgmt.; bd. trustees Univ. of St. Thomas. With Minnesota Air National Guard. Named Corp. Leader of Yr., Juvenile Diabetes Assn., 1999; named one of Top CEOs, Worth Mag., 1999; recipient Nat. Entrepreneur of Yr., Ernst & Young, 1999, America's Promise Red Wagon for Cmty. Svc., Gen. Colin Powell, 1999, Outstanding Mktg. Exec. of Yr., Minnesota DECA, 2000. Achievements include being named one of 400 richest Americans, among world's richest people and among America's most powerful people, Forbes Mag. Office: Best Buy 7601 Penn Ave S Minneapolis MN 55423-3645*

**SCHULZKI, ANTON G.,** history educator; b. Kearny, N.J., Oct. 17, 1959; s. Anton Fredrick and Clare Catherine Schulzki; m. Ann Michele Manhart, Aug. 2, 1986; children: Avery Rose, Analiese Clare Schuzki. BSc in Secondary Edn. and Social Studies, U. Colo., Colo. Springs, Colo., 1983, MA in History, 2001. Tchr. social studies West Jr. H.S., Colo. Springs, 1983—86; tchr. history Coronado H.S., Colo. Springs, 1986—89, William J. Palmer H.S., Colo. Springs, 1989—. Mem. standing com. U.S. History Exam 2006 NAEP, Princeton, NJ, 2004—06; asst. examiner Internat. Baccalaureate Program, Cardiff, Wales, 2003—; asst. lead tchr. S.W. Assessement Project, Colo. Springs, 1998—2001; presenter in field. Mem.: NEA, Nat. Coun. Social Studies, U.S. Lacrosse Assn. Home: 1421 Heidi Lane Colorado Springs CO 80907 Office: William J Palmer High School 301 North Nevada Avenue Colorado Springs CO 80903 Office Phone: 719-328-5054. Business E-mail: schulag@d11.org.

**SCHULZRINNE, HENNING G.,** computer science educator; b. Cologne, Germany; came to U.S., 1984; BS, Tech. U. Darmstadt, 1984; PhD, U. Mass., 1992. With AT&T Bell Labs., Murray Hill, N.J., 1992-94; GMD Fokus, Berlin, 1994-96; assoc. prof., prof., chair Columbia U., N.Y.C., 1996—. Editor: Jour. Communications and Networks. Mem.: IEEE (sr.; past editor Transactions on Networking, Internet Computing Mag., past mem., chmn. bd. gov., Comm. Soc.). Office: Dept Computer Sci Columbia Univ New York NY 10027 E-mail: hgs@cs.columbia.edu.*

**SCHUMACHER, BARRET,** motion picture propman, writer; b. Boulder, Colo., Sept. 16, 1965; s. Eugene Pierre and Mary Alice Schumacher; m. Beth Alice Edelstein, Mar. 24, 1996; 1 child, Tess Sara. BA screenwriting/film, San Francisco State Univ., Calif., 1990. Model maker Holt, Hinshaw, Peau Jones Arch., San Fransico, 1987—90, Clockwork Apple, Inc., N.Y., 1991—94, Cinergy Films "Judge Dredd", Lenox, Mass., 1994—95; motion picture propman I.A.T.S.E. Local 52, N.Y., 1995—. Author: (novels) Fear Itself, 2002. Avocations: guitar, hiking, skiing, drawing. Office Phone: 917-459-3079.

**SCHUMACHER, CYNTHIA JO,** retired elementary and secondary education educator; b. Sebring, Fla., Sept. 24, 1928; d. Floyd and Espage S. BA, Fla. State U., 1950, MA, 1951; MS, Nova U., 1978; postgrad., Fla. State U., 1968-69. English tchr. Grady County Sch. System, Cairo, Ga., 1951-53; elem. tchr. Brevard County Sch. System, Melbourne, Fla., 1953-55; elem. tchr., curriculum generalist, secondary tchr. Lake County Schs., Tavares, Fla. area, 1955-85; retired, 1985. Mem. Edn. Standards Commn., Fla., Fla., 1980—85, Quality Instrn. Incentives Coun., Fla., 1983—84. Author: (poetry) Seeds from Wild Grasses, 1988, Creekstone Crossings, 1993, Soul Candles, 1998, Wellspring Legacies, 2000; (poetry and stories) Butterfly Excursions, 1996; (children's books) Colorful Character, 1998, Searching for S, 1998. Pres. League of Women Voters of Lake County, 1989-91; mem. Lake Conservation Coun., The Nature Conservancy, Habitat for Humanity of Lake County. Named Fla. Tchr. of Yr., Fla. Fedn. Women's Clubs, 1966, Lake County Tchr. of Yr., Lake County Sch. Sys., 1985, East Cen. Fla. Tchr. of Yr. finalist, State of Fla., 1986; recipient Good Egg award, Leesburg Area C. of C., 1991, Lifetime Achievement award, Fla. Edn. Assn. United, 2000. Mem. Lake County Edn. Assn. (pres. 1971-72, cons. 1985—). Democrat. Roman Catholic. Avocations: gardening, creative writing, macrobiotic cooking, environmental support activities.

**SCHUMACHER, DIANE KOSMACH,** manufacturing executive, lawyer; b. Chgo., Aug. 13, 1953; BA with high honors, So. Ill. U., 1974; JD magna cum laude, DePaul U., 1977. Bar: Mo. 1977, Ill. 1978, Tex. 1983. Corp. atty. Belden Corp. (acquired by Cooper Industries Inc. 1981), 1980-81; sr. counsel Cooper Industries Inc., Houston, 1981-88, corp. sec., 1988-91, corp. v.p., 1991-93, v.p. adminstrn., corp. sec., 1993-95, sr. v.p., gen. counsel, sec., 1995—2003, sr. v.p., gen. counsel, chief compliance officer, 2003—. Bd. dirs. Gardner Denver, Inc. Mem. ABA, Am. Corp. Counsel Assn., Am. Soc. Corp. Secs. (pres. Houston chpt. 1992-93, bd. dirs. 1995-98), Am. Arbitration Assn. (bd. dirs. 1996—), State Bar Tex. Office: Copper Industries Inc Chase Tower 600 Travis St Ste 5800 Houston TX 77002-2912 E-mail: schumach@cooperindustries.com.

**SCHUMACHER, H(ARRY) RALPH,** internist, rheumatologist, medical educator, researcher; b. Montreal, Canada, Feb. 14, 1933; s. H. Ralph and Dorothy (Shreiner) S.; m. Elizabeth Jean Swisher, July 13, 1963; children: Heidi Ruth, Kaethe Beth. BS, Ursinus Coll., 1955; MD, U. Pa., 1959. Intern Denver Gen. Hosp., 1959-60; resident in medicine Wadsworth VA Hosp., LA, 1960-62, fellow in rheumatology, 1962-63, Robert B. Brigham Hosp. and Harvard U. Med. Sch., Boston, 1965-67; chief arthritis-immunology ctr. VA Med. Ctr., Phila., 1967—2006; faculty mem. U. Pa. Sch. Medicine, Phila. 1967—, prof. medicine, 1979—, acting arthritis divsn. chief, 1978-80, 91-95, prof. orthopaedics, 1998—2002. Vis. scholar NIH, 1994-99; lectr. in field. Author: (books) Gout and Pseudogout, 1978, Essentials of a Differential Diagnosis of Rhematoid Arthritis, 1981, Rheumatoid Arthritis, 1988, Case Studies in Rheumatology for the House Officer, 1989, Atlas of Synovial Fluid and Crystal Identification, 1991, A Practical Guide to Synovial Fluid Analysis, 1991, The Spondylarthropathies, 1998, Classic Papers in Rheumatology, 2001, Crystal-induced Arthropathies, 2006; editor: Primer on Rheumatic Disease, 1981—97, Jour. Clin. Rheumatology, 1994—, Crystal Diseases Section, 2005—; mem. editl. bd. Jour. Rheumatology, 1973—, Arthritis and Rheumatism, 1981—88, Revue du Rhumatisme (now Joint, Bone, Spine), 1992—, Internat. Jour. Clin. Practice, 1992—, New European Rheumatology, 1993—, Asian Pacific League Against Rheumatism Jour. Rheumatology, 1997—, Current Rheumatology Reports, 1999—, Indian Jour. Rheumatology, 2000—, Portuguese Jour. Rheumatology, 2000—; mem. editl. bd. Resident and Staff Physician, 2001—; mem. editl. bd.: Vojnosanitetski, 2005—; contbr. articles to profl. jours. Pres. Ea. Pa. chpt. Arthritis Found., 1980-82; chmn., founder Phila. Garden Tours, 1987—95; bd. dirs. Hemochromatosis Rsch. Found., 1984—, Am. Bd. Med. Advancement China, 1983-99. With M.C. USAF, 1963-65. Recipient VanBreeman award Netherland Rheumatism Soc., 1988, Philip Hench award Assn. Mil. Surgeons, 1986, Hollander award Arthritis Found., 1996; named Alumnus of Yr. Ursinus Coll, 1995; named to Sports Hall of Fame, 1997; Deposition VA grantee, 1967-95, NIH grantee, 1981, 94—. Fellow ACP; mem. AAAS, Am. Coll. Rheumatology (master; pres. Southeastern region 1981-82, Klemperer lectr. 2002), Phila. Rheumatism Soc. (pres. 1980), Phila. Electron Microscopy Soc. (chmn. 1975-76), Rheumatism Soc. Mex., Rheumatism Soc. Australia, Rheumatism Soc. Colombia, Rheumatism Soc. Chile, Rheumatism Soc. China, Rheumatism Soc. Argentina, Med. Soc. Argentina, Slovak Soc. Rheumatology, Fedn. Clin. Rsch. Office: VA Med Ctr 151 K University and Woodland Aves Philadelphia PA 19104 also: Hosp U Pa 8 Penn Tower 3400 Spruce St Philadelphia PA 19104-4206 Business E-mail: schumacr@mail.med.upenn.edu. *I try to teach meticulous observation and questioning of dogma both in daily care of patients and in laboratory investigation of the poorly understood rheumatic diseases.*

**SCHUMACHER, HARRY RICHARD,** lawyer; b. June 21, 1930; s. Henry Richard and Martha (Hagenburger) S.; m. Katherine E. Ware, June 8, 1991; children: Richard, Garry. BA, Yale U., 1951; JD magna cum laude, Harvard U., 1958. Bar: N.Y. 1959, U.S. Supreme Ct. 1964. Assoc. firm Cahill Gordon & Reindel and predecessor firms, N.Y.C., 1958—67, ptnr., 1968—97. Chmn. Legal Svcs. for N.Y.C., Inc., 1994—2003; dir. New York Legis. Svcs., 2000—. Mem. Manhattan Borough Pres.'s Cmty. Planning Bd. 6, 1962—66; Dem. candidate N.Y. State Assembly, 1962, 1963; warden Episcopalian Ch.; bd. dirs. Incarnation Camp, Ivoryton, Conn., 1961—72. Lt. (j.g.) USNR, 1951—54. Mem.: ABA, Am. Judicature Soc., N.Y. County Lawyers Assn. (bd. dirs. 1987—93, 1996—99), Fed. Comms. Bar Assn., Assn. Bar City of N.Y., N.Y. State Bar Assn. (mem. ho. dels. 1990—94, 2001—03), Yale (N.Y.C.). Union: Home: 47 E 88th St New York NY 10128-1152 Office: Cahill Gordon & Reindel 80 Pine St Fl 16 New York NY 10005-1790

**SCHUMACHER, HENRY JEROLD,** museum director, retired military officer; b. Torrance, Calif., June 17, 1934; s. Henry John and Rene S.; m. Barbara Howell, Aug. 24, 1958; children: Sheri Lynn, Henry Jerold II.

Student, Stanford U., 1953; BS, U.S. Mil. Acad., 1957; MS, Northeastern U., Boston, 1965; MBA, Auburn U., 1977. Commd. lt. U.S. Army, 1958, advanced through grades to maj. gen., 1982; army attaché Moscow, 1969-71; chief communications ops. Vietnam, 1971-72; exec. officer Office Chief of Staff, 1972-75; comdr. U.S. Army Communications Command, Panama, 1977-79; dir. network integration, Office Asst. Chief of Staff Automation and Communications, Dept. Army, 1979-81; comdr. The White House Communications Agy., Washington, 1981-82; chief U.S. Army Signal Corps, 1981-83; ret., 1983; sr. v.p. Visa Internat., 1983-86; chief oper. officer Fuel Tech., Inc., Stamford, Conn., 1986-87; pres. IMM Systems, Phila., 1987-89; exec. v.p. Cylink Corp., Sunnyvale, Calif., 1990-95; exec. dir. Hiller Mus. of No. Calif. Aviation History, Redwood City, 1995-98; mng. gen. ptnr. Distributed Sys. Ptnrs., 1999—2002, adv. bd. cranite sys., 2003—. Decorated Def. D.S.M., D.S.M., Legion of Merit. Home: 156 Normandy Ct San Carlos CA 94070-1519

**SCHUMACHER, JOEL,** film director, scriptwriter; b. NYC, Aug. 29, 1939; s. Francis and Marian (Kantor) S. BA, Parsons U., 1965. Costume designer: (stage) The Time of the Cuckoo, 1974, (films) Play It As It Lays, 1972, The Last of Sheila, 1972, Blume In Love, 1973, Sleeper, 1973, The Prisoner of Second Avenue, 1975, Interiors, 1978; screenwriter: Car Wash, 1976, Sparkle, 1976, The Wiz, 1978; screenwriter, dir.: (films) D.C. Cab, 1983, St. Elmo's Fire, 1985, Phantom of the Opera, 2004, (TV movies) The Virginia Hill Story, 1974, Amateur Night at the Dixie Bar and Grill, 1979; dir.: The Incredible Shrinking Woman, 1981, The Lost Boys, 1987, Cousins, 1989, Flatliners, 1990, Dying Young, 1991, Falling Down, 1993, The Client, 1994, Batman Forever, 1995, A Time to Kill, 1996, Batman & Robin, 1997, Bad Company, 2002, Phone Booth, 2002; writer, dir., prodr.: Flawless, 1999, 8MM, 1999; exec. prodr.: Foxfire, 1985, Slow Burn, 1986, The Babysitter, 1995; writer, exec. prodr.: (TV pilot) Now We're Cookin', 1983; prodn. designer: Killer Bees, 1974. also: Joel Schumacher Prodns 4000 Warner Blvd Burbank CA 91522-0001 Office: Joel Schumacher Productions 400 Warner Blvd Burbank CA 91522-0001

**SCHUMACHER, JON LEE,** lawyer; b. Rochester, NY, Feb. 28, 1937; s. Howard Alexander and Ruth S.; m. Katherine Truesdell, Apr. 22, 1967; children: Sara Wolff, Howard Alexander II. AB, Princeton U., 1959; JD, U. Va., 1964. Bar: N.Y. 1964. With Nixon Peabody LLP and predecessor firms, Rochester, 1964—; mem. mgmt. com. Nixon, Hargrave, Devans & Doyle, Rochester, 1986-90, mng. ptnr., 1988-90. Co-author Charitable Giving and Solicitation. Bd. dirs., officer Rochester Area Found., Inc., 1987-94, United Way, 1986—; pres. estate planning Coun. Rochester, 1986-87. Fellow Am. Coll. Trusts and Estate Counsel; mem. NY State Bar Assn. (exec. com. trusts and estates law sect. 1985-88, 94—, chmn. 1997, chmn. estate planning com. 1992-94), Monroe County Bar Assn. (found. pres. 1995-97), Country Club Rochester, Genesee Valley Club. Democrat. Methodist. Avocation: opera. Home: 550 Allens Creek Rd Rochester NY 14618-3406 Office: Nixon Peabody LLP Clinton Sq PO Box 31051 Rochester NY 14603-1051 Office Phone: 585-263-1263. Business E-Mail: jschumacher@nixonpeabody.com.

**SCHUMACHER, MABEL G.,** director, consultant; b. Milw., Sept. 14, 1944; d. Clarence F. and Mabel Baskin Smith; m. Vernon A. Schumacher, Nov. 1, 1984. EdB, U. Wis., Whitewater, 1968, MS in Edn., 1971; PhD, U. Wis., 1978. Cert. sch. dist. adminstr. Wis., 1975, dir. instrn. Wis., 1975, dir. spl. edn. Wis., 1975, reading specialist Wis., 1971, tchr. mentally retarded Wis., 1968, tchr. learning disabled Wis., 1971, dir. pupil svcs. Wis., 1980. Tchr. mentally retarded Racine County Handicapped Children's Edn. Bd., Burlington, Wis., 1970—71, tchr. learning disabled, 1973—74, assoc. dir. spl. edn. Union Grove, Wis., 1975—84, dir. spl. edn., 1984—88; coord. spl. edn. Wauwatosa (Wis.) Sch. Dist., 1988—90, Sheboygan (Wis.) Area Sch. Dist., 1990—92; dir. instrn. Sch. Dist. Ft. Atkinson, Wis., 1992—2002; ret. Program asst. dept. edn. U. Wis., Madison, 1974—75, adj. prof., Whitewater, 1978—84; adj. prof. programs in mgmt. for adults Cardinal Stritch U., Milw., 1980—88; rev. team mem. Sch. Evaluation Consortium, Madison, 1990; staff devel. adv. com. mem. Coop. Edn. Svc. Agy. (CESA) 2, Milton, Wis., 1994—97; rev. panel Project First View-Wis. Pub. Broadcasting, Madison, 1996; ednl. cons., 2001—; presenter in field. Bd. dirs. United Way, Ft. Atkinson, 1994—2000, campaign co-chairperson, 1995, campaign chairperson, 1996; ch. organist, instr., youth leader Ft. Atkinson, 1962—84; mem. Phi Delta Kappa, Whitewater, 1977—78; sec. Wis. Sch. Pub. Rels. Assn., Madison, 1997—99, v.p., 1999—2000, pres. elect, 2000—01, pres., 2001—02, sec., 2002—. Fellow Program Assistantship, U. Wis., Madison, 1974—75; scholar, State of Wis., 1973—75, U. Wis., Whitewater, 1967—68. Mem.: Wis. Sch. Educators Assn., Walworth County Area Ret. Educators Assn., Wis. Sch. Pub. Rels. Assn. (sec. and past pres. 2002—), Kennel Club of Ft. Atkinson. Achievements include development of variety of education-related computer databases; Facilitator of Concept-Based Curriculum Project. Avocations: travel, reading, computer, cooking, pets. Home: 848 Messmer St Fort Atkinson WI 53538

**SCHUMACHER, MICHAEL,** retired race car driver; b. Hürth-Hermühlheim, Germany, Jan. 3, 1969; s. Elisabeth and Rolf; m. Corinna Schumacher; children: Gina-Maria, Mick. Race car driver Jordan team, 1991, Benetton team, 1991—95, Ferrari team, 1996—2006. Named one of 100 Most Influential People, Time Mag., 2005; recipient Best Driver, ESPY awards, 2005. Achievements include winning the Formula 1 Driver's Championship a record 7 times, 1994, 95, 2000-04; 90 career Grand Prix wins since 1992; first to win a Formula 1 Grand Prix event 8 times, French Grand Prix, 1994, 95, 97, 98, 2001, 02, 04, 06; winner, Formula 3 German Championship, 1990. Office: Ferrari SpA Via Ascari 55-57 I-41053 Maranello Italy*

**SCHUMACHER, PAUL MAYNARD,** lawyer; b. Columbus, Nebr., Apr. 4, 1951; s. Maynard Mathew and Rita Bell (Jarosz) S.; m. Michele Suzanne Gassé, June 26, 1976; children: Nicah, Gavanna, Kristen Paulette. AA, Platte Coll., 1971; BS, Fort Hays U., 1973; JD, Georgetown U., 1976. Bar: Fla. 1976, Nebr. 1977, U.S. Dist. Ct. Nebr. 1977. Mem. staff U.S. Senate, Washington, 1974-76; sole practice Miami, Fla. and Columbus, 1976—; v.p. Community Lottery Systems, Inc., Columbus, 1990-92, pres., 1992—. V.p. Megavision Corp., Columbus, 1976—. Treas. prin. Rep. campaign com. U.S. Senate Candidate, Lincoln, Nebr., 1978-79; atty. Platte County, Columbus, 1979-87; chmn. Platte county Reps., 1988-94; mem. Nebr. Rep. State Ctrl. Com., 1994-96, 2000—; CEO Lotto Nebr., 1992—; CEO Cmty. Internet Sys., Inc., 1995-98, bd. dirs., 1995—; bd. dirs. Keep the Money in Nebr. Com. Mem. Nebr. Bar Assn., Fla. Bar Assn., Platte County Bar Assn. (pres. 1992-93), Nat. Republican small bus. adv. council, Nebr. Republican Legis. Com., Rotary, Elks. Roman Catholic. Avocation: physics. Home: 6255 Meyer Rd Columbus NE 68601-8044 Office: PO Box 122 Columbus NE 68602-0122 E-mail: pschumac@megavision.com.

**SCHUMACHER, PHILIP GERARD,** fundraising executive; b. Green Bay, Wis., Mar. 5, 1949; s. Peter John and June Elizabeth (Umberham) S.; m. Elizabeth Lucille Burke, Aug. 15, 1972 (div. Apr. 1985); children: Nicholas Philip, Eric Peter; m. Rebecca Satka, Jan. 3, 2003. BA, St. Norbert Coll., 1971; MA, St. Mary's U. Minn., 1974. Cert. fund raising exec. Tchr., coach Premontre H.S., Green Bay, 1971-73; assoc. dean students St. Mary's U. Minn., Winona, 1973-75, dir. residential life, 1975-77, v.p. student affairs, 1977-85; v.p. Maly & Co., Winona, 1985-87; dir. devel. Gundersen Med. Found., La Crosse, Wis., 1987-89; v.p. The Metanoia Group, Winona, 1989-90; dir. devel. St. Mary's U. Minn., Winona, 1989-90, v.p. instnl. advancement, 1990-93; exec. dir. devel. Gundersen Med. Found., La Crosse, 1993-96; grad. faculty St. Mary's U. Minn., 1994—2004; exec. dir. Gundersen Luth. Med. Found., La Crosse, 1996—. Editor: Memoirs of Jean Pierre Schumacher, 1975. Vol. Minn. Pvt. Coll. Found., St. Paul, 1987—97; bd. dirs. Winona Cath. Schs., 1989—95; mem. nat. bd. visitors St. Mary's U. Minn., Winona, 1993—; bd. dis. Riverfront, Inc., Assn. Fundraising Profls. Found., Canada, 2001—. Mem. Assn. Fundraising Profls. (chpt. pres. 1993-95, nat. nominating com. 1997, nat. bd. dirs., treas., exec. com.), La Crosse Club, Rotary (com. mem.). Roman Catholic. Avocations: tennis, travel. Business E-Mail: pgchuma@gundluth.org.

**SCHUMACHER, ROBERT DENISON,** banker; b. Evanston, Ill., Dec. 16, 1933; s. Frank Ade and Dorothy Ormonde (Hilton) S.; m. Mary Ann Montgomery, Aug. 25, 1956; children: Stephen Michael, Jeffrey Hilton. BA, Williams Coll., 1956; postgrad., Grad. Bus. Sch. N.Y. U., 1957-59; P.MD, Harvard Bus. Sch., 1966. With Irving Trust Co., N.Y.C., 1956-89, sr. v.p., 1977-89, mgr. adminstrv. services, 1976—89, ret., 1989. Treas. Calvary, Holy Communion and St. George's Episcopal Ch., 1976-79, warden, 1980-86, 89-93, 2001-05; trustee The Church Club, 1993-2003, treas., 1994-99; mem.Town of Chatham, Mass (summer residents adv. com.). Mem. The Church Club. Home: 431 E 20th St New York NY 10010-7502 Personal E-mail: rschumach@aol.com.

**SCHUMACHER, STANLEY E.,** composer, musician; b. Indpls., Aug. 9, 1942; s. Arnold and Lucille Schumacher; m. Susan Vetters, Sept. 9, 1967. MusB, Butler U., Indpls., 1964, MusM, 1966; PhD, Ohio State U., Columbus, 1976. Freelance composer and trombonist, 1976—; prof. C.C. RI, Warwick, 1978—80, Pikeville Coll., Ky., 1980—81; pvt. tchr., 1981—2000; prof. County Coll. Morris, Randolph, NJ, 1982—85, Lafayette Coll., Easton, Pa., 1988—89. Pres. Musikmacher Prodns., 2005—; artistic dir. Music Now Ensemble, 2003—, RASA Ensemble, Edison, NJ, 1984—95. Composer: (pub. composition) Symmetries (4 instruments); performer (trombonist): (CD) Zeppelins Erste Grosse Fahrt, Uber Brass, Poemusic, Sound Textures, (improvisation) Red Room, High Zero Festival; composer and trombonist (new arts program television series) New Arts Alive; composer: The Lecture (clarinet, piano, and narrator), Order (narrator and any number of brass, woodwind, and percussion), White on White (string quartet), No Technique (3 trombones), Musography (2 clarinets and 3 trombones), Brassman (trombone, soprano, clarinet, trumpet, violin, and piano). Mem.: Am. Fedn. Musicians, Internat. Trombone Assn., Am. Music Ctr. Roman Catholic. Avocations: travel, photography. Home: 4606 Cheryl Drive Bethlehem PA 18017

**SCHUMACHER, TARA,** biology educator; b. Chgo., July 17, 1973; d. Donald and Susann Schumacher. BS, Colo. State U., Fort Collins. Cert. secondary biology Nat. Coun. for Accreditation Tchr. Edn. Certification, 1999. Biology tchr. Windsor (Colo.) H.S., 1999—. Crisis response team mem. Windsor H.S., 1999—; mem. accreditation rev. com. Windsor Mid. Sch. Windsor Sch. Dist., 2002—, mem. curriculum devel. com. Poudre Learning Ctr., Greeley, Colo., 2005—. Mem. at large Hugh O'Brian Youth Leadership Orgn., Colo., 2005—06. Mem.: Windsor Edn. Assn. (treas. 2002—06), Nat. Sci. Tchrs. Assn. Office: Windsor High School 1100 W Main St Windsor CO 80550 Office Phone: 970-686-8100.

**SCHUMACHER, THOMAS,** film company executive; Grad., UCLA. Past mem. staff L.A. Music Ctr. Mark Taper Forum; past sr. v.p. feature animation Walt Disney Pictures, Burbank, Calif., exec. v.p. feature animation and theatrical prodns., 1996-98; pres. Walt Disney Feature Animation and Walt Disney Theatrical Prodns., 1999—2002, Buena Vista Theatrical Group, 1999—. Line prodr. Olympic Arts Festival, 1984; asst. gen. mgr. L.A. Ballet; co-founder, assoc. dir. L.A. Festival of the Arts, 1987; mem. edn. coun. L.A. Music Ctr.; bd. dirs. Rachel Rosenthal Co. Prodr. film The Rescuers Down Under, 1990; exec. prodr. film The Lion King, 1994. Office: Walt Disney Pictures 500 S Buena Vista St Burbank CA 91521-0006

**SCHUMAKER, WILLIAM THOMAS,** retired insurance company executive; b. Phila., Apr. 14, 1925; s. William John and Julia Ida Schumaker. BSc, Drew U., Madison, N.J., 1964, DD, 1980. Ordained to ministry Meth. Ch., 1974. V.p. New Amsterdam Casualty Co., Phila., 1947—59; gen. mgr. P.L.M. Ins. Co., 1959—79; min. Cortez United Meth. Ch.; chmn. Julia Ida Schumaker Found. Instr. Surety Bonds Ins. Soc. Phila., 1950-52; mem. adv. bd. P.L.M. Ins. Co., Phila., 1954-59. City ofcl. 34th ward City of Phila., 1955. Staff sgt. U.S. Army, 1943-46. Nat. acctg. fellow New Amsterdam Casualty Co., Phila., 1955, Paul Harris fellow Rotary of Nfld., Pa., 1990. Mem. Mensa, U.S. Army Infantry Divsn. (life). Avocations: antiques, stamp collecting/philately. Home: 603 Britt St Georgetown SC 29440-4003 E-mail: karpadopol@aol.com.

**SCHUMAN, ALLAN L.,** chemicals executive; b. 1937; BS, NYU, 1955. With Ecolab Inc., St. Paul, 1957—, v.p. mktg. and nat. acctg., 1972-78, v.p. mktg. devel., 1978-79, pres. svc. group, 1988—92, pres., COO, 1992—95, pres., CEO, 1995—2004, chmn., 2000—06, chmn. emeritus, 2006—. Bd. dir. Tanger Factory Outlet Ctr. Inc., Soap & Detergent Assn. Bd. dir. Ordway Ctr. Performing Arts, Guthrie Theater; bd. overseers Carlson Sch. Mgmt. at U. Minn.; trustee Hamline U., Minn., Culinary Inst. Am. Nat. Restaurant Assn. Office: Ecolab Inc Ecolab Ctr 370 N Wabasha St Saint Paul MN 55102*

**SCHUMAN, LEONARD M.,** medical educator, academic administrator; b. Cleve., Mar. 4, 1913; AB, Oberlin Coll., 1934; MSc, Western Reserve U., 1939, MD, 1940. Diplomate Am. Bd. Preventive Medicine. Teaching and rsch. fellow in hygiene and bacteriology St. Medicine Western Reserve U., 1937-39; intern U.S. Marine Hosp., Chgo., 1940-41; asst. epidemiologist Ill. Dept. Pub. Health, 1941-42, dist. health supt. dist. # 2, 1943, asst. chief divsn. local health adminstrn., 1943-45, chief divsn. venereal disease control, 1947-50, acting chief divsn. communicable disease, 1949-50, dep. dir. divsn. preventive medicine, 1950-51, 53-54; assoc. prof. Sch. of Pub. Health U. Minn., 1954-58, prof. epidemiology, 1958-83, Mayo prof. emeritus, dir. epidemiology emeritus Sch. Pub. Health, 1983—. Epidemiologist U.S. Dept. of Def., 1951-53; vis. lectr. U. Ill. Sch. of Medicine, Chgo., 1947-54; lectr. communicable diseases Springfield Meml. Hosp., Sch. of Nursing, 1947-54; cons. Communicable Disease Ctr., USPHS, 1955-83, Air Pollution Med. Program, 1958—, Nat. Cancer Inst., 1958-79, Divsn. Radiol. Health, 1961-69, Chronic Disease Divsn., 1964-72, mem. Adv. Com. Bio-Effects of Radiation, 1966-69, Grant Rev. Com. for Prevention Ctrs., Ctrs. for Disease Control 1986-93; conn. Minn. State Health Dept., 1955-90, mem. adv. com. cancer surveillance, 1981—, tech. adv. com. non-smoking and health, 1983—; cons. Hennepin County (Minn.) Gen. Hosp., 1955—. Contbr. articles to profl. jours. With USPHS, 1941-47. Rockefeller Found. fellow, 1946; recipient Samuel Harvey award Am. Assn. Cancer Edn., 1983, Wyeth award Pacific Coast Fertility Soc., 1983, Pioneer award Minn. Dept. of Health, 1991, Recognition award Hennepin County (Minn.) Cmty. Prevention Coalition, 1994, citation from Surgeon Gen. Jocelyn Elders, 1994, Recognition award Assn. Schs. Pub. Health, 1995; named Disting. Alumnus 2000, Case Western Reserve Sch. Medicine. Fellow APHA (chmn. infectious disease monograph subcom. 1961-68, mem. com. evaluations and standards 1962-66, governing coun. 1964-70, resolutions com. 1964-65, chmn. subcom. on drugs 1964-65, vice chmn. epidemiology sect. 1966, chmn. epidemiology sect. 1967, program area com. communicable diseases 1966-70, mem. tech. devel. bd. 1966-70, v.p. 1993-94, John Snow award 1983, Sedgwick Meml. medal 1996), Am. Coll. Epidemiology (bd. dirs. 1979-89, chmn. edn. com. 1985-92, Abraham H. Lilienfeld award 1989, cert. Appreciation 1991), Am. Heart Assn. (coun. epidemiology 1965, hon.); mem. AAAS, AAUP, Am. Assn. Pub. Health Physicians, Am. Coll. Preventive Medicine (sec. coun. rsch. 1956-59, chmn. 1959-64), Am. Epidemiol. Soc. (v.p. 1978), Am. Thoracic Soc. Am. Venereal Disease Assn., Am. Cancer Soc. (Minn. divsn.), Assn. Mil. Surgeons U.S., Assn. Tchrs. Preventive Medicine, Internat. Epidemiol. Soc., Internat. Soc. Cardiology, Internat. Soc. Thrombosis and Hemostasis, Mid. States Pub. Health Assn., Minn. Pub. Health Assn. (Pub. Health Achievement award 1987), N.Y. Acad. Scis., Pub. Health Cancer Assn., Soc. Epidemiol. Rsch. (exec. bd. 1980, award for Outstanding Contbns. to Field of Epidemiology 1992), Phi Beta Kappa, Alpha Omega Alpha, Phi Zeta, Sigma Xi, Phi Kappa Phi, Delta Omega (award selection com. 1985, pres. Pi chpt. 1985—, nat. pres.-elect 1990-92, pres. 1993-95). Office: U Minn Mayo Meml Bldg Box 197 420 Delaware St SE Minneapolis MN 55455-0374 Office Phone: 952-929-7012. Personal E-mail: schuman@mailstation.com.

**SCHUMAN, PATRICIA GLASS,** publishing company executive, educator; b. NYC, Mar. 15, 1943; d. Milton and Shirley Rhoda (Goodman) Glass; m. Alan Bruce Schuman, Aug. 30, 1964 (div. 1973); m. Stanley Robert Epstein, June 14, 1997 (dec. 2005) AB, U. Cin., 1963; MS, Columbia U., 1966. Libr. trainee Bklyn. Pub. Libr., 1963-65; tchr. libr. Brandeis High Sch., N.Y.C.,

1966; asst. prof. libr. N.Y. Tech. Coll., Bklyn., 1966-71; assoc. editor Sch. Libr. Jour., N.Y.C., 1970-73; sr. editor R.R. Bowker Co., N.Y.C., 1973-76; pres. Neal-Schuman Pubs., N.Y.C., 1976—. Vis. prof. St. John's U., Queens, N.Y., 1977-79, Columbia U., N.Y.C., 1981-90. Pratt Inst., 1993-2000, Syracuse U., 1997—; cons. N.Y. State Coun. on Arts, 1987, Office Tech. Assessment, U.S. Congress, 1982, 84, Coord. Coun. Lit. Mags., N.Y.C., 1987, NEH, 1980, Temple U., 1978-80; bd. visitors Sch. Libr. and Computer Studies Pratt Inst., 1987-2001; juror Best of Libr. Lit., 1980-88; mem. adv. bd. Sch. Libr. and Info. Studies, Queens Coll., 1989-91. Author: Materials for Occupational Education, 1973, 2d edit., 1983 (Best Edn. Book award 1973), Library Users and Personnel Needs, 1980, Your Right to Know: The Call to Action, 1993; editor: Social Responsibilities and Libraries, 1976; mem. editorial bd. Urban Acad. Libr., 1987-89, Multicultural Review, 1991-95; contbr. articles to profl. jours. Bd. dirs. Women's Studies Abstracts, Albany, N.Y., 1970-74, Pratt Inst. Sch. of Libr. and Info. Studies, 1993—2000, Ctr. for Publ., NYU, 1996—, Am. Libr. in Paris, 2004-; mem. Com. To Elect Major Owens to U.S. Congress, 1983, N.Y.C. Mayor's Com. for N.Y. Pub. Ctr., 1984-85; pres. Met. Reference and Research Coun./Met. N.Y. Libr. Coun, Neal Schumen Found., Inc. Recipient Fannie Simon award Spl. Librs. Assn., 1984, Disting. Alumni award Columbia U., 1992; U.S. Office Edn. fellow, 1969. Mem. ALA (councillor 1971-79, 84-88, exec. bd. 1984-88, 90-93, treas. 1984-88, chmn. legis. com. 1989-90, 94-96, chmn. internat. rels. com. 1998, 99, chmn. Libr. Advocacy NOW!, v.p., pres.-elect 1990-91, pres. 1991-92, Disting. Coun. Svc. award 1979, 88, Equality award 1993, hon. mem. Black Caucus, appreciation award 1993, Freedom to Read Found. Honor Roll 1999, Lippincott award for disting. svc. 2001), N.Y. Libr. Assn., Assn. for Libr. and Info. Sci. Edn., Spl. Librs. Assn. Office: Neal-Schuman Pubs Inc 100 William St Ste 2004 New York NY 10038 Business E-Mail: pgs@neal-schuman.com.

**SCHUMANN, GAIL L.,** plant pathologist, educator; BS in Botany, U. Mich., 1972; MS in Plant Pathology, Cornell U., 1976, PhD in Plant Pathology, 1978. From vis. lectr. to prof. U. Mass., Amherst, Mass., 1984—2001, prof. emerita, 2003—; prof. dept. biol. scis. Marquette U., Milw., 2023—. Sr. editor APS Press, 1992; chair APS Press Illustrations of Plant Pathogens and Disease Com.; editor-in-chief The Plant Health Inst., 2000—. Author: Plant Diseases: Their Biology and Social Impact, 1991; co-author: IPM Handbook for Golf Courses, 1998. Recipient APS Excellence in Tchg. award, 1993, Disting. Tchg. award U. Mass., 2994, award of merit MEDAPS, 1996. Mem.: APS (pres. N.E. divsn. 1995). Office: Marquette U Dept Biol Scis 202B Wehr Life Scis 530 N 15th St Milwaukee WI 53233 Business E-Mail: gail.schumann@marquette.edu.

**SCHUMANN, GAY LEE,** special education services professional, consultant; d. Harold Wayne Hamilton and Esther Elizabeth Sonnier, Woody Sonnier (Stepfather); m. Clint Aaron Schumann, June 3, 1995. B of Edn., U. Houston, 1992; MEd, U. Tex., Arlington, 2002. Cert. prin. Tex. Bd. Edn., elem. edn. Tex. Bd. Edn., spl. edn. Tex. Bd. Edn., English (lit.) edn. Tex. Bd. Edn., English as Second Lang. Tex. Bd. Edn., early childhood edn. Tex. Bd. Edn. Spl. edn. tchr. Houston Area Sch. Dist., 1993—95, Dallas/Ft. Worth Area Sch. Dist., 1995—, instrnl. specialist, 2002—. Author: Do You Think Teaching is Easy?. Mem.: Tex. Fedn. Tchrs., Assn. Tex. Profl. Educators, Nat. Assn. Edn. Young Children. Achievements include Personal interview with former Texas State Senator regarding advocacy for college students with leaning disabilities. Avocations: travel, reading, household finances, movies. Personal E-mail: dynastyed@sbcglobal.net.

**SCHUMANN, J. PAUL,** retired federal agency administrator; b. Kansas City, Mo., Dec. 10, 1937; s. Fred and Miriam E. (Penzotti) S.; m. Olva Kimmel Dorris, Dec. 23, 1960; 1 child, Robert Reynold. BA, MA, U. Miss., 1960; cert., Indsl. Coll. Armed Forces, 1966; PhD, U. Okla., 1982. Instr. polit. sci. Jacksonville (Ala.) State U., 1961-64; intelligence officer Missile and Space Intelligence Ctr., Huntsville, Ala., 1964-91, sr. intelligence officer, 1991—. Adj. asst. prof. U. Ala., Huntsville, 1981—2001; mem. Tenn dept. Coun. on Am's Mil. Past, Huntsville, 1971—82; adj. instr. Calhoun CC. Contbr. articles to profl. jours. V.p. external affairs Jaycees, Jacksonville, 1963-64. Recipient achievement medal for civilian svc. U.S. Army, 1992, letter of commendation South Korean Def. Intelligence Agy., 1992, Nat. Intelligence Cert. of Distinction, 2005, superior achievement medal Def. Intelligence Agy., 2006; Dept. Def. scholar, 1971-72. Mem. Nat. Mil. Intelligence Assn., Am. Polit. Sci. Assn., Phi Alpha Theta, Phi Kappa Psi (treas. 1957-58), Pi Sigma Alpha. Avocations: military history, collecting books. Home: 8204 Willowbrook Cir SE Apt A Huntsville AL 35802-3335 E-mail: paulschumann@comcast.net.

**SCHUMANN, JILL,** religious organization administrator; b. Pitts. m. Mark W. Oldenburg. BA, Ind. U. of Pa.; MBA, Mount St. Mary's Coll. Dir. outpatient svcs. Ctr. for Addictive Illnesses, Morristown, NJ; substance abuse program developer Gettysburg Coll., Pa.; dir., v.p. Craig and Assocs., York, Pa.; exec., v.p. planning and mktg. Tressler Luth. Svcs., Mechanicsburg; exec. v.p. Kairos Health Sys.; dir. mem. svcs. Luth. Svcs. in Am., Balt., pres., CEO, 2001—. Office: Luth Svcs in Am 700 Light St Baltimore MD 21230-3850 Office Phone: 410-230-2702. Office Fax: 410-230-2710. E-mail: jschumann@lutheranservices.org.*

**SCHUMANN, PAULA M. L.,** writer; b. Phila., Oct. 23, 1938; d. Paschal Francis and Paula Marie Libonati; m. Walter Francis Schumann, June 17, 1967; 2 children. MT, Philadelphia County Med. Soc., 1972. Cert. med. technologist Phila. Gen. Hosp. Sch. Med. Tech., Pa.; admitted to holy profession Secular Franciscan Order, 2004. Author and pub. Renaitre Press, King of Prussia, Pa., 1998—. Author (publisher): A Chapter in the Life of a Poet (a story in verse), 1995, With His Love, Prayers and Poems, 2002; author: (poetry) Les Saisons de la Vie, 1999, Pres. Legion of Mary, King of Prussia, Pa., 2000—02, Franklin Sci. and Arts scholar, 1960—61. Mem.: Internat. Soc. Poets (disting. mem.), Phila. Writers' Conf., Poetry Soc. Am., Acad. Am. Poets. Roman Catholic. Avocations: cooking, travel, swimming, piano, dance. Office: Renaitre Press P O Box 61163 King Of Prussia PA 19406-1163 Business E-Mail: renaitrepress@yahoo.com.

**SCHUMANN, WILLIAM HENRY, III,** corporate financial executive; b. Iowa City, Aug. 28, 1950; s. William Henry Jr. and Eunice Vere (Doak) S. BS, UCLA, 1972; MS, U. So. Calif., 1973. Program mgmt. analyst Hughes Helicopters, Culver City, Calif., 1973-75; mgr. fin. planning Sunkist Growers, Sherman Oaks, Calif., 1975-81; dir. N.Am. Ops. Agrl. Products Group, FMC Corp., Chgo., 1981—; treas. FMC Corp., 1987—, exec. dir. corp. development, 1990-93, v.p., 1995—, sr. v.p., CFO, 1999—2001, FMC Techs., 2001—. Bd. dirs. Gt. Lakes Advisors and DAP Holdings. Republican. Office: FMC Technologies 200 E Randolph Dr Chicago IL 60601

**SCHUMER, CHUCK (CHARLES ELLIS SCHUMER),** senator; b. Bklyn., Nov. 23, 1950; s. Abraham and Selma (Rosen) S.; m. Iris Weinshall, 1980; children: Jessica Emily, Alison. BA magna cum laude, Harvard U., 1971, JD with honors, 1974. Bar: NY 1975. Mem. staff US Senator Clairborne Pell, 1973; assoc. Paul, Weiss, Rifking, Wharton and Garrison, 1974; mem. NY State Assembly, 1975-80, chmn. subcom. on city mgmt. and governance, 1977, chmn. com. on oversight and investigation, 1979; mem. US Congress from 16th NY Dist., 1981—85, US Congresses from 10th (now 9th) NY Dist. Washington, 1985-98; US Senator from NY, 1998—. Com. banking, housing and urban affairs US Senate, com. fin., com. judiciary, com. rules and adminstrn., joint com. on Liberty of Congress. Bd. dirs. NY Philharmonic. Herbert Tenzer award for Pub. Service, Five Towns Jewish coun., 1995, Criminal Justice Legis. award, NY State Bar Assoc., 1999, Leadership in Govt. award, Columbia U. Bus. Sch., 1999, Travers J. Bell Mem award of Distinction, NY Dist. Econ. Edn. Found, Securities Industry, Assoc., 1999, Pub. Policy Achievement award, Amer. Cancer Society, 2000, Sound Guardian award, NY Audobon and Cons. Industry Coun. of Westchester, 2002 Mem. Jewish War Veterans, B'nai Brith, Phi Beta Kappa. Democrat. Jewish. Office: US Senate 313 Hart Office Bldg Washington DC 20515-0001 also: District Office Ste 17-02 757 Third Ave New York NY 10017 Office Phone: 202-224-6542, 212-486-4430. Office Fax: 202-228-3027, 212-486-7693.*

**SCHUMER, ROBERT B.**, lawyer; b. NYC, Mar. 8, 1958; BA magna cum laude, U. Mich., 1979; JD, Columbia U., 1982. Bar: NY 1983. With Paul, Weiss, Rifkind, Wharton & Garrison LLP, NYC, 1989—, ptnr., corp. dept., co-head mergers & acquisitions group, mem. mgmt. com. Named a Dealmaker of the Yr., Am. Lawyer mag., 2006; named one of 40 under 40, Crain mag., 1995, 45 under 45, Am. Lawyer mag., 1995. Mem.: ABA, Phi Beta Kappa. Office: Paul Weiss Rifkind Wharton & Garrison LLP 1285 Ave of the Americas New York NY 10019-6064 Office Phone: 212-373-3097. Office Fax: 212-757-2004. E-mail: rschumer@paulweiss.com.*

**SCHUMM, DARLA YZONNE**, religious-studies educator; b. Kitchner, Ontario, Can. d. Claire Floyd and Katie Ann Schumm; m. Jonathan Fisher Harris, Oct. 14, 2000. BA, Goshen Coll., NY, 1987; MA, Pacific Sch. Religion, 1992; PhD, Vanderbuilt U., Nashville, 2002. Case mgr. Cath. Charities, Washington, 1987—89; clin. dir. Gould Farm, Monterey, Mass., 1992—94; asst. prof. Hollins U., Roanoke, Va., 2001—. Fellow, Am. Ctr. Oriental Rsch., 2005. Mem.: Menoanite Scholars Network, Am. Acad. Religion, Delta Kappa Gamma. Avocations: knitting, reading, running. Office: Hollins Univ PO Box 9623 Roanoke VA 24020

**SCHUMM, STEVEN A**, former corporate financial executive; b. 1953; B in bus. administrn., St. Louis U. Now mng. ptnr. Ernst & Young, St. Louis, 1974—98, nat. dir. nat. tax. services; exec. v.p. Charter Communications, 1998—2002, interim CFO, 2002—, exec. v.p. chief admin. officer, 1998—2005. Mem. nat. tax com. Ernst & Young; dir. of TV Gateway LLC. Mem. St. Louis Regional Commerce and Growth Assn.; Repertory Theatre of St. Louis; Boy Scouts of Am.; mem. St. Louis U. Sch. of Bus.; archdiocese of St. Louis.

**SCHUNICHT, SHANNON ANTHONY**, retired military officer, political scientist; b. Miami, Fla., Nov. 17, 1961; s. Wayne Anthony Schunicht and Suzanne Chatin (Tindell) Fast. BA in Philosophy and Polit. Sci., Tex. State U., 1983; BA in Biology, Tex. A&M U., 1994, BS in Microbiology, 1994. Cert. real estate agt. Tex. With U.S. Army, 1983-90. Mem. Internat. Leprosy Assn., Am. Soc. for Microbiology. Office: 408 Eisenhower St College Station TX 77840-1715 Office Phone: 979-218-5764. Personal E-mail: mnemonicmind@alpha1.com.

**SCHUNK, DALE HANSEN**, dean; b. Chgo., Aug. 14, 1946; s. Elmer Charles and Mildred Augusta Schunk; m. Caryl Sue Cook, June 29, 1984; 1 child, Laura Christine. PhD, Stanford U., Calif., 1974—79. Asst. prof. edn. U. Houston, 1979—85, assoc. prof., 1985—86, U. NC, Chapel Hill, 1986—91, prof. edn., 1991—93; head dept. ednl. studies Purdue U., W. Lafayette, Ind., 1993—2001; dean sch. edn. U. NC, Greensboro, 2001—. Cons. chpt. 1 reading Br. Ind. Sch. Dist., Tex., 1981—94; mem. bd. trustees NC Tchr. Acad., Durham, 2002—; mem. task force tchr. retention NC State Bd. Edn., Raleigh, 2004—05. Author: (textbooks) Learning Theories: An Educational Perspective, Motivation in Education; editor: (profl. book) Educational Psychology: A Century of Contributions; contbr. articles to profl. jours., chapters to books. Sec. parent coun. W. Lafayette Sch. Corp., 1997—99; girls' softball coach W. Lafayette Little League, 1997—2000. Capt. USAF, 1968—74, Sewart AFB, Tenn., Naples, Italy. Recipient Disting. Svc. award, Purdue U. Sch. Edn., 1995, Fulbright Scholar award, New Zealand-US Ednl. Found., 1997, Univ. Honor Roll, W. Lafayette Sch. Corp., 2000. Fellow: APA (pres. divsn. ednl. psychology 1998—99, Early Career award 1982); mem. Am. Ednl. Rsch. Assn. (program chair 1999—2000). Avocations: tennis, travel. Home: 7007 Morganshire Ct Summerfield NC 27358 Office: Univ NC-Greensboro 1000 Spring Garden St Greensboro NC 27402 Office Fax: 336-334-4120. Business E-Mail: dhschunk@uncg.edu.

**SCHUNK, ROBERT WALTER**, space physics research administrator; b. N.Y.C. BS, NYU, 1965; PhD in Phys. Fluids, Yale U., 1970. Fellow space physics Inst. Sci. and Tech., U. Mich., 1970-71; rsch. assoc. geophysicist Yale U., 1971-73; rsch. assoc. space physics U. Calif., San Diego, 1973-76; assoc. prof. Utah State U., Logan, 1976-79, prof. physics, 1979—. Mem. Com. Solar Terrestrial Rsch., Geophys. Rsch. Bd., Nat. Acad. Sci., 1979-82, Nat. Ctr. Atmospheric Rsch. Computer Divsns. Adv. Panel, 1980-83; prin. invester Solar Terrestrial Theory Program, 1980—. Assoc. editor Jour. Geophys. Rsch., 1977-80. Recipient Gov.'s Medal Sci. & Tech., Utah, 1988. Fellow Am. Geophys. Union (Nicolet lectr. 2002); mem. AAAS. Home: Utah State U Ctr Atmospheric Space Logan UT 84322-4405 Office Phone: 435-797-2978. Business E-Mail: schunk@cc.usu.edu.

**SCHUNKE, HILDEGARD HEIDEL**, accountant; b. Indpls., Nov. 24, 1948; d. Edwin Carl and Hildegard Adelheid (Baumbach) S. BA, Ball State U., Muncie, Ind., 1971, MA in German, English, 1973, MA in Acctg., 1975. CPA Ind., Calif. Ech. tchg. grad. asst. Padagogische Hochschule, Germany, 1971-72; tchg. grad. asst. in German and acctg. Ball State U., 1972, 74-75, asst. prof. acctg., 1975-78; investing rschr. Family Partnership, Muncie, 1977-83; staff acct. Am. Lawn Mower Co., Muncie, 1984-88, G&J Seiberlich, CPAs, St. Helena, Calif., 1988-89, R.A Gullotta, MBA, CPA, Sonoma, Calif., 1989-90; plant acct. Napa (Calif.) Pipe Corp., 1990—2001; sys. engr. Napa Pipe Corp. Divsn. Oreg. Steel Mills, Napa, 2002—04; freelance acct. Fairfield, Calif., 2004—. ESOL instr. Napa County Project Upgrade, 1988-92; teaching and refreshments com. North Bay Philharm. Orch., Napa, 1988-2004, North Bay Wind Ensemble, Napa, 1988-2004; mem. steering com. Cordelia Cmty. Park, 2005—. Mem. AICPA, Calif. Soc. CPAs (continuing edn. instr. Redwood City 1990, bd. dirs. East Bay chpt. 1998-2000), Inst. Internal Auditors. Avocations: gardening, building computers, networks and websites. Home: 1117 Devonshire Ct Fairfield CA 94534-7443 Office: HH Schunke MA CPA 1117 Devonshire Ct Fairfield CA 94534-7443 Office Phone: 707-864-2640. Personal E-mail: hsg_1@juno.com.

**SCHUPAK, DONALD**, merchant banker, lawyer, strategic planner; b. NYC, Apr. 2, 1943; s. Sidney and Helen (Smith) S.; m. Leslie Silverman, June 21, 1964 (div. 1981); children: Andrew, Jessica; m. Cynthia Saul, Nov. 19, 1981; children: Amanda, Philip Nicholas. BA, Syracuse U., 1964, JD, 1966; LLM in Taxation, NYU, 1970. Bar: N.Y. Assoc. various law firms, N.Y.C., 1966-70; ptnr. Schupak, Rosenfeld, Fishbein, et al, N.Y.C., 1970-82; chmn. bd., chief exec. officer Donald Schupak and Co., Inc., N.Y.C., 1982—; Safety Harbor Corp., N.Y.C., 1985-90. Vice chmn. Horn and Hardart Co., N.Y.C., 1977-88, chmn. bd., chief exec. officer, pres., 1988—. Mem. Assn. of Bar of City of N.Y., N.Y. Bar Assn., Phi Kappa Phi, Order of Coif. Clubs: Rombout Hunt (Hyde Park, N.Y.). Office: Danskin Inc 530 7th Ave New York NY 10018 also: Hardart Cons Co 730 5th Ave New York NY 10019-4105 also: Learn2 dot com Inc 1311 Mamaroneck Ave White Plains NY 10605

**SCHUPAK, LESLIE ALLEN**, public relations company executive; b. Spokane, Wash., Apr. 5, 1945; s. Leo and Henrietta (Neumann) S.; m. Dianne Barbara Goldin, June 23, 1968; 1 child, Adam J. BS, Boston U., 1967, MS, 1971. Asst. to pres., account exec. Sperber Assocs., Inc., Boston, 1968-69; account supr. Wilcox & Williams, N.Y.C., 1969-70; v.p., mgr. Daniel J. Edelman, Inc., N.Y.C., 1970-72; mng. ptnr. Kanan, Corbin, Schupak & Aronow, Inc., N.Y.C., 1972—. Pres. Whippoorwill Lake Property Owners Assn., Chappaqua, N.Y., 1984-88; chmn. exec. com. Coll. Comm., Boston U., 1997-2005. With U.S. Army, 1968-73. Mem.: Golf Writers of Am. Assn., Nat. Investor Rels. Inst., Donald Ross Soc., Met. Golf Writers Assn. (v.p.), Met. Golf Assn. (pres.), U.S. Golf Assn. (comms. com.), Desert Mountain Club (Scottsdale, Ariz.), Metropolis Country Club (White Plains, NY). Avocations: golf, tennis. Office: KCSA Worldwide 800 2nd Ave New York NY 10017-4709 Office Phone: 212-682-6300. Business E-Mail: lschupak@kcsa.com.

**SCHUPP, JOYCE ELAINE**, elementary school educator; b. Jacksonville, Ill., Jan. 17, 1953; d. Clyde Delbert and Helen Louise (Petefish) B.; m. Terrence Joseph Schupp, Aug. 6, 1977; children: Natalie, Nicole. B of Music Edn., Ill. Wesleyan U., 1975; postgrad., Western Ill. U., 1976, Ill. State U. 1979. Gen. music educator East Peoria Elem., 1975-82; pre-sch. instr. Washington Christian Nursery Sch., Washington, Ill., 1982—. Piano instr. 1982—; organist, choir accompanist Washington Christian Ch., 1975—;

contest accompanist East Peoria Elem. Sch., 1975—86, Washington Mid. Sch., Washington Cmty. H.S. Mem. Music Tchrs. Nat. Assn., Ill. State Music Tchrs. Assn., Peoria Area Music Tchrs. Assn. Home: 917 E Guth Rd Washington IL 61571-9531

**SCHUPP, PAUL EUGENE**, mathematician, educator; b. Cleve., Mar. 12, 1937; s. Paul Eugene and Venna Marie Schupp; m. Elva Stewart, June 14, 1984 (div. June 14, 1984); 1 child, Jerome Oliver William. BA, Case Western Res. U., 1959; PhD, U. Mich., 1966. Asst. prof. U. Wis., Madison, 1966—67, U. Ill., Urbana, 1968—71, assoc. prof., 1971—75, prof., 1975—, assoc. mem. Ctr. for Advanced Study, 1976—77. Vis. prof. U. London, 1982, U. Paris VII, 1984—92, U. Singapore, 1982, U. Bordeaux, 1984, 96; exch. vis. USA-USSR Nat. Acads. Sci. Exch. Program, 1982. Author: (with R.C. Lyndon) Combinatorial Group Theory. Fellow, John Simon Guggenheim Found., 1977—78. Mem.: Am. Math. Soc. Greek Orthodox. Home: 310 Eliot Urbana IL 61801 Office: U Ill Dept Math Urbana IL 61801 Office Phone: 217-333-1610. Business E-Mail: schupp@math.uiuc.edu.

**SCHUPP, ROBERT WARREN**, law educator; b. Miami Beach, Fla., Jan. 21, 1947; s. Frederick Anthony Schupp and Mary June (Barefoot) Schupp Goodall. B.S. in Mgmt., U. Fla., 1969, J.D., 1973. Bar: Fla. 1973, U.S. Dist. Ct. (mid. dist.) Fla. 1974. Instr. Fla. Jr. Coll., Jacksonville, 1972-73; assoc. prof. U. N. Fla., Jacksonville, 1973—; cons. Sears, Roebuck & Co., Inc., 1974. Contbr. articles to legal jours. Participant Leadership Jacksonville, 1979. Recipient Fla. Disting. Service medal Fla. N.G., 1981. Mem. Fla. Bar Assns., Beta Gamma Sigma, Delta Sigma Pi. Republican. Office: U N Fla 4567 Saint Johns Bluff Rd S Jacksonville FL 32224-2646

**SCHUPP, RUSS**, computer professor; AA, State Fair C.C., Sedalia, Mo, 1974; MusB in Edn., Ctrl. Mo. State U., Warrensburg, 1976; MA, Webster U., Whiteman Air Force Base, 2003. Lan mgr. State Fair C.C., 1997—2000, coll. tchr., 2000—. Percussionist Sedalia Symphony, Sedalia 1971—2006; elder Broadway Presbyn. Ch., 2004—06; percussionist Broadway Presbyn. Ch. and Antioch Fellowship Praise and Worship groups, 1996—2006. Achievements include development of new curriculum and course requirements for computer programming, computer programming with emphasis in accounting, and Web development degrees. Office Phone: 660-530-5800.

**SCHUR, JEFFREY**, advertising executive; b. Capetown, South Africa, May 3, 1946; Canadian citizen; arr. USA, 1979. s. Lionel Harry and Dorothy (Siman) S.; m. Lucille Stella Breakey, Nov. 30, 1965; children: David Leon, Cynthia-Jean. Diploma in Mktg., Cape Coll. for Advanced Tech. Edn., Capetown, 1970. Account exec. J. Walter Thompson, Capetown and Johannesburg, Republic of South Africa, 1969-71; account dir. Ogilvy & Mather, Johannesburg, 1971-76, internat. vp. Latin Am. base N.Y.C., 1976-78, account dir. Toronto, Ont., Can., 1977-80; gen. mgr., pres. Saatchi & Saatchi, Toronto, 1980-84; pres., chief exec. officer Needham Harper Can., Toronto, 1985-86, Schur Peppler & Assocs., Toronto, 1986-89, Doner Schur Peppler, Toronto, 1989-92; exec. v.p. Earle Palmer Brown, N.Y.C., 1992-94; ptnr. Doig, Elliott, Schur Inc., N.Y.C., 1994—99; dir. integration Omnicon Group, N.Y.C., 1999—2006; dir. integrated mktg. JWT N.Y., 2006—. Dir. Outward Bound, Toronto, 1980-83, Can. Liver Found., Toronto, 1984-86, Toronto Family Svc. Assn., 1985, York Mills Valley Assn., Toronto, 1990-92, Children's Aid, Toronto, 1991-92, S.A. Defence Forces 1st Parachute Bn., 1964-73. Fellow Chartered Inst. Mktg. (lectr. 1971-73, examiner 1973-74, edn. chmn. 1974-75, rsch. award 1970); Vintage Sports Car Club Am., Old Greenwich Harbour Yacht Club, Sports Vintage Racing Assn., Yale Club N.Y. Avocations: skiing, scuba, vintage racing cars, gardening, sailing. Home: 10 Palmer Ter Riverside CT 06878-2103

**SCHUR, WALTER ROBERT**, physician; b. Webster, Mass., June 17, 1914; s. Robert O. and Alma L. (Gatzke) S.; m. Delta Jean Newman, June 17, 1944; children: Paul, David, Jonathan, Ruth, Timothy, Peter, Stephen, Mary, Joel, Daniel, Rhoda. Student, Valparaiso U., 1931-34; MD, Middlesex U.Sch. of Med., 1940. Resident Milford (Del.) Meml. Hosp., 1940-41, Grace Hosp., Cleve., 1942-43; intern Luth. Hosp., Cleve., 1941-42; pvt. practice Oxford, Mass., 1944—. Bd. dirs. Doctors Hosp., Worcester, Mass., chmn. bd., 1978-87; bd. dirs. AdCare Hosp., 1987—, chmn. bd. dirs., 1987-91, Atlantic dist. Luth. Ch.-Mo. Synod, 1978-87, mem., sec. edn. com., missions com., 1960-77, mem. stewardship com., youth com., 1951-57, chmn. edn. com. Atlantic dist., 1954-57, mem. commn. on mission and ministry in ch., named Dist. Layman of Yr., 1966, chmn. com. on ministry Atlantic dist., 1970; bd. dirs. Luth. Assn. Works of Mercy, assn. Evang. Luth. Chs.; bd. dirs. Valparaiso U., 1969-99, sec., 1984-99; pres., scholarship chmn. N.E. dist. Luth. Laymen's League, 1957; vice chmn. Luth. Hour Oper. Com., 1958, chmn., 1959-61; New Eng. bd. dirs. Assn. Evang. Luth. Chs., 1977-87, trustee East Coast Synod, 1977-87, mem. nat. bd. dirs., 1979-88; mem. coun. New Eng. Synod Evang. Luth. Ch. Am., 1988-94; bd. dirs., vice chmn. French River Dist. Ctr., 1985—; mem. Oxford Sch. Com., 1961-86, Mass. Commn. on Christian Unity; assoc. charter mem. Park Ridge Ctr., 1986. Recipient award of merit Internat. Luth. Laymen's League, 1963, Soli Deo Gloria award New Eng. Synod, Evang. Luth. Ch. Am., 1994. Fellow Am. Acad. Gen. Practice, Am. Acad. Family Physicians (charter); mem. AMA, Mass. Med. Soc., Worcester Dist. Med. Soc., Am. Geriatrics Assn., New Eng. Ob-gyn. Soc., Valparaiso U. Alumni assn. (past pres.), Luth. Acad. for Scholarship (bd. dirs. 1977-86), Concordia Hist. Inst., New Eng. Luth. Hist. Soc. (charter), Internat. Platform Assn., New Eng. Huguenot Soc., Rotary (past pres.). Home: 168 Charlton St Oxford MA 01540-2008 Office: 367 Main St Oxford MA 01540-1746

**SCHURE, ALEXANDER**, university chancellor; b. Can., Aug. 4, 1920; s. Harry Joshua and Bessie (Ginsberg) S.; m. Dorothy Rubin, Dec. 8, 1943 (dec. June 1981); children: Barbara, Matthew, Louis, Jonathan; m. Gail Doris Strollo, Sept. 12, 1984. AST in Elec. Engring, Pratt Inst., 1943; BS, CCNY, 1947; MA, NYU, 1948, PhD, 1950, EdD, 1953; D in Engring. Sci. honoris causa, Nova U., 1975; DSc, NY Inst. Tech., 1976; LLD, Boca Raton Coll., 1976, LI U., 1983; LHD, Columbia Coll., Calif., 1983; D of Pedagogy, NY Chiropractic Coll., 1985. Asst. dir. Melville Radio Insts., NYC, 1945-48; pres. Crescent Sch. Radio and TV, Bklyn., 1948-51, Crescent Electronics Corp., NYC, 1951-55; founder, pres., CEO NY Inst. Tech., Bklyn., 1955—82, chancellor, CEO, 1982-91, chancellor emeritus, 1991—, founder computer graphics lab., 1970-91; pres., CEO, chancellor The Univ. Fedn., Inc., 1995—; chancellor, CEO Nova U. (now NSU), 1970—85; mem. Fla. State Bd. Ind. Colls. and Univs., 1991—; pres. Vidbits, Inc., 1992, NY Coll. for Wholistic Health Edn. and Rsch., Syosset, LI, 2000—01. Cons. NY State Dept. Edn., US Office Edn., UNESCO, tech. educator sent to Venezuela to study needs, UNESCO, 1960; mem. Regents Regional Coordinating Coun. for Post-Secondary Edn. in NYC, 1973—; mem., 1st inductee Nassau County Consortia on Higher Edn., LI, 1971—, Alfred P. Sloan Found. adv. com. for expanding minority opportunities in engring., 1974; rep. to Nat. Assn. State Adv. Coun., 1975—; chmn. NY Title IV Adv. Coun., 1975-77; mem. steering com. LI Regional Adv. Coun. 1974—; chair Regents Adv. Coun. on Learning Techs., 1986-88; mem., trustee exec. com. Commn. Ind. Colls. and Univs.; mem. adv. coun. learning techs. NY State Dept. Edn., 1982—; co-founder NY Coll. Osteo Medicine, Old Westbury, 1977; mem. Accreditation Task Force for Coun.on Postsecondary Accreditation/SHEEBO Project on Assessing Long Distance Learning Via Telecoms. (Project ALLTEL), 1982—; mem. NY State Motion Picture and TV adv. bd.; chair tech. com.; dir. numerous rsch. projects; expert witness Ho. of Reps. com. of Commn. on Sci. and Astronautics; mem. adv. coun. Fla. State Bd. Ind. Colls. and Univs.; vis. tech. exec. Hofstra U., LI, NY, 1998, 99. Author and-or editor textbooks, film producer; prodr., dir. Tuby the Tuba; designer automatic teaching machine; built one of first computer-controlled anthropomorphic speech devices, 1959; contbr. articles to tech. publs.; patentee in field. Pres. bd. dirs., trustee LI Ednl. TV Coun., Channel 21, Garden City; bd. dirs. Coun. Higher Ednl. Instns., NYC, 1973-83; pres. The Univ. Fedns., Fla., 1995—. Served with Signal Corps AUS, 1942-45. Recipient (2) Clio awards; 1st inductee Fine Arts Mus. of Long Island's Computer Hall of Fame, 1986. Mem. IEEE (LI sect. Gruenwald award 1988), NY Acad. Sci., Am. Inst. Engring. Edn., N.E.A. Electronic Industries Assn. (chmn. task force curriculum devel.), Phi Delta

Kappa, Delta Mu Delta, Eta Kappa Nu. Personal E-mail: schure1ufi@aol.com. *The world is an ever changing, ever challenging reality, filled with opportunities for individual fulfillment and success. A positive philosophy toward life does much to make the realization of individual potential an actuality.*

**SCHURENBERG, ERIC**, magazine editor; b. Cin., Aug. 23, 1953; s. Carl Joseph and Lorraine Claire (Willows) S.; m. Judith Margaret Dowd, Apr. 30, 1983; 1 child, Emilie. AB in English, Brown U., 1975. Joined Money mag., NYC, 1984, sr. editor, 1990-95, asst. mng. editor, 1995—97, Fortune mag., 1997—2000; mng. editor Goldman.com, 2000—01; editor-at-large Business 2.0, 2001, deputy mng. editor, 2001—04; mng. editor Money mag., NYC, 2004—. Commentator Nightly Bus. Report, PBS, 1990—; former pers. fin. reporter WCBS News. Former pers. fin. editor Marketplace Radio, Mut. Broadcasting Sys., 1988-96. Author: (books) 401K Take Charge of Your Future, 1995. Recipient Nat. Mag. award Am. Soc. Mag. Editors, 1988, Page One award Newspaper Guild of N.Y., 1989, Gerald Loeb award Anderson Sch., UCLA, 1989. Office Phone: 212-522-0119. Office Fax: 212-522-3737.*

**SCHUR KAUFMAN, SUSAN**, retired public affairs consultant; b. Feb. 27, 1940; d. Norman and Jeanette (Handelman) Dorfman; m. Clayton Kaufman; children from previous marriage: Diana Elisabeth Schur, Erica M. Rydzewski. BA, Goucher Coll., 1961. Adminstr. fed. housing, fgn. aid, anti-poverty programs, 1961-67; mem. Mass. Housing Appeals Com., 1977-86; mem., v.p. Bd. of Alderman, Newton, Mass., 1974-81; mem. Mass. Ho. of Reps., 1981-94; pvt. pub. affairs cons., 1995—2000. Bd. dirs. Middlesex Bank & Trust Co. Bd. dirs. Newton Cmty. Devel. Found., 1995-99; overseer New Philharmonia Orch., 1997-99; mem. Newton Dem. City Com., 1970-99.

**SCHURMAN, DAVID JAY**, orthopedic surgeon, educator; b. Chgo., Apr. 25, 1940; s. Shepherd P. and Dorothy (Laskey) S.; m. Martha Ellen Rocker, Mar. 8, 1967; children: Hilary Sue, Theodore Shepherd. BA, Yale U., 1961; MD, Columbia U., 1965. Intern Baylor U., Houston, 1965-67; resident in gen. surgery Mt. Sinai Hosp., N.Y.C., 1966-67; resident in orthop. surgery UCLA, 1969-72; asst. rsch. surgeon UCLA Med. Sch., 1972-73; asst. prof. orthopedic surgery Stanford Med. Sch., 1973-79, assoc. prof., 1979-87, prof., 1987—. Acting chief divsn. orthop. surgery Stanford U. Med. Ctr., 1990-93, fellowship dir. total joint replacement, 1983—, fellowship dir. sports medicine, 1992-95, dir. orthop. rsch. lab., 1973—. Capt. USAF, 1967-69. Fellow NIH, 1972-73; grantee NIH, 1976-96; recipient Top Dr. award, San Francisco Mag., 02, 03, 05. Mem. Am. Orthopaedic Assn. (bd. dirs. 1994-95), Clin. Orthopaedics and Related Rsch. (bd. dirs. 1994-00), Assn. Bone and Joint Surgeons (v.p. 1996-97, pres. 1997-98). Office: Stanford U Sch Medicine R144 Divsn Orthop Surgery 300 Pasteur Dr Palo Alto CA 94304-2203 Office Phone: 650-723-7608.

**SCHURTZ, ORA SEARS**, hypnotist, educator; b. Indpls., July 30, 1919; d. Fred Harrison Sears and Stella; widowed; children: Carl Frederick, Penelope Ann. Student, Ind. Ctrl. Bus. Coll., 1939—40, Ind. U., 1943—44, Rutgers U., 1969—70; BS, Union U., 1978; PhD in Alternative Nutrition, Donsbach U., 1980. Ordained minister Alliance of Divine Love, West Palm, Fla., 1994; cert. hypnosis Hyphodyne Found., 1990, instr. Hyphodyne Found., 1996, master hypnotherapists Hyphodyne Found., 1998. Asst. to gen. foreman tool and dye dept. Gen. Motors, Indpls., 1942—43; with Pan Am. Airways, Miami, Fla., 1944—46; mgmt. Macy's, N.Y.C., 1946—47, Mandell Bros., Chgo., 1948—49; co-owner Renor Co., Milw., 1950—53; pub. rels. Bissill Corp., NJ; pres. Food Power Naturally, Inc., 1970—77; owner Survival, Inc., 1976—80; pvt. practice, 1980—. Instr. hypnotist ing. 1996—; workshop leader. Contbr. articles to profl. jours. Mem.: Palm Beach Ctr. Living, Internat. Assn. Counselors and Therapists (nat. mem. award 2000), Nat. Guild Hypnotists. Avocation: walking. Office: Bldg 3-1D 11811 Ave of Pga Palm Beach Gardens FL 33418 Office Phone: 561-627-6900. Business E-Mail: peg2490@aol.com.

**SCHURZ, SCOTT CLARK**, journalist; b. South Bend, Ind., Feb. 23, 1936; s. Franklin Dunn and Martha (Montgomery) S.; m. Kathryn Joan Foley, Aug. 5, 1967; children: Scott Clark, Alexandra Carol, John Danforth. BA, Denison U., 1957; LHD (hon.), Ind. U., 2000. Asst. instr. U. Md., 1957-58; adminstrv. asst. South Bend Tribune, 1960-66; circulation cons. Imperial Valley Press, El Centro, Calif., 1966; pres. Hoosier Times, Inc.; dir., v.p. Schurz Comms., Inc.; pub., editor-in-chief Sunday Hoosier-Times. Pres. Bloomington Boys' Club, 1970-71, Jr. Achievement Monroe County, 1971-73; bd. dirs. United Way Monroe County, 1979-81, Cmty. Found. Area Arts Coun. Served with U.S. Army, 1958-60. Mem.: Ind. U. Found. (bd. dirs. 1986—), Newspaper Advt. Bur. (bd. dirs. 1987—92), Internat. Press Inst., World Press Freedom Com. (exec. com.), Hoosier State Press Assn. (pres. 1989, 1997), Inter-Am. Press Assn. (bd. dirs. 1995—), Newspaper Assn. Am. (bd. dirs. 1992—95, 2002—, found. pres.), Inland Daily Press Assn. (pres. 1989), Internat. Newspaper Mktg. Assn. (pres. 1986, treas. 1997—2004), World Assn. Newspapers (bd. dirs.). Republican. Presbyterian. Office: Hoosier Times Inc 1900 S Walnut St Bloomington IN 47401-7720 Office Phone: 812-332-4401.

**SCHUSELKA, ELFI**, artist; Student, Graphic and Exptl. Inst., Vienna, Austria, 1958, 59, U. Vienna, 1958, 59, Acad. Applied Arts, Vienna, 1959-61, Sch. Vision, 1960, Oskar Kokoschka, 1960. Tchr., Italy, 1961, 62, 63; instr. Sch. Visual Arts, N.Y.C., 1970-72, Pratt Inst., N.Y.C., 1974, Rutgers U., 1976, Pratt Graphics Ctr., N.Y.C., 1978, 79, 80, CUNY, 1989. One-woman shows include U. Keele, Eng., 1974, 55 Mercer St. Gallery, N.Y.C., 1977, 1979, 1982, 1984, Condeso/Lawler Gallery, 1980, 1983, 1985, 1987, Neue Galerie, Vienna, 1988, N.Y. U. Broadway Windows, N.Y.C., 1988, Henry Chauncey Conf. Ctr., Princeton, N.J., 1990, Verita Gallery, Tokyo, 1990, AL Galerie Gerlinda Walz, Stuttgart, Germany, 1993, Glaskasten, Leonberg, Germany, 1996, Austrian Trade Commn., N.Y.C., 2000, exhibited in group shows at Bklyn. Mus., 1970, 1976, Internat. Print Biennale, Krakow, Poland, 1970, 1976, 1978, 1980, 1984, Internat. Brit. Print Biennale, Bradford, Eng., 1972, Betty Parsons Gallery, N.Y.C., 1974, Internat. Exhbn. Graphic Art, Ljubliana, Yugoslavia, 1975, 1979, 1981, 1983, 1985 (award, 1987), Frechen, Germany, 1976, 1978 (award), 1984, Aldrich Mus. Contemporary Art, Conn., 1978, Internat. Triennial Colored Graphics, Grenchen, Switzerland, 1979, 1982, 1985, European Biennale, Mulhouse, France, 1980, Rutgers U., 1980, Kyoto Mcpl. Mus. Art, Japan, 1980, 1982, 1984, Internat. Graphic Exhibit Taipei Fine Arts Mus., Taiwan, 1983, 1985, 1989, 1993, 1999, 2000, Mus. du Petit Format, Couvin, Niames-Viroinval, Belgium, 1983, 1985, 1987, 1989, 1989, 1991, 1993, 1998, 2000, 2002, 2004, Kanagawa Prefectural Gallery, Yokohama, Japan, 1989, 1991, 1992, 2001, Internat. Biennale Bharat Bhavan, Roopankar, India, 1989, 1991, 1995, 1997, 2001, Internat. Biennale Varna, Bulgaria, 1989, 2003, 2005, Internat. Triennial Graphic Art, Bitola, Macedonia, 1994, 1997, 2000, 2003, Internat. Festival Graphic Arts, Cluj-Napoca, Romania, 1999, 2001, 2003, 2005, Austrian Trade Commn., N.Y.C., 2000, Cheju Internat. Print Exhbn. Sungkyunkwan U., Korea, 2000, Y2K Met. Mus. Art, Iwasaki, Japan, 2000, Internat. Egyptian Print Triennale, Cairo, 2000, 2003, Festival EVORA, Portugal, 2001, 2004, Ural Print Triennial, Ufa, Russia, 2001, 2004, Triennial Graphic Arts, Sophia, Bulgaria, 2001, L'Enfant est un Artist, Niames, Belgium, 2002, Piero della Francesco "The Resurrection", Niames and San Sepolcro, Italy, 2003, Symbiotic Communication Internat. Exhibit, West Univ. Timisoara, Romania, 2003, Represented in permanent collections Graphische Sammlung Albertina, Vienna, Amon Carter Mus., Ft. Worth, Biblioteque Nationale, Paris, Calif. Coll. Arts and Crafts, San Francisco, Mus. Modern Art, N.Y.C., Nat. Mus. History, Taipei, Taiwan, Newark Pub. Libr., N.Y.C., Nat. Pub. Libr., U. R.I., USIA, U. Dallas. Address: 133 Eldridge St New York NY 10002-3710 E-mail: elfdom@earthlink.net.

**SCHUSSLER, IRWIN**, psychiatrist, educator; b. Bklyn., Nov. 14, 1943; s. Jack and Fannie Yetta (Blank) S.; m. Myra Yvette Paget, June 26, 1966; children: Jeffrey Mitchell, Doreen Robyn, Kimberly Beth, Howard, Brian. BS, Bklyn. Coll., 1964; DO, Chgo. Coll. Osteopathic Medicine, 1968. Diplomate Am. Bd. Psychiatry and Neurology, Am. Bd. Gen. Psychiatry and Child Psychiatry, Am. Osteopathic Bd. Neurology and Psychiatry, Am. Bd. Sexology. Intern Interboro Gen. Hosp., Bklyn., 1968—69; resident in gen. psychiatry U. Fla. Coll. Medicine, Gainesville, 1972—74, asst. prof. psychiatry and pediatrics, 1976—77, dir. in-patient psychotherapy, 1976—77, fellow in child and adolescent psychiatry, 1974—76; fellow in human sexual medicine U. Pa., Phila., 1975; practice medicine specializing in psychiatry Ft. Worth, 1977—; clin. assoc. prof., vice chmn. dept. psychiatry North Tex. State U. Health Scis. Ctr., North Tex. Coll. Osteo. Medicine, Ft. Worth, 1977—79. Past mem. bd. dirs. Osteo. Med. Ctr., former med. dir. psychiatry dept Contbr. articles to profl. jours. Bd. dirs. Mental Health Assn. Fellow Am. Coll. Neuropsychiatry, Am. Coll. Sexology; mem. Am. Psychiat. Assn., Am. Acad. Child Psychiatrists, Am. Acad. Clin. Psychiatrists, Am. Assn. Sex Educators, Counselors and Therapists, Tex. Soc. Psychiat. Physicians (pres. Tarrant County chpt.), Am. Osteo. Assn., Tex. Osteo. Med. Assn., Fla. Osteo. Med. Assn., Masters and Johnson Found. Jewish. Home: 3712 Myrtle Springs Rd Fort Worth TX 76116-9213 Office: Psychiat Cons Ft Worth 3704 Mattison Ave Fort Worth TX 76107-2619 also: Austin Psychiat cons 1500 W 38th St Ste 53 Austin TX 78731 Office Phone: 817-732-8441. E-mail: mschussler@charter.net, pcfw@sbcglobal.net.

**SCHUSTER, CARLOTTA LIEF,** psychiatrist; b. NYC, Sept. 16, 1936; d. Victor Filler and Nina Lincoln (Rayevsky) Lief; m. David Israel Schuster, Sept. 2, 1962; 1 child, Amanda. BA, Barnard Coll., 1957; MD, NYU, 1964. Cert. Am. Bd. Psychiatry and Neurology; cert. addiction psychiatry. Intern Lenox Hill Hosp., N.Y.C., 1964-65; resident St. Luke's Hosp., N.Y.C., 1965-68; fellow Inst. Sex Edn. U. Pa., Phila., 1968-69; instr. N.Y. Med. Coll., N.Y.C., 1969-72; asst. attending Met. Hosp., N.Y.C., 1969-72; assoc. attending St. Luke's-Roosevelt Hosp. Ctr., N.Y.C., 1972-95; staff psychiatrist Silver Hill Hosp., New Canaan, Conn., 1972-95; clin. assoc. instr. Columbia U., N.Y.C., 1990-95. Chief substance abuse svc. Silver Hill Hosp., New Canaan, 1976-95; dir. Recovery Clinic Bellevue Hosp., N.Y.C., 1995-2003; mem. faculty Dept. Psychiatry Sch. Medicine NYU, 1995—. Author: Alcohol and Sexuality, 1988; co-author: Chapter in Advances in Alcohol and Substance Abuse, 1987; contbr. chpts. to books. Mem. Am. Psychiat. Assn., Am. Med. Soc. on Addictions, Am. Acad. Addiction Psychiatry. Democrat. Jewish. Avocations: cooking, attending concerts, opera, films. Home: 130 E 30th St New York NY 10016-8230 Office Phone: 212-213-2513. Personal E-mail: carlotta_schuster@msn.com.

**SCHUSTER, CAROL JOYCE,** special education educator, consultant; d. Samuel Saul and Ruth Edna Levine; m. George M. Schuster, Sept. 18, 1964; 1 child, Robert Churchill. BS in Edn., SUNY, Oswego, 1952; MS in Edn., Queens Coll., SUNY, 1958. Lic. heath conservation for physcially handicapped NYC, 1963, tchr. orthop. handicapped NY, 1976, elem. tchr. NYC. Tchr. NYC Bd. Edn., 1953—62, tchr. physically handicapped, 1963—67, St. Francis Hosp., Roslyn; tchr. in charge Queens Gen. Hosp., Queens, NY; cons. in spl. edn. Dep. for handicapped, Huntington, NY, 1982—86; mem. adv. bd. and founding com. Dolan Family Health Ctr., Huntington, 1997—. Mem. prin. selection com. Half Hollow Hills Dist., Dix Hills, NY, 1979—80; cmty. activist Huntington, 1979—; mem. campaign com. election for US congressman Dix Hills, Huntington, LI, 1986—89; mem. Dem. campaign com. US pres. Huntington, 2003—04; youth edn. mentor AAUW; cert. instr. Literacy Vols. of Am. Recipient Lifetime award for Outstanding Achievement in Career and Cmty. Svc., SUNY, Oswego, 1997. Achievements include invention of an adjustable wheelchair desk in 1963. Avocations: reading, writing poetry and prose, painting, Sherlockian literature, travel.

**SCHUSTER, ELAINE,** retired civil rights professional; b. Detroit, Sept. 26, 1947; d. William Alfred and Aimee Isabelle (Cote) LeBlanc; m. James William Schuster, Sept. 6, 1969; 1 child, Cambrian James. BA, Wayne State U., 1972, postgrad., 1974-75, paralegal cert., 1991; student, Bay Mills Com. Coll., 2003—. Asst. payments Mich. Dept. Social Svcs., Detroit, 1972-73; rights rep. Mich. Dept. Civil Rights, Detroit, 1973-80, 82-87, 90, asst. dir. div., 1987-90, supr., 1993-97, dir. Svc. Ctr., 1997-99, contract coord., 1999—2002, ret., 2003; ct. adminstr. Chippewa-Ottawa Conservation Ct., Bay Mills, Mich., 1980-82; quality assurance coord. State Mental Health Facility, Southgate, Mich., 1991-93; acting interim dir. Mich. Indian Commn., Detroit, 1995; proprietor Good Things to Share, 2003—; trainer HIV/AIDS health support profls., 2004—. Author: Walking in Two Worlds, Delivering Culturally Competent Care in the American Indian Community, 2004, Critique, An Indian Tours Michilimackinac, 1981; contbr. articles and poems to mags. and profl. jours. Bd. dirs. Tri-County Native Ams., Warren, Mich., 1982-89, sec. Native Am. Sesquicentennial subcom., Mich., 1987; mem. Linking Lifetimes, mentor program for Native Am. youth, 1992-93; sec., newsletter editor various civic orgns.; also other polit. and civic activities. Native Am. fellow Mich. State U., 1989. Mem. NAACP (housing com. S. Oakland br. 2000), ACLU (bd. dirs. Union-Oakland county 1987-88, 2002-04). Democrat. Avocations: exploring local historical and natural places of interest, historical re-enactment, research, exercise. E-mail: ikwewe@comcast.net.

**SCHUSTER, INGEBORG IDA,** chemistry professor; b. Frankfurt, W. Ger., Oct. 30, 1937; came to U.S. 1947; d. Ludwig Karl and Mariluise (Lautetzky) S. BA, U. Pa., 1960; MS, Carnegie Inst. Tech., Pitts., 1963; PhD, Carnegie Inst. Tech., 1965. Postdoctoral fellow Bryn Mawr (Pa.) Coll., 1965-67; asst. prof. chemistry Pa. State U., Abington, 1967-73, assoc. prof. chemistry, 1973-83, prof. chemistry, 1983—. Contbr. articles to profl. jours. Huff fellow, 1966; E. Gerry fellow, 1982. Mem. Am. Chem. Soc. Republican. Roman Catholic. Avocations: skiing, violin, cartooning. Office: Pa State Univ 1600 Woodland Rd Abington PA 19001-3918 Business E-Mail: iis@psu.edu.

**SCHUSTER, MARVIN MEIER,** retired physician, educator; b. Danville, Va., Aug. 30, 1929; s. Isaac and Rosel (Katzenstein) S.; m. Lois R. Bernstein, Feb. 19, 1961; children: Roberta, Nancy, Cathy. BA, BS, U. Chgo., 1951, MD, 1955. Diplomate Am. Bd. Internal Medicine. Intern Kings County Hosp., Bklyn., 1955-56; resident Balt. City Hosps., 1956-58, founder divsn. digestive disease; resident John Hopkins Hosp., Balt., 1958-61; emeritus Janssen, Strauss Halbreich prof. medicine and psychiatry Johns Hopkins U. Sch. Medicine, Balt., 1976-97, chief emeritus digestive disease divsn.; dir. emeritus Marvin M. Schuster Ctr. for Digestive and Motility Disorders, Balt.; ret., 2004. Author: Gastrointestinal Disorders: Behavioral and Physiological Basis for Treatment; Keeping Control: Understanding and Managing Fecal Incontinence; editor: Gastrointestinal Motility Disorders, 1981, Atlas of Gastrointestinal Motility, 1st edit. 1994, 2d edit., 2002; mem. editl. bd. Gastroenterology, 1978-81, Gastrointestinal Endoscopy, 1979-81, Psychosomatics, 1979—, Am. Jour. Gastroenterology, 1993—; contbr. chpts. to textbooks and articles to profl. jours. Bd. dirs. Beth El Congregation, 1961-76, Am. Cancer Soc., 1975—, pres., 1984-86; chmn. med. adv. bd. Balt. Ostomy Assn., 1966—; chmn. phys. divsn. Assoc. Jewish Charities, 1961-76. Recipient St. George Disting. Svc. award Am. Cancer Soc., 1979, M. Rosenberg award, United Ostomy Assn. Fellow ACP, (life) Am. Psychiat. Assn., Am. Gastroent. Assn. (chmn. audiovisual com. 1975-78); mem. AAUP, Am. Soc. Gastrointestinal Endoscopy (governing bd. 1975-78), Am. Coll. Gastroenterology (master, pres. 1996), Am. Physiol. Soc. Democrat. Jewish. Achievements include research on gastrointestinal motility and application of biofeedback to gastrointestinal control. Home: 10 Red Cedar Ct Baltimore MD 21208-6305 E-mail: mschuster@comcast.net.

**SCHUSTER, PEGGY LINDNER (PRAVRAJIKA BRAHMAPRANA),** sister, nun; b. Seattle, Apr. 7, 1949; d. Philip Frederick Schuster and Ruth Elizabeth Robar. BA in History, Occidental Coll., Calif., 1970, U. Calif., Santa Barbara, 1973; solemn ordination (hon.), Vedanta Soc. So. Calif., 1984. Sr. monastic Vedanta Soc. So. Calif., 1973—. Convent bookstore mgr. Vedanta Soc., 1984—2004, interfaith dialog, 1984—, mem. monastic coun., 1995—2004; nun Ramakrishna Order of India; spkr. and presenter in field. Contbr. articles to religious and profl. jours.; editor: Vivekananda Swami: The Complete Works of Swami Vivekananda, 1997, of numerous works and works in progress. Interfaith seminar participant, Calcutta, India, 1977—98; lectr. Hospice, Santa Barbara, Calif., 1995—2004. Mem.: Amnesty Internat. Democrat. Avocations: swimming, writing, music, cooking. Home: Vedanta Convent 2027 Vine St Hollywood CA 90068 Personal E-mail: brahmaprana@yahoo.com. Business E-Mail: peggylschuster@yahoo.com.

**SCHUSTER, PHILIP FREDERICK, II,** lawyer, writer, educator; b. Denver, Aug. 26, 1945; s. Philip Frederick and Ruth Elizabeth (Robar) S.; m. Barbara Lynn Nordquist, June 7, 1975; children: Philip Christian, Matthew Dale. BA, U. Wash., 1967; JD, Willamette U., 1972. Bar: Oreg. 1972, Wash. 2002, U.S. Dist. Ct. Oreg. 1974, U.S. Ct. Appeals (9th cir.) 1986, U.S. Ct. Appeals (D.C. cir.) 2001, U.S. Supreme Ct. 1986. Dep. dist. atty. Multnomah County, Portland, Oreg., 1972; title examiner Pioneer Nat. Title Co., Portland, 1973-74; assoc. Buss, Leichner et al, Portland, 1975-76; from assoc. to prtnr. Kitson & Bond, Portland, 1976-77; pvt. practice Portland, 1977-95; prtnr. Dierking and Schuster, Portland, 1996—; adj. prof. law Lewis & Clark Coll., 2002. Arbitrator Multnomah County Arbitration Program, 1985—; student mentor Portland Pub. Schs., 1988—. Author: The Indian Water Slide, 1999; contbg. author OSB CLE Publ., Family Law; contbr. articles to profl. jours. Organizer Legal Aid Svcs. for Community Clinics, Salem, Oreg. and Seattle, 1969-73; Dem. committeeman, Seattle, 1965-70; judge Oreg. State Bar and Classroom Law Project, H.S. Mock Trial Competition, 1988—. Mem. ABA, ATLA, NAACP (exec. bd. Portland, Oreg. chpt. 1979-98), ACLU, Multnomah Bar Assn. (Vol. Lawyers Project), Internat. Platform Assn., Alpha Phi Alpha. Avocations: river drifting, camping, swimming, walking, writing. Office: 3565 NE Broadway St Portland OR 97232-1820 Office Phone: 503-335-7765. Business E-mail: schuster@pcez.com. *Hard work and perseverence are the keys to accomplishing any goal. Protecting and nurturing our children and our environment are life's most noble goals. Success is the pursuit of these goals.*

**SCHUSTER, REID S.,** advertising executive; m. Rachelle Schuster; 2 children. BA, U. Md. Founder Insite Strategies Corp., 1992; acct. exec. TDI (now Viacom Outdoor), 1997—99, nat. acct. mgr., 1999—2000, local sales mgr., 2000—02; exec. v.p. sales and mktg. Titan Worldwide, NYC, 2002—06, pres. sales and mktg., 2006—. Office: Titan Worldwide 850 Third Ave New York NY 10022 Office Phone: 212-644-6200. Office Fax: 212-644-2010.*

**SCHUSTER, ROBERT PARKS,** lawyer; b. St. Louis, Oct. 25, 1945; s. William Thomas Schuster and Carolyn Cornforth (Daugherty) Hathaway; 1 child, Susan Michele. AB, Yale U., 1967; JD with honors, U. Wyo., 1970; LLM, Harvard U., 1971. Bar: Wyo. 1971, U.S. Ct. Appeals (10th cir.) 1979, U.S. Supreme Ct. 1984, Utah 1990. Dep. county atty. County of Natrona, Casper, Wyo., 1971-73; pvt. practice Casper, 1973—76; assoc. Spence & Moriarity, Casper, 1976-78; prtnr. Spence, Moriarity & Schuster, Jackson, Wyo., 1978—2002; pvt. practice Jackson, Wyo., 2002—. Trustee U. Wyo., 1985-89; Wyo. Dem. nominee for U.S. Ho. of Reps., 1994; polit. columnist Casper Star Tribune, 1987-94; pres. United Way Natrona County, 1974; bd. dirs. Dancers Workshop, 1981-83; chair Wyo. selection com. Rhodes Scholarship, 1989-98; mem. bd. visitors Coll. Arts and Scis., U. Wyo., 1991-2000; mem. Dem. Nat. Com., 1992-2000; chair Wyo. Pub. Policy Forum, 1992-98; mem. Wind River Reservation Econ. Adv. Coun., 1998-99; bd. dirs. Internat. Edn. Found., 2005—. Ford Found. Urban Law fellow, 1970-71. Mem. ABA, ATLA, Wyo. Trial Lawyers Assn., Yale Club (pres. Wyo. chpt., 2004—). Home: PO Box 13160 Jackson WY 83002 Office: Robert P Schuster PC 250 Veronica Ln Ste 204 PO Box 13160 Jackson WY 83002 Office Phone: 307-732-7800.

**SCHUSTER, SEYMOUR,** mathematician, educator; b. Bronx, N.Y., July 31, 1926; s. Oscar and Goldie (Smilowitz) S.; m. Marilyn Weinberg, May 2, 1954; children: Paul Samuel, Eve Elizabeth. BA, Pa. State U., 1947; A.M., Columbia U., 1948; PhD, Pa. State U., 1953; postgrad. (fellow), U. Toronto, 1952-53. Instr. Pa. State U., 1950-52, Poly. Inst. N.Y., 1953-54, asst. prof., 1954-56, assoc. prof., 1956-58; vis. assoc. prof. Carleton Coll., Northfield, Minn., 1958-59, assoc. prof., 1959-63, prof. math., 1968—, chmn. dept., 1973-76, William H. Laird prof. math. and liberal arts, 1992-94, William H. Laird prof. emeritus, 1994— Vis. assoc. prof. U. N.C., Chapel Hill, 1961; research assoc. math. dept. U. Minn., Mpls., 1962-63, assoc. prof., 1963-65; assoc. prof. Minn. Math Center, 1965-68, dir. coll. geometry project, 1964-74; dir. Acad. Year Inst. for Coll. Tchrs., 1966-67, NSF Faculty fellow, 1970-71; vis. scholar U. Calif., Santa Barbara, 1970-71, U. Ariz., 1990; guest scholar Western Mich. U., 1976, 81; vis. prof. Western Wash. U., 1983, U. Oreg., 1986. Author: (with K. O. May) Undergraduate Research in Mathematics, 1961, Elementary Vector Geometry, 1962, (with P.C. Rosenbloom) Prelude to Analysis, 1966; also research articles on geometry, graph theory, and analysis.; cons. editor Xerox Pub. Co., 1962-71; assoc. editor, editorial bd.: Am. Math. Monthly, 1969-86; assoc. editor: Indian Jour. Math. Edn., 1976-86; co-producer 12 films on geometry. With USNR, 1944—46. Recipient Honor award Am. Film Festival, 1967, Golden Eagle award Cine Film Festival, 1967, 68; named found. fellow Inst. for Combinatorics and Applications. Mem. Math. Assn. Am., Am. Math. Soc., Nat. Assn. Math., Sigma Xi, Pi Mu Epsilon. Home: 316 Sumner St E Northfield MN 55057-2843 E-mail: schusters@charter.net.

**SCHUSTER, STEPHEN JOHN,** hematologist, oncologist; s. Andrew Matthew and Rose Schuster; m. Barbara Brennan; children: Stephen John, Matthew Martin. MD, Jefferson Med. Coll., Phila., Pa., 1981. Diplomate Am. Boards of Internal Medicine, Hematology and Oncology. Assoc. prof. of medicine U. Pa. Sch. of Medicine, Phila., 2005—. Dir. lymphoma program Abramson Cancer Ctr. of U. Pa., Phila. Achievements include research in Erythropoiesis; Therapy of Lymphomas. Office: Univ Pa 3400 Spruce St Philadelphia PA 19104 Office Phone: 215-614-1846.

**SCHUTSKY, KEITH BARRY,** neuroscientist, researcher; b. Summit, NJ, Jan. 10, 1979; s. Barry Abraham Schutsky and Ilene Pistilli; m. Christina Marie Reger, Aug. 27, 2005. BS in Biology and Psychology, Cornell U., Ithaca, NY, 2001. Lab. asst. dept. neurobiol. Cornell U., Ithaca, 1998—99; lab. intern Aventis Pharms Raritan NJ 1999; lab. asst. Ctr Molecular Medicine and Immunology, Belleville, 2001—03. Contbr. articles to profl. jours. Mem.: Nat. Honors Soc., Pre-Med. Honors Soc., Mensa. Avocations: tennis, running, basketball, weightlifting, football. Office: U Pa Dept Pharm 3620 Hamilton Walk Philadelphia PA 19104 Home: 3208 Aston Close Hillsborough NJ 08844-4892

**SCHUTTA, HENRY SZCZESNY,** neurologist, educator; b. Gdansk, Poland, Sept. 15, 1928; came to U.S., 1962, naturalized, 1967; s. Jakub and Janina (Zerbst) S.; m. Henryka Kosmal, Apr. 29, 1950; children: Katharine, Mark, Caroline. M.B., BS, U. Sydney, Australia, 1955, MD, 1968. Jr. resident, then sr. resident St. Vincent's Hosp., Sydney, 1956-58; acad. registrar, house physician Nat. Hosp. Nervous Diseases, London, 1958-62; neurologist Pa. Hosp., Phila., 1962-73; asso. prof. neurology U. Pa. Med. Sch., 1963-73; prof. neurology, chmn. dept. SUNY Downstate Med. Center, Bklyn., 1973-80; prof. U. Wis. Med. Sch., 1980-98, chmn. dept. neurology, 1980-95, prof. emeritus, 1999; prof. neurology U. Ariz., Tucson, 2001—. Achievements include research on bilirubin encephalopathy, cerebral edema, degeneration and regeneration of muscle, history of medicine. Office: U Hosp 600 Highland Ave Madison WI 53792-0001 Home: 506 Addison Street Philadelphia PA 19147-1404 E-mail: hsschutta@comcast.net.

**SCHUTTE, RICHARD DAVID,** diversified financial services company executive; b. Corona, Calif., Sept. 25, 1954; s. Richard A. and Cory M. Schutte; m. Karen M. Schutte, Sept. 8, 1984; children: Laura M., Michael R. BBA in Acctg., U. Wis., Eau Claire, 1976. CPA. Audit. mgr. Ernst & Young, Milw., 1976-83; contr. Hytek Internat. Corp., Brookfield, Wis., 1983-86; asst. contr. Autotrol Corp., Milw., 1986-89; v.p. fin., CFO Manu-Tronics Inc., Kenosha, Wis., 1989-2000; CFO Accutec, Oak Creek, Wis., 2000—01; pres. RDS & Assocs., Inc., Franklin, Wis., 2001—. Mem. Coun. Small Bus. Execs. Mem. AICPA, Wis. Inst. CPAs, Fin. Execs. Internat. (bd. dirs. 1992-95, treas. 1996, sec. 1997, v.p. 1998, pres. 1999), Kenosha Health Care Ptnrs, Inc. (bd. dirs. 1994-95, treas. 1994, pres. 1995), Metro. Milw. (Wis.) Assn. Commerce, CEO Roundtable, S.E. Chamber Small Bus. Execs. Avocations: reading, golf. Home: 2954 W Briarwood Dr Franklin WI 53132-9145 Office: RDS & Assoc Inc 2954 W Briarwood Dr Franklin WI 53132 Business E-Mail: richard@rdsassociates.com.

**SCHUTZ, DONALD FRANK,** geochemist, environmental corporate executive; b. Orange, Tex., Sept. 22, 1934; s. Theodore J. and Mildred Irene S.; m. Beatriz Valera, May 18, 1958; children: Delfino, Celita. BS in Geology cum laude, Yale U., 1956, PhD in Geology, 1964; MA in Geology, Rice U., 1958. Research staff geologist Yale U., New Haven, 1963-64; mgr. nuclear geochemistry dept. Teledyne Isotopes, Westwood, NJ, 1968-70, v.p., 1970-75, pres., 1975-93; engring. group exec. Teledyne, Inc., Westwood, 1989-92; chief scientist Teledyne Environ. Systems, 1992-93; gen. mgr. Teledyne Brown Engring. Environ. Svcs., 1993—99; v.p. Teledyne Environ., Inc., 1996-99; pres. Geonuclear, Inc., 1999—. Low level waste adv. com. N.J. Dept. Environ. Protection, Trenton, 1988-90; chmn. com. on radioactive materials N.J. BIA, Trenton, 1980-88. Pres. Children's Aid and Adoption Soc. N.J. Inc., Bogota, 1976-95, Am. Amateur Judo Found., River Vale, N.J., 1979-89; bd. visitors Berry Coll., 1985—; bd. dirs. Yale U. Alumni Fund, 1989-94; co-chmn. Children's Aid and Family Svcs. Inc., 1995-96, bd. dirs. emeritus, 2000—. Recipient Antarctic Service medal U.S. Congress, 1964. Mem.: World Fedn. Engring. Orgns. (mem. environ. com. 2005—, mem. energy com. 2006—), Am. Assn. Engring. Soc. (engrs. forum on sustainable devel. 1995—, internat. activities com.), Am. Nuc. Soc. (chmn. no. N.J. sect. 1988—89, pub. policy com. 1991—96, coord. climate change and sustainable devel. activities UN 1994—, chair environ. scis. divsn. 1995—96, vice chair 2000—01, chair 2001—02), Am. Assn. Radon Sci. and Tech. (life; pres. 1986—89, treas. 1990—95), Yale Sci. and Engring. Alumni Assn. (bd. dirs. Bergen County and vicinity chpt. 1989—), Sigma Xi. Office Phone: 201-391-2790. E-mail: donald.schutz@aya.yale.edu.

**SCHUTZER, KAREN ANN,** nurse; b. Detroit, Jan. 22, 1958; d. Melvin and Pauline Gordon; m. Robert Allen Schutzer, Apr. 22, 1989; children: Lauren Jean, Jake Maxwell. BSN, Mercy Coll. Detroit, 1977—81; MS, Fla. Atlantic U., Boca Raton, 1998—2004. RN State of Mich., 1981. Nursing asst. Children's Hosp. Mich., Detroit, 1979—81; med.-surg. nurse Henry Ford Hosp., Detroit, 1981—82; critical care, surg. ICU Jackson Meml. Hosp., Miami, Fla., 1985—88; cardiac rehab staff nurse Meml. Hosp., Hollywood, Fla., 1988—94; dir., cardiac rehab. Glades Gen. Hosp., Belle Glade, Fla., 1996—; adj. faculty, nursing Palm Beach C.C., Lake Worth, Fla., 2004—. Contbr. articles to profl. jours. Mem.: FACVPR. Avocations: travel, camping, running, gardening. Office Phone: 561-996-6571.

**SCHUTZKY, MARILYN HORSLEY,** artist; b. Soda Springs, Idaho, July 13, 1936; d. Earl James and Alta (Bollwinkel) Horsley; m. Victor Sergay Schutzky, Oct. 11, 1957; children: Allen Victor, Sandra Kristin. Student, U. Calif., Berkeley, 1954—55, U. Utah, 1955—57. Free-lance artist, 1957—. One-woman shows include Design Concepts, Alamo, Calif., 1991, Harbor Studio Gallery, Gig Harbor, 1991, Back Bay Gardens Gallery, Corte Madera. Calif., 1988, St. Paul Towers, Oakland, Calif., 1988, Marin Arts Guild, Larkspur, Calif., 1986, Two Birds, Forest Knolls, Calif., 1983, Avoir Gallery, Kirkland, Wash., 1993, 94, Andrea Schwartz Gallery, San Francisco, 1990, 95, Glendale (Ariz.) C.C., 1997, Sun Cities Mus. Art, 1997, Ch. of Beatitudes, Phoenix, 1994, 2003, Mayo Hosp. Gallery, 2001, Mayo Clinic Concourse Gallery, 2002, Chasby Sachs, 2005, El Dorado Gallery, 2003; exhibited in groups shows at Waterworks 1992, 93, 94, 95, Seattle Conv. Ctr., Grand Exhbn. 1992, Akron (Ohio) Soc. of Artists, Howard Mandeville Gallery, Kirkland, 1992, The Nut Tree, 1991, Kaiser Gallery, 1991, Ariz. Aqueous, Tubac, 1993, 95, 96, 97, 2002, 03, 06, Suncities Mus., Phoenix, 1994, 97, We. Fedn. Watercolor Socs., Phoenix, 1994, Ariz. State U., Frye Art Mus., 1999, Ariz. Watercolor Assn., 1999-2006 (10 awards including Best of Show), Chandler Ctr. for Arts (Merit award), Calif. Watercolor Assn. Art Inst. San Francisco, 1999, 2002, 03 (Pres.'s award 2001), Nat. Watercolor Soc. (Signature award 2003), Challenge of the Champions, Houston, 2003, Mo. Watercolor Soc., 2003, Hilton Head Nat., 2003, Rocky Mtn. Nat., 2003, San Diego Internat., 2003, 2004, NW Watercolor Soc. Waterworks, 2003, 04, 06 (award), Ga. Watercolor Nat., 2004, Emerald Art Ctr., Oreg., 2006, Pa. Watercolor Soc., 2006; Basic Flower Painting--Techniques in Watercolor, 1996, The Artistic Touch II-Chris Unwin, 1996, The Artistic Touch III-Chris Unwin, 1999, AWA Celebrating 40 Years of Watermedia Fine Arts, 2001, Watercolor Magic: Creativity, 2001, Painting from the Inside Out, 2002; regional exhbns. include D'Art, Dallas, 1993, Kimball Art Ctr., Park City, Utah, 2001, The Albuquerque Mus., 2002, Barrick Mus., Las Vegas, 2003; spl. exhbns include Foothills Art Ctr., 2000 (Friends of Art award), Frye Art Mus., Seattle, 2000, Foothills Art Ctr., 2003, Hilton Head Nat., 2003, Watercolor Art Soc., 2003, Calif. Watercolor Art Soc., 2003, Ga. Wateracolor Nat., 2004, Contemporary Watercolorists Ariz., 2000-06 (6 awards), Shemer Art Ctr. and Mus., 2005, Chandler Ctr. Arts, 2005, others. Recipient 1st award Frye Art Mus., 1990, James Copley Purchase award San Diego Watercolor Soc., 1988, 2d Pl. award The Artist's Mag., 1993, Excellence award We. Fedn. Watercolor Socs., 1993, award San Diego Internat. Watercolor Exhbn., 1998, award Kans. Watercolor Soc., 2006, award Watercolor Art Soc.-Houston, 2006, numerous others. Mem. N.W. Watercolor Soc. (Past Pres.'s award 1992, Signature award 1992, Merit award 1993), Marin Soc. Artists, Ariz. Watercolor Assn. (awarded Coatimundi Soc. membership, Royal Scorpion membership), Calif. Watercolor Soc. (Signature award 1989), Fedn. Can. Artists, Marin County Watercolor Soc., Watercolor West (Barr award 1995, Signature award 1995). Home: 7340 E Turquoise Ave Scottsdale AZ 85258-1220 also: Marilyn Schutzky Studio 7340 E Turquoise Ave Scottsdale AZ 85258-1220 Office Phone: 480-951-3472. E-mail: mschutzky@cox.net.

**SCHUUR, DIANE JOAN,** vocalist; b. Tacoma, Dec. 10, 1953; d. David Schuur. Singer: (albums) Pilot of My Destiny, 1983, Deedles, Schuur Thing, 1986, Timeless (Grammy award for female jazz vocal, 1986), Diane Schuur and the Count Basie Orchestra (Grammy award for female jazz vocal, 1987), Talkin' 'Bout You, 1988, Pure Schuur, 1991 (#1 on Billboard contemporary jazz chart, 1991, nominated for Grammy award, 1991), In Tribute, 1992, Love Songs, 1993 (Grammy nomination Best Traditional Vocal Grammy nomination for The Christmas Song), Love Walked In, 1996, Blues For Schuur, 1997, The Best of Diane Schuur, 1997, Music Is My Life, 1999, Friends for Schuur, 2000; singer: (with B.B. King) Heart to Heart, 1994 (No. 1 on Billboard contemporary jazz chart); singer: (with Maynard Ferguson) 'Swingin' for Schuur, 2001, Midnight, 2003; singer: Schuur Fire, 2005, (performances) White House, Monterey Jazz Festival, Hollywood Bowl, Carnegie Hall, Moscow Symphony, (tours) Japan, Far East, Near East, South Am., Europe, South Africa. Recipient 1st Ella Fitzgerald ann. award, Montreal Jazz Festival, 1999, Helen Keller Personal Achievement award, Am. Found. Blind, 2000. Office Phone: 949-240-4400. Personal E-mail: paulcantor@cox.net. *"There is no plateau that can't be reached, no obstacle that can't be overcome if you believe in yourself and your higher power".*

**SCHUURMAN, WILLEM GERHARD,** lawyer; b. June 21, 1940; s. William B. and Rina (Du Preez) S.; m. Karla Arnold, Feb. 15, 2001; children: Greg W., Bruce J., Angus D. D. Geordie. BS, U. Cape Town, South Africa, 1962, LLB, 1964; JD magna cum laude, South Tex. Coll. Law, 1981. Bar: Tex. 1981, U.S. Dist. Ct. (so. dist.) Tex. 1982, U.S. Dist. Ct. (we. dist.) Tex. 1985. Prtnr. Adams & Adams, Pretoria, South Africa, 1967—79; assoc. Arnold, White & Durkee, Houston, 1979—83, prtnr., 1983—98; prtnr., intellectual property sect. head Vinson & Elkins LLP, Austin, Tex., 1998—. Mem.: ABA, Internat. Assn. for the Protection of Indsl. Property, Travis County Bar Assn., Internat. Fedn. Indsl. Property Attys. U.S., Am. Intellectual Property Law Assn., Westwood Country Club. Office: Vinson & Elkins LLP Terrace 7 2801 Via Fortuna Ste 100 Austin TX 78746-7568 Office Phone: 512-542-8663. Business E-Mail: bschuurman@velaw.com.

**SCHWAAB, RICHARD LEWIS,** lawyer; b. Oconomowoc, Wis., Nov. 15, 1945; s. Thomas L. and Phyllis N. (Lord) S.; m. Lynn Louise Howie; children: Amy, William, Andrew, Matthew. BSChemE, U. Wis., 1967; JD with honors, George Washington U., 1971, LLM in Internat. Law with highest honors, 1979. Bar: Va. 1971, U.S. Dist. Ct. (ea. dist.) Va. 1979, U.S. Supreme Ct. 1980, U.S. Ct. Appeals (fed. cir.) 1982, D.C. 1998. Ptnr. Stepno, Schwaab & Linn, Arlington, 1974-78, Schwaab, Jeffrey, Schwaab, Mack, Blumenthal & Evans, P.C., Alexandria, 1978-88; ptnr. in charge, chair dept. intellectual property Foley & Lardner, Washington, 1988-99, ptnr., 1999—. Lectr. law George Washington U., 1978-88, George Mason U., 1989—. Max Planck

Inst. Fgn. and Internat. Patent, Copyright and Competition Law fellow, 1971-72. Co-author Patent Practice, 6 vols., 1976-99, International Patent Law: EPC & PCT, 3 vols., 1978; Intellectual Property Protection for Biotechnology Worldwide, 1987; contbr. articles to profl. jours. Mem. ABA, Am. Intellectual Property Law Assn., Va. State Bar (gov. 1974-78), Am. Soc. Internat. Law, Internat. Patent and Trademark Assn., Internat. Fedn. Indsl. Property Attys., Christian Legal Soc., Phi Kappa Phi, Tau Beta Pi. Home: 34205 Nashotah Rd Nashotah WI 53058-9534 Office: Foley & Lardner 3000 K St NW Ste 500 Washington DC 20007-5143 E-mail: rschwaab@foleylaw.com.*

**SCHWAB, ARTHUR JAMES,** lawyer; b. Pitts., Dec. 7, 1946; s. Earl Walter and Helen Alice (Gascoine) S.; m. Karen Jenny, Sept. 2, 1967; children: John Arthur, Ellen Katherine, David Earl. Student, Muskingum Coll., 1964-65; AB, Grove City Coll., 1968; JD, U. Va., 1972. Bar: Pa. 1972, N.J. 1985, U.S. Dist. Ct. (we. dist.) Pa. 1972, U.S. Dist. Ct. (ea dist.) Pa. 1978, U.S. Dist. Ct. (no. dist.) Ohio 1979, U.S. Dist. Ct. S.C. 1980, U.S. Dist. Ct. N.Mex. 1981, U.S. Dist. Ct. Mass. 1984, U.S. Dist. Ct. N.J. 1984, U.S. Ct. Appeals (3d cir.) 1972, U.S. Ct. Appeals (11th cir.) 1982, U.S. Ct. Appeals (4th cir.) 1982, U.S. Ct. Appeals (8th cir.) 1991, U.S. Ct. Appeals (9th cir.) 1995, U.S. Supreme Ct. 1975. Ptnr. Reed, Smith, Shaw and McClay, Pitts., 1973-90; ptnr., chair of litigation Buchanan Ingersoll, Pitts., 1990-99, chief counsel complex litig., 2000—. Mem. faculty Grove City Coll., U. Va. Trial Advocacy Program. Mem. editorial bd. Va. Law Rev., Sch. Law U. Va., Charlottesville, 1972. Bd. dirs. Grove City (Pa.) Coll. Mem. Pa. Bar Assn. (past chair civil litigation sect.), Acad. Trial Lawyers Allegheny County (past mem. bd. dirs.), Allegheny County Bar Assn., (past chair civil litigation sect.), Am. Inns of Ct. (past pres. Pitts. chpt.), Duquesne Club. Republican. Presbyterian. Office: Buchanan Ingersoll One Oxford Ctr 301 Grant St Fl 20 Pittsburgh PA 15219-1410 Home: 104 Applehill Ct Gibsonia PA 15044-8064

**SCHWAB, CHARLES R.,** brokerage house executive; b. Sacramento, 1937; m. Helen O'Neill; 5 children. BA in Economics, Stanford U., 1959, MBA, 1961. Formerly mut. fund mgr., Marin County, Calif.; founder, chmn. Charles Schwab Corp., San Francisco, 1971—, CEO, chmn., 1971—2003, chmn. 2003—04, CEO, chmn., 2004—. Bd. dirs. The Gap, Inc., 1986—2004, Seibel Systems, Inc. Author: How to be Your Own Stockbroker, 1984, Guide to Financial Independence, 1998, You're Fifty - Now What?, 2001; co-author (with Carrie Schwab Pomerantz): It Pays To Talk. Chmn. All Kinds of Minds Inst.; co-founder (with Helen Schwab) and chmn. Charles and Helen Schwab Found., 2001—; bd. trustees Stanford U. Named one of Top 200 Collectors, ARTnews Mag., 2004, 2005, 2006, 50 Most Generous Philanthropists, BusinessWeek, 2005, Forbes' Richest Americans, 2006. Republican. Achievements include pioneer in discount brokerage business since 1974. Avocation: collector of modern & contemporary art. Office: Charles Schwab & Co Inc 101 Montgomery St San Francisco CA 94104-4175*

**SCHWAB, DONALD PETER,** finance educator; s. Peter Franklin Earl and Verna A. Schwab; m. Lois A. Mangen, Sept. 10, 1960; children: Spencer E., Thomas W. BA, U. Minn., 1960, MS, 1964, PhD, 1967. Asst. prof. U. Wis., Madison, Wis., 1967—69, assoc. prof., 1970—73, prof., 1974—2004, emeritus prof., 2004—; vis. prof. U. Ky., Lexington, Ky., 1972—73, U. Minn., Mnpls., 1980—80, Purdue U., West Lafayette, Ind., 1986—86. Author: Research methods for organizational studies, 2005. Fellow: APA, Soc. Indsl. and Orgnl. Psychology, Acad. Mgmt. (life; chmn. personnel human resources divsn. 1980—81, Career Achievement award 1994). Office: University of Wisconsin - Madison 975 University Ave Madison WI 53706-1323 Personal E-mail: don_schwab@hotmail.com.

**SCHWAB, EILEEN CAULFIELD,** lawyer, educator; b. NYC, Feb. 11, 1944; d. James and Mary (Fay) Caulfield; m. Terrance W. Schwab, Jan. 4, 1969 (dec. Apr. 25, 2004); children: Matthew, Catherine Welykoridko, Claire. BA, Hunter Coll., 1965; JD, Columbia U., 1971. Bar: N.Y. 1972, U.S. Dist. Ct. (so. and ea. dists.) N.Y. 1975, U.S. Ct. Appeals (2d cir.) 1975, U.S. Tax Ct. 1980, U.S. Ct. Appeals (10th cir.) 1993. Assoc. Poletti Friedin, N.Y.C., 1971-72, Hughes Hubbard & Reed, N.Y.C., 1972-75, Davis Polk & Wardwell, N.Y.C., 1975-81; dep. bur. chief Charities Bur., Atty. Gen. of N.Y., 1981-82; counsel Sidley Austin LLP, N.Y.C., 1983—, ptnr., 1984. Adj. prof. N.Y. Law Sch. Trustee, sec., exec. com. Caramoor Ctr. Music and the Arts; trustee Cath. Communal Fund; chair planned gifts, bequests and endowment com. Archdiocese of NY; mem. profl. adv. com. Mus. Modern Art, Met. Mus. Art, Cen. Park Conservancy, Calvary Hosp., Mus. Arts and Design, N.Y. Pub. Libr., Meml. Sloan-Kettering Cancer Ctr.; chmn. adv. com. Ascension Sch.; trustee Cooke Ctr. Learning and Devel. Fellow Am. Coll. Trust and Estate Counsel; mem. N.Y. State Bar Assn., Phi Beta Kappa. Democrat. Roman Catholic. Office Phone: 212-839-5300. Personal E-mail: eschwab@sidley.com.

**SCHWAB, ERNEST ROE, III,** physiology educator, researcher; b. Denver, Colo., July 19, 1950; s. Ernest Roe and Mary Ellen (Murray) S.; m. Patty Ann Millspaugh, May 16, 1974. PhD, Loma Linda U., Loma Linda, California, 1981—89; M.S., Andrews U., Berrien Springs, MI, 1975—78; B.A., Union Coll., Lincoln, NE, 1969—75. Assoc. prof. Allied Health studies, assoc. dean academic affairs Sch. of Allied Health Professions, Loma Linda U., Loma Linda, Calif., 1996—; assoc. prof. of biology La Sierra U., Riverside, Calif., 1991—96; assist. prof. of biology Loma Linda U., Riverside, Calif., 1983—91. Author (secondary author): (published and presented research) Variety of Scientific Journals and Congresses. Mem. Calif. chpt. Nat. Wildlife Fedn., 1981. Recipient Godfrey T. Anderson Award for Excellence in Tchg., Loma Linda U., 1990, Cert. of Merit, Nat. Academic Advising Assn., 1994; grantee Rsch. Opportunity Award, NSF, 1989. Mem. AAAS, Entomol. Soc. Am. (news service liaison 1986—), Union Concerned Scientists, Scientists Action Network, Internat. Bee Research Assn., Internat. Union for the Study of Social Insects, N.Y. Acad. Scis., Sigma Xi (Grad. Student Research grantee 1979), Nat. Acad. Adv. Assn. (Cert. of Merit 1994), Soc. for Neurosci., Internat. Soc. for Neuroethology, Soc. Integrative of Comparative Biology. Democrat. Sda. Avocations: photography, travel, backpacking, piano. Home: 423 Marilyn Lane Redlands CA 92373 Office: Loma Linda University 11234 Anderson St Loma Linda CA 92350-0001 Personal E-mail: acheta1@earthlink.net. Business E-Mail: eschwab@llu.edu.

**SCHWAB, EVAN LYNN,** lawyer; b. Detroit, Apr. 13, 1938; s. Joe Schwab and Vanita Dobbs; m. Heidi Jensen, June 11, 1960 (div. Dec. 1975); children: Mari, Eric, Peter; m. Carole Fuller, Mar. 12, 1976; 1 child, William. BA, U. Wash., 1961, LLB with high honors, 1963. Bar: Wash. 1964, U.S. Dist. Ct. (we. dist.) Wash. 1966, U.S. Supreme Ct. 1967; CPA. Law clk. U.S. Supreme Ct. Justice William O. Douglas, Washington, 1963-64; assoc. Davis, Wright & Jones, Seattle, 1964-69, ptnr., 1969-88, Bogle & Gates, Seattle, 1988—99, co-chair dept. litigation, 1992—99; ptnr. trial group Dorsey & Whitney LLP, Seattle, 1999—; chair Seattle Trial Group, 2005—. 2d. lt. USAR, 1962-64. Fellow: Am. Coll. Trial Lawyers (chmn. Wash. state com. 2005—); mem.: ABA, Seattle-King County Bar Assn., Wash. State Bar Assn., Fed. Bar Assn. Western Dist. Wash. (pres. 1985—86), Wash. Athletic Club, Seattle Yacht Club (judge adv. 1986, 2005—). Avocations: sailing, skiing. Office: Dorsey & Whitney LLP Ste 3400 US Bank Ctr 1420 Fifth Ave Seattle WA 98101-4010 Office Phone: 206-903-8858. Office Fax: 206-903-8820. Business E-Mail: schwab.evan@dorsey.com.

**SCHWAB, FRANK, JR.,** management consultant; b. Brookline, Mass., Dec. 19, 1932; s. Frank Sr. and Phyllis (Robinson) F. BA, Rutgers U., 1952; MBA, Harvard Bus. Sch., 1956. Cert. mgmt. cons. Internal auditor Champion Paper, Inc., Hamilton, Ohio, 1956-57, mgmt. engr. Pasadena, Tex., 1957-58; cons., assoc. Booz Allen & Hamilton, N.Y.C., 1958-65; dir. trans. planning Planning Rsch. Corp., L.A., 1965; pres.; CEO F.R. Schwab & Assocs., N.Y.C., 1965-82; pres., co-CEO Fenvessy & Schwab, N.Y.C., 1982-87; pres., CEO Anderson & Schwab, N.Y.C., 1987—. Bd. dirs. Sugarland Oil Corp., N.Y.C., Nat. Mining Assn. (mfrs. and svcs. divsn.), Wash., D.C. Trustee Nat. Mining Hall of Fame and Mus., Leadville, Colo., 1992—. 1st lt. U.S. Army, 1952-54, Korea. Decorated Nat. Def. Svc. medal, Korean Svc. medal with bronze star, Commendation ribbon with medal pendant, UN Svc. medal; recipient medal for merit State of NY. Mem. Inst. Mgmt. Cons. (pres. N.Y. chpt. 1975-77),

Am. Arbitration Assn. (panel arbitrator), Mil. Order Fgn. Wars (vet. companion), Maidstone Club, Union Club, River Club, King Coal Club, Army and Navy Club. Republican. Avocation: tennis. Office: Anderson & Schwab Inc 444 Madison Ave New York NY 10022-6903 Fax: (212) 755-9576. Office Phone: 212-758-6800. Business E-Mail: fschwab@andersonschwab.com.

**SCHWAB, GEORGE DAVID,** social sciences educator, writer; b. Nov. 25, 1931; s. Arkady and Klara (Jacobson) S.; m. Eleonora Storch, Feb. 27, 1965; children: Clarence Boris, Claude Arkady, Solan Bernhard. BA, CCNY, 1954; MA, Columbia U., 1955, PhD, 1968. Lectr. Columbia Coll., N.Y.C., 1959, CUNY, 1960-68; asst. prof. history, 1968-72; assoc. prof. history, 1973-79; prof., 1980—2000; prof. emeritus, 2001—. Mem. Columbia U. Seminar on Law and Polit. Thought and Institutions; dir. Conf. History and Politics CUNY; with Nat. Com. Am. Fgn. Policy. Author: Dayez: Beyond Abstract Art, 1967, Enemy oder Foe, 1968, Switzerland's Tactical Nuc. Weapons Policy, 1969, The Challenge of the Exception: An Introduction to the Polit. Ideas of Carl Schmitt, 1970, 2nd edit., 1989, Appeasement and Detente, 1975, 81, Carl Schmitt: Polit. Opportunist?, 1975; translator: The Concept of the Polit. with Comments by Leo Strauss (Carl Schmitt), 1976, 96, Legality and Illegality as Instruments of Revolutionaries in Their Quest for Power, Remarks Occasioned by the Outlook of Herbert Marcuse, 1978, The German State in Hist. Perspective, 1978, Ideology: Reality or Rhetoric, 1978. Ideology and Fgn. Policy, 1978, 81, The Decision: Is the Am. Sovereign at Bay?, 1978, State and Nation: Toward a Further Clarification, 1980, Am. Fgn. Politics at the Crossroads, 1980, Carl Schmitt: Through a Glass Darkly, 1980, From Quantity and Heterogeneity to Quality and Homogeneity: Toward a New Foreign Policy, 1980, Toward an Open-Society Bloc, 1980, Eurocommunism: The Ideological and Political Theoretical Foundations, 1981, Am. Fgn. Policy at the Crossroads, 1982, A Decade of the Nat. Com. on Am. Fgn. Policy, 1984, (trans.) Polit. Theology: Four Chapters on the Concept of Sovereignty (Carl Schmitt), 1985, 88, 2005, The Destruction of a Family, 1987, Elie Wiesel: Between Jerusalem and New York, 1990, The Broken Vow, The Good Obtained, 1991, Thoughts of a Collector, 1991, Carl Schmitt Hysteria in the US, 1992, Contextualizing Carl Schmitt's Concept of Grossraum, 1994; (translator) The Leviathan in the State Theory of Thomas Hobbes (Carl Schmitt), 1996, Carl Schmitt, A Note on a Qualitative Authoritarian Bourgeois Liberal, 2000, The Nat. Com. on Am. Fgn. Policy's Focus on Russia, 2000, U.S. National Security Interests Today, 2003; editor Am. Fgn. Policy Interests; series Global Perspectives in History and Politics. Trustee, pres. mem. exec. com. Nat. Com. Am. Fgn. Policy; mem. Coun. on Fgn. Rels. Decorated Order of the Three Stars (Latvia); recipient Ellis Island medal of honor. Office: Nat Com Am Fgn Policy 320 Park Ave New York NY 10022-6815 Business E-Mail: george.schwab@ncafp.org, contact@ncafp.org.

**SCHWAB, HAROLD LEE,** lawyer; b. NYC, Feb. 5, 1932; s. Harold Walter and Beatrice (Braverman) S.; m. Rowena Vivian Strauss, June 12, 1953; children: Andrew, Lisa, James. BA, Harvard Coll., Cambridge, Mass., 1953; LLB, Boston Coll., 1956. Bar: NY 1957, U.S. Ct. Mil. Appeals 1958, U.S. Dist. Cts. (so. and ea. dists.) NY 1967, U.S. Dist. Ct. NY 1974, U.S. Dist. Ct. (we. dist.) NY 1988, U.S. Dist. Ct. Conn. 1995, U.S. Dist. Ct. (ea. and we. dists.) Ark. 2000, U.S. Ct. Appeals (2d cir.) 1971, U.S. Ct. Appeals (DC cir.) 1986, U.S. Ct. Appeals (11th cir.) 1988, U.S. Ct. Appeals (5th cir.) 1991, U.S. Supreme Ct. 1971. V.p. H.W. Schwab Textile Corp., NYC, 1959-60; assoc. Emile Z. Berman & A. Harold Frost, NYC, 1960-67, ptnr., 1967-74; sr. ptnr. Lester Schwab Katz & Dwyer, NYC, 1974—. Lectr. NY Jud. Seminars, 2000-02, 05, NY State Bar Assn., NY County Lawyers Assn.; examiner, Character and Fitness Com., First Jud. Dept., 2005. Contbr. articles to legal jours.; mem. editl. bd. Jour. Products and Toxics Liability, 1976-96. Served to lt. col. USAFR. Fellow Internat. Acad. Trial Lawyers; mem. ABA, ASTM, SAE, Assn. Advancement of Automotive Medicine, NY State Bar Assn. (chmn. trial lawyers sect. 1980-81, editor sect. newsletter 1981-84), Am. Bd. Trial Advs. (pres. NY chpt. 1982-83), Fedn. Ins. Counsel (v.p. 1979-80), NY State Trial Lawyers Assn., Def. Assn. NY, Harvard Club NY, Downtown Assn., Ft. Hamilton Officers Club. Home: 205 Beach 142 St Neponsit NY 11694 Office: Lester Schwab Katz & Dwyer 120 Broadway Fl 38 New York NY 10271-0071 Office Phone: 212-341-4234. Business E-Mail: hschwab@lskdnylaw.com.

**SCHWAB, HERMANN CASPAR,** banker; b. N.Y.C., Jan. 8, 1920; s. Hermann Caspar and Ruth (Bliss) S.; m. C. Meteer Shanks, July 5, 1955; children: Henry R., Lesley Schwab Forman, Margery Schwab Weekes, Stuart Taylor, George Bliss, Katharine Lambard Schwab Kimmick. Grad., St. Marks Sch., 1937, Yale U., 1941. With Hanover Bank, 1941-44, 46-55, asst. sec., 1949-53, asst. v.p., 1953-55; ptnr. Dick & Merle Smith, 1956; v.p. Empire Trust Co., 1957-66, sr. v.p., 1965-66; with Bank N.Y., 1966-67; sr. v.p. Schroder Trust Co., N.Y.C., 1967-73, dir., 1970-73; pres., dir. Cheapside Dollar Fund Ltd., N.Y.C., 1970-88; sr. v.p. Schroder Capital Mgmt. Inc., N.Y.C., 1973-84, cons., 1984-88. Chmn., dir. Schroder Capitol Funds Inc., 1988-98, trustee dir., 1998—. Mayor Oyster Bay Cove, N.Y., 1973-85, trustee, 1965-98; trustee St. Lukes-Roosevelt Hosp. Ctr., 1969-99. 2d lt. inf., AUS, 1943-46. Mem. Piping Rock Club (Locust Valley, N.Y.). Home: 34 Northern Blvd Oyster Bay NY 11771-4105

**SCHWAB, JOHN H.,** psychologist; b. NYC, Apr. 19, 1952; s. Armand Schwab Jr. and Lois F. Schwab; m. Robin Lynn Smith, Apr. 22, 1982; children: Peter, Rachel. BA in English, Middlebury Coll., Vt., 1975; MFA in Directing, Boston U., 1979; MA in Psychology, Seattle U., 1992; PhD in Clin. Psychology, Seattle Pacific U., 2001. Lic. clin. psychologist Wash., 2004. Pvt. practical clin. psychologist, Seattle, 1992—. Mem.: APA. Office Phone: 206-780-3976. E-mail: jhschwab@mindspring.com.

**SCHWAB, JOHN JOSEPH,** psychiatrist, educator; b. Cumberland, Md., Feb. 10, 1923; s. Joseph L. and Eleanor (Cadden) S.; m. Ruby Baxter, Aug. 4, 1945; 1 dau., Mary Eleanor. BS, U. Ky., 1946; MD, U. Louisville, 1946; MS in Physiology (Med. fellow), U. Ill., 1949; postgrad., Duke U., 1951-52, U. Fla., 1959-61. Diplomate: Nat. Bd. Med. Examiners. Intern Phila. Gen. Hosp., 1947-48; resident medicine Louisville Gen. Hosp., 1949-50; info. officer med. coll. U. Yokohama, 1952-54; internist, psychosomaticist Holzer Clinic, Gallipolis, Ohio, 1954-59; resident psychiatry U. Fla. Hosp., 1959-61; NIMH Career tchr. U. Fla., Gainesville, 1962-64, mem. faculty, 1961-73, prof. psychiatry and medicine, 1967-73, dir. cons. liaison program, 1964-67, resident tng. dir., 1965-71; prin. investigator Fla. Health Study, 1969-74; prof., chmn. dept. psychiatry and behavioral scis. Sch. Medicine U. Louisville, 1973-91, prof. psychiatry, 1991-93, prof. emeritus 1993—, assoc. dir. clin. psychopharm. rsch., 1991—. Chmn. epidemiologic studies rev. com. Ctr. for Epidemiologic Studies, NIMH, 1973-75, cons. psychiatry br., 1975-92; cons. Old Order Amish Study of Depression, 1978—; vol. vis. lectr. Howard U., 1992; ann. vis. lectr. U. Würzburg, Germany, hon. faculty, 1992—; vis. prof. El-Azar U., Cairo, 1991; prin. investigator LSVL Family Health Study, 1982—; dir. U. Fla. Coll. Med. Program: History and Philosophy of Medicine, 1967-72; mem. instn;. rsch. rev. bd. U. Louisville, 2003—. Author: Handbook of Psychiatric Consultation, 1968; also articles; co-author: Sociocultural Roots of Mental Illness: An Epidemiologic Survey, 1978, Social Order and Mental Health, 1979; assoc. editor Psychosomatics, 1965-86; co-editor: Man for Humanity: On Concordance V. Discord in Human Behavior, 1972, Social Psychiatry, vol. 1, 1974, The Psychiatric Examination, 1974, first author Family Mental Health History, Epidem, Clinical Health Issues, 1993, first author Family Functioning: The General Living Systems Research Model, 2000; co-edited 9 books, 11 Monographs, and over 250 articles. Capt. USAMC, 1949-54. Recipient Disting. Mental Health award Mental Health Assn. Ky., 1992. Fellow Am. Coll. Psychiatrists (regent 1977-79), Collegium Internat. Neuro-Psychopharmacologicum, World Assn. Social Psychiatry, AAAS, Am. Psychiat. Assn. (chmn. council research and devel. 1974-75); mem. AMA, Acad. Psychosomatic Medicine (exec. com. 1965-72, pres. 1970-71), Group for Advancement Psychiatry (bd. dirs. 1985-87), So. Assn., Jefferson County Med. Soc., Ky. Psychiat. Assn., Am. Assn. Social Psychiatry (pres. 1971-73), Alpha Omega Alpha, (Outstanding Performance award for Affirmative Action U. Louisville 1986), World Assn. Soc. Psychiatry (internat. adv. com., Rome, 1991), Psychiatrists for Better Psychiat. (pres.

1990-99), U. of the World (co-chair health, edn. com. 1992-98). Achievements include research on applicability of psychiatric concepts to general medicine, sociocultural aspects of mental illness; establishing guidelines for identification and management of medical patients with illnesses complicated by emotional stress; epidemiology of mental illness; depression and the family; clinical psychopharmacology, historical and epidemiologic perspectives on the family. Home: 6217 Innes Trace Rd Louisville KY 40222-6008

**SCHWAB, JUDITH,** artist, educator, sculptor; b. Phila., Feb. 22, 1935; d. Henry Ellick and Eleanor Adelman; m. Ralph Schwab, 1956; children: Linda Deutsch, Andrea Cohen. BA cum laude, Kean Coll., N.J., 1975; postgrad., Rutgers U., Union, N.J., 1978—79; MFA in Sculpture, U. Del., Newark, 1986. Cert. art tchr. Pa. Substitute art tchr. Manalapan-Englishtown Pub. Schs., Englishtown, NJ, 1970—77, art tchr., 1978—79; artist Sterk Sch. Hearing Impaired, Newark, Del., 1981, art tchr., 1982; vis. artist, facilitator Xian Art Sch., Xian, China, 1998; substitute art tchr. Del. Pub. Schs., Wilmington, 1990—93; art tchr. Shortlidge Elem. Sch., Wilmington, 1994—98. Initiator internat. exchanges Pacem in Terris, 1998; lectr. in field. One-woman shows include No. Ariz. U. Art Gallery, Flagstaff, 1985, Thompson Park Gallery, Lincroft, N.J., 1985, West Gallery and East Gallery, 1995, U. Tenn. Art Galleries I and II, Chattanooga, 1987, Susan Isaacs Gallery, Wilmington, 1990, U. Del. Clayton Hall Conv. Ctr. Gallery, 1990, Ctrl. House of Art, Tbilisi, Ga., Russia, 1991, Del. Ctr. for Contemporary Art, 1991, Jewish Cmty. Ctr. Art Gallery, 1993, Cecil CC Cultural Art Ctr., 2005, exhibited in group shows at Del. Art Mus., 1991—92, The Lorelton Gallery, Wilmington, 1999, U. Del., 1992—94, Xian Art Sch., 1998, Artemis Gallery, Richmond, Va., 1999—2001, Synergy Gallery, West Palm Beach, Fla. 2000—01, Del. Art Mus., Wilmington, 2001—04, Grace Gallery, 2005, Cecil Cultural Arts Ctr., Cecil C.C., 2005, East of the Bay Gallery, Md., 2006, Ft. Lauderdale History Mus., 2006, Represented in permanent collections Corp. Holding Svcs., One on One Fitness Ctr., Wilmington, Skadden Arps Slate Meagher and Flom, Salva Profl. Assn., The Arches, Del. History Mus. Mem. Nat. Mus. for Women in the Arts, NOW; bd. dirs. People to People Internat., 1993—2000, Jewish Family Svc., Wilmington, 1983—84, Grantee, U. Del., 1985; Emerging Artist fellowship in Sculpture, Del. Divsn. of the Arts, 1986—87, Established Artist fellow in Sculpture, 1993—94, Art fellow, Del. State Arts Coun., 1993—94, Opportunity grantee in Painting, Del. Divsn. of the Arts, 2005. Mem.: Del. Ctr. for Contemporary Art, Del. Art Mus. Avocations: dance, yoga, music, ceramics, voice. Office: 9325 Lagoon Pl #209 Fort Lauderdale FL 33324 Office Phone: 954-452-4615.

**SCHWAB, SHARON KAY,** language arts educator, drama educator; d. Edward Alvin Hutchins and Ida Lena Smith-Hutchins; m. Frank John Schwab, May 26, 2006; children: John, Michael, David. BS in Edn., So. Ill. U., Edwardsville, 1992; MA in Edn., Greenville Coll., Ill., 2005. 6th, 7th and 8th grade lang. arts tchr. Gillespie Mid. Sch., Ill., 1993—, 8th grade peer mediation tchr., 1997—2001, 6th grade drama tchr., 2003—. Mem. Ch. of the Ascension, Mt. Olive, Ill., 1973—. Roman Catholic. Avocations: travel, gardening, woodworking. Office: Gillespie Middle School 412 Oregon St Gillespie IL 62033 Office Phone: 217-839-2116.

**SCHWAB, STEWART JON,** dean, law educator; b. 1954; BA, Swarthmore U., 1975, JD, 1980; PhD, Mich. U., 1981. Bar: D.C. 1982. Law clk. to Hon. J. Dickson Phillips U.S. Ct. Appeals (4th cir.), 1981-82; law clk. to Hon. Sandra O'Connor U.S. Superior Ct, 1982-83; from asst. prof. to prof. law Cornell U. Law Sch., Ithaca, NY, 1983—2003, dean, 2004—; disting. visiting prof. U. Nebr. Coll. Law, Lincoln, 2003; Fulbright sr. scholar Australian Nat. Univ. Ctr. for Law & Econ., Canberra, 1998. Vis. fellow Centre Socio-Legal Studies Oxford U., 1990; vis. rsch. prof. U. Va. Law Sch., 1991; vis. prof. U. Mich. Law Sch., 1988, Duke Law Sch., 1999-2000. Editor: Jour. Empirical Legal Studies, 2004—. Mem. Am. Econ. Assn., Am. Judicature Assn., Order of Coif; City of Ithaca bd. zoning appeals, 1985-88. Office: Cornell Law Sch 263 Myron Taylor Hall Ithaca NY 14853-4901 Office Phone: 607-255-3527. Office Fax: 607-255-7193. Business E-Mail: stewart-schwab@postoffice.law.cornell.edu, sjs15@cornell.edu.

**SCHWAB, SUSAN CARROLL,** ambassador, former academic administrator; b. Washington, Mar. 23, 1955; d. Gerald and Joan Inga (Newton) Schwab. BA in Polit. Economy, Williams Coll., 1976; MA in Devel. Policy, Stanford U., 1977; PhD in Pub. Adminstrn., George Washington U., 1993. US trade negotiator Office of US Trade Rep., Washington, 1977-79; internat. economist & trade policy officer U.S. Embassy, Tokyo, 1980-81; chief economist, legis. asst. for internat. trade for Senator John C. Danforth, Washington, 1981-86, legis. dir., 1986—89; asst. sec. commerce, dir. gen. US and Fgn. Comml. Svc. US Dept. Commerce, Washington, 1989-93; dir. corp. bus. devel. Motorola, Inc., Schaumburg, Ill., 1993-95; dean U. Md. Sch. Pub. Affairs, College Park, 1995—2003; pres., CEO U. Md. Found., Adelphi, Md., 2004—05; vice chancellor U. Md. Sys., Adelphi, Md., 2004—05; US Trade Rep. Exec. Office of the Pres., Washington, 2005—06, US Trade Rep., 2006—. Bd. dirs. Calpine Corp., 1997—2005. Office: US Trade Rep 600 17th St NW Rm 200 Washington DC 20508 Office Phone: 301-445-1941.*

**SCHWALB, BRIAN L.,** lawyer; b. Washington, Sept. 24, 1967; married; 3 children. AB magna cum laude, Duke Univ., 1989; JD cum laude, Harvard Univ., 1992. Bar: Va. 1992, Md. 1993, DC 1998, US Dist. Ct. (ea. dist. Va., DC, Md.), US Ct. Appeals (4th, DC cir.), US Supreme Ct. Law clk. Judge John R. Hargrove, Sr., US Dist. Ct., Md. Dist., 1992—93. Asst. U.S. Dept. Justice, tax div., 1994—98, pvt. practice, 1998—2004; ptnr., Comml. Litigation practice Venable LLP, Washington, 2005—. Mem.: ABA, Md. State Bar Assn., Va. State Bar Assn., DC Bar Assn., Phi Beta Kappa. Office: Venable LLP 575 7th St NW Washington DC 20004 Office Phone: 202-344-4356. Office Fax: 202-344-8300. Business E-Mail: blschwalb@venable.com.

**SCHWALB, SUSAN AMELIA,** artist, educator; b. N.Y.C., Feb. 26, 1944; d. Morris and Evelyn C. Schwalb; m. Martin Boykan, Nov. 6, 1983. BFA, Carnegie-Mellon U., 1965. Designer Dell Pub. Co. N.Y.C., 1965—67; asst. art dir. Holt, Rinehart & Winston, N.Y.C., 1967—68; instr. art Kean Coll., Union, NJ, 1978—79; adj. lectr. CUNY, 1979—82; assoc. vis. prof. Mass. Coll. Art, Boston, 2002—91; spl. instr. Simmons Coll., 1988. Dir. Internat. Festival of Women Artists, Copenhagen, 1979-81; artist-in-residence Tel Aviv Artists Studios, 1994, Mishkenot Sha'ananim, Jerusalem, 1994. Represented in permanent collections Silverpoint Drawings, Norton Mus. Art, West Palm Beach, Fla., Fogg Art Mus., Harvard U., Chase Manhattan Bank, N.Y., Ark. Arts Ctr. Found., Little Rock, Mus. Modern Art, Belgrade, Sebria, Boston Pub. Libr., Brit. Mus., London, Bklyn. Mus., Israel Mus., Jerusalem, Mus. Fine Arts, Boston, Rose Art Mus., Yale U. Art Gallery, New Haven, RISD Mus. Art, Houghton Libr., Harvard U., Mus. Contemporary Religious Art, St. Louis, Yeshiva U. Mus., N.Y.C., Libr. of Congress, Wash., D.C., Nat. Mus. Women in Arts, Mus. Modern Art, N.Y.C., Mpls. Inst. Art, Nat. Gallery Art, Washington, D.C., Danforth Mus., Mass., Reed Coll., Oreg., Atheneaum, LaJolla, Calif. Del., Internat. Women's Yr. Conv., Houston, 1977, mem. Presdl. Continuing Commn. Conf., 1978; bd. dirs. Watertown Cultural Coun., 1991-96. Vis. Ctr. for Creative Arts fellow, 1973, 92; MacDowell Colony fellow, 1974, 75, 89; Yaddo fellow, 1981. Mem. Coalition Women's Art Orgns. (founding exec. com. 1977-78, v.p. 1985-87, nat. advd. bd. 1987—), Women's Caucus for Art (co-coord. Boston chpt. 1982-83), Coll. Art Assn. (com. on status of women 1991-94). Democrat. Jewish. Home: 10 Winsor Ave Watertown MA 02472-1460 Office: 233 E 21st St Apt 3 New York NY 10010-6444 Office Phone: 212-674-3434.

**SCHWALBE, LOWELL D,** secondary school educator; b. Waverly, Minn., July 29, 1938; s. Edward F Schwalbe and Alma Louise Splettstoezzer; children: Cameron, Elissa, Juddson, Deirdre, Rebecca, Robin, Melanie, Bret, Tisa, Keira. BS in Edn., U. Minn., 1961; MS in Edn., Mankato State Coll., 1971; MS in Adminstrn., U. Minn., Mankato, 1975; ABD, U. Northern Colo., 1985. Secondary sch. music tchr., adminstr., elem./secondary asst. supt. schs.; ret. Dir. Moose County Telecomms. Project; cert. real estate sales agt. Ctrl. Minn. Author: Educanese Rebuked, 2004, Educanese Revisited, 2005, (novels) Alma Louise, 2005, composer C16-26-16 and Deca. Bd. mem. East

Ctrl. Regional Libr., Cambridge, Minn., 2005—; ch. choir dir.; founder Mille Lacs County Kiosk Project; mem. east ctrl. regional libr. commn. Mem.: Am. Composers Forum. Office Phone: 612-859-8460. Personal E-mail: dearoled@ecenet.com.

SCHWALLER, JOHN FREDERICK, academic administrator, historian, educator; b. Hays, Kans., July 2, 1948; s. Henry and Juliette (Trembly) S.; m. Anne Cardot Taylor, Aug. 15, 1970; children: Robert Clemens, William Henry. AB, Grinnell (Ia.) Coll., 1969; MA, U. Kans., 1971; PhD, Ind. U., 1978. Asst. prof. Fort Hays State U., Hays, Kans., 1978-79, Fla. Atlantic U., Boca Raton, 1979-82, assoc. prof., 1982-86, prof. history, 1986—, asst. dean, 1989-90, assoc. dean, 1990-93; dir. Acad. Am. Franciscan History Franciscan Sch. Theology, Berkeley, Calif., 1993—2002; assoc. provost, prof. history U. Mont., Missoula, 1995—2001; vice chancellor academic affairs, dean U. Minn., Morris, 2001—06, prof. history, 2001—06; pres. SUNY, Potsdam, 2006—. Author: Partidos y parrocos bajo la real corona en la Nueva Espana, sigio XVI, 1981, Origins of Church Wealth in Mexico: Ecclesiastical Finances and Church Revenues, 1523-1600, 1985, The Church and Clergy in Sixteenth-Century Mexico, 1987; contbr. articles to profl. jours. Grantee Fla. Atlantic U., 1980, 81, 82, 83, 88, Am. Philos. Soc., 1982, NEH, 1989-90; fellow Newberry Library Assocs., 1982, Fulbright-Hays, 1982-83, Tulane U., 1983, Tinker Found., 1984-86. Mem. Am. Hist. Assn., Am. Cath. Hist. Assn., Conf. Latin Am. History, Latin Am. Studies Assn., Fullbright Assn., Hist. of Early Modern Europe, Rocky Mountain Conf. Latin Am. Studies, Phi Alpha Theta, Sigma Delta Pi. Democrat. Episcopalian. Office: SUNY at Potsdam Office of Pres 44 Pierrepont Ave Potsdam NY 13676 Office Fax: 315-267-2100, 315-267-2496. E-mail: schwaljf@potsdam.edu.

SCHWALM, LAURA, school system administrator; BA, U. Calif., Riverside; MA, Calif. State U., Fullerton; PhD, U. So. Calif. Tchr. Garden Grove Unified Sch. Dist., Calif., 1973—79, prin., dir. ednl. svcs., dir. pers. svcs., supt., 1999—. Finalist Broad Prize Urban Edn., 2003. Office: Garden Grove Unified Sch Dist 10331 Stanford Ave Garden Grove CA 92840

SCHWAN, ALFRED, food products executive; b. 1925; m. Doris Schwan; 5 children. CEO, chmn. Schwan Sales Enterprises, Inc., Marshall, Minn., 1965-2000; chmn., 1965—. Office: Schwan Sales Enterprises 115 W College Dr Marshall MN 56258-1747

SCHWAN, HOWARD W., manufacturing executive; From mgr. prodn. to pres. CTI Industries Corp., Barrington, Ill., 1983—97, pres., 1997—, dir. Office: CTI Industries Inc 22160 N Pepper Rd Barrington IL 60010

SCHWAN, LEROY BERNARD, artist, retired art educator; b. Dec. 8, 1932; s. Joseph L. and Dorothy (Papenfuss) S.; children from previous marriage: David A., Mark J., William R., Catherine L., Maria E. Student, Wis. State U., River Falls, 1951-53, Southeastern Signal Sch., Ga., 1954; BS, U. Minn., 1958, MEd, 1960, postgrad., 1961-64, No. Mich. U., 1965, Tex. Tech. U., 1970, So. Ill. U., 1978, U. Iowa, 1980, Ed.D (hon.), 1988. Head art dept. Unity Pub. Schs., Milltown, Wis., 1958-61; instr. art Fridley Pub. Schs., Mpls., 1961-64; asst. prof. art No. Mich. U., Marquette, 1964-66, Mankato (Minn.) State Coll., 1966-71, assoc. prof., 1971-74; tchr. off-campus grad. classes Northeast Mo. State U., John Wood Cmty. Coll.; dir. Art Workshop Educultural Ctr., 1968; dir. art edn. Quincy (Ill.) Pub. Schs., 1974-78, art tchr., 1978-88, ret., 1988. Tchr. art to mentally retarded children, Faribault, Minn., Owatonna, Minn., Mankato, Lake Owasso Children's Home, St. Paul; dir. art workshops, Mankato, 1970, St. Paul, 1972, 73, 74, 75; dir. workshops tchrs. mentally retarded Mankato, 1971, Faribault, 1972, Omaha, 1972-73, Quincy, 1974, 79, 82, 84-86, asst. adj. Ill. VA Home, 1980—. Author: Art Curriculum Guide Unity Public Schs., 1961, Portrait of Jean, 1974, Schwan's Art Activities, 1984, Poems of Life, 1995, LeRoy Remembers, 2003; co-author: Bryant-Schwan Design Test, 1971, Bryant-Schwan Art Guide, 1973; contbr. articles to profl. jours., author numerous poems; one-man shows: Estherville Jr. Coll., 1968, Mankato State Coll., 1968, 71, 73, 75, 77, Farmington, Wis., 1970-71, 91, Good Thunder, Minn., 1972, Quincy, 1975, 77, 84, Western Ill. U., 1979, St. Croix River Valley Arts Coun. Gallery, Osceola, Wis., 1993-96, The Northern Ctr. for the Arts, Amery, Wis., 1994, 2001, Borders Books Gallery, Woodbury, Wells Fargo Gallery, Woodbury, Health Ptnrs. Gallery, Woodbury, 2000, Gallery at Fortes Ins., Woodbury, 2001; exhibited in group shows at Pentagon, Washington, 1955, U. Minn., 1958, No. Mich. U., 1965, St. Cloud State Coll., 1967, Moorhead State Coll., 1967, Bemidji (Minn.) State Coll., 1967, MacNider Mus., Mason City, Iowa, 1969, 72-74, Gallery 500, Mankato, Minn., 1970, Rochester, Minn., 1972, Minn. Mus., St. Paul, 1973, Hannibal, Mo., 1976, 77-78, Quincy, Ill., 1976-77, 85, Ill. Art Educators Show, 1984-85, Tchrs. Retirement Art Show, Springfield, Ill., 1987, Phipps Ctr. Arts, Hudson, Wis., 1997-99, 2000-01, 03, 04; prodr. ednl. TV series, 1964-65, also 2 shows Kids Komments, Sta. WGEM, Quincy; mural commd. Gem City Coll., 1977. Webelos leader Twin Valley coun. Boy Scouts Am., 1968-69; bd. dirs. Quincy Soc. Fine Arts, 1975-85, Polk County Hist. Soc., 1993—. With Signal Corps., AUS, 1954-56. Recipient cert. of accomplishment Sec. Army, 1955, Golden Poet award, 1985, 86, 88, 90, 91, Silver Poet award 1989. Mem. Nat. Art Edn. Assn., Ill. Art Edn. Assn., Cath. Order Foresters, Am. Legion, Phi Delta Kappa. Home: 849 County Road H New Richmond WI 54017-6209

SCHWANAUER, FRANCIS, philosopher, educator; b. Zsámbék, Hungary, Jan. 20, 1933; arrived in US, 1959; s. Georg and Maria (Keller) S.; m. Johanna Maria Koelln, Sept. 29, 1957; children: Stephan Michael, Miriam Frances. Maturum, Ulrich von Hutten Gymnasium, Korntal, Germany, 1954; PhD, U. Stuttgart, Germany, 1959. Asst. prof. Lebanon Valley Coll., Annville, Pa., 1960—62, U. Maine, Orono, 1962—65, U. So. Maine, Portland Gorham, 1965—67, assoc. prof., 1967—72, prof., 1972—2006, prof. emeritus, 2006—. Author: Truth is a Neighborhood with Nothing in Between, 1977, Those Fallacies by Slight of Reason, 1978, No Many is not a One (Two the Cave is Comparison), 1001, The Flesh of Thought is Pleasure or Pain, 1982, To Make Sure is to Cohere, 1982, Philosophical Fact and Paradox, 1987, Fables from the Fox, 1991; contbr. articles to profl. jours. Grantee, John Anson Kittredge Ednl. Fund, 1991, 1993. Mem.: New Eng. Philos. Assn. Democrat. Roman Catholic. Avocation: fishing. Home: 4 Woodmont St Portland ME 04102-2709

SCHWANDA, GRACE ELAINE, music educator; b. Paterson, N.J. d. Cornelius Herbert and Matilda Dunning; m. Tom Schwanda, July 30, 1977; children: Rebecca, Stephen. BA, Montclair State U., 1972, MA, 1977; postgrad., Manhattan Sch. Music, 1977; phys. edn. cert., Calvin Coll., 1992; postgrad., Western Mich. U., 1999. Music educator Bloomingdale (N.J.) Pub. Schs., 1972—78; min. music Wanaque (N.J.) Reformed Ch., 1972—86; music literacy coach St. Cecilia Music Soc., Grand Rapids, Mich., 1987—98; children and youth choral dir. St. Robert Ch., Ada, Mich., 1992—2006; music instr. Grand Rapids C.C., 1995—. Music workshop presenter Grand Rapids Symphony, 1998, 2005. Contbr. articles to profl. jour. Vol. nursing home singer St. Cecilia Music Soc., Grand Rapids, 2000—06; knitting workshop presenter Gilda's Club, Grand Rapids, 2003—06; H.S. soccer referee. Recipient Mich. Compac award for svc. learning, 2002, Raider award, Grand Rapids C.C., 2003. Mem.: Choristers Guild, Am. Choral Dirs. Assn., Am. Orff Schulwerk Assn. Avocations: knitting, fitness. Office: Grand Rapds CC 143 Bostwick NE Grand Rapids MI 49503 Home: 1999 Nottingham Ln Wheaton IL 60187

SCHWANDA, TOM, religious studies educator; b. E. Stroudsburg, Pa., Oct. 23, 1950; s. Theodore Frank and Madlyn Betty (Backenso) S.; m. Grace Elaine Dunning, July 30, 1977; children: Rebecca Joy, Stephen Andrew. Student, Worcester Polytechnic Inst., 1968-69; BA in Econ., Moravian Coll., 1969-72; student, Gordon-Conwell Sem., 1972-74; MDiv, New Brunswick Sem., 1975; DMin, Fuller Theol. Sem., 1992. Ordained to ministry Reformed Ch. in Am., 1975. Pastor Wanaque (N.J.) Reformed Ch., 1975-87; pastor congl. care Immanuel Reformed Ch., Grand Rapids, Mich., 1987-92; interim sr. pastor Remembrance Reformed Ch., Grand Rapids, 1992-93; rsch. fellow H. Henry Meeter Ctr. for Calvin Studies Calvin Coll., Grand Rapids, 1993-95;

instr. spirituality and worship Bethlehem Ctr. for Spirituality, Grand Rapids, 1993—; dir. Reformed Spirituality Network, Grand Rapids, 1992—; assoc. for spiritual formation Reformed Ch. in Am., 1995-99; prof. spiritual formation Reformed Bible Coll., Grand Rapids, Mich., 1999—2006; assoc. prof. Christian formation and ministry Wheaton Coll., Ill., 2006—. Organizer, convener Gathering Reformed Spirituality, 1993, 94, 95, 97, 99, 2001, 2004; chair spirituality com. Synod of Great Lakes, 1989-2000, mem. Christian discipleship com., 1988-94; mem. ch. life, evangelism, missions com. South Grand Rapids Classics, chair, 1992; mem. commn. on worship Reformed Ch. in Am., 1978-94; mem. care of students com. Passaic Classis, 1975, 87, chair, 1978, 83-86, pres., 1979; adj. prof. spirituality and spiritual direction and worship Fuller Theol. Sem., San Francisco Theol. Sem., No. Bapt. Theol. Sem., Western Theol. Sem., Columbia Theol. Sem., Charlotte, Orlando, Reformed Theol. Sem., Charlotte. Author: Celebrating God's Presence: The Transforming Power of Public Worship, 1995; contbr. articles to religious jours.; author poetry; manuscript reader, evaluator religious pub. co. Established, managed Wanaque Cmty. Food Pantry, 1977-87; vol. Domestic Crisis Ctr., Grand Rapids, 1988—; bd. dirs. Nat. Inst. Rehabilitation Engring., Hewitt, N.J., 1984—, pres. bd. dirs., 1986—. Recipient Barnabas award Iglesia Cristiana Ebenezer, 1987. Mem. Czechoslovak Soc. Arts and Sci., Czechoslovak Hist. Conf., Soc. for Study of Christian Spirituality. Mem. Reformed Ch. Am. Avocations: running, landscaping, genealogy, amateur radio. Home: 1999 Nottingham Ln Wheaton IL 60187 Office: Wheaton College 501 College Ave Wheaton IL 60187 Office Phone: 616-988-3680. Business E-Mail: tschwanda@reformed.edu.

SCHWANTES, CARLOS ARNALDO, history professor, consultant; b. Wilmington, NC, Mar. 7, 1945; s. Arnaldo and Frances (Casteen) Schwantes; m. Mary Alice Dassenko, Sept. 4, 1966; children: Benjamin, Matthew. BA, Andrews U., 1967; MA, U. Mich., 1968, PhD, 1976. From instr. to prof. Walla Walla Coll., College Place, Wash., 1969-85; prof. history U. Idaho, Moscow, 1984—2002; St. Louis Merc. Libr. endowed prof. transp. studies U. Mo., St. Louis, 2001, 2002—. Cons. TV History Idaho, 1988. Author: Coxey's Army: An Amercian Odyssey, 1985, The Pacific Northwest: An Interpretive History, 1989, Railroad Signatures Across the Pacific Northwest, 1993, Going Places: Transportation Redefines the Twentieth Century West, 2003; mem. editl. bd.: Pacific NW Quart, 1982—97, Idaho Yesterdays, 1987—2002, Forest and Conservation History, 1988—95, Pacific Hist Rev 1991—95; contbr. articles to profl. jours. Fellow NEH, 1982—83, Research, Idaho Humanities Coun, 1989—90; grantee, Idaho State Bd Educ, 1990—91. Mem.: Mo. Hist. Soc., Lexington Soc., Mining Hist. Assn. (coun 1990—94), Western Hist. Assn., Am Hist. Assn. (pres Pacific Ct br 1999—2000). Republican. Seventh Day Adventist. Avocations: photography, backpacking. Personal E-mail: caschwantes@sbcglobal.net.

SCHWANTES, ROBERT SIDNEY, international relations executive; b. Beetown Township, Wis., July 11, 1922; s. Kurt John and Lillian Ellen (Walker) S.; m. Marion Laura Miles, July 15, 1943; children: Virginia, Janet, Ingrid. AB summa cum laude, Harvard U., 1943; MA, U. Colo., 1947; PhD, Harvard U., 1950. Instr. in history Harvard U., Cambridge, Mass., 1950-52; Carnegie resch. fellow Coun. on Foreign Rels., N.Y.C., 1952-54; various positions The Asia Found., San Francisco and Tokyo, 1954-66, dir. of programs San Francisco, 1966-69, v.p. for programs, 1969-84, exec. v.p., 1984-88; vis. rsch. scholar Hoover Inst., Stanford, 1988—. Mem. Am. adv. com. Japan Found., Tokyo, 1984-86, vis. History lectr. Harvard U., 1958. Author: Japanese and Americans, 1955, What Did You Do in the War, Daddy?, 1998; contbr. articles to profl. jours. Vestryman St. Paul's Episcopal Ch., Burlingame, Calif., 1993-95. Lt. (j.g.), USNR, 1942-46, PTO. Assn. Asian Studies, World Affairs Coun. No. Calif., Japan Soc. No. Calif. Democrat. Avocations: reading, travel. Home: 1432 Benito Ave Burlingame CA 94010-5550 Personal E-mail: robertschwantes@sbcglobal.net.

SCHWANTNER, JOSEPH, composer, educator; b. Chgo., Mar. 22, 1943; m. Janet Elaine Rossate; 2 children. B.Mus., Chgo. Conservatory Coll.; M.Mus., Northwestern U., 1966, D.Mus., 1968. Teaching fellow Northwestern U., 1966-68; mem. faculty Chgo. Conservatory Coll., 1967-68; asst. prof. Pacific Lutheran U., 1969-70, Ball State U., 1969-70; successively asst. prof., assoc. prof., prof. Eastman Sch. Music, U. Rochester, 1970—, prof. composition, 1970—. Composer-in-residence St. Louis Symphony Orch., 1982-84 Compositions include Aftertones of Infinity (Pulitzer prize for music 1979), Diaphonia Intervallum, Chronicon, Autumn Canticle, Consortium, In Aeternum, Modis Caelestis, Canticle for the Evening Bells, Elixir, Wild Angels of the Open Hills, And the Mountains Rising Nowhere, Sparrows. Recipient Faricy award, 1965, BMI Student award, 1965, 66, 67, Bearns prize Columbia U., 1967; Nat. Inst. Arts and Letters Charles Ives scholar, 1970; N.Y. State Council on Arts Creative Arts Public Service grantee, 1973; NEA grantee; Guggenheim fellow, 1978-79 Mem.: Am. Acad. Arts and Letters (v.p. 2006—). Mailing: c/o Amer Acad Arts and Letters Board of Directors 633 West 155th St New York NY 10032*

SCHWARCZ, STEVEN LANCE, lawyer, educator; b. NYC, Nov. 10, 1949; s. Charles and Elinor Schwarcz; m. Susan Beth Kolodny, Aug. 24, 1975; children: Daniel Benjamin, Rebekah Mara. BS summa cum laude in Aero. Engring., NYU, 1971; JD, Columbia U. 1974. Bar: N.Y. 1971, U.S. Dist. Ct. (so. dist.) N.Y. 1975. Assoc. Shearman & Sterling, N.Y.C., 1974-82, ptnr., 1983-89; ptnr., chmn. structured fin. Kaye, Scholer, Fierman, Hays & Handler, 1996—; prof. Duke U. Sch. Law, Durham, N.C., 1996—, Stanley A. Star prof., 2004—; spl. counsel Kaye, Scholer, Fierman, Hays & Handler, 1996—2004; faculty dir. Duke Global Capital Markets Ctr.; spl. cons. Kaye Scholer LLP, 2004—. Adj. prof. law Yeshiva U., Benjamin N. Cardozo Sch. Law, N.Y.C., 1983-92; vis. lectr. Yale Law Sch., 1992-96; lectr. Columbia Law Sch., 1992-96. Contbr. articles to profl. jours. Chmn. Friends of the Eldridge St. Synagogue, N.Y.C., 1979-96, Legis. Drafting Rsch. Fund George Granger Brown opholar, 1971. NSF grantee in Math., 1969. Fellow Am. Coll. Comml. Fin. Lawyers; mem. Am. Law Inst., Assn. of Bar of City of N.Y. (environ. law com. 1975-78, nuc. tech. com. 1979-81, sci. and law com. 1985—, chmn. 1987-90), Am. Law and Econs. Assn., Tau Beta Pi, Sigma Gamma Tau. Jewish. Office: Duke U Sch Law Box 90360 Science Dr & Towerview Rd Durham NC 27708 Office Phone: 919-613-7060. E-mail: schwarcz@law.duke.edu.

SCHWARCZ, VERA, historian, educator, poet; d. Elmer and Katherine Savin; m. Jason Wolfe, July 31, 1983; children: Elie, Esther. BA in French Lit. and Oriental Religions, Vassar Coll., 1969; MA in East Asian Studies, Yale U., 1971; PhD in Chinese History, Stanford (Calif.) U., 1977. Instr. Stanford U., 1973; lectr. Chinese history Wesleyan U., Middletown, Conn., 1975-77, asst. prof. Chinese history, 1975-83, assoc. prof. history, 1983-87, prof. history, 1987—, chair East Asian studies, 1985-88, 94-96, Mansfield Freeman prof. East Asian studies, 1987—; dir. Ctr. East Asian Studies, 1998—99. Dir. Mansfield Freeman for East Asian Studies, 1987-88, 94-96; exch. scholar Beijing U., 1979-80, vis. scholar, 1983, 86, 89; vis. scholar Ctr. de Documentation sur la Chine Contemporaine, Paris, 1985, DAO Assn., Cluj, Romania, 1993, Miskenot Sha'ananim, Jerusalem, 1991; vis. prof. East Asian studies Hebrew U., Jerusalem, 1996-97; presenter, referee in field Author: Long Road Home: A China Journal, 1984, Chinese Enlightenment: Intellectuals, and the Legacy of the May Fourth Movement in Modern China, 1986, Zhongguo de qimeng yundong, 1989, Time for Telling Truth is Running Out: Conversations with Zhang Shenfu, 1992, Bridge Across Broken Time: Chinese and Jewish Cultural Memory, 1998, Fresh Words for a Jaded World, 2000, A Scoop of Light: Poems, 2000, Zhonguo Oimeng Yundong, 2000, Zhang Shenfu Fangtan Lu, 2001, In the Garden of Memory, 2004, Truth is Woven, 2005; author numerous poems; co-editor: China: Inside the People's Republic, 1972; mem. editl. bd. History and Theory, 1981-84, 96-99, China Rev. Internat., 1994—; contbr. articles to profl. jours. Fellow Danforth Found., 1971-73, NDFL, 1973-74, NAS, 1979-80, Guggenheim Found. fellow, 1989-90, Great River Arts Inst. poetry fellow, 2000, Founders fellow AAUW, 1988-89, Faculty fellow Ctr. for Humanities Wesleyan U., 1988; grantee AAUW, 1974-75, Am. Philos. Soc., 1985, Am. Coun. Learned Socs., 1978, 96; finalist Nat. Jewish Book award in History, 1999; recipient Wesleyan Writers Conf. Poetry scholarship, 1999; poetry fellow Great River

Arts Inst., Mex., 2000; recipient Poetry prize Taproot Lit. Rev., 2002-03. Mem. Assn. for Asian Studies (coun. on confs. 1989—, mem. Levenson prize com. 1991-92, chair 1992-93), New Eng. Assn. for Asian Studies (pres. 1988-89). Home: 42 Seneca Rd West Hartford CT 06117-2245 Office: Wesleyan U History Dept Middletown CT 06459-0001 Office Fax: 860-685-2781.

SCHWARM, HAROLD CHAMBERS, artist; b. Fairmont, W.Va., May 5, 1925; s. Harold Chambers Schwarm and Ethel Eleanor Toothman; m. Claudia Beechum Chapline, Feb. 14, 1989; m. Margaret Elizabeth Collins Schwarm (div.); children: Mark, Eric, Kurt, Kim, Paul, Lisa, Karl, Mary. Student, U. Iowa, 1945—48; BFA, Bradley U., Peoria, Ill., 1951; MA, Bradley U., 1952. Instr. sculpture and drawing Bradley U., Peoria, Ill., 1952—55; supr. art svcs. So. Ill. U., Carbondale, 1955—59; asst. prof. graphic arts Calif. State U., Northridge, 1959—75; artist, 1973—. One-man shows include Claudia Chapline Gallery, Stinson Beach, Calif., 1989—2006, Bolinas Mus., Calif., 1998—99, Anagma Arte Contemporaneo, Valencia, Spain, 1994, Palais Maeterlinck, Nice, France, 1994, Represented in permanent collections Galeria del Ayantamienta, Naguera, Spain, Kaiser Hosp., Milpitas, Calif., Shriners Children's Hosp., Sacramento, Bolinas Mus., Calif., commd. paintings for, Ornick, Harrington and Sutcliffe, Kronick, Moskowitz, Tiedmann andGirard, Hyatt Regincy, U. Calif. Med. Ctr., others. Office: Claudia Chapline Gallery PO Box 1117 Stinson Beach CA 94970 Office Phone: 415-868-2308.

SCHWARTE, DAVID A., lawyer, travel company executive; b. 1950; BA, U. Ky.; JD, Salmon P. Chase Coll. Law. Atty. legal dept. Am. Airlines, 1979—98; dir. Kelly, Hart & Hallman, Ft. Worth, 1999—2000; exec. v.p., gen. counsel Sabre Holdings, Southlake, Tex., 2000—. Mem.: ABA (past chmn., forum on air and space law), Tex. State Bar Assn. Office: Sabre Holdings 3150 Sabre Dr Southlake TX 76092

SCHWARTZ, AARON ROBERT, lawyer, former state legislator; b. Galveston, Tex., July 17, 1926; s. Joseph and Clara (Bulbe) S.; m. Marilyn Cohn, July 14, 1951; children: Richard Austin, Robert Allen, John Reed, Thomas Lee. Pre-law student, Tex. A&M U., 1948; JD, U. Tex., 1951. Bar: Tex. 1951. Mem. Tex. Ho. of Reps., 1955-59, Tex. Senate, 1960-81, past chmn. rules, jurisprudence and natural resources coms. Chmn. Tex. Coastal and Marine Coun., U.S. Coastal States Orgn.; adj. prof. legis. and cosatal mgmt. law Bates Law Sch., U. Houston, Tex. A&M U., Corpus Christi. Contbr. articles to profl. jours. Mem. emeritus exec. com. Galveston Bay Fond.; apptd. to Tex. Oil Spill Oversight Commn., 1993. Served with USN, 1944-46, 2d lt. USAFR, 1948-53. Recipient conservation and legis. awards, Outstanding Citizen award Galveston Jr. C. of C., 1981, Man of Yr., People of Vision award Galveston chpt. Soc. for Prevention of Blindness, 1986, Disting. Service award Nat. Hurricane Conf., Tex. Coastal Mgmt. Adv. Com., 1987, Lifetime Coastal Achievement award, 1997. Mem. Tex. State Bar Assn., Galveston County Bar Assn. Democrat. Jewish. Address: 1122 Colorado St Apt 2102 Austin TX 78701-2142 Personal E-mail: ars71726@aol.com.

SCHWARTZ, ADAM J., elementary school educator; s. William G. and Mary Lou Schwartz; m. Laura J. Mammano, Apr. 10, 1999; children: Noah S., Lucas W. BS in Elem. Edn., Alfred U., NY, 1992; MS in Elem. Edn., Nazareth Coll. of Rochester, NY, 1999. Cert. advanced studies Oswego, NY, 2006. 5th grade tchr. Canandaigua (NY) City Sch. Dist., 1994—. Soccer coach NY State West Olympic Devel. Team, Rochester, 2002—, Rochester Jr. Rhinos, 2002—. Office: Canandaigua City Sch Dist 90 W Gibson St Canandaigua NY 14424 E-mail: schwartza@canandaiguaschools.org.

SCHWARTZ, ALAN, law educator; BS, Bates Coll., 1961; LLB, Yale U., 1964. Bar: NY 1965. Assoc. Rosenman, Colin, Kaye, Petschek, Freund & Emil, 1964—69; asst. prof. Ind. U., 1969—72, assoc. prof., 1972—75, prof. law, 1975—76; vis. prof. U. So. Calif. Law Ctr., 1976—77, prof., 1977—80, Maurice Jones, Jr. prof., 1980—87; vis. prof. law and social sci. Calif. Inst. Tech., 1979—81, prof., 1981—87; Townsend prof. Yale U., New Haven, 1987—99, Sterling prof. law, 1994—. Co-author: Commercial Law: Principles and Policies, 1982, 1991, Sales Law and the Contracting Process, 1982, 1991, Fundamentals of Contract Law, 1994, Payment Systems and Credit Instruments, 1996; contbr. articles to law jours. Office: Yale Law Sch PO Box 208215 New Haven CT 06520 E-mail: alan.schwartz@yale.edu.

SCHWARTZ, ALAN E., lawyer, director; b. Detroit, Dec. 21, 1925; s. Maurice H. and Sophia (Welkowitz) S.; m. Marianne Shapero, Aug. 24, 1950; children: Marc Alan, Kurt Nathan, Ruth Anne. Student, Wash. Mich. Coll., 1944-45; BA with distinction, U. Mich., 1947; LLB magna cum laude, Harvard U., 1950; LLD, Wayne State U., 1983, U. Detroit, 1985. Bar: NY 1951, Mich. 1952. Assoc. Kelley, Drye & Warren, N.Y.C., 1950-52; mem. Honigman, Miller, Schwartz & Cohn, Detroit, 1952—. Spl. asst. counsel N.Y. State Crime Commn., 1951; bd. dirs. Pulte Corp. Editor: Harvard Law Rev., 1950. Dir. Detroit Symphony Orch.; v.p. bd. dirs. United Found.; bd. dirs. Detroit Renaissance, New Detroit, Jewish Welfare Fedn. Detroit, Wayne State Univ. Found.; trustee Cmty. Found. for Southeastern Mich.; adv. mem. Arts Commn., City of Detroit; mem. investment com. Kresge Found., Skillman Found., Wayne State U. Found. Served as ensign Supply Corps, USNR, 1945-46. Recipient Mich. Heritage Hall of Fame award, 1984, George W. Romney award for lifetime achievement in volunteerism, 1994, Max M. Fisher Cmty. Svc. award, 1997; named one of Top 200 Collectors, ARTnews, 2004, 2005, 2006. Mem. Mich. Bar Assns. Clubs: Franklin Hills Country; Detroit, Economic (dir.). Avocation: collector of Old Masters, modern prints. Office: Honigman Miller Schwartz & Cohn 2290 1st National Bldg Detroit MI 48226

SCHWARTZ, ALAN GIFFORD, sport company executive; b. N.Y.C., Nov. 7, 1931; s. Kevie Wademar and Vera (Isaacs) S.; m. Roslyn Smulian, Sept. 6, 1958; children: Steven, Andrew, Sally, Elizabeth. BS, Yale U., 1952; MBA, Harvard U., 1954. Pmr. Gifford Investment Co., Chgo., 1954—; CEO Tennis Corp. of Am., Chgo., 1969—, chmn. bd., 1974—. Dir. Firstar Bank Ill., Comtrex Systems, Inc., Mt. Laurel, N.J.; trustee Roosevelt U., 1994—, Inst. European & Asian Studies, 1993—; v.p. U.S. Tennis Assn., 1994—. Contbr. articles to profl. jours.; editorial cons. Club Industry mag., 1985—. Bd. dirs. Grad. Sch. of Bus., Duke U., Durham, N.C., 1977—, McCormick Boys and Girls Club, 1989—. Elected to Club Industry Hall of Fame, 1987. Mem. Standard Club of Chgo., Exec. Club. Chgo. Jewish. Avocations: travel, tennis. Office: Tennis Corp of Am 3611 N Kedzie Ave Chicago IL 60618-4513

SCHWARTZ, ALAN LEIGH, pediatrician, educator; b. N.Y.C., Apr. 25, 1948; s. Robert and Joyce (Goldner) S.; m. Judith Child, June 22, 1974; 1 child, Timothy Child. BA, Case Western Res. U., 1974, PhD in Pharmacology, 1974, MD, 1976. Diplomate Am. Bd. Pediatrics. Intern Children's Hosp., Boston, 1976-77, resident, 1976-78, fellow Dana Farber Cancer Inst., 1978-80; instr. Harvard Med. Sch., Boston, 1980-81, asst. prof., 1981-83, assoc. prof., 1983-86; prof. pediatrics, molecular biology and pharmacology Washington U. Sch. Medicine, St. Louis, 1986—, chmn. dept. pediatrics, 1995—; chmn. faculty practice plan Washington U., 1999—2001. Vis. scientist MIT, Boston, 1979-82; mem. sci. adv. bd. Nat. Inst. Child Health and Human Devel., NIH, Bethesda, Md., 1988-94; investigator Am. Heart Assn. Alumni Endowed Prof. Pediats. Wash. U. Sch. Medicine, 1987-97, Harriet B. Spoehrer Prof. Pediats., 1997—. Mem. Inst. Medicine of NAS. Office: Washington U Sch Medicine Dept Pediatrics Box 8116 One Children's Pl Saint Louis MO 63110-1093 E-mail: schwartz@kids.wustl.edu.

SCHWARTZ, ALAN VICTOR, advertising executive; b. Detroit, July 12, 1948; s. Seymour and Adeline (Goldstein) S.; children: Stacy Ilana, Andrew Robert. BS with honors, Yale U. 1970; MBA with highest honors, Cornell U., 1972. CPA, N.Y. Mgr. Price Waterhouse, Huntington, NY, 1972-79; v.p., dir. fin. control Doyle Dane Bernbach, N.Y.C., 1979-81; v.p., CFO, Bernard Hodes Group, N.Y.C., 1981-84, sr. v.p., chief oper. and fin. officer, 1984-87, exec. v.p., COO, 1987—2001, pres., CEO, 2002—; trustee The Healthcare

Chaplaincy, 2005—. Bd. mgrs. Evans Tower, treas. 1991-92, pres. 1992-93. Campaign vice chmn. United Way L.I., 1978. Mem. Nat. Assn. Accts. (various directorships, treas.), N.Y. State Soc. CPAs, Lehigh Alumni Assn. (pres. L.I. chpt. 1977-79, treas. 1975-77). Office: Bernard Hodes Group 220 E 42d St New York NY 10017

**SCHWARTZ, ALFRED,** former dean; b. Chgo., Jan. 8, 1922; s. Isadore and Lena (Ziff) S.; m. Delle Weiss, Aug. 26, 1945; children: Reid Mitchell, Karen Ruth. B.Ed., Chgo. Tchrs. Coll., 1944; MA in Polit. Sci., U. Chgo., 1946, PhD in Ednl. Adminstrn., 1949. Tchr. Chgo. pub. schs., 1944-45; contact officer VA, 1946; instr. U. Chgo. Lab. Sch., 1946-50; assoc. prof. edn. Drake U., 1950-56, U. Del.; also exec. sec. Del. Sch. Study Council, 1956-58; dean (Univ. Coll.); prof. Coll. Edn., Drake U., 1958-85, dean, 1964-79, 80-84, dean emeritus, 1985—; acting v.p. acad. adminstrn. Coll. Edn., Coll. Edn. 1979-80; cons., 1985—. Adviser Iowa Dept. Pub. Instrn.; mem. coordinating bd. Nat. Council Accreditation for Tchr. Edn.; chmn. tchr. edn. and adv. com. Iowa Dept. Pub. Instrn. Author: (with Harlan L. Hagman) Administration in Profile for School Executives, 1954, (with Stuart Tiedeman) Evaluating Student Progress, 1957, (with Willard Fox) Managerial Guide for School Principals, 1965. Mem. Gov.'s Commn. State-Local Relations, pres. condo assn., 1987-97. Mem. World Council on Curriculum and Instrn., Iowa Assn. Colls. for Tchr. Edn. (pres., exec. sec.), Am. Profs. for Peace in Middle East, Am. Ednl. Research Assn., Iowa Ednl. Assn., NEA, Phi Delta Kappa, Kappa Delta Pi. Home: 3450 3rd Ave Apt 511 San Diego CA 92103-4939

**SCHWARTZ, ALLEN R.,** lawyer; b. Greeley, Colo., Oct. 13, 1951; s. David L. and Margaret L. Schwartz; m. Beverly S. Stephens, Mar. 23, 1985; 1 child, Christopher; 1 stepchild, Shawn Jensen. BA in Psychology and Sociology, U. Colo., 1973, JD, 1976. Bar: Colo. 1976, U.S. Dist. Ct. Colo. 1976, U.S. Ct. Appeals (10th cir.) 1983. Law clk. Denver Dist. Ct., 1976-77; assoc. Fischer & Wilmarth, Ft. Collins, Colo., 1977-79; ptnr. Dean, Martin, Mitchell & Schwartz, Ft. Collins, 1979-83; mng. ptnr. Nelson & Schwartz, Ft. Collins, 1983-90; ptnr. Nelson, Reid & Schwartz, Ft. Collins, 1990-96; pvt. practice Ft. Collins, 1996—. V.p., legal advisor acad. adv. com. Wingshadow Inc., Frontier H.S. and Frontier Med. Sch., Ft. Collins, 1994—. Asst. scoutmaster Boy Scouts Am., Ft. Collins, 1991-94. Mem. Colo. Bar Assn., Larimer County Bar Assn., Overland Sertoma (pres., chmn. bd., Sertoman of the Yr. 1994-95), High Plains Dist. Sertoma (dist. gov. 1996-98, Cmty. Achievement award 1991-92). Home: 1601 Centennial Rd Fort Collins CO 80525-2418 Office: 315 W Oak St Ste 501 Fort Collins CO 80521-2729 Office Phone: 970-493-0456. Business E-Mail: allen@allenschwartz.com.

**SCHWARTZ, ALLYSON Y.,** congresswoman; b. NYC, Oct. 3, 1948; d. Everett and Renee Perl Young; m. David Schwartz, 1970; children: Daniel, Jordan. BA in Sociology, Simmons Coll., Boston, 1970; MSW, Bryn Mawr Coll., Pa., 1972. Founder, exec. dir. Elizabeth Blackwell Health Ctr. for Women, 1975-88; acting commr., 1st dep. commr. Dept. Human Svcs., 1988-90; mem. Pa. State Senate, Harrisburg, 1990—2004, minority chmn. edn. com., 1994—2004; mem. US Congress from 13th Pa. dist., 2005—, mem. budget com., mem. transp. and infrastructure com. Mem. Pa. State Bd. Edn., Pa. Coun. Higher Edn., 2000, Pa. Hist. and Mus. Commn., Edn. Commn. States, Nat. Dem. Leadership Coun.; v.p. Women's Network; co-chair Pa. New Dem. Coalition; bd. trustees Arcadia U., Chestnut Hill Healthcare; chair Instl. Rev. Bd., Phila. Health Mgmt. Corpn.; bd. dirs. Nat. Jewish Dem. Coun.; adv. bd. Tuition Assistance (TAP) Democrat. Jewish. Office: US Ho Reps 423 Cannon Ho Office Bldg Washington DC 20515-3813 Office Phone: 202-225-6111.*

**SCHWARTZ, ANNA JACOBSON,** economist; b. NYC, Nov. 11, 1915; married; 4 children. BA, Barnard Coll., 1934; MA, Columbia U., 1935, PhD, 1964; LittD (hon.), U. Fla., 1987, Emory U., 2000; ArtsD (hon.), Stonehill Coll., 1989; LLD (hon.), Iona Coll., 1992, Rutgers U., 1998; LHD (hon.), CUNY, 2000; LLD (hon.), Williams Coll., 2002; LHD (hon.), Loyola U., Chgo., 2003; ScD (hon.), City U., London, 2006. Rschr. USDA, 1936, Columbia U. Social Sci. Rsch. Coun., 1936-41; sr. rsch. staff Nat. Bur. Econ. Rsch. Inc., N.Y.C., 1941—. Instr. Bklyn. Coll., 1952, Baruch Coll., 1959-60; adj. prof. econs. grad. CCNY, 1967-69, grad. sch. CUNY, 1986—, NYU Grad. Sch. Arts and Sci., 1969-70; hon. vis. prof. City U. Bus. Sch., London, 1984—; hon. fellow Inst. of Econ. Affairs, London, 1998. Mem. editorial bd. Am. Econ. Rev., 1972-78, Jour. Money, Credit and Banking, 1974-75, 84—, Jour. Monetary Econs., 1975—, Jour. Fin. Svcs. Rsch., 1993—; contbr. articles to profl. jours. Disting. fellow Am. Econ. Assn., 1993; hon fellow Inst. Econ. Affairs, London. Mem. Western Econ. Assn. (pres. 1987-88). Office: Nat Bur Econ Research 365 Fifth Ave 5th Fl New York NY 10016-4309 Business E-Mail: aschwartz@gc.cuny.edu.

**SCHWARTZ, ANTHONY,** veterinary surgeon, educator; b. Bklyn., July 30, 1940; s. Murray and Miriam Sarah (Wittes) S.; m. Claudia Rosenberg, July 21, 1963; children: Thomas Frederick, Eric Leigh. Student, Mich. State U., 1957—58; DVM, Cornell U., 1963; PhD, Ohio State U., 1972. Diplomate Am. Coll. Vet. Surgeons (bd. of regents 1989-92). Gen. practice vet. medicine, Huntington, NY, 1963—66; resident in surgery Animal Med. Ctr., N.Y.C., 1968—69, Ohio State U., Columbus, 1969—70, asst. prof., head sect. small animal surgery, 1973; asst. prof. then assoc. prof. comparative medicine Yale U. Sch. Medicine, New Haven, 1973—79; assoc. prof. then prof., chmn. dept. surgery, assoc. dean Tufts U. Sch. Vet. Medicine, Boston, 1979—89, assoc. dean clin. edn., 1989—93, prof., chmn. dept. surgery, assoc. dean acad. affairs, 1993—97, assoc. dean for acad. and outreach programs, 1997—2002, assoc. dean for continuing edu. and outreach programs, 2003—04, prof. emeritus, 2005—. Cons. U.S. Surg. Corp., Norwalk, Conn., 1975—; mem. Bd. Tufts Animal Expo LLC, program dir., 1999-2003; mem. vet. adv. bd. PetPlace.com, Intelligent Content Corp., 2000-03; exec. dir., chair bd. dirs. N.E. Vet. Conf., 2003-05, chair program com., 2003-04. Author: (with others) Small Animal Surgery, 1989, Complications in Small Animal Surgery, 1996; editl. bd. Vet. Surgery, 1987-90, Jour. Investigative Surgery, 1987-98; assoc. editor: Textbook of Small Animal Surgery, 1985; contbr. articles to profl. jours. Capt. U.S. Army Vet Corps, 1966-68. Recipient 1st prize N.Y. State Vet. Med. Soc., 1963; Robert Wood Johnson Health Policy fellow, Washington, 1988-89; NIH grantee, 1975-84. Mem.: AVMA (legis. planning com. 1989—92, coun. on govt. affairs 1992—97), Mass. Vet. Med. Assn. (chmn. 1990—91, animal welfare com. 1990-98, Merit award for leadership in pub. rels. and colleague devel. 2002), Nat. Acads. of Practice (co-chmn. acad. vet. medicine 2002—03), Am. Vet. Med. Colls. (treas. and exec. dir. 1992—93, Washington), Phi Kappa Phi, Sigma Xi. Democrat. Jewish. Office: Tufts U Sch Vet Medicine 200 Westboro Rd North Grafton MA 01536-1895 Personal E-Mail: tonyvet@comcast.net. Business E-Mail: Anthony.Schwartz@tufts.edu.

**SCHWARTZ, ARTHUR,** playwright, poet; b. N.Y.C., May 20, 1931; s. Harry and Sarah Pearl Schwartz; m. Joan Klenin, June 10, 1956; children: Jessy Ann, Rachel Freyda. Student, Champlain Coll., 1950, student, 1951, student, 1952. Minor league baseball player N.Y. Yankees, 1954—55; stand-up comedian, 1968—80; playwright, poet, 1976—. Prodr.: (plays) An Apple a Day, 1977, The King of Empire Boulevard, 1978, The General and the Jew, 1979, A Choice of Weapons, 1996, If The White House Calls, I'm Out, 2000, The Intruder-The National Pastime, 2001, Naked Batting Practice, 2004, A Song for Chaim Levy, 2004,; author poetry. Named one of Best Poets of 1994, Nat. Libr. Poetry, Best Poets of 1995, Best Poets of 1996, Best Poets of 1997; recipient Writers Digest Poetry award, 1995, Outstanding Achievement award, Nat. Libr. Poetry, 1994, 1995, 1996, 1997. Home: 420 Merrick Rd Rockville Centre NY 11570

**SCHWARTZ, BARRY FREDRIC,** lawyer, diversified holding company executive; b. Phila., Apr. 16, 1949; s. Albert and Evelyn (Strauss) S.; m. Sherry L. Handsman, Mar. 21, 1985; children: Fanny Rose, Abraham David. AB cum laude, Kenyon Coll., 1970; JD, Georgetown U., 1974. Bar: Pa. 1974, Ill. 1974, N.Y. 1992, U.S. Dist. Ct. (ea. dist.) Pa. 1974, U.S. Dist. Ct. (no. dist.) Ill. 1975, U.S. Dist. Ct. (so. dist.) N.Y. 1992, U.S. Ct. Appeals (7th cir.) 1977, U.S. Ct. Appeals (3d cir.) 1978, U.S. Ct. Appeals (4th cir.) 1979, U.S. Ct. Appeals (6th cir.) 1981, U.S. Supreme Ct. 1981, N.Y. 1992. Assoc.

Sachnoff, Schrager, Jones & Weaver, Chgo., 1974—76; ptnr. Wolf, Block, Schorr & Solis-Cohen, Phila., 1976—89; exec. v.p. gen. counsel MacAndrews & Forbes Holdings, Inc., N.Y.C., 1989—. Bd. visitors Georgetown U. Law Ctr., 2005—. Mem. Adv. Com. for Justices of the Comml. divsn. Supreme Ct., N.Y. County, 1999—, mem. adv. coun. Westchester Holocaust Commn., 2000—; trustee Kenyon Coll., 2000—; mem. bd.dirs. Sci. Games, 2003, REV Holdings LLC., 2004, Relvon Consumer Products, 2004. Mem.: Assn. Governing Bds. of Univs. and Colls. (bd. dirs. 2004), Revlon Consumer Products Corp. (bd. dirs. 2004), REV Holdings LLC (bd. dirs. 2004), Sci. Games Corp. (bd. dirs. 2003). Office: MacAndrews & Forbes Holdings Inc 35 E 62nd St New York NY 10021-8032

**SCHWARTZ, BART,** diversified financial services company executive; BA, Antioch Coll., 1975; JD, U. So. Calif., 1978; MBA, Vanderbilt U., 1991. Former assoc. atty. Debevoise and Plimpton, Skadden, Arps, Slate, Meagher & Flom; former exec. v.p., gen. counsel Werthan Packaging, Inc.; former sr. v.p., gen. counsel, sec. Willis Corroon Corp.; sr. v.p., gen. counsel The MONY Group, Inc., 2001—04; dep. gen. counsel, Marsh & McLennan Cos., Inc., NYC, 2004—. Mem.: ABA (com. corp. gen. counsel), Coun. Chief Legal Officers, Assn. Corp. Counsel (bd. dirs. global orgn. and N.Y. chpt.). Office: Marsh & McLennan Cos Inc 1166 Avenue of the Americas 3rd Fl New York NY 10036-2774

**SCHWARTZ, BENJAMIN MICHAEL,** gynecologist, oncologist; b. NYC, Mar. 17, 1969; s. Robert Sidney and Diane Carole Schwartz; m. Laura Ann Hendricks, July 20, 2002; children: Abigail Margot, Michael Henry, Andrew Zachary. BA in Govt., Dartmouth U., 1991; MD, George Washington U., DC, 1995. Diplomate Am. Bd. of Ob-gyn., 2004. Resident in ob-gyn. Albert Einstein Coll. of Medicine, Bronx, NY, 1995—99; fellow in gynecologic oncology Cleve. Clinic Found., Cleve., 1999—2002; asst. prof. of gynecol. oncology U. of Pitts., Magee Women's Hosp., Pitts., 2002—03; dir. of gynecol. oncology Nassau U. Med. Ctr., East Meadow, NY, 2003—; med. dir. Schwartz Gynecol. Oncology, PLLC, Babylon, NY. Fellow: Am. Coll. of Ob-gyn.; mem.: Am. Assn. of Gynecol. Laparoscopists, Am. Soc. of Clin. Oncology, Soc. of Gynecolo. Oncologists (assoc.), Internat. Soc. of Gynecol. Oncology, NY Yacht Club. Office: Schwartz Gynecol Oncology PLLC 500 West Main St Ste 209 Babylon NY 11702 Office Phone: 631-376-0055.

**SCHWARTZ, BERNARD,** physician; b. Toronto, Nov. 12, 1927; s. Samuel and Gertrude Schwartz; children: Lawrence Frederick, Karen Lynne, Jennifer Carla, Ariane Samara MD, U. Toronto, 1951; MS, State U. Iowa, 1953, PhD, 1959. Intern U. Hosps., State U. Iowa, 1951-52, resident ophthalmology, 1951-54; research fellow U. Iowa, 1954-58; asst. prof. to assoc. prof. Downstate Med. Center fo State U N.Y., 1958-68; prof. ophthalmology Tufts U., 1968-93, chmn. dept., 1968-90, prof. emeritus ophthalmology, 1993—. Author: Syphilis and the Eye; editor-in-chief Survey of Ophthalmology, 1968—, Comprehensive Ophthalmology Update, 1998—; contbr. articles to profl. jours. Fellow Am. Acad. Ophthalmology, ACS; mem. Assn. Rsch. in Ophthalmology, New Eng. Ophthalmol. Soc., N.Y. Acad. Medicine, Sigma Xi. Home: 180 Beacon St Boston MA 02116-1408 Office: 7 Kent St Ste 3 Brookline MA 02445 Office Phone: 617-232-4442. Business E-Mail: glaucomares@mva.net.

**SCHWARTZ, BERNARD JULIAN,** lawyer; b. Edmonton, Alberta, Can., July 29, 1960; came to U.S., 1982; s. Sol and Anne (Motkovici) S. BA, U. Alberta, 1981; JD, McGeorge Sch. Law, 1986. Bar: U.S. Supreme Ct. 1991. Atty. Ropers, Majeski, San Francisco, 1987-88, Riverside County Pub. Defenders, Riverside, Calif., 1988-89; pvt. practice Riverside, 1990—. Coach Riverside County H.S. Mock Trial Team, 1990, 96, 97. Mem. Calif. Attys. Criminal Justice, Calif. Pub. Defenders Assn., Riverside County Bar Assn., Criminal Cts. Bar Assn. (pres.)

**SCHWARTZ, BERNARD LEON,** retired space and communications company executive; b. Dec. 13, 1925; BBA, CCNY, 1948. Ptnr. Schnee, Hover & Schwartz, 1948—52; sr. v.p. APL Corp., Fla., 1962—68; chmn. bd., CEO Leasco Corp., Miami Beach, 1969—72; chmn., CEO Loral Corp., N.Y.C., 1972—96, pres. NYC, 1973—81; chmn., CEO, bd. dirs. Loral Space & Comm., 1996—2006; chmn., CEO Globalstar Telecomms. Ltd., 1996—, K&F Industries, Inc. Trustee Mt. Sinai NYU Med. Ctr. and Health Systems. With U.S. Army, 1943—45.*

**SCHWARTZ, BRIAN MICHAEL,** philosopher, think-tank executive; b. N.Y.C., Aug. 4, 1952; s. Bernard and Aileen Schwartz. BA, Oxford U., Eng., 1971; JD, Yale U., 1975. Law clk. to Hon. Irving R. Kaufman U.S. Ct. Appeals (2d cir.), N.Y.C.; famine relief coord. UNICEF, Namalu, Uganda, 1981—2002; treas. Prometheus Soc., 2003—. Author: China Off the Beaten Track, 1983, A World of Villages, 1986. Mem.: Lincoln's Inn, Lewis M. Terman High IQ Soc. (pres. 2006—), Omega Soc., Aleph 3, Oxford Union, Polonia Club.

**SCHWARTZ, CARL EDWARD,** artist, printmaker; b. Detroit, Sept. 20, 1935; s. Carl and Verna (Steiner) S.; m. Kay Joyce Hofmann, June 18, 1955 (div.); children: Dawn Ellen, Cari Leigh. BFA, Art Inst. Chgo. Sch.-U. Chgo. 1957. Past tchr. art, Chgo., N. Shore Art League, Suburban Fine Arts Center, Deerpath Art League; faculty art Edison C.C., Fla. Gulf Coast U. One-man shows include, South Bend (Ind.) Art Center, Feingarten Gallery, Chgo., 1960, Bernard Horwich Center, Chgo., Covenant Club, Chgo., Barat Coll., Chgo. Pub. Library, Alverno Coll., 1020 Art Center, Rosenberg Gallery, Peoria (Ill.) Art Guild, 1977, Ill. State Mus., 1977 Ill. Inst. Tech., 1978, Miller Gallery, Chgo., 1979, Union League Club, Chgo., 1982, Art Inst. Rental and Sale Gallery, Chgo., 1982, Horwich Gallery, Chgo., 1983, Lake Forest (Ill.) Coll., 1983, Campanile-Capponi Contemporary Gallery, Chgo., 1987, Nagata Gallery, Ft. Myers, Fla., 1988, Jan Cicero Gallery, Chgo., 1990, Neopolitan Gallery, Naples, Fla., 1996, 97; numerous group shows include 9th Ann. Michigana Exhbt, Detroit (Cloetingh and Deman award 1959), Hyde Park Art Center, Chgo., 1960 (5th Ann. Jury Exhbn. prize), Spectrum Exhbn. '63, Chgo. (1st prize), New Horizons Exhbt., Chgo., 1960 (Joseph Shapiro award), Nat. Design Center, Chgo., 1965 (New Horizons in Painting 1st prize), 3d Ann. Chgo. Arts Competition, 1962 (1st prize), Union League Club, Chgo., 1967 (2d prize), N. Shore Art League Ann. Drawing and Print Show, Chgo., 1965 (1st prize), Artists Guild Chgo., 1965 (prize), McCormack Pl., Chgo., 1965 (1st prize), Detroit Art Inst., 1965 (Commonwealth prize), Park Forest (Ill.) Art Exhbn, 1969 (Best of Show), 14th Ann. Virginia Beach (Va.) Show, 1969 (Best of Show), Suburban Fine Arts Center, Highland Park, Ill., 1970 (prize), 15th Ann. Virginia Beach Show, 1970 (prize), 32d Ann. Artists Guild, Chgo., 1970 (2d prize), N. Shore Art League Print and Drawing Show, 1970 (prize), 16th Ann. Virginia Beach Show, 1971 (2d prize), Ill. State Fair, 1972 (prize), Artists Guild Chgo., 1972 (1st prize), 17th Ann. Virginia Beach Exhbt, 1972 (1st prize), Artists Guild 50th Fine Art Exhbn., Chgo., 1973 (prize), Dickinson State U., 1973 (prize), N. Shore Art League Print Exhbn, 1973 (prize), Lakehurst Exhbt, 1974 (prize), Union League Art Exhbt, 1974 (1st prize), Artists Guild Fine Arts Exhbn., 1974 (best of Show), Bluegrass Painting Exhbn, Louisville, 1975 (award), Union League Art Exhbn, 1976 (prize); represented in permanent collections, Brit. Mus., London, Smithsonian Inst., Washington, Art Inst. Chgo., K. Van Ella, Chgo., Gardner-Colby Gallery, Naples, Fla. Home: 5825 Briarcliff Rd Fort Myers FL 33912-4204 Office Phone: 239-590-7249. *I am a painter of light. I'm intrigued and fascinated with form. To me, there are two worlds-the one we all live in, and the one that I create. Painting is the discipline by which I constantly rediscover both of these worlds.*

**SCHWARTZ, CAROL LEVITT,** government official; b. Greenville, Miss., Jan. 20, 1944; d. Stanley and Hilda (Simmons) Levitt; m. David H. Schwartz (dec.); children: Stephanie, Hilary, Douglas. BS in Spl. and Elem. Edn., U. Tex., 1965. Mem. transiton team Office of Pres. Elect, 1980-81; con. office presdl. personnel The White House, Washington, 1981; cons. U.S. Dept. Edn., Washington, 1982; pres. sec. U.S. Ho. Reps., Washington, 1982-83; mem.-at-large Coun. of D.C., Washington, 1985-89, 97—; candidate for mayor, Washington, 1986, 1994, 1998, 2002. Vice chmn. Nat. Edn. Commn. on Time

and Learning, 1992-94, Nat. Adv. Coun. on Disadvantaged Children, 1974-79; lectr. in field; radio commentator, 1990-91; chair transp., vice-chair planning bd. Coun. Govts. Regional columnist Washington Jewish Week, 1995-97. Mem. D.C. Bd. Edn., 1974-82, v.p., 1977-80; bd. dirs. Met. Police Boys and Girls Club, 1st v.p., 1989-93, pres., 1994-96, chmn. membership com., 1984-93; mem. adv. com. Am. Coun. Young Polit. Leaders, 1982-90; mem. Nat. Coun. Friends Kennedy Ctr., 1984-91; bd. dirs. Whitman-Walker Clinic, 1988-2006, v.p., 1995-96; bd. dirs. St. John's Child Devel. Ctr., 1989-91, Hattie M. Strong Found., 1995—; trustee Kennedy Ctr. Cmty. and Friends Bd., 1991—, chmn. ednl. task force, 1993—; trustee Jewish Coun. on Aging, 1991-93; v.p. adv. bd. Am. Automobile Assn., 1988-06; bd. dirs. Washington Hebrew Congregation, 1995-98. Mem. Cosmos Club. Republican. Jewish.

**SCHWARTZ, CHARLES WALTER,** lawyer; b. Brenham, Tex., Dec. 27, 1953; s. Walter C. and Annie (Kuehn) S. BS, U. Tex., 1975, MA, 1980, JD, 1977; LLM, Harvard U., 1980. Bar: Tex. 1977; bd. cert. civil appellate law Tex. Bd. Legal Specialization. Law clk. U.S. Ct. Appeals (5th cir.), Austin, Tex., 1977-79; assoc. Vinson & Elkins LLP, Houston, 1980—86, ptnr., 1986—2003, Skadden, Arps, Slate, Meagher & Flom, 2003—. Contbr. articles to law revs. Fellow: Am. Bar Found., Tex. Bar Found. (sustaining life), Coll. State Bar Tex., Houston Bar Found. (sustaining life); mem.: ABA, Tex. Law Rev. Assn., Am. Law Inst., Bar Assn. of 5th Cir., State Bar Tex. (former chmn. grievance com. 1993—99, bd. dirs. 2000—04, exec. com. 2001—04, chmn. 2002—03, immediate past chmn. 2003—04). Home: 2154 Chilton Rd Houston TX 77019 Office: Skadden Arps Slate Meagher & Flom LLP 1000 Louisiana St Ste 6800 Houston TX 77002 Office Phone: 713-655-5160. Business E-Mail: schwartz@skadden.com.

**SCHWARTZ, DANIEL BENNETT,** artist; b. N.Y.C., Feb. 16, 1929; s. Bennett Henry and Lillian (Blumenthal) S.; m. Judith Nancy Kass, June 12, 1955 (div. 1980); 1 child, Claudia Bennet. Grad., High Sch. of Music and Art, N.Y.C., 1946; student, Art Students League, 1946, Y. Kuniyoshi; BFA, R.I. Sch. Design, 1949. Instr. pvt. painting class, 1965-81, 90-95, Parsons Sch. Design, 1983. One man shows include Davis Galleries, N.Y.C., 1955, 56, 58, 60, Hirschl & Adler Galleries, N.Y.C., 1963, Maxwell Galleries, San Francisco, 1964, Babcock Galleries, N.Y.C., 1967, F.A.R. Galleries, N.Y.C., 1970, Armstrong Galleries, N.Y.C., 1985, 87, Hammer Galleries, N.Y.C., 1994, Hudson River Gallery, Dobbs Ferry, N.Y., 2001; exhibited in group shows at Albany Inst. History and Art, Am. Fedn. Arts, Butler Inst. Am. Art, Libr. of Congress, Nat. Acad. Design, Pa. Acad. Fine Art, Whitney Mus. Art, Collection Nat. Portrait Gallery, Munson-Williams-Proctor Inst., Bates Coll., Brit. Mus., Century Assn., others; subject of various articles and monograph. Louis C. Tiffany Found. grantee, 1956, 60; recipient Purchase prize Am. Acad. Arts and letters, 1964, 84, 11 Gold medals Soc. Illustrators, N.Y.C., 1960-85, Obrig prize for painting Nat. Acad. Design, 1990, winner 1st Benjamin Altman Figure prize, 1992; named to Soc. of Illustrators Hall of Fame, 2002. Mem. NAD, Century Assn. Avocation: jazz piano. E-mail: dschwartz17@nyc.rr.com.

**SCHWARTZ, DANIEL C.,** lawyer; b. Pa., 1943; AB, Stanford U., 1965; JD, George Washington U., 1969. Bar: D.C. 1969. Asst. to dir. Bur. Competition, FTC, Washington, 1973-75, asst. dir. evaluation, 1975-77, dep. dir., 1977-79; gen. counsel Nat. Security Agy., Washington, 1979-81; ptnr., group leader Corp. Compliance and Defense Bryan Cave LLP, Washington. Mem. ABA. Office: Bryan Cave LLP 700 13th St NW Fl 7 Washington DC 20005-5921 Office Phone: 202-508-6025. Business E-Mail: dcschwartz@bryancave.com.

**SCHWARTZ, DAVID A.,** federal agency administrator; m. Louise Sparks; 3 children. BA in biology, U. Rochester, 1975; MD, U. Calif., San Diego, 1979; MPH in occupational medicine, Harvard U., 1985. Diplomate Nat. Bd. Med. Examiners, 1981, Am. Bd. Internal Medicine, 1984, Am. Bd. Occupational Medicine, 1986, Am. Bd. Internal Medicine Subspecialty Bd. Pulmonary Disease, 1988, lic. NC, Iowa, DC, Tex. Training in tropical medicine Walter Reed Army Inst. Rsch., 1979; Pub. Svc. Sci. Resident NSF, 1979—80; intern then resident Boston City Hosp., 1980—83, chief resident in medicine, 1983—84; rsch. fellow Robert Wood Johnson Clin. Scholars Program U. Wash., Seattle, 1985—87, pulmonary and critical care fellow, 1985—88; asst. prof. Pulmonary Disease Divsn., Dept. Internal Medicine U. Iowa, Iowa City, 1988—92, assoc. prof. Pulmonary Disease, Critical Care, and Occupational Medicine Divsn., Dept. Internal Medicine, 1992—96, prof., 1996—2000, dir. occupational medicine, 1988—2000, assoc. chair program devel. Dept. Internal Medicine, 1996—2000, dir. Ctr. Environ. Lung Disease, 1997—2000, co-PI, assoc. dir. Environ. Health Sciences Rsch. Ctr., 1997—2000, mem. med. Scientist Training Program, 1999—2000, mem. Genetics Program, 1999—2000; staff physician VA Med. Ctr., Iowa City, 1989—2000; chief Divsn. Pulmonary and Critical Care Medicine Duke U. Med. Ctr., Durham, NC, 2000—05, dir. Ctr. Environ. Genomics, Inst. Genome Sci. and Policy, 2000—05, prof. medicine and genetics, 2000—05, Walter Kempner Prof. Medicine, 2001—05, vice chair. rsch. Dept. Medicine, 2003—05; prof. environ. sciences and policy Nicholas Sch. Environment and Health Sciences, Duke U., 2001—05, adj. prof., 2005—; staff physician VA Med. Ctr., Durham, 2000—04; dir. Nat. Inst. Environ. Health Sciences, NIH, Rsch. Triangle Pk., NC, 2005—. Nat. Toxicology Program, NIH, 2005—. Mem.: APHA, Am. Thoracic Soc. (Sci. Accomplishment Award 2003), Soc. Gen. Internal Medicine, Am. Soc. Human Genetics, Assn. Am. Physicians, Am. Soc. Clin. Investigation, Am. Fedn. Clin. Rsch., Am. Coll. Physicians, Am. Coll. Chest Physicians. Office: Nat Inst Environ Health Sciences PO Box 12233 111 TW Alexander Dr Research Triangle Park NC 27709 Office Phone: 919-541-3201. Office Fax: 919-541-2260. E-mail: david.schwartz@niehs.nih.gov.

**SCHWARTZ, DAVID JAY,** lawyer; b. 1967; s. Rand and Sandy Schwartz; m. Amy Roslyn Divak, June 1, 1996; 2 children. BA in economics, Duke U., 1989; JD, U. Pa., 1992; MBA, Columbia U., 1999. Bar: 1992. Corp. atty. Anderson, Kill & Olick PC, NYC; v.p., corp. counsel Toys "R" Us Inc., Wayne, NJ, 2001—02, sr. corp. counsel, 2002—03, sr. v.p., gen. counsel, 2003—. Office: Toys R Us Inc 1 Geoffrey Way Wayne NJ 07470-2030

**SCHWARTZ, DONALD FRANKLIN,** communication scientist; b. Jamestown, N.D., 1935; m. Lois Carolyn Schwartz, June 26, 1965; children: Daria, Karin, Marc. BS, ND State U., 1957, MS, 1961; PhD, Mich. State U., 1968. Asst. dir. pub. rels. ND State U., Fargo, 1959-66, social scis., 1969-71, chmn. comm., 1977-79; instr. comm. Mich. State U., East Lansing, 1966-67; vis. scientist US Dept. Agr., Washington, 1979-80; prof. comm. Cornell U., Ithaca, NY, 1980-98, chmn. dept., 1980-85, dir. undergraduate studies, 1995-98, prof. emeritus, 1998—. Vis. scholar U. N.Mex., 1994. Contbr. articles to profl. jours. Recipient Outstanding Svc. award Future Farmers Am., 1976, Svc. award USDA, 1980, A.D. White Prof. of Yr. award, 1993; named Alumni of Yr., Alpha Gamma Rho, 2005. Mem. AAUP, Internat. Comm. Assn. (sec., pub. rels. interest group 2004), Acad. Mgmt., Am. Soc. Pers. Adminstrn. (chpt. pres. 1976-77), Pub. Rels. Soc. Am. (nat. faculty advisor student assn. 1989-90, vice-chair educators sect. 1992, Pres.'s Citation for Leadership 1990, nat. ednl. affairs com. 1993-96). Roman Catholic. Office: Cornell U Dept Communication 331 Kennedy Hall Ithaca NY 14853-4203

**SCHWARTZ, DONALD LEE,** lawyer; b. Milw., Dec. 8, 1948; s. Bernard L. and Ruth M. (Marshall) S.; m. Susan J. Dunst, June 5, 1971; children: Stephanie Jane, Cheryl Ruth. BA, Macalester Coll., 1971; JD, U. Chgo., 1974. Bar: Ill. 1974. Assoc. Sidley & Austin, Chgo., 1974-80, ptnr., 1980-88, Latham & Watkins, Chgo., 1988—. Chmn. Ill. Conservative Union, 1979-81, bd. dirs. 1977-85. Served with U.S. Army, 1971-77. Mem. ABA (uniform comml. code com., comml. fin. svcs. comm.), Ill. Bar Assn. (sec. coun. banking and bankuprtcy sect. 1982-83), Chgo. Bar Assn. (chmn. comml. law com. 1980-81, fin. insts. com. 1982-83), Ivanhoe Country Club, Sea Pines Country Club, Colleton River Country Club, Met. Club. Republican. Episcopalian. Avocation: golf. Home: 191 Park Ave Glencoe IL 60022-1351 Office: Latham & Watkins Ste 5800 Sears Tower Chicago IL 60606 Office Phone: 312-876-7631. Business E-Mail: donald.schwartz@lw.com.

**SCHWARTZ, EDWARD ARTHUR,** lawyer; b. Boston, Sept. 27, 1937; s. Abe and Sophie (Gottheim) S.; m. Sheila Kauffman, Apr. 5, 1997; children: Eric Allen, Jeffrey Michael. AB, Oberlin Coll., 1959; LLB, Boston Coll., 1962; postgrad., Am. U., 1958—59, Northeastern U., 1970; postgrad. exec. program, Stanford U., 1979. Bar: Conn. 1962, Mass. 1965. Legal intern Office Atty. Gen. Commonwealth of Mass., 1961; assoc. Schatz & Schatz, Hartford, Conn., 1962—65, Cohn, Reimer & Pollack, Boston, 1965—67; v.p., gen. coun., sec. Digital Equipment Corp., Maynard, Mass., 1967—88; pres. New Eng. Legal Found., Boston, 1990—98. Vis. prof. law Boston Coll., 1986, adj. prof., 1987-89 bd. dirs. vice chmn. SatelLife Corp. Editor Boston Coll. Indsl. and Comml. Law Rev, 1960-62, Ann. Survey Mass. Law, 1960-62. Home: PO Box 1148 West Tisbury MA 02575

**SCHWARTZ, ELEANOR BRANTLEY,** academic administrator; b. Kite, Ga., Jan. 1, 1937; d. Jesse Melvin and Hazel (Hill) Brantley; children: John, Cynthia. Student, U. Va., 1955, Ga. Southern Coll., 1956-57; BBA, Ga. State U., 1962, MBA, 11963, DBA, 1969. Adminstrv. asst. Fin. Agy., 1954, Fed. Govt., Va., Pa., Ga., 1956-59; asst. dean admissions Ga. State U., Atlanta, 1961-66, asst. prof., 1966-70; assoc. prof. Cleve. State U., 1970-75, prof. and assoc. dean, 1975-80; dean, Harzfeld prof. U. Mo.-Kansas City, 1980-87, vice chancellor acad. affairs, 1987-91, interim chancellor, 1991-92, chancellor, 1992-99; prof. mgmt. U. Mo. Block Sch., Kansas City, 1999—2003, prof. emeritus, 2003—. Disting. vis. prof. Berry Coll., Rome, N.Y. State U. Coll., Fredonia, Mons U., Belgium; cons. pvt. industry U.S., Europe, Can.; bd. dirs. Roch. Med. Ctr., Waddell & Reed Funds, Inc., Toy and Miniature Mus., Menorah Med. Ctr. Found., NCAA, NCCJ, Econ. Devel. Corp. of Kansas City, Silicon Prairie Tech. Assn. Author: Sex Barriers in Business, 1971, Contemporary Readings in Marketing, 1974; (with Muczyk and Smith) Principles of Supervision, 1984. Chmn., Mayor's Task Force in Govt. Efficiency, Kansas City, Mo., 1984; mem. comm. unity planning and rsch. coun. United Way Kansas City, 1983-85; bd. dirs. Jr. Achievement, 1982-86. Named Jones Store Career Woman of Yr., Kansas City, Mo., 1989, Ctrl. Exch. Woman of Yr., 1995; named one of 60 Women of Achievement, Girl Scouts Coun. Mid Continent, 1983; recipient Disting. Faculty award, Cleve. State U., 1974, Disting. Svc. award, Kans. State U., 1992, YWCA Hearts of Gold award, 2002. Mem.: Alpha Iota Delta, Golden Key, Phi Kappa Phi. Office Phone: 816-942-1840.

**SCHWARTZ, ELEANORE ANITA,** retired elementary school educator, small business owner; b. Milw., Aug. 24, 1934; d. Arthur Eric Hageleit and Anna Wurth; m. James W. Schwartz, July 28, 1956; children: Ray Eric, Ted William. BA, San Francisco State Coll., 1955. Cert. tchr. Calif., 1966. Elem. sch. tchr. Millbrae Sch. Dist., Calif., 1955—59; substitute tchr. Cupertino Sch. Dist., Calif., 1960—67, elem. sch. tchr. Calif., 1961; substitute tchr. San Jose Unified Sch. Dist., 1967—85; tchr. needle art West Valley C.C., Saratoga, Calif., 1986—92; ret. Gift shop mgr. Good Shepherd Auxiliary, Saratoga, 1989—92. Chmn. bd. dirs. The Lace Mus., Sunnyvale, 1999—. Named Citizen of the Day, Radio KABL, San Francisco, 1993; recipient Cross & Bell award, Good Sheperd Cmtys., 1992, 2005. Mem.: DEA, Internat. Old Lacers, Inc., Calif., Nev., Hawaii Dist. Luth. Women's Missionary League (v.p. mission svcs. 1988—2006, v.p. convention planning 1988—2006, treas. 1978—86). Christian. Avocations: lacemaking, needlecrafts. Office: The Lace Mus 552 S Murphy Ave Sunnyvale CA 94086

**SCHWARTZ, ELI,** retired economics professor, writer; b. N.Y.C., Apr. 2, 1921; s. Israel and Tillie (Shapiro) S.; m. Renee S. Kartiganer, Aug. 29, 1948; children: Pamela F., Alan G. BS, Denver U., 1943; MA, U. Conn., 1948; PhD, Brown U., 1952. Instr. U. R.I, Kingston, 1947-48; asst. instr. Brown U., Providence, 1948-51; chief regional economist Office Price Stblzn., Boston, 1951-53; lectr. Mich. State U., East Lansing, 1953-54; asst. prof. econs. Lehigh U., Bethlehem, Pa., 1954-58, assoc. prof., 1958-62, prof., 1962-91, Charles Macfarlane prof. econs., 1978-91, chmn. dept. econs., 1978-84, ret., 1991; cons. econs. and fin., expert witness Schwartz-Aronson Assocs., Bethlehem, 1965—. Author: Corporate Finance, 1962, Trouble in Eden, 1980; editor: Managing Municipal Finance, 1980, 83, 87, 96, 2004, Restructuring the Thrift Industry, 1989, Theory and Application of the Interest Rate, 1993; columnist Allentown Moring Call. With U.S. Army, 1943-46, ETO. Recipient sr. teaching Lehigh U., 1972; Earhart Found. grantee, 1978 Mem. Am. Econs. Assn., Am. Fin. Assn., Nat. Assn. Forensic Econs. (founding mem.). Jewish. Home: 3185 W Cedar St Allentown PA 18104-3441 Office: Lehigh U Dept Econs Rauch Ctr 621 Taylor St Bethlehem PA 18015-3107 Office Phone: 610-758-3410. *If I have achieved any success it is because I am interested in the subject matter of my field. I am fortunate to enjoy reading, teaching, consulting and writing.*

**SCHWARTZ, ELLIOTT SHELLING,** composer, writer, music educator; b. Bklyn., Jan. 19, 1936; s. Nathan and Rose (Shelling) S.; m. Dorothy Rose Feldman, June 26, 1960; children: Nina, Jonathan. AB, Columbia U., 1957, MA, 1958, EdD, 1962. Instr. music U. Mass., Amherst, 1960-64; from asst. prof. music to assoc. prof. Bowdoin Coll., Brunswick, Maine, 1964-75, prof. music, 1975—. Vis. prof. music Ohio State U., Columbus, 1988-92; vis. composer Trinity Coll. Music, London, 1967, U. Calif. Coll. Creative Studies, Santa Barbara, 1970, 73, 74; composer, pianist, commentator British Broadcast Corp, London, 1972, 74, 78, 83; vis. research musician Center Music Expt., La Jolla, Calif., 1978-79; disting. vis. prof. Ohio State U., 1985-86; music cons. Holt, Rinehart & Winston, Random House, Oxford Univ. Press, Schirmer Books, N.Y.C., 1977—; vis. fellow Robinson Coll., Cambridge U., U.K., 1993-94, 99. Composer: Island, 1970 (Internat, Gaudeamus prize 1970), Chamber Concerto IV, 1977-81, Extended Piano, 1980, Dream Music With Variations, 1983, Four Ohio Portraits, 1986, Memorial in Two Parts, 1989, Elan, 1990, Rows Garden, 1993, Equinox, 1994, Timepiece, 1994, Chiaroscuro, 1995, Reflections, 1995, Rainbow, 1996, Tapestry, 1996, Alto Prisms, 1997, Vienna Dreams, 1998, Kaleidoscope, 1999, Jack O'Lantern, 2000, Mehitabel's Serenade, 2000, Rain Forest with Birds, 2001, Voyager, 2002, Downtown Crossing, 2004, Summer's Journey, 2005; author: Electronic Music: A Listener's Guide, 1973, Music: Ways of Listening, 1982, (with Daniel Godfrey) Music Since 1945: Issues, Materials and Literature, 1993; editor: (with Barney Childs) Contemporary Composers on Contemporary Music, 1967, rev. edit., 1998; contbr. articles to profl. jours. Nat. Endowment for Arts composition grantee, 1974, 76, 82; Rockefeller Found. residence fellow Bellagio, Italy, 1980, 89; MacDowell Colony resident fellow, 1965, 66; Yaddo residence fellow, 1977; recipient Maine State award Maine Commn. Arts and Humanities, 1970, McKim Commn., 1986 Mem.: Am. Composers Alliance (governing bd. 1994—2000), Am. Soc. Univ. Composers (nat. coun. 1968—72, nat. chmn. 1983—88), Coll. Music Soc. (nat. coun. 1984—88, pres. 1988—90), Am. Music Ctr. (v.p. 1981—87). Home: PO Box 451 South Freeport ME 04078-0451 Office: Bowdoin Coll Dept Music Brunswick ME 04011 Office Phone: 207-725-3320. Office Fax: 207-725-3748. E-mail: eschwart@bowdoin.edu.

**SCHWARTZ, ESTAR ALMA,** lawyer; b. Bklyn., June 29, 1950; d. Henry Israel and Elaine Florence (Scheiner) Sutel; m. Lawrence Gerald Schwartz, June 28, 1976 (div. Dec. 1977); 1 child, Joshua (dec.); m. James Frances Edward Stuart, Sept. 25, 1999 (div. Aug. 2001). JD, NYU, 1980. Mgr., ptnr. Scheiner, Scheiner, DeVito & Wytte, N.Y.C., 1966-81; social security fraud specialist U.S. Govt., 1982—83; pensions Todtman, Epstein, et al, 1983—85; office mgr., sec. Sills, Beck, Cummins, 1985—86; office mgr., bookkeeper Philip, Birnbaum & Assoc., 1986—87; office mgr., sec. Stanley Posses, Esq., Queens, 1989—90. Owner Estaris Paralegal Svc., Flushing, N.Y., 1992—; Sutel Creative Mgmt. Agy., Flushing, 1999—; Democrat. Jewish. Avocations: needlepoint, horseback riding, tennis, bowling, writing books and cookbooks. Home and office: 67-20 Parsons Blvd Apt 2A Flushing NY 11365-2960 Office Phone: 718-820-0432. Personal E-mail: sutelmmgmt12345@msn.com. Business E-mail: sutel@email.com, estaris@email.com.

**SCHWARTZ, FRANCIS,** music educator, composer; b. Altoona, Pa., Mar. 10, 1940; s. Isidore Joseph Schwartz and Simone Klughaupt; m. Martha Elena Moreno, Nov. 17, 1990; 1 child, Gabriela Raquel. BS, Juilliard Sch., 1961, MS, 1962; PhD, U. Paris, 1979. Prof. music U. of PR, San Juan, PR, 1966—99, dean Humanities Coll., 1995—99. Vis. prof. of music U. of Paris, 1977—79. Composer: (multi-sensorial sculpture-instrument) Mon Oeuf de Centre Pompidou. V.p. U. PR Press, San Juan, 1990—2000. Named Chevalier, Ordre des Arts et Lettres, French Govt., 1986. Mem.: ASCAP. Avocations: tennis, wine and food studies, travel. Home and Office: 435 South Gulfstream Ave Sarasota FL 34236 E-mail: maqroll40@yahoo.com.

**SCHWARTZ, GEORGE R.,** physician, researcher; b. Caribou, Maine; m. Colleen Jill Schwartz; children: Ruth, Rebekah, Rachel, Moses, Abigail, John Gabriel, Aaron. BS in Chemistry with honors, Hobart Coll., 1963; MD magna cum laude, SUNY, Bklyn., 1967. Diplomate Am. Bd. Family Practice, Am. Bd. Emergency Medicine; cert. CPR instr. Intern King County Hosp., Seattle, 1967-68; instr. dept. medicine U. Wash., Seattle, 1967-68; resident in psychiatry Hillside Hosp., Glen Oaks, NY, 1968-69; resident in surgery Ind. U. Med. Ctr., Indpls., 1971-72; instr. emergency medicine Med. Coll. Pa., Phila., 1972-76, dir. emergency svcs., asst. dir. emergency medicine program, 1972-74; dir. emergency medicine West Jersey Hosp., 1974-76; pvt. practice, 1977; assoc. prof. divsn. emergency medicine U. N.Mex., Albuquerque, 1978-83; staff mem. emergency medicine Heights Gen. Hosp., Albuquerque, 1983-85; with Los Alamos (N.Mex.) Med. Ctr., 1985-90. Vis. assoc. prof. Med. Coll. Pa., 1991—; co-founder Allied Genomics; ptnr. Brain Resuscitation Rsch. LLC; pres. Schwartz Pharm. and Med. Rsch. LLC. Author: Geriatric Emergencies, 1984; Co-author: (with Tandberg) Emergency Medicine Continuing Edn. Rev., 1981, 2d edit, 1984, (with Bosker) Geriatric Emergency Medicine, 1990; editor: Principles and Practice Emergency Medicine, 1978, 3d edit., 1992, 4th edit., 1999; co-editor Trauma Rounds, 1973-75; editorial bd. Annals Emergency Medicine, 1972-81, Resident and Staff Physician, 1978—, Emergency Med. Abstracts, 1978-85, Med. Exam. Publ. Co., 1981-87; contbr. articles to profl. jours., chpts. to textbooks. Med. dir. The Bridge Counselling Ctrs., Los Alamos, N.Mex., 1988-91, N.Mex. Poison Ctr., 1978-83; dir. planning com. disaster exercise Phila. Internat. Airport, 1974, Camden County Poison Ctr., 1974-76. Recipient Gallup award, 1973, Giraffe award, 1990. Mem. AAAS, AMA, Am. Coll. Emergency Physicians (charter mem.; pres. N.Mex. chpt. 1980-81), N.Mex. Med. Soc., Univ. Assn. Emergency Physicians (chmn. socio-econ. com. 1976-77), Internat. Emergency Care Assn., Am. Trauma Soc. (founding mem.), Am. Acad. Clin. Toxicology, Am. Acad. Emergency Medicine (founding mem., sec. 1994, bd. dirs. 1998—), Internat. Assn. for Study of MSG and Food Additives (pres. 1988). Achievements include patents in field; research in computer applications in medicine, new medical diagnostic instruments. Address: Rsch Inst/Schwartz Pharm LLC Santa Fe NM 87504-1968 Business E-Mail: drgschwartz@healingresearch.org.

**SCHWARTZ, GERALD,** public relations and fundraising agency executive; b. NYC, June 22, 1927; s. George and Martha F. S.; m. Felice P. Schwartz, June 25, 1950; children: Gary R., Gregg R., Wendy L. Student, NC State U., 1944-45; AB, U. Miami, Fla., 1949, BS, 1950, postgrad., 1966-67. Staff writer Miami Herald, 1941-44; publicity dir. U.S. Army in Europe, 1946-48; editor Miami Beach Sun, 1950-51; fund raising and pub. rels. counselor Miami, 1952-58; press sec. to Gov. Nebr., 1959—60; exec. v.p. Bar-Ilan U., Ramat Gan, Israel, 1960-61; prin. Gerald Schwartz Agy., Miami, Fla., 1962—. Editor, pub. Jewish Herald Newspaper, 1999-2000; editor, pub. emeritus Jewish Star-Times, 2000-2003. Nat. v.p. Am. Zionist Fedn., 1985—89, 1991—93; pres. Press.'s coun. Zionist Orgn. Am., 1983—85; nat. chmn. Friends of Pioneer Women/Na'amat, 1984—98; pres. Am. Zionist Fedn. So. Fla., 1970—73, 1986—92; vice chmn. Urban League of Greater Miami, 1983—87, City of Miami Beach Planning Bd., 1953—55; bd. dirs. Greater Miami Symphony, 1982—87, Miami Beach Taxpayers Assn., 1988—89; pres. Civic League Miami Beach, 1985—87; pres. Greater Miami chpt. Assn. Welfare of Soldiers in Israel, 1983—86; chmn. City of Miami Beach Hurricane Def. Com., 1978—86, 1990—97; trustee South Shore Hosp. and Med. Ctr., Miami, 1987—2004, exec. vice-chmn. Miami Beach, 1989—2004; vice chmn. South Shore Med. Ctr. Found., 1980—2004; bd. govs. Barry U., 1985—86; chmn. Econ. Devel. Coun. City of Miami Beach, 1985—91; bd. dirs. Crimestoppers of Dade County, 1991—94; mem. exec. bd. State of Israel Bonds Orgn., 1996—; dep. chmn. Dem. Midwest Conf., 1958—60; bd. dirs. adminstrv. com. Jewish Nat. Fund of Am., 1995—, v.p. Greater Miami region, 1996—97; bd. dirs. Temple Emanu-El of Greater Miami, Papanicolaou Cancer Rsch. Inst., Miami, 1962—80. With U.S. Army, 1944—46. Recipient Jerusalem Peace award State of Israel Bonds, 1978, Jerusalem 3000 award State of Israel, 1996. Mem. Pub. Rels. Soc. Am. (accredited; treas. So. Fla. chpt. 1962-64), Am. Pub. Rels. Assn. (pres. chpt. 1960-61), Am. Assn. Polit. Cons., Nat. Assn. Fund Raising Execs. (pres. chpt. 1977-78), Miami Beach Taxpayers Assn. (bd. dirs. 1994-2000), Miami Internat. Press Club (bd. dirs. 1991-99), Miami Beach C. of C. (v.p. 1978-80, 81-84, 86-87, pres.-elect 1988-90, trustee 1990—), Lead and Ink, Tiger Bay Club (pres. 1986-88), Prime Minister's Club of State of Israel (Greater Miami chmn. 1997—), B'nai B'rith (pres. lodge 1964-66), Theta Omicron Pi, Omicron Delta Kappa, Alpha Delta Sigma (pres. 1965-67), Zeta Beta Tau. Office: Gerald Schwartz Agy 18909 NE 5th Ave Miami FL 33179 Office Phone: 305-249-3032. Personal E-mail: geraldsch62227@aol.com.

**SCHWARTZ, GERALD WILFRED,** business executive; b. Winnipeg, Man., Can., Nov. 24, 1941; s. Andrew O. and Lillian Arkin (Leith) S.; m. Heather Reisman, May 15, 1982; children: Carey, Jill, Andrea, Anthony. B.Commerce, U. Man., 1962, LLB, 1966; MBA, Harvard U., 1970. V.p. Estabrook & Co., Inc., N.Y.C., 1970-73, Bear Stearns & Co., N.Y.C., 1973-77; pres., dir., mem. exec. com. CanWest Capital Corp., Winnipeg, 1977-83; chmn., pres., CEO ONEX Corp., Toronto, 1984—; bd. dirs. Celestica Internat. Holdings Inc. Bd. trustees Simon Wiesenthal Ctr. Bd. dirs. Can. Coun. Christians and Jews; vice chmn., mem. exec. com. Mt. Sinai Hosp. Toronto; trustee Simon Wiesenthal Ctr.; founder, mem. adv. bd. HSEG; cofounder, vice-chmn. Can. Coun. Israel and Jewish Advocacy. With RCAF, 1958. Decorated Order of Can. Office: Onex Corp 161 Bay St 49th Fl PO Box 700 Toronto ON Canada M5J 2S1

**SCHWARTZ, GIL (STANLEY BING),** broadcast executive, writer; b. Ill., 1951; children: Nina, Will. BA in Theater Arts and English, Brandeis Univ. Humor writer Boston Phoenix; theater co. mgr. Boston, Mass.; news columnist. Teleprompter Corp. (Westinghouse Group W HBO forerunner), 1981—84; dir., com. Group W Cable, NYC, 1984—87, Group W TV, NYC, 1987—89; v.p. com. Group W TV station group, NYC, 1989—93; v.p., corp. com. Westinghouse Broadcasting, NYC, 1993—96; sr. v.p., com. to exec. v.p. com. CBS Network TV, NYC, 1996—. Author: (plays) Ferocious Kisses, Love As We Know It; columnist (as Stanley Bing) Esquire Mag., 1984—95, Fortune Mag., 1995—; author (as Stanley Bing): (books) Crazy Bosses: Spotting Them, Serving Them, Surviving Them, 1992, Lloyd: What Happened, 1998, What Would Machiavelli Do: The Ends Justify the Meanness, 2000, Throwing the Elephant: Zen and the Art of Managing Up, 2002, You Look Nice Today, 2003, The Big Bing: Black Holes of Time Management, Gaseous Executive Bodies, Exploding Careers, and Other Theories on the Origins of the Business Universe, 2003, Sun Tzu Was A Sissy, 2004, 100 Bullshit Jobs...And How to Get Them, 2006, Rome, Inc.: The Rise and Fall of the First Multinational Corporation, 2006. Author: Stanley Bing HarperCollins Author Mail 10 E 53rd St New York New York 10022 Office: Communications Dept CBS TV 51 W 52nd St New York New York 10019*

**SCHWARTZ, GORDON FRANCIS,** surgeon, educator; b. Plainfield, NJ, Apr. 29, 1937; s. Samuel H. and Mary (Adelman) S.; m. Rochelle DeG. Krantz, Sept. 5, 1959; children— Amory Blair, Susan Leslie AB, Princeton U., 1956; MD, Harvard U., 1960; MBA, U. Pa., 1990. Intern N.Y. Hosp.-Cornell Med. Ctr., N.Y.C., 1960-61; resident in surgery Columbia-Presbyterian Med. Ctr., N.Y.C., 1963-68; instr. surgery Columbia U., N.Y.C., 1966-68; assoc. in surgery U. Pa., Phila., 1968-70; dir. clin. services Breast Diagnostic Ctr., Jefferson Med. Coll., Phila., 1973-78, asst. prof. surgery, 1970-71, assoc. prof., 1971-78, prof., 1978—; dir. breast surgery fellowship

2003—. Practice medicine specializing in surgery and diseases of breast, Phila., 1968—; founder, chmn. acad. com. sec. of Med. bd. Breast Health Inst., 1990—; edtl. bd. The Breast Jour., 1994—. Author: (with R.H. Guthrie, Jr.) Reconstructive and Aesthetic Mammoplasty, 1989, (with Douglas Marchant) Breast Disease: Diagnosis and Treatment, 1981; mem. editl. bd. The Breast-Ofcl. Jour. of the European Soc. of Mastology, 1996—, Cancer, 1997—; co-editor Seminars Breast Disease, 1997; mem. editl. bd. ONE, Oncology Econs., 1999—; contbr. mroe than 200 articles to profl. jours. Mem. Pa. Gov.'s Task Force on Cancer, 1976-82; mem. breast cancer task force Phila. chpt. Am. Cancer Soc.; mem. clin. investigation rev. com. Nat. Cancer Inst., 1992-95. Served to capt. AUS, 1961-63. NIH Cancer Control fellow, 1968-69 Mem. ACS, AMA, AAUP, Assn. for Acad. Surgery, Allen O. Whipple Surg. Assn., Soc. Surg. Oncology, Internat. Cardiovasc. Soc., Soc. for Surgery Alimentary Tract, John Jones Surg. Soc., Am. Soc. Clin. Oncology, Am. Soc. Breast Diseases (pres. 1981-83), Soc. Internat. Senologie (treas. 1982-90, v.p. 1990-92, sci. com. 1992—), Am. Soc. Breast Surgeons, N.Y. Acad. Scis., Am. Soc. Artificial Internal Organs, Am. Radium Soc., Philadelphia County Med. Soc. (chmn. com. on econs. 1999-2000, bd. dirs. 1999-2000), Internat. Sentinel Node Soc. (founding mem. 2003), Italian Soc. Senology (hon.), Greek Surg. Soc. (hon.), The Phila. Club, Union League, Princeton Club Phila. (pres. 1989-91), Princeton Club (N.Y.C.), Princeton Terrace Club, Nassau Club, Phi Beta Kappa, Sigma Xi, Alpha Omega Alpha, Nu Sigma Nu. Republican. Jewish. Office: 1015 Chestnut St Ste 510 Philadelphia PA 19107-4305 Office Phone: 215-627-8487.

**SCHWARTZ, HERBERT FREDERICK,** lawyer; b. Bklyn., Aug. 23, 1935; s. Henry and Blanche Theodora (goldberg) S.; m. Gail Lubets, Jan. 23, 1960; children: Wendy Helene, Karen Anne, Peter Andrew; m. Nan Budde Chequer, Mar. 13, 1987; stepchildren: Elizabeth Guthrie, Anne Hamilton, Laura Dunham. BSEE, MIT, 1957; MA in Applied Econs., U. Pa., 1964, LLB, 1964. Assoc. Fish & Neave, NYC, 1964-70, jr. ptnr., 1970-71, mng. ptnr., 1985-91, ptnr., 1972—2004, Ropes & Gray, 2005—. Lectr. law U. Pa., Phila., 1980-89, adj. prof., 1990—, NYU, 2003-. Author: Patent Law and Practice, Federal Judicial Center, 1988, 2d edit., 1995, Bureau of National Affairs, 2d edit., 1996, 5th edit., 2006; co-author: Principles of Patent Law, 1998, 2d edit., 2001; contbr. articles to profl. jours. Vice-chmn. Jr. Yacht Racing Assn. of L.I. Sound, 1985-88. 1st lt. U.S. Army, Signal Corps, 1957-59. Mem. Assn. of Bar of City of N.Y., Am. Intellectual Property Lawyers Assn., N.Y. Intellectual Property Lawyers Assn. (pres. 1999-00), Woods Hole Oceanographic Instn. (mem. corp. 2003-, trustee 2006-), Am. Coll. Trial Lawyers, Am. Bar Found., Am. Law Inst., Order of Coif, N.Y. Yacht Club, Riverside Yacht Club, Cruising Club of Am. Avocation: racing and cruising sailboats. Home: 24 Cherry Tree Ln Riverside CT 06878-2629 Office: Ropes & Gray LLP 1251 Avenue Of The Americas New York NY 10020-1105 Business E-Mail: herbert.schwartz@ropesgray.com.

**SCHWARTZ, HOWARD S.,** lawyer; BA magna cum laude, Brown U., 1988; JD, U. Va., 1992. Bar: Md. 1993, D.C. 1993. Ptnr., co-chmn. Life Sciences practice group DLA Piper Rudnick Gray Cary, Balt. Bd. mem. Balt. City Cmty. Coll. Found.; mem. adv. bd. Torah Inst. Balt. Mem. ABA, DC Bar Assn., Md. State Bar Assn., Phi Beta Kappa. Office: DLA Piper Rudnick Gray Cary 6225 Smith Ave Baltimore MD 21209-3600 Office Phone: 410-580-4251. Office Fax: 410-580-3001. Business E-Mail: howard.schwartz@dlapiper.com.

**SCHWARTZ, HOWARD WYN,** business and marketing educator, consultant; b. Mpls., June 12, 1951; s. Jerry Schwartz and Geraldine (Berg) Brooks; m. Jeannie Marie Holtzmann, Aug. 2, 1975; children: Abigail Jorene, Rachel Elizabeth. BA cum laude, U. Minn., 1973, MBA, 1982, MEd, 1999. Cert. tchr. Minn. Acct. Med. Sch., U. Minn., 1973-77, bus. mgr. dept. neurology, 1977-79, adminstr. found. edn. dept., 1979-82, assoc. to chmn. dept. radiology, 1982-99; chmn. bus./mktg. edn. dept. Robbindale-Cooper H.S., New Hope, Minn., 1999—. Adj. instr. dept. radiology U. Minn., 1982—; pres. Bus. Mgmt. Svcs., Golden Valley, Minn., 1979—; lectr., author topics in bus./mktg. edn., 2000—. Editor-in-chief: RADWORKS Workload Measurement Manual, 1985-87; editor: Radiology Management, 1985-87, Purchasing the Radiology Information System, 1991, Current Concepts in Radiology Management, 1991; contbr. articles to profl. jours. Active Cystic Fibrosis Found., Minn., 1980—; chmn. Human Rights Commn., Robbinsdale, 1982-84; sec. Coord. Coun. Minority Concerns, 1984-85; chmn. imaging tech. adv. com. U. Hosp. Consortium, 1989-92; dir. U. Hosp. Consortium Svcs. Corp., 1990-92, Nat. Summit on Manpower, 1989-92; treas. Tech. Learning Campus Site Coun. Dist. 281, 1990-91, chmn. Bond Referendum campaign, 1995; pres. Armstrong HS Parent Assn., Dist. 281, 1991-92. Recipient In the Spirit of Youth Role Model award, Cmty. Ahead, 2004, Tchr. of Excellence award, Best Prep, 2004. Fellow: Am. Healthcare Radiology Adminstrn. (regional pres. 1986—87, nat. pres. 1988—89, sec. edn. found. 1990—91, edn. found. 1993—95, 1997—98, Outstanding Author award 1990, 1993, 1996, Midwest Region Disting. Mem. award 1991, Gold award 1991); mem.: NEA, Assn. Career and Tech. Edn., Assn. for Supervision and Curriculum Devel., Am. Fedn. Tchrs., Nat. Bus. Edn. Assn., Minn. Bus. Educators, Inc., Delta Pi Epsilon, Delta Kappa Epsilon. Home: 7400 Winnetka Heights Dr Golden Valley MN 55427-3549 Office: PO Box 27405 Minneapolis MN 55427-0405 Office Phone: 612-327-4165. Personal E-Mail: hwschwartz@comcast.net.

**SCHWARTZ, IRVING DONN,** architect; b. Chgo., June 11, 1927; s. Simon S. and Rose P. S.; children: Charles, Linda. BS, U. Ill., 1949, BS in Architecture, 1965, MS in Architecture, 1972. Registered architect, Ill., Ind., Fla., D.C., Ohio, Ga., Ala., Calif., N.H., Va., Md., Pa, Tenn., La., N.J., Tex., Mo., N.C., S.C., Ark. Chief standard cost and indsl. engring. Lanzit Corrugated Box Co., Chgo., 1950-53; pres. Kaufman, Inc., Champaign, Ill., 1953-60; v.p. Hart Mirror Plate Co., Grand Rapids, Mich 1953-60; assoc. Richardson, Severns, Scheeler & Assos., Inc., Champaign, 1960-71; pres. IDS, Inc., Champaign, 1971-83, ADI, Dallas, 1983-86, IDS/B, Inc., Dallas, 1986—. Prof. architecture Grad. Sch. Architecture, U. Ill., 1976-83; assoc. prof. design U. North Tex.; cons. in field. Mem. Champaign County Devel. Council; mem. Model Community Coordinating Council, Champaign; co-chmn. bldg. com. Mercy Hosp.; bd. frat. affairs U. Ill.; bd. dirs. United Fund. Served to 2d lt. U.S. Army, 1945-47. Recipient archtl. design research award, graphic design citation Progressive Architecture mag., 1974, Gold Key Design award Hospitality Mag., 1994, John Robinson award, 2001. Fellow Am. Soc. Interior Designers (treas. 1976, nat. pres. 1978, Louis Tregre award 1992, Nat. design award 1983); mem. AIA (Design award 1983), Nat. Council Archtl. Registration Bds., Nat. Council Interior Design Qualifications (bd. dirs., pres. 1980), Tex. Assn. Interior Design (pres. 1993). Clubs: Standard (Chgo.). Home: 4928 Briarwood Pl Dallas TX 75209-2004 Office: IDS/B Inc 2777 N Stemmons Fwy Ste 1650 Dallas TX 75207-2502 Office Phone: 214-630-6999. E-mail: idschwartz@idsb.com.

**SCHWARTZ, IRVING LEON,** internist, educator, research scientist; b. Cedarhurst, NY, Dec. 25, 1918; s. Abraham and Rose (Doniger) S.; m. Felice T. Nlerenberg, Jan. 12, 1946; children: Cornelia Ann, Albert Anthony, James Oliver. AB, Columbia U., 1939; MD, NYU, 1943. Diplomate Am. Bd. Internal Medicine. Intern, then asst. resident Bellevue Hosp., N.Y.C., 1943-44, 46-47; NIH fellow physiology NYU Coll. Medicine, N.Y.C., 1947-50; Am. Physiol. Soc. Porter fellow, also Gibbs meml. fellow in clin. sci. Rockefeller Inst., N.Y.C., 1950-51, mem. Am. Heart Assn. fellow, 1951-52, asst., then assoc., 1952-58; asst. physician, then assoc. physician Rockefeller Inst. Hosp., N.Y.C., 1950-58; sr. scientist Brookhaven Nat. Lab., Upton, NY, 1958-61, rsch. collaborator, 1961—97; attending physician Brookhaven Nat. Lab. Hosp. Upton, NY, 1958-97; Joseph Leidy prof. physiology, dir. dept. U. Cin. Coll. Medicine, 1961-65; dean grad. faculties Mt. Sinai Med. and Grad. Schs., CUNY, 1965-80, prof. physiology and biophysics, chmn. dept., 1968-79, exec. officer biomed. scis. doctoral program, 1969-72, Dr. Harold and Golden Lamport disting. prof., 1979-99; dir. Peptide and Membrane Research Mt. Sinai Med. Ctr., 1979-87; dean emeritus Mt. Sinai Grad. Sch. Biol. Scis., 1980—. Contbr. articles to sci. publs. Pres. Life Scis. Found., 1962-98, pres. emeritus, 1998—. Served from 1st lt. to capt. M.C. AUS, 1944-46. Recipient Solomon A. Berson Med. Alumni Achievement award NYU Sch. Medicine, 1973. Fellow ACP; mem. Am. Physiol. Soc., Soc. Exptl.

Biology and Medicine, Am. Soc. Clin. Investigation, Am. Fedn. Clin. Rsch.; Biophys. Soc., Endocrine Soc., Aspberger Internat. Found. (bd. mem.), Harvey Soc., Soc. for Neurosci., Am. Heart Assn, John Jay Assocs. Columbia Coll., AAAS, N.Y. Acad. Sci., N.Y. Acad. Medicine, Sigma Xi, Alpha Omega Alpha. Home: 1120 5th Ave # 14B New York NY 10128-0144 Office: Mt Sinai Med Ctr Grad Sch Biol Scis Box 1022 100th St & 5th Ave New York NY 10029 also: Brookhill Group 501 Madison Ave 18th Fl New York NY 10022 Personal E-mail: tj52414@sbcglobal.net. *The excitement and stimulation that comes from a productive collaboration with other people has been a major source of satisfaction in my life. I feel privileged to have had the opportunity to interact with a wide range of imaginative and inspiring colleagues, students and friends, including my wife of 50 years, whose extraordinary career emphasized the importance of idealism, commitment, persistence and a felicitous blending of focus and flexibility.*

**SCHWARTZ, JEFFREY BYRON,** lawyer; b. Phila., Dec. 3, 1940; s. Carl Sidney and Tessie Claire (Cohen) S.; m. Joan S. Weinman, Aug. 4, 1963; children: Kevin, Jill. BS, Pa. State U., 1962; JD, U. Pa., 1965; MBA, Am. U., 1967. Bar: Pa. 1965, D.C. 1968, La. 1969. Staff acct. Price Waterhouse & Co., Washington, 1962; trial atty. SEC, Washington, 1965-68; sr. atty. New Orleans Legal Assistance, 1968-70; gen. counsel Nat. Tenants Orgn., Washington, 1970-73; litigation atty. Nat. Health and Environ. Law Project, Washington, 1971-74; chief counsel Pa. Dept. Health, Harrisburg, 1974-79; ptnr. Berriman & Schwartz, King of Prussia, Pa., 1979-85; sr. ptnr. Wolf, Block, Schorr & Solis-Cohen, Phila., 1985-92; ptnr. Cohen, Shapiro, Polisher, Shiekman & Cohen, Phila., 1992-95, Fox Rothschild, O'Brien & Frankel, LLP, Phila., 1995-99; sr. legal advisor USAID Assistance Program Bulgarian Securities and Stock Exch. Commn., 1999—; atty. Schwartz Law LLC, 2000—; v.p., gen. counsel Crossover Med. Tech., 2000—. Guest lectr. on welfare and health law U. Pa. Sch. Law, Tulane U. Law Sch., Wayne State U. Law Sch. and Georgetown U. Law Sch.; instr. Catholic U. Am. Law Sch., 1972-73; course planner Pa. Bar Inst., 1980—. Contbr. articles to profl. jours. Reginald Heber Smith fellow, 1968-70. Mem. Am. Soc. Hosp. Attys., Am. Health Lawyers Assn. (dir.), Pa. Soc. Hosp. Attys. (pres. 1983-85, bd. dirs. 1983-89), Hosp. Attys. Southeastern Pa., Am. Pub. Health Assn. (chmn. health law com. 1978-81), Pa. Bar Assn., D.C. Bar Assn. Democrat. Jewish. Home: 10 Radcliff Rd Bala Cynwyd PA 19004-2631

**SCHWARTZ, JEFFREY H.,** distribution facilities executive; BS with honors, Emory Univ., 1981; MBA, Harvard Univ., 1985. CPA. Acct. Arthur Anderson, Atlanta, 1981—83; with Anderson Properties, Atlanta; co-founder, mng. ptnr. Krauss/Schwartz Co.; mgr. global develop. ProLogis, Denver, 1994—96, vice-chmn. internat. ops. Mexico, 1996, Amsterdam, Netherlands, 1997—2000; CEO Vizional Technologies, 2001; pres., COO Asia ProLogis, Denver, 2002—05, pres. internat. ops., 2003—05, CEO, 2005—. Office: ProLogis 4545 Airport Way Denver CO 80239*

**SCHWARTZ, JOHN J.,** association executive, consultant; b. New Rochelle, N.Y., Aug. 28, 1919; s. Edwin Benner and Marjorie Helen (James) S.; m. Katharine S. Sprackling, Jan. 6, 1942; children: Christopher Louis. Grad. high sch., New Rochelle; student, Mercersburg Acad., 1938. Campaign dir. John Price Jones Inc., N.Y.C., 1946-50; dir. pub. relations and fund raising Travelers Aid Soc. N.Y., N.Y.C., 1950-55; dir. devel. Community Service Soc., N.Y.C., 1955-57, Near East Found., N.Y.C., 1957-60; v.p. G.A. Brakeley & Co. Inc., N.Y.C., 1960-61; dir. devel. Fgn. Policy Assn., N.Y.C., 1962-64; founding pres. Greater N.Y. Nat. Soc. of Fund Raising Execs., 1964; asst. v.p. for crusade Am. Cancer Soc., N.Y.C., 1964-66; exec. dir. Am. Assn. Fund Raising Counsel, N.Y.C., 1966-68, exec. v.p., 1968-72, pres., 1972-87. Founding bd. mem. Ind. Sector, Washington, 1980-85, mem. com. to measurably increase giving; mem., former pres. Com. on Nat. Ctr. for Charitable Stats.; spl. cons. to Com. on Pvt. Philanthropy and Pub. Needs., 1973; chair pvt. adv. group Nat. Assn. Attys. Gen. Model Law Project. Author: Modern American Philanthropy; A Personal Account, 1993. Mem. adv. bd. mgmt. fund-raising cert. program NYU; mem. adv. coun. Grad. Sch. Mgmt. and Urban Professions, New Sch. Social Rsch.; active formation of 5 borough coalitions Daring Coals for Caring Soc., N.Y.C., 1987; cons. Ind. U. Ctr. on Philanthropy, 1988—91, Cmty. Counselling Serv. Co., Inc., 1988—91; pres. Nat. Philanthropy Day, 1988—90, mem. hon. com., 1981; pres. Friends of Westport Libr., 1995—98; bd. dir.-at-large USA World Fund Raising Coun., 1993; bd. dirs. Norwalk Sr. Ctr., 2001—. Capt. PTO USAF, 1941—46. Recipient Disting. Profl. Service to Philanthropy award Am. Assn. Fund-Raising Counsel, N.Y., 1976, Outstanding Agy. Profl. award United Way Am., Alexandria, 1982, Henry A. Rosso Lifetime Achievement in Ethical Fundraising award Ind. U. Ctr. on Philanthropy, 1997. Mem.: Assn. Fund Raising Profls. Fairfield County (bd. dirs. emeritus), Am. Assn. Ret. Persons (bd. of Andrus Found. 1983-90), Fairfield County Assn. Fundraising Profls. (bd. dir. 1992-2000, bd. dir. emeritus 2000-02), Nat. Soc. Fund Raising Execs. (bd. dirs. 1964-90, past pres.), Nat. Charities Info. Bur. (bd. dirs. 1978-94), VFW, Princeton Club (N.Y.C.), 501C-3 Soc. Democrat. Unitarian Universalist. Avocations: writing history, ship models. E-mail: jschwarz227@aol.com.

**SCHWARTZ, JONATHAN D.,** lawyer; b. LI, NY, 1961; BS in Fin. and Polit. Sci. summa cum laude, U. Pa.; JD with honors, Stanford U.; MA in Internat. Rels. with hons., Cambridge U., Eng. Bar: DC, NY. Law clk. to Judge Harry T. Edwards US Ct. Appeals DC Cir.; law clk. to Justice Thurgood Marshall US Supreme Ct., 1988—89; with Jones Day Reavis & Pogue, NY, 1989—91; fed. prosecutor Office US Atty., Manhattan, NY, 1991—95; sr. positions Dept. Justice, Washington, 1995—2001, prin. assoc. dep. atty. gen., 2000—01; gen. counsel Napster, Inc., 2001—02; sr. v.p., dep. gen. counsel Time Warner Inc., 2002—03; exec. v.p., gen. counsel Cablevision Systems Corp., Bethpage, NY, 2003—. Named one of Top 40 Lawyers Under Age 40, Washingtonian Mag., 1998; recipient Edmund J. Randolph award, Dept. Justice, 2001; fellow, Harvard U. Inst. Politics, 1999; Fulbright scholar, 1986—87. Office: Cablevision Systems Corp 1111 Stewart Ave Bethpage NY 11714 Office Phone: 516-803-1125.

**SCHWARTZ, JONATHAN IAN,** information technology executive; b. Oct. 20, 1965; Student, Carnegie-Mellon U., 1983—84; BS in Econ. and Math., Wesleyan U., 1986. Cons. McKinsey & Co., Inc., 1987—89; co-founder, CEO Lighthouse Design (acquired by Sun Microsystems, Inc.), 1989—96; dir. investment group, devel. tools & Java product mktg. orgn. Sun Microsystems, Inc., Santa Clara, Calif., v.p. venture & strategic investments, 1999—2000, sr. v.p. corp. strategy & planning, 2000—02, exec. v.p. software group, 2002—04, pres., 2004—, COO, 2004—06, CEO, 2006—. Bd. dirs. Dorado Corp. Office: Sun Microsystems Inc 4150 Network Cir Santa Clara CA 95054 Office Phone: 650-960-1600, 800-555-9786. Office Fax: 408-276-3804. E-mail: jonathan.schwartz@sun.com.*

**SCHWARTZ, JONATHAN ROYAL LEE,** medical educator, researcher; MD, U. Okla., Okc, 1979. Cert. Am. Bd. Internal Medicine, Am. Bd. Sleep Medicine. Med. dir., integris sleep disorders Integris Health, Ctr. of Okla., Okc, 1988; clin. prof. U. Okla. Health Scis. Ctr., Okc, 1997—. Home and Office: Okla Pulmonary Physicians Inc 4200 S Douglas Ave Ste 313 Oklahoma City OK 73109 Office Phone: 405-636-1111.

**SCHWARTZ, JORDAN M.,** lawyer; b. NYC, Oct. 17, 1957; AB, Stanford Univ., 1978; JD, Univ. Chgo., 1981. Bar: Ill. 1981, NY 1988. V.p., gen. counsel Ticketmaster Corp., Chgo., 1985—86; assoc. Cadwalader Wickersham & Taft LLP, NYC, 1987—91, ptnr., corp. structured fin., 1991—. Mem.: ABA, Mortgage Bankers Assn. (mem. secondary & capital markets com.). Office: Cadwalader Wickersham & Taft 1 World Financial Ctr New York NY 10281 Office Fax: 212-504-6136, 212-504-6666. Business E-Mail: jordan.schwartz@cwt.com.

**SCHWARTZ, JUDY ELLEN,** thoracic surgeon; b. Mason City, Iowa, Oct. 5, 1946; d. Walter Carl and Alice Nevada (Moore) Schwartz. BS, U. Iowa, 1968, MD, 1971; M.P.H., Johns Hopkins U., 1996. Diplomate Am. Bd. Surgery, Am. Bd. Thoracic Surgery, Am. Bd. Med. Mgmt., cert. physician exec. Cert. Commn. Med. Mgt. Intern Nat. Naval Med. Ctr., Bethesda, Md.,

1971-72, gen. surgery resident, 1972-76, thoracic surgery resident, 1976-78, staff cardiothoracic surgeon, 1979-82, chief cardiothoracic surgeon, 1982-83; chmn. cardiothoracic surg. dept. Naval Hosp., San Diego, 1983-85, quality assurance program dir., 1985-88. Exec. office Rapidly Deployable Med. Facility Four, 1986—88; asst. prof. surgery Uniformed Svcs. U. Health Sci., Bethesda, 1983—99; sr. policy analyst quality assurance Profl. Affairs and Quality Assurance, 1988—90, drp. dir. quality assurance, 1990; dir. clin. policy Health Svcs. Ops., Washington, 1990—94; head performance evaluation and improvement Nat. Naval Med. Ctr., 1994—99; cardiothoracic splty. cons. to naval med. command USN, Washington, 1983—84; Dept. Def. rep. to task force info. mgmt. Joint Commn. Accreditation Health Care Orgn., 1990—93, chmn., 1991—93, mem. task force IMS Tech., 1993—94; chmn. info. mgmt. workshop Fed. Health Care Study Commn.'s Coord. Fed. Health Care, 1993; corp. med. dir. Medcenter One Health Sys., 1999—2002, trustee, 1999—2003; corp. med. dir. ND Dept. Corrections & Rehab., 1990—2002; v.p. med. affairs Medcenter One, 2002; v.p. Surg. Svc. and Electronic Med. Records Informatics, 2003—05, Surg. Svc., 2005—; bd. dirs. SCCI; mem. adv. com. Blue Cross Blue Shield Care Mgmt., 1999—2002, v.p. med. affairs, 2002; chmn. rsch. and bioethics com. Instnl. Rev. Bd., 2000—; mem. exec. adv. bd. Surg. Info. Sys., 2005—. Contbr. articles to various publs. Mem. nat. physician's leadership coun. VHA, 2000—02; trustee St. Vincent's Nursing Home, 2001—05. Capt. USN, 1969—99, ret. USN, 1999. Decorated Legion of Merit, Commendation Medal Navy and Marine Corps, Meritorious Unit Commendation; recipient Baldrige award, Examiner, 2006. Fellow: ACS (mem. com. allied health pers. 1985—91, mem. exec. com. 1987—91, mem. accreditation rev. com. edn. physician asst. 1987—94, treas. accreditation rev. com. 1991—93, sr. mem. com. allied health pers. 1991—94), Am. Coll. Cardiology; mem.: AMA, Am. Coll. Physician Execs., Am. Mgmt. Assn., Am. Med. Women's Assn., Am. Thoracic Soc. Office: Medcenter One Health Systems PO Box 5525 300 N 7th St Bismarck ND 58506-5525 Business E-Mail: jschwartz@mohs.org.

**SCHWARTZ, KESSEL,** modern language educator; b. Kansas City, Mo., Mar. 19, 1920; s. Henry and Dora (Tennenbaum) S.; m. Barbara Lewin, Apr. 3, 1947; children: Joseph David, Deborah, Edward, Michael. BA, U. Mo., Columbia, 1940, MA, 1941; PhD, Columbia U., N.Y.C., 1953. Asst. instr. U. Mo., 1940-42; dir. cultural ctrs. in Nicaragua, Ecuador, cultural observer in Costa Rica State Dept., 1946-48; instr. Hofstra, Hamilton, Colby colls., 1948-53; asst. prof. U. Vt., 1953-57; assoc. prof., then prof. modern langs., chmn. dept. U. Ark., 1957-62; prof. modern langs. U. Miami, Fla., 1962-90, chmn. dept., 1962-64, 74-83, dir. grad. studies, 1964-65, 83-90, now emeritus prof. Vis. prof. U. N.C., Chapel Hill, 1966-67 Author: The Ecuadorian Novel, 1953, An Introduction to Modern Spanish Literature, 1967, The Meaning of Existence in Contemporary Hispanic Literature, 1969, Vicente Aleixandre, 1970, Juan Goytisolo, 1970, A New History of Spanish American Fiction, 1972 (named Outstanding Acad. Book of Year, Am. Assn. Coll. and Research Librarians), Studies on Twentieth Century Spanish and Spanish American Literature, 1983; co-author: A New History of Spanish Literature, 1961, rev. edit., 1991, A New Anthology of Spanish Literature, 1968; assoc. editor Hispania, 1965-84; editorial adv. bd.: Anales de la Literatura Española Contemporánea Folio; Fiestas (Goytisolo), notes and introduction, 1964; contbr. numerous articles to profl. jours., chpts. to books, ency. Nat. patronato Letras de Oro Spanish Literary Prizes. Served with AUS, 1942-46. July 14, 1989 declared Kessel Schwartz Day in Coral Gables, Miami and Dade County by mayors' proclamation. Mem. MLA (group sec. 1964, group chmn. 1965, chmn. nominating com. for modern Spanish lit. 1966-68), Am. Assn. Tchrs. Spanish and Portuguese (chmn. Peninsular lit. sect. 1972), Internat. Assn. Hispanists, Phi Beta Kappa (pres. So. Fla. chpt. 1977), Phi Sigma Iota, Sigma Delta Pi (nat. Order of Don Quijote award 1984, Order of Discoverers award 1989), Pi Delta Phi, Delta Phi Alpha, Omicron Delta Kappa. Home: 6400 Maynada St Miami FL 33146-3318 Personal E-mail: edschwar@bellsouth.net. *If men loved one another sufficiently, we might not need our legal systems. Given our imperfect nature as human beings, we must believe in some higher goals to give meaning to our lives but be ever vigilant that in the pursuit of success we do not infringe upon the happiness of others or confuse the means with the end.*

**SCHWARTZ, LANCE,** music educator; s. John and Pam Schwartz; m. Mindy Johnson, June 12, 2002. MusB in Edn., Ea. Ky. U., Richmond, 2000, MusM, 2002. Lic. tchg. Ohio, 2005. Band and chorus dir. St. Mark Sch., Richmond, Ky., 2001—02; asst. band dir. Elgin Local Sch., Marion, Ohio, 2004—06, head band dir., 2006—. Advisor Elgin Music Booster, Marion, 2002—06. Scholar, IBEW Local 683, 1995—2000, Ea. Ky. U. Dept. Music, 1995—2000. Mem.: MENC, Phi Mu Alpha Sinfonia (life; collegiate province rep, pres., v.p., warden, alum. sec. 1996—2002). Democrat-Npl. Home: 1400 Columbus-Sandusky Rd S Marion OH 43302 Office: Elgin Local Sch 1239 Keener Rd S Marion OH 43302 Office Phone: 740-383-5118. Personal E-mail: lance_s@adelphia.net. E-mail: lance_s@treca.org.

**SCHWARTZ, LAURIE,** special education educator; b. Bklyn., Feb. 20, 1951; d. Paul and Marilyn Rosenthal Kamen; m. Paul M Schwartz, Nov. 4, 1972; children: Michael J, Faith J. BA in History, Bklyn. Coll., 1973; MS in Edn., Adelphi U., Garden City, N.Y., 1987. Cert. tchr. history, spl. edn., elem. edn. NY. Asst. office mgr. Gen. Elec. Credit Corp., NYC, 1972—76; tchr. Connetquot Sch. Dist., Bohemia, NY, 1987—. Class advisor Connetquot H.S., 1993—96. Youth mem. Sayville Jewish Cmty. Ctr., 1985—92. Mem.: Women's Am. ORT (pres. chpt. 1983—87). Home: 39 Arleen Ave Holbrook NY 11741 Office: Connetquot HS 190 7th St Bohemia NY 11716

**SCHWARTZ, LEON,** foreign language educator; b. Boston, Aug. 22, 1922; s. Charles and Celia (Emer) S.; m. Jeanne Gurtat, Mar. 31, 1949; children: Eric Alan, Claire Marie. Student, Providence Coll., 1939-41; BA, UCLA, 1948; certificat de phonetique, U. Paris, 1949; MA, U. So. Cal., 1950, PhD, 1962. Tchr. English, Spanish and Latin Redlands Jr. High Sch., Calif., 1951—54; high sch. tchr. Spanish and French Redlands Jr. High Sch., Calif., 1954—59; prof. French Calif. State U., L.A., 1959—87, chmn. dept. fgn. langs. and lit., 1970—73, prof. emeritus, 1987—; instr. Osher Learning Inst., 2006—. Author: Diderot and the Jews, 1981; co-author: Mortier-Tresson, Dictionnaire de Diderot, 1999. Served as 2d lt. USAAF, 1942-45. Decorated Air medal with 5 oak leaf clusters; recipient Outstanding Prof. award Calif. State U. L.A., 1976. Mem. Am. Assn. Tchrs. French, Am. Soc. 18th Century Studies, Calif. State U. L.A. Emeriti Assn. (pres. 1998-2000), Phi Beta Kappa, Phi Kappa Phi, Pi Delta Phi, Sigma Delta Pi, Alpha Mu Gamma. Business E-Mail: lschwar@calstatela.edu.

**SCHWARTZ, LEONARD JAY,** retired lawyer; b. San Antonio, Sept. 23, 1943; s. Oscar S. and Ethel (Eastman) S.; m. Sandra E. Eichelbaum, July 4, 1965; 1 child, Michele Fay. BBA, U. Tex., 1965, JD, 1968. Bar: Tex. 1968, Ohio 1971, U.S. Supreme Ct. 1971, U.S. Dist. Ct. (no., ea., wes. and so. dists.) Tex., U.S. Dist. Cts. (no. and so. dists.) Ohio, U.S. Dist. Ct. Nebr., U.S. Ct. Appeals (5th, 6th, 7th and 11th cirs.). Assoc. Roberts & Holland, N.Y.C., 1968-70; ptnr. Rigely, Schwartz & Fagan, San Antonio, 1970-71; staff counsel ACLU of Ohio, Columbus, 1971-74; ptnr. Schwartz & Fishman, Columbus, 1974-79; elections counsel to sec. of state State of Ohio, Columbus, 1979-80; ptnr. Waterman & Schwartz and successor firms, Austin, Tex., 1981-85; mng. dir. Schwartz & Eichelbaum, PC, Austin and other cities, 1985—99, 2000—01, shareholder Austin, various locations, 1985—2001, ret., 2001. Gen. counsel various sch. dists., cities and counties; adj. prof. law U. Tex. Sch. Law, Austin; labor and employment law com. and sch. law Tex. Assn. Sch. Administrs.; condr. workshops in field; mem. com. on fed. judiciary rels. Tex. Bar. Contbr. articles to profl. jours. Mem. chancellor's coun. U. Tex. Sys.; mem. U. Tex. Pres.'s Assocs., Littlefield Soc., Sch. of Law Keeton Fellows. Recipient Outstanding Tchg. Quiz Master award, U. Tex. Sch. Law, 1968. Fellow Tex. Bar Found.; mem. ABA, FBA, Tex. Bar Assn., Bar Assn. 5th Cir., Phi Delta Phi. Democrat. Jewish. Personal E-mail: lennyjay@sbcglobal.net.

**SCHWARTZ, LILLIAN FELDMAN,** artist, filmmaker, critic, nurse, writer; b. Cin., July 13, 1927; d. Jacob and Katie (Green) Feldman; m. Jack James Schwartz, Dec. 22, 1946; children: Jeffrey Hugh, Laurens Robert. BSE, U.

Cin., 1947; Dr. honoris causa, Kean Coll., 1988. Nurse Cin. Gen. Hosp., 1947; head supr. premature nursery St. Louis Maternity Hosp., 1947-48; cons. AT&T Bell Labs., Murray Hill, NJ, 1968-97; pres. Computer Creations Corp., Watchung, NJ, 1989—2004; cons. Bell Communications Research, Morristown, NJ, 1984-92, Lucent Technologies/Bell Labs. Innovations, 1996—2001. Artist-in-residence WNET, N.Y.C., 1972-74; cons. T.J. Watson Rsch. Lab. IBM Corp., Yorktown, N.Y., 1975, 82-84; vis. mem. computer sci. dept. U. Md., College Park, 1974-80; adj. prof. fine arts Kean Coll., Union, N.J., 1980-82, Rutgers U., New Brunswick, N.J., 1982-83; adj. prof. dept. psychology NYU, N.Y.C., 1985-86, assoc. prof. computer sci.; guest lectr. Princeton U., Columbia U., Yale U., Rockefeller U.; mem. grad. faculty Sch. Visual Arts, N.Y.C., 1990-91; dir. team from Rutgers U. to create world's first computer-generated 3-D model of Leaning Tower of Pisa to test structures, 1999; invited com. mem. info. tech. and creativity NAS, 2000-03; invited juror L'Oreal/Color/Internat., 2000-01; film retrospective Leeds, Eng. Lumen-Evolution, 2002, 2003-04. Co-author: Information Technology and Creativity, 2001, The Computer Artist's Handbook; contbd. articles to profl. jours including Scientific Am., 1995; contbr. chpts. to books, also Trans. Am. Philos. Soc., vol. 75, Part 6, 1985; one-woman shows of sculpture and paintings include Columbia U., 1967, 68, Rabin and Krueger Gallery, Newark, 1968, Computer Animation, Amsterdam, 2006, Florence, Italy, 2006, Pacific Film Archive, 20056 films shown at Met. Mus., N.Y.C., Franklin Inst., Phila., 1972, U. Toronto, 1972, am. Embassy, London, 1972, L.A. County Mus., Corcoran Gallery, Washington, 1972, Whitney Mus., N.Y.C., 1973, Grand Palais, Paris, Musee d'Art Moderne, Paris, IBM, (digital print show) Bklyn. Mus. Art, 2001, Chelsea Mus. Art, N.Y.C., 2004, Computer Animation Retrospective, U.K., U.S., 2005, Holland, Italy, U.S., 2006, others; dir.: Save the Leaning Tower. Recipient numerous art and film awards, Emmy award Mus. Modern Art, 1984, Computer Graphics World Smithsonian awards for virtual reality, art analysis, inventing computer medium for art and animation, 1993; named Outstanding Alumnus, U. Cin., 1987; grantee Nat. Endowment for Arts, 1977, 81, Corp. Pub. Broadcasting, 1979, Nat. Endowment Composers and Librettists, 1981, Arts Coun. Eng., 2003. Fellow World Acad. of Art and Sci.; mem. NATAS, Am. Film Inst., Internat. Film Prodrs. Am., Soc. Motion Picture and TV Engrs., Internat. Sculptors Assn., Centro Studi Pierfrancescani (Sansepolcro, Italy, founding mem.). Achievements include discovery of morphing algorithms to determine Leonardo's creative decision-making steps in transforming the Duchess of Aragon into the Mona Lisa using his own features to segue; reason for position of Christ's right hand and Judas's left hand in Leonardo da Vinci's Last Supper. Personal E-mail: lillianschwartz@lillian.com. *I have always been provoked by and concerned with the mechanical and technological world around me. I enjoy experimenting with traditional media and combining them with technology today. For example, I used computers as an art medium when computers were solely programmed for scientific purposes. By using the computer to understand the creative process I have made clear the intent of the great masters and applied their decision-making steps to my own work. The excitement in creating is to discover and to make a new world. My present success was achieved in part by being able to make new rules and not be hindered by old or obvious solutions.*

**SCHWARTZ, LLOYD,** music critic, poet; b. NYC, Nov. 29, 1941; s. Sam and Ida (Singer) Schwartz. BA, Queens Coll., N.Y.C., 1962; MA, Harvard U., 1963, PhD, 1976. Classical music editor Boston Phoenix, 1977—; dir. creative writing U. Mass., Boston, 1982—, 1990—2002; classical music critic Fresh Air Nat. Pub. Radio, Phila., 1987—. Prof. English U. Mass., Boston, 1986—. Author (poems): These People, 1981, Goodnight, Gracie, 1992, Cairo Traffic, 2000, Lloyd Schwartz: Greatest Hits 1973-2000, 2003; author: (plays) These People: Voices for the Stage, 1990; editor: Ploughshares, 1979, Elizabeth Bishop and Her Art, 1983; actor: The Spider's Web, 1975—82; dir.: These People: Voices for the Stage, 1990; (Operas) L'Heure Espagnol (Ravel), 1972, Mavra (Stravinsky), 1973. Recipient Pulitzer prize for criticism, 1994; NEA creative writing fellow in poetry, 1990. Mem.: MLA, PEN, Associated Writing Programs, New Eng. Poetry Club, Poetry Soc. Am., PEN Am. Avocations: collecting old recordings, books. Home: 27 Pennsylvania Ave Somerville MA 02145-2217 Office: Boston Phoenix 126 Brookline Ave Boston MA 02215-3920 Business E-Mail: lloyd.schwartz@umb.edu. E-mail: lschwartz@phx.com.

**SCHWARTZ, LYLE HOWARD,** materials scientist, science administrator; b. Chgo., Aug. 2, 1936; s. Joseph K. Schwartz and Helen (Shefsky) Bernards; divorced; children: Ara, Justin; m. Celesta Sue Jurkovich, Sept. l, 1973. BS in Sci. Engring., Northwestern U., 1959, PhD in Materials Sci., 1964. Prof. materials sci. Northwestern U., Evanston, Ill., 1964-84, dir. Materials Research Ctr., 1979-84; dir. materials sci. and engr. lab. Nat. Inst. Standards and Tech., Dept. Commerce, Gaithersburg, Md., 1984-97; pres. Associated Univs., Inc., Washington, 1997-98; interim dir. Brookhaven Nat. Lab., Washington, 1997; cons., 1998-99; dir. aerospace and material scis. Air Force Office Sci. Rsch., Arlington, Va., 1999-2001, dir., 2001—. Cons. Argonne Nat. Labs., Ill., 1965-79; vis. scientist Bell Telephone Labs., Murray Hill, N.J., 1971-73 Author: (with J.B. Cohen) Diffraction From Materials, 1977, 2d edit., 1987; also numerous articles and papers NSF fellow, 1962-63; recipient Presdl. Rank Award of Meritorious Exec. for outstanding govt. svc., 1990. Fellow Am. Soc. for Metals; mem. AAAS, AIME, Nat. Acad. Engring., Am. Phys. Soc., Am. Crystallography Assn., Materials Rsch. Soc., Sigma Xi. Office: 801 N Randolph St Ste 732 Arlington VA 22203-1977 E-mail: lyle.schwartz@afosr.af.mil.

**SCHWARTZ, LYNNE SHARON,** freelance/self-employed writer; b. NYC, Mar. 19, 1939; d. Jacob M. and Sarah (Slatus) Sharon; m. Harry Schwartz, Dec. 22, 1957; children: Rachel Eve, Miranda Ruth. BA, Barnard Coll., 1959, MA; Woodrow Wilson Nat. fellow, Bryn Mawr Coll., 1961; postgrad., NYU, 1967-72. Asso. editor The Writer mag., Boston, 1961-63; editorial dir. Calliope Records, spoken records, Boston, 1962-64; pub. relations writer Operation Open City, N.Y. Urban League, N.Y.C., 1965-67. Adj. lectr. English Hunter Coll., 1971-77; vis. lectr. U. Iowa Writers' Workshop, 1982-83, Columbia U., 1983, Boston U., 1984, 87, Rice U., 1987. Author: (novel) Rough Strife, 1980, Balancing Acts, 1981, Disturbances in the Field, 1983, Acquainted with the Night, 1984, The Fatigue Artist, 1995, Ruined by Reading, A Life in Books, 1996, In the Family Way, 1999, Face to Face, 2000, The Writing on the Wall, 2005, In Solitary, 2002, (stories) We are Talking about Homes, 1985, The Melting Pot and Other Subversive Stories, 1987, Leaving Brooklyn, 1989, Referred Pain, 2004, (transl.) Smoke Over Birkenau by Liana Millu, 1991, A Place to Live by Natalia Ginzburg, 2002; author short stories, numerous poems; contbr. articles to popular mags. Recipient James Henle award for prose Vanguard Press, 1974-75, Lawrence Found. award for fiction in Mich. Quar. and Prarie Schooner, 1987, N.Y. State Found. for the Arts award, 1988, 2002, Renato Poggioli award PEN, 1991; grantee Guggenheim Found., 1984, Nat. Endowment for the Arts, 1985, 2002; fiction selected for inclusion The Pushcart Prize III: Best of the Small Presses, The Best American Short Stories, 1978, 1979, 1996, 1998, 2005, O. Henry Prize Stories, 1979.

**SCHWARTZ, MARSHALL ZANE,** pediatric surgeon; b. Mpls., Sept. 1, 1945; s. Sidney Shay and Peggy Belle (Lieberman) S.; m. Michele Carroll Walker, Oct. 16, 1971; children: Lisa, Jeffrey. BS, U. Minn., 1968, MD, 1970. Diplomate Am. Bd. Surgery, Am. Bd. Pediatric Surgery. Intern NY Hosp., NYC, 1970—71; resident gen. surgery U. Minn., Mpls., 1971—73, 1975—76, rsch. fellow, 1974—75; jr. resident in pediat. surgery Children's Hosp. Med. Ctr., Harvard Med. Sch., 1973—74, sr. resident in pediat. surgery, 1976—77, chief resident in pediat. surgery, 1977—78; instr. Med. Sch. Harvard U., Boston, 1978—79; asst. surgery Children's Hosp. Med. Ctr., Boston, 1978—79; asst. prof. Med. Br. U. Tex., Galveston, 1979—81, assoc. prof., 1981—83, chief. pediat. surgery 1980—83; assoc. prof. U. Calif., Davis, 1983—86, prof., 1986—92, chief pediat. surgery, 1983—92, vice chmn. faculty Sch. Medicine, 1990—91, chmn. faculty Sch. Medicine, 1991—92; prof. surgery and pediat. George Washington Sch. Medicine, 1992—96; surgeon-in-chief, chmn. dept. pediatr.surgery Children's Nat. Med. Ctr., Washington, 1992—96; assoc. med. dir. Dupont Hosp. for Children, Wilmington, Del., 1996—2001, vice chmn. dept. surgery,

1996—2003; prof. surgery and pediat. Thomas Jefferson U., 1996—, vice chmn. dept. surgery, 1996—2003, sr. scholar dept. health policy, 2005—; mem. staff St. Christopher Hosp. for Children, Phila., 2004—06, surgeon-in-chief divsn. pediat. surgery, 2006—; prof. surgery and pediat. Drexel U. Sch. Medicine, Phila., 2004—; bd. dirs. Phila. Acad. Surgery, 2005—. Bd. dirs. Am. Bd. Surgery, Phila. Acad. Surgery, 2005—; exec. com. Internat. Soc. Surgery, 2005—. Mem. editl. bd. Jour. Pediat. Surgery, 1988—, Jour. ACS, 1999—. Vice chmn. Bd. of Childrens Faculty Assocs., Childrens Nat. Med. Ctr.; bd. dir. Am. Pediat. Surg. Assn., 2001—04; pres. bd. dir. Sacramento Children's Hosp. Found., 1990—92; chmn. bd. dir. Delaware Valley Transplant Program, 2000—02; bd. dirs. Gift of Life, 2005—. Recipient Basil O'Connor Rsch. award March of Dimes Found., 1981, Young Investigator award NIH, 1982, Found. for Children Rsch. award, 1982, James W. McLaughlin award U. Tex., 1983, ASPEN-Rhodes Rsch. award, 1999, Rsch. award Am. Colon and Rectal Surg. Assn., 2000. Fellow: ACS (chmn. adv. coun. pediat. surgery 2004—); mem.: Internat. Soc. Surgery (exec. com. 2004—), Pacific Assn. Pediat. Surgeons (pres. 1997—98), Soc. Surgery Alimentary Tract, Am. Pediat. Surg. Assn. (bd. govs. 2001—04), Soc. Univ. Surgeons, Am. Surg. Assn. Awards. Avocations: skiing, fishing, wood working. Office: St Christopher Hosp for Children Erie Ave at Front St Philadelphia PA 19134 Office Phone: 215-427-6698. Personal E-mail: mzschwartz@msn.com.

**SCHWARTZ, MARVIN,** lawyer; b. Phila., Nov. 3, 1922; s. Abe and Freda (Newman) S.; m. Joyce Ellen Sidner, Sept. 7, 1947; children: Daniel Bruce, Pamela Louise Pier. LL.B., U. Pa., 1949. Bar: Pa. 1950, N.Y. 1951, D.C. 1955. Law sec. to judge U.S. Ct. Appeals, 3d Circuit, Phila., 1949-50; law sec. to Justice Burton U.S. Supreme Ct., Washington, 1950-51; assoc. Sullivan & Cromwell, N.Y.C., 1951-60, ptnr., 1960-92, sr. counsel, 1993—. Mediator U.S. Dist. (so. dist.) N.Y., N.Y. Supreme Ct. Comml. Divsn.; arbitrator Am. Arbitration Assn., N.Y. Stock Exch., Nat. Assoc. Securities Dealers. Spl. master appellate divsn. 1st dept. Supreme Ct. N.Y.; chmn. Zoning Bd. of Adjustment, Alpine, N.J., 1966-74; mem. Planning Bd., Alpine, 1966-67; bd. overseers emeritus U. Pa. Law Sch.; bd. dirs. Conn. Cmty. Found. With Signal Corps U.S. Army, 1943-46. Mem. ABA, N.Y. Bar Assn., D.C. Bar Assn., Am. Coll. Trial Lawyers (sec. 1986-88, bd. regents 1981-86, chmn. Downstate N.Y. com. 1976-78), Am. Law Inst. (adviser complex litigation project), Univ. Club (N.Y.C.), Litchfield (Conn.) Country Club. Democrat. Jewish. Office: Sullivan & Cromwell 125 Broad St Fl 28 New York NY 10004-2489 Personal E-mail: mvnsch@aol.com.

**SCHWARTZ, MATTHEW BARAHAL,** historian; b. Detroit, Mich., Aug. 3, 1945; s. William and Pauline Schwartz; m. Nehama Nussbaum, Nov. 16, 1975; children: Margalit Gottlieb, Avigail, Asher. PhD, Wayne State U., Detroit, 1975; BHL in Rabbinics, Yeshivah Gedolah, Oak Park, Mich., 1977. Adj. Wayne State U., Detroit, Mich., 1976—, Ctrl. Mich. U., Mich., 1998—. Cons. Holocaust Meml. Ctr., Farmington Hills, Mich., 2004—. Author: (history book) Roman Letters:History from a Personal Point of View, 1991, (book) A Psychology of Hope: An Antidote to the Suicidal Pathology of the Western Civilization, 1993; author: (editor) Jewish Approaches to Suicide, Martyrdom and Euthanasia, 1998; author: Biblical Stories For Psychotherapy and Counseling, 2004, The Seven Habits of the Good Life, 2006, Greek and Biblical Families; contbr. articles to profl. jours. Mem.: Assn. for Jewish Studies, Assn. of Ancient Historians. Office: Wayne State Univ Hist Dep't Detroit MI 48202 Office Phone: 313-577-2525.

**SCHWARTZ, MAX J.,** lawyer; b. NYC, 1949; BA, Institut d'Etudes Politiques, Paris, 1970; JD, Univ. Mich., 1973. Bar: NY 1975. Ptnr. exec. compensation and benefits practice group Sullivan & Cromwell, NYC. Editl. adv. bd. Jour. of Pension Planning and Compliance. Mem.: ABA (tax section, former chair, exec. compensation subcom. of employee benefits com.), Practising Law Inst. (employee benefits adv. com.), NY State Bar Assn. (exec. com. of section of taxation). Office: Sullivan & Cromwell LLP 125 Broad St New York NY 10004-2498 Office Phone: 212-558-4000. Office Fax: 212-558-3588.

**SCHWARTZ, MICHAEL ROBERT,** music educator, department chairman; b. Huntington, Ny, Nov. 30, 1959; s. Herbert Lewis and Edith Dube; m. Jill Ann Glembourtt; children: Matthew Richard, Daniel Aaron. MusB, Mannes Coll. Music, 1983; MusM, Manhattan Sch. Music, 1990. Cert. in Adminstry. Supervision Hunter Coll, 1993. Music tchr. P.S. 217, N.Y.C, 1983—84, O'Henry Sch. Arts, N.Y.C, 1985—86, Robert Wagner Jr. H.S 167, N.Y.C, 1986—92, Great Neck Sch. Dist., NY, 1992—. Dir. summer music Great Neck Sch. Dist., NY, 1994—; music chmn. Great Neck South H.S., NY, 1996—, rep., 1996—. Mem.: LI String Festival Assn., Nassau Music Educators Assn., N.Y. Music Educators Assn., N.Y. State Coun. Adminstrs. Music, Music Educators Nat. Conf., NY Sch. Music Assn. Home: 32 Roberta Ln Syosset NY 11791 Office: Great Neck South HS 341 Lakeville Rd Great Neck NY 11020 Office Phone: 516-773-1631. Business E-mail: mschwartz@greatneck.k12.ny.us.

**SCHWARTZ, MICHAEL ROBINSON,** insurance company executive; b. St. Louis, Mar. 18, 1940; s. Henry G. and Edith C. (Robinson) Schwartz; m. Kathleen Nowicki, Dec. 9, 1989; children from previous marriage: Christine, Richard. AB, Dartmouth Coll., 1962; MHA, U. Minn., 1964. Asst. in adminstrn. Shands Tchg. Hosp., Gainesville, Fla., 1966-67, asst. dir., 1967-68, assoc. dir., 1968-73; assoc. adminstr. St. Joseph Mercy Hosp., Pontiac, Mich., 1973-76, pres., 1976-85; exec. v.p. Mercy Health Svcs., Farmington Hills, Mich., 1985-96, COO, 1988-96; exec. v.p. Ea. Mich. region Sisters of Mercy Health Corp., 1991-92; pvt. practice Birmingham, Mich., 1996—2004; dir. provider rels. Blue Cross Blue Shield of Mich., 2003—04, sr. v.p. network rels. Mich., 2005—. Non-resident lectr. U. Mich., 1982—93; cons. prof. Oakland U., 1980—88; asst. prof. hosp. adminstrn. U. Fla., 1967—73; pres. Eastern Mich. Regional Bd. Sisters of Mercy Health Corp., 1976—79; v.p. Lourdes Nursing Home, 1981-84; United Way-Pontiac/North Oakland, 1982—84; treas. Oakland Health Edn. Program, 1978—79; bd. dirs. Vis. Nurse Assn., Inc., 1997—2005; coms. Blue Cross/Blue Shield of Mich., 1978—86, chair hosp. committee to participating hosp. agreement adv. com., 1989—96; treas. Vis. Nurse Assn., Inc., 1998—99, 2003—04, vice chair, 1999—2000, chair, 2000—02; chmn. bd. dirs., pres. Accord Ins. Co. Ltd., 1983—88; chmn. bd. dirs. Mercy Health Plans, 1986—96, Venzke Svc. Co., 1983—88, pres., 1983—84; chmn. bd. dirs., pres. Venzke Ins. Co. Ltd. 1988—96; mem. audit and fin. com. Am. Healthcare Sys., 1988—92; mem. S.E. Mich. Hosp. Coun., chmn. pub. rels. com., 1983—85; mem. Commonfund Healthcare Coun., 1999—2005; trustee Sisters of Mercy Health Corp., 1991—93, sec. bd. trustees, 1993; bd. dirs. Hosp. Fund, 1986—96. Mem. charitable trust Sisters of Mercy, Regional Cmty. Detroit, 1999—2004. With U.S. Army, 1964—66. Fellow: Am. Coll. Healthcare Execs. (mem. exec. com. higher edn. 1990—93, Mich. Regent's award 1992); mem.: Comprehensive Health Planning Coun. (com. mem. 1976—81), Am. Healthcare Sys. Risk Retention Group (bd. dirs. 1990—91), Mich. Hosp. Assn. (at-large rep. corp. bd. 1990—96, exec. com. 1992—96), Pontiac Urban League (pers. com. 1979). Office: 600 Lafayette E MCJ 744 Detroit MI 48226 Office Phone: 313-225-9101. Business E-mail: mschwartz@bcbsm.com.

**SCHWARTZ, MISCHA,** electrical engineering educator; b. NYC, Sept. 21, 1926; s. Isaiah and Bessie (Weinstein) S.; m. Lillian Mitchnick, June 23, 1957 (div.); 1 son, David; m. Charlotte F. Berney, July 12, 1970. B.E.E., Cooper Union, 1947; M.E.E., Poly. Inst. Bklyn., 1949; PhD in Applied Physics (Sperry Gyroscope grad. scholar), Harvard U., 1951. Project engr. Sperry Gyroscope Co., 1947-52; mem. faculty Poly. Inst. Bklyn., 1952-74, prof. elec. engring., 1959-74, head dept., 1961-65; prof. elec. engring. and computer sci. Columbia U., N.Y.C., 1974-88, Charles Batchelor prof. elec. engring., 1988-96, Charles Batchelor prof. emeritus, 1996—, dir. Ctr. for Telecommunications Research, 1985-88. Part-time tchr. Adelphi Coll., 1951-52, CCNY, 1952; cons. radiation physicist Montefiore Hosp., N.Y.C., 1954-56; vis. prof. sys. sci. dept. UCLA, 1964; vis. prof. dept. elec. engring. and computer sci. Columbia U., 1973-74; vis. prof. dept. electronic and elec. engring. U. Coll., London, 1995; vis. prof. dept. elec. and computer engring. U. Calif., San Diego, 1997; chmn. Commn. C, U.S. Nat. Com. Internat. Union Radio Sci.,

1977-80; vis. scientist IBM Rsch., 1980, 94, NYNEX Sci. and Tech., 1986; vis. mem. tech. staff AT&T Bell Labs., 1995; cons. in field. Author: Information Transmission, Modulation and Noise, 4th edit., 1990, (with L. Shaw) Signal Processing, 1975, Computer Communication Network Design and Analysis, 1977, Telecommunications Networks, 1987, Broadband Integrated Networks, 1996; editor, contbr.: Communication Systems and Techniques, 1966, reissued, 1995; Mobile Wireless Comm., 2005. Trustee Gt. Neck Libr., 1997-2001, pres., 1998, 99. With U.S. Army, 1944—46, with AUS, 1944—46. NSF sci. faculty fellow, 1965-66; recipient Disting. Vis. award Australian-Am. Ednl. Found., 1975, Vis. Scientist award Nippon Tel. & Tel., 1981, Tchg. award Columbia U., 1984, Gano Dunn award Cooper Union, 1986, Mayor's award for excellence in tech., City of N.Y., 1995; finalist Mayor's Awards for Excellence in Sci. & Tech., City of N.Y., 1992, recipient Okawa award for contbns. comm., computer networks, engring. edn., 2003. Fellow AAAS, IEEE (chmn. adminstrv. com. profl. group info. theory 1964-65, bd. dirs. 1978-79, bd. govs. Comm. Soc. 1973-79, v.p. 1982-83, pres. 1984-85, Edn. medal 1983, IEEE Centennial Hall of Fame 1984, Region 1 award for leadership in mgmt. Ctr. for Telecom. Rsch. 1990, Edwin Armstrong award for contbns. to telecomm. 1994, Millennium medal 2000); mem. NAE, AAUP (chpt. pres. 1970-72), Soc. History Tech., Tau Beta Pi, Eta Kappa Nu (eminent mem. 1999). Home: 66 Maple Dr Great Neck NY 11021-1928 Office: Columbia U Schapiro CEPSR Rm 806 New York NY 10027 Office Phone: 212-854-3125. Personal E-mail: mcschw66@aol.com. Business E-mail: schwartz@ctr.columbia.edu.

**SCHWARTZ, NEENA BETTY,** endocrinologist, educator; b. Balt., Dec. 10, 1926; d. Paul Howard and Pauline (Shulman) S. AB, Goucher Coll., 1948, DSc (hon.), 1982; MS, Northwestern U., 1950, PhD, 1953. From instr. to prof. U. Ill. Coll. Medicine, Chgo., 1953-72, asst. dean for faculty, 1968-70; prof. physiology Northwestern U. Med. Sch., Chgo., 1973-74; Deering prof. Northwestern U., Evanston, Ill., 1974—99, chmn. dept. biol. scis., 1974-78, acting dean, Coll. Arts and Scis., 1996-97, prof. emeritus, 2000—. Contbr. articles to profl. jours., chapters to books. NIH rsch. grantee, 1955—. Fellow: AAAS (exec. bd. 1998—2002, Lifetime Mentor award 2003); mem.: Soc. for Neurosci., Am. Physiol. Soc., Soc. for Study of Reproduction (dir. 1975—77, exec. v.p. 1976—77, pres. 1977—78, Carl Hartman award 1992), Endocrine Soc. (v.p. 1970—71, mem. coun. 1979—83, pres. 1982—83, Williams award 1985, Disting. Educator award 1998), Am. Acad. Arts and Scis. Home: 1511 Lincoln St Evanston IL 60201-2338 Office Phone: 847-491-5529. Business E-Mail: n-schwartz@northwestern.edu.

**SCHWARTZ, NORTON A.,** career military officer; B in Polit. Sci. and Internat. Affairs, USAF Acad., Colorado, 1973; grad., Squadron Officer Sch., Alabama, 1977; MBA, Cen. Mich. U., 1983; grad., Armed Forces Staff Coll., Virginia, 1984; Nat. War Coll., Washington, DC, 1989; seminar fellow, Mass Inst of Tech, 1994. Commd. 2d lt. USAF, 1973, advanced through grades to gen., 2005, C-130E aircraft comdr. 776th & 21st tactical airlift squadrons Clark AFB, Philippines, 1975—77, C-130E/H flight examiner 61st Tactical Airlift Squadron Little Rock AFB, Ark., 1977—79, intern Air Staff Training Program, Office of the Dep. Chief of Staff for Plans, Ops, & Readiness, USAF Hdqs., 1979—80, MC-130E flight examiner, 8th Spl. ops. Squadron Hurlburt Field, Fla., 1980—83; action officer Directorate of Plans Hdqs. USAF, Office of Dep. Chief of Staff Plans & Ops., Washington, 1984-86; comdr. 36th Tactical Airlift Squadron, McChord AFB, Wash., 1986-88; dir. plans & policy Spl. Ops. Command Europe, Stuttgart-Vaihingen, Germany, 1989-91; dep. comdr. for ops., comdr. 1st Spl. Ops. Group, Hurlburt Field, Fla., 1991-93; dep. dir. ops., dep. dir. forces Office Dep. Chief of Staff for Plans and Ops., Hdqs. USAF, Washington, 1993-95; comdr. 16th Spl. Ops. Wing, Hurlburt Field, Fla., 1995-97, Spl. Ops. Command, Pacific, Camp H.M. Smith, Hawaii, 1997-98; dir. strategic planning Dep. Chief of Staff for Plans & Programs, Hdqs. USAF, Washington, 1998—2000; dep. comdr. in chief US Spl. Ops. Command, USAF, MacDill AFB, Fla., 2000; comdr. Alaskan Command, Alaskan N. Am. Def. Command Region & 11th Air Force, Elmendorf AFB, 2000—02; dir. ops. The Joint Staff, The Pentagon, Washington, 2002—04, dir., 2004—05; comdr. US Transp. Command, Scott AFB, Ill., 2005—. Decorated Def. Superior Svc. medal with oak leaf cluster, Def. Disting. Svc. medal, Disting. Svc. medal, Legion of Merit with two oak leaf clusters, Def. Meritorious Svc. medal, Meritorious Svc. medal with two oak leaf clusters, Air Force Commendation medal with oak leaf cluster, Army Commendation medal; Seminar XXI fellow MIT, 1994. Office: 300 Joint Staff The Pentagon Washington DC 20318*

**SCHWARTZ, PEPPER JUDITH,** sociologist, educator; b. Chgo., May 11, 1945; d. Julius J. and Gertrude (Puris) Schwartz; m. John A. Strait, June 19, 1971; m. Arthur M. Skolnick, Jan. 9, 1982 (div. 2001); children: Cooper, Ryder. BA, Washington U., St. Louis, 1968, MA, 1970; M in Philosophy, Yale U., 1972, PhD, 1974. Assoc. prof. sociology, adj. assoc. prof., 1972—88; prof. psychiatry and behavioral sci. U. Wash., Seattle, 1988—. Chmn. rev. com. NIMH; bd. dirs. Women's Rsch. Ctr.; frequent guest and host local and network TV shows; appt. to Pres. Reagan's ad hoc adv. roundtable on the family, 1984; expert appearance in NBC Sacred Sexless, 1987, Some Thoughts on Being Single, 1984, ABC After The Sexual Revolution, 1986; relationship expert LifetimeTV.com, 1998—, PerfectMatch.com, 2003—. Author: Women at Yale, 1976; author: (with Judith Laws et al) Sexual Scripts, 1977; author: (with P. Blumstein) American Couples, 1983; author: (with V. Rutter) The Gender of Sexuality, 1995; author: (with D. Cappello) Ten Talks Parents Must Have with their Children About Sex and Character, 2002; author: Everything You Know About Love & Sex is Wrong, 2002, Lifetime Book of Love & Sex Quizzes, 2003, Finding Your Perfect Match, 2006; contbr. numerous articles to mags. and jours.; profiles in Savvy, Ladies Home Jour., Playboy, Cosmopolitan, NY Times, Newsweek, others, articles on work in Time, Redbook, New West, American Baby Mag., news; co-author, editor: A Student's Guide to Sex on Campus, 1971. Guardian Ad-Litem Program: bd. dirs. Empty Arms, Theater, Seattle, pres., 1990, past mem. Gov. & Commn. Venereal Disease; mem. Presdl. Adv. Rountable on Family, 1984; bd. dirs. Nat. Abortion Rights Action League, Anti-Defamation League, ACLU; nat. bd. dirs. YWCA, Jewish Family Svc. Named Oustanding Young Woman of the Future, Time-Life mag., 1978; named one of Most Powerful People of the 1980s, Next mag., 1981. Fellow: Internat. Acad. Sex Rsch.; mem.: Lluminari Women's Expert Health Network, Nat. Conf. Family Relations, Am. Sociol. Assn. (chairperson com. on comms., Outstanding Contbn. Pub. Understanding Sociology 2005), Soc. for Sci. Study of Sexuality (pres. 1998—), Pacific Sociol. Assn. (mem. coun., pres. 2004—), Yale Club (N.Y.C.), The Diet Club. Office: Dept Sociology Dk 40 U Seattle WA 98195-0001 Office Phone: 206-543-4036. E-mail: pepperschwartz@hotmail.com.

**SCHWARTZ, PHILIP,** lawyer; b. June 7, 1930; s. Louis and Kate (Brodsky) S.; m. Iris M. Ballin, Nov. 28, 1953 (div. 1979); children: David, Elyse, Donna; m. Monique W. Wagner, July 26, 1982 (div. 1991); m. Carol J. Pruett, Aug. 14, 1992. BA, George Washington U., 1952, JD, 1959; LLM in Taxation, Georgetown U., 1961; postgrad., U. Paris, London Sch. Econs., Harvard U. Bar: Va. 1959, D.C. 1966, U.S. Tax Ct. 1966, U.S. Ct. Appeals (D.C. cir.) 1966, U.S. Ct. Mil. Appeals 1966, U.S. Supreme Ct. 1966, U.S. Ct. Appeals (4th cir.) 1982, U.S. Ct. Internat. Trade 1988, N.Am. Coun. London Ct. Internat. Arbitration 1988; diplomate Am. Coll. Family Law Trial Lawyers; fellow Am. Acad. Matrimonial Lawyers, Internat. Acad. Matrimonial Lawyers. Sr. intelligence analyst Nat. Security Agy., Washington, 1952-54, 76-83; assoc. Varoutsos, Koutoulakos & Arthur, Arlington, Va., 1963—68; ptnr. Schwartz & Ellis, Ltd., Arlington, 1968—2002, Schwartz & Assocs., LLC, 2002—. Instr. No. Va. Life Underwriters Tng. Coun., 1974, No. Va. Paralegal Inst., Arlington, 1976; moot ct. judge George Washington U., Washington, Georgetown U., Washington, Jessup Internat. Law Competition; commr. Chancery Arlington Cir. Ct., judge Pro Tempo; spkr. in field. Contbr. articles to profl. jours. Mem. U.S. Sec. of State Adv. Com. on Pvt. Internat. Law; mem. Arlington County Bd. Zoning Appeals, 1972-85, Arlington County Coun. Human Rels., 1973; del. to Hague Conf. Pvt. Internat. Law; bd. dirs. Jewish Cmty. Ctr. Greater Washington, 1975. With M.I., U.S. Army, 1954-56. Master Barrister Am. Inns of Ct.; Diplomate Am. Coll. of Family Law Trial Lawyers; fellow Internat. Acad. Matrimonial Lawyers (pres. 1996-97), Am. Acad. Matrimonial Lawyers (bd. govs., v.p.);

mem. ABA (chmn. family law sect. com. internat. laws 1983-86, chmn. internat. law sect. com. enforcement fgn. judgments), Internat. Bar Assn. (chmn. family law divsn. 1988-92, governing coun. gen. practice sect., liaison officer to IMF), Am. Coll. Family Trial Lawyers (diplomate), Va. Trial Lawyers Assn. (instr. 1984), Assn. Trial Lawyers Am. (vice chmn. internat. practice sect.), Va. State Bar (bd. govs. internat. law sect., liaison to ABA internat. law sect., spl. com. reducing litigation delay and costs, com. on bench/bar rels.), Calif. Bar Assn. (internat. law sect.), N.Y. State Bar Assn. (internat. law, family law sect.), D.C. Bar (internat. law, family law sect.), Arlington County Bar Assn. (cts. com., legis. com., jud. selection com.), Fairfax County Bar Assn. (family law and internat. law sects.), Brit. Inst. Internat. and Comparative Law, Am. Soc. Internat. Law, Union Internationale des Avocats, Inter-Am. Bar Assn., Internat. Soc. Family Law, Solicitors Family Law Assn. Eng. and Wales, Soc. English and Am. Lawyers, Am. Fgn. Law Assn. Internat. Law Assn., Asia-Pacific Lawyers Assn., Arlington Jaycees, Kiwanis, Phi Epsilon Pi, Delta Phi Epsilon, Phi Delta Phi. Office: Schwartz & Assocs LLC Ste 101 8221 Old Courthouse Rd Vienna VA 22182-3839 Office Phone: 703-883-8035. Business E-Mail: pschwartz@maddoxlawoffice.com.

**SCHWARTZ, RENEE GERSTLER,** lawyer; b. Bklyn., June 18, 1933; d. Samuel and Lillian (Neulander) Gerstler; m. Alfred L. Schwartz, July 30, 1955; children: Carolyn Susan, Deborah Jane. AB, Bklyn. Coll., 1953; LLB, Columbia U., 1955. Bar: N.Y. 1956, U.S. Dist. Ct. (so. and ea. dists.) N.Y. 1956, U.S. Ct. Appeals (2d cir.) 1956, U.S. Dist. Ct. D.C. 1983, U.S. Supreme Ct. 1986. Assoc. Botein, Hays & Sklar, N.Y.C., 1955-64, ptnr., 1965-89, Kronish, Lieb, Weiner & Hellman, N.Y.C., 1990—. Bd. dirs. New Land Found., N.Y.C., 1965—. Mem. Bar Assn. City of N.Y. Home: 115 Central Park W New York NY 10023-4153 Office: Kronish Lieb Weiner & Hellman 1114 Avenue Of The Americas New York NY 10036-7703 Office Phone: 212-479-6040. Business E-Mail: rschwartz@kronishlieb.com.

**SCHWARTZ, RICHARD BRENTON,** English language educator, dean, writer; b. Cin., Oct. 5, 1941; s. Jack Jay and Marie Mildred (Schnelle) S.; m. Judith Mary Alexis Lang, Sept. 7, 1963; 1 son, Jonathan Francis. AB cum laude, U. Notre Dame, 1963; AM, U. Ill., Urbana, 1967; instr. English, U.S. Mil. Acad., 1967-69; asst. prof. U. Wis.-Madison, 1969-72, assoc. prof., 1972-78, prof., 1978-81, assoc. dean Grad. Sch., 1977, 79-81; prof. English, dean Grad. Sch., Georgetown U., Washington, 1981-98, interim exec. v.p. for main campus academic affairs, 1991-92; interim exec. v.p. for the main campus Georgetown U., Washington, 1995-96; dean Coll. Arts and Sci. U. Mo., Columbia, 1998—2006, prof. English, 1998—. Mem. exec. bd. Ctr. Strategic and Internat. Studies, 1981-87. Author: Samuel Johnson and the New Science, 1971 (runner-up Gustave O. Arlt prize), Samuel Johnson and the Problem of Evil, 1975, Boswell's Johnson: A Preface to the Life, 1978, Daily Life in Johnson's London, 1983, Japanese edit., 1990, After the Death of Literature, 1997, Nice and Noir: Contemporary American Crime Fiction, 2002, (novels) Frozen Stare, 1989, The Last Voice You Hear, 2001, After the Fall, 2002, Into the Dark, 2002 (hon. mention genre fiction Writer's Digest); short stories, The Biggest City in America, 1999 (Choice Mag. citation); editor: The Plays of Arthur Murphy, 4 vols., 1979, Theory and Tradition in Eighteenth-Century Studies, 1990; contbr. articles to profl. jours. Served to capt. U.S. Army, 1967-69. Decorated Army Commendation medal; recipient Presdl. medal Georgetown U., 1998; Nat. Endowment Humanities grantee, 1970, 87; Inst. for Research in Humanities fellow, 1976; Am. Council Learned Socs. fellow, 1978-79; H.I. Romnes fellow, 1978-81. Mem. Mystery Writers Am., Johnson Soc. So. Calif., Johnson Soc. of London, Am. Soc. Eighteenth-Century Studies, Coun. Grad. Schs., N.E. Assn. Grad. Schs. (exec. com. 1986-88), Assn. Grad. Schs. in Cath. Univs. (exec. com. 1984-87), Assn. Literary Scholars and Critics, Nat. Assn. Scholars, N.Am. Conf. Brit. Studies, Jefferson Club, Mosaic Soc., Alpha Sigma Nu, Alpha Sigma Lambda. Roman Catholic. Home: 5800 Highlands Pkwy Columbia MO 65203-5125 Office: U Mo Dept English 236 Tate Hall Columbia MO 65211-6080 Office Phone: 573-884-7038. Business E-Mail: schwartzrb@missouri.edu.

**SCHWARTZ, RICHARD DEAN,** retired astronomer; b. Hutchinson, Kans., Apr. 17, 1941; s. Herbert and Elnora Leoti Schwartz; m. Eleanor Irene McIntyre, Dec. 31, 1987. BS, Kans. State U., Manhattan, 1963; MDiv, Union Theol. Sem., NYC, 1966; PhD, U. Wash., Seattle, 1973. Postdoctoral rsch. astronomer Lick Obs., U. of Calif., Santa Cruz, 1973—75; prof. of astronomy U. of Mo.i-St. Louis, 1975—2003, chair dept. physics and astronomy, 1996—2000; ret., 2003. Recipient Chancellor's Award for Excellence in Rsch. and Creativity, U. of Mo.-St. Louis, 1999. Mem.: Am. Astron. Soc. (Chretien Award 1987). Achievements include research in Observational study of Herbig-Haro Objects and T Tauri stars, and the theoretical interpretation of their relation to star formation. Avocations: travel, jogging, gardening. Personal E-mail: protostellarjet@yahoo.com.

**SCHWARTZ, RICHARD EDWARD DERECKTOR,** retired sociologist, educator; b. Newark, Apr. 26, 1925; s. Selig and Tillie (Derecktor) S.; m. Emilie Zane Rosenbaum, June 30, 1946; children: David, Margaret Jane, Deborah. BA, Yale U., 1947, PhD in Sociology, 1952. Rsch. fellow Inst. Human Rels., Yale U., 1951—54, instr., asst. prof. sociology and law, 1953—61; faculty Northwestern U., Evanston, Ill., 1961—71; prof. sociology, 1964—71; prof. sociology and law, 1966—71; dir. Coun. Intersocietal Studies, 1965—70, co-dir. law and social sci. program, 1967—70; dean, provost Faculty of Law and Jurisprudence, SUNY Buffalo, 1971—76; Ernest I. White rsch. prof. law Syracuse U., 1977—2004, Ernest I. White prof. emeritus, 2004—. Mem. com. law enforcement and adminstrn. of justice NAS, 1975-85; fellowship referee Russell Sage Found., 1970-77, NEH, 1972-77, NSF, 1978-81; exec. dir. NESCO, 1995-2001; sr. rsch. scholar Yale Law Sch., 2002— Author: (with others) Society and the Legal Order, 1970, Criminal Law, 1974, Handbook of Regulation and Administrative Law, 1994, Unobtrusive Measures, 2000; founding editor: Law and Soc. R., 1966-99. With U3NR, 1943—45. Ctr. for Advanced Study in Behavioral Scis. fellow, 1989—90, sr. rsch. scholar, Yale U. Law Sch., 2002—. Fellow AAAS, Am. Acad. Polit. and Social Sci.; mem. Am. Sociol. Assn. (Disting. Career award 2006), Law and Soc. Assn. (pres. 1972-75) Jewish. Home: 40 Beach Ave Milford CT 06460-8154 Office Phone: 203-874-4586. Personal E-mail: emnred@aol.com. *I believe that we could create a better way of life if we structured society to encourage-rather than to penalize-altruism. Although I have not yet contributed much toward achieving such a society, the effort to do so has been satisfying.*

**SCHWARTZ, RICHARD EVAN,** mathematician, educator; b. Aug. 11, 1966; BS in Math., UCLA, 1987; PhD in Math., Princeton U., 1991. Postdoctoral staff CUNY, IHES, MSRI, 1992—93; asst. prof. U. Chgo., 1993; assoc. prof. U. Md., 1997—2000, prof., 2000—04, Ruth Davis Prof., 2004—05; prof. Brown U., 2005—. Contbr. articles to profl. jours. Fellow, John Simon Guggenheim Meml. Found., 2003; grantee, NSF, 1998—; grad. fellow, 1988—90, postdoctoral fellow, 1993—95, Sloan Dissertation fellow, 1990—91, Sloan Rsch. fellow, 1996—99. Office: Dept Math Brown Univ Providence RI 02912*

**SCHWARTZ, RICHARD HARVEY,** pediatrician; b. Bklyn., July 6, 1938; s. Hy and Ruth (Marshak) S.; m. Rose Lynne Hass, May 29, 1960; children: Lisa, Keith, Keira. BA, George Washington U., 1960; MD, Georgetown U., 1965. Diplomate Am. Bd. Pediat., Am. Soc. Addiction Medicine. Intern U.S. Army, 1965-66, resident in pediat., 1969-71; prt. practice, Vienna, Va., 1972—. Contbr. articles to profl. jours. Maj. U.S. Army, 1965-69. Mem. AMA (Outstanding Contbn. in Adolescent Medicine award 1990), Am. Acad. Pediatrics (rsch. award 1989). Jewish. Avocations: walking, travel. Office: Advanced Pediatrics 100 East St SE Ste 301 Vienna VA 22180

**SCHWARTZ, RICHARD JOHN,** electrical engineering educator, researcher; b. Waukesha, Wis., Aug. 12, 1935; s. Sylvester John and LaVerne Mary (Lepien) S.; m. Mary Jo Collins, June 29, 1957; children: Richard, Stephen, Susan, Elizabeth, Barbara, Peter, Christopher, Margaret. BSEE, U. Wis., 1957; SM, MIT, 1959, ScD, 1962. Mem. tech. staff Sarnoff Rsch. Labs. RCA, Princeton, NJ, 1957-58; instr. MIT, Cambridge, 1961-62; v.p. Energy Conversions, Inc., Cambridge, 1962-64; assoc. prof. Purdue U., West Lafayette, Ind., 1964-71, prof., 1972—, head dept., 1985-95, dean engring., 1995—2001, dir. Optoelectronic Ctr., 1986-89. Co-dir. Nano Tech. Ctr. Purdue U., W. Lafayette, Ind.; cons. solar cells, 1965—. Contbr. chpts. to books, articles to profl. jours. Served to 2nd lt. U.S. Army, 1957-58. Recipient Disting. Svc. medal U. Wis., 1989, Centennial medal, 1991. Fellow: IEEE (William R. Cherry award 1998), Internat. Electronics Con.; mem.: Nat. Elec. Engring. Dept. Heads Assn. (bd. dirs.). Achievements include development of high intensity solar cells, of surface charge transfer device, and of numerical models for solar cells. Office: Purdue U 1285 Electrical Engring West Lafayette IN 47907 Office Phone: 765-494-0619.

**SCHWARTZ, ROBERT,** finance educator; b. N.Y.C., Feb. 12, 1937; s. Fred J. Schwartz and Shirley Liebowitz; m. Jody Silver Schwartz; 1 child, Emily. BA, NYU, 1959; MBA, Columbia U., N.Y.C., 1962, PhD, 1966. Asst. prof. econs. NYU, 1965—70, assoc. prof. econs., 1970—77, prof. econs., 1977—83, prof. econs. and fin., 1983—91; prof. econs. and fin., Yamaichi Faculty fellow Stern Sch. Bus., NYU, 1991—97; Speiser prof. fin., Univ. Disting. prof. Zicklin Sch. Bus. Baruch Coll., CUNY, 1997—. Chmn. econ. adv. bd. NASDAQ, 1995—97, mem. econ. adv. bd., 1997—99. Author (with Kalman J. Cohen, Steven F. Maier and David K. Whitcomb): The Microstructure of Securities Markets, 1986; author: Equity Markets: Structure, Trading and Performance, 1988, Reshaping the Equity Markets: A Guide for the 1990s, 1991, reissue, 1993; author: (with R. Francioni) Equity Markets in Action, 2004; author: (with R. Francioni and B. Weber) The Equity Trader Course, 2006; editor (with Ernest Bloch): Impending Changes for Securities Markets: What Role for the Exchanges?, 1979; editor: (with Yakov Amihud and Thomas Ho) Market Making and the Changing Structure of the Securities Industry, 1985; editor: (with Henry Lucas) The Challenge of Information Technology for the Securities Markets: Liquidity, Volatility and Global Trading, 1989; editor: Global Equity Markets: Technological, Competitive and Regulatory Challenges, 1995, The Electronic Call Auction: Market Mechanism and Trading, Building a Better Stock Market, 2001; editor: (with Antoinette Colaninno) Regulation of U.S. Equity Markets, 2001; editor: (with John A. Byrne and Antoinette Colaninno) Call Auction Trading: New Answers to Old Questions, 2003; editor: A Trading Desk's View of Market Quality, 2004, Coping with Institutional Order Flow, 2004; editor: (with John A. Byrne and Antoinette Colaninno) Electronic vs. Floor Based Trading, 2006; assoc. editor Jour. Fin., 1983—88, Rev. Quantitative Fin. and Acctg., Rev. Pacific Basin Fin. Markets and Policies, Jour. Entrepreneurial Fin. and Bus. Ventures, mem. adv. bd. Internat. Fin.; contbr. articles to profl. jours. Mem.: Am. Fin. Assn. Office: Baruch Coll CUNY 55 Lexington Ave Box B10-225 New York NY 10010

**SCHWARTZ, ROBERT,** epidemiologist; b. Racine, Wis., July 11, 1943; s. Ben and Elisheva Iushewitz Schwartz; m. Eileen Joan Lerner, Dec. 9, 1972; children: Sarianne Marissa Schwartz Hild, Hilary Joy, Max. BA, Boston U.; MD, U.A.G., Guadalajara, Mex. Intern Maimonides Med. Ctr., Bklyn., 1973, Lincoln Hosp., Bronx, NY, 1974, resident, 1976; fellow in infectious disease U. Miami, Fla.; pvt. practice infectious disease and internal medicine, 1978—. Med. dir. AIDS Resource Coun. S.W. Fla., Inc., ARC, 1995—; med. dir., founder Comprehensive Clinic, 1988—95; pres. Assocs. in Rsch. 1989—; pres. founder Lee County AIDS Task Force, 1986—93; mem. staff Lee Meml. Hosp., Health Park Hosp., Cape Coral Hosp., S.W. Fla. Regional Med. Ctr., Gulf Coast Hosp.; presenter in field; prin. investigator studies with pharm. cos. Contbr. articles to profl. jours. Named News-Press Person of Yr., 1987, Man of Yr., Kiwanis, 1989, Rotary, 1990; named to USA Today Man Who Made A Difference, 1987; recipient award for outstanding cmty. svc., dedication and support, Am. Legion, 1989, Marina Caper Corner Stone award, 1995, award for outstanding svc., Kiwanis Internat., 1995. Mem.: Assn. Practitioners in Infection Control, Am. Soc. Tropical Medicine and Hygiene, Am. Soc. Microbiology, Fla. Med. Soc., Lee County Med. Soc., Am. Acad. HIV Medicine, Assn. Clin. Rsch. Profls., HIV Medicine Assn. Infectious Diseases Soc. Am. Office: Schwartz & Schwartz 3677 Central Ave Fort Myers FL 33901

**SCHWARTZ, ROBERT GEORGE,** retired insurance company executive; b. Czechoslovakia, Mar. 27, 1928; came to U.S., 1929, naturalized, 1935; s. George and Frances (Antoni) S.; m. Caroline Bachurski, Oct. 12, 1952; children: Joanne, Tracy, Robert G. BA, Pa. State U., 1949; MBA, NYU, 1956. With Met. Life Ins. Co., N.Y.C., 1949-93, v.p. securities, 1962-70, v.p., 1970-75, sr. v.p., 1975-78, exec. v.p., 1979-80, vice chmn. bd., 1980-83, chmn. investment com., 1980-83, chmn. bd., 1983-93, chmn. bd., pres., chief exec. officer, 1989-93. Bd. dirs., mem. Horatio Alger Assn. Trustee Com. for Econ. Devel. With U.S. Army, 1950—52. Mem.: Alpha Chi Rho. Office: MetLife Bldg 200 Park Ave 32d Fl New York NY 10166-0005

**SCHWARTZ, ROBERT M.,** lawyer; b. LA, 1959; BS, U. Calif., Los Angeles, 1981; JD, U. So. Calif., 1984. Bar: Calif. 1984, US Dist. Ct., Ctrl. Dist. Calif. 1984, US Ct. Appeals, 9th Cir., DC 1987, US Dist. Ct., No. Dist. Calif. 2000, US District Ct., Ea. Dist. Calif. 2001. Litig. ptnr. O'Melveny & Myers LLP, LA, co-chair entertainment and media litig. practice group, mem. class action and appellate practice group. Bd. dir., mem. exec. com. Bet Tzedek- The House of Justice, LA. Mem.: Assn. of Bus. Trial Lawyers, ABA (mem. litig. sect.), LA County Bar Assn., Beverly Hills Bar Assn. (co-chair, entertainment law sect. 1998—99, 1999—2000). Office: O'Melveny & Myers LLP 1999 Avenue of the Stars 7th Fl Los Angeles CA 90067-6035 Office Phone: 310-246-6835. Office Fax: 310-246-6779. Business E-Mail: rschwartz@omm.com.

**SCHWARTZ, ROBERT TERRY,** industrial designer, director; b. Irvington, NJ, Sept. 29, 1950; s. Edward Herman and Harriet Selma (Rosenstein) S.; m. Carol Fawn Mullenix, July 27, 1975; children: Zachary Jacob, Allison Lizabeth. BFA, Kansas City Art Inst., 1973; M of Indsl. Design, R.I. Sch. Design, 1975. Red Cross project dir. R.I. Sch. Design, Providence, 1975-76; head indsl. design/architecture Red Cross Nat. Hdqrs., Washington, 1976-88; dir. sci. and tech. Health Industry Mfrs. Assn., Washington, 1988-90; exec. dir., COO Worldesign Found., Great Falls, Va., 1990-96, Indsl. Designers Soc. Am., Great Falls, 1990-99; dir. indsl. design Motorola, Inc., Ft. Lauderdale, Fla., 1999—2003; v.p. new product devel. Levolor Kirsch, High Point, NC, 2003; assoc. dir. global design orgn. Procter and Gamble, 2003—. Provider expert testimony before Congress, 1994, commencement address, Kansas City Art Inst., 1995; sr. tech. advisor to Peoples Republic of China, UN, 1998. Contbr. chpts. to books, articles to profl. jours.; presenter in field; holder 5 patents, 1 trademark. Recipient Project of Merit award Indsl. Design Mag., 1985, Cert. of Achievement, ARC, 1988, Louis B. Tiffany award ARC 1987, numerous others; Nat. Endowment for the Arts grantee, 1984, 92, 94; EPA grantee, 1992. Mem. Indsl. Designers Soc. Am. (Personal Recognition award 2000). Avocations: edison antiquities collecting, sailing. Office: Procter and Gamble One P&G Plz Cincinnati OH 45202 E-mail: designo@att.net.

**SCHWARTZ, ROBERT WILLIAM,** management consultant; b. NYC, Oct. 23, 1944; s. Edward and Bertha R. S.; m. Gail Beth Greenbaum, Mar. 18, 1967; children: Jill, Evan. BS, Cornell U., 1967; postgrad., SUNY, Albany, 1970. Assoc. IBM, 1967-68; cons. Peat, Marwick, Mitchell & Co., Albany, 1970-71; v.p. Security Gen. Svcs., Inc., Rochester, 1971—77; v.p. fin. and adminstrn. Gardenway Mfg. Co., Troy, NY, 1973-77; exec. v.p. United Telecommunications Corp., Latham, NY, 1977-79, pres., 1980-82, also bd. dir.; pres., chmn. Winsource, Inc., Albany, 1982-85, Schwartz Heslin Group, Inc., 1985—. Bd. dirs. Docucon, Inc., San Antonio, State Zone Capital Corp., Albany, NY, State Industries for Disabled, Donnkenny, NY; adj. prof. Rochester Inst. Tech., 1971—73; adj. prof., SUNY Albany, 1998—. Vice chmn. United Cerebral Palsy of Capital Dist., 1973—; trustee Newman Found., Rensselaer Poly. Inst., 1974-78, Gov. Clinton coun. Boy Scouts Am., SUNY Found. Mem. Am. Mgmt. Assn., Esarco Internat., N.Am. Tel. Assn., Assn. for Systems Mgmt., Ft. Orange Club, Econ. Club, Cornell Club (N.Y.C.). Republican. Home: 2 Myton Ln Albany NY 12204-1310 Office: 8 Airport Park Blvd Latham NY 12110-1441 Office Phone: 518-786-7733. Business E-mail: rschwartz@shggroup.com.

**SCHWARTZ, SHIRLEY E.,** retired chemist, researcher; b. Detroit, Aug. 26, 1935; d. Emil Victor and Jessie Grace (Galbraith) Eckwall; m. Ronald Elmer Schwartz, Aug. 25, 1957; children: Steven Dennis, Bradley Allen, George Byron. BS, U. Mich., 1957, Detroit Inst. Tech., 1978; MS, Wayne State U., 1962, PhD, 1970. Asst. prof. Detroit Inst. Tech., 1973—78, head divsn. math. sci., 1976—78; mem. rsch. staff BASF Wyandotte Corp., Mich., 1978—81, head sect. functional fluids, 1981; sr. staff rsch. scientist GM Rsch., Warren, Mich., 1981—99; materials engr. GM Powertrain, 1999—2003; ret., 2003. Contbr. articles to profl. jours.; patentee in field. Recipient Gold award Engring. Soc. Detroit, 1989 Fellow Soc. Automotive Engrs. (Excellence in Oral Presentation award 1986, 91, 94, Arch T. Colwell Merit award 1991, Lloyd L. Withrow Disting. Spkr. award 1995), Soc. Tribologists and Lubrication Engrs. (treas. Detroit sect. 1981, vice chmn. 1982, chmn. 1982-83, chmn. wear tech. com. 1987-88, bd. dirs. 1985-91, assoc. editor 1989-90, contbg. editor 1989—2003, Wilbur Deutsch award 1987, P.M. Ku award 1994); mem. Am. Chem. Soc., Soc. In Vitro Biology, Soc. Women Engrs. Life Achievement award 1989), Mich. Women's Hall of Fame (lifetime achievement award 1996), Women of Wayne (headliners award 2000), U.S. Nat. Acad. Engring., Mensa, Classic Guitar Soc. Mich., U.S. Power Squadrons, Detroit Navigators, Sigma Xi. Lutheran. *I've spent a number of very pleasant hours trying to make water behave like oil and alcohol behave like gasoline—a quest not much different from that of the ancient alchemists, who also spent their time trying to convert one substance to another.*

**SCHWARTZ, STEPHEN BLAIR,** retired information technology executive; b. Chgo., Oct. 19, 1934; s. Herbert S. and Gertrude Schwartz; m. Nancy Jean Astrof, Dec. 18, 1955; children: Debra Lee Schwartz Zaret, Susan Beth Schwartz Derene. BS in Indsl. Engring., Northwestern U., 1957. With IBM Corp., 1957-92; various mgmt. positions, dir. product programs Harrison, NY, to 1977; v.p. Systems Communications div., 1977-81; v.p. Armonk, NY, 1982-90; v.p. Am. Far East Corp. subs. IBM Corp. Tokyo, 1982-84; pres., CEO Satellite Bus. Systems, McLean, Va., 1984; v.p., asst. group exec. Telecommunications, 1985-86; v.p., pres. Systems Products Div., 1986-88; v.p., gen. mgr. Application Bus. Systems, 1988-90; sr. v.p. market driven quality Stamford, Conn., 1990-92. Bd. dirs. MFRI, Inc. Mem.: PGA Nat. Golf Club (Palm Beach Gardens, Fla.). Republican. Jewish. E-mail: sbsone@aol.com.

**SCHWARTZ, STEPHEN GREGORY,** ophthalmologist; b. Queens, NY, Nov. 28, 1969; s. Charles F. and Patricia Schwartz; m. Melanie Rebak, June 15, 1996; children: Jessica Hope, Reid Alexander. BS with honors, Cornell U., Ithaca, NY, 1991; MD, NYU, NYC, 1995. Diplomate Am. Bd. Ophthalmology. Intern Lenox Hill Hosp., NYC, 1995—96; resident NYU Sch. Medicine, NYC, 1996—99; fellow Baylor Coll. Medicine, Houston, 1999—2001; asst. prof. ophthalmology Va. Commonwealth U. Sch. Medicine, Richmond, 2001—04, program dir. ophthalmology, 2002—04; asst. prof. clin. ophthalmology U. Miami (Fla.) Miller Sch. Medicine, 2004—; med. dir., divsn. chief Bascom Palmer Eye Inst., Retina Ctr., Naples, Fla., 2004—. Bd. govs. Prevent Blindness Fla., Tampa, 2006; bd. dirs. Va. Voice for Print Handicapped, Inc., Richmond, 2002—04. Grantee Investigator award, Prevent Blindness Am., 2005; Nat. Glaucoma Rsch. grantee, Am. Health Assistance Found., 2003. Fellow: Am. Acad. Ophthalmology; mem.: AMA, Collier County Med. Soc. (bd. govs. 2006), Fla. Soc. Ophthalmology (bd. dirs. 2006), Fla. Med. Assn., Assn. Rsch. in Vision and Ophthalmology (members in mtg. com. 2002), Am. Soc. Retina Specialists. Office: Bascom Palmer Eye Inst 311 9th St N # 100 Naples FL 34102 Office Phone: 239-659-3937. Office Fax: 239-659-3982. Business E-mail: sschwartz2@med.miami.edu.

**SCHWARTZ, STEPHEN LAWRENCE,** composer, lyricist; b. NYC, Mar. 6, 1948; s. Stanley Leonard and Sheila Lorna (Siegel) Schwartz; m. Carole Ann Piasecki, June 6, 1969; children: Scott Lawrence, Jessica Lauren. Student, Juilliard Sch. Music, 1960—64; BFA, Carnegie-Mellon U., 1968. Composer (works include): title song for Butterflies Are Free, 1969; composer: (theatre) music and lyrics Godspell, 1971, Pippin, 1972, The Magic Show, 1974, The Baker's Wife, 1976, Children of Eden, 1991, Wicked, 2003, Mit Eventyr (Denmark), 2005, four songs, adaptation and direction Working, 1978; composer: (with Leonard Bernstein) English texts for Leonard Bernstein's Mass, 1971; composer: lyrics Rags, 1986, (films) lyrics Pocahontas, 1995 (Acad. award best original score, 1996, Acad. award best original song, 1996), The Hunchback of Notre Dame, 1996, (music and lyrics) The Prince of Egypt, 1998 (Acad. award best original song, 1999), (TV, music and lyrics) Geppetto, 2000, (juvenile) The Perfect Peach, 1977, Captain Louie, 1983, (recording) Reluctant Pilgrim, 1997, Uncharted Territory, 2001. Recipient Drama Desk awards, 1971, 1978, 2004, Grammy awards, 1971, 1996, 2005, Golden Globe award, 1996. Mem.: ASCAP (bd. dirs.), Am. Motion Picture Arts Soc., Dramatists Guild (coun.). Business E-mail: schwartz@stephenschwartz.com.

**SCHWARTZ, STEVE WENDELIN,** physician; b. Bethesda, Md., May 16, 1955; s. Wallace John and Gwynne June (Lingenfelter) S. AB in Chemistry summa cum laude, Duke U., 1977, MD, 1981. Diplomate Am. Bd. Family Practice. Rotating intern Med. U. S.C., Charleston, 1981-82, resident in family practice, 1982-84; emergency rm. physician Coastal Emergency Svc., 1985-86; family physician Carolina Health Care, Myrtle Beach, SC, 1984—; CEO Cactus Internat., Inc. Data processing dir. HMI, 1984—; pres. Unitrends Software Corp., 1989-2003, chief tech officer, 2004-05; pvt. Symbol Theory; programmer langs. Columnist SCO World Mag.; contbr. articles to profl. jours. Del. ann. meeting N.C. Med. Soc., 1980; participant Intramural Soccer, 1977-80; mem. Intramural Track, 1980, Blacknall Meml. Presbyn. Ch., 1977-80; coord. Boy Scouts Phys. Exam. Program, 1983; vol. cmty. health care project for poor East End Cmty. Health Ctr.; tchr. seminars on alcoholism for drug edn. project Holistic Medicine Group, 1980; Bible study coord. Valley of Achor. With USAF. 1973-75. First Place Durham Open Chess Tournament, 1974; recipient Grand Strand Leadership, 1986. Fellow Am. Acad. Family Physicians; mem. AMA (Physicians Recognition award 1986), So. Med. Assn., Horry County Med. Soc., Phi Beta Kappa, Upsilon Pi Epsilon. Avocations: chess, soccer. Office: Carolina Health Care 4605 Hwy 17 Byp S Myrtle Beach SC 29577-6681 Personal E-mail: steves@sc.rr.com.

**SCHWARTZ, STEVEN H.,** lawyer; b. Indpls., July 27, 1959; BA with distinction, Ind. U., 1981; JD with honors, George Washington U. Law Sch., DC, 1984. Bar: DC 1986, Mo. 1988, Ill. 1988. Investigative atty. US Internat. Trade Commn., Washington, 1984—87; assoc. Brown & James, PC, St. Louis, 1987—93, prin., 1993—. Chairperson Mo. Bar Computer Law Com., Jefferson City, 2000—02. Mem.: Phi Beta Kappa. Office: Brown & James PC 1010 Market Stt 20th Floor Saint Louis MO 63101 Office Phone: 314-242-5280. Office Fax: 314-242-5480.

**SCHWARTZ, STEVEN MARK,** marketing executive; b. Phila., Feb. 26, 1948; s. Edward and Erika (Schneier) S.; m. Paula Mae Levine, May 15, 1979; 1 child, Roger. AB magna cum laude, Bowdoin Coll., 1970; MFA in Writing, Columbia U., 1973. Writer, account exec. Schneider & Rich Assocs., N.Y.C., 1973-76; sr. account exec. Richard Weiner Inc., N.Y.C., 1976-78; account supr., v.p. The Rowland Co., N.Y.C., 1978-79; project mgr. exec. comm. GE, Fairfield, Conn., 1979-83, mgr. exec. comm., 1983-84; v.p. corp. comm. Interleaf Inc., Cambridge, Mass., 1984-86, v.p. mktg. programs and comm., 1986-88, v.p. mktg., 1989-90; pres. Schwartz Comm. Inc., Waltham, Mass., 1990—. Trustee Bowdoin Coll. Mem. Appalachian Mountain Club (bd. dirs.), Am. Alpine Club (bd. dirs.), Phi Beta Kappa, Theta Delta Chi. Republican. Avocations: kayaking, climbing. Office: Schwartz Comm Inc 230 3rd Ave Waltham MA 02451-7528

**SCHWARTZ, THEODORE H.,** neurosurgeon; MD, Harvard Med. Sch., 1993. Dir. brain tumor surgery NY Prebyn. Hosp., NYC, 2001—. Dir. inst. minimally invasive skull base and pituitary surgery NY Presbyn. Hosp. Office: New York Presbyterian Hospital 525 East 68th St Box #99 New York NY 10021 Office Phone: 212-746-5620.

**SCHWARTZ, VICTOR ELLIOT,** lawyer, educator; b. NYC, July 3, 1940; AB summa cum laude, Boston U., 1962; JD magna cum laude, Columbia U., 1965. Bar: NY 1965, Ohio 1974. Law clk. to judge So. Dist. N.Y., 1965-67; from asst. to assoc. prof. law U. Cin., 1967-72, prof., 1972-79, acting dean, 1973-74; vis. prof. U. Va. Law Sch., 1970-71; dist. vis. scholar U. Cin., 2002—; ptnr. firm Crowell & Moring, Washington, 1980—2001; sr. ptnr. firm Fed. Interagy. task Force on Products Liability, 1976; ptnr., chair firm's pub. policy group Shook Hardy & Bacon, Washington, 2001—. Bd. visitors U. Cin. Sch., 1998—; disting. vis. scholar U. Cin., 2003—; gen. counsel, bd. dirs. Am. Tort Reform Assn.; chmn. Civil Justice Task Force, Am. Legis. Exch. Coun.; chmn. Dept. of Commerce Task Force on Product Liability and Accident Compensation, 1977-80. Author: Comparative Negligence, 1974, 4th edit., 2002; (with Kelly and Partlett) Cases and Materials on Torts, 1976, 11th edit., 2005, How to Prepare for the Multi-State Bar Examination, 1977, Products Liability: Cases and Trends, 1987, Products Liability: Asset Trends, 1988, (with Lee and Kelly) Multistate Legislation, 1985; editor: Columbia Law Rev., 1965; prin. draftsman: Model Uniform Product Liability Act. Recipient Sec. of Commerce award for disting. svc., Burton award for best law rev. writing in U.S., Tort Summit award, Am. Tort Reform Assn., 2002; named One of 100 Most Influential Attys. in U.S., Nat. Law 3, 1994, 97, Pvt. Sector Person of Yr., Am. Legis. Exch. Coun., 2003. Mem. ABA (chmn. products liability com. 1979, uniform laws com. 1981, torts and ins. practice sect.), Am. Law Inst. (life, adv. com. Restatement Third of Torts), Phi Beta Kappa. Office: Shook Hardy & Bacon LLP 600 14th St NW Ste 800 Washington DC 20005-2004 Office Phone: 202-662-4880. Business E-Mail: vschwartz@shb.com. *The greatest joys in life are found in one's relationships, be it business, romance or friendship, with other people.*

**SCHWARTZ, WALLACE L.,** lawyer; b. Poughkeepsie, NY, 1952; BA, Harvard U., 1974; JD, Cornell U., 1977. Bar: N.Y. 1978. NY office leader Skadden, Arps, Slate, Meagher & Flom, NYC, chair, hiring com. Office: Skadden Arps Slate Meagher & Flom Four Times Sq New York NY 10036 Office Phone: 212-735-2640. Office Fax: 212-735-2000, 212-777-2640. Business E-Mail: wschwart@skadden.com.

**SCHWARTZ, WILLIAM,** lawyer, educator; b. Providence, May 6, 1933; s. Morris Victor and Martha (Glassman) S.; m. Bernice Konigsberg, Jan. 13, 1957; children: Alan Gershon, Robin Libby. AA, Boston U., 1952, JD magna cum laude, 1955, MA, 1960; postgrad., Harvard Law Sch., 1955-56; LHD (hon.), Hebrew Coll., 1996, Yeshiva U., 1998. Bar: D.C. 1956, Mass. 1962, N.Y. 1989. Prof. law Boston U., 1955-91, Fletcher prof. law, 1968-70, Roscoe Pound prof. law, 1970-73, dean Sch. of Law, 1980-88, dir. Ctr. for Estate Planning, 1988-91; univ. prof. Yeshiva U., N.Y.C., 1991—; of counsel Swartz & Swartz, 1993-98; v.p. for acad. affairs, chief acad. officer Yeshiva U., N.Y.C., 1993-98; counsel Cadwalader, Wickersham and Taft, N.Y.C., Washington, Charlotte, London, Beijing, 1988—; mem. faculty Frances Glessner Lee Inst., Harvard Med. Sch., Nat. Coll. Probate Judges, 1970, 77, 78, 79, 88; gen. dir. Assn. Trial Lawyers Am., 1968-73; reporter New Eng. Trial Judges Conf., 1965-67; participant Nat. Met. Cts. Conf., 1968; dir. Mass. Probate Study, 1976—; chmn. spl. com. on police procedures City of Boston, 1989, 91. Chmn. UST Corp., 1993—94; bd. dirs. Viacom Inc., chmn. governance and nominating com., compensation com.; legal adv. bd. NY Stock Exch. Author: Future Interests and Estate Planning, 1965, 77, 81, 86, Comparative Negligence, 1970, A Products Liability Primer, 1970, Civil Trial Practice Manual, 1972, New Vistas in Litigation, 1973, Massachusetts Pleading and Practice, 7 vols., 1974-80, Estate Planning and Living Trusts, 1990, The Convention Method: The Unused Amending Superhighway, 1995, Jewish Law and Contemporary Dilemmas and Problems, 1997, Does Time Heal All Wrongs?, 1999, Amending Irrevocable Trusts, 2003, The Art of Effectuating a Donor's Wishes, 2005; others; note editor: Boston U. Law Rev., 1954-55; property editor: Annual Survey of Mass. Law, 1960—; contbr. articles to profl. jours. Rep. Office of Pub. Info., UN, 1968—73; chmn. legal adv. panel Nat. Commn. Med. Practice, 1972—73; examiner of titles Commonwealth of Mass., 1964—; spl. counsel Mass. Bay Transp. Authority, 1979; pres. Fifth Ave. Synagogue, N.Y.C., 1997—2001, hon. pres., 2001—; trustee Hebrew Coll., 1975—, Salve Regina U., Yeshiva U. Recipient Homer Albers award Boston U., 1955, John Ordronaux prize, 1955, Disting. Svc. award Religious Zionists Am., 1977; William W. Treat award, William O. Douglas award Fellow Am. Coll. Probate Counsel; mem. ABA, Am. Law Inst., Mass. Bar Assn. (chmn. task force tort liability), N.Y. State Bar Assn., Bar City N.Y., Nat. Coll. Probate Judges (hon. mem.), Phi Beta Kappa. Office: Cadwalader Wickersham Taft One World Fin Ctr New York NY 10281 Office Phone: 212-504-6399. Personal E-mail: william.schwartz@cwt.com. *I have been guided by the maxim: "Ideals are like stars. You cannot touch them with your hands, but like the seafaring man, if you choose them as your guide and follow them, you will reach your destiny".*

**SCHWARTZBACH, M. GERALD,** lawyer; b. Wilkes-Barre, Pa., Oct. 6, 1944; m. Susan Schwartzbach; 1 child, Micah. BA in History, Washington and Jefferson Coll., 1966; JD, George Washington U., 1969. Bar: Mich. 1970, Calif. 1974, US Supreme Ct. 1982, US Ct. Appeals 9th Circuit 1980, US Dist. Ct. Eastern Dist. Mich. 1970, US District Ct. No. Dist. Calif. 1974, US Dist. Ct. So. Dist. Calif. 1978. Staff atty. Legal Aid and Defenders Office, Detroit, 1970—71, Mich. State Appellate Defender Office, Detroit, 1971, Bayview Hunter's Point Cmty. Defender, San Francisco, 1974—76; pvt. practice Detroit, 1971—72, San Francisco, 1977—87, 1989—96, Law Office of M. Gerald Schwartzbach, Civil Trial, Plaintiffs and Personal Injury, 1999—; assoc. Law Offices of Sheldon Otis, San Francisco, 1976—77, Joseph W. Carcione, Jr., Redwood City, Calif., 1996—99; ptnr. Garry, McTernan, Stender, Walsh & Schwartzbach, San Francisco, 1987—89. Lectr. in field. Vol. Svc. To Am., 1969—70; bd. dir. La Casa de Las Madres, shelter for battered women, 1981—90. Named one of Best Lawyers in Am., Woodward/White; recipient Outstanding Svc. award, No. Calif. Innocence Project, 2003. Mem.: Marin County Bar Assn., Calif. Pub. Defenders Assn., Nat. Lawyers Guild, No. Calif. Criminal Trial Lawyers Assn. (mem. bd. gov. 1989—95), Nat. Assn. Criminal Def. Lawyers, Calif. Atty. Criminal Justice (mem. bd. gov. 1986—93, Skip Glen Outstanding Lawyer award), State Bar Calif., Bar Assn. Calif. (chair criminal justice section 1988—91, mem. criminal justice adv. coun. 1988—92). Achievements include the successful defense of actor Robert Blake in the 2004-05 murder trial. Office: 655 Redwood Hwy Ste 277 Mill Valley CA 94941 Office Phone: 415-388-2343. Office Fax: 415-388-2353. Business E-Mail: mgslaw@pacbell.net.

**SCHWARTZBERG, ALLAN ZELIG,** psychiatrist, educator; b. Cleve., Dec. 5, 1930; s. Joseph and Jeanette (Eisenman) S.; m. Katherine Weiss, June 19, 1955; children: Shana, Robert. BS cum laude, Case Western Res. U., 1951; MD, Ohio State U., 1955. Diplomate Am. Bd. Psychiatry and Neurology, Am. Bd. Forensic Medicine. Intern, resident in psychiatry Johns Hopkins Hosp., Balt., 1955—59; pvt. practice Gaithersburg, Md.; assoc. clin. prof. psychiatry Georgetown U. Sch. Medicine, Washington, 1979—89, clin. prof., 1989—. Vis. prof. faculty seminar in cmty. psychiatry Harvard U. Med. Sch., Boston, 1965-67; cons. Dept. Energy, 2002. Editor-in-chief Internat. Annals Adolescent Psychiatry, 1988—2000; co-editor Adolescent Psychiatry, Vols. 8-19; contbr. articles to med. jours. Recipient Vicennial medal Georgetown U., 1984. Fellow AMA, Am. Psychiat. Assn. (disting. life), Am. Soc. for Adolescent Psychiatry, Am. Soc. Psychoanalytic Physicians (pres. 1986-87, 2000-01), Am. Coll. Psychiatrists; mem. Am. Group Psychotherapy Assn., B'nai B'rith, Phi Beta Kappa. Republican. Jewish. Home: 6616 Kenhill Rd Bethesda MD 20817-6014 Office: Comprehensive Behavioral Svcs 9021 Shady Grove Ct Gaithersburg MD 20877-1308 Office Phone: 301-590-9000. E-mail: azsmd@aol.com.

**SCHWARTZEL, CHARLES BOONE,** lawyer; b. Louisville, Jan. 4, 1950; s. Charles Joseph and Rosemary Jane (Redens) S.; m. Rose Marie Carlisi, June 20, 1980; children: Sally Ann, Charles Gerard. BA, Vanderbilt U., 1972; JD, U. Tex., 1975. Bar: Tex. 1975. Atty. Vinson & Elkins L.L.P., Houston, 1975-98, ptnr., 1983-98; pvt. practice Houston, 1998—. Contbr. articles to profl. jours. Councilman City of West University Place, Tex., 1985-89. Fellow Am. Coll. Trust and Estate Counsel; mem. Tex. Bar Assn. Roman Catholic. Office: Attorney at Law 1010 Lamar St Ste 1520 Houston TX 77002-6315

**SCHWARTZHOFF, GARY R.,** music educator; s. Clarence and Wenifred Schwartzhoff; m. Nancy Schwartzhoff; children: Rebecca Johnson, Jenifer. BA, Ctrl. Coll., 1974; MusM, U. No. Iowa, 1981; DMA, U. Mo., Kansas City, 1990. Music tchr. St. Ansgar (Iowa) H.S., 1974—77, Charles City, Iowa, 1977—85, Ames (Iowa) H.S., 1987—91; dir. choral activities U. Wis., Eau Claire, Wis., 1991—. Bd. mem. Intercollegiate Men's Choruses. Mem.: North Ctrl. Am. Choral Dirs. Assn. (pres. 1992—94). Office: Univ Wis Eau Claire 105 Garfield Ave Eau Claire WI 54701

**SCHWARTZMAN, ANDREW JAY,** lawyer; b. NYC, Oct. 4, 1946; s. Joel Jay and Theresa (Greenhauff) S.; m. Linda Lazarus, June 8, 1986. AB, U. Pa., 1968, JD, 1971. Bar: N.Y. 1972, D.C. 1974, Temporary Emergency Ct. Appeals 1977, U.S. Dist. Ct. D.C. 1978, U.S. Ct. Appeals (D.C. cir.) 1981, U.S. Ct. Appeals (2d cir.) 1987, U.S. Ct. Appeals (3rd, 4th, 7th, 8th, 9th cirs.) 1991, U.S. Supreme Ct. 1980. Staff counsel United Ch. of Christ Office of Comm., N.Y.C., 1971-74; atty. adviser Fed. Energy Office, Washington, 1974-77; sr. atty. adviser U.S. Dept. Energy, Washington, 1977-78; bd. dirs. Safe Energy Comms. Coun., pres. bd. dirs., 1989—2003; dir. Media Access Project, Washington, 1978-96, pres., CEO, 1996—. Mem. adv. panel Study on Comms. Systems for an Info. Age; mem. adv. bd. Ctr. for Democracy and Tech., 1996—; lectr. Fairleigh Dickinson U., 1972-73; instr. Johns Hopkins U., 2003—; mem. comms. coun. forum Aspen Inst. on Comms. and Soc., 1992—; bd. dirs. Min. Media and Telecomms. Coalition, 1994—; mem. adv. bd. Nat. Inst. Entertainment and Media Law, Southwestern U. Sch. Law, 2000—, dist. lectr. in residence Southwestern U. Sch. Law Summer Entertainment and Media Law Program, Fitzwilliam Coll., Cambridge U., 2004. Contbg. author: Les Brown's Dictionary of Television, 3d edit., Ency. of the Consumer Movement, 1997; contbr. articles to legal jours. Recipient Everett Parker award United Ch. of Christ, 1994, Just Media Lifetime Achiev. award, 2004. Mem. ABA, Fed. Comms. Bar Assn., U. Pa. Alumni Assn., Sci. Am. Soc (leader in technology policy 2004). Office: Media Access Project # 1000 1625 K St NW Washington DC 20006-1604 Office Phone: 202-232-4300. E-mail: info@mediaaccess.org.

**SCHWARTZMAN, PETER DAVID,** environmental scientist, educator; s. Barbara Ann Major and David William Schwartzman; m. Huong Minh Hua, June 27, 1998; children: Camellia Nai, Juniper Rose Nai. BS in Physics, Harvey Mudd Coll., Claremont, Calif., 1991; MS in Sci. and Tech. Studies, Va. Poly. Inst., Blacksburg, Ill., 1993; PhD in Environ. Sci., U. Va., Charlottesville, 1997. Assoc. prof. environ. studies Knox Coll., Galesburg, Ill., 1998—. Exec. bd. mem. Assoc. Coll. of Midwest, Chgo., 2000—04. Author: (book) One's Power, The Word Nerd Workbook #1; contbr. articles to profl. jours. Bd. mem. Western Ill. Nature Group, Galesburg, Ill., 2001—06; vol. educator Knox County Sch. Dist. 205, Galesburg, Ill., 1998—2006. Mem.: Union of Concerned Scientists (assoc.), Amnesty Internat. (assoc.). Office: Knox Coll 2 E South St Galesburg IL 61401 Office Phone: 309-341-7142. Personal E-mail: drearth1@gmail.com.

**SCHWARTZSTEIN, ADAM,** lawyer; b. NYC, Jan. 4, 1969; BS, Boston U., 1990; JD, Quinnipiac U., 1994. Bar: NY 1995, US Dist. Ct. Ea. Dist. NY, US Dist. Ct. So. Dist. NY. Ptnr. Wilson, Elser, Moskowitz, Edelman & Dicker LLP, NYC. Mem.: Assn. of the Bar of the City of NY. Office: Wilson Elser Moskowitz Edelman & Dicker LLP 150 E 42nd St 23rd Fl New York NY 10017-5639 Office Phone: 212-490-3000 ext. 2778. Office Fax: 212-490-3038. Business E-Mail: schwartzsteina@wemed.com.

**SCHWARY, RONALD LOUIS,** motion picture producer; b. The Dalles, Oreg., May 23, 1944; s. Mitchell Louis and Lorraine (Ablan) S.; children: Brian L., Neil L. BS, U. So. Calif., 1967. Pres. Red Truck Prodns., Inc., L.A., 1985—. Prodr. (motion pictures) Ordinary People, 1980 (Golden Globe award 1981, Acad. award 1981), Absence of Malice, 1981, Tootsie, 1982, A Soldier's Story, 1984, Batteries Not Included, 1987, Havana, 1990, Scent of a Woman, 1992, Cops and Robbersons, 1994, Sabrina, 1995, Mirror Has Two Faces, 1996, Meet Joe Black, 1997, Random Hearts, 1999; (TV series) Tour of Duty, 1987, Now and Again, 1999, Medium, 2004—. Mem. Dirs. Guild Am. Republican. Roman Catholic.

**SCHWARZ, BARBARA RUTH BALLOU,** elementary school educator; b. East Orange, N.J., Aug. 8, 1930; d. Robert Ingram Ballou and Ruth Edna Sweeney; m. Eugene A. Schwarz, Dec. 24, 1954 (div. 1977); children: Ruth Ellen, Eugene A. III. BS, Trenton State Coll., 1952. Tchr. West Orange N.J. Schs., 1952-54, Franklin Sch., Ft. Wayne, Ind., 1955-56, Parliament Place Sch., North Babylon, N.Y., 1965-91. Trustee welfare trust fund North Babylon Tchrs. Orgn., N.Y., 1988-91. Vol. Safe Home, Suffolk County Coalition Against Domestic Violence, Bayshore, NY, 1979—90; sec. Victims Info. Bur., Suffolk, 1987—88, v.p., 1989—90, pres. bd. dirs., 1990—94, rep. to Women's Equal Rights Coalition, Suffolk County Human Rights Commn., 1989—94; mem. adv. bd. Suffolk County Women's Svcs., 1990—96, vice-chair, 1991—93; rep. LD 14 Suffolk County Women's Adv. Commn., 2001—06; bd. dirs. Suffolk Abortion Rights Coun., 1992—96; mem. Suffolk-Nassau Abortion Def., 1991—94; pub. affairs com. Planned Parenthood Suffolk County, 1990—92; mem. Long Islanders for Fairness and Equality, 1994—97; mem. subcom. Islip Presbyn. Ch. on Legis. Com. of N.Y. State Coalition Against Domestic Violence, 1999—2001; steering com. Save Our Svcs., Long Island, 1998—2001; mem. coun. on women L.I. Presbytery, 2002—; sec. sr. lunch program Presbyn. Ch. of Islip. Women's History Month Community Svc. honoree Town of Babylon, 1997. Mem. AAUW (mem. v.p. Islip area br. 1982-84, pres. 1984-88, legis. chair 1988-93, mem. com. promoting individual liberties Nassau-Suffolk dist. VI 1989-91, pro-choice coord. N.Y. state 1990-92, rep. to women on job task force 1986-98, chair dist. VI inter-br. 1991-92, chair N.Y. state pub. policy 1992-96, rep. on L.I. and N.Y. State Pro-Choice Coalitions, chair N.Y. state voter edn. campaign, 1995-98, assoc. pub. policy com. 1996-98, L.I. Achievement award 1996), N.Y. State Rel Tln Avm., Western Suffolk Rel Tclns. Assn., Coalition Ret. Tchrs. L.I., North Babylon Tchrs. Orgn. (retirees chpt.). Republican. Avocations: lobbying, reading, handcrafts, gourmet cooking, volunteer activities. Home: 23 Wyandanch Ave Babylon NY 11702-1920 E-mail: bbschwarz@optonline.net.

**SCHWARZ, BERTHOLD ERIC,** psychiatrist; b. Jersey City, Oct. 20, 1924; s. Berthold Theodore Dominick and I. Thyra W. (Ericson) Schwarz; m. Ardis Marilyn Peterson, Jan. 22, 1955; children: Lisa Thyra, Eric Rolf. AB, Dartmouth Coll., 1945; MD, NYU, 1950; MS, Mayo Grad. Sch. Medicine, 1957. Intern Mary Hitchcock Meml. Hosp., Hanover, NH, 1950-51; psychiatrist, researcher pvt. practice, Montclair, NJ, 1955-82; Mayo Found., Rochester, Minn., 1951-55; psychiatrist, researcher pvt. practice, Vero Beach, Fla., 1982—. Cons. Essex County Hosp. Ctr., Cedar Grove, N.J., 1965-82, Med. Correctional Assn., Ossining, N.Y., 1960-72; exec. dir. Internat. Psychosomatics Inst., Mountain Lakes, N.J., 1995—. Contbr. articles to med. jours. With USNR, 1943-45. Fellow AAAS, Am. Psychiat. Assn., Am. Soc. Psychical Rsch., Am. Geriatric Soc. Republican. Avocations: ufos, paranormal aspects, swimming, walking. Home: 1070 Reef Rd Apt 305 Vero Beach FL 32963-4342 Office: 642 Azalea Ln Vero Beach FL 32963-1832 Office Phone: 772-231-5220. Personal E-mail: ardisps@aol.com.

**SCHWARZ, CARL A., JR.,** lawyer; b. NYC, Apr. 27, 1936; s. Carl A. and Genevieve C. Byrne; m. Maryellen McG., Apr. 30, 1966; children: Peter Thomas, Elizabeth Anne. BS, Fordham U., 1957, JD, 1960. Bar: N.Y. 1960, U.S. Dist. Ct. (so., ea., we. and D.C. dists.) N.Y. 1960, U.S. Ct. Appeals (2d cir.) 1960, U.S. Supreme Ct. 1965. Ptnr. Schwarz & DeMarco, Garden City, N.Y. Chmn., bd. trustees N.Y. Sch. Interior Design. Trustee Cath. Charities; Capt. USAF, 1961-65. Mem. Manhasset Bay Yacht Club (vice commodore), Order of Malta. Roman Catholic. Office: Schwarz & DeMarco LLP 300 Garden City Plz Ste 404 Garden City NY 11530-3332

**SCHWARZ, EGON,** language educator, writer, critic; b. Vienna, Aug. 8, 1922; arrived in U.S., 1949, naturalized, 1956; s. Oscar and Erna S.; m. Dorothea K. Klockenbusch, June 8, 1950; children— Rudolf Joachim, Caroline Elisabeth, Gabriela Barbara. PhD, U. Wash., 1954; PhD (hon.), U.

Vienna, 1997, U. Örebro, Sweden, 2002. Mem. faculty Harvard U., 1954-61; mem. faculty dept. Germanic langs. and lit. Washington U., St. Louis, 1961—, prof. German, 1963—, Rosa May Disting. Univ. prof. in the Humanities, 1975-93, prof. emeritus, 1993—. Vis. prof. U. Hamburg, Fed. Republic Germany, 1962-63, U. Calif., Berkeley, 1963-65, Middlebury Coll., 1969, U. Calif., Irvine, 1977, U. Tübingen, 1986; William Evans prof. U. Otago, Dunedin, N.Z., 1984; Disting. scholar Ohio State U., Columbus, 1987, U. Graz, Austria, 1989, 93, U. Siegen, 1993-94. Author: Hofmannsthal und Calderon, 1962, Joseph von Eichendorff, 1972, Das verschluckte Schluckzen-Poesie und Politik bei Rainer Maria Rilke, 1972, Keine Zeit für Eichendorff: Chronik unfreiwilliger Wanderjahre; an autobiography, 1979, rev., 1992, Dichtung, Kritik, Geschichte: Essays zur Literatur 1900-1930, 1983, Literatur aus vier Kulturen: Essays und Besprechungen, 1987, Ich bin Kein Freund allgemeiner Urteile über ganze Volker: Essays über österreichische, deutsche und jüdische Literatur, 2000, Die japanische Mauer: Ungewöhnliche Reisegeschichten, 2002, Refuge-Chronicle of a Flight from Hitler, 2002, Unfreiwillige Wanderjahre, 2005, others. Recipient Joseph von Eichendorff medal, 1986, Austrian Medal of Honor for Arts and Scis., 1991, Alexander von Humboldt prize for fgn. scholars, 1995; Guggenheim fellow, 1957-58, Fulbright fellow, 1962-63, sr. fellow NEH, 1970-71, fellow Ctr. for Interdisciplinary Studies, Bielefeld, Germany, 1980-81; grantee Am. Coun. Learned Socs., 1962-63. Mem.: MLA, German Acad. Lang. and Letters, Am. Assn. Tchrs. German, German Acad. Lang. and Lit. (hon.). Home: 1036 Oakland Ave Saint Louis MO 63122-6565 Office: Washington U German Dept Saint Louis MO 63130 Personal E-mail: gabrielas@aol.com. *When I was young, heroic phantasies were closer to my heart than ethical ones, desires of self-fulfillment stronger than the hopes for an equitable world. Today my horizon is broader in that I wish for a society where personal satisfactions are not achieved at the expense of others, where the earth which one generation inherits is not left more depleted to the next, a society which does not coerce other societies.*

**SCHWARZ, ERNST RUEDIGER,** cardiologist, researcher; s. Ernest Johann Ferdinand and Friedel Elise Schwarz; m. Juana Rocio Angel, Nov. 19, 1999; children: Aubriana d'Iwana Angel, Lujain Vanessa. MD, Philipps U. Marburg, Germany, 1987, U. Vienna, Austria, 1989; PhD, RWTH U. of Tech., Aachen, Germany, 2000. Diplomate in internal medicine German Physicians Chamber, in cardiology German Physicians Chamber, in intensive care medicine German Physicians Chamber. Assoc. prof. RWTH U. Hosp., Aachen, 1998—2000; chmn. cardiology Dr. S. Fakeeh Hosp.-Harvard Med. Internat., Jeddah, Saudi Arabia, 2000—03; prof. medicine U. Tex. Med. Br., Galveston, 2003—06, dir. cardiology clinics, 2005—06; prof. medicine UCLA, 2006—. Co-dir. cardiac transplant Cedars Sinai Med. Ctr., LA, 2006; dir. heart failure and transplantation U. Tex. Med. Br., Galveston, 2003—06, dir. heart failure fellowship program, 2004—06, dir. multidisciplinary clinic for sexual health, 2005—06; spkr. in field. Contbr. articles to profl. jours., chapters to books. Recipient Young Investigator award, Internat. Soc. Nuc. Cardiology, 1995. Fellow: Soc. Coronary Angiography and Interventions, European Soc. Cardiology, Am. Coll. Cardiology; mem.: Saudi Heart Assn., German Cardiac Soc., Heart Failure Soc. Am. Achievements include first in transesophageal echocardiography with IVUS catheters in rodent model; research in intensive invasive hemodynamic work in myocardial bridges; clinical and morphologic work in hibernating myocardium; evaluation, assessment and treatment of sexual dysfunction in patients with severe cardio-vascular diseases. Office: Cedars Sinai Med Ctr 8700 Beverly Blvd 6215 Los Angeles CA 90048 Office Phone: 310-423-1876. Office Fax: 310-423-1498. E-mail: schwarze@cshs.org.

**SCHWARZ, FREDERICK A.O., JR.,** lawyer; b. NYC, Apr. 20, 1935; s. Frederick August Otto and Mary Delafield (DuBois) S.; m. Marian Ladd, June 19, 1959; children: Frederick August Otto III, Adair L., Eliza Ladd; m. Frederica Perera, May 11, 1996. BA in History magna cum laude, Harvard Coll., 1957, LLB magna cum laude, 1960; LLD (hon.), N.Y. Law Sch., 1987, CUNY, 1993. Bar: N.Y. 1961, U.S. Dist. Ct. (so. dist.) N.Y. 1963, U.S. Ct. Appeals (2nd cir.) 1978, U.S. Ct. Appeals (9th cir.) 1972, U.S. Ct. Appeals (10th cir.) 1973, U.S. Supreme Ct. 1973. Law clk. to chief judge J. Edward Lumbard U.S. Ct. of Appeals, 2d Circuit, 1960-61; asst. commr. for law revision Govt. of No. Nigeria, 1961-62; assoc. firm Cravath, Swaine & Moore, N.Y.C., 1963-68, ptnr., 1969—81, 1987—2003; sr. counsel, 2003—; sr. counsel Brennan Ctr. for Justice NYU, 2001—. Chief counsel Senate Select Com. on Intelligence, 1975—76; corp. counsel, N.Y.C., 1982—86; chmn. Charter Revision Commn., N.Y.C., 1989. Author: Nigeria: The Tribes, The Nation, or the Race, 1966; Editor Harvard Law Sch. Law Review. Contbr. articles to profl. jours. Chmn. Found. for the City of N.Y., 1977-81, 87-97; pres. Vera Inst. Justice, 1978-81, chmn. 1987—; mem. bd. overseers Harvard U., 1977-83; mem. com. to Visit Harvard Coll., N.Y.-N.J. Citizens Commn. on AIDS; trustee Experiment in Internat. Living, 1965-82; bd. dirs. NAACP Legal Def. Fund. Constl. Edn. Found., Manhattan Bowery Corp., 1970-81, Lawyers for the Public Interest, 1976-81, FAO Schwarz, 1970-85; chair leadership N.Y. Adv. Coun., 1989—; trustee Nat. Resources Def. Coun., 1987-92, chmn., 1992—, Legal Action Center, 1973-81, N.Y.C. Criminal Justice Agy., 1977-81, Town Sch., 1972-80, Am. Com. on Africa, 1965-79, Milton Acad., 1960's, NAACP Legal Def. Fund, Constitutional Edn. Found., William Nelson Cromwell Found.; chmn. N.Y.C. Campaign Fin. Bd., 2003—. Recipient Liberty award Lambda Legal Def. and Edn. Fund, 1987, The Louis Lefkowitz award Fordham Urban Law Jour. 1990, Civic Leadership award Citizens Union City of N.Y., 1990, The Whitney North Seymour Pub. Svc. award Fed. Bar Coun., 1991., Lifetime Achievement award The Am. Lawyer, 2004. Fellow N.Y. Bar Found.; mem. ABA, Assn. of Bar of City of N.Y. (mem. exec. com. 1986-90, coun. on criminal justice, juvenile justice com. 1980-81, chmn. nominating com. 1983, Cardozo lectr. 1991), Am. Law Inst., Harvard Law Sch. Assn. of N.Y.C. (pres. 1983-84), N.Y. State Bar Assn., N.Y.C. Bar Assn. Office: Cravath, Swain & Moore 825 8th Ave Fl 30 New York NY 10019-7475

**SCHWARZ, GERARD,** conductor, musician, music director; b. Weehawken, NJ, Aug. 19, 1947; m. Jody Greitzer, June 23, 1984; children: Alysandra, Daniel, Gabriella, Julian. BS, MA, Juilliard Sch., 1972; DFA (hon.), Fairleigh Dickinson U., Seattle U.; MusD (hon.), U. Puget Sound. Trumpet player Am. Symphony Orch., 1965—72, Am. Brass Quintet, 1965—73, N.Y. Philharm., 1973—77; trumpet player, guest condr. Aspen Music Festival, 1969—75, bd. dirs., 1973—75; music dir. Erick Hawkins Dance Co., 1967—72, SoHo Ensemble, 1969—75, Eliot Feld Ballet Co., N.Y.C., 1972—78, Music Sch. Princeton (N.J.) U., 1977—2002, N.Y. Chamber Symphony, 1977—, L.A. Chamber Orch., 1978—86, White Mountains (N.H.) Music Festival, 1978—80; music advisor Mostly Mozart Festival, Lincoln Ctr., N.Y.C., 1982—84, music dir., 1984—2001, Music Today at Merkin Concert Hall, N.Y.C., 1988—89. Music advisor Seattle Symphony, 1983—84, prin. condr., 1984—85, music dir., 1985—, Royal Liverpool Philharm. Orch., 2001—06; artistic advisor Tokyu Bunkamura's Orchard Hall, Japan, 1994—98; mem. faculty Juilliard Sch., N.Y.C., 1975—83, Mannes Coll. Music, 1973—79, Montclair (N.J.) State Coll., 1975—80; guest condr. various orchs. including Phila. Orch., L.A. Philharm., St. Louis, Buffalo, Detroit, San Francisco, Atlanta, Houston, Pitts., Minn., Jerusalem Symphonies, Israel Chamber Orch., Moscow Philharm., Moscow Radio Orch., Orch. Nat. de France, Paris, London Symphony Orch., Frankfurt Radio, Stockholm Radio, Helsinki Philharm., Ensemble InterContemporain, Monte Caarlo Philharm., Nat. Orch. Spain, English Chamber Orch., London Symphony, Scottish Chamber Orch., City of Birmingham (Eng.) Symphony, Nouvel Orchestre Philharmonique, Sydney (Australia) Symphony, Melbourne (Australia) Symphony, Orchestre Nat. de Lyon, Orchestre Philharm. de Montpellier, France, Washington Opera, Da Capo Chamber Players, 20th Century Chamber Orch., Chamber Music Soc. Lincoln Ctr., San Francisco Opera, Seattle Opera, Tokyu Bunkamura, Japan, Rseidentie Orch. of The Hague, Netherlands, St. Louis Symphony, London Mozart Players, Kirov Orch., St. Petersburg, Russia, Tokyo Philharm., Royal Liverpool Philharm., Vancouver (Can.) Symphony Orch., City of London Symphonia, Evian Festival in France; artistic adv. Tokyo Philharm., 1994—98; mem. Nat. Coun. on the Arts Nat. Endowment for the Arts, 2005—. Rec. artist Columbia, Nonesuch, Vox, MMO, Desto, Angel, Delos Records, Season 1995. Nominee

·10 Grammy awards; named Condr. of Yr., Musical Am. Internat. Directory of Performing Arts, 1994; recipient award for concert artists, Ford Found., 1973, Mumms Ovation award, Record of Yr. awards, Ditson Condrs. award, Columbia U., 1989, Seattle Mayors Arts award, 2006. Mailing: Nat Endowment for Arts 1100 Pennsylvania Ave NW Washington DC 20506

**SCHWARZ, GLENN VERNON,** newspaper editor; b. Chgo., Nov. 24, 1947; s. Vernon Edward and LaVerne Louise (Schuster) S.; m. Cynthia Frances Meisenhoelder, June 17, 1984; 1 child, Chloe. BA, San Francisco State U., 1970. Sports writer San Francisco Examiner, 1970—87, sports editor, 1988—2000, San. Francisco Chronicle, 2000—. Fundraiser San Francisco Zoological Soc., 1987—. Mem. AP Sports Editors, Baseball Writers Assn. Am. (bd. dirs. 1986-87). Avocation: nature travel. Office: San Francisco Chronicle 901 Mission St San Francisco CA 94103

**SCHWARZ, JOHN J.H. (JOE SCHWARZ),** congressman, physician; b. Battle Creek, Mich., Nov. 15, 1937; s. Frank William and Helen Veronica (Brennan) S.; m. Anne Louise Ennis, Jan. 16, 1971 (dec. Feb. 1990); 1 child, Brennan Louise. BA in History, U. Mich., 1959; MD, Wayne State U., 1964. Operative CIA, 1968—70; physician, surgeon Battle Creek, Mich., 1974—; mayor City of Battle Creek, 1985-87; mem. Mich. Senate from 24th dist., Lansing, 1987—2002; pres. pro tempore of the Senate, 1993—2002; mem. US Congress 7th Mich. dist., 2005—. mem. com. agr., com. armed services, com. sci. Trustee Leila Y. Post Montgomery Hosp. (now Battle Creek Health Sys.), Mich., 1980-82, Olivet Coll., 1991—, Wayland Acad., 1992-96, Libr. Mich., 1994-2003; trustee, treas. Am. Legacy Found; bd. directors Artrain, Ann Arbor, Detroit Receiving Hosp., Kellogg Cmty. Coll. Found., Univ. Musical Soc., Ann Arbor, Wayne State U. Found. Lt. Comdr. USN, 1965—67, Vietnam. Fellow ACS; mem. AMA, Am. Soc. for Head and Neck Surgery, Calhoun County Mich. Med. Soc. (pres. 1971), Mich Otolaryngological Soc., Mich State Med. Soc., Soc. Med. Consultants to Armed Forces, U. Mich. Club of Battle Creek. Republican. Roman Catholic. Office: US Congress 128 Cannon House Office Bldg Washington DC 20515-2207 also: District Office 249 Michigan Avenue W Battle Creek MI 49017-3601 Office Phone: 202-225-6276, 269-965-9066. Office Fax: 202-225-6281, 269-965-9036.*

**SCHWARZ, KATHRYN J.,** gifted and talented educator; b. Pitts., Pa., May 28, 1977; d. Scott Alan Schwarz and Kathryn Geary. BA in Psychology, Villanova U., 1999; MEd, Immaculata U., 2006. Cert. elem. edn. Rosemont Coll., 1999, spl. edn. Immaculata U., 2004. Tchr. Holy Trinity Catholic, Bridgeport, Pa., 1999—2001, Woolmore Primary, London, 2001—02, St. Luke's Primary, London, 2002—03; gifted support tchr. Daniel Boone Sch. Dist., Douglasville, Pa., 2003—. Master: Kappa Delta Pi; mem.: Pa. Sch. Edn. Assn., Assn. of Supr. and Curricular Devel. Avocations: travel, singing, theater, reading. Office: Amity Intermediate Ctr 200 Boone Dr Douglassville PA 19518 Office Phone: 610-689-6240.

**SCHWARZ, LOUIS JAY,** financial advisor; s. Milton J. and Anita S.; m. Doris Ethel Schwarz, May 31, 1969; children: Jovialis Ona, Iris Nana, Janis Anna. BA, Gallaudet U., 1968; postgrad., Ill. Inst. Tech., 1968-69, U. Md., 1970-72. CFP, registered fin. cons., registered investment advisor, qualified fin. planner, chartered fed. employees benefit cons. Tchr. Ill. Sch. for Deaf, Jacksonville, 1969-70; tax preparer Income Tax Svc. for the Deaf, Silver Spring, Md., 1971—; chemist U.S. Geol. Survey, Reston, Va., 1970-85; agt. Nat. Fraternal Soc. of Deaf, Mt. Prospect, Ill., 1975-93; owner, fin. planner Schwarz Fin. Svcs. LLC, Bethseda, Md., 1983—; pres. Schwarz & Giuntoli, Inc., Gaithersburg, Md., 1987—91. Stockbroker Integrated Resources Equity Corp., N.Y.C., 1984—89; cons. instr. Nat. Ctr. for Fin. Edn., San Francisco, 1986—; pres. Met Washington Telecomm. Directory for the Deaf Inc., Silver Spring, 1988—2003; registered rep. Royal Alliance Assocs., Inc., N.Y.C., 1989—; adj. prof. Gallaudet U. Sch. Mgmt., 1993—94, 1997—2002. Author: (with L. Dunton) About Your Future, 1988; columnist NAD Broadcasters, 1984-95, Silent News, 1984-95, Deaf Nation, 1996-2000, Newswaves, 1996-2000, Deaf Digest, 1999—, Deaf Seniors of Am. New Horizons, 2002—. Active Nat. Assn. of Deaf, 1972—, Md. Assn. of Deaf, 1972—, Montgomery County Assn. Deaf, 1990—; consumer adv. C&P Tel. Co., 1981-84; bd. dirs. Telecomms. for Deaf Inc., 1976-82; commr. Montgomery County Commn. for Handicapped Individuals, 1979-83; adv. coun. Telecomms. Exch. of the Deaf, Inc., 1981-87; rep. Md. Gov.'s Adv. Bd. for Telecomms. Relay, 2004—; Named Top Prodr., Nat. Fraternal Soc. of Deaf, 1979, 83, Outstanding Handicapped Fed. Employee, U.S. Dept. Interior, 1974, 77; recipient Internat. Yr. of Disabled Persons Honor award U.S. Dept. Interior, 1981, Montgomery County Coun. Bus. Svc. award, 1988, 89, Knight of Flying Fingers award Nat. Assn. Deaf, 1990, 92, Disting. Svc. award Md. Assn. Deaf, 1993, Bus. of Yr. award Montgomery County Assn. of Deaf, 1997, Cmty. Svc. award Md. Assn. Deaf, 2001. Mem. Nat. Deaf Bus. Inst., Inc. (bd. dirs. 2001—), Internat. Assn. Registered Fin. Cons., Fin. Planning Assn., Deaf and Hard of Hearing Entrepreneurs Coun. (pres. 1993-96, bd. dirs. 1989-96). Jewish. Avocations: photography, swimming, bicycling, hiking, gardening. Office: Schwarz Fin Svcs LLC 4405 East-West Hwy Ste 502 Bethesda MD 20814-4536 Office Phone: 866-753-0333. Business E-Mail: louis@schwarz-financial.com.

**SCHWARZ, M. ROY,** physician, administrator; b. American Falls, Idaho, July 30, 1936; s. Frank and Hulda Christina (Rast) S.; m. Thelma Constance Schwarz, June 9, 1957; children: Ryan Merle, Tanna Berit. BS, Pacific Luth. U., 1959; MD, U. Wash., 1963; DS, Mont. State U., 1994, U. Idaho, 1995; LHD (hon.), Pacific Luth. U., 2002. From asst. to full prof. medicine U. Wash., Seattle, 1963-79; dean, prof. U. Colo., Denver, 1979-83; sr. v.p. Am. Med. Assn., Chgo., 1984-96; pres. China Med. Bd. N.Y.C., 1997—2006. Co-author (with C. Everett Koop, Clarence E. Pearson): Critical Issues in global Health, 2001; editor: Proceedings of the VI Leukocyte Culture Conf., 1971; contbr. over 175 articles to profl. jours. Office: China Med Bd NYC Business E-Mail: tcandmr@adelphia.net.

**SCHWARZ, MICHAEL,** lawyer; b. Brookline, Mass., Oct. 19, 1952; s. Jules Lewis and Estelle (Kosberg) S.; m. Rebecca Handy; 1 child, Patrick Joshua Charles. BA magna cum laude, U. No. Colo., 1975; postgrad., U. N.Mex., 1977, JD, 1980; reader in Negligence Law, Oxford U., 1978; diploma in Legal Studies, Cambridge U., 1981. Bar: N.Mex. 1980, US Dist. Ct. N.Mex. 1980, US Ct. Appeals (10th, DC and Fed. cirs.) 1982, US Ct. Internat. Trade 1982, US Tax Ct. 1982, NY 1987, US Supreme Ct. 1983, cert.: N.Mex. Supreme Ct. (Employment and Labor Law) 2000. Vol. VISTA, Albuquerque, 1975-77; rsch. fellow N.Mex. Legal Support Project, Albuquerque, 1978-79; supr. law Cambridge (Eng.) U., 1980-81; law clk. to chief justice Supreme Ct. N.Mex., Santa Fe, 1981-82; pvt. practice Santa Fe, 1982—. Spl. pros. City of Santa Fe, 1985, spl. asst. atty. gen., 1986-88; mem. west editl. adv. com. Social Security Reporting Svc., 1983-95; mem. N.Mex. Supreme Ct. Com. Profl. Responsibility, 1990—, chmn., 1998—, domestiv rels. task force com., 2004—, chmn. legal specialization com., employment and labor law, 2005—. Author: New Mexico Appellate Manual, 1990, 2d edit., 1996; contbr. articles to profl. jours. Vice-dir. Colo. Pub. Interest Rsch. Group, 1974; scoutmaster Ctr. S.W. Area coun. Boy Scouts Am., 1977—79; mem. N.Mex. Acupuncture Lic. Bd., 1983; master's coaching level U.S.A. Hockey Assn.; head coach Squirt Gold Santa Fe Trailrunners, 2001—03, Santa Fe Huskies, 2003—04, 2004—05; dir. N.Mex. U.S.A. Hockey Assn. Coaching Edn., 2004—05. Recipient Cert. of Appreciation Cambridge U., 1981, Nathan Burke Meml. award, 1980, N.Mex. Supreme Ct. Cert. Recognition, 1992, 93, 95, N.Mex. Supreme Ct. Cert. Appreciation Outstanding Svc. to Legal Sys., 2001. Mem.: ATLA, ABA (10th cir. editor 1998, litigation coms. on profl. responsibility, mem. Ctr. Profl. Responsibility, litigation com. on pretrial practice and discovery), Am. Law Inst. (mem. restatement employment law), N.Mex. State Bar (chmn. 1990—91, bd. dirs. employment law sect. 1990—96, family law sect. bd. 1999—2001), Bar Assn. US Dist. Ct. Dist. N.Mex. (1st judicial dis. bar assoc. pres. 1990—91), Assn. Coaching Edn. (dir., assoc. coach-in-chief Rocky Mt. dist. 2004—), Santa Fe Trailrunners Hockey Assn. (bd. dirs. 2001—02). Home and Office: PO Box 1656 Santa Fe NM 87504-1656 E-mail: barrister@pobox.com.

**SCHWARZ, NORBERT,** psychology professor; b. Annweiler, Germany, Mar. 28, 1953; Dipl. Sociol., Universität Mannheim, Germany, 1977, D. Phil., Sociol. & Psychol. summa cum laude, 1980; D. Phil. Habil., Universität Heidelberg, Germany, 1986. Lectr. Universität Mannheim, 1978—80; post-doctoral fellow Univ. Ill., 1980—81; fellow Decision Rsch., Universität Mannheim, 1981—83; asst. prof. Universität Heidelberg, 1981—86, privat-dozent, 1986—92; sci. dir. Zentrum für Umfragen Methoden & Analysen, Mannheim, 1987—92; prof. psychol. & rsch prof. Univ. Mich., Ann Arbor, 1993—, prof. mktg., 2002—; rsch. prof. Joint Univ. Md. & Univ. Mich. prog. in survey methodology, 1995—. Contbr. articles to profl. jour.; author: Stimmung als Information, 1987, Cognition and Communication, 1996; co-author: Thinking About Answers, 1996. Recipient Heinz Maier-Leibnitz prize, Fed. Republic of Germany, 1986. Fellow: Soc. Personality & Social Psychol., Am. Psychol. Soc., Am. Acad. Arts & Sci.; mem.: World Assn. Public Opinion Rsch., Assn. Consumer Rsch. (France Nicosia award 2004), Am. Assn. Public Opinion Rsch., Soc. Personality & Social Psychol., Soc. Judgement & Decision Making, German Psychol. Soc. (hon. Wilhelm Wundt medal 2004), Soc. Experimental Social Psychol., Soc. Applied Rsch. Memory & Cognition, Midwestern Psychol. Assn., Internat. Soc. Rsch. on Emotion, European Assn. Experimental Social Psychol., Am. Psychol. Assn. Office: Institute for Social Research 426 Thompson St PO Box 1248 Ann Arbor MI 48106-1248 Office Phone: 734-647-3616. Business E-Mail: nschwarz@umich.edu.

**SCHWARZ, RICHARD HOWARD,** obstetrician, gynecologist, educator; b. Easton, Pa., Jan. 10, 1931; s. Howard Eugene and Blanche Elizabeth (Smith) S.; m. Patricia Marie Lewis, Mar. 11, 1978; children by previous marriage: Martha L., Nancy Schwarz Tedesco, Paul H., Mary Katherine Schwarz Murray. MD, Jefferson Med. Coll., 1955; MA (hon.), U. Pa., 1971. Diplomate Am. Bd. Ob-Gyn. (examiner 1977-95), Divsn. Maternal Fetal Medicine 1974. Intern, then resident Phila. Gen. Hosp., 1955-59; prof. U. Pa., Phila., 1963-78; prof., chmn. Downstate Med. Ctr., Bklyn., 1978-90, dean, v.p. acad. affairs, 1983-89, provost, v.p. clin. affairs, 1988-93, interim pres., 1993-94, prof. ob.-gyn., 1990-96, disting. Svc. prof. ob.-gyn. emeritus, 1996; chmn. ob.-gyn. N.Y. Meth. Hosp., Bklyn., 1996—2002; prof. ob.-gyn. Cornell U. Med. Coll., N.Y.C., 1996—2002; vice chair for clin. svc. dept Ob/GYN Maimonides Med. Ctr., 2002—; prof. ob-gyn. and reproductive sci. Mt. Sinai Sch. Medicine, NY, 2005—. Obstetrical cons. March of Dimes Birth Defects Found., 1995— Author: Septic Abortion, 1968. Editor: Handbook of Obstetric Emergencies, 1984, mem. editorial bd. jour. Ob-Gyn., Milw., 1983-87; contbr. over 200 articles to profl. jours. Bd. dirs. March of Dimes, N.Y.C., 1985-95. Capt. USAF, 1959-63. Recipient Career Achievement award, Infectious Disease Soc. Ob-Gyn., 1999, Founder's award, 2004, Wyeth Ayerest Career Achievement award, 2000. Fellow Royal Coll ObGyn (ad eundem), 1999; mem. ACOG (chmn. dist. 2 1984-87, v.p. 1989-90, pres. elect 1990-91, pres. 1991-92, Lifetime Achievement award dist. II 2005). Republican. Presbyterian. Office: Maimonides Med Ctr 967 48th St Brooklyn NY 11219-3645

**SCHWARZ, THOMAS J.,** lawyer; b. NYC, 1945; BA, Hamilton Coll., 1966; JD cum laude, Fordham U., 1969. Bar: NY 1969. Sr. ptnr., former nat. practice leader, litigation dept. Skadden, Arps, Slate, Meagher & Flom, LLP, NYC, of counsel. Counsel Governor's Judicial Screening Com., First Judicial Dept., 1983—87, 1988—95; spl. counsel NY State Commn. on Govt. Integrity, 1987—90; counsel Governor's Statewide Judicial Screening Com., 1988—95. Articles editor Fordham Law Rev., 1968-69. Bd. trustee Hamilton Coll., 1987—; Citizens' Rsch. Found., 1991—, The Arts Connection, 1998—, NY Preservation League, 1999—, The Riverside Park Fund, 1999—; acting pres. Hamilton Coll., 1999; pres. Purchase Coll., 2003. Mem.: ABA (mem. litigation com. 1989—). Office: Skadden Arps Slate Meagher & Flom LLP Four Times Sq New York NY 10036 Office Phone: 212-735-3400. Office Fax: 917-777-3400. Business E-Mail: tschwarz@skadden.com.

**SCHWARZ, WOLFGANG,** psychologist; b. Stuttgart, Germany, Oct. 30, 1926; came to U.S., 1934, naturalized, 1940; s. Mole and Edith (Gutstein) S.; m. Cynthia Mae Johnson, Sept. 12, 1949 (div.); children: Amy Maria, Casey Andrew, Darcy Lynn, Priscilla Anne, Lydia Beth, Emily Jane; m. Susan Decker, 1976; children: Jaime Bartholomew, Noah. AB, NYU, 1948, AM, 1949, PhD, 1956. Diplomate Am. Bd. Profl. Psychology. Intern Bellevue Med. Ctr., N.Y.C., 1949-51; chief psychology Rip Van Winkle Med. Found., Hudson, N.Y., 1951-53; dir. psychology Hillcrest Med. Ctr., Tulsa, 1953-56, Hollywood Presbyn. Hosp., L.A., 1956-58; cons. psychology Cedars Lebanon Hosp., L.A., 1956-58; spl. cons. D.C. Govt., 1959-61, NIH, Bethesda, Md., 1962-64; dir. psychol. rsch. Mass. Dept. Mental Health, Boston and Malden, 1965-68; individual practice clin. psychology Tulsa, 1953-56, Beverly Hills, Calif., 1956-59, Washington, 1959-63, Malden and Concord, Mass., 1963-73, Mt. Kisco, N.Y., 1973—. Lectr. U. Tulsa, 1953-54, L.A. State Coll., 1956-57; asst. prof. Howard U., 1961; assoc. prof. George Washington U., 1961-62; vis. rsch. asst. Harvard Psychiatry Lab., 1966-68; prof. Malden Hosp., 1968-71; cons. No. Westchester Hosp., 1974—, United Hosp., 1975—, Four Winds Hosp., 1975-80; cons. psychology Peace Corps, Mass., 1969—. Author: A Survey of the Mental Health Facilities in the Disctict of Columbia, 1961; contbr. articles to profl. jours. and chpt. to book. Exec. com. Mayor's Model City Program, Malden, 1967-68. With USNR, 1945-46. Recipient Founder's Day award NYU, 1956, Individual award USPHS/NIH, 1960-64 Mem. APA, NY Psychol. Assn., Mass. psychol. Assn., Washington Soc. Hist. Medicine (exec. com. 1963-64), NY Acad. Sci. (honoree 2001), Psi Chi, Beta Lambda Sigma. Home: 249 Martling Ave Tarrytown NY 10591-4707 Office: 191 King St Chappaqua NY 10514 Office Phone: 914-238-0438. Personal E-mail: drwschwarz@aol.com.

**SCHWARZENEGGER, ARNOLD ALOIS,** governor; b. Thal, Styria, Austria, July 30, 1947; came to U.S., 1968, naturalized, 1983; s. Gustav and Aurelia (Jedrny) S.; m. Maria Owings Shriver, Apr. 26, 1986; children: Katherine Eunice, Christina Aurelia, Patrick, Christopher. BA in Bus. and Internat. Econs., U. Wis., Superior; doctorate (hon.), U. Wis. Superior, 1996, Chapman U., 2002. Owner prodn. co. and real estate; gov. State of Calif., Sacramento, 2003—. Speaker Republican Nat. Convention, NYC, 2004. Actor: (films) Stay Hungry, 1976 (Golden Globe award 1976), Pumping Iron, 1977, The Villain, 1979, Conan, The Barbarian, 1982, Conan, The Destroyer, 1983, The Terminator, 1984, Commando, 1985, Red Sonja, 1985, Raw Deal, 1986, Predator, 1987, Running Man, 1987, Red Heat, 1988, Twins, 1988, Total Recall, 1990, Kindergarten Cop, 1990, Terminator 2: Judgement Day, 1991, True Lies, 1994, Junior, 1994, Terminator 2: 3-D, 1996, Jingle All the Way, 1996, Eraser, 1996, Batman & Robin, 1997, End of Days, 1999, Collateral Damage, 2002, Terminator 3: Rise of the Machines, 2003, Around the world in 80 Days, 2004, The Kid al 2005; actor, prodr. The Last Action Hero, 1993, The 6th Day, 2000; (TV spl.) Sinatra: 80 Years My Way, 1995; (TV movies) The Jayne Mansfield Story, 1980; dir. TV movie Christmas in Connecticut, 1992; host A Very Special Christmas Story; dir. The Switch, Tales from the Crypt, HBO, 1990; author: Arnold: The Education of a Bodybuilder, 1977, Arnold's Bodyshaping for Women, 1979, Arnold's Bodybuilding for Men, 1981, Arnold's Encyclopedia of Modern Bodybuilding, 1985, 2d edit. 1998; prodr. bodybuilding video tape; exec. editor Muscle & Fitness Mag., Flex Mag. Nat. weight tng. coach Spl. Olympics; vol. prison rehab. programs; chmn. Pres.'s Coun. on Phys. Fitness and Sports, 1990-93. Bodybldg. champion, 1965-80; named Jr. Mr. Europe, 1965, Best Built Man of Europe, 1966, Mr. Europe, 1966; Internat. Powerlifting Championship, 1966, German Powerlifting Championship, 1968; IFFB (Internat. Fedn. Body Builders) Mr. Internat., 1968, IFFB Mr Universe (amateur), 1969; NABBA (Nat. Assn. Body Builders) Mr. Universe (amateur), 1967, NABBA Mr. Universe (profl.), 1968, 69, 70; Mr. World, 1970; IFFB Mr. Olympia, 1970, 71, 72, 73, 74, 75, 80; recipient Golden Globe award for Best Newcomer in Films, 1976, Timmie award The Touchdown Club, 1990; named Video Star Yr. VSDA, 1990; voted Internat. Star of 1984, ShoWest; recipient, Muhammad Ali Humanitarian award; Nat. Leadership award, Simon Wiesenthal Ctr.; Father Flanagan Svc. to Youth award, Boys and Girls Town. Republican. Roman Catholic. Office: Office of Governor State Capitol Sacramento CA 95814-4906 Office Phone: 916-445-2841. Office Fax: 916-445-4633.*

**SCHWARZER, WILLIAM W.,** federal judge; b. Berlin, Apr. 30, 1925; came to U.S., 1938, naturalized, 1944; s. John F. and Edith M. (Daniel) S.; m. Anne Halbersleben, Feb. 2, 1951; children: Jane Elizabeth, Andrew William. AB cum laude, U. So. Calif., 1948; LLB cum laude, Harvard U., 1951. Bar: Calif. 1953, U.S. Supreme Ct. 1967. Teaching fellow Harvard U. Law Sch., 1951-52; asso. firm McCutchen, Doyle, Brown & Enersen, San Francisco, 1952-60, ptnr., 1960-76; judge U.S. Dist. Ct (no. dist.) Calif., San Francisco, 1976—; dir. Fed. Jud. Ctr., Washington, 1990-95. Sr. counsel Pres.'s Commn. on CIA Activities Within the U.S., 1975; chmn. U.S. Jud. Conf. Com. Fed.-State Jurisdiction, 1987-90; mem. faculty Nat. Inst. Trial Advocacy, Fed. Jud. Ctr., All-ABA, U.S.-Can. Legal Exch., 1987, Anglo-U.S. Jud. Exch., 1994-95, Salzburg Seminar on Am. Studies; ret. disting. prof. Hastings Coll. Law U. Calif., ret. Author: Managing Antitrust and Other Complex Litigation, 1982, Civil Discovery and Mandatory Disclosure, 1994, Federal Civil Procedure Before Trial, 1994; contbr. articles to legal publs., aviation jours. Trustee World Affairs Coun. No. Calif., 1961-88; chmn. bd. trustees Marin Country Day Sch., 1963-66; mem. Marin County Aviation Commn., 1969-76; mem. vis. com. Harvard Law Sch., 1981-86. Served with Intelligence, U.S. Army, 1943-46. Recipient Edward J. Devitt Disting. Svc. to Justice award, 2004. Fellow Am. Coll. Trial Lawyers (S. Gates award 1992), Am. Bar Found.; mem. ABA (Meador Rosenberg award 1995), Am. Law Inst., San Francisco Bar Assn., State Bar Calif., Coun. Fgn. Rels. Office: 450 Golden Gate Ave San Francisco CA 94102-3661 Office Phone: 415-522-4660.

**SCHWARZMAN, STEPHEN ALLEN,** investment banker; b. NYC, Feb. 14, 1947; s. Joseph and Arline (Horelley) S.; children: Elizabeth, Edward. BA, Yale U., 1969; MBA, Harvard U., 1972. Mng. dir. Lehman Brothers, NYC, 1978—84; co-founder, chmn., CEO The Blackstone Group, NYC, 1985—. Mem. nat. adv. com. JP Morgan Chase. Bd. dirs. NYC Ballet, New York Pub. Libr., NYC Partnership, Frick Collection; chmn. bd. trustees Kennedy Ctr. Performing Arts, Washington, 2004-; mem. vis. com. Harvard Bus. Sch. Named one of Forbes' Richest Americans, 2006. Mem. Coun. on Fgn. Rels. Jewish. Office: The Blackstone Group 345 Park Ave Ste 3101 New York NY 10154-0004 Office Phone: 212-583-5823. E-mail: schwarzman@blackstone.com.

**SCHWARZROCK, SHIRLEY PRATT,** author, educator; b. Mpls., Feb. 27, 1914; d. Theodore Ray and Myrtle Pearl (Westphal) Pratt; m. Loren H. Schwarzrock, Oct. 19, 1945 (dec. 1966); children: Kay Linda, Ted Kenneth, Lorraine V. BS, U. Minn., 1935, MA, 1942, PhD, 1974. Sec. to chmn. speech dept. U. Minn., Mpls., 1935, instr. in speech, 1946, team tchr. in creative arts workshops for tchrs., 1955—56, guest lectr. Dental Sch., 1967—72, asst. prof. (part-time) practice administrn. Sch. Dentistry, 1972—80; tchr. speech, drama and English Preston H.S., Minn., 1935—37; tchr. speech, drama and English, dir. dramatics Owatonna H.S., Minn., 1937—39; tchr. creative dramatics and English, tchr.-counselor Webster Groves Jr. H.S., Mo., 1939—40; dir. dramatics and tchr.-counselor Webster Groves Sr. H.S., 1940—43; exec. sec. bus. and profl. dept. YWCA, Mpls., 1943—45; tchr. speech and drama Convent of the Visitation, St. Paul, 1958; editor pro-tem Am. Acad. Dental Practice Adminstrn., 1966—68. Guest tchr. Coll. St. Catherine, St. Paul, 1969; vol. mgr. Gift Shop, Ethel Hosp., Mpls., 1981-83, Edina Cmty. Resource Pool, 1992-95; cmty. citizen mem. planning, evaluating, reporting com. Edina Pub. Sch. Sys., 1993-96; tutor for reading, writing, and speaking, 1993-96; condr. tutorials in speaking and profl. office mgmt., 1985-96; owner Shirley Schwarzrock's Exec. Support Svc., 1989—, 2003—; cons. Ergodyne Corp., St. Paul, 1991-92; freelance editor med. support bus., 1992; cons., lectr. in field. Author: Coping With Personal Identity, Coping With Human Relationships, Coping With Facts and Fantasies, Coping With Teenage Problems, 1984; individual book titles (Coping With series) include: Do I Know the "Me" Others See?, My Life-What Shall I Do With It?, Living With Loneliness, Learning to Make Better Decisions, Grades, What's So Important About Them, Anyway?, Facts and Fantasies About Alcohol, Facts and Fantasies About Smoking, Food as a Crutch, Facts and Fantasies About the Roles of Men and Women, You Always Communicate Something, Appreciating People-Their Likenesses and Differences, Fitting In, To Like and Be Liked, Can You Talk With Someone Else?, Coping With Emotional Pain, Some Common Crutches, Parents Can Be a Problem, Coping With Cliques, Crises Youth Face Today; (with L.H. Schwarzrock) Effective Dental Assisting, 1954, 1st edit., 1967, (with J.R. Jensen) 1973, 3d edit., 1982; (with J.R. Jensen, Kay Schwarzrock, Lorraine Schwarzrock) 1990, 7th edit., 1991, Workbook for Effective Dental Assisting, 1968, 5th edit., 1991; (with Donovan F. Ward) Effective Medical Assisting, 1969, 2d edit., 1976, Manual for Effective Medical Assisting, 1969, 2d edit., 1976; (with C.G. Wrenn) The Coping With Series of Books for High School Students, 1970, The Coping With Manual, 1973, Contemporary Concerns of Youth, 1980, Shirley's Supergoodies: An Old Fashioned Cookbook for the Modern Cook, 2002; cons. editor: North Country Pages, St. Paul, 2003—; contbr. articles to profl. jours. Pres. Univ. Elem. Sch. PTA, 1955-56; vol. judge Minn. State Hist. Day Program, 1994-98. Mem. Minn. Acad. Dental Practice Adminstrn. (hon.), Minn. Geneal. Soc., Zeta Phi Eta (pres. 1948-49), Eta Sigma Upsilon. Home: 7448 W Shore Dr Edina MN 55435-4022 *Growing up as a latch key child, challenged to accomplish adult tasks accompanied by "You can do it, Kid", provided me with the ability to face challenges from scrubbing floors to delving deeply into reseach. Assured that there is a solution to every problem, I absorbed the knowledge and skills my professors taught, developed my creativity and spiritual awareness, and learned to listen sensitively and compassionately. This training enabled me to draw forth creative expression from adolescents, respond to their many needs, and to develop adults' communication skills in numerous settings.*

**SCHWARZSCHILD, JANE L.,** lawyer; b. Richmond, Va., 1949; BA, Smith Coll., 1971; JD, Univ. Va., 1974. Bar: Va. 1974. Ptnr. practice group leader trusts and estates Troutman Sanders LLP, Richmond, Va. Named one of Best Lawyers in Am. Trusts and Estates, 1993—2005; named to Legal Elite in Taxes, Estates, and Trusts, Va. Bus. Mag., 2000—05; recipient Spl. Achievements and Contributions award, Va. Women Attys. Assn., 1986. Mem.: Am. Coll. Trusts and Estate Counsel, Richmond Estate Planning Coun., Va. State Bar, Va. Bar Assn. Home and Office: Troutman Sanders LLP PO Box 1122 Richmond VA 23218 Office Phone: 804-697-1382. Office Fax: 804-698-5183. Business E-Mail: jane.schwarzschild@troutmansanders.com.

**SCHWARZSTEIN, RICHARD JOSEPH,** lawyer; b. Yonkers, NY, July 6, 1934; s. Jack H. and Beatrice (Florman) S.; m. Ann Sanford Adsley, Sept. 19, 1959; children: Cynthia L. Monahan, Alisa J. Cairns, Amy B. Capron. AB, Columbia U., 1956; JD, Harvard U., 1959. Bar: N.Y. 1960, U.S. Dist. Ct. (ea. and so. dists.) N.Y. 1960, U.S. Ct. Appeals 2d cir.) N.Y. 1960, U.S. Dist. t. (ctrl. dist.) Calif. 1976. Assoc. Kramer & Lans, N.Y.C., 1960-62; assoc., then ptnr. Delson & Gordon, N.Y.C., 1962-74; pvt. practice, Newport Beach, Calif., 1974—. Lectr. George Washington U. Law Sch., U. Calif., Irvine, Calif. State U., Fullerton, Long Beach, Orange Coast Coll., U. So. Calif. Am. Grad. Sch. Internat. Mgmt., Chapman Law Sch. Whitter Law Sch. Contbr. articles to law jours. Bd. dirs. Philharm. Soc. Orange County, 1978-2005, pres., 1993-94, chmn., 1994-95; bd. dirs. Econ. Devel. Corp. Orange County, 1983-85, Econ. Devel. Corp. Santa Ana, Calif., 1990-95, Multicultural Arts Coun. Orange County, 1985-99; mem. coun. Laguna Art Mus., 1997—. Mem. ABA, Calif. Bar Assn. (exec. com. econ. and law sect.) 1977-80, internat. practice com. 1986-87), N.Y. State Bar Assn. (com. on ctrl. Europe internat. law and practice com. 1993-96), Orange County Bar Assn. (chmn. internat. law sect. 1984—), World Trade Ctr. Assn. Orange County (bd. dirs. 1976-99, vice chmn., chmn. 1983-93), Am. Arbitration Assn. (nat. panel), Assn. Bar City N.Y. Home: 441 El Bosque Laguna Beach CA 92651-2532 Office: 1151 Dove St Ste 130 Newport Beach CA 92660-2852 Office Phone: 949-752-9152. Personal E-mail: legalrjs@aol.com.

**SCHWARZTRAUBER, SAYRE ARCHIE,** former naval officer, maritime consultant; b. Zion, Ill., June 23, 1929; s. Archie Douglas and Eleanor Miriam (Sayrs) S.; m. Beryl Constance Stewart, June 27, 1953; children: Sayre Archie, Beryl Ann, Heidi, Holly. BS cum laude, Maryville Coll., 1951; MA, Am. U., 1964, PhD, 1970. Commd. ensign USN, 1952; advanced through grades to rear adm., 1976; comdr. River Squadron 5, Vietnam, 1968-69;

U.S.S. Decatur guided missile destroyer, 1970-71, Navy Recruiting Area 4, 1974-76; dep. chief staff Supreme Command Atlantic (NATO), 1976-79; co-dir. U.S.-Spanish Combined Staff, Madrid, 1979-81; dir. Inter-Am. Def. Coll., Washington, 1981-83; ret., 1983; apptd. rear adm. U.S. Maritime Svc., 1984; pres. Maine Maritime Acad., 1984—86. Mem. Sec. of Navy Adv. Com., 1986-90; nat. and internat. lectr. strategic naval and maritime matters, 1973—. Author: The Three-Mile Limit of Territorial Seas, 1972, Schwarztrauber, Stewart and Related Families, 1995; editor Mass. Maritime Mag., 1987-90; contbr. articles, essays and revs. to profl. jours. Ruling elder Presbyn. Ch. U.S.A., 1965-86. Decorated Def. Disting. Svc. Medal, Legion of Merit, Cross of Gallantry (Vietnam), Gran Cruz de Merito (Spain); recipient Alfred Thayer Mahan award Navy League, 1974. Mem. SAR (pres. Cape Cod chpt. 1993-95, state reg. and genealogist 1992-2003, state pres. 1998-99, nat. trustee 1999-2000), Gamewardens of Vietnam, Nat. Geneal. Soc., U.S. Naval Inst., Am. Legion, Masons (adjutant Aleppo Temple), VFW, Mil. Order World Wars, Mensa, Travelers' Century Club, Phi Kappa Phi, Pi Gamma Mu, Pi Sigma Alpha, Theta Alpha Phi. Home and Office: PO Box 589 Osterville MA 02655-0589

**SCHWEBEL, MILTON,** psychologist, educator; b. Troy, N.Y., May 11, 1914; s. Frank and Sarah (Oxenhandler) S.; m. Bernice Lois Davison, Sept. 3, 1939; children: Andrew I., Robert S. AB, Union Coll., 1934; MA, SUNY, Albany, 1936; PhD, Columbia U., 1949; Cert. in Psychotherapy, Postgrad. Ctr. Mental Health, N.Y.C., 1958. Lic. psychologist, N.Y., N.J.; diplomate Am. Bd. Examiners Profl. Psychology. Asst. prof. psychology Mohawk Champlain Coll., 1946-49; asst. to faculty edn., dept. chmn., assoc. dean NYU, 1949-67; dean, prof. Grad. Sch. Edn., Rutgers U., New Brunswick, NJ, 1967-77; prof. Grad. Sch. Applied and Profl. Psychology, 1977-85, prof. emeritus, 1985—. Vis. prof. U. So. Calif. U. Hawaii; postdoctoral fellow Postgrad. Ctr. Mental Health, NYC, 1954-58, lectr. psychology, 1958-90; cons. NIMH, US, state and city depts. edn., UNESCO, edni. ministries in Europe, Asia, univs. and pub. schs., UNESCO; pvt. cons. psychologist and psychotherapist, 1953—; disting. cons. & faculty Saybrook Grad. Sch. & Rsch. Ctr., 1999—. Author: A Guide to a Happier Family, 1989, Personal Adjustment and Growth, 1990, Student Teachers Handbook, 3d edit., 1996, Interests of Pharmacists, 1951, Health Counseling, 1953, Who Can Be Educated?, 1968. Remaking America's Three School System: Now Separate and Unequal, 2003; editor: Mental Health Implications of Life in the Nuclear Age, 1986, Facilitating Cognitive Development, 1986, Promoting Cognitive Growth Over the Life Span, 1990, Behavioral Science and Human Survival, 1965, The Impact of Ideology on the I.Q. Controversy, 1975; editor Peace & Conflict: Jour. Peace Psychology, 1993-2000 (vol. 9, no. 4. named Pioneer in Peace Psychology: Milton Schwebel); co-editor Bull. Peace Psychology, 1991-94; mem. editl. bd. Am. Jour. Orthopsychiatry, Readings in Mental Health, Jour. Contemporary Psychotherapy, Jour. Counseling Psychology, Jour. Social Issues, others. Mem. sci. adv. bd. Internat. Ctr. for Enhancement of Learning Potential, 1988—; trustee Edn. Law Ctr., 1973-81, Nat. Com. Employment Youth, Nat. Child Labor Com., 1967-75, Union Exptl. Colls. and Univs., 1976-78; pres. Nat. Orgn. for Migrant Children, 1980-85; pres. Inst. of Arts and Humanities, 1984-95. Served with AUS, 1943-46, ETO. Met. Applied Rsch. Coun. fellow, 1970-71. Fellow APA, Am. Psychol. Soc., Am. Orthopsychiatry Assn., Soc. Psychol. Study Social Issues, Jean Piaget Soc. (trustee), Am. Ednl. Rsch. Assn., N.Y. Acad. Scis., Psychologists for Social Responsibility (pres.), Sigma Xi. Achievements include being a pioneer in peace psychology. Home: Apt 17L 1050 George St New Brunswick NJ 08901-1068 Office: Rutgers U Grad Sch Applied and Profl Psychology 152 Frelinghuysen Rd Piscataway NJ 08854-8085 Business E-Mail: mschwebe@rci.rutgers.edu.

**SCHWEBEL, RENATA MANASSE,** sculptor; b. Zwickau, Germany, Mar. 6, 1930; came to U.S., 1940, naturalized, 1946; d. George and Anne Marie (Simon) Manasse; m. Jack P. Schwebel, May 10, 1955; children: Judith, Barbara, Diane. BA, Antioch Coll., 1953; MFA, Columbia U., 1961; student, Arts Students League, 1967-69. Cartographer Ecostate Inc., Ridgewood, NJ, 1949; display artist Silvestri Inc., Chgo., 1950-51; asst. Mazzolini Art Foundry, Yellow Springs, Ohio, 1952. One-woman shows include Columbia U., 1961, Greenwich Art Barn, Conn., 1975, Sculpture Ctr., N.Y.C., 1979, Pelham Art Ctr., N.Y., 1981, New Rochelle Libr. Gallery, 1980, Outdoor Installations Katonah Gallery, 1986, 1989, Berman/Daferner Gallery, N.Y.C., 1992—93; artist (group shows) Stamford Mus., Conn., 1967, 1996, Hudson River Mus., Yonkers, N.Y., 1972, 1974, Wadsworth Atheneum, Hartford, 1974, Silvermine Art of the Northwest U.S.A. Anns., 1972, 1976, 1980, 1995, 1998, Silvermine Gallery, 1986, 1991, 2000, 2001, 2002, 2003, New Britain Mus. Am. Art, Conn., 1974, Imprimatur Gallery, St. Paul, 1985, 1986, Bergen County Mus., N.J., 1983, Sculpture Ctr., 1978—88, Katonah Gallery, N.Y., 1986—90, Cast Iron Gallery, N.Y.C., 1991, 1993, Kyoto (Japan) Gallery, 1993; exhibitions include Sculptors Guild Anns., 1974—, traveling show exhibitions, in Am. cultural ctrs. in Egypt and Israel, 1981, 3 Rivers Art Festival, Pitts., 1994, FFS Gallery, N.Y.C., 1994, 1995, Russian Consulate, 1998, Long Beach Island Assn. Arts and Scis., N.J., 1999, Grounds for Sculpture, Hamilton, N.J., 1999, Chesterwood Mus., Stockbridge, Mass., 2000, Troy Arts Ctr., N.Y., 2000—01, Rockland Ctr. for Arts, 2001—02, No. Westchester Arts Coun., 2002, 2003, Westport Arts Ctr., 2003, Ednl. Alliance Gallery, N.Y.C., 2003, Carriage Barn Arts Ctr., New Canaan, Conn., 2005, Pleiades Gallery, N.Y.C., 2006, Represented in permanent collections S.W. Bell, Columbia U., Colt Industries, Am. Airlines, Comcraft Industries, Nairobi, Gruber Haus, Berlin, Mus. Fine Art, Sofia, Bulgaria, Housatonic Mus., Jule Collins Smith Mus. Fine Art, Auburn, Ala. Bd. dirs. Fine Arts Fedn., N.Y., 1985-87; trustee Sculpture Ctr., 1980-88, chmn. exhbn. com., 1986-88; adv. bd. Pehlham Art Ctr., 1982. Mem.: N.Y. Artists Equity, Silvermine Guild, Conn. N.Y. Soc. Women Artists, Conn. Acad. Fine Arts, Audubon Artists (Chaim Gross award 1980, Medal of Honor 1982, Rennick award 1986, 1990, 1992, 1995), Nat. Assn. Women Artists (Willis Meml. prize 1974, Medal of Honor 1981, Paley Meml. award 1979), Sculptors Guild (bd. dirs. 1975—94, pres. 1980—83, bd. dirs. 1995—2004), Katonah Gallery (artist mem. 1986—90), Ams. for Peace Now (bd. dirs. 1991—2001), Antioch Coll. Assn. (bd. dirs. 1971—77). Home: 10 Dogwood Hills Pound Ridge NY 10576-1508 Personal E-mail: RENATA99M@aol.com.

**SCHWEBEL, STEPHEN MYRON,** arbitrator, mediator, legal advisor; b. N.Y.C., Mar. 10, 1929; s. Victor and Pauline (Pfeffer) S.; m. Louise Ingrid Nancy Killander, Aug. 2, 1972; children: Jennifer, Anna. BA in Govt. magna cum laude with highest honors in govt., Harvard U., 1950; postgrad., Cambridge U., 1950—51; LLB, Yale U., 1954; LLD (hon.), Bhopal U., 1983, Hofstra U., 1991, 2002. Bar: N.Y. 1955, U.S. Supreme Ct. 1965, D.C. 1976. Dir. UN hdqrs. office World Fedn. UN Assns., 1950—53; lectr. Am. fgn. policy various univs. U.S. Dept. State, India, 1952; rsch., drafting asst. Trygve Lie for writing of In the Cause of Peace, 1953; assoc. White & Case, N.Y.C., 1954—59; asst. prof. law Harvard U., Cambridge, Mass., 1959—61; asst. legal advisor U.S. Dept. State, Washington, 1961—66, dep. legal advisor, 1973—81; exec. dir. Am. Soc. Internat. Law, Washington, 1967—72; Burling prof. internat. law Sch. of Advanced Internat. Studies, Johns Hopkins U., Washington, 1967—81; pres. Adminstrv. Tribunal IMF, Washington, 1994—; judge Internat. Ct. Justice, The Hague, Netherlands, 1981—2000, v.p., 1994—97, pres.; 1997—2000; jurist-in-residence John's Hopkins Sch. Adv. Internat. Studies, 2000—01. Hon. fellow Cambridge U. Ctr. for Rsch. in Internat. Law, 1983—; mem. bd. electors Whewell Professorship in Internat. Law U. Cambridge, 1983—; hon. bencher Gray's Inn, London, 1998—; spl. rep. Micronesian claims U.S. Dept. State, 1966—71; legal adv. U.S. del. 16th-20th and 4th Spl. Gen. Assemblies UN; U.S. assoc. rep. Internat. Ct. Justice, 1962, U.S. dep. agt., 1979, U.S. counsel, 1980; U.S. rep., chmn. U.S. del. to 1st session UN Spl. Com. on Principles Internat. Law concerning friendly rels. and coop. among states, Mexico City, 1964; US rep. numerous other UN coms.; pres. So. Blue Fin Tuna Arbitration, 2000; mem. Eritrea-Yemen Arbitration Tribunal, 1998—2000, Eritrea-Ethiopia Boundary Commn., 2001—; pres. Barbados-Trinidad & Tobago Arbitration, 2004—; mem. panels arbitrators and conciliators Internat. Ctr. Settlement of Investment Disputes World Bank, 2000—; chmn. or party-apptd. arbitrator 45 internat. comml. arbitrations, 1982—2006; cons. Ford Found., 1990; chmn. supr. bd. Telders Internat. Law Moot Ct. Competition,

The Hague, The Netherlands, 1993—98; chmn. Hauser Scholars Selection Bd., N.Y.U. Law Sch., 1997—2000; bd. dirs. Am. Arbitration Assn., 2006—; vis. lectr. in field. Author: The Secretary-General of the United Nations, 1952, International Arbitration: Three Salient Problems, 1987, Justice in International Law, 1994; editor: The Effectiveness of International Decisions, 1971; mem. editorial bd. Am. Jour. Internat. Law, 1967-81, hon. mem., 1996—; chmn. editorial adv. com. Internat. Legal Materials, 1967-73. Mem. UN Internat. Law Commn., Geneva, 1977—81. Frank Knox fellow Harvard U., 1950-51, Hallows Jud. fellow Marquette U. Law Sch., 2000, Hon. fellow Trinity Coll., Cambridge U., 2005; recipient Gherini prize Yale Law Sch., 1954, medal of Merit, 1997, Pres. medal Johns Hopkins U., 1992, Harold Weill medal NYU, 1992, Wolfgang Friedmann award Columbia U., 1998. Mem. ABA, Am. Soc. Internat. Law (exec. v.p. 1967-73, hon. v.p. 1982-95, hon. pres. 1996-2001, Manley O. Hudson medal 2000), Internat. Law Assn., Inst. Droit Internat., Coun. Fgn. Rels., Acad. of Experts (v.p. 1995—), Harvard Club (N.Y.C.), Athenaeum (London), Met Club (Washington), Phi Beta Kappa. Avocation: music. Office: 1501·K St NW Washington DC 20005 Office Phone: 202-736-8328. Personal E-mail: judgeschwebel@aol.com.

**SCHWEBLER, STEPHEN,** retired chemist; b. Flemington, N.J., Dec. 5, 1928; s. Philip and Elizabeth (Pratscher) S.; m. Marian Finch, May 3, 1953; children: Bradley Stephen, Susan Elizabeth, Nancy Carol. AS, Columbia-Greene C.C., Hudson, N.Y., 1974; BS, SUNY, Saratoga, 1982. With Marshall's Chrysler-Plymouth, Ravena, N.Y., 1953-56; owner/mgr. Steve's Auto Svc., Coxsackie, N.Y., 1956-58; svc. mgr. Jackson & Boone Chrysler-Plymouth, West Coxsackie, N.Y., 1958-66; sr. lab. technician N.Y. State Dept. Health, Albany, 1966-72, N.Y. State Dept. Environ. Conservation, Albany, 1972-85; phys. chemist N.Y. State Office Gen. Svcs., Albany, 1985-88, specification writer, 1988-90, N.Y. State Thruway Authority, Albany, 1990-94; ret. Deacon New Baltimore Ref. Ch., N.Y., 1985-90; rsch. vol. Greene County Hist. Soc., West Coxsackie, 1996—. Democrat. Reformed Ch. Achievements include developing first confirmatory test for the birth defect, galactosemia, by paper chromatography; research in improved methods of sewage treatment and toxic substance monitoring of all bodies of water in N.Y. state. Home: 3931 Rt 51 Hannacroix NY 12087-9708 E-mail: sschweb@aol.com.

**SCHWED, ROGER E.,** lawyer; b. N.Y.C., Jan. 3, 1958; s. Peter and Antonia Holding Schwed; m. Laura F. Dukess, Feb. 26, 1989; children: Benjamin, Stephen. AB cum laude, Princeton U., 1979; JD, Columbia U., 1986. Bar: NY 1987, US Dist. Ct. (ea. dist.) NY 1987, US Dist. Ct. (so. dist.) NY 1988. Subs. rights assoc. Doubleday & Co., Inc., N.Y.C., 1979—83; mgr. subs. rights Harper & Row, N.Y.C., 1983—83; jud. clk. to Hon. Eugene H. Nickerson U.S. Dist. Ct. (ea. dist.), N.Y.C., 1986—87; assoc. Cleary, Gottlieb, Steen & Hamilton, N.Y.C., 1987—95; coun. Skadden, Arps, Slate, Meagher & Flom, N.Y.C., 1995—96; exec. v.p., gen. coun. Maxcor Fin. Group Inc., N.Y.C., 1996—2005. Bd. dirs. I Challenge Myself, Inc., N.Y.C. Coach West Side Little League, N.Y.C., 1998—2003, 2005—, West Side Soccer League, N.Y.C., 1999—2004. Avocations: bicycling, computers, reading. Business E-Mail: roger@rschwed.com.

**SCHWEICKERT, RICHARD JUSTUS,** psychologist, educator; b. Madison, Wis., July 19, 1946; s. Carl E. and Marie E. (Dilzer) S.; m. Carolyn M. Jagacinski, Dec. 27, 1980; children: Patrick, Kenneth. BS in Math. U. Santa Clara, 1968; MA in Math., Ind. U., 1972; PhD in Psychology, U. Mich., 1979. Statistician Bellevue Psychiatric Hosp., N.Y.C., 1969-71; asst. prof. Purdue U., West Lafayette, Ind., 1978-83, assoc. prof., 1984-91, prof., 1992—. Adv. panel on human cognition and perception NSF, 1993-96. Author (with others): Handbook of Human Factors; editor Jour. Math. Psychology, 2000—04, mem. editl. bd., 1986—94, 2004—, assoc. editor Psychol. Bull. and Rev., 1993—98, mem. editl. bd. Jour. Exptl. Psychology, Learning, Memory and Cognition, 1985—89, 1991—94; contbr. articles to profl. jours. Grantee NSF, 1981-84, 92-2000, NIMH, 1983-89, Air Force Office Sci. Rsch., 2006—. Fellow AAAS, Am. Psychol. Soc.; mem. Soc. for Math. Psychology (pres. 1990-91, bd. dir.), Psychonomic Soc., Informs. Office: Purdue U Dept Psychol Scis Lafayette IN 47907

**SCHWEIGER, PEGGY,** physics educator; b. Temple, Tex., July 24, 1949; d. John Edwin and Virginia Easterwood; m. Jerald Schweiger, July 24, 1971; children: Tina, Jerry. BS in Chemistry, U. Tex., Austin, 1971; MA in Counseling, Prairie View A&M U., Tex., 1997. Physics tchr. Klein Oak H.S., Spring, Tex., 1987—, Recipient Presdl. award for Excellence in Tchg. Math. and Sci., 2001. Mem.: Am. Assn. Physics Tchrs. (assoc.). Office: Klein Oak High School 22603 Northcrest Dr Spring TX 77389 Office Phone: 832-484-4893.

**SCHWEIKER, MARK S.,** former governor; b. Bucks County, Pa., Jan. 31, 1953; s. John and Mary S.; m. Katherine Schweiker; children: Brett, Eric, Kara. BS, Bloomsburg U., 1975; MA in Adminstrn., Rider U., 1983. Merrill Lynch; McGraw Hill; supr. Middletown Twp., 1979; commr. Bucks County, Pa., 1987-94; elec. lt. gov., 1994—2001; lt. gov., pres. of the Senate, chmn. of the bd. of pardons Commonwealth of Pa., 1995—2001, gov., 2001—03; former chmn. prime coun., chmn. local govt. adv. coun., chmn. gov.'s exec. coun. recycling devel. & waste reduction, dir. Pa. weed and seed program, gov., 2001—03; pres. & CEO Greater Phila. Chamber of Commerce, 2003—. Former chmn. Dela. Valley Regional Fin. Authority. Former bd. dirs. Bucks County United Way. Recipient Alumnus of Yr. Bloomsburg U., 1990, Outstanding Svc. to Conservation award Nature Conservancy Pa. Branch, 1993, Tech. Advocate of Yr. Tech. Coun. Ctrl. Pa., 1996, Outstanding Achievement award Citizens Against Govt. Waste, 1997, Commitment to Excellence in Local Govt. award Pa. Economy League, 1998. Republican. Office: Greater Phila C of C 200 Broad St Ste 700 Philadelphia PA 19102

**SCHWEIKER, RICHARD SCHULTZ,** former trade association administrator, former secretary of health & human services, former senator; b. Norristown, Pa., June 1, 1926; s. Malcolm Alderfer and Blanche (Schultz) S.; m. Claire Joan Coleman, Sept. 10, 1955; children: Malcolm C., Lani, Kyle, Richard S. Jr., Lara Kristi. BA, Pa. State U., 1950; D of Pub. Svcs. (hon.), Temple U., 1970; D.Sc. (hon.), Georgetown U., 1981. Bus. exec., 1950-60; mem. 87th-90th congresses from 13th Dist. Pa., mem. house armed services and govt. ops. coms., 1961—69; U.S. senator from Pa., 1969-80; mem. appropriations com., ranking mem. Labor-HEW subcom., ranking mem. health and human resources com., ranking mem. health subcom.; sec. US Dept. Health & Human Services, Washington, 1981—83; pres. Am. Council Life Ins., Washington, 1983-94. Chmn. Partnership for Prevention, 1991—97. Alt. del. Nat. Rep. Conv., 1952, 56, del., 1972, 80; designated v.p. candidate with Reagan for Pres. of U.S., 1976. Served with USNR, World War II. Recipient Disting. Alumnus award Pa. State U., 1970, Dr. Charles H. Best award Am. Diabetes Assn., 1974, Outstanding Alumnus of Yr. award Phi Kappa Sigma, 1982, Gold medal Pa. Assn. Broadcasters, 1982, Nat. Outstanding Svc. award Headstart, 1983, Pub. Svc. Gold medal Surgeon Gen. U.S., 1988, Govt. Achievement award Juvenile Diabetes Found., 1990, Disting. Achievement award Nat. Coun. on Aging, 1991, John Newton Russell award Nat. Assn. Life Underwriters, 1992; named Outstanding Young Man of Yr., Jr. C. of C., 1960. Mem. Phi Beta Kappa.

**SCHWEIKERT, EDGAR OSKAR,** dentist; b. Heidelberg, Germany, Aug. 30, 1938; came to U.S., 1972; s. Oskar and Priska (Zehr) S.; m. Mary Lou Como, Apr. 7, 1969; 1 child, Marisa. Degree, Hamburg Dental Sch., 1966; Dr. Med. Dentistry, U. Munich, 1969. Lic. dentist, Germany, UN Dentist, U.S. Army, Frankfurt, Fed. Republic Germany, 1969-72; gen. practice dentistry, LA, 1972-73, Bklyn., 1973—; lectr. in field. Author: Multiple Cantilevers in Fixed Prosthesis, 1988, Spanish edit., 1990; contbr. articles to profl. jours. Served as capt. German Air Force, 1967-69. Mem. ADA, German Dental Assn., Second Dist. Dental Assn., Bay Ridge Dental Soc., Guild Dental Craftsmen. Home and Office: 429 77th St Brooklyn NY 11209-3205 Office Phone: 718-680-4717.

**SCHWEIKERT, NORMAN CARL,** retired musician; b. L.A., Oct. 8, 1937; s. Carl Albert and Hilda (Meade) S.; m. Sally Hardin Haizlip, July 22, 1961; 1 son, Eric Carl. Mus.B. performer's certificate in horn, Eastman Sch. Music, 1961. Teaching assoc. Northwestern U., 1973-75, assoc. prof. (part-time), 1975-98; horn instr. Nat. Music Camp, Interlochen, 1967; curator Leland B. Greenleaf Collection Mus. Instruments, Interlochen, 1970-71 Successively 4th, 2d and 3d horn with, Rochester Philharmonic, Civic and Eastman-Rochester symphonies, 1955-62, 64-66, instr. horn, mem., Interlochen (Mich.) Arts Quintet, Interlochen Arts Acad., 1966-71, 1st horn, Rochester Chamber Orch., 1965-66, Midland (Mich.) Symphony Orch., 1969-71, 1st horn, soloist, Northwestern Mich. Symphony Orch., 1966-71, Chgo. Little Symphony, tours, 1967, 68, asst. 1st horn, soloist, Chgo. Symphony Orch., 1971-75, 2d horn, Chgo. Symphony Orch., 1975-97; appearances with, Eastman Chamber Orch., Rochester Bach Festival, Aspen Festival Orch., Moravian Music Festival, Alaska Festival, Peninsula Music Festival, Rochester Brass Quintet, Canterbury Wind Quintet, Westchester Brass Quintet, Eastman Wind Ensemble, Chgo. Symphony Winds, Quadrangle Chamber Players, Washington Island Music Festival; soloist, New Japan Philharmonic, rec. artist for, Mercury, Columbia, Everest, C.R.I., Capitol. Mark Ednl., London-Decca, DGG, RCA Victor records, Sheffield Lab, Koch; recitals, also lecture demonstrations.; Contbr. articles to profl. jours. Served with AUS, 1962-64. Recipient certificate of merit City Chgo., 1971 Mem. Internat. Horn Soc. (hon., chmn. organizing com., sec.-treas. 1970-72, adv. coun. 1972-76), Am. Mus. Instrument Soc., Phi Mu Alpha Sinfonia (life alumni mem.), Pi Kappa Lambda. Home: 1727 White Trillium Trail Washington Island WI 54246-9026

**SCHWEINSBURG, JANE DUBERG,** librarian; b. Chgo., Oct. 24, 1946; d. John Edward and Mary Andrews Duberg; m. Richard Lyle Schweinsburg, Sept. 3, 1977. BA in Math., Goucher Coll., Towson, Md., 1967; MLS, SUNY, Albany, 1996. Reference libr. Schenectady County C.C., Schenectady, NY; reference libr. and instr. Coll. of St. Rose, Albany, NY, 1996—98; reference libr. Johnson and Wales U., Providence, 1998—99, East Providence Pub. Libr., 1999—2000; asst. dir. Coventry Pub. Libr., Coventry, RI, 2000—. Contbr. articles to encys. and publs. Co-chair Episcopal charities campaign Episcopal Diocese of R.I., Providence, 1999—2000. Recipient Profl. Achievement award, Coll. of St. Rose, 1997. Mem.: R.I. Libr. Assn. (intellectual freedom com.). Episcopalian. Home: 46 Fairway Dr Coventry RI 02816-5775 Office: Coventry Pub Libr 1672 Flat River Rd Coventry RI 02816 Office Phone: 401-822-9104. Business E-Mail: js@coventrylibrary.org.

**SCHWEITZER, BRIAN,** governor; b. Havre, Mont., Sept. 4, 1955; s. Adam and Kay Schweitzer; m. Nancy Hupp, 1981; children: Ben, Khai, Katrina. BS in Internat. Agronomy, Colo. State U., 1978; MS in Soil Sci., Mont. State U., 1980. Agronomist Kaercherv Agr., Libya, 1980—81; crop supt. Alfa Laval Engring. Co., Saudi Arabia, 1981—84; farm owner, rancher Flathead, Sanders Rosebud and Judith Basin counties, Mont.; mem. Mont. state farm svc. agency com. USDA, 1993—99; gov. State of Mont., Helena, 2005—. Apptd. Mont. Rural Devel. Partnership Bd., 1996, Nat. Drought Task Force. Recipient Award for outreach efforts to Native Americans, U.S. Sec. Agr., 1995. Democrat. Achievements include development of various immigration systems in Africa, Asia, Europe, and South America; over 28,000 acres of irrigated cropland in Saudi Arabia. Office: Office of the Gov PO Box 200801 Helena MT 59620-0801 Office Phone: 406-444-3111. Office Fax: 406-444-5529.

**SCHWEITZER, CAREN S.,** social worker; b. N.Y.C., Aug. 1, 1931; d. Robert David and Margaret Lane Steefel; m. Ulrich Schweitzer, Jan. 27, 1984; m. Austin K. Haldenstein, Nov. 26, 1953 (div. June 1970); children: Susan Federspiel, Kenneth Haldenstein. BA, Wellesley Coll., Mass., 1953; MSW, Hunter Sch. Social Work, NYC, 1974. LCSW Acad. Cert. Social Workers, N.Y. Job placement for people with disabilities Just One Break, N.Y.C., 1953—56; job placement Cmty. Action Program, Mamaroneck, NY, 1965—70; asst. to psychologist, 1970—72; program dir. West Assn. for Retarded Citizens, White Plains, NY, 1974—80; supr. group homes Westchester Jewish Cmty. Svcs., White Plains, NY, 1980—85; program coord., Tel. support networks Westchester Self-Help Clearinghouse, Hartsdale, NY, 1985—. Author: (column) Westchester Women's News, 1990—99. Campaign mgr. several Dem. party candidates, Westchester, NY, 1960—69. Phi Beta Kappa, Wellesley Coll., Mass., 1953. Democrat. Jewish. Avocations: tennis, bridge, singing. Home: 214 Dogwood Ln Hartsdale NY 10530 Office Phone: 914-761-0600 314. E-mail: ulcare@aol.com.

**SCHWEITZER, GEORGE KEENE,** chemistry professor; b. Poplar Bluff, Mo., Dec. 5, 1924; s. Francis John and Ruth Elizabeth (Keene) S.; m. Verna Lee Pratt, June 4, 1948; children: Ruth Anne, Deborah Keene, Eric George. BA, Central Coll., 1945, ScD in Philosophy, 1964; MS, U. Ill., 1946, PhD in Chemistry, 1948; MA, Columbia U., 1959; PhD in History, NYU, 1964. Asst. Central Coll., 1943-45; fellow U. Ill., 1946-48; asst. prof. chemistry U. Tenn., 1948-52, assoc. prof., 1952-58, prof., 1960-69, Alumni Distinguished prof., 1970—. Cons. to Monsanto Co., Proctor & Gamble, Internat. Tech., Am. Cyanamid Co., AEC, U.S. Army, Massengill, CTI-Siemens; lectr. colls. and univs.; mem. adv. bd. East Tenn. Hist. Soc. Achievements include chemical expertise in solvent extraction, ion exchange, lanthanide chemistry, stable isotope concentration, radiochemistry, inductively-coupled plasma mass spectroscopy, the chemical implementation of positron-emission tomography and history and philosophy of science. Genealogical expertise in Revolutionary War, War of 1812, Civil War, Georgia, Kentucky, Illinois, Indiana, Massachusetts, Maryland, Missouri, New Jersey, New York, North Carolina, Ohio, Pennsylvania, South Carolina, Tennessee, Virginia, Germany, Ulster Ireland, migration routes, immigration and emigration records, settlement patterns, and tracing ancestors back across the Atlantic Ocean. Theological expertise in science and religion, religious epistemology, comparative religion, American colonial and frontier religion. Author: Radioactive Tracer Techniques, 1950, The Doctorate, 1966, Genealogical Source Handbook, 1992, Civil War Genealogy, 1993, Tennessee Genealogical Research, 1981, Kentucky Genealogical Research, 1981, Revolutionary War Genealogy, 1982, Virginia Genealogical Research, 1982, War of 1812 Genealogy, 1983, North Carolina Genealogical Research, 1983, South Carolina Genealogical Research, 1984, Pennsylvania Genealogical Research, 1985, Georgia Genealogical Research, 1987, New York Genealogical Research, 1988, Massachusetts Genealogical Research, 1989, Maryland Genealogical Research, 1991, German Genealogical Research, 1992, Ohio Genealogical Research, 1994, Indiana Genealogical Research, 1996, Illinois Genealogical Research, 1997, Missouri Genealogical Research, 1997; also 170 articles. Faculty fellow Columbia U., 1958-60. Mem. Am. Chem. Soc., Am. Physics Assn., History Sci. Soc., Soc. Genealogists, Phi Beta Kappa, Sigma Xi. Home: 407 Ascot Ct Knoxville TN 37923-5807

**SCHWEITZER, PETER,** advertising agency executive; b. Chgo., Aug. 31, 1939; children: Mark, Cynthia, Jenifer, Samantha; m. Elaine Elkin, 1986; children: Dana, Taylor. BA, U. of Mich., 1961; MBA, W. Mich. U., 1967. With Post div. Gen. Foods, 1961-69; v.p. Grey Advt., 1969-76; sr. v.p. J. Walter Thompson, 1976-79; sr. v.p. mktg. Burger King Corp., 1990; sr. v.p., gen. mgr., then exec. v.p., gen. mgr. J. Walter Thompson USA, Inc.-Detroit, 1995; v. chmn. of agency ops. J. Walter Thompson Co., Detroit, 1988-95, pres., 1995—, CEO, 2001—. Pres. Internat. Fedn. Multiple Sclerosis. Office: J Walter Thompson Co 500 Woodward Ave 14th Fl Detroit MI 48226-3416 also: 466 Lexington Ave New York NY 10017-3140

**SCHWEITZER, THEODORE GOTTLIEB, III,** government agency administrator; b. Hannibal, Mo., Aug. 28, 1942; s. Theodore Gottlieb Jr. and Dorothy Lois (Burnett) S. Cert. in French Lang., U. Paris, 1968; BA, U. Iowa, 1970, MA, 1974; student, Hanoi (Vietnam) Fgn. Langs. U., 1992-94. Cert. Thai Lang. Am. Univ. Alumnae Assn., Bangkok, 1976, profl. tchr., Iowa Tchr., librarian Lewis County Schs., Ewing, Mo., 1971-73; head librarian Internat. Sch., Bangkok, 1974-76; info. officer U.S. Army, Udorn, Thailand, 1974-76; dir. media services Am. Sch., Teheran, 1976-77, dir. media svcs. Isfahan, Iran, 1977-78; refugee officer UN HCR, Geneva and Bangkok,

1979—. Founder S.E. Asia Rescue Found., Ft. Walton Beach, Fla., 1981—, Hanoi Fgn. Langs. U., 1992-94. Author: (with Malcolm McConnell) Inside Hanoi's Secret Archives-Solving the MIA Mystery, 1995. Spl. rep. to Vietnam, Office of the Sec. of Def., Washington, 1992-94. With USAF, 1959-62. Recipient Award of merit SOS Boat people Com., San Diego, 1982, replica of Nobel Peace Prize, UN High Commr. for Refugees, 1981. Mem. Mensa, BPOE. Republican. Baptist. Avocations: writing, reading, scuba diving, photography, flying.

**SCHWEIZER, GREGORY PAUL,** music educator; b. St. Louis, Jan. 14, 1955; s. Marvin Bernard and Lois Joan Schweizer; m. Diane Marie Stipanovich, June 2, 1978; children: Matthew Gregory, Eric Michael. MusB in Edn., Webster U., 1981. Cert. tchr. K-12 Mo., 1981. Music dir./tchr. St. Dominic Savior Ch., St. Louis, 1978—87, Mary, Queen of Peace Sch., St. Louis, 1979—85; music dir. St. Roch Cath. Ch., St. Louis, 1986—94, St. Lucas United Ch. of Christ, St. Louis, 1994—96, Our Lady of Sorrows Cath. Ch., St. Louis, 1997—; music dir., tchr., dept. chair Visitation Acad., St. Louis, 2000—; music dir. Mo. Athletic Club Apollo Men's Chorus, St. Louis, 1985—. Adj. prof. Webster U., St. Louis, St. Louis Symphony Music Sch.; founder, dir. Camerata Singers. Composer: (composition for tv spot) Variety Club of St. Louis Promo; dir.: (theatrical) Music Director for Shooting Star Productions; condr. (chamber concert series) David & Beatrice Kornblum Concert Series, vocalist nat. comml. Chicken of the Sea Tuna, writer, performer (exercise videos) Martha Rounds; performer: (play with Vikki Carr) I'm Getting My Act Together and Taking It On the Road, G.F. Handel's Saul, St. Louis Bach Soc., St. Louis Symphony Orch.; condr., accompanist, arranger: with Ken Page, accompanist: with Donald O'Conner, Georgia Frontierre, Lou Rawles, Tommy Tune, The Manhattan Rhythm Kings, Rita Moreno, Bernadette Peters, Kathy Rigby, pianist: VP Ball Orch., pianist: Variety Club Telethon. Mem. Ind. Sch. of St. Louis, 2004—05. Mem.: Am. Guild Organists, Nat. Assn. of the Tchrs. of Singing (assoc.), Musicians' Assn. of St. Louis (assoc.). Avocations: photography, carpentry. Home: 5801 Westcliffe Dr Saint Louis MO 63129-4267 Office: Visitation Academy 3020 North Ballas Rd Saint Louis MO 63131 Office Phone: 314-625-9193. Personal E-mail: gregschweizer@hotmail.com. Business E-Mail: gschweizer@visitationacademy.org.

**SCHWEIZER, KARL WOLFGANG,** historian, educator, author; b. Mannheim, Fed. Republic Germany, June 30, 1946; came to U.S., 1988; 1 child, Paul. BA in History, Wilfrid Laurier U., Can., 1969; MA, U. Waterloo, Can., 1970; MA, PhD, Cambridge U., 1976. Prof. history Bishop's U., Lenoxville, Que., Canada, 1976-88, chmn. dept., 1978-79, 82-84, 86; prof., chmn. humanities dept. NJ Inst. Tech., Newark, 1988-93, prof. dept. social sci. and policy studies, 1993—, chmn. dept. humanities and social scis., 2000—03, prof. dept. humanities, 2003—; assoc. Ctr. for Study of Global Change Rutgers U., 1995—. Grad. faculty Rutgers U., 1993—; vis. lectr. U. Guelph, Can., 1978-80; rsch. assoc. Russian Rsch. Ctr., Ill., 1979-80, 99; acad. visitor London Sch. Econs., 1986, 94, vis. scholar, 1986-87, Queens U., Ont., Can., 1986-87; vis. fellow Darwin Coll., Cambridge U., 1997, 98, 2003, Princeton U., 1994, Yale U., 1994; vis. prof. dept. polit. sci. Rutgers U., 1997—; sr. rsch. assoc. Peterhouse Coll., Cambridge, 2003. Author: The Art of Diplomacy 1983, Lord Bute: Essays in Reinterpretation, 1988, England, Prussia and the Seven Years War, 1989, Frederick the Great, William Pitt and Lord Bute, 1991, Lord Chatham, A Biography, 1993, François de Callières: Diplomat and Man of Letters, 1995, War, Politics and Diplomacy: The Anglo Prussian Alliance, 1756-1763, 2001, Seeds of Evil: The Gray/Snyder Murder Case, 2001, Statesmen, Diplomats and the Press, 2003, Parliament and the Press 1688-1936, 2005, The International Thought of Herbert Butterfield, 2006; co-author: British Literary Periodicals, 1983, The Origins of War in Early Modern Europe, 1987; co-author: (with J. Osborne) Cobbett in His Times, 1990; co-author: paperback edit., 1993, The War of the Spanish Succession, 1994, British Prime Ministers, 1997, Hanoverian Britain and Empire, 1998, A Global Encyclopedia of Historical Writing, 1998, Oxford Dictionary of the Enlightenment, 2003, ScribnersEncyclopedia of Modern European History, 2004, Dictionary of National Biography, 2004, International Military Encyclopedia, Encyclopedia of Russia and the Soviet Union, 1980, 1983; editor: The Devonshire Political Diary, 1757-1762, 1982, Diplomatic Thought 1648-1815, 1982, Warfare and Tactics in the 18th Century, 1984, Herbert Butterfield: Essays on the History of Science, 1998, rev. paperback edit., 2005, In Defense of Australia's Constitutional Monarchy, 2004, Parliament and the Press, 1688-1936, 2005; co-editor: Essays in European History 1648-1815 in Honour of Ragnhild Hatton, 1985, Politics and the Press in Hanoverian Britain, 1989; gen. editor: Studies in History and Politics, 1980—91, editl. cons.: Scribner's Encyclopedia of Modern European History, Oxford Dictionary of National Biography; editl. cons. Internat. Mil. Ency.; contbr. articles to profl. jours. Mem. NJ Gov.'s Adv. Panel on Higher Edn. Restructuring, 1994; chmn. ho. majority trust N.J. Rep. Party, 2006—; trustee NJ Literary Hall of Fame, 1988—92. Named Wilfred Laurier Proficiency scholar, 1966—69; recipient Thesis Def. award, Can. Coun., 1976, travel awards, Peterhouse Coll., 1971—73, Adelle Mellen prize for outstanding contbn. to scholarship, Edwin Mellen Press, 1989, Author's award, NJ Writers' Conf., 1993, Tchg. award, NJ Inst. Tech., 2000, Congl. Order of Merit, 2005; fellow U. Waterloo, 1969—70, Province of Ont., 1969—70, Can. Coun., 1970—75; grantee Inter-Univ. Ctr. for European Studies, 1978, 1981; rsch. grantee, Bishop's U., 1977, 1978, 1980, 1982, 1983, postdoctoral rsch. grantee, Can. Coun., 1977—78, 1982—83, conf. grantee, S.S.H.R.C., 1985, travel grantee, NEH, 1991, NJ Com. for Humanities, 1988—92, Mellon fellow, Harvard U., 1978. Fellow Royal Hist. Soc.; mem. Internat. Commn. on History of Internat. Rels., Hist. Soc., Cambridge Hist. Soc., North American Conf. on Brit. Studies, Can. Assn. Scottish Studies, Can. Assn. 18th Century Studies. Inst. Hist. Rsch. Avocations: music, writing, reading. Home: 49 3 Passaic Ave Apt 24 Chatham NJ 07928 Office: NJ Inst Tech Dept HUmanities Newark NJ 07102 Office Phone: 973-596-3274. Business E-Mail: schweizer@adm.njit.edu.

**SCHWEIZER, KENNETH STEVEN,** physics professor; b. Phila., Jan. 20, 1953; s. Kenneth Paul and Grace Norma (Fischer) S.; m. Janis Eve Pelletier, Oct. 18, 1986; children: Gregory Michael, Daniel Patrick. BS, Drexel U., 1975; MS, U. Ill., 1976, PhD, 1981. Postdoctoral rsch. assoc. AT&T Bell Labs., Murray Hill, NJ, 1981-83; sr. mem. tech. staff Sandia Nat. Labs., Albuquerque, 1983-91; prof. materials sci. engring. and chemistry U. Ill., Urbana, 1991—, prof. chem. engring., 1998—, G. Ronald and Margeret H. Morris prof. materials sci., 2001—. Contbr. articles to profl. jours. Recipient Sandia award for Excellence, 1990, R&D 100 award, 1992, Award for Scientific Achievement in Materials Chemistry DOE, 1996, Burnett Tchg. award, 1997, Everitt Tchg. award, 2002. Fellow Am. Phys. Soc. (John H. Dillon medal 1991); mem. Am. Chem. Soc., Soc. Rheology, Sigma Xi, Pi Mu Epsilon. Office: U Ill Dept Materials Sci Engring 1304 W Green St Urbana IL 61801-2920 E-mail: kschweiz@uiuc.edu.

**SCHWEIZER, PAUL DOUGLAS,** museum director; b. Bklyn., Nov. 26, 1946; s. Alvin Charles and Marie Gertrude (Scholtz) S.; m. Jane Kulczycki, June 10, 1978 (div. 2004). BA, Marietta Coll., Ohio, 1968; MA, U. Del., 1975, PhD, 1979; postgrad. Mus. Mgmt. Inst., U. Calif., Berkeley, 1990. Instr. art history St Lawrence U., Canton, NY, 1977-78; asst. prof. St. Lawrence U., Canton, NY, 1978-80; curator St. Lawrence U. (Brush Gallery), Canton, NY, 1977-78; dir. St. Lawrence U., Canton, NY, 1979-80; dir. and chief curator Munson-Williams-Proctor Arts Inst. Mus. Art, Utica, 1980—; adj. prof. art history Pratt at Munson-Williams-Proctor, 2000—. Mem. vis. com. Picker Art Gallery, Colgate U., 1999-05. Author exhbn. catalog; contbr. articles to profl. jours. Bd. dirs. Remington Art Mus., Ogdensburg, N.Y., 1979-80; bd. dirs. Williamstown (Mass.) Regional Art Conservation Lab., 1981-92, pres., 1988-92. Rsch. grantee Nat. Endowment for Arts, 1978. Mem. Coll. Art Assn., Assn. Art Mus. Dirs., N.Y. State Assn. Art Mus. (trustee 1993-95), Mus. Assn. N.Y. (councilor 1995-2002), Gallery Assn. of N.Y. (bd. dirs. 1996-2002, pres. 1999), Otsego Sailing Club, Alpha Sigma Phi, Omicron Delta Kappa. Office: Munson-Williams-Proctor Arts Inst Mus Art 310 Genesee St Utica NY 13502-4799 Business E-Mail: pschweiz@mwpai.org.

**SCHWELB, FRANK ERNEST,** judge; b. Prague, Czechoslovakia, June 24, 1932; came to U.S., 1947; s. Egon and Caroline (Redisch) S.; m. Taffy Wurzburg, Apr. 9, 1988. BA, Yale U., 1949-53; LLB, Harvard U., 1958. Bar: N.Y. Ct. Appeals 1958, U.S. Dist. Ct. (so. and ea. dists.) N.Y. 1960, U.S. Ct. Appeals (2d cir.) 1961, U.S. Supreme Ct. 1965, U.S. Ct. Appeals (4th cir.) 1968, D.C., D.C. Ct. Appeals, U.S. Dist. Ct. D.C. 1972. Assoc. Mudge, Stern, Baldwin & Todd, N.Y.C., 1958-62; trial atty. Civil Rights Div. U.S. Dept. Justice, Washington, 1962-79, chief eastern sect., 1969, chief housing sect., 1969-79, spl. counsel for litigation, 1979; spl. counsel rev. panel on new drug regulation HEW, Washington, 1976-77; assoc. judge Superior Ct. D.C., Washington, 1979-88, D.C. Ct. Appeals, Washington, 1988—2006, sr. judge, 0206—. Instr. various legal edn. activities. Contbr. articles to profl. jours. With U.S. Army, 1955-57. Recipient Younger Fed. Lawyer award, Fed. Bar Assn., 1967. Mem. Bar Assn. D.C., World Peace Through Law Ctr., World Assn. Judges, Czechoslovak-Am. Orgns., De Tocqueville Soc., Order of the Battered Boot. Achievements include proficiency in Czech, French and German. Avocations: tennis, ping pong/table tennis, sports, gilbert and sullivan operettas, shakespeare. Office: DC Ct Appeals 500 Indiana Ave NW Washington DC 20001-2138 Office Phone: 202-879-2779. Business E-Mail: fschwelb@dcca.state.dc.us.

**SCHWEMM, JOHN BUTLER,** printing company executive, lawyer; b. Barrington, Ill., May 18, 1934; s. Earl M. and Eunice (Butler) S.; m. Nancy Lea Prickett, Sept. 7, 1956; children: Catherine Ann, Karen Elizabeth. AB, Amherst Coll., 1956; JD, U. Mich., 1959. Bar: Ill. 1959. With Sidley & Austin, Chgo., 1959-65; with legal dept. R.R. Donnelley & Sons Co., Chgo., 1965-69, gen. counsel, 1969-75, v.p., 1971-75, pres., 1981-87, chmn., 1983-89, dir., 1980-92. Bd. dirs. William Blair Mut. Funds, Inc., Walgreen Co., USG Corp. Life trustee Northwestern U., Chgo. Mem. Law Club Chgo., Order of Coif, Phi Beta Kappa. Clubs: Chgo., Univ., Hinsdale (Ill.) Golf, Old Elm. Home (Summer): 2 Turvey Ln Downers Grove IL 60515-4530 Home and Office: 565 Sanctuary Dr Ste A401 Longboat Key FL 34228

**SCHWENDEMAN, PAUL WILLIAM,** lawyer; b. Chgo., Apr. 7, 1945; s. Oscar and Edna Dorothy (Ellis) S.; m. Shirley Anne Starke; children: Paul A., John E., Thomas D. BA in Econs., Carleton Coll., 1966; MSJ, Northwestern U., 1967; JD, Duquesne U., 1978. Bar: Pa. 1978. Mgr. divsn. ops. Greater Waterbury (Conn.) Ct. of C., 1971-75; v.p. Greater Pitts. C. of C., 1975-78; assoc. Kirkpatrick & Lockhart, Pitts., 1978-84, ptnr., 1984—. Lt. USNR, 1971. Office: Kirkpatrick & Lockhart 1500 Oliver Bldg Pittsburgh PA 15222-2312

**SCHWENGER, WILBUR JOHN,** mathematics educator, mathematics professor; s. John William and Helen Elizabeth Schwenger; m. Barbara Ann Silvis, Aug. 15, 1970; children: Karin Christine, Lauralee Ruth, John Daniel, William James. AA, Palm Beach CC, West Palm Beach, Fla., 1967; BA, U. Fla., Gainesville, 1969, MEd, 1971. Tchr. St. Lucie County Sch. Bd., Fort Pierce, Fla., 1971—. Scoutmaster Boy Scouts Am., Ft. Pierce, 1973—88, cubmaster, 1988—94, scoutmaster, 1995—; jr. civitan advisor Civitan, 1973—90. A1C USAF, 1961—65. Recipient Dist. award of Merit, Boy Scouts Am., Silver Beaver, Civitan, Outstanding Jr. Civitan Advisor Fla. Dist., 2001, Dist. award of Merit, 1976, Silver Beaver award, 1976, Tchr. of Yr. award, St. Lucie County Sch. Bd., 1983, Lamb award, Lutheran Ch. Mem.: Am. Math. Assn., Math. Ass. Ft. Pierce, Nat. Coun. Tchrs. Math. Lutheran. Avocations: hiking, camping, scouting. Home: 5207 Citrus Ave Fort Pierce FL 34982 Personal E-Mail: schwenw@netscape.net.

**SCHWENK, SANDRA MATES,** secondary school educator; b. Pottsville, Pa., Sept. 13, 1953; d. Donald E. and Georgine (Connelly) Mates; m. Ray T. Schwenk Jr., June 17, 1977; 1 child, Matthew T. BS, Pa. State U., 1975; postgrad., Wilkes U., DeSales U., Pa. State U. Cert. Instrnl. II, Pa. Dept. Edn. Tchr. grades 5 & 6 St. Nicholas Ukranian Cath. Grade Sch., Minersville, Pa., 1975—77; tchr. French lang. Nativity Blessed Virgin Mary H.S., Pottsville, Pa., 1983—, tchr. art, 2000—, distance learning instr. French for elem. students, 2002—. Mem. ednl. adv. bd. Pottsville Rep., 1991—; liaison newspaper in edn. Pottsville Rep. and Evening Herald Cultural Heritage Alliance, Phila., 1985—. Counselor ednl. tours. Mem. Am. Assn. Tchrs. French, Nat. Cath. Ednl. Assn., Pa. State Alumni Assn., Pa. State MLA, Allentown Diocese Lay Tchr.'s Assn. Roman Catholic. Avocations: travel, drawing, painting, swimming, reading. Home: 441 E Deerview Dr Auburn PA 17922-8915 Office: Nativity BVM HS One Lawton's Hill Pottsville PA 17901

**SCHWENKE, ROGER DEAN,** lawyer; b. Washington, Oct. 18, 1944; s. Clarence Raymond and Virginia Ruth (Gould) S.; m. Carol Lynne Flenniken, Nov. 29, 1980; 1 child: Matthew Robert; stepchildren: Tracy L. Wolf Dickey, Mary M. Wolf. BA, Ohio State U., 1966; JD with honors, U. Fla., 1969. Bar: Fla. 1970. Instr. Coll. Law U. Fla., Gainesville, 1969—70; assoc. Carlton Fields, P.A., Tampa, Fla., 1970—74, ptnr., 1975—; administr., dept. head Real Estate, Environ. and Land Use Dept., 1978—99. Adj. prof. Coll. Law, Stetson U., St. Petersburg, Fla., 1979-80; mem. faculty U. Miami Coll. of Law Master of Law's in Real Estate Devel. Program, 1994-96. Author chpt. in Environmental Regulation and Litigation in Florida, 1987, chpt. in Florida Real Property Complex Transactions, 1997, 2000; contbr. articles to profl. jours., chpt. to book. Mem. diocesan coun. Episc. Diocese SW Fla., 1978-86, mem. standing com., 1989-92, chief judge Eccles. Ct., 1996—. Recipient Gertrude Brick Law Rev. prize, U. Fla., 1969. Fellow Am. Coll. Real Estate Lawyers (bd. govs. 1985-88), Am. Law Inst.; mem. ABA (liaison to standong com. on environ. law 1980-87, mem. coun. real property sect. 1988-95), Fla. Bar Assn., Air and Waste Mgmt. Assn., Order of Coif, Greater Tampa C. of C. (chmn. environ. coun. 1980-81), Tampa Club. Democrat. Office: Carlton Fields PO Box 3239 Tampa FL 33601-3239 Office Phone: 813-229-4152. E-mail: rschwenke@carltonfields.com.

**SCHWENN, LEE WILLIAM,** retired health facility administrator; b. Morrisonville, Wis., Dec. 23, 1925; s. LeRoy William and Vivian Mae (Kramer) S.; m. Glenna Edith Mehne, Jan. 16, 1947; 1 son, William Lee. BS, U. Wis., 1948; M.P.H., U. N.C., 1956. Tchr. pub. schs., Appleton, Wis., 1948-52; teaching cons. Wis. Health Dept., 1952-53; administrv. asst. Madison (Wis.) Health Dept., 1953-57; administrv. cons. U.S. Children's Bur., Atlanta Regional Office, 1957-58; administr. USPHS, Washington, 1958-66; assoc. dir. D.C. Dept. Health, 1966-70, D.C. Dept. Human Resources, 1970-71; exec. v.p. Maimonides Med. Center, Bklyn., 1971-88, pres., 1988-89, spl. cons. Bd. Trustees, 1989-96. Recipient Distinguished Pub. Service award D.C. Govt., 1970. Mem. Delta Omega. Home: 1007 Westminster Dr Greensboro NC 27410-4551

**SCHWENTERLY, STANLEY WILLIAM,** physicist, researcher; b. Phila., Aug. 18, 1945; s. Stanley William and Ruth Dorothy Schwenterly. BS, Yale U., 1967; PhD, Cornell U., 1972. Sr. rsch. staff Oak Ridge Nat. Lab., Tenn., 1972—. Editor IEEE Transactions on Applied Superconductivity, NYC, 1999—. Contbr. articles to profl. jours. Prin. mem Oak Ridge Symphony Orch., Oak Ridge, Tenn., 1975—. Recipient Tech. Achievement award, Martin Marietta Energy Systems, 1991, UT-Battelle, 2000, Engr. of the Yr.award, 2000. Mem.: IEEE, Cryogenic Soc. Am., Internat. Horn Soc., Knoxville Ski Club, Concord Yacht Club. Achievements include research in investigations of cryogenic dielectric materials and development of high voltage components for superconducting utility equipment, superconductor ac loss measurements; cryopumping studies for fusion applications, and development of superconducting motors, transformers, generators, and cables. Avocations: music, skiing, bicycling, sailing. Office: Oak Ridge Nat Lab PO Box 2008 Oak Ridge TN 37831 Office Phone: 865-574-1460. Personal E-mail: schwenterly@ieee.org.

**SCHWERDTFEGER, HENRY DOUGLAS,** military officer, physiologist; b. Alva, Okla., Jan. 20, 1972; m. Cindy Schwerdtfeger; children: Jeremy Lee, Justin Henry. BS, U. Kans., Lawrence, 1995. Commd. ensign USN, 1995, advanced through grades to It. NAS Lemoore, Calif. Decorated Navy and Marine Corps Commendation medal, Navy and Marine Corps Achievement medal. Mem.: Am. Coll. Sports Medicine. Avocations: flying, travel,

sports. Office: ASTC Lemoore 961 Franklin Ave Lemoore CA 93246 Office Phone: 559-998-3205. Personal E-mail: hdschwerdtfeger@aol.com. Business E-Mail: schwerdtfeger@astclem.med.navy.mil.

**SCHWERDTNER, FREDERICK HOWARD,** lawyer, retired police commander, real estate broker; b. Chgo., Oct. 13, 1949; s. Fred and Lydia (Tatz) S.; m. Julie Anne Carramusa, Oct. 21, 1990; 1 child, Sarah Elizabeth. BS, Loyola U., Chgo., 1973, JD, 1989; MBA with distinction, DePaul U., 1983. Bar: Ill. 1989, U.S. Ct. Appeals (7th cir.) Ill. 1989. Officer Oak Park (Ill.) Police Dept., 1973-93, commdr., 1989-93; with DuPage County Vets. Assistance Commn., 1995—, pres., 1997—99; lawyer Pvt. Practice, Ill. Contbr. articles to profl. jours. Tutor inner city high sch. students, Chgo., 1988; apptd. local bd. mem. Selective Svc. Sys., police commr. Bd. Police Commr., Village of Glendale Heights, Ill., 1999-, chmn. 2002-. Served USMC, 1965-69, Vietnam, 1967-68. Mem. ABA, Fraternal Order Police, Marine Corps League (Band of Bros. Detachment), VFW, Vietnam Vets of Am., Ill. State Bar Assn., Chgo. Bar Assn., DuPage County Bar Assn., Beta Gamma Sigma. Republican. Lutheran. Avocations: hiking, tennis, racquetball, golf. Office Phone: 630-653-3494. E-mail: vet-star@comcast.net.

**SCHWERIN, HORACE S.,** marketing research consultant; b. NYC, Jan. 18, 1914; s. Paul and Rose (Lewis) S.; m. Lorraine Roth, June 14, 1941 (div. Dec. 1969); children— Barbara, Bruce; m. Enid May Highton, Apr. 28, 1973. BS, Lafayette Coll., 1935; MA, London U., 1936; MS, U. Paris, 1937. Gen. mgr., research dir., cons. N.Y. advt. agys., 1936-41; pres. Research Analysts, Inc., 1946; chmn. bd. Schwerin Research Corp., N.Y.C., Toronto, London, Hamburg, to 1968; chmn., pres. Horace Schwerin & Assos., Englewood Cliffs, NJ, 1968-72; dir. marketing devel. Campbell Soup Co., Camden, NJ, 1972—, v.p market planning Canned Food div., 1977-82, mktg. strategy cons., 1982—; CEO, chmn. Schwerin Murphy, Inc., 1991-98; ret., 1998. Author: (with Henry H. Newell) Persuasion in Marketing, 1981; also articles on market research, nutrition, use of govt. data bases. Served as capt. U.S. Army, 1946. Decorated Legion of Merit with oak leaf cluster; inducted into Market Rsch. Coun. Hall of Fame, 1992. Mem. Am. Mktg. Assn., Market Rsch. Coun., Can. Club (N.Y.C.), Penn Club (N.Y.C.). Methodist. Home: 5D Toll Gate Of Moorestown 633 E Main St Moorestown NJ 08057-3059 Office: 633 E Main St Moorestown NJ 08057-3059 E-mail: hschwerin@comcast.net.

**SCHWERIN, KARL HENRY,** anthropology educator, researcher; b. Bertha, Minn., Feb. 21, 1936; s. Henry William and Audrey Merle (Jahn) S.; m. Judith Drewanne Altermatt, Sept. 1, 1958 (div. May 1975); children: Karl Frederic, Marguerite DelValle; m. Partha Louise Hake Buell, Jan. 25, 1979; stepchildren: Tamara, Brent, Taryn. BA, U. Calif., Berkeley, 1958; PhD, UCLA, 1965. Instr. Los Angeles State Coll., 1963; asst. prof. anthropology U. N.Mex., Albuquerque, 1963-68, assoc. prof., 1968-72, prof., 1972-2001, asst. chmn. dept. anthropology, 1983-85, chmn. dept. anthropology, 1987-93, prof. emeritus, 2001—. Prof. invidado Inst. Venezolano de Investigaciones Cientificas, Caracas, 1979. Author: Oil and Steel Processes of Karinya Culture Change, 1966, Antropologia Social, 1969, Winds Across the Atlantic, 1970; editor: Food Energy in Tropical Ecosystems, 1985; contbr. articles to profl. jours. V.p Parents without Ptnr., Albuquerque, 1976-77. Grantee Cordell Hull Found., Venezuela, 1961-62, N.Y. Zool. Soc., Honduras, 1981; Fulbright scholar Cañar, Ecuador, 1969-70, Paris, 1986; founded Karl H. Schwerin Fellowship in Ethnology. Fellow Am. Anthropol. Assn.; mem. Am. Ethnol. Soc., Am. Soc. Ethnohistory (pres. 1975), Southwestern Anthropol. Assn. (co-editor Southwestern Jour. Anthropology 1972-75), N.Mex. Cactus and Succulent Soc. (v.p 1970-71), Internat. Congress of Americanists (35th-40th, 43d, 46th, 48th, 49th, 50th), Netherwood Pk. Neighborhood Assn. (pres. 2005-), Sigma Xi (chpt. pres. 1980-81) Avocations: photography, gardening, hiking, camping, bicycling. Office: U NMex Dept Anthropology MSC01-1040 Albuquerque NM 87131-0001 Office Phone: 505-277-4614. E-mail: schwerin@unm.edu.

**SCHWERING, FELIX KARL,** electronics executive, researcher; b. Cologne, Nordrhein-Westfalen, Federal Republic of Germany, June 4, 1930; came to U.S., 1964; s. Felix Bernhard and Maria (Heinrichs) S. BS, U. Aachen, Federal Republic of Germany, 1951, Diplom-Ingenieur, 1954, PhD, 1957. Asst. prof. U. Aachen, Federal Republic of Germany, 1956-58; electronic scientist U.S. Army R & D Labs., Fort Monmouth, NJ, 1958-61; project leader AEG-Telefunken, Ulm, Federal Republic of Germany, 1961-64; rsch. scientist U.S. Army Communication Electronics Command (CECOM), Fort Monmouth, NJ, 1964-96, ret., 1996, cons., 1996—. Vis. lab. assoc. U.S. Army Rsch. Office, Rsch. Triangle, N.C., 1984-85; vis. prof. N.J. Inst. Tech., Newark, 1986—; Rutgers U., New Brunswick, N.J., 1973-87, Monmouth U., 1996—. Author: (with others) Millimeter Wave Antennas, 1988; author and editor (with others) Microwave Antennas, 1989; mem. editorial bd. Microwave and Optical Tech. Letters, 1988—; contbr. over 40 articles to profl. jours.; patentee in field. Fellow IEEE (Best Paper award Antennas and Propagation Soc. 1961, 82), Internat. Sci. Radio Union, Am. Geophys. Union, Armed Forces Comm. Electronics Assn., Sigma Xi. Roman Catholic. Office: US Army CERDEC Attn AMSRD-CER-ST-WL Fort Monmouth NJ 07703-5203 Office Phone: 732-532-0469. Business E-Mail: schwerin@mail1.monmouth.army.mil.

**SCHWERT, G(EORGE) WILLIAM, III,** finance educator; b. Durham, N.C., Jan. 26, 1950; s. George William Jr. and Margaret (Houlton) S.; m. Camille Matthews, Dec. 19, 1970 (div. 1983); 1 child, Lisa Margaret; m. Patricia Michel, Dec. 23, 1983; children: Michael William, Andrew Patrick. AB in Econs. with honors, Trinity Coll., 1971; MBA, U. Chgo., 1973, PhD in Fin., 1975. Asst. prof. Grad. Sch. Bus. U. Chgo., 1975-76; asst. prof. to prof. Simon Sch. Bus. U. Rochester, N.Y., 1976-86, Gleason prof. fin. N.Y., 1986-98, Disting. U. prof. N.Y., 1998—. Chmn. Knollwood Cons. Group, Inc., Rochester, 1987—. Co-editor Jour. Fin. Econs., 1979-86, 89-95, adv. editor, 1986-89, mng. editor 1995—; assoc. editor Jour. of Fin., 1983-2000, Jour. Monetary Econs., 1984—; contbr. articles to econs. jour. Recipient Smith-Breeden Disting. Paper prize Jour. Fin., 1990, Graham and Dodd plaque Fin. Analysts Jour., 1990. Mem. Am. Fin. Assn. (bd. dirs. 1987-89), Am. Econs. Assn., Econometrics Soc., Am. Statis. Assn. (chair bus. econs. sect. 1990-91). Avocations: tennis, boating, fishing, golf. Home: 71 Knollwood Dr Rochester NY 14618-3512 Office: U Rochester W E Simon Grad Sch Bus Adminstrn Rochester NY 14627 Office Phone: 585-275-2470. Business E-Mail: schwert@schwert.ssb.rochester.edu.

**SCHWETZ, BERNARD ANTHONY,** toxicologist; b. Cadott, Wis., Nov. 27, 1940; married; 4 children. BS in Biology, U. Wis., Stevens Point, 1962; DVM, U. Minn., 1967; MS in Pharmacology, U. Iowa, 1968, PhD in Pharmacology, 1970. Diplomate Am. Bd. Toxicology. USPHS trainee dept. vet. physiology and pharmacology U. Minn., 1964-66; USPHS trainee dept. pharmacology U. Iowa, 1966-70; toxicologist Dow Chem. U.S.A., Midland, Mich., 1970-78, dir. toxicology rsch. lab., 1978-82; chief sys. toxicity br. divsn. toxicology rsch. and testing NIEHS, Research Triangle Park, N.C., 1982-92, acting dir. environ. toxicology program, 1993; dir. Nat. Ctr. for Toxicol. Rsch., Jefferson, Ark., 1993—2000; assoc. commr. for sci. FDA, Rockville, Md., 1994—; sr. advisor. Adj. U. Ark. for Med. Scis., 1993—; Mich. State U., East Lansing, 1973-82, N.C. State U., Raleigh, 1985-93. Assoc. editor Fundamental and Applied Toxicology, 1983-86, editor, 1986-92; editl. adv. bd. Environ. Health Perspectives, 1984-93, Critical Revs. in Toxicology, 1984—; contbr. numerous articles to profl. publs. Recipient Arnold J. Lehman award Soc. of Toxicology, 1991, Dir.'s award NIH, 1991, Founders award Chem. Industry Inst. of Toxicology, 1994, FDA Commr.'s Spl. citation, 1995. Mem. AVMA, Soc. Toxicology (charter mem. Mich. chpt., councilor 1984-86, pres. N.C. chpt. 1987, pres. reproductive toxicology speciality sect. 1986, pres.-elect south ctrl. chpt. 1997), Teratology Soc. (treas. 1978-82), Behavioral Teratology Soc., Phi Zeta. Avocations: fishing, photography. Office: Nat Ctr Toxicol Rsch HFT-1 3900 Nctr Rd Jefferson AR 72079-9501 Home: 17601 Conoy Rd Barnesville MD 20838-9751

**SCHWIEBERT, DEBORAH JOHNSON,** marketing executive; b. Moline, Ill., Apr. 26, 1952; d. Robert B. and Ruth E. Cronin; m. Mark W. Schwiebert, Oct. 10, 1987. BA in English, St. Mary's Coll., 1974. Dealer mgmt. rep. John

Deere co., East Moline, Ill., 1975-77, territory mgr., 1977-85; mktg. cons. John Deere Info. Systems, East Moline, Ill., 1985-91, mgr. quality assurance, 1991-93; project mgr., product safety mktg. Deere & Co., Moline, Ill., 1993-97, divsn. mgr. retail customer, 1997-98, mgr. Deere.com, 1998—2005, dir. communication svcs., 2005—. Deere & Co. Credit Union, 1996-2001 Mem. St. Mary's Coll. Alumni (pres. 1998-2000, bd. dirs. 1994-2000, bd. trustees 1998—, chair bd. trustees 2004—) Roman Catholic. Avocations: reading, travel. Home: 3913 14th St Rock Island IL 61201-6016 Office: Deere & Co One John Deere Pl Moline IL 61265-1373

**SCHWIETZ, ROGER L.,** archbishop; b. St. Paul, Minn., July 3, 1930; MA in Philosophy, U. Ottawa; MA in Sacred Theology, Loyola U.; STL in Sacred Theology, Gregorian U., Rome; HHD (hon.), Lewis U., 1998. Ordained priest Roman Cath. Ch., 1967, consecrated bishop, 1990. Assoc. pastor St. Thomas Aquinas Parish, International Falls, Minn., 1975—78; dir. Coll. Seminary prog. for Oblates of Mary Immaculate Creighton U., Omaha, 1978—84; pastor Holy Family Parish, Duluth, Minn., 1984—89; bishop Diocese of Duluth, 1989—2000; archbishop Archdiocese of Anchorage, 2001—. Episcopal moderator Teens Encounter Christ (TEC) movement, 1991—. Home and Office: Archdiocese of Anchorage 225 Cordova St Anchorage AK 99501-2409

**SCHWIMMER, DAVID,** actor; b. Queens, N.Y., Nov. 12, 1966; BS in Speech/Theater, Northwestern U., 1988. Co-founder The Lookingglass Theater Co., Chgo., 1988. Actor: (films) Flight of the Intruder, 1991, Crossing the Bridge, 1992, The Waiter, 1993, Twenty Bucks, 1993, The Party Favor, 1995, The Pallbearer, 1996, Breast Men, 1997, The Thin Pink Line, 1998, Kissing a Fool (also exec. prodr.), 1998, Six Days Seven Nights, 1998, Apt Pupil, 1998, All the Rage, 1999, Picking Up the Pieces, 2000, Hotel, 2001, Duane Hopwood, 2005, (voice) Madagascar, 2005, (TV films) A Deadly Silence, 1989, Since You've Been Gone, 1998, Uprising, 2001, (TV miniseries) Band of Brothers, 2001, (TV series) The Wonder Years, 1992, Friends, 1994-2004, Monty, 1994, (stage appearances) West, The Odyssey, Of One Blood, In the Eye of the Beholder, The Master and Margarita, Some Girls, 2005; dir. The Jungle, The Serpent, Alice in Wonderland (TV appearances) LA Law, NYPD Blue, 1993, L.A. Law, 1992, 93, ER, 1996, The Single Guy, 1997, Curb Your Enthusiasm, 2004; exec. prodr. Humanoid, 2003, Shoot the Moon, 1996

**SCHWIMMER, SIGMUND,** food enzymologist; b. Cleve., Sept. 20, 1917; s. Solomon and Sarah (Brown) S.; m. Sylvia Klein, Dec. 18, 1941; children: Susan, Elaine. Student Ohio State U., 1935-36; B.S., George Washington U., 1940; M.S., Georgetown U., 1941, Ph.D., 1943. From lab. asst. to research chemist USDA, Washington and Berkeley, Calif., 1936-62; adj. prof. biology Calif. Inst. Tech., Pasadena, 1963-65; chief research biochemist USDA, Berkeley, 1966-72, collaborator emeritus, 1975-; adj. prof. dept. nutritional scis. U. Calif.-Berkeley, 1985-87; sr. expert biochemistry UN Indsl. Devel. Orgn., Haifa, Israel, 1973-74; cons. food enzymology, Berkeley, 1980-; lectr. dept. biotech. food engring. Israel Inst. Tech., Haifa, 1973; vis. scientist Food Industry Rsch. and Devel. Inst., Hsinchu, Taiwan, 1992. Contbr. articles to profl. jours.; editor, Biochem. Sci. Biotech., Cambridge, Eng., 1983—, Trends in Biochemistry, Trends in Biotechnology, 1983—, Jour. Food Biochemistry, 1977-98; author: Source Book of Food Enzymology, 1982 (Jour. Assn. Coll. and Rsch. Librs. award 1983). John S. Guggenheim fellow; NSF fellow; Carlsberg Biol. Inst. fellow, Copenhagen; recipient Superior Service award USDA, 1949, 59, Lifetime Achievement award, 1993, Agrl. and Food Chemistry Divsn. award Am. Chem. Soc., 1996. Fellow Inst. Food Technologists, inductee USDA's ARS Sci. Hall of Fame, 2005; mem. Am. Soc. Biochemistry Molecular Biology, Sigma Xi. Office: Western Regional Ctr USDA 800 Buchanan St Albany CA 94710-1105 also: U Calif Dept Nutritional Sci Berkeley CA 94720-0001 Office Phone: 510-559-5873. Business E-Mail: sig@pw.usda.gov.

**SCHWIND, MICHAEL ANGELO,** law educator; b. Vienna, July 2, 1924; came to U.S., 1951; s. Siegfried and Sali (Salner) S. JD, U. Central, Ecuador, 1949; LL.M. in Internat. Law, NYU, 1953, LL.B., 1957. Bar: Ecuador 1949, N.Y. 1957, U.S. Supreme Ct. 1967. Pvt. practice, N.Y.C., 1957-69; Lectr. law NYU Sch. Law, 1959-63, adj. asst. prof., 1963-64, assoc. prof., 1964-67, prof., 1967-94, prof. emeritus, 1994—. Dir. Inter-Am. Law Inst., Inst. Comparative Law, NYU Sch. Law, 1967-71. Contbr. International Encyclopedia of Comparative Law, vol. 5; Bd. editors Am. Jour. Comparative Law, 1971-97. Mem.: Am. Fgn. Law Assn. (bd. dirs. 1980—83, v.p. 1983—84, bd. dirs. 1984—87, 1988—91, v.p. 1991—93, bd. dirs. 1993—96, v.p. 1996—97, bd. dirs. 1997—, v.p. 2000—01), Am. Assn. Comparative Study Law (NYU rep. on bd. dirs. 1971—2000). Office: NYU Sch Law 40 Washington Sq S New York NY 10012-1005 Personal E-Mail: maschwind@msn.com.

**SCHWIND, WILLIAM F., JR.,** lawyer, oil industry executive; b. Chgo., 1944; BS, JD, Loyola U., Chgo. Bar: Tex. 1969. With Marathon Oil Corp., Findlay, Ohio, 1974—83; commd. contract mgr. Jakarta, Indonesia, 1983—84; gen. atty. Marathon Oil Corp., Houston, 1984—91, gen. counsel, sec., 1992—; sr. v.p. adminstrn., gen. counsel, sec. Dehli Gas Pipeline Corp., Dallas, 1991—92. Mem.: ABA, Am. Petroleum Inst. (chmn. gen. com. law), Am. Corp. Counsel Assn. Office: Marathon Oil Co PO Box 4813 5555 San Felipe Rd Houston TX 77210-4813

**SCHWINGER, DAVID,** lawyer; b. Phila., Nov. 8, 1956; BS summa cum laude, U. Pa., 1977; JD with high honors, George Washington U., 1982. Bar: DC 1982. Mng. ptnr. Katten Muchin Zavis Rosenman, Washington, DC. Mem.: Nat. Reverse Mortgage Lenders Assn., Mortgage Bankers Assn. of Am. Office: Katten Muchin Zavis Rosenman East Lobby, Ste 700 1025 Thomas Jefferson St, NW Washington DC 20007 Office Phone: 202-625-3600. Office Fax: 202-298-7570. E-mail: david.schwinger@kmzr.com.

**SCHWINGHAMER, MARY DENISE,** veterinarian; b. Jasper, Ind., Aug. 25, 1953; DVM, Auburn U., 1978. Preceptor Brentwood Vet. Clinic, Tenn., 1978—79; staff veterinarian Birmingham Humane Soc., Ala., 1980—81; emergency animal clinician Emergency Animal Clinic, Birmingham, 1980—83; small animal clinic propr. Companion Animal Clinic, Irondale, Ala., 1981—94; tech. writer, 1994—. Contbr. articles to profl. jours. Roman Catholic. Achievements include invention of; research in treatment for canine parvovirus enteritis; treatment for HIV-AIDS and Systemic Viremias in human population with companion animals as in vivo models. Avocations: swimming, dog breeding, horse breeding. Home: 78 Cromer St Talladega AL 35160 Office Phone: 256-362-1664.

**SCHWISTER, JAY EDWARD,** portfolio manager; b. Milw., Apr. 16, 1962; s. Jerome Charles and Carol Christina (Keeler) Schwister; m. Sara M. Schlaudecker; children: Katharine Claire, William Edward. BS in Fin. cum laude, Marquette U., 1984. Chartered fin. analyst. Sr. investment officer First Wis. Trust Co., Milw. 1984-87; sr. v.p., sr. portfolio mgr. Putnam Investments, Boston, 1987—2002; pres., CIO, Juneau Fund Advisors, 2002—04; sr. portfolio mgr. Baird Advisors, Milw., 2004—. Fin. com. mem. Hills Bd. Trustees, Wayland, Mass., 1990—; pres. coun. Marquette U., Milw., 1990—. Chmn. fund raising com. Marquette U. Alumni Fund, Boston, 1989—. Mem. CFA Inst., Milw. Investment Analysts Soc., Bond Analysts Soc., Inc., Beta Gamma Sigma. Avocations: golf, tennis, travel, woodworking, music. Home: 14655 Juneau Blvd Elm Grove WI 53122-1669 Office: Baird Advisors 777 E Wisconsin Ave Milwaukee WI 53202-5391 Office Phone: 414-298-1038. E-mail: Jschwister@rwbaird.com.

**SCHWITTERS, ROY FREDERICK,** physicist, researcher; b. Seattle, Wash., June 20, 1944; s. Walter Frederick and Margaret Lois (Boyer) S.; m. Karen Elizabeth Chrystal, June 18, 1965; children: Marc Frederick, Anne Elizabeth, Adam Thomas. S.B., MIT, 1966, PhD, 1971. Research asso. Stanford U. Linear Accelerator Center, 1971-74, asst. prof., then asso. prof., 1974-79; prof. physics Harvard U., 1979-90; scientist Fermi Nat. Accelerator Lab., Batavia, Ill., 1980-88, dir. superconducting supercollider, 1989-93; prof. physics U. Tex., Austin, 1994—. Author papers on high energy physics; asso. editor: Ann. Rev. Nuclear and Particle Sci; div. asso. editor: Phys. Rev.

Letters. Recipient Alan T. Waterman award NSF, 1980. W.K.H. Panofsky Prize, Am Physical Soc., 1996, Humboldt Rsch. prize, 1999. Fellow AAAS, Am. Phys. Soc. (W. K. H. Panofsky Prize, 1996), Am. Acad. Arts and Scis. Home: 1115 W 7th St Apt 300 Austin TX 78703-5350 Office: U Tex Dept Physics Austin TX 78712-1081

**SCHWOCH, ROBERT WILLIAM,** public affairs director; b. Milw., May 30, 1960; s. A. Darrell and Luciana Romani Schwoch; life ptnr. Hal Koenig. BA, U. Wis., 1982; MS in Journalism, Northwestern U., 1990; postgrad., Bennington Coll., 2005—. Sports writer Milw. Jour., Milw., 1983—88; legis. and comm. asst. Wis. State Legislature, Madison, 1992—2001; dir. pub. affairs AIDS Resource Ctr. Wis., Milw., 2001—03. Contbr. stories to lit. publs. Comm. officer Episcopal Diocese Milw., 2003—05.

**SCIAINO, MARIA ANN,** counseling educator; d. Rose Sciaino. BA, Stetson U., 1985, MEd, 1990; EdD, U. Ctrl. Fla., 2005. Cert. tchr. Fla. Dept. Edn., 2006. Classroom tchr. Seminole County Pub. Schs., Lake Mary, Fla., 1985—90, guidance counselor, 1990—. Named Tchr. of Yr., Seminole County Schs., 1986, 1992, 1993, 2006. Mem.: Assn. Moral Edn. Home: 2314 Abalone Blvd Orlando FL 32833 Office: Carillon Elementary School 3200 Lockwood Blvd Oviedo FL 32765 Office Phone: 407-320-4665. Personal E-mail: mariasedd@aol.com.

**SCIALDO, MARY ANN,** music educator, musician; b. Westchester, NY, Sept. 21, 1942; d. Camille George Scialdo. MusB, Seton Hill Coll., 1963; MusM, Pius XII Inst. Fine Arts, Florence, Italy, 1964; profl. diploma, Manhattan Sch. Music, 1978; postgrad., Peabody Cons. Cert. tchr. NY, Fla. Supr. music Great Barrington (Mass.) Sch. Sys., 1967—68; music, theater prof. Simons Rock Coll., Great Barrington, 1968—70, Cath. U. PR, Ponce, 1971; performing arts instr. Briarcliff Sch. Dist., 1981, Ossining (NY) Sch. Dist., 1982, Albert Leonard Jr. H.S., 1983, Pleasantville (NY) Sch. Dist., 1984; theater and music tchr. Briarcliff Manor Schs., 1984—98; music tchr. Hillsborough County Schs., Tampa, Fla., 1999—. Dir., prodr., mus. and vocal dir., set and costume numerous student prodns. Debut concert: Merkin Hall, N.Y.C., internat. debut concert: Glinka Mus.; performer: (fund raising concert) Chopin Found. NY, (Giannini retrospective) WQXR, WNCN, (CD) Scriabin 24 Preludes, Opus 11, 1998—99. Recipient Outstanding Drama Tchr. award, Emerson Coll., 1st place award, Young Artist Nat. Competition, Nat. Fedn. Music Clubs competition, Disting. Alumna Leadership award, Seton Hill U. Mem.: Sigma Alpha Iota (life). Democrat. Roman Catholic. Office: Webb Middle Sch 6035 Hanley Rd Tampa FL 33634-4913

**SCIAME, JOSEPH,** university administrator; b. Bklyn., Sept. 9, 1941; s. Joseph and Sophie (Pintacuda) S. EdB, St. John's U., 1971. Fla. aid officer, asst. to dean of admissions St. John's U., Jamaica, NY, 1967-71, dir. fin. aid, 1971-82, dean fin. aid, 1982, v.p. fin. aid and student svcs., 1982-94, v.p. for govt. and cmty. rels., 1994—2002, v.p. for cmty. rels., 2002—. Mem. Gov. Commn. on Sch. Achievement, 1971—, chairperson, 1993—; pres. N.Y. Assn. Student Fin. Aid Adminstr., 1980-82, Ea. Assn. Student Fin. Aid Adminstrn., 1986-87. Chmn. bd. ethics Town of North Hempstead, N.Y., 1984—; nat. chmn., bd. dirs. Garibaldi-Meucci Mus., N.Y., 1987-93, 97-99, pres., CEO, 1999-2002; mem. Providence Rest Found., 1995—; bd. dirs. St. John's Prep, 1996—; bd. mem. Queens Symphony Orch., 2000—, Boy Scouts Am., 2000—, v.p. membership, 2001—; bd. mem. Holocaust Resource Ctr., 2002—. Decorated Cavaliere Ufficiale del Merito della Repubblica Italiana, Cavaliere Ufficiale Order Merit House of Savoy; recipient Lifetime Membership award Ea. Assn., 1995, Achievement award N.Y. State Fin. Aid Adminstrs., 1982, Congl. Record award, 1979, 91, 93, 94, 95. Mem. Nat. Assn. Student Fin. Aid Adminstrs. (chmn. 1987-88, Disting. Svc. award 1988, Leadership award 1994), Assn. Equestrian Order Holy Sepulchre (knight grand cross 1991, knight invested 1980), Order Sons of Italy in Am. (lodge pres. 1974-75, state pres. 1993-97, nat. v.p. 1997—2003, nat pres. 2003—), Futures in Edn. Found. (vice chair 1991-93, chair 1994-97), Jamaica C. of C. (bd. dirs.), Queens Symphony Orch. (bd. dirs.), Boy Scouts Am.(v.p. membership com. 2001—), Holocaust Rejourne Ctr. (bd. dirs.) Roman Catholic. Avocations: walking, cooking, gardening, reading, lecturing. Home: 6 Jones St New Hyde Park NY 11040-1616 also: Trout Ln Southampton NY 11968 Office: St John's Univ Off Vp Cmty Rels 8000 Utopia Pky Jamaica NY 11439-0001 Business E-mail: sciamej@stjohns.edu.

**SCIANCE, CARROLL THOMAS,** chemical engineer, educator; b. Oke-mah, Okla., Feb. 16, 1939; s. Carroll Elmer and Winifred (Black) Sciance; m. Anita Ruth Fischer, Jan. 30, 1960; children: Steven, Frederick, Thomas, Erica. BSChemE, U. Okla., 1960, M in Chem. Engring., 1964, PhD, 1966. With E.I. duPont de Nemours & Co., Inc., 1966-95, planning mgr. nylon intermediates divsn., petrochem. dept. Wilmington, Del., 1978-80, tech. mgr., 1980-83, dir engring. rsch., engring. dept., 1983-87, prin. cons. corp. rsch. and devel. planning divsn., 1987-89; mgr. petroleum products R & D divsn. Conoco, Inc., 1989-93; dir. environ. tech. partnerships ctrl. R & D dept. DuPont, 1993-95; pres. Sci. Cons. Svcs., Inc., 1995—. Math. scis. and edn. bd. NRC, 1987—89; adv. bd. chem. sci. and tech. NIST, 1988—94; sr. lectr. U. Tex., Austin, 1996—; mem. Travis County Appraisals Rev. Bd., Tex., 1999—2004; instr. U. Phoenix, Austin, Tex., 2005—. Pres. Hudson Bend Colony Homeowners Assn., 2004—06. Officer USAR, 1961—63. Fellow: AIChE (bd. dirs. material engring. and scis. divsn. 1986—92, chmn. new tech. com. 1990—92, mem. govt. rels. com. 1993—96); mem. Am. Chem. Soc. (mem. environ. R & D com. 1995—99), Fedn. Materials Soc. (v.p. 1988—92, pres. 1993—94), Sigma Xi. Home: 16658 Forest Way Austin TX 78734-1110 Personal E-mail: scscorp@earthlink.net.

**SCIARRA, JOHN J.,** obstetrician, gynecologist, educator; b. West Haven, Conn., Mar. 4, 1932; s. John and Mary Grace (Sanzone) S.; m. Barbara Crafts Patton, Jan. 9, 1960; chidren: Vanessa Patton, John Crafts, Leonard Chapman. BS, Yale U., 1953; MD, Columbia U., N.Y.C., 1957, PhD, 1963. Asst. prof. Columbia U., N.Y.C., 1964-68; prof. dept head U. Minn. Med Sch, Mpls., 1968-74; prof. Northwestern U. Med. Sch., Chgo., 1974—; chmn. ob-gyn Northwestern Meml. Hosp. and Northwestern U. Med. Sch., Chgo., 1974—2003. Guest prof. Peking U., China, 2005. Editor Gyn-Ob Reference Series, 1973—2005, Internat. Jour. Gyn-Ob, 1985—. V.p. med. affairs Chgo. Maternity Ctr., Chgo., 1974—2003; treas. Soc. Family Planning, 2005. Fellow ACS, Am. Coll. Ob-Gyn. (chmn. internal affairs com. 1985-89), Royal Coll. Ob-Gyn. (ad eundem); Internat. Fedn. Gyn-Ob. (pres. 1991-94, pres. Supporters Assn. 1994-2000); mem. Assn. Profs. Gyn-Ob. (sec. 1976-79, pres. 1980-81, Achievement award 1998, Tchg. award 2003), Am. Assn. Maternal and Neonatal Health (pres. 1980-89), Coun. Resident Edn. in Ob-Gyn., Am. Fertility Soc. (Hartman award 1965, bd. dirs. 1971-73), Assn. Profs. Gyn-Ob. Med. Edn. Found. (sec.-treas. 1987-91, pres. 1991-93), Ctrl. Assn. Ob-Gyn. (trustees 1986-90, pres. 1990-91), Chgo. Gynecol. Soc. (pres. 1990-91), Internat. Soc. Gynecol. Endoscopy (hon. 2005, v.p. 1997-99, pres. 1999-01), Am. Gynecol. Club, Internat. Acad. Human Reprodn., Yale Club N.Y.C., Carleton Club (Chgo.). Avocations: photography, travel. Office: Northwestern U Med Sch Dept Ob-Gyn 680 N Lake Shore Dr Ste 1015 Chicago IL 60611-8702 Office Phone: 312-695-5107. Business E-mail: jsciarra@northwestern.edu.

**SCIBELLI, ANDREW M.,** academic administrator; BA, St. Anselm Coll., MEd, Boston State Coll.; EdD, U. Mass. Tchr. Springfield (Mass.) Pub. Schs., 1965-69; prof. biology Springfield Tech. Community Coll., 1969-70, 78-83, registrar, 1970-73, asst. to pres., 1974-78, dir. community rels., 1981-83, pres., 1983—. Bd. dirs. Mfg. Partnership of Western Mass., Springfield Ctr.; trustee Pioneer Valley Planning Commn.; mem. chancellor's coun. U. Mass.; chmn. New Eng. Tech. Edn. Project New Eng. Bd. Higher Edn., Statewide Collective Bargaining Negotiating Team for Mass. C.C.s; presenter nat. convs. Alliance for C.C. Innovation, 1991, 94, 95; active Toronto Trade Mission, 1992, Hartford Trade Mission, 1992; corporator Chicopee Savs. Bank. Apptd. commr. MASSJOBS West Commn., mem. Massjobs Coun.; chmn., co-host United Cerebral Palsy Telethon, 1981—, past. pres. bd. dirs. western Mass. chpt.; mem. exec. com. & bd. dirs. Pvt. Industry Coun. and Regional Employment Bd.; dir. Italian Cultural Ctr.; pres. Make-A-Wish Found. Western Mass.; chmn. maj. firms unit United Way, 1989; bd. dirs.

Springfield Edn. Ptnrship, Corp. Pub. Mgmt.; numerous other civic roles and activities. Mem. Am. Assn. Community and Jr. Colls. (presenter nat. conv.), Nat. Coun. Resource Devel., Nat. Inst. Staff and Organizational Devel. (Outstanding Chief Exec. Officer Mass. 1987), Nat. Coun. Community Svcs. and Continuing Edn. (Regional Person of the Yr. awd., 1993), Am. Assn. Higher Edn., Nat. Coun. Occupational Edn. (rep. New Eng.), Nat. Coalition Advanced Tech. Ctrs., Nat. Coun. Pres., Coop. Colls. Greater Springfield (chmn. 1987-88). Avocations: golf, sailing, bicycling, skiing. Office: Springfield Tech C C Office Pres Armory Sq Springfield MA 01105

**SCIFRES, DONALD RAY,** finance company executive; m. Carol Scifres. BS, Purdue U., 1968; MS, U. Ill., 1970, PhD, 1972; Doctorate (hon.), Purdue U., 2001. Rsch. and tchg. asst. U. Ill., Urbana, 1968-72; rsch. fellow, area mgr. Xerox Corp., Palo Alto, Calif., 1972-83; founder, pres., CEO SDL, Inc., San Jose, Calif., 1983-2001, dir., 1983-2001, chmn., 1992-2001; co-chmn., chief strategy officer JDS Uniphase Corp., 2001—03; mng. dir. SDL Capital, LP, 2003—; mng. dir. SDL Ventures, LLC, 2003—. Nat. lectr. IEEE Quantum Electronics Soc., 1979 Bd. editors Jour. Fiber and Integrated Optics, 1978; mem. editorial adv. bd. Photonics Spectra, 1992—; contbr. articles to tech. jours.; patentee in field. Recipient Disting. Engring. Alumni award, Purdue U., 1990, Outstanding Elec. Engr. award, 1992, The Gov. Nobert T. Tiemann award, Beta Sigma Pi, 2002, Engring. Alumni award, U. Ill., 1991, Alumni Honor award, 1993, Distinction in Photonics award, Laurin Pub. Co., 1999, Rank prize, Rank Found., (U.K. 2001; fellow U. Ill., 1968, Gen. Telephone and Electronics, 1970—72. Fellow IEEE (Jack Morton award 1985, 3d Millenium award 2000, Robert N. Noyce medal 2003, John Tyndall award 2006), IEEE Lasers and Electro-Optics Soc. (pres. 1992, Engring. Achievement award 1994), Optical Soc. Am. (Edward H. Land medal 1996); mem. Am. Phys. Soc. (George E. Pake prize 1997). Lasers and Electro Optics Mfg. Assn. (bd. dirs. 1992-, sec. 1994, pres. 1996), Nat. Acad. Engring., Tau Beta Pi, Eta Kappa Nu (Eminent Mem. award 2003), Phi Eta Sigma. Office: One First St Ste 14 Los Altos CA 94022

**SCIFRES, STEPHANIE L.,** psychologist; d. John Wesley Scifres and Patricia Ann Robinson; children: Derek Wesley Jones, Elizabeth Ann Jones. PhD in clin. psychology, Pacific Grad. Sch. Psychology, 2002. Prof. Ind. U., Purdue U., Columbus, Ind., 1997—; clin. psychologist Clin. Psychol. Assessment & Cons., PC, Crothersville, Ind., 2005—. Mem.: APA, Ind. Psychol. Assn., Nat. Psychologists Tng. Register. Office: Clin Psychological Assessment & Cons 139 S E St Crothersville IN 47229 Office Phone: 812-793-2570. Business E-mail: sscifres@insightbb.com.

**SCIFRES, TERESA ELLEN,** reporter, educator; b. Boston, Jan. 28, 1955; d. Charles Gregory Carver and Elda Fae Jones; children: Wesley, Garrett. BA, U. Ark., Monticello, 1977. Lic. tchr. Ark. Tchr. Grady H.S., Ark., 1978, Star City H.S., 1978—; reporter Lincoln Ledger Newspaper, 2000—. Mem.: Star City C. of C., Ark. Tchr. Assn. Democrat. Methodist. Avocations: reading, writing, acting. Home: 1307 E Bradley Star City AR 71667

**SCILEPPI, JOHN A.,** psychologist, educator; b. Bklyn., Aug. 30, 1946; s. Adolph G. and Marie Theresa (Saccaro) S.; m. Lynn A. Ruggiero, Nov. 27, 1982; 1 child, Luke M.R. BA magna cum laude in Psychology, Marist Coll., Poughkeepsie, 1967; MA, Loyola U., Chgo., 1969, PhD in Social Psychology, 1973. Lic. psychologist, N.Y. NDEA rsch. and tchg. fellow Loyola U., Chgo., 1969—71; asst. prof. St. Xavier Coll., Chgo., 1971—73; v.p. acad. affairs Oglala Sioux C.C., Pine Ridge, SD, 1975—76; assoc. prof. psychology Marist Coll., Poughkeepsie, NY, 1973-75, 76-88, prof., 1988—, chair psychology dept., 2005—. Dir. MA Psychology program, 1990-2002; psychol. cons. for program evaluation, survey research and interpersonal communication. Abstractor: Psychological Abstracts, 1977-81; author: A Systems View of Education: A Model of Change, 1984, rev. edit., 1988, Community Psychology: A Common Sense Approach to Mental Health, 2000, The Community Mental Health System: A Navigational Guide for Providers, 2006, Applications Of A System Approach to Education: Models for Change, 2006. Chmn. bd. Sch. of the New Cmty. of Chgo., 1970-72; bd. dirs. Rehab. Programs Inc., Poughkeepsie, 1981-94, Hyde Park Free Libr., 1996-2002, pres. 2001-02, Anderson Sch., Staatsburg, N.Y., 2003—; mem. planning com. United Way of Dutchess County (N.Y.), 1979-80. Mem. Am. Psychol. Assn., Eastern Psychol. Assn., Psi Chi, Alpha Sigma Nu. Democrat. Roman Catholic. Home: 1 River Rd Hyde Park NY 12538-1323 Office: Marist Coll Psychology Dept Poughkeepsie NY 12601 Office Phone: 845-575-3000. Business E-Mail: john.scileppi@marist.edu.

**SCIOLARO, CHARLES MICHAEL,** cardiothoracic and vascular surgeon; b. Kansas City, Kans., July 5, 1958; s. Gerald Michael and Charleen Gwen Sciolaro; m. Vicki Lynn Mizell, Sept. 29 BA Biology and Chemistry magna cum laude, Mid Am. Nazarene U., 1980; MD magna cum laude, U. Kans., Kansas City, 1984. Diplomate Am. Bds. Gen. Surgery, Thoracic and Cardiac; lic. Ariz., Calif., La., Fla., Kans., Mo.; cert. ACLS, instr., advanced trauma life support, Calif. x-ray supr. and operator, transesophageal echocardiography. Intern gen. surgery Tucson hosps. surg. program U. Ariz., 1984—85, resident gen. surgery, 1985—86, 1987—89, chief resident gen. surgery, 1989—90; instr. surgery Loma Linda U. Med. Ctr., Tucson, 1991—93; physician divsn. cardiac, thoracic and vascular surgery MacArthur Surg. Clinic, Alexandria, 1993-96; staff physician Bethany Med. Ctr., 1996—2001, Overland Park Med. Ctr., 2001—. Emergency rm. physician, cons. Nat. Emergency Corp., Tucson, 1986-87; emergency care attendent Vets. Med. Ctr., Tucson, 1985-89, Cigna Urgent Care, 1985-89; staff physician Kanza Multispecialty Clinic, Kansas City, 1996-2003, Rapides Regional Med. Ctr., Alexandria, 1993-96, Providence Med. Ctr., Kansas City, 1996-2000, Bapt.-Luth. Med. Ctr., 2003—; pres. Kans. Heart and Lung Surgery, Chartered, 2003—; rschr., lectr., presenter in field Author: (manuscripts) Aortic Coarctation in Infants, 1991 Mem. First Family Ch. Overland Park, Kans. Named America's Top Surgeons, 2005; recipient Congl. Order of Merit, 2005, Proudl. Dus Common, 2003, Bionemistry Rsch. fellow, U. Kans., Kansas City, 1978—79. Mem. ACS, AMA, Am. Coll. Cardiologists, Am. Coll. Chest Physicians, La. Med. Soc., Kans. Med. Soc., Wyandotte Med. Soc., Rapides Med. Soc., Southea. Surg. Congress, Soc. Thoracic Surgery, Internat. Soc. Intraoperative Cardiovasc. Ultrasound, Internat. Coll. Surgeons, Kans. Med. Soc., Wyandotte County Med. Soc., Internat. Platform Assn., Am. Heart Assn. (bd. dirs. Kansas City chpt.), Phi Delta Lambda Republican. Avocations: photography, golf, athletist. Office: 8919 Parallel Pky Ste 203 Kansas City KS 66112 also: 10550 Quivira Rd Ste 480 Overland Park KS 66215 also: 6650 Troost Ste 205 Kansas City MO 64131 also: 3550 South Fourth Ste 282 Leavenworth KS 66048 Office Phone: 913-660-0438. Business E-Mail: csciol@kc.rr.com.

**SCIOLI, ANTHONY,** psychologist, educator; b. Cantalupo, Italy, Apr. 20, 1959; arrived in US, 1963; s. Felice and Filomena Scioli. BS with honors, U. Mass., 1982; MA in Clin. Psychology, U. RI, 1987, PhD in Clin. Psychology, 1990. Lic. clin. psychologist Mass. Rsch. assoc. Brown Med. Sch./Bradley Hosp., Providence, 1986—90; rsch. fellow Harvard U., Cambridge, Mass., 1990—91; psychology prof. Keene (NH) State Coll., 1991—; clin. fellow in behavioral medicine Harvard Med. Sch., Somerville, Mass., 2000—01; grad. faculty mem. U. RI, Kingston, 2005—. Presenter in field. Contbr. articles to profl. jours. Sponsor Christian Children's Fund, 2000—. Mem.: APA, Assn. Applied Psychophysiology and Biomedicine, Phi Kappa Phi, Psi Chi, Phi Beta Kappa. Democrat. Roman Catholic. Achievements include creation of a comprehensive hope assessment scale. Avocations: tennis, literature, philosophy, comparative religion. Office: Keene State Coll 229 Main St Keene NH 03455 Office Phone: 603-358-2541. Office Fax: 603-358-2184. E-mail: tscioli@keene.edu.

**SCIOLINO, ELAINE,** reporter; m. Andrew Plump; children: Alessandra, Gabriela. M of History, NYU, 1971; D (hon.), Syracuse U., Canisius Coll., Dowling Coll. Vaious positions Newsweek, 1970—84, foreign corr. Paris, 1978—80, bur. chief Rome, 1980—82, internat. corr. NYC, 1983—84; metropolitan reporter UN Newspapers, 1984, bur. chief, 1985-87; diplomatic corr. The NY Times, 1987-91, covered intelligence beat, 1991-92, chief diplomatic corr., 1992-96, sr. writer, Washington bur.; sr. fellow U.S. Inst. Peace, Washington, 1998. Edward R. Murrow Press Fellow Coun. on Foreign

Rels., 1982—83. Author: The Outlaw State: Saddam Hussein's Quest for Power and the Gulf Crisis, 1991, Persian Mirrors: The Elusive Face of Iran, 2000. Recipient Page One Award, 1978, Nat. Headliners Award, 1981, Overseas Press Club citation, 1983, Helen Bernstein Book Award for Excellence in Journalism, NY Public Library, 2001.

**SCIORRA, ANNABELLA,** actress; b. Wethersfield, Mar. 24, 1964; Appeared in films, including True Love, 1989, Internal Affairs, 1990, Cadillac Man, 1990, Reversal of Fortune, 1990, The Hard Way, 1991, Jungle Fever, 1991, The Hand That Rocks the Cradle, 1992, Whispers in the Dark, 1992, The Night We Never Met, 1993, Romeo is Bleeding, 1994, The Cure, 1995, The Addiction, 1995, The Funeral, 1996, Underworld, 1996, Copland, 1997, Mr. Jealousy, 1997, Highball, 1997, Underworld, 1997, Destination Anywhere, 1997, What Dreams May Come, 1998, New Rose Hotel, 1998, Little City, 1998, Sam the Man, 1999, King of the Jungle, 1999, American Crime, 2003, Chasing Liberty, 2004; (TV series) The Sopranos, 1999, 2001, 2002, Queens Supreme, 2003; (TV miniseries) Asteroid, 1997.

**SCIPIO, L. ALBERT, II, (LOUIS ALBERT SCIPIO II),** retired aerospace science engineering educator, historian; b. Juarez, Mex., Aug. 22, 1922; s. Louis Albert and Marie Leona (Richardson) S.; m. Katherine Ruth Jones, Aug. 15, 1942; children: Louis Albert, Karen R. BS, Tuskegee Inst., 1943; B.Civil Engring., U. Minn., 1948, MS, 1950, PhD, 1958. Archtl. draftsman McKissack & McKissack, Tuskegee, Ala., 1943; instr. Tuskegee Inst., 1946; designer Long & Thorshov, Mpls., 1948-50; lectr. U. Minn., Mpls., 1950-59; research physicist Hughes Aircraft Co., Culver City, Calif., 1954; Fulbright prof. Cairo U., Giza, Egypt, 1955-56; assoc. prof. mechanics Howard U., Washington, 1959-61; Fulbright prof. Cairo U., Giza, Egypt, 1955-56; dir. grad. studies for engring. and architecture, prof. aerospace engring. Howard U., Washington, 1967-70, Univ. prof. space scis., 1970-87, Disting. Univ. prof. emeritus, 1987—; prof. phys. scis. U. PR, Mayaguez, 1961-63; prof. aerospace engring. U. Pitts., 1963-67; pub. Roman Publs., Silver Springs, Md., 1981—; cons. in field. Author: Compendium of Aircraft Stress Analysis and Design, 1956, Principles on Continua with Applications, 1966, Structural Design Concepts, 1967, E.M. Collar Insignia, 1907-1926, 1981, Last of the Black Regulars, 1983, With the Red Hand Division, 1985, The 24th Infantry at Fort Benning, 1986, Pre-War Days at Tuskegee, 1987, The Collar Disk Story (1907-1999), 1999. Bd. visitors Air Force Inst. Tech., 1979-83. Served with AUS, 1943-46. Mem. NY Acad. Scis., Internat. Assn. Bridge and Structural Engrs., Soc. Natural Philosophy, AIAA, AAAS; mem. Am. Phys. Soc.; mem. NSPE, Co. of Mil. Historians, Coun. on Am. Mil. Past, Phi Beta Kappa, Sigma Xi, Alpha Kappa Mu, Pi Mu Epsilon, Sigma Pi Sigma, Sigma Gamma Tau, Pi Tau Sigma. Home: 12511 Montclair Dr Silver Spring MD 20904-2053

**SCIRICA, ANTHONY JOSEPH,** federal judge; b. Norristown, Pa., Dec. 16, 1940; s. A. Benjamin and Anna (Sclafani) Scirica; m. Susan Morgan, May 6, 1966; children: Benjamin, Sarah. BA, Wesleyan U., 1962; JD, U. Mich., 1965; postgrad. Fulbright Scholar, Central U., Caracas, Venezuela, 1966. Bar: Pa. 1966, U.S. Dist. Ct. (ea. dist.) Pa. 1984, U.S. Ct. Appeals (3d cir.) 1987. Ptnr. McGrory, Scirica, Wentz & Fernandez, Norristown, Pa., 1966—80; asst. dist. atty. Montgomery County, Pa., 1967—69; mem. Pa. Ho. of Reps, Harrisburg, 1971—79; judge Montgomery County Ct. Common Pleas, Pa., 1980—84, U.S. Dist. Ct. (ea. dist.) Pa., Phila., 1984—87, U.S. Ct. Appeals (3d cir.), 1987—, chief judge, 2003—. Chmn. Pa. Sentencing Commn. 1980—85; bd. dir. William Penn Found.; trustee Temple Univ. (chmn, exec. com.); chmn. com. on rules of practice & procedure, Jud. Conf. of US; prof. Penn State U. Sch. of Law, 2004—. Scholar Fulbright scholar, Ctrl. U., Caracas, Venezuela, 1966. Mem.: ABA, Am. Law Inst., Montgomery Bar Assn., Pa. Bar Assn. Roman Catholic. Office: 22614 US Courthouse Independence Mall W Philadelphia PA 19106-1715*

**SCISM, DANIEL REED,** lawyer; b. Evansville, Ind., Aug. 27, 1936; s. Daniel William and Ardath Josephine (Gibbs) S.; m. Paula Anne Sedgwick, June 21, 1958; children: Darby Claire, Joshua Reed. BA, DePauw U., 1958; JD, Ind. U., 1965. Bar: Ind. 1965, U.S. Dist. Ct. 1965, U.S. Ct. Appeals (7th cir.) 1967, U.S. Supreme Ct. 1976. Reporter Dayton (Ohio) Jour.-Herald, 1958-59; editor Mead Johnson & Co., Evansville, 1961; first assoc., then ptnr. Roberts, Ryder, Rogers & Scism and predecessor firms, Indpls., 1965—86; ptnr. Barnes & Thornburg, Indpls., 1987—2002, of counsel, 2003—. Cons. Ind. Pers. Assn., 1984-2002. Treas. Marion County chpt. Myasthenia Gravis Found., Indpls., 1970; v.p. Marion County Mental Health Assn., Indpls., 1970-71; pres. The Suemma Coleman Agy., Indpls., 1973-74; bd. dir. Humanities Coun., 1995-2000, chmn. bd., 1997-98; trustee Indpls. Mus. Art, 2001—; bd. dirs. Westminster Village North, Inc., 2003—; pres. Persimmon Woods Homeowners Assn., 2001-03, sec. 2003-. With U.S. Army, 1959—62. Edwards fellow Ind. U., 1964. Mem. ABA, Ind. Bar Assn., Indpls. Bar Assn., Woodland Country Club (bd. dirs. 1984-88, sec. 1998-99). Methodist. Home: 10909 300 Yard Dr Fishers IN 46037-9306 Office: Barnes & Thornburg 11 S Meridian St Indianapolis IN 46204-3535

**SCITOVSKY, ANNE AICKELIN,** economist, researcher; b. Ludwigshafen, Germany, Apr. 17, 1915; arrived in U.S., 1931, naturalized, 1938; d. Hans W. and Gertrude Margarete Aickelin; 1 child, Catherine Margaret. Student, Smith Coll., 1933—35; BA, Barnard Coll., 1937; postgrad., London Sch. Econs., 1937—39; MA in Econs., Columbia U., 1941. Mem. staff legis. reference svc. Libr. of Congress, 1941—44; mem. staff Social Security Bd., 1944—46; with Palo Alto (Calif.) Med. Found./Rsch. Inst., 1963—, chief health econs. div., 1973—94, sr. staff scientist, 1994—. Lectr. Inst. Health Policy Studies, U. Calif., San Francisco, 1975—94; mem. Inst. Medicine of NAS, Nat. Acad. Social Ins., Pres.'s Commn. for Study of Ethical Problems in Medicine and Biomed. and Behavioral Rsch., 1992, U.S. Nat. Com. on Vital and Health Statistics, 1975—78, Health Resources and Svcs. Adminstrn., AIDS adv. com., 1990—94; cons. HHS, Inst. Medicine Coun. on Health Care Tech. Assessment, 1986—90. Home: 161 Erica Way Portola Valley CA 94028-7439 Office: Palo Alto Med Found Rsch Inst Ames Bldg 795 El Camino Real Palo Alto CA 94301-2302 Personal E-mail: ascitovsky@aol.com.

**SCIVALLY, BART MURNANE,** accountant, auditor; b. Oklahoma City, Mar. 13, 1944; s. Louis Frensley and Mary Helen (Boadway) S.; divorced; children: Amy D., Robyn M., Louis Francis. BS in Bus. Adminstrn., U. Ark., 1969. CPA Ark. Auditor Div. of Legis. Audit, Little Rock, 1968-73, audit supr., 1974—. Named Acct. of Yr. U. Ark., 2000. Mem.: AICPA, Assn. Govt. Accts. (cert. govt. fin. mgr. 1995). Roman Catholic. Office: Div of Legis Audit 172 State Capitol Little Rock AR 72201-1033 E-mail: bscivally@lapo.state.ar.us.

**SCLAFANI, ANTHONY PAUL,** plastic surgeon, educator, biomedical researcher; b. Bklyn., Oct. 3, 1963; BA, Columbia U., 1985; MD, U. Pa., 1989. Diplomate Am. Bd. Otolaryngology, Am. Bd. Facial Plastic and Reconstructive Surgery. Intern in gen. surgery Beth Israel Med. Ctr., N.Y.C., NY, 1989-91; from resident in otolaryngology, head and neck surgery to prof. N.Y. Eye and Ear Infirmary, N.Y.C., 1991—2004, prof., 2004—, dir. facial plastic surgery, 1996—; fellow in facial plastic and reconstructive surgery St. Louis U. Sch. Medicine, 1995-96; pvt. practice N.Y.C., 1996—, Chappaqua, NY, 1998—. Editor-in-chief Facial Plastic Surgery; assoc. editor Facial Plastics Clinics N.Am.; contbr. articles to profl. jours. Fellow ACS, Am. Acad. Facial Plastic and Reconstructive Surgery (Sir Harold Delf Gillies award 1996, Ira Tresley Rsch. award 2002, 04); mem. Am. Acad. Otolaryngology and Head and Neck Surgery, Am. Soc. for Laser Medicine and Surgery. Office: NY EE Infirm/Facial Pl Surg Dept Otolaryng/Head Neck 310 E 14th St 6th Fl New York NY 10003-4201 also: 59 S Greeley Ave Chappaqua NY 10514-3321 also: 1430 2d Ave Ste 110 New York NY 10021 Office Phone: 914-238-5500. Personal E-mail: docs@nyface.com.

**SCLAFANI, CHARLES CARLO,** language educator, department chairman; b. Sciacca, Italy, Apr. 13, 1941; arrived in US, 1954; s. Leonardo and Leonarda Sclafani; m. Emilia Sclafani, June 11, 1967; children: Dina, Sandra. BA, CCNY, 1964; MA, Rutgers U., New Brunswick, NJ, 1971. Prof. Italian and Spanish Westchester C.C., Valhalla, NY, 1971—, dir. lang. lab., 1975—99, chair dept. modern langs., 1999—. Office: Westchester CC 75 Grasslands Rd Valhalla NY 10595 Office Phone: 914-606-6794. Business E-Mail: carlos.sclafani@sunywcc.edu.

**SCLAFANI, JOSEPH L.,** diversified financial services company executive; Exec. v.p., contr. J.P. Morgan Chase & Co. Office: JP Morgan Chase & Co 270 Park Ave New York NY 10017-2070*

**SCLAFANI, SUSAN K.,** educational consultant, former federal agency administrator; b. Albany, NY, Sept. 22, 1944; AB in German and Math., Vassar Coll., 1966; MA in German Lang. and Lit., U. Chgo., 1967; ME in Ednl. Adminstrn., U. Tex., Austin, 1985, PhD, 1987. Cert. Tchr.Math. Ill., N.Y., Lifetime Tchr. Math. and German 6-12 Tex., Adminstr., Supt., Supr., Midmgr. Tex. Tchr. Ctrl. YMCA H.S., Chgo., 1971—72, Woodson Jr. H.S. Houston Ind. Sch. Dist., Tex., 1972—74, H.S. for Engring. Professions, Houston Ind. Sch. Dist., Tex., 1975—78; coord. magnet sch. Washington H.S. Houston Ind. Sch. Dist., 1978—83; ctrl. office coord. instrnl. tech. Houston Ind. Sch. Dist., Tex., 1983—84, exec. dir. curriculum devel., 1987—89, asst. supt. constrn. mgmt. and program planning, 1989—92, assoc. supt. dist. adminstrn., 1992—94, chief of staff, 1994—96, chief of staff ednl. svcs., 1996—2001; counselor to sec. US Dept. Edn., Washington, 2001—06, acting sec., vocational & adult edn., 2003—04, asst. sec., vocational & adult edn., 2004—06; mng. dir. Chartwell Education Group LLC, NYC, 2006—. V.p. and gen. mgr. Quantum Access, Inc., 1986—87; adj. prof. dept. curriculum and instrn. U. Houston, Tex., 1988—94, adj prof. dept. ednl. leadership, 1999—2001; presenter to numerous ednl. groups. Co-author (with R. Paige): (Book) Strategies for Reforming Houston's Schools; School Choice or Best Systems, What Improves Education, 2001; contbr. articles to profl. jours. Vol. Star of Hope Women and Family Shelter, Houston, 1988—90; mem. com. Tex. Alliance for Minorities in Engring., Houston, 1975—85; activity vol., conf. spkr. Coun. for Exceptional Children, Houston, 1989—91; com. mem. Tex. Task Force for the Homeless, 1990—92; mem. Hispanic Youth Leadership Forum Steering Com., Houston, 1990—, Pub. Policy, Comty. and Agy. Support, Success by Six Coms., United Way, Houston, 1997—2001; chair Children's Policy Com. United Way, Houston, 1987—2001. Office: Chartwell Education Group LLC Empre State Bldg Ste 7506 New York NY 10118 E-Mail: sclafani@chartwelleducation.com.*

**SCLAVOS, STRATTON,** information technology executive; BS in Elec. and Computer Engring., U. Calif., Davis. Various exec. positions Megatest Corp., 1982—87; various exec. and sr. mgmt. positions MIPS Computer Systems, 1987—92; v.p. worldwide sales and bus. devel. GO Corp., 1992—93; v.p. worldwide mktg. and sales Taligent, Inc., 1994—95; chmn., CEO VeriSign, 1995—. Bd. dirs. Juniper Networks, Intuit, Keynote Systems, Marimba, Inc.; mem. Nat. Security Telecomm. Adv. Com. (NSTAC). Named Entrepreneur Yr., Silicon Valley Bus. Jour., 1998, No. Calif. Ernst & Young, 2002; named to Top 50 CEO's List, Forbes, 2001; recipient Leadership award Global Commerce, Morgan Stanley, 2001, Excellence award Online Encryption, Info. Security Mag., 2001, Editor's Choice award Managed PKI Svc., Network Computing, 2001. Achievements include the formation of the Sclavos Family Found. with wife Jody to support charitable efforts in children's edn. and med. rsch. Mailing: Investor Rels Dept 487 E Middlefield Rd Mountain View CA 94043*

**SCOBEY, DAVID W., JR.,** telecommunications industry executive; b. Nashville; BSEE, Auburn U.; postgrad., Harvard U. With Bellsouth Advt. and Pub. - The Real Yellow Pages, Bellsouth Telecomm.; pres. long distance Bellsouth Corp., pres. small bus. svcs., Atlanta, 2001—. Mem. indsl. adv. bd. Auburn U. Sch. Elec. Engring.; mem. pres. coun. Harvard U.; mem. bd. elders North Atlanta Ch. Christ.

**SCOBLE, ROBERT,** podcast network company executive, blog writer; b. Jan. 18, 1965; m. Maryam Ghaemmaghami; 1 child from previous marriage, Patrick. Degree in Journalism, San Jose State U. Sch. Journalism and Mass Comm., 1993. Dir. mktg. UserLand Software; sales support mgr. NEC Mobile Solutions; technical evangelist Microsoft Corp., 2002—06; v.p. media develop. PodTech.net (PodTech.Network, Inc.), Menlo Park, Calif., 2006—. Author: Naked Conversations: How Blogs are Changing the Way Businesses Talk with Customers, 2006; blog writer Scobleizer.wordpress.com. Office: PodTechNetwork Inc 2735 Sand Hill Rd Menlo Park CA 94025 Office Phone: 950-292-2500.*

**SCOBLIC, J. PETER,** magazine editor; b. NYC, July 29, 1974; s. Joseph Michael and Barbara Scoblic. BA, Brown U., 1997. Editor-in-chief Brown Jour. World Affairs, Providence, 1994-96; rsch. dir. Hedrick Smith Prodns., Bethesda, Md., 1998-99; editor Arms Control Today, Washington, 1999—2003; mng. editor The New Republic, Washington, 2003—04, exec. editor, 2004—. Office: The New Republic 1331 H St NW Ste 700 Washington DC 20005

**SCODARI, JOSEPH C.,** health products executive; Bd. dirs. Centocor, 1997—, pres., COO; pres. Centocor Johnson & Johnson, 1999—2001, co. grp. chmn. North Am. pharm. bus., mem. pharms. grp. oper. com., 2001, co. grp. chmn. biopharmaceutical businesses, 2003—05, worldwide chmn. Pharms. Grp., mem. exec. com., 2005—. Office: Johnson & Johnson 1 Johnson & Johnson Plz New Brunswick NJ 08933*

**SCOFIDIO, RICARDO,** artist, educator, architect; Ptnr. Diller & Scofidio (now Diller Scofidio & Renfro), NYC, 1979—; prof. arch. The Cooper Union for the Advancement of Sci. and Art, NY. Works include Blur Bldg. (Progressive Architecture Design award), media pavillion for Swiss EXPO 2002, design viewing platform for Ground Zero, NYC, Brasserie Restaurant, NY (James Beard Found. award for Best New Restaurant Design), Slither, Gifu, Japan, Loophole, Mus. Contemporary Art, Chgo., 1992, Apparatus Drawing, Mus. of Modern Art, NY, 1993, Case #00-17164, New Mus., 1993, Dysfunction, Ctr. d'Art Contemporaion de Castres, France, 1993, Desiring Eye, I'dentity and Difference, Triennale, Milan, 1994, Pelts, Thaddeus Ropac Gallery, Paris, France, 1997, Non-Place, San Francisco Mus. Modern Art, 1997, Slow House, At the End of the Century: One Hundred Years of Architecture, Mus. Contemporary Art, LA, 1998, The American Lawn: Surface of Everyday Life, Canadian Centre for Architecture, Montreal, 1998, Public Faces/Private Places, Pusan Internat. Arts Festival, Korea, 1998, His/Her Bathroom, Thomas Healy Gallery, NY, 1998, Dress Code, Landesmuseum, Linz, Austria, 1998, (permanent collections) Travelogues, Internat. Arrivals Terminal 4, JFK Airport, NY, (installation) The Desiring Eye: Reviewing the Slow House, Gallery MA, Tokyo, 1992, Master/Slave, Fondation Cartier, Paris, InterClone Hotel, Ataturk Airport for Istanbul Biennial, 1997, (dance collaborations with the Lyon Ballet Opera of France and Charlerol/Danses of Belgium (touring exhbn.) EJM1: Man Walking at Ordinary Speed and EJM2:Inertia, 1998, (web project) Refresh, Dia Art Found., (video installation) Pageant, Johannesburg Biennial & Rotterdam Film Festival, 1997, (permanent installation) X,Y, Kobe, Japan, 1997, (multi-media work for stage in collaboration with Builders Assn.) Jet Lag, 1998 (Obie award for Creative Achievement), (pub. art commn., permanent video marques) Jump Cuts, United Artists Cineplex, San Jose, Calif., (collaborative dance work with Charlerol/Danses) Moving Target, (collaborative theater work with Dumb Type and Hotel Pro Forma) Business Class, Copenhagen Cultural Capital, (interactive video installation) Indigestion, Barbican Art Gallery, London, Walter Phillips Gallery, Banff, Canada, Biennial Nagoya, Japan, 1997, (electronic project) Subtopia, ICC Gallery, Tokyo, 1997, and several others, (installations commissioned by) Mus. of Modern Art, Whitney Mus., New Mus. of Contemporary Art, Walker Art Ctr., Minn., Cartier Found., Palais des Beaux-Arts Brussels, and Gallery Ma Tokyo, (works are in permanent collections of) Mus. of Modern Art, Mus. of Modern Art San Francisco, Fond Nat. d' Art Contemporian, several FRACs in France, Musee de la Mode in Paris, and many private collections, co-pub. with Elizabeth Diller Back to the Front: Tourisms of War, FRAC Basse-Normandie, 1994, Flesh: Architectural Probes, Princeton Architectural Press,

1995, Blur: The Making of Nothing, Abrams, 2002. Recipient Chrysler award for Innovation in Design, 1988—89, MacArthur Found. award, 1999, Brunner prize in Arch., AAAL, 2003, McDermott award for Creative Achievement, MIT; fellow, N.Y. Found. Arts, 1998—99, Graham Found. Fellowship, 1998—99, Chgo. Inst. for Architecture and Urbanism Fellowship. Office: Diller Scofidio & Renfro 36 Cooper Sq New York NY 10003-7971 Address: The Cooper Union for the Advancement Dept Arch Cooper Sq New York NY 10003-7120 Office Phone: 212-260-7971.

**SCOFIELD, DAVID WILLSON,** lawyer; b. Hartford, Conn., Oct. 17, 1957; s. Leslie Willson and Daphne Winifred (York) S. AB, Cornell U., 1979; JD, U. Utah, 1983. Bar: Utah 1983, U.S. Dist. Ct. Utah 1983, U.S. Dist. Ct. Ariz. 1993, U.S. Dist. Ct. Hawaii 1995, U.S. Ct. Appeals (10th cir.) 1990, U.S. Ct. Appeals (9th cir.) 1995, U.S. Supreme Ct. 1996, U.S. Ct. Claims 1997. Assoc. Parsons & Crowther, Salt Lake City, 1983-87, Callister, Duncan & Nebeker, Salt Lake City, 1987-89, ptnr., 1989-92; founding ptnr. Parsons, Kinghorn, Peters, Salt Lake City, 1992—2004, pres., 1996-97; founding ptnr. Peters Scofield Price, Salt Lake City, 2004—. Mem. adv. com. on Utah rules of civil procedure Utah Supreme Ct., 2002—, mem. adv. com. on professionalism, 2003—. Author: Trial Handbook for Utah Lawyers, 1994; mem. Utah Law Rev., 1981-83; contbr. articles to legal jours. Bd. dirs. Westminster Coll. Found., 1994-96, chmn. cultivation com., 1995-96. Named to Outstanding Young Men of Am., 1986. Mem. ABA, Assn. Trial Lawyers Am., Utah Trial Lawyers Assn., Salt Lake County Bar Assn., Zeta Psi. Congregationalist. Avocations: american history, writing, sports. Home: 2331 Scenic Dr Salt Lake City UT 84109-1432 Office: Peters Scofield Price 111 East Broadway Ste 340 Salt Lake City UT 84111-5225 Office Phone: 801-322-2002 102. E-mail: dws@psplawyers.com.

**SCOFIELD, GORDON LLOYD,** mechanical engineer, educator; b. Huron, S.D., Sept. 29, 1925; s. Perry Lee and Zella (Reese) S.; m. Nancy Lou Cooney, Dec. 27, 1947; children: Cathy Lynn, Terrence Lee. B.M.E., Purdue U., 1946; M.M.E., U. Mo., Rolla, 1949; PhD in M.E, U. Okla., 1968. Instr. mech. engring. S.D. State Coll., Brookings, 1946-47; successively grad. asst., instr., asst. prof., asso. prof., prof. U. Mo., Rolla, 1947-69; prof., head mech. engring.-engring. mechs. dept. Mich. Technol. U., Houghton, 1969—80; disting. prof. mech. engring. S.D. Sch. Mines and Tech., Rapid City, 1981-88, asst. v.p. for acad. affairs, 1981-83, v.p., dean engring., 1984-86; pres. S.D. Sch. Mines and Tech. Found., 1982-90. Cons. U.S. Naval Ordnance Test Sta., China Lake, Calif., 1956-71; bd. dirs. Accreditation Bd. for Engring. and Tech., 1994-2000; cons. to industry. Served with USNR, 1943-46. NSF sci. faculty fellow, 1966-67; recipient alumni achievement award U. Mo., Rolla, 1975 Mem. ASME, Soc. Automotive Engrs. (pres. 1977, Excellence in Engring. Edn. award, 1999), Am. Soc. Engring. Edn., Sigma Xi, Tau Beta Pi, Pi Tau Sigma, Phi Kappa Phi. Home: PO Box 1085 Rapid City SD 57709-1085 *Satisfaction comes from sharing achievements. By acknowledging and sharing the importance of others in our success it is possible to accomplish more that is worth remembering.*

**SCOFIELD, LOUIS M., JR.,** lawyer; b. Brownsville, Tex., Jan. 14, 1952; s. Louis M. and Betsy Lee (Aiken) S.; children: Christopher, Nicholas, Emma. BS in Geology with highest honors and high distinction, U. Mich., 1974; JD with honors, U. Tex., 1977. Bar: Tex. 1977, US Dist. Ct. (ea. and so. dists.) Tex., US Ct. Appeals (5th cir.) 1981, US Supreme Ct. 1984. Ptnr. Mehaffy/Weber, Beaumont, Tex., 1982—. Spkr. CNA Ins., Dallas, Jefferson County Ins. Adjusters, S.E. Tex. Ind. Ins. Agts., Gulf Ins. Co., Dallas, Employers Casualty Co., Beaumont, Tex. Employment Commn., Jefferson County Young Lawyers Assn., Jefferson County Bar Assn., South Tex. Coll. of Law, John Gray Inst., Lamar U., 1991, Tex. Assn. Def. Counsel, 1991; cert. arbitrator Nat. Panel of Consumer Arbitrators; presenter Forest Park HS, Martin Elem. Sch., St. Anne's Sch. Contbr. columns in newspapers, articles to profl. jours. Patron Beaumont Heritage Soc., John J. French Mus.; bd. dirs. Beaumont Heritage Soc., 1983-84, endowment fund com., 1988; chmn. lawyers divsn. United Appeals Campaign, 1984; grand patron Jr. League of Beaumont, 1989-90 Recipient Tex. Super Lawyer, Tex. Monthly Mag., 2005. Fellow: Tex. Bar Found. (life); mem.: ABA, Jefferson County Bar Assn. (disaster relief project 1979, outstanding young lawyer's com. 1980, dir. 2005), Def. Rsch. Inst., Tex. Assn. Defense Counsel (dir. at large 1986—87, v.p. 1987—89, program chmn. San Diego 1989, adminstrv. v.p. 1989—90), Assn. Defense Trial Attys. (chmn. Tex. membership com. 1999—, exec. coun. 1999—2002, conv. host 2005), State Bar of Tex. (mentors com. 1995), Beaumont County Country Club, Phi Beta Kappa. Democrat. Episcopalian. Avocations: golf, reading, fishing. Home: 4790 Littlefield St Beaumont TX 77706-7748 Office: Mehaffy & Weber PO Box 16 Beaumont TX 77704-0016 Office Phone: 409-835-5011.

**SCOFIELD, VIRGINIA LEE,** research scientist; b. Lincoln, Nebr., May 14, 1948; d. Louis Morris and Betsy Aiken Scofield; m. Michael Edward Barish, Nov. 23, 1984 (div. May 15, 2000); m. Jeffrey Andrew Elliott, Aug. 22, 1971 (div. May 15, 1980). BA, U. Tex., Austin, 1970, PhD, 1977. Asst. prof. UCLA Sch. Medicine, LA, 1984—89; rsch. assoc. prof. U. Calif., 1995—2000; scientist M.D. Anderson Cancer Ctr. Sci. Pk., Smithville, Tex., 2000—. Vis. prof. dept. biology Pomona/Claremont Colls., Calif., 1995—97. Mem. editl. bd.: Biol. Bull., 1984—88; contbr. articles to profl. jours. Fellow, U. Tex., Genetics Found., 1972—77, Stanford U. Sch. Medicine, Calif., 1977—83, NIH, 1978—81; grantee, 1987—90, US CDC, 1987—90, NSF Task Force AIDS, 1985—90, Am. Cancer Soc., 1987—90. Mem.: Am. Soc. Cell Biology, Am. Assn. Immunologists, Sigma Xi, Phi Kappa Phi, Angel Flight (sec. 1969—70), Alpha Phi (pledge class pres. 1967—68). Liberal. Episcopalian. Achievements include patents for sperm as immunogen carriers. Home: 303 Quail Run Smithville TX 78957 Office: MD Anderson Cancer Science Park 1808 Park Road 1-C PO Box 389 Smithville TX 78957 Office Phone: 512-237-9344. Home Fax: 512-237-2444; Office Fax: 512-237-2444. Business E-Mail: vscofield@mdanderson.org.

**SCOGGIN, BLAINARD ELMO,** religious educator; b. Harris, N.C., Oct. 17, 1915; ls. Johnnie E. and Julia Pearl (McEntyre) S.; m. Hannah Belle Pearlman, Jan. 30, 1941; 1 child, Scarlett. BA, Furman U., Greenville, S.C., 1942; ThM, So. Bapt. Sem., Louisville, 1945, ThD, 1954. Minister Bapt. Ch., Owensboro, Ky., 1943-48, Canal Point, Fla., 1948-49; Bapt. rep. Jerusalem Bapt. Community, Israel, 1949-54; prof. Hebrew and O.T. Southeastern Bapt. Theol. Sem., Wake Forest, N.C., 1955-84; prof. emeritus Heberew and O.T., 1984—. Announcer WCPE. Author: Commentary on Micah-Broadman Commentary Vol. 7, Historical Geography of Holy Land, Broadman Commentary Vol. 1; contbr. articles to profl. jours. Chmn. Friends of Raleigh Wake, 1974, N.C. Coun. on Holocaust, 1980-90; trustee Am. Schs. Oriental Rsch., Phila., 1979. Named Disting. Alumnus, Gardner Webb U., 1964, Outstanding Alumnus award, 1978. Mem. Rotary (pres. 1971). Avocations: flying, fishing, gardening, golf. Home: 2230 Lash Ave Raleigh NC 27607-3137 E-mail: scoggin88@earthlink.net.

**SCOGIN, MACK,** architect, educator; BArch, Ga. Inst. Tech., Atlanta, 1966. Registered Ga., Mass., Tex., NY, Conn., cert. NCARB. Sr. design architect Heery & Heery Architects and Engrs., Inc., 1967—81, v.p., coord., 1978—81, pres, COO, dir. design, 1981—84; prin. Scogin Elam and Bray Architects, Inc., Atlanta, 1984—2000, Mack Scogin Merrill Elam Architects, Inc., Atlanta, 2000—. Vis. critic Rice Univ., Houston, 1984, Ga. Inst. Tech., Atlanta, 1987—89, Harvard Univ. Grad. Sch. Design, 1989, chmn. dept. arch., 1990—95, Kajima adj. prof. arch., 1990—; Herbert Baumer disting. vis. prof., prof. of arch. Ohio State Univ., 2003—04. Prin. works include Buckhead Branch Libr., Atlanta (Ga. AIA award of excellence, 1990, Urban Design Commn. award of excellence, 1990, Nat. AIA/ALA award of excellence, 1991, Nat. AIA award of excellence, 1993), Clark Atlanta Univ. Art Galleries (Architectural Record Interiors award, 1996, Atlanta Urban Design Commn. award of excellence, 2000), Lee B. Philmon Branch Libr. (Ga. AIA Design award of excellence, 1999, Nat. AIA/ALA award of excellence, 2003, So. Atlantic Region AIA honor award, 2003). Mem.: NAD (assoc. fellow), Arch. Soc., Atlanta (founding mem., mem. bd. sponsors

1983—88), AIA (nat. com. on design, chmn. steering com. 1987). Office: Mack Scogin Merrill Elam Architects Inc 111 JW Dobbs Ave NE Atlanta GA 30303 Office Phone: 404-525-6869. Office Fax: 404-525-7061.

**SCOGLAND, WILLIAM LEE,** lawyer; b. Moline, Ill., 1949; s. Maurice William and Harriet Rebecca S.; m. Victoria Lynn, 1976; 1 child, Thomas. BA magna cum laude, Augustana Coll., 1971; JD cum laude, Harvard U., 1975. Bar: Ill. 1975, U.S. Dist. Ct. (no. dist.) Ill. 1975. Assoc. Wildman, Harrold, Allen & Dixon, Chgo., 1975-77, Hughes Hubbard & Reed, Milw., 1977-81; from assoc. to ptnr. Jenner & Block, Chgo., 1981—. Lectr. in law U. Chgo. Law Sch., 2000—; bd. dirs. Am. Benefits Coun., 2004—; adv. coun. employee welfare and pension benefits U.S. Dept. Labor, Phila., 2006—. Author: Fiduciary Duty: What Does It Mean?, 1989; co-author Employee Benefits Law, 1987; contr. Tort and Ins. Law Jour., 1989, and others. Fellow: Am. Coll. Employee Benefits Counsel; mem.: Omicron Delta Kappa, Phi Beta Kappa. Republican. Office: Jenner & Block LLP 330 N Wabash Chicago IL 60611 Office Phone: 312-923-2878. Business E-Mail: wscogland@jenner.com.

**SCOGNAMIGLIO PASINI, CARLO,** economics and finance professor, senator; b. Varese, Italy, Nov. 27, 1944; s. Luigi and esther (Pasini) S.; m. Cecilia Pirelli, May 28, 1980; children: Filippo, Elisabetta Thea. D.Econs., U. Bocconi, Milan, Italy, 1968; spl. student, London Sch. Econs., 1970-71. Asst. prof. U. Bocconi, 1968-73, prof., 1973-79, U. Rome-Luiss, 1979—, dean and rector, 1984—. Senator Constituency of Milan, 1992—, pres. of senate, acting pres. of Republic, 1994-96, defense minister, 1998-99; pres. Corriere della Sera, 1983, Aspens Inst. Italia, 1995—. Author: The Stock Exchange, 1973, Industrial Crises, 1976, Industrial Economics, 1987, Theory of Finance, 1987, The Liberal Project, 1996. Winner prize for econs. French Acad., 1988. Avocations: golf, sailing, skiing. Office: Senato della Repubblica 00100 Rome Italy Office Fax: 3906 67063825. E-mail: c.scognamiglipasini@senato.it.

**SCOLES, CLYDE SHELDON,** library director; b. Columbus, Ohio, Apr. 14, 1949; s. Edward L. and Edna M. (Ruddock) S.; m. Diane Francis, July 14, 1976; children: David, Kevin, Karen, Stephen. BS, Ohio State U., 1971; MLS, U. Mich., 1972. Librarian Columbus Pub. Library, 1972-74; library dir. Zanesville Pub. Library, Ohio, 1974-78; asst. dir. Toledo-Lucas County Pub. Library, 1978-85, dir., 1985—. Adj. lectr., libr. bldg. cons. U. Mich.; v.p. bd. dirs. Read for Literacy. Mem. ALA, Ohio Libr. Assn., Ohio Libr. Coun., Toledo C. of C., Com. of 100, Maumee Hist. Soc. Clubs: Torch (Toledo). Lodges: Rotary. Office: Toledo-Lucas County Pub Libr 325 Michigan St Toledo OH 43624-1628 Office Phone: 419-259-5207.*

**SCOLES, EUGENE FRANCIS,** lawyer, educator; b. Shelby, Iowa, June 12, 1921; s. Sam and Nola E. (Leslie) S.; m. R. Helen Glawson, Sept. 6, 1942; children— Kathleen Elizabeth, Janene Helen. AB, U. Iowa, Iowa City, 1943, JD, 1945; LLM, Harvard U., Cambridge, Mass., 1949; JSD, Columbia U., N.Y.C., 1955. Bar: Iowa 1945, Ill. 1946. Assoc. Seyfarth-Shaw & Fairweather, Chgo., 1945-46; asst. prof. law Northeastern U., 1946-48, assoc. prof., 1948-49, U. Fla., 1949-51, prof., 1951-56, U. Ill., Champaign, 1956-68, Max Rowe prof. law, 1982-89, prof. emeritus, 1989—; vis. prof. McGeorge Law Sch. U. Pacific, Sacramento, 1989-92; prof. U. Oreg., 1968-82, dean Sch. Law, 1968-74, disting. prof. emeritus, 1982—. Vis. prof. Khartoum U., Sudan, 1964-65. Author: (with H.F. Goodrich) Conflict of Laws, 4th edit., 1964, (with R.J. Weintraub) Cases and Materials on Conflict of Laws, 2d edit., 1972, (with E.C. Halbach, Jr., P.G. Roberts, H.D. Begleiter) Problems and Materials on Decedents' Estates and Trusts, 7th edit., 2006, Problems and Materials on Future Interests, 1977, (with P. Hay, P.J. Borchers, S.C. Symeonides) Conflict of Laws, 4th edit., 2004; contbr. articles to profl. jours.; notes and legislation editor Iowa Law Rev., 1945; reporter Uniform Probate Code Project, 1966-70; mem. joint editorial bd. Uniform Probate Code, 1972— Mem. ABA, Soc. Pub. Tchrs. Law, Am. Law Inst., Ill. Bar Assn., Assn. Am. Law Schs. (pres. 1978), Order of Coif Office: U Oreg Sch Law 1515 Agate St Eugene OR 97403-1221 Office Phone: 541-346-3862.

**SCOLLARD, PATRICK JOHN,** hospital executive; b. Chgo., Apr. 20, 1937; s. Patrick J. and Kathleen (Cooney) S.; m. Gloria Ann Carroll, July 1, 1961; children: Kevin, Maureen, Daniel, Thomas, Brian. BS in Econs., Marquette U., 1959; grad. sr. exec. program, MIT, 1976. With Equitable Life Assurance Soc. U.S., N.Y.C., 1962-79, asst. v.p., 1969-71, v.p., personnel dir., 1971-75, v.p. corp. adminstrv. svcs., 1975-79; v.p. Chem. Bank, N.Y.C. 1979-80, exec. v.p., 1980-87, chief adminstrv. officer, 1987-92; pres., CEO St. Francis Hosp., Roslyn, NY, 1992-99; pres. Scollard Assocs. LLC, Garden City, NY, 1999—; pres., CEO Cath. Health Svcs. of L.I., Melville, NY, 2003—04, also bd. dirs. Bd. dirs. Curaspan, Inc. Bd. dirs. Cath. Health Svcs. L.I., North Fork C.C. Office: Scollard Assocs LLP 1461 Franklin Ave Garden City NY 11530-1648 Office Phone: 516-739-5107.

**SCOMMEGNA, ANTONIO,** obstetrician, gynecologist, educator; b. Barletta, Italy, Aug. 26, 1931; came to U.S., 1954, naturalized, 1960; s. Francesco Paola and Antonietta (Maresca) S.; m. Lillian F. Sinkiewicz, May 3, 1958; children: Paola, Frank, Roger. BA, State Lyceum A. Casardi, Barletta, 1947; MD, U. Bari, Italy, 1953. Diplomate: Am. Bd. Obstetrics and Gynecology, also sub-bd. endocrinology and reprodn. Rotating intern New Eng. Hosp., Boston, 1954-55; resident obstetrics and gynecology Michael Reese Hosp. and Med. Center, Chgo., 1956-59, fellow dept. research human reprodn., 1960-61, research asso., 1961; fellow steroid tng. program Worcester Found. Exptl. Biology, also Clark U., Shrewsbury, Mass., 1964-65; asso. prof. obstetrics and gynecology Chgo. Med. Sch., 1965-69; mem. staff Michael Reese Hosp. and Med. Center, 1961—, attending physician obstetrics and gynecology, 1961—, dir. sect. gynecologic endocrinology, 1965-81; dir. ambulatory care obstetrics and gynecology Mandel Clinic, 1968-69, chmn. dept., 1969-89; attending, chief svc. U. Ill. Chgo. Hosp. and Med. Ctr. 1989-98; trustee Mandel Clinic, 1977-80; prof. dept. ob-gyn. Pritzker Sch. Medicine, U. Chgo., 1969-89; prof., head dept. ob-gyn. Coll. Medicine, U. Ill. Chgo., 1989-98, prof. emeritus, 1999—. Author numerous articles in field. Fulbright fellow, 1954-55 Fellow Am. Coll. Obstetricans and Gynecologists, Endocrine Soc., Chgo. Inst. Medicine, Am. Gynecol. and Obstet. Soc.; mem. AMA, Ill., Chgo. med. socs., Am. Fertility Soc., Chgo. Gynecol. Soc. (sec. 1976-79, pres. 1981-82), Soc. Study Reprodn., AAAS, Soc. for Gynecologic Investigation. Home: 1023 W Vernon Park Pl Apt E Chicago IL 60607-3447 Office Phone: 312-996-0222. Business E-Mail: anmis@uic.edu.

**SCOPPETTA, NICHOLAS,** fire commissioner; b. NYC; married; 2 children. BS, Bradley U., 1958; JD, Bklyn. Law Sch., 1962. Investigator Soc. Prevention of Cruelty to Children; asst. dist. atty. New York County; assoc. counsel Knapp Commn.; asst. U.S. atty. So. Dist. NY; commr. Adminstrn. for Children's Svcs., NYC; fire commr. NYC Fire Dept., 2001—. Past pres., former chmn. bd. trustees Children's Aid Soc.*

**SCORSESE, MARTIN,** film director; b. Flushing, N.Y., Nov. 17, 1942; s. Charles and Catherine (Cappa) S.; m. Laraine Marie Brennan, May 15, 1965 (div.), 1 daughter: Catherine Terese Glinora Sophia; m. Julia Cameron, 1975 (div.), 1 daughter: Domenica Elizabeth; m. Isabella Rosellini, Sept. 29, 1979 (div. 1983); m. Barbara DeFina, Feb. 9, 1985 (div.); m. Helen Morris, 1999; 1 child, Francesca Kingsland Scorsese. BS in Film Communications, NYU, 1964, MA in Film Communications, 1966, Doctorate (hon.), Princeton U., Wesleyan U., Bard Coll., Williams Coll., Royal Coll. Art. Faculty asst., then instr. film NYU, N.Y.C., 1963-70. Dir. (films) Who's That Knocking at My Door?, 1968, (also writer, assoc. prodr., actor) Boxcar Bertha, 1972 (also actor), Mean Streets, 1973 (also co-writer, actor), Alice Doesn't Live Here Anymore, 1975, Taxi Driver, 1976 (also actor) (Palme d'Or Cannes Internat. Film Festival), New York, New York, 1977, The Last Waltz, 1978, Raging Bull, 1980, The King of Comedy, 1983, After Hours, 1985, The Color of Money, 1986, The Last Temptation of Christ, 1988, New York Stories (Life Lessons segment), 1989, Goodfellas, 1990 (also co-writer), Cape Fear, 1991, The Age of Innocence, 1993 (also co-writer), Casino, 1995 (also writer), Kundun, 1997, Bringing Out the Dead, 1999, The Gangs of New York, 2002, The Aviator, 2004 (also exec. prodr.), The Departed, 2006 (also prodr.); prodr.

(films) The Grifters, 1990, Mad Dog and Glory, 1993; (exec. prodr.): Naked in New York, 1994, Clockers, 1995, Grace of My Heart, 1996, You Can Count On Me; documentaries include: (editor) Woodstock, 1970 (also asst. dir.), Elvis on Tour, 1973; (assoc. prodr.): Medicine Ball Caravan, 1971; (dir.): The Big Shave, 1968 (also writer), Street Scenes 1970, 1970, Italianamerican, 1974, American Boy: A Profile of Steven Price, 1979, Made in Milan, 1990; dir., prodr. (documentary) No Direction Home: Bob Dylan (Banff Rockie award, 2006), 2005; co-dir. A Personal Journey with Martin Scorsese Through American Movies, 1997, Il Mio Viaggio in Italia, 1999, The Blues, 2002; other film appearances include: Cannonball, 1976, Pavlova: A Woman for All Seasons, 1983, 'Round Midnight, 1986, Akira Kurosawa's Dreams, 1990, Guilty by Suspicion, 1991, Quiz Show, 1994, Search and Destroy, 1995 (also prodr.), The Muse, 1999, (TV films) La Memoire Retrouvee, 1996, (exec. prodr.) Kicked in the Head, 1997, The Hi-Lo Country, 1998. Decorated Legion of Honor (France); recipient Edward L. Kingsley Found. award, 1963-64, 1st prize Screen Prodrs. Guild, 1965, Best Dir. Cannes Film Festival, 1986. Am. Cinematheque award, 1991, Britannia award Brit. Acad. Film and TV Arts, 1993, Golden Lion award Venice Film Festival, 1995, Wexner prize Wexner Ctr. for the Arts, Columbus, Ohio, 1996, Life Achievement award Am. Film Inst., 1997, Lifetime Career award Lincoln Ctr. Film Soc., 1998, Ray of Light award Dalai Lama, 1998, Golden Globe, 2003, Evelyn F. Burkey award Writers Guild Am. East, 2003, Lifetime Achievement award Dirs. Guild Am., 2003, Ellis Island Family Heritage award, 2004, Grammy award for No Direction Home: Bob Dylan, 2006. Fellow: Am. Acad. Arts and Sciences; mem.: AAAL (hon.).

**SCORZELLI, JAMES FRANCIS,** counseling psychology educator; b. Detroit, June 19, 1943; s. Joseph Ernest and Loretta Barbara (Wolynski) S.; m. Mary Margaret Reinke, Nov. 27, 1970; children: Christopher, Miriam, Caroline, Jonathan. BS, Mich. State U., 1965, MA, 1967; PhD, U. Wis., 1973. Lic. psychologist, Mass.; cert. rehab. counselor. Counselor for deaf Mich. Assn. for Better Hearing, East Lansing, 1965-66; vocat. evaluator, counselor Nev. Rehab. Svcs., Las Vegas, 1967-68; program coord. Ighamn County Jail Rehab. Program, Mason, Mich., 1969-70; rsch. assoc. U. Wis., Madison, 1972-73; prof. dept. counseling psychology, rehab. and spl. edn. Northeastern U., Boston, 1973—. Cons. psychologist, Newton, 1976—. Author: Drug Abuse: Prevention and Rehabilitation in Malaysia, 1987; contbr. articles to profl. jours. Sgt. U.S. Army, 1968-69. Fulbright scholar Coun. Internat. Exch. of Scholars, Malaysia, 1984-85, India, 1993, Thailand, 1998; WHO fellow, Malaysia, 1987, 90. Mem. AACD (ad hoc editor 1990—), AAAS, APA, Am. Rehab. Counselors Assn. (newsletter editor, rsch. award 1974), Nat. Rehab. Assn., Nat. Rehab. Counseling Assn., Mass. Psychol. Assn., Fulbright Alumni Assn. Lutheran. Avocation: running. Home: 19 Adella Ave Newton MA 02465-1901 Office: Northeastern U 207 Lake Hall Boston MA 02115 Office Phone: 617-373-5919. E-mail: j.scorzelli@neu.edu.

**SCOTCHMER, SUZANNE ANDERSEN,** economics professor; b. Seattle, Jan. 23, 1950; d. Toivo Matthias and Margaret (Sangder) Andersen. BA in Econ., U. Wash., 1970; MA in Stats., U. Calif., Berkeley, 1979, PhD in Econ., 1980. From asst. to assoc. prof. econ. Harvard U., Cambridge, Mass., 1981-86; prof. econ. and pub. policy U. Calif., Berkeley, 1986—. Vis. prof. Toronto Sch. Law, 1993, Tel Aviv U., 1994, U. Paris, Sonbonne, 1992, New Sch. of Econ., Moscow, 1993, U. Aukland, 2002; prin. investigator NSF, 1986-2002; lectr. in law. Mem. editl. bd. Am. Econ. Rev., 1991-95, Jour. Pub. Econ., 1986-2001, Jour. Econ. Perspectives, 1994-97, Regional Sci. and Urban Econ., 1991—, Jour. Econ. Lit., 1998—; contbr. articles to profl. jours. Hoover Nat. fellow Stanford U., 1989, Olin fellow Yale Sch. Law, 1993, Sloan fellow, 1979, Phi Beta Kappa fellow, 1978; France/Berkeley Fund grantee, 1994-95. Office: Univ Calif 2607 Hearst Ave Berkeley CA 94720-7320 Business E-mail: scotch@socrates.berkeley.edu.

**SCOTT, A. TIMOTHY,** lawyer; b. Natchez, Miss., Feb. 16, 1952; s. John William and Patricia (O'Reilly) S.; m. Nancy E. Howard, June 7, 1976; children: Kevin Howard, Brian Howard. BA in Psychology, Stanford U., 1974, JD, 1977. Bar: Calif. 1977, U.S. Tax Ct. 1978. Assoc. then ptnr. Agnew, Miller & Carlson, L.A., 1977-83; assoc. Greenberg, Glusker, Fields, Claman & Machtinger, L.A., 1983; ptnr. Sachs & Phelps, L.A., 1983-91; mem. Heller, Ehrman White & McAuliffe, L.A., 1991-96, of counsel, 1996-99; sr. v.p., tax counsel Pub. Storage, Inc., Glendale, Calif., 1996—. Speaker in field. Note editor Stanford Law Rev., 1976-77; contbr. article to profl. publs., chpt. to book. Mem. ABA, L.A. County Bar Assn. (chmn. real estate taxation com. 1988-91, exec. com., taxation sect. 1989-91), Order of Coif. Democrat. Avocations: volleyball, gardening, art, skiing. Office: Pub Storage Inc 701 Western Ave Glendale CA 91201-2349 E-mail: tscott@publicstorage.com.

**SCOTT, ADAM,** professional golfer; b. Adelaide, Australia, June 7, 1980; Amateur tour golfer, 1996—2000; profl. golfer PGA Tour, 2001—. Achievements include 9 first place finishes, PGA Tour, 2001-; top ten World Ranking, 2006. Office: PGA 100 Ave of Champions West Palm Beach FL 33401-9601*

**SCOTT, ALASTAIR IAN,** chemistry professor; b. Glasgow, Scotland, Apr. 10, 1928; came to U.S., 1968; s. William and Nell (Newton) S.; m. Elizabeth Wilson Walters, Mar. 4, 1950; children: William Stewart, Ann Walker. BSc, Glasgow U., 1949, PhD, 1952, DSc, 1964; MA (hon.), Yale U., 1968; DSc (hon.), U. Coimbra, Portugal, 1990, U. Pierre & Marie Curie, Paris, 1992. Lectr. organic chemistry Glasgow U., 1957-62; prof. U. B.C., Vancouver, Canada, 1962-65. Sussex (Eng.) U., 1965-68, Yale U., 1968-77; disting. prof. Tex. A&M U., 1977-80; prof. dept. chemistry U. Edinburgh, Scotland, 1980-82; Davidson prof. sci. Tex. A&M U., 1982—2001, Welch & Barton chair in chemistry, 2002—. Cons. in field. Author: Interpretations of Ultraviolet Spectra of Natural Products, 1964; contbr. articles to profl. jours. Recipient Rsch. Achievement award, Am. Soc. Pharmacognosy, 1993, Robert A. Welch award in chemistry, 2000, Disting. Tex. Scientist of Yr. award, Tex. Acad. Sci., 2002. Fellow: Royal Soc, Edinburgh (Royal medal 2001), Royal Soc. (Hofmann lectr. 1996, Davy medal 2001); mem.: Tex. Acad. Sci. (Tex. Scientist of Yr. 2002), Japan Pharm. Soc. (hon.), Chem. Soc. (Corday-Morgan medal 1964, Centenary lectr. 1994, Tetrahedron prize for creativity in organic chemistry 1995, Natural Products Rsch. award 1996), Am. Chem. Soc. (Ernest Guenther award 1976, A.C. Cope scholar 1992, Nakanishi prize 2003). Office: Tex A&M U Dept Chemistry College Station TX 77843-0001 Office Phone: 979-845-3243. Business E-mail: scott@mail.chem.tamu.edu.

**SCOTT, ANNA MARIE PORTER WALL,** sociology educator; b. South Fulton, Tenn. d. Thomas Madison and Jevvie Roggie (Porter) P.; m. John T. Scott Sr. (dec.); 1 child, Harvey G. BA, MEd, MSW, U. Ill. Cert. tchr. and social worker, Ill. Caseworker Dept. Pub. Aid, Champaign, Ill.; psychiat. social worker Vets. Hosp., Danville, Ill.; prof. sociology Parkland Coll., Champaign, Ill. Head Dem. 21st Congl. Dist., 1974-78; del. Nominating Conv./Mini Conv., 1975, 76; commr. Ill. Banking Bd.; mem. AME Ch., Hadassah; mem. Vet. of Armed Svcs. Named Outstanding Black Alumni, U. Ill., Urbana. Mem. LWV, NAACP, Nat. Coun. Negro Women (past pres.), Am. Legion (past comdr. post 559, past commdr. Champaign County coun.), AMVETS, Champaign-Urbana Symphony Guild, Order Ea. Star (grand organist Eureka Grand chpt.). Avocations: piano, baking, gardening, politics, public speaking. Home: 309 W Michigan Ave Urbana IL 61801-4945 Office: Parkland Coll 2400 W Bradley Ave Champaign IL 61821-1806

**SCOTT, ANNE BYRD FIROR,** history professor; b. Montezuma, Ga., Apr. 24, 1921; d. John William and Mary Valentine (Moss) Firor; m. Andrew Mackay Scott, June 2, 1947; children: Rebecca, David MacKay, Donald MacKay. AB, U. Ga., 1941; MA, Northwestern U., 1944; PhD, Radcliffe Coll., 1958; LHD (hon.), Lindenwood Coll., 1968, Queens Coll., 1985, Northwestern U., 1989, Radcliffe Coll., 1990, U. of the South, 1990, Cornell Coll., 1991. Congressional rep., editor LWV of U.S., 1944-53; lectr. history Haverford Coll., 1957-58, U. N.C., Chapel Hill, 1959-60; asst. prof. history Duke U., Durham, N.C., 1961-67, assoc. prof., 1968-70, prof., 1971-80, W.K. Boyd prof., 1980-91, W.K. Boyd prof. emerita, 1992—, chmn. dept., 1981-85; Gastprofessor Universität, Bonn, Germany, 1992-93. Vis. prof. Johns Hopkins U., 1972-73, Stanford U., 1974, Harvard U., 1984, Cornell Coll., 1993, Williams Coll., 1994, U. Miss., 2000; Times-Mirror scholar

Huntington Libr., 1995; vice chmn. Nat. Humanities Ctr., 1991-98; mem. adv. com. Schlesinger Libr.; lectr. in field. Author: The Southern Lady, 1970, 25th anniversary edit., 1995, (with Andrew MacKay Scott) One Half the People, 1974, Making the Invisible Woman Visible, 1984, Natural Allies, 1991; editor: Jane Addams, Democracy and Social Ethics, 1964, The American woman, 1970, Women in American Life, 1970, Women and Men in American Life, 1976, Unheard Voices, 1993; mem. editl. bd. Revs. in Am. History, 1976-81, Am. Quar., 1974-78, Jour. So. History, 1978-84; contbr. articles to profl. jours. Chmn. Gov.'s Commn. on Status of Women, 1963-64; mem. Citizens Adv. Council on Status of Women U.S., 1964-68; trustee Carnegie Corp., 1977-85, W.W. Ctr. for Scholars, 1977-84; chmn. bd. dirs. Nat. Cmty. Investment Fund, 1996—2002. AAUW fellow, 1956-57; grantee NEH, 1967-68, 76-77, Nat. Humanities Ctr., 1980-81; grad. medal Radcliffe Coll., 1986, Duke U. medal, 1991, John Caldwell medal N.C. Humanities Coun., 1994; fellow Ctr. Advanced Study in Behavioral Sci., 1986-87; Fulbright scholar, 1984, 92-93. Fellow Am. Acad. Arts & Sci; mem. Am. Antiquarian Soc., Orgn. Am. Historians (exec. bd. 1973-76, pres. 1983, Disting. Pub. Svc. award 2002), So. Hist. Assn. (exec. bd. 1976-79, pres. 1989), Soc. Am. Historians, Phi Beta Kappa. Democrat. E-mail: ascott2@email.unc.edu, ascott@duke.edu.

**SCOTT, BERTRAM,** insurance company executive; Degree, DePaul U. Former claims ops. and acct. exec. Prudential Ins. Co., Chgo., v.p. mktg. and mng. care ops., 1989; pres., CEO Horizon Mercy, 1996; pres. TIAA-CREF Life Ins., N.Y.C. Mem. Robert Wood Johnson Pediat. Hosp. Project, State of N.J. Black Infant Mortality adv. com.; chmn. United Way, Essex and West Hudson, NJ, 2000. Mem.: Nat. Assn. Urban Based HMOs, Am. Heart Assn. Office: TIAA-CREF Life Ins 730 3rd Ave New York NY 10017

**SCOTT, BLACK,** investment company executive; B in Applied Math. and Econs., John Hopkins U., 1968; MBA, Harvard U. With William O'Neill Co., 1978—80; founder, pres. Delphi Mgmt., 1980—, portfolio mgr. Delphi Value Fund, 1980—. Recipient Corp. Goodwill award, Northwestern U. Ctr. for the Study Sport in Soc., 1996. Office: Delphi Mgmt Ste 540 50 Rowes Wharf Boston MA 02110

**SCOTT, BRIAN WALTER,** management consultant; b. Melbourne, Victoria, Australia, Apr. 23, 1935; s. Walter and Dorothy Ada (Ransom) S.; m. Dorothy Yvonne Allen, Aug. 15, 1959; children: David, Mark, Jennifer, Susan. B of Econs., Sydney (Australia) U., 1955; MBA, Stanford U., 1959; D of Bus. Adminstrn., Harvard U., 1963. Asst. prof. U. So. Calif., Los Angeles, 1961-62; cons. mgmt. W.D. Scott and Co. Pty. Ltd., Sydney, 1963-69, dir., 1969-74, mng. dir., 1974-79, chmn., 1979-85; dep. chmn. A.C.I. Internat. Ltd., Sydney, 1985-86, chmn., 1986-88; dir., mgmt. rev. Edn. Portfolio, New South Wales, 1988-90. Chmn. Mgmt. Frontiers Pty. Ltd., Sydney, 1985—, Found for Devel. Cooperation Ltd., Brisbane, 1990—; bd. dirs. James N. Kirby Found. Ltd. Chmn. Trade Devel. Coun., Canberra, 1984-90, chmn. Australian-Korean Found., 1992-2000; chmn. coun. Knox Grammar Sch., Sydney, 1981-89, Australia-Asean Bus. Coun., Canberra, 1980-82; mem. governing bd. Asian Inst. Mgmt., Manila, 1990—; co-chmn. Australia-Korea Forum, 1989-91. Named Officer, Order of Australia, 1985; recipient Australian Mfrs. Export Coun. award, 1989. Fellow Inst. Dirs. Australia (fed. pres. 1982-86), Internat. Acad. Mgmt., Australian Inst. Mgmt. Inst. Mgmt. Cons.; mem. Trade Policy Rsch. Ctr. (coun. mem. 1985-90), Sydney U. (senate 1990-95), Royal Sydney Yacht Squadron Club, Am. Club (Sydney). Avocations: reading, travel. Home: PO Box 829 Avalon Beach NSW 2109 Australia Office: Mgmt Frontiers Pty Ltd PO Box 494 North Sydney 2059 Australia Business E-Mail: brian.scott@mgtfrontiers.com.au. E-mail: brianwscott@aol.com.

**SCOTT, BYRON ALTON,** professional basketball coach, retired professional basketball player; b. Ogden, Utah, Mar. 28, 1961; m. Anita Scott; children: Thomas, Londen. Student, Ariz. State U., 1979-85. With L.A. Lakers, 1983-93, 96-97; shooting guard Indiana Pacers, Indpls., 1993-95, Vancouver Grizzlies, 1995-96; asst. coach Sacramento Kings, Sacramento, 1998-00; head coach New Jersey Nets, East Rutherford, 2000—04, New Orleans Hornets (now New Orleans/Okla. City Hornets), 2004—. Mem. NBA Championship Team, 1985, 87, 88. Office: New Orleans/Okla City Hornets Okla Tower Ste 1850 210 Park Ave Oklahoma City OK 73102*

**SCOTT, C. PAUL,** psychiatrist, educator; b. Pitts., June 2, 1943; m. Nancy Ipp, Aug. 17, 1969; children: Rebecca, John. AB, U. Pa., 1964; MD, Case Western Res. U., 1968; postgrad., Pitts. Psychoanalytic Inst., 1984. Diplomate Am. Bd. Psychiatry and Neurology. Intern Mt. Sinai Hosp., Cleve., 1968-69; resident in gen. medicine Univ. Hosp., Cleve., 1969-70; resident in psychiatry Western Psychiat. Inst., Pitts., 1972-75, pres. med. staff, 1985-87; v.p. med. staff U. Pitts. Med. Ctr., 1995-97, clin. prof. Nch. Medicine; clin. assoc. prof. psychiatry M.C.P. Hahnemann U. With USPHS, 1970-72. Disting. life fellow Am. Psychiat. Assn. (Falk lecture 1972-75); mem. Pa. Psychiat. Assn., Pitts. Psychiat. Assn., Am. Balint Soc. (pres.). Avocation: golf. Office: 401 Shady Ave Apt C202 Pittsburgh PA 15206-4800 Office Phone: 412-661-2354.

**SCOTT, CAMPBELL,** actor; b. NYC, July 19, 1961; s. George C. Scott and Colleen Dewhurst; m. Anne Scott, 1991; 1 child. BA, Lawrence U., 1983. Appearances include (theatre) The Queen and the Rebels, 1982, The Real Thing, 1984, Our Town, 1984, Hay Fever, 1985, A Man For All Seasons, 1986, Dalliance, 1986, Copperhead, 1987, Ah, Wilderness!, 1987-88, Long Day's Journey Into Night, 1987-88; (TV movies) The Kennedys of Massachusetts, 1990, The Perfect Tribute, 1991, Would You Kindly Direct Me to Hell?: The Infamous Dorothy Parker, 1994, The Love Letter, 1998, The Tale of Sweeney Todd, 1998; (TV miniseries) LIBERTY! The American Revolution, 1997; (films) Five Corners, 1987, From Hollywood to Deadwood, 1988, Longtime Companion, 1989, Ain't No Way Back, 1990, The Sheltering Sky, 1990, Dying Young, 1991, Dead Again, 1991, Singles, 1992, Mrs. Parker and the Vicious Circle, 1994, The Innocent, 1994, Let It Be Me, 1995, Big Night, 1996 (also dir., co-prodr.), The Daytrippers, 1996 (also exec. prodr.), The Spanish Prisoner, 1996, The Imposters, 1998, Hi-Life, 1998, Top of the Food Chain, 1999, Spring Forward, 1999, Lush, 1999, Other Voices, 2000, Delivering Milo, 2000, The Secret Lives of Dentists, 2002 (also prodr.), Marie and Bruce, 2004, Loverboy, 2004, Duma, 2005, The Exorcism of Emily Rose, 2005; (TV movies) Follow the Stars Home, 2001, The Pilot's Wife, 2002; actor, exec. prodr. (film) Roger Dodger, 2002; dir., prodr. (films) Off the Map, 2003; prodr. (films) The Dying Gaul, 2005. Address: Richard Parks Agy 138 E 16th St New York NY 10003*

**SCOTT, CARLA ANNE,** music educator, musician; b. Elmhurst, Ill., Feb. 6, 1951; d. William Frederick and Clara Lou Sommer; m. Kinney Duane Scott, Dec. 22, 1984; 1 child. Joelle Lynn Jewell. BA, Adams State Coll., Alamosa, Colo., 1973; Kodaly level 1, Colo. Coll., 1998; Kodaly Level 2, U. Colo. Boulder, 1999. Asst. libr., music instr. Lamar C.C., Colo., 1974—75; tchr. elem. band and gen. music Harrison Sch. Dist. 2, Colorado Springs, 1975—. Prin. oboist Pueblo Symphony Orch., Pikes Peak Philharm.; 2d oboe and English horn Chamber Orch., Colo. Springs; free lance musician, Colo. Springs, 2002—; mem. Pueblo Symphony Orch., Colo. Recipient 25 Yr. award, Colo. Music Educators Assn., 2004. Music Educators Assn.; 2004. Home: 3267 Teardrop Cir Colorado Springs CO 80917-3319 Office: Ivywild Elem Sch 1604 S Cascade Colorado Springs CO 80906 Office Phone: 719-328-4349. E-mail: casoboe@pcisys.net.

**SCOTT, CAROL SEELEY,** retired librarian, researcher; b. Phila., Aug. 10, 1921; d. Walter James and Emetta Susan (Weed) Seeley; m. Harley Augustus Scott, Jr., Feb. 2, 1943; children: Michael H., Elisabeth, Sally, David W., John S BA, Duke U., 1941; BS Libr. Sci., U. N.C., 1942; MA Tchg., Winthrop Coll., Rock Hill, S.C., 1967. Cert. in Libr. Sci. Libr. Pittsyvania County Pub. Libr., Chatham, Va., 1942—43; jr. profl. asst. D.C. Pub. Libr., Washington, 1943—44; libr. Winthrop Tng. Sch., Rock Hill, 1956—57, Rock Hill H.S., 1959—70, 1973—84, Castle Heights Jr. H.S., Rock Hill, 1970—73; part-time libr. Winthrop Coll. Libr., Rock Hill, 1984—85. Author: William Scott

1732-33 to 1800 of Cabarrus County, North Carolina and Some of His Descendants, 1987, The Rev. Samuel Suther 1722-1788 German Reformed Minister of the Two Carolinas and Some of His Descendants to the Fifth and Sixth Generations, 1993; contbr. articles to geneal. publs Pres. Guild of Mus. York County, S.C., 1988-89; vol. ARC Blood Svcs Mem. AAUW, AARP, DAR, S.C. Libr. Assn. (pres. 1966-70, v.p.), S.C. Assn. Sch. Librs. (bd. dirs., regional network 1980-81), Sierra Club, Phi Beta Kappa, Soc. Mayflower Descendants Democrat.

**SCOTT, CATHERINE DOROTHY,** librarian, library and information scientist, consultant; b. June 21, 1927; d. Leroy Stearns Scott and Agnes Frances (Meade) Scott Schellenberg. AB in English, Cath. U. Am., 1950, MS in Libr. Sci., 1955. Asst. libr. Export-Import Bank USA, Washington, 1951-55, Nat. Assn. Home Builders, 1955-62, reference libr., 1955-62; founder, chief tech. libr. Bellcomm, Inc., subs. AT&T, 1962-72; chief libr. Nat. Air, Space Mus. Smithsonian Instn., 1972-82, chief libr. Mus. Reference Ctr., 1982-88, sr. reference libr., 1989-95; info. cons., 1995—. Presdl. appointee, mem. Nat. Commn. Librs., Info. Sci., 1971—76; bd. visitors Cath. U. Am. Libr. Sci. Sch., Librs., 1984—93. Editor: International Handbook of Aerospace Awards and Trophies, 1980, 81; guest editor: Aeronautics and Space Flight Collections, 1985, in Spl. Collections, 1984. Vice chmn. DC Rep. Com., Washington, 1960—68; mem. platform com. Rep. Nat. Com., 1964; del. Rep. Nat. Conv., San Francisco, 1964; sec. Rep. Nat. Com., Washington, 1968; del. Rep. Nat. Conv., Miami, Fla., 1968. Named to Hon. Order Ky. Cols., 1968; recipient Sec.'s Disting. Svc. award Smithsonian Instn., 1976, Alumni Achievement award Cath. U. Am., 1977, Century Circle, 1998—, Disting. Fed. Svc. Nat. Commn. Libr. and Info. Sci. medal, 1985. Mem.: DC Libr. Assn. (cons. com. 1976—91, bd. dirs. 1987—90, award com. 1990—91, pres.-elect 1991—92, bd. dirs. 1991—94, immediate past pres. 1993—94, chpt. cons. com. 1994—98, conf. program facilitator 1998—2006), Am. Soc. Info. Sci, League Rep. Women DC (bd. dirs. 1995—97, nominating com. 1996—97, contbg. 1999—), Nat. Fedn. Rep. Women, Cath. U. Am. Devel. Com., Friends of Cath. U. Librs. (founder, pres. 1984—88, exec. coun. 1984—96, sustaining 1998—), Internat. Fedn. Libr. Assns. (del. 1976, 1983, 1985, 1988—89), Nat. Mus. Women in Arts, Am. Soc. Assn. Execs., Spl. Librs. Assn. (Washington chpt. pres. 1973—74, chair aerospace divsn. 1974—75, pres. 1992—93, past pres. 1993—94, chair assn. awards and honors 1994—95, convenor ret. caucus 1997—99, conf. planner 1996—2006, Hall of Fame 1996), Cath. U. Century Club, Spl. Librs. Assn. Legacy Club, Capital Yacht Club. Fax: 202-488-9223. Office Phone: 202-554-3928.

**SCOTT, CHARLES DAVID,** chemical engineer, consultant; b. Chaffee, Mo., Oct. 24, 1929; s. Charles Perry and Alma Gertrude (Kendall) S.; m. Alice Reba Bardill, Feb. 11, 1956; children: Timothy Charles, Mary Alice, Lisa Ann. BS in Chem. Engring., U. Mo., 1951; MS in Chem. Engring., U. Tenn., 1961, PhD, 1966. Registered profl. engr., Tenn. Devel. engr. Union Carbide Corp., Oak Ridge, 1953-57; rsch. engr. Oak Ridge Nat. Lab., 1957-73, sect. chief, 1973-76, assoc. divsn. dir., 1976-83, rsch. fellow, 1983-86, sr. rsch. fellow, 1987-94; dir. bioprocessing rsch. and devel. ctr., 1991-94; engirng. R&D cons. Oak Ridge, 1994—. Adj. prof. chem. engring. U. Tenn., Knoxville. Contbr. articles to profl. jours.; patentee in field. 1st lt. AUS, 1951-53. Recipient U.S. Dept. Energy E.O. Lawrence award, 1980, U. Tenn. Nathan W. Doughtery award, 1987, U. Mo. Honor award, 1988, David Perlman award Am. Chem. Soc., 1994; Union Carbide Corp. fellow 1983; Martin Marietta Sr. Corp. fellow, 1987. Mem. Am. Chem. Soc. (chmn. separation sci. subdivsn.), Am. Assn. Clin. Chemistry (chmn. com. advanced analytical concepts, nat. award 1980), Am. Inst. Chem. Engrs. (bd. dirs.), Nat. Acad. Engring., Sigma Xi, Alpha Chi Sigma. Lutheran. Personal E-mail: cdscott1@aol.com.

**SCOTT, CHARLES LEWIS,** retired photojournalist; b. Grayville, Ill., Aug. 18, 1924; s. Marvin Joseph and Prudence (Blood) S.; m. Jane Turner, Jan. 14, 1945 (dec. 1983); children— Lyntha Ann, Thomas Marvin; m. Martha McDonald, Aug. 23, 1986. BS in Journalism, U. Ill., 1948; MS, Ohio U., 1970. Photographer Champaign-Urbana (Ill.) Courier, 1946-50, chief photographer, 1953-56; photographer Ill. Natural History Survey, 1946-51, Binghamton (N.Y.) Press, 1951-53; asst. picture editor Milw. Jour., 1956-58; picture editor, 1958-66; graphics dir. Chgo. Daily News, 1966-69; instr. Sch. Journalism, Ohio U., Athens, 1969-70, asst. prof., 1971-72, asso. prof., 1972-74, 76-77, prof., 1977—; dir. Sch. Visual Communication, 1987-95, prof. emeritus visual comm., 1995; picture editor Chgo. Tribune, 1974-76; dir. photography Rocky Mountain News, Denver, 1987-88; ret., 1995. Served with U.S. Navy, 1942-45. Decorated D.F.C., Air medal (3); recipient numerous awards in regional and nat. news photo contests. Mem. Nat. Press Photographers Assn. (charter mem., Newspaper Photographer of Yr. 1963, Editor of Yr. 1966, Joseph Sprague Meml. award 1975, Robin F. Garland Educator award 1979), Soc. Profl. Journalists, Ohio News Photographers Assn. (Lifetime Achievement award 1995). Presbyterian. Home: 8559 Lavelle Rd Athens OH 45701-9190

**SCOTT, CHARNETA CLAUDETTA,** psychologist, educator; b. Jacksonville, Fla., May 3, 1963; d. Charles Alexander Scott and Venetia Lemar McLemoure. BS, U. of Fla. 1981—85; MA, Ea. N.Mex U., 1985—86; PhD, Howard U., 1992—2003. Lic. Professional Counselor D.C. Dept. of Health Health and Licensing, 2004. Clin. psychologist D.C. Dept. of Mental Health, 1996—; coord. of ct. services, therapist Francis and Associates, P.C., Washington, 2001—; adj. faculty Trinity U., Washington, 2000—. Assoc. dir. for conf. adminstrn. WBC Learning Conf., Washington, 2005—. Team mem. Capitol Area Crisis Response Team, Washington, 2004. Recipient Dedication to Work with Children, Francis and Associates, 2001, U. of Fla. Hall of Fame, 1984—85; Walter and Theodora Daniel Endowed Ednl. Rsch. Grant, Walter and Theodora Daniel Ednl. Rsch. Fund, 1998. Mem.: APA, Assn. for Play Therapy, Inc., The Am. Acad. of Experts in Traumatic Stress. D-Liberal. Roman Cath. Avocation: dance. Home: 520 U St NW Washington DC 20001 Office Phone: 202-409-7100. Personal E-mail: charneta@aol.com.

**SCOTT, CHERYL M.,** foundation administrator, healthcare educator; BA, U. Wash., 1975, MA in Health Adminstrn., 1977. Joined Group Health Coop., Seattle, 1979, regional v.p., exec. v.p., COO, pres., CEO, 1997—2004, pres. emerita, 2004—; COO Bill and Melinda Gates Found., Seattle, 2006—. Clin. assoc. prof. Dept. Health Svcs. U. Wash. Sch. Pub. Health and Cmty. Medicine, 2004—; past bd. mem. Am.'s Health Insurance Plans; past chair Alliance of Cmty. Health Plans and Healthcare Forum; bd. chair Health Tech. Ctr.; mem. Com. on Redesigning Health Insurance Benefits, Payment and Performance Improvement Programs Inst. Medicine. Past chair Alliance for Edn. U. Wash. Health Adminstrn. Program, chair External Adv. Com.; chair King County's Blue Ribbon Com. on Election Reform; trustee Wash. State Life Scis. Discovery Found. Office: Bill and Melinda Gates Found 1551 Eastlake Ave E Seattle WA 98101 Office Phone: 206-448-6755. Office Fax: 206-448-6464. E-mail: scott.cm@ghc.org.*

**SCOTT, D. DWIGHT,** corporate financial executive; BA, U. NC, Chapel Hill; MBA, U. Tex. Mng. dir. Donaldson, Lufkin and Jenrette; sr. v.p. fin. and planning El Paso Corp., Houston, 2002, exec. v.p., CFO, 2002—.

**SCOTT, DALE ALLAN,** major league umpire; b. Springfield, Oreg., Aug. 14, 1959; s. Jesse Lee and Betty Ann (Potts) S. AS, Lane C.C., 1979. Radio disc jockey Sta. KBDF, Eugene, Oreg., 1976-81; minor league umpire various orgns., 1981-85; umpire Am. League, 1986-99, Major League Baseball, 2000—. Instr. Golden State Umpire Camp, 1990—99; umpire All Star Game Am. League Baseball, 1993, 2001, umpire World Series, 1998, 2001, 04; crew chief Major League Baseball, 2001—. Mem.: World Umpires Assn. (bd. dirs. 2003—), Lane County Baseball Umpire Assn. (ofcl. 1975—81), Portland Football Ofcls. Assn. (ofcl. H.S. football 1989—96), Lane County Football Ofcls. Assn. (ofcl. 1976—88), Portland Basketball Assn. (86 1996), Lane County Basketball Ofcls. Assn. (ofcl. 1977—85). Democrat. Office: Office of Commr of Baseball 245 Park Ave New York NY 10167-0002

**SCOTT, DAVID ALBERT,** congressman; b. Aynor, SC, June 27, 1945; s. Albert and Mamie (Polite) S.; m. Alfredia Aaron, Oct. 26, 1969; children: Dayna Dorienda, Marcye Michelle. BA, Fla. A&M U., 1967; MBA, U. Pa., 1969. Pres., owner Dayn-Mark Advt., Atlanta; mem. Ga. Ho. of Reps., Atlanta, 1975-82, Ga. Senate, Atlanta, 1983—2002, chmn. edn. com., 1993, chmn. rules com., 1994—2002; mem. US Congress from 13th Ga. dist., 2003—; mem. Agriculture com., Fin. Svcs. Com. Chmn. Atlanta Fulton Senate Del., 1992-94. Creator, prodr., dir. (film) Langston! (4 Emmy awards, best cultural affairs program award NATAS, spl. recognition Congl. Black Caucus, Bronze Jubilee award), (nat. radio program) Inside Black America (spl. cmty. svc. award Mayor of Chgo., James Weldon Johnson journalism award NAACP, spl. citation City of Highland Park, Mich., spl. broadcasting cmty. svc. award Detroit City Coun., spl. tribute Mich. Ho. of Reps.). Mem. exec. bd. dirs. U. Pa. Wharton Sch. Recipient Silver Microphone award, 1986, 1992, 1993, 1994, Amy awards, 1993, Gov.'s award for excellence in edn., Telly award 1994; named one of Most Influential Black Americans, Ebony mag., 2006. Mem. Ga. Bus. Coun., Ga. C of C. (bd. dirs.), Nat. Assn. Black Elected Ofcls., Black Caucus, NAACP, Alpha Phi Alpha. Democrat. Baptist. Avocations: reading, writing, movies, theater. Office: US Ho Reps 417 Cannon Ho Office Bldg Washington DC 20515-1013 Office Phone: 202-225-2939. Office Fax: 202-225-2939.*

**SCOTT, DAVID CLINTON,** research scientist; b. Brighton, Colo., Sept. 5, 1960; s. Robert Glenn and Janice Elizabeth (Smith) S.; m. Dana Jungschaffer, Aug. 7, 1988; children: Clinton P., Alexander J., Eric O. BA, U. Colo., 1986; PhD, U. So. Calif., 1993. R & D chemist ICI, Hawthorn, Calif., 1987-88; rsch. asst. chemistry dept. U. So. Calif., L.A., 1988-93; rsch. scientist Jet Propulsion Lab, Pasadena, Calif., 1993-2000; sr. mem. tech. staff Atmospheric Scis., Pasadena, Calif., 2000—. Contbr. articles to profl. jours. Mem. AAAS, Am. Geophys. Union, Am. Chem. Soc., Applied Optics, Phi Beta Kappa. Avocations: mountain biking, running, swimming, skiing, hiking. Office: Jet Propulsion Lab M/S 183-401 4800 Oak Grove Dr Pasadena CA 91109

**SCOTT, DAVID J.,** lawyer; Bachelor, St. Lawrence U.; JD, Cornell Law Sch. Sr. v.p., gen. counsel, sec. Amgen Inc., Thousand Oaks, Calif., 2004—, Medtronic Inc. Office: Amgen Inc One Amgen Ctr Dr Thousand Oaks CA 91320-1799

**SCOTT, DAVID WARREN,** statistics educator; b. Oak Park, Ill., July 16, 1950; s. John V. and Nancy (Mellers) S.; m. Jean Charlotte Madera, June 15, 1974; children: Hilary Kathryn, Elizabeth Alison, Warren Robert. BA, Rice U., 1972, MA, PhD, Rice U., 1976. Asst. prof. Baylor Coll. Medicine, Houston, 1976—79, Rice U., Houston, 1979—80, assoc. prof., 1980—85, chmn. stats. dept., 1990—93, Noah Harding prof. stats., 2001—; vis. prof. Stanford U., Palo Alto, Calif., 1985—86. Vis. prof. Dept. Def., Ft. Meade, Md., 1993-94, 99-2000. Author: Multivariate Density Estimation, 1992; mem. editl. bd. John Wiley & Sons Probability and Stats. Series, 1994—; past editor jour. Computational Stats. and Jour. Statis. Scis.; editor Jour. Computational and Graphical Stats., 2000-03; contbr. articles to profl. jours. Applied and theoretical stats. com. Nat. Rsch. Coun., 2001-2005 Grantee NASA, 1982-84, Office Naval Rsch., 1985-93, 2005—, NSF, 1993—; Wilks award U.S. Army, 2004 Fellow Internat. Stats. Inst., Inst. Math. Stats., Am. Statis. Assn. (assoc. editor jour. 1983-94); mem. Inst. Math. Statis. (cons.). Avocations: woodworking, hiking. Home: 4143 Marlowe St Houston TX 77005-1953 Office Phone: 713-348-6037.

**SCOTT, DAVID WINFIELD,** artist, museum administrator; b. Fall River, Mass., July 10, 1916; s. Benjamin David and Edith May (Romig) S.; m. Tirsa Lilia Saavedra, July 10, 1947 (dec. Jan. 1986); children: Tirsa Margaret, Edith Elizabeth; m. Doris Jean Fitch White, Aug. 19, 1988. AB, Harvard Coll., 1938; MA, Claremont Grad. Sch., 1940, MFA, 1951; PhD, U. Calif., Berkeley, 1960; DFA, Corcoran Sch. Art, 1991. Instr. art Riverside (Calif.) Jr. Coll., 1940-41; from lectr. to prof. Scripps Coll., Claremont, Calif., 1947-63; dir. Nat. Collection Fine Art, Washington, 1964-69; planning officer Nat. Gallery Art, Washington, 1969-84; acting dir. Corcoran Gallery Art, Washington, 1990; artist, cons. pvt. practice, Whitehaven, Md., 1991—. Cons. in field. Capt. USAF, 1945. Home: 11403 Costakes Dr Austin TX 78750-2517 E-mail: scotfree@intercom.net, scottfreeaustin@sbcglobal.net.

**SCOTT, DEBORAH ELIZABETH,** school system administrator, poet; b. Middletown, Conn., July 6, 1969; d. Donald William Troxler, Sr. and Celeste Elizabeth Troxler (Jennings by later remarriage); m. Ashley Van Scott, May 13, 1967; children: Brittney Elizabeth, Ashley Celeste, Destiney Monae'. Cert. Completion Adminstrn. and Typing, Marine Corps Svc. Support Sch., Camp Lejeune, N.C., 1988; cert. Tng., Basic Mil. Police Sch., Ft. Jackson, S.C., 1995. Adminstrv. clk. USMC, Camp Lejeune, 1988—89; adminstrv. asst. Mayor's Office City Hall, Baker, La., 1991—92; officer mil. police U.S. Army N.G., Sacramento, 1994—97; adminstr. O Happy Day Christian Acad., Yuba City, Calif., 1996—97, Learning Light Acad., Lompoc, Calif., 1998—2002, Victorville, Calif., 2003—. Spl. guest poet/spkr. Buena Vista Elem. Sch., Lompoc, 2001—02; bd. dirs. Learning Light Acad. Author: Debbie ES Poetry Journals, 2002, Debbie ES Poetry, 2005, numerous poems. Mem. /hostess First Assembly of God, Victorville, 2003—05. Lance cpl. USMC, 1988—89. Mem.: Spring Valley Lake Country Club. Democrat. Avocations: poetry, sketch art, swimming, camping. Office: Learning Light Acad 8370 S V L Box Victorville CA 92392-5168

**SCOTT, DEBORAH EMONT,** curator; b. Passaic, N.J. d. Harold and Rhoda (Baumgarten) Emont; m. George Andrew Scott, June 4, 1983; children: Meredith Suzanne, Diana Faith. BA, Rutgers U., 1973, Livingston Coll.; MA, Oberlin Coll., 1979. Asst. curator Allen Meml. Art Mus., Oberlin, Ohio, 1977-79; curator collections Memphis Brooks Mus. Art, 1979-83; curator The Nelson-Atkins Mus. Art, Kansas City, 1983—, chief curator, 1998—. Project dir. Kansas City Sculpture Pk., 1986-01. Author: (catalogue) Alan Shields, 1983, (essay) Jonathan Borofsky, 1988, (essay) Judith Shea, 1989, (interview) John Ahearn, 1990, (essay) Gerhard Richter, 1990, (essay) Kathy Muehlemann, 1991, (essay) Nate Fors, 1991, (essay) Julian Schnabel, 1991, (essay) Louise Bourgeois, 1994, (essay) Joel Shapiro, 1995, (essay) Lewis deSoto, 1996, (catalogue) Ursula von Rydingsvard, 1997; contbr.: Celebrating Moore: Works from the Collection of the Henry Moore Foundation, Selected by David Mitchinson, 1998, Modern Sculpture at The Nelson-Atkins Museum of Art: An Anniversary Celebration, 1999, (CD ROM) Masterworks for Learning: A College Collection Catalogue, Allen Memorial Art Museum, Oberlin College, 1998. Office: Nelson-Atkins Mus Art 4525 Oak St Kansas City MO 64111-1873

**SCOTT, DONALD ALLISON,** retired lawyer; b. Phila., Oct. 7, 1929; s. Garfield and Grace Louise (Nevin) S.; m. Jeanne Marie Cooper, June 25, 1955; children: Allison Cooper, Andrew Garfield, John Wallace, Lindsay Nevin. AB, Princeton U., 1951; JD, Harvard U., 1956. Bar: Pa. 1958. Law clk. Judge Learned Hand, U.S. Ct. Appeals, 2d Circuit, 1956-57; assoc. Morgan, Lewis & Bockius, LLP, Phila., 1957-64, ptnr., 1964-98, counsel, 1998—. Served with USNR, 1951-53. Mem. ABA, Am. Law Inst., Merion Cricket Club, Paupack Hills Golf Club, Sunnybrook Golf Club. Presbyterian. Home: 714 W Mt Airy Ave Philadelphia PA 19119-3326

**SCOTT, DONALD LAVERN,** city manager, former army officer; b. Hunnewell, Mo., Feb. 8, 1938; s. William Edward and Amanda Beatrice (Dant) S.; m. Betty Jean Forte, Mar. 3, 1962; children: Jeffrey Jerome, Merriell Edward Lavern. BA in Graphic Arts, Lincoln U., 1960; MA in Counseling and Human Devel., Troy State U., 1982. Commd. 2d lt. U.S. Army, 1960, advanced through grades to brig. gen., 1991; bn. comdr. 3d Bn., 47th Inf. Div., Ft. Lewis, Wash., 1978-80; prof. mil. sci. Tuskegee (Ala.) U., 1980-81; dep. insp. gen. U.S. Army Europe, Heidelberg, Fed. Republic Germany, 1982-83; comdr. Hohenfels (Germany) Tng. Ctr., 1983-85; insp. gen. VII U.S. Corps, Stuttgart, Fed. Republic Germany, 1985-86; asst. div. comdr. 1st Cav. Div., Ft. Hood, Tex., 1986-88; chief of staff 2d U.S. Army, Ft. Gillem, Ga., 1988-91; ret. U.S. Army, 1991; chief of staff City of Atlanta,

1991, COO, 1991—; dir., founder AmeriCorps Nat. Civilian Cmty. Corps, 1993—96; mem. Five Star Coun., Vets. History Project, 1996—. Bd. dirs. Atlanta Conv. and Bus. Bur., 1991—; advisor Jimmy Carter's Atlanta Project, 1992; mem. 100 Blackmen, Atlanta, 1992; dep. Libr. of Congress, 1996—; mem. Leg. Br. Coun. Chief Adminstrn. Officers, 1996-. Decorated D.S.M., Legion of Merit, Bronze Star (6), Meritorious Svc. medal. Mem. Assn. U.S. Army, Atlanta C. of C., Kappa Alpha Psi (reporter 1980-82). Avocations: golf, reading, jogging. Office: City of Atlanta Office of Mayor 55 Trinity Ave SW Atlanta GA 30303-3520 Home: 1515 Jefferson Davis Hwy Apt 1510 Arlington VA 22202-3317 Office Phone: 202-707-5215. E-mail: dscott@loc.gov.

**SCOTT, DONALD MICHAEL,** writer, educator; b. L.A., Sept. 26, 1943; s. Bernard Hendry and Margherita (Baroni) Scott, Barbara (Lannin) Scott (Stepmother); m. Patricia Ilene Pancoast, Oct. 24, 1964 (div. June 1971); children: William Bernard, Kenneth George. BA, San Francisco State U., 1965, MA, 1986. Cert. tchr. Calif. Tchr. Mercy H.S., San Francisco, 1968-71; pk. ranger Calif. State Pk. Sys., Half Moon Bay, 1968-77; tchr. adult divsn. Jefferson Union HS Dist., Daly City, Calif., 1973-87; dir. NASA-NPS Project Wider Focus, Daly City, 1983-90, also bd. dirs., dir. Geo.S. Spl. Projects, San Francisco, 1990—; nat. pk. ranger, naturalist Grant-Kohrs Ranch Nat. Hist. Site, Deer Lodge, Mont., 1987-88; nat. pk. ranger pub. affairs fire team Yellowstone Nat. Pk., 1988. Rsch. subject NASA, Mountain View, Calif., 1986—90; guest artist Yosemite (Calif.) Nat. Pk., 1986; nat. pk. ranger Golden Gate Nat. Recreation Area Nat. Pk. Svc., San Francisco, 1986, nat. pk. svc. history cons. to Bay Dist., 1988—94; adj. asst. prof. Skyline Coll., 1989—94, Coll. San Mateo, 1992—94; aerospace edn. specialist NASA/OSU/AESP, 1994—2004; state rep. Mont. and Nev. AESP, 1999—2003; cons. Friends Eastern State Penitentiary Project, Phila., 1993. Author: The Man Who Named the Wind, 2003, From Montana to Mars, 2003, From GeoS to Mars, 2004; contbr. articles and photographs to profl. jours., mags., chapters to books. Panelist Cmty. Bds. San Francisco, 1978—87; active CONTACT Orgn., 1991—, bd. dirs., 1995—; mem. edn. working group Case for Mars VI, Boulder, 1996; hon. bd. dirs. T-Rex Discovery Ctr, Canada, 2006—; pres Youth for Kennedy, Lafayette, Calif., 1960; city chair Yes on A Com., So. San Francisco, San Mateo County, Calif., 1986. Mem.: Friends George R. Stewart, Wider Focus, Yosemite Assn. (life). Avocations: photography, hiking, camping, travel. Home and Office: PO Box 978 Oceano CA 93475 Personal E-mail: dscott943@sbcglobal.net.

**SCOTT, DOROTHY,** writer; b. Rochester, Pa., July 21, 1951; d. Mildred Boettner and James Frantz; m. Thomas C.H. Scott, June 10, 1978; children: Margaret, T.A. Malcolm. BA, U. Pitts., 1973. Asst. editor Learning Rsch. & Develop. Ctr., U. Pitts., 1973—79; manuscript editor Eye Rsch. Inst. Retina Found., Boston, 1979—81; freelance med. copy editor Pitts., 1981—86; project mgr., editor Physicians World, Secaucus, NJ, 1987—88; mng. editor Health Learning Sys., Lyndhurst, NJ, 1988—89; med. editor Discovery Internat., Deerfield, Ill., 1990—91, dir. editl. svcs., 1991—95, sr. mng. med. editor, 1995—2001; sr. med. writer CPE Comm., Chgo., 2001—03; med. writer Med. Media Comm., Rosemont, Ill., 2002—04, Sg2, LLC, Skokie, 2004—. Mem.: Am. Med. Writers Assn. Episcopalian. Avocations: bead work, singing. Office Phone: 847-779-5393. E-mail: dorothy.scott@comcast.net.

**SCOTT, DOUGLAS EDWARD,** lawyer; b. Evanston, Ill., Jan. 20, 1957; BA magna cum laude, U. Ill., 1979, MBA, 1981; JD, UCLA, 1984. Bar: Calif., 1984; U.S. Dist. Ct. (cen. dist.) Calif.; CPA, Ill. Assoc. O'Melveny & Myers, 1984-87; sr. v.p., gen. counsel, asst. sec. Sci. Applications Internat. Corp., San Diego, Calif., 1987—. James scholar. Mem. ABA, State Bar of Calif. (sr. v.p., gen. counsel and asst. sec.), Phi Beta Kappa. Office: Sci Applications Internat Corp Mail Stop F 3 10260 Campus Point Dr San Diego CA 92121

**SCOTT, EARLINE,** school system administrator; b. Gary, Ind., May 25, 1953; d. Eddie and Ethel Mae Holman; m. Angelo Byron Scott, Mar. 26, 1976; children: Angelo Byron Jr., Tiffany Latrese, Quincy Dwayne. EdD, Loyola U., Chgo., 2005. Asst. supt. Country Club Hills (Ill.) Sch. Dist., 2003—. Treas. St. Philip Luth. Ch. Gary, 1991—2001. Named Adminstr. of the Yr., J/P Associates, Inc., 2001. Mem.: ASCD (assoc. Exemplary Leadership in Sch. Improvement award South Suburban chpt. 1997, 2001), Nat. Staff Devel. Coun. (assoc.). Achievements include research in leadership and student achievement, study of high performing, high poverty and high minority schools. Office: Country Club Hills Sch Dist 160 4411 West 185th St Country Club Hills IL 60478 Office Phone: 708-957-6200. Personal E-mail: escott58@yahoo.com.

**SCOTT, EDWARD WILLIAM, JR.,** computer company executive; b. Panama City, Panama, May 25, 1938; s. Edward William and Janice Gertrude (Grimison) S.; m. Cheryl S. Gilliland, apr. 23, 1988; children: Edward William, Heather Yolanda Deirdre, Reece Donald; 1 stepson, Erik Veit. BA, Mich. State U., 1959, MA, 1963; BA, Oxford U., Eng., 1962. Personnel specialist Panama Canal Co., 1962-64, staff asst. to dir. personnel, 1964-66; personnel officer IRS, Detroit, 1966-68; staff personnel mgmt. specialist U.S. Dept. Justice, Washington, 1968-69, chief personnel systems and evaluation sect., 1970-72, dir. Office Mgmt. Programs, 1972-74, assoc. dep. commr. planning and evaluation U.S. Immigration and Naturalization Svc., 1974-75, dep. asst. atty. gen., 1972-75, asst. sec. for adminstrn. Trans. Dept., 1977-80; pres. Office Power, Inc., Washington, 1980-81; dir. mktg. Computer Consoles, Inc., 1981-84; v.p. mktg. Dest Systems, 1984-85; dir. govt. mktg. Sun Microsystems, Mountain View, Calif., 1985-88; exec. v.p. Pyramid Tech., Mountain View, 1988-95; founder, pres. BEA Sys., Inc., San Jose, Calif., 1995—. Founder, chmn. Ctr. for Global Devel., Washington, (with Bill Gates and George Soros) Data-Debt, AIDS, and Trade-Africa; founder, chmn. Friends of the Global Fight, Wash.; founder, pres. escottVentures, Inc.; pres. U.S. Dept. Justice Fed. Credit Union, 1970-73. Recipient Presdl. Mgmt. Improvement certificate, 1971; Spl. Commendation award Dept. Justice, 1973; also Spl. Achievement award, 1976; William A. Jump Meml. award, 1974; presdl. sr. exec. service rank of Disting. Exec., 1980; Mich. State U. scholar, 1957-60. Mem.: Phi Kappa Phi, Phi Eta Sigma. Office: BEA Sys Inc 2315 N 1st St San Jose CA 95131-1010 Business E-Mail: ed@escottventures.com.

**SCOTT, ELIZABETH S.,** law educator; b. Washington, 1945; BA, Coll. William and Mary, 1967; JD, U. Va., 1977. Bar: Va. 1977. Atty. Michie, Hamlett, Donato & Lowry, Charlottesville, Va., 1977—78; legal dir. Forensic Psychiatry Clinic of Inst. Law, Psychiatry, and Pub. Policy U. Va., 1979—87, Univ. prof., 1992—; Robert T. Taylor rsch. prof., 1997—2001, Joseph C. Carter, Jr. rsch. prof., 2003—; now Class of 1962 prof. law, also founder & co-dir. Ctr. for Children, Families and the Law. Vis. prof. Columbia U. Sch. Law, 1987—88, 2001—02. Co-author: Children in the Legal System, 1997, Family Law: Cases, Text, Problems, 1998. Mem. rsch. ethics com. U. Va. Med. Sch.; bd. dirs. Children, Youth and Family Services, Charlottesville. Mem.: John D. and Catherine T. MacArthur Found. Rsch. Network on Adolescent Devel. and Juvenile Justice. Office: U Va Sch Law 580 Massie Rd Charlottesville VA 22903-1789 Office Phone: 434-924-3217. E-mail: es@virginia.edu.

**SCOTT, EUGENIE CAROL,** science foundation director, anthropologist; b. LaCrosse, Wis., Oct. 24, 1945; d. Allen K. and Virginia Meliss (Derr) S.; m. Robert Abner Black, Oct. 18, 1965 (div. 1970); m. Thomas Charles Sager, Dec. 30, 1971; 1 child, Carrie Ellen Sager. BS, U. Wis., Milw., 1967, MS, 1968; PhD, U. Mo., 1974; DSc (hon.), McGill U., 2003, Ohio State U., 2005, Mt. Holyoke Coll., 2006. Asst. prof. anthropology U. Ky., Lexington, 1974-82; postdoctoral fellow U. Calif., San Francisco, 1983-84; asst. prof. U. Colo., Boulder, 1984-86; exec. dir., pub. newsletter NCSE Reports, Nat. Ctr. Sci. Edn., Oakland, Calif., 1987—. Vis. prof., U. Kans., 1976; bd. dirs. Biol. Scis. Curriculum Study, Colorado Springs, Colo., 1993-99; pub. Bookwatch Revs., 1988-92. Author, editor: Biology Textbooks, The New Generation, 1990, Evolution and Creationism: An Introduction, 2004; co-author: Teaching About Evolution and the Nature of Science, 1998; prodr. videotape series

How Scientists Know About...; featured guest as sci. authority on creationism and/or pseudosci. Mem. nat. adv. bd. Ams. United for Separation of Ch. and State, Washington, 1995—. Recipient Disting. Alumnus award U. Mo. Arts and Scis., 1993, Isaac Asimov Sci. award Am. Humanist Assn., 1998, James Randi Skeptic of Yr. award Skeptic Soc., 1999, Bruce Alberts award Am. Soc. Cell Biology, 1999, 1st Amendment award Playboy Found., 1999, Nat. Sci. Bd. Pub. Svc. award, 2003, Geol. Soc. Am. Pub. Svc. award, Calif. Sci. Tchr. Margaret Nicholson Dist. Svc. award, Ctr. for Inquiry Def. Sci. award. Fellow Com. for Sci. Investigation Claims of Paranormal (Sci. and Edn. award 1991), Calif. Acad. Scis. (elected 1994); mem. AAAS, Am. Assn. Phys. Anthropology (bd. dirs., exec. com. 1988-93, sec.-treas. 1993-97, pres. 2001-2003), Am. Anthropol. Assn. Office: Nat Ctr Sci Edn PO Box 9477 Berkeley CA 94709-0477 also: Nat Ctr Sci Edn 420 40th St Ste 2 Oakland CA 94609-2509 Office Phone: 510-601-7203. E-mail: scott@ncseweb.org.

**SCOTT, FRAN,** adult education educator; b. Gainsville, Fla., July 16, 1971; s. Robert and Rutha Scott; m. Leslie Scott, Mar. 11, 2000; 1 child, Alexis. BS in Health Admin., Albany State U., Ga., 1994. Lic. barber Lively Tech. Inst. Mental health asst. Apalachee Ctr. Human Svcs., Tallahassee, 1996—97, adult edn., 1997—; tchr. basic skills Adult and Cmty. Edn. Ctr. Asst. coach Football Teams, 1996—; bass guitarist; active Big Bros. Big Sisters; minister music True Gospel Mission Ministry. Recipient Glen-Howell Disting. Minority Educator, Adult and Cmty. Edn., 2002, Glen-Howell Disting. Minority Tchr. of Yr. Mem.: NAACP. Democrat. Pentecostal. Avocations: Bible study, chess, fishing, football. Home: 2756 Sandalwood Dr N Tallahassee FL 32305 Office Phone: 850-320-2307. Personal E-mail: fflascott@aol.com.

**SCOTT, GARY LEROY,** small business owner, photographer; b. Portland, Oreg., May 14, 1954; s. Glenn Howard and Esther Ruth (Robinson) S. Grad., USN Sch. Photography, Pensacola, Fla., 1974; BS, U. Oreg., 1979, MS, 1982. Pres., photographer, filmmaker Scott Cinema and Visual, Inc., various locations, 1969—; computer traffic operator Burlington No. R.R., Portland, 1979-81; instr. U. Oreg., Eugene, 1981-82; S.E. dist. sales mgr. E. Leitz, Inc., 1984-87; mgr. profl. products Fla. divsn. Fuji Photo Film USA, Inc., Lake Mary, Fla., 1987-2000, mgr. profl. products Pacific N.W. divsn. Vancouver, Wash., 2000—05; owner, pres. Scott Cinema and Visual, Inc., Vancouver, Wash., 2005—. Media cons., advt. copywriter, TV and film script writer, 1984—; lectr. in field. Served with USN, 1972-76. U. Oreg. Sch. Journalism research grantee, 1981. Mem. Am. Soc. Media Photographers, Profl. Photographers of Am. Republican. Avocations: history, photography, outdoor activities. Home and Office: 14300 NE 20th Ave Ste D102-349 Vancouver WA 98686 Personal E-mail: GaryL.Scott@att.net, garyl.scott@comcast.net.

**SCOTT, GARY THOMAS,** historian; b. Wichita Falls, Tex., Mar. 9, 1944; s. Thomas Clifford, Jr. and Lillian (Hanks) Fecher. BA, Southwestern U., Georgetown, Tex., 1966; MA, U. N.C., Chapel Hill, 1969. History instr. Tusculum Coll., Greeneville, Tenn., 1969-70, Herringswell Manor Sch., Bury St. Edmunds, UK, 1970-71; asst. to clk. of the works Washington Nat. Cathedral, 1971-75; archtl. historian Nat. Park Svc., Washington, 1976-82, regional historian, 1982-95, historian Nat. Capital area, 1995—; chief historian Nat. Capital Region, 1996—. Lectr., tour leader Smithsonian Inst., Washington, 1981—; prin. N.Am. rep. in course on archtl. conservation hist. bldgs. Property Svcs. Agy. and English Heritage of Brit. Govt., West Dean Coll., Chichester, Sussex, Eng., 1982-90. Author: The Kappa Alpha Order-1865-1897, 1994, Aquia and Seneca Stone, White House History, 1998. Rep. Nat. Park Svc., D.C. Bicentennial, Washington, 1991—; mem. Com. of One Hundred, Washington, 1993—, U.S. Capitol Cornerstone Bicentennial, Washington, 1993, Washington Monument Cornerstone Centennial, 1998; active Hist. Soc. Washington, 1977—, So. Hist. Assn., 1980—; mem. Friends Attingham Summer Sch., N.Y.C., 1981—, Preservation Roundtable, Washington, 1989—; pres. Victorian Soc., Washington, 2002—04. Mem. Masons (33 degree), Scottish Rite, Cosmos Club Washington, Kappa Alpha Order (chief alumnus 1991-95, Disting. Pub. Svc. award 1988, DC Mayor's Hist. Preservation award 2005). Episcopalian. Avocations: book collecting, antiques. Office: Nat Park Svc National Capital Region 1100 Ohio Dr SW Washington DC 20242-0001

**SCOTT, GENEVA LEE SMITH,** nursing educator; b. Codell, Kans., Nov. 2, 1943; d. Lester Lee and Lennicejean Leota (Lynch) Smith; m. Dennis G. Scott, Feb. 20, 1965; children: J.D., Shane, Deminy. BS, Fort Hays Kans. State Coll., 1965; BS in Nursing, Fort Hays State U., 1979; MS in Nursing, West Tex. State U., San Marcos, 1986. Charge nurse Hadley Regional Med. Ctr., Hays, Kans.; sch. nurse Borger (Tex.) Ind. Sch. Dist.; clin. and classroom instr. North Cen. Kans. Area Vocat. Tech. Sch., Hays; nursing instr. St. Philip's Coll., San Antonio; sch. nurse Bryan Ind. Sch. Dist., 1993-97; instr. nursing edn. Blinn Coll., Bryan, Tex., 1997-98, Weatherford Coll., 1998, vocat. nursing instr., 1998-2000, instr. associates degree in nursing program, 2000—03, dir. ADN program, 2003—04. Scholarship grant, 1983. Mem. Am. Nurses Assn., Phi Delta Kappa, Beta Sigma Phi (membership chairperson, Girl of Yr. 1978). Home: 405 W Spring St Weatherford TX 76086 E-mail: dgsgls@yahoo.com.

**SCOTT, GEORGE ALFRED,** advertising executive, writer; b. Detroit, Feb. 9, 1925; s. Frederick Harry and Irene Lottie Scott; m. Audrey Jil Scott, Dec. 16, 1950; 1 child, George A. IV; children: Mrs. Michel Princess Martin, James Sellers, Gary Sellers, Monty Sellers. BA, Mich. State Univ., Ea. Lansing, Mich., 1948. Reporter The Marion Star, Marion, Ohio, 1948—50, sports editor, 1952—53; acct. exec. Jay Maish Co., Marion, Ohio, 1953—57; adv. staff Dow Chem. Co., Midland, Mich., 1957—59; v.p. Barnes Chase Adv., San Diego, 1959—65; assoc. creative dir. MacManus, John & Adams, Bloomfield Hills, Mich., 1965—72; v.p., creative dir. D'Ary, MacManus & Masivs, Bloomfield Hills, Mich., 1972—83; sr. v.p., creative dir. D'Ary, Masium, Benton & Bowles, Bloomfield Hills, Mich., 1979—86; pres., owner Encore South, Ft. Myers, Fla., 1986—, Encore North, Lupton, Mich., 1986—. Author: (book) Ribbons & Roses & Rice, 1984, More Ribbons, Roses & Rice, 1994, Secrets of an Ad Pro, 2001, Laughing Your Way Through Life, 2003, (books) 2 books of poetry; co-author: Unlocking the T-Code, 2005. Worker Habitat for Humanity, Ft. Myers, Fla., 1996—2000. 1st Lt. USMC, 1943—46, 1st Lt. USMC, 1950—52. Recipient Aid to Advt., Ed. Award, Am. Advt., Ed., 1984, DMM Ad of the Yr., D'Avery, McManus & Masius, 1982. Avocations: marathons, poetry. Home: 17325 Birchwood Ln Fort Myers FL 33908-6102 Office Phone: 979-473-3564. E-mail: adpro29@yahoo.com.

**SCOTT, GEORGE GALLMANN,** accountant; b. Hattiesburg, Miss., July 8, 1928; s. John Havers and Rebecca Evelyn (Gallmann) S.; m. Patsy T. Womack, June 27, 1953; 1 child, George Gallmann. BS, Millsaps Coll., 1949. Accredited bus. acct., tax advisor, 1992; accredited in acctg. and taxation Nat. Accreditation Coun. for Accountancy. Clk. Spanish Trail Transport, Mobile, Ala., 1949—50, asst. auditor, 1953—55; bookkeeper Met. Engraving & Electrotype Co., Richmond, Va., 1952—53; chief clk. Mobile (Ala.) office Ctrl. Truck Lines of Tampa, Fla., 1955—56; gen. auditor M.R.&R. Trucking Co., Crestview, Fla., 1956—66, sec.-treas., 1967—77; pub. acct. enrolled to represent taxpayers before IRS, 1979—. Mem. data processing adv. com. Okaloosa-Walton Col., Niceville, Fla., 1965- 66, 72-73; mem. Okaloosa County Gen. Advisory Com. for Devel. Vocat. Edn., 1973, 79. Bd. dirs. Okaloosa Cmty. Concert Assn., 1982-87; chmn. Crestview Downtown Devel. Bd., 1988-89; bass-baritone soloist, 1953—, choir dir. Meth. Ch., 1966-83, chmn. ofcl. bd., 1971-73, chmn. fin. com., 1974-75, 79-81, audit com., 1977-86, mem. com. on lay personnel, 1979-87, chmn., 1983-87, 89-90, mem. com. on pastor-parish rels., 1980-86, coun. on ministries, 1985, trustee, 1985-87, 1990-95; mem. Walton Co. C. of C. With U.S. Army, 1950-52. Mem. Nat. Assn. Accts., Nat. Assn. Enrolled Agts., Am. Trucking Assn. (nat. acctg. and fin. coun. 1956-77), Southeastern Acctg. and Fin. Coun. (bd. dirs. 1974-77), Fla. Assn. Enrolled Agts., Crestview Downtown Merchs. Assn. (bd. dirs. 1980-84, treas. 1980-84), Greater Crestview C. of C. (chmn. bus. ethics com. 1973-74, bd. dirs. 1981-83, treas. 1982-83), Fla. Accts. Assn. (bd. govs. 1979-80, pres. N.W. Fla. chpt. 1979-80), DeFuniak Springs Bus. and Profl. Assn., Kiwanis (past treas., past sec., past pres.), Pi Kappa Alpha. Home: 244 Seminole Trail Crestview FL 32536-2326

**SCOTT, GLORIA RANDLE,** former college president; b. Apr. 14, 1938; d. Freeman and Juanita (Bell) Randle; m. Will Braxton Scott. AB, Ind. U., 1959, MA, 1960, PhD, 1965, LLD, 1977; DHL, Fairleigh Dickinson U., 1978, Westfield State Coll., 1992, Wilson Coll., 1992, Mt. Vernon Coll., Marian Coll., 1999. Rsch. assoc. in genetics Inst. Psychiat. Rsch. Ind. U. Med. Ctr. Indpls., 1961-63; instr. biology Knoxville (Tenn.) Coll., 1965-67; asst. to pres. N.C. Agrl. and Tech. State U. 1967-68, prof., 1967-76, dir. planning Inst. Rsch., 1973-76; prof. Tex. So. U., 1976-78; v.p., prof. Clark Coll., 1978-86; prof. Grambling State U., 1987; pres. Bennett Coll., Greensboro, NC, 1987-2001, founder Women's Leadership Inst., 1989; owner Scott's Bau Enterprises on Baffin Bay, Riviera, Tex., 1973-98. Sec. bd. dirs., founder Africa U., Mutare, Zimbabwe, 1988-97; bd. dirs. Loew Corp.; vice chair Women's Coll. Coalition, 1990-94; bd. dirs. Nat. Assn. Ind. Colls. and Univs., 1992-96, Nat. Assn. Schs. and Colls. of the United Meth. Ch., 1993-95. Del. UN Decade for Women Internat. Forum, Nairobi, Kenya, 1985; chmn. del. UN Decade for Women Conf., Beijing, 1995; chmn. bd. Nat. Scholarship Fund for Negro Students, 1984-85; 1st v.p. Girl Scouts U.S., 1972-75, pres., 1975-78; bd. dirs. Wilson Coll., 1978-83, Nat. Urban League, 1976-85; mem bd. visitors Ind. U. Sch. Edn., Bloomington, 1988-94; bd. dirs. United Negro Coll. Fund, 1993-95, chair golden anniversary com., 1992-95; chair edn. adv. com. Delta Sigma Theta, 1989—; mem. adv. bd. James McGregor Leadership Acad., Md., 2000—; mem. divsn. III pres.'s coun. NCAA, 1998-2001; founder Nat. African Am. Women's Leadership Inst., 1999; mentor Leadership Inst., 1997-98; mem. Internat. Women's Forum; chmn. Coun. Presidents Black Coll. Fund, UMC, 1997-99. Recipient Drum Major for Justice award, 1993, N.C. Gov's. award for Outstanding N.C. Women, 1991, Achievement award Delta Sigma Theta, 1994. Mem. Rotary (organizing founder East Greensboro 2000-01). Office Phone: 361-297-5307. E-mail: randle@rivnet.com.

**SCOTT, GREGG ALAN,** civil engineer; b. Ft. Collins, Colo., July 29, 1953; s. William Andrew and Marian Ramona Scott; m. Ellen Fredricka Scott, June 2, 1979; children: Devin Colin, Tanner Adam. BS, U. Colo., Boulder, 1976, MS, 1982. Registered profl. engr., Colo., 1980. Civil engr. Bur. Reclamation, Denver, 1976—88, prin. designer, civil engr., 1988—92, design mgr., civil engr., 1992—94, sr. tech. specialist, civil engr., 1994—. Named Reclamation Engr. Yr., Bur. Reclamation, Nat. Soc. Profl. Engr., 2002—03; recipient Superior Svc. award, Dept. Interior, 1999. Mem.: ASCE (chmn. rock mechanics com. 1993—96), Assn. State Dam Safety Ofcls., U.S. Soc. Dams (mem. foundations com. 1988—98), GeoInstitute (editl. bd. Geostrata mag. 1998—2000), Am. Rock Mechanics Assn. (bd. mem. 1997—99). Achievements include research in Earthquake stabillity of concrete dam foundations. Office: Bureau of Reclamation PO Box 25007 Denver CO 80225 Office Phone: 303-445-3233.

**SCOTT, GREGORY ALAN,** pharmacist, writer; b. Newport, Vt., June 10, 1954; s. S. Gerald Scott Sr. and Elizabeth A. Scott; m. Linda M. Scott, Apr. 21, 1996; children: Matthew, Ryan. BA in Chemistry, U. N.H., 1976, MS in Analytical Chemistry, 1979; PharmD, U. Pacific, 1981. Registered pharmacist. Clin./staff pharmacist Dartmouth-Hitchcock Med. Ctr., Hanover, NH, 1982—83; instr. in clin. pharmacology, dept. of medicine Dartmouth Med. Sch., Hanover, 1982—93; clin. pharmacist for drug info. Dartmouth-Hitchcock Med. Ctr., Hanover, 1982—89; asst. dir. clin. and informational pharmacy svcs., 1989—93; v.p. sci. affairs Clin. Comm. Inc., Greenwich, Conn., 1993—98; dir. continuing edn. Sci. Exch. Inc., Greenwich, 1993—2000; pres. and owner WriteHealth, LLC, Stamford, Conn., 2000—. Cons. to the therapeutic agts. and pharmacy rev. com. VA Med. and Regional Office Ctr., White River Junction, Vt., 1986—90; surveyor Accreditation Coun. for Continuing Med. Edn., Chgo., 2000—. Contbg. author: book Clinical Pharmacology Basic Principles in Therapeutics, 3rd edit., 1992; contbr. articles to profl. jours. Mem. bd. of ch. devel. First Congl. Ch. Stamford, 2002—04; bd. of trustees First Congl. Ch. of Stamford, 1996—2001. Mem.: Am. Coll. Clin. Pharmacy (reviewer Pharmaco Therapy 1989—98), Am. Soc. Health-Sys. Pharmacists (reviewer Am. Jour. Hosp. Pharmacy 1989—98), Am. Soc. Clin. Pharmacology and Therapeutics, Am. Med. Writers Assn., Alliance for Continuing Med. Edn. Avocations: carpentry, travel. Office: WriteHealth LLC 110 van Rensselaer Ave Stamford CT 06902 Office Phone: 203-325-9414. Personal E-mail: gscott@writehealth.com.

**SCOTT, GREGORY KELLAM,** former state supreme court justice, lawyer; b. San Francisco, July 30, 1943; s. Robert and Althea Delores Scott; m. Carolyn Weatherly, Apr. 10, 1971; children: Joshua Weatherly, Elijah Kellam. BS in Environ. Sci., Rutgers U., 1970, EdM in Urban Studies, 1971; JD cum laude, Ind. U., Indpls., 1977. Asst. dean resident instrn. Cook Coll. Rutgers U., 1972-75; trial atty. U.S. SEC, Denver, 1977-79; gen. counsel Blinder, Robinson & Co., Inc., Denver, 1979-80; asst. prof. coll. law U. Denver, 1980-85, assoc. prof., 1985-93, prof. emeritus, 1993—, chair bus. planning program, 1986-89, 92-93; justice Colo. Supreme Ct., Denver, 1993-2000; gen. counselor Kaiser-Hill Co., Golden, Colo., 2000—; judge trial referee Colo. Supreme Ct., Colo., 2000. Of counsel Moore, Smith & Bryant, Indpls., 1987-90; v.p., gen. counsel Comml. Energies, Inc., 1990-91; presenter in field. Author: (with others) Structuring Mergers and Acquisitions in Colorado, 1985, Airport Law and Regulation, 1991, Racism and Underclass in America, 1991; contbr. articles to profl. jours. Mem. ABA, Nat. Bar Assn., Nat. Assn. Securities Dealers, Inc., Nat. Arbitration Panel (arbitrator), Colo. Bar Found., Sam Cary Bar Assn., Am. Inn Ct. (founding mem. Judge Alfred A. Arraj inn). Avocations: golf, reading, travel. Office: Kaiser Hill Lle 12101 Airport Way Unit B Broomfield CO 80021-2507

**SCOTT, GREGORY W.,** health care company executive; B in Math. Econ., Colgate U.; MS, U. Mich. cert. CLU. Sr. v.p. Prudential Capital Corp.; gen. ptnr. RRV Pims.; v.p. corp. fin. Salomon Brothers, Inc.; exec. v.p., CFO Prudential Securities; pres. no. ctrl. group, healthcare & employee benefits ops. Prudential Ins. Co., v.p., treas., sr. v.p., CFO health care group; COO, CFO Medsite, 1999-01; exec. v.p., CFO PacifiCare Health Sys. Inc., Cypress, Calif., 2001—. Mem. Fin. Exec. Inst. Office: PacifiCare Health Sys 5995 Plaza Dr Cypress CA 90630*

**SCOTT, H. LEE, JR., (HAROLD LEE SCOTT JR.),** retail executive; b. Joplin, Mo., Mar. 14, 1949; s. Harold Lee and Avis Viola (Parsons) S.; m. Linda Gale Aldridge, June 7, 1969; children: Eric Sean, Wyatt Parson. BBA, Pitts. State U., Kans., 1971. Br. mgr. Yellow Freight System, Springdale, Ark., 1972-78; mgr. Queen City Warehouse, Springfield, Mo., 1978-79; dir. transp. Wal-Mart Stores, Inc., Bentonville, Ark., 1979-83, v.p. distbn. to sr. v.p. logistics, 1983—93, exec. v.p. logistics, 1993—95, exec. v.p. merchandise and sales, Wal-Mart Stores Divsn., 1995—98, pres., CEO, Wal-Mart Stores Divsn., 1998—99, COO, vice-chmn. Bentonville, Ark., 1999—2000, pres., CEO, 2000—. Bd. dirs. Pvt. Truck Council, Washington, 1985-86. Named one of World's 100 Most Influential People, Time Mag., 2005. Republican. Methodist. Avocations: reading, quail hunting. Office: Wal-Mart Stores Inc 702 SW 8th St Bentonville AR 72716-6299*

**SCOTT, HAL S.,** law educator; b. Chgo., Nov. 25, 1943. AB, Princeton U., 1965; MA, Stanford U., 1967; JD, U. Chgo., 1972. Bar: Mass., 1982. Law clk. to Hon. Harold Leventhal, US Ct. Appeals DC Cir., Washington, 1972-73, to Justice Byron R. White, US Supreme Ct., Washington, 1973-74; acting prof. law U. Calif., Berkeley, 1974-75; asst. prof. law Harvard Law Sch., Cambridge, Mass., 1975-80, prof., 1980-90, Nomura prof. internat. fin. systems, 1990—, dir. program internat. fin. systems, 1986-; bd. dir. Lazard Ltd., 2006-; cons. IBM, NYC, 1977. Contbr. articles to legal journals. Author: Euro: Law and Market Practices, 1999, International Finance: Law and Regulation, 2004; co-author: (with Philip A. Wellons) International Securities Regulation, 2002, International Finance: Transactions, Policy, and Regulation, 2000, 01, 02, 03, 04. Mem.: International Acad. Consumer and Comml. Law (past pres.). Office: Harvard Law Sch 1563 Massachusetts Ave Cambridge MA 02138 Office Phone: 617-495-4590. Office Fax: 617-495-9593. Business E-Mail: hscott@law.harvard.edu.

**SCOTT, HELEN S.,** law educator; b. 1949; BA, Barnard Coll., 1970; JD, Columbia U., 1977. Bar: NY 1978, DC 1978. Atty., adviser Office of Chmn. FTC, Washington, 1977-78, atty., adviser Office of Commr., 1978-79; assoc. Shearman & Sterling, NYC, 1980-82; asst. prof. law NYU Sch. Law, NYC, 1983—85, assoc. prof., 1985—88, prof., 1988—. Co-chair Listing and Hearing Rev. Coun. NASDAQ. Recipient Legal Adv. of Yr. award, US Small Bus. Adminstrn. Office: NYU Sch Law Vanderbilt Hall Rm 338 40 Washington Sq S New York NY 10012-1099 Office Phone: 212-998-6206. E-mail: helen.scott@nyu.edu.

**SCOTT, HUGH PATRICK,** former surgeon, military officer, medical advisor; b. Phila., Feb. 12, 1938; s. Hugh Patrick and Martha (Papiana) S.; m. Diane Marie Lopatzie, July 1, 1961; children: Karen, Brendan, Catherine. BA, LaSalle Coll., 1960; DO, Phila. Coll. Osteo. Medicine, 1964, LLD (hon.), 1991. Diplomate Am. Osteo. Bd. Ophthalmology and Otolaryngology. Intern Detroit Osteo. Hosp., Highland Park, Mich., 1964-65, resident otorhinolatyngology, 1965-68; lt. med. corps USNR, 1967, advanced through grades to rear adm., 1991; naval med. officer U.S. Naval Dispensary N.O.B., Norfolk, Va., 1968-70, Submarine Squadron 10, Groton, Conn.; Submarine Group 2; naval med. officer Naval Submarine Med. Ctr., New London, Conn., 1975-83; dir. undersea medicine and radiation health Naval Med. Command, Washington, 1983-86; comdg. officer Naval Hosp., Groton, 1986-88, Camp Lejeune, NC, 1988-90; fleet surgeon Comdr. in Chief, U.S. Pacific Fleet, Pearl Harbor, Hawaii, 1990-91; asst. chief for operational medicine and fleet support Bur. Medicine and Surgery, Washington, 1991-92; dir. med. resources, plans and policy Office Chief of Naval Ops., Washington, 1992-94; sr. med. advisor Northrop Grumman Info. Tech. Health Solutions, 2000—. Asst. clin. prof. medicine Mich. State U., Lansing, 1970—75; pvt. practice, Madison Heights, Mich., 1970—75; cons. Am. Coll. Undersea and Hyperbaric Medicine, Washington, 1985—86, 1994—96; sr. program mgr. Data Sys. & Svcs. divsn. Northrop Grumman Co., 1998—99; sr. med. advisor Northrop Grumman Info. Tech.; sr. v.p. Geo-Ctrs. Inc., 2000—01; mem. sr. exec. med. adv. com. for mil. medicine Johns Hopkins U. Applied Physics Lab.; mem. faculty U. So. Calf. Health Scis. Campus for Advanced Bioetlecomms. and Bio Informatics. Decorated Legion of Merit, Gold Star (3). Fellow Osteo. Coll. Ophthalmology and Otolaryngology, Am. Acad. Otolaryngology and Head and Neck Surgery; mem. Am. Osteo. Coll. Otolaryngology--Head and Neck Surgery (past pres.), Assn. Mil. Osteopathic Physicians and Surgeons (2nd v.p.). Republican. Roman Catholic. Home: 3707 Merlin Way Annandale VA 22003-1326 Office: Northrop Grumman Info Tech 5113 Leesburg Pike Ste 3090 Falls Church VA 22041 Office Phone: 703-575-5172. Business E-Mail: hugh.scott@ngc.com.

**SCOTT, ISADORE MEYER,** retired energy executive; b. Wilcoe, W.Va., Nov. 21, 1912; s. David and Libby (Roston) S.; m. Joan Rosenwald, Feb. 14, 1943; children: Betsy Scott Kleeblatt, Peggy, Jonathan D. AB, W.Va. U., 1934, MA, 1938, LLD, 1983; JD, Washington and Lee U., 1937. Bar: Va. 1937. Practiced law, Richmond, Va., 1937-38; v.p. Lee I. Robinson Hosiery Mills., Phila., 1938-42; with Winner Mfg. Co., Inc., Trenton, NJ, 1947-61, v.p., 1947-51, pres., 1951-61; chmn. bd. Tri-Instl. Facilities, Inc., Phila., 1962-78, TOSCO Corp., L.A., 1976—83, vice-chmn. bd., 1983—87, chmn. bd. Bd. dirs., chmn. Univ. City Assocs., Inc.; founder, mem. U.S. Adv. Bd. Brit.-Am. Project. Bd. dirs. S.E. Pa. chpt. ARC, Univ. City Sci. Ctr., Phila.; mem. adv. com. Urban Affair Partnership; bd. dirs. emeritus, former mem. exec. com., vice-chmn. Phila. Mus. Art; former chmn. World Affairs Coun. Phila.; mem. Phila. Coun. Fgn. Rels.; trustee emeritus Washington and Lee U.; emeritus trustee George C. Marshall Found.; former chmn. Christ Ch. Preservation Trust, Phila., Jefferson House Restoration, Phila. With inf. U.S. Army, 1942-46, NATOUSA, ETO. Decorated Legion of Merit, Silver Star, Purple Heart, Bronze Star; Crown of Italy; medal of merit Czechoslovakia; Mentioned-in-dispatches, Eng.; fellow Mus. Am. Jewish History Mem. Va. State Bar, Phila. Club, Gulph Mills Golf, Anglers of Phila., Masons, Phi Beta Kappa, Omicron Delta Kappa, Order of Coif. (hon.). Democrat. Jewish.

**SCOTT, JACQUELINE DELMAR PARKER,** educational association administrator, consultant; b. L.A., May 18, 1947; d. Thomas Aubrey and Daisy Beatrice (Singleton) Parker (div.); children: Tres Mali, Olympia Ranee, Stephen Thomas. AA in Theatre Arts, L.A. City Coll., 1970; BA in Econs., Calif. State U., Dominguez Hills, Carson, 1973; MBA, Golden Gate U., 1979; EdD, Pepperdine U., 1999. Cert. parenting instr., 2000; holder various Microsoft certs. Sales clk. Newberry's Dept. Store, L.A., 1963-65; long distance operator Pacific Telephone Co., L.A., 1965-66; PBX operator Sears, Roebuck & Co., L.A., 1966-68; retail clk. Otey's Grocery Store, Nashville, 1968-69; collector N.Am. Credit, L.A., 1970-71; office mgr. Dr. S. Edward Tucker, L.A., 1972-74; staff coord. sch. edn. dept. Calif. State U., 1973-74; from bank auditor to corp. loan asst. Security Pacific Bank, L.A., 1974-77; from dist. credit analyst to asst. v.p. Crocker Nat. Bank, L.A., 1977-80; from capital planning adminstr. to project bus. mgr. TRW, Inc., Redondo Beach, Calif., 1980-87, lab. sr. bus. adminstr., 1984-86, project bus. mgr., 1986-87, div. sr. bus. adminstr., 1987-92; ptnr., co-author, co-facilitator, cons. Diversified Event Planners, Inc., L.A., 1990-93; asst. area devel. dir. United Negro Coll. Fund, L.A., 1993-96; cons. parenting edn., 1994—. Cmty. coll. instr., dissertation coach, 1999-; cons. in field Co-founder career growth awareness com. TRW Employees Bootstrap, Redondo Beach, Calif., 1980, pres., 1983-84; role model Inglewood High Sch., TRW Youth Motivation Task Force, Redondo Beach, 1981-83, Crozier Jr. High Sch., 1981-83, Monroe Jr. High Sch., Redondo Beach, 1981-83, Frank D. Parent Career Day, TRW Affirmative Action Com., Redondo Beach, 1987, St. Bernard's Career Day, 1991; chairperson community involvement com., 1981, chairperson disaster com., 1989-90; chairperson gen. and local welfare com. TRW Employees Charitable Orgn., 1989-90, disaster com. chair, 1988-89, bd. dirs. 1987-89; pres. Mgmt. Effectiveness Program Alumnae, L.A., 1982-83, TRW Employees Bootstrap Program Alumnae, 1983-84; group leader Jack & Jill of Am., Inc., South L.A., 1980-81 parliamentarian, 1986-87, v.p. 1991-87, chm. pres., 1984-86, regional dir., 1987-89, nat. program dir., 1992-96, liaison to Young Black Scholars Program, 1986—; bd. dirs. Adolescent Pregnancy Child Watch, 1993—; nat. program dir., bd. dirs. Jack & Jill Am. Found., 1992-96; L.A. mem. Nat. Black Child Devel. Inst., 1994—; vol. ARC, 1994, parenting instr. Am. Red Cross, 1994-96; founder Jack & Jill of Am. Leadership Devel. Program, 1993. Recipient commendation NAACP, 1985, United Negro Coll. Fund, 1986, United Way, 1988, Austistic Children's Telephon, 1980, Inglewood Sch. Dist., 1981, Pres. award Harbor Area Chpt. Links, Inc., 1985, Women of Achievement award City of L.A., Black Pers. Assn., 1994. Mem. Black Women's Forum (sponsor), Phi Delta Kappa, Delta Sigma Theta. Avocations: reading, dance. Personal E-mail: jscott4@earthlink.net.

**SCOTT, JASON ROBERT,** social studies educator; s. Robert Carlton and Lee Ann Scott. BA, Stonehill Coll., Mass., 2004. Cert. tchr. Mass. Social studies tchr. Abington (Mass.) HS, 2004—. Mem.: Mass. Tchrs. Assn.

**SCOTT, JEAN A.,** university president; B in History, U. Richmond, 1968; M in History, Harvard U., 1969, PhD in History, 1974. Asst. prof. history Duke U., dir. admission; dean undergrad. admission Case We. Res. U., Ohio; assoc. provost acad. adminstrn., dean admissions Coll. William and Mary, Williamsburg, Va., 1989-94; v.p. enrollment and student svcs. SUNY, Potsdam, 1994—. Office: Potsdam Coll Pierrepont Ave Potsdam NY 13676-2294

**SCOTT, JEFFREY LYLE,** protective services official; b. Toledo; s. Mylous and Florastine S. Student, U. Toledo, 1977-80. Dist. mgr. DuBois Chems., Detroit, 1988-90; pres. F&S Chems., Detroit, 1991-94; police officer City of Toledo (Ohio), 1994—. Candidate Toledo City Coun., 1993, Ohio State Senate, Toledo, 1994. With Civil Air Patrol, 1995—. Recipient Lifesaving medal, Civil Air Patrol, 1994, Cert. of Appreciation, Safety Coun. NW Ohio, 2002. Mem. Smithsonian Inst.

**SCOTT, JEFFREY RYAN,** music educator; b. Pikeville, Ky., Aug. 25, 1964; s. Larry and Peggy Ann Scott; m. Sabrina Salles. May 21, 2006. MusB, U. Ky., 1987; MusM, So. Oreg. U., 2005. Dir. bands John T. Hoggard H.S., Wilmington, NC, 1987—89, Sedgefield Mid. Sch., Goose Creek, SC,

1989—94, Goose Creek (S.C.) H.S., 1994—2000, Cario Mid. Sch., Mt. Pleasant, SC, 2005—. Clinician, adjudicator in field; guest condr. various univs. and festivals. Mem.: Music Educators Nat. Conf., S.C. Music Educators Assn., Phi Mu. Avocations: travel, hiking, tennis, reading, basketball. Home: 1061 Law Ln Mount Pleasant SC 29464 Office: Cario Middle School 3500 Thomas Cario Blvd Mount Pleasant SC 29466 Office Phone: 843-856-4595.

**SCOTT, JILL,** poet, musician; b. Phila., 1952; Founder, pres. Blues Babe Found. Singer (with Eric Benet, Will Smith, Roots, Common), musician Who is Jill Scott? albums, Beautifully Human: Words and Sounds vol. 2; actor: (plays) Rent. Recipient Grammy Award, 2003. Office: Hidden Beach Recordings 3030 Nebraska Ave Santa Monica CA 90404

**SCOTT, JIM,** radio personality; b. Bridgeport, Conn. m. Donna Scott. With WSAI, Cin., 1968—84; radio host 700 WLW, Cin., 1984—. Active United Way, The Wellness Cmty. Recipient Marconi Radio award for Large Market Personality of Yr., Nat. Assn. Broadcasters, 2002. Avocation: running. Office: WLW 700 AM The Big One 8044 Montgomery Rd Cincinnati OH 45236-2919 Office Phone: 513-241-9597.*

**SCOTT, JOAN WALLACH,** historian, educator; b. Bklyn., Dec. 18, 1941; d. Samuel and Lottie (Tanenbaum) Wallach; m. Donald M. Scott, Jan. 30, 1965; children: Anthony Oliver, Elizabeth Rose. BA, Brandeis U., 1962; MA, U. Wis., 1964, PhD, 1969; LittD (hon.), SUNY, Stony Brook, 1989, Brown U., 1992; D honoris causa (hon.), U. Bergen, Norway, 2004. Asst. prof. history U. Ill., Chgo., 1970—72; asst. prof. Northwestern U., 1972—74; assoc. prof. U. NC, Chapel Hill, 1974—77, prof., 1977—80; Nancy Duke Lewis prof. history Brown U., Providence, 1980—85; Harold F. Linder prof. Sch. Social Sci., Inst. for Advanced Study, Princeton, NJ, 1985—. Dir. Pembroke Ctr. for Tchg. and Rsch. on Women, 1981—85, NEH Seminar for Coll. Tchrs., 1977, 1980—81; mem. Inst. for Advanced Study, Princeton, 1978—79; mem. editl. bd. Jour. Modern History, 1980—83; chair adv. com. Princeton U. Women's Studies Program, 1985—97; adv. com. Stanford Humanities Ctr., 1987; bd. govs. U. Calif. Humanities Rsch. Inst., 1998—2000. Author: The Glassworkers of Carmaux, 1974; author: (with Louise Tilly) Women Work and Family, 1978, rev. edit., 1987, Gender and the Politics of History, 1988; author: Only Paradoxes to Offer: French Feminists and the Rights of Man, 1996; editor (with Brian Tierney): Western Societies: A Documentary History, 1984; editor: (with Jill Conway and Susan Bourque) Learning About Women: Gender, Power and Politics, 1987; editor: (with James Gilbert) The Myth Making Frame of Mind: Social Imaginations of American Culture, 1992; editor: (with Judith Butler) Feminists Theorize the Political, 1992, Love and Politics in Wartime: Letters to My Wife, 1943-45, 1992 (Benedict S. Alper); editor: (with Cora Kaplan and Debra Keates) Transitions, Environments, Translations: Feminisms in International Politics; editor: (with Debra Keeates) Schools of Thought: Twenty-five Years of Interpretive Social Science, 2001; contbr. articles to profl. jours. Fellow NEH, 1975—76; grantee, Am. Coun. Learned Socs., 1978; Rsch. Tng. fellow, Social Sci. Rsch. Coun., 1966—68. Fellow: Sch. Criticism and Theory (sr.); mem.: AAUP (mem. Com. A (Acad. Freedom) 1993—), chmn. Com. A 1999—), Soc. French Hist. Studies, Berkshire Conf. Women Historians, Am. Hist. Assn. (chair com. on women historians 1978—80, Joan Kelly prize com. 1987—88, sec. Mod. European Sect. 1988—89, Joan Kelly prize 1989). Office: Inst for Advanced Study Einstein Dr Princeton NJ 08540-1914

**SCOTT, JOHN BELDON,** art history educator, writer; BA in history, Ind. U., 1968; MA in art history, Rutgers U., 1975, PhD in art history, 1982. Lectr. U. Pa., 1981—82; asst. prof. to prof. art history U. Iowa, Iowa City, 1982—; Elizabeth M. Stanley Prof. of the Arts, 2004—, head art history divsn. Sch. Art and Art History. Vis. mem. Inst. Advanced Study, Princeton, NJ, 1991—92; mem. US Nat. Com. for the History of Art Internat. Congress of the History of Art, 2001—02. Author: Images of Nepotism: The Painted Ceilings of Palazzo Barberini, 1991, Architecture for the Shroud: Relic and Ritual in Turin, 2003 (Charles Rufus Morey Book Award, Coll. Art Assn., 2004), (articles have appeared in) Art Bulletin, Burlington Mag., Memoirs of Am. Acad. Rome, Storia dell'Arte, Jour. of the Warburg and Courtauld Institutes, Jour. of Soc. Archtl. Historians. Served USAF, 1969—73. Samuel H. Kress Found. Rome Prize Fellowship, Am. Acad. Rome, 1979—81, Gladys Krieble Delmas Found. for Venetian Studies Grant, 1979, Andrew W. Mellon Postdoctoral Rsch. Fellow, U. Pa., 1984—85, Rsch. Fellowship for Recent PhD Recipients, Am. Coun. Learned Societies, 1984, Am. Philos. Soc. Rsch. Grant, 1984, 1989, NEH Travel to Collections Grant, 1986, Gladys Krieble Delmas Found. for Venetian Studies Grant, 1986, Nat. Humanities Ctr. Fellow, 1993—94, Trinity Coll. Barbieri Grant in Italian History, Barbieri Endowment for Italian Culture, 1994, Marta Sutton Weeks Fellow, Stanford Humanities Ctr., Stanford U., 1999—2000, Graham Found. for Advanced Studies in the Visual Arts Rsch. Grant, 1999, Am. Philos. Soc. Sabbatical Fellowship, 2000. Mem.: Midwest Art History Soc. (bd. dirs. 1986—89), Coll. Art Assn. (bd. dirs. nominating com. 1998), Soc. Archtl. Historians (bd. dirs. 1997—2000). Office: U Iowa Sch Art and Art History 120 N Riverside Dr #100 Art Bldg Iowa City IA 52242-1706

**SCOTT, JOHN BROOKS,** retired research and development company executive; b. Morenci, Ariz., Aug. 8, 1931; s. Brooks and Lucile (Slagle) S.; m. Jo Ann Rohrbach, June 5, 1987; children from previous marriage: Janice, Steven, Sarah. BS, U. Ariz., 1957, MA, 1959. Asst. prof. systems engring. U. Ariz., Tucson, 1959—61; mgr. Bell Aerosystems Co., Tucson, 1961—62; sr. v.p. IIT Rsch. Inst., Annapolis, Md., 1963—90, pres. Chgo., 1990-97. Author papers on computer software, electromagnetic compatibility. Past pres. bd. dirs. Md. Hall for Creative Arts, Inc.; past chmn. Md. Hall Found.; past mem. bd. govs. IIT Rsch. Inst.; past trustee Ill. Inst. Tech. Mem. Greater Annapolis C. of C. (pres. 1987); mem. Phi Kappa Phi, Sigma Pi Sigma, Pi Mu Epsilon. Home: Apt 903 3145 S Atlantic Ave Daytona Beach FL 32118-6045 E-mail: jscott2030@cfl.rr.com.

**SCOTT, JOHN CONSTANTE,** marketing company executive; b. Charleston, S.C., Jan. 31, 1941; s. John C. and Annabelle (Holmes) S.; m. Mary Frances Turner. BS in Psychology, St. Joseph's U., Phila., 1975; JD, Temple U., 1979. Commd. USAF, 1962, advanced through grades to lt. col.; served in Vietnam; resigned, 1972; personnel mgr. Campbell Soup Co., Camden, NJ, 1972-79, corp. mgr. employee relations, 1980-84; v.p. ops. Insilco Corp., Meriden, Conn., 1984-89; v.p. human resources Howmet Corp., Greenwich, Conn., 1989-92; pres. StarMedia, Inc. Greenwich, 1992—. Mem. pres.'s coun. St. Joseph's U., 1985-90. Mem. ABA, N.J. Bar Assn., Pa. Bar Assn., Res. Officers Assn. (life), Greater Meriden C. of C. (bd. dirs. 1986-89). Roman Catholic. Avocations: mountain hiking, chess. Office: 15 E Putnam Ave Ste 320 Greenwich CT 06830-5424 Personal E-mail: starmedia@optonline.net. *Peace: The product of justice; politics: the major subset of religion; law (human) rules that institutionalize political power (often as not related to justice).*

**SCOTT, JOHN D.,** pharmacologist; b. Edinburgh, Scotland, Apr. 13, 1958; married; 2 children. BSc in Biochemistry with honors, Herriot-Watt U., Edinburgh, 1980; PhD in Biochemistry, U. Aberdeen, 1983. NIH postdoctoral fellow dept. pharmacology U. Wash., Seattle, 1983—86, rsch. asst. prof. dept. biochemistry, 1986—88; asst. prof. dept. physiology and biophysics, dept. biol. chemistry U. Calif., Irvine, 1988—89; asst. scientist Ctr. Rsch. Occupl. & Environ. Toxicology Oreg. Health Scis. U., 1989—90, asst. scientist Vollum Inst. Advanced Biomed. Rsch. dept. biochemistry and molecular biology, 1990—92, scientist 1993—97, sr. scientist 1997—; investigator Howard Hughes Med. Ctr. (known as Vollum Inst.), 1997—. Spkr. in field. Mem. editl. bd. Jour. Biol. Chemistry; contbr. articles to profl. jours. Recipient John J. Abel award, Am. Soc. Pharmacology and Exptl. Therapeutics, 1996; scholar Med. Endowments Hon., U. Aberdeen, 1980—83. Fellow: Royal Soc.; mem.: Protein Soc., Biochem. Soc., Am. Soc. Biochemistry and Molecular Biology. Office: Vollum Inst Oreg Health Scis U 3181 SW Sam Jackson Park Rd Portland OR 97239-3011

**SCOTT, JOHN EDWARD SMITH,** lawyer; b. St. Louis, Aug. 6, 1936; s. Gordon Hatler and Luella Margarite (Smith) S.; m. Beverly Joan Phillips, Dec. 17, 1960; 1 dau., Pamela Anne. AB, Albion Coll., 1958; JD, Wayne State U., 1961. Bar: Mich. 1961, U.S. Dist. Ct. (ea. dist.) Mich. 1962, U.S. Dist. Ct. (we. dist.) Mich. 1970, U.S. Tax. Ct. 1979, U.S. Ct. Appeals (6th cir.) 1964, U.S. Supreme Ct. 1966. Law clk. Supreme Ct. Mich., Lansing, 1961-62; assoc. Dickinson, Wright, Moon, Van Dusen & Freeman, Detroit, 1962-69, ptnr., 1970—. Adj. prof. U. Detroit Law Sch., 1967-71. Supreme Ct. appointee State Bar Rep. Assembly, Detroit, 1972-77; mayor City of Pleasant Ridge, Mich., 1973-81; commr. Mich. Appellate Defender Commn., Detroit, 1979—, chmn., 1992—; hearing referee Mich. Civil Rights Commn., Detroit, 1974-80; chmn. Detroit Legal Aid & Defender Commn., 1972-77; chmn. case flow mgmt. com. Mich. Supreme Ct., 1989-90. Fellow Am. Coll. Trial Lawyers, Internat. Soc. Barristers, Internat. Acad. Trial Lawyers; mem. ABA (chmn. trial evidence com. sect. litigation 1988-91), Am. Bar Found., Mich. Bar Found., Detroit Golf Club, Order of Coif (hon.). Office: Dickinson Wright PLLC 500 Woodward Ave Ste 4000 Detroit MI 48226-3416 Office Phone: 313-223-3622. Business E-Mail: jscott@dickinson.wright.com.

**SCOTT, JOHN JOSEPH,** lawyer; b. Chgo., Dec. 30, 1950; s. John Joseph and Alice (Pierzhala) S.; m. Maria Crawford, Aug. 17, 1974. BA, Yale U., 1972; JD, U. Chgo., 1975. Bar: Ill. 1975, U.S. Dist. Ct. (no. dist.) Ill. 1976. Assoc. Kirkland & Ellis, Chgo., 1975-82, ptnr., 1982-91; asst. gen. counsel CF Industries Holdings, Inc., Long Grove, Ill., 1991—2006, sr. litig. counsel, 2006—. Mem. ABA, Chgo. Bar Assn., Order of Coif. Roman Catholic. Avocations: reading, swimming, bike riding, playing tennis. Office: CF Industries Holdings Inc One Salem Lake Dr Lake Zurich IL 60047-8401

**SCOTT, JOYCE,** writer; d. Charles William and Emma Reardon; m. Edward Dale Scott, Sept. 13, 1971; 1 child, Tonia Louise. Student, Inst. Children's Lit., 1984, student, 1993, Long Ridge Writers Group, 1994. Mem.: The Internat. Women's Writing Guild, Soc. Children's Book Writers and Illustrators.

**SCOTT, JOYCE ALAINE,** academic administrator; b. Long Beach, Calif., May 21, 1943; d. Emmett Emery Scott and Grace (Evans) Wedum. BA, U. Conn., 1964; MA, U. Va., 1966; PhD, Duke U., 1973. From instr. to assoc. prof. U. Wyo., Laramie, 1971-74, asst. dean, 1974-78, asst. v.p. acad. affairs, 1976-81, assoc. v.p. acad. affairs, 1981-84; provost, v.p. SUNY-Potsdam, 1984-86; exec. v.p. Wichita (Kans.) State U., 1986-90, v.p. on spl. assignment, 1990-91; sr. cons. Am. Assn. State Colls. and Univs., 1991-92, v.p. acad. and internat. programs, 1992-97; dep. commr. Mont. U. Sys., Helena, 1998—2003; provost, v.p. acad. and student affairs Tex. A&M U., Commerce, 2003—06, assoc. prof., dept. ednl. leadership, 2004—06, assoc. prof. ednl. leadership, 2005—. Mem. Commn. on Ednl. Credit and Credentials of Am. Coun. on Edn., Washington, 1982-87; cons. faculty Am. Open U., Lincoln, Nebr., 1981-82. Contbr. articles to profl. jours. Trustee Jones Internat. U. Mem. MLA, Am. Assn. Tchrs. French, Phi Beta Kappa, Phi Kappa Phi, Phi Sigma Iota. Republican. Presbyterian. Office: Dept Educational Leadership PO Box 3011 Commerce TX 75429-3011 Office Phone: 903-886-5503. Business E-Mail: Joyce_Scott@tamu-commerce.edu.

**SCOTT, KAREN BONDURANT,** consumer catalog company executive; b. East Orange, NJ, June 4, 1946; d. Walter James and Wanda (French) Schmidt; m. Ian James Anderson, May 12, 1982; children: Steven, Michael. BS, U. Mass., 1968; MBA, Northwestern U., 1977. Bus. analyst Dun & Bradstreet, N.Y.C., 1968-69; asst. mgr. Shay Med. Employment, Chgo., 1970-72; mgr. recruitment Michael Reese Med. Ctr., Chgo., 1972-76; brand mgmt., new bus. devel., dir. mergers & acquisitions Kraft Foods, Inc., Glenview, Ill., 1977-95; pres. Chelsea & Scott dba One Step Ahead, Lake Bluff, Ill., 1987—. Sec.-treas. adv. bd. Lincolnshire (Ill.) Nursery Sch., 1987-89; co-leader Boy Scouts Am., Lincolnshire, 1991. Mem. Juvenile Product Mfrs. Assn. (new product judge 1992-99, speaker nat. catalog conf.), Nat. Assn. Women Bus. Owners (mem. Lake Forest cmty. task force). Office: Chelsea & Scott Ltd 75 Albrecht Dr Lake Bluff IL 60044-2226

**SCOTT, KAREN ELIZABETH,** advocate; b. Buffalo, July 21, 1957; children: James Kenneth-Mark, Alexis Victoria Scott-Davis. BA, Empire State Coll., Buffalo, N.Y., 2002. Adminstrv. asst. WNY Libr. Resources Coun., Buffalo, 1990—97; tech. administr. U. Buffalo. Civil rights and human rights advocate; bd. dirs. Langston Hughes Inst., Buffalo, 2000. Avocations: interior decorating, fashion design, current affairs.

**SCOTT, KAREN LOU,** systems analyst; b. Rantoul, Ill., Aug. 3, 1965; d. David Edson Bishop Jr. and Maxine Helen Bishop; m. Daniel Joseph Scott; 1 child, Margaret Helen. AS, Clinton C.C., Clinton, Iowa, 1988; BS, U. Mary Hardin-Baylor, 1992; MS, Ga. So. U., 1994; postgrad., Baylor U. Instr. Math. Ogeechee Tech. Inst., Statesboro, Ga., 1994—95, Ctr. Tex. Coll., Ft. Steward, Ga., 1995—97, Clinton C.C., Clinton, Iowa, 1997; asst. instr. U. Tex. Austin, 1998; software engr., sci. sys. analyst Comarco Inc., Ft. Hood, Tex., 1998—2000; sci. sys. analyst EWA Svcs. Inc., Ft. Hood, 2000—. Instr. Math. Ga. So. U., Statesboro, 1995, Armstrong Atlantic State U., Savannah, Ga., 1995—97; tchg. asst. Baylor U., Waco, Tex., 1998—2000; adj. prof. Math. Tarleton State U., Killeen, Tex., 2002—; guest lectr. Clinton H.S., Ellison H.S., Killeen. Contbr. articles to profl. jours. Mem.: Am. Math. Soc., Soc. Indsl. and Applied Math., Math. Assn. Am. (Presentation award), Am. Statis. Assn., Kappa Mu Epsilon. Avocations: horseback riding, sports, cooking, stained glass, animals. Office: TESCO/EWA PO Box 5400 Fort Hood TX 76544

**SCOTT, KENNETH ELSNER,** mechanical engineering educator; b. Webster, Mass., May 18, 1926; s. Henry Anderson and Amanda (Elsner) S.; m. Elizabeth Ann Oldham, June 21, 1952; children— Kenneth Elsner, Cynthia Lynne, Jeffrey Alan, Donald Leighton. BSMechE, Worcester Poly. Inst., 1948, MS, 1954. Faculty Worcester Poly. Inst., 1948-91, prof. mech. engring., 1966-91, prof. emeritus, 1991—, George I. Alden prof. engring., 1971-75, inst. dir. audio-visual devel., 1971-74, dir. instructional TV, 1974-90, dir. CAD Lab., 1981-93, acting head dept. mech. engring., 1988-89. Active Bd. Health, Holden, Mass., 1963-70. With AUS, 1944-46. Recipient Trustees' award for Outstanding Tchr. of Year, 1971, Tchg. Excellence and Campus Leadership award Sears-Roebuck Found., 1990-91, William R. Grogan award in recognition of support for Mission of Worcester Poly. Inst., 1998. Fellow ASME (exec. com. Worcester sect. 1952-57, sec.-treas. 1955-56, chmn. 1956-57, region I chmn. profl. divns. com. 1957-58, chmn. agenda, audit, budget and nominating com. Worcester 1957-58, chmn. symposium lubrication Worcester sect. 1957-58, chmn. Adm. Earle award com. 1958-59, chmn. devel. com. 1960-61); mem. Am. Soc. Engring. Edn. (sec.-treas. New Eng. chpt., Western Electric Fund award 1972), Sigma Xi, Pi Tau Sigma, Tau Beta Pi. Home: 7054 W Brandywine Cir Fort Myers FL 33919-7317 Personal E-mail: easkes@aol.com

**SCOTT, KENNETH EUGENE,** lawyer, educator; b. Western Springs, Ill., Nov. 21, 1928; s. Kenneth L. and Bernice (Albright) S.; m. Viviane H. May, Sept. 22, 1956 (dec. Feb. 1982); children: Clifton, Jeffrey, Linda; m. Priscilla Gay, July 30, 1989; children: Ashley (dec. Apr. 2002), Shaler. BA in Econs., Coll. William and Mary, 1949; MA in Polit. Sci., Princeton U., 1953; LLB, Stanford U., 1956. Bar: N.Y. 1957, Calif. 1957, D.C. 1967. Assoc. Sullivan & Cromwell, N.Y.C., 1956-59; Musick, Peeler & Garrett, L.A., 1959-61; chief dep. savs. and loan commr. State of Calif., L.A., 1961-63; gen. counsel Fed. Home Loan Bank Bd., Washington, 1963-67; Parsons prof. law and bus. Stanford (Calif.) Law Sch., 1968-95, emeritus, 1995—; sr. rsch. fellow Hoover Instn., 1978-95, emeritus, 1995—; fellow Am. Acad. Berlin, 2001. Mem. Shadow Fin. Regulatory Com., 1986—, Fin. Economists Roundtable, 1991—. Author: (with others) Retail Banking in the Electronic Age, 1977; co-editor: The Economics of Corporation Law and Securities Regulation, 1980. Mem. Calif. Bar Assn., Phi Beta Kappa, Order of Coif, Pi Kappa Alpha, Omicron Delta Kappa. Home: 610 Gerona Rd Stanford CA 94305-8453 Office: Stanford Law Sch Stanford CA 94305-8610 Office Phone: 650-723-3070. E-mail: kenscott@stanford.edu.

**SCOTT, LIONEL FRANKLIN,** psychologist, educator; s. Charles Scott and Anna Lee Whitehead; children: Robert, Lewis, Karl, James. BA, CCNY, 1972, MS in Edn., 1991; MPA, John Jay Coll., NYC, 1985; PhD, Berne U., Switzerland, 1998. Assoc. prof. psychology Coll. New Rochelle, NY, 1984—; asst. prof. psychology Hofstra U., NY, 1990—; sr. psychologist NYC Dept. Edn., 1992—. Author: Tales of the Ancestors, 1994, Beads of Glass Beads of Stone, 1996, The Book of Ode, 1998, The Amber Talisman, 2003, Facets of the Diamond, 2005. Fellow, Harvard U., 2002; Schaumberg Inst. fellow, Schaumberg Rsch. Ctr., NYC, 1995. Mem.: APA, Ochosi Rsch. Group and Cultural Inst. (bd. dirs.). Office: NYC Dept Edn 11-11 Hazen St East Elmhurst NY 11370 Office Phone: 718-626-7835. Fax: 718-274-9651. E-mail: lionelodufora@aol.com.

**SCOTT, LORI DENISE,** music educator, musician; b. Springfield, Mo., May 16, 1958; d. Leo Franklin and Emma June Burrell; m. David Lee Scott, July 5, 1980; children: Christa Denise, Craig Loren. MusB in Edn., Drury U., Springfield, Mo., 1980, BMusArts, 1980; M in Music Edn., U. Kansas, Lawrence, 1987. Lifetime tchg. cert. Music educator Bonner Springs Schs., Kans., 1980—85, State Fair Cmty. Coll., Sedalia, Mo., 1985—87, Benton County R-9 Schs., Warsaw, 1987—2004, Oregon County R-4 Schs., Alton, 2004—. Bd. mem Habitat Humanity, Warsaw, Mo., 2000—04. Named Outstanding Sr. Woman, Drury U., 1980. Mem.: Mo. Choral Dirs. Assn. (mem. state adv. bd. 2002—04), Music Educators Nat. Conf. (pres. West Ctrl. Mo. chpt. 1998—2000). Republican. Methodist. Avocation: gardening. Office: Alton Schs Rt 2 Box 2181 Alton MO 65606 Personal E-mail: scottys@centurytel.net.

**SCOTT, LOUIS EDWARD,** advertising executive; b. Waterbury, Conn., June 17, 1923; s. Louis Arthur and Ellen (Eckert) S.; m. Phyllis Corrine Denker, Jan. 27, 1942; children: Susan Louise, Eric Richard, Jane Lynn. BS, U. Calif., Berkeley, 1944. Sr. account exec. McCarty Co., L.A., 1946-50; from mem. staff to dir. Foote, Cone & Belding, 1950—61; dir. Foote, Cone & Belding/Honig, 1961—98. Bd. dirs. Smart and Final Corp., Casino Internat., True North Comm. Chmn. publicity com. Los Angeles Community Chest, 1960; patron mem. Los Angeles YMCA; mem. Freedoms Found.; chmn. So. Calif. advisory bd. Advt. Council; mem. exec. advisory bd. Art Center Coll. Design. Served with U.S. Maritime Service, also USNR, World War II. Named Western Advt. Man of Year, 1972 Mem. Am. Assn. Advt. Agys. (dir., past chmn. Western region), Coronado Cays Yacht Club, Rio Verde Country Club, Seattle Yacht Club, Cruising Club Am. Home: 19119 E Tonto Trail Rio Verde AZ 85263 also: PO 682 Imperial Beach CA 91933 Office Phone: 480-390-9890. Personal E-mail: scottlophyl@aol.com

**SCOTT, MARCUS LEWIS ELLIOT,** music educator; b. Atlanta, Ga., July 22, 1981; s. Bernard Raymond and Brenda Foster Scott. BS in Music Edn., Fla. A&M Univ., 2004. Wardrobe asst. Men's Warehouse, Tallahassee, 2003—04; tchr. R. Frank Nims Mid. Sch., Tallahassee, 2004—. Mem. Family Worship and Praise Ctr., Tallahassee, 2000—05. Mem.: Music Educators Nat. Conf., Fla. Bandmasters Assn. Avocations: travel, music, automobiles. Office: R Frank Nims Mid Sch 723 W Orange Ave Tallahassee FL 32305

**SCOTT, MARGARET SIMON,** retired mortgage broker; b. Boston, May 12, 1934; d. Frank A. and Margaret Alice (Gotham) Simon; m. Walter Neil Scott, Nov. 21, 1959 (div. June 1997); 1 child, Walter David Kimbley; m. Stephen E. Michelman, Feb. 8, 2003. BA in Polit. Sci., Wellesley Coll., Mass., 1956; MA in Polit. Sci., Boston U., 1965; MS in Human Resources Mgmt., U. Utah, Salt Lake City, 1974. Rsch. asst. Bell Tel. Labs., Whippany, N.J., 1956-58; rsch. asst. med. sch. U. Louisville, 1959-60, Harvard U., Boston, 1960-64; instr. polit. sci. Trinity U., San Antonio, 1966-67; cons. info. systems U.S. Dept. Labor, Washington, 1968; dir. manpower planning N.Y.C. Human Resources Adminstrn., 1968-71; asst. v.p. First Nat. City Bank, N.Y.C., 1972-77; v.p. Citibank, N.A., N.Y.C., 1978-86, AMEV Asset Mgmt., Inc., N.Y.C., 1986-88; pres. Mortgage Adv. Svcs., Inc., N.Y.C., 1988-99. Vol. Jr. League, Louisville, 1957; bd. mgr. N.Y. Jr. League, N.Y.C., 1970—74; sec. 1095 Park Ave Corp., N.Y.C., 1977—86; bd. mgrs. McBurney YMCA, N.Y.C., 1995—2000, chmn., 1998—2000; trustee United Adult Ministries, 1998—, mem. exec. com., 1999—, chair, fin. com., 1999—; mem. Affordable Housing Task Force of N.Y. City Cmty. Bd., 2006—; mem. housing task Cmty. Bd. 4, N.Y.C., 2006—; trustee First Presbyn. Ch. in the City N.Y., 1995—98, pres., 1997—98; trustee N.Y. City Presbytery, 1996—98, treas., 1998—2002, chair coun. adminstrn. and support svcs., 2003—05, mem. com. on ministry, 2005—; ruling elder First Presbyn. Ch., 2000—03; mem. steering com. Presbyn. Welcome, 1999—2004, co-moderator, 2001—03; trustee Presbyn. Synod of Northeast, 2002—05; bd. dirs. YWCA, N.Y.C., 1980—85. Named Outstanding Vol. of Yr., Jr. League of City of NY, Inc., 2005. Mem.: Wellesley Club. Democrat. Home: 441 W 24th St New York NY 10011-1253 E-mail: margaretsnyc@mac.com.

**SCOTT, MARIAN ALEXIS,** journalist; b. Atlanta, Feb. 4, 1949; d. William Alexander and Marian (Willis) Scott; m. Marc Anthony Lewis, Sept. 14, 1968 (div. 1973); m. David Leslie Reeves, Mar. 16, 1974 (div. 1978); children: Cinque Scott, David Leslie Jr. Student, Barnard Coll., 1966-68, Spelman Coll., 1989-90, Regional Leadership Inst., 1992; LHD, Argosy U., 2003. Reporter, asst. city editor, cable TV editor, mgr., video, v.p. cmty. affairs Atlanta Jour. and Constn., 1974-93; dir. diversity Cox Enterprises Inc., 1993-97; pub. Atlanta Daily World, 1997—. Bd. dirs. Atlanta Life Ins. Co.; vis. instr. summer program for minority journalists, Berkeley, Calif., 1980, 81, 84, 85, 87 Grady High Sch., Atlanta, 1982-83; journalist-in-residence Clark Coll., Atlanta, 1983. Rschr., writer: The history of Atlanta NAACP, 1983 (NAACP award 1984). Moderator First Congl. Ch., 1982-92. Named one of 100 Top Black Bus. and Profl. Women, 1986, 20 Women Making a Mark in Atlanta, Atlanta Mag., 1998, Top 25 Women in Bus., The Network Jour., 2004; recipient Disting. Urban Journalism award, Nat. Urban Coalition, 1980, Acad. Achievement award, YWCA, 1989, Media of Yr. award, Ga. Legisl. Black Caucus, 2001, Citizen of Yr. award, Southwest Hosp., 2001, 1st Place Column Writing award, Ga. Press Assn., 2004, Millennium Pacesetter award, Atlanta Bus. League, 2005; Michele Clark fellow, Columbia U. Sch. Journalism, 1974, Grimes fellow, Cox Family Enterprise Ctr., Kennesaw State U. Mem.: Nat. Assn. Black Journalists, Atlanta Assn. Black Journalists (Commentary Print award 1983, Pioneer Black Journalist award 1998), Nat. Assn. Media Women (pres Atlanta chpt. 1985—87, Media Woman of Yr. award 1983, Media Woman of Yr. nat. award 1993), Atlanta Press Club (pres. 2000), Sigma Delta Chi (bd. dirs. 1980—84, treas. 1985—88). Office: Atlanta Daily World 145 Auburn Ave NE Atlanta GA 30303-2503

**SCOTT, MARIANNE FLORENCE,** retired librarian, educator; b. Toronto, Dec. 4, 1928; d. Merle Redvers and Florence Ethel (Hutton) Scott. BA, McGill U., Montreal, Que., Can., 1949, BLS, 1952; LLD (hon.), York U., 1985, Dalhousie U., 1989; DLitt (hon.), Laurentian U., 1990. Asst. librarian Bank of Montreal, 1952-55; law librarian McGill U., 1955-73, law area librarian, 1973-75, dir. libraries, 1975-84, lectr. legal bibliography faculty of law, 1964-75; nat. librarian Nat. Library of Can., Ottawa, Ont., 1984-99, ret., 1999. Co-founder, editor: Index to Can. Legal Periodical Lit., 1963—; contbr. articles to profl. jours. Decorated officer Order of Can.; recipient Queen Elizabeth II Silver Jubilee medal, 1977, IFLA medal, 1996, Queen Elizabeth II Golden Jubilee medal, 2002. Mem. Internat. Assn. Law Libraries (dir. 1974-77), Am. Assn. Law Libraries, Can. Assn. Law Libraries (pres. 1963-69, exec. bd. 1973-75, honored mem. 1980—), Can. Library Assn. (coun. and dir. 1980-82, 1st v.p. 1980-81, pres. 1981-82), Corp. Profl. Librarians of Que. (v.p. 1975-76), Can. Assn. Rsch. Librs. (pres. 1978-79, past pres. 1979-80, exec. com. 1980-81, sec.-treas. 1983-84), Can. Writers Found. (bd. dirs. 1999—, treas. 2003—), Ctr. for Research Libraries (dir. 1980-83), Internat. Fedn. Library Assns. (honor com. for 1982 conf. 1979-82, chair com. on copyright and other legal matters 1998-2003, hon. fellow 2003), Conf. of Dirs. of Nat. Libraries (chmn. 1988-92). Home: 119 Dorothea Dr Ottawa ON Canada K1V 7C6 E-mail: mfscott@rogers.com.

**SCOTT, MARIETTE A.,** marketing executive; b. Darien, Conn., July 18, 1953; d. Vincent Charles Arguimbau and Carmen Perez de Guzman de Arguimbau; m. Edward Barton Scott, Sept. 6, 1986. BA cum laude, Skidmore

Coll., 1976; MA, Johns Hopkins U., 1980; PhD, NYU, 1985. Instr. Goucher Coll., Towson, Md., 1977, Johns Hopkins U., Balt., 1978—80, NYU, NYC, 1981—83, Princeton U., NJ, 1984—85; dir. Latin Am. Cultural Ctr., NYC, 1980—84; mng. dir. Tucker Capital Corp., Princeton, 1984—85; mktg. mgr. Univision Inc., NYC, 1985—89; pres. Silk Serum Enterprizes, Greenwich, Conn., 1986—; ptnr. Argoimbau Co., Greenwich, 1989—. Dir. US-Spain C. of C., NYC, 2002—; trustee Hispanic Soc. Am., NYC, 2000—. Fulbright scholar, 1976. Mem.: Wee Burn Country Club. Republican. Roman Catholic. Avocations: calligraphy, clothing design, sewing, tennis, skiing. Home: 444 E 57th St New York NY 10022 Office: Argoimbau Co 4 Davenport Ave Greenwich CT 06830

**SCOTT, MCGREGOR W.,** prosecutor, lawyer; b. 1962; m. Jennifer Urbanski Scott; 3 children. BA History, Santa Clara Univ.; JD, Hastings Coll. of Law, Univ. of Calif. Dep. dist. atty. Contra Costa County, 1989—97; dist. atty. Shasta County, 1997—2003; US atty. (ea. dist.) Calif. US Dept. Justice, Sacramento, 2003—. Chair Rural Counties Commn., Calif. Dist. Atty. Assn.; bd. dirs. Calif. Dist. Atty. Assn.; mem. US Atty. Gen. Adv. Com. Lt. col. USNG. Avocations: reading, basketball, golf, exercise, college football, hunting. Office: US Attys Office Sacramento Fed Courthouse 501 1 St Ste 10-100 Sacramento CA 95814*

**SCOTT, MELLOUISE JACQUELINE,** retired media specialist; b. Sanford, Fla., Mar. 1, 1943; d. Herbert and Mattye (Williams) Cherry; m. Robert Edward Scott, Jr., July 1, 1972; 1 child, Nolan Edward. BA, Talladega Coll., 1965; MLS, Rutgers U., 1974, EdM, 1976, EdS, 1982. Media specialist Seminole County Bd. Edn., Sanford, 1965-72, Edison (N.J.), 1972-98; ret. Edison (N.J.) Bd. Edn., 1999. Mem. ALA, N.J. Ret. Educators Assn., NEA. Baptist. Home: PO Box 1771 Sanford FL 32772-1771

**SCOTT, MICHAEL DENNIS,** lawyer; b. Mpls., Nov. 6, 1945; s. Frank Walton and Donna Julia (Howard) S.; children: Michael Dennis, Cindal Marie, Derek Walton. BS, MIT, 1967; JD, UCLA, 1974. Bar: Calif. 1974, U.S. Dist. Ct. (no., so. and ctrl. dists.) Calif. 1974, U.S. Patent Office 1974, U.S. Ct. Appeals (9th cir.) 1974, U.S. Supreme Ct. 1978, U.S. Ct. Appeals (fed. cir.) 1989. Systems programmer NASA Electronics Rsch. Lab., Cambridge, Mass., 1967-69, Computer Scis. Corp., El Segundo, Calif., 1969-71, Univac, Valencia, Calif., 1971; from assoc. to ptnr. Smaltz & Neelley, LA, 1974-81; exec. dir. Ctr. for Computer/Law, LA, 1977-94; pvt. practice LA, 1981-86, 88-89; pres. Law and Tech. Press, 1981-94; ptnr. Scott & Roxborough, LA, 1986-88, Graham & James, 1989-93; v.p., gen. counsel Sanctuary Woods Multimedia, Inc., San Mateo, Calif., 1993-94; of counsel Steinhart & Falconer, San Francisco, 1995-97; ptnr. Hosie Wes Sacks & Brelsford, Menlo Park, Calif., 1997-98, Perkins Coie LLP, 1998—2003; prof. law Southwestern U., LA, 2003—. Adj. assoc. prof. law, Southwestern U., LA, 1975-80, 01-03, Loyola U., L.A., 1997-99, 02-04, Pepperdine U., LA, 2001-03; chmn. World Computer Law Congress, LA, 1991, 93; co-chmn. Internat. IT Law Conf., 2005. Author: (with David S. Yen) Computer Law Bibliography, 1979, Computer Law, 1984, Scott on Computer Law, 1991, Multimedia Law and Practice, 1993, Scott on Multimedia Law, 1996—, (with Warren S. Reid) Year 2000 Computer Crisis: Law Business Technology, 1998, Internet and Technology Law Desk Reference, 1999—, Intellectual Property and Licensing Law Desk Reference, 2001—, Telecommunications Law Desk Reference, 2003—, Scott on Outsourcing Law and Practice, 2006—; editor-in-chief: Computer/Law Jour., 1978-94, Software Protection, 1982-92, Software Law Jour., 1985-94, Internat. Computer Law Adviser, 1986-92, Cyberspace Lawyer, 1996—, E-Commerce Law Report, 1998—. Mem. Computer Law Assn. (bd. dirs. 1994-99), Calif. State Bar Assn. Office: 675 S Westmoreland Ave Los Angeles CA 90005

**SCOTT, MIMI KOBLENZ,** psychotherapist, actress, journalist, playwright; b. Albany, NY, Dec. 15, 1940; d. Edmund Akiba and Tillie (Paul) Koblenz; m. Barry Stuart Scott, Aug. 13, 1961 (dec. Nov. 1991); children: Karen Scott Zantay, Jeffrey B. BA in Speech and English Edn., Russell Sage Coll., 1962; MA in Speech Edn., SUNY, Albany, 1968; M in Social Welfare, SUNY, 1985; PhD in Psychology, Pacific Western U., Encino, Calif., 1985. Cert. tchr., social worker. Tchr. English, speech Albany Pub. Schs., 1961-63; hostess, producer talkshow Sta. WAST-TV 13, Albany, 1973-75; freelance actress N.Y.C., 1975-77; producer, actress Four Seasons Dinner Theater, Albany, 1978-82; instr. of theatre Albany Jr. Coll., 1981-83; pvt. practice psychotherapy Albany, NY, 1985-92, N.Y.C., 1992—; exec. producer City of Albany Park Playhouse, 1989-92; actor self-employed N.Y.C., 1992—; actor Off Broadway show Grandma Sylvia's Funeral, 1996-98, Split Ends, 2004. Guest psychotherapist Sally Jessy Raphael Show, 1992, 93, Jane Whitney Show, 1994, A Current Affair, 1995, News Talk TV, 1995; founder Manhattan Playwrights Inc., 2001—, producing artistic dir., 2001—06. Scriptwriter, dir., actor (TV films) To Liberty and Justice for All, 1985, featured writer Backstage, 1995—96, featured in ind. film Mr. Vincent, Sundance, 1997, book and lyricist (musical) Dressing Room, Soho Playhouse, N.Y.C., 2000; author: Mind Tricks, 2003; dir.: Mind Tricks, 2003; featured on NBC Dateline, 2005, VH1's So Jewtastic, 2006. Event organizer AmFar, 1985; co-chmn. March of Dimes Telethon, 1985-86; fundraiser Leukemia Found., 1987, AIDS Benefit, North Miami Beach, Fla., 1988; elected to SUNY Albany U. Found., 1990. Recipient FDR Nat. Achievement award March of Dimes, 1985, Recognition Cert. Capital Dist. Psychiat. Ctr., 1983-85; named Woman of Yr. YWCA, 1986, Commr. Albany Tricentennial Celebration, 1986; named Mimi Scott Day in her honor Mayor of Albany, 1989. Mem.: NASW, AFTRA, SAG, AEA, Drama League of N.Y., N.Y. League Profl. Theatre Women. Jewish. Avocations: boating, golf, tennis. Home and Office: 155 W 70th St PH2A New York NY 10023-3767 Office Phone: 212-721-2979. Personal E-mail: mscott13@aol.com.

**SCOTT, NANCY L.,** health facility administrator, consultant; b. Berwyn, Ill., Sept. 11, 1962; d. Kenneth N. and Lolita L. Unger; m. Paul A. Scott, Dec. 29, 1990 (div. Sept. 1995). BS, Univ. of Ill., 1983; MBA with hons., U. of Chgo., 1991. Cert. CHE Am. Coll. of Healthcare Execs., Chgo., 2000. Various positions including implementation consultant to fin. product mgr. Enterprise Systems, Inc., Wheeling, Ill., 1993—96; cytogenetics technologist Univ. of Chgo., 1986—88; supr. Reproductive Genetics Inst., Chgo., 1988—90; dist. agt. The Prudential, Des Plaines, Ill., 1992; mgr., sr. cons. Cap Gemini Ernst & Young U.S., Chgo., 1996—2003; acct. exec. AHA Fin. Solutions, Inc., Chgo., 2003—. Home: 3238 Elm Ave Brookfield IL 60513 Office: AHA Financial Solutions Inc 1 N Franklin 30th Fl Chicago IL 60606-3421 E-mail: NLScott@aol.com.

**SCOTT, NATHAN ALEXANDER, JR.,** minister, literary critic, religious educator; b. Cleve., Apr. 24, 1925; s. Nathan Alexander and Maggie (Martin) S.; m. Charlotte Hanley, Dec. 21, 1946; children: Nathan Alexander III, Leslie K. AB, U. Mich., 1944; BD, Union Theol. Sem., 1946; PhD, Columbia U., 1949; LittD, Ripon Coll., 1965, St. Mary's Coll., Notre Dame, Ind., 1969, Denison U., 1976, Brown U., 1981, Northwestern U., 1982, Elizabethtown Coll., 1989; LHD, Wittenberg U., 1985; DD, Phila. Div. Sch., 1967; STD, Gen. Theol. Sem., 1968; LHD, U. D.C., 1976; DD, The Protestant Episcopal Theological Seminary in Va., 1985; HumD, U. Mich., 1988; LHD, Wesleyan U., 1989, Bates Coll., 1990; STD, Univ of the South, 1992; DD, Kenyon Coll., 1993, Wabash Coll., 1996; Ordained priest Episcopal Ch., 1960; canon theologian Cathedral St. James, Chgo., 1967-76. dean of chapel, U. Union U., 1946-47; instr. humanities, Howard U., 1948-51, asst. prof., 1951-53, assoc. prof., 1953-55; asst. prof. theology and literature, U. Chgo., 1955-58, assoc. prof., 1958-64, prof., 1964-72, Shailer Mathews prof. of theology and lit., 1972-76, prof. English, 1967-76; Commonwealth prof. religious studies, U. Va., 1976-81, William R. Kenan prof. religious studies, 1981-90, prof. English, 1976-90, prof. emeritus, 1990—. Author: Rehearsals of Discomposure: Alienation and Reconciliation in Modern Literature, 1952, The Tragic Vision and the Christian Faith, 1957, Modern Literature and the Religious Frontier, 1958, Albert Camus, 1962, Reinhold Niebuhr, 1963, The New Orpheus: Essays toward a Christian Poetic, 1964, The Climate of Faith in Modern Literature, 1965, The Broken Center: Studies in the Theological Horizon of Modern Literature, 1966, Ernest Hemingway, 1966, The Modern Vision of Death, 1967, Adversity and Grace: Studies in Recent American

Literature, 1968, Negative Capability: Studies in the New Literature and the Religious Situation, 1969, The Unquiet Vision: Mirrors of Man in Existentialism, 1969, The Wild Prayer of Longing: Poetry and the Sacred, 1971, Nathanael West, 1971, Three American Moralists: Mailer, Bellow, Trilling, 1973, The Poetry of Civic Virtue: Eliot, Malraux, Auden, 1976, Mirrors of Man in Existentialism, 1978, The Poetics of Belief: Studies in Coleridge, Arnold, Pater, Santayana, Stevens and Heidegger, 1985, Visions of Presence in Modern American Poetry, 1993; co-editor Jour. Religion, 1963-77, (with Ronald Sharp) Reading George Steiner, 1994; adv. editor Religion and Lit., Literature and Theology, Callaloo. Fellow Am. Acad. of Arts and Scis.; mem. Soc. Arts, Religion and Contemporary Culture, Soc. for Values in Higher Edn. (Kent fellow), MLA., Am. Acad. Religion (pres. 1986), Century Assn. (N.Y.C.), Quadrangle Club, Arts Club (Chgo.), Greencroft Club (Charlottesville, Va.). Office: U Va Dept Religious Studies Charlottesville VA 22903 Personal E-mail: chs5a@ntelos.net.

**SCOTT, NINA ELIZABETH RAY,** music educator; b. Anniston, Ala., May 9, 1947; d. Douglas Marvin Sr. and Carrie Elizabeth Ray; m. Frank B. Scott (div.); 1 child, Charlotte E. Scott Askew. BA, Rust Coll., 1969; MA, Ea. Mich. U., 1976. Cert. tchr. Mich. Vocal music tchr. Whittier Jr. HS, Flint, Mich., 1969, Mandeville Mid. Sch., Flint, 1969–70, Myers Elem. Sch., Grand Blanc, Mich., 1970—73, Smuuit Mid. Sch., Beecher, Mich., 1972—85, Beecher HS, Mich., 1976—85, Northwestern HS, Flint, 1985—90, Renaissance HS, Detroit, 1990—. Choir dir. Brazeal Dennard Youth Chorale, Detroit, 1992—, Ctrl. United Meth. Ch., Detroit, 1998—. Author: (musical) Jam Tempo 12.0, 1989, (musical dramatization) A Call for Unification, 1994. Recipient Apple for the Tchr. Award, Iota Phi Lambda, Prin.'s and Educators Achievement award, Booker T. Washington Bus. Assn., Nat. award of excellence, Nat. Media Women, Sigma's Excellence Recognition for Vols. in Edn. award. Mem.: Am. Choral Dirs. Assn. (former mem. state bd. dirs.), Nat. Assn. Negro Musicians, Mich. Sch. Vocal Music Assn. (state honors choir dir. 2001, 2006, former dist. mgr., Tchr. of Yr. 2001, State). Home: 18600 Steel St Detroit MI 48235 Office: Renaissance HS 6565 W Outer Dr Detroit MI 48235

**SCOTT, NORMAN ROY,** academic administrator, agricultural engineer, educator; b. Spokane, Wash., Sept. 6, 1936; s. Roy Samuel and Agnes Sarafia (Lilljegren) S.; m. Sharon R. Cogley, June 17, 1961; children: Robin, Nanette, Shirlene. BS in Agrl. Engring., Wash. State U., 1958; PhD, Cornell U., 1962. Mem. faculty agrl. engring dept. Cornell U., Ithaca, NY, 1962—, chmn. agrl. engring. dept., 1978-84, dir. office for rsch. agrl. experimentation sta., 1984-89, v.p. rsch. and advanced studies, 1989-98. Mem. bd. on agriculture NRC, Nat. Acad. Scis., 1993-96. Contbr. articles to profl. jours.; patentee in field. Recipient Alumni Achievement award Wash. State U., 1995. Fellow ASHRAE, Am. Inst. for Med. and Biol. Engring. (founding 1991), Am. Soc. Agrl. Engrs. (tech. v.p. 1989-92, pres. elect 1992-93, pres. 1993-94, Henry Giese award 1989, McCormick-Case Gold Medal award 2002); mem. AAAS, N.Y. Acad. Scis., Nat. Acad. Engring., Inst. Biol. Engring. (pres. 2001), Am. Soc. for Engring. Edn., Instrument Soc. Am. (sr.) Democrat. Methodist. Avocations: sailing, golf. Home: 1662 Taughannock Blvd Trumansburg NY 14886-9120 Office: Cornell U 216 Riley Robb Hall Ithaca NY 14853-5701 Office Phone: 607-255-4473. Business E-Mail: nrs5@cornell.edu.

**SCOTT, OLOF HENDERSON, JR.,** priest; b. Phila., May 13, 1942; s. Olof Henderson and Julia Irene (Rutroff) S.; m. Eva Jakowenko, Sept. 13, 1969; children: Lisa Ann, Christopher Olof, Timothy Nicholas. BA in Physics, Franklin and Marshall Coll., 1964; MS in Nuclear Engring., Pa. State U., 1966; postgrad., St. Vladimir's Orthodox Theol. Sem., 1975-76. Ordained deacon Antiochian Orthodox Christian Ch., 1975, priest, 1976, archpriest, 1988. Ops. engr. S3G ops. Knolls Atomic Power Lab., GE Co., Schenectady, N.Y., 1966-68, project engr. S3G ops., 1968-69; lead nuclear engr. Seabrook Nuclear project Pub. Svc. Co. of N.H., Manchester, 1969-70; project engr. VEPCO projects Nuclear Energy Sys. divsn. Westinghouse Elec. Co., Monroeville, Pa., 1970-72, project mgr. VEPCO projects Nuclear Energy Sys. divsn., 1972-74, regional sales mgr. mktg., 1974-75; pastor St. George Orthodox Ch., Charleston, W.Va., 1976—; dean of clergy Appalachian-Ohio Valley Deanery, 1976—2005, W.Va. Deanery, 2005—. Spiritual advisor NAC-SOYO of Archdiocese, 1977-82, vice-chmn. inter-orthodox and interfaith rels., 1987-2005, chmn., 2005—; exec. bd. W.Va. Coun. Chs., 1977—; bd. govs. Nat. Coun. Chs., 1977-2005, nominating com., 1979-81, exec. com., 1985-96, membership com., 1988-91, unity and rels., 1989-92, ch. world svc., 1997-2005; active West Va. Ecumenical Coalition on Infant Mortality, 1992-96. Contbr. articles to profl. jours. Bd. dirs. Religious Coalition for Cmty. Renewal in Charleston, 1987-95, Charleston Ch. Recreation Assn., 1998—, Kanawha Home for Children, 1986-89, pres., 1989; long-range planning com. W.Va. State Rep. Exec. Com., 1985-87; adv. bd. Nat. Ctr. for Human Rels., 1997-98, Charleston Area Religious Leaders Assn., 2004—; del. 8th Assembly of WCC, Harare, Zimbabwe, 1998. Named Hon. West Virginian, 2001; Olof H. Scott Day named in his honor, City of Charleston, W.Va., 2001. Mem. Acad. Parish Clergy (pres. W.Va. chpt. 1983-85), Am. Nuclear Soc., St. Vladimir's Theol. Found., Charleston Ministerial Assn., Order of St. John of Jerusalem-Knights Hospitellers (chaplain 1998—), Order of St. Ignatius of Antioch, Soc. for Preservation and Encouragement Barbershop Quartet Singing in Am. Inc. (v.p. 1984-85), Pa. State Club W.Va. (pres. 1984-88), Alden Kindred of Am., Sigma Pi Sigma, Delta Sigma Phi. Avocations: camping, barbershop quartet, motorcycling. Home: 4409 Staunton Ave SE Charleston WV 25304-1743 Office: St George Orthodox Ch PO Box 2044 Charleston WV 25327-2044 E-mail: frolof@charter.net. *My thoughts on life are but mere recitations of the Holy Scripture and my feeble attempts at making Those words and Thoughts my own.*

**SCOTT, PAMELA J.,** educational consultant; b. Chehalis, Wash., Dec. 24, 1948; d. Jean Jones; m. Paul Alan Scott, June 6, 1970; children: Craig A., Ryan T. Eric I. Meghan MEd, Heritage U. Toppenish, Wash., 1991, MoI. Bd. Cert. tchr. 2004. Educator Kennewick Sch. Dist., Wash., 1987—2005, consulting peer educator, 2005—. Adj. prof. Heritage U., Toppenish, 2005—. Recipient Curriculum Quill award, Kennewick Sch. Dist., 2004. Mem.: ASCD, Nat. Coun. Tchrs. Math. Office: Kennewick Sch Dist 524 S Auburn St Kennewick WA 99336 Personal E-mail: pscott2b@charter.net. E-mail: pam.scott@ksd.org.

**SCOTT, PAMELA SUE,** middle school educator; d. James John and Norma Jean Williamson; m. Stanley Allen Scott; children: Nolan William Jackson, Parker Lucas Lee. MA in Mid. Level Edn., U. No. Colo., Greeley, Colo., 1996; MusB, U. Iowa, Iowa City, Iowa, 1985. Lic. tchr/ Dept. Edn., Colo., 2001. Tchr. elem. music Albert Lea (Minn.) Sch. Dist., 1985—88; tchr. mid. sch. choir Bookcliff Mid. Sch., Grand Junction, Colo., 1988—92; tchr. Redlands Mid. Sch., Grand Junction, 1992—. Guide, dir. Cheley Camps, Estes Park, Colo., 1982—89; guide, cook, counselor Sonlight Christian Camps, Pagosa Springs, Colo., 1991—97. Dir.(co-founder): Grand Valley Children's Choir. Recipient Outstanding Tchr. of Yr. award, Grand Junction (Colo.) C. of C., 1992, Grand Junction (Colo.) Masonic Lodge, 1992, 1997. Mem.: ASCD, Nat. Coun. Social Studies, Nat. Mid. Sch. Assn. Republican. Avocations: backpacking, jogging, music. Office: Mesa County School District # 51 2200 Broadway Grand Junction CO 81503 Office Phone: 970-254-7000. Office Fax: 970-245-1985. Personal E-mail: pscott@bresnan.net. Business E-Mail: pams@mesa.k12.co.us.

**SCOTT, RALPH MASON,** retired radiologist, educator; b. Leemont, Va., Nov. 23, 1921; s. Benjamin Thomas and Marion Hazel (Mason) S.; m. Alice Latine Francisco, Dec. 21, 1946; children: Susan Taylor, Ralph Mason, John Thomas. BA, U. Va., 1947; MD, Med. Coll. Va., 1950. Diplomate Am. Bd. Radiology (trustee 1965-76, treas. 1969-70, v.p. 1970-72, pres. 1972-74). Intern Robert Packer Hosp., Sayre, Pa., 1953-54, resident, 1954-57, dir. radiation therapy and nuclear medicine sect., 1957-59; fellow Christie Hosp. and Holt Radium Inst., Manchester, England, 1956-57; asst. prof. radiology U. Chgo. Med. Sch., 1959-60; assoc. prof. radiology, dir. radiation therapy and radioisotopes U. Louisville Med. Sch., 1960-64, prof., dir. radiation therapy, 1964-77; prof. and chmn. dept. rad. oncology U Louisville, 1974-77; prof. radiation therapy U. Louisville Med. Sch., 1981-82; prof. emeritus U.

Louisville, 1995; dir. J. Graham Brown Regional Cancer Ctr., Health Scis. Ctr. U. Louisville Med. Sch., 1981-82; dir. dept. radiation medicine Christ Hosp., Cin., 1982-93; ret. Clin. prof. radiology U. Cin. Coll. Medicine. 1982-93; prof., chmn. dept. therapeutic radiology U. Md. Sch. Med., 1977-80; dir. radiation therapy program div. cancer rsch. resources and ctrs., Nat. Cancer Inst. (on leave from U. Louisville), 1976-77. Pres. Ky. divsn. Am. Cancer Soc., 1972-73; bd. dirs. Living Arrangements for the Developmentally Disabled, 1993-95, No. Ky. Assn. for the Retarded, 1993-95, Day Spring Inc., 1993-95, United Health Care, 1994-95, Seven Counties Svcs., Inc., 1997-2003, J. Graham Brown Regional Cancer Ctr. Corp., 1997—. Lt. (j.g.) USNR, 1943-45. Fellow Christie Hosp. and Holt Radium Inst., Manchester, Eng., 1956-57. Mem. Am. Roentgen-Ray Soc. (exec. coun. 1968—, chmn. exec. coun. 1972-73), AMA, Am. Coll. Radiology (vice chmn. commn. on cancer 1968-69), Am. Radium Soc., Am. Soc. Therapeutic Radiologists, Assn. U. Radiologists, Radiol. Soc. N.Am., Pi Kappa Alpha, Phi Chi. Home: Treyton Oak Towers 211 W Oak St Apt 922 Louisville KY 40203 Personal E-mail: ramsco1@earthlink.net.

**SCOTT, RAYMOND PETER WILLIAM,** chemistry professor, writer; b. Erith, Eng., June 20, 1924; came to U.S., 1969; s. Ronald and Annie (Hoadley) S.; m. Barbara Winifred Doreen Strange, Apr. 20, 1946; children: Kerry Raymond, Kevin Francis. B.Sc., U. London, 1946, D.Sc., 1958. Lab. leader Burroughs Welcome, Dartford, England, 1946-48; chief chemist APCM, 1948-52; research mgr. Benzole Producers, Watford, England, 1952-60; divisional mgr. Unilever, Sharnbrook and Bedfordshire, England, 1960-69; dir. phys. chemistry Hoffman La Roche, Nutley, NJ, 1969-80; dir. applied rsch. Perkin-Elmer, Norwalk, Conn., 1980 86; sometime rsch. prof. dept. chemistry Georgetown U., Washington, 1986-2000; writer, cons., 2001—. Rsch. prof. dept. chemistry Birkbeck Coll., London. Author: Liquid Chromatography Detectors, 1977, 3d edit., 1987, Contemporary Liquid Chromatography, 1976, Liquid Chromatography Column Theory, 1991, Silica Gel and Bonded Phases, 1993, Liquid Chromatography for the Analyst, 1994, Chromatography Techniques, 1995, Chromatography Detectors, 1996, Tandem Techniques, 1996, Introduction to Analytical Gas Chromatography, 1997, Chiral Chromatography, 1998, Quantitative Chromatographer Analysis, 2000, Chromatography Theory, 2002; editor: Gas Chromatography, 1960, Small Bore Columns in Liquid Chromatography, 1983. Recipient Tswett medal Am. Internat. Symposia on Chromatography, 1978; recipient Tswett award USSR Tech. Inst. Moscow, 1978, Martin medal in chromatography Chromatography Group Gt. Britain, 1982 Fellow Royal Soc. Chemistry (chartered, Analysis and Instrumentation award 1988), Am. Inst. Chemists (cert.), Am. Chem. Soc. (Chromatography award 1977). Home: Great Sanders House Hurst Ln London TN33 0PE England

**SCOTT, REBECCA J.,** law educator; AB, Radcliffe Coll.; MPhil in econ. history, London Sch. Econs.; PhD, Princeton U. Charles Gibson Disting. Univ. Prof. of History, prof. law U. Mich. Law Sch., Ann Arbor. Author: Degrees of Freedom: Louisiana and Cuba after Slavery, 2005; contbr. articles to profl. jours. Grantee Guggenheim fellowship, 2004. Mem.: Am. Acad. Arts and Scis. Office: Mich U Law Sch 969 Hutchins Hall 625 S State St Ann Arbor MI 48109-1215 Office Phone: 734-615-2082. Office Fax: 734-764-8309. E-mail: rjscott@umich.edu.

**SCOTT, RENAY MARIE,** academic administrator, educator; b. Columbus, Ohio, Aug. 11, 1962; d. Douglas and Joan Scott. BA, Calvin Coll., Grand Rapids, Mich., 1984; MA, Mich. State U., Lansing, 1988; PhD, Wayne State U., Detroit, 1995. Tchr. secondary social studies Freedom Bapt. Acad., Hudsonville, Mich., 1984—89; instr. Grade Sch. of Bible, Grand Rapids, 1990—94; asst. prof. Grace Bible Coll., Wyoming, Mich., 1994—96; assoc. prof. Cornerstone U., Grand Rapids, 1996—98; chairperson Cen. Mich. U., Mt. Pleasant, 2003—, prof., 1998—2006; dean Owens CC, 2006—. Editor: Mich. Social Studies Jour., 2001—. Recipient Provost award, Cornerstone U., 1998. Mem.: Nat. Coun. for Social Studies (bd. dirs. 2006—07), Mich. Coun. for Social Studies (pres. 2001—06, bd. dirs. 2007). Avocations: bicycling, running, travel, reading. Office: Cen Mich U Roran Hall 208 Mount Pleasant MI 48859

**SCOTT, RICHARD ELTON,** health facility administrator; b. St. Louis, Oct. 3, 1930; s. Earl Ray and Celeste (Roark) Scott; m. Carol Jenkins, Sept. 3, 1960; children: Suzanne Scott Abbe, Richard E. Jr. BA, Baylor U., 1971; MS, Trinity U., 1978. Various positions Hillcrest Bapt. Med. Ctr., Waco, Tex., 1961-78, asst. adminstr., 1973-78, v.p., 1978-90, exec. v.p., 1990-92, pres., CEO, 1992—; adminstrv. resident Scott & White Clinic, Temple, Tex., 1973—. Chmn. VHA S.W., Inc., Dallas, 1997—98; exec. Bapt. Hosp. Assn., 1999—2001; co-founder, bd. dirs. Cmty. Health Action Ptnrs.; bd. dirs. Waco Family Practice Found. Pres. exec. com., bd. Dr. Pepper Mus., Waco, 1996; chmn. Waco Bus. League, 1989; chmn. bd. United Way, Waco, 1989; chmn. Greater Waco C. of C., 1991; chmn. bd. trustees First Bapt. Ch., Waco, 2000. Named Leonard A. Duce award, Trinity U. Healthcare Alumni Assn., San Antonio, 1997, Vol. or Yr., United Way, Waco, 1991. Mem.: Vol. Hosps. Am. Southwest, Tex. Hosp. Assn., Rotary. Office: Hillcrest Health Sys 3000 Herring Ave Waco TX 76708-3239

**SCOTT, RICHARD MALACHI,** psychologist; b. Bklyn., Dec. 15, 1968; s. David Malachi and Olive Scott. AA in Gen. Studies, Mira Costa Coll., 1990, AS in Psychology, 1990, AA in Visual Arts, 1990; BA in Psychology, U. Calif., San Diego, 1991; MA in Clin. Psychology, We. Am. U., 1993; MA in Psychology, Saybrook Inst., 1995, PhD in Clin. Psychology, 2000; postgrad., St. Luke Sch. Medicine. Lic. clin. psychologist. Social worker, case worker Salvation Army, Family Svcs. Divsn., San Diego, 1993; intern Dept. Pub. Social Svcs., Riverside, Calif., 1996—98; psychol. asst. various orgns., Calif., 1997—2000; clin. psychologist Calif. Dept. Corrections, Chino, Calif., 2000—04; pvt. practice San Diego, 2004—. Project and clin. dir. So. Calif. Alcohol and Drug Program, Inc., Downey, Calif., 2004; clin. psychologist Geriatric Cons., Inc., San Diego, 2003—05; sr. psychologist supr. Dept. of Corrections, Calif., 2005—06. Mem.: Nat. Acad. Sports Medicine, San Diego Psychol. Assn., APA. Avocations: dance, drawing, painting, sculpting, singing. Home: 11672 Ramsdell Ct San Diego CA 92131-3607 Office Phone: 619-405-6422. E-mail: research2005@hotmail.com.

**SCOTT, RICHARD THOMAS, JR.,** reproductive endocrinologist; b. Selma, Ala., Nov. 28, 1958; s. Richard Thomas and Cynthia Marvin (Coleman) S.; m. Blair MacKerer, June 16, 1979; children: Whitney Blair, Katherine Leigh, Richard Thomas III. BS in Chemistry, Randolph Macon Coll., 1979; MD, U. Va., Charlottesville, 1983. Diplomate Nat. Bd. Med. Examiners, Am. Bd. Ob-Gyn., reproductive endocrinology divsn; bd. cert. high complexity lab dir. embryology, andrology, endocrinology, Am. Bd. Bioanalysts. Commd. 2nd Lt. USAF, 1979, advanced through grades to lt. col., 1993; intern Wilford Hall USAF Med. Ctr., San Antonio, 1983-84, resident, 1984-87, chief reproductive endocrinology Lackland AFB, Tex., 1989-93; fellow Jones Inst. for Reproductive Medicine, Ea. Va. Med. Sch., Norfolk, 1987-89; chief reproductive endocrinology Uniformed Svcs. U. Health Scis., Bethesda, Md., 1993—, asst. prof., 1990—, assoc. prof., 1993—. Adj. scientist S.W. Found. Biomed. Rsch., 1990—, dir. Assisted Reproductive Technology, Reproductive Medicine Assocs. of N.J., Morristown, N.J. Ad hoc reviewer Fertility and Sterility, Jour. Clin. Endocrinology and Metabolism, Ob-Gyn., Am. Jour. Ob-Gyn., Contraception, Maturitas, Jour. Pediatric and Adolescent Gynecology, Internat. Jour. Infertility, Jour. In Vitro Fertilization and Embryo Transfer; contbr. articles to profl. jours. and abstracts. Lt Col USAF, 1993—95, Uniformed Services University of the Health Sciences. Grantee Surgeon Gen., Wyeth Rsch., Solvay Pharm. Rsch., Hitachi of Am., Tap Pharms. Fellow Am. Coll. Obstetricians and Gynecologists (chmns. award Armed Forces dist. meeting 1988, Searle award 1989, Prof. of Yr. 1991); mem. Am. Fertility Soc. (Best Poster award 1988), N.Am. Menopausal Soc., Am. Air Force Clin. Surgeons, Endocrine Soc., Soc. Developmental Endocrinologists, Phi Beta Kappa, Chi Beta Phi, Omicron Delta Kappa. Achievements include receiving several awards for research. Office: RMA of NJ 111 Madison Ave Ste 100 Morristown NJ 07960-6083 Home: 170 Post Kennel Rd Far Hills NJ 07931-2408

**SCOTT, RIDLEY,** film director; b. South Shields, Tyne and Wear, Eng., Nov. 30, 1937; m. Felicity Heywood, 1964 (div.); 2 children; m. Sandy Watson, 1979 (div. 1989); 1 child. BA, Royal Coll. Art; grad., London Internat. Film Sch. Dir.: (films) The Duellists, 1977, Alien, 1979, Legend, 1985, Black Rain, 1989; prodr.: The Browning Version, 1994, Clay Pigeons, 1998, Where the Money Is, 2000, Six Bullets from Now, 2002, All the Invisible Children, 2005, In Her Shoes, 2005; exec. prodr.: Monkey Trouble, 1994, The Hire: Hostage, 2002, The Hire: Beat the Devil, 2002, The Hire: Ticker, 2002; (films) Tristan & Isolde, 2006; dir.(and prodr.): Thelma & Louise, 1991, 1492: Conquest of Paradise, 1992, G.I. Jane, 1997, Black Hawk Down, 2001, Matchstick Men, 2003, Kingdom of Heaven, 2005; writer, dir., prodr. Boy on a Bicycle, 1965; dir.(and co-prodr.): Blade Runner, 1982, (and exec. prodr.): Someone to Watch Over Me, 1987, White Squall, 1996, Gladiator, 2000; dir., prodr., exec. music prodr. Hannibal, 2001; dir.: (TV series) Z Cars, 1962, Adam Adamant Lives, 1966, The Informer, 1966; exec. prodr.: The Hunger, 1997, AFP: American Fighter Pilot, 2002, Numb3rs, 2005—; (TV films) RKO 287, 1999, The Last Debate, 2000, The Gathering Storm, 2002 (Emmy award, 2002). Winner Design scholarship, N.Y.; named one of 50 Most Powerful People in Hollywood Premiere mag., 2004, 2005. Address: William Morris Agency One William Morris Pl Beverly Hills CA 90212*

**SCOTT, ROBERT ALLYN,** academic administrator; b. Englewood, NJ, Apr. 16, 1939; s. William D. and Ann. F. (Waterman) S.; children: Ryan Keith, Kira Elizabeth. BA, Bucknell U., 1961; PhD, Cornell U., 1975; LLD, Ramapo Coll., 2000. Mgmt. trainee Procter & Gamble Co., Phila., 1961-63; asst. dir. admissions Bucknell U., Lewisburg, Pa., 1965-67; asst. dean Coll. Arts and Scis. Cornell U., Ithaca, 1967-69, assoc. dean, 1969-79, anthropology faculty, 1978-79; dir. acad. affairs Ind. Commn. for Higher Edn., Indpls., 1979-84, asst. commr., 1984-85; pres. Ramapo (N.J.) Coll., 1985-2000, Adelphi U., 2000—. Cons. Sta. WSKG Pub. TV and Radio, 1977-79, also to various colls. and univs., pubs., 1966—; mem. curriculum adv. com. Ind. Bd. Edn., 1984-87, Lilly Endowment Think Tank, 1984-86; mem. nat. adv. panel Ind. 21st Century Schooling Project, 1990-92; U.S. rep. to creation of U. Mobility Asian-Pacific, 1993—; U.S. rep. to meetings of Coun. European Rectors, 1991—; sr. advisor to U.S. State Dept. on Higher Edn. in Unesco European Region, 1997—; U.S. del. to UNESCO N.Am. and World Confs. on Higher Edn., 1998; sr. cons., chair N.J. Higher Edn. Restructuring Team, 1994. Author books and monographs; editl. bd. Cornell Rev., 1976-79; book rev. editor Coll. and Univ., 1974-78; cons. editor Change mag., 1979-95; cons. editor Jour. Higher Edn., 1985—; exec. editor Saturday Evening Post book div. Curtis Pub. Co., 1982-85; contbr. articles to sociols., ednl. and popular publs. Trustee Bucknell U., 1976-78, First Unitarian Ch., Ithaca, 1970-73, 78-79, chmn., 1971-73, Unitarian Universalist Ch. of Indpls., 1980-85. With USNR, 1963-65. Spencer Found. rsch. grantee, 1977; recipient Sagamore of the Wabash award, 1986, Leader of Yr. award Prudential Found., 1987, Disting. Svc. award West Bergen Mental Health Ctr., 1991, Presdl. medal NYU, 1994, Sci. and Edn. award Boy Scouts Am., 1993, Raoul Wallenberg Humanitarian Leadership award, 2000, Disting. Svc. award ACIT, 2002, Disting. Svc. award Harbor Child Care, 2003, Excellence in Higher Edn. award Huntington Chamber, 2003, Telly award for Excellence in Cable TV Programming, 2003, Cmty. Svc. award Garden City Chamber, 2004, Annual Svc. award Hispanic Counseling Ctr., 2004, Martin Luther King, Jr. Cmty. Svc. award, 2005, Outstanding Paper Excellence award Emerald Group Publishing, Ltd., 2003, 04. Fellow Am. Anthrop. Assn.; mem. Am. Sociol. Assn., Am. Assn. Higher Edn., Coun. on Liberal Arts and Scis. (chair 1990-93), Am. Coun. on Edn. Commn. On Internat. Edn. (chair 1991-93), L.I. Assn., Global Kids, Inc., Coun. Fgn. Rels., Regional Plan Assn., Nat. Fgn. Lang. Ctr., Brookings Instn. Study Group, Higher Edn. Colloquium (chmn. 1982-84, 96-98), N.J. Assn. of Coll. and Univs. (chair 1991-92), Bucknell U. Alumni Assn. (bd. dirs. 1976-80, pres. 1976-78, Outstanding Achievement 1991), Indian Trail Club, Century Assn., Phi Kappa Psi, Phi Kappa Phi. Office: Adelphi U Garden City NY 11530 Office Phone: 516-877-3838.

**SCOTT, ROBERT CORTEZ,** congressman, lawyer; b. Washington, Apr. 30, 1947; s. Charles Waldo and Mae (Hamlin) Scott. BA, Harvard U., Cambridge, Mass., 1969; JD, Boston Coll. Sch. Law, 1973; LLD (hon.), Commonwealth Coll., Hampton, Va., 1988. Lawyer pvt. practice, Newport News, 1973—91; mem. Va. State Ho. Dels., Richmond, 1978—83, Va. State Senate, Richmond, 1983—93, US Congress from 3rd Va. dist., 1993—, mem. edn. and the workforce com., mem. judiciary com., ranking minority mem. crime, terrorism and homeland security subcommittee. Br. pres. NAACP, Newport News, 1974-80; pres. bd. Peninsula Legal Aid Ctr., Hampton, 1977-81; mem. state exec. bd. March of Dimes, Va., 1987—; chmn. 1st dist. Dem. Party Va., 1980-85; bd. dirs. Hampton Roads March of Dimes; adv. com. Peninsula Boy Scouts Am. Served in USAR, 1970—74, served in Mass. N.G., 1974—76. Recipient Brotherhood Citation award Nat. Conf. Christians & Jews, 1985, Child Adv. award Va. Acad. Pediat., 1987, Disting. Svc. award Va. State Fraternal Order Police, 1987, Outstanding Legislator award So. Health Assn., 1989; named one of 100 Most Influential Black Americans, Ebony mag., 2006. Mem. Peninsula C. of C., Alpha Phi Alpha, Sigma Pi Phi. Democrat. Episcopalian. Office: US Ho Reps 1201 Longworth Ho Office Bldg Washington DC 20515 Office Phone: 202-225-8351.*

**SCOTT, ROBERT EDWIN,** law educator; b. Nagpur, India, Feb. 25, 1944; came to U.S., 1955; s. Roland Waldeck and Carol (Culver) S.; m. Elizabeth (Loch) Shumaker, Aug. 14, 1965; children: Christina Elaine, Robert Adam. BA, Oberlin Coll., 1965; JD, Coll. of William and Mary, 1968; LLM, U. Mich., 1969, SJD, 1973. Bar: Va. 1968. Asst. prof. William and Mary Sch. Law, Williamsburg, Va., 1969—71, assoc. prof., 1971—72, prof., 1973—74; prof. law U. Va. Sch. Law, Charlottesville, 1974-82, Lewis F. Powell, Jr. prof. 1982—2003, dean and provost H. Leon prof. 1991—2001, William L. Mathanon and Robert M. Morgenthau disting. prof., 2001—03, David & Mary Harrison disting. prof. Law, 2003—. Vis. assoc. prof. U. Va. Sch. Law, 1972—73; vis. prof. Columbia U. Law Sch., 1987—88, Justin W. D'Atri vis. prof. law, bus. & soc., 2001—. Co-author: Commercial Transactions, 1982, 91, Sales Law and the Contracting Process, 1982, 91, Contract Law and Theory, 1988, 93, 2002, Payment Systems and Credit Instruments, 1996. Recipient Thomas Jefferson Award, U. Va., 2004. Fellow Am. Bar Found., Am. Acad. Arts and Sciences; mem. Am. Law Inst. Democrat. Methodist. Office: U Va Sch Law 580 Massie Rd Charlottesville VA 22903-1789 Office Phone: 434-924-3551. Personal E-mail: res8f@virginia.edu.

**SCOTT, ROBERT HAYWOOD, JR.,** lawyer; b. Hazelton, Pa., Mar. 1941; s. Robert Haywood and Marjorie Jane Scott; m. Sandra Lou Carroll, June 6, 1966; children: Paige Carroll, Robert Haywood. AB magna cum laude, Kenyon Coll., 1963; JD with distinction, Duke U., 1966. Bar: Mo. 1969, Kans. 1966, Ohio 1972. Assoc. Hoskins King Springer McGannon and Hahn, Kansas City, Mo., 1970-72; operating v.p., sr. counsel Federated Dept. Stores, Cin., 1972-83; prin. Roberts Fleischaker & Scott, Joplin, Mo., 1983-88; chief exec. officer W&S Mfg., Inc., Joplin, 1988-92, also chmn. bd. dirs.; CEO Robert Scott Investment Banking, 1988—. Chmn. Deep Sea Archaeology Rsch. Coun., 1994—. Contbr. articles to profl. jours. Capt. USAF, 1966—70. Mem. Mo. Bar Assn., Order of the Coif, Phi Beta Kappa. Home: 1330 Valle Dr Joplin MO 64801-1074

**SCOTT, ROBERT LANE,** chemist, educator; b. Santa Rosa, Calif., Mar. 20, 1922; s. Horace Albert and Maurine (Lane) S.; m. Elizabeth Sewall Hunter, May 27, 1944; children: Joanna Ingersoll (dec.), Jonathan Armat, David St. Clair, Janet Hamilton. S.B., Harvard U., 1942; MA, Princeton U., 1944, PhD, 1945. Sci. staff Los Alamos Lab., 1945-46; Frank B. Jewett fellow U. Calif., Berkeley, 1946-48; faculty UCLA, 1948—, prof. chemistry, 1960-92, prof. emeritus, 1993—, chmn. dept., 1963-67. Author: (with J.H. Hildebrand) Solubility of Nonelectrolytes, 3d edit, 1950, rev., 1964, Regular Solutions, 1962, Regular and Related Solutions, 1970; Contbr. articles to profl. jours. Guggenheim fellow, 1955; NSF sr. fellow, 1961-62; Fulbright lectr., 1958-59 Fellow AAAS, Am. Phys. Soc.; mem. Am. Chem. Soc. (Joel Henry Hildebrand award 1984), Royal Soc. Chemistry (London), Sigma Xi. Home: 11128 Montana Ave Los Angeles CA 90049-3509 Business E-Mail: scott@chem.ucla.edu.

**SCOTT, ROSA MAE,** art educator, artist; b. East Hampton, NY, Apr. 12, 1937; d. James Alexander and Victoria (Square) Nicholson; m. Frank Albert Hanna, Apr. 1, 1957 (div. Mar. 1985); 1 child, Frank Albert Hanna III; m. Warner Bruce Scott, Aug. 3, 1985 (dec. Oct. 2002); children: Bernadine, John, Patricia, Charlene, Lawrence. AA, Dabney Lancaster, 1989; BA, Mary Baldwin, 1992. Cosmetologist Rosa's Beauty Shop, East Hampton, 1962-68; sec. Frank Hanna's Cleaning Co., East Hampton, 1962-77; cashier, clk. Brook's Pharmacy, East Hampton, 1992; lead tchr. East Hampton Day Care, 1992-94, 97-98; substitute tchr. Lexington (Va.) Schs., 1994—; lead tchr. Suffolk C.C. Child Care Ctr., River Head, N.Y., 1999; substitute tchr. East Hampton Sch., 2000—03; lead tchr. after sch. program Springs Sch. 2000—02, 2004—05, substitute tchr. 2000—03. Substitute tchr. East Hampton Sch., 1996-97, 2000-04; sec. Lylburn Downing Cmty. Ctr., Inc., Lexington, 1985-97; arts and crafts tutor, supr. East Hampton Town Youth After Sch. Program, 1996—. Pres. Rockbridge Garden Club, Lexington, 1996; co-organizer Va. Co-op. Ex. Garden Clubs, Lexington, 1995; bd. dirs. Rockbridge Area Pres. Homes, 1996, Fine Arts of Rockbridge, 1985-92, Friends of Lime Kiln, Lexington, 1985-92. Mem.: Guild Hall, East End Arts, Montauk Artists Assn. (receptionist 2003—05), Artist Alliance East Hampton, L.I. Black Artists (v.p. 2000—05), Rockbridge Arts Guild (pres. LI Black Artists 2006—). Avocations: collecting emmett kelly clowns, art, reading, theater, tennis. Home: PO Box 1265 East Hampton NY 11937-0708 Personal E-mail: rosahannascott@aol.com.

**SCOTT, SAMUEL C.,** food products executive; B in Engring., Fairleigh Dickinson U., 1966, MBA. V.p. CPC Internat. Inc., 1991; pres. N. Am. corn refining Bestfoods, 1989—97, pres. worldwide corn refining, 1995-97; pres. COO Corn Products Internat., Westchester, Ill., 1997—2001, chmn., pres., CEO, 2001—. Bd. dir. Motorola Inc. Dir. ACCION USA; trustee Chgo. Symphony. Office: Corn Products International 5 Westbrook Corporate Ctr Westchester IL 60154*

**SCOTT, SANDRA J.,** not-for-profit executive; b. Kansas City, Kans., Jan. 12, 1959; d. Eartha Lee and Herman Scott; children: Sonya Lynn Allen, Jonelle Melissa Allen, Michael Lee Hunter, Jr. Exec. dir. Your Empowerment Source, Inc., Kansas City, 2003—. Author: (autobiography) Lord, Let There Be Light, Becoming Whole Before Becoming One, Baggage Handlers: My Road to Letting Go of Life's Painful Luggage. E-mail: sandra_j_scott59@yahoo.com.

**SCOTT, SHIRLEY CLAY,** dean; PhD, Kent State U., 1973. Dean Grad. Coll. Western Mich. U.; dean Coll. Liberal Arts Southern Ill. U., 1999—, prof. Office: Office of the Dean Coll Liberal Arts So Illinios U Mailcode 4522 Carbondale IL 62901 Office Phone: 618-453-2466. E-mail: scotts@siu.edu.

**SCOTT, SIDNEY BUFORD,** finance company executive; b. Richmond, Va., Mar. 3, 1933; s. Buford and Mary (Nixon) S.; m. Susan Elder Bailey, Sept. 19, 1959; children: Sidney Buford Jr., Elizabeth Scott Cech, George Reily Bailey. Student, Yale U., 1951-53; BA, U. Va., 1955; LLD (hon.), St. Paul's Coll., 1982. Chmn. Scott & Stringfellow Inc., Richmond, 1974—. Bd. dirs. New Market Corp.; mem. regional firms adv. com. N.Y. Stock Exch., 1982-85; chmn. bd. trustees Securities Industry Found. for Econ. Edn., 1976-86; trustee Va. Retirement Sys., 1984-94; dir. Nat. Coun. Econ. Edn. Bd. dirs. Hollywood Cemetery, Police Benevolent Assn.; trustee, chmn. Elk Hill Farm, Inc.; bd. visitors U. Va., 1987-94; former vice rector, bd. visitors Va. Commonwealth U.; past chmn. United Way Greater Richmond; vestryman, past sr. warden St. Paul's Episcopal Ch.; past pres. Sheltering Arms Hosp; past bd. dirs., v.p. Big Bros. Am.; past bd. dirs., chmn. Big Bros. Richmond, Met. Found., also others. Sgt. U.S. Army, 1956-58. Recipient Outstanding Young Man of Yr. award Richmond Jr. C. of C., 1964, outstanding svc. award Va. Coun. on Econ. Edn., 1976, 80, Brotherhood award NCCJ, 1981, George P. Baker medal Joint Coun. on Econ. Edn., 1986, Bd. Mem. of Yr. award Va. Assn. Children's Homes, 1987. Mem. Securities Industry Assn. (governing coun. 1976-78), Raven Soc., Beta Gamma Sigma. Democrat. Home: 4919 Lockgreen Cir Richmond VA 23226-1748 Office: PO Box 1575 Richmond VA 23218-1575

**SCOTT, STANLEY DEFOREST,** real estate executive; b. Hudson County, NJ, Nov. 2, 1926; s. Stanley DeForest and Anne Marie (Volk) Scott; m. Mary Elizabeth Hazard, Dec. 30, 1953. BA, U. So. Calif., 1950. Gen. mgr. Alfred Scott Pubs., N.Y.C., 1951-56; chmn., pres. S.D. Scott Printing Co. Inc., N.Y.C., 1956-92; gen. ptnr. 145 Hudson St. Assocs. Co-chmn. mus. and art com. Fraunces Tavern Mus., 1973—87, 1998—; assoc. J. Carter Brown Libr.; former mem. Mayor's Industry Adv. Com.; former bd. dirs. Bus. Relocation Com. With USNR, 1944—46. Fellow, Frick Collection. Mem.: Friends of Canterbury Cathedral in U.S., Am. Assocs. Royal Acad. Arts (patron), World Monuments Fund (internat. coun.), Am. Friends of the Brit. Libr., Am. Mus. Britain (coun. 1986—), Mus. Modern Art, Am. Friends Hermitage Mus., Am. Friends Brit. Mus. (patron), Royal Oak Found. English-Speaking Union N.Y. (patron), Am. Friends English Heritage, Sir John Soane's Mus. Found. (patron), Met. Mus. Art, Morgan Libr. (patron), N.Y. Hist. Soc., Mt. Vernon Ladies Assn. (adv. com.), Am. Numismatic Soc. (trustee), Church Club N.Y., Union Club, Knickerbocker Club, Grolier Club, St. George's Soc., S.R. (bd. mgrs., v.p.), Pilgrims U.S., Soc. Colonial Wars (mem. coun.), Soc. Mayflower Descs. Republican. Episcopalian. Home: One Sutton Pl South New York NY 10022-2471 Office: 145 Hudson St New York NY 10013-2103

**SCOTT, STEPHEN BRINSLEY,** theater producer; b. Pitts., Aug. 27, 1950; s. Robert Crawford and Lucille (Henrickson) Scott. BS in Edn., U. Kans., 1972; MA, U. Denver, 1973. Artistic dir. Creede (Colo.) Repertory Theatre, 1976-78; chair dept. theatre Baker U., Baldwin, Kans., 1978-80; dir. edn. and cmty. svcs. Goodman Theatre, Chgo., 1980-84, dir. arts in edn., 1986-88, artistic assoc., 1988-94, assoc. producer, 1994—; dir. ednl. programs Chgo. Internat. Theatre Festival, 1985-86. Spl. instr. Loyola U. Chgo., 1987-95; instr. Columbia Coll., Chgo., 1981-85, 92-97, Latin Sch. Chgo., 1984-86, Roosevelt U., 1997—; mem. arts in edn. panel Nat. Endowment for Arts, Washington, 1990-91. Mem. adv. panels Ill. Arts Coun., Chgo., 1984-87; mem. com. League Chgo. Theatres, 1990—; cmty. rep. local sch. coun. Franklin Schs., Chgo., 1990-94. pres. Chgo. Coalition for Arts in Edn., 1983-85. Named Outstanding Lectr., Chgo. Cultural Ctr., 1981, 84, Outstanding Dir., Joseph Jefferson Citation Nominations, 1987, 97, 2005, award for outstanding ensemble Joseph Jefferson Award Com., 1999, After Dark award for outstanding dir., 2001. Mem. Ill. Theatre Assn. (exec. com. 1987-97), Soc. Stage Dirs. and Choreographers, Ill. Alliance for Arts in Edn., Ill. Arts Alliance, Phi Beta Kappa. Democrat. Home: 118 N Elk St Apt 207 Chicago IL 60605-1766 Office: Goodman Theatre 170 N Dearborn St Chicago IL 60601 Office Phone: 312-443-8478. Business E-Mail: stevescott@goodmantheatre.org.

**SCOTT, STEPHEN CARLOS,** academic administrator; b. Greenville, S.C., Sept. 20, 1949; s. Carlos O'Dell and Christina (Nikitas) S.; m. Patsy Jordan, Apr. 13, 1968; children: Stephanie Christina, Lance Stephen. BA, Clemson (S.C.) U., 1971, MEd, 1975, EdD, 1987. Owner, mgr. Scotty's Inc., restaurant, Clemson, 1967-71; tchr. math. Pickens (S.C.) Sr. High Sch., 1972-74; instr. bus. Tri-County Tech. Coll., Pendleton, SC, 1974-76, head dept., 1976-78, dir. bc campus Easley, SC, 1978-80; dean bus. Greenville Tech. Coll., 1980-85, assoc. v.p., 1985-88; pres. Southeastern C.C., Whiteville, NC, 1988-99; exec. v.p N.C. C.C. Sys., 1999—2002; pres. Lenoir C.C., Kinston, N.C., 2002—. Cons. P.C.E. Fed. Credit Union, Liberty, S.C., 1975-88, Jacobs Mfg. Co., Clemson, 1979-80, Flat Rock Shelter Ctr., Easley, 1980-85; bd. mem. N.C. Rural Ctr. Contbr. articles to profl. jours. and mags. Pres. So. Shelter Ctr., Greenville, 1986—88, Good Shepherd Found., Whiteville, 1990—92; bd. dirs. Good Shepherd, 1988—91; chmn. Columbus County Sch. Bond. Dr., 1989. Am. Heart Fund Drive Columbus County, 1992; co-chmn. Columbus County Long Range Planning Com., 1989—91; vice chmn. Pvt. Industry Coun. Region O, 1992—99; funding dir. Habitat for Humanity Columbus County, 1992; pres. bd. dirs. Columbus County Rural Health Ctr., 1994; bd. dirs. N.C. Rural Ctr., 2000—02. Recipient award for patriotism U.S. Savs. Bonds Program, 1987. Mem. Am. Assn. Cmty. and Jrs. Colls. (Pres.'s Acad.), Greater Kinston C. of C. (exec. bd. 2003—), Rotary

(bd. dirs. Whiteville 1990-92, pres. 1992-93). Presbyterian. Avocations: running, chess, coin collecting/numismatics, reading. Home: 1417 Wynncrest Ct Raleigh NC 27603-8770 Personal E-mail: scs320@lenoircc.edu.

**SCOTT, STUART,** sports anchor; b. Chgo., July 19, 1965; married; 1 child. BA in Speech Comms. and Radio/TV/Film, U. N.C., 1987. News reporter, weekend anchor WPDE-TV, Florence, S.C., 1987-88; news reporter WRAL-TV, Raleigh, N.C., 1988-90; sports reporter, sports anchor WESH-TV, Orlando, Fla., 1990-93; sports anchor, sports reporter ESPN, Bristol, Conn., 1993—, co-host NFL Primetime, 1997—, former anchor SportSmash, 1993. Anchor reporter SportsNight: College Football Edition, 1995—, co-host SportsNight, 1994. Office: ESPN ESPN Plaza Bristol CT 06010*

**SCOTT, SUSAN CRAIG,** plastic surgeon; b. NYC, 1948; MD, Columbia U., 1974. Diplomate Am. Bd. Plastic Surgery with subspecialty in hand surgery. Intern Roosevelt Hosp., N.Y.C., NY, 1974—75, resident in gen. surgery, 1975—79; resident in plastic surgery NYU Med. Ctr., 1979—81; fellow in hand surgery Roosevelt Hosp., 1981—82; pvt. practice plastic surgery N.Y.C., 1987—. Office: 150 E 77TH St New York NY 10021-1922 Office Phone: 212-288-9922. Personal E-mail: smcscott@verizon.net.

**SCOTT, SYLVIA JANE,** small business owner; b. Charleston, S.C., Jan. 31, 1945; d. John Mitchell and Christabelle Lillian Johnson; m. Nathanial Myers, 1960 (dec. Mar. 9, 1998); children: Tia Johnson, Nathanial Myers, Norma Griffin, Tralane Mason, Sonia Melton, Troi Mack, Michael Myers. Student, Trident Tech. Coll., 1975; cosmetology cert., 1987. Owner Shear Beauty, Charleston, 1988—, Rental Units, Charleston, 1997—, Scott Supplies, Charleston, 1999—. Author: The Bookdweller, 2002. Recipient cert., Carolina Monority Supplier Council, Inc. Roman Catholic. Achievements include patents for multi-page doll bookmarks; scheduling board. Business E-Mail: scottsupplies@bellsouth.net.

**SCOTT, T. GORDON,** chemistry and math educator, writer; b. Laconia, N.H., Nov. 27, 1941; s. William Stafford and Jeanne Richardson Scott; m. Elizabeth Mary Winterberg, Mar. 11, 1995. BA, U. Pa., 1963; BA with honours, Cambridge U., England, 1965, MA, 1970; PhD, U. Ill., 1969. Profl. tchg. cert., Pa.; postgrad. tchg. lic., Va. Tchg. asst. U. Ill., Champaign-Urbana, 1965-66; asst. prof. chemistry Oberlin Coll., Ohio, 1969-70; lectr. biochemistry U. Calif., Santa Barbara, 1971; cons. Sci-Math Cons., Uniontown, Pa., 1972-75; supr. secondary studies Westminster Acad., Carmichaels, Pa., 1975-79; asst. prof. chemistry Alderson-Broaddus Coll., Philippi, W.Va., 1981-84; assoc. prof. chemistry Bryan Coll., Dayton, Tenn., 1984-86, Knoxville Coll., Tenn., 1987-89, Union Coll., Barbourville, Ky., 1989-91, Jarvis Christian Coll. Hawkins, Tex., 1992-98; with Chem. Edn. Cons. USA, Hawkins,Tex., 1998-2000; instr. math. Winona Ind. Sch. Dist., Tex., 1998-99; instr. math, chemistry and astronomy Pittsylvania County Schs., Va.; tchr. Dan River HS, Ringgold, Va., 2000—02; adj. prof. chemistry and natural sci-biochemistry Danville CC, Va., 1999—2004; adj. instr. pharmacology Nat. Coll., Danville, 2001—03; assoc. prof. chemistry Winston-Salem State U., NC, 2004—. Rsch. assoc. DuPont Chem. Co., Inc., Phila., 1963, EPA, Phila., 1988, Edgewood-Aberdeen Rsch. US Army, Aberdeen Proving Ground, Md., 1993; vis. prof. La. Coll., Pineville, 1992; adj. sci. instr. Hargrave Mil. Acad., Chatham, Va., 2003; undergrad. rsch. mentor NSF, New Orleans, 2004; cons. with Transition State Assocs., Danville, Va. Author: (with others) Synthetic Procedures in Nucleic Acid Chemistry, 1968, Spectroscopic Model Studies of NAD, 1969; contbr. articles to Jour. Am. Chem. Soc., 1967, 1970, 1972, 2003. Musician with Danville Recorder Consort, Danville Area Choral Arts Soc. Thouron fellow to Cambridge U., 1963-65; Thouron scholar Gonville & Caius Coll., Cambridge U.; grantee NSF, 1996-97, Army Rsch. Orgn., 1993-95, Robert A. Welch Found., 1996-98, NSF, 1997-99. Mem. Am. Chem. Soc., Cambridge U. Chem. Soc., Am. Sci. Affiliation (dir. 1998), Rotary Internat. (chmn. internat. edn. com. 1977-81). Achievements include determined the fluorescent lifetime of coenzyme NADH. Avocations: baritone vocal solos, exploring ideas, renaissance music (treble and tenor blockflute), astronomy. Office Phone: 336-750-3179. Business E-Mail: scottg@wssu.edu.

**SCOTT, TERRY LEE,** communications executive; b. Rockford, Ill., Oct. 21, 1950; s. Wilson C. and Marie G. (Bunger) S.; divorced; children: Andrea, Brady, Tiffany. BS in Acctg. magna cum laude, Bradley U., 1972. CPA Ill. Tex. Audit prin. Arthur Young and Co., Dallas, 1972-82; v.p. fin. and administrn., treas. Paging Network Inc., Dallas, 1982-90; sr. v.p. Paging Network, Inc., Dallas, 1990-92, pres., CEO, bd. dirs., 1993-95, Terion Inc. Melbourne, Fla., 1995-97, chmn., CEO, 1997-99, Terry Scott Enterprises, Plano, Tex., 1997—; dir. Chameleon Tech., Inc., Seattle, 2002—, Metasolv Software, Inc., Dallas, 2003—04; CFO, v.p. Fin. of Chase Med., Inc., 2003—04; pres., CEO, dir. Airimba Wireless, Inc., Plano, Tex., 2004—. Bd. dirs. XY Point Corp., Terion, Inc., Locate Networks, Inc., MobileStar Inc. Peoples Choice TV Corp. Mem. AICPA, Tex. Soc. CPAs, Phi Kappa Phi, Zeta Pi. Methodist. Office: 5816 Gallant Fox Ln Plano TX 75093-2910 Personal E-mail: tscott1704@aol.com. E-mail: tscott@airaba.com.

**SCOTT, THEODORE R.,** retired lawyer; b. Mount Vernon, Ill., Dec. 7, 1924; s. Theodore R. and Beulah (Flannigan) S.; m. Laurene Anne Laurence, Sarah Buckland, Daniel, Barbara Gomon. AB, U. Ill., 1947, JD, 1949. Bar: Ill. 1950. Law clk. to judge U.S. Ct. Appeals, 1949-51; pvt. practice Chgo., 1950—2000; assoc. Spaulding Glass, 1951-53, Loftus, Lucas & Hammand, 1953-58, Ooms, McDougall, Williams & Hersh, 1958-60; ptnr. McDougall, Hersh & Scott, Chgo., 1960-87; of counsel Jones, Day, Reavis & Pogue, 1987-97, Rockey, Milnamow & Katz, 1998—2000. 2nd lt. USAAF, 1943-45. Decorated Air medal. Fellow Am. Coll. Trial Lawyers; mem. ABA, Ill. Bar Assn., Chgo. Bar Assn., 7th Cir. Bar Assn., Chgo. (past pres.), Legal Club Chgo., Law Club Chgo., Patent Law Assn. Chgo. (past pres.), Union League Club, Exmoor Country Club (Highland Park, Ill.), Phi Beta Kappa. Home: 1569 Woodvale Ave Deerfield IL 60015-2350

**SCOTT, THOMAS JEFFERSON, JR.,** lawyer, electrical engineer; b. Montgomery, Ala., Dec. 30, 1943; s. Thomas Jefferson Sr. and Irene (Feagin) S.; m. Betsy Sue Mackta, Apr. 25, 1981; children: Elspeth Watts, Marguerita Taylor, Thomas Jefferson III. BEE, Yale U., 1966, BA in Econs., 1967; JD, Vanderbilt U., 1974. Bar: Va. 1974, D.C. 1975, N.Y. 1980, U.S. Dist. Ct. D.C. 1986, U.S. Dist. Ct. (ea. dist.) Va. 1993, U.S. Tax Ct. 1981, U.S. Ct. Fed. Claims, 1982, U.S. Ct. Appeals (fed. cir.) 1982, U.S. Ct. Appeals (4th cir.) 1993, U.S. Supreme Ct. 1984. Trial atty. civil div. U.S. Dept. of Justice, Washington, 1974-78; assoc. Cooper & Dunham, Washington, 1978-80, sr. trial counsel civil div., 1980-85; ptnr. Pennie & Edmonds, Washington, 1985-90, Howrey & Simon, Washington, 1990-97, Hunton & Williams, Washington, 1997—. Capt. USNR, 1966-71. Decorated D.F.C. Mem. ABA, Am. Intellectual Property Law Assn. Office: Hunton & Williams 1900 K St NW Washington DC 20006-1110 Office Phone: 202-955-1685. Business E-Mail: tscott@hunton.com.

**SCOTT, TONY,** film director; b. Stockton-on-Tees, England, July 21, 1944; m. Donna Wilson. Degree in Fine Arts, Sunderland Art School; postgrad., Leeds Coll. Art, 1969; MFA, Royal Coll. Arts, 1972. Film dir. Totem Prodn., L.A., 1972—. Dir. films including One of the Mission (half-hour film, Brit. Film Inst.), Loving Memory (1-hour feature), The Hunger, 1983, Top Gun, 1986, Beverly Hills Cop II, 1987, Revenge, 1990, Days of Thunder, 1990, The Last Boy Scout, 1991, True Romance, 1993, Crimson Tide, 1995, The Fan, 1996, Enemy of the State, 1998, Spy Game, 2001, Agent Orange, 2004, dir., exec. prodr.: The Hire: Beat the Devil (short film), 2002; dir., prodr. Man on Fire, 2004, Domino, 2005; exec. prodr.: Clay Pigeons, 1998, Where the Money Is, 2000, Big Time, 2001, The Hire: Hostage, 2002, The Hire: Ticker, 2002, Six Bullets From Now, 2002, Tristan & Isolde, 2005, In Her Shoes, 2005; exec. prodr. (TV movies) RKO 281, 1999, The Last Debate, 2000, The Gathering Storm, 2002; dir. (TV series episode) The Hunger, 1997; exec. prodr (TV series)The Hunger, 1997-2000, Numb3rs, 2005-. Recipient numer-

ous Clios, Gold and Silver Lions and various other awards. Avocation: mountain climbing. Office: Totem Prodns 8009 Santa Monica Blvd Los Angeles CA 90046-5008 also: Creative Artists Agy 9830 Wilshire Blvd Beverly Hills CA 90212-1804

**SCOTT, VERONICA L.,** middle school educator; d. Evelyn Scott; children: Carletta Maria, Caryn Michelle. BA, Spelman Coll., 1987; Masters, Cambridge Coll., 2000. Cert. tchr. SC., 1988. Music specialist Andrews H.S., SC, 1988—94, Rosemary Mid. Sch., Andrews, SC, 1994—. Mem.: Alpha Kappa Alpha (assoc.; membership chairperson, corr. sec., Soror of Yr.). Office: Georgetown County Sch Dist 12804 County Line Rd Andrews SC 29510 Personal E-mail: vlscott@rm.gcsd.k12.sc.us.

**SCOTT, VICKI SUE,** school system administrator; b. Pine Bluff, Ark., Feb. 16, 1946; d. John Wesley and Ruby Gray (Whitehead) and Hannah (Lewis) S. BA, Henderson Coll., 1968; MS in Edn., U. Cen. Ark., 1978, postgrad., 1979-84, U. Ark., 1983-85, Ark. State U., 1993-94. Cert. adminstrn., secondary sch. prin., middle sch., secondary health and phys. edn. Tchr., coach Brinkley (Ark.) Pub. Schs., 1968-76, Lonoke (Ark.) Jr. and Sr. High Schs., 1976-77, S.E. Jr. High Sch., Pine Bluff, 1978-92, asst. prin., 1992-2000, dir. summer sch., 1991, 92; prin. White Hall (Ark.) Jr. H.S., White Hall, Arkansas, 2000—. AIDS educator Arkansas River Edn. Svc. Coop., Pine Bluff, 1989-92. Active Leadership Pine Bluff, 1993-94. Scholar Assn. Women Ednl. Suprs., 1985; named Outstanding Young Women of Am., 1974, Ark. Leadership Acad., 2000. Mem.: DAR, ASCD, Nat. Mid. Sch. Assn., Nat. Assn. Sch. Secondary Prins., Ark. Activities Assn., Ark. Assn. Ednl. Adminstrs., Ark. Assn. Mid. Level Administrs. (bd. dirs. 2002—04), Order Ea. Star, Phi Delta Kappa, Delta Kappa Gamma (Epsilon chpt. pres., scholar 1994). Baptist. Avocations: tennis, reading, hiking, travel, golf. Home: 3215 S Cherry St Pine Bluff AR 71603-5983 Office: White Hall Jr HS 8106 Dollarway Rd White Hall AR 71602-6999 Office Phone: 870-247-2711. Personal E-mail: foghorn@cableynx.com. Business E-Mail: scottv@whjr.arsc.k12.ar.us.

**SCOTT, WALTER, JR.,** telecommunications industry executive; b. May 21, 1931; m. Suzanne Scott. BS, Colo. State U., 1953; LittD, U. Nebr., 1983; LHD, Coll. St. Mary, 1988; D of Commerce, Bellevue U., 1996. With Peter Kiewit Sons, Inc., Omaha, 1953—, engr., project engr., dist. engr., Cleve. dist., 1959—61, asst. dist. mgr., Cleve. dist., 1961—62, dist. mgr. Cleve. dist. Omaha, 1962-64, v.p., 1964, exec. v.p., 1965-79, chmn. bd., 1964, pres., 1979, chmn. bd. dirs., pres., CEO, 1979-97, chmn. emeritus, 1997—; chmn. Level 3 Communications Inc. (former subs. PKS), Broomfield, Colo., 1997—. Bd. trustee Open World Leadership Ctr.; dir. Berkshire Hathaway, Burlington Resources, Commonwealth Telephone Enterprises, MidAmerican Energy Holdings, RCN Corp., Valmont Industries. Served with USAF, 1954-56. Named Philanthropist of Yr., Nat. Soc. Fund-Raising Execs., 1987, Man of Yr., Mid-Am. Coun. Boy Scouts Am., 1988, King Ak-Sar-Ben XCII, Knights of Ak-Sar-Ben, 1988, Disting. Eagle Scout, Boy Scouts Am., 1991, Citizen of Yr., United Way of the Midlands, 1993, Air Force Assn., 1993, Person of Yr., Pmaha Club, 1996; named one of Forbes Richest Americans, 2006; named to Nebr. Bus. Hall Fame, Nebr. C. of C. and Industry, 1995, Omaha Bus. Hall Fame, Greater Omaha C. of C., 1995; recipient Nebr. Builder award, U. Nebr., 1983, Outstanding Achievement in Construction award, The Moles, 1986, Brotherhood award, Nat. Conf. Christians and Jews, 1986, Horatio Alger award, Horatio Alger Assn., 1997, Spirit Youth award, Uta Halee Girls Village, 1988, Perry W. Branch Disting. Svc. award, U. Nebr. Found., 1989, Golden Beaver for Mgmt., The Beavers, 1990, Order of Tower, U. Nebr., Omaha, 1991, Golden Plate award, Am. Acad. Achievement, 1991, Golden Apple award, Met. Cmty. Coll. Found., 1993, Headliner award, Greater Omaha C. of C., 1996, Nebraskalander award, Nebraskaland Found., 1998, Manresa award, Creighton U., 1998, Cmty. Builder award, Greater Omaha C. of C., 1999, Bus. Vol. of Yr., Nat. Alliance Bus., 1999, Midlander of Yr., Omaha World-Herald, 2000. Mem.: Chi Epsilon Soc. (hon.). Office: Peter Kiewit Sons Inc 1000 Kiewit Plz Omaha NE 68131-3302 also: Joslyn Art Mus 2200 Dodge St Omaha NE 68102-1208 Office: Level 3 Communications Inc 1025 Eldorado Blvd Broomfield CO 80021*

**SCOTT, WALTER, JR.,** business consultant; b. Balt., July 24, 1925; s. Walter and Margaret Catherine (Pfeiffer) S.; m. Barbara Main, July 6, 1946 (dec. 1964); children: Stephen Walter, Susan Marjorie, Cynthia Margaret, Christopher Main; m. Mary Joan Braun, Aug. 5, 1966 (dec. 1986); m. Helene Lyda Burke, May 1, 1987. AB, Duke U., 1945; MBA with distinction, Harvard U., 1949. Advtg. mgr. The Quaker Oats Co., Chgo., 1950-57; v.p. mktg. J.H. Filbert, Inc., Balt., 1957-67, pres., 1968-77; div. gen. mgr. Cen. Soya Co., Ft. Wayne, Ind., 1972-77; exec. v.p. Fairmont Foods Co., Des Plaines, Ill., 1978-81; pres. McKeon, Scott, Woolf & Assocs., Palo Alto, Calif., 1982-84; chmn. bd. Integral Cons. Group, Mill Valley, Calif., 1986-87, Scott, Woolf & Assocs., Palo Alto, 1984—2001, Mulford Moreland & Assocs., San Jose, Calif., 1986-89. Chmn., speaker pres. courses, Am. Mgmt. Assn., N.Y.C., 1970-90; trustee Calif. Inst. Integral Studies, San Francisco, 1983-89; bd. dirs. West Marine, Inc., Watsonville, Calif., 1995-2001. With USNR, 1943-46, PTO. Mem. Phi Beta Kappa. Home and Office: 1450 Redford Dr Palm Springs CA 92264 Office Phone: 760-416-0851.

**SCOTT, WALTER DILL,** management educator; b. Chgo., Oct. 27, 1931; s. John Marcy and Mary Louise (Gent) S.; m. Barbara Ann Stein, Sept. 9, 1961; children: Timothy Walter, David Frederick, Gordon Charles. Student, Williams Coll., 1949-51; BS, Northwestern U., 1953; MS, Columbia U., 1958. Cons. Booz, Allen & Hamilton, NYC, 1956—58; assoc. Glore, Forgan & Co., NYC, 1958—63, ptnr. Chgo., 1963-65; pntr. Lehman Bros, Chgo., 1965-72, sr. ptnr., 1972-73, also bd. dirs.; assoc. dir. econs. and govt. Office Mgmt. and Budget, Washington, 1973-75; sr. v.p. internat. and fin. Pillsbury Co., Mpls., 1975-78, exec. v.p., 1978-80, also bd. dirs.; pres., CEO, Investors Diversified Svcs., Inc., Mpls., 1980-84; group mng. dir. Grand Met. PLC, Mpls., 1984-86, also bd. dirs.; chmn. Grand Met USA, Mpls., 1984-86; prof., sr. Austin fellow Kellogg Sch. Mgmt., Northwestern U., Evanston, Ill., 1988—. Bd. dirs., vice chmn. Intermatic, Inc. Bd. dirs. Chgo. Cmtys. in Schs., Ctr. for Exec. Women Imagine Schs., Inc. Lt. (j.g.) USN, 1953-56. Home: 55 Meadowview Dr Northfield IL 60093-3547 Office: Northwestern U Kellogg Sch Mgmt 2001 Sheridan Rd Evanston IL 60208-0814 E-mail: wds@kellogg.northwestern.edu.

**SCOTT, WILL T.,** state supreme court justice; b. Ratliff's Creek, Ky., July 20, 1947; s. John H. H. and Betty (Thompson) Scott. Attended, Eastern Ky. U.; BA, Pikeville Coll.; JD, U. Miami, 1974, MS in Taxation, 1975. Bar: Ky., Fla. With trust dept. Pikeville Nat. Bank, 1975—76; atty. priv. practice, 1976—2004; asst. atty. Pike County, 1981—82; judge Pike County Cir. Ct., 1984—88; justice Ky. Supreme Ct., 2005—, dep. chief justice, 2006—. Served to First Lt. U.S. Army, 1966—69. Decorated Bronze Star, Vietnamese Cross of Gallantry, Combat Infantryman's Badge. Mem.: Ky. Circuit Judges' Assn. (second v.p. 1986). Office: Ky Supreme Ct 700 Capital Ave Frankfort KY 40601 Office Phone: 502-564-4168.*

**SCOTT, WILLIAM CLEMENT, III,** investor; b. NYC, Apr. 25, 1934; s. William Clement and Susan L. (Cameron) S.; m. Cindy L. Taylor, Dec. 5, 1981; children by previous marriage: Katherine Louise, David Campbell. AB, Coll. William and Mary, Williamsburg, Va., 1956. Self-employed, 1956-64; v.p. Booz-Allen & Hamilton, N.Y.C., 1964-69; group v.p. Cordura Corp., Los Angeles, 1969-72; exec. v.p. Western Pacific Industries, N.Y.C., 1972-76, pres., chief operating officer, 1977-87; pvt. investor N.Y.C., 1987-88; chmn., CEO Panavision Inc., N.Y.C., 1988-98. Bd. dirs. Edison Control Corp. Bd. dirs. Opera Orch. of N.Y., pres., 1988-97; bd. dirs. Met. Opera Club N.Y.C., pres., 2002-04. Mem. Met. Opera Club, Racquet and Tennis Club, Knickerbocker Club, Hay Harbor Club, Fishers Island Country Club, Coral Beach Club (Bermuda), Royal Bermuda Yacht Club. Republican. Episcopalian. Office: 445 Park Ave Ste 1905 New York NY 10022 Office Phone: 212-688-4748. E-mail: wcscott@att.net.

**SCOTT, WILLIAM FLOYD,** accountant; b. Woodland, Miss., Feb. 26, 1936; s. Robert Fulton and Sarah Etta (Watson) S.; m. Carolyn Marie Pierce, Dec. 12, 1958; children: David, Ricky, Stephen, Julie. BS in Bus. Adminstrn., Delta State U., Cleveland, Miss., 1957. Staff acct. Reynolds Elec. & Engring., Las Vegas, Nev., 1957-62, sr. auditor, 1962-65, dir. internal auditing, 1965-70; sr. staff acct. Davis & Mosher, CPAs, Pasadena, Tex., 1970-72; owner Scott & Co., CPAs, Pasadena, 1972–2001; mng. dir. Scott, Forrest, Adams & Co., PLLC, CPAs, Pasadena, 2002—. Chmn. fin. com. Meml. Bapt. Ch., Pasadena, Pasadena, 1974—80, treas., 2001-. Mem. AICPA, Tex. Soc. CPAs, Pasadena Noon Optimist Club (treas. 1973-75), Neighborhood Assn. Three Villas (treas. 2000-). Avocations: reading, gardening, sports. Office: Scott Forrest Adams & Co PLLC CPAs 4620 Fairmont Pky Ste 200 Pasadena TX 77504-3328 Office Phone: 281-487-2501. E-mail: wmfscott@swbell.net.

**SCOTT, WILLIAM PAUL,** lawyer; b. Staples, Minn., Nov. 8, 1928; m. Elsie Elaine Anderson, Feb. 7, 1968; children: Jason Lee, William P., Mark D., Brian D., Scott; stepchildren: Thomas J. (dec.), Terri L. Weeding-Berg. ALA, U. Minn., 1949; BSL, St. Paul Coll. Law, 1952, JD, 1954. Bar: Minn. 1954. Atty., right of way divsn. Minn. Hwy Dept., 1945-52, civil engr., traffic and safety divsn., 1953-55; practice law Arlington, Minn., 1955-61, Gaylord, Minn., 1963-67; sr. ptnr. Scott Law Offices and predecessors, Pipestone, Minn., 1967—. Probate, juvenile judge Sibley County, Minn., 1956-61; Minn. pub. examiner, 1961-63; county atty. Sibley County, 1963-68, city atty., Pipestone, 1979-2002. Sibley County Rep. chmn., 1961. Served with USMCR, 1946-50, from 2d lt. to lt. col. USAF Res., 1950-88, ret. Recipient George Washington Honor medal Freedoms Found., 1970, 72. Mem. MOAA, VFW, DAV, Minn. Bar Assn., Mensa, Am. Legion, Mil. Officers Assn. Am. Home: PO Box 689 Pipestone MN 56164 0689 Office: Park Plz Offices Pipestone MN 56164 Office Phone: 507-825-5496. Office Fax: 507-825-3528. E-mail: scottlaw@rconnect.com.

**SCOTT, WILLIAM PROCTOR, III,** lawyer; b. Berkeley, Calif., Dec. 1, 1946; s. William Proctor Jr. and Marcia (Wood) S.; children: William Proctor IV, Jennifer Anne Simon. BS, MIT, 1968; JD cum laude, U. Pa., 1975. Assoc. Ballard Spahr Andrews & Ingersoll LLP, Phila., 1975-82, ptnr., 1982-2000, Nixon Peabody LLP, Albany, NY, 2000—. Regional chmn. MIT Edni. Coun., 1988-2000. Bd. dirs. Cathedral Village, 1998—, vice chair, 2003-; Lt. (j.g.) USNR, 1969-72. Office: Nixon Peabody LLP 30 S Pearl St 9th Fl Albany NY 12207-3425 Office Phone: 518-427-2700. Business E-Mail: wscott@nixonpeabody.com.

**SCOTT, W(ILLIAM) RICHARD,** sociology educator; b. Parsons, Kans., Dec. 18, 1932; s. Charles Hogue and Hildegarde (Hewit) S.; m. Joy Lee Whitney, Aug. 14, 1955; children: Jennifer Ann, Elliot Whitney, Sydney Brooke. AA, Parsons Jr. Coll., 1952; AB, U. Kans., 1954, MA, 1955; PhD, U. Chgo., 1961; PhD in Econs. (hon.), Copenhagen Sch. Bus., 2000, Helsinki Sch. Econs., 2001. From asst. prof. to assoc. prof. sociology Stanford (Calif.) U., 1960-69, prof., 1969-99, prof. emeritus, 1999—, chair dept. sociology, 1972-75; sr. scholar John Gardner Ctr./Stanford U., 2002—; sr. rschr. Collaborating for Rsch. on Global Projects, 2003—. Courtesy prof. Sch. Medicine, Stanford U., 1972—, Sch. Edn., Grad. Sch. Bus., 1977—; fellow Ctr. for Advanced Study in Behavioral Scis., 1989-90; dir. Orgns. Rsch. Tng. Program, Stanford U., 1972-89, Ctr. for Orgns. Rsch., 1988-96; mem. adv. panel Sociology Program NSF, Washington, 1982-84; mem. epidemiol. and svc. rsch. rev. panel NIMH, Washington, 1984-88; mem. Commn. on Behavioral and Social Scis. and Edn., NAS, 1990-96; vis. prof. Kellogg Grad. Sch. Mgmt., Northwestern U., winter 1997, Hong Kong U. Sci. and Tech., fall 2000. Author: (with O.D. Duncan et al) Metropolis and Region, 1960; (with P.M. Blau) Formal Organizations, 1962, 2003, Social Processes and Social Structures, 1970; (with S.M. Dornbusch) Evaluation and the Exercise of Authority, 1975, Organizations: Rational, Natural and Open Systems, 1981, rev. edit., 2003; (with J.W. Meyer) Organizational Environments: Ritual and Rationality, 1983, edit., 1992; (with A.B. Flood) Hospital Structure and Performance, 1987; (with J.W. Meyer), Institutional Environments and Organizations: Structural Complexity and Individualism, 1994, Institutions and Organizations, 1995, rev. edit., 2001; (with S. Christensen) The Institutional Construction of Organization, 1995; (with M. Ruef et al) Institutional Change and Healthcare Organizations: From Professional Dominance to Managed Care, 2000; editor Ann. Rev. of Sociology, 1986-91; (with R. Cole) The Quality Movement and Organization Theory, 1999, (with G.F. Davis et al) Social Movements and Organization Theory, 2005. Fellow Woodrow Wilson, 1954-55; mem. Nat. Commn. Nursing, 1980-83; chair Consortium Orgns. Rsch. Ctrs., 1989-91; elder First Presby. Ch., Palo Alto, Calif., 1977-80, 83-86. Named Edmund P. Learned Disting. Prof., Sch. Bus. Adminstrn., U. Kans., 1970—71; recipient Cardinal Citation for Disting. Svc., Labette C.C., Parsons, 1981, Disting. Scholar award, Mgmt. and Orgn. Theory divsn. Acad. Mgmt., 1988, Richard D. Irwin award for scholarly contbns. to mgmt., Acad. Mgmt., 1996; Social Sci. Rsch. Coun. fellow, U. Chgo., 1959, resident fellow, Bellagio Conf. Ctr., 2002. Fellow Acad. Mgmt.; Mem. Inst. Medicine, Am. Sociol. Assn. (chmn. sect. on orgns. 1970-71, mem. coun. 1989-92), Sociol. Rsch. Assn. (exec. com. 2003—, pres. 2006—), Macro-Organizational Behavior Soc., Phi Beta Kappa. Democrat. Presbyterian. Home: 940 Lathrop Pl Stanford CA 94305-1060 Office: Stanford U Dept Sociology Bldg 120 Stanford CA 94305 Business E-Mail: scottwr@stanford.edu.

**SCOTTO, CIRO GERARD,** composer, educator; b. Bklyn., Sept. 16, 1955; s. Michael and Anne Marie Grace Scotto; m. Anne Marie Irvine, Apr. 24, 1983; children: Gabriel Gerard, Zachary Augustus. MusD, U. Wash., 1995. Instr. Cornish Coll. Arts, Seattle, 1990—91; lectr. U. Calif., Santa Barbara, 1991—92; vis. asst. prof. music theory U. Tex., Austin, 1995—97; assoc. prof. music theory Eastman Sch. Music, Rochester, NY, 1997—. Dir. New Music Ensemble U. Tex. Austin, 1996 Composer: (songs) Confessions for chamber ensemble, Tetralogy, Three Words for Three Guitars. Recipient Olga Brose Valente Meml. prize, U. Calif., Davis, 1983, The Warren Babb Music by People award, U. Wash., 1990; fellow, U. Rochester, 2000; grantee, Meet the Composer, 1996; scholar, Schweitzer Inst., 1991; Bridging fellowship, U. Rochester, 2001. Mem.: Soc. Music Theory. Independent. Avocations: computers, auto racing, hiking. Home: 61 Antlers Drive Rochester NY 14618 Office: Eastman School of Music 26 Gibbs St Rochester NY 14618 Office Phone: 585-274-1562. Personal E-mail: cscotto1@rochester.rr.com. Business E-Mail: cscotto@mail.rochester.edu.

**SCOTTO, ROSANNA,** newscaster; b. Bklyn. BA in Fine Arts, Catholic U. Reporter, assoc. prodr. WTBS, Atlanta; reporter WABC-TV NY, reporter Eyewitness News N.Y.C.; corr., anchor FOX 5/WNYW News, N.Y.C., 1986—. Co-owner Fresco by Scotto, 1993—. Co-author: Fresco: Modern Tuscan Cooking for All Seasons, 1997; actor: (films) Miracle on 34th Street, 1994, Ransom, 1996, The Object of My Affection, 1998, Famous, 2000. Nominee Emmy award, 1990, 1995; recipient First Place award for indiv. reporting, NY St. Associated Press Assoc., 1995. Office: WNYW-TV/Fox Broadcasting Co 205 E 67th St New York NY 10021-6050

**SCOTT-THOMAS, KRISTIN,** actress; b. Redruth, Cornwall, England, United Kingdom, May 24, 1960; m. Francois Olivennes, 3 children, Hannah, Joseph, George. Student, Cen. Sch. Speech and Drama, Ecole Nat. des Arts. Stage debut in Schnitzler's La Lune Déclinante Sur 4 ou 5 Personnes Qui Danse; stage appearances include La Terre Etrangère, Naive Hirondelles, Yes Peut-Etre, Bérénice, 2001, Three Sisters, 2003, As You Desire Me, 2005; appearances on French, German, Australian, U.S. and Brit. TV include L'Ami d'Enfance de Maigret, Blockhaus, Cameleon La Tricheuse, Sentimental Journey, The Tenth Man, Endless Game, Framed, Titmuss Regained, Look at it this Way, Body and Soul; film appearances include Djamel et Juliette, L'Agent Troublé, La Méridienne, Under the Cherry Moon, A Handful of Dust, Force Majeure, Bille en Tete, The Bachelor, Bitter Moon, Four Weddings and a Funeral (B.A.F.T.A. award), Angels and Insects (Evening Standard Film award), Richard III, 1995, Angels & Insects, 1996, Somebody to Love, 1996, The Pompatus of Love, 1996, Mission: Impossible, 1996, The English Patient, 1996, Amour et confusions, 1997, Souvenir, 1998, The Revenger's

Comedies, 1998, The Horse Whisperer, 1998, Up at the Villa, 1999, Random Hearts, 1999, Life as a House, 2001, Gosford Park, 2001. Office: c/o Kevin Huvane & Bryan Lourd Creative Artists Agy 9830 Wilshire Blvd Beverly Hills CA 90212*

**SCOTT-WILLIAMS, MILDRED P.,** food service specialist; b. Americus, Ga., Mar. 21, 1928; d. Bouie Lee and Mary (Jackson) Paschal; m. Mar. 10, 1986 (div.); 1 child, Alan Meadows. BS, Fort Valley State Coll., 1949; MA, Antioch U., 1980. Tchr. elem. schs., Ga., 1949-54; asst. dietitian Met. Hosp., Phila., 1954-57, head dietitian, 1957-67; tchr. home econs. Phila. Bd. Edn., 1967-68, food svc. mgr., 1969-71; dietitian Germantown Hosp., Phila., summer 1968; supr. tng. H.E.A.R.T. (Household Employment Assn. Reevaluation Tng.), Phila., 1968-69; tchr. food svc. Camden (N.J.) Bd. Edn., 1971-73, adminstrv. asst., 1973-81, food svc. supr., 1981-99; ret., 1999. Author: Metropolitan Diet Manual, 1965. Cub mother Boy Scouts Am., Phila., 1970-71; block chairperson 5900 Neighborhood Assn., Phila., 1980-89; Dem. committeewoman 17 Ward 28th Divsn.; mem. Phila. Dist. Atty. Panel for Youth. Recipient award The Chapel of Four Chaplains, Phila., 1977, Disting. Svc. Key award LKM Sorority, 2000, Cert. of Appreciation, USDA, 2000, Recognition of Svc. award Camden City Fedn. Sch. Adminstrs., 2000. Mem. Am. Fedn. Sch. Adminstrs. (merit award 1987), Am. Sch. Food Svc. Assn. (cert., Star Club cert. 1999), N.J. Food Svc. Assn. (sec. 1980-82, appreciation award Elizabeth 1987, President's award New Brunswick 1989), Order Ea. Star (sec. 1979-84). Home: 5956 N 21st St Philadelphia PA 19138-2922 Personal E-mail: mscott9837@aol.com

**SCOTT-WILLIAMS, WENDY LEE,** library and information scientist; b. Buffalo, Jan. 22; d. Arthur Raymond and June Amelia Schutt; m Nigel Simon Scott-Williams, Feb. 29, 1980. BA cum laude, SUNY, Buffalo, 1975; MA with honors, Cambridge U., 1979; MLIS with honors, CUNY-Queens Coll., 1987. Applications rep. Barrister, N.Y.C., 1983-87; coord. computer systems Stroock & Stroock & Lavan, N.Y.C., 1983-87; tech. svcs. mgr. Batten, Barton, Durstein & Osborn (BBDO) Worldwide, N.Y.C., 1987-92; adminstr. mgr. info. resources Fairchild Publs., N.Y.C., 1992-96; info. resource mgr. March of Dimes Birth Defects Found., White Plains, NY, 1996—. Active N.Y. Zool. Soc. Mem. Spl. Librs. Assn., Cambridge Union Soc., Oxford-Cambridge Soc., Nature Conservancy, Greenpeace. Presbyterian. Avocations: travel, gardening. Office: March of Dimes Birth Defects Found Nat Hdqs 1275 Mamaroneck Ave White Plains NY 10605-5298

**SCOULAR, ROBERT FRANK,** lawyer; b. Del Norte, Colo., July 9, 1942; s. Duane William and Marie Josephine (Moloney) Scoular; m. Donna V. Scoular, June 3, 1967; children: Bryan T., Sean D., Bradley R. BS in Aero. Engring., St. Louis U., 1964, JD, 1968. Bar: Mo. 1968, Colo. 1968, ND 1968, U.S. Supreme Ct. 1972, Calif. 1979. Law clk. to chief judge U.S. Ct. Appeals (8th cir.), 1968-69; ptnr. Bryan, Cave, McPheeters & McRoberts, St. Louis, 1969-89, mng. ptnr. L.A., 1979—85, exec. com., 1984-85, sect. leader tech., computer and intellectual property law, 1985-89; ptnr. Sonnenschein, Nath, Rosenthal, L.A., 1990—, mng. ptnr., 1990—, mem. policy and planning com., 1995—. Co-leader intellectual property practice, 1990—98; dir. Mo. Lawyers Credit Union, 1978—79. Contbr. articles to profl. jours. Bd. dirs. St. Louis Bar Found., 1975—76, 1979, bd. dirs., pub. counsel, 2004—; bd. dirs., vice chmn., gen. counsel LA area coun. Boy Scouts Am.; league commr. Am. Youth Soccer Orgn.; mem. alumni coun. St. Louis U., 1979—82, dean's coun. Sch. Law, 2000—; hon. dean Dubourg Soc. Recipient Nat. Disting. Eagle Scout award. Mem.: ABA (sect. adv. dir. young lawyers divsn. 1977—78), Fed. Bar Assn., Mo. Bar Assn. (chmn. young lawyers sect. 1976—77, Disting. Svc. award), Calif. Bar Assn., Assn. Bus. Trial Lawyers (bd. dirs. 2004—), LA County Bar Assn., Bar Assn. Met. St. Louis (chmn. young lawyers sect. 1975—76, v.p. 1978—79, sec. 1979), Chancery Club. Home: 1505 Lower Paseo La Cresta Palos Verdes Peninsula CA 90274-2066 Office: Sonnenschein Nath & Rosenthal LLP 601 S Figueroa St Ste 1500 Los Angeles CA 90017-5720 Office Phone: 213-892-5003. Business E-Mail: rscoular@sonnenschein.com.

**SCOVANNER, DOUGLAS,** retail executive; BS, Washington and Lee U., 1977; MBA, U. Va., 1979. With Coca-Cola Enterprises and affiliates, Atlanta, 1980-92, v.p., treas., 1989-92; sr. v.p. fin. Fleming Cos., Oklahoma City, 1992-94; sr. v.p. fin., CFO Target Corp., Mpls., 1994—2000, exec. v.p., CFO, 2000—. Office: Target Corporation 1000 Nicollett Mall Minneapolis MN 55403-2467*

**SCOVILLE, JAMES GRIFFIN,** industrial relations professor; b. Amarillo, Tex., Mar. 19, 1940; s. Orlin James and Carol Howe (Griffin) S.; m. Judith Ann Nelson, June 11, 1962; 1 child, Nathan James. BA, Oberlin Coll., 1961; MA, Harvard U., 1963, PhD, 1965. Economist ILO, Geneva, 1965-66; instr. econs. Harvard U., Cambridge, Mass., 1964-65, asst. prof., 1966-69; assoc. prof. econs. and labor and indsl. relations U. Ill.-Urbana, 1969-75, prof., 1975-80; prof. indsl. rels. Indsl. Rels. Ctr., U. Minn., Mpls., 1979—, dir., 1979-82, dir. grad. studies, 1990-97. Cons. ILO, World Bank, U.S. Dept. Labor, Orgn. for Econ. Cooperation and Devel., USAID; labor-mgmt. arbitrator. Author: The Job Content of the US Economy, 1940-70, 1969, Perspectives on Poverty and Income Distribution, 1971, Manpower and Occupational Analysis: Concepts and Measurements, 1972, (with A. Sturmthal) The International Labor Movement in Transition, 1973, Status Influences in 3rd World Labor Markets, 1991, (with H. Buds) The Ethics of Human Resources and Industrial Relations, 2005. Mem. Am. Econ. Assn., Indsl. Rels. Rsch. Assn. (v.p. internat. sect. 1998, pres. 1999), Internat. Indsl. Rels. Assn. Office: U Minn Ind Rels Ctr 3-289 CSOM Minneapolis MN 55455 Office Phone: 612-624-1579. Business E-Mail: jscoville@csom.umn.edu.

**SCOW, AARON ARNEY,** lawyer; b. Shelby, N.C., Jan. 16, 1973; s. Steven Davis and Vickie Lynn Scow; m. Margo Jean Scow, July 15, 1995; 1 child, Trevor Abbott. BS in Acctg., U. Nebr., 1995; JD, U. Minn., 1998. CPA; bar: Tex. Atty. Akin Gump Strauss Hauer, Dallas, 1998—. Bd. dirs. Star Sponsorship Program, Ft. Worth. Bd. dirs. Greater Dallas Comty. Rels. Commn., 2002—05. Named Tex. Super Lawyer Rising Star in Law and Politics, 2004, 2005, 2006. Mem.: Timmon Country Club. Avocations: golf, politics, reading. Home: 2180 Pinehurst Dr Grapevine TX 76051 Office: Akin Gump Strauss Hauer and Feld LLP Ste 4100 1700 Pacific Ave Dallas TX 75201

**SCOWCROFT, BRENT,** former national security advisor, retired military officer; b. Ogden, Utah, Mar. 19, 1925; s. James and Lucile (Ballantyne) S.; m. Marian Horner, Sept. 17, 1951 (dec. 1995); 1 dau., Karen. BS, U.S. Mil. Acad., 1947; MA, Columbia U., 1953, PhD, 1967; postgrad., Georgetown U., 1958. Commd. 2d lt. USAF, 1947, advanced through grades to lt. gen., 1974; asst. prof. dept. social sci. U.S. Mil. Acad., 1953-57; asst. air attache Am. Embassy, Belgrade, Yugoslavia, 1959-61; assoc. prof. dept. polit. sci. USAF Acad., Colorado Springs, Colo., 1962-63, prof., head dept., 1963-64; mem. staff long range planning div. Office Dep. Chief Staff Plans and Ops., Washington, 1964-67; assigned Nat. War Coll., 1967-68; staff asst. Western Hemisphere region Office Asst. Sec. Def. Internat. Security Affairs, Washington, 1968-69; dep. asst. dir. plans for nat. security matters office Dep. Chief Staff Plans and Ops., Washington, 1969-70; spl. asst. to dir. Joint Staff, Joint Chiefs of Staff, Washington, 1970-71; mil. asst. to Pres. The White House, Washington, 1972-73; dep. asst. to Pres. for nat. security affairs NSC, Washington, 1973-75, asst. to Pres. for nat. security affairs, 1975-77, 1989-93; mem. Pres.'s Gen. Adv. Com. on Arms Control, Washington, 1977-80; vice chmn. Kissinger Associates, Inc., Washington, 1982-89; pres. Forum for Internat. Policy, Washington, 1993—. Bd. dirs. Nat. Bank Washington, Qualcomm, Inc., Am. Coun. on Germany; chmn. Pres.'s Commn. on Strategic Forces; mem. Pres.'s Commn. on Def. Mgmt., Pres. Spl. Rev. Bd. on Iran/Contra Affair; pres. The Scowcroft Group, 1994—. Bd. dirs. Atlantic Coun. U.S., 1977—; bd. visitors U.S. Air Force Air U., 1977-79; bd. dirs. Internat. Rep. Inst., 1994—; chmn. Pres. Fgn. Intelligence Adv. Bd.; chmn. Am.-Turkish Coun., 2000—; Eisenhower Inst., 2004-05; mem. adv. bd. Georgetown Ctr. for Strategic and Internat. Studies; pres. George Bush Presdl. Libr. Foun.; bd. dirs. Gerald R. Ford Found., Nat. Def. U.; mem. Internat.

Rep. Inst. Decorated D.S.M. with two oak leaf clusters, Legion of Merit with oak leaf cluster, Air Force Commendation medal, D.S.M. Dept. Def., Nat. Security medal; recipient Medal of Freedom, 1991; named Hon. Knight Brit. Empire, 1993. Mem. Coun. Fgn. Rels. (bd. dirs.), UN Assn. U.S. (vice chmn.), Am. Polit. Sci. Assn., Acad. Polit. Sci. Mem. Ch. Jesus Christ of Latter-day Saints. Office: # 500 900 17th St NW Ste 500 Washington DC 20006-2507

**SCRAGG, THOMAS WILLIAM,** librarian, historian, solicitor; b. Wirral, Cheshire, Eng., Sept. 19, 1940; s. Joseph and Norah Scragg; m. Isabel Mary Thomas, Apr. 3, 1972; children: Maximian Rhys Joseph, Halcyon Rosemary Louise, Sophia Isabel Hannah, Mortimer Henry Thomas. BA with honours, Sch. Slavonic and E. European Studies, U. London; B.Phil., U. Liverpool; MA, Manchester Poly., Eng.; postgrad., King's Coll., U. London, U. Wales, Aberystwyth; Dipl.Lib., F.L.A., Manchester Libr. Sch. Solicitor Supreme Ct., 1968—; music adviser, hist. rschr., program annotator Chester Festival, 1967, 1986—88, Festival in Gt. Irish Houses, 1970—81, Queen's Festival, U. Belfast, 1971, 1972, Newcastle-upon-Tyne Festival, 1972—75, Portsmouth Festival, 1977—78, Dublin Festival, Royal Dublin Soc., 1979, Alfred Beit Found., 1979—81, Leeds Castle Festival, 1987, Music Assn. Ireland, others. Phonographic cons., cataloguer Sir Compton MacKenzie's Jethou Record Collection, 1973—75; music libr. cons. Granada TV Ltd., 1973—75; libr., archivist Knowsley Libr., 1974—91. Author: festival program material, Claudio Arrau Discography, 1978, 2d edit., 1982; author: (joint) Library Association Standards for Local Studies Provision in Public Libraries, 1989; contbr. articles to profl. jours. Fellow: Libr. Assn. (Charles Nowell Meml. prize 1992), Soc. Antiquaries of Scotland, Royal Soc Arts, Royal Geog. Soc.; mem.. E.S.U., Anglo-Polish Music Circle Gt. Britain (hon. v.p. 1970), Polish Inst. Arts and Scis. Am. (assoc.), Soc. Genealogists, Royal Mus. Assn., Soc. Archivists, Law Soc., Internat. Assn. Religious Freedom. Avocations: travel, history of public concerts, historical discography. Home: The Woodcroft Barnston Wirral CH6 11BU England

**SCRIBNER, CHARLES, III,** art historian, writer; b. Washington, May 24, 1951; s. Charles IV, Christopher Markoe. AB, Princeton U., 1973, MFA, 1975, PhD, 1977. Editor Charles Scribner's Sons, NYC, 1975—2004, dir. subs. rights, 1978-82, pub. paperback divsn., 1982-83, exec. v.p., 1983-84; v.p. Macmillan Pub. Co., NYC, 1984-94. Instr. dept. art and archaeology Princeton U., 1976-77; mem. adv. coun. Princeton U. Libr., 1981-90; mem. adv. coun. dept. art and archaeology Princeton U., 1983-91, 99-2003, 05—; trustee Princeton U. Press, 1984-90, Homeland Found., 1987—; bd. advisors Wethersfield Inst., 1985—; bd. dir. Met. Opera Guild, 1990-92; dir. Cath. Edn. Inst., 2004-. Author: The Triumph of the Eucharist-Tapestries by Rubens, 1982, Rubens, 1989, Bernini, 1991, The Shadow of God, 2006. Trustee St. Paul's Sch., Concord, NH, 1994-2006. Mem. Assn. Princeton U. Press, NYC Racquet and Tennis Club, Ivy Club (Princeton). Roman Catholic. Office: 155 E 72d St #5D New York NY 10021-4371 Office Phone: 917-623-0890. E-mail: cscribner3@yahoo.com.

**SCRIGGINS, LARRY PALMER,** lawyer, director; b. Englewood, NJ, Nov. 27, 1936; s. Thomas Dalby and M. Patricia (Fowler) S.; m. Victoria Jackola, Feb. 17, 1979; children: Elizabeth J., Thomas P. AB, Middlebury Coll., 1958; JD, U. Chgo., 1961. Bar: Md. 1962. Law clk. to chief judge Md. Ct. Appeals, 1962; assoc. Piper & Marbury, LLP, Balt., 1962-69, ptnr., 1969-98, vice chmn., 1988-93, mem. exec. com., CFO, 1993-98; sr. counsel Piper Rudnick, LLP, Balt., 1999-2001; ptnr. emeritus DLA Piper Rudnick Gray Cary US LLP, Balt., 2001—. Mem. legal adv. com. N.Y. Stock Exch., 1992-96; bd. dirs. USF & G Corp., 1979-98, Center Stage Assocs., 1979-89, Balt. Choral Arts Soc., 1979-96, Balt. Conv. Bur., 1982-95, YMCA of Greater Balt., 1987-94, Fund for Ednl. Excellence, 1990-98, bd. trustees, 1993-98; bd. dirs. Nat. Aquarium in Balt., bd. govs. 1987-93; bd. dirs. Balt. Symphony Orchestra, 1996-2001. Contbr. articles to profl. jours. Fellow: Am. Bar Found.; mem.: ABA (sect. on bus. law coun. 1972—76, chmn. law and acctg. com. 1985—88, vice chair and editor-in-chief The Bus. Lawyer 1989—90, chair 1991—92, chmn. com. corp. laws 1996—2000, chmn. ad hoc com. on ethics 2000 1999—2002), AICPA (planning com. 1989—92), Fin. Acctg. Stds. Bd., Task Force in Fin. Instruments, Am. Law Inst., Am. Judicature Soc., Md. Bar Assn. (coun. 1976—78, chmn. 1977—78, mem. com. corp. laws 1981—84). Office: DLA Piper Rudnick Gray Cary US LLP 6225 Smith Ave Baltimore MD 21209-3600 Office Phone: 410-580-4252. Office Fax: 410-580-3001. Business E-Mail: larry.scriggins@dlapiper.com.

**SCRIMPSHIRE, JENNIFER SUZANNE,** music educator; b. Laurel, Miss., June 27, 1980; d. Keith Doyle and Sheree Stewart Buckhaults; m. Jason Eric Scrimpshire, July 7, 2001. B of Music Edn., William Carey Coll., Hattiesburg, Miss., 2001. Tchr. music Columbus Mcpl. Schs., Miss., 2002—05, West Jones Mid. Sch., Laurel, Miss., 2005—. Dir. concert choir, freshman choir, advanced ensemble, show choir Columbus Mcpl. Schs., Miss., 2002—05; dir. 7th and 8th gr. chorus West Jones Mid. Sch., Laurel, Miss., 2005—. Mem.: Am. Choral Dir.'s Assn., Music Educator's Nat. Conf. Baptist.

**SCRIMSHAW, NEVIN STEWART,** physician, nutritionist, educator; b. Jan. 20, 1918; m. Mary Ware Goodrich, 1941; 5 children. BA with honors, Ohio Wesleyan U., 1938; MA in Biology, Harvard U., 1939, PhD in Physiology, 1941, MPH, 1959; MD with honors, U. Rochester, 1945. Intern Gorgas Hosp., 1945-46; Rockefeller postdoctoral fellow U. Rochester, NY, 1946—47, Merck NRC fellow NY, 1947—49; asst. resident in ob-gyn. Strong Meml. Hosp., Genesee Hosp., NY, 1948—49; dir. Inst. Nutrition C.Am. and Panama, Guatemala, 1949—61, cons. dir., 1961—65, cons., 1965—. Cons. nutrition Pan-Am. San Bur. WHO, 1948—49, regional advisor on nutrition, 1949—53; dir. Clin. Rsch. Ctr. MIT, 1962—66, 1979—83, dir. internat. food and nutrition program, 1976—80, prof. human nutrition, 1961—76, head dept. nutrition and food sci., 1961—79, inst. prof., 1976—87, emeritus, 1988—; vis. prof. Columbia U., N.Y.C., 1976—88, vis. lectr., 1961—66, Harvard U., 1968—85; adj. prof. Tufts U.; mem. govt. adv. com. NIH; chmn. internat. com. NRC; dir. food studies divsn. UN U., 1985—86, food nutrition program, 1975—97, sr. advisor, 1998—; mem. adv. com. WHO, Nutrition Found., others. Editor (with others): Amino Acid Fortification of Protein Foods, 1971, Nutrition, National Development and Planning, 1973, The Economics, Marketing and Technology of Fish Protein Concentrate, 1974, Development: Significance and Potential for the Tropics, 1976, Single-Cell Protein: Safety for Animal and Human Feeding, 1979, Nutrition Policy Implementation: Issues and Experience, 1983, Diarrhea and Malnutrition: Interactions, Mechanisms and Interventions, 1983, Chronic Energy Deficiency, 1987, Acceptability of Milk and Milk Products in Populations with Lactose Intolerance, 1988, Nutrition in the Elderly, 1989, Activity, Energy Expenditure and Energy Requirements of Infants and Children, 1990, RAP: Rapid Assessment Procedures: Qualitative Methodologies for Planning and Evaluation of Health Related Programs, 1992, Protein-energy Interactions, 1992, Community-based Longitudinal Nutrition and Health Studies: Classical Examples from Guatemala, Haiti, and Mexico, 1995, The Effects of Improved Nutrition in Early Childhood: The Institute of Nutrition of Central American and Panama Follow-up Study, 1995, The Nutrition and Health Transition of Democratic Costa Rica, 1995, Energy and Protein Requirements, 1996, Causes and Consequences of Intrauterine Growth Retardation, 2000; contbr. articles to profl. jours. Trustee Rockefeller Found., 1971—83, Pan-Am. Health and Edn. Found., 1986—92; pres. Internat. Nutrition Found. for Developing Countries, 1982—. Recipient Osborne and Mendal award, 1960, Internat. award, Inst. Food Technologists, 1969, medal of honor, Fundacion F. Cuenca Villoro, Spain, 1978, Bristol-Myers prize, 1988, Alan Shawn Feinstein award, 1991, World Food prize, 1991, Kellogg award in internat. nutrition, 2002, Lifetime Achievement and Svc. award, UN, 2004. Fellow: APHA (v.p. 1978, award of excellence in promoting and protecting health of people 1974), AAAS, Am. Soc. Clin. Nutrition, Royal Soc. Health, Am. Soc. Nutritional Scis.; mem.: NAS (chair applied biol. sect. 1973—76, 1988—91), others, Internat. Epidemiol. Assn., Internat. Union Nutritional Scis. (pres. 1978—81), Am. Epidemiol. Soc., Am. Physiol. Soc., Mass. Med. Soc., New Eng. Pub. Health Assn., Mass. Pub. Health Assn., Am. Bd. Nutrition, Am. Coll. Preventive Medicine, Am. Coll. Nutrition, Am. Acad.

Arts and Scis., Inst. Medicine NAS. Home and Office: Sandwich Mountain Farm 115 Sandwich Notch Rd PO Box 330 Campton NH 03223-0330 Fax: 603-726-4614. Office Phone: 603-726-4200. E-mail: nevin@cyberportal.net.

**SCRIMSHAW, SUSAN CROSBY,** academic administrator; b. Nov. 12, 1945; m. Allan Stern; 1 child from previous marriage, Mary Corey March. AB, Barnard Coll., 1967; MA, Columbia U., 1969, PhD in Anthropology, 1974. Rsch. assoc. Internat. Inst. for Study of Human Reproduction, 1969—75; asst. prof. health adminstrn. Columbia U., 1975; asst. prof. pub. health Div. Population, Family and Internat. Health, Sch. Pub. Health UCLA, 1975—80, assoc. prof. Div. Population and Family Health, 1980—85, assoc. dir. Latin Am. Ctr., 1984—88, prof. pub. health and anthropology, 1985—96, acting chair Dept. Pub. Health, 1988—89, assoc. dean Academic Programs, 1988—94, acting dean, 1991—92, 1992—93; dean, prof. cmty. health scis. and anthropology U. Ill. Sch. Pub. Health, Chgo., 1995—2006; pres. Simmons Coll., Boston, 2006. Co-editor: The Handbook of Social Studies in Health & Med. Recipient Margaret Mead award, 1985. Fellow: AAAS; mem.: Nat. Soc. Med. Anthropology (pres. 1985), Soc. Applied Anthropology, Am. Anthropology Assn., Inst. Medicine NAS. Office: Simmons Coll Office of Pres 300 The Fenway Boston MA 02115*

**SCRIPPS, DOUGLAS JERRY,** music educator, conductor; b. Grand Rapids, Mich., Aug. 25, 1942; s. Kenneth Witvoet and Marguerite F. (Rottier) Scripps; m. Betty Ann Broersma Porter, July 24, 1963 (div. Aug. 1974); children: Elisabeth Ann Scripps Blue, Theodore Jon; m. Collins Merilee Evelyn, Apr. 5, 1975; children: Daniel Collins, Taylor Douglas, Adam Rottier. Student, Eastman Sch. Music, 1961, 62; BA, Calvin Coll., 1965; student, U. Music and Dramatic Art, Vienna, 1965—66; MM, U. Mich., 1970. Prin. trumpet player Grand Rapids Symphony Orch., 1961—65, assoc. conductor, 1976—85; dir. music Grand Rapids City Coll., 1967—78; conductor Lake St. Clair Symphony, Detroit, 1970—72, Alma (Mich.) Symphony Orch., 1985—2002; music dir. Grand Rapids Ballet, 1979—99; asst. prof. music Ctrl. Mich. U., Mt. Pleasant, 1981—84; prof. music, dept. chair Alma Coll., 1985—2002, prof. emeritus, 2003—. Guest condr. Interlochen Ctr. Arts, Joffrey Balley, Bay View Music Festival, Blue Lake Fine Arts Camp, Czech Music Camp; vis. prof. Grand Valley State U., Calvin Coll., 1977—81; condr. Ctrl. European Youth Symphony Orch., 2004—05. Recipient Am. Heritage Assn. study abroad lectr., Vienna, 1999. Avocations: reading, travel, sailing. Home: PO Box 476 Northport MI 49670-0476 E-mail: scripps@alma.edu.

**SCRIVEN, L. E(DWARD),** engineering educator; b. Battle Creek, Mich., Nov. 4, 1931; s. L. Edward and Esther Mabel (Davis) S.; m. Dorene Bates Hayes, June 19, 1952; children: Ellen Dorene, Teresa Ann, Mark Hayes. BS, U. Calif., Berkeley, 1952; PhD, U. Del., 1956. Rsch. engr. Shell Devel. Co., Emeryville, Calif., 1956-59; asst. prof. chem. engring. and fluid mechanics U. Minn., Mpls., 1959-62, assoc. prof., 1962-66, prof., 1966-89, Regents' prof., 1989—, assoc. dept. head, 1975-78, program dir. Ctr. Interfacial Engring., 1988-90. Cons. in fields; advisor to Humboldt Found., Fed. Republic of Germany; vis. com. to chem. engring. MIT, sci. assoc. Jet Propulsion Lab., 1977, 79; tech. expert UN Indsl. Devel. Orgn., Vienna, Austria, 1979-88; exec. com. on chem. engring. frontiers NRC, 1984-87; mem. NRC Bd. on Chem. Scis. and Tech., 1987-92, chmn., 1992; mem. NRC Commn. on Phys. Scis., Math. and Applications, 1994—; sci. adv. com. Packard Found., 1988—. Editor: Physico-chemical Hydrodynamics (V.G. Levich), 1992; assoc. editor Jour. Fluid Mechanics, 1970-75; adv. editor Jour. Coll. Interfluid Sci., Physics of Fluids, L.Am. Jour. Chem. Engring. and Applied Chemistry, Internat. Jour. Numerical Methods in Fluid Mechanics; contbr. numerous articles to sci. jours.; patentee in field. Recipient chem. engring. award Am. Soc. Engring. Edn., 1968, Minn. Achievement award, 1989, Murphree award Am. Chem. Soc., 1990; named Fairchild disting. scholar Calif. Inst. Tech., 1989; Guggenheim fellow, 1969-70, fellow Minn. Supercomputer Inst., 1984—. Mem. NAE, Am. Inst. Chem. Engrs. (mem. nat. program com. 1964-69, Colburn award 1960, Walker award 1977, Tallmadge award 1992, Founders award 1997), Am. Phys. Soc., Soc. Petroleum Engrs., Gordon Rsch. Confs., Chem. Soc. (Faraday div.), Soc. Indsl. and Applied Math., Soc. Rheology. Achievements include research in capillarity, fluid mechanics and coating processes, porous media, cold-stage electron microscopy, microstructured fluids and interfaces, origins of pattern and form, supercomputer-aided analysis. Office: Univ Minn 151 Amundson Hall 421 Washington Ave SE Minneapolis MN 55455-0373

**SCRIVENER, LOIS DOING,** principal, educator; b. Mineola, N.Y., Oct. 10, 1945; d. Park Atkinson and Mary Houser Doing; m. James W. Scrivener, Jan. 21, 1967; children: Patricia, James Jr., Andrew. BA in English and Edn., St. Bonaventure U., 1967; MA in Theology, Immaculate Conception, 1982; EdS in Ednl. Leadership U. Ctrl. Fla., 1996; MS in Brain Rsch., Nova Southeastern U., 2006. Cert. tchr. N.Y., tchr. English, ednl. leadership Fla. Substitute tchr. Nassau County, NY, 1970—82; tchr. St. Edward the Confessor, Syosset, NY, 1982—84; tchr., part-time adminstr. Holy Child, Old Westbury, NY, 1984—89; tchr. theology Ctrl. Cath. H.S., Melbourne, Fla., 1989—92; prin. Holy Name of Jesus, Indiatlantic, Fla., 1992—. Adj. prof. Barry U., Miami, Fla., 2000—04; mem. salary scale com. Brevard County Cath. Sch., 1993—2004. Regent NSDAR, Satellite Beach, Fla., 1974—2006; youth min. St. William the Abbot, Seaford, NY, 1975—88. Named Catechist Prin. of Yr., Diocese Orlando, 1996, Nat. Disting. Prin., U.S. Dept. Edn., 2001, Blue Ribbon Sch. Excellence, 2001, U.S. Dept. Edn. No Child Left Behind, 2003; recipient St. Piux X CCD award, 1988, Schs. of Tomorrow Innovations in Tech. award, Today's Cath. Tchr., 1999, Outstanding Sch. Bd. award, NABE, 2000. Mem.: Nat. Cath. Edn. Assn. (Disting. Home and Sch. award 2000, Disting. Prin. 2001, Oustanding Sch. Bd. award 2001). Home: 421 Mallard Ln Indialantic FL 32903

**SCRIVER, CHARLES ROBERT,** medical researcher, human geneticist, retired medical educator; b. Montreal, Que., Can., Nov. 7, 1930; s. Walter deM. and Jessie (Boyd) S.; m. E.K. Peirce, Sept. 8, 1956; children: Dorothy, Peter, Julie, Paul. BA cum laude, McGill U., Montreal, 1951, MDCM cum laude, 1955; DSc (hon.), U. Man., 1992, U. Glasgow, 1993, U. Montreal, 1993, Utrecht U., 1999, U. B.C., 2002. Intern Royal Victoria Hosp., Montreal, 1955-56; resident Royal Victoria and Montreal Children's Hosps., 1956-57, Children's Med. Ctr., Boston, 1957-58; McLaughlin travelling fellow Univ. Coll., London, 1958-60; chief resident pediat. Montreal Children's Hosp., 1960-61; asst. prof. pediat. McGill U., 1961, prof. biology Faculty of Sci., prof. pediat. Faculty of Medicine, 1969—, Alva prof. human genetics, 1994—2002, prof. emeritus, 2002—. Mem. med. adv. bd. Howard Hughes Med. Inst., 1981-88; dir. Med. Rsch. Coun. Group in Genetics, 1972-94; assoc. dir. Can. Genetic Diseases Network, 1989-98. Co-author: Amino Acid Metabolism and Its Disorders, 1973, Garrod's Inborn Factors in Disease, 1989; sr. online editor Metabolic and Molecular Bases Inherited Disease, 1986—; contbr. more than 550 rsch. publs. in field. Decorated Order of Can., Que., Mont.; named Royal Coll. lectr., 1992, Disting. Scientist, Med. Rsch. Coun., 1995—; named to Can. Med. Hall of Fame, 2001, Can. Sci. Engring. Hall of Fame, 2001; recipient Wood Gold medal, McGill U., 1955, Gairdner Internat. award, Gairdner Found., 1979, Prix Michel-Sarrazin, Club de Rech Clin du Que., 1988, Ross award, Can. Pediatric Soc., 1990, Award of Excellence, Genet Soc. Can., 1992, Prix d'Excellence, Inst. Rsch. Clin. de Montreal, 1993, Prix du Quebec, Wilder Penfield, 1995, Lifetime Achievement award, Montreal Children's Hosp., 1995, Medal of Merit, Can. Med. Assns., 1996, Lifetime Achievement award, March of Dimes Birth Defects Found., 1997, Querci Found. prize, Italy, 2001, Founders award, Can. Coll. Med. Geneticist, 2003; Markle scholar, 1962—67. Fellow: AAAS, Royal Soc. London (Can. Rutherford lectr. 1983), Royal Soc. Can. (McLaughlin medal 1981), Royal Coll. Physicians of Ireland (hon.), Am. Coll. Med. Genetics (hon.); mem.: Am. Acad. Pediat. (Mead Johnson award for rsch. in pediat. 1968), Soc. Francaise de Pediat., Brit. Pediat. Assn. (50th Anniversary lectr. 1978), Assn. Am. Physicians, Am. Soc. Clin. Investigation, Am. Pediat. Soc. (pres. 1994—95), Am. Soc. Human Genetics (dir. 1971—74, pres. 1986—87, William Allan award 1978, Award of Excellence in Human Genetics Edn. 2001), Soc. Pediat. Rsch. (pres. 1975—76), Can. Soc. Clin. Investigation

(pres. 1974—75, G. Malcolm Brown Meml. award 1979, Henry Friesen award 2001). Office: McGill Univ-Montreal Childrens Hosp Rsch Inst 2300 Tupper St Montreal PQ Canada H3H 1P3 Business E-Mail: charles.scriver@mcgill.ca.

**SCRIVNER, B(ARBARA) E.,** piano educator; b. Medford, Oreg., May 25, 1931; 4 children. Student (piano student Lawrence Morton), Bob Jones U., 1962-66; corr. student, Inst. Children's Lit., Redding Ridge, Conn., 1974-76. Part time sec., Oreg., 1948-50, 60-62; S.C., 1974-76, 80-86, Census Bur., S.C., 1980-82; piano tchr. Greenville, SC, 1963—2003. Contbr. column A Life Within, also by-line columns-opinion to Times Examiner, Greenville, 1995-97; writer for monthly newsletter From Whence We Came, 1997—; contbr. articles to local newspapers. Mem. Nat. Presdl. Task Force; active Rep. Nat. Com., S.C. Rep. Party; mem. Nat. Rep. Congl. Com.; coord. hdqs. Greenville County Rep. Party, 1993—94.

**SCRIVNER, ELLEN M.,** psychologist; d. John P. O'Shea and Dorothy Mary O'Shea-Hanley; m. Peter C. Scrivner, Aug. 25, 1962; children: Anne Collins (Scrivner) Kuban, Thomas C. BS, St. Louis U., 1961, MS, 1963; PhD in Psychology, Cath. U. Am., 1986. Lic. psychologist Bd. of Examiners, Md. Police psychologist, Fairfax County, Va., Prince Georges County, Md.; dep. dir. COPS Office, U.S. Dept. of Justice, Washington, 2000—02; sr. advisor FBI Office Law Enforcement Coords., 2002—04; dep. supt. bur. of adminstrv. svcs. Chgo. Police Dept., 2004—. Pres. Pub. Safety Innovations, Washington, 2003—04; vis. fellow Nat. Inst. Justice, U.S. Dept. Justice. Author: Law Enforcement Families: Issues and Answers, 1994, Police Psychology Into The 21st Century, 1995. Mem. adv. bd. Local Initiatives Support Corp., N.Y.C., 2003—05. Recipient Women of Courage and Vision award, U.S. Dept. of Justice, 2001, Lifetime Achievement award, 2000. Mem.: APA (life; divsn. pres. 1991—92, Disting. Svc. award 1990). Achievements include research in excessive force/violence, community policing, police psychology. Home: 700 New Hampshire Ave NW Washington DC 20037 Office Phone: 312-745-6288. Personal E-mail: ellenscrivner284@msn.com. E-mail: ellen.scrivner@chicagopolice.org.

**SCRIVNER, THOMAS WILLIAM,** lawyer; b. Madison, Wis., Sept. 10, 1948; s. William H. and Jane (Gehrz) S.; m. Meredith Burke, Aug. 16, 1980; children: Allison, David. AB, Duke U., 1970, MAT, 1972; JD, U. Wis., 1977. Assoc. Michael, Best & Friedrich LLP, Milw., 1978-85, ptnr., 1985—. Mem. ABA, Wis. Bar Assn., Milw. Bar Assn. (labor sect.), Corp. Practice Inst. (pres. 1989-92). Episcopalian. Home: 4626 N Cramer St Milwaukee WI 53211-1203 Office: Michael Best & Friedrich LLP 100 E Wisconsin Ave Ste 3300 Milwaukee WI 53202-4108 Office Phone: 414-271-6560. Business E-Mail: twscrivner@michaelbest.com.

**SCROCCA, ANTHONY CHARLES,** bank executive; b. Bristol, Pa., Aug. 28, 1966; s. Henry Richard and Marian Jeanette Scrocca; m. Lori Lee Cantell, Sept. 19, 1987; children: Austin James, Gina Lynn, Luke Anthony. AA, Bucks County CC, Newtown, Pa., 1987; student, LaSalle U. Assoc. Bucks County (Pa.) Bank, 1985—87; asst. v.p. First Union Bank, Phila., 1988—99; v.p. Citizens Bank, Horsham, Pa., 1999—2001; gen. mgr. Pa. Auto Credit, Fairless Hills, Pa., 2002—. Author: Rising Son, 1999. Republican. Roman Catholic. Avocations: boating, coin collecting/numismatics. Home: 454 Pheasant Ln Fairless Hills PA 19030 Office: Pa Auto Credit 327 Lincoln Hwy Fairless Hills PA 19030 Office Phone: 800-736-4450. Personal E-mail: ascrocca@aol.com.

**SCROGGINS, M. SUZANNE PAONESSA,** budget analyst; b. Albany, N.Y., May 1, 1974; d. Thomas and Mary Laura (Maresca) Paonessa; m. Josh Scroggins. BS in Fin., Siena Coll., 1996. Fin. mgmt. specialist U.S. Dept. Energy, Schenectady (N.Y.) Naval Reactors Office, 1996-99; assoc. dir. fin. aid Siena Coll., 1999-2001; assoc. dir. budget and bus. svcs. U. Maine, Orono, 2001—, instr., Profl. Employees Adv. Coun. (PEAC), mem. athletic adv. bd., site coord. wellness program. Treas. Schenectady Naval Reactors Office Employee Assn., 1997—98. Vol. YMCA; ch. lector, greeter; co-chr. Siena Coll. Friendly's Fanfest, 1997—98; mem. Siena Coll. Career Adv. Network. Mem.: Nat. Youth Sports Coaches Assn., DOE Women's Golf League (treas. 1998—, named Most Improved Player 1998), Fin. Mgmt. Assn., 21st Century Leaders Soc., Kensho-Bo Karate Club (asst. instr. 1998—2000, brown belt), Sigma Beta Delta, Delta Epsilon Sigma, Alpha Kappa Alpha. Roman Catholic. Avocations: golf, softball, dancing. Home: 398 Old County Rd Apt 9 Hampden ME 04444-1936 Personal E-mail: sqboo@yahoo.com.

**SCROGGS, LARRY KENNETH,** lawyer, state legislator; b. Beebe, Ark., Oct. 8, 1941; s. Kenneth Chalmers and Mildred Lorene (McDonald) S.; m. Mary Patricia Rushing, Aug. 25, 1967; children: Larry Kenneth Jr., James Kevin, Michael Kyle. BA, Harding U., 1963; JD, Vanderbilt U., 1971. Bar: Tenn. 1971, U.S. Dist. Ct. (we. dist.) Tenn. 1971, U.S. Ct. Appeals (8th cir.) 1982, U.S. Ct. Appeals (6th cir.) 1989, U.S. Supreme Ct. 1981. Assoc. Law Firm of Leo Bearman, Memphis, 1971-72, Holt, Batchelor, Spicer, Memphis, 1972-76, ptnr., 1976-80, Less & Scroggs, Memphis, 1980-92; pvt. practice, Germantown, Tenn., 1992-96; ptnr. Scroggs & Rogers, Collierville, Tenn., 1997—2003, Burch, Porter & Johnson, Memphis, 2003; mem. Tenn. Ho. of Reps., Nashville, 1996—2002. Mcpl. ct. judge City of Germantown, 1980-86; atty. for County Trustee, Shelby County, Memphis, 1990—. Mem. campaign steering com. George Bush for Pres., Memphis, 1987-92; vol. Ed Bryant for Congress campaign, Memphis, 1994, Don Sundquist for Gov. campaign, Memphis, 1994. Lt. U.S. Navy, 1964-67; Vietnam. Mem. ABA, Tenn. Bar Assn., Memphis Bar Assn. (bd. dirs. 1990-91). Republican. Mem. Ch. of Christ. Avocations: photography, boating, tennis. Office: Burch Porter & Johnson 130 N Court Ave Memphis TN 38103

**SCRUGGS, EARL EUGENE,** entertainer; b. Cleveland County, NC, Jan. 6, 1924; s. George Elam and Georgia Lula (Ruppe) Scruggs; m. Anne Louise Certain, Apr. 18, 1948; children: Gary Eugene, Randy Lynn, Steven Earl. HHD in Folk Music (hon.), Gardner-Webb U., 1986; Mus D (hon.), Berklee Sch. Music, Boston, 2005. Recorded album MCA Records released 2001 with guest stars Elton John, Dwight Yoakam, Billy Bob Thornton, Gary Scruggs, Travis Tritt, Melissa Etheridge, Sting, Glen Duncan, Randy Scruggs, Steve Martin, Vince Gill, Marty Stuart, Albert Lee, Paul Shaffer, Jerry Douglas, Leon Russell, Rosanne Cash, John Fogerty, Don Henley and Johnny Cash. Album titled "Earl Scruggs and Friends". Banjo player, 1945—, rec. artist Columbia Records, 1950—, recorded theme song (TV) The Beverly Hillbillies, 1962; author: Earl Scruggs and the 5-String Banjo, 1968; banjo player formed Earl Scruggs Revue, 1969—, major performances Carnegie Hall, NYC, Wembley Festival, London, Washington Moratorium for Peace, also rock festivals, coll. concerts, 1969—, appearances (TV series) NET-TV Spl. Earl Scruggs: His Family and Friends, 1971; composer (with others): (movie score) Where The Lilies Bloom, 1973; star (films) Banjo Man, 1975, appearances (TV series) Midnight Spl., NBC-Harper Valley U.S.A. Spl., NBC Country Music Awards Show, Phil Donahue Show, Mike Douglas Show, Austin City Limits, 1977, The Grand Ole Opry's 60th Anniversary Show, 1985, The Nashville Network spl. The Am. Music Shop, 1990, The Grand Ole Opry's 65th Anniversary Show, Country Music Assn. Awards Show, 1991, guest appearance (TV films) Return of the Beverly Hillbillies, 1981, appearances (TV series) Country Music Assn. Hall of Fame 25th Anniversary TV show, 1992, The Legend of The Beverly Hillbillies, CBS-TV, 1993, Folk Sound USA-Revlon Revue, The Tonight Show, Les Crane Show, Mac Davis Special, The Johnny Cash Show, The Hootenanny Show, Frank McGee's Here and Now, Ernie Ford Show, Jimmy Dean Show, The Anatomy of Pop, Kraft's Am. Profile, The Roots of Country, CBS-TV, 1994, Red Hot and Country, TNN-TV, A Night at the Ryman, TNN-TV, 1995, An Evening of Country Grt., TNN-TV, CMA 40th Anniversary Celebration, CBS-TV, 1998, albums Nashville Rock, Dueling Banjos, Kans. State, I Saw the Light, Earl Scruggs Revue, Rockin' Across the Country, Family Portrait, Top of the World, Anniversary Spl. Vol. I and Vol. II, Live! At Austin City Limits, Earl Scruggs: His Family and Friends Soundtrack, Today and Forever, Bold and New, Am.-Made, World-Played, others, guest appearances (TV series) The Beverly Hillbillies, Earl Scruggs Revue rec. music soundtrack for (films) Where The Lilies Bloom; composer (instrumental) Foggy Mountain Breakdown (used in

movie Bonnie and Clyde) (Grammy award, 1968, 2001, Broadcast Music, Inc., 1969, Grammy award, 2003); appearance (radio program) John Boy & Billy, 2001, BBC Radio Network, London, Eng., 2001, (TV show) The Late Show with David Letterman, 2001; appearance; (TV show) The Tonight Show with Jay Leno, 2002. Apptd. hon. mem. Lt. Gov.'s Staff State of Tenn. 1987. Nominee 16 Grammy nominations; named Artist of Yr., Hi-Fi Inst., 1975; named to Gibson Hall of Fame, 1981, Country Music Assn. Hall of Fame, 1985, Internat. Bluegrass Music Assn. Hall of Honor, 1991, Starwalk-Nat. Acad. Recording Arts & Scis., 1997, NC Hall of Fame on Grand Ole Opry, 1999; recipient Country Music award best instrumental group, Billboard Mag., 1975, Best Country and Bluegrass Banjoist, Frets mag, 1980, Cert. of Merit, Internat. Bluegrass Music Assn., 1988, Order of the Long Leaf Pine award, Gov. State of N.C., 1988, cert. appreciation, Tenn. Gov. Ned McWherter, 1990, Nat. Medal of Arts award, Pres. George Bush, 1992, Spl. Citation of achievement recognition of nat. popularity over 1 million broadcasts of Foggy Mountain Breakdown, Broadcast Music, Inc., 1993, NC Folk Heritage award, N.C. Arts Coun. Dept Cultural Resources, others, NC Heritage award, NC Arts Coun. Dept. Cultural Resources, 1996, Grammy award vocal collaboration Same Old Train, 1998, lifetime achievement award, Gibson Guitar Corp., 2002, Star, Hollywood Walk of Fame, 2003; Nat. Heritage fellow NEA, 1989. Achievements include development of Scruggs style of banjo playing; invention of Scruggs Tuning Pegs; honored with a star in Hollywood Walk of Fame, Hollywood, Calif., 2003; 13 Grammy nominations.

**SCUDDER, THAYER,** anthropologist, educator; b. New Haven, Aug. 4, 1930; s. Townsend III and Virginia (Boody) S.; m. Mary Eliza Drinker, Aug. 26, 1950; children: Mary Eliza, Alice Thayer. Grad., Phillips Exeter Acad., 1948; AB, Harvard U., 1952, PhD, 1960; postgrad., Yale U., 1953-54, London Sch. Econs., 1960-61. Rsch. officer Rhodes-Livingstone Inst., No. Rhodesia, 1956-57, sr. rsch. officer, 1962-63; asst. prof. Am. U., Cairo, 1961-62; rsch. fellow Ctr. Middle East Studies, Harvard U., 1963-64; asst. prof. Calif. Inst. Tech., Pasadena, 1964-66, assoc. prof., 1966-69, prof. anthropology, 1969-2000, prof. emeritus, 2000—; dir. Inst. for Devel. Anthropology, Binghamton, NY, 1976—2002; commr. World Commn. on Dams, 1998-2000. Cons. UN Devel. Program, FAO, IBRD, WHO, Ford Found., Navajo Tribal Coun., AID, World Conservation Union, Lesotho Highlands Devel. Authority, South China Electric Power Joint Venture Corp., U.S. Nat. Rsch. Coun., Que.-Hydro, Environ. Def. Fund, Ministry of Industry and Handicrafts, Lao People's Dem. Republic, The Nature Conservancy Author: The Ecology of the Gwembe Tonga, 1962, The Future of Large Dams: Dealing with Social, Environmental, Institutional and Political Costs, 2005; co-author: Long-Term Field Research in Social Anthropology, 1979, Secondary Education and the Formation of an Elite: The Impact of Education on Gwembe District, Zambia, 1980, No Place to Go: The Impacts of Forced Relocation on Navajos, 1982, For Prayer and Profit: The Ritual, Economic and Social Importance of Beer in Gwembe District, Zambia, 1950-1982, 1988, The IUCN Review of the So. Okavango Integrated Water Development Project, 1993. Recipient (1st) Lucy Mair medal for applied anthropology, Royal Anthropol. Inst., 1998, John Phillips award, Phillips Exeter Acad., 2005; John Simon Guggenheim Meml. fellow, 1975. Mem. Am. Anthrop. Assn. (1st recipient Solon T. Kimball award for pub. and applied anthropology 1984, Edward J. Lehman award 1991), Soc. Applied Anthropology (Bronislaw Malinowski award 1999). Office: Calif Inst Tech # 228 77 Pasadena CA 91125-0001 Office Phone: 626-395-4207. Business E-Mail: tzs@hss.caltech.edu.

**SCUDIERE, DEBRA HODGES,** lawyer; b. Columbus, Ohio, Sept. 18, 1954; d. L.L. and Anita Lillian (Campbell) Hodges; m. William A. Scudiere, July 16, 1988; 1 child, Rachel Giovanna. BA magna cum laude, W.Va. U., 1976, JD, 1982. Bar: W.Va. 1982, U.S. Dist. Ct. (no. and so. dists.) W.Va. 1982, U.S. Supreme Ct. 1989. With Furbee, Amos, Webb & Critchfield, Morgantown, W.Va., 1982—2001; atty. Kay Casto & Chaney, PLLC, Morgantown, W.Va., 2001—. Mem. W.Va. Law Rev., 1981-82; adj. lectr. trial advocacy W.Va. U., Morgantown, 1991—. Staff mem. W.Va. Law Rev., 1981-82; rsch. editor Jour. Coll. and Univ. Law, 1981-82. Pres., chmn. bd. dirs. North Cen. W.Va. Legal Aid Soc., Morgantown, 1989-95; bd. dirs. W.Va. Sr. Legal Aid, Inc., 1999—. Mem. Def. Rsch. Inst., Def. Trial Counsel W.Va., Marion County Bar Assn., Monongalia County Bar Assn., W.Va. Bar Assn., W.Va. State Bar (mem. bd. govs., v.p., pres.-elect 2004-05, pres. 2005—), So. Conf. Bar Pres. (pres. 2005—), Nat. Conf. Bar Pres., Order of Barrister, Pi Delta Phi, Phi Delta Phi. mem. Lds Ch. Office: 50 Clay St Morgantown WV 26501 Office Phone: 304-296-1100. Business E-Mail: debras@kaycasto.com.

**SCULCO, THOMAS PETER,** surgeon; b. NYC, Feb. 20, 1944; s. Alfred Francis and Mary Jacqueline Sculco; m. Cynthia Davis, June 4, 1966; children: Sarah Jane, Peter. BA in Classics, Brown U., 1965; MD, Coll. of Physicians and Surgeons Columbia U., 1969. Intern in gen. surgery Roosevelt Hosp., NYC, 1969-70, resident in orthopedic surgery, 1970-71; orthop. fellowship London Hosp., 1974—75; asst. attending orthopedic surgery Meml. Hosp., NYC, 1977-83; resident in orthopedic surgery Hosp. for Spl. Surgery, 1971-74, asst. attending orthopedic surgery, 1977-83, assoc. attending orthopedic surgery, 1983-91, attending surgeon in orthopedics, 1991—, Korein-Wilson prof. orthopedic surgery, surgeon-in-chief, med. dir.; asst. attending orthopedic surgery NY Hosp., 1977-83, attending surgeon in orthopedics, 1991—; cons. orthopedic surgeon Mary Manning Walsh Nursing Home, 1978—, Meml. Hosp., 1983—, Bronx Vets. Adminstrn. Hosp., 1987—; from asst. to assoc. prof. clin. surgery Cornell U., 1977-91; dept. chmn., prof. clin. surgery in orthopedics Weill Med. Coll., Cornell U., 1991—. Chief surg. arthritis svc. Hosp. for Spl. Surgery, 1993-2003, dir. orthopedic surgery, 1993-2003, surgeon-in-chief, 2003—; sr. scientist Hosp. for Spl. Surgery, 1996—. Mem. editl. bd. Surg. Blood Mgmt. Forum, 1997. Trustee NY chpt. Arthritis Found., 1997—; mem. Carnegie Hill Assn., St. Bernard's Sch.; bd. dirs. Westerley (RI) Cmty. Chorus, 190-96; sponsor Westerley Pub. Libr., 1996; patron Met. Opera, Carnegie Hall. MC maj. USAF, 1975—77. Recipient Clint Compere award Twentieth Century Orthopedic Assn., 1997, Lifetime Achievement award Arthritis Found., 1999.; recipient numerous grants; named Best Doctors in NY, NY Mag., 2003 Mem. AMA, NY County Med. Soc., Am. Acad. Orthopedic Surgeons (com. on data svcs. chmn. 1981-85, coun. musculoskeletal specialty socs. 1986-90, coord. com. on health policy 1986-89, task force on data chmn. 1987, com. on clin. policies 1991—, patent edn. com. 1999—, liaison to bd. trustees Arthritis Found. 1999—, bd. dirs. 1999-2001), NY Acad. Medicine, NY State Orthopedic Soc., Eastern Orthopedic Soc., Am. Orthopedic Soc., Austrian Orthop. Soc. (hon.), Interurban Orthopedic Assn., Am. Rheumatism Assn., Orthopedic Rsch. and Edn. Found., Knee Soc. (founding mem. 1983, exec. com. 1983-84, program chmn. 1986, membership com. 1986-93, chmn. 1992-93, edn. com. 1990-94, chmn. 1993-94), Assn. VA Orthopedic Surgeons (founder 1986, sec.-treas. 1986-88), Assn. for Arthritis Hip and Knee Surgery, Acad. Orthopedic Soc., Physicians Sci. Soc., Med. Strollers, Internat. Soc. Tech. in Arthroplasty, Am. Austrian Found. (bd. dirs. 2000—), Hip Soc. (membership com. 2000—, Otto Aufranc Rsch. award 1991, Charnley Rsch. award 1995), Austrian Orthop. Assn. (hon.). Office: The Hosp for Spl Surgery 535 E 70th St New York NY 10021 Address: Belaire Bldg 525 East 71st St 2nd Fl between York Ave and East River New York New York NY 10021 Office Phone: 212-606-1475. Office Fax: 212-734-9572. Business E-Mail: sculcot@hss.edu.

**SCULL, ANDREW T.,** sociologist, educator; b. Edinburgh, Scotland, May 2, 1947; arrived in US, 1969; s. Alan Edward and Marjorie Therese Scull; m. Nancy Theresa Principi, Aug. 16, 1970; children: Anna, Andrew, Alexander. BA with first class honours, Oxford U., Eng., 1969; MA, Princeton U., 1971, PhD, 1974. Asst. prof. sociology U. Pa., Phila., 1977—78; vis. assoc. prof. Princeton U., Princeton, NJ, 1978—79; assoc. prof., sociology U. Calif., La Jolla, Calif., 1978—82, prof. sociology, 1982—94, disting. prof. sociology and sci. studies, 1994—. Author: Museums of Madness, 1979, Madhouses, Mad-Doctors, and Madmen, 1981, Decarceration, 1984, Social Order/Mental Disorder, 1989, The Most Solitary of Afflictions: Madness and Society in Britain, 1700-1900, 1993, Masters of Bedlam, 1996, Madhouse: A Tragic Tale of Megalomania and Modern Medicine, 2005, The Race of Insanity, 2006, The Insanity of Place/The Place of Insanity, 2006; co-author (with Steven Lukes): Durkheim and the Law, 1983; co-author: (with Jonathan Andrews)

Customers and Patrons of the Mad Trade: The Management of Lunacy in Eighteenth Century London, 2003, Undertaker of the Mind: John Monro and Mad-Doctoring in Eighteenth-Century England, 2001; co-editor (with Stanley Cohen): Social Control and the State, 1983. Office: 401 Social Science Bldg U Calif San Diego 9500 Gilman Dr La Jolla CA 92093-0533 Office Phone: 858-534-0492. Business E-Mail: ascull@ucsd.edu.

**SCULLEY, PATRICK DAVID,** retired army officer, science honor society director; b. Jamestown, NY, Sept. 12, 1947; s. Claude Francis and Hildegarde Ruth (Anderson) S.; m. Peggy Ann Carroll, Aug. 26, 1967; children: Patricia, Paul, Perry, Peter. BA, Washington and Jefferson Coll., 1969; DDS, SUNY, Buffalo, 1973; MA in Health Svcs. Mgmt., Webster U., 1994. Diplomate Fed. Svcs. Bd. Gen. Dentistry, Am. Bd. Oral Medicine, Am. Bd. Gen. Dentistry; cert. Am. Coll. Health Care Execs. Commd. U.S. Army, advanced through grades to maj. gen., 1999; gen. practice resident Kimbrough Army Hosp., Ft. Meade, Md., 1973-74; gen. dentist U.S. Army MEDDAC, White Sands Missile Range, N.Mex., 1974-76; gen. dentistry resident U.S.Army DEN-TAC, Ft. Knox, Ky., 1977-79, clinic chief Ft. Riley, Kans., 1979-81; comdr. 576th Med. Detachment, Bad Kreuznach, West Germany, 1982-85; staff officer U.S. Army Health Svcs. Command, Ft. Sam Houston, Tex., 1985-86, asst. inspector gen., 1986-88; dental cons. Dept. Army Surgeon Gen.'s Office, Washington, 1988-90; student U.S. Army War Coll., Carlisle Barracks, Pa., 1990-91; comdr. U.S. Army Dental Activity, Ft. Bragg, NC, 1991-92; dir. dental svcs. Health Svcs. Command U.S. Army, 1992-93, comdr. Dental Command, 1993-95, asst. surgeon gen. pers., 1996, commdg. gen. U.S. Army Ctr. Health Promotion and Preventive Medicine, 1996-99, acting dep. surgeon gen., 1998-99, dep. surg. gen./chief Army Dental Corps, chief of staff U.S. Army Med. Command, 1999—2002, ret., 2002; exec. dir. Sigma Xi, 2002—. Instr. oral medicine gen. practice residency, Ft. Riley, 1980-81; mem. bd. examiners Fed. Svcs. Bd. Gen. Dentistry, Washington, 1986-90; mem. bd. examiners Am. Bd. of Gen. Dentistry, 1991-95. Asst. high sch. football coach Bad Kreuznach Am. High Sch., 1982-83; basketball coach Vienna (Va.) Youth Inc., 1988-89, Cath. Youth Orgn., San Antonio, 1985-86; softball coach Girls Recreation Softball League, Manhattan, Kans., 1981; mem. adv. coun. Raleigh-Durham USO, 2004—; mem. steering com. N.C. Project Lead the Way, 2004-. Fellow: Internat. Coll. Dentists; mem.: ADA (alt. del. Ho. Dels. 1999—2000), Assn. Mil. Surgeons U.S. (Fed. Healthcare Adminstr. of Yr. 2001), Am. Bd. Gen. Dentistry, Acad. Gen. Dentistry (chmn. self-assessment com. 1988—91, pres. Army chpt. 1988—91, ho. of dels. 1988—91, examination coun. 1988—92, chmn. reference com. on adminstrn. comm. and constrn. bylaws 1990, long range planning coun. 1997—98, chmn. long range planning coun. 1998—99, chmn. strategic advancement com. 1999—2002, Disting. Svc. award 1999), Am. Coll. Health Care Execs., Triangle Area's Rsch. Dirs. Club (vice chmn. 2004—, chmn. 2005), Sigma Xi, Omicron Kappa Upsilon. Independent. Roman Catholic. Avocation: coaching athletics. Office: Sigma Xi 3106 E NC Hwy 54 Research Triangle Park NC 27709

**SCULLIN, FREDERICK JAMES, JR.,** federal judge; b. Syracuse, NY, Nov. 5, 1939; s. Frederick James and Cleora M. (Fellows) S.; m. Veronica Terek, Aug. 31, 1984; children: Mary Margaret, Kathleen Susan, Kellie Anne, Rebecca Rose; 1 stepchild, Angel Jenette Godleski. BS in Econs., Niagara U., 1961; LLB, Syracuse U., 1964. Bar: N.Y. 1964, Fla. 1976, U.S. Dist. Ct. (no. dist.) N.Y. 1967, U.S. Supreme Ct. 1971. Assoc. Germain & Germain, Syracuse, 1967-68; asst. dist. atty. Onondaga County, Syracuse, 1968-71; asst. atty. gen. NY State Organized Crime Task Force, 1971-78, dir. regional office Albany, 1974-78; chief prosecutor, dir. Gov.'s Coun. on Organized Crime State of Fla., Tallahassee, 1978—; sole practice Syracuse, 1979-82; U.S. atty. for No. Dist. N.Y., 1982-92; judge US Dist. Ct. (No. Dist.) NY, 1992—2000, chief judge, 2000—05; judge Fgn. Intelligence Surveillance Ct., 2005—. With U.S. Army, 1964-67, Vietnam; col. USAR. Decorated Air medal, Bronze Star; Cross of Gallantry (Vietnam); recipient Meritorious Svc. Cross, Vietnam Svc. medal, Vietnam Campaign medal, 5 stars; Nat. Def. medal, N.Y. State Dist. Svc. medal, various others. Mem. Am. Judicature Soc., Fla. Bar Assn., Fed. Bar Assn., Fed. Bar Assn., Onon City Bar Assn., Fgn. Intelligence Surveillance Ct Office: US Dist Ct US Courthouse 100 S Clinton St Syracuse NY 13261-6100 Office Phone: 315-234-8560.

**SCULLION, ANNETTE MURPHY,** lawyer, educator; b. Chgo., Apr. 6, 1926; d. Edmund Patrick and Anna (Nugent) Murphy; 1 child, Kevin. BEd, Chgo. Tchrs. Coll., 1960; JD, DePaul U., 1964, MEd, 1966, Loyola U., Chgo., 1970; EdD, No. Ill. U., 1974. Bar: Ill. 1964, U.S. Dist. Ct. (no. dist.) Ill. 1965, U.S. Ct. Appeals (D.C. cir.) 1978. Lectr. Chgo. C.C., 1964-68; pvt. practice Chgo., 1964—; from asst. prof. bus. edn. to prof. Chgo. State U., 1966-98. Founder, adviser Bus. Edn. Students Assn., Chgo. State U., 1976—; sch. law workshop coord. Ill. Divsn. Vocat. and Tech. Edn., 1981, coord. edn. workshops, 1990—. Mem. ABA, Nat. Bus. Edn. Assn., Womens Bar Assn. Ill., Am. Tchr. Edn., Beta Gamma Sigma. Home: 386 Muskegon Ave Calumet City IL 60409-2347

**SCULLION, TONY,** pharmaceutical executive; BSc in physiology, U. London, England; MSc in pharm., U. London. With Hoechst Roussel; sr. mktg., strategic oper. Pfizer Inc., England; v.p., head global bus. devel. Glaxo Wellcome plc; dir., CEO Memory Pharm., Montvale, NJ, 2001—. Bd. dirs. Dynogen Pharm., Inc. Office: Memory Pharm 100 Philips Pkwy Montvale NJ 07645

**SCULLY, JOHN CARROLL,** life insurance marketing research company executive; b. Springfield, Mass., Mar. 16, 1932; s. James and Frances (Carroll) S.; m. Barbara A. Fougere, Sept. 7, 1953; children: Kathleen, Margaret, John, James, Patricia, Mary Ellen, Susan. BA, Holy Cross Coll., 1953; C.L.U., Boston U., 1963; postgrad., Dartmouth Inst., 1977. With John Hancock Mut. Life Ins. Co., 1953-92, gen. agent Indpls., 1966-75, sr. v.p. agency dept. Boston, 1975-80, pres. retail sector, 1980-92; pres. emeritus Life. Ins. Mktg. Rsch. Assoc., Windsor, Conn., 1992-97. Bd. dirs. Greater Boston YMCA, 1975-91; chmn. Mass. Campaign Holocaust Meml. Mus., 1985—; chmn. United Way, 1985—; bd. dirs. Cath. Charities, 1986—; trustee Springfield Coll., 1986, Suffolk U., 1986, Am. United Life Ins. Co. With U.S. Army, 1954-56. Mem. Am. Coll. Life Underwriters, Nat. Assn. Life Underwriters (v.p. indl. 1973-75), Life Ins. Mktg. and Rsch. Assn. (past chmn.), Gen. Agts. and Mgrs. Assn. (past pres. Indpls.), Nat. Mgmt. award 1973-75), Life Underwriter Tng. Coun. (past chmn.), Greater Boston C. of C. (bd. dirs. 1985—), Wellesley Club, Executives Club (past pres.), Algonquin Club (bd. dirs.), KC. Roman Catholic. Home: Unit 414 4800 N AIA Vero Beach FL 32963 Office: Limra Internat PO Box 208 Hartford CT 06141-0208 Personal E-mail: jscully@limra.com.

**SCULLY, JOHN EDWARD, JR.,** banker; b. Chgo., Jan. 18, 1943; s. John Edward and Ann Berenice (Allenbrand) S.; m. Mary Julia Purvin, June 11, 1966; children: Melissa, Julie, John Edward III. BA, U. Notre Dame, 1964; MA, DePaul U., 1966. Supr., No. Trust Co., Chgo., 1968-69, with personnel dept., 1969-74, personnel officer, 1974-77, bond investment officer, 1977-80; asst. v.p. First Nat. Bank of Chgo., 1980-82, v.p., 1982-87; first v.p. Exch. Nat. Bank, 1987-90; sr. v.p. ABN AMRO, 1990-2005, group sr. v.p., 2005—; mem. mgmt. com. LaSalle Bank, Chgo., 1991-2002. Bd. dirs. Chgo. Heart Assn., 1987-98; trustee Village of Riverside, 1991—; chmn. Ill. Employer Support of Guard and Res. Mil. gen., 1964-96. Mem. Soc. for Human Resource Management, Mil. Officers Assn., Mil. Order World Wars, Assn. U.S. Army, Am. Legion, VFW, USO of Ill., Riverside Swim Club, Union League Chgo. (dir. 1993-96, 2d v.p. 1999-2000). Roman Catholic. Home: 258 Lawton Rd Riverside IL 60546-2337 Office: LaSalle Bank Corp Chicago IL 60603 Office Phone: 312-904-8183. Personal E-mail: john.scully@abnamro.com.

**SCULLY, JOHN THOMAS,** obstetrician, gynecologist, educator; b. NYC, Mar. 11, 1931; s. John Thomas and Mildred Frances (Dunstrop) S.; m. Kimberly Ann Stamberger; children: John, Helen Mary, Thomas, Nora, James, Sara, Megan, Devin. BS, Georgetown U., 1952; MD, U. Mex., 1959. Diplomate Am. Bd. Ob-Gyn. Intern Nassau Hosp., 1959-60, resident, 1960-63; practice medicine specializing in ob-gyn, 1963—; sr. attending dept. ob-gyn St. Peter's U. Hosp., 1971—75, chmn. dept. ob-gyn., 2003—. Fellow ACS, Am. Coll. Ob-Gyn; mem. NJ Med. Soc., Middlesex County Med. Soc., NJ Ob-Gyn Soc., NJ Right to Life (charter) Republican. Roman Catholic. Office: 215 Union Ave Ste A Bridgewater NJ 08807

**SCULLY, MARLAN ORVIL,** physics professor; b. Casper, Wyo., Aug. 3, 1939; s. Orvil O. and Thelma G. (Thoms) Scully; m. Judith Bailey, Aug. 16, 1958; children: James, Robert, Steven. AS, Casper Coll., 1959; BS, U. Wyo., 1961; MS, Yale U., 1963, PhD, 1966. Instr. Yale U., New Haven, 1967-69; asst. prof. MIT, Cambridge, 1969-71, assoc. prof., 1971-72; prof. U. Ariz., Tucson, 1972-80; disting. prof. physics U. N.Mex., Albuquerque, 1980—92; prof. physics Tex. A&M U., 1992—96; dir. Ctr. Theoretical Physics, Tex. A&M U., 1995—; Burgess disting. prof. Tex. A&M U., 1996—, prof. elec. engring., 1999—; disting. rsch. chair TEES, 2000—; dir. Inst. Quantum Studies, Tex. A&M U., 2001—. Dir., co-founder Radtech, 1984; mem. Joint coun. on Quantum Electronics, Internat. Commn. on Optics; mem. program com. VIIth and VIIIth Internat. Conf. on Quantum Electronics (co-chmn. program com.); panel mem. Internat. Conf. on Hot Electrons in Semiconductors, North Tex. State U.; co-dir. VIIth Course of NATO Internat. Sch. Quantum Electronics; mem. program com. for OSA sponsored topical meeting on Picosecons Phenomena, Hilton Head, S.C., 1978; invited lectr. U.S.-Japan Coop. Seminar on Laser Spectroscopy, Hakone, Japan, 1977; mem. NRC panel on electron, atomic and molecular physics; advisor to ARO Nat. Acad. Panel, Los Alamos Physics Div. Author: (with others) Laser Physics, 1974; contbr. articles to profl. jours. Recipient Elliott Cresson medal The Franklin Inst., 1990; John S. Guggenheim fellow, 1970, Alfred P. Sloan fellow, 1972. Fellow AAAS, Optical Soc. Am. (dir. at large 1978-80, publs. com. 1972, Ives medal com. 1976, chmn. Wood prize com. 1978, Adolph E. Lomb medal 1970; mem. Max Planck Soc., Nat. Acad. Scis., Academia Europa. Avocations: cattle ranching, inventing.

**SCULLY, MARTHA SEEBACH,** speech and language pathologist; b. S.I., Nov. 1, 1951; d. Henry F. and Rose Anne (Callahan) Seebach; m. Roger Tehan Scully, Dec. 29, 1979; 1 child, Roger Tehan. BA, Trinity Coll., 1972; MS, George Washington U., 1974; postgrad., Syracuse (N.Y.) U., 1976-79. Lic. speech-lang. pathologist, Md. Clin. supr. Syracuse U., 1976-79; speech-lang. pathologist Fairfax (Va.) County Pub. Schs., 1979—. Bd. dirs. Trinity Coll., Washington, Nat. Children's Choir, 1987-91; trustee Davis Meml. Goodwill Industries, 1994-96, bd. dirs. Goodwill Guild, 1990—, chair ball; donate Folger Shakespearean Libr.; chmn. Nat. Challenge Com. of Disabled, 1985; mem. Ear Ball, 1988, 89; mem. Internat. Children's Festival, 1990, 91; co-chmn. Jr. League of Washington Capital Collection, 1990; chmn. Salvation Army Garden Party, 1992, Washington Embassy Tour, 1993; mem. bd. edn. Holy Cross Sch., Garrett Park, Md., 2001-. Recipient First Order Affiliation Order of Franciscans mirror, 1985; named Outstanding Woman in Am., 1987, 88. Mem. Am. Biog. Inst., Am. Speech-Lang.-Hearing Assn., Coun. for Exceptional Children, Montgomery County Assn. for Hearing Impaired Children, Benevolent and Protective Order Elks (mem. Washinton-Rockville lodge, lecturing knight 1999, esteemed loyal knight 2000). Home: 10923 Wickshire Way Rockville MD 20852-3220

**SCULLY, ROBERT WILLIAM (BOB SCULLY),** diversified financial services company executive; b. Boston; m. Nancy Beth Peretsman, Sept. 17, 1988. AB, Princeton U., 1972; MBA, Harvard Bus. Sch., 1977. Joined Salomon Brothers, 1979, v.p. domestic products capital markets svc. group, mng. dir., 1984—88; co-founder Scully Brothers & Foss, 1988—93; mng. dir. industrials investment banking, mem. investment banking mgmt. com. Lehman Brothers, 1993—96; joined Morgan Stanley, 1996, vice chmn. investment banking, 1999, chmn. global capital markets, 2004, co-pres., 2006—. Bd. dirs. Global Fund for Children. Office: Morgan Stanley 1585 Broadway New York NY 10036*

**SCULLY, ROGER TEHAN, II,** lawyer; b. Washington, Jan. 10, 1948; s. James Henry and Marietta (Maguire) S.; m. Martha Anne Seebach, Dec. 29, 1979. BS, U. Md., 1977; JD, Cath. U., 1980. Bar: Md. 1980, D.C. 1981, U.S. Tax Ct. 1982, U.S. Supreme Ct. 1988. V.p. Bogley Related Cos., Rockville, Md., 1971-75; law clk. to presiding justice Superior Ct. of D.C., Washington, 1979-81; assoc. Lerch, Early & Roseman, Bethesda, Md., 1981-82; gen. counsel Laszlo N. Tauber, M.D. & Assocs., Bethesda, 1982-94, Jefferson Meml. Hosp., Alexandria, Va., 1982-94; spl. counsel Venable, Baetjer, Howard & Civiletti, Washington, 1991-96. Cons. in real estate Order of Friar Minor, N.Y.C., 1977—; lectr. Mortgage Bankers Assn., Washington, 1984—; bd. dirs. Nozzoli Constrn. Co., Washington; exec. com., spl. counsel to bd. dirs., bd. dirs. Chromachron Technology Corp.; Toronto; bd. dirs. Music-Works, N.Y.C.; vice chair Sayett Tech., Inc., Rochester, N.Y.; vice chair, bd. dirs., exec. com. MediaShare, Inc., Rochester; mng. dir. Jefferson Meml. LLC, Washington. Author: (with Quarles & Howard) Summary Adjudication Dispositive Motions and Summary Trials, 1991. Mem. pres.'s coun. St. Bonaventure U., Olean, N.Y., 1995—, chmn. pres.'s coun., 1986-96; trustee Belmont Abbey Coll., Charlotte, N.C., 1993-95; bd. trustees Edmund Burke Sch., Washington, 1984-2001, trustees emeritus, 2001-; bd. dirs. Nat. Children's Choir, Washington, 1980-94. Recipient First Order Affiliation Order of Friars Minor, 1985; named one of Outstanding Young Men in Am., 1982. Fellow D.C. Bar Assn.; mem. ABA, ATLA, FBA, Md. Bar Assn. (chmn. corp. counsel sect.), Am. Judicature Soc., Assn. Governing Bd. of Univs. and Colls., Am. Inns of Ct., Irish Legal Soc., Selden Soc., U.S. Jud. Conf. of 4th Cir. (permanent mem.), U.S. Jud. Conf. Fed. Cir. (del.), Jud. Conf. of D.C. (del.). Office: 7712 Greentree Rd West Bethesda MD 20817-1428 Office Phone: 202-299-7524. Business E-Mail: rts2esq@yahoo.com.

**SCULLY, SEAN PATRICK,** orthopaedic surgeon, educator; s. Michael A. and Anne Rita Scully; m. Kristi Griffin Scully, Aug. 11, 1979; children: Patrick, Colin. BS in Biochemistry, SUNY, Binghamton, 1978; MD, PhD in Biophysics, U. Rochester, 1986. Cert. Am. Bd. Orthop. Surgery 1995. Residency Duke U. Durham, NC, 1986—92; intramural rsch. fellowship Nat. Inst. Health, Bethesda, Md., 1989—90; asst. prof. cell biology Duke U. Medical Ctr., 1994—2000, assoc. prof. orthop., 1997—2000; clin. orthop. oncology fellow Mass. Gen. Hosp., Boston, 1992—93; assoc. prof. orthop. Mayo Medical Sch., Rochester, Minn., 2001—03, prof. orthop., 2003—04; prof. orthop., cell biology and cellular molecular pharmacology U. Miami, 2004—. Mem. advisory panel Musculoskeletal Transplant Found., 1994—2001; vice-chmn. Shriners Rsch. Advisory Bd., 1996—; Ad Hoc reviewer, orthop. study section NIH, 1997—, OBM-2, NIH, 2001—; presenter in field. Dep. editor Clinical Orthopaedics and Related Research, 2003—; contbr. articles to prof. jours., chpts. to books. Named one of America's Top Doctors for Cancer, Cantle Connolly's LTD, 2005; recipient William F. Neuman award in biophysics, 1984, George H. Whipple award, 1986, Marshall R. Urist award, 1999; grantee John J. Fahey N.Am. Traveling fellowship, 1993, Austrian Swiss German Traveling fellowship, AM. Orthop. Assn., 2000. Mem.: Nat. Inst. Arthritis, Musculoskeletal and Skin Diseases Nat. Inst. Health (FDA panel on cartilage repair 2005—), Internat. Skeletal Soc., Internat. Soc. Limb Salvage, Soc. Surgical Oncologists, Am. Orthop. Assn. (Howard Hatcher fellowship com. 2000), ASG fellowship com. 2000), Assn. Bone and Joint Surgeons (co-chair symposium on gene therapy in orthop. 2000, awards com. 2002—), Musculoskeletal Tumor Soc. (strategic planning com. 2001, specialty day organizer 2001), Orthop. Rsch. Soc., Am. Acad. Orthop. Surgeons (subcom. basic sci. evaluation 1995—, program com. 1999—, clinician scientist com. 2001—, fellowship issues task force 2003—), Howard Hatcher pathology fellowship com. 2003—), ASG fellowship ex-change com. 2003—). Achievements include research in tumor biology. Office: U Miami 1400 NW 12th Ave Miami FL 33136 Fax: 305-325-3928.

**SCULLY, THOMAS A.,** lawyer, former federal agency administrator; b. 1957; BA, U. Va., 1979; JD, Cath. U., 1986. Staff atty. Fed. Election Commn., 1979—81, U.S. Senator Slade Gorton, 1981—85; atty. Akin, Gump, Strauss, Hauer & Feld, LLP, 1986—88; comm. staff Bush-Quayle Campaign, 1988, dep. dir. congl. affairs; assoc. dir. human resources, vets. and labor Office Mgmt. & Budget, Washington, 1989—92, counselor to the dir., 1992—93; pres., CEO Fedn. Am. Hosps., 1995—2001; ptnr. Patton Boggs, LLP, Washington; dep. asst. to the pres. The White House, Washington, 2001—03; CEO, adminstr. Centers. for Medicare and Medicaid Services US Dept.

Health & Human Services, Washington, 2001—03; sr. counsel Alston & Bird LLP, Washington, 2003—. Mem.: bd. dirs., SHPS, Inc., 2004-. Republican. Office: Alston & Bird LLP 10th Fl N Bldg 601 Pennsylvania Ave NW Washington DC 20004-3606 Office Phone: 202-756-3459. Business E-Mail: tscully@alston.com.

**SCULLY, VINCENT JOSEPH, JR.,** architectural historian, educator, writer; b. New Haven, 1920; m. Susannah (Nancy) Keith, 1942 (div. 1965); m. Marian La Follette Wohl (div. 1978); m. Catherine Lynn, 1980. Entered Yale U. at age 16; BA in English, Yale U., 1940; MA in art history, Yale U., 1947, PhD in art history, 1949. Mem. faculty art history Yale U., New Haven, 1949—91, prof. art history, 1961-91, Sterling Prof. Emeritus of the History of Art, 1991—, master Morse Coll., 1969—75; disting. vis. prof. Sch. Architecture U. Miami, 1992—. Author: (books) The Shingle Style: Architectural Theory and Design from Richardson to the Origins of Wright, 1955, Frank Lloyd Wright, 1960, Modern Architecture: The Architecture of Democracy, 1961, Louis I Kahn, 1962, The Architectural Heritage of Newport, Rhode Island, 1640-1915, 1967, American Architecture and Urbanism, 1969, Pueblo Architecture of the Southwest, 1971, The Shingle Style and The Stick Style: Architectural Theory and Design from Richardson to the Origins of Wright, 1971, The Shingle Style Today: Or the Historian's Revenge, 1974, Pueblo: Mountain, Village, Dance, 1975, The Earth, the Temple, and the Gods: Greek Sacred Architecture, 1979, Robert Stern, 1981, Studies and Executed Buildings by Frank Lloyd Wright, 1986, The Villas of Palladio, 1986, New World Visions of Household Gods and Sacred Places: American Art and the Metropolitan Museum, 1650-1914, 1988, The Architecture of the American Summer: The Flowering of the Shingle Style, 1989, The Architecture of Robert Venturi, 1989, The Great Dinosaur Mural at Yale: The Age of Reptiles, 1990, Architecture: The Natural and the Man-Made, 1991, French Royal Gardens: The Design of Andre Le Notre, 1992, (book of essays) Modern Architecture and Other Essays, 2003; co-author: (with C. Lynn, E. Vogt, P. Goldberger) Yale in New Haven: Architecture & Urbanism, 2004. Served USMC, 1941—46. Named Jefferson Lectr., NEH, 1995; recipient Wilbur Lucius Cross Medal, Yale Grad. Sch. Alumni Assn., 1994, inaugural Vincent Scully Prize, Nat. Bldg. Mus., Washington, DC, 1999, J.C. Nichols Prize, Urban Land Inst., 2003, Nat. Medal of Arts, 2004; Fulbright Fellow, 1950. Office: Yale U Dept History of Art 56 High St PO Box 208272 New Haven CT 06520

**SCURICH, KELLY LEMOS,** music director; b. Sharon, Pa., Sept. 21, 1960; d. John and Mildred Novak Lemos; m. Thomas Michael Scurich, Oct. 10, 1987; children: Jenna Christine, Jonathan Frank. MusB, Youngstown State U., Ohio, 1983; MusM, Youngstown State U., 1985. Tchr. St. Mary's Mid. Sch., Warren, Ohio, 1985—86; dir. music Holy Trinity Luth. Ch., Hermitage, Pa., 1983—88; choral music dir. West Branch HS, Beloit, Ohio, 1987—93, Hickory HS, Hermitage, 1993—94, Canfield HS, Ohio, 1994—; dir. music First Covenant Ch., Boardman, Ohio, 1988—94. Named Tchr. of the Yr., Mahoning County Fine Arts Coun., 1992. Mem.: Ohio Choral Dirs. Assn. (show choir chair, bd. dirs. 1988—92), Ohio Music Educators Assn., Am. Choral Dirs. Assn., Nat. Assn. Tchrs. Singing, Music Educators Nat. Conf. Office: Canfield High School 100 Cardinal Dr Canfield OH 44406

**SCURLOCK, JO ANN,** history professor, researcher; b. Kansas City, Mo., Sept. 22, 1953; d. John Edward and Jean Lorraine Scurlock; m. Richard Henry Beal, May 13, 1978. BA, U. Chgo., 1975; PhD, U. of Chgo., 1988. Prof. of history Elmhurst (Ill.) Coll., 1984—. Author: (scholarly book) Diagnoses in Assyrian and Babylonian Medicine, Magico-Medical Means of Treating Ghost Induced Illnesses in Ancient Mesopotamia; contbr. articles to scholarly jours. Grantee, NEH, 2000—03. Mem.: Chgo. Soc. for Bibl. Rsch., Am. Hist. Assn., Soc. of Bibl. Lit., Am. Oriental Soc. Avocations: travel, architectural and ethnographic photography. Office: Elmhurst Coll 190 Prospect Elmhurst IL 60126 Office Phone: 630-617-3569. Home Fax: 773-702-9853.

**SCURRY, BRIANA COLLETTE,** professional soccer player; b. Mpls., Sept. 7, 1971; BS in Polit. Sci., U. Mass., 1995. Goalkeeper U.S. Women's Nat. Soccer Team, Chgo., 1994—99, 2002—; profl. soccer player Atlanta Beat (WUSA), 2001—03. Mem. U.S. Olympic Soccer Team, Athens, 2004. Named Goalkeeper of Yr., Mo. Athletic Club Sports Found., 1993; recipient Gold medal, Atlanta Olympics, 1996, Athens Olympic games, 2004, World Cup champion, 1999, Silver medal, Sydney Olympic games, 2000. Office: US Soccer Fedn US Soccer House 1801 S Prairie Ave Chicago IL 60616-1319

**SCUSERIA, GUSTAVO ENRIQUE,** theoretical chemist; b. San Fernando, Buenos Aires, Argentina, July 30, 1956; arrived in US, 1985, naturalized; s. Eraldo L. and Alicia (Capitanelli) S.; m. Ana Inés Ilvento, Apr. 17, 1982; children: Ignacio, Tomás. BS, MS, U. Buenos Aires, 1979, PhD in Physics, 1983. Grad. asst. U. Buenos Aires, 1979-83, asst. prof., 1983-85; rsch. assoc. U. Calif., Berkeley, 1985-87; sr. rsch. assoc. U. Ga., Athens, 1987-89; asst. prof. Rice U., Houston, 1989-93, assoc. prof., 1993-95, prof., 1995-2000, Robert A. Welch prof. chemistry, 2000—. Recipient IBM Partnership award IBM Corp., 1998-99; Camille and Henry Dreyfus Teacher scholar Camille and Henry Dreyfus Found., 1992; John Simon Guggenheim Meml. Found. fellow, 2003. Fellow AAAS, Am. Phys. Soc.; mem. Am. Chem. Soc., Materials Rsch. Soc. Office: Rice U Dept Chemistry PO Box 1892 Houston TX 77251-1892 E-mail: guscus@rice.edu.

**SCZUDLO, WALTER JOSEPH,** lawyer; b. Fairbanks, Alaska; s. Walter and Dolores J. Sczudlo; children: Lauren Hall, Elizabeth Fairbanks, Walter Christopher; m. Rebecca Grey Tucker. AB, Middlebury Coll.; JD, Golden Gate U.; LLM, Georgetown U.; post grad., U. Calif., Santa Barbara, Tulane U., Vt. Law Sch. Bar: Alaska, Calif., U.S. Ct. Appeals (9th cir.), U.S. Dist. Ct. Alaska, US Ct. Claims, US Tax Ct. Law clk. to presiding justice Alaska Supreme Ct.; assoc. atty. Merdes, Schaible, Staley and Delisio, Anchorage; legis. dir., gen. counsel U.S. Senator Murkowski, Washington; sr. tax assoc. Schramm and Raddue, Santa Barbara, Calif.; dir. congl. rels., counsel Natural Gas Supply Assn., Washington; Washington counsel Shell Oil Co., 1988-96; v.p., Washington counsel Intercontinental Energy Corp., 1996-99; gen. counsel, exec. v.p. Assn. Fundraising Profls., Washington, 1999—; prin. ptnr. WEBK Broadcasting 105.3 FM, Killington, Vt., 1985—. Dir. Sun's Edge, Inc., Santa Barbara, 1987—, Natural Gas Roundtable, Washington, 1987—. Author: (with other) Washington Legal Foundation, 1988. Com. chmn. Steve Cowper for Gov., Anchorage, 1982. Recipient Am. Jurisprudence award Bancroft-Whitney Pub. Co. Office Phone: 800-666-3863.

**SDERKSEN, MARY LOU,** writer, retired secondary school educator; b. Colorado Springs, Colo., June 12, 1937; d. George David and Frances Amelia (Bradley) Doty; m. Donald Earl Derksen, Aug. 31, 1956 (div. 1988), remarried, 1996; children: Paul, Deborah, Peter, Philip. BA in Anthropology, Wheaton Coll., Ill., 1957; MS in Counseling and Human Resource, SD State U., 1990. Cert. med. transcription Med. Transcription Advantage Career Ctr. Tchr. Head Start, Rapid City, SD, 1987-88; youth coordinator First Presbyn. Ch., Rapid City, 1988-89; counselor Community Coll. of the Air Force, Ellsworth AFB, SD, 1989-90; rsch. asst. Black Hills Coop. SD State U., 1989-90; psychotherapist in cmty. mental health ctr. Sturgis and Spearfish, 1990-95; customer svc. rep. Conseco Ins. Group, 2002—03; collections agt. and underwriter GE Consumer Credit Card Co., 2002—. Descriptive linguist-Bible tutor. Summer Inst. Linguistics/Wycliffe Bible Translators, Santa Ana, Calif., 1959-65; tchr., librarian, bookkeeper Rapid City Christian Acad., 1978-86; owner, operator magnamics.com, 2006. Author: AD/HD, What We Know, What We Think We Know, What We Don't Know, What We Should Know, 2002, Path to Destruction, 2002, Parenting Tales, 2002, monthly internet column. Mem. soloist Black Hills Voices in Concert, Rapid City, 1986-90; mem. Rapid City Symphony Concert Choir, 1986-90. Republican. E-mail: magnamics@rushmore.com.

**SEABAUGH, WILLIAM F.,** lawyer; BS magna cum laude, U. Mo., 1978; JD magna cum laude, U. Mich., 1981. Bar: Mo. 1981. Ptnr., group co-leader Transactions Bryan Cave LLP, St. Louis. Office: Bryan Cave LLP One Metropolitan Sq 211 N Broadway, Ste 3600 Saint Louis MO 63102 Office Phone: 314-259-2450. E-mail: wfseabaugh@bryancave.com.

**SEABERG, ERIC DAYLE,** audio engineer; b. San Diego, Oct. 20, 1953; s. William Eric and Marilyn Carolyn (Oberg) S.; m. Nancy Ellen Amerian-Omachi, Feb. 24, 1973 (div. 1984); children: Robin Eric, Sean Arthur; m. Deborah Ellen Harris, June 1, 1992. Grad., Fresno (Calif.) H.S., 1971. Chief audio engr. Kenjo Audio, Inc., Fresno, 1971-79; chief engr., ptnr. Triad Recorders, Fresno, 1979-83, chief engr., 1983-85, Maximus Recording, Fresno, 1985-88; owner, operator Seaberg Audio Svcs., Fresno, 1988-99; dir. audio Turning Point Ministries, San Diego, 1999—. Mem. NARAS, Audio Engring. Soc., Soc. Motion Picture and TV Engrs., Soc. Profl. Audio Rec. Studios. Home: 4117 Conrad Dr Spring Valley CA 91977-1312 Office: 10007 Riverford Rd Lakeside CA 92040 E-mail: eseaberg@seaberg.com, eseaberg@turningpointonline.net.

**SEABOLT, RICHARD L.,** lawyer; b. Chgo., Aug. 28, 1949; BGS with distinction, U. Mich., 1971; JD, U. Calif., Hastings, 1975. Bar: Calif. 1975. With Hancock, Rothert & Bunshoft, San Francisco, 1975—; ptnr. Hancock, Rothert & Bunshoft (merged with Duane Morris LLP), San Francisco, 1981—. Frequent speaker and author profl. jours.; author: (California Pretrial Civil Procedure and Discovery. Mem. Am. Arbitration Assn. (mem. large complex case panel), State Bar Calif. (chair litig. sect., mem. Calif. jud. coun. jury instrn. adv. com.), Assn. Bus. Trial Lawyers (bd. govs.). Office: Duane Morris LLP One Market Spear Tower San Francisco CA 94111 Office Phone: 415-957-3212.

**SEABOLT, ROBERT D.,** lawyer; b. Newport News, Va., 1955; BA magna cum laude, Univ. Richmond, 1977; JD, Univ. Va., 1980. Bar: Va. 1980. Adminstrv. ptnr. Troutman Sanders LLP, Richmond, Va., and mem. exec. com. Named one of Virginia's Legal Elite, Civil Litig. Mag., 2003. Mem.: ABA, Va. State Bar, Va. Bar Assn., Richmond Bar Assn. Office: Troutman Sanders LLP Bank of Am Ctr 1111 E Main St Richmond VA 23219 Office Phone: 804-697-1328. Office Fax: 804-698-5100. Business E-Mail: bob.seabolt@troutmansanders.com.

**SEABORG, DAVID MICHAEL,** evolutionary biologist; b. Berkeley, Calif., Apr. 22, 1949; s. Glenn Theodore and Helen Lucille (Griggs) S.; m. Adele Fong Yee, June 17, 1990. BS, U. Calif., Davis, 1972; MA, U. Calif., Berkeley, 1974. Biology tchr. U. Calif., Berkeley, 1972-73; biol. rschr., photographer Trans Time Labs, Berkeley, 1978; pvt. practice, 1974—; hypnosis and self-hypnosis tchr. Open Edn. Exchange, Oakland, Calif., 1978—81; biol. tchr. Oakland Mus., Calif., 1983-87; rsch. biologist, dept. ecology and evolutionary biology U. Calif., Irvine, 1987; pres. dir. Rsch. Found. for Biol. Conservation and Rsch., Walnut Creek, Calif., 1983—; radio talk show host Sta. KPFA, Berkeley, 1996; biology and life sci tchr. Phillip and Sala Burton Acad. H.S., San Francisco, 1996-97; lab. chem. Biodynamics U. Calif., Berkeley, 1975; comedian, 1969—. Vol. asst. to curator Smithsonian Instn. 1966-67; lectr. sci, philos., environ. issues, 1974—; Inventor game, Sum-It, 1981; originator, theory of evolution based on organisms as integrated systems; chmn. Com. for Arts and Lectures, U. Calif., Berkeley, 1974-75; chmn. Bastilla Day, Lafayette (Calif.)-Langeac Soc., 1982, master of ceremonies, 1982-86, 98-2000. Contbr. articles to profl. sci. jours. Environ. organizer, founder, pres. U Turn Soc., Glenn Seaborg Open Space Fund, World Rainforest Fund, Found. for Biol. Conservation and Rsch.; creator, organizer press conf. on global environ. and social issues 100th Nobel Prize Festivities, Stockholm, 2001. Recipient Meritorius Svc. award Smithsonian Inst., 1967, Animal Photograph award Soc. Photographic Scientists and Engrs., 1967, Best of Show Photo Contest award Klamath Basin Audubon Soc., 1991; award Nat. Libr. Poetry, 1997, 99. Mem.: Nat. Resources Def. Coun., Earth Island Inst., World Wildlife Fund, Calif. Aggie Alumni Assn., Population Connection, Save the Bay Assn., Desert Tortise Preserve Com., Greenpeace, Rainforest Action Network, Nature Conservancy, Calif. Alumni Assn., Sierra Club, Club of Rome USA (v.p. 1998—2001, bd. dirs. 1995—). Democrat. Address: 1888 Pomar Way Walnut Creek CA 94598-1424 Office Phone: 925-938-9206. E-mail: davidseaborg@juno.com.

**SEABRA, JAMES JOSEPH,** music educator, musician; b. Providence, Oct. 16, 1953; s. Dolores T. Case; m. Seabra (div. May 25, 1995); children: Jonathan, James, Trafford. BS applied music, Berklee Coll. of Music, Boston, Mass., 1972—76; post grad., UCLA, Los Angeles, CA, 1987—88, Calif. State Univ., Northridge, 1987—88; MATC, R.I. Coll., 1993. Educator Foster/Gloster Pub. Sch., Foster/Gloster, RI, 1989, Cranston (RI) Pub. Sch., 1989—90; band dir. Smithfield HS, Smithfield, RI, 1990—2002; music dir. RI Coll., Providence, 1998—2002, Providence Coll., 2003—. Mem. Percussive Arts Soc., Cawtow, Okla., 1976—2002, Am. Feb. of Musicians, Providence, 1976—2002, Music Ed. Nat. Conf. (MENC), 1989—2002. Home: 84 Cottage Ave North Providence RI 02911-2113 Office: Smithfield HS 90 Pleasantview Ave Smithfield RI 02917

**SEABROOK, JOHN MARTIN,** retired food products executive, chemical engineer; b. Seabrook, N.J., Apr. 16, 1917; s. Charles Franklin and Norma Dale (Ivins) S.; m. Anne Schlaudecker, Apr. 5, 1939 (div. 1951); children: Carol Ormsby (Mrs. Jacques P. Boulanger), Elizabeth Anne; m. Elizabeth Toomey, 1956; children: John Martin, Bruce Cameron. BS in Chem. Engring. Princeton, 1939; LL.D. (hon.), Gettysburg Coll., 1974. Registered profl. engr., N.J., Del. Engr. Deerfield Packing Corp., 1939-41; v.p. Seabrook Farms Co., 1941-50, exec. v.p., 1950-54, dir., 1941-59, pres., 1954-59, chief exec. officer, 1955-59; dir. Pa. Reading & Seashore Line, 1950-63, N.Y. Ctrl. R.R., 1964-69, Penn Ctrl. R.R., 1968-71; cons. IU Internat. Corp., Wilmington, Del., 1959, v.p., 1960-65, dir., 1963-87, pres., 1965-73, 74-78, chief exec. 1967-80, chmn. bd., 1969-82, chmn. exec. com., 1982-87. Pres., bd. dirs. Cumberland Automobile & Truck Co., 1954-59, Cumberland Warehouse Corp., 1954-59, Salem Farms Corp, N.J., 1948—; chmn. bd. dirs. Frick Co., Waynesboro, Pa., 1959-68; chmn., bd. dirs. S.W. Fabricating & Welding Co., Inc., Houston, 1964-68; chmn. Divcon, Inc., Houston, 1967-69; pres. bd. dirs. Internat. Utilities Overseas Capital Corp., Wilmington, 1966-82, chmn., 1970-80; v.p. Gen. Waterworks Corp., Phila., 1959-66, pres., 1966-68, chmn., 1968-71; chmn. bd. dirs. GWC Inc., Phila., 1971-73; pres. Brown Bros. Contractors, Inc., Phila., 1960, chmn. bd. dirs., 1965-67; pres. Am. Portable Irrigation Co., Eugene, Oreg., 1961, chmn. bd. dirs., 1966-68; chmn. bd. dirs. Gotaas-Larsen Shipping Corp., 1963, chmn., 1979, pres., CEO, 1982-88; chmn. bd. dirs. Amvit Corp., Cleve., 1964-68; bd. dirs. Echo Bay Mines Ltd., South Jersey Gas Co., Folsom, N.J., South Jersey Industries, Inc., Folsom, Bell Atlantic Corp.; dir. emeritus Bell Atlantic-N.J., Inc. Mem. N.J. Migrant Labor Bd., 1945-67, chmn., 1955-67; mem. N.J. Bd. Higher Edn., 1967-70, Pres.' Air Quality Adv. Bd., 1968-70; bd. dirs. Brandywine Conservancy, Inc., 1972-95, pres., 1992-93, hon. dir., 1997—; trustee Eisenhower Exch. Fellowships, 1974-85; trustee Hitchcock Found., 1991-96, chmn., 1993-96. Mem.: Coaching Club (N.Y.C. and U.K.), Wilmington (Del.) Club, Phila. Club, Knickerbocker Club (N.Y.C.), Racquet and Tennis Club (N.Y.C.), Phi Beta Kappa. Home: PO Box 3338 Aiken SC 29802 Office Phone: 856-935-5200, 800-358-5201. E-mail: jmsdrives@snip.net.

**SEABROOK, RAYMOND J.,** corporate financial executive; b. Toronto, Mar. 1, 1950; married; 2 children. Cert. in arch., Humber Coll., Toronto, 1972; B in Bus., McMaster U., Hamilton, Ontario, 1975. With Coopers and Lybrand, Toronto, Canada, 1976—85; v.p. fin. control Onex Packaging and Am. Can Can., 1985—91; from sr. v.p., CFO to sr. v.p. fin. Ball Packaging Products Can., Inc., Broomfield, Colo., 1991—2000, sr. v.p., CFO, 2000—. Office: Ball 10 Longs Peak Dr Broomfield CO 80021

**SEACREST, RYAN (RYAN JOHN SEACREST),** television and radio personality, entrepreneur; b. Atlanta, Dec. 24, 1976; s. Gary and Connie Seacrest. Attended, U. Ga., 1994—95. DJ WSTR/Star 94, Atlanta, 1992—94, 102.7 KIIS-FM morning show. Launched fashion line, R Line, 2005; part owner at Katana, Sushi Roku and Boa. Host (TV series) Gladiators 2000, 1994, Radical Outdoor Challenge, ESPN, 1995, The New Edge, 1996, The Click, 1997, American Idol, 2002—, American Juniors, 2003, host, exec. prodr. On-Air With Ryan Seacrest, 2004, corr. Extra Weekends, 2002, The Tonight Show, 2005—, host (TV) Wild Animal Games, 1995, (radio) Live from the Lounge, Star 98.7, 1995—2001, Ryan Seacrest for the Ride Home, Star 98.7, L.A., 1995—2004, American Top 40, 2004—, On-Air With Ryan Seacrest, 102.7 KIIS-FM, L.A., 2004—, New Year's Eve: Live From Times Square With Ryan Seacrest, 2004, New Year's Rockin' Eve Live From Times Square With Ryan Seacrest, 2004, New Year's Rockin' Eve 2006, 2005; actor: (TV series) Reality Check, 1995; voice Hey Arnold!, 1999, Robot Chicken, 2005, guest appearances Beverly Hills, 90210, 2000, Mad TV, 2002, 2005, Player$, 2003, guest host Good Day Live, 2003, Larry King Live, 2003, 2004, 2005. Named one of 50 Most Beautiful People, People Mag., 2003.*

**SEADEN, GEORGE,** civil engineer; b. Cracow, May 26, 1936; s. Simon and Mary (Guttman) S.; m. Linda Helen Mutch, Mar. 18, 1978; children: Amy Elisabeth, Maia Claire. BE, McGill U., Montreal, Que., Can., 1958; MS, Harvard U., 1968; postgrad., Northwestern U., 1992. Engr. Gatineau Power, Hull, Que., 1958-59, Ent. Fougerolle, Paris, 1960-62; mgr. Warnock Hersey Ltd., Montreal, 1959-60; assoc. Cartier, Coté, Piette, Montreal, 1962-67; sr. advisor Ministry Urban Affairs, Ottawa, Ont., Canada, 1969-71; pres. Archer, Seaden & Assoc., Inc., Montreal, 1971-84; dir. gen. Inst. Rsch. in Constrn. Nat. Rsch. Coun., Ottawa, 1985-97, chief Constrn. Tech. Group, 1995-97; exec.-in-residence Faculty Adminstrn. U. Ottawa, 1997—2001. Vis. prof. U. Ottawa, 1968-73; mem. Can. Constrn. Rsch. Bd., 1985-91, Constrn. Industry Devel., Can., 1988-93, Civil Engring. Rsch. Found., 1993—, Rsch. Bd. Am. Pub. Works Assn., 1994-97; dir. Continental Automated Bldg. Assn., 1995-97, Can. Rsch. Mgrs. Assn., CERIU; pres. Conseil Internat. du Batiment, Rotterdam, The Netherlands, 1989-92; vice chair Constrn. for Sustainable Devel. in the Twenty First Century Conf., Washington, 1996; chair INFRA 2000, Montreal; mem. jury to select best Can. Constrn. projects and engring. design; lectr. numerous univs. and rsch. ctrs.; chmn. Internat. Symposium on Innovation, Ottawa, 2001. Contbg. author: Buildings, Culture and Environment, 2003; co-editor: Trends in Building Construction Worldwide, 1989, Innovation in Construction, 2001; mem. editl. bd. Bldg. Rsch. and Practice, Constrn. Bldg. Rev., 1991—; contbr. numerous articles to profl. publs. Chmn. bd. dirs. St. Andrew's Sch., Westmount, Que., 1975-82; dir. SJCC, 2002— Fellow Am. Soc. Civil Engrs. E-mail: george.seaden@rogers.com.

**SEADER, JUNIOR DEVERE (BOB SEADER),** retired chemical engineering professor; b. San Francisco, Aug. 16, 1927; s. George Joseph and Eva (Burbank) S.; m. Joyce Kocher, Aug. 12, 1950 (div. 1960); m. Sylvia Bowen, Aug. 11, 1961; children: Steven Frederick, Clayton Mitchell, Gregory Randolph, Donald Jeffrey, Suzanne Marie, Robert Clark, Kathleen Michelle, Jennifer Anne. BS, U. Calif., Berkeley, 1949, MS, 1950; PhD, U. Wis., 1952. Instr. chem. engring. U. Wis., Madison, 1951-52; group supr. chem. process design Chevron Rsch. Corp., Richmond, Calif., 1952-57, group supr. engring. rsch., 1957-59; prin. scientist heat transfer and fluid dynamics rsch. Rocketdyne div. N.Am. Aviation, Canoga Park, Calif., 1959-65, sr. tech. specialist, summer 1967; prof. chem. engring. U. Idaho, 1965-66, U. Utah, Salt Lake City, 1966—2003, chmn. dept. chem. engring., 1975-78. Tech. cons.; trustee CACHE Corp., Austin, Tex., 1969—2002. Author 13 books; assoc. editor IEC Rsch. jour., 1986-99; contbr. more than 100 articles to tech. publs. With USNR, 1945—46. Recipient Disting. Tchg. award U. Utah, 1975, Donald L. Katz lectureship, 1990, Dean's Tchg. award U. Utah, 1998, CACHE award for excellence in computing in chem. engring. edn. Am. Soc. Engring. Edn., 2004. Fellow: AIChE (Inst. lectr. 1983, bd. dirs. 1983—85, Computing in Chem. Engring. award 1988, Warren K. Lewis award for chem. engring. edn. 2004). Heat transfer research connected with the development of rocket engines associated with the Apollo and Space Shuttle projects, 1960-65. E-mail: j.seader@utah.edu.

**SEADLER, STEPHEN EDWARD,** philosopher, writer; s. Silas Frank and Doris Amy Seadler; m. Ingrid Linnea Adolfsson, 1954 (div. 1997); children: Einar Austin, Anna Carin. AB in Physics, Columbia U., N.Y.C., 1947, postgrad., 1947; student in Big Bang Cosmology under George Gamow, George Washington U., Washington, D.C., 1948—50. Electronic engr. Cushing & Nevell, Warner Inc., N.Y.C., 1951—54; seminar leader, leader trainer world politics Am. Found. for Continuing Edn., N.Y.C., 1955—57; exec. dir. Medimetric Inst., 1957—59; mem. long range planning com., chmn. corporate forecasting com., mktg. rsch. dir. W.A. Sheaffer Pen Co., Ft. Madison, Iowa, 1959—65; founder Internat. Dynamics Corp., Ft. Madison and N.Y.C., 1965, pres., 1965—70; originator DELTA program for prevention and treatment of violence, 1970; founder, pres. ID Ctr., Ft. Madison, Dover, N.J., 1968—. Mgmt. cons. in human resources devel. and conflict reduction, N.Y.C., 1970-73; pres. UNICONSULT computer-based mgmt. and computer scis., N.Y.C., 1973-76; speaker on decision support systems, internat. affairs and ideological arms control; author/speaker (presentation) Holocaust, History and Arms Control; originator social sci. of ideologics and ideotopology; spl. works collection accessible via On-line Computer Lib. Ctr. Instr. polit. sci. Ia. State Penitentiary, 1959-62; guest speaker on radio and television. *In retrospect, a single predominant thread has woven through my life since childhood: to gain such learning and skills as to revolutionize mankind's thinking, slay the dragons of racism, religionism, ethnicism, and other ideologies of malevolence, oppression, and war and bring true peace for the first time. To accomplish that mission I have developed a comprehensive framework, the new field of ideologics, and comprehensive works presenting and employing that framework, beginning with the book, Principia Ideologica: A Treatise on Combatting Human Malignance.* Author: Principia Ideologica: A Treatise on Combatting Human Malignance, 1999, Ending the Bronze Age, 2001, Terror War and Peace, 2003, Bloodshed Trilogy, 2006, Slaying the Hydra: The Real War - And How to Win It, 2006; contbr. ideologics and ideotopology sects. to Administrative Decision Making, 1978, Management Handbook for Public Administrators, 1978, statement on ideological arms control in Part 4 of Sen. Fgn. Rels. Com. hearing on Salt II Treaty, 1979, Ideologics Extended to treat ethnic, racial, religious conflict, 1992, with first call for Abrahamic Reformation, Morristown (N.J.) Unitarian Ch., 1993; contbr. articles to profl. jours. With AUS, 1944—46. Recipient 20th Century Achievement Award medal Internat. Biographical Ctr., U.K., 1995; named to The Wisdom Hall of Fame by The Wisdom Soc., 1997. Mem.: IEEE, UN Assn.-USA, Forum on Physics and Soc., Fgn. Policy Assn., Am. Mgmt. Assn. (lectr. 1963—68), Am. Sociol. Assn., N.Y. Acad. Scis., Acad. Polit. Sci., Am. Statis. Assn., Am. Phys. Soc., Naval Intelligence Profls., Union Concerned Scientists, West Point Soc. NJ, Friends of West Point, Scottish Rite. Unitarian Universalist. Office: ID Ctr PO Box 824 Dover NJ 07802-0824 Business E-Mail: ses146@columbia.edu.

**SEAGAL, STEVEN,** actor; b. Lansing, Mich., Apr. 10, 1951; m. Miyako Seagal, 1975 (div. 1986); children: Kentaro, Ayako; m. Adrienne La Russa (div.); m. Kelly LeBrock (div. 1994); children: Annaliza, Dominic San Rocco, Arissa, Savannah. Studied martial arts under masters, Japan. Founded Aikido Ten Shin Dojo, L.A. Martial arts choreographer The Challenge, 1982; actor, prodr., martial arts choreographer Above the Law, 1988, Marked for Death, 1990, My Giant, 1998; actor, martial arts choreographer Hard to Kill, 1990; actor, prodr. Out for Justice, 1991, Under Siege, 1992, Under Siege 2, 1995, Half Past Dead, 2002, The Foreigner, 2003, Out for a Kill, 2003, Belly of the Beast, 2003; actor, dir., co-prodr. On Deadly Ground, 1994; fight scene choreographer various films; appeared in films The Glimmer Man, 1996, Executive Decision, 1996, Fire Down Below, 1997, The Patriot, 1998, Get Bruce, 1999, Blood on the Moon, 2000, Exit Wounds, 2001, Ticker, 2001, Out of Reach, 2004. Achievements include first non-Asian to open martial arts acad. in Japan; black belt numerous martial arts.

**SEAGLE, EDGAR FRANKLIN,** environmental engineer, consultant; b. Lincolnton, N.C., June 27, 1924; s. Franklin Craig and Lillie Mae (James) S.; m. Doris Elaine Long, Mar. 23, 1958; children: Rebecca Jane, Mary Elaine, James Craig, William Franklin. AB in Chemistry, U. N.C., 1949, MS in Pub. Health, 1954; BCE, U. Fla., 1961; DPH, U. Tex., 1974. Registered profl. engr., Ala. Sr. sanitarian Health Dept., City of Charlotte, NC, 1950-52, chief indsl. hygiene sect. NC, 1956-59; sanitation cons. N.C. State Bd. Health, Raleigh, 1954-56; engr. dir. USPHS, Rockville, Md., 1961-78; asst. dir. Fellowship Office Nat. Acad. Scis., Washington, 1978-83; pub. health engr. Dept. of Environ., State of Md., Balt., 1985-88; ind. engring. cons. Rockville, 1984-85, 88—. Contbr. articles to profl. publs. With USN, 1943-46, PTO. Mem. ASCE, APHA, Am. Acad. Environ. Engrs. (diplomate). Methodist. Home and Office: 14108 Heathfield Ct Rockville MD 20853-2760 Personal E-mail: efseagle@mindspring.com.

**SEAGLE, J. HAROLD,** lawyer; b. Marion, N.C., May 9, 1947; s. Rufus James and Alma Rhoda (McMahan) S.; m. Linda Jean Cranford, June 3, 1967; 1 child, James Mark. BA, U. NC, 1973, JD, 1977. Bar: N.C. 1977; U.S. Dist. Ct. (ea., middle, we. dists.) N.C. 1977, U.S. Ct Appeals (4th cir.) 1982; U.S. Supreme Ct. 1982. Assoc. atty. Rountree & Newton, Wilmington, NC, 1977-79; ptnr. Rountree & Seagle, L.L.P., Wilmington, 1979—2001. Past pres. Fifth Jud. Dist. Bar. Active Ctrl. United Meth. Ch.; past moderator Wilmington Baptist Assn.; bd. dirs. Rescue Mission of Cape Fear; past adv. Bd. Coastal Bioethics Network; past chmn. annual fund drive Am. Cancer Soc.; past sect. chmn. Cape Fear United Way. Mem.: 28th N.C. Jud. Dist. Bar, N.C. Bar Coun. of Pres. Wilmington Inns of Ct. (exec. com., master), Maritime Law Assn. of U.S. (proctor), Southeastern Admiralty Law Inst. (past chmn., chmn. adv. coun.), N.C. Coll. of Advocacy, N.C. Acad. Trial Lawyers, N.C. State Bar, N.C. Bar Assn., New Hanover County Bar Assn. Avocations: motorcycle racing, guitar. Home and Office: 311 Bradenton Knoll Fletcher NC 28732 Office Phone: 828-545-7777. E-mail: haroldseagle@charter.net.

**SEAGO, JEAN ANN,** science educator; b. Durant, Okla., Nov. 10, 1948; d. Louis Eugene and June Ette Seago; m. Haruo Minney Kuartei, Aug. 15, 1985; 1 child, Stefny Suellen Hutchinson. BSN, San Jose State U., Calif., 1974; MS, U. of Okla., Oklahoma City, 1979; PhD, U. of Calif., San Franciso, 1995. RN Calif. Assoc. prof. U. of Calif., San Francisco, 1995—. Contbr. articles to profl. jours. Capt. Navy Nurse Corps, Res., 1986. Office: U Calif Rm N505 2 Koret Way San Francisco CA 94143-0608 Office Phone: 415-502-6340. Office Fax: 415-476-6042. Business E-Mail: jean.ann.seago@nursing.ucsf.edu.

**SEAGREN, ALICE,** school system administrator, former state legislator; b. 1947; m. Fred Seagren; 2 children. BS, SE Mo. State U. Mem. Minn. Ho. of Reps., 1993—2004, actide min. fin., 1999—2004; commr. of edn. State of Minn., 2004—. Active Bloomington (Minn.) Sch. Bd., 1989-92. Mem. Bloomington C. of C. (bd. dirs. 1990-92), Phi Gamma Nu, Alpha Chi Omega. Republican. Home: 9730 Palmer Cir Bloomington MN 55437-2017 Office: Minn Dept Children, Famlies, Learning 1500 Highway 36 W Roseville MN 55113-4035 Office Phone: 651-582-8204. E-mail: mde.commissioner@state.mn.us.

**SEAGREN, STEPHEN LINNER,** oncologist; b. Mpls., Mar. 13, 1941; s. Morley Raymond and Carol Christine (Linner) S.; m. Jill Garrie; 1 child, Sean Garrie. AB, Harvard U., 1963; MD, Northwestern U., 1967. Diplomate Am. Bd. Internal Medicine, Am. Bd. Med. Oncology, Am. Bd. Radiology. From asst. prof. to assoc. prof. radiology and medicine U. Calif., San Diego, 1977-88, prof., 1988—, chief divsn. radiation oncology. Contbr. over 80 articles to profl. jours. Bd. dirs., chmn. profl. adv. com. Wellness Cmty., San Diego, 1988-2003; chmn. radiol. oncology com. Cancer and Acute Leukemia Group, Chgo., 1986-98; assoc. dir. U. Calif. San Diego Cancer Ctr., 1998-2000. Lt. comdr. USNR, 1971-73. Fellow ACP. Avocations: physical fitness, bridge, skiing, golf, tennis. Office: Moores Cancer Ctr 3855 Health Scis Dr #0843 La Jolla CA 92093-0843 Office Phone: 858-822-6040. Business E-Mail: sseagren@ucsd.edu.

**SEAL, MANUEL, JR.,** music company executive, composer; Staff songwriter, prodr. So So Def Recordings, Atlanta. Co-writer, co-prodr. (hit singles including) Always Be My Baby, Every Little Bit Hurts, It's Like That, Just Kickin' It, My Boo, My Way, Nice & Slow, You Make Me Wanna, We Belong Together (Grammy award, Best R&B Song, 2006). Office: So So Def Recordings 1946 Briarwood Ct NE Atlanta GA 30329 Office Phone: 404-638-5684.*

**SEAL,** musician; b. London, Jan. 3, 1963; m. Heidi Klum, May 10, 2005. Albums Seal, 1992, 1994, Being Human, 1998, Waiting for You, 2003, Seal IV, 2003, The Acoustic Session, 2003, singles Crazy, Killer, 1991, song Kiss From a Rose, included in Batman Forever, 1995. Recipient Grammy award Song of Yr., 1996, Grammy award Record of Yr., 1996, Grammy award Best Male Pop Vocal Performance, 1996. Office: Warner Bros Records Inc 75 Rockefeller Plz New York NY 10019-6908 also: Warner Bros Records 3300 Warner Blvd Burbank CA 91505-4632

**SEALE, JAMES LAWRENCE, JR.,** agricultural studies educator, trade association administrator, researcher; b. Memphis, Tenn., Mar. 12, 1949; s. James Lawrence and Mary Helen (Keefe) S.; divorced. BA, U. Miss., 1972; postgrad., U. Chgo., 1978-79; PhD, Mich. State U., 1985. Agrl. vol. Peace Corps, Tondo, Zaire, 1973-75; agrl. advisor Harvard Inst. for Internat. Devel., Abyei, Sudan, 1978; specialist Mich. State U., Fayoum, Arab Republic of Egypt, 1980-83; asst. prof. agrl. econs. U. Fla., Gainesville, 1985-90, assoc. prof. agrl. econs., 1990-95, prof. agrl. econs., 1995—. Vis. prof. U. Leicester (Eng.), 1992, 94, hon. vis. fellow, 95. Author: (with H. Theil and C.F. Chung) International Evidence on Consumption Patterns, 1989; editor: Journal of Agricultural and Applied Economics, 1998-2001, spl. editl., 2002-03; contbr. articles to profl. jours. Vol. Farmer to Farmer, UOCA, Namibia, 1994, Farmer to Farmer, Wenrock Internat., 1994; vol. agrl. bus. svcs. Wenrock Internat., Far Eastern Russia, 1998. NIMH scholar U. Chgo., 1978-79; traveling scholar U. Mich., 1979; rsch. fellow Cairo U., 1980-83; McKethan-Matherly rsch. fellow, 1986-88, McKethan-Matherly sr. rsch. fellow, 1991-94. Mem. Am. Econs. Assn., Am. Agrl. Econs. Assn., Internat. Assn. Agrl. Economists, Econometrics Soc., Caribbean Agro-Econ. Soc., Internat. Agrl. Trade Rsch. Consortium, Gamma Sigma Delta. Episcopalian. Avocations: scuba diving, karate. Home: 408 W University Ave 7D Gainesville FL 32601 Office: Univ Fla Dept Food and Resource G-125 McCarty PO Box 110240 Gainesville FL 32611-0240 Office Phone: 352-392-1845 ext 414. Business E-Mail: jseale@ufl.edu.

**SEALE, JAMES MILLARD,** retired religious organization administrator, minister; b. Middlesboro, Ky., Oct. 4, 1930; s. Albert Tyler and Edith Josephine (Buchanan) S.; m. Mary Dudley Harrod; children: William Alan, Ann Lynn Seale Hazelrigg. BA, Transylvania U., 1952; BD, Lexington Theol. Sem., 1955, MDiv, 1963, D Ministry, 1981. Ordained to ministry Christian Ch. (Disciples of Christ), 1951. Student pastor various Christian Chs., Ky., 1949-54; pastor 1st Christian Ch., Pikeville, Ky., 1954-58, Erlanger (Ky.) Christian Ch., 1958-61; sr. minister 1st Christian Ch., Mt. Sterling, Ky., 1961-70, Paris, Ky., 1978-82; stewardship sec. Gen. Office Christian Ch. Indpls., 1970-74; adminstr. Christian Ch. Home of Louisville, 1974-78; dir. devel. Christian Ch. Homes Ky., Louisville, 1978; pres. Disciples of Christ Hist. Soc., Nashville, 1983-95, pres. emeritus, 1995. Author: A Century of Faith and Caring, 1983, Forward From The Past, 1991; editor: (jour.) Discipliana, 1983—92. Pres. Kiwanis Club, Pikeville, 1957, Mt. Sterling, 1963, lt. gov., Ctrl. Ky., 1965. Mem. Christian Ch. Avocations: writing, photography, golf, fishing.

**SEALE, ROBERT ARTHUR, JR.,** lawyer; b. Shreveport, La., July 17, 1942; s. Robert Arthur Sr. and Lucille (Frank) S.; m. Chalon Fontaine, Feb. 24, 2001; children: Robert A. III, John Meyers. BBA, La. State U., 1964, JD, 1967. Bar: La. 1967, Tex. 1969. Mem. La. Law Rev., 1965—67; rsch. asst. La. Law Inst., Baton Rouge, 1967; law clk. U.S. Dist. Ct. (we. dist.) La., Shreveport, 1967-68; atty./ptnr. Vinson & Elkins, Houston, 1968—97; sr. ptnr. Phelps Dunbar LLP, Houston, 2002—04; of counsel Liskow & Lewis, Houston, 2005—. Trustee, legal counsel The Mus. of Fine Arts, Houston, 1981-89, The Creel Found., Augusta, Ga., 1989-97; pres., trustee The Lyons Found., Houston 1986—. Sr. Warden St. Martin's Episcopal Ch., Houston,

1990; pres. Pine Shadows Civic Assn., Houston, 1991; trustee Episcopal High Sch., Houston, 1985-88; bd. dir. Boys' and Girls' Country, Houston, 1990-94; mem. U. Tex. Houston Health Sci. Ctr. Devel. Bd. Fellow Houston Bar Found. (life); mem. ABA, Tex. Bar Assn., Coronado Club (pres. 1991), Omicron Delta Kappa, Vivian Smith Found. For Neurologic Rsch. (pres., trustee). Avocations: civic and charitable activities, golf. Office: 333 Clay St Ste 3485 Houston TX 77002-4102 Office Phone: 713-651-2910. Business E-Mail: raseale@lisrow.com.

**SEALE, RONALD ARMBRUST,** lawyer; b. Baton Rouge, La., June 24, 1948; s. Armbrust Gordon Seale and Lois Idell Petty; m. Saundra Ann Jordan, Dec. 23, 1972; children: Stephanie, Michael. BA, Niagara State U., 1970; JD, Samford U., 1974. Bar: La. 1974. Lawyer Seale, Smith, Zuber and Barnette, Baton Rouge, 1974—2003; sovereign grand comdr. Supreme Coun., 33 So. Jurisdiction A & A Scottish Rite of Freemasonry, Washington, 2003—. Youth coord.,del. La. Ann. Conf. United Meth. Ch., Baton Rouge; active mem. Supreme Coun. Order of DeMolay, Baton Rouge. Capt. U.S. Army, 1970—77. Mem.: ABA, Internat. Assn. Def. Counsel, La. State Bar Assn., Baton Rouge (La.) Bar Assn. Methodist. Avocations: amateur radio operator, flying. Office: Supreme Council 33 1733 16th Streeet NW Washington DC 20009 Office Phone: 202-777-3135. Office Fax: 202-464-0487. E-mail: grandcmdr@srmason-sj.org.

**SEALL, STEPHEN ALBERT,** lawyer; b. South Bend, Ind., Oct. 24, 1940; s. Stephen Henry and Mildred Rita (MacDonald) S.; m. Barbara Ann Halloran, June 25, 1966; children: John Paul, Edward Andrew, Ann Marie. BA, Purdue U., 1963; postgrad., Cornell U. Grad. Sch. Bus. Adminstrn., 1963; LLB, U. Notre Dame, 1966. Bar: Ind. 1966, U.S. Claims Ct. 1973, U.S. Tax Ct. 1968, U.S. Ct. Appeals (6th cir.) 1980, U.S. Ct. Appeals (7th cir.) 1969, U.S. Supreme Ct. 1973. Assoc. Thornburg, McGill, Deahl, Harman, Carey & Murray, South Bend, 1966-71; ptnr. Barnes & Thornburg LLP and predecessor firm Thornburg, McGill, Deahl, Harman, Carey & Murray, 1972—2005, vice chmn. and mgmt. com., mng. ptnr. South Bend office, 1985—2001. Spkr. in field. (Mem. editl. bd.) Notre Dame Law Rev., 1964—66. Mem. Mayor's Com. on Downtown Devel., South Bend, 1975-77, Mayor's Com. on Utilization of Downtown Bldgs., South Bend, 1988-96; trustee Project Future, South Bend, 1986-02; exec. com. Meml. Hosp. South Bend, Inc., 1999-03; dir. Meml. Health Found., 1992-98, Meml. Health Sys., 1997-03, United Way of St. Joseph County, Inc., 1992-98, Conv. and Tourism Industry Coun., 1994-00, CASIE Ctr., Inc., 1998-, Home Mgmt. Resources, Inc. 2003-06. Fellow Am. Coll. Tax Counsel, Am. Bar Found., Ind. Bar Found.; mem. ABA (taxation sect.), Ind. State Bar Assn. (chmn. taxation sect. 1977-78), Summit Club (chmn. 1976-77), Morris Park Country Club (bd. dirs., sec. 1998-2001). Democrat. Roman Catholic. Avocations: golf, softball, weightlifting. Home: 17705 Waxwing Ln South Bend IN 46635-1328 Office: Barnes & Thornburg LLP 600 1st Source Bank Ctr 100 N Michigan St Ste 600 South Bend IN 46601-1632 Office Phone: 574-233-1171.

**SEALS, MARGARET LOUISE CRUMRINE,** managing editor; b. Buckhannon, W.Va., Oct. 27, 1944; d. James Richard and Helen Margaret (Brown) Crumrine; m. Harry Eugene Seals, Jan. 10, 1975. BS in journalism, W. Va. U., 1966; MS in mass. comm., Va. Commonwealth U., 1983. Reporter, copy editor Democrat & Chronicle, Rochester, NY, 1966-67, Dayton (Ohio) Daily News, 1967-68; copy editor Richmond (Va.) Times-Dispatch, 1968-75, copy desk slot editor, 1975-81, exec. news editor, 1981, asst. mng. editor, 1982-92, dep. mng. editor, 1992-93, mng. editor, 1994—. Mem. Leadership Metro Richmond, 1986, mem. alumni adv. bd. sch. mass. comm. Va. Commonwealth U., 1988-93, 04-; mem. vis. com. Sch. Journalism, W.Va. U., 1999—. Named Outstanding Woman in Comms. YWCA Met. Richmond, 1989; recipient Perley Isaac Reed award W.Va. U. Journalism Sch. Alumni Assn., 1996; inducted into Va. Comm. Hall of Fame, 2003. Mem.: Va. Press Assn. (dir. 2001—03, treas. 2003—04, sec. 2004—05, v.p. 2005—), AP Mng. Editors (editor APME News 1993—94, dir. 1993—95, treas. 1996—97, dir. 1998—2001, Disting. Svc. award 2002), Va. Press Women (treas. 1986—88, 2d v.p. 1988—90, pres. 1990—92, Press Woman of Yr. 1986, Communicator of Achievement award 1997), Soc. Profl. Journalists (bd. dirs. Va. profl. chpt. 1998—2003, pres. Va. profl. chpt. 2000—02), Nat. Fedn. Press Women (bd. dirs. 1990—92, Communicator of Achievement award 1997), Phi Kappa Phi. Avocations: history, historical fiction, jazz. Office: Richmond-Times Dispatch PO Box 85333 Richmond VA 23293-5333 E-mail: lseals@timesdispatch.com.

**SEAMAN, ALFRED BARRETT,** journalist, writer; b. Rockville Center, N.Y., July 4, 1945; s. Alfred Jarvis and Mary Margaret (Schill) S.; m. Laura Powers Maxwell Apr. 25, 1970; children: Katherine Maxwell, Margaret Elise, Elizabeth Barrett. BA, Hamilton Coll., 1967; MBA, Columbia U., 1971. Reporter Life mag., N.Y.C., 1971-72, Fortune mag., N.Y.C., 1972; corr. Time mag., N.Y.C., 1972-73, Chgo., 1973-76, Bonn, Germany, 1976-78, bur. chief Detroit, 1978-81, dep. bur. chief Washington, 1981-83, White House corr., 1984-88, dep. chief corrs. N.Y.C., 1988-91, sr. editor, 1991-94, spl. projects editor, 1994—2001. Co-author: Going for Broke: The Chrysler Story, 1981; author: Binge: Campus Life in an Age of Disconnection and Excess, 2005. Alumni trustee Hamilton Coll., Clinton, N.Y., 1990-93, 94-95, charter trustee, 1997—; trustee Village of Irvington, N.Y., 1992-94. With USNR, 1969-71. Mem.: U.S. Sr. Golf Assn., Univ. Glee Club N.Y.C., Ardsley County Club. Episcopalian. Avocations: squash, tennis, golf. Home: Ardsley Ave W Ardsley On Hudson NY 10503 Personal E-mail: absea@aol.com.

**SEAMAN, ALFRED JARVIS,** retired advertising agency executive; b. Hempstead, L.I., N.Y., Sept. 17, 1912; s. Alfred J. and Ellen (Delaney) S.; m. Mary M. Schell, Sept. 26, 1937 (dec. June 1975); children: Marilyn Hollingsworth, Susan, Barry, Deborah; m. Honor S. Mellor, July 16, 1977. BS, Columbia U., 1935; LittD, U.S. Internat. U., 1987. Account exec. Fuller & Smith & Ross, Inc., N.Y.C., 1937-41; partner Knight & Gilbert Inc., Boston, 1941-41 with Compton Advt., Inc., N.Y.C., 1946-59, exec. v.p., creative dir., dir., 1954-59; vice chmn. bd., chmn. exec. com. SSC & B, Inc., 1959-60, pres., chief exec. officer, 1960-79, chmn., chief exec. officer, 1979-81. Dir., mem. exec. com. Interpublic Group of Cos., Inc. Hon. bd. dirs., adv. council, founding chmn. Advt. Ednl. Found.; bd. dirs., non. dir. com. Advt. Council.; chmn. planning bd., 1962—, mayor Village Upper Brookville, 1966-98; chmn. emeritus Samuel Waxman Cancer Research Found.; dir. Jupiter Hosp., 1991-2002. Lt. USNR, 1943-46. Named to Advt. Hall of Fame, 1983 Mem.: U.S. Sr. Golf Assn., Creek (Locust Valley, L.I.) (pres.), Piping Rock (Locust Valley, L.I.), Racquet and Tennis (N.Y.C.), Jupiter Island (Fla.), Nat. Golf Links Am. (Southampton, N.Y.), Seminole (Fla.), Hobe Sound Yacht (Fla.). Home: Wolver Hollow Rd Upper Brookville Oyster Bay NY 11771 also: Jupiter Island 126 Gomez Rd Hobe Sound FL 33455-2424 Office: 220 E 42nd St New York NY 10017-5806

**SEAMAN, ARLENE ANNA,** retired musician; b. Pontiac, Mich., Jan. 21, 1918; d. Roy Russell and Mabel Louise (Heffron) S. BS, life cert., Ea. Mich. U., 1939; MMus, Wayne State U., 1951; postgrad., Colo. Coll. 1951-52, Acad. Music, Zermatt Switzerland, 1954, 58, U. Mich. Guest conductor Shepherds and Angels, Symphonie Concertante, 1951; asst. conductor Detroit Women's Symphony, 1960-68; adjudicator Mich. State Band and Orch. Festivals, Solo and Ensemble Festivals, 1950-70, Detroit Fiddler's Band Auditions, 1948-52, Mich. Fedn. Music Clubs, 1948-55; tchr. Ea. Mich. U., 1939-42, Hartland Sch. Music, 1939-42, Pontiac (Mich.) Pub. Schs., 1942-45, Detroit Pub. Schs., 1945-73, pvt. studio, 1973-90. Performer cello South Oakland Symphony, 1958-65, Detroit Women's Symphony, 1951-68, Riviera Theatre Orch., 1959, 60, Masonic Auditorium Opera, Ballet Assocs, 1959-65, Toledo Ohio Symphony, 1963-70, others; performer trumpet Detroit Brass Quartet, 1974-78; piano accompanist various auditions, recitals, solo and ensemble festivals; composer: Let There Be Music, 1949, Fantasy for French Horn and Symphonic Band, 1951. Mem. Quota Internat., Delta Omicron. Home: 6231 N Montebella Rd #347 Tucson AZ 85704

**SEAMAN, BARBARA (ANN ROSNER),** author; b. NYC, Sept. 11, 1935; d. Henry Jerome and Sophie Blanche (Kimels) Rosner; m. Gideon Seaman, Jan. 13, 1957 (div.); children: Noah Samuel, Elana Felicia, Shira Jean. BA

(Ford Found. scholar), Oberlin Coll., 1956, LHD (hon.), 1978; cert. in advanced sci. writing (Sloan-Rockefeller fellow), Columbia U., 1968. Columnist Brides Mag., NYC, 1964-68; columnist, contbg. editor Ladies' Home Jour., NYC, 1965-69; editor child care and edn. Family Ctr., NYC, 1970-73; contbg. editor Omni mag., 1978; cons. FYI, ABC-TV, 1979-80; v.p. for devel. David Brooks Prodn., 1990-94; contbg. editor MS Mag., 1993—; columnist Hadassah Mag., 2000—03. Cons. US Senate subcom. on monopoly: Nelson pill hearings, 1970; presented testimony to Senate and Congl. coms., 1970—; lectr. in field; participant TV discussion shows; tchr. Coll. New Rochelle, 1975, Sagaris Inst., 1975, CUNY, 1993; founding mem. NY Women's Forum, 1973-99; co-founder Nat. Women's Health Network, 1975—, Comm. Consultants for Choice, 1985-86, Nat. Task Force Sexual Malpractice, 1985-86, Families Against Sexually Abusive Therapists and Other Profl., 1992—; v.p. Women's Med. Ctr., NYC, 1971-73; mem. ERA Emergency Task Force, 1979; adv. coun. Feminist Press, Old Westbury, NY, 1975; adv. bd. Feminist Ctr. for Human Growth and Devel., 1979, Women's History Libr., Berkeley, Calif., 1973-75; steering com. Women's Forum, 1974; adv. bd. NOW, NY, 1973, Women's Guide to Books, 1974, Jewish Women for Affirmative Action, Evanston, Ill., 1973—, Jour. Women and Health, 1975, Jewish Feminist Orgn., NYC, 1975; chair com. domestic violence Nat. Coun. Women's Health, 1993-98; judge for various journalism awards. Author: The Doctors' Case Against the Pill, 1969, rev. edit., 1980, 25th anniversary edit., 1995, Free and Female, 1972; (with G. Seaman) Women and the Crisis in Sex Hormones, 1977, Lovely Me: The Life of Jacqueline Susann, 1987, anniversary edit., 1996; (with Gary Null) For Women Only: Your Guide to Health Empowerment, 2000; The Greatest Experiment ever Performed on Women: exploding the Estrogen Myth, 2003; contbg. author: foreword to Lunaception, 1975; The Bisexuals, 1974, Career and Motherhood, 1979, The Menopause Industry, 1994; author (play) I Am a Woman, 1972; (movie) Scandalous Me: The Jackie Susann Story, 1998; contbr. (anthologies) Rooms with No View, 1974, Women and Men, 1975, Seizing Our Bodies, 1978, Women's Health Care: A Guide to Alternatives, 1984; Encyclopaedia of Childbirth, 1992, Lawyers Manual on Domestic Violence: Representing the Victim, 1995, The Conversation Begins, 1996, Real Majority Media Minority, 1997, The Reader's Companion to US Women's History, 1997, Jewish Women in America: An Historical Encyclopedia, 1997, Textbook of Women's Health, 1997, Women's Health, 1999, Routledge International Encyclopedia of Women,2001; George Mag., 250 ways to make Am. Better, 1999; Hands On! 33 More Things Every Girl Should Know, 2001, Sexual Revolution, 2003, Controversies in Science and Technology, 2005, Jewish Women's Archive: Feminism and Jewish Women Web Exhibit; cons. (film) The Pill, 1999; PBS Am. Experience the Pill, 2003; narrator (film) Taking Our Bodies Back, 1974; contbr. articles to newspapers, popular mags.; books and articles translated into Spanish, German, Dutch, Turkish, Japanese, Hebrew, French, Italian. Alumni cons. women's studies program Oberlin Coll., 1975; motivation com. Am. Cancer Soc., 1973; adv. com. Older Women's Health Project, NYU Med. Ctr., 1980; bd. dir. Safe Transp. of People, NYC, 1975, Women's Health Newsletter, 1983; adv. bd. DES Action, 1977, 7 Stories Press, 1997-; cons. Nat. Task Force on DES, 1978; contraceptive rsch. br. HEW, 1980; v.p. bd. dir. ARM (Abortion Rights Moblzn.), 1981—; hon. bd. dir. Carcinogen Info. Program, St. Louis, 1981, Am. Friends of Rabin Med. Ctr., 1998—;; trustee Nat. Coun. on Women in Medicine, 1989-1991, Nat. Coun. on Women's Health, 1992-2000; chmn. adv. bd. Coalition for Family Justice, 1991—; co-chair Domestic Violence com. NY Women's Agenda, 1992-93, del. Can.-USA Women's Health Forum, 1996; host com. Women's Health Day, Beijing, Plus-Five UN Reunion, 2000; cons. FDA Patient Labels on Oral Contraceptives, 2000-01; nat. judge Project Censored Award, 1997-. Recipient citation for books as first to raise issue of sexism in health care as world-wide issue Libr. of Congress, 1973, citation as author responsible for patient package inserts on prescriptions HEW, 1970, Matrix award, 1978, Pioneer Woman award Resources Divsn. of Am. Assn. Retired Persons, 1986, Athena award Nat. Coun. Women's Health, 1992, Health Advocacy award Health Policy Adv. Ctr., APHA, 1994, Project Censored award, 1996, Postal Service Women's Rights Movement stamp, 2000; Poynter Journalism Fellow, Yale U., 2003; inviting com. Am. Writers Congress. Mem. PEN, Authors Guild, Nat. Assn. Sci. Writers. Address: 110 W End Ave Apt 5D New York NY 10023-6348

**SEAMAN, DARYL KENNETH,** oil industry executive; b. Rouleau, Sask., Can., Apr. 28, 1922; BSME, U. Sask., 1948, LLD (hon.), 1982, U. Calgary, 1993. Cert. mech. engr. CEO Bow Valley Industries Ltd., Calgary, Alta., Canada, 1962-70, 85-91, chmn., chief exec. officer, 1970-82; chmn. Box Valley Industries Ltd., Calgary, Alta., Canada, 1982-85; pres. Bow Valley Industries Ltd., Calgary, Alta., Canada, 1985-87, chmn., 1991-92. Bd. dir. Far West Mining Ltd., Pure Techs. Ltd., Western Lakota Energy Svcs. Inc., Bow Valley Energy Ltd.; co-owner Calgary Flames Hockey Club, bd. dir.; chmn., pres. Dox Investments, Inc.; hon. regent Athol Murray Coll. of Notre Dame, 2001—. Mem. Royal Commn. Econ. Union and Devel. Prospects for Can., 1982-85; active numerous coms. for fundraising U. Sask.; Served with RCAF, 1941-45, North Africa, Italy. Can. Oilmen's Hall of Fame, 1997, Calgary Bus. Hall of Fame, 2004. Mem. Assn. Profl. Engrs., Geologists and Geophysicists (hon. life, Frank Spragins award, 1985, McGill Mgmt. Achievement award, 1979), Order of Canada 1993, Ranchmen's Club, RAF Club, Earl Grey Golf Club, Calgary Petroleum Club, Calgary Golf and Country Club, U. Calgary Chancellor's Club. Progressive Conservative. Mem. United Ch. Can. Avocations: ranching, golf, hunting. Home and Office: Dox Investments Inc 2320 300-5 Ave SW Calgary AB Canada T2P 3C4 Office Phone: 403-290-1884. E-mail: admin@doxinvestments.com.

**SEAMAN, DONNA JEAN,** editor, writer; b. Seattle, July 5, 1955; d. Harold A. and Elayne S. BFA, Kansas City Art Inst.; MA in English Lit., DePaul U. Assoc. editor, reviewer Booklist, Am. Libr. Assn., Chgo.; host, radio show, Open Books WLUW, Chgo., NW U., Chgo., Columbia Coll., Chgo. Vis. faculty Glencher Coll. Dak., 9th of the Art Inst. of Chgo., dir.; judge Claudia Ann Seaman Poetry award, 1984—; judge Carl Sandburg Lit. Arts Coun., 1997. Author: In Our Nature, 2000, Writers on the Air, 2005, contbr. essays and revs. to Chgo. Tribune, 1996—; author, host, prodr.: (radio program) Open Books (Ill. Arts Coun. award 1997). Recipient James Friend Meml. award for lit. criticism, Writers Who Make a Difference award, The Writer's Mag. Mem. Nat. Book Critics Cir. Address: Booklist Am Libr Assn 50 E Huron St Chicago IL 60611-5295 Business E-Mail: dseaman@ala.org.

**SEAMAN, IRVING, JR.,** banker; b. Milw., July 14, 1923; s. Irving and Anne (Douglas) S.; m. June Carry, June 24, 1950, (dec. 2001); children: Peter Stewart, Marion Carry, Irving Osborne, Anne Douglas; m. Barbara P. Gardner, May 22, 2002. BA, Yale U., 1944. With Continental Ill. Nat. Bank & Trust Co., Chgo., 1947-61, v.p., 1959-61; pres., chief exec. officer, dir. Nat. Boulevard Bank, Chgo., 1961-65, chmn. exec. com., chief exec. officer, dir., 1966-76; vice chmn. bd., dir. Sears Bank and Trust Co., Chgo., 1976-77, pres., chief operating officer, dir., 1977-82; sr. cons. Burson-Marsteller, Chgo., 1982-94. Chmn. bd. Associated Bank Chgo., 1985-05. Mem. Northwestern U. Assn.; life mem. bd. dirs. Lake Forest Hosp.; bd. dirs. United Way of Chgo., 1975-89, pres., 1979; bd. dirs. United Way/Crusade of Mercy, 1980-89, 94-95, vice chmn., 1980-81; trustee Chgo. Symphony Orch., 1987—. Lt. (j.g.) USNR, WWII. Mem. Commonwealth Club, Econ. Club, Chgo. Club, Comml. Club, Racquet Club, Onwentsia Club, Old Elm Club (Highland Park, Ill.), Shoreacres Club (Lake Bluff, Ill.), Augusta Nat. Golf Club (Ga.), Marsh Landing Club (Fla.), Sawgrass (Fla.) Country Club. Home: 666 N Sheridan Rd Lake Forest IL 60045-1410

**SEAMAN, JEFFREY,** consumer products company executive; Grad., U. Pa., 1984. Pres. Rooms to Go, Feffner, Fla., 1990—. Office: Rooms to Go 11540 Us Highway 92 E Seffner FL 33584-7346*

**SEAMANS, ROBERT CHANNING, JR.,** retired astronautical engineering educator; b. Salem, Mass., Oct. 30, 1918; s. Robert Channing and Pauline (Bosson) S.; m. Eugenia Merrill, June 13, 1942; children: Katherine (Mrs. Louis Padulo); Robert Channing III, Joseph, May (Seamans Baldwin), Daniel M. BS, Harvard U., 1939; MS, MIT, 1942, ScD, 1951; grad. exec. program bus. adminstrn., Columbia U., 1959; DSc, Rollins Coll., 1962, NYU, 1967;

DEng, Norwich Acad., 1971, Notre Dame U., 1974, Rensselaer Poly. Inst., 1974, U. Wyo., 1975, George Washington U., 1975, Lehigh U., 1976, Thomas Coll., 1980, Curry Coll., 1982. Successively instr. dept. aero. engring., staff engr. instrumentation lab., asst. prof., project leader instrumentation lab., asso. prof. Mass. Inst. Tech., 1941-55; chief engr. Project Meteor, 1950-53, dir. flight control lab., 1953-55; mgr. airborne systems lab., chief systems engr. airborne systems dept. RCA, 1955-58, chief engr. missile electronics and controls div., 1958-60; asso. adminstr. NASA, 1960-68, dep. adminstr., 1965-68, cons., 1968-69; vis. prof. MIT, 1968, Hunsaker prof., 1968-69; sec. air force, 1969-73; pres. Nat. Acad. Engring., 1973-74; adminstr. ERDA, Washington, 1974-77; Henry R. Luce prof. environment and pub. policy MIT, 1977-84, sr. lectr. dept. aeros. and astronautics, 1984-96, dean Sch. Engring., 1978-81. Mem. sci. adv. bd. USAF, 1957-62, assoc. adviser, 1963-67. Bd. overseers Harvard U., 1968—74; trustee emeritus Mus. Sci., Boston, Sea Edn. Assn., Nat. Geog. Soc., Carnegie Inst., Washington, Woods Hole Oceanographic Inst. Recipient naval ordnance devel. award 1945, Godfrey L. Cabot award Aero Club New Eng., 1965, disting. svc. medal NASA 1965, 69, Robert H. Goddard meml. trophy, 1968, disting. pub. svc. medal Dept. Def., 1973, exceptional civ. svc. award Dept. Air Force, 1973, Gen. Thomas D. White U.S. Air Force Space Trophy, 1973, Ralph Coats Roe medal ASME, 1977, achievement award Nat. Soc. Profl. Engrs., Thomas D. White Nat. Def. award, 1980, exceptional svc. award Dept. Air Force, 1985. Fellow Am. Acad. Arts and Scis., Am. Astron. Soc., IEEE, AIAA (hon., Lawrence Sperry award 1951); mem. Internat. Acad. Astronautics, Am. Soc. Pub. Adminstrn., Nat. Acad. Engring. (Arthur M. Bueche Award, 1994, Daniel Guggenheim award 1996), AAAS, Air Force Acad. Found., Fgn. Policy Assn., Coun. on Fgn. Rels., Sigma Xi. Clubs: Harvard (Boston); Manchester Yacht (Mass.); Essex County (Mass.), Chevy Chase, Metropolitan (Washington); Cruising of Am. (Boston Sta.).

**SEAMANS, WILLIAM,** writer, retired reporter, commentator; b. Providence, July 8, 1925; s. William and Mary Seamans; m. Jane Kingsbury, Sept. 15, 1951; children: Laurie, Jonathan, Adam. AB, Brown U., 1949; MS, Columbia U., 1952. Freelance journalist, 1952-53; journalist CBS News, 1953-63; producer evening news ABC News, 1963-65, European producer London, 1965-70, field producer N.Y.C., 1970-72, corr., bur. chief Tel Aviv, 1972-92; commentator Vt. Pub. Radio, lectr., freelance writer, 1992—. Producer Nightline in Israel Week (including Palestinian-Israeli town meeting) (Emmy award, Dupont award). Served with inf. AUS, 1942-45. Decorated Bronze Star medal; CBS Murrow News fellow Columbia U., 1961-62. Mem. Writers Guild Am., Nat. Acad. TV Arts and Scis. (Emmy award 1961, 89), Overseas Press Club Am. (award for best radio reporting invasion of Cyprus 1974, award for best fgn. affairs documentary Yitzhak Rabin biography 1975), Nat. Press Club (Washington), Fgn. Corrs. Assn. in Israel. E-mail: wmseamans@verizon.net.

**SEAN PAUL, (SEAN PAUL HENRIQUES),** singer; b. Kingston, Jamaica, Jan. 8, 1973; Grad., U. Tech. Jamaica. Former mem. Jamaican Nat. Water Polo Team. Singer: (albums) Stage One, 2000, Dutty Rock, 2002 (Billboard Top Reggae Album, 2003, 2004, Source award for Dancehall Reggae Album of Yr., 2003, Grammy award for Best Reggae Album, 2004), The Trinity, 2005 (Billboard Top Reggae Album, 2005), (songs) Gimme the Light, 2002, Get Busy, 2003, Like Glue, 2003, We Be Burnin', 2005 (Best Crossover Song, Internat. Reggae & World Music awards, 2006), Temperature, 2006. Named Top Reggae Artist, Billboard, 2003—05; recipient MTV Europe award for Best New Act of Yr., 2003, Bob Marley award for Entertainer of Yr., Internat. Reggae & World Music Awards, 2004, Spl. award for Cmty. Svc., 2005, Top Selling Reggae Artist of Yr., Billboard Music Awards, 2005, Rhythm & Soul Music award, ASCAP, 2005. Office: Atlantic Records 28th Fl 1290 Ave of the Americas New York NY 10104*

**SEAPKER, JANET KAY,** museum administrator, historic site director, consultant; b. Pitts., Nov. 2, 1947; d. Charles Henry and Kathryn Elizabeth (Dany) Seapker; m. Edward F. Turberg, May 24, 1975. BA, U. Pitts., 1969; MA, SUNY, Cooperstown, 1975. Park ranger Nat. Park Svc., summers 1967-69; archtl. historian N.C. Archives and History, Raleigh, 1971—76, hist. preservation adminstr., 1976—77, grant-in-aid adminstr., 1977—78; dir. Cape Fear Mus. (formerly New Hanover County Mus.), Wilmington, NC, 1978—2000, ret.; archtl. historian-preservation/mus. cons.; curator U. N.C. Wilmington's Kenan House, 2003—04. Bd. dirs. Bellamy Mansion Found., Wilmington, 1986-89, 91-97, Lower Cape Fear Hist. Soc., Wilmington, 1985-88; N.C. rep. S.E. Mus. Conf., 1986-90; bd. dirs. Cape Fear Coast Conv. and Vis. Bur., 1997-2001, sec., 2001, Wrightsville Beach Mus., 2004-05; field reviewer Inst. Mus. Svcs., 1982-2001 Contbr. articles to profl. jours. Bd. dirs. Downtown Area Revitalization Effort, Wilmington, 1979-81, Thalian Hall Ctr. for Performing Arts, 1996-98; bd. dirs. Hist. Wilmington Found., 1979-84, pres., 1980-81; mem. Cmty. Appearance Commn., Wilmington, 1984-88, 250th Anniversary Commn., Wilmington, 1986-90; mem. Wilmington Historic Preservation Commn., 2005-; pres. Friends of Oakdale Cemetery, Inc., 2004-. Grad. program fellow SUNY, Cooperstown, 1969-70; recipient Profl. Svc. award N.C. Mus. Coun., 1982, Woman of Achievement award YWCA, 1994. Mem. Am. Assn. Mus. (accreditation vis. com. 1983-2001, reviewer mus. assessment program 1982-2002), Nat. Trust Hist. Preservation, Southeastern Mus. Conf. (N.C. state rep. 1986-90), N.C. Mus. Coun. (sec.-treas. 1978-84, pres. 1984-86; recipient William T. Anderson award 2004), Hist. Preservation Found N.C. (sec. 1976-78). Presbyterian. Home and Office: 307 N 15th St Wilmington NC 28401-3813 Office Phone: 910-762-6301. Personal E-mail: jseapker@ec.rr.com.

**SEARBY, RICHARD HENRY,** academic administrator, lawyer; b. July 23, 1931; s. Henry and Mary Searby; m. Caroline McAdam, 1962; 3 sons. MA (hons.), U. Oxford. Bar: London 1956, Victoria, Australia 1957. Assoc. to Chief Justice of Australia Rt. Hon. Sir Owen Dixon, 1956-59, ind. lectr. law relating to executors and trustees U. Melbourne, Australia, 1961-72; bd. dirs. News Corp. Ltd., Australia, 1977-92, chmn., 1981-91; bd. dirs. Equity Trustees Executors and Agy. Co. Ltd., 1975—2000, S. China Morning Post, 1987—92; bd. dirs. Times Newspapers Holdings Ltd., 1981—, dep. chmn., 1981—92; bd. dirs. Rio Tinto Ltd., 1977-97, Shell Australia Ltd., 1977—98, News Internat. plc, U.K., 1981-92, Reuters Founders Share Co., Ltd., 1987—93, Tandem Australua Ltd., 1992—98, Amrad Corp. Ltd., 1992—2001, BRL Hardy Ltd., 1992—2003, Rio Tinto plc, 1995—97, Woodside Petroleum Ltd., 1998—2004; chancellor Deakin U., 1997—. Chmn. Geelong Grammar Sch., 1983-89; mem. coun. Nat. Libr. Australia, 1992-95, Mus. of Victoria, 1993-98. Decorated Queen's Counsel (Australia) 1971. Mem.: Melbourne Club. Avocations: reading, music, tennis, history. Office: 25 Flinders Ln Melbourne 3000 Australia also: 23A Hampden Rd Armadale 3143 Victoria Australia

**SEARCEY, PAUL W.,** music educator; b. Norman, Okla., 1958; s. Forest LaBoyd and Frances Anne Searcey; m. Nancy S. Riedl, 1989; children: Nathan, Adam. B in Music Edn. Okla. Bapt. U., 1980; MEd in Computers in Edn., Lesley Coll., 1993. Vocal music educator Natrona County Sch. Dist. #1, Casper, Wyo., 1980—; sound reinforcement instr. Casper Coll., 1998—. Sound and rec. engr. Searcey Music, Casper, 1985—. Author: (computer manuals) Clariworks 1 & 2. Negotiator NCEA, Casper, 1994—96; musician, sound technician Highland Park Cmty. Ch., Casper, 1996—. Recipient Unsung Hero award, No. Life Ins., 2001, Acad. Achievement award, Natrona County Sch. Dist. # 1, 2000—02. Mem.: NEA, Nat. Music Educator Com., Phi Mu Alpha. Avocations: reading, music. Home: 2202 Shattuck Ave Casper WY 82601

**SEARCY, WILLIAM NELSON,** lawyer, director; b. Moultrie, Ga., June 26, 1942; s. Floyd Hartsfield and Anna (Pidcock) Searcy; m. Camille Heery, June 17, 1967; 1 child, Amelia Ashburn. AB, U. Ga., 1964, JD, 1967; LLM in Taxation, Washington U., St. Louis, 1968. Bar: Ga. 1967, U.S. Dist. Ct. (so. dist.) Ga. 1970, U.S. Ct. Appeals (5th and 11th cirs.) 1976, U.S. Tax Ct. Assoc. Bouhan, Williams & Levy, Savannah, Ga., 1970-73; prnr. Brannen, Searcy & Smith LLP, Savannah, 1973—. Sec. Am. Fed. Savs. and Loan Assn., 1978—81; mem. adv. bd. Liberty Savs. Bank, 1984—88; chmn. bd. dirs. Citizens Bank, 1991—. Pres. Chatham-Savannah Voluntary Action Ctr.;

Inc., 1978—80. Served to maj. gen. Ga. N.G. USAF, 1967—2004, comdr. Ga. N.G. USAF, 2000—04. Mem.: ABA (sec. spl. liaison tax com. S.E. region 1983—85, chmn. 1984—85), Inst. Continuing Legal Edn., Savannah Estate Planning Coun., Am. Judicature Soc., Savannah Bar Assn. (pres. Younger Lawyers sect. 1975—76), State Bar Ga. (mem.-at-large exec. coun. Young Lawyers sect. 1975—78, chmn. conf. with Ga. Soc. CPAs 1979—81, chmn. sect. taxation 1983—84, Ga. commn. continuing lawyer competency 1989—95, vice chmn. 1995), N.G. Assn. U.S. (chmn. air resolution com. 2001—03, bd. dirs. 2002—04, chmn. resolutions com. 2003—, spl. adv. com. 2005—), Georgian Club, Savannah Golf Club, Oglethorpe Club, Rotary (pres. Savannah West 2004—05). Office: PO Box 8002 Savannah GA 31412-8002

**SEARE, PAUL DEARDEN,** music educator; b. Salt Lake City, Dec. 29, 1957; s. Roswell Heiner and Joyce (Dearden) Seare; children: Miriam, Linda, Sariah, Bryan. MusB in Music Composition, Brigham Young U., 1984; MusM in Music Composition, Cin. Conservatory Music, 1987; DMA, U. Oreg., 1991. Tchr. music K-12 South Umpqua Sch. Dist., Tri-City, Oreg., 1991—94; choral condr. grades 9-12 and tchr. Spanish Preston Sch. Dist., Idaho, 1994—. Composer: (songs) Pacha Mama, 1987, Metamorphis, 1988, I Saw You Yesterday, 1990. Missionary, La Paz, Bolivia. Scholar, U. Cin., 1984. Mem.: Am. Choral Dirs. Assn., Music Educators Nat. Conf. (mem. All State Choir 1996). Republican. Mem. Lds Ch. Avocations: hiking, model railroading, architecture. Home: 40 S 4th East Preston ID 83263 Office: Preston HS 151 E 2d St Preston ID 83263 Office Phone: 208-852-0280. E-mail: paul.seare@preston.k12.id.us.

**SEARL, HANFORD WILLIAMS, JR.,** communications executive, journalist, actor; b. Buffalo, Mar. 2, 1947; s. Dorothy Selma Cavin and Hanford Sr. WIlliams Searl; life prtnr. Keith Douglas Todtenhagen. BA in Broadcast Journalism, Brigham Young U., 1973. Reporter, staff writer Las Vegas Rev.-Jour., 1973—76; corr. Billboard Mag., Las Vegas, Nev., 1975—79; entertainment editor The Valley Times, North Las Vegas, 1976—79; west coast editor: radio/tv Billboard Mag., Los Angeles, Calif., 1979—80, corr. Buffalo, 1980—91; staff writer The Buffalo News/Gusto, 1982—84; upstate editor The Connection Newspaper, N.Y.C., 1982—85; editor, co-publisher Vol.' Newspaper, Buffalo, 1987—96; editor Roycroft Assoc., East Aurora, NY, 1990—93; publicist Galerie Alexi, Beverly Hills, Calif., 1997—98; entertainment editor Orange County/Long Beach Blade, Laguna Beach, Calif., 1998—99; publicist, writer Norman Winters PR Assoc., L.A., 1998—99, Lee Solters Agy., L.A., 1999—2000; co-creator, writer aH-Ha! Prodns., Palm Desert, Calif., 1999—. Publicist, writer Lee Solters Agy., L.A., 1999—2000; editor East Aurora (Ill.) Advertiser, 2001—03. Editor (writer, reporter): We're Not in Kansas Anymore Dorothy (Natl. Gay & Lesbian Press Assn. award, 1985); editor: (publicist) Featherweight, Inc. Benefit; editor: (writer) Roycrofters-at-Large Association Newsletter, (autobiography) Pink Seagulls. Editor newsletter Gay Profl. Buffalo, 1983—86; chpt. pres. Affirmation: Gay & Lesbian Mormons, Buffalo, 1985—89. Recipient award for coverage of 1st gay rights case at U.S. Supreme Ct., Nat. Gay & Lesbian Press Assn., 1985, William award, Gay Profl. Buffalo, 1986. D-Liberal. Presbyterian. Avocation: singing. Office Phone: 716-655-0696.

**SEARLE, PHILIP FORD,** banker; b. Kansas City, Mo., July 23, 1924; s. Albert Addison and Edith (Thompson) S.; m. Jean Adair Hanneman, Nov. 22, 1950 (dec. Nov. 1990); 1 child, Charles Randolph; m. Jean Walker, Oct. 4, 1992 (dec. oct. 1993); m. Elizabeth Gordon, Nov. 4, 1994. AB, Cornell U., 1949; grad. in banking, Rutgers U., 1957, 64. With Geneva (Ohio) Savs. & Trust Co., 1949-60, pres., 1959-60; sr. trust officer Northeastern Ohio Nat. Bank, Ashtabula, 1960-69; pres., CEO BancOhio Corp., Columbus, 1969-75; chmn., CEO Flagship Banks, Inc., Miami, 1975-84; chmn. bd. Sun Banks, Inc., Orlando, 1984-85, cons., 1986-94. Mem. faculty Sch. Banking, Ohio U., 1959-70, Nat. Trust Sch., Northwestern U., Evanston, Ill., 1965-68; corp. adv. com. Nat. Assn. Securities Dealers, 1981-83; v.p., fed. adv. coun. to bd. govs. FRS, 1983-85; chmn. Nat. Adv. Bd. to Oversight Bd. for Resolution Trust Corp., 1991-92. Co-author: The Management of a Trust Department, 1967. Past mem. bd. regents Stonier Grad. Sch. Banking, Rutgers U., 1974-76, past mem. faculty; trustee Fin. Acctg. Found., Norwalk, Conn., 1989-93. Capt. AUS, 1943-46, ETO. Decorated Bronze Star; named outstanding citizen in Ashtabula County, 1967. Mem. Am. Bankers Assn. (bd. dirs. 1972-74, governing coun.), Bank Adminstrn. Inst. (nat. chmn. 1987-88, bd. dirs. Chgo. 1985-89), Fla. Bankers Assn. (bd. dirs. 1979-81, coun. 1981), Ohio Bankers Assn. (pres. 1970-71), Assn. Bank Holding Cos. (pres. 1979-81), Fla. C. of C. (bd. dirs. 1978-82), Royal Poinciana Golf Club (Naples, Fla.), Naples Yacht Club, Catawba Island Club (Port Clinton, Ohio), Phi Kappa Tau.

**SEARLE, ROBERT FERGUSON,** minister; b. Auburn, NY, July 13, 1951; s. Loren Rawson and Esther Lucille (Ferguson) Searle; m. Elizabeth Jane Anderson, 1981; children: Joshua Michael Anderson, Nathanael Jeremiah Ferguson. BS, Cornell U., 1973; MDiv, Princeton Theol. Sem., 1977; DMin, Asbury Theol. Sem., 1997; MA, St. John's Coll., 2005. Ordained deacon United Meth. Ch., 1978, ordained elder United Meth. Ch., 1980, cert. in pastoral care 1981, in pastoral edn., bd. cert. chaplain Nat. Assn. Vet. Affairs Chaplains, 2004, Assn. Profl. Chaplains. Pastor of Blodgett Mills Freetown and McGraw (NY) United Meth. Ch., 1978-84; pastor Pennsylvania Ave. United Meth. Ch., Pine City, NY, 1984-98; chaplain U.S. Army Res., 1991—; chaplain resident Duke U. Med. Ctr., 1998-99; pastor Clyde United Meth. Ch., 1999—2003; adj. prof. spiritual formation Northeastern Sem., Rochester, NY, 2000—; contract chaplain Canandaigua and Syracuse VA Hosp., 2000—; mobilized as chaplain Operation Enduring Freedom, 2003; pastor Red Creek Westbury Sterling United Meth. Ch., 2004—. Mem. dist. bd. Ordained Ministry, Syracuse, NY, 1980-84, mem. conf. bd., 1980-85, dist. youth dir., Syracuse, 1981-84; mem. Cortland County Youth Bur., 1980-81; mem. hosp. com. Cortland County Coun. of Chs., 1980-84. Mem. McGraw Bd. Edn., 1981-84; bd. dirs. Meals on Wheels, Elmira, 1985-88, CPC, Elmira, 1985-93; mem. edn. and rsch. instl. rev. bd. Arnot Ogden Hosp., Elmira, 1995-98; mem. cmty. bd. Southport Correctional Facility, 1987-98; spiritual dir. Spiritual Exercises, High Acres, Geneva, NY, 1986-98, 99-2003, spiritual dir. Walk to Emmaus, Rome, NY, 1993; mem. design team Ctrl. Lakes Dist. Acad. Spiritual Devel., 1999-2003. Mem.: Charles Wesley Soc., Masons, KT. Republican. Avocations: reading, exercise, travel, music. Home: 5905 Draper St Wolcott NY 14590-1148 Office Phone: 315-754-8853. E-mail: r0027@aol.com.

**SEARLE, RODNEY NEWELL,** state legislator, farmer, insurance agent; b. Camden, N.J., July 17, 1920; s. William Albert and Ruby Marie (Barrus) S.; m. Janette Elizabeth Christie, May 17, 1941 (dec.); children: R. Newell Jr., Linda Jennison Grant, Alan John; m. Ruth Anne Bartlett, May 6, 2001. BA, Mankato State U., 1960; DHL, Winona State U., 2001. Prodn. coordinator Johnson & Johnson, New Brunswick, NJ, 1940-47; farmer Waseca, Minn., 1947—; spl. agt. John Hancock Mut. Ins. Co., Waseca, Minn., 1961-84; mem. Minn. Ho. of Reps., St. Paul, 1957-80, speaker, 1979—. Bd. pres. Minn. Legis. Soc., 1996—. Author: Minnesota Standoff-The Politics of Deadlock, 1990. Lay reader St. John's Episcopal Ch., 1952—; chmn. Upper Mississippi River Basin Commn., 1981-82; mem. Minn. State U. Bd., 1981-92; chmn. Minn. Higher Edn. Bd., 1991-92; bd. dirs. Minn. Wellsprings, 1984-90; emeritus mem. bd. Hubert H. Humphrey Inst.; emeritus mem. coun. Minn. Hist. Soc.; bd. dirs. Minn. Agrl. Interpretive Ctr., 1983-02; mem. Waseca County Hist. Bd., 1995—; capt. Minn. Wing of the Civil Air Patrol. Named Minn. State Tree Farmer of Yr., 1978 Mem. Am. Tree Farm Sys., Nat. Conf. State Legislators, Minn. Forestry Assn. (bd. dirs. 1991-01), Masons, Rotary (pres. club 1968). Independent.

**SEARLES, EDNA LOWE,** artist, illustrator, composer, poet; b. Minden, La., Sept. 10, 1936; m. Thomas B. Searles. AA, Mont. Coll., 1975; BA in Edn., La. Poly., 1958. Tchr. pub. sch., 1958—65. Guest curator Delaplaine Visual Arts Ctr., Frederick, Md., 1995, East Meets West. Illustrator Soy for the 21st Century, 1984, ABC Coloring Book, 1994, Mind Children, 1995, Mind Travel, 1998, About You, 1998, Choose Life, 2002, Animal Alphabet Coloring Book, 2003, Creator and Creativity, 2004; illustrator: Music ABC Book, 2006; illustrator Musical Alphabet Coloring Book, 2006; one-woman

shows include Arnot Art Mus., Elmira, N.Y., 1988, Va. Tech State U. Grad. Ctr., 1989, Gwinnett County Art Gallery, Ga., 1990, VA Honorarium, 1990, Other: Affiliation and Exhibits, Janice Aldridge Gallery (Cat Series), Washington, 1996, Sculpture on the Ground, Md., 1994, 1999, The Artist's Gallery, Frederick, Md., 1997—2002, The Garden Gallery, Carlisle, Pa., 1999—, Nancy Stamm's Galleria, 1999—, Gallery of New Masters, Sandy Spring, Md., 2000—01, Millinneum Exhibit Music for the Eyes, 1999—2000, Musicians and All that Jazz, Frederick, Md., 2000, Gallery of New Masters, Olney, Md., 2000—01, others, exhibited in group shows at Boarman Art Ctr., Martinsburg, W.Va., 2001, Nat. League Am. Pen Women, 2003, Summer Sch. Mus., Washington, 2004, Sandy Spring Mus., Md., 2004, Friendship Gallery, Chevy Chase, 2004, Ratner Mus., 2005, murals, Ambrosia Restaurant, 1991, Still Lake Greenhouse and Florist, 1999, Damascus United Meth. Ch., 2000, The Original Ambrosia Greek Restaurant, 2004, Baronessa Italian Restaurant, 2005, jazz poster for, Mel Brown and Western Oreg. U., 2001. Past pres. Clarksburg (Md.) Cmty. Assn. Recipient Juror's award for painting Montgomery County Art, 1993, Internat. Gold medal for painting Accademia Italia, 1973, 4 grants Crabtown Fund of Balt. Cmty. Found., 2005, others; named Wilson Wims Citizen of Yr., Clarksburg Comm. Assn.—1974. Mem.: DAR (vice regent Pleasant Plains of Damascus chpt. 2001—), Nat. League Am. Pen Women (pres. Chevy Chase br. 1980—82, 2002—04, Md. state pres. 2004—05, 3d v.p. Chevy Chase br. 2004—, 2005, Poetry award). Methodist. Achievements include invention of music system for the deaf to "see" music as art "Music for the Eyes". Avocations: hammered dulcimer, music, folk singer, harp, piano.

**SEARS, DAVID O'KEEFE,** psychology professor; b. Urbana, Ill., June 24, 1935; s. Robert R. and Pauline (Snedden) S.; married; children: Juliet, Olivia, Meredith. BA in History, Stanford U., 1957; PhD in Psychology, Yale U., 1962. Asst. prof. to disting. prof. psychology and polit. sci. UCLA, 1961—, dean social scis., 1983-92. Dir. Inst. for Social Sci. Rsch., 1993—. Author: Public Opinion, 1964, Politics of Violence, 1973, Tax Revolt, 1985, Political Cognition, 1986, Social Psychology, 12th edit., 2005, Racialized Politics, 2000, Oxford Handbook of Political Psychology, 2003. Recipient Edward L. Bernays award, Soc. for Psychol. Study of Social Issues, 1979, Warren E. Miller Career award, Am. Polit. Sci. Assn., 2003; fellow, Guggenheim, 1988—89. Fellow Am. Acad. Arts and Scis.; mem. Soc. for Advancement Socio-Econs. (pres. 1991-92), Internat. Soc. Polit. Psychology (pres. 1994-95, Harold D. Lasswell award 1994). Office: UCLA Psychology Dept Los Angeles CA 90095-0001 Office Phone: 310-825-2160. Business E-Mail: sears@psych.ucla.edu.

**SEARS, DEREK WILLIAM GEORGE,** education educator, researcher; b. Maidstone, Kent, Eng., Dec. 18, 1948; came to U.S., 1979; s. Sidney and Eileen Ida (Bird) S.; m. Hazel Bent, July 31, 1971; children: Andrew, Christopher, David. BS, U. Kent, Canterbury, Eng., 1970; diploma in space sci., U. Coll., London, 1971; PhD, U. Leicester, Eng., 1974. Postdoctoral rsch. assoc. U. Manchester, Eng., 1974-77; rsch. fellow U. Birmingham, Eng., 1977-79; asst. rsch. chemist U. Calif., LA, 1979-81; asst. prof. chemistry U. Ark., Fayetteville, 1981-84, assoc. prof. chemistry, 1984-88, prof. chemistry 1988—2005, W.M. Keck prof. space and planetary sci., 2005—. Vis. scientist NASA, Houston, 1986-89, NASA/NSF, Washington, 1986-89, dir. Ark. Ctr. for Space and Planetary Sci., 2000-. Author: Nature and Origin of Meteorites, 1978, Thunderstones, 1988; editor Meteoritics, 1992 (named changed Meteoritics and Planetary Science, 1996), Origin of Clondrules and Clondrites. Avocations: local history, photography, figure drawing, theater, music. Office: U Ark Dept Chemistry Fayetteville AR 72701 Office Phone: 479-575-7625. Business E-Mail: dsears@uark.edu.

**SEARS, EDWARD MILNER, JR.,** newspaper editor; b. Bluefield, W.Va., Dec. 28, 1944; s. Edward Milner and Helene (Stras) S.; m. Jo Ann Langworthy, May 15, 1971; 1 child, Helene Mateer. BS in Journalism, U. Fla., 1967. Makeup editor Atlanta Constn., 1970, news editor, 1971-73, feature editor, 1974, city editor, 1975-76, asst. mng. editor, 1977, mng. editor, 1978-80, Atlanta Jour., 1980-82, Atlanta Jour. and Atlanta Constn., 1982-85; editor Palm Beach Post, 1985—2005. Served with U.S. Army, 1968-69. Named Editor of the Yr., Editor & Pub., 2000 Mem. Fla. Soc. Newspaper Editors, Am. Soc. Newspaper Editors, Sigma Delta Chi. Home: 230 Dyer Rd West Palm Beach FL 33405-1218 Office Phone: 561-820-4133. E-mail: esears@pbpost.com.

**SEARS, JOHN PATRICK,** lawyer; b. Syracuse, N.Y., July 3, 1940; s. James Louis and Helen Mary (Fitzgerald) Sears; m. Carol Jean Osborne, Aug. 25, 1962; children: James Louis, Ellen Margaret, Amy Elizabeth. BS, Notre Dame U., 1960; LLB, JD, Georgetown U., 1963. Bar: N.Y. 1963. Clk. N.Y. Ct. Appeals, 1963-65; assoc. Nixon, Mudge, Rose, Guthrie, Alexander & Mitchell, 1965-66; mem. staff Richard M. Nixon, 1966-69; dep. counsel to U.S. Pres. Richard Nixon Washington, 1969-70; ptnr. Gadsby & Hannah, Washington, 1970-75, Baskin & Sears, Washington, 1977-84; pvt. practice Washington, 1984—. Polit. analyst NBC Today Show, 1984—89; mem. bd. polit. experts Wall St. Jour., 1984—. Columnist: LA Times, Newsday, 1992—. Mgr. Ronald Reagan's Presdls. Campaign, 1975—76, 1979—80; sr. advisor Jack Kemp for V.P. Campaign, 1996. Fellow, Kennedy Inst. Politics, Harvard U., 1970. Office: 2801 New Mexico Ave NW Washington DC 20007-3921

**SEARS, JOHN WINTHROP,** lawyer; b. Boston, Dec. 18, 1930; s. Richard Dudley and Frederica Fulton (Leser) S.; m. Catherine Coolidge, 1965 (div. 1970). AB magna cum laude, Harvard U., 1952, JD, 1959; MLitt, Oxford U., 1957. Bar: Mass. 1959, U.S. Dist. Ct. Mass. 1982. Rep. Brown Bros. Harriman, N.Y.C., 1959-63, Boston, 1963-66; mem. Mass. Ho. Reps., 1965-68; sheriff Suffolk County, Mass., 1968-69; chmn. Boston Fin. Commn., 1969-70, Met. Dist. Commn., 1970-75; councilor-at-large Boston City Coun., 1980-82; trustee Sears Office, Boston, 1975—. Contbr. articles to profl. jours. Apptd. bd. dirs. Fulbright Scholarship, 1991-93; trustee Christ's Ch., Longwood, Brookline, Mass., 1965—, Sears Trusts, Boston, 1975—; hon. trustee J. F. Kennedy Libr., 1991—; bd. dirs. Am. Mus. Textile Heritage, 1987-97, Shirley-Eustis Assoc., Environ. League, Mass., 1994-97; Rep. candidate Sec. State, Mass., 1978, Gov. of Mass., 1982; vice chmn. Ward 5 Rep. Com., 1965-69, 75-85; chmn. Rep. State Com., 1975-76, mem., 1980-85; del. Rep. Nat. Conv., 1968, 76, State Conv., 1966-92; mem. U.S. Electoral Coll., 1984; bd. dirs. United South End Settlements, 1966—, chmn., 1977-78. Lt. comdr. USNR, 1952-54, 61-62. Recipient Outstanding Pub. Servant award Mass. Legis. Assn., 1975; Rhodes scholar, 1955 Mem. Mass. Bar Assn., New Eng. Hist. and Geneal. Soc. (bd. dirs., councillor 1977-82), Mass. Hist. Soc., Handel and Haydn Soc. (gov. 1982-87), Signet Soc., Boston Atheneum, Tennis and Racquet Club, Somerset Club, The Country Club (Brookline), St. Botolph Club, Club of Odd Vols., Wednesday Evening Club of 1777, Thursday Evening Club of 1846 (pres. 1999-2004), Spee Club (Cambridge chpt., pres., trustee), Longwood Cricket Club (hon.), Phi Beta Kappa. Republican. Home: 7 Acorn St Boston MA 02108-3501 *As the working years come to an end, some of us look for ways to teach, to help neighbors, especially those in need, to build up the beauty and excellence we may have encountered in our own lives, and do our best to pass them on to others.*

**SEARS, LEAH WARD,** lawyer; b. June 13, 1955; d. Thomas E. and Onnye J. Sears; married; children: Addison, Brennan. BA, Cornell U., 1976; JD, Emory U., 1980; M in Apellate Jud. Process, U. Va.; JD (hon.), Morehouse Coll., 1993. Judge City Ct. Atlanta; atty. Alston & Bird, Atlanta; trial judge Superior Ct. Fulton County, Atlanta; justice Ga. Supreme Ct., Atlanta, 1992—, current presiding justice, chief justice, 2005—. Contbr. articles to profl. jours. Bd. dirs. Sadie G. Mays Nursing Home, Ga. chpt. Nat. Coun. Christians & Jews; mem. adv. bd. United Way Drug Abuse Action Ctr., Outdoor Activity Nature Ctr.; mem. Cornell U. Women's Coun.; mem. steering com. Ga. Women's History Month, Children's Def. Fund Black Cmty. Crusade Children; founder Battered Women's Project, Columbus, Ga. Recipient Outstanding Young Alumna award Emory U., One of 100 Most Influential Georgians Ga. Trend mag., Excellence in Pub. Svc. award Ga. Coalition Black Women, 1992, Outstanding Woman of Achievement YWCA Greater Atlanta, One of Under Forty & On the Fast Track, 1993. Mem. ABA

(chair bd. elections), Nat. Assn. Women Judges, Ga. Bar Assn., Women's Forum Ga., Gate City Bar Assn., Atlanta Bar Assn. (past chair jud. sect.), Ga. Assn. Black Women Attys. (founder, pres.), Fourth Tuesday Group, Jack & Jill Am. (Atlanta chpt.), Links Inc. (Atlanta chpt.), Alpha Kappa Alpha. Office: Ga Supreme Ct 244 Washington Street Atlanta GA 30334-9007*

**SEARS, MARY HELEN,** lawyer; b. Syracuse, N.Y. d. James Louis and Helen Mary (Fitzgerald) Sears. AB, Cornell U., 1950; JD with honors, George Washington U., 1960. Bar: Va. 1960, D.C. 1961, U.S. Supreme Ct. 1963. Chemist Allied Chem. and Dye Corp., Syracuse, 1950-52, Hercules Powder Co., Wilmington, Del., 1952-55; patent examiner U.S. Patent Office, Washington, 1955-60; pvt. practice Washington, 1960-61; assoc. Irons, Birch, Swindler & McKie, Washington, 1961-69; mem. firm Irons and Sears, Washington, 1969-84; chmn. trade regulation practice dept. Memel, Jacobs, Pierno, Gersh & Ellsworth, Washington, 1984-87; ptnr., chmn. intellectual property and unfair competition practice dept. Ginsburg, Feldman & Bress, Washington, 1987-91; ptnr., chmn. intellectual property and telecomm. practice group Reid & Priest, Washington, 1991-94; founder, chmn. M. H. Sears Law Firm, 1994—. Mem. adv. bd. Boardroom Reports, Inc., N.Y.C., 1980-85; mem. Cornell U. Coun., 1981-87, 89-93, life mem., 1995—, mem. adminstrv. bd., 1984-86. Contbr. articles to various publs. Named to Guide to the World's Leading Patent Law Experts Euromoney Publs., PLC, 1995, 1997, 2005; recipient Outstanding Performance award, U.S. Dept. Commerce, 1957. Mem.: ABA (co-chmn. appellate practice com., litigation sect. 1989—92), D.C. Bar Assn., Va. State Bar Assn., Internat. Trademark Assn., Am. Soc. Internat. Law, Am. Intellectual Property Law Assn., George Washington U. Law Alumnae Assn. (bd. dirs. 1995—2001), Order of Coif, Phi Alpha Delta. Republican. Office: MH Sears Law Firm Chartered NW Ste 800 910 17th St Washington DC 20006-2601 Office Phone: 202-463-3892. Business E-Mail: mhsears@mhsears.com.

**SEARS, SANDRA JONES,** medical/surgical nurse, consultant; b. Auburn, Mass., 1945; d. Harold Douglas Jones and Margaret Catherine Buckley; m. Raymond R. Johnson (div.); 1 child, Sharon Rae; m. Norman Allen Sears, June 22, 1980; 1 child from previous marriage, Allen Norman. AS with hons., Quinsigamond CC, 1975; BS in Psychology with hons., Worcester State Coll., Mass., 1978; BSN, Fitchburg State Coll., 1981. RN Mass., Ariz., cert. operating room nurse, Ariz., 2004, legal nurse consultant, Ariz., 2002. Registered nurse Meml. Hosp., Worcester, 1975—81; staff nurse John C. Lincoln Hosp., Phoenix, 1982—83, Paradise Valley Hosp., 1983—, charge nurse, 1985—86; owner Horizon Light Legal Nurse Cons., Phoenix. Lectr. in field; prin., owner HorizonLight Legal Nurse Cons. Mem.: Assn. Operating Rm. Nurses, Nat. Alliance Certified Legal Nurse Cons., Am. Assn. Legal Nurse Cons., Assn. Perioperative Nurses. Roman Cath. Avocations: reading, baseball, travel, history of lighthouses, stamp collecting/philately. E-mail: horizonlightInc@aol.com.

**SEARY, LAWRENCE ANTHONY,** cinematographer, editor; b. N.Y.C., June 13, 1951; m. Phyllis Cole, Oct. 2, 1976; children: Tara Ann, Paul Anthony. BFA, NYU, 1973. News cameraman, assignment desk supr., prodr. NBC, N.Y.C., 1974—. Recipient N.Y. State Broadcast award UPI, 1987. Mem. Nat. TV Acad. (bd. govs. 1996-2000, 03-05, nat. bd. trustees 2003-06, awards com., 9 Emmy award nominations 1978, 82, 94, 95, 2003, 05, Emmy awards 1978, 2 Emmy awards 2003), Mensa, N.Y. Press Club (1st v.p., 2002—, Feature Video award 1994). Democrat. Roman Catholic. Office: NBC 30 Rockefeller Plz Rm 728E New York NY 10112-0002 E-mail: larry.seary@nbc.com.

**SEASE, CATHERINE,** conservator, consultant; b. Middletown, Conn., Sept. 19, 1947; d. John William and Mary Lieurance Sease; m. David Stephen Reese, Jan. 7, 1984. AB, Bryn Mawr Coll., Pa., 1965—69; BSc, U. London, 1974—77. Assoc. conservator Met. Mus. Art, N.Y., 1979—82; assoc. conservator field mus. Field Mus., Chgo., 1986—88, head of conservation, 1988—2000; sr. conservator Peabody Mus. Natural History, New Haven, 2000—. Recipient Rome Prize, Am. Acad. in Rome, 1995. Fellow: Am. Inst. for Conservation. Office: Peabody Mus Natural History PO Box 208118 New Haven CT 06520 Office Phone: 203-432-3965. E-mail: catherine.sease@yale.edu.

**SEASE, GENE ELWOOD,** communications executive; b. Portage, Pa., June 28, 1931; s. Grover Chauncey and Clara Mae (Over) S.; m. Joanne D. Cherry, July 20, 1952; children: David Gene, Daniel Elwood, Cheryl Joanne. AB, Juniata Coll., 1952; B.D., Pitts. Theol. Sem., 1956, Th.M., 1959; PhD, U. Pitts., 1965, M.Ed., 1958; LL.D., U. Evansville, 1972, Butler U., 1972; Litt.D., Ind. State U., 1974; DD, U. Indpls., 1989. Ordained to ministry United Methodist Ch., 1956; pastor Grace United Meth. Ch., Wilkinsburg, Pitts., 1952-63; conf. dir., supt. Western Pa. Conf. United Meth. Ch., Pitts., 1963-68; lectr. grad. faculty U. Pitts., 1965-68; mem. staff U. Indpls., 1968-89, asst. to pres., 1968-69, pres., 1970-88, chancellor, 1988-89, pres. emeritus, 1989—; chmn. Sease, Gerig & Assocs., Indpls., 1989—. Bd. dirs. Bankers Life Ins. Co. of N.Y. Author: Christian Word Book, 1968; also numerous articles. Pres. Greater Indpls. Progress Com., 1972-75, Marion County Sheriff's Merit Bd.; mem. Ind. Scholarship Commn.; cons. Time Warner; bd. dirs. Indpls. Conv. Bur., Ind. Law Enforcement Tng. Acad., 500 Festival, Crossroads coun. Boy Scouts Am., Community Hosp. Indpls., St. Francis Hosp.; chmn. Ind. State Fair Commn. Mem. Internat. Platform Assn., English Speaking Union, Japan-Am. Soc. Ind., Ind. C. of C. (bd. dirs.), Indpls. C. of C. (bd. dirs.), Ind. Schoolmen's Club, Ind. State Fair Commn. (chmn.), Econ. Club of Indpls. (bd. dirs.), Skyline Club (bd. dirs.), Phi Delta Kappa, Alpha Phi Omega, Alpha Psi Omega. Clubs: Mason (Indpls.) (33 deg., Shriner), Kiwanian. (Indpls.), Columbia (Indpls.).

**SEASHORE, MARGRETTA REED,** physician, educator; b. Red Bank, NJ, June 20, 1939; d. Robert Clark and Lillie Ann (Heaviland) Reed; m. John Seashore, Dec. 26, 1964; children: Robert H., Carl J., Carolyn L. BA, Swarthmore Coll., 1961; MD, Yale U., 1965. Diplomate Am. Bd. Pediatrics, Am. Bd. Med. Genetics, Nat. Bd. Med. Examiners. Intern in pediat. Yale U. Sch. Medicine, New Haven, 1965-66, asst. resident in pediat., 1966-68, postdoctoral fellow in genetics and metabolism, depts. pediat. and medicine, 1968-70, asst. clin. prof. human genetics and pediat., 1974-78, from asst. prof. to assoc. prof., 1978-90, prof. genetics and pediatrics, 1990—; clin. asst. prof. pediat. U. Fla. Coll. Medicine, Gainesville, 1970-71, asst. prof., 1971-73; attending physician Duvall Med. Ctr., U. Hosp. Jacksonville, 1970-73, asst. prof., 1970-71; attending physician Hope Haven Children's Hosp., Jacksonville, Fla., 1970-73, Shands Tchg. Hosp., Gainesville, 1971-73, Danbury (Conn.) Hosp., 1977—, Yale-New Haven Hosp., 1974—, dir. Genetic Consultation Svc., 1977-86, 1989—; cons. physician Bridgeport (Conn.) Hosp., 1974—, Lawrence and Meml. Hosp., New London, Conn., 1979—, Norwalk (Conn.) Hosp., 1981—. Contbr. chapters to books. Fellow: Am. Coll. Med. Genetics (founding fellow), Am. Acad. Pediat. (mem. screening com. Conn. chpt. 1977—, mem. genetics com. 1989—94, chair com. genetics 1990—94); mem.: AAAS, AMA, New Eng. Genetics Group (chmn. outreach com. 1979—89, mem. steering com. 1979—98, chmn. screening com. 1989—93, co-dir. 1992—95), Soc. Study Inborn Errors of Metabolism, Am. Bd. Med. Genetics (bd. dirs. 2004—), Soc. Inherited Metabolic Disorders (bd. dirs. 1989—, sec. 1991—96, pres. 1997), Am. Soc. Human Genetics (mem. genetic svcs. com. 1986—91). Avocations: music, gardening, sewing, computers. Office: Yale U Sch Med Dept Genetics 333 Cedar St New Haven CT 06510-3289 Office Phone: 203-785-4938. Business E-Mail: margretta.seashore@yale.edu.

**SEATON, CAROLLE CARTER,** writer, educator; b. Oklahoma City, Okla., Sept. 18, 1939; d. Robert Henry and Claire (Haggard) Carter; m. James Cagney Seaton, Oct. 24, 1959 (dec.); children: Jene, James II, Ernest. BA in Early Childhood Edn. and Supervision, U. West Fla., 1975, MA in Early Childhood Edn. and Supervision, 1980, cert. edn. specialist, 1990. Kindergarten tchr. Santa Rosa Schs., Gulf Breeze, Fla., 1975-83, head gifted programs, 1983-85, staffing specialist Milton, Fla., 1985-95, program facilitator, 1995—. Editor: One Kid at a Time; author poetry. Chairperson Interagy. Coun., Milton, 1995-96; comdr. Gulf Breeze Sail and Power Squadron,

2002--. Mem. Fla. Assn. for the Gifted (regional rep. 1985-95), NEA. Avocations: diving, photography, charter boat captain, biking. Home: 907 Aquamarine Dr Gulf Breeze FL 32563-3001 Office: Santa Rosa Sch Dist 6751 Berryhill St Milton FL 32570-4824

**SEATON, EDWARD LEE,** editor, publishing executive; b. Manhattan, Kans., Feb. 5, 1943; s. Richard Melvin and Mary (Holton) Seaton; m. Karen Mathisen, Sept. 4, 1965; children: Edward Merrill, John David. AB cum laude, Harvard U., 1965; postgrad., U. Ctr., Quito, Ecuador, 1965-66, U. Mo., 1966—67. Staff writer Courier-Jour., Louisville, 1968—69; editor-in-chief, pub. Manhattan Mercury, 1969—. Bd. dirs., officer 8 newspaper and broadcasting affiliates; mem. Pulitzer Prize Bd., 1992—2001, chmn., 2001; mem. adv. com. Knight Internat. Press Fellowship Program, 1994—2006; mem. Cabot Awards bd. Columbia U., 1995—2003. Contbr. articles to profl. jours. Chmn. Alfred M. Landon lecture patrons Kans. State U.; chmn. Latin Am. Scholarship Program Am. Univs., Cambridge, Mass., 1986—87. Decorated comendador Order Christopher Columbus (Dominican Republic); recipient Cabot prize, Columbia U., 1993; Fulbright scholar, 1965. Mem.: Internat. Press Inst., Internat. Ctr. Journalists (bd. dirs. 1990—2001), Inter-Am. Press Assn. (pres. 1989—90, exec. com. 1976—), Am. Soc. Newspaper Editors (Found. pres. 1994—, pres. 1998—99), Kans. C. of C. and Industry (pres. 1987), Fly Club (Harvard U.). Avocations: tennis, cooking. Office: 318 N 5th St Manhattan KS 66505-0787

**SEATON, JAMES,** humanities educator; s. John Everett and Frances Kopecky Seaton; m. Sandra Cecelia Harris-Browne, Nov. 9, 1966; children: Ann Louish, James Everett Seaton, Jr., Amanda Cecelia Webster, Jeremy Evans Francis. BA, U. Ill., Urbana-Champaign, 1966; MA, PhD, U. Iowa, Iowa City, 1971. Asst. prof. Dept. Humanities Mich. State U., East Lansing, Mich., 1976—81, assoc. prof. Dept. English, 1981—91, prof. Dept. English, 1991—. Mem. academic bd. Nat. Humanities Inst., Washington, 1999—; reviewer NEH, Washington, 2006. Author: Cultural Conservatism, Political Liberalism, A Reading of Vergil's Georgics; editor: Beyond Cheering and Bashing: New Perspectives on The Closing of the American Mind; mem. editl. bd.: Humanitas, 1998—2006; contbr. essays to publications. Recipient Essay prize, Midwest Heritage, 1991. Mem.: Soc. Study Midwestern Lit. (pres. 2006—). Office: Michigan State University Dept of English Morrill Hall East Lansing MI 48824 Office Phone: 517-355-1730. Home Fax: 517-355-1730; Office Fax: 517-355-1730. Business E-Mail: seaton@msu.edu.

**SEATON, ROBERT FINLAYSON,** retired finance company executive; b. Hancock, Mich., Nov. 28, 1930; s. Donald W. and Mary Lucille (Finlayson) S.; m. Helen Jean Roberts, Apr. 18, 1954; children: Scott, Sandy. BS, Mich. Technol. U., 1952; MBA, Stanford, 1956; postgrad., Ind. U., 1966, U. So. Calif., 1973. Asst. sec. Palo Alto (Calif.) Mut. Savs. and Loan Assn., 1956-60; asst. v.p. Am. Savs. and Loan Assn. No. Calif., 1960-63; v.p. 1st Western Savs. and Loan Assn., Las Vegas, 1963-67; v.p., sec. Fed. Home Loan Bank, Cin., 1967-72; pres., chief exec. officer 2d Fed. Savs. and Loan Assn., Cleve., 1973, Cardinal Fed. Savs. Bank, Cleve., 1973-87, chmn., 1987-88; sr. v.p. Planned Giving Solutions, Inc., Cleve., 1989-90, pres., 1990-94. Trustee, v.p. Cmty. Housing Solutions; trustee N.E. Ohio Coun. Higher Edn.; hon. trustee ParkWorks. Lt. USNR, 1952—54. Republican. Methodist. Home: 16 Pepper Creek Dr Cleveland OH 44124-5248

**SEATON, SHIRLEY SMITH,** academic administrator, consultant; b. Cleve. d. Kibble Smith and Cecil Wright; m. J. Lawrence Seaton, Oct. 2, 1965; 1 child, Eric Dean BA, MA History, Howard U., 1949; MEd, Case We. Res. U., 1956; EdD, U. Akron, 1981; cert. Chinese history and culture, Beijing Normal U. Tchr. Cleve. Dist., 1950—59, dir. social studies, 1976—87; prin. Lafayette, Dike, Cleve., 1959—63, 1965—78; with Stas. WEWS-TV, WVIZ-TV, Cleve., 1963—67; adj. prof. Cleve. State U., 1988—90; administr. John Carroll U., University Heights, Ohio, 1990—. Program dir. OEO, Cleve., 1965; peer rev. Ohio Proficiency Test, 1986—2005; cons. Basics and Beyond, Cleve., 1990— Coord. Ctr. Civic Edn., 11th Congress Dist., 1987—; peer interview chair Fulbright tchr. exch. U.S. Dept. State, 1994-99, 2001-05; trustee We. Res. Hist. Soc., Cleve., 1996—. Ret. Vol. Program, Cleve., 1997-2003; commr. City of Cleveland Heights, 1997— Recipient Ohio Humanitarian award Govt. of Ohio, 1992; Fulbright grantee USIA, 1959, 82 Mem. AAUW, Fulbright Assn., Nat. Alliance Black Edn., Coalition 100 Black Women, Phi Delta Kappa, Alpha Kappa Alpha, Phi Beta Delta, Alpha Sigma Nu Episcopalian. Avocation: bridge. Home: 3680 Bendemeer Rd Cleveland Heights OH 44118 Office: John Carroll U 20700 North Pk Blvd University Heights OH 44118 Office Phone: 216-397-1604. Personal E-mail: sseaton664@aol.com. Business E-Mail: sseaton@jcu.edu.

**SEATON, VAUGHN ALLEN,** retired veterinary pathology educator; b. Abilene, Kans., Oct. 11, 1928; m. Clara I. Bertelrud; children: Gregory S., Jeffrey T. BS, DVM, Kans. State U., 1954; MS, Iowa State U., 1957. Pvt. practice, Janesville, Wis., 1954; instr. pathology Vet. Diagnostic Lab. Iowa State U., Ames, 1954-57, from asst. to assoc. prof. pathology Vet. Disgnostic Lab., 1957-64, prof., head Vet. Diagnostic Lab., 1964-94. Lab. coord. regional emergency animal disease eradication orgn. Animal and Plant Health Inspection Svc. USDA, 1974—; mem. rsch. com. Iowa Beef Industry Coun., 1972-85; mem. adv. bd. Iowa State Water Resources Rsch. Inst., 1973-80; cons. several orgns. Co-author: (monographs) Feasibility Study of College of Veterinary Medicine, 1972, Veterinary Diagnostic Laboratory Facilities-State of New York, 1970; bd. dirs. Iowa State U. Press, 1985-88, mem. manuscript com., 1982-85; contbr. articles to profl. jours. Trustee Ames Pub. Libr., 1979-85; mem. Iowa State Bd. Health. 1971-77, v.p., 1976-77; bd. dirs. Masonic Edn. Found., 1985-88; v.p. Iowa Scottish Rite Masonic Found. Recipient Disting. Alumnus award, Coll. Vet. Medicine, Kans. State U., 2005. Mem. AVMA, Am. Assn. Vet. Lab. Diagnosticians (bd. govs. 1973-88, pres. 1968, E.P. Pope award 1980), Am. Coll. Vet. Toxicologists, U.S. Animal Health Assn., Iowa Vet. Med. Assn. (pres. 1971), North Ctrl. Assn. Vet. Lab. Diagnosticians, Western Vet. Conf. (exec. bd. 1986-90, v.p. 1994, pres.-elect 1995, pres. 1996), World Assn. Vet. Lab. Diagnosticians (pres. 1980-86), Ames C. of C. (bd. dirs. 1970-73), Phi Kappa Phi, Phi Zeta (pres. 1964), Alpha Zeta, Gamma Sigma Delta. Office: Iowa State U Coll Vet Medicine Vet Diagnostic Lab Ames IA 50011-0001

**SEATS, PEGGY CHISOLM,** public affairs executive; b. Lisman, Ala., Oct. 12, 1951; d. William H. and Bernice (Berry) Chisolm; m. Melvin Seats (dec.). BA in Communications cum laude, Lewis U., 1974; grad. cert. in event mgmt., George Washington U., 1995; MA in Pub. Comm., Am. U., 1997; grad. cert. in intercultural comm., Vaxjo (Sweden) U., 1997; Master's cert. in Pub. Affairs & Exec. Non-profit mgmt., Georgetown U., 2005. Account exec. Globe Broadcasting, Chgo., 1976-78, Merrill Lynch, Chgo., 1978-79, Transp. Displays, Inc., Chgo., 1979-81; with Reverie, Inc., 1981—; nat. accounts mgr. Soft Sheen Products Co., Chgo., 1981-83; mktg. cons. Reverie, Inc., Chgo., 1983-85; pub. rels., mktg. mgr. Proctor & Gardner Advt., Chgo., 1985-86; dir. pub. rels., mktg. Morris Brown Coll., Atlanta, 1985-87; mgr. mktg. Howard U. Press, Washington, 1989-90; cons. White House Initiative on Historically Black Colls., Univs., 1990-92. State advisor U.S. Congl. Adv. Bd., Ill., 1982. Contbr. numerous articles to newspapers and mags. Founder Benjamin Banneker Meml. Found., Washington, 1996; organizer S.W. Waterfront Initiative, 2000—; facilitator L'Enfant Plaza Revitalization Project, 1997—; bd. dir. Congl. Award Found. Recipient Kizzie award Black Women Hall of Fame, Chgo., 1981, Svc. award Nat. Assn. Women in Media, Chgo., 1982. Mem. Internat. Platform Assn., Internat. Assn. Bus. Communicators, Internat. Spl. Events Soc., Pub. Rels. Soc. Am., Black Pub. Rels. Soc. (founder Atlanta chpt.), Nat. Assn. Market Developers, World Affairs Coun., Committee of 100, Lewis U. Alumni Assn. (bd. dirs. Ill. 1979). Washington Interdependence Coun. (founder, CEO 1996), Benjamin Banneker Inst. Math. and Sci. (founder). Unitarian Universalist. Avocations: music, art collecting, reading. Home: 2020 Pennsylvania Ave NW Washington DC 20006-1811 Office Phone: 202-387-3380. Business E-Mail: info@bannekermemorial.org.

**SEAU, JUNIOR (TIANA SEAU JR.),** retired professional football player; b. Samoa, Jan. 19, 1969; Student, U. So. Calif. Linebacker San Diego Chargers, 1990—2003, Miami Dolphins, 2003—06; ret., 2006. Player Super Bowl XXVIV, 1994. Named to Sporting News Coll. All-Am. Team, 1989, to Pro Bowl Team, 1991-2000, 2002, to Sporting News NFL All Pro Team, 1992, 93.*

**SEAVEY, WILLIAM ARTHUR,** lawyer, vintner; b. LA, Aug. 28, 1930; s. Arthur Jones and Dorothy (Keyes) S.; m. Mary van Beuren, June 25, 1955; children: Dorothy K., Arthur V.B., William G., Frederic A., Charles K. AB, Princeton U., 1952; LLB, Harvard U., 1955; grad. Inst. Internat. Studies, U. Geneva, Switzerland, 1956, D in Polit. Sci., 1970. Bar: Calif. 1957, U.S. Dist. Ct. (so. and no. dist.) Calif. 1957, U.S. Ct. Appeals (9th cir.) 1957. Assoc. Luce, Forward, Kunzel & Scripps, San Diego, 1956-57; asst. U.S. atty. U.S. Dist. Ct. (so. dist.) Calif., 1957-59; with Noon & Seavey, San Diego, 1959-65; lectr. in internat. law and econ., asst. to pres. Mills Coll., Oakland, Calif., 1968-74; ptnr. Richards & Seavey, San Francisco, 1974-76, Davis, Stafford, Kellman & Fenwick, San Francisco, 1976-78; of counsel Friedman, Olive, McCubbin, Spalding, Bilter, Roosevelt etal, San Francisco, 1987—2004. Proprietor Seavey Vineyard, Napa County, 1981—. Author: Dumping Since the War: The Gatt and National Laws, 1970. Councilman City of Coronado, Calif., 1960-62, mayor 1962-64; trustee French-Am. Internat. Sch., San Francisco, 1968-96; pres. English Speaking Union, San Francisco, 1982-85, Alliance Francaise, San Francisco, 1979-81; chair Javits Fellowship Bd., Washington, 1989-92; mem. Columbus Fellowship Found. Bd., Washington, 1993-99; dir. San Francisco Com. on Fgn. Rels., 1995-98, 2001—, chmn., 1998-2001. Mem. ABA, Calif. Bar Assn., Am. Soc. Internat. Law. Clubs: Pacific Union, Cercle de l'Union, World Trade (San Francisco), The Met. (Washington). Republican. Avocations: skiing, jazz, piano. Home: 90 Hazel Ln Piedmont CA 94611-4033 Office: 1310 Conn Valley Rd Saint Helena CA 94574-9624 Business E-Mail: info@seaveyvineyard.com.

**SEAWELL, DONALD RAY,** lawyer, performing company executive; b. Jonesboro, NC, Aug. 1, 1912; s. A.A.F. and Bertha (Smith) S.; m. Eugenia Rawls, Apr. 5, 1941; children: Brook Ashley, Donald Brockman. AB, U. NC, 1933, JD, 1936, DLitt, 1980; LHD, U. No. Colo., 1978. Bar: NC 1936, NY 1947. With SEC, 1939-41, 45-47, Dept. Justice, 1942-43; chmn. bd., dir., pub., pres. Denver Post, 1966-81; chmn. bd., dir. Gravure West, LA, 1966-81; dir. Swan Prodns., London; of counsel firm Bernstein, Seawell, Kove & Maltin, NYC, 1979—; chmn. bd., chief exec. officer Denver Ctr. for Performing Arts, 1972—. Ptnr. Bonfils-Seawell Enterprises, NYC; bd. vis. U. NC Chmn. bd. ANTA, 1965—; theatre panel Nat. Coun. Arts, 1970-74; bd. govs. Royal Shakespeare Theatre; trustee Am. Acad. Dramatic Arts, 1967—, Hofstra U., 1968-69, Cen. City Opera Assn., Denver Symphony; bd. dirs., Air Force Acad. Found., Nat. Ints. Outdoor Drama, Walter Hampden Meml. Library, Hammond Mus.; pres. Helen G. Bonfils Found., 1972-97, pres. emeritus, 1997—, chmn. fin. com., 1997—; Denver Opera Found.; Population Crisis Com., 1982-91; bd. dirs Family Health Internat., Found. for Internat. Family Health; bd. visitors NC Sch. Arts, 1992-98; pres. Frederick G. Bonfils Found., 1972-92; chmn. Civilian Mil. Inst. Named Officer, Most Excellent Order of the Brit. Empire, 2002; recipient Am. Acad. Achievement award, 1980, Tony award for producing, On Your Toes, 1983, Vocie Rsch. and Awareness award, Voice Found., 1983, Arts and Entertainment Cable Network award, 1987, Third Millennium Leadership award, Am. Diabetes Assn., 1996, Colo. Tourism Hall of Fame award, 1999, Thomas Degaetani award, U.S. Inst. for Theatre Tech., 2000, Benjamin F. Stapleton, Jr. award, 2000. Disting. Svc. award, U. Colo., 2000, Downtown Denver award for Tantalus, 2001, AWARE Honoree award, 2001, Donald Seawell Outstanding Achievement in Theatre award, Colo. Festival World Theatre, 2005, Founders award for Outstanding Contbn. to Am. Theater, Theater Hall of Fame, NYC, 2005, Theatre Hall Fame, NYC, 2006. Mem. Bucks Club (London), Dutch Treat Club (NYC), Denver Country Club, Denver Club, Cherry Hills Country Club, Mile High Club (Denver), Garden of Gods Club (Colorado Springs, Colo.). Office: Denver Ctr for Performing Arts 1101 13th St Denver CO 80204 E-mail: geary@dcpa.org.

**SEAWELL, THOMAS ROBERT,** artist, retired art educator; b. Balt., Mar. 17, 1936; s. Robert James and Cynthia Edith (Bass) S.; m. Barbara Louise Frey, Nov. 30, 1985; children: James Bradford, Lee Thomas, Gustin Charles, Jay Turner Frey. B.F.A., Washington U., 1958; M.F.A., Tex. Christian U., 1960. Mem. faculty dept. art SUNY-Oswego, 1963-91, prof., 1973-91; tchg. adj. Tex. A&M, Commerce, 1999—2006. Juror 50th Cooperstown Nat., 1985, Nat. Print Exhbn. Minot State U., ND, 1985, Rochester Print Club Ann. Meml. Art Gallery U., Minn., 1988; vis. artist Ox Bow Print Symposium, 1985, Ann. Matrix Artist U. Dallas, 1989, Midwestern State U., Wichita Falls, 1993, East Tenn. State U., Knoxville, 1997; guest spkr. L.A. Coll., 2004. One-man exhbns. include retrospective U. Md., Baltimore County, 1983, Retrospective Tyler Art Gallery, SUNY, Oswego, 1991, Univ. Gallery, Tex. A&M U., Commerce, 1995, Brazos Gallery, Dallas, 1997, La. Coll., Pineville-Alexandria, 2004; group exhbns. include Contemporary Am. Prints in Leningrad, USSR, 1983-84, The Collagraph, U. Mont., 1987, The Streets Suite, Rochester Meml. Art Gallery, 2005; traveling exhbn. So. Arts Fedn. Traveling Exhbn. "A Sense of Place," 1986—, Columbia Coll., 1996-97, Art in the Metroplex, J.M. Moudy Gallery, Ft. Worth, Tex., 1997, Contemporary Tex. Clay, Dallas Visual Arts Ctr., 1997, To Have and to Hold, Irving (Tex.) Arts Ctr. Main Gallery, 1998, Kennedy-Douglass Ctr. for the Arts Nat. Ceramic Competition, 1999, Woodmere Art Mus., 1999, San Angelo Mus. Fine Arts, 2000, 2004, Ark. State U., 2000, U. Wis., Parkside, 2000, 2003, 2005, Oxford Gallery, Rochester, N.Y., 2000; represented in permanent collections Bklyn. Mus., DeCordova Mus. Art, Rochester Meml. Art Gallery, Pushkin Mus., USSR, Brit. Mus., Munson-Williams-Proctor Inst., Library of Congress, Portland Art Mus., Ark. Arts Ctr., Alexandria Mus. Art, La., Phila. Watercolor Soc., 2005, Roberson Art Mus., Binghamton, NY 2005, Phila. Water Color Soc., Burman Mus., 2005, commd. print editions: Geldermann Securities Ltd., 1985-92, 8 Stock Exchange Images, The Print Club Albany, N.Y., 2004. Recipient Joseph A. Cain Meml. Purchase award for sculpture Del Mar Coll., 1999, 2d prize 15th Internat. Miniature Print Exhbn. Roberson Art Mus., Binghamton, N.Y. 2005. Mem. Boston Printmakers, Phila. Water Color Soc. Am. Graphic Artists, Tex. Sculpture Assn. E-mail: tseawell@9plus.net.

**SEAWRIGHT, JAMES L., JR.,** sculptor, educator; b. Jackson, Miss. May 22, 1936; s. James L. and Josephine (Power) S.; m. Mabelle M. Garrard, June 22, 1960; 1 child, James Andrew. Student, U. of South, 1954-54, Delta State Coll., 1954-55; BA in English, U. Miss., 1957; postgrad., Art Students League of N.Y., 1961-62. Tech. supr. Columbia-Princeton Electronic Music Center, N.Y.C., 1963-69; tchr. Sch. Visual Arts, 1967-69; dir. visual arts program Princeton U., 1972-2001, prof. coun. of humanities and visual arts, 1992—. Asst. to choreographer, Henry St. Playhouse, N.Y.C., 1962-63, spl. effects, tech. cons., Mimi Garrard Dance Co., N.Y.C., 1964—; sculptor represented in permanent collections, Mus. Modern Art, N.Y.C., Whitney Mus., N.Y.C., N.J. State Mus., Trenton, Guggenheim Mus., N.Y.C., Wadsworth Atheneum, Hartford, Conn., others; pub. commns. for SEA-TAC Internat. Airport, Seattle, Logan Internat. Airport, Boston; also put. collections. Served with USN, 1957-61. Recipient Theodoron award Guggenheim Mus., 1969, Am. Acad. Arts and Letters Art award, 1997, Lifetime Achievement award Miss. Inst. Arts and Letters, 2003, Howard T. Behrman award for disting. accomplishment in humanities Princeton U., 2004; Graham Found. Advanced Study in Arts fellow, 1970. Mem. Am. Abstract Artists, Phi Delta Theta. Democrat. Episcopalian. Office: 185 Nassau St Princeton NJ 08544-2003 Office Phone: 609-258-5098. Personal E-mail: james@seawright.net. Business E-Mail: jims@princeton.edu.

**SEAY, CHARLOTTE J.,** artist; d. Charles Ervin and Imogene Touchstone Craig; m. John Randolph Seay, Mar. 20, 1964; children: Daniel Thomas, Steven Lee, Sheri Lynn Smith, Scott Craig. Student, Midland Coll., Tex., 1986—88, U. of Tex. of the Permian Basin, Odessa, 1988—90. Designer Midland Country Club/Wildcatter, 1976—77; painter, printmaker, 1980—; curator Midland/Wirral, Eng. art exhbn. City of Midland, 1999—2000; cover designer Tumbleweed Publs. Jr. League of Midland, 2003; label designer

Messina Hof Winery, Bryan, Tex., 2005—. Tchr. Pecos Arts Assn., Snyder Arts Assn., Paint and Palette, West Texas Area, 1992—2001; juror Monahans Art Assn., Tex., 1994; lectr. Del Rio Old Firehouse Art Mus., Tex., 1997; juror Watercolor Horizons Group, Odessa, Tex., 1998; instr. secondary sch. art tchrs. workshop Midland Ind. Sch. Dist., 1999; illustrator Sweet Mischief Press, Midland, 2001—02, Midland, 2003—04; juror Carlsbad Art Assn., N.Mex., 2003; illustrator Author's Pub. House, Midland, 2005, Midland, 06. Contbr. essays to publs. Bd. dirs. Midland Tourism Bd., 2003—04; chmn. hotel/motel tax adv. bd. Midland City Coun., 2002—06; mem. City of Midland and Chamber Planning Retreat, 2004—06, Visions 2000 of Midland, 1999; elder Grace Presbyn. Ch., Midland, 2001—04; pres. Midland Opera Theater, 2003—04, Opportunity Ctr. of Midland, 1973—74. Named Disting. Artist, Arts Assembly of Midland, 1997, Best In Show, Odessa Arts Assn., 1994, Best in Show, 1995, Best In Show, Arts Assembly of Midland/Celebration of the Arts, 1992; recipient Merit award, Midland Arts Assn. and Midland Coll., 2005, Daniel Smith award, So. Watercolor Soc., 1998, Paul Harris fellowship, Dist. 5530, Rotary Clubs Internat., 1994, Swartz Framing award, Midland Arts Assn. and Mus. of the S.W., 2005. Mem.: Midland Arts Assn. (pres. 1995—96), Tex. Watercolor Soc. (chmn. 47th ann. exhbn. 1996—97), Tex. Watercolor Soc. (pres. 1996—97), Arts Assembly of Midland (Vol. of the Yr./Midland Opera Theater 2004), Midland Country Club Ladies Assn. (bd. of directors 1998—99). Republican. Presbyterian. Avocations: travel, writing essays, writing poetry, photography, reading. Home Fax: 432-570-1875. Personal E-mail: seayart@sbcglobal.net.

**SEAY, JOSEPH DANIEL,** music educator; b. Macon, Ga., Feb. 10, 1981; s. Joseph Mitchell and Deborah Burton Seay. BS in Music Edn., U. Ala., 2004. Cert. tchr. Va. Band dir. L.F. Addington Mid. Sch. and J.J. Kelly H.S., Wise, Va., 2004—. Mem.: MENC. Office: JJ Kelly HS 716 Birchfield Rd Wise VA 24293 Home: 118 W First St S Big Stone Gap VA 24219

**SEAY, MARLAINA JOAN,** theater educator, set designer; b. Paducha, Ky., May 16, 1978; d. Hal Gordon and Patricia Joan Vanmetre; m. Marlaina Joan Vanmetre, Oct. 10, 1999; children: Regan Elizabeth, Madeline Avigail. BA in Theater, Austin Peay State U., Clarksville, Tenn., 1999; MFA in Scenography, U. N.C., Greensboro, 2003. Instr. Lynchburg (Va.) Coll., 2003—. Set designer: (plays) Camelot; Mousetrap; The Fantasticks; Children's Theatre Productions; scenic artist: Central Piedmont Summer Theatre; set and lighting designer, technical dir: Lynchburg Coll. Ctr. Aging Tchg. grantee, Lynchburg Coll., 2006. Mem.: Popular Culture Assn., South Ea. Theatre Conf., Alpha Psi Omega (hon.). Constitution. Presbyterian. Office: Lynchburg Coll 1501 Lakeside Dr Lynchburg VA 24501 Office Phone: 434-544-8351.

**SEBASTIAN, PETER,** political scientist, consultant, retired diplomat; b. June 19, 1926; m. Harvel Huddleston, Dec. 11, 1951; 1 child, Christopher. BA, U. Chgo., 1950; postgrad., U. d'Aix-Marseille, Nice, France, 1949. New Sch. for Social Research, N.Y.C., 1950, Nat. War Coll., 1969-70. Dir. owner cons. co., N.Y.C., 1950-57; U.S. Fgn. Service officer Dept. State, Washington, 1957-76, dep. exec. sec., 1976-77, sr. seminar, 1977-78; U.S. consul gen. Casablanca, Morocco, 1978-80; minister, counselor Am. embassy, Rabat, Morocco, 1980-82; dir. for North Africa Dept. State, Washington, 1982-84; ambassador to Tunisia Tunis, 1984-87; ambassador-in-residence Ctr. for Strategic Internat. Studies, Georgetown U., Washington, 1987-88; cons in fgn. affairs to the public and pvt. sector, lectr., 1988—. Mem. V.P. Bush's task force on border control, 1988—89. Contbr. poems to Osmose, 1949; author studies for the pvt. sector U.S. Dept. State and other U.S agys. Bd. dirs. Santa Fe Coun. on Internat. Rels., 2005, chair spl. events com. Served to sgt. AUS, 1944-46 Decorated Ouissam Alaouite (Morocco), numerous U.S. mil. decorations; recipient Presdl. Meritorious Service award, 1985. Mem. Am. Fgn. Svc. Assn., Nat. Geog. Soc., Mid. East Inst. Episcopalian. Avocations: painting, drawing, photography. Office Phone: 505-983-6364. Personal E-mail: Batuta@aol.com.

**SEBASTIAN, PHYLIS SUE (INGRAM),** real estate broker, antique appraiser, real estate appraiser; b. Childersburg, Ala., Jan. 24, 1945; d. Albert Freeman and Era Mae (McGowin) Ingram; m. Robert Emmett Martin, March 31, 1965 (div. Sept. 1976); children: Connie, Michael, Toni, Steve; m. Thomas Haskell Sebastian III, June 26, 1985; stepchildren: Shellie, Tabatha, Cherie, Thomas IV. Ordained minister Progressive Universal Life Ch., 2002; lic. real estate broker Mo., real estate appraiser Tenn., Mo., PREA, CIMA. Owner, broker Phylis Sebastian Real Estate, Farmington, Mo., 1989—, U.S. Auto Sales, Park Hills, Mo., 1993—96; owner Bus. Legal Svc., Park Hills, Mo., 1993—; ptnr. La Femme Fine Antique Auction Svc., Ironton, Mo., 1997—. Owner Astrology Cons., 1970—; numerous appearances St. Louis TV; hostess radio show, St. Louis. Contbr. articles to newspapers; author: Marriages in Madison County Missouri for 1848-1868, 1998, 1910 Census for Madison County Missouri, 1998, numerous poems. Co-founder Astrological Assn., St. Louis, 1976-77, Mo. Mental Health Consumer Network, 1989-93, Mineral Area chpt. 1989-93. Mem. Nat. Gardening Club, Libr. Congress, Smithsonian, Nat. Hist. soc., Geneal. Assn. Madison County, Mo. (founder, sec., treas., genealogist). Mem. Lds Ch. Avocations: reading, walking, gardening, piano, guitar. Home: 5231 West 72 Highway Fredericktown MO 63645 Office: Arcadia Valley Auction Company Inc and Real Estate 315A W Russell St Ironton MO 63650-1316 Office Phone: 573-546-3900, 573-546-7440. Personal E-mail: phylis@phylissebastian.com. E-mail: avac@myway.com.

**SEBASTIAN, SUZIE,** television producer; b. Redding, Calif., Aug. 2, 1962; d. Richard Werner and Hildegard (Goettel) Guenther; m. Ted Sebastian, June 6, 1984 (div. July 1990). AA, Shasta Coll., 1985. Freelance tv prodr., prodn. mgr. commls., 1985-91; freelance underwater model, stunt woman; expedition leader, hostess Adventures on Scuba Dive Travel, Santa Barbara, Calif. 1991—; documentary TV prodr. Discovery Channel, 1998-2000. Asst. instr. Filming Sharks in the Wild. Nassau, Bahamas, 1996—. Prodr.: documentaries, ednl. videos; picture editor, underwater model: Tom Campbell's Film and Video Prodns., 1991—; prodr.: Navy Seals: In Harms Way; (films) How to Survive Hellweek, FBI: Critical Incident Class 234, Breathe, 2006. Mem.: Internat. Documentary Assn., Divers Alert Network, Aquatic Bodyworks. Avocations: skiing, triathlon. Home: 919 Veronica Springs Rd Santa Barbara CA 93105-4500 Office: Adventures on Scuba 238 Las Alturas Rd Santa Barbara CA 93103-2170 E-mail: suzies@silcom.com.

**SEBASTIANELLI, MARIO JOSEPH,** internist, nephrologist, health facility administrator; b. Jessup, Pa., Sept. 14, 1935; s. Carlo and Antonia (Antonelli) S.; m. Alena Marie Drazdauskas, June 26, 1993 (div. July 2004); children: Mario, Alexa, Marco. BS in Biology, U. Scranton, 1958; MD, Jefferson Med. Coll., 1962. Diplomate Am. Bd. Internal Medicine. From sr. instr. to assoc. prof. medicine Hahnemann U., Phila., 1969—87; pvt. practice Scranton, Pa., 1971—; chief nephrology, founding dir. hemodialysis Moses Taylor Hosp., Scranton, 1972—76; founding med. dir. Pa. Regional Tissue Bank, Scranton, 1983—91; founding dir. inpatient hemodialysis svcs. Comty. Med. Ctr., Scranton, 1996—; founding med. dir. Fresenius Med. Care Dialysis Svcs. Dunmore, Scranton, 2001—. Mem. senateconfirmed gov. apptd. Govs. Renal Disease Adv. Com., Harrisburg, Pa., 1973-76; creator, owner Comprehensive Health Svcs. Ctr., Dunmore, Pa., 1979—; founding med. dir. Diagnostic Lab., Dunmore, 1981-95. Contbr. articles to profl. jours. Bd. dirs. Scranton Lackawanna Human Devel. Agy., Scranton, 1977-82. Lt. USNR, 1963-65. Fellow: ACP; mem.: KC (4th degree), AMA, Renal Physicians Assn., Internat. Soc. Nephrology, Am. Soc. Nephrology, Alpha Omega Alpha. Republican. Roman Catholic. Avocations: fishing, swimming, travel, sports cars, reading. Office: Comprehensive Health Svcs Ctr 1416 Monroe Ave Ste 206 Dunmore PA 18509-2477 Office Phone: 570-347-5212. E-mail: drsebjsj@hcrn.com.

**SEBASTIEN, ANYA CELITA,** academic administrator, consultant; d. Errol Olliver Sebastien and Grace Elma Audain Sebastien. BS in Elem. and Spl. Edn., Lesley Coll., 1975; MS in Exceptional Citizen Edn. and Learning Disabilities. U. Miami, Fla., 1979; EdD in higher Edn. Administrn., George Washington U., 1989. Spl. edn. tchr. Govt. of V.I., Dept. Edn., St. Thomas, 1975—78, resource specialist, 1983—84; dean's grant coord. Coll. of V.I., St.

Thomas, 1979—81; info. and referral specialist Info. Ctr. for Handicapped Individuals, Inc., Washington, 1981—82; asst. prof. edn. U. V.I., St. Thomas, 1990—91, exec. asst. to v.p. acad. affairs, 1992—95; sec. to bd. trustees, exec. asst. to pres. Chgo. State U., 1995—97; assoc. provost St. Petersburg (Fla.) Coll., Seminole Campus, 1998—. Mem. selection com. Leadership Pinellas, Clearwater, Fla., 2002—. Grantee, U.S. Dept. Edn., 1991; participant Nat. Identification Program for Advancement of Women in Higher Edn., Am. Coun. Edn., 1996. Mem.: AAUW (assoc.), Coun. for Exceptional Children (assoc.; pres. St Thomas, V.I. chpt. 1977—78), Am. Assn. Higher Edn. (assoc.), Caribbean Studies Assn. (assoc.). Office: St Petersburg Coll PO Box 13489 Saint Petersburg FL 33733 Personal E-mail: acseb@aol.com. E-mail: sebastiena@spcollege.edu.

**SEBBA, ROSANGELA YAZBEC,** music educator, musician; b. Goiania, Goias, Brazil, Jan. 1, 1971; d. Taufic Jose and Leila (Yazbec) Sebba. BMus, U. Fed. de Goias, Goiania, 1991; MuxM, U. Wyo., 1996; DMA, U.So. Miss., 2000. Pianist MMTA, 2001. Prof. Conservatorio Estadual Gustav Ritter, Goiania, Goias, Brazil, 1989—94; adj. prof. U. of So. Miss., Hattiesburg, 2000; adj. professor Pearl River C.C., Poplarville, Miss., 2000—01; asst. prof. Miss. State U., Starkville, Miss., 2001—. Pianist, accompanist etc. Freelance, 1996—; lectr./recital Coll. Music Soc. Internat. Conf., Costa Rica, 2003; founder, coord. Brazilian Music Festival. Concert tour Teatro Goiania, Teatro Pirinopolis, Teatro Sao Joaquim, Orche. Camara Goyazes, Brazil, 2003; concert tour Mexico. Performer. Recipient First prizes in Brazilian Nat. Competitions, 1986-1994; grantee, Humanities and Arts Rsch. Program, 2002, Schillig, H.A.R.P., Office Rsch. Mem.: Music Tchrs. Nat. Assn., Miss. Music Tchrs. Assn., Coll. Music Soc. Office Phone: 662-325-2854. Business E-Mail: rys3@colled.msstate.edu.

**ŠEBEK, MICHAEL,** research scientist, entrepreneur; b. Prague, Czech Republic, Jan. 25, 1954; s. Antonín and Jana (Hanzlová) S.; m. Ivana Ornestová, Nov. 21, 1992; children: Michael, Natalie. Diploma in elec. engring., Czech Tech. U., Prague, 1978; PhD, Czech Acad. Scis., Prague, 1981, DSc, 1995. Scientist Inst. Info. Theory and Automation, Prague, 1981-88, sr. scientist, 1988-90, chief scientist, chmn. of Control Theory Dept., 1991-98, head Control Theory Dept., 1998—2005. Vis. prof. Swiss Fed. Inst. Tech., Zurich, 1994-95; mem. policy com. Internat. Fedn. Automatic Control, 1993—2005; coord. of EUROPOLY (Europen Network of Excellence for Indsl. Applications of Polynomial Methods 1998; co-founder and CEO of PolyX, Ltd. (world-wide producer of software for polynomial methods in systems, signals and control), 1998, head control engring. dept., 2003—; mgr. Ctr. applied cybernetics Control, Czech Tech. U. Prague, 2000—, prof., 2004—; lectr. in field. Contbr. numerous articles to profl. jours. Mgr., coach Medicina Baseball Club, Prague, 1985-90. Recipient Czech Nat. prize Czech Parliament, 1989. Mem. IEEE (sr., mem. exec. com. Czech sect. 1996—), IEEE Control Sys. Soc. (mem. conf. editl. bd. 1994-2000, chmn. Czech chpt. 1996-2000), Am. Math. Soc., N.Y. Acad. Scis. Avocations: jogging, baseball, photography. Home: Jarní 4 16000 Prague 6 Czech Republic Office: Czech Tech U Prague Technicka 2 166 27 Prague 6 Czech Republic also: Inst Info Theory & Automation 18208 Prague 8 Czech Republic E-mail: m.sebek@polyx.cz, m.sebek@c-a-k.cz.

**SEBEK, MIKLÓS LÁSZLÓ,** sculptor, educator; b. Sóskút, Hungary, Dec. 6, 1941; arrived in U.S., 1970; s. Rudolf Sebek and Mária Zámecsnik; m. Villö Katalin Varga, June 18, 1993. BA in Sculpture, Montclair State U., N.J., 1978; Diploma in Architecture, Budapest Inst. Architecture, Hungary, 1968. Exhbn. com. chair Audubon Artists, NY, 2003—, Allied Artists of Am., NY, 2006—. Wood sculpture, Origin No. 2, 2004 (Excellence award, 2004), bronze sculpture, Freedom, 2005 (Best in Show, 2005), marble sculpture, Baroque, 2005 (Best Sculpture, 2005). Mem. Southwestern Vt. Arts Ctr., Manchester, 2005—. Recipient Best in Show, West Essex Art Assn., 2005, Best Sculpture, West Essex Art Ann. Exhbn., 2005, Best in Show, State Show. Mem.: So. Vt. Arts Ctr., Allied Artists of Am. Inc., Audubon Artists Inc. Home: 112 Lafayette Ave Passaic NJ 07055

**SEBELIUS, KATHLEEN GILLIGAN,** governor; b. Cin., May 15, 1948; d. John J. and Mary K. (Dixon) Gilligan; m. Keith Gary Sebelius, 1974; children: Edward Keith, John McCall. BA, Trinity Coll., 1970; MA in Pub. Adminstrn., U. Kans., 1977. Exec. dir. Kans. Trial Lawyers Assn., 1978—86; mem. Kans. Ho. of Reps., 1987-95; ins. commr. State of Kans., 1995—2002, gov., 2003—. Founder Women's Polit. Caucus; precinct committeewoman, 1980-86; mayor, Potwin, 1985-87; appointed Presdl. adv. commn. consumer protection and quality in Health Care, 1997. Mem. Common Cause (state bd., nat. gov. bd. 1975-81), Nat. Assn. Ins. Commrs. (chair). Democrat. Roman Catholic. Office: Office of the Gov State Capitol 2nd Fl Topeka KS 66612-1590 Office Fax: 785-296-7973.*

**SEBESTA, HENRY R.,** engineering executive, researcher; b. Rosharon, Tex., Nov. 20, 1938; s. Henry C. and Olga Emma Sebesta; m. Mary M. Mumberson, Aug. 31, 1963; children: David Patrick, Robert Ellis. BSME, U. Tex., Austin, 1962; MSME, U. Tex., 1964, PhD, 1966. Registered profl. engr., Okla. Asst. prof. mech. and aero. engring. Okla. State U., Stillwater, 1966—69, assoc. prof. mech. and aero. engring., 1969—71, prof. mech. and aero. engring., 1971—75; chmn. mech. engring. U. Tex., Arlington, 1975—79; v.p. Applied Tech. Assocs., Albuquerque, 1979—94, pres., CEO, 1994—98, chief scientist, 1998—. Contbr. articles to profl. jours. Asst. scoutmaster Boy Scouts Am., Stillwater, 1968—75. Mem.: IEEE, AIAA (sect. pres. 1978—79), ASME (life), Internat. Soc. Optical Engring., Pi Tau Sigma, Tau Beta Pi. Republican. Achievements include patents for line-of-sight stabilization. Avocations: travel, fishing, reading. Office: Applied Tech Assocs 1300 Britt St SE Albuquerque NM 87123 Office Phone: 505-767-1202. Office Fax: 505-768-1379. E-mail: henry.r.sebesta@aptec.com.

**SEBHATU, MESGUN,** physics professor; b. Menoxeito, Eritrea, Ethiopia, Jan. 6, 1946; came to U.S., 1970; s. Sebhatu and Mehret (Tesfay) S.; m. Almaz Yilma, July 21, 1984; children: Emnet, Temnete. BS in Physics, Haile Selassie I U., Addis Ababa, Ethiopia, 1969; PhD in Physics, Clemson (S.C.) U., 1975. Vis. asst. prof. N.C. State U., Raleigh, 1975-76; asst. prof. physics Pensacola (Fla.) Jr. Coll., 1976-78, Winthrop Coll., Rock Hill, S.C., 1978-84, assoc. prof. physics, 1984-91; King-Chavez-Parks vis. prof. physics Mich. State U., East Lansing, 1991-92; prof. Winthrop U., Rock Hill, 1992—. Textbook reviewer Prentice Hall, 1987, Little Brown, 1989. Contbr. articles to profl. jours. Rsch. initiation and devel. grantee NSF, 1989, Cottrel grantee Rsch. Corp., 1982; Kavli Inst. for Theoretical Physics scholar U. Calif., Santa Barbara, 2002-04. Mem. Am. Phys. Soc., Am. Assn. Physics Tchrs. Democrat. Roman Catholic. Achievements include derivation of two-nucleon relative wave exchange potentials. Office: Winthrop U 101 Sims Bldg Rock Hill SC 29733-0001 Office Phone: 803-323-4935. Business E-Mail: sebhatum@winthrop.edu.

**SEBO, STEPHEN ANDREW,** electrical engineer, educator, researcher, consultant; b. Budapest, Hungary, June 10, 1934; s. Emery Sebo and Elizabeth Thieben; m. Eva Agnes Vambery, May 25, 1968. MSEE, Budapest Poly-tech. U., 1957; PhD, Hungarian Acad. Sci., 1966. Engr. Budapest Elec. Co., 1957-61; asst. prof. Budapest Poly. U., 1961-66, assoc. prof., 1966-68, Ohio State U.: Columbus, 1968-74, prof., 1974—82, Am. Electric Power prof. in power sys. engring., 1982—2003, Neal A. Smith prof., 1995—2003, prof. emeritus, 2003—. Recipient Power Educator award Edison Elec. Inst., 1981, Tech. Person of Yr. award Columbus Tech. Coun., 1994. Fellow IEEE (Prize Paper award 1981). Office: Ohio State U Elec Engring 2015 Neil Ave Columbus OH 43210-1272 Business E-Mail: sebo.1@osu.edu.

**SEBOLD, ALICE,** writer; b. Madison, Wis., 1963; d. Jane and Russell Sebold; m. Glen David Gold, 2001. BA, Syracuse U., 1984; studied poetry, U. Houston, 1984—85; MFA in fiction, U. Calif., Irvine, 1998. Author: (memoir) Lucky, 1999, (novels) The Lovely Bones, 2002. Office: c/o Steven Barclay Agy 12 Western Ave Petaluma CA 94952

**SEBOLD, RUSSELL PERRY, III,** Romance languages educator, writer; b. Dayton, Ohio, Aug. 20, 1928; s. Russell Perry and Mary (Kiger) Sebold; m. Jane Norvell Hale, Nov. 24, 1955; children: Mary Norvell, Alice Hale. Student, U. Chgo., 1945—47; BA, Ind. U., 1949; MA (Woodrow Wilson fellow), Princeton U., 1951, PhD, 1953; D.Phil. and Letters (hon.), U. Alicante, Spain, 1984. Instr. Spanish, Duke U., 1955-56; instr. Spanish, U. Wis., 1956-58, asst. prof., 1958-62, assoc. prof., 1962-66; prof. Spanish, chmn. dept. fgn. langs. and lits. U. Md., 1966-68; prof. Spanish, U. Pa., 1968-88, chmn. dept. Romance langs., 1968-78, Edwin B. and Leonore R. Williams prof. Romance langs., 1988—. Mem. adv. soc. Ibero-Am. Enlightenment, 1968—, treas., 1969—; mem. steering com. Am. Soc. Eighteenth Century Studies, 1970—; corr. academician Royal Spanish Acad., 1993—, Royal Acad. Humane Letters of Barcelona, 1993—. Author: Tomás de Iriarte: poeta de rapto racional, 1961, El rapto de la mente, 1970, 1989, Colonel Don José Cadalso, 1970, Cadalso: el primer romántico europeo de España, 1974, Novela y autobiografía en la Vida de Torres Villarroel, 1975, Trayectoria del romanticismo español, 1983, Descubrimiento y fronteras del neoclasicismo español, 1985, Bécquer en sus narraciones fantásticas, 1989, De ilustrados y románticos, 1992, La novela romantica en España, 2000, La perduración de la modalidad clásica, 2001, Lírica y poética en España, 1536-1870, 2003, Ensayos de meditacion y crítica literaria, 2004; author, editor Fray Gerundio de Campazas (José Francisco de Isla) 4 vols., 1960—64, 2d edit., 1992, Visiones y visitas de Torres con don Francisco de Quevedo por la Corte (Diego de Torres Villarroel, 1966, 2d edit., 1991, Numancia destruida (Ignacio López de Ayala, 1971, 2d edit., 2005, Poética (Ignacio de Luzán), 1977, Comedias (Tomás de Iriarte), 1978, 2d edit., 1986, Gustavo Adolfo Bécquer (antología crítica), 1985, Vida (Diego de Torres Villarroel), 1985, Rimas (Gustavo Adolfo Bécquer), 1991, author, editor (with David T. Gies) Ilustración y neoclasicismo, 1992, Noches Iúgubres (José de Cadalso), 1993, author, editor (with Jesus Perez Magallon) El hombre practico (Conde de Fernán Nuñez), 1996, Cartas marruecas, Noches Iúgubres (Jose de Cadalso), 1999, 5th edit., 2005, gen. editor Hispanic Rev., 1968—97, adv. editor Eighteenth Century Studies, 1983—, Cuadernos para Investigación de la Literatura Hispánica, 1987—, El Gnomo, 1992—, Dieciocho, 1994—, Siglo XIX, 1995—, Salina, 1999—, columnist ABC newspaper, Madrid, 1985—; contbr. articles to profl. jours. Recipient Elio Antonio de Nebrija Internat. prize, U. Salamanca, 2001; grantee, Am. Philos. Soc., 1971, 1976, 1982; Guggenheim fellow, 1962—63, Am. Coun. Learned Socs. fellow, 1979—80. Mem.: Hispanic Soc., Am., Sociedad de Literatura Española del Siglo XIX, Ctr. 18th Century Studies (Oviedo, Spain), Am. Assn. Tchrs. French, Am. Assn. Tchrs. Spanish and Portuguese, Sigma Delta Pi, Phi Gamma Delta, Phi Beta Kappa. Episcopalian. Home: 16 Flintshire Rd Malvern PA 19355-1108 Office: U Pa Dept Romance Langs Philadelphia PA 19104-6305 E-mail: rpsebold@earthlink.net.

**SEBOROVSKI, CAROLE,** artist; b. San Diego, June 16, 1960; d. Stanley and Eleanor Ononsko S. BFA, Calif. Coll. Arts and Crafts, 1982; MFA, Hunter Coll., 1987. Artist: solo exhibitions include: Damon Brandt Gallery, N,Y.C., 1986, Hunter Coll. Art Gallery, N,Y.C., 1986, Lorence-Monk Gallery, N,Y.C., 1988, 89, Galerie Karsten Greve, Paris, 1991, 94, 2003, Cologne, 1992, 2004, Milan, 1995, 2001, Angles Gallery, Santa Monica, Calif., 1991, 92, 93, 96, Betsy Senior Contemporary Prints, N,Y.C., 1993, John Weber Gallery, N,Y.C., 1993, 95, John Berggruen Gallery, San Francisco, 1994, Locks Gallery, Phila., 1997, Karsten Greve, Koln, 1997, Galerie Karsten Greve, Milan, Italy, 1997, 2001, John Weber Gallery, N,Y.C., 1998, Cheryl Haines Gallery, San Francisco, 2000, 2002, Mitchell-Innes and Nash Gallery, N,Y.C., Miller Block Gallery, Boston, 2001; group exhbns. at: Willard Gallery, N,Y.C., 1984, Nora Haime Gallery, N,Y.C. 1985, 86, 93, 95, 2002, Manhattan Arts Ctr., N,Y.C., 1985, Hillwood Art Gallery L.I. Univ., Brookville, N.Y., 1985, Damon Brandt Gallery, 1985, 86 (2), 87, Mus. de Arte, La Tertuila, Columbia, 1986, Weatherspoon Gallery, Greensboro, N.C., 1986, Barbara Krakow Gallery, Boston, 1986, 88, 90 (travels to John C. Stoller & Co., Mpls.), Anne Plumb Gallery, N,Y.C., 1987, Am. Acad. and Inst. Arts and Letters, 1987, Bklyn. Mus., 1987, Lorence-Monk Gallery, 1987, 89 (3), 90, 91 (2), Carnegie Mellon U. Art Gallery, Pitts., 1988, Reynolds/ Minor Gallery, Richmond, Va., 1988, John Good Gallery, N,Y.C., 1988, 92, Pamela Auchincloss Gallery, N,Y.C., 1988, Dart Gallery, Chgo., 1988, Angles Gallery, 1989, Persons & Lindell Gallery, Helsinki, Finland, 1989, Anderson Gallery Va. Commonwealth U., Richmond, 1989, Baxter Gallery, Richmond, 1989, Hillwood Art Gallery, Brookville (travels through 1991 to Blum Helman Gallery, N,Y.C., Richard F. Brush Gallery, Canton, N.Y., Contemporary Mus. Art, Caracas, Venezuela), Cheryl Haines Gallery, San Francisco, 1989, 94, 96, 2003, Security Pacific Corp. Gallery, Santa Monica, 1990, Meml. Art Gallery U. Rochester, N.Y., 1990, Hood Mus. Art Dartmouth Coll., Hannover, N.H., 1990, San Francisco Mus. of Art, 1991, Pfizer, Inc. (Mus. Modern Art, N.Y. Collection), 1991, John Berggruen Gallery, 1991, travelling exhbn. to Anthony Ralph Gallery at Earl McGrath, L.A., Mars Gallery, Tokyo, Katonah Mus. Art, N.Y., Ind. U. Fine Arts Gallery, Kerr Gallery, Alberta Coll. of Art, Can., Huntsville Mus. Art, Ala., Worcester Art Mus., Mass., Lamont Gallery N.H., San Diego State U. Gallery, 1992, Barbara Mathes Gallery, N,Y.C., 1993, Transamerica Pyramid Lobby, San Francisco, 1993, travelling exhbn. to The Drawing Ctr., N.Y., Corcoran Gallery Art, Washington, Santa Monica Mus., L.A., The Forum, St. Louis, Am. Ctr., Paris, 1993, Addison Gallery Andover, Mass., 1994, John Weber Gallery, 1994, 96, Huntington Gallery Mass. Coll. Art, Boston, 1995, Rice U. Art Gallery, Houston, 1995, The Altered Stages, N.Y., 1995, Brooke Alexander Gallery, N,Y.C., 1995, Thread Waxing Space, N.Y., 1996, Duchess County C.C., N.Y., 1996, Gallery 7, Hong Kong, 1996, Century Club, N,Y.C., 1996, Dutchess Coll., N.Y., 1997, Vassar Coll., Poughkeepsie, N.Y., 1997, Mus. Cantonale d'Arte, Lugano, Switzerland, 1997, Kunst-Mus., Aiken, Germany, 1998, Kunstmus., Winterhur, Switzerland, 1998, Acad. der Kunste, Berlin, 1999, Mitchell-Innes and Nash, N,Y.C., Nohra Haime Gallery, N,Y.C., 2002, Maragaret Thatcher Projects, N,Y.C., 1999, 2002, San Francisco Mus. Modern Art, Calif., 2000, Block Mus., Chgo., 2000, Contemporary Mus., Honolulu, 2000, Fogg Art Mus., 2000, Neuberger Mus. Art, Purchase, NY, 2000, Lyman Allyn Mus, Conn., 2000, Yale Art Gallery, 2002, Bertha and Karl Leubsdorf Art Gallery, N,Y.C., 2002, Charles Cowles Gallery, N,Y.C., 2002, Krannert Art Gallery, Ill., 2002, Anthony Grant, Inc., 2003, Cin. Art Mus., 2003, The Workspace, N,Y.C., 2003, others; represented in permanent collections including Whitney Mus. Art, N.Y., Paine Webber, N.Y., Weatherspoon Art Gallery, Greensboro, N.C., J. Walter Thompson, N.Y., Refco Collection, Chgo., Panza Collection, Italy, San Francisco Mus. Modern Art, Mus. Modern Art, N.Y., Mus. Cantonale d'Arte, Lugano, Switzerland, Met. Mus. Art, N.Y., Merril Lynch Inc., N.Y., MIT Visual Ctr., Hood Mus. Art, Hanover, N.H., Fogg Art Mus., Harvard U., Cambridge, Mass., Cleve. Ctr. Contemporary Art, Chase Manhattan Bank, N.Y., Carnegie Mus. Art, Pitts., Bklyn. Mus., Balt. Mus., Anderson Collection, Calif., Addison Gallery, Phillips Acad., Andover, Mass., Bklyn. Mus., Yale U. Art Gallery, Wadsworth Atheneum, Conn., Tel Aviv Mus., Nat. Gallery Art, Washington. Grantee Pollock-Krausner Found., 1986, NEA, 1991, Art Devel. Com., 1997; named Artist in Residence, Villa Monalvo, Saratoga, Calif., 1989, Djerassi Found., Calif., 1990; Agnes Bourne fellow in visual arts, 1990. Home: 171 E 81st St Apt #3A New York NY 10028

**SEBRANEK, JOSEPH G.,** science educator; b. Richland Center, Wis., Feb. 22, 1948; s. Marvin Joseph and Elsie Margaret Sebranek; m. Annette Kay Marshall, Jan. 17, 1970; children: Amy Christina, Abby Joanna Theresa. BS, U. Wis., Platteville, 1970; MS, U. Wis., Madison, 1971, PhD, 1974. Asst. prof. Iowa State U., Ames, 1975—79, assoc. prof., 1979—84, prof., 1984—. Fellow: Inst. Food Techs.; mem.: Am. Soc. Animal Sci. (Meat Rsch. award 2005), Am. Meat Sci. Assn. (pres. 2002—03, Disting. Tchg. award 1995). Office: Iowa State U 215 Meat Lab Ames IA 50011 Business E-Mail: sebranek@iastate.edu.

**SEBRIS, ROBERT, JR.,** lawyer; b. NYC, May 20, 1950; s. Robert and Ruth (Kagis) Sebris; m. S. Lawson Hollweg, Sept. 8, 1973; children: Jared Matthew, Bryan Taylor. BS in Indsl. Labor Rels., Cornell U., 1972; JD, George Washington U., 1978. Bar: DC 1978, Wash. 1980. Labor rels. specialist Onondaya County Office labor rels., Syracuse, NY, 1973-74, U.S. Dept. Labor, Washington, 1972-75; labor rels. mgr. U.S. Treasury Dept.,

Washington, 1975-78, employee rels. mgr., 1978-80; assoc. Davis, Wright, Todd, Riese & Jones, Seattle, 1980-84; ptnr. Davis, Wright, Tremain, Bellevue, Wash., 1985-92, Sebris Busto James, Bellevue, 1992—. Expert witness Amendments NLRA US Senate hearing, 1997. Co-author: (book) Employer's Guide to Strike Planning, 1985; contbr. articles to profl. jours. Mem. Bellevue CC Found., 1988—95, pres., 1995—96; chair employment law cert. program U. Wash. Law Sch., 1996—97. Mem.: ABA (health law forum, labo and employment law sect., mem. com. employee rights), Soc. Human Resource Mgmt., Am. Health Lawyers Assn., Pacific Coast Labor Law Conf. (planning com. 1980—93, chmn. 1991—92), Seattle/King County Bar Assn. (chmn. labor law sect. 1991—92), DC Bar Assn., Wash. Bar Assn. Avocation: golf. Home: 16301 Mink Rd NE Woodinville WA 98072-9463 Office: Sebris Busto James Ste 325 14205 SE 36th St Bellevue WA 98006 Office Phone: 425-450-0300. Business E-Mail: rsebris@sebrisbusto.com.

**SECCHIA, PETER F.,** forest products executive, former United States ambassador to Italy; b. Englewood, NJ, Apr. 15, 1937; s. Charles P. and Valerie Margaret (Smith) S.; m. Joan Peterson, 1960; children: Mark, Charles, Sandra, Stephanie. BS, Mich. State Univ., 1962; AA (hon.), Grand Rapids Cmty. Coll., 1993; LLD (hon.), Grand Valley State Univ., 1990, Davenport Coll., 1993, Cooley Law Sch., 1993; HHD (hon.), Mich. State Univ., 1997. Positions through v.p. sales Universal Forest Products, Grand Rapids, Mich., 1962—71, dir., 1967—, chmn., pres., CEO, 1971—89, chmn. 1993—2006, chmn. emeritus, 2006; U.S. Amb. to Italy, 1989—93. Chmn. River City Food Co.; mng. ptnr. SIBSCO LLC. Mem. exec. com. Gerald R. Ford Found., past chmn. endowment com.; trustee Bush Presdl. Libr. Found., James A. Baker III Inst. Pub. Policy, Rice Univ, John Cabot Univ., Rome; Mich. del. Rep. Nat. Convention, 1976, 1980, 1984; mem. Rep. Nat. Com., 1980—89, vice chmn. Midwest region, 1984—89; co-chmn. Dole for Pres. Nat. Campaign, 1995—96. Served to sgt. USMC, 1956—59. Named Master Entrepeneur of the Year, 1994, Businessman of the Year, Econ. Club We. Mich., 1995; recipient Cavaliere di Gran Croce, Govt. of Italy, Disting. Honor award, U.S. Dept. State, 1993, Louis A. Smith Disting. Jurist award, Cooley Law Sch., 1993, Michelangelo D'Oro Children of the World award, 1993, Peace award, Internat. Commn. for Peace. Mem.: Council of Am. Ambassadors. Republican. Methodist. Office: Universal Forest Products 2801 East Beltline NE Grand Rapids MI 49525*

**SECHREST, LARRY JAMES,** economist, educator; b. Detroit, Oct. 12, 1946; s. Howard J. and Frances C. Sechrest; children: J. Kyle R. Tara. BA in History, U. Tex., Arlington, 1968, MA in Econs., 1985, PhD in Econs., 1990. Instr. U. Tex., Arlington, 1985-90; prof. econs. Sul Ross State U., Alpine, Tex., 1990—. Adj. scholar Ludwig von Mises Inst., Auburn, Ala., 1996—; rsch. fellow Ind. Inst., Oakland, Calif.; found. scholar Found. Advancement of Monetary Edn., 1996—; bd. advisors Def. of Freedom Found., Newport Beach, Calif. Author: Free Banking, 1993; co-editor (with Jorg Guido Hulsmann): Capital and Production, 2000; co-editor: (with Chris M. Sciabarra) (spl. issue) Jour. Ayn Rand Studies, —; mem. editl. bd.: Quar. Jour. Austrian Econs., 1996—, ICFAI Jour. Pub. Fin., —, bd. advisors: Jour. Ayn Rand Studies, 1999—; contbr. chapters to books, articles to profl. jours. Fellow Inst. Humane Studies, Fairfax, Va., 1987-88; listed Guide to Pub. Policy Experts, Heritage Found., Washington, 2000. Mem. Nat. Assn. Scholars, U.S. Naval Inst., Assn. Pvt. Enterprise Edn., The Hist. Soc., Soc. Devel. Austrian Econs., Internat. Maritime Econ. History Assn., So. Econ. Assn., N.Y. Acad. Scis. Libertarian. Avocations: maritime history, yacht design, firearms, marine art, golf. Office: Sul Ross State U 400 N Harrison St Alpine TX 79832-8300 Office Phone: 432-837-8069. Business E-Mail: larrys@sulross.edu.

**SECHRIST, CHALMERS FRANKLIN, JR.,** electrical engineering educator; b. Glen Rock, Pa., Aug. 23, 1930; s. Chalmers F. and Lottie V. (Smith) S.; m. Lillian Beatrice Myers, June 29, 1957; children: Jonathan A., Jennifer N. BE in Elec. Engring., Johns Hopkins U., 1952; MS, Pa. State U., 1954, PhD in Elect. Engring., 1959. Sr. engr. Bendix Corp., summers 1952, 53, 54; instr. elec. engring. Pa. State U., 1954-55; staff engr. HRB-Singer, Inc., State College, Pa., 1959-65; from asst. prof. to prof. elec. engring. U. Ill., Urbana, 1965-96, assoc. head instructional programs dept. elec. and computer engring., 1984-86, asst. dean engring. 1986-96, prof. Emeritus, 1996—; program dir. divsn. undergrad. edn. NSF, Washington, 1992-96; adj. prof. engring. Fla. Gulf Coast U., 1998—. Acting sci. sec. Sci. Com. on Solar-Terrestrial Physics, 1981; chmn. publs. com. Middle Atmosphere Program, 1980-86, editor handbook, 1981-86; mem. adv. com. on tech. edn. Fla. Dept Edn., 2001-2005 Editor: Proc. Aeronomy Confs, 1965, 69, 72; contbr. articles to profl. jours. Grantee NSF. Fellow: IEEE (edn. activities bd. 1990, tech. activities bd. 1991—92, edn. activities bd. 1992—93, chmn. com. on pre-coll. edn. ednl. activities bd. 1997—99, edn. activities bd. 1997—99, awards and recognition com. edn. activities bd. 2000—01, oversight subcom. Virtual Mus. 2000—02, precoll. edn. coord. com. edn. activities bd. 2000—03, Millennium medal 2000); mem.: Internat. Tech. Edn. Assn., Am. Soc. Engring. Edn., Am. Meteorol. Soc., Am. Geophys. Union, Edn. Soc. of IEEE (v.p. 1989—90, pres. 1991—92, Achievement award 1993). Office Phone: 239-454-0640. Personal E-mail: csechrist@comcast.net.

**SECK, MAMADOU MANSOUR,** ambassador, military officer; b. Dakar, Senegal, July 3, 1935; children: Ndeye, Safi, Makana, Astou Dior, Sonia Penda. Attended. St. Cyr Milit. Acad., France, Salon Air Force Acad., French Air War Coll., Institut des Hautes Etudes de la Def. Nat. Commanding officer 1st Senegalese Air Force Squad, 1966; comdr. 1st Senegalese Air Force, 1972; dep. chief gen. staff, 1980-84; spl. chief of staff to Pres. of Republic of Senegal, chief of staff of Sene-Gambia Confedn., 1984; gen. chief of staff, gen. chief Confedn., 1988; chmn. Joint Chiefs of Staff of Senegal, 1988-93; amb. to U.S. Govt. of Republic of Senegal, 1993—; amb. to Mex., Argentina, Jamaica, Haiti, Trinidad and Tobago, Barbados, 1993—. Decorated Senegal, France, Gabon, Hollan, Luxembourg. Office: Embassy of Republic of Senegal 2112 Wyoming Ave NW Washington DC 20008-3926

**SECORD, LLOYD DOUGLAS,** health facility administrator; b. Lachine, Que., Can., Nov. 22, 1946; s. George William and Gladys Mable (Wilson) S.; m. Louise Margaret Morrison, Dec. 21, 1966; children: Steven Lloyd, Gordon Arthur, Mary Elizabeth. BS in Chemistry, U. New Brunswick, 1968; M of Adminstrn., U. Toronto, Ont., Can., 1970. Cert. accreditation surveyor Can. Coun. on Health Facilities, 1990-92. Adminstrv. resident Toronto East Gen. and Orthopaedic Hosp., 1969-70; adminstrv. asst. Moncton Hosp., summer 1968, asst. adminstr., 1970-75; exec. dir. Kiwanis Nursing Home Inc., 1975—; facility adminstr. Region 2 Hosp. Corp., Sussex, N.B., Canada, 1992-98; sec. Sussex Health Ctr. Svcs. Inc., Bryant Dr. Holdings Inc., 1975—, CEO, adminstr. Sussex Hosp., 1975-98; region dir. capital projects Atlantic Health Scis. Corp., 1999—2003. Chmn. adv. com. Min. Health; mem. Fundy Linen Svcs. Inc., 1976-92; mem. regional hosp. planning com. Health Region II, 1974-76; commr. of oaths, 1975—. Bd. dirs. Atlantic Bapt. Sr. Citizen's Home Inc., 1973-79, original bldg. com., 1971-74, rec. sec., 1971-74, plng. bldg. com.; founding chmn. County. Based Svcs. Coord. Com. for Sussex, 1981; founding pres. Sussex Sr. Housing Inc., 1981, 82; established Sussex Health Ctr. Svcs. Inc., 1991, Bryant Dr. Holdings Inc., 1992-93; founding sec. Kings County Wellness Ctr., 1997; bd. trustees, bd. deacons Sussex United Bapt. Ch.; dir. Sussex br. Order of St. John, 1976-78, 90-92; trombonist Sussex Comty. Adult Band, 1989—; sec. Kings County Wellness Ctr., 1997—. Lord Beaverbrook scholar, Leonard Found. scholar. Fellow Can. Coll. Health Svc. Execs., Soc. Mgmt. Accts. Can. (cert., mem. provincial coun. 1977-88, provincial sec-treas. 1982, provincial chmn. 1987, nat. edn. svcs. com. 1985, 86, nat. bd. dirs. 1986, 87, nat. strategic planning com. 1986); mem. New Brunswick Hosp. Assn. (numerous provincial coms.), New Brunswick Assn. Nursing Homes (numerous provincial coms.), Northeastern Can./Am. Health Coun. (Can. co-chmn 1991-94, co-chair internat. mini conf. on rural health care New London, N.H. 1988, chair bi-nat. conf. Montreal 1991), Provincial Ambulance Operators Assn. (exec. com. 1990-96), Sussex and Dist. C. of C. (pres. 1985, 2005), Kiwanis Club Sussex Inc. (pres. 1985, 99). Avocations: band, golf, gardening, painting, education. Office: Kiwanis Nursing Home 11 Bryant Dr Sussex NB Canada E4E 2P3 Office Phone: 506-432-3207. Personal E-mail: l2secord@nbnet.nb.ca.

**SECREST, GEORGE MCCALL, JR.,** lawyer; b. Laredo, Tex., Jan. 5, 1952; BA, U. Houston, 1974; JD with distinction, St. Mary's U. Sch. Law, 1977. Admitted: Tex. 1977, US Ct. Appeals, 5th Cir. 1981, US Dist. Ct., No. So., Ea. & We. Dists. Tex. 1982, US Supreme Ct. 1984, US Ct. Appeals, 11th Cir. 1989, US Ct. Appeals 6th Cir. 1990. Briefing atty. Tex. Ct. Criminal Appeals, 1977—78; asst. dist. atty. Harris County, Tex., 1978—81; asst. fed. pub. defender So. Dist. Tex., 1981—83; adj. prof. law So. Tex. Coll. Law, 1984, U. Houston, 1994—2003; mem. Bennett & Secrest, LLP, Houston, 2003—. Mem. Gov.'s Ad Hoc Com. to Revise the Tex. Code of Criminal Procedure, 1995—96, Tex. Bd. Legal Specialization Exam Commn., Criminal Law. Named one of Best Lawyers in Am., 1997—2005. Mem.: Nat. Assn. Criminal Def. Lawyers, Tex. Criminal Def. Lawyer's Assn., Harris County Criminal Lawyers Assn. (treas. 1996—97), Houston Bar Assn., State Bar Tex. (Criminal Def. Lawyer of Yr. 1998), Bar Assn. 5th Fed. Cir., John Harlan Soc. Office: Bennett & Secrest LLP 24th Fl Esperson Bldg 808 Travis St Houston TX 77002 Office Phone: 713-757-0679. Office Fax: 713-650-1602.*

**SECREST, GLENDA,** music educator; MusB, Ariz. State U., 1978, MusM, 1985; DMA, U. of Memphis, 2000. Asst. prof. music Manhattan (Kans.) Christian Coll., 1984—87; instr. music Chandler/Gilbert (Ariz.) C.C., 1989—90, Cameron U., Lawton, Okla., 1990—93; assoc. prof. music Ouachita Bapt. U., Arkadelphia, Ark., 1995—. Recipient M. May Robertson scholarship, So. Bapt. Found., 1997—2000, doctoral fellowship, U. of Memphis, 1997. Mem.: Nat. Assn. Tchrs. of Singing (pres.-elect 2002—04, chosen to perform and lectr. at nat. conf. 2004), Nat. Assn. of Teachers of Singing (pres. Ark. chpt. 2004—06), Pi Kappa Lambda, Sigma Alpha Iota Alumni Assn. Office Phone: 870-245-5131.

**SECULA, JENNIFER MICHELE,** psychologist; b. Annapolis, Md., May 20, 1973; d. George Melvin and Bonnie Jean Kellenbenz; m. Andrew John Secula, Aug. 8, 1998; children: Andrew John III, Julian Lucas. BA, Salisbury State U., 1975; MA, Towson State U., 1997, CAS, 1998. Sch. psychologist Balt. City Pub. Sch. Sys., 1997—2006, Lincoln Intermediate Unit, 2006—. Mem.: Md. Sch. Psychologists Assn., Nat. Assn. Sch. Psychologists, Balt. City. Assn. Sch. Psychologists (sec. 2002—03, pres. 2004—05), Phi Kappa Phi, Phi Eta Sigma, Psi Chi. Avocations: violin, choral singing, reading, travel. Home: 4 Stonewood Dr Jacobus PA 17407 also: Lincoln Intermediate Unit 12 65 Billerbeck St New Oxford PA Business E-Mail: jmsecula@iu12.org.

**SECULAR, SIDNEY,** actor, writer, fundraiser, consultant; b. N.Y.C., Dec. 20, 1940; s. Benjamin and Mollie (Stern) Secular; m. Mildred Vance, Oct. 31, 1969. BA, SUNY, Stony Brook, 1962. Cert. HS tchr. Contract asst. U.S. Army, Bklyn., 1962-66; contract specialist USN, Washington, 1966-67, FDA, Washington, 1967-68; contracting officer Dept. Justice, Washington, 1968-81; conf./expo organizer, counselor to small bus. SBA, Washington, 1986-97; govt. mktg. cons. to small bus. Silver Spring, Md., 1997—. Mem. consumer bd. Giant Food corp., WSSC Water Utility; freelance writer, Silver Spring, Md., 1985—; weathercaster NOWCAST Weather, Bethesda, Md., 1982—91; weather broadcaster Comprehensive Weather Svcs., 1982—85, Verizon Comm., 1991—; total quality mgmt. cons., 1995—. Activist East Sliver Spring Citizens Assn., 1981—; chief election judge Montgomery County, Md., 1998—. With U.S. Army, 1963—90. Recipient Performance and Suggestion awards, U.S. DEA and SBA. Mem.: Nat. Assn. Active and Retired Fed. Employees, ASPA, Area Small and Disadvantaged Bus. Coun., Am. Meteorol. Soc., Nat. Contract Mgmt. Assn., Ctr. Hiking Club (trails dir. 1975), Masons. Avocations: weather forecasting, entrepreneurial activities, history, voiceovers, musical recording restoration. Home: 740 Silver Spring Ave Silver Spring MD 20910-4661 Office Phone: 301-588-7668. Personal E-mail: SidSecular1@aol.com.

**SECUNDA, EUGENE,** marketing professional, educator; b. Bklyn., June 15, 1934; s. Sholom and Betty (Almer) Secunda; m. Shirley Carol Frummer, Sept. 23, 1961; children: Ruthanne, Andrew. Comml. degree, N.Y. Inst. Photography, 1955; BS, NYU Sch. Bus., 1956; MS, Boston U., 1962; PhD, NYU, 1988. News editor Sta.-WBMS, Boston, 1956-57; reporter New London (Conn.) Daily Day, 1958-59; publicist various Broadway shows, 1959-62; sr. publicist 20th Century Fox Film Corp., N.Y.C., 1962-65; with J. Walter Thompson Co., N.Y.C., 1965-73; dir. corp. and pub. affairs, 1974-78, sr. v.p., dir. entertainment group, 1974-80, dir. entertainment divsn., 1978-80; sr. v.p., dir. comm. svcs. N.W. Ayer Internat., N.Y.C., 1980-82; pres. Barnum/Secunda Assocs., N.Y.C., 1982-85, Secunda Mktg. Comm., N.Y.C., 1985—2005. Adj. prof. media studies NYU, N.Y.C., 1972—2003, prof. mktg. and advt. Grad. Sch. Bus., 1985—88, prof. mktg., 1993—96, adj. prof. mktg. and media studies, 1996—; prof. mktg. and advt. Baruch Coll. CUNY, 1988—93; prof. mktg. Adelphi U., Garden City, NY, 1993—96; guest lectr. FBI Acad., Columbia U., UCLA; Fulbright scholar U. Ljubljana, Slovenia, 2006—. Contbr. articles to profl. jours. Mem. Greenwich Village Hist. With USAR, 1957—63. Mem.: NATAS, Am. Mktg. Assn., Mcpl. Arts Soc., Am. Acad. Advt., Internat. Advt. Assn., Internat. Comm. Assn., Greenwich Village Preservation Soc., Mooring Mates. Address: 30 5th Ave New York NY 10011-8859

**SEDAGHAT-HERATI, REZA,** chemistry professor; b. Yazd, Iran, Nov. 22, 1947; s. Mohammad Sedaghat-Herati and Soltan Farzin; m. Fatemeh Hosseini Firoozabadi, Feb. 17, 1956; children: Ramin, Amin. PhD in Chemistry, U. [illegible], Sep. 1977 Asst. prof. Esfahan U. Tech., Iran, 1977—84, rsch. asst. prof. U. Ala., Huntsville, 1984—90; prof. chemistry Mo. State U., Springfield, 1990—. Author: (rsch.) Synthesis of poly(ethylene glycol) propionaldehyde (Cert. of recognition, NASA, 1992). Achievements include patents for Preparation and use of poly(ethylene glycol) propionaldehyde; Poly(ethylene glycol) Diene Derivatives. Office: Mo State Univ 901 S National Springfield MO 65897 Office Phone: 417-836-6772. Office Fax: 417-836-5507. Business E-Mail: sedaghat-herati@missouristate.edu.

**SEDARIS, AMY,** writer, actress; b. Endicott, NY, Mar. 19, 1961; d. Lou Sedaris. Performer: (TV series) Exit 57, 1995—96; co-writer (TV series) Exit 57, 1995—96, co-creator, 1995—96; performer: (TV series) Strangers With Candy, 1999—2000; co-writer (TV series) Strangers With Candy, 1999—2000, co-creator, 1999—2000; actor(guest appearances): (TV series) Just Shoot Me, Monk, Sex and the City, Ed, Cracking Up.; (films) Commandments, 1997, Bad Bosses Go to Hell, 1997, Six Days Seven Nights, 1998, Jump Tomorrow, 2001, Maid in Manhattan, 2002, The School of Rock, 2003, Elf, 2003, My Baby's Daddy, 2004, Strangers with Candy, 2005, Stay, 2005, Bewitched, 2005, Romance and Cigarettes, 2005, (voice) Chicken Little, 2005, Full Grown Men, 2006; (TV films) Untitled New York Pilot, 2003; (plays) Jamboree, 1993; co-author (with brother David Sedaris): (plays) Jamboree, 1993; actor: (plays) Stump the Host, 1993; co-author (with brother David Sedaris): (plays) Stump the Host, 1993; actor: (plays) One Woman Shoes, 1995; co-author (with brother David Sedaris): (plays) One Woman Shoes, 1995; co-author (with brother David Sedaris): (plays) Froggy, The Country Club, 1998—99 (nominated Drama Desk award, 1999), The Most Fabulous Story Ever Told, 1998—99, The Little Freida Mysteries, 1999; co-author (with brother David Sedaris): (plays) The Little Freida Mysteries, 1997; actor: (plays) The Book of Liz; co-author (with brother David Sedaris): (plays) The Book of Liz, 2001; co-author: (book), 2002; actor: (plays) Drama Department, 2001, Wonder of the World, 2001—02 (Lucille Lortel award for outstanding featured actress League of Off-Broadway Theatres and Prodrs., 2002), (short film) Wheels of Fury, 1998; co-writer (short film) Wheels of Fury, 1998; co-author (with brother David Sedaris): (plays) Stitches, Incident at Cobbler's Knob; co-author: (books) Wigfield: The Can-Do Town That Just May Not, 2003; author: I Like You, 2006. Office: c/o Jonathan Bluman Paradigm 10100 Santa Monica Blvd 25th Fl Los Angeles CA 90067*

**SEDARIS, DAVID RAYMOND,** writer; b. Johnson City, NY, Dec. 26, 1956; s. Lou and Sharon Sedaris. Student, Kent State U.; BFA, Art Inst. Chgo. 1987. Tchr. writing Art Inst. Chgo., 1987—90; commentator Nat. Pub. Radio, 1992—. Author: (books) Barrel Fever: Stories and Essays, 1994, Holidays on Ice, 1997, Naked, 1997, Me Talk Pretty One Day, 2000 (Thurber Prize for Am. Humor, 2001), Dress Your Family in Corduroy and Denim, 2004 (Publishers Weekly Bestseller); co-author (with sister Amy under the name The Talent Family): (plays) Stump the Host, Stitches, 1994, One Woman Shoe, 1995 (Obie award, 1995), Incident at Cobbler's Knob, 1997, The Little Freida Mysteries, 1997, The Book of Liz, 2001; writer: (TV series) Exit 57, 1995; contbg. writer Esquire, The New Yorker. Named Humorist of Yr., Time mag., 2001; recipient Lambda Award, 2001.

**SEDDON, JOHANNA MARGARET,** ophthalmologist, epidemiologist; b. Pitts. BS, U. Pitts., 1970, MD, 1974; MS in Epidemiology, Harvard U., 1976. Intern Framingham (Mass.) Union Hosp., 1974-75; resident Tufts New Eng. Med. Ctr., Boston, 1976-80; fellow ophthalmic pathology Mass. Eye and Ear Infirmary, Boston, 1980-81, clin. fellow vitreoretinal Retina Svc., 1981-82; instr. clin. ophthalmology Harvard Med. Sch., Boston, 1982-84, asst. prof., asst. surgeon ophthalmology, 1984, assoc. prof., 1989—; assoc. surgeon, dir. ultrasound svc. Mass. Eye and Ear Infirmary, Boston, 1989—, founder epidemiology rsch. unit, 1984-85, dir. epidemiology unit, 1985—, surgeon in ophthalmology, 1992—; assoc. prof. faculty dept. epidemiology Harvard Sch. Pub. Health, Boston, 1992—. Mem. com. vision Commn. Behavioral and Social Scis. and Edn., NRC, NAS, Washington, 1984; mem. divsn. rsch. grants NIH, 1987-89, 94—; mem. sci. adv. bd. Found for Fighting Blindness, 1994—, Macular Degeneration Internat., 1994—, adv. panel, Age-Related Macular Degeneration Alliance Internat., spkr. in field; lectr. in field. Author books and articles in field, especially in field of ocular tumors and macular degeneration; mem. editl. staff ophthalmic jours. Recipient NIH Nat. Svc. Rsch. awards, 1975, 80-81, Lewis R. Wasserman Merit award Rsch. to Prevent Blindness for contbns. to ophthalmic rsch., 1996, 1st Maurice Rabb, Jr. award Prevent Blindness Am. Orgn., 2005; grantee, prin. investigator Nat. Eye Inst., 1984—, Nat. Cancer Inst., 1986; med. sch. scholar, 1970-74, Henry H. Clark Med. Edn. Found. scholar, 1973, voted one of Am.'s top ophthalmologists, Consumer Rsch. Coun. Am., 2004. Mem. AMA (Sr. Honor award 2003), APHA, Am. Acad. Ophthalmology (Honor award 1990, Sr. Honor award 2003), Am. Med. Women's Assn., Assn. Rsch. in Vision and Ophthalmology (elected, chair epidemiology com. 1990, trustee clin. vision epidemiology sect. 1992-97, v.p. 1996-97, Spl. Recognition award 1997), Soc. Epidemiologic Rsch., New Eng. Ophthal. Soc., Am. Coll. Epidemiology, Retina Soc., Macula Soc. (mem. com. 2006—), Mass. Soc. Eye Physicians and Surgeons (v.p. 2000-02, mem. com. 2006—), Am. Epidemiol. Soc., Am. Soc. Ret. Surgeons (Hon. award 2005). Achievements include being first to evaluate association between nutrition, dietary antioxidants, and inflammatory biomarkers and age-related macular degeneration. Home: 4 Louisburg Sq Boston MA 02108-1203 E-mail: jseddon@earthlink.net.

**SEDDON, PRISCILLA TINGEY,** painter; b. Boston, Apr. 1, 1938; d. Richard Hume and Mildred Gurina (Lundgren) Tingey; m. James Alexander Seddon, Jr., Nov. 28, 1959; children: Amy, Sarah, Carroll, Alice. BFA, Tufts U., 1989; Cert., Sch. of the Mus. of Fine Arts, Boston, 1990, Postgrad. 5th Yr., 1991. Associated with Imagining Angels: World AIDS Day Show, Howard Yezersky Gallery, Boston, 1995, others. Exhbns. include: U. Bridgeport, Conn., 1997, Gallery 84, N.Y.C., 1996, Erector Square Gallery, New Haven, Conn., 1996, Harvard U., Cambridge, Mass., 1996, ArtsWorcester Gallery, Worcester, Mass., 1995, Wellesley Coll., Mass., 1994, Grove Street Gallery, Worcester, 1993, Carvajal Sculpture Gallery, Boston, 1992; works include metal work, paintings and sculptures. Grantee MIT Coun. for Arts, Cambridge, 1988, Firstnight, Inc., Boston, 1991, Hingham Edn. Found., Mass., 1993. Mem. Womens Caucus for Art, Visual AIDS. Avocation: watercolour.

**SEDEI RODDEN, PAMELA JEAN,** psychologist, director; b. Johnstown, Pa., Jan. 31, 1956; d. Joseph and Betty Ruth (Watkins) Sedei; m. William Eugene Rodden, Dec. 4, 1982; 1 child, Gretchen Jean Rodden. BA, Southwestern Coll., Winfield, Kans., 1977; MS, Pittsburg (Kans.) State U., 1979; PhD, Western Colo. U., 1983. Lic. profl. counselor Colo., diplomate in psychotherapy, cert. cognitive behavior therapist, nat. cert. counselor, domestic violence counselor, criminal justice specialist. Staff psychologist Autumn Manors Inc., Florence, Kans., 1982-83; clin. psychologist Richmond (Tex.) State Hosp., 1984-86; unit psychologist Wheat Ridge (Colo.) Regional Ctr., 1986-89, acting unit dir., 1989; dir. behavioral svcs. Colo. State Divsn. Devel. Disabilities, Denver, 1989-97; dir. Forensic Mental Health Svcs., Boulder, Colo., 1997—2001, Pamela JS Rodden & Assocs., Fort Collins, Colo. 2001—. Dir. Rodden Consultants, Longmont, Colo., 1986—90, Rodden Assocs., 2001—. Co-author: A Model For Interdisciplinary On Site Evaluation of People Who Have Dual Diagnosis, 1991. Fellow: Am. Coll. Forensic Examiners; mem.: ACA, Assn. Treatment of Sexual Abusers (clin. mem.). Republican. Roman Catholic. also: 315 W Oak St Ste 204 Fort Collins CO 80521-2724 Office Phone: 970-482-8553. E-mail: Pjsrodden@juno.com.

**SEDELMAIER, J. J.,** filmmaker; b. Chgo., Mar. 11, 1956; s. John Josef and Marie S.; m. Patrice Estella Masters, Nov. 4, 1981. Student, Millikin U., 1974-75; BS in Art, U. Wis., 1979. Asst. animator Perpetual Motion Pictures, N.Y.C., 1981-82; asst. animator, animator Buzzco Prodns., N.Y.C., 1982-84, The Ink Tank Corp., N.Y.C., 1984-85, producer, 1985-86, exec. producer, 1986-88, assoc. dir., dir., exec. producer rep., 1989-91; pres., producer, dir. J. J. Sedelmaier Prodns., White Plains, N.Y.. 1991—. Launched Beavis and Butthead for MTV-(Art Dirs. Club gold medal, BDA awards, Comm. awards, Hatch awards; subject of retrospectives: Ottawa Animation Festival, 1997, Cinematique Quebecoise, 1997; acclaimed series of cartoons for "Saturday Night Live", animated peacocks for NBC, Captain Linger series for Cartoon Network: co-creator Ambiguously Gay Duo, X Presidents, Fun with Real Audio; prodr. (3 episodes) Schoolhouse Rock; prodr., dir. Harvey Birdman Attorney@Law; vis. artist Sch. Visual Arts, assisted in saving and restoration of Dempster St. terminal, Skokie, Ill., adv. bd., Mercy Coll. Prodr., dir. Saturday TV Funhouse, Captain Linger, Harvey Birdman-Attorney at Law. Recipient Annecy Film Festival, France, N.Y. Festivals, Annie award, Mobius award, medal Multiple N.Y. Festivals, Multiple Worldfest. Mem. Am. Inst. Graphic Artists, Assn. Internat. Film Animation, Art Dirs. Club (2 Gold medals, honored guest San Diego Comic Conv., 2005), Shore Line Interurban Hist. Soc., Chgo. Transit Posters Archtl. Restoration. Achievements include successful in arranging landmark status on National Register of historic places for studio building in White Plains, N.Y. Avocations: collecting illustrations, animation art, animation film cons, architecture. Office: 199 Main St White Plains NY 10601-3200 Office Phone: 914-949-7979. Personal E-mail: sedelmaier@aol.com.

**SEDELMAIER, JOHN JOSEF,** filmmaker; b. Orrville, Ohio, May 31, 1933; s. Josef Heinrich and Anne Isabel (Baughman) S.; m. Barbara Jean Frank, June 6, 1965; children: John Josef, Nancy Rachel, Adam Frederich. BFA, Art Inst. Chgo. at U. Chgo., 1955. Dir. art Young and Rubicam, Chgo., 1955-61; dir. art, assoc. creative dir. Clinton E. Frank, Chgo., 1961-64; dir. art, producer J. Walter Thompson, Chgo., 1964-67; pres. Sedelmaier Film Prodns., Chgo., 1967—. Spkr. Brit. design and art direction Lectr. Series, London, 1998; spkr. Harvard Bus. Sch., 2003. Exhibitions include Mus. Broadcast Comms., Chgo., 1988, Mus. Broadcasting, LA, 1991, Mus. TV and Radio, NYC, 1992, Represented in permanent collections Acad. TV Arts and Scis. Archive; dir.: (films) OpenMinds, 2003 (Sundance Film Festival Official Selection, 2003). Recipient Golden Ducat award for short film MROFNOC Mannheim Film Festival, 1968, Golden Gate award for short film Because That's Why, San Francisco Film Festival, 1969, 82 Clio awards, 1968-92, numerous Gold, Silver and Bronze Lion awards Cannes Film Festival, 1972-90, Gold Hugo award Chgo. Film Festival, 1976, 91, 2d Ann. IDC Creative award, Chgo., 1980, Internat. Broadcasting award for world's best TV comml., 1980, 86, Clio award for dir. of yr., 1981, London Internat. Advt. awards, 1986-88, numerous awards Internat. Festival of NY, 1984-93, Ann. Achievement award Assn. Ind. Comml. Producers, 1988; named Advt. Person of Yr., Chgo. Advt. Club, 1984, Jewish Communicator of Yr., 1985; named one of 50 Pioneers & Visionaries Who Made TV America's Medium, Advt.

Age Mag., 1995; profiled in Communication Arts mag., Mar. 1976, Print mag., Jan. 1982, Fortune mag., June 1983, Newsweek mag., Nov. 1986, numerous others; featured on 60 Minutes, 48 Hours; subject of cover story Esquire mag., Aug. 1983; included in Arts & Entertainment's Top 10 Greatest Commls. of All Time, 1999; inducted The Art Dirs. Hall Fame, 2000; body of work and interview made part of permanent collections Acad. TV Arts and Scis. Archive, 2006. Office: Sedelmaier Film Prodns Inc 858 W Armitage Ave # 267 Chicago IL 60614-4329 Office Phone: 312-822-0110. Personal E-mail: sedelmaier@hotmail.com.

**SEDEÑO, EUGENE RAYMOND,** electrical engineer, consultant; b. Honolulu, Aug. 31, 1952; s. Josephine Marie Sedeño Rosa; m. Theresa Ann Contreras, Dec. 28, 1980; children: Roxanne Guadelupe, Raymond Contreras, Darrell Kealoha Albright. ASET, Heald Engring. Coll., 1974; BSEE, Coll. Allied Sci., 1980; MBA, Calif. Coast U., 2002. Field svc. engr. Bausch & Lomb, San Leandro, Calif., 1974—81; project mgr. Tylan Corp., Carson, Calif., 1981—85; field svc. supr. Sci. Atlanta, Santa Fe Springs, Calif., 1985—86; facilities and systems engr. Refractory Composites, Inc., Whittier, Calif., 1986—90, cons., 1985—91; supr. test and integration Thermco Systems, Orange, Calif., 1989—90; field engring. So. Calif. Edison, 1990—. With U.S. Army, 1970—76. Mem. Am. Mgmt. Assn., Mensa. Democrat. Roman Catholic. Avocations: kenpo karate, kobudo, kajukenbo, photography, collecting antique books. Home: 16137 Minnetonka St Victorville CA 92395-9146 Office: So Calif Edison 12353 Hesperia Rd Victorville CA 92395-4797 Office Phone: 760-951-3132. Office Fax: 760-951-3115. Business E-Mail: Eugene.Sedeno@sce.com.

**SEDERBAUM, ARTHUR DAVID,** lawyer; b. N.Y.C., Sept. 14, 1944; s. William and Harriet (Warschauer) Sederbaum; m. Francine Haba, Dec. 30, 1967 (div. Aug. 1982); children: Rebecca, David; m. Phyllis Padow, Jan. 18, 1988 (div. Aug. 2002); 1 child, Elizabeth. AB cum laude, Columbia U., 1965, JD, 1968; LLM, NYU, 1972. BAr: N.Y. 1968, Fla. 1980, U.S. Dist. Ct. (so. and ea. dists.) N.Y. 1972. Assoc. Zissu Nelper & Martin, N.Y.C., 1968-70, Berlack, Israels & Liberman, N.Y.C., 1970-72, Rubin Baum Levin Constant & Friedman, N.Y.C., 1972-76; ptnr. Certilman, Haft, Balin, Buckley, Kremer & Hyman, N.Y.C., 1976-88, Olshan, Grundman, Frome, Rosenzweig & Orens, N.Y.C., 1988-92, Patterson, Belknap, Webb & Tyler, L.L.P., N.Y.C., 1992—. Mem. adv. bd. Bur. Nat. Affairs Estates, Gifts and Trusts Jour.; mem. adv. bd. NYU Inst. Fed. Taxation, CCH Fin. and Estate Planning. Author: Setting Up and Executing Trusts, 1988; contbr. articles to Tax Mgmt. Estates, Gifts and Trusts Jour. Recipient J.K. Lasser Tax prize NYU Inst. Fed. Taxation, 1968. Fellow Am. Coll. Trusts and Estates Coun.; mem. ABA, N.Y. State Bar Assn. (vice chmn. com. on estate planning trustees and estates law sect.), Assn. Bar City N.Y. (com. surrogates cts.), Practicing Law Inst. (chmn. income taxatin of estates and trusts program). Office: Patterson Belknap Webb & Tyler LLP Ste 1405 1133 Avenue Of The Americas New York NY 10036-6710 Home: 91 High St Armonk NY 10504-1226 Office Phone: 212-336-2550. E-mail: adsederbaum@pbwt.com.

**SEDERBAUM, WILLIAM,** marketing professional; b. NYC, Dec. 22, 1914; s. Harry and Sarah (Steingart) S.; m. Harriet Warschauer, Aug. 29, 1940 (dec. Mar. 1980); children: Arthur David, Caroline Joan; m. Pearl Lebowitz, Jan. 11, 2003. BS, NYU, 1936, MA, 1943, PhD. Assoc. Sigmund Pines Co., Pub. Accts., 1935-38; tchr. N.Y.C. pub. schs., 1935-39; restaurant propr., 1939-41; v.p. Schenley Distillers Co., N.Y.C., 1941-61; pres. Distbrs. New Eng., 1956-61, Melrose Distillers Co., 1959-60, Park & Tilford Distillers Co., 1959-61; exec. v.p. Meade & Co., 1961-62; v.p., mktg. dir. J. T. S. Brown Distillers Co., 1962-65; mktg. cons., 1965-67; exec. v.p., gen. mgr. Fulton Distbg. Co., 1967-77; asst. gen. mgr., dir. spl. projects Am. Distbrs. Fla., 1977—. Instr. acctg. Fla. Jr. Coll., 1984-89 Mem. Eleanor Roosevelt Cancer Com.; mem. U.S. Olympic Games Com.; exec. com. Fedn. Jewish Charities, March of Dimes; bd. dirs. Jacksonville Urban League, 1975-87; mem. Com. of 100; bus. cons. Jr. Achievement Project, Jacksonville; chmn. bd. trustees, pres. men's club Reform Cong. of Merrick, L.I. Recipient Arch award NYU; named Chevalier, Confrerie de la Chaine des Rotisseurs, Bailliage de Jacksonville, Fla. Mem. Jacksonville Wholesale Liquor Assn. (pres. 1970-76), Jacksonville Symphony Assn., Jacksonville Civic Music Assn., Jacksonville C. of C. (econ. edn. com., airline svc. com., hon. adm. of flag ship Am. Airlines), Kappa Phi Kappa. Clubs: River, Carriage (N.Y.C.); NYU, Playboy, Key. Office: So Wine and Spirits 6867 Stuart Ln S Jacksonville FL 32254-3438 Home: 3820 La Vista Cir Unit 108 Jacksonville FL 32217 *Live life the way it should be-not the way it is.*

**SEDERBURG, WILLIAM ALBERT,** academic administrator, former state senator; b. Chadron, Nebr., Aug. 1, 1947; s. Marion E. and Viola A. (Shalender) S.; m. Joyce I. Witte, July 29, 1972; children: Matthew E., Karl A. BS, Mankato State Coll., 1969; MA, Mich. State U., 1972, PhD, 1974. Faculty dept. polit. sci. Mich. State U., East Lansing, 1973-75; dir. rsch. Ho. Rep. Office, Lansing, 1975-78, exec. dir., 1978; mem. Mich. Senate, Lansing, 1978—90; pres. Ferris State U., Big Rapids, Mich., 1994—2003, UT Valley State Coll., Orem, Utah, 2003—. Mem. appropriations com., 1983-95, chmn. higher edn. and tech. com., health policy com., 1987-95, Mich. Capitol com., 1989-95. Contbr. articles to profl. jours. Bd. dirs. Luth. Social Svcs. Mich. NSF fellow, 1970-73. Mem. Phi Beta Kappa, Kappa Delta Pi. Republican. Office: UT Valley State Coll 800 W Univ Pkwy Orem UT 84058 Business E-Mail: William.Sederburg@uvsc.edu.

**SEDGWICK, ALEXANDER,** retired historian, educator; b. Boston, June 8, 1930; s. William Ellery and Sarah (Cabot) S.; m. Charlene Mary Maute, June 24, 1961; children— Catherine Maria, Alexander Cameron BA, Harvard U., 1952, PhD in History, 1963. Asst. prof. history Dartmouth Coll., 1962-63; assoc. prof. U. Va., Charlottesville, 1963-66, 1966-74, prof., 1974—, chmn. history dept. 1979-83, dean Coll. Arts and Scis., 1985-90, dean grad. studies Charlottesville, 1990-95, univ. prof., 1995-97, univ. prof. emeritus, 1997—; ret., 1997. Mem. adv. com. in history Sr. Fulbright Awards Council for Internat. Exchange of Scholars. Author: The Ralliment in French Politics 1890-98, 1965, The Third French Republic, 1870-1914, 1968, Jansenism in Seventeenth Century France, Voices in the Wilderness, 1977, The Travails of Conscience. The Arnauld Family and the Ancien Regime, 1998; co-author: Church, State and Society Under the Bourbon Kings of France, 1982, For Want of a Horse, 1985, That Gentle Strength, 1980, Les Discour sur les Révolutions, 1991, History Today, 1991, Chroniques de Port-Royal, 1993, 95. Served with U.S. Army, 1952-54. Fulbright fellow, 1960-62; recipient Am. Coun. Learned Socs. grant-in-aid, 1967-68, Am. Philos. Soc. grant-in-aid, 1971. Mem. AAUP (nat. council 1976-79), Soc. French Hist. Studies (sec. 1979-83, pres. 1983-84), Am. Hist. Assn., Century Assn. Home: 1409 Rugby Rd Charlottesville VA 22903-1240 E-mail: as6d@virginia.edu.

**SEDGWICK, JEFFREY LEIGH,** federal agency administrator, political science professor; b. Columbus, Ohio, Dec. 11, 1951; married; 2 children. AB, Kenyon Coll., 1973; MAPA, U. Va., 1975, PhD, 1978. Instr. polit. sci. U. Va., 1975, acting asst. prof., 1977—78; asst. prof. U. Mass., 1978—84, assoc. prof., 1984—2006, grad. program dir., 1987—90, undergrad. program dir., 1997—2001; dep. dir. data analysis Bur. Justice Statistics, US Dept. Justice, Washington, 1984—85, dir., 2006—. Asst. dean Coll. Arts and Scis., 1991—93; assoc. dean, acting dir. Coll. Arts and Scis. Info. and Advising Ctr., 1993—94; vis. assoc. prof. govt. Smith Coll., 1985, 88, 94. Office: US Dept Justice Bur Justice Statistics 810 Seventh St NW Washington DC 20531*

**SEDGWICK, KYRA,** actress; b. NYC, Aug. 19, 1965; m. Kevin Bacon, Sept. 4, 1988; children: Travis, Sosie. Appeared in off-Broadway prodns. Time Was, 1981, Dakota's Belly Wyoming, 1989; stage appearances in Ah Wilderness!, 1988 (Theatre World award), Maids of Honor, 1990, Oleanna, 1994; Actress (films) War and Love, 1985, Tai-Pan, 1986, Kansas, 1988, Born on the Fourth of July, 1989, Mr. and Mrs. Bridge, 1990, Pyrates, 1991, Singles, 1992, Heart and Souls, 1993, Murder in the First, 1995, Something to Talk About, 1995, Losing Chase, 1996, Phenomenon, 1996, Montana, 1997, Critical Care, 1997, Twelfth Night, 1998, The Red Door, 1999, Labor Pains, 1999, What's Cooking, 2000, Just a Kiss, 2002, Behind the Red Door, 2002, Secondhand Lions, 2003, The Woodsman, 2004, Loverboy, 2005; (TV movies) The Man Who Broke 1,000 Chains, 1987, Women & Men II, 1991, Hallmark Hall of Fame, 1992 (Golden Globe award nomination 1993), The Wide Net, 1997, Door to Door, 2002, Cavedweller, 2004, Something the Lord Made, 2004, (TV series) Another World, 1982-83, Talk to Me, 2000, The Closer, 2005-; (mini-series) Family Pictures, 1983; (TV appearances) ABC Afternoon Spls., 1985, Am. Playhouse, 1987, 88, Miami Vice, 1985, Amazing Stories, 1986, Ally McBeal, 2002, Queens Supreme, 2003 Address: WMA 151 S El Camino Dr Beverly Hills CA 90212-2704

**SEDGWICK, TIMOTHY FOSTER**, religion educator; b. Melrose Park, Ill., Dec. 6, 1946; s. Roger Stanley and Virginia May (Karau) S.; m. Martha Wallace Wilkinson, Aug. 24, 1968; children: Sarah Wallace, Ellen Foster. AB, Albion Coll., 1969; PhD, Vanderbilt U., 1975. Asst. prof. Denison U., Granville, Ohio, 1975-76, Marshall U., Huntington, W.Va., 1976-77, Blackburn Coll., Carlinville, Ill., 1977-78; prof. Christian ethics and moral theology Seabury-Western Theol. Sem., Evanston, Ill., 1978—. Mem. adv. bd. Westminster Libr. Theol. Ethics; mem. nat. couns. and coms. Episcopal Ch. Author: Sacramental Ethics, 1987; mem. editorial bd. Anglican Theol. Rev.; also articles. Mem. Soc. Christian Ethics, Conf. Anglican Theologians. Home: 2135 Orrington Ave Evanston IL 60201-2936 Office: Seabury-Western Theol Sem 2122 Sheridan Rd Evanston IL 60201-2976

**SEDIGHI, ARTIN**, application developer, researcher; b. Shiraz, Iran, July 13, 1976; arrived in U.S., 1990; s. Mousa and Flora Sedighi. BSEE, Rensselaer Poly Inst., 1998, MS, 2004. Software engr. GTE, Waltham, Mass., 1999—2000, Lavastorm.com, Waltham, Mass., 2000—01; cons. Tibco Software, N.Y., 2001—03; software arch. SIAC/NYSE, N.Y., 2003—04, Tibco Software, N.Y., 2004—05, DataSynapse, NY, 2005—. Contbr. articles to profl. jour., scientific papers to meetings, workshops and confs. Mem.: IEEE, Assn. for Computing Machinery, Eta Kappa Nu, Chi Phi. Republican. Jewish. Avocations: jazz, photography. Office Phone: 917-856-5892. Business E-Mail: sediga@alum.rpi.edu.

**SEDIGH SARVESTANI, SAHRA**, engineering educator; b. Shiraz, Iran; d. Rahmat Sedigh Sarvestani and Mahboobeh Ayatollahzadeh; m. Shoukat Ali. BSEE, Sharif U. Tech., Iran, 1995; MSEE, Purdue U., 1998, PhD, 2003. Cert. Applied Management Principles Krannert Grad. Sch. Mgmt. Purdue U., 2001. Grad. rsch. asst. Purdue U., West Lafayette, Ind., 1996—2003, Cisco Sys., Inc., San Jose, Calif., 1997—2000; instr. Purdue U., West Lafayette, 2002—03; lectr. U. Mo., Rolla, 2003—04, asst. prof., 2004—. Author: (article) IEEE Computer, (book chpt.) Component-Based Software Quality: Methods and Techniques. Recipient Student award, Internat. Symposium on Software Reliability Engring., 2000; Grad. Rsch. fellow, Purdue Rsch. Found., 1996, 1997, 1999, 2000. Mem.: IEEE, Am. Soc. Engring. Edn., Assn. Computing Machinery, Eta Kappa Nu. Achievements include research in cost and quality management of component-based software; structural and environmental monitoring systems; embedded systems. Office: Univ of Missouri 135 Emerson Electric Co Hall Rolla MO 65409

**SEDLACEK, SARAH LYNN**, publishing executive; b. Kettering, Ohio, Feb. 7, 1971; d. Jerry A. and Marjorie W. Sedlacek. BA cum laude, Kent State U., Ohio, 1993; M.A, U. Cin., Ohio, 1996. Tour coord. Cin. Art Mus., 1996—99, publs. and web site coord., 1999—2003, asst. dir. publs., 2003—. Artist, designer, Dayton, Ky., 2005—. Founder, editor (jour.) Art Words: U. Cin. Studies in Art. Toy shop aux. Salvation Army, Cin., 2003; mktg. com. co-chair No. Ky. Legacy, Covington, 2004; site host Habitat for Humanity, Cin., 2004. Recipient Outstanding Svc. award, U. Cin. Grad. Student Governance Assn., 1995, Outstanding Art History Grad. student, U. Cin. Coll. of DAAP, 1995, 2000 Visual Comm. award, Ohio Museums Assn., 2001. Mem.: Am. Assn. of Museums. Office Phone: 513-639-2952.

**SEDLACK, KASHANNIA LYNN**, history educator; b. Eufaula, Okla., Sept. 6, 1974; d. Doyle Wayne and Nadine M. Shaver; m. Mark Lester Sedlack, Jan. 16, 1999; children: Devan, Kyle, Brett, Kaitlyn. AA in Criminal Justice, Tulsa C.C., Okla., 1999; BA in History, Langston U., Tulsa, 2002. Tchr. and coach Tulsa Pub. Schs., Okla., 2003—04, band Sprngs Schs., 2004—. Coach soccer and basketball ages 6 to 18 yrs. Mem.: Okla. Soccer Coaches Assn., Okla. Secondary Schs. Activities Assn. Office: Sand Springs Schs 305 W 35th St Sand Springs OK 74063 Office Phone: 918-246-1535. Office Fax: 918-246-1544.

**SEDLAK, ROBERT**, academic administrator; BS, Calif. State Coll., Pa., 1968; M Ed, Pa. State Univ., 1970, PhD, 1973. Prof. spl. edn., dir. Office Rsch. U. Wis.-Stout, Menomonie, asst. to dean Sch. Ed. and Human Svcs., 1983—85, asst. dean rsch., 1985—89, assoc. vice chancellor, provost, vice chancellor, 1999—. Office: U Wis-Stout Office of Provost 303 Adminstrn Bldg 712 Broadway Menomonie WI 54751-0790

**SEDLAK, VALERIE FRANCES**, retired English language educator, retired academic administrator; b. Balt., Mar. 11, 1934; d. Julian Joseph and Eleanor Eva (Pilot) Sedlak; 1 child, Barry. AB in English, Coll. Notre Dame of Md., 1955; MA, U. Hawaii, 1962; PhD, U. Pa., 1992. Grad. tchg. fellow East-West Cultural Ctr. U. Hawaii, 1959-60; adminstrv. asst. Korean Consul Gen., 1959-60; tchr. Boyertown (Pa.) Sr. H.S., 1961-63; asst. prof. English U. Balt., 1963-69; assoc. prof. Morgan State U., Balt., 1970-2000, assoc. prof. English emerita, 2001—, asst. dean Coll. Liberal Arts, 1995-2000, sec. to faculty, 1981-83, faculty rsch. scholar, 1982-83, 92-93, comm. officer, 1989-90, dir. writing for TV program, 1990-97; exec. dir. Renaissance Inst. Coll. of Notre Dame of Md., 2000—03, ret., 2003—. Cons. scholar Md. Humanities Coun., 1992—; adj. prof. York (Pa.) Coll., 2004- Author numerous poems and lit. criticism; editor Liberal Arts Rev., 1996-2000; assoc. editor Md. English Jour., 1994-2000; assoc. editor Morgan Jour. Rsch., 1995-2000, CEA mag., 2002—; mem. editl. bd. CEA Critic, 2003—; contbr. articles to lit. jours. Coord. Young Reps., Berks County, Pa., 1962-63; chmn. Md. Young Reps., 1964; election judge Baltimore County, Md., 1964-66; regional capt. Am. Cancer Soc., 1978-79; mem. adv. bd. Md. Our Md. Anniversary, 1984, The Living Constitution: Bicentennial of the Fed. Constitution, 1987. Morgan-Penn Faculty fellow, 1977-79, NEH fellow, 1989; named Outstanding Tchg. prof., U. Balt. Coll. Liberal Arts, 1965, Outstanding Tchg. Prof. in English Dept., Morgan State U., 1987. Mem. MLA, South Atlantic MLA, Coll. Lang. Assn., Coll. English Assn. (Mid-Atlantic Group v.p. 1987-90, pres. 1990-92, exec. bd. 1992-2005, nat. bd. dir. 2001-04, nat. liaison officer 1993-2004), Women's Caucus for Modern Langs., Md. Coun. Tchrs. English, Md. Poetry and Lit. Soc., Md. Acad. Depts. English (bd. dir. 1992—), Mid. Atlantic Writers' Assn. (founding 1981, exec. editor Mid. Atlantic Writers' Assn. Review 1989-2000), Delta Epsilon Sigma (v.p. 1992-94, pres. 1994-96), Pi Kappa Delta Roman Catholic. Home: 17049 Keeney Mill Rd New Freedom PA 17349 Personal E-Mail: vfsedlak@aol.com.

**SEDLER, ROBERT ALLEN**, law educator; b. Pitts., Sept. 11, 1935; s. Jerome and Esther (Rosenberg) S.; m. Rozanne Friedlander, Jan. 24, 1960; children: Eric, Beth. BA, U. Pitts., 1956, JD, 1959. Bar: D.C. 1959, Ky. 1968, Mich. 1979; U.S. Supreme Ct. 1969. Asst. prof., assoc. prof. law St. Louis U., 1961-65; assoc. prof. law, asst. dean Addis Ababa U., Ethiopia, 1963-66; assoc. prof. to prof. law U. Ky., Lexington, 1966-77; prof. law Wayne State U., Detroit, 1977—; disting. prof. law, Gibbs chair civil rights & civil liberty Wayne State Acad. Scholars, Detroit, 2005—06. Author: Across State Lines, 1989: Applying the Conflict of Law to Your Practice, 1989, American Constitutional Law, 2005; (with R. Cramton) The Sum and Substance of Conflict of Laws, 1987, Ethiopian Civil Procedure, 1968; contbr. articles to profl. jours. Gen. counsel ACLU Ky., 1971-76. Named Gershenson Disting. Faculty fellow, Wayne State U., 1985—87. Mem. ABA, AAUP, Phi Beta Kappa, Order of the Coif. Democrat. Jewish. Home: 18851 Capitol Dr Southfield MI 48075-2680 Office: Wayne State U 471 W Palmer Detroit MI 48202-3620 Office Phone: 313-577-3968. Personal E-Mail: rsedler@aol.com. Business E-Mail: rsedler@wayne.edu.

**SEDLER, ROZANNE FRIEDLANDER**, social worker, educator; b. Greensburg, Pa., June 16, 1938; d. Ernest and Belle (Marchel) Friedlander; m. Robert Allen Sedler, Jan. 24, 1960; children: Eric Mark, Beth Ellen. BA, U. Pitts., 1960; MSW, St. Louis U., 1962. Social worker Family & Children's Svc., St. Louis, 1962—63; lectr. Sch. of Social Work Haile Selassie U., Addis Ababa, Ethiopia, 1963—66; social worker U. Ky. Med. Ctr., Lexington, 1966—68, Renaissance Home Health Care, Detroit, 1984—86; geriatric social worker Jewish Family Svc., Southfield, Mich., 1986—. Mem.: AFSME (chair Jewish Family Svcs. bargaining unit 1998—2006, bd. dir. 2000—06, exec. bd. local 1640 2000—06), ACLU Mich. (chpt. pres. 2001—04, chmn. bd. dir. Oakland County, Mich.). Democrat. Jewish. Home: 18851 Capitol Dr Southfield MI 48075-2680 Office: Jewish Family Svc 24123 Greenfield Rd Southfield MI 48075-3116 Office Phone: 248-592-2348. Personal E-Mail: rozsedler@aol.com.

**SEDLIN, ELIAS DAVID**, orthopedist, educator; b. NYC, Jan. 21, 1932; s. Arnold Boris and Sonia Lipschitz Sedlin; m. Barbara Sue Zidell, July 9, 1960; children: Faith Avril, Adrian. BS in Biology, U. Ala., 1951; MD, Tulane U., 1955; D.Med. Sci., U. Gothenburg, Sweden, 1966. Diplomate: Am. Bd. Orthopedic Surgery. Intern Mobile (Ala.) Gen. Hosp., 1955-56; resident Charity Hosp., New Orleans, 1956-57; chief resident Bronx (N.Y.). Mcpl. Hosp., 1959-60; sr. resident Henry Ford Hosp., Detroit, 1960-61, rsch. assoc., emergency room lectr., 1961-63, NIH fellow, 1963-64; jr. attending physician Detroit Receiving Hosp., 1962-63; spl. NIH fellow dept. orthopedic surgery Sahlgrenska Sjukhuset, Gothenburg, 1964-66; asst. prof. dept. orthopaedic surgery Albert Einstein Coll. Medicine, 1966-69, assoc. prof., 1969-75, prof., 1975—, dir. orthopaedic surgery, 1969-79; prof. orthopaedic surgery Mt. Sinai Sch. Medicine, 1980—. Contbr. to multiple symposia, profl. meetings, also articles to profl. jours. Served to capt. AUS, 1957-59. Fulbright scholar, 1962; NSF postdoctoral fellow, 1964; recipient P.D. McGehee award Mobile Gen. Hosp., 1956; Ludvic Hektoen gold medal AMA, 1963; Nicholas Andry award Assn. Bone and Joint Surgeons, 1964 Fellow ACS, AAAS, Am. Acad. Orthopaedic Surgeons; mem. Orthopaedic Rsch. Soc., Phi Beta Kappa. Office: 133 E 73d St New York NY 10021 Office Phone: 212-410-2719. Personal E-Mail: edsedlin@hotmail.com.

**SEDMAK, DANIEL D.**, academic administrator; b. Columbus, Ohio, Apr. 18, 1952; m. Peggy Sedmak; 5 children. BS in biology, U. Cin.; MD, Ohio State U., 1980. Resident in pathology Cleveland Clinic Found., 1980—84, fellow in immunopathology, 1984—85; joined faculty Ohio State U., 1985; dir. nephropathology and transplant pathology programs Ohio State U. Hosp.; prof. and chair pathology Coll. Medicine and Pub. Health, Ohio State U., 1997, interim dean, sr. assoc. v.p. health sci. and exec. vice dean; exec. dean Georgetown U. Sch. Medicine, 2003—04, exec. v.p. health sci., 2003—04; exec. vice dean, assoc. v.p. health sciences Ohio State Med. Ctr., Columbus, 2003—. Office: Ohio State Univ Med Ctr 200 Meiling Hall 370 West 9th St Columbus OH 43210 Office Phone: 202-687-4600. Business E-Mail: sedmak@georgetown.edu.*

**SEDO, MANUEL ARTURO**, neuropsychologist, researcher; b. Barcelona, Catalonia, Spain, 1932; s. Manuel Sedo and Manuela Garcia-Tunon; m. Asuncion Sastre, July 10, 1965; children: Silvia Johnson, Natalia C., Arturo. PhD, Boston Coll., Chestnut Hill, 1978; CAGS, Inst. Psychology, Sorbonne. Lic. psychologist, sch. psychologist Commonwealth of Mass. Staff psychologist Children's Hosp. Med. Ctr., Boston, 1975—78; sch. psychologist Boston Pub. Schs., 1980—2000; dir. of test devel. MultiLingual Testing, Natick, Mass., 2000—. Author, rschr.: multicultural multilingual psychol. tests Five Digit Test, Oral Trials, Animal Span, Kiddy Words (Edith Kaplan award, 2004). Recipient Fulbright Fellowships, 1990, 1991; fellow, Harvard Coll., 1972, Harvard U., 1972—73. Mem.: APA (mem. bd.), Mass. Neuropsychol. Soc. Achievements include design of Tests of Minimal Language Load (elementary cognitive units); Neuropsych tests based on school materials (EXP.RE.S.S.); Language tests based on Sentence Repetition (Spanish sentences with simple and with complex syntax); Kiddy Words: Naming Tests ages 2, 3, 4, 5, 6; Neuropsych tests from school curriculum materials (EXP.RE.S.S.); Naming test ages 2, 3, 4, 5 or 6; Language test: Senence Repetition, sentences; Neuropsych test from curriculum materials (EX-P.RE.S.S.); Language test, Spanish sentence repetition comparing sentences of equal length and different language complexity. Office: MultiLingual Testing 9 Ingleside Rd Natick MA 01760 Office Phone: 508-655-6970. Business E-Mail: manuel@sedo.net.

**SEDRA, ADEL SHAFEEK**, engineering educator, academic administrator; b. Assuout, Egypt, Nov. 2, 1943; arrived in Can., 1966; s. Chafik and Hélène (Monsour) S.; m. Doris M. Barker, May 5, 1973; children: Paul Douglas, Mark Andrew. BSEE, Cairo U., 1964; MASc in Elec. Engring., U. Toronto, Ont., Can., 1968, PhD in Elec. Engring., 1969; DSc (hon.), Queen's U., 2003; LLD (hon.), U. Toronto, 2005. Registered profl. engr., Ont. Instr. Cairo U., 1964-66; asst. prof. elec. engring. U. Toronto, 1969-72, assoc. prof., 1972-78, prof., 1978—2003, chmn. dept., 1986-93, v.p., provost, chief acad. officer, 1993—2002; prof. elec. engring., dean faculty of engring. U. Waterloo, Ont., Canada, 2003—. Pres. Elec. Engring. Consociates Ltd., Toronto, 1979-81; bd. dirs. Info. Tech. Rsch. Ctr., Toronto, 1988-93; mem. rsch. coun. Can. Inst. for Advanced Rsch., 1994—; del. Oxford U. Press, 1995—. Co-author: Filter Theory and Design, 1978, Microelectronic Circuits, 1982, 5th edit., 2004 (also Spanish, Korean, Greek, Italian, Portuguese, Chinese, Persian, and Hebrew transls.), SPICE, 1997; contbr. over 120 articles to sci. jours. Operating grantee Nat. Scis. and Engring. Rsch. Coun. Can., 1970—; Ryerson Poly. Inst. fellow, 1988. Fellow IEEE (Darlington best paper award 1984, Edn. medal 1996, Cir. and Sys. Soc. Edn. award 1994, Guillemin Cauer Best Paper award 1987, Golden Jubilee medal 2000, 3d Millennium medal 2000), Can. Acad. Engrs., Royal Soc. Can., Am. Soc. Engring. Edn. (Terman award 1988); mem. Info. Tech. Assn. Can. (Tech. Achievement award 1993), Assn. Profl. Engrs. Ont. (Engineering Excellence award 2002). Home: 18 High Park Blvd Toronto ON Canada M6R 1M4 Office: U Waterloo Dean of Faculty of Engring 200 University Ave W Waterloo ON Canada N2L 3G1 Office Phone: 519-888-4567 ext. 33348. Business E-Mail: sedra@uwaterloo.ca.

**SEDWAY, LYNN MASSEL**, real estate economist; b. Washington, Nov. 26, 1941; d. Mark S. and Jean M. (Magnus) Massel; m. Paul H. Sedway, June 12, 1966; children: Mark, Carolyn, Jan. BA in Econs., U. Mich., 1963; MBA, U. Calif., Berkeley, 1976. Economist San Rafael (Calif.) Redevel. Agy., 1976-78; prin. Sedway Group, San Francisco, 1978—99; exec. mng. dir. CB Richard Ellis, San Francisco, 1999—. Instr. Appraisal Bus. Sch. U. Calif., Berkeley; corporate bd. mem. Hunting Gate Capital, Swig Co., AMB Alliance Fund III Bride Housing. Bridge housing bd., exec. com. trust Public Land Real Estate Coun. 1984-86, Internat. Coun. of Shopping Ctrs.; chmn San Rafael Downtown Retail Com., 1985; former trustee Urban Land Inst., former chmn. retail comml. coun., San Francisco District Council. Fellow, Homer Hoyt. Mem. Counselors of Real Estate, San Francisco Chamber of Commerce (former bd. of dirs.), City Club, Intl. House, Lambda Alpha (past pres., bd. dirs.), Internat. Land Econs. Soc., San Francisco Mayors Mcpl. Fiscal Advisory Com. Avocation: tennis. Home: 765 Market St Apt 26G San Francisco CA 94103-2038 Office Phone: 415-733-5321. Personal E-Mail: lynn.sedway@cbre.com.

**SEE, CAROLYN**, English language educator, writer, book critic; b. Pasadena, Calif., Jan. 13, 1934; d. George Newton Laws and Kate Louise (Sullivan) Daly; m. Richard Edward See, Feb. 18, 1955 (div. June 1959); 1 child, Lisa Lenine; m. Tom Sturak, June 11, 1959; 1 child, Clara Elizabeth Marya. BA, Calif. State U., L.A., 1958; PhD, UCLA, 1963. Prof. English Loyola Marymount Coll., L.A., 1970-85, UCLA, 1985—; book critic L.A. Times, 1981-93, Washington Post, 1999—. Author: Rhine Maidens, 1980, Golden Days, 1986, Making History, 1991, Dreaming: Hard Luck and Good Times In America, 1995, The Handyman, 1999, Making a Literary Life, 2002, There Will Never Be Another You, 2006 Bd. dirs. Calif. Arts Coun., L.A., 1987-91, Day Break, for homeless, Santa Monica, Calif., 1989—, Friends of English, UCLA, 1990—; buddy for life AIDS Project L.A., AIDS relief, L.A., 1990—. Recipient award Sidney Hillman Found., 1972, Robert Kirsch award L.A. Times, 1994; PEN Ctr. USA West Lifetime Achievement award 1998;

grantee Nat. Endowment for Arts, 1980, Guggenheim fellow, 1990-91. Mem. Writers Guild Am., Libr. Found. Calif., PEN Ctr. USA West (pres. 1990-91), Nat. Book Critics Cir. (bd. dirs. 1986-90). Democrat. Avocations: gardening, sailing, dance, brush clearing. Home: 17339 Tramonto Dr Pacific Palisades CA 90272-3124 Office: UCLA Dept English 405 Hilgard Ave Los Angeles CA 90095-9000 Office Phone: 310-454-7724. Business E-Mail: csee@ucla.edu.

**SEE, EDMUND M.**, lawyer; b. Marietta, Ohio, Oct. 9, 1943; s. Edgar Thorpe and Katherine M. (Merriam) S.; m. Ellen Engler, June 5, 1976; children: Kevin, Gregory, Tyler. BA, Wesleyan U., Middletown, Conn., 1965; JD, Harvard U., 1971. Bar: Conn. 1971. Assoc. Day, Berry & Howard LLP, Hartford, Conn., 1971-77, ptnr., 1978—. Chmn. Mcpl. Fin. Practice Group. Vol. Peace Corps, Gabon, 1965-67, Vista, 1968-69; pres. bd. dirs. Legal Aid Soc., 1977-85, Hartford Arch. Conservancy, 1983-86; trustee St. Joseph Coll., 1991-2003, 2004—; dir. Conn. Bar Found., 1994-; corporator Hartford Sem., 1994-. Mem. ABA, Conn. Bar Assn., Hartford County Bar Assn., Nat. Assn. Bond Lawyers, Conn. Govtl. Fin. Officers Assn., U.S. Govtl. Fin. Officers Assn., Phi Beta Kappa. Office: Day Berry & Howard LLP Cityplace 25th Fl Hartford CT 06103-3499 Office Phone: 860-275-0100. Business E-Mail: emsee@dbh.com.

**SEE, HAROLD FREND**, state supreme court justice; b. Chgo., Nov. 7, 1943; s. Harold Frend and Corinne Louise (Rachau) S.; m. Brenda Jane Childs, Dec. 2, 1978; children: Callie Suzanne, Garrett Brittain; children by previous marriage: Mary Elisabeth, Eric Palmer. Student, U. Chgo., 1962-63; BA, Emporia State U., 1966; MS, Iowa State U., 1969; JD, U. Iowa, 1973. Bar: Ill. 1973, U.S. Dist. Ct. (no. dist.) Ill. 1973, Ala. 1981, U.S. Ct. Appeals (fed. cir.) 1991; U.S. Supreme Ct. Instr. econs. Iowa State U., Ames, 1967-69; asst. prof. econs. Ill. State U., Normal, 1969-70; assoc. Sidley & Austin, Chgo., 1973-76; assoc. prof. law U. Ala., Tuscaloosa, 1976-78, prof., 1978-97; justice Supreme Ct. Ala., 1997—. Contbr. to books, also articles and book reviews. Mem. ABA, Ala. Bar Assn., Am. Econ. Assn., Am. Law and Econs. Assn., Soc. Profls. in Dispute Resolution, Am. Law Inst., Ala. Law Inst. Baptist. Office: Supreme Ct Ala 300 Dexter Ave Montgomery AL 36104-3741*

**SEE, MILES TODD**, animal scientist, educator; b. Mt. Clemens, Mich., Sept. 23, 1965; s. Larry Jay and Judith Sharon See; m. Leslie Murphy, Dec. 30, 1989; children: Garrett, Emma. BS, Mich. State U., East Lansing, 1987; MS, U. Ga., Athens, 1990, PhD, 1992. Asst. prof., ext. swine specialist N.C. State U., Raleigh, 1992—98, assoc. prof., ext. swine specialist, 1998—2002, prof., 2002—, swine commodity coord., 2002—. Dir. Nat. Swine Improvement Fedn., Columbus, Ohio, 1994—99, pres., 1998—99; vice chmn. Nat. Swine Registry, West Lafayette, Ind., 2002—02, chmn., 2003—05; pork checkoff fellow Nat. Pork Bd., Des Moines, 2004—04; pork info. gateway editor U.S. Pork Ctr. of Excellence, Ames, Iowa, 2005—. Author: (textbook) The Swine AI Book; contbr. articles to profl. jours. Ex officio N.C. Pork Coun., Raleigh, 2002—06. Named Outstanding Young Animal Scientist, Am. Soc. Animal Sci., 2004; recipient Early Career award, Epsilon Sigma Phi, 2002, Charles Stanislaw Dist. Svc. award, Nat. Swine Improvement Fedn., 2004, Lois G. Britt Svc. to N.C. Pork Industry, N.C. Pork Coun., 2006; Pork Checkoff fellow, Nat. Pork Bd., 2004. Mem.: Am. Soc. Animal Sci. (Swine Industry award for Innovation 1995, 1997, 2003), Phi Kappa Phi, Gamma Sigma Delta, Epsilon Sigma Phi. Office: NC State Univ Animal Sci Dept Campus Box 7621 Raleigh NC 27695-7621 Office Phone: 919-515-8797. Office Fax: 919-515-6316. E-mail: todd_see@ncsu.edu.

**SEE, ROBERT FLEMING, JR.**, lawyer; b. Kansas City, Mo., Apr. 23, 1942; s. Robert Fleming and Betty (Conard) S.; m. Leslie, Apr. 26, 1985 (dec.). BA with honors, U. Tex., 1964, JD with honors, 1966. Bar: Tex. 1966. Assoc. Locke, Purnell, Rain, Harrell and predecessor, Dallas, 1966-72, ptnr., 1972-89, pres., 1989-96; ptnr. Locke, Liddell & Sapp LLP and predecessor, Dallas, 1996—2001; pres., owner Robert F. See, Jr. & Assocs., P.C., Dallas, 2001—. Spkr. in field. Contbg. author: Loan Documentation Guide, 1990. Chmn. bd. commrs. Dallas Housing Authority; bd. dirs. The Real Estate Coun., Dallas Citizens Coun. Mem. Tex. Bar Assn., Dallas Bar Assn., Greater Dallas C. of C., North Dallas C. of C., Salesmanship Club Dallas. Office: Robert F See Jr & Assocs PC 901 Main St Ste 3601 Dallas TX 75202 Office Phone: 214-761-3001. E-mail: rsee@rseelaw.com.

**SEE, SAWTEEN**, structural engineer; b. Georgetown, Penang, Malaysia, Mar. 23, 1954; came to US, 1974; d. Hock-Eng and Ewe-See (Lim) S.; m. Leslie Earl Robertson, Aug. 11, 1982; 1 child, Karla Mei. BSCE, Cornell U., 1977, MCE, 1978. Registered profl. engr., NY, Calif., Conn., Fla., Mass., Md., NJ, Ohio, Pa., Wash., Ark., Ill., Tex., NC. Design engr. Leslie E. Robertson Assocs., R.L.L.P., NYC, 1978-81, assoc., 1981-85, ptnr., 1986—, mng. ptnr., 1990—. Cons. M of Engring. class Cornell U., 1994-95, mem. adv. coun. Sch. Civil and Environ. Engring., 1999—; project dir., project mgr. Miho Mus., Kyoto, Japan, West Side HS, NYC, Jr. HS 234, Bklyn., Jewelry Trade Ctr., Bangkok, Bilboa (Spain) Emblematic bldgs., Internat. Trade Ctr., Barcelona, Spain, Seattle Art Mus., San Jose (Calif.) Convention Ctr., San Jose Arena; project dir. Hong Kong Sta. South West & North East Tower Structural Audit, Balt. Conv. Ctr., Rock 'N Roll Hall of Fame and Mus., Cleve., Pontiac Marina Hotel and Retail, Singapore, acad. bldgs. and greenhouse, SUNY, Binghamton, NY; project mgr. Coll. of Law bldg. U. Iowa, Iowa City, Neiman-Marcus store, San Francisco, AT&T Exhbn. bldg., NYC, Bank of China Tower, Hong Kong; ptnr.-in-charge Nat. Constn. Ctr., Phila. Contbr. articles to profl. jours. Named to Those Who Made Marks in the Constrn. Industry in 1988, Engring. News Record, NYC, 1989, Spl. Recognition award Profl. Women in Constrn., 2002. Fellow ASCE (hon., performance study team World Trade Ctr. with FEMA), N.Y. Acad. Sci.; mem. Archtl. League, Coun. on Tall Bldgs. and Urban Habitat (chair com. on gravity loads and temperature effects 1982-85), Architects, Designers, Planners for Social Responsibility, N.Y. Assn. Cons. Engrs. (dir. 1989-93, structural codes com. 1991—). Avocations: sailing, skiing, reading, photography. Home: 45 E 89th St Apt 25C New York NY 10128-1230 Office: Leslie E Robertson Assocs RLLP 30 Broad St Fl 47 New York NY 10004-2304 Office Phone: 212-750-9000. E-mail: sawteen.see@lera.com.

**SEEBACH, LYDIA MARIE**, physician; b. Red Wing, Minn., Nov. 9, 1920; d. John Henry and Marie (Gleusen) S.; m. Keith Edward Wentz, Oct. 16, 1959; children: Brooke Marie, Scott. BS, U. Minn., 1942, MB, 1943, MD, 1944, MS in Medicine, 1951. Diplomate Am. Bd. Internal Medicine. Intern Kings County Hosp., Bklyn., 1944; fellow Mayo Found., Rochester, Minn., 1945-51; pvt. practice Oakland, Calif., 1952-60, San Francisco, 1961—. Asst. clin. prof. U. Calif., San Francisco, 1981—; mem., vice chmn. Arthritis Clinic, Presbyn. Hosp., San Francisco, 1961-88, pharmacy com., 1963-78; chief St. Mary's Hosp. Arthritis Clinic, San Francisco, 1968-72; exec. bd. Pacific Med. Ctr., San Francisco, 1974-76. Contbr. articles to med. jours. Fellow ACP; mem. AMA, Am. Med. Womens Assn. (pres. Calif. chpt. 1968-70), Am. Rheumatism Assn., Am. Soc. Internal Medicine, Pan Am. Med. Womens Assn. (treas.), Calif. Acad. Medicine, Calif. Soc. Internal Medicine, Calif. Med. Assn., San Francisco Med. Soc., San Francisco Med. Assn., San Francisco Soc. Internal Medicine, No. Calif. Rheumatism Assn., Internat. Med. Women's Assn., Mayo Alumni (bd. dirs. 1983-89), Iota Sigma Pi. Republican. Lutheran. Avocations: music, cooking, gardening, needlepoint. Office: 490 Post St Ste 939 San Francisco CA 94102-1414 Office Phone: 415-397-9571. Personal E-Mail: lseebach@sbcglobal.net.

**SEED, BRIAN BRUCE**, music educator; b. Anchorage, Alaska, Jan. 4, 1966; s. Gerald Bruce and Marilyn Marie Seed; m. Stephanie Louise Brown, June 24, 1995; children: James, Mark. Grad., Armored Forces Sch. of Music, Norfolk, Va., 1984—85; BMus Edn., Willamette U., 1990, MA Tchg., 1991. Cert. tchr. Oreg., 1991. Announcer KSJJ - KPRB Radio, Redmond, Oreg., 1987—88; announcer/news reporter KBND-KLRR Radio, Bend, Oreg. 1989—91; youth program dir. Holland Am. Cruise Line, Seattle, 1992—95; advt./tech. cons. The Mattress Factory, Inc., Bend, 1997—2002; band dir. Molalla H.S./Molalla River Sch. Dist., Oreg., 1991—2001, Summit H.S./Bend-LaPine Sch. Dist., Bend, 2001—; v.p. The Mattress Factory, Inc.,

2002—. Dir. band exch. program with Matsudo Mcpl. HS, Japan, 1996—. Chair North Lancaster Neighborhood Assn., Salem, Oreg., 1994—98; founder, pres. Molalla River Cmty. Concert Assn., 1998—2001. Specialist 4 U.S. Army, 1984—87, Ft. Hood, Tex. Recipient Army Commendation Medal, U.S. Army, 1987, Army Achievement Medal, 1986—87, Good Conduct Medal, 1987. Mem.: Oreg. Edn. Assn., Oreg. Music Educators Assn., Music Educators Nat. Conf., Arthritis Found., Am. Legion. Conservative. Mem. Christian Ch. (Disciples Of Christ). Avocation: music, computers, movies, history, travel. Home: 2446 NE 6th St Bend OR 97701 Office: Summit HS 2855 NW Clearwater Dr Bend OR 97701 Personal E-mail: seedb@bendnet.com.

**SEED, PATRICIA,** historian, educator; b. Balt., Sept. 20, 1949; d. John Cathro and Pauline (Sullivan) S.; m. George E. Marcus, June 22, 1984. B.A., Fordham U., 1971; M.A., U. Tex., 1975; Ph.D., U. Wis., 1980. Lectr. Ohio U., Athens, 1979; asst. prof. Coll. Charleston, S.C., 1980-82; asst. prof. history Rice U., Houston, 1982-2005, assoc. prof., 1987-1994; prof. U. Calif., Irvine, 1994-2005; vis. researcher Nat. Anthropology Inst., Mex., 1976-78. Author: To Love Honor and Obey in Colonial Mexico, 1987, Ceremonies of Possession in Europe's Conquest of the New World, 1995, American Pentissiento: The Invention of Indians and the Pursuit of Riches, 2001. Fellow Tinker Found., 1984, NEH, 1981, 86, Social Sci. Research Council, 1976-78, Fulbright Found., 1976-77, 88—. Mem. Am. Hist. Soc., Latin Am. Studies Assn., Conf. Latin Am. History. Avocations: ballet; modern dance. Office: Univ Calif Irvine 200 Murray Kreiger Hall Irvine CA 92697-3275 Business E-Mail: seed5@uci.edu.

**SEEDS, SHARON LYNN,** bank processor; d. Don A. and Marguerite Morairty Seeds. BA in Edn., Ariz. State U., 1972. Tchr. gen. and vocal music edn. Paradise Valley Unified Sch. Dist. # 69, Phoenix, 1973—76; advt. coord. Greater Phoenix Jewish News, 1976—83; disbursements/loan rev. processor Merabank, Phoenix, 1984—88; loan processor II Citibank, Scottsdale and Mesa, Ariz., 1989—91; acctg. specialist, ops. processor I and II, store acctg. support, mortgage lending home equity Internet divsn. Wells Fargo & Co., Phoenix, 1992—. Festival adjudicator Ariz. Solo and Ensemble Festival, Phoenix, 1973—; jr. choir dir. Christ Ch. of the Ascension, Paradise Valley, 1983—87; soloist and sect. leader Congregation Ch., Tempe, Presbyn. Ch., Phoenix, Ch. of Divine Sci., Trinity Episcopal Cathedral, St. Barnabas-on-the-Desert, 1976—2002. Contr.ghost editor: textbook Arizona Construction Lending and the Law, 1988. Vol. libr. catalog and music areas Lillian Valley Sch., Blackfoot, Idaho, 2002, 2004; neighborhood activist on hist. preservation com. Sunview Estates II, Phoenix, 2002—; vol. press release area Episcopal Ch. Gen. Conv., Phoenix, 1991. Mem.: Am. Choral Dirs. Assn., Music Educators Nat. Conf., Phi Kappa Phi, Kappa Delta Pi, Pi Lambda Theta, Sigma Alpha Iota (local chair/co-chair for nat. bazaar at triennial conv. 1987—, nat. elections chair triennial conv. 2003, Sword of Honor 1972, Rose of Honor 1995, Rose of Dedication 2003). Episcopalian. Avocations: music theater/liturgical drama, needlecrafts, reading. Personal E-mail: seedssl@hotmail.com.

**SEEGAL, JOHN FRANKLIN,** lawyer; b. Newton, Mass., May 21, 1946; s. Samuel Melbourne and Martha (Lewenberg) S.; m. Barbara Ellen Wayne, Apr. 2, 1982; children: Sarah Rachel, Laura Rose. BA in econ. summa cum laude, Harvard U., MBA with distinction, 1973, JD magna cum laude, 1973. Bar: Calif. 1973. Assoc. Orrick, Herrington & Sutcliffe, LLP, San Francisco, 1973-78, ptnr., 1979—, practice leader mergers & acquisitions. Co-chmn. Inst. on Securities Regulation, 2001. Author: Bargaining Power, Acquiring or Selling the Privately Held Co., 1999, Private Co. M&A: Deal Structures, Execution & Related Issues, 2001. Mem.: ABA, Practicing Law Inst. (co-chmn. Securities Regulation Inst. 2001), Calif. Bar Assn. Republican. Jewish. Fluent in french. Office: Orrick Herrington & Sutcliffe LLP 405 Howard St San Francisco CA 94105 Office Phone: 415-773-5797. Office Fax: 415-773-5759. Business E-Mail: jseegal@orrick.com.

**SEEGER, GUENTER OTTO,** chef; b. Loffenau, Baden, Germany, Mar. 23, 1949; s. Otto Emil and Margarete (Temme) S.; m. Marion Boehmlander (div. Aug. 1991); children: Diana, Denise. Student, Cook and Hotel Sch., Lucerne, Switzerland. Apprentice Hotel Funk, Dobel, Germany, 1963-66; cook various locations, Switzerland, 1966-77; owner, operator restaurant Pforz Heim, Germany, 1977-84; exec. chef maifar Regent Hotel, Washington, 1984-85; exec. chef dining rm. Ritz-Carlton Hotel, Atlanta, 1985—. Pres., cons. produce developer Smi, Inc., Atlanta, 1993. Editor calendars, 1982, 83 (award 1982). Named Best Chef of Atlanta, Atlanta Mag., 1993. Mem. Chefs Collaborative 2000 (bd. overseers 1994). Avocation: Kung Fu. Office: The Ritz-Carlton Buckhead 3434 Peachtree Rd NE Atlanta GA 30326-1172

**SEEGER, LAUREEN E.,** health products executive; BBA, U. Wis., Eau Claire, 1983; JD, U. Wis., Madison, 1986. Atty. Jones, Day, Reavis & Pogue, 1986—92; ptnr.-in-charge tech. litigation sect. Morris, Manning & Martin, LLP, 1992—2000; v.p., gen. coun. McKesson Provider Technologies, 2000—06; exec. v.p., gen. counsel, sec. McKesson Corpn., San Francisco, 2006—. Office: McKesson Corpn 1 Post St San Francisco CA 94104*

**SEEGERS, HARVEY,** retail executive; B. U. Va.; JD, Cath. U.; MBA, Harvard Bus. Sch. With GE, 1991—96; pres., CEO Global Exch. Svcs., 1996; tchr. internet commerce U. Md. Grad. Bus. Sch.; pres. Home Depot Direct Home Depot, 2005—. Faculty adv. internet commerce rsch. U. Md. Served in USMC. Decorated 2 Meritorious Svc. medals. Office: Home Depot 2455 Paces Ferry Rd Atlanta GA 30339*

**SEEHAFER, BRENDA ANN,** elementary school educator; b. Minot, ND, Dec. 18, 1969; d. Kenneth Bernard and Lila Lou (Ehrman) Seehafer. BS in elem. edn., Minot State U. ND, 1992. Assoc. libr. U. ND Lake Region Coll., Devils Lake, ND, 1992—95; gifted and talented instr. Lake Region Spl. Edn., Devils Lake, ND, 1994—95; elem. tchr. Wolford Pub. Sch., Wolford, ND, 1995—2003; title I tchr. Mt. Pleasant Sch., Rolla, ND, 2003—. Sub. tchr. Devils Lake Pub. Sch., Devils Lake, ND, 1992—95. V.p. Dollars for Scholars, Wolford, ND, 1994—95; mem. Parent/Teacher Orgn., Wolford, ND, 1995—2003. Mem.: NEA, Chautauqua Reading Coun., Rolla Edn. Assn., Internat. Reading Assn., ND Reading Assn., ND Edn. Assn. (bd. dirs. 2004—), Thrivent Fin. for Luth., Merrymakers Homemakers (v.p. 1999, pres. 2000), Kappa Delta Pi, Delta Kappa Gamma (first v.p.Lambda chpt. 2004—06, pres. Lambda chpt. 2006—). Luth. Home: PO Box 951 Rolla ND 58367 Office: Mt Pleasant Sch 201 5th St NE Rolla ND 58367 Office Phone: 701-477-3151. E-mail: brenda.seehafer@sendit.nodak.edu.

**SEEHAUSEN, RICHARD FERDINAND,** architect; b. Indpls., Mar. 17, 1925; s. Paul Ferdinand and Melusina Dorothea (Nordmeyer) S.; m. Phyllis Jean Gates, Dec. 22, 1948; children: Lyn, Dirk. Student, DePauw U., 1943, Wabash Coll., 1944, State U. Iowa, USN Pre Flight, 1944; BArch, U. Ill., 1949. Registered prof. arch., 1951. Ptnr. Johnson, Kile, Seehausen & Assocs. archs., engrs., Rockford, Ill., 1955-82, pres., 1974-82, Richard F. Seehausen-Arch., Inc., Rockford, Ill., 1983—2001. Mem. com. jail planning and constrn. stds. Bur. Detention Facilities, Ill. Dept. Corrections, 1970-73; analyst Dept. Def., 1962-66; analyst Fed. Fall-Out Shelter, 1962—. Prin. works include No. Ill. U. Ctr, Harrison Hall, Lorado Taft, Oreg., Health Svc. Bldg., No. Ill. U., (Renovation) Old Winnebago County Pub. Safety Bldg., Rockford, Ill., St. Mark Luth. Ch., Christ Meth. Ch., Forest Hills Free Ch., Page Park Spl. Edn. Sch., Winnebago County Courthouse, Court Street Meth. Ch., Willows Personal Care Ctr., 1st Presbyn. Ch., Rochelle, Ill., Messiah Luth. Ch., Rock Falls, Ill., Rockford Mut. Ins. Home Office Bldg., Ch. of the Nazarene, Freeport, Ill., Stephenson County Courthouse, LDS Temple, McHenry County Ct. House, Woodstock, Ill., Ogle County Pub. Safety Bldg., Oreg., DeKalb Hills Ch., Freeport YWCA Bldgs., renovation Carroll County Ct. House, DeKalb Area Retirement Ctr., Oak Crest Retirement Ctr., Sycamore/DeKalb, Ill., St. Paul Ch. of Christ, Davis, Ill., Savanna Meth. Ch., Savanna, Ill., others. Bd. dir. Rockford Boys Club, Lincoln Pk. Boys Club, past dir.; trustee Emmanuel Luth. Ch., Rockford, 1989-92; mem. Nat. Trust Hist. Preservation, 2000—. Served with USN, 1943-45, USNR, 1945-47, lt. USAF, 1949-55.

Mem. AIA (dir. No. Ill. chpg. 1966-68, 75-77, pres. chpt. 1978-79, nat. design com. 2005—), Ill. Coun. of Am. Inst. Archs., U. Ill. Alumni Assn., Mason (Shriner), Kiwanian, Forest Hills Country Club (gov. 1970-72), Saddle Brooke Country Club, Saddle Brooke Arc. Com., Lambda Chi Alpha. Lutheran. Office: Richard F Seehausen Arch Inc 65297 E Emerald Ridge Dr Tucson AZ 85739-1434

**SEEHRA, MOHINDAR SINGH,** physics professor, researcher; b. Panjab, Pakistan, Feb. 14, 1940; came to U.S., 1963; s. Bakhshish Singh and Rattan (Kaur) S.; m. Harbhajan Kaur, May 12, 1963; children: Jasmeet, Parveen. BS, Panjab U., 1959; MS, Aligarh (India) U., 1962; PhD, U. Rochester, 1969. Instr. chemistry Arya Coll., Nawanshahr, India, 1959-60; lectr. physics Jain Coll., Ambala City, India, 1962-63; asst. prof. physics W.Va. U., Morgantown, 1969-73, assoc. prof., 1973-77, prof., 1977-91, Eberly disting. prof. physics, 1992—. Contbr. more than 200 articles to profl. jours. Rsch. fellow A.P. Sloan Found., 1973-75, ORAU Summer fellow, 1976, 77, 84, 85; recipient Outstanding Rsch. award Coll. Arts and Scis., U. W.Va., 1985. Fellow Am. Phys. Soc., Inst. Physics (Eng.). Office: WVa State U Dept Physics PO Box 6315 Morgantown WV 26506-6315 Business E-Mail: mseehra@wvu.edu.

**SEELAN, SANTHOSH KUMAR,** science educator, department chairman; b. India; arrived in U.S., 1998; BS in Geology, Annamalai U., India, 1971; MS in Applied Geology, IIT Bombay, India, 1974; diploma in Groundwater, Hebrew U. Jerusalem, Israel, 1975; PhD, Jawaharlal Nehru Technol. U., India, 1994. Cert. in remote sensing GTZ, Germany, 1978. Sr. rsch. analyst Ops. Rsch. group, Baroda, India, 1975—77; scientist Nat. Remote Sensing Agy., Hyderabad, India, 1977—89, head data ctr. Dept. Space, 1990—95; prof. Terralink, Wellington, New Zealand, 1996—98; rsch. faculty Upper Midwest Aerospace Consortium U. N.D., Grand Forks, ND, 1998—2003, chair Dept. Earth Sys. Sci. and Policy, 2003—05, prof., applied remote sensing Dept. Space Studies, 2005—. Contbr. articles to profl. jours. Recipient Silver medal, Indian Inst. Tech., 1974, Best Spkr. award, Asian Conf. Remote Sensing, 1986; fellow, UNESCO, 1974-75. Mem.: AM. Soc. Photogrammetry and Remote Sensing, Indian Nat. Cartography Assn. (life), Indian Soc. Photointerpretation and Remote Sensing (life). Office: University of North Dakota Clifford Hall Grand Forks ND 58202

**SEELAND, ARTHUR DAVID,** bishop; b. Jersey City, Oct. 31, 1931; s. Theodore Arthur and Dorothea Augusta (Thomas) Seeland; m. Mary Ann Hove, Apr. 10, 1954; children: John Robert, Eric David, Tellef Martin, Karen Victoria. BA, Houghton Coll., 1953; MDiv, Temple U., 1958; D Ministry, McCormick Theol. Sem., 1978; grad. with highest distinction, U.S. Naval War Coll., 1981; ThM, Princeton Theol. Sem., 1973. Diplomate Am. Bd. Med. Psychotherapists. Pastor NJ United Meth. Conf., 1953—64; commd. lt. (j.g.) USN, 1963, advanced through grades to comdr., 1975, chaplain, 1964—87; clin. dir. Family and Psychol. Svcs., Cherry Hill, NJ, 1987—90; rector Holy Sacraments Anglican Cath. Ch., King of Prussia, Pa., 1988—93; archdeacon Diocese of the Resurrection, Quakertown, Pa., 1990—93; bishop Diocese of the Pacific and SW of the Anglican Rite Cath. Ch., L.A., 1993—. Lectr. med. ethics Med. Sch. Uniformed Services U., Bethesda, Md., 1980—84; lectr. ethics U.S. Nat. War Coll., Washington, 1980—84; asst. prof. Pa. State U., Hershey; pres. Holy Cross Seminary, Hereford, Ariz., 2005—. Contbr. articles to profl. jours. Editl. bd. Jour. of Christian Bioethics, Waco, Tex., 1994—99; pres. Houghton (NY) Coll. Alumni, 1981—83. Master: Mason (life; grand chaplain NJ 1963—, grand chaplain France 1977—); mem.: Assn. of Mil. Surgeons of the U.S. (life), NY Acad. of Scis. (life). Anglican Catholic. Avocations: sailing, travel, hiking, hunting. Home: 764 West Bay Ave Barnegat NJ 08005 Office: Diocese of the Pacific and Southwest 6752 East Ramsey Rd Hereford AZ 85615

**SEELBACH, ANNE ELIZABETH,** artist; b. Detroit, July 27, 1944; BA, NYU, 1967; MFA, CUNY, 1985. Curator Monhegan (Maine) Mus., 1992—95; art instr. The Victor d'Amico Inst. of Art, Napeague, N.Y., 1994—, Arts Pro Tem, Hancock, NH, 1991—95. One-woman shows include Tower Gallery, Southampton, N.Y., 1981, Newark (N.J.) Mus., 1984, Tower Gallery, N.Y.C., 1985, The Conn. Gallery, Marlborough, 1989, Radcliffe Inst. Advanced Studies, Cambridge, Mass., 1990, Frick Gallery, Belfast, Maine, 1991, Simmons Coll., Boston, 1991, The Painting Ctr., N.Y.C., 1994, Kouros Gallery, 1996, exhibited in group shows at Met. Mus. and Art Ctr., Coral Gables, Fla., 1986—, Kommunale Galerie, Berlin, 1987, Frauenmuseum, Bonn, Germany, 1988, Northeastern U., Boston, 1990, Fed. Res. Bank, 1995, Kouros Gallery, N.Y.C., 1995—96, Wheaton Coll., Norton, Mass., 2004, others, —, Represented in permanent collections Newark Mus., Frauenmuseum, Bonn, Germany, Centrum Frans Masereel, Kasterlee, Belgium, Lyman Allyn Mus., New London, Conn., Radcliffe Inst. Advanced Studies, Prudential Ins. Co., Newark, Continental Grain Corp., N.Y.C., Phoenix Mut. Life Ins. Co., Hartford, Conn., The Hillier Group, Princeton, N.J., one-woman shows include Alva Gallery, New London, Conn., 2002, Wheaton Coll., Norton, Mass., 2004, exhibited in group shows at Attleboro Mus., Mass., 1996, Alva Gallery, New London, Conn., 2002, Norwalk Mus., Conn., 2002. Recipient painting fellowship Radcliffe Inst. Advanced Studies, 1989-90, artist fellowship Triangle Artists' Workshop, Pine Plains, N.Y., 1988, MacDowell Colony, Peterborough, N.H., 1987; artist-in-residence I-Park, East Haddam, Conn., 2003. Mem.: Soc. Bunting Fellows. Address: PO Box 0812 Amagansett NY 11930

**SEELE, PERNESSA C.,** immunologist, health science association administrator; b. Lincolnville, SC, 1954; MS, Clark Atlanta Univ. Rschr. Rockefeller Univ., NYC; immunologist Harlem Hosp.; founder, CEO Balm In Gilead non-profit AIDS edn. program, NYC, 1989—. Organizer Week of Prayer for the Healing of AIDS, Harlem, 1989—. Named one of 35 Most Beautiful Women, Ebony Mag., 2005, 100 Most Influential People, Time mag., 2006. Office: The Balm In Gilead Inc Ste 450 130 W 42nd St New York NY 10036 Office Phone: 212-730-7381. Office Fax: 212-730-2551. Business E-Mail: pseele@balmingilead.org.

**SEELENFREUND, ALAN,** retired pharmaceutical company executive; b. NYC, Oct. 22, 1936; s. Max and Gertrude (Roth) S.; m. Ellyn Bolt; 1 child, Eric. BME, Cornell U., 1959, M. in Indsl. Engring., 1960; PhD in Mgmt. Sci., Stanford U., 1967. Asst. prof. bus. adminstrn. Grad. Sch. Bus. Stanford U., Palo Alto, Calif., 1971-75; various mgmt. positions McKesson Corp., San Francisco, 1975-84, v.p., chief fin. officer, 1984-86, exec. v.p., chief fin. officer, 1986-89, chmn., CEO, 1989-97, chmn., 1997-99, also bd. dirs., chmn., 1997—2002; ret., 2002. Mem. Nature Conservancy, St. Francis Yacht Club, Villa Taverna Club, Pacific Union Club, Francisco Yacht Club. Avocations: sailing, skiing, hiking. Office: McKesson Corp 1 Post St Ste 2625 San Francisco CA 94104-5296

**SEELER, RUTH ANDREA,** pediatrician, educator; b. NYC, June 13, 1936; d. Thomas and Olivia Seeler. BA cum laude, U. Vt., 1959, MD, 1962. Diplomate Am. Bd. Pediat., Am. Bd. Pediatric Hematology/oncology. Intern Bronx (N.Y.) Mcpl. Hosp., 1962—65; pediats. hematology/oncology fellow U. Ill., 1965—67; dir. pediatric hematology/oncology Cook County Hosp., 1967—84; prof. pediatrics and pediatric edn. Coll. Medicine U. Ill., Chgo., 1984—; assoc. chief pediatrics Michael Reese Hosp., Chgo., 1990—97, acting chief pediatrics, 1997—99; pediatrician St. Anthony's Hosp./U. Ill. Coll. Medicine, 1999—2001. Course coord. pediatrics Nat. Coll. Advanced Med. Edn., Chgo., 1987-96; mem. subboard Pediatric Hematology/Oncology, Chapel Hill, 1990-95; chief Midwest Am. Bd. Pediat., 1990-, Mem. editl. bd. Am. Jour. Pediatric Hematology/Oncology, 1985-95. Founder med. dir. camp for hemophiliacs Ill. Hemophilia Found., 1973—2000, pres. Ill., 1981—85; sec. exec. com. U. Vt. Med. Sch. Alumna Assn.; jr. and sr. warden, treas. Ch. Our Saviour, Chgo., 1970—92. Mem.: U. Vt. Med. Sch. Alumna Assn. (pres.-elect), Phi Beta Kappa, Gamma Phi Beta Found. (trustee 1994—2000, 2002—). Avocations: triathalons, biking, swimming. Office: U Ill Coll Medicine Pediats M/C 856 840 S Wood St Chicago IL 60612-7317 Office Phone: 312-355-1021. Business E-Mail: seeler@uic.edu.

**SEELIG, GERARD LEO,** management consultant; b. Schluchtern, Germany, June 15, 1926; came to U.S., 1934, naturalized, 1943; s. Herman and Bella (Bach) S.; m. Lorraine Peters, June 28, 1953; children: Tina Lynn, Robert Mark and Carol Ann (twins). BEE, Ohio State U., 1948; MS in Indsl. Mgmt, N.Y. U., 1954. Registered profl. engr., Ohio. Electronics engr. Martin Corp., Balt., 1948-50; sr. engr. Fairchild Aircraft Co., Farmingdale, NY, 1950-54; program mgr. RCA, Moorestown, NJ, 1954-59, Van Nuys, Calif., 1959-61; div. mgr. Missile & Space Co. div. Lockheed Aircraft Corp., Van Nuys, 1961-63; v.p., gen. mgr. Lockheed Aircraft Corp. (Lockheed Electronics div.), Los Angeles, 1963-68; exec. v.p. Lockheed Electronics Co., Inc., Plainfield, NJ, 1968-69, pres., 1969-71; group exec., exec. asst. to office of pres. ITT, N.Y.C., 1971-72, corp. v.p., 1972-79, sr. v.p., 1979-81, exec. v.p., 1981-83; pres. indsl. and tech. sector Allied Corp., exec. v.p. Morristown, NJ, 1983-87. Disting. exec. lectr. Rutgers Grad. Sch. Mgmt.; exec.-in-residence, vis. prof. Columbia U. Grad. Sch. Bus.; bd. dirs. 5 corps.; cons. various investment firms. Served with AUS, 1944-46. Recipient Disting. Alumnus award Ohio State U., 1987. Fellow AIAA (assoc.); mem. IEEE (sr.).

**SEELIG, JILL,** publishing executive; MBA, Fordham U., NY. With fin. svcs. ind., 1984—89; sales rep. NY Mag.; advt. sales rep. Self Mag., 1993—94, beauty dir., 1994—95; nat. sales mgr. Self Mag., 1996—99; advt. dir. Vanity Fair, 1998—99, O, The Oprah Mag., 1999—2000, pub., 2000—. Office: O, The Oprah Magazine 1700 Broadway New York NY 10019*

**SEELING, PATRICK,** research scientist, educator; b. Berlin, Mar. 29, 1976; s. Kurt Heinz and Angelika Ingrid Seeling; m. Jody Irene Platt, Aug. 7, 2005. Engring. diploma, Tech. U. of Berlin, 2002; PhD, Ariz. State U., Tempe, 2005. Rsch. assoc. Ariz. State U., Tempe, 2003—05, faculty rsch. assoc., 2005—. Author: (book chpts.) Wireless Internet; contbr. articles to profl. jours. Recipient 2nd Pl. award for Best Conf. Paper, IEEE Consumer Comm. and Networking Conf., 2005. Mem.: ACM, IEEE. Achievements include research in Video Traces for Network Performance Evaluation; Engineering Education; Header Compression; Multimedia Networking; development of Software Tools for Video Traces. Office: Ariz State Univ Dept Elec Engring Tempe AZ 85287-5706 Office Phone: 480-965-7280. E-mail: patrick.seeling@asu.edu.

**SEELMAN, JANNET GENEVIEVE,** secondary school educator; b. Constableville, NY, Sept. 23, 1954; d. Carl Francis and Genevieve Eve (Jarecki) S. AA, Jefferson Community Coll., 1974; BA, SUNY, Potsdam, 1976, MS, 1979. Cert. elem. and secondary tchr., N.Y. Para-tchr. Potsdam Middle Sch., 1978-79; 5th-12th grade tchr. remedial reading, writing, math. Harrisville (N.Y.) Cen. Sch., 1979. Tchr. computer word-processing PSEN students; tchr. alternative English, math. and social studies to learning disabled students; GED tchr. regular and learning disabled students, 2004—. Troop leader Girl Scouts U.S., 1980-96, mem. secondary shared decision making com. Mem. ASCD, Internat. Reading Assn., Lewis County Opportunities, Inc. (bd. dirs. 1980-2006, sec., 1987-91, 97-2001, 2003), Parent-Tchr. Orgn. (sec. 1997-2006) Office: One Pirate Ln Harrisville NY 13648-0200 Home: 5434 Park Pl Apt 4 Lowville NY 13367-1338 Office Phone: 315-543-2920. Business E-Mail: jseelman@hcsk12.org.

**SEELMAN, KATHERINE DOLORES,** institute administrator; b. Boston, May 26, 1938; d. Frederick George and Loretta (Tetu) S. BA, Hunter Coll., 1964; MA, NYU, 1970, PhD, 1982. Tchr. N.Y.C. Schs., 1966-73; instr., rschr. N.Y. Inst. Tech., NSF, N.Y.C., 1973-75; project mgr. Nat. Coun. Chs., N.Y.C., 1976-82; cons. Am. Assn. Retired Persons, Washington, 1982-83; rsch. scholar Gallaudet U., Washington, 1984-86; dir. pub. edn. Mass. Comm. for Deaf and Hard of Hearing, Boston, 1986-89; rsch. specialist Nat. Coun. on Disability, Washington, 1989-93; dir. program devel. Adminstrn. on Devel. Disability, Washington, 1993-94; dir. Nat. Inst. on Disability and Rehab. Rsch., Washington, 1994—. Switzer scholar Nat. Rehab. Assn., 1991, Disting. Switzer fellow Dept. Edn. Nat. Inst. Disability and Rehab. Rsch., 1985-86; recipient Scholarships NYU, 1973, Am. Law Inst./ABA, 1977, Fellowships NSF, 1974, Resources for the Future, 1976; named to Hall of Fame Alumni Assn. Hunter Coll., 1995; recipient pub. svc. award Assn. Acad. Physiatrists, 2000. Mem. RESNA, AAAS, Am. Pub. Health Assn. (Disability Achievement award 1999), Assn. for Advancement of Sci., Soc. for Disability Studies, Self-Help for Hard of Hearing.

**SEELY, DENNIS M.,** secondary school educator; m. Vivian D. Gaden, July 4, 1996. BA in Speech and Theater, U. LaVerne, La., 1971; postgrad., Ball State U., 1975, U. Okla., Norman, 1987; MS in Comm., Lacross U., Covington, La., 2004, PhD, 2005. Cert. tchr. Ariz. Commd. 2d lt. US Army, 1971, advanced through grades to maj., 1991; congrl. press sec. Rep. Jim Kolbe, Tucson, 1991—92; tchr. Santa Rita HS, Tucson, 1994, Blue Ridge HS, Lakeside, Ariz., 1994—. Mem.: US Inst. Theater Tech., Nat. Coun. Tchrs. English, Alpha Psi Omega. Mailing: PO Box 1445 Lakeside AZ 85929 Office: Blue Ridge HS 1200 W White Mountain Blvd Lakeside AZ 85929

**SEELY, JAMES MICHAEL,** retired military officer, defense consultant, small business owner; b. L.A., Oct. 15, 1932; s. Louis K. and Mary Edith (Gleason) S.; m. Gail Margaret Deverman, July 13, 1957; children: Ted Andrew, Nina Marie. BS, UCLA, 1955; MS, George Washington U., 1976. Commd. ensign USN, 1955, advanced through grades to rear adm.; student pilot, 1955-56; attack pilot, 1957-75; comdg. officer Attack Squadron 165, Naval Air Sta. Whidbey Island, Wash., 1972-73; comdr. Carrier Air Wing 9, Naval Air Sta. Lemoore, Calif., 1974-75; comdg. officer U.S. Naval Air Sta., Whidbey Island, 1977-79; dep. dir. DCNO (Air Warfare, OP-50), Pentagon, Washington, 1979-82; dir. Joint Analysis Directorate, Office Joint Chiefs Staff, Washington, 1982-84; comdr. Medium Attack Tactical Electronic Warfare Wing Pacific Fleet, Naval Air Sta. Whidbey Island, 1984-86; dir. DCNO (Air Warfare, OP-50), Pentagon, 1986-88; dep. comptr. of Navy, Pentagon, 1988-89; ret., 1989; with RRP Def. Cons. Assocs., Arlington, Va., 1989—2002; owner, pres. JMS Cons., 2002—. Vietnam combat duty with Attack Squadrons 93, 152, 165 flying from aircraft carriers USS Enterprise, Hancock, Bon Homme Richard, Shangri-La and Constellation; 447 combat missions. Decorated Defense Superior Service, Legion of Merit (3), D.F.C. (4), Bronze Star, Air Medal (43), Navy Commendation medal with combat v (7). Mem. Naval Inst., Tailhook Assn., Assn. Naval Aviation, Marine Corps Aviation Assn., Red River Valley Fighter Pilots Assn., Navy League, Assn. Old Crows, Golden Eagles, Sigma Pi. Republican. Roman Catholic. Avocations: sports, automobiles. Home: 15552 Legacy Way Haymarket VA 20169-6117 Office Phone: 703-753-2618. E-mail: jimseely@regancydv.com.

**SEELY, MARIBETH WALSH,** elementary school educator; d. William F. and Agnes C. Walsh; m. Thomas P. Seely; children: Timothy Patrick Francis, Keribeth Francis. BS in Elem. Edn., Lowell U., 1966. Cert. reading specialist Mass. Tchr. Town of Methuen, Mass., 1966—71, City of Lawrence, Mass., Sandyston-Walpack Sch., Layton, NJ. Testified to Ho. Reps. Am. Legion and Citizens Flag Alliance, Washington, 1997; testified for Am. flag Senate Judiciary Com., Washington, 1999. Nominee Gov.'s Tchr. Recognition award, State N.J., 1994; named Woman of Distinction, Lenni-Lenape Girl Scouts, 1995, Woman of the 90's, N.J. Herald Newspaper, 1995; recipient Inspiring Tchr. award, Sussex County C.C., 2005, Cert. Appreciations, Vietnam Vets. Am., 2005. Mem.: Sierra Club (assoc.). Roman Catholic. Avocations: hiking, art museums, travel, baseball. Home: 19 Summit Dr Branchville NJ 07826 Office: Sandyston-Walpack School PO Box 128 Layton NJ 07851

**SEELY, ROBERT DANIEL,** cardiologist, medical association administrator; b. Woodmere, NY, Nov. 4, 1923; s. Harry and Ethel (Weil) S.; m. Marcia Ann Wells, June 19, 1953; children: Ellen Wells, Anne Wells. BS, NYU, 1943; MD, Columbia U., 1946. Intern Mt. Sinai Hosp., N.Y.C., 1946-47, asst. resident in medicine, 1950-51, resident in pathology, 1951-52, chief resident in medicine, 1952-53; Sara Welt fellow in cardiovascular research Presbyn. Hosp., N.Y.C., 1953-54; instr. cardiovascular research Western Res. U., Cleve., 1947-48; chief rheumatic heart disease clinic Mt. Sinai Hosp., N.Y.C., 1961-70, attending physician medicine and cardiology, 1978—, chief of service dept. medicine, 1979—, clin. prof. medicine, cardiology Sch. Medicine, 1970—; practice medicine specializing in cardiovascular disease N.Y.C., 1953—. Contbr. articles to profl. jours. Served to capt. M.C. AUS, 1948-50. Recipient Solomon Berson Meml. award Mt. Sinai Hosp., 1977 Fellow Am. Coll. Cardiology, ACP; mem. N.Y. Heart Assn., AMA, N.Y. County Med. Soc., Soc. Cert. Internists N.Y., Phi Beta Kappa, Alpha Omega Alpha, Beta Lambda Sigma Office: 49 E 96th St # 11D New York NY 10128-0782 Personal E-mail: billybobseedy@gmail.com.

**SEELY, ROBERT EUGENE,** management consultant; b. Bangor, Mich., Oct. 23, 1941; s. Leroy W. and Ruth A. Seely. Cert., A&M U., 1961; BBA, West Mich. U., 1969. Officer Am. Nat. Bank, Kalamazoo, 1969-74; v.p. mktg. and fin., gen. mgr. Portage Rapid Cut, 1974-78; chief exec. officer Sutliff & Case, Inc., Peoria, Ill., 1978-81; chief oper. officer Allied Material Handing Co., Peoria, 1981-83; pres. S.E.R., Inc., Kalamazoo, 1983-86; bus./mgmt. cons. Seely & Assocs., L.L.C., Kalamazoo, 1986—. Mem. adv. com. C & S Plastic Climax, Mich., 1986—88; advisor to bd. dirs. Simpson Enterprises, 1990—2003; bd. dirs. Maro, Inc., Venureprise, Inc., Kalamazoo, Portage Rapid Cut, Allied Material Handling, New World Condo Assn., Champion Furnace Pipe, Wonder Makers, Inc., Exhibit House, Portage Dist. Libr. Contbr. articles to profl. publs. First chmn. Kalamazoo Valley Quality Coun., 1993-95; bd. dirs. city of Portage Economic Devel. Fin. Authority, 1998-, Portage Dist. Libr.; mem. City of Portage Devel. Authority. With U.S. Army, 1966-68, Vietnam. Recipient Cert. of Appreciation Gov. of Mich., Cert. South Mich. Water Quality Commn., 1978, Cert. of Achievement Entrepreneurial Inst., 1983. Mem. Nat. Assn. Corp. Dirs., Austin Lake Riparian (pres. 1991-93, bd. dirs.), C. of C. (chmn. small bus. week 1990, chmn. small bus. coun. 1991-92, organizer and 1st chmn. mfg. coun. 1992-96, Portage dir. Kalamazoo county)), Kal Valley Cmty. Quality Coun. (1st chmn. 1993, 94), Kal County C. of C. (bd. dirs. 1996-99). Avocations: golf, racquetball, skiing. Home: 9930 E Shore Dr Portage MI 49002-5879 Office: PO Box 924 Portage MI 49081-0924

**SEENITH, SIVASUNDARAM,** mathematician, educator; s. Sam Seenith and Tham Kanaga; m. Irene M Siva, May 21, 1973; 1 child, Diantha A Siva. PhD, U. Tex., 1987. Prof. Embry-Riddle Aero. U., Daytona Beach, Fla., 1989—. Organizer Conf. Nonlinear Problems in Aviation and Aerospace, Internat. Conf. Math. Problems in Engring. and Aerospace Scis., Budapest, Hungary, 2006. Author: Vector Lyapunov Functions and Stability Analysis of Nonlinear Systems, 1991, College Mathematics for Aviation I, 1992, College Mathematics for Aviation II, 1993, Dynamics Systems on Measure Chain, 1996, Advances in Nonlinear Dynamics, 1997, Nonlinear Problems in Aviation and Aerospace, 2000, Advances in Dynamics and Control, 2004; editor-in-chief Jour. Nonlinear Studies; editor-in-chief: Nonlinear Systems in Aviation, Aerospace and Astronautics Book Series; editor: Proceedings of Nonlinear Problems in Aviation Aerospace, Proceedings of Mathematical Problems in Engineering and Aerospace Sciences; editor: (in Chief) Nonlinear Systems in Aviation, Aerospace and Astronautics Series. Mem.: AAUP, Soc. Indsl. and Applied Math., Internat. Fedn. Nonlinear Analysts (charter), Math. Assn. Am. (charter math. for bus., industry and govt. 1999), Acad. Nonlinear Scis., Am. Math. Soc. Avocations: travel, cricket. Office: Embry-Riddle Aero U 600 S Clyde Morris Blvd Daytona Beach FL 32114 Business E-Mail: siva@erau.edu.

**SEEP, DOROTHY M.,** music educator; d. Frederick Henry and Estelle May Muller; m. Ralph Vincent Seep, Nov. 11, 1978; children: Jessica, Jeremy. MusB, Eastman Sch. Music, 1969, MusM, 1972. Music tchr. Taft Elem. Sch., Washingtonville, NY, 1969—71, Wayne Cent. Sch., Ontario, NY, 1972—81, Rochester Christian Sch., Penfield, NY, 1987—92; sr. choir dir. Rochester Christian Reformed Ch., Penfield, NY, 1988—91; music tchr. Annapolis Area Christian Sch., 1998—. Founder and dir. children's chorale Annapolis Area Christian Sch., Md., 1998—; founder and dir. adult cmty. choir and orch., 2003. Mem. choir Nat. Presbyn. Ch., Washington, 2004—; music dir. Safe Harbor Presbyn. Ch., 2000—03. Mem.: Music Educators Nat. Conf., Am. Choral Dir. Assn., Phi Kappa Lambda, Sigma Alpha Iota. Presbyterian. Avocations: sewing, gardening, reading, cooking. Office: Annapolis Area Christian Sch 710 Ridgely Ave Annapolis MD 21401 Office Phone: 410-266-8255.

**SEETALA, NAIDU V.,** physics professor, researcher; s. Subba Rao and Veerayamma Seetala; m. Sailaja Bandi, Nov. 25, 1987; children: Prasant, Kiran Sai. PhD, Calcutta (India) U., 1985. Lectr., postdoctoral rsch. assoc. U. Tex., Artington, 1986—88; prof. Grambling State U., La., 1988—. Rsch. grantee, NSF, ONR, Dept. of Energy, USAF, 1988—2006. Mem.: Materials Rsch. Soc., Am. Chem. Soc. (sr. 2000). Office: Grambling State U Dept Physics RWE Jones Dr Carver Hall 81 Grambling LA 71245 Office Phone: 318-274-2574. Office Fax: 318-274-3281. E-mail: naidusv@gram.edu.

**SEETHALER, WILLIAM CHARLES,** international business executive, consultant; b. N.Y.C., Dec. 4, 1937; s. William Charles and Catherine Frances (Flaherty) Seethaler. Student, Quinnipiac Coll., Conn., 1955-56, Ohio State U., 1956-58; BSBA, U. San Francisco, 1977; MBA in Internat. High Tech., Pepperdine U., 1982; grad. tech. mktg. program, Stanford U., 1990; grad. global enterprise mgmt. program, Oxford U., Eng., 2000. Lic. real estate salesperson Calif. Asst. to v.p. sales T Sendzimir, Inc., Waterbury, Conn. and Paris, 1960-66; mgr. internat. sales Dempsey Indsl. Furnace Co., East Longmeadow, Mass., 1966-67; mgr. internat. sales Yoder Co., Cleve., 1967-74; mng. dir., owner Seethaler & Assocs., Palo Alto, Calif., 1974—; owner, chief exec. officer Seethaler Internat. Ltd., Palo Alto, Calif., 1982-92; ptnr. DFS Computer Assocs., San Jose, Calif., 1976-87; v.p. mktg. and sales Telewave Inc., Mountain View, Calif., 1996—2001; rep. IMSM, Malmesbury, Wiltshire, England, 2002—; Spacesonic, San Carlos, Calif., 2004—; assoc. prof. Internat. Mktg. Mission Coll., Santa Clara, Calif., 2006—. Bd. dirs. Palo Alto Fund, 1979—93, chmn., 1986—88; cmty. rels. advisor Stanford U., 1986—2003; mem. Friends of Rewley House, Oxford U., 2001—. Mem.: Soc. Mfg. Engrs., Joint Venture: Silicon Valley (bd. dirs. 1992—95), Assn. MBA Execs., Assn. Iron and Steel Engrs. (life), Inst. Indsl. Engrs. (sr.; v.p. profl. rels. Peninsula chpt. 1988—90, bd. dirs. 1988—, del. to Silicon Valley Engring. Coun. 1991—97), Ohio State U. Alumni Assn., Stanford U. Alumni Assn. (life), Pepperdine U. Alumni Assn., U. San Francisco Alumni Assn., Palo Alto C. of C. (bd. dirs. 1975—79, v.p. orgn. affairs 1976—77, pres. 1977—78), Stanford Diamond Club. Office: 345 Stanford Shopping Ctr #144 Palo Alto CA 94304-1412

**SEEVERS, ROBERT H.,** chemist; b. N.Y.C., Nov. 2, 1954; s. Robert H. and Hannah Rose Seevers; m. Arlene R. Kurz, Aug. 11, 1984; children: Anne Elizabeth, Deborah Grace, Matthew Robert, David Daniel. BS, Lehigh U., 1976; PhD, U. Mich., 1981. Radiopharmacy dir. Michael Reese Hosp. and Med. Ctr., Chgo.; chemistry reviewer U.S. FDA, Rockville, Md., 1994—98, chemistry rev. team leader, 1998—2001; tech. advisor Eli Lilly and Co., Indpls., 2002—. Mem., expert com. and packaging, storage, and distbn. US Pharmacopeia, Rockville, 2001—05; presenter in field. Author: (sci. regulatory consensus) FDA-Industry Consensus on Site-Specific Stability (FDA-CDER Excellence in Communication award, 2000); editor: (draft regulatory guidance) Stability Testing of Drug Substances and Drug Products; contbr. articles to profl. publs. Mem.: Am. Chem. Soc. Office: Eli Lilly and Co Lilly Corporate Center Indianapolis IN 46285 Office Phone: 317-651-4193.

**SEEWALDT, VICTORIA L.,** medical educator, researcher; b. Jackson Heights, N.Y., Jan. 9, 1959; d. Alfred and Elizabeth Seewaldt; m. Eric Carl Dietze, Aug. 25, 1993; 1 child, Erin Rebecca Seewaldt-Dietze. BA, Cornell U., Ithaca, N.Y., 1980; MD, U.Calif., Davis, 1989. Assoc. prof. Duke U. Sch. of Medicine, Durham, NC, 2000—. Dir. breast cancer rsch. Duke U. Sch. of Medicine, Durham, 2002—06. Cons. Susan G. Komen, Dallas, 2000—06. Recipient 3 basic/translational R01 rsch. awards, NIH, 2001—. Achievements include research in early events in breast cancer. Avocation: gardening. Office: Duke Univ Sch Medicine Box 2628 Rm 221A MSRB Research Drive Durham NC 27710 Office Phone: 919-668-3051. Office Fax: 919-668-2458. Business E-Mail: seewa001@mc.duke.edu.

**SEFF, JAMES M.,** lawyer; b. NYC, Jan. 27, 1941; AB with honors, U. Mich., 1963; JD, U. Calif., 1966. Bar: Hawaii 1969, Calif. 1970, US Dist. Ct. (no., ctrl. dist Calif., Hawaii), US Supreme Ct. Mem. Pillsbury Winthrop Shaw Pittman LLP, San Francisco, ptnr., chmn. Wine Beer & Spirits practice, co-chair restaurant, food & beverage group. Lectr. Univ. Calif., Davis; co-chmn. CLE Internat. Seminar on Wine Beer & Spirits Law; mem. adv. com. Columbia Univ. Legis. Drafting Rsch. Fund. Author (contributing): Univ. Calif. / Sotheby Book of California Wine; contbr. articles to profl. jours. Dir. Carmel Bach Festival; counsel Soc. Medical Friends of Wine; dir. Lasallian Edn. Fund; past v.p. Jewish Family & Children's Svc., San Francisco. Capt. USNR. Recipient Disting. Cmty. Svc. award, Jewish Family & Children's Svc. of San Francisco. Fellow: Am. Bar Found.; mem.: ABA (past chmn. alcoholic beverage practice com.), Barristers Club San Francisco (past pres.), San Francisco Bar Found. (past pres.), State Bar Calif. (past v.p., gov., vice chmn. conf. del.), Bar Assn. San Francisco (past pres., Award of Merit), Assn. Internationale des Juristes pour le Droit de la Vigne et du Vin, Am. Soc. Enology & Viticulture. Office: Pillsbury Winthrop Shaw Pittman 50 Fremont St San Francisco CA 94105 Office Phone: 415-983-7441. Office Fax: 415-983-1200. Business E-Mail: james.seff@pillsburylaw.com.

**SEFF, KARL,** chemistry educator; b. Chgo., Jan. 23, 1938; s. Joseph and Rose (Hauser) S. BS, U. Calif., Berkeley, 1959; PhD, MIT, 1964. Asst. rsch. chemist UCLA, 1965—67; asst. prof. chemistry U. Hawaii, Honolulu, 1968—73, assoc. prof. chemistry, 1973—75, prof. chemistry, 1975—. Cons. Filtrol Corp., L.A., 1966-73, Mitsubishi Heavy Industry, Nagasaki, Japan, 1992-94; vis. scholar Princeton (N.J.) U., 1974-75, Oxford (Eng.) U., 1988, 89, Pusan and Kyungpook Nat. Univs., Korea, 1996; assoc. rschr. U. Mex, 1981-82; vis. prof. Dartmouth U., 1989; lectr. Tokyo Inst. Tech., 1980, 91, U. Salford, Eng., 1983, U. Bristol, 1988, ETH, Zurich, Switzerland, 1988, Goethe U., Frankfurt, Germany, 1988, Imperial Coll., London, 1989, Cambridge U., 1989, Kyungpook Nat. U., Korea, 1990, Acad. Sci. Leningrad, 1990, Pusan Nat. U., Korea, 1990, Northwestern U., 1994, others; assoc. chair chemistry dept. U. Hawaii, 2000, chair, 2000-03. Contbr. numerous articles to profl. jours. NATO sr. fellow, NSF, 1975, Rsch. Travel award, 1988-90; grantee Army Rsch. Office, 1969-72, NIH, 1972-75, 75-78, NSF, 1973-76, 75, 77, 78-81, Petroleum Rsch. Fund, 1974-76, 95-98, Gordon Conf., 1976, U.S.-Korea Coop. Rsch., NSF, 1982, 84-86, Mitsubishi Industries, 1992-93. Mem. Am. Chem. Soc. (local sect. chair, award 1983, councilor 1992-94, 2005—, pres. 1983), Am. Crystallographic Assn., Vegetarian Soc. Honolulu (exec. com. 1993—), Internat. Peolite Assn., Sigma Xi. Democrat. Avocations: travel, gardening. Office: U Hawaii Dept Chemistry 2545 The Mall Honolulu HI 96822-2233 Business E-Mail: seff@hawaii.edu.

**SEFF, RICHARD,** actor, writer; b. N.Y.C., Sept. 23, 1927; s. Chester and Henrietta (Levy) Siff. BA, NYU, 1947. Agt. MCA, Inc., N.Y.C., 1954-62; sec., treas. Hesseltine, Bookman & Seff, N.Y.C., 1962-69; v.p. Creative Mgmt. Assn., N.Y.C., 1969-74. Staff writer Theater Week Magazine, N.Y.C., 1988—. Author: (musical book) Shine!, 2001; (plays) Paris Is Out, 1969-70, The Whole Ninth Floor starring Alan Alda, 1966; appeared on Broadway in Darkness At Noon, 1950-52, Herzl, 1976, The Seagull, 1982, End of the World, 1984, Musical Comedy Murders of 1940, 1987; off-Broadway in Modigliani, 1979-80, Childe Byron, 1981, Richard II, 1982, Angels Fall, 1984, Only You, 1987, Summer and Smoke, 1988, Established Price, 1990, Countess Mitzi, 1991, Lend Me a Tenor, 1991, The Cocktail Hour, 1992, The Truth Teller, 1995, The Countess, 1999-2000; appeared in films The Onion Field, 1979, Being There, 1979, Where The Buffalo Roam, 1980, A Stranger is Watching, 1982, Quiz Show, 1994, The Hours, 2002. Recipient Carbonell award for best featured actor in play Angels Fall, Carbonell (Fla.) Com., 1984. Avocations: financial planning, theatrical investment, travel.

**SEFFKER COPE, ANGELA ROSE,** librarian; b. West Allis, Wis., May 26, 1965; d. Allen Herman Seffker and Mary Ann Wenzel; m. Daniel Lee Cope; children: Margaret Rose Cope, Brandon Lee Cope; m. Charles Scott Yates (div.); 1 child, Frederick Augustus Yates. BS, SW Mo. State U., 1989, MS, 1992; M in Libr. and Info. Sci., U. Wis., 1994. Map libr. Am. Geog. Soc. Libr., Milw., 2002—. Citizen adv. Ozaukee County Comprehensive Planning, Port Washington, Wis., 2003—06. Office: Am Geographical Soc Libr 2311 E Hartford Ave Milwaukee WI 53211 Office Phone: 414-229-6282. Office Fax: 414-229-3624. Business E-Mail: acope@uwm.edu.

**SEFFRIN, JOHN REESE,** health science association administrator, educator; b. Hagerstown, Ind., May 19, 1944; s. Theodore H. and Mary Ellen (Reese) Seffrin; m. Carole Sue Washburn, Apr. 16, 1966; 1 child, Mary. BS in Edn., Ball State U., 1966, DSc (hon.), 1994; MS, U. Ill., 1967; PhD in Health Edn., Purdue U., 1970, D (hon.) in Social Sci., 2003. Asst. prof. health edn. Purdue U., West Lafayette, Ind., 1970—76, assoc. prof., 1976—79; prof., chmn. dept. applied health sci. Ind. U., Bloomington, 1979—92; CEO Am. Cancer Soc., Atlanta, 1992—. Trustee Am. Cancer Soc. Found., 1992—; guest lectr. various pub. health orgns. and schs., 1970—; bd. dirs. Healthcare Inc.; mem. subcom. on cessation Dept. HHS, Washington, 2002—03; charter mem., mem. steering com. C-Change (formerly Nat. Dialog on Cancer), 1999. Nat. bd. dirs. Am. Lung Assn., 1980—90; treas. Partnership for Prevention of Premature Death, Disease and Disability, 1991—; mem. Pres.'s Commn. on Improving Econ. Opportunity in Cmtys. Dependent on Tobacco Prodn. While Protecting Pub. Health, 2000—01; trustee Ctr. for Advancement of Health; pres. State Welfare Bd. Ind. Dept. Pub. Welfare, 1979—80, 1982—84; treas. Midwest Nuc. Bd., 1973—75; chmn. cmty. edn. com. Am. Lung Assn., 1981—83, v.p., 1980, pres., 1982; bd. dirs. Nat. Ctr. Tobacco-Free Kids, 1997—2000; chmn. bd. dirs. Nat. Health Coun., 1998—2000; bd. advisors Discovery Health Media, 2000—; bd. dirs. Wabash Ctr. for the Mentally Retarded, 1970—73. Named Commr.-at-large. Nat. Commn. Health Edn. Credentialing, 1995—2000, Sagamore of Wabash, State of Ind., 1980, 1988; recipient Cert. appreciation, Surgeon Gen. Pub. Health Svc., 1992, Outstanding Alumnus award, Ball State U., 1982. Fellow: Am. Sch. Health Assn. (mem. governing coun. 1979—81, 1982—89, pres. 1987—88, Howe award 1991); mem.: NAS (Nat. Cancer Policy Bd. 1997—2002), AMA, Am. Acad. Family Physicians (pub. adv. bd. 1999—), Rsch. Am. (bd. dirs. 1996—), Independent Sector (bd. dirs. 1997—, 1997—), Nat. Interagy. Coun. on Smoking and Health (bd. dirs. 1979—), Internat. Union Against Cancer (ex-officio mem. U.S. nat. com. 2000—, pres. 2002—06), Nat. Assn. for Health, Phys. Edn. and Recreation (pres. 1976, Cert. of Appreciation 1977, Honor award 1982), Am. Cancer Soc. (dir. Ind. Divsn. 1977—90, chmn. Ind. Divsn. 1982—85, dir.-at-large to nat. bd. dirs., chmn. nat. pub. edn. com. 1984—87, nat. v.p. 1986—87, chmn. nat. bd. dirs. 1989—91), Ind. Thoracic Soc. (mem. governing coun. 1977—84), Ind. Family Health Coun. (dir. 1979—81, v.p. 1980—81, pres. 1981), Ind. Assn. Health Educators (pres. 1975—76, chair 1997—2000), Assn. for Advancement Health Edn. (bd. dirs. 1989—92), Nat. Assn. State Bds. of Edn. (commn. on sch. cmty. role in improving adolescent health 1989—90), Eta Sigma Gamma, Phi Delta Kappa. Roman Catholic. Office: Am Cancer Soc 1599 Clifton Rd NE Atlanta GA 30329-4251

**SEGA, A. CHRISTOPHER,** lawyer; b. Frankfurt, Germany, Oct. 12, 1954; AB, Dartmouth Coll., 1976; MBA, George Washington Univ., 1981; JD with cert. in Comparative & Internat. Law, Catholic Univ. Am., 1991. Bar: Md. 1991, DC 1992, US Tax Ct. 1993. Ptnr., Trusts & Estates, Taxation practices Venable LLP, Washington. Adj. prof. Catholic Univ. Am., 1993—95, Georgetown Univ., 2004—. Contbr. articles to profl. jours. Named a Top Washington Lawyer, Washingtonian Mag., 2004. Fellow: Am. Coll. Trust & Estate Counsel; mem.: ABA (vice chmn. com. fiduciary income tax, chmn. subcom. grantor trusts), DC Bar Assn. Office: Venable LLP 575 7th St NW Washington DC 20004 also: Venable LLP 5th Fl 1 Church St Rockville MD 20850 Office Phone: 202-344-8565, 301-217-5658. Office Fax: 202-344-8300. Business E-Mail: acsega@venable.com.

**SEGA, RONALD MICHAEL,** civilian military employee, former dean; b. Cleve., Dec. 4, 1952; m. Bonnie Dunbar. BS in Math. and Physics, USAF Acad., 1974; MS in Physics, Ohio State U., 1975; grad., Squadron Officers Sch., 1979; PhD in Elec. Engring., U. Colo., 1982; grad., Air Command and Staff Coll., 1985, Air War Coll., 1991; Ph.D (hon.), Clarkson U., 1993; grad.

Mgmt. Inst., Harvard U., 1997; Ph.D (hon.), Bridgewater State Coll., 1998; exec. program in global security, Harvard U., 2001. Commd. 2d lt. USAF, 1974, advanced through grades to maj. gen., 2001, ret., 2005, instr. pilot Williams AFB, Ariz., 1976—79; mem. faculty USAF Acad., 1979—82, asst. prof., 1982—85, assoc. prof., 1985—90, tech. dir. Lasers & Aerospace Mechanics Directorate, Frank J. Seiler Rsch. Lab, 1987—88; astronaut Space Shuttle Discovery, 1990; dir. ops. Gagarin Cosmonaut Training Ctr. NASA, Russia, 1994—95; payload comdr. 3d Shuttle/Mir docking mission Atlantis, 1996; dean Coll. Engring. & Applied Sci. U. Colo., Colorado Springs, 1996—2001; dir. def., rsch. & engring. US Dept Def., Washington, 2001—05, under sec. USAF, 2005—. Contbr. articles to tech. publs. Decorated Legion of Merit, Def. Meritorious Svc. medal, Meritorious Svc. medal with oak leaf cluster; named a Air Force rsch. fellow, Air Force Office Sci. Acad., 1980; named to Ohio Vets. Hall of Fame, 1994; recipient Outstanding Leadership medal, NASA, 1997. Fellow: AIAA (assoc. Achievement award 1996), Inst. for Advancement of Engring.; mem.: IEEE (sr.), Aerospace Edn. Found. (trustee 2000). Office: USAF 1670 Air Force Pentagon Rm 4E886 Washington DC 20330

**SEGAL, BERNARD LOUIS,** cardiologist, educator; b. Montreal, Feb. 13, 1929; came to U.S., 1961, naturalized, 1966; s. Irving and Fay (Schecter) S.; m. Idajane Fischman, Feb. 17, 1963; 1 dau., Jody Segal Reinbold. BSc cum laude, McGill U., 1950, postgrad., 1950-51, MD, C.M. high standing, 1955. Diplomate Am. Bd. Internal Medicine. Intern Jewish Gen Hosp., Montreal, 1955-56; resident Balt. City Hosp., 1956-57, Beth Israel Hosp., Boston, 1957-58, Georgetown Med. Ctr., Washington, 1958-59, St. George's Hosp., London, 1959-61; pvt. practice internal medicine and cardiology Phila., 1961—; prof. medicine Med. Coll. Pa., Hahnemann U., 1996—; prof. medicine, sr. attending physician Jefferson Med. Coll./Thomas Jefferson U., 1998—. Dir. cardiology Thomas Jefferson U., 1998. Author: Auscultation of the Heart, 1965; Editor: Theory and Practice of Auscultation, 1964, Engineering in the Practice of Medicine, 1966, Your Heart, 1972, Arteriosclerosis and Coronary Heart Disease, 1972; mem. editl. bd. Am. Jour. Cardiology, 1970—, Clin. Echocardiography, 1978; contbr. articles to profl. jour. Fellow ACP, Am. Coll. Cardiology (chmn. scholar-trainee com., trustee 1969-71), Am. Coll. Chest Physicians; mem. NY Acad. Sci., Alpha Omega Alpha. Home: 1156 Red Rose Ln Villanova PA 19085-2121 Office: Jefferson Heart Inst 925 Chestnut St Mezzanine Philadelphia PA 19107-4824 also: 401 E City Line Ave Ste 525 Bala Cynwyd PA 19004-1125 Office Phone: 215-955-8145, 610-667-5555.

**SEGAL, JACK,** mathematics professor; b. Phila., May 9, 1934; s. Morris and Rose (Novin) S.; m. Arlene Stern, Dec. 18, 1955; children: Gregory, Sharon. BS, U. Miami, 1955, MS, 1957; PhD, U. Ga., 1960. Instr. math. U. Wash., Seattle, 1960-61, asst. prof., 1961-65, assoc. prof., 1965-70, prof., 1970-1999, prof. emeritus, 2000—, chmn. dept., 1975-78. Author: Lecture Notes in Mathematics, 1978, Shape Theory, 1982. NSF postdoctoral fellow Inst. Advanced Study, Princeton, N.J., 1963-64; Fulbright fellow U. Zagreb, Croatia, 1969-70, U. Coll. London hon. rsch. fellow, 1988; NAS exch. prof. U. Zagreb, 1979-80. Mem. Am. Math. Soc. Home: 8711 25th Pl NE Seattle WA 98115-3416 Office: U Washington Dept Mathematics Seattle WA 98195-0001 Office Phone: 206-543-1914. E-mail: segal@math.washington.edu.

**SEGAL, JONATHAN BRUCE,** editor; b. NYC, May 12, 1946; s. Clement and Florence Lillian (Miller) S.; m. Haidi Kuhn, June 30, 1974. BA, Washington Coll., 1966. Writer, editor NY Times, NYC, 1966-73; editor Quadrangle/NY Times Book Co., NYC, 1974-76; sr. editor Simon & Schuster, NYC, 1976-81; exec. editor, editor-in-chief, editl. dir., v.p. Times Books, NYC, 1981-89; editor-at-large Random House, NYC, 1985-89; v.p., sr. editor Alfred A. Knopf, NYC, 1989—. Contbr. articles to popular jour. Democrat. Jewish. Home: 115 E 9th St Apt 12E New York NY 10003-5420 Office: Alfred A Knopf 1745 Broadway New York NY 10019 E-mail: jsegal@randomhouse.com.

**SEGAL, LORE,** writer; b. Vienna, Mar. 8, 1928; came to U.S., 1951, naturalized, 1956; d. Ignatz and Franzi (Stern) Groszmann; m. David I. Segal, Nov. 3, 1960 (dec.); children: Beatrice Ann, Jacob Paul. BA in English, Bedford Coll., U. London, Eng., 1948. Prof. writing div. Sch. Arts, Columbia U., also Princeton U., Sarah Lawrence Coll., Bennington Coll.; founder guest lectr. U. Ill., Chgo., 1978-92, Ohio State U., 1992-97. Author: Other People's Houses, 1964; Lucinella, 1976, Her First American, 1985; (children's book) Tell Me A Mitzi, 1970, All the Way Home, 1973, Tell Me a Trudy, 1977; The Story of Mrs. Brubeck and How She Looked for Trouble and Where She Found Him, 1981, The Story of Mrs. Lovewright and Purrless Her Cat, 1985, Morris the Artist, 2003, Why Mole Shouted and Other Stories, 2004, More Mole Stories and Little Gopher Too, 2005; translator: (with W.D. Snodgrass) Gallows Songs, 1968, The Juniper Tree and Other Tales from Grimm, 1973, The Book of Adam to Moses, 1987, The Story of King Saul and King David, 1991; contbr. short stories, articles to N.Y. Times Book Rev., Partisan Rev., New Republic, The New Yorker, others5 Guggenheim fellow, 1965-66; Council Arts and Humanities grantee, 1968-69; Artists Public Service grantee, 1970-71; CAPS grantee, 1975; Nat. Endowment Arts grantee, spring 1982, 1987; NEH grantee, 1983; Acad. Arts and Letters award, 1986. Fellow: Acad. Arts & Scis. Address: 280 Riverside Dr New York NY 10025-9010 Office Phone: 212-663-1524. E-mail: Lore@usa.net.

**SEGAL, MARTIN ELI,** retired actuarial and consulting company executive; b. Vitebsk, Russia, Aug. 15, 1916; came to U.S., 1921, naturalized, 1928; s. Isidor and Anna (Title) S.; m. Edith Levy, June 17, 1937; children: Susan Segal Rai, Paul. LHD (hon.), Pratt Inst., 1976; MusD (hon.), Mannes Coll. Music, 1976; LHD (hon.), Grad. Ctr. CUNY, 1979, L.I. U., 1986, NYU, 1988, The Julliard Sch., 2006; D in Music (hon.), Manhattan Sch. Music, 1999. Various positions ins. industry, 1935-39; founder The Segal Co., consultants and actuaries, N.Y.C., 1939, pres., CEO, 1939-67, chmn. bd., 1967-91, cons., 1991—. Pres. Wertheim Asset Mgmt. Svcs., Inc., N.Y.C., 1972-75, chmn. bd., 1975-82; ptnr. Wertheim & Co., investment bankers, N.Y.C., 1967-82; comdr. Order of Arts and Letters, Ministry of Culture of French Govt., 2005, officer, 1984-05. Former columnist: Associated Press. Founding chmn. The N.Y. Internat. Festival of the Arts, Inc., 1985-02; chmn. bd. Lincoln Ctr. Performing Arts, Inc., 1981-86, chmn. emeritus, 1986—; gen. chmn. Night of 100 Stars (first ever AIDS Benefit), Actors' Fund Am., 1985; organizing co-chmn. Internat. Conf. on Future of Arts Edn., 1999; bd. dirs., founding mem. Pub. Radio Internat., 1981-94, dir. emeritus, 1994-98; counselor at large, 1998—; co-chmn. Conf. on Intellectual Property The Arts and Tech., 1994; chmn. arts and culture com., N.Y. 92, N.Y. 93, N.Y. 94, N.Y. 95; chmn. First Equal Opportunity Day Dinner, Nat. Urban League, 1961, nat. bd. mem., 1961-70, v.p. 1967-70; mem., bd. dirs. Nat. Bldg. Mus., 1983-91; founding mem., bd. advisers Libr. of Am., 1984—, sole hon. mem. bd. dirs., 2005—; trustee Am.-Scandinavian Found., 1986-91, adv. trustee, 1991—; bd. visitors Grad. Sch. and Univ. Ctr., CUNY, 1983-96; bd. trustees The Grad. Ctr. Found., Inc., 1996—, vice chmn. bd. trustees, 2003—; bd. dirs. ASCAP Found., 1997-03, S.L.E. Lupus Found., 2000—; mem. adv. bd. French Am. Cultural Exch.; mem. arts adv. com. Harvard, 1993-94, consultant, 1999—; bd. trustees, chmn. exhbns. com. Mus. Modern Art, 1978-81; trustee Inst. for Advanced Study, Princeton, N.J., 1972-91, trustee emeritus, 1991—; bd. dirs. City Ctr. Music and Drama, 1971-74, trustee N.Y. City Ctr., 1974—; founder, pres. Cultural Assistance Ctr., Inc., 1974-82, chmn., 1982-84, hon. chmn., 1984—; founding pres. Film Soc. of Lincoln Ctr., 1968-78, pres. emeritus, 1978—; mem. adv. com. Tony voter Am. Theater Wing, 2000—; mem. adv. coun. Theatre Devel. Fund, 1972—; Town Hall Found., 1986-; mem. nat. bd. Young Audiences, Inc., 1979—; mem. adv. bd. Concert Artists Guild, 1983-00; founding mem. trustees. The Pub. Interest, 1965-2002; mem. vis. com. Harvard U. Sch. Pub. Health, 1979-92, dean's coun. Sch. Pub. Health, 1990—; mem. adv. bd. Studio in a Sch. Assn., 1988—; bd. dirs. Helena Rubinstein Found., 1972-95; chmn. mayor's Com. on Cultural Policy, 1974; founding chmn. Commn. for Cultural Affairs City of N.Y., 1975-77; chmn. pub. svc. exam. bd. Fund for City of N.Y., 1978, 79, bd. dirs. 1978-87; co-chair China cultural exch. mission, Ctr. US-China Arts Exchange, 1979; bd. mem. Bd. Hosps. City N.Y., 1962-70, N.Y. City Health and Hosps. Corp., chmn. fin. com., exec. com. mem., 1970-72; founder Film Guild N.Y., 1940-41. Decorated Royal Swedish Order of Polar Star; recipient Spl. award, Internat. Film Importers and Distbrs. Am., 1973, Cert. of Merit, Mcpl. Art Soc., 1974, award for Svc. to Music, Third Street Music Sch. Settlement, 1981, award of Honor for Arts and Culture, N.Y.C. Mayor, 1982, Ann. award of Distinction, Mus. City of N.Y., 1982, Concert Artists Guild award, 1983, Edn. Fund award, LWV of NYC, 1984, Disting. Am. Fgn. Birth award, Internat. Ctr. NYC, 1985, John H. Finley medal, Alumni Assn. CCNY, 1985, Annual Arts Leadership award, Alumni and Friends of LaGuardia H.S., 1985, Friend of the Arts award, Town Hall, 1987, Dirs. Emeriti award, Lincoln Ctr. for Performing Arts, Inc., 1987, Patron of the Arts award, Songwriters' Hall of Fame, 1988, NY State Gov.'s Arts award, 1989, Presdl. Citation award, Nat. Fedn. Music Clubs, 1989, Pub. Spirit award, Creative Arts Rehab. Ctr., 1989, Pres.'s award, Grad. Sch. and Univ. Ctr. of City Univ. of N.Y., 1990, Honor medal, Nat. Arts Club, 1992, Laureate award, Lincoln Ctr., 1997, Our Town Treasure award, Mus. City of N.Y., 1998, Civic Leadership award, Citizens Union of City of N.Y., 1998, award of Honor, Arts Roundtable, 1998, CUNY Graduate Ctr., Martin E. Segal Theatre Ctr., 2000, Acting Co. Joan Warburg Humanitarian award, 2001, S.L.E. Lupus Found. award, 2001, Honoree, Am.-Scandinavian Found., 2004, Alliance for Arts, 2004, Chamber Music Soc. Lincoln Ctr., 2005, Living Landmark Honoree, NY Landmarks Conservancy, 2005. Mem.: The Pilgrims of the U.S., Century Assn. Democrat. Jewish. Office: 375 Park Ave Ste 2602 New York NY 10152-2699

**SEGAL, PHYLLIS NICHAMOFF,** mediator; b. Apr. 18, 1945; d. Sidney and Theresa Helen (Uroff) Nichamoff; m. Eli J. Segal, June 13, 1965; children: Jonathan, Mora. Student, Brandeis U., 1962-65; BA, U. Mich., 1966; JD, Georgetown U., 1973. Bar: N.Y. 1974, U.S. Dist. Ct. (so. and ea. dists.) N.Y. 1975, Mass. 1983, U.S. Supreme Ct. 1979. Deputy atty. gen. Commonwealth Mass., 1986—88; assoc. Weil, Gotshal and Manges, N.Y.C., 1973-77; legal dir. NOW Legal Def. and Edn. Fund., N.Y.C., 1977-82, gen. counsel, 1986—94; mediator ADR Assoc., L.L.C., Boston, 2001—. Chmn. Fed. Labor Rels. Auth., Washington, 1994-2000; gen. counsel Exec. office Transp. and Constrn., Commonwealth of Mass., 1984-86; adj. asst. prof. law NYU, 1980-82; fellow Bunting Inst. Radcliffe Coll., 1982-83; cons. U.S. Commn. Civil Rights. Contbr. articles to profl. jours. Mem. Commn. on Party Reform Nat. Dem. Party, 1972-73, mem. Compliance Rev. Commn., 1974-76; mem. adv. bd. Mass. Commn. Against Discrimination, 1983—; bd. chmn. Handgun Control Inc./Ctr. to Prevent Handgun Violence; former chairwoman Nat. Labor Rels. Authority. Mem. ABA, Fedn. Women Lawyers Jud. Screening Panel, Mass. Bar Assn.

**SEGAL, RENA BETH,** artist; b. New Brunswick, N.J., May 27, 1953; d. George and Helen (Steinberg) S BFA, Montclair State Coll., 1975; MFA, Rutgers U., 1977. One person shows include Ocean County Coll., Toms River, N.J., 1978, Piscataway (N.J.) Mcpl. Bldg., 1983, Johnson and Johnson, New Brunswick, 1985, N.J. State Mus., Trenton, 1989, Mystic Knight Gallery, New Brunswick, 1990, Advocate Bldg., Stamford, Conn., 1991, Gratz Gallery, New Hope, Pa., 2001, Rutgers U. Art Libr., New Brunswick, 2004, Princeton U., 2004, CAS Gallery Kean U., Union, NJ, 2005.; exhibited in group shows Dumont Landis Gallery, New Brunswick, 1981, Sidney Janis Gallery, N.Y.C., 1984, Laforet Mus. Harajunku, Tokyo, 1986, Morris Mus., Morristown, N.J., 1987, Hunterdon Art Ctr., Clinton, N.J., 1990, Phoenix Group, Metuchen, N.J., 1993, Sound Shore Gallery, Stamford, 1994, 95, 96, The Gallery at Bristol-Meyer Squibb, Princeton, 1995, 98, Collectors Edge Summit, N.J., 1999, N.J. Ctr. Arts, Summit, 1999, Marsh Ins. Co., Morristown, 2000, Rutgers U. Art Libr., New Brunswick, 2003, Gallery at StageWorks Hudson, N.Y., 2005, others; represented in permanent collections Pub. Svc. and Electric, Newark, Pepsico, Purchase, N.Y., Bristol-Meyers Squibb, Lawrenceville, N.J., Johnson & Johnson, New Brunswick, Chase Manhattan Bank, N.Y., Marsh Ins. Co., Morristown, Frederick R. Weisman Found., L.A. N.J. State Coun. on Arts fellow, 1985

**SEGAL, ROBERT MARTIN,** lawyer; b. Atlantic City, Apr. 7, 1935; s. Nathan Albert and Edna (Dutkin) S.; m. Rhoda Sue Luber, June 8, 1958; children— Deborah Ann, William Nathan, Elizabeth Ann Student, Cornell U., 1953-54; BS in Econs., U. Pa., 1957; LLB cum laude, Harvard Law Sch. 1960. Bar: Pa. 1961. Assoc. Wolf, Block, Schorr & Solis-Cohen LLP, Phila., 1960-69, ptnr., 1969—, chmn., exec. com., 1978-79, 82-83, 86-87, 89-98. Hon. pres. Jewish Employment and Vocat. Svc.; bd. dirs. Orleans Homebuilders, Inc. Contbr. articles to profl. jours. and mags. Constable of elections Lower Merion Twp., Pa., 1970-72; bd. dirs. Jewish Family and Children's Agy., Am. Jewish Com., Feinstein Ctr. for Am. Jewish History at Temple U., Greater Phila. Urban Affairs Coalition; bd. govs. Rep. Jewish Coalition; past trustee Hahnemann U., Fedn. Jewish Agys., Phila. Rehab. Plan, Inc., Rosenbach Mus. and Libr. Mem. ABA, Pa. Bar Assn., Phila. Bar Assn., Internat. Coun. Shopping Ctrs., Urban Land Inst. (assoc.), Am. Coll. Real Estate Lawyers, Phila. Bar Found. (trustee 1981-87), Am. Law Inst., Harvard Law Sch. Assn. Phila., Federalist Soc., Wharton Club, Chaine des Rotisseurs, L'Ordre Mondial, Sunday Breakfast Club, La Coquille Club, Harvard Club, Beta Gamma Sigma. Avocations: golf, swimming. Office: Wolf Block Schorr & Solis-Cohen LLP 1650 Arch St Fl 22 Philadelphia PA 19103-2097 Office Phone: 215-977-2230. Personal E-mail: rsegal@wolfblock.com.

**SEGAL, ROBERT S.,** retail executive; b. New Haven, Conn., Nov. 4, 1954; s. Leonard and Barbara Segal; m. Mariquita A.K. Segal, Aug. 7, 1977; 1 child, James Q. AB, Ripon Coll., 1975; MA, NYU, 1977; postgrad., U. Ill., 1981. Buyer Hecht Co., Arlington, Va., 1981-87; mktg. mgr. Lechmere, Woburn, Mass., 1987-89; v.p. merchandising Rickel Home Ctr., Plainfield, NJ, 1989-90; dir. merchandising Best Products, Richmond, Va., 1990-93; sr. v.p. merchandising Fresh Fields, Rockville, Md., 1993-94; v.p. merchandising Shopko, Green Bay, Wis., 1995—2004, Big Lots, Inc., Columbus, Ohio, 2004— Mem. adv. bd. Internat. Housewares Show, Chgo., 1998. Contbr. articles to profl. jours. Bd. dirs. Autism Soc. of Am. Found., 2000-2001, Orgn.for Autism Rsch., 2002—. Mem. Phi Beta Kappa. Office Phone: 614-278-7042. Business E-Mail: rsegal@biglots.com.

**SEGAL, SHELDON JEROME,** biologist, educator, foundation administrator; b. NYC, Mar. 15, 1926; s. Morris M. and Florence (Bogen) S.; m. Harriet Ellen Feinberg, May 22, 1961; children: Amy Robin, Jennifer Ann, Laura Jane. BA, Dartmouth Coll., 1947; postgrad., U. Geneva, 1947-48; MS, U. Iowa, 1951, PhD, 1952; MD (hon.), U. Tampere, Finland, 1984, U. Uppsala, Sweden, 1985; LHD (hon.), Mercy Coll. Rsch. scientist William S. Merrill Co., Cin., 1952-53; rsch. assoc., asst. prof. U. Iowa, 1953-56; asst. med. dir. Population Coun., N.Y.C., 1956-63, med. dir., 1963-78, v.p., 1969-76, sr. v.p., 1976-78; affiliate Rockefeller U., N.Y.C., 1956-76, adj. prof., 1977-87; dir. population scis. Rockefeller Found., 1978-91; disting. scientist Population Coun., N.Y.C., 1991—. Lectr. Columbia U., 1959-61; vis. prof. All-India Inst. Med. Scis., New Delhi, 1962-63, Amir Chand lectr., 1975; mem. Marine Biol. Lab, Woods Hole, Mass.; cons. World Bank, WHO, NIH, Ford Found., Indian Govt., UN Office Sci. and Tech., UN Fund Population Activities; mem. com. on contraceptive tech. NAS, 1977-80, com. on health effects of marijuana Inst. Medicine, 1981-82, NAS com. on demographic impact of contraceptive tech., 1988-89, nat. rsch. com., overview com. for Indo-U.S. initiative, 1985-89; adv. com. on human reproduction FDA; cons. to dir. Nat. Inst. Child Health and Human Devel., 1978-80; plenary lectr. 3d World Congress Endocrinology, 1968, Upjohn lectr. Am. Fertility Soc., 1971, plenary lectr. World Fertility Congress, 1975, Sigma Xi lectr. U. Idaho, 1976, plenary lectr. World Congress on Ob-Gyn., 1976, lectr. Chinese Acad. Scis., 1977, Carl Gemzell lectr. U. Uppsala, 1982, Pierre Soupart lectr. Axel Munthe Found., 1988, Alpha Omega Alpha lectr. U. Pa. Coll. Medicine, 1989, plenary lectr. World Congress on Human Reproduction, 1990, 2005; hon. prof. Peking Union Med. Coll., Beijing, 1987, Chinese Acad. Scis., 1988; trustee Marine Biol. Lab., 1985—, chmn. bd. trustees, 1991-2004; pres. 10th World Congress on Human Reproduction, 1990, 2004. Co-editor 8 books; author 3 books; contbr. 300 articles to profl. jours. Trustee Rye Country Day Sch., 1979-85, pres. bd. trustees, 1981-85; trustee Ctr. for Reproductive Law and Policy, 1992—. Lt. (j.g.) USNR, 1943-45. Decorated Order Comdr. of Lion (Finland); recipient Honor award Innsbruck U., Austria, hon. citation Pres. of India, 1978, Clarence J. Gamble award World Acad. Arts and Scis., 1980,

Joseph C. Wilson award Rochester Assn. for UN, 1981, UN Population award, 1984, Axel Munthe award in medicine Axel Munthe Found., Italy, 1985, Sci. award Planned Parenthood Fedn. Am., 1990, Dmitirus N. Chorafas award in medicine Swiss Acad. Scis., 1995. Fellow AAAS, Royal Coll. Obstetricians and Gynecologists (hon.); mem. Am. Reproductive Med. Soc. (hon. v.p. 1975-76, trustee found. 1975-77), Endocrine Soc., Internat. Soc. for Study Reprodn. (pres. 1968-72), Coun. Fgn. Rels., Internat. Acad. Human Reproduction (hon. pres. 2005), Mexican Acad. Medicine (hon.), Inst. Medicine, Dartmouth Club N.Y., Woods Hole Yacht Club. Home: 515 E 72nd St New York NY 10021 Office: Population Coun One Dag Hammarskjold Plz New York NY 10017 E-mail: ssegal@popcoun.org.

**SEGAL, STEVEN E.,** retired lawyer; b. Norfolk, Va., May 19, 1941; AB, Coll. William & Mary, 1963; MBA, U. Miami, 1965; JD, U. Houston, 1971. Bar: Tex. 1971. Mem. Fulbright & Jaworski L.L.P., Houston, 1971—2001; ret., 2001. Mem. State Bar Tex., Houston Bar Assn., Phi Delta Phi, Omicron Delta Kappa Office: Fulbright & Jaworski LLP 1301 Mckinney St Ste 5100 Houston TX 77010-3031 Office Phone: 713-651-5554. Business E-Mail: ssegal@fulbright.com.

**SEGAL, THEODORE D.,** lawyer; b. Washington, Aug. 7, 1955; BA magna cum laude, Duke Univ., 1977; JD magna cum laude, Georgetown Univ., 1984. Bar: Md. 1985, DC 1986. Law clk. Chief Judge William C. Pryor, DC Ct. Appeals, 1984—86; ptnr., co-chmn. Health Care practice group, office mng. ptnr. DLA Piper Rudnick Gray Cary, Washington. Mem.: ABA, Am. Health Lawyers Assn. Office: DLA Piper Rudnick Gray Cary 1200 19th St NW Washington DC 20036-2412 Office Phone: 202-861-3838. Office Fax: 202 223-2085. Business E-Mail: theodore.segal@dlapiper.com.

**SEGALL, PAUL,** geologist, educator; BA/MS in Earth Scis., Case Western Reserve U., 1976; PhD in Geology, Stanford U., Calif., 1981. Geologist US Geol. Survey, 1981—93, project chief mechanics of faulting and fracturing, 1983—93; assoc. prof. rsch. Stanford U., Calif., 1989—93, assoc. prof., 1993—98, prof., 1998—. Consulting prof. Stanford U., Calif., 1987—89, assoc. chair geophysics dept., 2003—04; vis. assoc. prof. U. Grenoble, France, 1991; sci. adv. team Long Valley caldera US Geol. Survey, 1994—; vis. prof. Inst. Earth Physics, Paris, 2000; mem. Calif. Earthquake Prediction Evaluation Coun., 2002—; mem. sci. earthquake adv. com. Dept. Interior, 2002—06. Contbr. articles to sci. jours. Fellow: Am. Geophys. Union (pres. tectonophysics sect. 2003—04, J.B. Macelwane medal 1990), Geol. Soc. Am. Office: Stanford U Dept Geophysics Mitchell Bldg 397 Panama Mall Stanford CA 94305-2215 E-mail: segall@pangea.stanford.edu.*

**SEGALL, ROBERT D.,** lawyer; b. Chgo., 1946; BA, Vanderbilt Univ., Nashville, 1968; JD summa cum laude, Univ. Ala. Sch. of Law, Tuscaloosa, 1971; LLM, Harvard Univ. Law Sch., Cambridge. Law clerk Hon. Frank M. Johnson Jr., 1971—72; shareholder Copeland, Franco, Screws & Gill PA, Montgomery, Ala. Mem.: ABA, Am. Coll. Trial Lawyers, Ala. Bar Assn. (pres.-elect 2004—05), U.S. Supreme Ct., 1975, U.S. Ct. of Appeals 11th Cir., U.S. Ct. of Appeals 5th Cir., 1974, U.S. Dist. Ct. Middle Dist. Ala., 1972, Am. Bd. Trial Advocates, Ala. Bd. of Bar Commrs., Montgomery Bar Assn. (pres. 1989), Ala. Law Found. (life). Office: Copeland Franco Screws & Gill PA PO Box 347 Montgomery AL 36101-0347 Office Phone: 334-834-1180. Business E-Mail: segall@copelandfranco.com.

**SEGALL, WYNN H.,** lawyer; b. Phila. AB cum laude, U. Pa., 1983; JD, U. Chgo., 1989; MPhil, Oxford U., 1985. Bar: NY 1990, DC 1991, US Ct. Internat. Trade, US Ct. Appeals, Fed. Cir. Polit. risk analyst Middle East; ptnr. internat. trade Akin Gump Strauss Hauer & Feld LLP, Washington, DC. Contbr. articles to profl. jours. Thowon scholar, 1985. Mem.: ABA (mem. internat. sec.), NY State Bar Assn., DC Bar Assn. Office: Akin Gump Strauss Hauer & Feld LLP Robert S Strauss Bldg 1333 New Hampshire Ave NW Washington DC 20036-4288 Office Phone: 202-887-4573. Office Fax: 202-955-7823. E-mail: wsegall@akingump.com.

**SEGALLA, THOMAS FRANCIS,** lawyer; b. Lee, Mass., Apr. 7, 1943; s. Stanley John and Ann (Finnegan) S.; m. Mary Louise, Aug. 5, 1967. BBA, U. Miami, Coral Gables, Fla., 1965; JD cum laude, SUNY-Buffalo, 1972. Bar: N.Y. 1973, U.S. Dist. Ct. (we.dist.) N.Y. 1973, U.S. Supreme Ct. 1983. Prodn. mgr. UniRoyal Inc., Naugatuck, Conn., 1966-69; law asst. N.Y. Atty. Gen., Buffalo, 1971; ptnr. Saperston & Day, PC, Buffalo, 1972-2001, Goldberg Segalla, Buffalo, 2001—. Lectr. Erie C.C., Buffalo, 1970-73, Bryant & Stratton Inst., Buffalo, 1975; assoc. prof. SUNY, 1985-90. Editor SUNY Buffalo Law Rev., 1971-72. Mem. ABA, Def. Rsch. Inst., Erie County Bar Assn., Fed. Def. and Corp. Counsel, Internat. Assn. Def. Counsel, Kappa Sigma (pres. Miami 1964-65). Roman Catholic. Home: 25 Westfield Rd Buffalo NY 14226-3492 Office: Goldberg Segalla 665 Main St Ste 400 Buffalo NY 14203 Office Phone: 716-566-5480. Business E-Mail: tsegalla@goldbergsegalla.com.

**SEGARS, KELLY SCOTT, SR.,** physician, banker; b. Red Bay, Ala., Mar. 11, 1930; s. Dock and Ora (Sims) S.; m. Martha Ann Thompson, oct. 3, 1952; children: kelly Scott, Jr., Mark Thompson, Leigh Ann. BS in Pharmacy, Auburn U., 1952; MD, U. Miss.-Jackson, 1959. Diplomate Am. Bd. Fam. Practice. Intern USPHS Hosp., Norfolk, Va., 1959-60; physician Segars Clinic, Iuka, Miss., 1960—. Founder, pres., chmn. First Am. Nat. Bank, Iuka, 1964—; pres. Tri-State Savs. & Loan, 1963-64; chief med. staff Tishominga County Hosp., Iuka, 1968, 76, 82, dir. coronary care unit, 1970—; chmn. constrn. com. Iuka Airport, 1964, Iuka Mcpl. Library, 1971. Exec. coun. Boy Scouts Am., Tupelo, Miss., 1971—. 1st lt. U.S. Army, 1953-55. Decorated Army Commendation medal. Fellow Am. Acad. Family Physicians; mem. AMA, Miss. Med. Assn., Flying Physicians assn., Ole Miss Med. Alumni, Rotary (paul Harris Fellowship). Republican. Methodist. Address: Segars Clinic 1507 W Quitman St Iuka MS 38852-1132

**SEGEBARTH, MARSHA LYNN,** biology professor; d. William Milton and Margaret McLeish Craft; m. Ronald James Segebarth, Aug. 31, 1968; children: James Andrew, Christopher Scott, Paul Bradley, Cynthia Suzanne Spencer, Mary Kathryn Soria, Jenifer Meagan. B, Ind. State U., Terre Haute, 1969; M, U. Evansville, Ind., 1975; PhD, U. Ky., Lexington, 2000. Cert. Am. Soc. Clin. Pathologists. Instr. biology U. So. Ind., Evansville, 1990—. Mem.: AAUW. Office: U So Ind 8600 University Blvd Evansville IN 47712 Office Phone: 812-465-1272. Personal E-mail: msegebar@usi.edu.

**SEGELHORST, CINDY MARIE,** pre-school educator; b. St. Louis, Oct. 2, 1957; d. Bernard Anthony and Marjorie Ann Engler; children: April Christine Brooks, Kenneth Andrew. BS in Edn., U. Mo., St. Louis, 1994; MA, Lindenwood U., 1998. Cert. early childhood edn. Dept. Elem. and Secondary Edn., Mo., 1994, elem. edn. Dept. Elem. and Secondary Edn., Mo., 1994, middle sch. social studies Dept. Elem. and Secondary Edn., Mo., 1994, early childhood spl. edn. Dept. Elem. and Secondary Edn., Mo., 1998, trainer work sampling sys. assessment. Early childhood educator Francis Howell Sch. Dist., St. Charles, Mo., 1995—; adj. instr. St. Charles C.C., St. Peters, Mo., 2001—. Cooperating tchr. for student teachers Lindenwood U. and U. of Mo. at St. Louis, St. Charles, 1997—; chairperson for cmty. wellness fair Francis Howell Pub. Sch. Dist., St. Charles, 1998—; mentor for new educators Francis Howell Sch. Dist., St. Charles, 1998—, mem. mentor-mentee coms. 2003—; contbg. mem. Pub. Sch. Kindergarten Transition Team, St. Charles, 2000—; adv. bd. mem. St. Charles C.C. Child Care and Early Childhood, St. Peters, 2001—; contbg writer for fine arts and math curriculum Francis Howell Sch. Dist., St. Charles, 2001—; adv. bd. mem. for pre-kindergarten math stds. Dept. Elem. and Secondary Edn., Jefferson City, Mo., 2001—; dist. rep. Francis Howell Sch. Dist. Profl. Devel. Com., St. Charles, 2002—; presenter Crucial Early Years Confs., 1998—, Young Years Confs., 1998—. Mem. Citizens for a Healthy Environment, St. Charles, 2001—; vol. Vacation Bible Sch., 2004, 2005. Named Tchr. of Yr., Walmart Stores, 1997—98, Tchr. of Week, St. Charles Jour., 2002; recipient Golden Apple for Early Childhood, St. Peters C. of C., 1996—97, Tchr. of Yr., Francis Howell Sch. Dist., 2004,

Bldg. Tchr. of Yr., 2004. Mem.: Mo. C.C. Assn., Nat. Assn. Edn. Young Children (presenter Mo. conf.), Womens Small Group Study. Avocations: remodeling, reading, travel, tennis, gardening. Home: 1312 Presidents Landing Dr O Fallon MO 63366-8480 Office: Francis Howell Sch Dist 2555 Hackmann Rd Saint Charles MO 63303

**SEGELMAN, ALVIN BURTON,** pharmaceutical executive, educator, research scientist; b. Boston, Sept. 27, 1931; s. Joseph Theodore and Anna (Klein) Segelman; m. Florence Hannah Pettler, Apr. 27, 1972 (dec. Jan. 7, 1994); children: Lauren Beth, Sheera Toba. BS, Mass. Coll. Pharmacy, 1954, MS, 1967; PhD, U. Pitts., 1971. Registered pharmacist Mass., cert. nutritional specialist Am. Coll. Nutrition. Chief pharmacist Kenmore Pharmacy, Boston, 1954—61; pres. Bell Pharmacy, Stoughton, Mass., 1961—67; instr. pharmacognosy and microbiology pharmacognosy dept. U. Pitts., 1967—71; asst. prof. pharmacognosy dept. Rutgers U., Piscataway, NJ, 1971—74, assoc. prof., chmn. pharmacognosy dept., 1974—90; v.p. R&D health scis. Nature's Sunshine Products, INc., Provo, Utah, 1990—2000; CEO Pharmacognosy Rsch. Inst., Orem, Utah, 2001—. Prin. investigator rsch. Rutgers Biomed. Rsch. Grants, New Brunswick, 1972—85, U.S. Pub. Health Svc. Grant, Washington, 1973; co-prin. investigator rsch. Am. Cancer Soc., Washington, 1987—88; expert med. cons. U.S. Congress Select Com. on Aging, Washington, 1981—83; vis. prof. Jagellonian U., Cracow, Poland, 1989, Patrice Lamumbe U., Moscow, 1999; cons. in field. Co-author: Antibiotics in Historical Perspective, 1981; contbr. articles to profl. jours.; sci. reviewer: various profl. and sci. jours. Mem. various coms. Acad. Pharm. Scis., Washington, 1976—89; mem. med. adv. com. Planned Parenthood Middlesex County, New Brunswick, NJ, 1979—90 Served to 2d lt. U.S Army NJ, 1949—59. Avocations: small arms pistol competition, ethnopharmacognosy research and writing, mountain climbing. Home and Office: Pharmacognosy Rsch Inst 54 West 680 South Orem UT 84058 Office Phone: 801-226-2184. Personal E-mail: herbdoctoralvin@aol.com.

**SEGERSTEN, ROBERT HAGY,** lawyer, investment banker; b. Boston, June 24, 1941; s. Wendell C. and Claire H. Segersten; m. Marie E. Makinen, Feb. 13, 1965; children: Amanda Beth, Vanessa Bryce. AB, Bates Coll., 1963; JD, Boston U., 1970. Bar: Mass. 1970. Assoc. Nessen & Csaplar, Boston, 1970-75; v.p. March Co., Boston, 1975-77; pres. March-Eton Corp., Concord, Mass., 1977-82; ptnr. Nessen, Goodwin & Segersten, Concord, 1977-82, Kane & Segersten, Dedham, Mass., 1983-85; pres. Woodbine Optical Corp., Boston, 1990—2006; pres., CEO Solos Endoscopy, Boston, 2006—. Officer, bd. dirs. Friends of Jimmy Fund, Boston. Served to lt. USN, 1963—67. Mem.: ACLU, Mass. Bar Assn. Democrat. Episcopalian. Home: 64 Folsom Ave Hyannis MA 02601-4823 Business E-Mail: rsegersten@solosendoscopy.com.

**SEGERSTRALE, ULLICA CHRISTINA,** social sciences educator, researcher; d. Curt Olof Segerstrale and Dagny Cecilia Flodin; m. Val Jason Martin, Dec. 6, 1991. MS in Sociology, U. Helsinki, Finland, 1973; MA in Comm., U. Pa., Phila., 1975; PhD, Harvard U., Cambridge Mass., 1983. Vis. asst. prof. Smith Coll., Northampton, Mass., 1984—86; prof. and acting chair Abo Akademi U., Finland, 1986—87; sr. rschr. Acad. of Finland, Helsinki, 1988—91; asst. prof. Ill. Inst. Tech., Chgo., 1988—93, assoc. prof., 1993—2000, chair dept. social sci., 2000—, prof. sociology, 2003—. Adv. bd. Ctr. for the Study of Ethics in the Professions, IIT, Chgo., 1989—; sr. fellow Ctr. on Nanotechnology and Soc., IIT, Chgo., 2005—; assoc. editor Sci. Studies, Helsinki, 1988—; mem. editl. bd. Social Epistemology, Pitts., 2002—, Jour. Biosics., Bangalore, India, 2002—05. Author: Defenders of the Truth: The Battle for Science in the Sociobiology Debate and Beyond, 2000; editor: Nonverbal Communication: Where Nature Meets Culture, 2000, Beyond the Science Wars, 2000. Recipient Julia Beveridge award, Ill. Inst. Tech., 2006, Hon. Fgn. Mem., Finnish Soc. of Sciences and Letters, 2003; fellow, Salzburg Seminar in Am. Studies, 1974, Fulbright Program, 1974, Guggenheim Meml. Found., 2002—03, Am. Philos. Soc., 2002—03, Bellagio Residency, Rockefeller Found., 2003; grantee, Sloan Found., 2004. Mem.: AAAS, Am. Sociol. Assn., Soc. for the Social Studies of Sci., Sigma Xi. Achievements include research in underlying reasons for the sociobiology controversy research, travel, languages. Office: Ill Inst Tech 3301 S Dearborn Ste 116 Chicago IL 60616 Office Phone: 312-567-5128. Office Fax: 312-567-6821. Business E-Mail: segerstrale@iit.edu.

**SEGGER, MARTIN JOSEPH,** museum director, educator, art historian; b. Felixtowe, Eng., Nov. 22, 1946; s. Gerald Joseph and Lillian Joan (Barker-Emery) S.; m. Angele Cordonier, Oct. 4, 1968; children: Cara Michelle, Marie-Claire, Margaret Ellen. BA, U. Victoria, 1969, diploma in edn., 1970; MPhil, U. London, 1973. Prof. art history U. Victoria, BC, Canada, 1970—74; museologist Royal B.C. Mus., Victoria, 1974—77; dir. Maltwood Art Mus., prof. art history U. Victoria, 1977—, dir. cmty. rels., 2001—. Cons. Nat. Mus. Corp., Ottawa, 1977, UNESCO, O.E.A., Cairo, 1983; bd. dirs. Canadian Cultural Rsch. Network, Victoria Coll. Art, Can. Rsch. Alliance; bd. advisors Greater Victoria Econ. Devel. Commn.; pres. Pacific northwest chpt. Soc. Archtl. Historians, 2002— Author: exhbn. catalogue House Beautiful, 1975, Arts of the Forgotten Pioneers, 1971, Victoria: An Architectural History, 1979, (commendation Am. Assn. State and Local History 1980), This Old House, 1975, This Old Town, 1979, British Columbia Parliament Buildings, 1979, The Heritage of Canada, 1981, Samuel Maclure: In Search of Appropriate Form, 1986 (Hallmark award 1987, 98), (a guide) St. Andrew's Cathedral, 1990, The Development of Gordon Head Campus, 1988, An Introduction to Museum Studies, 1989, An Introduction to Heritage Conservation, 1990, Botswana Live, 1994, Exploring Victoria's Architecture, 1996; contbr., cons. British Columbia Encyclopedia, 2000. Mem. heritage policy rev. com. Govt. Can., 2001—; Canadian Decorative Arts Soc., 2001—; mem. cultural diversity experts com. Govt. Can., 2002—; v.p. Commonwealth Museums Assn., 2003—, bd. govs. Heritage Can. Found., 1979—85; chmn. City of Victoria Heritage Adv. Com., 1975—79; bd. dirs. Downtown Victoria Cmty. Alliance, Heritage Trust, 1977—86, B.C. Touring Coun., Sta. CFUV Radio, B.C. Govt. Ho. Found., Royal B.C. Mus., 1996—99; co-chair B.C. Arts Festival; mem. B.C. Heritage Adv. Bd., 1973—83; councillor City of Victoria, 1987—93; vice-chair Provincial Capital Commn., 1991—2001; pres. Assn. Vancouver Island Municipalities, 1993—94; chmn. B.C. Festival of the Arts, 1999; bd. dirs. Internat. Coun. Mus.-Can., 1999, Victoria Coll. Art, 2001—, Victoria Harbour Authority, 2002—, dir. Decorated knight Equestrian Order of Holy Sepulchre of Jerusalem; named Hon. Citizen, City of Victoria, 2000, Arts Citizen of Yr., 2000; recipient award, Heritage Can. Comm., 1976, Heritage Conservation award, Lt. Gov. B.C., 1989, Harley J. McKee award, Assn. Preservation Tech., 1994, Queen's Golden Jubilee medal. Fellow Royal Soc. Arts, Can. Mus. Assn. (counsellor 1975-77); mem. Internat. Coun. Mus. (chair internat. com. for tng. pers. 1995-98), Internat. Coun. Monuments and Sites (bd. dirs 1980-82), Soc. Study Architecture Can. (bd. dirs. 1979-81), Can Mus. Dirs. Orgn., Commonwealth Assn. Museums (pres. 2005—), Union Club Victoria. Roman Catholic. Avocations: travel, motor mechanics, water color painting. Office Phone: 604-721-8298. Business E-Mail: msegger@uvic.ca.

**SEGGERMAN, ANNE CRELLIN,** foundation executive; b. Los Angeles, May 13, 1931; d. Curtis Vergil and Yvonne (LaGrave) Crellin; m. Harry G.A. Seggerman, Apr. 14, 1951; children: Patricia, Henry, Marianne, Yvonne, Suzanne, John. Studies with Albert Levesque, Paris, 1948-50; Student, Sch. Decorative Arts, Paris, 1950, Sch. of the Louvre, 1950, Albertus Magnus Coll., 1951; D.H.L. (hon.), Sacred Heart U., 1980. French tchr., Beverly Hills, Calif., 1950-60; translator World Affairs Council, Los Angeles, 1958-60; staff mem. West Side Sch. Gifted Children, Beverly Hills, 1958-60; pres. Huxley Inst. for Bio-Social Research, Fairfield, Conn., 1972—, 4th World Found. Interfaith Media Action, Fairfield, 1977—, Steiner Prodns., Fairfield, 1981—; founder The Com. for Guadalupe Research, Fairfield, 1982—. Bd. dirs. Anuk, Inc. Financer with Lee Edwards Kahn (documentaries) The Bronx Frontier, 1985. Co-founder Christian/Jewish Ctr. Understanding Sacred Heart U., Fairfield, Conn.; active Pres. Reagan's Health Task Force Resources Com. on Health Adv. Couns. of U.S. Dept. Health and Human Svcs.; mem. Pres.'s Com. Mental Retardation, 1981-86, Com. Housing Handicapped Families, 1989; mem. Nat. Coun. on Disability, 1992-95; bd. dirs. Easter Seal Rehab.

Ctr., Fairfield, Internat. Coll. Applied Nutrition, World Health Med. Group, Cath. League for Religion and Civil Rights. Recipient Am. Assn. Sovereign Mil. Order of Malta, 1991, Cmdr. of Equestrian Order of Holy Sepulchre of Jerusalem, 1991. Mem. Nat. Health Fedn., The Inst. for Study of Human Knowledge, Am. Holistic Med. Inst., Internat. Acad. Preventive Medicine, Calif. Orthomolecular Soc., Am. Phys. Rsch., Fairfield County Organic Gardeners.

**SEGLER, CHRISTOPHER PAIGE,** surgeon, researcher; s. David Otis and Julia Cate Segler; m. Paige Elizabeth Clem, May 29, 2004. BA in English, U. Houston, 1996; DPM in podiatric medicine, Calif. Coll. Podiatric Medicine, 2003. Rsch. asst. U. Houston, Dept. Chemistry, 1994—97; hospice vol. Hospice at the Tex. Med. Ctr., Inpatient Unit, Houston, 1994—95; psychiat. tech. Sharpstown Gen. Hosp., Houston, 1995—97; psychiat. technician Harris County Psychiat. Ctr., Houston, 1997—98; med. illustrator Calif. Coll. Podiatric Medicine, Dept. Basic Scis., San Francisco, 2000—02; sr. editor Nat. Foot and Ankle Rev., Oakland, Calif., 2002—03; podiatric surg. resident Dept. Veterans Affairs Health Care Sys., Salt Lake City, 2003—; design prin., co-founder Orthovation, LLC, Houston, 2003—; pvt. practice Chattanooga. Chief resident U. Utah/VAMC, 2005—06. Contbr. articles to profl. jours., chapters to books. Named 1st place, Outstanding Resident Rsch Abstract Competition, Am. Podiatric Med. Assn., 2006; recipient Excellence in Rsch. award, Calif. Coll. of Podiatric Med., 2003; grantee, Gilkey Meml. Fund, 2000. Mem.: Soc. for Exptl. Biology and Medicine, Am. Podiatric Med. Writers Assn., Utah Podiatric Med. Assn., Am. Podiatric Med. Assn., Am. Coll. Foot and Ankle Surgeons (assoc. 2nd pl. Sci. Rsch. Post Competition, Instnl. Category 2005, 3rd pl. Sci. Rsch. Post Competition, Instnl. Category 2006, others), Omicron Delta Kappa (life), Alpha Epsilon Delta (life), Sigma Tau Delta (life). Achievements include invention of Tarsal Joint Space Distractor, surgical instrument for use in foot and ankle surgery. Avocations: rock climbing, kayaking, writing, painting, running. Office: Ankle & Foot Ctr Chattanooga 5870 Highway 153 Hixson TN 37343 Office Phone: 423-877-8870. Home Fax: 801-486-7464. Personal E-mail: chris@orthovation.com. Business E-Mail: drsegler@anklecenter.com.

**SEGLER, LYNN CCHANDLER,** elementary school educator; b. Guntersville, Ala., June 23, 1955; d. John Haden and Florence Schultz Chandler; m. Jimmy W. Segler, Dec. 28, 2004; 1 child, Malissa Clay. BS in Elem. Edn., Ala. A&M U., 1978, MS in Elem. Edn., 1980. Tchr. Claysville Jr. H.S., Ala., 1978—89, Union Grove Jr. H.S., Union Grove, 1989—97; tchr. English DAR Mid. Sch., Grant, 1997—99, tchr., 1999—2004, reading coach, 2004—. Named Mid. Sch. Tchr. of Yr., DAR Mid. Sch., Grant, 1999, 2003. Baptist. Avocations: baking, sewing, reading. Home: 304 2d Ave W Grant AL 35747 Office: Kate Cundan Smith Dar Elem Sch 6077 Main St Grant AL 35747

**SEGLIN, JEFFREY L.,** columnist, educator; b. Plattsburgh, N.Y., Dec. 26, 1956; s. Lester L. and Beverly K. Seglin; m. Nancy L. Long, Jan. 18, 1986; children: Edward Coleman, Bethany Whitemyer. BA, Bethany Coll., 1978; cert., Radcliffe Pub. Course, Cambridge, Mass., 1978; MTS, Harvard Divinity Sch., 1981. Exec. editor Inc. Mag., Boston, 1989—98; asst. prof. Emerson Coll., Boston, 1999—, dir. grad. writing & pub. program, 2004—. Author: (NY Times Syndicated Column) The Right Thing, 1998—, (books) The Good, the Bad and Your Business, 2000, The Right Thing: Conscience, Profit, & Personal Responsibility in Today's Bus., 2003. Fellow, Ctr. for the Study of Values in Pub. Life at Harvard U., 1998-1999; Poynter Ethics fellow, Poynter Inst. for Media Studies, 2001. Office: Emerson Coll 120 Boylston St Boston MA 02116 also: NY Times Syndication Sales Corp 14th Fl 122 E 42nd St New York NY 10168 E-mail: jseglin@post.harvard.edu, rightthing@nytimes.com.*

**SEGOTA, ENA,** hematologist; b. Zagreb, Croatia, Dec. 12, 1969; arrived in U.S., 1998; d. Anton and Mira Jambrisak; m. Branko Segota, Sept. 8, 1994; children: Ashley, Anton. MD, U. Zagreb, Croatia, 1995. Intern Cmty. Health Care Ctr., Zagreb, 1996—97, Univ. Hosps., Zagreb, 1997—98; intern/resident dept. internal medicine Huron Hosp.-Cleve. Clinic Health Sys., 1999—2002; rsch. fellow exptl. therapeutics Taussig Cancer Ctr., Cleve. Clinic Found., 2002—03; fellow dept. hematology and med. oncology Cleve. Clinic Found., 2003—. Mem.: Am. Soc. for Blood and Marrow Transplantation (assoc.), Am. Soc. Clin. Oncology (assoc.). Office: Cleve Clinic Found 4500 Euclid Ave Cleveland OH 44195 Mailing: 1033 NE 17th Way 2002 Fort Lauderdale FL 33304 Office: Michael and Dianne Bienes Cancer Ctr 4725 N Federal Hwy Fort Lauderdale FL 33308 Fax: 216-444-9464.

**SEHILI, MAHMOUD,** artist; b. Tunis, July 27, 1931; m. Gabriele Buth, Apr. 11, 1959; children: Thouraya, Lilia, Raouf. Student, Fine Arts Sch., Tunis; diploma supérieur des arts plastiques, Ecole des Beaux-Arts, Paris. Tchr. Inst. Technol. Art, Arch., Urbanisme, Tunis; dir. Irtissem Art Gallery, Tunis, 1977—. Recipient Golden medal, Cagnes sur Mer, 1st prize, Town of Tunis, 1963, others. Avocations: music, playing the luth, composition of arabic music, fishing. Home: 4 Rue Victor Hugo Carthage Tunisia Office Phone: 71-740-515, 00216-48-305-007.

**SEIB, BILLIE MCGHEE RUSHING,** nursing administrator, consultant; b. Brookport, Ill., Mar. 04; d. Frank and Ila (Paris) McGhee; m. Alfred Rushing, Jan. 2, 1958 (dec.); children: Lisa, Libbi; m. Bob Seib, Mar. 21, 1986 (dec. Mar. 17, 2006) Diploma, DePaul Sch. Nursing, St. Louis, 1947; postgrad. in oper. rm. nursing, Washington U., St. Louis, 1950; BS, U. St. Francis, Joliet, 2002. Cert. nurse: cert. legal nurse cons., 2005. Dir. oper. rm. Jennie Stuart Med. Ctr., Hopkinsville, Ky.; clin. mgr. oper. rm. Meml. Med. Ctr., Savannah, Ga.; mgr. oper. rm. Meth. Med. Ctr., Oak Ridge, Tenn.; coord. oper. rm. Parkwest Hosp., Knoxville, Tenn.; mem. oper. rm. pool Ft. Sanders Park West Hosp., Knoxville, 1992-93; geriat. nurse Briarcliff Health Care Ctr., Oak Ridge, Tenn., 1993-96, Windwood Health Care Ctr. (now Beverly Health & Rehab. Ctr.), Clinton, Tenn., 1996—, asst. dir. nursing, 1996—2001. Cons. Washington, Fla., Ky., New.; mgr. Oak Ridge, Tenn., 1997—; owner New York New York Ladies Boutique. Mem. Assn. Oper. Rm. Nurses (cert., bd. dirs., past pres. East Tenn. chpt.), Am. Gerontol. Nursing Assn. Home: 133 Lakeview Hills Ln Clinton TN 37716-5957 Office Phone: 865-254-5879. E-mail: B23P@comcast.net.

**SEIBER, RICHARD ALLAN,** retired minister; b. L.A., Nov. 15, 1932; s. Edward Maurice and Dorothy Mildred (Ball) S.; m. Wilma Ellen Shook, Sept. 24, 1955; children: Bruce Wayne, Roger Kent, Dale Eugene, Michael Allan. BA in History, U. Puget Sound, 1958; MDiv, Garrett Bibl. Inst., 1962, grad. Air Command & Staff Coll., 1962, Air War Coll., 1970. Ordained elder United Meth. Ch., 1960. Enlisted USAF, 1950, advanced through grades to lt. col., ret., 1976, chaplain, 1960—76; student pastor Meth. Ch., Algona-Pacific, Wash., 1955—57, Sciota-Friendship, Ill., 1957—60; pastor United Meth. Ch., Spanaway, Wash., 1976—83, Epworth-LeSourd United Meth. Ch., Tacoma, 1983—97; ret. United Meth. Ch., Tacoma, 1997. Mem. editl. bd. Meth. History United Meth. Ch., Madison, NJ, 1982—86, mem. gen. conf. archives and history, 1980—88, mem. jurisdictional conf. archives and history, 1980—, pres. jurisdictional conf. archives and history, 1980—84; chmn. com. on chaplains Pacific N.W. Conf., 1977—88, archivist, 1978—2004. Editor: Memoirs of Puget Sound: David Blaine, 1978 (Wash. Gov.'s Writer's award), Methodist History Index: Oct. 1962-July 1982, 1984, Jour. Henry Bridgeman Brewer, 1839-48, 1986; contbr. Sprague, Lamont, Edwall, WA, 1881-1981, 1982; contbr. Religious Heritage of Washington State, 1988, Illustrated History of Methodism, 1999; co-editor: William Roberts: Circuit Riding Superintendent of the Oregon-California Mission Conference, 1847-1853, 2004. Mem. Tacoma Mayor's Task Force on Vets. Affairs, 1986-91; chmn. Ministry with Service People—Co-NeXion, Tillicum, Wash., 1976-79, 87-90; mem. Wesley Homes Corp., Des Moines, Wash., 1984—; v.p. exploring, exec. com. Mount Rainier Coun., Boy Scouts Am., 1976-81, v.p. rels., 1981-92, mem. nat. coun., rep. Pacific Harbors coun., 1999-2005 Recipient Silver Beaver award Boy Scouts Am., 1977, God and Svc. recognition award Boy Scouts Am., 1988, James E. West fellow, 1997. Mem.: SAR (life; chpt. pres. 1989—91), Air Force Hist. Found., Mil. Chaplain's Assn. (Puget Sound chpt. pres. 1985—93, 2002, chmn. Pacific NW Nat. Security Forum 2006), Mil. Officers' Assn. (life), Nat. Eagle Scout Assn. (life), Air Force Assn. (life;

chpt. pres. 1980—84, state pres. 1994—98, Exceptional Svc. award 1999, 2005, Presdl. citation 2006), Scouting Heritage Assn. (life; charter), Air War Coll. Alumni Assn. (life), Sigma Chi. Avocations: stained glass, genealogy, clocks, early northwest church history, collecting royal doulton. Home: 5514 89th Avenue Ct W University Place WA 98467-1532 Office Phone: 253-564-3757. Personal E-mail: raseiber@nventure.com.

**SEIBERG, NATHAN,** physics professor; b. Israel, Sept. 22, 1956; married; two children. BSc with high distinction, Tel-Aviv U., 1977; PhD, Weizmann Inst. Sci., Israel, 1982. Sr. scientist Weizmann Inst., 1985-86, assoc. prof., 1986-89, prof., 1989-91, Rutgers U., 1989-90, prof. II, 1990-97; prof. Inst. Advanced Study, Princeton, NJ, 1997—. Vis. mem. Inst. for Advanced Study, 1994-95. With Israeli Def. Force, 1977-82. Recipient Israel Phys. Soc. prize, 1976, Mifal Hapais prize, 1979, Michael Landau prize, 1981, J.F. Kennedy prize, 1982, N.J. Pride award N.J. Monthly Mag., 1996, Bd. Trustees award Rutgers U. for Excellence in Rsch., 1996, Dannie Heineman prize Am. Inst. of Physics, 1998; named Racah lectr. Weizmann Inst. Sci., 1985, Oskar Klein lectr. and Oskar Klein medal, 1995, Disting. IFT lectr. U. Fla., 1996; Amos de-Shalit Found. scholar, 1976; John D. and Catherine T. MacArthur Found. fellow, 1996. Fellow: Am. Acad. Arts and Scis. Office: Inst for Advanced Study Sch Natural Sci Einstein Dr Princeton NJ 08540 Business E-Mail: seiberg@ias.edu.

**SEIBERLING, DAVID WILLIAM,** retired music educator; b. Barberton, Ohio, Aug. 16, 1944; s. Robert William and Jean (Marcellus) Seiberling; m. Linda Ayers, July 10, 1976; 1 child, Ellis. MusB, Appalachian State U., Boone, NC, 1971, MusM, 1975. Dir. bands North Stokes HS, Danbury, NC, 1971—78, Union Pines HS, Cameron, NC, 1978—2002; ret., 2002. Adj. instr. U. NC, Pembroke, 2002—; music dir.; condr. Moore County Concert Band, Pinehurst, NC, 1982—. Arranger: numerous CD soundtracks, concert band titles; composer: (concert band piece) The Carolina March, 2006. Pres. Arts Coun. Moore County, Southern Pines, NC, 2002—; elder Cameron (NC) Presbyn. Ch. With U.S. Army, 1966—69. Recipient award of excellence, NC Music Educators, 2002. Avocations: golf, reading, composing/arranging.

**SEIBERLING, JOHN FREDERICK,** retired congressman, lawyer, educator; b. Akron, Ohio, Sept. 8, 1918; s. J. Frederick and Henrietta (Buckler) S.; m. Elizabeth Pope Behr, June 4, 1949; children— John B., David P., Stephen M. AB, Harvard U., 1941; LLB, Columbia U., 1949. Bar: N.Y. 1950, Ohio 1955. Assoc. mem. firm Donovan, Leisure, Newton, Lumbard & Irvine, N.Y.C., 1949-53; atty. Goodyear Tire & Rubber Co., Akron, 1954-71; mem. 92d-99th Congresses from 14th Ohio Dist.; mem. com. on judiciary, com. on interior and insular affairs, chmn. subcom. on public lands; vis. prof. law U. Akron, 1987, 90, dir. Ctr. for Peace Studies, 1991-96; ptnr. Goldman, Seiberling, Davis & Tsarnas, Akron, 1988-89. Served to maj. AUS, 1942-46. Mem. United Ch. of Christ. Home: 154 Tecumseh Ln Akron OH 44321-2753

**SEIBERLING, KRISTIN ANN,** otolaryngologist; b. Redlands, Calif., June 4, 1976; d. Monroe and Pat Seiberling. MD, Northwestern Feinberg Sch. of Medicine, Chgo., 2002. Tchg. asst. biology dept. U. Calif., San Diego, 1996—98; otolaryngology resident Northwestern U., Chgo., 2002—. Cermack health srvcs. dept. Cook County, Chgo., 2006; physician Cermack Health Svc. Ctr., Chgo., 2006—. Contbr. articles. Recipient Alpha Omega Alpha, Northwestern Med. Sch., 2002, Resident rsch. award 2nd Pl., Chgo. Laryngo-Otologic Soc., 2005, Resident rsch. award 1st Pl., Northwestern U., Dept Otolaryngology, 2005; fellow Summa Cum Laude, U. Calif., San Diego, 1998. Home Fax: 312-503-1616. Personal E-mail: kristinseiberling@gmail.com.

**SEIBLE, FRIEDER,** structural engineer, educator; b. Schwaebisch Gmuend, Germany, 1952; m. Betsy Seible; children: Michael, Daniel, Anika. Dipl. Ing. in civil engring., U. Stuttgart, Germany, 1976; MCE, U. Calgary, Alta., Can., 1978; PhD in civil engring., U. Calif., Berkeley, 1982. Registered profl. engr., 1985. Mem. faculty U. Calif.-San Diego, La Jolla, 1983—, founding chair dept. structural engring., 1995—2001, Eric and Johanna Reissner Prof. Applied Mechanics and Structural Engring., dir. Charles Lee Powell Structural Rsch. Laboratories; prof. Structural Engring., interim dean Irwin & Joan Jacobs Sch. Engring., 2002—03, dean, 2003—. Mem. seismic adv. bd. Calif. Dept. Transp. (Caltrans). Recipient Best paper award Can. Soc. Civil Engring., 1982, K.B. Woods award Transp. Rsch. Bd., 1983, 92, Presdl. Young Investigator award Pres. Reagan, 1986, Japanese Govt. Rsch. award for fgn. rsch. specialists Sci. and Tech. Agy., 1987, Outstanding Paper award N.Am. Masonry Conf. award, 1990, 93, Best Paper award Internat. Conf. on Short and Medium Span Bridges, 1990, Raymond C. Reese Rsch. prize ASCE, 1992, Outstanding Jour. Paper award Masonry Soc., 1993, Shiley Achievement award Chancellor's Assocs., 1994, Outstanding Concrete Project award Am. Concrete Inst., 1994, Orchid award for design of Scripps Crossing pedestrian bridge San Diego Cmty. Awareness Program, 1994, citation for Lighting Design, Internat. Assn. Lighting Designers, 1994, Alan H. Yorkdale award ASTM, 1994, Concrete Bridge award Portland Cement Assn., 1994, Moisseiff award ASCE, 1995, Charles Pankow award for innovation CERF, 1996, Best Paper award ASCE, 1997. Mem.: NAE. Achievements include being one of the world's foremost seismic structural engineers. Office: U Calif San Diego Sch Engring 9500 Gilman Dr La Jolla CA 92093-0403*

**SEIBOLD, JAMES RICHARD,** physician, educator; b. Washington, Apr. 5, 1950; s. Herman Rudolph and Clara Bond (Taylor) S.; m. Margaret Frances Bennett, Jan. 20, 1968; children: Jon Drew, Zachary Bennett. BS, La. State U., 1972; MD, SUNY, Stony Brook, 1975. Diplomate Am. Bd. Internal Medicine, Am. Bd. Rheumatology. Intern in medicine L.I. Jewish Hosp., New Hyde Park, NY, 1975-76, resident in medicine, 1976-78; fellow in rheumatology U. Pitts., 1978-80; asst. prof. medicine Robert Wood Johnson Med. Sch. U. Medicine and Dentistry N.J., New Brunswick, 1980-86, assoc. prof., 1986-92, prof., 1992—, chief rheumatology, 1986-91, dir. clin. rsch. ctr., 1989-95; prof., dir. scleroderma program U. Mich., Ann Arbor, 2004—. Mem. adv. bd. Ctr. for Advanced Biotech. and Medicine, Piscataway, N.J., 1989-95, dir. Scleroderma program 1995—; W.H. Conzen chair clin. pharmacology Schering-Plough Found., 1989; prof. internal medicine Scleroderma Program U. Mich., 2006, Marvin and Betty Danto rsch. prof., 2006—, dir. Author: (chpt.) Rheumatology, 1988, 91, 94, 95, 99, 2001, 03, 05; contbr. over 300 articles to profl. jours. Mem. bd. dirs. Arthritis Found. Fellow ACP, Am. Coll. Rheumatology (regional coun. 1985), Scleroderma Clin. Trials Consortium (founder 1994, pres. 2004—). Mem. Soc. Of Friends. Home: 1622 Kriss Crossing Brighton MI 48114 Office: U Mich Health Sys 3918 Taubman Ctr 1500 E Medical Center Dr Ann Arbor MI 48109-0358 Office Phone: 734-736-3110. Business E-Mail: jseibold@umich.edu.

**SEIDE, PAUL,** civil engineering educator; b. N.Y.C., July 22, 1926; s. Julius David and Sylvia (Eiler) S.; m. Joan Cecilia Matalka, Jan. 7, 1951; children: Richard Laurence, Wendy Jane Seide Kielsmeier. B.C.E., CCNY, 1946; M. Aero. Engring, U. Va., 1952; PhD, Stanford U., 1954. Aero. research scientist Nat. Adv. Commn. for Aeros., Langley AFB, Va., 1946-52; research asst. Stanford Calif. U., 1952-53; research engr. Northrop Aircraft Co., Hawthorne, Calif., 1953-55; head methods and research sect. TRW Inc., Los Angeles, 1955-60; head methods and research sect. Aerospace Corp., El Segundo, Calif., 1960-65; prof. civil engring. U. So. Calif., L.A., 1965-91, prof. emeritus, 1991—, assoc. chmn. dept. civil engring., 1971-73, 81-83; Albert Alberman vis. prof. Technion-Israel Inst. Tech., Haifa, 1975; vis. prof. U. Sydney, Australia, 1986, U. Canterbury, N.Z., 1986. Cons. Northrop Inc., 1972-77, Aerospace Corp., 1966-68, Rockwell Inc., El Segundo, 1982-85 Author: Small Elastic Deformations of Thin Shells, 1975; contbr. numerous articles to profl. jours. NSF fellow, 1964-65 Fellow (life) ASME, Am. Acad. Mechanics; mem. ASCE (life), Tau Beta Pi, Sigma Xi. Democrat. Jewish. Home: 300 Via Alcance Palos Verdes Estates CA 90274-1105

**SEIDEL, ARTHUR HARRIS,** lawyer; b. N.Y.C., May 25, 1923; s. Philip and Pearl (Geller) S.; m. Raquel Eliovich, Aug. 21, 1949; children: Stephen A., Paul B., Mary Beth Sharp. BS, CCNY, 1942; A.M., U. Mich., 1943; JD

with honors, George Washington U., 1949. Bar: D.C. 1949, Pa. 1956, N.Y. 1957. Atty. patent dept. Gulf Oil Corp., Washington and Pitts., 1947-52; individual practice law, 1952-64; sr. ptnr. firm Seidel & Gonda, 1964-68, Seidel, Gonda & Goldhammer (P.C.), Phila., 1968-72, pres., 1972-84, Seidel, Gonda, Goldhammer & Abbott, P.C., Phila., 1984-88, Seidel, Gonda, Lavorgna & Monaco, Phila., 1988-2001; of counsel Drinker, Biddle & Reath, Phila., 2001—. Lectr. in Intellectual Property Temple U. Law Sch., 1973-86, Am. Law Inst. Editor: George Washington Law Rev, 1949; author: (with others) Trademark Practice, 2 vols, 1963, Monographs on Patent Law and Practice, 5th edit, 1993, Trademarks and Copyrights, 6th edit., 1992, Trade Secrets and Employment Agreements 3d edit, 1995; also articles. Mem. Adv. Com. for Restatement of Law of Unfair Competition. Mem. ABA, Am. Law Inst., Pa. Bar Assn., Phila. Bar Assn., Am. Intellectual Property Law Assn., Phila. Intellectual Property Law Assn., Order of Coif. Home: The Quadrangle C104 3300 Darby Rd Haverford PA 19041-1095 Office: Drinker Biddle & Reath LLP Ste 300 1000 Westlakes Dr Berwyn PA 19312-2409 Office Phone: 610-993-2218. Business E-Mail: arthur.seidel@dbr.com. *My entire professional career has been devoted to the question of innovation, patents for inventions, trademarks for new businesses and copyrights for new writings. I have seen the United States become the world's leader in technology and business.*

**SEIDEL, CARL WILLIAM,** pharmaceutical executive, consultant; b. Hempstead, NY, Aug. 18, 1938; s. Charles Francis and Wilma Marie Seidel; m. Suzanne Winslow Dana (dec. June 22, 2005); children: Lisa Marie, Michael Dana, Rebecca Suzanne, Elaine Marie. BS in Chemistry, U. Wis., 1959; MS in Chemistry, U. Notre Dame, 1962. Chemist, mktg. mgr. Nuclear Sci. and Engring., Pitts., 1962-69; product mgr. New England Nuclear, Billerica, Mass., 1969-73, asst. divsn. mgr., 1973-79, gen. mgr. new products, 1979-81; various positions, mfg. mgr. pharm. divsn. DuPont, Billerica, 1981-91; assoc. dir. DuPont Merck, Billerica, 1991-97; pres., CEO Internat. Isotopes, Denton, Tex., 1997-99; pres. Carl W. Seidel & Assocs., Cons., 2000—. Cons. Dept. of Energy, Washington, 1990-2001; tech. advisor U.S. Pharmocpiea, Bethesda, 1995-2000; com. mem. Am. Nat. Stds. Inst., Gaithersburg, 1975. Co-editor Mössbauer Effect Methodology, Vol. 8, 1973, Vol. 9, 1974, Vol. 10, 1976; editor: The Mössbauer Effect and Its Application in Chemistry, 1967. Town rep., Chelmsford, Mass., 1980-97. Mem. Internat. Isotope Soc., Am. Coll. Nuclear Physicians, Legatus, Soc. of Nuclear Medicine (sec.-treas. therapy coun.), Am. Chem. Soc., European Soc. of Nuclear Medicine, Russell Mill Swim and Tennis (pres. 1972-75), C. of C. Republican. Roman Catholic. Avocations: tennis, travel. Home and Office: 4 Thresher Rd Nashua NH 03063 E-mail: carl.w.seidel@mindspring.com.

**SEIDEL, CHARLES KENNETH,** military officer; s. Barry Dewees Seidel and Judith May Burger; m. Cynthia Ann Crout, Apr. 9, 1988; children: Brittany Elizabeth, Brandon Charles. BS in Bus. Mgmt. summa cum laude, N.H. Coll., 1995; MSA in Human Resource Mgmt., Ctrl. Mich. U., 2002. Cert. level III program mgr. Def. Acquisition U. Commd. 2d lt. USAF, 1988, advanced through grades to capt., 1999, orderly room clk. 73rd Tactical Control Squadron Myrtle Beach, SC, 1988—92, chief info. mgmt. 319th Recruiting Squadron Portsmouth, NH, 1992—2005, sect. comdr. 305 Aircraft Generation Squadron McGuire AFB, NJ, 1995—98, program mgr. home office ASC/SY Dayton, Ohio, 1998—99, F-15 Link 16 program mgr. F-15 Sys. Program Office, 1999—2001, SIAP assessment program mgr. SIAP Task Force Crystal City, Va., 2001—02, exec. officer SAF/AQP Rosslyn, Va., 2002—03, F/A-22 budget program element monitor SAF/AQPB, 2003—04, F-117 & A-10 program element monitor SAF/AQPB, 2004—. Sec. Air Force Sgts. Assn. Chpt. 376, Myrtle Beach AFB, SC, 1989—90, sec./treas., 1990—91, v.p., 1991—92. Republican. Baptist. Office: SAF/AQPB 1500 Wilson Blvd Rosslyn VA 20333 E-mail: charles.seidel@eglin.af.mil.

**SEIDEL, FREDERICK LEWIS,** poet; b. St. Louis, Feb. 19, 1936; s. Jerome Jay and Thelma (Cartun) S.; children: Felicity, Samuel. AB, Harvard U., 1957. Occasional lectr., Rutgers U., New Brunswick, 1964—; Paris editor, Paris Review, 1961, advisory editor, 1962. Author: (poetry) Final Solutions, 1963, Sunrise, 1979 (Lamont Poetry prize Acad. Am. Poets 1980, Am. Poetry Rev. prize 1980, Nat. Book Critics Circle award for poetry 1981), Men and Woman: New and Selected Poems, 1984, Poems 1959-1979, 1989, These Days, 1989, My Tokyo, 1993, Going Fast, 1998, The Cosmos Poems, 2000, Life on Earth, 2001, Area Code 212, 2002, The Cosmos Triology, 2003, Barbados, 2004. Guggenheim Fellow, 1993, Pen/Voelcker award for poetry, 2002.

**SEIDEL, GEORGE ELIAS, JR.,** zoology educator; b. Reading, Pa., July 13, 1943; s. George E. Sr. and Grace Esther (Heinly) S.; m. Sarah Beth Moore, May 28, 1970; 1 child, Andrew. BS, Pa. State U., 1965; MS, Cornell U., 1968, PhD, 1970; postgrad., Harvard U. Med. Sch., Boston, 1970-71. Asst.-prof. physiology Colo. State U., Ft. Collins, 1971-75, assoc. prof., 1975-83, prof., 1983-93, univ. disting. prof., 1993—. Vis. scientist Yale U., 1978-79, MIT, 1986-87; mem. bd. on agr. NRC. Co-editor: New Technologies in Animal Breeding, 1981; contbr. articles to profl. jours. Recipient Alexander Von Humboldt award, N.Y.C., 1983, Animal Breeding Research award Nat. Assn. Animal Breeders, Columbia, Mo., 1983, Clark award Colo. State U., 1982, Upjohn Physiology award, 1986; Gov's. award for Sci. and Tech., Colo., 1986. Mem. AAAS, NAS, Am. Dairy Sci. Assn., Am. Soc. Animal Sci. (Young Animal Scientist award 1983), Soc. for Study of Reprodn., Internat. Embryo Transfer Soc. (pres. 1979, disting. svc. award 2001). Home: 3101 Arrowhead Rd Laporte CO 80535-9374 Office: Colo State U Animal Repro Biotech Lab Fort Collins CO 80523-1683 Office Phone: 970-491-5287. Business E-Mail: gseidel@colostate.edu.

**SEIDEL, JAMES P.,** manufacturing executive; s. Robert A. and Mary Ann Seidel; m. Deborah J. Aziz, Nov. 14, 1998; children: Allison J., Grace C. BS, U. Wis., LaCrosse, 1989. Regional fleet mgr. Bridgestone Corp., Nashville, 1991—2002; nat. sales mgr. Gt. Am. Tire & Auto, Denver, 2002; dir. sales Continental Tire N.Am., Charlotte, NC, 2003—05; v.p., COO Stamford Tires & Wheels, Inc., Charlotte, 2005—, also sec., bd. dirs. Avocations: bicycling, running, gardening, antique cars, cooking. Office: Stamford Tires & Wheels Inc 929 Jay St Charlotte NC 28208 Office Phone: 704-409-7300. Business E-Mail: jseidel@stamford-tires.com.

**SEIDEL, JOAN BROUDE,** securities dealer, investment advisor; b. Chgo., Aug. 16, 1933; d. Ned and Betty (Treiger) Broude; m. Arnold Seidel, Aug. 18, 1957; children: David, Craig. BA, UCLA, 1954; postgrad., N.Y. Inst. Fin. Registered prin., investment advisor Morton Seidel & Co. Inc., L.A. 1970-74, v.p., 1974-93; pres., 1993—; also bd. dirs. Morton Seidel & Co. Inc., L.A. Instr. UCLA Extension, 1979—84; bd. overseers Hebrew Union Coll. Treas. City of Beverly Hills, Calif., 1990-2001, chmn. rent adjustment bd., 1989-90, mem., 1983-89; investment com. YWCA of greater LA, 1987-2002, treas. 1992-95; bd. dirs. Discovery Fund for Eye Rsch., LA, 1987—, treas., 1999—; corp. bd. dirs. Queen's Care, 1999-2005, fin. com., 1999-2005, audit com., 2004-05; bd. dirs. LA Opera, 2002—; CFO Maple Couns. Ctr., 2002-04; bd. govs. Cedars Sinai Med. Ctr. Named Citizen of Yr. Beverly Hills C. of C. 1993. Fellow Assn. for Investment Mgmt. and Rsch., Israel Inst. Tech. (hon.); mem. Am. Technion Soc. (v.p. 1998-2002, nat. pres. So. Calif. chpt. 2001-04, nat. bd. dir. 2002—, internat. bd. 2003—, nat. pres. 2006—), Nat. Assn. Security Dealers (dist. bus. conduct com. 2S 1993-95, 98-2000, small firm adv. bd. 1998-2000, chair dist. 2 1999-2000), LA Soc. Fin. Analysts, Orgn. Women Execs., Rotary. Phi Sigma Alpha. Avocations: reading, travel. Office: Morton Seidel & Co Inc 8730 Wilshire Blvd Ste 530 Beverly Hills CA 90211-2792 Office Phone: 310-360-7541. Personal E-mail: seidel350@aol.com.

**SEIDEL, ROBERT WAYNE,** science historian, educator; b. Kansas City, Mo., June 9, 1945; s. Wayne Herman and Harriet Anita (Day) S.; m. Alison Publicover, Aug. 26, 1972 (div. 1989); 1 child, Mary Ruth; m. Christine Ruth Stack, July 1, 1993. BA, Westmar Coll., 1967; MA, U. Calif., Berkeley, 1968, PhD, 1978. Exhibit designer Lawrence Hall Sci., Berkeley, 1970-72; specialist Poland 4-city tour USIA, Warsaw, 1971-72; grad. rsch. and teaching asst. U. Calif., 1972-78; asst. prof. Tex. Tech U., Lubbock, 1978-83, dir. rsch.

history of engring. program, 1979-83; rsch. historian U. Calif., Berkeley, 1980-82, Laser History Project, Albany, Calif., 1983-85; adminstr. Bradbury Sci. Mus., Los Alamos, N.Mex., 1985-90, overview project leader, 1990-92; sr. staff mem. Ctr. Nat. Security Studies, Los Alamos, N.Mex., 1992-94; dir. Charles Babbage Inst., U. Minn., Mpls., 1994-99; ERA Land Grant prof. History of Tech. U. Minn., Mpls., 1994-99, prof. chem. engring., 1999—. Author: Lawrence and His Laboratory: A History of the Lawrence Berkeley Laboratory, 1989, Los Alamos and the Making of the Atomic Bomb, 1995. Mem. N.Mex. Sci. Ctr. Commn., 1989-92; bd. dirs. The Bakken Mus., 1994-2004. Woodrow Wilson fellow, 1967, U. Calif. Regent's fellow, 1968, German Marshall Fund fellow, Grenoble, France, 1975, Sr. fellow Dibner Inst., MIT, 2001; recipient Bicentennial Essay prize Nat. Sci. Tchrs. Assn., 1976. Mem. AAUP, History Sci. Soc., Soc. for History Tech. Democrat. Avocation: computer simulations. Home: 5625 Woodlawn Blvd Minneapolis MN 55417-2667 Office: 151 Amundson Hall/U Minn Minneapolis MN 55455 Office Phone: 612-624-8003. Business E-Mail: rws@tc.umn.edu.

**SEIDEL, SELVYN,** lawyer, educator; b. Long Branch, N.J., Nov. 6, 1942; s. Abraham and Anita (Stoller) S.; m. Deborah Lew, June 21, 1970; 1 child, Emily. BA, U. Chgo., 1964; JD, U. Calif., Berkeley, 1967; diploma in law, Oxford U., 1968. Bar: N.Y. 1970, D.C. Ct. Appeals 1982. Ptnr. Latham & Watkins, N.Y.C., 1985—. Adj. prof. Sch. Law, NYU, 1974-84; instr. Practicing Law Inst., 1980-81, 84. Contbr. articles to profl. jours. Bd. dirs. Citizen Scholarship Fund Am., 1995-2000. Mem. ABA, N.Y. County Bar Assn., N.Y.C. Bar Assn. (mem. fed. cts. com. 1982-85, internat. law com. 1989-92, 95-96, exec. v.p. 1997-2000), Boalt Hall Alumni Assn. (bd. dirs. 1980-82). Office: Latham & Watkins 885 3rd Ave New York NY 10022-4802 Office Phone: 212-906-1312. Business E-Mail: selvyn.seidel@lw.com.

**SEIDELMANN, PAUL KENNETH,** astronomer, educator; s. Paul Emil and Esther (Momberg) S.; m. Roberta Jane Buck, Aug. 27, 1960; children: Holly Marie Flippen, Alan David. BSEE, U. Cin., 1960, MS, 1962, PhD, 1968. Dir. US. Naval Obs., Washington, 1975—2000; rsch. prof. U. Va., Charlottesville, Va., 2000—. Vis. assoc. prof. U. Md., College Park, 1972-90, vis. prof., 1992—; pres. Celestial Mechanics Inst., Washington, 1986—. Contbr. over 100 articles to profl. jours. Pres. Emmanuel Luth., Bethesda, Md., 1985-86, chmn. bldg. com., 1986-91. 1st lt. U.S. Army, 1963-65. Lt U.S. Army, 1963—65, Redstone Arsenal. Recipient Norman P. Hays award I.O.N., 1992; named Disting. Alumni, U. Cin. Engring. Coll., 1975; minor planet 3217 named Seidelmann in his honor. Fellow AAAS (co-recipient 2005 AAAS Internat. Scientific Cooperation award, 2006); mem. AIAA, Internat. Astron. Union (pres. com. 4 1988-91, pres. divsn. I 1997-00), Inst. Navigation (pres. 1979-80), Am. Astron. Assn. (pres. divsn. on dynamical astronomy). Luth. Achievements include co-discovery of Saturn Satellite XIV Calypso; design of star map, Einstein statue, Nat. Acad. Scis. Home: 129 Fontana Ct Charlottesville VA 22911-3531 Office Phone: 434-243-5567.

**SEIDEN, HENRY (HANK SEIDEN),** advertising executive; b. Bklyn., Sept. 6, 1928; s. Jack S. and Shirley (Berkowitz) S.; m. Helena Ruth Zaldin, Sept. 10, 1949; children: Laurie Ann, Matthew Ian. BA, Bklyn. Coll., 1949; MBA, CCNY, 1954. Trainee Ben Sackheim Advt. Agy., 1949-51; nat. promotion mgr. NY Post Corp., 1951-53; promotion mgr. Crowell-Collier Pub. Co., Inc., 1953-54; copy group head Batten, Barton, Durstine & Osborn, Inc., 1954-60; v.p., creative dir. Keyes, Madden & Jones, 1960-61; sr. v.p., assoc. creative dir. McCann-Marschalk, Inc., 1961-65, chmn. plans bd., 1964-65; creative dir., dir. Hicks & Greist, Inc., NYC, 1965—, sr. v.p., 1965-74, exec. v.p., 1974-83, COO, 1983—, pres., 1986—; CEO Ketchum/Hicks & Greist Inc., 1987-89; chmn., CEO Ketchum Advt., 1989-91; exec. v.p. Ketchum Comm. Inc., also bd. dirs.; vice chmn. Jordan, McGrath, Case & Taylor, Inc., 1992—97; chmn., CEO The Seiden Group, Inc. Bd. dirs. Ketchum Internat. Inc.; guest lectr. Bernard M. Baruch Sch. Bus. and Pub. Administrn., CCNY, 1962—, Baruch Coll., 1969—, New Sch. Social Scis., 1968, 72,73, Sch. Visual Arts, 1979, 80—, Lehman Coll., CCNY, 1980—, Ohio U., 1981, Newhouse Grad. Sch., Syracuse U., 1981, NYU, 1983; cons. pub. rels. and comm. to mayor City of New Rochelle, NY, 1959—; cons. mktg. dept. Ohio State U.; cons. to pres. NYC City Coun., 1972-73; cons. Postmaster Gen. US, 1972-74; comm. advisor to commr. NYC Police Dept., 1973—; hon. dept. commr., 1991—, spl. cons. to commr., 1992—; mem. bd. advisors Stillman Sch. Bus., Seton Hall U., 2002; adv. circle, Columbia U., Health Sci. Divsn., 2003. Author: Advertising Pure and Simple, 1976, Advertising Pure and Simple: The New Edition, 1990; contbg. editor: Madison Ave. mag, 1966-, Advt. Age, Mag. Age; guest columnist: NY Times, 1972. Vice commr. Little League of New Rochelle; bd. dirs. Police Res. Assn. NYC, 1973—; pres. exec. com.; bd. dirs. Cancer Rsch. and Treatment Fund, Inc., pres., 1992—; bd. dirs. Am. Heart Assn., 2002, Transmedia Network, Inc.; bd. dirs., chmn. New York's Finest Found., 1975—, pres., 1996, chmn., 2002; bd. dirs., chmn., sr. v.p. Drug Enforcement Agy. Found., 1995—; advisors cir. Columbia Presbyn. Hosp., 2002; assoc. Marine Corps Univ. Found., 2004. Recipient award Four Freedoms Found., 1959, award Printers Ink, 1960, promotion award Editor and Pub., 1955, Am. TV Commls. Festival award, 1963-69, Effie award Am. Mktg. Assn., 1969, 70, award Art Dirs. Club NY, 1963-70, award Am. Inst. Graphic Arts, 1963, Starch award, 1969, spl. award graphic art lodge B'nai B'rith Greater NY, 1971, 87, award of highest honor FBI Nat. Acad., 1994, Commendation, 1995. Mem. NATAS, Am. Inst. Graphic Arts. Avocations: reading, sports, travel. Office: The Seiden Group 708 3rd Ave New York NY 10017-4201 Office Phone: 212-655-1051. Personal E-mail: hankruthseiden@aol.com. Business E-Mail: handseiden@theseidengroupadv.com. *Be yourself but don't take yourself too seriously.*

**SEIDEN, STEVEN ARNOLD,** executive search consultant; b. N.Y.C., Feb. 18, 1936; s. Leon and Eleanor (Troy) S.; m. Katherine Cohen, June 8, 1965; children: Lisa Brooke, Hilary Anne. AB, Yale U., 1958. Pres. Seiden Krieger Assocs., 1984—. Mem. N.Y. Stock Exch. Regulatory Adv. Com., 1981-83, policy com. Am. Coun. for Capital Formation, 1982-87. Mem. adv. bd. Registered Rep. Mag., 1982-84. With U.S. Army, 1961—62. Mem.: U.S. C. of C. (small bus. coun. 1985—89), Internat. Assn. Corp. and Profl. Recruiters (editl. bd. 1993—95), N.Y. Biotech. Assn., Turnaround Mgmt. Assn. (program co-chair N.Y. chpt. 1991—92), N.Y. Soc. Security Analysts, Securities Industry Assn. (bd. dirs. 1981—83), Assn. Corp. Growth (asst. v.p. 1987—88, bd. dirs.), Wall St. Tax Assn. (bd. dirs. 1981—83), Bond Club, Century Country Club. Republican. Office: Seiden Krieger Assocs 375 Park Ave New York NY 10152-0002 Business E-Mail: steven@seidenkrieger.com.

**SEIDENBERG, IVAN G.,** telecommunications industry executive; b. NYC, Dec. 10, 1946; s. Howard and Kitty (Zaretsky) S.; m. Phyllis A. Maisel, Dec. 13, 1969; children: Douglas, Lisa. BS in Math., CUNY, 1972; MBA in Mkt. Mgmt., Pace U., 1980. Various engring. positions NY Tel., 1966-74; dist. mgr. transmission design AT&T, Basking Ridge, NJ, 1974-76, dist. mgr. tech. planning, 1976-78, div. mgr. fed. regulatory NYC, 1978-81, asst. v.p. mktg., 1981-83; v.p. fed. relations Nynex Corp., 1983-86, v.p. external affairs, pres., vice chmn., chmn., CEO, 1995-98, Bell Atlantic Corp, NYC, 1999-2000; pres., co-CEO Verizon Comm., Inc. (formerly Bell Atlantic Corp.), NYC, 2000—02; pres, CEO Verizon Comm. (formerly Bell Atlantic Corp.), NYC, 2002—05, chmn., CEO, 2005—. Bd. dirs. Boston Properties Inc., CVS Corp., Honeywell, Wyeth, Viacom, Inc. Bd. dirs. NY Hall Sci., Nat. Urban League., Pace U., Mus. TV and Radio, Verizon Found. Sgt. U.S. Army, 1966—68, Vietnam. Mem. US Telephone Assn. (bd. dirs. 1985—), Rockland Bus. Council (trustee 1987). Office: Verizon Communications Ste 200b 1095 Avenue of the Americas New York NY 10036-6704*

**SEIDENSTICKER, EDWARD GEORGE,** Japanese language and literature educator; b. Castle Rock, Colo., Feb. 11, 1921; s. Edward George and Mary Elizabeth (Dillon) S. BA, U. Colo., 1942; MA, Columbia U., 1947; postgrad., Harvard U., 1947-48; LittD (hon.), U. Md., 1991. With U.S. Fgn.

Service, Dept. State, Japan, 1947-50; mem. faculty Stanford U., 1962-66, prof., 1964-66; prof. dept. Far Eastern langs. and lit. U. Mich., Ann Arbor, 1966-77; prof. Japanese Columbia U., 1977-85, prof. emeritus, 1986—. Author: Kafu the Scribbler, 1965, Japan, 1961, Low City, High City, 1983, Tokyo Rising, 1990, Very Few People Come This Way, 1994; transl.: (by Murasaki Shikibu) The Tale of Genji, 1976. Served with USMCR, 1942-46. Decorated Order of Rising Sun Japan; recipient Nat. Book award, 1970; citation Japanese Ministry Edn., 1971; Kikuchi Kan prize, 1977; Goto Miyoko prize, 1982; Japan Found. prize, 1984; Tokyo Cultural award, 1985; Yamagata Banto prize, 1992. Home: 1350 Ala Moana Blvd Apt 3103 Honolulu HI 96814-4229 Office Phone: 808-591-1795. *"Make yourself a routine and stick to it," said my childhood piano teacher when I went off to college. I have never had, as some people seem to have, great plans for my future; but if a person has a serious routine and sticks resolutely with it, something is bound to get accomplished.*

**SEIDL, LYNN ANN,** music director, educator; b. Green Bay, Wis., Aug. 1, 1955; d. Ervin R. and Barbara A. (Blahnik) Stahl; m. Joseph D. Seidl, Sept. 13, 1975; children: Kimberly, Gregory, Molly. BA, U. Wis., Green Bay, 1977; MS, Viterbo U., LaCrosse, Wis., 2005. Music tchr. Luxemburg Area Cath. Schs., Wis., 1978—89; vocal music dir. Luxemburg-Casco Mid. Sch., Wis., 1990—. Mem.: Wis. Sch. Music Assn. (master adjudicator 1978—), Music Educators Nat. Confs., Wis. Choral Dirs. Assn. (pres. 2003—05). Avocations: reading, sports, travel. Office Phone: 920-837-2205 ext. 330. Office Fax: 920-837-7517. Business E-Mail: lseidl@luxcasco.k12.wi.us.

**SEIDL, SUSAN KATHRYN,** secondary school educator; b. Menominee, Mich., June 18, 1951; d. Roger Paul and Frances Mary Seidl. BA, Mt. Mary Coll., 1973; MA, Cardinal Stritch U., 1992. Cert. English, speech, drama, art Dept. Pub. Instrn., Wis. Tchr. English, speech, drama, art St. Mary's H.S., Burlington, Wis., 1973—74, Oconto (Wis.) H.S., 1974—. Dir. drama Oconto H.S. and St. Mary's, Oconto and Burlington, 1973—; com. mem. Oconto H.S., 1974—, mentor, tchr., 2000—02; mus. dir. The Machickanee Players. Named H.S. Tchr. of Yr., Oconto Unifed Sch. Dist., 2002; recipient Tchr. Fellowship award, Dept. Instrn., 1997. Mem.: NEA (mem. secondary divsn.), Nat. Coun. Tchrs. of English, Wis. Theater Assn. (chair secondary edn. com. 1970—90), Oconto County Hist. Soc., Delta Kappa Gamma (Beta Sigma chpt.) (com. mem., pres., chpt. photographer, Woman of Distinction 1989). Roman Catholic. Avocations: reading, writing, photography, walking, bicycling. Office: Oconto H S 1717 Superior Ave Oconto WI 54153 Office Phone: 920-834-7812 ext. 322. Business E-Mail: seidsuet@oconto.k12.wi.us.

**SEIDLER, ALAN RICHARD,** composer, musician, music company executive; b. N.Y., Dec. 4, 1951; s. Jack Seidler and Martha Kahn; m. Jean Alyson Godden, Feb. 16, 1977 (div. Jan. 1980). Student, Juilliard Sch., 1969—72; MusB, Manhattan Sch. Music, NY, 1988; student, New Sch. U., 1972—73, UCLA, 1975. Adj. instuctor musical theatre Inst. for Arts Iona Coll., New Rochelle, NY, 1970—71; chmn., pres. Ook Ook Productions, Inc., N.Y., 1974—75; faculty voice and piano N.Y. Schs. Music, N.Y., 1978—79; chmn., pres. New Classics Entertainment N.Y., 1995—, Furhoof Enterprises, Ltd., N.Y., 2001—, Hoove Ape Records, 2006—. Cons. programming Radio Pacifica WBAI-FM, N.Y., 1971—72; musical dir. Roundabout Theatre, N.Y., 1967—68; musical, faculty creative arts Iona Coll. Summer Inst. Composer: (films) He Outta Be Committed (Audience Appreciation award Louisville Film Festival, 2000); composer: (singer, songwriter, pianist) (albums) Alan Seidler: The Duke of Ook; composer: (pianist, singer) Morning Impromptus/Evening Bacchanals; musician I'm In Love, Ragtime Millionaire; composer Alan Seidler: Chamber Music, From The Soul-Sonata for Violin and Piano, Five English Poems for Voice and Piano, (choral works) Three Profundities for Unison Chorus, (chamber music) Quartet for Piano and Strings, (choral symphony) The Mystic Trumpeter, (songs) String Quartet #1, Sonata for Violin and Piano, Two Sacred Pieces for a capella chorus, Four Poems of William Blake for a capella chorus, Four Preludes on Playthings of the Wind, In The Arc of Your Mallet: 4 Love Poems of Jelaluddin Rumi, Oh, On An Early Morning; musician: (debut piano soloist) Philharmonic, 1968. Scholar, Young Artists New Rochelle, N.Y., 1969. Mem.: Nat. Composers, Inc., Chamber Music Am., Am. Music Ctr., Am. Fedn. TV and Radio Artists, Soc. of Composers, Inc., Am. Soc. Composers, Authors and Publishers (grantee 1997—2006). Avocations: swimming, ping pong/table tennis. Office: c/o Carole Sorell Inc Ste 24H 395 S End Ave New York NY 10280 Business E-Mail: alanseidler@gmail.com.

**SEIDLER, B(ERNARD) ALAN,** lawyer; b. N.Y.C., Nov. 26, 1946; s. Aaron H. and Ethel T. (Berkowitz) S.; m. Lynne Aubrey, Jan. 21, 1978; children: Jacob A., Morgan H., Lily R. BA, Colgate U., 1968; JD, Seton Hall U., 1972. Bar: N.Y. 1973, U.S. Dist. Ct. (ea., no. and so. dists.) N.Y. 1975, U.S. Ct. Appeals (2d cir.) 1976, U.S. Ct Appeals (3d cir.) 1984,U.S. Ct Appeals (4th cir.) 2004, U.S. Supreme Ct. 1977. Staff atty. N.Y. Legal Aid Soc., N.Y.C., 1972-75; sole practitioner N.Y.C., 1975—. Mem. Snedens Landing Tennis Assn. (Palisades, N.Y.), Palisades Swim Club. Office: 580 Broadway New York NY 10012 Office Phone: 212-334-3131. Personal E-mail: snedens66@aol.com.

**SEIDLER, DORIS,** artist; b. London, Nov. 26, 1912; m. Bernard Seidler, Sept. 5, 1935; 1 child, David. Exhibited in group shows at Bklyn. Mus. Bi-Ann., Vancouver Internat., Honolulu Acad. Arts, Pa. Acad. Fine Arts, Phila., Soc. Am. Graphic Artists, assoc. Am. Artists Gallery, Jewish Mus., N.Y.C., Albright-Knox Mus., 1994, Brit. Mus. Recent Acquisitions, 1997, Whitworth Gallery, Manchester, Eng., 2003, Represented in permanent collections Libr. of Congress, Smithsonian Instn., Washington, Phila. Mus. Art, Bklyn. Mus., Seattle Mus. Art, Whitney Mus., Nat. Gallery Art, Nassau County (N.Y.) Mus. Fine Arts, Brit. Mus., London, Victoria and Albert Mus. London, Pallant House Coll., Eng., Portland Mus. Art, Oreg., Birmingham Mus., Eng. Address: 14 Stoner Ave Great Neck NY 11021 2101

**SEIDMAN, CHRISTINE E.,** medical educator; BA, Harvard U.; MD, George Washington U., 1978. Resident in internal medicine Johns Hopkins U., Balt.; resident in cardiology Mass. Gen. Hosp., Boston; staff Brigham and Women's Hosp. Harvard U., Boston, 1987, dir. cardiovasc. genetics svc., prof. Dept. Medicine and Dept. Genetics; assoc. investigator Howard Hughes Med. Inst., 1994, investigator. Recipient Bristol-Myers Squibb award, 2002. Mem.: NAS, Inst. Medicine. Office: Harvard U Med Sch Genetics NRB 256 77 Avenue Louis Pasteur Boston MA 02115 Business E-Mail: cseidman@genetics.med.harvard.edu.*

**SEIDMAN, DAVID N(ATHANIEL),** materials scientist, engineer, educator; b. NYC, July 5, 1938; s. Charles and Jeanette (Cohen) S.; m. Shoshanah Cohen-Sabban, Oct. 21, 1973; children: Elie, Ariel, Eytan. BS, NYU, 1960, MS, 1962; PhD, U. Ill., Urbana, 1965. Postdoc. assoc. Cornell U., Ithaca, NY, 1964-66, asst. prof. materials sci. and engring., 1966-70, assoc. prof. materials sci. and engring., 1970-76, prof. materials sci. and engring., 1976-85, Northwestern U., Evanston, Ill., 1985-96, Walter P. Murphy prof. materials sci. and engring., 1996—, founder., dir. Ctr. for Atom-Probe Tomography, 2004—. Vis. prof. Technion, Haifa, 1969-70, Tel-Aviv U., Ramat-Aviv, 1972; Lady Davis vis. prof. Hebrew U., Jerusalem, 1978, 80-81, prof. materials sci., 1983-85; vis. scientist C.E. de Grenoble, 1981, C.N.E.T.-Meylan, 1981, C.E. de Scalay, 1989, U. Goettingen, 1989, 92; sci. cons. Argonne Nat. labs., Ill., 1985-94. Editor: Jour. Materials Sci., 2004—; mem. editl. bd., editor spl. issues (jour.) Interface Sci., 1993—2001, editor-in-chief, 2002—04, mem. editl. bd. Materials Sci. Forum, 1996—; contbr. numerous articles to profl. jours. Recipient Max Planck Rsch. prize Max-Planck-Gesellschaft and the A. von Humboldt-Stiftung, 1993; Guggenheim fellow, 1972-73, 80-81, Humboldt fellow, 1989, 92; named chair for phys. metallurgy Gordon Conf., 1982. Fellow Am. Phys. Soc., TMS (mem. fellows award com. 2002-2005, chair, 2006-, Hardy Gold medal 1966), Am. Soc. Metals Internat. (Grossman and Howe awards com. 2005-, fellow awards com., 2006—), Albert Sauveur Achievement award, 2006), AAAS (Washington achievement award com., 2006); mem. Materials Rsch. Soc., Microscopy Soc. Am., A. von Humboldt Soc. Am., Internat. Field-Emission Soc. (mem. steering com. 1997-2002, pres. 2000-2002), Böhmische Phys. Soc Democrat. Jewish.

Achievements include research in nanostructural temporal evolution, internal interfaces, atomic-scale imperfections in metals and semiconductors, radiation in metals three-dimensional atom-probe tomography and electron microscopy. Avocations: reading, history, travel. Home: 9056 Tamaroa Ter Skokie IL 60076-1928 Office: Northwestern U MS&E Dept Cook Hall Evanston IL 60208-3108 Business E-Mail: d-seidman@northwestern.edu.

**SEIDMAN, ELLEN SHAPIRO,** lawyer, government official; b. NYC, Mar. 12, 1948; d. Benjamin Harry Shapiro and Edna (Eysen) Stern; m. Walter Becker Slocombe, June 14, 1981; 1 child, Benjamin William. AB, Radcliffe Coll., 1969; JD, Georgetown U., 1974; MBA, George Washington U., 1988. Bar: D.C., 1975. Law clk. US Ct. of Claims, Washington, 1974-75; assoc. Caplin & Drysdale, Washington, 1975-78; atty., advisor US Dept. Transp., Washington, 1978-79, dep. asst. gen. counsel, 1979-81; assoc. gen. counsel Chrysler Corp Loan Guaranty Bd., Washington, 1981-84; atty., advisor US Dept. of Treasury, Washington, 1981-86, spl. asst. to the Under Sec. Fin., 1986-87; dir. strategic planning Fed. Nat. Mortgage Assn., Washington, 1987-88, v.p., asst. to chmn., 1988-91, sr. v.p. regulation rsch. and econs., 1991-93; spl. asst. to the pres. for econ. policy The White House, Washington, 1993-97; dir. Office Thrift Supervision US Dept. Treasury, Washington, 1997—2001; sr. counsel, Minority Staff, fin. svcs. com. US Ho. of Reps., Washington, 2002; sr. mng. dir. nat. practice Shorebank Adv. Svcs., 2002—05; exec. v.p. Shorebank Corp., 2006—. Office Phone: 202-822-9146. Business E-Mail: ellen_seidman@sbk.com.

**SEIDMAN, GLENN ELLIOTT,** sales executive, marketing professional, consultant; b. June 18, 1951; m. Charlene Goldberg, 1988; children: Brooke, Michelle. BA, CUNY, 1975; MA, NYU, 1977. Asst. dir. student activities Columbia U., N.Y.C., 1978-83; assoc. dean students Poly. U., Bklyn., 1983-88; territory mgr. Quality Products & Svcs., Reading, Pa., 1988—2000; pres. Oxford Bus. Cons. Group, LLC, Huntington, NY, 2000—. Mem. Ind. Cons. Assn., Inst. Mgmt. Cons., U.S. C. of C., Queens Coll. Alumni Assn. (pres. 1987-89), Huntington C. of C. E-mail: oxfordbcg@aol.com.

**SEIDMAN, L(EWIS) WILLIAM,** television commentator, publisher; b. Grand Rapids, Mich., Apr. 29, 1921; s. Frank E. and Esther (Lubetsky) S.; m. Sarah Berry, Mar. 3, 1944; children: Thomas, Tracy, Sarah, Carrie, Meg, Robin. AB, Dartmouth Coll., 1943; LL.B., Harvard U., 1948, MBA, U. Mich., 1949. Bar: Mich. 1949, D.C. 1977. Spl. asst. fin. affairs to gov. of Mich., 1963-66; nat. mng. partner Seidman & Seidman C.P.A.s, N.Y.C., 1969-74; asst. for econ. affairs to Pres. Gerald R. Ford, 1974-77; dir., chief fin. officer Phelps Dodge Corp., N.Y.C., 1977-82, vice chmn., 1980-82; dean Coll. Bus. Adminstrn. Ariz. State U., Tempe, 1982-85; chmn. RTC FDIC, Washington, 1985—91; chief commentator Sta. CNBC-TV, 1991; pub.-bd. Bank Dir. Mag., 1992. Chmn. Detroit Fed. Res. Bank Chgo., 1970, RTC, 1989-91; co-chair White House Conf. on Productivity, 1983-84. Lt. USNR, 1942-46. Decorated Bronze Star. Mem. D.C. Bar Assn., Chevy Chase Club (Md.), Univ. Club (N.Y.C.), Crystal Downs Club (Mich.), Nantucket Yacht Club (MA). Office: CNBC 8th Flr 1025 Connecticut Ave NW Washington DC 20036-5405 Office Phone: 202-530-0910. Personal E-mail: lws1025@aol.com.

**SEIERSEN, NICHOLAS STEEN,** management consultant; b. Geneva, June 23, 1955; s. Ove Steen and Kamini Shoshiela (Bhandari) S.; m. Sylvie Jacqueline Fenouillet, Nov. 7, 1981. BSc with honors, U. Sussex, 1976; MBA, Pacific State U., L.A., 1987. Project chief Metra Proudfoot Internat. Mgmt. Cons., Brussels, 1977-81; unit mgr. Auchan Hypermarkets, Paris, 1981-83; internat. controller Pain Jacquet Group, Paris, 1983-85; sr. cons A.T. Kearney Mgmt. Cons., Paris, 1985-88; European mktg. mgr. Digital Equip. Corp., Paris, 1988-95; dir. sales, mktg., logistics and distbn. European Mfg. Expertise Ctr., Digital Equipment Corp., Paris, 1995-96; prin. KPMG Mgmt. Consulting (now BearingPoint, LP), Toronto, Ont., Canada, 1996—99, sr. mgr., 1999—2005; sr. mgr. adv. svcs. KPMG, Toronto, Canada, 2005—. Sci. bd. Logistique & Mgmt. Jour. (in French); editl. com. Global Supply Chain Forum mgmt. jour., Logistics Quarterly. Editl. adv. bd.: Logistics Quar. Jour., 2001—03, Can. exec. editor.; 2003—; contbr. articles to profl. jours. Mem. U.S. Bus. Logistics Assn. (coun. supply chain mgmt. profls., v.p. 1998-2000, pres. Toronto Roundtable 2000-02), Can. Assn. for Supply Chain and Logistics Mgmt., French Assn. Logistics Mgmt. (bd. dirs. 1994-96, v.p. internat. affairs 1994-96). Office: KPMG Ste 3300 Commerce Ct W 199 Bay St Toronto ON Canada M5L 1B2 Office Phone: 416-777-8391. Business E-Mail: nseiersen@kpmg.ca.

**SEIFE, HOWARD,** lawyer; b. NYC, Apr. 10, 1952; BA cum laude, Union Coll., NY, 1973; JD cum laude, Georgetown U., 1978; LLM, U. London, 1983. Bar: NY 1979, US Dist. Ct. (Ea. Dist.) NY 1980, US Dist. Ct. (So. Dist.) NY 1980, US Ct. Appeals (2nd Cir.) 1982, US Ct. Appeals (9th Cir.) 1990, US Ct. of Claims 1985, US Supreme Ct. 2001. Ptnr. Chadbourne & Parke LLP, NYC, chmn., Fin. Restructuring and Bankruptcy Practice Group. Mediator Bankruptcy Ct. (So. Dist.) NY, 1996—; arbitrator US Dist. Ct. (Ea. Dist.) NY, 1985—. Contbr. articles to profl. jour.; spkr. in field. Mem.: INSOL Internat. (chmn. tech. rsch. com. 2003—). Office: Chadbourne & Parke LLP 30 Rockefeller Plaza New York NY 10112 Office Phone: 212-408-5361. Office Fax: 212-541-5369. Business E-Mail: hseife@chadbourne.com.

**SEIFERT, BETTY L.,** conservator, consultant; d. Marvin Leon Morris and Cleo Mae Betel; m. Walter Seifert, May 31, 1970; children: Eli, Sara Marguerite. BA, BS, Tex. Woman's U., 1962; MLS, Rutgers U., 1964. Libr. N.Y. Pub. Libr., N.Y.C., 1962—64, Bronx Vet.'s Hosp., N.Y.C., 1965—68; exhibit preparator Maine State Mus., Augusta, 1975—76, conservation technician, 1976—82; conservator Profl. Svc. Industries, Groton, Mass 1982—85; cons. conservator various orgns., 1985—89, chief conservator Jefferson Patterson Pk. and Mus., St. Leonard, Md., 1989—; dep. dir. Md. Archaeol. Conservation Lab., St. Leonard, 1997—. Weaving instr. Riverside Ch. Arts and Crafts, N.Y.C., 1968—73. Author: (stds.a and guidelines) Standards and Guidelines for Archaeological Investigations in Maryland: Technical Update No. 1 - Collections and Conservation Standards. Adv. bd. mem. for conservation of the USS Monitor Mariner's Mus., Newport News, Va., 2003—06; bd. mem. adv. coun. for underwater archaeology Soc. for Hist. Archaeology, 1990—2001. Recipient full tuition and textbooks scholarship, N.Y. Pub. Libr., 1962—64, Gov.'s Disting. Svc. award, Gov. of Maine, 1978, 2004 Spl. Recognition award, Md. Dept. of Housing and Cmty. Devel., 2004. Mem.: Am. Inst. for Conservation. Achievements include development of Standards and Guidelines for Curation and Conservation of Archaeological Collections; Technical Lead in Design of the Maryland Archaeological Conservation Laboratory. Avocations: weaving, spinning, basketry. Office: Maryland Archaeol Conservation Lab 10515 Mackall Rd Saint Leonard MD 20685 Office Phone: 410-586-8578. E-mail: bseifert@mdp.state.md.us.

**SEIFERT, CAROLINE HAMILTON,** community health nurse; b. Warren, Ohio, May 28, 1937; d. Oliver L. and Martha (Moran) Hamilton; m. Dale E. Seifert, Sept. 5, 1959; children: Brian Dale, Joan Kimberly. Diploma, Youngstown (Ohio) Hosp. Assn., 1959; BSN, U. Cin., 1964, MEd, 1979. Cert. sch. nurse, health educator, spl. edn. educator. Caseworker Children's Svcs. div. Dept. Health and Human Svcs., Batavia, Ohio, 1966-68; dir. Happy Days Nursery Sch. Bethel (Ohio) United Meth. Ch., 1970-73; social worker Clermont County Bd. Mental Retardation/Devel. Disabilities, Batavia, 1973-97; sch. nurse, health educator Thomas A. Wildey Sch., Owensville, Ohio, 1973-97; retired, 1997. Instr. Sch. Health Svcs. U. Cin., 1976, preceptor nursing students, 1992-97. Mem. Hamilton/Clermont Sch. Nurses Orgn. (v.p.), S.W. Ohio Sch. Nurses Assn. (program chmn.), Profl. Assn. for Retardation (v.p. nursing div., Nurse of Yr.). Home: 2631 Oldforge Ln Cincinnati OH 45244-2831 Office: Thomas A Wildey Sch PO Box 8 Owensville OH 45160-0008

**SEIFERT, FRANK C.,** thoracic surgeon; b. Chgo., Feb. 27, 1948; MD, U. Chgo. Pritzker Sch. Medicine, 1974. Cert. Thoracic Surgery, Surgical Critical Care. Intern, gen. surgery U. Chgo. Hospitals, 1974—75, resident, cardiothoracic surgery, 1976—80; resident, anatomy Stanford U. Med. Ctr., 1980—83;

fellow U. Goteborg, 1977—78; hosp. appt. U. Hosp., Stony Brook, NY; assoc. prof. surgery SUNY-Stony Brook, NY. Named one of Medical Marvels, New York Mag., 2006. Fellow: Am. Coll. Cardiology, Am. Coll. Surgeons. Office: Health Sciences Center T19-080 SUNY Stony Brook Surgery Stony Brook NY 11790 Office Phone: 631-444-1820. Business E-Mail: fseifert@notes.cc.sunysb.edu.*

**SEIFERT, JEFFREY W.,** political scientist, researcher; s. Edward C.W. and Marilyn G. Seifert. BA summa cum laude, Towson State U., Md., 1992; MA, Syracuse U., NY, 1995, PhD, 2001. Global programs coord. Syracuse (N.Y.) U., 1999—2000; specialist info. sci. and tech. policy Congl. Rsch. Svc., Washington, 2000—. Vis. instr. Va. Tech. U., Blacksburg, Va., 2001—. Co-author: The New International Studies Classroom, 2000; mem. editl. bd.: Jour. E-Gov., 2004—; Govt. Info. Quar., 2003—; contbr. articles to profl. jours.; contbg. author: Comparative Perspectives on E-Government, 2006. Mem.: Midwest Polit. Sci. Assn., Internat. Studies Assn. (active learning internat. affairs sect. 2000—01, Jr. scholar 1999), Internat. Soc. Polit. Psychology, Assn. Am. Geographers, Am. Polit. Sci. Assn. (bd. dir. info. tech. politics sect. 2002—04, pres. info. tech. politics sect. 2005—), Gamma Theta Upsilon. Office: Congressional Research Service 101 Independence Avenue SE Stop 7450 Washington DC 20540-7450 Office Phone: 202-707-0781. Office Fax: 202-707-7000. E-mail: jseifert@crs.loc.gov.

**SEIFERT, KATHI P.,** manufacturing executive; b. Appleton, Wis., 1949; m. Steve Seifert; children: Erin, Andrew. BA Valparaiso U., 1971. Various mgmt. positions P&G, Beatruce Foods, Fort Howard Paper Co., 1972—78; from product mgr. to mktg. dir. feminine care products Kimberly-Clark, Inc., Neenah, Wis., 1978—92, pres. feminine care sectory, 1992—94, group pres. N. Am. consumer products, 1994—95, group pres. N. Am. personal care products, 1995—98, group pres. personal care products, 1998—99, exec. v.p., group pres. global personal care products, 1999—, ret.; with Pinnacle Perspectives, LLC. Bd. dirs. Eli Lilly and Co. Bd. dirs. U.S Fund for UNICEF; bd., dirs. Fox Cities Performing Art Ctr., 1999—, chmn. of bd., 2003—; bd, dirs. Theda Health Care Group, Wis. Commn. in Arts Edn. Office: Pinnacle Perspectives LLC Ste 303 330 W College Ave Appleton WI 54911

**SEIFERT, SHELLEY JANE,** bank executive, human resources specialist; b. Aug. 12, 1954; BS in Consumer Econs. and Journalism, U. Mo., 1976; MBA in Fin. with honors, U. Louisville, 1980. Fin. analyst Nat. City Bank, Ky., 1979-81, compensation analyst 1981-85, mgr. compensation, 1985-86 mgr. compensation, recruiting and tng., 1986-91; mgr. compensation and devel. Nat. City Corp., Cleve., 1988-91, human resource dir., 1991-94, sr. v.p., 1994—2000, corp. human resource dir., 1994—2004, exec. v.p., 2000—. Spkr. in field; bd. dirs., Blair Corp., 2006- Grad. Leadership Cleve.; vice chair bd. dirs. Bus. Vols. Unlimited, Vis. Nurse Assn. Greater Cleve.; bd. dirs. Arthritis Found.; mem. Cleve. Commn. on Econ. Partnership and Inclusion. Recipient Woman of Distinction award YMCA. Mem. Urban League (bd. dirs., chair employment com., Ohio labor adv. com.). Office: Nat City Corp Nat City Ctr 1900 E 9th St Cleveland OH 44114-3401*

**SEIFERT, THOMAS LLOYD,** lawyer; b. Boston, June 6, 1940; s. Ralph Frederick and Hazel Bell (Harrington) S.; m. Ann Cecelia Berg, June 19, 1965. BS cum laude, Ind. U., Bloomington, 1962; JD cum laude, Ind. U., 1965. Bar: Ill. 1965, Ind. 1965, N.Y. 1979. Assoc. law firm Keck, Mahin & Cate, Chgo., 1965-67; atty. Essex Group, Inc., Ft. Wayne, Ind., 1967-70, Amoco Corp., Chgo., 1970-73; assoc. gen. counsel, asst. sec. Canteen Corp. Chgo., 1973-75; sec., gen. counsel The Marmon Group, Inc. (and predecessor cos.), Chgo., 1975-78; v.p., gen. counsel, sec. Hanson Industries, Inc., N.Y., 1978-82; sr. v.p. law, chief fin. officer Petrie Stores Corp., N.Y.C., 1982-83; mem. Finley, Kumble, Wagner, Heine, Underberg, Manley, Myerson & Casey, N.Y.C., 1983-87, Paul, Weiss, Rifkind, Wharton & Garrison, N.Y.C., 1987-91; gen. counsel, chief legal officer Sterling Grace Capital Mgmt., L.P. and affiliated cos., N.Y.C., 1991—. Note editor Ind. Law Jour., 1964-65. Named to Ind. Track and Cross Country Hall of Fame, 1993. Mem. ABA, N.Y. State Bar Assn., Order of Coif, The Creek, Beta Gamma Sigma. Home: Museum Tower 15 W 53d St Apt 31 E New York NY 10019-5401 Office: Sterling Grace Capital Mgmt 405 Park Ave Ste 1203 New York NY 10022 Office Phone: 212-644-5067. Personal E-Mail: tlseifert@msn.com.

**SEIFF, GLORIA LOUISE,** volunteer; b. Denver, Apr. 3, 1929; d. Edward Hyatt and Lilliian Pearl (Blend) Holtzman; m. Stephen S. Seiff, Apr. 16, 1950; children: Stuart R., Sherri P. Seiff Sloane, Karen E. Seiff Sacks. Student, Washington U., 1947-48. Commr. Pub. Works Commn., Beverly Hills, Calif., 1990-98, bd. pres. 1993, 96; pres. Beverly Vista Elem. Sch. PTA, Beverly Hills, lif.,968-69, PTA Coun., Beverly Hills, 1972-73; bd. dirs. Beverly Hills S.W. Homeowners Assn., 1985—, Braille Inst Aux., L.A., 1998—; founding mem., bd. dirs., trustee Beverly Hills Edn. Found., 1975-79; v.p. devel. Assistance League So. Calif., L.A., 1994-98, bd. dirs., 1994—; trustee L.A. County Mosquito Abatement Dist., 1984-92, bd. pres. 1988; pres. LWV, Beverly Hills, 1985-87; mem. long range planning com. Assistance League So. Calif., 1997-98, 2005—, mem. endowment com., 1995—, v.p. pub. rels., 1999-2002; chmn. Beverly Hills Groundwater Tech. Adv. Com., 1999—; commr. Beverly Hills Traffic and Parking Commn., 2000—, vice chmn., 2002, chair 2002-2003; mem. City of Beverly Hills Gen. Plan Topics Com./Residential, 2002-04. Recipient Hon. Svc. award PTA, Beverly Hills, 1972, Outstanding Cmty. Svc. award, Beverly Hills City Coun., 1984-87, Resolution Cmty. Svc. award Beverly Bd. Edn., 1986. Mem. Calif. Yacht Club, Las Doñas UCLA Alumni Assn., Beverly Hills Unified Sch. Dist. Citizens Oversight Com. "Measure K". Avocation: sailing.

**SEIFF, STEPHEN S.,** ophthalmologist; b. LA, Sept. 30, 1925; s. Max and Minnie F. (Feldman) S.; m. Gloria Louise Holtzman, Apr. 16, 1950; children: Stuart R., Sherri Seiff Sloane, Karen Seiff Sacks. AA, UCLA, 1945; AB, U. Calif., Berkeley, 1946; MD, U. Calif., San Francisco, 1949. Diplomate Am. Bd. Ophthalmology. Intern County Gen. Hosp., L.A., 1949-50; fellow in anesthesiology Lahey Clinic, Boston, 1950-51; resident in ophthalmology U. Calif., San Francisco, 1952-55; clin. prof. ophthalmology UCLA, 1956—2002, emeritus clin. prof., 2002—; pvt. practice Beverly Hills, Calif., 1955—; clin. chief divsn. ophthalmology Cedars/Sinai Med. Ctr., L.A., 1957—; attending ophthalmologist Children's Hosp., L.A., 1956-94. Lectr. in field; assoc. examiner Am. Bd. Ophthalmology. Collaborating author: Clinical Anticoagulant Therapy, 1965; contbr. articles to profl. jours. Bd. dirs. Found. That Man May See Inc., San Francisco; former exec. com. mem. UCLA Hosp. Lt. M.C. USNR, 1950-52. Recipient Sr. Honor award UCLA Dept. Ophthalmology, 1994. Fellow ACS, Am. Acad. Ophthalmology; mem. L.A. Soc. Ophthalmology (past pres.), Frederick Cordes Eye Soc. (past nat. pres.), Am. Soc. Cataract and Refractive Surgery (founding mem.). Avocation: sailing. Office: 435 N Roxbury Dr Ste 107 Beverly Hills CA 90210-5003 Personal E-mail: sseiff@aol.com.

**SEIFMAN, BARRY A.,** lawyer; b. Oct. 14, 1946; m. Marcia Kirschbaum, Sept. 11, 1966; 2 children. BA, Wayne State U., 1968, JD magna cum laude, 1972. Bar: Mich., 1973, U.S. Dist. Ct. (we. & ea. dists.) Mich., U.S. Ct. Appeals (6th cir.), U.S. Supreme Ct. Claim rep. personal injury Traveler's Ins. Co., 1968-70; sr. claim rep. multi-line Fireman's Fund Ins. Co., 1970-72; pvt. practice Farmington Hills, Mich., 1998—; owner Seifman & Assocs., P.C. City atty. City of Woodhaven, 1997-2001, City of Romulus 1998-2001—; asst. city atty. City of Dearborn Heights, 1991-98, Garden City, 1972-75; past tchr. Detroit Bus. Inst.; guest spkr., lectr. Monteith Coll. Tort Law; neutral mediator negligence and employment law Mediation Tribunal Assn., Wayne County, 1977; mediator Oakland County, 1984—; spl. products liability panelist. Past pres. Southfield Little League, mgr.; past mem. rep. student bd. govs. Wayne State U. Law Sch.; past trustee Southfield Hockey Assn.; mgr. North Farmington Little League, West Bloomfield; mem. grievance bd. State Mich. Mem. ABA, ATLA (sustaining mem.), Mich. Trial Lawyers Assn., State

Bar Mich., Oakland County Bar Assn., Detroit Bar Assn., Millionaires Club. Home: 30069 High Valley Rd Farmington Hills MI 48331-2144 Office: Ste 255 30665 Northwestern Hwy Farmington Hills MI 48334-3144 Office Phone: 248-538-0711.

**SEIGEL, JERROLD EDWARD,** historian, writer; b. St. Louis, June 9, 1936; s. William and Katherine (Ginsberg) S.; m. Jayn Rosenfeld, Aug. 28, 1966; children: Micol, Jessica. AB, Harvard U., 1958; PhD, Princeton U., 1963. Instr. Princeton (N.J.) U., 1962-65, asst. prof., 1965-68, assoc. prof., 1968-78, prof. history, 1978-88, NYU, N.Y.C., 1988—, Kenan prof., 1994—2006, emeritus, 2006—. Vis. prof. history Maitre d'Etudes, Ecoles des hautes études, Paris, 1988-94; finalist Nat. Book Critics Cir., 1987. Author: Rhetoric and Philosophy, 1968, Marx's Fate, 1978, Bohemian Paris, 1986, Private Worlds of Marcel Duchamp, 1995, The Idea of the Self, 2005. Fulbright fellow Inst. Internat. Edn., 1961-62; NEH fellow, 1979-80, 87-88; resident Am. Acad. Rome, 2000; Guggenheim fellow, 2004-05. Mem. N.Y. Inst. for Humanities, Phi Beta Kappa. Home: 48 Horatio St New York NY 10014-1614 Business E-Mail: jes3@nyu.edu.

**SEIGEL, RICHARD M.,** consumer products company executive; Chmn., CEO SYSCO Food Svcs., L.A., 1990-97; dir. Indsl. Distbn. Group, Atlanta, 1997—, chmn., acting CEO, 1998—. Office: Indsl Distbn Group 950 E Paces Ferry Rd NE Atlanta GA 30326-1180

**SEIGEL, STUART EVAN,** lawyer; b. NYC, Mar. 25, 1933; s. Philip Herman and Betty Sarah (Leventhal) S.; m. Joyce Roberta Meyers (div.); children: Charles Meyers, Lee Bennett, Suzanne Marcie; m. Sherry Diane Jackson,Sept. 24, 1989. BS, NYU, 1953, LLB, 1957; LLM in Taxation, Georgetown U., 1960. Bar: N.Y. 1958, D.C. 1958. Atty. Office Chief Counsel, IRS, Washington, 1957—65, Office Tax Legis. Counsel, Dept. Treasury, Washington, 1965—69, assoc. tax legis. counsel, 1968—69; ptnr. Cohen and Uretz, Washington, 1969—77; chief counsel IRS, Washington, 1977—79; ptnr. Williams and Connolly, Washington, 1979—89, Arnold and Porter, N.Y.C., 1989—2002. Lectr. George Washington U. Sch. Law, 1970-73; adj. prof. law Antioch Sch. Law, 1973-76, Georgetown U. Sch. Law, 1981. Mem. ABA, Am. Law Inst., Am. Coll. Tax Counsel, N.Y. State Bar Assn., Met. Club Washington E-mail: mdllb@nyc.rr.com.

**SEIGLER, DAVID STANLEY,** botanist, educator, chemist; b. Wichita Falls, Tex., Sept. 11, 1940; s. Kenneth R. and Floy M. (Wilkinson) S.; m. Janice Kay Cline, Jan. 20, 1961; children: Dava, Rebecca. BS in Chemistry, Southwestern State Coll., Okla., 1961; PhD in Organic Chemistry, U. Okla., 1967. Postdoctoral assoc. USDA No. Regional Lab., Peoria, Ill., 1967-68; postdoctoral fellow dept. botany U. Tex., Austin, 1968-70; asst. prof. botany U. Ill., Urbana, 1970-76, assoc. prof., 1976-79, prof. botany, 1979—, head dept. plant biology, 1988-93. Curator U. Ill. Herbarium, 1993—. Author: Plant Secondary Metabolism, 1999; editor: Crop Resources, 1977, Phytochemistry and Angiosperm Phylogeny, 1981; contbr. numerous articles to profl. jours. Recipient Fulbright Hays Lecturer award Fulbright Commn., Argentina, 1976, (alternate) Germany, 1995-96, study award Deutsche Akademischer Austauschdienst, Germany, 1995, Rupert Barneby award NY Bot. Garden, 1997. Mem. Phytochem. Soc. N.Am. (pres. 1988-89), Bot. Soc. Am., Am. Chem. Soc., Am. Soc. Plant Taxonomists, Internat. Soc. Chem. Ecology (pres. 1990-91). Mem. Assembly of God Ch. Avocation: genealogy. Home: 510 W Vermont Ave Urbana IL 61801-4931 Office: U Ill Dept Plant Biology 265 Morrill Hall 505 S Goodwin Ave Urbana IL 61801-3707 Office Phone: 217-333-7577. Business E-Mail: seigler@life.uiuc.edu.

**SEIGLER, MICHAEL EDWARD,** lawyer, librarian; b. Tallahassee, Oct. 14, 1948; s. Claude Milo and Roberta Bradford (Whitfield) S.; m. Janet Cummings, Feb. 19, 1971; children: Kelly Elizabeth, Megan Whitfield. AA, Lake Sumter C.C., 1968; BS, Fla. State U., 1970, MS, 1974; JD, Atlanta Law Sch., 1980. Bar: Ga. 1980, U.S. Ct. Appelas (5th cir.) 1980, U.S. Ct. Appeals (11th cir.) 1980, U.S. tax Ct. 1985, U.S. Supreme Ct. 1985, Cert. tchr. Libr., tchr. Sumter Correctional Inst., Bushnell, Fla., 1970—73; asst. libr. dir. Leesburg Pub. Libr., Fla., 1974—75, libr. dir., 1975—77, Atlanta Law Sch., 1979—81; atty. Brooks & Brock, Marietta, Ga., 1981—83; libr. Port Charlotte Pub. Libr., 1983—84; assoc. Brooks & Brock, Marietta, 1985, Brock & Barr, Marietta, 1985—86, Brock & Clay, 1987; judge pro hoc vice State Ct. of Cobb County, 1986; pvt. practice, 1986—, Asst. dir. Pine Mountain Regional Libr., 1988-95; libr. dir. Smyrna Pub. Libr., 1995—; design judge Ben Franklin Awards, 2001, 03, 04. Columnist Smyrna Vinings Living, 2000-02; contbr. articles to jours. Vol. worker ACLU, Atlanta, 1979; mem. Fla. State U. Libr. Com., Tallahassee, 1974, Children's Program Com., Port Charlotte, 1983, Port Charlotte Cultural Ctr. Adv. Com., 1984, Pine Mountain Arts Coun., past bd. dirs.; mem. Cobb County Dem. Exec. Com., 1986-87; exec. mem. Cobb Christmas, 1986-87; com. mem. Smyrna Cmty. Culture, 2000-2002; sec. program com. WRFG Cmty. Radio, 2002, bd. dirs., 2003--, chair fin. com., 2003--. Named Tchr. of Yr., Sumter Correctional Inst., 1973. Mem. Nat. Libr. Assn. (com. chmn. 1975-76), Fla. Libr. Assn. (caucus chmn. 1976-77), Ga. Libr. Assn. (mem. com. chmn. 1990—; sec. 1993-94, parliamentarian 1997, 1st v.p. 1999, pres. 2000), Metro Atlanta Libr. Assn. (v.p. 1997, pres. 1998), Southeastern Libr. Assn. (mem. com. 1988—, convention chair 2000, com. chair 2001—), ALA (con. spkr.), Atlanta Law Sch. Alumni Assn. (treas. 1996-90), Fla. State U. Alumni Assn. (life), Ga. Libr. Video Assn. (pres. 1991-92), Mensa (sec. 1987, 89, pres. Ga. chpt. 1988, mediator Ga. chpt. 2000-02, regional vice chmn. 2003—, trustee Mensa Edn. and Rsch. Found. (v.p. 1993), Ga. Coun. Media Orgn. (chair steering com. 2000), Leadership Meriwether (pres. 1993). Office: 100 Village Green Cir SE Smyrna GA 30080-3478 Home: 192 Katrina Dr Powder Springs GA 30127 Office Phone: 770-431-2860. E-mail: mjseigler@msn.com.

**SEIGLER, RUTH QUEEN,** college nursing administrator, educator, consultant, nurse; b. Conway, S.C., July 31, 1942; d. Charles Isaac and Berneta Mae (Weaks) Queen; m. Rallie Marshall Seigler, Sept. 1, 1963; children: Rallie Marshall Jr., Scot Monroe. ADN, Lander Coll., 1962; BSN, U. S.C. 1964, M of Nursing, 1980. Pub. health nurse Richland County Health Dept., Columbia, SC, 1964—66; dir. nurses Columbia Area Mental Health Ctr. 1966—69; program nurse specialist Midlands Health Dist., 1969—72; discharge planner Richland Meml. Hosp., 1972—73, clin. dir., 1973—75; exec. dir. S.C. State Bd. Nursing, 1976—83; v.p. nursing dept. Self Meml. Hosp., Greenwood, SC, 1983—86; exec. dir. S.C. Commn. on Aging, Columbia, 1986—95; asst. dean Coll. Nursing U. S.C., Columbia, 1995—96, assoc. clin. prof., 1996—. Cons. intergenerational family studies, 1999—; dir. Cockcroft Leadership Program for Nurse Execs., 2002—, Ctr. for Nursing Leadership, 2004-05, sr. cons., 2005—; bd. dirs. Queen Gas Co., Barnwell, S.C.; nurse cons. Creative Nursing Mgmt., Mpls., 1984—. Advisor: The Role of Cmty. Mental Health Nurse, 1971. Moderator Trinity Presbytery, 2003—. Recipient Disting. Alumni award Lander Coll., 1978, Career Woman Recognition award Columbia YWCA, 1980, William S. Hall award S.C. Assn. Residential Care Homes, 1988, U.S.C. Coll. Nursing Disting. Alumni award, 1993, award for excellence S.C. League for Nursing, 1995, Svc. Recognition award S.C. AARP, 1995; named one of Ten Women of Achievement, S.C. March of Dimes, 1987, hon. fellow AVC Leadership, 2002, Excellence in Leadership award, 2004, Ordie P. Taylor Humanitarian award, 2005, Palmetto Gold award Top 100 Nurses in S.C., 2006. Mem. ANA, APHA, S.C. Nurses Assn. (sec. 1965-68, bd. dirs. 1986-88, Excellence award 1984, Recognition award 1984), S.C. Hosp. Assn., S.C. Gerontol. Soc., S.C. Nurses Found., S.C. Healthy People 2000 (vice chair), Partnership for Older South Carolinians (founder, chair bd. dirs.), Columbia Luncheon Club (pres. 1997-98), S.C. Fedn. Older Ams., Evening Mission Action Group, Bd. Nursing Home Examiners, Pilot Club, Inc. (pres. 1988-89, 97-98), Vols. of Am.-Carolinas (bd. dirs., chair 1998-00, elder, 1999-01), Rotary Internat., Sigma Theta Tau, Beta Sigma Phi. (mem. chpt. 1997-98). Presbyterian. Avocations: gardening, travel. Home: 6 Beaver Dam Ct Columbia SC 29223-3100 Office: U SC Coll Nursing Ctr Nursing Leadership Columbia SC 29208-0001

**SEIL, FREDRICK JOHN,** retired neuroscientist; b. Nove Sóve, Yugoslavia, Nov. 9, 1933; s. Joseph and Theresa (Krieger) S.; m. Daryle Faith Wolfers, July 2, 1955; children: Jonathan Fredrick, Joel Philip Timothy. BA, Oberlin

Coll., 1956; MD, Stanford U., 1960. Intern Kaiser Found. Hosp., San Francisco, 1960-61; resident in neurology Stanford U., Calif., 1961-64, fellow in neurology, 1964-66; staff neurologist VA Med. Ctr., Palo Alto, Calif., 1969-76, clin. investigator Portland, Oreg., 1976-79, staff neurologist, 1979-81, dir. VA office regeneration research programs, 1981—2001, ret., 2001. Asst. prof. neurology Stanford U., 1969-75, assoc. prof. neurology Oreg. Health and Sci. U., Portland, 1976-78, prof. neurology, 1978-2001, prof. cell and devel. biology, 1990-2001, prof. emeritus neurology, 2001—. Editor: Nerve, Organ and Tissue Regeneration: Research Perspectives, 1983, Neural Regeneration, 1987, 94, Current Issues in Neural Regeneration Rsch., 1988, Current Issues in Neural Regeneration and Transplantation, 1989, Advances in Neural Regeneration Research, 1990, Neural Injury and Regeneration, 1993, Multiple Sclerosis: Current Status of Research and Treatment, 1994, Neural Regeneration, Reorganization, and Repair, 1997, Neural Plasticity and Regeneration, 2000; contbr. articles to profl. jours. Capt. US Army Med. Corps, 1966—68. Grantee VA, 1970-2001, NIH, 1986-95. Mem. Internat. Brain Rsch. Orgn., Internat. Soc. Develop. Neurosci., Am. Neurol. Assn., Am. Assn. Neuropathologists, Soc. Neurosci., Soc. Exptl. Neuropathology. Democrat. Achievements include founding of biennial International Symposium on Neural Regeneration; co-founding of biennial Asia Pacific Symposium on Neural Regeneration. Home: 1 Twain Ave Berkeley CA 94708 Personal E-mail: seilf@comcast.net.

**SEIL, MICHAEL JAMES,** music educator; b. Carrington, N.D., Feb. 10, 1973; s. James Warren Seil and Linda Marie Donlin; m. Sheri Lynn Schwindt, July 20, 1996; 1 child, Harrison Michael. MusB in Edn., U. N.D., 1995. Educator's profl. lic. N.D. Edn. Stds. and Practices Bd. Choral dir. Simle Mid. Sch., Bismarck, ND, 1996—2004; secondary choral dir. Cen. Dakota Children's Choir, Bismarck, 2001—; dir. of choral activities, instr. music theory Bismarck H.S., 2003—. Adj. prof. music U. Mary, 2005—. Music director: (mus. theater prodn.) West Side Story; vocal director Oklahoma; Annie. Named Educator of Distinction, Nat. Soc. of H.S. Scholars, 2004; recipient Golden Apple award, Sta. KXMB-TV, 2002. Mem.: N.D. Music Educators Assn., Music Educators Nat. Conf., Am. Choral Dirs. Assn. (chair ethnic and multicultural repertoire and stds. 2004). Office: Bismarck H S 800 N 8th St Bismarck ND 58501 Office Phone: 701-221-3510 144. Personal E-mail: mike_seil@hotmail.com. E-mail: mike_seil@educ8.org.

**SEILACHER, ADOLF,** special education educator; b. Stuttgart, Germany, Feb. 24, 1925; came to U.S., 1987; s. Adolf and Frida (Pfitzer) S.; m. Edith Drexler, July 20, 1957; children: Ulrike, Peter. PhD, U. Tübingen (Germany), 1951. Asst. prof. Tübingen U., 1951-57; docent Frankfurt (Germany) U., 1957-59; lectr. Baghdad (Iraq) U., 1959-61; prof. Göttingen (Germany) U., 1961-64, Tübingen U., 1964-90; adj. prof. geology & geophysics Yale U., New Haven, 1987—. Mem. adv. bd. Senckenberg Mus., Frankfurt, Naturkunde Mus., Berlin. Editor Neues Jahr Geol. Paleontol., Stuttgart, 1965—. With German Navy, 1943-45. Recipient Crafoord prize Swedish Acad. Sci., Stockholm, 1992. Fellow AAAS; mem. Acad. Scis. Heidelberg, Geol. Soc. London (hon.), Royal Phys. Soc. Lund (hon.), Paleontology Assn. (hon.). Avocation: ballroom dancing. Home: 25 Engelfriedslhalde D-72076 Tübingen Germany Office: Dept Geology Yale U 210 Whitney Ave New Haven CT 06511-8902 Office Phone: 203-432-3173. Business E-Mail: geodolf@tuebingen.netsurf.de.

**SEILER, FRITZ ARNOLD,** physicist; b. Basel, Switzerland, Dec. 20, 1931; came to U.S., 1980; s. Friedrich and Marie (Maibach) S.; m. Mary Catherine Coster, Dec. 22, 1964; children: Monica, Simone, Daniel. BA in Econs., Basel Sch. of Econs., 1951; PhD in Physics, U. Basel, 1962. Rsch. assoc. U. Wis., Madison, 1962-63; scientific assoc. U. Basel, 1963-69, privat dozent, 1969-75, docent, 1975-80; sr. scientist Lovelace Inhalation Toxicology Inst., Albuquerque, 1980-90; sr. tech. assoc. IT Corp., Albuquerque, 1990-92, disting. tech. assoc., 1992-96; v.p. Inst. Regulatory Sci., Albuquerque, 1996-97; prin. Sigma Five Cons., Los Lunas, N.Mex., 1997—. Cons. Swiss Dept. Def., 1968-74; vis. scientist Lawrence Berkeley Labs., 1974-75. Contbr. numerous articles to profl. jours. With Swiss Army staff, 1964-75. Fellow Am. Phys. Soc., Health Physics Soc., Soc. for Risk Analysis, Fachverband fuer Strahlenschutz, Am. Nat. Stds. Inst. (mgmt. const. 1987-2002, com. N14 1986-2002), Internat. Hormesis Soc Office: Sigma Five Consulting PO Box 1709 Los Lunas NM 87031-1709 Office Phone: 505-866-5193. Office Fax: 505-866-5197. Business E-Mail: faseiler@nmia.com.

**SEILS, WILLIAM GEORGE,** lawyer; b. Chgo., Aug. 9, 1935; s. Harry H. and Hazel C. (Sullivan) S.; m. Evelyn E. Oliver, Sept. 8, 1956; children: Elizabeth Ann, Ellen Carol, Eileen Alison. AB, JD, U. Mich., 1959. Bar: Ill. bar 1959. Since practiced in, Chgo.; ptnr. Arvey, Hodes & Costello & Burman, 1968-87; gen. counsel, sec., sr. v.p. Richardson Electronics, Ltd., LaFox, Ill., 1986—2006, of counsel, 2006. Contbr. articles to profl. jours.; asst. editor: Mich. Law Rev, 1958-59. Mem. Ill. State Bar Assn., Order of Coif. Office: Richardson Electronics Ltd PO Box 393 40w267 Keslinger Rd Lafox IL 60147-0393 Office Phone: 630-208-2370. Business E-Mail: wgs@rell.com.

**SEINFELD, JERRY,** comedian, actor, television producer, scriptwriter; b. Bklyn., Apr. 29, 1954; s. Kalman and Betty S.; m. Jessica Sklar, Dec. 25, 1999; children: Sascha, Julian, Shepherd Kellen Grad. with degree in theatre communications, Queens (N.Y.) Coll., 1976. Former salesman. Stand-up comedian, 1976—; joke-writer (TV series) Benson, ABC, 1980; actor, co-writer, prod. (TV series) Seinfeld, NBC-TV, 1990-97 (Emmy award Outstanding Comedy Series, 1993, Emmy nomination, Lead Actor - Comedy Series, 1994, Golden Globe winner, 1994, best actor comedy series,) (TV movie) The Ratings Game, 1984, I'm Telling You for the Last Time, 1999; (TV specials) The Tommy Chong Roast, 1986, The Seinfeld Chronicles, 1989; (film) Comedian (also exec. prodr.), 2002; writer Jerry Seinfeld-Stand-Up Confidential, 1987; author: Sein Language, 1993; guest appearances The Larry Sanders Show, 1992, News Radio, 1995. Recipient Am. Comedy award funniest male comedy stand-up, 1988, funniest actor in a TV series, 1992, 93; Screen Actors Guild award, Outstanding Performance by an Ensemble in a Comedy Series, 1994, 96, 97; People's Choice award, Favorite TV Comedy Series, 1998. Jewish. Avocations: zen, yoga.

**SEINFELD, JOHN HERSH,** chemical engineering professor; b. Elmira, NY, Aug. 3, 1942; s. Ben B. and Minna (Johnson) S. BS, U. Rochester, 1964; PhD, Princeton U., 1967. DSc honoris causa, U. Patras, Greece, 2002, Carnegie Mellon U., 2002. Assoc. prof. chem. engring. Calif. Inst. Tech., Pasadena, 1967-70, assoc. prof., 1970-74, prof., 1974—, Louis E. Nohl prof., 1980—, exec. officer for chem. engring., 1973-90, chmn. engring. and applied sci. div., 1990-2000. Allan P. Colburn meml. lectr. U. Del., 1976; Camille and Henry Dreyfus Found. lectr. MIT, 1979; mem. coun. Gordon Rsch. Confs., 1980-83; Donald L. Katz lectr. U. Mich., 1981; Reilly lectr. U. Notre Dame, 1983; Dean's Disting. lectr. U. Rochester, 1985; Katz lectr. CUNY, 1985; McCabe lectr. N.C. State U., 1986; Lewis lectr. MIT, 1986; Union Carbide lectr. SUNY, Buffalo; Van Winkle lectr. U. Tex., 1988; Bicentennial lectr. La. State U., 1988; Ida Beam lectr. U. Iowa, 1989, David Mason lectr. Stanford U., 1989; Julian Smith lectr. Cornell U., 1990; Merck lectr. Rutgers U., 1991; Henske Disting. lectr. Yale U., 1991; lectr. AIChE, 1980; Centennial lectr. U. Pa., 1993; Miles Disting. lectr. U. Pitts., 1994; Kelly lectr. Purdue U., 1996; Disting. rsch. lectr. Carnegie Mellon U., 1998; Berkeley lectr. U. Berkeley, 1998; Sigma Xi lectr., 1998—, Merck Sharp & Dohme lectr. U. P.R., 1996; Hess lectr. U. Va., 1998; inaugural disting. lectr. U. Toledo, 1999; Priestley lectr. Commonwealth Scientific and Indsl. Rsch. Orgn., 2000; Amundson lectr. U. Houston, 2002, Hottel lectr. MIT, 2002, Lowrie lectr. Ohio State U., 2004; Fingerson/TSI lectr. U. Minn., 2004; Frontiers lectr. U. Conn., 2005; ICI disting. lectr. U. Alberta, 2005. Author: Numerical Solution of Ordinary Differential Equations, 1971, Mathematical Methods in Chemical Engineering, Vol. III, Process Modeling, Estimation and Identification, 1974, Air Pollution: Physical and Chemical Fundamentals, 1975, Lectures in Atmospheric Chemistry, 1980, Atmospheric Chemistry and Physics of Air Pollution, 1986, Fundamentals of Air Pollution Engineering, 1988, Distributed Parameter Systems--Theory and Applications, 1989, Atmospheric Chemistry and Physics, 1998, 2nd edit., 2006; assoc. editor Environ. Sci., Tech.,

1981-97; mem. editorial bd. Computers, Chem. Engring, 1974-96, Jour. Colloid and Interface Sci, 1978-95, Advances in Chem. Engring, 1980-03, Revs. in Chem. Engring, 1980—, Aerosol Sci. and Tech., 1981-93; assoc. editor: Atmospheric Environment, 1976—. Recipient Donald P. Eckman award Am. Automatic Control Coun., 1970, Pub. Svc. medal NASA, 1980, Disting. Alumnus award U. Rochester, 1989, Nev. medal Desert Rsch. Inst., 2001, Haagen-Smit Clean Air award Calif. Air Resources Bd., 2003, Haagen-Smit award, Atmos Environ., 2004; Camille and Henry Dreyfus Found. Tchr. Scholar grantee, 1972. Fellow AIChE (dir. dirs. 1988-91, mem. editl. bd. jours. 1985—, Allan P. Colburn award 1976, William H. Walker award 1986, Warren K. Lewis award 2000), NAE, AAAS, Japan Soc. Promotion Sci., Am. Geophysical Union; mem. Am. Soc. Engring. Edn. (Curtis W. McGraw Rsch. award 1976, George Westinghouse award 1987), Assn. Aerosol Rsch. (bd. dirs. 1983—, v.p. 1988-90, pres. 1990-92), Am. Acad. Arts and Scis., Am. Chem. Soc. (Svc. through Chemistry award 1988, Creative Advances in Environ. Sci. and Tech. award 1993), Internat. Aerosol Rsch. Assembly (Fuchs award 1998), Sigma Xi, Tau Beta Pi. Home: 4409 Beulah Dr La Canada CA 91011 Office: Calif Inst Tech Divsn Engring Applied Sci 210-41 Pasadena CA 91125-0001 E-mail: seinfeld@caltech.edu.

**SEINUK, YSRAEL A.,** architectural engineer; b. Cuba; Grad. in civil engring., Univ. Havana, 1954. Lic. in 15 states, DC, Puerto Rico, United Kingdom. Founder, CEO Ysrael A. Seinuk P.C., NYC, 1977—; co-founder, CEO Cantor Seinuk, NYC; CEO WSP New York, NYC; prof., chmn. structural dept. Irwin S. Chanin Sch. Architecture, Cooper Union, NYC, 1969—. Supv. structural design of Trump World Tower, NYC, Bear Stearns World Headquarters, NYC, Time Warner Centre at Columbus Cir., NYC, Riverside So. apartments, NYC, New York Mercantile Exch., Four Times Sq., NYC, 7 World Trade Cu., NYC, Trump Tower 5th Ave., NYC, Lipstick Bldg., NYC, Arthur Ashe Tennis Stadium, NYC, Torre Mayor, Mexico City. Named one of 25 Most Influential Hispanics, Time Mag., 2005; recipient Leader of Industry award, Concrete Industry Bd., Urban Visionary award, Cooper Union. Fellow: Inst. Civil Engineers (U.K.), Am. Soc. Civil Engineers, Am. Concrete Inst. Office: Ysrael A Seinuk PC 2d Fl 228 E 45th St New York NY 10017

**SEIPLE, JOHN W., JR.,** corporate financial executive; b. July 20, 1958; married; 3 children. BA in Econs., Davidson Coll.; MBA, Tex. Christian U. With Interfirst Bank Dallas, N.A.; ptnr., sr. v.p. Trammell Crow Co.; v.p., market officer Prologis, Houston, 1993—94, sr. v.p., regional dir., 1994—97, mng. dir. S.E. region, 1997—99, COO, 1999, pres., chief investment officer N.Am. Denver, 2004—, chair N.Am. mgmt. com., chair N.Am. investment com., mem. Office of the Chmn. Office: Prologis 14100 E 35th Pl Denver CO 80011

**SEITEL, FRASER PAUL,** public relations executive; b. Jersey City, June 6, 1946; s. Robert and Helen (Barmad) S.; m. Rosemary Kierstein, Dec. 20, 1969; children: Raina, David. BJ, U. Mo., 1964; MA, U. ND, 1970; MBA, NYU, 1977. Pub. rels. officer Chase Manhattan Bank, NYC, 1970-73, v.p., 1974-85, sr. v.p./dir. pub. affairs, 1985-92; mng. ptnr. Emerald Ptnrs., Ft. Lee, NJ, 1992—; sr counselor Burson Marsteller, NYC, 1992—; asst. prof. pub. rels. NYU, 2006—; vis. prof. reputation mgmt. Fla. Internat. U., 2005—; sr. counselor investor rels. and mktg. communications Greater NY Savs. Bank, 1994-97. Pub. rels. con. Hill and Knowlton, NYC, 1973; instr. Profl. Devel. Inst., NYC, Ragan Comms., Chgo., Estes Park Inst., Colo.; columnist US Banker, 1989—94, Odwyerpr.com, 2001—, Profit Mag., 1993—95, Tech Central Station, 2003—; adj. asst. prof. NYU, 2006—. Author: The Practice of Public Relations, 9th edit., 2003; co-author: Idea Wise, 2002; pub. editor: The Public Relations Strategist, 1995—2001, columns editor: PRSA Tactics mag., 1994—95, columnist: odwyerpr.com, 2001—; contbr. ABC Good Morning America, CNN, MSNBC, Fox News Channel, CNBC. Named among Top 100 Pub. Rels. Profls. of 20th century PR Week. Mem. Pub. Rels. Soc. Am., Bank Mktg. Assn. Avocations: baseball, football, basketball, tai chi, rugby. Office: 177 Main St Ste 215 Fort Lee NJ 07024-6936 Office Phone: 201-784-8880. E-mail: yusake@aol.com.

**SEITMAN, JOHN MICHAEL,** arbitrator, mediator, lawyer; b. Bloomington, Ill., Feb. 9, 1942; BS, U. Ill., 1964, JD, 1966. Bar: Calif., U.S. Dist. Ct. (so., ctrl., no. and ea. dists.) Calif., U.S. Ct. Appeals (9th cir.). Prin. Lindley, Lazar & Scales, San Diego, 1966-97; full-time neutral affiliated with JAMS, 1997—. Lectr. in continuing legal edn. Bd. dirs. San Diego County Bar Found., 1983-89, treas., 1983-84, pres., 1988-89; del. to 9th Cir. Jud. Conf., 1986, 88. Fellow Am. Bar Found.; mem. ABA, State Bar Calif. (pres. 1991-92), San Diego County Bar Assn. (pres. 1986). Office: PO Box 2156 Del Mar CA 92014-1456 Office Phone: 858-793-4555. Personal E-mail: jseitman@pacbell.net.

**SEITSINGER, ANNE M.,** education educator; b. Argentia, Nfld., Can., Apr. 3, 1954; arrived in U.S., 1954; d. Emile G. and Claire E. Cote; m. Roy M. Seitsinger Jr., July 16, 1977; children: Alyson K., Julie A. BS, Bridgewater State Coll., 1976; MS Edn., R.I. Coll., 1983; PhD Edn., U. R.I., 2000. Cert. provisional tchr. elem. grades 1-6 R.I. Tchr. Brockton Pub. Schs., Mass., 1977—85, Am. Cmty. Schs., London, 1980—81; instr. Elem. Edn. Dept. R.I. Coll., Providence, 1993—94; lectr., faculty coord. Providence Coll., 1994—96; rsch. assoc. East Bay Ednl. Collaborative, Portsmouth, RI, 1996—97; lectr. Sch. Edn. U.R.I., Kingston, 1997—98, rsch. assoc. Nat. Ctr. Pub. Edn. and Pub. Policy, 1998—99, asst. prof. Edn. Nat. Ctr. Pub. Edn. and Pub. Policy, 1999—. Field observer Program Evaluation Rsch. Group Lesley Coll., Cambridge, Mass., 1996; supr. student tchrs. R.I. Coll., Providence, 1997; acting dir. Nat. Ctr. Pub. Edn. and Pub. Policy U. R.I., 2004—. Contbr. articles to profl. jours. Recipient Outstanding Contbn. award, Bridgewater State Coll., 1997; grantee, R.I. Dept. Edn., Nat. Ctr. Pub. Edn. and Pub. Policy, 2004—06, 2002—03, 2001—02, prin. investigator, R.I. Dept. Edn., 2004—, R.I. Sch. 2003—06, Narr Bay Ednl. Collaborative, 2004—03, U. R.I., 2003—04, 2000—01, 2001 Nat. Ctr. Pub. Edn. and Pub. Policy, 1997—98, 1998—99. Mem.: ASCD, R.I. Math. Tchrs. Assn., Assn. Tchrs. Math. New Eng., Nat. Coun. Tchrs. Math., Assn. Math. Tchrs. Educators, Am. Ednl. Rsch. Assn., Phi Delta Kappa, Kappa Delta Pi. Avocations: skiing, golf, reading. Office: Univ Rhode Island Nat Ctr Pub Edn and Social Policy 608 Chafee Hall Kingston RI 02881

**SEITZ, CAROLE JANE,** composer, educator; d. Charles N. Hicks and Ermagene Virginia Hicks, nee Riley; m. Richard John Seitz, Aug. 10, 1991; children: Kimberly Ann Santora, Jeffrey Ward Bean. MusM Edn., MusB Edn., Wichita State U., Wichita, Kansas, 1956—61. Assoc. chair of performing arts Creighton U., Omaha, Nebr., 1976—, assoc. prof. of music. Asst. condr., chorus master Opera Omaha, 1976—89; violinist Omaha Symphony, 1961—75; musical dir. Coun. Bluffs Cmty. Chorus, Council Bluffs, Iowa, 1969—73, Chanticleer Theatre, Council Bluffs; violinist Wichita Symphony, 1958—60, Lincoln Symphony, Nebr., 1972—79, Des Moines Symphony, 1972—79; dir. of music St. John's Luth. Ch., Council Bluffs; jr. choir dir., soprano soloist St. Andrews Episc. Ch., Omaha, 1980—89. Composer: (play) The Devils, (choral compositions) Midwinter Carol Two Wee Girls Christmas Eve Prayer Alleluia He is Risen, (music for indiv. ballet practice, dance compositions) Dances for the Young Ballerina, (dance compositions) Music for Individual Practice, (string orchestra) Little Fugue, (ballet music) Requiem inspired by poem by Desmond Egan. Founder and pres. Coun. Bluffs Arts Coun., 1970—73. Recipient Citizenship award, AAUW. Mem.: Am. Choral Dirs. Assn. (life; iowa bd. mem. 1968—69), Mortar Bd., Mu Phi Epsilon. Episcopalian. Avocations: horseback riding, travel, reading, knitting. Home: 1705 Laguna Drive Fremont NE 68025 Office: Creighton University 2500 California Plaza Omaha NE 68178 Office Phone: 402-280-2766. Office Fax: 402-280-2320. Business E-mail: cseitz@creighton.edu.

**SEITZ, FREDERICK,** former university administrator; b. San Francisco, July 4, 1911; s. Frederick and Emily Charlotte (Hofman) S.; m. Elizabeth K. Marshall, May 18, 1935. AB, Leland Stanford Jr. U., 1932; PhD, Princeton U., 1934; Doctorate Hon. Causa, U. Ghent, 1957; DSc (hon.), U. Reading, 1960, Rensselaer Poly. Inst., 1961, Marquette U., 1963, Carnegie Inst. Tech., 1963, Case Inst. Tech., 1964, Princeton U., 1964, Northwestern U., 1965, U.

Del., 1966, Poly. Inst. Bklyn., 1967, U. Mich., 1967, U. Utah, 1968, Brown U., 1968, Duquesne U., 1968, St. Louis U., 1969, Nebr. Wesleyan U., 1970, U. Ill., 1972, Rockefeller U., 1981; LLD (hon.), Lehigh U., 1966, U. Notre Dame, 1962, Mich. State U., 1965, Ill. Inst. Tech., 1968, N.Y. U., 1969; LHD (hon.), Davis and Elkins Coll., 1970, Rockefeller U., 1981, U. Pa., 1985, U. Miami, 1989. Instr. physics U. Rochester, 1935-36, asst. prof., 1936-37; physicist research labs. Gen. Electric Co., 1937-39; asst. prof. Randal Morgan Lab. Physics, U. Pa., 1939-41, assoc. prof., 1941-42; prof. physics, head dept. Carnegie Inst. Tech., Pitts., 1942-49; prof. physics U. Ill., 1949-57, head dept., 1957-64, dir. control systems lab., 1951-52, dean Grad. Coll., v.p. research, 1964-65; exec. pres. Nat. Acad. Scis., 1962-69; pres. Rockefeller U., N.Y.C., 1968-78; dir. Richard Lounsbery Found., N.Y.C., 1980—, pres., 1995—2002, U. Miami (Fla.), 1989. Trustee Ogden Corp., 1977—; dir. tng. program Clinton Labs., Oak Ridge, 1946-47; chmn. Naval Rsch. Adv. Com., 1960-62; vice chmn. Def. Sci. Bd., 1961-62, chmn., 1964-68; sci. adviser NATO, 1959-60; mem. nat. adv. com. Marine Biomed. Inst. U. Tex., Galveston, 1975-77; mem. adv. group White House Conf. Anticipated Advances in Sci. and Tech., 1975-76; mem. adv. bd. Desert Rsch. Inst., 1975-79, Ctr. Strategic and Internat. Studies, 1975-81; mem. Nat. Cancer Adv. Bd., 1976-82; dir. Akzona Inc. Author: Modern Theory of Solids, 1940, The Physics of Metals, 1943, Solid State Physics, 1955, The Science Matrix, 1992, On the Frontier: My Life in Science, 1994, Stalin's Captive: Nikolaus Riehl and the Soviet Race for the Bomb, 1995, Electronic Genie: The Tangled History of Silicon. Trustee Rockefeller Found., 1964-77, Princeton U., 1968-72, Lehigh U., 1970-81, Rsch. Corp., 1966-82, Inst. Internat. Edn., 1971-78, Woodrow Wilson Nat. Fellowship Found., 1972-82, Univ. Corp. Atmospheric Rsch., Am. Mus. Natural History, 1975—; trustee John Simon Guggenheim Meml. Found., 1973-83, chmn. bd., 1976-83; mem. Belgian Am. Edn. Found. Decorated Order of the Brilliant Star (Republic of China); recipient Franklin medal Franklin Inst. Phila., 1965, Hoover medal Stanford U., 1968, Nat. Medal Sci., 1973, James Madison award Princeton U., 1978, Edward R. Loveland Meml. award ACP, 1983, Vannevar Bush award Nat. Sci. Bd., 1983, J. Herbert Holloman award Acta Metallurgica, 1993, Von Hippel award Materials Rsch. Soc., 1993, Joseph Henry medal Smithsonian Instn., 1997. Fellow Am. Phys. Soc. (pres. 1961); mem. NAS, Am. Acad. Arts and Scis., AIME, Am. Philos. Soc., Am. Inst. Physics (chmn. govorning bd. 1954-59), Inst. for Def. Analysis, Finnish Acad. Sci. and Letters (fgn. mem.), Phi Beta Kappa Assocs.; mem. GM Adv. Council, Cancer Rsch. Found. Address: Rockefeller U 1230 York Ave New York NY 10021-6307 Office Phone: 212-327-8423.

**SEITZ, JAMES EUGENE,** retired college president, freelance writer; b. Columbia, Pa., July 27, 1927; s. Joseph Stoner and Minnie (Frey) S.; m. Florence Arlene Dutcher, Apr. 6, 1950; children: Diane Louise, Ellen Kay, Linda Marie, Karl Steven. BS, Millersville State Coll., 1950; MEd, Pa. State U., 1952; PhD, So. Ill. U., 1971. Tchr. pub. schs., Pa., 1950-56; lectr. Temple U., Phila., 1956-62; asst. prof. engr. tech. Kans. State U., Pitts., 1962-65; dean Mineral Area Coll., Flat River, Mo., 1965-69, Coll. of Lake County, Gravslake, Ill., 1969-73; founding pres. Edison State Community Coll., Piqua, Ohio, 1973-85; freelance writer Sidney, Ohio, 1985—. Founding sec.-treas. Ohio Tech. and C.C. Assn., Columbus, 1976; speaker in field. Author: Woodcarving: A Designer's Notebook, 1989, Country Creations, 1991, Selling What You Make, 1992, Effective Board Participation, 1993, Substance for the Soul, 1999, Practical Woodcarving Design and Application, 2003; contbr. articles to profl. jours. Founding pres. Exch. Club Grayslake, 1970; pres. Epicurian Soc., Sidney, Ohio, 1978-79; mediator Mcpl. Ct., Sidney, 1992-2003; sr. citizens' steering com. Arbor Day Found.; founding pres. Sr. Ctr. of Sidney-Shelby Co., 1996—, choir, 2001—04; trustee Sidney Meml. Bldg., 2003—; named Outstanding Sr. Citizen, 2001; mem. Ret. Srs. Vol. Program, 2005—. Recipient Leadership and Svc. award, Pa. State U. Alumni Soc., 1990. Mem. Am. Assn. Ret. Persons (founding chpt. pres. 1990-91), Assn. for Career & Tech. Edn., VFW (charter Post 8757), Am. Legion (scholarship com. and judge Post 217 1996-97, exec. com. 1997—, publicity dir. 1998-2000), Sidney Singing Soldiers (pres., 1998), AmVets, Shelby Woodcarvers Guild (founding pres. 1999), Iota Lambda Sigma. Avocations: woodworking, lecturing. Home: 55 Brown Rd Sidney OH 45365-8949 E-mail: jseitz@netpenny.net.

**SEITZ, KARL RAYMOND,** editor; b. Corpus Christi, Tex., Sept. 26, 1943; s. Kerlin McCullough and Martha Elisabeth (Tillman) S.; m. Patricia Jean Floyd, June 13, 1970; 1 child, Lee Kerlin. BA, Birmingham So. Coll., 1970. Copy editor Birmingham (Ala.) Post-Herald, 1967-70, asst. news editor, 1970-73, chief editorial writer, 1973-78, editor editorial page, 1978—2005. Dir. Birmingham Post-Birmingham Typographical Union Pension Plan, 1983-90, chmn., 1986-90; v.p. Goodfellow Fund, Inc., Birmingham, 1986—2005. Active exec. in residence Birmingham So. Coll., 1987, Leadership Birmingham, 1986—, mem. mem.'s coun., 1998—2001. With USN, 1961—64. Mem. Nat. Conf. Editl. Writers, Acad. Polit. Sci. Home: 1212 30th Street S Birmingham AL 35205-1910 E-mail: kseitz@earthlink.net.

**SEITZ, MARY LEE,** mathematics professor; BS in Edn. summa cum laude, SUNY, Buffalo, 1977, MS in Edn., 1982. Cert. secondary tchr., N.Y. Prof. math. Erie C.C.-City Campus, Buffalo, 1982—. Reviewer profl. jours. and coll. textbooks. Vol. Buffalo (N.Y.) Philharmonic Orch. Mem. NY Maths. Assn. Two Yr. Colls., Assn. Maths. Tchrs. NY, NY Assn. Two Yr. Colls., Inc., Buffalo (N.Y.) Philharmonic Orch., Commerative AF, Pi Mu Epsilon. Avocations: gardening, photography, bird watching. Office: Erie C C-City Campus 121 Ellicott St Buffalo NY 14203-2601 E-mail: seitzm@ecc.edu. *Quotable quote from Alfred Lord Tennyson, "To strive, to seek, to find, and not to yield".*

**SEITZ, NICHOLAS JOSEPH,** editor, journalist; b. Topeka, Jan. 30, 1939; s Frank Joseph and Lydia Natalie (Christi) S.; m. Velma Jean Pannenstiel, Sept. 12, 1959; children: Bradley Joseph, Gregory Joseph. BA, U. Okla. 1966. Sports editor Manhattan (Kans.) Mercury, 1960-62, Norman (Okla.) Transcript, 1962-64, Okla. Jour., Oklahoma City, 1964-67; staff Golf Digest mag., Norwalk, Conn., 1967—, editor, 1973-82; editorial dir. Golf Digest and Tennis, 1982-90; editorial dir. Sports/Leisure divsn. N.Y. Times Co. Mag. Group, 1991-92, sr. v.p., editor in chief, 1992-98, editor at large, 1999—. Syndicated golf instrn. and commentary CBS Radio Network; commentary ESPN TV Network. Author: Superstars of Golf, 1978; (with Dave Hill) Teed Off, 1977; (with Tom Watson) Getting Up and Down, 1983, Getting Back to Basics, 1991, Tom Watson's Strategic Golf, 1993; contbr. articles to profl. jours.; anthologized in: Best Sports Stories. Named Okla. Sports Writer of Year Nat. Sportswriters and Sportscasters Assn., 1965; winner contests Nat. Basketball Writers Assn.; winner contests Golf Writers Assn.; recipient Lincoln A. Werden award for outstanding contbn. to golf journalism, 1993, Meml. Tournament Golf Journalism award, 2000, PGA Lifetime Achievement in Journalism award, 2002. Home: 36 Hunt St Norwalk CT 06853-1015 Office: 20 Westport Rd Wilton CT 06897-0850 Personal E-mail: nseitz@optonline.net.

**SEITZ, PATRICIA ANN,** judge; b. Washington, Sept. 2, 1946; d. Richard J. and Bettie Seitz; m. Alan Graham Greer, Aug. 14, 1981. BA in History cum laude, Kans. State U., 1968; JD, Georgetown U., 1973. Bar: Fla. 1973, D.C. 1975, U.S. Dist. Ct. (no., mid., so. dists., trial bar) Fla., U.S. Ct. Appeals (5th and 11th cirs.), U.S. Supreme Ct. Reporter Dallas Times Herald, Washington, 1973-74; law clk. to Hon. Charles R. Richey U.S. Dist. Ct., Washington, 1973-74; assoc. Steel, Hector & Davis, Miami, Fla., 1974-79, ptnr., 1980-96; dir. office legal counsel Office of Nat. Drug Control Policy, Exec. Office of Pres., Washington, 1996-97; judge U.S. Dist. Ct. (so. dist.) Fla., 1998—. Adj. faculty U. Miami Law Sch., Coral Gables, Fla., 1984-88; faculty Nat. Inst. Trial Advocacy, Boulder, Colo., 1982, 83, 95, Chapel Hill, N.C., 1984, 87. Fla. region, 1989; lectr. in field. Contbr. numerous articles to law jours. Mem. Dade Mouron Mental Health Bd., Miami, 1982-84, United Way of Greater Miami comty. devel. com., 1984-87; chmn. family abuse task force United Way of Greater Miami, 1986; chmn. devel. com. Miami City Ballet, 1986-87, bd. dirs., 1986-90. Fellow Am. Bar Found.; mem. Am. Bd. Trial Advocacy, Internat. Soc. Barristers; mem. ABA (chmn. various coms. 1979-85, Ho. Dels. 1992-96), Am. Arbitration Assn. (nat. bd. dirs. 1995-97, complex case panel

arbitrator), The Fla. Bar (bd. govs. young lawyer divsn. 1981-82, bd. govs. 1986-92, pres. 1993-94, bd. cert. civil trial), Fla. Assn. Women Lawyers, Dade County Bar Assn. (pub. interest law bank). Roman Catholic. Avocations: travel, art. Office: Fed Courthouse Square 301 N Miami Ave Fl 5 Miami FL 33128-7702

**SEIVERS, LANA C.,** school system administrator; b. Clinton, Tenn, 1951; BEd, Middle Tenn. State U.; MA in Ednl. Adminstrn., U. Tenn., D in Ednl. Leadership. Speech pathologist Spl Edn. Oak Ridge Sch. System, Tenn.; adminstr. early childhood and edn programs Oak Ridge Sch. System, prin. Linden Elem. Sch.; supt. Clinton City Schs., Tenn., 1989—2003; commr. Tenn. Dept. Edn., Nashville, 2003—. Design cons. Inst. Sch. Leaders; mem. adv. coun. Edn of Childen with Disabilities. Mem.: Assn. Ind. and Mcpl. Schs. (bd. dirs.), Tenn. Orgn. Sch. Supts. (treas.), E. Tenn. Supts. Study Coun. (chair), So. Assn. Colls. and Schs. (chair). Office: Tenn Dept Edn 6th Fl Andrew Johnson Twr 710 James Robertson Pkwy Nashville TN 37243*

**SEIZER, FERN VICTOR,** retired mental health services administrator; b. N.Y.C., Oct. 29, 1934; d. David L. and Florence Maisel Victor; m. Robert J. Seizer, Aug. 28, 1955; children: Steven P., Susan A. BA, UCLA, 1956. Dir. pub. affairs and edn. Nat. Coun. Jewish Women, LA, 1968—80; exec. dir. Fair Housing Coun. San Fernando Valley, LA, 1980—82, Venice Family Clinic, LA, 1982—94, exec. advisor, 1994; dir. cmty. rels. Didi Hirsch Cmty. Mental Health Ctr., Culver City, Calif., 1994—2000; ret., 2000. Mng. editor, city editor UCLA Daily Bruin, 1953—54; mem. corp. coun. execs. United Way of Greater L.A., 1991—93; mem. Adminstrs. Forum and Cmty. Outreach Task Force UCLA Sch. Medicine, 1990—93. Adv com on primary care Calif. State Dept. Health Svcs., Sacramento, 1990—93; mem. managed care planning coun. L.A. County, 1989—90; mem. social svcs. commn. City of Santa Monica, 1998—99; bd. dirs. Nat. Multiple Sclerosis Soc., L.A., 1995—, St. John's Hosp. and Health Ctr., Santa Monica, Calif., 1994—2000, Venice Family Clinic, 1996—. Recipient Alumni Award for excellence in Profl. Achievement, UCLA, 1995, Unsung Hero award, Calif. Cmty. Found., 2000, Most Valuable Trustee award, Nat. Multiple Sclerosis Soc., 1999, Outstanding Contbn. to the Cmty. award, L.A. City and County, 2000. Mem.: Phi Beta Kappa. Avocations: movies, theater, travel, bridge. Home: 257 S Rodeo Dr Beverly Hills CA 90212

**SEJNOWSKI, TERRENCE JOSEPH,** science educator; b. Cleve., Aug. 13, 1947; s. Joseph Francis and Theresa (Cudnik) Sejnowski; m. Beatrice Alexandra Golomb, Mar. 24, 1990. BS, Case Western Res. U., 1968; PhD, Princeton U., 1978. Rsch. fellow Harvard Med. Sch., Boston, 1979-82; prof. biophysics Johns Hopkins U., Balt., 1982-90; prof. Salk Inst. U. Calif. San Diego, La Jolla, 1988—, dir. computational neurobiology tng. program, 2001—; Francis Crick prof. Salk Inst., 2005—. Investigator Howard Hughes Med. Inst., 1991—; bd. dirs. San Diego McDonnell-Pew Ctr. for Cognitive Neurosci., 1990-98, Inst. for Neural Computation, U. Calif. San Diego., 1990—. Editor-in-chief Neural Computation, 1989—; co-inventor: (with others) the Boltzmann machine and NET talk; mem. editl. bd. Sci. Mag., 1990—. Pres. Neural Info. Processing System Found. Recipient Presdl. Young Investigator award NSF, 1984, Wright prize Harvey Mudd Coll., 1996; Sherman Fairchild Disting. scholar Calif. Inst. Tech., 1993. Fellow IEEE (Neural Network Pioneer award 2002; mem. Soc. for Neurosci., Am. Phys. Soc., Internat. Neural Network Soc. (governing bd. 1988-92, Hebb prize 1999), Am. Math. Soc., Assn. Rsch. in Vision and Ophthalmology, Am. Assn. Artificial Intelligence, Biophys. Soc., Optical Soc. Am., Am. Psychol. Soc., Am. Psychol. Assn., N.Y. Acad. Scis., Fedn. Am. Soc. Exptl. Biophysics, Soc. Neuroscience, Internat. Soc. Neuroethology, Soc. Math. Biology, Johns Hopkins U. Soc. of Scholars. Achievements include co-invention of the Boltzmann machine, of NETtalk, a neural network for text-to-speech. Office: Salk Inst PO Box 85800 San Diego CA 92186-5800 E-mail: sejnowski@salk.edu.

**SEKANINA, ZDENEK,** astronomer; b. Mlada Boleslav, Czechoslovakia, June 12, 1936; came to U.S., 1969; s. Frantisek Sekanina and Hedvika Sekaninova; m. Jana Soukupova, Apr. 1, 1966; 1 child, Jason. Diploma, Charles U., Prague, Czechoslovakia, 1959, PhD in Astronomy, 1963. Astronomer Stefanik Obs., Prague, 1959-66, Ctr. for Numerical Math., Charles U., Prague, 1967-68; vis. scientist Inst. d'Astrophysique, Univ. de Liege, Cointe-Ougree, Belgium, 1968-69; physicist Smithsonian Astrophys. Obs., Cambridge, Mass., 1969-80; mem. tech. staff Jet Propulsion Lab., Pasadena, Calif., 1980-81, rsch. scientist, 1981-84, sr. rsch. scientist, 1984—. Assoc. Harvard Coll. Obs., Cambridge, 1969-80; mem. NASA Comet Sci. Working Group, 1977-80; cons. Jet Propulsion Lab., 1977-80; prin. U.S. co-investigator Particulate Impact Analyzer Experiment, Dust Impact Detector Sys. Experiment, European Space Agy.'s Giotto Mission to Comet Halley, 1980-89; mem. NASA-European Spacy Agy. Comet Halley Environ. Working Group, 1980-89; discipline specialist Near Nucleus Studies Network, Internat. Halley Watch, 1982-90; mem. imaging sci. subsys. team Comet Rendezvous Asteroid Flyby Mission, 1986-92; mem. sci. definition team ESA/NASA Comet Nucleus Sample Return Mission, 1988—; co-investigator STARDUST Discovery Mission, 1994—. Editor Comet Halley Archive, 1982-91; mem. editorial bd. Kosmicke Rozhledy, 1963-69. Recipient Exceptional Sci. Achievement medal NASA, 1985, 2005; minor planet named Sekanina, 1976. Mem. Internat. Astron. Union (mem. commns. 15, 20, 22, mem. organizing commn. 22 1976-82, organizing commn. 15 1979-85, mem. working group on comets 1988—, assoc. dir. Ctrl. Bur. for Astron. Telegrams 1970-80), COSPAR (working group 3, panel C, exec. mem. 1980-82), Learned Soc of Czech Republic (hon. 1996—), Czech Astron. Soc. (hon. 2001-, Nušl prize 2006). Roman Catholic. Office: Jet Propulsion Lab 4800 Oak Grove Dr Pasadena CA 91109-8001 Business E-mail: zs@sek.jpl.nasa.gov.

**SEKERKA, ROBERT FLOYD,** physics and mathematics professor; b. Wilkinsburg, Pa., Nov. 27, 1937; s. John Jacob and Vivian Mae (Smith) S.; m. Dianne Thompson, Apr. 30, 1960 (div. Apr. 1981); children: Lee Ann, Robert Thompson; m. 2d Carolyn Lee Confer, May 24, 1981. BS in Physics, U. Pitts., 1960; AM, Harvard U., 1961, PhD, 1965; PhD (hon.), U. Timisoara, Romania, 1996. Engr. Westinghouse Rsch. Labs., Pitts., 1965-68, mgr. materials growth and properties dept., 1968-69; lectr. Carnegie-Mellon U., Pitts., 1967-69, assoc. prof., 1969-72, prof. metallurgy and materials sci., 1972-82, dept. head, 1976-82, prof. physics and math., dean Mellon Coll. Sci., 1982-91, prof., 1991—. Mem. space studies bd. NRC, 1989-91. Assoc. editor Jour. Crystal Growth, 1971-94; Metallurgical Trans., 1970-76; editorial bd. Applied Microgravity Tech., 1987-90. Past bd. dirs. Forbes Health Sys., Pitts., Pitts. Regional Ctr. for Sci. Tchrs.; past vice chmn. bd. dirs. NMR Inst.; past mem. rsch. com. Allegheny Singer Rsch. Inst., Pitts. Recipient A.G. Worthing award U. Pitts., 1959, Philip M. McKenna Meml. award, 1980, Bruce Chalmers award TMS, 1998; Woodrow Wilson fellow, 1960, NSF fellow, 1962-65. Fellow: Am. Phys. Soc., Am. Soc. Metals, Japanese Soc. for Promotion of Sci.; mem.: Internat. Orgn. Crystal Growth (pres. 2001—, Frank prize 1992), Am. Assn. Crystal Growth (mem. exec. com.), Minerals Metals Materials Soc., Edgewood Country Club, Sigma Xi, Phi Beta Kappa, Omicron Delta Kappa. Home: 307 S Dithridge St Atrium 911 Pittsburgh PA 15213-3519 Office: Carnegie Mellon U Dept Physics 6416 Wean Hall Pittsburgh PA 15213-3890 Office Phone: 412-268-2362. Business E-mail: sekerka@cmu.edu.

**SEKIGUCHI, EUGENE,** dentist; BSEE; DDS, U. So. Calif., MS in elec. engring. Pvt. practice dentist, Monterey Park, Calif.; clinical prof., assoc. dean internat. profl. and legis. affairs U. So. Calif. Sch. Dentistry Pres. ADA, 2003—04, former trustee; past. pres., interim exec. dir. Calif. Dental Assn.; past pres. San Gabriel Valley Dental Soc. Office: 823 S Atlantic Blvd Ste 1 Monterey Park CA 91754 Office Phone: 323-283-3662.*

**SEKOWSKI, CYNTHIA JEAN,** health products executive, medical consultant, contact lens specialist; b. Chgo., Feb. 14, 1953; d. John L. and Celia L. (Matusiak) S. PhD in Health Svcs. Adminstrn., Columbia Pacific U., 1984, PhD in Health Scis., 1984; grad., Realtor Inst., 1998. Chief contact lens dept. Lieberman & Kraff, Chgo., 1974—87; pres., CEO Seko Eye Care, Inc.,

Chgo., 1988—; realtor Country Club Realty Group, Naples, Fla., 1995—2002, John R. Wood, Inc. Realtors, 2002—. Rschr., technologist U. Ill., Chgo., 1976-78. Mem. Chgo. Zool. Soc., 1984—, Little City Inner Circle, 1991—, ptnrs. coun., Habitat for Humanity; sponsor Save the Children Orgn.; 1983—; asst. to campaign mgr. Rep. state senatorial candidate, Chgo., 1972; pres. Compass Point Condo Assn., Naples, Fla., 1996-99; budget com. Windstar Country Club Master Homeowner's Assn., Naples, 1996-99; mem. ptnrs. cir. Habitat for Humanity. Fellow: Contact Lens Soc. Am.; mem.: Women's Coun. Realtors, Naples Area Bd. Realtors, Nat. Assn. Realtors, Fla. Assn. Realtors, Nat. Contact Lens Examiners, Better Vision Inst., Opticians Assn. Am., Ill. Soc. Opticianry, Wis. Hist. Soc., Geneva Lakes Conservancy, Soc. of the Little Flower, Nat. Wildlife Fedn., S.W. Fla. Conservancy, Nat. Geog. Soc., U.S. Golf Assn., Columbia Pacific U. Alumnae Assn., The Phoenix Soc. (med. profl.), Bear's Paw Country Club (mktg. com. 2002—), Vanderbilt Country Club (residents adv. bd. 1999—2001, vice-chmn. adminstrn. com. 2001—03). Roman Catholic. Avocations: gardening, reading, photography, poetry, golf. Office: John R Wood Inc Realtors 3255 Tamiami Trl N Naples FL 34103 Office Phone: 239-269-5000. E-mail: luvfla@mindspring.com.

**SEKULER, ROBERT WILLIAM,** psychologist, educator; b. Elizabeth, N.J., May 7, 1939; s. Sidney and Mary (Siegel) Sekuler; m. Susan Pamela Nemser, June 25, 1961; children: Stacia, Allison, Erica. AB, Brandeis U., 1960; MSc, Brown U., 1963, PhD, 1964; postgrad. (NIH postdoctoral fellow), MIT, 1964-65. Prof. psychology Northwestern U., Evanston, Ill., 1973-89, prof. ophthalmology Med. Sch., 1978-89, prof. neurobiology and physiology, 1982-89, John Evans prof. neuroscience, 1986-89, chmn. dept., 1975-79, assoc. dean Coll. Arts and Scis., 1985-89; v.p. Optronix, Inc., 1980-82; Louis and Frances Salvage prof. psychology Brandeis U., Waltham, Mass., 1989—, provost, dean faculty, 1989-91, dir. program cognitive scis., 1998—, chair program on neurosci., 2003—; mem. Ctr. Complex Sys., 1990—. Rsch. prof. biomed. engring. Boston U., 1992—, adj. prof. cognitive and neural sys., 1994—2001; vis. prof. psychology U. Toronto, 2000; cons. NWSF, NIH, AAAS, USAF, U. Calif., APA; chmn. vision com. NRC-NAS; chmn. working group on visual function and aging NRC, chmn. working group on aging workers and visual impairment; scientist Rotman Inst. Baycrest Geriatric Ctr., 2000. Author (with D. Kline and K. Dismukes): (book) Aging and Human Visual Function, 1981; author: Star Trek on the Brain, 1998, Star Trek on the Brain, paperback edit., 1999, Star Trek on the Brain, Japanese edit., 2000; author: (with R. Blake) Perception, 1985, Perception, Hungarian edit., 2000, Perception, 4th edit., 2001; editor: Perception & Psychophysics, 1971—86, Jour. Exptl. Psychology, 1973—74, Vision Rsch. Jour., 1974—79, 1980—92, Optics Letters, 1977—79, Am. Jour. Psychology, Ophthalmic and Physiol. Optics, 1989—99, Intelligent Sys., 1986—92, Psychology and Aging, 1987—92; co-author: Oxford Textbook of Geriatric Medicine, 1992, 1999, Ency. Psychology, 1999; contbr. articles to profl. jours. Grantee, Nat. inst. Neurol. Diseases and Stroke, USAF, NSF, Nat. Eye Inst., Nat. Inst. Aging, USN, James McDonnell Found., Alzheimer's Found. Fellow: AAAS, Am. Psychol. Soc., Optical Soc. Am.; mem.: Knowles Inst. for Hearing Rsch. (bd. dirs. 1988—90), Psychonomic Soc., Neurosci. Soc., Assn. Rsch. in Vision and Ophthalmology, Sigma Xi. Home: 64 Strawberry Hill Rd Concord MA 01742-5502 Office: Brandeis U Ctr for Complex Systems Waltham MA 02454

**SEKULIC, DUSAN P.,** science educator, engineering educator, researcher; b. Novi Sad, Vojvodina, Yugoslavia, June 21, 1949; s. Petar and Djurdjinka Sekulic; m. Gorana Jesic, Dec. 17, 1949; children: Visnja, Aleksandar. B in Engring., U. Novi Sad, 1972, BS in Physics, 1976; MME, U. Belgrade, 1976, DSc, 1981. Cert. profl. mech. engr., Yugoslavia, 1973. Prof. U. Novi Sad, 1976—95; vis. rschr. Tech. U. Munich, 1977; vis. scholar Duke U., Durham, NC, 1988—89; vis. scientist MIT, Cambridge, Mass., 1989; vis. prof. Marquette U., Milw., 1994—96; sr. rsch. scientist U Ky. Ctr. for Mfg., Lexington, 1997—; prof. U Ky., Lexington, 2002—. Author: Fundamentals of Heat Exchanger Design, 2003; contbr. articles to profl. jours. Grantee Materials Sci. and Advanced Mfg., NSF, 1999—2003, Heat Exch. and Boundary Layer Phenomena, KFA-Julich, Germany, 1989—91, Ky. Sci. and Engring. Found., 2003—; Cryogenics Rsch. grant, Dept. of Energy, 1988—91, Sr. Fulbright scholar, 1988—89. Fellow: ASME; mem.: Yugoslav Soc. Physicists, Mathematicians and Astronomers, Yugoslav Assn. Engrs., Am. Welding Soc. Avocations: rowing, scuba diving, skiing. Home: 1064 Albert Ln Lexington KY 40514 Office: University of Kentucky 210 CRMS Bldg Lexington KY 40506 Office Phone: 859-257-2972. Business E-Mail: sekulicd@engr.uky.edu.

**SEKULOVICH, MALDEN See MALDEN, KARL**

**SEKULOW, JAY ALAN,** lawyer; b. 1956; BA cum laude, Mercer U, JD; PhD in Am. Legal History, Regent U. Bar: Ga. 1980. Chief counsel Am. Ctr. for Law and Justice, Virginia Beach, 1990—, European Ctr. for Law and Justice, 1998—. Adj. prof. law Regent U. Author: From Intimidation to Victory, 1990, Knowing Your Rights, 1993, Students Rights and the Public School, And Nothing But The Truth, 1996, Christian Rights in the Workplace, 1997. Office: Am Ctr for Law & Justice 1000 Regent University Dr Virginia Beach VA 23464-5037

**SELANDER, LUCY MAE,** librarian; b. Mpls., June 26, 1946; d. Gustav Martinus and Marion (Aagaard) Svang; m. Dennis Duane Selander, June 9, 1973; children: Andrea Marie, Adrian Francis (dec.), Christina Louise, Elizabeth Mae. BA, U. Minn., 1969. Libr. aide I history dept Mpls. Pub. Libr., 1969-70; libr. asst. adult sect. Mpls. Pub. Libr.-East Lake Br., 1970-73; libr. asst. children's sect. Mpls. Pub. Libr.-Roosevelt br., 1973-82, Mpls. Pub. Libr.- Nokomis br., 1982—. Mem. ALA, Minn. Libr. Assn. Home: 3921 27th Ave S Minneapolis MN 55406-3043 Office: Mpls Pub Libr Nokomis 5100 34th Ave S Minneapolis MN 55417-1545 E-mail: lselander@mplib.org.

**SELANDER, ROBERT W.,** finance company executive; BS, Cornell Univ., 1972; MBA, Harvard Univ., 1974. Mgmt. positions through dir. global retail strategy Citicorp., 1974—94; exec. v.p., pres. Europe, Middle East/Africa & Canada regions MasterCard Inc., 1994—97, pres., CEO Purchase, NY, 1997—. Bd. dir. The Hartford, 1998—. Mem. Com. to Encourage Corp. Philanthropy. Office: MasterCard Inc 2000 Purchase St Purchase NY 10577*

**SELANNE, TEEMU,** professional hockey player; b. Helsinki, Finland, July 3, 1970; Right wing Winnipeg Jets, 1992—95, Phoenix Coyotes, 1995—97, Anaheim Ducks (formerly Mighty Ducks of Anaheim), 1997—2001, 2005—, San Jose Sharks, 2001—03, Colo. Avalanche, 2004—05. Mem Finnish Nat. Olympic Team, 1992, 98, 2002, Finnish Nat. Team, World Cup of Hockey, 1996, 2004, Finnish Nat. Team, World Championships, 1996, 99; player NHL All-Star game, 1993, 94, 1996—2000, 2002, 03. Named World Championships Tournament MVP, 1999; named to All-Rookie Team, 1993, First All-Star Team, NHL, 1993, 1997; recipient Calder Meml. Trophy, 1993, Maurice Richard Trophy, 1999, Bill Masterton Trophy, 2006. Office: Anaheim Ducks PO Box 61077 2695 E Katella Ave Anaheim CA 92803-6177*

**SELBERG, ATLE,** retired mathematician; b. Langesund, Norway, June 14, 1917; came to U.S., 1947; married, 1947. D, U. Oslo, 1943; postgrad. Inst. Advanced Study, Princeton U., 1947-48, 49. Rsch. fellow U. Oslo, 1942-47; assoc. prof. math. Syracuse U., 1948-49; prof. Inst. Advanced Study, Princeton U., 1949-87, prof. emeritus, 1987—. Editor: (with others) Axel Thue's Selected Mathematical Papers, 1977; author: Reflections Around the Ramanujan Centenary, 1989, Number Theory, Trace Formulas & Discrete Groups, 1989, Collected Papers, 1991. Recipient Fields medal Internat. Congress Math., Harvard U., 1950, Wolf prize in math. Wolf Found., Israel, 1986. Mem. Norwegian Acad. Sci., Royal Danish Acad. Scis. and Letters, Am. Acad. Arts and Scis. Achievements include elementary proof of the prime number theorem, with a generalisation to prime numbers in an arbitrary arithmetic progression. Office: Inst Advanced Studies Sch Math 1 Einstein Dr Princeton NJ 08540

**SELBY, CECILY CANNAN,** dean, science educator; b. London, Feb. 4, 1927; d. Keith and Catherine Anne Cannan; m. Henry M. Selby, Aug. 11, 1951 (div. 1978); children: Norman, William, Russell; m. James Stacy Coles, Feb. 21, 1981. AB cum laude, Radcliffe Coll., 1946; PhD in Phys. Biology, MIT, 1950. Teaching asst. in biology MIT, 1948-49; adminstrv. head virus study sect. Sloan-Kettering Inst., N.Y.C., 1949-50, asst. mem. instr., 1950-55; instr. microscopic anatomy Cornell U. Med. Coll., 1955-57; tchr. sci. Lenox Sch., N.Y.C., 1957-58, headmistress, 1959-72; nat. exec. dir. Girl Scouts U.S.A., N.Y.C., 1972-75; adv. com. Simmons Coll. Grad. Mgmt. Program, 1977-78; mem. Com. Corp. Support of Pvt. Univs., 1977-83; spl. asst. acad. planning N.C. Sch. Sci. and Math., 1979-80, dean acad. affairs, 1980-81, chmn. bd. advisors, 1981-84. Cons. U.S. Dept. Commerce, 1976-77; dir. Avon Products Inc., RCA, NBC, Loehmanns Inc., Nat. Edn. Corp. pres. Am. Energy Ind., 1976; co-chmn. commn. pre-coll. math. and sci. Nat. Sci. Bd., 1982-83; adj. prof. NYU, 1984-86, prof. sci. edn., 1986-94; mem. policy steering com. Gov. Cuomo's Conf. on Sci. and Engring., 1989-90; affil. scholar Radcliffe Pub. Policy Ctr. of Harvard U., 2000-2001. Contbr. articles to profl. jours., chapters to books. Founder, chmn. N.Y. Ind. Schs. Opportunity Project, 1968-72; mem. invitational workshops Aspen Inst., 1973, 75, 77, 79; trustee MIT, Bklyn. Law Sch., Radcliffe Coll., Woods Hole Oceanographic Instn., Women's Forum N.Y., N.Y. Hall of Sci., 1982—, vice chmn., 1989—, trustee Girls Inc., 1992—. Nat. Coun. Women in Medicine, 1990-94; mem. Yale U. Peabody Mus. Adv. Coun., 1981-89; co-chair program in sci., soc. and gender Radcliffe Inst. of Harvard U., 1999-2001. Named affiliated scholar, Harvard U., 2001; recipient Woman Scientist of Yr. award, N.Y. chpt. Am. Women in Sci., 1992, Alumnae Achievement award, Radcliffe Coll., 2001. Fellow: Am. Women Sci., N.Y. Acad Scis.; mem.: Century Assn. Club, Woods Hole Golf Club, The Explorers Club, Cosmopolitan Club, Sigma Xi, Phi Delta Kappa. Home and Office: 1 E 66th St New York NY 10021-5854 also: 100 Ransom Rd Falmouth MA 02540-1652 E-mail: selbyc@aol.com.

**SELBY, CORA NORWOOD,** retired elementary school educator; b. Nassau, Del., July 15, 1920; d. Clarence Paige and Martha Loretta (Maull) Norwood; m. Paul Myron Selby, Sr., May 26, 1945; children: Paul M.N., Clarence P.N., Clyde L.N., Clyde L.N., Adrian L.N., Terence P.N. BS in Elem. Edn., Del. State U., 1940; MS in Edn., U. Del., 1959, degree (hon.), 1987. Tchr. Ross Point 215-C, Laurel, Del., 1941—64, Paul Laurence Dunbar, Laurel, 1964—66, N. Laurel Sch., 1964—68, faculty adv. Head Start, 1968—80; adult educator Laurel Sch. Dist., 1968—2002, migrant specialist, 1980—87; ret., 2002. Mentor Read Aloud N. Laurel, 1999—; tchr. Elem. Start Program Lake Forest, 1993—2002. Bd. trustees Del. State U., Dover, Del., 1997—; pres. Laurel Sr. Ctr., 2000—; mem. Laurel C. of C.; bd. dirs. Laurel Gardens, 1999—. Mem.: Nat. Assn. Equal Opportunity Higher Edn., Retired Educators Assn., Delaware Assn. Adult and Continuing Edn. (life), Exchange Club, Phi Delta Kappa, Alpha Delta Kappa. Home: 34385 Whaleys Rd Laurel DE 19956

**SELBY, DIANE RAY MILLER,** fraternal organization administrator; b. Lorain, Ohio, Oct. 11, 1940; d. Dale Edward and Winifred (Ray) Miller; m. David Baxter Selby, Apr. 14, 1962; children: Elizabeth, Susan, Sarah. BS in Edn., Ohio State U., 1962. Sec. Kappa Kappa Gamma Frat., Columbus, Ohio, 1962-63, editor, 1972-86, dir. Hilliard (Ohio) High Sch., 1963-65; exec. dir. Mortar Bd., Inc. Nat. Office, Columbus, Ohio, 1986—. Editor The Key of Kappa Kappa Gamma Frat, 1972-86 (Student Life award, 1983, 84, 85). Founding officer Community Coordinating Bd., Worthington, Ohio, 1983; pres. PTA Coun., Worthington, 1984, Worthington Band Boosters, 1985; sec., treas. Sports and Recreation Facilities Bd., Worthington, 1986-90; mem. sustaining com. Jr. League Columbus, 1991-93, docent Kelton House, 1979—. Mem.: Assn. Coll. Honor Soc. (exec. com. 1999—2001, 2003—04, 2004—, chmn. bylaws com., trustee 2004—), v.p. 2005—06, pres. 2006—), Mortar Bd., Inc., Ladybugs and Buckeyes, Twig 53 Children's Hosp. (assoc.), Kappa Kappa Gamma (House Bd. v.p. 1997—2000). Republican. Lutheran. Home: 6750 Merwin Pl Columbus OH 43235-2838 Office: Mortar Bd Inc 1200 Chambers Rd Ste 201 Columbus OH 43212-1754 Business E-Mail: selby.1@osu.edu.

**SELBY, GAIL DIANA,** computer scientist; b. Tenn. m. Douglas Selby, 1975; children: Jason, Joshua. BA, Mid. Tenn. State U., Murfreesboro, 1971; MA Tchg., Mid. Tenn. State U., 1972. Libr. Coffee County Tenn., 1972—73; tchr. Paxon H.S., Duval County, Fla., 1973—81, 1986—91; tchr., chair Social Studies dept. Southwest DeKalb H.S., Decatur, Ga., 1991—. Named Social Studies Tchr. of Yr., Paxon Sr. H.S., 1988. Mem.: Nat. Coun. Social Studies. Office: Southwest DeKalb HS 2863 Kelley Chapel Rd Decatur GA 30034

**SELBY, JEROME M.,** mayor; b. Wheatland, Wyo., Sept. 4, 1948; s. John Franklin and Claudia Meredith (Hudson) S.; m. Gloria Jean Nelson, June 14, 1969; children: Tyan, Cameronn, Kalen. BS in Math., Coll. Idaho, 1969, MA in Ednl. Adminstrn., 1974; MPA, Boise State U., 1978. Assoc. engr. Boeing Co., Seattle, 1969-71; dir. evaluation WICHE Western States Regional Med. Program, Boise, 1971-74; dir. rsch., evaluation Mountain States Health Corp., Boise, 1974-76, with health policy analysis and accountability, 1976-78; dir. health Kodiak (Alaska) Area Native Assn., 1978-83; mgr. Kodiak Island Borough, 1984-85, mayor, 1985-98, 2004—, mcpl. and fisheries cons., 1998—; regional dir. planning and devel. Providence Health System, 1998—2003. Propr. Kodiak Tax Svc., 1978—, Registered Guide, Kodiak, 1987—; cons. Nat. Cancer Inst., Washington, 1973-78, others. Contbr. articles to profl. jours. Treas. ARC, Kodiak, 1978-93, bd. dirs., 1978-95, chmn., 1989-90, mem. western ops. hdqrs. adv. bd., 1986-92, mem. group IV and V nat. adv. coj., 1986-89, nat. bd. govs., 1989-95, chmn. chpt. rels. com., 1994-95, mem. Alaska statewide chpt. bd. dirs., 2002—; pres. S.W. Alaska Mcpl. Conf., Anchorage, 1988-89, v.p., 1986-87, treas., 1996-98, bd. dirs., 1986-98; pres. Alaska Mcpl. League Investment Pool, Inc., 1992-98; v.p. Alaska Mcpl. League, 1988-90, pres., 1990-91, bd. dirs., 1988-98, 2004—; bd. dirs. Alaska Mcpl. League Jt. Ins. Assn. Bd., 1995—, v.p., 1996-98, pres., 1998-2000; mem. Coun. on Econ. Policy for Rural Alaska, 2006-; mem. Alaska State C. of C., 2004—, exec. com., 2002-06; mem. policy com. of outer continental shelf adv. bd. U.S. Dept. Interior, 1990-2004, vice chair, 1996-98, chair, 1998-2000; chmn. Natural Gas Subcom., 2000-01; co-chair Alaska Task Force, 1995-2004; mem. Com. on Oil Pollution Act, 1995; mem. Nat. Assn. Counties, Cmty. and Econ. Devel. Steering Com., 1990-98, Alaska govtl. roles task force, 1991-92; mem. Alaska state/local govt. task force, 1996-98; chmn. Kodiak Island Exxon Valdez Restoration Com., 1991-95; bd. dirs. Kodiak Health Care Found., 1992—; v.p. 1992—; co-chmn. Arctic Power, 1993-2005; bd. dirs. Western Interstate Region Nat. Assn. Counties, 1993-98; bd. dirs. Alaska Oceans, Seas, Fisheries Rsch. Found., 1998-2005, pres., 1998-2005; mem. environment, energy and land use steering com. Nat. Assn. Counties, 1997-98; mem. grad. edn. com. Alaska Family Practice Residency, 2000-01; mem. Koniag Edn. Found., 2002-03; mem. Oiled Regions of Alaska, 2001—, pres., 2002—. Paul Harris fellow, 1987, 88, 91, 92, 96, 2005; recipient Outstanding Contbn. award Alaska Mcpl. League, 1994, Disting. Alumni award Albertson Coll. of Idaho, 1997, Lifetime Achievement award Alaska Mcpl. League, 1998, Mem. Yr., Kodiak C. of C., 2005. Mem. Alaska Conf. Mayors, Nat. Soc. Tax Profls., Acad. Polit. Sci., Alaska Mcpl. Mgrs. Assn., Kodiak C. of C. (dir. 1983-99, Mem. of Yr. 2005), Rotary (bd. dirs. 1989-97, 2004—, treas. 1989-93, v.p. 2005—, pres.-elect 1994-95, pres. 1995-96). Office: Kodiak Tax Svc 1120 Baranof St Kodiak AK 99615 Office Phone: 907-486-4833. E-mail: jselby@ptialaska.net.

**SELBY, JOHN BAYNE, SR.,** retired radiologist, medical educator; b. Cheyenne, Wyo., Feb. 17, 1924; s. John Edwin Selby and Caroline Lansdale Duckett; m. Jane Claire Dentry, June 11, 1950; children: John Bayne Jr., Henry Gordon, Rebecca Jane. BS, U. Tenn., 1948, MD, 1946; MS in Medicine, U. Minn., 1957. Diplomate Am. Bd. Internal Medicine, Am. Bd. Nuc. Medicine. Asst. in pathology Johns Hopkins U., Balt., 1950—51; intern Evanston (Ill.) Hosp., 1947—48; resident Garfield Hosp., Washington, 1948—50; fellow in pathology Johns Hopkins U., Balt., 1950—51, Mayo Clinic, Rochester, Minn., fellow in medicine, 1954—57, asst. staff mem., 1957; assoc. prof. medicine U. Ky., Lexington, 1958—75; chief nuc. medicine VA Hosp., Lexington, 1966—75, Charleston, SC, 1975—89; prof.

radiology Med. U. SC, Charleston, 1995—2000, emeritus prof. radiology, 2001—. Mem. editl. bd. Clin. Nuc. Medicine, Phila., 1985—, Jour. SC Med. Assn., Columbia, 2000—. Author: Self Assessment Nuclear Medicine, 1977, 1981, Mission in Space, 1994. Mem. Med. Discipline Commn., SC, 1985—88; pres. Ky. Diabetes Assn., Lexington, 1968—69; bd. dirs. Sch. Applied Radiol. Sci., Med. U. SC, Charleston, 1984—86. Capt. U.S. Army, 1952—54, Korea, col. USAR, 1956—74. Fellow: ACP; mem.: Soc. Nuc. Medicine, Endocrine Soc., Alpha Omega Alpha. Avocation: tennis. Home: 2602 Atlantic Ave Sullivans Island SC 29482 E-mail: selbysr2@aol.com.

**SELBY, JOHN GREGORY,** history professor; b. Detroit, Mich., Dec. 6, 1955; s. John LaVerne and Mary Jean Selby; m. Deborah Holder, Oct. 13, 1990; children: Margaret Mary, John Le. BA, U. of Ariz., Tucson, 1980; MA, Duke U., Durham, N.C., 1981, PhD, 1984. Vis. asst. prof. Guilford Coll., Greensboro, NC, 1984—85, Duke U., Durham 1985—86; prof. Roanoke Coll., Salem, Va., 1986—, dir. Henry H. Fowler pub. affairs program, 1987—92. Author: Virginians at War: The Civil War Experiences of Seven Young Confederates. Specialist 4th class U.S. Army, 1975—77. Recipient NATO Discussion Series Travel grant, Atlantic Coun., 1989, Albert J. Beveridge Grant for Rsch. in Am. History, Am. Hist. Assn., 1983—84. Mem.: Salem Hist. Soc. (corr.), Hist. Soc. of Western Va. (corr.), Va. Hist. Soc. (corr.), So. Hist. Assn. (corr.), Orgn. of Am. Historians (corr.), Phi Beta Kappa. Methodist. Office: Roanoke Coll 221 College Ln Salem VA 24153 Office Phone: 540-375-2425. Office Fax: 540-375-2577. E-mail: selby@roanoke.edu.

**SELBY, LELAND CLAY,** lawyer; b. Granite City, Ill., July 4, 1944; s. William Edward and Agnes (Newell) S.; m. Diane Schryver, Aug. 20, 1966; children: Leland Clay, Timothy Schryver, Amanda Elizabeth. BA, U. Richmond, 1966; LLB, U. Va., 1969. Bar: Conn. 1969, NY 1989. Assoc. Hirschberg, Pettengill & Strong, Greenwich, Conn., 1969-74; ptnr. Hirschberg, Pettengill, Strong & Nagle, Greenwich, 1974-78, Whitman & Ransom, Greenwich, 1978-93, Whitman Breed Abbott & Morgan, Greenwich, 1993-95; mem. Fogarty Cohen Selby & Nemiroff LLC, Greenwich, 1995—. Bd. dirs., v.p. Stamford Ctr. for Arts, Conn., 1989—2003; chmn. adv. coun. Stamford Ctr. for Arts, 2003-05; chmn. bd. govs. Greenwich Found. for Cmty. Gifts, 1980-90; pres. United Way of Greenwich, 1978-80; bd. dirs. Retirement Sys., Town of Greenwich, 1993-2001, Greenwich Symphony Orch., 1986-95; co-pres. Greenwich chpt. English-Speaking Union; bd. dirs. exec. com. English-Speaking Union US Named Greenwich Young Man of Yr., Greenwich Jaycees, 1974. Fellow Am. Coll. Trust and Estate Counsel; mem. ABA, Conn. Bar Assn., NY State Bar Assn., Greenwich Bar Assn., Preston Mountain Club (sec. 1999-04), Riverside Yacht Club, Indian Harbor Yacht Club, Va. Club NYC, Harpoon Club of Greenwich. Episcopalian. Avocations: fly fishing, sporting clays, hiking, reading, travel. Home: 155 Field Point Rd 3 S Greenwich CT 06830 Office: Fogarty Cohen Selby & Nemiroff 88 Field Point Rd Greenwich CT 06836-2508

**SELBY, RONALD M.,** orthopedic surgeon; b. New Brunswick, N.J., Feb. 24, 1951; s. Raymond V. and Louise Selby; m. Rosemary Selby. AB, Rutgers U., 1973; postgrad., U. Vt., 1974; MD, Autonomous U. Guadalajara, Mex., 1979. Diplomate Am. Bd. Orthop. Surgery, Am. Bd. Forensic Medicine, cert. advanced shoulder arthroscopy. Intern Muhlenberg Hosp., Plainfield, NJ, 1979—80; resident in gen. surgery NY Med. Coll./Westchester County Med. Ctr. and Met. Hosp. Ctr. 1980—81; resident, chief resident in orthop. surgery St. Vincent's Hosp. and Med. Ctr. NY, 1981—84; James A. Dickson fellow in adult reconstructive surgery Cleve. Clinic Found., 1984—85; clin. asst. prof. orthop. surgery N.Y. Med. Coll., Valhalla, 1988—; attending dept. surgery divsn. orthop. surgery St. Peter's U. Hosp., New Brunswick, NJ; attending CARES Ambulatory Surgery Ctr., New Brunswick; attending dept. orthop. surgery Robert Wood Johnson U. Hosp., New Brunswick. Team physician N.Y.C. Marathon, Spl. Olympics World-Wide Games, NC, 1999; orthop. surgery team cons. St. Bartholomew's Pop Warner Football and Cheerleaders, 1992—; orthop. surgery cons. jr. divsn. U.S. Tennis Assn., 1998—; orthop. team cons. New Brunswick (NJ) H.S. Athletics, 1998—; instr. Coll. Medicine Drexel U., Phila., 2005—; orthop. cons. various athletic orgns. and teams.; presenter in field. Assoc. editor Arthroscopy: The Jour. Arthroscopic and Related Surgery, 2003—; contbr. articles to profl. jours. Hon. co-chmn. physician's adv. bd. Nat. Congl. Com. Named Physician of Yr., Nat. Congl. Com.'s Physician's Adv. Bd., 2002; named one of Am.'s Top Surgeons, Consumer's Rsch. Coun. Am., 2002—05, Best Drs., Better Living Mag., 2002—03; named to Best Doctors, Better Living mag., 2002—03; recipient Nat. Leadership award, Physician's Adv. Bd., Nat. Congl. Com., Order of Merit cum laude, Orthop. Rsch. and Edn. Found., Honors, Arthritis Found. Fellow: Royal Soc. Medicine, Am. Acad. Orthop. Surgeons (spkr. mgr. 2004, mem. comms. coun. 2005—), mem. sports medicine/arthroscopy program subcom. 2005—, mem. ctrl. program subcoms. 2005—, mem. sports medicine evaluation subcom., chmn. subcom. arthroscopy and sports medicine), Am. Coll. Sports Medicine; mem.: Nat. Assn. Sports Physicians, Athletic Trainers' Soc. NJ, Irish Am. Orthop. Assn., Internat. Fedn. Sports Medicine, European Soc. Sports Traumatology, Knee Surgery and Arthoscopy, Nat. Athletic Trainer's Assn., Internat. Cartilage Repair Soc., Am. Med. Soc. Sports Medicine, Osteoarthritis Rsch. Soc. Internat., Internat. Soc. Arthroscopy, Knee Surgery and Orthop. Sports Medicine (mem. program com. 2005—, mem. editl. bd. 2005—, chmn. comms. com. 2005—), Am. Orthop. Soc. for Sports Medicine (mem. subcom. of edn. com.), Arthroscopy Assn. N.Am. (advisor comm. 2005—, presenter, bd. dirs., archives com., rsch. com. learning ctr. com., edn. com., Cert. for Dedication and Svc.), St. Vincent's Hosp. and Med. Ctr. Alumni Assn., Cleve. Clinic Found. Alumni Assn. Office: 20 W 13th St New York NY 10011 also: 330 Livingston Ave New Brunswick NJ 08901 Office Phone: 212-255-8000, 732-846-4900.

**SELDEN, JANE TIBBS,** biology educator; b. Lynchburg, Va., Aug. 19, 1947; 1 child, William Douglas III. MEd, U. Va., Charlottesville, 1976. Tchr. Tucker HS, Richmond, Va., 1979—. Recipient, U. Va. Curry Sch. Edn., 2005. Office: John Randolph Tucker HS 2910 Parham Rd Richmond VA 23294 Office Phone: 804-527-4600.

**SELDEN, ROBERT WENTWORTH,** physicist, consultant; b. Phoenix, Aug. 11, 1936; s. Edward English and Mary Priscilla (Calder) S.; m. Mary Tania Hudd, June 1958 (div. 1976); 1 child, Ian Scott; m. Marjorie Anne Harmon, Feb. 20, 1977; children: Brock, Thane, Shawna, Kirsten. BA in Physics cum laude, Pomona Coll., 1958; MS in Physics, U. Wis., 1960, PhD in Physics, 1964. Rsch. assoc. Lawrence Livermore Nat. Lab., Calif., 1965—67, staff mem. Calif., 1967—73, group leader Calif., 1973—83, asst. assoc. dir., 1978—80; div. leader applied theoretical physics Los Alamos Nat. Lab., N.Mex., 1980—83, dep. assoc. dir. strategic def. rsch. N.Mex., 1983—84, assoc. dir. theoretical and computational physics, 1984—86, dir. Ctr. for Nat. Securities Studies, 1988—88, assoc. dir. for lab. devel., 1991—94; chief scientist USAF, Washington, 1988—91, panel chmn. sci. adv. bd., 1984-88, 91-96, 1991—96, 2002—05, chmn. sci. adv. bd., 1999—2002, mem., 2002—05; cons. Los Alamos, 1994—. Chmn. study group on reactor materials and nuclear explosives U.S. Dept. Energy, 1976-78; mem. ballistic missile def. techs. adv. panel U.S. Congress Office Tech. Assessment, 1984-85, The Pres.'s Defensive Tech. Study Team, Washington, 1983; strat. adv. group U.S. Strat. Command, 1996—, panel chair, 2003—; strat. adv. group jt. adv. com. Sec. Def., Sec. Energy, 1996—. Editor Rsch. Jour. Lawrence Livermore Nat. Lab., 1976-77; contbr. sci. and tech. papers to profl. jours. Pres. Livermore Cultural Arts Coun., 1969-72; chmn. Livermore Sister City Orgn., 1973, Planning Commn. City of Livermore, 1971-76; bd. dirs. Orch. of Santa Fe, 1986-88. Capt. U.S. Army, 1964-67. Grad. fellow Edward John Noble Found., 1958-62; recipient Theodore von Karman award for outstanding contbn. to def. sci., 1989, medal for outstanding pub. svc. U.S. Sec. Def., 1996; decorated for exceptional civilian svc. USAF, 1988, 91, 96, 2005. Mem. AAAS, Am. Phys. Soc., N.Y. Acad. Sci., Air Force Assn. Avocations: tennis, hiking, music. Office: 624 La Bajada Los Alamos NM 87544-3805 E-mail: selden@cybermesa.com.

**SELDERS, JEAN E.,** retired psychology professor; b. La Junta, Colo., Nov. 6, 1942; d. Samuel Allen and Dorothy Jean Selders; m. Paul J. Fraker (div.); m. James R. Powell (div.). BA, U. No. Colo., 1964, MA, 1967; PhD, U. Denver, 1980. Cert. Colo. Dept. Edn., Colo. Soc. Sch. Psychologists, Nat. Assn. Sch. Psychologists, Nat. Cert. Sch. Psychologist. Spl. edn. tchr. Jefferson Co. Pub. Schs., Lakewood, Colo., 1964—65; elem. tchr. Mt. Cam Pub. Schs., Tex., 1965—66; spl. edn. tchr. Dept. Def. Overseas Schs., Tokyo, 1967—70, Cumberland County Schs., Fayetteville, NC, 1970—72; Ednl. diagnostician NC Dept. Pub. Health, 1972—78; sch. psychologist Littleton Pub. Schs., Littleton, Colo., 1980—2004; coll. instr. Arapahoe CC, 1990—2004; ret., 2005. Bd. dirs. Mental Fragile X Found., Denver, 1988—92; pres., bd. dirs. Arapahoe Assn. Retarded Citizens, Littleton, 1980—88; state sec., bd. Colo. Soc. Sch. Psychologists, 1984—89. Vol. Opera Corado, Denver, 1980—, Central City Opera, Central City, 1980—. Recipient State Champion-Toastmistress, NC, 1976, Sch. Psychologist Yr., Colo. Soc. Sch. Psychologists, 1985. Mem.: APA, Arapahoe/Douglas Mental Health Assn., Colo. Soc. Sch. Psychologists (state bd. sec. 1980—85), Alpha Gamma Delta (rec. sec. 1963—64, panhellenic del. 1982—84). Republican. Lutheran. Avocations: travel, reading, theater, opera.

**SELDES, MARIAN,** actress; b. NYC; d. Gilbert and Alice (Hall) S.; m. Julian Claman, Nov. 3, 1953 (div.); 1 child, Katharine; m. Garson Kanin, June 19, 1990 (dec. Mar. 1999). Grad., The Dalton Sch., N.Y.C., 1945, Neighborhood Playhouse, 1947; DHL, Emerson Coll., 1979; DFA (hon.), Julliard Sch., 2003. Faculty drama and dance divsn. Juilliard Sch. Lincoln Ctr., NYC, 1969-91; faculty drama dept. Fordham U., 2003, 2005. Appeared with Cambridge (Mass.) Summer Theatre, 1945, Boston Summer Theatre, 1946, St. Michael's Playhouse, Winooski, Vt., 1947-48, Bermudiana Theatre, Hamilton, Bermuda, 1951, Elitch Gardens Theatre, Denver, 1953, The Cretan Woman, Lysistrata, 1955 (actress/artist-in residence Stanford U.), The Flowering Peach, L.A., 1956, Witness for the Prosecution, The Players' Ring, L.A., 1957; Broadway appearances include Medea, 1947, Crime and Punishment, 1948, That Lady, 1949, Tower Beyond Tragedy, 1950, The High Ground, 1951, Come of Age, 1952, Ondine, 1954, The Chalk Garden, 1955, The Wall, 1960, A Gift of Time, 1962, The Milk Train Doesn't Stop Here Any More, 1964, Tiny Alice, 1965, A Delicate Balance, 1967 (Tony award for best supporting actress), Before You Go, 1968, Father's Day, 1971 (Drama Desk award, Tony nomination), Mendicants of Evening (Martha Graham Co.), 1973, Equus, 1974-77, The Merchant, 1977, Deathtrap, 1978 (Tony nomination), Ivanov (Drama Desk nomination), 1997, Ring Round the Moon, 1999 (Tony nomination), 45 Seconds from Broadway, 2001 Dinner At Eight, 2003 (Tony nomination); off-Broadway appearances include Diff'rent, 1961, The Ginger Man, 1963 (Obie award), All Women Are One, 1964, Juana LaLoca, 1965, Three Sisters, 1969, Am. Shakespeare Festival, Stratford, Conn., Mercy Street at Am. Place Theater, N.Y.C., 1969, Isadora Duncan, 1976 (Obie award), Painting Churches, 1983, 84 (Outer Critics Circle award 1984), Other People, Berkshire Theatre Festival, 1969, The Celebration, Hedgerow Theater, Pa., 1971, Richard III, N.Y. Shakespeare Festival, 1983, Remember Me, Lakewood Theatre, Skowhegan, Maine, Gertrude Stein and a Companion, White Barn Theatre, Westport, Conn., 1985, Lucile Lortel Theatre, N.Y.C., 1986, Richard II, N.Y. Shakespeare Festival, 1987, The Milk Train Doesn't Stop Here Anymore, WPA Theatre, N.Y.C., 1987, Happy Ending, Bristol (Pa.) Riverside Theatre, 1988, Annie 2 John F. Kennedy Ctr., Washington, 1989-90, Goodspeed Opera House, Chester, Conn., 1990, A Bright Room Called Day, N.Y. Shakespeare Festival, 1991, Three Tall Women, River Arts, Woodstock, N.Y., 1994, Another Time, Am. Jewish Theatre, 1993, Breaking the Code, Berkshire Theatre Festival, 1993, Three Tall Women, Vineyard Theatre, N.Y.C., 1994, Promenade Theatre, 1994-95, nat. tour, 1995-96, Boys From Syracuse, City Ctr., N.Y.C., 1997, Dead End: Williamstown, 1997, Dear Liar, Irish Repertory Theater, 1999, The Matchmaker: Williamstown, 1998, Tongue of a Bird, Mark Taper Forum, 1998, Sail Away, Carnegie Hall, 1999, Mad About The Boy, Carnegie Hall, 1999, The Torch-Bearers, 2000, Ancestral Voices, 2000, The Skin of our Teeth, 2000, Williamstown, The Play About the Baby, Alley Theatre, Houston, 2000, The Butterfly Collection, Playwrights Horizon, NY, 2000, The Play About the Baby, Helen, NY Shakespeare Festival, 2001, Play Yourself, N.Y. Theater Workshop, 2002, Beckett/Albee, Century Ctr. Theatre, N.Y.C., 2003, The Royal Family Ahmanson Theatre, L.A., 2004, Dedication or the Stuff of Dreams, 2005; nat. tour Three Tall Women, 1995-96; film appearances include The Greatest Story Ever Told, Gertrude Stein and a Companion, 1988, In a Pig's Eye, 1988, The Gun in Betty Lou's Handbag, 1992, Tom and Huck, 1995, Digging to China, 1997, Home Alone 3, 1997, Affliction, 1997, Celebrity, 1998, The Haunting, 1999, Town and Country, 1999, Duets, 1999, Hollywood Ending, 2002, Mona Lisa Smile, 2003, (documentary) Golden Age of Broadway, 2005, (narrator documentary) Ballet Russes, 2005, August Rush, 2006; (TV series) Good and Evil, 1991, Murphy Brown, 1992, Truman, 1995, Cosby, 1996, 98, Trinity, 1998, Remember WENN, 1999, The Others, 2000, If These Walls Could Talk 2, 2000, Nero Wolfe, 2001 (A&E), The Education of Max Bickford, 2002, American Masters PBS "Juilliard Documentary, 2003", Hallmark Hall of Fame, 2004, Frasier, 2004, TV: The Book of Daniel, 2005; also appeared on radio CBS Mystery Theater, 1976-81, Theatre Guild on The Air; author: The Bright Lights, 1978, Time Together, 1981; appeared in soap opera One Life to Live, 1998. Bd. dirs. Neighborhood Playhouse, The Acting Co., Nat. Repertory Theatre, Theatre Hall of Fame, 1996; bd. trustees Broadway Cares/Equity Fights Aids. Winner Ovation award Theater L.A. for Three Tall Women, 1996, Conn. Critics award for Three Tall Women, 1996; recipient Madge Kennedy/Sidney Kingsley award Dramatists Guild Fund, 2000, Obie award for sustained achievement, Lucille Lortel award for Sustained Achievement, 2003, Edwin Booth award, Players Club, 2003, Lifetime Mem. award Theatre Lit. Assn., 2003, Breukelein Inst. Gaudium award, 2003, Julliard Sch. medal svc. to arts, 2005, Drama League award sustained achievement, 2006, Dutch Treat Gold medal award, 2006, Rebekah Kohl award Nat. Coun. Jewish Women, 2006. Mem. Players Club, Century Assn. Home: 210 Central Park S Apt 19D New York NY 10019-1426

**SELDES, RICHARD M.,** orthopedist, consultant; MD, U. Pa., 1994; BA, Johns Hopkins U., 2000. Diplomate Am. Bd. Orthop. Surgeons; 2003. Dir., orthop. surgery Forest Hills (N.Y.) Hosp., 2003—. Fellow: Am. Acad. Orthop. Surgeons; mem.: N.Y. Med. Soc., Arthroscopy Assn. N.Am. Achievements include development of surgical technique for shoulder surgery. Office: Forest Hills Hosp 102-01 66th Rd Forest Hills NY 11375 Office Phone: 718-830-1290.

**SELDMAN, NEIL NORMAN,** cultural organization administrator; b. Bklyn., Aug. 2, 1945; s. Fred Herman and Sylvia (Flaster) S.; m. Laura Jane Klugherz, Feb. 22, 1968; children: Oliver, Chloe. BS in Indsl. and Labor Rels., Cornell U., 1966; MS in Internat. Communism, George Washington U., 1968, PhD in Internat. Rels., 1974. Asst. to pres. B.H. Krueger Co., Bklyn., 1969-72; assoc. prof., lectr. George Washington U., Washington, 1974-76, asst. dir. exptl. program, 1976-77; founder Inst. for Local Self-Reliance (ILSR), Washington, 1974—, pres., 1980—. Cons.: UN/UN Environ. Program, Washington, 1980-81, City Coun., Phila., 1984-90. Author: Common Sense Radicalism, 1976, Waste to Wealth: A Guide for Community Enterprise, 1985; co-author: Integrated Resource Recovery-Recycling from Municipal Refuse: A State-of-the-Art Review and Annotated Bibliography, 1985, Proven Profits from Pollution Prevention, 1986, Garbage in Europe: Economics, Technologies, Trends, 1987, Deconstruction, 1999, State of Wasting and Recycling in the U.S., 2000; contbr. article to Ency. of Energy Tech. and the Environment, 1995; contbg. editor International Dialogue on Zero Waste, 2005 Fabrangen Cheder Jewish Community Orgn.; elected chair Neighborhood Planning Coun., Washington, 1976-82; co-founder D.C. Interracial Coalition for Environ. Equity, Washington, 1989; Nat. Recycling Coalition, 1980, Grass Roots Recycling Network, 1996. With NG, 1968-74. Grantee Moriah Fund, 1990-95, Pew Charitable Trusts, 1991, NSF, 1979-80, H. Heinz Endowment, 1995-96, EPA, 1993-98, Turner Found., 1995-98, Ford Found. Environl. Justice Program, 2002-03 Jewish. Avocations: fast pitch softball, nineteenth-century literature, French and Russian revolutions. Office Phone: 202-898-1610 x210. Business E-Mail: nseldman@ilsr.com.

**SELDNER, BETTY JANE,** environmental engineer, consultant, aerospace transportation executive; b. Balt., Dec. 11, 1923; d. David D. and Miriam M. (Mendes) Miller; m. Warren E. Gray, June 20, 1945 (div. 1965); children: Patricia, Deborah; m. Alvin Seldner, Nov. 15, 1965; children: Jack, Barbara. BA in Journalism, Calif. State U., Northridge, 1975, MA in Communications, 1977. Dir. pub. info. United Way, Van Nuys, Calif., 1958-63, dir. edn. Los Angeles, 1963-68; dir. pub. relations, fin. San Fernando Valley Girl Scout Council, Reseda, Calif., 1968-73; asst. dir. pub. info. Calif. State U., Northridge, 1973-75; dir. environ. mgmt. HR Textron Corp., Valencia, Calif., 1975-87; environ. engr. Northrop Aircraft, Hawthorne, Calif., 1987-88, EMCON Assocs., Burbank, Calif., 1988-92, Atkins Environ., 1992-93, Seldner Environ., Valencia, Calif., 1993—; pres. Seldner Environ. Svcs. 1993—. Author non-fiction. Named Woman of Yr., Santa City C. of C. and vol. orgns., 2000. Mem. Santa Clarita Valley Environ. Mgrs. Soc. (chmn. bd. dirs. 1984), San Fernando Valley Round Table (pres. 1971-72), Hazardous Materials Mgrs.' Assn., Zonta Internat., Valencia Indsl. Assn. (environ. chair). Republican. Jewish. Avocation: sailing. Office Phone: 661-255-6427. Personal E-Mail: Betty13ix@comcast.net.

**SELES, MONICA,** professional tennis player; b. Novi Sad, Yugoslavia, Dec. 2, 1973; arrived in US, 1996; d. Karolj and Esther Seles. Profl. tennis player, 1989—. Mem. U.S. Fed Cup Team, 1996, 99, 2000, WTA Tour Players' Coun., 1998—99. Author: (novels) From Fear to Victory, 1996. Active Spl. Olympics. Named Sportswoman of Yr., Yugoslavia, 1985, Female Rookie of Yr., TENNIS Mag./Rolex Watch, 1989, Most Improved Player, WTA Tour, 1990, Player of Yr., 1991, Female Athlete of Yr., AP, 1991, 1992, Comeback Player of Yr., TENNIS Mag., 1995, Female Pro Athlete of Yr., Fla. Sports Hall of Fame, 1998, Player Who Makes a Difference, Family Circle Cup, 1999; recipient Ted Tinling Diamond Award, 1990, Rado Topspin Award, 1990, Comeback Player of Yr. Award, WTA Tour, 1995, 1998, Committment to Cmty. Award, Fla. Times-Union, 1999, Flo Hyman Meml. Award, Women's Sports Found., 2000, Sanex Hero of Yr. Award, WTA Tour, 2002. Achievements include 3rd player in the Open-era to capture the Australian and Roland Garros in same calendar year; World #1 ranked player, 1991, 92, 95; youngest #1 ranked player in tennis history for women and men at 17 years, 3 months, 9 days; Winner Grand Slam titles: Roland Garros, 1990, 91, 92, French Open, 1990, 91, 92, U.S. Open, 1991, 92, Australian Open, 1991, 92, 93, 96; Winner 53 Career Singles Titles and 6 Career Doubles Titles, WTA Tour. Office: c/o Internat Mgmt Group 1 Erieview Plz Cleveland OH 44114-1715

**SELFE, EDWARD MILTON,** lawyer; b. St. Paul, Sept. 26, 1921; s. Edward Milton and Eleanor (Moen) S.; m. Rena Hill McMurry, July 10, 1950 (div. Oct. 1979); children: Murry, Edward, James; m. Jane Comer Bowron, Dec. 31, 1979. BA, Presbyn. Coll., Clinton, S.C., 1943; LLB, U. Va., 1950. Bar: N.Y., Va., Ala. Asst. prof. law Law Sch., U. Va., Charlottesville, 1950-51; assoc. Shearman & Sterling, N.Y.C., 1951-52, Bradley Arant Rose White, Birmingham, Ala., 1952-57, ptnr., 1957-2000, of counsel, 2000—; vice chmn. Secor Bank, Birmingham, 1988-91, gen. counsel, 1991-93. Lectr. Law Sch., U. Ala., Tuscaloosa, 1968—90. Chmn. Birmingham-Jefferson County Transit Authority, 1972-82. Served to capt., inf. U.S. Army, 1943-47, ETO. Decorated Silver Star, Bronze Star (V) with oak leaf cluster, Purple Heart. Fellow Am. Coll. Tax Counsel; mem. ABA, Ala. Bar Assn., Birmingham Bar Assn. Democrat. Avocation: tennis (ranked 5th nationally USTA in men's singles-age 80). Home: 84 Arlington Crest 2600 Arlington Ave S Birmingham AL 35205-4167 Office: Bradley Arant Rose & White One Federal Pl 1819 Fifth Ave N Birmingham AL 35203-2104 Office Phone: 205-521-8280. Business E-Mail: eselfe@bradleyarant.com.

**SELFRIDGE, GEORGE DEVER,** retired dentist, retired military officer; b. Pitman, N.J., Sept. 24, 1924; s. William John and Edith (Gorman) S.; m. Ruth Motisher, 1948; children: Pamela Ruth, Kimberly Dawn, Cheryl Beth. Student, Gettysburg Coll., 1942-43, Muhlenburg Coll., 1943-45; DDS, U. Buffalo, 1947; MA, George Washington U., 1974. Commd. lt. (j.g.) USN, 1948, advanced through grades to rear adm., 1973; intern Naval Dental Sch., Bethesda, Md., 1948-49, Naval Hosp., St. Albans, NY, 1949-50; asst. dental officer U.S.S. Midway, 1949-51; with USN, 1951-64; sr. dental officer U.S.S. Randolph, 1958-60, U.S.S. Cadmus, 1964-65, U.S.S. Vulcan, 1965-66, Svc. Force, 1964-66, Submarine Force, Atlantic Fleet, 1967-69; from asst. dir. grad. edn. to comdg. officer Navy Grad. Dental Sch., Bethesda, 1969-76; exec. officer Norfolk (Va.) Navy Dental Clinic, 1972-73; ret. USN, 1976; dean Dental Sch., Washington U., St. Louis, 1976-86; dir. dental services Barnes Hosp., St. Louis, 1976—87, Children's Hosp., St. Louis, 1976-87; exec. dir. Am. Bd. Orthodontics, 1986-97; ret., 1998. Adv. bd. VA Hosp., St. Louis, 1977-79; mem. exec. coun. Cen. Region Testing Svc., 1976-86; adv. com. St. Louis Jr. Coll. Dist., 1976-86. Contbr. articles to med. jours. Decorated Legion of Merit; recipient commendation medals, Greater St. Louis Gold Medallion award, 1995, Spl. Recognition award Am. Bd. Orthopedics, 1996. Mem. ADA, Am. Coll. Dentists (past pres.), Internat. Coll. Coll. Dentists (dep. registrar, sec. U.S. sect., Spl. Recognition award), Assn. Mil. Surgeons U.S., Omicron Kappa Upsilon. Republican. Home: 14545 Foxham Ct Chesterfield MO 63017-5620

**SELI, EMRE UTKU,** reproductive endocrinology and infertility specialist, physician researcher; s. Kemal Ali Seli and Ayla Zeliha Hungen; m. Meltem Solak, Dec. 10, 1994; children: Devin Murat, Denis Adrian. MD, Istanbul U., Turkey, 1984—92. Postdoctoral rsch. fellow, dept. ob-gyn. Divsn. Reproductive Endocrinology and Infertility, Yale U. Sch. Medicine, New Haven, 1995—97, resident, dept. ob-gyn., 1997—2001, instr. and fellow, dept. ob-gyn., 2001—04, asst. prof., dept. ob-gyn. Contbr. articles to profl. jours. Reciplent Oustanding Laparoendoscopic Surgeon Award, Soc. Laparoendoscopic Surgeons, 2001; grantee, Am. Coll. Obstetrics and Gynecology, 1999, 2000, N.Am. Menopause Soc., 1999, 2000, NIH, 2004—. Achievements include discovery of a mammalian embryonic polyA binding protein that regulates gene expression during mammalian oocyte and embryo development; research in gene expression during gamete and embryo development; infertility; and fertility preservation in women with cancer. Business E-Mail: emre.seli@yale.edu.

**SELICK, HOWARD E. (BARRY SELICK),** biotechnology executive; BA in Biophysics, U. Pa., PhD in Molecular Biology. Am. Cancer Soc. fellow U. Calif. San Francisco Sch. Medicine; Damon Runyon-Walter Winchell Cancer Fund fellow Protein Design Labs.; former v.p. rsch. Affymax Rsch. Inst.; pres., CEO Camitro Corp., Menlo Park, Calif.

**SELIG, BUD (ALAN H. SELIG),** major league baseball commissioner; b. Milw., July 30, 1934; s. Ben and Marie Selig; m. Suzanne Lappin Steinman, Jan. 18, 1977; children: Sari, Wendy. Grad., U. Wis., Madison, 1956; LHD (hon.), Lakeland Coll., 1989. With Selig Ford (became Selig Chevrolet 1982), West Allis, Wis., 1959-90, pres., owner, 1966-90; with Selig Exec. Leasing Co., West Allis, 1959—, pres., owner, 1977—; part owner Milw. Braves (became Atlanta Braves 1965), 1963-65; co-founder Teams, Inc., 1964; co-owner, pres., chief exec. officer Milw. Brewers Baseball Club, Inc., 1970-98; interim commr. Maj. League Baseball, 1991-98, commr., 1998—. Bd. dirs. Green Bay Packers Profl. Football Team., Marcus Corp., Oil-Dri Corp. Am.; coord. World Baseball Classic, 2006 Co-founder Child Abuse Prevention Fund, 1988. With U.S. Army, 1956-58. Recipient Major League Exec. of Yr. award UPI, 1978, Internat. B'nai B'rith Sportsman of Yr. award 1981, Sportsman of Yr. award U.S. Olympic Com., 1988, August A. Busch, Jr. award for long and meritorious svc. to baseball, 1989, Ellis Island Congl. medal of honor, 1993, Anti-Defamation League's "A World of Difference Award" 1994, Herbert Hoover Humanitarian award Boys and Girls Clubs for Outstanding Svc. to Benefit Am.'s Youth 1998, Sports Leadership Award, March of Dimes NYC Chpt. 2000, Sports Torch of Learning American Friends of Hebrew Univ. 2001, Inducted Wisconsin Athletic Hall of Fame 2001. Office: Office of the Commr Major League Baseball 245 Park Ave New York NY 10167-0002*

**SELIG, KARL-LUDWIG,** literature and language professor; b. Wiesbaden, Germany, Aug. 14, 1926; naturalized, 1948; s. Lucian and Erna (Reiss) S. BA, Ohio State U., 1946, MA, 1947; postgrad., U. Rome, Italy, 1949—50; PhD, U. Tex., 1955. Asst. prof. Romance langs. and lit. Johns Hopkins U., Balt., 1954-58; assoc. prof. U. N.C., Chapel Hill, 1958-61, U. Minn., Mpls., 1961-63; vis. prof. U. Tex., Austin, 1963-64, prof. Romance langs. and lit., 1964-65; Hinchliff prof. Spanish lit. Cornell U., Ithaca, NY, 1965-69, dir. grad. studies in Romance lit., 1966-69; prof. Spanish lit. Columbia U., N.Y.C., 1969—. Brown Found. fellow, vis. prof. Spanish and comparative lit. U. of the South, Sewanee, Tenn., 1990; vis. prof. U. Munich, 1963-64, U. Berlin, 1967; vis. prof. U. Greifswald, Germany, 1991-96, hon. prof., 1996—; cons. prof. Ohio State U., Columbus, 1967-69; vis. lectr. U. Zulia, Maracaibo, Venezuela, 1968; dir. summer seminar NEH, 1975, cons., 1975-77; vis. scholar Ga. U. Sys., 1977; vis. rsch. scholar Fondation Hardt, Vandoeuvres, Switzerland, 1959, Herzog August Bibliothek Wolfenbüttel, Fed. Republic Germany, 1979—; mem. com. grants-in-aid Am. Coun. Learned Soc., 1969-73; chmn. Comparative Lit. Program and Colloquia, Columbia Coll., 1976-88. Author: (books) The Libr. of Vincencio Juan de Lastanosa, Patron of Gracián, Geneva, 1960, Studies on Alciato in Spain, 1990, Studies on Cervantes, 1993, also numerous articles, revs.; editor: (books) (Thomas Blundeville) of Councils and Counselors, 1963; editor: (with A.G. Hatcher) Studia Philologica et Litteraria in Honorem L. Spitzer, 1958; editor: (with J.E. Keller) Essays in Honor of N.B. Adams, 1966; editor: (with R. Brinkmann) Theatrum Europaeum. Festschrift E.M. Szarota, 1982; editor: (with S. Neumeister) Theatrum Mundi Hispanicum, 1986; editor: (with R. Somerville) Florilegium Columbianum: Essays in Honor of Paul Oskar Kristeller, 1987; editor: (with E. Sears) The Verbal and the Visual: Essays in Honor of William Sebastian Heckscher, 1990; editor: Polyanthea Essays on Art and Lit. in Honor of William Sebastian Heckscher, 1993, Mira de Amescua, La hija de Carlos Quinto, 2002; assoc. editor: Modern Lang. Notes, 1955—58, mng. editor: Romance Notes, 1959—61; editor: U. NC Studies in Comparative Lit., 1959—61, Bull. Comediantes, 1959—64; assoc. editor:, 1964—68, mem. editl. bd.:, 1978—88; co-editor: Yearbook of Comparative Lit., vol. IX, 1960; mem. editl. bd.: Colección Támesis, 1962—79, Romanic rev., 1969—89, Yale Italian Studies, 1976—80, Tchg. Lang. Through Lit., 1978—88, Edición Reichenberger, 2002—, assoc. editor: Hispania, 1969—74, Ky. Romance Quar., 1973—85, gen. editor: Revista Hispánica Moderna, mem. nat. adv. com.; MLA Internat. Bibliography, 1978—88. Recipient Mark Van Doren award Columbia, 1974, spl. citation Columbia Coll. Alumni Assn., 1991, Festschrift, Über Texte, 1997; fellow Fulbright Found., Rome, 1949-50, Newberry Libr., 1958, Folger Shakespeare Libr., 1959, 63, Belgian Am. Ednl. Found., 1961, 62; sr. fellow Mediaeval and Renaissance Inst. Duke U., 1978; Fulbright rsch. scholar Utrecht, The Netherlands, 1958-59; DAAD rsch. grantee, 1979; Karl-Ludwig Selig scholarship named in his honor, Columbia Coll., 2001. Mem. MLA (sec., then chmn. Romance sect. 1965-66, chmn. comparative lit. 1973, James Russell Lowell prize com. 1989-90, chmn. 1990), Internat. Assn. Hispanists, Acad. Lit. Studies, Am. Friends Herzog August Bibliothek (bd. dirs. 1996—), Phi Beta Kappa (hon.). Home: 333 W 86th St Apt 406 New York NY 10024

**SELIG, OURY LEVY,** port financial consultant; b. Galveston, Tex., Sept. 24, 1924; s. Andrew Lionel and Freda (Schreiber) S.; m. Miriam Claire Pozmantier, Aug. 22, 1948; children: Michael, Debra, Madeline, James. BBA, U. Tex., 1949, postgrad., 1950, U. Houston, 1953-56. Asst. bus. adminstr. of hosp. U. Tex. Med. Br., Galveston, 1952-54; acct. Port of Galveston, 1954-57, asst. auditor, 1957-64, asst. to gen. mgr., 1964-69, dir. fin. and adminstrn., 1966-74, dep. exec. dir., 1974-88; lectr. in marine transp. Tex. A&M U., Galveston, 1998-2000. Author: (with E. Kalketenidou) Public Port Financing in the United States, 1994, An Analysis of U.S. Public Port Profitability and Self-Sufficiency 1985-1994, 1997; editor: (book series) The Road to Scientific Success: Inspiring Life Stories of Prominent Researchers, 2004—. Life mem. Bay Area coun. Boy Scouts Am., Galveston, 1963—; v.p. Galveston County Jewish Welfare Assn., 1982-84; trustee Galveston Wharves, 1994-97. Sgt. USAF, 1943-46. Recipient Nehemiah Gitelson award, Alpha Epsilon Pi, 1948, Silver Beaver award Boy Scouts Am., 1968, Shofar award, Boy Scouts Am., 1968, Disting. Service award, Galveston Jaycees, 1968. Mem. Am. Assn. Port Auths. (hon. life, chmn. fin. com. 1972-76, chmn. risk mgmt. com. 1981-85, vice chmn. task force on tax reform 1985-86, Important Svc. award 1987), Tex. Water Conservation Assn. (life, pres. 1979-80), Galveston Hist. Found., Friars Club. Democrat. Avocations: gardening, reading. Home and Office: 11 Colony Park Cir Galveston TX 77551-1737 Office Phone: 409-744-1235. E-mail: olselig@wt.net.

**SELIG, WILLIAM GEORGE,** academic administrator; b. Prince Rupert, B.C., Can., Sept. 25, 1938; s. George Oliver Selig and Minerva Junuetta (Brand) Goodale; m. Judith Margaret Sprague, June 20, 1964; children: Cheryl, Cynthia. BA, Cen. Washington State Coll., 1961, MA, 1968; CAGS, U. Mass., 1972, EdD, 1973. Tchr. Sharon (Mass.) High Sch., 1963-64, Hydaburg (Alaska) Grade Sch., 1964-65, W. Puyallup (Wash.) Jr. High Sch., 1966-69; dir. spl. edn. Northampton (Mass.) Schs., 1969-73, 1974-76; asst. prof. Westfield (Mass.) State Coll., 1973; dir. pupil svcs. Longmeadow (Mass.) Pub. Schs., 1976-80; prof. Regent U., Virginia Beach, Va., 1980-83, dean, prof., 1984-89; provost, 1989-2000; Disting. prof. ednl. leadership, 2000—. Bd. dirs. Set Net, Virginia Beach; pres. Motivational Teaching Systems, Inc.; spl. edn. adv. bd. dirs. Virginia Beach Pub. Schs.; bd. trustees Klingberg Family Ctrs., New Britain, Conn., 1991—2000. Author: Training for Triumph, 1984, Loving Our Differences, 1989, Handbook of Individualized Strategies for Classroom Discipline, 1995, Handbook of Individualized Strategies for Building Resilience in At Risk Students, 2005; contbr. chpt. to book. Episcopalian. Avocations: skiing, tennis. Office: Regent University 1000 Regent University Dr Virginia Beach VA 23464-9800 Business E-Mail: georsel@regent.edu.

**SELIGA, CHARLES G.,** airport administrator; BS, MBA, Seton Hall U. Mgmt. analyst Port Authority of N.Y. and N.J., N.Y.C., 1966, exec. asst. to dep. dir. World Trade Ctr., sr. exec. asst. to dir. World Trade Dept., project dir. World Trade Ctr.; asst. gen. mgr. aviation mktg. econs. N.Y.-N.J. Regional Airport Sys., N.Y.C., gen. mgr. ctrl. bus. adminstrn.; mgr. bus. adminstr. JFK Internat. Airport, Jamaica, N.Y., 1987-94, mgr. security and landside ops., 1994-96, gen. mgr., 1996—2000; mng. dir., pres., CEO Nat. Express Corp., Stewart Internat. Airport, Newburgh, NY, 2000—.

**SELIGER, CHARLES,** artist; b. NYC, June 3, 1926; s. George Zekowski and Hortense S.; m. Ruth Lewin, June 20, 1948 (dec. May 1975); children: Robert, Mark; m. Lenore Kelebanow, 1975. Student in pvt. art instrn., WPA Sch., 1940. Robert H. and Clarice Smith Disting. vis. prof. George Washington U., Washington, 1990; lectr. Katonah Art Mus., 1990; panelist Terra Mus. Art, Chgo., 1990, Whitney Mus. Am. Art, N.Y.C., 1990, Michael Rosenfeld Gallery, N.Y.C., 1994. One man shows include Peggy Guggenheim Gallery, N.Y.C., 1945-46, Carlebach Gallery, 1948, DeYoung Meml. Mus., San Francisco, 1949, Whitney Mus. am., 1949-57, Willard Gallery, N.Y.C., 1951, 53, 55, 57, 61, 62, 66, 68, Seligman Gallery, Seattle, 1955, 58, 65, Nassau Community Coll., N.Y.C., 1965, Wooster Community Art Center, Conn., 1969, Andrew Crispo Gallery, 1973, 75, 76, 78, 80, 81, 83, Mus. Modern Art, Hayden Calhoun Gallery, Dallas, Makler Gallery, Phila., 1979, Miami-Dade Community Coll., 1981, Jacksonville (Fla.) Art Mus., 1981, Gallery Schlesinger-Boisanté, 1985, 86, Guggenheim Mus., 1986, Galerie Lopes, Zurich, Switzerland, 1986, 89, 95, 97, 99, 2003, 2006, Greenville County Mus. Art, S.C., 2003, others; exhibited in Norlyst Gallery, N.Y.C., 1942, 67 Gallery, N.Y.C., 1943, David Porter Gallery, Washington, 1945, Four Arts Club, Palm Beach, Fla., 1946, Va. Mus. Fine Arts, 1946, U. Iowa, 1946, Salon des Realites Nouvelle, Paris, France, 1948, Bklyn. Mus., 1949, Cornell U., 1951, Art Inst. Chgo., 1961, 64, Syracuse Mus. Fine Arts, 1953, Nebr. Art Assn., 1953, Am. Acad. Arts & Letters, 1965, 67, 68, Smithsonian Inst., 1968, Taft Mus., Cin., 1981, Okla. Art Ctr., 1981, Saidenberg Gallery, N.Y.C., 1983, 89, Wight Art Gallery, UCLS, traveling to Nat. Gallery Modern Art, New Delhi, 1987, 88, Frances Wolfson Art Gallery, Miami, Fla., 1987, Guggenheim Mus., traveling to Venice, Italy, 1987, 88, Sid Deutsch Gallery, N.Y.C., 1989, 90, Weatherspoon Gallery, Greensboro, N.C., 1989, Nat. Acad. Mus., NYC, 2005, many others.; exhbn. Abstract Expressionism: Other Dimensions traveling to Lowe Art Mus., Coral Gables, Fla, Terra Art Mus., Chgo. (also panelist), Jane Voorhees Zimmerli Art Mus., Rutgers, New Brunswick, 1990, 92; works in permanent collections Herbert F. Johnson Mus., Cornell U., Ithaca, N.Y., Norton Mus. Art, West Palm Beach, Fla., Addison Gallery, Andover, Mass., Munson Williams Proctor Mus., Utica, N.Y., Guggenheim Mus., Miss. Mus. Art, Whitney Mus., High Mus., Atlanta, Terra Mus. Am. Art, Evanston, Ill., Mus. Modern Art, Chgo. Art Inst., Newark Mus. Art, Iowa State U., Municipal Art Mus., The Hague, Holland, Tel Aviv Mus., Balt. Mus. Art, Hirshhorn Mus. and Sculpture Garden, Met. Mus. Art, N.Y.C., Phillips Collection, Washington, Carnegie Inst., Pitts., Rutgers U., Jane Voorhees Zimmerli Art Mus., New Brunswick, N.J., Worcester (Mass.) Art Mus., Nat. Mus. Am. Art Smithsonian Inst., Washington, Met. Mus. Art, NYC, Peggy Guggenheim Collection, Venice, Italy, others, also numerous pvt. collections; artist, 1960—. Recipient Pollock-Krasner Lifetime Achievement Award. Office: Michael Rosenfeld Gallery 24 W 57th St New York NY 10019-3918

**SELIGMAN, BRAD,** lawyer; b. Cin., Aug. 25, 1951; s. Selig J. and Muriel (Bienstock) S.; children: Corina Kasten, Mariana Campos, Sofia Maya Campos. BA, Sonoma (Calif.) State U., 1975; JD, U. Calif., San Francisco, 1978. Bar: Calif. 1978, U.S. Dist. Ct. (no. dist.) Calif. 1978, U.S. Dist. Ct. (ea. dist.) Calif. 1979. Teaching fellow Law Sch. Stanford (Calif.) U., 1978-79; sr. law clk. to Hon. Lawrence K. Karlton U.S. Dist. Ct. (ea. dist.) Calif., Sacramento, 1979-80; assoc. Farnsworth, Saperstein & Brand, Oakland, Calif., 1981-85; ptnr. Farnsworth, Saperstein & Seligman, Oakland, 1985-89; mng. dir. Saperstein, Seligman & Mayeda, Oakland, 1989-91; of counsel Saperstein, Mayeda, Larkin & Goldstein, Oakland, Calif., 1991-94; exec. dir. The Impact Fund, Berkeley, Calif., 1992—. Advisor Disability Rights Edn. and Def. Fund, Inc., 1992—; trustee Calif. Rural Legal Assistance, San Francisco, 1982-88; bd. dirs. Equal Rights Advisors, San Francisco, 1989-92. Author: (with others) CEO: Wrongful Employment Termination Practice, 1987, Tax Aspects of Litigation and Settlements, 1989. Office: The Impact Fund 125 University Ave Berkeley CA 94710 E-mail: bs@impactfund.org

**SELIGMAN, DANIEL,** editor; b. N.Y.C., Sept. 25, 1924; s. Irving and Clare (O'Brien) S.; m. Mary Gale Sherburn, May 23, 1953; children: Nora, William Paul. Student, Rutgers U., 1941-42; MB, NYU, 1946. Editl. asst. New Leader, 1946; asst. editor Am. Mercury, 1946-50; assoc. editor Fortune, 1950-59, editl. bd., 1959-66, asst. mng. editor, 1966-69, exec. editor, 1970-77, assoc. mng. editor, 1977-87, contbg. editor, 1988-97, Forbes, 1997—. Sr. staff editor all Time, Inc. (publs.), 1969-70. Author: A Question of Intelligence: The IQ Debate in America, 1992. Home: 190 E 72nd St New York NY 10021-4370 Office Phone: 212-249-5650, Personal E-mail: ad453@aol.com.

**SELIGMAN, JOEL,** academic administrator; b. NYC, Jan. 11, 1950; s. Selig Jacob and Muriel (Bienstock) Seligman; m. Friederike Felber Seligman, July 30, 1981; children: Andrea, Peter. AB in polit. sci. magna cum laude, UCLA, 1971; JD, Harvard U., 1974. Bar: Calif. 1975. Atty., writer Corp. Accountability Rsch. Group, Washington, 1974-77; prof. law Northeastern U. Law Sch., 1977-83, George Washington U., 1983-86, U. Mich., Ann Arbor, 1987—95; dean law sch. U. Ariz., Tucson, 1995-99, Samuel M. Fegtly prof. law, 1995—99; dean law sch. Washington U., St. Louis, 1999—2005, Ethan A. H. Shepley prof. law, 1999—2005; pres. Rochester U., NY, 2005—. Cons. Fed. Trade Commn., 1979-82, US Dept. Transp., 1983, Office Tech. Assessment, 1988—89; chair adv. com. on mktg. info. SEC, 2000—01; reporter Nat. Conf. of Commrs. on Uniform State Laws, Uniform Securities Act, 2002. Co-author: Constitutionalizing the Corporation: The Case for the Federal Chartering of Giant Corporations, 1976, The High Citadel: The Influence of Harvard Law School, 1978, The Transformation of Wall Street: A History of the Securities and Exchange Commission and Modern Corporate Finance, 1982, The SEC and the Future of Finance, 1985, Securities Regulation, The New Uniform Securities Act, 2002; contbr. articles to profl. jour. Mem.: Am. Law Inst. (adv. com., adv. corp. governance project), State Bar Calif., NASD (bd. govs.), AICPA (profl. ethics exec. com. 2000—02). Office: Pres 240 Wallis Hall Univ Rochester Rochester NY 14627 Office Phone: 585-275-8356. Office Fax: 585-256-2473. E-mail: seligman@rochester.edu.

**SELIGMAN, MARTIN E.P.,** psychologist, educator; b. Albany, N.Y., Aug. 12, 1942; s. Adrian and Irene Seligman; m. Mandy M. Seligman; children: Amanda, David, Lara, Nicole, Darryl, Carly, Jenny. AB, Princeton U., 1964; PhD in psychology, U. Pa., 1967; PhD (hon.), Uppsala U., Sweden, 1989, Mass. Coll. Profl. Psychology, 1997, Complutense U., Madrid, 2004. Asst. prof. Cornell U., 1967-70; assoc. prof. psychology U. Pa., 1972-76, prof., 1976—, Fox Leadership prof., 1999—, dir. clin. program, 1980-94. Vis. fellow Maudsley Hosp. Inst. Psychiatry, U. London, 1975; hon. prof. psychology U. Wales, Cardiff. Author: Helplessness, 1975, Learned Optimism, 1991, What You Can Change & What You Can't, 1993, The Optimistic Child, 1995, Authentic Happiness, 2002 (Best Psychology Book 2003), (with Christopher Peterson) Character Strengths and Virtues, 2004; contbr. numerous articles to profl. jours. Recipient MERIT award, 1991, William James fellow award Am. Psychol. Soc., 1992, James McKeen Cattell Fellow award, 1995; NIMH grantee, 1969—; NSF fellow, 1963-64, Woodrow Wilson fellow, 1964-65, Guggenheim fellow, 1974-75, Ctr. Advanced Study in Behavioral Scis. fellow, 1978-79, Theodore Roosevelt fellow, 2002, Am. Acad. Polit. and Social Sci. Fellow AAAS, APA (pres. divsn. clin. psychology 1993-95, pres. 1997-99); mem. Ea. Psychol. Assn. (bd. dirs.), Psychonomic Soc., Assn. Advancement Behavior Therapy, Am. Psychopthol. Assn., Am. Psychosomatic Soc., Phi Beta Kappa, Sigma Xi. Office: Positive Psychology Ctr 3701 Market St Ste 200 Philadelphia PA 19104 Business E-Mail: seligmaninfo@psych.upenn.edu.

**SELIGMAN, NICOLE K.,** broadcast executive, lawyer; BA magna cum laude, Harvard Coll., Radcliffe, 1978; JD magna cum laude, Harvard Law Sch., 1983. Assoc. editl. page editor The Asian Wall St. Jour., Hong Kong, 1978—80; law clk. to Judge Harry T. Edwards U.S. Ct. of Appeals, Wash., DC, 1983—84; law clk. to Justice Thurgood Marshall U.S. Supreme Ct., 1984—85; ptnr., litig. Williams & Connolly LLP, Wash., DC; exec. v.p., gen. counsel Sony Corp. of Am., 2001—; corp. exec. Sony Corp., Tokyo, 2003—, group deputy gen. counsel, 2003—.

**SELIG-PRIEB, WENDY,** sports team executive; JD, Marquette U., 1988. With broadcasting dept. Milw. Brewers, from 1982; exec. trainee Office of Baseball Commr.; corp. atty. Foley & Lardner, to 1990; gen. counsel Milw. Brewers, 1990-95, v.p., gen. counsel, 1995-98, now pres., CEO, 1998—. Office: Milw Brewers Baseball % Miller Park 1 Brewers Way Milwaukee WI 53214-3651

**SELIGSON, CARL HAROLD,** corporate financial executive; b. NYC, Feb. 25, 1935; s. Harold P. and Lilian (Yohalem) Seligson; m. Bonnie Laskin, Mar. 6, 1983; children: Susan S. Pattenaude, Barbara S. Zweig, Nina Priven, Eric M. Drath. AB, Brown U., 1956; postgrad., NYU Grad. Sch. Bus. Adminstrn., 1961—63. Textile salesman Cohn, Hall, Marx Co., Montreal, Canada, 1958—61; security analyst Burnham & Co., NYC, 1961—67, Kuhn, Loeb & Co, NYC, 1967—71; mng. dir. Merrill Lynch, NYC, 1971—87, Kidder, Peabody & Co., NYC, 1987—90; sr. exec. cons. regulated industries Deloitte & Touche, NYC, 1990—92; mng. dir. Prudential Securities, NYC, 1992—95; sr. advisor Andersen Consulting, NYC, 1996—2000; sr. v.p. energyLeader-.com, NYC, 2000; sr. advisor Prospect St. Ventures, NYC, 2001, K Rd. Power, NYC, 2002—05; fin. cons. Edison Electric Inst., Washington, 2003—. Contbr. articles to profl. jours. including Pub. Utilities Fortnightly, Telephony, Fin. Exec., The So. Banker, Coal Monthly and Energy News. Chmn. Regulatory Industry Com., Securities Industry Assn., 1985—87; mem. strategic issues com. and coun. Elec. Power Rsch. Inst., Palo Alto, Calif., 1998—2006; mem. adv. coun. Nat. Assn. Registry Utilities Commrs. Edn. & Rsch. Found., 2005—; bd. dirs. Nuc. Energy Inst., Washington, 1988—95. With Counter Intelligence Corps U.S. Army. Fellow Fin. Analysts Fedn.; mem. Univ. Club. NY. Avocations: water sports, travel, theater. Office Phone: 212-410-9718. Personal E-mail: cseligson@nyc.rr.com.

**SELIGSON, JUDITH,** artist; b. Phila., July 8, 1950; d. David and Harriet Tutelman Seligson; m. Allan M. Greenberg, Sept. 7, 1938; 1 child, Hannah Leah. BA cum laude, Harvard U., 1973. One-woman shows include Jane Haslem Gallery, Washington, 1992, Anita Friedman Fine Art, N.Y.C., 1997, Schlesinger Libr., Radcliffe Coll., Cambridge, Mass., 1997, exhibited in group shows at Gary Snyder Fine Art, N.Y.C., 1998, 2002, Signal 66, Washington, 2001, Exit Art, N.Y.C., 2002, Amram Sunday Scholars Series, Washington, 2000; contbr. articles to profl. jours. and pubs.

**SELIGSON, MITCHELL ALLAN,** political science educator; b. Hempstead, NY, Nov. 12, 1945; m. Susan Berk, June 18, 1967; 1 child, Amber Lara. BA cum laude, Bklyn. Coll., 1967; MA, U. Fla., 1968; PhD, U. Pitts., 1974. Vol. U.S. Peace Corps, Costa Rica, 1968-70; asst. prof./assoc. prof. U. Ariz., Tucson, 1974-85; prof. U. Pitts., 1986-93, Daniel H. Wallace prof. polit. sci., 1994—2004, dir. Latin Am. studies, 1986-92, rsch. prof., 1992—2004; Centennial prof. polit. sci. Vanderbilt U., Nashville, 2004—. Fellow Ctr. Ams.; dir. pub. opinion project, L.Am.; cons. to World Bank, UN Devel. Program, US AID, Inter-Am. Devel. Bank, Guatemala, Honduras, Nicaragua, Costa Rica, Colombia, Dominican Republic, Mex., Ecuador, Jamaica, Panama, El Salvador, Peru, Bolivia, Paraguay, 1980—. Author, editor: Peasants of Costa Rica and the Development of Agrarian Capitalism, 1980, The Gap Between Rich and Poor, 1984, Authoritarians and Democrats, 1987, Elections and Democracy in Central America, 1989, rev. edit. 1995, Development and Underdevelopment, 1993, The Political Economy of Global Inequality, 2003. Fulbright fellow, Costa Rica, 1986, Rockefeller Found. fellow, 1985-86; grantee Social Sci. Rsch. Coun., Ford Found., NSF, Mellon Found., Heinz Endowment. Mem. Am. Polit. Sci. Assn., Latin Am. Studies Assn. (chmn. fin. com. 1991). Office: Vanderbilt U Dept Polit Sci Nashville TN 37235 Office Phone: 615-322-6238. E-mail: m.seligson@vanderbilt.edu.

**SELIGSON, THEODORE H.,** architect, interior designer, urban planner; b. Kansas City, Mo., Nov. 10, 1930; s. Harry and Rose (Haith) S.; m. Jacqueline Rose, Dec. 27, 1964 (div. 1976). BArch, Washington U., St. Louis, 1953. Registered architect, Mo., Kans. Intern Marshall & Brown, Kansas City, Mo., 1949-54; designer, head design Kivett & Myers, Kansas City, Mo., 1954-62; prin. Design Assocs., 1955—, Atelier Seligson, Kansas City, Mo., 1962-64; pres. Seligson, Eggen, Inc., Kansas City, 1964-73, Seligson Assocs., Inc. Architects Planners, Kansas City, 1973-97; prin. Foss, Seligson, Lafferty, 1997—. Vis. lectr. adult edn. U. Mo.-Kansas City, 1958-61, vis. prof. arch., 1989—, vis. prof. urban design, 2002—; tchr., critic Kansas City Art Inst., 1961-64, 71-72, adj. prof., 1986, 89, 91, 92; adj. prof. Kans. State U., 1991-92, 97; vis. prof. Washington U., St. Louis, 1975, 77, 78, 81, 86, 91, U. Kans., Lawrence, 1978, 79, 80, 91, 92; art cons. Design Assocs., Kansas City, Mo., 1955—. Projects pub. in archtl. jours. V.p. Friends of Art Nelson-Atkins Mus. Art, Kansas City, bd. dirs. 1994—; chmn. selections com., 1981, vis. curator, 1972, 87; chmn. Capitol Fine Arts Commn. Mo., 1983-90, Kansas City Worlds Fair goals and themes subcom., 1985-90; bd. dirs. Westport Tomorrow, Kansas City, 1980-87, Hist. Kansas City Found., 1984-90; pres. Native Sons of Kansas City, 1989, bd. dirs. 1978-94, Westport Cmty. Coun., 1973-75; bd. govs. Truman Med. Ctr., Kansas City, 1998-2002, mem. bd. advisors, 2002—; mem. Kansas City Key to City Commn., 2001-02; bd. dirs. Sacred Structures, 2003—. Recipient Urban Design award Kansas City Mcpl. Art Commn., 1968, 74, 78; Nat. Archtl. award Am. Inst. Steel Constrn., 1970; Nat. award ASID/DuPont Corian, 1989. Fellow AIA (Kansas City chpt. pres. 1983, bd. dirs. 1979-84, Design Excellence award 1966, 68, 70, 74, Ctrl. States Regional award 1974, 78, Honor award for outstanding svc. to chpt. and profession 1982-83); mem. Mo. Coun. Archs., Am. Soc. Interior Designers, Nat. Coun. Archtl. Registration Bds. (task analysis adv. com. 1988-90), Soc. Archtl. Historians (pres. 1973-75, bd. dirs. 1994-97). Jewish. Office: Foss Seligson Lafferty 450 E 4th St Kansas City MO 64106 Office Phone: 816-421-4133, 816-235-6655.

**SELIN, IVAN,** entrepreneur; b. NYC, Mar. 11, 1937; s. Saul and Freda (Kuhlman) Selin; m. Nina Kallet, June 8, 1957; children: Douglas, Jessica. BE, Yale U., 1957, ME, 1958, PhD, 1960; DSc, U. Paris, 1962. Rsch. engr. Rand Corp., Santa Monica, Calif., 1960-65; sys. analyst Dept. Def., Washington, 1965-67, dep. asst. sec. def., 1967-69, acting asst. sec. for systems analysis, 1969-70; founder, chmn. bd. Am. Mgmt. Systems, Inc., Arlington, Va., 1970-89; undersec. state Dept. State, Washington, 1989-91; chmn. Nuc. Regulatory Commn., Washington, 1991—95; chmn., CEO Phoenix Internat., Washington, 1995—; chmn. BZL Biologics, Inc., 1998—, Enumerale Solutions, Inc., 1998—. Lectr. UCLA, 1961-63; chmn. mil. econ. adv. panel to CIA, 1978-89. Author: Detection Theory, 1964; contbr. articles to profl. jours. Pres. Corp. Against Drug Abuse, 1988-95; bd. dirs., gov. UN Assn. U.S., 1979-89; exec. com. Greater Washington Research Ctr., Fed. City Council; trustee Asia Soc., 1996-98; chmn., bd. dirs. Smithsonian Nat. Mus. of Am. History, 1996—, Yale U. Coun., 2000—. Recipient Disting. Civilian Svc. medal, 1970, Disting. Svc. medal Sec. of State, 1991; Fulbright scholar, 1959-61; Ford Found. grantee, 1952-54. Mem. IEEE (editor Trans. on Info. Theory 1960-65), Coun. Fgn. Rels., Yale Club, Sigma Xi, Tau Beta Pi. Office: Phoenix Internat Inc PO Box 58277 Washington DC 20037-5503 Home: 1455 Ocean Dr Apt 1602 Miami FL 33159 Office Phone: 202-337-2337. Business E-Mail: ixs@phnx-intl.com.

**SELIN, LISA K.,** physician; b. Helsinki, Finland, Jan. 8, 1952; d. Lauri Oscar and Hilma K Selin. BSc, Dalhousie Univ, 1970—74; MD, Dalhousie U., 1974—79, FRCP, 1980—84; PhD, Univ. Man., 1986—93. Med. intern Dalhousie U., Halifax, Canada, 1979—80, resident in internal medicine, 1980—84; fellow in infectious diseases Univ. of Man., Winnipeg, Canada, 1984—86; doctoral student Univ of Man., 1986—91; postdoctoral fellow Univ. Mass. Med. Sch., 1992—95, instr., 1995—96; asst. prof. Univ. Mass. Med Sch., 1996—2001; assoc. prof. Univ. Mass. Med. Sch., 2001—. Contbr. articles to profl. jours. Med. Coun. of Can. Student fellowship, Med. Coun. of Can., 1986—91, Dalhousie Entrance schoarship, Dalhousie Univ, 1970, Izaak Walton Killam scholarship, Izaak Walton Killam Found., 1984—86, Clin. Investigator award, Nat. Inst. of Health, 1996—99, Rsch. grant, NIH- NIAID, 2000—, NIH-NIAID, 2001—, 1999—2003. Mem.: Can. Infectious Disease Soc., Am. Assn. of Immunologists. Achievements include research in T cell-mediated heterologous immunity in viral infections. Avocations: painting, cross country skiing, swimming, gardening, travel. Office: Univ Mass Med Sch 519 Lake Ave North Worcester MA 01655 E-mail: liisa.selin@umassmed.edu.

**SELIN, NINA EVVIE,** museum director, electric power industry executive, volunteer; b. N.Y.C., Dec. 16, 1935; d. Louis Harry and Ida Canto; m. Ivan Selin, June 8, 1957; children: Douglas Scott, Jessica Beth. BS, Boston U., 1957. Tchr., Conn., 1957-60; dir. Nat. Consumers League, Washington, 1968-75; propr. Relax-Relocation Cons., Washington, 1975-80; vice chmn. Phoenix Internat. Power Plant Co., Washington, 1995-98; chmn. Nat. Aquarium, Washington, 1986—. Bd. dirs. Am. Cancer Soc., 1972-87, Nat. Geog. Soc., 1995—, Mt. Sinai Hosp. Found., Miami Beach, Fla., 1998-2004, Smithsonian Environ. Rsch. Ctr., 2004—, Rep. Nat. Com., 1991—, Nat. Aquarium, Balt., 2003—; chmn. Selin Family Found., Del., 1995; judge Nathan Davis award AMA, Washington, 2001. Recipient Disting. Svc. award, Am. Cancer Soc., 1987, Mt. Sinai Found., 1999. Mem. Internat. Club III, Welcome to Washington Internat. Club. Avocations: exotic travel, scuba diving, reading, public service. Home: 1455 Ocean Dr Apt 1602 Miami FL 33139 E-mail: nselin@phnx-intl.com.

**SELINGER, PATRICIA GRIFFITHS,** computer science professional; b. Cleve., Oct. 15, 1949; d. Fred Robert and Olive Mae (Brewster) Priest; m. James Alan Griffiths, Aug. 29, 1970 (div. 1973); m. Robert David Selinger, July 22, 1978; children: David Robert, Thomas Robert. AB, Harvard U., 1971, MS, 1972, PhD, 1975. Rsch. staff IBM Rsch. Lab, San Jose, Calif., 1975-78, mgr., 1978-83, mgr. computer sci., 1983-86, program dir. Database Technology Inst., 1986, with devel. team, 1997, v.p. Rsch. Area Strategy, Info. and Interaction. Patentee in field; co-author numerous tech. papers. IBM fellow, 1994; recipient YWCA Tribute to Women in Industry award, 1989; named to Hall of Fame, Women in Tech. Internat., 2004. Mem. NAE, Assn.

for Computing Machinery (System Software award 1989, former vice-chmn. spl. interest group for mgmt. data). Avocations: cooking, reading. Office: IBM Almaden Rsch Ctr 650 Harry Rd San Jose CA 95120-6099

**SELIX, KAREN ELIZABETH,** writer, artist, vocalist; b. Alice, Tex., Jan. 10, 1960; d. LeRoy Albert; 3 children. Owner, designer Spark a Link, Inc., 1999—. Author: (children's stories) Rainbow's End, 2000, Black Rainbow, 2003; co-author (with LeRoy Selix): (cassette recording) The Easter Bunny That Wasn't a Rabbit, 1988; musician: (albums) I'll Be There, 2005, Until We Meet Again, 2005. Recipient Gift of Life award, Ben Taub Gen. Hosp., 1973. Roman Catholic. Home: 236 Sharon Terr Hot Springs National Park AR 71913

**SELJESETH, CAROL H.,** physics educator; d. Charles Henry and Mable Jorgena Heitzeg; children from previous marriage: Chad Heitzeg, Malla Kari. BA, BS, Minn. State U., Mankato, 1966; EdM, U. Ctrl. Okla., Edmond, 1975; post grad., Nat. Microscale Chem. Ctr. Merrimac Coll., Boston, 1994—95, Tulsa U., Okla., 2001. Tchr. biology, chemistry and physiology St. Mary's Hall, Faribault, Minn., 1966—67; tchr. sci. Hefner Jr. H.S., Oklahoma City, 1967—72; pvt. tutor, 1970—93; tchr. intro. and intermediate algebra Okla. State U., 1981—91; tchr. biology, physics, chemistry and geometry Piedmont (Okla.) H.S., 1990—91; tchr. physics Putnam City H.S., Oklahoma City, 1991—. Participant World Yr. Einstein Fermi Nat. Accelerator Lab, Chgo., 2005. Mem.: NEA, Nat. Sci. Tchrs. Assn. Office: Putnam City HS 5300 NW 50th St Oklahoma City OK 73122-5399 Office Phone: 405-789-4350.

**SELKIRK, ALEXANDER MACDONALD, JR.,** lawyer; b. Jamaica, N.Y., Oct. 2, 1943; s. Alexander MacDonald and Anne (Roth) S.; m. Joanne Patrician Diskant, July 21, 1974; children: Marianne E., Victoria L. BA in Polit. Sci., St. Johns U., Jamaica, 1965; JD, N.Y. Law Sch., 1970; LLM in Trade Regulation, NYU, 1973. Bar: N.Y. 1971, U.S. Dist. Ct. (so. and ea. dists.) N.Y. 1972, U.S. Ct. Appeals (2d cir.) 1972, U.S. Supreme Ct. 1976, Fla. 1991. Sr. staff atty. Hartford Ins. Co., N.Y.C., 1971-74; assoc. Richard C. Mooney, Esq., Hempstead, NY, 1974-77; sr. trial atty. Home Ins. Co., Huntington Sta., NY, 1978-80; asst. county atty. Suffolk County, Hauppauge, NY, 1980-88; assoc. Garcia & Stallone Esqs., Melville, NY, 1988-90, CIGNA Ins. Co., Woodbury, NY, 1990-95; trial counsel Martin Fallon Mulle, Huntington, NY, 1995—2004; asst. atty. Town of Huntington. Arbitrator Suffolk County Dist. Ct. 10th Jud. Dist., 1982-88; instr. N.Y. State JAG's Sch., 1997—. Feature writer Ronkonkoma Rev., 1986-90; contbr. articles to legal publs. Committeeman Suffolk Country Rep. Com., Ronkonkoma, N.Y., 1977-92; del. 10th Jud. Dist. Conv. Suffolk County, 1981-84; v.p. Holbrook Rep. Club, 1979-81, pres., 1981-83; bd. dirs. Holbrook Youth Devel. Corp., 1985-91; pilot legal officer Nassau sr. squadron CAP, 1978-84; counsel. Com. for A Drug Free Holbrook, 1988-90. Maj. JACG, N.Y. Army N.G., 1983-2003. Mem. Am. Arbitration Assn. (comml. arbitrator), N.Y. State Bar Assn., Internat. Platform Assn., Suffolk County Bar Assn., NYU Alumni Assn. Holbrook C. of C. (bd. dirs. 1981-92, v.p. 1987-89, pres. 1984-91, 92-93), Gt. Neck (N.Y.) Sportsman's Club (pres. 1998), KC (adv. 1981-84, 87—, trustee 1984-87), Lions (bd. dirs. 1981-92, v.p. 1987-89, pres. 1987-88). Roman Catholic. Home: 12 Glen Summer Rd Holbrook NY 11741-5006 Office: 100 Main St Huntington NY 11743 Office Phone: 631-351-3342. Personal E-mail: flyallaw@hotmail.com.

**SELKIRK, JAMES KIRKWOOD,** biochemist, researcher; b. N.Y.C., Dec. 3, 1938; s. James Kirkwood and Doris (Schuler) S.; m. Carole Ann Bozzone, Sept. 16, 1961; children: James Kirkwood, David Edward. BS, Coll. Environ. Sci. and Forestry, Syracuse U., NY, 1964; PhD, Syracue U. Upstate Med. Ctr., Syracuse, 1969. Postdoctoral fellow McArdle Lab. Cancer Rsch., U. Wis., Madison, 1969-72; staff fellow Nat. Cancer Inst., NIH, Bethesda, Md., 1972-74, sr. staff fellow, 1974-75; sr. staff scientist unit leader chem. carcinogenesis biology divsn. Oak Ridge (Tenn.) Nat. Lab., 1975-85; chief carcinogenesis and toxicology evaluation br. nat. toxicology program Nat. Inst. Environ. Health Scis., 1985-89, assoc. dir. divsn. toxicology rsch. and testing, 1989-92, chief carcinogen mechanism group Lab. Molecular Carcinogenesis, 1992—97; spl. asst. to sci. dir. for technology devel. Nat. Inst. Environ. Health Scis., 1997-2000; deputy dir. Nat. Ctr. Toxicogenomics, 2000—; adj. prof. Oak Ridge Biomed. Grad. Sch., U. Tenn., 1975-85; mem. breast cancer task force NIH, 1979-82; mem. com. on pyrenes and analogs NAS, 1981-83; chmn. Interagy. Testing Commn., 1986-90. Author rsch. articles, chpts. in books; mem. editl. bd. Carcinogenesis Jour., 1984-87, 91-93, Cancer Rsch., 1981-86, Environ. Health Perspectives, 1993-98, contbg. editor, 2003—. Mem. Orange County Planning Bd., 1997—; chmn. Weaver Dairy Precinct, Dem. Party Orange County, 1996-99. With AUS, 1959-61. Recipient U.S. Interagy. Testing Com. Exemplary Svc. award, 1992. Mem. Am. Cancer Soc. (carcinogenesis study sect. 1975-78, 92-96). Home: 30119 Settle Dr Chapel Hill NC 27517 Office: Nat Inst Environ Health Scis PO Box 12233 Research Triangle Park NC 27709 Office Phone: 919-541-2548. Business E-Mail: selkirk@niehs.nih.gov.

**SELKOE, DENNIS JESSE,** neurologist, researcher, educator; b. N.Y.C., Sept. 25, 1943; s. Herbert E. and Mary P. (Lille) S.; m. Polly Ann Strasser, June 24, 1967; children: Gregory, Kimberly. BA, Columbia U., 1965; MD, U. Va., 1969. Diplomate Am. Bd. Psychiatry and Neurology, Nat. Bd. Med. Examiners. Intern in medicine Hosp. U. Pa., Phila., 1969-70; rsch. assoc. NIH, Bethesda, Md., 1970-72; resident in neurology Peter Bent Brigham/Children's Hosp., Boston, 1972-74, chief resident in neurology, 1974-75; rsch. assoc. Harvard Med. Sch., Boston, 1975-78, asst. prof. neurology, 1978-82, assoc. prof., 1982-85, assoc. prof. neurology and neurosci., 1985-90, faculty mem. divsn. on aging, 1980—, prof. neurology and neurosci., 1990—, Vincent and Stella Coates prof. neurol. diseases, 2001—; co-dir. Ctr. Neurologic Diseases Brigham and Women's Hosp., Boston, 1985—. Mem. sci. adv. bd. Alzheimer's Disease Assn., Chgo., 1983-89; mem. Gov.'s Commn. on Alzheimer's Disease, Mass., 1985-87; neurosci. adv. com. Howard Hughes Med. Inst., 1996—. Author over 200 articles, book chpts. on biochemistry and molecular biology of Alzheimer's Disease. Recipient Wood-Kalb Found. prize Alzheimers Disease Assn., 1984, Med. Rsch. award Met. Life Found., 1986, LEAD award Nat. Inst. on Aging, 1988, NIH Merit award, 1991—, Arthur Cherkin award UCLA, 1995, Mathilde Solowey award in neurosci. Found. for Advanced Edn. in Scis., NIH, 1998, Rita Hayworth award Alzheimer's Assn., 1995, Boerhaave medal U. Leiden, 1998, Pioneer award Alzheimer's Assn., 1999; grantee Bristol-Myers Squibb Neurosci., 1990. Fellow AAAS, Am. Acad. Neurology (Potamkin prize 1989, Dr. A.H. Heineken prize for Medicine 2002); mem. Am. Neurol. Assn., Soc. for Neurosci., Am. Assn. Neuropathologists, World Fedn. Neurologists, Inst. Medicine NAS. Office: Harvard Med Sch Brigham & Womens Hosp 77 Avenue Louis Pasteur Boston MA 02115-5727

**SELKOWITZ, ARTHUR,** retired advertising executive; b. N.Y.C., May 26, 1943; s. Harry and Anne (Lichten) S.; m. Betsey Wattenberg, Apr. 15, 1967; children: Adam, Jed. AB, Syracuse U., NY, 1965. Account exec. Dancer Fitzgerald Sample, 1969-71; with Benton & Bowles, Inc., N.Y.C., 1971-82, v.p., account supr. 1972-75, sr. v.p., mgmt. supr., 1975-81, sr. v.p., account dir., 1981-82; founder, pres. Penchina, Selkowitz Inc., N.Y.C., 1982-90; exec. v.p. internat. D'Arcy, Masius, Benton & Bowles, N.Y.C., 1990-94, pres. Asia and Pacific, 1995-96, pres. N.Am., 1996-97, chmn., CEO, 1997-2000; vice chmn., chief client officer BCom3 Group, Inc., N.Y.C., 2001—02, Publicis Groupe, 2002. Lectr. Columbia U., 2003—; mem. adv. bd. Spot Runner, Inc. Dancer Fitzgerald Sample, N.Y.C., 1966—71. Mem.: Lotos (N.Y.) Club. E-mail: arthur@sunrockholdings.com.

**SELL, CLAY (JEFFREY CLAY SELL),** federal agency administrator; BS, Tex. Tech. U.; JD, U. Tex. Staff mem. to Congressman Mac Thornberry US Ho. Reps., Washington, 1995—97, adminstrv. asst. to Congressman Mac Thornberry, 1997—99; majority clk. & staff dir. for energy & water sub com. of the Senate Com. on Appropriations US Senate, Washington, 2000—03; spl. asst. to Pres. for econ. policy The White House, Washington, 2003—04, spl. asst. to Pres. for legis. affairs, 2004—05; dep. sec. US Dept. Energy, Washington, 2005—. Office: US Dept Energy Forrestal Bldg 1000 Independence Ave SW Rm 7B-252 Washington DC 20585

**SELL, JAMES DOUGLAS,** music educator; b. Albany, N.Y., Oct. 31, 1966; s. James Edwin and Avagene Aaron Sell. MusB in Edn., We. Ky. U., 1988, MA in Edn., 1992; MA in Leadership, Ea. Ky. U., 2004, cert. in Rank I in Leadership, 2004. Dir. bands Clinton County Schs., Albany, Ky., 1988—. Pvt. practice music educator, Albany, Ky., 1988—. Scholar, We. Ky. U., 1984. Mem.: Music Educators Nat. Conf., Ky. Music Educators. Republican. Avocations: agriculture, cattle breeding. Home: Rt 5 Box 664 Albany KY 42602 Office: Clinton County Schs Hwy 127N Albany KY 42602

**SELL, JEFFREY EDWARD,** heart surgeon; b. June 5, 1954; s. William Edward and Cordelia Isabel (Fulton) S.; m. Christine Marie Fulner, June 2, 1984. BS in Chemistry summa cum laude, Yale U., 1976, BS in Physics summa cum laude, 1976; MD, MIT, 1980. Diplomate Am. Bd. Thoracic Surgeons, Am. Bd. Surgery, Nat. Bd. Med. Examiners; cert. thoracic organ transplant surgeon; lic. physician, Va., Md., D.C. Intern Brigham and Women's Hosp., Boston, 1980-81, jr. resident gen. surgery, 1981-82, sr. resident gen. surgery, cardiac surgery, 1984-86, 87, chief resident cardiac surgery, 1988; fellow clin. assoc. surgery br. NIH, Nat. Heart Lung and Blood Inst., Bethesda, Md., 1982-84; fellow cardiac surgery Children's Hosp. Boston, 1986-87, chief resident cardiac surgery, 1989; attending cardiac surgeon Alexandria (Va.) Hosp., 1993-95, Washington VA Hosp., 1991-95; dir. heart transplant program, attending surgeon Children's Hosp. Nat. Med. Ctr., Washington, 1990—2000; with Midlantic Carciovasc. Assocs., 2000—; attending surgeon St. Joseph's Med. Ctr., Towson, Md., 2000—. Dir. pediatric cardiac surgery U. Md. Hosp., Balt., 1989-90; asst. prof. surgery and pediatrics George Washington U., Washington, 1990—2000; investigator varoius rsch., 1986-87, 91—. Contbr. articles to profl. jours., chpts. to books. Fellow ACS, Am. Coll. Cardiology; mem. Soc. Thoracic Surgeons, Andrew G. Morrow Soc. Cardiovascular Surgeons, Internat. Soc. Heart and Lung Transplantation, Soc. Cardiac Surgeons. Pediatric Cardiac Surgery. Avocation: flying. Home: 13020 Jerome Jay Dr Cockeysville MD 21030-1522 Office: O'Day Med Office Bldg Ste 410 7505 Osler Dr Towson MD 21204 Office Phone: 410-583-1175. E-mail: jeffreysellmd@earthlink.net.

**SELL, ROBERT EMERSON,** electrical engineer; b. Apr. 23, 1929; s. Cecil Leroy and Ona Arletta (Stevens) S.; m. Ora Lucile Colton, Nov. 7, 1970. BS, U. Nebr., 1962. Registered profl. engr., Nebr., Mo., Ill., Ind., Ohio, W.Va., Ky., Ark., Tex., Oreg., Wash., Calif. Chief draftsman Dempster Mill Mfg. Co., Beatrice, Nebr., 1949-53; designer-engr. U. Nebr., Lincoln, 1955-65; elec. design engr. Kirkham, Michael & Assocs., Omaha, 1965-67, Leo A. Daly Co., Omaha and St. Louis, 1967-69; mech. design engr. Hellmuth, Obata, Kassabaum, St. Louis, 1969-70; chief elec. engr. Biagi-Hannan & Assocs., Inc., Evansville, Ind., 1971-74; elec. project engr. H.L. Yoh Co. under contract to Monsanto Co., Creve Coeur, Mo., 1974-77, Dhillon Engrs., Inc., Portland, Oreg., 1978-85; project coord. Brown-Zammit-Enyeart Engring., Inc., San Diego, 1985-88; elec. engr. Morgen Design, Inc., San Diego, 1988; lead elec. engr. Popov Engrs., Inc., San Diego, 1988-89; mech. and elec. specialist Am. Engring. Labs., Inc. divsn. Profl. Svc. Industries, Inc., San Diego, 1990—. Instr. Basic Inst. Tech., St. Louis, 1971. Mem. ASHRAE, IEEE. Home and Office: PO Box 261578 San Diego CA 92196-1578

**SELLA, ANTHONY,** film company executive; Joined advt. dept. Diener Hauser Bates, NYC, 1980; v.p. creative svcs. Walt Disney, Touchstone Pictures, Hollywood Pictures; sr. v.p. creative advt. Twentieth Century Fox Film Corp., LA, 1991—94, sr. v.p. mktg. and creative advt., 1994—2002, co-pres. domestic theatrical mktg., 2002—. Office: Twentieth Century Fox Film Corp 10201 W Pico Blvd Los Angeles CA 90035 Office Phone: 310-277-2211. Office Fax: 310-203-1558.*

**SELLECCA, CONNIE,** actress; b. Bronx, N.Y., May 25, 1955; d. Primo and Ann; m. Gil Gerard, 1979 (div. 1987); 1 child, Gilbert Vincent Gerard; m. John Tesh, Apr. 4, 1992; 1 child, Prima Sellechia Tesh. Attended, Boston Coll. Appeared in The Bermuda Depths, TV films include Somebody's Killing the World's Greatest Models, Captain America, The Last Fling, Flying High, 1978, Captain America II, 1979, Circus of the Stars #5, 1980, Hotel, 1982, International Airport, 1985, Downpayment on Murder, 1987, Brotherhood of the Rose, 1989, Turn Back the Clock, 1989, Miracle Landing, 1990, People Like Us, 1990, P.S.I. Luv U, 1991, House of Secrets and Lies, 1992, Passport to Murder, 1993, She Led Two Lives, 1994, The Surrogate, 1995, Holiday to Remember, 1995, A Dangerous Affair, 1995, While My Pretty One Sleeps, 1997, Something Borrowed, Something Blue, 1997, Domesday Rock, 1997, Dangerous Waters, 1999, Anna's Dream, 2002; TV series include Beyond Westworld, Flying High, The Greatest American Hero, Arthur Hailey's Hotel, PS I Luv U; films I Saw Mommy Kissing Santa Claus, 2002. Address: William Morris Agcy 151 El Camino Dr Beverly Hills CA 90212 also: Richard Grant and Assocs 8489 W Third St Los Angeles CA 90048

**SELLECK, TOM,** actor; b. Detroit, Jan. 29, 1945; s. Robert D. and Martha S.; m. Jacquelyn Ray, 1970 (div. 1982); 1 stepson, Kevin; m. Jillie Joan Mack, Aug. 7, 1987; 1 child, Hannah Margaret. TV appearances include The Rockford Files, Simon & Simon, 1982, Friends, 1996, 2000, Boston Legal, 2006; star TV series Magnum P.I. 1980-88, The Closer, 1998; films include Midway, 1976, Coma, 1982, High Road to China, 1983, Lassiter, 1984, Runaway, 1985, Three Men and a Baby, 1987, Her Alibi, 1989, An Innocent Man, 1989, Quigley Down Under, 1990, Three Men and a Little Lady, 1990, Folks!, 1992, Mr. Baseball, 1992, In and Out, 1997, The Love Letter, 1999; TV films include The Sacketts, 1979, Divorce Wars, 1982, Louis L'Amour's "The Shadow Riders", 1982, Broken Trust, 1995, Ruby Jean and Joe, 1996, Last Stand at Saher River, 1998, Louis l'Amour's Crossfire Trail, 2000, Monte Walsh, Reversible Errors, Ike: Countdown to D Day, 2004, Stone Cold, 2005, Jesse Stone: Night Passage, 2006. Office: care Esme Chandlee 2967 Hollyridge Dr Los Angeles CA 90068-1949 Office Phone: 323-962-3704.*

**SELLER, GREGORY EROL,** marketing executive, consultant, writer; b. Denver, Oct. 4, 1953; s. Otto Gustave and Dolores Louise (Crawford) S. BBA, U. Colo., 1975. Account exec. Gt.-West Life, L.A., 1975-79, asst. v.p. group devel. Denver, 1980-84; v.p. govt. mkts. and nat. accts. Great-West Life, L.A., 1988—; pres., chief exec. officer Benefits Communication Corp., Denver, 1985-87, sr. v.p. govt. mkts., 1991—. Bd. dirs. Benefits Communication Co., Fascorp, Emjoy Corp Editor newsletter Focus on 457, 1988—. Mem. vestry, treas. St. Thomas Episc. Ch., Hollywood, Calif., 1990-93 Mem. Delta Upsilon. Democrat. Office: Great West Life Ste 560 18111 Von Karman Ave Irvine CA 92612-7131

**SELLER, ROBERT HERMAN,** cardiologist, physician; b. Phila., Mar. 21, 1931; s. David and Elsie (Straussman) S.; m. Maxine Schwartz, June 3, 1956; children: Michael, Douglas, Stuart. AB, U. Pa., 1952, MD, 1956. Intern. Grad. Hosp. of U. Pa., Phila., 1956-57; research asst. dept. pharmacology U. Pa., 1953-55; resident in cardiology, research fellow Am. Heart Assn., Phila. Gen. Hosp., 1957-58; resident in internal medicine Albert Einstein Med. Ctr. Phila., 1958-59, chief resident, 1959-60; instr. medicine Hahnemann Med. Coll. and Hosp., Phila., 1960-64, asst. prof., 1964-69, assoc. prof., 1969-72, dir. Service F, 1962-67, asst. coordinator mil. edn. for nat. def., 1961-64, dir. div. family medicine, 1967-72, acting chmn. dept. family medicine and community health, 1972-74, prof. medicine, family medicine and community health, 1973-74; practice medicine, specializing in cardiology Buffalo, 1974—; prof., chmn. dept. family medicine, prof. medicine SUNY-Buffalo, Deaconess Hosp., 1974-82, chmn. dept. family practice and dir. family practice residency program, 1974-82; prof. medicine and family medicine SUNY-Buffalo, 1974-2000; emeritus prof. medicine and family medicine, 2000—. Author: Differential Diagnosis of Common Complaints, 1986, 4th edit., 2000, Diagnosis of Common Complaints, 2004; contbr. articles to profl. jours. NIH grantee, 1972-75; Deaconess Hosp. family practice resident tng. grantee, 1975-; health professions spl. projects grantee, 1975- Fellow ACP, Am. Coll. Cardiology, Am. Acad. Family Physicians, Phila. Coll. Physicians; mem. AMA, N.Y. Med. Soc., Erie County Med. Soc., Am. Fedn. Clin.

Research, Am. Heart Assn., Soc. of Tchrs. of Family Medicine, N.Y. Acad. Sci., N.Y. Acad. Family Physicians. Home: 125 Crestwood Ln Buffalo NY 14221-1462 Office: 1542 Maple Rd Buffalo NY 14221-3625 Office Phone: 716-568-3402.

**SELLERS, BARBARA JACKSON,** federal judge; b. Richmond, Va., Oct. 3, 1940; m. Richard F. Sellers; children: Elizabeth M., Anne W., Catherine A. Attended, Baldwin-Wallace Coll., 1958-60; BA cum laude, Ohio State U., 1962; JD magna cum laude, Capital U. Law Sch., Columbus, Ohio, 1979. Bar: Ohio 1979, U.S. Dist. Ct. (so. dist.) Ohio 1981, U.S. Ct. Appeals (6th cir.), 1986. Jud. law clk. Hon. Robert J. Sidman, U.S. Bankruptcy Judge, Columbus, Ohio, 1979-81; assoc. Lasky & Semons, Columbus, 1981-82; jud. law clk. to Hon. Thomas M. Herbert, U.S. Bankruptcy Ct., Columbus, 1982-84; assoc. Baker & Hostetler, Columbus, 1984-86; U.S. bankruptcy judge So. Dist. Ohio, Columbus, 1986—. Lectr. on bankruptcy univs., insts., assns. Recipient Am. Jurisprudence prize contracts and criminal law, 1975-76, evidence and property, 1976-77, Corpus Juris Secundum awards, 1975-76, 76-77. Mem. Columbus Bar Assn., Am. Bankruptcy Inst., Nat. Conf. Bankruptcy Judges, Order of Curia, Phi Beta Kappa. Office: US Bankruptcy Ct 170 N High St Columbus OH 43215-2403 Office Phone: 614-469-6638 ext. 250. Business E-Mail: barbara_sellers@ohsb.uscourts.gov.

**SELLERS, DONALD R.,** biotechnology company executive; AB, Lafayette Coll.; M.Internat. Mgmt., Am. Grad. Sch. Internat. Mgmt. Counter-intelligence spl. agt. Spl. Forces U.S. Mil. Intelligence; country mgr. Vietnam and Hong Kong Pfizer Pharm., 1973; dir. worldwide exports Revlon Health-care Group, Pacific area dir.; v.p. mktg. and ops. Asia Sterling Drug Internat., 1983—90, pres. L.Am. Andina Group; corp. v.p. Getz Bros., 1990—93, pres. Japanese ops.; mng. dir. SciClone Pharms. Internat., Ltd., 1993—; CEO, pres., dir. SciClone Pharms., Inc., San Mateo, Calif., 1996—.

**SELLERS, FRED EVANS,** accounting educator; b. Lexington, Mo., Feb. 28, 1941; s. James MacBrayer and Rebekah Hall (Evans) S.; m. Katherine Ann Griggs, May 3, 1969; children: Mark Griggs, Rebekah Field. BA in History, Yale U., 1965; MBA, U. Kans., 1976, PhD in Bus., 1984. CPA Tex. Reporter Kansas City (Mo.) Star, 1965-66, copy editor, 1966-70, Washington Star, 1970-72, asst. nat. editor, 1972-73; asst. prof. U. Tulsa, 1979-87; assoc. prof. Southwestern U., Georgetown, Tex., 1987—, chmn. dept. econs. and bus., 1994—2004. Sec., treas. planning com. U. Tulsa Conf. Accts., 1980-87. Contbr. articles to profl. jours. Trustee Wentworth Mil. Acad., Lexington, Mo., 1986—, pres., 1990-92; trustee Williamson County (Tex.) Literacy Coun., 1989-91; treas., bd. dirs. St. John's Presch., Tulsa, 1984-87; conv. del. Episc. Diocese Okla., 1984, 85; audit com. St. John's Episc. Ch., Tulsa, 1983-87; bishop's com. Grace Episc. Ch., 1989, jr. warden, 1989, bishop's warden, 1990, chmn., audit com., 2004, treas., 2004-05, mem. rector search com., 2004; alt. Tex. State Rep. Conv., 1988; treas. Georgetown Area United Way, 1993-99; mem. Georgetown Ethics Commn., 2004—, vice chair, 2004-06, chair, 2006—. Mem. Inst. Mgmt. Accts. (dir. manuscripts Austin chpt. 1988-96), Am. Acctg. Assn. (membership com. 1980-81), AICPA, Tex. Soc. CPAs (edn!. instns. com. Austin chpt.), Rotary. Avocations: bridge, piano, trombone, singing, jogging. Home: 1610 E 15th St Georgetown TX 78626-7206 Office: Southwestern U Dept Econs and Bus Adminstrn Georgetown TX 78627-0770 Office Phone: 512-863-1574. Business E-Mail: sellersf@southwestern.edu.

**SELLERS, GREGORY JUDE,** physicist; b. Far Rockaway, N.Y., June 20, 1947; s. Douglas L. and Rita R. (Dieringer) S.; m. Lucia S. Kim, Nov. 26, 1983; 1 child, Kristin Kim. AB in Physics, Cornell U., 1968; MS, U. Ill., 1970, PhD, 1975. Sr. scientist B-K Dynamics, Inc., Rockville, Md., 1974-76; with Allied-Signal Corp., Morristown, NJ, 1976-88, applications physicist, 1977-88; product supr. Amphenol Fiber Optic Products, Naperville, Ill., 1985-88; mgr. Cinch Connectors, Elk Grove, Ill., 1988-91; pres. Forss, Inc., Naperville, 1991-96, Fotron, Inc., Naperville, 1995—. Bd. dirs. Fotron; lectr. Benedictine U., 2004—. Mem. AAAS, IEEE, Am. Phys. Soc. Achievements include development and commercialization of electronic connectors and fiber optic products; development of applications for polymeric materials and glassy metals in the electrical and electronics arena. Co-inventor adhesive bonding metallic glass, electromagnetic shielding, testing of thermal insulation, amorphous antipilferage marker, amorphous spring-shield, multiple fiber positioner for optical fiber connection, raised rib waveguide ribbon for precision optical interconnects. Home and Office: Fotron Inc 7S 515 Oak Trails Dr Naperville IL 60540 Office Phone: 630-983-4146. E-mail: fotron1gs@aol.com.

**SELLERS, JIMMIE,** construction executive; b. Florence, S.C., Aug. 4, 1951; s. Kisar and Evell Sellers; m. Lorraine Conley Sellers, Aug. 25, 1996; children: Jimmy, Nikita Renee 1 stepchild, Teran Correia. Advanced welding cert., Coosa Valley Vocat.-Tech. Sch., 1971; small bus. mgmt. course, Floyd Jr. Coll., 1974. Cardiac care provider Am. Heart Assn., Rome, Ga., 1997; medic 1st aid EMP Am., Catersville, Ga., 2002. Author: (poetry) America at the Millennium, 2000. Min. Pentecostal Assembly of the World. Sgt. 1st class U.S. Army, 1988. Mem.: Handyman Club Am., VA Assn. Pentecostal. Avocations: drawing, wood carving, playing guitar, writing, building. Home: 117 Simpson Dr Nw Rome GA 30165-1031

**SELLERS, KATE M.,** art museum director; From dir. devel. and comm. to acting dir. Walters Art Gallery, Balt., 1987-94; dir. devel. and external affairs Cleve. Mus., 1995-97, dep. dir., 1997-2000; dir. Wadsworth Atheneum, Hartford, Conn., 2000—. Office: Wadsworth Atheneum Mus Art 600 Main St Hartford CT 06103-2990

**SELLERS, LARRON F.,** and educator, minister, b. Orangeburg, S.C., Nov. 21, 1950; s. George E. and Janie S. Sellers; m. Mary E. Denard, Apr. 7, 1979; children: Christian T., LaBron C., Tramon C. BA, Claflin U., 1973; MA, U. S.C., 1986; design cert., Art Inst. Atlanta, 1990. Grad. asst. U. S.C., Columbia, 1974. Pastor Mt. Calvary Ch. of God, Orangeburg, SC, 1979—2005; dist. youth dir. St. James Ch. of God Dist., Orangeburg, 1980—2005. Mentor Big Bro., Orangeburg, 1974; mentor/tchr. St. Paul Complex, Orangeburg, 1990; art educator Boys Club, Orangeburg, 2003. Mem.: Nat. Geog. Soc., S.C. State Mus., Nat. Art Edn. Assn. Democrat. Avocations: collecting old books and coins, jogging, tennis, fishing, carpentry. Home: 124 Goucho Rd Orangeburg SC 29115 Office: Edisto HS PO Box 1001 500 RM Foster Dr Cordova SC 29039-0101

**SELLERS, PETER HOADLEY,** mathematician, educator; b. Phila., Sept. 12, 1930; s. Lester Hoadley and Therese (Tyler) S.; m. Lucy Bell Newlin, June 21, 1958; children: Mortimer, Therese, Mary, Lucy Bell BA, U. Pa., 1953, MA, 1958, PhD, 1965. Math. tchr. Kanagwa Sch., Embu, Kenya, 1961-63; programmer U. Pa., Phila., 1958-61; mem. faculty Rockefeller U., N.Y.C., 1966—. Johnson Found. postdoctoral fellow, 1963-65 Mem. editl. bd. Genomics, 1986-97; author: Combinatorial Complexes, 1979; contbr. articles to profl. jours. Trustee Coll. of the Atlantic, Bar Harbor, Maine, 1985-96; curator Rockefeller Hist. Instrument Collection, 1997—. Lt (j.g.) USNR, 1953-55 Mem. Am. Math. Soc., Math. Assn. Am., Soc. Indsl. and Applied Math. Democrat. Episcopalian. Avocations: boat building, sailing. Home: 413 W Stafford St Philadelphia PA 19144-4407 Office: Rockefeller Univ 1230 York Ave New York NY 10021-6399 Business E-Mail: sellers@rockefeller.edu.

**SELLERS, PIERS J.,** astronaut; b. Crowborough, Sussex, Eng., Apr. 11, 1955; married; 2 children. BS in Ecol. Sci., U. Edinburgh, Scotland, 1976; PhD in Biometeorology, Leeds U., Eng., 1981. Astronaut, mission specialist NASA, Johnson Space Ctr., Houston, 1996—. Mem. flight team STS-112 Atlantis, 2002; crew mem. STS-121 (Discovery), a return-to-flight test mission and assembly flight to the Internat. Space Station, 2006. Recipient Arthur Fleming award, 1995. Fellow: Am. Meteorology Soc. (Houghton award 1997), Am. Geophys. Union. Achievements include research in how the earth's biosphere and atmosphere interact, computer modeling of climate

system, satellite remote sensing studies; field work utilizing aircraft, satellites and ground teams in Kansas, Russia, Africa, Canada and Brazil. Office: Astronaut Office/CB NASA Johnson Space Ctr Houston TX 77058*

**SELLERS, WAYNE CHADICK,** retired publisher, retired editor; b. Brady, Tex., Mar. 10, 1916; s. Marcellus Stephenson Sellers and Martha Jane Chadick; m. Camilla Ann Browning, June 29, 1946 (dec. June 1996). BA, Tex. Tech U.; 1938; postgrad., U. Tex., 1940-41. Statistician Ft. Worth Star-Telegram, 1943-50; prodn. mgr. San Francisco News, 1951-52; bus. mgr. Sherman (Tex.) Democrat, 1953-59; pub. Rock Hill (S.C.) Herald, 1959-66; editor, pub. Palestine (Tex.) Herald-Press, 1966-80. Mem. bd. mgrs. Tex. State R.R., 1969-73; mem. adv. coun. U. Tex. Coll. communication, Austin, 1979—. Chmn. Palestine United Way, 1968, Northeast Tex. Lib. Sys. Adv. Coun., Garland, 1986—, Palestine Pub. Libr. Bd., 1979—; vol. lobbyist Tex. Libr. Assn., 1983; chmn. Reporter Bd., United Meth. Ch., Dallas, 1980-82. Named to Hall of Fame Tex. Tech U. Sch. Mass Commn., Lubbock, 1979; named Trustee of Yr. Tex. Libr. Assn., Houston, 1981, Nat. Advocacy Honor Roll Mem., Am. Libr. Assn., chgo., 2000, Builder of Palestine, Palestine C. of c., 1982, Mr. Books, Tex. State Libr. and Archives Commn., Austin, 1983. Democrat. Methodist. Avocations: amateur radio, travel, collecting books. Home: 215 Stephanie Dr Palestine TX 75803-8505 E-mail: wcsellers@earthlink.net.

**SELLES, ROBERT HENDRIKUS,** retired actuary; b. Amsterdam, Nov. 8, 1938; arrived in U.S., 1969; s. Albertus Henrikus and Jansje Suzanna (Cordes) Selles; m. Manuela Ioana Comnene, Aug. 26, 1966 (div. Mar. 1978); 1 child, Melina Joanna. B of Commerce with honors, U. Manitoba, 1961. Actuarial asst. Can. Premier Life Ins. Co., Winnipeg, Man., Canada, 1961-62; asst. actuary Sun Life Assurance Co. Can., Montreal, 1962-69; sr. v.p. Hay/Huggins Co., Inc., Phila., 1969—91, ret., 2004. Fellow: Soc. Actuaries; mem.: Gavel Soc., Western Pension and Benefits Conf., Am. Acad. Actuaries, Conf. Cons. Actuaries, Netherlands Am. Assn. Delaware Valley (bd. dirs. 1993—96), Rainbow River Inc. (pres. 1995—2005), Netherlands Soc. Phila. (bd. dirs. 1991—, pres. 1993—96, 1999—2000), Internat. Benefits Found., Actuaries Club San Francisco. Home: 1420 Locust St Apt 34-A Philadelphia PA 19102-4220 Personal E-mail: rselles@aol.com.

**SELLEY, MICHAEL L.,** pharmaceutical company executive; b. Woking, Surrey, U.K., Jan. 20, 1948; s. Stanley John and Rosina Lillian Selley; m. Angela Grace Charlton, July 30, 1966 (div. Sept. 1976); 1 child, Michelle Louise; m. Pamela Kay Foulser, Oct. 29, 1977; 1 child, Timothy Michael. BSc, U. London, 1968; MSc, U. Alta., Edmonton, 1971; PhD, U. Sydney, 1975. Sr. rsch. scientist Sandoz Pharma Ltd., Basle, Switzerland, 1975-84; sr. rsch. fellow John Curtin Sch. Med. Rsch. Inst. Advanced Studies, Australian Nat. U., Canberra, 1985-95; chief of staff Office of the Min. for Sci., Parliament Ho., Canberra, 1996-97; chmn. and mng. dir. Pan Australia Labs Pty. Ltd., Symonston, 1997—99; chmn., CEO Angiogen Pharms. Pty. Ltd., Sydney, 1999—. Cons. Asia/Pacific region Panlabs Inc., Seattle, 1988-95. Contbr. articles to profl. jours. Anutech Canberra Tech. Partnership grantee, 1991-93. Fellow Royal Australian Chem. Inst. Achievements include patents for new drugs for the treatment of autoimmune and neurodegenerative diseases. Avocations: horseback riding, golf, classical music, wine. Home: 19 Holmes St Turramurra NSW 2074 Australia Office: Level 31 ABN AMRO Tower 88 Phillip Street Sydney NSW 2000 Australia Office Phone: 61 2 8211 0662. Home Fax: 61 2 9144 3175. Business E-Mail: mlselley@angiogen.com.au.

**SELLICK, KATHLEEN A.,** hospital administrator; b. Phoenix; m. Phil Sellick; 1 child, Grace. BS, Ariz. State U.; MBA, U. Chgo. Grad. Sch. Bus., 1984. With Am. Med. Internat., Beverly Hills, Calif., Westgate Med. Ctr., Denton, Tex.; adminstrv. resident Mayo Clinic, Rochester, Minn.; v.p. adminstrn. and dir. outreach devel. Hoag Meml. Hosp. Presbyn., Newport Beach, Calif.; exec. v.p. and COO St. Joseph Hosp., Orange, Calif., 1995—99; assoc. exec. dir. and COO U. Wash. Med. Ctr., Seattle, 1999—2001, acting exec. dir., 2000—01, exec. dir., 2001—. Clin. asst. prof., dept. health services U. Wash. Sch. of Public Health and Community Medicine. Office: U Wash Med Ctr 1959 NE Pacific St Box 356151 Seattle WA 98195-6151 Office Fax: 206-598-6292.*

**SELLIN, THEODORE,** diplomat, consultant; b. Phila., June 17, 1928; s. Thorsten and Amy (Anderson) S.; m. Taru Jarvi, July 10, 1965; 1 child, Derek. Student, U. Uppsala, Sweden, 1946-48; BA, U. Pa., 1951, MA, 1952. Joined Fgn. Svc., Dept. State, 1952; vice consul Copenhagen, 1952-56; rsch. analyst Dept. State, Washington, 1956-58; program officer Office Internat. Confs., 1965-67; acad. tng. staff U. Ind., 1958-59; 2d sec. Am. Embassy, Helsinki, Finland, 1959-64, 1st sec. polit. officer, 1971-73, 1st sec., labor-polit. officer Oslo, 1967-71; polar affairs officer Dept. State, 1975; consul gen. Goteborg, Sweden, 1978-80; fgn. rels. cons. Dept. State, Washington, 1980—. Office: Dept State A/ISS/IPS/CR/IR Washington DC 20520

**SELLKE, FRANK WILLIAM,** cardiothoracic surgeon, researcher; b. Ft. Wayne, Ind., Feb. 5, 1956; s. Erwin A. and Anna Luise (Schumacher) S.; m. Amy Marie Brill, Jan. 31, 1987; children: Michelle, Eric, Nicholas, Amanda. AB summa cum laude, Wabash Coll., 1978; MD, Ind. U., Indpls., 1981. Diplomate Am. Bd. Thoracic Surgery, Am. Bd. Surgery. Intern Ind. U. Hosp., Indpls., 1981-82; emergency physician Culver Union Hosp., Crawfordsville, Ind., 1982-83; resident in surgery Akron (Ohio) City Hosp., 1983-87; postdoctoral fellow cardiac surgery U. Iowa, Iowa City, 1987-90; from instr. to asst. prof. surgery Harvard Med. Sch., Boston, 1990-95, assoc. prof. surgery, 1995—2000, prof. surgery, 2000—; cardiothoracic surgeon Beth Israel Hosp., Boston, 1990—; chief cardiothoracic surgery Beth Israel Deaconess Med. Ctr., Boston, 1999—2006, vice chmn. dept. surgery, 2006—. Mem. editl. bd. Jour. Thoracic and Cardiovascular Surgery, Jour. Surg. Rsch., Jour. Cardiac Surgery, Shock; contbr. rsch. articles to profl. jours. Fellow Am. Coll. Cardiology, Am. Coll. Surgeons; mem. AMA, Am. Surg. Assn., Am. Heart Assn., Am. Physiol. Soc., Am. Coll. Chest Physicians, Soc. Univ. Surgeons, Assn. Acad. Surgeons, Am. Assn. for Thoracic Surgery, Soc. Thoracic Surgeons, Phi Beta Kappa. Lutheran. Home: 121 Monadnock Rd Chestnut Hill MA 02467-1136 Office: Beth Israel Deaconess Med Ctr 110 Francis St Boston MA 02215 Office Phone: 617-632-8383. Business E-Mail: fsellke@bidmc.harvard.edu.

**SELLMANN, MEINOLF,** computer science educator; b. Holzminden, Lower Saxony, Germany, Dec. 7, 1971; s. Paul and Marianne Elisabeth Sellmann. D, U. Paderborn, Germany, 2002. Postdoctoral assoc. Cornell U., Ithaca, NY, 2003—04; asst. prof. Brown U., Providence, 2004—. Assoc. editor Informs Jour. Computing, 2005—. Fellow German Nat. Merit Found., 1994—98. Achievements include co-invention of several combinatorial methods, including CP-based Lagrangian Relaxation, Streamlining and Symmetry Breaking by Dominance Detection. Office Phone: 401-863-6057.

**SELLMYER, DAVID JULIAN,** physicist, researcher; b. Joliet, Ill., Sept. 28, 1938; s. Marcus Leo and Della Louise (Plumhoff) S.; m. Catherine Joyce Zakas, July 16, 1962; children: Rebecca Ann, Julia Maryn, Mark Anthony. BS, U. Ill., 1960; PhD, Mich. State U., 1965. Asst. prof. MIT, Cambridge, 1965-72, assoc. prof., 1972, U. Nebr., Lincoln, 1972-75, prof., 1975—, chmn. dept. physics, 1978-84, George Holmes disting. prof., 1987—, dir. Ctr. Materials Rsch., 1988—. Cons. Dale Electronics, Norfolk, Nebr., 1980-. Contbr. articles, book revs. to refereed jours. Recipient tech. award NASA, 1972; disting. vis. prof. S.D. Sch. Mines and Tech., Rapid City, 1981. Fellow Am. Phys. Soc. Office: U Nebraska Lincoln Dept Physics and Astronomy 112 Brace Lab Lincoln NE 68588-0111*

**SELLS, BOAKE ANTHONY,** private investor; b. Ft. Dodge, Iowa, June 24, 1937; s. Lyle M. and Louise (Gadd) S.; m. Marian S. Stephenson, June 20, 1959; children: Damian, Brian, Jean Ann. BSc, U. Iowa, 1959; MBA, Harvard U., 1969. Bus. office mgr. Northwestern Bell Tel., Des Moines, 1959-63; salesman Hydraulic Cos., Ft. Dodge, 1964-67; pres. Cole Nat. Corp., Cleve., 1969-83; vice chmn. Dayton Hudson Corp., Mpls., 1983-84, pres., 1984-87; chmn., pres., chief exec. officer Revco D.S., Inc., Twinsburg, Ohio, 1987-92. Bd. dirs. Promus Cos. (name changed to Harrah's Entertainment, Inc. Trustee Cleve. Play House, Mus. Contemporary Art, Cleve., dir.

**SELLS, FAWN LEIGH,** paralegal, writer; b. Martins Ferry, Ohio, Jan. 17, 1974; d. Jim and Penny Leigh Raha; 1 child, Andrew Michael Finefrock. AA, W.Va. Bus. Coll., 2002. Lic.: Nat. Paralegal Assn. (paralegal) 2002. Commd. lt. USAF, advanced through grades to sgt., office adminstrn. Scott AFB, Ill., 1992—2000; paralegal Palm Beach (Fla.) County Atty., 2000—03. Author: You're All Right.By God, Learning in the Light. Decorated AF Achievement medal USAF, Humanitarian Svc. award, Nat. Def. Svc. Ribbon. Office Phone: 724-602-4378. Personal E-mail: fawnsells@msn.com.

**SELMAN, RUSSELL BERTRAM,** lawyer; b. Oceanside, N.Y., May 31, 1954; s. Leon Daniel and Lorraine Thelma (Leichter) S.; m. Elizabeth Friedgut. BA, New Coll., 1975; MPA, Syracuse U., 1978; JD, Washington U., 1980. Bar: Ill. 1987, D.C. 1981, Mo. 1980. Asst. enforcement counsel U.S. Environ. Protection Agy., Washington, 1980-82, atty., advisor, 1983; atty. McKenna, Conner & Cuneo, Washington, 1983-86, Schiff, Hardin & Waite, Chgo., 1986-88, Bell, Boyd & Lloyd, Chgo., 1988-93; ptnr., chmn. environ. law dept. Katten Muchin Rosenman, Chgo., 1993—. Contbr. Chicago Lawyer mag. Office: Katten Muchin Rosenman 525 W Monroe St Ste 1600 Chicago IL 60661-3693 Office Phone: 312-902-5390. Business E-Mail: russell.selman@kattenlaw.com.

**SELOLWANE, DIPHETOGO (DIPSY SELOLWANE),** professional soccer player; b. Jan. 27, 1978; s. Gertrude Selolwane and Leslie Ramasodi. Attended, Harris Stowe State Coll. Played one season Harris Stowe State Coll., St. Louis; forward Chgo. Fire, Major League Soccer, 2002—. Mem. Botswana Nat. Team, 1998—. Achievements include top goal-scorer, 23-and-under nat. team, Four Nation's Cup, South Africa, 1998. Office: Soldier Stadium 425 E McFetridge Dr Chicago IL 60605-279

**SELOVER, R. EDWIN,** lawyer; b. Norman, Okla., Aug. 18, 1945; BA, Union Coll., 1967; JD, U. Minn., 1972. Bar: NJ 1972. Atty. Pub. Svc. Electric & Gas Co. (PSE&G), Newark, 1972-75, asst. gen. counsel, 1975-79, assoc. gen. counsel, 1979-80, gen. counsel, 1980-83, v.p., gen. counsel, 1983-88, sr. v.p., gen. counsel, 1988—; v.p., gen. counsel Pub. Svc. Enterprise Group Inc. (PSEG), Newark, 1988—2002, sr. v.p., gen. counsel, 2002—, PSEG Services Corp., 1999—. Bd. trustees NJ Conservation Found., NJ Future, 1998—, Stockton Alliance, NJ; nuclear ind. sector chmn., Infrastructure Adv. Com. NJ Office of Counterterrorism. Served U.S. Army, 1969—71. Mem.: NJ Bar Assn., ABA. Office: Pub Svc Enterprise Group Inc 80 Park Plz Newark NJ 07102

**SELTSER, RAYMOND,** epidemiologist, educator; b. Boston, Dec. 17, 1923; s. Israel and Hannah (Littman) S.; m. Charlotte Frances Gale, Nov. 16, 1946; children: Barry Jay, Andrew David. MD, Boston U., 1947; MPH, Johns Hopkins U., 1957. Diplomate Am. Bd. Preventive Medicine (trustee, sec.-treas. 1974-77), Am. Bd. Med. Specialties (mem. exec. com. 1976-77). Asst. chief med. info. and intelligence br. U.S. Dept. Army, 1953-56; epidemiologist divsn. internal health USPHS, 1956-57; from asst. prof. to prof. epidemiology Johns Hopkins U. Sch. Hygiene and Pub. Health, Balt., 1957-81, assoc. dean, 1967-77, dep. dir. Oncology Ctr., 1977-81; dean U. Pitts. Grad. Sch. Pub. Health, 1981-87, prof. epidemiology, 1981-88, emeritus dean, emeritus prof. epidemiology, 1988—; assoc. dir. USPHS Ctrs. for Disease Control, Rockville, Md., 1988-90; assoc. dir. Ctr. for Gen. Health Svcs. Extramural Rsch. Agy. for Health Care Policy and Rsch., Rockville, 1990-95, sr. advisor spl. population rsch. Ctr. Primary Care Rsch., 1995-98; med. and healthcare advisor Dept. Va Office Inspector Gen. Office Health Care Inspections, Chevy Chase, Md., 1997—2000. Cons. NIMH, 1958-70, also various govtl. health agys., 1958-79; expert cons. Pres.'s Commn. on Three Mile Island, 1979-80; mem. Three Mile Island Adv. Panel Health, Nat. Cancer Inst. Cancer Control Grant Rev. Com., Pa. Dept. Health Preventive Health Service Block Grant Adv. Task Force, Gov.'s VietNam Herbicide Info. Commn. Pa.; chmn. Toxic/Health Effects Adv. Com. 1982-87. Trustee, exec. com., chmn. profl. adv. com. Harmarville Rehab. Ctr., Pitts., 1982-87; bd. dirs. Health Edn. Ctr., Media Info. Svc.; chmn. USPHS Task Force on Improving Med. Criteria for SSA Disability Determination, 1988-92. Capt. AUS, 1951-53, Korea Decorated Bronze Star; recipient Centennial Alumni citation Boston U. Sch. Medicine, 1973; elected to Johns Hopkins Soc. of Scholars, 1986. Fellow AAAS, APHA (mem. governing coun. 1975-77, chmn. EPI sect. coun. 1979-80), Pa. Pub. Health Assn. (bd. dirs. 1985-88, pres.-elect 1986-88), Am. Coll. Preventive Medicine, Am. Heart Assn.; mem. Am. Epidemiol. Assn., Internat. Epidemiol. Assn., Am. Soc. Preventive Oncology, Am. Cancer Soc. (bd. dirs. Pa. divsn. 1985-87, exec. com. 1986-87), Socs. Pub. Health (sec. 1969-71, exec. com., chmn. edn. com. 1983-87), Soc. Med. Cons. Armed Forces, Soc. Epidemiologic Rsch., Nat. Coun. Radiation Protection and Measurements (consociate), Johns Hopkins Alumni Coun. (exec. com. 1994-97), Sigma Xi, Delta Omega. E-mail: rseltser@comcast.net.

**SELTZER, BARRY S.,** federal judge; b. 1954; BA magna cum laude, Hamilton Coll., 1976; MBA, JD, NYU, 1980, LLM in Taxation, 1984. Atty. Trenam, Simmons, Kemker, Scharf, Barkin, Frye & O'Neill, Tampa, Fla., 1980-82; asst. U.S. atty. So. Dist. Fla., 1984-88; judge Broward County Ct., 1988-91; magistrate judge U.S. Dist. Ct. (so. dist) Fla., Ft. Lauderdale, 1991—. Comment editor NYU Law Rev. of Law and Social Change. Recipient Spl. Achievement award Dept. Justice, plaques and commendations Drug Enforcement Agy., US Secret Svc., Bur. of Alcohol, Tobacco and Firearms, Postal Inspection Svc., US Customs Svc., USDA. Mem. ABA, Fed. Bar Assn., Fla. Bar, Broward County Bar Assn., Fed. Magistrate Judges Assn., Stephen Booher Inn of Ct. (past pres.), B'nai B'rith Justice Unit (past pres.), Beta Gamma Sigma. Office: 109 US Courthouse 299 E Broward Blvd Fort Lauderdale FL 33301-1944

**SELTZER, LEO,** cinematographer, educator; b. Montreal, Que., Can., Mar. 13, 1910; came to U.S., 1916; s. Boris and Atalia (Gerowitz) S.; m. Elaine Basil, Apr. 15, 1941 (div. 1950); children: Jeanie, John; m. Dicky Ransohoff, 1951 (div. 1963). BA, U. Mass., 1979. Faculty CCNY, 1949-54, New Sch. Social Rsch., 1949-51; pres. Leo Seltzer Assocs., Inc., N.Y.C., 1950-90; faculty Columbia U., 1954-60, Phila. Coll. Art, 1955-56, NYU, N.Y., 1966-67; dir. audio-visual therapy program pediatrics ward Univ. Hosp., N.Y.C., 1970-76; instr. film prodn. workshop Sch. Visual Arts, N.Y.C., 1969-84; adj. prof. performing and creative arts Coll. S.I., NY, 1977-78; prof. film Bklyn. Coll., 1978-83, prof. emeritus film, 1983—. Lectr. in U.S. and abroad, including Mus. Modern Art, N.Y.C., Marymount Coll., Ghent U., Belgium, Libr. Congress, others. Prodr., dir. over 60 social documentaries and TV films in 35 countries, including First Steps, UN Divsn. Social Affairs, 1946 (Acad. award for best documentary 1947), Fate of a Child, UN Divsn. Tech. Assistance, 1949, For the Living, City of N.Y., 1952, (with Walter Cronkite) Conquest of Aging, 1958, All the Years, 1959, Jacqueline Kennedy's Asian Journey, 1962, Progress Through Freedom (pres. Kennedy's visit to Mex.), 1962, (with Edward R. Murrow) The American Commitment, USIA, 1963, Report on Acupuncture, 1977, (with John Huston) Let There Be Light; prodr., dir.: Nat. Film Bd. Can., 1941, films include Air-Sea Rescue Techniques; chief cons. visual aids City of N.Y., 1941-42; prodr.: N.Y.C. Mcpl. Film and TV Unit Sta. WNYC, 1949-50; film biographer to White House for Pres. Kennedy, 1962; exec. prodr. Quadrant Comms., Inc., 1973-75 (7 citations Cannes and Edinburgh Film Festivals 1948-63); films are in U.S. Nat. Archives, Libr. of Congress, in collection and distributed by Mus. Modern Art; photographs are in Houston Mus. Fine Arts collection, Nat. Gallery Can., Visual Studies Workshop, Rochester, N.Y., N.Y.C. 5th Ave. Libr.; reconstructed 6 Am. social documentary films of 1930's in 1978 for Mus. Modern Art Film Archives, 1976-77,: edited and filmed much of original footage; subject of TV program by Bill Moyers, A Walk Through the Twentieth Century, Blackside Prodns., CBC, BBC TV; contbr. film footage to Nat. Geographic, History Channel, others. 1st lt. Signal Corps. U.S. Army; directed tng. and information films for U.S. Army and public; officer in charge of Film and Equipment Depot, ETO, 1947. Recipient Acad. award for best

documentary, 1948, Silver medals Venice Film Festival, 1949, Freedom's Found. award, 1953, Golden Reel award Scholastic Mag., 1955, Robert Flaherty award CCNY, 1956, Silver medal Atlanta Internat. Film Festival, 1977; honored in tribute Mus. Modern Art, 1990; oral history N.Y. Fifth Ave. Libr. Archives. Mem. Dirs. Guild Am. (charter). Achievements include research on Early American social documentary films. Home and Office: 368 E 69th St New York NY 10021-5706 Office Phone: 212-879-0990.

**SELTZER, RICHARD WARREN, JR.,** writer, editor, consultant; b. Clarksville, Tenn., Feb. 23, 1946; s. Richard Warren and Helen Isabella (Estes) S.; m. Barbara Ann Hartley, July 28, 1973; children: Robert, Heather, Michael, Timothy. BA, Yale U., 1969; MA in Comparative Lit., U. Mass., 1972. Editor Benwill Pub., Boston, 1973-79; sr. communications cons., Internet cons. Digital Equip. Corp., Maynard, Mass., 1979-98; ind. internet cons. and writer, 1998—. Pub. B&R Samizdat Express, Boston, 1974—. Author: Name of Hero, 1981, Lizard of Oz, 1974, Now and Then, 1976, The Alta Vista Search Revolution, 1997, Shop Online the Lazy Way, 1999, Ethiopia Through Russian Eyes, 2000, Take Charge of Your Website, 2001, Web Business Boot Camp, 2001, My Internet: A Personal View of Internet Business Opportunities; editor: Internet-on-a-Disk, 1994—, Please Copy This Disk, 1993—; author short stories. With USAR, 1969-75. Mem. Internat. Assn. Bus. Communicators, U.S. Chess Fedn. Avocations: chess, internet, russian translation. Home: PO Box 320161 West Roxbury MA 02132-0002 E-mail: seltzer@samizdat.com

**SELTZER, VICKI LYNN,** obstetrician, gynecologist; b. June 2, 1949; d. Herbert Melvin and Marian Elaine (Willinger) Seltzer; m. Richard Stephen Brach, Sept. 2, 1973; children: Jessica Lillian Brach, Eric Robert Brach. BS, Rensselaer Poly. Inst., 1969; MD, NYU, 1973. Diplomate Am. Bd. Ob-Gyn. (examiner 1988-2001). Intern Bellevue Hosp., N.Y.C., 1973—74, resident ob-gyn., 1974—77; fellow gynecol. cancer Am. Cancer Soc., N.Y.C., 1977—78, Meml. Sloan Kettering Cancer Ctr., N.Y.C., 1975—79; assoc. dir. gynecol. cancer Albert Einstein Coll. Medicine, N.Y.C., 1979—83, prof. ob-gyn., 1989—. Assoc. prof. ob-gyn SUNY, Stony Brook, 1983—89; Edie and Marvin H. Shur prof. ob-gyn and women's health Albert Einstein Coll. Medicine, N.Y.C., 2003—; dir. ob-gyn. Queens Hosp. Ctr., Jamaica, NY, 1983—93, pres. med. bd., 1986—89; chair ob-gyn L.I. Jewish Med. Ctr., 1993—; v.p. women's health svcs. North Shore-L.I. Jewish Health Sys., 1999—; chair ob-gyn North Shore U. Hosp., 1999—, chair med. bd., 2001—; mem. steering com. N.Y. State Coun. Grad. Med. Edn., 2005—, chair subcom. primary care; mem. U.S. Coun. Grad. Med. Edn., 2006—. Author: Every Woman's Guide to Breast Cancer, 1987; editor: Women's Primary Health Care, 1995, 2000; editor-in-chief: Primary Care Update for the Ob-Gyn, 1993—; mem. editl. bd. Women's Life mag., 1980—82, Jour. Jacobs Inst. Women's Health, 1990—95, Ob-Gyn. Survey, 2005—, Jour. Reproductive Medicine, 2005—, mem. internat. editl. bd. Jour. Soc. Obstetricians and Gynecologists Can., 2000—; contbr. articles to profl. jours.; host (TV series) Weekly Ob-Gyn. program, Lifetime Med. TV. Mem. Mayor Beame's Task Force on Rape, N.Y.C., 1974—76; chair health com. Nat. Coun. Women, N.Y.C., 1979—84; bd. govs. Nat. Coun. Women's Health, 1985—94; chair Coun. Resident Edn. Ob-Gyn., 1987—93. Recipient citation, Nat. Safety Coun., 1978, Achiever award, L.I. Ctr. Bus. and Profl. Women, 1987; Galloway Fund fellow, 1975. Fellow: ACOG (gynecol. practice com. 1981, v.p. 1993—94, pres.-elect 1996—97, pres. 1997—98), N.Y. Obstet. Soc. (pres. 1999—2000); mem.: Am. Hosp. Assn. (governing coun. maternal and child health 2004—), N.Y. Cancer Soc., Am. Med. Women's Assn. (com. chair 1975—79, editl. bd. jour. 1986—2002, citation 1973), Internat. Fedn. Gynecology and Obstetrics (internat. steering com. to reduce maternal mortality 2000—02), Women's Med. Assn. (v.p. N.Y. 1974—79, resident rev. com. ob-gyn 1993—98, Lila Wallis Lifetime Achievement award 2002), NYU Sch. Med. Alumni Assn. (bd. govs. 1979—, v.p. 1987—91, pres. 1992—93), Alpha Omega Alpha. Office: LI Jewish Med Ctr New Hyde Park NY 11040 Office Phone: 718-470-7660. Business E-Mail: vseltzer@lij.edu.

**SELTZER, WILLIAM,** statistician, social science administrator; b. NYC, Sept. 22, 1934; s. William B. Seltzer and Edith S. (Goldman) Alt.; m. Jane E. Berger, Nov. 20, 1970; children: Benjamin, Ezra. BA, U. Chgo., 1956. Rsch. asst. Health Info. Found., N.Y.C., 1957-60; statistician U.S. Bur. Census, Suitland, Md., 1960-64; advisor Pakistan Inst. Devel., Econs. and Cen. Statis. Office, Karachi, 1964-68; staff assoc. Population Assn., N.Y.C., 1968-74; br. chief UN Statis. Office, N.Y.C., 1974-86, dir., 1986-94; sr. advisor to under-sec.-gen. Dept. Econ. and Social Info. and Policy Analysis, N.Y.C., 1993-94; sr. rsch. schlar Fordham U., N.Y.C., 1995—. Mem. com. on population and demography, chair panel on data collection NAS, Washington, 1977-82, mem. Roundtable on the Demography of Forced Migration, 2001-04; cons. UN Population Fund, 1995, Internat. Criminal Tribunal for Rwanda, 1996, UN Stats. Divsn., 1996-98, Internat. Labor Office, 1997, World Bank, 1997-98; mem. panel of Ind. Experts, Metagora Project Orgn. for Econ. Cooperation and Devel., 2005—. Author: Poems, 1960, Politics and Statistics, 1994; co-author: Population Growth Estimation, 1973; also various UN documents, jour. articles, reports. Fellow Am. Statis. Assn. (chair social stats. sect. 1983-84, chair com. on internat. rels. 1986-87, chair com. on profl. ethics 2000—05), Royal Statis. Soc. (hon.:); mem. Population Assn. Am., Internat. Statis. Inst., Internat. Assn. Ofcl. Statisticians. Mem. Soc. Of Friends. Office: Fordham U Dept Sociology and Anthropology 441 E Fordham Rd Bronx NY 10458-5149 Office Phone: 718-817-3868. E-mail: seltzer@fordham.edu.

**SELTZNER, RACHEL,** museum administrator, science educator; d. Gary Dennis Seltzner and Beth Ann Murray; m. Brian Wayne Meixner, Sept. 23, 2002; 1 child, Carson Annan Meixner. BS in Environ. Edn. and Interpretation, U. Wis., Stevens Point, 2001; post grad. in Natural Health, Clayton Coll. Natural Health, Birmingham, Ala., 2006—. Naturalist Peninsula State Park Wis. Dept. Natural Resources, Fish Creek, 1999, 2001; tchr. Countryside Montessori Sch., Madison, 2001—02; camp dir. Dane County Humane Soc., 2002; mus. coord. Nat. Wild Turkey Fedn., Edgefield, SC, 2002—. Mem. Ctrl. Savannah River Area Environ. Sci. Edn. Coop., Augusta, Ga., 2002—. Vol. tchr. Roots and Shoots Jane Goodall Inst., Stevens Point, 1998—2001; pres. Environ. Coun., 2000—01; coord. Moonlight Delight Festival, Edgefield, SC, 2002—05. Recipient U. Leadership award, U. Wis. Stevens Point, 2001; scholar, Wis. Rural Opportunities Found., 2000—01. Mem.: Am. Assn. Museums, S.C. Fedn. Museums, Nat. Assn. Interpretation. Achievements include development of expansion plan doubling size of Nat. Wild Turkey Fedn. Winchester museum. Avocations: backpacking, canoeing, snowshoeing, camping, travel. Office: 3829 Coyt Dr Cottage Grove WI 53527 Office Phone: 262-327-0617.

**SELVADURAI, ANTONY PATRICK SINNAPPA,** civil engineer, educator, mathematician, consultant; b. Matara, Sri-Lanka, Sept. 23, 1942; arrived in Can., 1975; s. Kanapathiyar Sinnappa and W. Mary Adeline (Fernando) S.; m. Sally Joyce; children: Emily, Paul, Mark, Elizabeth. Diploma in Engring., Brighton Poly., 1964; Diploma, Imperial Coll./London U., 1965; MS, Stanford U., 1967; PhD in Theoretical Mechanics, U. Nottingham, 1971, DSc in Theoretical Mechanics, 1986. Registered profl. engr., Can.; chartered mathematician, UK. Staff rsch. engr. Woodward Clyde Assoc., Oakland, Calif., 1966-67; rsch. assoc. dept. theoretical mechanics U. Nottingham, 1969-70; lectr. dept. civil engring. U. Aston, Birmingham, England, 1971-75; asst. prof. civil engring. Carleton U., Ottawa, Ont., Canada, 1975-76, assoc. prof., 1976-81, prof., 1982-93, chmn. dept., 1982-90, Davidson Dunton Rsch. lectr., 1987; prof., chmn. dept. civil engring./applied mechanics McGill U., Montreal, Canada, 1993-96, William Scott prof., 2004, James McGill prof., 2005. Vis. rsch. sci. Bechtel Group, Inc., San Francisco 1981-82; vis. prof. U. Nottingham, 1986, Inst. de Mécanique de Grenoble, France, 1990; cons. Atomic Energy of Can. Ltd., Pinawa, Man., 1983-96—, Ministry of Transp. Ont., Toronto, 1984-97, Fleet Tech., Ottawa, 1988—, Atomic Energy Control Bd., 1987—. Author: Elastic Analysis of Soil Foundation Interaction, 1979, (with R.O. Davis) Elasticity and Geomechanics, 1996, (with R.O. Davis) Plasticity and Geomechanics, 2002; editor: Mechanics of Structured Media, 1981, (with G.Z. Voyiadjis) Mechanics of Material Interfaces, 1986, Developments of Mechanics, 1987, (with M.M. Zaman and C.S. Desai) Recent

Accomplishments and Future Trends in Geomechanics in the 21st Century, (with M.J. Boulon) Mechanics of Geomaterial Interfaces, 1995, Mechanics of Poroelastic Media, 1996, Partial Differential Equations in Mechanics, Vol. 1, Fundamentals, Laplace's Equation, Diffusion Equation, Wave Equation, 2000, Vol. 2, The Biharmonic Equation, Poisson's Equation, 2000, (with J.M. Hill) Mathematics and Mechanics of Granular Materials, 2005. Recipient Rsch. award Alexander von Humboldt Found., 1997; King George VI Meml. fellow English Speaking Union of Commonwealth, 1965, rsch. fellow SRC, UK, 1969, Erskine fellow U. Canterbury, New Zealand, 1992, 98, Killam rsch. fellow Can. Coun. for Arts, 2000-02. Fellow Am. Acad. Mechanics, Can. Soc. Civil Engring. (Leipholz medal 1991), Assoc. Prof. Engrs. of Ont. (Engring. medal for rsch. 1993), Engring. Inst. Can., Inst. Math. and Its Applications, Can. Acad. Engring.; mem. Internat. Assn. for Computer Methods and Advances in Geomechanics (award for significant paper in the category theory computational analytical 1994, paper prize computational and analytical theory category 1997, John Booker medal 2001), Max Planck Soc. (Max Planck Rsch. prize 2003). Roman Catholic. Office: McGill U Dept Civil Engring Montreal PQ Canada H3A 2K6 E-mail: patrick.selvadurai@mcgill.ca.

**SELVER, PAUL DARRYL,** lawyer; b. NYC, May 28, 1947; s. Rene T. Selver and Marilyn (Steiner) Pomerance; m. Ellen J. Roller, Jan. 22, 1984; children: Adam, Max, Katelyn. BA magna cum laude, Harvard U., 1969, JD, 1972. Bar: N.Y. 1973. Assoc. Hale Russell & Gray, N.Y.C., 1972-74; ptnr. Brown and Wood (formerly Tufo and Zuccotti), N.Y.C. 1974-94, Battle Fowler, N.Y.C., 1994-2000, Paul Hastings Janofsky & Walker, N.Y.C., 2000—05, Kramer Levin Naftalis & Frankel LLP, N.Y.C., 2005—. Lectr. law Columbia U. Law Sch., 1994-97; assoc. adj. prof. Sch. Architecture, Planning and Preservation Columbia U., NYC, 1986-88; chmn. zoning and design com. Real Estate Bd. NY, 2000— Edit. bd. Metropolis Mag., 1983-86; author: (guide book) Real Estate: Land Use Regulations, 1986. Mem. ordinance com. Borough of Mountain Lakes Planning Bd., 2004; mem. adv. bd. Cityland, Ctr. for N.Y.C. Law at N.Y. Law Sch., 2004—. Mem.: ABA, Assn. of Bar of City of N.Y. Office: Kramer Levin Naftalis & Frankel LLP 1177 Avenue of the Americas New York NY 10036

**SELVIG, JETTIE PIERCE,** lawyer; b. Bee Branch, Ark., Dec. 16, 1932; d. Jefferson Davis Pierce and Ruba Ann Bivens; m. Rolf S. Selvig Sr., Jan. 27, 1962; children: Rolf S. Jr., Erik K., John L. LLB, U. Ark., 1954. Bar: Ark. 1953, Calif. 1961, U.S. Supreme Ct. 1969. Pvt. practice, 1961—. Bd. dir. San Francisco Neighborhood Legal Assistance Found., 1975. Named Hidden Heroine, San Francisco Bay Girl Scout Coun., 1976; recipient cert. of honor, Bd. Suprs. of City and County of San Francisco, 1969, Countess of Pulaski Proclamation, Quorum Ct. of Pulaski County, 1969, Silver Bowl of Appreciation, Girl Scouts Am. Mem.: Legal Aid Soc. San Francisco (bd. dirs. 1976), Women's Equity Action League (treas. Calif. divsn. 1970—72, pres. Calif. divsn. 1973), Calif. Applicants' Attys. Assn. (dir. No. Calif. chpt. 1974, v.p. 1975, pres. 1976, 1977, sec. and pres.-elect statewide assn., pres. statewide assn. 1981—82, Lifetime Achievement award 2005), Calif. State Bar (disciplinary com. 1972—74), Lawyer's Club San Francisco (life; del. to state bar conv.), Queen's Bench (life; asst. sec.-treas., dir. 1972, treas. 1973, Law Day com., chmn. publicity com., v.p. 1974, pres. Queen's Bench Found. 1974—76, pres. 1975, Lifetime Achievement award 1995), Nat. Assn. Women Lawyers (life; state del., assembly del., bus. mgr., treas., v.p., pres.-elect, pres. 1969—70, chairperson, mem. women in pub. svc. com. 1971—75). Democrat. Home and Office: 469 Molino Ave Mill Valley CA 94941-3380 Office Phone: 415-383-9105. Office Fax: 415-383-6605. Personal E-mail: jettiecoleen@msn.com.

**SELVY, BARBARA,** dance instructor; b. Little Rock, Jan. 20, 1938; d. James Oliver and Irene Balmat Banks; m. Franklin Delano Selvy, Apr. 15, 1959; children: Lisa Selvy Yeargin, Valerie Selvy Miros, Lauren Kroll, Franklin Michael, Madison Banks Selvy. Student, U. Calif. Ark., 1955—57. Founder, dir. Carolina Ballet Theater, Greenville, SC, 1973—; pres. Dance Arts Inc. and Incentives, Inc. Mem. adv. bd. dirs. Met. Arts Coun., and S.C. Govs. Sch., St. Marys Cath. Sch. Appeared in numerous TV commls., on Goodson-Toddman game show Play Your Hunch, 1958-59; toured Far East with TV show Hit Parade, 1958; named Miss Ark., 1956, Mrs. S.C., 1981; dir. and staged Mrs. Va., Mrs. N.C., Mrs. S.C. pageants; choreographed Little Theater prodns., Furman U. Opera. Mem. Nat. Rep. Congl. Com., 2003, Pres. Bush Small Bus. Adv. Coun., 2003. Mem. So. Assn. Dance Masters (ballet adviser, regional dir.), Dance Educators Am., Dance Masters of Am., Profl. Dance Tchrs. Home: 18 Oglethorpe Lane Hilton Head Island SC 29926

**SELWYN, DONALD,** engineering administrator, researcher, inventor, educator; b. NYC, Jan. 31, 1936; s. Gerald Selwyn and Ethel (Waxman) Selwyn) Moss; m. Delia Nemec, Mar. 11, 1956 (div. Mar. 1983); children: Laurie, Gerald, Marcia; m. Myra Rowman Markoff, Mar. 17, 1986 BA, Thomas A. Edison Coll. N.J., 1977. Svc. engr. Bendix Aviation, Teterboro, NJ, 1956-59; svc. mgr. Bogue Electric Mfg. Co., Paterson, NJ, 1959; proposal engr. advanced design group Curtiss-Wright Corp., East Paterson, NJ, 1960-64; ind. bioengr., rehab. engring. cons. N.Y.C., 1964-67; pres. bd. trustees, exec. tech. and tng. dir. Nat. Inst. for Rehab. Engring., Hewitt, NJ, 1967—. Cons. N.Y. State Office Vocat. Rehab., 1964—, Pres.'s Com. on Employment of Handicapped, 1966—; bus. and industry and for Am. with Disabilities Act compliance, also numerous state rehab. agys., health depts., vol. groups, agys. for handicapped in fgn. countries; cons., trainer computer applications. Contbr. articles on amateur radio, rehab. of severely and totally disabled to profl., gen. mags. Trustee Nat. Inst. for Rehab. Engring., Rehab. Research Center Trust. Decorated Knight of Malta; recipient Humanitarian award U.S. Ho. of Reps., 1972, Bicentennial Pub. Service award, 1975. Mem. Am. Acad. Consultants, I.E.E.E. (sr.), Soc. Tech. Writers and Pubs. (sr.), Nat. Rehab. Assn., N.Y. Acad. Scis., Mensa. Achievements include being the developer or co-developer field-expander glasses for hemianopsia, tunnel and monocular vision, electronic speech clarifiers, electronically guided wheelchairs, off-road vehicles and cars for quadriplegics, others; patentee indsl., mil. and handicapped rehab. inventions; expert, cons. on handicapped employment, handicapped product safety including design, manufacture, labelling and user instrnl. material, 1990—. Office: Nat Inst Rehab Engring PO Box T Hewitt NJ 07421-1020 Office Phone: 973-853-6585, 800-736-2216. Personal E-mail: dons@warwick.net. Business E-Mail: dons@theoffice.net. *As I travel the road of life, it becomes more and more evident to me that people matter most, and technology is useful and good only so long as it serves man, and man is not made to serve technology. From technician I have evolved to humanist, using technology only as a tool. Always think positive. Don't waste your time or emotional energy on people who do not appreciate your good will. Think only about those who do, and you'll achieve more and enjoy life.*

**SELYA, BRUCE MARSHALL,** federal judge; b. Providence, May 27, 1934; s. Herman C. and Betty (Brier) S.; children: Dawn Meredith Selya Sherman, Lori Ann BA magna cum laude, Harvard U., 1955, JD magna cum laude, 1958. Bar: D.C. 1958, R.I. 1960. Law clk. U.S. Dist. Ct. R.I., Providence, 1958-60; assoc. Gunning & LaFazia, Providence, 1960-62; ptnr. Gunning, LaFazia, Gnys & Selya, Providence, 1963-74, Selya & Iannuccillo, Providence, 1974-82; judge U.S. Dist. Ct. R.I., Providence, 1982-86, U.S. Ct. Appeals (1st cir.), Providence, 1986—. Judge Lincoln Probate Ct., R.I., 1965-72; mem. R.I. Jud. Council, 1964-72, sec., 1965-70, chmn., 1971-72; mem. Gov.'s Commn. on Crime and Adminstrn. Justice, 1967-69; del. Nat. Conf. on Revisions to Fed. Appellate Practice, 1968-82; mem. various spl. govtl. comms. and adv. groups Chmn. bd. trustees Bryant Coll., Smithfield, R.I., 1986-92; bd. dirs. Lifespan Health Sys., chmn. bd. dirs., 1994—, mem. bd. trustees R.I. Hosp. subs. Recipient Louis Dembitz Brandeis medal for disting. legal svc. Brandeis U., 1988, Neil Houston award Justice Assistance of Am., 1992. Mem. ABA, FBA, Fed. Judges Assn.; R.I. Bar Assn. (chmn. various coms.), R.I. Bar Found., U.S. Jud. Conf. (mem. com. on jud. br.), Am. Arbitration Assn., Am. Judicature Soc. (bd. dirs.). Jewish. Home: 224 George St Providence RI 02906-3115 Office: US Ct Appeals US Courthouse 1 Exchange Terr Rm 316 Providence RI 02903*

**SELZ, PETER HOWARD,** art historian, educator; b. Munich, Mar. 27, 1919; arrived in US, 1936, naturalized, 1942; s. Eugene and Edith S.; m. Thalia Cheronis, June 10, 1948 (div. 1965); children: Tanya Nicole Eugenia, Diana Gabrielle Hamlin; m. Carole Schemmerling, Dec. 18, 1983 Student, Columbia U., U. Paris; MA, U. Chgo., 1949, PhD, 1954; DFA, Calif. Coll. Arts and Crafts, 1967. Instr. U. Chgo., 1951-56; asst. prof. art history, head art edn. dept. Inst. Design, Ill. Inst. Tech., Chgo., 1949-55; chmn. art dept., dir. art gallery Pomona Coll., 1955-58; curator dept. painting and sculpture exhbns. Mus. Modern Art, 1958-65; dir. univ. art mus. U. Calif., Berkeley, 1965-73, prof. history of art, 1965—; Zaks prof. Hebrew U., Jerusalem, 1976. Vis. prof. CUNY, 1987; pres.'s coun. on art and architecture Yale U., 1971-76 Author: German Expressionist Painting, 1957, New Images of Man, 1959, Art Nouveau, 1960, Mark Rothko, 1961, Fifteen Polish Painters, 1961, The Art of Jean Dubuffet, 1962, Emil Nolde, 1963, Max Beckmann, 1964, Alberto Giacometti, 1965, Directions in Kinetic Sculpture, 1966, Funk, 1967, Harold Paris, 1972, Ferdinand Holder, 1972, Sam Francis, 1975, The American Presidency in Political Cartoons, 1976, Art in Our Times, 1981, Art in a Turbulent Era, 1985, Chillida, 1986, Twelve Artists from the GDR, 1989, Max Beckmann: The Self Portraits, 1992, William Congdon, 1992, Beckmann, 1996, Gottfried Helnwein, 1997, Beyond the Mainstream, 1997; co-author: Theories and Documents of Contemporary Art, 1996, Beyond the Mainstream, 1998, Barbara Chase-Riboud, 1999, Nathan Oliviera, 2001, The Art of Engagement, 2005; editor: Art in Am., 1967—, Art Quar., 1969-75, Arts, 1981-92, Cross-Currents in Modern Art, 2000; contbr. articles to profl. jours. Trustee Am. Crafts Coun., 1985—89; mem.adv. coun. archives Am. Art, 1971—; mem. acquisitions com. Fine Arts Mus., San Francisco, 1993; pres. Berkeley Art Project, 1988—93; project dir. Christo's Running Fence, 1973—76; commr. Alameda County Art Commn., 1990—95; bd. dirs. Richmond Art Ctr., 1998—2004; chair Berkeley Arts Festival, 1997 2000; trustee Neue Galerie, New York, 2001—, Amster Kala Inst., 2004. Decorated Order of Merit Fed. Republic Germany; Fulbright grantee Paris, 1949-50; fellow Belgian-Am. Ednl. Found.; Sr. fellow NEH, 1972; resident Rockefeller Found. Study Ctr., Bellagio, 1994. Mem. Coll. Art Assn. Am. (dir. 1959-64, 67-71), AAUP, Internat. Art Critics Assn. Office: U Calif Dept Art History Berkeley CA 94720-0001 Office Phone: 510-524-5402.

**SEMAK, MICHAEL WILLIAM,** photographer, educator; b. Welland, Ont., Can., Jan. 9, 1934; s. John and Lena (Keselsky) S.; m. Annette Antoniuk, Jan. 30, 1960; children: James, Arlene. Student archtl. tech., Ryerson Poly. Inst., 1956-58. Freelance photographer Toronto-Pickering, 1961—; mem. faculty York U., Toronto, 1971—, assoc. prof. photography, 1977—. Exhibitor one-man shows, Image Gallery, NYC, 1972, Il Diaframma Canon Gallery, Milan, Italy, 1976, Enjay Gallery, Boston, 1977, Ukraina Soc., Kiev, U.S.S.R., 1980, 81, Can. Mus. Contemporary Photography, Ottawa, 2005, Mus. Contemporary Photography, Fed. Govt. Can., Ottawa, Ont., 2005; group shows, Ont. Art Gallery, 1967, Expo '67 Internat. Exhbn., Montreal, 1967, Neikrug Gallery, NYC, 1971; represented in permanent collections, Nat. Film Bd. Can., Ottawa, Nat. Gallery Can., Ottawa, Mus. Modern Art, NYC, UN, Geneva. Recipient Photo Excellence Gold medal Nat. Film Bd., 1969; recipient Excellence award Pravda newspaper, Moscow, 1970, 71, Excellence diploma Fedn. Intenationale de l'art Photographique, Switzerland, 1972 Achievements include first to be included in a speech of the federal government's member of parliament regarding photographs at solo show at The Canadian Museum of Contemporary Photography in Ottawa, 2005. Home: 1796 Spruce Hill Rd Pickering ON Canada L1V 1S4 Office: Dept Photography York U 4700 Keeles St Toronto ON Canada M3J 1P3 *I see mass contradictions around us, social realities which I believe rob us of our self-esteem and individuality. Must we continually accept and succumb to the never-ending hot baths for the mind society offers us? I wish my photography and words to disturb the complacent and the sleeper. I offer you cold showers for the mind.*

**SEMALI, LADISLAUS,** education educator; arrived in U.S., 1976; s. John K. and Martha N. Semali. MA, Stanford U., 1977; PhD, UCLA, 1991. Prof. curriculum theory, comparative and internat. edn. Pa. State U., University Park, 1992—. Author: Literacy in Multimedia America, 2000. Mem.: Internat. Visual Literacy Assn. (v.p. 1995—96, pres. 2004—05). Democrat. Roman Catholic. Office: Pa State U 257 Chambers Bldg University Park PA 16802 Office Phone: 814-865-2246. Business E-Mail: lms22@psu.edu.

**SEMANS, MARY DUKE BIDDLE TRENT,** foundation administrator; b. N.Y., Feb. 21, 1920; d. Anthony Joseph Drexel and Mary (Duke) B.; m. Josiah Trent; m. James H. Semans. Attended, Hewitt Sk., N.Y.; AB in History, Duke U.; LLD (hon.), N.C. Cen. U., 1963; HHD (hon.), Elon Coll., 1965; degree (hon.), Davidson Coll., N.C. Wesleyan Coll., 1982, U.N.C. at Chapel Hill, Duke U., 1983; LLD (hon.), Furman U., 1993. Trustee emeritus Duke U., 1961-81; chmn. The Duke Endowment, 1960-2001; various positions N.C. Sch. Arts, 1981—; former trustee Davidson Coll., N.C. Mus. Art, 1961-83, Shaw U., Converse U., Lincoln Hosp.; vice chmn. The Mary Duke Biddle Found., 1960—; chmn. Angier B. Duke Meml., Exec. Mansion Fine Arts Com., 1965—, Friends of Duke U. Library; pres. Durham Homes, Inc., 1968; mem. bd. dirs. Goodwill Industries of the Rsch. Triangle Area, 1964—, First Union Corp., 1980-82, N.C. State Library, 1958-61, Durham Pub. Library; numerous other positions. Mem. Durham City Coun., 1951-55; mayor pro-tem City of Durham, 1953-55; commencement speaker Duke U., 1983. Recipient Merit award Duke U. Health and Hosp. Adminstrn. Alumni Assn., 1989, Giannini medal for meritorious svc. to N.C. Sch. of the Arts, 1990, Alan Keith-Lucas Friend of Children award N.C. Childcare Assn., 1991, Elna Spaulding award Women-in-Action, 1993, Outstanding Philanthropist award Triangle Chpt. Nat. Soc. Fund Raising Execs., 1993, Sam Ragan award St. Andrews Coll., 1993. Mem. LWV, Bus. and Profl. Women's Club, Altrusa Club, Half Century Club, Rotary Club. Democrat. Methodist. Home: 1415 Bivins St Durham NC 27707-1519 Office: The Mary Duke Biddle Found 1044 W Forest Hills Blvd Durham NC 27707-1678*

**SEMAS, PHILIP WAYNE,** editor; b. Gilroy, Calif., Feb. 23, 1946; s. Louis Alexander and Marian (Crapper) S.; m. Robin Lucille Tuttle, Sept. 7, 1967; children: Katherine Lucille, Anna Marian, Ellis Jeremy. Student, U. Oreg., 1963-67. Editor Coll. Press Service, Washington, 1967-68; free-lance writer Berkeley, Calif., 1968-69; asst. editor Chronicle of Higher Edn. Inc., Balt. and Washington, 1969-76, 1976-78, mng. editor, 1978-88, editor, new media, 1995—2002, editor in chief Washington, 2002—; editor Chronicle of Philanthropy, Washington, 1988—95. Recipient Higher Edn. Writers award, AAUP, 1974 Mem. Am. Soc. Mag. Editors Office: Chronicle of Higher Edn 1255 23rd St NW Ste 700 Washington DC 20037-1125 Office Phone: 202-466-1000.

**SEMBLER, MELVIN F.,** former ambassador, real estate developer; b. St. Joseph, Mo., 1930; m. Betty Schlesinger; children: Steve, Brent, Greg. BS, Northwestern U., 1952. Developer shopping ctrs.; chmn. bd. The Sembler Co., St. Petersburg, Fla., 1962—; US amb. to Australia & Nauru US Dept. State, Canberra, 1989-93, US amb. to Italy Rome, 2001—05. Trustee George Bush Presdl. Libr. Found., Internat. Coun. Shopping Ctrs.; bd. dirs. Am. Momentum Bank, Am. Enterprise Inst., Am.-Australian Edn. Leadership Found., Rep. Jewish Coalition, Moffitt Cancer Ctr.; resident mem. Fla. Coun. of 100. Mem. Internat. Coun. Shopping Ctrs. (pres. 1986-87). Office Phone: 727-384-6000.

**SEMEL, GEORGE HERBERT,** plastic surgeon; b. NYC, Apr. 20, 1938; s. Louis Bennett and Sara Sonja (Eutis) S. AB, Columbia U., 1959; MD, Boston U., 1963. Diplomate Am. Bd. Plastic Surgery. Intern L.A. County Gen. Hosp., 1963-64; resident gen. surgery Long Beach (Calif.) VA Hosp., 1964-67; residency in plastic surgery Mayo Clinic, Rochester, Minn., 1967-69; chief resident plastic surgery Med. U. S.C., Charleston, 1969-70; pvt. practice L.A., 1970—; staff Midway Hosp. Founder L.A. Music City, 1978, Mus. Contemporary Art, 1980. With Calif. NG, 1964-69, USNG, 1969-73. Mem. AMA, Am. Soc. Plastic Surgery, Am. Lipoplasty Soc., L.A. Soc. Plastic Surgeons, Phi Gamma Delta. Office: 450 S Beverly Dr Beverly Hills CA 90212-4402 Office Phone: 310-274-7547. E-mail: drsemel@drsemel.com.

**SEMEL, TERRY S.,** Internet company executive; b. NYC, Feb. 24, 1943; s. Ben and Mildred S.; m. Jane Bovingdon, Aug. 24, 1977; children: Eric Scott, Courtenay Jane, Lily Bovingdon Semel, Kate Bovingdon Semel. BS in Acctg., L.I.U., 1964; postgrad. in market research, CCNY, 1966-67. Domestic sales mgr. CBS Cinema Center Films, Studio City, Calif., 1970-72; v.p., gen. mgr. Walt Disney's Buena Vista, Burbank, Calif., 1972-75; pres. W.B. Distbn. Corp., Burbank, 1975-78; exec. v.p., chief operating officer Warner Bros., Inc., Burbank, 1979-80, pres., chief operating officer, 1980-94, chmn., co-CEO, 1994-99, Warner Music Group Inc, 1995-99; chmn., CEO Yahoo! Inc., 2001—. Bd. dirs. Revlon., Polo Ralph Lauren Corp. Vice chmn. Pres.'s Com. for the Arts and Humanities; vice chair San Diego Host Com. for 1996 Rep. Nat. Conv.; bd. trustee Solomon R. Guggenheim Mus., Edn. First, Cedars Sinai Med. Ctr., Environ. Media Assn. Pioneer of the Year, 1990, Found. of Motion Pictures Pioneers. Office: Yahoo! Inc 701 First Ave Sunnyvale CA 94089*

**SEMERJIAN, HRATCH GREGORY,** federal agency administrator; b. Istanbul, Turkey, Oct. 22, 1943; came to U.S., 1966; s. Krikor and Diruhi (Semerciyan) S.; m. Sona Kohar Kurkciyan, July 12, 1969 (dec. 1983); children: Tamar, Ara; m. Ayda Karabal, Feb. 8, 1986 (div. 1994). BSME, Robert Coll., Istanbul, 1966; MSc in Engring., Brown U., 1968, PhD in Engring., 1972. Rsch. asst. div. engring. Brown U., Providence, 1966-70; lectr. chemistry U. Toronto, Ont., Can., 1971-73; rsch. engr. Pratt & Whitney Aircraft United Technologies Corp., East Hartford, Conn., 1973-77; group leader Ctr. for Chem. Tech. Nat. Bur. Standards (now Nat. Inst. Standards and Tech.), Gaithersburg, Md., 1977-87, divsn. chief Chem. Sci. and Tech. Lab., 1987-92, dir. Chem. Sci. and Tech. Lab., 1992—2003, dep. dir. Gaithersburg, 2003—, acting dir. Gaithersburg, Md. 2004—05. Organizer tech. sessions, confs. and symposiums for various profl. orgns., 1978—. Contbr. rsch. articles to profl. publs.; editor numerous conf. procs. Mem. parish coun. St. George Armenian Apostolic Ch., Hartford, Conn., 1975-77; chmn. parish coun., dir. choir St. Mary Armenian Apostolic Ch., Washington, 1977—; coach youth soccer Montgomery Soccer Inc., Rockville, Md., 1978-81; mem. Ani Armenian Choral Group, Washington, 1988—. Hagopian scholar Robert Coll., 1961-64, A.M.&F. corp. fellow, 1965, C.B. Keen fellow Brown U., 1969; recipient Silver medal Dept. Commerce, Washington, 1984, Gold medal US Dept. Commerce, Washington, 1995, Brown Engring. Alumni medal, 1997; named Fed. Engr. of Yr., NSPE, Washington, 1991. Fellow ASME; mem. AAAS, AIAA, AIChE, Am. Chem. Soc., Combustion Inst., NAE. Avocations: soccer, singing, boating. Office: Nat Inst Standards and Tech 100 Bur Dr Gaithersburg MD 20899-0001

**SEMINARA, LYNDA ANNE,** editor; b. Needham, Mass., Jan. 17, 1961; d. Donald Cecil Garaventi and Lois Ann Pichulo Garaventi; children: Daniel Joseph, Robert James. BA cum laude, U. Pa., 1985. Writer, editor, tour coord. Cultural Heritage Alliance, Phila., 1985—88; from prodn. editor to sr. ops. mgr. W.B. Saunders Co., Phila., 1988—93; self-employed editor and writer, 1993—; pres. and owner The WordShop, Cherry Hill, NJ, 1993—; sr. editor OCC N.Am., N.Y.C., 2003—. Game creator Senior Sez trivia games, 2002—. Vol. sr. citizens and children, 1996—2001; sponsor Children Internat., 2003—; music ministry, 1974—. Mem.: Internat. Scleroderma Network (sr. editor 2004—), Soc. Children's Book Writers and Illustrators. Roman Catholic. Avocations: volunteer work, writing, guitar, languages.

**SEMLIES, LORI R.,** lawyer; b. LI, NY, 1969; BA, SUNY, Albany, 1991; JD magna cum laude, Touro Coll., 1994. Bar: NY 1995, NJ 1995, US Dist. Ct. Ea. Dist. NY, US Dist. Ct. So. Dist. NY. Ptnr. Wilson, Elser, Moskowitz, Edelman & Dicker LLP, NYC. Mem.: NY State Bar Assn. Office: Wilson Elser Moskowitz Edelman & Dicker LLP 150 E 42nd St 23rd Fl New York NY 10027-5639 Office Phone: 212-490-3000 ext. 2390. Office Fax: 212-490-3038. Business E-Mail: semliesl@wemed.com.

**SEMMEL, BERNARD,** historian, educator; b. NYC, July 23, 1928; s. Samuel and Tillie (Beer) S.; m. Maxine Loraine Guse, Mar. 19, 1955; 1 child, Stuart Mill. BA, CCNY, 1947; MA, Columbia U., N.Y.C., 1951; PhD, Columbia U., 1955; postgrad., London Sch. Econs., 1959—60. With Nat. Citizens Commn. for Pub. Schs. and Coun. for Fin. Aid to Edn., N.Y.C., 1951-55; asst. prof. history Park Coll., Parkville, Mo., 1956-60; mem. faculty SUNY, Stony Brook, 1960-91, prof. history, 1964-91, chmn. dept., 1966-69; Disting. prof. Grad. Sch. CUNY, 1991-96. Vis. prof. Columbia U., 1966-67. Author: Imperialism and Social Reform, 1960, Jamaican Blood and Victorian Conscience, 1963, The Rise of Free Trade Imperialism, 1970, reprinted, 2004, The Methodist Revolution, 1973, John Stuart Mill and the Pursuit of Virtue, 1984, Liberalism and Naval Strategy, 1986, The Liberal Ideal and The Demons of Empire, 1993, George Eliot and the Politics of National Inheritance, 1994; editor: Occasional Papers of T.R. Malthus, 1963; editor, translator: Halévy's The Birth of Methodism in England, 1971; editor Jour. Brit. Studies, 1969-74, Marxism and the Science of War, 1981. Rockefeller Found. grantee, 1959-60; Am. Council Learned Socs. fellow, 1964-65; Guggenheim fellow, 1967-68, 74-75; Nat. Humanities Ctr. fellow, 1986-87 Fellow Royal Hist. Soc.; mem. Am. Hist. Assn. (profl. divsn. 1984-86), Conf. Brit. Studies, Cosmos Club, Phi Beta Kappa. Home: PO Box 1162 Stony Brook NY 11790-0749

**SEMMEL, STUART,** history professor; s. Bernard and Maxine Semmel; m. Tina Lu. AB, Harvard Coll., 1988; AM, Harvard U., 1988, PhD, 1997. Asst. dir. history and lit. Harvard U., Cambridge, Mass., 1995—98; fellow Pa. Humanities Forum, Phila., 1999—2000; vis. asst. prof. Dept. History Am. U. Washington, 2000—01; asst. prof., 2005—; fellow Nat. Humanities Ctr., 2004—05. Author: Napoleon and the British, 2004. Mem.: Am. Hist. Assn., North Am. Conf. Brit. Studies. Office: University of Delaware Dept of History Newark DE 19716 Office Phone: 302-831-0794 Personal E-mail: ssemmel@udel.edu.

**SEMMLER, CARL D.,** lawyer; b. New Bern, N.C., Feb. 2, 1958; s. Henry C. and Gene P. Semmler; m. Diane K. Kett, Aug. 25, 1990; children: Sean A., Nathan D. BA, U. N.C., Chapel Hill, 1980; JD, Wake Forest U., Winston-Salem, N.C., 1987. CLU The Am. Coll., 2001, FLMI Life Office Mgmt. Assn., Inc., 1991. Intern Friends Com. on Nat. Legislation, Washington, 1980—81; ho. parent Presbyn. Children's Home of Highlands, Wytheville, Va., 1983—84; law clk. White & Crumpler, Winston-Salem, 1986—87; asst. v.p., assoc. counsel Lincoln Fin. Group, Greensboro, NC, 1987—. Mem. electronic commerce com. Am. Coun. Life Insurers, Washington, 2003—04, mem. privacy com., 2003—. Vice chair Jefferson-Pilot Fed. Credit Union, Greensboro, 1991—98; bd. dirs. Quaker Lake Camp, Greensboro, 2001—06; chmn. admissions com. Friends Homes, Inc., Greensboro, 2002—. Mem.: ABA (licentiate). Avocations: reading, gardening. Office: Lincoln Fin Group 100 N Greene St Greensboro NC 27401 Office Phone: 336-691-3369.

**SEMON, MARK DAVID,** physicist, researcher; b. Milw., Mar. 27, 1950; s. Milton K. and Joyce Gloria (Kupper) S. Student, Imperial Coll., London, 1973-74; AB magna cum laude, Colgate U., 1971; PhD, U. Colo., 1976. Rsch. asst. Kitt Peak Nat. Obs., Tucson, 1970, Los Alamos (N.Mex.) Sci. Lab., 1974; asst. prof. physics Bates Coll., Lewiston, Maine, 1976-83, assoc. prof., 1983-88, prof. physics, 1990—. Vis. prof. physics Amherst (Mass.) Coll., 1988-90; accident reconstructionist Med. and Tech. Cons., Portland, Maine, 1986—; referee Am. Jour. Physics, 1988—, Founds. of Physics, 1989—. Asst. editor Am. Jour. Physics, 1988-90; contbr. articles to Phys. Rev., Il Nuovo Cimento, other profl. jours. Woodrow Wilson fellow, 1971; grantee NSF, 1980, Nat. Rsch. Corp., 1978. Mem. Am. Phys. Soc., Am. Acad. Forensic Scientists, Am. Assn. Physics Tchrs., Am. Coll. Forensic Examiners, Coun. Undergrad. Rsch., Soc. Woodrow Wilson Fellows. Achievements include evaluation of expectation values in Aharonov-Bohm Effect; co-authoring new equation of state for liquid/gas systems near critical point, alternative formulation of quantum electrodynamics; new interpretation of the electromagnetic vector potential, new geometric model of velocity addition in special relativity. Office: Bates Coll Dept Physics 44 Campus Ave Lewiston ME 04240-6018 Office Phone: 207-786-6324. Business E-Mail: msemon@bates.edu.

**SEMON, WARREN LLOYD,** information scientist, educator; b. Boise, Ida., Jan. 17, 1921; s. August and Viola Lorreta (Eastman) S.; m. Ruth Valerie Swift, Dec. 1, 1945; children— Warren Lloyd, Nolan David, Jonathan Richard, Sue Anne. Student, Hobart Coll., 1943-45; S.B., U. Chgo., 1944 MA, Harvard, 1949, PhD, 1954. Instr. math. Hobart Coll., 1946-47; lectr. applied math. Harvard U., Cambridge, Mass., 1956-61, asst. dir. computation lab., 1954-61; head applied math. dept. Sperry Rand Research Ctr., Sudbury, Mass., 1961-64; mgr. computation and analysis lab. Burroughs Research Ctr., Paoli, Pa., 1964-67; prof. computer sci. Syracuse (N.Y.) U., 1967-84, prof. emeritus, 1984—, dir. system and information sci., 1968-76, dean Sch. Computer and Info. Sci., 1976-84. Cons. USAF, 1957, NSA, 1957, Lockheed Electronics Corp., 1967, Monsanto Co., 1972. Contbr. profl. jours. Served to 1st lt. USAAF, 1943-46, MTO. Fellow IEEE; mem. Assn. Computing Machinery, Math. Assn., IEEE Computer Soc. (chmn. publs. com. 1972-74, bd. govs. 1973-74, editor-in-chief 1975-76), Sigma Xi. Home: 1035 Scott Drive Apt 224 Prescott AZ 86301

**SEMONIN, RICHARD GERARD,** retired state official; b. Akron, Ohio, June 25, 1930; s. Charles Julius and Catherine Cecelia (Schooley) S.; m. Lennie Stuker, Feb. 3, 1951; children: Cecelia C., Richard G. Jr. (dec.), James R., Patricia R. BS, U. Wash., 1955. With Ill. State Water Survey, Champaign, 1955-91, chief, 1986-91, chief emeritus, 1991—; co-chmn. Ill. Water Rsch. & Land Use Planning Task Force, 1992-94. Adj. prof. U. Ill., 1975-91; chmn. Ill. Low-Level Radioactive Waste Task Group, 1994-96. Contbr. chpts. to books and articles to profl. jours.; co-editor: Atmospheric Deposition, 1983. Staff sgt. USAF, 1948-52. Grantee, NSF, 1957—76, US Dept. Energy, 1965—90. Fellow: AAAS, Am. Meteorol. Soc. (councilor 1983—86); mem.: Ill. Acad. Scis., Weather Modification Assn. Nat. Weather Assn. (councilor 1978—81), Sigma Xi. Roman Catholic. Avocations: civil war, golf, fishing, genealogy. Home: 1002 Devonshire Dr Champaign IL 61821-6620 Office: Ill State Water Survey 2204 Griffith Dr Champaign IL 61820-7495 E-mail: semonin@uiuc.edu.

**SEMPLE, CECIL SNOWDON,** retired manufacturing executive; b. Assam, India, Aug. 12, 1917; arrived in U.S., 1927, naturalized, 1948; s. Fordyce B. and Anne (Munro) Semple. BA, Colgate U. 1939. Buyer R.H. Macy & Co., 1939-42, 46-48; buyer, div. supt. Montgomery Ward, 1948-50; v.p. Nachman Corp., Chgo., 1950-55; sales mgr. radio receiver dept. GE, Bridgeport, Conn., 1955-60, mktg. cons. merchandising NYC, 1966-67, gen. mgr. audio products dept., 1967-68, dep. divsn. gen. mgr. housewares divsn., 1968-69, gen. mgr. housewares divsn., 1969, v.p., 1969-71, v.p. corp. customer rels., 1971-85; v.p. Rich's Inc. Atlanta, 1960-62, sr. v.p., dir., 1962-66, ret., 1985. Trustee Peoples Bank, 1975—89, trustee emeritus. Bd. dirs. Nat. Jr. Achievements Inc., Bridgeport Area Found., 1970—91, dir. emeritus, 1991—; bd. dirs. Bridgeport Hosp., 1970—93, chmn., 1983—89, dir. emeritus 1993—; trustee Colgate U., 1970—84, vice chmn., 1978—84; trustee emeritus, past pres., bd. dirs. Alumni Corp.; chmn. So. Conn. Health Svc. Inc., 1990—93. Serrved to maj. USAAF, 1942—46. Mem.: Fairfield Country Club, Brooklawn Country Club (Fairfield, Conn.), St. Andrews Soc. State of N.Y. (chmn. bd. mgrs. 1968—70), Delta Kappa Epsilon. Home: 25 Cartright St Bridgeport CT 06604-2047

**SEMPLE, JAMES WILLIAM,** lawyer; b. Phila., Nov. 18, 1943; s. Calvin James and Marie (Robinson) S.; m. Ellen Burns, Nov. 26, 1966; children: Megan Semple Greenberg, Luke Robinson. AB, St. Josephs U., Phila., 1965; JD, Villanova U., 1974. Bar: Del. 1974, U.S. Dist. Ct. Del. 1974, D.C. 1975, U.S. Ct. Appeals (3d cir.) 1982, U.S. Tax Ct. 1996. Ptnr. Morris, James, Hitchens & Williams, Wilmington, 1983—. Lectr. numerous seminars; mediator Superior Ct. Voluntary Mediation Program. Mem.: ABA, Fedn. Defense and Corp. Counsel, Am. Bd. Trial Advs. Office: Morris James Hitchens & Williams, LLP PO Box 2306 Wilmington DE 19899-2306 E-mail: jsemple@morrisjames.com.

**SEMPLE, JANE FRANCES,** health facility director; b. Lakewood, Ohio, Feb. 14, 1951; d. Frank Joseph and Margaret Eleanor (Carpenter) Semple; m. Nick N. Morana, June 24, 1977 (div. Sept. 1981). AAB, Cuyahoga CC, Cleve., 1977; BA, Baldwin-Wallace Coll., 1980; MBA, Case Western Res. U., 1984; ND, Trinity Coll. Natural Health, 1999. Diplomate Am. Bd. Naturopaths. Adminstry. asst. DeVilbiss Co., Cleve., 1969—77; project dir. Nat. Survey Rsch. Ctr., Cleve., 1977—80; market rsch. mgr. Sherwin-Williams Co., Cleve., 1980—85; instr. Cuyahoga CC, Cleve., 1986—92, Baldwin-Wallace Coll., Berea, Ohio, 1992—93; dir. Alternative Healing Inst., 1989—. Mem. S. B. Anthony Soc. Womenspace, Cleve., 1980—88. Mem.: Coalition for Natural Health, Am. Botanic Coun., Am. Assn. Nutritional Cons., Am. Naturopathic Med. Assn. Democrat. Home: 26969 Greenbrooke Dr Olmsted Falls OH 44138 Office Phone: 440-777-2665. Personal E-mail: drjane@bright.net.

**SEMPLE, ROBERT BAYLOR, JR.,** editor, journalist; b. St. Louis, Aug. 12, 1936; s. Robert B. and Isabelle Ashby (Neer) S.; m. Susan Riker Kirk, Aug. 19, 1961 (div. Feb. 1980); children: Robert Baylor III, Elizabeth, William, Mary; m. Lisa Pulling, Jan. 10, 1981. Grad., Phillips Acad., 1954; BA, Yale U., 1959; MA, U. Calif., Berkeley, 1961. Reporter Nat. Observer, 1961-63; corr. NY Times, 1963-68, White House corr., 1968-72, dep. nat. editor, 1973-75, London bur. chief, 1975-77, fgn. editor NYC, 1977-82, op-ed page editor, 1982-88, assoc. editor editl. page, 1988—, and editl. bd. mem. Recipient Pulitzer prize for editl. writing on environ. issues, 1996; Carnegie fellow, 1959-60; Woodrow Wilson fellow, 1960-61. Mem. Century Assn. (NYC), Yale Club (NYC). Episcopalian. Office: NY Times 229 W 43rd St New York NY 10036-3913 E-mail: semple@nytimes.com.

**SEMROD, T. JOSEPH,** banker; b. Oklahoma City, Dec. 13, 1936; s. L.J. and Theda Jo (Hummel) S.; m. Janice Lee Wood, June 1, 1968 (div. 1988); children: Ronald, Catherine, Christopher, Elizabeth; m. Jaye Patricia Hewitt, May 27, 1989; 1 child, Kelsey. BA in Polit. Sci., U. Okla., 1958, LLB, 1963. Bar: Okla. 1963. With Liberty Nat. Bank, Oklahoma City, 1963-67, sr. v.p., 1969-71, exec. v.p., 1971-73, pres., 1973-81, Liberty Nat. Corp., Oklahoma City, 1976-81; chmn. bd., pres., CEO United Jersey Banks (now UJB Fin. Corp.), Princeton, N.J., 1981-96; chmn., CEO Summit Bancorp. (merged with UJB Fin. Corp.), Princeton, 1996—; chmn., bd. dirs., CEO Summit Bank, Princeton, N.J., 1981—; vice chmn. Fleet Boston Fin., 2001—; chmn. Fleet Bank, N.J., 2001—. Bd. dirs. Fed. Res. Bank N.Y., Internat. Fin. Conf., chmn., 1994. Trustee, mem. exec. com. Nat. Urban League, 1963-95; mem. bd. advisors Outward Bound, Inc., 1984-2000, Ind. Coll. Fund NJ, 1986-90; commr. Citizens Commn. on Aids, 1988-90; chmn. bd. regents Stonier Grad. Sch. Banking, Rutgers U., 1983; mem. NJ Transp. Trust Fund Authority 1985-87; chmn. The Partnership for NJ, 1999-01, trustee; chmn. banking industry US Savs. Bonds campaign, 1992-93. 1st lt. U.S. Army, 1958-60. Mem. Am. Bankers Assn., NJ Bankers Assn., NJ Bar Assn., Okla. Bar Assn., Bankers Roundtable (bd. dirs. 1995-97), Regional Plan Assn. (bd. dirs. 1989-91), Youn Pres. Orgn., Am. Running and Fitness Assn. (bd. dirs. 1983-86), NJ C. of C. (bd. dirs., chmn. 1998-99, chair prosperity NJ 1998-00, chmn. 1999-00), Drumthwacket Found. (chmn. 1990-94), Bedens Brook Club (Skillman, NJ), River Club (NYC), Jasna Polana TPC (Princeton), Coral Beach Club (Bermuda), Nassau Club, Tournament Players Club, Adirondack League Club (Old Forge, NY), The Port Royal Club (Naples, Fla.). Democrat. Roman Catholic.

**SEMTNER, EMMA MARGARETTE,** music educator; b. Shawnee, Okla. d. David Anthony Semtner and Janice Virnell Hanson. B of Music Edn., U. of Pacific, 2004. Music lectr. Brentwood Union Sch. Dist., Calif., 2004—. Mus. dir.: children's mus. The Littlest Reindeer, Brentwood Mus. Music ministry for African children Every Child Ministries, Hebron, Ind., 2005; H.S. youth leader First Bapt. Ch., Stockton, Calif., 2004—. Office: Loma Vista Elem Sch 2110 San Jose Ave Brentwood CA 94513 Personal E-mail: treblec625@hotmail.com. Business E-Mail: esemtner@brentwood.k12.ca.us.

**SEMYONOV, OLEG G.**, research scientist; b. Abakan, Siberia, Russia, Jan. 3, 1944; arrived in U.S., 1997; s. Gabriel P. and Anna G. Semyonov; m. Eugenia V. Khorochilova, Oct. 15, 1971; children: Xenia, Nick. MS, Moscow State U., 1967; PhD, Lebedev Inst. Physics, Moscow, 1981. Rsch. scientist VNIIEF, Arzamas, Russia, 1967—70, Inst. Atomic Energy, Moscow, 1970—71; sr. scientist Lebedev Inst. Physics, Moscow, 1971—97; sr. rsch. engr. Applied Laser and Fusion Tech., Hull, Que., Canada, 1999—2001; sr. rsch. scientist SUNY, Stony Brook, 2001—. Cons. ALFT, Inc., Hull, 2001; tech. transl. KAHOT, Inc., Bklyn., 1998. Contbr. articles to profl. publs. Russian Orthodox. Achievements include discovery of effect of polarization of x-ray lines of highly ionized atoms in a high-current discharge and suggested a theoretical model to explain it; microrelief and internal structure modification of solid films irradiated by pulsed x-rays; fluorescent biomedical imaging of tumors in vivo; optical powering of sensors and actuators; fluroescence sensors; patents in field. Avocations: tennis, guitar, composing. Office Phone: 631-632-1402. Business E-Mail: osemyonov@ece.sunysb.edu.

**SEN, AMARTYA KUMAR**, economist, educator; b. Santiniketan, India, Nov. 3, 1933; s. Ashutosh and Amita Sen. BA, Calcutta U., 1953, Cambridge U., Eng., 1955; PhD, 1959; DLitt (hon.), U. Sask., 1979, Visva-Bharati U., 1983, U. Essex, 1984, Georgetown U., 1989, Jødavpur U., 1990, Kalyani U., 1990, Athens U. Econs. and Bus., 1991, Williams Coll., 1991, London Guildhall U., 1991, New Sch. Social Rsch., 1992, Calcutta U., 1992, Oberlin Coll., 1993, Syracuse U., 1994, Wesleyan U., 1995, Oxford, 1996; DSc (hon.), U. Bath, 1984, U. Edinburgh, 1995; D (hon.), U. Caden, 1987, U. Caen, 1987, Louvain, 1989, U. Valencia, 1994, U. Zurich, 1994, U. Antwerp, 1995, U. Stockholm, 1996, Bard Coll., 1997, Kiel U., 1997; dottore ad honorem, U. Bologna, 1988; LLD (hon.), U. Tulane, 1990, Queen's U., 1993. Prof. econs. Jadavpur U., Calcutta, 1956-58; fellow Trinity Coll., Cambridge U., 1957-63; prof. econs. Delhi U., 1963-71, London Sch. Econs., 1971-77, Oxford (Eng.) U., 1977-80, Drummond prof. polit. economy, 1980-88; prof. econs. and philosophy Harvard U., Cambridge, Mass., 1987-98, Lamont univ. prof., 1988-98, vis. prof., 1968-69; master Trinity Coll. Cambridge U., 1998—. Vis. prof. U. Calif., Berkeley, 1964-65; Andrew D. White prof.-at-large Cornell U., Ithaca, N.Y., 1978-84; chmn. expert group role advanced skill and tech. UN, 1967; hon. fellow Trintiy Coll., Cambridge Inst. Social Studies, The Hague, Inst. Devel. Studies, U. Sussex, London Sch. Econs., U. London. Author: Choice of Techniques, 1960, Collective Choice and Social Welfare, 1970, Growth Economics, 1970, Guidelines for Project Evaluation, 1972, On Economic Inequality, 1973, Employment, Technology and Development, 1975, Poverty and Famines: An Essay on Entitlement and Deprivation, 1981, Utilitarianism and Beyond, 1982, Choice, Welfare and Measurement, 1982, Resources, Values and Development, 1984, Commodities and Capabilities, 1985, On Ethics and Economics, 9187, The Standard of Living, 1987, Hunger and Public Action, 1989, The Political Economy of Hunger, 1990, Inequality Reexamined, 1992, Quality of Life, 1993, India: Economic Development and Social Opportunity, 1995, Indian Development: Selected Regional Perspectives, 1997, On Economic Inequality, 1997; contbr. articles to profl. jours. Recipient Adam Smith Prize, Cambridge U., 1954, Stevenson Prize, 1956, Mahalanobis award, 1976, Rank E. Seidman Disting. award in Polit. Economy, 1986, Agnelli Internat. prize, 1990, Alan Shawn Feinstein World Hunger award, 1990, Jean Mayer Global Citizenship award, 1993, Indira Gandhi Gold Medal award, Asiatic Soc., 1994, Edinburgh Medal, 1997, 9th Catalonia Internat. prize, 1997, Nobel prize in econ. scis., 1998; co-recipient Wassily Leontief prize for advancing frontiers econ. thought Tufts Global Inst. for Environ. and Devel., 2000; grantee Wrenbury Scholarship, Cambridge U., 1956. Fellow Brit. Acad., Econometric Soc. (past pres.); mem. AAAS (fgn. hon.), Am. Econ. Assn. (past pres.), Indian Econ. Assn. (past pres.), Royal Econ. Soc. (v.p.), Indian Econometric Conf., Devel. Studies Assn. (past pres.), Internat. Econ. Assn. (pres. 1986-89, hon. pres.), Accademia Nazionale dei Lincei, Am. Philosophical Assn. Office: Lamont U Prof Dept Econs Harvard U Cambridge MA 02138*

**SEN, ANJAN ANANDA**, physicist, researcher; b. Calcutta, West Bengal, India, May 17, 1971; s. Asokananda and Subhra Sen; m. Somasri Sen; 1 child, Aryaman. PhD, Jadavpur U., Calcutta, 1994—99; Diploma in Network Computing, NIIT, India, 1998. Rsch. assoc. Harish Chandra Rsch. Inst., Allahabad, India, 1999—2001; post doctoral fellowship Inst. Superior Tecnico, Lisbon, Portugal, 2001—04; rsch. assoc. Vanderbilt U., Nashville, 2004—. Contbr. articles to profl. jours. Mem.: Indian Assn. Gen. Relativity & Gravitation (life). Home: 7439 Hwy 70 S Apt 230 Nashville TN 37221 Office: Dept Physics & Astronomy Vanderbilt Univ Nashville TN 37235 Business E-Mail: anjan.sen@vanderbilt.edu.

**SENATOR, RONALD PAUL**, composer, writer, retired music educator; b. London, Apr. 17, 1926; arrived in US, 1981; m. Dita Branicky (dec.); m. Miriam Brickman, Aug. 15, 1986. BMus, Caford U., England, 1949; PhD, London U., England, 1950. Sr. lectr. London U., 1958—75; profl. Guildhall Sch. Music, London, 1976—82; vis. prof. MIT, USC, 1980—85; ret., 1985. Composer: Holocaust Requiem, 1986; author: Gaia of Music, 1980, Requiem Letters, 1988. Nominee Pulitzer Prize, 1991; recipient Rsch. Program award, Social Sci. Rsch. Coun., 1970—76. Mem.: ASCAP, Montserrat Sacred Music Assn. (founding mem.). Home: 81 Hillcrest Ave Yonkers NY 10705-1509 Office Phone: 914-476-1962. E-mail: ronaldsenator@hotmail.com.

**SENCHUK, DENNIS M.**, philosopher, educator; b. Chgo., Oct. 14, 1945; s. Michael and Loretta Senchuk; m. Karen Hanson, Aug. 22, 1970; children: Chloë Miranda, Tia Elizabeth. BA in Philosophy, U. Ill., Chgo., 1967; PhD in Philosophy, U. Minn., 1973; postgrad., Harvard U., 1975—76. Provisional elem. tchr. Chgo. Bd. Edn., 1966—67; psychiat. social worker Chgo. State Hosp., 1967; lectr. Northeastern U., Boston, 1971—75; asst. of continuing edn. Boston State U., 1975; tchg. asst. Harvard Grad. Sch. Edn., Cambridge, Mass., 1975; rsch. asst. Harvard Project Zero, Cambridge, 1975—76; assoc. prof. philosophy Ind. U., Bloomington, 1976—, adj. prof. edn. and Am. studies, 1976—. Mem. sci. com. Cognitio: Revista De Filosofia, Sao Paulo, Brazil, 2001—03. Editor: (other) Philosophical Studies in Education, 1981—83; author: Against Instinct: From Biology to Philosophical Psychology, 1991; contbr. articles to profl. jours. Grantee, NSF, 1979. Mem.: Ohio Valley Philosophy Edn. Soc. (pres. 1985), Ind. Philos. Assn. (pres. 1999—2000), Radical Philosophy Assn. (ctrl. divsn. pres. 1988—89, chair program com. ctrl. divsn. 1988—2003). Home: 3678 Sterling Ave Bloomington IN 47401 Office: Ind Univ Philosophy Dept 1033 E 3rd St Bloomington IN 47405 Office Phone: 812-855-3106. E-mail: senchuk@indiana.edu.

**SENDAK, MAURICE BERNARD**, writer, illustrator; b. Bklyn., June 10, 1928; s. Philip and Sadie (Schindler) S. Student, Art Students League, NYC, 1949-51; LHD, Boston U., 1977; degree (hon.), U. So. Miss., 1981, Keene State Coll., 1986. Window display artist Timely Svc., N.Y.C., 1946; display artist FAO Schwartz, N.Y.C., 1948-51; co-founder, artistic dir. The Night Kitchen, 1990—. One-man shows include Gallery Sch. Visual Arts, N.Y.C., 1964, Rosenbach Found., Phila., 1970, 75, Trinity Coll., 1972, Galerie Daniel Keel, Zurich, 1974, Ashmolean Mus., Oxford, 1975, Am. Cultural Center, Paris, 1978, Pierpont Morgan Library, N.Y.C., 1981; author, illustrator: Kenny's Window, 1956 (Spring Book Fesitval honor book 1956), Very Far Away, 1957, The Acrobat, 1959, The Sign on Rosie's Door, 1960, The Nutshell Library (contains Chicken Soup with Rice, One Was Johnny, Alligators All Around, Pierre: A Cautionary Tale), 1962, Where The Wild Things Are, 1963 (N.Y. Times Best Illustrated Book award 1963, Caldecott medal 1964, Lewis Carroll Shelf award 1964, Internat. Bd. on Books for Young People award 1966, Art Books for Children award 1973, 74, 75, Best Young Picture Books award Redbook Mag. 1984, Children's Choice award 1985), Hector Protector and As I Went Over the Water: Two Nursery Rhymes, 1965, Higglety, Pigglety, Pop!; or, There Must Be More to Life, 1967 (Am. Book award nomination 1980), In the Night Kitchen, 1970 (N.Y. Times Best Illustrated Book award 1970, Caldecott medal nomination 1971, Art Books for Children award 1973, 74, 75, Redbook Mag. award 1985), Ten Little Rabbits: A Counting Book with Mino the Magician, 1970, Pictures by Maurice Sendak, 1971, Maurice Sendak's Really Rosie, 1975, Some Swell Pup; or, Are You Sure You Want A Dog, 1976, Seven Little Monsters, 1977, Outside Over There, 1981 (N.Y. Times Best Illustrated Book

award 1981, Boston Globe/Horn Book award 1981, Caldecott medal nomination 1982, Am. Book award 1982), We Are All in the Dumps with Jack and Guy, 1993, Tsippi, 1994, Moishe, 1994, Max, 1994; illustrator: Atomics for the Millions, 1947, Good Shabbos, Everybody!, 1951, The Wonderful Farm, 1951, A Hole is to Dig, 1952 (N.Y. Times Best Illustrated Book award 1952), Maggie Rose: Her Birthday Christmas, 1952, The Giant Story, 1953, Hurry Home Candy, 1953, Shadrach, 1953, A Very Special House, 1953 (Caldecott medal nomination 1954), I'll Be You and You Be Me, 1954 (N.Y. Times Best Illustrated Book award 1954), Happy Hanukkah, Everybody, 1954, The Tin Fiddle, 1954, Magic Pictures, 1954, Mrs. Piggle-Wiggle's Farm, 1954, The Wheel on the School, 1954, Charlotte and the White Horse, 1955, The Little Cow and the Turtle, 1955, Singing Family of the Cumberlands, 1955, What Can You Do With a Shoe?, 1955, Happy Rain, 1956, The House of Sixty Fathers, 1956, I Want to Paint My Bathroom Blue, 1956 (N.Y. Times Best Illustrated Book award 1956), Birthday Party, 1957 (N.Y. Times Best Illustrated Book award 1957), Circus Girl, 1957, You Can't Get There From Here, 1957, Little Bear, 1957, Along Came a Dog, 1958, No Fighting, No Biting!, 1958, Somebody Else's Nut Tree, 1958, What Do You Say, Dear?, 1958 (N.Y. Times Best Illustrated Book award 1958, Caldecott medal nomination 1959), The Moon Jumpers, 1959 (Caldecott medal nomination 1960), Father Bear Comes Home, 1959 (N.Y. Times Best Illustrated Book award 1959), Seven Tales, 1959, Dwarf Long-Nose, 1960, Little Bear's Friend, 1960, Open House for Butterflies, 1960 (N.Y. Times Best Illustrated Book award 1960), Let's Be Enemies, 1961, The Tale of Gockel, Hinkel and Gackeliah, 1961, What Do You Do, Dear?, 1961, Little Bear's Visit, 1961 (Caldecott medal nomination 1962), Schoolmaster Whackwell's Wonderful Sons, 1962, Mr. Rabbit and the Lovely Present, 1962 (Caldecott medal nomination 1963), The Singing Hill, 1962 (N.Y. Times Best Illustrated Book award 1962), Nikolenka's Childhood, 1963, She Loves Me, She Loves Me Not, 1963, The Bat-Poet, 1964 (N.Y. Times Best Illustrated Book award 1964), How Little Lori Visited Times Square, 1964, Pleasant Fieldmouse, 1964, Lullabies and Night Songs, 1965, The Animal Family, 1965 (N.Y. Times Best Illustrated Book award 1965), Zlateh the Goat, 1966 (N.Y. Times Best Illustrated Book award 1966), The Golden Key, 1967, Poems from William Blake's Songs of Innocence, 1967, The Big Green Book, 1968, Griffin and the Minor Canon, 1968, A Kiss for Little Bear, 1968 (N.Y. Times Best Illustrated Book award 1968), The Light Princess, 1969 (N.Y. Times Best Illustrated Book award 1969), The Bee-Man of Orn, 1971, Sarah's Room, 1971, The Juniper Tree and Other Tales from Grimm, 1973 (N.Y. Times Best Illustrated Book award 1973), Fortunia: A Tale by Mme. D'Aulnoy, 1974, Fly by Night, 1976 (N.Y. Times Best Illustrated Book award 1976), King Grisly-Beard: A Tale from the Brothers Grimm, 1978, The Nutcracker, 1984 (N.Y. Times Best Illustrated Book award 1984), In Grandpa's House, 1985, The Children's Books of Randall Jarrell, 1988, Dear Mili: An Old Tale by Wilhelm Grimm, 1988, I Saw Esau, 1992, The Ubiquitous Pig, 1992; author: Fantasy Sketches, 1970, Collection of Books, Posters, and Original Drawings, 1984, The Love for Three Oranges: The Glyndebourne Version, 1984, Posters, 1986, Caldecott & Co.: Notes on Books and Pictures, 1988, Maurice Sendak Book and Poster Package: Wild Things, 1991, Bears, 2005 (Publishers Weekly children's picture book bestseller list); editor: Maxfield Parrish Poster Book, 1974, The Disney Poster Book, 1977; contbr.: The Publishing Archive of Lothar Meggendorfer, 1975, Babar's Anniversary Album, 1981, Masterworks of Children's Literature, Vol. 7, 1984, Victorian Color Picture Books, 1985, Winsor McCay: His Life and Art, 1987, Mickey Mouse Movie Stories, 1988; dir., lyricist: Really Rosie, 1975; lyricist, set designer: Really Rosie, 1978; lyricist, set designer, costume designer: Where the Wild Things Are, 1980, Higglety, Pigglety, Pop!, 1984; set designer, costume designer: The Magic Flute, 1980, The Cunning Little Vixen, 1981, Love for Three Oranges, 1982, The Goose of Cairo, 1984, Idomeneo, 1988, L'Enfant et les Sortileges, 1989, L'Heure Espagnol, 1989, It's Alive!, 1994, So, Sue Me, 1994; photographer: The Cunning Little Vixen, 1985; set designer: The Nutcracker, 1983, Hansel and Gretel, 1998, Brundibar, 2004; designer: (film) The Nutcracker, 1986. Recipient Chandler Book Talk Reward of Merit, 1967, Hans Christian Andersen Internat. medal, 1970, Laura Ingalls Wilder award Assn. Libr. Svc. to Children, 1983, Nat. Medal Arts, 1997, Lindgren award, 2003, Pell Lifetime Achievement award, 2003, Lifetime Achievement award Child mag., 2004. Office: Harper Collins Childrens Divsn 1350 Ave of the Americas New York NY 10019

**SENDAX, VICTOR IRVEN**, dentist, educator, dental implant researcher; b. NYC, Sept. 14, 1930; s. Maurice and Molly R. S.; m. Deborah deLand Cobb, Dec. 17, 1969 (div. June 1976); 1 child, Jennifer Reiland; m. Marcia Ayer Pearson, Dec. 13, 1986; children: Anneliese Chase, Cordelia Ayer. Grad., Tanglewood Music Ctr., 1953; BA, NYU, 1951, DDS, 1955; postgrad., Harvard U. Sch. Dental Medicine, Cambridge, Mass., 1969-72. Diplomate Am. Bd. Oral Implantology/Implant Dentistry (pres. 1996, dir.). Commr. N.Y. State Dental Svc. Corp., 1969-73; pres., dir. BioDental Rsch. Found., Inc., N.Y.C., 1975—; pres. Victor I. Sendax, D.D.S., P.C., N.Y.C., 1972—, Sendax Mini Dental Implant Ctrs. Mgmt., Inc., 1985—; assoc. attending implantologist mini-dental implant program St. Lukes-Roosevelt Hosp., N.Y.C., 1979—. Adj. assoc. prof. implant prosthodontics Columbia U. Sch. Dental and Oral Surgery, N.Y.C., 1974-92; vis. lectr. dept. implant dentistry NYU Coll. Dentistry; faculty N.Y. County Dental Soc. Sch. for Continuing Dental Edn.; mem. dental implant rsch. programs adv. com. Nat. Inst. Dental Rsch., HHS; cons. Julliard Sch. Voice and Drama, N.Y.C., 1972—, Vocal Dynamics Lab. Dept. Otolaryngology, Lenox Hill Hosp., N.Y.C., 1970-90; founder Sendax Seminars; 1st dir. implant prosthodontics resident program Columbia U. Sch. Dental and Oral Surgery and Columbia Presbyn. Hosp. Editor: Dental Clinics of North America: HA-Coated Dental Implants, 1992; mem. editl. bd. Oral Implantology, 1979-98; patentee in mini-implants, oral implant magnetics, implant abutments and sinus graft implant stabilizers; co-developer IMTEC/SENDAX mini-dental implant system. Bd. dirs. City Ctr. Music and Drama, Inc. divsn. Lincoln Ctr. Performing Arts, N.Y.C., 1966-75; mem. adv. bd. Amagansett (N.Y.) Hist. Assn., 1969-89; trustee Leukemia Soc. Am., N.Y.C., 1967; bd. dirs. Schola Cantorum, 1980-90, Soc. Asian Music, 1965-76. Capt. Dental Corps USAF, 1955-57. Recipient Cert. of Honor, Brit. Dental Implant Assn., 1988., Aaron Gershkoff Meml. award for Outstanding Contbns. and Dedication to Oral Implantology Am. Acad. of Implant Dentistry, 1996. Fellow: Royal Soc. Medicine Gt. Britain, Am. Acad. Implant Dentistry (nat. pres. 1981), Internat. Coll. Dentists, Am. Coll. Dentists; mem.: ADA (ho. of dels. 1969), Japan Soc., N.Y. Acad. Scis., Internat. Assn. Dental Rsch., Am. Dental Rsch. (implant group), Fedn. Dentaire Internat., Am. Analgesia Soc., Acad. of Osseointegration, Am. Dental Edn. Assn. (former chmn. spl. interest group on dental implant edn.), Century Assn. Home: 70 E 77th St Apt 6A New York NY 10021-1811 Office: Mini Dental Implant Ctr 30 Central Park S Ste 14B New York NY 10019-1628 Office Phone: 212-753-2775. Business E-Mail: vis@sendax-minidentimpl.com. *I stand in awe of mankinds' eternal need to innovate and push back the frontiers of knowledge, while tempering the harsher realities of existence with a perspective born of our cultural heritage.*

**SENDER, ADAM D.**, investment company executive, art collector; Gen. ptnr. Exis Capital Mgmt., N.Y.C., 1998—. Named one of Top 200 Collectors, ARTnews Mag., 2004, 2005, 2006. Avocation: Collector of Contemporary Art. Office: Exis Capital Management 29th Fl 875 Third Ave New York NY 10022*

**SENDERLING, JON TOWNSEND**, journalist, public relations executive, consultant; b. Phila. s. John Chester and Elizabeth (Nogle) S.; m. Elizabeth Marie Broadbent, Mar. 27, 1965; children: Jon, Tracy. Student, Ursinus Coll., 1960, Temple U., 1961-64; student (fellow), Stanford U., 1970. Reporter Bucks County Courier Times, Levittown, Pa., 1966-68, Wilmington (Del.) News-Jour., 1968-70; reporter, mag. writer, columnist, spl. projects editor Trenton (N.J.) Times, 1970-76; gen. assignments editor, state editor, nat.-fgn. editor Dallas Times Herald, 1976-80, editorial page dir., 1981-86; dep. fgn. editor Newsday, Melville, L.I., NY, 1987-89; pub. affairs mgr. EDS Corp., Dallas, 1989-97, mgr. corp. message strategy, 1997-99; pub. affairs mgr. LandSafe, Plano, Tex., 2000-01; exec. dir. news and info. U. Tex. at Dallas, Richardson, 2001—. Author: play The Trashman, 1970. Recipient disting.

service award for editorial writing Sigma Delta Chi, 1982, also 16 awards state press assns. Office: U Tex Dallas PO Box 830688 MS: AD38 Richardson TX 75093-0688 Business E-Mail: jsender@utdallas.edu. E-mail: jon.senderling@verizon.net.

**SENDO, TAKESHI**, mechanical engineering educator, researcher, writer; b. Ena City, Japan, Aug. 5, 1917; s. Shigeyoshi and Michie (Yamamoto) S.; m. Hide Okamoto, Apr. 16, 1945; children: Mitsuyoshi, Sachiko, Kazuyasu. B of Engring., Tokyo U., 1941. Prof. mech. engring. Meijo U., Nagoya City, Japan, 1959-90, hon. prof., 1990—. Curator libr. Meijo U., Nagoya City, 1975-80. Author: Treatise of High Speed Deformation of Metal, 1993, 2nd edit., 1994, Experiment: Behavior of Al Column by Drop Hammer Test, 1959-90; contbr. over 60 articles to profl. jours. Mem. cmty. activity com. Local Self-Governing Orgn., Moriyama City, Japan, 1990, 91. Served to lt. comdr. Japanese Navy, 1941-45. Fellow Japan Soc. Mech. Engring., Japan Soc. Precision Engring. Avocations: composing haiku and tanka, trying essay, jogging. Home: 21-8 Choei Moriyama-ku Nagoya 463 Japan

**SENECHAL, ALICE R.**, federal magistrate judge, lawyer; b. Rugby, N.D., June 25, 1955; d. Marvin William and Dora Emma (Erdman) S. BS, N.D. State U., 1977; JD, U. Minn., 1984. Bar: Minn. 1984, U.S. Dist. Ct. Minn. 1984, N.D. 1986, U.S. Ct. Appeals (8th cir.) 1987. Law clk. U.S. Dist. Judge Bruce M. Van Sickle, Bismarck, ND, 1984-86; with Robert Vogel Law Office, Grand Forks, ND, 1986—. U.S. magistrate judge, 1990—.

**SENEKER, CARL JAMES, II, (KIM SENEKER)**, lawyer; b. San Jose, Calif., Oct. 12, 1942; s. Carl James and Beth D. (Hearn) S.; m. Julie Marie Pardee, June 17, 1967; children: Mark Gwynn, Todd Christian. AB, Stanford U., 1964; JD, U. Calif., Berkeley, 1967. Bar: Calif. 1969, U.S. Dist. Ct. (no. dist.) Calif. 1973. Law clk. to Hon. William O. Douglas U.S. Supreme Ct., Washington, 1967-68; ptnr. Morrison & Foerster, San Francisco, 1971-84, 96—, LA, 1984—96. Adj. prof. law, lectr. law sch. Stanford U., Palo Alto, Calif., 1982-83. Co-editor: California Real Estate Law and Practice, Vols. 12 & 13, 1983-96; contbr. articles to profl. jours. Bd. dirs. L.A. Hdqs. City Assn., 1988-93. Capt. USAF, 1968-71. Mem. Am. Coll. Real Estate Lawyers (bd. govs. 1989-97, pres.-elect 1996-97, pres. 1997-98), State Bar Calif. (real property law sect., vice-chair exec. com. 1987-90), Am. Coll. Mortgage Attys., Anglo-Am. Real Property Inst., Lambda Alpha Internat. Roman Catholic. Avocations: golf, travel, music. Office: Morrison & Foerster 425 Market St Fl 32 San Francisco CA 94105-2467 Office Phone: 415-268-6619. Office Fax: 415-268-7522. Business E-Mail: cseneker@mofo.com.

**SENER MD, STEPHEN FRANCIS**, oncologist, surgeon; b. Chgo., Jan. 30, 1950; m. Sherri Abbott, June 0, 1971; children: Matthew Charles Sener, Michael Stephen Sener. BA in Chemistry, Northwestern U., Evanston, Illinois, 1972; MD, Northwestern U., Chgo., 1977. Lic. surgeon Am. Bd. Surgery, 1983, surg. oncologist Soc. of Surg. Oncology, 1988. Asst. prof. surgery Northwestern U., Chgo., 1987—92, assoc. prof. surgery, 1992—98; prof. of surgery Northwestern U. Dept. of Surgery, 1998—; head, divsn. gen. surgery Evanston Northwestern Healthcare, 1996—2001, attending surgeon, 1984—, vice-chairman, dept. surgery, 1999—. Recipient Departmental Honors award, Northwestern U. Dept. Chemistry, 1972, Faculty Tchr. Yr., Northwestern U. Dept. Surgery, 1998. Fellow: Soc. Surg. Oncology; mem.: Midwest Surg. Assn. (mem. exec. com. 2003—), Am. Cancer Soc. (pres. 1992—94, nat. bd. dirs. 1992—, nat. pres. 2004—05, immediate past pres. 2005—, pres. 2004—05, Sr. George medal 1998), Chgo. Surg. Soc. (sec. 1999—2003), Am. Soc. Clin. Oncology, Ctrl. Surg. Assn. Achievements include first to organize and lead six surgical teams from Evanston Northwestern Healthcare on humanitarian surgical missions to Moscow State University, Latvia Cancer Inst., and Peking University. Office: Evanston Northwestern Healthcare 2650 Ridge Walgreen Bldg 2545 Evanston IL 60201 Office Phone: 847-570-1328.

**SENESE, DANIEL**, professional society administrator; Various positions, including v.p., quality Bellcore (now Telecordia Tech.), 1985—95; exec. dir. Inst. of Elec. and Electronic Engr., 1995—, acting CIO, 2003—. Office: Exec Dir & CEO IEEE 3 Park Ave 17th Fl New York NY 10016-5997

**SENFT, MASON GEORGE**, musician; b. Bklyn., Nov. 1, 1942; s. Arthur and Ann (Nagel) S. BA cum laude, Adelphi U., 1964. Pvt. practice accompanist/vocal coach, Roslyn Heights, NY, 1964—. Tchr. Adelphi U., Garden City, NY, 1964-73; dir. Nat. Scholastic Aptitude Tng. Inst., Garden City, 1966-69; musical dir. Tibbits Opera House, Coldwater, Mich., 1972-73, Canal Fulton (Ohio) Playhouse, 1974-84, Island Lyric Opera, Garden City, 1980—, A Small Co. in America, Glen Cove, NY, 1984—; cons. Island Chamber Symphony Orch., Glen Head, NY 1985—, Nat. Grand Opera, Tilles Ctr., Greenvale, NY, 1988—, PBS TV spl. Christmas with Flicka, 1988, Dark Summer debut by Christine Berl, Lincoln Ctr. Chamber Soc., Alice Tully Hall, NY, 1989, Glimmerglass Opera, 1992—; accompanist to Frederica von Stade 350th Convocation Celebration, Harvard U., Cambridge, Mass., 1986; accompanist ARC benefit concert In Concert, Carnegie Hall, 1989, Met. Opera Gala, NYC, 1994; music coach The Aspern Papers, Dallas Opera, debut 1988; cons. NY Virtuoso Chamber Symphony, 1989—; music coach DiCapo Opera Co., 1975—; accompanist concert in honor of Queen Margrethe II of Sweden, The White House, 1991, hist. gala concert at Steinway Hall, NY, 1991, gala concert for Met. Opera Four Seasons Hotel, 1993. Author: Chimera, 1997, Elusive Thought, 1998, Windows, 1998; orchestrator: (films) Liberty Heights, 1998; prodr.: (CD) A Memorial Tribute-To the Fallen Heroes of September 11, 2001, Three Tenors-Home for the Holidays, 2004; musician (with violinist Jeremy Cushman): (TV broadcast) Madison Sq. Garden, N.Y.C., 2003. Apptd. to the Rep. Presdl. Ta*k Force, 2001. Recipient citation for lifetime achievement N.Y. State Assembly, 1994. Mem. Musicians Union Local 802, L.I. Singers Soc. (accompanist 1985-96), Mensa. Avocations: travel, writing, metaphysics. Home: 18 Osborne Ln Greenvale NY 11548 Personal E-Mail: msenft@optonline.net.

**SENG, COLEEN JOY**, mayor; b. Council Bluffs, Iowa, Feb. 8, 1936; d. Otis A. and Helen V. (Anderson) McElwain; m. Darrel E. Seng, Oct. 22, 1960 (dec. 1993); children: Marcee Lee, Christopher Charles, Phillip Scott. BA, Nebr. Wesleyan U., 1958. Dist. dir. Girl Scouts U.S.A., Saginaw, Mich., 1958-60, Lincoln, Nebr., 1960-62; cmty. ministry 1st United Meth. Ch., Lincoln, 1977-97; mem. Lincoln City Coun., 1987—2003; mayor City of Lincoln, 2003—. Mem. Mayor's first multi-cultural task force, co-chair of Gov. Nelson's urban adv. team, chmn. railroad transp. safety dist. Lincoln/Lancaster county joint budget com., mem. Lincoln/Lancaster county homeless coalition; active U. Place Cmty. Orgn. N.E. Family Resource Ctr.; past chair Lincoln/Lancaster county family resource ctr. bd.; past pres. Lincoln Fellowship of Chs.; mem. Lincoln Interfaith Coun.; mem Lincoln Urban Ministries com.; past pres. Homestead Girl Scouts Coun. Democrat. United Methodist. Avocations: reading, movies, gardening. Home: 6101 Walker Ave Lincoln NE 68507-2467 Office: County City Bldg 555 S 10th St Lincoln NE 68508-2810 Office Phone: 402-441-7511.

**SENGER, JEFFREY M.**, lawyer; b. 1962; AB magna cum laude, Harvard U., JD cum laude. Law clerk for Hon. Earl B. Gilliam U.S. Dist. Ct., So. Dist. Calif.; dir. training civil and appellate dept. lawyers U.S. Dept. Justice; sr. trial atty.; spl. asst. U.S. atty. U.S. Dept. Justice, asst. U.S. atty., sr. coun. Office Dispute Resolution. Fed. mediator U.S. Dist. Ct.; civil, family, and criminal misdemeanor mediator Superior Ct., Washington, DC; arbitrator Better Bus. Bur., DC Bar Assn.; tchr. negotiations Harvard Law Sch.; tchr. trial techniques Nat. Inst. Trial Advocacy, Harvard Law Sch. Author: Federal Dispute Resolution: Using ADR with the United States Government; contbr. articles to law jours. Office: US Dept Justice 950 Pennsylvania Ave NW Washington DC 20530-0001

**SENGERS, JOHANNA M. H. LEVELT**, physicist; b. Amsterdam, The Netherlands, Mar. 4, 1929; married, 1963; 4 children. Drs, U. Amsterdam, 1954, PhD in Physics, 1958; PhD (hon.), Delft U. Tech., 1992. Rsch. assoc. U. Amsterdam, Van der Waals Lab, 1954-58, 59-63, U. Wis., Inst. Theoretical

Chemistry, Madison, 1958-59; physicist heat divsn. Inst. Basic Stds., Nat. Bur. Stds., Gaithersburg, Md., 1963-78; group leader thermophysics divsn. Nat. Engring. Lab., 1978-87; sr. fellow thermophysics divsn. Nat. Inst. Standards and Tech., 1983-95, fellow emeritus, 1995—. Lectr Cath. U., Louvain, Belgium, 1971; rsch. assoc. Inst. Theoretical Physics, U. Amsterdam, 1974—75; regent's prof. chemistry U. Calif., LA, 1982. Chair working group A Internat. Assn. Properties Steam, 1985-90; pres. Internat. Assn. Properties Water and Steam, 1991-92. Recipient Silver medal U.S. Dept. Commerce, 1972, Gold medal, 1978, Wise award Interagy. Com. Women in Sci. and Engring., 1985, Alexander von Humboldt Rsch. award Alexander von Humboldt-Stiftung, Bonn, Germany, 1991, L'Oreal-UNESCO Women in Sci. award, 2003. Fellow: AAAS, ASME, Am. Phys. Soc., Internat. Assn. Properties Water and Steam (hon.); mem.: AIChE, Assn. Women in Sci., Royal Holland Soc. of Scis. and Humanities, Dutch Phys. Soc., Netherlands Royal Acad. Arts and Sci. (corr.), European Phys. Soc., Nat. Acad. Engring., Nat. Acad. Sci., Cosmos Club. Office: Phys & Chem Properties Div Nat Inst Stds & Tech 100 Bureau Dr Stop 8380 Gaithersburg MD 20899-8380 Office Phone: 301-975-2463. Business E-Mail: johanna.sengers@nist.gov.

**SENGPIEHL, PAUL MARVIN,** lawyer, former state official; b. Stuart, Nebr., Oct. 10, 1937; s. Arthur Paul and Anne Marie (Andersen) S.; B.A., Wheaton (Ill.) Coll., 1959; M.A. in Pub. Adminstrn., Mich. State U., 1961; J.D., Ill. Inst. Tech.-Chgo. Kent Coll. Law, 1970; m. June S. Cline, June 29, 1963; children— Jeffrey D., Chrystal M. Bar: Ill. 1971, U.S. Supreme Ct. 1982. Adminstrv. asst. Chgo. Dept. Urban Renewal, 1962-65; supr. Ill. Municipal Retirement Fund, Chgo., 1966-71; mgmt. officer Ill. Dept. Local Govt. Affairs, Springfield, 1971-72; legal counsel, Chgo., 1972-73; spl. asst. atty. gen. Ill. Dept. Labor, Chgo., 1973-76; asst. atty. gen. Ct. of Claims div. Atty. Gen. of Ill., 1976-83; hearing referee Bd. Rev., Ill. Dept. Labor, 1983-84; local govt. law columnist Chgo. Daily Law Bull., 1975-84; instr. polit. sci. Judson Coll., Elgin, Ill., 1963. Republican candidate for Cook County Recorder of Deeds, 1984; dep. committeeman Oak Park Twp Rep. Orgn.; elected alt. del., served del. Rep. Nat. Conv., 1992; People's Choice candidate pres. Oak Park Village, 1993; Rep. alt. state ctrl. committeeman 7th Congl. Dist.; Oak Park Twp., 1994-99; elected del. Rep. Nat. Convention, 1996; co-chmn. Cook County Jail Ministry Bd., chmn. 2003—; treas. Cook County Correctional Chaplaincy Coun., 2003-04, chmn., 2006-. Mem. Ill. Bar Assn. (local govt. law sect. council 1973-79, vice chmn. 1976-77, co-editor local govt. newsletter 1976-77, chmn. 1977-78, editor newsletter 1977-78, state tax sect. council 1979-82, 84-85), Chgo. Bar Assn. (local govt. com., chmn. legis. subcom. 1978-79, sec. 1979-80, vice chmn. 1980-81, chmn. 1981-82, state and mcpl. tax com.), John Ericsson Rep. League Ill. (state sec. 1983-85, 95—, hon. past pres. Cook County 1982-97, pres. 1997—), Oak Park-River Forest C. of C. (small bus. coun. 1991-00). Baptist (vice chmn. deacons 1973-76, 79-80, moderator 1983-86, supt. Sunday sch. 1986-93). Home and Office: 727 N Ridgeland Ave Oak Park IL 60302-1735 Office Phone: 708-383-8859. Business E-Mail: sengpiehllaw@aol.com.

**SENGUPTA, ABHIJIT,** molecular and optical physicist; PhD, Stanford U., 1995. Rsch. assoc. Stanford U., Calif., 1989—95; NSF postdoctoral fellow Mass. Inst. Tech., Cambridge, Mass., 1995—97; rsch. scientist Eastman Kodak Co., Rochester, NY, 1997—99; asst. prof., rsch. Jefferson Lab. Consortium, Old Dominion U., Norfolk, Va., 1999—2001; sr. scientist, project leader Bell Labs., Lucent Tech., Norcross, Ga., 2001—02, OFS, Norcross, Ga., 2002—03; prin. rsch. scientist SYSTIMAX Solutions, Richardson, Tex., 2004—; founder, pres. FEMTONIX, Alpharetta, Ga., 2003—. Vis. scientist Inst. Optics, U. Rochester, 1998—99; adj. asst. prof., physics Old Dominion U., 1999—2003, adj. asst. prof., elec. computer engring., 1999—2001; cons. SOLAREX, Va. Beach., 2000—01; panel reviewer NSF, Arlington, Va., 1999—2000; peer reviewer Internat. Sci. Tech. Ctr., Wash., DC, 2000—. One-man shows include Stanford U. Tressidor Union Gallery; co-author: Laser Techniques in Chemistry, 1995. Recipient Innovation award, Va. Ctr. Innovative Tech., 2000, US Patent award in Optical Comms. Mem.: AAAS, OSA, IEEE. Office Phone: 678-528-5109. E-mail: asengupta@femtonix.com.

**SENGUPTA, CHAITALI,** computer engineer; BS in Tech., Indian Inst. Tech., Kharagpur, 1992; MS in Elec. and Computer Engring., Rice U., 1995, PhD in Elec. and Computer Engring., 1999. Sr. mem. tech. staff Texas Instruments, Inc. Contbr. articles to profl. jours. Named one of Top 100 Young Innovators, MIT Tech. Review, 2004. Office: Texas Instuments Inc MS8723 12500 Texas Instruments Blvd Dallas TX 75243-4136

**SENGUPTA, SHOMIK,** internist; s. Dipankar and Saswati Sengupta; m. Anindita Sengupta, July 18, 1997; children: Shohaag, Aneek. MBBS, U. Melbourne, Australia, 2003. Urology registrar Royal Australasian Coll. Surgeons, Melbourne, Victoria, 2001—04; cons. urologist Urology Victoria, East Melbourne, 2006—. Contbr. articles to profl. jours. Recipient ESR Hughes prize, Cabrini Hosp., Melbourne, 2002, Kelalis prize, Minn. Urol. Soc., 2005—06; fellow, Mayo Clinic, Rochester, Minn., 2004—06; grantee, NIH, 2004; scholar, U. Melbourne, 2000. Fellow: Royal Australasian Coll. of Surgeons (RC Bennett medal 2000, Travel grantee 2004—05), Soc. Urologic Oncology (corr.; fellowship rep. exec. bd. 2005—06); mem.: Am. Urol. Assn. (corr.). Office Phone: (613) 8415 1500.

**SENGUPTA, SOMINI,** reporter; b. Calcutta, India; BA in English and Devel. Studies, U. Calif., Berkeley, 1988. With Newsday, N.Y.C.; West African bur. chief N.Y. Times, N.Y.C., 2003—. Recipient Feature Writing award, Newswomen's Club N.Y., 1997, SAJA Journalism award, 1999, George K. Polk award for fgn. reporting, 2004. Office: NY Times 229 W 43rd St New York NY 10036-3959

**SENHAUSER, JOHN CRATER,** architect; b. New Philadelphia, Ohio, Apr. 7, 1947; s. Edwin Crater and Margaret Jean (Huffman) S.; m. Teri A. Schleyer, June 25, 1988. BS in Architecture, U. Cin., 1971. Registered architect, Ohio, Ky., Fla. Designer Jones, Peacock, Garn & Ptnrs., Cin., 1971-72; project architect Smith Stevens Architects, Cin., 1972-76; project mgr. Herrlinger Enterprises, Cin., 1976-79; prin., owner John C. Senhauser, Architect, Cin., 1979—. Adj. assoc. prof. Sch. Architecture and Interior Design, U. Cin., 1992-98 Exhibited in group shows at Toni Birckhead Gallery, 1990, Contemporary Arts Ctr., Cin., 1993, 98, Canton (Ohio) Art Inst., 1993; prin. works include residences. Mem. historic conservation bd. City of Cin., 1986-98, chmn. 1998—; mem. urban design rev. bd., 1998—; mem. dean's adv. coun. Coll. Design Architecture Art and Planning U. Cin., 1990; mem. design rev. com. U. Cin., 1997—. Recipient Merit award Builder mag., 1985, 88, 94, 96, 99, Grand award, 1990, Grand Best in Region award Profl. Builder, 1988, 90, Grand award for Best Overall Design, Custom Home Mag., 1996, 97, Merit award, 1990, 94, other awards. Fellow AIA (pres. 1991, Honor award Cin. chpt. 1983, 85, 90-96, 2000, 04, Merit award 1990, 93-94); mem. AIA Ohio (bd. dirs., sec. 1997-98, v.p. 1999, pres. 2000, regional dir. nat. bd. dirs. 2001—03, Inst. sec. 2005-06, Honor award 1985, 90-91, 93-94, 99, 2003-04) Office: John Senhauser Architects 1118 Saint Gregory St Cincinnati OH 45202-1724

**SENIA, GRACE MELANIE,** language and music educator; d. Gibson Kenyon Davis and Gertrude Mae Cook; m. Anthony Joseph Senia, June 26, 1971; children: Carmella Grace Bullick, Filene Marie Travis. BA, U. Buffalo, 1965; MS in Reading summa cum laude, Marywood U., 2001; postgrad., SUNY, Binghamton. Cert. tchr. Latin and English NY, 1974, tchr. Latin Pa., 1980, English Pa., 1990, instr. reading NY, 2001, tchr. Latin NJ, 2001. Tchr. Latin and English Greene Ctrl. Sch., NY, 1964—68; tchr. English East HS, Rochester, NY, 1970—71, Hancock Ctrl. Sch., NY, 1971—87; tchr. Latin and English Scranton HS, Pa., 1993—94, Honesdale HS, Pa., 1999; adj. tchr. SUNY, Binghamton, 2001; instr. Latin Binghamton City HS, 2005—06. Tchr. after sch. program Hancock City. Edn. Found., 2002—06. Conf. del. Emory United Meth. Ch. Mem.: Internat. Honor Soc. in Edn., Nat. Scholar's Honor Soc., Kappa Delta Pi. Avocations: piano, golf. Home: 257 E Main St Hancock NY 13783 Office: Binghamton City Sch Dist 31 Main St Hancock NY 13783 Office Phone: 607-762-8200.

**SENIOR, DONALD PAUL,** religious organization administrator; b. Phila., Jan. 1, 1940; s. Vincent Edward and Margaret (Tiernan) S. BA in Philosophy, Passionist Sem. Coll., Chgo., 1963; Licentiate in Sacred Theology, U. Louvain, Belgium, 1970, STD, 1972. Prof. New Testament Cath. Theol. Union, Chgo., 1972—, dir. Israel program, 1980-88, acting dean, 1986-87, acting pres., 1988, pres., 1988—. Author books and articles on New Testament; assoc. editor The Bible Today, New Theology Rev., New Testament Message (22 vols.); gen. editor The Cath. Study Bible; writer, commentator, host radio and TV programs, Chgo. Mem. Cath. Bibl. Soc. Am., Soc. Bibl. Lit., Soc. for New Testament Studies, Cath. Theol. Soc. Am., Chgo. Soc. Bibl. Rsch. Democrat. Home and Office: 5401 S Cornell Ave Chicago IL 60615-5664*

**SENIOR, ENRIQUE FRANCISCO,** investment banker; b. Havana, Cuba, Aug. 3, 1943; came to U.S., 1960; s. Frank and Dolores (Hernandez) Senior; m. Robin Suffern Gimbel, Sept. 7, 1977; children: Tailer, Heather, Fern, Seanna. BA in Electrical Engring., Yale U., 1964, MS in Elec. Engring., 1967; MBA, Harvard U., 1969. Corp. fin. exec. White, Weld & Co., NYC, 1969-73; v.p. Allen & Co., Inc., NYC, 1973-80, exec. v.p., mng. dir., 1980—. Bd. dirs. Allen & Co., Inc., Televisa S.A. de CV, Coca Cola Femsa, Cinemark Inc. Mem. The Brook Club, Piping Rock Club, Sailfish Club, The Beach Club, Phi Beta Kappa, Tau Beta Pi. Avocations: flying, fishing, hunting, skiing, woodworking. Office: Allen & Co Inc 711 5th Ave Fl 8 New York NY 10022-3111

**SENIOR, RICHARD JOHN LANE,** linen and uniform services executive; b. Datchet, Eng., July 6, 1940; arrived in U.S., 1972, naturalized, 1977; s. Harold Dennis Senior and Jane Lane Dorothy (Chadwick) Senior Rigg; m. Diana Morgan, Dec. 19, 1966; children: Alden, Alicia, Amanda. BA, Oxford U., 1962, MA, 1966; MIA, Yale U., 1964. Jr. mgr. Tate & Lyle, London, 1964—66; mgmt. cons. McKinsey & Co., Inc., London, Chgo., 1967-74; pres., CEO Morgan Svcs., Inc., Chgo., 1974—2004, chair, CEO, 2004—. Bd. dirs. Northwestern Meml. Healthcare, 1992-2001, Chgo. Crime Commn., 1994-99, Ball Hort. Co., 1996-, Near South Planning Bd., 2001-2003, Northwestern Meml. Found., 2001-; regional adv. bd. Kemper Ins. Cos., 1994-96. Pres. bd. trustees Latin Sch., Chgo., 1979-83. Hon. scholar Oxford U., 1960-1962. Mem. Uniform and Textile Svc. Assn. (bd. dirs. 1996-99, exec. com. 2001-06, chmn. 2002-04); Textile Rental Svcs. Assn. Am. (pres. 1983-85, dir., exec. com. 1978-86); Northwestern U. Assocs., Racquet Club (bd. govs. 1983-91, 2006—), Chgo. Club, Glen View Club, Casino (bd. govs. 1991-96, treas. 1993-94), Econ. Club, Yale Club Chgo. (bd. dirs. 1991-95, AYA del. 1992-95, chmn. grad. sch. task force 1990-95). Home: 1500 N Lake Shore Dr Chicago IL 60610-6657 Office: Morgan Svcs Inc 323 N Michigan Ave Chicago IL 60601-3798 Office Phone: 312-346-3184. Business E-Mail: senior@morganservices.com.

**SENIOR, THOMAS BRYAN A.,** electrical engineering educator, researcher, consultant; b. Menston, Yorkshire, Eng., June 26, 1928; arrived in U.S., 1957; s. Thomas Harold and Emily Dorothy (Matthews) Senior; m. Heather Margaret Golby, May 4, 1957; children: Margaret, David, Hazel, Peter. B.Sc., Manchester U., 1949, M.Sc., 1950; PhD, Cambridge U., 1954. Sr. sci. officer Royal Radar Establishment, Malvern, Eng., 1952-57; rsch. scientist U. Mich., Ann Arbor, 1957-69, prof. elec. engring., 1969-84, prof. elec. and computer sci., 1984-98, Arthur F. Thurnau prof., 1990-98, prof. emeritus, 1998—, dir. radiation lab., 1975-87, assoc. chmn. elect. engring. & computer sci. dept., 1984-90, acting chmn., 1987-88, assoc. chmn. acad. affairs, 1991-98. Cons. in field. Author: (with Bowman and Uslenghi) Electromagnetic and Acoustical Scattering by Simple Shapes, 1969; Mathematical Methods in Electrical Engineering, 1986; (with Volakis) Approximate Boundary Conditions in Electromagnetics, 1995; contbr. articles to profl. jours. Fellow IEEE (3d Millennium medal, AP-S Disting. Achievement award 2000); mem. Internat. Sci. Radio Union (chmn. U.S. nat. com. 1982-84, vice chmn. Com. B. 1985-87, chmn. 1988-90, pres. 1996-99, Van der Pol Gold medal 1993). Home: 1919 Ivywood Dr Ann Arbor MI 48103-4527 Office: U Mich Dept Elec Engring Comp S Ann Arbor MI 48109 E-mail: senior@eecs.umich.edu.

**SENIORS, PAULA MARIE,** history professor, researcher; b. Cleve., Mar. 29, 1963; d. Audrey Proctor and Clarence Henry Seniors. BFA Dance, CCNY, 1985; MA Music, NYU, 1996; MA, PhD Ethnic Studies, U. Calif., San Diego, 2003. Tchg. asst. U. Calif., San Diego, 1998—2003; asst. prof. African Am. studies Coll. NJ, 2005—. Bd. mem. African and African-Am. Studies Rsch. project, San Diego; mem. book award com. Assn. Black Women Historians, Lansing, Mich., 2004—; rschr. Bldg. Curriculum Focused on S.Am. and the Caribbean: United Negro Coll. Fund Spl. Programs, Fla. Meml. Coll., Washington, 2004—; com. mem., rschr. creation history mng. Fla. Meml. Coll., Miami, 2004—; rschr. San Diego Urban League; presenter at confs. Contbr. book manuscripts for profl. seminars. Facilitator, organizer Themes in African Am., U.S. History, and Contemporary Soc. Student Conf. Fla. Meml. Coll., Miami, 2003—. Thelma Hill Meml. Dance scholar, CCNY, 1982, fellow, Dept. Ethnic Studies, U. Calif. San Diego, 1998—2002. Mem.: Nat. Coun. for Black Studies, Am. Studies Assn., Assn. Black Women Historians (book award com. 2004—), Assn. Study African Am. Life, Am. Hist. Assn. Avocation: rollerblading. Personal E-mail: pseniors@comcast.net. E-mail: seniors@tcnj.edu.

**SENKAYI, ABU LWANGA,** environmental scientist; b. Mpigi, Uganda, Oct. 16, 1943; came to U.S., 1973; s. Alamanzane Buza and Manjeri (Nalwoga) Abalyawo; m. Sunajeh Nansamba, Dec. 27, 1969; children: Ali K., Sala N. BS, Makerere U., Kampala, Uganda, 1971, MS, 1973; PhD, U. Calif., Davis, 1977. Rsch. scientist Tex. A&M U., College Station, 1977-87; sr. soil chemist Ebasco Environ. Svcs., Dallas, 1987-90; soil chemist PRC Environ. Mgmt., Inc., Dallas, 1990-96; sr. soil scientist Railroad Commn. of Tex. (Surface Mining/Reclamation Divsn.), Austin, Tex., 1996-97; environ. scientist U.S. EPA, Dallas, 1997—. Author 7 book chpts.; contbr. articles to Soil Sci. Soc. Am. Jour., Soil Sci. Jour., Clays and Clay Minerals Jour. Recipient PRC-EMI Exceptional Performance award, 1991, Fed. Ingeragy. Recognition award, 2000. Mem. Soil Sci. Soc. Am., Clay Mineral Soc., Mineral. Soc. Gt. Britain, Sigma Xi. Achievements include research on the chemistry and mineralogy of lignite, mineralogical weathering processes in soils, and problems associated with reclamation of surface-mined lands. Home: 1122 De Havilland Ave Duncanville TX 75137-4742 Office: US EPA Region 6 Compliance Assurance and Enforcement Divsn Dallas TX 75202-2733 E-mail: senkayi.abu@epa.gov.

**SENKLER, ROBERT L.,** insurance company executive; BA in Math. and Stats., Minn. Duluth Coll., 1974. Began Minn. Life Ins. Co., 1974—, v.p. Individual Ins. Divsn., 1987-94, pres., 1994—, CEO Minn—, chmn., 1995—. Past chmn. Ins. Fed. Minn.; pres. Minn. Bus. Prtnrshp., 2003; chmn. Cap. City Partnership. Recipient Univ. Minn.-Duluth Acad. Sci. Engring., 2003. Fellow Soc. Actuaries. Office: 400 Robert St N Saint Paul MN 55101-2015

**SENNEMA, DAVID CARL,** arts consultant; b. Grand Rapids, Mich., July 6, 1934; s. Carl Edward and Alice Bertha (Bieri) S.; m. Martha Amanda Dixon, Feb. 22, 1958; children: Daniel Ross, Julia Kathryn, Alice Dixon. BA, Albion Coll., 1956. Mgr. Columbia Music Festival Assn., 1964-67; exec. dir. S.C. Arts Commn., Columbia, 1967-70; assoc. dir. Fed.-State Partnership and Spl. Projects program Nat. Endowment for the Arts, Washington, 1971-73; prof. arts adminstrn., dir. cmty. arts mgmt. program Sangamon State U., Springfield, Ill., 1973-76; dir. S.C. State Commn., Columbia, 1976-85; bus. mgr. Palmetto Mastersingers, 1986—2004. Cons. in field. Co-author: Columbia, S.C. A Postcard History, 1997. Mem. adv. panel Nat. Endowment for the Arts Music, 1968-70; mem. Springfield Arts Commn., 1975-76. Served with U.S. Army, 1957-58. Mem. Rotary. Office Phone: 803-782-3581. E-mail: dsennema@sc.rr.com.

**SENNET, CHARLES JOSEPH,** lawyer; b. Buffalo, Aug. 7, 1952; s. Saunders M. and Muriel S. (Rotenberg) S. AB magna cum laude, Cornell U., 1974; JD with high honors, George Washington U., 1979. Bar: Ill. 1979, U.S. Dist. Ct. (no. dist.) Ill. 1979, U.S. Ct. Appeals (7th cir.) 1982, U.S. Ct. Appeals

(D.C. cir.) 1993. Assoc. Reuben & Proctor, Chgo., 1979-83; assoc. counsel Tribune Co., Chgo., 1984-91, sr. counsel, 1991—. Adj. faculty Medill Sch. Journalism, Northwestern U., 1991-94, 2004—; chmn. Television Music Lic. Com., 1995—. Contbr. articles to profl. jours. Chmn. cable royalty distbn. com. Nat. Assn. Broadcasters, 2005—. Mem. ABA (spkr. 1984-88, 91-97, 2000—, mem. gov. bd. Forum on Comms. Law 1995-98), NATAS, Ill. Bar Assn. (chmn. media law com. 1989-91), Chgo. Bar Assn., Fed. Comms. Bar Assn. Office: Tribune Co 435 N Michigan Ave Chicago IL 60611-4066 E-mail: csennet@tribune.com.

**SENNETT, JOHN O.,** lawyer; b. Broken Bow, Neb., Apr. 10, 1948; BS, Univ. Neb., 1970, JD, 1972. Mem.: ABA, Assn. of Trial Lawyers of Am., Neb. Trial Lawyers Assn., Custer County Bar Assn., Neb. State Bar Assn. (Ho. of Del. 1986—92, chmn. 1991—92, bd. trustees 1992—98, pres. 2004). Office: Sennett Duncan & Borders 425 S 7th St PO Box 326 Broken Bow NE 68822

**SENNETT, MICHAEL,** lawyer; b. Chgo., Oct. 24, 1951; BA with honors, Quincy U., 1973; JD cum laude, Loyola U., 1977. Bar: Ill. 1977, (US Supreme Ct.) 1984. Assoc. Bell, Boyd & Lloyd, Chgo., 1977—83, ptnr., 1984—; chair antitrust and trade regulation Bell, Boyd & Lloyd LLC, Chgo., 1996—. Exec. editor Loyola U. Chgo. Law Jour., 1976—77; adj. law faculty Loyola U., 1996—; bd. advisors Inst. for Consumer Antitrust Law Studies, Chgo., 1998—. Contbr. chpt. to book. Trustee Children's Home and Aid Soc. of Ill., Inc., Chgo., 2004—, Quincy U., Ill., 2006—. Mem.: Internat. Bar Assn., Chgo. Bar Assn. (chair, antitrust law com. 1996—97), ABA, Lawyers Club Chgo. Office: Bell Boyd & Lloyd LLC 70 W Madison St Ste 3100 Chicago IL 60602 Office Phone: 312-807-4243. Office Fax: 312-827-8161. E-mail: msennett@bellboyd.com.

**SENNETT, NANCY J.,** lawyer; b. Milw., Nov. 26, 1951; BS in English & comm. arts with honors, U. Wis., 1973; JD cum laude, Northwestern U., 1979. Bar: Wis. 1979. With Foley & Lardner LLP, Milw., 1979—, chair securities litig. practice group, mng. ptnr. Milw. office. Chair merit selection com. reappointment magistrate judges Ea. Dist. Wis. Notes and comments editor Northwestern U. Law Rev., 1978-79. Active Jr. Achievement. Mem.: ABA (securities litig. com.), Securities Industry Assn. (compliance & legal divsn.), State Wis. Bar Assn., Milw. Bar Assn. (Lawyer Year 2003), ABCD, Inc. (bd. dirs.), Betty Brinn Children's Mus. (founding bd. dirs.), Greater Milw. Com., Tempo & Rotary, U. Wis. Alumni Assn. (bd. dirs., Distinguished Alumni Award 2003). Office: Foley & Lardner LLP US Bank Ctr 777 E Wisconsin Ave Milwaukee WI 53202-5367 Office Phone: 414-297-5522. Business E-Mail: nsennett@foley.com.

**SENSENBRENNER, F. JAMES, JR., (FRANK JAMES SENSENBRENNER JR.),** congressman; b. Chgo., June 14, 1943; s. F. James and Margaret Sensenbrenner; m. Cheryl Warren, Mar. 26, 1977; children: F. James III, Robert Alan. AB in Polit. Sci., Stanford U., 1965; JD, U. Wis., Madison, 1968. Bar: Wis. 1968, US Supreme Ct. 1972. State rep. Wis. State Assembly, Madison, 1969-75; mem. Wis. State Senate, Madison, 1975-79, asst. minority leader, 1976-79; mem. US Congress from 5th Wis. dist., 1979—, chmn. sci. com., 1997—2001, chmn. judiciary com., 2001—. Mem. Friends of Milw. Mus., Riveredge Nature Ctr. Mem. Am. Philatelic Soc., Chenequa Country Club, Capitol Hill Club. Republican. Office: US Ho Reps 2449 Rayburn Ho Office Bldg Washington DC 20515-4905 Office Phone: 202-225-5101.*

**SENSENICH, ILA JEANNE,** judge; b. Pitts., Mar. 6, 1939; d. Louis E. and Evelyn Margaret S. BA, Westminster Coll., 1961; JD, Dickinson Sch. Law, 1964, JD (hon.), 1994. Bar: Pa. 1964. Assoc. Stewart, Belden, Sensenich and Harrington, Greensburg, Pa., 1964-70; asst. pub. defender Westmoreland (Pa.) County, 1970-71; U.S. magistrate judge We. Dist. Pa., Pitts., 1971—. Adj. prof. law Duquesne U., 1982-87. Author: Compendium of the Law of Prisoner's Rights, 1979; contbr. articles to profl. jour. Vis. fellow Daniel & Florence Guggenheim program in criminal justice Yale Law Sch., 1976-77. Mem. ABA, Fed. Magistrate Judges Assn. (sec. 1979-81, 88-89, treas. 1989-90, 2d v.p. 1990-91, pres.-elect 1992-93, pres. 1993-94), Pa. Bar Assn. (comn. on women in the profession 1998—), Nat. Assn. Women Judges, Westmoreland County Bar Assn., Allegheny County Bar Assn. (fed. ct. sect., com. women in law), Womens Bar Assn. We. Pa., Am. Judicature Soc. Democrat. Presbyterian. Avocations: skiing, sailing, bicycling, classical music, cooking. Office: US PO and Courthouse 3d Fl Pittsburgh PA 15219 Office Phone: 412-208-7480.

**SENSENIG, DANIEL SCOT,** music educator; b. Reamstown, Pa., Nov. 6, 1978; s. Thomas Eugene and Donna Lorraine Sensenig; m. Margaret Anne Ryan, June 17, 2006. BS in Music Edn. summa cum laude, Indiana U. Pa., 2001. Level I instrnl. tchg. cert. Pa. Secondary band, choral and gen. music educator Cameron County Sch. Dist., Emporium, Pa., 2002—. Composer, clinician Enloe (NC) HS Band, 1997—, Otto Eldred HS Band, Duke Center, Pa., 2002—; pvt. studio instr. Founder, dir. Emporium Cmty. Band, 2003—. Mem.: Pa. State Edn. Assn., Pa. Music Educators Assn. Republican. Lutheran. Avocations: fishing, gardening, model railroading. Home: 550 Poplar St Emporium PA 15834 Office: Cameron County HS 601 Woodland Ave Emporium PA 15834 Office Phone: 814-486-4000. Fax: 814-486-4006. E-mail: dansensenig@hotmail.com.

**SENSIPER, SAMUEL,** electrical engineer; b. Elmira, NY, Apr. 26, 1919; s. Louis and Molly (Pedolsky) S.; m. Elaine Marie Zwick, Sept. 10, 1950; children: Martin, Sylvia, David. BSEE, MIT, 1939, ScD, 1951; EE, Stanford U., 1941. Asst. project engr. to sr. project engr., cons. Sperry Gyroscope, Garden City, Great Neck, NY, 1941-51; sect. head and sr. staff cons. Hughes Aircraft, Culver City, Malibu, Calif., 1951-60; lab. divsn. mgr. Space Gen. Corp., Glendale, Azuza, L.A., 1960—67; lab. mgr. TRW, Redondo Beach, Calif., 1967—70; cons. elec. engr. L.A., 1970—73; dir. engring. Transco Products, Venice, Calif., 1973—75; cons. elec. engr. in pvt. practice L.A., 1975—95; cons., 1995—. Faculty U. So. Calif., L.A., 1955-56, 79-80. Contbr. articles to profl. jours.; patentee in field. Recipient Cert. of Commendation U.S. Navy, 1946; indsl. electronics fellow MIT, 1947-48. Fellow IEEE, AAAS; mem. Calif. Acad. Soc. Profl. Engrs., MIT Alumni Assn., Stanford Alumni Assn., Electromagnetics Acad., Sigma Xi, Eta Kappa Nu. Home and Office: 215 Moreton Bay Ln # 2 Goleta CA 93117-2206 Office Phone: 805-967-9264. Personal E-mail: sensiperl@ieee.org.

**SENSOR, MARY DELORES,** health facility administrator, consultant; b. Erie, Pa., July 20, 1930; d. Sergie Pavl Malinowski and Leocadia Mary Francis (Machalinski) Harner; m. Robert Louis Charles Sensor, Apr. 21, 1945; children: Robert Louis Paul, Stephen Maxmillian Augustus, Therese Blaze, Kathryn Anne. MS in Health Care Adminstrn., Gannon U., 1986, MS in Health Svc. Adminstrn., 1988; BS in Hosp. Adminstrn., Daemon Coll., 1972. Intern in hosp. adminstrn. Harvard U., Boston, 1972; dir. med. records St. Mary Hosp., Langhorne, Pa., 1972-74, Moses Taylor Hosp., Scranton, Pa., 1975-77, Erie County Geriatric Ctr., Fairview, Pa., 1988-92; dir. utilization rev. Millcreek Cmty. Hosp., Erie, Pa., 1983—. Cons. prof. in hosp. adminstrn. and med. records U. Pitts., 1972-74, Temple U., 1972-74; contbr. paper 6th World Congress Automated Med. Data, Washington, 2000; presenter paper Computer Adaptation of SNOMed to DRG Assignment, to 12th Ann. Symposium on Coomputer Application in Med. Care, Washington. Bd. dirs. St. John Kanty Prep. Sch., Erie, 1970-71, pres. Ladies Aux., 1970-71; mem. Siebenburger Singing Soc. Mem. Am. Med. Record Assn., Pa. Med. Record Assn., N.W. Pa. Med. Record Assn. (2d treas. 1982-84), Nat. Assn. Quality Assurance Profls., Pa. Assn. Quality Assurance Profls. Roman Catholic. Avocations: professional classical dancing, researcher early man's migration patterns, gourmet cooking, collecting jazz. Home: 2023 Harrison St Erie PA 16510-1403

**SENTELLE, DAVID BRYAN,** federal judge; b. Canton, NC, Feb. 12, 1943; s. Horace Richard Jr. and Maude (Ray) Sentelle; m. Jane LaRue Oldham, June 19, 1965; children: Sharon Lewis, Regan Herman, Rebecca Acheson. BA, U. N.C., 1965, JD with honors, 1968. Bar: N.C. 1968, N.C. (U.S. Dist. Ct. (we.

dist.)) 1969, (U.S. Ct. Appeals (4th cir.)) 1970. Assoc. Uzzell & Dumont, Asheville, NC, 1968—70; asst. U.S. atty. (we. dist.) NC US Dept. Justice, 1970—74; dist. judge City of Charlotte, NC, 1974—77; ptnr. Tucker, Hicks, Sentelle, Moon & Hodge, P.A., Charlotte, 1977—85; judge U.S. Dist. Ct. (we. dist.) N.C., Charlotte, 1985—87, U.S. Ct. Appeals (D.C. cir.), 1987—. Adj. prof UNC, 1991—92; adj. prof. Fla. State U. Coll. Law, 1993; presiding judge Spl. Divsn. for Appointment of Ind. Counsels, 1992—; Disting. adj. prof. Geroge Mason U. Sch. Law. Contbr. articles to profl. jours. Chmn. Mecklenburg County Rep. Com., 1978—80, N.C. State Rep. Conv., 1979—80. Fellow, Dameron Found., 1967. Mem.: Mecklenburg County Bar Assn., Shriners, Masons (Scottish Rite), Am. Inn of Ct. Found. (bd. dir.), Edward Bennett Williams Inn of Ct. (pres.). Baptist. Office: US Court of Appeals 333 Constitution Ave NW Washington DC 20001-2866*

**SENTER, LYONEL THOMAS, JR.,** federal judge; b. Fulton, Miss., July 30, 1933; s. L. T. and Eva Lee (Jetton) S. BS, U. So. Miss., 1956; LL.B., U. Miss., 1959. Bar: Miss. 1959. County pros. atty., 1960-64; U.S. commr., 1966-68; judge Miss. Circuit Ct., Circuit 1, 1968-80, U.S. Dist. Ct. (no. dist.) Miss., 1980-82, chief judge, 1982-98, sr. judge, 1998—. Mem. Miss. State Bar Office: 2012 15th St Ste 514 Gulfport MS 39501 Office Phone: 228-563-1755. Business E-Mail: lt_senter@mssd.uscourts.gov.

**SENTINEK, KELLY MARIE,** social studies educator; b. Painesville, Ohio, Nov. 17, 1979; d. Thomas Andrew and Elaine Marie Sentinek. BA in Social Studies Edn., Ohio No. U., Ada, 1998—2002; MA in Leadership Tchg., Adminstrn. & Supervision, Coll. of Notre Dame of Md., Balt., 2003—05. Social studies tchr. Patterson H.S., Balt., 2002—. Curriculum designer Balt. City Pub. Sch. Sys., 2003—. Coach Balt. Urban Debate League, Baltimore, Md., 2005—06. Recipient Reginald F. Lewis Tchr. Recognition cward, Balt. City CC, 2006. Democrat. Roman Catholic. Home: 107 Aspinwood Way Apt E Baltimore MD 21237 Office: Patterson High School 100 Kane St Baltimore MD 21224 Office Phone: 410-396-9276. Office Fax: 410-633-0179. Personal E-mail: kellysentinek@yahoo.com.

**SENTY, JAMES A.,** energy executive; BS metallurgical and mining engring., Univ. Wis. Chmn. bd. Western Gas Resources, Inc., 2003—. Chmn. State Wis. Investment Bd.; chmn. bd., pres. Midwest Bottle Gas Co.; chmn. Park Bark, Madison, Wis. Office: Western Gas Resources Ste 1200 1099 18th St Denver CO 80202

**SENZEL, MARTIN LEE,** lawyer; b. Rochester, N.Y., June 21, 1944; s. Albert Benjamin and Besse (Lipson) S.; m. Dagni Maren Belgum, Feb. 17, 1979; 1 child, Whitney. BA, Yale U., 1966, LLB, 1969. Bar: N.Y. 1971, U.S. Dist. Ct. (so. dist.) N.Y., U.S. Ct. Appeals (2nd cir.) 1973. Assoc. Cravath, Swaine & Moore LLP, N.Y.C., 1971; ptnr., 1977—2000. Bd. dir. Medinol Ltd. Mem.: ABA, N.Y. State Bar Assn., Assn. Bar City N.Y. Home: Apt 4-E 101 Central Park W New York NY 10023-4204 Office: Cravath Swaine & Moore LLP Worldwide Plz 825 8th Ave Fl 38 New York NY 10019-7475 Office Phone: 212-474-1520. E-mail: msenzel@cravath.com.

**SEO, BYUNG-IN,** literature and language educator; d. Woon-Young and Hyo-Kyoung Seo. BA, U. Ill., 1989; MA, Lewis U., 1994. Cert. Type 9 English and Gen. Sci. 1994, Type 75 Gen. Adminstrn. 1996. English tchr. Project Upward Bound, Romeoville, Ill., 1991—94, Driscoll Cath. HS, Addison, Ill., 1994—2005; writing coord. San Miguel Gary Comer Sch., Chgo., 2005—. Governing bd. ednl. cons. Depressive Bipolar Support Alliance, Hinsdale, Ill., 1989—93; rsch. asst. U. Ill., Chgo., 2004; lab. supr. Morton Coll., Cicero, Ill., 2005. Contbr. articles in field. Vol. tutor Children's Home and Aid Soc., Urbana, Ill., 1984—89; vol. Southeast Area Special Pks. and Recreation, Downers Grove, Ill., 1992—94. Named Tchr. of Yr., Driscoll Cath. HS, 1997, 1998; fellowship, Diversifying Faculty in Ill., 2002—04. Mem.: Ill. Assn. Tchrs. English, Nat. Coun. Tchrs. English, Am. Ednl. Rsch. Assn. Avocations: photography, reading, exercise.

**SEOL, DAI-WU,** geneticist, educator; PhD, U. Pitts., Pitts., Pa., 1998. Asst. prof. U. Pitts., 2000—. Cons. Genenmend Inc., Seoul, Republic of Korea, 2000—. Dir. Sunday Sch. Korean Ctrl. Ch. Pitts., 2003. Achievements include patents for cancer gene therapy using a secretable trimeric TRAIL. Office: University of Pittsburgh 200 Lothrop Street Pittsburgh PA 15261 Office Phone: 412-624-6704. Office Fax: 412-624-1172. Business E-Mail: seold@pitt.edu.

**SEON, YVONNE,** cultural educator, minister; d. George Raymond and Beatrice M. Reed; 3 children. BA, Allegheny Coll., 1959; MA, Am. U., 1960; PhD, Union Inst., 1974; MDiv, Howard U., 1981. Exec. dir. High Commn. Inga Dam Project, Kinshasa, Democratic Republic of Congo, 1961—63; program officer Office Internat. Confs., US Dept. State, Washington, 1964—67; dir. student life programs Wilberforce U., Ohio, 1967—71; dir. Bolinga Black Cultural Resources Ctr. Wright State U., 1971—73; student svcs. program coord. Prince Georges CC, Largo, Md., 1993—96, prof. African Am. studies, 1996—. Sec. del. US Del. 14th Gen. Assembly UNESCO, Paris, 1966; disting. vis. dir. Bolinga Black Cultural Resources Ctr., 2005—06. Pres. Capitol Hill Group Ministries, Washington, 1987—89; ordained min. Unitarian Universalist Assn., Boston, 1981—; bd. dirs. Africare, DC, 1977—2000, vice-chair, 2002—04; bd. dirs. Prince George's County So. Christian Leadership Conf., Largo, 1994—; mem. Bretton Woods Com., Washington, 2000—. Office: Prince Georges CC 301 Largo Rd Largo MD 20774 Business E-Mail: yvonne_seon@wright.edu.

**SEOW, MING-JUNG,** computer engineer, researcher; b. Kuala Lumpur, Selangor, Malaysia, Mar. 10, 1979; s. WanSeong Seow and AhChap Lim. BS in Computer Engring., Old Dominion U., 2001, MS in Computer Engring., 2002. Rsch. asst. Old Dominion U., Norfolk, Va., 2001—, tchg. asst., 2002—. Reviewer: sci. jours.; contbr. articles to profl. jours. Grad. Assistance in Areas of Nat. Need fellow, U.S. Dept. Edn., 2001—04. Mem.: IEEE Neural Networks Soc., IEEE, Eta Kappa Nu. Achievements include patents pending for color image characterization, enhancement and balancing process; development of a new architecture and learning algorithm for artificial neural network. Avocations: travel, reading, art, music, walking. Home: 101 Pearl St Strawberry Plains Williamsburg VA 23188 Office: Dept Electrical Engring Old Dominion Univ Norfolk VA 23529 Personal E-mail: mseow@gmail.com. Business E-Mail: mseow@odu.edu.

**SEPKOSKI, DARA HENNING,** museum educator; d. J. F. Henning and G. W. Wolf; m. David Henning Sepkoski, Jan. 2, 1972; 1 child, Ella. BA in Lit., Scripps Coll., Claremont, Calif., 1993; MA in Art Edn., Sch. of the Art Inst. of Chgo., 1996. Mus. educator Kidspace Mus., Pasadena, Calif., 1993—95, Natural History Mus. of L.A. County, 1994—96; coord. studio and family programs Terra Mus. of Am. Art, Chgo., 1996—99; program mgr. family programs Walker Art Ctr., Mpls., 1999—2002; curator of edn. MOCA Cleve. 2004—05, Allen Meml. Art Mus., Oberlin, 2005—. Mem. Am. Assn. of Museums. Democrat. Home: 39 North Cedar St Oberlin OH 44074 Office: Allen Meml Art Mus 87 N Main St Oberlin OH 44074 Office Phone: 440-775-8671. E-mail: dara.sepkoski@oberlin.edu.

**SEPP, PETER JOHN,** communications executive, writer; s. John Arthur and Patricia Florence Sepp; m. Cecilia Marie Blanke, Mar. 21, 1987. BA in History and Polit. Sci. cum laude, Webster U., 1986. Clk., election judge St. Louis County Bd. Elections, Clayton, 1984—86; intern Kit Bond for Senate, St. Louis, 1986; pub. info. officer Nat. Taxpayers Union, Washington, 1988—92, v.p. comm. Alexandria, Va., 1992—. Contbr. articles to profl. jours. Avocations: aviation, hiking, military history. Office: Nat Taxpayers Union 108 N Alfred St Alexandria VA 22314 Office Phone: 703-683-5700. E-mail: pressguy@ntu.org.

**SEPULVADO, JOSEPH MICHAEL,** computer information scientist; b. Cheyenne, Wyo., Aug. 16, 1952; s. Joseph Martin and Ann Mildred (Shipp) S.; m. Cynthia Marie Howell, July 31, 1982 (div. Aug. 1987); m. Shirley Rae Benham; children: Julie Ann, Angela Dyan. BS, U. Okla., 1972. Cert. data

processor, data educator, computer programmer. Sr. systems analyst Pub. Svc. Co. of Okla., Tulsa, 1978-80; application supr. Cotton Petroleum Corp., Tulsa, 1980-81; cons. Forte Info. Svcs., Tulsa, 1981-82; instr. Tulsa Jr. Coll., 1982-84; sr. systems analyst Citgo Petroleum Corp., Tulsa, 1984; cons. Computer Horizons, inc., Jacksonville, Fla., 1984-85, Computer Assistance, Inc., Dallas, 1985-87, IMI Systems, Inc., Dallas, 1987-97; ind. contractor, 1997—. With USAF, 1981. Roman Catholic. Avocations: reading, fishing. Home: 1701 Windmire Dr Mesquite TX 75181-1555

**SEPULVEDA, EDUARDO SOLIDEO,** chemical engineer; b. Loay, Philippines, Jan. 5, 1945; came to U.S., 1981; m. Consuelo S. Araneta, May 18, 1977; children: Edward, Josephus, Blaise. BSChE, De La Salle U., 1966; M of Chem. Engring., U. Philippines, 1972. Lic. profl. engr., Calif. Instr. U. Philippines, Quezon City, 1968-70; sr. instr. De La Salle U., Manila, Philippines, 1970-71, asst. prof., 1971-73; process engr. Philippines Petroleum Corp., Makati, 1973-74, sr. process engr., 1974-75, mgr. tech. svc., 1975-81; sr. engr. C F Braun & Co., Alhambra, Calif., 1981; prin. engr. Brown & Root Braun, Alhambra, Calif., 1987-94, L.G. Engineering Co., Ltd., Seoul, Korea, 1994-96; supervising process engr. Parsons, Martinez, Calif., 1997—. Reviewer chem. bd. De La Salle U., 1970-79. Mem. St. John Corregidor Lodge, Manila, 1979. Mem. AIChE, Phi Kappa Phi. Achievements include designed and engineered a fluid catalyst transport system to hydrocracker reactor. Home: 3700 Oaklawn Ln Pico Rivera CA 90660-5941 Office: Worley Parsons 2000 Marina Vista Ave Martinez CA 94553-1301 Office Phone: 925-313-5187. Personal E-mail: essep@aol.com. Business E-Mail: ed.sepulveda@worleyparsons.com.

**SEPÚLVEDA, SANDRA,** communications educator; b. N.Y.C., N.Y., Sept. 14, 1948; d. Samuel Sepúlveda and Maria Trinidad. PhD, U. P.R., Rio Piedras, 2000. Cert. life cert. Tchr. Dept. Edn., P.R. Prof. U. P.R., Rio Piedras, PR, 1986—. V.p. acad. affairs Nat. Coll., Bayamon and Arecibo, PR, 1994—95; dean acad. affairs Sch. Fine Arts, San Juan, PR, 1997—99; cons. in field, PR, 1996—; mem. consultative bd. Coun. Higher Edn., PR, 1996—. Pres. editl. bd.: Nat. Coll. Bull., 1989—95. Mem. P.R. chpt. ARC, 1990, Preservation Trust of P.R., 1995—. Mem.: AAUW, MLA, Phi Delta Kappa. Avocations: travel, photography, reading, decoration, cooking. Home: PO Box 195081 San Juan PR 00919-5081 Office: U PR Rio Piedras Campus Coll Bus Adminstrn PO Box 23332 San Juan PR 00931

**SÉQUIN, CARLO H.,** computer science educator; b. Winterthur, Switzerland, Oct. 30, 1941; came to U.S., 1970; s. Carl R. and Margrit (Schaeppi) S.; m. Margareta Frey, Oct. 5, 1968; children: Eveline, Andre. BS, U. Basel, Switzerland, 1965, PhD, 1969. Mem. tech. staff Bell Labs., Murray Hill, NJ, 1970-76; vis. Mackay lectr. U. Calif.-Berkeley, 1976-77, prof. elec. engring. computer scis., 1977—, assoc. chmn. computer sci., 1980-83, assoc. dean capital projects, 2001—. Author: First Book on Charge-Coupled Devices, Charge Transfer Devices, 1975; contbr. over 230 articles to profl. jours. Fellow IEEE (Tech. Achievement award 2003), Assn. Computing Machinery, Swiss Acad. Engring. Scis. Achievements include patents for integrated circuits. Office: U Calif Dept EECS Computer Scis Divsn Soda Hall Berkeley CA 94720-1776 Office Phone: 510-642-5103. Business E-Mail: sequin@cs.berkeley.edu.

**SERAFIM, PHILIP E.,** electrical engineer, computer engineer; b. Piraeus, Greece, July 10, 1937; s. Evangelos D. and Amalia Serafim; m. Leta Naugle, Nov. 27, 1976; children: Amalia, Anna-Maria. Diploma in Elec. and Mech. Engring., Nat. Tech. U., Greece, 1959; MSc in Elec. Engring., MIT, 1960, ScD in Elec. Engring., 1963. Profl. engr., Tech. Chamber of Greece, 1959. Prof. of elec. engring. Poly. U. NY, NYC, 1963—75; sr. rsch. scientist Naval Rsch. Lab., Washington, 1975—77; prof., chair elec. engring. Nat. Tech. U., Athens, Greece, 1977—84; prof. elec. engring. Grad. Mil. Acad., Athens, Greece, 1978—84; sr. rsch. fellow NAS, Washington, 1984—85; prof. elec. and computer engring. Northeastern U., Boston, 1985—. Cons. Naval Rsch. Lab., Washington, 1985—. Author: General Principles of Electrical Engineering, Electromagnetics Fields, 2 vols.; contbr. articles to profl. jours.; author tchg. notes. Trustee Maliotio Hellenic Cultural Ctr., Boston, 2001—; sci. adv., coord. New England chpt. Archidiocesan Adv. Com. on Sci. and Tech., NYC, 2002—. Named Most Outstanding Elec. and Computer Engring. Prof., Elec. and Computer Engring. Dept., 1999, 1998, 1997, 1995, 1994; recipient Outstanding Tchg. award, Coll. of Engring., Northeastern U., 1999, Excellence in Tchg. award, Northeastern U., 1990; Sr. Rsch. fellow, NAS, 1984-1985, NATO scholar, Greek Govt., 1961-1963, Fulbright scholar, 1959—60, IKY scholar, Greek Nat. Scholarship Found., 1954-1959. Mem.: IEEE (sr.), Electromagnetics Acad., Tau Beta Pi, Eta Kappa Nu, Sigma Xi. Greek Orthodox. Achievements include patents for system for conditioning an electron beam for improved free-electron laser operation. Home: 260 Peakham Rd Sudbury MA 01776-2732 Office: Northeastern U ECE Dept 360 Huntington Ave Boston MA 02150 Office Phone: 617-373-2063. Personal E-mail: serafim@ece.neu.edu.

**SERAFIN, DONALD,** plastic surgeon, educator; b. NYC, Jan. 18, 1938; s. Stephen Michael and Julia (Sopko) S.; m. Patricia Serafin; children: Allison Elizabeth, Christina Julia, Donald Stephen, Lara Leigh. AB, Duke U., 1960, MD, 1964. Diplomate Am. Bd. Surgery, Am. Bd. Plastic Surgery. Surg. intern Grady Meml. Hosp., Atlanta, 1964-65; resident in surgery Emory U. Hosp., Atlanta, 1965-69; asst. resident in plastic and reconstructive surgery Duke U. Med. Ctr., Durham, NC, 1971-73, chief resident, 1973-74; Christine Kleinert fellow in hand surgery U. Louisville Hosp., 1972-73; practice medicine specializing in plastic surgery, Durham. Mem. staff N.C. Splty. Hosp., Durham Regional Hosp., Maria Parham Hosp.; attending faculty Durham VA Med. Ctr.; asst. prof. plastic, reconstructive and maxillofacial surgery Duke U., 1974-77, assoc. prof., 1977-81, prof., 1981-2000, prof. emeritus, 2000—, chief divsn. plastic reconstructive and maxillofacial and oral surgery, 1985-95, chmn. Plastic Surgery Rsch. Coun., 1983. Assoc. editor Jour. Reconstructive Microsurgery; contbr. articles to profl. jours. Served to maj. M.C., USAF, 1969-71, to col. M.C., USAR. 1971-2004 Decorated Air Force Commendation medal, Army Commendation medal, Army Achievement medal. Fellow ACS; mem. AMA, Internat. Soc. Reconstructive Microsurgery, Am. Soc. Plastic Surgeons, Am. Assn. Plastic Surgeons, Am. Soc. Aesthetic Plastic Surgery, Am. Soc. Surgery Hand, Am. Assn. Hand Surgery, Am. Burn Assn., Plastic Surgery Rshc Coun., N.C. Soc. Plastic, Maxillofacial and Reconstructive Surgeons, Southeastern Soc. Plastic and Reconstructive Surgeons. Office: 511 Ruin Creek Rd Ste 104B Henderson NC 28350 Office Phone: 866-892-7711, 252-438-8152, 919-220-7711. Personal E-mail: seradonmd@aol.com.

**SERAFIN, ROBERT JOSEPH,** science center administrator, electrical engineer; b. Chgo., Apr. 22, 1936; s. Joseph Albert and Antoinette (Gazda) S.; m. Betsy Furgerson, Mar. 4, 1961; children: Katherine, Jenifer, Robert Joseph Jr., Elizabeth. BSEE, U. Notre Dame, 1958; MSEE, Northwestern U., 1961; PhDEE, Ill. Inst. Tech., 1972. Engr. Hazeltine Rsch. Corp. Ill. Inst. Tech. Rsch. Inst., 1960-62; assoc. engr., rsch. engr., sr. rsch. engr. Nat. Ctr. for Atmospheric Rsch., Boulder, Colo., 1962-73, mgr. field observing facility, 1973-80, dir. atmospheric tech. div. Boulder, Colo., 1981-89, dir. 1989-2000. Chair Nat. Weather Svc. Modernization Com. Author: Revised Radar Handbook, 1989; contbr. numerous articles to profl. jours.; editl. bd./com. Acta Meteorologica Sinica; editl. founder Jour. Atmospheric and Oceanic Tech.; patentee in field. Speaker various civic groups in U.S. and internationally. Fellow IEEE, Am. Meteorol. Soc. (pres.); mem. NAE, NAS (human rights com.), Boulder C. of C., Sigma Xi. Avocations: golf, fishing, skiing. Office: Nat Ctr Atmospheric Rsch 1850 Table Mesa Dr PO Box 3000 Boulder CO 80307-3000

**SERAFIN, THOMAS JOSEPH,** photographer; b. Buffalo, July 28, 1952; s. Joseph Thomas and Mary Helen Serafin; 1 child, Christine. Photographer Modernage, L.A., 1984—. Author: (book) Relics-The Forgotten Sacramental, 1999, The Simony Report, 1999. Founder Internat. Crusade Holy Relics, L.A., 1996—2002; dep. mem. assembly Internat. Parliament Safety & Peace, Palermo, Sicily, Italy, 2001—. With USAR, 1970-76. Decorated knight Order Immaculate Conception Vila Vicosa, Duke Braganca, 36th Titular King of Portugal, comdr. St. Michael of the Wing; named Officer,

Imperial Order of Dragon of Annam-Liaison to His Royal Highness Prince Nhiep Chinh Nguyen-Phuc Buu Chanh, Vietnam. Mem.: Apostolate Holy Relics (pres., CEO 2002). Roman Catholic. Office: Ichrusa/Apostolate Holy Relics PO Box 21301 Los Angeles CA 90021 Office Phone: 818-416-9279. Business E-Mail: tom@ICHRusa.com.

**SERAFINE, MARY LOUISE,** psychologist, educator, lawyer; b. Rochester, N.Y., July 2, 1948; BA in Music with honors, Rutgers U., 1970; PhD, U. Fla., 1975; JD, Yale U., 1991. Bar: Calif. 1992, D.C. 1993, U.S. Tax Ct. 1995, N.Y. 1999, Tex. 2005. Tchg. and rsch. fellow U. Fla., Gainesville, 1970-76; vis. asst. prof. U. Tex., San Antonio, 1976-77, asst. prof. Austin, 1977-79; postdoctoral fellow dept. psychology Yale U., New Haven, 1979-83, lectr., 1981-83; asst. prof. dept. psychology Vassar Coll., Poughkeepsie, N.Y., 1983-88; with O'Melveny & Myers, L.A., 1991-96, Chadbourne & Parke, L.A., 1996-97, Fried, Frank, Harris, Shriver & Jacobson, L.A., 1997-99; pvt. practice, 1999—. Author: Music as Cognition: The Development of Thought in Sound, 1988; editl. reviewer Child Devel., Devel. Psychology, Am. Scientist, Jour. Exptl. Child Psychology, Jour. Applied Developmental Psychology, Yale Law Jour.; contbr. articles to profl. jours. Grantee State of Fla. 1974-75, U. Tex.-Austin, 1977, Spencer Found., 1979-85. Office: PO Box 4342 Austin TX 78765 Office Phone: 512-220-5452. E-mail: mlserafine@earthlink.net.

**SERBAROLI, FRANCIS J.,** lawyer, educator, writer; b. NYC, Feb. 8, 1952; AB, Fordham U., 1973, JD, 1977. Bar: N.Y. 1978, U.S. Dist. Ct. (ea. and so. dists.) N.Y. 1978, U.S. Ct. Appeals (2d and D.C. cirs.) 1979, U.S. Supreme Ct. 1983. Asst. atty. gen. N.Y. State Dept. Law, 1978-80; ptnr. Cadwalader Wickersham & Taft, N.Y.C., 1995—. Vice chmn. N.Y. State Pub. Health Coun., 1995—; health law columnist The N.Y. Law Jour. Author: The Corporate Practice of Medicine Prohibition in the Modern Era of Health Care, 1999. Chmn. bd. trustees Loyola Sch., N.Y.C. Fellow N.Y. Acad. Medicine; mem. Am. Health Lawyers' Assn., N.Y. State Bar Assn., Assn. Bar City N.Y. Office: Cadwalader Wickersham Taft LLP One World Fin Ctr New York NY 10281

**SERCHUK, IVAN,** lawyer; b. N.Y.C., Oct. 13, 1935; s. Israel and Freda (Davis) S.; children: Camille, Bruce Mead, Vance Foster. BA, Columbia U., 1957, LLB, 1960. Bar: N.Y. 1961, U.S. Dist. Ct. (so. dist.) N.Y. 1963, U.S. Ct. Appeals (2d cir.) 1964, U.S. Tax Ct. 1966. Law clk. to judge U.S. Dist. Ct. (so. dist.) N.Y., NY, 1961-63; assoc. Kaye, Scholer, Fierman, Hays & Handler, 1963-68; dep. supt., counsel N.Y. State Banking Dept., N.Y.C., Albany, 1968-71; ptnr. Berle & Berle, 1972—73; spl. counsel N.Y. State Senate Banks Com., 1972; ptnr. Serchuk & Zelermyer LLP, White Plains, NY, 1976—2003, Todtman, Nachamie, Spizz & Johns, PC, 2003—. Lectr. Practising Law Inst., 1968-71. Mem. N.Y. State Bar Assn., Assn. of Bar of City of N.Y. Office: Todtman Nachamie Spizz & Johns 425 Park Ave New York NY 10022 Home: 100 United Nations Plaza New York NY 10017 Office Phone: 212-754-9400. Business E-Mail: iserchuk@tnsj-law.com.

**SERCK-HANSSEN, EILIF,** air transportation executive; BS in Civil Engring., U. Bergen; BA in Mgmt. Studies., U. Kent, Canterbury; MBA, U. Chgo. Former mgr. PricewaterhouseCoopers, London, PepsiCo; former mng. dir. fin., asst. treas. N.W. Airlines; sr. v.p.-fin., treas. US Airways Group, Inc., US Airways, Inc., Arlington, Va., 2003—. Mem.: Inst. Chartered Accts. Eng. and Wales. Office: US Airways 2345 Crystal Dr Arlington VA 22227

**SERDAHELY, DOUGLAS J.,** lawyer, former state judge; b. Rhinelander, Wis., June 1, 1946; AB with highest honors, Northwestern Univ., 1968; JD, Harvard Univ., 1972. Bar: Alaska 1972, US Dist. Ct. (Alaska dist.) 1972, US Ct. Appeals (9th & DC cir.) 1973, US Supreme Ct. 1994. Law clk. Chief Justice Jay A. Rabinowitz, Alaska Supreme Ct., 1972—73; judge Alaska Superior Ct., 1981—89, presiding judge, 1985—89; pro tem panelist Alaska Ct. Appeals, Alaska Supreme Ct., 1981—89; former ptnr. Bogle & Gates, Anchorage; ptnr. Litigation & Dispute resolution, Environ. Health & Safety, Antitrust practices, mem. mgmt. com., office mng. ptnr. Patton Boggs LLP, Anchorage. Instr. Nat. Inst. Trial Advocacy, 1981, Hastings Coll. Trial Advocacy, 1985; adj. prof. Puget Sound Law Sch., 1987. Mem.: ABA, Alaska Bar Assn., Phi Beta Kappa. Office: Patton Boggs LLP Ste 700 601 W Fifth Ave Anchorage AK 99501-2226 Office Phone: 907-263-6310. Office Fax: 907-263-6345. Business E-Mail: dserdahely@pattonboggs.com.

**SERDARI, THOMAÏ,** architect, historian; b. Athens, Greece, May 5, 1970; d. Vasilis Serdaris and Despina Serdari. MA in Architecture, Nat. Tech. U. of Athens, 1994; MA in Media studies, New Sch. for Social Rsch., N.Y.C., 1997; MA in Art History, NYU, 2001, PhD in Art History, 2005. Cert. archtl. engr., Hellenic Republic Tech. Chamber of Greece. Arch., Lamia, Greece, 1994—95; art and architecture libr. Dept. Fine Arts NYU, 1999—; prin. Novel May Properties LLC, NYC, 2006—. Founder, editor-in-chief (jour.) POLIS. Scholar, Pratt Inst., Bklyn., 1999—2000; Bogardus scholar, 1999—2000. Mem.: Art Librs. Soc. N.Am., Soc. Archtl. Historians, Documentation and Conservation of Bldgs., Sites and Neighborhoods of Modern Movement.

**SEREBRIER, JOSÉ,** musician, composer, conductor; b. Montevideo, Uruguay, Dec. 3, 1938; came to U.S., 1956; s. David and Frida (Wasser) S.; m. Carole Farley, Mar. 29, 1969; 1 child, Lara Adriana Francesca. Diploma, Nat. Conservatory, Montevideo, 1956, Curtis Inst. Music, 1958; BA, U. Minn., 1960; studied with Aaron Copland, Antal Dorati, Pierre Monteux. Ind. composer, condr., 1955—. Apprentice condr. Minn. Orch., 1958-60; assoc. condr. Am. Symphony Orch., N.Y.C., 1962-66; music dir. Am. Shakespeare Festival, 1966; composer-in-residence Cleve. Orch., 1968-71; artistic dir. Internat. Festival of Ams., Miami, 1984—; Festival Miami, 1985—; guest condr. numerous orchs. including London Symphony, London Philharm., Paris Radio, Cleve. Symphony Orch., Phila. Symphony Orch., Pitts. Symphony Orch.; founder, artistic dir. Festival Miami (internat. arts festival), 1984. Composer: (for orch.) Variations on a Theme from Childhood, (for chamber) Symphony for Percussion, Concerto for Violin and Orch. (recorded by Royal Phila. Orch. on ASV), (concerto for harp and orch.) Colores Magicos, 1970, Symphonie Mystique, 2003 (5 Grammy nominations including best new composition 2004), Symphony No. 3 (Grammy nomination for best new competition 2004), also works for chorus, voice, keyboard; recs. for RCA, CRI, ASV, KEM, Disc, Trax Classique, EMI, Tioch, Chandos, Varese-Sarabande Decca, IMG, Pickwick, BMG, BIS Records, Vox, Dinemec, Conifer Classics, Decca, Warner Classics, Naxos, with various orchs.; condr. for many recs. including Sibelius Symphony No. 1, Holst's The Planets, Carmen, Poulenc's opera La Voix Humaine, Shostakovich Film Suites vol. 1, 2 and 3(Deutsche Schallplatten award 1988), Carole Farley Sings French Songs (Deutsche Schallplaten award 1988), (home video) Kultur, Prokoviev's Alexander Nevsky, Beethoven's Eroica and Tchaikovsky Symphony No. 1 with Sydney and Melbourne Symphony Orch., Mendelssohn Symphonies, Beethoven Symphonies, Bloch's Violin Concerto and Serebrier's Poema Elegiaco CD, 1992, Le Orchestral Music of Tchaikovsky (several vols.), Laserdisc of Operas The Telephone by Menotti and La Voix Humaine by Poulenc with Scottish Chamber Orch., 1992, Royal Philharm. Orch., 1992, Dvořak Symphonies with Czech State Philharm. for Conifer/BMG, Music of Janacek and Chadwick (4 CDs) for R.R., Hindemith CD with Philharmonia Orch. for ASV; (first complete recording) Partita, Ned Rorem For Naxos; (world-premiere recordings) Winterreise, Fantasia; solo-violin sonata with London Philharm. Orch.; Gershwin CD with Royal Scottish Nat. Orch. for Dinemic; Delius songs and orch. works, Grieg songs, London Philharmonic Orch. recording for Dinemic; conductor Grammy Awards, 2003; recordings: music by William Schuman (2 Grammy nominations), Ives Symphony No. 4 (Grammy nomination), Carmen Symphony (Latin Grammy for best classical album 2004). Recipient Ford Found. Condr.'s award, Alice M. Ditson award, 1976, commn. award Nat. Endowment Arts, 1978, Deutsche Schall Platten Critics award, Music Retailers Assn. award for Best Symphony Rec., 1991, 2002; Guggenheim fellow, 1958-60; Rockefeller Found. grantee, 1968-70. Mem. Am. Symphony Orch. League, Am. Music Ctr., Am. Fedn. Musicians. Home: 270 Riverside Dr New York

NY 10025-5209 E-mail: caspi123@aol.com. *A composer has the duty to communicate with his audience. The academic-intellectual composer of the 50's has become obsolete. Writing just for one's colleagues has fortunately been proven a dead-end.*

**SERENBETZ, ROBERT,** manufacturing executive, financial planner; b. Rockville Centre, N.Y., Apr. 18, 1944; s. Raymond Robert Serenbetz and Mildred (Egner) Clapp; m. Karen Jeanne Jackson, Dec. 30, 1967; children: Todd, Gregg, Kathryn. AB, Dartmouth Coll., 1966; MBA, Harvard U., 1968. Cert. fin. planner. Mktg. staff asst. to group product mgr. Colgate-Palmolive Co., N.Y.C., 1968-75; dir. mktg. Colgate-Palmolive Colombia, Cali, Colombia, 1975-77; v.p. mktg. Colgate-Palmolive Canada, Toronto, Ont., Canada, 1977-81; v.p. mktg. western hemisphere Warner-Lambert Co., Morris Plains, NJ, 1981; pres. Warner-Lambert Can., Toronto, 1981-85; pres. Latin Am., Asia, Australia Warner-Lambert Co., Morris Plains, 1986-89; pres. Am. Chicle, Morris Plains, 1989-91; pres., COO DNA Plant Tech. Corp., Cinnaminson, NJ, 1991-92; pres., CEO Oakland, Calif., 1992-94, chmn., CEO, 1994-96; COO DNAP Holding Corp., Oakland, Calif., 1996-98; pvt. practice CFP, 2003—. Mem. adv. bd. Coun. Ams., N.Y.C., 1987-89; mem. steering com. Pharm. Mfrs. Assn., Washington, 1987-89; bd. dirs. Caribbean/Cen. Am. Com., Washington, 1989; mem. adv. bd. Coun. for Internat. Unity, N.Y.C., 1987-89; alumni coun. Dartmouth Coll., 2002-05, student life com. chmn., 2004-05. Bd. dirs. Notch Brook Resort Gen. Ptnrs. Condominium Assn., Stowe, Vt., 1988-94; pres. bd. dirs. Seaside Homeowners Assn., Isle of Palms, S.C., 1997—; mem. U.S. Postal Svc. Mktg. Adv. Bd., 1990-2004, vice chmn., 1998-2004. Mem. Nat. Candy Wholesalers Assn. (bd. dirs. 1989-91), Morris County C. of C. (bd. dirs. 1989-91), Leadership Inc. (bd. dirs. Phila. br. 1993-94), Fin. Planning Assn., Wild Dunes Club (Isle of Palms, SC), Trillium Links and Lake Club (Cashiers, NC). Republican. Episcopalian. Avocations: golf, stamp collecting/philately, photography, tennis. E-mail: bobserenbetz@prodigy.net.

**SERGENT, JOHN STANLEY,** hospital administrator, medical educator; m. Carole Sergent; children: Ellen, Katie. MD, Vanderbilt U., 1966. Pvt. practice; chair dept. medicine St. Thomas Hosp., Nashville, 1988—95; mem. faculty Vanderbilt U., Nashville, 1975—88, prof. medicine, 1988—; chief med. officer Vanderbilt U. Hosp. and Clinic, Nashville, 1995—2003; vice chmn. for edn. Vanderbilt U. Sch. of Medicine, Nashville, 2003—, prog. dir. resident tng., dept. medicine, 2003—. Mem.: Am. Coll. Rheumatology (pres. 1992—). Office: Vanderbilt U 1161 21st Ave S D 3100 MCN Nashville TN 37232-2358 Office Phone: 615-343-0339. E-mail: john.sergent@vanderbilt.edu.

**SERGEY, JOHN MICHAEL, JR.,** investment company executive, consultant; b. Chgo., Nov. 17, 1942; s. John Michael and Helen Ann (Bruchan) S.; m. Sharon Lee Ourada (div. 1982); children: John Michael III, Elisabeth Ann, Mark William, Tanya Ruth; m. Pamela Lynne Murphy, Aug. 8, 1987; children: Brian M., Sarah L. BA in Bus., Northwestern U., 1968; MBA, U. Chgo., 1976. Mgr. rolled products A. M. Castle, Chgo.; v.p. Dietzgen Corp., Chgo.; dir. sales and mktg. Avery Label, Azusa, Calif., 1978-80; v.p., gen. mgr. Fasson Roll div. Avery, Painesville, Ohio, 1980-84; group v.p. Soabar Products Group div. Avery, Phila., 1984-87, Materials Group div. Avery, Painesville, 1987-89; pres., CEO GAF Materials Corp., Wayne, N.J., 1989-96; CEO Strategic Distbn., Inc., Bensalem, Pa., 1997—2001; chmn. Sergey Enterprises, 2002—. Office: Sergey Enterprises 517 Falcon Point Dr New Hope PA 18938

**SERGI, VINCENT A.F.,** lawyer; Grad.: Beloit Coll.; JD with honors, Northwestern U. With fin. and reorganization dept. Katten Muchin Zavis Rosenman, 1974, dept. head, nat. mng. ptnr., 1996—, mem. bd. dirs., mem. exec. and operating com., chmn. compensation com. Bd. dirs. Goodman Theatre, Joffrey Ballet, Providence-St. Mel Sch. Achievements include mem. first assoc. class, Katten Muchin Zavis Rosenman. Office: 525 W Monroe St Chicago IL 60661-3693 Office Phone: 312-902-5255. Business E-mail: vincent.sergi@kmzr.com.

**SERIDO, JOYCE,** psychologist, researcher; b. Plainfield, N.J., May 13, 1953; d. Mary Ann Gibriano and John Carmen Serido; m. Barry Edward Runyon, Jan. 1, 1985; 1 child, Evan Tyler Runyon. BA, Rutgers U., 1971—75; MBA, Seton Hall U., 1976—81; MS, U. Ariz., 1999—2001, PhD, 2001—03. Programmer First Nat. State Bank, Newark, 1975—76; programmer/analyst A T & T, Piscataway, NJ, 1976—83; sr. ptnr. CSC Cons., Roseland, 1983—91; mng. ptnr. Egal Inc., Milford, 1991—94; pres. Methods & Solutions, Tucson, Ariz., 1994—98; project mgr. Sunquest Info. Sys., Tucson, 1998—2000; post-doctoral assoc. Cornell U., Ithaca, NY, 2004—05; rsch. scientist U. Ariz., 2005—. Author: (jour. article) Chronic Stressors and Daily Hassles: Unique and Interactive Relationships with Psychological Distress, Recipient Tribute to Women and Industry, YWCA, 1990; grantee Paolucci Rsch. grant, Kappa Omicron Nu / W. K. Kellogg Found., 2002; scholar Travel scholarship, APA, 2001, Ruth R. Cowden scholarship, U. Ariz., 2003. Mem.: AAUW (assoc.), Gerontol. Soc. Am. (assoc.), Am. Psychol. Assn. (assoc.), Nat. Coun. Family Rels. (assoc.). Avocations: hiking, travel, dance. Office: Univ Arizona PO Box 210033 Tucson AZ 85712-0033 Office Phone: 520-621-7127. Office Fax: 520-621-3401. Personal E-mail: jserido@email.arizona.edu, joyceserido@hotmail.com.

**SERIO, ROBERT FRANCIS,** lawyer; b. Oct. 27, 1957; BA cum laude, Harvard Coll., 1980; JD, UCLA, 1985. Bar: NY 1986, Calif. 1987. Assoc. Shearman & Sterling, NYC, 1985—87, Gibson Dunn & Crutcher LLP, NYC, 1987—94, ptnr. litig. dept., 1994—, and co-ptnr.-in-charge, NYC office. Mem.: ABA. Office: Gibson Dunn & Crutcher LLP 47th Fl 200 Park Ave New York NY 10166-0193 Office Phone: 212-351-3917. Office Fax: 212-351-5246, Business E-mail: rserio@gibsondunn.com

**SERKES, JEFFREY D.,** former energy executive; b. Dec. 24, 1950; BBA in Acctg., George Washington U.; MBA in Fin., Rutgers U. With RJR Nabisco; from v.p. fin, sales and distbn. to v.p., treas. IBM, 1995—2002; pres. JDS Opportunities, LLC, 2002—03; sr. v.p., CFO Allegheny Energy, Inc., Hagerstown, Md., 2003—06. Bd. adv. Rutgers U.; dir. chmn., audit com. compensation com. REFAC.

**SERLET, BERTRAND,** information technology executive; PhD in computer sci., U. Orsay, France. Rsch. engr. Xerox PARC, 1985—89; engring./managerial positions NeXT, 1989—97; sr. v.p. software engring. Apple Computer Inc., Cupertino, Calif., 1997—. Achievements include key player in the definition, development and creation of Mac OS X, the world's most advanced operating system. Office: Apple Computer Inc 1 Infinite Loop Cupertino CA 95014 Office Fax: 408-996-1010.

**SERLING, JOEL MARTIN,** educational psychologist; b. Seneca Falls; NY, Feb. 8, 1936; s. Philip and Cecil Serling; AA, U. Buffalo, 1957; BS in Edn., Ohio No. U., 1959; MA, Columbia U., 1960; children— Meredith Anne, Rebecca Lynne, Heather Lee. Instr. psychology West Liberty (W.va.) State Coll., 1961-63; vocat. psychologist, div. child welfare, Cleve., 1963-64; sch. psychologist Steuben County Bd. Coop. Ednl. Services, Bath, NY, 1964-65, Chenango County Bd. Coop. Ednl. Services, Norwich, NY, 1965-67, Delaware County Bd. Coop. Ednl. Services, Walton, NY, 1967-68; sch. psychologist Vestal (NY) Central Sch., 1968-70, Whitesboro (NY) Central Sch., 1970-92; adj. prof. psychology Utica Coll., Syracuse U., 1971-75, 86—, SUNY Coll. Tech., Utica-Rome, 1975—, Mohawk Valley Community Coll., 1971-91, C. C. of So. Nevada, 1995—; cons., mentor Empire Coll., SUNY, 1975—; instr. psychology Am. Inst. Banking, 1971—. Bd. edn., bd. dirs. Hillel Day Sch., Utica-Rome, 1971-75; bd. prof. advs. Mohawk Valley Learning Disabilities Assn., 1972-76. Recipient cert. of recognition Mohawk Valley Learning Disabilities Assn., 1973; cert. sch. psychologist, NY State, NC Mem. Am. Psychol. Assn., Nat. Assn. Sch. Psychologists (charter), NY Assn. Sch. Psychologists (cert. of recognition 1977), Sch. Psychologists of Upper NY, Central NY Psychol. Assn., United Univ. Professions, N.Y. State

United Tchrs. Assn., Whitesboro Tchrs. Assn., Phi Delta Kappa. Jewish. Clubs: Odd Fellows, Zeta Beta Tau. Co-author, co-developer; Early Identification Screening Index, 1971; contbr. articles to profl. publs., presenter in field E-mail: jssp@cox.net.

**SERMOS, SYBIL FALK,** retired artist; b. Boston, June 8, 1938; d. Edward I. and Etta (Goldman) Falk; m. Kemon A. Sermos, Apr. 4, 1968; children: Evan, Holly. BFA, Mass. Coll. Art, 1960. Tchr. Art Inst. Boston, 1962-69; pres. Holly Dolls by Sybil, Somerville, Mass., 1972-82; free-lance artist Harvard U. Med. Sch. News Office, Boston, 1981-89, Larkin Publs., Chestnut Hill, Mass., 1981-91. Tchr. pvt. classes in furniture painting, 1999—2006. Group shows include Art Inst. Boston, 1967, Boston City Hall, 1977, Marlborough House Boston, 1978; works include Family of Dolls quilt (pub. in the National Bicentennial Quilt Exposition, 1976, and The Big Book of Applique, 1978). Mem., past chairperson Somerville Arts Lottery Coun., 1980-86; mem. Mass. Coun. on Arts and Humanities, 1984-87, Mass. Cultural Coun., 1990-91, Mass. Arts Lottery Coun., 1985-90, vice chmn., 1988-90; vol. Perkins Sch. for Blind and Deaf. Recipient Richard R. Mitton award Jordan Marsh, 1960; 2d Place Crafts award Am. Mothers Com. Mass., 1976, 78; Best of Show Craft award Invitational Marblehead Art Festival, 1991, judges choice award, 1997, 1st prize Mixed Media award Winthrop Art Festival, 1978, 80, 82, 84, 90, 3d prize, 1989, 2nd prize Craft award, 1989, Spl. award for excellence in watercolor, 1984, 85, 86, 90, 3d prize, 1992. Mem. Winthrop Art Assn. (pres. 1981-83), Mass. Cultural Alliance, Boston Women's Caucus for Art. Democrat. Jewish.

**SERNA, PATRICIO,** state supreme court justice; b. Reserve, N.Mex., Aug. 26, 1939; m. Eloise Serna; children: Elena Patricia, Anna Alicia 1 stepchild, John Herrera. BSBA with honors, U. Albuquerque, 1962; JD, U. Denver, 1970; LLM, Harvard U., 1971; postgrad., Nat. Jud. Coll., 1985, postgrad., 1990, postgrad., 1992, postgrad., 1994; LLD (hon.), U. Denver, 2002. Bar: N.Mex. 1970, Colo. 1971, U.S. Dist. Ct. N.Mex. 1970. Probation and parole officer State of N.Mex., Santa Fe, Las Cruces, 1966—67; spl. asst. to comm. mem. Equal Opportunity Commn., Washington, 1971—75; asst. atty. gen. State of N.Mex., Santa Fe, 1975—79; pvt. practice Santa Fe, 1979—85; dist. judge First Jud. Dist., Santa Fe, 1985—96; justice N.Mex. Supreme Ct., Santa Fe, 1996—, chief justice, 2001—02. Adj. prof. law Georgetown U., Washington, 1973, Cath. U., Washington, 1974—75; faculty advisor Nat. Jud. Coll., Reno, 1987. Bd. dirs. Santa Fe Group Homes Inc. With U.S. Army, 1963—65. Mem.: Santa Fe Bar Assn., No. N.Mex. Am. Inns of Ct., Nat. Hispanic Bar Assn. (Judge of Yr. award 2002, Judge of Yr. 2002), N.Mex. Hispanic Bar Assn., N.Mex. Bar Assn., Elks, Phi Alpha Delta. Avocations: hiking, fishing, Ping Pong, chess, painting. Office: NMex Supreme Ct PO Box 848 Santa Fe NM 87504-0848 Office Phone: 505-827-4886. Business E-Mail: suppms@nmcourts.com.*

**SERNA, PHILLIP WOODROW,** music educator, musician; b. Houston, Aug. 12, 1976; s. Fred Louis and Kathleen Louise Serna; m. Magdalena Ewa Mikolajczyk, July 17, 2005. MusB, San Francisco Conservatory of Music, 1998; MusM, postgrad., Northwestern U., 2001—. Prin. double bass Northbrook (Ill.) Symphony Orch., 2003; sect. double bass Ill. Philharm. Orch., Park Forest, 2002; music faculty Sherwood Conservatory of Music, Chicago, 2002—04. Pvt. music tchr. Willowbrook H.S., Villa Park, Ill., 2003; adj. pvt. music tchr. Neuqua Valley H.S. Music Dept., Naperville, Ill., 2003; pvt. music tchr. Glenbard East H.S., Lombard, Ill., 2004, Glenbard South H.S., Glen Ellyn, Ill., 2004, Carl Sandburg H.S., Orland Park, Ill., 2004. Edn. com. Early Music Chgo., 2005; outreach adv. Northbrook Symphony, 2003. Mem.: Internat. Soc. Bassists (assoc.), Early Music Am. (assoc.), Viola da Gamba Soc. Am. (assoc.), Chgo. Fedn. Musicians (assoc.), Early Music Chgo. (assoc.), Ill. Music Educators Assn. (assoc.), Am. String Tchrs. Assn. (assoc.). Home: 22041 W Petoskey Ct Plainfield IL 60544 Personal E-mail: gallifrey76@hotmail.com.

**SERNETT, RICHARD PATRICK,** lawyer; b. Mason City, Iowa, Sept. 8, 1938; s. Edward Frank and Loretta M. (Cavanaugh) S.; m. Janet Ellen Ward, Apr. 20, 1963; children: Susan Ellen, Thomas Ward, Stephen Edward, Katherine Anne. BBA, U. Iowa, 1960, JD, 1963. Bar: Iowa 1963, Ill. 1965, U.S. Dist. Ct. (no. dist.) Ill. 1965, U.S. Supreme Ct. 1971. House counsel, asst. sec. Scott, Foresman & Co., Glenview, Ill., 1963-70, sec., legal officer, 1970-80; v.p., law sec. SFN Cos., Inc., Glenview, 1980-83, sr. v.p., sec., gen. counsel, 1983-85, exec. v.p., gen. counsel, 1985-87; pvt. practice Northbrook, Ill., 1988-90; v.p., sec., gen. counsel Macmillan/McGraw-Hill Sch. Pub. Co., 1990-92; ptnr. Sernett & Blake, Northfield, Ill., 1993-95; ret., 1995. Mem. U.S. Dept. State Adv. Panel on Internat. Copyright, 1972-75. Chmn. bd. dirs. Iowa State U., Broadcasting Co., 1987-94. Mem. ABA (chmn. copyright divsn. 1972-73, com. on copyright legis. 1967-70, com. on copyright office affairs 1966-67, 79-81, com. on program for revision copyright law 1971-72), Am. Intellectual Property Law Assn., Am. Soc. Corp. Secs., Ill. Bar Assn. (chmn. copyright com. 1971-72), Chgo. Bar Assn., Patent Law Assn. Chgo. (bd. mgrs. 1979-82, chmn. copyright law com. 1972-73, 77-78), Copyright Soc. U.S.A. (trustee 1972-75, 77-80), Wyndemere Country Club, Naples, Fla., Mission Hills Country Club, Northbrook, Ill. Home: 3741 Mission Hills Rd #409 Northbrook IL 60062

**SEROKA, JAMES HENRY,** social studies educator, academic administrator; b. Detroit, Mar. 5, 1950; s. Henry S. and Mary (Wyoral) S.; m. Carolyn Marie White, June 27, 1970; children: Mihail, Maritsa. BA, U. Mich., 1970; MA, Mich. State U., 1972, PhD, 1976. Labor mkt. analyst U.S. Dept. of Labor, Washington, 1970-71; asst. prof. U. N.C., Greensboro, 1976-77, Appalachian State U., Boone, N.C., 1977-79; Ill. Ill. U., Carbondale, 1979-81, assoc. prof., 1981-87, prof., dir., 1987-88; prof., head div. humanities and social scis. Pa. State U., Erie, 1988-90; prof. U. North Fla., Jacksonville, 1990-98; dir. Ctr. for Pub. Leadership, Jacksonville, 1991 98; vis. prof. country studies U.S. Air War Coll., Maxwell AFB, Ala., 1997-98, 2005—; prof. Auburn (Ala.) U., 1998—; dir. Ctr. for Govtl. Svcs., Auburn, 1998—2005. Dir. Master of Pub. Affairs Program Soc. Ill. U., 1987-88, Rural and Small Town Adminstrn. Project, 1980-85; asst. dir. Appalachian Regional Bur. Govts., Boone, N.C., 1977-79; manpower planning analyst U.S. Dept. Labor, Washington, 1970-71; exchange prof. Fakultet Politickih Nauka, Univerzitet u Beogradu, Yugoslavia, 1986; vis. prof. Air War Coll., Montgomery, Ala.; sr. researcher Coun. for the Internat. Exchange Scholars Yugoslavia, 1980; mem. state adv. com. Gov.'s Rural Affairs Coun. for State of Ill., 1988; dir. Ctr. Govt. Svcs., Auburn, 1998—. Co-author: Political Organizations in Social Yugoslavia, 1986 (Choice award 1987); editor Rural Public Adminstration, 1986; co-editor: Developed Socialism, 1982, Comparative Political Systems, 1990, Yugoslavia: The Failure of Democratic Transformation, 1992; contbr. numerous articles to profl. jours. Recipient Akademischer Austausch Dienst Lang. scholar Fed. Republic of Germany, 1988 and numerous other grants, traveling fellows. Mem. Am. Soc. Pub. Adminstrn., Am. Polit. Sci. Assn., Internat. Polit. Sci. Assn., Midwest Polit. Sci. Assn., So. Polit. Sci. Assn., Southwestern Polit. Sci. Assn., Western Polit. Sci. Assn., Policy Studies Orgn., Acad. Polit. Sci., Internat. Studies Assn., Am. Assn. Advancement of Slavic Studies, Western Social Sci. Assn., Cmty. Devel. Soc., Hon. Order of Ky. Colonels. Office: Auburn Univ Dept Political Sci 7080 Haley Ctr Auburn AL 36849 Business E-Mail: jseroka@auburn.edu.

**SEROTA, JAMES IAN,** lawyer; b. Chgo., Oct. 20, 1946; s. Louis Henry and Phyllis Estelle (Horner) S.; m. Susan Perlstadt, May 7, 1972; children: Daniel Louis, Jonathan Mark. AB, Washington U., St. Louis, 1968; JD cum laude, Northwestern U., 1971. Bar: Ill. 1971, US Dist. Ct. (no. dist.) Ill. 1972, DC 1978, US Supreme Ct. 1978, US Ct. Appeals (DC cir.) 1978, U.S. Dist. Ct. (DC dist.), US Ct. Claims 1980, NY 1981, US Dist. Ct. (ea. dist.) NY, 1981, US Dist. Ct. (no dist) NY, 2003, US Ct. Appeals (2d cir.) 1983. Trial atty. Antitrust div. US Dept. Justice, Washington, 1971—77; assoc. Bell, Boyd & Lloyd, Washington, 1977—81; ptnr. Werner, Kennedy & French, NYC, 1982—85, Levitsky & Serota, 1985-86, Huber, Lawrence & Abell, NYC, 1987—98, Vinson & Elkins, NYC, 1998—2002; shareholder Greenberg Traurig, NYC, 2003—. Contbr. articles to profl. jours.; editor Law Rev., Law bd., Northwestern U.; ed bd., antitrust columnist CCH Power and

Telecom Law jour. Recipient Spl. Achievement award U.S. Dept. Justice, 1976. Mem. ABA (chmn. ins. industry com. 1987-90, vice chair program com. 1990-91, chair annual mtg. program 1991-94, chair fuel & energy com. 1994-97, coun. 1997-2000), N.Y. State Bar Assn., Assn. of Bar of City of N.Y. (antitrust and trade regulation com. 1988-91), Fed. Bar Council. Office: Greenberg Traurig LLP 15th Fl 200 Park Ave Met Life Bldg New York NY 10166 Office Phone: 212-801-2277. Business E-Mail: serotaj@gtlaw.com.

**SEROTA, SCOTT,** medical association administrator; BA, Purdue U.; MA in Health Admin. and Planning, Wash. U. Sch. of Med., St. Louis. Creator, leader Physicians Preferred Health Inc., Mo.; v.p. health care mgmt. PruCare, St. Louis, 1980; v.p. group ops., v.p. health care mgmt. Prudential Ins. Co., Chgo.; pres., CEO Rush Prudential Health Plans, Chgo., 1990—96; exec. v.p. system devel. Blue Cross and Blue Shield Assn., COO, 1994—96, exec. v.p. sys. devel., 1996—2000, pres., CEO, 2000—. Founding mem. Inst. on Healthcare Costs and Solutions Wash. Bus. Group on Health; bd. mem. Council for Affordable Quality Healthcare, Nat. Ctr. for Healthcare Leadership, Partnership for Prevention, Nat. Alliance for Health Info. Tech., Accrediting Commn. on Edn. for Health Services Admin.; mem. Am. Coll. of Healthcare Executives. Office: Blue Cross Blue Shield Assn 225 N Michigan Ave Chicago IL 60601

**SEROTA, SUSAN PERLSTADT,** lawyer, educator; b. Chgo., Sept. 10, 1945; d. Sidney Morris and Mildred (Penn) Perlstadt; m. James Ian Serota, May 7, 1972; children: Daniel Louis, Jonathan Mark. AB, U. Mich., 1967; JD, NYU, 1971. Bar: Ill. 1971, DC 1972, NY 1981, US Dist. Ct. (no. dist.) Ill. 1971, US Dist. Ct. (so. dist.) NY 1981, US Dist. Ct. (ea, dist.) NY 1985, US Ct. Claims 1972, US Tax Ct. 1972, US Ct. Appeals (DC cir.) 1972. Ptnr. Pillsbury Winthrop Shaw Pittman LLP, NYC, 1982—, ptnr., chmn. Exec. Compensation & Benefits practice, 2001—. Adj. prof. Sch. Law, Georgetown U., Washington, 1974-75; mem. faculty Practicing Law Inst., NYC, 1983—. Editor: ERISA Fiduciary Law, 1995, Supplement, 2003; assoc. editor Exec. Compensation Jour., 1973—75, dep. editor Tax Mgmt., Estate and Gift Taxation and Exec. Compensation, 1973—75, mem. editl. adv. bd. Benefits Law Jour., 1973—, Tax Mgmt. Compensation Jour., 1993—, mem. bd. editors ERISA and Benefits Law Jour., 1992—; contbr. articles to profl. jours. Fellow: Am. Coll. of Employee Benefits Counsel (pres. 2004—05, ptnr., charter fellow), Am. Coll. Tax Counsel (regent 1999—2005); mem.: ABA (chmn. joint com. employee benefits 1987—88, chmn. com. employee benefits 1991—92, vice-chair taxation sect. 1999—2001, chair taxation sect. 2006—), Am. Bar Retirement Assn. (dir. 1994—2004, pres. 1999—2000), NY State Bar Assn. (exec. com. tax sect. 1988—92), Internat. Pension and Employee Benefit Lawyers Assn. (co-chair 1993—95). Democrat. Office: Pillsbury Winthrop Shaw Pittman 1540 Broadway New York NY 10036 Office Fax: 212-858-1500. Business E-Mail: susan.serota@pillsburylaw.com.

**SERRA, MATTHEW D.,** consumer products company executive; b. 1945; With R.H. Macy & Co., 1962—69, Bloomingdale's, 1969—76; divisional merchandising mgr. men's wear Lord & Taylor, 1976; v.p. & divisional merchandise mgr. Saks Fifth Ave, NYC, 1976—78, assoc. gen. merchandise mgr, men's and boys' wear, 1978—79, sr. v.p. & gen. merchandise mgr. men's and boys' wear, 1979—83; pres. Gimbels NY divsn., 1983, Gimbels East, 1983—86, CEO, 1985—86; pres. Sibleys, Rochester, NY, 1986—90, CEO, 1987—90; pres. CEO Seaman's Furniture Co., NY, 1991—92; chmn., CEO Sterns divsn. of Federated Dept. Stores Inc., 1993-98; pres., CEO Foot Locker Worldwide, 1998—2000; COO Foot Locker Inc. (formerly Venator Group Inc.), 2000—01, pres., 2000—, CEO, 2001—, chmn., 2004—. Office: Foot Locker Inc 112 W 34th St New York NY 10120*

**SERRA, RICHARD,** sculptor; b. San Francisco, Nov. 2, 1939; m. Clara Weyergraf-Serra. BA in English Lit., U. Calif., 1961; BFA, MFA, Yale U., 1964; DFA (hon.), Calif. Coll. Arts and Crafts, 1994. One-man shows include Galleria La Salita, Rome, 1966, Kunsthalle Tübingen, Germany, 1978, Richard Hines Gallery, Seattle, 1979, Venice Biennale, 1981, Pace Gallery, Leo Castelli Gallery, 1987, Musée Nat. d'Art Moderne, Paris, 1984, Mus. Haus Lange, Krefeld, Germany, 1985, Mus. Modern Art, NYC, 1986, Bonnefantenmuseum, Maastricht, 1990, Pace Gallery, 1992; exhbns. include Stedelijk Mus., Amsterdam, 1969, Kunsthalle, Bern, Switzerland, 1969, Solomon R. Guggenheim Mus., NYC, 1969, Pasadena Art Mus., Calif., 1970, Leo Castelli Gallery, NYC, 1970, 72, 74, 82, 84, ACE Gallery, LA, 1970, 72, 74, Whitney Mus. Am. Art, NYC, 1973, Akira Ikeda Gallery, Nagoya, Japan, 1982, Margo Levin Gallery, 1984, Visual Arts Mus., 1985, Mus. Modern Art, NYC, 1986; group shows include Tony Shafrazi Gallery, 1991-92, Pace Gallery, 1992, Dia Ctr. for Arts, NYC, Whitney Biennial: Day for Night, Whitney Mus. Am. Art, 2006; represented in permanent collections: Mus. Modern Art, NYC, Whitney Mus. Am. Art, Guggenheim Mus., NYC, Pasadena Mus. Art, LA County Mus. Art, Art Gallery Ont., Toronto, Stedelijk Mus.; also filmmaker. Recipient Praemium Imperiale, Japan Art Assn., 1994, Gold Medal for Sculpture, Am. Acads. Arts and Letters, 2001, Internat. Art award, Cristóbal Gabarrón Found., 2005. Fellow: Am. Acad. Arts and Sciences. Office: 173 Duane St Fl 5 New York NY 10013-3334*

**SERRAGLIO, MARIO,** architect; b. Bassano, Veneto, Italy, Apr. 13, 1965; arrived in U.S., 1972; s. Luciano G. and Maria P. (Bellon) Serraglio. BS in Architecture, Ohio State U., 1988. Real estate agt. Four Star Realty, Columbus, Ohio, 1984—2005; treas. Columbus Masonry, Inc., 1985-86; v.p. Serraglio Masonry, Inc., Columbus, 1986-87; pres. Serraglio Constrn., Columbus, 1988-89, Sullivan Gray Ptnrs., Columbus, 1989-92; project mgr. John Regan Archs., Columbus, 1992-93; prin. Architettura Serraglio, Inc., Reynoldsburg, Ohio, 1995—; real estate agt. WEBMLS.net, Columbus, Ohio, 2005—. Mem.: AIA, Nat. Assn. Realtors. Office: Architettura Serraglio 7404 E Main St Reynoldsburg OH 43068 2166 Office Phone: 614-759-6070. E-mail: mario@serraglio.com.

**SERRANO, JOSÉ ENRIQUE,** congressman; b. Mayagüez, PR, Oct. 24, 1943; arrived in US, 1950; s. Jose E. and Hipolita (Soto) Serrano; m. Mary Staucet; children: Lisa Marie, Jose Marco, Justine, Jonathan, Benjamin. Student, CUNY Lehman Coll., 1961. With Mfrs. Hanover Trust Co., 1961-69; mem. Bd. Edn., NYC, 1969-74, NY State Assembly, 1975—90, US Congress from 16th (formerly 18th) NY dist., 1990—, mem. appropriations com., 1993—95, 1996—, mem. Congl. Hispanic Caucus, co-vice chair Dem. steering and policy com. With 172nd Support Bn. Med. Corps U.S. Army, 1964—66. Recipient Congl. Recognition award, Nat. Coun. La Raza, 1993, Evelina Lopez Antonetty award, Disting. Pub. and Cmty. Svc., Hunter Coll. Ctr. Puerto Rican Studies, 2003, Man of Yr. award, Bronx Puerto Rican Day Parade, 2003, Friend of the Nat. Pks. award, Nat. Pks. Conservation Assn., 2005. Democrat. Roman Catholic. Office: US Ho Reps 2227 Rayburn Ho Office Bldg Washington DC 20515-3216 Office Phone: 202-225-4361.*

**SERRE, JEAN-PIERRE,** mathematician, scholar; b. Bages, France, Sept. 15, 1926; s. Jean and Adèle (Diet) S.; m. Josiane Heulot, Aug. 10, 1948; 1 child, Claudine. Baccalauréat, Lycée de Nîmes, France, 1944; agrégation, Ecole Normale Supérieure, France, 1948; PhD, Sorbonne, 1951; PhD (hon.), Cambridge U., Eng., 1978, U. Stockholm, 1980, U. Glasgow, Scotland, 1983, U. Athens, 1996, Harvard U., 1998, Durham U., 2000, London U., 2001, U. Oslo, 2002, U. Oxford, 2003, Acad. Bucharest, 2004, U. Barcelona, 2004, U. Madrid, 2006. With Centre Nat. de la Recherche Scientifique, Paris, 1948—54, U. Nancy, 1954—56; prof. Coll. de France, Paris, 1956—94, prof. emeritus. Author: Groupes algébriques et corps de classes, 1959, Corps Locaux, 1962, Lie Algebras and Lie Groups, 1965, Représentations linéaires des groupes finis, 1968, Cours d'arithmétique, 1970, Trees, 1980, Local Algebra, 2000, Collected Papers, 1986, 2000. Recipient Fields Medal, 1954, Prix Gaston Julia, Prix Balzan, 1985, Leroy P. Steele prize Am. Math. Soc., 1995, Wolf prize in math., Israel, 2000, Abel prize, 2003. Mem. Acad. Sci. U.S. (fgn.), Nederland Acad. Sci. (fgn.), Acad. Sci. Stockholm (fgn.), Russian Acad. Sci. (fgn.). Home: 6 Ave de Montespan 75116 Paris France Office: Coll de France 75005 Paris France Business E-Mail: serre@dma.ens.fr.

**SERRIE, HENDRICK,** retired anthropology and international business educator; b. Jersey City, July 2, 1937; s. Hendrick and Elois (Edge) S.; m. Gretchen Tipler Ihde, Sept. 3, 1959; children: Karim Jonathan, Keir Ethan. BA with honors, U. Wis., 1960; MA, Cornell U., 1964; PhD with distinction, Northwestern U., 1976. Dir. Solar Energy Field Project, Oaxaca, Mex., 1961-62; instr. U. Aleppo, Syria, 1963-64; asst. prof. Beloit (Wis.) Coll., 1964-69, Calif. State U., Northridge, 1969-70, Purdue U., West Lafayette, Ind., 1970-72, New Coll./U. South Fla., Sarasota, 1972-77; tchr. Pine View Sch., Sarasota, 1978; prof. anthropology, internat. bus. Eckerd Coll., St. Petersburg, Fla., 1978—2002, dir. internat. bus. overseas programs, 1981—2002; ret., 2002. Sr. rsch. assoc., Human Resources Inst., St. Petersburg, 1988—. Author, editor: Family, Kinship, and Ethnic Identity Among the Overseas Chinese, 1985, Anthropology and International Business, 1986, What Can Multinationals Do for Peasants, 1994, The Overseas Chinese: Ethnicity in National Context, 1998; writer, dir. films: Technological Innovation, 1962, Something New Under the Sun, 1963; contbr. articles to Wall Street Jour. and Wall Street Jour. Europe. Tchr. Sunday sch., North United Methodist Ch., Sarasota, 1977—. Exxon scholar, So. Ctr. for Internat. Issues, Atlanta, 1980-81; Presdl. fellow Am. Grad. Sch. Internat. Mgmt., 1991; recipient Leavy award, Freedoms Found., Valley Forge, Pa., 1989. Fellow Am. Anthropol. Assn., Soc. Applied Anthropology; mem. So. Ctr. Internat. Issues, Acad. Internat. Bus., Tampa Bay Internat. Trade Coun., Internat. Soc. Intercultural Edn., Tng. and Rsch. Republican. Avocations: singing, drawing, beach walking, bicycling, sailing. E-mail: serrieh@eckerd.edu.

**SERRIN, JAMES BURTON,** mathematics professor; b. Chgo., Nov. 1, 1926; s. James B. and Helen Elizabeth (Wingate) S.; m. Barbara West, Sept. 6, 1952; children: Martha Helen Stack, Elizabeth Ruth, Janet Louise Sucha. Student, Northwestern U., 1944-46; BA, Western Mich. U., 1947; MA, Ind. U., PhD, 1951; DSc, U. Sussex, 1972; DSc in Engring., U. Ferrara, Italy, 1992; DSc in Math., U. Padova, Italy, 1992; DSc, U. Tours, France, 2004. With MIT, Cambridge, 1952-54; mem. faculty U. Minn., Mpls., 1955—, prof. math., 1959-95, Regents prof., 1968—, head So. Sch. Math., 1964-65; emeritus, 1995. Vis. prof. U. Chgo., 1964, 75, Johns Hopkins U., 1966, U. Sussex, 1967-68, 72, 76, U. Naples, 1979, U. Modena, 1988, Ga. Inst. Tech., 1990. Author: Mathematical Principles of Classical Fluid Mechanics, 1957. Mem. Met. Airport Sound Abatement Council, Mpls., 1969—. Recipient Disting. Alumni award Ind. U., 1979 Fellow AAAS; mem. NAS, Am. Math. Soc. (G.D. Birkhoff prize 1973), Math. Assn. Am., Soc. for Natural Philosophy (pres. 1969-70), Finnish Acad. Sci. and Letters. Home: 4422 Dupont Ave S Minneapolis MN 55419-4739

**SERRITELLA, WILLIAM DAVID,** lawyer; b. Chgo., May 16, 1946; s. William V. and Josephine Dolores (Scalise) S. JD, U. Ill., Champaign, 1971. Bar: Ill. 1971, US Dist. Ct. (no. and cen. dists.) Ill. 1972, US Dist. Ct. (ea. and we. dists.) Wis. 1995, US Ct. Appeals (7th cir.) 1974, US Supreme Ct. 1979, US Dist. Ct. (so. dist.) 1997. Law clk. U.S. Dist. Ct., Danville, Ill., 1971-72; ptnr. Ross & Hardies, Chgo., 1972—2003, McGuire Woods, Chgo., 2003—. Arbitrator Am. Arbitration Assn. Named to Leading Lawyers Network, Ill. Super Lawyers, Top Best Lawyers Network. Fellow Am. Bar Found.; mem. ABA, Ill. Bar Assn., Chgo. Bar Assn., Internat. Assn. Def. Counsel, Soc. Trial Lawyers, Defense Rsch. Inst., Trial Lawyers Club (Chgo.), Lawyers Club Chgo. Office: McGuire Woods Ste 4100 77 W Wacker Dr Chicago IL 60601-7567 Office Phone: 312-750-8643. Business E-mail: wserritella@mcguirewoods.com.

**SERSTOCK, DORIS SHAY,** retired microbiologist, civic worker, educator; b. Mitchell, SD, June 13, 1926; d. Elmer Howard and Hattie (Christopher) Shay; m. Ellsworth I. Serstock, Aug. 30, 1952; children: Barbara Anne, Robert Ellsworth, Mark Douglas. BA, Augustana Coll., 1947; postgrad., U. Minn., 1966-67, Duke U., summer 1969, Communicable Disease Ctr., Atlanta, 1972. Bacteriologist Civil Svc., S.D., Colo., Mo., 1947-52; rsch. bacteriologist U. Minn., 1952-53; clin. bacteriologist Dr. Lufkin's Lab., 1954-55; chief technologist St. Paul Blood Bank of ARC, 1959-65; microbiologist in charge mycology lab. VA Hosp., Mpls., 1968-93; ret. Instr. Coll. Med. Scis., U. Minn., 1970-79, asst. prof. Coll. Lab. Medicine and Pathology, 1979-93. Contbr. articles to profl. jours. Mem. Richfield Planning Commn., 1965-71, sec., 1968-71; extended ministries commn. Wood Lake Luth. Ch., Richfield, 1993-94; rep. religious coun. Mall Am., Bloomington, Minn., 1993-94; chief nursery caregiver Christ the King Luth. Ch., Bloomington, 1994-99, Hope Presbyn. Ch., Richfield, Minn., 1994-2003; mem. Rep. Presdl. Task Force, Nat. Rep. Senatorial Com., 1997. Fellow Augusta Coll.; named to Exec. and Profl. Hall of Fame; recipient Alumni Achievement award Augustana Coll., 1977, Superior Performance award VA Hosp., 1978, 82, Cert. of Recognition, 1988, Golden Spore awards Mycology Observer, 1985, 87, Congl. Order of Merit Nat. Rep. Congl. Com., 2003; name engraved on founders' wall Ronald Reagan Rep. Ctr., 2000; named Minn. Rep. of Yr. Nat. Rep. Congl. Com., 2003; recipient Congl. Order Merit, NRCC, 2005. Mem. Richfield Women's Garden Club (pres. 1959), Wild Flower Garden (chmn. 1961). Republican. Home: 7201 Portland Ave Minneapolis MN 55423-3218

**SERTEL, KUBILAY,** engineer, researcher; s. Yavuz and Rukiye Sertel. PhD, U. Mich., 2002. Grad. rsch. asst. U. Mich., 1997—2002; rsch. scientist Ohio State U., 2003—. Contbr. articles to profl. jours. Recipient 3rd Pl., Best Student Paper award, ACES, 2006. Mem.: IEEE (v.p. Columbus chpt. 2006—). Office: ElectroScience Lab Ohio State Univ 1320 Kinnear Rd Columbus OH 43212 Office Phone: 614-688-5822. Business E-mail: sertel.1@osu.edu

**SERTICH, KELLI ANN,** land use planner; b. Riverside, Calif., Nov. 9, 1959; d. Robert Sr. and Lillian Patricia (Hale) S. AAS in Constrn. Drafting, Glendale C.C., 1981; BS in Design Urban Planning, Ariz. State U., 1983; MPA, Western Internat. U., 2002. Draftsman, facilities planner Washington Elem. Sch. Dist., Phoenix, 1980-83; planner various pvt. sector planning & archtl. firms, Phoenix, 1983-88; dir. planning & econ. devel. Town of Buckeye (Ariz.), 1988-93; dir. tourism & econ. devel. City of Williams (Ariz.), 1993-95; dir. cmty. devel., interim city mgr. City of Bisbee (Ariz.), 1995-98; sr. planner Cmty. Scis. Corp., Phoenix, 1998; sr. planner policy analyst Maricopa County Dept. Transp., Phoenix, 1998-2000; regional area planning mgr. Flood Control Dist. Maricopa County, Phoenix, 2000—. Pres. Bisbee Christmas in April, 1997; chmn. Ariz. Cmty. Found. Cochise County Team, Bisbee, 1997; chmn. Buckeye Clean and Beautiful, 1989-93. Mem. Am. Planning Assn. (sec. region 5 2006—), Ariz. Planning Assn. (dir.-at-large 1993-2001, sec. 1994-99, pres. 2003-04). Roman Catholic. Avocations: sewing, horseback riding, travel, gardening. Office: Maricopa County Flood Control 2801 W Durango St Phoenix AZ 85009-6357

**SERVAAS, BEURT RICHARD,** manufacturing executive; b. Indpls., May 7, 1919; s. Beurt Hans and Lela Etta (Neff) S.; m. Cory Jane Synhorst, Jan. 7, 1950; children: Eric, Kristin, Joan, Paul, Amy. Student, U. Mex., Mexico City, 1938-39; AB, Ind. U., 1940, MD, 1970; postgrad., Purdue U., 1941; D Bus. Mgmt., Ind. Inst. Tech.; LHD (hon.), Butler U. Agt. CIA, China, 1946; v.p. constrn. Vestar Corp., N.Y.C., 1948; founder, chief exec. officer, chmn. bd. No. Vernon Forge, Inc. Rev. Pub. Co., ServVaas Labs., Indpls., 1949—. Chmn. bd. ServVaas, Inc., Indpls. and affiliated cos. Curtis Pub. Co., Forge Mexicana, Edgerton Tool, Dependable Engring., ServVaas Mgmt., ServVaas Rubber, Premier, Indpls. Rubber Co., Bridgeport Brass Co.; bd. dirs. Bank One Ind. Pres. City-County Coun., Indpls.; chmn. Ind. State Commn. Higher Edn., Kirksville Coll. Osteo. Medicine; bd. dirs. Coll. Univ. Corp., Ind. Pub. Health Found., Robert Schuller Ministries; past chmn. bd. dirs. Ind. State Bd. Health, Ind. Fair Rels. Commn. With USNR, 1941—45. Decorated Bronze Star, Army Commendation medal; recipient Horatio Alger award, 1980. Mem. NAM, Am. Acad. Achievement (Golden Plate award 1973), Assn. Am. Med. Colls., Ind. C. of C., Indpls. C. of C., Marion County Hist. Soc., Ind. Hist. Soc., Newcomen Soc. N.Am., U.S. Naval Res. Assn., World Future Soc., Am. Legion, Columbia Club, Econ. Club, Indpls. Athletic Club, Indpls. Press Club, Meridian Hills Country Club, Phi Delta Kappa. Presbyterian. Home: 2525 W 44th St Indianapolis IN 46228-3249 Office: Office of the City County Coun 241 City-County Bldg 200 E Washington St Indianapolis IN 46204-3307 also: SerVaas Inc 1000 Waterway Blvd Indianapolis IN 46202-2155

**SERVAAS, CORY,** editor-in-chief; AB in Journalism, Univ. Iowa; MD, Ind. Univ.; PhD (hon.), Vincennes Univ. Chmn., pres., CEO Curtis Pub. Co., 1975—82; former chmn. Country Gentleman Pub. Co.; founder, pres., CEO Benjamin Franklin Literary and Med. Soc., 1976—; also editorial dir. Children's Better Health Inst. Indpls.; and editor Saturday Evening Post, Indpls., editor-in-chief, 2004—. Mem. Press Coun. on Phys. Fitness and Sports, 1990—94. Named to Univ. Iowa Journalism Hall of Fame; recipient Ind. Woman of Achievement award, Nat. Fedn. of Press Women, Kappa Tau Alpha award for outstanding svc., Nat. Journalism Scholarship Soc., Outstanding Bus. Leader award, Northwood Inst. Mem.: Nat. Women's Coalition, Women in Comm. Inc., Indianapolis Arthritis Guild, Am. Med. Women's Assn., Ind. State Med. Assn., AMA, Education CHOICE Charitable Trust, Epsilon Sigma Alpha. Office: Saturday Evening Post 1100 Waterway Blvd Indianapolis IN 46202-2174

**SERVIEN, LOUIS-MARC (COMTE DE BOISDAUPHIN, LORD OF QUENDON),** finance company executive, import/export company executive; b. Yverdon-les-Bains, Switzerland, Jan. 8, 1934; Doctorate, Acad. Tiberina, Rome. Pres., mng. dir. Soc. de Financement SA, Geneva, Compagnie des Grands Crus SA. Pres., mng. dir., Cmte. European Excellence. Author: Mutual Funds, Why Not? A Survey of International Investment Funds, 1968; "Gibraltar: Tax on the Rock" (Revue Premier Monte Carlo, Monaco, No. 17, 1985-86); several publications in German, French, Italian & Spanish; contbr. articles to profl. publs., journalist. Named hon. col. Confederate Air Force, Midland, Tex., Commendatore of the Concordia Order, Brazil, 1974, Commedador of Imperial Orden Hispanica de Carlos V, Spain, 1992; recipient cert. recognition. Mem. Manorial Soc. Gt. Britain, Com. European Excellence, Diplomat Club Geneva, Chow Chow Club Paris. Home and Office: Quendon Hall 23 chemin du Levant CH 1005 Lausanne Switzerland Office Phone: 0041 21 311 44 70.

**SERVODIDIO, PAT ANTHONY,** broadcast executive; b. Yonkers, NY, Nov. 9, 1937; s. Pasquale and Catherine (Verdisco) S.; children: Christian, Alexa. BS, Fordham U., 1959; postgrad., St. John's U., N.Y.C., 1960-63. Asst. to bus. mgr. Sta. WCBS-TV, N.Y.C., 1960-64; account exec. Sta. WTNH-TV, New Haven, 1964-66; account exec., N.Y. sales mgr. RKO TV Reps., N.Y.C., 1967-74; v.p., N.Y. sales mgr. Sta. WOR-TV, N.Y.C., 1974-79, v.p., gen. sales mgr., 1979-81; v.p., gen. mgr. Sta. WNAC-TV, Boston, 1981-82; pres. RKO TV, N.Y.C., 1982-87, RKO Gen., Inc., N.Y.C., 1987—91, also bd. dirs.; v.p., gen. mgr. Sta. WKYC-TV, Cleve., 1991-92; pres. Multimedia Broadcasting Co., Cin., 1992-94; broadcast cons., 1995—. Bd. regents St. Peter's Coll., 1983-99; mem. com. future financing Rutgers U., New Brunswick, N.J., 1983-85; dir. TV bur. Advt. Bd., 1993-94; bd. dirs. Internat. Radio and TV Found., 1983-93, Assn. for Maximum Svc. TV, Inc., 1993-95. With U.S. Army, 1959-62. Office: 380 Lexington Ave Ste 1700 New York NY 10168-0002

**SERVODIDIO, THOMAS GERARD,** lawyer; b. SI, NY, Sept. 14, 1962; s. Francis and Nina Servodidio; m. Julie Ann Luybli, Aug. 15, 1987; children: David, Daniel, Maria BA magna cum laude, Bucknell U., 1984; JD cum laude, U. Pa., 1987. Bar: Pa. 1987, NJ 1988, DC 1989, US Dist. Ct. Ea. Pa. 1987, US Dist. Ct. Dist. NJ 1988, US Ct. Appeals 3rd Cir. 1991, US Ct. Appeals 4th Cir., Supreme Ct. Pa., Supreme Ct. NJ. Assoc. Duane Morris LLP, Phila., 1987—96, ptnr., 1997—, chair legal recruitment & retention com., 1998—2000, chair firm employment, and immigration dept. Mem. ABA, Pa. Bar Assn., Phila. Bar Assn., DC Bar, Phi Beta Kappa. Republican. Office Phone: 215-979-1844. Office Fax: 215-979-1020. Business E-Mail: tgservodidio@duanemorris.com.

**SERWATKA, JUDY ANN,** computer and information systems educator; d. Carl Daniel and Mary Ellen Penovich; m. Conrad Mitchell Serwatka, Oct. 4, 1997. BS in Computer Tech., Purdue U. Calumet, Hammond, Ind.l, 1978, MS in Mgmt., 1983; EdD in Bus. Edn., No. Ill. U., 1993. Sys. engr. Bethlehem Steel Corp., Burns Harbor, Ind., 1979—85; assoc. prof. info. sys. and computer programming Purdue U. Calumet, Hammond, 1985—2002; assoc. prof. computer and info. tech. Purdue U. North Ctrl., Westville, Ind., 2002—06, prof. computer and info. tech., 2006—. Author: Business Data Communications: Introductory Concepts and Techniques, 2004; contbr. articles to profl. jours. Recipient cert. recognition, Ind. Partnership for Statewide Edn., 2002, 2004, Merlot Vol. of the Yr. award, Project Merlot, 2005. Mem.: Assn. Computing Machinery, Internat. Assn. Computer Info. Sys., Network and Sys. Profls. Assn. (dir. 2002—04), Sigma Xi. Office: Purdue U North Ctrl 1401 S US 421 Westville IN 46391 Office Phone: 219-785-5445. E-mail: jserwatka@pnc.edu.

**SERWER, ALAN MICHAEL,** lawyer; b. Detroit, Aug. 31, 1944; s. Bernard Jacob and Marian (Borin) S.; m. Laurel Kathryn Robbert, June 6, 1968; children: David Matthew, Karen Anne. BA in Econs., U. Mich., 1966; JD, Northwestern U., 1969. Bar: Ill. 1969, D.C. 1980, U.S. Dist. Ct. (no. dist.) Ill. 1970, U.S. Ct. Appeals (7th cir.) 1979, U.S. Supreme Ct. 1979, U.S. Ct. Appeals (6th cir.) 1982, U.S. Ct. Appeals (5th cir.) 1983, U.S. Ct. Appeals (9th cir.) 1986. Trial atty. U.S. Dept. Labor, Chgo., 1969-78, counsel safety and health, 1978-79; assoc. Haley, Bader & Potts, Chgo., 1979-82, ptnr., 1983-87; mem. Bell, Boyd & Lloyd, Chgo., 1987—. Ill. Bar Assn., Chgo. Bar Assn. Home: 233 Woodland Rd Highland Park IL 60035-5052 Office: Bell Boyd & Lloyd 70 W Madison St Ste 3200 Chicago IL 60602-4244 Office Phone: 312-372-1121. E-mail: aserwer@bellboyd.com.

**SESHADRI, SRIVATSAN,** optics scientist; b. Chennai, Tamil Nadu, India, July 26, 1969; s. Indira Seshadri and Seshadri S. PhD, U. So. Calif., 1998. Optical scientist Osmic Inc., Auburn Hills, Mich., 1998—2004; staff scientist Xradia, Inc., 2005—. Presenter: in field; contbr. articles to profl. jours. Recipient Disting. Scholar award, Microbeam Analysis Soc., U.S. Dept. of Commerce, 1995; Rsch. assistantship, Dept. of Materials Sci. and Engring., U. So. Calif., 1993-1998. Mem.: IEEE, Microbeam Analysis Soc., Soc. Photooptical Instrumentation Engrs. Achievements include patents for Protective Layers for Multilayers Exposed to X-rays; Protective Layers for Multilayers exposed to hard X-rays. Office: Xradia Inc 4075A Sprig Dr Concord CA 94520 E-mail: Srivatsan_Seshadri@yahoo.com.

**SESHAIYER, PADMANABHAN,** mathematician, educator; b. Chennai, Tamil Nadu, India; B. with honors in engring., Birla Inst. Tech. and Sci., India, 1994; MSc with honors, Birla Inst. Tech. and Sci., 1994; PhD, U. Md., 1998. Rsch. assoc. Tex. A&M U., Coll. Sta., Tex., 1998—2000; asst. prof. Tex. Tech U., Lubbock, Tex., 2000—. Recipient Grad. Prof. of Yr., SIAM Chpt., Tex. Tech U., 2002; Tex. Project NExT fellow, Math. Assn. of Am., Tex. Chpt., 2001-2002, Std. Rsch. grant, NSF, 2002-2005, Std. Conf. grant, 2003-2004, Whitaker Found., 2003-2004. Mem.: Tchg. Academy, Tex. Tech. U. Office: Tex Tech U Box 41042 Math Stats Lubbock TX 79409-1042 E-mail: padhu@math.ttu.edu.

**SESIN, MARIA CARMEN,** psychologist, researcher; b. Havana, Cuba, June 14, 1954; d. Cecilio Sesin and Balbina Vazquez; 1 child, Martin Manzanares-Sesin. BS, CUNY, 1979; MA, Columbia U., N.Y.C., 1981; PhD, Yeshiva U., N.Y.C., 1998. Tchr. gifted and talented Grants Mcpl. Sch., Grants, N.Mex., 1981—82; elem. tchr. N.Y.C. Bd. Edn., 1982—85; psychologist Luth. Med. Ctr., N.Y.C., 1988—. Psychologist Behavioral Medicine Assocs., N.Y.C., 2004—; sole proprietor The Healing Arts, N.Y.C., 2004—; presenter workshops on group therapy. Contbr. articles to profl. jours. Mem.: APA. Avocations: piano, poetry. Office: Lutheran Medical Ctr Sunset Park Mental Health Ctr 514 49th St Brooklyn NY 11220 Office Phone: 718-437-5229.

**SESONSKE, ALEXANDER,** nuclear and chemical engineer; b. Gloversville, NY, June 20, 1921; s. Abraham and Esther (Kreitzer) S.; m. Marjorie Ann Mach, Apr. 17, 1952 (dec. Jan. 1995); children: Michael Jan, Jana Louise. B.Chem. Engring., Rensselaer Poly. Inst., 1942; MS, U. Rochester, 1947; PhD, U. Del., 1950. Engr. Chem. Constrn. Corp., N.Y.C., 1942; chem. engr. Manhattan Project, 1943-45, Columbia Chem. Corp., 1945-46; staff Los Alamos Sci. Lab., 1950-54, 60-61, cons., 1961-63; faculty Purdue U.,

Lafayette, Ind., 1954, prof. nuclear and chem. engring., 1959-86, prof. emeritus, 1986—, asst. chmn. dept. nuclear engring., 1966-73. Cons. Oak Ridge Nat. Lab., 1963-67, Electric Power Research Inst., 1974; mem. rev. com. Argonne (Ill.) Nat. Lab., 1965-67, 75-81; ind. cons. 1986—. Author: (with Samuel Glasstone) Nuclear Reactor Engineering, 1963, 4th edit., 1994, Nuclear Power Plant Design Analysis, 1973; mem. editorial bd. Advances in Nuclear Sci. and Tech., 1972—; contbr. numerous articles to profl. jours. Recipient Wall of Fame award U. Del., 1988. Fellow Am. Nuclear Soc. (Arthur H. Compton award 1987); mem. Am. Inst. Chem. Engrs., Am. Soc. Engring. Edn., Sigma Xi, Omega Chi Epsilon. Achievements include research on nuclear fuel mgmt., liquid metal heat transfer and nuclear reactor engring. Home and Office: 700 Black Lake Blvd SW Apt 109 Olympia WA 98502 Office Phone: 360-943-5467.

**SESSIONS, BARBARA C.,** lawyer; b. St. Johns, Mich., Jan. 23, 1961; d. John C. and Patricia H. (Hyland) Cary; m. Rex. L. Sessions, Oct. 10, 1989; 1 child, Isabel P. BA in English, U. Mich., 1983; JD, DePaul U., 1986. Bar: Ill. Comml. litigator Hinshaw & Culbertson, Chgo., 1986-90; sr. acct. exec. Edelman Pub. Rels. Worldwide, N.Y.C., 1990-91; mgr. mktg. and comms. Skadden, Arps, Slate, Meagher & Flom, N.Y.C., 1991-94; ptnr., dir. bus. devel. mktg. and planning Winston & Strawn LLP, Chgo., 1994—. Mem. Jr. League, N.Y.C., 1990-94, Chgo., 1989-99. Mem. Law Mktg. Assn. (pres., pres-elect 1998, bd. dirs. 1996—), Info. Innovators (editl. bd.). Office: Winston & Strawn LLP 35 W Wacker Dr Chicago IL 60601-9703 Fax: 312-558-5700. Office Phone: 312-558-5834. E-mail: bsessions@winston.com

**SESSIONS, JEFF (JEFFERSON BEAUREGARD SESSIONS III),** senator, former state attorney general; b. Hybart, Ala., Dec. 24, 1946; s. Jefferson Beauregard and Abbie (Powe) S.; m. Mary Montgomery Blackshear, Aug. 9, 1969; children: Mary Abigail, Ruth Blackshear, Samuel Turner BA, Huntingdon Coll., Montgomery, Ala., 1969; JD, U. Ala., 1973. Bar: Ala. 1973. Assoc. Guin, Bouldin & Porch, Russellville, Ala., 1973-75; asst. U.S. atty. (so. dist.) Ala. US Dept. Justice, Mobile, Ala., 1975-77, US atty., 1981-93; assoc. then ptnr. Stockman & Bedsole Attys., Mobile, Ala., 1977-81; ptnr. Stockman, Bedsole & Sessions, Mobile, 1993-94; atty. gen. State of Ala., Montgomery, 1995—97; U.S. Senator from Ala., 1997—; mem. armed services com., budget com., health, edn., labor & pension com. Mem. U.S. Atty. Gen's. adv. com., 1987-89, vice-chmn. 1989 Presdl. elector State of Ala., 1972; trustee, mem. exec. com. Mobile Bay Area Partnership for Youth, 1981-95; chmn. adminstrv. bd. Ashland Pl. United Meth. Ch., Mobile, 1982; 1st v.p. Mobile Lions Club, 1993-94. Capt. USAR, 1975-85 Recipient U.S. Atty. Gen's. award for significant achievements in the war against drug trafficking, U.S Dept. Justice, 1992, George (Buck) Gillespie Congl. award, Blinded Americans Veterans Found., 2000, Nat. Leadership award, Civil War Preservation Trust, 2004, Disting. Eagle Scout award, Guardian of Small Bus. award, Minuteman of the Yr. award, Reserve Officers Assn., Svc. to Agrl. award, AL Farmers Fedn., Teddy Roosevelt Environ. award, Watchdog of the Treasury award Mem. ABA, Ala. Bar Assn., Mobile Bar Assn. Republican. Methodist. Office: 335 Senate Russell Office Bldg Washington DC 20510-0001 E-mail: senator@sessions.senate.gov.*

**SESSIONS, JOAN T.,** director, educator; d. David Pyper and Rose Smith Thomas; children: Linda Ann Hadley, Gina Louise. BS in Edn., Kent State U., 1962; postgrad., U. Akron, 1970; MA in Edn. with honors, Ohio State U., 1966; PhD in Edn., Kent State U., 1975; postgrad., U. Chgo., 1996, St. Michael's Coll., Burlington, Vt., 1998. Elementary Principal's Provisional State of Ohio, 1966, cert. elem. tchr., elem. prin. Ohio. Rsch. asst. Ohio State U., 1965—66; tchr. pub. schs., Wooster, Ohio, 1962—64, Elyria City Schs., 1966—67; dir. of info. systems, planning quality assurance Ctr. for Human Services, Cleve., 1974—91; program specialist UN Volunteers, Beijing, 1991—96; tutoring program dir. U. of Chgo., 1998—; Headstart dir. Elyria City Schools, 1967—70, elem. prin. Ohio, 1970—72; tchg. fellow Kans. State U., 1972—73; rsch. assoc. Bur. Ednl. Rsch., 1973—74; rsch. assoc. to dir. evaluation Ctr. for Human Svcs., Cleve., 1974—91; instr. John Carroll U., 1985—90; vol. UN, Beijing; lang. evaluation cons. Beijing Diplomatic Svc. Grad. sch. lectr. John Carroll U., Cleve., 1987—89; grad. tchg. fellow Kent State U., 1972—74; cons. and lectr. in field; tutor program dir., mgr. VISTA and AmeriCorps, 1999—2005; primary literacy tutoring cons. City Yr. Chgo., 2001—05; USI primary literacy tutor program tng. materials evaluation methodology dir. Dept. Neighborhood Schs., U. Chgo., 2006—. Pres. Ohio City Redevelopment Assn., Cleve., 1986—91; treas., pres., deacon, trustee and elder Fairmont Presbyn. Ch.; bd. dirs. 5000 S Cornell Condominium Assn., 2001—; Literacy Vols. of Ill. Recipient Descone award, Fairmond Frost Clare Ho., 1984, award, Luth. Med. Ctr. Women's Bd., 1988, Cmty. Svc. award, Mayor George Voinovich, City of Cleve., 1991, Moccasin award for cmty. svc., City Yr. Chgo., 2004; grantee, Cleve. Found., United Way of Cuyahoga County, Gund Found., Luth. Med. Ctr. Found., 1989, BP Am. Found., numerous others. Mem.: Wooster Edn. Assn., Ohio Fedn. Women, Wooster Jr. Women's Club. Avocations: collecting art, studying Chinese language and culture. Home: 5000 S Cornell #3A Chicago IL 60615 Office Phone: 773-834-3286. Office Fax: 773-702-2010. Personal E-mail: joansessions@comcast.net.

**SESSIONS, PETE,** congressman; b. Waco, Tex., Mar. 22, 1955; m. Juanita Diaz, 1984; children: Bill, Alex. BS in Polit. Sci., Southwestern U., Georgetown, Tex. Dist. mgr. mktg. Southwestern Bell Tel. Co., 1978—94; v.p. pub. policy Nat. Ctr. Policy Analysis, Dallas, 1994—95; mem. US Congress from 32nd (formerly 5th) Tex. dist., 1997—; mem. rules com., mem. budget com., chair Results Caucus. Bd. mem. YMCA; mem. exec. bd. Circle Ten Coun. of Boy Scouts Am.; active United Meth. Ch. Recipient Nat. Disting. Eagle Scout award, 1999. Mem. Rotary Club. Republican. Methodist. Avocations: hiking, mountain climbing, running. Office: US Ho Reps 1514 Longworth Ho Office Bldg Washington DC 20515-4305 Office Phone: 202-225-2231.*

**SESSIONS, ROY BRUMBY,** otolaryngologist, educator; b. Houston, July 28, 1937; s. Roy Brumby and Elizabeth (Compton) S.; m. Mary Cousart, Aug. 28, 1976; children: Kate, Elizabeth, Abigail, Matthew. BS, La. State U., Baton Rouge, 1958; MD, La. State U., New Orleans, 1962. Resident gen. surgery and otolaryngology Washington U. Sch. Medicine, St. Louis, 1965-69; asst. prof. Baylor Coll. Medicine, Houston, 1969-73, assoc. prof., 1973-83; prof. head and neck surgery Meml. Sloan Kettering Cancer Ctr., N.Y.C., 1983-89; prof., chmn. dept. otolaryngology, head and neck surgery Med. Sch. Georgetown U., Washington, 1989-97; chmn. dept. otolaryngology, head and neck surgery Beth Israel Med. Ctr., N.Y.C., 1998—, assoc. dir. Cancer Ctr., co-dir. Inst. Head and Neck Surgery, 1998—. Contbr. articles to profl. jours., chpts. to books; author one textbook. Lt. comdr. USN, 1962-65. Roman Catholic. Home: 411 Forest St Rye NY 10580 Office: Beth Israel Med Ctr 10 Union Sq E Ste 4J New York NY 10003-3314

**SESSIONS, WILLIAM K., III,** federal judge; b. Hartford, Conn., 1947; BA, Middlebury Coll., 1969; JD, George Washington U., 1972. Bar: 1973; Ct. of Appeals, D.C., 1973; Ct. of Appeals (2nd cir.) 1975; U.S. Dist. Ct., Vt., 1973; U.S. Supreme Ct., 1992. Law clk. Hon. Hilton Dier, Jr. Addison (Vt.) Dist. Ct., 1973; exec. dir. Addison County Youth Svcs. Bur., 1973-74; staff Addison County Pub. Defender, 1974-78; pvt. practice Middlebury, Vt., 1978-80; ptnr. Sessions, Keiner, Dumont & Barnes, P.c., Middlebury, Vt., 1980-95; judge U.S. Dist. Ct., Burlington, 1995—, chief judge, 2002—. Adj. prof. law Vt. Law Sch., 1978-95; vice chmn. U.S. Sentencing Commn., 1999—; chair Vt. State com. of selection for Rhodes Scholarship Trust, 2000; trustee Vt. Law Sch., 1999-2001. 1st Lt. U.S. Army, 1972—77. Mem.: Friends Children's Art Exch. Office: US Dist Ct PO Box 928 Burlington VT 05402-0928

**SESSIONS, WILLIAM STEELE,** lawyer, former FBI director; b. Ft. Smith, Ark., May 27, 1930; s. Will Anderson and Edith A. (Steele) S.; m. Alice Lewis, Oct. 5, 1952; children: William Lewis, Mark Gregory, Peter Anderson, Sara Anne. BA, Baylor U., 1956, LLB, 1958; degree (hon.), John C. Marshall Law Sch., St. Mary's U., 1989; LLD (hon.), Dickinson Coll., 1988, Flager Coll., 1990, Davis & Elkins Coll., 1992, McMurry U. 1997. Bar: Tex. 1959;

U.S. Dist Ct. (Western Dist.) Tex.; Ct. Appeals (5th Cir.). Ptnr. McGregor & Sessions, Waco, Tex., 1959-61; assoc. Tirey, McLaughlin, Gorin & Tirey, Waco, 1961-63; ptnr. Haley, Fulbright, Winniford, Sessions & Bice, Waco, 1963-69; sect. chief, govt. ops sect. criminal divsn. U.S. Dept. Justice, Washington, 1969-71; U.S. atty. U.S. Dept Justice, U.S. Dist. Ct., (we. dist), San Antonio, 1971-74; dist. judge U.S. Dist. Ct. (we. dist.) Tex., San Antonio, 1974-87, chief judge, 1980-87; dir. FBI, Washington, 1987-93; ptnr. Sessions & Sessions, San Antonio and Washington, 1995-2000, Holland & Knight, LLP, San Antonio and Washington, 2000—. Bd. dirs., chmn. book com. Fed. Jud. Ctr., Washington, 1981—; mem. Tex. Commn. on Judicial Efficiency, 1995, Tex. Commn. on a Representative Student Body, 1998, Gov.'s Task Force on Homeland Security, Gov.'s Anti-Crime Commn., Tex., 2002, ABA Standing Com. on the 21st Century Judiciary, ABA Standing Com. on the Libr. of Congress; mem. steering com. of coastal Tex.; mem. George W. Bush presdl. lib. steering com. Baylor U.; served on initiatives of Constitution Project; served as signatory The Ctr. for Study of Presidency; served as commr. Commn. on Safety & Abuse in America's Prisons. Contbr. articles to profl. jours. Active Dr. Martin Luther King Jr. Fed. Holiday Commn., 1991-96, hon. bd. dirs., 1993-94; bd. trustees Nat. Environ. Edn. & Tng. Found., Inc., 2001—. Lt. USAF, 1951-55; capt. USAFR. Recipient Rosewood Gavel award St. Mary's U. Sch. Law, San Antonio, 1982, Disting. Alumni award Baylor U., Golden Plate award Am. Acad. Achievement, 1988, Law Enforcement Leadership award Assn. Fed. Investigators, 1989, medal of honor DAR, 1989, Disting. Eagle Scout award Boy Scouts Am., 1990, Person of Yr. award Am. Soc. for Indsl. Security, 1990, Magna Charta award Baronial Order of Magna Charta, 1990, Price Daniel Disting. Pub. Svc. award Baylor U., 2002; named Lawyer of Yr., Baylor Law Sch., 1988, Father of Yr., Nat. Fathers Day Com., 1988, Ellis Island Congl. Medal of Honor, 1992; inducted into Eagle Scout Hall of Fame, 1998. Fellow ABA (chmn. spl. com. on judicial independence 1997—, Nat. Law Day chmn. 2000-02, hon. co chmn., pres. commn. on the 21st Century Judiciary, 2002-, mem. commn. on civic edn. and separation of powers); mem. Nat. Conf. U.S. (com. on ct. adminstrn., chmn. jud. improvements subcom. 1983-85, ad hoc com. on automation to state. reporter com. 1984-87, mem. ad hoc ct. reporter com. 1984-87), San Antonio Bar Assn. (bd. dirs. 1973-74), Fed. Bar Assn. (pres. San Antonio sect. 1974), Am. Judicature Soc. (exec. com. 1982-84), Dist. Judges Assn. of 5th Cir. (pres. 1982-83), State Bar of Tex. (chmn. com. to develop procedures for cert. state law questions to Supreme Ct. by Fed. Cts. 1983-85), Waco McLennan County Bar Assn. (pres. 1968), San Antonio Inns of Ct. (pres. 1986), William S. Sessions Inns of Ct. Republican. Methodist. Avocations: hiking, climbing, canoeing. Office: Holland & Knight LLP Ste 100 2099 Pennsylvania Ave NW Washington DC 20006 Office Phone: 202-955-3000. Office Fax: 202-955-5564. Business E-Mail: wsessions@hklaw.com, william.sessions@hklaw.com.

**SESSLE, BARRY JOHN,** adult education educator, researcher; b. Sydney, NSW, Australia, May 28, 1941; arrived in Can., 1971; s. Frederick George and Sadie Isobel (Lawson) S.; m. Mary Baldwin; children from previous marriage: Erica Jane, Claire Marie. BDS, Sydney U., New South Wales, 1963, MDS, MSc, Sydney U., New South Wales, 1965; PhD, U. New South Wales, 1969, DSc (hon.), 2000. Scholar Dental Found. Sydney U., 1963-64; tchg. fellow U. New South Wales, 1965-68; vis. assoc. U.S. Nat. Inst. Dental Rsch., Bethesda, Md., 1968-70; assoc. prof. U. Toronto Dental Sch., Ont., Canada, 1971-76, prof., 1976-85, chmn. divsn. biol. scis., 1978-84, assoc. dean rsch., 1985-90, dean, 1990-2001. Mem. com. on dental scis. Can. Med. Rsch. Coun., Ottawa, 1979-82; mem. com. grants rev. U.S. NIH, Bethesda, 1976-. Author: The Neural Basis of Oral and Facial Function, 1978; editor: Mastication and Swallowing, 1976, Oro-facial Pain and Neuromuscular Dysfunction, 1985, Effects of Injury of Trigeminal and Spinal Somatosensory Systems, 1987, Trigeminal Neuralgia: Current Concepts Regarding Pathogenesis and Treatment, 1991, Temporomandibular Joint and Masticatory Muscle Disorders, 1994, Temporomandibular Disorders and Related Pain Conditions, 1995, Neurobiology of Mastication, 1999, Orofacial Pain, 2001; mem. editl. bd. Arch. Oral Biol. Jour., 1988—, Pain Jour., 1986-90, Jour. Dental Rsch., 2003-05, Dysphagia Jour., 1990—, Pain Rsch. and Mgmt. Jour., 1995—, Oral Bioscis. and Medicine, 2003-2005, Jour. of Oral Rehab., 2003—; editor-in-chief Jour. Orofacial Pain, 1997—. Can. rsch. chair, 2001—. Recipient Tchr. award Can. Fund for Dental Edn., 1977, Disting. Career award Can. Pain Soc., 1999, Nat. Recognition award Am. Acad. Orofacial Pain, 2004; grantee Med. Rsch. Coun., 1971—, NIH, 1974—, Quality Life award Can. Inst. Health Rsch., 2005. Fellow Royal Soc. Can., Can. Acad. Sci., Internat. Coll. Dentists, Can. Acad. Health Scis.; mem. Internat. Assn. Study Pain (sec. Can. chpt. 1982-87, mem. coun. 1993-96, pres.-elect 1997-99, pres. 1999-2001), Can. orofacial pain group 2002-05), Soc. Neurosci. (pres. South Ont. chpt. 1982-83), Internat. Assn. Dental Rsch. (pres. Can. divsn. 1977-78, sec.-treas. 1976-79, pres. neurosci. group 1985-86, pres. 1994-95, Oral Sci. award 1976, Pindborg Oral Biol. prize 1994), Internat. Union Physiol. Sci. (sec. oral physiology commn. 1983-90). Office: Faculty Dentistry U Toronto 124 Edward St Toronto ON Canada M5G 1G6

**SESSLER, ANDREW MARIENHOFF,** physicist; b. Bklyn., Dec. 11, 1928; s. David and Mary (Baron) S.; m. Gladys Lerner, Sept. 23, 1951 (div. Dec. 1994); children: Daniel Ira, Jonathan Lawrence, Ruth. BA in Math. cum laude, Harvard U., 1949; MA in Theoretical Physics, Columbia U., 1951, PhD in Theoretical Physics, 1953. NSF fellow Cornell U., Ithaca, NY, 1953—54; asst. prof. Ohio State U., Columbus, 1954, assoc. prof., 1960; on leave Midwestern Univs. Rsch., 1955—56; vis. physicist Lawrence Radiation Lab., 1959—60; vis. physicist, summer Niels Bohr Inst., Copenhagen, 1961; lectr. theoretical physics Lawrence Berkeley Lab. U. Calif., Berkeley, 1961—73, rschr. energy and environment Lawrence Berkeley Lab., 1971—73, dir. Lawrence Berkeley Lab., 1973—80, sr. scientist plasma physics Lawrence Berkeley Lab., 1980—94, disting. sr. staff scientist Lawrence Berkeley Lab., 1994—2001, disting. vis. scientist Lawrence Berkeley Lab., 2001—02, disting. scientist Lawrence Berkeley Lab., 2002—, dir. emeritus, 2002-. U.S. advisor Punjab U. Physics Inst., Chandigarh, India; mem. US-India Coop. Program for Improvement Sci. Edn. in India, 1966, high energy physics adv. panel to U.S. AEC, 1969-72, adv. com. Lawrence Hall Sci., 1974-78; chmn. Stanford Synchrotron Radiation Project Sci. Policy Bd., 1974-77, EPRI Advanced Fuels Adv. Com., 1978-81, BNL External Adv. Com. on Isabelle, 1980-82; vis. sci. pol. bd. Stanford Synchrotron Radiation Lab., 1991-92; LJ. Haworth dist. scientist Brookhaven Nat. Lab., 1991-92; spokesperson Neutrino Factory and Muon Collider Collaboration, 1999-2002, assoc. spokesperson 2002—. Mem. editl. bd. Nuclear Instruments and Methods, 1969—2000, correspondent Comments on Modern Physics, 1969—71; contbr. over 300 articles to profl. jours.; editor: 5 books. Mem. Superconducting Super Collider Sci. Policy Com., 1991—93; mem. radiation effects rsch. bd. Nat. Rsch. Coun., 2001—04, mem. nuclear radiation studies bd., 2005—. Recipient E.O. Lawrence award US Atomic Energy Commn., 1970, US Particle Accelerator Sch. prize, 1988, Nicholson Medal for Humanitarian Svc., 1994, Robert R. Wilson prize 1997; fellow Japan Soc. for Promotion Sci. at KEK, 1985. Fellow AAAS (nominating com. 1984-87), Am. Phys. Soc. (chmn. com. internat. freedom scientist 1983-88, study of directed energy weapons panel 1985-87, chmn. panel pub. affairs 1988, chmn. divsn. physics of beams 1990, chmn. com. applications of physics 1993 councilor for divsn. physics of beams 1994-97, pres.-elect 1997, pres. 1998, past pres. 1999, vice-chmn. forum on physics and soc. 2001, chmn.-elect 2002, chmn. 2003). N.Y. Acad. Sci.; mem. NAS (bd. on radiation effects rsch. 2002-05, nuclear radiation studies bd., 2005-), IEEE (sr.), Fedn. Am. Scientists Coun. (vice chmn. 1987-88, chmn. 1988-92), Assoc. Univ. Inc. (bd. dirs. 1991-98), Sigma Xi. Avocations: skiing, hiking, jogging, exercise, flute. Office: Lawrence Berkeley Lab Univ Calif MS 71R0259 I Cyclotron Rd Bldg Berkeley CA 94720-8211 Office Phone: 510-486-4992. Business E-Mail: AMSessler@lbl.gov.

**SESSLER, JONATHAN LAWRENCE,** chemistry professor; b. Urbana, Ill., May 20, 1956; s. Andrew M. and Gladys Sessler; m. Carol Ann Rubel, Jan. 13, 1963; children: Jordan Elija, Chanan David. BS, U. Calif., Berkeley, 1973—77; PhD, Stanford U., Calif., 1977—82. Asst. prof. U. Tex., Austin, 1984—89, assoc. prof., 1989—92, prof. 1992—2001, Roland K. Pettit centennial prof., 2001—. Co-founder and cons. Pharmacyclics, Inc., Sunny-

vale, Calif., 1991—; editor Supramolecular Chemistry, Reading, 2000—; co-founder Anionics, Inc., Oakland, Calif., 2003—; standing mem., msfa study sect. NIH, Bethesda, Md., 2005—; assoc. editor ChemComm, Cambridge, England, 2005—; vis. prof. U. Southampton, England, 2006—; adj. prof. U. Calif., Santa Barbara, 2006—. Contbr. over 75 papers to profl. jours. and pubs. Mem. Temple Beth Shalom, Austin, Tex., 2002—06. Recipient Dreyfus Tchr. Scholar award, 1988, Cope Scholar award, Am. Chem. Soc., 1991, Sr. Scientist award, Alexander von Humboldt Found., 1992, Japanese Soc. for Promotion of Sci., 1992, 2004; fellow, AAAS, 1999; Sloan fellow, 1989. Jewish. Achievements include patents for Texaphyrin, Sapphyrin, Calixpyrrole And Related Inventions (75 Total). Avocation: languages. Office: Univ Texas 1 University Sta A5300 Austin TX 78712-0165 Office Phone: 512-471-5009. Home Fax: 512 471 7550; Office Fax: 512-471-7550. Business E-Mail: sessler@mail.utexas.edu.

**SESSOMS, ALLEN LEE,** academic administrator, physicist, educator, retired diplomat; b. NYC, Nov. 17, 1946; s. Albert Earl and Lottie Beatrice (Leff) Sessoms; children from previous marriage: Manon Elizabeth, Stephanie Csilla. BS, Union Coll., Schenectady, N.Y., 1968; PhD, Yale U., 1972; DSc (hon.), Union Coll., 1998; PhD (hon.), Soka U., Japan, 2000. Sci. assoc. CERN, Geneva, 1973-78; asst. prof. physics Harvard U., Cambridge, Mass., 1974-81; sr. tech. advisor OES, State Dept., Washington, 1980-82; dir. Office Nuclear Tech. & Safeguards, State Dept., Washington, 1982-87; counselor for sci. and tech. U.S. Embassy, Paris, 1987-89, polit. minister, counselor Mexico City, 1989-91, dep. chief of mission, 1991-93; exec. v.p., v.p. for acad. affairs U. Mass. Sys., Boston, 1993-95; pres. CUNY Queens Coll., Flushing, NY, 1995-2000; lectr., fellow Belfer Ctr. for Sci. and Internat. Affairs, JFK Sch. Govt., Harvard U., Cambridge, Mass., 2000—03; pres. Del. State U., 2003—. Adv. com. U.S. Sec Energy, 1995-2002; mem. NCAA Pres. Coun., 1996-2000; nuc. energy rsch. adv. com. U.S. Dept. Energy. Contbr. articles to profl. jours. Bd. dirs. Milestone Fund, Drawing Ctr., Big Apple Circus; mem. Del. Arts Coun.; mem. adv. coun. Toda Internat.; member bd. trustees Chapman U. Travel/study grant Ford Found., 1973-74; Alfred P. Sloan Found. fellow, 1977-81; recipient Wilbur Cross medal Yale Grad. Sch. Alumni, 1999, Medal of Highest Honor, Soka U., 1999; officer dans l'Order des Palmes Académiques, 1999. Mem. AAAS, Am. Phys. Soc., N.Y. Acad. Sci., Cosmos Club. Office: Office of the Pres Del State Univ 1200 N Dupont Hwy Dover DE 19901 Office Phone: 302-857-6001. Personal E-mail: allensessoms@aol.com. Business E-Mail: asessoms@desu.edu.

**SESSUMS, T. TERRELL,** lawyer; b. Daytona Bch., Fla., June 11, 1930; m. Neva Ann Steeves, Aug. 16, 1958; children: Thomas T. Jr., Richard H., Sandra Sessums Mooneyham. BA in polit. sci., U. Fla., 1952; JD, U. Fla. Coll. Law, 1958; grad., Fla. Exec. Mgmt. Program, 1993; LLD (hon.), Fla. So. Coll., 1973; D of pub. adminstrn. (hon.), Rollins Coll., 1974; LLD (hon.), Flagler Coll., 1988; LHD (hon.), U. So. Fla., 1995. Assoc. atty. Hardee & Ott, Tampa, 1958—60; legis. aide/legal asst. to State Senator Sam Gibbons, Fla. Senate, 1959—61; ptnr. Albritton, Sessums Gordon & Ryder, Tampa, 1961—84; shareholder, mng. ptnr. Macfairlane Ferguson & McMullen, 1984—97; ptnr. Salem Saxon, P.A., 1999—; of counsel Salem Law Group, P.A., Tampa, 2003—. Spkr. Fla. Ho. Reps., 1972—74; adj. prof. U. S. Fla., Tampa, 1974—75; gen. coun. Tampa Port Authority, 1974—89; colloquium bd., lectr., ednl. policy issues Harvard U. Grad. Sch. Edn., 1977; chmn. Fla. Bar Legis. Com., 1977—78; coun. Fla. Conf. Cir. Judges, 1978; spl. coun. Fla. Bar/Workers' Compensation Section, 1978—79, chmn., 1979—80; served on Fla. Bd. Regents, 1979—88, chmn., 1986—88; spl. coun. to US Senator Bob Graham, 1995; dir. GTE Fla., 1986—93; dir. region II, cons. bd. Southeast Bank, N.A., Tampa Bay, 1973—91; dir. Blue Cross Fla., 1977—78; trustee, exec. com., gen. coun. Time Warner Trust, Tampa, 1983—98; dir. Family TV Co. (WFTV, Channel 28), 1978—84; pres. Ashley St. Properties, Inc., 1986—89, Golden Pond Groves, Inc., Tampa, 1986—89, Halifax Mgmt. Co., 1994—97; v.p. Trouble Creek Properties, Inc., 1988—2001; mem. Tampa Bay Area Com. on Fgn. Rels., 1982—; state dir., sr. mem. Orange Bowl Com., 1991—; dir. Mus. Sci. and Industry (MOSI), Tampa, 1990—94, adv. coun., 1994—; founding pres. Georgia Seagle Alumni Assn., Inc., 1982—84, dir., 1984—94, adv. coun., 1994—2004. Contbr. articles to jour. Bd. trustees exec. com. U. S. Fla. Found., 1979—89; bd. dir. Moffitt Cancer Ctr., Inc., 1984—91; ednl. mission to coll. and U. in China and Japan U. S. Fla., 1986, life mem. pres. coun.; trustee Found. Eye Rsch., Inc., 1987—91; dir. Fla. State Fair Authority, 1995—96; pres. Greater Tampa C. of C., 1983—84, gen. coun., 1979—87, exec. com., 1988—91, chmn. com. of 100, 1986; dir. Fla. C. of C., 1987—96, v.p. pub. affairs, 1988—89, mem. project cornerstone adv. com., 1988—89, vice chmn. programs, 1989—90, chmn. rsch. and info. coun., 1990—91, chmn., 1992—93, exec. com., 1988—94, bd. gov., 1996—; pres. alumni coun. U. Fla. Coll. Law, 1984—85, mem. major gifts com./Hillsborough County chmn., 1989—91; trustee U. Tampa, 1978—91, chmn. strategic planning com., 1987—88, vice chmn. bd. trustees, 1987—88, chmn. bd. trustees, 1988—90, bd. overseers; trustee Fla. So. Coll., 1989—, chmn. long range planning com., 1990—2003, pres. coun., 1983—85, chmn. bd. trustees, 1993—2003, emeritus chmn. bd.; parents' coun. Wofford Coll. 1981—85, pres. coun., 1983—85; trustee Inter Am. Scholarship Found., Inc.; asst. scoutmaster Boy Scouts Am., Tampa, 1976—79; organizing com. mem. Tampa Bay Performing Arts Ctr., 1980, trustee, 1980—88; mem. Found. Excellence in Edn., 1987—90; dir. Fla. Independent College Fund, 1988—90; fed. judicial nom. com. Fla. (Middle Dist. Panel), 1997—2001; chmn. adv. coun. Tampa United Meth. Ctr., 1989—94; trustee United Meth. Found. Higher Edn., 1998—; dir. Nat. Conf. Christians and Jews, Tampa Bay Chpt., 1990—94. Named diplomat, Fla. Demolay Hall Fame, 1995; recipient Disting. Alumnus award, U. Fla., 1973, CHIEF award (Champion Higher Independent Edn. in Fla.), Pres. Independent Coll. and U. in Fla., 1974—75, Pres. Disting. Citizen award, U. So. Fla., 1975, Don L. and Ruth E. Smith Founders award, 1980, Nat. Football Found. award, Contbn. to Cmty. and Football Tampa Chpt., 1982, Person of Vision award, Nat. Soc. Prevent Blindness, 1986, "Class of 56" award, U. So. Fla. Alumni Assn., 1988, Silver Medallion award, Nat. Conf. Christians and Jews, 1990, Disting. Svc. award, Fla. Assn. Coll. and U., 1993, Francis Asbury award, Fla. Annual Conf., United Meth. Ch., 1998. Mem.: Fla. Bar Assn., Hillsborough Bar Assn., Tampa Bar Assn., Hall Fame Bowl Assn. (founding dir. 1986—88), Tampa Kiwanis Club, Tampa Yacht and Country Club, U. Club Tampa, Omicron Delta Kappa. Achievements include named in honor, Terrell Sessums Mall at U. So. Fla., 2001; named in honor, Terrell Sessums Elem. Sch., 2004. Office Phone: 813-224-9000.

**SESTINA, JOHN E.,** financial planner; b. Mar. 17, 1942; s. John J. and Regina Sestina; m. Mary Barbara Jezek, Dec. 20, 1970; 1 child, Alison. BS, U. Dayton, 1965; MS in Fin. Svc., Am. Coll., 1982. Cert. fin. planner, chartered fin. cons. With John E. Sestina and Co., Columbus, Ohio, 1967—. Author: Complete Guide to Professional Incorporation, 1970, Managing To Be Wealthy, 1988, 2d edit. 2000, Fee-Only Financial Planning, How to Make It Work For You, 1991, 2d edit. 2000; (video tape series) Managing To Be Wealthy (4 series), 1987; contbr. articles to profl. jours.; contbr. weekly fin. planning segment AM Columbus, WOSU-AM, 1979—. Named one of Nation's 200 Best Fin. Advisors of 1996-98, Worth Mag. Mem. Soc. Ind. Fin. Advisers (past pres., Fin. Planner of Yr. award 1982), Internat. Assn. Fin. Planners, Nat. Assn. Personal Fin. Advisors (founder, pres.), Inst. Cert. Fin. Planners, Fin. Planning Clubs Internat. (founder). Office: 1161 Bethel Rd Ste 201 Columbus OH 43220-2606 Office Phone: 614-326-3077. Business E-Mail: jsestina@sestina.com.

**SESTINI, VIRGIL ANDREW,** retired biology educator; b. Las Vegas, Nov. 24, 1936; s. Santi and Merceda Francesca (Borla) S. BS in Edn., U. Nev. 1959; postgrad., Oreg. State U., 1963-64; MNS, U. Idaho, 1995; postgrad. Ariz. State U., 1967; No. Ariz. U., 1969. Cert. tchr., Nev. Tchr. biology Rancho H.S., 1960-76; sci. chmn.; tchr. biology Bonanza H.S., Las Vegas, 1976-90, ret., 1990. Co-founder, curator exhibits Meadows Mus. Nat. History, 1993-94; part-time tchr. sci. chmn. Meadows Sch., 1987-94; ret., 1994; edn. specialist, cell biologist SAGE Rsch., Las Vegas, 1993, ret., 1998; founder Da Vinci Enterprises, Las Vegas, 1995. Author: Lab Investigations for High School Honors Biology, 1992, Laboratory Investigations in Microbiology, 1992, Genetics Problems for High School Biology, 1995, Science Laboratory

Report Data Book, 1995, Field and Museum Techniques for the Classroom Teacher, 1995, Selected Lab Investigations and Projects for Honors and AP Biology, Vol. I Microbiology, 1995, Telecommunications: A Simulation for Biology Using the Internet, 1995; co-author: A Biology Lab Manual for Cooperative Learning, 1989, Metrics and Science Methods: A Manual of Lab Experiments for Home Schoolers, 1990, Experimental Designs in Biology I: Botany and Zoology, 1993, Designs in Biology: A Lab Manual, 1993, Integrated Science Lab Manual, 1994, Supplemental Experiments and Field Studies for AP Biology, 1998; contbr. articles to profl. jours. including The Sci. Tchr., Am. Biology Tchr., Fine Scale Models, Ships in Scale, IPMS Jour. With USAR, 1959-65. Reciepient Rotary Internat. Honor Tchr. award, 1965, Region VIII Outstanding Biology Tchr. award, 1970, Nev. Outstanding Biology Tchr. award Nat. Assn. Biology Tchrs., 1970, Nat. Assn. Sci. Tchrs., Am. Gas Assn. Sci. Tchg. Achievement Recognition award, 1976, 80, Gustov Ohaus award, 1980, Presdl. Honor Sci. Tchr. award, 1983; Presdl. Award excellence in math. and sci. tchg., 1984, Celebration of Excellence award Nev. Com. on Excellence in Edn., 1986, Hall of Fame award Clark County Sch. Dist., 1988, Excellence in Edn. award, 1987, 88, Spl. Edn. award 1988, NSEA Mini-grants, 1988, 89, 92, World Decoration of Excellence medallion World Inst. Achievement, 1989, Cert. Spl. Congrl. Recognition, 1989, Senatorial Recognition, 1989, mini-grant Jr. League Las Vegas, 1989, Excellence in Edn. award Clark Country Sch. Dist., 1989; named Nev. Educator of Yr., Milken Family Found./Nev. State Dept. Edn., 1989; grantee Nev. State Bd. Edn., 1988, 89, Nev. State Edn. Assn., 1988-89. Mem. AAAS, NEA, Nat. Assn. Taxidermists, Nat. Sci. Tchrs. Assn. (life, Nev. state membership chmn. 1968-70), Nat. Assn. Biology Tchrs. (life, OBTA dir. Nev. state 1991-93), Am. Soc. Microbiology, Coun. for Exceptional Children, Am. Biographic Inst. (rsch. bd. advisors 1988), Nat. Audubon Assn., Nat. Sci. Suprs. Assn., Am. Inst. Biol. Scis., Nautical Rsch. Guild, Internat. Plastic Modelers Soc., So. Nev. Scale Modelers (Las Vegas coord., Modeloberfest, 1995), Silver State Scale Modelers Guild. Avocations: scale models, military figures, scale models circus, photography. Office Phone: 702-873-2900. E-mail: vsestini@cox.net.

**SESTRIC, ANTHONY JAMES,** lawyer; b. St. Louis, June 27, 1940; s. Anton and Marie (Gasparovic) Sestric; m. Carol F. Bowman, Nov. 24, 1966; children: Laura Antonette, Holly Nicole, Michael Anthony. Student, George-town U., 1958-62; JD, Mo. U., 1965. Bar: Mo. 1965, Minn. 1996, U.S. Ct. Appeals (8th cir.) 1965, U.S. Ct. Appeals (7th cir.) 1984, U.S. Dist. Ct. Mo. 1966, U.S. Dist. Ct. (no dist.) Tex. 1985, U.S. Dist. Ct. Ill. 1994, U.S. Tax Ct. 1969, U.S. Supreme Ct. 1970, U.S. Claims Ct. 1986. Law clk. U.S. Dist. Ct., St. Louis, 1965-66; ptnr. Sestric, McGhee & Miller, St. Louis, 1966-77, Fordyce and Mayne, 1977-78, Sestric & Garvey, 1978-96, Sestric Law Firm, St. Louis, 1996—. Spl. asst. to Mo. atty. gen., St. Louis, 1968; spl. asst. cir. atty., 2001—; mem. Fed. Jud. Selection Commn., 1993, U.S. Jud. Selection Commn., 1993—94, U.S. Magistrate Merit Selection Commn., 2005; gen. chmn. 22d jud. cir. bar com., 1995; mem. Region XI disciplinary com., 2001—. Contbr. articles to profl. jours. Hearing officer St. Louis Met. Police Dept.; active St. Louis Air Pollution Bd. Appeals and Varience Rev., 1966-73, chmn., 1968-73; active St. Louis Airport Commn., 1975-76; dist. vice-chmn. Boy Scouts Am., 1970-76; bd. dirs. Full Achievement, Inc., 1970-77, Legal Aid Soc. St. Louis, 1976-77, Law Libr. Assn. St. Louis, 1976-78, Thomas Dunn Memls., 1995-98, Marquette Learning Ctr., 1995-98, v.p. bd. St. Elizabeth Acad., 1985-86 Mem. ABA (state chmn. judiciary com. 1973-75, cir. chmn. com. condemnation, zoning and property use 1975-77, standing com. bar activities 1982-88), Nat. Conf. Bar Pres.'s (exec. coun. 1987-90), Mo. Bar Assn. (vice-chmn. young lawyers sect. 1973-76, bd. govs. 1974-77, chmn. law practice mgmt. com. 1997-99), Bar Assn. Met. St. Louis (chmn. young lawyers sect. 1974-75, exec. com. 1974-83, 94-95, pres. 1981-82, bd. govs. 1995-98, chmn. survey com. 1999). Home: 3967 Holly Hills Blvd Saint Louis MO 63116-3135 Office Phone: 314-351-2512. Personal E-mail: ajsestric@juno.com.

**SETEAR, JOHN K.,** law educator; BA, Williams Coll., 1981; JD, Yale Univ., 1984. Law clerk U.S. Ct. Appeals D.C. cir., Sandra Day O'Connor, U.S. Supreme Ct.; policy analyst RAND Corp.; prof. Univ Calif. Los Angeles, 1991—97; vis. prof. Univ. Va. Sch. Law, 1997—98, prof., 1998—, now Thomas F. Bergin prof. Dir. Internat. Environmental Cooperation Project, Ctr. Internat. Rel., Univ. Calif. Los Angeles. Editor (in chief): Yale Law Journal, 1984. Fellow Woodrow Wilson Internat. Ctr. Scholars, 1995—96. Office: Univ Va Law Sch 580 Massie Rd Charlottesville VA 22903

**SETH, ANIL KUMAR,** neuroscientist, researcher; b. Oxford, Oxfordshire, U.K., Nov. 6, 1972; s. Bhola Seth and Anne Delaney. MA, Cambridge U., Uk, 1991—94; DPhil, Sussex U., U.K., 2000. Assoc. fellow The Neurosciences Inst., San Diego, 2001—. Mem.: Soc. for Neuroscience. Achievements include research in the theoretical basis of brain function, including the biological foundation of consciousness and the construction of intelligent machines. Office: The Neurosciences Institute 10640 John Jay Hopkins Dr San Diego CA 92121 Office Phone: 858-626-2000. Office Fax: 858-626-2099. Personal E-mail: anil.k.seth@gmail.com.

**SETHALER, BERNARD A.,** secondary school educator; s. Perry T. and Susan M. Sethaler; m. Patricia A. Sethaler; children: Debora, Brian. BA, Western State Coll., Gunnison, Colo., 1968; 5th-Yr. degree, No. Mont. Coll., Havre, 1994. Cert. tchr. Colo., Ky., Ohio, Mont., Nev., Tex. Tchr., coach Newport (Ky.) H.S., 1968—77, Hays/Lodge Pole H.S., Hays, Mont., 1977—79; work coord., program dir. U.S. Fish and Wildlife, Potosboro, Tex., 1978—79; tchr., coach Henrietta (Tex.) H.S., 1979—81, Grass Range (Mont.) H.S., 1981—96; tchr. Elko (Nev.) H.S., 1996—. Adviser Skills USA-VICA, Elko, Grass Range, and Newport, Ky., 1970—. Councilman City of Grass Range, 1990—96; mem., dir. Gov.'s Panel Vocat. Edn., Helena, Mont., 1992—96. Named Vocat. Tl In of Yr., Ky. Vocat. Assn., 1974, Trade and Indsl. Tchr. of Yr., Mont. Vocat. Assn., 1995, Advisor of Yr., Mont. VICA, 1996. Mem.: NVEA, NEA, NVACTE, ACTE (v.p., pres. 1996—2005, Example by Performance award 2000), Nev. Assn. Career Edn. (pres. 2000—05, bd. dirs. 2003—), Lions Club (pres., sec. 1982—). Avocations: skiing, stock car racing, hunting, fishing. Office: Elko H S 987 College Ave Elko NV 89801

**SETHI, GAUTAM,** environmental professor; PhD, U. Calif., Berkeley, 2001. Rsch. assoc. Tata Energy Rsch. Inst., New Delhi, Delhi, 1989—93; fellow U. of Tex., Austin, 1993—94; adj. instr. U. of Calif., Berkeley, 1998; asst. prof. Bard Coll., Annandale, NY, 2001—. Mem. steering com. Hudson Valley Consortium of Schs. and Colls., Beacon, NY, 2004—06. Named Outstanding Grad. Student Instr., U. Calif., 1996; recipient Full tuition remission and tchg. assistantship, 1994—2001; fellow, U. of Tex., 1993—94. Achievements include research in Modeling uncertainty and complex systems. Office: Bard Ctr for Environ Policy 5 Hegeman Hall Tivoli NY 12583 Office Phone: 845-758-7386. Office Fax: 845-758-7636. E-mail: sethi@bard.edu.

**SETHI, RAJAT,** cardiologist, educator, research scientist; b. New Delhi, Sept. 2, 1964; arrived in US, 2005; s. Prabhu Dayal Sethi; m. Manjit Dhalla, Aug. 25, 1990; children: Vishal, Akshay. Pharm D. Univ. Delhi, India, 1985, MSc, 1987; PhD, U. Man., Winnipeg, Canada, 1994. Registered pharmacist Delhi. Asst. rsch. officer NRC, Canada, 1994—96; dir. preclin. rsch. Medicine Inc., Canada, 1996—2000; sr. scientist U. Manitoba, Canada, 2000—05; mem. faculty Tex. A&M Health Sci. Ctr., Irma Lerma Rangel Coll. Pharmacy, Kingsville, 2005—. Recipient Best Rsch. Trainee award, Heart and Stroke Found. Can., 1991—92, Prize for excellence in rsch., Man. Med. Svc. Found., 1993; scholar, U. Delhi, 1985—87, Man. Health Rsch. Coun., 1990—91, Heart and Stroke Found. Can., 1994—95; rsch. Cir. scholar, St. Boniface Gen. Hosp., 1989—90. Mem.: Can. Pharmacy Assn., Internat. Soc. Heart Rsch., Am. Assn. Colls. of Pharmacy. Achievements include patents pending for pyridoxine compounds for the treatment of diabetes and related compounds; therapeutic agent for ischemic reperfusion injury and therapeutic agent for cell dysfunction including cardiac insufficiency due to arrhythmias and cardiac infarction; beneficial effects of DDG on various cardiovascular pathologies; pyridoxine compounds in the treatment of cardiovascular pathologies. Home: 7425 Vaquero Dr Corpus Christi TX 78414 Office: Tex A&M Health Sci Ctr Irma Lerma Rangel Coll Pharmacy MSC 131 Kingsville TX 78363 Office Phone: 361-593-4275. Business E-Mail: rsethi@pharmacy.tamhsc.edu.

**SETHI, SHYAM SUNDER,** management consultant; b. Rawalpindi, Pakistan, July 11, 1942; s. Balraj and Shakuntala (Sawhney) Sethi; m. Kiran Nair, Oct. 17, 1972; children: Seema, Shana. B.E. in Mech. Engring., Birla Inst. Tech., Ranchi, India, 1964; MS1.E., U. Wis., 1970. Cert. mgmt. cons. V.p. Drake Sheahan/Stewart Dougall, NYC, 1970-80; pres., ptnr. Distbn. Mgmt. Assocs., Inc., Princeton, NJ, 1980-96; exec. dir. Dechert-Hampe & Co./DMA, 1996-2000; pres. Distbn. Mgmt. Assocs., Inc., 2001—. Cons. in supply chain, logistics, inventory mgmt., ops. for maj. consumer goods, indsl. and retail cos., Europe, S.Am. and US; spkr. internat. logistics conf. Contbr. articles to profl. jours. Pres. NJ chpt. Coun. Logistics Mgmt., 1987-88, NJ chpt. Inst. Mgmt. Consultants, 1987-88. Mem. Yacht Assn. India. Hindu. Avocations: tennis, sailing. Home: 4 Haelig Ct Bridgewater NJ 08807-2377 Office: DMA Inc PO Box 6843 Bridgewater NJ 08807-0843 Office Phone: 732-469-1885. Personal E-Mail: sethinj@optonline.net.

**SETHNA, BEHERUZ NARIMAN,** academic administrator, educator, management consultant; b. Bombay, July 31, 1948; came to U.S., 1973; s. Nariman Dhanjishaw and Mithu Nariman (Mistry) S.; m. Madhavi Kaji, May 25, 1974; children: Anita B., Shaun B. B in Tech. with honors, Indian Inst. Tech., Bombay, 1971; MBA, Indian Inst. Mgmt., Ahmedabad, 1973; MPhil, Columbia U., 1975, PhD in Bus., 1976; student, Ind. U., 1986, Harvard U. 1991. Cert. computing profl. Inst. for Cert. Computing Profls. Engring. and mgmt. trainee various corps., Bombay, 1968-69, 70-72; case writer, trainee Clarion Advt., Bombay, 1973; project mgr., cons. Lever Bros. Co., N.Y.C., 1974-76; prof., chair mktg. and mgmt. info. systems Clarkson U., Potsdam, NY, 1976-89, dir. grad. programs, 1978-80; mktg., rsch. and strategic planning mgr. Procter & Gamble (India)/Richardson Hindustan (Vicks), Bombay and Westport, Conn., 1980-81; interim exec. v.p. acad. and student affairs; dean Coll. of Bus., chief acad. officer Lamar (Tex.) U., 1989-94, Gulf States Utilities prof. bus., 1991-94; pres. West Ga. Coll., Carrollton, 1994—96, State U. West Ga., 1996—2005, U. West Ga., 2005—; interim sr. vice chancellor Univ. Sys. Ga., 1999—2000, exec. vice chancellor, chief acad. officer, 2006—; pres. Ga. Assn. Colls., 2000—01. Mem. adv. coun. SUNY-Canton (N.Y.) Coll., 1975-89; cons. in field. Author: Research Methods in Marketing, 1984; contbr. articles to profl. jours. Scoutmaster Boy Scouts Am., Potsdam, 1987—89, pack com. chair, den leader, 1987—89, mem. dist. bd., 1991—94, mem. exec. bd. Atlanta Area coun., 1997—2003, Pres.'s Scout Gold Cord, 1966; leader Girl Scouts U.S., Beaumont, 1989—94. Named one of 100 Most Influential Georgians, Ga. Trend, 2003, 2006; recipient Minority Achiever's award, Role Model award, 1991, Dean's Leadership award, Acad. Bus. Adminstrn., 1993, Nat. Svc. award, 1996, Alumnus award (hon.), 1999, Disting. Alumnus award, Indian Inst. Tech., Bombay, 2000, Carroll County Citizen of Yr., 1999, rated 1st among Carroll County's Movers, Shakers and Newsmakers, 2002, Resolution of Commendation, State Senate, 2003, Instrument Innovation award (hon.), 1984—89, 2004; grantee U.S. Dept. Energy, 1980, IBM Corp., 1984, AT&T, 1985; Fulbright scholar, U.S. Info. Agy., 1986—87, Paul Harris fellow, Rotary Internat., 1997. Mem. Rotary (polio plus edn. chair). Avocation: scouting. Home: 107 Windsong Ct Carrollton GA 30117-8978 Office: U W Ga Office Pres Carrollton GA 30118-0001 Office Phone: 678-839-6442. Business E-Mail: bsethna@westga.edu.

**SETLOW, JANE KELLOCK,** biophysicist; b. NYC, Dec. 17, 1919; d. Harold A. and Alberta (Thompson) Kellock; m. Richard Setlow, June 6, 1941; children: Peter, Michael, Katherine, Charles. BA, Swarthmore Coll., 1940; PhD in Biophysics, Yale U., 1959. With dept. radiology Yale U., 1959-60; with biology div. Oak Ridge Nat. Lab., 1960-74; biophysicist Brookhaven Nat. Lab., Upton, N.Y., 1974—. Mem. recombinant DNA molecule program adv. com. NIH, chmn., 1978-2005. Editor: Genetic Engineering, Principles and Methods; mem. editl. bd. various jours.:; contbr. articles to profl. jours. Predoctoral fellow USPHS, 1957-59; postdoctoral fellow, 1960-62 Mem. Biophys. Soc. (pres. 1977-78), Am. Soc. Microbiology. Democrat. Home: 57 Valentine Rd Shoreham NY 11786-1243 Office: Biology Dept Brookhaven Nat Lab Upton NY 11973

**SETLOW, RICHARD BURTON,** biophysicist, researcher; b. NYC, Jan. 19, 1921; s. Charles Meyer and Elsie Setlow; children: Peter, Michael, Katherine, Charles; m. Neva Delihas, Mar. 3, 1989. AB, Swarthmore Coll., 1941; PhD, Yale U., 1947; DSc, U. Toronto, 1985; MD, U. Essen, 1993. Assoc. prof. Yale U., 1956-61; biophysicist Oak Ridge (Tenn.) Nat. Lab., 1961-74, sci. dir. biophysics and cell physiology, 1969-74; dir. U. Tenn.-Oak Ridge Grad. Sch. Biomed. Scis., 1972-74; sr. biophysicist Brookhaven Nat. Lab., Upton, NY, 1974—, chmn. biology dept., 1979-87, assoc. dir. life scis., 1985-98, assoc. lab. dir., 1998. Prof. biomed. scis. U. Tenn., 1967-74; adj. prof. biochemistry SUNY, Stony Brook, 1975—. Author: (with E.C. Pollard) Molecular Biophysics, 1962; editor: (with P.C. Hanawalt) Molecular Mechanisms for Repair of DNA, 1975; contr. books to chap. Recipient Finsen medal Internat. Assn. Photobiology, 1980, Enrico Fermi award U.S. Dept. Energy, 1988, Environ. Mutagen Soc. award, 2002. Mem. NAS, Am. Acad. Arts and Scis., Biophys. Soc. (pres. 1969-70), Environ. Com. Photobiology (pres. 1972-76), Radiation Rsch. Soc., Am. Soc. Photobiology, Am. Assn. Biochemistry and Molecular Biology, Am. Soc. Cancer Rsch., Environ. Mutagen Soc., 11th Internat. Congress on Photobiology (hon. pres. 1992), Phi Beta Kappa. Home: 4 Beachland Ave East Quogue NY 11942-4941 Office: Brookhaven Nat Lab Dept Biology Upton NY 11973 Office Phone: 631-344-3391. Personal E-mail: setlow@optonline.net. Business E-Mail: setlow@bnl.gov.

**SETO, THEODORE PAUL,** lawyer, educator; b. Kermanshah, Iran, Feb. 18, 1951; came to U.S., 1951; s. Paul Susumu and Genevieve (Reynolds) S.; m. Lenore T. Rothman, Aug. 2, 1980 (div. 1999); 1 child, Kira Rothman Seto; m. Sande Lynn Buhai, July 8, 2000; children: Samantha Elizabeth, Genevieve Danielle. BA, Harvard U., 1973, JD, 1976. Bar: Mass. 1977, U.S. Dist. Ct. Mass. 1978, U.S. Dist. Ct. (ea. dist.) Pa. 1983, U.S. Tax Ct. 1985, U.S. Ct. Appeals (1st cir.) 1983, U.S. Ct. Appeals (3d cir.) 1990, U.S. Supreme Ct. 1983, U.S. Claims Ct. 1990. Law clk. to Hon. Judge Mansfield U.S. Ct. Appeals (2nd cir.), N.Y.C., 1976-77; assoc. Foley, Hoag & Eliot, Boston, 1977-83, Drinker Biddle & Reath, Phila., 1983-86, ptnr., 1986-91; assoc. prof. Loyola Law Sch., L.A., 1991-97, prof., 1997—. Vis. prof. U. Paris X, 1998, Cornell Law Sch., 2005. Author: A Uniform System of Citation, 12th edit. 1976; contbr. articles to profl. jours. Democrat. Office: Loyola Law Sch 919 Albany St Los Angeles CA 90015-1211 Office Phone: 213-736-1154. E-mail: tseto@lls.edu.

**SETRAKIAN, BERGE,** lawyer; b. Beirut, Apr. 14, 1949; came to U.S. 1976; s. Hemayak and Arminee S.; m. Vera L. Nazarian, Nov. 22, 1975; children: Ani, Lara. Diplome d'Etudes de Doctorat, U. Lyons, France, 1973; Diplome d'Etudes de Doctorat Droit Compare, F.I.E.D.C., Strasbourg, France, 1974; Licence en Droit Francais, U. St. Joseph, Beirut, 1972, Licence en Droit Libanais, 1972. Bar: Beirut 1972, N.Y. 1983. Assoc. Tyan & Setrakian, Beirut, 1972-76; ptnr. Whitman & Ransom, N.Y.C., 1976-93, Whitman, Breed, Abbott & Morgan, N.Y.C., 1993-2000, Winston & Strawn, N.Y.C., 2000—05, LeBoeuf, Lamb, Greene & MacRae, 2005—. Bd. dirs. Cedars Bank, Calif., 1987—, Interaudi Bank, NY, 1991; fgn. law cons., N.Y, 78. Pres. Armenian Gen. Benevolent Union, N.Y.C., 2002-; bd. dirs. Armenian Assn. of Am., Washington, 1978-87; bd. dirs. Am. Task Force for Lebanon, 1988—; bd. dirs. Am. U. Armenia, 1992—. Mem. ABA, N.Y. Bar Assn., Beirut Bar Assn., Am. Fgn. Law Assn., Englewood Field Club. Office: LeBoeuf, Lamb, Greene & MacRae 125 W 55th St New York NY 10019

**SETSER, CAROLE SUE,** food scientist, educator; b. Warrenton, Mo., Aug. 26, 1940; d. Wesley August and Mary Elizabeth (Meine) Schulze; m. Donald Wayne Setser, June 2, 1969; children: Bradley Wayne, Kirk Wesley, Brett Donald. BS, U. Mo., 1962; MS, Cornell U., 1964; PhD, Kans. State U., 1971. Grad. asst. Cornell U., Ithaca, NY, 1962-64; instr. Kans. State U., Manhattan, 1964-72, asst. prof., 1974-81, assoc. prof., 1981-86, prof., 1986-2001, prof.

emeritus, 2001—. Vis. prof. Bogazici U., Istanbul, Turkey, 2000—01. Recipient Rsch. Excellence award, Coll. of Human Ecology, Manhattan, 1990. Mem.: Inst. Food Techs. (chmn. sensory evaluation divsn. edn. com. 1989—92, continuing edn. com. 1992—95, sec. product devel. divsn. 1997—99, also other offices), Am. Assn. Cereal Chemists (assoc. editor 1989—93), Kappa Omicron Nu (Excellence for Rsch. award 1987), Sigma Xi, Phi Tau Sigma (Outstanding Food Scientist 1998), Gamma Sigma Delta, Phi Upsilon Omicron, Phi Kappa Phi (Scholar award 1998). Business E-Mail: setser@ksu.edu.

**SETTERHOLM, JEFFREY MILES,** systems engineer; b. Rochester, N.Y., May 8, 1946; s. Vernon Miles and Grace Lorraine (Bogema) S.; m. Donna Jean Stollenwerk, Aug. 6, 1974; children: Gregory Todd, Vincent Michael. BS in Engring., Applied Sci. cum laude, Yale U., 1968; MS in Sys. Sci. and Math., Washington U., 1976. Electronic engr. McDonnell Douglas Aircraft Divsn., St. Louis, 1974, sr. engr. flight simulation, 1976-78; prin. devel. engr. mil. avionics divsn. Honeywell Inc., Mpls., 1978-84; prin. engr. aerospace divsn. Rosemount, Inc., Burnsville, Minn., 1984-92; ind. software tech. cons. Lakeville, Minn., 1992-94; geodetic scientist Geospan Corp., Maple Grove, Minn., 1994—2003, contract engr., 2006—, Alliant Techsys., Plymouth, Minn., 2005—06. Author: The Philosophy Works Manual, 1993, Learning Together in a Diverse World, 2004. Capt. USAF, 1969-73. Decorated DFC. Mem. AIAA, Soc. Automotive Engrs. Lutheran. Achievements include patents in field; origination of the computer configurable six-axis hand controller concept; invention of surveying from non-coplanar images; research in virtual cockpit concepts. Home: 8095 230th St E Lakeville MN 55044-8287 Personal E-mail: jeff@setterholm.com.

**SETTIS, SALVATORE,** archaeologist, art historian; b. Rosarno, Italy, June 11, 1941; s. Rocco and Carmela (Megna) Settis; m. Chiara Frugoni, Dec. 9, 1965 (div. 1982); children: Silvano, Andrea, Marta; m. Maria Michela Sassi, Jan. 4, 1984; children: Bruno, Nicola. Degree, U. Pisa, Italy, 1963; PhD, Scuola Normale Superiore, Pisa, 1965. Asst. prof. U. Pisa, 1965—69, lectr. 1969—75, prof., 1976—84, dean Faculty Letters and Philosophy, 1978—81; prof. Scuola Normale Superiore, Pisa, 1984—, dean Faculty Letters and Philosophy, 1986—91, dir., 1999—, Getty Rsch. Inst. for History Art and Humanities, Santa Monica, Calif., 1994—99. Author: La Tempesta Interpretata, 1978, La Colonna Traiana, 1988, I Greci, 5 vols., 1996—2001, Laocoonte Fama e Stile, 1999, Italia SpA L'assalto al patrimonio culturale, 2002, Futuro del "Classico", 2004, Battaglia senza eroi, 2005. Office: Scuola Normale Superiore Piazza dei Cavalieri 7 56125 Pisa Italy Office Phone: +39050509215. E-mail: direttore@sns.it.

**SETTLE, MARK,** information technology executive; BS earth and planetary sci., MS earth and planetary sci., MIT; PhD geological sci., Brown Univ. CIO Occidental Petroleum, 1997—99; exec. v.p., systems and processing Visa Internat., 1999—2001; v.p., CIO Arrow Electronics, Inc., Melville, NY, 2001—. Retired USAF. Office: Arrow Electronics Inc 50 Marcus Dr Melville NY 11747-4210

**SETTLES, F. STAN, JR.,** engineering educator, manufacturing executive; b. Denver, Oct. 3, 1938; s. Frank S. and Dorothy Marie (Johnson) S.; m. Evelyn Brown, June 10, 1961; children: Frank S. III, Richard, Charles, Michael. BS in Prodn. Tech., Indsl. Engring., LeTourneau Coll., Longview, Tex., 1962; MS in Indsl. Engring., Ariz. State U., Tempe, 1967, PhD in Indsl. Engring., 1969. Sr. systems analyst AiResearch Mfg. Co., Phoenix, 1968-70, project mgr., 1970-74, mgr. operational planning, 1974-80; mgr. indsl. engrs. Garrett Pneumatic Systems, Phoenix, 1980-83; mgr. indsl. mfg. engring. Garrett Turbine Engring. Co., Phoenix, 1983-85; v.p. mfg. ops. AiResearch Mfg. Co., Torrance, Calif., 1985-87; dir. indusl. mfg. engring. The Garrett Corp., Phoenix, 1987-88; dir. planning Garrett Engine Div., Phoenix, 1988-92; asst. dir. White House Office of Sci. and Tech. Policy, 1992-93; program dir. NSF, 1992-94; prof., chmn. indsl. and systems engring. U. So. Calif., L.A., 1994—2003, IBM prof. indsl. engring. mgmt., dir. sys. arch. & engring. program, 2003—. Faculty assoc. Ariz. State U., Tempe, 1974-85, 90-92, rsch. prof., 1992-94. Mem. sch. bd. Tempe Elem. Sch. Dist., 1976-80; mem. YMCA Indian Guides, nat. chief, 1978-79. Fellow Inst. Indsl. Engrs. (pres. 1987-88, Ops. Rsch. award 1980), Inst. Ops. Rsch. and Mgmt. Sci., Nat. Acad. Engrs., Soc. Mfg. Engrs. (sr.), IEEE Engring. Mgmt. Soc., Am. Soc. Quality Control, Am. Soc. Engring. Edn. Republican. Presbyterian. Home: 1310 E Ocean Blvd Unit 1602 Long Beach CA 90802-6917 Office: U So Calif Dept Indsl Sys Engring Los Angeles CA 90089-0193 Office Phone: 213-740-0263. Business E-Mail: settles@usc.edu.

**SETTLES, JEANNE DOBSON,** retired librarian; b. Covington, Tenn., Nov. 21, 1928; d. Garrett Edward and Lula Mai (Birmingham) Dobson; m. Andrew Settles, Dec. 26, 1948; children: Thomas E., Anthony Dobson. BS, Memphis State U., 1966, MEd, 1977. Cert. tchr., Tenn. Libr. Memphis City Schs. 1966—72, 1977—91; ret. 1991. Mem. Delta Kappa Gamma (treas.). Avocations: painting, writing, sewing, travel.

**SETZER, ARLENE J.,** state representative, retired secondary school educator; b. Dayton, Ohio, Mar. 2, 1944; BS in Bus. Adminstrn., U. Dayton, 1966; MEd, Wright State U., 1973, postgrad. Tchr. bus. and computer applications Vandalia-Butler HS, 1967—2000; rep. Ohio State Ho. Reps., Columbus, 2000—. Mem. agr. and natural resources com. Ohio State Ho. Reps., chmn. edn. com., mem. ins. com. mem. ins. rev. com. and state govt. com. City of Vandalia, 1998—2000; chair Vandalia-Butler Food Pantry Bldg. Fund; pres. Pres.'s Club of Vandalia, 1997—99; mem. Ednl. Trust Project, Advocates for People with Devel. Disabilities, Montgomery County Ednl. Advancement Dialogue; precinct capt. Montgomery County Rep. Party, mem. ctrl. com., exec. com.; mem. Vandalia City Coun., 1982—2000, vice-mayor, 1986—88, 1995—2000. Named Rep. Woman of Yr., 1997, 2001, 2003; recipient Clara Weisenborn award, 1999, Horace M. Huffman Jr. Svc. to Bicyclists award, Ohio Bicycle Fedn., 2001, Appreciation award, S.W. Ohio Hemophilia Found. and W. Ctrl. Ohio Hemophilia Ctr., 2002, Rep. of Yr. award, Ohio Coll. Rep. Fedn., 2003; Martha Holden Jennings scholar, 1983—84. Mem.: Sister Cities of Vadalia, Montgomery County Farm Bur., Inc., Montgomery County Cattlemen's Assn., Montgomery Agrl. Soc., Sr. Citizens of Vandalia-Butler, Miami Valley Mil. Affairs Assn., Vandalia-Butler (Ohio) Hist. Soc. (v.p. 2000), Rotary (hon.; Dist. 6670 dir. 1992—96, pres. 1994—95, Dist. 6670 scholarship com. 1997, Dist. 6670 bd. dirs., asst. dist. gov. 1998—2000, named to Hall of Fame). Republican. Office: Ohio State Ho of Reps 77 S High St 13th Fl Columbus OH 43215-6111

**SETZLER, EDWARD ALLAN,** lawyer; b. Kansas City, Mo., Nov. 3, 1933; s. Edward A. and Margaret (Parshall) S.; m. Helga E. Friedemann, May 20, 1972; children: Christina, Ingrid, Kirstin. BA, U. Kans., 1955; JD, U. Wis., 1962. Bar: Mo. 1962, U.S. Tax Ct. 1962. Assoc. Spencer, Fane, Britt & Browne, Kansas City, 1962-67, ptnr., 1968-2000, mng. ptnr., 1974-77, 78-82, chmn. trust and estate sect., 1974-2000; ptnr. Husch & Eppenberger, LLC, 2000—06, Lathrop & Gage, 2006—. Co-author: Missouri Estate Administration, 1984, supplements, 1987—2004; contbg. editor: Understanding Living Trusts, 1990—2004; co-author: Missouri Estate Planning, 1986; co-author supplements, 1988—2004; contbg. editor: A Will is Not the Way--The Living Trust Alternative, 1988; bd. editors: Wis. Law Rev., 1961—62. Bd. govs., bd. dirs., chmn. found. com. Am. Royal, 1982—2006; mem. planning giving com. Nelson Atkins Mus. Art, 1984—95; mem. deferred giving com. Children's Mercy Hosp., 1991—; mem. Kansas City Estate Planning Symposium Com., 1984—92, chmn. 1991; mem. adv. com. Greater Kansas City Cmty. Found., 2000—; trustee Zoo Learning Fund, 2002—; mem. adv. bd. Children's Svc. League, 2003—. Fellow: Am. Coll. Trust and Estate Counsel (state chmn. 1992—97, mem. state membership com. 1986—2001); mem.: Assn. Conflict Resolutions, Estate Planning Soc. Kansas City (co-founder 1965, pres. 1983—84, dir. 1984—85, mem. social com. 1968—), Kansas City Met. Bar Assn. (lectr., chmn. probate and trust 1979, 1992, vice chmn. 1983—85, 1991, legis. rev. com. 1991—95), Mo. Bar

Assn. (lectr., vice chmn. probate and estate planning com. 1994—97), Sigma Xi, ORder of the Coif, Phi Delta Phi. Office: 2345 Grand Ste 2400 Kansas City MO 64108 Fax: 816-292-2001. Office Phone: 816-460-5412. Business E-Mail: esetzler@lathropgage.com.

**SETZLER, WILLIAM EDWARD,** retired chemicals executive; b. Bklyn., Dec. 20, 1926; s. William Edward and Gertrude A. (Seyer) S.; m. Dorothy C. Kress, Dec. 2, 1950 (dec. Mar. 1987); children: William John, Heather A.; m. Lenore Kelly, July 13, 1991. B of Chem. Engring., Cooper Union, 1950; MS in Liberal Studies, Columbia U., 1993. V.p. ops. Argus Chem. Corp., N.Y.C., 1950-66; v.p. engring., then group v.p. Witco Chem. Corp. (now Crompton Corp.), N.Y.C., 1966-75, exec. v.p., 1975-90, ret., 1990, also bd. dirs.; chmn. and CEO Faimount Chem. Inc., 1993-97. Author and patentee in field. Served with USAAF, 1945-46. Mem. Am. Inst. Chem. Engrs., Soap and Detergent Assn. (bd. dirs.), The Dorothy Setzler Fund (pres. 1991—). Home: 3921 Lincoln St Seaford NY 11783-2115 E-mail: billchair@att.net.

**SEUBERT, LORI A.,** elementary school educator; d. Harry Marx Seubert Jr. and Ruth Janice Seubert. BA in English and Elem. Edn. cum laude, U. Toledo, 1981, MEd in Sci. and Early Childhood cum laude, 1990. Tchr. Franklin Sch., Toledo, 1985—90; NSF-funded Toledo Area Partnership in Edn: Support Tchrs. as Resources to Improve Elem. Sci. sci. support tchr. Toledo City Schs., U. Toledo, Bowling Green State U., 1998—2002; TAPESTRIES summer inst. educator Bowling Green State U., Ohio, 2000, U. Toledo, 1999—2002; tchr. Toledo City Schs., 2002—04; tchr., grade 5 Reynolds Sch., Toledo, 1990—. Young exptl. scientist tchr. intern Columbus's Ctr. Sci. and Industry, Ohio Coun. for Elem. Sch. Sci., 1989, workshop coord., 1990—93; edn. cons., Toledo, 1996—; Full Option Sci. Sys. cons. Delta Edn., Nashua, NH, 1999—. Author: (book) A Unit on Physics of Flight for Third Graders, 1990; co-author, editor: guide TAPESTRIES's K-6 Science Curriculum Alignment to Ohio Outcomes for Toledo City Schools, 2001. Recipient Outstanding K-3 Tchr. award, Toledo Assn. for Edn. of Young Children, 2004, Impact II award, Ameritech Ohio Dept. Edn., 1995, 1996, Bd. Trustees award, U. Toledo, 1989—91; Award grant, Ohio Space Grant Consortium, 2000, 2 Ohio's BEST Practice Award grants, NSF-funded TAPESTRIES, 2002. Mem.: DAR, NSTA, Ohio Coun. Elem. Sch. Sci. (bd. dirs. 1992—95, pres.-elect to pres. 1994—96), Nat. Assn. for Edn. of Young Children, Assn. Supervision and Curriculum Devel., Kappa Delta Pi, Delta Delta Delta. Avocations: photography, hiking, reading, art and antique collecting, travel. Office: Toledo City Schs 420 E Manhattan Blvd Toledo OH 43608 Business E-Mail: lori.seubert@tps.org.

**SEUNG, THOMAS KAEHAO,** philosophy educator; b. Jungju, Korea, Sept. 20, 1930; m. Kwihwan Hahn, May 29, 1965; children: Hyunjune Sebastian, Kwonjune Justin, Haesue Florence. BA, Yale U., 1958, MA, 1961, PhD, 1965. Instr. Yale U., 1963-65; asst. prof. Fordham U., 1965-66; mem. faculty dept. philosophy U. Tex., Austin, 1966—, prof. in philosophy, 1972—, prof. in govt., 1985—, prof. in law, 1993—, Jesse H. Jones prof. liberal arts, 1987—. Author: The Fragile Leaves of the Sybil, 1962, Kant's Transcendental Logic, 1969, Cultural Thematics, 1976, Structuralism and Hermeneutics, 1982, Semiotics and Thematics, 1982, Intuition and Construction, 1993, Kant's Platonic Revolution, 1994, Plato Rediscovered, 1996, Nietzsche's Epic of the Soul, 2005, Goethe, Nietzsche, and Wagner, 2006. Served as officer Korean Army, 1950-53. Recipient Wilbur Lucius Cross medal Yale Grad. Sch. Alumni Assn., 1988; Soc. Religion in Higher Edn. fellow, 1969-70; Am. Council Learned Soc. fellow, 1977-71; NEH fellow, 1977-78 Office: U Tex Dept Philosophy Austin TX 78712 Mailing: PO Box 28055 Austin TX 78755 Business E-Mail: t.k.seung@mail.utexas.edu.

**SEURKAMP, MARY PAT,** college president; b. Pitts., Sept. 6, 1946; d. Frank H. and Loretta (Husic) Reuwer; m. Robert W. Seurkamp, Aug. 6, 1983; children: Kris, Robert, Brooke. BA, Webster U., 1968; MA, Washington U., 1969; PhD, SUNY, Buffalo. Counselor to dir. student living Gannon U., Erie, Pa., 1969-76; assoc. v.p. St. John Fisher Coll., Rochester, N.Y., 1976-92, adj. asst. prof. dept. psychology, 1992—, acting v.p. academic affairs, dean, 1992-98; pres. Coll. of Notre Dame of Md., Balt., 1998—. Mem. planning team Monroe County Ednl. Outcomes Conf.; bd. dirs. Bishop Kennedy High Sch.; cons. Women's Career Ctr., Rochester, N.Y., 1987—. Com. mem. various parish coms., Pittsford, N.Y., 1983—; Diocesan Com. Devel. of Mins. and Employees, Rochester, 1986-89, Internat. Alliance Leadership Conf., 1991; mentor Career Beginnings Program; vol. Career Connections Mentoring Program, 1988-90. Mem. AAUP, Am. Assn. High Edn., Nat. U. Continuing Edn. Assn., Rochester Women's Network. Republican. Roman Catholic. Home: 5502 Lombardy Pl Baltimore MD 21210-1420 Office: Office of the President Coll Notre Dame Md 4701 N Charles St Baltimore MD 21210-2404

**SEVART, DANIEL JOSEPH,** lawyer; b. Oswego, Kans., June 25, 1944; s. Vernon Joseph and Alma Bridget (Carland) S.; m. Shoko Kato, Apr. 17, 1968; 1 child, Eric J. AA, Parsons Jr. Coll., 1964; BA, Washburn U., 1973, JD with honors, 1975. Bar: Kans. 1976, U.S. Dist. Ct. Kans. 1976, U.S. Ct. Appeals (10th cir.) 1976. Assoc. Render & Kamas, Wichita, Kans., 1976-78, ptnr., 1978-82, Schartz & Sevart, Wichita, 1982-83, Sevart & Sevart, Wichita, 1983—. Bd. dirs. Wichita Symphony Soc., Inc., 1989—. Served to staff sgt. USAF, 1965-72. Mem. Assn. Trial Lawyers Am., Kans. Bar Assn. (bd. govs. 1995-98, 2000-01, sec.-treas. 1998-99, v.p. 2001-02, pres.-elect 2002-03, pres. 2003-04, Kans. Trial Lawyers Assn. (bd. govs. 1989—), Wichita Bar Assn. (bd. govs. 1988-90, sec.-treas. 1990-91, v.p. 1991-92, pres.-elect 1992-93, pres. 1993-94), Wichita C. of C. Democrat. Roman Catholic. Avocations: classical music, gardening, fishing, camping, travel. Office: Sevart & Sevart Ste 400 100 S Main St Wichita KS 67202-3208 also: 1900 L St NW Ste 500 Washington DC 20036-5031

**SEVCENKO, IHOR,** history professor, literature professor; b. Radosc, Poland, Feb. 10, 1922; came to U.S., 1949, naturalized, 1957; s. Ivan and Maria (Cherniatynska) S.; m. Oksana Draj-Xmara, Apr. 1945 (div. 1953); m. Margaret M. Bentley, July 16, 1953 (div. 1966); m. Nancy Patterson, June 18, 1966 (div. 1995); children: Catherine, Elisabeth. Dr.Phil., Charles U., Prague, 1945; Doct. en Phil. et Lettres, U. Louvain, Belgium, 1949; PhD (hon.), U. Cologne, Germany, 1994; D in Hist. Scis. (hon.), U. Warsaw, Poland, 2001; D in Liberal Arts (hon.), Cath. U., Lublin, Poland, 2005. Fellow in Byzantinology Dumbarton Oaks, 1949-50, dir. studies, 1966, prof. Byzantine history and lit., 1965-75, sr. research assoc., 1975—; lectr. Byzantine and ancient history U. Calif., Berkeley, 1950-51; fellow Byzantinology and Slavic lit., research program USSR, 1951-52; instr., then asst. prof. Slavic langs. and lit. U. Mich., 1953-57; mem. faculty Columbia U., 1957-72, prof., 1962-65, adj. prof., 1965-72; vis. prof. Harvard U., 1973-74, prof., 1974-92, emeritus, 1992. Vis. fellow All Souls Coll., Oxford U., 1979—80, Wolfson Coll., Oxford U., 1987, 93, Onassis Found., Athens, 2002; vis. mem. Princeton Inst. for Advanced Study, 1956; vis. prof. Munich U., 1969, Coll. de France, 1985, Cologne U., 1992, 96, Ctrl. European U., Budapest, 1995, 97; treas., acting treas., bd. dirs. Am. Rsch. Inst. in Turkey, 1964—66, 1967, 1975—; assoc. dir. Harvard Ukrainian Rsch. Inst., 1973—89, acting dir., 1977, 1985—86; chmn. Nat. Com. Byzantine Studies, 1966—77; mem. Internat. Com. for Greek Paleography, 1983—; guest of the rector Collegium Budapest, 1998. Author: Etudes sur la polémique entre Théodore Métochite et Nicéphore Choumnos, 1962, Society and Intellectual Life in Late Byzantium, 1981, Ideology, Letters and Culture in the Byzantine World, 1982, Byzantium and the Slavs in Letters and Culture, 1991, Ukraine Between East and West, 1996; co-author: Der Serbische Psalter, 1978, Life of St. Nicholas of Sion, 1984; contbr. articles to profl. jours. Recipient Hrusevs'kyj medal, Sci. Sevcenko Soc., 1996, Antonovych Lit. prize, Kiev, 2000; Guggenheim fellow, 1963, Humboldt-Forschungspreistraeger, 1985. Fellow Mediaeval Acad. Am., Brit. Acad. (corr.); mem. Am. Philos. Soc., Am. Acad. Arts and Scis., Ukrainian Acad. Arts and Scis. (hon. pres. 2003), Sci. Sevcenko Soc. (v.p. 1986-96, hon. pres. 1996—), Christian Archeological Soc. of Athens (hon.), Austrian Acad. Sci. (corr.), Accademia Pontaniana of Naples (fgn.), Nat. Acad. of Sci. Ukraine (fgn.), Acad. Humanities Rsch. (Moscow), Cosmos Club (Washington), Harvard Club (N.Y.C.), Signet Soc., Phi Beta Kappa. Office: Harvard Univ 204 Boylston Hall Cambridge MA 02138 Office Phone: 617-495-4027. Business E-Mail: sevcenko@fas.harvard.edu.

**SEVENING, DIANE KAY,** alcohol/drug abuse studies educator, researcher; b. Platte, SD, July 27, 1951; d. James Clayton (Stepfather) and Florence June Rommen; m. Douglas Lee Sevening, Aug. 15, 1981; children: Rodney Justin, Ryan Lee. D of edn., U. SD, 1998—99. Instr. U. SD Arts & Sciences Alcohol & Drug Abuse Studies Dept., Vermillion, 1984—89, 1989—99, asst. prof. Internat. pres. Internat. Coalition for Addiction Studies Edn. (INCASE), Vermillion, SD, 2000—02. Contbr. articles to profl. jours.; co-author: A Comparison of Traditional Teaching Methods and Problem-Based Learning in Addictions Studies Class, 2002. Sec. U. SD Student Affairs Com., 2001—03; mem. U. SD Academic Integrity Task Force, 2002—03; presenter Internat. Coalition for Addiction Studies Edn. (INCASE) Conf., Portland, Oreg., 2003, Nat. Drug and Alcohol Recovery Month, Sioux Falls, SD, 2003, Vol. Am., Sioux Falls, SD, 2003—03. Mem.: Internat. Coalition for Addiction Studies Educators (assoc.; immediate past pres. 2002—03), Gamma Sigma Delta (assoc.), Phi Delta Kappa (assoc.). Home: 602 W Dartmouth St Vermillion SD 57069 Office: Univ SD 414 E Clark St Vermillion SD 57069 Office Phone: 605-677-5519. Business E-Mail: dsevenin@usd.edu.

**SEVER, JOHN LOUIS,** medical researcher, educator; b. Chgo., Apr. 11, 1932; s. John Louis and Harriet (Link) Sever; m. Gerane Werle, Mar. 3, 1956; children: Kimberly, Beverly, Valerie. BA, U. Chgo., 1952; BS, MD, MS, PhD, Northwestern U., 1957. Head sect. infectious diseases NINDS, NIH, Bethesda, Md., 1960—71, chief infectious diseases, 1971—88; chmn. pediat. Children's Nat. Med. Ctr., Washington, 1988—90, prof. pediat., ob-gyn., immunology, microbiology and tropical medicine, 1988—. Cons. Rotary Internat., Evanston, Ill., 1964—; NIH, Bethesda, 1988—; WHO, Geneva, 1991—. Editor: 11 med. books; contbr. more than 600 articles to profl. jours. Capt. USPHS, 1960—88. Recipient Kimbel award, Am. Soc. for Microbiology, 1979, Wellcome Diagnostics award, Pan Am. Med. Virology, 1989, Meritorious Alumni award, Northwestern U., 1989, Pasteur award, Microbiology Soc., 1987, Abbott award, 1996, Soc. for Biomolecular Screening award, 2001. Mem.: Pan Am. Soc. Rapid Viral Diagnosis (pres. 1995—96), Assn. Med. Lab. Immunologists (pres. 1994—95, Erwin Niter award 1997), Teratology Soc. (pres. 1976—77), Assn. Med. Clin. and Lab. Immunologists (pres. 1992—94), Infectious Disease Soc. of Ob-gyn. (pres. 1994—96, Ortho-McNeill award 1998), Country Glen Club, Potomac Rotary Club. Avocation: gardening.

**SEVERANCE, DIANA LYNN,** curator; b. Wharton, Tex., Mar. 22, 1948; d. Arthur Walter Walzel and Dorothy Mae Kucera; m. Gordon Barker Severance, June 8, 1991. BA, Rice U., Houston, 1970, MA, 1972, PhD, 1974. Cert. secondary tchr. Tex. Tchr., dept. chair Klein (Tex.) Ind. Sch. Dist., 1976—97, mus. curator, 1995—2003; writer, hist. cons. Christian History Inst., Worcester, Pa., 1993—95; curator bible mus. Houston Bapt. U., Houston, 2003—. Editl. advisor Christian History & Biography, Christianity Today, Carol Springs, Ill., 1991—; hist. cons. Christian History Inst., Worcester, 1990—; adj. faculty, history curriculum writer LeTourneau U., 1994—. Author: Deep Roots, Strong Branches, 1999, Against the Gates of Hell: The Life and Times of Henry Perry, Christian Missionary in a Moslem World, A Cord of 3 Strands: Three Centuries of Christian Love Letters, 2004, 2004; contbr.: Faith in God and Generals, 2003. Named Outstanding Tchr. for State of Tex., DAR, 1982; recipient Leadership in Edn. award, Tex. State Hist. Assn., 1997. Mem.: Internat. Soc. Bible Collectors (sec.), Conf. on Faith and History, Am. Soc. Ch. History, The History Soc., Am. Hist. Assn. Evangelical. Office: Houston Bapt U 7502 Fondren Houston TX 77074 Office Phone: 281-649-3287. E-mail: dseverance@hbu.edu.

**SEVERDIA, ANTHONY GEORGE,** chemistry researcher; b. Sharon, Pa., Sept. 20, 1946; s. George Anthony and Angela Mary (Tomich) S. BS, Pa. State U., 1968; MS, Case Western Reserve U., 1971, PhD, 1974. Rsch., teaching assoc. Rensselaer Poly. Inst., Troy, NY, 1975-77; chemist N.Y. U., 1977-79, 82-83, Columbia U., N.Y.C., 1979-82; analytical chemist Mallinckrodt Group, Terre Haute, Ind., 1983-92; sr. chemist analytical sci. Sanofi-Aventis Rsch., St. Galley, Pa., 1992—. Presenter in field. Contbr. articles to profl. jours. Summer fellow NSF, Cleve., 1971. Mem. Am. Chem. Soc. (exec. com., treas. Terre Haute sect. 1991-92), Soc. Applied Spectroscopy, The Internat. Soc. for Optical Engring. Home: 301 Pritchard Ln Wallingford PA 19086-6104 Office Phone: 610-889-6103. Personal E-mail: aseverdia@comcast.net.

**SEVERIN-HANSEN, JEANNE ANNE,** poet; b. Delhi, NY, Aug. 29, 1948; d. Frank Rivers and Rosellen MacGowan; married; 1 child, Margaret Eun Sil. AA. Suffolk C.C., Selden, N.Y., 1975; BA, SUNY Empire State, Old Westbury, 1994. Adminstrv. asst. to pres. Go-Lo Resources, 1995—99; customer svc. asst. State Farm Ins., Melville, NY, 2000—02; freelance writer. Editor (monthly column): Threshold, Open Door Soc., 1985—87; author: numerous poems; contbr. articles to profl. jours. Dir. parent guild Infinity Ballet, Apex, NC. Recipient Pres. award, Nat. Author's Registry, 2002. Mem.: Hunting Sch. Ballet Guild. Office Phone: 919-266-4379. E-mail: nseverinhansen@netscape.net, jeanne4379@bellsouth.net.

**SEVERINO, ELIZABETH FORREST,** consulting company executive, animal communicator, spiritual healer; b. Bryn Mawr, Pa., Dec. 29, 1945; d. John Joseph and Elizabeth (Patton) Girard-diCarlo; m. Joseph Domenic Severino, Oct. 20, 1973 (div. Oct. 1983); 1 child, Nicole Marie. AB, Vassar Coll., 1967; MS in Computer Sci., Syracuse U., 1969; DD, Universal Life Ch., 1977; D of Religious Studies, U. Global Religious Studies, 2000. Ordained spiritual healer; cert. biofeedback therapist. Systems programmer IBM Corp., Poughkeepsie, N.Y., 1967-71, competitive analyst Phila., 1977-79; systems analyst Fidelity Bank, Phila., 1971-72; mng. editor Auerbach Pubs. Phila 1973 77; v.p. editorial and technology McGraw-IIIll Pubs., Delran, N.J., 1979-81; v.p Symcro Systems, Pennsauken, N.J., 1981-82; pres. The PC Group, Inc., Turnersville, NJ, 1982—, also bd. dirs.; pres. The Healing Connection, Cherry Hill, 1996—. Bd. dirs. Tech E-Writers, Cherry Hill, Simple Solutions, Inc., Cherry Hill. Author: Guide to International Computer Systems Architecture, 1976, Do-It-Yourself Vibrant Mind/Body/Spirit Health, 1995, Reiki: The Healer's Touch, 1995, Diet to Raise Your Spiritual Level, 1996, The Animals' Viewpoint on Dying, Death, and Euthanasia, 2001; (poetry) Garden of Life, 1995, 100 Breaths, 1998; contbr. over 200 articles to profl. jours.; choreographer Faust, Der Vampyr, Sound of Music. Vol. exec. dir. Nat. Reiki Assn., 1995—. Recipient Editors Choice award Nat. Libr. Poetry, 1995. Mem. Assn. Personal Computers Cons. (bd. dirs. Phila. chpt., pres. 1987-90), NAFE, Phila. Area Computer Soc., Inst. Noetic Scis., U.S. Amateur Ballroom Dancers Assn. (Phila. chpt. bd. dirs.), South Jersey Holistic Health Assn. (treas.). Republican. Episcopalian. Avocations: skiing, golf, competitive ballroom dancer. Personal E-mail: spirit1@beyond1.com.

**SEVERINO, ROBERTO,** language educator, academic administration executive; b. Catania, Italy, July 19, 1940; s. Giuseppe and Alba (Scroppo) S. Student, State U. Catania, Italy, 1960-62; BA, Columbia Union Coll., 1967; MA, U. Ill., 1969, PhD, 1973. Head acct., pres. dir. Industria Nazionale Apparecchiature Scientifiche, Milan, 1961-63; teaching asst., lang. lab. supv. Columbia Union Coll., Takoma Park, Md., 1965-67; grad. teaching asst. U. Ill., Urbana, 1967-70, coord. Corr. Sch., 1970-71; instr. dept. French and Italian U. Mass., Amherst, 1971-73; prof. dept. Italian Georgetown U., Washington, 1973—, acting chmn., 1987, chmn. dept., 1988—93; pres., co-founder Nat. Inst. Contemporary Italian Studies, 1986—; co-founder Associazione Internazionale del Diritto e dell'Arte, 1994—; pres. emeritus Am. U. of Rome, 1990-93, chair. U. dir. Georgetown U. Elec. Text Repository, Italian Archive, 1988-91, Ultramarina, 1992-96; mem. adv. bd. Nat. Italian Am. Found. Nat. Christopher Columbus 1992 Celebration; mem. U.S. delegation to 1st Conf. on Italian lang. and culture in U.S., 1987; founder Georgetown Poetry Series; pres. Coun. Promotion of Italian Lang. in Am. Schs., 1999—; hon. pres. U.S. Assn. Italian Studies, 2000—; pres. Italian Muse Found., Washington, 2003—; inst. dir. NEH "The Art of Tchg.

Italian Through Italian Art", 2004; elected mem. exec. com. Lista Unitalia Com. of Italians Residing Abroad; mem. selecting com. Washington Post Ednl. Found.; lectr., spkr. in field Author: Le soluzioni immaginarie, 1985, The Signs and Sounds of Italian, 1985, A carte scoperte, 1990, Presente imperfetto ed altri tempi, 1992, The Battle for Humanism, 1994, A Dumas: Mariano Stabile Sindaco di Palermo, 1994, My Dream-The Paintings of Gaetano N. Musto, 2002, Uga Martinotti, Io sono un pittore, 2005, Campania, Land of Myth and History, 2005; co-author: Periscopio, 1986, International Nuclear Agreements Multilingual Glossary, 1988, United Nations Organization Multilingual Glossary, 1988, Regularizing the Irregular Italian Verb, 1990, Preserving and Promoting Italian language and Culture in North America, 1997, Napoleon: One Image, Ten Mirrors, 2002; translator; The Next 6000 Days by Saverio Avveduto, 1987; editor: (serials) Segni, 1985-88, Hispano-Italic Studies, 1976, 79; mem. editorial bd. Educazione Comparata, 1993—; contbr. articles to profl. jours.; translator: Angelo Scandurra: The Hot-Tempered Musician and Other Poems, 1996, M. Rotelli's E. Sanguineti, If, For Me, You Write a Poem, 1999, Francesco Battiato: Amnesia of the Blue, 2000; editor: Giuseppe Severino: Ricordi di Castelnuovo primi '900. Scene di vita paesana, 1992; co-founder, U.S. editor: Colophon, An Internat. Jour. Arts and Letters, 1997-2003 Trustee Joel Nafuma Refugee Ctr., Rome, 1993—; chmn. Strega Lit. Prize, Washington D.C. Jury, 1997-2001; mem. jury Prima Parete in Concerto, Lion's Internat. Art Prize, Catania, 1998—, Spoleto Poetry Prize, 1999—. Rsch. grantee Interuniversity Ctr. European Studies, 1977; recipient Accademia Internazionale di Lettere, Scienze, Arti medal, 1983, Internat. Poetry prize, 1986, Gold Cross Cavaliere dell'Ordine al Merito della Repubblica Italiana, 1983, Gold medal Italian Ministries of Univs. and Sci. Rsch., 1988, Marranzano d'Argento prize, 1989, Gold Commander class Cross al Merito della Repubblica Italiana, 1990, Georgetown U. Vicennial Disting. Svc. medal, 1994, Telamone prize, 1995, Top Sprint: Siciliani nel Mondo award, 2000, Premio Internazionale "Castello di Pietrarossa" Caltanissetta, 2001, Gold Comdr. Cross Order "Stella della Solidarieta Italiana" by decree of Pres. of Italy, 2004 Mem. MLA, So. Atlantic Modern Lang. Assn., Nat. Assn. Secondary Sch. Prins. (mem. sch. partnerships internat. Italian adv. coun. 1988—), Italian Am. Cultural Found., Italian Cultural Soc. (pres. 1979-81, 83-85, Outstanding Svc. award 1983, chmn. acad. policy com. 1981—), Assn. Internationale Critiques Literaires and Associazione Italiana Critici Letterari, Greater Washington Assn. Tchrs. Fgn. Langs. (mem. award selection com. 1983-85), Manuscript Soc., Renaissance Soc. Am., Circolo Culturale Italiano (hon.), Am. Club (Rome), Touring Club Italiano (hon.), Gamma Kappa Alpha (v.p. 1990—, sec.-treas. and chpt. advisor 1985-90), World Jurist Assn. Ctr. Assocs. (U.S. pres. 1993—, chmn. program devel. and fin. com. 2000—), Associazione Internazionale del Diritto e dell'Arte (v.p. 1994—), Nat. Italian Am. Found. Coun. of 1100, Napoleonic Soc. Am., Soc. di Studi Valdesi, Istituto Internazionale di Epistemologia la Magna Grecia, Unione Nazionale per la lotta contro l'Analfabetismo, Sons of Italy. Home: 4949 Quebec St NW Washington DC 20016-3230 Office: Georgetown U Dept Italian 37th And O Sts NW ICC 307 Washington DC 20057-0001 E-mail: Severino@georgetown.edu.

**SEVERINSEN, DOC (CARL H. SEVERINSEN),** conductor, musician; b. Arlington, Oreg., July 7, 1927; m. Emöke Edith de Papp, Apr. 7, 1961. s. Thomas and Mary Theresa (Farina) S.; m. Emöke Edith de Papp. The Phoenix (Ariz.) Symphony Orchestra; prin. pops condr. Minn. Orch., Milw. Symphony Orch., Phoenix Symphony Orch. Mem. Ted Fio Rito Band, 1945, Charlie Barnet Band, 1947—49, Tommy Dorsey Band, Benny Goodman Band, Vaughn Monroe Band, soloist network band Steve Allen Show NBC-TV, 1954—55, mem. orch. Tonight Show, 1962—67, music dir. Tonight Show, 1967—92, host Midnight Spl., rec. artist Brass Roots album RCA Records, 1971, rec. artist Facets album, 1988, rec. artist The Tonight Show Band, Night Journey album. Address: Minn Orch 1111 Nicollet Mall Minneapolis MN 55403-2406 also: c/o William Morris Agency 151 S El Camino Dr Beverly Hills CA 90212-2704 also: c/o The Phoenix Symphony Orch 455 N 3rd St Ste 390 Phoenix AZ 85004-3942*

**SEVERO, RICHARD,** writer; b. Newburgh, NY, Nov. 22, 1932; s. Thomas and Mary Theresa (Farina) S.; m. Emöke Edith de Papp, Apr. 7, 1961. BA, Colgate U., 1954; postgrad., NYU Inst. Fine Arts, 1955-56, Columbia U. Sch. Architecture and Urban Planning, 1964-65. News asst. CBS, NYC, 1954-55; reporter Poughkeepsie New Yorker, NY, 1956-57, A.P., Newark, 1957-61, NY Herald Tribune, 1961-63; writer TV news CBS, NYC, 1963-66; reporter Washington Post, 1966—68; reporter, fgn. correspondent, feature writer, feature obituary reporter, sci. and environ. reporter NY Times, NYC, 1968—2006. Assoc. Seminar on the City, Columbia U., 1966-69; vis. lectr. Am. culture Vassar Coll., 1985-99; bd. dirs. Hudson Valley Philharm., 1998-99, Colgate U. Alumni Corp., 1988-92. Author: Lisa H., 1985; (with Lewis Milford) The Wages of War, 1989 (Am. Legion Nat. Comdr.'s award 1990); contbr. articles to mags. Established Thomas and Mary Severo Scholarship funds for majors in music and Italian Vassar Coll., 2002. Poynter fellow-in-residence Vassar Coll., 1974-75; CBS News fellow, 1964-65; Recipient Front Page award Washington-Balt. Newspaper Guild, 1967; Journalistic award H.A.V.E.N., 1969; Schaeffer Gold Typewriter award NY Newspaper Reporters Assn., 1969; Page One award Newspaper Guild of N.Y., 1970; hon. mention Mike Berger award Columbia U., 1970; Leone di San Marco award Italian Heritage and Culture Com., 1982; George Polk Meml. award L.I. U. Sch. Journalism, 1975; Hudson River Fisherman's Assn. award, 1976; Mike Berger award Columbia U., 1976; James Wright Brown award Deadline Club, Sigma Delta Chi, NYC, 1976; Feature award NY Press Club, 1977; Page One award Newspaper Guild NY, 1977, 82; Media award Am. Cancer Soc., 1977; hon. mention Heywood Broun Meml. award Am. Newspaper Guild, 1977; Penney-Mo. Newspaper award U. Mo. Sch. Journalism, 1978; Media award Agt. Orange Victims Internat., 1981 Page One award NY Newspaper Guild, 1982; Gift of Life award NY Blood Ctr., 1991, Spl. Writing award Soc. of the Silurians, 1992. Personal E-mail: richard.severo2@verizon.net.

**SEVERS, CHARLES A., III,** lawyer; b. N.Y.C., Sept. 16, 1942; s. Charles A. and Gertrude (O'Neill) S.; m. Regina Ferrone, Sept. 4, 1965; children: Charles A. IV, Cornelius Forsythe, Rudyard Pierrepont, Olivia Consuelo Poor. BA, Georgetown U., 1964, JD, 1967. Bar: N.Y. 1968, D.C. 1985. Ptnr. Dewey Ballantine, N.Y.C., 1967-96; gen. counsel, exec. v.p. Nat. Madison Group, N.Y.C., 1996-97. Lectr. various continuing legal edn. programs. Contbr. articles to profl. jours. Dir., trustee various orgns. Fellow Am. Coll. Trust and Estate Counsel; mem. ABA, N.Y. State Bar Assn., Assn. of Bar of City of N.Y., D.C. Bar Assn., Union Club. Address: High Meadow Old Chatham NY 12136

**SEVERS, WALTER BRUCE,** pharmacology educator, researcher; b. Pitts., June 10, 1938; s. Walter Bruce and Pauline Marie (Sever) S.; m. Anne Elizabeth Daniels, Apr. 25, 1970; children: Mary, Jane, Steven, William, Katherine. BS, U. Pitts., 1960, MS, 1963, PhD, 1965. Postdoctoral fellow NIH, Bethesda, Md., 1966-68; asst. prof. pharmacology Coll. Medicine, Pa. State U., Hershey, 1968-71, assoc. prof., 1971-77, prof., 1977-99, prof. emeritus, 1999—. Cons. pharmacology/toxicology, 1999—; v.p. for sci. affairs Ednl. Horizons, Inc., Lemoyne, Pa., 1998—; ad hoc grant cons. NIH, U.S. Army, NSF. Mem. editl. bd. Am. Jour. Physiology, 1978-98; assoc. editor Pharmacology Today 2000-2000; contbr. numerous articles, chpts., revs. to profl. publs. Recipient Disting. Alumnus award U. Pitts., 1978, I.M. Setchenov medal Acad. Med. Sci. USSR, 1983, Blue medal for sci. Acad. Med. Sci., Bulgaria, medal for sci. U. Belgrade; NASA grantee, 1976-98. Fellow Am. Coll. Clin. Pharmacology; mem. Am. Physiol. Soc., Am. Soc. Pharmacology and Exptl. Therapeutics, Soc. for Neurosci., Soc. for Exptl. Biology and Medicine, Sigma Xi (pres. Pa. State U. chpt. 1981-82), Kiwanis (pres. Hershey area 1980, bd. dirs.). Republican. Roman Catholic. Avocations: reading, camping, hiking. Home: 1011 Grubb Rd Palmyra PA 17078-3510 Office: Pa State U Coll Medicine Dept Pharm Mail Code H78 500 University Dr Hershey PA 17033-2360 Office Phone: 717-531-8291. Business E-Mail: wbs2@psu.edu.

**SEVERS, WILLIAM FLOYD,** actor; b. Britton, Okla., Jan. 8, 1932; s. Harry Lysander Fletcher and Katherine Lucinda (McAuliffe) S.; m. Mary Anne Proctor, Jan. 18, l964 (div. l971); 1 child, Pilar; m. Barbara Alice Schonger, Sept. 9, 1978; children: Katherine Meghan, Erin Christine. AA, Pasadena Playhouse Coll., 1956. Appeared on Broadway in Cut of the Axe, 1959-60, The Moon Is Blue, 1962, On Borrowed Time, 1991-92, nat. tour Look Homeward, Angel, 1960; co-star nat. tour Spoon River, 1964; actor Secret Storm, All My Children, One Life to Live, Guiding Light, Texas, Search for Tomorrow, Another World, Loving, 1963-93; other TV appearances include Armstrong Circle Theatre, 1963, The Defenders, 1964, World War II, A GI Diary, 1978, Nurse, 1980, Muggable Mary, 1986, Law and Order, recurring role as Hon. Henry Fillmore, 1990-2004, Hallmark Hall of Fame, Grace and Glorie, 1998, Law and Order: Criminal Intent, 2000; appeared in films including Funny Farm, 1988, Regarding Henry, 1991, Meet the Parents, 2000, Revolution #9, 2000, 13 Conversations About 1 Thing, 2001, The Departed, 2005; actor European tour West Side Story, 1990-91, 94, Asian tour West Side Story, 1999; actor, voice artist numerous commls., 1964— Staff sgt. USAF, 1946-53. Mem. SAG, AFTRA, Actors Equity Assn., Pasadena Playhouse Alumni Assn. Democrat. Avocations: reading, golf. Home: 10 Waterside Plz Apt 6F New York NY 10010-2610 Office: Hartig/Hilefo Agy Ltd 54 W 21st St New York NY 10010-7002 E-mail: wfsevers@rcn.com.

**SEVERSON, GARY R.,** bank executive; BA, MBA, Stanford U.; MS, U. So. Calif. Various positions Security Pacific Bank, Bank of Am.; former bd. chmn. First Interstate Bank of Wash., Seattle. Bd. dirs. Laird Norton Tyee, Inc., Wentworth, Hauser & Violich, Inc., Farmers New World Life Insurance, Inc.; former chmn., pres. Japan-Am. Soc. of Wash., Pacific Coast Banking Sch., Trade Development Alliance of Greater Seattle, Wash. Council on Internat. Trade. Trustee Casey Family Programs, 1996—, chair; bd. dirs. Marguerite Casey Found.; former chmn. bd. of Executive Svc. Corp. of Wash. Office: Casey Family Programs 1300 Dexter Ave N Seattle WA 98109

**SEVERSON, ROGER ALLAN,** bank executive; b. Thief River Falls, Minn., Sept. 2, 1932; s. Alfred Gerhard and Esther Olga (Landro) S.; m. Beverly Diane Hays, Aug. 30, 1953; children: Eric Hays, Holle Diane. BS, U. Minn., 1954. Group v.p. First Nat. Bank, Mpls., 1952-73; pres. FBS Fin., Inc., Mpls., 1974-77; exec. v.p. F&M Savs. Bank, Mpls., 1977-82; sr. v.p. First Nat. Bank, St. Paul, 1983-85; exec. v.p. Shelard Nat. Bank, Mpls., 1985-86, TCF Bank Savs., Mpls., 1986-92; ret., 1992. Mem. Robert Morris Assocs., 1980-92; trustee Heitman Mortgage Investors, Chgo., 1970-71, Mass. Mut. Mortgage Realty Investors, Springfield, 1972-85. Vice chmn. bd. of trustees The Am. Luth. Ch. Synod, Mpls., 1976-81; trustee Children's Health Ctr., Mpls., 1971-72; bd. dirs. Goodwill Industries, Mpls., 1967-70. Fellow Versterheim Mus.; mem. Ethics in Pub. Policy Ctr., Ctr. for Am. Experiment. Home: 8321 Essex Rd Chanhassen MN 55317-8705

**SEVIGNY, CHLOË,** actress; b. Darien, Conn., Nov. 18, 1974; Actor: (films) Kids, 1995, Trees Lounge, 1996, Gummo, 1997, Palmetto, 1998, The Last Days of Disco, 1998, Boys Don't Cry, 1999, Julien Donkey-Boy, 1999, A Map of the World, 1999, American Psycho, 2000, Ten Minutes Older: The Trumpet, 2002, Demonlover, 2002, Party Monster, 2003, Death of a Dynasty, 2003, Dogville, 2003, The Brown Bunny, 2003, Shattered Glass, 2003, Melinda and Melinda, 2004, Manderlay, 2005, Broken Flowers, 2005, 3 Needles, 2005, Mrs. Harris, 2005; (TV films) If These Walls Could Talk 2, 2000. Office: c/o William Morris Agency One William Morris Pl Beverly Hills CA 90212*

**SEVIK, MAURICE,** acoustical engineer, researcher; b. Istanbul, Turkey, Mar. 19, 1923; s. Benjamin and Esther (Barzilai) S.; m. Jacqueline Delannoy, June 2, 1953; children: Michele, Martine. DIC, Imperial Coll. Sci. Tech., London, 1946; PhD, Pa. State U., 1963. Registered profl. engr., Ont. With Bristol Aircraft Corp., U.K., 1946-51; sr. structures engr. Avro Aircraft Ltd., Can., 1952-59; prof. aerospace engring., dir. Garfield Thomas Water Tunnel, Pa. State U., University Park, 1959-72; mem. assoc. tech. dir. ship signatures directorate David Taylor Rsch. Ctr., Bethesda, Md., 1972-96, sr. rsch. scientist, 1996-99; ret., 1999. Vis. prof. Cambridge (Eng.) U., 1970; cons. USAF Office Sci. Rsch. 1965; cons. applied physics lab. U. Wash., Seattle, 1999—. Contbr. articles to profl. jours. Overseas fellow Churchill Coll., Cambridge U., 1970; recipient Gold Medal award The Am. Soc. of Naval Engrs., 1990, Disting. Alumni award Central Pa. chpt. Acoustical Soc. of Am., Charles B. Martell Tech. Excellence award Nat. Security Indsl. Assn., 1992, Robert Dexter Conrad award Office Naval Rsch., 1996, French decoration Ordre Nat du Mérite, 1997; Dr. M. M. Sevik Acoustic Data Analysis Ctr. Bldg. named in his honor. Fellow ASME (Rayleigh lectr. 1995, Per Bruel Gold medal for noise control and acoustics 1996), Acoustical Soc. Am., Sigma Xi; mem. Nat. Acad. Engring. Home: 2 Spruce Ct Hilton Head Island SC 29928 Office: David Taylor Model Basin 9500 Macarthur Blvd West Bethesda MD 20817-5700 Office Phone: 843-341-7994. Personal E-mail: msevik@aol.com.

**SEVILGEN, FATIH ERDOGAN,** computer scientist, educator; m. Rukiye Sevilgen. BS, Bogazici U., Istanbul, 1985—90; MS, Syracuse U., NY, 1993—96, PhD, 1996—2000. Rsch. asst. Syracuse U., 1999—2000; asst. prof. Gebze Inst. Tech., Kocaeli, Turkey, 2000—. Rsch. advisor Tubitak, Gebze, 2006—. mem: Bogazici Univ. Reunion Assoc. (assoc.). Office: Gebze Inst Tech Bilgisayar Muh Bol Cayirova Kampusu Gebze Kocaeli 41400 Turkey Business E-Mail: sevilgen@gyte.edu.tr.

**SEVILLA, EMERITA NEPOMUCENO,** writer; b. Manila, Philippines, Dec. 7, 1926; arrived in U.S., 1970; d. Perfecto Tuddulino und Dolores Mapa (Alvarez) Nepomuceno; m. Victor Jocson Sevilla, Dec. 10, 1949 (dec. May 20, 1993); children: Mary Therese Victoria, Victor, Mary Enid, Vincent, Vidal, Virgil, Valentin, Vinci, Mary Elaine. BJ, U. Santo Tomas, Manila, 1949. Writer, rschr. Red Cross Philippines, Manila, 1947—48; reporter Evening News, Manila, 1948—49; sec. to dept. head Dept. Commerce and Industry, Manila, 1949—51; owner, co-founder, treas. Sevilla Bookshop, Davao City, Philippines, 1951—67; mgr. Ency. Britannica, Manila, 1968—71; cons. Philamlife Ins. Co., Manila, 1972—92. Author: (poetry) Springs of Joy, 1992, Silver and Gold, 1995, (prayerbook) Treasures from Heaven, 1997. Mem.: DAV, Rancho Cucamonga Pub. Libr., Help Hospitalized Vets. (Donor of Yr. 2004), Trinitarians, Perpetual Rosary Assn. (life; Regina Coeli divsn.), Priests Sacred Heart, Rancho Cucamonga Sr. Citizen Club. Roman Catholic. Avocations: reading, collecting books and mugs.

**SEVILLA, STANLEY,** lawyer; b. Cin., Apr. 3, 1920; s. Isadore and Dienna (Levy) S.; m. Lois A. Howell, July 25, 1948; children: Stanley, Susan, Donald, Carol, Elizabeth. BA in Econs. with high honors, U. Cin., 1942; JD, Harvard U., 1948. Bar: Calif. 1949. Since practiced in. Los Angeles; assoc. Williamson, Hoge & Curry, 1948-50; mem. Axelrod, Sevilla and Ross, 1950-75, Stanley Sevilla (P.C.), 1975—. Gen. counsel La.-Pacific Resources, Inc., 1970-90. Bd. dirs. Caesars World, Inc., 1989-95. With USAAF, 1942-46. Mem. Beverly Hills Bar Assn., Phi Beta Kappa, Tau Kappa Alpha. Home: 16606 Merrivale Ln Pacific Palisades CA 90272-2236 Office: PO Box 308 Pacific Palisades CA 90272-0308 Office Phone: 310-459-8116.

**SEVILLA-SACASA, FRANCES ALDRICH,** bank executive; BA in Langs., U. Miami, 1977; MA in Internat. Mgmt., Am. Grad. Sch. Internat. Mgmt., 1978. Joined Bankers Trust, 1983; mng. dir. L.Am. pvt. banking Bankers Trust Internat. Pvt. Banking Group, Miami, Fla.; sr. v.p. pvt. client svcs. Lehman Bros., Miami, 1997—98; mng. dir. L.Am. pvt. bank divsn. Deutsche Bank; pres. Bankers Trust Internat. Pvt. Banking Corp., 1998—2000; mng. dir., S.E. region head Citibank Pvt. Bank, 2000—01; mng. dir., head L.Am. Citigroup, NYC, 2001—05; head Europe Citigroup Pvt. Bank, 2003—04, CEO Latin Am. Citigroup Private Bank, 2004—05; pres. US Trust Corp. Charles Schwab Corp., NYC, 2005—, exec. v.p. Office: US Trust Corp 114 W 47th St New York NY 10036 Office Phone: 415-627-7000. Office Fax: 212-852-1140.*

**SEVIN, DIETER HERMANN,** literature and language professor; b. Mühlanger, Germany, Nov. 5, 1938; arrived in US, 1958; s. Wolf-Dieterich and Erna (Brockmann) Sevin; m. Ingrid Antje Dirks, June 15, 1963; children: Sonja, Karen. BA, San Jose State U., 1963; MA, U. Wash., 1964, PhD, 1967. Asst. prof. Pacific Lutheran U., Tacoma, 1967-68, Vanderbilt U. Nashville, 1968-73, assoc. prof., 1973-82, prof., 1982—; chair dept., 2000—. Author: Individuum und Staat, 1972, Zur Diskussion: A Modern Approach to German Conversation, 3d edit., 1987, Teststrategien in DDR-Prosawerken zwischen Bau und Durchbruch der Berliner Mauer, 1994, Christa Wolf (interpretation), 4th edit., 2006, Wie Geht's? An Introductory German Course, 8th edit., 2006; editor: Die Resonanz des Exils, 1992; contbr. articles to profl. jours. Fellow: German Acad. Exch. Svc. (grantee 1980), Am. Coun. Learned Socs. (grantee 1981—82), Am. Philos. Soc. (grantee 1991). Avocations: travel, reading, music. Office: Vanderbilt U Dept Germanic And Slav Nashville TN 37235 Business E-Mail: dieter.h.sevin@vanderbilt.edu.

**SEVRUKOV, ALEXANDER BIRON,** radiologist, researcher; b. Moscow, Apr. 7, 1974; s. Boris Biron and Tatiana Fedorova Sevrukov. MD, Moscow Med. Acad., 1998; MHPE, U. Ill., Chgo., 2005. Sr. postdoctoral rschr. cardiology sect. U. Ill. Coll. Medicine, Chgo., 1999—2005, clin. instr. dept. radiology, 2004—; resident in diagnostic radiology Mallinckrodt Inst. Radiology/Washington U., St. Louis, 2005—. Contbr. articles to profl. jours. Mem.: Radiologic Soc. N.Am., Am. Roentgen Ray Soc. E-mail: sevrukova@mir.wustl.edu.

**SEWARD, GEORGE CHESTER,** lawyer; b. Omaha, Aug. 4, 1910; s. George Francis and Ada Leona (Rugh) S.; m. Carroll Frances McKay, Dec. 12, 1936 (dec. 1991); children: Gordon Day, Patricia McKay (Mrs. Dryden G. Liddle), James Pickett, Deborah Carroll (Mrs. R. Thomas Coleman). BA, U. Va., 1933, LLB, 1936. Bar: Va. 1935, N.Y., K.y., D.C., U.S. Supreme Ct. With Shearman & Sterling, N.Y.C., 1936-53, Seward & Kissel LLP, N.Y., 1953—. Dir. Witherbee Sherman Corp., 1952-66, pres. 1964-66, Howmet Corp., 1955-75, Chas. P. Young Co., 1965-72, Howmedica Inc., 1970-72, Benson Mines, Inc., 1980-85; trustee Benson Iron Ore Trust, 1969-80. Author: Basic Corporate Practice, 1977, Seward and Related Families, 1994; co-author: Model Business Corporation Act Annotated, 1960, We Remember Carroll, 1992. Trustee Arts and Scis. Coun. U. Va., 1983-93, pres., 1991-93; trustee Edwin Gould Found. for Children, 1955-96, Nature Conservancy of Ea. L.I., 1969-80, N.Y. Geneal. and Biog. Soc., 1991-2006. Named to Louisville Male H.S. Alumni Assn. Hall of Fame, 1991; commd. Ky. Col., 1993. Fellow: N.Y. State Bar Found., Am. Bar Found.; mem.: ABA (chmn. sect. com. corp. laws 1952—58, chmn. bus. law sect. 1958—59, ho. of dels. 1959—60, chmn. sect. banking com. 1960—61, ho. of dels. 1963—74, joint com. with Am. Law Inst. on continuing legal edn. 1965—74), Internat. Bar Assn. (hon. life pres., lectr. series by heads of state named in his honor, New Delhi 1988, Lisbon 1992, Budapest 1993, Geneva 1994), Downtown Assn. (N.Y.C.), Athenaeum Lit. Assn. (Louisville), Greencroft Club (Charlottesville, Va.), Univ. Club (Chgo.), Met. Club (Washington), Bohemian Club (San Francisco), Gardiner's Bay Country Club (Shelter Island, N.Y.), N.Y. Yacht Club, Knickerbocker Club, Delta Sigma Rho, Theta Chi, Phi Beta Kappa, Phi Beta Kappa Fellows (pres. 1969—75), Order of Coif, Raven Soc., Cum Laude Soc. Home: 48 Greenacres Ave Scarsdale NY 10583-1436 Office: Seward & Kissel LLP One Battery Park Plz New York NY 10004 also: Internat Bar Assn 1 Stephen St London W1T 1AT England

**SEWARD, LORI A.,** speech educator; d. Herbert and Carolyn Seward; m. Michael D. Fisher, July 16, 1993. PhD, NYU, NYC, 1992. Assoc. prof. speech South Ga. Coll., Douglas, Ga., 1992—2006. Office: South Georgia Coll 100 West College Park Dr Douglas GA 31533 Office Phone: 912-389-4426. E-mail: lseward@sga.edu.

**SEWARD, NATHAN WILLIAM,** biologist, researcher; b. Xenia, Ohio, May 10, 1975; s. William Arthur and Diana Lynn Seward; m. Kathleen Ann MacCarthy; 1 child, Reilly Alice. BS in Natural Resources, Ohio State U., Columbus, 2000; MS in Forestry, U. Ky., Lexington, 2003. Resource mgmt. intern Columbus and Franklin County Met. Pk. Dist., Columbus, Ohio, 1998—98; biol. scis. technician USDA Forest Svc., Gunnison, Colo., 1999; rsch. asst. U. Ky., Lexington, 2000—03; biol. scis. technician USDI Nat. Pk. Svc., Gunnison, 2003, USDA Nat. Wildlife Rsch. Ctr., Fort Collins, Colo., 2003—. Contbr. articles to profl. jours. Com. mem. Rocky Mountain Elk Found., Fort Collins, 2004. Recipient Performance award, USDA Nat. Wildlife Rsch. Ctr., 2006. Mem.: Wildlife Soc. (assoc.; cert.). Independent Methodist. Avocations: hunting, fly fishing, hiking, wildlife. Office: USDA Nat Wildlife Rsch Ctr 4101 LaPorte Ave Fort Collins CO 80521 Office Phone: 970-266-6174. Office Fax: 970-266-6083. Business E-Mail: nathan.w.seward@aphis.usda.gov.

**SEWARD, WILLIAM W(ARD), JR.,** writer, educator; b. Surry, Va., Feb. 2, 1913; s. William Ward and Elizabeth (Gwaltney) S.; m. Virginia Leigh Widgeon, Dec. 27, 1941 (dec. Feb. 2005); children: Virginia S. Godwin, Leigh S. Huston. AB, U. Richmond, 1934, MA, 1935. English tchr. pub. schs., 1935-38; instr. U. Richmond, 1939-40, summer 1944; head English dept. Greenbrier Mil. Sch., 1941-42; prof., head English dept. Tift Coll., 1942-45; faculty Old Dominion U., Norfolk, Va., 1945, 47—, prof., 1957-77, prof. emeritus, 1977—, head dept. English, 1947-61. Lectr. U. Va. extension div., 1952-54 Author: The Quarrels of Alexander Pope, 1935; editor: The Longer Thou Livest the More Fool Thou Art (W. Wager), 1939, Literature and War, 1943, Skirts of The Dead Night, 1950, Foreword to Descent of the White Bird (Barbara Whitney), 1955, Contrasts in Modern Writers, 1963, My Friend Ernest Hemingway: An Affectionate Reminiscence, 1969, 2003; contbr. to book: The True Gen: An Intimate Portrait of Hemingway by those Who Knew Him (Denis Brian), 1988, Remembering Ernest Hemingway (interviews by James Plath and Frank Simons), 1999; mem. editl. bd.: Lyric Virginia Today, 1956; contbr. articles to profl. jours. Grad. fellow Duke U., 1938-41; recipient Charles T. Norman medal U. Richmond, 1934 Mem. Poetry Soc. Va. (pres. 1952-55), Hemingway Soc., Internat. Mark Twain Soc. (hon.), Va. Writers Club (emeritus), Virginia Beach Sports Club, Phi Beta Kappa, Kappa Alpha, Pi Delta Epsilon. Methodist. Home: 701 Cavalier Dr Virginia Beach VA 23451-3837

**SEWELL, CAROL ANN,** artist; b. Dodge City, Kans., June 12, 1944; d. John Elbert and Mary Claire (Wetmore) Frazier; m. Herbert Carey Zortman, Aug. 21, 1960 (div. Jan. 1989); children: Elaine Marie, Anita Louise, Stanley Dale; m. George D. Rosel, Sept. 22, 1990 (div. June 1995), m. Maurice Sewell, June 4, 2004. Student, Ctrl. Coll., McPherson, Kans., 1961; BFA cum laude, Ft. Hays State U., 1994. Cert. machine embroidery instr. Dress designer Ms. Cosmo Ltd., Wichita, Kans., 1975-76; designer artistic embroidery garments, 1977-80, 99; owner Carol Ann's Gallery, Liberal, Kans.; part time music tchr. W. Mid. Sch., 1989—. Part-time art tchr. U.S. D 443, Dodge City, part-time music tchr. One-woman show Ft. Hays Libr., 1993; singer: A Touch of Class; developer: The Tour (the Life of Christ); performer: Wild West Dinner Theater. Mem. Baker Art Ctr., Liberal, 1989—, Hays (Kans.) Arts Coun., 1993, Carnegie Ctr. of Arts, Dodge City, Kans.; solo pianist ch. weddings and comty. functions; mem. Glory Rd. Singers, 1999; mem. cast Wild West Show, 2001—, Touch of Class Ladies Group; vol. Make A Wish Found.; tchr. Sunday sch. Recipient All Am. Scholar Collegiate award, 1994, Grand Champion award State Fair, 1989, 90, 95, 97, 98, Purple Champion award, 1990, 06, others; named Woman of World, 1995-96, Internat. Women of World, 1997, Internat. Woman of Yr., 1995-96. Mem.: So. Gospel Music Assn., Baker Art Ctr., Mid. Am. Arts and Crafts Assn., Christian Womens Club, Lions Club, Art Club, Pinnacle Honor Soc. Republican. Avocations: piano, singing, dramatics, painting. Home and Office: 2901 Westview Dodge City KS 67801

**SEWELL, GLORIANA,** music educator; b. Huntington, NY, June 6, 1948; d. Reavis Staggs and Evelyn (Vilches) Kurlowich; m. C. Eugene Sewell, Aug. 8, 1969; children: Keren Ligowski, Daniel Sewell. BA in Piano, Bob Jones U., 1970. Piano tchr. in pvt. practice, Santa Barbara, Calif., 1970-71, Sodus, N.Y., 1971-78; Suzuki piano tchr. in pvt. practice Quakertown, Pa., 1979-86, Milford Square, Pa., 1986—; Kindermusik tchr. Milford Square Music

Studio, 1996—. Piano accompanist ch. choir Assembly of the Word, Milford Square, 1993—. Recipient Tchr. award for 1st Pl. Winner, Baldwin Jr. Keyboard Competition, 1985, 1992, 2000, Tchr. of Yr. award, 1989, award, Music Tchrs. Nat. Assn. Student Composition Competition, 1993, 1994, 2001, Tchr. award 1st Pl., Yamaha H.S. Keyboard Competition, 2002. Mem.: Dalcroze Soc. Am., Nat. Guild Piano Tchrs., Am. Orff-Schulwerk Assn., Kindermusik Educations Assn., Suzuki Assn. of Am., Pa. Music Tchrs. Assn. (pres. Lehigh Valley chpt. 1991—92, co-dir. spring music festival 1997, v.p. 1999—2001, pres. 2001—03, immediate past pres. 2003—), Music Tchrs. Nat. Assn. (Disting. Svc. award 2003). Avocation: gardening. Home and Office: Milford Square Music Studio PO Box 199 2244 Milford Square Pike Milford Square PA 18935 Office Phone: 215-536-8142. Personal E-mail: gloriana.s@comcast.net.

**SEWELL, JOHN WILLIAMSON,** research association executive; b. Cleve., Dec. 19, 1935; s. William and Hilda F. (Gaunt) S.; m. Maryann Strauss, July 19, 1958; children: Gregory J., Michael P. BA, U. Rochester, 1957; MA, NYU, 1967. Fgn. service officer Dept. State, 1961-68; asst. to dir. Bur. Intelligence Research, Dept. State, Washington, 1968-70; asst. to pres. Brookings Inst., Washington, 1970-71; v.p. Overseas Devel. Council, Washington, 1971-77, exec. v.p., 1977-79, pres., 1980-2000; sr. scholar Woodrow Wilson Internat. Ctr., 2001—. Mem. Bretton Woods Com.; former vice-chair Internat. Ctr. for Rsch on Women; vice chair New Rules for Global Fin.; mem. Internat. Adv. Group for 1995 World Summit for Social Devel.; spl. advisor to the adminstrn. UNDP, 1988-99; chair Working Group on Devel. of Role of IMF; advisor UN Assn. USA. Author: U.S. Foreign Policy and the Third World Agenda, 1985-86, Growth, Exports, & Jobs in a Changing World Economy: Agenda 1988, The Real Politik of Poverty: An Action Plan for American Foreign Policy, 2005; co-editor: United States Budget for a New World Order, FY, 1992, Challenges and Priorities in the 1990s: An Alternative U.S. International Affairs Budget, FY, 1993; contbr. articles to jours. Pres. Nat. Choral Found., 1969-75. With U.S. Army, 1958-60. Mem. Coun. on Fgn. Rels. Home: 7614 Morningside Dr NW Washington DC 20012-1557 Business E-Mail: john.sewell@wilsoncenter.org.

**SEWELL, RICHARD HERBERT,** retired historian, retired educator; b. Ann Arbor, Mich., Apr. 11, 1931; s. Herbert Mathieu and Anna Louise (Broene) Sewell; m. Natalie Paperno, Jan. 13, 1971; 1 child, Rebecca Elizabeth. AB, U. Mich., 1953; MA, Harvard U., 1954, PhD, 1962. Asst. prof. No. Ill. U., DeKalb, 1962-64, U. Wis., Madison, 1965-67, assoc. prof., 1967-74, prof., 1974-95, prof. emeritus, 1995—; ret., 1995. Vis. lectr. U. Mich., Ann Arbor, 1964—65; adv. bd. Lincoln and Soldiers Inst. Gettysburg Coll., Pa., 1990—. Author: (book) John P. Hale and the Politics of Abolition, 1965, Ballots for Freedom, 1976, A House Divided, 1988; contbr. articles to profl. jours. Lt. (j.g.) USNR, 1954—57. Fellow: Wis. Hist. Soc. (hon.); mem.: Orgn. of Am. Historians, So. Hist. Assn., Soc. Civil War Historians, Phi Beta Kappa, Phi Kappa Phi. Home: 2206 Van Hise Ave Madison WI 53726 Business E-Mail: rhsewell@wisc.edu.

**SEWELL, ROBERT GEORGE,** librarian; b. Stillwater, Okla., Aug. 28, 1942; s. William Hamilton and Elizabeth Sewell; m. Barbara Judy Love, Jan. 27, 1963; 1 child, Jamin Robert. BS in Asian Studies, U. Wis., 1964; MA in Japanese Lit., Columbia U., 1967; PhD in Comparative Lit., U. Ill., 1976, MLS, 1982. Japanese bibliographer Asian libr. U. Ill., Urbana-Champaign, 1970-80, reader's svcs. coord., 1978-80, asst. to dir. libr. collections, 1983-86; asst. dir. for collection mgmt. and devel. SUNY, Stony Brook, 1986-89; assoc. univ. libr. for collection devel. and mgmt. Rutgers U. N.J., 1989—. Contbr. articles to profl. jours. Home: 29 Coan Pl Metuchen NJ 08840-2523 Office: Rutgers U 169 College Ave New Brunswick NJ 08901-1163 E-mail: rgsewell@rci.rutgers.edu.

**SEWELL, RODNEY MILTON,** biologist; b. Frederick, Md., July 5, 1946; BS in Psychobiology, Hood Coll., 1974. Operating room tech. USN, 1967-70; biologist NIMH/LBEB, 1974-79; systems integrator LAMDA, 1983—. Mem. IEEE Computer Soc., N.Y. Acad. Scis., AAAS, Am. Chem. Soc., Am. Psychol. Soc. Achievements include research in developmental and comparative aspects of neurobiology and behavior, computer-assisted learning devices. Office: Lab Med Devices PO Box 30634 Bethesda MD 20824-0634 E-mail: rodney.m.sewell@att.net.

**SEWELL, RUFUS,** actor; b. Twickenham, England, Oct. 29, 1967; s. William and Jo Sewell; m. Yasmin Abdallah, Mar. 24, 1999 (div. Mar. 2000); m. Amy Gardner, Feb. 2004; 1 child, William Douglas. Student, Ctrl. Sch. Speech & Drama, London. Actor theatrical debut As You Like It, Shefield's Crucible Theatre, (miniseries) Middlemarch, 1994, Arabian Nights, 1999, (films) Twenty-One, 1991, Dirty Weekend, 1993, Victory, 1995, Carrington, 1995, Hamlet, 1996, The Woodlanders, 1997, Dangerous Beauty, 1998, Dark City, 1998, Martha, Meet Frank, Daniel, and Laurence, 1998, Illuminata, 1998, In Sachem Farm, 1998, In a Savage Land, 1999, Bless the Child, 2000, A Knight's Tale, 2001, Extreme Oops, 2002, Victoria Station, 2003, The Legend of Zorro, 2005, The Illusionist, 2006, Tristan & Isolde, 2006, (TV films) Cold Comfort Farm, 1995, King Henry IV, 1995, Arabian Nights, 2000, Mermaid Chronicles Part 1: She Creature, 2001, Helen of Troy, 2003, The Taming of the Shrew, 2005. Office: UTA 9560 Wilshire Blvd Ste 500 Beverly Hills CA 90212-2427*

**SEWELL, WILLIAM GEORGE, III,** electronics engineer, writer; b. Roanoke, Va., Dec. 14, 1950; s. William George Jr. and Elizabeth Marie (Morrison) S.; m. Verna Landry, Aug. 25, 1970 (div. 1974); children: Ronald Allen, Bryan Joseph; m. Colleen Rose Gaynor, May 15, 1981 (div. 2005); m. Nancy A. Levy, Dec. 31, 2005. BS in Engring., U. Ill., Chgo., 1980; PhD, Calif. U., Modesto, 1983. Electronic technician 928 Airlift Group, Chgo., 1972-74; with FAA, Chgo., 1974-85, staff engr. Wheeling, Ill., 1980-82, regional nav. and landing systems engr. Chgo., 1982-85, nat. program engr., 1985—87; with Jerry Thompson & Assocs., Kensington, Md., 1987-88; v.p. Navcom Systems, Inc., 1988-89, B2 Software, Inc., 1988-89; v.p., CEO The Thinkk Corp., 1988-89; founder, CEO Software Coalition, 1989—99. Dir. comm. and info. systems group SEMA, Inc., 1990—93; dir. comm. solutions Jacobs Facilities, Inc., 1993—2000; Sverdrup fellow, 1998; v.p. Holmes & Narver, Inc., 2000—01; sr. v.p. DMJM Holmes & Narver, Inc., 2001—; pres. GEOLINC, 2002—04; cons. engr. W.G. Sewell & Assocs., Internat., Niles, Ill., 1981—88; chair TIA Indsl. Telecoms Standards Body, 1999—2001; sr. v.p. DMJM Tech., 2003—, gen. mgr., 2003—; mem. joint venture bd. LAnova Assoc. Contbr. articles to profl. jours., chapters to books. Mem. Chgo. Coun. Fgn. Rels., 1976-80. Served with USAF, 1972-73, Vietnam. Recipient 1st prize, Am. Soc. Electro-Surgery, 1982. Mem. IEEE Soc. Automotive Engrs., Aircraft Owners and Pilots Assn. Achievements include invention of high speed turn control for land vehicles, 1980; co-inventor child's hidden identification and location device, 1990. Office: 515 S Flower St Los Angeles CA 90071 Office Phone: 213-593-8487. E-mail: bill.sewell@dmjm.com.

**SEWELL, WILLIAM HAMILTON, JR.,** historian; b. Stillwater, Okla., May 15, 1940; s. William Hamilton and Elizabeth Lucille (Shogren) S.; m. Ellen Martha Wheeler, June 16, 1962 (dec. July 2001); children: Jessica Ellen, Adrienne Felicity; m. Jan Goldstein, Dec. 2004. BA, U. Wis., 1962; MA, U. Calif., 1963, PhD, 1971. Instr. history U. Chgo., 1968-71, asst. prof. history, 1971-75; assoc. prof. history U. Ariz., Tucson, 1980-83, prof. history, 1983-85; dir. d'etudes associe Ecole de Hautes Etudes en Scis. Sociales, Paris, 1984, 88; prof. history and sociology U. Mich., Ann Arbor, 1985-90; prof. polit. sci. and history U. Chgo., 1990—, Max Palevsky prof., 1996—2004, Frank P. Hixon disting. svc. prof., 2004—; fellow Ctr. for Advanced Study in Behavioral Scis., 1990-91. Mem. bd. editors Jour. Modern History, 1984-86, French Hist. Studies, 1985-88, Sociol. Theory, 2003—; mem., bd. dirs. Social Sci. Rsch. Coun., N.Y.C., 1986-92; dir. Program in Comparative Study of Social Transformations, U. Mich., Ann Arbor, 1987-90, Ctr. for Rsch. Social Orgn., 1988-90; dir. Wilder House Ctr. for Politics, History and Culture, U. Chgo., 1999-2004; mem. Social Sci. Inst. Advanced Study, Princeton, NJ, 1971-72, 75-80, 2002-03. Author: Work and Revolution in France, 1980, Structure and Mobility, 1985, A Rhetoric of Bourgeois Revolution, 1994, Logics of History, 2005. Recipient Herbert Baxter Adams prize Am. Hist.

Assn., 1981, William Koren Jr. prize Soc. French hist. studies, 1982; grantee Nat. Sci. Found., 1972-75; Guggenheim fellow, 1990-91, Nat. Humanities Ctr., 2006-. Fellow Am. Acad. Arts and Sci.; mem. Am. Hist. Assn., Soc. French Hist. Studies, Am. Sociol. Assn. (Best Article prize comparitive hist. sociology sect. 1991, culture sect. 1993, theory sect. 1997), Social Sci. History Assn., European Studies, Am. Polit. Sci. Assn. Office: U Chgo Dept Polit Sci 5828 S University Ave Chicago IL 60637-1515

**SEXSON, RICHMOND LOCKWOOD,** professional baseball player; b. Portland, Oreg., Dec. 29, 1974; m. Kerry Sexson. Player Milw. Brewers, 2000—03, Ariz. Diamondbacks, Phoenix, 2003—04, Seattle Mariners, 2004—. Achievements include third in Brewers franchise history to hit 40 home runs in a season; named to All-Star game, 2002-03. Office: c/o Seattle Mariners 1250 1st Ave Soth Seattle WA 98134

**SEXSON, WILLIAM ROBERT,** pediatrician, educator; b. Washington, Dec. 3, 1945; children: Sara Kristen, Ryan William. BS, USAF Acad., 1967; MD, U. Miss., 1971. Diplomate Am. Bd. Pediatrics, Am. Bd. Neonatal-Perinatal Medicine. Pediat. resident Wilford Hall USAF Med. Ctr., 1994; fellow in neonatology Vanderbilt U., Nashville, 1976; staff neurologist Crawford Long Hosp., Atlanta, 1984—, Egleston's Children's Hosp., Atlanta, 1984—; dir. nurseries Grady Meml. Hosp., Atlanta, 1987-94; vice-chair dept. pediatrics, assoc. prof. Emory U. Sch. Medicine, Atlanta, 1994—, interim assoc. dean clin. affairs, 1998-2000, assoc. dean clin. affairs, 2000—; chief pediatrics Grady Health Sys., Atlanta, 1994-2000. Contbr. articles to profl. jours. Active Ga. Policy Coun. for Children and Families, 1995-2000; co-chair Children's Health Com., 1998—, Ga. Dept. Med. Assts.; child health adv com., physicians adv. coun. Ga. Medicaid, 2001—; chmn. health and safety com. Boy Scouts Am. Atlanta Area Coun., 1998—. Col. USAFR. Named Outstanding Citizen of Ga., 1990, 2004. Fellow WHO (collaborating ctr. 2003—, asst. dir. collaborating ctr. 2005—); mem. Am. Acad. Pediatrics (v.p. Ga. chpt. 1990-92, pres. 1993-96, exec. com. 1996—, chair com. on bioethics for Ga., chair hosp. ethics com. 1987—, co-chair legis. com. 2000—), Coun. on Maternal and Infant Health (chair 1993-95), Ga. Perinatal Assn. Home: 804 Springdale Rd NE Atlanta GA 30306-4618 Office: Grady Health Sys 49 Jesse Hill Dr SE Atlanta GA 30303-3040 E-mail: wsexson@emory.edu.

**SEXSTONE, BRIAN THOMAS,** protective services official; b. Rochester, N.Y., Nov. 3, 1975; s. Thomas Joseph and Deirdre Cathrine Sexstone; m. Michelle Lynn Zinner, July 29, 2000; children: Kylie, Molly; 1 child, Bridget. Student, Finger Lakes C.C., Canandaigua, N.Y., 1995—97, Monroe C.C., Rochester, N.Y., 1997—98; grad., Police Acad., Valhalla, N.Y., 1999. Police officer SUNY Police Dept., Purchase, 1999—2000, Rochester Police Dept., NY, 2000—02, 2006—, Palmyra Police Dept., NY, 2002—06. Drug enforcement officer Palmyra Police Dept., Palmyra, NY, 2002—06, bike patrol officer, 2003—06. With U.S. Army, 1993—2001. Recipient Svc. award, Palmyra Police Dept., 2003, 2005, Police Commendation award, 2003. Mem.: Law Enforcement Assisting Fallen Families (sec. 2005—). Republican. Roman Catholic. Avocations: hunting, fishing. Office: Rochester Police Dept 185 Exchange St Rochester NY 14614 Office Phone: 315-597-9211. E-mail: bts1103@aol.com

**SEXTON, DAVID FARRINGTON,** lawyer, bank executive; b. Montclair, N.J., Aug. 20, 1943; s. Dorrance and Marjorie (McComb) S.; m. Ann Hemelright, Feb. 27, 1971; children: James, Ashley, Christopher. AB cum laude, Princeton U., 1966; JD cum laude, U. Pa., 1972. Bar: N.Y. 1972. Assoc. Sullivan & Cromwell, N.Y.C., 1972-77; with First Boston Corp., N.Y.C., 1977-90, v.p., gen. counsel, 1980-83, mng. dir., gen. counsel, 1983-86; mng. dir., pres. First Boston Internat. Ltd., 1986-90; sr. exec. v.p., dir. Yamaichi Internat. (America), Inc., N.Y.C., 1990-95, vice-chmn., 1995-98; pres., CEO The Farrington Group, LLC, Greenwich, Conn., 1998—. Global Alliance assoc. for N.Am. IBS Securities Co., Ltd., Tokyo; adj. prof. law Fordham U., 1985—86; mem. U.S.-Japan Friendship Commn., Washington, 1990—94; adv. bd. mem. Manifold Products, LLC; sr. advisor Milbank Roy & Co., NYC. Lt. USNR, 1966—69. Mem. Assn. Bar City N.Y., Racquet and Tennis Club, N.Y. Yacht Club, Ivy Club, Bucks Harbor Yacht Club (bd. govs. 1991-, commodore 2003-05), The Nat. Assn. of Japan Am. Socs. (bd. dirs. 1998-, dir. exec. com. 1997-). Republican. Presbyterian. Office: The Farrington Group 186 Field Point Rd Ste 1B Greenwich CT 06830

**SEXTON, DONALD LEE,** retired business administration educator; b. New Boston, Ohio, June 14, 1932; s. Benjamin Franklin and Virgie Marie (Jordan) S.; m. Levonne Bradley, June 1954 (div. June 1964); 1 child, Rhonda Jane; m. Carol Ann Schwaller, Dec. 18, 1965; children: David Lee, Douglas Edward BS in Math. and Physics, Wilmington Coll., 1959; MBA, Ohio State U., 1966, PhD in Mgmt., 1972. Indsl. engr. Detroit Steel Corp., Portsmouth, Ohio, 1959-61; sr. rsch. engr. Rockwell Internat., Columbus, Ohio, 1961-68; v.p. merchandising R.G. Barry Corp., Columbus, 1968-74; v.p., gen. mgr. Henri Fayette, Inc., Chgo., 1976; gen. mgr. M.H. Mfg. Co., Jackson, Miss., 1976-77; assoc. prof. Sangamon State U., Springfield, Ill., 1977-79; Caruth prof. entrepreneurship Baylor U., Waco, Tex., 1979-86; Davis prof. entrepreneurship Ohio State U., Columbus, 1986-94, prof. emeritus, 1994—; dir. Nat. Ctr. for Entrepreneurial Rsch. Kauffman Found., Kansas City, Mo., 1994-97, scholar-in-residence, 1997-2000. Adj. faculty Nova Southeastern U., Ft. Lauderdale, Fla., 1997-99; mem. adv. bd. SBA, Columbus, 1986-94; rsch. adv. bd. U. So. Calif., L.A., 1986-90 Co-author: Entrepreneurship Education, 1981, Experiences in Small Business, 1982, Starting A Business in Texas, 1983; co-editor: Encyclopedia of Entrepreneurship, 1981, Art and Science of Entrepreneurship, 1986, Women Owned Business, 1989, Entrepreneurship: Creativity and Growth, 1990, The State of the Art of Entrepreneurship, 1991, Leadership and Entrepreneurship, 1996, Entrepreneurship: 2000, 1996, The Handbook of Entrepreneurship, 1999, Strategic Entrepreneurship, 2002 Served to staff sgt. USAF, 1951-55 Recipient Leavy Free Enterprise award Freedoms Found. Valley Forge, 1985, Cert. Appreciation SBA, Washington, 1984, 85, Outstanding Contbn. to Entrepreneurship Edn. award Assn. Coll. Entrepreneurs, 1991, Disting. Alumni award Wilmington Coll., 1993, Entrepreneurship Adv. of the Yr., 1997; named Adv. of Yr.-Innovation SBA, Dallas, 1982, 83, 84 Mem. Internat. Coun. for Small Bus. (sr. v.p. 1986), U.S. Assn. for Small Bus. (v.p. pub. rels. 1987), Acad. Mgmt. (chmn. entrepreneurship com. 1981, mem. adv. bd. 1984-85), Masons, Shriners, Eagles, Am. Legion, Alpha Tau Omega Republican. Baptist. Avocation: golf. Home: 2940 West Bay Dr #303 Belleair Bluffs FL 33770 Personal E-mail: dlsexton@aol.com.

**SEXTON, DOUGLAS ROBERT,** education educator; b. St. Louis, Mar. 10, 1963; s. Robert Roy and Dorothy Jean Sexton; m. Cheryl Ann Jones, Apr. 11, 1992. BS in Edn., U. Mo.-St. Louis, 1986; MA in Edn., Maryville U., Ladue, Mo., 1994; EdD in Ednl. Leadership, St. Louis U., 2003. Cert. sch. adminstrn. Mo., 1997, elem. edn. Calif., Mo., social studies, 4-8 Mo., 1986, clear crosscultural, lang. and acad. devel. 2003. Elem. tchr. Pattonville Sch. Dist., Maryland Heights, Mo., 1986—97; prin. Riverview Sch. Dist., Bellfontaine Neighbors, Mo., 1997—2001; elem. tchr. Palm Springs Unified Sch. Dist., Calif., 2002—. Instr. edn. Chapman U., Palm Desert, Calif., 2004—. Editor: Emerald Reflection ist. mag., 1991—97. Participant Focus St. Louis, St. Louis, 1995—96; sec. Pattonville Teachers Assn., Maryland Heights, Mo., 1995—97, Dems. of the Desert, Palm Springs, Calif., 2002—05; treas. Coachella Coalition for Responsible Soverrnty, Palm Springs, Calif., 2003—04; bd. dirs. St. Charles Hist. Soc., St. Charles, Mo., 1990—92; coach Spl. Olympics, Wentzville, Mo., 1994—98. Named Tchr. of the Yr. Elem. Pattonville Sch. Dist., 1994. Mem.: Palm Springs Tchrs. Assn. (assoc.; chair), Phi Delat Kappa Club. Democrat. Presbyterian. Avocations: travel, astronomy, writing, fly fishing. Home: 51 Sutton Pl E Palm Desert CA 92211 Office: Palm Springs Unified School District 30-800 San Luis Rey Dr Cathedral City CA 92234 Office Phone: 760-416-8234. Personal E-mail: telescopes@verizon.net. E-mail: dsexton@psusd.us.

**SEXTON, J. STAN,** lawyer; b. Hays, Kans., 1948; BA, Univ. Kans., 1970, JD, 1977. Bar: Kans. 1977, Mo. 2001. Ptnr. complex litigation, toxic tort, insurance practices Shook Hardy & Bacon LLP, Kans. City, Mo. Editor (assoc., note & comment): Kans. Law Rev. Served to Lt. USN, 1970—74.

Mem.: Am. Coll. Trial Lawyers, ABA, Def. Rsch. Inst., Kans. Inst. Trial Advocacy, Kans. Assn. Def. Counsel, Kans. Bar Assn., Mo. Bar. Office: Shook Hardy & Bacon LLP 2555 Grand Blvd Kansas City MO 64108 Office Phone: 816-474-6550. Office Fax: 816-421-5547. Business E-Mail: jsexton@shb.com.

**SEXTON, JOE**, editor; Dep. met. editor NY Times. Office: NY Times 229 West 43rd St New York NY 10036 Office Phone: 212-556-7371. Office Fax: 212-556-3690.*

**SEXTON, JOHN EDWARD**, academic administrator, law educator; b. Bklyn., Sept. 29, 1942; s. John Edward and Catherine (Humann) S.; m. Lisa Ellen Goldberg; children: Jed, Katherine. BA in History, Fordham U., 1963, MA in Comparative Religion, 1965, PhD in History of Am. Religion, 1978; JD magna cum laude, Harvard U., 1979; PhD (hon.), Fordham U., 2005; degree (hon.), St. Francis Coll., Katholieke Universiteit, Leuven. Bar: NY 1981, US Supreme Ct. 1984. Prof. religion St. Francis Coll., Bklyn., 1966—75, religion dept. chair, 1970—75; law clk. to Hon. Harold Leventhal and Hon. David L. Bazelon US Ct. Appeals DC Cir., Wash., 1979—80; law clk. to Chief Justice Warren E. Burger US Supreme Ct., Wash., DC, 1980-81; assoc. prof. law NYU Sch. Law, NYC, 1981—84, prof., 1984—, Warren E. Burger prof. constl. law, 1994—2001, Benjamin F. Butler prof. law, 2001—, dean, 1988—2002, dean emeritus, 2002—; pres. NYU, 2002—. Dir. Washington Sq. Legal Services, NYC, 1983-2002, Pub. Interest Law Found., NYC, 1983-85, dep. chmn., Fed. Res. Bank NY, 2002-04, chmn., 2004-; past founding chmn. NASD Dispute Resolution; mem. exec. com. Consortium Ind. Colleges and Universities. Author: Modern Federal Jury Instructions-Civil, 1985, How Free Are We: A Non-Lawyer's Guide to the Constitution, 1986, Redefining the Supreme Court's Role: A Theory of Managing the Federal Court System, 1986, Civil Procedure, Cases and Materials, 1988. Dir. Root-Tilden Scholarship Program, 1984-88. Fellow Am. Acad Arts & Sciences; mem. Assn. Am. Law Schs. (pres. 1997-98), Assn. Am. Univ. Presidents, Coun. Fgn. Rels. Office: NYU Sch Law Vanderbilt Hall Rm 316 40 Washington Sq S New York NY 10012-1099 Office Phone: 212-998-2345. E-mail: john.sexton@nyu.edu.*

**SEXTON, JOHN JOSEPH**, oral and maxillofacial surgeon, educator; b. Boston, Dec. 4, 1947; s. Bernard Thomas and Margaret Theresa (Carrigg) S.; m. Judith Whelden, Aug. 21, 1971; 1 child, Benjamin. BS, Boston Coll., 1970; DMD, Tufts U., 1975; MScD, Boston U., 1978, CAGS, 1979. Diplomate Am. Bd. Oral and Maxillofacial Surgery. Orthognathic fellow Boston U. Inst. for Correction of Facial Deformities, 1976-77; intern, jr. resident, chief resident Boston U./Tufts U., 1975-79; asst. prof. Goldman Sch. Dental Medicine, Boston U., 1979-81; chief oral and maxillofacial surgery Beth Israel Hosp., Boston, 1981—2001, dir. maxillofacial trauma svc., 1990—2001, dir. mucosal disorders unit, 1990—2001; chief oral and maxillofacial surgery Lahey Clinic Med. Ctr., Burlington, Mass., 2001—04; dir. Maxillofacial Trauma Svc. Beth Israel Deaconess Med. Ctr., 2004—, chief oral and maxillofacial surgery emeritus, 2005—. Clin. dermatology Beth Israel Hosp.; asst. prof. oral and maxillofacial surgery Harvard Med. Sch., Boston. Contbr. numerous articles to profl. jours. Avocations: philosophy, physics, history, travel. Office: 372 Washington St Ste 2500 Wellesley MA 02481-6202 Office Phone: 781-235-4554. Business E-Mail: jsexton@bidmc.harvard.edu.

**SEXTON, JOSEPH A.**, editor; BA, Univ. Wis., 1982. Reporter The City Sun, Bklyn, NY, UPI, The Post-Standard, Syracuse, NY, The Record, Hackensack, NJ; sports reporter The NY Times, 1987—94, metro news. reporter, 1994—98, enterprise editor sports desk, 1998—99, dep. investigations & enterprise editor metro desk, 1999—2003, dep. metro editor, 2003—06, metro editor, 2006—. Contbr. articles to Best Am. Sports Writing 1992. Office: NY Times 229 W 43d St New York NY 10036*

**SEXTON, ROBERT FENIMORE**, educational organization executive; b. Cin., Jan. 13, 1942; s. Claude Fenimore and Jane (Wisenall) S.; m. Pam Peyton Papka, Sept. 15, 1985; children: Rebecca, Robert B., Ouita Papka, Paige Papka, Perry Papka. BA, Yale U., 1964; MA in History, U. Wash., Seattle, 1968, PhD in History, 1970; DHL (hon.), Berea Coll., 1990, Georgetown Coll., Ky., 1993, Eastern Ky. U., 2000. Asst. prof. history Murray (Ky.) State U., 1968-70; dir. Office Acad. Programs, Commonwealth of Ky., Frankfort, 1970-73; assoc. dean, exec. dir. Office Exptl. Edn. U. Ky., Lexington, 1973-80; dep. exec. dir. Ky. Coun. Higher Edn., Frankfort, 1980-83; exec. dir. Prichard Com. for Acad. Excellence, Lexington, 1983—; founder, pres. Ky. Ctr. Pub. Issues, Lexington, 1988—94. Vis. scholar Harvard U. Cambridge, Mass., 1992, 94; chair Nat. Ctr. for Internships, Washington, 1973-80, Coalition for Alternatives in Post-Secondary Edn., Washington, 1977-80; bd. dirs Editl. Projects in Edn., Consortium Policy Rsch. in Edn., Ky. Long Term Policy Rsch. Ctr., Edn. Trust, Trust for Early Edn., 1992-94. Pub. The Ky. Jour., 1988-2001; editor book series: Public Papers of Governors of Kentucky, 1973-86, Mobilizing Citizens for Better Schools, 5 books, 2004; contbr. articles to profl. jours. Co-chmn. Carnegie Ctr. for Literacy, Lexington, 1990-93; mem. Gov.'s Task Force on Health Care, Frankfort, 1992-99; bd. dirs. Ky. Inst. Edn. Rsch. Fund for Improvement in Postsecondary Edn., 1993-2000; chair Bluegrass Edn. Work Coun., Lexington, 1978-80; founder, steering com. Gov.'s Scholars Program, Frankfort, 1983-85. Recipient Charles A. Dana award for pioneering achievement, 1994. Mem. Am. Assn. Higher Edn. (bd. dirs. 1979-83). Democrat. Avocations: fishing, travel. Office: Prichard Com Acad Excell 167 W Main St Ste 310 Lexington KY 40507-1702

**SEXTON, SCOTTY EUGENE**, music educator, gifted and talented educator; b. Somerset, Ky., Apr. 19, 1973; s. Isaac Roy and Verna Gussie (Hunley) Sexton, BA of Music Edn. cumma cum laude, Cumberland Coll., 1996, MA in Edn., Ea. Ky. U., 1999. Dir. band, tchr. music Hart County Schs., Munfordville, Ky., 1996—98; dir. band, gifted & talented resource specialist Wayne County Schs., Monticello, 1998—. Chmn. adv. bd. Family Pl. Resource Ctr., Monticello, 2002—. Founder, dir. Cardinal Chorus, Monticello, 1998—, Cardinal Drama Club, 1998—; coach Turner Intermediate Sch. Acad. Team, 1998—. Mem.: NEA, Nat. Band Assn., Ky. Music Educators Assn. (chair elem./mid. sch. band 2004—), Hon. Order Ky. Cols. Democrat. Nazarene. Avocations: music, scrapbooks, reading, exercise. Home: 130 Golden Pond Rd Monticello KY 42633 Office: Wayne County Schs 534 Albany Rd Monticello KY 42633 Business E-Mail: scott.sexton@wayne.kyschools.us.

**SEXTON, TIMOTHY CURT**, music educator; b. Madisonville, Ky., Jan. 18, 1975; s. Donald Ray and Linda Ray Sexton; m. Jana Karol Ballard, Oct. 3, 1998 (div.). B Music Edn., Western Ky. U., 1997, M Music Edn., 2003. Cert. K-12 music tchr Ky. Dir. choirs Bowling Green H.S., 1999—; adult choir dir. Christ Episcopal Ch., Bowling Green, 2000—. Named H.S. Music Educator of Yr., 3rd Dist. Music Educators, 2004. Mem.: Ky. Music Educators Assn. (assoc.; 3rd dist. choral chmn. 2001—), Music Educators Nat. Conf. (assoc.), Am. Choral Dirs. Assn. (assoc.; state repertoire and stds. chmn. 2001—). Republican. Avocation: movies. Home: 1659 Smallhouse Rd Apt B Bowling Green KY 42104 Office: Bowling Green HS 1801 Rockingham Ln Bowling Green KY 42104 Office Phone: 270-746-2300. Personal E-Mail: tsexton1801@yahoo.com.

**SEYBERT, JOANNA**, federal judge; b. Bklyn., Sept. 18, 1946; BA, U. Cin., 1967; JD, St. John's U., 1971. Bar: N.Y. 1972, U.S. Dist. Ct. (ea. and so. dists.) N.Y. 1973. Trial staff atty. Legal Aid Soc., N.Y.C., 1971-73, sr. staff atty. Mineola, N.Y., 1976-80; sr. trial atty. Fed. Defender Svc., Bklyn., 1973-75; bur. chief Nassau County Atty's Office, Mineola, 1980-87; judge Nassau County Dist. Ct., Hempstead, N.Y., 1987-92, Nassau County Ct., Mineola, 1992-94, U.S. Dist. Ct. (ea. dist.) N.Y., Uniondale, 1994—. Mem.: Nassau Lawyers Assn. (past pres.), Fed. Judges Assn. (v.p.), Theodore Roosevelt A. Inns of Ct. (past pres.), Suffolk County Bar Assn., Internat. Assn. Judges (delc.). Office: 100 Federal Plz Central Islip NY 11722

**SEYBOLD, DAVID JAMES**, artist; b. Dunkirk, N.Y., Dec. 29, 1968; BFA in Painting, Edinboro U. of Pa., 1991. Publ. Susquehanna Editions, 2002—. Commns. include Pa. Coll. of Tech. Found., 1998; one-man show Susquehanna Gallery, Jersey Shore, Pa., 1999. Recipient Buyer's Choice award Gallery One, 1996; named one of Top 27 Artists to Watch, US Art mag., 1998. Home: 220 Beck St Lewisburg PA 17837-1118 Office Phone: 877-739-2053.

**SEYEDI, NAHID**, physiologist, researcher; b. Shiraz, Fars, Iran, Nov. 22, 1949; arrived in U.S., 1987; d. Abbas and Legha Seyedi. MS, Pahlavi Med. Coll., Shiraz, Iran, 1978, N.Y. Med. Coll., Valhalla, N.Y., 1993, PhD, 1994. Lectr. physiology Urima Univ., Urmia, Iran, 1978—78; tchg. asst. N.Y. Med. Coll., Valhalla, NY, 1988—94; rsch. assoc. Weill Med. Coll., Cornell Univ., 1998—. Mem.: APA, Am. Soc. for Pharmacology, Am. Heart Assn. Achievements include discovery of local Bradikimin production from isolated synaptosomes of guinea-pig heart; local nitric oxide production from coronary micro vessels of heart. Office: Weill Md Coll 1300 York Ave New York NY 10021

**SEYFANG, ANDREAS GEORG**, biochemist, educator; b. Essen, Northrhine-Westphalia, Germany, Apr. 4, 1960; arrived in U.S., 1993; s. Wolfdieter and Irmela S.E.G. Seyfang. BSc, U. Tübingen, 1983, MSc in Zoology and Parasitology, 1989, PhD magna cum laude in Biochemistry, 1993; student, Duke U., 1984—85. Postdoctoral fellow U. Bordeaux, France, 1993—95, Oreg. Health Sci. U., Portland, Oreg., 1995—99; asst. prof. Med. Coll. Ga., Augusta, Ga., 1999—2005, U. South Fla., Tampa, 2005—. Grant reviewer Am. Heart Assn., St. Petersburg, Fla., 2004—, The Wellcome Trust, London, 2004, Uniformed Svcs. U. Health Scis., Bethesda, Md., 2004, USDA, Washington. Co-author: Advances in Cell and Molecular Biology of Membranes: Membrane Traffic in Protozoa, 1993; contbr. articles to profl. jours. Fellow, Fondation pour la Recherche Medicale, 1994—95, Alexander-von-Humboldt Found., 1995—97, Am. Heart Assn., 1997—99; grantee, 2000—, MCG Rsch. Inst., 2000—01; scholar Duke U. Exch. Student, German Academic Exch. Svc., 1984—85. Mem.: AAAS, Am. Soc. Biochemistry and Molecular Biology, Am. Soc. Microbiology. Achievements include patents pending for method for multiple site-directed mutagenesis; development of reconstitution system for protozoan membrane transporters. Avocations: music, travel, birdwatching, skiing, horseback riding. Home: 6037 Catlin Dr Tampa FL 33647-2603 Office: U South Fla Med Microbiology MDC 10 Tampa FL 33612-4799 Office Phone: 813-974-2332. Personal E-mail: seyfang@earthlink.net. Business E-Mail: aseyfang@hsc.usf.edu.

**SEYFERT, PAUL**, social studies educator; b. Lebanon, Pa., Sept. 23, 1967; s. Richard A. Seyfert, Sr. and Kathryn A. (Morrisey) Seyfert; m. Beth A. Wolf, May 27, 1989; children: Benjamin, Luke, Hailey. BSc in Social Sci., Pa. State U., Harrisburg, Pa., 1994, MS in Curriculum and Tchg., 2001; MS in ESL, Turabo U., Puerto Rico, 2006; student in Instrl. Design, Capella U., on-line, 2006—. Cert. prin. Pa., tchr. Pa. Tchr. Lancaster-Lebanon (Pa.) IUB, 1994—2001, Lebanon (Pa.) Sch. Dist., 2001—. With USAF, 1987—92, with reserves USAF, 1992—95. Grantee, Pa. Dept. Edn., 2005. Mem.: Nat. Assn. Student Coun., Nat. Assn. Social Studies. Democrat. Meth. Home: 6 Monarch Cir Myerstown PA 17062 Office: Lebanon School Dist 1000 South 8th St Lebanon PA 17042

**SEYFERT, WAYNE GEORGE**, secondary education educator, anatomy educator; b. Roslyn Park, N.Y., Nov. 23, 1947; s. George William Seyfert and Helen Francis (Weiss) Marks; m. Kathleen A. Kearns, May 23, 1970 (div. 1980); children: Sean Francis, Kerry Noelle, Adam Wayne. BS in Biology, SUNY, Cortland, 1969; MS in Biology, L.I. U. at C.W. Post, 1973; profl. diploma in sch. adminstrn., CUNY at Queen's Coll., N.Y.C., 1988. Cert. biology and secondary sci. tchr., N.Y.; cert.-sch. adminstr. and supr., N.Y.; cert. sch. dist. administr., N.Y. Jr. h.s. sci. tchr. Port Washington (N.Y.) Schs., 1969-70; sci. tchr. Lawrence (N.Y.) Pub. Schs., 1970—2003; instr. North Shore Sci. Mus., Plandome, NY, 1973—75; adj. prof. human anatomy and physiology Nassau C.C., Garden City, NY, 1975—, N.Y. Inst. Tech., 1994—. Summer program dir. Sci. Mus. L.I., Plandome, 1976-85; environ. cons. Town of Brookhaven, L.I., 1978-80. Contbr. articles to profl. publs. Membership chmn. Boy Scouts Am., Sunrise dist., N.Y., 1978-79; mem. conservation adv. coun. Town of Brookhaven, 1977-79; mem. L.I. Sci. Congress exec. bd., 1985-88. Recipient Ednl. Leadership award Lawrence Ednl. Found., 1998, named L.I. Educator of Month, Hofstra U./TV Channel 12, L.I., 1995, Person of the Yr., Nassau Herald, 1998, STANYS Nassau County H.S. Sci. Tchr. of Yr., 1998. Mem. AAAS, Am. Fedn. Tchrs., Adj. Faculty Assn., Nat. Sci. Tchrs. Assn., Nat. Biology Tchr. Assn., Am. Philatelic Soc., Am. 1st Day Cover Soc., Am. Revenue Assn., Am. Perfin Soc., Am. Precanceled Stamp Soc., United Postal Stationary Soc., Meter Stamp Soc., State Revenue Assn., Am. Airmail Soc., Aerogramme Soc., Christmas Seal and Charity Seal Soc., N.Y. Acad. Scis., N.Y. State United Tchrs., Sci. Tchrs. Assn. N.Y. State, Lawrence Tchrs. Assn. (1st v.p. 1984-2001), MACUB Soc. for Neutobiology. Achievements include writing first history of America's first prairie and performance of first environmental study to trace an area's environmental change since first European encroachment. Home: PO Box 116 Woodmere NY 11598-0116

**SEYFERTH, DIETMAR**, chemist, educator; b. Chemnitz, Germany, Jan. 11, 1929; arrived in U.S., 1933; s. Herbert C. and Elisabeth (Schuchardt) S.; m. Helena A. McCoy, Aug. 25, 1956; children — Eric Steven, Karl Dietmar, Elisabeth Mary. BA summa cum laude, U. Buffalo, 1951, MA, 1953; PhD, Harvard, 1955; Dr. honoris causa, U. Aix-Marseille, 1979, Paul Sabatier Univ., Toulouse, France, 1992. Fulbright scholar Tech. Hochschule, Munich, Germany, 1954-55; postdoctoral fellow Harvard U., 1956-57; faculty MIT, 1957—, prof. chemistry, 1965-2000, prof. emeritus, 2000—, Robert T. Haslam and Bradley Dewey prof., 1983-99. Cons. to industry, 1957—. Author: Annual Surveys of Organometallic Chemistry, 3 vols, 1965, 66, 67; regional editor: Jour. Organometallic Chemistry, 1963-01; coordinating editor revs. and survey sects., 1964-81; editor: Organometallics, 1981—; contbr. research papers and articles to profl. lit. Recipient Disting. Alumnus award U. Buffalo, 1964, Alexander von Humboldt Found. sr. award, 1984, Clifford C. Furnas Meml. award SUNY-Buffalo, 1987; Guggenheim fellow, 1968. Fellow AAAS, Am. Inst. Chemists, Inst. Materials, Am. Acad. Arts and Scis.; mem. NAS, Am. Chem. Soc. (Frederic Stanley Kipping award in organosilicon chemistry 1972, disting. svc. award advancement inorganic chemistry 1981, award in organometallic chemistry, 1996, Arthur C. Cope Sr. Scholar award 2003), Materials Rsch. Soc., Am. Ceramic Soc., Royal Soc. Chemistry, Gesellschaft Deutscher Chemiker, German Acad. Scientists-Leopoldina, Phi Beta Kappa, Sigma Xi. Office: MIT 77 Massachusetts Ave Rm 4-382 Cambridge MA 02139-4307 Office Phone: 617-253-1861. Business E-Mail: seyferth@mit.edu.

**SEYHUN, HASAN NEJAT**, finance educator, department chairman; b. Ankara, Turkey, May 19, 1954; came to U.S., 1972; s. Niyazi and Serife (Sayilgan) S.; m. Tamara Z. Cleland, Aug. 10, 1992; children: Kent E., Jon C. and Evan G. BEE, Northwestern U., 1976; MA in Econs., U. Rochester, 1981, PhD in Fin., 1984. Elec. engr. Sungurlar, Istanbul, 1976-77; asst. prof. fin. U. Mich., Ann Arbor, 1983-91, assoc. prof., 1991-93, prof., 1993—; Jerome B. and Eilene M. York prof. bus. adminstrn., 1998—, chmn. fin. dept., 1994-95, 97-00. Vis. prof. Koc U. Istanbul, 2000-01, vis. assoc. prof. U. Chgo., 1988-89, 92, Wissenschaftliche Hochschule für Unternehmens führung, Koblenz, Germany, 1994; co-dir. banking and fin. svcs. program, cons. Citibank, Zurich, Switzerland, 1991; cons. Tweedy Brown, N.Y.C., 1993—, Towneley Capital, N.Y.C., 1994—. Mem. Am. Fin. Assn., Western Fin. Assn., European Fin. Assn., Beta Gamma Sigma. Avocations: volleyball, running. Office: U Mich 701 Tappan Ave Ann Arbor MI 48109-1217 E-mail: nseyhun@umiu.edu.

**SEYLER, MONIQUE GEORGINA**, artist; b. Jersey City, Dec. 3, 1956; d. John Joseph and Claude Marie (Jordan) S.; m. Chet Zoltak, May 25, 1985; children: Danielle, Matthew. Student, Art Students League, N.Y.C., 1976, 80-83; cert. of honors, U. Sorbonne, Paris, 1976. Fu Jen U., Hsinchu, Taiwan, 1978; BA in Asian Studies cum laude, Seton Hall U., South Orange, N.J., 1979; postgrad., Sch. Visual Arts, N.Y.C., 1983-85. Ind. curator Maxwell's

Hoboken, N.J., 1991, Westchester Land trust, Bedford Hills, N.Y., 1993, 94, Working Artists, Hastings-on-Hudson, N.Y., 1994; freelance China Hand (lang. and culture): China Inst., NYC, 1980-1985., Nat. Com. on U.S.-China rels., Lindblad Travel, Pan Am. World Airways, Phelps Stokes Fund; founder/dir. Gallery St. Martin, Phila., 2003—. One-woman shows include Westchester C.C., 1993, Westchester Arts Coun., 1995, NARDIN Gallery, 1997, Art as Spectacle, Katonah Mus., Thelma Golden, Whitney Mus., 1998; exhibited in group shows including Whitney Mus. Pace U., 1995, Nat. Assn. Women Artists, 1995, Nardin Gallery, 1995, Elaine Benson Gallery, Bridgehampton, N.Y., 1996; permanent collections include Zimmerli Mus., Rutgers U., New Brunswick, N.J., Sanford C. Bernstein, Inc.; author: China Nights. Founder and chair Concerned Somers (N.Y.) Residents, 1990-96; assoc. Westchester Land trust, Bedford Hills, 1992-94; bd. dirs. Valley Pond Assn., Somers, 1994-95, pres. 1996-98. Recipient hon. mention Putnam Arts Coun., 1993; painting scholar N.J. Ctr. for Visual Arts, 1988. Mem. Nat. Assn. Women Artists (Miriam E. Halpern award 1993, 2002), Katonah Mus. Art Artists Assn. (assoc. 1993-98). Home: 7811 Saint Martins Ln Philadelphia PA 19118-4212 E-mail: moniqueseyler@comcast.net.

**SEYMOUR, CHARLENA**, academic administrator; m. Harry Seymour. BA, Howard U., 1965; MA, Ohio State U., 1967, PhD in Speech and Hearing Sci., 1981. Asst. prof. U. Mass., Amherst, 1971—78, assoc. prof., 1978—89, chair dept. comm. disorders, 1984—92, dean Grad. Sch., 1994—2001, provost, 2001—. Chair Coun. Grad. Schs. Adv. Com. on Minorities in Grad. Edn. Creative editor: Communication Disorders Textbook Series. Recipient Disting. Alumni award, Sch. Intercultural and Race Rels., Harvard Found., Harvard U., 1997. Fellow: Am. Speech-Lang. Hearing Assn.; mem.: N.E. Assn. Grad. Schs. (pres.-elect). Office: U Mass Office of the Provost 362 Whitmore Bldg 181 Presidents Dr Amherst MA 01003

**SEYMOUR, DOROTHY Z. See MILLS, DOROTHY**

**SEYMOUR, EVERETT HEDDEN, JR.**, lawyer; b. Tuxedo Park, Apr. 16, 1958; s. Everett Hedden and Deborah (Robinson) S. BA, Yale U., 1980; JD, U. Va., 1986. Bar: N.Y. 1988, U.S. Dist. Ct. (so. and ea. dists.) N.Y. 1988, Conn. 1988, U.S. Dist. Ct. Conn. 1988. Law clk. to justice U.S. Dist. Ct., New Haven, 1986-87; assoc. Davis Polk & Wardwell, N.Y.C., 1987-97; mng. dir., assoc. gen. counsel J.P. Morgan Chase & Co., N.Y.C., 1997—. Articles rev. editor U. Va. Law Rev., 1984-86. Office: JP Morgan Chase & Co 270 Park Ave 40th Fl New York NY 10017-2014

**SEYMOUR, JANE**, actress; b. Hillingdon, Middlesex, Eng., Feb. 15, 1951; came to U.S., 1976; d. John Benjamin and Mieke Frankenberg; m. David Flynn, July 18, 1981 (div. 1991); 2 children; m. James Keach, May 15, 1993; 2 children (twins). Student, Arts Ednl. Sch., London. Appeared in films Oh What A Lovely War, 1968, The Only Way, 1968, Young Winston, 1969, Live and Let Die, 1971, Sinbad and the Eye of the Tiger, 1973, Somewhere in Time, 1979, Oh Heavenly Dog, 1979, Lassiter, 1984, Head Office, Scarlet Pimpernel, Haunting Passion, Dark Mirror, Obsessed with a Married Woman, Killer on Board, The Tunnel, 1988, The French Revolution, Tochiny Wild Horses, 2002; TV films include Frankenstein, The True Story, 1972, Captains and The Kings, 1976 (Emmy nomination), The Awakening Land, 1977, The Four Feathers, 1977, Battlestar Galactica, Dallas Cowboy Cheerleaders, 1979, Our Mutual Friend, PBS, Eng., 1975, Jamaica Inn, 1982, Sun Also Rises, 1984, Crossings, 1986, Keys to Freedom, Angel of Death, 1990, Praying Mantis, 1993; A Passion for Justice: The Hazel Brannon Smith Story, 1994; Broadway appearances include Amadeus, 1980-81, I Remember You, 1992, Matters of the Heart, 1991, Sunstroke, 1992, Praying Mantis, 1993, Heidi, 1993; TV mini-series include East of Eden, 1980, The Richest Man in the World, 1988 (Emmy award), The Woman He Loved, 1988, Jack the Ripper, 1988, War and Remembrance, 1988, 89; host PBS documentary, Japan, 1988; TV series: Dr. Quinn: Medicine Woman, 1993-98 (Emmy nomination, Lead Actress - Drama, 1994, 98, Golden Globe award 1996), A Marriage of Convenience, CBS, 1998, A Memory in My Heart, CBS, 1999, Murder in the Mirror, CBS, 2000, Enslavement: The True Life Story of Fanny Kemble, Showtime, 2000, Blackout, CBS, 2000, Yesterday's Children, CBS, Dr. Quinn Winters Heart, 2001, Heart of a Stranger, 2002; author: Jane Seymour's Guide to Romantic Living, 1986, Two at a Time, 2001; co-author: Yum, Splat, 1998, Boing, 1999. Decorated Order Brit. Empire; recipient OBE award, 2000; named Hon. Citizen of Ill., Gov. Thompson, 1977. Mem. Screen Actors Guild, AFTRA, Actors Equity, Brit. Equity. Office: Guttman Assocs 118 S Beverly Dr Ste 201 Beverly Hills CA 90212-3016

**SEYMOUR, JEFFREY ALAN**, governmental relations consultant; b. L.A., Aug. 31, 1950; s. Daniel and Evelyn (Schwartz) S.; m. Valerie Joan Parker, Dec. 2, 1973; 1 child, Jessica Lynn. AA in Social Sci., Santa Monica Coll., 1971; BA in Polit. Sci., UCLA, 1973; MPA, 1977. Councilman aide L.A. City Coun., 1972-74; county supr.'s sr. dep. L.A. Bd. Suprs., 1974-82; v.p. Bank of L.A., 1982-83; prin. Jeffrey Seymour & Assocs., L.A., 1983-84; prin. Morey/Seymour & Assocs., L.A., 1984—2002, Seymour Consulting Group, 2002—. Mem. comml. panel Am. Arbitration Assn., 1984—90. Chmn. West Hollywood Parking Adv. Com., L.A., 1983-84; chmn. social action com. Temple Emanuel of Beverly Hills, 1986-89, bd. dirs. 1988-93, v.p. 1990-93; v.p. Congregation N'Vay Shalom, 1995; mem. Pan Pacific Park Citizens Adv. Com., L.A., 1982-85; bd. dirs. William O'Douglas Outdoor Classroom, L.A., 1981-88; mem. bd. regents U. Calif., 2001-02; pres. Alumni Assns. U. Calif., 2000-02; chair UCLA Fund, 2002—; friend com. L.A. Free Clin., 2005—; mem.govtl. affairs com. Venice Family Clin., 2005—. Recipient plaques for svcs. rendered Beverlywood Cheviot Hills Dem. Club, L.A., 1981, Jewish Fedn. Coun. Greater L.A., 1983, certs. of appreciation, L.A. Olympic Organizing Com., 1984, County of L.A., 1984, City of L.A., 1987, Santa Monica Mountains Conservancy, 1999, UCLA Alumni Assn. 2002, others; commendatory revolutions, rules com. Calif. State Senate, 1987, Calif. State Assembly, 1987, 96, County of L.A., 1987, City of L.A., 1987; mem. bd. Regents of U. Calif., 2000-2002. Mem. ASPA, UCLA Alumni Assn. (mem. govtl. steering com. 1983-97, bd. dirs. 1995—, chair govtl. rels. steering com. 1995-97, pres. 1998-2000); exec. sect. Calif. Fedn. Young Dems., 1971; mem. Calif. Dem. Cen. Com., 1979-82; pres. Beverlywood-Cheviot Hills Dem. Club, L.A., 1978-81; co-chmn. Westside Chancellor's Assocs. UCLA, 1986-88; mem. L.A. Olympic Citizens Adv. Com.; mem. liaison adv. commn. with city and county govt. for 1984 Olympics, 1984; v.p. comty. rels. metro region, Jewish Fedn. Coun. of L.A., 1985-87, co-chmn. urban affairs commn., 1987-89, vice chmn., 1989-90, subcom. chmn. local govt. law and legislation commn., 1990, chmn. campus outreach task force, 1994; mem. adv. bd. Nat. Jewish Ctr. for Immunology & Respiratory Medicine, 1991-93; bd. dirs. Hillel Coun. of L.A., 1991; mem. platform on world peace and internat. rels. Calif. Dems., 1983; pres. 43d Assembly Dist. Dem. Coun., 1975-79; arbitrator BBB, 1984; trustee UCLA Found., 1989-97; pres. UCLA Jewish Alumni, 1992-95; mem. Santa Monica Mountains Conservancy adv. com., 1996-99; mem. cabinet Jewish Cmty. Rels. Com. Greater L.A., 1994, chair campus outreach task force, 1994-95, govtl. rels. commn., 1995-96, v. chair Jewish Cmty. Rels. com. Jewish Fedn. Coun. Greater L.A., 1998; mem. bd. dirs., Century City C of C, 1998-2000, adv. bd. L.A. Peace Now, UCLA Fund (chair 2002-04), Alumni Assn. U of Calif. (pres. 2001-2002, chmn. 2002-04). bd. govs. 2004—, mem. adv. com. 2004—). Office: 2815 Townsgate Rd Ste 140 Westlake Village CA 91361 Office Phone: 818-905-0283. Business E-Mail: jeff@jseymourgroup.com.

**SEYMOUR, KAREN PATTON**, lawyer, former prosecutor; b. Big Springs, Tex. m. Samuel Seymour; 2 children. BA, So. Methodist U., 1983; JD, U. Tex., 1986; LLM, U. London, 1987. Bar: NY 1988. Fed. prosecutor USA Attys. Office, So. Dist. NY, 1990—96, Asst. US Atty., Criminal Div. Chief, 2002—04; ptnr. Sullivan & Cromwell, New York, NY, 2004—2004. Office: Sullivan & Cromwell 125 Broad St New York NY 10004-2498

**SEYMOUR, McNEIL VERNAM**, lawyer; b. St. Paul, Dec. 21, 1934; s. McNeil Vernam and Katherine Grace (Klein) S.; children: Margaret, McNeil Vernam, James, Benjamin; m. Mary Katherine Velner, May 15, 1993. AB, Princeton U., 1957; JD, U. Chgo., 1960. Bar: Minn. 1960, U.S. Dist. Ct. Minn. 1960. Mem. Seymour & Seymour, St. Paul, 1960-71; mem. firm Briggs

& Morgan, St. Paul, 1971—, ptnr., 1976—2005, of counsel, 2005—. Pres. elect Thomas Irvine Dodge Nature Ctr.; sec., bd. dirs. Ramsey County Law Libr., 1972—76; pres., treas. White Bear Unitarian Ch., 1964—65; trustee Oakland Cemetery Assn. With U.S. Army, 1960—62. Mem. Minn. Bar Assn., Ramsey County Bar Assn., Somerset Country Club. Republican. Unitarian Universalist. Home: 886 S Highview Cir Mendota Heights MN 55118-3686 Office: Briggs & Morgan W-2200 1st Nat Bank Bldg Saint Paul MN 55101 Office Phone: 651-808-6601. E-mail: MSeymour@Briggs.com.

**SEYMOUR, MICHELLE GENE,** elementary school educator; b. Mpls., Jan. 27, 1946; d. Eugene John and Eileen Rose Giddings; m. Lewis Arthur Seymour, Aug. 3, 1968 (dec.); children: James Jon, Jennifer Gene Seymour Ludvigson. BS, U. Wis., Eau Claire, 1968; MS in Reading, U. Wis., 1995. Elem. tchr. Lancaster (Wis.) Sch. Dist., 1968—70, DeForest (Wis.) Sch. Dist., 1970—71, Rice Lake (Wis.) Area Schs., 1985—. Tchr. Head Start, Spooner, Wis., 1968; instr. Kid's Coll., Rice Lake, 1990—91, Kiddie Korner Pre-Sch., Rice Lake. Mem. ch. coun. Bethany Luth. Ch., 1983—84. Mem.: Internat. Reading Assn., Naomi Cir. Avocations: reading, walking, piano, violin. Home: 332 Mission Pl Rice Lake WI 54868 Office Phone: 715-234-8065.

**SEYMOUR, RICHARD DEMING,** technology educator; b. Shelby, Ohio, Oct. 3, 1955; s. G. Deming and Elizabeth (Peterson) S.; m. Vicki Stebleton; 1 child, Ryan. BS in Edn., Ohio State U., 1978; MA, Ball State U., 1982; EdD, W.Va. U., 1990. Tchr. Crestview Sr. High Sch., Ashland, Ohio, 1978-81; from instr. to assoc. prof. Ball State U., Muncie, Ind., 1982—. Vis. instr. W.Va. U., Morgantown, 1985, Oreg. State U., 1990-91. Co-author: Exploring Communications, 1987, rev. edit., 2000; co-editor: Manufacturing in Technology Education, 1993. Advisor 4-H Clubs, Richland County, Ohio, 1978-81; dir. tech. in-svc. workshops Ind. Dept. Edn., Indpls., 1988-2000. Named technology tchr. educator of yr. Coun. on Technology Tchr. Edn., 1998. Mem.: Tech. Edn. Collegiate Assn. (internat. advisor 1992—92, nat. contest coord. 1992—), Am. Soc. Engring. Edn., Tech. Educators Ind. (pres. 1995—96), Ind. Math., Sci., Tech. Alliance (bd. dirs. 1994—), Coun. on Tech. Tchr. Edn. (v.p. 2003—05), Soc. Mfg. Engrs., Internat. Tech. Edn. Assn. (bd. dirs. 1992—94, chmn. internat. conf. 1999, award of distinction 1999), Phi Delta Kappa, Epsilon Pi Tau. Methodist. Avocations: model railroads, sports, travel. Office: Ball State U Dept Industry Tech Muncie IN 47306-0255 E-mail: rseymour@bsu.edu.

**SEYMOUR, SAMUEL WHITNEY,** lawyer; b. Hanover, NH, 1957; AB, Dartmouth Coll., 1979; JD, Columbia U., 1982. Bar: NY 1983. Asst. US Atty. US Dist. Ct. (so. dist.) NY, 1988-91; instr. Sullivan & Cromwell, NYC, 1991—, and coord. criminal def. and investigations practice area. Bd. dir. Fund for Modern Courts, First Dept. Assigned Counsel Corp.; adj. lectr. trial advocacy Columbia Law Sch., NYC. Mem.: NY Coun. Def. Lawyers, Assn. of Bar City of NY (past v.p. and chair, exec. com.). Office: Sullivan & Cromwell 125 Broad St Fl 28 New York NY 10004-2489 Office Phone: 212-558-4000. Office Fax: 212-558-3588. Business E-Mail: seymours@sullcrom.com.

**SEYMOUR, SCOTT,** science administrator; BEE, Poly. U., Bklyn.; JD, Western State U. From engr. to v.p., B-2 program mgr. Northrop Grumman Corp., 1983—97, v.p. air combat sys., 1998—2001, corp. v.p., pres. integrated sys. El Segundo, Calif., 2001—. With USMC. Office: Northrop Grumman Corp Air Combat Sys Integrated Sys One Northrop Grumman Ave El Segundo CA 90245-2804

**SEYMOUR, SLOAN,** media specialist; BA summa cum laude, St. Lawrence U. With PC Mag. Medford, Mass.; v.p., pub. eWEEK; v.p. PC Computing; with Ziff Davis Media Inc., NYC, 1986—; sr. v.p. Enterprise Group, 2003—04, pres. Enterprise Group, 2004—. Office: Ziff Davis Media 28 E 28th St New York NY 10016 Office Phone: 212-503-3500.

**SEYMOUR, STEPHANIE KULP,** federal judge; b. Battle Creek, Mich., Oct. 16, 1940; d. Francis Bruce and Frances Cecelia (Bria) Kulp; m. R. Thomas Seymour, June 10, 1972; children: Bart, Bria, Sara, Anna. BA magna cum laude, Smith Coll., 1962; JD, Harvard U., 1965. Bar: Okla. 1965. Practice, Boston, 1965—66, Tulsa, 1966—67, Houston, 1968—69; assoc. Doerner, Stuart, Saunders, Daniel & Anderson, Tulsa, 1971—75, ptnr., 1975—79; judge US Ct. Appeals (10th Cir.), Tulsa, Okla., 1979—, chief judge, 1994—2000, sr. judge, 2005—. Mem.: U.S. Jud. Conf., 1994—, com. defender svcs., 1985—90, chmn., 1987—90, com. to review ctr. council conduct and disability, 1996—; joint fed. tribal rels. com. 9th and 10th cirs., 1993—; mem. Okla. State Fed. Tribal Judicial Coun., 1993—94. Task force Tulsa Human Rights Commn., 1972—76; legal adv. panel Tulsa Task Force Battered Women, 1971—77; trustee Tulsa County Law Libr., 1977—78. Mem.: ABA, Am. Inns of Ct. (Council Oak chpt.), Nat. Assn. Women Judges, Fed. Judges Assn., Tulsa County Bar Assn., Okla. Bar Assn. (assoc. bar examiner 1973—79), Phi Beta Kappa. Office: US Courthouse 333 W 4th St Ste 4-562 Tulsa OK 74103-3819*

**SEYMOUR, THADDEUS,** language educator; b. N.Y.C., June 29, 1928; s. Whitney North and Lola Virginia (Vickers) S.; m. Polly Gnagy, Nov. 20, 1948; children— Elizabeth Halsey, Thaddeus, Samuel Whitney, Mary Duffie, Abigail Comfort AB, U. Calif., 1950; MA, U. N.C., 1951, PhD, 1955; D.H.L. (hon.), Wilkes Coll., 1968; LL.D. (hon.), Butler U., 1971, Ind. State U., 1976; LLD (hon.), Wabash Coll., 1984, U. Cen. Fla., 1990, Stetson U., 1990; DHL (hon.), Rollins Coll., 1990. Mem. faculty Dartmouth Coll., 1954-69, prof. English, dean coll., 1959-69; pres. Wabash Coll., Crawfordsville, Ind., 1969-78, Rollins Coll., Winter Park, Fla., 1978-90, prof. English, 1978—. Pres. Nat. Conf. Higher Edn., 1977; v.p. Assoc. Colls. Ind., 1978; vice-chmn. Fla. Ind. Colls. Fund Past mem. Ind. Bicentennial Commn.; trustee Park-Tudor Sch., 1970-78, Bach Festival Soc., Winter Park Pub. Libr., 1998—; chmn. Fla. selection com. Rhodes Scholarship Trust, 1983-88; chmn. Habitat for Humanity of Winter Park, 1994—; sec.-treas. Winter Park Health Found., 1998—. Mem. Cmty. Found. Ctrl. Fla. (bd. dirs.), Ring 219 (charter), Internat. Brotherhood Magicians, Century Assn., Rotary, Omicron Delta Kappa. Home: 1804 Summerfield Rd Winter Park FL 32792 Office Phone: 407-646-1985. Business E-Mail: tseymour@rollins.edu.

**SEYOUM, BELAY,** business educator; s. Seyoum Anore and Memenasha Abay; m. Muwen Xu, Aug. 22, 2003. PhD, McGill U., 1986. Assoc. prof. Nova Southeastern U., Ft. Lauderdale, Fla., 1991—. Adj. prof. Concordia U., Montreal, Canada, 1986—91. Author: (book) Export-import Theories, Practices And Procedures, Notable Selections In Economics, The State Of The Global Economy. Fulbright scholar, 2006. Office: Nova Southeastern U 3301 College Ave Fort Lauderdale FL 33314 Office Phone: 954-262-8133. E-mail: seyoum@nova.edu.

**SFEKAS, STEPHEN JAMES,** lawyer, educator; b. Balt., Feb. 12, 1947; s. James Stephen and Lee (Mesologites) S.; m. Joanne Lorraine Murphy, May 27, 1973; children: James Stephen, Andrew Edward Stephen, Christina Marie; m. Elizabeth Ruff, Nov. 1, 1997. BS in Fgn. Svc., Georgetown U., 1968, JD, 1973; MA, Yale U., 1977. U.S. Dist. Ct. Md. 1974, U.S. Ct. Appeals (4th cir.) 1974. Law clk. U.S. Dist. Ct., Balt., 1973-74; assoc. firm Frank, Bernstein, Conaway & Goldman, Balt., 1974-75; asst. atty. gen. State of Md., Balt., 1975-81; assoc. firm Tydings & Rosenberg, Balt., 1981-82, ptnr., 1983-86; with firm Miles & Stockbridge, Balt., 1986-90; ptnr. Weinberg & Green, Balt., 1991-98, Saul, Ewing, LLP, Balt., 1998—2001; counsel Cook & Di Franco, LLC, 2001—05; sole practice Balt., 2005—. Instr. legal writing C.C. Balt., 1976-79; instr. legal ethics Goucher Coll., Balt., 1979; adj. prof. adminstrv. law U. Md., Balt., 1981-93, health, 1993—, law sch. U. Balt., 1993—. Editor Georgetown Law Jour., 1972-73; contbr. articles to legal publs. Bd. dirs. Md. region NCCJ, 1981-89, co-chmn. Md. region, 1986-89, Orthodox Christian Laity, 1990—98, ARC of Balt. Md. Ecumenical Coun., 1991—93, ARC of Balt. Vol. for Med. Engring., 2001-; mem. Piraeus Sister City Com., City of Balt., 1983-89; mem. parish coun. Greek Orthodox Cathedral of Annunciation, Balt., 1981-84; mem. internat. com. Balt. region ARC, 1984-85; mem. adv. com. on bread for the world Dept. Ch. and Soc.,

Greek Orthodox Archdiocese North and S.Am., 1984—; pres. Greek Orthodox Counseling and Social Svcs. of Balt., 1984-88; mem. bylaw com. Girl Scouts Ctrl. Md., 1989-91, Md. Leadership Program, 1997; mem. pres.'s adv. coun. U. Md., Baltimore County; mem. human rights com. ARC of the U.S., 2002—. Danforth fellow, Woodrow Wilson fellow, WHO fellow, London, 1979. Fellow: Md. Bar Found., Soc. for Values in Higher Edn. (bd. dir. 2002—); mem.: ABA (forum com. on health law, Grant Morris fellow 1979), Am. Health Lawyers Assn., Bar Assn. Balt. City, Md. Bar Assn. Democrat. Office: 111 S Cassler St Ste 2700 Baltimore MD 21202 Office Phone: 410-385-5322. Business E-Mail: stephen@sfekaslaw.com.

**SFERRAZZA, ANTHONY CARL,** historian, writer; b. N.Y.C., June 13, 1959; s. Carl Richard and Marie Jane (Martirano) Sferrazza. BA in History, George Washington U., 1983. Writer Presdl. Inaugural Book Com., Washington, 1980—81, 1984—85, 1988—89, Exec. Office of Pres., Washington, 1981—82, White House Preservation Fund, Washington, 1983—84; speechwriter Office of First Lady Nancy Reagan, Washington, 1985—86; instr. George Washington U., Washington, 1994; contbg. editor George Mag., N.Y.C., 1997—99; bibliographer, bd. dirs. Nat. First Ladies Libr., Canton, Ohio, 1996—. Freelance hist. writer Style sect. Washington Post, Washington, 1985—98; hist. cons. Nat. Mus. Am. History, Smithsonian Instn., Washington, 1990—92; hist. source Office of First Lady Hillary Clinton, Washington, 1993—2001; guest curator Richard Nixon Mus. and Birthplace, 1997, 2006—. Author: First Ladies: The Saga of the Presidents' Wives and Their Power, 1789,1990, 2 vols., 1990—91, As We Remember Her: Jacqueline Kennedy Onassis in the Words of Her Friends and Family, 1997, Florence Harding: The First Lady, The Jazz Age and the Death of America's Most Scandalous President, 1998, The Kennedy White House: Family Life and Pictures, 1961-1963, 2001, America's First Families, 2000, Heads of State: The Presidents as Everyday Useful, Household Objects, 2004, Nellie Taft: The Unconventional First Lady of the Ragtime Era, 2005. Named Bicentennial Honoree, U. Louisville, 1997; recipient Spl. Book Collections, Brandeis U. Libr., 2001. Episcopalian. Avocations: hiking, boxing, tennis.

**SFIKAS, PETER MICHAEL,** lawyer, educator; b. Gary, Ind., Aug. 9, 1937; s. Michael E. and Helen (Thureanos) S.; m. Freida Platon, Apr. 24, 1966; children: Ellen M., Pamela C., Sandra N. BS, Ind. U., 1959; JD, Northwestern U., 1962. Bar: Ill. 1962, US. Dist. Ct. (no. dist) Ill. 1963, US. Ct. Appeals (7th cir.) 1963, U.S. Supreme Ct. 1970, U.S. Ct. Appeals (9th cir.) 1976, U.S. Ct. Appeals (3d cir.) 1981, U.S. Ct. Appeals (D.C. cir.) 1984, U.S. Ct. Appeals (8th cir.) 1995, U.S. Dist. Ct. (cen. dist.) Ill. 1988. Atty. Legal Aid Bur., United Charities Chgo., 1962-63; sr. ptnr. Peterson & Ross, Chgo., 1970-95; chief counsel, assoc. exec. dir. divsn. legal affairs ADA, Chgo., 1995—; ptnr. Bell, Boyd & Lloyd, Chgo., 1996—. Prosecutor Village of LaGrange Park, Ill., 1969-74; mem. rules com. Ill. Supreme Ct., 1975-95, mem. spl. joint com. on discovery rules, 1995; arbitrator Nat. Panel Arbitrators, 1972—; adj. prof. Loyola U. Sch. Law, 1978—; guest lectr. U. Ill. Coll. Dentistry, 1988-95; lectr. corp. counsel inst. Northwestern U. Sch. Law, 1984, lectr. Ray Garret Jr. Corp. and Securities Law Inst., 1996. Co-author: Antitrust and Unfair Competition Practice Handbook, 1996; contbr. articles to profl. jours. Mem. Ill. steering com. Ct. Watching Project, LWV, 1975-77; pres. Holy Apostles Greek Orthodox Ch. Parish Coun., 1987-89; co-pres. Oak Sch. PTO, 1989-90; mem. com. to select sch. supr., dist. 86, DuPage County, Ill., 1993-94. Named Super Lawyer, Chgo. (Ill.) Mag., 2006; recipient Maurice Weigle award, Chgo. Bar Found., 1973, Fones award and hon. membership, Com. Dental Assn., 1998. Fellow Am. Bar Found., Am. Coll. Trial Lawyers, Chgo. Bar Found. (life); mem. ABA (editor in chief Forum Law Jour. sect. ins., negligence and compensation law 1972-76), Ill. Bar Found. (bd. dirs. 1975-77), Northwestern U. Law Alumni Assn. (1st v.p. 1985-86, pres. 1986-87, Svc. award 1990), Ill. State Bar Assn. (bd. govs. 1970-76, chmn. antitrust law sect. coun. 1986-87), Chgo. Bar Assn. (editl. bd. Chgo. Bar Record 1973-84), Bar Assn. 7th Fed. Cir. (chmn. com. on meetings 1973-75), Ill. Inst. Continuing Legal Edn. (chmn. profl. antitrust problems program 1976, author program on counseling corps., antitrust and trade regulation), Am. Nat. Standards Inst. (mem. copyright ad hoc group 2004-), Legal Club Chgo. (sec.-treas, 1984-86, v.p. 1989-90, pres. 1990-91). Office: Bell Boyd & Lloyd 70 W Madison St Ste 3300 Chicago IL 60602-4284 Office Phone: 312-807-4348. E-mail: psfikas@bellboyd.com.

**SFIROUDIS, GLORIA TIDES,** library and information scientist, educator; d. George and Mary Despotides; m. Harry Sfiroudis, June 30, 1957; children: Steven, Christina. BA in Geography and Geology, Hunter Coll., 1954, MS in Edn., 1957; Profl. Diploma in Adminstrn. and Supervision, Queens Coll., 1981. Cert. tchr. effectiveness instrn. N.Y. Tchr. North Babylon Sch., L.I., NY, 1954—55, P.S. 123, Bklyn., 1955—61; tchr. 2nd and 3rd grade P.S. 229, Queens, NY, 1970—72, tchr. libr., 1972—74, corrective reading tchr., 1974—82, talented and gifted tchr., 1982—89, acting asst. prin., 1989—90, ednl. enrichment specialist, 1991—2000, tchrs. coll. literacy coach 2000—04, libr./rsch. tchr., 2004—. Chairperson sch. bd. William Spyropolous Sch. of St. Nicholas, Flushing, NY, 1982—2000; mem., participant Law in a Free Soc., Albany, NY, 1985—89. Co-author: (handbook) The Opera, 1990. Vol. Hosp. Audiences, Inc., N.Y.C., 1975—; active fundraiser Reading Olympics, March of Dimes, UNICEF, Am. Cancer Soc.; mem. exec. bd. St. Nicholas Shrine Ch., Flushing, 1995—. Recipient Vol. Cmty. Action award, Hosp. Audiences, Inc., award, Audubon Soc., 1995; CVS Innovations Charitable Trust Inc. grant, TPI Philanthropic Initiative, 2002—05, Greenwich Conn. fellow, Korean Summer Inst. Yale U. fellow, 1997. Mem.: St. Nicholas Ladies Philoptochos Soc. (sec. 1999—, Pastor's award 2002). Avocations: piano, swimming. Office: Emanuel Kaplan Sch PS 229 67-25 51st Rd Woodside Woodside NY 11377 Office Phone: 718-446-2120.

**SFORZA, ALFRED VINCENT,** dentist, educator, writer; b. Huntington, N.Y., Aug. 26, 1939; s. Alfred Anthony and Lena Sforza; m. Barbara Joan Albin, June 10, 1961; children: Anthony V., Debra Ann Smith, Sharon Lee Buehrig. BA, N.Y. U. Heights N.Y., 1961; DDS, NYU, 1965. Cert. D.D.S. N.Y. Officer Suffolk County Police, L.I., NY, 1963—65; dentist pvt. practice, Huntington, NY, 1965—; assoc. clin. prof. NYU Coll. of Dentistry, N.Y.C., 1965—. Author: Portrait of a Small Town Huntington Station, 1996, Portrait of a Small Town II Huntington 'In the Beginning', 2001. Bd. of trustees Huntington Historical Soc., 1996—; Anniversary Com. Huntington 350th Anniversary, 2002—. Mem.: Dentist For A Better Huntington, Suffolk County Dental, Am. Dental Assn. (assoc.). Avocations: skiing, hiking, history. Office: Alfred V Sforza DDS PC 44 West Neck Road Huntington NY 11743

**SFORZINI, RICHARD HENRY,** aerospace engineer, educator; b. Rochester, N.Y., July 25, 1924; m. Corinne Lorenz, 1947; children: Richard Jr., Suzanne Simonelli, Deborah Pugh, Michael, Stephen, Andrew, Mark. Degree of Mech. Engr., MIT, 1954; BS, U.S. Mil. Acad., 1947. Instr. ordnance U.S. Mil. Acad., 1954-56, asst. prof., 1956-57; project dir. anti-tank missile sys. R&D Army Rocket and Guided Missile Agy., Redstone Arsenal, Ala., 1958-59; engr. Huntsville divsn. Thiokol Chem. Corp., Ala., 1959-62, mgr. engring. dept. Ala., 1962-64, vis. prof. Auburn (Ala.) U., 1966-67, 1967-85, prof. emeritus aerospace engring., 1985—. Home and Office: 912 Cherokee Rd Auburn AL 36830-2723

**SGARRO, DOUGLAS A.,** pharmaceutical executive, lawyer; b. NY, 1959; m. Breda Sgarro; 3 children. Grad. Hamilton Coll., 1981; law degree, Univ. of Va. Sch. of Law, 1984. Assoc. Brown & Wood LLP, New York, NY, 1984—93, ptnr., 1993—97; sr. v.p. and chief legal officer CVS Pharmacy, Woonsocket, RI, 1997—2000; pres. CVS Realty Co., Woonsocket, RI, 1999—; sr. v.p. and chief legal officer CVS Corp., Woonsocket, RI, 2000—04; dir. Econ. Devel. Corp., Woonsocket, RI, 2000—; exec. v.p. Strategy, Chief Legal Officer CVS Corp., CVS Pharmacy, 2005—. Dir. Providence Children's Mus., United Way, Rye, NY. Mem.: Am. Bar Assoc. Bus. Law Sect., Internat. Assoc. of Atty. Exec. in Corp. Real Estate. Avocations: reading, exercise. Office: Office Chief Legal Officer CVS Corp One CVS Dr Woonsocket RI 02895

**SGOUROS, THOMAS,** artist; b. Mass., 1927; s. Thomas and Rena (Vekos) Sgouros; m. Joan Sgouros (dec.); 3 children; m. Roxie Sgouros. BFA, RI Sch. Design; DFA (hon.), RI Coll., 2001. Comml. illlustrator, NYC; prof., illustration RI Sch. Design, Providence. One-man shows include RI Watercolor Soc., 2004, exhibited in group shows at Parkland Art Gallery, 1999. Recipient Claiborne Pell award for excellence in arts, 2001. Mem.: NAD (academician 1994—), Am. Watercolor Soc., RI Watercolor Soc. Renowned watercolorist despite macular degeneration since 1992. Studio: Providence Art Club 7 Thomas St Providence RI 02903-1314 Office: RI School of Design 2 College St Providence RI 02903 Office Phone: 401-454-6242. Business E-Mail: tsgouros@risd.edu.

**SGRO, JOSEPH ANTHONY,** retired psychologist, educator; b. New Haven, Nov. 22, 1937; s. Fred and Tullia (Francesconi) S.; m. Beverly Ann Huston, Feb. 1, 1964; children: Anthony, Jennifer. BA, Trinity Coll., 1959; MS, Lehigh U., 1961; PhD, Tex. Christian U., 1966. Asst. prof. Old Dominion U., Norfolk, Va., 1965-67, Va. Poly. Inst. & State U., Blacksburg, 1967-71, assoc. prof., 1971-79, prof., 1979-99; prof. emeritus, 1999—; dept. head psychology Va. Poly. Inst. & State U., Blacksburg, 1982-96, mem. exec. bd., sec.-treas. coun. grad. dept. psychology, 1990-92, chmn., 1992-93; adj. prof. Warren Wilson Coll., 2000, U. NC Asheville, 2004. Vice-chmn. Va. Bd. Psychologists Examiners, Richmond, 1970-75. Editor: Virginia Tech Symposium on Applied Behavioral Science, 1980. Mem. APA, Southeastern Psychol. Assn. (chmn. assn. heads depts. psychology 1987-89), Ea. Psychol. Assn., Va. Psychol. Assn. (pres. 1974-76), Soc. Indsl. and Orgnl. Psychology, Omicron Delta Kappa, Psi Chi, Sigma Xi. Avocations: golf, cooking, yoga. Home: 22 Hilltop Rd Biltmore Forest NC 28803 E-mail: jsgro@charter.net.

**SGUERRA, JAIME,** insurance company executive; Degree in systems engring., Universidad Piloto de Columbia. Joined Guardian Life Ins. Co. of Am., 2001, now 2nd v.p., chief arch., sr. bus systems officer for corp. mktg. Named one of Premier 100 IT Leaders, Computerworld, 2005. Office: Guardian Life Ins Co of Am 7 Hanover Sq New York NY 10004 Office Phone: 212-598-8000.*

**SHA, NAIJUN,** statistician; BS in Math., Fudan U., China, 1985; PhD, Tex. A&M U., 2002. Tchg. asst. Tex. A&M U., College Station; asst. prof. U. Tex., El Paso, 2002—. Mem.: Phi Kappa Phi. Achievements include research in relationship between individual behavior and their characteristics. Office: U Tex 500 W University Ave El Paso TX 79968 Office Phone: 915-747-6844. Business E-Mail: naijun@math.utep.edu.

**SHABANOV, NIKOLAY V.,** physicist, researcher; b. Novocherkassk, Rostovskaya, Russia, Dec. 2, 1972; arrived in U.S., 1997; MA in Physics, Moscow State U., 1996; PhD in Remote Sensing, Boston U., 2002. Rsch. asst. prof. Boston U., 2005—. Rsch. grantee, NASA, 2004. Avocations: reading, swimming, travel. Home: 1152 Commonwealth Ave # 36 Allston MA 02134 Office: Boston U Geography Dept 675 Commonwealth Ave Boston MA 02215

**SHABAZ, JOHN C.,** judge; b. West Allis, Wis., June 25, 1931; s. Cyrus D. and Harriet T. Shabaz; children: Scott J., Jeffrey J., Emily D., John D. LLB, Marquette U., 1957; BS in Polit. Sci., U. Wis., 1999. Comd. 2d lt. U.S. Army, 1954, assigned to inactive reserves as capt., 1964; pvt. practice law West Allis, Wis., 1957—82; mem. Wis. Assembly, 1965—81; judge U.S. Dist. Ct. (we. dist.) Wis., 1982—96, chief judge, 1996—2001. Office: US Dist Ct PO Box 591 Madison WI 53701-0591

**SHABAZZ, DAVID LORENZO,** vocational school educator; b. Clinton, SC, Oct. 26, 1969; s. Moses Jackson Dillard and Mary Leola Byrd. BA in Journalism, Benedict Coll., 1991; MA in Mass. Comms., U. SC, 1994; MEd, Wake Forest U., 1998. Reporter SC Black Media Group, Columbia, 1989—93, Clinton (SC) Chronicle, 1991, Winston-Salem (NC) Chronicle, 1993—95; news dir. WKWQ Radio FM, Batesburg, SC, 1990—91; author, lectr. Awesome Records, Clinton, 1995—; instr. Forsyth Tech. C.C., Winston-Salem, 2001—, Ky. State U. Author: Dolemite: The Story of Rudy Ray Moore, 1996, Public Enemy Number One, 1999, Discover Your Mind, 2001. Recipient Editor's Choice award, Internat. Soc. Poets, 1999. Home: 720 Ridgeview Dr Apt 909 Frankfort KY 40601 E-mail: info@DavidShabazz.com

**SHABESTARI, KHOSROW TOUTOUNCHI (T. SHABESTARI),** research scientist; arrived in US, 2003; s. Javad Shabestari; m. Azam Akhtari, Sept. 19, 1973; 1 child, Neda. BSc, Istanbul Tech. U., Dept. of Geophysics, Istanbul, 1989; MS, Istanbul Tech. U., Istanbul, 1993; PhD, U. Tokyo, Tokyo, 1999. Geophysical, Istanbul Tech. U./Istanbul, 1989. Rsch. assistance Istanbul Tech. U., Turkey, 1990—91; rsch. assoc. Internat. Inst. of Earthquake Engring. and Seismology, Tehran, Iran, 1993—96; post doctoral fellowship U. Tokyo, 1999—2000; rsch. scientist Earthquake Disaster Mitigation Rsch. Ctr., EDM, NIED, Kobe, 2000—03, Air Worldwide, Boston, 2003—. Referee Earthquake Engring. Rsch. Inst., Oackland, Calif., 2003—, Seismology Soc. of Am., Los Alamos, N.Mex., 2004—. Contbr. scientific papers pub. to profl. jour. Scholar (monbusho) rsch. scholarship, Japanese govtl., 1996—99. Mem.: Seismol. Soc. of Japan (assoc.), Japan Assn. for Earthquake Engring. (assoc.), Japan Soc. of Civil Engring. (assoc.), Seismol. Soc. of Am. (assoc.), Earthquake Engring. Reseach Inst. (assoc.). Achievements include first to time develop JMA intesity attenuation equation for Japan site application for entire Japans rapid generation of GM maps. Office: Air Worldwide Corp 131 Dartmouth st Boston MA 02116-5134 Office Phone: 617-267-6645. Office Fax: 617-267-8284. Business E-Mail: kshabestari@air-worldwide.com.

**SHABICA, CHARLES WRIGHT,** geologist, earth science educator; b. Elizabeth, N.J., Jan. 2, 1943; s. Anthony Charles and Eleanor (Wright) S.; m. Susan Ewing, Dec. 30, 1967; children: Jonathan, Andrew, Dana. BA in Geology, Brown U., 1965; PhD, U. Chgo., 1971. Prof. earth sci. Northeastern Ill. U., Chgo., 1971—; disting. prof., 1991; pres. Shabica & Assocs. Coastal Cons., Inc., Northfield, Ill., 1985—. Chmn. bd. dirs. Aesti Corp., 1991-96; rsch. collaborator Nat. Park Svc., 1978-82, 89—; adj. prof. Coll. V.I., St. Thomas, 1980, adj. prof. environ. sci. Northwestern U., Evanston, 1999-2003; Kellogg fellow Northeastern Ill. U., 1979—; chmn. Task Force on Lake Michigan, Chgo., 1986-89; mem. Chgo. Shoreline Protection Commn., 1987-88; cons. Shedd Aquarium, Chgo., 1991; mem. Ft. Sheridan Commn., 1989-90; bd. dirs. Winnetka (Ill.) Hist. Soc. Editor: (with Andrew A. Hay) Richardson's Guide to the Fossil Fauna of Mazon Creek, 1997. Commr., packmaster Boy Scouts Am., Winnetka, Ill., 1984-88. Coop. Inst. for Limnology and Ecosystems Rsch. Lab. fellow. Mem. ASCE, Internat. Assn. for Great Lakes Rsch., Am. Shore and Beach Preservation Assn. (bd. dirs., pres. Great Lakes chpt.), Sigma Xi. Home: 326 Ridge Ave Winnetka IL 60093-3842 Office: 550 W Frontage Rd Ste 3735 Northfield IL 60093-1246 Office Phone: 847-446-1436. Personal E-mail: charles@shabica.com.

**SHABOT, MYRON MICHAEL,** critical care educator; b. Houston, Aug. 5, 1945; s. Sam and Mona Doris (Stalarow) S.; 1 child, Samuel Laib. Student, Tulane U., 1963-64; BA, U. Tex., Austin, 1966; MD, U. Tex., Dallas, 1970. Intern Parkland Meml. Hosp., Dallas, 1970—71; resident Harbor Gen. Hosp., Torrance, Calif., 1973—78; lectr. surgery UCLA Sch. Medicine, 1977-78, asst. prof., 1978-82, clin. assoc. prof. surgery and anesthesiology, 1983-97, prof. surgery, 1997—; dir. surg. ICU, LA County Harbor Med. Ctr.-UCLA Sch. Medicine, 1980-82; med. dir. Enterprise Info. Svcs. Cedars-Sinai Med. Ctr., LA, dir. surg. ICU, 1982—, vice chief of staff, 2000—01, chief of staff, 2002—03, also bd. dirs. Sec. Cedars-Sinai Med. Ctr. Attending Staff, 1999-2000; bd. dirs. eHealth Initiative and Found., 2006-. Contbr. articles to profl. jours. Served to lt. comdr. USPHS, 1971-73. Fellow ACS (So. Calif. profl. assn. Served to lt. comdr. USPHS, 1971-73. Fellow ACS (So. Calif. chpt. bd. dirs. 1988—, pres. 1992-93, gov., 1992—), Am. Coll. Critical Care Medicine, Am. Coll. Med. Informatics; mem. Western Surg. Assoc., Pacific Coast Surg. Assn., Soc. Critical Care Medicine, Am. Assn. Surgery of Trauma, Soc. Computers in Critical Care and Pulmonary Medicine (bd. dirs.

1988—, treas. 1989—, pres., 1993-94), Soc. Clin. Data Mgmt. Systems (pres. 1985-86), L.A. Surg. Soc. (pres. 1997-98), Phi Eta Sigma. Jewish. Office Phone: 310-423-5873. Business E-Mail: michael.shabot@cshs.org.

**SHACHAR, AVISHAI,** lawyer; b. Bklyn., Oct. 29, 1953; s. Zeev and Natasha (Kisler) S. m. Orly Eylan, Sept. 6, 1977; children: Carmel, Tal, Abigail. LLB magna cum laude, Tel-Aviv U., 1980; SJD, Harvard U., 1984. Bar: Israel 1983, N.Y. 1984. With Prof. Yuval Levi Law Offices, Tel-Aviv, 1979-80, Herzog, Fox, Neeman & Co., Tel-Aviv, 1980-81; assoc. Davis, Polk & Wardwell, N.Y.C., 1984-86, ptnr., 1987—, head tax practice group. Recipient acad. award Yad Avi Ha-Yishuv, Israel, 1982. Mem. ABA, Internat. Fiscal Assn., Israeli Bar Assn. Office: Davis Polk & Wardwell 450 Lexington Ave New York NY 10017 Office Phone: 212-450-4638. Office Fax: 212-450-3638. Business E-Mail: avishai.shachar@dpw.com.

**SHACK, R. BRUCE,** plastic surgeon; b. Vernon, Tex., Oct. 7, 1947; s. Nathan Lee and Patsy Lee (Holliday) S.; m. Sharon Summers Frazier, Aug. 16, 1969 (div. 1982); children: Robert David, Nathan Andrew; m. Wanda Kaye, Nov. 11, 1984; children: Jerion Elizabeth, Austin Ryan. BS, Midwestern U., 1969; MD, U. Tex., 1973. Diplomate Am. Bd. Plastic Surgery. Resident in gen. surgery Vanderbilt U. Med. Ctr., Nashville, 1973-78, resident in plastic surgery, 1978-80; asst. prof. surgery Johns Hopkins Med. Sch., Balt., 1980-82; from asst. prof. to prof., chmn. plastic surgery Vanderbilt U. Med. Ctr., 1982—. Fellow Am. Coll. Surgeons, So. Surg. Assn.; mem. AMA, Am. Assn. Plastic Surgeons, Am. Soc. Maxillofacial Surgeons, Am. Soc. Plastic Surgeons, Am. Soc. Reconstructive Microsurgery, Am. Soc. Aesthetic Plastic Surgery, H. William Scott, Jr. Soc., John B. Lynch Soc., John Staige Davis Soc. Plastic Surgeons Md., Nashville Acad. Medicine, Nashville Surg. Soc., Southeastern Soc. Plastic and Reconstructive Surgeons, So. Med. Assn., Tenn. Soc. Plastic Surgeons. Republican. Methodist. Avocations: golf, travel, shooting. Office: Vanderbilt U Med Ctr Dept Plastic Surgery D-4207 Med Center North Nashville TN 37232-2345 Office Phone: 615-936-0169. Business E-Mail: bruce.shack@vanderbilt.edu.

**SHACK, TIMOTHY G.,** information technology executive; Various info. tech.-related positions PNC, Pitts., 1976—97; chief info. officer PNC Fin. Services Corp., Pitts., 1997—; and chmn., pres., & CEO PFPC Worldwide Inc. (subs. PNC), Pitts., 2002—. Adv. bd. mem. Sch. of Info. Sci. and Tech. Penn State Univ. Office: CIO PNC Fin Svcs One PNC Plz 249 Fifth Ave Pittsburgh PA 15222-2707 also: Pres & CEO PFPC Inc 301 Bellvue Pkwy Wilmington DE 19809

**SHACKELFORD, JAMES FLOYD,** materials science educator, researcher; b. Springfield, Mo., Sept. 1, 1944; s. Amos Franklin and Opal Leona Shackelford; m. Penelope Lea Openshaw, Dec. 11, 1971; 1 child, Scott. BS, U. Wash., Seattle, 1966, MS, 1967; PhD, U. Calif., Berkeley, 1971. Postdoctoral fellow U. Calif., Berkeley, 1971, McMaster U., Hamilton, Ont., Canada, 1972—73; asst. prof. U. Calif., Davis, 1973—79, assoc. prof., 1979—84, prof., 1984—, assoc. dean, 1984—2001, dir. integrated studies honor program, 2001—. Author: Introduction to Materials Science for Engineers, 1984, 6th edit., 2005, (book) Bioceramics, 1999; editor: CRC Handbook of Materials Science and Engineering, 1992, CRC Practical Handbook of Materials Selection, 1995, CRC Materials Science and Engineering Handbook, 2nd Edition, 1994, Bioceramics - Applications of Ceramic and Glass Materials in Medicine, 1999, CRC Handbook of Materials Science and Engineering, 3rd Edition, 2001. Fellow: Am. Ceramic Soc. (Outstanding Educator 1996); mem.: ASM Internat. Office: U Calif Dept Chem Engring and Materials Sci Davis CA 95616 Business E-Mail: jfshackelford@ucdavis.edu.

**SHACKELFORD, LOTTIE HOLT,** civic worker, former mayor; b. Pulaski County, Ark., Apr. 30, 1941; d. Curtis and Bernice Linzy Holt; m. Calvin H. Shackelford Jr. (div.); children: Russell, Karla, Karen. BS, Philander Smith Coll., 1979, LHD (hon.), 1988; student, Harvard U., 1983, U. Ark., Little Rock; LHD (hon.), Shorter Coll., 1987. City dir. City of Little Rock, 1978—, mayor, 1987—91; dir. Overseas Private Investment Corp., 1993—2002; vice chmn. DNC, 1989—. Del. Italian Econ. Trade Mission, 1987, U.S.-Soviet Women's Wilderness Dialogue, USSR, 1987; panelist Harvard U. Inst. Polits. Pub. Affairs Forum, 1987; bd. dirs. Little Rock Advt. and Promotion, Econ. Opportunity Agy., Little Rock Job Corps, Elizabeth Mitchell's Children Ctr., Links, Inc.; adv. com. Ark. Vocat. and Tech. Edn., Sta. KARK-TV; speaker in field. Del., mem. platform com. Dem. Nat. Conv., 1984; vice chmn. Dem. Nat. Com.; mem. Dem. Policy Commn.; bd. dirs. Nat. League Cities, Ark. Mcpl. League, Ark. Women's Polit. Coun., Urban League, ARC, ARK. PTA, YWCA; bd. dirs. So. Regional Coun., pres., 1988-90; regional bd. dirs. Nat. Black Caucus Local Elected Ofcls., 1979-92; youth dir. St. Peter's Bapt. Ch., 1969-73; pres. Little Rock PTA Coun., 1973; coord. human and civil rights workshops, 1975-77, others. Recipient Women of Style award Pulaski County Council, 1987. Mem. Nat. Assn. State Dem. Chairmen (sec.), Links, Delta Sigma Theta, Gamma Phi Delta, Alpha Kappa Mu.

**SHACKLETON, RICHARD JAMES,** lawyer, director; b. Orange, NJ, May 24, 1933; s. S. Paul and Mildred W. (Welsh) S.; m. Katharine L. Richards, June 16, 1956; children: Katharine Margaret, Julia Anne, Forrest Maxwell. Student, Kalamazoo Coll., 1957; JD, Rutgers U., 1961. Bar: N.J. 1961, U.S. Dist. Ct. N.J. 1967, U.S. Dist. Ct. (ea. dist.) N.Y. 1987, U.S. Dist. Ct. (so. dist.) N.Y. 1986, U.S. Dist. Ct. (we. and no. dists.) N.Y. 1997, U.S. Ct. Appeals (3rd cir.) 1983, U.S. Ct. Appeals (4th cir.) 1986, U.S. Supreme Ct. 1969, Fed. Bar Coun. N.J. 1988. Ltd. atty. Berry Whitson & Berry, 1961; practice Ship Bottom, NJ, 1961—; sr. ptnr. Shackleton, Hazeltine & Dasti, Ship Bottom, NJ, 1965—, Shackleton, Hazeltine & Bishop 1984—2003, Shackleton & Hazeltine, 2003—. Exec. com., bd. dirs. Mount Pocono Water Quality Com. Mem. ABA (litigation sect., product liability com.), Am. Judicature Soc., Fed. Bar Coun. N.Y., N.J. Bar Assn., N.Y. Bar Assn., Ocean County Bar Assn., Def. Rsch. Inst. (mem. med. device and products sect.), U.S. Dist. Ct. N.J. Hist. Soc., Ocean County Lawyers Club, Henryville Conservation Club (chmn. bd.), Henryville Flyfishers Club (pres., bd. dirs., chmn.), The Anglers' Club Phila., Phila. Gun Club (bd. dirs., sec.), Sandy Island Gun Club (life, bd. dirs., pres.), NRA (life), Gun Owners Am. (life), U.S. Sportsman's Alliance, Brodhead Watershed Assn. (bd. dirs., pres. 1997-98), Brodhead Protective Assn. (bd. dirs., v.p.), Ancient Inc. Order of the Beefeater. Home: 5614 West Ave Beach Haven NJ 08008-1059 Office: 2119 Long Beach Blvd Ship Bottom NJ 08008 Office Phone: 609-494-2136. Personal E-mail: shlaw@comcast.com.

**SHACKLEY, DOUGLAS JOHN,** fire alarm company executive; b. Oakland, Calif., Sept. 21, 1938; s. Floyd H. and Margret I. Shackley; m. Chloe Jeanne Olson, Sept. 11, 1965; children: Derek Todd, Darren James, Daniel John, Christina Louise. Student, San Jose State U., 1957, Chabot Coll., 1962-63; diploma in bus. mgmt., LaSalle Extension U., 1972. Officer mgr. service dept. Am. Dist. Telegraph Co., Oakland, 1961-67; office mgr. Pacific Aux. Fire Alarm Co., San Francisco, 1967-69, mgr., 1969-73, gen. mgr., 1974—2004, pres., CEO, 2004—, also bd. dirs. Mem. task force improved fire protection Gov. of Calif., 1989; contbg. mem. Alarm Industry Telecom. Com.; pres. Dad's Club Chabot Sch., 1969—70, pres. Paren'ts Club, 1971—72; mem. Eden area YMCA, San Francisco YMCA, Boy Scouts Am.; sustaining mem. Calif. Rep. Com.; mem. Rep. Presdl. Task Force, 1994—95; moderator Eden United Ch. of Christ, 1980—81, vice moderator, 1987—88. With USMC, 1957—61. Mem.: Calif. Automatic Fire Alarm Assn. (bd. dirs. 1986—87, v.p. No. Calif. 1987—88, pres. 1988—89, bd. dirs. 1994—95, v.p. No. Calif. 1996—2000, pres. 2003, 2003—, v.p. No. Calif. 2004—, Art Kane Meml. award 2000), Nat. Automatic Fire Alarm Assn. (bd. dirs. 2003—), Nat. Fire Prevention Assn., San Francisco C. of C. (mem. code com.), Lake Mont Pine Home Owners Assn. (bd. dirs. 1988—89), Rotary. Home: 1380 Carlton Pl Livermore CA 94550-6400 Office: Pacific Aux Fire Alarm Co 95 Boutwell St San Francisco CA 94124-1903 Office Phone: 415-467-9393. Personal E-mail: doug@shackley.us. Business E-Mail: doug@pafa.com.

**SHACKMAN, DANIEL ROBERT,** psychiatrist; b. NYC, Nov. 15, 1941; s. Nathan H. and Dorothy K. Shackman. BA, Columbia U., 1962, MD, 1966. Diplomate Am. Bd. Psychiatry and Neurology. Intern Mount Sinai Hosp., N.Y.C., 1966-67, resident, chief resident, fellow, 1967-70; psychiatrist USAF, Spokane, Wash., 1970-72; clin. and adminstrv. staff Brentwood VA Hosp., L.A., 1972-79; pvt. practice psychiatry L.A., 1975-87, Santa Barbara, Calif., 1984—. Asst. clin. prof. UCLA Sch. Medicine, L.A., 1975—87; psychiat. cons. Calif. Dept. Rehab., L.A., 1975—87; cons. psychiatrist Sanctuary Psychiat. Ctrs., Santa Barbara, 1984—2001; chmn. dept. psychiatry Santa Barbara Cottage Hosp., 1990—92. Bd. dirs. Family Counseling Svc., Spokane, 1971-72. Maj. USAF, 1970-72. Mem. Am Psychiat. Assn., Am. Acad. Child/Adolescent Psychiatry, So. Calif. Psychiat. Soc. (dist. councillor 1989-92), Am. Soc. Clin. Psychopharmacology. Avocations: photography, travel, music, computer science. Office: 924 Anacapa St Santa Barbara CA 93101-2115

**SHACKOULS, BOBBY S.,** oil and gas industry executive; b. Dec. 29, 1950; BSChemE, Miss. State U. Various mgmt. positions in oil and gas industry; sr. mgmt. positions Torch Energy Advisors affil. Torchmark Corp., Plains Resources, Houston Oil & Minerals; exec. v.p., COO Burlington Resources, 1993-95, exec. v.p. Meridian Oil subs., pres., CEO oil & gas subs., 1994, pres., CEO, 1995—97, chmn., pres., CEO, 1997—2005. Bd. dir. Conoco Phillips, 2006—, Kroger Co.; treas. Am. Petroleum Inst. Vice chmn. Tex. Heart Inst.; mem. nat. bd., mem. exec. bd. Houston area council Boy Scouts Am. Mailing: Conoco Phillips Bd Directors PO Box 2197 Houston TX 77252-2197*

**SHACTER, JAMES DETMERS,** editor, writer; b. Chgo., Apr. 14, 1926; s. Joseph Andrew and Helen Seidman Shacter; m. Nancy Louise Blankenberg, Dec. 30, 1997; m. Ruth Evelyn Bjorn, Aug. 1, 1958 (dec. Sept. 5, 1994); 1 child, Joseph Edwin. BS, U. Ill., 1948. Copy editor UP, Milw., Chgo., Detroit, Washington, N.Y.C., 1947—55; chief copy editor World Book Ency., Chgo., 1955—81; freelance editor, writer Chgo., 1981—. Author: Piano Man, 1975, Loose Shoes, 1994, Jazz Party, 2000. Yeoman 3d class USN, 1944—46. Avocation: traditional jazz.

**SHADDOCK, CARROLL SIDNEY,** lawyer; b. Beaumont, Tex., July 7, 1940; s. Carroll Bitting Jr. and Hulda Martha (Gaertner) S.; m. Dorothea Schulze, Nov. 30, 1963; children: Carroll Christian, Peter Eric, Matthew Nolan. BA, Rice U., 1962; JD, Yale U., 1965. Ptnr. Locke Liddell & Sapp LLP, Houston, 1967—. Chmn. Scenic Am., Washington, 1985-92, Scenic Tex., 1992—, Trees for Houston, 1982—; Billboards Limited, Houston, 1982-92. Republican. Avocations: music, golf, travel. Home: 1715 South Blvd Houston TX 77098-5419 Office: Locke Liddell & Sapp LLP JP Morgan Chase Tower 600 Travis St Ste 3400 Houston TX 77002-3095 E-mail: cshaddock@lockeliddell.com.

**SHADDOX, MICHAEL SCOTT,** social studies educator; b. Harrison, Ark., Jan. 6, 1967; s. Jack Rowland and Rebecca Sue Shaddox; m. Darlene Janette Rogers, Nov. 25, 1994; children: Rachel Darlene, Emily Katherine, Jackson Isaiah. AS, North Ark. Coll., Harrison, Ark., 1988; BS in Edn., U. Cntl. Ark., Conway, Ark., 1990. Cert. tchr. Ark., 1991. Tchr. Elmdale Elem. Sch., Springdale, Ark., 1991—93; tchr., coach Lead Hill (Ark.) Pub. Schs., 1993—95; tchr. Omaha (Ark.) Pub. Schs., 1995—, coach, 1994—2004. Named Tchr. of Yr., Southshore Found., 2005. Mem.: Son's Confederate Vets. Republican. Bapt. Home: 2552 Lacy Lane Harrison AR 72601 Office: Omaha Public Schools 522 W College Road Omaha AR 72601 Office Phone: 870-426-3366. Personal E-mail: badshad@alltel.net.

**SHADEGG, JOHN BARDEN,** congressman; b. Phoenix, Oct. 22, 1949; s. Stephen and Eugenia Shadegg; m. Shirley Shadegg; children: Courtney, Stephen. BA, U. Ariz., 1972, JD, 1975. Advisor U.S. Sentencing Commn.; spl. asst. atty. gen. State of Ariz., 1983-90; spl. counsel Ariz. State Ho. Rep. Caucus, 1991-92; pvt. practice; mem. U.S. Congress from 4th Ariz. dist., 1995—, asst. whip; mem. commerce com., fin. svcs. com., homeland sec. com. Mem. Victims Bill of Rights Task Force, 1989-90; mem. Fiscal Accountability and Reform Efforts Com., 1991-92; counsel Arizonian's for Wildlife Conservation, 1992; chmn. Proposition 108-Two-Thirds Tax Limitation Initiative, 1992. Rep. Party Ballot Security chmn., 1982; active Corbin for Atty. Gen., 1982-86; Rep. Precinct committeeman; chmn. Ariz. Rep. Caucus, 1985-87; chmn. Ariz. Lawyers for Bush-Quayle, 1988; mem. steering com., surrogate spkr. Jon Kyl for Congress, 1988-92; former pres. Crime Victim Found.; founding dir. Goldwater Inst. Pub. Policy; chmn. Ariz. Juvenile Justice Adv. Coun.; mem. adv. bd. Salvation Army; mem. vestry Christ Ch. of Ascension, 1989-91; mem. class II Valley Leadership; bd. dirs. Ariz. State U. Law Soc. Republican. Episcopalian. Office: US Ho Reps 306 Cannon Ho Office Bldg Washington DC 20515-0001

**SHADER, RICHARD IRWIN,** psychiatrist, pharmacologist, educator; b. Mt. Vernon, NY, May 27, 1935; s. Myer and Beatrice (Epstein) Shader; m. Aline Brown, Sept. 21, 1958 (dec. Aug. 10, 2002); children: Laurel Beth, Jennifer Robin, Robert Andrew; m. Cynthia H. Livingston, Dec. 6, 2003. Student, Harvard U., 1952-56; MD, NYU, 1960; grad., Boston Psychoanalytic Inst., 1970. Diplomate Am. Bd. Psychiatry and Neurology (dir. 1977-84, treas. 1982-83, pres. 1984). Intern Greenwich Hosp., Conn., 1960-61; resident in psychiatry Mass. Mental Health Ctr., Boston, 1961-62, 64-65, NIMH, Bethesda, Md., 1962-64; assoc. chief psychiatry Harvard Med. Sch., 1970-79; psychiatrist in chief New Eng. Med. Ctr. Hosp., Boston, 1979-91; prof. dept. psychiatry Tufts U. Med. Sch., Boston, 1979—, chmn. dept., 1979-91, prof. pharmacology, 1989—, chmn. dept. pharmacology and exptl. therapeutics, 1991-93, dir. grad. program dept. pharmacology and exptl. therapeutics, 1999—. Author (with A. DiMascio): Psychotropic Drug Sides Effects, 1970; author (with D. J. Greenblatt) Benzodiazepines in Clinical Practice, 1974; author: Manual of Psychiatric Therapeutics, 1975, 3d edit., 2004; editor: Psychiatric Complications of Medical Drugs, 1972; editor: (with A. DiMascio) Clinical Handbook of Psychopharmacology, 1970, Butyrophenones in Psychiatry, 1972; editor: (with D. J. Greenblatt) Pharmacokinetics in Clinical Practice, 1985, MAOI Therapy, 1988; editor: (with J. P. Tupin and D. S. Harnett) Handbook of Clinical Psychopharmacology, 1988; editor: (with D.A. Ciraulo) Pharmacotherapy of Depression, 2004; editor: (with others) Drug Interactions in Psychiatry, 1989, 3d edit., 2005; editor: Clinical Manual of Chemical Dependence, 1991; editor-in-chief Jour. Clin. Psychopharmacology, 1980—. Bd. dirs. Med. Found., Inc., 1980—87. With USPHS, 1962—64. Recipient Seymor Vestermark award, Am. Psychiat. Assn., 1988, 1990; fellow, Ctr. Advanced Study Behavioral Scis., Stanford, Calif., 1990—91; Joseph J. Michaels Merit scholar, 1968—69. Fellow: Am. Coll. Neuropsychopharmacology (v.p. 1984, pres. 1990, emeritus 2005, life emeritus); mem.: AMA (emeritus), Am. Soc. Pharmacology and Exptl. Therapeutics, Am. Soc. Clin. Pharmacology and Therapeutics (emeritus), Mass. Med. Soc. (emeritus,). Democrat. Jewish.

**SHADID, ANTHONY,** journalist; b. Okla. married; 1 child. Student, U. Okla.; B in journalism, U. Wis., Madison, 1990; postgrad., Columbia U., 1993—94. With AP, Milw., 1990—93; editor AP Internat. Desk, NYC, 1993—95; reporter, editor AP, Cairo, 1995—99, news editor LA, 1999—2000; reporter, diplomacy, State Dept. Boston Globe, 2000—03; Islamic affairs corr., Middle East Wash. Post, 2003—. Author: (book) Legacy of the Prophet: Despots, Democrats and the New Politics of Islam, 2002, Night Draws Near: Iraq's People in the Shadow of America's War, 2005. Named Joe Alex Morris Jr. Meml. Lectr., Nieman Found. Journalism, Harvard U., 2004; recipient Bob Considine award, Overseas Press Club, 1997, Ralph O. Nafziger award for disting. achievement, U. Wis., Madison, 2002, George Polk award for foreign reporting, 2003, Pulitzer Prize for internat. reporting, 2004, Michael Kelly Award, Atlantic Media Co., 2004; fellow in Arabic language, Am. U. Cairo, 1991—92. Fluent in Arabic. Office: Middle East Bur c/o Washington Post 1150 15th St NW Washington DC 20071

**SHADLEY, ROBERT D.,** retired army officer; b. Circleville, Ohio, Aug. 5, 1942; BS in Indsl. Engring., MS in Indsl. Engring., Purdue U.; M of Mil. Arts and Scis., Army Command/Gen. Staff Coll. Commd. 2d lt. U.S. Army, 1965, advanced through grades to maj. gen., 1997; served in Vietnam and Desert Shield/Desert Storm; exec.officer to the comdg. gen. U.S. Army Materiel Command, 1992-94; dir. for logistics U.S. Atlantic Command, 1994-95; chief of ordnance, comdg. gen. U.S. Army Ordnance Ctrs. and Schs., 1995-97; dep. comdg. gen. for ordnance U.S. Army Combined Arms Support Command, Aberdeen Proving Ground, Md.; dep. chief of staff for logistics Hdqrs. U.S. Army Forces Command, Ft. McPherson, Ga., 1997-2000. Decorated Disting. Svc. medal, Legion of Merit with 2 oak leaf clusters, Bronze Star medal with oak leaf cluster, others. Address: Alliant Techsystems MN07-ME10 4700 Nathan Ln North Plymouth MN 55442-2512

**SHADUR, MILTON IRVING,** judge; b. St. Paul, June 25, 1924; s. Robert and Mary Shadur; m. Eleanor Pilka, Mar. 30, 1946; children: Robert, Karen, Beth. BS, U. Chgo., 1943, JD cum laude, 1949. Bar: Ill. 1949, U.S. Supreme Ct. 1957. Pvt. practice, Chgo., 1949-80; assoc. Goldberg, Devoe & Brussell, 1949-51; ptnr. Shadur, Krupp & Miller and predecessor firms, 1951-80; judge U.S. Dist. Ct. (no. dist.) Ill., Chgo., 1980-92, sr. judge, 1992—. Commr. Ill. Supreme Ct. Character and Fitness, 1961-72, chmn., 1971; gen. counsel Ill. Jud. Inquiry Bd., 1975-80; chmn. adv. com. on evidence rules to Jud. Conf. of U.S., 1999-2002, mem. adv. com., 1992-99. Editor-in-chief: U. Chgo. Law Rev., 1948-49. Chmn. visiting com. U. Chgo. Law Sch., 1971-76, mem. vis. com., 1989-92, 99-2002; bd. dirs. Legal Assistance Found. Chgo., 1972-78; trustee Village of Glencoe, 1969-74, Ravinia Festival Assn., 1976-93, exec. com. 1983-93, vice chmn. 1989-93, life trustee, 1994— Lt (j g.) USNR, 1943-46. Fellow Am. Bar Found.; mem. ABA (spl. com. on youth edn. for citizenship 1975-79), Ill. State Bar Assn. (joint com. on rules of jud. conduct 1974), Chgo. Bar Assn. (chmn. legis. com. 1963-65, jud. com. 1970-71, profl. ethics com. 1975-76, sec. 1967-69), Chgo. Council Lawyers, Order of Coif. Office: US Dist Ct 219 S Dearborn St Ste 2388 Chicago IL 60604-1800 Office Phone: 312-435-5766.

**SHADYAC, THOMAS,** film director, producer; b. Falls Church, Va., 1960; m. Richard Shadyac. Grad., U. Va.; MA in Film, UCLA, 1989. Stand-up comedian Improv, L.A. Motion pictures include: (dir.) Ace Ventura: Pet Detective, 1994, The Nutty Professor, 1996, Liar, Liar, 1997; (dir., prodr.) Patch Adams, 1998, Dragonfly, 2002, Bruce Almighty, 2003; (prodr.) Nutty Professor II: the Klumps, 2000, Accepted, 2006; TV movies: (dir.) Frankenstein: The College Years, 1991. TV series: (exec. prodr.) 8 Simple Rules for Dating My Teenage Daughter, 2002-05. Office: United Talent Agy care Dan Aloni 9560 Wilshire Blvd Fl 5 Beverly Hills CA 90212-2400*

**SHAEFFER, JOHN NEES,** historian, educator; b. Wapato, Wash., Dec. 7, 1929; s. John Nees Shaeffer and Helen May Kerns. BA, Wash. State U., 1953; AM, Harvard U., 1957; PhD, U. Wis., 1968. Instr. history Columbia Basin Coll., Pasco, Wash., 1957—63; prof. history Calif. State U., Northridge, 1968—92, prof. emeritus, 1992—. Contbr. articles to profl. jours. 1st lt. USAF, 1953—57, Korea. Mem.: Orgn. Am. Historians (life), Am. Hist. Assn. (life), Phi Kappa Phi (life).

**SHAEVSKY, MARK,** lawyer; b. Harbin, Manchuria, China, Dec. 2, 1935; came to U.S., 1938, naturalized, 1944; s. Tolio and Rae (Weinstein) S.; m. Lois Ann Levi, Aug. 2, 1964; children: Thomas Lyle, Lawrence Keith. Student, Wayne State U., Detroit, 1952—53; BA with highest distinction, U. Mich., Ann Arbor, 1956; JD with highest distinction, U. Mich., 1959. Bar: Mich. 1959. Law clerk to presiding judge U.S. Dist. Ct., Detroit, 1960-61; assoc. Honigman Miller Schwartz & Cohn, Detroit, 1961-64; ptnr. Honigman, Miller, Schwartz & Cohn, Detroit, 1965-69, sr. ptnr., 1969—2001, of counsel, 2001—05; prin., owner Mark Shaevsky & Assocs., LLC, Detroit, 2006—. Instr. law Wayne State U. Law Sch., Detroit, 1961-64; comml. arbitrator Am. Arbitration Assn., Detroit; bd. dir. Charter One Fin. Inc., Charter One Bank, H.W. Kaufman Fin. Group, Inc., Freya Fanning Mgmt., LLC, USF Ins. Co. Contbr. Wayne State U. Law Rev., U. Mich. Law Rev., 1957-59, asst. editor, 1958-59. Dir. Detroit Mens Orgn. of Rehab. through Tng., 1969—79; trustee William Beaumont Hosp., 1997—, Beaumont Found., 1997—2005; Jewish Vocat. Svcs., 1973—76; mem. exec. bd. Am. Jewish Com., 1965—74; sec., dir. Am. Friends Hebrew U., 1976—84; mem. capital needs com. Jewish Welfare Fedn., 1986—97; bd. dir. William Beaumont Hosp., 2002—, Shaevsky Family Found., 2000—. With U.S. Army, 1959—60. Burton Abstract fellow, 1959. Mem. ABA, Mich. Bar Assn., Franklin Hills Country Club, Detroit Athletic Club, Order of the Coif, Phi Beta Kappa. Home: The Hills of Lone Pine 4750 N Chipping Gln Bloomfield Hills MI 48302-2390 Office: Mark Shaevsky & Assocs LLC 30883 Northwestern Hwy Ste 200 Farmington Hills MI 48334 Office Phone: 248-737-0808. Business E-Mail: advisors@honigman.com

**SHAFER, BARBARA HOUGH,** retired secondary school educator; b. Ft. Myers, Fla., Apr. 16, 1928; d. Wendell M. and Jeannette (Carmichael) Hough; m. Robert T. Shafer, Jr., Dec. 27, 1950; children: Richard, Janet, Charles. BA, Coll. Wooster, 1950; MA, U. South Fla., 1982. Tchr. Wooster High Sch. (Ohio), 1950-51; tchr. Ft. Myers High Sch., 1951—53, volleyball coach, 1969—85, tchr., coord. girls sports, 1969—91, ret., 1991; tchr. Withrow High Sch. (Cin.), 1953—55, Bishop Verot HS, Ft. Myers, 1965—69. Vol. ARC, 1970—; mem. steering com. for girls sports State of Fla., 1974—76; Lee County steering com. for girls sports, 1974—76. Republican. Presbyterian. Home: 5879 Key Lime Way Fort Myers FL 33919

**SHAFER, BYRON EDWIN,** American government educator; b. Hanover, Pa., Jan. 8, 1947; s. Byron Henry and Doris Marguerite (von Bergen) S.; m. Wanda Kathleen McFrn. Aug. 22, 1981. BA, Yale U., 1968, PhD U Calif. Berkeley, 1979; MA, Oxford U., 1985. Andrew W. Mellon prof. Am. govt. Oxford (Eng.) U., 1985-2001; Hawkins prof. public. sci. U. Wis., Madison, 2001—. Author: Presidential Politics, 1983, Quiet Revolution, 1983, Bifurcated Politics, 1988, Is America Different?, 1991, The End of Realignment?, 1991, The Two Majorities, 1995, Postwar Politics in the G-7, 1996, Present Discontents, 1996, Partisan Approaches to American Politics, 1998, Contesting Democracy, 2001, The State of American Politics, 2002, The Two Majorities and the Puzzle of Modern American Politics, 2003, The End of Southern Exceptionalism, 2005. Resident scholar Russell Sage Found., N.Y.C., 1977-85; recipient Schattschneider prize Am. Polit. Assn., 1980, Burdette prize, 1990, Party Politics prize, 2003. Mem.: Phi Beta Kappa. Lutheran. Avocations: gardening, livestock management, furniture restoration. Home: Nether Blenheim 10621 W Blue Mounds Rd Blue Mounds WI 53517 Office: U Wis Dept Polit Sci Madison WI 53706-1389 Office Phone: 608-263-1909. Business E-Mail: bshafer@polisci.wisc.edu.

**SHAFER, ERIC CHRISTOPHER,** minister; b. Hanover, Pa., Apr. 10, 1950; s. B. Henry and Doris M. (Von Bergen) S.; m. Kristi L. Owens, Nov. 24, 1973. BA, Muhlenberg Coll., 1972; MDiv, Hamma Sch. Theology, 1976. Ordained to ministry Luth. Ch. Am., 1976. Pastor Holy Trinity Meml. Luth. Ch., Catasauqua, Pa., 1976-83; asst. to Bishop Northeastern Pa. Synod, Wescosville, Pa., 1983-92; staff commr. for ministry Evang. Luth. Ch. in Am., Chgo., 1988-92, asst. dir. dept. for comm., 1992-93, dir. dept. for comm., 1993—. Contbg. editor The Lutheran mag., 1989-92. Trustee Muhlenberg Coll., Allentown, Pa., 1972-83; bd. dirs. Luth. Film Assn., 1993—; chmn. commn. commn. Nat. Coun. Chs. in USA, 1996—2003, mem. exec. bd., 1996—2003. Democrat. Lutheran. Avocations: running, computers, photography, travel. Office: Evang Luth Ch in Am 8765 W Higgins Rd Chicago IL 60631-4178 Office Phone: 773-380-2960. Business E-Mail: eric.shafer@elca.org.

**SHAFER, JOHN ERIC,** art educator; b. Lima, Ohio, Oct. 8, 1970; s. George Ronald and Kathleen Ann Shafer; m. Deborah Ann Ruhrkraut, Dec. 16, 1995; children: Maxwell, Ronald, Samuel, John. BA, Baldwin-Wallace Coll., 1993; M in curriculum and instruction, Ashland U., 2002. Lic. tchr. Ohio. Sub. tchr. Painesville Twp. Sch., Painesville, Ohio, 1995; art tchr. Willoughby-Eastlake City Sch., Willowick, Ohio, 1995—2003; art. tchr. Cuyahoga Heights City,

Cuyahoga Heights, Ohio, 2003—. Asst. coach Varsity Football, Eastlake, Ohio, 1997—2000. Nominee Nat. Outstanding Art Educator, Walt Disney, 2001. Mem.: Nat. Edn. Assns., Ohio Art Edn. Assn., Ohio Mid. Sch. Assn. Republican. Avocations: theater, hunting, sports. Office: Cuyahoga Heights HS 4820 E 71st St Garfield Heights OH 44125 Home: 18158 Treasure Isle Cir Strongsville OH 44136-8030 Office Phone: 216-429-5705 5740. E-mail: jshafer@cuyhts.k12.oh.us.

**SHAFER, JOHN MILTON,** hydrologist, consultant, data processing executive; b. Findlay, Ohio, Mar. 18, 1951; s. Paul Eugene and Mary Ethel (Schwyn) S.; m. Elise Ann Dunne, Apr. 11, 1980; children: Paul Emery, Jessica Elise, Elise Ann. BS in Earth Sci., Pa. State U., 1973; MS in Resource Devel., Mich. State U., 1975; PhD in Civil Engring., Colo. State U., 1979. Cert. hydrologist #218. Asst. rsch. prof. Colo. State U., Fort Collins, 1979-80; rsch. engr. Battelle Meml. Inst., Richland, Wash., 1980-83, sr. rsch. engr., 1983-84; hydrologist Ill. State Water Survey, Champaign, 1984-85, asst. head ground water sect., 1985-90, prin. hydrologist, 1988-91, head hydrology div., 1990-92; assoc. dir., rsch. prof. Earth Scis. and Resources Inst., U. S.C., Columbia, 1992-95, dir., 1995—. Cons. pvt. cos., 1984—; owner GWPATH, Columbia, S.C., 1992; v.p Environ. and Archtl. Signage, Findlay, Ohio; prin. hydrologist, co-owner Applied Hydrogeologic Rsch., Inc., Seattle, 1995-00. Developer software, 1987; contbr. articles to profl. jours. Recipient John C. Frye Meml. award in geology, 1991, Ill. Groundwater Sci. Achievement award, 1993. Mem. Intergovt. Coord. Com. Groundwater, Am. Geophys. Union, Am. Inst. Hydrology (pres. Ill. sect. 1985-92), Nat. Ground Water Assn., Ill. Groundwater Assn., Sigma Xi. Presbyterian. Avocations: tennis, handball, woodworking, model building. Home: 321 Lake Front Dr Columbia SC 29212-2426 Office: Earth Scis Resouces Inst U SC 901 Sumter St Columbia SC 29201-3961 Office Phone: 803-777-6484. Business E-Mail: jshafer@sc.rr.com.

**SHAFER, MICHAEL GALES,** priest; b. NYC, Mar. 12, 1941; s. Judson Bell Shafer and Helene Gales; m. Johanna Marie Bauby, June 17, 1967; children: Reuben, Gail. BA, Bard Coll., 1966; STB, Berkeley Div. Sch., 1969. Curate Holy Trinity Ch., Valley Stream, NY, 1969—71; rector St. John's Parish, Lewisboro, NY, 1971—85; asst. min. St. Peter's Ch., Albany, NY, 1986—88; priest-in-charge Trinity Ch., Watervliet, NY, 1989—95, St. Luke's Ch., Chatham, NY, 1995—2000, Episcopal Ch. Regeneration, Pine Plains, NY, 2000—. Coord. juvenile sex offender treatment program La Salle Sch., Albany, 1989—99. Author: (book) Old Values for a New Generation, 2002. Vol. chaplain Taconic Correctional Facility, Bedford Hills, NY, 1980—86; com. mem. Young Life Mid Hudson Valley. With USNR, 1960—62. Mem.: Am. Legion Chaplains, Rotary Club (pres. 1993). Democrat. Episcopalian. Avocations: tennis, golf. Home: 21 Decker Rd Stanfordville NY 12581 Office: Episcopla Ch Regeneration 18 Pine St Pine Plains NY 12567

**SHAFER, ROBERT TINSLEY, JR.,** judge; b. Cin., Sept. 11, 1929; s. Robert Tinsley and Grace Elizabeth (Welsh) S.; m. Barbara Jean Hough, Dec. 27, 1950; children: Richard Hough, Janet Lee Shafer Davis, Charles Welsh. BA, Coll. of Wooster, 1951; JD, U. Cin., 1956. Bar: Fla. 1956, U.S. Ct. Appeals (5th cir.) 1963, U.S. Dist. Ct. (so. dist.) Fla. 1961, U.S. Supreme Ct. 1965. Asst. trust officer 1st Nat. Bank, Ft. Myers, Fla., 1956-57; ptnr. Henderson, Franklin, Starnes & Holt, P.A., Ft. Myers, 1957-77; cir. judge 20th Jud. Cir. State of Fla., Ft. Myers, 1977-92, chief cir. judge, 1985-89, sr. judge, 1992—2004. Former mem. com. for ret. and sr. judges Nat. Conf. State Trial Judges. Contbr. article to Corp. Law, 1955-56 (Goldsmith Corp. Law prize, 1956). Elder Covenant Presbyn. Ch., 1982-85; mem. jud. commn. Fla. Presbyn. Synod, 1960-63; chmn. Lee County chpt. Red Cross, Ft. Myers, 1963; chair Permanent Judicial Commn., Peace River Presbytery, Presbyn. Ch. U.S.A., 2001-05, mem. Permanent Judicial Commn., South Atlantic Synod., Presbyn. Ch. U.S.A., 2005—, pres. S.W. Fla. Hist. Soc. 2003-2005. 2nd lt. USMCR, 1951-53, PTO, Korea. Mem. ABA, Fla. Conf. Cir. Judges (exec. com. 1986-88), Fla. Bar Assn. (bd. govs. Jr. Bar sect. 1961-64), Lee County Bar Assn. (pres. 1968), Am. Judicature Soc., Nat. Conf. Met. Cts. Calusa Inn of Ct. Republican. Avocations: bicycling, travel, reading, walking. Home: 5879 Key Lime Way Fort Myers FL 33919

**SHAFF, KAREN E.,** lawyer, insurance company executive; BA, Northwestern U., Evanston, Ill.; JD, Drake U., Des Moines. Atty. Austin and Gaudineer, Des Moines, 1979—82, Principal Fin. Group, 1982—83, asst. counsel, 1983—86, assoc. counsel, 1986—90, sr. v.p., gen. counsel, 1999—2004, exec. v.p., 2004—, gen. counsel, 2004—. Bd. mem. Hospice of Ctrl. Iowa Found., Sci. Ctr. of Iowa. Mem.: ABA, Am. Life Ins. Coun., Am. Corp. Counsel Assn., Polk County Bar Assn., Iowa Bar Assn., Am. Coun. Life Ins. Office: Principal Fin Group 711 High St Des Moines IA 50392

**SHAFFER, BERNARD WILLIAM,** mechanical and aerospace engineering educator; b. N.Y.C., Aug. 7, 1924; s. Abraham and Eva (Ellinsky) S.; m. Florence Solow, Feb. 23, 1947 (dec. Oct. 29, 1986); children: Janet Ilene, Roberta Franceen. BME, CCNY, 1944; MSME, Case Inst. Tech. (now Case W. Res. U.), 1947; PhD, Brown U., 1951. Registered profl. engr., N.Y., R.I. Aero. rsch. scientist flight propulsion rsch. lab. NACA (now NASA), Cleve., 1944-47; spl. lectr. applied mechanics Case Inst. Tech. (now Case Western Reserve Univ.), Cleve., 1946-47; rsch. assoc., grad. div. applied math. and engring. instr. Brown U., Providence, 1947-50; asst. prof. mech. engring. NYU, N.Y.C., 1950-53, assoc. prof., 1953-58, prof., project dir. rsch. divsn., 1958-73; prof. dept. mech. and aerospace engring. Poly. U., Bklyn. and Farmingdale, NY, 1973-93, prof. emeritus, 1993—. Cons. in field; mem. adv. coun. Coll. Aeros., N.Y.C., 1982—; vis. rsch. prof. mech. engring. Fla. Atlantic U., Boca Raton, 1992, Disting. vis. rsch. prof., 1993-95, 97—. Contbr. articles to profl. jours. Bd. dirs. Harbor Hills Civic Assn., Great Neck, N.Y., 1968-71. With USAAF, 1944-47. Recipient various govt. grants. Fellow ASME (Kraciech Meml. award 1968); mem. AIAA (assoc. fellow), Sigma Xi, Tau Beta Pi, Pi Tau Sigma. Avocations: golf, swimming.

**SHAFFER, DAVID JAMES,** lawyer; b. Springfield, Ohio, July 30, 1958; s. Frank James Shaffer and Martha Isabelle (Hardman) Matthews; children: Brynn Danielle, Jedediah Clay. BA, Wittenberg U., 1980; JD, Stanford U., 1983. Bar: Calif. 1984, U.S. Dist. Ct. (no. and ea. dists.) Calif. 1984, U.S. Ct. Appeals (9th cir.) 1984, U.S. Dist. Ct. (so. dist.) Calif. 1985, U.S. Dist. Ct. (we. dist.) Wash. 1986, D.C. 1988, U.S. Dist. Ct. D.C. 1988, U.S. Ct. Appeals (D.C. cir.) 1988, U.S. Dist. Ct. (no. dist.) Tex. 1991, U.S. Supreme Ct. 1993, Md. 1994, U.S. Dist. Ct. Md. 1997. Supr. field ops. U.S. Census Bur., Columbus, Ohio, 1980; legal intern Natural Resources Def. Coun., Inc., San Francisco, 1982-83; assoc. Gibson, Dunn & Crutcher, San Jose, Calif., 1983; law clk. to Judge Betty B. Fletcher, U.S. Ct. Appeals for 9th Cir., Seattle, 1983-84; assoc. Gibson, Dunn & Crutcher, San Jose, 1984-87, Arnold & Porter, Washington, 1987-92; ptnr. Semmes, Bowen & Semmes, Washington, 1992-94, Arter & Hadden, Washington, 1995-99, Thelen Reid & Priest LLP, Washington, 1999—. Contbr. articles to profl. and legal jours. Campaign mgr. Clark County Dem. Party, Springfield, 1978-80; organizer Citizens for Sensible County Planning, Fairfax, Va., 1989-94. Alumni scholar Wittenberg U., 1976. Mem. ABA, FBA (chmn. EEO com. 1992-94, individual rights and responsibilities 1994-95, co-chmn. alt. dispute resolution 1995-96, mem. governing bd. labor law and labor rels. sect., editor newsletter Labouring Oar, Outstanding Svc. award 1992), D.C. Bar Assn., Calif. Bar Assn., Order of Coif. Avocations: music, hiking, nature study. Office: Thelen Reid & Priest LLP 701 Pennsylvania Ave NW Washington DC 20004-2608 E-mail: dshaffer@thelenreid.com.

**SHAFFER, DENNY RICHARD,** small business owner; b. Altoona, Pa., Feb. 13, 1931; s. Melvin Anson and Mildred Catherine Shaffer; m. Kim Martin, May 6, 1984; 1 child, Francesca Martin; m. Betty Blair (dec. Dec. 1972); children: Robert Daniel, David Richard. BBA, U. Pitts., 1952; student, Inst. for Advanced Pastorial Studies, Bloomsfield Hill, Mich., 1968. Mar. One Hour Koretizing / One Hour Martinizing, Fayetteville, NC, 1954—66, Burlington, 1954—66, Durham, 1954—66, Rocky Mount, 1954—66, Charleston, SC, 1954—66; v.p. One Hour Koretizing, Lynchburg, NC, 1962—66; field mgr. One Hour Valet, Miami, Fla., 1963—65; pres. Kore-O-Mat of Fayetteville, 1965—2003, One Hour Koretizing, Fayetteville,

1966—99, Shaffer Mgmt. Co., Fayetteville, 1966—99; ptnr. Scots Hills Floral Nursery, Cameron, NC, 1968—75. Author: (oral history forward) Ted Synder, 1984, Brock Evans, 1987, (book forward) Images of Wilderness, 1993. Mem. Fayetteville City Coun., 1967—71; del. Sierra Club Coun., San Francisco, 1972—77; lobbyist Easter Wilderness Bill, Washington, 1974, chmn. nat. membership com., 1976—79; nat. bd. dirs. Sierra Club, Washington, 1977—84, bd. dirs., 1985—91, 1994—97; pres. Nat. Sierra Club, 1982—84, treas., CFO, 1978—82, 1985—86, 1994—95, sec., 1997, v.p. for planning, v.p. for electorial politics, 1982—85, 1987—94; mem. bd. trustees The Sierra Club Found., 1979—86, 1991—94; founding mem. Sierra Club of Fayetteville, NC Group, 1970; chmn. NC Conservation, 1972—74; exec. com. mem Sierra Club Coun., 1974—77; founding dir. Hillsboro St. Sch., 1958, Spainhour Sch., 1967—84, The People's Clinic, 1968—72. Recipient Gov.'s award, 1983, Realtor's Cup, Fayetteville C. of C., 1967, William Colby award, Sierra Club, 1996, Disting. Environ. Series, Bancroft Libr., 2003, U. Calif., Berkley, 2003, Order of the Long Leaf Pine, State of N.C., 2003. Democrat. Presbyterian. Avocations: golf, hiking. Home: 2910 Skye Dr Fayetteville NC 28303-5925

**SHAFFER, EARL E., JR.,** music educator; m. Ellen Shaffer. B of Music Edn., James Madison U., 1980. Dir. bands Covington HS, Covington, Va., 1980—89, Lloyd C. Bird HS, Chesterfield, Va., 1989—. Named to VBODA Honor Band Directors Hall of Fame. Home: 12207 Swift Crossing Dr Midlothian VA 23112 Office: Lloyd C Bird HS 10301 Courthouse Rd Chesterfield VA 23832 Office Phone: 804-768-6110. Office Fax: 804-768-6117. Business E-Mail: earl_shaffer@ccpsnet.net.

**SHAFFER, GAIL DOROTHY,** secondary school educator; b. Summit, N.J., May 7, 1936; d. Franklin Clifford Jr. and Mildred Edna (Burgmiller) S. AB, Hood Coll., 1958. Tchr. Sherman Sch., Cranford, N.J., 1959-60, Gov. Livingston High Sch., Berkeley Heights, N.J., 1960—. Vol. intake worker Covenant House, N.Y.C., 1982-92, spkrs. bur., 1986—, bd. dirs., Newark, 1993—; mem. juvenile conf. Family Ct. Union County, Elizabeth, N.J., 1968—; project dir. Berkeley Heights (N.J.) Alliance Against Drugs and Alcohol, 1990-95; active Berkeley Heights Youth Com., 1960-65. Named Berkeley Heights Citizen of Yr. by Jr. C. of C., Speaker of Yr. by Covenant House Corp., Vol. of Yr. by Covenent House, Union County Tchr. of Yr., 1992-93, N.J. State Tchr. of Yr., 1992-93. Mem. DAR (Beacon Fire chpt.), ASCID, NEA, N.J. Edn. Assn., N.J. State Tchrs. of the Yr. (pres.), Union County Edn. Assn. Republican. Methodist. Avocations: reading, travel, U.S. history, needlework, victoriana. Home: 522 Plainfield Ave Berkeley Heights NJ 07922-1919 also: 7 Embury Ave Ocean Grove NJ 07756-1354 Office: Gov Livingston High Sch 175 Watchung Blvd Berkeley Heights NJ 07922-2799

**SHAFFER, MARGARET MINOR,** retired library director; b. New Orleans, Sept. 20, 1940; d. Milhado Lee and Margaret Minor (Krumbhaar) S. BS, Nicholls State U., Thibodaux, La., 1962; MLS, La. State U., 1965. Asst. dir. Terrebonne Parish Pub. Libr., Houma, La., 1965-72, dir., 1973-95; ret., 1995. Named Woman of Yr., Houma Bus. and Profl. Women's Club, 1981. Mem. ALA, La. Libr. Assn. (chmn. pub. libr. com. 1986-87), Southeastern Libr. Assn. Democrat. Episcopalian. Avocations: crafts, travel. Home: 2678 Highway 311 Schriever LA 70395-3240

**SHAFFER, OREN GEORGE,** former manufacturing company executive; b. Sharpsville, Pa., Aug. 13, 1942; s. Oren G. and Alice Marie (Miller) S.; m. Evelyne Soussan, Oct. 2, 1965; children: Kathleen K., Oren O. BSBA, U. Calif., Berkeley, 1968; MS, MIT, 1985. Mem. internal tng. squad Goodyear Tire and Rubber Co., Akron, Ohio, 1968-69, asst. comptr., 1983-84, v.p., treas., 1985-87, exec. v.p., CFO, 1987-90; mem. fin. staff Goodyear SA, Diegem, Belgium, 1969-70, fin. mgr. Benelux, 1970-75; CFO, Goodyear France, Paris, 1975-80, pres., 1981-83; CFO, Goodyear Tyre and Rubber Co., Wolverhampton, England, 1980-81; exec. v.p., CFO Ameritech Corp., Chgo., 1994-2000; pres., COO Sorrento Networks Corp., San Diego, 2000—02, advisor, 2000—02; vice chmn., CFO Quest Communications Internat., Denver, 2002—. Bd. dir. Belgacom, Brussels, 2004—, Singapore Equity Fund. Bd. dirs. Akron Priority Corp., pres. 1987. Recipient Chevalier de L'Order du Merite, France, Commandeur de l'Ordre de Merite du Grand-Duche de Luxembourg. Mem. Nat. Assn. Accts., Fin. Execs. Inst., Officer's Conf. Group. Clubs: Firestone Country, Portage Country (Akron). Office: Quest Communications 1801 California St Denver CO 80202*

**SHAFFER, PAUL,** musician, bandleader; b. Thunder Bay, Ont., Can., Nov. 28, 1949; m. Cathy Vasapoli; children: Victoria Lily, William Wood Lee. BA Sociology & Philosophy, U. Toronto, Can., 1971; doctorate (hon.), Five Towns Coll., Dix Hills, NY, Lakehead U., Can. Mem. band Fabulous Fugitives, Thunder Bay, 1964-68; keyboardist NBC's Saturday Night Live, 1975-80; musical dir. Blues Bros. Band, 1978-79; leader, keyboardist The World's Most Dangerous Band NBC's Late Night with David Letterman, 1982-1993; music director The Late Show with David Letterman (CBS), 1993—. Mus. dir. (Toronto, Ont. prodn.) Godspell, 1972; musician: (N.Y.C. prodn.) The Magic Show, 1974, (Gilda Radner's mus. revue, also co-composer) Live in New York, 1979, (off-Broadway prodn.) Leader of the Pack, 1984, Olympic Games closing concert, Atlanta, 1996, The Concert for NYC, 2001; mus. prod. Blues Bros. 2000, 1998, Rock & Roll Hall of Fame Induction Ceremony, 1986-; rec. artist, keyboardist: (with Barry Manilow) This One's For You, 1976, (with National Lampoon) Good-Bye Pop, 1976, (with the Jeff Healey Band) Feel This, 1977, (Blues Bros.) Briefcase Full of Blues, 1978, Made in America, 1980, (with Jaon Armatrading) Me Myself, 1980, (with Nina Hagen) Nunsexmonkrock, 1980, (with Diana Ross) Silk Electric, 1981, (with Yoko Ono) It's Alright, 1982,(Honey Drippers) The Honey Drippers, 1985, (film soundtrack) The Karate Kid II, 1986, (with Dion, Ben. E. King, Bobby Womack and Wilson Pickett) Coast to Coast, 1991, (with Blues Traveler) Save His Soul, 1993, (with the Party Boys of Rock 'n' Roll) The World's Most Dangerous Party, 1993; co-writer (with Paul Jabara) It's Raining Men, 1983; regular mem. cast (TV series) A Year at the Top, 1977, Saturday Night Live, 1979-80, Flash Gordon, 1996, Disney's Hercules, 1998; film appearances include This Is Spinal Tap, 1984; Scrooged, 1988, Hercules, 1997, Blues Bros. 2000, 1998; solo album Coast to Coast, 1989 (2 Grammy nominations). Chmn. Am. Red Cross recruiting drive, 1990. Co-recipient Grammy award, Best Country Instrumental Performance, 2002; recipient Golden Jubilee Medal of Queen Elizabeth II, 2003. Office: Late Show w/ David Letterman CBS 530 W 57th St New York NY 10019-2902*

**SHAFFER, PEGGY S.,** music educator; b. South Bend, Ind., Dec. 25, 1951; d. Phyllis L. White. MusM, Ind. State U., 1970—76; M in Guidance, Purdue U.-Calumet, 1994—97. Music Ind. Dept. Edn., 1976. Tchr. Crown Point Schs., Ind., 1977—. Musician: (free-lance performer) drummer. Bd. mem. Ind. Music Educator's Assn., Crown Point, 1986—88. Mem.: Music Educators Nat. Conf., Nat. Band Assn., Ind. Bandmasters Assn., Ind. State Teachers Assn. Home: 702 W Sigler Hebron IN 46341 Office: Crown Point HS 1500 S Main St Crown Point IN 46307 Office Phone: 219-663-4885. Office Fax: 219-662-5661. Personal E-mail: pshaffer@cps.k12.in.us.

**SHAFFER, PETER (SIR PETER SHAFFER),** playwright; b. Liverpool, Eng., May 15, 1926; s. Jack and Reka (Fredman) S. BA, Cambridge U., Eng., 1950. Conscript coal mines, Eng., 1944-47; with N.Y. Pub. Libr., N.Y.C., 1951-54, Boosey & Hawkes, London, 1954-55; lit. critic Truth, 1956-57; music critic Time and Tide, 1961-62; freelance playwright, 1957—. Vis. prof. contemporary drama Oxford (Eng.) U., 1994-95. Author: (plays) Five Finger Exercise, 1958 (Evening Standard Drama award 1958, N.Y. Drama Critics Cir. award 1960), The Private Ear, 1962, The Public Eye, 1962, It's About Cinderella, 1963, The Royal Hunt of the Sun, 1964, Black Comedy, 1965, The White Liars, 1967, The Battle of Shrivings, 1970, Equus, 1973 (Best Play Tony award 1975, Outer Critics Cir. Best Play award 1975), Amadeus, 1979 (Evening Standard Drama award 1979, London Drama Critics award 1979, Best Play Tony award 1980, Plays and Players Best Play award 1980), Yonadab, 1985, Lettice and Lovage, 1987 (Evening Standard Drama award 1988), The Gift of the Gorgon, 1992, Whom Do I Have the Honor of Addressing?, Chichester Festival Theatre, 1996, (screenplays) Follow Me!, 1971, Equus, 1977 (Acad. award nomination for best screenplay adaptation

1977), Amadeus, 1984 (Acad. award for best screenplay adaptation 1984), (TV plays) The Salt Land, 1955, Balance of Terror, 1957, (radio plays) The Prodigal Father, 1955, Whom Do I Have the Honor of Addressing?, 1989, (novels) The Woman in the Wardrobe, 1951, (novels, with Anthony Shaffer), How Doth the Little Crocodile?, 1952, Withered Murder, 1955. Created knight, 2001; decorated comdr. Order Brit. Empire, 1987; recipient Hamburg Shakespeare prize, 1987, William Inge award for disting. achievement in Am. theatre, 1992; hon. fellow St. Andrews U., Scotland, emeritus fellow St. Catherine's Coll., Oxford, Eng. Fellow Royal Soc. Lt. (London chpt.). Address: 173 Riverside Dr New York NY 10024

**SHAFFER, RICHARD JAMES,** lawyer, retired manufacturing executive; b. Pe Ell, Wash., Jan. 26, 1931; s. Richard Humphrys and Laura Rose (Faas) S.; m. Donna M. Smith, May 13, 1956; children: Leslie Lauren Shaffer Litsinger, Stephanie Jane Athenton. BA, U. Wash.; LL.B., Southwestern U. Bar: Calif. Vice pres., gen. counsel, sec. NI, Inc., Long Beach, Calif., 1974—89; gen. counsel Masco Bldg. Products Corp., Long Beach, 1985—89; pvt. practice Huntington Beach, Calif., 1989—98; internat. ops. officer Newport Fin. Group; CFO Dream Quest Entertainment, Ltd., 2000—. Mem. ltd. liability co. drafting com. and task force Calif. State Bar, 1992-94; lectr. in field. Trustee Ocean View Sch. Dist., 1965-73, pres., 1966, 73; mem. fin. adv. com. Orange Coast Coll., 1966; mem. Long Beach Local Devel. Corp., 1978-89, Calif. Senate Commn. on Corp. Governance, Shareholders' Rights and Securities Transactions, 1986-97, chmn. drafting com. ltd. liability co. act for senate com., 1991-93; mem. Pers. Commn. City of Huntington Beach, 1996-98; mem. Huntington Beach clean water subcom. Huntington Beach; bd. dirs. Huntington Beach Libr. Patrons, 1996-98. Mem. ABA, Nat. Assn. Securities Dealers (bd. arbitrators), Calif. Bar Assn. (exec. com. corp. law dept. com. bus. sect. 1981-88), Orange County Bar Assn., Trinidad Island Homeowners Assn. (pres.), Huntington Harbour Yacht Club, Catalina Island Yacht Club, Wanderlust Skiers of Huntington Harbour (pres.).

**SHAFFER, SHERRILL LYNN,** economist; b. Tyler, Tex., Aug. 1, 1952; s. Douglas Marsene and Ethel Elizabeth (Green) S.; m. Margaret Jane Ahrens, Jun 20, 1987; 1 child, David Carsten. BA, Rice U., 1974; MA, Stanford U., 1978, PhD, 1981. Rsch. asst. Stanford U., Calif., 1976—79, instr., 1979—80; from economist to chief Fed. Res. Bank N.Y., N.Y.C., 1980—88; from rsch. officer, economist to asst. v.p/discount officer Fed. Res. Bank Phila., 1988—97; John A. Guthrie disting. prof. banking and fin. svcs. U. Wyo., Laramie, 1997—. Vis. scholar Stanford U., 2004; chmn. tenure and promotion com., grad. coun., 2000-02, MBA adv. com., grad. admissions com., 1999-2000, grad. program rev. com., 2000-02; violinist solo and with orchs., Calif., NY, 1976-88; cons. asst. Rosse & Olszewski, Palo Alto, Calif., 1978-80; cons. in field. Contbr. articles to profl. jours.; assoc. editor to editor Jour. Econs. and Bus., 1993—; mem. editl. bd. Jour. Regulatory Econs., 2002—. Sec. bd. dirs. N.Y. Arts Group, N.Y.C., 1982—83; mem. program com. So. Fin. Assn., 1996; exec. adv. coun. mem. dept. fin. Temple U., 1996—97; bd. advisors cultural programs series U. Wyo., 1999—; mem. fin. com. St. Matthew's Cathedral, Laramie, Wyo., 1998—2004, mem. vestry, 1999—2002; bd. dirs. artist selection com. Tri-County Concerts Assn., 1996—. Recipient Messier cert. Astronomical League, 1993; vis. scholar, Stanford Univ., 2004. Mem. AAAS, Am. Econ. Assn., Am. Math. Soc., Math. Assn. Am., N.Am. Econs. and Fin. Assn., Indsl. Orgn. Soc., N.Y. Acad. Scis., Fin. Mgmt. Assn. (program com. 1991, 01, 03, 04, 05, nat. awards com. 2000, 01), So. Fin. Assn. (program com. 1996), Delaware Valley Amateur Astronomers (observing chmn. 1993, publicity chmn. 1994-96), Chamber Music Am. Episcopalian. Avocations: hiking, astronomy, computer programming, theology, number theory. Home: 30 Silver Spur Rd Laramie WY 82072-9563 Office: U Wyo Dept Econs and Fin PO Box 3985 Laramie WY 82071-3985 Business E-Mail: shaffer@uwyo.edu.

**SHAFFER, SHIRLEY POLLACK,** secondary school educator, sales executive; b. Bklyn., Dec. 5, 1921; d. Harry Lionel and Sylvia Ruth (Smith) Pollack; m. Alfred Shaffer, Feb. 14, 1943 (dec. July 1995); children: Robert Stuart, Steven Michael. BA magna cum laude, Bklyn. Coll., 1955; MA, Calif. State U., 1967. Life certificates in elem. and secondary edn., Calif. Sec. Am. Foreign Credit, N.Y.C., 1939-41, Victor M. Calderon Co., N.Y.C., 1941-43, sales, 1943-46; tchr. Bklyn. Pub. Sch., 1955-56, West Covina (Calif.) S.D., 1957-83; retired, 1983; mem. Calif. St. Legis. Assembly, 1985-95. Mem. NEA, Calif. Tchrs. Assn. (local sec. 1983), Calif. Retired Tchrs. Assn. (legis. chair), Brandeis U. Women's Aux. Com., Phi Beta Kappa, Kappa Delta Pi, Sigma Delta Pi. Avocations: writing, reading, poetry, lecturing, local civic participation.

**SHAFFER, THOMAS LINDSAY,** lawyer, educator; b. Billings, Mont., Apr. 4, 1934; s. Cecil Burdette and Margaret Jeanne (Parker) S.; m. Nancy Jane Lehr, Mar. 19, 1954; children: Thomas, Francis, Joseph, Daniel, Brian, Mary, Andrew, Edward. BA, U. Albuquerque, 1958; JD, U. Notre Dame, 1961; LLD, St. Mary's U., 1983. Bar: Ind. 1961. Assoc. Barnes, Hickam, Pantzer, & Boyd, Indpls., 1961-63; prof. law U. Notre Dame, Ind., 1963-80, assoc. dean Ind., 1969-71, dean Ind., 1971-75, Robert and Marion Short prof. Ind., 1988-97; Robert and Marion Short prof. emeritus, 1997—; supervising atty. Notre Dame Legal Aid Clinic, 1991—; prof. law Washington and Lee U., 1980-87, Robert E.R. Huntley prof. law, 1987-88. Vis. prof. UCLA, 1970-71, U. Va., 1975-76, U. Maine, 1982, 87, 98, Boston Coll., 1992; mem. Ind. Constl. Revision Commn., 1969-70, Ind. Trust Code Study Commn., 1968-71; reporter Ind. Jud. Conf., 1963, 67. Author: Death, Property, and Lawyers, 1970, The Planning and Drafting of Wills and Trusts, 1972, 4th edit., 2001, On Being a Christian and a Lawyer, 1981, American Legal Ethics, 1985, Faith and the Professions, 1987, Moral Memoranda From John Howard Yoder, 2002; co-author: Lawyers, Law Students, and People, 1977, Cases in Legal Interviewing and Counseling, 1980, American Lawyers and Their Communities, 1991, Property Cases, Materials and Problems, 1992, 2nd edit., 1998, Lawyers, Clients, and Moral Responsibility, 1994, Legal Interviewing and Counseling, 1976, 4th edit., 2004; co-editor: The Mentally Retarded Citizen and the Law, 1976; contbr. articles to profl. jours. Served with USAF, 1953-57. Frances Lewis scholar Washington and Lee U., 1979; recipient Emil Brown Found. Preventive Law prize, 1966, Presdl. citation U. Notre Dame, 1975, St. Thomas More award St. Mary's U., 1983, Law medal Gonzaga U., 1991, Jour. Law and Religion award, 1993. Mem. Ind. State Bar Assn., Jewish Law Assn. Roman Catholic. Home: 1865 Champlain Dr Niles MI 49120-8935 Office: Notre Dame Legal Aid Clinic 725 Howard St South Bend IN 46617-1529 Office Phone: 574-631-7250. E-mail: shaffer@lnd.edu.

**SHAFFERN, ROBERT WILLIAM,** history professor; b. Chgo., Jan. 5, 1963; s. William and Joan Shaffern; m. Elizabeth Martin, Aug. 22, 1992; children: Thomas Martin, Monica Rose, Christina Loughlin, Caroline Grace. BA, De Paul U., Chgo., 1985; MA, U. Notre Dame, South Bend, 1987; PhD, U. Notre Dame, Ind., 1992. Vis. asst. prof. U. Notre Dame, South Bend, 1992—95; assoc. prof. U. Scranton, Pa., 1995—. Contbr. articles to profl. jours. Conservative. Roman Catholic. Office: U Scranton Dept History Scranton PA 18510 Office Phone: 570-941-4360. Business E-Mail: shaffernr1@scranton.edu.

**SHAFFNER, PATRICK NOEL,** retired architectural engineering executive; b. Burlington, N.C., Nov. 1, 1939; s. Samuel Hubert and Martha Jane (Noel) Shaffner; m. Patricia Anne Anders, June 12, 1961; children: Scott Anders, Kimberly Page, Melissa Hope. BS, Va. Poly. and State U., 1961. Registered profl. engr., Va. Structural engr. Hayes, Seay, Mattern & Mattern, Roanoke, Va., 1963-68; sr. structural engr. Sherertz & Franklin, Roanoke, 1968-72; ptnr. Sherertz, Franklin, Crawford, Shaffner, Roanoke, 1972-87; chmn., CEO Sherertz, Franklin, Crawford, Shaffner Inc., Roanoke, 1998-98. Bd. dirs. Mill Mountain Theatre; mem. adv. bd. Va. Tech. Coll. Engring. Com. 100; v.p. Roanoke Found. For Downtown, Inc.; trustee Va. Bapt. Children's Home and Family Svcs.; interim exec. dir. Downtown Roanoke, Inc., 2005-06. Capt. C.E., U.S. Army, 1961-63. Paul Harris fellow. Fellow ASCE; mem. AIA (assoc.), Roanoke Regional C. of C. (Small Bus. Person of Yr. 1991), Rotary (pres. Roanoke club 1986). Lodges: Rotary (Roanoke) (pres. 1986). Republican. Baptist. Home: 2635 Turnberry Rd Salem VA 24153-7483 E-mail: shaffner@adelphia.net.

**SHAFFNER, RANDOLPH PRESTON,** shop owner, educator, writer, publisher; b. Winston-Salem, N.C., Jan. 17, 1940; s. Emil Nathaniel and Anna Jackson (Preston) S.; m. Margaret Farmer Rhodes; children: Eric Randolph, Edward David, Joseph Andrew, Thomas Matthew, Jackson Rhodes. Student, Davidson Coll., 1958-60; BA in English with honors in writing, U. N.C., 1962, MA in Comparative Lit., 1969, PhD, 1973. Surveyor's lineman Joyce Mapping Co., Winston-Salem, 1955-58, 62; counselor, scoutmaster Camp Sequoyah, Weaverville, N.C., 1959; track repairman Alaska R.R., Anchorage, 1960; case handler Emard Packing Co., Anchorage, 1960, AYR Canneries, Seldovia, Alaska, 1961; tchr. U.S. Peace Corps., Chiengrai, Thailand, 1963-65, St. Christopher's Sch., Richmond, Va., 1969-71; instr. U. N.C., 1968-69, 71-73; asst. prof. Fairfield U., Conn., 1973-78, Western Carolina U., 1984, 87, Continuing Edn. program World Masterpieces, Highlands, NC, 1987—89; moderator Highlands lecture series Western Carolina U., 1989-92. Instr. carolina environ. program U. NC, Chapel Hill, 2003; editor John F. Blair Pub., Winston-Salem, 1966-68; bookseller, owner Cyrano's Bookshop, Highlands, NC, 1978-05; founder, pub. Faraway Pub., 2001; asst. to dean Sch. Libr. Scis. U. NC, Chapel Hill, 1973-74; literary mag. adv., various subcoms. Dept. Eng. Fairfield U., 1973-78. Author: Apprenticeship Novel, 1984, Tree Ordinance for Town of Highlands, 1987, Good Reading Material, Mostly Bound and New: The Hudson Library 1884-1994, 1994, Heart of the Blue Ridge: Highlands, North Carolina, 2001, 2d edit., 2004, Highlands Heritage Trail: A Walking Tour of Many Highlands Historical Buildings and Landmarks, 2003; (with others) Nineteenth Century Literature Criticism, Vol. 21, 1989; contbr. poetry to N.C. Poetry Soc. anthology Here's to the Land, 1992; contbr. short stories to mags; contbr. Heritage of Macon Co., N.C., Vol. 2, 1999. Lectr. with Alexander, String Quartet, Words & Music, 1989, 92, 94, for Western Carolina U., Highlands lectr. series, 1991-93, 2000; inaugural lectr. Chattooga Watershed Cultural Heritage Series, 2005; instr. Ctr. for Life Enrichment, 2000, 06; chmn. ARC Disaster Svcs., Fairfield, 1974-78, Zoning Bd. of Adjustment, Highlands, 1981-83, 85-90; pres., bd. trustees Hudson Libr., Inc., Highlands, 1987-90, 99-2001, admin. libr. com., 1995-99; trustee Hudson Libr. Bascom-Louise Art Gallery, 1987-90, 95-99, Highlands Land Trust, Inc., 1995-96; bd. dirs. ARC, Fairfield, 1974-78, Highlands Cultural Art Ctr., 1987; fundraising com. Highlands Permanent Endowment Scholarships, 1987-89; Town of Highlands Millennium Com., 1999; historian Highlands Hist. Soc., Inc., 1999—, adv. com., 2001—, archivist, 2005—; mem. Macon County Hist. Preservation Comm. Task Force, 2006, Macon County Heritage Coun., 2006—; bd. dirs. Friends Mtn. Hist., 2006—; vice-chmn. bd. missions Greenfield Hill Congl. Ch., Fairfield, Conn., 1977, chmn. scholarship co., 1975-77; chaperon Am. Inst. for Fgn. Study, Grenoble, France, 1970. Recipient God and Country award, 1955, Outstanding Pres. and Trustee award Hudson Libr. and Bascom-Louise Gallery, 1990, Daniel Boone Coun. Boy Scouts Am. Disting. Citizen award, 2002, Gertrude and Dolly Harbison award, Hudson Libr., 2004; Goethe Inst. scholar German Embassy, Munich, Fed. Rep. Germany, 1965, Univ. Besançon, France, 1965. Mem.: Am. Assn. for State and Local History (highlands greenways com. 2005—, ann. award for Heart of the Blue Ridge 2005), Highlands Biol. Found. (trustee 1981—2006, fund raising com. 1986, environ. protection com. 1986—88, exec. com. 1986—2004, treas. 1990—2004, adv. com. on Nature Ctr. 1992, hon. trustee 2006—), Highlands Mchts. Assn. (chmn. fin. com., treas. 1984—87, chmn. tree com. and beautification com. 1984—89, greenways com. 2004—), Southeastern Booksellers Assn., Am. Booksellers Assn., Am. Acad. Poets, N.C. Poetry Soc., Writers' Workshop, Am. Comparative Lit. Assn., Internat. Comparative Lit. Assn., Highlands-Cashiers Land Trust, N.C. Soc. Historians (History Book award 2002), Clan Morrison Soc., Highlands C. of C., Highlands Hist. Soc., Nat. Peace Corps Assn., Trail Hikers Am., Rotary (Outstanding Vol. award 1989), Lambda Iota Tau (faculty moderator Delta Omicron Ch. 1975—80, founder). Democrat. Moravian. Avocations: construction, reading, travel, hiking. Office: Highlands Hist Soc 524 N 4th St Highlands NC 28741-0670 Office Phone: 828-787-1050. Business E-Mail: anwil@nctv.com.

**SHAFII, BAHMAN,** statistician, educator, researcher; b. Tehran, Iran, Dec. 12, 1954; s. Mahmood and Akhtar Shafii; m. Sima Safaei; children: Omid, Farid children: Sara Azar. BS with hon., Rezaeyeh U., Rezaeyeh, Iran, 1977; MS, U. Idaho, 1980, MS, 1982, PhD, 1988. Lectr. Wash. State U., Pullman, Wash., 1984—88; dir. statis. programs U. of Idaho, Moscow, Idaho, 1988—. Contbr. articles over 70 to profl. jours. Recipient Paul Howe Shepard award, Am. Pomological Soc., 1998, award of Excellence, Weed Sci. Soc. Am., 2002. Mem.: AAAS, NCR-170 Coord. Rsch. Advances Agrl. Statistics (sec. 1995—2001), Am. Statis. Assn. (pres. 1995—96, Snake River chpt.), Internat. Biometric Soc., Sigma Xi. Avocations: travel, music, poetry. Office: Statistical Programs University of Idaho PO Box 442337 Moscow ID 83844-2337 Business E-Mail: bshafii@uidaho.edu.

**SHAFRITZ, DAVID ANDREW,** physician, research scientist; b. Phila., Oct. 5, 1940; s. Saul and Ethel (Kohn) S.; m. Sharon C. Klemow, Aug. 16, 1964; children: Gregory S., Adam B., Keith M. AB in Chemistry with honors, U. Pa., 1962, MD, 1966. Diplomate Nat. Bd. Med. Examiners, Am. Bd. Internal Medicine. Intern, then asst. resident U. Md. Hosp., Balt., 1966-68; rsch. assoc. NIH, Bethesda, Md., 1968-71; clin. and rsch. fellow Mass. Gen. Hosp., Boston, 1971-73; instr. Harvard Med. Sch., Boston, 1971-73, asst. prof. medicine, 1973; asst. prof. medicine and cell biology Albert Einstein Coll. Medicine, Yeshiva U., Bronx, NY, 1973-76, assoc. prof., 1976-81, prof. medicine and cell biology, 1981—; dir. Marion Bessin Liver Rsch. Ctr., 1985—; Herman Lapota prof. liver disease rsch. (endowed chair), 1992—. Cons. integrated Genetics, Inc., Framingham, Mass., 1981-86, Immuno, Vienna, Austria, 1986-91, Innovir, Inc., N.Y.C., 1991-98, Eugenetech Internat., Inc., Ramsey, N.J., 1991-93, Ctrs. for Med. Innovation, 1997-2001; temp. advisor WHO, Geneva, 1983; mem. Nat. Com. for Clin. Lab. Stds., Villanova Pa., 1983—, Renaissance Techs., 1996—, Affymetrix, Inc., 1997—; sci. adv. bd. com. liver cancer program Inst. for Cancer Rsch., Fox Chase and Phila., 1987—; mem. rev. panel U. study sect. Nat. Inst. Diabetes and Digestive and Kidney Diseases, 1988-92, chmn., 1991-92; mem. cen. coord. com. Liver Tissue Procurement and Distbn. Sys., 1986-95, Nat. Inst. Health Metabolic Pathology Study sect., 1995-99; mem. Nat. Bd. Med. Examiners and U.S. Med. Exam. Com., 1996-98. Co-author: The Liver: Biology and Pathobiology, 1982, 4th edit., 2001, Hepatobiliary Diseases, 1991; assoc. editor Hepatology, 1981-86; mem. editl. bd. Jour. Med. Virology, 1982-93, Hepatology, 1990-96, Jour. Virology, 1992-98; contbr. numerous rsch. articles and revs. to profl. publs.; contbr. chpts. to books; patentee in field. Trustee Westchester Jewish Ctr., Mamaroneck, N.Y., 1980-86. Lt. comdr. USPHS, 1968-71. Recipient Merck award U. Pa., 1962, Morton McCutcheon Meml. Rsch. prize Sch. Medicine, 1966, Career Scientist award Irma T. Hirschl Trust, N.Y.C., 1974-79, NIH Merit award, 1994, Disting. Rsch. Achievement award Am. Liver Found., 2000; European Molecular Biology Orgn. fellow, 1978; recipient Rsch. Career Devel. award NIH, 1975-80, spl. rsch. fellow, 1971-73, rsch. grantee, 1974—. Mem. Am. Assn. for Study of Liver Diseases, Internat. Assn. for Study of Liver, Am. Gastroenterol. Assn., Am. Soc. Biochemistry and Molecular Biology, Am. Soc. Investigative Pathology, Am. Soc. Clin. Investigation, Assn. Am. Physicians, N.Y. Acad. Scis., Harvey Soc., Interurban Clin. Club (sec./treas. 1996-99, pres. 1999-2000). Democrat. Jewish. Avocations: jogging, tennis. Home: 4 Pheasant Run Larchmont NY 10538-3423 Office: Yeshiva U Albert Einstein Coll Med Marion Bessin Liver Rsch Ctr 1300 Morris Park Ave Bronx NY 10461-1926 E-mail: shafritz@aecom.yu.edu.

**SHAFRITZ, KEITH MICHAEL,** psychology professor; b. Boston, Dec. 29, 1972; s. David A. and Sharon K. Shafritz; m. Donna J. Lutz, May 30, 1999; 1 child, Matthew. BA, Haverford Coll., 1995; MPhil, Yale U., 1999, PhD, 2002. Rsch. asst. Albert Einstein Coll. Medicine, Bronx, NY, 1996—97; grad. rsch. fellow Yale U., New Haven, 1997—2002, grad. tchng. fellow, 1998—2000, postdoctoral rsch. fellow, 2002—03; rsch. assoc. Duke U., Durham, NC, 2003—05; asst. prof. Drew U., Madison, NJ, 2005—06, Hofstra U., Hempstead, NY, 2006—. Adj. prof. Quinnipiac U., Hamden, Conn., 2002; sci. reviewer various profl. jours. Contbr. articles to profl. jours. Recipient Rsch. Travel award, Yale U., 1997—99, Nat. Rsch. Svc. award, NIMH, 2002—03, Rsch. Travel award, Drew U., 2005; Grad. Rsch. Tng. fellow, Yale U., 1997—2002, Tchg. fellowship, 2000, Postdoctoral rsch. fellow,

---

**SHAFTEL, MATTHEW ROBERT,** music educator, tenor, conductor; b. Tucson, Ariz., Sept. 10, 1973; s. Timothy L. Shaftel and Cassie L. Wesselius; m. Pascale R. Rodrigue, Aug. 16, 1994; children: Veronique, Alexandre, Genevieve. BA, Yale U., New Haven, Conn., 1991—95, MPhil, 1995—97, PhD, 1995—2000. Cert. music tchr. Conn., 1995. Dir. of music Good Shepherd Cath. Ch., Tallahassee, 2001—; music theory prof. Fla. State U., Tallahassee, 2001—. Treas. Music Theory SE, Tallahassee, 2004—. Author, editor (non-fiction book and edition) Anton Webern's Early Vocal Music, 2004; contbr. articles to profl. music jours. Recipient U. Tchg. award, Fla. State U., 2005. Mem.: Coll. Music Soc. (music theory adv. bd. 2004—), Soc. for Music Theory (com. on the status of women 2003—). Roman Catholic. Avocations: travel, cooking, basketball. Office: Fla State Univ Sch Music Tallahassee FL 32306-1180 Office Phone: 850-644-6271. Business E-Mail: mshaftel@fsu.edu.

**SHAFTMAN, FREDRICK KRISCH,** telephone communications executive, lawyer; b. Roanoke, Va., Apr. 9, 1948; s. Sydney and Rosalie (Krisch) S.; m. Diane Hasson, Dec. 27, 1970; children: Stephanie, Emily. BSBA, U. Ala., 1970, JD, 1973. Bar: Va. 1973. Gen. counsel Bell South Comm. Sys. (formerly Universal Comm. Sys., Inc.), Roanoke, 1973-74, v.p., gen. counsel, 1974-79, pres., 1979-84, CEO, 1984-99, also bd. dirs.; pres. Bus. BellSouth Corp, Atlanta, 2000—. V.p. Am. Motor Inns, Inc. Bd. dirs, United Way Roanoke Valley, Roanoke Mill Mountain Zoo; trustee North Cross Country Day Sch., Roanoke, Roanoke Valley Sci. Mus., Roanoke Valley ARC. Recipient President's Disting. Svc. award N.Am. Telecom. Assn., 1989, achievement award United Jewish Assn., 1989. Mem. ABA, N.Am. Tel. Assn. (bd. dirs.), Western Va. BBB (bd. dirs.), Va. Bar Assn., Rotary.

**SHAGAM, MARVIN HÜCKEL-BERRI,** private school educator; b. Monongalia, W.Va. s. Lewis and Clara (Shagam) S. AB magna cum laude, Washington and Jefferson Coll., 1947; postgrad., Harvard Law Sch., 1947—48, Oxford U., 1948—51. Tchr. Mount House Sch., Tavistock, England, 1951—53, Williston Jr. Sch., Easthampton, Mass., 1953—55, Westtown Sch., Pa., 1955—58, Thacher Sch., Ojai, Calif., 1958—; head English dept. Kurasini Internat. Edn. Centre, Dar-es-Salaam, Tanzania, 1966—67; head dept. Nkumbi Internat. Coll., Kabwe, Zambia, 1967—68. Vol. visitor Prisons in Calif., 1980-95, Calif. Youth Authority, 1983-93; sr. youth crisis counsellor InterFace, 1984-94. With U.S. Army, 1942-46, 1st lt. M.I. res.,1946-57. Danforth Found. fellow, 1942; Coun. for the Humanities fellow, Tufts U., 1983. Mem. We. Assn. Schs. and Colls. (accreditation com.), Great Tchg. (Cooke chair 1977—), Phi Beta Kappa, Delta Sigma Rho, Cum Laude Soc. Republican. Avocations: hiking, camping, travel. Home: 5025 Thacher Rd Ojai CA 93023-8304 Office: The Thacher Sch 5025 Thacher Rd Ojai CA 93023-9001 Fax: 805-646-4377. Office Phone: 805-646-4377. E-mail: mshagam@thacher.org.

**SHAGAN, STEVE,** scriptwriter, producer; b. NYC, Oct. 25, 1927; m. Elizabeth Florance, Nov. 1956. Film technician Consol. Film, Inc., N.Y.C., 1952-56, RCA, Cape Canaveral, Fla., 1956-59; asst. to publicity dir. Paramount Pictures, Hollywood, Calif., 1962-63. Prodr.: (TV series) Tarzan, 1966; prodr., writer movies for TV, Universal and CBS, Hollywood, Calif., 1968-70; writer original screenplay: Save the Tiger, 1972 (Writers Guild award, Acad. award nominee 1973); prodr. film, author screenplay: City of Angels (produced as movie Hustle), 1975, novel, screenplay The Formula, 1979, screenplay Voyage of the Damned, 1976 (Acad. award nominee); writer, prodr. film The Formula, 1980; author: (novels) Save the Tiger, 1972, City of Angels, 1975, The Formula, 1979, The Circle, 1982, The Discovery, 1985, Vendetta, 1986, Pillars of Fire, 1989, A Cast of Thousands, 1993, (screenplays) Primal Fear, 1996, Gotti, 1996 (Emmy nominee Best Screenplay). Served with USCG, 1944-46. Mem. Writers Guild Am. (bd. dirs. West chpt. 1978-82).

**SHAGGY, See BURRELL, ORVILLE**

**SHAH, ATIQUE R.,** gaming activities executive; Grad., Wittenberg U.; MBA, St. Thomas Aquinas U. With Uproar.com (later Vivendi Universal); dir. customer relations mgmt. (CRM)/employee relations mgmt. (ERM) NBA; v.p. CRM and mktg. tech. GSI Commerce, 2002—03; v.p. CRM and tech. solutions Churchill Downs Inc., 2003—. Named one of Premier 100 IT Leaders, Computerworld, 2005. Office: Churchill Downs Inc 700 Central Ave Louisville KY 40208 Office Phone: 502-636-4400. Office Fax: 502-636-4430.*

**SHAH, BHUPEN,** consumer electronics company executive; MS in Computer Sci. and Elec. Engring., U. Mich., Ann Arbor. V.p. software Dazzle (acquired by SCM Microsystems); v.p., products and tech. RealChip Communications, Sunnyvale, Calif.; co-founded, COO, exec. v.p. engring. to chief tech. officer, v.p. mktg. Emuzed, Inc. (acquired by Flextronics Internat. Ltd.), San Jose, Calif., 1999—2004; founder DiTango (acquired by Sling Media, Inc.), 2004; co-founder, COO, v.p. engring. Sling Media, Inc., San Mateo, Calif., 2004—. Former chmn. USB video and imaging device working group. Achievements include with other members of Slingbox Media, Inc., created Slingbox, a device that allows a person to watch their own TV from a laptop anywhere in the world; Slingbox Player named one of PC World Innovations in 2006, Business Week Best Products of 2005, Time Best Inventions of 2005, Popular Science Best of What's New 2005 & Laptop Best of CES 2005; Slingbox Player has won awards including Mobile Trax Mobility award Accessories III 2006 and International Consumer Electronics Show Innovations 2006 Design and Engrineering Finalist; Sling Media Inc. was chosen by Fortune as one of the 25 Breakout Companies of 2005 and 2006 ACE award Finalist-Start-up Company of Year. Office: Sling Media Inc 901 Mariners Island Blvd Ste 300 San Mateo CA 94404 Office Phone: 650-293-8000. Office Fax: 650-378-4422.*

**SHAH, DHAVAN VINOD,** communications educator; s. Vinod Kasturchand and Dharmishtha Vinod Shah; m. Christine Lynn Garlough, July 13, 1991; children: Gabriel Dhavan Garlough-Shah, Isabel Arya Garlough-Shah. BA, U. Wis., Madison 1989; MA, U. Minn., Twin Cities, 1995, PhD, 1998. Media buyer planner Leo Burnett Co., Chgo., 1990—92; cons. Fallon Worldwide, Mpls., 1997—2001; prin. Metascope, LLC, Madison, 2000—02; asst. prof. U. Wis., Madison, 1998—2002, assoc. prof., 2002—04, prof., 2004—06, Louis A. & Mary E. Maier-Bascom prof., 2006—. Prin. investigator Digital Media Forum, Ford Found., Washington, 2000—01, Pub. Broadcasting Svc., 2001—02, Nat. Ctr. for Outreach, Corp. for Pub. Broadcasting, 2002—04, Russell Sage Found., NYC, 2004—, Rockefeller Bros., 2004—, Carnegie Corp., 2004—, Pew Charitable Trusts, 2004—, C.I.R.C.L.E., 2004—, Jour. Found, 2004—. Editl. bd. mem. Comm. Methods and Measures, Human Comm. Rsch., Jour. of Comm., Journalism and Mass Comm. Quarterly, Mass Comm. Soc., Polit. Comm. Recipient Krieghbaum Under-40 award, Assn. for Edn. in Journalism and Mass Comm., 2005, Chancellor's Excellence award, U. Wis. Ext., 2003, Vilas Assoc. Award, U. Wis., Madison, 2003, 2004, 2005, Jour. Comm., Warren J. Heyse Faculty Excellence award, 2000, 2001, 2002, 2003, 2004, 2005, 2006. Mem.: Am. Assn. Pub. Opinion Rsch., Am. Polit. Sci. Assn., Nat. Comm. Assn., Internat. Comm. Assn., Assn. Edn. in Journalism and Mass Comm. Office: U Wis 821 University Ave Madison WI 53706 Office Phone: 608-262-0388. E-mail: dshah@wisc.edu.

**SHAH, JAMES M.,** actuary; b. Amadhara, India, Feb. 4, 1943; came to U.S.; 1980; s. Manekchand Keshrichand and Kamuben Manekchand Shah; m. Urmila Jashwantlal Shah, May 16, 1966; children: Meeta, Keena, Jatin. BS, Gujarat U., India, 1965; MS, Gujarat U., 1969; MA, Georgetown U., 1983; MS, U. Nebr. 1986. Sr. rsch. asst. Nat. Inst. Rural Devel., Hyderabad, India, 1972-74; rsch. officer Population Ctr. World Bank Population Project, Bangalore, India, 1974-77; actuarial analyst Shelby Ins. Co., Ohio, 1987-90;

---

actuary ins. dept. State of ND, Bismarck, ND, 1990-91; pres. A S D Consulting Svc., Mansfield, Ohio, 1991—2005; asst. actuary Blue Cross Blue Shield Utica, Utica, NY, 2000; ret., 2005. Contbr. articles to profl. jours. UN fellow Ministry of Fgn. Affairs, 1978; recipient Outstanding Young Person award Garden City Jaycees, 1977, 7th Summer Seminar award U. Hawaii, 1976. Mem. Internat. Actuarial Assn. (cert. 1996), Internat. Union for Sci. Study of Population, Soc. Actuaries (cert. 1994), Am. Acad. Actuaries (cert. 1994). Avocations: travel, reading, ping pong/table tennis. Home: 91 S Ireland Blvd Mansfield OH 44906-2220 Office: ASD Cons Svc 91 S Ireland Blvd Mansfield OH 44906 E-mail: shahjames@hotmail.com.

**SHAH, JATIN PREMANAND,** head and neck surgeon, educator; b. Visnagar, Gujarat, India, Dec. 31, 1940; came to U.S., 1967; s. Premanand C. and Sarla P. (Mehta) S.; m. Bharti N. Gandhi, May 11, 1967; 1 child, Mili MD, Baroda (India) Med. Coll., 1964, MS in Surgery, 1967. Diplomate Am. Bd. Surgery. Attending surgeon Meml. Sloan Kettering Cancer Ctr., N.Y.C., 1974—; chief head and neck svc., 1992—, E.W. Strong chair in head and neck oncology; prof. surgery Cornell U. Med. Coll., N.Y.C., 1987—. Vis. prof. Royal Soc. Medicine, London, 1997. Author: Head and Neck Surgery, 1996 (prize Royal Soc. Medicine 1996), rev. edit., 1997 (1st prize Brit. Med. Assn. 1997), 3d edit., 2003 (George D. Howells prize U. London 2003). Hon. fellow in dental surgery Royal Coll. Surgeons Eng. Fellow ACS, Royal Coll. Surgeons Edinburgh (hon.), Royal Australian Coll. Surgeons (hon.); mem. Soc. Head and Neck Surgeons (pres. 1991), Internat. Fedn. Head and Neck Oncological Socs. (bd. dirs. 2002), NY Cancer Soc. (pres. 1984), NY Head and Neck Soc. (pres. 1985), North Am. Skull Base Soc. (pres. 2003), Internat. Acad. Oraloncology (pres. 2005) Office: Meml Sloan Kettering Cancer Ctr 1275 York Ave New York NY 10021-6094

**SHAH, NANDLAL CHIMANLAL,** retired physiatrist; b. Sadra, Gujarat, India, July 3, 1933; came to U.S., 1969; s. Chimanlal D. and Dahiben C. (Shah) Shah; m. Indira N. Shah, May 15, 1960; children: Sandip N., Tushar N. Student, M.G. Sci. Inst., Ahmedabad, India, 1952; MB, BS, B.J. Med. Coll., Ahmedabad, India, 1957. Diplomate Am. Bd. Phys. Medicine and Rehab., Am. Bd. Quality Assurance and Utilization Review Physicians. Intern Yonkers (N.Y.) Gen. Hosp., 1970; resident in internal medicine St. Barnabas Hosp., Bronx, NY, 1971; resident in phys. medicine and rehab. Albert Einstein Coll. Medicine, Bronx, 1971-74; staff physiatrist, dir. med. svcs. Inst. Phys. Medicine and Rehab., Peoria, Ill., 1974-79; med. dir. Thomas Rehab. Hosp., Asheville, NC, 1979-81; staff physiatrist phys. medicine and rehab. Charlotte (N.C.) Inst. Rehab. (formerly Charlotte Rehab. Hosp.), 1981; pvt. practice Carolina Rehab. Clinic, Charlotte, 1981-99, ret., 2001. Mem. Greater Charlotte (N.C.) Assn. Physicians Indian Origin (chartered), N.C. Assn. Physicians Indian Origin (past pres.), Masons. Hindu. Avocations: Indian classical music, cultural and religious programs.

**SHAH, SHIRISH KALYANBHAI,** computer science, chemistry and environmental science educator; b. Ahmedabad, India, May 24, 1942; came to U.S., 1962, naturalized, 1974; s. Kayyanbhai T. and Sushilaben K. S.; m. Kathleen Long, June 28, 1973; 1 son, Lawrence. BS in Chemistry and Physics, St. Xavier's Coll. Gujarat U., 1962; PhD in Phys. Chemistry, U. Del., 1968; cert. in bus. mgmt., U. Va., 1986; PhD in Cultural Edn. (hon.), World U. West, 1986. Assoc. prof. Washington Coll., Chestertown, Md., 1967-68; dir. quality control Vita Foods, Chestertown, Md., 1968-72; asst. prof., assoc. prof. sci., adminstr. food, marine sci. and vocat. programs Chesapeake Coll., Wye Mills, Md., 1968-76; assoc. prof. chemistry Coll. Notre Dame of Md., 1991—2002. Chmn. computer sys. and engring. techs., 1982-89, project facilitator telecom. curriculum and lab., 1985-89, coord. tech. studies, 1989-91; adj. prof. Phys. Sci. Coppin State Coll., 1996-98; mem. Balt. City Adult Edn. Adv. Com., 1982-89, Distance Learning Task Force, 1996-97; chmn. Coll. wide computer user com., 1985-91; coun. mem. Faculty R&D, 1994-97; adj. prof. chemistry Villa Julie Coll., 2002-05; lectr./prof. chemistry Towson U., 1998—, Morgan State U., 1999—; cons. joint apprentice com. Baltimore City Govt., 1980-91. Contbr. articles to profl. jours. Permanent mem. Rep. Senatorial Com.; charter mem. Rep. Presdl. Task Force; mem. Congl. Adv. Com., 1983—; adviser Young Reps., 1992-2002. Recipient Phoenix award Am. Chem. Soc., 1996, 97, Pub. Rels. award, 1996, Sci. Policy award, 2000. Fellow Am. Inst. Chemists (co-chair internat. com. 2002); mem. IEEE, APHA, NSTA, Am. Lung Assn. (chair environ. affairs com., 1976-80), Am. Lung Assn. Md. (bd. dir. 1971-80), Am. Chem. Soc. (mem. mid. states higher edn. eval. teams 1987-, chmn.-elect Md. sect. 1995-96, chmn. 1996-98, chair kids and chemistry program Md. sect. 1996-99, sec. Mid-Atlantic regional conf., 2002-04, chmn. com. govt. rels. Md. sect. 1998-, chair pub. rels. com. 2000-, pres.-elect Chesapeake sect. 2002-03, co-coord. chemagination program 2005, Salute to Excellence award, 2004, Outstanding Coord. Chemagination, 2005), Indsl. Hygiene Assn. (pres. Chesapeake sect. 2003-04), Nat. Environ. Tng. Assn., Nat. Assn. Indsl. Tech. (dir. local region, bd. dir. 1989-95), Md. Pub. Health Assn. (bd. dir., chair pub. health nursing edn. 2005), Am. Vocat. Assn., Am. Tech. Edn. Assn., Am. Fedn. Tchrs., Md. State Tchrs. Assn., Md. Assn. Cmty. and Jr. Colls. (v.p. 1977-78, pres. 1978-97), Sigma Xi, Epsilon Pi Tau, Iota Lambda Sigma Nu. Roman Catholic. Home: 5605 Purlington Way Baltimore MD 21212-2950 Office: Chemistry Dept Towson University Towson MD 21252- Office Phone: 410-704-2720. Personal E-mail: dr.shah@juno.com. Business E-Mail: sshah@towson.edu.

**SHAH, SURENDRA POONAMCHAND,** engineering educator; b. Bombay, Aug. 30, 1936; s. Poonamchand C. and Maniben (Modi) S.; m. Dorothie Crispell, June 9, 1962; children: Daniel S., Byron C. BF, B V M Coll engring., India, 1959, MJ, Lehigh U., 1960; PhD, Cornell U., 1965. Asst. prof. U. Ill., Chgo., 1966-69, assoc. prof., 1969-73, prof., 1973-81; prof. civil engring Northwestern U., Evanston, Ill., 1981—, dir. Ctr. for Concrete and Geomaterials, 1987—, prof. civil engring., 1989—, Walter P. Murphy prof. of engring., 1992—. Cons. govt. agys. and industry, U.S.A., UN, France, Switzerland, People's Republic China, Denmark, The Netherlands; vis. prof. MIT, 1969, Delft U., The Netherlands, 1976, Denmark Tech. U., 1984, LCPC, Paris, 1986, U. Sidney, Australia, 1987; NATO vis. sci. Turkey, 1992; disting. vis. prof. Nat. Singapore U., 1999, vis. chair prof. Denmark Tech. U., 2002; hon. prof. Hongkong Poly. U., 2003. Co-author: Fiber Reinforced Cement Composites, 1992, High Performance Concrete and Applications, 1994, Fracture Mechanics of Concrete, 1995; contbr. more than 400 articles to profl. jours.; editor 20 books; mem. editorial bds. 2 internat. jours.; editor-in-chief Jour. Materials and Structures. Recipient Thompson award ASTM, Phila., 1983, Disting. U.S. Vis. Scientist awrd Alexander von Humboldt Found., 1989, Swedish Concrete award, Stockholm, 1993, Engring. News Record award of Newsmaker, 1995, Charles Perkow award, 1997. Fellow Am. Concrete Inst. (chmn. tech. com., Anderson award 1989, 99, Henry Crown award 2000, Symposium in his honor 2002, Robert Philbo award 2006), Internat. Union Testing and Rsch. Labs. Materials and Structures (chmn. tech. com. 1989—; mgmt. adv. bd. 1996—; Gold medal 1980, symposium in his honor 2002), mem. NAE, ASCE (past chmn. tech. com.; mem. exec. com., mem. adv. bd., Richard J. Caroll Meml. Lectr. 2001). Achievements include dedicated in his honor RILEM 7th international conference on fiber reinforced concrete and was given a special seventh award, Italy, 2004; symposium in his honor during the 13th European fracture conference in Greece, 2006. Home: 921 Isabella St Evanston IL 60201-1773 Office: Northwestern U Tech Inst Rm A130 2145 Sheridan Rd Evanston IL 60208-0834 Office Phone: 847-491-3858. Business E-Mail: s-shah@northwestern.edu.

**SHAH, VIJAY PRAVIN,** electrical engineer, researcher; b. Ahmedabad, Gujarat, India, Jan. 9, 1979; arrived in US 2000; s. Pravin Nemchand and Chandraprabha Pravin Shah. B Engring., Nirma Inst. Tech., Ahmedabad, 2000; MS, Miss. State U., 2002. Grad. rsch. asst. dept. elec. engring. Miss. State U., Mississippi State, 2001—02, 2003—04; patent searcher PatentComplete, LLC, Towson, Md., 2003; grad. rsch. asst. GeoResources Inst., Starkville, Miss., 2004—. Contbr. articles to profl. publs. Com. mem. Student Assn. Starkville, 2004—05. Barrier fellow, Dept. Elec. Engring., Miss. State

U., 2001—04. Mem.: IEEE. Home: 3 Vipul Apt Opp Naranpura PO Gujarat Ahmedabad 380013 India Office: Miss State U Dept Elec Engring Mississippi State MS 39762 Personal E-mail: vijaypshah@yahoo.com. Business E-Mail: shah@erc.msstate.edu.

**SHAH, Y. T.,** academic administrator; BSChemE, U. Mich.; MS, ChE, DSc, MIT. Prof. chem. engring. U. Pitts., 1969—87; dean engring. and sci. U. Tulsa, 1987—91; disting. prof., dean Coll. Engring. Drexel U., Phila., 1991—97; sr. vice provost for rsch. and grad. studies, chief rsch. scientist Clemon U., 1997; provost U. Mo., Rolla, 2002—. Mem.: AIChE, Am. Chem. Soc., Am. Soc. Elec. Engring. Office: Office of the Provost 204 Parker Hall 1870 Miner Cir Rolla MO 65409

**SHAHAN, SHERRY JEAN,** writer, educator; b. Long Beach, Calif., Aug. 14, 1949; d. Frank Rowe Webb and Sylvia Jean (Brunner) Benedict; m. Edgar Harold Shahan, Oct. 23, 1982; children: Kristina Michelle Beal, Kyle Shannon Beal. BS in Social Scis., Calif. Poly. State U., San Luis Obispo, 1978. Lectr. Saddleback Coll. Writers Conf., Orange County, Calif., 1992, Cuesta Community Coll., San Luis Obispo, 1988—, Calif. Reading Assn., 1998—, Nat. Coun. Tchrs. English, 1999—. Author: Dashing Through the Snow: The Story of the Jr. Iditarod (a photo essay, 1997), (mid. grade novel) Frozen Stiff, 1998, (photoessay) The Little Butterfly, 1998, (photoessays) The Sunflower Family, 1996, Feeding Time at the Zoo, 2000, (picture book) A Jazzy Alphabet, 2002, Working Dogs, 1999, Willie Covan Loved to Dance!, 2004; contbr. articles, photographs numerous regional and nat. newspapers and mags. Mem.: Children's Bookwriters and Illustrators, So. Calif. Children's Book Sellers, Am. Travel Writers, Authors Guild, Pi Gamma Mu. Home and Office: 2603 Richard Ave Cayucos CA 93430 E-mail: Kidbooks@thegrid.net.

**SHAHDA GERACI, CAROLE ANNE,** elementary school educator; d. Isaac Shahda and Mary LeGerda; children: Lorri Lee Geraci, Steven V. Geraci, Christopher B. Geraci, Christopher B. Geraci. BA, Bklyn Coll., 1956; MS, Addelphi U., 1975. Tchr. art P.S. 145, Bklyn., 1956—63; tchr. elem. sch. Oceanside Sch. Dist., 1965—80, tchr. program gifted children, 1980—88; dir. Oceanside Tchr. Ctr., 1980—90. Editor: (newsletters) LWV Beacon, Long Beach Hist. Soc. Heritage. Pres. LWV Nassau County, NY, 2001—04, Long Beach Hist. & Preservation Soc., 2004—, trustee. Named Trailblazer of Millenium, Nassau County Legis., 2002, Citizen of Yr., Kiwanis Club, Long Beach, 2003. Avocations: history, museum house restoration, travel. Home: 410 East Broadway Long Beach NY 11561

**SHAHEEN, ANTHONY JOSEPH,** lawyer; b. Battle Creek, Mich. children: Brett, Margaret. BA, U. Notre Dame, 1968; MA, U. Mich., 1973, PhD, 1977, JD, 1984. Ptnr. Davis, Graham, & Stubbs LLP, Denver, 1984—. Home: 3135 S Monaco Cir Denver CO 80222 Office: Davis Graham & Stubbs LLP 1550 17th St Ste 500 Denver CO 80202 Office Fax: 303-893-1379.

**SHAHEEN, C. JEANNE,** political organization administrator, former governor; b. St. Charles, Mo., Jan. 28, 1947; m. William H. Shaheen; 3 children. BA, Shippensburg U., 1969; M of Social sci. in Polit. Sci., U. Miss., 1973. Campaign mgr. Pres. Jimmy Carter, 1980, Gary Hart, 1984, Gov. Paul McEachon, 1986, 1988; mem. N.H. Senate, 1991-96; gov N.H., 1997—2003; vice chair Democratic Nat. Convention Com., 2004; nat. chair John Kerry Presidl. Campaign, 2004; dir. Inst. Politics Harvard Univ., 2005—. Democrat. Protestant. Office: Inst of Politics Harvard Univ 75 JFK St Cambridge MA 02138 Office Phone: 617-495-1363.

**SHAHEEN, CHRISTOPHER T.,** lawyer; b. 1962; BA in Internat. Rels. magna cum laude, Bucknell Univ., 1984; JD cum laude, Harvard Univ., 1987. Bar: Pa. 1989, Minn. 1994. Assoc. Bustamante & Crespo, Ecuador, 1987; law clerk, Hon. Samuel Conti US Dist Ct, No. Dist., Calif., 1988—89; trial atty. US Dept. Justice, civil rights divsn., 1989—94; assoc., litig. dept. Dorsey & Whitney LLP, Mpls., 1994—97, ptnr., trial dept., 1998—, and co-chair, tax, trust, estate litig. group. Bd. dir. Project for Pride in Living, Inc.; chmn. Kenwood Isles Area Assn. Grantee Humphrey Inst. Policy Fellow, Univ. Minn., 1999—2000. Mem.: ABA, Hennepin County Bar Assn., Minn. State Bar Assn. Office: Dorsey & Whitney LLP Ste 1500 50 S Sixth St Minneapolis MN 55402-1498 Office Phone: 612-340-2886. Office Fax: 612-340-2807. Business E-Mail: shaheen.christopher@dorsey.com.

**SHAHEEN, GEORGE T.,** software company executive; b. 1944; BS in Mktg., Bradley U., MBA. With Andersen Worldwide Orgn., 1967—89, mng. ptnr.-cons. for N.Am., 1977—89; mng. ptnr., CEO Andersen Cons. (now Accenture), Chgo., 1989-99; chmn., CEO Webvan Group, Inc., Foster City, Calif., 1999—2001; CEO Siebel Systems, Inc., San Mateo, Calif., 2005—. Bd. dirs. Memec, Siebel Systems, Inc., 1996—; mem. adv. bd. Marcus & Millichap Co. Mem. bd. advisors Northwestern Univ. J.L. Kellogg Grad. Sch. Bus. Office: Siebel Systems Inc 2207 Bridgepointe Pkwy San Mateo CA 94404 Office Phone: 650-295-5000.

**SHAHEEN, SHAHEEN AZEEZ,** minister, textiles executive; b. Chgo., Jan. 23, 1928; s. Azeez and Saleemeh (Balluteen) S.; m. Pierina Barbaglia, June 30, 1951; children: John A., David M. BS, Ill. Inst. Tech., 1949. Regional sales Katherine Rug, Dalton, Ga., 1949-53; chmn., pres., founder World Carpets, Inc., Dalton, Ga., 1954-92. Author: World Carpets-The First Thirty Years, 1984; mineral exhbn. Dalton State Coll., Ga., 2000-. Min. Jehovah's Witnesses, 1942—; helped establish Fed. Housing Authority carpet standards, Washington, 1970-75; mem. stay-in-sch. task force Dalwhichcom Found., Dalton, 1984-90; participant, bd. dirs. Harvest Outreach Rehab. Ctrs. for the Homeless, Dalton, 1990-2000; pres., treas. Dalton Land Co., 1982— Named Permanent Carpet Industry Elected Mem. of World Floor Covering Hall of Fame, World Floor Covering Assn., Anaheim, Calif. Established modern carpet production and technology, by pioneering methods and techniques for carpet production in areas of manufacturing, equipment development and innovation, quality assurance, continuous dyeing, product flow, distribution, marketing, merchandising, personell incentives and programs, profit sharing, direct private trucking, and related areas that resulted in common, everyday usage of wall to wall carpet worldwide.

**SHAHIED, ISHAK I.,** science educator; BA, Ea. Nazarene Coll., 1959; MS, U. Tenn., 1964; PhD, Colo. State U., 1973. Sr. rsch. chemist Aerospace Med. Rsch. Lab. USAF, Dayton, 1973—74; prof., dept. chmn. St. George's Med. Coll., Grenada, 1977—86; prof. Cleveland Coll., Kansas City, Mo., 1986—89; prof., head biochemist Life U., Marietta, Ga., 1989—94; prof. St. Matthew's Med. Coll., Belize, 1997—98, Ctrl. Bapt. Coll., Conway, Ark., 2001—02; prof., dean basic scis. St. James Sch. Medicine, Bonaire, Netherlands Antilles, 2002—, tchr. Cleve. Coll., Kansas City, Mo., 1976-77, 86-89. Author: Biochemistry of Foods and the Biocatalysts, 1977, (textbook) Physiology, 1980. Named Hon. fellow Truman Libr. Inst.; recipient Best Instr. award, 1984. Mem. N.Y. Acad. Sci. Avocations: writing, swimming. Office Phone: 011-599-717-2150, 011 599 717 2150. Personal E-mail: shahiedishak@hotmail.com.

**SHAHINIAN, HYRAYR K.,** surgeon; b. Beirut; Bachelor Degree in Biology and Chemistry with Distinction, Am. U. Beirut, Beirut, Lebanon, 1983; MD with Distinction, Am. U. Beirut and U. Chgo., Pritzker Med. Sch., 1985. Cert. Am. Bd. Surgery. Intern, rsch. assoc. U. Chgo., 1986—87; resident Vanderbilt U. Med. Ctr., Nashville, 1987—91, NYU Med. Ctr., 1991—92; fellow, plastic and reconstructive surgery, then craniofacial surgery NYU Med. Ctr., Inst. Reconstructive Plastic Surgery, NYC, 1992—93, asst. clin. prof., 1995—96; fellow, skull base surgery, dept. head and neck surgery U. Zurich, Switzerland, 1993—94; attending surgeon US Dept. Veterans Affairs Med. Ctr. Northport, NY, 1995—96; dir. Skull Base Inst., Cedars-Sinai Med. Ctr., LA, 1996—. Contbr. articles to profl. jours., chapters to books. Mem.: Alpha Omega Alpha. Office: Skull Base Inst 8635 W Third St Los Angeles CA 90048 Office Phone: 310-691-8888. Office Fax: 310-691-8877. Business E-Mail: staff@skullbaseinstitute.com.

**SHAHN, JONATHAN,** sculptor; s. Ben and Bernarda (Bryson) Shahn. One-man shows include Mary Porter Sesnon Gallery, UC Santa Cruz, 1980, Hackett-Freedman Gallery, NYC, 2001, exhibited in group shows at NAD, 1998, Cantor Fitzgerald Gallery, Harvard Coll., 2001, O'Hara Gallery, NYC. Represented in permanent collections Nat. Portrait Gallery, Washington, Vatican Mus., Rome, Art Mus., Princeton, NJ, prin. works include Martin Luther King Jr. commemt., NJ Transit, Jersey City, NJ, Franklin D. Roosevelt Meml., Roosevelt, NJ. Fellow: Nat. Sculpture Soc.; mem.: NAD (academician 1994—). Office: O'Hara Gallery Ste 1302 41 E 57th St New York NY 10022 E-mail: jonjeb@yahoo.com.

**SHAHSHAHANI, AHMAD,** economics professor; b. Tehran, Iran, Sept. 14, 1947; came to U.S., 1971; s. Housein Shahahshani and Zahra (Heshmat) Zommorodian; m. Shahla Mohtasham; 1 child, Ramina. Cert. in English, U. Cambridge, 1968; BS, U. Tehran, 1969; MA, U. Colo., 1973, PhD, 1976. Asst. prof. econs. Tehran U., 1976-80; research fellow Hoover Instn., Stanford, Calif., 1980-82; fin. analyst Unity in Diversity Council, L.A., 1983-84; asst. prof. Calif. State U., L.A., 1984-91, Northridge, 1985-87; economist U.S. Dept. Treasury, Glendale, Calif., 1991-93; economist, mgr. U.S. Dept. Treasury, IRS, L.A., 1993—. Mem. corp. fin. team Baraban Securities, Culver City, Calif., 1983-87; fellow Internat. Rsch. Ctr. Energy and Econ. Devel., Boulder, 1976-87; fin. advisor Tissurama-Knitex Industries, L.A., 1987-91. Author: Economics for Students, 1972, 2d edit., 1977, An Introduction to the Theory of Employment, 1974, 2d edit., 1977, An Econometric Model of Iran, And Its Application, 1978, Economist Report Writing Guide for Transfer Pricing, 2001, Economist Report Writing Guide for Intangible Assets, 2003, Economist Program website, 1999—; editor Econ. Issues, 1995-2000; also articles to profl. jours. Fellow Tehran U., 1974-76, scholar U. Colo., Boulder, 1973-74. Mem. Nat. Assn. Securities Dealers (series 7 lic.), Omicron Delta Epsilon. Avocations: tennis, jogging, travel. Home: 11939 Gorham Ave Apt 101 Los Angeles CA 90049-5362 Office: US Dept of Treasury IRS 225 W Broadway Glendale CA 91204-1331 Office Phone: 818-265-2323.

**SHAHZAD, M. AHMAD,** computer scientist; B.Computer Sci., U. Karachi, Pakistan. Cert. project mgmt. profl. System analyst Sidat Hyder Morshed Assocs., Karachi, 1996—98; database administr. Saudi Pak Leasing Co., Karachi, 1999—99; Oracle cons. Oracular System and Software, Inc., Oshkosh, Wis., 1999—2000; prin. cons. Blue Hammock Inc., Pitts., 2000—. Contbr. articles to profl. jours. Home: 2220 Meadowbrook Ct Unit A Oshkosh WI 54904

**SHAICH, RONALD M.,** food service executive; b. Newark, Dec. 30, 1953; s. Joseph and Pearl (Kalfus) S. AB in Govt., Clark U., 1976; MBA, Harvard U., 1978. Ea. regional mgr. Cole Nat. Corp., Cleve., 1978-80; pres. Targeting Systems, Inc., Washington, 1980-81; owner, pres. The Cookie Jar, Boston, 1981-82; co-founder, co-chmn., co-CEO Au Bon Pain Co., Inc., Boston, 1982—98; co-founder, chmn., CEO Panera Bread Co. (formerly Saint Louis Bread Co.), Richmond Heights, Mo., 1998—. Bd. dirs. Store 24, Inc., Boston. Trustee Clark U., Worcester, Mass., 1989—; incorporator Mt. Auburn Hosp., Cambridge, Mass.; treas. Mass. Dem. Party, Boston, 1990—. Recipient Golden Plate award, Internat. Foodservice Mfrs. Assn., 2005. Jewish. Avocation: swimming. Office: Panera Bread Co 6710 Clayton Rd Richmond Heights MO 63117*

**SHAIK, JAHANGHEER SHAREEF,** research scientist; b. Hyderabad, Andhra Pradesh, India, July 3, 1979; s. Hussain and Hussain Bee Shaik; m. Ishrat Nazneen, Dec. 12, 2005. Maste's degree, U. Memphis, 2003. Rsch. scholar U. Memphis, 2001—06; Herff Coll. Engring. fellow Herff Coll. Engring., Memphis, 2005—. Contbr. scientific papers to profl. jours. Achievements include research in Genomic scale analysis and visualization; Rotated Target Identification and Tracking Using Hilbert Wavelet Transform. Office: U Memphis EECE Dept Central Ave Memphis TN 38111 Office Phone: 901-678-4720. E-mail: jahangeer.shaik@gmail.com.

**SHAIKH, BAHU SULTAN,** physician, educator; b. Karachi, Sind, Pakistan, 1945; came to U.S., 1969; s. Noor Mohammad and Shahkhatoon Shaikh.; m. Yasmeen Khamisani, 1972 (div. Nov. 1995); children: Maheen, Sasha Ghulam Mohammad; m. Mona Sayed, July 1996; 1 child: Aneesa. Student, St. Patrick's Coll., Karachi, Pakistan, 1963; MBBS, Dow Med. Coll., Karachi, 1968. Intern Ellis Hosp., Schenectady, NY, 1969; resident in internal medicine Thomas Jefferson U., Phila., 1970-72, rsch. fellow, 1972-74; asst. prof. clin. medicine Penn State U., Hershey, Pa., 1974-80; assoc. prof. Med. Coll. Ohio, Toledo, 1980-87, clin. assoc. prof., 1987—99, clin. prof., 1999—. Cons. Toledo Clinic, Ohio, 1987—. Contbr. several chpts. in books related to cancer and AIDS, 1983-87, numerous articles to prof. jours. Recipient Key to the Golden Door award, Internat. Inst. Greater Toledo, 1999. Fellow. ACP, Pakistan Acad. Med. Scis.; mem. Am. Soc. Clin. Oncology, Am. Soc. of Hematology, Assn. Internat. Physicians of N.W. Ohio,; Assn. Pakistani Physicians N.Am. Office: Toledo Clinic 4235 Secor Rd Toledo OH 43623-4299

**SHAIKH, MUZAFFAR ABID,** management sciences educator; b. Bombay, Jan. 5, 1946; came to U.S., 1966; s. Shaikh A. Razzaque and Khudaija R. Shaikh; m. Farhat Anjum, Dec. 29, 1968; children: Mahjabeen, Shahbaaz, Shoaib. BS, U. Bombay, 1966; MS, Kans. State U., 1968; PhD, U. Ill., 1983. Mgmt. sci. rsch. analyst Caterpillar Inc., Peoria, Ill., 1968-85; sr. staff engr. Harris Corp., Melbourne, Fla., 1985-87; assoc. prof. Fla. Inst. Tech., Melbourne, 1987-92, prof. mgmt. sci., 1992—, assoc. dean Sch. Bus., 1992—97, head engring. sys. Coll. Engring., 1999—. Cons. Harris Corp., Melbourne, 1987-92, Grumman Corp., Melbourne, 1987-92. Assoc. editor Trans. of Simulation, 1989-96, INCOSE Sys. Engring. Jour., 1998-; N.Am. editor Bus. Process Mgmt. Jour., 2002-; contbr. over 1000 articles to profl. jours. Fellow Sigma Xi; sr. mem. Ops. Rsch. Soc., Am. Inst. Mgmt. Sci., Inst. Indsl. Engrs. Home: 409 Crystal Lake Dr Melbourne FL 32940-1934 Office: Fla Inst Tech 150 W University Blvd Melbourne FL 32901-6975

**SHAIKH, NAZRUL ISLAM,** industrial engineer, researcher; s. Nisar Ahmed and Deeba Shaikh. B in Chem. Engring., India Inst. Tech., Bombay, 2000; MSEE, Pa. State U., 2002, MS in Indsl. Engring., 2002, postgrad., 2002—. Intern Nat. Chem. Labs, Pune, Maharashtra, India, 1997—99; grad. lectr. Pa. State U., State College, 2001, tchg. asst., 2001, rsch. asst. indsl. engring., 2000—. Contbr. articles to profl. jours. Scholar Nat. Merit scholar, Govt. of India, Jit Paul scholar, Apeejay Edn. Soc. Mem.: IIE, INFORMS, Interact Club (dir.). Tau Beta Pi. Office: Dept Indsl Engring 310 Leonhard Bldg State College PA 16802 E-mail: nis109@psu.edu.

**SHAIN, IRVING,** retired chemicals executive, academic administrator; b. Seattle, Jan. 2, 1926; s. Samuel and Selma (Blockoff) S.; m. Mildred Ruth Udell, Aug. 31, 1947; children: Kathryn A., Steven T., John R., Paul S. BS in Chemistry, U. Wash., 1949, PhD in Chemistry, 1952. From instr. to prof. U. Wis., Madison, 1952-75, vice chancellor, 1970-75, chancellor, 1977-86; provost, v.p. acad. affairs U. Wash., Seattle, 1975-77; v.p. Olin Corp., Stamford, Conn., 1987-92, ret., 1992, also bd. dirs. Mem. tech. adv. bd. Johnson Controls, Inc., Milw., 1980-2003; trustee Univ. Rsch. Park, Inc. Madison, pres., 1984-86, v.p. 1987—; mem. Nat. Commn. on Superconductivity, 1989-90. Contbr. articles on electroanalytical chemistry to profl. jours. Bd. dirs. Madison Gen. Hosp., 1972-75; v.p. Madison Cmty. Found., 1984-86; mem. CEO adv. bd. Kamehameha Schs./Bishop Estates, 2002-04; mem. bd. dirs. Madison Symphony Orch., 2006-. With U.S. Army, 1943-46, PTO. Fellow AAAS, Wis. Acad. Scis., Arts and Letters; mem. Am. Chem. Soc., Electrochem. Soc., Coun. Acad. Sci. and Engring., Phi Beta Kappa, Sigma Xi, Phi Kappa Phi, Alpha Chi Sigma (Chemistry Hall of Fame 2006-). Home: 2820 Marshall Ct # 8 Madison WI 53705-2270 Office Phone: 608-441-8000. E-mail: i.shain@att.net.

**SHAIN, KENNETH STEPHEN,** management consultant, writer; b. Bridgeport, Conn., Sept. 24, 1952; s. Albert Benjamin and Gladys Ann (Lustig) S.; m. Nancie Ann Taylor, Apr. 1983 (div. Dec. 2002); children: Ian Alexander,

Kevin Mitchell, Andrew Thomas. BA, U. Mass., 1978. Prin. Shain Assocs., Atlanta, 1982—87, 1993—; chmn., pres. Geovision, Inc., Norcross, Ga., 1985—93, cons.; pres. Cyco Internat., Inc., Atlanta, 1995—98; CEO MENSI, Inc., Atlanta, 1999—2001; pres. XOBOX Corp., 2001—, cons.; v.p. sales, mktg. and bus. devel. Synaps, Inc., Atlanta, 2002—03; pres. SMB Automation, Inc., 2004—. Chmn. mech. engring. curriculum com. Gov.'s High-Tech Adv. Coun., State of Ga., 1984. Recipient Cert. Appreciation Gov.'s Office of Ga., 1985, Arthur Andersen Best Bus. Practices award, 1998. Mem. Soc. Mfg. Engrs. (sr., chmn. 1983-84), Computer and Automated Sys. Assn. (sr.), Nat. Info. Stds. Orgn., Southeastern Software Assn., ACM Siggraph. Office Phone: 770-841-0700. E-mail: kenshain@comcast.net.

**SHAINWALD, SYBIL,** lawyer; b. N.Y.C., Apr. 27, 1928; d. Samuel and Anne; m. Sidney Shainwald; children: Robert, Louise, Laurie, Marsha. BA, Coll. William and Mary, 1948; MA, Columbia U., 1972; JD, N.Y. Law Sch., 1976, LLD (hon.), 2000. Bar: N.Y. 1976. Pvt. practice, NYC, 2005—. Legal advisor Am. Found. for Maternal Child and Health; adj. prof. dept. law Baruch Coll., 1981—82. Co-editor: Jour. Women and Health; contbr. articles to profl. jours. Active Abortion Rights Action; co-founder, bd. mem. Trial Lawyers for Pub. Justice, 1982—88; bd. mem. Hysterectomy Edn. Resources and Svcs., 1985—, Dalkon Shield INfo. Network, Nat. Network to Prevent Birth Defects, No. Ariz. Sch. Midwifery, 1989—; bd. advisors Med. Legal Aspects of Breast Implants; bd. dirs. Consumer Interest Rsch. Inst.; fellow Roscoe Pound Inst., Morgan Libr.; trustee Civil Justice Found., 1998—99; bd. dirs. Am. Friends of Tel Aviv Mus., 2000, Friends of Tel Aviv Mus., 2000-; trustee N.Y. Law Sch., 2000—; adv. bd. Southampton The Hamptons Shakespeare Festival, 2000—; co-chair Take Home a Nude N.Y. Acad. Art, 2001; active Sybil Shainwald Charitable Found., N.Y.C. Comptrs. Health Task Force. Recipient Susan B. Anthony award, NOW; grantee, Nat. Endowment for the Humanities, Rockefeller Found., Gov. W. Averell Harriman; scholar Pres. Bryan scholar, Coll. of William and Mary, Edward Coles scholar. Mem.: ATLA (chair environ. and toxic tort sect. 1988—89, co-chair breast implant litigation group 1992—2000, mem. Dalkon shield litigation group 1995, mem. contraceptive implant litigation group 1995, co-chair DES litigation group, environ. law adv. com.), N.Y. State Trial Lawyers (bd. govs.), Assn. of the Bar of the City of N.Y. (judge nat. moot ct. competition 1988—2003), Soc. Med. Jurisprudence, Health Action Internat.-U.S. (co-founder, mem. steering com.), Lawyers Com. for Human Rights, Am. Soc. Law, Medicine and Ethics, Nat. Women's Health Alliance (pres.), Nat. Women's Health Network (bd. mem. 1980—86, chair litigation svc. 1980—86, chair health law and regulation 1981—88, chmn. bd. dirs. 1982—86, chair N.Y. state affiliate), Phi Beta Kappa. Avocations: art, music. Home: 955 5th Ave 15B New York NY 10021 Office: Law Offices of Sybil Shainwald 111 Broadway 4th Fl New York New York 10006 Business E-Mail: shainwaldlaw@aol.com.

**SHAKEEL, ARIF,** retail executive; BSME, Memphis State U.; MBA, Pepperdine U. From product mgr. to v.p. positions in various areas Western Digital Corp., Lake Forest, Calif., 1985—2001, pres., 2002—, COO, 2003—05, CEO, 2005—, also bd. dir., 2004—. Bd. dir. Share Our Selves, Calif. Office: Western Digital Corp 20511 Lake Forest Dr Lake Forest CA 92630-7741

**SHAKELY, JOHN BOWER (JACK SHAKELY),** foundation executive; b. Hays, Kans., Jan. 9, 1940; s. John B. and Martha Jean (Gaston) S.; 1 child, Benton. BA, U. Okla., 1962. Vol. Peace Corps., Costa Rica, 1963-64; editor publs. Dept. Def., 1967-68; dir. devel. U. Okla., 1968-70, Resthaven Mental Health Ctr., L.A., 1970-74; pres. Jack Shakely Assocs., L.A., 1974-75; sr. adv. Grantsmanship Ctr., L.A., 1975-79, Coun. on Founds., Washington, 1979; pres. Calif. Community Found., L.A., 1980—. Lectr. in field. Bd. dirs. Emergency Loan and Assistance Fund, 1985—, chair bd. dirs., 1988-93; mem., vice chair L.A. Am. Indian Commn.; bd. dirs. So. Calif. Assn. Philanthropy, 1980—, Comic Relief, 1987—; chmn. bd. dirs. Nonprofit Channel. Served to 1st lt. U.S. Army, 1965-68. Decorated Army Commendation medal; named Philanthropy Day Outstanding Exec., L.A. Com. Nat. Philanthropy Day, 1989. Office: 445 S Figueroa St Ste 3400 Los Angeles CA 90071-1638

**SHAKER, JOSEPH LOUIS,** internist, educator; b. Danbury, Conn., Apr. 23, 1954; s. George and Elizabeth Shaker; m. Sona Andrews, May 29, 1993; children: Elizabeth Marilyn, Christopher Andrews. BA, Colby Coll., Waterville, Maine, 1976; MD, Georgetown U., Washington, DC, 1976. Diplomate Am. Bd. of Internal Medicine, 1983, cert. clin. densitometrist Internat. Soc. for Clin. Densitometry, 1998. Intern in internal medicine Albany Med. Ctr., NY, 1980—81; resident in internal medicine Georgetown U. Med. Ctr., Washington, 1981—83; attending physician in internal medicine Cermak Health Svcs., Chgo., 1983—85; fellow in endocrinology U. Pa. Sch. of Medicine, Phila., 1985—87; asst. prof. medicine Med. Coll. of Wis., Milw., 1987—88; endocrinologist St. Luke's Med. Ctr., Milw., 1987—, chair sect. of endocrinology and metabolism, 1999—; clin. asst. prof. medicine U. Wis. Sch. of Medicine, Milw., 1988—92, clin. assoc. prof. medicine, 1992—2003, clin. prof. medicine, 2003—. Contbr. articles to profl. jours. Bd. mem. Paget Disease Found., N.Y.C., 2003—06. Mem.: Internat. Soc. for Bone Densitometry (sci. adv. com. 2003—06), Am. Soc. for Bone and Mineral Rsch., The Endocrine Soc. (clin. affairs com. 2003—06). Avocation: mountain biking. Home: 11435 W Oklahoma Ave West Allis WI 53227 Office: Midwest Endocrinology 2801 West KK River Pky Milwaukee WI 53217 Office Phone: 414-649-6421. Home Fax: 414-649-3763; Office Fax: 414-649-3763. Personal E-mail: joseph.shaker@aurora.org.

**SHAKER, WILLIAM HAYGOOD,** marketing professional, public policy reformer; b. Downey, Calif., Apr. 22, 1938; s. Elmer S. and Marylee Shaker; m. Joanna Drummond, Jan. 28, 1966; children: Catherine Patricia, Marylee, Marcus, Matthew. BS in Engring., U. So. Calif., 1964; MS in Engring., U. Mich., 1969. Registered profl. engr., Calif. Exec. Dow Chem. Co., Midland, Mich., 1966-78; v.p. Nat. Legal Ctr. for the Pub. Interest, Washington, 1979; exec. v.p. Nat. Tax Limitation Com., Washington, 1980-86; pres. Am. Coun. for Health Care Reform, Arlington, Va., 1982—, Heart to Heart Found., Arlington, 1982—; CEO Washington Mktg. Group, Arlington, 1987—; pres. Health PAC, Arlington, 1994—. Pres. RepublicanPac.com, 2000—, Rule of Law Com., 2001—. Author: Health Care Reform, 1994, also legis. and govt. publs.; editor: Electric Power Reform, 1979; editor, pub. millennium edit. The Man of Galilee, 2001; contbr. articles to profl. jours. Founder, chmn. Taxpayers United, Mich., 1972-84. Mem. Govtl. Rsch. Assn. (most effective presentation of govtl. rsch. award 1973), Direct Mktg. Assn. (Echo award 1982-97, Maxi award 1987-2001), Pub. Rels. Soc. (Silver Anvil 1979), Am. Conservative Union (Health Care Reform award 1995). Republican. Lutheran. Office Phone: 703-534-9331. E-mail: william.shaker@twmg.com.

**SHAKESPEARE, FRANK,** ambassador; b. N.Y.C., Apr. 9, 1925; s. Francis Joseph and Frances (Hughes) S.; m. Deborah Anne Spaeth, Oct. 9, 1954; children: Mark, Andrea, Fredricka. BS, Holy Cross Coll., 1947; D.Eng. (hon.), Colo. Sch. Mines, 1975; DCS (hon.), Pace U., 1979; LLD (hon.), Del. Law Sch., 1980, Sacred Heart U., 1985, U. Dallas, 1987, Pepperdine U., 1990, Nichols Coll., 1991, Marquette U., 1993; D of Pub. Svc. (hon.), Hillsdale Coll., 1996. Formerly pres. CBS-TV Services; exec. v.p. CBS-TV Stas.; dir. USIA, 1969-73; exec. v.p. Westinghouse Electric Corp., 1973-75; pres. RKO Gen. Inc., N.Y.C., 1975-85, vice chmn., 1983-85; U.S. ambassador to Portugal Lisbon, 1985-87; U.S. ambassador to The Holy See Vatican City, 1987-89. Chmn. Heritage Found., 1975-85, dir., 1989—; chmn. Radio Free Europe/Radio Liberty, Inc., 1976-85; dir. Bradley Founhd., 1989—. Served to lt. (j.g.) USNR, 1945-46. Mem.: Union League. Home: 303 Coast Blvd La Jolla CA 92037-4630

**SHAKIRA, (SHAKIRA ISABEL MEBARAK RIPOLL),** musician; b. Barranquilla, Colombia, Feb. 2, 1977; Actor: (TV series) El Oasis, 1996; musician: (albums) Magia, 1991, Peligro, 1994, Pies descalzos, 1995, The Remixes, 1995, Dónde Están Los Ladrones?, 1998, MTV Unplugged, 2000, Laundry Service, 2001, Grandes éxitos, 2002, Live & Off the Record, 2004, Fijación Oral Vol. 1, 2005 (Latin Pop Album of Yr., Billboard Music Awards,

2005, Grammy Award for Best Lation Rock/Alternative Album, 2006, Spanish Album of Yr., Nat. Coun. La Raza ALMA award (Am. Latin Media Arts), 2006, Latin Pop Album of Yr., Billboard Latin Music Awards, 2006), Oral Fixation Vol. 2, 2005, (songs) La Tortura (Latin Song of Yr., Billboard Music Awards, 2005, 4 Billboard Latin Music awards: Hot Latin Song, Hot Latin Vocal Duet, Latin Pop Airplay Song for Duo, Latin Ringtone, 2006), Hips Don't Lie (MTV Video Music award for Best Choreography, 2006). Global Goodwill Amb. UNICEF, 2003—; founder Pies Descalzos, 1996, 3 elementary schools, Colombia. Named Latin Pop Album Artist of Yr., Billboard Music Awards, 2005, Outstanding Female Musical Performer, Nat. Coun. La Raza ALMA award (Am. Latin Media Arts), 2006; recipient Eres award, pop singer of yr., 1997, Casandra award, best Latin female singer, 1997, Best Latin Artist, World Music Awards, 1998, Best Female Pop Artist, Billboard Latin Music Awards, 1999, Spirit of Hope award, 2006, Gardel award, 2006, Nickelodeon Kids Choice award, 2000, Echo award, best female pop artist, 2003, Best Latin Female Artist, World Music Awards, 2003, Luna award, best Latin pop artist, 2003, Favorite Latin Music Artist, Am. Music Awards, 2005, Best Female award, MTV Europe Music Awards, 2005, Best Latin Entertainer, Internat. Reggae & World Music Awards, 2006. Office: Sony Music Entertainment Inc 550 Madison Ave New York NY 10022 Office Phone: 212-833-8000.*

**SHAKLEY, ELAINE M.,** organist, department chairman; b. Boswell, Pa., Dec. 23, 1922; d. John Henry and Pearl Beatrice Morrison; m. Glenn Huling Shakley; children: Susan, Bonnie, Pam. MusB, Heidelberg Coll., Tiffin, Ohio, 1944; MA, Case Western Res. U., Cleve., 1965. Music supr. K-1 Northfield Pub. Schs., Ohio, 1944—45, music supr. K-12, 1959—74; music tchr. Roosevelt Jr. H.S, Cleveland Heights, Ohio, 1944—46; music cons. Cleveland Heights, 1959—74; adj. prof. Ch. Grace State U., 1961—99; music tchr. Chagrin Falls Pub. Schs., Ohio, 1974—83; tchr. WVIZ-TV, Cleve., 1965—66; organist Fed. Ch. Chagrin Falls, Ohio, 1965—93, Chagrin Falls United Meth. Ch., 1993—2004; music dir. First English Luth. Ch., Cleveland Heights, 1959—63; bell choir dir. Federated Ch., Chagrin Falls, Ohio, 1974—93. Chmn. Fortnightly Chagrin Valley Jr. Divsn., Cleve., 1996—2006, Chagrin Valley Nat. Piano Auditions, Cleve., 1998—2006. Composer: (songs) April, 1944, Mass in Pentatonic, 1970; prodr., writer script for songs; author: various music courses of study. Chmn. Musical Club Jr. Divsn., Cleve., 1996—2006. Recipient Alumni Excellence award, Heidelberg Coll., 2002; grantee, Martha Holden Jennings Found., 1966. Avocations: knitting, swimming, walking. Home and Office: 7662 Birchmont Dr Chagrin Falls OH 44022 Personal E-mail: eshakley@aol.com.

**SHAKNO, ROBERT JULIAN,** hospital and social services administrator; b. Amsterdam, Holland, Aug. 15, 1937; came to U.S., 1939, naturalized, 1944; s. Rudy C. and Gertrude S.; m. Linda, June 10, 1962; children: Steven Lee, Deborah Sue. BBA (scholar 1955), So. Methodist U., 1959; M.H.A., Washington U., St. Louis, 1961. Adminstrv. asst. Mt. Sinai Hosp., Chgo., 1961—63; asso. adminstr. Tex. Inst. Rehab. and Research, Houston, 1963—65; asst. adminstr. Michael Reese Hosp., Chgo., 1965—70, v.p., hosp. dir., 1970—73; asso. exec. dir. Cook County Hosp., Chgo., 1973—75; pres. Hackensack Med. Center, NJ, 1975—85, Mt. Sinai Med. Ctr., Cleve., 1985—96; dir. market strategy practice KPMG Peat Marwick, 1996-98; v.p. med. affairs, vice dean sch. of medicine Case Western Res. U., 1998—2002; pres., CEO Jewish Family Svc., Cleve., 2002—05; ptnr. Tatum Ptnrs., LLC, Deerfield, Ill., 2005—. Bd. dirs. Ohio Hosp. Inc. Co. Mem. editorial bd. Mgmt. Series, Am. Coll. Healthcare Execs. Mem. Leadership Cleve.; bd. dirs. Premier Hosp. Alliance, chmn., 1994-96; bd. dirs. The New Cleve. Inc., Univ. Circle Inc., Cleve., Cleve. Sight Ctr.; trustee Hope Lodge, Cleve. chpt. Am. Cancer Soc.; chmn. elect, bd. dirs. Jewish Family Svcs.; chmn. social svcs. divsn. United Jewish Appeal, Cleve., 1987-88, chmn. health cabinet, 1990, gen. co-chmn., 1990—; chmn. Hosp. Pacesetter campaign United Way, chmn. health svcs. portfolio, 1988-89, oversight commn., 1992-93. Served to 1st lt. USAR, 1960-66. Named Young Adminstr. of Yr., Washington U., 1968 Fellow Am. Coll. Hosp. Adminstrs.; mem. Am. Hosp. Assn. (coun. urban hosps., del. coun. on met. hosps., rep. regional policy bd.), Washington U. Alumni Assn. (past pres.), Greater Cleve. Hosp. Assn. (bd. dirs.), Ohio Hosp. Assn. (bd. dirs.), Cleve. Sight Ctr. (trustee, bd. dirs.), Sigma Alpha Mu (past pres.). Home: 908 Island Ct Deerfield IL 60015 Office Phone: 312-909-2022. Personal E-mail: lbs1shak@sbcglobal.net.

**SHAKOW, ALEXANDER,** economist, government official; b. Apr. 12, 1937; s. David and Sophie (Harap) S.; m. Patricia Connell, Dec. 26, 1967; children: John, Peter, Thomas. BA with honors, Swarthmore Coll., 1958; PhD in Internat. Rels./Econ. Devel., London Sch. Econs., 1962. Assoc., dep., then dir. Indonesia program U.S. Peace Corps, Washington and Jakarta, Indonesia, 1963-65, asst., dep. then dir. Office Vol. Tng. Washington, 1965-67; dir. Office Indonesia Affairs-Office Asia Devel. Planning, US AID, Washington, 1968-74, dep. asst. adminstr., then asst. adminstr. program-policy, 1974-81; spl. policy advisor, chief policy unit, sr. advisor internat. econ. affairs World Bank, Washington, 1981-85, chief internat. econ. affairs, 1985-87, dir. strategic planning and rev., dir. external affairs, 1987-94, exec. sec. World Bank/IMF devel. com., 1995—2002; dep. sec. World Bank group World Bank/IMF, 1997—2002, acting v.p., sec., 2001—02. Chmn. bd. sci. and tech. for internat. devel. NAS, Washington, 1989-95; bd. Enterprise Works/VITA, 2003—. Bd. trustees Inst. Devel. Studies, Sussex, Eng., 1991-2002, hon. gov., 2002—. Recipient William A. Jump Meritorious award for outstanding pub. svc. William A. Jump Meml. Found., 1967. Mem. Am. Friends London Sch. Econs. (founding). Avocations: carpentry, gardening, reading. Fax: 301-933-3218. E-mail: ashakow@comcast.net.

**SHAKOW, DAVID JOSEPH,** lawyer, educator; b. NYC, May 26, 1945; s. Jacob and Rae (Levine) S.; m. Rachel Pilich, Aug. 3, 1980; children: Rachel Esther, Chava Leah, Yaakov, Tuvia Simcha, Rivka Sara, Chana Miriam. BA, Harvard U., 1967, JD, 1970; LLM, NYU, 1976. Bar: NY 1971. Law clk. to Hon. William H. Hastie, Phila., 1970-71; assoc. Davis Polk & Wardwell, NYC, 1971-77; atty., adviser Office Tax Legis. Counsel US Treasury, Washington, 1977-79, assoc. tax legis counsel, 1979-80, dep. tax legis. counsel, 1980-81; assoc. prof. U. Pa., Phila., 1981-87, prof. law, 1987-2000, prof. law emeritus, 2000—; of counsel King & Spalding, Washington, 1998-99; dir. KPMG, Washington, 2000—05; of counsel McKee Nelson LLP. NYC, 2005—. Author: The Taxation of Corporations, Partnerships, and Their Owners, 2d edit., 1997; co-reporter Taxation of Pass-through Entities, Am. Law Inst. Fed. Income Tax Project, 1994-99. Office: McKee Nelson LLP One Battery Park Plz New York NY 10004 Business E-Mail: dshakow@mckeenelson.com.

**SHALALA, DONNA EDNA,** academic administrator, former secretary of health and human services; b. Cleve., Feb. 14, 1941; d. James Abraham and Edna (Smith) S. AB, Western Coll., 1962; MSSC, Syracuse U., 1968, PhD, 1970; 39 hon. degrees, 1981-91. Vol. Peace Corps, Iran, 1962-64; asst. prof. polit. sci. CUNY, 1970-72; assoc. prof. politics and edn. Tchrs. Coll. Columbia U., 1972-79; asst. sec. for policy devel. and research HUD, Washington, 1977-80; prof. polit. sci., pres. Hunter Coll., CUNY, 1980-87; prof. polit. sci., chancellor U. Wis., Madison, 1987-93; sec. US Dept. Health & Human Services, Washington, 1993-2001; pres. U. Miami, 2001—. Dir., treas. Mcpl. Assistance Corp. for the City of N.Y., 1975—77. Author: Neighborhood Governance, 1971, The City and the Constitution, 1972, The Property Tax and the Voters, 1973, The Decentralization Approach, 1974. Mem. Trilateral Commn., 1988—92, Knight Commn. on Intercollegiate Sports, 1989—91; bd. govs. Am. Stock Exch., 1981—87; trustee TIAA, 1985—89, Com. Econ. Devel., 1982—92, Brookings Inst., 1989—92; bd. dirs. Children's Def. Fund, 1980—93, Am. Ditchley Found., 1981—93, Spencer Found., 1988—92, M&I Bank of Madison, 1991—92, NCAA Found., 1991, Inst. Internat. Econs., 1981—; Gannett Co., Inc., McLean, Va., United Health Group, Mpls., Lennar Corp., Miami; trustee emeritus Kennedy Ctr. Bd. of Trustees, Washington. Ohio Newspaper Women's scholar, 1958, Western Coll. Trustee scholar, 1958-62; Carnegie fellow, 1966-68; Guggenheim fellow, 1975-76; recipient Disting. Svc. medal Columbia U. Tchrs. Coll.,

1989. Mem. ASPA, Am. Polit. Sci. Assn., Nat. Acad. Arts and Scis., Nat. Acad. Pub. Adminstrn., Coun. Fgn. Rels., Nat. Acad. Edn. (Spencer fellow 1972-73). Office: U Miami Office Pres 230 Ashe Bldg Coral Gables FL 33146

**SHALES, THOMAS WILLIAM,** television and film critic, writer, journalist; b. Elgin, Ill., Nov. 3, 1953; s. Clyde LeRoy and Hulda Louise (Reko) S. BA, Am. U., 1973. Entertainment editor Washington Examiner, 1968-71; writer style sect. Washington Post, 1972—77, chief TV critic, 1977—, TV editor, 1979—; film critic, modular arts service Nat. Public Radio, 1970-79, film critic, Morning Edit., 1979—. Adj. prof. Am. U., 1978; syndicated columnist On the Air, Washington Post Writers Group, 1979— Author: The American Film Heritage, 1972, On the Air!, 1982, Legends, 1989; Co author: Live from New York: An Uncensored History of Saturday Night Live, 2002. Recipient Disting. Alumnus award Am. U., 1978. Recipient Pulitzer Prize for criticism, 1988, Disting. Writing Award, Am. Soc. Newspaper Editors, 1988. Office: Washington Post Co 1150 15th St NW Washington DC 20071-0002

**SHALHOUB, TONY,** actor, television producer; b. Green Bay, Wis., Oct. 9, 1953; m. Brooke Adams, 1992; 1 child, Sophie 1 stepchild, Josie. Grad., U. So. Maine, 1977; attended, Yale U. Actor: (plays) Conversations with My Father, 1992; (films) Longtime Companion, 1990, Quick Change, 1990, Barton Fink, 1991, Honeymoon in Vegas, 1992, Searching for Bobby Fischer, 1993, Addams Family Values, 1993, I.Q., 1994, Big Night, 1996 (Nat. Soc. Film Critics award best supporting actor, 1996), Men in Black, 1997, Gattaca, 1997, A Life Less Ordinary, 1997, Primary Colors, 1998, Paulie, 1998, The Siege, 1998, The Impostors, 1998, A Civil Action, 1998, The Tic Code, 1998, The Man Who Wasn't There, 2001, Spy Kids, 2001, Thirteen Ghosts, 2001, Men in Black II, 2002, Life or Something Like It, 2002, Impostor, 2002, Something More, 2003, Against the Ropes, 2004, Spy Kids 3-D: Game Over, 2003, T for Terrorist, 2003, The Great New Wonderful, 2005, (voice) Cars, 2006; actor, dir.: (films) Made-Up, 2002; actor: (TV films) Alone in the Neon Jungle, 1988, Money, Power, Murder, 1989, Day One, 1989, Gypsy, 1993, Radiant City, 1996, That Championship Season, 1999, The Heart Department, 2001, (video game) Thralls: A Post-Nuclear Role-Playing Game, 1997; (TV series) Wings, 1991—97, Stark Raving Mad, 1999—2000, Monk, 2002— (Golden Globe award, 2002, Emmy award best actor in a comedy, 2003, Screen Actors Guild Award for best actor in a comedy series, 2004, Screen Actors Guild award, outstanding performance by male actor in comedy series, 2005, Emmy award for outstanding lead actor in a comedy series, 2005, Emmy award for Outstanding Lead Actor in a Comedy Series, 2006); (TV guest appearances) Late Late Show with Craig Kilborne, Ally McBeal, Frasier, Almost Perfect, The X Files, many others. Office: UTA 9560 Wilshire Blvd # 500 Beverly Hills CA 90291*

**SHALIKASHVILI, JOHN MALCHASE,** former Chairman of the Joint Chiefs of Staff; b. Warsaw, June 27, 1936; s. Dimitri and Maria (Ruediger) S.; m. Joan E. Zimpelman, Dec. 27, 1966; 1 child, Brant. BSME, Bradley U., 1958; attended, Naval War Coll., 1969—70, U.S. Army War Coll., 1977—78; MA in Internat. Affairs, George Washington U., 1970; LLD (hon.), U. Md., 1993, Bradley U., 1994. Joined U.S. Army, 1958, advanced through grades to gen., 1992, ret., 1997, various troop and staff assignments Alaska, U.S., Fed. Republic of Germany, Vietnam, Korea, Italy, Belgium, 1959-75, commdr. 1st bn. 84th field arty. Ft. Lewis, Wash., 1975-77; dep. chief of staff ops. So. European Task Froce U.S. Army, Vicenza, Italy, 1978-79; comdr. div. arty., 1st Armored Div. U.S. Army, Nuernberg, Fed. Republic of Germany, 1979-81, chief., politico-mil div., later dep. dir. ODCSOPS Washington, 1981-84, asst. div. comdr. 1st. Armored Div. Nuernberg, Fed. Republic of Germany, 1984-86, dir. strategy, plans, policy ODCSOPS Washington, 1986-87; comdg. gen. 9th inf. div. Ft. Lewis, Wash., 1987-89; dep. comdr.-in-chief Hdqrs. USAREUR and 7th Army, Heidelberg, Fed. Republic of Germany, 1989-91; asst. to chmn. Joint Chiefs of Staff, Washington, 1991-92; Supreme Allied Comdr. Europe, Comdr.-in-Chief NATO, Brussels, 1992-93; chmn. Joint Chiefs of Staff, US Dept. Def., Washington, 1993-97. Vis. prof. Ctr. Internat. Security and Cooperation, Stanford U.; bd. dirs. Boeing Co., 2000—, Frank Russell Trust Co., L-3 Comm. Holdings, Inc., Plug Power Inc. Bd. trustees Bradley U.; mem. Buffalo Soldier Meml. Hon. Com. Decorated Def. D.S.M. with 3 oak leaf clusters, D.S.M. (Army) with oak leaf cluster), D.S.M. (Navy), D.S.M. (Air Force), D.S.M. (Dept. Trans.), Legion of Merit with 2 oak leaf clusters, Bronze Star medal with V device, Meritorious Svc. medal with 3 oak leaf clusters, Air medal, Joint Svc. Commendation medal, Army Commendation medal, Nat. Def. Svc. medal with bronze svc. star, Armed Forced Expeditionary medal, Republic of Vietnam Svc. medal with silver service star, S.W. Asia Svc. medal with bronze svc. star, Humanitarian Svc. medal, Army Svc. Ribbon, Overseas Svc. Ribbon with bronze Arabic numeral 5, Inter-Am. Def. Bd. medal, Kuwait Liberation medal, Order of Combat Infantryman badge, Parachutist badge, Joint Chiefs of Staff Identification badge, Army Staff Identification badge, Brazilian Order of Mil. Merit with 1st and 2d award, French Grand Officer of Nat. Merit, Belgian Grand Cordon of Order of Leopold, German Order of Merit with star and sash, Japanese Order of Rising Sun, Argentine Order of May in Grade of Gt. Cross for Mil. Merit, Korean Order of Nat. Security Merit, Tong-IL medal, Bintang Yudha Dharama Utama Hon. Decoration (Indonesia), Kuwait Def. medal, Grand Cross of Royal Norwegian Order of Merit, Grand Cross of Mil. Merit medal of Portuguese Republic, Republic of Vietnam Gallantry Cross with 2 silver and 1 bronze star, Republic of Vietnam Armed Forces Honor medal 1st class, Republic of Vietnam Armed Forces Honor medal 1st class, Republic of Vietnam Campaign medal, Republic of Vietnam Chung My medal 2d class, Tng. Svc. medal 1st class, Netherlands Comdr. Order Orange Nassau with swords, Mexican U.S. Mil. Merit 1st class, Great Cross Repub. Poland; recipient Chilean Bernardo Higgins award, Dwight D. Eisenhower Dist. Svc. award Vets. Fgn. Wars. Dist. Alumni Achievement award George Washington U., Presdl. Medal of Freedom award, 1997*

**SHALITA, ALAN REMI,** dermatologist; b. Bklyn., Mar. 22, 1936; s. Harry and Celia; m. Simone Lea Baum, Sept. 4, 1960; children: Deborah (dec.) and Judith (twins). AB, Brown U., 1957; BS, U. Brussels, 1960; MD, Bowman Gray Sch. Medicine, 1964; DSc (hon.), L.I. U., 1990. Intern Beth Israel Hosp., N.Y.C., 1964-65; resident dept. dermatology NYU Med. Ctr., 1967-68, NIH tng. grant fellow dept. dermatology, 1968-70, instr. dermatology, 1970-71; asst. prof. NYU, 1971-73, Columbia U., 1973-75; assoc. prof. medicine, head divsn. dermatology SUNY Downstate Med. Ctr., Bklyn., 1975-79, prof., 1979—, head divsn. dermatology, 1979-80, chmn. dept. dermatology, 1980—, asst. dean, 1977-83, acting dean Queens campus, 1983-84; assoc. dean clin. affairs SUNY Health Sci. Ctr., Bklyn., 1989-92, assoc. provost for clin. affairs, 1992-93, assoc. v.p. clin. affairs, 1993—2005, assoc. dean grad. med. edn., 1994—2006. Disting. tchg. prof. SUNY Health Sci. Ctr., Bklyn., 1996—; asst. attending in dermatology U. Hosp., NYC, 1970-73, Bellevue Hosp. Ctr., 1970-73, Manhattan VA Hosp., 1971-73, Presbyn. Hosp., 1973-75; bd. dirs. Kings County Hosp., 1975—; cons. dermatology Bklyn. VA Hosp., 1975—; chief dermatology U. Hosp. Bklyn., 1975—, Brookdale Med. Ctr., 1977-90, Kings County Hosp. Ctr., Bklyn., 1975—, acting med. dir., 1989-92; med. dir. U. Hosp. Bklyn., 1992-96. Pres. Temple Shaaray Tefila, N.Y.C., 1982-86, chmn. bd. trustees, 1987-95. Lt. M.C. USNR, 1965-67. Recipient Torch of Liberty award Anti-Defamation League, 1987, Surg. and Pediat. awards Beth Israel Hosp., NYC, 1965, Leah Dickstein Man of Good Conscience award Women's Med. Assn. NY, 1999, Leadership in Urban Med. Edn. award Arthur Ashe Inst. for Urban Health, 1999; Spl. fellow NIH, 1970-73. Mem.: AMA, Venezuelan Dermatology Soc., Argentina Dermatology Soc., Brit. Assn. Dermatologists, N.Y. Dermatol. Soc. (pres. 1989—90), Dermatol. Soc. Greater N.Y. (pres. 1980—81), N.Y. State Dermatol. Soc., N.Y. Acad. Medicine, N.Y. State Med. Soc., N.Y. Acad. Scis., Internat. Soc. Dermatology, Assn. Profs. Dermatology (sec.-treas. 1988—94, pres. 1996—98), Am. Soc. Dermatol. Surgery (past bd. dirs.), Am. Dermatol. Assn. (sec.-treas. 1996—2001, pres. 2001—02), Dermatology Found. (past trustee), Soc. Investigative Dermatology, Am. Acad. Dermatology (bd. dirs. 1983—87, v.p. 1995—96), Polish Dermatology Soc. (hon.), Soc. Francaise de Dermatology (hon.), Alpha Omega Alpha. Republican. Home: 70 E 77th St New York NY 10021-1811 Office: 450 Clarkson Ave Brooklyn NY 11203-

2056 Office Phone: 718-270-1229. Business E-Mail: ashalita@downstate.edu. *Treat others with compassion, dignity and respect, add a little humor to everyone's life. Speak up for what you truly believe, be charitable.*

**SHALLCROSS, DEANNE J.,** finance company executive; Mktg. exec. TIAA-CREF, N.Y.C., 1996—. Office: TIAA-CREF 730 3d Ave New York NY 10017 E-mail: dshallcross@tiaa-cref.org.

**SHALLCROSS, DORIS JANE,** education educator; b. Cranford, N.J., Feb. 28, 1933; d. John William and Ethel Belle (Ruth) S. BA, Montclair State Coll., 1955; MA, Wesleyan U., Middletown, Conn., 1962; EdD, U. Mass., 1973. Tchr. Hunterdon Cen. High Sch., Flemington, NJ, 1955-61, Roosevelt Jr. High Sch., Cleveland Heights, Ohio, 1961-65, Cleveland Heights H.S., 1965-67; adminstr. Cleveland Heights Pub. Schs., 1967-69; dir. humanistic edn. Montague (Mass.) Pub. Schs., 1972-75; program devel. specialist Tchr. Corps., SUNY, Oneonta, NY, 1976-78; asst. prof. edn. divsn. home econs. U. Mass., Amherst, 1978-82, prof., dir. grad. studies in creativity, 1982-95; pres. Shallcross Creativity Inst., Haydenville, Mass., 1995—. Pres. bd. trustees Creative Edn. Found., Buffalo, 1988-94; co-dir. Global Odyssey, 1992—; bd. dir. Ctr. for Critical and Creative Thinking, Hartford, Conn., 1989-92, 95—; prof. internat. grad. program in creativity U. Santiago, Santiago de Compostela, Spain, 1999. Author: Teaching Creative Behavior, 1981; co-author: The Growing Person, 1985, Leadership: Making Things Happen, 1987, Intuition: An Inner Way of Knowing, 1989, Celebrating the Soul of CPSI, 2004; cons. editor Jour. Creative Behavior, 1967—; contbr. articles to profl. jours. Mem. Planning Dd., Town of Williamsburg, 1981-89; v.p. bd. dir. Pioneer Valley Performing Arts H.S., 1995-98, pres., 1998—; chair edn. com. Arts in Edn. Ctr., 1997—, pres. 2002-; bd. dir. Mass. Charter Schs. Assn., 2001—; mem. Creative Problem Solving Inst. Coun., co-chair, 2004—05. Recipient Disting. Leader award Creative Edn. Found., 1986; named to Creative Problem Solving Inst. Hall of Fame, 2004; grantee, NSF, 1987-89, U. Mass., 1987-89. Mem. NEA, Mass. Soc. Profs., Inst. for Noetic Scis., Am. Creativity Assn. (bd. dirs. 1990-93). Avocations: music, golf, reading, gardening. Home and Office: 26 S Main St Haydenville MA 01039-9735 E-mail: dshallx@highstream.net.

**SHALLCROSS, RICHARD,** corporate financial executive; BS in Acctg., U. Denver. CPA. Audit mgr. Arthur Andersen & Co.; v.p. fin., chief fin. officer Rose Health Care System, Denver; pres. fin. and managed care HCA, Inc., Colo., 1995—96, chief fin. officer Utah, 1996—97, Denver, 1997—2001, Nashville, 2001—. Mem.: Colo. Soc. CPA's, Health Care Fin. Mgmt. Assn. Office: HCA Inc 1 Park Plz Nashville TN 37203

**SHALOM, GALIT,** psychologist; b. Béer-Sheva, Israel, Dec. 26, 1969; arrived in US, 1992; d. Emil and Nourit Assor; m. Moshe Shalom, July 7, 1996; children: Nathan, Brit. BA in Edn. & Behavioral Scis., Ben-Gurion U. Negev, 1995; MA in Clinical Psychology, Forest Inst. Profl. Psychology, 1998, PsyD in Clinical Psychology, 2000. Lic. psychologist Fla., 2002. Evening news anchor ICS, Beer-Sheva, 1991—92; psychologist-in-tng. Forest Human Svcs. Ctr., Springfield, Mo., 1997—99, Neuropsychological & Assocs. SW Mo., 1999; intern Forest Inst. Profl. Psychology, Springfield Mo., 1999—2000, tchg. asst., 1999—2000, clinical supr., 1999—2000; clinical psychologist Greene County Jail, Springfield, 2000; adj. prof. psychology Fla. Internat. U., Miami, 2001—02, post-doctorate residence, 2001—02; postdoctoral resident Fla. Internat. U. Counseling and Psychol. Svcs. Ctr., Miami, 2001—02; licensed clinical psychologist S. Fla. State Hosp., Atlantic Shores Healthcare, Inc., Pembroke Pines, Fla., 2003, pvt. practice, Boca Raton, Fla., 2003—, Jewish Family Svc., Inc. Broward County, Plantation, Fla., 2004—. Guest spkr. various seminars & presentations, 1999—2001. With Israeli mil. comdr. naval divsn. Israeli Defence Force, 1988—90. Recipient Outstanding Psychological Trainee of Month, The Resident Com., Forest Human Svcs. Ctr., 1998. Mem.: APA, Soc. for Psychology of Women. Jewish. Avocation: reading. Office: 370 W Camino Gardens Blvd Ste 204 Boca Raton FL 33432 E-mail: drshalom@bellsouth.net.

**SHALOM, LILIANE WINN,** investment company executive, consultant; b. Casablanca, Morocco, May 28, 1940; d. Joseph and Madeleine Levy; 1 child, Dominique Winn. Brevet Etudes Premier Cycle, Alliance Israelite, Casablanca, 1956; cert. proficiency in English, U. Mich., 1960. English tchr. U.S. Info. Agy., Casablanca, 1959-61; multilingual guide, interpreter for VIPs, heads of state UN, N.Y.C., 1962-65; designer-ptnr., v.p. I.Q. Originals, Inc., N.Y.C., 1977-82; pres. EON Holdings, Inc., N.Y.C., 1981—, L.S. Cons., 1991—; cons. Applied Energy Svcs., Alexandria, Va., 1992—95, Airbus Industrie, Toulouse, France, 1999—2000. Editor, pub., contbr. The Sephardi World quar. mag., 1975-82. Fin. com. Carter for Pres., N.Y.C., 1975-76, Moynihan for Senate, N.Y.C., 1976, Dukakis for Pres., N.Y.C., 1987-88; chmn. fundraising Congl. Fgn. Rels. Com., N.Y.C. 1986. Recipient Louise Waterman Wise award Am. Jewish Congress, 1984, Stanley Isaacs Human Rels. award Am. Jewish Com., N.Y., 1986; named Comdr. of Ouissam Alaouite, King of Morocco, 1987. Mem. Am. Sephardi Fedn. (pres. 1975-82), World Zionist Congress (presidium 1971—), Moroccan Jewish Orgn. (founder, chmn. 1978), United Jewish Appeal (bd. dirs.), Hebrew Immigration Aid Soc. (v.p. 1990—), World Jewish Congress (econ. and social commn.). Democrat. Office: 645 5th Ave Ste 710 New York NY 10022-5910

**SHALOWITZ, ERWIN EMMANUEL,** civil engineer; b. Washington, Feb. 13, 1924; s. Aaron Louis and Pearl (Myer) S.; m. Elaine Mildred Langerman, June 29, 1952; children: Jane Janet, Aliza Beth, Jonathan Avram. Student, U. Pa., U. Notre Dame, 1941-43; BCE, George Washington U., 1947, postgrad., 1948-49; grad. soil mechanics, Cath. U., 1951; MA in Pub. Adminstrn. (fellow U.S. Civil Service Commn.), Am. U., 1954. Registered profl. engr., Washington. Engr. Klemitt Engring. Co., N.Y.C., 1947; with cons. firm Whitman, Requardt & Assos., Balt., 1947-48; chief structural rsch. engr., head def. rsch. sect., project officer and tech. adviser for atomic tests Bur. Yards and Docks, Dept. Navy, Washington, 1948-59; supervisory gen. engr. spl. asst. for protective constrn. programs, project mgr. for bldg. systems, chief rsch. br., chief mgmt. info, chief contracting procedures and support, chief contract evaluation and analysis, team leader/project mgr. acquisition sys., acquisition/procurement exec., Pub. Bldg. Svc., Gen. Svcs. Adminstrn., Washington, 1959—98; mgr. ednl. svc. for individual improvement Silver Spring, Md., 1998—. Chmn. fed. exec. tng. program U.S. Civil Service Commn., 1950; fallout shelter analyst Dept. Def.; chmn. GSA Fire Safety Com., GSA Fallout Protection Com., GSA Bldg. Evaluation Com.; mem. Interagy Com. on Housing Rsch. and Bldg. Tech.; mem. Nat. Evaluation Bd. Architect-Engr. Selections; mem. standing com. on procurement policy Nat. Acad. Sci. Bldg. Research Adv. Bd. and Interagency Com. on Procurement Curriculum Rev.; coordinator pub. bldgs. design and constrn. Small Bus. Program and Minority Enterprise and Minority Subcontracting Programs. Contbr. articles profl. jours. Served to engring. officer USNR, 1944-46. Recipient Commendable Svc. award GSA, 1968, Outstanding Performance recognition, 1976, 77, 79, 83, 87, 93-96, Superior Accomplishment award, 1995, others; Engr. Alumni Achievement award George Washington U., 1989. Fellow ASCE, Am. Biog. Inst.; mem. Soc. Advancement Mgmt., Am. Biog. Inst. (nat. bd. advisors), Soc. Am. Mil. Engrs., Sigma Tau, Pi Sigma Alpha. Jewish. Home: 3122 Gracefield Rd Apt 108 Silver Spring MD 20904-5801 Personal E-mail: shalowitz@aol.com. *PRINCIPLES: Look beyond the material for lasting values and meaning, optimize managerial effectiveness by creating an objective and challenging climate in an organization, delve into the underlying causes of problem areas for meaningful solutions, and persevere in spite of obstacles. IDEAS: Cultural pluralism; the intrinsic potential of each individual; and love, appreciation, and support of one's family as indispensable for real accomplishment. GOALS: To attain the highest level of professional accomplishment within my capabilities and to continue to have a rich, happy, and fulfilling family life. STANDARDS OF CONDUCT: To be fair, consistent, and straightforward; and to avoid over-reacting.*

**SHAM, LU JEU,** physics professor, physicist; b. Hong Kong, Apr. 28, 1938; s. T. S. and Cecilia Maria (Siu) Shen; m. Georgina Bien, Apr. 25, 1965; children: Kevin Shen, Alisa Shen. GCE, Portsmouth Coll., Eng., 1957; BS, Imperial Coll., London U., Eng., 1960; PhD in Physics, Cambridge U., Eng. 1963. Asst. rsch. physicist U. Calif., San Diego, 1963-66, assoc. prof., 1968-75, prof., 1975—, chair dept. physics, 1995-98, dean div. natural scis., 1985-89, Disting. physics prof., 2005—; asst. prof. physics Irvine, 1966-67; rsch. physicist IBM Corp., Yorktown Heights, NY, 1974-75. Reader Queen Mary Coll. U. London, 1967—68. Assoc. editor: Physics Letters A, 1992—; contbr. articles to profl. jours. Recipient Churchill Coll. studentship, Eng., 1960—63, U.S. Scientist award, Humboldt Found., 1978, Faculty Rsch. Letter award, 2000, Lamb medal, 2004, Chancellor Assocs. award for Excellence in Rsch., 1995; fellow, Guggenheim Found., 1984. Fellow: Am. Phys. Soc.; mem.: NAS, AAAS, Optical Soc. Am., Acad. Sinica Republic of China. Democrat. Avocations: tennis, folk dancing. Office: U Calif San Diego Dept Physics 0319 La Jolla CA 92093-0319 Office Phone: 619-534-3269. E-mail: lsham@ucsd.edu.

**SHAMASH, YACOV,** dean, electrical engineering educator; b. Iraq, Jan. 12, 1950; BSEE, Imperial Coll., London, 1970; PhD in Control Systems, Imperial Coll., 1973. Postdoctoral fellow in elec. engring. Tel-Aviv U., 1973-75, from lectr. elec. engring. to sr. lectr. elec. engring., 1975-78; prof. elec. engring. Fla. Atlantic U., Boca Raton, 1977-85; prof., chair dept. elec. engring. dept. Wash. State U., Pullman, 1985-92; dean engring. SUNY, Stony Brook, 1992—. Bd. dirs. KeyTronics, Spokane, Wash., 1990—; vis. asst. prof. U. Pa., Phila., 1976-77. Contbr. over 100 articles to profl. jours.; book chpts. Fellow IEEE (sr.). Office: SUNY Coll Engring & Applied Sci Stony Brook NY 11794-2200

**SHAMASK, RONALDUS,** fashion designer; b. Amsterdam, The Netherlands, Nov. 24, 1945; Window display artist, Melbourne, Australia, 1963-66; fashion illustrator The Times and The Observer, London, 1967-68; freelance stage set, costume designer for ballet, opera, Company of Man Buffalo, 1968-71; freelance interior and clothing designer N.Y.C., 1971-77; founder, ptnr. Moss Shamask Fashion Co., N.Y.C., 1978—; founder Moss Boutique, N.Y.C., 1979—. Contbr. design packing Revlon Cosmetics and Fragrances, 1993; launched cosmetic line, Fire & Ice Fragrance, Revlon, 1993—. Exhibit at MIT, 1982. Recipient Coty Fashion award, 1981; Fil d'Or award Conf. Internat. du Lin, 1982. Office: c/o Revlon 625 Madison Ave New York NY 10022*

**SHAMATAVA, IRMA,** physicist, researcher; arrived in U.S., 2000; d. Iuri and Tsiuri Shamatava; m. Fridon Shubitidze, July 20, 1993; children: Tornike Shubitidze, Salome Shubitidze. MS, Sukhumi br. of Tbilisi State U., Tbilisi, Georgia, 1993. Physicist (radio physics), Dept. Edn. of Ga. Tchr. Sukhumi U., Tbilisi; rsch. engr. Dartmouth Coll., Hanover, NH, 1996—. Cons. Cold Regions Rsch. and Engring. Lab., NH, 2005—. Contbr. scientific papers to profl. jours. Achievements include development of User friendly computer programs; research in unexploded ordnances detection and discrimination. Office Phone: 603-646-2685.

**SHAMBAN, AVA T.,** dermatologist; BS, Harvard U., 1977; MD, Case Western Res. U. Pvt. practice dermatology, Santa Monica, Calif.; asst. clin. prof. dermatology UCLA. Cons. ABC's Extreme Makeover; investigator Nat. Acne Rsch. Project; featured regarding cosmetic dermatology Discovery Channel. Bd. dirs. Santa Monica Coll. Found. Fellow: Am. Acad. Dermatology. Office: Laser Inst for Dermatology 2021 Santa Monica Blvd #600E Santa Monica CA 90404

**SHAMBAUGH, DAVID LEIGH,** political scientist, educator, writer; b. Chgo., Jan. 18, 1953; s. George E. Shambaugh, Jr. and Genevieve (Krum) Shambaugh; m. Ingrid Cecile Larsen, Aug. 7, 1982; children: Christopher Leigh, Alexander George. BA in East Asian Studies, George Washington U., 1977; MA in Internat. Affairs, Johns Hopkins U., 1980; PhD in Polit. Sci., U. Mich., 1989. Prof. U. London, 1988—96, George Washington U., Washington, 1996—; sr. fellow Brookings Instn., 1998—. Cons. in field. Editor China Quar., 1991—96, mem. editl. bd., 1989—, Studies on Contemporary China, 1991—, Internat. Security, 2003—, China Perspectives, 1998—, Current History, 1999—; author: The Making of a Premier: Zhao Ziyang's Provincial Career, 1984, Beautiful Imperialist: China Perceives America, 1991, China and Europe, 1996, Modernizing China's Military Progress, Problems, and Prospects, 2002, The Odyssey of China's Imperial Art Treasures, 2005; editor, contbr. American Studies of Contemporary China, 1993, Greater China: The Next Superpower?, 1995, Deng Xiaoping: Portrait of a Chinese Statesman, 1995, China's Military in Transition, 1997, Contemporary Taiwan, 1998, The Modern Chinese State, 2000, Is China Unstable?, 2000, co-editor Chinese Foreign Policy: Theory and Practice, 1994, co-editor, contbr. China's Military Faces the Future, 1999, The China Reader: The Reform Era, 1999, Making China Policy: Lessons from the Bush and Clinton Administrations, 2001, Power Shift: China and Asta's New Dynamics, 2005. Fellow, Smith Richardson Found., 2005—06; grantee, Brit. Acad./Econ. & Social Rsch. Coun. China Exch. Program, 1990, 1994, Chiang Ching-kuo Found., 1998—2000; Rsch. fellow, Pacific Cultural Found., 1998—2000, Woodrow Wilson fellow, 2002—03, others. Mem.: Council on Internat. Policy, Coun. on Fgn. Rels., Asia Soc., Internat. Studies Assn., Assn. for Asian Studies, Coun. on Security Coop. in the Asia Pacific, Nat. Com. U.S.-China Rels., Internat. Inst. Strategic Studies, World Econ. Forum. Avocations: travel, basketball, tennis, canoeing, bluegrass music. Home: 1600 N Highland St Arlington VA 22201 Office: George Washington Univ Elliott Sch Internat Affairs 1957 E St NW Ste 503 Washington DC 20052 Office Phone: 202-994-5887. Business E-Mail: shambaug@gwu.edu.

**SHAMBAUGH, IRVIN CALVIN, JR.,** aptitude test firm executive; b. Harrisburg, Pa., June 7, 1943; s. Irvin Calvin and Viola Mary (Deibler) Shambaugh; m. Amy Wilcox Shambaugh, Jan. 3, 1975. BS in Geol. Sci., Pa. State U., 1964; postgrad., MIT, Cambridge, Mass., 1964—65, Tex. Christian U., Ft. Worth, 1974—76, East Tex. State U., 1976—77. Rsch. coord. Johnson O'Connor Rsch. Found., Ft. Worth, 1965—76; pres., chief scientist Aptitude Inventory Measurement Svc., Dallas, 1976—. Centennial fellow Coll. Earth and Min. Scis., Pa. State U., 1996. Author: The Test-Taker's Guide to Career Literature, 1982, Test Manual for Selected AIMS Worksamples, 1986, Books About Careers, 1986, Career Facts: Where to Find Them and How to Use Them, 1992, The AIMS Guide to Career Facts, 1997; co-author: AIMS Information About Aptitudes, 1979, The Aptitude Handbook: A Guide to the AIMS Program, 1996, 2004, Career Facts: In Print and on the World Wide Web, 2003; co-prodr.: (e-pub.) AIMS Information Disk, 2004; editor: You and Your Aptitudes, 1983; developer Activity Preference Questionnaire, 1994, psychometric instrument III Interest Inventory, 1996; contbr. articles to profl. jours.; developer AIMS test battery, 1976—, digital version, 2005—, AIMS Measure of Color Perception, 2005—, AIMS Reasoning Measure, 2006, 3-D Mental Gymnastic Worksample, 2006. With USMC, 1966—68. Mem.: AAAS, ACA, APA (assoc.), Nat. Assn. Test Dirs., Nat. Assn. Coll. Admissions Counselors, Nat. Coun. Measurement in Edn., Am. Psychol. Soc., Assn. Assessment in Counseling and Edn. Achievements include development of psychometrics instruments. Home: 934 Westbrook Dr Garland TX 75043-5243 Office: Aptitude Inventory Measurement Svc 12160 Abrams Rd Ste 314 Dallas TX 75243-4525

**SHAMBAUGH, STEPHEN WARD,** lawyer; b. South Bend, Ind., Aug. 4, 1920; s. Marion Clyde and Anna Violet (Stephens) S.; m. Marilyn Louise Pyle (dec. 1993); children: Susan Wynne Shambaugh Hinkle (dec. 1998), Kathleen Louise Shambaugh Thompson. Student, San Jose State Tchrs. Coll., 1938-40. U. Ark., 1951; LLB, U. Tulsa, 1954. Bar: Okla. 1954, Colo. 1958. Mem. staff Reading & Bates, Inc., Tulsa, 1951-54; v.p., gen. mgr., legal counsel Reading & Bates Drilling Co. Ltd., Calgary, Alta., Canada, 1954-61; sr. attny. Bowman, Shambaugh, Geissinger & Wright, Denver, 1964-81; sole legal counsel various corps. Col. USAF ret. Mem. Colo. Bar Assn., Okla. Bar Assn., P-51 Mustang Pilots Assn., Masons, Elks, Phi Alpha Delta.

**SHAMBERG, MICHAEL,** film producer; m. Carla Santos, 1996. Grad., Washington U. Films produced include Heart Beat, 1980, Modern Problems, 1981, The Big Chill, 1983, Club Paradise, 1986, Salvation!, 1987, A Fish Called Wanda, 1988, How I Got Into College, 1989, 8 Seconds, 1994, (with Danny DeVito) Reality Bites, 1994, (with Danny DeVito and Stacey Sher) Pulp Fiction, 1994, Get Shorty, 1995, Sunset Park, 1996, Matilda, 1996, Feeling Minnesota, 1996, Fierce Creatures, 1997, Gattaca, 1997, Out of Sight, 1998, Living Out Loud, 1998, Drowning Mona, 2000, Erin Brockovich, 2000, The Caveman's Valentine, 2001, Ghost World, 2001, How High, 2001, Camp, 2003, Along Came Polly, 2004, Garden State, 2004, Be Cool, 2005, The Skeleton Key, 2005, World Trade Center, 2006, (TV films) The Pentagon Wars, 1998, The Funkhousers, 2002, (TV series) UC: Undercover, 2001-02, The American Embassy, 2002, Karen Sisco, 2003-04. Office: Jersey Films 10202 Washington Blvd Culver City CA 90232-3119*

**SHAMBROOM, PAUL,** artist, photographer; b. Teaneck, N.J., 1956; BFA, Mpls. Coll. Art Design, 1978. One-man shows include Film in the Cities, St. Paul, 1979, Minn. Hist. Soc., 1984, Bockley Gallery, Mpls., 1990, CEOA Gallery and Medaillel Coll., Buffalo, 1995, Walker Art Ctr., Mpls., 1995, Tanya Bonakdar Gallery, N.Y.C., 1997—98, Franklin Artworks, Mpls., 2001, Julie Saul Gallery, NYC, 2002, 2004, 2006, Le Mois de la Photo a Montreal, 2003, Mus. Contemporary Photography, Chgo., 2003, Arles Recontres de la Photographie, France, 2004, Nederlands Fotomuseum, Rotterdam, 2005, Howard Yezerski Gallery, Boston, 2005, Atomic Testing Mus., Las Vegas, 2005, Rocket Gallery, London, 2005, exhibited in group shows at Camerawork Gallery, San Francisco, 1979, Northlight Gallery, Tempe, Ariz., 1981, Forecast Pub. Artspace Prodns., Mpls., 1981, Univ. Gallery, U. Minn., 1986, Minn. Coll. Art Design, 1988, Film in the Cities, St. Paul, 1990, Mpls. Inst. Arts, 1990, 1996, Bockley Gallery, Mpls., 1991, Mus. Modern Art, N.Y.C. 1996, Whitney Mus. Am. Art, 1997, Madison Art Ctr., Wis., 2001, Ludwig Mus., Budapest, 2002—03, Univ. Art Mus., Santa Barbara, Calif., 2003—04, Ronald Feldman Fine Arts, NYC, 2003, Milw. Art Mus., 2004, Weinstein Gallery, Mpls., 2005, N.C. Mus. Art, 2005, Represented in permanent collections Whitney Mus. Am. Art, N.Y.C., San Francisco Mus. Modern Art, L.A. County Mus. Art, Mus. Modern Art, N.Y.C., Walker Art Ctr., Mpls., Mpls. Inst. Arts, Mus. Fine Arts, Houston. Fellow Photography fellow, McKnight Found., Mpls., 1985, 1989, 1995, Visual Arts fellow, Jerome Found., St. Paul, 1987, Artist Assistance fellow, Minn. State Arts Bd., 1988, 1993, Artist fellow, Bush Found., St. Paul, 1992; Dayton Hudson Found. grantee, Mpls., 1979, Jerome Found. grantee, St. Paul, 1996. Office: c/o Julie Saul Gallery 535 W 22nd St New York NY 10011 E-mail: paul@paulshambroomart.com.*

**SHAMBUREK, ROBERT DEAN,** gastroenterologist; b. Pensacola, Fla., Aug. 24, 1957; BS, Marquette U., 1979; MD, U. Va., 1984. Intern in internal medicine Med. Coll. Va., Richmond, 1984—85, resident in internal medicine, 1985—87, geriatric fellow, 1987—88, gastroenterology fellow, 1988—91, instr. in medicine, 1991—92, asst. prof., 1991—93; sr. staff fellow molecular disease br. Nat. Heart Lung and Blood Inst., NIH, Bethesda, Md., 1993—, head inpatient lipid. svc., 1995—, clin. scientist, 1999—. Office: Nat Heart Lung and Blood Inst NIH Molecular Disease Br Bldg 10 Rm 7N115 10 Center Dr Bethesda MD 20892-1666 Office Phone: 301-496-1500.

**SHAMBUREK, ROLAND HOWARD,** physician; b. Adell, Wis., June 7, 1928; s. William and Catherine (Illig) Shamburek; m. Gladys Irene Gibbons, June 21, 1952; children: Steven J., Robert D., Daniel J. BS, U. Wis., 1950, MD, 1953; MPH, Harvard U., 1960; grad., U. Army War Coll., Carlisle Barracks, Pa., 1972. Diplomate Am. Bd. Preventive Medicine. Commd. 1st lt. M.C., U.S. Army, 1953, advanced through grades to col., 1968; intern St. Joseph's Hosp., Marshfield, Wis., 1953-54; grad. U.S. Naval Sch. of Aviation Medicine, Pensacola, Fla., 1957; resident in preventive (aerospace) medicine USAF Sch. Aerospace Medicine, Brooks AFB, 1960-63; service in 216th Field Artillery (Atomic) Battalion, 1954—56, 1966, Office of Army Surgeon Gen., Washington, 1966—70, 1972—75; comdr. 67th EVAC Hosp., Vietnam, 1970-71, U.S. Army Med. Pers. Support Agy., 1975-77; ret. U.S. Army, 1977; exec. v.p. Aerospace Med. Assn., 1977-79; clin. practice Pentagon Health Clinic, Washington, 1981-85; med. researcher Office of Army Surgeon Gen., 1985-87. Med. monitor Canary Island Tracking Sta. for Gemini missions NASA, 1965—66. Contbr. scientific papers in field. Decorated Legion of Merit with oak leaf cluster, Army Commendation medal, Meritorious Svc. medal. Mem.: AMA (del. 1978), Internat. Acad. Aviation and Space Medicine, Soc. NASA Flight Surgeons, U.S. Army Flight Surgeons, Soc. Med. Cons. Armed Forces, Aerospace Med. Assn. (v.p. 1968—69), Am. Coll. Preventive Medicine (v.p. 1968—69), Assn. Mil. Surgeons (John Shaw Billings award 1968). Address: 3700 Moss Dr Annandale VA 22003-1915

**SHAMBURG, CHRISTOPHER,** education educator; b. Jersey City; s. James and Jacqueline Shamburg; m. Katherine Mazzetti, July 20, 1996; children: Emma Jeanne, Luke Robert. EdD, Columbia U., 2001. Prof. ednl. tech. dept. NJ City U., Jersey City, 2001—. Home: 39 Kensington Terr Maplewood NJ 07040 Office: NJ City U 2039 Kennedy Blvd Jersey City NJ 07305 Office Phone: 201-200-2435. Personal E-mail: cshamburg@comcast.net. Business E-Mail: cshamburg@njcu.edu.

**SHAMES, HENRY JOSEPH,** lawyer; b. Milw., Jan. 20, 1921; s. Aron and Jennie (Greenberg) S.; m. Beverly Cleveland Van Wert, June 9, 1972; children: Stephen H., Suzanne Shames Sattelmeyer, Sarah Shames Phillips, Diana Shames Strandberg. AB, U. Chgo., 1942; JD, Harvard U., 1948. Bar: Ill. 1949, Calif. 1962. Mem. firm Arvey, Hodes & Mantynband, Chgo., 1949-61; partner Pacht, Ross, Warne, Bernhard & Sears, Los Angeles, 1962-75, Grossman & Shames, Los Angeles, 1975-83, Rosenfeld, Parnell & Shames Inc., Los Angeles, 1984-86; counsel Patterson, Belknap, Webb and Tyler, Los Angeles, 1986-87. Chmn. bd. Switzer Center, Los Angeles, 1966-73 Served with USNR, 1943-46. Mem. Assn. Bus. Trial Lawyers (bd. govs. 1973-76, v.p. 1973-76), Calif. State Bar Assn., So. Calif. Def. Counsel, Los Angeles County Bar Assn., Phi Beta Kappa. Home: 4906 La Ramada Dr Santa Barbara CA 93111-1518 E-mail: westerner@verizon.net.

**SHAMMAS, NAZIH KHEIRALLAH,** environmental engineer, consultant, engineering educator; b. Homs, Syria, Feb. 18, 1939; arrived in U.S., 1991; s. Kheirallah Hanna and Nazha Murad (Hamwi) Shammas; m. Norma Massouh, July 28, 1968; children: Sarmed Erick, Samer Sam. Degree in engirng. with distinction, Am. U., Beirut, 1962; MS in Sanitary Engring., U. N.C., 1965; PhD in Civil Engring., U. Mich., 1971. Instr. civil engring. Am. U., Beirut, 1965-68; tchg. fellow U. Mich., Ann Arbor, 1966-71; asst. prof. civil engring. Am. U., Beirut, 1972-76, King Saud U., Riyadh, Saudi Arabia, 1976-78, assoc. prof., 1978-91; prof. environ. engring. Lenox (Mass.) Inst. Water Tech., 1991-2001, dean edn., 1992-93. Cons., ptnr. Cons. and Rsch. Engrs., Beirut, 1973—76; cons. Ar-Riyadh Devel. Authority, 1977—93, Riyadh Water and Sanitary Drainage Authority, 1979—83, Assoc. Cons. Engring. Team, 1994—99, Vikakis Internat., 1995—2002; adj. prof. environ. sci. Berkshire CC, 1995—; planning assoc. Berkshire Regional Planning Commn., 1999—2003. Co-author: Environmental Sanitation, 1988, Wastewater Engineering, 1988, Physicochemical Treatment Processes, 2005, Advanced Physicochemical Treatment Processes, 2006; contbr. articles to profl. jours. and confs. Recipient Excellence in Tchg. award, King Saud U., 1981, 1984; Block grantee, U. Mich., 1968—70. Mem.: ASCE, Assn. Environ. Engring. and Sci. Profs., Internat. Water Assn., New Eng. Water Works Assn., New Eng. Water Environ. Assn., Am. Water Works Assn., Water Environ. Fedn. Achievements include research in biological and physiochemical remediation processes; mathematical modeling of nitrification process; water and wastewater management in developing countries; water conservation, wastewater treatment and reuse; appropriate technology for developing countries; multidisciplinary studies in environmental management and planning. Home: 35 Flintstone Dr Pittsfield MA 01201 Personal E-mail: nazih413@aol.com.

**SHAMMAS, NICOLAS WAHIB,** internist, cardiologist; b. Amyoun, El-Koura, Lebanon, Jan. 31, 1963; arrived in U.S., 1988; s. Wahib Nicolas and Vera Yousuf (El-Helou) Shammas; m. Gail Ann Hanson, Feb. 22, 1991;

children: Waheeb John, Andrew Nicolas, Anna Elizabeth. BSc with distinction, Am. U. Beirut, 1983, MD, 1987, MSc in Physiology, 1987, Diploma in Computer Programming, 1985. Diplomate Am. Bd. Internal Medicine, Am. Bd. Cardiology and Interventional Cardiology. Postdoctoral rsch. fellow Am. U. Beirut, 1987-88; resident in internal medicine U. Iowa Hosps., Iowa City, 1988-91; instr. medicine, clin. fellow cardiology U. Rochester (N.Y.) Med. Ctr., 1991-94; fellow assoc. in cardiology U. Iowa Hosps., Iowa City, 1994—95; mem. staff Genesis Med. Ctr., Davenport, Iowa, 1995—; clin. asst. prof. U. Iowa. Founder Mastermind Pub., 1995, Phenix Realty Co., 1997; founder, pres. Midwest Cardiovasc. Rsch. Found., 2002. Author (with others): Flavors of Lebanon, 1995, Learn About Your Heart.Made Simple, 2004, Cardiovascular Interventions and Practice Guidelines, 2004; contbr. more than 100 articles to profl. jours. mem. Am. U. Beirut U. Rsch. Bd. award, 1986-87, John C. Sable Meml. Heart award J.C. Sable Fund, 1993, Trainee Investigator award, Balt., 1994, Extra-mile award Am. Heart Assn. 2002, First Poster award Internat. Congress of Angiology, 2003 Fellow: ACP, Acad. Transcatheter Therapeutics, Am. Coll. Chest Physicians, Internat. Coll. Angiology, Am. Coll. Cardiology, Soc. Cardiac Angiography and Interventions; mem.: AMA, Am. Soc. Echocardiography, Am. Soc. Nuclear Cardiology, Iowa Med. Soc., Am. Soc. Internal Medicine, Am. Fedn. Clin. Rsch. Achievements include research in basic cardiology: prostacyclin and transmembrane calcium movements; adrenergic binding sites; hypertension; myocardial ischemia and coronary flow reserve; inflammation and thrombosis. Avocations: writing, skiing, golf, travel. Office: Cardiovasc Medicine PC 1236 E Rusholme St Ste 300 Davenport IA 52803-2400 E-mail: shammas@mchsi.com.

**SHAMOO, ADIL ELIAS,** biochemist, educator; b. Baghdad, Iraq, Aug. 1, 1941; came to U.S., 1964, naturalized, 1973; s. Elias M. and Mariam T. (Mansour) S.; m. Joan Hutchison, Dec. 16, 1967 (div. Dec. 1997); children: Abraheem, Zachary, Jessica. B.Sc. in Physics, U. Baghdad, 1962; MS in Physics (grad. fellow), U. Louisville, 1966; PhD in Biophysics, CUNY, 1970. Instr. engring. physics Speed Sch., U. Louisville, 1965-68; asst. prof. physiology City U. N.Y., 1971-73; guest worker Lab. Biophysics and Neurochemistry, NIH, Bethesda, Md., 1972-73; asst. prof. radiation biology and biophysics U. Rochester, 1973-75; guest prof. Max-Planck Inst. Biophysics, Frankfurt, West Germany, 1977-78; assoc. prof. radiation biology and biophysics U. Rochester, 1975-79; prof., chmn. dept. biol. chemistry U. Md., Balt., 1979-82, prof. biochemistry and molecular biology, 1982—, prof. epidemiology and preventive medicine, 2003—, head membrane biochemistry research lab., 1982-90. Cons. div. biol. scis. Kodak Co., Rochester, 1976-77; NIH tng. fellow U. Louisville, 1967; investigator Am. Heart Assn., 1976-79; Neurosci. Rsch. Program fellow, Boulder, Colo., summer 1977; chmn. symposia, various coms. in field; mem. organizing coms. workshops in field; adj. prof. dept. physics East Carolina U., Greenville, N.C., 1996-2000; bd. dirs. Friends Rsch. Inst., 1994-2001; ethics coms. Armed Forces Epidemiol. Bd.; chair ethics adv. group GlaxoSmithKline Co., 2003. Editor (with M.W. Miller) Membrane Toxicity, 1977, Carriers and Channels in Biological Systems, 1975, Carriers and Channels in Biological Systems-Transport Proteins, 1980, Regulation of Calcium Transport Across Muscle Membranes, 1985, Principles of Research Data Audit, (with R. Verna) Biotechnology Today, 1995, Ethics in Neurobiological Research with Human Subjects, 1997; editor in chief Membrane Biochemistry, 1977-93, Accountability in Research: Policies and Quality Assurance, 1988—; mem. editl. bd. Molecular and Cellular Biochemistry, 1987-94, Quality Assurance: Good Practice Regulation and Law, 1991—; contbr. articles and abstracts to profl. jours., chpts. to books. Bd. dirs. Alliance for Mentally Ill of Md., 1990-93, Friends Rsch. Inst. Inc., 1994-2002; mem. rsch. monitoring com. Nat. Alliance for Mentally Ill, bd. dirs. Howard County Mental Health Authority, 1997-00, pres., 1997-2000; bd. dirs. Citizens for Responsible Care and Rsch., 1998—, v.p., 1998—; mem. Nat. Human Rsch. Protections Adv. Com., 2000-02. Recipient Advocacy award Mental Health Assn. Md., 1994, Disting. Svc. award Alliance for Mentally Ill of Md., 1994, Howard County Mental Health Auth., 1999. Mem. AAAS, AAUP (chpt. sec. 1971-72), Basic Sci. Council of Am. Heart Assn., Am. Soc. Biol. Chemists and Mol. Biol., Am. Coll. Sports Medicine, Am. Assn. Physics Tchrs., Am. Soc. Bioethics and Human Values, Am. Physiol. Soc., Biophys. Soc. (Cole Membrane Award Com. 1983-84, chmn. biophysics subgroup 1982-83, council 1986-89), Membrane Biophys. Group (chmn. 1982-83, sec.-treas. 1983-85, co-chmn. U.S. bioenergetics group 1979-80), Md. Acad. Scis. (chmn. com. programs and exhbns. 1986-87, sci. council 1985-89), N.Y. Acad. Scis., Coun. of Biology (editor 1989—), Soc. Quality Assurance. Achievements include patents for liquid scintillators. Office: 108 N Greene St Baltimore MD 21201-1503 E-mail: ashamoo@umaryland.edu.

**SHAMOUN, JOHN MILAM,** plastic surgeon; b. Greenville, Miss., Apr. 1, 1960; s. Joseph David Shamoun and Phyllis Ann Joseph. BS, U. Miss., 1982, MD, 1986. Bd. cert. Am. Bd. Surgery, Am. Bd. Plastic and Reconstructive Surgery, Am. Bd. Facial Plastic and Reconstructive Surgery, Am. Bd. Forensic Examiners. Gen. surgeon U. South Ala., Mobile, 1986-91; plastic surgeon U. Tex., Dallas, 1991-93, Mt. Sinai Hosp., Miami Beach, Fla., 1993-94, Plastic Surgery Ctr. of the Pacific, Honolulu, 1994-95, Atlanta Plastic Surgery, 1994-95, Newport Inst. Plastic Surgery, Newport Beach, Calif., 1995; solo practice Beverly Hills, Palm Springs, Newport Beach, Calif. Legal cons. Law Firm of Charles G. Shamoun, Dallas, 1995—. Author: (books) Aesthetic Surgery, 1996, Microvascular Atlas, 1997; contbr. articles to profl. jours. Fellow ACS; mem. Am. Soc. Plastic and Reconstructive Surgery, Calif. Soc. Plastic Surgery, Anti Aging Soc., Alpha Omega Alpha. Roman Catholic. Achievements include performed plastic surgery (facelift and forehead lift) on female celebrity, Christopher Templeton, live on the Internet, June 7, 1999. Avocations: skiing, hunting, fishing, horseback riding, golf. Office: 360 San Miguel Dr Ste 406 Newport Beach CA 92660-7822

**SHAMPO, MARC ANTHONY,** retired editor; b. Green Bay, Wis., Oct. 20, 1924; s. Norman Joseph Shampo and Antoinette Rondou; m. Norma Eileen Beyea, Oct. 23, 1945 (div. Oct. 1965); 1 child, Teresa; m. Lila Irene Mayhew, July 29, 1967; children: Barbara, Charles, Nancy, Scott. BS, U. Wis., 1948, MS, 1949; PhD, U. Wis., Madison, Wis., 1960. H.S. tchr., Pewaukee, Wis., 1949—51, Racine, Wis., 1951—58; prof. Duquesne U., Pitts., 1958—62; med. editor Mayo Clinic, Rochester, Minn., 1962—99; ret., 1989. Contbr. articles to profl. jours., chpts. to books. With U.S. Army, 1943—46, ETO. Mem.: Phi Delta Kappa, Phi Eta Sigma. Home: 2828 Wellington Ln SW Rochester MN 55902

**SHAMSHAM, FADI MICHEL,** cardiologist; b. Beirut, Nov. 28, 1968; arrived in U.S., 1994; s. Michel Salim Shamsham and Marie Assi Gemayel. BS, Am. U. of Beirut, 1989, MD, 1993. Diplomate Am. Bd. Internal Medicine, Am. Bd. Internal Medicine with subspecialties in cardiovascular diseases and interventional cardiology. Resident in internal medicine S.I. U. Hosp., S.I., NY, 1994—97; fellow in cardiovascular diseases SUNY, Bklyn., 1997—2000; fellow in interventional cardiology Kaiser Permanente Found. Hosp., L.A., 2000—01; fellow in vascular medicine Charleston Area Med. Ctr., W.Va., 2001—02; cardiologist Med. Group of North Fla., Tallahassee, 2002—; med. staff Tallahassee Meml. Hosp., 2002—, Capital Regional Med. Ctr., 2002—. Clin. inst. SUNY, Bklyn., 1997—2000. Contbr. articles to profl. jours. Fellow: Soc. Cardiac Angiography and Interventions, Am. Coll. Cardiology; mem.: AMA, ACP. Office: Med Group of North Florida 2626 Care Dr Ste 100 Tallahassee FL 32308 Personal E-mail: fshamsham@aol.com.

**SHAN, KESAVAN,** cardiologist, researcher; b. Jaffna, Sri Lanka, Dec. 6, 1965; s. Krishnambal and Shanmugananthan; m. Girija Shan, Nov. 28, 1992; children: Tamara, Devan, Evan. BSc with honors, U. London, 1987, MBBS MD with honors, 1990. Diplomate Am. Bd. Internal Medicine, 1996, Nat. Bd. Echocardiography, 1999, cardiovas. diseases Am. Bd. Internal Medicine, 2000, cert. nuc. cardiology Am. Bd. Nuc. Medicine, 2001. Clin. instr. medicine Baylor Coll. Of Medicine, Houston, 1998—2000; cardiologist Tex. Heart Inst., Houston, 1999—2001, Cardiology Of Houston, 2001; clin. asst. prof. medicine U. Tex., Houston, 2001—. Med. edn. com. S.W. Meml. Hosp., Affiliate U. Tex., Houston. Contbr. articles to profl. jours.; author: (multiple pubs. in peer-rev. jours. including) The Lancet, Circulation, Jour. Am. Coll. Cardiology, Annals Internal Medicine, Am. Jour. Cardiology. Fellow: Am. Coll. Cardiology (fellow, Merck award and Young Clin. Investigator award finalist 1999); mem.: Royal Coll. Physicians. Achievements include research in cardiovascular MRI echocardiography; discovery of tissue doppler changes and diastolic dysfunction in hibernating myocardium; cardiovascular MRI and nuclear cardiology. Office: Cardiology Of Houston 7737 SW Freeway Ste 780 Houston TX 77074 Office Phone: 713-988-9512. E-mail: shankg@att.net.

**SHAN, YUFENG,** research scientist; Faculty mem. Shandong U., Jinan, China, 1995—2000; vis. prof. French Nat. Inst. for Rsch. in Computer Sci. and Control, Sophia Antipolis, 2000; rsch. scientist U. Calif., Berkeley, 2001—02. Author: more than 20 rsch. papers. Mem.: IEEE. Home: 21 Beman Lane Troy NY 12180 Office: Rensselaer Polytechnic Inst 110 8th St Troy NY 12180 Office Phone: 518-276-8678. Personal E-mail: yfshan@yahoo.com. Business E-Mail: shany@rpi.edu.

**SHANAHAN, BETTY,** professional society administrator; BSEE, Mich. State. U.; M of Software Engring., Wang Inst. of Grad. Studies; MBA in Strategic Mgmt., U. Chgo. Grad. Sch. of Bus. Various positions in devel., engring. mgmt. and mktg. Data Gen., Alliant Computer Sys., 1978—90; mktg. mgmt., including v.p., prod. mgmt. and mktg., software components divsn. Stellent, Inc., 1990—2002; exec. dir. Soc. of Women Engr., Chgo., 2002—. Bd. dir. Women in Engring. Programs and Adv. Network. Fellow: Soc. Women Engr. (life); mem.: IEEE, Am. Soc. of Assn. Execs., Assn. for Computing Machinery. Office: Exec Dir Soc of Women Engr 230 E Ohio St Chicago IL 60611*

**SHANAHAN, BRENDAN FREDERICK,** professional hockey player; b. Mimico, Ont., Can., Jan. 23, 1969; Left wing NJ Devils, 1987—91, St. Louis Blues, 1991—95, Hartford Whalers, 1995—97, Detroit Red Wings, 1997—2006, NY Rangers, 2006—. Player NHL All-Star Game, 1994, 1996—2000, 2002. Named to First All-Star Team, NHL, 1994, 2000, Second All-Star Team, 2002; recipient King Clancy Meml. Trophy, 2003. Achievements include being a member of the Stanley Cup Champion Detroit Red Wings, 1997, 1998, 2002; being a member of gold medal Canadian Hockey team, Salt Lake City Olympic Games, 2002. Office: NY Rangers Hockey Club 2 Pennsylvania Plaza New York NY 10121*

**SHANAHAN, EDWARD J.,** headmaster; b. NYC; m. Sandra Podesta Shanahan; children: Tom, Nell, Kate. BA in Philosophy, St. Joseph's Coll., Yonkers, NY, 1965; MA in Eng. Lit., Fordham U., Bronx, NY, 1968; PhD in Eng. Lit., U. Wis., Madison, 1982. Prof. Eng. Fordham U., Bronx, 1970—71; hall adv. U. Wis., Madison, 1971—72; dir. housing Wesleyan U., Middletown, Conn., 1972—73, assoc. dean, 1973—77, dean of students, 1977—82; dean Dartmouth Coll., Hanover, NH, 1982—91; pres. & headmaster Choate Rosemary Hall, 1991—. Bd. mem. Conn. Assn. of Independent Schools, 1993—97, 2003—; bd. dirs. United Educators Inc., 1989—2004, chair, 1998—2004; chmn. commn. on institutions of higher ed. New England Assn. of Schools and Colleges, 1990. Mem.: NEASC (pres. 1992). Office: Choate Rosemary Hall 333 Christian St Wallingford CT 06492

**SHANAHAN, EUGENE MILES,** flow measurement instrumentation company executive; b. Great Falls, Mont., Sept. 18, 1946; s. Raymond Eugene and Helen Marjorie (Graham) S.; m. Beverly Ann Braaten, Sept. 8, 1967; children— Bret Allen, Shaun Eugene, Shae Erin BS in Mech. Engring., Mont. State U., 1968; MS, Mont. State U., 1969; MBA, Portland State U., 1976. Registered profl. engr., Oreg. Mech. engr. Tektronix, Beaverton, Oreg., 1968-71; mech. engr. Shell Oil Co., Martinez, Calif., 1967; chief mech. project engr. Mears Controls, Beaverton, 1971-76, mktg. mgr., 1976-79; v.p., gen. mgr. Eaton Corp., Beaverton, 1979-87; pres. Dieterich Std., 1987—99; v.p. Asia Pacific Rosemount, 1999—2002; v.p. mktg.-sales Micro Motion, 2002—03, pres., 2003—. Served with N.G.; 1969-73 NSF trainee, 1969 Mem. ASME, Instrumentation Soc. Am., Tau Beta Pi, Phi Kappa Phi, Pi Tau Sigma. Office: 7070 Winchester Cir Boulder CO 80301 Home: 5253 Bella Vista Dr Longmont CO 80503

**SHANAHAN, MICHAEL FRANCIS,** retired manufacturing executive; former hockey team executive; b. St. Louis, Oct. 29, 1939; m. Mary Ann Barrett; children: Megan Elizabeth, Michael Francis Jr., Maureen Patricia. BS in Commerce, St. Louis U.; postgrad., Washington U., St. Louis; LHD (hon.), St. Louis Rabbinical Coll., 1987; PhD (hon.), St. Louis U., 2002. With McDonnell Douglas Automation Co., St. Louis, 1962-73, sales mgr., 1969-71, br. mgr., 1971-72, mktg. dir. cen. region, 1972-73; mktg. v.p. Numerical Control Inc., St. Louis, 1973-74, pres., 1974-79; v.p. Cleve. Pneumatic Co. (formerly Numerical Control Inc.), St. Louis, 1979-82; chmn., chief exec. officer Engineered Air Systems Inc., St. Louis, 1982—; former chmn., ceo St. Louis Blues Hockey Team. Bd. dirs. Engineered Air Systems Inc. (chmn.), St. Louis Blues Hockey Inc. (chmn.); adv. com. Nat. Hockey League; mem. U.S. Senatorial Bus. Adv. Bd.; bd. dirs. Capital Bank and Trust of Clayton, The Graphic Arts Ctr. Inc., Kilo Rsch. Found. (vice chmn.). Bd. dirs. Am. Heart Assn., St. Louis Ambassadors, Catholic Charities of St. Louis, Galway Sister City Com., The Backstoppers, Christmas in St. Louis Found.; nat. bd. dirs. Boys Hope; bd. trustees, pres. coun. St. Louis U.; adv. bd. Safe Kids; hon. bd. Paraquad; hon. chmn. Small Bus. Week in St. Louis, 1989; hon. co-chmn. Veteran's Day Observance and Parade, 1989; co-chairpsn AMC Cancer Rsch. Ctr. Community Svc. award. Named St. Louis Ambassador of Yr., 1986, Olivette Businessman of Yr., 1987, St. Louis Bus. Leader of Yr. Coll. Bus. Adminstrn., So. Ill. U. at Carbondale, 1987,Outstanding Philanthropist St. Louis chpt., Nat. Soc. Fund Raising Execs., 1987; recipient Spirit of Life award City of Hope Labor Mgmt., 1987, St. Louis U. Alumni Merit award, 1987, Meritorious Svc. to Sports award MS Soc., 1987, Presdl. Sports award Maryville Coll., 1987 Jak's Day of Yr. award Sales and Mktg. Execs. of Met. St. Louis, 1988, St. Louis Man of the Yr. award Greater St. Louis Area and Vicinity Port Council, Maritime Trades Dept., AFL-CIO,, 1989. Mem. Alzeimer's Disease and Related Disorders Assn. (hon.), St. Louis Counts, Hawthorn Found., St. Louis Club, Mo. Athletic Club, Old Warson Country Club, Boone Valley Country Club. Home: 10 Trent Dr Saint Louis MO 63124-1033 Office: Engineered Air Systems Inc 201 Evans Ln Saint Louis MO 63121-1126

**SHANAHAN, MIKE,** professional football coach; b. Oak Park, Ill., Aug. 24, 1952; m. Peggy; children: Kyle, Krystal. BS Phys. Edn., Eastern Illinois U., Charleston, 1974; MS Phys. Edn., 1975. Student coach Eastern Illinois U.; asst. coach U. Oklahoma, 1975-76; offensive coord. No. Ariz. U., 1976-77, Ea. Ill. U., 1977—78, U. Minn., 1979—80, U. Fla., Gainesville, 1980—84, asst. head coach, 1983—84; receivers coach Denver Broncos, 1984-87; head coach LA Raiders, 1988-89; asst. coach Denver Broncos, 1989-91; offensive coord. San Francisco 49ers, 1992-94; head coach Denver Broncos, 1995—. Achievements include coaching the Super Bowl Champion Denver Bronco's, 1997, 1998. Avocations: golf, travel. Office: Denver Broncos 13655 Broncos Pkwy Englewood CO 80112-4150*

**SHANAHAN, REBECCA M.,** lawyer; b. 1953; BA, Ind. U., 1974, JD cum laude, 1977. Bar: Ind. 1977, Ill. 1997, Fla. 2003. Of counsel RCA Consumer Electronics, 1980—86; v.p., gen. counsel Cmty. Hosps. Ind., Inc., 1986—91; sr. v.p. Methodist Health Group, 1991—96; v.p. managed care and bus. devel. U. Chgo. Hosps. and Health Systems, 1997—2002; exec. v.p. adminstrn., gen. counsel, sec. Priority Healthcare Corp., Lake Mary, Fla., 2002—. Cons. The Shanahan Group, 1996—97; bd. dirs. SinusPharma. Office: Priority Healthcare Corp 250 Technology Pk Ste 124 Lake Mary FL 32746 Office Phone: 407-804-6700. Office Fax: 407-804-5675. E-mail: rebecca.shanahan@priorityhealthcare.com.

**SHANAHAN, SHEILA ANN,** pediatrician, educator; m. Justin Laurence Cashman Jr., Sept. 14, 1968; children: Justin III, Gillis. BA, Trinity Coll., 1963; MD cum laude, Med. Coll. Pa., 1969. Diplomate Nat. Bd. Med. Examiners, Am. Bd. Pediats. Intern Presbyn. Hosp., N.Y.C., 1969-70, resident

in pediats., 1970-72, asst. in clin. pediats., 1972-75, assoc. clin. pediats., 1975-78; pvt. practice specializing in pediats. Greenwich, Conn., 1972-78; asst. attending Greenwich Hosp., 1972-73, assoc. attending, 1973-78; from instr. to assoc. Columbia Coll. Physicians and Surgeons, N.Y.C., 1972-78; asst. prof. pediats. George Washington U. Sch. Medicine, Washington, 1980—, Georgetown U. Sch. Medicine, Washington, 1984—; pvt. practice specializing in pediats. Washington, 1984—. Attending dept. ambulatory medicine Children's Hosp. Nat. Med. Ctr., Washington, 1980—84; courtesy staff Georgetown U. Hosp., Washington, 1984—, Sibley Meml. Hosp., Washington, 1984—, Columbia Hosp. for Women, 1984—2002, Children's Hosp. Nat. Med. Ctr., 1984—. Fellow Am. Acad. Pediats.; mem. Am. Women's Med. Assn. Office: 4900 Massachusetts Ave NW Washington DC 20016-4358

**SHANAHAN, THOMAS M.,** judge; b. Omaha, May 5, 1934; m. Jane Estelle Lodge, Aug. 4, 1956; children: Catherine, Thomas M. II, Mary Elizabeth, Timothy F. AB magna cum laude, U. Notre Dame, 1956; JD, Georgetown U., 1959. Bar: Nebr., Wyo. Mem. McGinley, Lane, Mueller, Shanahan, O'Donnell & Merritt, Ogallala, Nebr.; assoc. justice Nebr. Supreme Ct., Lincoln, 1983-93; judge U.S. Dist. Ct. Nebr., Omaha, 1993—. Office: US Dist Ct 111 S 18th Plz Ste 3141 Omaha NE 68102

**SHANAHAN, TIMOTHY EDWARD,** urban education educator, researcher; b. Detroit, Aug. 10, 1951; s. Ignatius and Irene Alida (Duncan) S.; children: Erin Rachael, Meagan Rebecca; m. Cynthia Tullis Hynd. BA, Oakland U., 1972, MA in Tchg. of Reading, 1974; PhD, U. Del., 1980. Prof. U. Ill., Chgo., 1980—. Bd. dirs. Ctr. for Literacy, U. Ill., Chgo.; adv. panel Nat. Assessment Ednl. Progress, Princeton, NJ, 1991—; pres III Literacy Resource Devel. Ctr., Urbana, 1999-2001; mem. Nat. Reading Panel, 1998-2000; chair Nat. Literacy Panel for Language Minority Youth, 2002-,chair, Nat. Early Literacy Panel, 2002-; creator reading instrn. program Treasury of Literature, 1995, Elements of Reading: Fluency Author: Understanding REading and Writing Research, 1984, Academic Research Libraries in the Teaching of English, 1993; editor: Reading and Writing Together, 1990, Multidisciplinary Perspectives on Literacy Research, 1992, Teachers Thinking, Teachers Knowing, 1994, Dir. of reading, Chgo. Pub. Sch. 2001-2002. Mem. dels. assembly Sch. Dist. 101, LaGrange, Ill., 1991-93 Recipient Outstanding Tchr. award Amoco Found., 1982, Presdl. Citation for outstanding achievement U. Del., 1994, Albert J. Harris award for outstanding rsch., 1997, Ill. Reading Coun. Reading Hall of Fame, 2002. Fellow Nat. Conf. Rsch. in English (dir. coop. rsch. 1988-91); mem. Am. Ednl. Rsch. Assn., Internat. Reading Assn. (bd. dirs. 1998-2001, nat. English lang. arts stds. com. 1994-95, v.p. 2004-05, pres. 2004—), Milton D. Jacobson award 1982), Phi Kappa Phi. Democrat. Jewish. Home: 208 W Washington St #711 Chicago IL 60606 Office: Univ Ill Ctr for Literacy M/C 147 1040 W Harrison St Chicago IL 60607-7129 Office Phone: 312-413-1914. Business E-Mail: shanahan@uic.edu.

**SHANAHAN, WILLIAM STEPHEN,** consumer products company executive; b. Cin., Apr. 15, 1940; s. William Stephen and Dorothea (Murken) S.; children: Kimberly, Michael Erika, Alejandra. BA, Dartmouth Coll., 1962; postgrad., U. Calif.-Berkeley, 1962-63, Internat. Christian U., Tokyo, 1963-64, U. Philippines-Manila, 1964-65. Joined Colgate-Palmolive Co., 1965, pres., gen. mgr. Sao Paulo, Brazil, 1972-76, v.p. mktg. services div. Colgate U.S.A. N.Y.C., 1976-78; pres., CEO Helena Rubinstein, N.Y.C., 1978-80; v.p. western hemisphere, group v.p. Colgate-Palmolive Co., N.Y.C., sr. exec. v.p. ops., until 1989, chief oper. officer, 1989-2000, pres., 2000—. Office: Colgate-Palmolive Co 300 Park Ave New York NY 10022-7402

**SHANDLING, GARRY,** comedian, scriptwriter, actor; b. Chgo., Nov. 29, 1949; s. Irving and Muriel S. BA in Marketing, U. Ariz. TV screenwriter: Sanford and Son, Welcome Back Kotter, Three's Company; guest host The Tonight Show, 1986-88; host Emmy Awards 1987, 88, Grammy Awards 1990, 91, 92; writer, prodr. (comedy specials) Garry Shandling: Alone in Las Vegas, 1984; exec. prodr., writer (comedy specials) It's Garry Shandling's Show 25th Anniversary Special, 1986, (TV Series) It's Garry Shandling's Show, 1986-90 (CableACE award best comedy series 1989, 90, CableACE award best actor in a comedy series, 1990), Garry Shandling: Stand-Up, 1991; writer, exec. prodr.. dir. (TV Series) The Larry Sanders Show, 1992-98 (Emmy award for outstanding writing, 1998, CableACE award writing in a comedy series, 1993, 94, 95, 96, CableACE award best actor in a comedy series, 1995, 96); actor (films) Love Affair, 1994, Mixed Nuts, 1994, Doctor Doolittle (voice), 1998, Hurlyburly, 1998, What Planet Are You From? 2000 (also writer, prodr.), Town & Country, 2001, Run Ronnie Run!, 2002, Comedian, 2002, Over the Hedge (voice), 2006.*

**SHANE, JEFFREY NEIL,** federal agency administrator, lawyer; b. NYC, Mar. 27, 1941; s. Albert and Ann (Semanoff) S.; m. D. Jean Wu, June 27, 1992. AB, Princeton U., 1962; LLB, Columbia U., N.Y.C., 1965. Bar: D.C. 1966. Trial atty. FPC, Washington, 1966-68, Dept. Transp., Washington, 1968-70, spl. asst. to gen. counsel, 1970-72; traveled in Africa, Europe, 1972-73; researcher Environ. Law Inst., Washington, 1974-75; mem. UN Task Force on Human Environ., Bangkok, 1975-77; atty., cons. environ. law in developing countries, Washington, 1978-79; asst. gen. counsel internat. law Dept. Transp., Washington, 1979-83, dep. asst. sec. policy and internat. affairs, 1983-85, asst. sec. policy and internat. affairs, 1989—93, assoc. dep. sec., 2002—03, under sec. for policy, 2003—; dep. asst. sec. transp. affairs Dept. of State, Washington, 1985-89; counsel Wilmer, Cutler & Pickering, Washington, 1993-96, ptnr., 1997-2000; Hogan & Hartson, Washington, 2000—02. Adj. prof. law Georgetown U., Washington, 1985-89; cons. and lectr. transp. law and policy; mem. Archl. and Transp. Barriers Compliance Bd., 1989-93, 2005-06, vice-chmn., 1992-93; vice chmn. Adv. Com. on Confs. in Ocean Shipping, 1990-91; chmn. commn. on air transport Internat C of C, Paris, 1991 2001, chmn. mil. airlift com. Nat. Defense Transport Assn.; mem. Air Transp. Stabilization Bd., 2004-. Co-author: Developing Economies and the Environment, 1978; co-author-editor: NEPA in Action: The Impact of the National Environmental Policy Act on Federal Decision-Making, 1975, Environmental and Natural Resource Management in Developing Countries, 1979. Recipient Presdl. Meritorious Rank award, Dept. of State, 1988. Mem.: ABA (chmn. forum on air and space law 2001), Met. Club, Columbia Country Club (Chevy Chase, Md.), Wings Club (N.Y.C. bd. govs. 1995—98), Internat. Aviation Club (Washington pres. 1999—2000), Aero Club (Washington bd. govs. 1984—86), Cosmos Club (Washington). Home: 5015 Rockwood Pkwy NW Washington DC 20016-1913 Office: Dept Transp 400 7th St NW Washington DC 20590 Office Phone: 202-366-1815. Business E-Mail: jeff.shane@dot.gov.

**SHANE, JOHN MARDER,** endocrinologist; b. Kansas City, Mo., Oct. 5, 1942; s. Henry Kamsler and Ruth (Marder) S.; m. Eileen Goodart, June 18, 1967; children: Robert M., Edward G. BS, U. Okla., 1964, MD, 1967. Diplomate Am. Bd. Ob-Gyn., Am. Bd. Reproductive Endocrinology; cert. master gardener. Resident Harvard Med. Sch., Boston, 1970-73, fellowship, 1973-75, instr., 1970-75, asst. prof., 1975-78; pvt. practice Tulsa, 1978-99. Lectr., cons. Tutorial Svcs. Internat., England, 1984—; bd. dirs. St. Francies G.I.F.T. Lab., Tulsa; cons. to preimplantation genetics project Chapman Genetics Inst., Children's Med. Ctr., Tulsa. Author: CIBA Symposium Infertility: Diagnosis and Treatment; contbr. articles to profl. jours. and publs.; exhibitions include Okla. Woodturners, The Philbrook Mus. Active Tulsa Garden Ctr., 1988—; bd. dirs. Temple Israel, Tulsa, 1985-86, Up With Trees Found., 2000—, Tulsa. master gardener. Capt. USAF, 1967-69. Recipient Annual award Boston Obstet. Soc., 1977; named one of Best Doctor's in Am., Tulsa's Best Doctors, Tulsa People Mag. Mem. ACS, Tulsa Gynecol. Soc. (past pres. 1986-87), Soc. Reproductive Endocrinologists, Tulsa bonsai Soc. (bd. dirs. 1988—), Am. Coll. Ob-Gyn. (v.p. 1971-92, pres. New England Jr. divsn. 1972-73), Am. Bonsai Soc. (nat. bd. dirs.), Chanie des Rotisseurs (l'Ordre Mondial, Tulsa, v.p., advisor to bd.), Bronze Star 2001), Southside Rotary of Tulsa (bd. dirs., pres. 1997-98, Nat. Arboretum Bonsai Pavilion (nat. bd. dirs.), Rotary Club Tulsa (past pres. Southside club). Republican. Jewish. Avocations: gardening, cooking, bonsai, collector Oriental arts, woodturning.

**SHANE, PENNY,** lawyer; b. NYC, 1963; BA, Barnard Coll., 1985; JD, NYU, 1988. Bar: NY 1989, US Ct. of Appeal (2nd cir.) and (DC cir.), US Dist. Courts (so., ea., we. districts) NY, NY State Courts. Law clk. Judge Richard Owen US Dist. Ct. (so. dist.) NY, 1988—90; ptnr. and mem. litig. group, fin. institutions group, criminal def. and investigations group Sullivan & Cromwell, NYC. Office: Sullivan & Cromwell 125 Broad St New York NY 10004-2498 Office Phone: 212-558-4000. Office Fax: 212-558-3588. Business E-Mail: shanep@sullcrom.com.

**SHANE, PETER MILO,** law educator; b. Oceanside, NY, July 12, 1952; s. Albert and Ann (Semanoff) S.; m. Martha Elisabeth Chamallas, June 27, 1981; 1 child: Elisabeth Ann. AB, Harvard U., 1974; JD, Yale U., 1977. Bar: N.Y. 1978, U.S.C.t. Appeals (5th cir.) 1978, D.C. 1979, U.S. Ct. Appeals (8th cir.) 1983, U.S. Supreme Ct. 1984, Pa. 1995. Law clk. to judge U.S. Ct. Appeals (5th cir.), New Orleans, 1977-78; atty., advisor office of legal counsel U.S. Dept. Justice, Washington, 1978-81; asst. gen. counsel Office of Mgmt. and Budget, Washington, 1981; assoc. prof. law U. Iowa, Iowa City, 1981-85, prof., 1985-94; dean U. Pitts., 1994-98, prof., 1994—2001; Disting. Service prof. law & pub. policy, dir. Inst. for Study of Info. Tech. and Soc., Carnegie Mellon U., 2001—03, Disting. Service prof. law & pub. policy (adj.), 2003—, chair adv. bd., 2003—; Joseph S. Platt-Porter, Wright, Morris and Arthur prof law, dir. Ctr. Interdisciplinary Law & Policy Studies, Ohio State U., 2003—. Adj. lectr. Am. U., Washington, D.C., 1979-80; vis. prof. law Duke U., Durham, N.C., 1986, Boston Coll., Newton, Mass., 1999, Villanova (Pa.) U., 1999, Carnegie Mellon U., 2000-01; cons. U.S. Dept. Edn., Washington, D.C., 1980, MacArthur Justice Found., Chgo., 1987; active Administrv. Conf. U.S., 1991, pub. mem., 1995; cons. Nat. Commn. Jud. Discipline and Removal, 1992-93; cooperating atty. Iowa Civil Liberties Union, Des Moines, 1982-94, bd. dirs., 1987-89; active Coun. on Legal Edn. Opportunity, 1996-2004; reporter Civil Justice Adv. Group, U.S. Dist. Ct. (we. dist.) Pa. Author: (with H.H. Bruff) The Law of Presidential Power: Cases and Materials, 1988, (with H.H. Bruff) Separation of Powers Law, 1996, 2005, (with J. Mashaw and R. Merrill) Administrative Law: The American Public Law System, 2003, Democracy Online: The Prospects for Political Renewal Through the Internet, 2004, (with John Podesta and Richard C. Leone) A Little Knowledge: Security, Privacy and Public Information After September 11, 2004. Mem. Dem. cen. com. Johnson County, Iowa, 1982-88. Recipient citation for outstanding svc. Pa. House of Reps., 1998, Cleo Disting. Svc. award, 2004; named Young Leader of Higher Edn., Am. Assn. Higher Edn., 1998; Old Gold Summer fellow U. Iowa, 1981-84, Mellon Found. fellow, 1982. Mem. ABA (coun. sect. adminstrv. law and regulatory practice 1993-96, chmn. com. on govt. orgn. and separation of powers 1987-91), Assn. Am. Law Schs. (chair adminstrv. law 1990, chair remedies 1992, chair law sch. deans 1997), Am. Law Inst. Jewish. Office: Ohio State U Moritz Coll Law 55 W 12th Ave Columbus OH 43210 Office Phone: 614-688-3014. Business E-Mail: shane.29@osu.edu.

**SHANE, RITA,** opera singer, educator; b. NYC; d. Julius J. and Rebekah (Milner) S.; m. Thomas F. Tritter, June 22, 1958; 1 child, Michael Shane. BA, Barnard Coll., 1958; postgrad., Santa Fe Opera Apprentice Program, 1962-63, Hunter Opera Assn., 1962-64; pvt. study with Beverly Peck Johnson. Adj. prof. voice Manhattan Sch. of Music, 1993-95. Prof. voice Eastman Sch. Music Rochester U., 1989—, Aspen Music Sch., 1999, Hamamatsu, Japan, 2000—02; pvt. tchr., N.Y.C., 1978—; judge Richard Tucker Music Found.. Met. Opera Regional Auditions, Licia Albanese Puccini Found. Performer with numerous opera cos., including profl. debut, Chattanooga Opera, 1964, Met. Opera, San Diego Opera, Santa Fe Opera, Teatro alla Scala, Milan, Italy, Bavarian State Opera, Netherlands Nat. Opera, Geneva Opera, Vienna State Opera, Phila., New Orleans, Balt. Opera, Opera du Rhin, Strasbourg, Scottish Opera, Teatro Reggio, Turin, Opera Metropolitana, Caracas, Portland Opera, Minn. Opera, also others; world premiere Miss Havisham's Fire, Argento; Am. premieres include Reimann-Lear, Schat-Houdini, Henze-Elegy for Young Lovers; participant festivals, including Mozart Festival, Lincoln Center, N.Y.C., Munich Festival, Aspen Festival, Handel Soc., Vienna Festival, Salzburg Festival, Munich Festival, Perugia Festival, Festival Canada, Glyndebourne Festival, performed with orchs. including Santa Cecilia, Rome, Austrian Radio, London Philharmn., Louisville, Cin., Cleve., Phila., RAI, Naples, Denver, Milw., Israel Philharm., rec. artist, RCA, Columbia, Louisville, Turnabout, Myto labels, also radio and TV. Recipient Martha Baird Rockefeller award, William Matheus Sullivan award. Mem. Am. Guild Mus. Artists, Screen Actors Guild, Nat. Assn. Tchrs. Singing.

**SHANE, SANDRA KULI,** postal service administrator; b. Akron, Ohio, Dec. 12, 1939; d. Amiel M. and Margaret E. (Brady) Kuli; m. Fred Shane, May 30, 1962 (div. 1972); 1 child, Mark Richard; m. Byrl William Campbell, Apr. 26, 1981 (dec. 1984). BA, U. Akron, 1987, postgrad., 1988-90. Scheduler motor vehicle bur. Akron Police Dept., 1959-62; flight and ops. control staff Escort Air, Inc., Akron and Cleve., 1972-78; asst. traffic mgr. Keen Transport, Inc., Hudson, Ohio, 1978-83; mem. ops. and mktg. staff Shawnee Airways and Essco, Akron, 1983-86; in distbn. U.S. Postal Svc., Akron, 1986—. Sec. Affirmative Action Coun., Akron, 1988-90. Asst. art tchr. Akron Art Mus., 1979; counselor Support, Inc., Akron, 1983-84; com. chmn. Explorer post Boy Scouts Am., Akron, 1984-85. Mem. Bus. and Profl. Women's Assn. (pres.), Delta Nu Alpha. Democrat. Roman Catholic. Avocations: painting, sculpting, fabric design. Home: 745 Hampton Ridge Dr Akron OH 44313

**SHANE, WILLIAM WHITNEY,** astronomer; b. Berkeley, Calif., June 3, 1928; s. Charles Donald and Mary Lea (Heger) S.; BA, U. Calif., Berkeley, 1951, postgrad., 1953-58; ScD, Leiden U., The Netherlands, 1971; m. Clasina van der Molen, Apr. 22, 1964; children: Johan Jacob, Charles Donald. rsch. assoc. Leiden U., 1961-71, sr. scientist, 1971-79; prof. astronomy, dir. Astron. Inst., Cath. U. Nijmegen, The Netherlands, 1979-88; guest prof. astronomy Leiden U., 1988-93; C H Adams fellow Monterey Inst Rsch Astronomy, Calif., 1994—. With USN, 1951-53. Fellow AAAS; mem. Internat. Astron. Union (commns. 33, 34), Am. Astron. Soc., Astron. Soc. Netherlands, Astron. Soc. of the Pacific, Phi Beta Kappa. Achievements include rsch. on structure and dynamics of galaxies, observational astronomy. Home: 9095 Coker Rd Prunedale CA 93907-1401 Office: Monterey Inst Rsch Astronomy 200 8th St Marina CA 93933-6002

**SHANEFIELD, DANIEL JAY,** ceramic engineering educator; b. Orange, NJ, Apr. 29, 1930; s. Benjamin and Nan (Leichter) S.; m. Elizabeth Davis, June 28, 1964; children: Alison, Douglas. BS in Chemistry, Yale U., 1952; PhD in Chemistry, Rutgers U., 1962. Sr. project engr. ITT Group, Nutley, NJ, 1962-67; sr. mem. tech. staff AT&T Bell Labs., Princeton, NJ, 1967-86; disting. prof. Rutgers U., New Brunswick, NJ, 1986—. Adv. panel NSF, 1990—; course dir. Ctr. for Profl. Advancement, U.S. and The Netherlands, 1993—; cons., presenter in field. Author: Organic Additives and Ceramic Processing, 1996; co-author: Defects in Gold Plating, 1981, Industrial Electronics for Engineers, Chemists and Technicians, 2000; contbr. chpts. to books, articles to profl. jours.; co-inventor 17 patents; mem. editl. bd. Jour. Am. Ceramic Soc., 1987-99. With U.S. Army, 1952-54, Korea. Fellow Am. Inst. Chemists, Am. Ceramic Soc. (Best Paper award); mem. IEEE (life; chmn. stds. com. 1984-99), Am. Chem. Soc., Ceramic Assn. of N.J. (Man of Yr. award 1996). Republican. Avocations: modifying sports cars, writing audio, stereo articles. Office: Rutgers U Ceramics Engring Dept 607 Taylor Rd Piscataway NJ 08854-8065 Office Phone: 732-445-2226.

**SHANGRAW, ROBERT EDWARD,** medical educator, researcher; b. Troy, N.Y., Mar. 16, 1954; s. Robert Dixon and M. Janice (Bonacker) S.; m. Patricia Mary Ford, May 25, 1985; children: Kirsten Celanire, Sarah Elizabeth, Kathleen Ford. BS, Rensselaer Poly. Inst., 1976; PhD, Albany Med. Coll., NY, 1981, MD, 1985. Resident in surgery U. Wash., Seattle, 1985-86; rsch. assoc. U. Tex. Med. Br., Galveston, 1986-87; resident in anesthesia Hosp. U. Pa., Phila., 1987-90; asst. prof. anesthesiology Oreg. Health and Sci. U., Portland, 1990—96, assoc. prof., 1996—2001, prof., 2001—. Cons. NIH Study Sects., 1999—; contbr. articles on biomedicine to profl. jours. Fellow NIH, 1977-80, 82, 83. Mem. AMA, Am. Physiol. Soc., Am. Soc. Anesthesiologists, Internat. Anesthesia Rsch. Soc., Biochem. Soc., Assn. Univ. Anesthesiologists, Sigma Xi, Alpha Omega Alpha. Roman Catholic. Avocations:

skiing, sailing, hiking, kayaking, swimming. Home: 5776 SW Calusa Loop Tualatin OR 97062-9757 Office: Oreg Health and Sci U Dept Anesthesiology and Periop Medicine 3181 SW Sam Jackson Park Rd Portland OR 97239-3098 Office Phone: 503-494-7641. Business E-Mail: shangraw@ohsu.edu.

**SHANK, CHARLES VERNON,** science administrator, educator, physicist; b. Mt. Holly, NJ, July 12, 1943; s. Augustus Jacob and Lillian (Peterson) S.; m. Brenda Buckhold, June 16, 1969. BS, U. Calif., Berkeley, 1965, MS, PhD, 1969. Mem. tech. staff AT&T Bell Labs., Holmdel, NJ, 1969-76, head quantum physics and electronics dept., 1976-83, dir. Electronics Rsch. Lab., 1983-89; dir. Lawrence Berkeley Lab., prof. chemistry, physics, elec. enging. and computer scis. U. Calif., Berkeley, 1989—2004. Co-author over 200 sci. pubs. Recipient E. Longstreth medal Franklin Inst., Phila., 1982, Morris E. Leeds award IEEE, 1982, David Sarnoff award IEEE, 1989, Edgerton award Optical Soc. Engring., John Scott award, Edward P. Longstreth award Franklin Soc. Fellow AAAS, IEEE, Am. Phys. Soc. (George E. Pake prize 1996, Arthur L. Schawlow prize 1997), Optical Soc. Am. (R. W. Wood prize 1981); mem. NAS, NAE, Am. Acad. Arts and Scis. Numerous patents in field. Home: 118 S Kalaheo Ave Kailua HI 96734-2932

**SHANK, FRED ROSS,** food scientist; b. Harrisonburg, Va., Oct. 11, 1940; m. Peggy Anne Westbrook, June 1967; children: Virginia Anne, Fred Ross III. BS in Agriculture, U. Ky., 1962, MS in Nutrition, 1964; PhD, U. Md., 1969. Dep. dir. Office Nutrition and Food Sci. FDA, Washington, 1979-86, dir. Office Phys. Sci., 1986-87, dep. dir. Ctr. for Food SAfety and Applied Nutrition, 1987-89, dir., 1989-98, sr. advisor to FDA commr., 1998-99; sr. v.p. sci. Chocolate Mfrs. Assn., McLean, Va., 1999—2000; v.p. Sci. Inst. of Food Tech., Wash., DC, 2000. Fellow Inst. Food Technologists; mem. Am. Assn. Cereal Chemists, Am. Inst. Nutrition, Am. Soc. for Clin. Nutrition. Avocation: Food and Drug Ofcls. Home: 2621 Steeplechase Dr Reston VA 20191-2130 Office Phone: 202-466-5980.

**SHANK, GARY D.,** education educator; b. Charleston, W.Va., Aug. 16, 1949; s. William H. and Lorene A. Shank; m. Deborah L. Smith (div.); children: Bridget, Morgan. BS, Rensselaer Poly. Inst., 1971; MS, PhD, Ind. U., 1980. Assoc. prof. St. Meinrad (Ind.) Coll., 1980—91, No. Ill. U., DeKalb, 1991—97; prof. Duquesne U., Pitts., 1997—. Vis. prof. U Surrey, Guildford, England, 1999. Author: (2d edit.) Qualitative Research: A Personal Skills Approach, 2006. Scholar, Sears Found., 1967. Mem.: Semiotic Soc. Am., Am. Ednl. Rsch. Assn. Independent. Roman Catholic. Office: Duquesne Univ 410C Canevin Hall Pittsburgh PA 15282 Office Phone: 412-356-4154. Business E-mail: shank@duq.edu.

**SHANK, J. WILLIAM,** art conservator; Studied art history and art conservation, Villa Schifanoia, Florence, Italy; grad. studies, NYU Inst. Fine Arts; advanced tng. in art conservation, Harvard U. With We. Ctr. for the Conservation of Fine Arts; mem. staff San Francisco Mus. Modern Art, 1985—2000, chief conservator, 1991—2000; now with Conservation Resources Mgmt. Founder Rescue Pub. Murals (in cooperation with Heritage Preservation). Curator (conservation based exhbn.) A Hidden Picasso, Guggenheim Mus., Bilbao, Spain, 2004. Booth Family Rome Prize Fellowship for Historic Preservation and Conservation, Am. Acad. in Rome, 2004—05. Address: P O Box 410266 San Francisco CA 94141-0266

**SHANK, MAURICE EDWIN,** aerospace engineer, consultant; b. NYC, Apr. 22, 1921; s. Edwin A. and Viola (Lewis) S.; m. Virginia Lee King, Sept. 25, 1948; children: Christopher K., Hilary L. Shank-Kuhl, Diana L. Shank. BS in Mech. Engring., Carnegie-Mellon U., 1942; D.Sc., MIT, 1949. Registered profl. engr., Mass. Assoc. prof. mech. engring. MIT, Cambridge, 1949-60; dir. advanced materials R&D Pratt & Whitney, East Hartford, Conn., 1960-70; mgr. materials engring. and rsch., 1971-72; dir. engring. tech., 1972-80; dir. engine design and structures engring. Pratt & Whitney, East Hartford, Conn., 1980-81, dir. engring. tech., 1981-85, dir. engring. tech. assessment, 1985-86; v.p. Pratt Whitney of China, Inc., East Hartford, 1986-87; pvt. exec. cons. to industry and govt., 1987—. Cons. editor McGraw-Hill Book Co., N.Y.C., 1960-80; adv. com. to mechanics div. Nat. Bur. Standards, Washington, 1964-69; vis. com. dept. mech. engring. Carnegie-Mellon U., Pitts., 1968-78; corp. vis. coms. depts. materials sci. and engring., dept. aeros. and astronautics MIT, 1968-74, 79-92; mem. rsch. and tech. adv. coun. com. on aero. propulsion NASA, Washington, 1973-77; mem. aero. adv. com., 1978-86; mem. aero. and space engring. bd. NRC, 1989-92; lectr. in field. Contbr. articles to profl. jours. Served to maj. U.S. Army Corps. of Engrs., Ordnance Corps, 1942-46, Middle East/North Africa. Fellow AIAA, ASME, AIME, Am. Soc. Metals; mem. Nat. Acad. Engring., Conn. Acad. Sci. and Engring. Clubs: Cosmos. Episcopalian. Avocations: boating, fishing.

**SHANK, RUSSELL,** librarian, educator; b. Spokane, Wash., Sept. 2, 1925; s. Harry and Sadie S.; m. Doris Louise Hempfer, Nov. 9, 1951 (div.); children: Susan Marie, Peter Michael, Judith Louise. BS, U. Wash., 1946, BA, 1949; MBA, U. Wis., 1952; DrLS, Columbia U., 1966. Reference libr. U. Wash., Seattle, 1949; asst. engring. libr. U. Wis.-Madison, 1949-52; chief pers. Mil. Pub. Libr., 1952; engring.-phys. scis. libr. Columbia U., N.Y.C., 1953-59, sr. lectr., 1964-66, assoc. prof., 1966-67; asst. univ. libr. U. Calif.-Berkeley, 1959-64; dir. sci. libr. N.Y. Met. Reference and Rsch., 1966-68; dir. librs. Smithsonian Instn., Washington, 1967-77; univ. libr. prof. UCLA, 1977-89, asst. vice chancellor for libr. and info. svcs. planning, 1989-91, univ. libr., prof. emeritus, 1991—. Cons. Indonesian Inst. Sci., 1970; bd. cons. Pahlavi Nat. Library, Iran, 1975-76; pres. U.S. Book Exchange, 1975; bd. trustees Freedom to Read Found., 1989—. Trustee OCLC, Inc., 1978-84, 87, chmn., 1984; mem. library del. People's Republic of China, 1979; bd. dirs. Am. Council on Edn., 1980-81. Served with USNR, 1943-46. Recipient Disting. Alumnus award U. Wash. Sch. Librarianship, 1968, Role of Honor award Freedom to Read Found., 1990, Disting. Alumnus award Columbia U. Sch. Libr. Sci., 1992; fellow Coun. on Libr. Resources, 1973-74. Fellow AAAS; mem. ALA (coun. 1978-79, coun. 1961-65, 74-82, exec. bd. 1975-80, chmn. internat. rels. com. 1980-83, pres. info. sci. and automation div. 1968-69), Assn. Coll. and Rsch. Librs. (pres. 1972-73, Hugh Atkinson award 1990), Assn. Rsch. Librs. (bd. dirs. 1974-77), Beta Phi Mu. Home: 12919 Montana Ave Apt 101 Los Angeles CA 90049-4843 Business E-Mail: rshank@ucla.edu. *Intellectual freedom is the paramount human right. It is the American's premier heritage. Without it the claim to democracy is a sham. Should the principles of our society fade or perish, the survival of this freedom alone would justify the nation's experience. The freedom to think, to read, and to speak will be our enduring monument. Their diffusion throughout the world must be our unending crusade.*

**SHANK, SUZANNE ADAMS,** lawyer; b. Kansas City, Mo., Nov. 13, 1946; d. Howard Howe and Bettie Ann (Winkler) Hettick; m. Martin Smoler, May 18, 1991. BJ, U. Mo., 1972; MPA in Health Adminstrn., U. Mo., Kansas City, 1982, JD, 1982. Bar: Mo. 1982, U.S. Dist. Ct. (we. dist.) Mo. 1982. Journalist U. Kans. Med. Ctr., Kansas City, 1972-73; asst. editor Am. Family Physician, Kansas City, Mo., 1973-75; exec. dir. Lambert Med. Clinic, Kansas City, Mo., 1975-80; assoc. Shughart, Thomson & Kilroy, Kansas City, 1982-85; v.p. GE/Employers Reins. Corp., Overland Park, Kans., 1985-2000; sr. v.p. Attys. Liability Assurance Soc., Chgo., 2000—. Mem. Friends of Zoo, Kansas City, Mo., 1981—, Menorah Med. Ctr. Aux., Kansas City, 1982—, Women's Vision Internat., Kansas City, Mo., 1999—; mem. Internat. Rels. Coun., 1999—; bd. dirs. Friends Conservatory Music, Kansas City, 2002—, Found. on Aging, Kansas City, 2003—. Mem. ABA, Mo. Bar Assn., Kansas City Bar Assn. (chmn. ins. law com.), Soc. Profl. Journalists, Soc. CPCU (rsch. com.), Com. to Protect Journalists, Kappa Tau alpha. Home: 2703 W 66th Ter Shawnee Mission KS 66208-1810 Office: Attorneys Liability Assurance Soc 311 S Wacker 5700 Chicago IL 60606

**SHANK, WILLIAM O.,** lawyer; b. Hamilton, Ohio, Jan. 11, 1924; s. Horace Cooper and Bonnie (Winn) S.; m. Shirleen Allison, June 25, 1949; children—Allison Kay, Kristin Elizabeth. BA, Miami U., Oxford, Ohio, 1947; JD, Yale, 1950. Bar: Ohio, Ill., U.S. Supreme Ct. Pvt. practice, Hamilton, Ohio, 1951-55, Chgo., 1955—; mem. firm Shank, Briede & Spoerl, Hamilton, Ohio,

1951-55; assoc. Lord, Bissell & Brook, Chgo., 1955-58; atty. Chemetron Corp., 1958-60, sr. atty., 1960-61, gen. atty., asst. sec., 1961-71, sec., gen. counsel, 1971-78; v.p., gen. counsel, sec. Walgreen Co., Deerfield, Ill., 1978-89; ptnr. Burditt & Radzius, Chartered, Chgo., 1989-98; exec. v.p. Internat. Bus. Resources, Inc., Chgo., 1993—2000; ptnr. Williams Montgomery & John Ltd., Chgo., 1998—2003; of counsel Hinshaw & Culbertson, Crystal Lake, Ill., 2003—. Mem. bus. adv. coun. Miami U., Oxford, Ohio, 1975—; arbitrator 19th Jud. Cir., Ill., 1995—; adv. bd. eLawForum, Washington, 1999—. Bd. dirs. Coun. for Cmty. Svcs. Met. Chgo., 1973-77; trustee Libr. Internat. Rels., 1971-78; bd. dirs. Chgo. Civic Fedn., 1984-89, Walgreen Drug Stores Hist. Found., 1990—; mem. Chgo. Crime Commn., 1985-89. 1st lt., pilot 8th Air Force, USAAF, World War II, ETO. Fellow Am. Bar Found. (life) mem. ABA (com. corp. gen. counsel), Ill. State Bar Assn., Chgo. Bar Assn. (chmn. com. on corp. law depts. 1971-72, 89-90), Am. Soc. Corp. Secs. (pres. Chgo. regional group 1983-84, nat. bd. dirs. 1984-87), Yale U. Law Sch. Assn. (past pres. Ill. Alumni, exec. com. New Haven), Walgreen Alumni Assn. (pres. 1992-94), Legal Club (pres. 1979-80), Law Club, Lawyers Club (Chgo.), Univ. Club, Econ. Club, Yale Club of Chgo., Am. Air Mus. in Britain (sustaining mem. 2004—), Omicron Delta Kappa, Phi Delta Phi, Sigma Chi. Home: 755 S Shore Dr Crystal Lake IL 60014-5530 Office: Hinshaw & Culbertson 500 Coventry Ln Crystal Lake IL 60014 Office Phone: 815-459-5123. E-mail: wshank@hinshawlaw.com.

**SHANKAR, GAUTHAM,** associate, financial services & sales trader; b. Mumbai, Maharashtra, India, Sept. 6, 1974; s. A.G. Shankar, Lalitha Shankar. Bachelor of Pharmacy (Honors), Birla Institute of Technology & Science, Pilani, Pilani, Rajasthan, India 333031, 1992—96; Master of Business Administration, Pennsylvania State University, Smeal College of Business, State College, PA, 1996—98. Consultant i2 Technologies Inc., Dallas, 1998—2000; Associate Goldman, Sachs & Co., New York, NY, 2000—02; v.p. Soundview Tech. Group, Conn., 2003—. Author: (Publication) Impact of GATT on Indian Pharmaceutical Markets, 1996. Mem.: Penn State Alumni Association (Member 1998—2002).

**SHANKAR, RAVI,** composer, musician; b. Apr. 7, 1920; m. Sukanya Rajan; children: Shubho, Geetali, Anoushka. Studied under, Ustad Allauddin Khan of Maihar; trained in Guru-Shishya tradition, pupil of Ustad Allauddin Khan, 1938. Solo sitar player; former dir. music All India Radio, also founder Nat. Orch.; founder, dir. Kinnara Sch. Music, Bombay, 1962, Kinnara Sch. Music, L.A., 1967; many recordings of traditional and exptl. variety in India, U.K., U.S., including Tana Mana, 1987; concert tours in Europe, U.S., The East; vis. lectr. U. Calif., 1965; appeared in film Raga, 1974; fellow Sangeet Natak Akademi, 1976; responsible for music and choreography for ASIAD, 1982; film scores: Pather Panchali, The Flute and the Arrow, Nava Rasa Ranga, Charly, Gandhi, and many musical compositions including Concerto for Sitar No. 1, 1971, No. 2, 1981, Ghanashyam, 1989, and numerous ragas and talas; author: My Music, My Life, 1969, Rag Anurag (Bengali), (autobiography) Raga Mala, 1997. Recipient Deshikottam award, 1982; Silver Bear of Berlin; award of Indian Nat. Acad. Music, Dance and Drama, 1962; award of Padma Bhushan, 1967, Padma Vibushan, 1981, Internat. Music Coun. UNESCO award, 1975; elected to the Rajya Sabha, India, 1986; recipient 16 hon. doctorates around the world; recipient Grand prize Fukuoka Asian Cultural Prizes, Japan, 1991, Ramon Magsaysay award, The Philippines, 1992, Bharatiya Vidya Bhavan Mahatma Gandhi award, 1992, U.K. Ho. of Commons Shield, 1995, Crystal award, Switzerland, 1995, Premium Imperial Arts award, Japan, 1997, Light of Asia award, U.S., 1997, Juliet Hollister award, U.S., 1998, The Polar Music prize, Sweden, 1998, Bharat Ratna, India, 1999, Hon. KBE, 2000; named Commdr. of Legion of Honour, France, 2000. Address: care Sulivan Sweetland 28 Albion St London W2 2AX England*

**SHANKEL, DELBERT MERRILL,** microbiologist, biologist, educator; b. Plainview, Nebr., Aug. 4, 1927; s. Cecil Wilfred and Gladys Dalton (Dodd) Shankel; m. Carol Jo Mulford, Sept. 10, 1962; children: Merrill, Jill, Kelley. BA, Walla Walla Coll., 1950; PhD, U. Tex., 1959. Tchr. Walla Walla Coll. Acad., College Place, Wash., 1950-51; instr. San Antonio Coll., 1954-55; asst. prof., assoc. prof. microbiology and biology U. Kans., Lawrence, 1959-68, prof., 1968—, asst. dean, assoc. dean arts and sci., 1966-72, acting dean, 1973, exec. vice chancellor, 1974-80, 86, 90-92, acting chancellor, 1980-81, chancellor, 1994-95, chancellor emeritus, 1996. Commr. N. Ctrl. Assn. Colls. and Schs., Chgo., 1991—95, cons., evaluator, 1969—96, NW Comm. Coll., 1997—. Editor: Artimutagenesis and Anticarcinogenesis: Mechanisms vols. I-III, 1986, 1988, 1993; assoc. editor: Mutation Rsch., 1992—95. Active numerous civic orgns. With U.S. Army, 1952—54. Named Disting. Alumnus of the Yr., Walla Walla Coll., 1989; recipient Outstanding Educator award, Mortar Bd., U. Kans., 1982, 1985, 1990; numerous rsch. grantee. Fellow: Am. Acad. Microbiology; mem.: Radiation Rsch. Soc., Soc. Gen. Microbiology (Eng.), Genetics Soc. Am., Environ. Mutagen Soc. (chmn. pub. policy com. 1991—93, mem. nat. coun. 1994—97), Am. Soc. Microbiology (past chmn. edn. com., chmn. numerous coms.), U. Kans. Alumni Assn. (interim pres., edn. com., chmn. numerous coms.), Sigma Xi (pres. U. Kans. chpt. 1967). Republican. Unitarian Universalist. Avocations: sports, music, theater, reading. Office: U Kans 1002 Haworth Hl Lawrence KS 66045-0001 Office Phone: 785-864-3150. Business E-Mail: shankel@ku.edu.

**SHANKEN, EDWARD A.,** art educator, design educator; b. Phila., June 8, 1964; s. Mayor Shanken and Judy Fishman. PhD, Duke U., Durham, NC, 2001. Exec. dir. Info. Sci. and Info. Studies Program Duke U., 2001—04; prof. Savannah Coll. Art and Design, Ga., 2004—. Vice-chair Leonardo Edn. Forum, San Francisco, 2005—. Editor (author): Telematic Embrace: Visionary Theories of Art, Technology, and Consciousness. Mem. planning com. REFRESH!, 2004—. Luce/ACLS Doctoral Dissertation fellow in Am. art, Am. Coun. Learned Socs., 1998—99. Mem.: Coll. Art Assn. Am. (edn. com. 2005—). Office: Savannah Coll Art and Design Pepe Hall 212 W Taylor St Savannah GA 31402-3145 Office Phone: 912-525-6068. Office Fax: 912-525-6069. E-mail: eshanken@scad.edu.

**SHANKLIN, CAROL W.,** dietician, educator; BS in Home Econs. Edn., U. Tenn., Martin, 1973; MS in Food Sys. Adminstrn., U. Tenn., Knoxville, 1974, PhD in Food Sys. Adminstrn., 1976. Asst. prof. foods and nutrition Tex. Tech. U., 1977—86; asst. food svc. dir. Highland Hosp., Lubbock, Tex., 1978; asst. prof. food sys. mgmt. Tex. Women's U., 1978—82, assoc. prof. food sys. mgmt., 1982—88, assoc. prof., chair Dept. Nutrition and Food Scis., 1985—87, prof., chair Dept. Nutrition and Food Scis., 1987—90; tech. advisor, cons. Miss. Inst. Higher Learning, 1988—89; grad. program dir., prof. dept. hotel, restaurant, instn. mgmt. and dietetics Kans. State U., Manhattan, 1990—2001, asst. dean. Grad. Sch., prof. dept. hotel, restaurant, instn. mgmt. and dietetics, 2001—04, assoc. dean. Grad. Sch., prof. dept. hotel, restaurant, instn. mgmt. and dietetics, 2004—. Contbr. articles to profl. jours. Recipient Michael Olsen Rsch. Achievement award, U. Del. Mem.: Am. Dietetic Assn. (Medallion award 2001). Achievements include research in on environmental issues in the foodservice and hospitality industry; dietetics and hospitality education; quality service in foodservice operations; and foodservice management, food safety and nutrition in foodservice operations. Office: Kansas State U Graduate Sch 103 Fairchild Manhattan KS 66502-1404 Office Phone: 785-532-7927. Business E-Mail: shanklin@k-state.edu.

**SHANKLIN, KENNETH DALE,** plastic surgeon; b. Toluca, Ill., Dec. 21, 1931; s. Walter Arthur and Elsie Ida Josephine (Holz) S.; m. Doris Gay Minton, July 24, 1955 (div. Jan. 21, 1971); 1 child, Steven Dale; m. Colleen Jean Wheeler, July 30, 1978. BS, U. Ill., 1954; MD, U. Utah, 1967. Diplomate Am. Bd. Med. Specialists in gen. surgery, plastic surgery; lic. Calif. Commd. 2d lt. USAF, 1954, advanced through grades to lt. col., ret., 1977; intern Wilford Hall USAF Med. Ctr., San Antonio, 1967-68, resident in plastic surgery, 1972-74, resident in gen. surgery Travis AFB, Calif., 1968-72; assoc. clin. prof. plastic surgery U. Tex., San Antonio, 1974-77; asst. clin prof. plastic surgery U. Calif., Davis, 1977-84; pvt. practice plastic surgery Fresno, Calif., 1977-93; assoc. clin. prof. plastic surgery U. Calif., San Francisco, 1984—2004; acting chief med. officer Mil. Entrance Processing Sta., Sacramento, 1994—2001. Bd. dirs., pres. Valley Children's Hosp. Med. Staff,

Fresno; bd. dirs. Liga Flying Physicians, Fresno, 1995-98. Producer, dir. films for sci. meetings (Outstanding award 1976). Mem. Am. Soc. Plastic Surgeons, Internat. Congress Plastic and Reconstructive Surgeons (bd. dirs. 1983-91), Am. Med. Soc. Vienna, Mil. Order of the World Wars (dept. N. Calif. comdr. 1996-97, region 14 comdr. 1998-99, nat. surgeon gen. 2004—, Disting. Chpt. Comdr. 1997, Silver Patrick Henry Patriotism award, 1997), Am. Legion (dist. vice comdr. 1998-99, dist. comdr. 1999-2000, vice comdr. Calif. 2001-02), Rotarian. Avocations: teaching, flying. Home and Office: 5100 John D Ryan Blvd #2211 San Antonio TX 78245-3513 E-mail: shanklinken@aol.com.

**SHANKS, DAVID,** publishing executive; Grad, Holy Cross Coll., 1968. V.p., dir. of sales Berkley Pub. Co. (now known as Penquin Putnam Pub. Co.), 1979—82, sr. v.p., dir. of planning ops., 1982—85, sr. v.p., 1985—91, pres. N.Y.C., 1991—97, COO, 1997—2001; CEO Penguin Putnam Pub. Co., 2001—. Office: Penguin Group USA Inc 375 Hudson St New York NY 10014*

**SHANKS, EARL,** marketing professional; married; 2 children. BSc, U. Ill., MA in Acctg. CPA AICPA. Mgr. Peat Marwick Mitchell & Co., Chgo.; from dir. tax to v.p., treas. Farley Industries Inc., 1983—96; v.p. The Convergys Corp., Cin., 1996—, treas., 1996—, CFO, 2003—. Office: Convergys Corp 201 E 4th St Cincinnati OH 45202

**SHANKS, EUGENE BAYLIS, JR.,** banker; BA, Vanderbilt U., 1969; MA, PhD, Stanford U., 1974. With Bankers Trust Co., NYC, 1973—78, 1980—95, pres., dir., 1992-95; pres. NetRisk, Inc., Greenwich, Conn., 1997—2002. Treas. Tenn. Valley Bancorp, 1978—80, Commerce Union Bank, 1978—80. Trustee Vanderbilt U.; bd. dir. Posse Found, IFL, Ltd., New Power, Inc. Office: IFL Ste 450 630 Fifth Ave New York NY 10111 Office Phone: 212-209-2134. Business E-Mail: ebshanks@optonline.net.

**SHANKS, HERSHEL,** editor, writer; b. Sharon, Pa., Mar. 8, 1930; s. Martin and Mildred (Freedman) S.; m. Judith Alexander Weil, Feb. 20, 1966; children: Elizabeth Jean, Julia Emily. BA, Haverford Coll., Pa., 1952; MA, Columbia, 1953; LLB, Harvard, 1956. Bar: D.C. 1956. Trial atty. Dept. Justice, 1956-59; pvt. practice Washington, 1959-88; ptnr. Glassie, Pewett, Beebe & Shanks, 1964-88; editor Bibl. Archaeology Rev., Washington, 1975—. Pres. Bibl. Archaeology Soc., 1974—2004, Jewish Ednl. Ventures Inc., 1987—. Author: The Art and Craft of Judging, 1968, The City of David, 1973, Judaism in Stone, 1979, Jerusalem--An Archaeological Biography, 1995, The Mystery and Meaning of the Dead Sea Scrolls, 1998, also articles; co-author: (with Ben Witherington III) The Brother of Jesus, 2003; co-editor: Recent Archaeology in the Land of Israel, 1984; editor: Ancient Israel, A Short History, 1988, revised edit., 1999, Christianity and Rabbinic Judaism, 1992, Understanding the Dead Sea Scrolls, 1992; editor Bible Rev., 1985—2004, Moment mag., 1987—2004, Archaeology Odyssey, 1998—2004; contbr. articles to profl. jours. Fellow Royal Asiatic Soc.; mem. ABA, D.C. Bar Assn., Am. Schs. Oriental Rsch., Soc. Bibl. Lit., Cosmos Club, Phi Beta Kappa. Home: 5208 38th St NW Washington DC 20015-1812 Office: Bibl Archaeology Soc 4710 41st St NW Washington DC 20016-1706 Office Phone: 202-966-9888. E-mail: hshanks@bib-arch.org. *I try to take time to identify what is important in my life, to focus on that and ignore the rest when it conflicts. It takes conscious effort not to dissipate energy on activities and attitudes that don't matter in the big picture of my priorities. Free to concentrate on what I value most, I try to accomplish something each day in a regular, habitual way.*

**SHANKS, PATRICIA L.,** lawyer; b. Salt Lake City, Apr. 3, 1940; BA in Microbiology with honors, Stanford U., 1962; JD, U. Colo., 1978. Bar: Calif. 1978. Mng. ptnr. McCutchen, Doyle, Brown & Enersen, L.A., 1990-94, ptnr., 1985—. Trustee L.A. County Bar Found., 2001-04. Recipient West Publishing award; Stork scholar. Mem. Order of the Coif, Practice in Environ. Law. Office: Bingham McCutchen 355 S Grand Ave Ste 4400 Los Angeles CA 90071-3106

**SHANLEY, JOHN PATRICK,** playwright, screenwriter; b. NYC, 1950; s. Nicholas and Frances Shanley; m. Jayne Haynes (div.); adopted children: Nick, Frank. Grad., NYU. Disting. artist-in-residence The New Sch. for Drama, NYC, 2006—. Writer (plays) Rockaway, 1982, Welcome to the Moon, 1982, Danny and the Deep Blue Sea, 1984, Savage in Limbo, 1985, the dreamer examines his pillow, 1985, Women of Manhattan, 1986, All for Charity, 1987, Italian-American Reconciliation, 1988, The Big Funk, 1990, Beggars in the House of Plenty, 1991, Four Dogs and a Bone, 1993, Psychopathia Sexualis, 1996, Missing/Kissing, 1997, Cellini, 1998, Where's My Money, 2001, Dirty Story, 2003, Doubt, 2004 (Pulitzer Prize for drama, 2005, Tony Award for best play, 2005), Sailor's Song, 2004, Defiance, 2006, Down and Out, The Red Coat, Let Us Go Out Into the Starry Night, Out West, A Lonely Impulse of Delight, (screen adaptations) Alive, 1993, Congo, 1995, (teleplay) Live From Baghdad, 2002, (screenplays) Moonstruck, 1987 (Acad. Award for best writing- screenplay written directly for the screen, 1988), January Man, 1989, We're Back! A Dinosaur's Story, 1993, writer, assoc. prodr. Five Corners, 1987, writer, dir. Joe Versus the Volcano, 1990, Chain of Command, 2005, Appeared in film Crossing Delancey, 1988. Served USMC. Office: c/o William Morris Agy 151 S El Camino Dr Beverly Hills CA 90212-2704*

**SHANMAN, JAMES ALAN,** lawyer; b. Cin., Aug. 1, 1942; s. Jerome D. and Mildred Louise (Bloch) S.; m. Marilyn Louise Glassman, June 11, 1972; 1 child, Ellen Joan. BS, U. Pa., 1963; JD, Yale U., 1966. Bar: N.Y. 1967, Conn. 2004, U.S. Ct. Mil. Appeals 1971, U.S. Supreme Ct. 1971, U.S. Ct. Appeals (2d cir.) 1972, U.S. Dist. Ct. (so. and ea. dists.) N.Y. 1972, U.S. Ct. Internat. Trade 1976, U.S. Ct. Appeals (fed. cir.) 1987, U.S. Dist. Ct. (ea. dist.) Mich. 1989, U.S. Dist. Ct. Conn. 2006, U.S. Ct. Appeals (7th cir.) 1999. Assoc. Cahill Gordon & Reindel, N.Y.C., 1971-74, Freeman, Meade, Wasserman, Sharfman & Schneider, N.Y.C., 1974-76; mem. firm Sharfman, Shanman, Poret & Siviglia, P.C., N.Y.C., 1976-95; ptnr. Camhy Karlinsky & Stein LLP, N.Y.C., 1995-96; mem. firm Sharfman, Siviglia, Poret, Kook, Ross & Shanman, P.C., N.Y.C., 1996-98; ptnr. Edwards, Angell, Palmer & Dodge LLP (formerly Edwards & Angell LLP), NYC and Stamford, 1998—. Speaker on reins. law topics. Contbr. articles to profl. jours. Capt. USAF, 1966-71. Mem.: ABA, ARIAS.US (cert. arbitrator), Am. Arbitration Assn. (comml. panel arbitrators 1980—), Assn. of Bar of City of N.Y. (com. ins. law 1985—88, 1990—92, 1998—2001, com. profl. liability ins. 1988—92, com. on assn. ins. plans 1989—), N.Y. State Bar Assn. Office: Edwards & Angell LLP Three Stamford Plz 301 Tresser Blvd Stamford CT 06901 Office Phone: 203-975-7505. Business E-Mail: jshanman@eapdlaw.com.

**SHANMUGAM, GANAPATHY,** geologist, researcher; b. Sirkali, Tamil-nadu, India, Apr. 23, 1944; came to U.S., 1970; s. Ganapathy Mudaliar and Sambooranam; m. Jean Marie Barham, Aug. 21, 1976. BSc in Geology and Chemistry, Annamalai U., South India, 1965; MSc in Applied Geology, Indian Inst. Tech., Bombay, 1968; MS in geology, Ohio U., 1972; PhD in Geology, U. Tenn., 1978. Rsch. geologist Mobil Exploration & Product Tech. Ctr., Dallas, 1978-82, sr. rsch. geologist 1982-84, assoc., 1984-85, rsch. assoc., 1985-89, sr. rsch. assoc., 1993, assoc. geol. rsch. advisor 1993-96, geol. scientist, 1996-2000; adj. prof. geology U. Tex., Arlington, 2000—. Conf. chmn. Geol. Soc. London, 1996; debate panelist Am. Assn. Petroleum Geologists, Dallas, 1997. Author: Deep-Water Processes and Facies Models: Implications for Sandstone Petroleum Reservoirs, 2006; contbr. over 120 articles to profl. jours. Geology adv. bd. U. Tenn., Knoxville, 1985-89. Recipient Silver medal Indian Inst. Tech., 1968; Penrose grantee Geol. Soc. Am., 1976-78; recipient best Paper award Nigerian Assn. Petroleum Logorationists, 1995. Achievements include questioning of the deep-water turbidite paradigm and advocation of sandy debris flows in forming deep-water petroleum reservoirs. Avocation: photography. Office: U Tex Arlington Dept Geology PO Box 19049 Arlington TX 76019 E-mail: shanshanmugam@aol.com.

**SHANNON, CATHERINE BARBARA,** history professor; b. Hingham, Mass., Jan. 22, 1938; d. David Joseph and Catherine Patricia (Cannon) S. BA, St. Michael's U., Toronto, Can., 1960; MA, Nat. U. Ireland, Dublin, 1963; PhD, U. Mass., 1975. Tchr. Holbrook (Mass.) H.S., 1964-67; prof. history Westfield (Mass.) State Coll. 1967—2000, prof. emeritus history 2001—; adj. prof. history U. Mass., Amherst, 1995—2001. Cons. Boston Shakespeare Co., 1987; organizer com. New Ireland Conf., 1982-85; co-chair Com. for Irish Forum, 1982-92. Author: Arthur J. Balfour and Ireland, 1988; contbr. articles to profl. jours. Recipient Sr. fellowship Inst. Irish Studies, Queen's U., Balfast, No. Ireland, 1991-92; Achievement award Irish Immigration Ctr., Boston, 1994, Heritage Cup award Irish Am. Partnership, 1998, Dreamer of Dreams award Irish Voice Newspaper, 1999; NEH fellow U. Wa., 1976, Brown U., 1982, Irish Am. Cultural Inst. fellow Nat. U. Ireland, 2001-02; Phi Kappa Phi Faculty Lecture award Westfield Coll., 1997. Fellow Royal Hist. Soc. London; mem. Am. Conf. Irish Studies (treas., bd. rep. 1981-91), Eire Soc. (pres. 1983-84), Charitable Irish Soc. (pres. 1990-91), New England Hist. (exec. bd. 1986-89), Com. for New Ireland (bd. mem., editor 1986-89). Avocations: golf, sailing, reading.

**SHANNON, DAVID M.,** lawyer; b. Gardena, Calif., July 22, 1955; s. William R. Shannon and Delores Ann (Nettleton) DeBenedictis; m. Maureen Michelle Green, Feb. 18, 1978; 1 child, Ryan Edward. BA, Pepperdine U., 1976, JD cum laude, 1985. Law clk. Office of Dist. Atty. County of Ventura, Calif., 1984-85; assoc. Gibson, Dunn & Crutcher, L.A., 1985-87, San Francisco & San Jose, Calif., 1987—93; v.p., asst. gen. counsel Intel Corp., Santa Clara, Calif., 1993—2002; v.p., gen. counsel NVIDIA Corp., Santa Clara, Calif., 2002—. Mem. ABA, Calif. Bar Assn., L.A. County Bar Assn. Avocations: swimming, basketball. Office: NVIDIA Corp 2701 San Tomas Expressway Santa Clara CA 95050 Office Phone: 408-486-2000. Office Fax: 408-486-2200.

**SHANNON, DONALD HAWKINS,** retired editor; b. Auburn, Wash., Feb. 1, 1923; s. Ernest Victor and Fern (McConville) S.; m. Sally van Deurs, June 13, 1952; children— John McConville, Susanna Shepard. BA, Stanford, 1944; postgrad., Law Sch., 1946-47. Reporter Brazil Herald, Rio de Janeiro, 1947-48; Reporter UPI, London, 1949-51, Western Reporters, Washington, 1951-53; mem. staff L.A. Times, 1954-92, bur. chief Paris Paris, 1962-65, bur. chief Africa, 1965-66, bur. chief Tokyo Tokyo, 1966-71; bur. chief UN, NYC, 1971—75, Washington, 1975—92; sr. editor Georgetown and Country, Washington, 1996-99; ret., 1999. Served with AUS, 1944-46, PTO. Mem. Nat. Press Club, Fed. City Club, City Tavern Club, Overseas Press Club (N.Y.C.), Phi Gamma Delta. Address: 1068 30th St NW Washington DC 20007-3822

**SHANNON, IRIS REED,** health facility administrator, consultant; b. Chgo. d. Ira Paul and Iola Sophia Reed. BS in Nursing, Fisk U.-Meharry Med. Coll., 1948; MA, U. Chgo., 1954; PhD, U. Ill., Chgo., 1987; D in Pub. Svc. (hon.), Elmhurst Coll., 1993. Staff nurse Chgo. Bd. Health, 1948-50; instr. pub. health nursing Meharry Med. Coll., Nashville, 1951-56; tchr.-nurse, health coordinator child devel. Head Start, Chgo. Bd. Edn., 1957-66; dir. community nursing Mile Sq. Neighborhood Health Center, Presbyn.-St. Luke's Hosp., Chgo., 1966-69; co-dir. nurse assoc. programs Rush Presbyn.-St. Luke's Hosp., 1971-76; chairperson community nursing Rush U., Chgo., 1972-77, acting chairperson, 1988-90; asst. prof. pub. health nursing U. Ill., 1971-74; assoc. prof. cmty. nursing Rush U., 1974-97, health sys. mgr., 1988—, health cons., 1974—. Adj. faculty Sch. Pub. Health, U.N.C., 1977—85; mem. profl. adv. bd. Vis. Nurse Assn. Chgo., 1973—75; cons. Video Nursing, Inc.; mem. profl. adv. com. Mile Sq. Home Health Unit, Chgo., 1975—77; mem. nat. adv. coun. on nurse tng. HEW, 1978—81; mem. Nat. Task Force on Credentialing in Nursing, 1979—82; mem. Chgo. regional com. Ill. White House Conf. on Children, 1979—80; v.p. Chgo. Bd. Health, 1989—99. Named Prin. for a Day, Brownell Elem. Sch., Mayor's Office, City of Chgo., 1998—99, Englewood Tech. Prep. Acad., 2000—01; recipient award of merit, Ill. Pub. Health Assn., 1979, 1989—2000, Outstanding Achievement award, YWCA of Met. Chgo., 1988, Disting. Svc. award, Chgo. chpt. Meharry Alumni, 1989, Lowenberg Chair of Excellence in Nursing, Memphis State U., 1993, Bd. Trustees' Svc. medal, Rush-Presby. St. Luke's Med. Ctr., 1996, Lifeline award, Cmty. Mental Health Coun., 2002. Fellow: APHA (ntional. pub. health nursing sect. 1977—79, governing coun. 1980—82, exec. bd. 1985—87, pres. 1988—89, governing coun. 1989—99), Am. Acad. Nursing, Royal Soc. Health (hon. 1989); mem.: ANA (Pearl McIver Pub. Health Nurse award 1998), Inst. of Medicine of NAS, Delta Sigma Theta, Sigma Theta Tau. Home: 3100 S King Dr Chicago IL 60616-3634 Office Phone: 312-842-6164. E-mail: irisshannon@aol.com.

**SHANNON, JOE,** art critic, painter; b. Lares, Puerto Rico, 1933; Exhbn. technician Smithsonian Mus. Nat. History; former curator Hirshhorn Mus. & Sculpture Garden; prof. Corcoran Sch. Art, Md. Inst. Coll. Arts (MICA), Baltimore. Exhibitions include Studies Monuments & Variations, Haslem Gallery, 1983, Shoe Salesman, Corcoran Gallery, 1969; reviews art shows Art in America, writer (art related articles) Washington Times. Office: Md Inst Coll Arts (MICA) 1300 Mount Royal Ave Baltimore MD 21217

**SHANNON, JOHN SANFORD,** lawyer, retired rail transportation executive; b. Tampa, Fla., Feb. 8, 1931; s. George Thomas and Ruth Evangeline (Garrett) S.; m. Elizabeth Howe, Sept. 22, 1962; children: Scott Howe, Elizabeth Garrett, Sandra Denison. AB, Roanoke Coll., 1952; JD, U. Va., 1955. Bar: Va. 1955. Assoc. Hunton Williams Gay Powell & Gibson, Richmond, Va., 1955-56; solicitor Norfolk & Western Ry., Roanoke, Va., 1956-60, asst. gen. solicitor, 1960-64, gen. atty., 1964-65, gen. solicitor, 1965-68, gen. counsel, 1968-69, v.p. law, 1969-80, sr. v.p. law, 1980-82; exec. v.p. law Norfolk So. Corp., 1982-90, ret., 1996. Bd. dirs. Norfolk So. Ry. Co., Pocahontas Land Corp., Va. Holding Corp., Norfolk and Western Ry. Co. Editor-in-chief: Va. Law Rev, 1954-55. Chancellor Episcopal Diocese Southwestern Va., 1974-82; bd. trustees North Cross Sch., Roanoke, 1973-82; trustee, past chmn. exec. com. Roanoke Coll., Salem, Va., 1974-2005; bd. dirs. Legal Aid Soc., Roanoke Valley, 1969-80, pres., 1970-79; trustee Chrysler Mus., Norfolk, 1982-94, Norfolk Acad., 1987-99. Mem. Va. Bar Assn., Norfolk and Portsmouth Bar Assn., Shenandoah Club, Roanoke Country Club, Norfolk Yacht and Country Club, Order of Coif, Sigma Xi, Omicron Delta Kappa, Phi Delta Phi. Home: 7633 Argyle Ave Norfolk VA 23505-1701

**SHANNON, MARGARET ANNE,** lawyer; b. Detroit, July 6, 1945; d. Johannes Jacob and Vera Marie (Spade) Van De Graaf; m. Robert Selby Shannon, Feb. 4, 1967. Student, Brown U., 1963-65; BA in History, Wayne State U., 1966, JD, 1973. Bar: Mich. 1973. Housing aide City of Detroit, 1967-68; employment supr. Sinai Hosp., Detroit, 1968-69; assoc. gen. counsel regulatory affairs Blue Cross Blue Shield Mich., Detroit, 1969-80; ptnr. Honigman Miller Schwartz and Cohn, Detroit, 1980-95, of counsel, 1996—. Nat. Merit scholar, 1963-66. Mem. Mich. State Bar (chmn. health care com. 1991, 92, co-chmn. payor subcom. health law sect.). Home: 1111 Orinoco Way Palm Beach Gardens FL 33410 Office: Honigman Miller Schwartz and Cohn 2290 First National Bldg Detroit MI 48226-3583 Office Phone: 313-465-7552. E-mail: mshannon@honigman.com.

**SHANNON, MARY LOU,** adult health nursing educator; b. Memphis, Apr. 4, 1938; d. Sidney Richmond Shannon and Lucille (Gwaltney) Cloud. BSN, U. Tenn., 1959; MA, Columbia U., 1963, MEd, 1964, EdD, 1972. Staff nurse City of Memphis Hosps., 1959—60, instr. Sch. Nursing, 1960—62; asst. prof. U. Tenn., Memphis, 1964—70, assoc. prof., 1970—73, prof., 1973—89; prof., chair adult health dept. Sch. Nursing U. Tex., Galveston, 1989—98, prof., 1989—2000, prof. emeritus, 2000—. Bd. dirs. Nat. Pressure Ulcer Adv. Panel, Buffalo, 1987-96; vis. prof. U. Alta., Edmonton, Can., 1982, Union U., Memphis, 2001, Bapt. Coll. Health Scis., 2003, U. Tex., Galveston, 2004; mem. project adv. bd. RAND, Santa Monica, Calif., 1994. Contbr. chpts. to books in field and to periodicals; mem. editl. bd. Advances in Wound Care, 1987-2000. Trustee Nurses Edn. Funds, N.Y.C., 1972-86. Mem. AAAS,

ANA, Nat. League Nursing (bd. of rev. 1983-86), Orthopedic Nurses Assn., So. Nursing Rsch. Soc., Am. Assn. for History of Nursing, Sigma Xi, Sigma Theta Tau, Phi Kappa Phi. Avocations: travel, reading.

**SHANNON, PATRICK S.,** retail executive; Sr. acct. Arthur Andersen LLP; asst. controller AGCO Corp., Duluth, Ga., v.p., controller, v.p., dir. fin., v.p., CFO, 1998-2000; sr. v.p., CFO US Gifts Corp., Atlanta, 2000—.

**SHANNON, SAMUEL A.,** chemist; b. Meridian, Miss., July 13, 1927; d. Samuel A. Shannon, Sr. and Ruby Angelon Snowden; m. Carol Rose Shannon, Oct. 10, 1970; 1 child, Julia Angela Shannon Valerius; children: Bethany Jane Shannon Owens, David Samuel, Sean Michael. Student, Brigham Young U., 1961—67; degree in Edn., Utah State U.; degree in Arts and Scis., Tulane U. Chemist Brookley AFB, Mobile, Ala., Scott Paper Co., Mobile, Douglas Aircraft Co., Santa Monica, Calif., Plastic Age Co., Saugus, Calif.; tchr. Mobile (Ala.) County Pub. Schs.; chemist Courtaulds N.Am., Mobile, Sucro-Chem. Co., Gramercy, La. With U.S. Army, 1946—48, Germany. Home: 2116 North Christy Ln Las Vegas NV 89156

**SHANNON, STEPHEN CURTIS,** medical association administrator, occupational health physician; b. Frederick, Md., Dec. 9, 1948; s. James Lee and Mary Catherine (Fry) S.; m. Barbara Jean Winterson, Jul. 31, 1971; children: Joyce Megan Shannon-Winterson, Sally Catherine Shannon-Winterson. BA in hist., U. Md., 1971, MA in Am. hist., 1975; DO, U. New Eng. Coll. Osteopathic Medicine, 1986; MPH, Harvard U., 1990. Diplomate Am. Bd. Preventive Medicine and Family Practice. Program mgr. WESM-FM Radio, Prince Frederick, Md., 1971-73; instr. Am. hist. U. Md., College Park, 1973-79, congl. rels. analyst U.S. Dept. Energy, Washington, 1979-80; family practice resident Brighton Medical Ctr., Portland, Maine, 1986-88; preventive medicine resident U. Mass. Medical Ctr., Worcester, Mass., 1988-90; medical epidemiologist Mass. Dept. Pub. Health, Boston, 1990-92; asst. prof. U. New Eng. Coll. Osteopathic Medicine, Biddeford, Maine, 1990-95; medical dir. Ctr. Health Promotion Brighton Medical Ctr., 1991-95; dir. occupational health Maine Bureau of Health, Augusta, 1990-95; acting dean U. New Eng. Coll. Osteo. Medicine, 1995, dean & v.p. health services, 1995—2005; pres. Am. Assn. Colleges of Osteopathic Medicine, 2005—. Med. epidemiologist cons. Maine Bur. Health, 1990—91; chmn. occupational health sect. Brighton Med. Ctr., 1994; former pres. Maine Biomedical Rsch. Coalition, Maine Ctr. for Pub. Health. Editor: The Maryland Historian, 1976-78; contbr. articles to profl. jours. Exec. com. York County Health Services Bd., Saco, Maine; bd. dirs. Maine Inst. Occupational Health Edn., Waterville, Maine, 1993, Brighton Consortium, 1991. Recipient Dan Hanley Meml. Trust award, 2003, Disting. Svc. award in field of higher edn. Fin. Authority of Maine, 2002, New Eng. Found. Osteopathic Medicine award, 1986, U.S. Sec. Health & Human Svcs. award for Health Promotion, 1984, Ciby-Geigy award for Outstanding Comm. Svc., 1984, fellow William Randolph Hearst, U. Md., 1979. Mem. Am. Pub. Health Assn., Maine Pub. Health Assn. (bd. dirs. 1993), Am. Osteopathic Assn., Maine Osteopathic, Physicians for Nat. Health Program, Am. Coll. Occupational & Environ. Medicine. Democrat. Avocations: canoeing, hiking, camping, writing, reading. Office: American Assn Colleges Osteopathic Medicine Ste 310 5550 Friendship Blvd Chevy Chase MD 20815-7231*

**SHANNON, THOMAS A., JR.,** federal agency administrator; BA, Coll. William and Mary; M in Politics, Oxford U., doctorate. Consular/polit. rotational officer U.S. Embassy, Guatemala City, Guatemala, 1984—86; country officer Cameroon, Gabon, Sao Tome, Principe, 1987—89; spl. asst. to amb. U.S. Embassy, Brasilia, Brazil, 1989—92; regional labor attache U.S. Consulate General, Johannesburg, 1992—96; polit. counselor U.S. Embassy, Caracas, Venezuela, 1996—99; dir. Inter-Am. affairs Nat. Security Coun., 1999—2000; U.S. dep. permanent rep. OAS, 2000—01; dir. Andean affairs US Dept. State, 2001—02, dep. asst. sec. we. hemisphere affairs, 2002—03, asst. sec. for we. hemisphere affairs, 2005—; sr. dir. we. hemisphere affairs Nat. Security Coun., 2003—05; spl. asst. to Pres. The White House, 2003—05. Career mem. Sr. Fgn. Svc. Office: US Dept State 2201 C St NW Washington DC 20520*

**SHANNON, THOMAS ALFRED,** retired educational association administrator emeritus; b. Milw., Jan. 2, 1932; s. John Elwood and Eleanor Ann (Mitchell) S.; m. Barbara Ann Weidner, June 26, 1954; children: Thomas Alfred, Paul J., Suzanne L., Terrence D. BS, U. Wis, 1954; JD, U. Minn. 1961. Bar: Minn. 1961, Calif. 1963, U.S. Supreme Ct. 1965, D.C. 1977, Va. 1984; Life cert. as sch. administr., Calif.; cert. assoc. exec. Am. Soc. Assn. Execs. Pvt. practice law, Mpls., 1961-62; schs. atty. San Diego City Schs., 1962-73; dept. supt., gen. counsel, 1973-77; exec. dir. Nat. Sch. Bds. Assn., Washington, 1977-97, ret., 1997. Adj. prof. law and edn. U. San Diego; vis. prof. edn. U. Va.; adv. mem. Edn. Commn. of States; prof. Nat. Acad. Sch. Execs., 1971-77; legal counsel Am. Assn. Sch. Adminstrs., 1973-77; adj. prof. ednl. adminstrn. George Washington U., 1996-97. Exec. pub. The Am. Sch. Bd. Jour., 1977-96, Exec. Educator, 1978-96, Sch. Bd. News, 1981-96. Chmn. San Diego County Juvenile Justice Commn., 1973-74; mem. nat. coun. Boy Scouts Am., 1979-97; bd. dirs. Found. for Teaching Econ., San Francisco, 1993-2003. With USN, 1954—59. Mem. VFW (life), Am. Bar Assn. (chmn. com. public edn. 1978-82), Nat. Orgn. on Legal Problems of Edn. (pres. 1973), Nat. Sch. Bds. Assn. (chmn. council sch. attys. 1967-69) Home: 3811 26th St N Arlington VA 22207-5241 Office Phone: 703-525-8577. Personal E-mail: tombar2@juno.com.

**SHANNON, THOMAS FREDERIC,** German language educator; b. Cambridge, Mass., Mar. 16, 1948; m. Christine D. Höner. BA in German summa cum laude, Boston Coll., 1969; MA in German Lit., SUNY, Albany, 1973; MA in Theoretical Linguistics, Ind. U., 1975, PhD in Germanic Linguistics, 1982. Instr. in German Dndrui Coll, 1969-70, ... fellow in German SUNY, Albany, 1971-73; univ. fellow Ind. U., Bloomington, 1973-74, assoc. instr., 1974-76, 79-80; acting asst. prof. in Germanic linguistics U. Calif., Berkeley, 1980-82, asst. prof., 1982-87, assoc. prof., 1987-94, prof., 1994—; dir. lang. lab., 1989-92, assoc. dir. Berkeley Lang. Ctr., 1994-95, dir. edn. abroad study ctr. Germany, 2000—02. Co-organizer Berkeley Confs. on Dutch Lang. and Lit., 1987, 89, 91, 93, 95, 97, 10th Interdisciplinary Conf. Netherlandic Studies, 2000; econs. presenter and spkr. in field. Contbr. articles to profl. jours.; mem. editl. adv. bd. Am. Jour. Germanic Linguistics, 1998—. With USAR, 1970-76. Grantee Fulbright Found., 1976-78, U. Calif. Berkeley, 1983-84, 94-95, ACLS, 1987, Internat. Assn. Netherlandic Studies, 1988, 91, 94, 97, German Acad. Exch. Svc., summer 1996; NDEA fellow, 1969; Fulbright rsch./lectr. grantee Rijksuniversiteit Groningen, Netherlands, 1992-93; Inst. fuer deutsche Sprache summer rsch. grantee, Mannheim, Germany, 1997. Mem. MLA (exec. com. discussion group in Germanic philology 1989-94, discussion group for Netherlandic Studies 1995-99, divsn. on lang. change 1995-99), Am. Assn. Netherlandic Studies (exec. com. 1988—, editor newsletter 1989-95, series editor publs. 1994-2005), Am. Assn. Tchrs. German, Internat. Assn. Netherlandic Studies, Linguistic Soc. Am., Pacific Ancient and Modern Lang. Assn., European Linguistic Soc., Soc. Germanic Philology (v.p. 1991-92, 95-99), Internat. Cognitive Linguistics Assn., Alpha Sigma Nu. Home: 770 Rose Dr Benicia CA 94510-3709 Office: U Calif Dept German 5319 Dwinelle Hall Berkeley CA 94720-3243 Office Phone: 510-642-2004. E-mail: tshannon@berkeley.edu.

**SHANNON, THOMAS O.,** plastic surgeon; b. Pottstown, Pa., Aug. 25, 1962; s. John H. and Rosemary E. Shannon; m. Kelly R. Shannon, Nov. 4, 1995; children: Sydney, Mitchell. BA in Chemistry, U. Rochester, 1984; MD, Pa. State U., 1988. Diplomate Am. Bd. Surgery, dir. physician Tex., Pa. Surg. resident Lankenau Hosp. and Med. Rsch. Ctr., Phila., 1993; resident in plastic surgery U. Tex. Med. Br., Galveston, 1996; plastic surgeon Keystone Plastic Surgery, Conroe, Tex., 1996—, Woodlands, Tex., 1996—. Med. dir. Woodlands Meml. Woundcare Ctr., 1998—2001; med. dir. wound care Triumph N.W. Hosp., 2002; med. dir. woundcare Nexus Hosp., 2006—; presenter in field. Contbr. articles to profl. jours. Capt. U.S. Army, 1986—2004. Ames Rsch. Lab. fellow, 1983, Std. Oil Rsch. Profl. Program trainee, 1984, summer fellow, NIH, 1985. Mem.: AMA, Tex. Med. Assn., Montgomery County Med. Soc., Am. Chem. Soc., Am. Coll. Surgeons, Blocker-Lewis Plastic Surg. Soc.,

Singleton Surg. Soc., Galveston Hist. Found., Mixed Volleyball League, The Woodlands Mixed Bowling League. Republican. Presbyterian. Avocations: tennis, skiing, volleyball, bowling, choir. Home: 75 Pleasant Bend Pl The Woodlands TX 77382 Office: Keystone Plastic and Reconstructive Surgery LLC 3115 College Park Dr Bldg 101 The Woodlands TX 77384 also: 13628 Michael Rd Tomball TX 77375 also: 18955 Memorial N Ste 590 Humble TX 77338 Office Phone: 936-321-4345. E-mail: tshannon@keystoneplasticsurgery.com.

**SHANNON, W. PATRICK,** telecommunications industry executive; BSBA, U. Ga. CPA. With Arthur Andersen, Atlanta, 1983—91; dir. fin. planning, analysis, dir. investor rels., dir. tech. acctg. US West, Inc., 1991—94, v.p. corp. devel., 1994; v.p., chief fin. officer MediaOne, Inc., 1994—97, CFO domestic ops., contr., 1997—2004, sr. v.p. fin., 2004—05, CFO, 2006—.

**SHANNON, WILLIAM NORMAN, III,** finance educator, food service executive; b. Chgo., Nov. 20, 1937; s. William Norman Jr. and Lee (Lewis) S.; m. Bernice Urbanowicz, July 14, 1962; children: Kathleen Kelly, Colleen Patricia, Kerrie Ann. BS in Indsl. Mgmt., Carnegie Inst. Tech., 1959; MBA in Mktg. Mgmt., U. Toledo, 1963. Sales engr. Westinghouse Electric Co., Detroit, 1959-64; regional mgr. Toledo Scale, Chgo., 1964-70; v.p. J. Lloyd Johnson Assoc., Northbrook, Ill., 1970-72; mgr. spl. projects Hobart Mfg., Troy, Ohio, 1972-74; corp. v.p. mktg. Berkel, Inc., La Porte, Ind., 1974-79; gen. mgr. Berkel Products, Ltd., Toronto, Canada, 1975-78; chmn. Avant Industries, Inc., Wheeling, Ill., 1979-81; chmn., pres. Hacienda Mexican Restaurants, South Bend, Ind., 1978—95; chmn. Ziker Shannon Corp., South Bend, 1982-88, Hacienda Franchising Group, Inc., South Bend, Ind., 1987—92. Assoc. prof. mktg. and internat. bus. St. Mary's Coll., Notre Dame, Ind., 1982—; chmn. Hacienda Franchise Group, Inc., 1987-96, Hacienda Mex. Restaurants Mgmt., Inc., 1994-96; sr. chmn. Hacienda Mex. Restaurants, 1996-2004; mem. London program faculty, 1986, 89, 92, 94, coord. internat. bus. curriculum, 1989—; mktg. curriculum, 1983; advisor Coun. Internat. Bus. Devel. Notre Dame, 1991-2005; mng. dir. Alden & Torch Lake Railway, 1995—. Co-author: Laboratory Computers, 1971; columnist Bus. Digest mag., 1988-1994; mem. editl. bd. Jour. Bus. and Indsl. Mktg., 1986-1992, South Bend Tribune Business Weekly, 1990-1994; contbr. articles to profl. jours. V.p. mktg. Jr. Achievement, South Bend, Ind., 1987-90; pres. Small Bus. Devel. Coun., South Bend., 1987-90; bd. dirs. Ind. Small Bus. Coun., Indpls., 1986—, Mental Health Assn., South Bend, 1987-90, Michiana World Trade Orgn., Internat. Bus. Edn., 1989-91; Entrepreneurs Alliance Ind., 1988-92, Nat. Small Bus. United, Washington, 1989-92, Women's Bus. Initiative, 1986-90, dir. ednl. confs., 1986-90; chmn. bd. trustees, Holy Cross Coll., Notre Dame, Ind., 1987-1993, chmn. edn. com., 1993-1993; chmn. St. Joseph County Higher Edn. Coun., 1988-91, Nat. Coun. Small Bus., Washington, 1988-1994; Midwest region adv. coun. U.S. SBA, 1988-91; at-large mem. U.S. Govt. Adv. Coun. on Small Bus., Washington, 1988-90, 1994-1996, chmn. Bus. and Econ. Devel. Coun., 1988-90, 1994-1996; vice chmn. Internat. Trade Com., 1994-1996; nat. adv. coun. Women's Network for Entrepreneur Tng., 1991-1994; vice chmn. State of Ind. Enterprise Zone Bd., 1991-1994; elected del. White House Conf. Small Bus., Washington 1986; bd. dirs. Ind. Small Bus. Devel. Ctrs. Adv. Bd.; co-pres. Helena Twp. Downtown Devel. Authority, 2002—. Named Small Bus. Person of the Yr., City of South Bend, 1987, Small Bus. Advocate of the Yr., State of Ind., 1987, Ind. Entrepreneur Advocate of the Yr., 1988. Mem. Am. Mktg. Assn. (chmn. Mich./Ind. chpt., pres. 1985-86), U.S. Assn. Small Bus. and Entrepreneurship (nat. v.p. for entrepreneurship edn. 1991-92, nat. v.p. entrepreneurship devel. 1992-1996), Ind. Inst. New Bus. Ventures (mktg. faculty 1987-91), Michiana Investment Network (vice chmn. 1988-91), SBA (adminstrn. adv. coun. 1988-1992, contbg. editor Our Town Michiana mag. 1987-91), U.S.C. of C., Nat. Coun. Small Bus. (Washington), South Bend C. of C. (bd. dirs. 1987-1996, vice chmn. membership 1993-1996), Assn. for Bus. Communications (co-chmn. Internat. Conf. 1986), Univ. Club Notre Dame (vice chmn.), Shamrock Club Notre Dame (exec. dir., trustee 1993-1996), Rotary. Roman Catholic. Office: Saint Mary's Coll Dept Bus Adminstrn Eco Notre Dame IN 46556 Office Phone: 574-284-4508. *Enjoy good fortune resulting from LUCK, an acronym for (L) Learning how to (U)Use your talents with genuine (C) Concern on how your (K) Knowlege can benefit others.*

**SHANNON-GRAGG, TENITA LEANETTE,** computer scientist, educator; b. Centerville, Miss., Aug. 22, 1963; d. Eddie and Percy Lee Shannon; m. Kelvin B. Gragg, July 23, 1994; children: Christopher LeEdward Gragg, Shannon Williams Gragg. BS, U. Ark., Pine Bluff, Ark., 1985, MS in Engring., 1996. Cert. Mos expert Microsoft, instr. Microsoft, Nat. Cisco, 2000. Tchr., coach Milw. Pub. Schs., 1985—89; instrnl. supr. IMPAC, Inc, Little Rock, 1991—95; facilitator pc sys. Nat. Ctr. Toxicological Rsch., Jefferson, Ark., 1995—98; computer tng. specialist S.E. Ark. Coll., Pine Bluff, 1998—. Dir. conf. youth chrisitian edn. African Meth. Episc. Ch., East Northeast, Ark., 1989—91; vice chmn. Jefferson County Alliance, Pine Bluff, 2003—05. Fellow, Ark. Dept Higher Edn., 1994—97. Mem.: Delta Sigma Theta (life). Democrat. African Meth. Episc. Avocations: walking, cooking, motivational speaking. Home: PO Box 267 Dumas AR 71639 Office: Southeast Arkanas College 1900 Hazel Pine Bluff AR 71603 Office Phone: 870-543-5900. Home Fax: 870-543-5951; Office Fax: 870-543-5951. Personal E-mail: tgragg@seark.edu.

**SHANNY, RAMY,** physicist; b. Jerusalem, Nov. 6, 1935; s. Meir and Batia Shanny, Batia Shanny; m. Laura Eileen Hamilton; children: Emily, 0000 0000; m. Shula Dafny (div. Dec. 0, 1976); children: Ronnit, Micky. PhD, Princeton U. Rsch. physicist GE, Valley Forge, Pa., 1968—69, Naval Rsch. Lab., Washington, 1969—70, br. head, 1971—75; plasma physics dir., supt. NRL, 1971—75; pres. INESCO, Inc., Washington, 1977—84, LaJolla, Calif., 1977—84; pres., CEO Advanced Power Techs., Inc., 1986—2003; v.p., gen. mgr. AT, D&P Systems, 1980-2003. Recipient Ennr. Svc. award, Naval Rsch. Lab., 1974. Fellow: Am.Phys. Soc.; mem.: IEEE, N.Y. Acad. Sci. Office: Advanced Power Technologies, Inc 1250 24th St NW 8th Fl Washington DC 20037 Business E-Mail: shanny@yahoo.com.

**SHANOR, DONALD READ,** journalism educator, writer; b. Ann Arbor, Mich., July 11, 1927; s. William Wilson and Katherine Creamer (Read) S.; m. Constance May Collier, 1951; children— Rebecca, Donald (dec.), Elizabeth BS, Northwestern U., 1951; MA, Columbia U., N.Y.C. Corr. Am. Forces Network, Frankfurt, Fed. Republic Germany, 1952-54; corr. UPI, Frankfurt and London, 1954-59, Chgo. Daily News, Vienna and Bonn, 1967-71; editor UPI, N.Y.C., 1959-65; lectr. Columbia U., N.Y.C., 1965-67, prof. Grad. Sch. Journalism, 1971—92, Godfrey Lowell Cabot prof. emeritus, 1992—, prof. Internat. and Pub. Affairs, 1979-92, prof. Harriman Inst., 1985-92, prof. Inst. on East Cen. Europe, 1991—92. Vis. prof. Chinese Acad. Social Scis., Beijing, 1984-85, Charles U., Prague, 1992-93; online writing instr. U. Phoenix, 2002-. Author: Soviet Europe, 1975, The Soviet Triangle, 1980, Behind the Lines/The Private War Against Soviet Censorship, 1985, News From Abroad, 2003; co-author: News From Abroad, 1981, China Today, 1993, After the Russians, 2000; advisor Journalists in Europe, Paris, 1973—92; contbg. editor World Press Rev., 1974-93; mem. adv. panel Himal mag., 1988—92. Trustee Arthur F. Burns Internat. Fellowship Program, 1990—2004. Served with USNR, 1945-46 Recipient Fed. Republic of Germany Friendship award, 2005; U.S. Inst. Peace grantee, 1988-89. Mem. Soc. Profl. Journalists, Am. Council on Germany Democrat. Home: 13 Pierce Ln Edgartown MA 02539 Office: Columbia U New York NY 10027 E-mail: dcshan@vineyard.net.

**SHANSBY, JOHN GARY,** investor; b. Seattle, Aug. 25, 1937; s. John Jay and Jule E. (Boyer) S.; m. Joyce Ann Dunsmore, June 21, 1959 (div.); children: Sheri Lee, Kimberly Ann, Jay Thomas; m. Barbara Anderson De Meo, Jan. 1, 1983 (div.); m. Jane Robinson Dettner, May 1, 1990. BA, U. Wash., 1959. Mktg. exec. Colgate-Palmolive Co., N.Y.C., 1959-67; subs. pres. Am. Home Products Co., N.Y.C., 1968-71; v.p. Clorox Co., Oakland, Calif., 1972-73; ptnr. Booz, Allen & Hamilton, San Francisco, 1974-75; chmn. bd., chief exec. officer, pres. Shaklee Corp., San Francisco, 1975-86; co-founder, chmn. TSG Consumer Ptnrs., San Francisco, 1986—. Former chmn. Calif. State Commn. for Rev. of Master Plan Higher Edn.; founder J.

Gary Shansby chair mktg. strategy U. Calif., Berkeley, U. Wash., Seattle; trustee Calif. State U. Mem. San Francisco C. of C. (past pres.), Villa Traverna Club, Pennask Lake Fishing Club (B.C.), Sigma Nu Republican. Office: TSG Consumer Ptnrs 600 Montgomery St Ste 2900 San Francisco CA 94111

**SHAO, OTIS HUNG-I,** retired political science professor; b. Shanghai, July 18, 1923; came to U.S., 1949, naturalized, 1956; s. Ming Sun and Hannah (Chen) S.; m. Marie Sheng, Apr. 2, 1955. BA, St. John's U., 1946; MA, U. Colo., 1950; PhD, Brown U., 1957. From instr. to prof. polit. sci. Moravian Coll., Bethlehem, Pa., 1954-62; assoc. prof., then prof. polit. sci. Fla. Presbyn. Coll., St. Petersburg, 1962-68; prof. internat. politics, dean (Grad. Sch., U. Pacific), 1968-74; dir. Pub. Affairs Inst., 1969-74; provost Callison Coll., 1974-76; dean faculty, v.p. Occidental Coll., 1976-78; asso. exec. dir. sr. commn. Western Assn. Schs. and Colls., 1978-80; v.p., dean Hawaii Loa Coll., 1980-85; pres. Sheng Shao Enterprises Calif., 1985-92; CEO, chmn. D.S. Capital Internat., Calif., 1993-94. Mem. grad. students relations com. Council Grad. Schs., U.S., 1970-73; mem. exec. council undergrad. assessment program Ednl. Testing Service, 1978-80. Contbr. articles to profl. jours. Chmn. bd. dirs. Fgn. Policy Assn. Lehigh Valley, 1961-62; bd. dirs. World Affairs Council, San Joaquin County, 1969-77; trustee Inst. Med. Scis., Pacific Med. Center, San Francisco, 1968-72, optical scis. group of Profl. and Pub. Service Found., 1969-72; Resident fellow Harkness House, Brown U., 1953-54, Danforth Asso., 1958-85. Recipient Distinguished Service award Fgn. Policy Assn. Lehigh Valley, 1962 Mem. AAUP (pres. Fla. Presbyn. Coll. chpt. 1965-66), Am. Assn. Higher Edn., Rho Psi, Tau Kappa Epsilon. Democrat. Presbyterian. Home: 1784 Curtner Ave San Jose CA 95124

**SHAO, RONG,** research scientist, educator; s. Heming Shao and Guanying Le; m. Wei Yan, June 26, 1990; children: Jessica Nancy, William Frank. PhD, Phila. Coll. Pharmacy, 1997. Postdoctoral rschr. Duke U., Durham, NC, 1997—2004; scientist Pioneer Valley Life Scis. Inst., Springfield, Mass., 2004—. Asst. prof. U. Mass., Amherst, 2004—. Grantee, Rays of Hope, 2004—05. Home: 102 Ferncroft St Longmeadow MA 01106 Office: Pioneer Valley Life Scis Inst 3601 Main St Springfield MA 01107 Office Phone: 413-794-9568.

**SHAO, WEI,** writer, educator; BA, China; MA, NYU, 1998. Author: (nonfiction, poetry) Pulling A Dragon's Teeth (Agnes Lynch Starrett Poetry award, 2002). Recipient Rona Jaffe Found. Writers' award, 1999; N.Y. Found. Fellowship For Arts, 2001. Home: Apt 3LL 601 W 110st New York NY 10025 Personal E-mail: wendyshao7@yahoo.com.

**SHAO, ZHENHUA,** electrical engineer, consultant; arrived in U.S., 1989; s. Jinrui Shao and Rujing Hua. Diploma in elec. engring., Shanghai Jiao Tong U., 1983, MSME, 1989; MSEE, Wichita State U., 1991; PhD Elec. Engring., U. Kans., 1994. Registered profl. engr. Calif. Elec. engr. Shanghai Jiao Tong U., 1983—86; rsch. asst. Nat. Inst. Aviation Rsch., Wichita, 1990—92; tchg. asst. U. Kans., Lawrence, 1993—94; elec. design engr. Eastman Kodak, Kansas City, 1994; chief engr. NGK Insulators Inc., Torrance, Calif. 1996—2002; circuit design mgr. L.A. divsn. Ibiden USA Inc., Torrance, Calif., 2003—. Cons. Lawrence Paper Co., 1994—95; cons. engring., San Gabriel, Calif., 1997—; reviewer IEEE and Inst. Elec. Engring. Contbr. articles to profl. jours. Named Outstanding Rschr., Shanghai Jiao Tong U., 1985; named one of Top 50 Pairs in Open Pair Game, N.Am. Bridge Championships U.S., Am. Contract Bridge League, 1998, Top 50 Pairs in Open Pair Game, N.Am. Bridge Championships Can., 1999. Achievements include patents in field; design of high frequency integrated circuits. Home: PO Box 1083 San Gabriel CA 91778 E-mail: zshao2001@yahoo.com.

**SHAO, ZHIFENG,** biophysics educator; b. Beijing, Mar. 1, 1959; came to U.S., 1982; s. Hong Kui and Jie Hua (Dong) S. BS, U. Nanking, Nanjing, China, 1982; MS, U. Chgo., 1985, PhD, 1988. Rsch. assoc. U. Chgo., 1988-89; asst. prof. biophysics U. Va., Charlottesville, 1989-93, assoc. prof., 1993—. Cons. AT&T Bell Labs., Murray Hill, N.J., 1990-91. Contbr. over 100 articles and revs. to sci. jours. Mem. Am. Phys. Soc., Microscopy Soc. Am. (Presdl. scholar 1987), Biophys. Soc. Avocations: photography, gardening.

**SHAOHUA KEVIN, ZHOU,** research scientist; m. Chunhui Zhang, Mar. 20, 1998; 1 child, Darwin Zhou. PhD, U. of Md., College Park, 2004. Grad. rsch. asst. U. of Md., College Park, 2000—04; rsch. scientist Siemens Corp. Rsch., Princeton, NJ, 2004—. Reviewer over 15 jours. and confs. Author: (rsch. monograph) Unconstrained Face Recognition, Recognition of Humans and Their Activities Using Video; contbr. articles to profl. jours., chpts. to books. Named Finalist of U. Md. Invention of the Yr. award, 2003; recipient grad. rsch. assistantship, U. of Md., 2000—04, rsch. scholarship, Nat. U. of Singapore, 1999—2000, vis. rsch. sScholarship, Indian Inst. of Sci., 1999—2000. Mem.: IEEE (program chair Conf. CVPR 2006). Achievements include invention of echocardiography tracking using pairwise active appearance models; apparatus for real time visual tracking through hardware acceleration; patents pending for image-based recognition using boosting method. Office: Siemens Corp Rsch 755 College Rd E Princeton NJ 08540 Office Phone: 609-734-3325. Office Fax: 609-734-6565. E-mail: kzhou@scr.siemens.com.

**SHAOULOV, VESSELIN,** technologist; s. Iossif Shaoulov and Boyanka Apostolova. MSc, Sofia U., 1996; MS, Coll. of Optics and Photonics, Orlando, Fla., 2000, PhD, 2004. Rsch. scientist Bulgarian Acad. of Sci., Sofia, 1996—98; rsch. asst. Coll. of Optics and Photonics, Orlando, 1998—2004, cons., 2004; chief tech. officer Adastra Labs LLC, Orlando, 2004—. Mem. internat. optical design conf. program com. Internat. Soc. for Optical Engring. and Optical Soc. Am., Washington, 2004—; reviewer sci. jour. Optical Engring.; mem. William Price Scholarship Com., 2005. Contbr. scientific papers to profl. jours. Mem.: IEEE, Laser and Electro-Optics Soc., Am. Physics Soc., Internat. Soc. for Optical Engring. (pres. local chpt. 2001—04, William Price Meml. scholarship in the field of optical engring.), Optical Soc. of Am. Achievements include patents pending for compact microlenslet array imager; compact illumination system for head-mounted displays; first to develop imaging with multi-aperture micro-optics. Office: Coll Optics and Photonics 4000 Cen Florida Blvd Orlando FL 32186 Office Phone: 407-823-6851. E-mail: vesko@odalab.ucf.edu.

**SHAPEERO, LORRAINE G.,** physician, researcher, educator; d. Ezra and Goldine Shapeero. BA, U. Calif., Berkeley, 1964; MD, U. Calif., San Francisco, 1968. Diplomate Am. Bd. of Radiology, 1974. Resident to faculty U. Pa., Phila., 1970—74; fellowship Inst. of Orthop. Royal Nat. Orthop. Hosp., London, 1975—76; faculty U. Calif., San Francisco, 1977—82, 1984—95, Columbia U., NY, 1982—84, Institut Gustave Roussy, France, 1990—; chief Musculo-skeletal Radiology sect. Uniformed Svcs. U., Bethesda, Md., 1995—; attending radiologist Walter Reed Army Med. Ctr. Wash., 1995—; dir. Bone and Soft Tissue Sarcoma Program US Mil. Cancer Inst., Wash. 2004. Contbr. articles various profl. jours. and rsch. publs. Mem.: Musculoskeletal Radiology (mem. editl. bd. 1999—2002), Investigative Radiology (mem. editl. bd. 1990—94), Internat. Skeletal Soc. (chair, grants com.), Radiology (mem. editl. bd., cons. to editor 1995—2001), Acad. Radiology (mem. editl. bd. 1994—), Assn. U. Radiologists (bd. dirs.), Alliance Med. Student Educators in Radiology (mem. exec. com.), Am. Roentgen Ray Soc., Am. Coll. Radiology, Radiol. Soc. North Am., Internat. Soc. Magnetic Resonance in Medicine (sec.; Musculoskeletal Study Group), Connective Tissue Oncology Soc., Radiology Rsch. Alliance (pres.), Phi Beta Kappa. Office: Uniformed Svcs U 4301 Jones Bridge Rd Bethesda MD 20814

**SHAPELL, NATHAN,** financial and real estate executive; b. Poland, Mar. 6, 1922; s. Benjamin and Hela S. Shapell; m. Lilly Szenes, July 17, 1948; children: Vera Shapell Guerin, Benjamin(dec.). Co-founder Shapell Industries, Inc., Beverly Hills, Calif., 1955, now chmn. bd., CEO, 1989—. Mem. adv. bd. Union Bank, Beverly Hills, Calif.; mem. residential bldgs. adv. com. Calif. Energy Resources Conservation and Devel. Commn.; speaker in field.

Author: (novels) Witness to the Truth, 1974. Mem. adv. coun. Pres.'s Commn. on the Holocaust, 1979; pres. Am. Acad. Achievement, 1975—; prisoner in Auschwitz, 1943—45; Mem. Calif. Commn. Govt. Reform, 1978; Atty. Gen. Calif. Adv. Coun.; Dist. Atty. Los Angeles County Adv. Coun.; chmn. Calif. Govt. Commn. Orgn. and Economy, 1975—; mem. Gov.'s Task Force on Affordable Housing, 1980—; mem. dean's coun. UCLA Sch. Architecture and urban Planning, 1976—; trustee U. Santa Clara, Calif., 1976—; bd. councillors U. So. Calif. Med. Sch., 1973—. Recipient Golden Plate award, Am. Acad. Achievement, 1974, Fin. World award, 1977. Mem.: Hillcrest Country Club (Los Angeles). Jewish. Office: Shapell Industries Inc Ste 700 8383 Wilshire Blvd Beverly Hills CA 90211-2410 Office Phone: 323-651-4349.

**SHAPER, C. PARK,** energy executive; BA, BS, Stanford Univ.; MBA, Northwestern Univ. Cons. Boston Consulting Group, 1995—97; v.p., CFO First Data Corp., 1997—99; pres., bd. dir. Altair Corp., 1999; v.p., CFO Kinder Morgan Inc., Kinder Morgan Energy Partners LP, Kinder Morgan Mgmt. LLC, Houston, 2000—04, exec. v.p., CFO, 2004—05, pres., 2005—. Bd. dir., treas. Children's Fund, Houston. Office: Kinder Morgan Inc Ste 1000 500 Dallas St Houston TX 77002*

**SHAPER, CHRISTOPHER THORNE,** sales executive; b. Columbus, Ohio, Sept. 6, 1955; s. Charles R. and M. Caroline (Garringer) Shaper. BA, Wake Forest U., 1977; MA in Mgmt., Coll. of Notre Dame, 1992. Sales rep. Intex Products Inc., Winston-Salem, NC, 1978; tech. sales rep. Am. Can Co., Oak Brook, Ill., 1979-81, J.T. Baker Chem. Co., Atlanta, 1981-83; corp. accts. rep. Erachem Comilog, Inc., Balt., 1983-84, industry sales mgr., 1984-92, dir. mktg. and sales, 1992—2000, dir. sales, 2000—03, v.p. global manganese sales, 2003—, v.p. sales, 2005. Mem.: Am. Feed Industries Assn., Am. Chem. Soc. Republican. Roman Catholic. Avocations: sports, reading. Office: Southmountain Assoc LLC PO Box 1524 Hagerstown MD 21741 Office Phone: 410-636-7108, 301-665-1177. Business E-Mail: CShaper@Erachem-Comilog.com, cshaper@myactv.net.

**SHAPERE, DUDLEY,** philosophy educator; b. Harlingen, Tex., May 27, 1928; s. Dudley and Corinne (Pupkin) S.; m. Hannah Hardgrave; children: Hannah Elizabeth, Christine Ann; children by previous marriage: Alfred Dudley, Catherine Lucretia. BA, Harvard U., 1949, MA, 1955, PhD, 1957. Instr. philosophy Ohio State U., 1957-60; asst. prof. U. Chgo., 1960-65, assoc. prof., 1965-67, prof., 1967-72; mem. com. on evolutionary biology, 1969-72, chmn. undergrad. program in history and philosophy of sci., 1966-72, chmn. com. on conceptual founds. sci., 1970-72; prof. U. Ill., Urbana, 1972-75, chmn. program in history and philosophy of sci., 1972-75; prof. U. Md., College Park, 1975-84; Z. Smith Reynolds prof. philosophy and history of sci. Wake Forest U., 1984—2002; ret., 2002. Mem. com. on history and philosophy of sci. U. Md., 1975-84, chmn. program in history and philosophy of sci., 1983-84.; vis. prof. Rockefeller U., 1965-66, Harvard U., 1968; mem. Inst. Advanced Study, Princeton, N.J., 1978-79, 81, 89, Otto Neugebaur fellow, 2001; spl. cons. (program dir.) program in history and philosophy of sci. NSF, 1966-75; Sigma Xi nat. bicentennial lectr., 1974-77. Author: Philosophical Problems of Natural Science, 1965, Galileo: A Philosophical Study, 1974, Reason and the Search for Knowledge, 1984; editorial bd.: Philosophy of Sci., Studies in History and Philosophy of Sci.; rev. bd.: Philosophy Research Archives; contbr. articles to profl. jours. Served with AUS, 1950-52. Recipient Quantrell award for excellence in undergrad. tchg. U. Chgo., 1968; Disting. Scholar-Tchr. award U. Md., 1979-80. Fellow AAAS (sec. sec. 1972); mem. APA, Philosophy of Sci. Assn., History of Sci. Soc., Am. Philos. Assn., Acad. Internat. de Philosophie des Sci. Home: 3125 Turkey Hill Ct Winston Salem NC 27106-4951 E-mail: shapere@wfu.edu.

**SHAPERO, DONALD CAMPBELL,** physicist, government official; b. Detroit, Apr. 17, 1942; s. Donald Mayer and Lillian Emily (Campbell) S.; m. Diana B. Berner, Dec. 17, 1969 (div.); 1 child, Stephen B.; m. Linda J. Ravdin, Sept. 8, 1985; child, Daniel R. BS, MIT, 1964, PhD, 1970. Thomas J. Watson fellow IBM Corp., Yorktown Heights, N.Y., 1970-72; asst. prof. physics Am. U., Washington, 1972-73, Cath. U., Washington, 1973-75; exec. dir. energy rsch. adv. bd. U.S. Dept. Energy, Washington, 1978-79; sr. staff officer Nat. Acad. Scis., Washington, 1975-78, spl. assts. for program coord., 1979-82, dir. bd. physics and astronomy, 1982—. Exec. sec. com. effects on multiple nuclear weapon detonations Nat. Acad. Scis.-NRC, Washington, 1975-76, exec. sec. geophys. data panel, 1976, exec. sec. panel to assess nat. need for facilities dedicated to prodn. synchrotron radiation, 1976, sr. staff officer geophys. study com., 1976-78; dir. com. sci. and pub. policy nuclear risk survey Nat. Acad. Sci., 1976-78; sr. staff officer for five yr. outlook sci. and tech., 1979-82, sr. staff officer workshop sci. instrumentation, 1982; staff dir. physics survey Physics Through the 1990's, 1982-86, Materials Sci. and Engring. study for the 1990's, 1985-89. Contbr. sci. articles to profl. publs. V.p. Jewish Congregation, 1983-84, pres., 1984-85; sec. James Clark Maxwell Found., 1992—. NSF fellow, 1964-68; rsch. grantee Cottrell, 1975. Mem. Am. Phys. Soc., Am. Astronomical Soc., Internat. Astronomical Union, Am. Geophys. Union. Home: 7537 Heatherton Ln Rockville MD 20854-3232 Office: Nat Acad Scis KECK 956 500 5th St Washington DC 20001

**SHAPIRA, DAVID S.,** food products and retail grocery executive; b. 1942; married. BA, Oberlin Coll., 1964; MA, Stanford U., 1966. V.p. Giant Eagle, Inc. (formerly Giant Eagle Markets, Inc.), Pitts., 1974—81, pres., 1981—94, CEO, also bd. dirs.; chmn. & CEO Giant Eagle, Youngstown; now chmn. bd. Phar-Mor Inc., Youngstown. Mem. bd. Allegheny Conf. Community Devel.*

**SHAPIRO, ALEX,** composer; b. N.Y.C., Jan. 11, 1962; d. Ivan and Maria Shapiro; m. Charles Anthony Richardson, Oct. 4, 2003. Grad., The Juilliard Sch., 1980; MusB, Manhattan Sch. Music, NY, 1983. Composer-in-residence, moderator The Walden Sch., Dublin, 2004; judging panelist McKnight Found. Artist Fellowship Award, St. Paul, 2004; composer-in-residence New Music Festival Calif. State U. Sacramento, 2003; mem. alumni coun. Manhattan (N.Y.) Sch. Music, N.Y.C., 2001—. Composer: (songs) Piano Suite No. 1: The Resonance of Childhood, 1996, Trio for Clarinet, Violin and Piano, 1998 (named Best Instrumental Composition, The Composers Guild, 1999), Transplant, 1999, Of Breath and Touch, 1999, Evensong Suite, 1999, Piano Trio No. 1: Elegy, 1999, Sonata for Piano, 1999, Shiny Kiss, 1999, Music for Two Big Instruments, 2000, Of Bow and Touch, 2000 (award Internat. Soc. Bassists, 2002), Introspect, 2000, Re:pair, 2000 (Artist award Mu Phi Epsilon, 2001), Desert Passage, 2001, Slip, 2001, Celebrate, 2002, At the Abyss, 2003 (Best Original Composition award Mu Phi Epsilon, 2003), Current Events, 2003, Bioplasm, 2004 (Comml. Composer award The Calif. Assn. Profl. Music Tchrs., 2004, award Music Tchrs. Nat. Assn., 2005), Deep, 2005, Unabashedly, 2006, (recordings) For My Father on California Concert, 2005; contbg. composer: recordings Clariphonia, 1998, New American Piano Music, 1999, Music for Hammers and Sticks, 2003, Above and Beyond, 2005, Coast to Coast, 2005; translator: Beck and Call, 2005; contbr. articles to profl. jours. Co-founder The Clinic Def. Alliance, L.A., 1989—93; v.p. Inst.First Amendment Studies, L.A., 1990—92. Fellow, Alpha Chi Omega Found., 2003, The Calif. Arts Coun., 2000—01, The MacDowell Colony, Peterborough, N.H., 2003; Margaret Jory grantee, The Am. Music Ctr., 2003. Mem.: ACLU (chmn. state and nat. legis. action com. 1990—96, bd. dirs. So. Calif. chpt. 1992—96, v.p. So. Calif. chpt. 1992—96, Fundamental Right Reproductive Freedom award 1992, Chpt. Activist of Yr. award 1993), The Am. Soc. Composers, Authors and Pub. (co-chmn. internet rights com. 1997—98, Standard award 1998—), Meet the Composer, The Rec. Acad., Nat. Music Publishers Assn., Nat. Assn. Composers (sec. 1999—2002), Soc. Composers, Inc., The Coll. Music Soc. (sec. 1998—2002), Am. Fedn. Musicians, Local 47, The Am. Composers Forum (chmn. adv. coun. 2000—, moderator composer salon series 2001—; pres. bd. dirs. 2003—, Disting. Svc. award 2001, Subito award 2003, 2005), The Film Music Soc., The Soc. Composers and Lyricists (v.p. bd. dirs. 1994—96, chmn. film and TV music state of art confs. 1994—2000), Ctr. Promotion of Contemporary Composers, Chamber Music Am., Internat. Alliance Women in Music, Soc. Electro Acoustic Music,

The Am. Music Ctr., The Dominant Club, Sigma Alpha Iota Composers Bur., Mu Phi Epsilon. Avocations: sailing, marine biology, astronomy. Home: 106 Paradise Cove Road Malibu CA 90265 Home Fax: 270-916-0093. Personal E-mail: alex@alexshapiro.org.

**SHAPIRO, ARTHUR GILMAN,** science educator; b. Riverside, Calif., Oct. 18, 1964; s. Victor Lenard and Florence Gilman Shapiro; m. Sherri Marla Geller, Aug. 21, 1994; children: Sarah Mariam, Benjamin David, Joel Isaac. PhD, Columbia U., 1992; BA in Math. and Psychology, U. Calif., San Diego, 1987. Post-doctoral fellow U. Chgo., 1992—95; asst. prof. Lewis and Clark Coll., Portland, Oreg., 1995—98, Bucknell U., Lewisburg, Pa., 1998—2001, assoc. prof., 2002—; external dir. studies for exptl. psychology Corpus Christi Coll., Cambridge, England, 2000—01. Grantee Visual Adaptation at Mesopic Light Levels, NIH. Mem.: Psychonomics Soc., Internat. Colour Vision Soc., Visual Sciences Soc., Optical Soc. Am. Achievements include research in color vision and low-light-level vision; discovery of several varieties of visual illusions, most significantly a class of illusion referred to as contrast asynchronies. Office: Bucknell University O'Leary Center Lewisburg PA 17837 Office Phone: 570-577-7522. Business E-Mail: shapiro@bucknell.edu.

**SHAPIRO, BURTON LEONARD,** dentist, geneticist, educator; b. N.Y.C., Mar. 29, 1934; s. Nat Lazarus and Fay Rebecca (Gartenhouse) S.; m. Eileen Roman, Aug. 11, 1958; children— Norah Leah, Anne Rachael, Carla Faye. Student, Tufts U., 1951-54; D.D.S., NYU, 1958; MS, U. Minn., 1962, PhD, 1966. Faculty U. Minn. Sch. Dentistry, Mpls., 1962—, assoc. prof. div. oral pathology, 1966-70, prof., chmn. div. oral biology, 1970-79, prof., chmn. dept. oral biology, 1979-88, prof. dept. oral pathology and genetics, 1979-88, dir. grad. studies, mem. grad. faculty genetics, 1966—, prof. dept. oral sci., 1988—, mem. grad. faculty pathobiology, 1979; prof. dept. lab. medicine and pathology U. Minn. Sch. Medicine, 1985—, mem. Human Genetics Inst., 1988—, univ. senator, 1968-72, 88-93; also mem. med. staff U. Minn. Health Scis. Center; exec. com. Grad. Sch. U. Minn., chmn. health scis. policy rev. council, chmn. univ. faculty consultative com., 1988-92; chmn. univ. fin. and planning com. Grad. Sch. U. Minn., 1988. Hon. research fellow Galton Lab. dept. human genetics Univ. Coll., London, 1974; spl. vis. prof. Japanese Ministry Edn., Sci. and Culture, 1983 Mem. adv. editorial bd.: Jour. Dental Research, 1971—; Contbr. articles to profl. jours. Served to lt. USNR, 1958-60. Am. Cancer Soc. postdoctoral fellow, 1960-62; advanced fellow, 1965-68; named Century Club Prof. of Yr., 1988. Fellow Am. Acad. Oral Pathology, AAAS; mem. Internat. Assn. Dental Research (councilor 1969), Am. Soc. Human Genetics, Craniofacial Biology Soc. (pres. 1972), Sigma Xi, Omicron Kappa Upsilon. Home: 148 Nina St # 2 Saint Paul MN 55102-2160 Office: U Minn Sch Dentistry Dept Oral Sci Minneapolis MN 55455 Office Phone: 612-624-3991. Business E-Mail: burt@umn.edu.

**SHAPIRO, DAVID LOUIS,** law educator; b. NYC, Oct. 12, 1932; s. Louis and Sara (Grabelsky) Shapiro; m. Jane Wilkins Bennett, June 19, 1954; 1 child: Lynn Mayson. Grad., Horace Mann Sch., 1950; AB magna cum laude, Harvard U., 1954, LLB summa cum laude, 1957. Bar: DC 1957, Mass. 1964. Assoc. Covington & Burling, Washington, 1957-62; law clk. to Justice John M. Harlan US Supreme Ct., 1962-63; asst. prof. law Harvard Law Sch., Cambridge, Mass., 1963—66, prof., 1966—84, William Nelson Cromwell prof. law, 1984—2006, emeritus, 2006—, assoc. dean, 1971-76; dep. solicitor gen. US Dept. Justice, Washington, 1989—91. Vis. prof. NYU, 2003, U. Ariz., 2004. Author: Federalism: A Dialogue, 1995, Civil Procedure: Preclusion in Civil Actions, 2001; co-author: The Federal Courts and the Federal System, 1973, 88, 96, 2003; Editor: The Evolution of a Judicial Philosophy: Selected Opinions of Justice John M. Harlan, 1969, The Judicial Code and the Rules of Procedure in the Federal Courts, annually 1988-2000. Mem.: Am. Law Inst. Office: Harvard Law Sch 1563 Massachusetts Ave Cambridge MA 02138 Office Fax: 617-496-4880. Business E-Mail: dshapiro@law.harvard.edu.

**SHAPIRO, DAVID W.,** prosecutor; BA in English Lit. and Creative Writing, SUNY, Binghamton; JD, SUNY, Buffalo. Bar: Calif., NY, Ariz., admitted to practice: US Dist. Cts. (So. and Eastern Dists. NY, Dist. Ariz., No. and Ctrl. Dists. Calif.), US Ct. Appeals (2nd and 9th Cirs.). Fed. Prosecutor Eastern Dist., NY, 1986—92, chief organized crime unit NY; Fed. Prosecutor Dist. of Ariz., 1992—94; chief Appellate Div. Northern Dist., Calif., 1994—2001, chief Criminal Div. Calif., 1994—2001, U.S. Atty. Calif., 2001—02; administ. ptnr. Boies, Schiller & Flexner, Oakland, Calif., 2002—. Spkr. in field. Mng. editor Buffalo Law Review. Office: Boies, Schiller & Flexner 1999 Harrison Street Ste 900 Oakland CA 94612

**SHAPIRO, DIANNA J.,** school librarian; b. Grand Rapids, Mich., Jan. 12, 1959; d. Clarence Menninga and Irene June Van Prooyen; m. Richard Joseph Shapiro, Apr. 27, 2005. BA, Calvin Coll., Grand Rapids, Mich., 1982; M in Art Therapy, Wright State U., Dayton, Ohio, 1985; MS in Libr. and Info. Sci., U. Ill., Champaign, 2003. Reference libr. Grand Valley State U., Allendale, Mich., 2004—. Sec. Grand Rapids Cantata Choir, Mich., 2004—06, bd. dir., 2004—06. Avocations: knitting, needlecrafts.

**SHAPIRO, E. DONALD,** lawyer, educator; b. York, Pa., Nov. 1, 1931; s. Samuel Milton and Sarah (Lavetan) S.; m. Merle Judith Mandell, Aug. 12, 1956; children— Felicia, Rachel, Carol, Richard. Student, Sorbonne, Paris, 1952; AB summa cum laude, Dickinson Coll., 1953, LL.D., 1975; JD, Harvard U., 1956; LL.D., N.Y. Law Sch., 1973; H.L.D., York Coll., 1980; MA (hon.), Oxford U., 1986. Bar: Pa. 1957, D.C. 1957, Mich. 1967, N.Y. 1981. With Freedman, Landy & Lorry, Phila., 1956-57; instr. Boston U. Sch. Law, 1957-59; prof. law Detroit Coll. Law, 1959-60; dir. Inst. Continuing Legal Edn., U. Mich. Law Sch., Wayne State Law Sch.; mem. faculty U. Mich. Law Sch., 1960-68; adj. prof. law NYU Sch. Law, 1968-74; dean N.Y. Law Sch., 1973-83, Solomon Disting. Prof. law, 1982—, dean emeritus, 2000—. Vis. disting. prof. law Bar-Ilan U., 1986—; vis. prof. numerous ednl. instns. including Harvard Med. Sch., 1979-80 and Oxford U., 1983-84; Joseph C. Hostetler, Baker and Hostetler vis. prof. law Cleve. State U. Sch. Law; supernumerary fellow St. Cross Coll. Oxford U., 1984—; cons. in law numerous profl. and civic orgns.; bd. dirs., trustee various orgns. including Loral Corp., Bank Leumi, Rapitech Systems, Inc., TSS Ltd., Gamma Internat., The Jesup Group, Applied Laser Systems, Fountain Pharms., MelaRx Pharms., Interferon Scis. Author: (with Curran) Law, Medicine and Forensic Science, 3d edit., 1981; editor: Mich. Basic Practice Series, 1960; co-editor numerous legal works; editorial bd. Am. Jour. Law and Medicine, Jour. Medicine and Law, 1978—, numerous others; contbr. articles to profl. jours. Trustee Dickinson Coll., 1969-90; trustee The Milton Helpern Library, N.Y.C., 1970—, chairperson and pres., 1977-82, 88—; mem. bd. govs. Home Care, Group Health, Inc. Decorated Cavaliere Ufficiale Order of Merit (Italy). Recipient numerous awards; Sacks Meml. lectr. Oxford U., 1984. Fellow Am. Coll. Legal Medicine (hon.), Inst. Jud. Administrn.; mem. NAACP, Am. Bar Assn., Am. Acad. Forensic Sci., Am. Law Inst. (life), ABA, AAUP, Harvard Law Assn., Scribes (pres. 1981), Phi Beta Kappa, Omicron Delta Kappa, Tau Kappa Alpha, Phi Epsilon Pi (Nat. Achievement award 1967). Jewish. Home: 480 Park Ave New York NY 10022-1613*

**SHAPIRO, EDWARD MURAY,** dermatologist; b. Denver, Oct. 6, 1924; s. Isador Benjamin and Sara (Berezin) Shapiro; m. Ruth Young, Oct. 14, 1944; children: Adrian Michael, Stefanie Ann; m. Dorothy Rosmarin, July 22, 1990. Studied, U. Colo., 1941—43; AB with honors, U. Tex., 1948, MD, 1952. Diplomate Am. Bd. Dermatology. Intern Jefferson Coll. Medicine Hosp., Phila., 1952—53; resident in dermatology U. Tex. Med. Br., Galveston, 1953—55, Henry Ford Hosp., Detroit, 1955—56, assoc. in dermatology divsn., 1956—57; clin. instr. dermatology Baylor U. Coll. Medicine, Houston, 1957—68, assoc. clin. prof., 1968—; staff mem. Ben Taub Gen. Hosp., Houston, 1958—; active staff mem. Columbia Bayshore Hosp., Houston, 1957—68, assoc. clin. prof., 1968—; staff mem. Ben Taub Gen. Hosp., Houston, 1958—; active staff mem. Columbia Bayshore Hosp., 1962—, Meml. Hosp. S.E., Houston, 2000. Contbr. articles to profl. jours. With USAAF, 1943—46. Grantee, Henry J.N. Taub, 1958—60. Fellow: Am. Acad. Dermatology; mem.: AMA, Am. Physicians Art Assn., Am. Physicians Art Assn. (v.p. 1993, pres. 2003—04, 2003—04, 2004—05), Houston Dermatology Assn., Harris County Med. Assn. (pres., S.E. br. 1968—69), South Ctrl.

Dermatol. Assn. (bd. dirs. 1987—88), Tex. Dermatol. Soc. (pres.-elect 1988, pres. 1989—90), Tex. Med. Assn., Rotary Internat. (Paul Harris fellow 1995, 1997), B'nai B'rith. Office: 1020 Pasadena Blvd Pasadena TX 77506-4700 Office Phone: 713-477-8183.

**SHAPIRO, EDWARD ROBERT,** psychiatrist, educator, health facility administrator, psychotherapist; b. Boston, Sept. 13, 1941; s. Jacob and Ruth (Yankelovich) S.; m. Donna Elmendorf; 1 child, Joshua Jackson; 1 child from previous marriage, Jacob Matthew; 1 stepchild, Zachary Andrew Robbins. BA magna cum laude, Yale U., 1962; MA in Anthropology, Stanford U., 1966; MD, Harvard U., 1968. Diplomate Am. Bd. Psychiatry and Neurology. Intern in medicine Beth Israel Hosp., Boston, 1968-69; resident in psychiatry Mass. Mental Health Ctr., Boston, 1969-72, chief resident in psychiatry, 1971-72; clin. assoc. NIMH, Bethesda, Md., 1972-74; dir. Adolescent and Family Treatment and Study Ctr. McLean Hosp., Belmont, Mass., 1974-89, dir. Psychosocial Tng. and Consultation, 1989-91; bd. dirs. Ctr. for Study of Groups and Social Systems, Boston, 1983-90, A.K. Rice Inst., Washington, 1983-90, dir. Nat. Group Rels. Conf., 1989-91; faculty mem. Boston Psychoanalytic Inst., 1978—; assoc. clin. prof. psychiatry Harvard Med. Sch., Boston, 1982—; med. dir., CEO The Austen Riggs Ctr., Stockbridge, Mass., 1991—; tng. and supr. analyst Psychoanalytical Inst. of the Berkshires, 2003—. Dir. The Erik H. Erikson Inst. for Edn. and Rsch., 1994-2000. Co-author: (with A.W. Carr) Lost in Familiar Places: Creating New Connections Between the Individual and Society, 1991; editor: The Inner World in the Outer World: Psychoanalytic Perspectives, 1997; mem. editorial bd. Jour. Adolescence, 1977-82, Psychiatry, 1988—; assoc. editor Jour. Adolescence, 1982-84; contbr. articles to profl. jours. Mem. Yale Russian Chorus. With USPHS, 1972-74. Recipient Isenberg Teaching award McLean Hosp., 1980, Rsch. prize Soc. for Family Therapy and Rsch., 1984, Felix and Helen Deutsch Sci. prize Boston Psychoanalytic Inst., 1980. Fellow Am. Psychiat. Assn. (disting. life), Am. Coll. Psychoanalysis, A.K. Rice Inst.; mem. Am. Psychoanalytic Assn. Achievements include helping develop the Erik H. Erikson Inst. for Edn. and Rsch. as a vehicle for applying the clinical insights developed at Riggs to larger social issues. Avocation: music. Office: The Austen Riggs Ctr PO Box 962 25 Main St Stockbridge MA 01262-0962

**SHAPIRO, EDWIN STANLEY,** lawyer, judge; b. Bklyn., Jan. 14, 1931; s. Harry I. and Ann (Safanie) S.; m. Sandra I. Bernstein, Sept. 15, 1957; children: James A., Sarah E. BA, Trinity Coll., Hartford, Conn., 1952; LLB, JD, Harvard Law Sch., 1955. Bar: N.Y. 1956, U.S. Dist. Ct. (so. and ea. dist.) N.Y. 1956, U.S. Ct. Appeals 1957. Atty. Levin & Weintraub, N.Y.C., 1956—57; pvt. practice N.Y.C., 1957-59; ptnr. Smith, Shapiro & Scheier, N.Y.C., 1959—62; pvt. practice N.Y.C., 1962—69; ptnr. Basch, Seits & Shapiro, N.Y.C., 1970—74, Seits & Shapiro, N.Y.C., 1974—81; town justice Ossining, NY, 1980—; pvt. practice N.Y.C., 1981—95, Briarcliff Manor, NY, 1996—. Lawyer Staten Island Open Lands Found., 1965-67. Mem. Assn. of Bar of City of N.Y. (environ. law com. 1970-73, com. on state cts. 1982-83, corrections com. 1996-98), Ossining Area Bar Assn. (pres. 2003). Personal E-mail: shaplaw@verizon.net.

**SHAPIRO, ELI,** business consultant, educator, economist; b. Bklyn., June 13, 1916; s. Samuel and Pauline (Kushel) S.; m. Beatrice Ferbend, Jan. 18, 1946 (dec. July 1999); 1 child, Laura J. AB, Bklyn. Coll., 1936; MA, Columbia U., 1937, PhD, 1939. Instr. Bklyn. Coll., 1936-41; rsch. assoc. Nat. Bur. Econ. Rsch., 1938-39, cons., 1939-42, mem. rsch. staff, 1955-62; asst. prof. fin. U. Chgo., 1946-47, asso. prof., 1948-52, prof., 1952; prof. fin. Mass. Inst. Tech., 1952-61; assoc. dean Mass. Inst. Tech. (Sch. Indsl. Mgmt.), 1954-58, Alfred P. Sloan prof. mgmt., 1976-84, Alfred P. Sloan prof. emeritus, 1984—; prof. fin. Harvard Bus. Sch., 1962-72, Sylvan C. Coleman prof. fin. mgmt., 1968-72; chmn. fin. com., dir. Travelers Ins. Cos., Hartford, Conn., 1971-78, vice chmn. bd., dir., 1976-78; chmn. bd. Mass. Co., 1971-72; pres. Nat. Bur. Econ. Research, 1982-84. Chmn. bd. Fed. Home Loan Bank Boston, 1970-89; econ. analyst div. monetary rsch. US Dept. Treasury, 1941-42; economist rsch. div. OPA, 1941-42; staff cons. Com. Econ. Devel., 1950-51, mem. rsch. adv. com., 1961-64, 69—, project dir., 1966-69; cons. sec. treasury; mem. enforcement commn. WSB, 1952-53; cons. Inst. Def. Analyses; dep. dir. Rsch. Com. Money Credit, 1959-61. Author: (with others) Personal Finance Industry and Its Credit Standards, 1939, (with Steiner) Money and Banking, 1941, Development of Wisconsin Credit Union Movement, 1947, Money and Banking, 1953, (with others) 1958, (with D. Meiselman) Measurement of Corporate Sources and Uses of Funds, 1964, (with others) Money and Banking, 1969, (with Wolf) The Role of Private Placement in Corporate Finance, 1972; Editor: (with W.L. White) Capital for Productivity and Growth, 1977. Served from ensign to lt. USNR, 1942-46. Recipient Econ. Dept. award Bklyn. Coll., 1936, Honors Day award distinguished alumni, 1949 Fellow Am. Acad. Arts and Scis.; mem. Nat. Bur. Econ. Research (pres.), Am. Econ. Assn., Council Fgn. Relations, Am. Fin. Assn. Home and Office: 180 Beacon St Boston MA 02116-1408 Office Phone: 617-266-5512.

**SHAPIRO, EUGENE DAVID,** pediatrician, epidemiologist, educator; b. Jonah R. and Rita R. Shapiro; m. Susan K. Bowers; children: Lauren R., Amy E., Daniel J. BA, Yale Coll., New Haven, Conn., 1970; MD, U. Calif., San Francisco, 1976. Resident Children's Hosp. Pitts., 1976—79; asst. prof. pediat. Yale Sch. Medicine, New Haven, 1983—89, assoc. prof. pediat., 1989—93, prof. pediat., 1993—. Fellow, Children's Hosp. Pitts., 1979—81; grantee, NIH, 1983—; Robert Wood Johnson scholar, Yale Sch. Medicine, 1981—83. Fellow Am. Acad. Pediat.; mem.: Soc. Pediatric Rsch., Am. Pediatric Soc., Am. Bd. Pediatrics-Infectious Diseases. Achievements include research in assessment of clinical effectiveness of vaccines. Office: Yale U Dept Pediatrics 333 Cedar St PO Box 208064 New Haven CT 06520 8064 Office Phone: 203-688-4555.

**SHAPIRO, FLORENCE,** state legislator, advertising executive, public relations executive; b. N.Y.C., May 2, 1948; d. Martin Nmi and Ann (Spiesman) D.; m. Howard Nmi Shapiro, Dec. 28, 1969; children: Lisa, Todd, Staci. BS, U. Tex., 1970. Tchr. Richardson High Sch., Tex., 1970-72; advt., pub. rels. Shapiro & Co., Plano, Tex., 1982—; formerly mayor and mem. city coun. City of Plano, Tex.; now mem. Tex. Senate, 1992—, chmn. edn. com., mem. fin. com., adminstrn. com. and transp. and homeland security coms. Bd. dirs. Plano C. of C., Presbyn. and Children's Healthcare Ctr., Plano Econ. Devel. Bd., U. Tex. at Dallas Adv. Coun., The North Tex. Commn., The Dallas Regional Mobility Coalition; mem. nat. bd. dirs. Susan B. Komen Breast Cancer Found.; mem. adv. bd. Children's Edn. Fund Dallas, Dallas County Domestic Violence Task Force, Family Violence Prevention Coun. Injury Prevention Ctr. Greater Dallas. Recipient Plano Vol. of Yr. award, 1983, Plano Citizen of Yr. award, 1985, Athena award Plano C. of C. for Businesswoman of Yr., 1990, Child Advocate award Dallas Children's Advocacy Ctr., 1995, Legislator of Yr. award Tex. Mcpl. League, 1995, 97, Nat. Rep. Legislators Assn., 1997, Tex. Ct. Apptd. Spl. Advs., 1997; Outstanding Legislator of Yr. award Tex. Police Chiefs Assn., 1995, Legislator of Yr. award, 1997, Friend of the Taxpayer award Citizens for a Sound Economy, 1999, Centennial Hero award Plano Ind. Sch. Dist., 1999, Voice of Children award, Ct. Apptd. Spl. Advs. of Collin County, 2001, others; Outstanding Legislator award Tex. Assn. Dist. and County Attys., 1997, Leader of Excellence award Free Market Com., 1997, Senate Statesman award Lonestar Found., 1997, Polit. Courage award John Ben Sheppard Pub. Leadership Forum, 1997; named One of 10 Best Legislators family law session State Bar Tex., 1997, One of 3 State Senators on YCT Honor Roll, 1997, Legis. Star, Tex. Classroom Tchrs. Assn., 1997, Guardian of Free Enterprise, Nat. Fedn. Ind. Bus., 1999, Woman of Yr., Les Femmes du Monde, 2002, Woman of Yr., Women's Transp. Seminar Dallas-Ft. Worth, 2002, others; honored by Texans for Lawsuit Reform, 1997, Assn. Ob-Gyn. and Southwestern Med. Sch., 1997. Mem. Rotary (Paul Harris fellow 1990), Alpha Epsilon Phi (Nat. Outstanding Young Alumnae award). Republican. Jewish. Office: Tex Senate PO Box 12068 Austin TX 78711-2068 Home: 1500 Eastwick Ln Plano TX 75093-2443

**SHAPIRO, FRED DAVID,** lawyer; b. Cleve., Nov. 10, 1926; s. Isadore R. and Lottie (Turetsky) S.; m. Helen Solomon, Sept. 5, 1948; children— Gary N., Ira R., Diane S. BA cum laude, Ohio State U., 1949; LL.B., Harvard U. 1954. Bar: Ohio 1954. Since practiced in, Cleve.; sr. ptnr. Shapiro and Lodwick, Co., L.P.A, 1994—. Served with USNR, 1945-46. Mem. Ohio Bar Assn., Greater Cleve. Bar Assn., Cuyahoga County Bar Assn., The Rowfant Club, Phi Beta Kappa. Jewish. Home: 29226 S Woodland Rd Cleveland OH 44124-5737 Office Phone: 216-378-9730. Personal E-mail: fshapo@aol.com.

**SHAPIRO, GARY EVAN,** newspaper journalist; b. Lewiston, Maine, Feb. 5, 1964; s. Sherman George and Charlotte (Cominsky) S. AB, Harvard U., 1986; JD, Columbia U., 1993. Assoc. Skadden Arps Slate Meagher & Flom, N.Y.C., 1993-94; writer, event prodr. N.Y.C., 1994-99; journalist Forward newspaper, N.Y.C., 1999—. Contbg. editor Am. Scholar, 2000—; note editor Columbia Jour. Environ. Law, 1993; contbr. numerous articles to profl. jours.; prodr. numerous programs on diplomacy, history, arch., bus., arts and lit., politics and econs., sci., edn., philosophy. Recipient Charles William Eliot medal for Citizenship, 1986, Cox Medal, Phillips Exeter, 1982; John Finley Traveling fellow, 1986. Mem. Overseas Press Club, Nat. Arts Club (lit. com. 1997—), Harvard Club (program com. 1995-2000). Avocation: book collecting. Home: 27 W 44th St # 50 New York NY 10036-6613 Office: Forward Newspaper 45 E 33rd St New York NY 10016-5336

**SHAPIRO, GEORGE HOWARD,** retired lawyer; b. St. Louis, Nov. 10, 1936; s. Isadore T. and Alice (Schucart) S.; m. Mary Kenney Leonard, 1977 (div. 1994); m. Ray Ann Kremer, 1999; 1 child, Ellen. BA, Harvard U., 1958, LLB, 1961; postgrad., London Sch. Econs., 1961-62. Bar: Ga. 1960, D.C. 1963. Atty. U.S. Dept. Labor, Washington, 1962-63; assoc. Arent Fox Kintner Plotkin & Kahn, Washington, 1963-69, ptnr., 1970-99; ret., 2000. Co-author: 'Cable Speech' The Case for First Amendment Protection, 1983; editor: New Program Opportunities in the Electronic Media, 1983. Current Developments in CATV, 1981. With USAR, 1962-68. Frank Knox Meml. fellow Harvard U., 1961-62. Mem. D.C. Bar Assn., Fed. Communications Bar Assn. Democrat. Jewish. Avocation: skiing. Home: Apt 906 3180 Mathieson Dr NE Atlanta GA 30305-1871 E-mail: GHSinATL@aol.com.

**SHAPIRO, HAROLD TAFLER,** economics professor, former academic administrator; b. Montreal, Que., Can., June 8, 1935; s. Maxwell and Mary (Tafler) Shapiro; m. Vivian Bernice Rapoport, May 19, 1957; children: Anne, Marilyn, Janet, Karen. BComm, McGill U., Montreal, 1956; PhD in Econs. (Harold Helm fellow, Harold Dodds sr. fellow), Princeton U., 1964. From asst. prof. to assoc. prof. econs. U. Mich., 1964-72, prof., 1970-76, prof. econs. and pub. affairs, 1977, chmn. dept. econs., 1974-77, v.p. acad. affairs, 1977-79, pres. Mich., 1980-87; rsch. adv. Bank Can., 1965-72; pres. Princeton U., 1988-2001, pres. emeritus, prof. econ. and pub. affairs Woodrow Wilson Sch., 2001—. Mem. exec. com. Assn. of Am. Universities, 1985—89; trustee N.J. Commn. Sci. and Tech., 1988—91; mem. Pres.'s Coun. Advisors Sci. and Tech., 1990—92, Stem Cell Inst. of NJ Joint Bd. Mgrs., 2005—; chmn. com. employer-based health benefits Inst. Medicine, 1991; bd. overseers Robert Wood Johnson Med. Sch., 2000—; bd. dirs. Dow Chem. Co., 1985—, DeVry Inst., Hastings Ctr., HCA, Reading is Fundamental, 2002—, Knight Found. Comm. on Intercollegiate Athletics, 2004—, Merck Vaccine Adv. Bd., 2004—, U.S. Olympic Com., 2004—; bd. trustees U. Medicine & Dentistry NJ, 2006—; trustee tech. Israel Inst. Tech., 2002—; chmn. Orgn. NIH Nat. Sci., 2000—03. Editor (with William G. Bowen): (book) Universities and Their Leadership, 1998. Chair Nat. Bioethics Adv. Commn., 1996—2001; chmn. spl. Presdl. Coun. Rsch. Librs. Group, 1980—89; mem. Gov.'s High Tech. Task Force, Mich., 1980—87, Gov.'s Commn. Jobs and Econ. Devel., Mich., 1983—87, Carnegie Commn. Coll. Retirement, 1984—86; dir. Am. Coun. Edn., 1989—91; mem. Pres. Bush Coun. Advisors Sci. and Tech., 1990—93; trustee Alfred P. Sloan Found., 1980—, Interlochen Ctr. Arts, 1988—95, U. Pa. Med. Ctr., 1992—, Univ. Corp. Advanced Internet Devel., 2000, Am. Jewish Com., 2002—, U. Medicine and Dentistry NJ, 2006—, Ednl. Testing Svc., 1994—2000. Recipient Lt. Gov.'s medal in commerce, McGill U., 1956. Fellow: Am. Acad. Arts and Scis., Mich. Soc. Fellows (sr.); mem.: Am. Philos. Soc., Inst. Medicine of NAS (in conjunction w/NRC) mem. adv. com. Human Embryonic Stem Cell Rsch. 2006—), Univs. Rsch. Assn. (trustee 1988—2001). Office: Princeton U Woodrow Wilson School 355 Wallace Hall Princeton NJ 08544 Office Phone: 609-258-6184. Business E-Mail: hts@princeton.edu.

**SHAPIRO, HARRY DEAN,** lawyer; b. Louisville, June 21, 1940; s. Herman Shapiro and Toby (Spector) Levy; m. Linda Siegel, Dec. 19, 1970; 1 child, Deborah Anne. BS, U. Louisville, 1962, JD, 1964. Bar: Ky. 1964, D.C. 1968, Md. 1970. Trial and appellate atty. U.S. Dept. Justice, Washington, 1964-70; assoc. Venable, Baetjer & Howard, Balt., 1970-74, ptnr., 1975-87; sr. ptnr., head of tax practice Weinberg & Green, Balt., 1987—98, chmn. corp. dept., 1993-95; transaction group coord., 1995-98; head tax practice Saul Ewing LLP (formerly Saul, Ewing, Remick & Saul LLP), 1998-99; chmn. tax group Saul Ewing LLP (formerly Saul, Ewing, Remick & Saul LLP), 1999—. Author: Federal Tax Liens, 1981, The Successful Practice, 2005; contbr. articles to profl. jours. Mem. Md. State Bd. Edn., 1990-97; v.p. Assoc. Jewish Charities of Balt., Inc. 1991-94; vice chmn. The Assoc. Jewish Cmty. Fedn. Balt. 1987-89, asst. treas., 1989-91, mem. exec. com., 1993-97; trustee Sinai Hosp., Balt., 1987-90; counsel Balt. Mus. Art, 1984-97, trustee, 1984-96, sec., 1985-92, v.p., sec., 1992-94, v.p., 1994-96; dir., 1989-96; chmn. Joint Budgeting Coun., 1993-96, Coun. Jewish Fedns.; trustee Acad. Art Mus., Easton, 1998-2005. Capt. USAR, 1967-70. Recipient Disting. Alumni award Brandeis Sch. of Law, 1996, Chmn.'s award Balt. Mus. Art, 1996. Mem. ABA (tax sect.), Md. State Bar Assn., Ky. Bar Assn., D.C. Bar Assn., Md. Club, Center Club. Home: 717 S President St Unit 602 Baltimore MD 21202 Office: Saul Ewing LLP Lockwood Pl 500 E Pratt St Baltimore MD 21202 Office Phone: 410-332-8658. Business E-Mail: hshapiro@saul.com. *Our country is at a crossroads in its history, and it is becoming clear that a real change is necessary. Basic reforms must occur in our governmental and educational structures. The question is whether we have the intelligence to reject the cries for bigger government and more taxes to solve these problems when fundamental action is required.*

**SHAPIRO, HARVEY,** poet; b. Chgo., Jan. 27, 1924; s. Jacob J. and Dorothy (Cohen) S.; m. Edna Lewis Kaufman, July 23, 1953 (div.); children— Saul, Dan. BA, Yale U., 1947; MA, Columbia U., 1948. Instr. English Cornell U., 1949-50, 51-52; creative writing fellow Bard Coll., 1950-51; mem. editl. staff Commentary, New Yorker, 1955-57, N.Y. Times Mag., N.Y.C., 1957, asst. editor, 1964-75; editor N.Y. Times Book Rev., 1975-83; dep. editor N.Y. Times Mag., 1983-96, consulting editor, 1996—2002. Author: The Eye, 1953, The Book and Other Poems, 1955, Mountain, Fire Thornbush, 1961, Battle Report, 1966, This World, 1971, Lauds, 1975, Nightsounds, 1978, The Light Holds, 1984, National Cold Storage Company, 1988, A Day's Portion, 1994, Selected Poems, 1997, How Charlie Shaver Died and Other Poems, 2001; editor: Poets of World War II, 2003, The Sights Along the Harbor: New and Collected Poems, 2006. With USAAF, World War II. Decorated D.F.C., Air medal with 3 oak leaf clusters.; Rockefeller Found. grantee in poetry, 1967 Club: Elizabethan (New Haven), Century (N.Y.).

**SHAPIRO, HARVEY,** sales executive, journalist, writer, lyricist; b. Bklyn., Mar. 18, 1937; s. Louis and Pauline (Watson) S.; m. Judith Shapiro, June 16, 1962 (div. Dec. 1982); children: Eric, Elyse; m. Eileen Strachman, Apr. 20, 1985. BA in Journalism, L.I. Univ., 1958. Enlisted USAR, 1954; honorably discharged U.S. Army, 1962; reporter, editor various publs. including Pitts. Press, UPI, 1958-1982; sports writer, sports slotman Dayton (Ohio) Daily News, 1974-79; founder, editor, pub. World of Speed, Dayton, 1979-81; copy editor Lake County Telegraph, Painesville, Ohio, 1982; gen. sales mgr. Del Rey Plastics Corp., N.Y.C., 1982-95. Author: Faster Than Sound, 1975 (named 1st in book divsn. 1976), Sports Stars Cookbook, 1978, Where Eagles Fly, 1996, Man Against the Salt, 1997 (named 1st in book divsn. 1997), Class of '68, 1998, Dream Machine, 2005; composer: (with Haman Harchol) A Simple Silver Band, 1989, We Love You, Welcome Home, 1991, Where Are You America?, 1992, (folk) A Simple Silver Band (first Pl., Eventide Arts Festival), 2002,(pop) In The Middle of the Night, 2003, (country) Is It Me Or My Music?, 2004, (gospel/inspirational) Do We Ever Take the Time?, 2005, Can A Blanket Shield the Cold?, 2006; contbr. articles to profl. jours. Recipient numerous writing awards AP, 1972-82; mag. named Top Nat. Motorsports Mag., Dayton Auto Racing Fan Club, 1980. Mem. ASCAP, Am. Automobile Racing Writers and Broadcasters Assn. (writing awards 1974-98), Vietnam Vets. Am. (assoc. chpt. 151). Avocations: photography, golf, concerts, whale watching. Home: 370 Buckskin Path Centerville MA 02632-2206 Personal E-mail: harvey@sharpiroworldofspeed.com.

**SHAPIRO, HOWARD M,** lawyer, former prosecutor; b. May 8, 1960; BA magna cum laude, Williams Coll., 1982; JD, Yale Univ., 1985. Bar: NY 1986, DC 1997. Law clk. Judge Pierre N. Leval, US Dist. Ct. (so. NY dist.), 1985—87; asst. U.S. atty. U.S. Dept. Justice, so. NY dist., 1987—92; gen. counsel FBI, Washington, 1993—97; ptnr., co-chmn. Litigation dept., co-chmn. investigations & criminal litigation group Wilmer Cutler Pickering Hale & Dorr, Washington. Assoc. prof. Cornell Law Sch. Contbr. articles to newspapers. Named one of Top DC Lawyers, Washingtonian mag., 2002, 2004, DC Go-to Litigators, Legal Times, 2003; recipient Nat. Intelligence Disting. Svc. medal, dir. of Ctrl. Intelligence, 1997. Office: Wilmer Cutler Pickering Hale & Dorr 2445 M St NW Washington DC 20037 Office Phone: 202-663-6606. Office Fax: 202-663-6363. Business E-Mail: howard.shapiro@wilmerhale.com.

**SHAPIRO, IRWIN IRA,** physicist, researcher; b. NYC, Oct. 10, 1929; s. Samuel and Esther (Feinberg) S.; m. Marian Helen Kaplun, Dec. 20, 1959; children: Steven, Nancy. AB, Cornell U., 1950; A.M., Harvard U., 1951, PhD, 1955. Mem. staff Lincoln Lab. MIT, Lexington, 1954-70; Sherman Fairchild Distinguished scholar Calif. Inst. Tech., 1974; Morris Loeb lectr. physics Harvard, 1975; prof. geophysics and physics MIT, 1967-80, Schlumberger prof., 1980-84; Paine prof. practical astronomy, prof. physics Harvard U., 1982-97; sr. scientist Smithsonian Astrophys. Obs., 1982—; dir. Harvard-Smithsonian Ctr. for Astrophysics, 1983—2004; prof. Harvard U./Timken, 1997—. Cons. NSF, NASA. Contbr. articles to profl. jours. Recipient Albert A. Michelson medal Franklin Inst., 1975, award in phys. and math. scis. N.Y. Acad. Scis., 1982, Einstein medal Einstein Soc. Bern, 1994, Joseph Henry medal Smithsonian Instn., 2004; Guggenheim fellow, 1982. Fellow AAAS, Am. Geophys. Union (Charles A. Whitten medal 1991, William Bowie medal 1993), Am. Phys. Soc.; mem. AAAS, NAS (Benjamin Apthorp Gould prize 1979), Am. Astron. Soc. (Dannie Heineman award 1983, Dirk Brouwer award 1987, Gerard Kuiper award 1997), Am. Philos. Soc., Internat. Astron. Union, Phi Beta Kappa, Sigma Xi, Phi Kappa Phi. Home: 17 Lantern Ln Lexington MA 02421-6029 Office: Harvard-Smithsonian Ctr Astrophysics 60 Garden St Cambridge MA 02138-1516 Business E-Mail: ishapiro@cfa.harvard.edu.

**SHAPIRO, ISAAC,** lawyer; b. Tokyo, Jan. 5, 1931; arrived in U.S., 1946, naturalized, 1951; s. Constantine and Lydia (Chernetzky) S.; m. Jacqueline M. Weiss, Sept. 16, 1956; children: Tobias, Alexandra, Natasha. AB, Columbia U., 1954, LLB, 1956; postgrad., U. Paris, 1956—57. Bar: N.Y. 1957, U.S. Supreme Ct. 1971, Paris 1991. Assoc. Milbank, Tweed, Hadley & McCloy, N.Y.C., 1956-65, ptnr., 1966-86, resident ptnr. Tokyo, 1977-79; ptnr. Skadden Arps Slate Meagher & Flom LLP, N.Y.C., 1986—2001; resident ptnr. Skadden Arps Slate Meagher & Flom, Hong Kong, 1989-90, Paris, 1990—2001; of counsel Skadden Arps Slate Meagher & Flom LLP, N.Y.C., 2001—; ptnr. Skadden Arps Slate Meagher & Flom (Europe) LLP, 2006—; tchg. fellow comparative law NYU, 1959-61. Lectr. Soviet law, 1961-67; adj. asst. prof. NYU, 1967-69; adj. assoc. prof., 1969-71, 74-75; adj. prof. dir. Russian legal studies Columbia Law Sch., 1999-2000. Author: (with Hazard and Maggs) The Soviet Legal System, 1969; author: Japan: The Risen Sun (in Japanese), 1982; editor: The Middle East Crisis-Prospects for Peace, 1969; contbr. articles to profl. jours. Mem. Joint Com. US-Japan Cultural and Ednl. Cooperation, Washington, 1972—78, Japan-US Friendship Commn., 1976—78; mem. svcs. policy adv. com. to US Trade Rep., 1982—91; trustee Nat. Humanities Ctr., Triangle Park, NC, 1978—89, Bank of Tokyo Mitsubishi Found., 1986—; trustee, v.p. Chamber Music Soc. Lincoln Ctr., 1980—86; pres. Japan Soc., NYC, 1970—77; trustee Isamu Noguchi Zaidan, Japan, 1999—, Isamu Noguchi Found., NY, 1985—, pres., 1985—2005; trustee, chmn. Isa Cultural Found., 1984—90; bd. advisors Trust for Mutual Understanding, NYC, 1985—; dir. Bank of Tokyo-Mitsubishi Trust Co., NY, 1975—77, 1980—2001, Japan Soc., 1969—77, 1979—80; bd. dirs. Bus. Coun. for Internat. Understanding, 1989—95, Nat. Com. US-China Rels., 1989—95, Asian Cultural Coun., 1980—. With U.S. Army, 1950-52. Fulbright scholar, 1956-57; decorated Order of the Rising Sun with gold rays and neck ribbon Emperor Japan, 2006. Mem.: ABA, N.Y. State Bar Assn., Coun. Fgn. Rels., Japan Soc. N.Y. (trustee 1969—77, 1979—80), Century Assn. (N.Y.C.), Cercle de l'Union Interaliee (Paris), Royal Automobile Club (London). Office: Skadden Arps Slate Meagher & Flom LLP 4 Times Sq New York NY 10036-6522 Office Phone: 212-735-3480. Business E-Mail: ishapiro@skadden.com.

**SHAPIRO, ISADORE,** materials scientist, consultant; b. Mpls., Apr. 25, 1916; s. Jacob and Bessie (Goldman) Shapiro; m. Mae Hirsch, Sept. 24, 1938; children: Stanley Harris, Jerald Steven. BChemE summa cum laude, U. Minn., 1938, PhD, 1944. Registered metall. engr., Calif. Asst. instr. chemistry U. Minn., 1938—41; rsch. fellow, 1944—45; rsch. chemist E.I. duPont de Nemours and Co., Phila., 1946; head chem. lab. U.S. Naval Ordnance Test Sta., Pasadena, Calif., 1947—52; dir. rsch. lab. Olin-Mathieson Chem. Corp., 1952—59; head chemistry Hughes Tool Co., Aircraft divsn., Culver City, Calif., 1959—62; pres. Universal Chem. Sys. Inc., 1962—, Aerospace Chem. Sys., Inc., 1964—66; dir. contract rsch. HITCO, Gardena, Calif., 1966—67; prin. scientist Douglas Aircraft Co. of McDonnell Douglas Corp., Santa Monica, Calif., 1967, McDonnell Douglas Astronautics Co., 1967—70; head materials and processes AiResearch Mfg. Co., Torrance, Calif., 1971—82, cons., 1982—. Inaugurated dep. gov. Am. Biog. Inst. Rsch. Assn. 1988; dep. dir. gen. Internat. Biog. Ctr., 1989, vice consul, 2002—; eng. rater U.S. Civil Svc. Bd. Exam, 1948—52. Contbr. articles to tech. publs. 1st lt. AUS, 1941—44. Fellow: AIAA (assoc.), Am. Inst. Chemists; mem.: AIM, AAAS, Internat. Plansee Soc. for Powder Metallurgy, Am. Powder Metallurgy Inst., Nat. Inst. Ceramic Engrs., Am. Ceramic Soc., Am. Assn. Contamination Control, NY Acad. Scis., Am. Phys. Soc., Am. Inst. Physics, Soc. Advancement Materials and Process Engring., Soc. Rheology, Am. Chem. Soc., Am. Ordnance Assn., Phi Lambda Upsilon, Tau Beta Pi, Sigma Xi. Achievements include patentee, discoverer series of carborane compounds; created term "carborane"; formulator of universal compaction equation for powders (metals, ceramics, polymers, chemicals). Home: PO Box 16737 Beverly Hills CA 90209-2737

**SHAPIRO, JAMES EDWARD,** judge; b. Chgo., May 28, 1930; BS, U. Wis., 1951; JD, Harvard U., 1954. Bar: Wis. 1956, U.S. Dist. Ct. (ea. dist.) Wis. 1956, U.S. Ct. Appeals (7th cir.) 1962, U.S. Supreme Ct. 1971. Sole practice, Milw., 1956-57; resident house counsel Nat. Presto Industries, Eau Claire, Wis., 1957-60; ptnr. Bratt & Shapiro, Milw., 1960-64; sole practice Milw., 1964-74; ptnr. Frank, Hiller & Shapiro, Milw., 1974-82; judge U.S. Bankruptcy Ct., Milw., 1982—, chief judge, 1996-2000. Mem. Bayside Bd. Appeals, Wis., 1969-77; Milwaukee County Ct. commr., 1969-78; dir. Milw. Legal Aid Soc., 1969-77. Served to 1st lt. U.S. Army, 1954-56. Jewish. Office: US Courthouse 140 Fed Bldg 517 E Wisconsin Ave Milwaukee WI 53202-4500 Office Phone: 414-297-3291 ext. 3201. Business E-Mail: james_e_shapiro@wieb.uscourts.gov.

**SHAPIRO, JAMES STEPHEN,** English professor; b. NYC, Sept. 11, 1955; s. Herbert and Lorraine (Ackerman) S. BA, Columbia U., 1977; PhD, U. Chgo., 1982. Asst. prof. Columbia U., 1985, Larry Miller Prof. of English and Comparative Lit. Co-dir. NEH Summer Shakespeare Insts., 1989-91. Author: Rival Playwrights Marlowe, Shakespear, Jonson, 1991, Shakespears and the Jews, 1996, A Year in the Life of William Shakespeare 1599, 2005; contbr. Theater Week, 1989—; assoc. editor: Medieval and Renaissance Drama in England, 1989. Recipient Rsch. stipend NEH, NY 1988, Huntington Libr., San Marion Calif. 1988; grantee NEH, NY, 1989. Office: Eng Comp Lit MC 4954 606B Phil Columbia Univ 1150 Amsterdam New York NY 10027

**SHAPIRO, JARED,** freelance/self-employed emergency medical technician; A.Paramedic Sci., Ivy Tech. State Coll., Bloomington, Ind., 2004; BS in Liberal Arts, Ind. U., Bloomington, 2004; postgrad., N.Y. Med. Coll., Valhalla, 2006. Cert. EMT N.J., N.Y., Ind., firefighter N.Y., Ind., instr. EMT, bloodborne pathogens, inciden command system. Police dispatcher Tri-Boro Pub. Safety Comm., Park Ridge, NJ, 1997—2004; dir. Ind. U. Emergency Med. Svc., Bloomington, 2000—04; capt., tng. officer Woodcliff Lake Vol. Dept., Woodcliff Lake, NJ, 2004—; paramedic Monoc/Hackensack U. Med. Ctr., Hackensack, NJ, 2004—05; paramedic planner/sr. disaster rschr. St. Barnabas Health Care System, West Orange, NJ, 2005—. Instr. Cmty. Life Safety, Woodcliff Lake, 2001—. Office: Saint Barnabas Health Care System 95 Old Short Hills Rd West Orange NJ 07052

**SHAPIRO, JERALD STEVEN,** chemist, bank executive; b. Dec. 3, 1943; s. Isadore and Mae (Hirsch) S. BS, UCLA, 1964, student, 1970. Lic. real estate broker, Calif.; cert. review appraiser, real estate broker, mortgage banker, escrow officer, investment broker, investment specialist; registered mortgage underwriter. Mgr. process engrng., quality control Aerospace Chem. Sys., Inc., Gardena, Calif., 1963-66; chem. engr. HITCO, Gardena, Calif., 1966-67; materials and process engr. McDonnell Douglas Corp., Long Beach, Calif., 1967-70; chemist L.A. county Sanitation Dist., 1971-74; staff scientist TRW Def. and Space Sys. Group, Redondo Beach, Calif., 1975—86. Cons. Century 21 Beverlywood Realty, Inc., L.A., 1977-; pres. Nationwide Mortgage Corp., L.A., 1983-, Heritage Realty Group, L.A.; adv. bd. 1st Women's Bank of Calif., 1977-78; JSK Capital Group, Inc. Beverly Hills, 1990-94; trustee, prof. Internat. Coll. of Calif., Irvine, 1991-93; bd. dirs. Western Advanced Tech. Systems, Inc., Environ. Protection Polymers, Inc. Author: Aware and Beware Guide to Intelligent Home Buying, 1974; co-inventor particle discriminator, 1964. Bd. dirs. Internat. Wellness Inst., Beverly Hills, 1992-93. Mem. Nat. Assn. Mortgage Bankers, Nat. Assn. Rev. Appraisers and Mortgage Underwriters, Chem. Soc., Century 21 Investment Soc. (charter), Mortgage Bankers Assn., Calif. Escrow Assn., Calif. Assn. Realtors, L.A. Bd. Realtors, Alpha chi Sigma. Office: 2800 S Robertson Blvd Los Angeles CA 90034-2406

**SHAPIRO, JOAN ISABELLE,** lab administrator, medical/surgical nurse; b. Aug. 26, 1943; d. Macy James and Frieda Lockhart; m. Ivan Lee Shapiro, Dec. 28, 1968; children: Audrey, Michael. Diploma, Peoria Meth. Sch. Nursing, 1964. RN. Nurse Nurse Grant Hosp., Columbus, Ohio, 1975—76, Cardiac Thoracic and Vascular Surgeons Ltd., Geneva, Ill., 1977—, mgr. non-ivasive lab., 1979—. Owner operator Shapiro's Mastiff's 1976-82; sec.-treas. Sounds Svcs., 1990—, Mainstream Sounds Inc., 1980-84; co-founder Cardio-Phone Inc., 1982-99, Edgewater Vascular Inst., 1987-89, Associated Profls., 1989? v.p. Computer Specialists Inc., 1986-89; founder, pres. Vein Ctr., Edema Ctr. Ltd. Mem. DAR (sec. Katahdin Valley-Lydia Putman chpt. 2004—), Soc. Non-invasive Technologists, Soc. Peripheral Vascular Nursing (cmty. awareness com. 1984-2004), Kane County Med. Soc. Aux. (pres. 1983-84, adviser, 1984-85), Katahdin Valley Putnam Cpt. of DAR (sec. 2004-). Lutheran. Home: Cardiac Thoracic/Vas Surg PO Box 325 Fort Fairfield ME 04742-0325 Business E-Mail: joan@ivanshapiro.com.

**SHAPIRO, JOEL ELIAS,** artist; b. NYC, Sept. 27, 1941; s. Joseph and Anna (Lewis) S.; m. Ellen Phelan; 1 dau., Ivy Bess. BA, NYU, 1964, MA, 1969. One-man shows include Paula Cooper Gallery, NYC, 14 shows, 1970—90, The Clocktower Gall., Inst. Art and Urban Resources, NYC, 1973, Mus. Contemporary Art, Chgo., 1976, Albright-Knox Art Gallery, Buffalo, 1977, Gallery M. Bochum, W. Germany, 1978, Galerie Mukai, Tokyo, 1980, 1981, 1988, 1991, Asher/Faure, LA, 1980, 1989, 1991, Whitechapel Gallery, London, 1980, Haus Lange, Krefeld, W.Germany, 1980, Moderna Museet, Stockholm, 1980, Brown U., 1980, Ackland Art Mus., Chapel Hill, NC, 1981, Contemporary Arts Ctr., Cin., 1981, Israel Mus. Jerusalem, 1981, Portland Ctr. Visual Arts, Oreg., 1982, Whitney Mus. Am. Art, NYC, 1982, Galerie Aronowitsch, Stockholm, 1984, Delahunty Gallery, Dallas, 1980, Donald Young Gallery, Chgo., 1987, Stedelijk Mus., Amsterdam, 1985, Kunstmuseum, Dusseldorf, 1985, Staatliche Kunsthalle, Baden-Baden, 1986, Seattle Art Mus., 1986, Galerie Daniel Templon, Paris, 1986, 1988, The John and Mable Ringling Mus., Sarasota, 1986, John Berggruen Gallery, San Francisco, 1987, Hirshhorn Mus. and Sculpture Garden, Washington, 1987, Hans Strelow, Dusseldorf, Germany, 1988, Toledo Mus. Art, 1989, Waddington Gallery, London, 1989, Museet I Varberg, Sweden, 1990, Balt. Art Mus., 1990, Des Moines Art Ctr., 1990, Ctr. for Fine Arts, Miami, 1991, IVAM Centre Julio Gonazlez, Valencia, Spain, 1990, John Berggruen Gallery, San Francisco, 1991, Pace Gallery, 1993, Galerie Karsten Greve, Cologne, Germany, 1993, Gallery Seomi, Seoul, 1994, 1996, Galerie Aronowitsch, Stockholm, 1995, Karsten Greve, Paris, 1995, Walker Art Ctr./Mpls. Sculpture Garden, 1995, Nelson-Atkins Mus. Art/Kansas City Sculpture Park, 1996, Pace Wildenstein Gallery, NY, 1995, 1996, 1998, 2001, 2002, 2003, 2005, Galerie Biedermann, Munich, Germany, 1997, Addison Gallery, Andover, Mass., 1997, Haus der Kunst, Munich, 1997, Barlach Halle K, Hamburg, 1998, Galerie Jamileh Weber, Zurich, Switzerland, 1997, Pace Wildenstein, LA, 1999, Am. Acad. in Rome, 1999, Boston Mus. Fine Arts, 1999, New Art Ctr., Salisbury, Eng., 1999, Yorkshire Sculpture Park, Wakefield, Eng., 1999—2000, Nat. Gallery Can., 1999—2000, John Berggruen Gallery, San Francisco, 2000, Timothy Taylor Gallery, London, 2000, Spoleto Festival USA, Charleston, SC, 2000, McNay Art Mus., San Antonio, 2000—01, Denver Art Mus., 2001, Galerie Daniel Templon, Paris, 2001, 2004, Met. Mus. Art, NY, 2001, Gerald B. Cantor Rooftop Galleries, 2001, L.A. Louver Gallery, 2004, Musee d'Orsay, Paris, 2005, numerous group exhibits, Represented in permanent collections Mus. Modern Art, NYC, Whitney Mus. Art, Walker Art Ctr., Mpls., Met. Mus. Art, NYC, Albright Knox Art Gallery, Buffalo, Detroit Inst. Art, Stedelijk Mus., Amsterdam, Moderna Museet, Stockholm, Dallas Mus. Art, Centre Pompidou, Paris, Nat. Gallery Art, Washington, Brit. Mus., London, Bklyn. Mus., Cocoran Gallery, Washington, Fogg Art Mus. at Harvard U., Cambridge, Mass., High Mus. Art, Atlanta, Hirshhorn Mus. and Sculpture Garden at Smithsonian Instn., Washington, Israel Mus., Jerusalem, Kunsthaus Zürich, Switzerland, Mus. Contemporary Art, LA, Mus. Fine Arts, Boston, Mus. Modern Art, Friuli, Italy, Parrish Art Mus., Southampton, NY, Phila. Mus. Art, Tate Gallery, London, Cleve. Mus. Art, NC Mus. Art, Raleigh, Des Moines Art Ctr., commns. include, Cigna Corp., Phila., 1983—84, Fukuoka (Japan) Sogo Bank, 1988, Creative Artists Agy., LA, 1988—89, Kawamura Meml. Mus. Art, Chiba, Japan, 1988—89, Govt. Svc. Adminstrn., LA, 1988—90, Hood Mus. Art at Dartmouth Coll., Hanover, N.H., 1989—90, U.S. Holocaust Meml. Mus., Washington, 1993, Sony Music Entertainment, NYC, 1994—95, Friedrichstadt Passagen, Berlin, 1994—95, Kansas City (Mo.) Internat. Airport, 1995—96, Embassy of U.S.A., Ottawa, 1999, Koln Skulpture Park, 1999, The Principal Riverwalk, Des Moines, 2005. Recipient Nat. Endowment for Arts award, 1975, Brandeis award, 1984, Skowhegan medal, 1986. Mem. Am. Acad. and Inst. Arts and Letters (merit award 1990), Am. Acad. Arts and Letters, Swedish Royal Acad. Art. Office: care Pace Idenstein 32 E 57th St New York NY 10022-2513

**SHAPIRO, JUDITH R.,** academic administrator, anthropology educator; b. NYC, Jan. 24, 1942; Student, Ecole des Haute Etudes Inst. d'Etudes Politiques, Paris, 1961—62; BA, Brandeis U., 1963; PhD, Columbia U., 1972. Asst. prof. U. Chgo., 1970—75; fellow U. Calif., Berkeley, 1974—75; Rosalyn R. Schwartz lectr., asst. prof. anthropology Bryn Mawr Coll., Pa., 1975—78, assoc. prof. Pa., 1978—85, prof. Pa., 1985—94; pres. Barnard Coll., 1994—. Chmn. dept. Bryn Mawr Coll., 1982—85, acting dean undergrad coll., 1985—86, provost, 1986—94; bd. dir. Fund for City of NY; ptnr. NYC Partnership and C. of C.; exec. com. NY Bldg. Congress. Contbr. articles to profl. jours. Nat. adv. com. Woodrow Wilson Nat. Fellowship Found.; chair bd. dirs. Consortium on Financing Higher Edn.; bd. dirs. Fund for the City of N.Y.; chair bd. dirs. Women's Coll. Coalition. Recipient Gold Medal, Nat. Inst. of Social Sciences, 2002; fellow, Woodrow Wilson Found., 1963—64, Columbia U., 1964—65, Younger Humanist fellow, NEH, 1974—75, Am. Coun. Learned Socs., 1981—82, Ctr. for Advanced Study in the Behavioral Scis., 1989; grantee Summer Field Tng. grant, NSF, 1965, Ford Found., 1966, NIMH, 1974—75, Social Sci. Rsch. Coun., 1974—75. Mem.: NY State Leadership Coun. (devel. of World's Mus., NYC), Am.

Philos. Soc., Social Sci. Rsch. Coun. (com. social sci personnel 1977—80), Am. Anthrop. Assn. (ethics com. 1976—79, bd. dirs. 1984—86, exec. com. 1985—86), Am. Ethnol. Soc. (nominations com. 1983—84, pres. elect 1984—85, pres. 1985—86), Phila. Anthrop. Soc. (pres. 1983), Morningside Area Alliance (pres. 2003—04), adv. com, Save the Children, Women's Forum, Sigma Xi, Phi Beta Kappa. Office: Barnard Coll Office of Pres 109 Milbank Hall New York NY 10027 Office Phone: 212-854-2021.*

**SHAPIRO, KEITH J.,** lawyer; b. Chgo., Nov. 14, 1958; BS, Univ. Ill., 1980; JD, Emory Univ., 1983. Bar: Ill. 1983. Former chmn., pres. Am. Bankruptcy Inst.; co-mng. shareholder, co-chair nat. reorganization, bankruptcy and restructuring practice Greenberg Traurig LLP, Chgo. Fellow: Am. Coll. Bankruptcy; mem.: Am. Bankruptcy Bd. of Certification (founder, first chmn. 1992—95), R3, London, Chgo. Bar Assn. (chair, bankruptcy and reorganization com. 1999—2000), Am. Bankruptcy Inst. (pres. 2000—01, chmn.bd. 2002—03). Office: Greenberg Traurig Ste 2500 77 W Wacker Dr Chicago IL 60601 Office Phone: 312-456-8405. Office Fax: 312-456-8435. Business E-Mail: shapirok@gtlaw.com.

**SHAPIRO, KENNETH N.,** neurosurgeon; b. Bklyn., Aug. 7, 1943; Degree in politics, Princeton U., 1965; MD, U. Pitts., 1970. Diplomate Am. Bd. Neurol. Surgery, Am. Bd. Pediat. Neurol. Surgery. Intern Montefiore Hosp. Med. Ctr., Bronx, NY, 1970—71, resident in neurol. surgery, 1971—72, Albert Einstein U. Hosp., NY, 1972—74, 1977—78, fellow in neurol. surgery, 1974—76; registrar Hosp. for Sick Children, Gt. Ormond St., London; dir. pediat. neurosurgery Albert Einstein Coll. Medicine, 1978—86; founder Neurosurgeons for Children, Dallas, 1985—; attending neurosurgeon Children's Med. Ctr., Dallas, 1987—, med. dir. pediat. neurooncology program, 1991—; attending neurosurgeon Med. City Dallas Hosp., 1987—, Parkland Meml. Hosp., 1987—. Consulting neurosurgeon Tex. Scottish Rite Hosp. for Children, 1987—; asst. prof. pediat. Albert Einstein Coll. Medicine, 1978—83, assoc. prof. neurol. surgery, 1983—87, assoc. prof. pediat., 1984—87; clin. assoc. prof. U. Tex. Southwestern Med. Sch., Dallas, 1987—; presenter in field. Editor: (books) Pediatric Head Trauma, 1983, Hydrocephalus, 1984; editor Pediat. Neurosurgery jour. Office: Children's Med Ctr - Neurosurgery 1935 Motor St Dallas TX 75235

**SHAPIRO, LARRY J.,** pediatrician, educator, scientist, dean; b. July 6, 1946; s. Philip and Phyllis Shapiro; m. Carol-Ann Uetake; children: Jennifer, Jessica, Brian. AB, Washington U., St. Louis, 1968, MD, 1971. Diplomate Am. Bd. Pediat., Am. Bd. Med. Examiners, Am. Bd. Med. Genetics. Intern St. Louis Children's Hosp., 1971—72, resident, 1971—73; rsch. assoc. NIH, Bethesda, Md., 1973—75; asst. prof. Sch. Medicine UCLA, 1975—79, assoc. prof., 1979—83, prof. pediat. and biol. chemistry, 1983—91; investigator Howard Hughes Med. Inst., 1987—91, investigator, W.H. and Marie Wattis Disting. prof.; prof., chmn. dept. pediat. U. Calif.-San Francisco Sch. Medicine, 1991—2003; chief pediat. svcs. U. Calif.-San Francisco Med. Ctr., 1991—2003; Spencer T. and Ann W. Olin Disting. prof., exec. vice chancellor for med. affairs, dean Washington U. Sch. Medicine, St. Louis, 2003—. Contbr. numerous articles to profl. publs. Served to lt. comdr. USPHS, 1973—75. Fellow: AAAS, Am. Acad. Pediat. (E. Mead Johnson award in rsch. 1982); mem.: Am. Acad. Arts and Scis., Am. Pediatric Soc. (coun. mem. 1999—2001, pres. 2003—04), Soc. Clin. Investigation, Am. Soc. Human Genetics (coun. 1985—88, pres.-elect 1995, pres. 1997), Assn. Am. Physicians, Soc. for Inherited Metabolic Disease (coun. 1983—88, pres. 1986—87), Western Soc. for Pediatric Rsch. (coun. 1983—87, pres. 1989—90, Ross award in rsch. 1981), Soc. Pediatric Rsch. (coun. 1984—87, pres. 1991—92), Inst. Medicine of NAS. Office: Wash U 660 S Euclid campus box 8106 Saint Louis MO 63110

**SHAPIRO, LELAND,** epidemiologist, educator; b. Memphis, Tenn., June 26, 1958; s. Norman Shapiro and Ruth Kramer. MD, U. Mass., Worcester, Mass., 1986. Diplomate in internal medicine Bd. Med. Examiners, 1989. Assoc. prof. medicine Health Scis. Ctr. U. Colo., Denver, 1996—; staff physician Denver Vets. Affairs Med. Ctr., Denver, 1999—2006. Recipient Clin. Tchg. award, Moses H. Cone Meml. Hosp., 1990, Maxwell Finland Rsch. Excellence award, Tufts-New Eng. Med. Ctr., 1994, Young Investigator award, Internat. Cytokine Soc., 1996, Clin. Tchg. award, U. Colo. Infectious Diseases Divsn., 1997. Fellow: ACP; mem.: AMA, Com. Sci. Investigation Claims of Paranormal, Counsel Sci. Medicine, Infectious Diseases Soc. Am. Libertarian. Jewish. Achievements include research in novel therapies for HIV infection, viral and bacterial infections. Avocations: speed skating, ping pong/table tennis, comic books, trivia. Home: 3070 Ash Street Denver CO 80207 Office: University of Colorado 4200 East 9th Avenue Denver CO 80220 Office Phone: 303-315-7233. Office Fax: 303-315-8681. Business E-Mail: leland.shapiro@uchsc.edu.

**SHAPIRO, LEO J.,** social researcher; b. N.Y.C., July 8, 1921; m. Virginia L. Johnson, Feb. 9, 1952; children: David, Erik, Owen, Amy. BA, U. Chgo., 1942, PhD, 1952. Survey specialist Fed. Govt. Agy., Washington, 1941-45, Sci. Rsch. Assn., Chgo., 1948-52; prin., founder Leo J. Shapiro and Assocs., Chgo., 1952-91; pres. Greenhouse, Inc., 1991—2001, SAGE LLC Survival & Growth Enterprise, Chgo., 2002—. Bd. dirs. Field of Flowers. Fellow U. Chgo., 1949. Fellow Social Sci. Rsch. Coun.; mem. Am. Sociol. Assn., Phi Beta Kappa.

**SHAPIRO, LUCY,** molecular biology educator; b. NYC, July 16, 1940; d. Philip and Yetta (Stein) Cohen; m. Roy Shapiro, Jan. 23, 1960 (div. 1977); 1 child, Peter; m. Harley H. McAdams, Aug. 28, 1978; stepchildren: Paul, Heather. BA, Bklyn. Coll., 1962; PhD, Albert Einstein Coll. Medicine, 1966. Asst. prof. Albert Einstein Coll. Medicine, N.Y.C., 1967-72, assoc. prof., 1972-77, Kramer prof., chmn. dept. molecular biology, 1977-86, dir. biol. scis. divsn., 1981-86; Eugene Higgins prof., chmn. dept. microbiology, Coll. Physicians and Surgeons Columbia U., N.Y.C., 1986-89; Joseph D. Grant prof. devel. biology Stanford (Calif.) U. Sch. Medicine, 1989-97, chmn. dept. devel. biology, 1989-97, Virginia and D.K. Ludwig prof. cancer rsch., dept. devel. biology, 1998—; dir. Beckman Ctr. Molecular and Genetic Medicine, Stanford U., 2001—. Mem. bd. sci. counselors NIH, Washington 1980—84; mem. bd. sci. advisors G.D. Searle Co., Skokie, Ill., 1984—86; trustee Scientists Inst. for Pub. Info., 1990—94; mem. sci. adv. bd. SmithKline Beecham, 1993—2000, Anacor Pharms., Inc., 2001—, PathoGenesis, 1995—2000, Ludwig Found., 2000—, Glaxo Smith Kline, 2001—; mem. adv. bd. Biodesign Inst., Ariz. State U., 2006—, Singapore Inst. Molecular and Cell Biology, 2006—, Lawrence Berkeley Nat. Labs., 2006—; bd. dirs. Anacor Pharms. Inc. Editor: Microbiol. Devel., 1984; mem. editl. bd. Jour. Bacteriology, 1978-86, Trends in Genetics, 1987—, Genes and Development, 1987-91, Cell Regulation, 1990-92, Molecular Biology of the Cell, 1992-98, Molecular Microbiology, 1991-96, Current Opinion on Genetics and Devel., 1991—; contbr. articles to profl. jours. Mem. sci. bd. Helen Hay Witney Found., N.Y.C., 1986-94, Biozentrum, Basel, 1999-2001, Hutchinson Cancer Ctr., Seattle, 1999; mem. grants adv. bd. Beckman Found., 1999—; co-chmn. adv. bd. NSF Biology Directorate, 1988-89; vis. com., bd. overseers Harvard U., Cambridge, Mass., 1987-90, 2003—; mem. sci. bd. Whitehead Inst., MIT, Boston, 1988-93; mem. sci. rev. bd. Howard Hughes Med. Inst., 1990-94, Cancer Ctr. of Mass. Gen. Hosp., Boston, 1994; mem. Presidio Coun. City of San Francisco, 1991-94; mem. press. coun. U. Calif., 1991-97. Recipient Hirschl Career Scientist award, 1976, Spirit of Achievement award, 1978, Alumna award of honor Bklyn. Coll., 1983, Excellence in Sci. award Fedn. Am. Soc. Exptl. Biology, 1994; Jane Coffin Child fellow, 1966; resident scholar Rockefeller Found., Bellagio, Italy, 1996. Fellow AAAS, Am. Acad. Arts and Scis., Am. Acad. Microbiology, Calif. Coun. on Sci. and Tech.; mem. NAS (Selman A. Waksman award 2005), Inst. Medicine of NAS, Am. Philos. Soc., Am. Soc. Biochemistry and Molecular Biology (nominating com. 1982, 87, coun. 1990-93), Am. Heart Assn. (sci. adv. bd. 1984-87). Avocation: watercolor painting. Office: Stanford U Sch Medicine Beckman Ctr Dept Devel Biology Stanford CA 94305 Office Phone: 650-725-7678.*

**SHAPIRO, MARC S.,** lawyer; b. NYC, Oct. 12, 1960; BA, NYU, 1980; JD, Syracuse U., 1983. Bar: NY 1984, NJ 1987. Ptnr. Real Estate Department Katten Muchin Rosenman LLP, NYC.

**SHAPIRO, MARK HOWARD,** physicist, educator, dean; b. Boston, Apr. 18, 1940; s. Louis and Sara Ann (Diamond) S.; m. Anita Rae Lavine, June 8, 1961; children: David Gregory, Diane Elaine, Lisa Michelle. AB with honors, U. Calif., Berkeley, 1962; MS (NSF coop. fellow), U. Pa., 1963, PhD, 1966. Research fellow Kellogg Radiation Lab., Calif. Inst. Tech., Pasadena, 1966-68; vis. assoc. divsn. math., physics and astronomy Calif. Inst. Tech., 1976—; research assoc. Nuclear Structure Research Lab. U. Rochester (N.Y.), 1968-70; mem. faculty Calif. State U., Fullerton, 1970—2002, prof. physics, 1978—2002, acting assoc. dean Sch. Math., Sci. and Engring., 1985-86, acting dir. Office Faculty Research and Devel., 1986-87, chmn. physics dept., 1989-96, 98-01, prof. physics emeritus, 2002—; dir. tchr. enhancement program NSF, Washington, 1987-88. Tour speaker Am. Chem. Soc., 1983-85 Editor, publisher: The Irascible Professor, 1999; contbr. over 125 articles to profl. jours. Pres. Pasadena Young Democrats, 1967-68; mem. pub. info. and edn. com. Calif. Task Force on Earthquake Preparedness, 1981-85; bd. dirs. Calif. State U. Fullerton Found., 1982-85. Grantee Research Corp., 1971-74, Calif. Inst. Tech., 1977-78, U.S. Geol. Survey, 1998-85, Digital Equipment Corp., 1982, NSF, 1985-87, 90—. Mem. AAAS, Am. Phys. Soc., Am. Assn. Physics Tchrs. (profl. concerns com. 1990-93, chmn. 1991-93), Materials Rsch. Soc., Coun. on Undergrad. Rsch. (physics/astronomy councillor 1993—). Achievements include research in experimental nuclear physics, experimental nuclear astrophysics, geophysics and atomic collisions in solids. Office: Calif State Univ Physics Dept Fullerton CA 92834-6866 Business E-Mail: mshapiro2@adelphia.net.

**SHAPIRO, MARTIN,** law educator; b. 1933; BA, UCLA, 1955; PhD, Harvard U., 1961. Instr. polit. sci. Harvard U., Cambridge, Mass., 1960-62, prof., 1971-74; asst. prof. Stanford U., Calif., 1962-65; assoc. prof. U. Calif., Irvine, 1965-70, prof. Berkeley, 1970, prof. law, 1977—, prof. San Diego, 1974-77. Author: Law and Politics in the Supreme Court, 1964, Freedom of Speech, The Supreme Court and Judicial Review, 1966, Supreme Court and Administrative Agencies, 1968, Courts, 1981, Who Guards the Guardians, 1987, Law, Politics and Judicialization, 2002. Mem. Law and Soc. Assn. (trustee 1992-95), Western Polit. Sci. Assn. (pres. 1978), Am. Acad. Arts and Scis., Am. Polit. Sci. Assn. (v.p. 1988). Office: U Calif Law Sch 886 Simon Hl Berkeley CA 94720-0001 Office Phone: 510-642-7190.

**SHAPIRO, MARVIN LINCOLN,** communications company executive; b. Erie, Pa., Feb. 12, 1923; s. Hyman and Flora (Burstein) S.; m. B. Gertrude Berkman, Oct. 25, 1946; children: Susan Jo, Barbara Ann, Jonathan David. BS, Syracuse U., 1948; postgrad., Williams Coll., 1966, Columbia U., 1975. Account exec. WSYR, Syracuse, 1948-50; account exec. sta. WCAU-TV, Phila., 1950-55, nat. sales mgr., 1956-58; account exec. CBS TV Spot Sales, Chgo., 1955-56, N.Y.C., 1958-60; with TV Advt. Reps., Inc., N.Y.C., 1961-66, exec. v.p., 1965-66, pres., 1968-69, dir., vice chmn., 1969-77, chmn., 1978; pres. Radio Advt. Reps., Inc., N.Y.C., 1966-68, dir., vice chmn., 1969-77; exec. v.p., COO, pres. sta. group Westinghouse Broadcasting Co., Inc., N.Y.C., 1969-77, sr. v.p., 1978-83, also dir., 1969-83; pres., dir. Foxwood Comm. Inc., N.Y.C., 1983—; mng. dir. Veronis Suhler Stevenson, N.Y.C., 1983—; pres., dir. Farragut Comm., Inc., N.Y.C., 1992-99, Columbia Empire Broadcasting Corp., Yakima, Wash., 1992-96. Bd. dirs. Broadcasting Ptnrs. Holdings, L.P., 1996-2000, VS&A Spectrum, Inc., 1997-2000; chmn. bd. Micro-Relay, Inc., 1974-83; chmn. bd. dirs., pres. CATV Enterprises, Inc., 1970-83. Boxing official Pa. Athletic Commn., 1952-55; Bd. dirs. TV Bur. Advt., 1974-81, chmn., 1977-79; bd. dirs. Radio Advt. Bur., 1970-77; With USAAF, 1942-45. Decorated Air medal with 9 oak leaf clusters.; recipient Communications Alumni award Syracuse U., 1960 Mem. Internat. Radio and TV Soc., DAV, Alpha Epsilon Rho (hon.). Clubs: Long Ridge (Stamford). Home: 26 Foxwood Rd Stamford CT 06903-2207 Office: Veronis Suhler Stevenson 350 Park Ave New York NY 10022-6022

**SHAPIRO, MATTHEW DAVID,** economist, educator; b. Mpls., Apr. 11, 1958; s. Irving and Janet (Reinstein) S.; m. Susan L. Garetz, Oct. 21, 1989; children: Benjamin Avigdor, Molly Kendall. BA summa cum laude, Yale U., 1979, MA, 1979; PhD, MIT, 1984. Jr. staff economist Coun. Econ. Advisers, Washington, 1979-80, sr. economist, 1993-94; asst. prof. Yale U., New Haven, 1984-89; assoc. prof. U. Mich., Ann Arbor, 1989-95, prof., 1995—, L.R. Klein Collegiate prof., 2004—, sr. rsch. scientist, 2000—, chair, 2003—. Rschr. Nat. Bur. Econ. Rsch., Cambridge, Mass., 1986—; mem. acad. adv. coun. Fed. Res. Bank Chgo., 1995-; mem. com. on nat. stats. NAS, 1999-2002; mem. Fed. Econ. Stats. Adv. Com., 2000—, chmn., 2006—. Bd. editors Am. Econ. Rev., 1993-96, 2000-02, co-editor, 1997-2002; contbr. articles to profl. jours. Recipient Paul A. Samuelson Cert. of Excellence, TIAA-CREF, 1997; Olin fellow Nat. Bur. Econ. Rsch., Cambridge, 1986-87, Alfred P. Sloan fellow Sloan Found., 1991-93. Mem. Am. Econ. Assn., Econometric Soc., Phi Beta Kappa. Office: U Mich Dept Econs 611 Tappan Ave Ann Arbor MI 48109-1220

**SHAPIRO, MAURICE MANDEL,** nuclear astrophysicist; b. Jerusalem, Nov. 13, 1915; came to U.S., 1921; s. Asher and Miriam R. (Grunbaum) S.; m. Inez Weinfield, Feb. 8, 1942 (dec. Oct. 1964); children: Joel Nevin, Elana Shapiro Ashley Naktin, Raquel Tamar Shapiro Kislinger; m. Ruth Auslander, Nov. 30, 2002. BS, U. Chgo., 1936, MS, 1940, PhD, 1942. Instr. physics and math. Chgo. City Colls., 1937-41; chmn. dept. phys. and biol. scis. Austin Coll., 1938-41; instr. math. Gary Coll., 1942; physicist Dept. Navy, 1942-44; lectr. physics and math. George Washington U., 1943-44; group leader, mem. coordinating council of lab. Los Alamos Sci. Lab., U. Calif., 1944-46; sr. physicist, lectr. nucleonics tng. sch. Oak Ridge Nat. Lab., Union Carbon and Carbide Corp., 1946-49. Cons. div. nuc. energy for propulsion aircraft Fairchild Engine & Aircraft Corp., 1948-49; head cosmic ray br. nucleonics div. U.S. Naval Research Lab., Washington, 1949-65, supt. nucleonics div., 1953-65, founder, chief scientist Lab for Cosmic Physics, 1949-82, apptd. to chair of cosmic ray physics, 1966-82, chief scientist emeritus, 1982—; lectr. U. Md., 1949-50, 1952—, assoc. prof., 1950-51, vis. prof. physics and astronomy, 1986—; vis. prof. physics and astronomy U. Iowa, 1981-84; vis. prof. astrophysics U. Bonn, 1982-84; vis. scientist Max Planck Inst. für Astrophysik, W. Ger., 1984-85; cons. Argonne Nat. Lab., 1949; cons. panel on cosmic rays U.S. nat. com. IGY; lectr. physics and engring. Nuclear Products-Erco div. ACF Industries, Inc., 1956-58; lectr. E. Fermi Internat. Sch. Physics, Varenna, Italy, 1962; vis. prof. Weizmann Inst. Sci., Rehovoth, Israel, 1962-63, Inst. Math. Scis., Madras, India, 1971; Inst. Astronomy and Geophysics Nat. U. Mex., 1976; vis. prof. physics and astronomy Northwestern U., Evanston, Ill., 1978, exec. dir. Astrophysics Assoc. 1995—; cons. space rsch. in astronomy Space Sci. Bd., Nat. Acad. Scis., 1965; cons. Office Space Scis., NASA, 1965-66, 89; prin investigator Gemini S-9 Cosmic Ray Expts., NASA, 1964-69, Skylab, 1967-76, Long Duration Exposure Facility, 1977—; mem. Groupe de Travail de Biologie Spatiale, Council of Europe, 1970—; mem. steering com. DUMAND Consortium, 1976—; mem. exec. com., 1979-82, mem. sci. adv. com., 1982—; lectr. Summer Space Inst., Deutsche Physikalische Gesellschaft, 1972; founder, dir. Internat. Sch. Cosmic-Ray Astrophysics, Ettore Majorana Centre Sci. Culture, Erice, Italy, 1977—; chmn. U.S. IGY com. on interdisciplinary research, mem. nuclear emulsion panel space sci. bd.; Nat. Acad. Scis., 1959—; chief U.S. rep., steering com. Internat. Coop. Emulsion Flights Cosmic Ray Rsch.; cons. CREI Atomics, 1959—; vis. com. Bartol Rsch. Found., Franklin Inst., 1967-74; mem. U.S. organizing com. 13th and 19th Internat. Confs. on Cosmic Rays; mem. sci. adv. com. Internat. Confs. on Nuclear Photography and Solid State Detectors, 1966—; mem. Com. of Honor for Einstein Centennial, Acad. Naz. Lincei, 1977; mem. Internat. Organizing com. Tex. Symposia on Relativistic Astrophysics, 1976—; Regents lectr. U. Calif. Riverside, 1985; Edison lectr. Naval Rsch. Lab award, 1990; plenary lectr. Oppenheimer Centennial, Gamow Centennial, 2004. Mem. editorial bd. Astrophysics and Space Sci., 1968-75; assoc. editor: Phys. Rev. Letters, 1977-84; editor (NATO) ASI Series on Cosmic-Ray Astrophysics; contbr. to Am. Inst. Handbook of Physics, various encys. Mem. exec. bd. Cong. Beth Chai, Washington 1987—; trustee Nat. Capital Astronomers, Washington, 1989—; mem. internat. panel Chernobyl World Lab., 1988. Recipient Disting. Civilian Svc. award Dept. Navy, 1967, medal of honor Soc. for Encouragement au Progrés, 1978, Sr. U.S. Scientist award Alexander von Humboldt Found., 1982, Profl. Achievement citation U. Chgo., 1992; Guggenheim fellow, 1962-63. Fellow Am. Phys. Soc. (chmn. organizing com. div. cosmic physics, chmn. 1971-72, com. on publs. 1977-79), AAAS, Washington Acad. Scis. (past com. chmn., Disting. Career in Scis. award, 1993); mem. Am. Astron. Soc. (exec. com. div. high-energy astrophysics 1978—, chmn., 1982), Philos. Soc. Washington (past pres.), Am. Technion Soc. (Washington bd.), Alexander von Humboldt Assn. of Am. (pres. Washington area chpt. 2000—), Assn. Los Alamos Scientists (past chmn.), Assn. Oak Ridge Engrs. and Scientists (past chmn.), Fedn. Am. Scientists (past mem. exec. com., nat. council), Internat. Astron. Union (organizing com. commn. on high-energy astrophysics), Internat. Conf. on Cosmic Rays (Victor Hess Meml. lectr., Rome, 1995), Phi Beta Kappa, Sigma Xi (Edison lectr. 1990). Clubs: Cosmos (Washington). Achievements include patents in field; discovery of first definitive evidence for production of cosmic ray secondaries in the interstellar medium; first determination of the source composition of cosmic rays; prediction of isotopic composition of "arriving" cosmic rays, co-discovery of the sigma hyperon; research in cosmic radiation, composition, origin, propagation, and nuclear transformations, high-energy astrophysics, particles and fields, nuclear physics, neutron physics and fission reactors, hydrodynamics and piezoelectricity, gamma-ray and neutrino astronomy; design of a low-enrichment nuclear reactor for submarines used at Shippingport and in various naval ships; identification of the fissile fuel in the first Soviet atomic explosion as plutonium. Address: 5809 Nicholson Ln # 801 Rockville MD 20852 Personal E-mail: mmshapiro@mailaps.org. *In scientific achievement, good judgement (e.g., in choice of research problems)is sometimes more important than brilliance.*

**SHAPIRO, MEL,** playwright, educator, theater director; b. Bklyn., Dec. 16, 1935; s. Benjamin Shapiro and Lillian (Lazarus) Bestul; m. Jeanne Elizabeth Shapiro, Feb. 23, 1963; children: Joshua, Benjamin. BFA, MFA, Carnegie-Mellon U., 1961. Resident dir. Arena Stage, Washington, 1963-65; producing dir. Tyrone Guthrie Theater, Mpls., 1968-70; master tchr. drama NYU, N.Y.C., 1970-80; guest dir. Lincoln Ctr. Repertory, N.Y.C., 1970; dir. N.Y. Shakespeare Festival, N.Y.C., 1971-77; prof. Carnegie Mellon U., Pitts., 1980-90, head. dept., 1980-87. Disting. prof. theater UCLA Sch. Theater, Film and TV, 1990—. Dir. N.Y.C. prodns. The House of Blue Leaves, 1970, Bosoms and Neglect, 1978, Marco Polo Sings a Solo, 1998, Taming of the Shrew, 1999, Big Love (L.A.), 2002; co-adaptor mus. Two Gentlemen of Verona, 1971 (Tony award); author: (plays) The Price of Admissions, 1984 (Drama-Logue mag. award), The Lay of the Land (Joseph Kesselring award 1990), A Life of Crime, 1993; (books) An Actor Performs, 1996, The Director's Companion, 1998. With U.S. Army, 1955-57. Recipient N.Y. Drama Critics award, 1971, 72, Obie award Village Voice, 1972, Drama Desk award, 1973, Drama-logue award, 1993. Mem. Soc. Stage Dirs. and Choreographers (founder, editor The Jour. 1978). Office: UCLA Sch Theatre Film & TV 405 Hilgard Ave Los Angeles CA 90095-9000 Business E-Mail: mshapiro@ucla.edu.

**SHAPIRO, MERYL,** lawyer; d. Robert M. and Thelma Shapiro. JD, NY Law Sch., 1978. Atty. Guggenheimer & Untermyer, NYC, 1978—79, Law Offices of Henry R. Simon, NYC, 1979—81, Toberoff & Tessler, NYC, 1981—86, Katz, Katz & Brand, NYC, 1986—87, Law Offices of Henry R. Simon, White Plains, NY, 1988—91, Wiesen, Gurfein & Jenkins, NYC, 1991—93, Weinstein, Chase, Messinger & Peters, P.C., Bklyn., 1995—2005; founder Meryl Shapiro, Atty.-at-Law, NYC, 2005—. Supporter Sylvia Rivera LAw Project, NYC, Soka U. of Am., Aliso Viejo, Calif.; com. mem. Dem. Party County Com., 74th Asssembly Dist., NYC; NE zone legal divsn. chair, women's divsn. chpt. leader Soka Gakkai Internat.-USA, NYC. Mem.: Nat. Lesbian and Gay Law Assn., Bars of the So. and Ea. Dists. of NY, NY State Trial Lawyers' Assn., NY State Bar Assn. (com. on women in the law 2006—), Assn. of Bar of City of NY (civil rights com. 2001—03). Buddhist. Office: Meryl Shapiro Atty at Law Ste 7F 305 East 24th St New York NY 10010 Office Phone: 212-213-9252. Business E-Mail: mshapiro@merylshapiro.com.

**SHAPIRO, MICHAEL EDWARD,** museum director; b. NYC, Nov. 15, 1949; s. Edward Aaron and Sylvia (Fishman) S.; m. Elizabeth Harvey, 1977; 2 children. BA, Hamilton Coll., 1972; MA, Williams Coll., 1976, Harvard U., 1978, PhD, 1980. Asst. prof. dept. art history Duke U., Durham, NC, 1980-84; curator 19th-20th century art St. Louis Art Mus., 1984-92, chief curator, 1987-92; dir. Los Angeles County Mus. Art, 1992-93; dir. mus. programs, chief curator High Mus. Art, Atlanta, 1994-95, dep. dir., chief curator, 1996-99, dir., 2000—. Author: Bronze Casting and American Sculpture, 1985; contbg. author: Frederic Remington: The Masterworks, 1988, George Caleb Bingham, 1990; mng. curator, editor Rings: Five Passions in World Art, 1996; co-curator Impressionism: Paintings Collected by European Museums, 1998, mng. curator, 1999. Office: High Museum Art 1280 Peachtree St NE Atlanta GA 30309

**SHAPIRO, NEAL,** broadcast executive, television producer; s. Sumner and Mildred Shapiro; m. JuJu Chang, Dec. 2, 1995; 1 child. BA in History and Polit. Sci., Tufts U., 1980. With ABC News, 1980—93; spl. segment prodr. World News Tonight, 1986—89; broadcast prodr. PrimeTime Live, 1989—93; exec. prodr. NBC News, Dateline, NYC, 1993—2001; pres. NBC News, NYC, 2001—05. Recipient George Polk award, 1992, 2000, 2 Emmy awards, Investigate Reporter and Editor award. Office: NBC Universal 30 Rockefeller Plz New York NY 10112-0036

**SHAPIRO, NELLA IRENE,** surgeon, educator; b. NYC, Nov. 13, 1947; d. Eugene and Ethel (Pearl) Shapiro; m. Jack Schwartz, Oct. 16, 1977; children: Max Schwartz, Molly Schwartz. BA, Barnard Coll., 1968; MD, Albert Einstein Coll., 1972. Resident in gen. surgery Montefiore Hosp., NYC, 1972-76; mem. staff N. Ctrl. Hosp., Bronx, NY, 1976-77, Bronx Mcpl. Hosp., 1977-87 chief gen surgery 1983-87; mem staff gen surgery Albert Einstein Coll. Hosp., Bronx, 1977-93, chief gen. surgery, 1991-93; atty. Lear Surg. Assocs., 1993-94; pvt. practice Bronx, 1994—; dir. breast surgery Eastchester Ctr. Cancer Care, Bronx, 2004—. Asst. prof. surgery Albert Einstein Coll., Bronx, 1980—; assoc. clin. prof. surgery Weller Hosp., Bronx, 1991—93; co-founder Whaecom Breast Ctr., Bronx, 1991—. Fellow: ACS. Avocations: travel, opera. Office: Eastchester Ctr Cancer Care 2330 Eastchester Rd Bronx NY 10469 Office Phone: 718-405-0400, 718-732-4000.

**SHAPIRO, NORMA SONDRA LEVY,** federal judge; b. Phila., July 27, 1928; d. Bert and Jane (Kotkin) Levy; m. Bernard Shapiro, Aug. 21, 1949; children: Finley, Neil, Aaron. BA in Polit. Theory with honors, U. Mich., 1948; JD magna cum laude, U. Pa., 1951. Bar: Pa. 1951, U.S. Supreme Ct. 1978. Law clk. to presiding justice Pa. Supreme Ct., 1951-52; instr. U. Pa. Law Sch., 1951-52, 55-56; assoc. Dechert Price & Rhoads, Phila., 1956-58, 67-73, ptnr., 1973-78; judge U.S. Dist. Ct. 3rd circuit (ea. dist.) Pa., 1978—. Assoc. trustee U. Pa. Law Sch., 1978-93; former trustee Women's Law Project, Albert Einstein Med. Ctr.; v.p. Jewish Pub. Soc.; trustee Fedn. Jewish Agys., 1980-83; mem. lawyers adv. panel Pa. Gov.'s Commn. on Status of Women, 1974; legal adv. regional Coun. Child Psychiatry, bd. dirs. Women Judges' Fund for Justice. Guest editor: Shingle, 1972. Mem. Lower Merion County (Pa.) Bd. Sch. Dirs., 1968-77, pres., 1977, v.p., 1976; v.p. Jewish Community Relations Council of Greater Phila., 1975-77; chmn. legal affairs com., 1978; pres. Belmont Hills Home and Sch. Assn., Lower Merion Twp.; legis. chmn. Lower Merion Sch. Dist. Intersch. Council; mem. Task Force on Mental Health of Children and Youth of Pa.; treas., chmn. edn. com. Human Relations Council, Lower Merion; v.p., parliamentarian Nes Ami Penn Valley Congregation, Lower Merion Twp. Named Woman of Yr., Oxford Circle Jewish Community Center, 1979, Woman of Distinction, Golden Slipper Club, 1979; Gowen fellow, 1954-55; recipient Hannah G. Solomon award Nat. Coun. Jewish Women, 1992; Disting. daughter of Pa.; Liberty Bell award, Berks County Bar Assn. Mem. Am. Law Inst., Am. Bar Found., ABA (ho. dels. 1990-96, conn./chmn. conf. fed. judges 1986-87, chmn. jud. divsn. 1996-97, Margaret Brent Women Lawyers Achievement award 1999, bd. govs. 2003-), Pa. Bar Assn. (ho. of dels. 1979-81), Phila. Bar Assn. (chmn. women's rights 1972, 74-75, chmn. bd. govs. 1977-78, chmn. pub. rels. com. 1978, Sandra Day O'Connor award), Fed. Bar Assn. (Bill of Rights award 1991), Nat. Assn. Women Lawyers, Phila. Trial Lawyers Assn., Am. Judica-

ture Soc., Phila.; Nat. Assn. Women Judges (exec. comm. bd. dir.), Fellowship Commn., Order of Coif (chpt. pres. 1973-75), Tau Epsilon Rho. Office: US Dist Courthouse Independence Mall West 601 Market St Rm 10614 Philadelphia PA 19106-1714

**SHAPIRO, NORMAN RICHARD,** literature and language professor; b. Boston, Nov. 1, 1930; s. Harry Alexander and Eva (Goldberg) Shapiro. BA, Harvard U., 1951, MA, 1952, PhD, 1958; diplôme in French lang. and lit., U. d'Aix-Marseille, 1956, MA (hon.), Wesleyan U., 1972. Instr. French Amherst Coll., 1958-60; asst. prof. romance langs. and lits. Wesleyan U., Middletown, Conn., 1960-65, assoc. prof., 1965-71, prof., 1971—. Writer-in-residence Adams House, Harvard U., 2003—. Editor: Echos, 1965, Palabres, 1973; translator, editor: Négritude, 1971; translator: Four Farces (Georges Feydeau), 1970 (nominated for Nat. Book award), Comedy of Eros, 1971, Kamouraska (Anne Hébert), 1973, Virginie, or the Dawning of the World (Joseph Majault), 1974, The Camp of the Saints (Jean Raspall), 1975, Feydeau, First to Last, 1982, Fables from Old French: Aesop's Beasts and Bumpkins, 1983, A Fitting Confusion (Georges Feydeau), 1985, The Pregnant Pause, or Love's Labor Lost (Georges Feydeau), 1987, The Brazilian (Henry Melhac and Ludovic Halévy), 1987, A Slap in the Farce (Eugène Labiche), 1988, A Matter of Wife and Death (Eugène Labiche), 1988, Fifty Fables of La Fontaine, 1988, The Fabulists French: Verse Fables of Nine Centuries, 1992, La Fontaine's Bawdy: Of Liberties, Louts and Lechers, 1992, A Flea in Her Rear, or Ants in Her Pants, and Other Vintage French Farces, 1994, Fifty More Fables of La Fontaine, 1998, Selected Poems from Les Fleurs du Mal, 1998, One Hundred and One Poems of Paul Verlaine, 1999 (MLA Scaglione award), All Gall: Malicious Monologues and Ruthless Recitations, 1999, Once Again (La Fontaine), 2001, Take Her, She's Yours, or Till Divorce do Them Part (Georges Feydeau), 2001, The Jew of Seville (Victor Sèjour), 2002, The Fortune Teller (Victor Sèjour), 2002, Lyrics of the French Renaissance: Marot, Du Bellay and Ronsard, 2002, revised edit., 2006, Creole Echoes: Francophone Poetry of 19th Century Louisiana, 2003; composer: Three Songs, 1961; mem. editl. bd. Tex. Rev.; contbr. articles, transls. and revs. to profl. jours. Mem.: Acad. Am. Poets, Poetry Soc. Am., Beast Fable Soc. (mem. editl. bd. Bestia), Dramatist Guild, Am. Translators Assn., Am. Lit. Transl. Assn. (Disting. Transl. award 1992), Signet Soc. Harvard, Delta Kappa Epsilon. Jewish. Office: Wesleyan U Dept Romance Langs & Lit 300 High St Middletown CT 06459-3233 Office Phone: 860-685-3089. Business E-Mail: nshapiro@wesleyan.edu.

**SHAPIRO, RICHARD CHARLES,** publishing executive, sales executive, marketing professional; b. Bklyn., May 28, 1936; s. Isidore and Sylvia (Rappaport) Shapiro; m. Marilyn Joyce Baily, Feb. 17, 1957 (div. 1974); children: Joseph, Scott; m. Francine L. Shaw, Sept. 19, 1975. BS in Edn., Golden State U., 1978, MBA, 1981; PhD in Bus. Adminstrn. and Mktg., Honolulu U., 1987. Lic. real estate broker Ill. Sales mgr. Coca Cola Bottling Co. of N.Y., 1955-62; affiliate Effective Motivation Assocs./Success Motivation inst., Bethpage, N.Y., 1965-68; v.p. sales, dir. Field Enterprises, Chgo., 1962-78; pres., CEO Snack-In, Inc., Detroit, 1978-82; sr. ptnr. Directions Growth and Strategy Cons., Chgo., 1982-95; v.p. domestic & internat. mktg. & sales, oper. officer Ency. Brit.-Compton's Learning Co., 1991-93, specialist network mktg. & relationship mktg., CEO, pres., bd. dirs.; CEO Am.'s Home Detailing Corp., 1995—, CEO, chmn. bd., 2001—; pres., COO Am.'s Deep Clean Divsn., Deerfield, Ill., 1995—2000; CEO, chmn. emeritus Am.'s Home Detailing Corp., Deerfield, Ill.; instr. grad. studies mktg. mgmt., instr. human resources mgmt. Robert Morris Coll., Chgo., 2001—; owner, operator PennyPincherDepot.com, 2005—. Instr. planning Life Underwriter Tng. Coun., L.I., 1965—66; assoc. editor Media Technics Pub. Assn., Lake Forest, 1988; bd. dirs. Master Deep Clean Co., Nat. Video Libr.; spkr. on mktg., sales and leadership; cons. in field; liaison Chgo. Daily News, Chgo. Sun Times, Sta. WFLD-TV; founder Discovery Toy Divsn.; tennis pro, instr. Frank Sacks Tennis Camps, Chgo., 2001—; profl. tennis registry tennis instr., 2002—; asst. e-bay Auction Svcs., Deerfield, Ill., 2001—; continuing edn. instr. Gen. Contracting, Highland Pk., Ill., 2005—; founder Pennyincberdepot.com, 2005—. Pub.: Real Estate Property Marketing News; author: self-improvement cassettes; contbr. articles to profl. jours. Active Explorers, high schs., youth clubs, 1965—74; founder, pres. Abundance and Goodwill Soc., 1968—. With USAF, 1957—60. Named Sales/Mktg. Execs. Leadership Recruiter/Trainder of Decade award, Profl. Tennis Assocs. Singles champion, 1957, 1958, 1960; recipient Leadership award, Am. Sales Masters, 1968, 1999—2000, POPAI-OMA Best Industry Point of Purchase Display and Mktg. award, 1992. Mem.: Chgo. Computer Soc., Effective Motivation Assocs., Salesman with a Purpose, Deercreek Tennis Club (tchr., mem. rels. 2000—). Avocations: white-water rafting, canoeing, camping, tennis, writing. Office Phone: 847-459-3435. Personal E-mail: ahd10@yahoo.com, leadership_01@yahoo.com. E-mail: richard@pennyincberdepot.com, richard@tennis2win.com.

**SHAPIRO, RICHARD GERALD,** retail executive, consultant; b. NYC, Apr. 24, 1924; s. David and Sophie (Hayflich) S.; m. Lila Eig, July 27, 1951; children—Judith, Amy, Donald. BA, U. Mich., 1946; MBA, Harvard, 1948. With Lord & Taylor, N.Y.C., 1948-64, v.p., 1959-63, sr. v.p., 1963-64; also mem. adv. bd.; pres. Wm. Filene's Sons Co., Boston, 1965-68, chief exec. officer, chmn. bd., 1968-73; pres. Gimbel Bros. Corp., N.Y.C., 1973-76; v.p. W.R. Grace & Co., pres. sporting goods div., 1977-79, pres. splty. store div., 1979-84; pres. Richard Shapiro Assocs., 1979—; sr. v.p. Montgomery Ward, Inc., 1986-88. Bd. dirs. Assoc. Merchandising Corp., Nitrotec Corp., Capital Market Fund; retail chmn. Greater N.Y. Fund, 1963; chmn. merc. div. Mass. Bay United Fund, 1967 Mem. corp. Simmons Coll., Boston Mus. Fine Arts (permanent); bd. dirs. Mass. Mchts.; bd. dirs Family Counseling and Guidance Centers, 1969-72, v.p., 1970; trustee Brandeis U. fist vol with AUR 1942-46. Mem.: Harvard Bus. Sch. Assn. (gov.). Home: 10019 Gable Manor Ct Potomac MD 20854-5000 Office Phone: 301-299-3545. Personal E-mail: rgsle@webtv.net.

**SHAPIRO, RICHARD STANLEY,** physician; b. Moline, Ill., June 11, 1925; s. Herbert and Esther Dian (Grant) S.; m. Arlene Blum, June 12, 1949; children: Michele Pamela, Bruce Grant, Gary Lawrence; m. Mary Lou Coook, Oct. 11, 1971. BS in Pharmacy, U. Iowa, 1951, MS in Preventive Medicine & Environ., 1951, MD, 1957. Diplomate Am. Bd. Allergy and Immunology. Pharmacist, Rock Island, Ill., 1951-53; rsch. asst. U. Iowa Coll. Medicine, Iowa City, 1950-51, 53-57; practice medicine specializing in allergy Beverly Hills, Calif., 1958-62, Lynwood, Calif., 1962—. Attending physician Good Hope Found. Allergy Clinic, Los Angeles, 1958-62, Cedars of Lebanon Hosp., Hollywood, Calif., 1959-68, U. So. Calif.-Los Angeles County Med. Center, 1962—; physician St. Francis Hosp., Lynwood, 1962—; assoc. clin. prof. medicine U. So. Calif., 1978-84, emeritus, 1984—. Contbr. articles to profl. jours.; bd. dirs. Westside Mental Hlth. Ctr., 1961—65, Camp JCA, 1964—65. With USNR, 1943—46. Fellow Am. Geriatric Soc., Am. Coll. Allergy, Am. Assn. Clin. Immunology & Allergy; mem. AMA, AAAS, Am. Soc. Tropical Medicine and Hygiene, Am. Acad. Allergy, Am. Soc. Internal Medicine, Am. Heart Assn., West Coast Allergy Soc., Calif. Med. Assn., Calif. Soc. Internal Medicine, Calif. Soc. Allergy, L.A. County Med. Assn., L.A. Allergy Soc., Sierra Club, B'nai B'rith, Masons, Sigma Xi. Jewish. Office: 8301 Florence Ave Ste 104 Downey CA 90240-3946 Office Phone: 562-862-1991.

**SHAPIRO, ROBERT,** lawyer; b. Plainfield, NJ, Sept. 2, 1942; BS in Fin., UCLA, 1965; JD, Loyola U., L.A., 1968. Bar: Calif. 1969, U.S. Ct. Appeals (9th cir.) 1972, U.S. Dist. Ct. (ctrl., no. and so. dists.) Calif. 1982. Dep. dist. atty. Office of Dist. Atty., L.A., 1969-72; sole practice L.A., 1972—87; of counsel Bushkin, Gaims, Gaines, Jonas, L.A., 1987-88, Christensen, Miller, Fink & Jacobs, L.A., 1988-95; ptnr. Christensen, Miller, Fink, Jacobs, Glaser, Weil & Shapiro (formerly known as Christensen, Glaser, Fink, Jacobs, Weil & Shapiro), L.A., 1995—. Founder legal-com. Author: Search for Justice, 1996, Misconception, 2001. Recipient Am. Jurisprudence award Bancroft Whitney, 1969. Mem. Nat. Assn. Criminal Def. Lawyers, Calif. Attys. for Criminal Justice, Trial Lawyers for Pub. Justice (founder 1982),

Century City Bar Assn. (Best Criminal Def. Atty. 1993). Office: 10250 Constellation Blvd Fl 19 Los Angeles CA 90067 Office Phone: 310-553-3000, 310-556-7886. Business E-Mail: rs@chrisglase.com.

**SHAPIRO, ROBERT B.,** former food products manufacturing executive; b. NYC, Aug. 4, 1938; s. Moses and Lilly (Langsam) Shapiro; m. Berta Gordon, Mar. 27, 1964; children: James Gordon, Nina Rachel. AB, Harvard U., 1959; LLB, Columbia U., 1962. Bar: N.Y. 1963. Assoc. in law Columbia U., 1962—63; atty. firm Poletti Freidin Prashker Feldman & Gartner, N.Y.C., 1963—67; spl. asst. to gen. counsel and undersec. U.S. Dept. Transp., Washington, 1967—69; assoc. prof. law Northeastern U., Boston, 1969—71; asst. prof. law U. Wis., Madison, 1971—72; v.p., gen. counsel Gen. Instrument Corp., N.Y.C., 1972—79, G.D. Searle & Co., Skokie, Ill., 1979—82; pres. NutraSweet Group divsn. G.D. Searle & Co., Skokie, Ill., 1982—85; chmn., pres., CEO Nutra Sweet Co. subs. Monsanto, Skokie, Ill., 1985—95, also bd. dirs, 1992—; chmn., CEO Monsanto Co., St. Louis, 1995—2000; chmn. Pharmacia Corp., St. Louis, 2000—01. Bd. dirs. NY Stock Exch., 2003—06, NYSE Group, Inc., 2006—. Mem. bus. adv. com. White House Domestic Policy Rev. on Indsl. Innovation, 1978—79; nat. bd. trustees Boys Clubs of Am.; mem. Mass. Gov.'s Transp. Task Force, 1970—71; mem. com. on procedure CAB, 1975—76. Recipient John R. Miller award as outstanding corp. mktg. exec., 1984, Outstanding Achievement award, Sales and Mktg. Mgmt. Mag., 1984. Mem.: ABA (vice chmn. com. on corp. counsel 1981—82), NY State Bar Assn., U.S. C. of C. (coun. on antitrust policy 1981—82).

**SHAPIRO, ROBERT FRANK,** investment company executive; b. St. Louis, Dec. 19, 1934; s. Eugene J. and Clara (Katz) S.; m. Anna Marie Susman, Dec. 21, 1960; children: Albert Andrew, Robert Jr., Jeanne Savitt. Grad., St. Louis Country Day Sch., 1952; BA, Yale U., 1956. Assoc. Lehman Bros., N.Y.C., 1956-67, ptnr., 1967-73, dir., sr. mng. dir., 1970-73; ptnr. Wertheim & Co., 1974; exec. v.p. Wertheim & Co., Inc., N.Y.C., 1974-75, pres., 1975-86; co-chmn. Wertheim Schroder & Co., Inc., 1986-87; chmn. RFS and Assocs., Inc., N.Y.C., 1988—2004, New Street Capital Corp., 1992-94; vice-chmn. Klingenstein, Fields & Co., L.P., N.Y.C., 1997—. Bd. dirs. TJX Cos., Inc.; Genaera Corp., The Burnham Fund, chmn. nominating com. N.Y. Stock Exch., 1980, mem. regulatory adv. com., 1988—; surveillance com., 1989—; bd. govs. Am. Stock Exch., 1970-76. Trustee Lenox Hill Hosp., Skowhegan; mem. gov. bd. Yale U. Art Gallery, New Haven, 1993—; trustee Louis Comfort Tiffany Found. Named one of Top 200 Collectors, ARTnews Mag., 2004. Mem. Securities Industry Assn. (chmn. 1985, Bond Club N.Y. (pres. 1987-88, Yale Club, Century Country Club, Knickerbocker Club. Avocation: Collector of Contemporary Art, especially American. Office: Klingenstein Fields & Co LLC 787 7th Ave New York NY 10019-6018 Office Phone: 212-492-6143.

**SHAPIRO, ROBERT N.,** lawyer; b. June 18, 1950; AB cum laude, Harvard Univ., 1972; postgraduate, Trinity Coll., Cambridge Univ., England; JD cum laude, Harvard Univ., 1978. Bar: Mass. 1978. Law clk. US Dist. Ct. (Conn.), Judge Jon O. Newman, US Ct. Appeals 2d cir.; assoc. Ropes & Gray, Boston, 1979—87, ptnr., 1987—, head private client grp. Pres. Harvard Law Sch. Assn.; past pres. Harvard Alumni Assn.; chmn. Friends of Philip Exeter Acad. Libr.; trustee Noble & Greenough Sch., Dedham, Mass., Peabody Essex Mus., Salem, Mass.; overseer Handel & Haydn Soc., Boston. Fiske scholar. Office: Ropes & Gray I International Pl Boston MA 02110-2624 Office Phone: 617-951-7217. Office Fax: 617-951-7050. Business E-Mail: robert.shapiro@ropesgray.com.

**SHAPIRO, ROBYN SUE,** lawyer, educator; b. Mpls., July 19, 1952; d. Walter David and Judith Rae (Sweet) S.; m. Charles Howard Barr, June 27, 1976; children: Tania Shapiro-Barr, Jeremy Shapiro-Barr, Michael Shapiro-Barr. BA summa cum laude, U. Mich., 1974; JD, Harvard U., 1977. Bar: D.C. 1977, Wis. 1979, U.S. Supreme Ct. 1990. Assoc. Foley & Lardner, Washington, 1977-79; ptnr. Barr & Shapiro, Menomonee Falls, Wis., 1980-87; assoc. Quarles & Brady, Milw., 1987-92; ptnr. Michael Best & Friedrich, Milw., 1992—2005, chair health law practice, 2003–05; ptnr. Gardner Carton & Douglas LLP, Milw., 2005—. Adj. asst. prof. law Marquette U., Milw., 1979-83; assoc. dir. bioethics ctr. Med. Coll. Wis., Milw., 1982-85, dir., 1985—; asst. prof. bioethics Med. Coll. Wis., 1984-89, assoc. prof. bioethics, 1989-97, prof. bioethics, 1997—, Ursula Von der Ruhr prof. bioethics, 2000—; dir. Wis. Ethics Com. Network, 1987-98, Midwest Ethics Com. Network, 1998-2004, Med. Ethics Com. Network, 2004—; bd. dirs. Wis. Health Decisions, 1990-93; drug safety and risk mgmt. adv. com. FDA, 2003—; mem. data and safety monitoring bd. Med. Coll. Wis., 2003—; mem. recombinant DNA adv. com. NIH, 2005—. Mem. editl. bd. Cambridge Quar., 1991—, HEC Forum, 1988—91, Human Rights, 1998—; contbr. articles to profl. jours. Mem. ethics com. St. Luke's Med. Ctr., Milw., 1983—, Elmbrook Meml. Hosp., Milw. 1983-86, Cmty. Meml. Hosp., Menomonee Falls, 1984—, Aurora Sinai Med.Ctr., Milw., 1986—, Milw. County Mental Health Complex, 1984—, Froedtert Meml. Luth. Hosp., 1985—; mem. subcom. organ transplantation Wis. Health Policy Coun., Madison, 1984, bioethics com., 1986-89; mem. com. study on bioethics Wis. Legis. Coun., Madison, 1984-85; bd. dirs. Jewish Home and Care Ctr., 1994—, chair ethics com., 1994—; chair Bayside Ethics Bd., 1994—; bd. dirs. Milw. area chpt. Girl Scouts U.S., Am. Bioethics Assn., 1995-97, Wis. Perinatal Found., 1996-99, Am. Soc. Bioethics and Humanities, 1997-00, Manor Park Found., 2002—; mem. sec.'s adv. com. on xenotransplantation U.S. Dept. Health and Human Svcs., 2001-05; mem. sci. adv. com. Alzheimer's Assn. Southeastern Wis., 1997—; mem. data and safety monitoring bd. GlaxoWellcome, 1995-03; mem. med. and cmty. adv. bd. After Breast Cancer Diagnosis, 1999—. James B. Angell scholar, 1971—72. Mem. ABA (health law sec., coordinating com. on bioethics and law 1993—, individual rights and responsibilities sect., 1999—, mem. working group on health info. privacy 2000-02, adv. nat. conf. of commrs. on uniform state laws, misuse of genetic info. study group 2002—, sec. 2004-05, vice chair 2005-06, chair-elect 2006—, AIDS coordinating com. 2003—), Am. Health Lawyers Assn., Am. Hosp. Assn. (bioethics tech. panel 1991-94, spl. com. HIV practitioners 1991-93), Wis. Bar Assn. (chair Wis. health law sect. 1988-89, individual rights sect. coun. 1987-90), Assn. Women Lawyers, ACLU, Wis. Found. (Atty. of Yr. 1988), Assn. Post-Doctoral Programs in Clin. Neurophysiology (bd. dirs.), Am. Soc. Law, Medicine, and Ethics, Milw. Acad. Medicine (coun. 1992-98, chair bioethics com. 1992-98), Milw. AIDS Coalition (steering com. 1988-91), Am. Soc. Transplant Surgeons (ethics com. 1999—), Internat. Bioethics Assn. (chair task force on ethics coms.), Profl. Dimensions (Golden Compass award 1994), Phi Beta Kappa (Wis. chpt. scholarship com. chair 1990-93), Susan G. Komen Breast Cancer Found., others. Home: 9474 N Broadmoor Rd Milwaukee WI 53217-1309 Office: Med Coll Wis Bioethics Ctr 8701 Watertown Plank Rd Milwaukee WI 53226-3548 Office Phone: 414-221-6040. Business E-Mail: rshapiro@mcw.edu, rshapiro@gcd.com.

**SHAPIRO, RONALD GARY,** psychologist; b. Providence, Oct. 10, 1953; s. Nathan and Raquel (Rebe) S. BA, U. Rochester, 1975; MA, Ohio State U., 1977, PhD, 1981. Cert. human factors profl. Teaching, rsch. assoc. Ohio State U., Columbus, 1975-81; asst. prof. Denison U., Granville, Ohio, 1981-82; prin. assoc. Dunlap and Assocs. Inc., Norwalk, Conn., 1982-85; sr. engring. mgr. IBM, Poughkeepsie, N.Y., 1985-96, cons. human resources profl., 1996—, program mgr. enterprise-wide tech. and strategic learning curricula, US external edn. univ. programs, 2002—, new employee orientation, career counseling, 2006—. Evening faculty U. Conn., Stamford, 1983-85, Dutchess C.C. Poughkeepsie, 1986-94; bd. dirs. cert. Profl. Ergonomics Recert. Com. Contbr. articles to Psychol. Rev., Jour. Exptl. Psychology and other profl. jours. Recipient Grad. Sch. Leadership award Ohio State U., 1979; recipient Sr. Engring. Mgr. promotion IBM, 1993. Fellow Human Factors and Ergonomics Soc. (nat. program com. 1994-97, tech. program com. 1997-2000, chair computer sys. tech. group 1999-2000, chair coun. tech. groups 2001-02, vol. chair 2003-05, chair nat. ergonomics month 2003-05, chair spkrs. bur., 2004-05, Human Factors & Ergonomics Soc. Oliver Keith Hansen Outreach award, 2005); mem. APA (pres. divsn. 21 applied experimental and engring. psychology), Soc. Indsl. Orgnl. Psychologists, SHARE, Inc. (IBM rep. 1987-91), Sigma Xi, Phi Kappa Phi. Achievements include design of computer products for easy use by people. Home and Office: 17 Brookway Rd Providence RI 02906 Office Phone: 401-272-4664. E-mail: rshapiro@us.ibm.com.

**SHAPIRO, ROSE,** elementary school educator; b. Passaic, N.J., Feb. 10, 1945; d. Max and Ida Shapiro. BA, William Paterson Coll., 1966; MA, Kean Coll., 1982. Cert. advanced elem. tchr., adminstr., supr., N.J. Elem. tchr., tchr. math. lab. Passaic Bd. Edn., 1966—. Adj. instr. Kean Coll., Union, N.J., 1988—; fellow Project for Resourceful Instrn. Math. in Elem. Schs. Recipient Gov.'s Tchr. Recognition Award State of N.J., 1988. Mem. NEA, Nat. Coun. Tchrs. Math., N.J. Edn. Assn., Edn. Assn. Passaic, Phi Delta Kappa. Avocations: hiking, reading.

**SHAPIRO, SANDER WOLF,** retired lawyer; b. St. Louis, Sept. 24, 1929; s. Robert and Bess (Fisher) S.; m. Lottie F. Frankel, Aug. 14, 1955; children: Julie A. Shapiro Schechter, Susan B. Shapiro Schmitz. BA, Rice U., 1951; postgrad., Columbia U., 1951-52; JD, U. Tex., 1954. Atty. tax div. Dept. Justice, Washington, 1955-57; atty. advisor U.S. Tax Ct., Washington, 1957-58; ptnr. Clark, Thomas, Winters & Shapiro, Austin, Tex., 1958-84; sr. prtnr. Shapiro, Edens & Cook, Austin, 1984-91; of counsel Jenkens & Gilchrist, P.C., Austin, 1991-2000; ret. Adj. prof. law U. Tex., 1975-2000; lectr. in tax field. Author, editor Tex. Franchise Earned Surplus and Tax, 1985, Family Solutions to Family Concerns, 1991, A Walk Through Form 706, 1991; co-editor Tex. Tax Svc., 1986-94. Bd. dirs. Austin Symphony Orch. Soc., 1974-97, dir. emeritus 1997—, fin. v.p., 1980-95; bd. dirs. U. Tex. Coll. Fine Arts Adv. Coun., 1987-95, hon. bd. dirs., 1995—, pres., 1991-94; bd. dirs. Capital of Tex. Pub. Telecomm. Coun., 1988-97, pres., 1994-95; bd. dirs. Ronald McDonald House of Ctrl. Tex., Austin, 1990-98, pres., 1994-95; bd. dirs. Capital Met. Transit Authority, 1988-91, chair, 1990; bd. dirs. Austin Cmty. Found., 1985-92, pres., 1991; adv. coun. U. Tex. Press, 1998—, vice chmn. 1999, chmn. 2000. Sander W. Shapiro Presdl. Scholarship in Law at U. Tex. endowed in his honor by Jenkens & Gilchrist, 1992; recipient Disting. Lawyer award Travis County, 1999. Fellow Am. Bar Found. (life), Am. Coll. Tax Counsel, Tex. Bar Found. (sustaining life); mem. ABA, State Bar of Tex., Am. Law Inst., Nat. Assn. State Bar Tax Sects. (bd. dirs., chair 1997, dir. emeritus 2002—), Tex. Law Rev. Assn. (pres. 1992-93). Avocations: reading, music, golf. E-mail: sws@austin.rr.com.

**SHAPIRO, SANDRA,** lawyer; b. Providence, Oct. 17, 1944; d. Emil and Sarah (Cohen) S. AB magna cum laude, Bryn Mawr Coll., Pa., 1966; LLB magna cum laude, U. Pa., 1969. Bar: Mass. 1970, U.S. Dist. Ct. Mass. 1971, U.S. Ct. Appeals (1st cir.) 1972, U.S. Supreme Ct. 1980. Law clk. U.S. Ct. Appeals (1st cir.), Boston, 1969-70; assoc. Foley, Hoag & Eliot LLP, Boston, 1970-75, ptnr., 1976—. Mem. bd. bar overseers Mass. Supreme Judicial Ct., 1988-92, mem. gender bias study com., 1986-89; dir. Mass. Govt. Land Bank, 1994-96; dir. Lex Mundi, 2004—. Contbr. articles to profl. jours. Bd. dirs. Patriots' Trail coun. Girl Scouts U.S., 1994—97; mem. bd. overseers Boston Lyric Opera, 1993—99, New Eng. Conservatory of Music, 1995—2001, Celebrity Series of Boston, 1997—, chair, 2003—. Woodrow Wilson fellow, 1966. Mem.: ABA (ethics, profl. and pub. edn. com. 1994—), U. Pa. Law Sch. Alumni Assn. (bd. mgrs. 1990—94), Boston Bar Assn. (mem. coun.), Mass. Bar Assn. (chmn. real property sect. coun., com. on profl. ethics), Nat. Women's Law Ctr. Network, New Eng. Women in Real Estate, Women's Bar Assn. Mass. (pres. 1985—86), Boston Club, Order of Coif. Office: Foley Hoag LLP 155 Seaport Blvd Boston MA 02110-2600 Office Phone: 617-832-1156. Business E-Mail: sshapiro@foleyhoag.com.

**SHAPIRO, STEPHEN MICHAEL,** lawyer; b. Chgo., May 3, 1946; s. Samuel H. and Dorothy A. (D'Andrea) S.; m. Joan H. Gately, Oct. 30, 1982; children: Dorothy Henderson, Michael Clifford. BA magna cum laude, Yale U., 1968, JD, 1971. Bar: Ill. 1971, Calif. 1972, D.C. 1991, U.S. Dist. Ct. (no. dist. trial bar) Ill. 1992, U.S. Ct. Appeals (all cirs.), U.S. Supreme Ct. 1975. Law clk. U.S. Ct. Appeals (9th cir.), San Francisco, 1971—72; with Mayer Brown & Platt, Chgo., 1972—78; asst. to solicitor gen. U.S. Dept. Justice, Washington, 1978-80, dep. solicitor gen., 1981—83; sr. mem. Supreme Ct. and Appellate Ct. practice Mayer Brown Rowe & Maw LLP, Chgo., 1983—, ptnr., 1983—. Trustee Product Liability Adv. Found. Co-author: Supreme Court Practice, 2002; contbr. articles to profl. jours. Mem. ABA, Am. Law Inst. (life), Am. Acad. Appellate Lawyers, 7th Cir. Bar Assn., Inst. Jud. Adminstrn. (bd. dirs.), Phi Beta Kappa. Republican. Jewish. Office: Mayer Brown Rowe & Maw LLP 71 S Wacker Dr Ste 4430 Chicago IL 60606 Office Phone: 312-782-0600, 312-701-7327. Business E-Mail: sshapiro@mayerbrownrowe.com.

**SHAPIRO, STEVEN A.,** lawyer; b. Chgo., Oct. 22, 1950; BS, U. Ill., 1971; JD, Ill. Inst. Tech., 1975. Bar: Ill. 1975, Fla. 1983. Ptnr. Katten Muchin Zavis Rosenman, Chgo. Mem.: ABA. Office: Katten Muchin Zavis Rosenman 525 W Monroe St Chicago IL 60661 Office Phone: 312-902-5545. Office Fax: 312-577-8881. E-mail: steven.shapiro@kmzr.com.

**SHAPIRO, STEVEN J.,** energy executive; BS, Union Coll.; MBA, Harvard U. Formerly with treasury and bus. devel. depts. ARCO, former v.p. corp. planning, former pres. ARCO Coal Australia; sr. v.p., CFO, bd. dirs. Vastar Resources, Inc., 1993—2000; sr. v.p., CFO Burlington Resources, Inc., Houston, 2000—02, exec. v.p., CFO, 2002—. Office: Burlington Resources 717 Texas St Ste 2100 Houston TX 77002-2753

**SHAPIRO, STEVEN R.,** legal association administrator; JD, Harvard U., 1975. Law clk. to Hon. J. Edward Lumbard US Ct. Appeals 2nd Cir., 1975—76; with ACLU, 1976—, staff counsel Children's Rights Project, gen. staff counsel, assoc. legal dir., 1987—93, legal dir., 1993—. Adj. prof constl. law Columbia U.; bd. dirs. Human Rights First (previously Lawyers Com. for Human Rights); mem. Asia Adv. Com. Human Rights Watch, mem. policy com. Named Civil Rights Lawyer of Yr., Am. Lawyer, 1981. Office: ACLU 125 Broad St 18th Fl New York NY 10004

**SHAPIRO, STUART CHARLES,** computer scientist, educator; b. NYC, Dec. 30, 1944; s. Louis M. and Bertha (Rubinstein) S.; m. Caren Dee Knight, July 16, 1972. BS, MIT, 1966; MS, U. Wis., 1968, PhD, 1971. Lectr. computer scis. dept. U. Wis., Madison, 1971; vis. asst. prof. Ind. U., Bloomington, 1971-72, asst. prof., 1972-77, assoc. prof., 1977-78; asst. prof. SUNY, Buffalo, 1977-78, assoc. prof., 1978-83, prof., 1983—, chmn., 1984-90, 96-99, dir. Ctr. for Cognitive Sci., 2004—. Pres. Principles of Knowledge Representation and Reasoning, Inc., 1998-2000; rsch. scientist Nat. Ctr. for Geographic Info. and Analysis, 1989—. Author: Techniques of Artificial Intelligence, 1979, LISP: An Interactive Approach, 1986, Common Lisp: An Interactive Approach, 1992; editor: Encyclopedia of Artificial Intelligence, 1987, paperback edit., 1990, 2d edit., 1992, (with Lucja Iwanska) Natural Language Processing and Knowledge Representation: Language for Knowledge and Knowledge for Language, 2000; contbr. articles to profl. jours. Grantee NSF, 1971—; recipient numerous grants for computer sci. research, 1971—. Fellow Am. Assn. Artificial Intelligence; mem. IEEE (sr.), Assn. Computing Machinery (chmn. spl. interest group on artificial intelligence 1991-95), Assn. Computational Linguistics, Cognitive Sci. Soc., Sigma Xi. Home: 142 Viscount Dr Buffalo NY 14221-1770 Office: Univ at Buffalo Dept of Comp Sci & Engring 201 Bell Hall Buffalo NY 14260-2000 Office Phone: 716-645-3180 ext. 125. Personal E-mail: shapiro@adelphia.net. Business E-mail: shapiro@cse.buffalo.edu.

**SHAPIRO, SUMNER,** consulting firm executive, retired naval officer; b. Nashua, NH, Jan. 13, 1929; s. Maurice David and Hannah (Goodman) S.; m. Eleanor S. Hymen, June 14, 1949; children: Martha, Steven, Susan. BS, U.S. Naval Acad., 1949; MS, George Washington U., 1966; postgrad., Naval War Coll., 1966, U.S. Army Inst. Advanced Soviet and Eastern European Studies, 1961. Commd. ensign U.S. Navy, 1949; advanced through grades to rear adm.; asst. naval attache U.S. Am. embassy), Moscow, 1963-65; dep. asst. chief of staff for intelligence U.S. Naval Forces Europe, London, 1967-69; comdg. officer Naval Intelligence Processing System Support

Activity, Washington, 1969-72; asst. chief staff for intelligence U.S. Atlantic Command and U.S. Atlantic Fleet, Norfolk, Va., 1972-76; dep. dir. naval intelligence, 1976-77; comdr. Naval Intelligence Command, Washington, 1977-78; dir. naval intelligence Washington, 1978-82; ret., 1982; v.p. for advanced planning BDM Internat., 1983-89; pres. The Sumner Group Inc., 1989—. Pres. Naval Intelligence Found. Decorated D.S.M., Legion of Merit and others., Nat. Intelligence D.S.M., Netherlands Order Orange-Nassau, Brazil Order Naval Merit, French Nat. Order Merit, others Mem. Naval Intelligence Found. (pres.), Naval Intelligence Profs. (bd. dirs.), U.S. Naval Inst., Assn. Former Intelligence Officers, Nat. Mil. Intelligence Assn., Nat. Security Industries Assn., U.S. Naval Acad. Alumni Assn., Naval Submarine League. Office Phone: 703-448-8538. Personal E-mail: sumnergp@att.net.

**SHAPIRO, THEODORE,** psychiatrist, educator; b. N.Y.C., Feb. 26, 1932; s. Herman Alexander and Nettie (Rosenblatt) S.; m. Joan May Itkin, June 26, 1955; children: Susan, Alexander Herman. BA, Wesleyan U., 1953; MD, Cornell U., 1957. Diplomate Am. Bd. Psychiatry and Neurology, Am. Bd. Child Psychiatry, Am. Psychoanalytic Assn. Intern Montefiore Hosp., N.Y.C., 1957—58; resident in psychiatry NYU-Bellevue Hosp., 1958—61; instr. to prof. NYU Sch. Medicine, 1960—76; rsch. assoc. child psychiatry NYU-Bellevue Hosp., 1961—65; asst. lectr. N.Y. Psychoanalytic Inst., N.Y.C., 1970—86; prof. psychiatry and pediatrics Cornell U. Med. Coll., N.Y.C., 1976—2002; tng. and supervising analyst N.Y. Psychoanalytic Inst., N.Y.C., 1986—; vice chair for child and adolescent psychiatry, 1995—2002; emeritus prof. Cornell U. Med. Coll., N.Y.C., 2002—. Cons. alcohol, drug abuse and mental health adminstrn. WHO, Washington, Geneva and Copenhagen, 1980—82, Am. Acad. Child and Adolescent Psychiatry, Washington; chair com. on stewardship Task Force Future, 1980—82, acad. sec., 1981—83, chair work group on sci. issues, 1988—89, chair com. editorship and stewardship of jour., 1984—86, 1990—92; participant APA bilateral exch. in Ea. Europe, 1992; mem. reviewer child psychopathology and treatment rev. com. NIMH, 1994—98; lectr. in field. Author: Clinical Psycholinguistics, 1979; co-editor: Infant Psychiatry, 1976; editor: Psychoanalysis and Contemporary Science, 1976, Structure in Psychoanalysis, 1991, Affect: Psychoanalytic Perspectives, 1992; co-author: Manual of Panic-Focused Psychodynamic Psychotherapy, 1996, Psychodynamic Treatment of Depression, 2004, Psychodynamic Approaches to the Adolescent with Panic Disorder, 2004; editor Jour. Am. Psychoanalytic Assn., 1984-93; book rev. editor Internat. Jour. Psychoanalysis, 1993-2002; co-editor Research in Psychoanalysis, 1995; contbr. articles to profl. jours. Keynote lectr. Am. Psychoanalytic Assn., Boston, 2003, H. Hartmann Meml. NY Psychoanalytic Inst., 2004. Recipient Wilfred C. Hulse award, N.Y. Coun. Child Psychiatry, 1982, Harry Bakwin Meml. award, NYU, 1982, Heinz Hartmann award, N.Y. Psychoanalytic Inst., 2004; grantee, NIMH, 1976—86. Fellow Am. Acad. Child Psychiatry (sec. 1981-83), Am. Psychiat. Assn.; mem. Soc. Profs. Child Psychiatry (chmn. com. on edn. 1982-90, keynote spkr. 1999), Group for Advancement of Psychiatry (chmn. com. on child psychiatry 1985-90), Am. Bd. Psychiatry & Neurology (com. on child and adolescent psychiatry 1987-93, chmn. 1992-93), N.Y. Psychoanalytic Soc. Jewish. Office: Weill Med Coll Cornell U Payne Whitney Clinic PO Box 140 New York NY 10021-0012 Office Phone: 212-746-5713. E-mail: tshapiro@med.cornell.edu.

**SHAPIRO, VICTOR LENARD,** mathematics professor; b. Chgo., Oct. 16, 1924; s. Joseph E. and Anna (Grossman) S.; m. Florence Gilman, Mar. 21, 1948; children: Pamela Sue Shapiro Baer, Laura Fern Shapiro Young, Charles R., Arthur G. BS, U. Chgo., 1947, MS, 1949, PhD, 1952. Mem. faculty Rutgers U., 1952-60, prof. math., 1959-60; mem. Inst. Advanced Studies, Princeton, N.J., 1953-55, 58-59; mem. faculty U. Oreg., Eugene, 1960-64; prof. math. U. Calif., Riverside, 1964—, faculty research lectr., 1978. Author: Topics in Fourier and Geometric Analysis, 1961, Contemporary Mathematics, Vol. 208, 1997, Singular Quasilinearity and Higher Eigen Values, 2001; contbr. articles to profl. jours. and publs. Served with AUS, 1943-46. NSF postdoctoral fellow, 1954-55 Fellow AAAS; mem. Am. Math. Soc., Math. Assn. Am., Am. Soc. Indsl. and Applied Math. Office: U Calif Math Dept Riverside CA 92521-0001 Office Phone: 951-827-3113. Business E-Mail: shapiro@math.ucr.edu.

**SHAPIRO, WALTER ELLIOT,** columnist; b. NYC, Feb. 16, 1947; s. Salem Seeley and Edith Geraldine (Herwitz) S.; m. Meryl Gordon, Aug. 24, 1980. BA, U. Mich., 1970, postgrad., 1970-71. Reporter Congl. Quarterly, Washington, 1969-70; editor Washington Monthly, 1972-76; spl. asst. U.S. Sec. Labor, Washington, 1977-78; Presdl. speechwriter The White House, Washington, 1979; reporter Washington Post, 1979-83; gen. editor Newsweek, NYC, 1983-87; sr. writer Time Mag., NYC, 1987-93; White House corr. Esquire mag., 1993-97; polit. columnist USA Today, 1995—2004; fellow Joan Shorenstein Ctr. on the Press, Politics and Pub. Policy Kennedy Sch. Govt. Harvard U., Boston, 2005; chief Washington bur. Salon.com, 2006—. Contbg. editor Washington Monthly, 1976—. Author: (book) One-Car Caravan: On the Road with the 2004 Democrats Before America Tunes In, 2003. Leadership fellow Japan Soc., U.S.-Japan, 1991. Mem.: White House Correspondents Assn., Judson Welliver Soc., Author's Guild. Jewish. Avocations: standup comedy, rotisserie baseball. Office: Salon Media Group 3417 1/2 M St NW Washington DC 20007 Office Phone: 202-333-5695. Business E-Mail: wshapiro@salon.com.

**SHAPIRO-MATHES, ANGELA,** broadcast executive; BA, St. Peter's Coll. Co-owner Brookville Mktg/Greybark Advt.; owner, oper. several businesses; co-founder, pub. Soap Opera Digest, 1975, Soap Opera Update, 1988; co-prodr. Soap Opera Awards; sr. v.p. mktg. and promotion ABC Daytime, 1995, pres., 1998, Buena Vista Prodns., 2000; pres. ABC Family Channel Walt Disney Co., Burbank, Calif., 2002—03; pres. Fox TV Studios, 2004—. Office: Fox Television Studios Po Box 900 Beverly Hills CA 90213*

**SHAPIROV, SALIZHAN SHAKIROVICH,** cosmonaut; b. Uzgen, Kirghizia, Aug. 24, 1964; s. Shakirzhan Sharipov; m. Nadezhda Mavlyanovna Sharipova; 2 children. Grad., Air Force Pilot Sch., 1987; degree in cartography, Moscow State U., 1994. Pilot/instr. Russian Air Force, 1987—90; cosmonaut candidate Y.A. Gagarin Cosmonaut Tng. Ctr., Russia, 1990—92, cosmonaut, 1992—; mission specialist STS-89 8th Shuttle-Mir docking mission, 1998. Office: NASA/Johnson Space Ctr c/o Astronaut Office Houston TX 77058

**SHAPLEY, GREGORY PAUL,** head of religious order, music director; b. Ft. Worth, Tex., Nov. 22, 1965; s. Darrell DeWayne and Beverly Ann Shapley; m. Sessalie Alma Kidwell, July 16, 1988; children: Savannah Michelle, Abigail Ann, Benjamin Gregory. MusB, Ariz. State U., 1988; MusM, U. of Cin., 1990. Cert. Microsoft sys. engr. Dir. music and worship 1st United Meth. Ch. of Hurst, Tex., 2003—. Mem.: Tex. Choral Dirs. Assn. United Methodist. Avocations: running, fishing, skiing, avigation. Office: 1st United Methodist Ch Hurst 521 W Pipeline Rd Hurst TX 76053 Office Phone: 817-282-7384. E-mail: gshapley@fumchurst.org.

**SHAPO, HELENE S.,** law educator; b. NYC, June 5, 1938; d. Benjamin Martin and Gertrude (Kahaner) Seidner; m. Marshall S. Shapo, June 21, 1959; children: Benjamin Mitchell, Nathaniel Saul. BA, Smith Coll., 1959; MA in Teaching, Harvard U., 1960; JD, U. Tex. Bar: Va. 1976, U.S. Dist. Ct. (we. dist.) Va. 1977, Ill. 1993. Tchr. Dade County, Miami, Fla., 1960-64; assoc. Robert Musselman & Assocs., Charlottesville, Va., 1976-77; law clk. to presiding justice U.S. Dist. Ct. Va., Charlottesville, 1977-78; asst. prof. law Northwestern U., Chgo., 1978-81, assoc. prof. law, 1981-83; prof. law, 1983—, Perkins-Bauer prof., 1987. Instr. Sweet Briar Coll., Va., 1976-77, U. Va., Charlottesville, 1976-78; vis. fellow Wolfson Coll., Cambridge U., 2001, vis. scholar, 1992; mem. law sch. admissions coun./testing and devel., 1983—; cons. in field. Author (with Walter and Fajans): Writing and Analysis in the Law, 1989, 4th edit., 2003; author: (with Marshall Shapo) Law School Without Fear, 1996, 2d edit., 2003; author: Writing for Law Practice, 2004; contbr. articles to legal jours. Recipient award, sect. on legal writing, Assn. Am. Law Schs., 2002, award for disting. achievement, Assn. Legal Writing

Dirs., 2005. Mem. ABA, Va. Bar Assn., Assn. of Am. Law Schs. (sect. chairperson 1985—), Women's Bar Assn. Chgo. Office: Northwestern U Sch Law 357 E Chicago Ave Chicago IL 60611-3059 E-mail: h-shapo@law.northwestern.edu.

**SHAPO, MARSHALL SCHAMBELAN,** lawyer, educator; b. Phila., Oct. 1, 1936; s. Mitchell and Norma (Schambelan) S.; m. Helene Shirley Seidner, June 21, 1959; children: Benjamin, Nathaniel. AB summa cum laude, U. Miami, 1958, JD magna cum laude, 1964; AM, Harvard U., Cambridge, Mass., 1961, SJD, 1974. Bar: Fla. 1964, Va. 1977, Ill. 1993. Copy editor, writer Miami News, Fla., 1958-59; instr. history U. Miami, 1960-61; asst. prof. law U. Tex., 1965-67, asso. prof., 1967-69, prof., 1969-70; prof. law U. Va., 1970-78, Joseph M. Hartfield prof., 1976-78; Frederic P. Vose prof. Northwestern U. Sch. Law, Chgo., 1978—; of counsel Sonnenschein, Nath & Rosenthal, Chgo., 1991-2001. Vis. prof. Juristisches Seminar U. Gottingen (Fed. Republic Germany), 1976; cons. on med. malpractice and tort law reform U.S. Dept. Justice, 1978-79; mem. panel on food safety Inst. Medicine, NAS, 1978-79; vis. fellow Centre for Socio-legal Studies, Wolfson Coll., Oxford, vis. fellow of Coll., 1975, Wolfson Coll. Cambridge, 1992, 2001; mem. Ctr. for Advanced Studies, U. Va., 1976-77; cons. Pres.'s Commn. for Study of Ethical Problems in Medicine and Biomed. and Behavioral Rsch., 1980-81; reporter Spl. Com. on Tort Liability System Am. Bar Assn., 1980-84; del. leader People to People Citizen Amb. program delegation to East Asia Tort and Ins. Law, 1986; lectr. appellate judges' seminars ABA, 1977, 83, 90; reporter symposium on legal and sci. perspectives on causation, 1990; advisor Restatement of the Law, Third, Torts: Products Liability, 1992-97. Author: Towards a Jurisprudence of Injury, 1984, Tort and Compensation Law, 1976, The Duty to Act: Tort Law, Power and Public Policy, 1978, A Nation of Guinea Pigs, 1979, Products Liability, 1980, Public Regulation of Dangerous Products, 1980, The Law of Products Liability, 1987, Tort and Injury Law, 1990, (with Richard Peltz) 3d edit., 2006, The Law of Products Liability, 2 vols., 2d edit., 1990, 4th edit., 2001, supplements, 1991, 92, 93, 95, 96, 97, 98, 99, 2002, 03, 04, 05, 06, Products Liability and the Search for Justice, 1993, (with Helene Shapo) Law School Without Fear, 1996, 2d edit., 2002, Basic Principles of Tort Law, 1999, 2d edit., 2003, Tort Law and Culture, 2003, Compensation for Victims or Terror, 2005; (with Page Keeton) Products and the Consumer: Deceptive Practices, 1972, Products and the Consumer: Defective and Dangerous Products, 1970, (with D. Jacobson & A.N. Weber) International e-Commerce: Business & Legal Issues, 2001, (with G. Hernandez & others) eBusiness & Insurance, 2001, Concise Hornbook on Tort Law, 2003; mem. editl. bd. Jour. Consumer Policy, 1980-88, Products Liability Law Jour.; author: A Representational Theory of Consumer Protection: Doctrine, Function and Legal Liability for Product Disappointment, 1975; mem. adv. bd. Loyola Consumer Law Reporter; contbr. articles to legal and med. jours. Recipient Andrew J. Hecker award Fedn. Ins. and Corp. Counsel, 2001, Robert B. McKay Prof. award Am. Bar Assn., 2005, Disting. Alumnus award U. Miami Sch. Law, 2005; NEH sr. fellow, 1974-75 Mem. Am. Law Inst., Am. Assn. Law Schs. (chmn. torts compensation systems sect. 1983-84, torts round table coun. 1970). Home: 1910 Orrington Ave Evanston IL 60201-2910 Office: Northwestern U Sch Law 357 E Chicago Ave Chicago IL 60611-3059 E-mail: m-shapo@law.northwestern.edu.

**SHAPPERT, GRETCHEN C. F. (GRETCHEN CECILIA FRANCES SHAPPERT),** prosecutor, lawyer; b. 1956; AB, Duke U.; JD, Washington & Lee U. Bar: 1980. Assoc. Maupin, Taylor, & Ellis, P.A., Raleigh, 1980—81, Tucker, Hicks, Sentelle, Moon, & Hodge, P.A., Charlotte, 1981—83; asst. pub. defender Mecklenburg County, NC, 1983—88, asst. dist. atty., 1988—90; asst. US atty. (we. dist.) NC US Dept. Justice, 1990—2004, acting US atty., 2004—05, US atty. (we. dist.) NC, 2005—. Republican. Office: US Attys Office 227 West Trade St Ste 1650 Charlotte NC 28202 Office Phone: 704-344-6222.*

**SHARAPOVA, MARIA,** professional tennis player; b. Nyagan, Russia, Apr. 19, 1987; d. Yuri and Yelena Sharapova. Trained, Bollettieri's Acad., 1996. Prof. tennis player WTA Tour, 2001—; model IMG Modeling Agy., 2003—; winner Wimbledon, 2004. Nominee Laureus World Newcomer Yr., 2004; named Sports-Choice Athlete (Female), Teen Choice Awards, 2006. Achievements include 12 career singles WTA championships; 3 career doubles championships; 4 career ITF Women's Circuit singles titles; first Russian woman to win at Wimbledon, 2004; signed endorsement deals with Parlux Fragrances Inc and Motorola. Avocations: singing, reading, stamp collecting/philately, fashion, Russian music. Mailing: WTA Tour One Progress Plz Ste 1500 Saint Petersburg FL 33701*

**SHARBAUGH, THOMAS J.,** lawyer; b. June 18, 1947; BS, Pa. State U., 1973; JD, U. Mich., 1976. Bar: Pa. 1976. Ptnr., mem. firm mgmt. com. (ops.) Morgan, Lewis & Bockius LLP, Phila. Mem.: Pa. Bar Assn., ABA (bus. law sect.). Office: Morgan Lewis & Bockius One Logan Sq Ste 2000 Philadelphia PA 19103-6993 Office Phone: 215-963-5004. Office Fax: 215-963-5001. Business E-Mail: tsharbaugh@morganlewis.com.

**SHARBEL, JEAN M.,** editor; b. Lansford, Pa. d. Joseph and Star S. BA in Journalism, Hunter Coll. Editl. dir., v.p. Dauntless Books, N.Y.C., 1962-75; editor romance mags., True Confessions mag. Macfadden Holdings, Inc., N.Y.C., 1976-92; freelance editor fiction and non-fiction books, N.Y.C., 1989—. Home: 165 E 66th St New York NY 10021-6132

**SHARER, JOHN DANIEL,** lawyer; b. Bklyn., Sept. 19, 1950; s. Albert Robert and Alda Loretta (Tapiro) S.; m. Kathleen Gail Donaldson, Feb. 14, 1981; 1 child, Stephanie Erin. AB, Dartmouth Coll., Hanover, N.H., 1972; JD, U. Pa., 1975. Bar: Pa. 1975, NJ 1975, DC 1976, NY 1989, Va. 1994. Law clk. Superior Ct. Pa., Hon. Edmund B. Spaeth, Jr., Phila., 1976-77; assoc. Sutherland, Asbill & Brennan, Washington, 1976-82, ptnr., 1982-94; counsel Christian & Barton, L.L.P., Richmond, Va., 1994-95, ptnr., 1996-99; sr. counsel Dominion Resources Svcs. Inc., Richmond, 1999—2001, mng. counsel electric delivery, 2001—06, asst. gen. counsel, 2006—. Faculty Va. State Bar Professionalism Course, 2001—04; mem. Third Dist. Disciplinary Comm. Sect. III, 2003—06; grader Va. State Bar Examination, 2003—; mem. Va. State Bar Coun., 2005—. Bd. dirs. Wakefield Sch., Marshall, Va., 1990-94; pres. Dartmouth Club of Cen. Va., 1997-2003. Fellow Va. Law Found.; mem. Phi Beta Kappa. Republican. Avocations: classical music, judicial biographies, computers, Norfolk Terriers. Home: 12317 Northlake Ct Richmond VA 23233-6635 Office: 120 Tredegar St PO Box 26532 Richmond VA 23261-6532 Office Phone: 804-819-2271. E-mail: john_d_sharer@dom.com.

**SHARER, KEVIN W.,** medical products company executive; b. Clinton, Iowa, Mar. 2, 1948; m. Faye M. Sharer (div.); children: Heather, Keith; m. Carol Sharer. BS in Aero. Engring., US Naval Acad., 1970; MS in Aero. Engring., US Naval Postgraduate Sch., 1971; MBA, U. Pitts., 1982. Commd. lt. to lt. comdr. USN, 1970—78; with AT&T, 1978-82; cons. McKinsey & Co., 1982-84; pres., chief exec. officer GE, Princeton, NJ, 1984-89; exec. v.p., pres. bus. markets divsn. MCI Comm., Washington 1989—92; pres., COO, bd. dirs. Amgen Inc., Thousand Oaks, Calif., 1992-2000, pres., CEO, 2000—, chmn., 2001—. Bd. dirs. UNOCAL, 3M, Northrup Grumman Corpn., 2003—, US Naval Acad. Found. Chmn. bd. trustees LA County Mus. Natural Hist. Office: Amgen Inc 1 Amgen Ctr Dr Thousand Oaks CA 91320-1799*

**SHARER, ROBERT JAMES,** archaeologist; BA, Mich. State Univ.; PhD, Univ. Pa., 1968. Sally & Alvin V. Shoemaker prof. Univ. Pa., 1972—, curator Am. sect., Mus. Archaeology & Anthropology. Author: Prehistory of Chalchuapa, El Salvador, 1978, Fundamentals of Archaeology, 1979, Quirigua: A Classic Maya Center and Its Sculptures, 1990, Daily Life in Maya Civilization, 1996; co-author: Archaeological Investigations in the Northern Maya Highlands, Guatemala, 1987, The Ancient Maya, 1994, Discovering Our Past: A Brief Introduction to Archaeology, 1995, Archaeology: Discovering Our Past, 2002, Understanding Early Classic Copan, 2003; co-editor: Olmec and the Development of Formative Mesoamerican Civilization, 1989, River of

Gold: Precolumbian Treasures from Sitio Conte, 1992, New Theories on the Ancient Maya, 1992. Fellow: Am. Acad. Arts & Sci. Office: Department of Anthropology University Museum Room 323 3260 South St Philadelphia PA 19104-6398 Office Phone: 215-898-7461. Business E-Mail: rsharer@sas.upenn.edu.

**SHARF, STEPHAN,** automotive executive; b. Berlin, Dec. 30, 1920; came to U.S., 1947; s. Wilhelm and Martha (Schwartz) S.; m. Rita Schantzer, June 17, 1951. Degree in Mech. Engring., Tech. U., Berlin, Fed. Republic Germany, 1947. Tool and die maker Buerk Tool & Die Co., Buffalo, 1947-50; foreman Ford Motor Co., 1950-53, gen. foreman Chgo., 1953-58; with Chrysler Corp., Detroit, 1958-58, master mechanic Twinsburg stamping plant, 1958-63, mfg. engring. mgr., 1963-66, mfg. prodn. Twinsburg stamping plant, 1966-68, plant mgr. Warren stamping plant, 1968-70, plant mgr. Sterling stamping plant, 1970-72, gen. plants mgr. stamping, 1972-78, v.p. Engine and Casting div., 1978-80, v.p. Power Train div., 1980-81, exec. v.p., mfg., div., 1981-85, exec. v.p. internat., 1985-86, also bd. dirs.; pres. SICA Corp., Bloomfield Hills, Mich., 1986—. Bd. dirs. Jr. Achievement, Detroit council Boy Scouts Am.; trustee, v.p. Oakland U. Mem. Soc. Auto Engrs., Detroit Engring. Soc. Clubs: Wabeek Country. Home: 966 Adams Castle Dr Bloomfield Hills MI 48304-3713 Office: SICA Corp PO Box 623 Troy MI 48099-0623 Office Phone: 248-642-8364. Personal E-mail: sharfsteve@yahoo.com.

**SHARFSTEIN, JOSHUA M.,** city health department administrator, pediatrician; s. Steven Sharfstein and Margaret Shiling; m. Yngvild Olsen; 2 children. Grad., Harvard, 1991; MD, Harvard Med. Sch., 1996. Pediatrician Children's Nat. Med. Ctr., Mt. Wash. Pediatric Hosp.; sr. public health aide for Rep. Henry A. Waxman Calif.; commr. Balt. Health Dept., 2005—. Office: Balt Health Dept 210 Guilford Ave Baltimore MD 21202*

**SHARGEL, GERALD L.,** lawyer; b. New Brunswick, N.J., Oct. 5, 1944; BA, Rutgers U., 1966; JD, Bklyn. Law Sch., 1969. Bar: N.Y. 1969, U.S. Dist. Ct. (ea. and so. dists.) N.Y. 1969, U.S. Ct. Appeals (2nd, 3rd, 5th and 9th cirs.) 1969. Pvt. practice, N.Y.C., 1970—. Faculty mem. Practising Law Inst., 1976—77; adj. assoc. prof. law NYU, 1977—82; adj. prof. law Bklyn. Law Sch.; mem. adv. bd. NYU Sch. Law, Ctr. for Rsch. in Crime and Justice, 1984—88. Mem.: ABA, Fed. Bar Coun. N.Y. State Trial Lawyers Assn., N.Y. County Lawyers Assn., Assn. Bar City N.Y. N.Y. State Bar Assn., Criminal Bar Assn. Office: 16th Fl 570 Lexington Ave New York NY 10022

**SHARGIN, YURI GEORGUEVICH,** flight engineer, cosmonaut; b. Engels, Russia, Mar. 20, 1960; 2 children. Grad., Mil. Engring. Acad. for Aeronautics and Astronautics, Leningrad. Officer Cosmic Armed Forces; cosmonaut GMVK, 1996; cosmonaut basic tng. OKP, 1996—98; flight engr., cosmonaut, Russian Space Forces NASA. Broke a nearly 30 year tradition of having at least one crewman with previous experience in piloting the capsule. Flight Engr. of Expedition-10 headed for the International Space Station with Russian-US crew (with Leroy Chiao and Salizhan Sharipov) in the Soyuz TMA-5 on October 14, 2004.

**SHARICK, MERLE DAYTON, JR.,** sales executive; b. Bloomington, Ill., May 5, 1946; s. Merle Dayton and Joyce Madeline (Reed) Sharick; m. Cheryl Jean Easterday, Dec. 28, 1966; children: Amber Dawn, Cami Nicole. BA, Southwestern Coll., Winfield, Kans., 1968; MS in Edn., U. Kans., 1970. Tchr., coach Kans. High Schs., Lawrence, Hutchinson, 1968-73, asst. prin., prin. Buhler, Inman, Leoti, 1973-77; auctioneer, real estate salesman R.E.I.B., Inc., Hutchinson, 1977-78; acct. exec. Mortgage Guaranty Ins. Co., Hutchinson, 1978-81, regional sales mgr. Shawnee Mission, Kans., 1981-83, Houston, 1983-86, divsn. risk mgr. Atlanta, 1986-90, regional dir. Charlotte, NC, 1990-93; v.p., mgr. risk mgmt. Republic Mortgage Ins. Co., Winston-Salem, NC, 1993-99; mgr. S.E. divsn. Sheldon Good & Co. Auctions, Charlotte, 1999-2001; sr. v.p. Infinity Info. Solutions and Gen. Info. Svcs., Chapin, SC, 2001—03; dir. sales Mortgage Asset Rsch. Inst., Prosperity, SC, 2003—. Sports editor Winfield (Kans.) Daily Cour., 1966—68; owner, operator Riverside Home Style Laundry, South Hutchison, 1975—79; founder, owner Sport Shack, Hutchison, 1977—79; mem. UNBOG adv. group Freddie Mac, 1995—; spkr. in field. Active Rep. support groups, Houston, Atlanta, 1983—. Fellow: Inst. Devel. Ednl. Adminstrs.; mem.: Charlotte Region Comml. Bd. Realtors, Nat. Auctioneers Assn., Nat. Assn. Realtors, Housing Roundtable, Charlotte Mortgage Bankers, Tex. Mortgage Bankers, Fla. Mortgage Bankers, S.C. League Savs. Instns., N.C. Alliance Cmty. Fin. Instns., N.C. Bankers Assn., Mortgage Bankers Carolinas, Ga. Mortgage Bankers, Mortgage Bankers Am., Nat. Assn. Rev. Appraisers and Mortgage Underwriters, Charlotte Touchdown Club, Town Club. Methodist. Office Phone: 803-364-9048. Personal E-mail: msharick@mari-inc.com.

**SHARIF, BEHZAD,** research scientist; s. Abdolreza Sharif and Khojaste Salehi. BS, Sharif U. Tech., Iran, 2002; MS, U. Ill., Urbana, 2004. Rsch. asst. Coordinated Sci. Lab, U. of Ill., Urbana, 2002—. Computational Sci. and Engring. Fellowship, U. Ill., 2006. Mem.: Internat. Soc. Magnetic Resonance in Medicine (New Entrant award 2006), Soc. for Indsl. and Applied Math., IEEE. Achievements include patents pending for Method and Appartus for Patient Adaptive Reconstruction and Acquisition in Cardiac MRI. Office: Univ of Ill Urbana-Champaign 1308 W Main St Urbana IL 61801 Office Phone: 217-265-8234. Business E-Mail: sharif@uiuc.edu.

**SHARIFI, AZALEA A.,** orthodontist and general dentist; b. Hays, Kans., Mar. 2, 1967; d. Iraj Alagha Sharifi and Sara D. Salehian; m. Ramin Farmand; 1 child, Shayan-Daniel Farmand. DDS, Westfalian U., Muenster, Germany, 1995. MSc in Orthodontics and Dentofacial Orthopedics, 2001; PhD, U. Muenster Dental Sch., 1997; DMD, U. Pa., Phila., 2004. Cert. orthodontics. Orthodontics fellow Clinic for Orthodontion, Osnabrueck Germany 1996—98; pvt. practice Collegeville, 2004—. Interdisciplinary cons. dentofacial anomalies and clefts dept. maxillo-facial surgery U. Muenster Dental Sch., 1998—2001, instr., 1998—2001; instr. restorative dentistry dept. U. Pa., 2004—. Translator dentistry articles in internat. jours. Mem.: ADA, Acad. Gen. Dentistry, Montgomery-Bucks (Pa.) Dental Assn., Pa. Dental Assn., German Dental Assn. Avocations: travel, arts, skiing. Office: Market Place at Collegeville 201 S 2nd Ave Collegeville PA 19426 Office Phone: 610-454-7991. Personal E-mail: azaleasharifi@yahoo.com.

**SHARIFI, NIMA,** oncologist, researcher; s. Mohammad and Roghieh Sharifi. BS, Va. Tech., Blacksburg, 1992—95; MD, U. Pitts., Pa., 1996—2001. Res. Cleve. Clinic Found., Cleve., 1998—99; res., internal medicine Yale New Haven Hosp., Conn., 2001—03. Grantee fellowship, Howard Hughes Med. Inst., 1998, Med. Oncology fellowship, NIH, 2006. Mem.: AAAS, Am. Assn. Cancer Rsch., Am. Soc. Clin. Oncology. Home: 13215 Dairymaid Dr Unit 201 Germantown MD 20874 Office: Nat Cancer Inst Bldg 560 Rm 21-81 Frederick MD 21702

**SHARIFY, NASSER,** librarian, educator, writer; b. Tehran, Iran, Sept. 23, 1925; came to U.S., 1953, naturalized, 1972; s. Ebrahim and Eshraf (Saghafy) S.; m. Homayoun Taslimy, June 14, 1950 (div. 1978); children: Sharareh, Shahab. Licencie es Lettres, U. Tehran, 1947; MS, Columbia U., 1954, Dr. L.S., 1958. Editorial staff Teheran jours. Rah-e Now, Jahan-e Now, Saba, Jonb va Josh, 1943-51; translator, announcer All India Radio, 1948-49; librarian, dep. dir. Library of Parliament Iran, Tehran, 1949-53; cataloger Library of Congress, 1954-55; program asst. libraries devel. sect. UNESCO, Paris, 1959-61; acting chief servicing sect. Dept. Edn., Iran, 1962-63; dir. gen. Ministry Edn., Tehran, 1961-62; asst. prof. library and info. scis. and internat. edn. U. Pitts., 1963-66; founder, dir. Internat. Library Info. Center, 1964-66; vis. lectr. SUNY Albany Sch. Library Sci., summer, 1966; dir. internat. librarianship and documentation, internat studies and world affairs SUNY, Oyster Bay, 1966-68; dean, prof. grad. sch. library and info sci. Pratt Inst., Bklyn., 1968-87, chmn. inst. research council, 1971-89, dean emeritus sch. computer, info. and library scis., 1987—; pres. B.E.L.T., Inc., internat planning cons., 1981—. Dir. Grad. Library Tng. Program, UNESCO Mission, Nat. Tchrs. Coll., Tehran, 1960; Iran's Ofcl. del. to UNESCO Conf. Ednl.

Pubs., Geneva, 1961, SE Asia Edn. Secs. Conf., Murree, Pakistan, 1961, Internation Conf., on Cataloging Prins., Paris, 1961, CENTO Libr. Devel. Conf., Ankara, Turkey, 1962; chmn. standing com. for preparation reading materials for new literates UNESCO, Tehran, 1961-62; mem. U.S. AID Mission, Turkey, Iran, Pakistan, 1966; dir. Conf. on Internat. Responsibility Coll. and Univ. Librarians, Oyster Bay, 1967; U.S. del. 33d Conf. and Internat. Congress on Documentation, Tokyo, 1967; ALA del. UN Conf. on Non-Govtl. Orgn., 1969; cons. U.S. AID, Conf. on Book Devel., 1967; mem. adv. bd. Ency. Libr. and Info. Scis., 1969—; chmn. Pre-Am. Library Assn. Conf. Inst. on Internat. Libr. Manpower, Edn. and Placement in N.Am., Detroit, 1970; mem. Am. del. Internat. Fedn. Libr. Assn. Conf., Liverpool, Eng., 1971, Budapest, 1972, Grenoble, France, 1973, Washington, 1974, Brussels, 1977, Montreal, 1982, Chgo., 1985, Barcelona, 1992; organzier USAID sponsored Global Info. Village Conf., Rabat, Morocco, Bklyn., N.Y., 1997, spkr., 1997; bldg. cons. Learning Resources Center, Nat. Tchrs. Coll., Iran, 1972-73; cons. campus planning, 1972-73; UNESCO cons. missions to plan and evaluate Nat. Sch. Info. Sci., Morocco, 1973-74, 79-81, 89, 96-; cons. U.S. Info. Agy., Morocco, 1991, 92, 95; chmn. Conf. on Orgn. and Control of Info for Islamic Research, 1982; chmn. bd. cons. to Nat. U. Iran, 1974-75, Pahlavi Nat. Library of Iran, 1975-77; speaker Symposium Internat. sur l' information Economique, Casablanca, Morocco, 1990; inaugural speaker Ctr. Documentation et D'Information Multimedia, Rabat, Morocco, 1995. Author: cataloging of Persian works Including Rules for Transliteration Entry and Description, 1959, Book Production, Importation and Distribution in Iran, Pakistan and Turkey, 1966; Beyond the National Frontiers: The International Dimension of Changing Library Education for a Changing World, 1973; The Pahlavi National Library of the Future., 17 vols., 1976, other books; contbr. to Ency. of Library and Info. Sci., 1969, ALA World Ency. Library and Info. Services, 1980, 86, library jours., 1973—, Bookmark, 1972, Library Education in the Middle East, 1991; contbr. poetry to various jours. and anthologies, 1947-51, 67, 91-93 lyrics to Iranian motion pictures and recs., 1948-52; works on display at Archieves of Hoover Inst. on War Revolution and Peace, Stanford U.; Contbr. to: film script for motion picture Morad, 1951-52. Trustee Bklyn. Public Library, 1970-82; pres. Maurice F. Tauber Found., 1981—. Recipient Taj (crown) medal and citation for disting. svc. Mohammad Reza Shah Pahlavi, Shah of Iran, 1978, Kaula Gold medal and citation for disting. svc. to internat. librarianship, 1985; named for Annual Nasser Sharify Lecture Series, Sch. of Computer Info. and Libr. Scis., Pratt Inst., 1988—; writings by and about Nasser Sharify are preserved at Archives of Hoover Instn. on wars, revolutions and peace., Stanford U., Stanford, Calif. Mem. ALA (chmn. com. equivalencies and reciprocity 1966-71, mem. UNESCO panel, mem. nominating com. 1970-71, chmn. Pakistan, Iran, Turkey, Morocco, and Middle East Resource panels, internat. libr. edn. com. 1973—, mem. com. internat. libr. schs. div. libr. edn. div. 1973-78, Citation extraordinary and exemplary svc. internat. librarianship 1999, John Ames Humphry OCLC Forest Press award 2004), NY Libr. Assn. (dir. library edn. sect. 1969-72), Pub. Libr. Assn. (task force on internat. relations 1981-86), Am. Assn. Libr. Schs. (chmn. govtl. relations com., 1984-88), Am. Soc. Info. Sci., Spl. Libr. Assn., Internat. Fedn. Libr. Assns. (adv. group libr. edn. 1971-73, v.p. libr. schs. sect. 1973-77). Home: 252 Jericho Tpke Westbury NY 11590-1213 Office: Pratt Inst Sch Info and Libr Sci 200 Willoughby Ave # 4 Brooklyn NY 11205-3899 Office Phone: 212-647-7691. Personal E-mail: nsharify@aol.com. *If I am asked to wash a car, I try to make it spotless. If I am to write a book, I try to make it faultless. But it seems that I always find spots on the shining surface of the car, and faults in many well-written pages of the book. This gives me another reason to live for another day.*

**SHARIPOV, SALIZHAN SHAKIROVICH,** cosmonaut; b. Uzgen, Oshsk region, Kirghizia, Aug. 24, 1964; m. Nadezhda Mavlyanovna Sharipova; 2 children. Grad., Air Force Pilot Sch., 1987, Moscow State U. Pilot-instr. teaching 5 cadets; mission specialist STS-89, 1998; cosmonaut-candidate Gagarin Cosmonaut Tng. Ctr., 1990; cosmonaut NASA, 1992—. Broke a nearly 30 year tradition of having at least one crewman with previous experience in piloting the capsule. Soyuz Comdr. and Flight Engineer of Expedition-10 headed for the International Space Station with Russian-US crew (with Leroy Chiao and Yuri Shargin) in the Soyuz TMA-5 on October, 2004, landed April, 2005 (with Leroy Chiao and Roberto Vittori). Office: NASA JSC 2101 NASA Rd 1 Houston TX 77058-3691 Office Phone: 281-483-0123.

**SHARKAWY, AHMED SAMIR,** engineering company executive; b. Abu Kebeer, Sharkia, Egypt, Jan. 26, 1972; s. Samir Ibrahim and Fatma Ahmed Sharkawy; m. Stamatia J. Piteris, Dec. 17, 1997; 1 child, Mu'min Ahmed Samir. BSEE, Benha Inst. Tech., Egypt, 1994; M in Elec. Engring., Pa. State U., 1998; PhD in Elec. Engring., U. Del., 2003. Instr. Benha Inst. Tech., 1994—96; sr. engr. W.L. Gore and Assocs., Newark, Del., 1998—2000; rsch. assoc. U. Del., Newark, 2000—03; sr. engr. EM Photonics, Newark, 2001—04, dir. neophotonics applications, 2004—. Application engr. EM Photonics, Newark, 2002—, cons., 2001—02. Author: (book chpt.) Handbook of Nanotechnology, 2001, (book) Photonic Crystals, 2005. Mem.: IEEE, SPIE, Optical Soc. Am.

**SHARKEY, CATHERINE MOIRA,** law educator; b. Balt., May 1, 1970; BA in Economics, summa cum laude, Yale U., 1992; JD, Yale U., 1997; MS in Economics for Devel., Oxford U., 1994. Bar: Md. 1998, DC 2000, NY 2000. Jud. clk. to Hon. Guido Calabresi US Ct. Appeals 2nd Cir., New Haven, 1997—98; jud. clk. to Hon. David H. Souter US Supreme Ct., Washington, 1998—99; Supreme Ct. & appellate litig. assoc. Mayer, Brown Rowe & Maw, NYC, 2000—02, cons., 2002; assoc. prof. law NYU, NYC, 2003—. Rhodes Scholar, 1992—94. Office: Columbia U Sch Law 435 W 116th St New York NY 10027 Office Fax: 212-854-0739, 212-854-7946. Business E-Mail: cshark@law.columbia.edu.

**SHARKEY, LEONARD ARTHUR,** automobile company executive; b. Detroit, May 21, 1946; s. Percy and Lillian (Peros) S.; m. Irene Johnson, Aug. 9, 1969 (div. Nov. 1991); children: Michelle, Wesley Tucker (step-son). Cert. pvt. pilot. Tool and diemaker Ford Motor Co., Dearborn, Mich., 1965-85; indsl. hazardous substance educator Ford Motor co., Dearborn, Mich., 1985-86, indsl. health, safety and energy control educator, 1987-88, tool and diemaker leader, 1989—; non-fiction author Individual Initiative, Brighton, Mich., 1989—. Author: Journey Into Fear (reprinted title Split Decision, 1997), 1995, Hidden Shadows - An Opening to the Windows of the Mind, 1996. Mem. Nat. Geog. Soc., Nat. Rifle Assn., Boat U.S., Drummond Island Sportsman's Club, Mich. United Conservation Clubs. Avocations: boating, shooting sports, political awareness studies, biblical prophetic studies, theater.

**SHARKEY, ROBERT EMMETT,** lawyer; b. Chgo., Oct. 21, 1942; s. Edward Francis and Catherine Christine (Grundhoefer) S.; m. Phoebe Dadakis, July 28, 1963 (div.); children: Siobhan, Edward, Catherine, James. BA, Georgetown U., 1964, JD, 1967. Bar: Md. 1967, D.C. 1995, U.S. Dist. Ct. Md. 1967, U.S. Ct. Appeals (4th cir.) 1972, U.S. Ct. Appeals (2nd cir.) 1973, U.S. U.S. Supreme Ct. 1973, U.S. Ct. Appeals (fed. cir.) 1986, U.S. Ct. Fed. Claims 1986, D.C. 1995, D.C. Ct. Appeals 1995, U.S. Dist. Ct. D.C. 1996. Mem. staff subcom. fed., state, local rels. Commn. for Re-orgn. Exec. Branch Md. Govt., College Park, 1967; law clerk for Chief Judge Edward S. Northrop U.S. Dist. Ct. Md., Balt., 1967-68; assoc. Gordon, Feinblatt, Rothman, Hoffberger & Hollander, Balt., 1968-74, ptnr., 1974—. Mem. counsel Balt. Hist. Soc., 2000. Mem. Md. Bar Assn. (profl. ethics 1987—, vice chmn. com. profl. ethics 1991-93, chmn. com. profl. ethics 1993), Bar Assn. Balt. City (com. profl. ethics 1984-86), St. Thomas More Soc. Md. (pres. 1982-83), Georgetown U. Alumni Assn. (law alumni rep. 1992), Ice Club Balt. (v.p. 1981-83), Phi Delta Phi. Avocation: figure skating. E-mail: rsharkey@gfrlaw.com.

**SHARKEY, THOMAS DAVID,** botanist, educator; b. Detroit, Jan. 28, 1953; s. Robert Hugh and Patricia June (Elliott) S.; m. Paulette Marie Bochnig June 21, 1974; 1 child, Jessa Sung. BS in Biology with honors, Mich. State U., 1974, PhD in Botany and Plant Pathology, 1980. Postdoctoral

fellow Australian Nat. U., Canberra, 1980-82; assoc. rsch. prof. Desert Rsch. Inst., Reno, Nev., 1982-87; asst. prof. U. Wis., Madison 1987-88, assoc. prof., 1988-91, prof., 1991—. Assoc. dir. Biolog. Scis. Ctr., Reno, Nev., 1983-87; chmn. dept. botany U. Wis., Madison, 1992-94; dir. Inst. Cross-Coll. Biology Edn. Editor: Trace Gas Emissions from Plants, 1991, Photosynthesis: Physiology and Metabolism, 2000; contbr. more than 140 articles to profl. peer-reviewed jours. Mem.: AAAS, Internat. Soc. Photosynthesis Rsch., Am. Soc. Plant Biologists. Home: 5901 S Highlands Ave Madison WI 53705-1108 Office: Univ Wis Dept Botany 430 Lincoln Dr Madison WI 53706-1313 Office Phone: 608-262-6802. Business E-Mail: tsharkey@wisc.edu.

**SHARKEY, VINCENT JOSEPH,** lawyer; b. Newport, R.I., May 25, 1944; s. Vincent Joseph and Dorothy (Auvil) S.; m. Joyce Toomey, Dec. 27, 1969; children: Alison, Christina, John, Julia. BA in Econs., Yale U., 1966; JD, U. Va., 1971. Bar: N.J. 1971, U.S. Ct. Appeals (3d cir.) 1985. Asst. prosecutor Bergen County Prosecutor's Office, Hackensack, NJ, 1971-72; pvt. practice, Bergen County, 1972-75; ptnr. Riker, Danzig, Scherer, Hyland & Perretti, Morristown, NJ, 1979—. U.S. Army, 1966-68. Mem. ABA, N.J. Bar Assn., Yale U. Alumni Assn. (pres. Bergen County chpt. 1986-88). Office Phone: 973-451-8509. E-mail: vsharkey@riker.com.

**SHARLACH, JEFFREY,** public relations executive; b. Conn., June 11, 1953; BA, Northwestern U., 1974; JD, NYU, 1977. V.p., client svc. mgr. Burson-Marsteller, N.Y.C., 1982-85; v.p., dir. creative svcs. Carl Byoir & Assocs., N.Y.C., 1986-88; exec. v.p. internat. ops. Rowland Worldwide, N.Y.C., 1988-93; chair, CEO Jeffrey Group, Miami Beach, Fla., 1993—. Mem Pub Rels Soc. Am. Office: Jeffrey Group 1111 Lincoln Rd Ste 800 Miami Beach FL 33139-2451

**SHARMA, ANAND,** manufacturing executive; BS in mech. engring., Roorkree U., India; MS in bus. adminstrn., Boston U.; adv. mgmt. studies, Wharton Sch. Mgmt. With Am. Standard, Inc., v.p. ops.; exec. v.p. Productivity Inc.; co-founder, pres., CEO TBM Consulting Group, Durham, NC, 1991—. Spkr. AME Annual Conf. Author: The Perfect Engine: How to Win in the New Demand Economy by Building to Order With Fewer Resources, 2001; monthly columnist The Manufacturer. Recipient Hero of U.S. Mfg., Fortune, 2001, Donald Burnham Mfg. Mgmt. Award, Soc. Mfg. Engrs., 2002. Office: TBM Consulting Group 4400 Ben Franklin Blvd Durham NC 27704

**SHARMA, ARJUN DUTTA,** cardiologist; b. Bombay, June 2, 1953; came to U.S., 1981; s. Hari D. and Gudrun (Axelsson) S.; m. Carolyn D. Burleigh, May 9, 1981; children: Allira, Eric, Harrison. BSc, U. Waterloo, Ont., Can., 1972; MD, U. Toronto, Ont., 1976. Intern Toronto Gen. Hosp., 1976-77, resident in medicine, 1978-80, St. Michael's Hosp., Toronto, 1980-81; residency medicine Toronto Gen. Hosp., 1977-78; Rsch. assoc. Washington U., St. Louis, 1981-83; asst. prof. pharmacy and toxicology U. Western Ont., London, 1985-89, asst. prof. medicine, 1983-89, assoc. prof. medicine, 1989-90; dir. interventional electrophysiology Sutter Meml. Hosp., Sacramento, 1990-95. Assoc. clin. prof. U. Calif., Davis, 1990—96, clin. prof. medicine, 1997—2002; cons. Medtronic Inc., Mpls., 1995—2000, Telectronics Pacing Sys., Inc., 1990—94, Cardiometrics, 1995, Ela Med., 2000—03, Guidant, 2000, Cyberknife, 2006, Cardema, 2003, St. Jude Med., 2003; mem. rsch. com. Sutter Inst. Med. Rsch., 1991—97; mem. exec. com. Sutter Heart Inst., 1992; faculty ann. sci. sessions N.Am. Soc. Pacing and Electrophysiology, 1993—97, Heart Rhythm Soc., 2005, Am. Coll. Cardiology, 2005; program dir. Update in Tachyarrhythmia Mgmt., Palm Springs, 1996, Pacing Defibrillation and Electrophysiology, Squaw Valley, Calif., 1997; resynchronization co-chair Am. Heart Ann., 2003; mem. atrial fibrillation adv. bd. Guidant Inc.; mem. steering com. David I, II and Rathin Q Clin. Trials; abstract reviewer. Reviewer profl. jours., including Circulation, Am. Jour. Cardiology; contbr. articles to profl. pubs. Recipient John Melady award, 1972, Dr. C.S. Wainwright award, 1973-75, Rsch. prize Toronto Gen. Hosp., 1979, 80, Ont. Career Scientist award Ont. Ministry of Health, 1983-89; Med. Rsch. Coun. Can. fellow, 1981-83. Fellow ACP, Am. Coll. Cardiology; mem. Am. Fedn. Clin. Rsch., Canadian Cardiovasc. Soc., N.Y. Acad. Scis., Sacramento Eldorado Med. Soc. Avocations: skiing, tennis, stamp collecting/philately, genealogy. Office: 3941 J St Ste 260 Sacramento CA 95819-3633 Office Phone: 916-736-2323. E-mail: asharma@rcamd.com.

**SHARMA, BRAHAMA D.,** chemistry professor; b. Sampla, Punjab, India, June 5, 1931; naturalized Am. citizen; s. Des Raj and Kesara Devi (Pathak) S.; m. Millicent M. Hewitt, Dec. 22, 1956 (div. 1996); children: Nalanda V. Sharma Bowman, Renuka D; m. Katharine A. McAfee, June 17, 2001. BS with honors, U. Delhi, India, 1949, MS, 1951; PhD, U. So. Calif., 1961. Chemist Govt. Opium Factory, Ghazipur, India, 1951-52; lab. assoc., sci. asst. Nat. Chem. Lab., Poona, India, 1952-55; lab. assoc. U. So. Calif., L.A., 1955-61; research fellow Calif. Inst. Tech., Pasadena, 1961-65; asst. prof. chemistry U. Nev., Reno, 1963-64, Oreg. State U., Corvallis, 1965-70, Calif. State U., Northridge, 1973-75, assoc. prof., 1975-76; prof. L.A. Pierce Coll., Woodland Hills, Calif., 1976-96. Part-time assoc. prof. chemistry Calif. State U., L.A., 1973-85, prof., 1985—; vis. assoc. Calif. Inst. Tech., 1979, 82; pres. L.A. Pierce Coll. Senate, 1981-82, chmn. profl. and acad. stds., 1989-92. Contbr. articles to profl. jours. Key leader sci. and tech. 4-H U. Calif., San Luis Obispo County. Grantee E.I. duPont de Nemours, L.A., 1961, NSF, 1967-69. Mem. Am. Chem. Soc. (chmn. edn. com. So. Calif. chpt. 1981-82, rsch. grantee 1965-69), Royal Soc. Chemistry (chartered chemist), Am. Inst. Parliamentarians (sec., adminstr., lt. gov. region VII, exec. lt. gov.), Nat. Assn. Parliamentarians (registered parliamentarian, life), Calif. Assn. Parliamentarians (pub. rels. chmn., statewide edn. chmn. So. area, pres. Calif. Sigma unit), San Luis Obispo Gem and Mineral Club Inc. (pres. 1998, sec. 1999, v.p. 2000). Avocations: playing bridge, reading, history, classical music, crystal models, Office: LA Pierce Coll Chem Dept Woodland Hills CA 91371-0001 E-mail: mercury610@aol.com.

**SHARMA, DINESH KUMAR,** management science educator; arrived in U.S., 1988; s. Phool W. Sharma; m. Preeti R. Rani; children: Amit K., Rajat K. BS in Math., M.D. U., Rohtak, India, 1985; PhD, Chaudhary Charan Singh U., India, 1999. Asst. prof. U. Md. Ea. Shore, Princess Anne, 1999—2002, assoc. prof., 2002—. Contbr. articles to profl. pubs. (Received 6 Best Paper awards). Mem.: N.E. Decision Scis. Inst., S.E. Decision Scis. Inst., Decision Sciences Inst., Operational Rsch. Soc. India (life), Amer. Inst. Mgmt. Sci. (life), Sigma Beta Delta (hon.; chpt. pres.). Office: U Md Ea Shore Dept Bus Mgmt and Acctg Princess Anne MD 21853 Office Phone: 410-861-6523.

**SHARMA, GAURAV,** imaging scientist, electrical engineer; b. Dehradun, India, Oct. 12, 1968; came to U.S. 1992; s. Sohan Lal and Santosh Sharma. B Engring. U. Roorkee, India, 1990; M Engring., Indian Inst. Sci., Bangalore, 1992; MS, N.C. State U., 1995, PhD, 1996. Rsch. engr. Ctr. for Devel. Telematics, Bangalore, 1992; rsch. asst. N.C. State U., Raleigh, 1992-96, tchg. asst., 1995; summer rsch. intern Webster (N.Y.) Rsch. Ctr. Xerox Corp, 1993, 94, 95, main rsch. staff Ditigal Imaging Tech. Ctr. Webster, 1996—. Contbr. articles to profl. jours. Vol. Adopt-A-Hwy., Webster, 1997. Mem. IEEE (referee trans. on signal/image processing/comms. 1995—), Soc. Imaging Sci. and Tech., Sigma Xi, Phi Kappa Phi, Pi Mu Epsilon. Achievements include patent for automatic calibration of halftones and patents pending on tangetless scanner calibration, show-through compensation, and marking process identification. Office: ECE Dept U Rochester PO Box 270126 Rochester NY 14627-0126 Office Phone: 585-275-7313. E-mail: gsharma@ece.rochester.edu.

**SHARMA, MARTHA BRIDGES,** geography educator; b. Balt., Feb. 2, 1945; d. Gail and S. Evelyn Bridges; m. Narendra P. Sharma, Aug. 16, 1968; 1 child, Stephanie. BA in Geography, Internat. Studies, U. N.C., 1967; postgrad., U. Hawaii, 1967—68; George Washington U., 1984. Tchr. geography Washington Internat. Sch., 1976—80; dir. records/accounts Washington Internat. Sch., 1981—82, adminstrv. dean, 1983—84; tchr. geography Nat. Cathedral Sch., Washington, 1984—2004. Mem. AP Human Geography Test Devel. Com., 1996—2005; geography cons.; lectr. in field. Joint author: 7-12 Geography: Themes, Key Ideas, and Learning Opportunities, 1989;

co-author: The National Council for Geographic Education: The First Seventy-Five Years and Beyond, 1990, Using Internet Primary Sources to Teach Critical Thinking Skills in Geography, 2000; contbg. author: Revisiting the Americas: Teaching and Learning the Geography of the Western Hemisphere, 1992; author: (online) Making Population Real, 2005; contrb. articles to profl. jours. Mem. Nat. Coun. Geographic Edn. (Region VIII awards com. 1988-90, dir. spl. pub.s 1989-92, gender/ethnicity project task force 1991-92, v.p. curriculum and instrn. 2002-04, pres. 2005), Assn. Am. Geographers, Soc. Woman Geographers. Avocations: reading, music, needlecrafts, travel. E-mail: geogsharma@yahoo.com.

**SHARMA, NAWAL K.,** bioengineering educator, researcher; s. Bhagwan Singh and Jai Devi Sharma; m. Pooja Sharma, Nov. 29, 1993; children: Nishtha, Pratishtha. MPhil, U. Delhi, 1990, PhD, 1995. Sr. scientist Poly. U., Bklyn., 2001—02; rsch. instr. U. Pitts., 2002—03, asst. prof. bioengring., 2003—, instr. medicinal chemistry, biotech., 2003—. Vis. scientist Odense U., Denmark, 1992; post-doctoral fellow U. Antwerp, Belgium, 1995—96; sr. scientist, group leader Ranbaxy Rsch. Labs., Gurgaon, Haryana, India, 1996—2000. Contrb. articles to internat. jours. Mem.: AAAS, NY Acad. Sci, Soc. Pest Sci., Indian Sci. Congress Assn., Am. Soc. Pharmacognosy, Soc. for Neurosci., Soc. for Neurosci., Am. Physiol. Soc., Am. Assn. Pharm. Scientists, Am. Chem. Soc. (assoc.; assoc.), Sigma Xi. Home: 4353 Saline St #1 Pittsburgh PA 15217 Office: Univ Pitts 260 Kappa Dr Ste 106 Pittsburgh PA 15238 Fax: 412-521-3442. Office Phone: 412-967-6512.

**SHARMA, OM PRAKASH,** clinical research and development executive; s. Babu Lal and Sushila Sharma; m. Manju Sharma, July 1, 1968; 1 child, Himanshu. BSc, U. Rajasthan, Jaipur, India, 1977, MSc, 1979, PhD, 1984. Rsch. officer med. sch. faculty All India Inst. of Med. Scis., New Delhi, 1984—87; Alexander von Humboldt fellow Max Plank Inst. of Medicine, Muenster, Westfalia, Germany, 1987—89; rsch. assoc. Johns Hopkins U., Balt., 1989—91; rsch. asst. prof. U. Va., Charlottesville, 1991—93; asst. dir. Organon Inc. subs. of AKZO-NOBEL, West Orange, NJ, 1993—94, assoc. dir., 1994—98; sr. clin. rsch. scientist Wyeth, Madison, NJ, 1998—2000; dir. clin. devel. Ono Pharma USA, Inc. subs. of Ono Pharm. Co., Osaka, Japan, Lawrenceville, NJ, 2000—05; dir. project mgmt. Memory Pharmaceutical Corp., Montvale, NJ, 2005; dir. clin. rsch. Johnson & Johnson, Raritan, NJ, 2005—. Cons. Long Range Internat., Inc., Bridgewater, NJ, 1998. Reviewer for sci. jours.; contrb. articles to profl. jours. V.p. Indian Assn., Charlottesville, Va., 1991—93; v.p., exec. com. Shri Sanatan Mandir, Parsippany, NJ, 1996—2003; asst. scout master Boys Scout of Am., Parsippany, NJ, 1998—2001; mgr. Sunday sch. Shri Sanatan Mandir, Parsippany, NJ, 1998—2003. Mem.: Am. Diabetes Assn., Brahman Samaj of N.Am. (treas. 2004—), Assn. Reproductive Health Profls., Drug Info. Assn., Am. Acad. Asthma, Allergy and Immunology, Soc. for Study of Reprodn., Am. Soc. for Reproductive Medicine, Am. Soc. of Andrology, The Endocrine Soc., Indian Soc. for Study of Reprodn. and Fertility (life), Primatological Soc. India (life), Klinische Forschungsgruppe fuer Reproduktionsmedizin (life). Achievements include research in reproductive medicine, reproductive endocrinology, diabetes, urology; development of two hormonal oral contraceptives; research in analgesic, antihistamine and antiasthematic drugs for respiratory illnesses; drugs for the treatment of benign prostatic hyperplsia; drugs for the treatment of overactive bladder, incontinence; drugs for the treatment of type 2 diabetes; drugs for the treatment of ctrl. nervous sys. diseases such as alzhimer's disease, schizophrenia, etc. Avocations: swimming, walking, travel, reading. Home: 65 Squirrel Dr Skillman NJ 08558 Office Phone: 908-927-4695. Personal E-mail: omsharma@patmedia.net. Business E-mail: osharma@prdus.jnj.com.

**SHARMA, SURENDRA PRASAD,** aerospace engineer, scientist; b. Gorakhpur, India, Feb. 3, 1943; came to U.S., 1971; s. Suresh Dutt and Dhanpati (Devi) S.; m. Prabha Durgapal; 1 child, Seema. BS, U. Gorakhpur, 1962; MS in Engring., Peoples' Friendship U., Moscow, USSR, 1968; PhD, MIT, 1978. Scientist Scientists' Pool, Coun. of Sci. and Indsl. Rsch., New Delhi, 1968-70; lectr., Dept. of Aeronautics Indian Inst. Tech., Bombay, India, 1970-71; rsch. asst. MIT, Cambridge, Mass., 1972-78; adj. rsch. prof. aeronautics Naval Postgrad. Sch. Monterey, Calif., 1979; rsch. engr. U. Tenn. Space Inst., Tullahoma, Tenn., 1979-81; sr. engr. Brown & Root, Inc., Houston, 1981-82, Sii Drilco, Smith Internat., Houston, 1982-85; rsch. scientist NASA Ames Rsch. Ctr., Moffett Field, Calif., 1986—. Contrb. articles profl. jours. Mem. PTA, Cupertino, Calif. Assoc. fellow Am. Inst. Aeronautics and Astronautics; mem. Soc. Petroleum Engrs., IEEE, Sigma Xi (MIT chpt.). Avocations: gardening, classical music. Office: MS 230-2 NASA Ames Rsch Ctr Moffett Field CA 94035-1000 Home: 2111 Jefferson Davis Hwy Apt 720 N Arlington VA 22202

**SHARMA, SUSHIL K.,** medical educator; b. Bharmar, India, Dec. 2, 1952; arrived in Can., 1988, naturalized, 2000; s. Shri Ram and Ram Piari Sharma; m. Kusum Sharma, June 27, 1983; 1 child, Aditya. BSc with honors in biophysics, Panjab U., India, 1974; MSc with honors in biophysics, Panjab U., 1976; PhD in neuroscience, All India Inst. of Med. Scis., India, 1986; postgraduate diploma in med. radio tech. (hon.), Bhabha Atomic Rsch Ctr., India, 1978. Rsch. officer All India Med. Inst., New Delhi, 1979—88; rsch. assoc. U. Manitoba, Winnipeg, 1988—93; sr. scientist U. Montreal, Montreal, Canada, 1993—97; deputy dir. Defence Inst. Physiology, New Delhi, 1997; rsch. scientist U. Manitoba, Winnipeg, 1997—2000; assoc. prof. U. ND Sch. Medicine, Grand Forks, ND, 2000—; dir. Cyclotron /microPET Labs. Author: (med. rsch. operation) Reputed Internat. Jours. of Med. Rsch. Certified, 1978. Mem.: Soc. of Neuroscience. Home: 715 N 4oth St 204J Grand Forks ND 58203 Office: Positron Imaging Rsch Lab 501 N Columbia Rd Grand Forks ND 58203 Office Phone: 701-777-6295. Business E-Mail: skumar@medicine.nodak.edu.

**SHARMA, TINA,** lawyer; b. New Delhi, Sept. 25, 1968; BS, Georgetown U., 1990; JD, Fordham U., 1993. Bar: NY 1994, NJ 1994, Md. 1996, US Dist. Ct. Dist. Md. 1996, US Ct. Appeals 4th Cir. 1996, DC 2005. Shareholder, immigration practice group Jenkens & Gilchrist, P.C., Washington, mng. shareholder Washington DC office. Mem.: ABA, Assn. Am. Lawyers from the Indian Subcontinent, NY State Bar Assn., Md. State Bar Assn., Network of Indian Professionals, Am. Immigration Lawyers Assn. Office: Jenkens & Gilchrist PC Ste 900 901 15th St NW Washington DC 20005-2301 Office Phone: 202-326-1516. Office Fax: 202-326-1555. Business E-Mail: tsharma@jenkens.com.

**SHARMA, VENKATANARAYANAN,** surgeon, consultant, medical educator; s. Sreekrishna and Kamalam Sharma; m. Sunita Subramanian, Feb. 10, 1991; children: Adrika V, Arvind V. PhD, Cancer Inst., U. Madras, India, 1989. Pre-doctoral fellow Cancer Inst., U. Madras, Chennai, 1986—89; project investigator MD Anderson Cancer Ctr., Houston, 1989—92; rsch. scientist Ohio State U., Columbus, 1992—95; asst. prof. U. West Fla., Pensacola, 1995—97, assoc. prof., 1999—2005. Head, lab. cytokine rsch. U. West Fla., 1995—, dir., health sci. adv. programs, 2001—; adminstrv. fellow, 2006—. Contbr. articles to profl. jours.; mem. editl. bd. Jour. of Alternative and Complementary Medicine. Pres. India Cultural Ctr., Inc., Pensacola, 2004—06. Recipient Awards for excellence in tchg., U. West Fla., 1998, 2003, Disting. U. Rsch. and Creative Activities award, 2001, Excellence in Undergrad. Tchg. and Advising award, 2005, 2001, Escambia County Father of Yr. award, Chief Judge's Children's Coun., Pensacola, 2002, Nautilus Excellence award, U. West Fla., 2004, Ann. Disting. Tchg. award, U. West Fla. Student Govt. Assn., 2005, Pres.'s award for Leadership in Diversity, U. West Fla., 2006; fellowship, U. Grants Commn., India, 1986—89, grants, Merck Pharm. Co., 2004. Mem.: NAAHP. Independent. Hindu. Achievements include research in identification of B-cell secreted cytokines and MNP transcription factor. Avocations: travel, gardening, woodworking. Home: 3243 Moss Point Lane Cantonment FL 32533-4844 Office: U West Fla 11000 University Parkway Pensacola FL 32514 Office Phone: 850-474-2649. Office Fax: 850-474-2749. E-mail: vsharma@uwf.edu.

**SHARMAN, RICHARD LEE,** telecommunications executive, consultant; b. Warren, Pa., Oct. 23, 1932; s. Scott Albert Sr. and Viola Lena Marie (Kittner) S.; m. Diane Lee Van Patten, Nov. 3, 1973; children: Daria Lee, Deedra Lee; children by previous marriage: Suzanne Annette, Cynthia Lee. BS in Engring. Physics, U. Toledo, 1959; MSEE, Cornell U., 1961. Project engr. advanced electronics ctr. GE, Ithaca, NY, 1959—64, Syracuse, N.Y., 1965-68, mgr. infrared and optics, electronics lab., 1965-68, mgr. info. networks, info. sys. divsn. Bethesda, Md., 1968-73; mgr. comml. analysis Xerox Corp., Rochester, N.Y., 1973-78, mgr. mktg. sys., 1978-80; v.p. bus. sector GTE Corp., Stamford, Conn., 1980-84; v.p. mktg. GTE Mobilnet Inc., Houston, 1984-87, gen. mgr. Tex. region, 1987-90; v.p. ops. GTE Mobilnet Inc. Hdqrs., Houston, 1990-92; pres., owner Mgmt. Consulting Svcs. Co., The Woodlands, Tex., 1993—. Adj. faculty Montgomery Coll., Conroe, Tex., 1997—; mem. Svc. Corps of Ret. Execs., 1998-2003 Contbr. articles to profl. jours. With USCG, 1951-54. Mem. Am. Mktg. Assn. (exec.), Cornell Alumni Assn. (admissions amb.), Tau Beta Pi. Republican. Episcopalian. Avocation: photography. Home and Office: 26 Fernglen Dr The Woodlands TX 77380-3955 Personal E-mail: rshar45854@aol.com. Business E-Mail: RLS36@cornell.edu.

**SHARMAN, WILLIAM,** professional basketball team executive; b. Abilene, Tex., May 25, 1926; m. Joyce Sharman; children from previous marriage: Jerry, Nancy, Janice, Tom. Student, U. So. Calif. Basketball player Washington Capitols, 1950-51, Boston Celtics, 1951-61; coach LA/Utah Stars, 1968-71, LA Lakers, 1971-76, gen. mgr., 1976-82, pres., 1982-88, spl. cons., 1991—. Author: Sharman on Basketball Shooting, 1965. Named to All Star 1st Team, NBA, 1956-59, 2nd Team, 1953, 55 (game MVP), 60, All League Team, 7 times, named Coach of Yr., 1972, One of Top Players in NBA History, league 50th anniversary, 1997, league leader free-throw percentage, 7 times; named to Basketball Hall of Fame, 1976, Naismith Basketball Hall of Fame (as player), 2004, as coach (3d man ever as both player and coach), 2004; named All-Am., twice; inductee U. So. Calif. Hall of Fame, 1994; Porterville H.S. gymnasium renamed in his honor, 1997; recipient John Wooden All-Time All-Am. award, 2003.

**SHAROFF, LEIGHSA,** nursing educator, researcher; d. Burton and Geraldine Sharoff; 1 child, Brody. BSN, Adelphi U., NY, 1983; MSN, Hunter Coll., NY, 1995; EdD, Columbia U., NYC, 2004. RN NY State Licensing, 1983, cert. psychiatric nurse practitioner, NY State Licensing, 1996, advanced cert. holistic nurse, Am. Holistic Nurses Assn., 2004. With Columbia U. Med. Ctr., NYC, 1983—84, Cedars Sinai Med. Ctr., LA, 1984—85, NY Hosp. Med. Ctr., NYC, 1985—91, Rockefeller U. Hosp., NYC, 1991—92; prof. nursing LI U., Bklyn., 1999—2004, Hunter Coll., NYC, 2004—. Contbr. articles to jour. Grantee Holistic Nurses Experience with Modalities, PSC-CUNY Rsch. Awards Grant, 2005, Use of PDA's in the Clin. Setting, Tech. Grant/CUNY, 2005; scholar Academic Fed. Grant Scholarship, CUNY/Hunter Coll., 1993-1995. Mem.: Am. Holistic Nurses Assn. (chair edn. approval com. 2004, Charlotte McGuire Scholarship 1994), Sigma Theta Tau. Office: Hunter Coll 425 E 25th St New York NY 10010

**SHARON, MOMANY,** retired elementary school educator, retired music educator; b. Gary, Ind., Aug. 9, 1936; d. Peter Garhardt Miller and Leona Trump; m. Frank Momany, Jan. 23, 1960 (div. Jan. 1990); children: Cory, Shelley. BM, DePauw U., 1958; MM, Memphis State U., 1984, D in Mus. Arts, 1990; postgrad., Ind. U., 1060-61. Cert. tchr., Tenn. PE: piano tchr., 1964-97; class piano asst. Cont. Edn. Memphis State U., 1981-87; staff accompanist Lambuth U., Jackson, Tenn., 1987-88; organist St. Paul the Apostle, Humboldt, Tenn., 1990-94; tchr. Bethel Coll., 1990-94; tchr. Capa keyboard Colonial Middle Sch., Memphis, 1997—2006; ret., 2006. Adj. faculty various colls., 1987-96; accompanist dance, opera, chamber groups. Contbr. articles to profl. jours. Pres. Germantown Symphony Orch., Tenn., 1980, pres.-elect, 2005-2006, pres., 2006-; v.p. Germantown Arts Coun., 1980; coord. Cornell Performers Group, Ithaca, N.Y., 1968. Grantee various orgns. including Rotary Club, Tenn. Arts Coun. Mem. Music Educators Nat. Conf., Nat. Middle Sch. Assn., Tenn. Music Tchrs. Assn., Pi Kappa Lambda, Mu Phi Epsilon. Episcopalian. Avocations: reading, baseball, football, arts and crafts. Home: 1155 Dearing Rd Memphis TN 38117-6147 Personal E-mail: drmomis@hotmail.com.

**SHARON, YITZHAK YAAKOV,** physicist, researcher; b. Tel Aviv, Feb. 29, 1936; came to U.S., 1948; s. Abraham Sharon-Schwadron and Dina Freidenberg; m. Sandra Brook, Jan. 13, 1991; 1 child, Dina Avrahama Jennie. AB with highest honors, Columbia U., 1958; MA in Physics, Princeton U., 1960, PhD in Physics, 1966. Rsch. asst. Inst. for Advanced Study, Princeton, NJ, 1965-66; asst. prof. Northeastern U., Boston, 1966-72; assoc. prof. Richard Stockton Coll., Pomona, NJ, 1972-75, prof. physics, 1975—, trustee fellow in scis., 2000-01. Cons. Edml. Svcs., Inc. Phys. Sci. Study Commn., 1962-63; vis. prof. Temple U., Phila., 1970-71, U. Montreal, 1970; vis. fellow Princeton U., 1980-82, 91-92; summer physicist Nat. Bur. Standards, Washington, 1971, Oak Ridge (Tenn.) Nat. Lab., 1969, Lawrence Radiation Lab., Berkeley, Calif., 1968; vis., cons. Rutgers U., 1995—. Contbr. articles to profl. jours. Grantee NSF, N.J. Dept. Higher Edn., Ctr. for Theology and Natural Scis. Mem. Am. Phys. Soc., Am. Assn. Physics Tchrs. (NJ exec. bd., NJ Lifetime Contbn. Physics Edn. award 2005), Sigma Xi, Phi Beta Kappa. Jewish. Home: 19 James Ave Kendall Park NJ 08824-1620 Office: Richard Stockton Coll NJ Dept Physics Pomona NJ 08240 Office Phone: 609-652-4500. Business E-Mail: sharon@physics.rutgers.edu.

**SHARP, ALLEN,** federal judge; b. Washington, D.C., Feb. 11, 1932; s. Robert Lee and Frances Louise (Williams) S.; children: Crystal Catholyn Sharp Bauer, Scarlet Frances Thomas. Student, Ind. State U., 1950-53; AB, George Washington U., 1954; JD, Ind. U., 1957; MA, Butler U., 1986. Bar: Ind. 1957. Practiced in Williamsport, 1957-68; judge Ct. of Appeals Ind., 1969-73, U.S. Dist. Ct. (no. dist.) Ind., South Bend, 1973—. Served to JAG USAF, Res. Mem.: Ind. Judges Assn., Phi Delta Kappa, Tau Kappa Alpha, Pi Gamma Mu, Blue Key. Republican. Mem. Christian Ch. Club: Mason. Office: US Dist Ct 124 Fed Bldg 204 S Main St South Bend IN 46601-2122

**SHARP, ANNE CATHERINE,** artist, educator; b. Red Bank, NJ, Nov. 1, 1943; d. Elmer Eugene and Ethel Violet (Hunter) S. BFA, Pratt Inst., 1965; MFA, Bklyn. Coll., CUNY, 1973. Tchr. art Sch. Visual Arts, 1978-89, NYU, 1978, SUNY, Purchase, 1983, Pratt Manhattan Ctr., N.Y.C., 1982-88, Parsons Sch. Design, N.Y.C., 1984-90, Visual Arts Ctr. of Alaska, Anchorage, 1991, Anchorage Mus. Hist. and Art, 1991, 93, 94, 95, U. Alaska, Anchorage, 1994-96, Fashion Inst. Tech., SUNY, 1997-98; lectr. AAAS, The 46th Arctic Divsn. Sci. Conf., U. Alaska, Fairbanks, 1995, Cmty. Ch., Ho-Ho-Ku, N.J., 2005. One-person shows Pace Editions, N.Y.C., Ten/Downtown, N.Y.C., Katonah (N.Y.) Gallery, 1974, Contemporary Gallery, Dallas, 1975, Art in a Public Space, N.Y.C., 1979, Eatontown Hist. Mus., N.J., 1980, N.Y. Pub. Library Epiphany Br., 1988, Books and Co., N.Y., 1989, The Kendall Gallery, N.Y.C., 1990, Alaska Pacific U., Carr-Gottstein Gallery, Anchorage, 1993, Internat. Gallery Contemporary Art, Anchorage, 1993, Art Think Tank Gallery, N.Y.C., 1994, U.S. Geol. Survey, Reston, Va., 1994, Stonington Gallery, Anchorage, 1994, on TV Lid. Benefit, N.Y.C., 1998-2000; group shows include Arnot Art Mus., Elmira, N.Y., 1975, Bronx Mus., 1975, Mus. Modern Art, N.Y.C., 1975-76, Nat. Arts Club, N.Y.C., 1979, Calif. Mus. Photography, Riverside, 1983-92, Jack Tilton Gallery, N.Y.C., 1983, Lincoln Ctr., N.Y.C., 1983, Cabo Frio Print Biennale, Brazil, 1983, Pratt Graphic Ctr., N.Y.C., 1984, State Mus. N.Y., Albany, 1984, Kenkeleba Gallery, N.Y.C., 1985, Hempstead Harbor Art Assn., Glen Cove, N.Y., 1985, Mus. Mod. Art, Weddel, Fed. Republic of Germany, 1985, Kenkeleba Gallery, N.Y.C., 1985, Paper Art Exhbn. Internat. Mus. Contemporary Art, Bahia, Brazil, 1986, Mus. Salon-de-Provence, France, 1987, Mus. Contemporary Art, Sao Paulo, Brazil, 1985-86, Salon de Provence, France, 1987, Adirondack Lakes Ctr. for Arts, Blue Mountain Lake, N.Y., 1987, Kendall Gallery, N.Y.C., 1988, Exhibition Ctr. Parsons Sch. Design, N.Y.C., 1989, F.M.K. Gallery, Budapest, Hungary, 1989, Galerie des Kulturbundes Schwarzenberg, German Dem. Republic, Q Sen Do Gallery, Kobe, Japan, 1989, Anchorage Mus. History and Art, 1990-91, 94, U. Alaska, Anchorage, 1990, 91, Coos Art Mus., Coos Bay, Oreg., 1990, Spaceship Earth, Mus. Internat. de Neu Art, Vancouver, Can., 1990, Councourse Gallery, Emily Carr Coll. Art and Design, 1990, Nat. Mus.

Women in the Arts, Washington, 1991, Visual Arts Ctr. Alaska, 1991, 92, Nomad Mus., Lisbon, Portugal, 1991, Mus. Ostdeutsche Gallery, Regensberg, Germany, 1991, Mcpl. Mus. Cesley Krumlov (So. Bohemia) CSFK, Czechoslovakia, 1991, Böltmiche Dörter Exhbn. Hochstrass 8, Munich, 1992, BBC-TV, Great Britain, U.K., Sta. WXXI-TV, Rochester, N.Y., 1992-93, Site 250 Gallery Contemporary Art., Fairbanks, 1993, Santa Barbara (Calif.) Mus. Art, 1993, The Rochester (N.Y.) Mus. and Sci. Ctr., 1990-94, Space Arc: The Archives of Mankind, Time Capsule in Earth Orbit, Hughes Comm., Divec TV Satellite Launch, 1994, Stonington Gallery, Anchorage, 1994, 95, UAA Art Galley U. Alaska, 1995, Arctic Trading Post, Nome, Alaska, 1995, Allan P. Kikbuarts Ctr. Gallery at the Lawrenceville (N.J.) Sch., 1996, Blue Mountain Gallery, N.Y., 1998, The Book Room, Jersey City, 2000, 01, A.I.R. Gallery, 2002, 03, 04, 05, 06-, others; represented in permanent collections Smithsonian Instn., Nat. Air and Space Mus., Washington, Albright Knox Gallery, Buffalo, St. Vincent's Hosp, N.Y.C., N.Y. Pub. Libr., N.Y.C., U.S. Geol. Survey, Reston, Va., White House (Reagan, Bush adminstrns.), Site 250 Gallery Contemporary Art, Fairbanks, Alaska, Anchorage Mus. History and Art, others; Moon Shot series to commemorate moon landing, 1970-76, Cloud Structures of the Universe Painting series, 1980-86, Am. Landscape series, 1987-89, Thoughtlines, fall 1986, Swimming in the Mainstream with Her, U. Va., Charlottesville; author: Artist's Book - Travel Dreams U.S.A., 1989, Artworld-Welt Der Kunst, Synchronicity, 1989—, Art Think Tank: Projects in Art and Ecology, 1990—, The Alaska Series, 1990—, Portraits in the Wilderness, 1990—, Family History Project J. Lindemann, 2004—; columnist: Anchorage Press, 1995. Sponsor Iditorod Trail Com., Libby Riddles. Tchg. fellow Bklyn. Coll., 1972; Artist-in-residence grantee Va. Ctr. for Creative Arts, 1974, Artpark, Lewiston, N.Y., 1980, Vt. Studio Colony, 1989; recipient Pippin award Our Town, N.Y.C., 1984, certificate of Appreciation Art in Embassy program U.S. Dept. State, 1996. Mem. Mus. Women in Arts, Pratt Inst. Alumni Assn., Internat. Assn. Near-Death Studies. Address: Murray Hill Station PO Box 1776 New York NY 10156-1776 also: On Television Ltd 388 Broadway New York NY 10013-3542 *As an active painter I explore the mysteries of the 21st century space adventure in my American landscapes, painted directly from nature and in planetary landscapes, fantastic pictures of the cosmos. I believe it is in the reconciliation between inner and outer experience, through a personal sense of humor and use of universal symbols that a mystical or cosmic harmony can be expressed in art.*

**SHARP, BARRY J.,** school system administrator; BBA, Coll. of William and Mary, 1981. CPA. Dir. fin. and adminstrn. The AES Corp., Arlington, Va., 1986—87, v.p., CFO, 1987—2006, sr. v.p., 1998, exec. v.p., 2001—06, COO, 2002, cons., 2006—; bd. dirs. Imagine Schools, Arlington, Va., 2005—, CFO, 2006—. Bd. mem. Coll. William and Mary Bus. Found. Office: Imagine Schools 1005 N Glebe Rd Ste 610 Arlington VA 22201 Office Phone: 703-527-2600. Office Fax: 703-527-0038.

**SHARP, CHRISTINA KRIEGER,** retired nursing educator; b. Ft. Montgomery, N.Y., Aug. 4, 1928; d. Joseph Lewis and Mary Agnes Krieger; m. Andrew Asa Sharp, Jr., Feb. 3, 1957 (dec. Jan. 31, 1969); children: Shawn Patrick, Sharon Paula Zegers. RN, cadet nurse, St. Lukes Hosp., Newburgh, N.Y., 1948; BS, Coll. William and Mary, 1955; MA, NYU, 1974. RN N.Y. Staff nurse Vets. Hosp., Richmond, Va., 1948—53, Army Hosp., West Point, NY, 1954—56; instr. nursing Orange County CC, Middletown, NY, 1956—57, Santa Rosa (Calif.) Jr. Coll., 1961—62; supr. nursing Vocat. Edn. and Extension Bd., New City, NY, 1957—60; coord. practical nursing program Newburgh Sch. Dist., 1963—83. Cons. N.Y. State Edn. Dept. Nursing, Albany, 1983—84. Mem.: VFW, AFL-CIO, AAUW (sec. 1999—2001), Fla. Educators Assn., N.Y. State United Tchrs. (Cmty. Svc. award 1998), Fla. Alliance Ret. Ams. (bd. mem. 2002—, sec. ctrl. Fla. chpt. 2004—), Fla. Soc. RNs Ret., Inc. (Orlando dist. pres. 1994—97, editor yearbooks 1997—, state pres. 1998—2002, Fla. state coun. 43 pres. 2001—), Widow and Widowers Soc. Ctrl. Fla. (pres. 1999—2002), Orange County Ret. Educators Assn., Tchr. Retirees Fla., Golden Rod Civic Club (bd. dirs. 2001—), Am. Legion Aux. Avocations: travel, opera, ballet, Broadway shows, ice shows. Home: 2735 Mystic Cove Dr Orlando FL 32812-5344 E-mail: tisharp@aol.com.

**SHARP, DAN STEVEN,** epidemiologist; s. Darrell Dean Sharp and Stella Louise Morrison-Sharp; m. Carol Lee Thomas, Dec. 26, 1996; m. Caroline Stanley Johnson, June 20, 1970 (div. Apr. 16, 1996); children: Sarah Elizabeth, David Henry. BS in Chemistry, U. Redlands, Calif., 1972; MD, U. Calif., Irvine, 1975; MPH, U. Calif., Berkeley, 1984; PhD in Epidemiology, U. Calif., 1987. Board Certified in Public Health and General Preventive Medicine Am. Bd. of Preventive Medicine, 1990, diplomate Nat. Bd. of Med. Examiners, 1977, Physician's and Surgeon's Certificate Bd. of Med. Quality Assurance, State of Calif., 1977, Certificate of Registration as a Visiting Overseas Doctor Gen. Med. Coun., UK, 1989. Flight surgeon US Army, Natick, Mass., 1977—80; sr. med. epidemiologist Med. Rsch. Coun., Cardiff, Wales, 1988—90; dir., Honolulu heart program Nat. Heart, Lung and Blood Inst., 1992—97; assoc. dir. sci. Health Effects Lab., Nat. Inst. for Occupl. Safety and Health, Morgantown, W.Va., 2000—. Contbr. scientific papers. Capt. US Army, 1977—80, Natick, Massachusetts. Mem.: Soc. for Epidemiologic Rsch. Achievements include research in cardiovascular disease in populations. Office Phone: 304-285-6260.

**SHARP, DAVID HOWLAND,** physicist; b. Buffalo, Oct. 14, 1938; s. Russel Howland and Margaret (Dorries) E.; m. Gloria Evanitsky, Jan. 9, 1982; children: Lisa E., Michelle L.; stepchildren: Brian P. Riepe, Michael A. Riepe. AB, Princeton U., 1960; PhD, Calif. Inst. Tech., 1964. Mem. staff Los Alamos Nat. Lab., N.Mex., 1974—84, fellow, 1984—, group leader complex systems group, theoretical divsn., 2002—04, sr. sci. advisor applied physics divsn., 2002—04, dep. chief sci. officer, 2004—. Vis. fellow Ctr. for Theoretical Neurosci., Salk Inst., 1995—98; mem. indsl. adv. bd. Inst. Math. and Its Applications, 2002—. Mem. editl. bd.: Jour. Math. Physics, 1985—87. Recipient def. programs award of excellence, U.S. Dept. Energy, 2001; Postdoctoral fellow, NSF, 1963—64. Fellow AAAS, Am. Phys. Soc.; mem. Am. Math Soc. (mem. editl. bd. Jour. Procs. 1992-2003), Internat. Assn. Math. Physicists, Internat. Soc. for Gen. Relativity and Gravitation, N.Y. Acad. Scis., Soc. Indsl. and Applied Math., Soc. Petroleum Engrs., N.Mex. Acad. Scis. Home: 174 Laguna St Los Alamos NM 87544-2603 Office Phone: 505-667-5266. Personal E-Mail: davidandglory@msn.com. Business E-Mail: dcso@lanl.gov.

**SHARP, J(AMES) FRANKLIN,** finance educator, portfolio manager; b. Johnson Count, Ill., Sept. 29, 1936; s. James Albert and Edna Mae (Slack) S. BS in Indsl. Engring., U. Ill., 1960; MS, Purdue U., 1962, PhD, 1966, cert. mgmt. acctg., 1979. Chartered fin. analyst, 1980; cert. in fin. mgmt., 1997. Asst. prof. engring., econs. Rutgers U., New Brunswick, NJ, 1966-70; assoc. prof. NYU Grad. Sch. Bus., N.Y.C., 1970-74; supr. bus. research AT&T, N.Y.C., 1974-77; dist. mgr. corp. planning, 1977-81, dist. mgr. fin. mgmt. and planning, 1981-85; prof. fin. Grad. Sch. Bus. Pace U., N.Y.C., 1975-91; chmn. Sharp CFA Rev. & Inst. for Investment Edn., 1987-96, Sharp Seminars, 1996—. Speaker, moderator meetings, 1965—; cons. Sharp Investment Mgmt., 1967—. Contbr. numerous articles to profl. publs.; corr.: Interfaces, 1975-78; fin. editor: Planning Rev., 1975-78. Mem. N.Am. Soc. Corp. Planning (treas. 1976-77, bd. dirs. at large 1977-78), Inst. Mgmt. Sci. (chpt. v.p. acad. 1972-74, chpt. v.p. program 1974-75, chpt. v.p. membership 1975-76, chpt. pres. 1976-77), Internat. Affiliation Planning Socs. (coun. 1978-84), N.Y. Soc. Security Analysts (CFA Rev. 1985-87), Ops. Rsch. Soc. Am. (pres. corp. planning group 1976-82), AAUP (v.p. U. chpt. 1988-90), Theta Xi. Republican. Office: 315 E 86th St Apt 7H New York NY 10028-4740

**SHARP, JANE SHRIVER,** artist; b. Dechard, Tenn., Oct. 14, 1931; d. Paul and Jane (Brown) Shriver; m. Benjamin Thomas Sharp, Sept. 26, 1953; children: Jane Ashton Sharp, Anne Dudley, Julia Shriver. Student, Art Acad., Cin., 1948, Wesleyan Women's Coll., Macon, Ga., 1949-52, U. Chattanooga, 1953, Ecole Beaux Arts, Geneva, 1968-70. Transp. line designer TVA, Chattanooga, 1952-55. Founder Artist's Studio Gallery, Palos Verdes Art Ctr., Palos Verdes Estates, Calif., 1987, bd. dirs., 1985-88; coord. art displays Hall of Adminstrn., L.A., 1987—. One-woman show includes Security Pacific Bank, Palos Verdes Estates, 1988; juried shows include Palos Verdes Art Ctr., 1988, 89; group exhbns. include The Artist's Studio Gallery, Rancho Palos Verdes, 1991; permanent collections include Wesleyan Coll., Macon, Ga., City Hall Palos Verdes Estates; pvt. collections in Geneva, Switzerland and Wilmington, Del.; executed mural Children at Play, Nemours Inst., 1961. Artistic cons. Peninsula Beautification Com., Palos Verdes Estates, Calif., 1987—. Recipient Profl. Artist award Los Angeles County Suprs., 1989; tchr.'s scholar Art Acad., 1948. Mem. Los Angeles County Mus. Art, Mus. Contemporary Art (charter), Armand Hammer Mus. (charter), Beverly Hills Art League, 242 Art Gallery Palos Verdes, Jr. League L.A. (sustaining), Pacific Arts Group (pres. 1976-78), Peninsula Six Artists Groups (pres. 1985-88). Republican. Episcopalian. Avocations: tennis, swimming, skiing. Home: 2405 Via La Selva Palos Verdes Estates CA 90274-1017

**SHARP, JOAN DIANE,** biology professor; d. Jack Roger and Doris Jean Fehseke; m. Charles Leonard Sharp, May 22, 1976; children: Carolynn Joan Dwight, Charles Leonard III. AS, Southeastern C.C., West Burlington, Iowa, 1973; BS, U. Iowa, 1976; MS, Western Ill. U., 2001. Instr. biol. scis. Southeastern C.C., West Burlington, 2001—. Mem.: Iowa Assn. C.C. Tchrs., Am. Inst. Biol. Scis., Des Moines County Nature Trail Assn., Art Guild Burlington, Phi Kappa Phi. Avocations: bicycling, fishing, sketching. Home: 12356 S Prairie Grove Rd West Burlington IA 52655 Office: Southeastern CC 1500 W Agency Rd West Burlington IA 52655 Office Phone: 319-753-2731 ext. 8318.

**SHARP, JOSHUA S.,** biochemist; b. Brownsville, Tenn., July 10, 1977; s. John Michael (Stepfather) and Elizabeth Newman; m. Shannon R. Stone, July 25, 1999; children: Chloe A., Aaron M. BS, U. of Tenn., Knoxville, 1999; PhD, 2003. IRTA fellow Nat. Inst. Environ. Health Scis., Research Triangle Park, NC, 2003—. Recipient Intramural Rsch. Tng. award, NIH, 2003—06. Mem.: Am. Soc. for Mass Spectrometry, Am. Chem. Soc. Achievements include development of technique to study structural effects of oxidation-induced protein unfolding. Office Phone: 919-541-0192.

**SHARP, LEWIS INMAN,** museum director, curator; b. NYC, Dec. 22, 1941; BA, Lewis & Clark Coll., 1965; MA, U. Del., 1968, PhD. Asst. curator paintings & sculpture Met. Mus. Art, NYC, 1972—75, assoc. curator, 1975—82, curator, adminstr. Am. Wing, 1982—89; dir. Denver Art Mus., 1989—. Office: Denver Art Mus 100 W 14th Ave Pkwy Denver CO 80204-2749

**SHARP, PAUL DAVID,** institute administrator; b. Youngstown, Ohio, Nov. 3, 1940; s. Robert Henderson and Kathryn (Tadsen)S.; m. Carole G. Graff, Sept. 16, 1967; children: David Allen, Kathryn Sharp Snyder. BA cum laude, Kenyon Coll., Gambier, Ohio, 1962; MPA, Auburn U., 1974. Commd. 2d lt. USAF, 1962, advanced through grades to col., 1983, comdr. Detachment 1, 7450th Intelligence Squadron Neubruecke, Germany, 1980-83, comdr. 480th Reconnaissance Tech. Group Langley AFB, Va., 1983-85, dir. intelligence systems HQ Tactical Air Command, 1985-86, dep. chief intelligence Tactical Air Command, 1986-88; mgr. operational intelligence group Battelle Meml. Inst., Columbus, Ohio, 1988-89, mgr. fgn. tech. assessment group, 1989-91, mgr. intelligence projects/programs, 1991-92, v.p. bus. devel. fgn. sci. and tech., 1992-95, dir. fgn. sci. and tech. programs, 1995-98; dir. Air Force spl. programs Batelle Meml. Inst., Columbus, Ohio, 1998-99, mgr. spl. programs office, 1999-2000; mgr. Internat. Tech. Assessments Product Line, 2000—. Student career coun. Kenyon Coll., Columbus, 1992—. Trustee Brandywine Assn., Yorktown, Va., 1987, Chase Assn., Powell, Ohio, 1991. Decorated Legion of Merit. Mem. Nat. Mil. Intelligence Assn., Armed Forces Communications and Electronics Assn., Air Force Assn., Retired Officers Assn., Sigma Pi (pres. Lambda chpt. 1961-62). Republican. Episcopalian. Avocations: golf, woodworking, photography, music. Office: Battelle Meml Inst 505 King Ave Columbus OH 43201-2681 Personal E-mail: sharppd@aol.com.

**SHARP, PAUL FREDERICK,** retired academic administrator, educational consultant; b. Kirksville, Mo., Jan. 19, 1918; s. Frederick J. and L. Blanche (Phares) S.; m. Rosella Ann Anderson, June 19, 1939; children: William, Kathryn, Paul Trevor. AB, Phillips U., 1939; PhD, U. Minn., 1947; LLD (hon.), Tex. Christian U., 1961, Austin Coll., 1978, Drake U., 1980; LHD (hon.), Buena Vista Coll., 1967, U. Nev., Towson State U., 1980, Oklahoma City U., 1996, U. Okla., 1997; LittD (hon.), Limestone Coll., 1971; HHD, Okla. Christian U. Sci. & Arts, 1992. Instr. U. Minn., 1942, 46-47, vis. lectr., 1948; asso. prof. Am. history Iowa State U., 1947-54; prof. Am. history, chmn. Am. Instns. program U. Wis., 1954-57, vis. lectr., 1953, San Francisco State Coll., 1950, U. Oreg., 1955; Fulbright lectr. Am. Instns., univs. Melbourne, Sydney, 1952; pres. Hiram Coll., 1957-64; chancellor U. N.C., Chapel Hill, 1964-66; pres. Drake U., Des Moines, 1966-71, U. Okla., Norman, 1971-78, pres. emeritus, Regents' prof., 1978-88, pres. emeritus, Regents' prof. emeritus, 1988—; disting. prof. history U. Sci. and Arts, Okla., 1990—96. Dir. Am. Coun. on Edn. Insts. for Coll. and Univ. Presidents, 1977-79; vis. lectr. Harvard U. Bus. Sch. summer session 1970-72. Author: Agrarian Revolt in Western Canada, 1948, Old Orchard Farm, Story of an Iowa Boyhood, 1952, Whoop-Up Country, Canadian American West, 1955; cons. author: Heritage of Midwest, 1958; editor: Documents of Freedom, 1957; contbr. articles to profl. jours. Pres. Norman Cmty. Found., 1995-97, Okla. State Coun. Aging, 1997-99. USN liaison officer His Majesty's Australian Ship, Hobart, 1943-46. With USNR, 1943-47. Recipient Iowa State U. Alumni Fund award, 1952, award of merit Am. Assn. State and Local History, 1955, Silver Spur award Western Writers Am., 1955, Fulbright award to Australia, 1952; named to Okla. Higher Edn. Hall of Fame, 1995; Minn. Hist. Soc. grantee, 1947, 48, Social Sci. Rsch. Coun. grantee, 1949, 51; Ford Faculty fellow, 1954, Guggenheim fellow, 1957. Mem. Phi Beta Kappa, Phi Kappa Phi, Phi Delta Kappa, Pi Gamma Mu, Phi Alpha Theta. Mem. Christian Ch. (Disciples Of Christ). Home: 701 Mockingbird Ln Norman OK 73071-1829

**SHARP, PHILLIP ALLEN,** biologist, educator; b. Ky., June 6, 1944; s. Joseph Walter and Katherin (Colvin) S.; m. Ann Christine Holcombe, Aug. 29, 1964; children: Christine Alynn, Sarah Katherin, Helena Holcombe. BA, Union Coll., Barbourville, Ky., 1966; PhD, U. Ill., 1969; LHD (hon.), Union Coll., Barbourville, Ky., 1991; DSc (hon.), U. Ky., 1994, Bowdoin Coll., 1995, U. Tel Aviv, Israel, 1996, Albright Coll., 1996; degree (hon.), U. Glasgow, 1998, U. Uppsala, 1999, Thomas Moore Coll., 1999, U. Buenos Aires, 1999, No. Ky. U., 1999, PhD (hon.), 2001. NIH postdoctoral fellow Calif. Inst. Tech., 1969—71; sr. research investigator Cold Spring Harbor (N.Y.) Lab., 1972—74; assoc. prof. MIT, Cambridge, 1974—79, prof. biology, 1979—99, dir. Ctr. Cancer Rsch., 1985—91, head dept. biology, 1991—99, inst. prof., 1999—. Co-founder, bd. dirs. BIOGEN IDEC, 1978—, chmn. sci. bd., 1987—2002, pres. adv. coun. sci. and tech., 1991—97; mem. presdl. appt. Nat.Cancer Adv. Bd. NIH, 1996—2000; chmn. GM Cancer Rsch. Found. Awards Assembly, 1994—; mem. sci. bd. Ludwig Inst., 1998—; mem. bd. sci. govs. Scripps Rsch. Inst., 1999—; trustee Mass. Gen. Hosp., 2001—; co-founder, chair of sci. bd. and mem. of bd. dirs. Alnylan Pharm. Inc., 2002—; bd. advisors Polaris Venture Ptnrs., 2002; mem. Corp. Ptnrs. HealthCare Systems, Inc., 2003—; sci. adv. bd. Fidelity Bioscis. Group, 2004—; dir. sci. bd. Sirtus Pharm. Inc., 2005—; co-founder, dir. sci. bd. Magen Pharmaceuticals Inc., 2006—. Mem. editl. bd.: Cell, 1974—95, Jour. Virology, 1974—86, Molecular and Cellular Biology, 1974—85, RNA, 1995—. Trustee Alfred P. Sloan Found., 1995—2004. Co-recipient Nobel Prize in Physiology or Medicine, 1993; named Class of '41 chair, 1986—87, John D. MacArthur chair, 1987—92, Salvador E. Luria chair, 1992—99; recipient awards, Am. Cancer Soc., 1974—79, Eli Lilly, 1980, Nat. Acad.Sci./U.S. Steel Found., 1980, Howard Ricketts award, U.Chgo., 1985, Alfred P. Sloan Jr. prize, Gen. Motors Rsch. Found., 1986, award, Gairdner Found. Internat., 1986, N.Y. Acad.Scis., 1986, Louisa Horwitz prize, 1988, Albert Lasker Basic Med. Rsch. award, 1988, Dickson prize, U. Pitts., 1990, Fourth Ann. Biotech. Heritage award, 2002, Alumni Achievement award, U. Ill., 2003, Nat. Medal in Biol. Scis., 2004. Fellow: AAAS, Royal Soc. Edinburgh (hon.); mem.: NAS (councilor 1986, Nat. Medal of Sci. 2004), Corp. Ptnrs. HealthCare Systems, Inc. (elected mem.), Inst. of Medicine of

NAS (elected mem.), Am. Philos. Soc. (elected mem.) (The Benjamin Franklin medal 1999), Am. Soc. Biochemistry and Molecular Biology (elected mem. coun.), European Molecular Biology Orgn. (assoc.), Am. Acad. Arts and Scis., Am. Soc. Microbiology, NAS Republic of Korea (hon.). Office: MIT Rm E17529B Ctr for Cancer Rsch 40 Ames St Cambridge MA 02139-4307 Business E-Mail: sharppa@mit.edu.

**SHARP, RICHARD L.,** retail company executive; b. Washington, Apr. 12, 1947; Student, U. Va., 1965-66, Coll. of William and Mary, 1968-70. Programmer Group Health Inc., Washington, 1970-75; founder, pres. Applied Systems Corp., Washington, 1975-81; with Circuit City Stores, Inc., Richmond, Va., 1982—2002, exec. v.p., 1982-84, pres., 1984-86, pres., CEO, 1986-94, chmn., pres., CEO, 1994-97, chmn., CEO, 1997-2000, chmn., 1997—2002, CarMax Inc., Glen Allen, Va., 2002—, Flextronics Internat. Ltd., 2003—. Bd. dirs. Flextronics Internat. With USAF, 1967-70. Office: Carmax 12800 Tuckahoe Creek Pkwy Richmond VA 23238-1115*

**SHARP, ROB,** investment company executive; BA summa cum laude, Union Coll.; MBA, Columbia Bus. Sch. Assoc. mergers and acquisitions group Drexel Burnham Lambert; exec. v.p. Remsen Ptnrs. Ltd.; v.p. BT Securities; prin. Investcorp Internat. Inc.; mng. dir. DB Capital Ptnrs.; ptnr. MidOcean Ptnrs. Bd. dirs. Jenny Craig, Inc., Jostens, Inc., Prestige Brands Internat., Inc., Stratus Tech., Global Sight, Illumin. Mem.: Phi Beta Kappa. Office: MidOcean Ptnrs 320 Park Ave Ste 1700 New York NY 10022

**SHARP, RON,** secondary school educator; b. Shawnee, Okla., May 15, 1952; s. Halbert K. and Virginia Pauline Sharp; m. Debbie Marie Buckmaster (div.); 1 child, Kara Meli. BA in Social Studies, Southeastern Okla. State U., Durant, 1974; MEd in Polit. Sci., U. Ctrl. Okla., Edmond, 1979; PhD in Polit. Sci., Kensington U., Glendale, Calif., 1988. Cert. tchr. Okla. Instr. social scis. Shawnee (Okla.) Pub. Schs., 1974—. Instr. U.S. Profl. Tennis Assn., Shawnee, 1978—; mem. adv. bd. Pottawatomie County Jail Trust, Shawnee, 2002—06. Author: Clarisa Leflore/Choctaw Princess, 2004. Adv. Nat. Youth Leadership Forum, Washington, 2005; parliamentarian Rep. Party, Pattawatomie, Okla., 1996—99, chmn. precinct, 1996—2004. Named Tennis Coach of Yr., Okla. State Tennis Coaches Assn., 1976, 1977, 1979, 1984, 1996, Nat. Tennis Coach of Yr., Nat. H.S. Athletic Coaches Assn., 1987, All-American Tennis Coach of Yr., 1987, Tchr. of Yr., Shawnee (Okla.) H.S., 1996, 1997, 1998, Masonic Lodge, 1998; recipient Pres.'s award, U.S. Interpreunmenal and Interagency Affairs, 2001, Leadership award, Heritage Found., 2002, Am. Medal Hon., 2002. Mem.: Nat. Coun. Social Studies, Okla. States Tennis Coaches Assn. (pres. 1977—82), U.S. Profl. Tennis Assn. (mentor 1983—), Shawnee Assn. Classroom Tchrs. (legis. liaison 1996—2004). Republican. Bapt. Avocations: tennis, genealogy, politics. Home: 1835 N Oklahoma Ave Shawnee OK 74804 Office: Shawnee High School 1001 N Kennedy Shawnee OK 74801 Office Phone: 405-275-3084.

**SHARP, RONALD ALAN,** language educator, writer, dean; b. Cleve., Oct. 19, 1945; s. Jack Trier and Florence (Tenenbaum) S.; m. Inese Brutans, June 22, 1968; children: Andrew Janis, James Michael. BA, Kalamazoo Coll., 1967; MA, U. Mich., 1968; PhD, U. Va., 1974. Instr. in English Western Mich. U., Kalamazoo, 1968-70; from instr. to prof. English Kenyon Coll., Gambier, Ohio, 1970—2002, assoc. provost, provost, acting pres., 1998—2003; prof. English, dean of faculty Vassar Coll., Poughkeepsie, NY, 2003—. Dir. Keats Bicentennial Conf., Harvard U., 1995. Author: Keats, Skepticism and the Religion of Beauty, 1979, Friendship and Literature: Spirit and Form. 1986; translator: Teatro Breve (Garcia Lorca), 1979, editor (with Eudora Welty) The Norton Book of Friendship, 1991, (with Nathan Scott) Reading George Steiner, 1994, (with Robert Ryan) The Persistence of Poetry: Bicentennial Essays on John Keats, 1998, Selected Poems of Michael Harper, 2002; co-editor Kenyon Rev., 78-82; contbr. articles to profl. jours. Recipient award for editl. excellence Ohioana Assn., 1980; fellow Nat. Humanities Ctr., 1981, 86, NEH, 1981, 84-87, 93, 94, 96, 98, Ford Found., 1971, Mellon Found., 1980, Danforth Found., 1971, English Speaking Union, 1973, Am. Coun. Learned Socs., 1986. Mem. MLA, NEH (chmn.'s adv. group humanities edn. 1987), Wordsworth-Coleridge Assn., Keats-Shelley Assn. Jewish. Office: Dean of Faculty Vassar Coll Box 4 Poughkeepsie NY 12604 Office Phone: 845-437-5300. Business E-Mail: sharp@vassar.edu.

**SHARP, RONALD ARVELL,** sociology educator; b. Vivian, La., Sept. 29, 1941; s. Walter Arvell and Virginia (Refield-King) S.; m. Imelda Idalia Pena, Sept. 16, 1967; children: Ronald Arvell II, Donald Allen. BS in Edn. Cameron U., 1976; BA in Sociology, SUNY, Albany, 1977; MEd in Counseling Psychology, U. Okla., 1978; PhD in Sociology, Clayton U., 1985. Ret. radiologic technologist and instr. U.S. Army, 1960-82; radiologic technologist VA Hosp., Temple, Tex., 1983-84; vets. counselor Vets. Outreach Program, San Antonio, 1982-83; dir. personnel & mktg. Heran Pharms., San Antonio, 1988-91; prof. sociology Ctrl. Tech. Coll., Killeen, 1991-95; instr. sociology Tex. State Tech. Coll., Waco, 1995-96, Academia Assocs., 1996—. Part-time instr. Ctrl. Tex. Coll., 1980-82, City Coll. Chgo., 1981, Big Bend C.C., Mannheim, Germany, 1981-82; instr. Acad. Health Scis., 1977-79. Contbr. articles to profl. jours. Coach Youth Soccer Orgns., San Antonio and Mannheim, 1976-82. Nat. Coll. Radiologic Technologists fellow, 1968. Mem. AAUP, DAV (past comdr.), VFW (past comdr.), Uniformed Svcs. Disabled Retirees (nat. vice-commdr., treas.), Am. Sociol. Assn., Soc. Applied Sociology, Nat. Assn. Medics and Corpsmen (PNC), Am. Mil. Ret. Assn. (PNVP), Combat Medics Assn. (nat. dir.), La. Archeol. Soc., Choctaw Nation of Okla., Okla. Anthrop. Soc., La. Archeol. Conservancy, Caddoan Hist. Soc., Okla. Anthropol. Survey, Order of Alhambra, KC, Masons, Soc. for the Study of Social Problems, Four Winds Intertribal Soc., Hickshichankiya Soc., Psi Beta (chpt. sponsor), Alpha Kappa Delta, Psi Chi, Sigma Eta Sigma (nat. dir.). Roman Catholic. Avocations: soccer, golf, paleo-historic anthropology. Home: 9310 Oak Hills Dr Temple TX 76502-5272 Office: Academia Assocs Waco TX 76705

**SHARP, WALTER L. (GARY SHARP),** career military officer; Grad., US Mil. Acad., 1974; MS in Ops. Analysis and Engring., Rensselaer Poly. Inst. 1981; grad., Command and Gen. Staff Coll., 1986, Army War Coll. Advanced through grades to lt. gen. US Army, 2003, platoon leader A Company, later exec. officer, B Company, later S-3 (Air), 1st Bn., 67th Armor, 2d Armored Divsn. Fort Hood, Tex., 1975—77; armor co. comdr. 1st Bn., 67th Armor, 2nd Armored Divsn., Fort Hood, Tex., 1978—80; combat devel. analysis officer Office of Dir. Combat Developments US Army Armor Sch., Fort Knox, Ky., 1981—84; combat devel. officer, Deep Attach Programs Office, Office Dep. Chief of Staff for Ops. & Plans US Army, 1984—85; exec. officer, 2nd Squadron, 11th Armored Cavalry Regiment US Army Europe/Seventh Army, Germany, 1986—88; combat devel. analysis officer, A3 Task Force, Office Chief of Staff US Army, Washington, 1988—89, dir. analysis, Force Devel Divsn, Office Dep. Chief of Staff for Ops. & Plans., 1989—90; comdr., 7th Cavalry Squadron, 1st Cavalry divsn., Desert Shield/Storm, 1990—93; dir., models & simulations directorate US Army Combined Arms Command, Nat. Simulations Ctr., Fort Leavenworth, 1993—94; comdr., 2d Armored Cavalry Regiment Operation Uphold Democracy, Haiti, 1994—96; exec. officer to comdr.-in-chief UN Combined Forces Command/US Forces Korea, Republic of Korea, 1996—97; asst. divsn. comdr. for maneuver 2nd Infantry Divsn., Camp Red Cloud, Republic of Korea, 1997—98; comdr. 3rd Infantry Divsn. (Mechanized), Fort Stewart, 1999—2001; dep. dir. for Global/Multilateral Issues/Internat. Am. Affairs (J-5) The Joint Staff, Washington, 1998—99, vice dir. for force structure, resources & assessment (J-8), 2001—03 dir. strategic plans and policy (J-5), 2003—05, dir., 2005—. Decorated Disting. Svc. Medal, Defense Superior Svc. Medal with Oak Leaf Clusters, Bronze Star, Legion of Merit with Oak Leaf Cluster, Meritorious Svc. Medal with 5 Oak Leaf Clusters, Army Commendation Medal, Army Achievement Medal. Office: The Pentagon 300 Joint Staff Washington DC 20318*

**SHARP, WILLIAM WHEELER,** geologist; b. Shreveport, La., Oct. 9, 1923; s. William Wheeler and Jennie V. (Benson) S.; m. Rubylin Slaughter, 1958; children: Staci Lynn, Kimberly Cecile; 1 child from previous marriage, John E. BS in Geology, U. Tex., Austin, 1950, MA, 1951. Lic. pvt. pilot. Geol. Socony-Vacuum, Caracas, Venezuela, 1951-53; surface geol. chief Creole,

1953-57; dist. devel. geologist, supr. exploration, devel. unitization of 132 multi-pay oil and gas fields, expert geol. witness, coll. recruiter, rsch. adviso ARCO, 1957—85. Discovered oil and gas at Bayou Boullion, Bayou Sale, Jeanerette, La., Chandeleur Sound and Beauregaurd Parish, La.; petroleum exploration in Alaska, Aus., Can., U.S. and S.A. Contbr. articles to profl. jours.; author numerous corp. rsch. and ops. reports; included in From Acorn to Oakbourne—History of Oakbourne Country Club, 1998.; contbr. artifacts/photos to Nimitz Mus., Fredricksburg, Tex., Nat. Mus. Pacific War, Nat. WWII Meml., Washington, Tex. Meml. Mus., Benson Latin Am. Libr., U. Tex., Austin. Past dir. and chmn. U.S. Tennis Assn. Tournaments; pres. Lafayette Tennis Adv. Com., 1972; pres. Oakbourne Tennis Assn.; past dir. Jr. Achievement and United Fund Programs; contbr. to various mus. With USAF, 1943-46, PTO. Winner and finalist more than 75 amateur tennis tournaments including Confederate Oil Invitational, Gulf Coast Oilmen's Tournament, So. Oilmen's Tournament, Tex.-Ark.-La. Oilmen's Tournament, top La. State Ranking; named Hon. Citizen of New Orleans, 1971, recipient Key to New Orleans; named in Registry of Remembrances Nat. WWII Meml., Washington. Mem. Dallas Geol. Soc., Lafayette Geol. Soc. (bd. dirs. 1973-74), Am. Assn. Petroleum Geologists (emeritus, co-author Best of SEG conv. 1982), Tex. Astron. Soc., VFW, Am. Legion, Lafayette Petroleum Club, Appaloosa Horse Club, Collin County Hist. Soc., Am.'s Nat. World War II Mus. (charter, Brookhaven Country Club (Dallas), Oakbourne Country Club Tennis Assn. (pres. 1976, organizer USTA nat. boys tennis tournament 1976). Republican. Methodist. Achievements include drilling of more than 30 successful wells at Bayou Boullion Field; report/recommendations that resulted in Atlantic Refining Co. office at Anchorage, 1962. Avocations: sports, music, history. Home: 7312 Mimosa Ln Dallas TX 75230-5446

**SHARPE, CONSTANTINE,** engineer, consultant, mathematics professor; b. Bacau, Romania, Aug. 27, 1941; s. Constantin and Elisabeta; m. Antonina Casam-Sharpe, Nov. 10, 1971; children: Christian Tiberius, Patricia Sorina. MSEE in Math., Polytech. U., Bucharest, 1967; MS in Econ., Acad. Econ. Studies, Bucharest, 1974; PhD in Energy Conservation Engring., Acad. Econ. Studies, 1978. Sr. rschr., devel. engr. scientist Ctrl. Rsch. and Design Inst. for Electrotechnics, Bucharest, 1978—89; cons. engr. Engring. Design, Costa Mesa, Calif., 1991—95; hs. math tchr. Tustin and Santa Ana Unified Sch. Dist., Calif., 1996—99; math. prof. Irvine (Calif) Valley Coll., 1999—2005. Assoc. prof. Polytech. U., 1975—79, Acad. Econ. Studies, 1979—88; math. instr. Nat. U., San Diego, 1997—99; founder Math Master, Costa Mesa, Calif., 1997—. Author: (novels) Running Hope, 1999, Unfamiliar Ground, 2004, Energy Conservation Engineering, vol. I and vol.II; contbr. over 60 articles to profl. jours. Mem.: Mathematical Assn. Am., Internat. Assn. Conservation of Natural Resources and Energy, Assn. Profl. Engrs. and Scientist. Republican. Greek Orthodox. Avocations: writing, politics, history, physics. Address: 170 E 17th St # 207 Costa Mesa CA 92627 Office Phone: 949-515-4710. Personal E-mail: casoumsharpe@adelphia.net.

**SHARPE, JAMES SHELBY,** lawyer; b. Ft. Worth, Sept. 11, 1940; s. James Henry and Wanzel (Vanderbilt) S.; m. Martha Moudy Holland, June 9, 1962; children: Marthanne Freeman, Caren Sharp, Stephen. BA, U. Tex., 1962, JD, 1965. Bar: Tex. 1965, U.S. Dist. Ct. (no. dist.) Tex. 1966, U.S. Dist. Ct. (ea. dist.) Tex. 1993, U.S. Dist. Ct. (ea. and we. dists.) Ark. 1997, U.S. Ct. Appeals (5th and 6th cirs.) 1982, U.S. Ct. Appeals (fed. cir.) 1983, U.S. Ct. Appeals (10th cir.) 1992, U.S. Supreme Ct. 1972. Briefing atty. for chief justice Supreme Ct. of Tex., Austin, 1965-66; ptnr. Brown, Herman, Scott, Dean & Miles, Ft. Worth, 1966-84, Gandy Michener Swindle Whitaker & Pratt, Ft. Worth, 1984-87; shareholder Sharpe Tillman & Melton, Ft. Worth, 1988—. Adj. prof. polit. sci. Tex. Christian U., Ft. Worth, 1969-79, Dallas Bapt. U., 1987, 1992-94; gen. counsel U.S.A. Radio Network, Internat. Christian Media, Denton Pub. Co. Pres. Ft. Worth-Tarrant County Jr. Bar, 1969-70, bd. dirs., sec., 1968, v.p., 1968-69; head marshal USA-USSR Track and Field Championships, Ft. Worth, USA-USSR Jr. Track and Field Championships, Austin, Tex., Relays, Austin, 1963—, NCAA Nat. Track and Field Championships, 1976, 80, 85, 92, 95, S.W. Conf. Indoor Track and Field Championships, 1987-96, Olympic Festival, San Antonio, 1993, Colorado Springs, 1995; 12 time head marshal S.W. Conf. Track and Field Championships, Big 12 Outdoor Conf. Track and Field Championship, 1997-99, 2001-03, head marshall Olympic Trials in Track and Field, 2000, 04. USA/Mobil Track Championship, 1994, 95; USA Nat. Jr. Track Championship, 1994, 95, 98, USA Track and Field Track Championship, 1997, 2001-03, Master's Nat. Track and Field Nat. Championship, 1996, 98, 2002. Mem. ABA, State Bar of Tex. (dist. 7-A grievance com. 1983-85, com. adminstrn. of justice 1985-92, com. on ct. rules 1992-2003, chmn. 1992-93, 93-94). Baptist. Office: Sharpe & Tillman 6100 Western Pl Ste 1000 Fort Worth TX 76107-4679 Office Phone: 817-338-4900. Personal E-mail: utlawman@aol.com.

**SHARPE, KATHRYN MOYE,** retired psychologist; b. Barnesville, Ga., Nov. 27, 1922; d. Herbert Johnston and Henri Lucile (Winter) Moye; m. William Herschel Sharpe, Mar. 2, 1946; children: William Herschel Jr., Mark Stephens. AB, Piedmont Coll., Demorest, Ga., 1942; MA, U. N.C., 1947; PhD, U. S.C., 1975. Tchr., guidance counselor Charleston (S.C.) Pub. Schs., 1947-66; prof. sociology, chmn. dept. Bapt. Coll. at Charleston, 1966-88, prof. emeritus, 1988—; ret., 2005. Pvt. practice psychology, Charleston, SC, 1975-2005. Named One of Twelve Outstanding Women in Greater Charleston by The Ctr. for Women; Kathryn Moye Sharpe scholarship given in her honor Bapt. Coll. at Charleston, 1988. Fellow Am. Assn. for Marriage and Family Therapy (approved supr., pres. S.C. div. 1975-77, disting. svc. award S.C. chpt. 1999). Congregationalist. Home and Office: 6 Cavalier Ave Charleston SC 29407-7702

**SHARPE, KEITH YOUNT,** retired lawyer, writer; b. Hiddenite, NC, July 11, 1930; s. Ruel Yount and Eileen Lois (Lackey) S.; m. Margaret Joyce Land, Aug 27, 1955 (div.); children: Jonathan, Matthew, Leonora, Felicia. AB, Duke U., 1952; JD, Wake Forest U., 1957, MBA, 1982; MLA, U. NC, Asheville, 2001. Bar: NC 1957. Pvt. practice law, Winston-Salem, NC, 1957-62, 82-94; asst. solicitor Mcpl. Ct. of Winston-Salem, 1958-60; with Pilot Freight Carriers Inc., Winston-Salem, 1962-82, sr. v.p., 1967-76, exec. v.p., 1976—82, also dir.; v.p., dir. Commil. Automotive Co., 1967-76, Terminal Warehouse Corp., 1967-82. Bd. govs. So. Motor Carriers Rate Conf., 1977-81. Served with inf. U.S. Army, 1952-54. Mem. Assn. Transp. Practitioners, Phi Alpha Delta, Theta Chi. Democrat. Episcopalian. Home: 5932 Fox Ridge Ln Winston Salem NC 27104

**SHARPE, MARTHA ANNE SMITH,** academic administrator, consultant; b. Crossnore, NC, June 26, 1955; d. Virginia Sutherland and Eustace Henry Smith; m. Leo Francis Smith, May 15, 1993. BA, Davidson Coll., 1977; MA, U. NC, Greensboro, 1979; EdD, Coll. William and Mary, 1992. Devel. counselor, evaluation specialist U. Del., Newark, 1981—82; assoc. dir., enrollment analyst Old Dominion U., Norfolk, Va., 1983—93, dir. instl. rsch., 1993—2002, asst. v.p. for instl. rsch. and assessment, 2002—. Commr. Montessori Accreditation Coun. for Tchr. Edn., Commn. on Accreditation, Racine, Wis., 1999—; assoc. Hermitage Cons. Assoc., Ltd., Virginia Beach, Va., 2002—. Named Adminstr. of Yr., Old Dominion U., 2000; recipient Paschall HIgher Edn. award, Coll. of William and Mary, 1990, Armand and Mary Faust Galfo Rsch. award, 1991. Mem.: Kappa Delta Pi, Phi Beta Kappa. Avocations: photography, swimming, art, music. Office: Old Dominion Univ 5115 Hampton Blvd 218 Koch Hall Norfolk VA 23529 Office Phone: 757-683-4046.

**SHARPE, MYRON EMANUEL,** publishing executive, writer; b. Chester, Pa., Sept. 10, 1928; s. Abraham Maxwell and Emma (Friedman) S.; m. Jacqueline Steiner, 1959 (div.); children: Susanna, Matthew; m. Carole S. Brafman, 1983; children: Elizabeth, Hannah. BA, Swarthmore Coll., 1950; MA, U. Mich., 1951; PhD, Madison U., 2000. Pres. Modern Factors Corp., Phila., 1957; founder, comn. bd., pres. M.E. Sharpe, Inc. (Pub.), Armonk, NY, 1958—, writer, editor, 1955—. Founder, exec. dir. Com. to Save the Life of Henry Spetter, 1974-76; co-founder, coord. Initiative Com. for Nat. Econ. Planning, 1974-76; participant in drafting Full Employment and Balanced Growth Act of 1978; co-founder, pres. M.E. Sharpe, Ltd. (Arts and Antiques), New Canaan, Conn., 1981-83. Author: John Kenneth Galbraith and the Lower

Economics, 1973, Thou Shalt Not Kill Unless Otherwise Instructed, 2005, Requiem for New Orleans, 2006. Chmn. Pro Arte Chamber Singers of Conn., 1982-83; pres. Waveny Chamber Music Soc., 1987-98; econ. advisor to Senator Birch Bayh for presdl. campaign, 1975. Office: M E Sharpe Inc 80 Business Park Dr Armonk NY 10504-1715 Office Phone: 914-273-1800.

**SHARPE, ROBERT FRANCIS, JR.,** food products company executive; b. 1952; m. Rebecca Ann Gillan, Feb. 23, 1991. BA, DePauw U., 1974; JD, Wake Forest U. V.p. Tyco Internat. Ltd.; with RJR Nabisco Holdings Corp., sr. v.p., gen. counsel; sr. v.p. pub. affairs, gen. counsel, sec. Pepsico Inc., Purchase, NY, 1998—2002; ptnr. Brunswick Group LLP, 2002—05; exec. v.p., legal & external affairs ConAgra Foods, Inc., Omaha, 2005—. Bd. dirs. Ameriprise Fin. Office: ConAgra Foods Inc 1 ConAgra Dr Omaha NE 68102*

**SHARPE, ROBERT KENT,** writer, director, producer, photographer; b. Chgo., Nov. 17, 1930; s. Byron C. and Helen Lee Sharpe; m. Mary Kahn, 1955 (div. 1971); m. T Tina Ditta, Apr. 26, 1980; children: Steven W., Sharon E., Jonathan K., Julia A. BA in English, Brown U., 1953. Writer, dir. Ford Found., NYC, 1956-57, CBS, NYC, 1957-58, NBC Spl. Projects Dept., NYC, 1959-61, freelance dir., 1962-63; pres. RKS Devel. Corp., Ardsley, 1963-75, Robert K. Sharpe Prodns., Inc., Ardsley, NY, 1965—, Hastings on Hudson, NY, 1965—. Prodr., writer, dir.: (documentary) Before the Mountain Was Moved, 1969 (awards 1969-70); writer, dir.: (shorts) Night in a Pet Ship, 1959 (awards 1959-60), prodr., writer, dir. (shorts) Pancho, 1966-67 (awards 1966-67), Joe, 1965 (awards 1965), Face of Excellence, 1962, The Forgotten, 1958 (awards 1958-59); screenwriter: (films) WFAT, 1982, The Long Night, 1962, Barbero, 1983, A Dead Issue, 1963, Computer, 1965, A Letter Home, 1965, Squaw Gap Speaking, 1976; dir.: (TV) The Twentieth Century Series, 1962-63, Keep It Cool, Rhodes Scholar, The Jazz of Dave Brubeck, The Songs of Harold Arlen, Fire Brand on Ice - Stan Mikita, Here is New York, Buildings for Business and Government, Call it Courage, Equestrianism, others; staff writer, dir.: (TV) Wisdom Series, 1959-61, The Ordeal of Woodrow Wilson as Told by President Herbert Hoover, The Seven Lively Arts Series, Omibus Series, 1956-57; prodr., dir. (films) The Great Debate, 1963; writer, dir. (films) Light as You Like It, 1958; photographic series Assisi, 1953, Spanish Patterns, 1990, Interplay, 1998, The Unseen, 1999, Changes, 2003, Portugal, 2003, Glimpses of the Gates, 2005 Mem. Am. Soc. Media Photographers, Dirs. Guild Am., Photographic Adminstrs., Inc., Phi Beta Kappa. Democrat. Jewish. Avocations: amateur radio, hi-fi & electronics, wood working. Home and Office: 765 N Broadway Apt 15E Hastings On Hudson NY 10706 Office Phone: 914-478-3434. Personal E-mail: rksharpe@optonline.net.

**SHARPE, ROLAND LEONARD,** structural engineer, consultant; b. Shakopee, Minn., Dec. 18, 1923; s. Alfred Leonard and Ruth Helen Sharpe; m. Jane Esther Steele, Dec. 28, 1946; children: Douglas Rolfe, Deborah Lynn, Sheryl Anne. BSCE, U. Mich., 1947, MSE, 1949. Registered civil engr., structural engr. Designer Cummins & Barnard, Inc., Ann Arbor, Mich., 1947-48; instr. engring. U. Mich., 1948-50; exec. v.p. John A. Blume & Assocs., engrs., San Francisco, 1950-73; chmn., founder Engring. Decision Analysis Co., Inc., Cupertino, Calif., 1974-87; cons. earthquake engr. Sharpe Structural Engrs., Los Altos, Calif., 1987—. Mng. dir. EDAC, GmbH, Frankfurt, Germany, 1974—82; pres. Calif. Devel. & Engring. Co., Inc., Las Vegas, Nev., 1973—81; mem. nat. earthquake hazard reduction program adv. com. overviewing Fed. Emergency Mgmt. Agy., U.S. Geol. Survey, NSF and Nat. Inst. Stds. and Tech., 1990—93. Author (with J. Blume, E. G. Kost): (book) Earthquake Engineering for Nuclear Facilities, 1971; co-author: DOE Seismic Safety Manual, 1996; contbr. articles to profl. jours. Mem. Planning Commn., Palo Alto, 1955—60; mng. dir. Applied Tech. Coun., Palo Alto, 1973—83; dir. Earthquake Engring. Rsch. Inst., 1972—75, mem.; project dir., editor Tentative Provision Devel. Seismic Regulations Bldgs., 1978; tech. mgr., contbr., editor Data Processing Facilities: Guidelines Earthquake Hazard Mitigation, 1987. With USMC, 1942—46. Recipient citation for contbn. to constrn. industry, Engring. News Record, 1978—79, 1986—87, chmn. U.S. Joint Com. Earthquake Engring., 1982—88, citation for devel. of improvements in structural design and constrn. practices, Applied Tech. Coun., Japan Structural Cons. Assn., 1990. Fellow: ASCE (hon.; chmn. dynamic effects com. 1978—80, exec. com. structural divsn. 1980—84, chmn. 1983, exec. com. structural divsn. 1989—93, mgmt. group B 1989—93, Earnest E. Howard award 1994); mem.: Structural Engrs. World Congress (pres. 1995—, chair 1988), Structural Engrs. Assn. Calif. (coll. of fellows dir. 1971—73, chmn. seismology com. 1972—74), Earthquake Engring. Rsch. Inst. (hon.; dir. 1972—75), Structural Engrs. No. Calif. (hon.; dir. 1969—71), Japan Structural Cons. Assn. (hon.), Am. Concrete Inst. (life). Avocations: gardening, hiking, fly fishing. Home: 10320 Rolly Rd Los Altos CA 94024-6568 Office: Sharpe Struct Engrs 10320 Rolly Rd Ste 1 Los Altos CA 94024-6568 Office 650-948-9095. Personal E-mail: rsharpe3@mindspring.com. *Personal philosophy: One's conduct should be beyond reproach both morally and ethically and I should serve each of my clients to the best of my ability.*

**SHARPE, SHANNON,** commentator, retired professional football player; b. Chgo., June 26, 1968; Student, Savannah State U. Tight end Denver Broncos, 1990—99, Balt. Ravens, 2000—02, Denver Broncos, 2002—04; commentator NFL Today, CBS, 2004—. Named to Pro Bowl Team, 1992—98, 2001. Achievements include being ranked first in NFL history in recieving yards, receptions, and touchdowns for a tight end; being a member of Superbowl Championship Team, Denver Bronco's, 1997, 1998, Baltimore Ravens, 2000. Office: NFL Today 51 W 52nd St New York NY 10019

**SHARPE, WILLIAM FORSYTH,** economics professor; b. Cambridge, Mass., June 16, 1934; s. Russell Thornley Sharpe and Evelyn Forsyth (Jillson) Maloy; m. Roberta Ruth Branton, July 2, 1954 (div. Feb. 1986); children: Deborah Ann, Jonathan Forsyth; m. Kathryn Dorothy Peck, Apr. 5, 1986. AB, UCLA, 1955, MA, 1956, PhD, 1961; DHL (hon.), DePaul U., 1997; D (hon.), U Alicante, Spain, 2003, U. Vienna, Austria, 2004. Economist Rand Corp., 1957—61; asst. prof. econs. U. Wash., 1961—63, assoc. prof., 1963—67, prof., 1967—68, U. Calif., Irvine, 1968—70; Timken prof. fin. Stanford (Calif.) U., 1970—89, Timken prof. emeritus, 1989—92, prof. fin., 1993—95, STANCO 25 prof. fin., 1995—99, prof. emeritus, 1999—; prin. William F. Sharpe Assocs., 1986—92; chmn. Fin. Engines, Inc., 1996—2003. Author: The Economics of Computers, 1969, Portfolio Theory and Capital Markets, 1970; co-author: Fundamentals of Investments, 1989, 3d edit., 2000, Investments, 6th edit., 1999. With U.S. Army, 1956—57. Recipient Graham and Dodd award, Fin. Analysts' Fedn., 1972, 1973, 1986—88, Nicholas Molodovsky award, 1989, Nobel prize in econ. scis., 1990, UCLA medal, 1998. Mem.: Am. Econ. Assn., Ea. Fin. Assn. (Disting. Scholar award 1991), Western Fin. Assn. (Enduring Contbn. award 1989), Am. Fin. Assn. (v.p. 1979, pres. 1980), Phi Beta Kappa.*

**SHARPE-TAYLOR, LINDA,** psychologist; m. Blaine Sharpe, Sept. 21, 1980; children: Cassandra Rae, Elizabeth Ryan, Jeremy Nathaniel. BA in Psychology, Case Western Res. U., 1978; MA in Clin. Cmty. Psychology, Cleve. State U., 1980; PhD, Mo., St. Louis, 1994. Pres. Urban Behavioral HealthCare Inst., Saint Louis, 1997—. Office: Urban Behavioral HealthCare Institute 1104 South Jefferson Ave Saint Louis MO 63104 Office Phone: 314-577-5000.

**SHARPLES, RUTH LISSAK,** communications executive; b. N.Y.C., Feb. 3, 1952; d. Saul and Nettie (Field) Lissak; m. Winston Sharples, June 26, 1981; stepchildren: Hadley, John, Gillian. BA, CUNY, 1973; MFA, Columbia U., 1975. Rschr. Am. Film Inst./Motion Picture Divsn. of Libr. of Congress, Washington, 1977-79; mgr. audio-visual programs Am. Soc. Microbiology, Washington, 1979-82; mgr. video tech. Am. Gas Assn., Arlington, Va. 1982-96; dir. comm. Am. Gas Cooling Ctr., 1996—; exec. asst., gen. counsel Quaker Cooling Corp., Fall River, Mass., 2005—06; exec. office dir. chancellor U. Mass., Dartmouth, 2006—. V.p., corp. sec. Cantab Motors, Ltd., Purcellville, Va., 1988—; corp. sec. Am. Gas Cooling Ctr., Arlington, 1996—.

---

Editor Cool Times Newsletter, 1996-98. Mem. Nat. Trust Historic Preservation, Nature Conservancy, Mass. Audubon Soc., English Heritage, Nat. Trust, Internat. TV Assn. Avocations: hiking, archaeology.

**SHARPLES, WINSTON SINGLETON,** automobile importer and distributor; b. Springfield, Mass., Oct. 24, 1932; s. Winston Singleton and Carmela (Parrino) S.; m. Jeanette Williams, July 196l (div. Apr. 1981); children: John, Hadley, Gillian; m. Ruth Emily Lissak, June 26, 1981. BA, Harvard Coll., 1953; postgrad. drama, Yale U., 1956-57; MFA, Carnegie Mellon U., 1959; postgrad., Univ. Md., 1978-80. Freelance writer, 1959—; producer, dir. Mon. Valley Playhouse, Charleroi, Pa., 1959, Robin Hood Theater, Arden, Del., 1960-61; pres., film and music editor Synchro-Sound Inc., N.Y.C., 1961-71; prof. CUNY, N.Y.C., 1969-74, Temple Univ., Phila., 1974-76, U. Md., College Park, 1978-79; adminstr. film preservation and documentation Am. Film Inst., Washington, 1976-78; prof. Howard Univ., Washington, 1978-80; pres. Cantab Motors, Ltd., Puncellville, Va., 1984— Author: (with others) A Primer for Film-Making, 197l—; editor, music editor films and cartoons; contbr. articles to profl. jours. and mags. With U.S. Army, 1953-56. Nat. Endowment for the Humanities grantee, 1977. Mem. ASCAP, Archeol. Soc. Va., Am. Studies Assn., Univ. Film Assn. (v.p 1975-76), Soc. for Cinema Studies, Soc. Automotive Engrs., Washington Automotive Press Assn., Morgan Car Club, Land Rover Owners Assn. Va., British Automobile Mfrs. Assn., Harvard Club (N.Y.C.). Democrat. Avocations: forestry, archeology. Office: Cantab Motors Ltd Valley Indsl Park 37251 E Richardson Ln Purcellville VA 20132-3505 Home: 15 Gerrish Rd Rochester MA 02770-1815

**SHARPLESS, JOSEPH BENJAMIN,** retired county official; b. Takoma Park, Md., Feb. 4, 1933; s. William Raiford and Julia Maude (Rouse) Sharpless; m. Nancy Kathleen Steffen, July 28, 1962 (dec. Feb. 1988); 1 child, Carole Marie. BA, Earlham Coll., 1955; MS, Pa. State U., 1960. Instr. recreation Montgomery County Recreation Dept., Rockville, Md., 1957—58; from program supr. to dir. Recreation and Parks Dept., Livingston, NJ, 1959—70; chief recreation svc Md.-Nat. Capital Park and Planning Commn. Prince George's County, Riverdale, Md., 1970—77, parks and recreation div. chief, 1977—95; ret., 1995. Mem. bd. regents, instr. Sch. Sports Mgmt. N.C. State U., 1989—92. Contbr. articles to profl. jours. Dir. volleyball Spl. Olympics Inc., 1994—; tech. del. Spl. Olympics World Summer Games, 1995, 1999, 2003, Spl. Olympics World Summer Nat. Games, 2006; trustee U.S. Volleyball Edn. Found., 1976—2005, sec., 1996—2005; nat. volleyball chmn. AAU, 1966—69, 1972; nat. commr. U.S. Volleyball, 1976—81; mem. volleyball games staff 1996 Olympic Games, Atlanta; staff World Volleyball Congress, Atlanta, 1996; v.p. Montpelier Cmty. Assn., South Laurel, Md., 1983—84, pres., 1985; mem. Md. Sports Adv. Com., 1988—92, Md. State Games Commr., 1986—91; volleyball chmn. N.J. assn., 1961—70, Potomac Valley Assn., 1971—73; pres. NJAAU, 1968—70. Recipient Pioneer award, AAU, 1998, Athletic Hall Fame, Earlham Coll., 2005, Breitkeutz Leadership award, AAU, 1972. Fellow: Nat. Recreation Pks. Assn. (life Berman Profl. Citation award Mid-Atlantic Regional Coun. 1995, Disting. Svc. award 1995, Disting. Fellow award 1996); mem.: N.J. Soccer Ofcls. Assn. (sec., treas. 1966—70), Nat. Capitol Area Bd. Volleyball Ofcls. (sec. 1985—89), Sch. and Coll. Soccer Ofcls. Assn. (sec., treas. 1965—70, del. Mid-Atlantic NRPA regional coun. 1969—79), Md. Recreation and Pk. Assn. (v.p. 1975—77, pres. 1977—78, Mem. of the Yr. 1975, citation 1985), N.J. Recreation and Pks. Assn. (sec. 1965, v.p. 1966, pres. 1967), Am. Pk. and Recreation Soc. (bd. dirs. 1977—80, nat. coun., coun. affiliate pres.), Nat. Intercollegiate Soccer Ofcls. Assn. (sec. 1966—68, treas. 1968—70), U.S. Volleyball Assn. (regional commr. 1965—78, nat. ofcl. 1967—96, v.p. 1973—90, bd. dirs. 1973—, exec. com. 1976—80, 1985—89, exec. cons. 1989—2004, exec. com. 1992—96, corp. sec. 1992—96, mng. editor publs. 1994—98, v.p. 1996—2004, regional commr., referee, scorekeeper emeritus 2000, v.p. 1996—2004, numerous awards). Independent. Mem. Soc. Of Friends. Home: 26205 S Cedarcrest Dr Sun Lakes AZ 85248-7206 Personal E-mail: chessycrab@aol.com.

**SHARPLESS, K. BARRY,** chemist, educator; b. Phila., Apr. 28, 1941; m. Jan Dueser, Apr. 28, 1965; children: Hannah, William, Isaac. BA, Dartmouth Coll., 1963; PhD, Stanford U., 1968; doctorate (hon.), Dartmouth Coll., 1995, Swedish Royal Inst. Tech., 1995, Tech. U. Munich, 1995, Cath. U. Louvain, Belgium, 1996. Postdoctoral assoc. Harvard U., Stanford U., to 1970, faculty dept. chemistry, 1977-80; faculty MIT, Cambridge, 1970-77, 1980-90; W. M. Keck prof. chemistry Scripps Rsch. Inst. and Skaggs Inst. of Chem. Biology, La Jolla, Calif., 1990—. Recipient Pual Janssen prize for Creativity in Organic Chemistry, Chem. Pioneer award, Am. Inst. Chemists, 1988, Prelog medal, Swiss Fed. Inst. Tech., Zurich, 1988, Scheele medal and prize, Swedish Acad. Pharm. Scis., Tetrahedron prize for Creativity in Organic Chemistry, 1993, King Faisal Internat. prize for sci., 1995, Microbial medal, Kitasato Inst., Tokyo, 1997, Harvey medal, Technion-Israel Inst. Tech., 1998, Carothers award, 1999, John Scott Medal, City of Phila, 2001, Benjarmin Franklin medal in chemistry, 2001, Wolf prize in chemistry, Wolf Found., Israel, 2001, Nobel prize in Chemistry, 2001; fellow A. P. Sloan, 1987—88, Guggenheim, 1987—88; scholar Camille and Henry Dreyfus Tchr. Fellow: AAAS, Am. Acad. Arts and Scis., Royal Soc. Chemistry (hon.); mem.: NAS (Award in Chemical Sciences 2000), Am. Chem. Soc. (Creative Work in Synthetic Organic Chemistry award 1983, Harrison Howe award Rochester chpt. 1987, Remsen award Md. sect. 1989, Arthur C. Cope award 1992, Roger Adams award 1997, Richards medal Northeastern sect. 1998, Top 75 Contbrs. to Chem. Enterprise 1998). Office: Scripps Rsch Inst BCC 315 10550 N Torrey Pines Rd La Jolla CA 92037-1000*

**SHARPLEY, NORMA GERALDINE,** music educator; b. Houston, Jan. 3, 1929; d. John Quitman and Nancy Pearl (Wright) Knighton; m. James Wesley Sharpley, Oct. 17, 1953; children: John Stephen, Nancy Ann Sharpley Hutchinson, Janet Kay. MusB in Piano, So. Coll. Fine Arts, Houston, 1950. Profl. cert. in piano Music Tchrs. Nat. Assn. Organist, pianists Gulfgate Christian Ch., Houston, 1956—92; organist Forest Pk. Lawndale Funeral Home, Houston, 1978—; pvt. piano tchr. Houston, 1949—. Recipient Outstanding Music award, Gulfgate Christian Ch., 1968; Paul Harris fellow, Gulfway Hobby Rotary Club, Houston, 1999. Mem.: Gulf Coast Music Tchrs. Assn. (v.p.), Bay Area Music Tchrs. Assn. (charter), Houston Music Tchrs. Assn. (v.p., other offices, Tchr. Svc. award 1984), Tex. Congress Parents and Tchrs. (hon. life), Houston Tuesday Musical Club (performer 1976—). Home: 11454 Sagestaney Dr Houston TX 77089 E-mail: glovespiano@sbcglobal.net.

**SHARPLEY, ROBERT LOUIS,** performing arts educator, language educator; s. Doris Mae Sharpley; m. Gayle Elaine Sharpley, Dec. 17, 1983. MusB in Edn., U. North Tex., Denton, 1985. Cert. bilingual, ESL elem. cert. Tex., 1989, all-level, music, choral cert. Tex., 1997, secondary, advanced cert in Spanish Tex., 2004. Bilingual tchr. 1st grade East Ctrl. Ind. Sch. Dist., San Antonio, 1991, bilingual tchr. 5th grade, 1991—97, choir dir., 1997—2001, North East ISD, 2001—. Choir dir. Northwood Presbyn. Ch., 1985—86; participant Nat. Tchr. Cert. Rater, PsychCorp, 1997; site mgr. SW Winner, Summer Youth Employment Training, 1997—99; training developer Syscom, 2000. Musician (baritone): (oratorio) Handel's Messiah; musician: (bell choir member) (entertainment) Bells-a-Poppin'. Mem. San Antonio Wheelmen, 2004—06, Cycle Logic, 2003—06; mem., contbr. ChoralTalk, 2001—06; mem. Bike City Chain Reaction, 2005—06; mem., contbr. Dead Runners Soc., 1992—2006; donor South Tex. Blood and Tissue, 1989—2006; baker San Antonio Loafers, 2001—06; skilled labor Northwood Presbyn. Mission Team, 1989—2006; elder Northwood Presbyn. Ch., 1989—2006; skilled labor Habitat for Humanity, 1997—2006; choir director Northwood Presbyn. Ch. Men's Chorus #1, 2001—06; choir mem. Northwood Presbyn. Ch. Chancel Choir, 1985—2006; bell choir mem. Northwood Presbyn. Ch. Bells Angels, 1997—2006; actor, singer, chorus dir. Northwood Presbyn. Ch. Players, 1985—2006; leader Northwood Presbyn. Ch. Hike and Bike, 2003—06. Named Margaret Fund scholar, Fgn. Mission Bd., 1979—85; recipient John Philip Sousa award Musicianship, Escola Americana Rio de Janeiro, 1979, Professionalism award, Chili's, Inc., 1987, Bilingual Tchr. Hall Fame, San Antonio Assn. Bilingual Educators, 1993—94, Professionalism award, Sin-

---

clair Elem. Sch., 1995—96, Making a Difference award, East Ctrl. Ind. Sch. Dist., 2000—01, Tchr. Yr., East Ctrl. Heritage Mid. Sch., 2001, Trinity prize Excellence, Trinity U./HEB, 2001, Dist. Tchr. Yr., East Ctrl. Ind. Sch. Dist., 2001, Lakeshore Tchr. Yr., Lakeshore, Inc., 2001, Falcon award, Krueger Mid. Sch., 2004; grantee Future Teacher Loan Program, 1989. Mem.: Parent Tchr. Assn. (assoc.), Tex. Music Educators Assn. (assoc.; facilities com. mem. 2004—05), Tex. Choral Dirs. Assn. (assoc.; hospitality com. 1997—98), Fellowship Christian Musicians (sponsor 2004—06), Krueger Bike Club (sponsor 2004—06). Republican. Presbyterian. Avocations: singing, cycling, running, swimming, hiking. Office: Krueger Mid Sch 438 Lanark San Antonio TX 78218-1899 Office Phone: 210-650-1350. Personal E-mail: sharpner@metrogate.com

**SHARPNACK, RAYONA,** management consultant; b. 1952; 1 child, Chelsea. Grad., U. Nev., Reno. Founder, pres. Inst. Women's Leadership, Redwood City, Calif., 1992—. Faculty Mills Coll., Women in Mgmt. program, 1994; bd. dirs. Profl. Bus. Women Calif. Conf., 1994—99; co-chair State of World Forum, Investing in Women Initiative, 1998—99; pres. Profl. Bus. Women in Calif., 1999; adv. coun. mem. Internat. Mus. Women, 1999—2001; player, mgr. Internat. Women's Profl. Softball League, 1979; shortstop Calif. Express. Office: Inst Women's Leadership PO Box 58 Redwood City CA 94064-0058

**SHARPTON, ALFRED CHARLES, JR.,** minister, political activist; b. Bklyn., Oct. 3, 1954; m. Kathy Lee Jordan, 1980; children: Dominique, Ashley. Student, Bklyn.Coll., 1973—75. Cert. ordained a Rev. 1964. Youth dir. Operation BreadBasket, 1969; founder Nat. Youth Movement, 1971—; road mgr. James Brown concert tours, 1973—80; founder, pres., CEO Nat. Action Network, Inc., Bklyn., 1991—. Candidate NY State Senate, 1978, US Senate, 1988, 92, 94, NYC mayor, 1997, Pres., 2004. Co-author (with Anthony Walton): Go Tell the Pharaoh: The Autobiography of Reverend Al Sharpton, 1996; co-author: (with Karen Hunter) Al on America, 2002. Named one of 100 Most Influential Black Americans, Ebony mag., 2006. Pentecostal. E-mail: info@sharpton2004.org.*

**SHARPTON, THOMAS,** physician; b. Augusta, Ga., July 15, 1949; s. Thomas and Elizabeth (Dozier) S. BA, Northwestern U., 1971; MS, Stanford U., 1973, MD, 1977. Intern Martinez (Calif.) VAMC, 1977-78, resident, 1978-80; mem. staff Kaiser Permanente Med. Group, Oakland, Calif., 1980—; asst. clin. prof. medicine U. Calif., San Francisco, 1994—. Cons. Berkeley (Calif.) Free Clinic, 1977—; chmn. peer review Kaiser Permanente Med. Group, Oakland, 1985-86; clin. mem. faculty U. Calif., San Francisco, 1992, asst. clin. prof., 1994; chair AIDS therapeutics com. No. Calif. Kaiser Hosps., 1996-2000. Mem. Rep. Nat. Com., 1996—, Alameda County Profl. Adv. Com., Oakland, 1984-88, Alameda County AIDS Task Force, Oakland, 1985-88, Alameda County Pub. Health Adv. Com., 2000-. Fellow ACP; mem. Calif. Med. Assn., Alameda-Contra Costa Med. Assn., Am. Soc. Microbiology, Mensa, Sigma Pi Sigma, Phi Beta Kappa. Clubs: Phi Beta Kappa of No. Calif. Republican. Avocation: classical piano. Office: Kaiser Permanente 280 W Macarthur Blvd Oakland CA 94611-5642 Business E-Mail: thomas.sharpton@kp.org.

**SHARROCK (WRENTMORE), ANITA KAY,** information technology specialist; b. Logan, Ohio, Dec. 3, 1955; d. Lloyd Earl and Gayle Irene (Daubenmier) W. BS, Ohio U., Lancaster, 1978; MS, Ohio U., Athens, 1979; postgrad., Ohio State U., 1985, Cen. Ohio Tech. Coll., 1987. Cert. tchr. Vis. lectr. Denison U., Granville, Ohio, 1980; lectr. Ohio State U., Newark, 1980-83; instr. Cen. Ohio Tech. Coll., Newark, 1983-86; substitute tchr. Newark City Schs., 1986-87, Northfork Sch. Dist., Utica, Ohio, 1987, Lakewood Sch. Dist., Hebron, Ohio, 1987; with Kelly Services, Reynoldsburg, Ohio, 1986-87; computer specialist Def. Constrn. Supply Ctr., Columbus, 1987—92, DLA Sys. Automation Ctr., 1992—2000, DLA Sys. Integration Office, 2000—04, DLA Info. Ops., Columbus, 2004—. Mem. exec. bd. Newark-Licking County Coun. Tchrs. Math., Newark, 1985-88. Mem. Nat. Coun. Tchrs. Math., Ohio Coun. Tchrs. Math., Am. Math. Soc., Assn. for Computing Machinery, Phi Kappa Phi, Kappa Delta Pi. Independent. Methodist. Avocations: swimming, dance, hiking, tv, reading. Home: 103 Ramona Ave Newark OH 43055-1334 Office Phone: 614-692-8347. Business E-Mail: asharrock@alltel.net.

**SHARROW, MARILYN JANE,** library administrator; b. Oakland, Calif. d. Charles L. and H.Evelyn Sharrow; m. Larry J. Davis. BS in Design, U. Mich., 1967, MALS, 1969. Libr. Detroit Pub. Libr., 1968-70; head fine arts dept. Syracuse U. Librs., NY, 1970-73; dir. libr. Roseville Pub. Libr., Mich., 1973-75; asst. dir. librs. U. Wash., Seattle, 1975-77, assoc. dir. librs., 1978-79; dir. librs. U. Man., Winnipeg, Canada, 1979-82; chief libr. U. Toronto, Canada, 1982-85; univ. libr. U. Calif., Davis, 1985—. Chair bd. North Regional Libr. Facility, 1999—2001; bd. dirs. press U. Calif., 2005—. Recipient Woman of Yr. in Mgmt. award Winnipeg YWCA, 1982; named Woman of Distinction, U. Calif. Faculty Women's Rsch. Group, 1985. Mem. ALA, Assn. Rsch. Librs. (bd. dirs., v.p., pres.-elect 1989-90, pres. 1990-91, chair sci. tech. work group 1994-98, rsch. collections com. 1993-95, 2000-2002, preservation com. 1997-99, 2003-05, ARL leadership devel. task force 2006—), OCLC-Rsch. Librs. Adv. Com. (vice-chair 1992-93, chair 1993-94), Calif. State Network Resources Libr. Com., Cau. Assn. Rsch. Libr. (pres. 1984-85). Office: U Calif Shields Libr 100 NW Quad Davis CA 95616-5292 Office Phone: 530-752-2110. E-mail: mjsharrow@ucdavis.edu.

**SHARRY, JANICE VYN,** lawyer; b. Toledo, Aug. 1, 1951; d. John Cameron and Patricia Mae (Hammontree) Vyn; m. Michael Sharry, Aug. 14, 1976; children: Jessica, Greg, Melanie. Grad. cum laude, Knox Coll., 1973; JD magna cum laude, So. Meth. U., 1977. Atty. Haynes & Boone, L.L.P., Dallas, 1977—, head corp. fin. sect., 1989—, ptnr., corp. fin., bd. dir. Rsch. editor Southwester Law Jour. Bd. dirs. Dallas Children's Theatre, 1989-93; edn. com. Greenhill Sch., Dallas, 1990; active Dallas Summer Mus. Guild, 1989—, Dallas Dem. Forum, 1993. Named a Texas Super Lawyer, Tex. Monthly Mag., 2003; named one of Best Lawyers in Dallas, D Magazine, 2003. Mem. ABA (mem. ad hoc com. on form of model simplified indenture, bus. law sect., com. on devels. in bus. fin. 1991—), Tex. Bar Assn.(bus. law sect.), Tex. Bus. Law Found. (bd. trustees 1990—), Dallas Bar Assn., Dallas C. of C. (chair, Executive Women's Roundtable), Phi Beta Kappa, Order of Coif. Presbyterian. Avocations: reading, sports, politics. Office: Haynes and Boone LLP 901 Main St Ste 3100 Dallas TX 75202-3789 Office Phone: 214-651-5562. Office Fax: 214-200-0620. Business E-Mail: janice.sharry@haynesboone.com.

**SHARTLE, STANLEY MUSGRAVE,** engineering executive, consultant, surveyor; b. Brazil, Ind., Sept. 27, 1922; s. Arthur Tinder and Mildred C. (Musgrave) Shartle; m. Anna Lee Mantle, Apr. 7, 1948; 1 child, Randy. Student, Purdue U., 1947—50. Registered profl. engr., land surveyor. Ind. chief dep. surveyor Hendricks County, Danville, Ind., 1941—42, dep. county surveyor, 1944—50, county engr., surveyor, 1950—54, county hwy. engr., 1975—77; asst. hydrographer Fourteenth Naval Dist., Pearl Harbor, Hawaii, 1942—44; staff engr. Ind. Toll Rd. Commn., Indpls., 1954—61; chief right of way engring. Ind. State Hwy. Commn., Indpls., 1961—75; owner, civil engr. Shartle Engring., Indpls., 1977—89; prin. Parsons Cunningham & Shartle Engrs., Inc., Indpls., 1990—. Right of way engring. cons. Gannett Fleming Transp. Engrs., Inc., Indpls., 1983—88; part-time lectr. Purdue U. Ind. State Hwy. Commn., 1965—67. Author: Shartle Genealogy, 1955, 2d edit., 2005, Musgrave Family History, 1961, 2d edit., 1995, Right of Way Engineering Manual, 1975, (novel) Her Word of Honor, 2001; contbr. articles to profl. jours. Ex-officio mem., charter mem. exec. sec. Hendricks County Planning Commn., 1951—54; mem. citizen adv. com. Hendricks County Subdivision Control Ordinance, 1988—. Named Stanley Shartle Day, Hendricks County, 1997; recipient Outstanding Contbn. award, Hendricks County Soil and Water Conservation Dist., 1976. Mem.: Geog. and Land Info. Soc., Internat. Right of Way Assn. (founder chpt. 10), Ind. Toll Rd. Employees Assn. (pres. 1959—60), Nat. Soc. Profl. Surveyors, Ind. Soc. Profl. Land Surveyors (life; bd. dirs. 1979), Am. Congress Surveying and Mapping (life). Avocations: astronomy, genealogy, geodesy. Office Phone: 317-837-9900.

**SHASHKIN, PAVEL NIKOLAYEVICH,** biochemist; b. Ulyanovsk, Russia, Sept. 23, 1957; s. Nikolay I. Shashkin and Maria Ya Shashkina; m. Tamara S. Varfolomeeva; children: Alexey, Alice Shashkina, Veronika. M in Physics, M.V. Lomonosov Moscow State U., 1980; PhD in Biology, Cancer Rsch. Ctr., Moscow, 1990. Rsch. scientist Cancer Rsch. Ctr., Moscow, 1991—97, sr. rsch. scientist, 1997—99; vis. instr. U. Md., Balt., 1998—2000; rsch. assoc. U. Winnipeg, Man., Canada, 2000—01, U. Va., Charlottesville, 2002—04, Cleve. Clinic, 2004—. Contbr. articles to profl. jours. Grantee, Karolinska Inst. Stockholm, Sweden, 1995, 1996. Mem.: Am. Heart Assn., Am. Diabetes Assn. Avocations: tennis, travel. Office: Cleve Clin 9500 Euclid Ave Cleveland OH 44195 Home: 6589 Maplewood Rd Apt 304 Mayfield Heights OH 44124-1930 Office Phone: 216-445-5492. Personal E-mail: pshashkin@hotmail.com. Business E-Mail: shashkp@ccf.org.

**SHASSIAN, DONALD R.,** telecommunications company executive; b. Sept. 2, 1955; m. Pamela; children: Brian, Daniel. BSBA, Bucknell U., 1977. Ptnr.-in-charge Arthur Anderson & Co., 1977-93; sr. v.p., CFO So. New England Telecomms. Corp., New Haven, 1993—98; exec. v.p., CFO RSL Communications, Ltd., 1998—2000, COO, 2000—01; ind. cons., 2001—05; CFO Health Net of the Northeast, Inc., Shelton, Conn., 2005—06, Citizens Communications Co., Stamford, Conn., 2006—. Office: Citizens Communications Co Three HIgh Ridge Pk Stamford CT 06905*

**SHASTEEN, DONALD EUGENE,** government official; b. Englewood, Colo., Dec. 3, 1928; s. George Donald and Frances True (Meyers) S.; m. Shirley Mae Johnson, Aug. 8, 1954; children: Jon Randolph, Ron Winston, Sherilyn Sue Kosman. BA in Journalism, U. Colo., 1950. Reporter Omaha World-Herald, Des Moines, 1954-58, Lincoln, Nebr., 1958-66; exec. asst. to Senator Carl T. Curtis of Nebr., Washington, 1966-73, administrv. asst., 1973-78, to Sen. Gordon J. Humphrey, 1979-80; with transition group Senate Republican Conf., 1980; dep. under sec. for legislation and intergovtl. affairs Dept. Labor, 1981-83, dep. asst. sec. for vets. employment, 1983-85, asst. sec. for vets. employment and tng., 1985-89. Pres. Shasteen Assocs. Rep. nominee for U.S. Senate Nebr., 1978. Served with U.S. Army, 1951-52. Mem. Am. Legion, VFW, Am. Vets., Disabled Am. Vets., Phi Delta Theta. Republican. Lutheran. Office Phone: 240-876-3366. E-mail: shasteens@juno.com, shasteen@msn.com.

**SHATILA, AHMAD HUSSAIN,** surgeon, oncologist; arrived in U.S., 1970; s. Hussain Ahmad and Yisir Omar Shatila; m. Bonnye Lynn Oliver, June 24, 1972; children: Suzanne, Sarah, David. BS in Biology, Am. U. Beirut, 1965, MD, 1970. Diplomate Am. Bd. Surgery. Resident surgery U. Louisville, 1970—72, SUNY, Syracuse, 1972—75; fellow surg. oncology U.N. Med. Ctr., Cleve., 1975—76, Cleve. Met. Health Med. Ctr., Case We. Res. U., 1976—78; pvt. practice Cleve., 1976—. Asst. clin. prof. surgery Case Western Res. U., Cleve., 1984—; chmn. dept. surgery S.W. Gen. Health Ctr., Middleburg Heights, Ohio, 1989—91, chief surg. oncology, 1990—, co-founder cancer program; dir., founder Cleve. Breast Clinic, Middleburg Heights; pres. S.W. Med. Corp., 1986—94, 2000—; presenter in field. Contbr. articles to profl. jours. Com. mem. S.W. Cmty. Health Found., Middleburg Heights, 1990—. Fellow: ACS, U.S. Soc. Surg. Oncology; mem.: Ea. Coop. Oncology Group (investigator 1976—2005, mem. breast steering com. 1980—86, vice chair toxicity com. 1983—88, mem. surgery steering com. 1984—87), Ohio State Med. Assn., Am. Cancer Soc. (med. adv. com.), Am. Soc. Clin. Oncology. Moslem. Avocations: golf, photography, boating. Office: Cleve Breast Clinic 18660 E Bagley Rd Cleveland OH 44130 Office Phone: 440-234-2988.

**SHATIN, JUDITH,** composer, educator; b. Boston, Nov. 11, 1949; d. Leo and Harriet Evelyn (Sommer) S.; m. Michael Kubovy, June 28, 1992. AB, Douglass Coll., 1971; MM, Julliard Sch., 1974; PhD, Princeton U., 1979. Asst. prof. U. Va., Charlottesville, 1979-85, assoc. prof., 1985-92, prof., 1992—, chmn. McIntire dept. music, 1995—2002, William R. Kenan Jr. prof., 1999—. Dir. Va. Ctr. Computer Music, 1988—. Composer: (orch.) Aura, 1981, (piano concerto) Passion of St. Cecilia, 1985, (flute concerto) Ruah, 1985, (piano trio) View from Mt. Nebo (commd. by Garth Newel Chamber Players), 1985, (piano trio) Ignoto Numine (commd. Monticello Trio), 1986, (flute, clarinet, violin, cello) Secret Ground (commd. by Roxbury Chamber Players), 1990, (soprano and tape) Three Summers Heat, 1989 (Barlow Found. Commn.), (orch.) Piping the Earth (commd. by Women's Philharm.), 1990, (flute and piano) Gabriel's Wing (commd. by Julia Bogorad and the Upper Midwest Flute Assn.), 1990, (flute and electronics) Kairos (Commd. Va. Commn. for the Arts), 1991, (chorus, brass quintet, tympani) We Hold These Truths (commd. U. Va., for Thomas Jefferson's 250th birthday), 1992, (string orch.) Stringing the Bow (commd. Va. Chamber Orch.), 1992, COAL (commd. as part of 2-yr. retrospective of work, sponsored by Lila Wallace- Readers Digest Arts Ptnrs. Program), 1994, (piano and percussion) 1492 (commd. Arioso Ensemble), 1992, (piano) Chai Variations on Eliahu HaNavi, 1995, (flute and guitar) Dreamtigers (commd. Ekko!), 1996, (chorus) Adonai Roi, 1995, (string quartet) Janus Quartet (commd. for the Arcata Quartet), 1994, (string quartet and electronic playback) Elijah's Chariot (commd. Kronos Quartet), 1995, (amplified clarinet with PVC extensions effects processor, foot pedals and playback sys.) Sea of Reeds (commd. F. Gerard Errante), 1997, (chorus and piano) Songs of War and Peace, 1998, (brass quintet) Fantasia sobre el Flamenco, 1998, (piano, cello, percussion) Houdini: Memories of a Conjurer, 1999 (commd. Core Ensemble), (wind quintet and piano) Ockeghem Variations (commd. Hexagon Ensemble), 2000, Run (piano quintet) (commd. Currents) 2001, (SATB chorus) Allelulia, 2001, Singing the Blue Ridge (commd. Wintergreen Performing Arts through Ams. for the Arts), 2002, Tree Music (commd. U. Va. Art Mus., interactive electronics), 2003, Penelope's Song (viola and electronics), 2003, Amulet (commd. N.Y. Treble Singers, SSA Chorus), 2005, Civil War Memories (commd. Jane Franklin Dance, electronics), 2005, Clave (commd. New Ear, flute, clarinet, saxophone, violin, viola, piano, percussion), 2006, Jabberwocky, 2006, (amplified cello and electronics) For the Birds, 2006. Nat. Endowment for Arts Composer fellow, 1980, 85, 89, 92; recipient award Va. Commn. for the Arts, 1989, 02. Mem. Am. Music Ctr., Am. Women Composers (pres. 1989-93), Am. Composers Alliance (bd. dirs. 1993-98), Internat. Alliance for Women in Music (chair nominating com. 1996-98, adv. bd. 1999-). Business E-Mail: shatin@virginia.edu, asst@judithshatin.com.

**SHATNER, WILLIAM,** actor; b. Montreal, Que., Can., Mar. 22, 1931; s. Joseph and Anne S.; m. Gloria Rosenberg, Aug. 12, 1956 (div. Mar. 1969); three children; m. Marcy Lafferty, Oct. 20, 1973 (div. 1996); m. Nerine Kidd, Nov. 15, 1997 (dec. Aug. 1999); m. Elizabeth Anderson, Feb. 2001. BA, McGill U., 1952. Stage debut, 1952; appeared Montreal Playhouse, summers 1952, 53; played juvenile roles Canadian Repertory Theatre, Ottawa, 1952-53, 53-54; appeared Stratford Shakespeare Festival, Ont., 1954-56; Broadway appearances include Tamburlaine the Great, 1956, The World of Suzie Wong, 1958, A Shot in the Dark, 1961; films include The Brothers Karamazov, 1958, The Explosive Generation, 1961, Judgement at Nuremburg, 1961, The Intruder, 1962, The Outrage, 1964, Dead of Night, 1974, The Devil's Rain, 1975, Star Trek: The Motion Picture, 1979, The Kidnapping of the President, 1979, Star Trek: The Wrath of Khan, 1982, Airplane II: The Sequel, 1982, Star Trek III: The Search for Spock, 1984, Star Trek IV: The Voyage Home, 1986, (dir.) Star Trek V: The Final Frontier, 1989, Star Trek VI: The Undiscovered Country, 1991, National Lampoon's Loaded Weapon, 1992, Star Trek: Generations, 1994, Trekkies, 1997, Free Enterprise, 1998, Shoot or be Shot, 2000, Groom Lake, 2000, Miss Congeniality, 2000, American Psycho II, 2001, Osmosis Jones, 2001, Dodgeball: A True Underdog Story, 2004, Miss Congeniality 2: Armed and Fabulous, 2005, The Wild, 2006, Over the Hedge (voice), 2006; also TV movies and appearances on The Andersonville Trial, The Bastard, 1978, Disaster on the Coastliner, 1979, Secrets of a Married Man, 1984, North Beach and Rawhide, 1985, Columbo, 1993; TV series Star Trek, 1966-69, animated series, 1973-75, Barbary Coast, 1975-76, The Babysitter, 1979, T.J. Hooker, 1982-86; host (TV series) Rescue 911, CBS, 1989—96, Third Rock From the Sun, 1996, The Practice, 2004 (Emmy award for Outstanding Guest Actor in a Drama Series 2004), Boston Legal (Golden Globe award for best supporting actor series, miniseries or TV movie, 2005, Emmy award for outstanding supporting actor in a drama series,

2005), 2004-, (TV spls.) Invasion Iowa, 2005, How William Shatner Changed the World, 2006, William Shatner in Concert, 2006; dir. TV movie TekWar; author: (novels) TekWar, 1989, TekLords, 1991, TekLab, 1991, Tek Vengeance, 1992, Tek Secret, 1993, (memoirs) Star Trek Memories, 1993, Star Trek Movie Memories, 1994, Tek Power, 1994, Tek Money, 1995, The Ashes of Eden, 1995, Man O' War, 1996, Tek Kill, 1996, The Return, 1996, Avenger, 1997, Delta Search: Quest for Tomorrow, 1997, Delta Search: In Alien Hands, 1998, Delta Search: Step Into Chaos, 1999, I'm Working on That, 2002; albums: Transformed Man, 1968, Has Been, 2004. Recipient Tyrone Guthrie award, 1956, Theatre World award, 1958; named to Acad. TV Arts & Sciences Hall of Fame, 2006 Mem. Actors Equity Assn., AFTRA, SAG, Dirs. Guild. Office: care Melis Prodns Ste 500 8383 Wilshire Blvd Beverly Hills CA 90211

**SHATTER, SUSAN LOUISE,** artist; b. NYC, Jan. 17, 1943; d. Aubrey and Florence (Breines) S.; m. Paul Brown (div. June 1975); 1 child, Scott Brown. Student, Skowhegan Sch. Sculpture, Maine, 1964; BFA, Pratt Inst., 1965; MFA, Boston U., 1972. Artist in residence Skowhegan (Maine) Sch Painting and Sculpture, 1977, 79; art instr. Sch. Visual Arts, NYC, 1980-84, Tyler Sch. of Art, Phila., 1985, San Francisco Art Inst., 1989, Vt. Studio Ctr., Johnson, 1989, Bklyn. Coll., 1991-95. Vis. critic, U. Pa., 1974-85, acting co-chair, 1983-84; bd. govs. Skowhegan Sch. Painting and Sculpture, 1979—, chair, 1988-91. One-woman shows include Catalogue by D. Kuspit, SUNY Fine Arts Ctr., 2003, Fischbach Gallery, N.Y.C., 1973-97, Harcus Gallery, Boston, 1975-87, Mattingly Baker Gallery, Dallas, 1981, John Berggruen Gallery, San Francisco, 1986, Heath Gallery, Atlanta, 1987, SECCA, Winston-Salem, NC, 2001, Lyons Wier Gallery, N.Y.C., 2002, Staller Ctr. Arts, 2003, Lyonswier Gallery, 2005, Ancocisco Gallery, Portland, Maine, 2006; works reproduced in America '76: A Bicentennial Exhibition, 1976, Boston Watercolor Today, 1976, Realist Drawings and Watercolors: Contemporary Works on Paper, 1980, Contemporary Realism Since 1960, 1981, Perspectives on Contemporary American Realism: Works of Art on Paper from the Collection of Jalane and Richard Davidson, 1983, Eireland, McMullen Mus. of Art, Boston Coll., 2003, New Vistas: Contemporary American Landscapes, 1984, American Realism: Twentieth Century Drawings and Watercolors from the Glenn C. Janss Collection, 1984, A Graphic Muse: Prints by American Women, 1987, Spirit of Place: Contemporary Landscape Painting & the American Tradition, 1989, Twentieth Century Watercolors, 1990, American Realism and Figurative Art: 1952-1991, 1991, (catalogue) Meridian Shift, 12 yrs. of paintings by Susan Shatter, U. Tex., San Antonio, 1998; represented in permanent collections Art Inst. Chgo., Mus. Fine Arts, Boston, MIT, Cambridge, Currier Gallery of Art, Manchester, N.H., Hood Art Mus., Dartmouth Coll., Hanover, N.H., Phila. Mus. Art, Utah Mus. Fine Art, Salt Lake City, Farnesworth Mus., Maine, Buffalo Bill Hist. Soc., Cody, Wyo., U. Tex., San Antonio, Nat. Mus. Am. Art, Washington, Yale U. Art Gallery, Boise (Idaho) Mus. Recipient grants Mass. Creative Artists Humanities, Radcliff Inst., Ingram-Merrill Found., NEA, N.Y. State Found. for the Arts, Yaddo Corp., Ballinglen Artists Fellowship, Ireland, 1999, Pollock-Krasner Found, 2004-05; Brittany fellow Rochefort-en-Terre, 2002; recipient Childe Hassam Purchase award, Am. Acad. Arts and Letters, 2003; Yaddo resident, Saratoga Springs, NY, 2001, 02. Mem. NAD (W. Paten Prize 2003, treas. 1998-05, pres. 2005-), The Century Club. Office: DFN Gallery 176 Franklin St New York NY 10013-2806 E-Mail: sshatter@mindspring.com.

**SHATTUCK, CATHIE ANN,** lawyer, former government official; b. Salt Lake City, July 18, 1945; d. Robert Ashley S. and Lillian Culp (Shattuck). BA, U. Nebr., 1967, JD, 1970. Bar: Nebr. 1970, U.S. Dist. Ct. Nebr. 1970, Colo. 1971, U.S. Dist. Ct. Colo. 1971, U.S. Supreme Ct. 1974, U.S. Ct. Appeals (10th cir.) 1977, U.S. Dist. Ct. D.C. 1984, U.S. C. Appeals (D.C. cir.) 1984. V.p., gen. mgr. Shattuck Farms, Hastings, Nebr., 1967-70; asst. project dir. atty. Colo. Civil Rights Commn., Denver, 1970-72; trial atty. EEOC, Denver, 1973-77, vice chmn. Washington, 1982-84; pvt. practice law Denver, 1977-81; mem. Fgn. Svc. Bd., Washington, 1982-84, Presdl. Pers. Task Force, Washington, 1982-84; ptnr. Epstein, Becker & Green, L.A. and Washington, 1984—. Lectr. Colo. Continuing Legal Edn. Author: Employer's Guide to Controlling Sexual Harrassment, 1992; co-editor Nat. Employment Law Insider, 2004-; mem. editl. bd. The Practical Litigator, 1988-2003. Bd. dirs. KGNU Pub. Radio, Boulder, Colo., 1979, Denver Exch., 1980-81, YWCA Met. Denver, 1979-81. Named Nebr. Young Career Woman, Bus. and Profl. Women, 1967, Outstanding Nebraskan, Daily Nebraskan, Lincoln, 1967. Fellow Am. Coll. of Labor and Employment Lawyers; mem. ABA (mgmt. chair labor and employment law sect. com. on immigration law 1988-90, mgmt. chair com. on legis. devels. 1990-93), Nebr. Bar Assn., Colo. Bar Assn., Colo. Women's Bar Assn., D.C. Bar Assn., Nat. Women's Coalition, Delta Sigma Rho, Tau Kappa Alpha, Pi Sigma Alpha, Alpha Xi Delta, Denver Club. Office Phone: 202-861-0900. Business E-Mail: cshattuck@ebglaw.com.

**SHATTUCK, GEORGE CLEMENT,** retired lawyer; b. Syracuse, N.Y., Sept. 2, 1927; s. Frank M. and Genevieve Mary (Hannon) S.; m. Sheila Eagan, Sept. 21, 1957 (div. 1985); children: Edward, George, Frank, Mark, Patrick; m. Carla A. Amussen, June 16, 1987; 1 dau., Morgan. BS in Mgmt., Syracuse U., 1950, JD, 1953. Bar: N.Y. 1954, U.S. Supreme Ct. 1973. Retired ptnr., estate planning splty. practice group Bond, Schoeneck & King Law Firm, Syracuse, 1954—94. Author: Oneida Land Claims, 1991. Mem. Syracuse Bd. Edn., 1968-75. Roman Catholic. Avocations: writing, reading history and philosophy, fishing. Home: 5158 W Lake Rd Cazenovia NY 13035-9616

**SHATTUCK, JOHN,** diplomat, civil rights lawyer, educator; b. Pownal, Calif., Sept. 22, 1943; s. H. Francis Jr. and Ruth (Murphy) S.; m. Petra Tölle, May 17, 1970 (dec. Mar. 1988); m. Ellen Hume, Feb. 14, 1991; children: Jessica, Rebecca, Peter, Susannah. BA magna cum laude, Yale U., 1965, JD, 1970; MA with 1st class hon. in internat. law, Cambridge U., Eng., 1967; doctorate (hon.), CUNY, 1995, Kenyon Coll., 2001, U. R.I., 2002, U. Western Bohemia, Czech. Rep., 2002. Law clk. to Hon. Edward Weinfeld U.S. Dist. Ct. (so. dist.) N.Y., 1970-71; nat. counsel ACLU, 1971-77, dir. Washington office, 1977-84; v.p. govt., community and pub. affairs Harvard U., 1984-93, sr. assoc. sci. tech. and pub. policy program John F. Kennedy sch. govt., 1984-93; asst. sec. of state bur. democracy, human rights and labor Dept. of State, Washington, 1993-98; U.S. amb. Czech Republic, 1998-2000; CEO John F. Kennedy Presdl. Libr. Found., 2001—. Lectr. Harvard Law Sch., 1986—93. Author: Freedom on Fire: Human Rights, Wars and America's Response, 2003; contbr. articles to profl. jours. Bd. dir. The Petra Fedn., Am. Friends of Czech Republic, ABA Ctrl. & E. Law Inst., Common Cause. Recipient UN Assn. Human Rights award 1998, Am. Bar Assn. Ambassador award 2000, H.L. Mencken award Free Press Assn. 1988, Pub. Svc. award Yale U. Law Sch. 1988, Roger Baldwin medal 1984, Global Leadership award Tufts U., 2003. Office: John F Kennedy Presdl Libr and Found/Columbia Point Boston MA 02125 Personal E-mail: john.shattuck@ifklfoundation.org.

**SHATTUCK, MAYO ADAMS, III,** utilities executive; b. Boston, Oct. 7, 1954; s. Mayo Adams Jr. and Jane (Bergwall) S.; m. Molly Anne George, Sept. 29, 1997; children: Mayo Adams IV, Kathleen Elizabeth, Spencer George, Wyatt Augustus, Lillian Jessie. BA, Williams Coll., 1976; MBA, Stanford U., 1980. Analyst Morgan Guaranty Trust Co., N.Y.C., 1976-78; mgr. Bain & Co., Menlo Park, Calif., 1980-83; v.p. to mng. dir. and head of corp. fin. Alex Brown & Sons, San Francisco, 1985-91, pres. and COO Balt. 1991-97; co-chmn., CEO BT Alex Brown Inc., from 1997; vice chmn. Bankers Trust N.Y., from 1997; co-chmn., co-CEO, Deutsche Banc Alex Brown Inc., Balt., 1999—2001; pres., CEO, chmn. bd. Constellation Energy Group, Balt., 2001—02, chmn., pres., CEO, 2002—. Bd. dirs. Constellation Energy, Gap Inc., Nuc. Energy Inst., Edison Electric Inst., Capital One Fin. Trustee Noble & Greenough Sch.; adv. dir. U. Md. Balt. County, Johns Hopkins Medicine. Avocations: tennis, golf. Office: Constellation Energy Group 750 E Pratt St 18th Floor Baltimore MD 21202*

**SHATZ, CARLA J.,** biology professor; b. NYC; BA in Chemistry, Radcliffe Coll., 1969; MPhil, Univ. Coll., London, 1971; PhD, Harvard U., 1976, postdoc., 1976—78. Assoc. prof. neurobiology Sch. Medicine Stanford U., Palo Alto, Calif., 1985—89, prof. neurobiology, 1989—92; investigator Howard Hughes Med. Inst., 1994—2000; Class of 1943 prof. neurobiology U. Calif., Berkeley, 1992—2000; prof., chair dept. neurobiology Harvard Med. Sch., Boston, 2000—. Mem. commn. on life scis. NRC, 1996—96; nat. adv. NIH, 1996—99; mem. coun. NAS, 1998—2001. Fellow: Inst. Medicine, Am. Philos. Soc., NAS, AAAS. Office: Harvard Med Sch Dept Neurobiology 220 Longwood Ave Boston MA 02115-5701

**SHAUD, GRANT,** actor; b. Evanston, Ill., Oct. 17; s. Edward Jr. and Ann Barbara (Dougherty) S. BA in Liberal Arts, U. Richmond, 1983. Appeared on Broadway in Torch Song Trilogy, 1984; other appearances include (plays) Today I Am a Fountain Pen, Pilgrims, Laughing Wild, 1990, A Ripe Banana, Diphthong, After Ashley, 2005 (TV) Murphy Brown, Murder, She Wrote, Kate & Allie, (film) Wall Street. Mem. Ensemble Studio Theatre. Democrat. Roman Catholic.

**SHAUGHNESSY, EDWARD LOUIS,** language educator; b. Sewickley, Pa., July 29, 1952; s. James Francis and Marie Rosalia (Kraus) S.; m. Gina Lynn Look, May 15, 1976 (div. Sept. 1992); m. Elena Valussi, Sept. 6, 1997. BA, U. Notre Dame, 1974; MA, Stanford U., 1980, PhD, 1983. Asst. prof. U. Chgo., 1985-90, assoc. prof., 1990-96, prof., 1996—, Lorraine J. and Herrlee G. Creel prof. of early China. Assoc. editor: Early China, 1985-88, editor, 1988-96; editor: New Sources of Early Chinese History: An Introduction to the Reading of Inscriptions and Manuscripts, 1997, (with Michael Loewe) The Cambridge History of Ancient China: From the Origins of Civilization to 221 R.C., 1999, China Empire and Civilization, 2000; author: Sources of Western Zhou History: Inscribed Bronze Vessels, 1991, I Ching, The Classic of Changes: The First English Translation of the Newly Discovered Second-Century B.C. Mawangdui Manuscripts, 1996, Before Confucius: Studies in the Creation of the Chinese Classics, 1997, Ancient China: Life, Myth and Art, 2005, Rewriting Early Chinese Texts, 2006, (with Robert Poor and Harrie A. Vanderstappen) Ritual and Reverence: Chinese Art at the University of Chicago, 1989, (with Cai Fangpei and James F. Shaughnessy) A Concordance of the Xiaotun Nandi Oracle-Bone Inscriptions, 1988; contbr. essays to books. Andrew W. Mellon fellow for Chinese studies, 1984-85; Divsn. of Humanities jr. faculty fellow U. Chgo., 1986; J. William Fulbright fellow in China, 2003-04. Office: U Chgo East Asian Langs/Civilizat 1050 E 59th St Chicago IL 60637-1559 Home: 1050 E 59th St Chicago IL 60637-1559 Business E-Mail: e-shaughnessy@uchicago.edu.

**SHAUGHNESSY, MARIE KANEKO,** artist; b. Detroit, Sept. 14, 1924; d. Eishiro and Kiyo (Yoshida) Kaneko; m. John Thomas Shaughnessy, Sept. 23, 1959. Assocs. in Liberal Arts, Keisen U., Tokyo, 1944. Ops. mgr. Webco Alaska, Inc., Anchorage, 1970-88; ptnr. Webco Partnership, Anchorage, 1983-98, also bd. dirs. Faculty Art League Sch., Alexandria, Va., Fairfax County Pub. Sch. Adult Continuing and Cmty. Edn. Paintings, Lilacs, 1984, Blooms, 1985, The Fence, 1986 (Purchase award, 1986). Bd. dirs. Alaska Artists Guild, 1971—87; commr. Mcpl. Anchorage Fine Arts Commn., 1983—87; organizing com. Japanese Soc. Alaska, 1987. Recipient Art Affiliate award, Anchorage C. of C., 1975, 1978, 1984, Univ. Artists award, Alaska Pacific U., 1986, Am. Juror's Choice award, Sumi-E Soc. Am., 1994, Ikebana Internat. award, 1994, Dorothy Klein Meml. award, 1995, Yasutomo Calligraphy award, 1997, 1998, Oriental Calligraphy award, 1997, 1998, Sarasota Chpt Painting award, 1999, Paul Schwartz Meml. award, 2001, Sm. Works Exhibit 1st Pl. award, Wash. Watercolor Assn., 2001, Wang Chi Yuan award, 2000. Mem.: Washington Water Color Assn. (1st place award Strathmore Mansion summer exhbn. 2005), Nat. League Am. Penwomen (Grumbacher Gold medal award excellence 1993), Vienna Art Soc. (bd. dir. 1995—96), Sumi-E Soc. Am. (past pres. 1992—94, bd. dir., Nat. Capital Area chpt. past pres. awards 1990, Nat. Capital Area chpt. award 1990—92, Purchase award 1993, Nat. Capital Area chpt. award 1994), Va. Watercolor Soc. (pres. 1993, co-chmn. 2004 All State Juried Show), Potomac Valley Watercolorists (exhibits chair 1989—93, bd. dir. 1989—99, newsletter editor 1993—96, v.p., workshop chair 1996—2001, historian 2003, awards 1989, 1991, Spl. award 1995), Alaska Watercolor Soc. (life; chmn. Grumbacher Silver medal 1989), McLean Art Soc. (pres. 2006—, 1st pl. award 1991). Republican. Roman Catholic. Personal E-mail: markaneko@aol.com.

**SHAUGHNESSY, MEGHANN,** professional tennis player; b. Richmond, Apr. 13, 1979; d. Bill and Joy. Profl. tennis player, 1996—. Recipient WTA Tour Doubles Title, Quebec City, 2000, German Open, 2001, Gold Coast, 2002, Moscow, 2003, WTA Tour Single Title, Shanghai, 2000, Quebec City, 2001, Canberra, 2003, Grand Prix SAR, 2006, Forest Hills Women's Tennis Classic, 2006, Ranked #17, WTA, Ranked #6 Among U.S. Players, Highest Season Ending Single's Ranking #12, 2001, Resident Pro, Scottsdale Hyatt Gainey Ranch Resort, 6 Internat. Women's Circuit Singles Titles. Mem.: U.S. Fedn. Cup Team. Office: WTA Tour Corporate Headquarters One Progress Plz Ste 1500 Saint Petersburg FL 33701*

**SHAUGHNESSY, THOMAS WILLIAM,** retired librarian; b. Pitts., May 3, 1938; s. Thomas W. and LaVerne (O'Brien) Shaughnessy; m. Marlene D. Reuben, Aug. 11, 1968; 1 child, Mark Andrew. BS at St. Vincent Coll., 1961; MLS, U. Pitts., 1964; PhD, Rutgers U., 1970. Asst. dean Rutgers U., New Brunswick, NJ, 1969-71, libr. dir. Newark, 1971-74; assoc. dean U. So. Calif., L.A., 1974-78; asst. libr. dir. U. Houston, 1978-82; libr. dir. U. Mo., Columbia, 1982-89; univ. libr. dir. U. Minn., Mpls.-St. Paul, 1989—2002; dir. Metronet, St. Paul, 2005—. Rsch. dir. Chgo. Pub. Libr. Survey, 1968—69; cons. U. Tulsa Libr., 1982—83; mem. faculty exch. USIA, Poland, 1998; trustee OCLC, Inc. 1997—2004. Author (with Lowell A. Martin): (book) Library Response to Urban Change, 1969, Developing Leadership Skills: A Source Book for Librarians, 1990. Recipient Hugh C. Atkinson Meml. award, 1996; fellow, Coun. Libr. Resources, 1973; U.S. Office Edn. grantee, Rutgers U., 1971, Sr. fellow, Coun. Libr. Resources, 1985. Mem.: ALA, Minn. Libr. Assn. (Disting. Achievement award 2002), Assn. Rsch. Librs. (cons. tng. fellow 1981, bd. dirs. 1989—92), Assn. Coll. and Rsch. Librs. Home: 5705 Wycliffe Rd Minneapolis MN 55436-2264 E-mail: tws@umn.edu.

**SHAVELL, STEVEN M.,** law educator; b. Wash., May 29, 1946; AB in Math. and Economics, U. Mich., 1968; PhD in Economics, MIT, 1973. Lt. j.g. US Pub. Health Svc. Centers for Disease Control, 1968—70; asst. prof. economics Boston Coll., 1973—74, Harvard U., Cambridge, Mass., 1974—79, assoc. prof., 1979—80; asst. prof. law and economics Harvard Law Sch., 1980—82, prof., 1982—, Samuel R. Rosenthal prof., 2000—, dir. John M. Olin Ctr. for Law, Economics, and Bus., 1985—. Vis. prof. U. Chgo. Law Sch., 1984—85, NYU Law Sch., 1999; assoc. editor Geneva Risk and Ins. Rev., 1990—; bd. editors Internat. Rev. Law and Economics, 1987—; Jour. Law, Economics, and Orgn., 1989—, Rsch. in Law and Economics, 1990—, Am. Law and Economics Rev., 1999—, Ency. Law and Economics, 1999—; bd. advisors Ctr. for Law, Economics, and Fin. Institutions, Copenhagen Bus. Sch., 2001—; bd. faculty advisors Jour. Law, Economics, and Policy, 2003—. Author: Economic Analysis of Accident Law, 1987, Foundations of Economic Analysis of Law, 2004; co-author: Fairness versus Welfare, 2002, Analytical Methods for Lawyers, 2003. NSF Grad. Fellowship, 1968, NSF Nat. Needs Postdoctoral Rsch. Fellowship, 1977—78, Harvard Law Sch. Liberal Arts Fellow, 1977, Liberty Fund Summer Fellow in Law and Economics, 1979, Guggenheim Meml. Found. Fellowship, 1983—84. Fellow: Econometric Soc.; mem.: Am. Law and Economics Assn. (bd. dirs. 1990—94, pres. 2001—02), Am. Acad. Arts and Sciences. Office: Harvard Law Sch 1563 Massachusetts Ave Cambridge MA 02138 Office Phone: 617-495-3668. Office Fax: 617-496-2256. Business E-Mail: shavell@law.harvard.edu.

**SHAVELLE, ROBERT,** medical researcher, consultant; PhD, U. of Calif., Riverside. Tech. dir. Life Expectancy Project, San Francisco, 1994—. Office: Life Expectancy Project 1439 - 17th Ave Cerritos CA 90703 E-mail: shavelle@lifeexpectancy.com.

**SHAVELSON, MELVILLE,** scriptwriter, theater producer, director; b. NYC, Apr. 1, 1917; s. Joseph and Hilda (Shalson) S.; m. Lucille T. Myers, Nov. 2, 1938; children: Richard, Lynne. AB, Cornell U., 1937. Mem. faculty sch. profl. writing U. So. Calif., 1998—2006. Author: How to Make a Jewish Movie, 1970, Lualda, 1975, The Great Houdinis, 1976, The Eleventh Commandment, 1977, Ike, 1979, Don't Shoot, It's Only Me, 1990, How To Succeed in Hollywood Without Really Trying, P.S. You Can't, 2006; writer Bob Hope Pepsodent Show, NBC radio, 1938-43; screenwriter The Princess and the Pirate, 1944, Wonder Man, 1944, Room for One More, 1951, I'll See You in My Dreams, 1952; screenwriter, dir. The Seven Little Foys, 1954, Beau James, 1956, Houseboat, 1957, The Five Pennies, 1958, It Started in Naples, 1959, On the Double, 1960, Yours, Mine and Ours, 1968, The War Between Men and Women, 1972, The Legend of Valentino, 1975, Deceptions, 1985; screenwriter, dir., producer The Pigeon That Took Rome, 1962, A New Kind of Love, 1963, Cast a Giant Shadow, 1966, Mixed Company, 1974, The Great Houdinis, 1976, Ike, 1979; dir. The Other Woman, 1983; creator TV shows including Danny Thomas Show, ABC-TV, 1953, My World— and Welcome To It, NBC-TV, 1969; author Broadway mus. Jimmy, 1969. Recipient Screen Writers Guild award, 1959, Christopher award, 1959, Sylvania TV award, 1953, Acad. Award nominations (screenplay), 1955, 58, Screen Writers Ann. award nominations (screenplay), 1952 (2), 58, 59, 62, 68, 72, 75, Screen Writers award (best written Am. mus.), 1959, Award of Merit United Jewish Appeal, 1966. Mem. Dirs. Guild Am., Writers Guild Am. (exec. bd. dirs 1960-75, 78, pres. screen writers br. 1967, pres. found. 1975-96, pres. emeritus 1997—, v.p. 1996—), Acad. Motion Picture Arts and Scis. (mem. bd. govs.), Writer Guild Am. West (pres. 1969-70, 79-81, 85-87, Valentine Davies award 1979, Laurel award 1984, Morgan Cox award 1998), Writers Guild Found. Shavelson-Webb Libr., Sigma Delta Chi. Home and Office: 11947 Sunshine Ter Studio City CA 91604-3708 E-mail: melshavelson@earthlink.net.

**SHAVELSON, RICHARD,** education educator; BA in Psychology, U. Oreg., 1964; MA in Psychology, San Jose State Coll., 1967; PhD in Ednl. Psychology, Stanford U., 1971. Asst. prof. edn. UCLA, 1973—75, assoc. prof. edn., 1975—79; dean Grad. Sch. Edn. U. Calif., Santa Barbara, 1987—93, prof. edn., 1987—96, affiliated appointment in stats. and applied probability, 1993—96; prof. edn. Stanford (Calif.) U., 1995—. Mem.: Spencer Found. (bd. dirs.), Am. Ednl. Rsch. Assn. (bd. dirs. grants bd. com.), Yosemite Nat. Insts. (bd. dirs.). Office: Stanford Edn Assessment Lab 485 Lasuen Mall Room 336 Stanford CA 94305-3096*

**SHAVENDER, MARILYN FAYE,** retired elementary school educator; b. Washington, Feb. 22, 1938; d. Redden Hudnell and Alice Gray Shavender; 1 child, Annette Byrd (dec.). BS in Elem. Edn., East Carolina U., 1959. 2d grade tchr. Virginia Beach Sch. Sys., Va., 1959—, lang. arts com., 1988—2003; ret., 2003. Author: (book) Poetry by Grammy, 2000, Marsh Winds...A Sentimental Journey. Mem.: DAR, Virginia Beach Edn. Assn. Republican. Mem. Church of Christ. Avocations: piano, writing, antiques, gardening. E-mail: Twingrand@aol.com.

**SHAVER, JAMES PORTER,** retired education educator, dean; b. Wadena, Minn., Oct. 19, 1933; BA magna cum laude, U. Wash., Seattle, 1955; MA in Teaching, Harvard U., 1957, EdD, 1961. Instr. Grad. Sch. Edn., Harvard U., 1961-62; assoc. prof., dir. Social Studies Curriculum Ctr., Ohio State U., Columbus, 1964-65; mem. faculty Utah State U. Coll. Edn., Logan, 1962-64, prof., 1965—, chmn. Bur. Rsch. Svcs., 1965-93, assoc. dean rsch., 1978-93, acting dean Sch. Grad. Studies, 1990-91, 92-93, dean, 1993-99, prof. emeritus secondary edn., 1999—. Mem. Commn. Youth Edn. for Citizenship, ABA, 1975-81; mem. edn. task force Am. Hist. Assn.-Am. Polit. Sci. Assn. Project '87, 1981-84; tech. advisor Nat. Ctr. on Effective Secondary Schs., 1988-91; mem. adv. bd. program in civic and moral edn. Inst. for Philosophy and Pub. Policy, U. Md., 1992—; mem. steering com. Nat. Assessment Ednl. Progress Civics Consensus Project, 1995-96. Co-author: Teaching Public Issues in the High School, 1966, 2d edit., 1974, Facing Value Decisions: Rationale-building For Teachers, 1976, 2d edit., 1982; editor: Building Rationales for Citizenship Education, 1977, Handbook of Research on Social Studies Teaching and Learning, 1991; co-editor: Democracy, Pluralism, and the Social Studies, 1968; also others. Recipient Outstanding Svc. and Tchg. award, Utah Coun. for the Social Studies, 1975, 1978, Lifetime Achievement award, 1998. Mem. AAAS, AAUP, Nat. Coun. Social Studies (pres. 1976, Exemplary Rsch. award 1977, Exemplary Rsch. Editor award 1991), Am. Ednl. Rsch. Assn., Phi Beta Kappa, Phi Kappa Phi. Home: PO Box 176 Hyrum UT 84319-0176 Office: Utah State U 2800 Old Main Hill Logan UT 84322-2800 Office Phone: 435-797-1469. Business E-mail: jim.shaver@usu.edu.

**SHAVER, JOAN LOUISE FOWLER,** dean, women's health nurse; BS in Nursing, U. Alberta, Can., 1966; M in Nursing, U. Wash., 1968-70, PhD in Physiology and Biophysics, 1976. Nursing instr. chair med. surgical prog. Holy Cross Hosp. Sch. Nursing, Calgary, Canada, 1966-68; staff nurse Virginia Mason Hosp., Seattle, 1970-71; asst. prof. Sch. Nursing U. Ariz., Tucson, 1976-77; assoc. prof. U. Calgary, Canada, 1977-80; asst. prof. Dept. Physiological Nursing U. Wash., Seattle, 1980-85, rsch. affil. Regl. Primate Rsch. Ctr., 1983-86, assoc. prof., 1985-89, chair Dept. Physiological Nusring, 1988-95, prof., 1989-95, prof. chair Dept. Biobehavioral Nursing & Health Systems, 1995-96, co-dir. Ctr. Women's Health Rsch., 1989-96; prof., dean Coll. Nursing U. Ill., Chgo., 1996—, co-dir. Rsch. Core Nat. Ctr. Excellence in Women's Health, 1997—. Mem. editl. bd. Health Care for Women Internat., 1984—, Heart and Lung: The Jour. of Critical Care, 1988-90, Jour. of Applied Nursing Rsch., 1988-91, IMAGE: Jour. Nursing Scholarship, editl. adv. bd. Nursing Rsch., 1997—, Biol. Rsch. for Nursing, 1999—, Jour. Nursing Scholarship, 2000—; contbr. artilces to profl. jours. Abe Miller Meml. scholar Alberta Assn. Registered Nurses, 1968-69; Kathryn McLaggen Meml. fellow Can. Nurses Found., fellow Am. Acad. Nursing. Mem. Nurses Assn., 1988—. Office: U Ill Coll Nursing 845 S Damen Ave # Mc802 Chicago IL 60612-7350*

**SHAVERS, CHERYL L.,** technology and business consultant; married; 3 children. BS in Chemistry, Ariz. State U., PhD in Solid State Chemistry; degree in engring. mgmt. (hon.), Calif. Poly. State U., 1996. Practicing registered patent agent Patent and Trademark Office of Dept. of Commerce. Prod. engr. Motorola; process devel. engr Hewlett-Packard, patent agent, tech. legal dept.; microelectronics sect. mgr. Wiltron Co.; engring. mgr., thin films devel. lab. Varian Associates; sector mgr. microprocessor div., corp. bus. devel. div. Intel Corp.; under sec. commerce for tech. U.S. Dept Commerce, 1999—2001; chmn., CEO Global Smarts, Inc., Santa Clara, Calif., 2001—. Spkr., workshop leader in field; non-exec. chmn. BitArts Ltd., 2001—03; bd. dirs. Rockwell Collins, Inc., 2002—. Weekly columnist San Jose Mercury News Bus. Sect.; contbr. articles to profl. publs.; featured in articles, books and Web sites; TV appearances include documentary Wizards and Alchemists, 1995, Real Science Program, Sta. KTEH-TV, NBC New Media News, Women in Technology, 1997 Active numerous outreach programs, including Real Sci., Wizards and Alchemists, KTEH Silicon Valley Report, KRON New Media News programs; bd. dirs. San Jose Tech Mus. of Innovation, 1996—; former bd. dirs. Internat. Network Women in Tech., 1995-96, ARC, 1995-96. Recipient Janet Gray Hayes award, award Phi Lambda Upsilon, Outstanding Presenter of Yr., San Francisco Bay Area chpt. Nat. Assn. of Black MBAs, 1998; Henry Crown fellow Aspen Inst.'s Crown Fellowship Program; inductee Internat. Women in Tech. Hall of Fame, Coll. Liberal Arts and Scis. Hall of Fame, Ariz. State U., 1997, Internat. Network of Women in Tech. Hall of Fame, 1996. Mem. Libr. of Congress (assoc.). Office: Global Smarts Inc 3333 Bowers Ave Ste 130 Santa Clara CA 95050

**SHAVERS, CLYDE,** electrical engineer, researcher; s. Solomon Rube and Lelar W. Shavers; m. Lora Scottsly Brown, Aug. 14, 1994; children: Melissa C., Felicia N., Christina C., Clyde Jr., Savonna J., Quinten R., Keisha R. BS, So. U., Baton Rouge, 1977; MS, So. Meth. U., Dallas, 1994; PhD, NC A & T State U., Greensboro, 2006. Sr. sys. engr. Tex. Instruments Inc., Richardson, 1995—97; sr. staff mgr. GTE Comm. (now Verizon), 1997—98; regional prin. cons. Architel Sys. Corp., Richardson, 1998—99; pvt. practice Richardson,

Tex., 1999—2000; prin. design engr. DNA Computing Solution, Richardson, 2000—02; tech. staff Alcatel Network Sys., Richardson; electronic circuits engr. govt. electronics E-Systems, Inc. (now Raytheon), Garland, Tex.; electronic sys. engr. govt. electronics Electrospace Sys. Inc., Richardson. Presenter in field. Mem.: IEEE, Nat. Soc. Black Engrs., Am. Soc. Engring. Edn., Etta Kappa Nu.

**SHAVIN, HELENE B.,** venture capital company executive; b. 1954; BA, Queens Coll.; MBA, Baruch Coll. Sr. acct. KPMG Peat Marwick, Hawaii; CPA Citicorp Venture Capital Ltd., NY, 1986—2000, v.p. NY, 1999—2000; v.p., controller Harris & Harris Group, Inc., NY, 2001—. Office: Harris & Harris Group Inc 111 W 57th St Ste 1100 New York NY 10019 also: Harris & Harris Group Inc 11150 Santa Monica Blvd Ste 1200 Los Angeles CA 90025 Office Phone: 212-582-0900, 310-479-2595. Office Fax: 212-582-9563, 310-312-1868. Business E-mail: admin@tinytechvc.com.

**SHAW, ALAN,** lawyer; b. Long Branch, N.J., July 23, 1930; m. Margaret Knight, Oct. 15, 1959; children: Andrew Macbeth, Adriane Macbeth. AB, U. Mich., 1952; LLB, Harvard U., 1955. Bar: Mass. 1955, N.Y. 1958. Atty. Skadden, Arps, Slate, Meagher & Flom, N.Y.C., 1958-65; v.p., gen. counsel, sec. Athlone Industries Inc., Parsippany, NJ, 1966-93, also bd. dirs. Adj. prof. law Fordham U.; arbitrator Am. Arbitration Assn., NASD Dispute Resolution, N.Y. Stock Exch.; panelist Contract Dispute Resolution Bd., N.Y.C. Mem. co-chair fundraising Jefferson Soc. Morristown Meml. Hosp. With U.S. Army, 1955-57. Mem. ABA (sect. on corps., litig., alt. dispute resolution sect.), NJ Gen. Counsel Group, Assn. Bar City NY (mem. arbitration com.), Soc. Profls. Dispute Resolution, Morristown (NJ) Club, Washington Assn. Morristown (trustee, 2d v.p.), Morris County Golf Club, Harvard Club, Churchill Ctr. (charter mem.), Alexander Hamilton Hist. Soc. Home: 490 S Maple Ave Basking Ridge NJ 07920-1327 Office: 1812 Front St Scotch Plains NJ 07076

**SHAW, ALAN BOSWORTH,** geologist, retired paleontologist; b. Engle-wood, N.J., Mar. 28, 1922; s. Carroll Harper and Natalie Frederique (Howe) S.; m. Helen Louise Wilson, Nov. 2, 1945 (div. Apr. 1952); m. Marian Tavenner Stoll, Mar. 11, 1954 (dec. Apr. 1981); children: Nancy Jeanne, Sally Ann; m. Mary Elizabeth Merrem, Sept. 3, 1982. AB magna cum laude, Harvard Coll., 1946; AM, PhD, Harvard U., 1949. Asst. prof. geology U. Wyo., Laramie, 1949-55; paleontologist Shell Oil Co., Denver, 1955-60; owner Nat. Elec. Svc., N.Y.C., 1960-61; freelance cons. geologist Denver, 1961; supr. Pan Am. Rsch. (now BP), Tulsa, Okla., 1961-68; various positions Pan Am. Petroleum, Denver, 1968-76; chief paleontologist Amoco Prodn., Chgo., 1976-77, chief geologist, 1977-81; geol. rsch. cons. Amoco Rsch., Tulsa, 1981-85; ret., 1985. Oil industry rep. NRC Com. on Paleontology, Washington, 1963-69; mem. Com. on Paleontology and Stratigraphy Deep Sea Drilling Program, 1973-75. Author: Time in Stratigraphy, 1964; contbr. numerous articles to profl. jours. Served to 1st lt., USAAF, 1943-45. Recipient Moore Paleontology medal Soc. Sedimentary Geology, 1996. Achievements include invention of graphic correlation system for use of fossils in making time correlations of sedimentary rocks. Home: 210 Kamira Kerrville TX 78028 Personal E-mail: shaw99@ktc.com.

**SHAW, ALAN ROGER,** retired finance company executive, finance educator; b. Bklyn., July 7, 1938; s. Sewall S. and Vera (Dimmick) S.; children: Stephen S., Todd J., Bradley C.; m. Mary Elizabeth Hogg, May 30, 1987. Student, Susquehanna U., 1957, Adelphi U., 1963-66; LLD (hon.), Susquehanna U., 1999. Analyst Harris Upham & Co., N.Y.C., 1958-71, asst. v.p., 1971-73, v.p., 1973-75; 1st v.p. Smith, Barney, Harris, Upham & Co., N.Y.C., 1975-80; sr. v.p., mng. dir. Smith Barney, N.Y.C., 1980—2004. Tchr. N.Y. Inst. Fin., 1966— Mem. Market Technicians Assn. (pres. 1974), N.Y. Soc. Security Analysts, Securities Industry Assn. Inst. (trustee 1986-92), South-ward Ho Country Club, Unqua Corinthian Yacht Club (commodore 1988-90). Home: PO Box 322 79 N Midway Rd Shelter Island NY 11964 E-mail: almed@optonline.net.

**SHAW, ANNITA LOUISE,** art educator; b. Scottsbluff, Nebr., Feb. 13, 1941; d. Harold Kenneth and Velma Loraine Shaw; m. Max Le Roy Shaw, June 29, 1968; 1 child, Justin Owen. BS in Elem. Edn., Chadron State Coll., Nebr., 1963; MA in Art Supervision and Direction, NYU, 1969. Tchr. 2d grade Bridgeport Sch. Dist., Nebr., 1961—64; tchr. 3rd grade Geneva Sch. Dist., Nebr., 1964—66; elem. art specialist Omaha Sch. Dist., 1966—68; tchr. jr. high sch. New London Sch. Dist., Conn., 1968—70; tchr. jr. and sr. high visual arts and visual arts curriculum specialist Ctrl. Kitsap Sch. Dist., Silverdale, Wash., 1974—2003; owner A.Shaw Originals. Mem. adv. com. Wash. State Commn. on Student Learning, Olympia, 1993—95; mem. assessment cert. team Nat. Bd. Profl. Tchg. Stds., San Francisco, 1996; mem. People to People Art Edn. Delegation to Russia, 2006; presenter in field. Prodr.: (video) Whistle Wisdom, 1993, Perspective: More than Converging Line, 1999, Roll, Pinch, Shake and Rattle, 2001; contbr. articles to mags. and profl. jours. Mem.: Nat. Art Edn. Assn. (mem. dels. assembly 1994, historian Wash. chpt. 1994, pres. Wash. chpt., treas. Wash. chpt., Pacific Region Elem. Art Educator 1988, Christa McAliffe Excellence in Edn. 1990, Pacific Region Mid. Level Art Educator 2001, Wash. Art Educator of Yr. 2000, Nat. Mid. Level Art Educator of the Yr. 2002), Women in the Arts (charter mem. 2006). Avocations: sculpting, designing pins and medallions, writing. Home: PO Box 737 Silverdale WA 98383-0737 Personal E-mail: mashaw@mindspring.com.

**SHAW, ANTHONY,** pediatric surgeon, retired educator; b. Shanghai, Oct. 31, 1929; s. Bruno and Regina (Hyman) S.; m. Iris Violet Azian, Mar. 12, 1955; children: Brian Anthony, Diana Shaw Clark, Daniel Aram. BA cum laude, Harvard Coll., 1950; MD, NYU, 1954. Diplomate Am. Bd. Surgery; cert. spl. competence pediat. surgery. Intern and resident in surgery Columbia-Presbyn. Med. Ctr., N.Y.C., 1954-56, 58-62; resident in pediat. surgery Babies Hosp., N.Y.C., 1962; asst. prof. surgery Columbia U. Coll. Physicians and Surgeons, N.Y.C., 1965-70; chief pediat. surgery St. Vincent's Hosp., N.Y.C., 1963-70, Harlem Hosp. Ctr., N.Y.C., 1965-70; prof. surgery U. Va., Charlottesville, 1970-81, chief pediat. surgery Med. Ctr., 1970-81; prof. surgery UCLA, 1981-2001, emeritus prof. surgery, 2001—; chief pediat. surgery Olive View-UCLA Med. Ctr., Sylmar, 1986-2001, cons. surgeon, 2003—. Expert witness on child abuse L.A. Superior Ct., 1986—; chmn. gov.'s adv. com. child abuse and neglect Commonwealth of Va., 1975-80; vis. prof. pediat. surgery People's Republic of China, 1985. Contbr. more than 220 articles to profl. jours. Mem. Gov.'s Task Force on Child Abuse Va., 1973-74. Capt. U.S. Army, 1956-58. Recipient Commrs. award Va. Dept. Social Svcs., 1980, award Gov.'s Adv. Bd., Cert. of Recognition HEW, 1978. Fellow Am. Pediat. Surg. Assn. (sec. 1982-85), ACS (v.p. 1987-89); mem. AMA, Pacific Coast Surg. Assn. (v.p. 1989-90), Am. Soc. Law, Medicine, and Ethics, Am. Profl. Soc. on Abuse of Children, Alpha Omega Alpha. Avocation: writing humor. Home and Office: One S Orange Grove Blvd # 9 Pasadena CA 91105 Office Phone: 626-796-8588. Personal E-mail: shawpas@pacbell.net.

**SHAW, ANTHONY RAYMOND, JR.,** research company executive; b. NYC, Dec. 26, 1942; s. Anthony Raymond and Isabelle Leone (Bisson) S.; m. Diane Lynn Tomason, Nov. 1986; children: Amy, Anthony Raymond III (dec.), Danielle, Devon Young. BA cum laude, St. John's Sem. Coll., Boston, 1964; postgrad. Loyola U., Chgo., 1970-71, Rutgers U., 1975, Brookings Instn., 1987-88. Positions in personnel, purchasing and service ops. AT&T Bell Labs., Chgo., Denver and N.J., 1969-77, head adminstrn. network planning div., Holmdel, N.J., 1977-81, mgr. adminstrn. pers. svcs., 1981-85, dir. research and devel. security and spl. projects, Whippany, N.J., 1986-94, dir. info. svcs, ret.; prin., bus. ops. GeoPartners Rsch., Cambridge, Mass.; dir. labs., co-dir. grad. studies dept. chemistry Harvard U., Cambridge, 2001—. Sgt. Westfield (N.J.) Spl. Police Force. Capt. USMC, 1965-69. Decorated Purple Heart. Mem. South Coastal Hockey League. Republican. Roman Catholic. Author: Low/High Altitude Instrument Approach Procedures, 1969. Office: Harvard U Dept Chemistry 12 Oxford St Cambridge MA 02138 Office Phone: 617-495-4283. Business E-mail: shaw@chemistry.harvard.edu.

**SHAW, BILLY,** retired professional football player; b. Natchez, Miss., Dec. 15, 1938; Student, Ga. Inst. Tech. Guard Buffalo Bills, 1961—69. Named All-Am. lineman, Ga. Inst. Tech., 1961; named to 1st team All-AFL, 1962—66, 2d team All-AFL, 1968, 1969, 8 AFL All-Star Games, All-Time AFL Team, All-Decade Team of '60's, Pro Football Hall of Fame, 1999. Home: Pro Football Hall of Fame 2121 Geore Halas Dr NW Canton OH 44708-2630

**SHAW, BRAD,** communications executive; b. Apr. 10, 1966; B in Journalism, Washington and Lee U., Lexington, Va. Account mgr. Doremus Pub. Rels., NYC; sr. account mgr. Ketchum Pub. Rels., NYC; sr. mgr. comm. N.Am. Pepsi-Cola Co., Puchase, NY, dir. worldwide comm. Purchase, NY; v.p. corp. comm. Gateway, Inc., Poway, Calif., 1999; sr. v.p. corp. comm.; sr. v.p. corp. comm. and external affairs Home Depot, Inc., Atlanta, 2004—. Chair coordinating com. Bus. Roundtable Partnership for Disaster Response Task Force. Bd. mem. Hands On Network; bd. dirs. San Diego Regional C. of C.; bd. mem. Homer Fund, KABOOM!. Mem.: Arthur W. Page Soc. Office: Home Depot Inc 2455 Paces Ferry Rd Atlanta GA 30339

**SHAW, CAROLE,** editor, publisher; b. Bklyn., Jan. 22, 1936; d. Sam and Betty (Neckin) Bergenthal; m. Ray Shaw, Dec. 27, 1957; children: Lori Eve Cohen, Victoria Shaw Locknar. BA, Hunter Coll., 1962. Singer Capitol Records, Hilton Records, Rama Records, Verve Records, 1952-65; TV appearances Ed Sullivan, Steve Allen, Jack Paar, George Gobel Show, 1957; owner The People's Choice, L.A., 1975-79; founder, editor-in-chief Big Beautiful Woman mag., Beverly Hills, Calif., 1979—. Creator Carole Shaw and BBW label clothing line for large-size women. Author: Come Out, Come Out Wherever You Are, 1982. Avocations: piano, painting, swimming, travel. Office: BBW Mag 6666 Brookmont Ter Ste 412 Nashville TN 37205-4622 Personal E-mail: bibewa@comcast.net.

**SHAW, CHARLES ALDEN,** engineering executive; b. Detroit, June 8, 1925; s. Fred Alden and Amy (Ellis) S.; m. Barbara Loveland, Mar. 9, 1963 (div. 1979); children: Amy Elizabeth, Polly Nicole; m. Jeanne Steves Partridge, Apr. 22, 1989. BS, Harvard U., 1945; MSEE, Syracuse U., 1958. Test and design engr. G.E., Syracuse-Schenectady, NY, 1947-51; chief engr. electronics divsn. Onondaga Pottery Co., Syracuse, 1951-60; mgr. semiconductor div. G.E., Syracuse-Schenectady, 1960-66; cons. to gen. dir. Bull-G.E., Paris, 1966-69; mgr. CAD sect. integrated cir. product dept. G.E., Syracuse, 1969-71, mgr. CAD ctr. solid state applied ops., 1971-78, mgr. computer support solid state applied ops., 1978-81; dir. CAD G.E. Intersil, Cupertino, Calif., 1981-88; cons. in field Cupertino, 1988-89; mgr. tech. program Cadence Design Systems, Santa Clara, Calif., 1989—. Trustee Hidden Villa, Los Altos Hills, Calif., 1986—92; bd. dirs. Unitarian Universalist Ch., Livermore, 1999—2002. With USN, 1942—45, PTO. Mem. IEEE (officer 2003—, bd. govs. 2005—), Assn. Computing Machinery (chmn. spl. interest group SIGDA 1986-91), Design Automation Conf. (exec. bd. 1985-95), Harvard Club of Silicon Valley. Democrat. Unitarian Universalist. Home and Office: 4925 Monaco Dr Pleasanton CA 94566-7671 Office Phone: 925-426-0513. Personal E-mail: shawcha@comcast.net.

**SHAW, CHARLES ALEXANDER,** judge; b. Jackson, Tenn., Dec. 31, 1944; s. Alvis and Sarah S.; m. Kathleen Ingram, Aug. 17, 1969; 1 child, Bryan Ingram. BA, Harris Stowe State U., 1966; MBA, U. Mo., 1971; JD, Cath. U. Am., 1974. Bar: D.C. 1975, Mo. 1975, U.S. Ct. Appeals (8th and D.C. cirs.) 1975, U.S. Dist. Ct. (ea. dist.) Mo. 1976, U.S. Ct. Appeals (6th and 7th cirs.) 1976. Tchr. St. Louis Pub. Schs., 1966-69, D.C. Pub. Schs., Washington, 1969-71; law clk. U.S. Dept. Justice, Washington, 1972-73, NLRB, Washington, 1973-74, atty., 1974-76; assoc. Lashly, Caruthers, Theis, Rava & Hamel, St. Louis, 1976-80, asst. U.S. atty., 1980-87; judge Mo. Cir. Ct., St. Louis, 1987-94, asst. presiding judge, 1993-94; judge U.S. Dist. Ct., St. Louis, 1994—. Hearing officer Office of the Mayor, Washington, 1973-74; instr. U. Mo., St. Louis, 1980-81. State bd. dirs. United Negro Coll. Fund, St. Louis, 1979-83; trustee St. Louis Art Mus., 1979-82, 89-96; bd. dirs. Arts and Edn. Coun., 1992-96, Metro Golf Assn., 1993-2000, Landmarks Assn., St. Louis, 1980-82. Recipient Silver Gavel award Fed. Def. Bar, 2005; named Disting. Alumnus, Cath. U., 2001; fellow Danforth Found., 1978-79; scholar Cath. U. Am., 1971-74. Mem. D.C. Bar Assn., Mo. Bar Assn., Mound City Bar Assn., Bar Assn. Met. St. Louis, Harris-Stowe State Coll. Alumni Assn. (Disting. Alumni 1988), Nat. Assn. Guardsmen (sec. St. Louis chpt. 1999-2001), Phi Alpha Delta (svc. award 1973-74), Sigma Pi Phi (pres. St. Louis chpt. 1999-2001). Avocation: golf. Office: 111 S 10th St Saint Louis MO 63102 Office Phone: 314-244-7480.

**SHAW, CHARLES RAYMOND,** journalist; b. Phila., Feb. 2, 1951; s. Charles Raymond Sr. and Dorothy Blanche (Buckman) S.; m. Francine Ruth Pennock, Jan. 14, 1983. BS in Journalism, Temple U., 1972; MS in Journalism, Columbia U., 1973. Staff writer Intelligencer Jour., Lancaster, Pa., 1973-83, asst. news editor, 1983-88, news editor, 1988-97, editor, 1997—. Mem. Pa. Soc. of Newspaper Editors, Am. Soc. Newspaper Editors, Pa. Assoc. Press (bd. dirs.). Office: Lancaster Newspaper PO Box 1328 Lancaster PA 17608-1328 Office Phone: 717-291-8650. E-mail: rshaw@lnpnews.com.

**SHAW, CHARLES RUSANDA,** retired government investigator; b. Detroit, Aug. 17, 1914; s. Leonard George and Harriet (Kratzer) S.; m. Sally Madeline Jock, May 3, 1947 (dec. June 1996); children: Patrick R., Sandra L. Keding (dec.), Janice L., Lisa Keding. Cert., Wicker Sch. of Fine Arts, 1936, Mich. Acad. Advt. Art, 1937; student, Intelligence Corps Sch., 1947. Freelance artist, Detroit, 1936-39; spl. agt. U.S. Army Counter Intelligence Corps, Washington, 1947-48, Office Spl. Investigations, USAF, Washington, 1948-66; pvt. investigator Charles Shaw Assocs., Mt. Clemens, Mich., 1966-84; contract investigator USAF & U.S. Customs Svc., Washington, 1984-94; prin. C.R. Shaw Assocs., New Haven, Mich., 1994—. Author: Immaculate Misconception, 1999. Master sgt. U.S. Army, 1939-45, PTO, ETO. Mem. Assn. Former OSI Spl. Agts. (chartered), VFW, Pearl Harbor Survivors Assn. Democrat. Roman Catholic. Achievements include invention of neoteric products; patents pending for. Avocations: fine arts, photography, gardening. Home and Office: 59295 Bates Rd New Haven MI 48048-1728 Office Phone: 586-749-9223.

**SHAW, CURTIS S,** lawyer; b. 1948; BA in Econ. with honors, Trinity Coll., 1970; JD, Columbia U. Sch. of Law, 1973. Assoc. gen. counsel Occidental Chemical Corp., 1983—88; v.p., gen. counsel divsn. of Occidental Chemical Corp.; corp. counsel NYNEX, 1988—96; sr. v.p., gen. counsel and sec. Charter Commn., 1997—2003, exec. v.p., gen. counsel, sec., 2003—.

**SHAW, DAVID ELLIOT,** financial executive; b. Chgo., Mar. 29, 1951; s. Charles B. Jr. and Marilyn (Baron) Shaw. BA, U. Calif., San Diego, 1972; MS, Stanford U., 1975, PhD, 1980. Pres. Stanford Systems Corp., Palo Alto, Calif., 1976-79; assoc. prof. Columbia U., NYC, 1980-86; v.p. Morgan Stanley & Co., NYC, 1986-88; chmn. D.E. Shaw & Co., Inc. and Juno Online Svcs., Inc., NYC, 1988—, Schrödinger, Inc., NYC, 1988—. Contbr. articles to profl. jours. Chmn. NYC Mayor's Panel on Tech. and Fin., 1987; mem. NYC Partnership Subcommittee on Tech. and Fin., 1987; apptd. to Pres. Clinton's Com. of Advs. on Sci. and Tech., 1994; chmn. Pres. Clinton's Panel on Ednl. Tech., 1995. Named one of 400 Richest Ams., Forbes mag., 2006. Mem. AAAS (bd. dirs. 1999), NY Acad. Scis. (bd. govs. 1993-95), Coun. on Competitiveness (exec. com.). Democrat. Jewish. Office: DE Shaw and Co 39th Fl Tower 45 120 W 45th St New York NY 10036-4041*

**SHAW, DAVID TAI-KO,** electrical and computer engineering educator, academic administrator; b. China, Mar. 13, 1938; came to U.S., 1960, naturalized, 1972; m. Katharine Lin-Yee Yang; children: Albert, Stanley. BSM.E., Nat. Taiwan U., Taipei, 1959; MS in Nuclear Engring., Purdue U., 1961, PhD, 1964. Asst. prof. div. interdisciplinary studies and research Sch. Engring., SUNY-Buffalo, 1964-67, assoc. prof. faculty engring. and applied scis., 1967-74, prof. elec. engring. and nuclear engring. aerospace and engring. sci., 1974-77, prof. elec. engring., 1974—, dir. lab. for power and environ. studies, 1978—90. Exec. dir. State Inst. on Superconductivity, 1987-97; vis. prof. U. Paris, 1976-77; vis. scientist Centre d'Etudes Nucleairs de Fontenay-aux-Roses (France) Commissariat a L'Energie Atomique, 1976-77; vis. assoc. dept. environ. health engring. Calif. Inst. Tech., 1970-71; mem. U.S. del. French Commissariat a L'energie ATomique, 1974, U.S. del. Joint Nuclear Energy Agy. IAEA Internat. Liaison Group on Thermionic Elec. Power Generation, Paris, 1974; mem. U.S. vis. team USSR Acad. Scis. Editor: Fundamentals of Aerosol Science, 1978, Recent Developments in Aerosol Science, 1978, Assessment of Airborne Radioactivity, 1978; editor-in-chief: Jour. Aerosol Sci. and Tech., 1982-93; contbr. numerous articles to profl. publs. Mem. IEEE, ASME, AAAS, Am. Assn. Aerosol Rsch. (pres. 1982-85, Assn. award 1984, Internat. Aerosol Fellow award 1994), Sigma Xi, Sigma Pi Sigma. Office: SUNY-Buffalo Materials Rsch Lab/Ctr for Innovation Engring 330 Bonner Hall Buffalo NY 14260-1900 E-mail: dshaw@buffalo.edu.

SHAW, DENNIS FREDERICK, former library director, chartered physicist, consultant; b. Teddington, Middlesex, Eng., Apr. 20, 1924; s. Albert and Lily Florence (Hill) S.; m. Joan Irene Chandler, June 25, 1949; children: Peter James, Margaret Denise, Katherine Joan, Deborah Mary. BA in Physics, U. Oxford, 1945, MA, 1950, DPhil in Nuc. Physics, 1950. Sr. rsch. officer Oxford (Eng.) U., 1950-75; tutor in physics Keble Coll., 1956-75, professorial fellow, 1977—, keeper of sci. books, 1975-91, emeritus, 1991. Vis. scientist CERN, Geneva, 1961-62; vis. prof. U. South Tenn., 1974; chmn. IFLA Sci. and Tech. Librs., 1987-91, hon. treas. spl. librs. div., 1991-93, cons., 1993—; mem. Home Office Sci. Adv. Coun., London, 1966-78; mem. Home Def. Sci. Adv. Com., London, 1978-95; mem. Hebdomadal Coun., Oxford U., 1980-89; mem Com. for the Internat. Coun. of Sci. Unions Press, 1991-96, mng. editor electronic pub., 1997-2002. Author. Introduction to Electronics, 1962, 70, Information Sources in Physics, 1985, 95; editor: Proceedings of ICSU/UNESCO Internat. Conferences on Electronic Publishing in Sci., 1996, 2001, Guidelines for Scientific Publishing, 1999; contbr. articles to profl. jours. Gov. Christ's Hosp., London, Almoner, 1980-98, chmn. edn. com., 1993-96; mem. Oxford City Coun., 1963-67; freeman City of London, 1998. Decorated Comdr. Brit. Empire, 1974. Fellow Inst. Physics, Zool. Soc. London; mem. Am. Inst. Physics (sr.), Internat. Assn. Tech. Univs. Librs. (hon., sec. 1983-85, pres. 1986-90, chmn. pub. bd. 1991-93), N.Y. Acad. Sci., Oxford and Cambridge Club. Anglican. Home: 29 Davenant Rd Oxford OX2 8BU England Office: Keble Coll Parks Rd Oxford OX1 3PG England Business E-Mail: dennis.shaw@keb.ox.ac.uk.

SHAW, DONALD HARDY, lawyer; b. Oelwein, Iowa, June 1, 1922; s. John Hardy and Minnie (Brown) S.; m. Elizabeth Jean Orr, Aug. 16, 1946; children: Elizabeth Ann, Andrew Hardy, Anthony Orr. BS, Harvard U., 1942; JD, U. Iowa, 1948. Bar: Ill. 1949, Iowa 1948, cert. fin. planner 1983. With firm Sidley & Austin, Chgo., 1948-55; with Iowa-Ill. Gas & Electric Co., Davenport, Iowa, 1956-87, treas., 1960-72, v.p. finance, 1973-87, also dir.; of counsel Walton, Creen, Curry and Robertson, Davenport, Iowa, 1987-88, Newpor, Bell, Leon & Martinez, Davenport, 1989-98. Author: As We Were, 2006. Mem. Iowa State Bd. Regents, 1969-81, Iowa State TV-Radio Com., 1976-81; trustee St. Luke's Hosp., Davenport, 1966-91. Served to capt. USAAF, 1942-45. Recipient Philo Sherman Bennett award, 1942 Mem.: Order of Coif, Delta Theta Phi. Congregationalist. Home: Vantage House #P11 Columbia MD 21044

SHAW, DONALD KEITH, physical therapist, educator; s. Eugene Leigh and Bernice Margarette Shaw; m. Mary Bleve Hegi, Dec. 10, 1994. BS in Health and Phys. Edn., George Williams Coll., Downers Grove, Ill., 1969, MS in Health and Phys. Edn., 1971; PhD in Exercise Physiology, Kent State U., Ohio, 1986; BS in Phys. Therapy, Tex. State U., San Marcos, 1997. Lic. phys. therapist Tex. From asst. prof. to assoc. prof. dept. phys. therapy SW Tex. State U., San Marcos, 1995—2002; assoc. prof. dept. phys. therapy Tex. State U. (formerly SW Tex. State U.), San Marcos, 2002—. Mgr. exercise physiologist cardiopulmonary testing Universal Testing Svcs., Seattle, 1972—75; site dir. exercise physiologist cardiac rehab. Cardiopulmonary Rsch. Inst., Seattle, 1975—78; adj. prof. dept. health, phys edn., recreation and dance Kent State U., Ohio, 1986—88; adj. prof. dept. health, phys edn. and recreation Akron U., Ohio, 1986—88; adj. prof. dept. edn. Vanderbilt U./Peabody Coll., Nashville, 1989—94; adj. prof. dept. phys therapy Trevecca Nazarene U., Nashville, 1993—94, East Carolina U., Greenville, NC, 1999—2002; program dir. exercise physiologist cardiac rehab. Aultman Hosp., Canton, Ohio, 1981—88, St. Thomas Hosp., Nashville, 1988—94, clin. dir. exercise physiologist, 1995—96; lectr., presenter, cons. reviewer in field. Contbr. articles to profl. jours. Recipient Deans award, East Carolina U., 2001; grantee, United Way Health Found., 1984, Physiodyne, Inc., 1997, ScottCare Corp., 1998, 2002, 2005, HealthCare Vision, Inc., 2004, Tex. Dept. Info. Resources, 2004, Spectrum Fitness Ctrs., 2004, Scotty Group, 2005, CenturyTel, 2005; Tchg. fellow, Kent State U., 1981, Resident Rsch. grant, United Way Health Found., 1983, Rsch. grant, Aultman Hosp. Divsn. Edn., 1988, East Carolina U., 1998—2000, PSH Found., 2003—, Devel. grant, St. Thomas Found., 1992, Ednl. grant, Astra/Merck, Inc., 1993—94, Genetech, Inc., 1994. Office: Tex State Univ 601 University Dr San Marcos TX 78666-4693

SHAW, DONALD LESLIE, Spanish language educator; b. Feb. 11, 1930; s. Stephen Leslie and Lily (Hughes) S.; m. Maria Concetta Cristini, June 30, 1958; children: Andrew Leslie, Sylvia Maria Pierina. BA, U. Manchester, Eng., 1952, MA, 1953; PhD, U. Dublin, Ireland, 1960. Asst. lectr. U. Dublin, 1955-57, U. Glasgow, Scotland, 1957-64, U. Edinburgh, Scotland, 1964-69, sr. lectr., 1969-72, reader, prof. spanish, 1972-86; prof. spanish U. Va., Charlottsville, 1986—. Vis. prof. Brown U. Providence, 1967, U. Va., Charlottesville, 1983. Author: Historia de la Literatura Española, Siglo XIX, 1973, La Generación del 98, 1977, Nueva Narrativa Hispanoamericana, 1981, Alejo Carpentier, 1985, Borges' Narrative Strategies, 1992, Antonio Skármeta and the Post-Boom, 1994, The Post-Boom in Spanish American Fiction, 1998, A Companion to Spanish American Fiction, 2001. Served with RAF, 1953-55. Avocation: cycling. E-mail: dls6h@virginia.edu. Home: 1800 Jefferson Park Ave Charlottesville VA 22903-3554 Office: U Va 115 Wilson Hall Charlottesville VA 22903-3238 Office Phone: 434-924-4658. Business E-mail: dls6h@virginia.edu.

SHAW, E. CLAY, JR., (CLAY SHAW), congressman; b. Miami, Apr. 19, 1939; s. E. Clay and Rita (Walker) S.; m. Emilie Costar, Aug. 22, 1960; children: Emilie, Jennifer, E. Clay, John C. BS, Stetson U., 1961, JD, 1966; MBA, U. Ala., 1963. Bar: Fla. 1967; CPA, Fla. Asst. city atty. City of Ft. Lauderdale, 1968, chief city pros., 1968-69, assoc. mcpl. judge, 1969-71, city commr., 1971-73, vice mayor, 1973—75, mayor, 1975-80; mem. U.S. Congress from 22d (formerly 15th) Fla. dist., 1981—; mem. ways and means com.; chmn. subcom. on human resources, 1995-98; chmn. social security subcom., 1999—. U.S. spl. ambassador to Papua New Guinea Independence; pres. U.S. Conf. Republican Mayors; mem. adv. and exec. bd. U.S. Conf. Mayors.; former chmn. mcpl. div. Ft. Lauderdale United Fund Campaign, 1971; former Young Rep. Club Broward County, Ft. Lauderdale Rep. Exec. Com.; past mem. exec. com. Fla. Rep. Assn.; former mem. house select com. narcotics abuse and control; past bd. dirs. Broward County Traffic Assn.; mem judiciary com. Pub. Workers and Youth Found. Bd. overseers Stetson Coll. Law. Republican. Home: 700 Coral Way Fort Lauderdale FL 33301-2532 Office: US Ho Reps 1236 Longworth Ho Office Bldg Washington DC 20515-0922

SHAW, ELEANOR JANE, newspaper editor; b. Columbus, Ohio, Mar. 23, 1949; d. Joseph Cannon and Wanda Jane (Campbell) S. BA, U. Del., 1971. With news local newspapers, Wilmington, Del., 1970-82, editor HEW desk, asst. met. editor, 1977-80, bus. editor, 1980-82; topics editor USA Today, 1982-83; asst. city editor The Miami Herald, 1983-85; projects editor The Sacramento Bee, 1985-87, news editor, 1987-91, exec. bus. editor, 1991-93, editor capitol bur. news, 1993-95, state editor, 1995-99; mng. employee comm. The McClatchy Co., Sacramento, 1999—2004; associate HartMedia, 2004—. Bd. dirs. Del. 4-H Found., 1978-83; bd. dirs. Safety Ctr., Inc., Sacramento, 2003—, sec., 2005—. Mem. Calif. Soc. Newspaper Editors (bd.

dirs. 1990-96), No. Calif. Wine Soc. (v.p. 1987-93, pres. 1993-2002). Office: 11682 Gold Country Blvd Gold River CA 95670 Office Phone: 800-732-1722. Personal E-mail: ellieshaw@sbcglobal.net. E-mail: ellie@hartmedia.com.

SHAW, HAROLD, retired performing arts association administrator; b. Hebron, N.Y., June 11, 1923; Student, Ithaca Coll., 1942, Columbia, 1944, N.Y. U. Extension, 1948. Former assoc. Hurok Concerts, Inc., N.Y.C.; chmn., owner Shaw Concerts, Inc., N.Y.C., 1969-99; ret., 1999; performing arts dir. Seattle World's Fair, 1961-62. Former concert mgr. Nathan Milstein, Vladimir Horowitz, Dame Janet Baker, Jessye Norman, Helen Donath, Jacqueline duPre, Wolfgang Holzmair, Jard van Nes, Mitsuko Uchida, Garrick Ohlsson, Shura Cherkassky, Horacio Gutiérrez, Julian Bream, John Williams, Elmar Oliveira, Kyoko Takezawa, Robert Shaw, Andrew Davis, and over 100 artists and attractions; exec. dir. President's Shakespeare Ann. Com., 1964. Dir. exec. staff, mem. performing arts com. Cultural Commn., N.Y.C., 1966; nat. chmn. Performing Arts Energy Commn., 1974; chmn. bd. trustees Am. Shakespeare Theatre, Stratford, Conn., 1974. With USAAF, 1942-43. Mem.: Am. Summer Stock Mgrs. Assn. (co-founder), Actors Equity Assn., Assn. Coll., Univ. and Cmty. Arts Administrs., Am. Symphony Orch. League, Internat. Performing Arts Adminstrs., Athletic Club, Phi Mu Alpha Sinfonia. E-mail: hshaw611@msn.com.

SHAW, HELEN LESTER ANDERSON, nutrition educator, researcher, retired dean; b. Lexington, Ky., Oct. 18, 1936; d. Walter Southall and Elizabeth (Guyn) Anderson; m. Charles Van Shaw, Mar. 14, 1988. BS, U. Ky., Lexington, 1958; MS, U. Wis., Madison, 1965, PhD, 1969. Registered dietitian Dietitian Roanoke (Va.) Meml. Hosp., 1959-60, Santa Barbara (Calif.) Cottage Hosp., 1960-61; dietitian, unit mgr. U. Calif., Santa Barbara, 1961-63; rsch. asst., NIH fellow U. Wis., Madison, 1963-68; from asst. prof. to prof. U. Mo., Columbia, 1969-88, assoc. dean, prof., 1977-84; prof., chair dept. food and nutrition U. N.C., Greensboro, 1989-94, dean Sch. Human Environ. Scis., 1994-2000; ret., 2000. Cluster leader Food for 21st Century rsch. program U. Mo., 1985-88. Contbr. articles to rsch. publs. Elder First Prebsbyn. Ch., Columbia, Mo., 1974—89, Greensboro, NC, 1992—. Recipient Teaching award Home Econ. Alumni Assn., 1981, Gamma Sigma Delta, 1984; rsch. grantee Nutrition Found., 1971-73, NIH, 1972-75, NSF, 1980-83. Mem. Am. Soc. for Nutrition, Am. Bd. Nutrition, Am. Soc. for Clin. Nutrition, Am. Dietetic Assn., Sigma Xi, Phi Upsilon Omicron, Kappa Omicron Nu. Democrat. Avocations: tennis, singing, volunteering, watercolor painting. E-mail: shaw713helen@aol.com.

SHAW, JACK ALLEN, communications company executive; b. Auburn, Ind., Jan. 1, 1939; s. Marvin Dale and Vera Lucille (Harter) S.; m. Martha Sue Collins, Aug. 24, 1963; 1 child, Mark Allen. BSEE, Purdue U., 1962; DSc (hon.), Capitol Coll., 1994, DSc (hon.), 1995; D in Engring. (hon.), Purdue U., 1998. Project engr. Hughes Aircraft Co., El Segundo, Calif., 1962-69; dir. program mgmt. ITT Space Comms., Ramsey, NJ, 1969-74; v.p., corp. devel. Digital Comms. Corp., Gaithersburg, Md., 1974-78, exec. v.p., COO Germantown, Md., 1978-81, pres., CEO, 1981-84, M/A-com Telecom divsn., Germantown, Md., 1984-87; chmn., CEO Hughes Network Sys., Inc., 1988—, chmn., also bd. dirs., 1978—, Germantown, 1987-2000, corp. sr. exec. v.p. enterprise sector, 2000—; pres., CEO Hughes Elecs., 2001. Bd. dirs. XM Satellite Radio, Guidant Corp.; exec. v.p. Hughes Electronics, 1999. Mem.: IEEE (sr.), Radio Club Am. (hon.). Republican. Personal E-mail: jackbrasshat@aol.com.

SHAW, JEANNE OSBORNE, editor, poet; b. Stone Mountain, Ga., June 1, 1920; d. Virgil Waite and Daisy Hampton (Scruggs) Osborne; m. Harry B. Shaw, Dec. 10, 1982; children from previous marriage: Robert Allan Gibbs, Marilyn Osborne Gibbs Barry. BA, Agnes Scott Coll., 1942. Editl. staff Atlanta Constitution, 1942; feature writer New London Day, Conn., 1943; book reviewer Atlanta Constitution, 1940—42, Atlanta Jour., 1945—48; poetry Banner Press Emory U., Atlanta, 1957—59; book editor Georgia Mag., Decatur, 1957—73. Author: The Other Side of the Water, 1970 (author of yr. in poetry award Dixie Coun. Authors and Journalists), From Cowslip to Cobalt, 1971, Unravelling Yarn, 1979, Faithbuilders, 1982—84, Third Millennium Christmas, 2001, The First Easter Parade, 2003; co-author: Noel: Poems of Christmas, 1979, They Continued Steadfastly, History of Druid Hills Baptist Church, 1987; contbr. poems, pen and ink sketches to mags.; author: Serious Poem, 2005. Mem. nat. arts and humanities com. Learning Life Boy Scouts Am., 2000—; pres. Newton class Druid Hills Bapt. Ch., 1973—74, dir. ch. tng., 1978—79, ch. clk., 1995—2001. Recipient Internat. Narrative Poem award, Poets and Patrons, Inc., 1992, Robert Martin, Burke, Otto in Praise of Poetry award, N.Y. Poetry Forum, 1973, 1979, 1981, Westbrook award, Ky. Poetry Soc., 1976, Ariz. award, 1981, Ind. State Fedn. Poetry Clubs award, Ala. State Poetry Soc. award, 1990, Rev. Earl M. Smith Meml. award, 1997, Joseph V. Hickey Meml. award, Nat. Fedn. State Poetry Socs., 1998. Mem.: Ga. Poetry Soc. (artistic dir. 2000, judge Nat. River of Words Contest 2002—05, Traditional award 1984, Cole and Ledford award 1986, Goreau award 1987, Melissa Henry award 1989, Charles and Virginia Dickson award 1990, Jo Ann Yeager Adkins award 1991, Poem About Atlanta award 1992, Goreau award 1993, Free Verse award 1993, My Very Best Poem award 1995, Traditional award 1997, Jabberwocky award 1997, Annette Peery award 1998, 1999, Charles Bruehler award 2000, Annette Peery award 2001, 22d Anniversary award 2002, Mikki Morris award 2002, Reece award 2002, Poems in Reach of Song award 2004—06), Atlanta Writers Club (pres. 1949—50, Aurelia Austin Writer of Yr. in poetry 1971, Wyatt award 1986, Light Verse award 1989, 1990, Daniel Whitehead Hicky award 1991, F. Levering Neely award 1991, Poet Laureate's award 1993, Wyatt award 1995, Daniel Whitehead Hicky award 1995, Gerry Crocker award 1995, Villanelle award 1997, 1998, Virginia Cole Veal award 1999, Light Verse award 2001, 2005, Serious Poetry award 2005, Formal Verse award 2006, Ben Willingham award), Poetry Soc. Ga. (John Clare prize 1935, Katharine H. Strong prize 1975, Eunice Thomson prize 1976, Jimmy Williamson prize 1977, Capt. Frank Spencer prize 1985, Conrad Aiken prize 1987, Capt. Frank Spencer prize 1988, Conrad Aiken prize 1988, Sarah Cunningham prize 1989, Soc. prize 1989, Lucy McEntire prize 1990, Grace Schley Knight prize 1991, Gerald Chan Sieg prize 1991, Eunice Thomson prize 1992, Grace Schley Knight prize 1993, Sarah Cunningham prize 1994, Lucy McEntire prize 1994, Harriet Ross Colquitt prize 1994, Gerald Chan Sieg prize 1995, Harriet Ross Colquitt prize 1995, Eva Tennyson Forbes Meml. prize 1996, Sarah Cunningham prize 1997, About Holes prize 1998, Soc. prize 2001, Formal prize 2005, Monday prize 2005, Grace Schley Knight prize 2005, Critics' Com. prize 2006), Ga. Writers Assn. (Lit. Achievement award 1971, Ga. Sr. Poet Laureate award 2006), Phi Beta Kappa. Home: 809 Pinetree Dr Decatur GA 30030-2332

SHAW, JEFFREY WILLIAM, gas industry executive; b. Salt Lake City, Nov. 9, 1958; s. William R. Jr. and Janet (Engar) S.; m. Cynthia Roberts, July 3, 1984; children: Morgan, Lauren, Catherine, Michael. BA in Acctg., U. Utah, 1983. CPA, Nev. With audit div. Arthur Andersen & Co., Dallas, 1983-85, Las Vegas, Nev., 1985-88; dir. internal audit SW Gas Corp., Las Vegas, Nev., 1988—91, controller, chief acctg. officer, 1991—93, v.p., controller, chief acctg. officer, 1993—94, v.p., treas., 1994—2000, sr. v.p. fin., treas., 2000—02, sr. v.p. gas resources & pricing, 2002—03, pres., 2003—04, CEO, 2004—. Active Boy Scouts Am., Dallas, 1985, Las Vegas, 1987—. Mem. AICPA, Am. Law Assn. (bd. dirs.), Nev. Soc. CPAs., U. Nev. Las Vegas Found. (bd. trustees). Republican. Mem. Lds Ch. Avocations: writing, guitar, composing music, golf, basketball. Office: SW Gas Corp PO Box 98510 Las Vegas NV 89193-8510

SHAW, JIM, painter; b. Midland, Mich., Aug. 8, 1952; BFA, U. Mich., Ann Arbor, 1974; MFA, Calif. Inst. Arts, 1978. Exhibitions include What Exactly is a Dream and What Exactly is a Joke, Donna Beam Fine Art Gallery, 1995, Galerie Praz-Delavallade, Paris, 1997, 1999, 2002, Frankfort Kunstverein, 1998, From Head to Toe: Concepts of the Body in 20th Century Art, LA County Mus. Art, 1998, Jim Shaw: Thrift Store Paintings, Inst. Contemporary Art, London, 2000, La Biennale de Montreal 2000, 2000, The Artist's World, Calif. Coll. of Arts and Crafts, 2000, Biennale of Sydney, Mus. Contemporary

Art, 2002, one-man shows include The Goodman Image File and Study, Swiss Inst., 2002, O, Kunsthaus Glarus, Germany, 2004. Fellow Guggenheim Meml. Found., 2004. Office: Metro Pictures Gallery 519 West 24th St New York NY 10011 Office Phone: 212-206-7100.

SHAW, JOHN FREDERICK, retired naval officer; b. Dallas, Oct. 14, 1938; s. John Frederick and Sarah E. (Crouch) S.; m. Janice Muren, July 14, 1962; children: Elizabeth Lee, Suzanne Michele. BS, U.S. Naval Acad., 1960; MS in Mgmt. with distinction, Naval Postgrad. Sch., Monterey, Calif., 1970; grad., Armed Forces Staff Coll., 1971. Commd. ensign USN, 1960, advanced through grades to rear adm., 1983; exec. officer USS Long Beach (CGN 9), 1978-79; comdg. officer USS Bainbridge (CGN 25), 1980-83; dir. guided missile destroyer 51, Arleigh Burke program Comdr. Naval Sea Systems Command, Washington, 1983-85, mgr. AEGIS shipbldg. program, 1985-87; comdr. Cruiser-Destroyer Group One, San Diego, 1987-88; dep. chief staff plans and policy Supreme Allied Comdr., Atlantic, Norfolk, Va., 1988-89, chief staff, 1989-91; ret., 1991; profl. mil. ops. Coll. Continuing Edn. Naval War Coll., San Diego, 1992-94. Bd. advisors United Svc. Benefit Assn., Kansas City, Kans., 1987-93; mem. cmty. bd. advisors Sam and Rose Stein Inst. for Rsch. on Aging, 1998-2004; membership chmn., 1999-2000, sec.-treas., 2000-2004, mem. bd. mem., 2006—; tax. cons. for elderly, AARP, 2000—. Trustee Coronado Libr., 1998—, exec. sec., 2001—02, pres., 2002—04. Decorated Def. D.S.M., Legion of Merit with two gold stars, Meritorious Svc. medal with gold star, Navy Commendation medal with gold star, Meritorious Unit Commendation (civilian) USN. Mem. AARP, U.S. Naval Inst. (life), U.S. Naval Acad. Alumni Assn. (life, pres. Washington chpt. 1986, bd. govs. San Diego/Coronado chpt. 1996-99), Surface Navy Assn. (life), San Diego Navy League (dir. 1997-2002), Coronado Men's Golf Club. Avocations: golf, reading, economics, travel. Personal E-mail: jshaw14@aol.com.

SHAW, JOHN W., lawyer; b. Mo., 1951; BA, MA, U. Mo., 1973, JD, 1977. Bar: Mo. 1977. Ptnr. Bryan Cave, Kansas City, 1977-92, Lathrop & Norquist, 1983-92, Bryan Cave LLP, 1992-98, Berkowitz Oliver Williams Shaw & Eisenbrandt LLP (formerly Berkowitz Stanton Brandt Williams and Shaw LLP), Kansas City, 1998—. Named Best of the Bar, Kansas City Bus. Jour., 2003. Mem. ABA, Securities Industry Assn. (legal and compliance group), Mo. Bar, Def. Rsch. Inst. (chmn. firearms litigation subcom.), Order of Coif. Office: Berkowitz Oliver Williams Shaw & Eisenbrandt LLP 2600 Grand Blvd Ste 1200 Kansas City MO 64108 Office Phone: 816-561-7007. Business E-mail: jshaw@bowse-law.com.

SHAW, JOSEPH THOMAS, Slavic languages educator; b. Ashland City, Tenn., May 13, 1919; s. George Washington and Ruby Mae (Pace) S.; m. Betty Lee Ray, Oct. 30, 1942 (dec. Sept. 2002); children: David Matthew, Joseph Thomas (dec. Dec. 2005), James William (dec. Jan. 1999). AB, U. Tenn., 1940, AM, 1941, Harvard, 1947, PhD, 1950. Asst. prof. Slavic langs. Ind. U., 1949-55, assoc. prof., 1955-61; prof. Slavic langs. U. Wis., 1961-89, prof. emeritus, 1989—, chmn. dept. Slavic langs., 1962-68, 77-86, chmn. div. humanities, 1964-65, 72-73, assoc. dean Grad. Sch., 1965-68. Author: The Letters of Alexander Pushkin, 1963, Pushkin's Rhymes: A Dictionary, 1974, Baratynskii: A Dictionary of the Rhymes and a Concordance to the Poetry, 1975, Batiushkov: A Dictionary of the Rhymes and a Concordance to the Poetry, 1975, Pushkin: A Concordance to the Poetry, 1985, American Association Teachers Slavic and East European Languages: The First Fifty Years 1941-91, 1991, Pushkin's Poetry of the Unexpected: The Nonrhymed Lines in the Rhymed Poetry and the Rhymed Lines in the Nonrhymed Poetry, 1994, Pushkin, Poet and Man of Letters, and His Prose (collected works vol. 1), 1995, Pushkin Poems and Other Studies (collected works vol. 2), 1996, The Letters of Alexander Pushkin (collected works vols. 3-5), 3d edit., 1997, Konkordans k stikham Pushkina, 2000, Pushkin's Rhymes: A Dictionary (collected works, vol. 6-7), 2d edit., 2001, Batiushkov: A Dictionary of the Rhymes & A Concordance to the Poetry (collected works, vol. 8), 2d edit., 2001, Baratynskii: A Dictionary of the Rhymes & A Concordance to the Poetry (collected works, vol. 9), 2d edit., 2001, Poeziia neozhidannogo u Pushkina, 2002, Studies in Pushkin's Rhyming: Theory from Practice (collected works, vol. 10), 2002, The Letters of Alexander Pushkin(vol. 10-12 in The Complete Works of Alexander Pushkin 15 vols.1999-2003) 4th edit.; editor: The Slavic and East European Jour., 1957-70; contbr. articles to profl. jours. Served to capt. USNR, 1942-46, 51-53. Mem. Am. Assn. Tchrs. Slavic and East European Langs. (mem. exec. council 1953-70, 73-80, pres. 1973-74) Home: 4505 Mineral Point Rd Madison WI 53705-5071 Personal E-mail: jtshaw@wisc.edu.

SHAW, JUDITH ANN, secondary school educator, human resources specialist, consultant; b. Detroit, Jan. 16, 1956; d. Harry Edward Yuschak and Gertrude Pauline (Pankovits) Hannah; m. Christopher Quayle, Aug. 9, 1975 (div.); children: Christopher Alan, Kendra Lynn; m. David Shaw, Oct. 13, 2000. AS in Mktg. and Applied Mgmt., Schoolcraft Coll., 1986; BS in Humanities, Lawrence Tech. U., 1990; postgrad., U. Mich., 1990-91; MA, U. Phoenix, 2003. Cert. corp. trainer. Sr. acctg. clk. Comml. Credit Bus. Loans, Southfield, 1974-80; cmty. edn. instr. Southfield, Troy and Livonia (Mich.) Pub. Schs., 1986—; mktg. dir., trainer Magna Carta Inst., 1988-90; instr. Am. Inst. of Motivation (formerly Acquire Corp.), 1990; corp. trainer Evelyn Wood Reading Dynamics, 1990-95. Contractor/trainer A.I.M., Evelyn Wood Reading Dynamids, Brian Tracy Learning Systems, 1990-95; exec. dir. edn., tng. Internat. Network Mktg. Alliance, 1993, 95-96; tng. specialist Mich. Paperboard Co., 1995-96, tng. specialist, ISO mgmt. rep., 1996-99, safety and tng. mgr., 1998-99, safety and human resource mgr. Advanced Design & Packaging, 1999—. Active various civic groups, Livonia; mem. parish coun. Sacred Heart Byzantine Cath. Ch., Livonia, 1988-90, catechism instr. 1986-89, coord. ednl. program, 1987-89; cons., coord. ednl. program United Cerebral Palsy Detroit. Beautiful Id. 1987, dir. cheerleading program St. Damian Ch., Westland, Mich., 1982-85. Mem. ASTD, Am. Mktg. Assn. (dir. speakers bur. Detroit chpt.), Schoolcraft Coll. Alumni Assn., Phi Theta Kappa. Home and Office: 43 Brookcrest Dr Marietta GA 30068-3703 Office Phone: 404-699-1952. E-mail: judeshaw@bellsouth.net.

SHAW, KENDALL (GEORGE SHAW), artist, educator; b. New Orleans, Mar. 30, 1924; s. George Kendall and Florence Gladys (Worner) S.; m. Frances (Glenn) Fort, Oct. 31, 1955. Student, Ga. Inst. Tech., 1944-46; BS in Chemistry, Tulane U., 1949, MFA, 1959; postgrad., La. State U., 1950. Instr. Columbia U., 1961-66, Hunter Coll., 1966-68, Parsons Sch. Design, N.Y.C., 1966-86, Lehman Coll., 1968-70, Bklyn. Mus. Art Sch., 1970-76; US del. to UNESCO Conf. London, 1965. One-man shows include Orleans Gallery, New Orleans, 1960, 61, 63, Columbia U., 1962, 65, Bienville Gallery, New Orleans, 1968, Tibor de Nagy Gallery, N.Y.C., 1964, 65, 67, 68, Southampton Coll., 1969, John Bernard Myers Gallery, 1972, Alessandra Gallery, 1976, Lerner Heller Gallery, N.Y.C., 1979, 81, 82, Nature Morte, N.Y.C., 1983, Bernice Steinbaum Gallery, N.Y.C., 1991, Artists Space, N.Y.C., 1992, The Gallery of South Orange, NJ, 1997, U. Richmond, Va., 1999, Tulane U., 2001; group shows include Downtown Gallery, New Orleans, 1959, Orleans Gallery, 1959, 60, 61, Mus. Contemporary Art, Nagaoka, Japan, 1965, Alessandra Gallery, N.Y.C., 1976, Gallerie simonne Stern, New Orleans, 1968, Albright-Knox Gallery, Buffalo, 1970, P.S.I., N.Y.C., 1977, Gladstone Villani Gallery, N.Y.C., 1978, Galerie Habermann, Cologne, 1979, Modern Art Gallery, Vienna, 1980, Jacksonville Art Mus..Fla., 1983, The Ogden Mus. So. Art, New Orleans, 2001-04, others; represented in permanent collections Sammlung Ludwig, Aachen, Bklyn. Mus., Mus. Contemporary Art, Nagaoka, Japan, Everson Mus., Syracuse, Chase Bank, N.Y.C., N.Y. Univ., Polk Mus. Art, Lakeland, Fla., Orlando Mus. Art, Weathersport Art Gallery, Greensboro, NC, Marsh Art Gallery, Richmond, Va., Tulane U., New Orleans, New Orleans Mus. Art, Miss. Mus. Art, The Ogden Mus. So. Art, New Orleans. Served in USN, 1943—46. Named Disting. Alumnus, Tulane Coll., 2001. Mem.: NY Artists Equity Assn., Coll. Art Assn. Address: 916 President St Brooklyn NY 11215-1604 Personal E-mail: kendallshaw@aol.com.

SHAW, L. EDWARD, JR., lawyer; b. Elmira, NY, July 30, 1944; s. L. Edward and Virginia Anne (O'Leary) S.; m. Irene Ryan; children: Christopher, Hope, Hillary, Julia, Rory BA in Econs., Georgetown U., Washington,

1966; JD, Yale U., New Haven, 1969. Bar: N.Y. 1969. Assoc. Milbank, Tweed, Hadley & McCloy, N.Y.C., 1969—76, ptnr., 1976—82; sr. v.p., gen. counsel Chase Manhattan Corp., N.Y.C., 1982—85, exec. v.p., gen. counsel, 1985-96; vice chmn., gen. counsel Natwest Markets, N.Y.C., 1996-97, pres., 1997-99; exec. v.p. and gen. counsel Aetna Inc., 1999—2004; of counsel Gibson Dunn & Crutcher LLP, 2004—. Bd. dirs. HealthSouth Corp., Birmingham, Ala., 2005—. Mem.: Am. Law Inst., Phi Beta Kappa. Roman Catholic. Office Phone: 212-351-3846. Business E-Mail: eshaw@Gibsondunn.com.

**SHAW, LACY,** academic consultant; b. Bklyn., Sept. 29, 1947; s. Lacy Shaw and Callie Currie; 1 child, Nzinga. AA, Kingsborough C.C., Bklyn., 1967; BA, Bklyn. Coll., 1970; MA, Morgan State U., 1973; postgrad., NYU. Lic. elem. and secondary educator NY. Mentor Empire State Coll., Westbury, NY, 1991—92; prof. Medgar Evars Coll., Bklyn.; adminstr. Adelphi Inst., Bklyn., 1985—91; tchr. Pub. Sch. 197, Bklyn., 1977—2001; academic advisor Touro Coll., NYC, 2001—. Author: Not a Slave!, 1996, Reading Women's Lives, 2005, Reinventing the American Past, 2006. Staff sgt. U.S. Army, 1972—90. Recipient NY Times Publ. award. Mem.: NY Hist. Soc., Orgn. Am. Historians, Am. Hist. Assn. Democrat. Baptist. Avocations: reading, jogging, swimming. Home: 141 Wyckoff St Brooklyn NY 11217 Office: Touro Coll 27-33 W 27th St New York NY 10010 Office Phone: 212-469-0200 ext 511. Office Fax: 212-627-9542. E-mail: lshaw@touro.edu.

**SHAW, LEONARD GLAZER,** retired electrical engineering educator, consultant; b. Toledo, Aug. 15, 1934; s. A. Daniel and Mary (Glazer) S.; m. Susan Gail Weil, Dec. 24, 1961; children: Howard Benjamin, Mitchell Bruce, Jenny Louise. BSEE, U. Pa., 1956; MSEE, Stanford U., 1957, PhD, 1961. From asst. to assoc. prof. Polytech. U. N.Y., Bklyn., 1960-75, prof., 1975—99, prof. emeritus, 1999—, head dept. elec. engring. and computer sci., 1982-90, dean Sch. Elec. Engring. and Computer Sci., 1990-94, vice provost for undergrad. studies, 1995-96. Vis. prof. Tech. U., Eindhoven, Netherlands, 1970, Ecole Nationale Superieure de Mecanique, Nantes, France, 1977, U. Sussex, Brighton, Eng., 1998; cons. Sperry Systems Mgmt. Div., Great Neck, N.Y.; mem. grant rev. panels NSF, 1986-98. Co-author: Signal Processing, 1975; contbr. articles to profl. jours. Rsch. grantee NSF, 1973, 81. Fellow: IEEE (mem. pub. bd. 1961—92, mem. various coms., editor-in-chief IEEE Press 1988—91, gen. chmn. Conf. of Decision and Control 1989, chmn. Tech. Field Award Coun. 1995—97), Control Sys. Soc. of IEEE (fin. v.p. 1992—93, 2000, pres.-elect 2001, pres. 2002). Office: Polytech U 6 Metrotech Ctr Brooklyn NY 11201-3840 Business E-Mail: lshaw@poly.edu.

**SHAW, MELVIN PHILLIP,** physicist, engineering educator, psychologist; b. Bklyn., Aug. 16, 1936; s. Harry and Yetta (Stutsky) S.; m. Carol Joan Phillips, Sept. 5, 1959 (div. Feb. 1987); children: Adam, Evan; m. Bernetta Berger, May 16, 1987. BS, Bklyn. Coll., 1959; MS, Case Western Res. U., 1963, PhD, 1965; MA, Ctr. for Humanistic Studies, 1988. Research scientist United Techs. Research Labs., E. Hartford, Conn., 1964-68, scientist-in-charge, 1966-70; prof. Wayne State U., Detroit, 1970-96, prof. emeritus, 1997—; adminstrv. dir. Assocs. of Birmingham/Kingswood Hosp., 1991-93. Cons. Energy Conversion Devices, Troy, Mich., 1970-92. Co-author: The Gunn-Hilsum Effect, 1979, The Physics and Applications of Amorphous Semiconductors, 1988, The Physics of Instabilities in Solid State Electron Devices, 1992, Creativity and Affect, 1994. Fellow Am. Phys. Soc.; mem. IEEE (sr.), Am. Psychol. Assn. (assoc.). Avocations: cooking, walking, exercise, travel. Office Phone: 248-644-8330. E-mail: bunny3336@aol.com.

**SHAW, MICHAEL,** biologist, educator; b. Barbados, W.I., Feb. 11, 1924; s. Anthony and Myra (Perkins) S.; m. Jean Norah Berkinshaw, Oct. 16, 1948; children: Christopher A., Rosemary E., Nicholas R., Andrew L. BSc, McGill U., 1946, MSc, 1947, PhD, 1949, DSc (hon.), 1975, U. B.C., 2003. NRC Can. postdoctoral fellow Botany Sch., Cambridge U., 1949-50; assoc. prof. biology U. Sask., Canada, 1950-54, prof., 1954-67, prof., head dept. biology, 1961-67; dean faculty agrl. scis. U. B.C., Canada, 1967-75, v.p. acad. devel., 1975-81, acad. v.p., provost, 1981-83, univ. prof., 1983-89, univ. prof. emeritus, 1989—. Mem. Sci. Coun. Can., 1976-82, Natural Scis. and Engring. Rsch. Coun. Can., 1978-80. Contbr. articles to profl. jours. Recipient Queen's Silver Jubilee medal, 1977, Gold medal Biol. Coun. Can., 1983. Fellow Royal Soc. Can. (Flavelle medal 1976), Can. Phytopath. Soc., Am. Phytopath. Soc.; mem. AAAS, Can. Bot. Assn., Can. Soc. Plant Physiologists (Gold medal 1971), Am. Soc. Plant Biologists. Home: 1792 Western Pky Vancouver BC Canada V6T 1V3

**SHAW, MICHAEL JOSEPH,** automotive executive; b. Fort Wayne, Ind., Aug. 30, 1946; s. Robert Brons and Eva (Fernandez) S.; m. Nancy Merrill James, June 21, 1969; children: Michael Joseph Jr., Eleanor Merrill, Robert Richardson. BBA, Tex. A&M U., 1968; MBA, Lamar Tech. U., 1970. With sales dept. David Taylor Buick, Beaumont, Tex., 1969-70; sales mgr. Tommy Vaughn Motors, Houston, 1972; gen. sales mgr. Boggus Motors, McAllen, Tex., 1973; owner, pres. Tradewinds Ford, Corpus Christi, Tex., 1973-88, Tradewinds Subaru, Corpus Christi, 1984-88, Tradewinds Chrysler Imports, Corpus Christi, 1985-88, Tradewinds Suzuki, Corpus Christi, 1987-88, Tradewinds Mgmt. Group, Corpus Christi, 1987-88; v.p., gen. mgr. David Taylor Cadillac, Houston, 1989; now pres. Mike Shaw Automotive Group, Denver. Bd. dirs. Subaru Nat. Dealer Coun., San Antonio, 1985-88, Suzuki Nat. Advt. Coun., Atlanta, 1987-88, Ford Dealer Advt. Coun., Houston. 1st lt. U.S. Army, 1970—72. Named Entrepreneur of Yr. Heavy Industry Category, Hispanic Bus. Mag., 2005. Mem. Tex. Automobile Dealers Assn., Houston Automobile Dealers Assn., Rotary. Episcopalian. Avocations: reading, golf, skiing. Office: Mike Shaw Automotive Group 1080 S Colorado Blvd Denver CO 80246

**SHAW, MILTON CLAYTON,** mechanical engineering educator; b. Phila., May 27, 1915; s. Milton Fredic and Nellie Edith (Clayton) S.; m. Mary Jane Greeninger, Sept. 6, 1939; children: Barbara Jane, Milton Stanley. BSME, Drexel Inst. Tech., 1938; M of Engring. Sci., U. Cin., 1940, ScD, 1942; PhD (hon.), U. Louvain, Belgium, 1970; DEng (hon.), Drexel U., 1996. Rsch. engr. Cin. Milling Machine Co., 1938-42; chief materials br. NACA, 1942-46; with MIT, 1946-61, prof. mech. engring., 1953-61, head materials processing divsn., 1952-61; prof., head dept. mech. engring. Carnegie Inst. Tech., Pitts., 1961-71; univ. prof. (hon.) Carnegie-Mellon U., 1974-77; prof. engring. Ariz. State U., Tempe, 1977-86, emeritus prof. engring., 1986—. Cons., lectr. in field; pres. Shaw Smith & Assos., Inc., Mass., 1951-61; Lucas prof. Birmingham (Eng.) U., 1961; Springer prof. U. Calif., Berkeley, 1972; Distinguished guest prof. Ariz. State U., 1977; mem. Nat. Materials Adv. Bd., 1971-74; v.p. conf. com. Engring. Found., 1976-78. Recipient Outstanding Research award Ariz. State U., 1981, Am. Machinist award, 1972, Schlesinger award German Govt., 1997; P. McKenna award, 1975; Guggenheim fellow, 1956; Fulbright lectr. Aachen T.H., Germany, 1957; OECD fellow to Europe, 1964—. Fellow Am. Acad. Arts and Scis., ASME (Hersey award 1967, Thurston lectr. 1971, Outstanding Engring. award 1975, ann. meeting theme organizer 1977, Gold medal 1985, hon. 1980), Am. Soc. Lubrication Engrs. (hon., nat. award 1964), Am. Soc. Metals (Wilson award 1971, fellow 1981); mem. Internat. Soc. Prodn. Engring. Research (pres. 1960-61, hon. mem. 1975), Am. Soc. for Engring. Edn. (G. Westinghouse award 1956), Soc. Mfg. Engrs. (hon. mem. 1970, Gold medal 1958, Internat. Edn. award 1980, M.C. Shaw award 1999), Nat. Acad. Engring., Polish Acad. Sci., Am. Soc. Precision Engrs. (hon.), Japan Soc. Precision Engrs. (Internat. award 1999), Drexel 100. Home: Unit C119 2625 E Southern Ave Tempe AZ 85282-7633

**SHAW, MONTGOMERY THROOP,** chemical engineering professor; b. Ithaca, N.Y., Sept. 11, 1943; s. Robert William and Charlotte (Throop) S.; m. Stephanie Habel, Sept. 5, 1966 (dec. 1989); 1 child, Steven Robert; m. Maripaz Nespral, June 25, 1994. BChemE, MS, Cornell U., 1966, Princeton (N.J.) U., 1968, PhD, 1970. Engr., project scientist Union Carbide Corp., Bound Brook, N.J., 1970-76; assoc. prof. Dept. Chem. Engring., U. Conn., Storrs, 1977-83, prof., 1983—; sabbatical prof. Sandia Nat. Labs., Albuquerque, 1983-84. Vis. scientist E.I. Dupont de Nemours and Co., Experimental

Station, Wilmington, Del., 1991-92; adv. bd. Jour. of Applied Polymer Sci., 1984-89. Co-author: Polymer-Polymer Miscibility, 1977, Computer Programs for Rheologists, 1994, Introduction to Polymer Viscoelasticity, 2005. Grantee Alcoa Found., 1985, Exxon Edn. Found., 1986. Mem. IEEE (sr. mem., assoc. editor transactions on dielectrics and elec. insulation), Soc. Rheology (sec. 1977-81, treas. 1997—), Am. Chem. Soc., Am. Phys. Soc. Achievements include patents on rheological measurement method and apparatus and low density microcellular foams. Office: U Conn IMS 97 N Eagleville Rd Storrs Mansfield CT 06269-3136 Business E-Mail: montgomery.shaw@uconn.edu.

**SHAW, NINA L.,** lawyer; b. NYC; BA, Barnard Coll., 1976; JD, Columbia U., 1979. Bar: Calif. 1981. Founding ptnr., entertainment law Del, Shaw, Moonves, Tanaka & Finkelstein, Santa Monica, Calif. Bd. dirs. The Montel Williams MS Found.; mem. Barbara A. Black Professorship Com. Named one of 100 Most Powerful Women in Entertainment, Hollywood Reporter, 2003, 2004, 100 Most Influential Blacks in America; recipient Disting. Alumna/us Award, Columbia Black Law Students Assn., 2002, Women in Film Crystal award, 2005. Mem.: State Bar Calif., LA County Bar Assn., Kernochan Ctr. Law, Media and Arts (West Coast adv. bd.), Black Women Lawyers Assn.*

**SHAW, RICHARD EUGENE,** cardiovascular researcher; b. Springfield, Ohio, Jan. 20, 1950; s. Eugene Russell and Marjorie Caroline Shaw; m. Nov. 26, 1976; 2 children. BA, Duquesne U., 1972; MA, U.S. Internat. U., San Diego, 1977; PhD, U. Calif., San Francisco, 1984. Cert. nuc. med. technologist. Nuclear Medicine Tech. Cert. Bd. Staff nuc. med. technologist Scripps Meml. Hosp., La Jolla, Calif., 1978-79; rsch. asst. U. Calif. San Francisco Sch. Medicine, 1980-85; mgr. rsch. programs San Francisco Heart Inst., Daly City, Calif., 1985-87, dir. rsch., 1988-90, dir. rsch. and ops., 1991—2003; dir. rsch., quality and edn. Sutter Pacific Heart Ctrs., 2003—. Sr. advisor steering com. for databases Daus. of Charity Nat. Health Sys., St. Louis, 1993-96. Editor-in-chief Jour. Invasive Cardiology, 1989—; contbr. articles to profl. jours; chpts. to books. Coach Am. Youth Soccer Orgn. and Youth Baseball Assn., bd. dirs., Burlingame, Calif., 1990-94; pres. Burlingame H.S. Athletic Boosters, 2000—. Fellow Am. Coll. Cardiology (nat. cardiac database com., outcomes assessment subcom. 1998—, NCDR task force 2001—, publs. subcom. 2001—), Am. Coll. Angiology; mem. Am. Heart Assn. (sec. for Clin. Trials, N.Y. Acad. Scis., Am. Statis. Assn., Am. Med. Informatics Assn., Soc. Behavioral Medicine. Avocation: music. Office: Sutter Pacific Heart Ctr CPMC 2340 Clay St #120 San Francisco CA 94115 Business E-Mail: shawr@sutterhealth.org.

**SHAW, ROBERT GILBERT,** retired state legislator, food service executive; b. Erwin, N.C., Nov. 22, 1924; s. Robert Gilbert B. and Annie Elizabeth (Byrd) S.; m. Grace Lee Wilson, Jan. 29, 1951 (div. 1976); children: Ann Karlen, Barbara Jean; m. Linda Owens, May 27, 1982. AA, Campbell U., 1948; postgrad., U. N.C., 1948-50. Restaurateur, 1951—. County commr. County of Guilford, Greensboro, N.C., 1968-76; chair N.C. Rep. Party, Raleigh, 1975-77; minority leader N.C. Senate, Raleigh, 1984-2002; chair Guilford County Rep. Party, 1973-75; mem. Rep. Nat. Com., Washington, 1975-77. With USAAC, 1943-46. Named Legislator of Yr. Nat. Fedn. Wildlife, 1990. Mem. Elks (time bd. govs. 1953—). Presbyterian. Avocations: fishing, hunting, politics. Home: 5105 Bennington Dr Greensboro NC 27410 Personal E-mail: RGB112224@aol.com.

**SHAW, ROBERT WILLIAM, JR.,** management consultant, venture capitalist; b. Ithaca, NY, Aug. 10, 1941; s. Robert William and Charlotte G. (Throop) Shaw; m. Anne P. Meads, Aug. 29, 1964; children: Mark James, Christopher Matthew. B of Engring. Physics, Cornell U., 1964, MSEE, 1964; PhD, Stanford U., 1968; MPA, Am. U., 1981. Postdoctoral fellow Cavendish Lab., Cambridge, Eng., 1968-69; mem. tech. staff Bell Tel. Labs., Murray Hill, NJ, 1969-72; with Booz Allen Hamilton, Bethesda, Md., 1972-83, sr. v.p. energy and environ. divsn., 1979-83, mem. oper. coun., 1981-83, also bd. dirs.; pres. Arete Ventures, Inc., 1983-97, Utech Venture Capital Corp., 1985—2003, Utech, LLC, 2003—05; gen. ptnr. Utech Venture Capital Corp. Fund I, 1985—2000, Utech Venture Capital Corp. Fund II, 1988—2003, Utech Venture Capital Corp. I Parallel Fund L.P., 1988—2001, Utech Venture Capital Corp. II Parallel Fund, L.P., 1991—2003, Utech Climate Challenge Fund, L.L.C., Bethesda, 1995—2005; v.p. Can. Energy and Environment Ventures, Inc., 1993-95; pres. Arete Corp., Center Harbor, NH, 1997—; ptnr. Atrium Capital/Honda Ventures, 2004—. Spl. ltd. ptnr. Nth Power Techs. Fund II; mem. investment com. Sustainable Asset Mgmt. Pvt. Equity Fund, Commons Capital LLC; mng. ptnr. Micro-Generation Tech. Fund, LLC, 1997—; mem. bd. energy and environ. sys. Nat. Rsch. Coun., 1998—2004; ptnr. Atrium Capital LLC, 2004—; mem. energy com. Aspen Inst. Humanistic Studies, Investor's Cir., Solar Cir.; bd. councillors China-U.S. Ctr. Sustainable Devel.; chmn. bd. dirs. Distributed Energy Sys. Corp., CTP Hydrogen Corp., H2Gen Innovations, Inc.; mem. adv. coun. Cornell U. Engring. Coll., 2005—; mem. hydrogen tech. adv. com. The US Dept. of Energy, 2006—. Contbr. articles to profl. jours. Named NASA trainee; Office Sci. Rsch. fellow, USAF, 1968—69. Mem.: AAAS, Social Venture Network, Inst. Noetic Scis., Assn. Humanistic Psychology, Orgnl. Devel. Network, Nat. Venture Capital Assn., Am. Phys. Soc., Tau Beta Pi, Sigma Xi, Kappa Delta Rho, Pi Alpha Alpha, Phi Kappa Phi. Home: PO Box 1664 Center Harbor NH 03226-1664 Office: PO Box 1299 Center Harbor NH 03226-1299 Office Phone: 603-253-9797. Business E-Mail: aretecorp@cyberportal.net.

**SHAW, RODERICK KIRKPATRICK, III,** dentist; b. Tallahassee, Fla., Dec. 15, 1956; s. Roderick Kirkpatrick, Jr. and Floride Wilkinson Shaw; m. Kathleen Bentley, Jan. 11, 1991; children: Carolyn Floride children: Roderick Kirkpatrick VIII. BS in Biochemistry, Auburn U., 1981; DMD, U. Fla. Coll. Dentistry, 1986, cert. comprehensive dental program #22, 2003. Pvt. practice, Madison, Fla., 1997—. Contbr. articles to profl. jours. Chmn. Madison campaign Davis for Gov., 2006; elder Madison Presbyn. Ch., Fla., 1996—2000; fin. chmn. First United Meth. Ch. of Madison, Fla., 2003; treas. Madison Presbyn. Ch., Fla., 1998—2000. Master: Acad. Gen. Dentistry (CE com.); mem.: ADA, Comprehensive Dental Program 22, NE Dist. Dental Assn., Fla. Dental Assn., Fla. Acad. Cosmetic Dentistry (charter). Conservative. Methodist. Avocations: boating, running. Office: 317 N Duval St Madison FL 32340 Home: 2678 NW Jersey Rd Greenville FL 32331

**SHAW, ROGER WALZ,** physicist, educator; b. Chgo., May 29, 1934; s. Everett Jesse Shaw and Florence Margaret Walz; m. Joan Ann Petrunick, Sept. 9, 1933; children: Gordon Roger, Beverly Joan, Martha Ann. BSc, U. Rochester, 1955; MSc in Physics, U. Ill., 1956, PhD in Physics, 1959. Postdoctoral rschr. U. Ill., Champaign, Ill., 1959—60; asst. prof. physics Rensselaer Polytech Inst., Troy, NY, 1960—62, assoc. prof. physics, 1962—66; sr. rsch. specialist Monsanto Co., St. Louis, 1967—84; fellow MEMC Elec. Materials, St. Peters, Mo., 1984—94, ret., 1994. Vis. staff Los Alamos (N.Mex.) Nat. Lab., 1966—67; mem. grant rev. com. NSF, 1985—88. Contbr. articles to profl. jours.; musician: Kirkwood (Mo.) Symphony, 1968—92. Co-founder Grand County Wilderness Group, Fraser, Colo., 1995—; treas. Mid. Pk. Land Trust, Grand County, Colo., 1999—2002. Mem.: Am. Phys. Soc. Home: PO Box 2200 Fraser CO 80442

**SHAW, RONALD AHREND,** physician, educator; b. Toledo, July 20, 1946; s. Harold Michael and Eve Helen (Ganch) S.; m. Carol Ann Rapp, June 13, 1970; children: Robert, Benjamin, Daniel. BS, U. Toledo, 1968; MD, Washington U., 1972. Diplomate Am. Bd. Emergency Medicine. Intern, then resident in surgery St. Luke's Hosp., St. Louis, 1972-73, resident in surgery, 1973; mem. staff Bapt. Med. Ctr.-Montclair, Birmingham, Ala., 1976-81, chief emergency svc., 1979-81; assoc. dir. lifesaver flight ops. Caraway Meth. Med. Ctr., Birmingham, 1981-85; dir. emergency sch. medicine U. Ala. 1985-89; asst. dir. emergency svc. R.I. Hosp., Providence, 1989-95; attending physician emergency dept. Bapt. Med. Ctr., Montgomery, Ala., 1996—; med. dir. emergency dept. Jackson Hosp., 2000—01; svc.-treas., med. staff Bapt. Med. Ctr., 2001—03. Cons. U. Tex., Houston, 1986, Bell Helicopter, Ft. Worth, 1986, Mut. Assurance, Birmingham, 1988-89, NYU, 1988-89, R.I. State Med. Examiners Office, 1991-96, Fla. Dept. Health, EMS Office, 1991—, Joint Underwriters Assocs. of R.I., 1991-96; chmn. adv. bd. emergency svc. Ala. Dept. Pub. Health, 1986-89; med. dir. Emergency Med.

Svcs. div. R.I. Dept. Health, 1990-95; med. dir. Health Care Rev., Inc., 1995-96. Bd. dirs. MADD, Ala., 1986, Univ. Emergency Medicine Found., 1995-96; mem. planning com. Youth Baseball, Vestavia Hills, ala., 1986, 87; mem. disaster com. City of Birmingham, 1984-89; mem. 911 Commn., State of R.I., 1991-96. Recipient Disting. Achievement award Birmingham Emergency Med. Svc., 1988. Fellow Am. Coll. Emergency Physicians (bd. dirs. Ala. chpt. 1984-89, steering com. EMS sect. 1991-94, sec.-treas. R.I. chpt. 1995-96); mem. AAAS, ACS (state com. on trauma R.I. chpt. 1990-96), N.Y. Acad. Sci., Med. Assn. Ala. (mem. coun. med. svc. 1985-86). Republican. Avocations: hunting, stamp collecting and computer programming. Office Phone: 334-272-1050. Personal E-mail: kd1hp@msn.com.

**SHAW, ROSLYN LEE,** small business owner, retired elementary school educator; b. Bklyn., Oct. 1, 1942; d. Benjamin Biltmore and Bessie (Banilower) Deretchin; m. Stephen Allan Shaw, Feb. 1, 1964; children: Laurence, Victoria, Michael. BA, Bklyn. Coll., 1964; MS, SUNY, New Paltz, 1977, cert. advanced study, 1987; cert. gifted edn., Coll. New Rochelle; 1986. Cert. sch. adminstr., supr., sch. dist. adminstr., reading tchr., tchr. N-6. Tchr. Hillel Hebrew Acad., Beverly Hills, Calif., 1965-66, P.S. 177, 77, Bklyn., 1964-65, 66-67, Middletown (N.Y.) Sch. Dist., 1974-77, reading specialist, 1977-99, compensatory edn. reading tchr., 1977-99, tchr. gifted children, 1984-87, asst. project coord. pre-K, 1988-89, instrnl. leader, 1989-93; ret., 1999; pres. Maxwell Enterprises Ltd. Adj. assoc. prof. SUNY, Coll. at New Paltz, 1997-98; newspaper in edn. coord. The Times Herald Record, 1999-2001, ednl. cons., 2001-; pres. Rotary Club of New Brunswick, 2005- Pres. Middletown H.S. Parents' Club, 1983-86; bd. dirs. Mental Health Assn., Goshen, N.Y., 1980-81; mem. Middletown Interfaith Coun., 1983-85. Mem. Amy Bull Crist Reading Coun. (pres. 1989-91, 93-95, 2001), N.Y. State Reading Assn. (Coun. Svc. award 1990, regional dir. 1991-94, bd. dirs. 1991—, chair reading tchrs. spl. interest group 1993-94, pres.-elect 1999—, pres. 2000-01, past pres. 2001, regional dir. 2001, newsletter editor The Empire State Reading Scene), Internat. Reading Assn., Univ. Women's Club, Delta Kappa Gamma. Avocations: photography, walking, reading. Home: 21 Thatchwood Ct North Brunswick NJ 08902 E-mail: iconsult@optonline.net.

**SHAW, RUSSELL BURNHAM,** writer, journalist; b. Washington, May 19, 1935; s. Charles Burnham and Mary (Russell) S.; m. Carmen Hilda Carbon, July 19, 1958; children: Mary Hilda, Emily Anne, Janet, Charles, Elizabeth. BA, Georgetown U., 1956, MA, 1960. Staff writer Cath. Standard, Washington, 1956-57; reporter Nat. Cath. News Svc., 1957-66; dir. publs., pub. info. Nat. Cath. Ednl. Assn., 1966-69; dir. Nat. Cath. Office for Info., 1969-73; assoc. sec. for communication U.S. Cath. Conf., 1973-74, sec. for pub. affairs Nat. Conf. Cath. Bishops, 1975-87; dir. pub. info. KC, 1987-97; assoc. prof. Pontifical Univ. of the Holy Cross, 1996—. Consultor Pontifical Coun. for Social Comms., 1984—89, 2001—06; editor The Pope Speaks, 1998—2005. Author: The Dark Disciple, 1961, Abortion on Trial, 1968, Church and State, 1979, Choosing Well, 1982, Why We Need Confession, 1986, Renewal, 1986, Signs of the Times, 1986, Does Suffering Make Sense?, 1987, To Hunt, To Shoot, To Entertain, 1993, Understanding Your Rights, 1994, Papal Primacy in the Third Millennium, 2000, Ministry or Apostolate—What Should the Catholic Laity Be Doing?, 2002, Catholic Laity in the Mission of the Church, 2005; co-author: S.O.S. for Catholic Schools, 1970, Beyond the New Morality, 3d edit., 1988, Fulfillment in Christ, 1991, Personal Vocation, 2003, Good News, Bad News, 2006, others; editor Ency. of Cath. Doctrine, 1997; columnist monthly mag. Washington Report, 1966-2006; columnist weekly newspaper Cath. Herald, 1999—; contbg. editor Crisis Mag., 2002—, Columbia Mag., 2002-06, Our Sunday Visitor, 2006—. Mem. Equestrian Order of Holy Sepulchre of Jerusalem, Phi Beta Kappa. Roman Catholic. Home and Office: 2928 44th Pl NW Washington DC 20016-3555 Office Phone: 202-363-9566. Personal E-mail: rshaw10290@aol.com.

**SHAW, RUTH G.,** energy company executive; m. Colin Stuart Shaw; 2 children. BA in English magna cum laude, East Carolina U.; PhD, U. Tex. Pres. Central Piedmont Cmty. Coll., 1986—92; v.p. corp. comms. Duke Energy Corp., Charlotte, NC, 1992-94, sr. v.p. corp. resources, 1994-97, exec. v.p., chief adminstrv. officer, 1997—2002, pres., 2003—, El Centro Coll., Dallas. Dir. Wachovia Corp., MedCath Corp.; mem. bd. dirs. Edison Electric Inst., Nuclear Energy Inst., S. E. Electric Exchange; chair Charlotte Rsch. Inst.; mem. Palmetto Bus. Forum. Mem. Order of the Long Leaf Pine; trustee U. N.C., Charlotte; bd. dirs. Rsch. Triangle Found. of N.C.; mem. Conf. Bd. Chief Adminstrv. Officer's Coun.; chmn. Found. for the Carolinas; elder 1st Presbyn. Ch., Charlotte; active United Way, Arts and Scis. Coun., YMCA, Boy Scouts Am. Named Outstanding Alumni, East Carolina U., disting. grad. U. Tex., Charlotte Woman of Yr., 1992, Businesswoman of Yr., 1995; recipient award for comms. excellence, 1997. Office: Duke Energy Corp 526 S Church St Charlotte NC 28202-1802

**SHAW, STANLEY MINER,** pharmacist, educator; b. Parkston, S.D., July 4, 1935; s. George Henry and Jensina (Thompson) S.; m. Excellda J. Watke, Aug. 13, 1961; children: Kimberly Kay, Renee Denise, Elena Aimee. BS, S.D. State U., 1957, MS, 1959; PhD, Purdue U., 1962. Instr. S.D. State U., 1960-62; asst. prof. bionucleonics Purdue U., West Lafayette, Ind., 1962-66, assoc. prof., 1966-71, prof. nuclear pharmacy, 1971—2005, prof. emeritus nuclear pharmacy, 2005—, head. divsn. nuclear pharmacy, 1990—2004, acting head Sch. Health Scis., 1990-93. Bd. pharm. spltys. Splty. Council Nuclear Pharmacy, 1978-82. Contbr. articles to profl. jours. Recipient Lederle Pharmacy faculty award, 1962, 1965, Parenteral Drug Assn. Rsch. award, 1970, Henry Heine Outstanding Tchr. award, Sch. Pharmacy Purdue U., 1989, 1993, 1999, Disting. Alumnus award, S.D. State U., 1991, Coll. Pharmacy Disting. Alumnus award, 2006, Disting. Pharmacy Educator award, Am. Assn. Colls. Pharmacy, 1994. Fellow Acad. Pharmacy Practice (chmn. sect. nuclear pharmacy 1979-80, historian 1981-85, mem.-at-large 1993-95, chmn.-elect 1995-96, chmn. 1996-97, Disting. Achievement award 1998); Am. Soc. Hosp. Pharmacy, Am. Pharm. Assn. (ho. of dels. 1977, 79, 86, 92, Founder's award, Daniel B. Smith Practice Excellence award 2000); mem. Health Physics Soc., Sigma Xi, Phi Lambda Upsilon, Phi Lambda Sigma, Rho Chi. Home: 7208 W Greenview Dr Battle Ground IN 47920-9732 Office: Purdue U Sch Pharmacy West Lafayette IN 47907-1336 Business E-Mail: sshaw@pharmacy.purdue.edu.

**SHAW, STEVEN A.,** information technology executive; BBA, MBA, Univ. So. Calif. Mgmt. positions with Volt Info. Sciences Inc., NYC, 1995—97, pres. ProcureStaff subs., 1997—2005, bd. dir., 1998—, sr. v.p., 2000—05, exec. v.p., COO, 2005, co-CEO, 2005—06, pres., CEO, 2006—. Office: Volt Info Sciences 560 Lexington Ave New York NY 10022*

**SHAW, SUE ANN,** church organist; b. Tiffin, Ohio, July 31, 1949; d. Orval Dale and Suzanne Mae Loucks; m. Herbert Allen Shaw, Aug. 4, 1973; children: Lisa Ann Shaw Deakins, Jennifer Lee. BS in Edn., Bowling Green State U., 1971, MS in English and Libr. Sci., 1973. Tchr. Tiffin City Schs. 1971; tchr., libr. Marion (Ohio) City Schs., 1971—73; tchr. Shawnee Local Schs., Lima, Ohio, 1973—77; ch. organist Shawnee United Meth. Ch., Lima, 1991—; staff accompanist Bluffton (Ohio) Coll., 2000—03. Co-owner Anndale Mgmt., LLC. Contbr. poetry to anthologies. Mem.: AAUW (treas. 1999—2001), Am. Guild Organists (treas. 1998—2005). Avocations: painting, piano, sewing, reading. Home: 2944 Yoakam Rd Lima OH 45806

**SHAW, TALBERT O.,** university president; BD, Andrews U., 1963; MA, U. Chgo., 1968, PhD, 1973. Dean of students Oakwood Coll., Huntsville, Ala., 1965-71; dean Howard U., Washington, 1971-76; dean Coll. Arts and Scis. Morgan State U., Balt., 1976-87; pres. Shaw U., Raleigh, NC, 1987—2003.

**SHAW, THEODORE MICHAEL,** legal association administrator; b. NYC, Nov. 24, 1954; s. Theodore and Jean Audrey (Churchill) Shaw; m. Cynthia E. Muldrow; children: T. Winston, Zora Jean. BA with honors, Wesleyan U., 1976; JD, Columbia U., 1979. Bar: Calif. Trial atty. Civil Rights Divsn. U.S. Dept. Justice, 1979—82; dir. ednl. docket NAACP Legal Def. and Ednl. Fund, 1982—87; assoc. dir.-counsel NAACP Legal Def. Edn. Fund, Inc., NYC, 1993—2004, pres., dir.-counsel, 2004—; founder, counsel Legal Def.

and Edn. Fund's Western Regional Office, 1987—90. Asst. prof. law U. Mich. Law Sch., 1990—93; adj. prof. Columbia U. Sch. Law, 1993—. Named one of Most Influential Black Americans, Ebony mag., 2006; recipient Lawrence A. Wein prize for social justice, Columbia U., Baldwin medal, Wesleyan U. Mem.: ABA, Langston Bar Assn., L.A. County Bar Assn., Nat. Bar Assn. (A. Leon Higginbotham Jr. Meml. award Young Lawyers Divsn.). Office: NAACP Legal Def and Ednl Fund Inc Ste 1600 99 Hudson St New York NY 10013 Office Phone: 212-965-2200.*

**SHAW, THERESA S. (TERRI SHAW),** federal official; married; 2 children. BS, George Mason U., 1960; Grad. Exec. Devel. Program, George Washington U., 1991. From staff to sr. v.p. and chief info. officer SLM Corp., Reston, Va., 1988—99; exec. v.p., COO eNumerate Solutions, Inc, McLean, Va., 2000—02; COO Fed. Student Aid US Dept. Edn., Washington, 2002—. Office: Office of Federal Student Aid US Dept Edn 830 First St NE Rm 112G1 Washington DC 20202 Office Phone: 202-377-3003. E-mail: terri.shaw@ed.gov.

**SHAW, THOMAS,** conductor, director; b. Whichita Falls, Tex., May 25, 1930; s. Lloyd L. Shaw and Flora Mabry; m. Joan H. Shaw, June 26, 1957; children: Thomas Jr., Kenneth Mark, Sara Lynn. MusB in Edn., Midwestern State U., Tex., 1951; MusM in Edn., U. North Tex., 1952, D of Edn., 1971. Choral dir. Wichita Falls H.S., Tex., 1957—65; asst. prof. music Okla. Coll. of Liberal Arts, Chickasha, 1966—69; assoc. prof. music Fla. So. Coll., Lakeland, 1972—76; choral dir. Whichita Falls H.S., 1976—78; supr. of music, dir. fine arts Wichita Falls Ind. Sch. Dist., 1978—91; retired. Ch. choir dir., Wichita Falls, Tex., Chickasha, Lakeland, Fla.; pvt. voice lessions tchr. E-4 USAF, 1952—57, San Antonio and Japan. Republican. Presbyterian. Avocations: woodworking, stained glass.

**SHAW, TIMOTHY MILTON,** political science professor; b. Frimley, Surrey, Eng., Jan. 27, 1945; came to Can., 1971; s. Arnold J. and Margaret E. (Milton) S.; m. Jane L. Parpart, Sept. 2, 1983; children: Laura, Lee Parpart; m. Susan M. Sturt, July 8, 1967 (div. 1980); children: Benjamin, Amanda. BA, Sussex U., 1967; MA, East Africa U., 1969, Princeton U., 1971, PhD, 1975. Prof. polit. sci. Dalhousie U., Halifax, Canada, 1971—2002; dir. Ctr. African Studies, Halifax, 1983—89, Ctr. for Fgn. Policy Studies, Halifax, 1993—2000, Internat. Devel. Studies Program, 1986—89, dir. BA and MA program, 1998—2000; dir. Pearson Inst., Halifax, 1985—87, Can. Internat. Devel. Agy., 1994—95. Vis. faculty Makerere U., Kampala, 1968-70, U. Zambia, Lusaka, 1973-74, Carleton U., Ottawa, Ont., Can., 1978-79, U. Ife, Nigeria, 1979-80, U. Zimbabwe, 1989, Rhodes U., South Africa, 1993, 2002-03, Warwick U., U.K., 1997, U. Western Cape & Stellenbosch U., South Africa, 1998—, Mbarara U. Sci. and Tech., 1998—, Aalborg U., 2000-01, Bus. Sch., Makerere U., 2006-; cons. UN Econ. Commn. for Africa, Addis Ababa, Ethiopia, 1983-88. Editor: Palgrave Macmillan Internat. Polit. Economy Series, 1984—, Ashgate Publishing Series on the International Political Economy of New Regionalisms, 2001—; author: Reformism and Revisionism in Africa's Political Economy in the 1990s, 1993; author: (with Julius Ihonvbere) Illusions of Power: Nigeria in Transition, 1998; co-editor (with Julius Nyangoro): Beyond Structural Adjustment in Africa, 1992; co-editor: Corporatism in Africa, 1988; co-editor: (with Kevin Dunn) Africa's Challenge to International Relations Theory, 2001; co-editor: (with Sandra Maclean & John Harker) Advancing Human Security & Development in Africa, 2002; co-editor: (with Fredrik Soderbaum) Theories of New Regionalism: A Palgrave Reader, 2003; co-editor: (with Natalie Mychajlyszyn) Twisting Arms & Flexing Muscles: Humanitarian Intervention & Peacebuilding in Perspective, 2005; co-editor: (with Morten Boas & Marianne Marchand) The Political Economy of Regions & Regionalisms, 2005; co-editor: (with Sandra Maclean and David Black) A Decade of Human Security, 2006; co-editor: others. Mem. New Dem. Party, Halifax, 1984—. Grantee, Social Sci. & Humanities Rsch. Coun. Can., Africa, 1981—, Ford Found., 1999—2001. Mem. Internat. Polit. Sci. Assn. (chair rsch. com. #40 on New World Orders, 1997-2003), Can. Assn. Devel. Studies (pres. 1993-94), European Assn. Devel. Inst. (co-chmn. working group on new regionalisms), Can. Assn. African Studies (pres. 1984-85), Internat. Studies Assn. (pres. global devel. sect. 1995-96), Waegwoltic Club (Halifax). Avocations: jogging, cooking, building, travel. Home: 1701-751 Fairfield Rd Victoria BC V8W 4A4 Canada Office: Royal Roads Univ Victoria BC V9B 5Y2 Canada Office Phone: 250-391-2600 ext. 4786. Office Fax: 250-391-2500. Business E-Mail: tim.shaw@royalroads.ca.

**SHAW, WILLIAM FREDERICK,** statistician; b. Bklyn., Feb. 24, 1920; s. Charles Peter and Josephine Veronica (Seusing) S.; m. Josephine Cannington Kerbey, Jan. 18, 1947; children— William Frederick, Teresa Anne. BBA, U. Miami, 1949; MA, George Washington U., 1953; postgrad. studies in econometrics, math. and computer scis., U.S. Dept. Agr. Grad. Sch., 1964-74; PhD (fellow), Walden U., 1977. Rsch. asst. U. Miami, 1948—49; with Rsch. and Stats. divsn. FHA, Washington, 1950—73, chief statistician Rsch. and Stats. divsn., 1969—; chief statistician, dir. Advanced Statis. Analysis and Computer Applications Staff HUD, 1974—82, chief statistician, dir. housing stats. divsn., 1982—89, chief statistician, dir. info. sys. divsn., 1990—91, chief statistician, dir. Office of Evaluation, 1991—. Pres. Kerbey-Shaw Assos. Served with F.A. AUS, 1943-45. Decorated Bronze Star; recipient Superior Performance award HUD, 1977; named by Info. Resources Adminstrn. Coun. as Fed. Office Sys. Profl. of Yr., 1983. Mem. AAAS, Am. Statis. Assn., Am. Risk and Ins. Assn., Am. Real Estate and Urban Econ. Assn., Am. Econ. Assn., Am. Fin. Assn., N.Y. Acad. Scis., Nat. Assn. Rev. Appraisers and Mortgage Underwriters, Soc. Cost Estimating and Analysis, Res. Offcers Assn. U.S., 101st Airborne Divsn. Assn., Air Force Assn., Alpha Kappa Psi. Roman Catholic. Home: 6527 Byrnes Dr Mc Lean VA 22101-5227 Office: HUD 7th and D Sts SW Washington DC 20411-0001

**SHAW, WILLIAM J.,** hotel facility executive; b. Arlington, Va., Oct. 3, 1945; married; 3 children. BBA, U. Notre Dame, 1967; MBA, Washington U., 1972. With Arthur Andersen & Co., 1972-74, Marriott, 1974-79, corp. controller, 1979-82, corp. v.p., 1982-85, sr. v.p.-fin., head dept. tax and risk mgmt., 1985-88, treas., 1986, CFO, exec. v.p., 1988-92; pres. Marriott's Svc. Group, 1992-97; pres., COO Marriott Internat., Inc., Washington, 1997—; chmn. bd. Host Marriott Svcs. Corp., Bethesda, Md., 1995-99, Sodexho Marriott Svcs., Gaithersburg, Md., 1998. Bd. trustees Suburban Hosp. Found., U. Notre Dame, South Bend, Ind.; mem. NCAA Leadership Adv. Bd.; bd. dirs. World Trap Found. for Performing Arts. Office: Marriot Internat Marriot Dr Washington DC 20058-0001*

**SHAW, WILLIAM J.,** religious organization administrator; BA summa cum laude in Philos. and Relig., Bishop Coll.; MDiv, Union Theol. Seminary; DMin, Colgate Rochester Div. Sch. Supply pastor New Bethel Baptist Church, Marshall, Tex.; pastor White Rock Baptist Church, 1956—; pres. Nat. Baptist Conv. USA, Inc., 1999—. Chmn. bd. dir. Jr. Achievement Del. Valley, Inc., Cmty. Legal Svcs. Phila., Med. Ctr. Univ. Pennn., Phila. Airport Adv. Bd. Named one of 100 Most Influential Black Americans, Ebony mag., 2006. Mem.: Baptist Min. Conf. Phila. (pres.), Greater Phila. Urban Affairs Coalition. Office: White Rock Baptist Church Office 5240 Chestnut St Philadelphia PA 19139 Office Phone: 215-474-5785. Office Fax: 215-474-3332. E-mail: president@nationalbaptist.com.*

**SHAW-EAGLE, JOANNA,** art critic; Art critic Washington Times. Contbr. articles to profl. jours. Office: Washington Times 3600 New York Ave NE Washington DC 20002-1947

**SHAWEN, DANIEL ALLAN,** engineer; s. Harold Eugene and Rosa Pauline Shawen. BS, U. Md., College Park, 1974. Test engr. Fairchild Aerospace, Germantown, Md., 1980; mem. tech. staff Comsat Labs., Clarksburg, Md., 1981—2001; software engr. Lockheed Martin Global Telecom, Clarksburg, 2001—02; ops. mgr. LKC Systems, Gaithersburg, Md., 2003—03; engr. Ensco Inc, Falls Church, Va., 2004—06. Provisional judge 2002 Election, Middletown, Md., 2002—02. Recipient Cert. of Appreciation, Md. Mensa, 2006. Mem.: IEEE (assoc.), Am. Mensa (assoc. Cert. of Appreciation 2006).

**SHAWN, WALLACE,** playwright, actor; b. NYC, Nov. 12, 1943; s. William and Cecille (Lyon) S.; m. Twink Caplan. BA., Harvard U., 1965; BA, Oxford U., Eng., 1968, MA, 1975. Instr. English Indore Christian Coll., Madhya Pradesh, India, 1965-66; tchr. English, Latin, drama Ch. of Heavenly Rest Day Sch., N.Y.C., 1968-70; shipping clk. Laurie Love Ltd., N.Y.C., 1974-75; machine operator Hamilton Copy Ctr., N.Y.C., 1975-76. Author: (plays) Our Late Night, 1975 (Obie award for disting. playwriting 1975), Summer Evening, 1976, The Youth Hostel, 1976, Mr. Frivolous, 1976, (libretto) In the Dark, 1976, (trans.) The Mandrake, 1977, Marie and Bruce, 1980, The Hotel Play, 1981, Aunt Dan and Lemon, 1985, The Music Teacher, 2006; (monologue) The Fever, 1990 (Obie award for best play 1991); (screenplay) My Dinner with Andre, 1981; actor: (theatre) The Mandrake, 1977, The Master and Margarita, 1978, Chinchilla, 1979, The First Time, 1983, Ode to Napoleon Bonaparte, 1984, Aunt Dan and Lemon, 1985, The Fever, 1991; (films) Manhattan, 1979, Starting Over, 1979, All That Jazz, 1979, Simon, 1980, Atlantic City, 1981, My Dinner with Andre, 1981, A Little Sex, 1982, The First Time, 1983, Deal of the Century, 1983, Lovesick, 1983, Strange Invaders, 1983, Saigon-Year of the Cat, 1983, Crackers, 1984, The Hotel New Hampshire, 1984, The Bostonians, 1984, Micki and Maude, 1984, Heaven Help Us, 1985, Head Office, 1986, Radio Days, 1987, The Bedroom Window, 1987, Nice Girls Don't Explode, 1987, Prick Up Your Ears, 1987, The Princess Bride, 1987, The Moderns, 1988, She's Out of Control, 1989, Scenes From the Class Struggle in Beverly Hills, 1989, We're No Angels, 1989, Shadows and Fog, 1992, Mom and Dad Save the World, 1992, Nickel and Dime, 1992, The Cemetary Club, 1993, Un-Becoming Age, 1993, The Meteor Man, 1993, Vanya on 42nd Street, 1994, Mrs. Parker and the Vicious Circle, 1994, Canadian Bacon, 1995, Clueless, 1995, (voice) Toy Story, 1995, All Dogs Go to Heaven 2, 1996, House Arrest, 1996, Vegas Vacation, 1997, Critical Care, 1997, My Favorite Martian, 1999, (voice) Toy Story 2, 1999, The Prime Gig, 2000, The Curse of the Jade Scorpion, 2001, Love Thy Neighbor, 2002, Duplex, 2003, The Haunted Mansion, 2003, Melinda and Melinda, 2004, (voice) The Incredibles, 2004, Chicken Little, 2005; (TV films) How to Be Perfect In Three Days, 1983, Saigon: Year of the Cat, 1983, Just Like Dad, 1995, Blind Men, 1998, Noah, 1998, Mr. St. Nick, 2002, Monte Walsh, 2003, Karroll's Christmas, 2004, (TV series) One Life to Live, 1992, Clueless, 1996-97, (voice) The Lionhearts, 1998. Fulbright scholar, India, 1956-66, PEN/Laura Pels Found. award for drama, 2005. Mem.: Am. Acad. Arts and Letters. Office: care Rosenstone/Wender 3 E 48th St New York NY 10017-1027*

**SHAWVER, LAURA K.,** biotechnology company executive; PhD Pharmacology, U. Iowa, 1983. With Triton Bioscis., 1989—92; from dir. preclin. devel. to sr. v.p. preclin. & pharm. devel. Sugen, Inc., San Francisco, 1992—2002. Office: 5871 Oberlin DR #200 San Diego CA 92121-3702

**SHAY, ALBERT W.,** lawyer; b. Cherry Hill, NJ, May 17, 1959; BA, U. Md., 1982; MHA, St. Louis U., 1987, JD magna cum laude, 1987. Bar: Va. 1987, DC 1988. Ptnr., health care practice group Sonnenschein Nath & Rosenthal LLP, Washington. Mem.: Am. Health Lawyers Assn. (vice chair fraud and abuse, self-referrals, and false claims substantive law com.). Office: Sonnenschein Nath & Rosenthal LLP Ste 600, E Tower 1301 K St NW Washington DC 20015 Office Phone: 202-408-6401. Office Fax: 202-408-6399. Business E-Mail: ashay@sonnenschein.com.

**SHAY, ANTHONY VICTOR,** choreographer, dance historian; b. L.A., Oct. 31, 1936; s. Jack Wendell Shay and Margaret Martha Read. MLS, UCLA, L.A., 1963; MA anthropology, Calif. State Univ., L.A., 1970; MA, UCLA, 1971; PhD dance hist. and theory, Univ. Calif. Riverside, Riverside, Calif., 1997. Artistic dir. Aman Folk Ens., L.A., 1960—77, Avaz Internal. Dance Theatre, L.A., 1977—. Author: Choreographic Politics, 2002 (Outstanding dance svc., 2002), Choreophobia, 1999, Choreographing Identities, 2006; choreographer over 250 works (Calif. Arts Coun. Lifetime Acheivement award, 2001); author, co-editor: Belly Dance, 2005. James Irvine Choreographic fellow, 1998, Soc. Sci. Rsch. Coun. fellow, 2000, NEH fellow, 2003. Home: 3756 Aloha St Los Angeles CA 90027

**SHAY, KATHLEEN M.,** lawyer; b. Drexel Hill, Pa., Feb. 21, 1952; AB, Villanova U., 1974, JD, 1977. Bar: Pa. 1977, US Ct. Appeals 3rd Cir., US Dist. Ct. Ea. Dist. Pa., Supreme Ct. Pa. Ptnr. Duane Morris LLP, Phila., chair firm corp. practice group, 1998—. Bd. consultors Villanova U. Sch. Law, 1992—, vice chair, 2001—04, chair, 2004—; bd. trustees Acad. Notre Dame de Namur, 1995—2001, 2004—, chair, 1999—2001. Mem.: ABA (bus. law sect.), Phila. Bar Assn. (exec. com. bus. sect. 2001—, sec. 2002, treas. 2003, vice chair 2004, chair 2005), Pa. Biotech. Assn., Pa. Bar Assn. (corp., banking & bus. law sect.), Tech. Coun. Ea. Pa., Women's Investment Network (bd. dirs. 2000—), Greater Phila. Venture Group, Assn. Corp. Growth (bd. dirs. Phila. chpt. 2004—), Order of Coif. Office: Duane Morris LLP 30 S 17th St Philadelphia PA 19103-4196 Office Phone: 215-979-1210. Office Fax: 215-979-1020. Business E-Mail: kmshay@duanemorris.com.

**SHAYE, ROBERT KENNETH,** film company executive; s. Max and Dorothy S.; m. Eva G., 1970; children: Katja, Juno. BBA, U. Mich., 1960; postgrad., Sorbonne U., 1961; JD, Columbia U., 1964. Bar: N.Y. 1967. Chmn. of the bd., CEO New Line Cinema Corp., N.Y.C., 1967—. Bd. trustees Am. Film Inst. Bd. trustees Legal Aid Soc., NYC, Neurosci. Inst. Recipient 1st prize Rosenthal competition Soc. Cinematologists, 1964; recipient cert. of merit Inst. Copyrights and Patents, U. Stockholm, 1966; Recipient award ASCAP/Nathan Burkan Meml. competition, 1964; Fulbright scholar, 1964-66; named one of 50 Most Powerful People in Hollywood, Premiere mag., 2002-06. Mem. Motion Picture Pioneers (bd. dirs.), Friar's Club (N.Y.C.). Office: New Line Cinema 116 N Robertson Blvd West Hollywood CA 90048-3103 also: New Line Cinema Corp 888 7th Ave Fl 19 New York NY 10106 2599 Office Phone: 310-854-5811, 212-649-4900. *Life is a lot tougher than television watching in the '50's led me to believe.*

**SHAYS, CHRISTOPHER,** congressman; b. Darien, Conn., Oct. 18, 1945; m. Betsi deRaismes, 1968; 1 child: Jeramy Alice. BA, Principia Coll., 1968; MBA, NYU, 1974, MPA, 1978. Vol. US Peace Corps, 1968-70; state rep. State of Conn. (Dist. 147), Stamford, 1974—87; mem. US Congress from 4th Conn. dist., Washington, 1987—, mem. fin. svcs. com., vice chmn. govt. reform com., vice chmn. budget com., mem. select com. on homeland securitychmn. subcom. on nat. security. Republican. Office: US Ho Reps 1126 Longworth Ho Office Bldg Washington DC 20515-0704 also: Bridgeport Dist Office 11th Fl 10 Middle St Bridgeport CT 06604 also: Government Center 888 Washington Blvd Stamford CT 06901

**SHAYWITZ, BENNETT ARTHUR,** medical educator; MD, Yale U., 1963. Prof. pediats. and neurology Sch. Medicine Yale U., 1972—; co-founder, co-director National Inst. Child Health & Human Development-Yale Ctr. for the Study of Learning and Attention. Mem.: Inst. Medicine. Office: Yale New Haven Hosp LMP 3089 20 York St New Haven CT 06504-8900

**SHAYYA, WALID H.,** natural resources engineer; b. Saoufar, Lebanon, Apr. 21, 1963; s. Hani and Salwa Shayya; m. Cathleen M. Shayya, Apr. 3, 1993; children: Hani John, Caitlin, Ashley. Diploma of Agrl. Engring., Am. U. Beirut, 1984, BSc, 1984, MSc, 1986; PhD, Mich. State U., 1991. Rsch. asst. Mich. State U., 1986—91, vis. asst. prof., 1991—94; asst. prof. Sultan Qaboos U., Al-Khod, Oman, 1994—98, assoc. prof. and head of dept. 1998—2000, asst. dean for resident instrn., 1996—99; assoc. prof. of natural resources engring. SUNY at Morrisville, NY, 2000—. Editor: (book series) Water Management, Conservation, and Purification in Arid Climates, 2000; contbr. articles to profl. jours. Named Coll. Tech. Educator of Yr., Tech. Alliance Ctrl. NY, 2005; recipient award of Merit, Nat. Assn. Colls. and Tchrs. of Agr., 2001—03; Disting. Svc. award, Sultan Qaboos U., 1999; US AID grad. scholar, 1984—86. Mem.: Nat. Assn. Coll. and Tchrs. of Agr., Am. Soc. Agrl. and Biol. Engrs., Phi Kappa Phi, Phi Beta Delta, Alpha Epsilon, Signa Xi, Gamma Sigma Delta. Avocations: tennis, volleyball. Office: State Univ of New York at Morrisville 134 Marshall Hall Morrisville NY 13408 Office Phone: 315-684-6526. Business E-Mail: shayyaw@morrisville.edu.

**SHCHERBAKOVA, ESTELLA,** chemist, mathematician, educator; b. Dnepropetrovsk, Ukraine, Oct. 15, 1938; arrived in Russia, 1951, arrived in U.S., 1994; d. Stepan and Fira (Poltorak) Masko; m. Stanislav Shcherbakov; 1 child, Yuriy Shcherbakov. MA math and drawing, State Pedagogical Inst., Moscow, Russia, 1956—61; PhD chem. sci., Post grad. Sch. of L. Karpov Rsch. Physical Chem. Inst., Moscow, Russia, 1968—74. Math tchr. HS #79, Moscow, 1961—62; engr. State Inst. of Caouchouc, Moscow, 1962—64; sci. worker from jr. to maj. L. Karpov Rsch. Phys. Chem. Inst., Moscow, 1964—94. Cons. and joint rsch. Inst. of Thin Chem. Tech., Moscow, 1971—89, State External Polytech. Inst., Moscow, 1978—90. Co-author: 113 articles, SU Jour. Miscellaneous reports, 1961—91, (book, monograph) Math Matters of Investigation of Chem. Equilib., 1978, (3 inventions) SU Bull. of Inventions, 1985, 1992—93. Recipient Semicentennial, L. Karpov Inst./ Moscow, Russia, 1988. Finding common math technology for investigation of the multiple equilibriums in solutions and applying it to various chemical systems, including solutions of bromine and iodine that brought to inventions of industrial modus of their deriving from a leach. Finding the method for nonlinear optimizations, as to apply non-equilibrium thermodynamics to processes of polymerizations. Home: 2820 W 32nd St Apt 3E Brooklyn NY 11224 E-mail: shchest@aol.com. *She evacuated in Kuybishev (Samara) Russia, 1941-1945; resided in Moscow from 1951 because of father's job in aerospace engineering.*

**SHE, CHIAO-YAO,** physics professor, researcher; s. Young-Chi She and I-Jung Fang; m. Lucia Shumai Yein, Feb. 8, 1964; children: Colleen Suelie Kirtland, Fannie Camille. BS, Taiwan U., 1957; MS, N.D. State U., 1961; PhD, Stanford U., 1964. Asst prof elec engring U Minn., Mpls., 1964—68; from asst. to prof. physics Colo. State U., Fort Collins, 1968—. Editor: (book) Selected Papers on Laser Applications in Remote Sensing, SPIE Milestone Series, MS 141 (1997); contbr. articles to profl. jours. Recipient, Fulbright scholarship, 2000, Lecture prize, NSF/Coupling, Energetics and Dynamics of Atmospheric Regions Sci. Steering Com., 2003. Fellow: Optical Soc. of Am.; mem.: Am. Phys. Soc., Am. Geophys. Union. Achievements include invention of Two high-spectral-resolution atmospheric lidars. Office: Colo State U Dept Physics 200 W Lake St Fort Collins CO 80523-1875 Office Phone: 970-491-6261. Office Fax: 970-491-7947.

**SHEA, ANDREW BRENDAN,** film director, film producer; b. NYC, May 27, 1954; s. John Joseph Brendan and Felice Klau Shea; m. Melissa Anna Gerrero, May 2, 1998; 1 child, Sadie Catherine. BA, Hampshire Coll., Amherst, Mass., 1976; JD, Northeastern U., Boston, 1982; MFA, Calif. Inst. Arts, LA, 1985, U. So. Calif., 1994. Bar: Mass. 1982, NY 2005. Founder, artistic dir. N.Mex Repertory Theatre, Santa Fe, Albuquerque, 1983—91; ind. dir., writer, 1991—2004; asst. prof. dept. radio-TV-film U. Tex., Austin, 2004—. Dir., prodr.: (films) Forfeit; dir., prodr., screenwriter, editor The Corndog Man (Ofcl. Selection, Sundance Film Festival, 1999); dir. prodr., screenwriter Santa Fe (Ofcl. Selection, Sundance Film Festival, 1997); dir., screenwriter Take My Breath Away (Ofcl. Selection, Cannes Film Festival, Semaine de la Critique, 1993). Recipient Directing award, Drama-Logue, 1996, Emerging Filmmaker award, St. Louis Film Festival, 1999, Best Film award, Northampton Film Festival, 1999, Phila. Internat. Film Festival, 1999. Mem.: Soc. Stage Dirs and Choreographers, Writers Guild Am., Directors Guild Am. Office: Univ Texas Austin 1 University Station A0800 Austin TX 78712 Office Phone: 512-471-5303. Business E-Mail: ashea@mail.utexas.edu.

**SHEA, BERNARD CHARLES,** retired pharmaceutical executive; b. Bradford, Pa., Aug. 7, 1929; s. Bernard and Edna Catherine (Green) S.; m. Marilyn Rishell, Apr. 12, 1952; children— David Charles, Melissa Leone. BS in Biology, Holy Cross Coll., Worcester, Mass. Dir. mktg. Upjohn Co., Kalamazoo, 1954-80; pres. pharm. div. Pennwalt Corp., Rochester, NY, 1980-86, v.p. health div. Phila., 1986, sr. v.p. health div., 1987-88, sr. v.p. chemicals, 1988-89; group pres. Atochem N.Am., Inc., Phila., 1989-90, pharm. cons., 1990-93. Served to It. (j.g.) USN, 1951-54, Korea Personal e-mail: Berniemari@comcast.com.

**SHEA, CHRISTINE M.,** education educator; d. Harold Gordon Shea and Jacqueline Pauline Harvey. BA, Wilfrid Laurier U., 1980, MBA, 1984; PhD, U. Western Ont., 1995. Ops. mgr. Grantech divsn. Devtek Aerospace, Waterloo, Canada, 1980—90; prof. tech. and ops. mgmt. U. NH., Durham, 1994—. Strategic planning chair Homemakers Health Svcs., Rochester, NH, 2005—06, treas., 2006—. Doctoral fellowship, Social Sciences and Humanities Rsch. Coun. of Can., 1991—94; Rsch. fellowship, Whittemore Sch. of Bus. & Economics, UNH, 1999, 2003, 2005. Mem.: Internat. Assn. for Mgmt. of Tech., Decision Sciences Inst., Acad. of Mgmt. Office: U NH McConnell Hall Durham NH 03824 Office Phone: 603-862-3322. E-mail: christine.shea@unh.edu.

**SHEA, DION WARREN JOSEPH,** academic administrator, fundraiser; b. New London, Conn, June 10, 1937; s. Frank Steven and Violette Marie (Dion) S.; m. Elizabeth M. Siaba, Dec. 31, 1986; children from previous marriage: Dion Warren Joseph, Nancy Wallace. AB, ScB in Physics, Brown U., 1959; MA in Physics, Boston U., 1962; PhD in Physics, U. Colo., 1968. Mem. tech. staff RCA, 1959-62; asst. prof. physics Creighton U., 1967-68; NRC/Environ. Sci. Svc. Adminstrn. fellow, rsch. assoc. Environ. Sci. Svc. Adminstrn., Boulder, Colo., 1968-70; exec. dir. Soc. Physics Students, Am. Inst. Physics, 1970-87, mgr. edn. div., 1972-87; cons. ednl. and computer sytems, 1988—; dir. alumni affairs US Mcht. Marine Acad., Kings Point, NY, 1989-93; asst. dir. devel. CUNY Grad. Sch., 1993-99. Author sci. articles. Fellow AAAS; mem. Am. Phys. Soc., Am. Assn. Physics Tchr., Assn. Coll. Honor Soc. (exec. com. 1984-86), Am. Soc. Assn. Exec., Assn. Fundraising Profl., Planned Giving Group Greater NY, Coun. Advancement and Support Edn., Sigma Xi, Sigma Pi Sigma, Sigma Chi, Huntington Bicycle Club (treas. 2000-01), Colo. Mountain Club, Port Dive Club (treas. 1980-83). Home: 11821 Lionel Ln Golden CO 80403 Office Phone: 303-642-0699. Personal E-mail: dion_shea@yahoo.com.

**SHEA, EDWARD EMMETT,** lawyer, educator, writer; b. Detroit, May 29, 1932; s. Edward Francis and Margaret Kathleen (Downey) S.; m. Ann Marie Conley, Aug. 28, 1957; children: Michael, Maura, Ellen. AB, U. Detroit, 1954; JD, U. Mich., 1957. Bar: Mich. 1957, Fla. 1959, N.Y. 1961. Assoc. Simpson Thacher & Bartlett, N.Y.C., 1960-63, Dykema, Wheat, Spencer, Detroit, 1963-69, Cadwalader Wickersham & Taft, N.Y.C., 1969-71; v.p., gen. counsel, chmn. Reichhold Chems., White Plains, NY, 1971-81; adj. prof. Pace U. Grad. Sch. Bus., N.Y.C., 1982—; counsel, ptnr. Windels, Marx, Davies & Ives, N.Y.C., 1982-84; ptnr. Windels, Marx, Lane & Mittendorf, N.Y.C., 1986—; sr. v.p., gen. counsel GAF Corp., 1984-86. Sec. Peridot Chems., 1988-97; lectr. N.Y. Inst. Fin., 1995—. Author: An Introduction to the U.S. Environmental Laws, 1995, The Lead Regulation Handbook, 1996, The McGraw-Hill Guidebook to Acquiring and Divesting Businesses, 1998, Environmental Law and Compliance Methods, 2002; editor: The Acquisitions Yearbook, 1991-93; contbr. articles to profl. jours. Mem. bd. N.Y. State Small Bus. Ctr. Program, 1988-93. 1st It. JAGC, USAF, 1957-60. Mem. N.Y. Athletic Club. Office: Windels Marx Lane & Mittendorf 156 W 56th St Fl 23 New York NY 10019-3867 Office Phone: 212-237-1140. Business E-Mail: eshea@windelsmarx.com.

**SHEA, GWYN,** former state official; 2 children. Student, U. North Tex.; student, Dallas Baptist U.; grad., Dallas Baptist U. Police Acad. Served Tex. Ho. Reps., 1982—92, Ho. Ways and Means Com., Ho. Ins. Com.; pres. Nat. Coun. Ins. Legislators; apptd. Tex. Worker's Compensation Ins. Facility, 1995; Sec. of State of State of Tex., 2002—03. Constable Dallas County Precint 2 Irving, Coppell, North Dallas, 1994, 96, 2000. Pres. Tex. Healthy Kids Corp., 1997; former dir. Irving C. of C.; past pres. Women's Divsn. of C.; mem. adv. bd. Irving CARES. Profl. Secs. Internat.; 1st Baptist Ch., Irving; mem. adv. bds. Irving Infant Intervention Ctr. Named to legis. commitment to people of Tex., Tex. Mun. League, Tex. Assn. Bus., Tex. Civil Justice League, Tex. Assn. Concerned Tax Payers; recipient Legislative Leadership award, Tex. C. of C. Republican.

**SHEA, JAMES BRYAN,** writer; b. Newark, N.J., Sept. 19, 1954; s. Francis V. and Jeanne R. Shea. BA in History, Mt. St. Mary's Coll., 1976. Supr. Bayshore Cmty. Hosp., Holmdel, N.J. Author: SERIAL, 2000, Diary of the Unspoken, 2002. Bd. dirs. Cmty. YMCA, Red Bank, NJ, 1990—. Mem.: Affiliated Rep. Club Monmouth County. Republican. Roman Cath. Home: PO Box 183 Hazlet NJ 07730

**SHEA, JAMES L.,** lawyer; b. Balt., June 19, 1952; Ab cum laude, Princeton U., 1974; JD, U. Va., 1977. Bar: Md. 1977, DC 1998. Law clk. to Hon. Joseph H. Young US Dist. Ct. Md., 1977-78; asst. atty. gen. State of Md., 1981-83; mng. ptnr. Venable LLP, Washington, 1994—2006, chmn. Balt., 2006—. Chmn. bd. Empower Balt. Mgmt. Corp., Downtown Partnership of Balt., Downtown Mgmt. Authority; bd. mem. Greater Balt. Com., Mercantile Safe-Deposit and Trust Co., Balt. Symphony Orchestra, Nat. Capital Area Chap., Leukemia/Lymphoma Soc.; trustee U. Md., College Park. Named Power 50: The Men and Women Who Rule, Balt. Mag., 2003; recipient Leadership in Law Award, The Daily Record. Fellow Am. Coll. Trial Lawyers; mem. ABA, Md. State Bar Assn., Bar Assn. Balt. City, Defense Rsch. Inst., Md. Assn. of Defense Trial Counsel, Order of Coif. Address: Venable LLP 1800 Mercantile Bank & Trust Bldg 2 Hopkins Plz Baltimore MD 21201-2930 Office Fax: 410-244-7742. E-mail: jshea@venable.com.

**SHEA, JAMES WILLIAM,** lawyer; b. NYC, July 10, 1936; s. William P. and Mildred E. (McCaffrey) S.; m. Ann Marie Byrne, June 6, 1964; children: James T., Kathleen A., Tracy A. BS, St. Peters Coll., 1957; JD, Fordham U., 1962; LLM in Taxation, NYU, 1965. Bar: N.Y. 1962, U.S. Dist. Ct. (so. and ea. dists.) N.Y. 1966, U.S. Supreme Ct. 1967. Revenue agt. U.S. Treasury Dept., N.Y.C., 1961-63; tax atty. Kennecott Copper Corp., N.Y.C., 1963-67; tax counsel CBS Inc., N.Y.C., 1968-71; ptnr. Hunton & Williams and predecessor firm Conboy, Hewitt, O'Brien & Boardman, N.Y.C., 1971—2001, sr. counsel, 2001—. Rep. committeeman, S.I., N.Y., 1980; mem. adv. com. tax and fin. N.Y. State Charter Commn. City of S.I. Served to 1st lt. U.S. Army, 1957-61, to capt. USAR, 1962-72. Mem. N.Y. State Bar Assn. Richmond County Country Club S.I. (sec. 1993-96, v.p. 1996-98, pres. 1998-2000, bd. dirs. 1993-2004). Republican. Roman Catholic. Home: 399 Tysens Ln Staten Island New York NY 10166-0091 Office Phone: 718-987-9798. E-mail: jws@si.rr.com.

**SHEA, JIM,** Olympic athlete; b. Hartford, Conn., June 10, 1968; Mem. U.S. Skeleton Team. Vol. fireman, Lake Placid, NY. Named Athlete of Month, USA Today, 1995, Rookie of Yr., 1995; recipient Gold medal, Nat. Championships, Lake Placid, 1996, 1st pl., Push Championships, 1995, 1997, 1998, Gold medal, Skeleton World Cup, 1998, Stubai Cup, 1999, 1st pl., Skeleton World Championship, Winterberg, Germany, 1999, Gold medal, Winter Goodwill Games, Lake Placid, 2000; mem., US Nat. Team and World Cup Team, 9502, 1st American to win World Cup, 10 World Cup medals worldwide. Address: PO Box 681367 Park City UT 84068 Office Phone: 435-602-6786. E-mail: dkeletonwc@aol.com.

**SHEA, JOSEPH LAWRENCE, JR.,** lawyer; b. New Orleans, Aug. 30, 1952; s. Jerry Lawrence and Nellie (MAxwell) S.; m. Jane Stillwell, Dec. 29, 1973; children: Shawn Stillwell, Shannon Catherine. BA, Tulane U., 1974; JD, La. State U., 1978. Bar: La. 1978, U.S. Dist. Ct. (we. dist.) La. 1980, U.S. Ct. Appeals (5th and 11th cirs.) 1981, U.S. Dist. Ct. (ea. dist.) La. 1984, U.S. Supreme Ct. 1988, U.S. Dist. Ct. (mid. dist.) La. 1988, U.S. Dist. Ct. (ea. and we. dists.) Ark. 1992, U.S. Ct. Appeals (8th cir.) 1994. Ptnr. Hargrove, Guyton, Ramey & Barlow, Shreveport, La., 1978-94, Barlow & Hardtner, Shreveport, La., 1994—2001, Lemle & Kelleher, Barlow & Hardtner, Shreveport, La., 2001—02, Lemle & Kelleher, LLP, Shrevenport, 2003—. Editor: Lousffisiana Law Review, 1977-78. Dir. Peter Pan Players, Shreveport, 1996—. Mem. ATLA, Am. Bd. Trial Advocates (v.p. 1997), Nat. Inst. Trial Advocates, Mid-Continent Oil & Gas Assn., La. State Bar Assn. (disciplinary bd.), East Ridge Country Club (v.p., bd. dirs.), Order of Coif. Avocations: golf, reading, basketball. Home: 508 Wilder Pl Shreveport LA 71104-4432 Office: Lemle & Kelleher LLP 401 Edwards St Fl 10 Shreveport LA 71101-3289 Office Phone: 318-227-1131. E-mail: jlshea@lemle.com.

**SHEA, KEVIN MICHAEL,** lawyer; b. Indpls., Dec. 23, 1951; s. James Louis and Elizabeth (Walker) S.; children: Brendan Alkire, Maura Kathryn. BS, U. Colo., 1973; JD, U. Detroit, 1976. Bar: Colo. 1976, U.S. Dist. Ct. D.C. 1976, U.S. Ct. Appeals (10th cir. 1980), U.S. Supreme Ct. 1982. Dep. dist. atty., Boulder, Colo., 1976—79; shareholder, dir., assoc. Roath & Brega P.C., Denver, 1980—84; spl. counsel, ptnr. Holme Roberts & Owen, Denver, 1984—94; ptnr. Ballard, Sphar, Andrews & Ingersoll, Denver, 1995—. Named in Best Lawyers in Am., Leading Lawyers Bus. Chambers USA. Mem. ABA (vice chair environ. crime sect. 1991—), Colo. Bar Assn. (chair criminal law sect. 1990-91), Denver Country Club (bd. dirs.). Democrat. Avocation: fishing. Office: Ballard Sphar Andrews Inger 1225 17th St Ste 2300 Denver CO 80202-5596 Office Phone: 303-299-7337. Business E-Mail: shea@ballardspahr.com.

**SHEA, MARTIN M.,** communications executive; BS, U. Harford. Various positions, investor relations Paramount Comm. Inc. (formerly Gulf & Western), 1977—94; v.p. investor relations Viacom, Inc. (formerly Triarc Companies, Inc.), 1994; sr. v.p., corp. comm. Viacom, Inc., sr. v.p., investor relations, 1998—. Mem.: Nat. Inst. Investor Relations (NIRI) (past pres. N.Y. Chpt.). Office: Viacom Inc 1515 Bdwy New York NY 10036

**SHEA, WILLIAM J.,** former insurance company executive; With Coopers & Lybrand, 1974—93; vice chmn., CFO BankBoston Corp., Boston, 1993—98; CEO View Tech, Camarillo, Calif., 1999—2000; pres., CEO Conseco, 2001—04; chmn. Demoulas Supermarkets, Tewksbury, Mass., 1998—99. Office: Demoulas 875 East St Tewksbury MA 01876*

**SHEA, WILLIAM RENE,** historian, history and philosophy professor; b. Gracefield, Que., Can., May 16, 1937; s. Herbert Clement and Jeanne (Lafreniere) S.; m. Evelyn Fischer, May 2, 1970; children: Herbert, Joan-Emma, Louisa, Cecilia, Michael. BA, U. Ottawa, 1958; LPh, Gregorian U., Rome, 1959; LTh, Gregorian U., 1963; PhD, Cambridge U., Eng., 1968. Assoc. prof. U. Ottawa, 1968-73; fellow Harvard U., Cambridge, Mass., 1973-74; prof. history and philosophy of sci. McGill U., Montreal, 1974—; dir. d'etudes Ecole des Hautes Etudes, Paris, 1981-82. Sec.-gen. Internat. Union of History and Philosophy of Sci., 1981-89, pres., 1990-93; mem. gen. com. Internat. Coun. of Sci. Union, 1983-89; cons. Killam Found., Ottawa, Ont., 1983-85; mem. McGill Centre for Medicine, Ethics and Law, 1990-95; Hydro Que. prof. environ. ethics, 1992—; vis. prof. U. Rome, 1992; dir. Inst. History of Sci., U. Louis Pasteur, Strasbourg, 1995-2003; Galilean chair history of sci. U. Padua, 2003—. Author: Galileo Intellectual Revolution, 1972, The Magic of Numbers and Motion, 1991, Copernico, 2001, Designing Experiments and Games of Chance, 2003; co-author: Galileo Florentine Residences, 1979, Galileo in Rome, 2003, Galileo Observed, 2006; editor: Nature Mathematized, 1983, Otto Hahn and the Rise of Nuclear Physics, 1983, Revolutions in Science, 1988, Creativity in the Arts and Science, 1990, Persuading Science: The Art of Scientific Rhetoric, 1991, Interpreting the World, Science and Society, 1991, Energy Needs in the Year 2000: Ethical and Environmental Perspectives, 1994, Science and the Visual Image in the Enlightenment, 2000. Recipient The Alexandre Koyre medal, Internat. Acad. of History of Sci., 1993, Knight of the Order of Malta, 1993; Can. Coun. fellow, 1965—68, Can. Cultural Inst. fellow, Rome, 1973, Social Scis. and Humanities Rsch. Coun. Can., 1980—81, Inst. of Advanced Studies in Berlin fellow, 1988—89. Fellow Royal Soc. Can.; mem. Royal Swedish Acad. Scis. (fgn.), Acadmie D'Alsace, Academia Europaea (mem. coun., 2003-), History of Sci. Soc. (coun. 1973-76), European Sci. Found. (standing com. for humanities 1989-95, chmn. 1999-2003), Can. Nat. Com. of History and Philosophy of Sci. (vice pres. 1982-93), Can. Philos. Assn., Internat. Acad. History of Sci. (pres. 1997-2001), Rotary. Home: 35 Via Guglielmo Marconi 35122 Padua Italy Fax: +39-049-827-5068. Office Phone: +39-049-827-5073. E-mail: william.shea@unipd.it.

**SHEAFFER, RICHARD ALLEN,** electrical engineer; b. Bronxville, NY, May 30, 1950; BSEE, Pa. State U., 1972; MSEE, U. So. Calif., 1975; MBA, Pepperdine U., 1996. Registered profl. engr., Calif. Fla. Elec. engr. So. Calif. Edison Co., Rosemead, 1973-79, 80-90, Harris Controls divsn., Melbourne, Fla., 1979-80; cons. to elec. utility industry, 1990-91; sr. transmission planner San Diego Gas & Electric, 1991-2000; San Diego Gas & Electric rep. for decommissioning San Onofre Nuc. Generating Sta. Unit 1, 2000—; prin. engr. San Diego Gas & Elec., 2004—. Project leader nomogram study for Pacific and S.W. transfer subcom. Western Systems Coordinating Coun., 1988, 91; project leader Ariz.-Calif. 7550 NW Path Rating, 1994-97. Author: 1984 West-of-the-River Operating Study, 1985, December 22, 1982 Disturbance Study, 1983. Mem. IEEE (Power Engring. Soc., Engring. Mgmt. Soc.), Am. Nuc. Soc., Phi Eta Sigma.

**SHEAFFER, WILLIAM JAY,** lawyer; b. Carlisle, Pa., Jan. 18, 1948; s. Raymond Jay and Barbara Jean (Bell) S.; m. Carol Ann Madison, Jan. 5, 1974. BA cum laude, U. Cen. Fla., 1975; JD, Nova U., 1978. Bar: Fla. 1978, U.S. Dist. Ct. (mid. dist.) Fla. 1979, U.S. Dist. Ct. (so. and no. dists.) Fla. 1981, U.S. Ct. Appeals (5th and 11th cirs.) 1981, U.S. Supreme Ct. 1983. Atty. State of Fla., Orlando, Fla., 1978-79; pvt. practice, 1979—. Apptd. to merit selection panel to consider U.S. Magistrate Judge Applicants, 1995, 97, 99. Pres. City Coun. Edgewood, Fla., 2000—02, coun. mem., 2003—04. Served to ensign class 4 USN, 1967—71. Named Fla. Trend Mag. Legal Elite, 2004, 2005. Mem.: ACLU, NACDL, ABA, The Federalist Soc., Assn. Fed. Def. Attys., Ctrl. Fla. Assn. Criminal Def. Attys., Nat. Bd. Trial Advocacy (bd. cert. criminal trial specialist), Am. Inns of Ct. (ctrl. Fla. master), Fed. Trial Lawyers Assn., Fla. Assn. Criminal Def. Lawyers Inc., Fed. Bar Assn., Orange County Bar Assn. (Guardian Ad Litem of Yr. 1994, award of excellence 1995), Fla. Bar Assn. (cert. criminal trial specialist, vice chmn. 9th jud. cir. grievance com. 1997, 1998). Democrat. Avocations: boating, running, skiing. Office: 609 E Central Blvd Orlando FL 32801-2916 Fax: 407-648-0683. Office Phone: 407-423-1066. Business E-Mail: mail@defenselaw.net.

**SHEAHAN, JOHN BERNARD,** economist, educator; b. Toledo, Sept. 11, 1923; s. Bernard William and Florence (Sheahan) S.; m. Denise Eugénie Morlino, Nov. 29, 1946; children: Yvette Marie, Bernard Eugene. BA, Stanford U., Calif., 1948; PhD, Harvard U., Cambridge, Mass., 1954. Econ. analyst Office Spl. Rep. in Europe, ECA, Paris, France, 1951-54; mem. faculty Williams Coll., 1954-94, prof. econs. Williamstown, Mass., 1966-94, prof. emeritus. Mem. devel. adv. service Colombia adv. group Harvard, 1963-65; nat. research prof. Brookings Instn., 1959-60; vis. prof. El Colegio de México, Mexico City, 1970-71; Fulbright research scholar Institut de recherche économique et de planification, Université de Grenoble, France, 1974-75; vis. scholar Inst. Devel. Studies, U. Sussex, 1981-82; vis. fellow Ctr. for U.S.-Mexican Studies, U. Calif. at San Diego, 1991. Author: Promotion and Control of Industry in Postwar France, 1963, The Wage-Price Guideposts, 1967, An Introduction to the French Economy, 1969, Patterns of Development in Latin America, 1987, Conflict and Change in Mexican Economic Strategy, 1992, Searching for a Better Society: The Peruvian Economy from 1950, 1999. Mem. Presdl. Price Adv. Com., 1979-80 Mem. Latin Am. Studies Assn., New England Coun. Latin Am. Studies (pres. 1989-90), Phi Beta Kappa. Home: Syndicate Rd Williamstown MA 01267

**SHEAHAN, ROBERT EMMETT,** lawyer, consultant; b. Chgo., May 20, 1942; s. Robert Emmett and Lola Jean (Moore) S.; m. Pati Smith, Mar. 20, 1991. BA, Ill. Wesleyan U., 1964; JD, Duke U., 1967; MBA, U. Chgo., 1970. Bar: Ill. 1967, La. 1975, N.C. 1978. Vol. VISTA, N.Y.C., 1967-68; trial atty. NLRB, Milw., New Orleans, 1970-75; ptnr. Jones, Walker, Waechter, Poitevent, Carrere & Denegre, New Orleans, 1975-78; pvt. practice High Point, NC, 1978—. Bd. dirs. Inst. for Effective Mgmt., Bus. Publs. Inst. Author: Employees and Drug Abuse: An Employer's Handbook, 1994, The Encyclopedia of Drugs in the Workplace, Labor and Employment Law in North Carolina, 1991, Personnel and Employment Law in North Carolina, 1992, Desk Book of Labor and Employment Law for Healthcare Employers' Desk Manual, 1995, North Carolina Lawyers' Desk Book; contbg. author: The Developing Labor Law, 1975—; editor: The World of Personnel; contbg. editor: Employee Testing and the Law; contbr. periodic supplements N.C. Gen. Practice Deskbook, 1992—. Bd. dirs. High Point United Way, 1979-83; mem. congl. action com. High Point C. of C., chmn., 1991—, bd. dirs., 1996—. Mem. ABA, N.C. Bar Assn., High Point Bar Assn., Ill. Bar Assn., La. Bar Assn., Sedgefield (N.C.) Country Club, String and Splinter Club, Bald Head Island Club. Republican. Roman Catholic. Home: 101 Bellwood Ct Jamestown NC 27282 Office: Robert E Sheahan & Assocs 603 Eastchester Dr Ste B High Point NC 27262-7647 Office Phone: 336-889-2711.

**SHEAKS, BARCLAY,** artist; b. Oct. 22, 1928; s. Earl Leroy and Jeanie Rice Sheaks; m. Deborah Mae Joyner; 1 child, Owen James. BFA, Va. Commonwealth U., 1948; LHD (hon.), Christopher Newport U., 1997. Disting. resident artist Va. Wesleyan Coll., Norfolk, 1990—2005. Author: (poetry book) Stretching the Eyes Distance, 1980, (book) The Acrylics Book, 1995; Represented in permanent collections Va. Mus. Fine Arts, Chrysler Mus., Butler Inst. Am. Art, Valentine Mus., Mobile Mus., Mead Coll. Va., Christopher Newport U., others. Mem.: Peninsula Fine Arts Ctr. Avocation: boating. Home: 51 Hopkins St Newport News VA 23601

**SHEAN, TIMOTHY JOSEPH,** manufacturing executive; b. Norfolk, Va., Sept. 19, 1945; s. Hobart Philip S.; m. Adriana Bergo, July 12, 1970; children: Jonathan Michael, Arianne Marie. BSME, U. Notre Dame, 1967; postgrad., U. Va., 1991. Sales engr. Shean Equipment Co., Syracuse, NY, 1967-69; application engr. Gen. Electric Co., Schenectady, 1970-71, prodn. control supr., 1972-75, process devel. engr., 1975-78, project mgr., 1978-80, mgr. facilities and engring., 1980-83; plant mgr. Hughes Tool Co., Bristol, Va., 1983-85; mgr. mfg. Sandvik Rock Tools, Inc., Bristol, 1985-89, gen. mgr., 1989-92, v.p., 1992-2000; pres. Sandvik Mineral Tools USA, Bristol, 2000—02, Sandvik CPD-MTD Prodn. Co., Bristol; pres., CEO R.P. Abrasives and Machine, Inc., Milton, NH, 2002—. Sr. patrolman Nat. Ski Patrol Sys., Wilminton, Vt., 1970-80; instr., trainer first aid ARC, Schenectady, 1975-78, vice-chmn. disaster svcs., 1976-77; mem. sch. bd. Schalmont Ctrl. Sch. Dist., Schenectady, 1979-82; cmty. involvement com. Bristol Sch. Dist., 1990; chmn. Literacy Acad. Bristol, 1991-92; chmn. fin. coun. St. Anne's Cath. Ch. 1992-96; mem. Va. Atty. Gens. Commn., 1995-96, Commn. on Future S.W. Va., 1995-97; bd. fellows Va. Intermont Coll., 1996-99; mem. pres.'s adv. bd. King Coll., 1997-2002; bd. dirs. Mfg. Tech. Ctr. S.W. Va., 1998-2002, Va. Mfg. Assn., 1999-2000. Named one of Outstanding Young Men of Am., U.S. Jaycees, 1979. Mem. Soc. Mfg. Engrs., Nat. Mining Assn. (chmn. resins group 1989-95, tech. com. 1990-96), Va. Coal Coun. (bd. dirs. 1993-2002), Bristol C. of C. (bd. dirs. 1994-2000). Roman Catholic. Avocation: skiing. Office: R P Abrasives & Machine Inc 61 Old Wakefield Rd Milton NH 03851 Office Phone: 603-335-2132. Business E-Mail: joe@pabrasives.com.

**SHEAR, NATALIE PICKUS,** conference and event management executive; b. N.Y.C., Oct. 18, 1940; d. Sam and Mildred (Shulman) Pickus; m. Daniel H. Shear, Dec. 14, 1968 (dec. Apr. 1989); children: Adam Brian, Tamara Beth; m. Henry D. Lewis, Jan. 10, 1999. BA in Journalism, Fairleigh Dickinson U., 1962. Editl. asst. Show Bus. Newspaper, N.Y.C., 1962-64, Jewish News, Newark, 1964-66; dir. Manhattan women's divsn., program asst. Am. Jewish Congress, N.Y.C., 1966-68; mng. editor Jewish Week, Washington, 1971-73; dir. pub. rels. United Jewish Appeal, Washington, 1973-74; pub. affairs dir. Leadership Conf. Civil Rights, Washington, 1977-83; pres. Natalie P. Shear Assocs., Inc., Washington, 1983—. Editor: (newspaper) Books Alive 1973—74; editor, pub.: newsletter Trends, Inc., 1989—94. V.p. Nat. Child Rsch. Ctr., Washington, 1974—76; bd. dirs. Urban Philharm. Soc., 1998—99; vol., bd. dirs. Nat. Jewish Dem. Coun., Washington, 1996—; vol. nat. bd. Ams. Dem. Action, 2001—; pres. Ohr Kodesh Sisterhood, Chevy Chase, Md., 1980—82; chairperson women's task force Am. Jewish Congress, Washington, 1984—86. Mem.: Nat. Press Club. Avocation: needlecrafts. Home: 4701 Willard Ave Chevy Chase MD 20815-4643 Office: 1730 M St NW Ste 801 Washington DC 20036 Office Phone: 202-833-4456. Business E-Mail: natalie@natalieshear.com.

**SHEAR, THEODORE LESLIE, JR.,** archaeologist, educator; b. Athens, Greece, May 1, 1938; s. Theodore Leslie and Josephine (Platner) S.; m. Ione Doris Mylonas, June 24, 1959; children: Julia Louise, Alexandra. AB summa cum laude, Princeton U., NJ, 1959, MA, 1963, PhD, 1966. Instr. Greek and Latin Bryn Mawr (Pa.) Coll., 1964-66, asst. prof., 1966-67; asst. prof. art and archaeology Princeton U., 1967-70, assoc. prof., 1970-79, chmn. program in classical archaeology, 1970-85, assoc. chmn. dept. art and archaeology, 1976-78, 82-83, prof. classical archaeology, 1979—; prof. archaeology Am. Sch. Classical Studies, Athens, 1988-94. Mem. mng. com. Am. Sch. Classical Studies, Athens, 1972—; mem. archaeol. expdns. to Greece and Italy, including Mycenae, 1953-54, 58, 62-63, 65-66, Eleusis, 1956, Perati, 1956, Corinth, 1960, Morgantina, Sicily, 1962; mem. Ancient Agora of Athens, 1955, 67, field dir., 1968-94; trustee William Alexander Procter Found., 1982-89, Princeton Jr. Sch., 1983—, pres., 1994—. Author: Kallias of Sphettos and the Revolt of Athens in 286 B.C., 1978; contbr. articles to profl. jours. White fellow Am. Sch. Classical Studies, 1959-60. Mem. Archaeol. Inst. Am., Am. Philol. Assn., Coll. Art Assn., Archaeol. Soc. Athens (hon.), Century Assn. Club (NYC); Nassau Club (Princeton), Princeton Club (NYC), Hellenic Yacht Club (Piraeus, Greece), Phi Beta Kappa. Republican. Episcopalian. Home: 87 Library Pl Princeton NJ 08540-3015 also: 30 Deinokratous St Athens Greece

**SHEARD, CHARLES, III,** dermatologist; b. Toronto, Ont., Can., Nov. 22, 1914; came to U.S., 1945; s. Charles Jr. and Alice Elizabeth (Ramsay) S.; m. Katherine Patricia Murphy, Nov. 19, 1937; children: Joan Virginia Sheard Cumming (dec.), Pamela Carol Sheard McGuiness, Wendy Alice Sheard Geyer. Sr. matriculation, Upper Can. Coll., Toronto, 1933; MD, U. Toronto, 1939. Diplomate Am. Bd. Dermatology. Intern Toronto Gen. Hosp., 1939-40; instr. physiology, anatomy U. Toronto Med. Faculty, 1940-41; surgical asst. resident Hosp. for Sick Children, Toronto, 1945; from resident to chief resident dermatologist Columbia Presbyn. Hosp., N.Y.C., 1945-49; assoc. prof. medicine Cornell U. Med. Coll., N.Y.C., 1950-94, assoc. prof. emeritus, 1994—. Author: (textbook) Treatment in Dermatology, 1978; contbr. articles to profl. jours. Flight lt. RCAF, 1941-45. Fellow ACP, Royal Coll. Physicians (Can.); mem. Metro-Manhattan Dermatol. Soc. N.Y.C. (sec. 1970-80), Royal Can. Yacht Club, Muskoka Lakes Golf and Country Club. Republican. Episcopalian. Avocations: sailing, fishing, golf.: 10 Merry Meeting Ln Lloyd Harbor NY 11743

**SHEARER, DEREK NOCROSS,** political science professor, diplomat, academic administrator; b. LA, Dec. 5, 1946; s. Lloyd and Marva (Peterson) S.; m. Sue Toigo; 1 child, Casey (dec.); stepchildren: Anthony, Julie. BA, Yale U., 1968; PhD, Union Grad. Sch., Yellow Springs, Ohio, 1977. Lectr. U. Calif., L.A., 1979-81; dir. internat. and pub. affairs ctr., prof. of pub. policy Occidental Coll., L.A., 1981-94, 98—; dep. undersec. U.S. Dept. Commerce, Washington, 1993; U.S. amb. to Finland U.S. Dept. State, Washington, 1994-97; prof. internat. affairs Occidental Coll. L.A., 1997—; internat. advisor Ziff Bros. Investments, 1998—. Fellow Econ. Strategy Inst., Washington, 1993; policy adv. to Presidential Candidate Bill Clinton, 1990-92; adv. on NATO peace keeping USN, 1997—; pub. policy fellow Woodrow Wilson Internat. Scholars Ctr., 1999-2000; dir. global affairs Occidental Coll., 2001—, Chevalier prof. diplomacy and world affairs, 2002—; founder Pacific Coun. Internat. Policy, 1994—; sr. fellow USC Inst. Public Diplomacy. Contbr. articles to profl. publs. Planning commr. City of Santa Monica (Calif.), 1984; bd. mem. Nat. Consumer Bank, Washington, 1991. Fellow Guggenheim Found., 1984, U.S.-Japan Leadership fellow Japan Soc., 1991. Democrat. Avocations: basketball, tennis, travel, mysteries. Office: Global Affairs Occidental Coll Los Angeles CA 90041 Office Phone: 323-259-1459. Business E-Mail: dshearer@oxy.edu.

**SHEARER, HARRY JULIUS,** scriptwriter, actor, television director; b. LA, Dec. 23, 1943; s. Mack Shearer and Dora (Kohn) Warren; m. Penelope Joyce Nichols, Oct. 1974 (div. 1977); m. Judith Owen, March 28, 1993. BA in polit. sci., UCLA, 1964; postgrad. in urban govt., Harvard U., 1964-65. Cert. secondary tchr., Calif. Reporter Newsweek mag., LA, Boston, 1964-65; legis. intern Calif. State Assembly, Sacramento, 1965-66; tchr. Compton (Calif.) Unified Sch. Dist., 1966-68; writer, actor, producer The Credibility Gap, LA, 1968-76; creator nat. pub. radio show Sta. KCRW, Santa Monica, Calif., 1983—. Co-creator, co-producer (recs.) A Great Gift Idea, 1974, A Star is Bought, 1975; author: (weekly column) Man Bites Town, 1990—; actor: (films) Cracking Up, 1977, American Raspberry, 1977, Fish That Saved Pittsburgh, 1979, Loose Shoes, 1980, The Right Stuff, 1983, Plain Clothes, 1988, Oscar, 1991, Pure Luck, 1991, Blood and Concrete, 1991, The Fisher King, 1991, A League of Their Own, 1992, Wayne's World 2, 1993, I'll Do Anything, 1994, Little Giants, 1994, Speechless, 1994, My Best Friend's Wedding, 1997, Godzilla, 1998, Almost Heroes, 1998, The Truman Show, 1998, Edtv, 1999, Dick, 1999, Haiku Tunnel, 2001, Out There, 2001, (voice) Animalympics, 1980, Flicks, 1987, My Stepmother is an Alien, 1988, Small Soldiers, 1988, Encounter in the Third Dimension, 1999, Ghost Dog: The Way of the Samurai, 1999, Edward Fudwupper Fibbed Big, 2000, Haunted Castle, 2001, Chicken Little, 2005; actor, writer, composer: This is Spinal Tap, 1984; actor, dir. Portrait of a White Marriage, 1988; actor, writer, dir., exec. prodr. Teddy Bears' Picnic, 2002; actor, composer A Mighty Wind, 2003; actor: (TV films) Serpico: The Deadly Game, 1976, Million Dollar Infield, 1982, Hometown By Makes Good, 1990, (voice) Spitting Image: Down and Out in the White House, 1986, Spitting Image: The Ronnie and Nancy Show, 1987; actor, writer, composer, prodr. (TV films) The T.V. Show, 1979; actor, dir.: (TV films) The History of White People in America, 1985; The History of White People in America: Volume II, 1996; actor: (TV series) The Simpsons, 1989—; Sunday Best, 1991, The News Hole, 1995, State of the Union Undressed, 1996; actor, writer (TV series) Saturday Night Live, 1979—80 (Emmy award nomination for Outstanding Writing Variety or Music Program, 1980), 1984—85, Likely Stories, Vol. 1, 1981; actor(voice): (TV specials) The Simpsons Christmas Special, 1989; actor, writer, composer: videos Spinal Tap: Break Like the Wind - The Videos, 1992; actor: (numerous TV guest appearances); writer, composer, prodr.: (TV films) A Spinal Tap Reunion: The 25th Anniversary London Sell-Out, 1992; composer: (films) Waiting for Guffman, 1996; writer (TV films) Disco Beaver from Outer Space, 1978, Real Life, 1979, (TV series) America 2-Night, 1978 (Emmy award nomination for Outstanding Writing Comedy-Variety or Music Series, 1978); author: (novels) Not Enough Indians, 2006. Recipient Cable ACE award for Best Game Show Series or Special, 1995. Mailing: Author Mail Justin Charles & Co 236 Huntington Ave Boston MA 02115*

**SHEARER, LINDA,** museum director; b. Long Island, NY, Feb. 13, 1946; BA, Sarah Lawrence Coll., 1968. Assoc. curator Solomon R. Guggenheim Mus., NYC; exec. dir. Artists Space, NYC; curator painting and sculpture Mus. of Modern Art, NYC; dir. Williams Coll. Mus. Art, Mass., 1989; Alice & Harris Weston dir. Contemporary Arts Ctr., Cin. Tchr. contemporary art Williams Coll., Sch. Visual Arts, NYC. Bd. trustees Am. Fedn. of Arts; adv. com. Skowhegan Sch. of Painting and Sculpture; chair Phila. Exhibition Initiative, 2003. Office: Contemporary Arts Ctr 44 E Sixth St Cincinnati OH 45202 Office Phone: 513-345-8412.

**SHEARER, PAUL SCOTT,** federal agency administrator, trade association administrator; b. Clinton, Ill., Feb. 27, 1948; s. Lloyd Jr. and Pauline Lucille (Glosser) S.; m. Barbara Boston, July 3, 1981; children: Jason J. Brunk, Carrie K. Premo. BS, U. Ill., 1970, MS, 1975. Asst. dir. cash mgmt. State Treas. Ill., Springfield, 1973-74, asst. CFO, 1974-77, chief fiscal officer, 1977-78; dir. vehicle svc. State of Ill., Springfield, 1978-81; legis. asst. Senator Dixon US Senate, Washington, 1981-84; exec. dir. Nat. Corn Growers Assn., St. Louis, 1984-90; dir. govt. rels. Halfpenny, Hahn Roche & Marchese, 1990-93; dep. asst. sec. congl. rels. USDA, 1993-96; dir. nat. rels. Farmland Industries, Inc., Washington, 1996—2003; v.p. Bockorny Group, 2003—. Mem. adv. com. U.S. Atty.'s Gen. Agr., State of Ill., 1985-91; dean Coll. Agr., U. Ill., 1989-90, U. Ill. Dept. Agrl. Econs., 1986-89; mem. agrl. tech. com. for trade in animals and animal products USDA/U.S. Trade Rep., 1998-2002; U.S. del. to WTO Ministerial Conf., 1999; food security adv. com. USAID, 1998-2002. Del. Dem. Nat. Conv., 1978, Mo. Dem. State conv., 1988, Va. Dem. State Conv., 1992, 93, 94, 96, 97, 2000; mem. Police

Bd. Commrs., Chesterfield, Mo., 1988-90; pres. Mo. River Dem. Club, 1987-89. Named to Hon. Order of Ky. Cols., 1990, Alpha Gamma Sigma nat. merit award, 1991; named to Villa Grove (Ill.) HS Alumni Hall of Fame. Mem. St. Louis Agr.-Bus. Club (sec.-treas. 1987-88, 2d v.p. 1988-89, v.p. 1989-90, pres. 1990), Ill. Group (chmn. 1993, 04-05), Ill. State Soc. (bd. dirs. 1996—, pres. 2002-03), Mo.-Kans. Forum (chmn. 1998-00), Alpha Zeta (Honor Roll), Nat. Democrat Club. Methodist. Home: 2744 Clarkes Landing Dr Oakton VA 22124-1120 Office: Bockorny Group 1101 16th St NW Ste 500 Washington DC 20036 E-mail: sshearer@bockornygroup.com.

**SHEARER, RONALD ALEXANDER**, economics professor; b. Trail, BC, Can., June 15, 1932; s. James Boyd and Mary Ann (Smith) S.; m. Renate Elizabeth Selig, Dec. 20, 1956 (dec.); children: Carl, Bruce. BA, U. B.C., 1954; MA, Ohio State U., 1955, PhD, 1959. Asst. prof. econs. U. Mich., 1958-62; economist Royal Commn. Banking and Fin., Toronto, Canada, 1962-63; mem. faculty U. B.C., Vancouver, 1963—, prof. econs., 1970-98, emeritus prof., 1998—, head dept., 1972-76. Co-author: Money and Banking, 1975, The Economics of the Canadian Financial System, 1994; editor: Trade Liberalization and a Regional Economy, 1971. Mem. Can. Econs. Assn. Office: U BC Dept Econs Vancouver BC Canada Business E-Mail: rshearer@interchange.ubc.ca.

**SHEARER, WILLIAM THOMAS**, pediatrician, educator; b. Detroit, Aug. 23, 1937; BS, U. Detroit, 1960; PhD, Wayne State U., 1966; MD, Washington U., St. Louis, 1970. Diplomate Am. Bd. Pediat., Am. Bd. Allergy and Immunology (chmn. 1994 95, dir. 1990 95, chair nominations com., clin. immunology soc.), Nat. Bd. Med. Examiners, cert. in diagnostic lab. immunology. Post-doctoral fellow in biochemistry dept. chem. Indiana U., Bloomington, 1966—67; intern in pediat. St. Louis Children's Hosp., 1970—71, resident in immunology in pediat., 1971—72, dir. divsn. allergy and immunology, 1974—78; fellow in immunology Barnes Hosp., Washington U., St. Louis, 1972—74; spl. USPHA sci. rsch. fellow in medicine dept. medicine Washington U., 1972—74, assoc. prof., 1978, prof., 1978; prof. pediat., microbiology, immunology Baylor Coll. Medicine, Houston, 1989—, dir. AIDS rsch. ctr., 1991—; head sect. allergy & immunology Tex. Children's Hosp., Houston, 1978—. Mem. ACTU Cmty. Adv. Bd. Tex. Children's Hosp., Houston, 1991—; chmn. pediat. core com. pediat. AIDS clin. trial group Nat. Inst. Allergy and Infectious Diseases, NIH, Bethesda, Md., 1989—, ad hoc reviewer, 1991, mem. therapeutics subcom. AIDS rsch. adv. com., 1993—, chmn. pediat. AIDS clin. trial group immunology com., 1994—, mem. pediat. AIDS clin. trials group exec. Com., 1991—95, mem. spl. rev. com. persons affected by chronic granulomatous disease, 1992; site visitor Gen. Clin. Rsch. Ctr. NIH, Bethesda, Md., 1993, vice chmn. pediat. AIDS clin. trials group exec. com., 1996—; chmn. study populatoin/patient mgmt. com. Clin. Ctrs. for the Study of Pediat. Lung and Heart Complications of HIV Infection, Nat. Heart, Lung and Blood Inst., NIH, Bethesda, Md., 1989—, mem. AIDS ad hoc work group, 1991; dir. Pediat. HIV/AIDS Clin. Rsch. Ctr., Houston, 1988—; chmn. exec. com. clin. trial intravenous gammaglobulin in HIV infected children Nat. Inst. Child Health and Human Devel., Bethesda, 1989—; dir. Am. Bd. Allergy and Immunology, 1990—95, chair, 1994—95; vice-chair exec. com. Pediat. AIDS Clin. Trials Group, 1996—2001. Editor: Pediatric Asthma, Allergy, and Immunology, 1989; editl. bd. Jour. Allergy and Clin. Immunology, 1993—, Clin. and Diagnostic Lab. Immunology, 1994—, editor Pediatric Allergy and Immunology, 1995—, Allergy and Immunology Tng. Program Dir.; assoc. editor: Jour. Allergy and Clin. Immunology, 2003—; guest editor Seminar Pediatric Infectious Disease, 1990, contbr. intro. Allergy: Princples and Practice, 1992, contbr. articles to profl. jours. including New Eng. Jour. Medicine. AIDS cons. Houston Ind. Sch. Dist., 1986—; med. adv. Spring Br. Ind. Sch. Dist., Houston, 1987—; chmn. cmty. HIV/AIDS adv. group Tex. Med. Ctr., 1991—. Recipient faculty rsch. award, Am. Cancer Soc., 1977—79, Myrtle Wreath award, Hadassah, 1985, spl. recognition award, Am. Acad. Allergy and Immunology, 1994; grantee NIH, 1988—; scholar rsch., Cystic Fibrosis Found., 1974—77. Mem.: Clin. Immunology Soc. (chair Am. Bd. Allergy and Immunology nominations com. 1994—96, pres. 2001—02), Am. Acad. Allergy, Asthma and Immunology (assoc. chmn. for planning of 1997-98 internat. meetings, profl. ednl. coun.), Am. Acad. Allergy and Immunology (chmn. clin. and lab. immunology com. 1994—96, chmn. tng. program dirs. nat. issues subcom. 1994—96), Tex. Allergy and Immunology Soc. (chmn. nat. issues com. 1992—96, pres. 1994—96), Tex. Allergy Soc. (exec. com. 1990—), Am. Acad. Pediat. (exec. com. sect. allergy and immunology 1991—), Am. Soc. Clin. Investigation. Achievements include research in half-matched T-cell-depleted bone marrow transplants; membrane signal pathway of human B lymphcytes. Office: Baylor Coll Med Allergy/Immun Clinic 6621 Fannin MC FC 330 01 Houston TX 77030-2600

**SHEARING, GEORGE ALBERT**, pianist, composer; b. London, Aug. 13, 1919; arrived in U.S., 1947, naturalized, 1956; s. James Philip and Ellen Amelia (Brightman) Shearing; m. Beatrice Bayes, May 1, 1941 (div.); 1 child, Wendy Ann; m. Eleanor Geffert, July 28, 1984. Student, Linden Lodge Sch. for Blind, London; D Music (hon.), Westminster Coll., Salt Lake City, 1975, Hamilton Coll., 1994. Composer: (songs) Lullaby of Birdland, numerous other popular songs; recs. English Decca and Parlophone, Am. Savoy, London, MGM Capitol, Sheba Records, Concord Jazz, Telarc, albums An Evening with George Shearing and Mel Torme, 1982 (Grammy, 1982), Top Drawer, 1983 (Grammy, 1983), An Evening at Charlie's, 1984, Grand Piano, 1985, An Elegant Evening, 1986, George Shearing and Barry Tuckwell Play the Music of Cole Porter, 1986, More Grand Piano, 1987, (with Marian McPartland) Alone Together, 1981, George Shearing and Dakota Staton: In the Night, A Vintage Year, 1987, George Shearing In Dixieland, 1989, I Hear a Rhapsody, Live at the Blue Note, 1994, On a Clear Day, 1980, How Beautiful Is Night, Best of George Shearing, 1993, That Shearing Sound, 1994, Walkin' - Live at the Blue Note, The George Shearing Quintet: By Request, Jazz Moments, 1995, Paper Moon: Music of Nat King Cole, George Shearing and Friends, 1996, appearance London Symphony Pops Concerts, 1986, 1987, London Paladium, Concord Jazz Festival, Japan, 1987, Hong Kong Cultural Ctr., 1992, European Jazz Festivals, 1995, Birmingham (Eng.) Symphony with Sir Simon Rattle, 1995, Can. Tour, 1995, Japan Tour, New Eng. Jazz Festival, Tanglewood, Mass., US Tour, 1996, others, 1996; author: (autobiography) Lullaby of Birdland. Bd. dirs. Guide Dogs for Blind San Rafael, Hadley Sch. for Blind, Winnetka, Ill. Named top English pianist, 1941—47; recipient all Am. jazz polls, also many pvt. awards, Golden Plate award, Am. Acad. of Achievement, 1968, Helen Keller Achievement award, 1995. Mem.: Broadcast Music Inc., Bohemian Club (San Francisco), Lotos Club (N.Y.), Friars Club. Avocations: walking, listening to tennis and cricket matches, bridge, quiet dinners.

**SHEARING, MIRIAM**, retired state supreme court chief justice; b. Waverly, NY, Feb. 24, 1935; BA, Cornell U., 1956; JD, Boston Coll., 1964. Bar: Calif. 1965, Nev. 1969. Justice of peace Las Vegas Justice Ct., 1977-81; judge Nev. Dist. Ct., 1983-92, chief judge, 1986; justice Nevada Supreme Ct., Carson City, 1993—2005, chief justice, 1997, 2004, st. justice, 2005—. Mem. ABA, Am. Judicature Soc. (chair 2001-03), Nev. Judges Assn. (sec. 1978), Nev. Dist. Ct. Judges Assn. (sec. 1984-85, pres. 1986-87), State Bar Nev., State Bar Calif., Clark County Bar Assn. Democrat. Office Phone: 775-831-9158. E-mail: shearing@nvcourts.state.nv.us.

**SHEARMUR, ALLI**, broadcast executive; married. V.p. prodn. Walt Disney Co., 1994—97; exec. v.p. prodn. Universal Pictures, Paramount Pictures, co-pres. prodn., 2005—. Office: Paramount Pictures 5555 Melrose Hwy West Hollywood CA 90038 Office Phone: 323-956-5000.*

**SHEARROW, SAMUEL CARL**, mathematics professor; b. New Philadelphia, Ohio, Jan. 24, 1946; s. Lloyd Ray Shearrow and Lena Mae Reneker; m. Karen Jean Kinnaman, Nov. 26, 1969; children: Rebecca Lynn Petersen, Roger Lee, Rochelle Leanne. BS, Grand Canyon Coll., Ariz., 1969; EdM, U. Ariz., Tucson, 1981. Endorsement No. Ariz. U., 1989, ESL endorsement No. Ariz., 1989. Educator Murphy Elem. Sch., Phoenix, 1969—75, Wellton

Elem. Sch., Ariz., 1975—2002; prof. math. Ariz. Western Coll., Yuma, 1989—; math instr. Yuma Elem. Dist. 1, 2004—05. Mem.: NEA. Avocations: remodeling, automotive enthusiast, travel.

**SHEA-STONUM, MARILYN**, federal bankruptcy judge; b. 1947; AB, U. Calif., Santa Cruz, 1969; JD, Case Western Res. U., 1975. Law clk. to Hon. Frank J. Battisti, Cleve., 1975-76; pvt. pactice, Jones, Day, Reavis & Pogue, Cleve., 1984—94; bankruptcy judge U.S. Dist. Ct. (no. dist.) Ohio, Akron, 1994—. Editor-in-chief Am. Bankruptcy Law Jour. Mem. Nat. Conf. Bankruptcy Judges. Mem. Order of Coif. Office: US Bankruptcy Ct No Dist Ohio 240 Fed Bldg 2 S Main St Akron OH 44308-1813 Office Phone: 330-252-6130.

**SHEATH, ROBERT GORDON**, botanist, educator; b. Toronto, Can., Dec. 26, 1950; arrived in U.S., 1978; s. Harry Gordon and Shirley Irene (Rose) Sheath. BSc, U. Toronto, 1973, PhD, 1977. Nat. Rsch. Coun. Can. postdoctoral fellow U. B.C., 1977-78; asst. prof. aquatic biology U. RI, Kingston, 1978-82, assoc. prof., 1982-86, chmn. dept. botany 1986-90, prof., 1987-91; head dept. biology Meml. U., St. Johns, Canada, 1991-95; dean coll. biol. sci. U. Guelph, Ont., 1995-2001; provost Calif. State U. San Marcos, 2001—. Mem. evolution and ecology grant selection com. NSERC, 1994—97, chair, 1996—97, selection com. life scis., 1996, chair maj. facilities access life scis. subcom., 2001; mem. Can. Rsch. Chairs Coll. of Reviewers, 2000—01. Editor (with M. M. Harlin): Freshwater and Marine Plants of RI, 1988; editor: (with K. M. Cole) Biology of the Red Algae, 1990; editor: (with J.D. Wehr) Classification and Ecology of Freshwater Algae of North America, 2003; contbr. 131 articles to profl. jours. Recipient G. A. Cox Gold medal, U. Toronto, 1973, Darbaker prize, Bot. Soc. Am., 1997, T. Christensen prize panel, 2000; grantee, NSF, 1980—91, 2001—05, NSERC, 1991—2002. Mem.: Japanese Phycological Soc. (editl. bd. 2000—05), Brit. Phycological Soc. (freshwater flora com. 1993—2002, overseas v.p. 1997—99, assoc. editor 1999—2001), Arctic Inst. N.Am., Phycological Soc. Am. (editl. bd. 1983—86, assoc. editor 1984—89, pres. 1991—92, editl. bd. 1996—2000, publs. com. chair 2001—, bd. trustees 2001—, Bold award 1976), Internat. Phycological Soc. (editl. bd. 1993—95, T. Christensen prize panel 2000, nominating com. 2000—01). Office: Calif State U San Marcos Office of Provost San Marcos CA 92096-0001 Office Phone: 760-750-4050. E-mail: rsheath@csusm.edu.

**SHEBEL, HEATHER A.**, editor; d. Jack Raymond and Martha Ann Heminger; m. Shebel John M., Oct. 10, 2001. BA in math., U. Chgo., 1996. Rsch. tech. U. Chgo. Hosp., 1996—2001; sr. manuscript editor Jour. AMA, Chgo., 2001—. Editor (copy editor): (cd-rom) Multimedia Textbook of Coronary Arteriography and Interventions, 1997; co-author: Journal of Hand Surgery, 2002 (Joseph B. Boyes award, 1998). Mem.: Coun. Sci. Editors (cert.). Office: Am Med Assn 515 N State St Chicago IL 60610 Personal E-mail: haheming@hotmail.com.

**SHECHET, ARLENE J.**, artist; BA, NYU, Skidmore Coll.; MFA, RI Sch. Design. Artist-in-residence Pilchuck Glass Sch. One-man shows include Bernard Toale Gallery, Boston, 1997, John Berggruen Gallery, San Francisco, 1997, Mirror Mirror, Elizabeth Harris Gallery, 1999, Galerie Rene Blouin, Montreal, 2000, Flowers Found, Elizabeth Harris Gallery, 2002, Harbor Cultural Ctr., 2003, Out of the Blue, Shoshana Wayne Gallery, 2004, exhibited in group shows at Water, Water, Rotunda Gallery, 2003, Vessels, Greenwich House Poetry, 2003, Mystic, Mass. Coll. Art, 2003, Adlrich Contemporary Art Mus., 2004, pub. collections, Brooklyn Mus. Art. Fidelity Investments, Boston, NY Pub. Libr., Drawings & Prints Collection, Banff Sch. Fine Arts, Can. Fellow Guggenheim Meml. Found., 2004; grantee NY Found. for Arts, Artist Fellowship. Office: 52 White St New York NY 10013 Office Phone: 212-941-0749. E-mail: ray@rlemes.com.

**SHECKLER, ROSS DAVID**, engineering executive; b. Cato, NY, Mar. 24, 1966; m. Cynthia Rose Delaney, June 1, 1996. MS in Aerospace Engring., Iowa State U., 1991. Sr. engr. Boeing Comml. Aircraft, Seattle, 1991—95; mem. tech. staff 5 Dynacs Engring., Seattle, 1995—97; mgr. Dynacs, Inc., Cato, 1997—2002; pres. Calmar Rsch. Corp., Cato, 2002—. Adj. prof. Aerospace Engring., Ames, 2001—. Mem. bd. trustees Lang Meml. Libr., Cato, 2000. Mem.: AIAA, Soc. Automotive Engrs., Exptl. Aircraft Assn. Conservative. Achievements include patents for Ltd. injection cycle safety syringe. Office: Calmar Rsch Corp PO Box 247 Cato NY 13033

**SHECTER, HOWARD L.**, lawyer; b. Boston, May 13, 1943; AB, Harvard U., 1965; JD, U. Pa., 1968. Bar: Pa. 1968, N.Y. 1996. Assoc. Morgan, Lewis & Bockius LLP, Phila., 1968-73, ptnr. NYC, 1973—, bus. and fin. practice group leader, firm mng. ptnr., 1979—84, chmn., 1985—86. Founder & former chmn. seminar series, Acquiring or Selling the Privately Held Company, Practicing Law Inst. Office: Morgan Lewis & Bockius LLP 101 Park Ave New York NY 10178-0060 Office Phone: 212-309-6384. Office Fax: 212-309-7044. Business E-Mail: hshecter@morganlewis.com.

**SHEDD, DENNIS W.**, federal judge; b. 1953; BA, Wofford Coll., 1975; JD, U. S.C., 1978; LLM, Georgetown U., 1980. Bar: S.C. Law clerk Harry Dent & Assoc., 1977—78; admin. asst. US Senator Strom Thurmond, 1978—88; chief counsel US Senate Jud. Com., Washington, 1985-86; of counsel Bethea, Jordan & Griffin, Columbia, S.C., 1988-90; pvt. practice, 1989-90; judge U.S. Dist. Ct. S.C., Greenville, 1990—2002, US Ct. of Appeals (4th cir.), 2002—. Adj. prof. U. SC, 1989-92. Mem. SC Bar Assn., Richland County Bar Assn., Phi Beta Kappa. Office: US Courthouse 1100 Laurel St Columbia SC 29201-2431*

**SHEDD, DONALD POMROY**, surgeon; b. New Haven, Aug. 4, 1922; s. Gale and Marion (Young) S.; m. Charlotte Newsom, Mar. 17, 1946; children: Carolyn, David, Ann, Laura BS, Yale U., 1944, MD, 1946. Diplomate Am. Bd. Surgery. Intern Yale New Haven Hosp., 1946-47, asst. resident, resident, 1949-53; instr. surgery Yale U. Med Sch., New Haven, 1953-54, asst. prof., 1954-56, assoc. prof., 1956-67; chief dept. head and neck surgery Roswell Park Cancer Inst., Buffalo, 1967-96, prof. emeritus, 1996—; rsch. prof. emeritus SUNY at Buffalo, 1996—. Co-editor: Surgical and Prosthetic Speech Rehabilitation, 1980, Head and Neck Cancer, 1985, The Early History of Hospice Buffalo, 2003; author: Historical Landmarks in Head and Neck Cancer Surgery, 2000; contbr. numerous articles to profl. jours. Founding bd. dirs. Hospice Buffalo, Inc., 1973—83. Served to capt. U.S. Army, 1947—49. Mem. Am. Head and Neck Soc., Soc. Univ. Surgeons, Soc. Surg. Oncology, New Eng. Surg. Soc., Soc. Head and Neck Surgeons (pres. 1976-77). Avocations: sailing, windsurfing, tennis, history of medicine. Home: 671 Lafayette Ave Buffalo NY 14222-1435 Office Phone: 716-845-3158.

**SHEDLARZ, DAVID L.**, pharmaceutical executive; b. NYC, 1948; m. Patricia Shedlarz; 1 child, Danielle. BS in Econs. and Math., Mich. State U., 1970; MBA in Fin. and Acctg., NYU, 1975. Various position including sr. fin. analyst, Pharmaceutical divsn., fin. mgr. & controller mktg/sales/prodn., Diagnostics divsn. Pfizer Inc., N.Y.C., 1976-79; prodn. contr. U.S. pharms. divsn., 1979-81, asst. group contr. U.S. Pharms. divsn., 1981-84, group contr., 1984-89, v.p. fin. U.S. pharms. group, 1989-92, corp. officer, v.p. fin. planning and anal., 1992-95, CFO, 1995—2005, ex. v.p. 1997—99, exec. v.p., 1999—2005, vice chmn., 2005—. Bd. dirs. Pitney Bowes Inc., 2001—, Nat. Multiple Sclerosis Bd.; mem. NYU Stern Sch. Bd. Overseers, J.P. Morgan Chase & Co. Nat. Adv. Bd., Nat. Assn. Mfrs. Bd., Internat. Acctg. Standards Bd., Standing Adv. Group, Pub. Acctg. Oversight Bd. Mem. Nat. Jr. Achievement Bd.; chmn. Nat. Jr. Achievement NY. Office: Pfizer Inc 235 E 42d St New York NY 10017-5755*

**SHEDLOCK, JAMES**, library director, consultant; b. Detroit, Nov. 25, 1950; BA in English, U. Notre Dame, 1974; AM in LS, U. Mich., 1977. Reference and serials libr. St. Joseph Mercy Hosp., Pontiac, Mich., 1977-79; document delivery libr. Wayne State U. Med. Libr., Detroit, 1979-81; coord. online search svc. U. N.C. Health Scis. Libr., Chapel Hill, 1982-84; head pub. svcs. Med. Libr. Northwestern U., Chgo., 1985-88, assoc. dir., 1988-91, dir.

Galter Health Scis. Libr., 1991—. Cons. U.N. High Commr. for Refugees, Cyprus, 1993-94, Med. Coll. Wis. Libr., 1996-97, La Porte (Ind.) Hosp., 1998. Mem. ALA, Med. Libr. Assn. (bd. dirs. 1997-99), Am. Med. Informatics Assn., Assn. Acad. Health Scis. Libr. Dirs. (rep.), Acad. Health Info. Profls. (disting.). Office Phone: 312-503-8133. E-mail: j-shedlock@northwestern.edu.

**SHEDROFF, SHARON D.**, psychologist, researcher, anthropologist, consultant; b. Middletown, Conn., Feb. 7, 1952; d. Leon and Sylvia Shedroff. BA summa cum laude, Syracuse U., N.Y., 1974; MA, Calif. Sch. Profl. Psychology, San Diego, 1979. Lic. marriage, family and child counselor Calif., 1981. Psychology intern T.R.I. Cmty. Svcs., San Diego, 1978—81, marriage, family & child counselor, 1981—82; rsch. psychologist Grid Rsch., San Diego, 1983—85; founder, ptnr. Edwards Assocs., San Diego, 1985—, Strategic Vision Inc., San Diego, 1989—, Inst. for Value-Centered Life, San Diego, 1999—. Author: (novels) Dakota Dreams, 2003; contbr. articles to profl. jours. Mem.: Am. Morgan Horse Assn., U.S.A. Equestrian. Avocations: skiing, competitive horseback riding. Home: PO Box 420036 San Diego CA 92142 Office: The Edwards Assocs PO Box 420429 San Diego CA 92142 Office Phone: 858-576-7141.

**SHEEDER, ROBERT ELWOOD**, lawyer; b. Ind., Pa., Apr. 8, 1951; s. Elwood B. and Alice (Poole) Sheeder; m. Martha Ann Painter. BA with high honors, U. Va., 1973; JD cum laude, U. Mich., 1976. Bar: Tex. 1976, Pa. 1978, US Dist. Ct. We. Dist. Pa. 1980, US Ct. Appeals 3rd Cir. 1981, US Dist. Ct. No. Dist. Tex. 1985, US Dist. Ct. Ea. Dist. Tex. 1986, US Ct. Appeals 5th Cir. 1988, US Dist. Ct. So. Dist. Tex. 1989, US Ct. We. Dist. Tex. 1991, US Supreme Ct. 1996. Assoc. Reed, Smith, Shaw & McClay, Pitts., 1977-84; ptnr. Winstead, McGuire, Sechrest & Minick, Dallas, 1984-92; shareholder Jenkens & Gilchrist, P.C., Dallas, 1992—, firm leader labor/employment practice group. Lectr. labor law So. Meth. U., 1988-90. Editor-in-chief: Tex. Labor Letter, 1994-01. Mem.: ABA, Dallas Bar Assn., Tex. State Bar Assn. (governing coun. labor & employment law sect. 2002—04, Best Lawyers in Am. 2001—). Republican, Presbyterian. Office: Jenkens & Gilchrist PC 1445 Ross Ave Ste 3200 Dallas TX 75202-2799 Office Phone: 214-855-4371. Office Fax: 214-855-3400. Business E-Mail: rsheeder@jenkens.com.

**SHEEDY, ALLY (ALEXANDRA ELIZABETH SHEEDY)**, actress; b. NYC, June 13, 1962; d. John and Charlotte (Baum) S.; m. David Lansbury, Oct. 10, 1992; 1 child, Rebecca. Student, U. So. Calif. Past ballet dancer. Film debut in Bad Boys, 1983; other films include Wargames, 1983, Oxford Blues, 1984, The Breakfast Club, 1985, St. Elmo's Fire, 1985, Twice in a Lifetime, 1985, Short Circuit, 1986, Blue City, 1986, Maid to Order, 1987, Heart of Dixie, 1989, Betsy's Wedding, 1990, Only the Lonely, 1991, Home Alone II: Lost in New York, 1992, The Pickle, 1992, Man's Best Friend, 1993, Tattle Tale, 1993, One Night Stand, 1995, Groupies, 1997, Highball, 1997, Crossroads of Destiny, 1997, Country Justice, 1997, Amnesia, 1997, High Art, 1998 (Best Actress award Nat. Soc. Film Critics 1998, Ind. Spirit award for best female lead 1999), Autumn Heart, 1998, I'll Take You There, 1999, Advice From a Caterpillar, 1999, Just a Dream, 2002, Happy Here and Now, 2002, A Good Night to Die, 2003, Shelter Island, 2003, Noise, 2004, Shooting Livien, 2005; TV films include The Best Little Girl in the World, 1981, The Day the Loving Stopped, 1981, The Violation of Sarah McDavid, 1981, Splendor in the Grass, 1981, Dead Lessons, 1983, We Are the Children, 1987, Fear, 1990, The Lost Capone, 1990, Lethal Exposure, 1993, Chantilly Lace, 1993, The Hauting of Sea Cliff Inn, 1994, Ultimate Betrayal, 1994, Parallel Lives, 1994, Tin Soldier, 1995, Hijacked: Flight 285, 1996, Sleeping With the Devil, 1997, Buried Alive 2, 1997, Amnesia, 1997, Myth America, 1998, High Art, 1998, (TV) The Fury Within, 1998, Sugar Town, 1999, Autumn Hart, 1999, (TV) Our Guys, 1999, The Warden, 2001, The Interrogation of Michael Crowe, 2002, Life On the Line, 2003, (TV guest appearances) The Dead Zone, 2002; author (children's book) She Was Nice to Mice, 1975, (poetry) Yesterday I Saw the Sun, 1991. Address: Don Buchwald & Assocs Ste 2200 6500 Wilshire Blvd Los Angeles CA 90048 also: PO Box 523 Topanga CA 90290-0523 also: 11766 Wilshire Blvd #1610 Los Angeles CA 90025-6555

**SHEEDY, PATRICK THOMAS**, judge; b. Green Bay, Wis., Oct. 31, 1921; s. Earl P. and Elsie L. (Brauel) S.; m. Margaret P. Mulvaney, Sept. 6, 1952; children: Michael, Mary, Kathleen, Patrick Thomas, Ann, Maureen. BS in Bus. Adminstrn., Marquette U., 1943, JD, 1948; LLM in Taxation, John Marshall Law Sch., 1972. Bar: Wis. 1948. Pvt. practice, Milw., 1948-80; judge Wis. Cir. Ct., Milw., 1980-90; chief judge 1st Jud. Dist., Milw., 1990-98. Past vice chmn. Archdiocesean Sch. Bd., Milw., chairperson, 1986—. Served to col. USAR, 1942-73. Decorated Legion of Merit. Mem.: ABA (state del. 1983—85, 1989—92, bd. govs. 1985—88), Wis. Bar Assn. (pres. 1974—75, bd. govs., exec. com.), Exchange (pres.). Roman Catholic.

**SHEEHAN, CHARLES VINCENT**, investment banker; b. London, Dec. 19, 1930; came to U.S. 1931; s. Charles Vincent and Mary Margaret (Stokes) S.; m. Susan Ellen Rosar, May 5, 1962. BS, Georgetown U., 1952. Chief fin. officer Gen. Electric Co., Tokyo, Sydney, Australia and Sao Paulo, Brazil, 1962-64, 64-66, 67-71, staff exec. Fairfield, Conn., 1972-83, v.p. corp. exec. office, 1983-87; sr. v.p., chief fin., adminstrn. officer Kidder, Peabody Group, Inc., N.Y.C., 1987-90. Bd. dirs. Fleet Trust Co.; mem. bd. dirs. Indian River Meml. Hosp. Chmn. Non-partisan Polit. Action Com. for Gen. Electric Co. employees, Fairfield, 1982-83. Served to lt. USN, 1952-54. Mem. Johns Island Club (Vero Beach, Fla.), Quail Valley Golf Club (Vero Beach, Fla.), Wildcat Cliffs Country Club (Highlands, N.C.) (pres. 1998-99). Republican. Roman Catholic. Avocations: golf, boating. Home (Winter): 884 Indian Lane Vero Beach FL 32963 1131 E-mail: gecharlie@earthlink.net

**SHEEHAN, DEBORAH HARDICK**, lawyer; b. Glens Falls, NY, July 11, 1961; d. Frank Clark and Jean Ogden Hardick; m. John Francis Sheehan, Nov. 5, 1994; 1 child, Hannah Elizabeth. BA cum laude, Coll. New Rochelle, NY, 1983; JD, Union U. Albany Law Sch., NY, 1986. Bar: NY 1987, US Supreme Ct. 2003. Lawyer Duggan Crotty & Dunn, P.C., New Windsor, NY, 1987—88, Law Office of Paul M. Whitaker, Albany, 1988—98; sole practice Albany, 1998—. Pro bono atty. The Legal Project, Inc., Albany, 1993—; mem. Harriet Tubman March 10 Coalition, Albany, 2000—03; mem., cookie coord. Girl Scouts USA Troop 593, Albany, 2003—; bd. dirs. The Women's Bldg., Inc., Albany, 1998—2003. Recipient Pro Bono award, The Legal Project, Inc., 1994—95. Mem.: Exec. Women's Golf Assn. Democrat. Methodist. Home and Office: 20 W Meadow Dr Albany NY 12203 Office Phone: 518-456-5644. Fax: 518-456-4512. E-mail: deblawofc@aol.com.

**SHEEHAN, EDWARD JAMES**, retired night vision and electro-optics specialist; b. Johnstown, Pa., Dec. 31, 1935; s. Louis A. and Ethel F. (Schaefer) S.; m. Florence Ann Hartnett, June 17, 1958; children: Edward, James, John, William, Mary. BS in Physics, St. Francis Coll., 1959; MS (Sloan fellow), Mass. Inst. Tech., 1972. Project engr. Electronics Command, Dept. Army, 1959-61, project team leader electro-optic equipment for tanks, 1961-63, project team leader electro-optic equipment for infantry, 1963-65, tech. area dir. electro-optic night vision equipment, 1965-73, assis. lab. dir. for devel. engring., 1973-76; lab. dir. Night Vision Lab., Fort Belvoir, Va., 1976-79; founder, pres. Sheehan Assos. Inc., Alexandria, Va., 1979-92; founder, CEO, chmn. Stardyne, Inc., Johnstown, 1990-96; ret., 1996. Chmn. Nat. and Internat. Symposia for Electro-Optical Tech. and Applications. Recipient numerous awards including Meritorious Civilian Svc. award Dept. Army, Disting. Alumnus award in sci. St. Francis Coll., 1989; named Man of Yr., Combined Svc. Clubs, Johnstown, Pa., 1993. Home: 809 Luzerne St Johnstown PA 15905-2301

**SHEEHAN, GEOFFREY**, theater educator; b. Bridgeport, Conn., Mar. 31, 1962; s. John and Lorraine Sheehan; m. Laura Sheehan, May 27, 1988; children: Jeremiah, Ethan, Kiera, Jackson. BFA, U. Conn., Storrs, 1980—84; MALS, Wesleyan U., Middletown, Conn., 2000—06. Program coord., asst. prof. theater arts Housatonic CC, Bridgeport, 1999—. Co-founder Capital

Classics Shakespeare Festival. Bd. dirs. Capital Classics, Inc., Hartford, Conn., 1991—2006. Office: Housatonic CC 900 Lafayette Blvd Bridgeport CT 06604 Office Fax: 203-332-5123. Business E-Mail: gsheehan@hcc.commnet.edu.

SHEEHAN, GREGORY D., lawyer; AB magna cum laude, Harvard Univ., 1977; JD, Univ. Calif., Berkeley, 1980. Bar: Mass. 1980, Calif. 1981. Law clk. Judge Walter J. Skinner, US Dist Ct. (Mass.), 1980—81; ptnr. corp. dept & chmn. investment mgmt. practice group Ropes & Gray, Boston. Editor (exec.): Calif. Law Rev. Pres. French-Am. C. of C. of New England, 1993—95. Mem.: Phi Beta Kappa, Order of the Coif. Office: Ropes & Gray 1 International Pl Boston MA 02110-2624 Office Phone: 617-951-7621. Office Fax: 617-951-7050. Business E-Mail: gsheehan@ropesgray.com.

SHEEHAN, JAMES JOHN, historian, educator; b. San Francisco, May 31, 1937; s. James B. and Sally W. (Walsh) S.; m. 1960; 1 child, Michael L.; m. Margaret L. Anderson, Sept. 2, 1989. BA, Stanford U., 1958; MA, U. Calif., Berkeley, 1959, PhD, 1964. From asst. to assoc. prof. Northwestern U., Evanston, Ill., 1964-79; prof. Stanford (Calif.) U., 1979-86, chmn. dept., 1982-89, Dickason prof. in humanities, 1986—. Author: Lujo Brentano, 1966, German Liberalism, 1978, German History 1770-1866, 1989, Der Ausklang des alten Reiches, 1994, Museums in German Artworld, 2000; editor: The Boundaries of Humanity, 1991; contbr. articles to profl. jours. Decorated officer's cross Order of Merit; fellow Am. Council Learned Socs., 1981-82, NEH, 1985-86, Wissenschaftskolleg Berlin; Guggenheim fellow, 2000—. Fellow AAAS (Humboldt Rsch. prize 1995), Am. Acad. Berlin; mem. Royal Hist. Soc. (corr.), Am. Hist. Assn. (nominating com. 1979-81, chmn. com. group on Ctrl. European history 1985-86, pres. 2005), Am. Philos. Soc. Office: Stanford U Dept History Stanford CA 94305 Business E-Mail: sheehan@stanford.edu.

SHEEHAN, JAMES JOSEPH, social studies educator; m. Olivia Sheehan; children: Ryan, Matthew. BBA, Ohio U., Athens, 1988; MA in Internat. Affairs, Ohio U., 1990, MEd, 1992, MA, 1996, PhD, 1998. Cert. tchr. social studies Ohio. Instr. Ohio U., Athens, 1993—97; asst. prof. U. N.D., Grand Forks, 1997—98, Cleve. State U., 1998—2003, Miami U., Oxford, Ohio, 2003—06, assoc. prof. social studies, 2006—. Author: Justice, Idealogy and Education, 2001, NCSS Presidential Addresses, 2002, 2003. Grantee Sr. Rsch. awardee, Fulbright Found./U.S. Dept. State, 2005—06. Mem.: Ohio Coun. for the Social Studies (exec. dir. 2005—, conf. dir. 2001—06), Nat. Coun. for the Social Studies (pubs. chair 2005—06). Office: Miami University 401 J McGuitey Hall Oxford OH 45056

SHEEHAN, JAMES PATRICK, printing company executive, former media company executive; b. Jersey City, June 6, 1942; s. John Patrick and Helen Teresa (Woods) S.; m. Mary Ellen Finnell, July 1, 1967; children: James, Christopher. BS, Seton Hall U., 1965; MBA, Wayne State U., 1973. Contr. Otis Elevator Co. N.Am., Farmington, Conn., 1976-78, dir. mfg. Yonkers, N.Y., 1978-80; v.p., contr., Pratt & Whitney Aircraft, East Hartford, Conn., 1980-82; sr. v.p. A. H. Belo Corp., Dallas, 1982-84; CFO, A.H. Belo Corp., Dallas, 1984-86, pres., COO, 1987-93, CEO, 1993-99; pres., CEO, chmn. Goss Graphic Systems, Westmont, Ill., 1999—. Mem. devel. bd. U. Tex.-Dallas, 1985—; bd. dirs. United Way, The Dallas Partnership, The Dallas Morning News Charities; trustee St. Paul Med. Ctr. Found. Served to Lt. (j.g.) USN, 1967-69, Vietnam. Mem. Am. Newspaper Pubs. Assn., So. Newspaper Pubs. Assn. Roman Catholic. Avocations: tennis, racquetball, golf, running. Office: Goss International 3 Territorial Ct Bolingbrook IL 60440-3557

SHEEHAN, KEVIN EDWARD, venture capitalist; b. Deerfield, Mass., June 17, 1945; s. Walter Francis and Lillian (Fontaine) S.; m. Barbara Ann Frank, July 6, 1974; children: Timothy John, James Frank. BA, Williams Coll., 1966; MBA, Harvard U., 1971. Traffic mgr. New England Tel., Boston, 1966-69; foreman H Block Line Cummins Engine Co., Columbus, Ind., 1971, employee rels. mgr., 1972-75, dir. employee rels., 1975-77, mgr. engine plant, 1977-80, v.p. mgmt. systems, 1980-83, v.p. parts, 1984, v.p. parts and distbn., 1984-86, v.p. components group, 1986; gen. ptnr. CID Equity Partners, 1994—. Bd. dirs. One Call Comm., Hetsco, Inc., SPS Commerce; bd. observer SmartSignal, Emerald BioAg.; non-exec. chmn. Flowserve Corp. Pres., bd. dirs. Quinco Mental Health Ctr., Columbus, 1976-80, St. Agnes Parish, Nashville, Ind., 1980-84. Mem. Country of Brown County Club (Nashville, Ind.), pres., bd. dirs. 1984-88). Avocations: golf, reading, nature study. Office: CID Capital 1 American Sq Ste 2850 Indianapolis IN 46282 Office Phone: 317-269-2350. Business E-Mail: kevins@cidcap.com.

SHEEHAN, LAWRENCE JAMES, lawyer; b. San Francisco, July 23, 1932; BA, Stanford U., 1957, LLB, 1959. Bar: Calif. 1960. Law clk. to chief judge U.S. Ct. Appeals 2d Cir., N.Y.C., 1959-60; assoc. O'Melveny & Myers, L.A., 1960-68, ptnr., 1969-94, of counsel, 1995—2004. D. dirs. FPA Mut. Funds, Source Capital, Inc. Mem. ABA, Los Angeles County Bar Assn., Calif. Bar Assn., Order of Coif. Office: O Melveny & Myers 1999 Avenue Of The Stars Los Angeles CA 90067-6035 also: 400 S Hope St Los Angeles CA 90071-2801 Office Phone: 310-246-6895. Business E-Mail: lsheehan@omm.com.

SHEEHAN, MICHAEL ANDREW, former protective services official, former federal agency administrator; b. Red Bank, N.J., Feb. 10, 1955; s. John M. and Janet M. (Purcell) S.; m. Sita Sheehan; children: Alexandra, Michael BS, US Mil. Acad., 1977; MS in Fgn. Svc., Georgetown U., 1988. Commd. 2d lt. U.S. Army, 1977-97, advanced through grades to lt. col., ret., 1997; intelligence analyst The White House, Washington, 1989-91; dir. internat. programs NSC, Washington, 1992-93, dir. global issues, 1995-97; dir. POLMIL affairs U.S. Mission to UN, N.Y.C., 1993-95; dept. asst. sec. for internat. org. affairs US Dept. State, Washington, 1997-98, coord. for counter terrorism, 1998-2000; asst. sec. gen. Dept. Peacekeeping Ops. UN, NYC, 2001—03; dep. commr. counter-terrorism NY Police Dept., NYC, 2003—06; Disting. Fellow, Ctr. for Law & Security NYU Sch. Law, NYC, 2006—. Mem.: Coun. on Fgn. Rels., Spl. Forces Assn. Roman Catholic. Office: NYU Sch Law 110 W 3rd St Ste 224/5 New York NY 10012*

SHEEHAN, MICHAEL JARBOE, archbishop; b. Wichita, Kans., July 9, 1939; s. John Edward and Mildred (Jarboe) Sheehan. MST, Gregorian U., Rome, 1965; D of Canon Law, Lateran U., Rome, 1971. Ordained priest Roman Cath. Ch., 1964. Asst. gen. sec. Nat. Coun. Cath. Bishops, Washington, 1971—76; rector Holy Trinity Sem., Dallas, 1976—82; pastor Immaculate Conception Ch., Grand Prairie, Tex., 1982—83; bishop Diocese of Lubbock, Tex., 1983—93; archbishop Archdiocese of Santa Fe, Albuquerque, N.Mex., 1993—. Bd. dirs. Tex. Conf. of Chs.; past chmn. Am. Bd. Cath. Missions 1989—91. Contbr. articles to profl. jours. Trustee St. Mary Hosp., Lubbock, Tex., 1983—89, Cath. Relief Svcs., 1992—. Mem.: Serra Club (chaplain 1983—93, chmn. NCCB com. on Evangelization 1996—99, NCCB adminstrv. com. Washington). Avocations: skiing, racquetball. Office: Archdiocese Santa Fe 4000 Saint Josephs Pl NW Albuquerque NM 87120-1714

SHEEHAN, MIKE, advertising executive; m. Maureen Sheehan. Student, U.S. Naval Acad.; BA in English, St. Anselm Coll. With Leo Burnett, Chgo., Clarke Goward and Ingalls Quinn & Johnson, Boston; exec. creative dir. Hill Holliday, Connors, Cosmopolos Interpub. Group, Boston, DDB, Chgo., Hill Holliday, Connors, Cosmopulos Interpub. Group, NYC, 2000—02, pres., 2002—, CEO, 2003—. Vice chmn., bd. trustees St Anselm Coll. Named Nat. Creative Dir. of Yr., Adweek, 1998; recipient Grand Clio award, One Show Gold award, Cannes Lions award, Best of Show award, Hatch, Communication Arts award. Office: Hill Holliday Franfurt Balkind 622 3RD Ave #15 New York NY 10017-6710

SHEEHAN, NEIL, reporter, writer; b. Holyoke, Mass., Oct. 27, 1936; s. Cornelius Joseph and Mary (O'Shea) Sheehan; m. Susan Margulies, Mar. 30, 1965; children: Maria Gregory, Catherine Fair. AB cum laude, Harvard, 1958; LittD (hon.), Columbia Coll., Chgo., 1972; LHD (hon.), Am. Internat. Coll., 1990, U. Lowell, 1991. Vietnam bur. chief UPI, Saigon, 1962—64; reporter

N.Y. Times, N.Y.C., Djakarta, Saigon, Washington, 1964—72. Author: The Arnheiter Affair, 1972, A Bright Shining Lie: John Paul Vann and America in Vietnam, 1988 (Nat. Book award, 1988, Pulitzer Prize for gen. non-fiction, 1989, Robert F. Kennedy Book award, 1989, Vetty award Vietnam Vets. Ensemble Theatre Co., 1989, Spl. Achievement award Vietnam Vets. Am., 1989, Outstanding Investigative Reporting award Investigative Reporters and Editors Inc. of U. Mo. Sch. Journalism, 1989, Amb. award English Speaking Union, 1989, John F. Kennedy award Holyoke, Mass., 1989, selected by Modern Libr. as one of the 100 best works of non-fiction of the 20th century 1999, After the War Was Over: Hanoi and Saigon, 1992; contbr. articles and book revs. for popular mags., The Pentagon Papers, 1971. With U.S. Army, 1959—62. Recipient Louis M. Lyons award for conscience and integrity in journalism, 1964, Silver medal, Poor Richard Club, Phila., 1964, Cert. of Appreciation for best article on Asia, Overseas Press Club Am., 1967, 1st Ann. Drew Pearson prize for excellence in investigative reporting, 1971, Columbia Journalism award, 1972, 1989, Sidney Hillman Found. awards, 1972, 1988, Page One award, Newspaper Guild N.Y., 1972, Disting. Svc. award and Bronze medallion, Sigma Delta Chi, 1972, Citation of Excellence, Overseas Press Club, 1972, Lit. Lion award, N.Y. Pub. Libr., 1992; Guggenheim fellow, 1973—74, Adlai Stevenson fellow, 1973—75, Lehrman Inst. fellow, 1975—76, Rockefeller Found. fellow in humanities, 1976—77, Woodrow Wilson Internat. Ctr. for Scholars fellow, 1979—80. Mem.: Am. Acad. Achievement, Soc. Am. Historians, Lansdowne Club (London). Achievements include obtaining Pentagon Papers, 1971. Home and Office: 4505 Klingle St NW Washington DC 20016-3580

SHEEHAN, PATTY, professional golfer; b. Middlebury, Vt., Oct. 27, 1956; 4th ranked woman LPGA Tour, 1992; winner U.S. Women's Open, 1992, 94, McDonald's LPGA Championship, 1983-84, 93. Inductee LPGA Hall of Fame, 1993, Sports Illustrated Sportsman of the Yr., 1987. Achievements include being the winner for 31 LPGA Tournaments including Mazda Japan Classic, 1981, 88, Inamori Classic, 1982-83, 86, Orlando Lady Classic, 1982, Safeco Classic, 1982, 90, 95, LPGA Corning Classic, 1983, LPGA Championship, 1983-84, 93, Henredon Classic, 1983-84, Elizabeth Arden Classic, 1984, McDonald's Kids Classic, 1984, 90, Sarasota Classic, 1985-86, 88, J&B Scotch Pro AM, 1985, Konica San Jose Classic, 1986, Rochester Internat., 1989-90, 92, 95, Jamaica Classic, 1990, Ping-Cellular One Championship, 1990, Orix Hawaiian Ladies Open, 1991, Jamie Farr Toledo Classic, 1992, Weetabix Women's Brit. Open, 1992, U.S. Women's Open, 1992, 94, Mazda LPGA Championship, 1993, The Nabisco Championship, 1996; in 17 tournaments earning $179,453, 1997, 16 tournaments earning $342,391, 1996, 35th victory, Nabisco Dinah Shore earning 6th major champ. title, crossed $5 million mark in career earnings, 1996, winner Michelob Light Front Runner Awd. for leading most rounds in season, 1996. Office: LPGA 100 International Golf Dr Daytona Beach FL 32124-1092

SHEEHAN, ROBERT C., lawyer; b. NYC, Oct. 12, 1944; s. John Edward and Mary Elizabeth (Trede) Sheehan; m. Elizabeth Mary Mammen, Aug. 17, 1968; children: Elizabeth, Robert, William. Ba, Boston Coll., 1966; LLB, Univ. Pa., Phila., 1969. Bar: NY 1970. Joined Skadden, Arps, Slate, Meagher & Flom LLP, 1969, ptnr. NYC, 1978—94, exec. ptnr., 1994—. Head, founder, Financial Institutions Merger & Acquisition Group Skadden, Arps, Slate, Meagher & Flom LLP; counsel for fin. institutions in connection with their rels. with various state and fed. banking regulatory authorities; bd. dir. Lawyers'. Com. for Civil Rights Under Law; co-chair, Law Firm Pro Bono Project Pro Bono Inst. Mem. bd. overseers U. Pa. Law Sch.; bd. dir. Harlem RBI. Mem.: Assn. of the Bar of City of NY. Office: Skadden Arps Slate Meagher Flom LLP 4 Times Sq New York NY 10036-6595 Office Phone: 212-735-3350. Office Fax: 212-735-2000, 917-777-3350. Business E-Mail: rsheehan@skadden.com.

SHEEHAN, ROBERT JAMES, II, management and market research consultant; b. Pitts., May 13, 1937; s. Regis James and Helen Lillian (O'Leary) S.; m. Marie Elizabeth Yoskovich, Apr. 24, 1964; children: Stephanie Ann, Robert James III. AB in Econs., U. Pitts., 1967, MA, 1970; postgrad., Am. U. Cert. mgmt. cons. Rsch. analyst Action Housing Inc., Pitts., 1960-63; from project rep. to dir. rehab. Urban Redevel. Authority Pitts., 1963-73; assoc. chief economist, dir. econ. rsch. Nat. Assn. Homebuilders, Washington, 1973-82, v.p econ. policy analysis, 1982-83; v.p. Regis J. Sheehan & Assocs., McLean, Va., 1983-96, pres., 1997—. Founding dir. Georgetown Cons., Inc., 1993—; vice-chmn. Fairfax County Housing and Redevel. Authority, 1988-92, chmn. 1993-95. cons. in field. Author: The Basics of Land Acquisition, 1985; co-pub., prin. contbr. Mgmt./Econs. & Constrn. Real Estate newsletters; contbr. articles to profl. jours. Pres. bd. dirs. Touchstone Theatre Co., 1984-2003; pres. Caths. for Housing, 1998-2003; founding mem. Supporter Bus. Roundtable. Mem. ASTD, Nat. Economists Club, Inst. Mgmt. Cons. (pres. Washington chpt. 1989-96), Nat. Assn. Bus. Econs., KC Soc. for Human Resource Mgmt. Roman Catholic. Avocations: walking, jogging, reading. E-mail: rjscmc@erols.com.

SHEEHAN, SAMANTHA, gymnast; b. Cin., May 20, 1986; d. Kevin and Cindy Sheehan. Gymnast Cincinnati Gymnastics/U.S. Natl. Team, 2002—. Achievements include Level 10 National Bar Champion; Level 10 State Champion; Qualified to 2001, 02 U.S. Gymnastics Championships, World Championships, 2002; Bronze Medal Floor Exercise, World Championships, 2002; 1st place All Around, USA-Belgium dual competition, 2003. Office: 3635 Woodbridge Blvd Fairfield OH 45014

SHEEHAN, SOPHIA ANN, marriage and family therapist, director; b. San Gabriel, Calif., May 13, 1972; d. Mary Angela and Henry C. Gonzalez; m. Joseph Scott Sheehan, Apr. 13, 1996. BA, U. of So. Calif., 1990—94; M, Peperdine U., 1994—96. Lic. Marriage and Family Therapist Bd. of Behavioral Sci., Calif., 2000. Marriage and family therapist trainee Family Assessment Counseling and Ednl. Services, Fullerton, Calif., 1996—97; marriage and family therapist intern Mid Valley Learning Ctr., Baldwin Park, Calif., 1997—99; clin. social worker Canyon Acres Children's Services, Anaheim Hills, Calif., 1999—2002; clin. program supr. Canal St. Elm. Sch. (TEC/Olive Crest), Orange, Calif., 2002—04; site dir. Therapeutic Edn. Ctr., Bellflower, Calif., 2004—. Mem.: Am. Assn. of Marriage and Family Therapists. Catholic. Avocations: crocheting, dance, travel.

SHEEHAN, SUSAN, writer; b. Vienna, Aug. 24, 1937; arrived in U.S., 1941, naturalized, 1946; d. Charles and Kitty C. (Herrmann) Sachsel; m. Neil Sheehan, Mar. 30, 1965; children: Maria Gregory, Catherine Fair. BA, Wellesley Coll., 1958; DHL (hon.), U. Lowell, 1991. Editl. rschr. Esquire-Coronet, N.Y.C., 1959-60; freelance writer N.Y.C., 1960-61; staff writer New Yorker mag., N.Y.C., 1961—; contbg. writer Archtl. Digest, 1997—. Writer-in-residence, lectr. Georgetown U., 1999. Author: Ten Vietnamese, 1967, A Welfare Mother, 1976, A Prison and a Prisoner, 1978, Is There No Place on Earth for Me?, 1982, Kate Quinton's Days, 1984, A Missing Plane, 1986, Life For Me Ain't Been No Crystal Stair, 1993, The Banana Sculptor, the Purple Lady, and the All-Night Swimmer, 2002; contbr. articles to various mags., including N.Y. Times Sunday Mag., Washington Post Sunday Mag., Harper's, Atlantic, New Republic, McCall's, Holiday, Boston Globe Sunday Mag., Life. Judge Robert F. Kennedy Journalism awards, 1980, 84; mem. lit. panel D.C. Commn. on Arts and Humanities, 1979-84; mem. pub. info. and edn. com. Nat. Mental Health Assn., 1982-83; mem. adv. com. on employment and crime Vera Inst. Justice, 1978-86; chair Pulitzer Prize nominating jury in gen. non-fiction for 1988, 1994, mem., 1991. Recipient Sidney Hillman Found. award, 1976, Gavel award ABA, 1978, Individual Reporting award Nat. Mental Health Assn., 1981, Pulitzer prize for gen. non-fiction, 1983, Feature Writing award N.Y. Press Club, 1984, Alumnae Assn. Achievement award Wellesley Coll., 1984, Carroll Kowal Journalism award NASW, 1993, Disting. Grad. award Hunter Coll. H.S., 1995, Pub. Awareness award Nat. Alliance for Mentally Ill, 1995, Casey medal for meritorious journalism, 1997; Durant scholar Wellesley Coll., 1958; fellow Guggenheim Found., 1975-76, Woodrow Wilson Internat. Ctr. for Scholars, 1981, Open Soc. Inst., 1998-99. Mem.: Soc. Am. Historians, Authors Guild, Lansdowne Club (London), Phi Beta Kappa. Home: 4505 Klingle St NW Washington DC 20016-3580 Office: New Yorker Mag 4 Times Sq New York NY 10036-7441

SHEEHAN, TIMOTHY J., lawyer; b. Beacon, NY, Apr. 28, 1959; BA magna cum laude, SUNY, Buffalo, 1981; JD, U. Buffalo, 1984. Bar: NY 1985, US Dist. Ct. Ea. Dist. NY, US Dist. Ct. So. Dist. NY. Ptnr. Wilson, Elser, Moskowitz, Edelman & Dicker LLP, White Plains, NYC. Mem.: NY State Med. Malpractice Def. Bar, NY State Bar Assn., Westchester County Bar Assn. Office: Wilson Elser Moskowitz Edelman & Dicker LLP 3 Gannett Dr White Plains NY 10604 Office Phone: 914-323-7000 ext. 4243. Office Fax: 914-323-7001. Business E-Mail: sheehan@wemed.com.

SHEEHY, BARRY MAURICE, management consultant; b. Nov. 17, 1951; came to the U.S., 1991; BA in History, Econs. cum laude, Loyola Coll., 1975; MA in History, McGill U., 1977; Comms. & Electronics and Engring., Can. Forces Sch. Comm. Electronic Engring. Officer Canadian Armed Forces, Savannah, Ga., 1975-80; quality mgr. City of Calgary, 1980-85; mgr. orgnl. efectiveness No. Telecom, 1985-87; pres. Achieve Internat., 1987-91, CPC Econometrics, Inc., 1991-94, CPC Econometrics Inc., Savannah, Ga., 1997—; ptnr. The Atlanta Cons. Group, 1994-96, Sentry Technology Group, 1996-97; pres. & CEO CPC Econometrics Inc., Savannah, Ga., 1998—. Mem. faculty Estes Pk.(Healthcare) Inst., Healthcare Governance Inst., Healthcare Forum; guest spkr. U.S.C. of C., Quality Coun. Can., Quality Coun. Mex., Microsoft Healthcare Forum, INC 500, Am. Express Bank Global Forum, others. Author: In Search of Quality: 4 Unique Perspectives, 43 Different Views (Exec. Excellence 1995); (with others) Firing on All Cylinders, 1992, Game Plans for Success, 1995, Economic Divide: Winners and Losers in an Age of Abundance, 1996, Winning the Race for Value, 1996, Smart Business, 2001; contbr. articles to profl. jours. Guest spkr. SCLC, Savannah Found. Officer Can. Armed Forces. Co-recipient Am. Soc. Indsl. Engrs. award, 1985. Office: CPC Econometrics Inc 38 Mulberry Bluff Dr Savannah GA 31406-3269

SHEEHY, BETTY JO, real estate company executive, investment advisor; b. Baileysville, W.Va., Oct. 1, 1936; d. Virgil and Virginia Graham Lester; m. John D. Sheehy, Sept. 21, 1963 (div. 1976); children: John, Peter, Barbara. Student, Marshall U., 1956; lic. in real estate, Southampton Coll., 2002. Fin. cons. Merrill Lynchnnnnn, Short Hills, NJ, 1984—90; fin. adv., assoc. v.p. Morgan Stanley, Southampton, NY, 1991—2002; owner, broker Betty Jo Sheehy Real Estate, Southampton, 2002—. Chpt. pres. NJ Symphony Women League, Short Hills, 1977—81; vol. Red Cross of the Oranges, NJ, 1970; benefactor Parish Art Mus., Southampton, 1999—. Named Bus. Woman of Yr., Nat. Congressional Com., 2006; recipient Leadership Devel. award, Merrill Lynch, 1985—86. Avocations: golf, music, reading, running. Home and Office: PO Box 2363 Southampton NY 11969 Office Phone: 516-318-5647.

SHEEHY, JEROME JOSEPH, electrical engineer; b. Hartford, Conn., Dec. 3, 1935; s. Jeremiah and Anna (Foley) S.; m. Jean Ann Baldassari, Oct. 13, 1962; children: Caroline, Jerome, Daniel, Carlene. BSEE, U. Conn., 1962, MSEE, 1967. Electronic engr. USN Underwater Sound Lab., New London, Conn., 1962-69; mem. tech. staff Rockwell Internat., Anaheim, Calif., 1969-74; staff engr. Hughes Aircraft Co., Fullerton, Calif., 1974-83; systems engr. Norden Systems, Santa Ana, Calif., 1983-89; advanced engring. specialist Lockheed Martin Aircraft Svc., Ontario, Calif., 1990-97. Contbr. articles to Jour. Acoustical Soc. Am. With USAF, 1954-57. Mem. Tau Beta Pi, Eta Kappa Nu Achievements include research in detection and estimation theory for non-gaussian noise, non-normal statistics. Home: 8 Sagitta Way Coto De Caza CA 92679-5102 Personal E-mail: jandjsheehy@cox.net.

SHEEHY, RICK, lieutenant governor; m. Connie Sheehy; children: Maggie, Joel. Attended, Ctrl. CC, U. Nebr.-Lincoln. City coun. mem., Hastings, Nebr., 1994—2005; mayor, 2000—05; lt. gov. State of Nebr., 2005—, dir. Homeland Security, chmn. Nebr. Info. Tech. Commn., presiding officer Nebr. Legislature, 2005—. Market gen. mgr., paramedic Rural/Metro Ambulance, 1982—; Exec. com. mem. Cottonwood Festival, mem. Nebr. State Trauma Adv. Bd., Mary Lanning Hosp. Found. Bd., Crane Meadows Bd. Dirs., Nebr. Rural Health Assn. Mem.: Hastings C. of C. (former chair), Hastings Noon Rotary, Hastings Sertoma Club (past pres.). Republican. Office: Lt Gov State Capitol, Rm 2315 PO Box 94863 Lincoln NE 68509-4863 Office Phone: 402-471-2256. Office Fax: 402-471-6031.

SHEEHY, ROBERT J., insurance company executive; V.p., gen. mgr. Lincoln Nat. Corpn.; with UnitedHealthcare, UnitedHealth Grp., Minnetonka, Minn., 1992—, CEO, UnitedHealthcare Ohio, 1994—98, pres. UnitedHealthcare, 1998—2000, CEO UnitedHealthcare, 2000—. Office: UnitedHealth Grp 9900 Bren Rd E Minnetonka MN 55343

SHEELER, JIM, journalist; b. Tex., 1969; m. Annick Sheeler; 1 child, James. BA, Colo. State U., 1990. With Boulder (Colo.) Daily Camera, 1991—96; sr. staff writer Boulder Planet, 1996—2000; freelance writer Denver Post, 1999—2003; staff writer Rocky Mountain News, Denver, 2004—. Contbr. (books) Life On the Death Beat, 2005. Recipient Pulitzer Prize for feature writing, 2006. Office: Rocky Mountain News 100 Gene Amole Way Denver CO 80204 Office Phone: 303-892-2561. Office Fax: 303-892-2841. E-mail: sheelerj@rockymountainnews.com.*

SHEEN, CHARLIE (CARLOS IRWIN ESTEVEZ), actor; b. NYC, Sept. 3, 1965; s. Ramon (Martin Sheen) and Janet Estevez; m. Donna Peele, Sept. 3, 1995 (div. 1996); m. Denise Richards, June 15, 2002 (separated); children: Sam, Lola; 1 child, Cassandra. Appearances include (film) Grizzly II: The Predator, 1984, Red Dawn, 1984, The Boys Next Door, 1985, Ferris Bueller's Day Off, 1986, Lucas, 1986, Platoon, 1986, Wisdom, 1986, The Wraith, 1986, A Life in the Day, 1986, Wall Street, 1987, No Man's Land, 1987, Three for the Road, 1987, Eight Men Out, 1988, Young Guns, 1988, Major League, 1989, Never on Tuesday, 1989, (also prodr.) Comicitis, 1989, Courage Mountain, 1990, Navy SEALS, 1990, Backtrack, 1990, Hot Shots!, 1990, Men At Work, 1990, The Rookie, 1990, Cadence, 1991, Beyond the Law (aka Fixing the Shadow), 1992, Hot Shots, Part Deux, 1993, The Three Musketeers, 1993, Loaded Weapon I, 1993, Deadfall, 1993, (also exec. prodr.) The Chase, 1994, Major League 2, 1994, Terminal Velocity, 1994, The Shadow Conspiracy, 1995, Shockwave, 1995, Loose Women, 1996, (voice) All Dogs Go to Heaven 2, 1996, The Arrival, 1996, Postmortem, 1997, Bad Day On the Block, 1997, Money Talks, 1997, (also writer, narrator) Mission to Mars, 1997, (also exec. prodr., writer) No Code of Conduct, 1998, Free Money, 1998, Letter From Death Row, 1998, Five Acres, 1999, Being John Malkovich, 1999, Rated X, 2000, Famous, 2000, Good Advice, 2001, Scary Movie 3, 2003, Deeper Than Deep, 2003, The Big Bounce, 2004; (TV movies) Execution of Private Slovik, 1974, Silence of the Heart, 1984, The Fourth Wise Man, 1985, Out of the Darkness, 1985; (tv series) Sugar Hill, 1999, Spin City, 2000-02 (Golden Globe award bext actor, 2001), Two and a Half Men, 2003-.*

SHEEN, MARTIN (RAMON ESTEVEZ), actor; b. Dayton, Ohio, Aug. 3, 1940; s. Francisco and Mary Ann (Phelan) Estevez; m. Janet Sheen, Dec. 23, 1961; children: Emilio, Ramon, Carlos, Renee. Grad. high sch. Made NY stage debut as mem. Living Theatre in The Connection, 1959; Broadway debut in Never Live Over a Pretzel Factory, 1964; other stage appearances include The Subject Was Roses, 1964-66, The Wicked Crooks, 1967, Hamlet, 1967, Romeo and Juliet, 1968, Hello and Goodbye, 1969, The Happiness Cage, 1970, Death of a Salesman, 1975, Julius Caesar, 1988; film appearances include The Incident, 1967, The Subject Was Roses, 1968, Catch-22, 1970, No Drums, No Bugles, 1971, Rage, 1972, Badlands, 1973, The Legend of Earl Durand, 1974, The Cassandra Crossing, 1976, The Little Girl Who Lives Down the Lane, 1977, Apocalypse Now, 1979, The Final Countdown, 1980, Gandhi, 1982, That Championship Season, 1982, The King of Prussia, 1982, No Place to Hide, 1983, The Dead Zone, 1983, Man, Woman, and Child, 1983, Enigma, 1983, Eagle's Wing, 1983, Firestarter, 1984, The Believers, 1987, Wall Street, 1987, Siesta, 1987, Judgement in Berlin, 1988, Walking After Midnight, 1988, Da, 1988 (exec. producer, dir.), Beverly Hills Brats, 1989, Cadence, 1991 (dir.), JFK, 1991 (narrator), Hot Shots, Part Deux!, 1993 (cameo), Hear No Evil, 1993, Gettysburg, 1993, The Break, 1995, The

American President, 1995, The War At Home, 1996, Truth or Consequences, 1997, Spawn, 1997, Letter From Death Row, 1998, Stranger in the Kingdom, 1998, Storm, 1998, Monument Avenue, 1998, Free Money, 1998, Catch Me If You Can, 2002, The Departed, 2006; TV series include As the World Turns, The Edge of Night, The West Wing, 1999-2006 (Golden Globe award, 2001, SAG award, 2001, 2002); TV movies and miniseries include Then Came Bronson, 1969, The Subject Was Roses, 1969, Mongo's Back in Town, 1971, Welcome Home, Johnny Bristol, 1972, That Certain Summer, 1972, Catholics, 1973, The Execution of Private Slovik, 1974, The California Kid, 1974, The Story of Pretty Boy Floyd, 1974, The Missiles of October, 1974, Sweet Hostage, 1975, The Last Survivors, 1975, Blind Ambition, 1979, Taxi!!, 1978, The Long Road Home, 1980, Fly Away Home, 1981, Kennedy, 1982, Choices of the Heart, 1983, The Atlanta Child Murders, 1985, Consenting Adult, 1985, Out of Darkness, 1985, Shattered Spirits, 1986, Samaritan, 1986, News at Eleven, 1986, Babies Having Babies (dir.), 1986, Conspiracy: The Trial of the Chicago 8, 1987, No Means No (exec. producer), Night Breaker, 1989, Project Alf, 1996, Marlon Brando: The Wild One, 1996, D.R.E.A.M. Team, 1999; TV appearances include Mannix, 1967, The Streets of San Francisco, 1972, Murphy Brown, 1988 (Emmy award, Guest Actor - Comedy Series, 1994), The Simpsons (voice), 1989, The Great War, 1996, The Elevator, 1996, Entertaining Angels, 1996, Spin City, 1996, Medussa's Child, 1997, 187 Documented, 1997, Titanic: Anatomy of a Disaster (narrator), 1997, Tudjman (narrator), 1997 Babylon 5: The River of Souls, 1998, Letter From Death Row, 1998, Ambrose Chapel, 1998, Gunfighter, 1998, No Code of Conduct, 1998, Shadrach (voice), 1998, Stranger in the Kingdom, 1998, Talk of the Town, 1998, Voyage of Terror, 1998, Celebrity Poker Showdown, 2003. Named Favorite Actor in a New Series, TV Guide Awards; recipient Lifetime Achievement award, Imagen Found., 1998. Roman Catholic.*

**SHEERAN, MAUREEN FLYNN,** retired secondary school educator; b. Lewiston, N.Y., May 10, 1946; d. Edward and Ursula (Trank) Flynn; m. Thomas J. Sheeran, June 27, 1970; children: Meaghan, Brendan. BA in English, Niagara U., 1968, MEd in Counseling, 1973, MEd in Administrn., 1993, CEA, 1975. Cert. tchr. elem. edn., secondary English, counseling, adminstrn., N.Y. Secondary English tchr. Niagara Falls (N.Y.) City Sch. Dist. 1968-87, 90—, tchr. on spl. assignment, instructional team leader, 1987-90, guidance and couseling, 1994—2001; ret., 2003. Publs. chmn./editor: College Club, Niagara Falls, 1986-88. Mem. exec. com. Porter Cup Golf Tourney; v.p. Lewiston Svc. Guild. Mem. Niagara Falls C. of C., Niagara County Decorative Painters Soc., Youngstown Garden Club, Alpha Delta Kappa, Phi Delta Kappa. Home: 5230 Hewitt Pky Lewiston NY 14092 Business E-Mail: tjs@niagara.edu.

**SHEERAN, MICHAEL JOHN LEO,** priest, academic administrator; b. NYC, Jan. 24, 1940; s. Leo John and Glenna Marie (Wright) Sheeran. AB, St. Louis U., 1963, PhL, 1964, AM in Polit. Sci., 1967, AM in Theology, 1971, STL, 1971; PhD, Princeton U., 1977. Joined Soc. of Jesus, 1957, ordained priest Roman Cath. Ch., 1970. Exec. editor Catholic Mind., N.Y.C., 1971-72; assoc. editor Am. Mag., N.Y.C., 1971-72; assoc. chaplain Aquinas Inst., Princeton, NJ, 1972-75; asst. dean Regis U., Denver, 1975-77; dean Regis Coll., Denver, 1977-82, v.p. acad. affairs, 1982-92, acting pres., 1987-88, pres., 1993—. Retreat dir., cons. governance religious cmtys., 1970—. Author: Beyond Majority Rule, 1984; contbr. articles and editls. to publs. Trustee Regis Jesuit HS, 1999—2005; chmn. Mile High United Way, Denver, 1999—2000; nat. bd. dirs. Campus Compact, 2002—; trustee Rockhurst Coll., Kansas City, Mo., 1982—91, Creighton U., Omaha, 1985—95, U. San Francisco, 1985—94, 2001—, Loyola U., New Orleans, 1994—96, Rocky Mountain Coll. Art and Design, Denver, 1994—99; mem. adv. bd. Cmty. Coll. Aurora, Colo., 2001—; bd. dirs. Colo. Inst. Tech., 2001—. Ford Found. scholar, 1963. Democrat. Roman Catholic. Home: 3333 Regis Blvd Denver CO 80221-1099 Office: Regis U 3333 Regis Blvd Denver CO 80221-1099 Office Phone: 303-458-4190. Business E-Mail: president@regis.edu.

**SHEETS, BEN,** professional baseball player; b. Baton Rouge, La., July 18, 1978; Attended, Northeast La. State. Pitcher Milw. Brewers, 2001—. Named to NL All-Star Team, 2001, AL All-Star Team, 2004. Office: Miller Park 46th St Milwaukee WI 53201*

**SHEETS, NELDA,** artist; b. Roger Mills County, Okla., Oct. 31, 1931; d. Merril Ezra and Alice (Tucker) Johnson; m. Willis Davis Sheets, Nov. 12, 1949; children: Steve, Dana. Instr. Silva Method of Mind Devel., Laredo, Tex., 1967—; lectr., author Creativity Workshop, Tex., 1968—; artist Sunset Art Gallery, Amarillo, Tex., 2005—. Trainer of instrs. Silva Method, 1971-85, conv. dir., 1973-80. Author: (book) Creative Study Skills, 1990, The Creativity Workshop, 1968, Silva Stories, 2006; presenter workshop Creative Parenting. Pres. Area Arts Found., Amarillo, 1986; adv. com. Amarillo Coll. Adult Program, 1991. Democrat. Methodist. Personal E-mail: nelsheets@aol.com.

**SHEETS, THOMAS R.,** lawyer, gas industry executive; BA, Ashland U., 1973; JD, U. Toledo, 1975. Bar: Ohio 1975, Nev. 1982, Tex. 1986. Sr. atty. Tex. Eastern Corp., 1985—87; litig. atty. Southwest Gas Corp., Las Vegas, 1987—89, assoc. gen. counsel, 1989—90, dir. regulatory affairs, 1990—94, asst. gen. counsel, 1994—96, v.p., gen. counsel, 1996—98, sr. v.p., gen. counsel, 1998—. Mem. Nev. Tax Commn., chair; former mem. Nev. Standing Com. Jud. Ethics. Mem.: ABA, Am. Arbitration Assn., Energy Bar Assn., Am. Gas Assn., Clark County Bar Assn. (pres. 1995). Office: Southwest Gas Corp 5241 Spring Mountain Rd Las Vegas NV 89193-8510 E-mail: thom.sheets@swgas.com.

**SHEETZ, STANTON R.,** grocery retail executive; b. May 26, 1955; BS, Bentley Coll.; MBA, Pace U., NY. With Colt Industries, 1977-81; exec. v.p., dir. Sheetz Inc. Altoona, Pa, 1981—91, CEO, 1997—; dir. Dir. Omega Bank, 1994—, Hollidaysburg Trust, 1996—, PBS. Mem.: Nat. Assn. Convenience Stores (vice chmn. 2000—). Office: Sheetz Inc 5700 6th Ave Altoona PA 16602*

**SHEFFER, CHRISTOPHER RYAN,** land surveyor; b. Harrisonburg, Va., Dec. 15, 1951; s. Jerry Lewis and Donna Kaye Sheffer. Correctional officer Va. Dept. Corrections, Staunton, 2001—02; security officer Mary Baldwin Coll., Staunton, Va., 2002—03; land surveyor Hamrick Engring., Verona, Va., 2003—. Vol. firefighter Churchville Fire Dept., Va., 1997—2005. Cpl. USMC, 2000—06. Republican. Methodist. Avocations: backpacking, hiking, canoeing. Office Phone: 540-248-7407. E-mail: ffemt455@aol.com.

**SHEFFER, JAMES THOMAS,** music educator, elementary school educator; b. Phila., May 27, 1970; s. James F. and Antoinette Patricia Sheffer; m. Terri Lynn Huffman, June 25, 1994; children: Victoria Lynn, Jamie Lynn. BS in Music Edn., West Chester U., 1992; MA in Edn. Adminstrn. and Supervision, U. Phoenix, 2004, MA in Edn. Curriculum and Instrn., 2005. Cert. music tchr. grades K-12 State of NJ., 1992, Commonwealth of Pa., 1992. Tchr. music, band dir. Medford Lakes Neeta Sch., NJ, 2001—04; dir. instrumental music Medford Meml. Mid. Sch./Haines 6th Grade Ctr., 2004—. Dir. instrumental music Manchester Twp. H.S., Lakehurst, NJ, 1996—2001. Dir.: (marching band director) Salute to the 50s and 60s (US Scholastic Band Assn. Group I Champions, 2001). Grantee Excellence in Edn., Medford Lakes Edn. Found., 2003. Mem.: ASCD, NAESP, N.J. Music Educators Assn., Music Educators Nat. Conf., Olympic Conf. Band Dirs. Assn., Internat. Assn. Jazz Edn., South Jersey Band and Orch. Dirs. Assn. (treas. 1996—2000). Roman Catholic. Achievements include development of Scales, Chorales, and Arpeggios for Band Warm-up. Avocations: music, fishing, swimming, travel. Home: 218 Kihade Trail Medford Lakes NJ 08055 Office: Medford Township Memorial Middle Sch 55 Mill St Medford NJ 08055 Office Phone: 609-654-7707 8231. Home Fax: 609-953-6929. Personal E-mail: jimsheffer@aol.com. E-mail: jsheffer@medford.k12.nj.us.

**SHEFFERY, MICHAEL B.,** investment company executive; BA in biology, Princeton U.; PhD in molecular biology. Head of lab, gene structure and expression Meml. Sloan-Kettering Cancer Ctr.; sr. analyst, biotechnology

Mehta, 1996, Isaly, 1997; dir. NeoGenesis Pharm., Biosynexus Inc., Memory Pharm. Corp.; mng. gen. ptnr. Orbimed Advisors, LLC, N.Y.C., 1996—. Office: Orbimed Advisors LLC 767 Third Ave 30th Fl New York NY 10017

**SHEFFEY, RUTHE T.,** language educator; m. Vernon R. Sheffey, Dec. 29, 1950; children: Illona Sheffey Rawlings, Renata Sheffey Strong. BA, Morgan State U., Balt., 1947; MA, Howard U., 1949; PhD, U. Pa., 1959. Prof. English Morgan State U., Balt., 1949—, chair dept. English, 1970-76. Author: Impressions in Asphalt, 1969, Trajectory (My Collected Essays), 1989; editor Zora Neale Hurston Forum, 1986—. Named Mid. Outstanding Faculty Mem. of Yr., 1994, Disting. Scholar in African-Am. Studies for Yr., Towson State U., 2002, Sheroe as Honor, Women for Responsive Govt., Inc., 2003; named to Morgan State U. Hall of Fame, 2000. Mem. Nat. Coun. Tchrs. English (past mem. coll. bd.), Coll. English Assn. (past pres. Mid. Atlantic Group), Zora Neale Hurston Soc. (founder, 1984, pres.), Langston Hughes Soc. (past pres.), other lit. socs., Alpha Kappa Alpha (Golden mem.). Mem. United Ch. of Christ. Avocations: reading, theatre-going, dance. E-mail: rsheffey@moac.morgan.edu.

**SHEFFI, YOSSI,** engineering educator, researcher; b. Jerusalem, 1948; BSc, Technion, 1975; MS, Mass. Inst. Tech., 1976, PhD, 1978. Prof. civil and environ. engring., dir. ctr. transp. and logistics Mass. Inst. Tech., Cambridge, Mass., founder Master of Engring. Logistics Program, 1997. Co-founder Logicorp, 1988, co-owner, 1991—94; co-founder Princeton Transp. Consulting Group, 1987, owner, chmn., cons., 1992—96; co-founder Syncra, 1997, e-Chemicals, 1997, Home Preview Channel; founder, CEO Logistics.com, 1999—2000, chmn. bd., 2000—; spkr. in field. Author: Urban Transportation Networks: Equilibrium Analysis with Mathematical Programming Methods, 1995, The Resilient Enterprise: Overcoming Vulnerability for Competitive Advantage, 2005; contbr. articles to profl. jours. Capt. Israeli Air Force, 1966—71. Recipient Disting. Svc. award, Coun. Logistics Mgmt., 1997. Achievements include development of computerized decision support systems for LTL and TL motor carrier operations, rail car distribution, vehicle routing and scheduling, and other various carrier problems; decision support systems used by shippers. Office: Mass Inst Tech 77 Massachusetts Ave Rm E40-275 Cambridge MA 02139-4307 Office Phone: 617-253-5316. Business E-Mail: sheffi@mit.edu.

**SHEFFIELD, GARY ANTONIAN,** professional baseball player; b. Tampa, Fla., Nov. 18, 1968; Baseball player Milw. Brewers, 1986-92, San Diego Padres, 1992-93, Florida Marlins, 1993-98, L.A. Dodgers, 1999—2001, Atlanta Braves, 2002—03, N.Y. Yankees, 2004—. Named Nat. League All-Star Team, 1992-93, 96, 98, 99, 2000, 2003, Am. League All-Star Team, 2004; Sporting News Player of the Year, 1992; Comeback Player of Yr., Sporting News, 1992; Silver Slugger award, MLB, 2005. Nat. Batting League Champion, 1992. Office: c/o NY Yankees Yankee Stadium E 161 St and River Ave Bronx NY 10451*

**SHEFFIELD, GREG,** liberal media blogger; Co-founder RatherBiased.com, 2000; editor NewsBusters.org, 2005—. Work has been featured by CNN, MSNBC, Fox News Channel, NY T. Office: Media Rsch Ctr 325 S Patrick St Alexandria VA 22314 E-mail: gsheffield@mediaresearch.org.*

**SHEFFIELD, JEFFREY T.,** lawyer; b. Oct. 1954; BA phi beta kappa, U. Chgo., 1976; JD, Harvard Law Sch., 1979. Bar: Ill. 1980. Law clk. Mass. Supreme Jud. Ct., Mass., 1979—80; ptnr., mem. firm mgmt. com. Kirkland & Ellis LLP, Chgo. Former adj. prof. IIT/ Chgo. Kent Coll. Law; former lecturer U. Chgo. Sch. Law. Achievements include author, "Organizing the Corp. Venture" (Aspen Law & Bus. 1988); co-author, "How VC/PE Funds Can Deliver Spl. LTCG Tax Benefits to Individual LPs & GPs". Office: Kirkland & Ellis LLP 200 E Randolph Dr Chicago IL 60601 Home: 125 Laurel Ave Wilmette IL 60091-2830 Office Phone: 312-861-2454. Office Fax: 312-861-2200. Business E-Mail: jsheffield@kirkland.com.

**SHEFFIELD, JUSTIN,** hydrologist, researcher; b. Basingstoke, Hampshire, Nov. 24, 1968; arrived in US, 2000; s. Brian Sheffield and Davina Long; m. Catherine Jones, June 30, 2001; children: Talle, Medi. BSc in Math. & Oceanography, U. Southampton, Eng., 1986—89; MSc in Engring. Math., U. Newcastle, Eng., 1990—91. Rsch. assoc. Newcastle U., England, 1991—99, sr. rsch. assoc., 1999—2000; profl. specialist Princeton U., NJ, 2000—. Contbr. articles to profl. jours. Mem.: Am. Geophys. Union. Office: Princeton Univ Dept Civil Eng Olden St Princeton NJ 08544

**SHEFFIELD, MATTHEW,** liberal media blogger; Co-founder RatherBiased.com, 2000; media and tech. cons., exec. editor NewsBusters.org, 2005—. Lectr. in field. Work has been featured in NY Times, Washington Post, BBC, Fox News Channel, CNN, MSNBC and the New Yorker; maintains personal blog site matthewsheffield.org. Mormon. Office: Media Rsch Ctr 325 S Patrick St Alexandria VA 22314*

**SHEFFIELD, NANCY,** city agency administrator; b. Mpls. BA in Sociology and Psychology, U. Minn., 1969; postgrad., U. Wis., 1992. Participant City of Aurora (Colo.) Supervisory Cert. Series Program, 1988-90. Social worker LeSueur County Human Svcs., Le Centre, Minn., 1969-71; quality control reviewer Minn. Dept. Human Svcs., St. Paul, 1971-74, quality control supr., 1974-75; neighborhood-planner City of Aurora, 1987, neighborhood support supr., 1987-94, acting mgr. Original Aurora Renewal, 1994-95, acting mgr. neighborhood support divsn., 1995, dir. neighborhood svcs., 1996—. Mem. PTO, vol. elem. sch. media ctr., 1980-86. Office: City Aurora Dept Neighborhood Svcs 15151 E Alameda Pkwy Aurora CO 80012 Office Phone: 303-739-7280. E-mail: nsheffie@auroragov.org.

**SHEFFIELD, SCOTT D.,** oil industry executive; BS in Petroleum Engring., U. Tex. Prodn. and reservoir engr. Amoco Prodn. Co.; petroleum engr. Parker & Parsley Devel. Co., 1979—85, v.p. engring., 1981—85, pres., bd. dirs., 1985—89, chmn., CEO, 1989; pres., bd. dirs. Parker & Parsley Petroleum Co., 1990—97, chmn., CEO, 1990—97; pres., CEO Pioneer Natural Resources, 1997—2000, chmn. bd. dirs., 1999—. Office: 1400 Williams Sq W Irving TX 75039

**SHEFFIELD, VAL C.,** medical geneticist; MD, PhD, U. Chgo. Pediat. resident U. Calif. San Francisco, med. genetics fellow; with U. Iowa, 1990—; prof. pediatrics U. Iowa Roy J. & Lucille A. Carver Coll. Medicine, Iowa City, dir. med. genetics div.; investigator Howard Hughes Med. Inst., 1998—. Mem.: Inst. Medicine. Office: U Iowa Hosp Med Genetics Div 200 Hawkins Dr Iowa City IA 52242 Office Phone: 319-356-2674. Office Fax: 319-356-3347. E-mail: val-sheffield@uiowa.edu.*

**SHEFTEL, ROGER TERRY,** merchant banker; b. Denver, Sept. 10, 1941; s. Edward and Dorothy (Barnett) S.; m. Phoebe A. Sherman, Sept. 7, 1968; children: Tisha B., Ryan B. BS in Econs., U. Pa., 1963. Comml. lending officer Provident Nat. Bank, Phila., 1963-65; asst. to pres. Continental Fin. Corp., Denver, 1965-68; v.p. Eastern Indsl. Leasing Corp., Phila., 1968-71, exec. v.p., dir., 1971-73; HBE Leasing Corp., Phila., 1971-73; dir. Kooly Kupp, Inc., Boyertown, Pa., 1974-77, pres., dir., 1977; prin. Trivest, Phila., 1973-77, pres., 1977-78, 1670 Corp., 1978-82, Am. Cons. Group, Inc., 1982-83; exec. v.p., dir. Argus Rsch. Labs., Inc., 1982-83; pres. Leasing Concepts, Inc., 1983-87, Brice Capital Corp., 1987-92, Rhodes Fin., Inc., 1992—. Dir. strategic planning Wharton Sch., U. Pa., 1999; pres. AttendBy-Web, Inc., 1999—, AssignByWeb, Inc., 1999—; CEO, chmn. FlyOff, Inc., 1998—. Mem.: Friars Club. Home: 414 Barclay Rd Bryn Mawr PA 19010-1218 Office: Rhodes Fin Inc PO Box 7338 Saint Davids PA 19087-7338

**SHEHAN, GERALDEAN HARRISON,** ESL educator; b. Dallas, Sept. 4, 1950; d. Jerrold Harrison and Violet Elizabeth Herndon; m. Thomas Nelson Shehan, Dec. 13, 1986; children: David Harrison Hardy, Daniel Patrict Hardy. BS in edn., Stephen F. Austin State U., 1973; MEd, North Tex. State U., 1984. Cert. Elem. Tchr. Self Contained grades 1-8 Tex. Edn. Agy., 1973, ESL grades

1-8 Tex. Edn. Agy., 1996, Reading Recovery Tex. Woman's U. 1998. Educator reading and ESL specialist Irving Ind. Sch. Dist., Tex., 1973—2003; testing diagnostician Knowledge Point Tutoring, Colleyville, Tex., 2004—; educator reading specialist NW Ind. Sch. Dist., Fort Worth, Tex., 2005—. Chairperson Elliott Campus Improvement Com., Irving, Tex., 1997—2002; adv. mem. IISD Dist. Improvement Com., Irving, Tex., 1999—2003; pres. elect Alpha Delta Kappa Tex. Beta Omicron Chpt., Irving, Tex., 1998—; mentor and grade level chair Irving ISD, Tex., 1990—2003. Mem. PTA; tchr. First United Meth. Ch., Irving, Tex., 1984—98. Recipient Irving Dist. Elem. Tchr. of the Yr., Irving Ind. Sch. Dist., 1999—2000, Outstanding Grad., 1990; grant, Irving Schools Found., 1988, 1988, 1995, 1997. Mem.: Internat. Reading Assn., Tex. Teachers of English to Speakers of Other Languages, Reading Recovery Coun. of N.Am., Parent Tchr. Assn. (life; bd. mem. 1990—2000), Kappa Delta Pi, Alpha Chi, Tex. Beta Omicron Chpt. of Alpha Delta Kappa (pres. elect 2004—). R-Conservative. Methodist. Avocations: outdoor activities, reading, travel, farming. Home: 1812 Krokus Dr Keller TX 76248 Office: Northwest Ind Sch Dist PO Box 77070 Fort Worth TX 76177-0070 Personal E-mail: gerishehan@verizon.net.

**SHEHI, LYLE EDWARD, JR.,** psychiatrist; b. Asheville, N.C., Jan. 15, 1947; s. Lyle Edward Shehi Sr. and Rebecca Hyatt Shehi; m. Jean Waide, Dec. 29, 1989. BA, U. Tenn., 1970, MD, 1973. Diplomate Am. Bd. Psychiatry. Commd. 2d. lt. U.S. Army, 1970, psychiatrist Ft. Polk, La., 1977—78, child and adolescent fellow Walter Reed Army Med. Ctr., 1978—80, chief psychiatry Ft. Polk, La., 1977—78, psychiatrist Ft. McCellan, Ala., 1980—82, dep. commdr. Noble Army Hosp., 1980—82, advanced through ranks to lt. col., 1981, ret., 1982; psychiatrist Birmingham Psychiatry PA, 1982—2004, v.p., 2000—04; psychiatrist Ctrl. Ala. Psychiatry, Birmingham, 2004—, mng. ptnr., 2004—. Chief psychiatry Brookwood Med. Ctr., Birmingham, 1995—2000. Fellow: Am. Psychiatry Assn.; mem.: Birmingham Psychiatry Soc., Ala. Psychiatry Soc. Methodist. Avocations: bowling, golf. Office: Ctrl Ala Psychiatry 2100 A South Bridge Pl #540 Birmingham AL 35209 Home: 611 Renaissance Dr Birmingham AL 35226 Office Phone: 205-871-9898. Personal E-mail: dreshehi@aol.com.

**SHEIK, DUNCAN,** singer, songwriter; b. Montclair, N.J., Nov. 18, 1969; Degree in semiotics, Brown U., New Providence, RI, 1992. Performed with bands His Boy Elroy, 1993, Liz and Lisa. Singer, musician: (albums) Duncan Sheik, 1996; singer, musician, co-prodr.: albums Humming, 1998, Phantom Moon, 2001, Daylight, 2002, songs "Wishful Thinking", 1998; TV Appearances: Boston Public, 2003, American Dreams, 2003; composer: (plays) (musical score) Spring Awakening. Office: c/o Atlantic Records Inc 1290 6th Ave Flr 28 New York NY 10104

**SHEIKH, FAZAL,** photographer, writer; b. NYC, 1965; BA, Princeton U., 1987. Author: (books) A Sense of Common Ground, 1996, The Victor Weeps, 1998, A Camel for the Son, 2001, Ramadan Moon, 2001, Moksha, 2005; photographer (exhibitions) Art Inst. Chgo., Seattle Art Mus., Internat. Ctr. Photography, NYC, Corcoran Gallery of Art, Washington, Tate Modern, London, Fondation Cartier-Bresson, Paris, Mus. Fine Arts, Orleans, France, Mus. Contemporary Art, Moscow, UN, NYC. Named MacArthur fellow, John D. and Catherine T. MacArthur Found., 2005; recipient Ruttenberg Award, The Friends of Photography, 1995, Ferguson Award, 1995, Mother Jones Internat. Documentary Award, 1995, Infinity Award, Internat. Ctr. of Photography, 1995, Leica Medal of Excellence, 1995, Volkart Found. Grant, 2000, Recontres d'Arles, Le Prix Dialogue de l'Humanité, 2003, Henri Cartier-Bresson Internat. Grand Prize, 2005; grantee Fulbright Fellowship, 1992, Fellowship in Photography, NEA, 1994, NJ State Coun. on Arts Fellowship, 1994.

**SHEIKHI, M. REZA H.,** engineering educator; PhD in Engring., U. Pitts., 2005. Registered profl. engr., Pa., 2005. Grad. rsch. asst. U. Pitts., 2002—05, rsch. assoc., 2006—. Rsch. assoc. U. of Pitts., Pittsburgh, 2006—. Mem.: ASME, Am. Phys. Soc. Achievements include research in computational fluid dynamics, turbulence and combustion modeling. Office: University of Pittsburgh 648 Benedum Hall 3700 Ohara st Pittsburgh PA 15261 Office Phone: 412-624-9755. Office Fax: 412-624-4846.

**SHEILS, DENIS FRANCIS,** lawyer; b. Ridgewood, NJ, Apr. 7, 1961; s. Denis Francis and Anna Marie (Clifford) Sheils; m. Harriet A. Bonawitz, Sept. 17, 1988; children: Denis F., Dylan I., Matthew D. BA, La Salle Coll., 1983; JD, Fordham U., 1986. Bar: NY 1987, Pa. 1987, U.S. Dist. Ct. (ea. dist.) Pa. 1987, U.S. Ct. Appeals (3d cir.) 1987, U.S. Dist. Ct. (so. and ea. dists.) NY 1992, U.S. Supreme Ct. 1994, U.S. Dist. Ct. (no. dist.) NY 1997, U.S. Ct. Appeals (2d cir.) 1999, Nev. 2003, U.S. Dist. Ct. Nev. 2003. Assoc. Kohn, Swift & Graf, PC, Phila., 1987—97, shareholder, 1997—. Mem.: ABA, Phila. Bar Assn. Roman Catholic. Office: Kohn Swift & Graf PC 21st Fl One South Broad St Philadelphia PA 19107 Home: The Dorchester Unit Number 1613 226 W Rittenhouse Sq Philadelphia PA 19103 Office Phone: 215-238-1700. E-mail: dsheils@kohnswift.com.

**SHEILS, PAUL T.,** lawyer; b. N.Y.C., Aug. 17, 1954; s. James Henry and Margaret (Lambert) S.; m. Theresa V. Sheils; children: Erin Margaret, James Henry II. BA, Williams Coll.; JD, Fordham U. Assoc. Patterson, Belknap, Webb & Tyler, NYC, 1980-84; counsel Dow Jones & Co., Inc., Princeton, NJ, 1984, exec. dir., 1993—94, v.p. interactive publishing, 1994—98; CEO, pres., dir. Medscape, Inc. (negotiated merger into MedicaLogic, Inc.), 1998—2000; chmn. Medscape / MedicaLogic, Inc.; CEO Mayo Health Ventures; CEO, pres., dir. InterCure, Inc., 2001; pres., CEO Aetna Health Solutions Aetna Inc.—. Mem. ABA, N.Y. State Bar Assn., N.Y. County Lawyers Assn. Achievements include the team that launched The Wall Street Journal Online in 1996 which has over 700,000 subscribers and is among the most successful subscription-based publications on the Web. Office: Aetna 151 Farmington Ave Hartford CT 06156*

**SHEIMAN, RONALD LEE,** lawyer; b. Bridgeport, Conn., Apr. 26, 1948; s. Samuel Charles and Rita Doris Sheiman; m. Deborah Joy Lovitky, Oct. 16, 1971; children: Jill, Laura. BA, U. Mich., 1970; JD, U. Conn., 1973; LLM in Taxation, NYU, 1974. Bar: Conn. 1973, US Ct. Appeals (2d cir.) 1975, US Supreme Ct. 1977, DC 1978, NY 1981. Tax atty. Office Regional Counsel IRS, Phila., 1974-78; pvt. practice Westport, Conn., 1978—. Mem.: ABA, Conn. Bar Assn., Fed. Bar Assn. Home: 128 Random Rd Fairfield CT 06432-1408 Office: 1804 Post Rd E Westport CT 06880-5607

**SHEINBAUM, GILBERT HAROLD,** international management consultant; b. N.Y.C., Apr. 20, 1929; s. Herman and Selma (Klimberg) S.; m. Inger Fredebo Thomsen, Aug. 28, 1971; children: Neil, Britt. AB in History, NYU, 1950; postgrad., CUNY, 1954-55, New Sch. for Social Rsch., 1955-56. Various fgn. svc. posts, Washington, Laos, France, Vietnam, Denmark, 1957-72; polit. officer U.S. Dept. of State, Washington, 1972-75; chargé d'affaires Am. Embassy, Antananarivo, Madagascar, 1975-77, dep. chief of mission Lilongwe, Malawi, 1977-79; Am. consul Cebu, Philippines, 1979-83; polit. counselor U.S. Mission to the UN, Geneva, 1983-86; dir. Colombo Plan (internat. orgn.), Colombo, Sri Lanka, 1986-91; cons. Nat. Security Edn. Program, Washington, 1992-95. Internat. Found. for Election Sys., Washington, 1995-96; sr. cons., advisor U.S. Dept. State, 1997—. Internat. observor Sri Lankan elections, 1993, 94; convenor Shepherd's Ctr. World Affairs Program, Vienna, Va. Co-founder, trustee George Keyt Cultural Found., Colombo, 1987-91; bd. chmn. Overseas Children's Sch., Colombo, 1987-90; commr. Boy Scouts Am., Geneva, 1984-86; stage mgr., bd. dirs. Am. Light Opera Co., Washington, 1962-64. 1st lt. U.S. Army, 1951-53. Recipient Award of Recognition, Mindanao State U., Marawi, Philippines, 1983. Mem.: Assn. Diplomatic Studies, UN Assn. of U.S., Diplomatic and Consular Officers Ret. (treas. 1995—2000), Asia Soc., World Affairs Coun. of Washington DC, Am. Fgn. Svc. Assn., Soc. Internat. du Mékong (founder, pres. 1957—59). Avocations: tennis, running, touring, reading, public speaking. Home: 407 East St NE Vienna VA 22180-3577 Personal E-mail: gsheinbaum@aol.com.

**SHEINDLIN, JUDITH (JUDGE JUDY),** television personality, judge; b. Bklyn., Oct. 21, 1942; d. Murray and Ethel Blum; m. Ronald Levy, 1964 (div. 1976); children: Jamie, Adam; m. Gerald Sheindlin, 1977 (div. 1990); stepchildren: Greg, Jonathan, Nicole; m. Gerald Sheindlin, 1991. BA, Am. U., Wash., DC, 1963; JD, NY Law Sch., 1965; LLD (hon.), Elizabethtown Coll. Pros. atty. Family Ct., NYC, 1978—82, judge Bronx, 1982—86; supervising judge Manhattan, NYC, 1986—96. Appeared as herself (TV films) ChiPs '99, 1998, (TV series) Judge Judy, 1996— (nominee Daytime Emmy for outstanding special class series, 1999, 2000, 2001, 2002, 2003); author: Don't Pee on My Leg and Tell Me It's Raining: America's Toughest Family Court Judge Speaks Out, 1996, Beauty Fades, Dumb is Forever: The Making of a Happy Woman, 1999, Keep It Simple, Stupid: You're Smarter Than You Look: Uncomplicating Families in Complicated Times, 2000, Judge Judy Sheindlin's Win or Lose by How You Choose, 2000, You're Smarter Than You Look: Uncomplicating Relationships in Complicated Times, 2001, Judge Judy Sheindlin's You Can't Judge a Book By Its Cover: Cool Rules for School, 2001.

**SHEINGOLD, DANIEL H.,** electrical engineer; b. Boston, Sept. 26, 1928; s. Louis S. and Elsie Sheingold; m. Ann Silverman, Aug. 2, 1953 (dec. Feb. 1995); children: Mark J., Laura S. Duffy. BSEE with distinction, Worcester Poly. Inst., 1948; MSEE, Columbia U., 1949. Engr. George A. Philbrick Rschs. Inc., Boston, 1949-55, application engring. mgr., 1957-63; v.p. George A. Philbrick Researches, Inc., Dedham, Mass., 1964-67; staff cons. Teledyne Philbrick, Dedham, 1967-68; tech. mktg. mgr. Analog Devices, Inc., Norwood, Mass., 1969—. Editor: Analog-Digital Conversion Handbook, 1972, 3d edit., 1986, Nonlinear Circuits Handbook, 1974, Transducer Interfacing Handbook, 1980; editor Analog Dialogue jour., 1969—, others. With AUS, 1955-57. Fellow IEEE; mem. IEEE Instrumentation and Measurement Soc. (sec.-treas. 1976, v.p. 1977, pres. 1978), AAAS. Jewish. Avocations: music, walking, reading. Office: Analog Devices Inc PO Box 9106 3 Technology Way Norwood MA 02062-9106 Office Phone: 781-461-3294. Business E-Mail: dan.sheingold@analog.com.

**SHEININ, ROSE,** biochemist, educator; b. Toronto, Ont., May 18, 1930; d. Harry and Anne (Szyber) Shuber; m. Joseph Sheinin, July 15, 1951; children: David Matthew Khazanov, Lisa Basya Judith, Rachel Sarah Rebecca. BA, U. Toronto, 1951, MA (scholar), 1953, PhD in Biochemistry, 1956, LHD, 1985; DHL (hon.), Mt. St. Vincent U., 1985; DSc (hon.), Acadia U., 1987, U. Guelph, 1991. Demonstrator in biochemistry U. Toronto, Ont., Canada, 1951-53, asst. prof. microbiology Ont., 1964-75, asst. prof. med. biophysics Ont., 1967-75, assoc. prof. microbiology Ont., 1975-90, assoc. prof. med. biophysics Ont., 1975-78, prof. med. biophysics Ont., 1978-90, chmn. microbiology and parasitology Ont., 1975-82, vice dean Sch. Grad. Studies Ont., 1984-89; vice-rector acad. Concordia U., Montreal, Que., Canada, 1989-94, prof. dept. biology, 1989-2000. Mem. Health Scis. Com.; vis. rsch. assoc. chem. microbiology Cambridge U., 1956-57, Nat. Inst. Med. Rsch., London, 1975-58; rsch. assoc. fellow divsn. biol. rsch. Ont. Caner Inst., 1958-67; sci. officer cancer grants panel Med. Rsch. Coun. Can.; mem. Can. Sci. Del. to People's Republic of China, 1973; mem. adv. com. Provincial Lottery Health Rsch. Awards; mem. adv. com. on biotech. NRC Can., 1984-87; mem. Sci. Coun. Can., 1984-87; adv. com. on sci. and tech. CBC, 1980-85; mem. bd. dirs. Can. Bacterial Disease Network, 1989-94; vis. prof. biochemistry U. Alta., 1971. Assoc. editor Can. Jour. Biochemistry, 1968-71, Virology, 1969-72, Intervirology, 1974-85; editl. bd. Microbiol. Revs., 1977-80; author, co-author various publs. Nat. Cancer Inst. Can. fellow, 1953-56, 58-61; Brit. Empire Cancer Campaign fellow, 1956-58; recipient Queen's Silver Jubilee medal, 1978, Woman of Distinction award Health and Edn., YWCA, 1988, Josiah Macy Jr. faculty scholar, 1981-82; fellow Ligue Contre le Cancer, France, 1981-82, Massey Coll., U. Toronto, 1981—, continuing sr. fellow, 1994—; hon. fellow Ryerson Polytech. U., 1993. Fellow Am. Acad. Microbiology, Royal Soc. Can. (chair women in scholarship com. 1990-93); mem. Can. Biochem. Soc. (pres. 1974-75), Can. Soc. Cell Biology (pres. 1975-76), Am. Soc. Virology, Am. Soc. Microbiologists, Can. Assn. Women in Sci., Internat. Assn. Women Bioscientists, Sigma Xi Rsch. Soc., Scitech. Soc. Complex Carbohydrates, Toronto Biochem. and Biophys. Soc. (pres. 1960-70, coun. 1970-74). E-mail: roseshenin@sympatico.ca.

**SHEINMAN, MORT,** editor, consultant, writer, photographer; b. NYC, Oct. 7, 1933; s. Irving and Molly (Feigenblatt) S.; m. Claire Rosenfeld, Aug. 27, 1967 (div.). BA in English, CCNY, 1954. Sports tabulator New York Daily News, 1956-58; reporter Women's Wear Daily, N.Y.C., 1960-69, news editor, 1970-71, mng. editor, 1971-2000, W Mag., N.Y.C., 1972-82, assoc. editor, 1982-2000; editl. dir. Publicis Dialog N.Y., N.Y.C., 2000-01; journalism instr. Fashion Inst. Tech., 2001—. Cons., writer ATT Summer Olympics Exhibit, L.A., 1984, Pru Ctr. Obs., Boston, 1995. Co-author Fashion Retailing and a Bygone Era: Inside Women's Wear Daily, 2005; contbr. articles and photographs to various publs. including Ency. Judaica, 2005. With U.S. Army, 1954-56. Mem.: CCNY Comm. Alumni (Hall of Fame 2003), Soc. of the Silurians, Nat. Arts Club. Home: 60 Gramercy Park N New York NY 10010-5423 E-mail: mortone@aol.com.

**SHEKAR, SAM S.,** federal agency administrator; MD, MPH, U. Mich. Asst. surgeon gen., rear admiral USPHS Commd. Corps.; assoc. adminstr. field ops. Bur. Health Professionals Health Resources and Services Adminstrn., HHS, 1998—2000, assoc. adminstr. health professions, 2000—02, assoc. adminstr Bur. Primary Health Care, 2002—05, dir. Ctr. for Quality, HIV/AIDS Bur., 2005—. Fellow: Am. Coll. Preventive Medicine. Office: US HHS Health Resources and Services Adminstrn 5600 Fishers Ln Rockville MD 20857 Office Phone: 301-443-0458.*

**SHEKHAR, STEPHEN S.,** obstetrician, gynecologist; b. New Delhi, Jan. 13, 1944; arrived in U.S., 1972; s. S.P. Jain and Shakuntala Mithal; m. Claudette Dorita, Jan. 6, 1978; children: Sasha, Stephen. MBBS, Punjabi U., Patiala, India, 1966. Surgeon Nat. Health Svc. U.K., 1966-72; intern Roosevelt Hosp.-Columbia Coll. Physicians and Surgeons, N.Y.C., 1972-73; resident in ob-gyn. St. Clare's Hosp., N.Y. Med. Coll., N.Y.C., 1973-76, Harlem Hosp.-Columbia U., N.Y.C., 1976-77; pvt. practice Studio City, Calif., 1977—. Mem. staff L.A. County-U. So. Calif. Med. Sch.; clin. prof. ob-gyn. and family medicine U. So. Calif. Sch. Medicine, Oreg. Health Scis. U. Sch. Medicine. Fellow ACS, Am. Coll. Ob-Gyn., L.A. Soc. Ob-Gyn.; mem. AMA, Calif. Med. Assn., L.A. County Med. Assn., Oreg. Med. Assn., Jackson County Med. Assn. Home and Office: PO Box 1742 Medford OR 97501-0136 Office Phone: 541-608-6199. Office Fax: 541-608-6199. Personal E-mail: drsshekhar@yahoo.com.

**SHEKHAWAT, DUSHYANT,** chemical engineer; b. Jakhal, Rajasthan, India, June 30, 1966; s. Indra S. and Ichraj Shekhawat; m. Archana K. Solanki; children: Suveer S., Pragya K. BS, U. Minn., 1995; PhD, Mich. State U., 2000. Registered profl. engr., W.Va. Rsch. assoc. U.S. Dept. Energy, Pitts., 2001—02, chem. engr. Morgantown, W.Va., 2002—. Contbr. articles to profl. jours. Mem.: AIChE (assoc.), Am. Chem. Soc. (corr.). Achievements include patents for catalysts and processes for the conversion of succinates to citraconates or itaconates; patents pending for hexaaluminate-type catalysts for the reforming of hydrocarbon fuels to hydrogen and carbon monoxide. Home: 131 Village Crest Dr Morgantown WV 26508 Office: US Department of Energy 3610 Collins Ferry Rd Morgantown WV 26507 Office Phone: 304-285-4634. Office Fax: 304-285-0903. Personal E-mail: shekhawa@hotmail.com. Business E-mail: shekhawa@netl.doe.gov.

**SHELANSKI, MICHAEL L.,** cell biologist, educator; b. Phila., Oct. 5, 1941; s. Herman Alder and Bessie B.; m. Vivien Brodkin, June 9, 1963; children: Howard, Samuel, Noah. Student, Oberlin Coll., 1959-61; MD (Life Ins. Med. Research Fund fellow), U. Chgo., 1966. PhD, 1967. Intern in pathology Albert Einstein Coll. Medicine, N.Y.C., 1967-68, fellow in neuropathology, 1968-70, asst. prof. pathology, 1969-74; staff scientist NIH, Bethesda, Md., 1971-73; vis. scientist Inst. Pasteur, Paris, 1973-74; assoc. prof. neuropathology Harvard U., Cambridge, Mass., 1974-78; sr. research assoc., asst. neuropathologist Children's Hosp. Med. Center, Boston, 1974-78; prof., chmn. dept. pharmacology N.Y. U. Med. Center, N.Y.C., 1978-86;

Delafield Prof., chmn. dept. pathology Coll. Physicians and Surgeons, Columbia U., N.Y.C., 1987—; dir. pathology services Presbyn. Hosp., N.Y.C., 1987—; co-dir. Taub Inst. for Rsch. on Alzheimer's Disease and the Aging Brain, N.Y.C., 1998—. Mem. Neurology A study sect. NIH, 1974-78; Pharmacological Scis. study sect., 1986-90; mem. sci. and med. adv. bd. Alzheimer's Disease and Related Disorders Assn., 1985-92, sec., 1987-92, mem. Zenith award panel, 1993-95; chmn. overhead powerline adv. panel State of N.Y., 1981-87; dir. Alzheimer's disease rsch. ctr. Columbia U., 1989—; mem. Am. Cancer Soc. IRG Panel, 1989-93, sci. adv. bd. Dystonia Assn., Amyotrophic Lateral Sclerosis Assn; elected mem., Inst. of Medicine, 1999. Mem. editl. bd. Jour. Neurochemistry, 1982-90, Jour. Neuropathology and Exptl. Neurology, 1983-85, Neuroscis., 1985—, Neurobiology of Aging, 1988-95, Lab. Investigation, 1989—, Brain Pathology, 1990-93. Served as sr. asst. surgeon USPHS, 1971-73. Guggenheim fellow, 1973-74 Mem. Am. Soc. Cell Biology, Inst. Medicine NAS, Am. Assn. Neuropathologists, Assn. Med. Coll. Pharmacologists, Am. Soc. Neurochemistry, Am. Assn. Physicians. Achievements include research on fibrous proteins of brain, aging of human brain, devel. neurobiology. Office: Columbia U Coll Physicians and Surgeons Dept Pathology 630 W 168th St New York NY 10032-3702

**SHELBURNE, JOHN DANIEL,** pathologist; b. Washington, Aug. 27, 1943; s. Clarence Daniel and Edith (McDanel) S.; m. Katherine Howard Parrish, June 17, 1966; children: Mark, Kerri. BA, U. N.C., 1966; PhD, Duke U., 1971, MD, 1972. Intern, then resident Duke U. Med. Ctr., Durham, NC, 1972-76; asst. prof. Duke U., Durham, 1973-78, assoc. prof., 1978-85, prof. pathology, 1985—; dir. electron microscopy lab. VA Med. Ctr., Durham, 1976-92, chief lab. svc., 1983-99, chief of staff, 1999—. Adv. WHO, Manila, 1990; panel mem. VA Program, Washington, 1987—; participant Nordrhein/Westfalen Exchange, Germany, 1988. Editor: Basic Methods in Biological X-Ray Microprobe, 1983; author, editor: Microprobe Analysis in Medicine, 1989, Biomedical Applications of Microprobe Analysis, 1999. Mem. Appalachian Trail Conf., Harpers Ferry, West, Va., 1970—; bd. dirs. Cen. Carolina Youth Soccer, Durham, 1987-90; founding mem. N.C. Soc. for Electron Microscopy and Microprobe, Research Triangle Park, N.C., 1980—. Recipient Morehead scholarship, 1961-66, AOA Med. Honorary Duke Med. Sch., 1970; named Med. Scientist Tng. Program participant NIH, 1966-72, Shelley Meml. lectr., 1985, Florey Meml. lectr., 1988. Fellow Coll. Am. Pathologists; mem. Am. Assn. Pathologists, Microscopy Soc. Am., Microbeam Analysis Soc. Democrat. Episcopalian. Home: 4302 Malvern Rd Durham NC 27707-5451 Office: Duke U Dept Pathology PO Box 3712 Durham NC 27710-3712 Business E-mail: john.shelburne@med.va.gov.

**SHELBY, BRYAN ROHRER,** information systems management consultant; b. Bryn Mawr, Pa., June 26, 1952; s. Albert Rohrer and Elizabeth Ellen (Griffinger) S.; m. Linda Yale Pole, Sept. 9, 1972; children: Caroline Belle, Christina Marie, Heather Lynn. AB in Math. cum laude, Harvard U., 1974. Programmer Litton Industries, Morris Plains, N.J., 1974-75; mgr. info. svcs. The Becker Co., East Orange, N.J., 1975-81; mgr. design and devel. Key Fin. Sys., Pine Brook, N.J., 1982-85; v.p., group project mgr. Bankers Trust Co. Jersey City, N.J., 1985-93; pres. Contek Sys., Inc., Madison, N.J., 1993—; prin ITR Group LLC, Madison, 2002—, Total Rights Mgmt., Inc., Madison, 2003—. Process reengring., project mgmt. and strategic tech. planning cons.; program mgmt. and life cycle methodology specialist; corp. expert in enterprise project mgmt. setup and adminstrn.; designer, project mgr., sys. integrator fin., portfolio mgmt., trust acctg., telecom., pub. Designer/project mgr./sys. integrator fin./portfolio mgmt./trust acctg./telecom./pub. Mem. IEEE, Am. Soc. Pension Actuaries. Democrat. Avocations: reading, building sandcastles. Office: ITR Group LLC 235 Main St # 307 Madison NJ 07940-0292 Office Phone: 973-966-1845. Business E-mail: brian.shelby@itrgrouplic.com.

**SHELBY, CARROLL HALL,** automotive designer; b. Leesburg, Tex., Jan. 11, 1923; s. Warren Hall Shelby and Eloise Lawrence; m. Jeanne Fields (separated 1960); children: Sharon Anne, Michael Hall, Patrick Boyke. Profl. race car driver Cad-Allard, Aston Martin, and Maserati teams, 1954—60; founder Carroll Shelby Sports Cars, Dallas, 1957, Shelby School of High Performance Driving, 1961, Shelby-Dowd Wheel Co., 1973, Shelby-Am. Automobile Club, 1975, Carroll Shelby Internat., Inc., LA; automobile designer, 1961—, Shelby-Am., 1962—; Ford Motor Co., Chrysler Corp., GM; tech. advisor Ford GT project, 2003. Co-founder Original Tex. Chili Co., 1969, Internat. Chili Soc. Founder Carroll Shelby Children's Found., 1991. 2nd lt. US Army Air Corps. Named winner, Torrey Pines, 1955, 24 Hours of LeMans, 1959, Continental Divide Raceways, 1960, Sports Car Driver of Yr., Sports Illustrated, 1956, 1957; named to Internat. MotorSports Hall of Fame, 1991, Automotive Hall of Fame, 1992; recipient Kruse Internat. Collector Car Hall of Fame Award, 2002, Robert E. Petersen Lifetime Achievement Award, 2003. Achievements include design of original Shelby Cobra Roadster, Ford Motor Co., 1962; Shelby Mustang, 1964; Dodge Viper, 1989; Shelby GT500, 2005. Office: 11150 W Olympic Blvd, Ste 1050 Los Angeles CA 90064 also: Carroll Shelby Children's Found 19021 S Figueroa St Gardena CA 90248

**SHELBY, JAMES STANFORD,** surgeon, researcher; b. Ringgold, Tex., June 15, 1934; s. Jesse Audrey and Mable (Martin) S.; m. Susan Rainey, July 15, 1967; children: Bryan Christian, Christopher Linden. BS in Liberal Arts, La. Tech. U., 1956; MD, La. State U., 1958. Diplomate Am. Bd. Surgery, Am. Bd. Thoracic Surgery. Intern Charity Hosp. La., New Orleans, 1958-59, resident in surgery and thoracic surgery, 1959-65; fellow in cardiovasc. surgery Baylor U. Coll. Medicine, Houston, 1965-66; practice medicine specializing in cardiovasc. surgery Shreveport, La., 1967—2004; mem. staff Schumpert Med. Ctr., Highland Hosp., Willis-Knighton Med. Ctr.; assoc. prof. surgery La. State U. Sch. Medicine, Shreveport, 1967—; pres. Shelby Oil and Gas. With M.C., AUS, 1961-62. Recipient Medallion award La. Tech. U., 1982. Mem. AMA, Am. Coll. Cardiology, Soc. Thoracic Surgeons, Am. Heart Assn., Southeastern Surg. Congress, So. Thoracic Surgery Assn Home: 6003 E Ridge Dr Shreveport LA 71106-2425 Office: 2751 Albert Bicknell Dr Ste 2G Shreveport LA 71103-3970 Office Phone: 318-632-9438. E-mail: jshelby@worldnet.att.net.

**SHELBY, NINA CLAIRE,** special education educator; b. Weatherford, Tex., Oct. 23, 1949; d. Bill Hudson and Roselle (Price) S.; m. Richard Dean Powell, May 29, 1971 (div. 1973); 1 child, Stoney Hudson. BA in English, Sul Ross State U., 1974, MEd, 1984; MA in English, U. Tex., 1995. Jr. high lang. arts educator Liberty Hill, Tex., 1974-75; H.S. resource educator Georgetown (Tex.) I. S. D., 1976-77; intermediate resource educator Raymondille (Tex.) I. S. D., 1977-81; educator of severe profound Napper Elem. Pharr (Tex.) San Juan Alamo Ind. Sch. Dist., 1981-90; H. S. life skills educator Pharr (Tex.) San Juan Alamo ISD North H.S., 1990-93; intermediate inclusion educator Carman Elem. Pharr (Tex.) San Juan Alamo Ind. Sch. Dist., 1993—2000, chair dept. spl. edn. Carman Elem., 1998—2000; primary resource/inclusion educator Elgin (Tex.) Elem. Sch., 2000—, chair dept. spl. edn., 2002—. Coach asst. Tex. Spl. Olympics, Pharr, 1981-2000, sponsor vocat. adj. club, 1990-93, adaptive asst. device team, Edinburg, Tex., 1993-95; spl. edn. rep. to Elgin Primary Campus Performance Adv. Coun., 2000—. Asst. cub scout leader Boy Scouts Am., 1994-95, sec. parental com. bd. rev., 1997—; parent vol. boy's and girl's Club McAllen, 1992-96. Mem. DAR, Daus. Republic of Tex., Assn. Tex. Profl. Educators, Alpha Delta Kappa. Democrat. Mem. Ch. Of Christ. Avocations: reading, horticulture, piano, opera. Home: PO Box 426 Elgin TX 78621-0426 Office: Elgin Elem Sch Elgin ISD 1001 W 2d St Elgin TX 78621 Office Phone: 512-281-3457. Business E-Mail: nshelby@elginisd.com.

**SHELBY, RICHARD CRAIG,** senator, former congressman; b. Birmingham, Ala., May 6, 1934; s. O.H. and Alice L. (Skinner) S.; m. Annette Nevin, June 11, 1960; children: Richard Craig, Claude Nevin. AB, U. Ala., 1957, LLB, 1963. Bar: Ala. 1961, DC 1979. Law clk. Supreme Ct. of Ala., 1961-62; practice law Tuscaloosa, Ala., 1963—78; prosecutor City of Tuscaloosa, 1963—71; spl. asst. atty. gen. State of Ala., 1968—71; U.S. magistrate No. Dist. of Ala., 1966—70; mem. Ala. State Senate, 1971—78, 96th-99th Congresses from 7th Ala. dist., 1979-87; mem. energy and commerce com., mem. vets. affairs com.; US Senator from Ala., 1987—. Mem. com.

appropriations US Senate, chmn. com. banking, housing, and urban affairs, spl. com. aging. Active Boy Scouts Am.; pres. Tuscaloosa County Mental Health Assn., 1969-70; bd. govs. Nat. Legis. Conf., 1975-78. Recipient Taxpayer's Friend award, Nat. Taxpayers Union, 1998, Congressional Leadership award, Airports Coun. Internat.-N.Am., 2003. Mem. ABA, Ala. Bar Assn., Tuscaloosa County Bar Assn., DC Bar Assn., Am. Judiciary Soc., Exch. Club, Tuscaloosa County Mental Heatgh Assn.(former pres.) Republican. Presbyterian. Office: US Senate 110 Hart Senate Bldg Washington DC 20510-0001 also: Federal Bldg Ste 240 1118 Greensboro Ave Tuscaloosa AL 35401-2816 Office Phone: 202-224-5744, 205-759-5047. Office Fax: 202-224-3416, 205-759-5067.*

**SHELBY, RONALD VAN DORN,** information technology executive, consultant; b. Covington, Ind., Jan. 14, 1948; s. Richard Van Dorn and Edna Belle Shelby; m. Susan Gail Bamford, Dec. 28, 1984; 1 child, Richard James Harold. BA, Wabash Coll., 1970; MAT, Ind. U., 1973; MBA, U. Toronto, 1984. Project leader Travelers Ins. Co., Toronto, Ont., 1976-79, mgr. data adminstrn., 1979—84; data adminstr. U.S. Dept. Interior, Washington, 1984—86; prin. Am. Mgmt. Sys., Arlington, Va., 1986—89; v.p. info. and tech. svcs. Conn. Mut. Life, Hartford, 1989—96; v.p. tech. leader Am. Express Co., Phoenix, 1996—98; chief tech. officer General Motors corp., Detroit, 1998—2000; CEO XML Solutions corp., McLean, Va., 2000—01, e Fusion Solutions, LLC, Vienna, Va., 2001—. Author: Selecting a DBMS, 1984, Project Manager's Guide to System Development, 1985, also chpts. to books; reviewing editor Data Resource Mgmt., 1989—. Mem. Data Adminstrn. Mgmt. Assn. (adv., bd. dirs., founder Washington chpt. 1988—, internat. pres. 1990). Episcopalian. Avocations: photography, baseball, jogging. Home: 10831 W Broad St # 213 Glen Allen VA 23060-3311 E-mail: ron@theshelbys.com.

**SHELBY, ROSELLE PRICE,** writer, retired special education educator; b. Granbury, Tex., Sept. 6, 1929; d. Ernest Blanton and Alice Parthenia (Merrill) Price; m. Billy Hudson Shelby, May 5, 1948; 1 child, Nina Claire. AA, Weatherford Coll., 1948; BA, Tex. Wesleyan U., Ft. Worth, 1960; NDEA diploma, U. Minn., 1963; MEd, Sul Ross State U., Alpine, Tex., 1974. Cert. tchr., Tex. Tchr. Waka Ind. Sch., Tex., 1956-57, 60-65, 69-72, Hart Ind. Sch., Tex., 1957-60, Eagar Ind. Sch., Ariz., 1966-67, New Waverly Ind. Sch., Tex., 1967-68, Willis Ind. Sch., Tex., 1968-69, Georgetown Ind. Sch., Tex., 1972-87. Author: Frogs in the Milk, 1967; editor: Quick and Easy Way to Riches, 1980. Active local Democratic Party, 1968—, precinct chair, Georgetown, 1980-90, election judge, 1991-2000; mem. sch. bd., Alpine, Ariz. Fulbright scholar U. Costa Rica, 1964; Reynolds fellow U. NC, 1971. Mem. AAUW (br. pres. Perryton 1971-72, state bd. dirs. 1971-73, 75-77, br. pres. Georgetown 1975-77), DAR, Daughters of Republic of Tex. (charter mem. Brazos River Chpt.), Am. Assn. Ret. Persons, Beta Sigma Phi, Delta Kappa Gamma (v.p. 1979-81). Mem. Ch. of Christ. Avocations: bible study, reading, cooking, travel. Home: 2006 Terry Ln Georgetown TX 78628-3338

**SHELDON, EDITH LOUISE THACH,** writer; b. Walsenburg, CO, Nov. 28, 1941; d. William Mason Thach and Jeannette Violet Faris-Thach; m. John Michael Sheldon, June 27, 1964; children: Michael Mason, William David. Student, Pueblo Jr. Coll., Colo. State Coll., Adam's State Coll., Colo., 1959—74. Assoc. pub. Valley Courier Newspaper, Alamosa, Colo., 1974—81; adminstrv. mgr. Colo. Press Assn., Denver, 1981—83; office mgr. The Villager Newspaper, Englewood, Colo., 1983—85; assoc. pub. The Littleton Times, Littleton, Colo., 1986—87; ad exec. The Denver Parent Newspaper, Denver, 1988—94; editor, pub. Denver Parent News Mag., Denver, 1994—. Pres. Parenting Pub. of Am., San Antonio, 1989—91; mem. Gov.'s Coun. on Edn. of Young Children, 1991—94; pres. Huerfano County Hist. Soc., 1995—97; active numerous orgns. and polit. campaigns; mayor City Walsenburg, 2005—06; v.p., bd. trustees Huerfano County Hosp. Dist.

**SHELDON, ELEANOR HARRIET BERNERT,** sociologist, writer; b. Hartford, Conn., Mar. 19, 1920; d. M.G. and Fannie (Myers) Bernert; m. James Sheldon, Mar. 19, 1950 (div. 1960); children: James, John Anthony. AA, Colby Jr. Coll., 1940; AB, U. N.C., 1942; PhD, U. Chgo., 1949. Asst. demographer Office Population Rsch., Washington, 1942-43; social scientist USDA, Washington, 1943-45; assoc. dir. Chgo. Community Inventory, U. Chgo., 1947-50; social scientist Social Sci. Rsch. Coun., N.Y.C., 1950-51, rsch. grantee, 1953-55, pres., 1972-79; rsch. assoc. Bur. Applied Social Rsch. Columbia U., 1950-51, lectr. sociology, 1951-52, vis. prof., 1969-71; social scientist UN, N.Y.C., 1951-52; rsch. assoc., lectr. sociology UCLA, 1955-61; assoc. rsch. sociologist, lectr. Nursing U. Calif., 1957-61; sociologist, exec. assoc. Russell Sage Found., N.Y.C., 1971—72; vis. prof. U. Calif., Santa Barbara, 1971. Author: (with L. Wirth) Chicago Community Fact Book, 1949, America's Children, 1958, (with R.A. Glazier) Pupils and Schools in N.Y.C., 1965; editor: (with W.E. Moore) Indicators of Social Change, Concepts and Measurements, 1968, Family Economic Behavior, 1973; contbr. articles to profl. jours. Bd. dirs. Colby-Sawyer Coll., 1979-85, UN Rsch. Inst. for Social Devel., 1973-79; trustee Rockefeller Found., 1978-85, Nat. Opinion Rsch. Ctr., 1980-87, Inst. East-West Security Studies, 1984-88, Am. assembly, 1976-95. William Rainey Harper fellow, U. Chgo., 1945—47. Fellow AAAS, Am. Acad. Arts and Scis., Am. Sociol. Assn., Am. Statis. Assn.; mem. U. Chgo. Alumni Assn. (Profl. Achievement award), Sociol. Rsch. Assn. (pres. 1971-72), Coun. on Fgn. Rels., Am. Assn. Pub. Opinion Rsch., Ea. Sociol. Soc., Internat. Sociol. Assn., Internat. Union Sci. Study of Population, Population Assn. Am. (2d v.p. 1970-71), Inst. of Medicine (chmn. program com. 1976-77), Cosmopolitan Club. Home and Office: 630 Park Ave New York NY 10021-6544 E-mail: ehbsheldon@aol.com.

**SHELDON, GEORGE FRANK,** medical educator; b. Dec. 20, 1934; s. Richard Robert and Helen Irene (Zerzan) S.; m. Ruth Guy, Aug. 28, 1959; children: Anne Anderson, Elizabeth, Julia. BA, U. Kans., 1957, MD, 1961; postgrad., Mayo Clinic Grad. Sch., 1965. Asst. instr. we. civilization U. Kans., 1955—57; intern Kans. U. Med. Ctr.; resident in surgery U. Calif., San Francisco, 1965-69; fellow in surg. biology Harvard Med. Sch. of Peter Bent Brigham Hosp., 1969-71; from asst. to prof. U. Calif., 1971-82; Dr. Zack D. Owens Disting. prof. surgery, dept. chmn. U. N.C., Chapel Hill, 1984—2001. Chmn. residency rev. com. accreditation Coun. for Grad. Med. Edn.; mem. Coun. Grad. Edn. of Health and Human Svcs., 1986, chmn. 1998; mem. adminstrv. bd. Coun. Acad. Socs., chair, 1998-99; chmn. Merit Rev. Bd. for Surgery Va., AAMC, 2000, 01; pres. vis. bd. UN Formed Svcs. U. Health Scis., 2002-03. Author: (with J.B. Runnell) Pictorial History of Kansas Medicine, 1961; (with Jill Ridky) Managing in Academics, 1993; editor: (with J.B. Davis) Clinical Surgery, 1995; editor-in-chief: E-Facs.org. With USPHS, 1962-64. Recipient Surgeon's award for Svc. to Safety, Nat. Safety Coun., 1993, Douglass Stubbs award Nat. Med. Assn., 1991, Disting. Faculty award Med. Alumni Assn. U. N.C., 2001; named Disting. Med. Alumnus, Kans. U., 2000. Fellow Royal Coll. Surgeons of Edinburgh (hon.), Royal Coll. Surgeons Eng., European Surg. Assn., Assn. of Surgeons of Gt. Britain and Ireland, Phila. Acad. Surgeons (Hunterian Orator 2001); mem. ACS (sec. bd. govs., regent 1984-93, pres. 1998, editor-in-chief e.facs.org web portal 2004—, Surgeon of Yr. 2001, Fitts Orator, 1987, Scudder Orator Honored Surgeon, editor E facs.org web porta 2004-), Am. Bd. Surgery (chmn. 1989-90), Nat. Bd. Med. Examiners (test com 1981-84), Am. Assn. Surgery of Trauma (pres. 1984, Fitts medal), Am. Surg. Assn. (sec. 1989-94, pres. 1994-95), Assn. Am. Med. Colls. (exec. com., chair elect 1999, chair 2000-01, disting. svc. mem.), Soc. Surg. Chmn. (pres.), Coun. Acad. Socs. 1998—, com. on gender equity and com. on health workforce), Inst. Medicine (sec. com. on employer based health ins. and tech. assessment edn. bds., Fluid Resuscitation com. on Nation's Physician Workforce 1996, Reviewer Poison Ctrs). Office: U NC at Chapel Hill Med Surgery Campus Bx 7050 136 Burnett-Womack Bldg Chapel Hill NC 27599-7228 Office Phone: 919-966-4052. Business E-Mail: gsheldon@med.unc.edu.

**SHELDON, GILBERT IGNATIUS,** clergyman; b. Cleve., Sept. 20, 1926; s. Ignatius Peter and Stephanie Josephine (Olszewski) S. Student, John Carroll U.; M.Div., St. Theol. Sem. 1970; D.Min., St. Mary Sem. and Ohio Consortium of Sems., 1974; HHD, Jesuit U. of Wheeling, 1993; STD, Franciscan U., Steubenville, 1994. Ordained priest Roman Cath. Ch., 1953, bishop, 1976. Assoc. pastor Cleve. Diocese, 1953-64, diocesan dir. propagation of faith, 1964-74; pastor, Episcopal vicar Lorain County, Ohio, 1974-76; aux. bishop Cleve., 1976—; vicar for Summit County, 1979-80, So. Region, 1980-92; bishop Steubenville, 1992—. Bd. dirs. Soc. Propagation of Faith, 1968-74, Diocesan Presbyteral Coun.; instr. theology St. John Coll.; clergy adv. bd. econ. edn. Akron U.; mem. Bishop's Com. Latin Am.; adv. bd., Franciscan U.; bd. trustees St. Mary Seminary, Diocesan Health Ins. Adv. Bd., Cath. Charities Corp.; former mem. bd. trustees Borromeo Coll.; mem. acad. bd. St, Mary Seminary; bd. dirs. Bishops' Com. Latin Am., adminstrv. com. Nat. Conf. Cath. Bishops/USCC, Nat. Adv. Coun., Bishops' Com. for Missions, Nat. Bd. Soc. for Propagation of Faith; bd. trustees Pontifical Coll. Josephinum, Bishop Emeritus of Steubenville, 2002, Adj. Faculty, Franciscan U. of Steubenville, 2003. Goals for Greater Akron. With USAF, 1944—45. Mem. Nat. Conf. Cath. Bishops (adminstrv. bd. 1985—), Am. Legion, Cath. War Vets., Knights of Columbus, Order of Alhambra., Rotary Club Akron and Steubenville. Clubs: K.C. Lodges: Rotary (Akron). Roman Catholic. Avocations: golf, astronomy, photography, history, travel. Home: 609 N 7th St Steubenville OH 43952-1748 Business E-Mail: lnichols@diosteub.org.

**SHELDON, INGRID KRISTINA,** retired mayor, controller; b. Ann Arbor, Mich., Jan. 30, 1945; d. Henry Ragnvald and Virginia Schmidt Blom; m. Clifford George Sheldon, June 18, 1966; children: Amy Elizabeth, William David. BS, Eastern Mich. U., 1966; MA, U. Mich., 1970; doctorate (hon.), Cleary U., 2001. Cert. tchr., Mich. Tchr. Livonia (Mich.) Pub. Schs., 1966-67, Ann Arbor Pub. Schs., 1967-68; bookkeeper Huron Valley Tennis Club, Ann Arbor, 1978—; acct. F.A. Black Co., Ann Arbor, 1984-88; coun. mem. Ward II City of Ann Arbor, 1988-92, mayor, 1993-2000. Commr. Housing Bd, Appeals, Ann Arbor, 1988—91; vice chmn. fin. and budget com. S.E. Mich. Coun.Govts.; treas. Huron Valley Child Guidance Clinic, Ann Arbor, 1984—, Ann Arbor Hist. Found., 1985—, Parks Adv. Commn., 1987—92, Ann Arbor Planning Commn., 1988—89; excellence com. Ann Arbor Pub. Schs. reorgn., 1985; treas. SOS Cmty. Crisis Ctr., Ypsilanti, Mich., 1987—93; chair United Meth. Retirement Cmty., Ann Arbor, 2003—06; trustee Cmty. Found., 2001—05; chair Ann Arbor Summer Festival, 2005. Recipient Cmty. Svc. award Ann Arbor Jaycees, 1980, DAR Cmty. Svc. award, 1997; AAUW fellow, 1982. Mem.: Mich. Mcpl. League (life; del. 1989—97, hon. life mem. 1994, trustee 1997—2000, pres. 1999—2000), Ann Arbor Rotary (pres.-elect 2005), Ann Arbor Women's City Club (fin. com. 1987—90, chair endowment com. 1989—90, treas. 2003), Alpha Omicron Pi, Kappa Delta Pi. Republican. Methodist. Avocation: musical theatre. Home: 1416 Folkstone Ct Ann Arbor MI 48105-2848 E-mail: aasheldon@aol.com.

**SHELDON, J. MICHAEL,** lawyer, educator; b. Mt. Carmel, Pa., Sept. 1, 1951; s. Lloyd Loomis and Helen Roberta (Sosnowski) S. AA, Harrisburg (Pa.) Community Coll., 1978; BS, Pa. State U., 1980; M in Journalism, Temple U., 1991; JD, Widener U. Sch. Law, 1996. Bar: U.S. Ct. Appeals 2004, U.S. Surpeme Ct. 2006. News announcer Sta. WNUE-AM, Ft. Walton Beach, Fla., 1974-76, Sta. WFEC-AM, Harrisburg, 1977-78; announcer Sta. WCMB-AM, Wormleysburg, Pa., 1979-80; writer newspaper Pa. Beacon, Harrisburg, 1982-85; media specialist Commonwealth Media Svcs., Harrisburg, 1982-86; dir. communications Pa. Poultry Fedn., Harrisburg, 1986-89; news anchor Sta. WGAL-TV, Lancaster, Pa., 1989-90; dir. pub. rels. Profl. Ins. Agts. - Pa., Md., Del., Mechanicsburg, Pa., 1990-92; v.p. comm. and mktg. United Way of the Capital Region, Harrisburg, Pa., 1992-93, Widener U. Sch. of Law, 1994-96; pres. Open Mike Comm., Harrisburg, 1994—. Mem. adj. faculty dept. journalism Temple U., 1992; mem. faculty dept. humanities Pa. State U., 1995-97, 99-04. Contbg. author: Pa. 12th Annual Civil Litigation Update, Spoliation of Evidence: Why You Can't Have Your Cake and Eat it Too, 1999; contbg. editor: A Practical Guidebook to Massachusetts Aviation Law, 1999; Contbr. articles to profl. jours. Pub. rels. advisor Cen. Pa. Leukemia Soc., Harrisburg, 1989-90; media advisor Polit. Campaign, Hershey, Pa., 1990. With USAF, 1969-73. Mem. Pa. Bar Assn., Pa. Criminal Def. Lawyers Assn., Dauphin County Bar (bd. dirs. 2006—), VFW (life), Am. Legion, Loyal Order of Moose, Chi Gamma Iota, Delta Tau Kappa. Republican. Roman Catholic. Avocations: motorcycles, music, electronics, martial arts. Office: 6059 Allentown Blvd Harrisburg PA 17112-2672

**SHELDON, Mrs. JOHN** See GIBBONS, CELIA

**SHELDON, KATHLEEN EDDY,** historian; b. Hartford, Conn., June 9, 1952; d. Austin Mather and Sylvia Desmond Sheldon; m. Stephen Tarzynski, Dec. 28, 1974; children: Mercie DiGangi, Benjamin Sheldon-Tarzynski. PhD, U. of Califorina, Los Angeles, 1977—88; MA, African Area Studies, U. of Calif., Los Angeles, 1975—77; BA, History, Northwestern U., Evanston, Ill. 1970—74. Vis. rsch. scholar UCLA Ctr. for the Study of Women, 1988—. Editor: Courtyards, Markets, City Streets: Urban Women in Africa, 1996; author: Pounders of Grain: A History of Women, Work, and Politics in Mozambique, 2002, Historical Dictionary of Women in Sub-Saharan Africa, 2005; contbr. articles to profl. jours. Commr. Commn. on the Status of Women, Santa Monica, Calif., 1992—2002. Recipient Catherine Prelinger Prize, Coordinating Coun. for Women in History, 1999. Mem.: Lusophone African Studies Orgn. (founding chair 1999—, editor h-luso-africa listserve 2002—), African Studies Assn. (women's caucus treas. 1997—2003, bd. dirs. 2004—07).

**SHELDON, LOIS ELIZABETH,** social services administrator; b. Marion, Va., Oct. 20, 1942; d. Godfrey Hudson Coombs, Margaret Lillian Coombs; m. Jack Maurice Sheldon, Nov. 24, 1985. BS, San Diego State U., 1968; MPH, Loma Linda U., 1982; MDiv, Fuller Sem. Cert. med. technologist Calif. Med. technologist Sharp Hosp., San Diego, 1979—82; staff mem. Cmty. Health Agy., Romona, Calif., 1982—84, Health Sys. Agy., San Diego, 1984—86; dir. Christian Social Concerns, San Diego, 1986—99; cons, Ministries Enterprises, San Diego, 1999—. Author: The Rape of Ariel House, 1998; contbr. articles to profl. jours. Recipient Leadership award, Channel 10, 1996, Brad Truax award, San Diego AIDS Assn., 1994. Mem.: APHA, Jr. League (Award 1992). Home: 6662 Del Cerro Blvd San Diego CA 92120

**SHELDON, MARK,** assistant dean; b. Camp Blanding, Fla., Dec. 17, 1944; s. Marvin and Georgianna Sheldon; children: Ivan, Noah. AB, Shimer Coll., Ill., 1968; PhD, Brandeis U., Mass., 1975; Sachar Fellow, Wadham Coll., Oxford U., Eng., 1973. Prof. philosophy Ind. U., Gary, Ill., 1982—2002; sr. policy analyst AMA, Chgo.; asst. dean, sr. lectr. Northwestern U., Evanston, Ill., 2002—. Med. ethics cons. Rush U. Med. Ctr., Chgo., 1986—. Contbr. articles various profl. jours., chapters to books. Adv., program on genetics Ill. Humanities Coun., Chgo., 2005—. 2nd lt U.S. Army, 1967—69. Recipient Sachar award, Brandeis U., 1972-73. Mem.: Am. Philos. Assn. (co-editor, newsletter on philosophy and medicine 2000). D-Liberal. Jewish. Avocations: reading, music. Home: 611 Sheridan Rd Evanston IL 60202 Office: Northwestern U 1922 Sheridan Rd Evanston IL 60208 Office Phone: 847-491-8918. Business E-Mail: sheldon@northwestern.edu.

**SHELDON, MARY ANNE,** composer, music educator; d. Henry W. and Katharina M. Seeger; m. Terry Lynn Sheldon, Sept. 5, 1959; children: Mary Lynn Abbott, Kathleen Marie Lonero, Stephen Michael. Cert. piano tchr. Utica Conservatory of Music. Piano tchr. Mary Anne Sheldon Piano Studio, Clark Mills, NY, 1970—. Composer: (piano music) Springtime, The Vagabond. Mem.: Nat. Guild of Piano Tchrs., Nat. Soc. DAR (rec. sec. Oneida chpt. 2002—06), B Sharp Musical Club (assoc.). Office Phone: 315-853-8124.

**SHELDON, SIDNEY,** writer, television director, television producer; b. Chgo., Feb. 11, 1917; s. Otto and Natalie (Marcus) S.; m. Jorja Curtright, Mar. 28, 1951 (dec. 1985); 1 dau., Mary; m. Alexandra Kostoff, 1989. Student, Northwestern U. Started as reader, Universal and 20th Century Fox Studios; author: (novels) The Naked Face, 1970, The Other Side of Midnight, 1975, A Stranger in the Mirror, 1976, Bloodline, 1977, Rage of Angels, 1980, Master of the Game, 1982, If Tomorrow Comes, 1985, Windmills of the Gods, 1987, The Sands of Time, 1988, Memories of Midnight, 1990, The Doomsday Conspiracy, 1991, The Stars Shine Down, 1992, Nothing Lasts Forever, 1994,

Morning, Noon and Night, 1995, The Best Laid Plans, 1997, Tell Me Your Dreams, 1998, The Sky is Falling, 2000, Are You Afraid of the Dark?, 2004 (Publishers Weekly Bestseller); creator, writer, producer: Nancy, The Patty Duke Show, I Dream of Jeannie; created TV show Hart to Hart; author: plays including Roman Candle, Jackpot, Dream With Music, Alice in Arms, Redhead; writer: screenplays including Billy Rose's Jumbo, The Bachelor and the Bobby-Soxer, 1947, Easter Parade (Box Office Blue Ribbon award), Annie Get Your Gun; writer, dir.: screenplays including Dream Wife, Buster Keaton Story; writer: screenplays including Anything Goes, Never Too Young; recipient Acad. award for screenplay The Bachelor and the Bobby-Soxer 1947, Tony award for Redhead 1959, Writers Guild Am. Screen awards for Easter Parade 1948, Annie Get Your Gun 1950, Edgar Allan Poe award Mystery Writers Am. for Naked Face, 1970. Served with USAAF, World War II. Inducted into the Guinness Book of Records as the Most Translated Author for 1997; recipient Will Rogers Meml. award, 2002. Address: care Warren Cowan Warren Cowan & Assocs 8899 Beverly Blvd # 919 Los Angeles CA 90048

**SHELDON, STEPHEN,** pediatric sleep medicine educator, researcher; b. Miami Beach, Fla., Nov. 4, 1947; s. Murray M. and Sally (Lee) Sheldon; m. Rebecca Sheldon, May 17, 1996; children: David Patrick, Susan Victoria, Mara Elyn, Amy Michel. BS, U. Fla., 1969; DO, Chgo. Coll. Osteo. Medicine, 1975. Diplomate Am. Bd. Physicians and Surgeons, Am. Bd. Sleep Medicine, Am. Bd. Pediat. Resident in pediatrics Rush-Presbyn.-St. Luke's Med. Ctr., Chgo., 1975-78, chief pediatric resident, 1977-78, coord. pediatric residency, 1978-80, dir. pediatric residency, 1980-83; dir. pediatric research Mt. Sinai Hoop. Med. Ctr., Chgo., 1983-85; chmn. dept. pediatrics Chgo. Coll. Osteo. Medicine, 1985—. Cons. pediatrician Rush-Presbyn.-St. Lukes Med. Ctr., 1983—; prof. pediat. Feinberg Sch. Medicine Northwestern U., 2006—; assoc. dept. neurology U. Chgo., 1986—. Author: Pediatric Differential Diagnosis, 1979, 1986, Manual of Practical Pediatrics, 1981, Diagnosis and Management of the Hospitalized Child, 1984, Pediatric Sleep Medicine, 1992, Atlas of Sleep Medicine in Infants and Children, 1999, Evaluating Sleep in Infants and Children, 1996; sr. editor: Principles and Practice of Pediatric Sleep Medicine. Fellow: Am. Acad. Pediat. (cert. merit 1985); mem.: AMA, Ambulatory Pediatric Assn., Am. Acad. Sleep Medicine. Avocations: painting, ship building, cabinetry, writing, photography. Business E-Mail: ssheldon@northwestern.edu.

**SHELDON, TERRY EDWIN,** lawyer, investment advisor; b. Sacramento, June 22, 1945; s. Earl M. and Christine M. S.; m. Jan L. Winters, Aug. 26, 1966; children: Jeffrey, Tiffini, Melissa. BS magna cum laude, Abilene Christian U., 1967; JD, So. Meth. U., 1970. Bar: Calif. 1970. Assoc. Bronson, Bronson & McKinnon, San Francisco, 1970-74; gen. counsel, also dir. Consol. Capital Cos., Emeryville, Calif., 1974-83, exec. v.p., chief oper. officer, 1984-85, cons., advisor, 1986-87; pres, trustee Consol. Capital Spl. Trust, 1980-85; exec. v.p., trustee Consol. Capital Realty Investors, 1975-85, Consol. Capital Income Trust, 1978-85, Consol. Capital Income Opportunity Trust, 1983-85, Consol. Capital Income Opportunity Trust 2, 1985; chmn. Nat. Syndication Forum (a div. of RESSI), 1981-82; real estate securities specialist RESSI. V.p., prin. Alpha Venture Corp., Walnut Creek, Calif., 1987; bus. cons., 1988—. Chmn. bd. visitors adv. com. Coll. of Bus. Adminstrn. Abilene Christian U., 1990. Mem. ABA, Calif. Bar Assn., Nat. Assn. Securities Dealers (direct participation programs com., real estate com., standing adv. com. to bd. govs. 1980-83), Nat. Syndication Forum. Republican. Mem. Ch. of Christ.

**SHELDON, THOMAS DONALD,** academic administrator; b. Canastota, NY, July 15, 1920; s. Harry Ellsworth and Sadie Joyce (McNulty) S.; m. Helen Elizabeth Kyser, Aug. 29, 1941; children: Thomas, Paul, Edward, Patricia, Curtis, Roberta, Kevin, Kelly. BS, Syracuse U., 1942, MS, 1949, Ed.D., 1958; grad., Air Command and Staff Coll., 1972. Tchr. sci., coach Split Rock (N.Y.) High Sch., 1942-43; tchr. sci., coach vice prin., prin. Minoa (N.Y.) High Sch., 1946-59; prin., asso. supt. Hempstead (N.Y.) High Sch., 1959-63; supt. Hempstead Pub. Schs., 1963-68, Balt. City Schs., 1968-71; dep. commr. N.Y. State Edn. Dept., Albany, 1971-77; pres. Utica Coll. of Syracuse U., 1977-82; interim pres. Mohawk Valley Community Coll., 1983; then interim pres. Onondaga Community Coll., 1984, now hon. pres. emeritus; prof. ednl. adminstrn. Syracuse U., NY, 1984-85; supt. Sewanhaka Central High Sch. Dist., 1985-86; interim pres. Munson-Williams-Proctor Inst., 1990-91; exec. dir. Syracuse U. Relations, N.Y.C., 1987-93; chmn. Edn. Profls. Internat., 1977-9. Co-author and editor various N.Y. State Regents publs., 1971-76. Served with U.S. Army, 1943-46; served to col. USAF, 1972-77, Berlin; to brig. gen. Air N.G. 1955-77. First recipient Outstanding Grad. award Syracuse U. Sch. Edn., 1977; recipient Outstanding Md. Educator award Maryland Found., 1966; Conspicuous Service medal N.Y. State Gov., 1976; N.Y.C. PSAL medal, 1978; named to Balt. Afro-Am. Honor Roll, 1970 Mem. VFW (life), N.Y. State PTA (hon. life), N.Y. State Coaches Assn. (pres. 1957), Am. Legion, Phi Delta Kappa. Clubs: Lions (hon. life). Office Phone: 315-633-8052.

**SHELDON-MORRIS, TIFFINI ANNE,** clinical psychologist, consultative examiner; b. Berkeley, Calif., Apr. 20, 1976; d. Terry E. and Jan L. Sheldon; m. John Christopher Morris, Aug. 6, 2000. BS in Psychology, Abilene Christian U., 1997; MS in Psychology, Fla. Inst. Tech., 2001, D of Psychology, 2001. Licensed Clinical Psychologist Tex., 2004. Postdoctoral fellow Houston Veterans Affairs Med. Ctr., Houston, 2001—02; team leader and counselor Sr. Connections, Houston, 2003—04; clin. psychologist VeriCare, 2004—. Consultative examiner Dept. of Assistive and Rehabilitative Svcs., Austin, Tex., 2004—. Active mem. Monterey Ch. Christ, Lubbock, Tex., 2001 ; Scholar Grad. Student Tchg. Assistantship Fla. Inst. of Tech. 1998-2000. Mem.: APA, Alpha Kappa Delta Internat. Hon. Soc., Alpha Chi Nat. Honor Soc., Girls Aiming Toward Achievement. Avocations: travel, reading, swimming, music, theater. Home: 6508 89th St Lubbock TX 79424 Office: VeriCare 4715 Viewridge Ave Ste 230 San Diego CA 92123 Office Phone: 806-577-3050. Home Fax: 806-698-8994; Office Fax: 800-819-1655. Personal E-mail: drtiffini@yahoo.com.

**SHELDRICK, GEORGE MICHAEL,** chemistry professor, crystallographer; b. Huddersfield, Great Britain, Nov. 17, 1942; s. George and Elizabeth S.; m. Katherine E. Herford, 1968; 4 children. Student, Huddersfield New Coll., Jesus Coll., Cambridge. Lectr. Cambridge U., Eng., 1966-78; prof. structural chemistry U. Göttingen, Germany, 1978—; with Inst. Anorg Chemie, Göttingen, Germany. Contbr. numerous articles to profl. jours. Recipient Meldola and Corday-Morgan medals, Royal Soc. Chemistry, Leibniz prize, Deutsche Forschungsgemeinschaft, A.L. Patterson award, Am. Crystallographic Assn., 1993, Carl-Hermann medal, Deutsche Gesellschaft fur Kristallographie, 1999, Hodgkin prize, Brit. Crystallographic Assn., 2004, Perutz prize, European Crystallographic Assn., 2004. Fellow: Royal Soc. (London). Achievements include authorship of widely used computer programs for crystal structure determination; mineral sheldrickite named in his honor. Office: Lehrstuhl Strukturchemie Tammannstrasse 4 D-37077 Göttingen Germany

**SHELITE, LESLIE MICHELLE,** vocational school educator; d. Joyce Merle Oakes and Chester Henry Shelite; children: Chandra Dawn Murrow, Cynthea Diane Baker, Caleb Tip Murrow. BS, Northwestern Okla. State U., 1993; MS, US Sports Acad., 1994. Cert. tchr. Okla. State Dept. Edn., 1993. Vocat. svc. mgr. Arrowhead West, Inc., Medicine Lodge, Kans., 1994—97; case mgr. Okla. Dept. Corrections, 1997—98; tchr. South Barber Pubic Schs., Kiowa, Kans., 1998—99, Okla. City Pub. Schs., 1999—2000, Putnam City Pub. Schs., 2000—. Recipient Tchr. of Yr. Mayfield Mid. Sch., 2005; grantee Schools for Healthy Lifestyles, Okla. Med. Assn., Schools for Healthy Lifestyles, 2000—01. Mem.: Okla. Secondary Schools Activities Assn., PCACT (bldg. rep. 2005—06), NEA, OEA. D-Conservative. Christian. Avocation: walking. Home: 1200 Glenwood Dr Yukon OK 73099 Office: Mayfield Mid Sch 1600 N Purdue Oklahoma City OK 73127 Office Phone: 405-947-8693.

**SHELKROT, ELLIOT L.,** library director; b. Pitts., June 24, 1943; m. Evelyn Minick; children: Benjamin, Max, Daniel. BA, Oberlin Coll., 1965; MLS, U. Pitts., 1966. Trainee Pa. State Libr., 1965-66; branch head, young adult svcs. librarian Free Libr. Phila., 1966-69, pres., dir., 1987—; specialist cmty. svcs. divsn. libr. devel. Md. State Dept. Edn., 1969-76; chief pub. svcs. support Balt County Pub. Libr., 1976-80; state librarian Commonwealth Pa., 1980-87. Mayor's commn. literacy, 1987-99; bd. dirs. Ctr. Literacy, trustee, 1987-00. Mem. Mayor's Cultural Adv. Coun., 1987-92, Ben Franklin Pkwy. Coun., 1997—, chair, 2000; mem. Phila. Citizens Children and Youth, 1997—, Greater Phila. Urban Affairs Coun., 1998—, Greater Phila. Cultural Alliance, 1999—; bd. dirs. Fellowship Commn., 1989-92, Nat. Conf. Christians Jews, 1991-94. Mem. ALA (coun. 1972-78, 83-91, intellectual freedom com. 1975-79, nat. libr. week com. 1983-85, councilor at large 1988-91, legis. com. 1989-91), Urban Libr. Coun. (bd. dirs. 1997—, pres. 2000—), Pub. Libr. Assn. (goals, guidelines and stds. task force com. 1979-83, dir.-at-large, new stds. task force 1983-86, v.p., rsch. com. 1983-84, pres. 1991-93), Assn. Specialized Coop. Libr. Agys. (legis. com. 1982-85, chair 1984-85, bd. dirs. 1985-91), Chief Officers State Libr. Agys. (chair com. liaison Nat. Commn. Librs. Info. Sci. 1981-85, bd. dirs. 1983-84), Pa. Libr. Assn. Avocations: clarinet, biking, reading, skiing. Office: Free Libr Phila 1901 Vine St Philadelphia PA 19103-1189 Office Phone: 215-686-5300. E-mail: shelkrote@library.phila.gov.*

**SHELL, ART (ARTHUR SHELL JR.),** professional football coach; b. Charleston, SC, Nov. 26, 1946; m. Janice Shell; children: Arthur III, Christopher. BS in Industrial Arts, Md. State Coll., 1968. Player Oakland Raiders, 1968-83; coach L.A. Raiders (formerly Oakland Raiders), 1983-89, head coach, 1989-94, offensive line coach Kans. City Chiefs, 1995-96, Atlanta Falcons, 1997—2000; appeals officer NFL, NYC, 2001—04, sr. v.p. football ops. & devel., 2004—06; head coach Oakland Raiders, 2006—. Inducted into Pro Football Hall of Fame, 1989; recipient, Jackie Robinson Award for Athletics (Ebony mag.), 1990; named All-Pro, 1973, 1974, 1976, 1977; named to Pro Bowl, 1972-78, 1980; named N.F.L. Coach of Yr., 1991 Office: Oakland Raiders 1220 Harbor Bay Pkwy Alameda CA 94502*

**SHELL, OWEN G., JR.,** retired bank executive; b. Greenville, S.C., June 19, 1936; s. Owen and Katherine S.; m. Mary Ruth Trammell, Aug. 9, 1980; children: Katherine Sloan, Mary Carroll, Robert Owen, James Walker. BS, U. S.C., 1960; postgrad., Stonier Grad. Sch. Banking, 1971; grad., Advanced Mgmt. Program, Harvard U., 1979. V.p. Citizens & So. Nat. Bank S.C., Columbia, 1968-71, sr. v.p., 1971-74, exec. v.p., 1974-79; pres., dir., chief exec. officer First Am. Nat. Bank, Nashville, 1979-86; vice chmn. bd., dir. First Am. Corp., 1979-86; chmn., pres., chief exec. officer Sovran Bank/Tenn., Nashville, 1986-91; pres. Nations Bank of Tenn. (formerly Sovran Bank), Nashville, 1992-96; pres. asset mgmt. group NationsBank Corp., St. Louis, 1997-99; pres. Asset Mgmt. Bank of Am., Charlotte, 1997—2002; ret., 2002. Bd. dirs. Nashville br. Fed. Res. Bank, Atlanta; chmn. bd. Lifepoint Hosp. Inc., Ctrl. Parkins, inc. Chmn. Leadership Nashville, Tenn. Performing Arts Found., Mid. Tenn. coun. Boy Scouts Am., Vanderbilt U. Owen Grad. Sch. Mgmt.; trustee Met. Nashville Pub. Edn. Found.; chmn. bd. INROADS/Nashville; bd. dirs. Tenn. Bus. Roundtable, Tenn. Tomorrow. Mem.: Assn. Res. City Bankers, Old Warson Country Club (St. Louis), Harvard Club N.Y.C., Belle Meade Country Club (Nashville), Kappa Alpha. Presbyterian. Home: 4412 Chickering Ln Nashville TN 37215-4915 also: 114 Tern Dr Anna Maria FL 34216

**SHELL, ROBERT J.,** construction executive; b. Honolulu, Oct. 16, 1930; s. Roscoe and Gladys Rose (Callahan) Shell; m. Virginia Louise Brooks, Apr. 7, 1973; children: Linda Shell Squires, Vickie Doss, Scott, Cathy Gammill, Allison Nelson. Grad. high sch., Little Rock, 1947. Project mgmt. acct. The Baldwin Co., Little Rock, 1950-61, sec., treas., 1961-76, exec. v.p., 1976-83, pres., 1983—, also bd. dirs.; pres. Baldwin & Shell Constrn., Little Rock, 1980—. Chmn. Little Rock Censor Bd., 1969, Little Rock Bd. Adjustment, 1979; pres. Pulaski Acad., Little Rock, 1984—85, Ark. Arthritis Assn. 1991—; treas. Metro YMCA; bd. dirs., pres. Bapt. Med. Sys. Found.; pres. 50 for the Future, 2000; charter mem. Ark. Constrn. Hall of Fame, 2000; chmn. found. bd. U. Ark., Little Rock, 2004; bd. dirs. Twin City Bank. Mem.: Associated Gen. Contractors Am. (nat. bd. dirs. 1982—, Disting. Svc. award 1984, Ark. Bus. Exec. of the Yr. 1991), Am. Inst. Constructors, Am. Arbitration Assn., Alzheimer Ark. (bd. dirs. 1999—), Pleasant Valley Country Club (Little Rock) (sec. 1985—86). Baptist. Home: 4 Bretagne Cir Little Rock AR 72223-9136 Office: Baldwin & Shell Constrn 523 Ringo PO Box 1750 Little Rock AR 72203-1750 Office Phone: 501-374-8677.

**SHELLEDY, JAMES EDWIN, III,** newspaper editor; b. Spencer, Iowa, Nov. 11, 1942; s. James E. Jr. and Patricia L. (Cornwall) S.; m. Susan Emily Thomas, Mar. 7, 1986; 1 child. Ian Whittaker. BA, Gonzaga U., 1966. Reporter Spkesman-Rev., Spokane, Wash., 1963-66; tchr., coach Kootenai High Sch., Harrison, Idaho, 1967-71; reporter AP, Boise, Idaho, 1971-72; reporter, editor Lewiston (Idaho) Morning Tribune, 1973-80; editor, pub. Moscow, Idaho, 1981-91; editor The Salt Lake Tribune, Salt Lake City, 1991—; editor, pub. Daily News, Pullman, Wash., 1981—91. Juror Pulitzer Prize Com., Columbia U., 1987-88; dir. Investigative Reporters and Editors, 1978-82; bd. dirs. New Directions for News, 1989-96, Newspaper Agy. Corp., 1994-99; mem. AP audit com., N.Y.C., 1982-91. Dir. Idaho Parks Found., Boise, 1978-58, Idaho-Washington Symphony, Pullman, Wash., 1986-89; commr. Idaho Lottery Commn., Boise, 1989-91; adv. bd. Utah YWCA, 1992-97; bd. visitors La. State U. Sch. Comms., 1995—, mem. Utah Alliance for Unity, 2001--, adv. bd, comm. dept. Utah State U., 2002--. Roman Catholic. Avocations: golf, sailing.

**SHELLER, JOHN WILLARD,** lawyer; b. LA, Oct. 29, 1950; s. Willard and Barbara S.; m. Mary Elizabeth Hodor, Aug. 9, 1975; children: Matthew John, James Henry. BA, Stanford U., 1972; JD, Loyola U., L.A., 1975. Bar: Calif. 1975. With Hinshaw & Culbertson, L.A. Mem. Am. Bd. Trial Advs. Contbr. articles to profl. jours. Mem. Calif. State Bar Assn., L.A. County Bar Assn., L.A. Country Club. Avocation: golf. Office: Hinshaw & Culbertson 11601 Wilshire Blvd Ste 800 Los Angeles CA 90025 Home: 16 Park Ave Venice CA 90291-3222 Office Phone: 310-909-8000. Business E-Mail: jsheller@hinshawlaw.com.

**SHELLEY, BONNIE J.,** voice educator; b. Sullivan, Mo., Nov. 15, 1926; d. Earl William Sperry and Erma Laura Trout; m. Peter Lipkan (dec.); children: Kathleen, Michael, Christopher, Charissa, Brian; m. Clark C. Shelley (dec.); m. Dean F. Hollister, Nov. 15, 1990. MusB, U. Ariz., 1965; MA in Music, Calif. State U., Fullerton, 1976. Adj. prof. voice Yavapai Coll., Prescott, Ariz., 1986—93, 1998—, No. Ariz. U., Flagstaff, 1989—93. Youth choir dir. St. Francis Episcopal Ch., Palos Verdes, Calif., 1982—85; choir dir., bell dir. 1st Congl. Ch./St. Lukes Episcopal, Prescott, 1989—93, Prescott, 1994—96; choir dir. First Meth. Ch., Prescott Valley, 2000—05. Mem.: Nat. Assn. Tchrs. Singing. Home: 5325 N Bremont Way Prescott Valley AZ 86314

**SHELLEY, CAROLE,** actress; b. London, Aug. 16, 1939; arrived in U.S., 1964; d. Curtis and Deborah (Bloomstein) Shelley; m. Albert G. Woods, July 26, 1967 (dec.). Student, Arts Edul. Sch., 1943-56, Prepatory Acad. Royal Acad. Dramatic Art, 1956-57; studies with Iris Warren and Eileen Thorndike. Trustee Am. Shakespeare Theatre, 1974—82. Actor: (plays) The Odd Couple, 1965, Absurd Person Singular, 1973, The Norman Conquests (L.A. Drama Critics Cir. award, 1975), As You Like It, King Lear, She Stoops to Conquer, 1972, The Country Wife, 1973, A Doll's House, Man and Superman, 1977, Misalliance, 1980, Grand Hunt, 1980, The Play's the Thing, 1978, Lion in Winter, 1987, The Elephant Man (Outer Critics Cir. award, 1979, Tony award for Best Actress, 1979), What the Butler Saw, 1989, Broadway Bound, 1987—88, Lettice and Lovage, 1989—90, The Miser, 1990, Cabaret Verboten, 1991, The Destiny of Me, 1992—93, Later Life, 1993 (Outer Critics nominee), Richard II, 1994, London Suite, 1995, Show Boat, 1995—96, 1998, The Film Society, 1997, The Last Night of Ballyhoo, 1997—98, Cabaret, 1999—2002, Wicked, 2002—04, 2005—, The Importance of Being Earnest, 2005—, Ring Round the Moon, 2006; (films) The Boston Strangler, The Odd Couple, 1968, The Super, 1990, Devlin, 1991, Quiz Show, 1993,

The Road to Wellville, 1993, Bewitched, 2005, others; (TV series) The Odd Couple, Robin Phillips Grand Theatre Co., 1983—84, Nat. Co. The Royal Family (L.A. Drama Critics Cir. award, 1977); (Broadway plays) Noises Off, 1985, Stepping Out, 1986 (Tony nominee, 1986), Waltz of the Toreadors, 1986, Oh Coward, 1986—87, Broadway Bound, 1987—88; voice actor: (films) Robin Hood; The Aristocats; Hercules. Recipient Obie award for Twelve Dreams, N.Y. Shakespeare Festival, 1982. Jewish. Office: Robert Duva 277 W 10th St New York NY 10014

**SHELLEY, HERBERT CARL,** lawyer; b. Stamford, Tex., Jan. 28, 1947; s. Carl B. and Lourena A. (Whitley) S.; m. Jerilyn S. Ray, Aug. 9, 1969; children: Megan, Caitlyn, Daniel. BA, Columbia Coll., 1969; JD, Vanderbilt U., 1972; LLM in Internat. and Comparative Law magna cum laude, Vrije U. Brussels, 1973. Bar: D.C. 1973, Md. 1985, U.S. Ct. Appeals (fed. cir.) 1981, U.S. Ct. Internat. Trade 1982, U.S. Supreme Ct. 1987. Atty./adv. U.S. Tariff Commn., Washington, 1973-74; Internat. trade specialist, asst. Office dir. Office Tariff Affairs U.S. Dept. Treasury, Washington, 1974-76; internat. trade negotiator Office Spl. Trade Reps., Geneva, Switzerland, 1976-79; prtr. Plaia & Schaumberg, Washington, 1979-86, Howrey & Simon, Washington, 1986-99, Steptoe & Johnson LLP, Washington, 1999—. Mem. ABA, D.C. Bar Assn., Md. Bar Assn. Avocations: skiing, golf, cooking, travel. Office: 1330 Connecticut Ave NW Washington DC 20036-1704 Office Phone: 202-429-8146. Business E-Mail: hshelley@steptoe.com.

**SHELLEY, KEVIN FRANCIS,** former state official; b. Washington, Nov. 16, 1955; s. John Francis and Thelma (Smith) Shelley; m. Dominique Shelley; 1 child, Jack. BA in Polit. Sci., U. Calif., Davis, 1978; JD, Hastings Coll. Law, 1983. Asst. to U.S. Congressman Phil Burton US Ho. Reps., 1978—87; mem. bd. suprs., pres. bd. San Francisco Bd. Suprs., 1990—96; mem., majority leader Calif. State Assembly, 1996—2002; sec. state State of Calif., 2003—05; atty. Calif., 2005—. Mem.: Calif. State Bar.*

**SHELLEY, LORE,** writer, small business owner, realtor; b. Lubbecke, Nordrhein Westfalen, Germany, Feb. 19, 1924; d. Siegfried and Meta Weinberg; m. Sucher Szaldajewski, Aug. 19, 1951; 1 child, Gabriela. Student, U. Bonn, 1955; Certificat Propedeutique, U. Geneva, 1956; MA in Exptl. Psychology, New Sch. Social Rsch., 1958; MSW, San Francisco State U., 1978; PhD in Philos., The Fielding Inst., 1984. Author: Secretaries of Death, Criminal Experiments on Human Beings in Auschwitz and War Research Laboratories, Auschwitz - the Nazi Civilization, The Union Kommando in Auschwitz, Post Auschwitz Fragments, The Fatherland's Gratitude is Guaranteed. Vol. tutor adults and children The Jewish Agy., Jerusalem, 1974—75, Maalot, 1974—75; mem. San Francisco Commn. Aging, 1977—83; vol., active mem. Bay Area Coun. on Soviet Jewry, 1971—80; co-founder The Shelley Charitable Trust Hasidim Gur, Jerusalem, 1976—2004; cofounder, bd. mem. Tikva (a support orgn. for aging Holocaust survivors), San Francisco, 1997—2002. Democrat. Jewish. Avocations: travel, yoga, bicycling, dog training.

**SHELLEY, WALTER BROWN,** dermatologist, educator; b. St. Paul, Feb. 6, 1917; s. Patrick K. and Alfaretta (Brown) S.; m. Marguerite H. Weber, 1942 (dec.); children: Peter B., Anne E. Kiselewich, Barbara A. (dec.); m. E. Dorinda Loeffel, 1980; children: Thomas R., Katharine D., William L. BS, U. Minn., 1940, PhD, 1941, MD, 1943; MA honoris causa, U. Pa., 1971; MD honoris causa, U. Uppsala, Sweden, 1977; DSc (hon.), Med. U. Ohio, 2006. Diplomate: Am. Bd. Dermatology (pres. 1968-69, dir. 1960-69). Instr. physiology U Pa., Phila., 1946-47, asst. instr. dermatology and syphilology, 1947-49, asst. prof. dermatology, 1950-53, assoc. prof., 1953-57, prof., 1957-80, chmn. dept., 1965-80; prof. dermatology U. Ill. Peoria Sch. Medicine, 1980-83; prof. medicine (dermatology) Med. Coll. Ohio, 1983-97, emeritus prof. medicine, 1997—. Instr. dermatology Dartmouth Coll., 1949-50; Regional cons. dermatology VA, 1955-59; mem. com. on cutaneous system NRC, 1955-59, Commn. Cutaneous Diseases, Armed Forces Epidemiological Bd., 1958-61, dep. dir., 1959-61; cons. dermatology Surgeon Gen. USAF, 1958-61, U.S. Army, 1958-61; mem. NRC, 1961-64 Author (with Crissey): Classics in Clinical Dermatology, 1953, 2003; author (with Pillsbury, Kligman) Dermatology, 1956; author: Cutaneous Medicine, 1961; author: (with Hurley) The Human Apocrine Sweat Gland in Health and Disease, 1960; author: (with Botelho and Brooks) The Endocrine Glands, 1969; author: Consultations in Dermatology with Walter B. Shelley, 1972, 2006, Consultations II, 1974; author: (with Shelley) Advanced Dermatologic Therapy, 1987; author: Advanced Dermatologic Diagnosis, 1992, A Century of International Dermatological Congresses, 1992, Advanced Dermatological Therapy II, 2001, Shelley's 77 Skins, 2001, Consultations in Dermatology, 2006; mem. editl. bd. Jour. Investigative Dermatology, 1961—64, Archives of Dermatology, 1961—62, Skin and Allergy News, 1970—93, Excerpta Medica Dermatologica, 1960—, Cutis, 1972—, Jour. Geriatric Dermatol, 1993; assoc. editor: Jour. Cutaneous Pathology, 1972—81; editl. cons. Medcom, 1972—. Served as capt. M.C. AUS, 1944-46. Recipient Spl. award Soc. Cosmetic Chemists, 1955, Hellerstrom medal, 1971, Am. Med. Writers Assn. Best Med. Book award, 1973, Dohi medal, 1981, Rothman medal Soc. for Investigative Dermatology, 1987, Rose Hirschler award, 1990, Humane Dermatologist award, 2005. Master ACP; fellow Assn. Am. Physicians, St. John's Dermatol. Soc. London (hon.); mem. AMA (chmn. residency rev. com. for dermatology 1963-67, chmn. sect. dermatology 1969-71), Assn. Profs. Dermatology (pres. 1972-73), Pacific Dermatol. Assn. (hon.), Am. Dermatol. Assn. (hon., dir., pres. 1975-76), Soc. Investigative Dermatology (hon. pres. 1961-62), Am. Physiol. Soc., Phila. Physiol. Soc., Brit. Dermatol. Soc. (hon.), Phila. Dermatol. Soc. (pres. 1960-61), Mich. Dermatol. Soc., Ohio Dermatol. Soc. (hon.), Am. Acad. Dermatology (Gold medal 1992, hon. pres. 1971-72), Pa. Acad. Dermatology (pres. 1972-73), Am. Soc. Dermatologic Surgery, N.Am. Clin. Dermatol. Soc. (hon.), Noah Worcester Dermatol. Soc., Royal Soc. Medicine; corr. mem. Nederlandse Vereniging Van Dermatologen, Israeli Dermatol. Assn., Finnish Soc. Dermatology, Swedish Dermatol. Soc., French Dermatologic Soc.; fgn. hon. mem. Danish Dermatol. Assn., Japanese Dermatol. Assn., Dermatol. Soc. S.Africa, Austrian Dermatol. Assn. Home: 21171 W River Rd Grand Rapids OH 43522-9703 Office: Med Univ Ohio 3120 Glendale Ave Toledo OH 43614-2595 Office Phone: 419-383-3720. Business E-Mail: wshelley@meduohio.edu.

**SHELLHORN, RUTH PATRICIA,** landscape architect; b. LA, Sept. 21, 1909; d. Arthur Lemon and Lodema (Gould) S.; m. Harry Alexander Kueser, Nov. 21, 1940. Student dept. landscape architecture, Oreg. State Coll., 1927—30; BA in Landscape Arch., Cornell U., 2005, BArch, 2005. Pvt. practice landscape architecture, various cities, Calif., 1933—; exec. cons. landscape arch. Bullocks Stores, Calif., 1945-78, Fashion Sqs. Shopping Ctrs., Calif., 1958-78, Marlborough Sch., L.A., 1968-93, El Camino Coll., Torrance, Calif., 1970-78, Harvard Sch., North Hollywood, Calif., 1974-90. Cons. landscape arch., site planner Disneyland, Anaheim, Calif., 1955, U. Calif., Riverside Campus, 1956-64, numerous others, also numerous gardens and estates; landscape arch. Torrance (Calif.) City Goals Com., 1969-70; cons. landscape arch. City of Rolling Hills (Calif.) Cmty. Assn., 1973-93. Contbr. articles to garden and profl. publs.; subject of Oct. 1967 issue Landscape Design & Constrn. mag. Named Woman of Year, L.A. Times, 1955, Woman of Year, South Pasadena-San Marino (Calif.) Bus. Profl. Women, 1955; recipient Charles Goodwin Sands medal, 1930-33, Landscape Architecture award of merit Calif. State Garden Clubs, 1984, 86, Horticulturist of the Yr. award So. Calif. Hort. Inst., numerous nat., state, local awards for excellence. Fellow Am. Soc. Landscape Archs. (past pres. So. Calif. chpt., Lifetime Achievement award, 2005), Phi Kappa Phi, Kappa Kappa Gamma (Alumni Achievement award 1960, 2006), Garden Club Am. (Civic Improvement award 2006). Achievements include oral history and biography published by Pasadena Heritage, 2002. Home and Office: 362 Camino De Las Colinas Redondo Beach CA 90277-6435 Integrity, honesty, dependability, sincerity, dedication, and a willingness to give more than is expected in service, are the basic principles which have guided my career. Never losing sight of the importance of the individual, I have tried to create total environments of harmony and beauty to which each individual can relate in a very personal and pleasureable way, and for a little while, can find a calm oasis in a busy and demanding world.

**SHELLMAN-LUCAS, ELIZABETH C.,** special education educator, researcher; b. Thomas County, Ga., Feb. 5, 1937; d. Herbert and Juanita (Coleman) Smith; m. John Lee Lucas, Jr. (div.); 1 child, Sandie Juanita Lucas Boyce; m. Eddie Joseph Shellman; 1 child, Eddie Joseph Shellman, Jr. MS in Edn., CUNY, 1990. Cert. tchr. NY. Pvt. practice cosmetologist, N.Y.C., 1959—; tchr. N.Y.C. Bd. of Edn. High Sch. Dist., 1984—. Vol. various cmty. orgns.; citizen amb. del. People to People Internat., 1994; ch. sch. tchr., supt. Canaan Bapt. Ch., Harlem, 1990-2002. Mem. Coun. for Exceptional Children. Avocations: reading, music, dance, jogging, languages.

**SHELOV, STEVEN PATRICK,** pediatrician, educator; b. Honolulu, Nov. 19, 1944; s. Sidney M. and Faith R. S.; m. Marsha Liberman, Aug. 30, 1968; children: Joshua, Danielle, Eric. BS, Yale, 1966; MD, Med. Coll. Wisc., 1971; MS in Med. Admin., U. Wisc., 1995. Diplomate Am. Bd. Pediatrics. Intern, then resident Montefiore Med. Ctr., Bronx, 1971-74, chief resident, 1974-75; asst. dir. amb. pediat. Albert Einstein Coll. Med., Bronx, NY, 1977-79; dir. pediat. edn. Montefiore Med. Ctr., Bronx, 1980—, prof. and vice chmn. pediat., 1989-97; chmn. pediat. Infants and Children's Hosp. of Bklyn., Maimonides Med. Ctr., Bklyn., 1997—; prof. Mt. Sinai Sch. Medicine. Editor: Caring for Your Baby and Young Child: Birth to 5, 1991, 1996, 2004, Pediatrics for Medical Students, 2003, Guide to Your Child's Symptoms, 1997, The First Year of Life, 2004. Recipient Geo. Armstrong award Ambulatory Pediat. Assn., 1996, Lifetime Achievement in Edn. award Am. Acad. Pediat., 2002. Mem.: Am. Acad. Pediats. (Holroyd-Sherry award 2004). Office: Maimonides Med Ctr 4802 10th Ave Brooklyn NY 11219-2844 Office Phone: 718-283-6150. Business E-Mail: sshelov@maimonidesmed.org.

**SHELTON, CAROLYN JOHNSON,** professional society administrator; d. Ernest Gustav Johnson and Anne Mabel Nemergut; m. Philo Sherwood Shelton, June 27, 1962; children: Philo Sherwood, Anne F. Mele. AS (hon.), U. Bridgeport, 1962. Dir. membership Conn. Audubon Soc., Fairfield, 1984—. V.p. Fairfield Women's Club, Conn., 1980—82. Recipient 10 Yr. Award for Volunteerism on the Four Seasons Ball Com. to raise money for the mentally challenged, The Kenndey Ctr., 10. Mem.: Greenfield Hill Garden Club. R-Consevative. Catholic. Achievements include design of Designed the pussy willow stencils and applied the stencils for a suite in a National Historic Restoration inn called the Inn at National Hall located in Westport, Conn. Home and Office: Conn Audubon Soc 2325 Burr St Fairfield CT 06824 Business E-Mail: cshelton@ctaudubon.org.

**SHELTON, CRAIG,** food service executive; b. Rye, N.H. naturalized, U.S., naturalized, France; trained with Joel Rubochon, trained with Ferran Adriá, trained with Paul Haeberlin. Chef Ma Maison, L.A., Rainbow Rm., Le Chantilly, Le Bernardin, Bouley; chef, owner Ryland Inn, Whitehouse, NJ, 1991—. Named Relais Gourmand, Relais & Chateaux, 1999; recipient Best award Excellence, Wine Spectator's, 1994—, James Bears award, 2000. Mem.: N.J. Restaurant Assn. (bd. dirs.), Internat. Assn. Culinary Profls. Office: Ryland Inn Rt 22 W Whitehouse NJ 08888

**SHELTON, DARLENE,** psychologist, consultant; d. Harvey Clinton and Opal Lyles Shelton; m. David Weinberg, Oct. 10, 2003. BA in Psychology, So. Ill. U., 1979, MA in Psychology, 1986, PhD in Behavioral Medicine and Psychology, 1990. Lic. clin. psychologist State of Ky., State of Conn. Dir. coord. psychol. svcs. Econ. Opportunity Family Health Ctr., Miami, 1991—94; rsch. asst. prof. dept. psychiatry U. Miami Sch. Medicine, 1993—94; assoc. prof., dir. diversity and minority affairs Spalding U. Sch. Profl. Psychology, Louisville, 1995—2003; assoc. rsch. scientist dept. psychiatry Yale U. Sch. of Medicine, New Haven, 2003—04; CEO Ctr. for Humanitarian Initiatives, Guilford, Conn., 2004—; sr. fellow Garrison Inst., NY, 2005—; assoc. of the Chaplain's Office, Yale U., New Haven, 2006—. Rsch. cons. U.S. HHS, Pub. Health Svc., Health Resources and Svcs. Adminstrn., Bur. Health Resources Devel., Washington, 1991—93; forensic psychology cons. Thematix Group, Guilford, Conn., 2001—; program cons. Garrison Inst., Garrison, 2004—; rsch. cons. Ctr. for Women Policy Studies, Washington, 1993; mem. adv. com. Pediat. AIDS Health Care Demonstration Project of U. Miami/Jackson Meml. Hosp., 1992—94; grant reviewer Women's Initiative for HIV Care and Reduction of Perinatal HIV Transmission, Maternal and Child Health Bur., Health Resources and Svcs. Adminstrn., Rockville, Md., 1995; mem. Ky. HIV Prevention Cmty. Planning Group, State of Ky. Dept. of HIV Prevention, Frankfort, 1996—98; mem. African-Am. adv. com. Ky. HIV Prevention Cmty. Planning Group, State of Ky., Dept. HIV Prevention, Frankfort, 1996—98, advisor, 1998—99; psychol. cons. State of Fla. Dept. Juvenile Justice Dist. XI, Miami, 1994—95; rsch. cons. R.E.A.C.H., Louisville, 1995—96, Coun. on Prevention and Edn.: Substances, Inc. (COPES) Family Connection Demonstration Project, Louisville, 1996—2000; psychologist U. Louisville Sch. Medicine WINGS (HIV/AIDS) Clinic Aux. Support Team, Louisville, 1996—2000; co-process evaluator Ky. Incentives for Prevention, Louisville, 1997—2000; psychologist site supr. Americana Cmty. Ctr., Louisville, 1999—2003; adj. asst. prof. dept. psychology Barry U., Miami Shores, Fla., 1995; presenter, lectr., spkr. in field. Author: (nonfiction book) Babies Mamas, (booklet) Health Care Utilization and Medical Adherence Issues Among Prenatal HIV Seropositive African American Women in Miami: The Role of The Family and The Extended Kinship Networks.; panelist (television program) KENTUCKY TONIGHT; Coping Emotionally with the Aftermath of September 11th; author: (public service television script) Make Your Next Move Count, (public service TV script) Child Abuse: Sticks and Stones and Words Can Hurt; contbr. articles to scholarly jours. Mem. planning com. Ann. Nat. Conf. on the Black Family in Am., Louisville, 2001—03; judge panelist ABA Regional Client Counseling Competition, Louisville, 2002; facilitator One Louisville, 2001—02; bd. dirs. Ctr. for Haitian Studies, Miami, 1993—95. Named Outstanding Leader and Mentor, Spalding U. Black Student Assn., 1997, Nat. Inst. of Drug Abuse Sponsored Jr. Minority Investigator, APA, 1992; recipient White Ho. Briefing Honoring World AIDS Day invitation, 2005, NIMH Postdoctoral fellowship in psychoimmunology, Ctr. for the Biopsychosocial Study of AIDS, Dept. Psychiatry, U. Miami Sch. of Medicine, 1990—91, Cert. Appreciation for Contbns. in Devel. of Creative AIDS Edn. Programs, U.S. Dept. VA, 1990, Ill. Minority Grad. Incentive Program fellowship, State of Ill., 1986—90, So. Ill. U. Grad. Dean's fellowship, 1984—85, Cert. of Appreciation, Omega Psi Phi, 1997, 1998, 1999, 2000; grantee Ongoing Program of Stress Mgmt. for Spl. Immunology Unit Staff., U.S. Dept. VA, Office Acad. Affairs, and Regional Med. Edn. Ctr., 1989, Five-year Plan for Ethnic Minority Recruitment, Retention and Tng. in Psychology, APA, 2002, Qualitative studies addressing the sexual behaviors and biopsychosocial issues of patients in the Women's HIV/AIDS Clinic at the U. of Miami, U. Miami Sch. of Medicine Ctr. for Comprehensive Study of HIV/AIDS, 1990—92; scholar Non-Traditional Student Scholarship award, Delta Sigma Theta, Carbondale Alumnae Chpt., 1989. Mem.: APA, Inst. Noetic Scis., Kentuckiana Assn. of Black Psychologists (pres. 2002—03), Ky. Psychol. Assn., Conn. Psychol. Assn. (ethnic diversity task force 2004, co-chair 2005—), Nature Conservancy. Achievements include research in Ethnographic Study of Miami-area HIV Positive Expectant Mothers with Previous Children. Office: Ctr for Humanitarian Initiatives Deep River Center 3 Taliar Ridge Rd Guilford CT 06437 Office Phone: 203-458-3244. E-mail: darlene.shelton@chiglobal.org.

**SHELTON, DAVID HOWARD,** economics professor; b. Winona, Miss., Nov. 30, 1928; s. Tuttle M. and Kate (Moss) S.; m. Margaret Murff, Feb. 4, 1951; children: David Keith, Sarah Katherine, Susan Esther. BA, Millsaps Coll., 1951; MA, Ohio State U., 1952, PhD, 1958. Instr. Ohio State U., 1958; asst. prof. U. Del., 1958-63, assoc. prof., 1963-65; prof. U. N.C. Greensboro, 1965—93, head dept. econs., bus. adminstrn., 1967-70, dean Sch. Bus. and Econs., 1970-83, head dept. econs., 1988-93, prof. emeritus, 1993—. Cons. Joint Coun. on Econ. Edn., 1969-72, N.C. Dept. Pub. Instrn., 1970-73. Trustee N.C. Coun. on Econ. Edn., 1971-96, chmn., 1971-75, pres., 1975-85. Served with USN, 1946-48. M.D. Lincoln fellow, 1956-57; H.L. and Grace Doherty fellow, 1957. Mem. Beta Gamma Sigma, Omicron Delta Kappa, Kappa Sigma. Episcopalian. Home: 3609 Dogwood Dr Greensboro NC 27403-1010 Office: UNC 462 Bryan Bldg Greensboro NC 27412-0001

**SHELTON, DOROTHY AUBINOE,** interior designer; b. Washington, Feb. 19, 1927; d. Alvin Love and Dorothy (Barron) Aubinoe; m. William Roy Shelton, (dec. 1985); children: June, Paul, Tod, Holly. A.B., Rollins Coll., 1948; grad. teaching cert. U. Md., 1949; diploma Internat. Inst. Interior Design, 1958. Owner, interior designer Griffith Assos., Inc., Bethesda, Md., 1958-78; owner, dir. Griffith Gallery, Miami, Fla., 1978-84; owner, pres. Griffith Investments. Mem. alumni council Rollins Coll., 1983—, trustee, 1983-86, nat. dir. Coll. Fund, 1985-87. Recipient Disting. Service award Rollins Coll. Alumni Assn., 1988. Mem. Am. Soc. Interior Designers. Home: 322 Tollgate Shores Dr Islamorada FL 33036-4222 Office Phone: 305-664-9239. Personal E-Mail: dottieshelton@msn.com.

**SHELTON, HUGH (HENRY HUGH SHELTON),** former Chairman of the Joint Chiefs of Staff; b. Tarboro, N.C., Jan. 2, 1942; m. Carolyn L. Johnson; children: Jon, Jeff, Mark. BS, N.C. State U.; MS, Auburn U.; grad., Air Command and Staff Coll., Nat. War Coll. Commd. 2d lt. U.S. Army, 1963, advanced through grades to gen., 1996, ret., 2001; with 5th Spl. Forces Group, Vietnam, 173d Airborn Brigade, Vietnam; comdr. 3d Bn., 60th Infantry, 9th Infantry Divsn., Ft. Lewis, asst. chief of staff for ops.; comdr. 1st Brigade, 82d Airborne Divsn., Ft. Bragg, N.C.; chief of staff 10th Mountain Divsn., Ft. Drum, N.Y.; with ops. directoratie Joint Staff, Washington, 1987—89, asst. divsn. comdr. for ops. 101st Airborne Divsn., 1989-91; comdr. 82d Airborne Divsn., Ft. Bragg, N.C., XVIIIth Airborne Corps., 1993, Chief of U.S. Spl. Ops. Comman, 1996—97; chmn. Joint Chiefs of Staff, US Dept. Def., Washington, 1997—2001; pres., internat. ops. M.I.C. Industries, 2002—. Bd. dirs. Anheuser-Busch Companies Inc., 2001—, Red Hat, Inc., 2003—. Decorated Def. D.S.M. with two oak clusters, D.S.M., Bronze Star with V device with three oak clusters, Purple Heart, Legion of Merit with oak leaf cluster. Office: MIC Industries Inc 11911 Freedom Dr Reston VA 20190

**SHELTON, JAMES D. (DENNY SHELTON),** hospital management company executive; b. in Polit. Sci. and History, La. State U.; MS in Pub. Adminstrn., U. Mo. Hosp. adminstr. La., Iowa, NC, Ga., Ill., Mo.; exec. dir. Westbank Hosp. Ops. Nat. Med. Enterprises (now Tenet Healthcare Corp.), New Orleans, 1984—86, v.p. ops., 1986—90, sr. v.p. ops., 1990—93, exec. v.p. ctrl. divsn., 1993—94; pres Ctrl. Group Columbia/HCA, 1994—98, pres. Pacific Group, 1998—99; chmn., pres., CEO Triad Hosps. Inc., 1999—. Chmn. Fedn. Am. Hosps., 1999, mem. bd. govs., 1999—2002; bd. dirs. Am. Hosp. Assn. Office: Triad Hosp Inc 5800 Tennyson Pwy Plano TX 75024-3548*

**SHELTON, JAMES DOUGLAS,** banker; b. Boynton Beach, Fla., Feb. 28, 1939; s. Clarence Wilton and Lou Anna (Ward) S.; m. Claudia Ellen Marshall, Oct. 20, 1973; children: Christopher John, Ryan Marshall. BA, Duke U., 1961; MDiv, Union Sem., 1965; STM, Boston U., 1966; SEP, Stanford U., 1975. Adj. prof. NY Sem., NYC, 1966-68; asst. treas. Bankers Trust Co., NYC, 1968-71; v.p. Chase Manhattan Bank, NYC, 1971-84; sr. v.p. Conn. Bank & Trust, Hartford, Conn., 1984-88; chmn., pres., chief exec. officer First Fed. Savs., East Hartford, Conn., 1988-2001. Bd. dirs. Conn. On-Line Computer Ctr., Avon, chmn., 1989-2001; bd. dirs. Cmty. Bank League of New Eng., Boston, chmn., 1989-96; mem. Conn. Legislature Interstate Banking Task Force, Hartford, 1989-90. Bd. dirs. Jr. Achievement North Ctrl. Conn., Windsor, 1986-90, Sci. Ctr. Conn., West Hartford, 1988-94, Riverfront Recapture, Inc., Hartford, 1994-98, Charter Oak State Coll. Found., New Britain, Conn., 2004—; corporator Am. Sch. for the Deaf, West Hartford, 1986-2001; trustee Noah Webster House, West Hartford Hist. Soc., 2005—. Mem. Am. Cmty. Bankers Assn. (bd. dirs. 1995-2001), New Eng. Automated Clearing House Assn. (bd. dir. 1983-98), The Country Club of Farmington, Old Guard of West Hartford.

**SHELTON, KATHRYN H.,** librarian; d. Bruce Whittington and Edna Poyas (Hall) Martin; m. L. Jev Shelton, Aug. 27, 1970; children: Kirsten Anna, Martin Harold, Andrew Olaf. BA in English, Randolph-Macon Woman's Coll., 1963; MS in Libr. Sci., Simmons Coll., 1966; MA in Am. Studies, U. Minn., 1969; postgrad., U. Alaska SE; cert., Modern Archives Inst., 1986. Profl. libr. asst. Boston Pub. Libr., 1965-67; substitute libr. Mpls. Pub. Libr., 1967-68; teaching assoc. Gen. Coll. U. Minn., Mpls., 1968-69; asst. libr., reader svcs. libr. Carleton Coll., Northfield, Minn., 1969-70; part-time libr. III Dept. Environ. Conservationand Dept. Edn. Alaska State Libr., Juneau, 1975-76; assoc. prof. libr. sci., head libr. U. Alaska, Juneau, 1970-75, 76-78; libr. II. State Legislature, Juneau, 1979—85; archivist I Alaska State Archives Dept. Administrn., Juneau, 1985-86; libr. III head pub. svcs. sect. Dept. Edn. Alaska State Libr., 1986-87, libr. III head Hist. Dept. Edn., 1987—2005, Alaska state libr., dir. divsn. librs., archives and museums, 2005—. Spkr. in field. Editor: Alaskana Books, 1993, Some Books About Alaska Received in..., 1988—2001; contbr. articles to profl. jours. Project dir. Alaska Newspaper Project, 1991-98; mem. Gold Rush Centennial Task Force, 1993-2003, Alaska Geographic Names Bd., 1973-93, Alaska Gov.'s Adv. Coun. on Libr., 1973-74. Recipient Kudo award Office of Ombudsman State of Alaska, 1985. Mem. ALA, Alaska Libr. Assn. (pres. 1973-74, v.p. program chmn. annual conf. 1973, continuing edn. com. 1984, Alaska collection devel. com. 1986-88, Alaska subcom. 1987-95, chair 1987-93), Alaska Hist. Soc. (pres. 2000-2002), Gastineau Channel Hist. Soc. (sec. 1991, Cert. Appreciation 1989), Soc. Am. Archivists, Acad. Cert. Archivists (cert. 1991), Polar Librs. Colloquy (co-editor Polar Librs. Bull. 1989-98). Home: 1670 Evergreen Ave Juneau AK 99801-1458 Office: Alaska State Libr PO Box 110571 Juneau AK 99811-0571 Office Phone: 907-465-2911.

**SHELTON, KENNETH N.,** bishop; b. Phila., Jan. 26, 1959; Baccalaureate, Am. Coll., Geneva, Switzerland, 1982, LHD, 1995; MA in Polit. Sci., Human Behavior, Webster U., Geneva, Switzerland, 1984; Alliance Francais, Ecole Schulz, Geneva, Switzerland, 1985. Elder of oversight for nat. youth dept. Ch. of the Lord Jesus Christ of the Apostolic Faith, Phila., 1976-91, elder (adminstrv.) of Pa., 1976-91, bishop (gen. overseer), 1991—. Home: 2401 Pennsylvania Ave Apt 21a4 Philadelphia PA 19130-3007 Office: 701 S 22d St Philadelphia PA 19146

**SHELTON, KENNETH R., JR.,** real estate company executive, artist; b. Galveston, Tex., Aug. 29, 1946; Pres. Moore Climatic Inc., 1984—87; gen. ptnr. Various Real Estate Ltd. Partnerships, 1978—, Moore-Shelton, LP, 1984—; pres. Polybus, Inc., 1989—; gen. ptnr. Video Lane Ltd., 1983—. Exhibited in group shows at Rosenberg Gallery, Galveston, 1982, one-man shows include Galveston Art Ctr., 1991, exhibited in group shows at Island Inspired, Galveston Art Ctr., 1992. Mem. Galveston Bd. Realtors, 1983—; pres. Galveston County Apt. Assn., 1984—85; chmn. Cancer Crusade, 1983—84; pres. Galveston Acad. Excellence Booster Club, 2000—03, v.p., 1999—2000, 2003—; founding pres. Galveston Fencing Club, 1999—2001, Knights of Momus, 1984—85. Mem.: Galveston Fencing Club (dir.). Episcopalian. Avocations: painting, fencing, furniture making. Office: Kenneth R Shelton Jr 2002 450th St Ste 103 Galveston TX 77550 Mailing: PO Box 3123 Galveston TX 77552 Office Phone: 404-765-5600. E-mail: krskrs@swbell.net.

**SHELTON, MICHAEL PATRICK,** principal; b. Seymour, Ind., July 16, 1972; s. John Michael Shelton and Paula Michelle Kemp, William Newt Kemp (Stepfather); m. Stacy Leigh Conway, Aug. 12, 1995; children: Brendan Patrick, Kelsey Rae, Katelyn Grace. MusB, Culver-Stockton Coll., 1994—94; MS in Edn., So. Ill. U., Edwardsville, 2002. Dir. of vocal music Staunton (Ill.) Cmty. Unit Sch. Dist., 1994—2002; prin. Wood River (Ill.) -Hartford Elem. Sch. Dist., 2002—. Pres. St. Paul United Ch. of Christ, Staunton, 2001—02. Mem.: ASCD, Nat. Assn. of Elem. Sch. Prin., Ill. Alliance Adminstrs. Spl. Edn., Internat. Reading Assn., Ill. Music Educators Assn., Ill. Principals Assn., Staunton Optimist Club (pres. 2000—02), Delta Upsilon (vice-president 1993—94). Avocations: golf, music, travel. Home: 610 Stone Creek Dr Staunton IL 62088 Office: Lewis and Clark Elem Sch 501 E Lorena Ave Wood River IL 62095 Office Phone: 618-254-9814. Business E-Mail: pshelton@madison.k12.il.us.

**SHELTON, RICHARD CHARLES,** psychiatrist, educator; b. Louisville, Ky., Jan. 12, 1954; m. Judith Lee, July 20, 1975; children: Abigail, Amelia, Kathryn Maureen. MD, U. Louisville, 1979. Diplomate Am. Bd. Psychiatry and Neurology. Prof. dept. psychiatry Vanderbilt U., Nashville, 1985—, Vanderbilt U., Dept. of Pharmacology, Nashville, 1985–2006. James G. Blakemore rsch. prof. dept. psychiatry Vanderbilt U., Nashville, 2001—, vice-chmn. rsch. dept. psychiatry, 2006—. Contbr. articles to profl. jours. Rsch. grant, NIH. Presbyterian. Office Phone: 615-343-9669.

**SHELTON, ROBERT ARTHUR,** lawyer; b. Atlanta, July 15, 1941; s. James Hill and Julia Elizabeth (Gemmill) S. AB, Oberlin Coll., 1963; LLB, Harvard U., 1966. Bar: Md. 1966. Law clk. to judge U.S. Dist. Ct. Md., 1966-67; assoc. Venable LLP, Balt. & Washington, 1967—72, ptnr., Health Care, Nonprofit Organizations, Pub. Fin. practices, 1973—. Perm. mem. Judicial Conf., US Ct. Appeals (4th cir.); assoc. spl. counsel impeachment inquiry staff, com. on judiciary, Ho. of Reps., Washington, 1974; counsel to RI Ho. Reps. in impeachment of State Chief Justice; bd. dirs. Dome Corp., Balt. Mem. Revenue Bond Adv. Bd., Md. Dept. Housing & Cmty. Devel.; past chmn. & trustee Md. Inst. Coll. Art, Balt. Episcopalian. Office: Venable LLP 1800 Merc Bank & Trust Bldg 2 Hopkins Plz Ste 2100 Baltimore MD 21201 also: Venable LLP 575 7th St NW Washington DC 20004 Office Phone: 410-244-7660, 202-344-4973. Office Fax: 410-244-7742. Business E-mail: rashelton@venable.com.

**SHELTON, ROBERT NEAL,** academic administrator, physics professor, researcher; b. Phoenix, Oct. 5, 1948; s. Clark B. and Grace M. (McLaughlin) S.; m. Adrian Ann Millar, Aug. 30, 1969; children: Christian, Cameron, Stephanie. BS, Stanford U., 1970; MS, U. Calif., San Diego, 1973, PhD, 1975. Postdoctoral researcher U. Calif.-San Diego, La Jolla, 1975-76, asst. rsch. physicist, 1976-78; asst. prof. Iowa State U., Ames, 1978-81, assoc. prof., 1981-84, prof. physics, 1984-87; prof. physics, chmn. dept. U. Calif.-Davis, 1987-90, vice chancellor for rsch., 1990-96, vice provost for rsch., 1996-2001; exec. vice chancellor, provost U. N.C., Chapel Hill, 2001—06; pres. U. Ariz., Tucson, 2006—. Contbr. over 200 articles to profl. jours. Fellow Am. Phys. Soc., Calif. Coun. on Sci. and Tech.; mem. AAAS, Materials Rsch. Soc., Sigma Xi, Phi Beta Kappa. Office: Univ Ariz Adminstrn Bldg Rm 712 PO Box 210066 Tucson AZ 85721-0066

**SHELTON, SAMANTHA,** psychologist; b. Chgo., Ill., July 16, 1974; d. Emmett and Marie Shelton. BS, Xavier U. La., New Orleans, La., 1996; Clin. Psychology, Forest Inst. of Profl. Psychology, Springfield, Mo., 2000. Mental health provider Sinai-Mile Sq. Mental Health Clinic, Chicago, Ill., 2000—01; clin. psychologist Fed. Bur. of Prisons, Beaumont, Tex., 2001—03, drug abuse program coord. Las Vegas, Nev., 2003—. Treas. Fed. Bur. of Prisons Non Profit Orgn., Las Vegas, Nev., 2003—04. Contbr. scientific papers. Mem.: APA, Black Psychologist Assn. Office: Fed Bureau of Prisons - Nellis PO Box 9910 Las Vegas NV 89191 Office Phone: 702-644-5001. Office Fax: 702-644-7253. Business E-Mail: sshelton@bop.gov.

**SHELTON, STEPHANI,** broadcast journalist, consultant; b. Boston; d. Phil and Babette (Belloff) Saltman; m. Frank Herold. BS, Boston U. Corr. CBS News, N.Y.C., 1973—84; news corr. WWOR-TV, N.Y.C., 1984—88; corr., anchor Fin. News Network, N.Y.C., 1989—91. Freelance reporter Sta. WPIX-TV, 1991-95, Sta. WNBC-TV, 1993-96, WWOR-TV, 1999-02; writer, prodr., radio anchor CNBC, 2003—; cons. trainer Ctrl. and Eastern Europe broadcast journalists, 1998—; med. health prodr.-reporter PBS, The Learning Channel, 1997-99; owner The Fred Group Ltd., video/internet prodn. co., 1998—; freelance radio documentary writer Westinghouse Grwf W Broadcasting, NYC, 1970-73. Recipient Peabody award, 1972, N.J. Best Spot News award AP, 1987, 88, N.J. Working Press award, 1993-94; Emmy nominee, 1995, 96, 99, 2000. Mem. Soc. Profl. Journalists (award 1999), Radio and TV News Dirs. Assn., N.Y.C. Press Club, Investigative Reporters and Editors, Com. to Protect Journalists. E-mail: backbay38@aol.com, fred@fredgroupltd.com. *Guiding principles: a questioning mind, a refusal to take no for an answer and the memory of 28 marathons. If you don't ask "why", you are not a journalist.*

**SHELY, JOHN B.,** lawyer; b. Detroit, 1958; BA magna cum laude, Albion Coll., 1980; JD, U. Houston, 1986. Bar: Tex. 1986, admitted to practice: US Dist. Ct. (No. Dist.) Tex., US Dist. Ct. (So. Dist.) Tex., US Dist. Ct. (Ea. Dist.) Tex., US Dist. Ct. (We. Dist.) Tex., US Ct. Appeals (5th Cir.), US Ct. Appeals (9th Cir.), US Supreme Ct. Ptnr., Litig. Andrews Kurth LLP, Houston, mem. mgmt. com. Mem. Houston Law Rev., 1985—86. Mem.: Fed. Bar Assn. (dir. South Tex. Chpt.), State Bar Tex., Houston Bar Assn., Order of Coif, Phi Delta Phi, Phi Beta Kappa, Phi Eta Sigma. Office: Andrews Kurth LLP 600 Travis St Ste 4200 Houston TX 77002-3090 Office Phone: 713-220-4105. Office Fax: 713-238-7228. Business E-Mail: jshely@andrewskurth.com.

**SHEMCHUK, MARY ELIZABETH,** occupational therapist; b. Meriden, Conn., Dec. 17, 1954; d. Paul John and Rose Virginia (Piccolo) S. AS, Middlesex C.C., Middletown, Conn., 1977; BS, Eastern Mich. U., 1983. Registered occupl. therapist Minn. Staff occupl. therapist Gaylord Rehab. Hosp., Wallingford, Conn., 1985-89, sr. staff occupl. therapist, 1989-95; clin. supr. occupl. therapy Sundance Rehab. Corp., East Berlin, Conn., 1995; lead therapist in occupl. therapy Symphony Rehab. Svcs., Minnetonka, Minn., 1995—. Guest spkr. Bridgeport (Conn.) Arthritis Support Group, 1992; cons. for hearing impaired Gaylord Hosp., Wallingford, 1992-94. Former church organist Our Lady of Mt. Carmel Ch., Meriden, Conn.; guest spkr. Quota Club of Hamden (Conn.), 1986; vol. St. Vincent DePaul Soc. of Meriden Shelter, Inc., 1988. Mem. Am. Occupl. Therapy Assn. (cons. on hearing impaired 1992—), Minn. Occupl. Therapy Assn., Conn. Occupl. Therapy Assn., Self Help for Hard of Hearing, Inc., Minn. Arthritis Found. Avocations: horseback riding, nature walks, playing piano and organ, handicrafts. Home: 9350 Collegeview Rd Apt 103 Minneapolis MN 55437-2174

**SHEMIN, BARRY L.,** actuary; b. Bklyn., Dec. 17, 1942; AB magna cum laude, Brown U., 1963; MA, U. Mich., 1964. With John Hancock Life Ins. Co., Boston, 1968—2003, sr. v.p., corp. actuary; cons actuary. Chmn. bd. dirs. ARC of Mass. Bay; bd. dirs. Harvard Pilgrim Health Care Fellow: Soc. Actuaries (bd. govs.); mem.: Am. Acad. Actuaries, Sigma Xi, Phi Beta Kappa. Office: PO Box 111 Boston MA 02117-0111

**SHEMWELL, MARY ANNE,** adapted physical education specialist; b. Shreveport, La., Mar. 16, 1942; d. James Dee Jr. and Frances (Oden) Youngblood; children from previous marriage: Dee Wade, Charles James. BS, Centenary Coll., 1965; postgrad., La. Poly. Inst. Phys. edn. tchr. Midway Jr. H.S., Shreveport, 1965-69; adapted phys. edn. specialist Caddo Parish Pub. Schs., 1982—. Phys. edn. tchr. for track and field events for physically handicapped State of La.; v.p., fundraising chmn. Games Uniting Mind and Body. Coach United Cerebral Palsy of La.; mem. Rep. Women's Orgn., 1989—; treas. Rep. Profl. Women's Club, 1993—94. Named G.U.M.B.O. coach of the Yr., State of La., 1994. Mem.: La. Fedn. Tchrs., La. Assn. Heath Phys. Edn. and Recreation, Coun. Exceptional Children, Jr. League Shreveport, Plantation Club, Cotillion Club. Republican. Methodist. Avocations: reading, tennis, walking, swimming, coaching handicapped students. Home: 4431 Fern Ave Shreveport LA 71105-3103

**SHEMWELL, ROBERT H.,** federal judge; b. 1941; BA, La. State U., 1963, JD, 1967. Assoc. Seale, Smith, Baine & Phelps, 1967-70; asst. U.S. atty. U.S. Dist. Ct. (we. dist.) La., 1970-75, clk. of ct., 1975—; part-time magistrate judge Shreveport, 1984—; acting clk. of ct. U.S. Bankruptcy Ct., 1986-87. Office: US Dist Ct We Dist 1167 US Courthouse 300 Fannin St Shreveport LA 71101-3141 Fax: 318-676-3966.

**SHEN, BA-ZHONG,** mathematician, computer scientist; s. Min-De Shen and Jia-Hua Wu; m. Qi Zhang; 1 child, Siyu Shen. MS, Xidian U., Xi'an, China, 1988; PhD, Eindhoven U. Tech., The Netherlands, 1992. Asst. lectr. Xidian U., Xi'an, 1988; adj. asst. prof. and rsch. scientist Lehigh U.,

Bethlehem, Pa., 1993—96; prin. engr. Quantum Corp., Shrewsbury, Mass., 1996—99; sr. staff scientist Broadcom Corp., Irvine, Calif., 1999—. Mem. IEEE. Achievements include patents for parallel concatenated code with soft-in soft-out interactive turbo decoder; modified Reed-Solomon error correction system using (W+i+1)-bit representations of symbols of GF(2.sup.W+i); two-level error correction encoder; error correction encoder/decoder; modified Reed-Solomon code selection and encoding system; patents pending for variable code rate and signal constellation turbo trellis coded modulation code; close two constituent trellis of a turbo encoder within the interleave block; metric calculation design variable code rate decoding of broadband trellis, TCM, or TTCM; turbo coding for upstream and downstream transmission in cable system; low density parity check(LDPC) decoder using min*, min*-, min*, abd/or min*; the inverse of Min*: Min*-(The inverse of Max&: Max*-); patents for stopping criteria for iterative decoding; patents pending for 8-PSK rotationally invariant turbo trellis coded modulation without parallel transitions; true bit-level decoding of turbo trellis coded modulation; method and apparatus for parallel decoding of turbo encoded data; patents for parallel input output combined system for producing error correction code redundancy symbols and error syndromes; error correction system for five or more errors; combined system for producing error correction code symbols and error syndromes; system for finding roots of degree three and degree four error locator polynomials over GF(2M); galois field multiplier; Five-error correction system; pub. numerous sci. papers on the subjects of algebraic-geometric codes, turbo codesx, decoding error-correcting codes and etc. on the jour: IEEE transaction on Info. Theory. Office: Broadcom Corp 16215 Alton Pky Irvine CA 92619 Office Phone: 949-926-6019. E-mail: bzshen@broadcom.com.

**SHEN, BENJAMIN SHIH-PING,** astrophysicist, educator; b. Hangzhou, China, Sept. 14, 1931; s. Nai-cheng and Chen-chiu (Sun) S.; m. Lucia Elisabeth Simpson, 1971; children: William, Juliet. AB, Assumption Coll., Mass., 1954, ScD (hon.), 1972; AM in Physics, Clark U., 1956; DSc d'Etat in Physics, U. Paris, 1964; MA (hon.), U. Pa., 1971. Tchr. Assumption Prep Sch., Mass., 1954-56; asst. prof. physics SUNY, Albany, 1956-59; assoc. prof. space sci., dept. aeros. and astronautics NYU, 1964-66; assoc. prof. astronomy and astrophysics U. Pa., Phila., 1966-68, prof., 1968-72, Reese W. Flower prof. astronomy and astrophysics, 1972-96, Reese Flower prof. emeritus, 1996—, chmn. coun. grad. deans, 1979-81, assoc. provost, 1979-80, provost, 1980-81, chmn. dept. astronomy and astrophysics, 1973-79, dir. Flower and Cook Obs., 1973-79, mem. Ctr. for Energy and Environment, 1976-93, chmn. roundtable on sci., industry and policy, 1976-96, hon. prof. Sch. Engring. and Applied Sci., 1980-85; ret., 1996. Mem. U.S. Nat. Sci. Bd., 1990-94, chmn. U.S. sci. and engring. indicators, 1990-92, chmn. Task Force on Sci. Literacy, 1992-94; mem. Nat. Coun. on Sci. and Tech. Edn., 1996-2001; cons. GE, 1961-68, Office Tech. Assessment, U.S. Congress, 1977-78; sci. and tech. adviser U.S. Senate Budget Com., 1976-77; guest staff Brookhaven Nat. Lab., 1963-64, 65-70; chmn. Commn. on Pub. Understanding of Sci., N.Y. Acad. Scis., 1972-75; mem. adv. com. Mt. John Obs., New Zealand, 1978-84. Author: Nuclear Problems in Radiation Shielding in Space, 1963, Passage des Protons dans les Milieux Condenses, 1964; co-editor, co-author: High-Energy Nuclear Reactions in Astrophysics, 1967; Spallation Nuclear Reactions and Their Applications, 1976, Research in the Age of the Steady-state University, 1982; mem. editorial bd. Earth and Extraterrestrial Scis., 1974-78, assoc. editor, 1978-79; assoc. editor: Comments on Astrophysics, 1978-95; contbr. articles to profl. jours. Mem. Hayden Planetarium com. of bd. trustees Am. Mus. Natural History, 1978—; mem. sci. adv. bd. Children's TV Workshop, N.Y.C., 1977, 79-00; mem. ABA-AAAS Nat. Conf. Bd. Lawyers and Scientists, 1986-92; former trustee or bd. dirs. NSF, N.Y. Acad. Scis., Pa. Ballet Co., Assumption Coll., University City Sci. Ctr., Phila., U. Pa. Rsch. Found., Morris Arboretum, Phila., Univ. Mus., Phila. Decorated Ordre des Palmes Academiques (France); recipient Vermeil medal for sci. Soc. d'Encouragement au Progres, France, 1978. Fellow emeritus AAAS, Am. Phys. Soc., Royal Astron. Soc. (U.K.); mem. Internat. Astron. Union. Office: U Pa Dept Physics & Astronomy Philadelphia PA 19104-6396 Business E-mail: bshen@sas.upenn.edu.

**SHEN, BO,** research scientist; arrived in US, 1993; s. Heyong Shen and Shixiang Zhao; m. Weiwei Liang, Sept. 8, 2001; 1 child, Tammy Y. PhD, Wayne State U., Detroit, 1997. Sr. rsch. scientist Hewlett-Packard Labs., Palo Alto, Calif., 1997—. Mem. program com. internat. conf. ACM Multimedia 2005, 2005; mem. program com. Internat. Conf. on Distributed Computing Sys., 2005, Internat. Conf. on Parallel Processing, 2005; session chair Internat. Web Content Caching and Distbn. Workshop, 2004; mem. program com., session chair SPIE Conf. on Storage and Retrieval for Image and Video Databases, 1999; mem. program com. Internat. Conf. on Multimedia Modeling, 2006—, Pacific-Rim Conf. on Multimedia, 2006—. Author: (book chpt.) Handbook of Video Database, Design and Applications; contbr. scientific papers to profl. jours. Recipient rsch. fellowship, Wayne State U., 1996, tchg. fellowship, 1993, 1994, 1995. Mem.: IEEE (sr.; assoc. editor IEEE Transactions on Multimedia 2006—). Achievements include patents for; patents pending for. Office: 1501 Page Mill Rd 1181 Palo Alto CA 94301 Business E-Mail: bo.shen@hp.com.

**SHEN, CHIA THENG,** retired water transportation executive, religious organization administrator; b. Chekiang, China, Dec. 15, 1913; came to U.S., 1952, naturalized, 1964; s. Foo Sheng and Wen Ching (Hsai) S.; m. Woo Ju Chu, Apr. 21, 1940; children: Maria May Shen Jackson, Wilma Way Shen George, David Chuen-Tsing, Freda Foh. BEE, Chiao Tung U., 1937; LittD (hon.), St. John's U., 1973. With Central Elec. Mfg. Works, China, 1937-44, factory mgr., 1942-44; dep. coordinating dept. Nat. Resources Commn., Govt. of China, 1945-47; pres. China Trading and Indsl. Devel. Corp., Shanghai, 1947-49; mng. dir. China Trading & Indsl. Devel. Co. Ltd., Hong Kong, 1949-53; with TransAtlantic Financing Corp., 1954-67, pres., 1950-67; Pan-Atlantic Devel. Corp., N.Y.C., 1955-70; with Marine Transport Lines Inc., N.Y.C., 1958-70, sr. v.p., 1964-70; with Am. Steamship Co., Buffalo, 1967-80, chmn. bd., chief exec. officer, 1971-80. Trustee Inst. Advanced Studies World Religions, N.Y., 1970—, chmn. bd., chief exec. officer, 1970-92, pres., 1970-84, 90—; trustee China Inst. in Am., N.Y.C., 1963-90, vice chmn., 1970-79, chmn., 1979-80, mem. exec. com., 1963-84; trustee, v.p. Buddhist Assn. U.S., N.Y.C., 1964—. Mem. Chinese Inst. Engring. Home and Office: 2020 Route 301 Carmel NY 10512-3426 Fax: (845) 225-0447. E-mail: chiatshen@yahoo.com. *To benefit all human beings and to work toward freeing them from fear is my goal. The collective wisdom of all world religions furnishes us the direction and means to achieve that goal. To introduce such wisdom into the daily life of mankind in general and America in particular, is therefore what I devote my energy to.*

**SHEN, HUA-QIONG (JOAN),** clinical research director; d. Zhongzao Shen and Deli Wen; m. Yonggang Wu, Sept. 28, 1987; children: Johnna Nan Wu, Shana Wu. MD, Nanjing Rlwy. Med. Coll., 1983; MS, West China Univ. Med. Scis., 1989; PhD, Ind. U. Sch. Medicine, 1996. Cert. Am. Bd. Neurology & Psychiatry, 2003. Surgeon Chengdu Second Hosp., Sichuan, China, 1989—91; staff psychiatrist Wabash Valley Hosp., West Lafeyette, Ind., 2001—; staff psychiatrist Mental Health Ctr. Wishard Meml. Hosp., Indpls., 2002—03; clin. rsch. physician Eli Lilly & Co., Indpls., 2003—05; dir. neuroscience clin. R & D Wyeth Pharm., Collegeville, Pa., 2005—. Professorship The Learning Disabilities Rsch. Assn. China, Beijing, 2003—. Editor: (physiology jour.) Selective Reviewer; contbr. articles to profl. jours. Bd. mem. Lilly Chinese Culture Network Eli Lilly & Co., 2003; coun. mem. Ind. Assn. Chinese Am. Inc., Indpls. Recipient Exemplary Young Physician award, Ziyiang Rlwy. Factory Hosp., 1985, APA Travel Fellowship award, Wyeth Pharm. Co., 2002. Mem.: Ind. Chinese Med. Assn. (chair), Am. Endocrine Soc., Am. Psychiat. Assn. (assoc.). Achievements include design of clinical trials for drugs pre- and post-marketing. Office: Wyeth Pharm 500 Arcola Rd Collegeville PA 18426 Home: 1550 Knobb Hill Ln Paoli PA 19301 Business E-Mail: shenj1@uyeth.com.

**SHEN, MICHAEL,** lawyer; b. Nanking, Jiangsu, Peoples Republic of China, Aug. 15, 1948; came to U.S. 1951; s. James Cheng Yee and Grace (Pai) S.; m. Marina Manese (div.); m. Pamela Nan Bradford, Aug. 12, 1983; 1 child,

Jessica Li. BA, U. Chgo., 1969; MA, U. Pa., 1970; JD, Rutgers U., 1979. Bar: U.S. Dist. Ct. N.J. 1979, N.Y. 1980, U.S. Dist. Ct. (so., no. and ea. dists.) N.Y. 1980, N.J. 1981, U.S. Ct. Appeals (2d cir.) 1987, U.S. Supreme Ct. 1988, U.S. Ct. Appeals (3rd cir.) 1996. Staff atty. Bedford Stuyvesant Legal Svcs., Bklyn., 1979-80, Com. for Interns and Residents, N.Y.C., 1980-81; ptnr. Michael Shen & Assocs., PC, N.Y.C., 1981—. Bd. dirs. Asian Am. Legal Def. and Edn. Fund, N.Y.C.; pres. bd. dirs. Anti-Discrimination Ctr. Metro New York. Pres. bd. dirs. Nat. Employment Law Project; past bd. dirs. N.Y. Civil Liberties Union, N.Y.C., Nat. Asian Pacific Am. Legal Consortium. Mem. Internat. Platform Assn., Nat. Employees Lawyers Assn., N.Y. State Bar Assn., N.Y. County Bar Assn., Nat. Lawyers Guild. Avocations: arts, reading. Office: 225 Broadway Ste 2515 New York NY 10007 Office Phone: 212-227-0300. E-mail: mslaw@alumni.uchicago.edu.

**SHEN, SHIHUI,** research assistant; d. Qiyou Shen and Zhenhua Ma; m. Hai Huang, Jan. 7, 2004; 1 child, Sarah Huang. PhD, Rutgers U., 2006. Rsch. asst. U. Ill., Urbana, 2001—. Rsch. asst. Jiangsu Transp. Rsch. Inst., Nanjing, Jiangsu Province, China, 2000—01. Recipient 1st prize Student Poster Contest award, FAA Ann. Conf., 2003; fellow, U. Ill., 2003; scholar, SE U., Nanjing, China, 1995—96; Helene M. Overly Meml. Grad. scholar, Chgo. chpt. Women's Transp. Seminar, 2005. Achievements include design of Moisture Permeability Test Equipment For Pavement.

**SHEN, SIN-YAN,** physicist, acoustical engineer, musicologist; b. Singapore, Nov. 12, 1949; came to the U.S., 1969, naturalized, 1984; s. Shao-Quan and Tien-Siu (Chen) S.; m. Yuan-Yuan Lee, Aug. 4, 1973; children: Jia, Jian. BSc, U. Singapore, 1969; MS, Ohio State U., 1970, PhD, 1973. Concert recitalist on Erhu Chinese fiddle, 1963—; instr. math. U. Singapore, 1969; asst. prof. physics Northwestern U., Evanston, Ill., 1974-77, assoc. prof., 1977-81; faculty assoc. Argonne (Ill.) Nat. Lab., 1974-77, scientist, 1977-83, sr. rsch. leader, 1983—. Dir. rsch. divsn. natural resource mgmt. SUPCON Internat. 1988—; prof. Harvard U., 1989—; meeting series reviewer NSF, Washington, 1981—; coord. Tech. Rev., Argonne, Atlanta, Phoenix, Portland, Oreg., 1983—; dir. Global Warming Internat. Ctr., 1991—, chmn. Internat. Conf. Chgo., 1990-93, San Francisco, 1994-95, Vienna, 1996, Columbia U., N.Y.C., 1997, Hong Kong U. Sci. and Tech., 1998, Yamanashi Inst. Environ. Scis., 1999, Harvard U., 2000, Cambridge U., 2001, Max Planck Inst., 2002, Mass. Inst. Tech., 2003; Chinese Music Internat. Conf., 1991, 94, 2002; advisor Internat. Energy Agy., 1986—, Gas Rsch. Inst., 1984—, SUPCON Internat. 1986—, Nat. Geog., 1986—, Internat. Boreal Forest Rsch. Assn., 1991—, Electric Power Rsch. Inst., 1992—, World Climate Rsch. Programme WMO, 1993—, UN Devel. Program, 1993—, World Bank, 1994—, US Dept. Energy and US EPA, 1995—; prof. Chinese Acad. Forestry, 1986—; panel on biol. diversity Nat. Acad. Scis., Smithsonian Instn., 1986; chmn. internat. program com. Austrian Acad. Scis., 1995-96, Columbia U., 1996-97, Japan Environ. Agy., 1998-99, Intergovt. Panel on Climate Change, 1999—; music dir. Orch. Chinese Music Soc. N.Am., 1976—, Silk & Bamboo Ensemble, 1981—; adv. Ctrl. Traditional Orch., 1984—; del. leader, UN Conf. Environ. and Devel., Rio, 1992; del. chmn. Third All China Arts Festival, Kunmin, 1992; panelist Nat. Endowment for Arts, 1981—, New Eng. Found. for Arts, 1987—, Arts Midwest, 1985—, Ill. Arts Coun., 1982—, Chgo. City Arts, 1990—, Ill. Art's Alliance Found., adv. coun., 1992—, adv. coun. Mid-Am. Arts Alliance, 1992—, bd. dirs., adv. Shanghai Nat. Musical Instrument Co., 1985—; adv. West Lake Qin Soc., Hangzhou, China, 1991—. Author: Superfluidity, 1982, Acoustics of Ancient Chinese Bells, 1987, Chinese Music and Orchestration: A Primer on Principles and Practice, 1991, Global Warming Science and Policy, 1992, The Boreal Forests and Global Change, 1993, Global Warming Elucidated, 1994, Chinese Musical Instruments, 1999, Global Warming and Public Health, 1999, China: A Journey through Its Musical Art, 1999, Chinese Music in the 20th Century, 2001; editor-in-chief Chinese Music Internat. Jour., 1978—; mem. internat. editl. bd. World Resource Rev., 1989—, Internat. Boreal Forest Rsch., 1992—, Ency. of Life Support Sys., 1994—; adv. Ency. Brit., 1983—; contbr. over 300 articles to profl. jours.; patentee molten liquids, 1974, 80. Recipient Mich. Heritage award, 1992; Fulbright scholar U.S. State Dept., 1969; merit scholar Govt. Singapore, 1967; named Artistic Treasure Gov. Jim Edgar of Ill., 1998. Mem. AAAS, Am. Phys. Soc., Ops. Rsch. Soc. Am., Acoustical Soc. Am., Chinese Music Soc. N.Am. Achievements include rsch. in renewable energy and materials techs.; global change and global warming; extreme event index; indsl. sonic techs.; energy policy, planning and economics; acoustics; cultural acoustics; also: SUPCON Internat PO Box 5275 Woodridge IL 60517-0275 Office Phone: 630-910-1551.

**SHEN, TSUNG YING,** medicinal chemistry educator; b. Beijing, Sept. 28, 1924; came to U.S., 1950; s. Tsu-Wei and Sien-Wha (Nieu) S.; m. Amy T.C. Lin, June 20, 1953; children: Bern, Hubert, Theodore, Leonard, Evelyn, Andrea. B.Sc., Nat. Ctrl. U., Chongqing, China, 1946; diploma, Imperial Coll. Sci. and Tech., London, 1948; PhD, U. Manchester, Eng., 1950, D.Sc., 1978. Research assoc. Ohio State U., Columbus, 1950-52, MIT, Cambridge, 1952-56; sr. research chemist Merck, Sharp & Dohme Research Labs., Rahway, NJ, 1956-65, dir. synthetic chem. research, 1966-76, v.p. membrane chem. research, 1976-77, v.p. membrane and arthritis research, 1977-86; A. Burger prof. medicinal chemistry U. Va., Charlottesville, 1986-96, emeritus and rsch. prof., 1996—2001. Vis. prof. U. Calif., Riverside, 1973, U. Calif., San Francisco, 1985; adj. prof. Stevens Inst. Tech., Hoboken, NJ, 1982-85; hon. prof. Beijing Med. U., Chinese Acad. Med. Sci., Inst. Material Medica, China Pharm. U.; mem. sci. bd. CytoMed, 1989-96, T Cell Sci, 1988-93, Gene Labs., 1989-94, Osteo Arthritis Sci, 1993-95, Argonex, 1994-98; advisor Academica Sinica Taiwan, 1992-97. Mem. editl. bd. Clinica Europa Jour., 1977, Prostaglandins and Medicine, 1978, Medicinal Rsch. Revs., 1979-94, Jour. Medicinal Chemistry, 1980-83, Medicinal Chem. Rsch., 1991—; pub aut in field Recipient Outstanding Patent award NJ Research and Devel. Council, 1975, Merck Dirs. sci. award, 1976, Galileo Meml. medal, U. Pisa, 1976, Rene Descartes medal U. Paris, 1977, medal of Merit Giornate Mediche Internazionali del Collegium Biologicum Europea, 1977, cert. of merit Spanish Soc. Therapeutic Chemistry, 1983, achievement award Chinese Inst. Engrs.-USA, 1984. Mem. AAAS, Am. Chemistry Soc. (1st Alfred Burger award in medicinal chemistry 1980), NY Acad. Scis., Acad. Pharm. Assn. (hon.), Chinese Am. Chem. Soc. (bd. dirs. 1995-97), Acad. Pharm. Scis. (hon.). Achievements include discovery of indomethacin, sulindac, diflunisal and other antiinflammatory agents; synthesis of bioactive natural product derivs and drug targeting ligands. Home: 238 Eliot St Chestnut Hill MA 02467-1447 Business E-Mail: tjs2b@virginia.edu.

**SHEN, WEI-CHIANG,** medical educator; b. Wenzhou, Zhejiang, China, May 3, 1942; s. Tze-Ping and Yi-Ching Shen; m. Daisy Hsia, Jan. 13, 1968; children: Howard, Jerry. PhD, Boston U., 1972. Assoc. prof. Boston U. Sch. Medicine, 1983—87; prof. pharm. scis. U. So. Calif. Sch. Pharmacy, LA, 1987—. Contbr. scientific papers to profl. jours. Recipient Eurand award for Outstanding Novel Rsch. in Oral Drug Delivery, Controlled Release Soc., 2002. Fellow: AAPS; mem.: ASCB, ASBMB, ASPET, AAAS, CRS, Chinese-American Faculty Assn. So. Calif. (pres. 2004—05). Achievements include research in protein and peptide drug delivery; patents in field. Office: U So Calif 1985 Zonal Ave PSC 404B Los Angeles CA 90033 Office Phone: 1-323-442-1902. Office Fax: 1-323-442-2263. Business E-Mail: weishen@usc.edu.

**SHEN, WEIXING,** meteorologist; b. Huzhou, Zhejiang, China, Oct. 9, 1964; s. Agen and Meifeng Shen; m. Yan Wu, July 19, 1995; children: Emily, Kimberly. PhD, SUNY, 1995. Rsch. asst. Stony Brook U., NY, 1991—95; from postdoctoral rschr. to asst. marine scientist U. RI, Kingston, 1996—2001; vis. rsch. scientist U. Corp. Atmospheric Rsch., Camp Springs, Md., 2001—05; vis. rsch. scientist U. Md., College Park, 2005—. Named Environ. Hero, NOAA, 2002. Mem.: Am. Geophys. Union (assoc.), Am. Meteorol. Soc. (assoc.). Achievements include development of a simple physical model for hurricane intensity research and prediction; discovery of environmental circulation-associated zonal variability of transient atmospheric waves in the tropics; nonlinear responses of stratospheric Quasi-Biennial Oscillation to sea surface temperature changes; modeling of standing surface water's effects on landfall hurricanes. Home: 10627 Alison Dr Burke VA 22015 Office: U Md 2207 CSS Bldg 224 College Park MD 20742-2465 Office Phone: 301-405-8245. Personal E-mail: wshenhz@yahoo.com. E-mail: wshen@essic.umd.edu.

SHEN, XIAOHUI, application developer, researcher; s. Decheng Shen and Youfen Liang; married. MS, Tsinghua U., Beijing, 1994; PhD, Northwestern U., 2001. Rsch. assist. Northwestern U., Evanston, Ill., 1997—2001; sr. software engr. Motorola Inc., Libertyville, Ill., 2001—. Program com. mem., session chair numerous internat. confs. Contbr. articles to profl. jours., 2001. Recipient Guanghua prize, Guanghua Edn. Found., 1990. Mem.: IEEE (sr.). Office: Motorola Inc 1000 Technology Way Libertyville IL Home: 28975 Sky Crest Dr Mundelein IL 60060-5310 Personal E-mail: shen_xh@yahoo.com. Business E-Mail: axs095@email.mot.com.

SHEN, XIAOPING, science educator; b. China; 1 child, Jane An. BS, Beijing Normal U., China, 1983, MS; PhD, U. Ottawa, Canada, 1995. Lectr. Beijing Normal U., Beijing, 1986—89; prof. Ctrl. Conn. State U., New Britain, 1995—. Adj. prof. Grad. Sch. Chinese Acad. Scis., Beijing, 2003—06. Contbr. articles various profl. jours., chapters to books. Activity coord. Conn. Chinese Culture Ctr., Hartford, 2000—03. Faculty Rsch. grants, Conn. State U., 2000, 2001, 2002, 2003, 2004, 2006. Mem.: Assn. Am. Geographers (chair, china splty. group 2002—03), Gamma Theta Upsilon Internat. Geog. Honor Soc. (regional councilor for New Eng. - St. Lawrence Valley 2000—06). Office: Ctrl Conn State U 1615 Stanley St New Britain CT 06050 Office Phone: 860-832-2794.

SHEN, XUEMIN SHERMAN, engineering educator, researcher; b. AnShan, Liaoning, China, Dec. 30, 1958; s. Zhong Shen; m. Weihua Zhuang, Feb. 2, 1962; children: Alan, Alvin. PhD, Rutgers U., 1990. Cert. profl. engr., Profl. Engineers Ont., 2002. Prof. U. Waterloo, Ont., Canada, 1993—. Assoc. chair grad. studies U. Waterloo, Ont. Mem.: IEEE. Office: U Waterloo 200 University Ave West Ontario Waterloo Canada N2L 3G1 Office Phone: 5198884567 ext 2691. Office Fax: 5197463077. Business E-Mail: xshen@bbcr.uwaterloo.ca.

SHEN, YU-CHU, economics professor; b. Kaohsiung, Taiwan, Jan. 25, 1974; MA, Harvard U., PhD, 2001. Asst. prof. econs. Naval Postgrad. Sch., Monterey, Calif., 2004—. Faculty rsch. fellow Nat. Bur. Econ. Rsch., Cambridge, Mass., 2004—.

SHENDE, RAJESH V., chemical engineer, materials scientist, researcher; b. Nagpur, Maharashtra State, India, Mar. 13, 1965; arrived in U.S., 1999; s. Vitthalrao Ganpatrao and Kamaltai Kashikae Shende; m. Anuradha Rajesh Deshmukh, Mar. 31, 1996; 1 child, Shaunak Rajesh Shende. BS in Physics, Chemistry, Math.h.), U. of Nagpur, 1986; PhD in Chem. Engring., MS in Chem. Tech., U. of Bombay, Matunga, 1995. Dep. mgr. Khatau Dyes Ltd., Ankleshwar, Gujarat, India, 1995—96; asst. mgr., process tech. cell devel. incharge Indian Dyestuff Industries Ltd., Kalyan, Maharashtra, 1996—98; rsch. scientist Inst. of Chemistry, Ljubljana, Slovenia, U. of Mo., Columbia. Contbr. rsch. publs. to sci. jours. Recipient postdoctoral fellowship, U. of Mo., 1999—, Inst. of Chemistry, Lab. for Catalysis and Chem. Reaction Engring., 1998—99, sr. rsch. fellowship for PhD, Univ. Grants Commn., 1991—95, His-Holiness the Pope Merit scholarship for MS, U. of Bombay, 1989. Mem.: Am. Chem. Soc. (reviewer Jour. Indsl. and Engring. Chemistry Rsch., reviewer Jour. Environ. Sci. and Tech.), Sigma Xi. Home: 2601 Hillshire Dr Columbia MO 65203 Office: U Mo Dept Chem Engring Columbia MO 65211 Personal E-mail: shender@missouri.edu. E-mail: rajeshshende@hotmail.com.

SHENEFELT, ARTHUR B., transportation executive, consultant; b. Boston, May 5, 1920; s. Arthur Merle and Martha Marion (Baird) S.; m. Gloria May Willis, Apr. 28, 1948; 1 child, Michael Baird. BA, Miami U., Oxford, Ohio, 1942; student, Garrett Theol. Sem., Evanston, Ill., 1942-44, Columbia U., 1946-47. Dir. pub. rels. Brotherhood of Locomotive Engrs., Cleve., 1951-56; dir. press rels. N.Y. Cntrl. R.R., N.Y.C., 1956-57; transp. editor Jour. of Commerce, N.Y.C., 1957-59; asst. tp pres. for pub. affairs Freight Forwrders Inst., Washington, 1959-71; dir. comms. N.Y. State Trucking Assn., N.Y.C., 1960-61, Trucking Employers Inc., Washington, 1970-71; press sec. to chmn. U.S. Senate Transp. Com., Washington, 1971-73; personal transp. adviser to Gov. of Pa., Harrisburg, 1973-77. Cons. Fed. Appalachian Regional Commn., Harrisburg and Washington, 1977-79, Japanese Nat. Ry., N.Y.C. and Tokyo, 1980-85; chmn. Bucks HUB Conf., Bristol, Pa., 1985—; chmn. Super Mag. Coalition, Washington, 1988—; chmn. Amtrak for Profit Coalition, Washington, 1995-97; pres. Interstate Maglev Inc., Bristol, 1992—; dir., chmn. Office of Transp. Tech., Strategy and Planning, 1998—. Contbr. articles, stories and features to most maj. Am. newspapers and trade jours. Lt. (j.g.), pub. info. officer USN, 1944-46, PTO. Avocation: music. Office: Bucks HUB Conf 1200 New Rodgers Rd Bristol PA 19007-2525 E-mail: shenefelt@surface-transportation.com.

SHENEFELT, PHILIP DAVID, dermatologist; b. Colfax, Wash., July 31, 1943; s. Roy David and Florence Vanita (Cagle) S.; m. Debrah A. Levenson; children: Elizabeth, Sara, Shaina. BS with honors, U. Wis. Madison, 1966, MD, 1970, MS in Adminstrv. Medicine, 1984. Intern U.S. Naval Hosp., Bethesda, Md., 1970-71; gen. practice Oreg. (Wis.) Clinic, 1975; resident in dermatology U. Wis. Hosp., Madison, 1975-78, mem. staff, 1978-87; asst. prof. dermatology U. South Fla., Tampa, 1987—97; assoc. prof., 1997—. Chief dermatology sect. VA Hosp., Bay Pines, Fla., 1987—89, assoc. chief, Tampa, 1988—2002, chief, 2002—; dermatologist Univ. Health Svc. U. Wis., Madison, 1978—87, VA Hosp., Madison, 1982—85. Served to lt. comdr. USN, 1969-74; capt. USNR (ret.). Kellogg fellow, 1980-82. Mem.: AMA, Fla. Med. Assn., Soc. Clin. Exptl. Hypnosis, Noah Worcester Dermatol. Soc., Fla. West Coast Dermatol. Soc., Fla. Dermatol. Soc., Am. Soc. Clin. Hypnosis, Am. Coll. Physician Execs., Am. Acad. Dermatology. Home: 15919 Notting Hill Dr Lutz FL 33548-6147 Office: U South Fla Dermatol # 79 12901 Bruce Downs Blvd Tampa FL 33612-4742 Office Phone: 813-974-2188. Business E-Mail: pshenefe@health.usf.edu.

SHENG, QIN, mathematics professor; s. Re and Sh Sheng; m. Helen Huang, Jan. 1, 1962; children: Andy, Danny. PhD, U. Cambridge, England, 1990. Prof. U. Dayton, Ohio, 2001—04, Baylor U., Waco, Tex., 2004—. Fellow, U.S. Air Force, 2005—06. Mem.: Am. Math Soc. Achievements include research in applied mathematics and computer simulation. Avocations: music, paintings, sight-seeing, mountain walks. Office: Dept Math Baylor Univ One Bear Pl Waco TX 76798-7328 Office Phone: 254-710-1241. Office Fax: 254-710-3569. E-mail: qin_sheng@baylor.edu.

SHENG, QUAN, chemist; b. Changzhou, China, Nov. 7, 1947; arrived in U.S., 1997; s. Benyu Sheng and Yuru Lu; m. Chimin Jiang, Oct. 28, 1982; 1 child, Yiqing. BSc, Nanjing U., China, 1982, MSc in Polymer Chemistry, 1985; MSc, Laurentian U., Sudbury, Ont., Canada, 1992; PhD in Polymer Chemistry, McMaster U., Hamilton, Ont., Canada, 1997. Technician Jiangsu Jintan Pharm. Factory, Jintan, China, 1973-78; lectr., vice dir. Polymer Chemistry Inst. Dept. Chemistry Nanjing (China) U., 1985-91; rsch. chemist postdoctoral fellow Nat. Ctr. for Agrl. Utilization Rsch. USDA, Peoria, Ill., 1997-98; chemist OMG Ams., Research Triangle Park, NC, 1998—2003; tech. devel. mgr. Microbond EPM, UMICORE, Raleigh, 2003—. Vice dir. Polymer Chemistry Inst. Nanjing U., China, 1985-91. Contbr. articles to profl. jours.; solder paste trade secrets and patents. Coord. Canada-China Friendship Assn., Hamilton, Ont., Canada, 1995-97. Mem.: Am. Chem. Soc. Achievements include research in polyurethanes, ionomers, polysulfone and selective functionalization of polymers; development of anti-corrosive coatings, no-clean solder paste, water-soluble solder paste, RMA solder paste and lead free solder paste for SMT and die attach applications. Avocations: Chinese finger calligraphy, ping pong/table tennis, travel, reading. Office: Microbond EPM, Umicore 3420 Tarheel Dr Ste 100 Raleigh NC 27609 Home: 807 Bristol Blue St Apex NC 27502 Office Phone: 919-876-9231. Business E-Mail: quan.sheng@am.unicore.com.

SHENK, DENA, social sciences educator; b. N.Y.C., Feb. 22, 1952; d. Jerome and Rose (Weber) S.; m. Kenneth Quilty, June 18, 1977; children: Adam, Shayna. BA, SUNY, Stony Brook, 1973; MA, U. Mass., 1976, PhD, 1979. Asst. prof. St. Cloud (Minn.) State U., 1979-85, assoc. prof., 1985-88, chair dept. interdisciplinary studies, 1987-91, prof., 1988-91; dir. gerontology program, prof. dept. sociology and anthropology U.N.C., Charlotte, 1991—. Dir. gerontology program, St. Cloud (Minn.) State U., 1980-91. Author: The Aging Experience in a Lebanese-American Community, 1991, Gender and Race Through Education and Political Activism-The Legacy of Sylvia Helen Forner, 1995, Someone to Lend a Helping Hand - Women Growing Old in Rural America, 1998, Teaching About Aging, Interdisciplinary and Cross-Cultural Perspectives, 1999, Aging Education in a Global Context, 2005; mem. editl. bd. Jour. Cross-Cultural Aging, 1985-87, Jour. Applied Gerontology, 2003—, Jour. Ednl. Gerontology, 2005—, Jour. Gerontology and Geriatrics Edn., 2005—; contbr. articles to profl. jours. Mem. bd. advs. various orgns.; bd. dirs. Charlotte-Mecklenburg Coun. on Aging, 1991-2001, mem. exec. bd., 1992-2001. Grantee for rsch., curriculum devel. and creation of photog. exhibits. Fellow Assn. Gerontology in Higher Edn. (charter, sec. 2000-02, treas. 2003-05), Gerontol. Soc. Am.; mem. Assn. for Anthropology and Gerontology (pres. 1985-86, editor newsletter 1983-85), Minn. Gerontol. Soc. (chairperson program com. 1983-84, sec. 1991), Am. Anthropol. Assn., Nat. Coun. Aging, Nat. Women's Studies Assn., Internat. Comm. on Study of Aging and the Aged (charter). Office Phone: 704-687-4349. E-mail: DShenk@email.uncc.edu.

SHENK, GEORGE H., lawyer; b. NYC, Sept. 10, 1943; BA, Princeton U., 1965; M in Internat. Affairs, Columbia U., 1967; JD, Yale U., 1970. Bar: N.Y. 1971, Calif. 1985. Assoc. Coudert Bros., Paris, 1970, N.Y.C., 1970-73, Hong Kong, 1973-75, Tokyo, 1975-78, ptnr. N.Y.C., 1977-91, San Francisco, 1991-94, Heller Ehrman LLP, 1994—. Exec. dir. San Francisco Com. on Fgn. Rels. Contbr. articles to publs. Mem. Bar Assn. City of N.Y., Calif. State Bar Assn., Coun. Fgn. Rels., Pacific Coun. on Internat. Policy. Office: Heller Ehrman LLP 333 Bush St San Francisco CA 94104-2806

SHENK, LOIS ELAINE LANDIS, writer; b. Ephrata, Pa., May 30, 1944; BA in English, Eastern Mennonite Coll., 1966; MSc in Edn., Temple U., 1984. English mistress Githumu Secondary Sch., Thika, Kenya, 1966-68; English tchr. Kraybill's Jr. High, Mount Joy, Pa., 1976-77; freelance writer, 1978—; religious news corr. Gospel Herald, Scottdale, Pa., 1978-82. Observer, corr. The U.S. Senate, Washington, 1987-2001. Author: Out of Mighty Waters, 1982 (R.I.M. excellence award 1983), The Story of Ephrata Mennonite School, 1996; (one act play) A House for David in (anthology) Swords into Plowshares, 1983; (study guide for Christian edn.) Hebrews, 1988; contbr. poems, stories & features to jours.; editl. work Mennonite Ctrl. Com., Akron, Pa., 1977. Cmty. living advisor Friendship Cmty., Lititz, Pa., 1997-99; Sunday sch. tchr. Ephrata Mennonite Ch., 1997-99; tutor English as a Second Lang., 2004. Recipient Rep. Senatorial Medal of Freedom, many other honors and awards. Avocations: reading, cooking, music. Home and Office: 444 W Marion St Lancaster PA 17603 Personal E-mail: lshenk@verizon.net.

SHENK, THOMAS EUGENE, molecular biology educator, academic administrator; b. Bklyn., Jan. 1, 1947; s. Eugene Richard and Helen Marie (Deffenbaugh) S.; m. Susan Mary Hillman, July 4, 1979; children— Christopher Thomas, Gregory Thomas BS, U. Detroit, 1969; PhD, Rutgers U., 1973. Asst. prof. molecular biology U. Conn., Farmington, 1975-80; prof. molecular biology SUNY, Stony Brook, 1980-84; Elkins prof. molecular biology Princeton U., 1984—. Am. Cancer Soc. prof., 1986—, chmn. dept. molecular biology, 1996—. Bd. dirs. Merck & Co., Inc., 2001—. Co-editor Enhancers and Eukaryotic Gene Expression, 1983. Mem. Am. Soc. Microbiology (Eli Lilly award 1982) Office: Princeton U Dept Molecular Biology Lewis Thomas Lab 203 Princeton NJ 08544-0001*

SHENKER, IRA RONALD, physician; b. July 8, 1934; s. Morris and Rose (Wilner) Shenker; m. Caroline Cabin, June 27, 1958; children: Diane Amy, Mitchell Steven. BS, U. Wis., 1955, MD, 1958. Diplomate Am. Bd. Pediatrics. Intern L.I. Jewish Med. Ctr., New Hyde Park, NY, 1958—59, resident pediats., 1959—61; resident pub. health Hassau County Health Dept., NY, 1961—62; coll. health physician Mt. Holyoke Coll., 1962—64; chief adolescent medicine L.I. Jewish Med. Ctr., 1965—; assoc. prof. pediat. SUNY-Stony Brook, 1979—; prof. pediat. Albert Einstein Coll. Medicine, 1989—. Author: Human Figure Drawings in Adolescence, 1972; editor: Adolescent Medicine, 1981, Clinical Monographs in Pediatrics: Adolescent Medicine, 1994; contbr. articles to profl. jours. Bd. dirs. Roslyn Sr. Citizens, NY, 1975—78. Recipient Adele Hoffman award, 2001; grantee USPHS, 1965—82. Fellow: Am. Acad. Pediats.; mem.: Soc. Adolescent Medicine (pres. 1986), N.Y. Pediat. Soc., Nassau Pediat. Soc., N.Y. Pediat. Soc. (pres. 1986—87), Queens Pediat. Soc. (pres. 1981—82). Home: 5 Fairway Rd Roslyn NY 11576-1099 Address: 270-05 76th Ave New Hyde Park NY 11040-1433 Office: Schneider Children's Hosp of LI Jewish Med Ctr New Hyde Park NY 11042 Office Phone: 516-465-3270. Business E-Mail: rshenker@lij.edu.

SHENKER, JOSEPH, academic administrator; b. NYC, Oct. 7, 1939; s. George and Isabelle (Schwartz) S.; m. Adrienne Green (div. 1979); children: Deborah, Karen; m. Susan Armiger, Jan. 2, 1988; children: Sarah Gabrielle, Jordan. BA in Psychology, Hunter Coll., 1962, MA in Econ., 1963; EdD in High Edn., Tchrs. Coll., 1969. Dean, community coll. affairs CUNY, 1967-69; acting pres. Kingsborough Community Coll., N.Y.C., 1969-70; chief negotiator for mgmt. CUNY, 1977; acting pres. Hunter Coll., N.Y.C., 1979-80; founding pres. LaGuardia Community Coll., N.Y.C., 1970-88; pres. Bank St. Coll. Edn., N.Y.C., 1988-95; provost C.W. Post Campus, L.I. U., 1995—. Bd. dirs. Sch. & Bus. Alliance, N.Y.C.; ptnr. N.Y.C. Partnership, 1990—; advisor Consortium for Worker Edn., 2001-; bd. dirs. DeWitt Wallace Reader's Digest Fund, 2001-. Chmn. Liberty Scholarship Adv. Com., Albany, N.Y., 1989—; co-chmn. Task Force on Early Childhood Edn., N.Y.C., 1989—; Agenda for Children Tomorrow, 1989—; chmn. Chancellor's Com. on U./Sch. Collaboratives, N.Y.C., 1988; trustee UNICEF Am., 1993-97. Recipient Distinguished Alumni award Tchrs. Coll. Columbia, N.Y.C. Office: C W Post Campus Long Island U 720 Northern Blvd Greenvale NY 11548-1319*

SHENKER, JOSEPH C., lawyer; b. NYC, Nov. 6, 1956; BS in Acctg., CUNY, 1977; JD, Columbia U., 1980. Bar: NY 1981, US Dist. Ct. (ea. and so. dists.) NY 1981, US Claims Ct. 1982, US Tax Ct. 1982, US Supreme Ct. 1988. Assoc. Sullivan & Cromwell, NYC, 1980-86, ptnr., 1986—; also mem. mgmt. com. and coord. comml. real estate practice area, vice chmn., 2006—. Contbr. articles to profl. jours. Pres. Met. Coun. on Jewish Poverty, bd. dir. Jewish Cmty. Rels. Coun. Fellow Am. Bar Found.; mem. ABA, NY State Bar Assn., Assn. Bar City NY Office: Sullivan & Cromwell 125 Broad St Fl 33 New York NY 10004-2400 Office Phone: 212-558-3768. Office Fax: 212-558-3588. E-mail: shenkerj@sullcrom.com.

SHENKER, STEPHEN, physics professor; BA, Harvard U., 1975; PhD, Cornell U., 1980. Faculty U. Chgo., 1981—89; prof. Rutgers U., 1989—98; prof. and dir. Stanford Inst. Theoretical Physics, 1998—; Richard Herschel Weiland prof. Sch. Humanities Stanford U., 2004—. Recipient Young Investigator award, Nat. Sci. Found., 1985; fellow Sloan Found., 1983, MacArthur Found., 1987. Fellow: Am. Acad. Arts and Sciences, Am. Physical Soc. Office: Stanford Univ Varian Physics Bldg Rm 354 382 Via Pueblo Mall Stanford CA 94305-4060 Office Phone: 650-723-4615. Office Fax: 650-725-6544. E-mail: sshenker@stanford.edu.*

SHENKIR, WILLIAM GARY, business educator; b. Three Rivers, Tex., June 27, 1938; s. William and Lydia (Jancik) S.; m. Missy Smith, Jan 1, 1973. BBA, Tex. A & M U., 1960; postgrad. (Rockefeller Bros. Theol. fellow), Drew U. Sem., 1960-61; MBA, U. Tex., 1962, PhD, 1964. Asst. prof. McIntire Sch. Commerce, U. Va., Charlottesville, 1967-69, assoc. prof. 1969-72, prof., 1972—75, dean, 1977-92, Paul Goodloe McIntire prof. Charlottesville, 1977—82; William Stamps Farish prof. McIntire Sch. Commerce U. Va., 1982—. Project dir. Fin. Acctg. Stds. Bd., Stamford, Conn.,

1973—76; vis. prof. NYU Grad. Sch. Bus., N.Y.C., 1976—77; bd. dirs. ComSonics Corp., Harrisburg, Va. Editor: Carman Blough: His Professional Career and Accounting Thought, 1978; co-author: The University of Virginia's McIntire School of Commerce: The First 75 Years, 1921-96, 1996, Open-Book Management: Creating an Ownership Culture, 1998, Making Enterprise Risk Management Pay Off, 2001, Making Enterprise Risk Management Pay Off: How Leading Companies Implement Risk Management, 2002, Enterprise Risk Management: Pulling It All Together, 2002; contbr. articles to profl. jours. Capt. USAF, 1964—67. Mem. AICPA, Am. Acctg. Assn. (former v.p.), Acctg. Edn. Change Commn. (former vice chmn.), Am. Assembly Collegiate Schs. of Bus. (former bd. dirs., pres. 1990-91), Fin. Execs. Inst., Va. Soc. CPAs, Raven Soc., Landfall Club, Farmington Country Club, Phi Delta Kappa, Beta Gamma Sigma, Phi Kappa Phi. Presbyterian. Home: 420 Rookwood Dr Charlottesville VA 22903-4732 Office Phone: 434-924-4146. E-mail: wgs2Z@virginia.edu.

SHENKMAN, MARK RONALD, investment and finance executive; b. Providence, Aug. 17, 1943; s. George and Florence (Littman) S.; children: Andrew Harris, Gregory Alexander; m. Rosalind Stanski, Aug. 10, 1997; 1 stepson, Justin Warren Slatky. BA, U. Conn., 1965; MBA, George Washington U., 1967. Security analyst New Eng. Mchts. Bank, Boston, 1969-71; fin. analyst Stone & Webster Securities Corp., Boston, 1971-73; rsch. analyst, portfolio mgr. Fidelity Mgmt. & Research Co., Boston, 1973-79; v.p. Lehman Bros. Kuhn Loeb, N.Y.C., 1979-83; pres. First Investors Asset Mgmt. Co., N.Y.C., 1983-85; pres., chief exec. officer Shenkman Capital Mgmt. Inc., N.Y.C., 1985—. Vice chmn. bd. trustees Wilbraham (Mass.) and Monson Acad.; bd. dirs. U. Conn. Found.; bd. visitors, trustee George Washington U. Sch. Bus.; bd. govs. Hillel Found.; bd. adv. Coll. William and Mary Sch. Bus. 1st lt. U.S. Army, 1967-69. Mem. Am. Bankruptcy Inst., N.Y. Soc. Security Analysts, Boston Security Analysts Soc., Am. Statis. Assn., CFA Inst. Home: Gaston Farm Rd Greenwich CT 06831 Office: 461 Fifth Ave New York NY 10017-6234 also: 462 Harbor Dr Stamford CT 06902

SHENON, PHILIP, journalist; b. San Francisco, June 26, 1959; s. Peter and Philippa (Richards) Shenon. BA in English Lit., Brown U., 1981. Reporter N.Y. Times, N.Y.C., 1983—85, corr. Washington, 1985—90, S.E. Asia corr. Bangkok, 1991—95, def. corr. Washington, 1996—97, diplomatic corr., 1997—99, investigative corr., 2000—. Office: NY Times Washington Bur 1627 I St NW Washington DC 20006-4007

SHEON, AARON, art historian, educator; b. Toledo, Oct. 7, 1937; s. Benjamin William and Katherine (Rappoport) S.; m. Martine Bruel, Jan. 26, 1963 (div. 1986); children: Sandrine, Nicolas; m. Jill Belasco, Nov. 11, 2000. BA, U. Mich., 1959, MA, 1960; M.F.A. (Wilson fellow), Princeton U., 1962, PhD, 1966; postgrad., U. Paris, 1962-63. Staff officer, dir. gen.'s cabinet UNESCO, Paris, 1963-66; asst. prof. U. Pitts., 1966-69, assoc. prof., 1969-78, acting chmn. dept. fine arts, 1969, 79-80, dir. univ. program Rouen, France, 1974-75, prof. art history, 1979—2003, prof. emeritus, 2004; vis. prof. Carnegie-Mellon U., 1981, 2002—03. Vis. exhbn. curator Mus. Art, Carnegie Inst., Pitts., 1977-81; program cons. Nat. Endowment Arts and Humanities, 1978-85; visual arts cons. Pa. Arts Council, 1981; vis. mem. Inst. for Advanced Study, Princeton, 1984-85 Author: The Gosman Collection, 1969, Monticelli, His Contemporaries, His Influence, 1978, Organic Vision, The Architecture of Peter Berndtson, 1980, Monticelli, 1986, Paul Guigou, 1987. Recipient Charles E. Merrill faculty award, 1968; Chancellor Bowman award, 1976; Honor award Pa. Soc. Architects, 1982, Innovation award in tchg. Art History Course for Blind Students U. Pitts., 2001, Bellet Teaching award, 2002, Innovation in Tchg. award, 2003; grantee Ford Found., 1967, NEH, 1979, European Union grantee, 2006; Gould Arts Found. fellow, 1986 Mem. Coll. Art Assn., Société de l'histoire de l'art français, Am. Assn. of Mus. Office: U Pitts Dept History Arts & Arch Pittsburgh PA 15260 Office Phone: 412-648-2400. E-mail: ash2@pitt.edu

SHEPARD, ANNA RICHARDSON, elementary school educator; b. Portsmouth, Va., Dec. 1, 1947; d. Curtis Leo and Lois (Bailey) Richardson; m. Ronald Lee Shepard, Dec. 28, 1968 (div. 1985) m. Feb. 14, 1990; 1 child, Kelly Suzanne. BA in Elem. Edn., U. Ky., Lexington, 1969. Tchr. 4th grade Churchland Elem., Portsmouth, Va., 1969-70, tchr. 5th grade, 1970-72; substitute tchr. Monterey (Calif.) Unified Sch. Dist., 1972, Prince Georges County Pub. Schs., Laurel, Md., 1973-76; tchr. 2d grade Lakeview Elem., Portsmouth, Va., 1976-80; substitute tchr. Portsmouth Pub. Schs., 1980-83, Chesapeake (Va.) Pub. Schs., 1980-83; tchr. 6th grade Churchland Elem., Portsmouth, 1983-90; tchr. 7th grade math. Churchland Jr. High., Portsmouth, 1990—96; founder Shepard's Tutoring Svc., 1996—2005, Shepard's Transcription Svc., 2005—. Author: What Could Our Child Possibly Teach Us?, 2002. Sunday sch. tchr. Aldersgate United Meth. Ch., Chesapeake, 1990-2005 Mem. Tidewater Coun. Tchrs. Math. (bd. mem. 1990-91), Delta Kappa Gamma (recording sec. 1986-88). Republican. Methodist. Avocations: needlecrafts, reading, writing. Office Phone: 757-484-8439.

SHEPARD, BEATRICE L., retired microbiologist, historian; b. Hillsdale, Mich., May 15, 1919; d. James Wesley Shepard and Ona Ola Kinney. AB in Zoolog., U. Calif., Berkeley, 1940. Regional lab. dir. L.A. County Health Dept., L.A., 1945-46; sr. biologist, sr. chemist S.E. Regional Lab., Juneau, Alaska, 1946-67; acting chief of labs. Alaska Dept. Health & Social Svcs., Juneau, 1967-70; microbiologist in charge S.E. Regional Lab., Alaska Dept. Health and Social Svcs., 1970-77; ret., 1977. Chemist L.A. County Health Dept., 1944-45, L.A. County Gen. Hosp., 1943-44; dir. pub. health lab. Health Dept. Riverside (Calif.) County, 1942-43. Author: Praise the Lord and Pass the Penicillin, 1979; co-author: Have Gospel Tent, Will Travel, History of 100 Years of Alaskan Methodism, 1986; editor: (newsletter) Western Cir. Rider, 1998—2005, Eagle River United Meth. Camp, 1998—; contbr. articles to profl. jours., chapters to books. Docent Alaska State Mus., 1992—2004; mem. Juneau Borough Commn. on Aging, 1997—; curator Alaska State Mus. 2003; mem. gen. commn. archives and history United Meth. Ch. Archives Ctr., Madison, NJ, 1988—96; historian Alaska Meth. Ch., Alaska Missionary Conf., Anchorage, 1980—; bd. dirs., advocacy chair Mus. Alaska, 1992—2005; sec. bd. dirs. Eagle River Meth. Camp, 1955—2005; bd. dirs. Western Jurisdictional Commn. on Archives and History, 1984—2005; chair Alaska Missionary Conf. Commn. on Archives and History, 1980—2004. Named Outstanding Lay Person of Yr. award Alaska Missionary Conf. of United Meth. Ch., 1986; recipient Meritorious Health Svc. award Alaska Pub. Health Assn., 1990. Mem.: Friends of Alaska State Mus. (hon.; life), Museums Alaska (hon.; life). Avocation: photography. Home: 12585 Glacier Hwy Juneau AK 99801 E-mail: BShep98308@aol.com.

SHEPARD, CHRISTY J., special education educator; d. William E. and Shirley M. Shepard. BS in Spl. Edn., U. Houston, 1974, MS in Occupl. Edn., 1989. Salesperson/customer svc. Sears, Roebuck & Co., Houston, 1968—93; sec. Preston Exterminating Co., Houston, 1971—74; tchr. Aldine Ind. Sch. Dist., Houston, 1974—76; tchr. of students with visual impairments Cypress-Fairbanks Ind. Sch. Dist., Houston, 1976—. Facilitator Region IV Edn. Svc. Ctr., Houston, 1999—. Asst. sec./treas. Harris County MUD #23, Houston, 1989—. Mem.: Assn. of Tex. Profl. Educators, Assn. for Edn. and Rehab. of the Blind and Visually Impaired (treas. 2000—). Avocations: reading, travel, cross stitch. Office Phone: 281-897-6490.

SHEPARD, DAVID HASPEL, film restoration specialist; b. N.Y.C., Oct. 22, 1940; s. Bertram David Shepard and Marjorie (Haspel) Markley; m. Kimberly Fetter, Mar. 26, 1977 (div.); 1 child, Benjamin Baker. AB, Hamilton Coll., 1962; MA, U. Pa., 1963. Asst. prof. theatre Pa. State U., State College, 1965-68; film restorations mgr., programmer Am. Film Inst., Washington, 1968-73; v.p. Blackhawk Films, Inc., Davenport, Iowa, 1973-76; spl. projects officer Dirs. Guild Am., Hollywood, Calif., 1976-87; adj. prof. cinema-TV U. So. Calif., L.A., 1982—2002; owner Film Preservation Assocs., Hat Creek, Calif., 1989-2000; managing dir. Film Preservation Assocs., Inc., 2000—. Trustee Internat. Film Seminars, NYC, 1972-82; adv. bd. Hollywood (Calif.) Entertainment Mus., 1984—, San Francisco Silent Film Festival, 1998—. Prodr. (video series) Chaplin: A Legacy of Laughter, 1992-93, Masterworks of D.W. Griffith, 1992/2002, Landmarks of Early Soviet Cinema, 1992—,

Great British Documentary Movement, 1993-2003, Golden Age of German Cinema, 1994—, Art of Buster Keaton, 1995, Douglas Fairbanks: King of Hollywood, 1996, Cecil B. De Mille: The Visionary Years, 1997-2005, Slapstick Encyclopedia, 1998, Les Vampires (1915 serial), 1998, Lon Chaney: Behind the Masks, 1997-2003, Valentino Lives!, 2002, Unseen Cinema: American Avant-Garde Films 1894-1941, 2005. Recipient Preservation award Soc. Cinephiles, 1970, 95, 2 Emmy awards Acad. TV Arts & Scis., 1973, Scholarship and Preservation award Internat. Documentary Assn., 1989, Prix Jean Mitry, Giornate des Cinema Muto, Pordenone, Italy, 1993, Saturn award Acad. Sci. Fiction, Horror and Fantasy Films, 1999, Mel Novikoff award San Francisco Internat. Film Festival, 2000, Preservation award Anthology Film Archives, 2005, Heritage award Nat. Soc. Film Critics, 2006, Hubbard award Niles Essanay Film Mus., 2006. Mem.: Soc. Cinema and Media Studies (hon. life), Acad. Motion Picture Arts and Scis. Home: PO Box 71 Hat Creek CA 96040-0071 Office Phone: 530-335-7420. Personal E-mail: dshepfilm@aol.com.

**SHEPARD, DONALD J.,** insurance company executive; MBA, U. Chgo. Various mgmt. positions Life Investors, Inc., 1970-85; exec. v.p., COO Life Investors, Inc. (consolidated with AEGON), 1985-89; chmn., pres., CEO AEGON USA, Balt., 1989—2002; chmn., 2002—. Bd. dirs. AEGON USA, Mercantile Bankshares Corp., CSX Corp., U.S. C. of C. Bd. dirs. Balt. Symphony Orch.; trustee Johns Hopkins Health Sys. Corp., Johns Hopkins Hosp., Johns Hopkins U., Walters Art Gallery. Office: AEGON NV AEGON plein 50 PO Box 202 2501 CE The Hague Netherlands

**SHEPARD, DONALD SLOANE,** public policy research educator; b. NYC, Sept. 15, 1947; s. Bertram David Shepard and Marjorie (Haspel) Markley; m. Emily A. Maitin, Aug. 17, 1980; children: Melissa R. Maitin-Shepard, Jeremy B. Maitin-Shepard. BA (magna cum laude) with highest honors, Harvard U., 1969, M in Pub. Policy, 1973, PhD, 1976. Lectr. U. Nairobi, Kenya, 1970—71; sr. economist Mass. Dept. Pub. Health, Boston, 1977—79; dir. econ. rsch. VA, West Roxbury, Mass., 1979—85; lectr. Harvard U., Cambridge, Mass., 1977—80, assoc. prof., 1980—91; prof. Brandeis U., Waltham, Mass., 1991—. Mem. pub. policy adv. com. Am. Found. for AIDS Rsch., Washington, 1991-95; vis. lectr. Harvard U., 1992-99; adj. faculty Boston U., 1986-2004; affiliated faculty Brown U., Providence, 1995—; dir. cost and value work group Inst. Health Policy Brandeis U., 2000-. Author: Assessing Costs for Cost-Effectiveness Analysis, 1988, Analysis of Hospital Costs: A Manual for Managers, 2000; mem. editl. bd. Scientific Evaluation and Program Planning, 1977-92; guest editor Adminstrn. and Policy in Mental Health, 2005; contbr. more than 100 articles to profl. jours. Bd. sci. advisors Sabin Vaccine Inst., Washington DC, 2004—; bd. councilors Pediat. Dengue Vaccine Initiative, 2002—2005, spl. adviser, 2006—; health svcs. rsch. study sects. of Nat. Inst. Alcohol Abuse and Alcoholism, 1998-2002, Nat. Inst. Drug Abuse, 2004-06. Grad. fellow NSF, 1971; prin. investigator Nat. Inst. on Drug Abuse and Nat. Inst. on Alcohol Abuse and Alcoholism, 1993—, Ctrs. for Medicine & Medicaid Svcs., 2000—. Mem. APHA, Mass. Pub. Health Assn., Acad. Health, Internat. Health Econs. Assn., Phi Beta Kappa. Avocations: cross country skiing, swimming. Home: 16 Cranmore Rd Wellesley MA 02481-1329 Office: Brandeis U Heller Sch 415 South St Waltham MA 02454-9110 Office Phone: 781-736-3975. Business E-Mail: shepard@brandeis.edu.

**SHEPARD, GEOFFREY CARROLL,** insurance company executive; b. Santa Barbara, Calif., Nov. 7, 1944; s. James J. and Barbara (Hoose) S.; m. Saundra Gayle Carlton, Jan. 10, 1973; children: Jonathan Pettus, William Dabney. BA, Whittier Coll., 1966; JD, Harvard U., 1969. Bar: D.C. 1972, Pa. 1977, U.S. Supreme Ct. 1973. White House fellow, 1969-70; staff asst. to Pres. White House, 1970-72, assoc. dir. domestic coun., 1972-75; sr. assoc. Steptoe & Johnson, Washington, 1975-77; sr. v.p., assoc. gen. counsel CIGNA Corp., Phila., 1977-91; sr. v.p., gen. counsel, corp. sec. Reliance Ins. Group, Phila., 1991-94; pres. corp. divsn. Karr Barth Assocs., Phila., 1994—. Trustee Whittier Coll., 2002—. Office: Karr Barth Assocs Inc 40 Monument Rd Bala Cynwyd PA 19004-1797

**SHEPARD, JEAN HECK,** retired publishing consultant; b. NYC, Feb. 2, 1930; d. Chester Reed and Anna S. (Charig) Heck; m. Lawrence Vaeth Hastings, Mar. 29, 1950 (div. 1953); 1 child, Lance Clifford Hastings; m. Daniel A. Shepard, July 26, 1954 (div. 1981); 1 child, Bradley Reed. BA, Barnard Coll., 1950; postgrad., Columbia U., 1952. Mem. sch. and libr. svc. Viking Press, N.Y.C., 1956-57; asst. dir. sch. and libr. promotion E.P. Dutton, N.Y.C., 1957-58; dir. advt. publicity and promotion Thomas Y. Crowell Co., N.Y.C., 1958-62; dir. advt. and promotion Charles Scribner's Sons, N.Y.C., 1962-67; cons. Stephen Greene Press, Brattleboro, Vt., 1970-73; mktg. mgr. A&W Publishers, N.Y.C., 1979-80, Franklin Watts Publ., N.Y.C., 1980-82; pub. 2 mags., divsn. advt. & promotion mgr. McGraw Hill Book Co., N.Y.C., 1983-85; cons. Monitor Publ. Co., N.Y.C., 1988-2000. Author: Simple Family Favorites, 1971, Herb and Spice Sampler, 1972, Cook With Wine!, 1973, Earth Watch: Notes on a Restless Planet, 1973, Harvest Home Steak Cookbook, 1974, Fresh Fruits and Vegetables, 1974, Yankee Magazine, 1972, Let Them be Sea Captains. Mem.: Authors Guild, Am. Libr. Assn., Women's Nat. Book Assn., Pub. Ad Club. Methodist. Avocations: reading, writing, travel, music, dance. Home: 73 Kingswood Dr Bethel CT 06801-1834 Office Fax: 203-798-2924. E-mail: shepardagcy@mindspring.com.

**SHEPARD, JEAN M.,** city health department administrator; b. San Diego; BA in Sociology, San Diego U. Employee San Diego County, 1976—, adminstrv. dept. Auditor, Contr., 1978—85, asst. chief adminstrv. officer, 1985—89, various positions Dept. Social Services, 1989—95, asst. dir. health, 1995—98, COO health and human services agy., 1998; dir. County of San Diego Health and Human Services Agy. Office: Health and Human Services Agy 1700 Pacific Hwy Rm 207 San Diego CA 92101*

**SHEPARD, JUDITH BETHEA,** librarian; b. Tuscaloosa, Ala., Apr. 12, 1947; d. Odis Hamner Reynolds and Audrea Earle Thomas; m. James Crenshaw Shepard, Feb. 19, 1978; children: Angela Elaine Ashcraft, Penelope Lea Taylor. BA, Ala. Coll., 1969; MLS, U. Ala., 1974. Tchr., libr. Decatur City Schs., Ala., 1969—71; libr. Gadsden Pub. Libr., Ala., 1974—76; libr., head of info. svcs. Ala. Pub. Libr. Svc., Montgomery, 1976—. Contbr. articles to profl. jours. Mem. Montgomery Mus. Fine Arts, Ala., 1999—, Montgomery Zool. Soc., Ala., 2002—; St. Peter's Parish Coun. Mem.: Ala. Libr. Assn. (moderator ref. and adult svcs. roundtable 2000—03). Republican. Roman Catholic. Achievements include development of State of Ala. Resource Sharing Sys. Avocations: painting, travel, reading. Home: 30 Tecumseh Dr Montgomery AL 36117 Office: Ala Pub Libr Svc 6030 Monticello Dr Montgomery AL 36130

**SHEPARD, KATHERINE,** science educator, consultant; d. Johnnie B. (Stepfather) and Jessie Beatrice Wright; m. Franklin Delano McKinney, Apr. 10, 1971 (div. Oct. 1985). BA, Goshen Coll., Ind., 1964; MA, Atlanta U., Ga., 1971; post grad., Case Western Res. U., Cleve., 1971—; Kent State U., Ohio, Hiram Coll., Suffolk U., Boston, Miami U., Oxford, Ohio. Cert. scuba diver. Summer recruiter Goshen Coll., 1967; tchr. HS physical edn. Cleve. Mcpl. Sch. Dist., 1964—65, tchr. HS health, 1993—94, tchr. HS sci., 1964—95, cons. and mentor to entry level tchrs., 1997—. Grant com. mem. Cleve. Pub. Schs. and NSF, 1993; mem. tchr. adv. com. Cleve. Pub. Schs. and Sci. Mus., 1994; mem. sch. governance com. Cleve. Pub. Schs., 1996; founder and dir. George E. Mills Gallery of Excellence, 1994; faculty adv. student coun.; faculty adv. Youth Coun. on Human Rels.; faculty adv. extracurricular clubs. Photographer (talent, fashion shows and Hall of Fame). Vol. Exec. Bd. Alumni Goshen Coll., 1981—84; newsletter publ. Shakerwood Assn., Warrensville Heights, Ohio, 1972—75, 2000—03; trustee Lee Heights Cmty. Ch., Cleve., 1986—89. Named to Gradsnet Found. Hall of Fame, 2001; recipient Inspirational Tchr. award, BP Am., 1996, Lifetime Achievement award, Harvard - Lee Times, 1996; scholar, Martha Holden Jennings Found., 1974—75. Mem.: Com. Political Edn., Assn. Supervision and Curriculum Devel., Cleve. Tchrs. Union. Avocations: photography, gardening, travel, sports, puzzles.

**SHEPARD, LANCE HASTINGS,** marketing professional, consultant, newscaster; b. NYC, Dec. 11, 1950; s. Lawrence Vaeth Hastings and Jean Heck Hastings Shepard. Student, Boston U., 1969—70; BS in Psychology, Franklin Pierce Coll., Rindge, NH, 1973. Cert. radio operator NY. Mgmt. tng. Waltham Savs. Bank, Mass., 1974—75; news and sports anchor Ch. 10 Cable TV, Danbury, Conn., 1975—76; guest rels. reception Plaza Hotel, Waldorf Astoria, NYC, 1978—90; owner DJ-on-Call, NYC, 1981—88; v.p., dir. Hin Shepard Agy., Brewster, NY, 1988—2000, exec. v.p., treas. Bethel, Conn., 2000—. Umpire Nat. Assn. Baseball Umpires, NH, 1970, Babe Ruth Baseball, Conn., 1978, Little League, Conn., 1978; referee Accredited NH Basketball Ofcls., 1973. Mem.: Princeton Club. Avocations: French horn, trumpet, reading, sports, films. Home: 73 Kingswood Dr Bethel CT 06801 Office: Shepard Agy M&T Bank Bldg Brewster NY 10509 Office Phone: 845-279-2900. Office Fax: 203-798-2924. Personal E-mail: shepardagcy@mindspring.com.

**SHEPARD, LAURA ANN,** microbiologist, researcher; b. Ft. Worth, Tex., Dec. 30, 1962; d. Larry and Montie Hopkins; m. Brett David Shepard, May 2, 1998; m. Dale Alan Utt, Jr., May 27, 1984 (div. Apr. 12, 1996); children: Dale Alan Utt, III, Amanda Leigh Utt. Student, Coll. of William and Mary, 1984; BHS summa cum laude, U. Mo., 1986; PhD, U. Okla., Oklahoma City, 1999. Cert. med. technologist Am. Soc. for Clin. Pathology, 1986. Med. technologist Boone Hosp. Ctr., Columbia, Mo., 1986—89; adj. faculty Okla. Bapt. U., Shawnee, Okla., 1991—94; postdoctoral rsch. fellow U. Okla., Oklahoma City and Norman, Okla., 2000—03; rschr. Mayo Clinic, Rochester, Minn., 2004—. Contbr. articles to profl. jours. Grad. fellow, NSF, 1995—98. Mem.: Assn. for Rsch. in Vision and Ophthalmology, Am. Soc. for Microbiology, Am. Soc. for Clin. Pathology, Lambda Tau, Golden Key, Alpha Eta, Alpha Epsilon Lambda, Phi Kappa Phi. Home: 1710 11th Ave NE Rochester MN 55906

**SHEPARD, MICHAEL J.,** prosecutor; Atty. U.S. Dept. Justice, Chgo., 1993—, asst. atty. Office: US Attys Office E M Dirksen Bldg 1500 South 219 S Dearborn St Ste 1500 Chicago IL 60604-1700

**SHEPARD, RANDALL TERRY,** state supreme court chief justice; b. Lafayette, Ind., Dec. 24, 1946; s. Richard Schilling and Dorothy Ione (Donlen) S.; m. Amy Wynne MacDonell, May 7, 1988; one child, Martha MacDonell. AB cum laude, Princeton U., 1969; JD, Yale U., 1972; LLM, U. Va., 1995; LLD (hon.), U. So. Ind., 1995, U.S.C., 1996. Bar: Ind. 1972, U.S. Dist. Ct. (so. dist.) Ind. 1972. Spl. asst. to under sec. U.S. Dept. Transp., Washington, 1972-74; exec. asst. to mayor City of Evansville, Ind., 1974-79; judge Vanderburgh Superior Ct., Evansville, 1980-85; assoc. justice Ind. Supreme Ct., Indpls., 1985-87, chief justice, 1987—. Instr. U. Evansville, 1975-78, Indiana U., 1995, 99; pres. Nat. Conference of Chief Justices, 2005—. Author: Preservation Rules and Regulations, 1980, Indiana Legal History, 2005; contbr. articles to profl. publs. Bd. advisors Nat. Trust for Hist. Preservation, 1980-87, chmn. bd. advisors, 1983-85, trustee, 1987-96; dir. Hist. Landmarks Found. Ind., 1983—, chmn., 1989-92, hon. chmn., 1992—; chmn. State Student Assistance Commn. Ind., 1981-85; chmn. Ind. Commn. on Bicentennial of U.S. Constn., 1986-91; vice chmn. Vanderburgh County Rep. Ctrl. Com., 1977-80. Recipient Disting. Svc. award Evansville Jaycees, 1982, Herbert Harley award Am. Judicature Soc., 1992, Wickler award Nat. Assn. Women Judges, 2004. Mem. ABA (coun. mem. sect. on legal edn. 1991—; chair sect. on legal actn. 1997-98, chair appellate judges conf. 1996-97), Ind. Bar Assn., Ind. Judges Assn., Princeton Club (N.Y.), Capitol Hill Club (Washington), Columbia Club (Indpls.), Woodstock Club (Indpls.). Republican. Methodist. Home: 3644 Totem Ln Indianapolis IN 46208-4171 Office: Ind Supreme Ct 315 State House Indianapolis IN 46204-2213 Office Phone: 317-232-2550.*

**SHEPARD, RICHARD BLOUNT,** surgeon, educator; b. Birmingham, Ala., May 9, 1926; m. Winyss Renee Acton, Mar. 26, 1955; children: Winyss Elizabeth, Richard Kesniel, Kathryn Bouchelle, Karen Acton. BS in Physics, Pa. State U., 1949; MD, U. Pa., 1953. Intern, resident in surgery U. Pa. Hosp., Phila., 1953-59; instr., rsch. assoc. in physiology U. Pa., Phila., 1954-56; chief resident Fitkin Hosp. Hahnemann Med. Coll., Neptune, NJ, 1959-60; from instr. to prof. surgery U. Ala., Birmingham, 1960-98, prof. surgery, emeritus, 1998—. Engr. Victoreen Instrument Co., Cleve., 1946; engr. Haller, Raymond & Brown, State College, Pa., 1948; cons. for device implant mfrs. and electronics mfr., 1960-2004; chmn. USRA-NASA biomed. com. for studies selection, shuttle orbital flight tests, 1981-83. Contbr. articles to profl. jours. and chpts. to books. With U.S. Army, 1943—46, spl. engr. detachment Manhattan Project U.S. Army, 1945—46. Grantee Heart Assn. S.E. Pa., NIH. Fellow ACS, Am. Coll. Cardiology, Soc. for Vascular Surgery (disting.); mem. IEEE (life), Heart Rhythm Soc., Soc. Thoracic Surgeons. Achievements include research in blood flow and energy characteristics, especially as related to cardiopulmonary bypass operations and underlying physiology; one of the first to implant cardiac pacemakers and investigational defibrillators; application of physics and cellular biology to clinical and laboratory implantable device development, teaching and problem solutions. Office Phone: 205-934-4672. Business E-Mail: RShepard@uab.edu.

**SHEPARD, ROBERT M.,** lawyer, investment banker, engineer; b. Amityville, N.Y., Feb. 15, 1932; s. Sidney M. and Undine L. (Lehmann) Shapiro; m. Barbara S. Stannard, June 25, 1955 (div. 1980); children: Karen Michele Shepard Sweer, Daniel Robert; m. Joanne E. Devlin, May 16, 1981 (div. 1993); m. Martha Kothe, Nov. 24, 1999. B.C.E., Cornell U., 1954; MBA, Hofstra Coll., 1960; LL.B., Yale U., 1963; LLM, NYU, 1988. Bar: N.Y. 1964; registered profl. engr., N.Y., Conn. Project engr. Lockwood Kessler & Bartlett, Syosset, NY, 1956-60; assoc. atty. Cravath, Swaine & Moore, N.Y.C. and Paris, 1963-70; gen. ptnr. Kuhn, Loeb & Co., N.Y.C., 1970-77; sr. v.p. Donaldson, Lufkin & Jenrette, N.Y.C. 1977-83; gen. ptnr. Donovan Leisure Newton & Irvine, N.Y.C., 1983-89, Adler & Shepard, N.Y.C., 1989-91, Shepard & van Essche, N.Y.C., 1991, Ballon Stoll Bader & Nadler, P.C., N.Y.C., 1992—. Note and comment editor: Yale Law Jour., 1962-63. Bd. dirs. N.Y. Grand Opera, Regency Whist Club. Recipient Fuertes Medal Cornell U., 1953 Mem. ABA, Am. N.Y. State Bar Assn., Pub. Power Assn., Nat. Assn. Bond Lawyers, Order of Coif, Union League Club, Regency Whist Club, Inc., Tau Beta Pi, Chi Epsilon. Home: 750 Park Ave Apt 2C New York NY 10021-4252 Office: Ballon Stoll Bader & Nadler 1450 Broadway New York NY 10018-2201 Office Phone: 212-575-7900 x248.

**SHEPARD, SAM (SAMUEL SHEPARD ROGERS),** playwright, actor; b. Ft. Sheridan, Ill., Nov. 5, 1943; s. Samuel Shepard and Jane Elaine (Schook) Rogers; m. O-Lan Johnson Dark, Nov. 9, 1969 (div. 1984); 1 child, Jesse Mojo; life ptnr. Jessica Lange; children: Hannah Jane, Samuel Walker. Student, Mt. San Antonio Jr. Coll., Walnut, Calif., 1961-62. Playwright-in-residence Magic Theatre, San Francisco. Author: (plays) Cowboys, The Rock Garden, 1964, 4-H Club, Up to Thursday, Dog, Rocking Chair, 1965, Chicago, 1965 (Obie award, 1966), Icarus's Mother, 1965 (Obie award, 1966), Fourteen Hundred Thousand, 1966, Red Cross, 1966 (Obie award, 1966), Melodrama Play, 1966 (Obie award, 1968), La Turista, 1967 (Obie award, 1967), Cowboys #2, 1967, Forensic and the Navigators, 1967 (Obie award, 1968), The Holy Ghostly, The Unseen Hand, 1969, Operation Sidewinder, Shaved Splits, 1970, Mad Dog Blues, Terminal, (with Patti Smith) Cowboy Mouth, Black Bog Beast Bait, 1971, The Tooth of Crime, 1972 (Obie award, 1973), Blue Bitch, (with Megan Terry and Jean-Claude van Itallie) Nightwalk, 1973, Geography of a Horse Dreamer, Little Ocean, Killer's Head, 1974, Action, 1974 (Obie award, 1975), Starving Class, 1977, Buried Child, 1978 (Obie award, 1977; Pulitzer Prize in drama, 1979, Obie award, 1979), Tongues, Savage/Love, Seduced, 1979, True West, 1981, Fool for Love, 1983 (Obie award, 1984), Superstitions, The Sad Lament of Pecos Bill on the Eve of Killing his Wife, 1983, A Lie of the Mind, 1985 (New York Drama Critics' Circle award, 1986), States of Shock, 1991, Simpatico, 1993, The Late Henry Moss, 2000, (collections of plays) Five Plays by Sam Shepard, 1967, The Unseen Hand and Other Plays, 1971, 1986, Mad Dog Blues and Other Plays, 1972, The Tooth of Crime and Geography of a Horse Dreamer, 1974, Angel City, Curse of the Starving Class and Other Plays, 1976, Buried Child, Seduced, Suicide in B-Flat, 1979, (collection of plays)

Four Two-Act Plays by Sam Shepard, 1980, Chicago and Other Plays, Seven Plays, 1981, Fool for Love and The Sad Lament of Pecos Bill on the Eve of Killing His Wife, 1983, Fool For Love and Other Plays, 1984, 1986, contbr. to Oh! Calcutta, 1976, (with Bob Dylan) Renaldo and Clara, 1978, (collection of plays) Paris, Texas, 1984, (other writings) Rolling Thunder Logbook, 1977, Hawk Moon: A Book of Short Stories, Poems and Monologues, 1981, Motel Chronicles, 1982; dir.:(writer): (plays) Fool for Love, 1983, A Lie of the Mind, 1985; (screenplays) Far North, 1988, Silent Tongue, 1993; actor: (plays) A Number, 2004—05; (films) Renaldo and Clara, Days of Heaven, 1978, Resurrection, 1980, Raggedy Man, 1981, Frances, 1982, The Right Stuff, 1983 (Academy award nomination best supporting actor, 1984), Country, 1984, Fool for Love, 1985, Crimes of the Heart, 1986, Baby Boom, 1987, Steel Magnolias, 1989, Hot Spot, 1990, Bright Angel, Defenseless, 1991, Thunderheart, 1992, The Pelican Brief, 1993, Safe Passage, 1994, The Good Old Boys, 1995, Curtain Call, The Only Thrill, 1997, All the Pretty Horses, 2000, The Pledge, 2001, Swordfish, 2001, Black Hawk Down, 2001, Leo, 2002, Blind Horizon, 2003, The Notebook, 2004, Don't Come Knocking, 2005, Stealth, 2005; (TV films, performance) Streets of Laredo, 1995, Lily Dale, 1996, Purgatory, Dash & Lilly, 1999, Hamlet, 2000 (nominated for Golden Globe, Best Actor). Named to Theater Hall of Fame, 1994; recipient Nat. Inst. and Am. Acad. Arts and Letters award for lit., 1974, Creative Arts award Brandeis U., 1975; grantee Rockefeller Found., 1967, Guggenheim Found., 1968, 1971; Fellow, U. Minn., 1966, Yale U., 1967. Mem.: Am. Acad. and Inst. of Arts and Letters.

**SHEPARD, STEPHEN BENJAMIN,** journalist, educator, former magazine editor; b. NYC, July 20, 1939; s. William and Ruth Shepard; m. Lynn Povich, Sept. 16, 1979; children: Sarah. Ned. B3, CCNY, 1961; MS, Columbia U., 1964. Reporter, editor, writer Bus. Week, NYC, 1966—75; asst. prof.; dir. Walter Bagehot fellowship program econs. and bus. journalism Columbia U., NYC, 1975—76; sr. editor Newsweek, NYC, 1976—81; editor Saturday Rev., NYC, 1981—82; exec. editor Bus. Week mag., NYC, 1982—84, editor in chief, 1984—2005; dean Grad. Sch. Journalism CUNY, NYC, 2005—. Adj. prof. Columbia Grad Sch. Journalism, 1971—75. Mem. visitors Columbia Grad. Sch. Journalism. Recipient Lifetime Achievement award, Gerald Loeb Found., 1999, Henry Johnson Fisher award, Mag. Publs. Am., 2000, President's award, Overseas Press Club, 2003. Mem.: Coun. Fgn. Rls., Am. Soc. Mag. Editors (v.p. 1990—92, pres. 1992—94, Hall of Fame 1999), Century Assn. Office: CUNY Grad Sch Journalism 230 West 41st St New York NY 10036 Business E-Mail: steve.shepard@journalism.cuny.edu.

**SHEPARD, STEVE,** graphic educator, painter; b. Port Arthur, Texas, Mar. 23, 1955; Attended, Workshops Contemporary Art, Santa Fe, 1976; BFA (hon.), U. South Ala., 1977. One-man shows include Chgo. Pub. Libr., 1987, Wake Forest U., Winston - Salem, 1988, Southeastern Ctr. for Contemporary Art, 1997, U. West Fla., 1998, Miss. Mus. Art, Jackson, 1999, Represented in permanent collections Mobile Mus. Art, Ala., prin. works include J.L. Scott Marine Edn. Ctr., Biloxi, Miss., George Ohr Mus., exhibited in group shows at U. South Ala., 1988, 2002, Mont. Mus. Art, 2003, works pub. in various publ.; author, illustrator Elvis Hornbill: Internat. Bus. Bird, 1991. Mem.: Nat. Assn. Ind. Artists. Address: America Oh Yes Gallery Joe Adams PO Box 3078 Hilton Head Island SC 29928-0078 Personal E-Mail: shepart@datasync.com.

**SHEPARD, SUZANNE V.,** language educator; b. Montour Falls, N.Y., Mar. 4, 1958; d. William Henry III and A. Louisa (Stenberg) S.; m. Tredwell Burch Jr., May 29, 1982. BA in Music and Lit., Eisenhower Coll., Seneca Falls, N.Y., 1980; MA in English, Binghamton U., 1983, PhD in English, 1995. Tchg. asst. Binghamton U., N.Y., 1981-87, adj. prof., 1987; from adj. prof. to prof. Broome C.C., Binghamton, 1991—2003, prof., 2003—, dept. chair, 2005—. Author: The Patchwork Quilt: Ideas of Community in Nineteenth Century American Women's Fiction, 2001. Elder Presbyn. Ch., Binghamton, 1988—, lay preacher, 1993—; mem. Multicultural Reading Group, Binghamton, 1995—. Mem. MLA, Nat. Coun. Tchrs. English, Phi Kappa Phi. Presbyterian. Business E-Mail: shepard_s@sunybroome.edu.

**SHEPARD, THOMAS ROCKWELL, III,** advertising executive; b. Greenwich, Conn., Apr. 21, 1951; s. Thomas Rockwell Jr. and Nancy (Crandall) S.; m. Margaret O'Neal, Sept. 1, 1972; children: Amanda Marie, Thomas Rockwell IV, Brian Dickinson. BA, Amherst Coll., 1973. Salesman Union Carbide Battery Products, N.Y.C., 1974-78; advt. dir. Good Housekeeping mag., 1984—90; pub. Country Living mag., 1990—93, Redbook mag., 1993—97; v.p. network advt. sales Manursing Club, N.Y. Athletic Club; v.p. network advt. sales Hearst HomeArts, 1997—99; pres. King Features Syndicate, N.Y.C., 1999—. Office: King Features Ltd 2nd Fl 888 7th Ave New York NY 10106-0003 E-mail: trshepano@hearst.com.

**SHEPARD, W. BRUCE,** academic administrator; m. Cyndie Shepard. BA in Polit. Sci., U. Calif., Riverside, 1969, MS in Polit. Sci., 1970, PhD in Polit. Sci., 1972. Prof. polit. sci., provost, v.p. acad. affairs Ea. Oreg. U., LaGrande, 1995—2002; mem. faculty dept. polit. sci. Oreg. State U., Oreg.; chancellor U. Wis., Green Bay, Wis., 2002—. Vis. scientist Population Study Ctr., Seattle; vis. fellow Sch. Comm. and Liberal Studies MItchell Coll. Advanced Edn., Bathurst, Australia. Office: U Wis Office Chancellor 2420 Nicolet Dr Green Bay WI 54311-7001

**SHEPARD, WILLIAM SETH,** diplomat, writer; b. Boston, June 7, 1935; s. Robinson and Myra Ellen (Foster) S.; m. Lois Rosalie Burke, Sept. 25, 1960; children— Stephanie Lee, Cynthia Robin, Warren Burke (dec.) AB cum laude, Wesleyan U., Middletown, Conn., 1957; JD, Harvard U., Cambridge, Mass., 1961. Bar: N.H. 1961, U.S. Ct. Mil. Appeals 1962 U.S. Supreme Ct., 1970. Aide to ambs. Henry Cabot Lodge and Ellsworth Bunker, Am. embassy, Saigon, Vietnam, 1966-67; staff officer Exec. Secretariat Dept. of State, Washington, 1967-69; consul, polit. officer Am. Embassy, Budapest, Hungary, 1970-73; desk officer Hungarian affairs Dept. State, Washington, 1973-75; desk officer Singapore and Malaysian affairs Dept. of State, Washington, 1975-77; dep. polit. counselor Am. embassy, Athens, Greece, 1978-80; consul gen. Am. Consulate Gen., Bordeaux, France, 1983-85; dir. Office Congl. Affairs, ACDA, Washington, 1987-89; cons. to gen. counsel USDA, Washington, 1991-92. Lectr. internat. law U. Singapore, 1965-66; CEO The Shepard Internat. Group, Inc., 1994—. Author: Consular Tales, 2001, Murder on the Danube, 2001, Vintage Murder, 2002, Foreign Service Tales, 2002, Shepard's Guide to Mastering French Wines, 2003, Murder in Dordogne, 2005, Diplomatic Tales, 2006; wine editor: Bonjour Paris, 2002—. Candidate for Rep. nomination 8th Md. Congl. Dist., 1985-86, Rep. nominee for Gov. of Md., 1990, candidate, 1994; del. Rep. Nat. Conv., 1992; Md. co-chmn. Dole Presdl. Campaign, 1996; apptd. mem. citizens adv. com. Chesapeake Exec. Coun., by Gov. Md., 2004. Recipient Pro Libertate Hungariae Commemorative medallion, 1981, Pub. Svc. Leadership award U.S.-Baltic Found., 1996, George L. Plimpton Pub. Svc. award Tilton Sch., 2003; French Govt. teaching asst. and Fulbright travel grantee, 1957-58; Congl. fellow Am. Polit. Sci. Assn. and fgn. policy legis. asst. to Senator Robert Dole, 1982-83. Mem. Soc. Mayflower Desc., Gov. Bradford Compact, Soc. Desc. Colonial Govs. (chancellor gen. 1993-95), Soc. Desc. Colonial Wars, Montesquieu Acad. France (corr.), City Tavern Club (Washington), Flagon and Trencher (Trencher award 2003), Les Chevaliers de Bretvin, Ordre des Compagnons de Bordeaux, Connetablie de Guyenne, La Jurade de St. Emilion, Bontemps Medoc et des Graves, Tred Avon Players. Republican. Unitarian Universalist. Avocations: reading, vintage Bordeaux, travel, gastronomy. Home: 4540 Boone Creek Dr Oxford MD 21654 *I remember Himalayan peaks, Asian sunsets, Greek islands and Bordeaux vineyards. Along the way, hard work in a principled cause is its own reward. In the end, family life and friends, a foyer, pets, a book worth reading, and a glass of wine matter most.*

**SHEPHARD, BRUCE DENNIS,** obstetrician, educator, medical writer; b. San Francisco, Apr. 21, 1944; s. Richard G. and Madelyn (Rogers) S.; children: Christopher, Carleton, Elizabeth. BA in History, U. Calif., Berkeley, 1966; MD, U. Calif., San Francisco, 1970. Diplomate Am. Bd. Ob-Gyn. Intern Jackson Meml. Hosp.-U. Miami (Fla.), 1970-71, resident in ob-gyn., 1971-74; pvt. practice Tampa, 1976—; clin. assoc. prof. obstetrics U. So. Fla. Sch. Medicine, Tampa, 1976—. Bd. dirs. Ctr. of Excellence, Humana

Women's Hosp., Tampa, Fla., 1983-90, Gulf Coast Health Systems Agy., 1980-83; mem. midwifery adv. com. Fla. Dept. Health and Human Resources, Tallahassee, 1982-86. Prin. author: The Complete Guide to Women's Health, 1982, 3d rev. edit., 1997; prin., writer, spokesperson (series of TV commls.) The Healthy Woman (Gold Link award 1987); mem. med. adv. bd. Baby Talk mag., 1992—; bd. dirs. PBS affiliate WEDU, 1998-2005; contbr. articles to profl. jours. and women's mags. Lectr. Continuing Edn., Inc., 2002—; mem. Agy. Health Care Adminstrn., Dept. Health and Rehab. Svcs., Fla., cert. med. expert Fla., 2001—; med. adv. bd. Welcare HMO, 1996—; prostr. coun. AVMED HMO, 1999—2002. Served as maj. USAF, 1974—76. Mem. AMA, Am. Coll. Ob-Gyn. (patient com. 1984-86, John McCain fellow 1981), Hillsborough County Med. Assn. (v.p. 2003-04, pres. 2006—), Phi Beta Kappa. Democrat. Lutheran. Avocations: tennis, photography, golf, antique glass collecting, running. Home: 14516 Nettle Creek Rd Tampa FL 33624 Office: 4302 N Habana Ave Ste 300 Tampa FL 33607

**SHEPHARD, MARK SCOTT,** civil and mechanical engineering educator; b. Buffalo, Oct. 27, 1951; s. William N. and Beatrice (Hass) S.; m. Sharon L. Nirschel, Nov. 25, 1972; children: Steven W., Kari L. BS, Clarkson U., 1974; PhD, Cornell U., 1979. Asst. prof. civil engring. and mech. engring. Rensselaer Poly. Inst., Troy, N.Y., 1979-84, assoc. prof., 1984-87, prof., 1988—, dir. Sci. Computation Rsch. Ctr., 1990—, Samuel A. and Elisabeth C. Johnson Jr. prof. engring., 1993—; assoc. dir. Rensselaer Design Rsch. Ctr., Troy, N.Y., 1980-90. Vis. rsch. fellow GE Corp., R & D Schenectady, 1985, cons., 1984-87; cons. GM Rsch. Lab., Detroit, 1980—, others; tech. adv. bd. Aries Tech., Lowell, Mass., 1987-89. Editor: Engring. with Computers; mem. editl. bd. Internat. Jour. Numerical Methods Engring., Computer Methods in Applied Mechanics and Engring., Engring. Applications of Artificial Intelligence, Internat. Jour. Engring. Analysis and Design, Computational Mechanics; contbr. articles to profl. jours., chpts. to books. Fellow ASME, AIAA (assoc.), U.S. Assn. for Computational Mechanics (past pres.), Internat. Assn. for Computational Mechanics (exec. bd.); mem. Am. Soc. Engring. Edn., Am. Acad. Mechanics, Sigma Xi, Tau Beta Pi, Phi Kappa Phi. Home: 305 Algonquin Beach Rd Averill Park NY 12018-6007 Office: Rensselaer Poly Inst 110 8th St Troy NY 12180-3522 Office Phone: 518-276-8044. Business E-Mail: shephard@scorec.rpi.edu.

**SHEPHERD, ALAN J.,** construction executive, management consultant; b. Bklyn., Jan. 15, 1942; s. Morris Elijah and Jean (Birnbaum) Shapiro; children: Robin Elyse, Kevin Peter BS in Mech. Engring., Mich. State U.; MS in Indsl. Engring., Wayne State U., 1966. Mgmt. trainee Chrysler Corp., Detroit, 1964-65, product engr., 1965-66; exec. v.p. Bruce Erts & Assocs., Southfield, Mich., 1966-70; pres. Creative Mgmt. Group, Inc., Southfield, Mich., 1970-76, chmn. bd., 1976, pvt. cons., 1976-79. Dir. planning and coordination Mgmt. Support Assocs., Tel Aviv, Israel, 1979-81, gen. mgr., 1981-82; mgmt. cons. MSA Consortium, Washington, 1982-83; regional mktg. dir. Hill Internat., Washington, 1983-84; mng. v.p. spl. projects CRS Sirrine, Inc., Washington, 1984-85; dir. advanced mgmt. program BDM Corp., McLean, Va., 1986-89; v.p. Hill Internat., Inc., Willingboro, N.J., 1989-90; v.p. mktg. and bus. devel. AWD Techs., Inc., Rockville, Md., 1990-94; dir. bus. devel. and cons. Brown & Root, Inc., Washington, 1994-98; v.p. Montgomery Watson, Washington, 1998—. Mem. Am. Inst. Indsl. Engrs., Project Mgmt. Inst., Soc. Am. Mil. Engrs. Office: Montgomery Watson Harza 1133 21st St NE Ste 710 Washington DC 20036-3390

**SHEPHERD, BOBBY E.,** federal judge; b. Arkadelphia, Ark., Nov. 18, 1951; BA, Ouachita Bapt. U., 1973; JD, U. Ark., 1976. Ptnr. Spencer & Spencer, El Dorado, Ark., 1976—81; Spencer, Spencer & Shepherd, 1981—84, Landers & Shepherd, 1987—90; pvt. law practive, 1984—87; circuit-chancery judge Ark. 13th Jud. Dist., 1991-93; magistrate judge US Dist. Ct. (we. dist.) Ark., El Dorado, Ark., 1993—2006; judge US Ct. Appeals (8th Cir.), Little Rock, 2006—. Served with U.S. Army Res., 1976-81.

**SHEPHERD, BRUCE P.,** lawyer; BA, Harvard Univ., 1979; MBA, JD, Univ. Calif., Berkeley, 1983. Bar: Calif. 1984. Mng. ptnr. Latham & Watkins LLP, San Diego, and mem. fin. and real estate dept. Bd. dir. San Diego County Big Brothers and Big Sisters, Coronado Schools Found.; elected sch. bd. mem. (pres. 2001-02) Coronado Sch. Dist., 1998—2002. Mem.: ABA. Office: Latham & Watkins LLP Ste 1800 600 W Broadway San Diego CA 92101-3375 also: Latham And Watkins Llp 12636 High Bluff Dr Ste 400 San Diego CA 92130-2071

**SHEPHERD, CYBILL LYNNE,** actress, singer; b. Memphis, Feb. 18, 1950; d. William Jennings and Patty Shobe (Micci) S.; m. David Ford, Nov. 19, 1978 (div., 1982); 1 child, Clementine; m. Bruce Oppenheim, March 1, 1987 (div., 1990); children: Molly Ariel and Cyrus Zachariah (twins) Shubert, Hunter Coll., 1969, Coll. of New Rochelle, 1970, Washington Sq. Coll., NYU, 1971, U. So. Calif., 1972, NYU, 1973. Appeared in motion pictures Last Picture Show, 1971, The Heartbreak Kid, 1973, Daisy Miller, 1974, At Long Last Love, 1975, Taxi Driver, 1976, Special Delivery, 1976, Silver Bears, 1977, The Lady Vanishes, 1978, Earthright, 1980, The Return, 1986, Chances Are, 1988, Texasville, 1990, Alice, 1990, Once Upon a Crime, 1992, Married to It, 1993; star TV series The Yellow Rose, 1983-84, Moonlighting, 1985-89, Cybill, 1994-98 (also prodr.); TV films include A Guide for the Married Woman, 1978, Secrets of a Married Man, 1984, Seduced, 1985, The Long Hot Summer, 1985, Which Way Home, 1991, Memphis, 1992 (also co-writer, co-exec. prodr.), Stormy Weathers, 1992, Telling Secrets, 1993, There Was a Little Boy, 1993, Journey of the Heart, 1997, Due East, 2002, Martha, Inc.: The Story of Martha Stewart, 2003, Martha Behind Bars, 2005; record albums include Cybill Does It To Cole Porter, 1974, Cybill and Stan Getz, 1977, Vanilla with Phineas Newborn, Jr, 1978; appeared in stage plays A Shot in the Dark, 1977, Picnic, 1980, Vanities, 1981, The Muse, 1999, Marine Life, 2000; co-author Cybill Disobedience, 2000.

**SHEPHERD, DONNA LOU,** interior designer; b. Uvalde, Tex., Sept. 25, 1948; d. Herbert Quarrels Jr. and Wanna Lou (Ray) Haile; m. Richard Ray Shepherd, June 2003; children from previous marriage: Laura Anne Howell, Christopher J. Huffman. BS, U. Houston, 1969, MEd, 1973. Owner Rainbow Design LLC, Greenwood Village, Colo., 1975—. Ptnr. Health By Design; spkr. in field. Designer Parade of Homes, 1989, Jr. Symphony Guild Showhome, 1996, designs featured in Colo. Homes and Lifestyles, Denver Post. Founder, pres. Prime Time Today, Littleton. Republican. Baptist. Avocations: water fitness, fly fishing, white-water rafting. Office: PO Box 3285 Littleton CO 80161-3285

**SHEPHERD, GAAL,** artist; b. Gainesville, Fla., Jan. 25, 1951; d. Charles Claypoole and Ruby Frances (Grogan) S.; m. John Allen Crowl. Student, Stella Adler Theater Studio, 1968-73, U. Tampa, 1974-75, Corcoran Sch. Art, 1985-88. Artist, Atlanta, Tampa, Ga., Fla., 1973-76; graphic designer Art Prodn., Inc., Washington, 1976-79; art dir. illustrations editor Chronicle Higher Edn., Washington, 1979-88; painter, sculptor North Pomfret, Vt., 1988—; dir. Cooler Gallery, White River Junction, Vt., 1996—. Exhbn. agt. The Carving Studio, West Rutland, Vt., 1996—. One-woman shows include Pierre Antoine Gallery, Washington, 1987, 1989, Beside Myself Gallery, Arlington, Vt., 1993, Bromfield Gallery, Boston, 1993, Colby-Sawyer Coll., New London, NH, 1993, Lyndon State Coll., Lyndonville, Vt., 1993, Chaffee Art Ctr., Rutland, Vt., 1994, 1997, 1998, 2002, Vt. Coun. on Arts, Montpelier, 1995, Clarke Galleries, Stowe, Vt., 1995, Between the Muse Gallery, Rockland, Maine, 1996, No B.I.A.S. Gallery, Bennington, Vt., 1997, Steinway Gallery, Chapel Hill,NC, 1998, Red Mill Gallery, Johnson, Vt., AVA Gallery, Lebanon, N.H., 2003, Vt. Supreme Ct., Montpelier, 2003, Cooler Gallery, White River, Vt., 2004, exhibited in group shows at Middletown (NY) Arts Ctr., 1994, Vt. State Craft Ctr. at Frog Hollow, Middlebury, 1994, Attleboro (Mass.) Mus., 1996, Helen Day Art Ctr., Stowe, 1996, Vt. Coun. on Arts, West Rutland, 1996, AVA Gallery, Lebanon, NH, 1996, Harvard U., Cambridge, Mass., 1996, Ashuah-Irving Gallery, Boston, 1996, Ctr. for Contemporary Arts, Santa Fe, N.Mex., 1997, Guadalupe Fine Arts, Santa Fe, 1997, State Capitol Rotunda, 1997, Vt. Inst. Natural Sci., Woodstock, 1997, Beside Myself Gallery, Arlington, Vt., 1998, Maine Coast Artists, Rockport, 1999, Shelburne Farms, Vt., 2001, N.Mex. State Capitol, Santa Fe, 2002,

two-person shows, Colby-Sawyer Coll., New London, NH, 1997, Milton Acad., Mass., 1998, The Munson Gallery, Chatham, Mass., 2001, exhibited in group shows at N.Mex. State Capital, Santa Fe, 2002, Rosewood Gallery, Sunapee, N.H., 2002, Munson Gallery, Chatham, Mass., 2002, Woodstock (Vt.) Folk Art, 2002, Elements Gallery, Rockland, Maine, 2002, Alliance for Visual Arts, Lebanon, N.H., 2003; author: Tranquil Vermont, 2000. Democrat. Avocations: mycology, gardening. Home: Thistle Hill Rd PO Box 307 North Pomfret VT 05053-0307 E-mail: coolergallery@together.net.

**SHEPHERD, GILLIAN MARY,** physician; b. Mar. 12, 1948; d. John Thompson and Helen (Johnston) S.; m. Eduardo Goar Mestre, Aug. 4, 1973; children: Laura Elena, Cristina Alicia, Eduardo Goar. BA, Wheaton Coll., Norton, Mass., 1970; postgrad., Tufts U., 1970-73; MD, N.Y. Med. Coll. 1976. Diplomate Am. Bd. Internal Medicine, Am. Bd. Allergy and Immunology. Intern, resident Lenox Hill Hosp., N.Y.C., 1976-79; fellow in allergy and immunology N.Y. Hosp./Cornell Med. Sch., N.Y.C., 1979-81; assoc. prof. medicine Cornell U. Med. Coll., N.Y.C., 1988—; clin. assoc. prof. medicine 1995—. Assoc. attending physician N.Y. Hosp., N.Y.C.; cons. allergy and immunology dept. medicine Meml. Sloan-Kettering Cancer Ctr., N.Y.C., 1982—. Contbr. articles in field to profl. jours. Fellow ACP, Am. Acad. Asthma, Allergy and Immunology (chair Edn. and Rsch. Trust 1999-2001, bd. dirs. 2000-2003); mem. AAAS, Am. Fedn. for Clin. Rsch., Joint Coun. Allergy and Immunology, N.Y. Allergy Soc. (exec. com. 1982-94, pres. 1991-92), N.Y. County Med. Soc. Office: 235 E 67th St Rm 203 New York NY 10021-6040 Office Phone: 212-288-9300.

**SHEPHERD, GORDON GREELEY,** space physics educator, researcher; b. Senate, Sask., Can., June 19, 1931; s. George Fredrick and Irene Eleanor (Thompson) S.; m. Marian Margaret Morgenroth, Aug. 15, 1953; children: Theodore Gordon, David Michael, Paul Ronald; m. Marianna Genova Gerdjikova, Dec. 19. 1987. BSc in Engring. Physics, U. Sask., 1952, MSc in Physics, 1953; PhD in Physics, U. Toronto, 1956. Asst. prof. physics U. Sask., 1957-64, assoc. prof., 1964-69; prof. York U., Toronto, 1969—, dir. Ctr. for Rsch. in Earth and Space Sci., 1994—. Author: Spectral Imaging of the Atmosphere, 2002. Recipient John H. Chapman award of excellence, Canadian Space Agy., 2003. Fellow Royal Soc. Can., Can. Aeronautics and Space Inst. (Alouette award 2004), Am. Geophys. Union; mem. Can. Assn. Physicists. Mem. United Ch. of Can. Avocations: travel, swimming, skiing. Home: 14 E Humber Dr King City ON Canada L7B 1B6 Office: York Univ/Ctr Rsch E/S Sci 4700 Keele St Toronto ON Canada M3J 1P3 E-mail: gordon@yorku.ca.

**SHEPHERD, GORDON MURRAY,** neuroscientist, educator; Faculty mem. med. sch. Yale U., 1967—, prof. neurobiology, prof. emeritus. Editor-in-chief Jour. Neurophysiology, Jour. Neuroscience; mem. adv. com. for cyberinfrastructure Nat. Sci. Found. Mem. Am. Acad. Arts and Sciences. Office: Dept Neurobiology Yale Sch Med PO Box 208001 333 Cedar St SHM C303 New Haven CT 06520-8001 Office Phone: 203-785-4323. E-mail: gordon.shepherd@yale.edu.*

**SHEPHERD, IAIN THOMAS,** biologist, educator; s. Alistar and Janette Shepherd. DPhil, Oxford U., Eng., 1994. Post-doctoral fellow U. Pa., Phila., 1994—98; sr. rsch. fellow Wash. U., Seattle, 1998—2002; asst. prof. Emory U., Atlanta, 2002—. Contbr. articles to profl. jours. Grantee, NIH, 2004—; Basil O'Connor fellow, Mar. Dimes, 2003—05. Mem.: Brit. Soc. Devel. Biology, Soc. Neuroscience, Devel. Biology. Office: Emory University Dept of Biology 1510 Clifton Road Atlanta GA 30322

**SHEPHERD, JOHN FREDERIC,** lawyer; b. Oak Park, Ill., May 22, 1954; s. James Frederic Shepherd and Margaret Joanne (Crotchett) Woollen; m. Jane Lowell Montgomery; children: Eliza Marion, Justine Catherine, Austin Frederic, Jack Lowell. AB magna cum laude, Dartmouth Coll., Hanover, N.H., 1976; JD, U. Denver, 1979. Bar: Colo. 1979, U.S. Dist. Ct. Colo. 1979, D.C. 1981, Okla. 2005, U.S. Dist. Ct. D.C. 1981, U.S. Ct. Appeals (10th cir.) 1981, U.S. Ct. Appeals (D.C. cir.) 1982, U.S. Supreme Ct. 1984, U.S. Ct. Appeals (9th cir.) 1990. Assoc. Holland & Hart, Denver, 1979-81, Washington, 1981-85, ptnr., 1985-87, Denver, 1987—; natural resources disting. practitioner in residence U. Denver Coll. Law, 1998. Reporter Mineral Law Newsletter, 1985-92. Mem. 50 for Colo., Denver, 1989. Mem. ABA (chmn. pub. lands and land use com. 1991-93, mem. coun. for sect. of natural resources energy and environ. law 1993-96), Rocky Mountain Mineral Law Found. (mem. long-range planning com. 1988—, trustee 1993-95), Dartmouth Alumni Club (pres. Washington chpt. 1985-86, trustee Rocky Mt. chpt., 1998-2001), Denver Athletic Club Avocations: fly fishing, basketball, running. Home: 320 Clermont St Pky Denver CO 80220-5642 Office: Holland & Hart 555 17th St Ste 3200 Denver CO 80202-3950 Office Phone: 303-295-8309. Business E-Mail: jshepherd@hollandhart.com.

**SHEPHERD, JON GLEN,** lawyer; b. Des Moines, May 22, 1968; s. Jerry Wayne and Vicki Jean (Clark) S.; m. Stacy Kenna York, May 23, 1992. BA, U. No. Iowa, 1990; JD magna cum laude, U. Mich., 1992. Bar: Tex. 1993, U.S. Ct. Appeals (5th cir.) 1994, U.S. Dist. Ct. (no. dist.) Tex. 1994, U.S. Dist. Ct. (ea. dist.) Tex. 1995. Jud. clk. U.S. Ct. Appeals (5th cir.), San Antonio, 1993-94; assoc. Gibson, Dunn & Crutcher LLP, Dallas, 1994—2003, ptnr., 2003—05. Mem. edit. bd. Sequoia, Inc., 2005—. Exec editor U. Mich. Law Rev., 1992; sr. editor ABA Antitrust Sec. Antitrust Law Jour., 1997—2006. Mem. Tex. Bar Assn., Dallas Bar Assn., Order of Coif. Avocation: sports. Office: Crews Shepherd & McCarty LLP 2200 Ross Ave Ste 4650W Dallas TX 75201 Office Phone: 214-432-7766. Office Fax: 214-432-7771. Business E-Mail: jshepherd@csm-lawyers.com.

**SHEPHERD, KAREN,** retired congresswoman; b. Silver City, N.Mex., July 5, 1940; m. Vincent P. Shepherd. BA, U. Utah, 1962; MA, Brigham Young U., 1963. Former instr. Brigham Young U., Am. U., Cairo; former pres. Webster Pub. Co.; former adminstr. David Eccles Sch. Bus., U. Utah; former dir. Salt Lake County Social Svcs., Utah; former dir. continuing edn. Westminster Coll.; former mem. Utah Senate; mem. 103d Congress from 2d Utah dist., Washington, 1993—94; exec. dir., U.S. rep. European Bank for Reconstruction Devel., London, 1996—2002; mem. exec. com., chair East West Trade and Investment Forum Am. C. of C., England, 1998—2002; dir. EMILY's List, 2002. Mem. nat. governing bd. Common Cause, Washington, 1995-96, Internat. Delegation to Monitor Elections in West Bank and Gaza, Israel, Nat. Planned Parenthood Action Fund, 2004—; founder Karen Shepherd Fund; founding mem. Utah Women's Polit. Caucus, Project 2000; mem. trustee KeyBank Victory Funds; bd. dirs. UBS Bank, USA., O.C. Tanner. Former mem. United Way, Pvt. Industry Coun.; former mem. adv. bd. U.S. West Grad. Sch. Social Work; trustee Westminster Coll.; bd. dirs. Utah Red Cross, 2003—; chair Grad. Sch. Social Work, U. Utah, 2002—. Recipient Women in Bus. award U.S. Small Bus. Assn., Woman of Achievement award, Pathfinder award, YWCA Leadership award, 1st place award Nat. Assn. Journalists, Disting. Alumni award U. Utah Coll. Humanities, Eleanor Roosevelt award Utah Dem. Party, 2002, Merit of Honor award U. Utah, 2004. Fellow Inst. Politics Kennedy Sch. Govt., Internat. Women's Forum, Salt Lake Area C. of C. (pub. rels. com.), Coun. on Fgn. Rels. Home: PO Box 1049 Salt Lake City UT 84110-1049

**SHEPHERD, KEVIN L.,** lawyer; b. Wichita, Kans., Aug. 4, 1957; BA magna cum laude, Frostburg State Coll., 1979; JD magna cum laude, Univ. Balt., 1984. Bar: Md. 1985, U.S. Dist. Ct. 1985. Law clk. judge Harry A. Cole, Md. Ct. Appeals, 1984—85; ptnr., co-chmn. Real Estate practice group Venable LLP, Baltimore & Washington. Editor (in chief): Balt. Law Rev., Probate & Property; contbr. articles to profl. jours. Recipient Am. Jurisprudence awards. Mem.: ABA (vice chmn. real property divsn., chair real property, probate and trust law sects.), Anglo-Am. Real Property Inst., Am. Coll. Real Estate Lawyers (bd. gov.), Md. State Bar Assn., Bar Assn. Balt. City, DC Bar Assn., Phi Alpha Theta, Pi Sigma Alpha, Heuslier Honor Soc. Office: Venable LLP

1800 Mercantile Bank & Trust Bldg 2 Hopkins Plz Baltimore MD 21201 also: Venable LLP 575 7th St NW Washington DC 20004 Office Phone: 410-244-7772, 202-344-4881. Office Fax: 410-244-7742. Business E-Mail: klshepherd@venable.com.

**SHEPHERD, MARK, JR.,** retired electronics company executive; b. Dallas, Jan. 18, 1923; s. Mark and Louisa Florence (Daniell) S.; m. Mary Alice Murchland, Dec. 21, 1945; children: Debra Aline Shepherd Robinson, MaryKay Theresa, Marc Blaine. BSEE, So. Meth. U., 1942; MSEE, U. Ill., at Urbana, 1947. Registered profl. engr., Tex. With GE, 1942-43, Farnsworth TV and Radio Corp., 1947-48, Tex. Instruments, Dallas, 1948-88, v.p., gen. mgr. semicondr.-components div., 1955-61, exec. v.p., chief operating officer, 1961-66, pres., chief operating officer, 1967-69, pres., chief exec. officer, 1969-76, chmn. bd. dirs., chief exec. officer, 1976-84, chmn. bd. dirs., chief corp. officer, 1984-85, chmn., 1985-88; ret. Hon. trustee Com. for Econ. Devel.; councillor conf. Bd.; mem. Bus. Coun. Lt. (j.g.) USNR, 1943-46. Fellow IEEE; mem. NAE, Sigma Xi, Eta Kappa Nu.

**SHEPHERD, MILDRED ROOF,** retired secondary school educator, art restorer; d. Charles Kiel Roof and Sarah Fields Finter; m. John Tyler Shepherd, Aug. 5, 1945; children: James Scott, Janet Anne, BA, San Francisco State U., 1936; MA in Music Edn., MA in Tchg. Music, Stanford U., 1942. Cert. tchr. Calif., lic. Internat. Soc. Appraisers. Tchr. All-Chinese Sch., San Francisco, 1938—39; tchr. music and drama Everett Jr. High, San Francisco, 1939—41; tchr. Sunset Elem., San Francisco, 1942—44; tchr. music Ruffner HS, Norfolk, Va., 1947—48, Glen Burnie (Md.) High, 1948—49; tchr. English Japanese Officers' Sch., Yokosaka, Japan, 1964—65; proprietor, resident artist Shepherd Studio, Arlington, Va. Chief appraiser St. John's Thrift Shop, Bethesda, Md., 1970—2001. Organizer, dir. girls' choir Hollywood Meth. Ch., Md. Lt. j.g. USNR, 1944—45. Mem.: Am. Inst. Conservation. Home: 5527 3d St S Arlington VA 22204 Office Phone: 703-671-1789. E-mail: johnmilshep@aol.com.

**SHEPHERD, STORMY,** talent agency executive; Bachelor, U. Utah, 2005. Pres. Leave Home Booking, Inc., Salt Lake City, 1990—. Tchr. LDS Ch., Salt Lake City, 2004—06; vol. El Nido, Compton, Calif., 2000—02. Recipient Small Agy. of Yr. award, Pollstar, 1995. Mem.: Am. Hist. Assn. (assoc.), Amnesty Internat., Ft. Douglas Mil. Mus. (life).

**SHEPHERD, TERRY L.,** health facility administrator; BS, Purdue U.; MBA, Ind. U. V.p., CFO Cardiac Pacemakers, Inc.; dir. bus. devel. med. devices and diagnostics divsn., CFO Lilly Industries, Ltd., U.K.; pres. Hybritech Eli Lilly and Co.; pres. heart valve divsn. St. Jude Med. Inc., St. Paul, 1994, mgr. internat. ops., 1996, pres., CEO, 1999—, chmn., 2002—. Office: St Jude Med Inc 1 Lillehei Plz Saint Paul MN 55117-9983

**SHEPHERD, TERRY LYNN,** special education educator; b. Knox, Ind., Feb. 22, 1958; s. A.B. Shepherd and Verona Darlene Preston; m. Melanie Ann Mullet; children: Jared, Samuel; m. Penny Kaye Price (div. Feb. 12, 1985); children: Shaun, William. EdD, Ball State U., Muncie, Ind., 1998. Social studies tchr. Houston Ind. Sch. Dist., Houston, 1982—85; tchr. Family and Children's Ctr., Mishawaka, Ind., 1985—90; spl. edn. tchr. Joint Svcs. for Spl. Edn., Plymouth, Ind., 1990—98; assoc. prof. spl. edn. Tex. A&M Internat. U., Laredo, Tex., 1998—2005. Contbr. articles to profl. jours. Grantee McCay Sch. of Edn. Rsch. Funds, U. Utah, 2000, Regents' Initiative Collaborative Rsch. Grant, State of Tex., 2001; Regents' Initiative Fellowship Grant, 2001. Mem.: Coun. for Exceptional Children, Pi Lambda Theta. Republican. Baptist. Achievements include research in over representation of Limited English Proficient students in special education; working conditions of special education teachers in Texas. Avocations: music, genealogy, model building. Office: Tex A&M Internat Univ 5201 University Blvd KL3 435C Laredo TX 78041-1900 Home: 9843 Spindrift Dr Laredo TX 78045-6337 Office Phone: 956-326-2689. Personal E-mail: terrys2956@aol.com. Business E-Mail: tshepherd@tamiu.edu.

**SHEPHERD, WILLIAM MICHAEL,** music educator, musician; b. Ft. Knox, Ky., Mar. 26, 1949; s. Elisha and Zella Shepherd; m. Shelley Alice Jaffe, Feb. 10, 1985; children: Kevin, Marc. Student, Vallejo Jr. Coll., Calif., 1968—70; B in Music Edn., Ea. Ky. U., 1975; postgrad., U. Calif., Davis, 1986; MusM., U. Oreg., 1987. Music tchr. Dayton (Ohio) City Schs., 1975—77; profl. musician Stan Kenton, Les Brown, 1977—80; music tchr. Vallejo Unified Schs., 1980—83, Ukiah (Calif.) Unified Schs., 1983—94, Brookings (Oreg.)-Harbor Schs., 1994—. Dir. Curry Big Band, Brookings; leader Banana Belt Brass Quintet, Brookings. Mem.: Internat. Assn. Jazz Educators, Internat. Trumpet Guild, Phi Mu Alpha. Avocations: shooting, sports, fishing, model aviation. Home: 337 Mill Beach Rd Brookings OR 97415 Office Phone: 541-469-2108. Personal E-mail: shepherd@nwtec.com. Business E-Mail: shepherd@harborside.com.

**SHEPHERDSON, JAMES A. (JAMIE),** diversified financial services company executive; Past COO McGuinness; mng. dir. Equitable Distbrs., Inc., 1994—2000, sr. v.p., 1996—2000; co-CEO, Security First Group Met. Life Ins. Co., 2000—02; sr. v.p. and pres., retirement svcs. John Hancock Fin. Svcs., Inc., Boston, 2003—04, exec. v.p. mutual funds, 2004—. Office: John Hancock Fin Svcs Inc John Hancock Pl PO Box 111 Boston MA 02117

**SHEPLEY, HUGH,** architect; b. Boston, Mar. 17, 1928; s. Henry Richardson and Anna Lowell (Gardiner) S.; m. Mary Waters Niles, Dec. 27, 1950; children: Hamilton Niles, Philip Foster. BA, Harvard U., 1951; BArch., Boston Archtl. Ctr., 1958; postgrad., Mass. Inst. Tech., 1958-59. Mem. archtl. firm Shepley, Bulfinch, Richardson & Abbott, Boston, 1955-63, ptnr., 1963-91. Bd. dirs. Greater Boston Red Cross, 1967-73, mem. exec. com., 1968-69; bd. dirs. Cmty. Music Ctr., Boston, 1968-72, Boston Ctr. for Blind Children, 1979-87; trustee New Eng. Conservatory Music, 1978-83, overseer, 1983—; trustee Univ. Hosp., 1980-96, mem. exec. com., 1981-92, vice chmn. bd. dirs., 1985-89, chmn. bd. dirs., 1989-92; trustee Am. Coll. of Greece, 1983-92, treas., 1986-88; trustee, sec. Rotch Travelling Scholarship, 1987-93, v.p., 1993-2006; mem. adv. coun. Boston U. Med. Ctr., 1990-96, Corp. Old South Assn., 1993-2002; bd. dirs. Manchester (Mass.) Hist. Soc., 1994-2002; overseer Spaulding Rehab. Hosp., 2003—. Fellow AIA; mem. Mass. Assn. Architects (pres. 1972), Boston Soc. Architects (pres. 1974), Boston Archtl. Ctr. (pres. 1969-71), Tavern Club (Boston), Manchester Yacht Club (commodore 1985-87), Essex County Club. Independent. Episcopalian. Home: 8 Andover Ct Bedford MA 01730 E-mail: hshepley@verizon.net.

**SHEPLEY, MARDELLE MCCUSKEY,** architect, educator; b. Bethesda, Md., June 28, 1949; d. E. Scott McCuskey (father) & James R. and Yvonne Hudson S.; m. Laurence Berger, 1974 (div. 1978); m. Michael Curtis Blair, 1981 (div., 2004); children: Colin, Ian, Teal. BA, Columbia U., 1971, MArch, 1974; MA, U. Mich., 1979, DArch, 1981. Registered architect Calif. Urban designer N.Y.C. Dept. City Planning, 1972—74; planner Min. Planning & Econ. policy, Panama, Panama, 1975—77; lectr., teaching asst. U. Mich., Ann Arbor, 1977—81; assoc. Tai Assocs. Architects, San Francisco, 1981—85, The Design Partnership, San Francisco, 1985—93; asst. prof. Tex. A&M U., College Station, 1993—97, assoc. prof., 1997—2003, prof., 2003—, coord. PhD program, 1999-2001, assoc. dean for students, 2001—05, interim head dept. architecture, 2005—. Rsch. com. Ctr. Health Design, Martinez, Calif., 1993—; assoc. dir. Ctr. Health Sys. and Design, 1995—2004, interim dir., 2004—05, dir., 2005—. Co-author: Healthcare Environments for Children and Their Families, 1998. Bd. dirs. Assn. for Care of Children's Health, Mt. Royal, N.J., 1994-2000; mem. parent bd. Oakland (Calif.) Montessori Sch. 1991-93. Recipient Health Facilities Rsch. award AIA, 1992, Tex. A&M U. scholar, 1998; Tex. A&M U. faculty fellow, 2001-, William Pena Endowed Prof., 2003-. Office: Tex A&M U Dept Architecture College Station TX 77843-3137 Business E-Mail: mardelle@tamu.edu.

**SHEPP, BRYAN EUGENE,** psychologist, educator; b. Cumberland, Md, Sept. 13, 1932; s. Bryan Evert and Dorothy Lorene (Stell) S.; m. June Lee Langeluttig, Jan. 31, 1953; children— Karen Suzanne, David Bryan. BS, U.

Md., 1954, MS, 1956, PhD, 1960; MS with honors, Brown U., 1966. Rsch. prof. U. Conn., 1961-63; asst. prof. psychology George Peabody Coll., Nashville, 1963-64, Brown U., Providence, 1964-66, assoc. prof., 1966-69, prof., 1969-98, prof. emeritus, 1998—, chmn. dept. Providence, 1983-88, assoc. dean faculty, 1988-91, dean faculty, 1991-96. Cons. in field; vis. scientist Oxford (Eng.) U., 1970 Contbr. numerous articles to profl. publ.; ad hoc editor for several psychol. jour. Served with USN, 1955-59. Decorated letter of commendation Sec. of Navy; USPHS postdoctoral fellow, 1959-61; Nat. Inst. Child Health and Human Devel. grantee, 1965—82. Fellow APA, Am. Psychol. Soc. (founding fellow); mem. AAAS, AAUP, Psychonomic Soc., Univ. Club. Personal E-mail: beshepp@yahoo.com.

**SHEPPARD, BEN H., JR.,** lawyer; b. Amarillo, Tex., Jan. 18, 1943; BA, U. North Tex., 1965; LLB, U. Tex., 1968. Bar: Tex. 1968. Mem. Vinson & Elkins L.L.P., Houston. Adj. prof. U. Houston Law Ctr. Editor-in-chief: Internat. Arbitration News. Adv. bd. Inst. Transnat. Arbitration. Mem. Chancellors, Order of Coif, Phi Delta Phi. Office: Vinson & Elkins 3300 First City Tower 1001 Fannin St Ste 3300 Houston TX 77002-6706

**SHEPPARD, DOUGLAS G.,** manufacturing project engineer; b. Spartanburg, SC; s. E. Gene and Priscilla S.; m. Donna Lowder; children: Andy, Hannah, Kristina. BS in Bus., Lenoir Rhyne Coll., 1986; BS in Mech. Engring., U. S.C., 1988. Registered profl. engr., S.C. Process engr. Dana Corp., Morganton, N.C., 1989; applications and design engr. Carbis Access and Safety Sys., Florence, S.C., 1990; mfg. engr. Automatic Switch Co., Aiken, S.C., 1990-91; mfg. engr., assembly automation Pass and Seymour/LeGrand, Concord, N.C., 1992—. Active Mallard Creek Presbyn. Ch., Charlotte, N.C. Mem. Nat. Soc. Profl. Engrs. Achievements include development of hospital grade receptacle, "maxgrip" plugs and connectors, thermoplastic switch plates; designer new compressed air system. Office: Pass and Seymour 4515 Enterprise Dr Concord NC 28027-6437

**SHEPPARD, JOHN WILBUR,** computer research scientist; b. Pitts., Aug. 21, 1961; s. Harry Reid and Mary Jane (Amon) S.; m. Justina Anne Pape, Oct. 29, 1988; children: Jesse Carl, Jeannette Alida. BS, So. Meth. U., 1983; MS, Johns Hopkins U., 1989, PhD., 1996. Systems analyst Sheppard Internat., Inc., Hermitage, Pa., 1979-86; fellow ARINC Inc., Annapolis, Md., 1986—; lectr. Johns Hopkins U., 1994—2005, asst. rsch. prof., 2005—. Co-author: System Test and Diagnosis, 1994; author, editor: Research Perspectives and Case Studies in System Test and Diagnosis; contbr. articles to profl. jours. Mem. YMCA, Hermitage, 1979-85, Md. Hall for the Creative Arts, Annapolis, 1988-90; pres. Univ. Chapel Campus Ministry, Dallas, 1982-83. Mem. IEEE (sr.), Mensa, Kappa Mu Epsilon. Achievements include development of explanation-based learning approach for fault diagnosis; multi-agent learning approaches for solving Markov games; Bayesian approach to system diagnosis and prognosis; patents for methods and apparatus for diagnostic testing. Office: ARINC Inc 2551 Riva Rd Annapolis MD 21401-7461 E-mail: jws@cablespeed.com, jsheppar@arinc.com.

**SHEPPARD, SCOTT S.,** astronomer; b. Buffalo, Feb. 19, 1976; s. Fred and Margaret Sheppard. PhD, U. Hawaii, 2004. Rschr. U. Hawaii, Honolulu, 1998—2004, Carnegie Inst. Wash., Washington, 2004—. Achievements include discovery of over 70 new moons of Jupiter, Saturn, Uranus and Neptune. Office: Carnegie Institution of Washington 2541 Broad Branch Rd NW Washington DC 20015 Office Phone: 202-478-8854.

**SHEPPARD, VANESSA B.,** medical educator; d. Primus Waverly Banks and Winifred Lavene Reid; m. Earle Edward Sheppard, Nov. 16, 1991; children: Aaron Edward, Erik Alexander. BA, James Madison U., Harrisonburg, Va., 1988; MA, Norfolk State U., Norfolk, Va., 1990; PhD, Old Dominion U., Norfolk, Va., 1997; student, La. Va. Med. Sch., Norfolk, Va., 1997—99. Sr. health policy analyst Va. Dept. Health, Richmond, Va., 1995—96; sr. rsch. analyst Med. Sch. Ea. Va. U., Norfolk, Va., 1997—2001, from instr. to asst. prof. Med. Sch., 2001—02; asst. prof. oncology Georgetown U., Washington, 2002—. Dir. evaluation Va. Healthy Start Initiative, Richmond, 1998—2002. Contbr. articles to profl. jours. Health ministry leader First Ch. Seventh-Day Adventists, Washington, 2005—06. Fellow, Agy. Healthcare Rsch. and Quality, 1999—2001, Moffit Cancer Ctr., 2004; grantee, Nat. Cancer Inst., 2003, 2003—06, Susan G. Komen Found., 2005—, 2006—, Am. Cancer Soc., 2006—; scholar, Va. Coun. Higher Edn., 1990—95. Mem.: Assn. Am. Med. Colls. (Herbert Nickens award 2005), Latin Am. Cancer Rsch. Coalition (dir. 2002—03), Minority Health Rsch. Coalition (co-founder 1999), Cmty. Health Partnership (v.p. 2003—05). Achievements include research in decision support intervention for minority women with breast cancer. Office Fax: 202-687-0305. Business E-Mail: vls3@georgetown.edu.

**SHEPPARD, WILLIAM J.,** lawyer; b. Portland, Oreg., Nov. 4, 1941; BS, Fla. State U., 1963; JD, U. Fla., 1967. Bar: Fla. 1968, U.S. Dist. Ct. Fla. (Middle and No. Dist.) 1968, U.S. Ct. Appeals (5th cir.) 1971, U.S. Supreme Ct. 1973, U.S. Ct. Appeals (11th cir.) 1981, U.S. Ct. Appeals (4th cir.) 1982, U.S. Ct. Appeals (7th cir.) 1991, U.S. Ct. Appeals (Fed. cir.) 1995, U.S. Tax Ct. 1999, bd. cert. criminal trial lawyer: Fla. Bar Bd. Legal and Specialization Edn. Ptnr. Sheppard, White & Thomas, P.A., Jacksonville, Fla. Mem. Gov.'s Adv. Com. on Corrections, 1982—86; chmn. Jud. Nomm. Commn. Fourth Jud. Cir., 1992—96; mem. civil justice reform act commn. Middle Dist. Fla., 1996—98. Exec. editor: U. Fla. Law Rev., 1966—67; contbr. articles to profl. jours. 1st lt. U.S. Army, 1963—65. Decorated Commendation Medal U.S. Army; recipient Disting. Svc. award, Nat. Fedn. Blind Fla., 1978, Nelson Poynter Civil Liberties award, 1982, Tobias Simon Pro Bono Svc. award, Fla. Supreme Ct., 1985, Civil and Human Rights award, Internat. Assn. Official Human Rights Agencies, 1990, Nelson Poynter Civil Liberties award, 2000. Mem. NACDL, Chester Bedell Inn of Ct. (master of the bench), Am. Coll. Trial Lawyers, Fla. Assn. Criminal Def. Lawyers (Steven M. Goldstein Criminal Justice award 2001), Fla Bar. Assn. (mem. criminal law cert. com. 1986—88, Pres. Pro Bono Svc. award 1984, Selig I. Golden Meml. award 1993), Jacksonville Bar Assn. (mem. 4th jud. cir. professionalism com. 1999—2000), Fla. Bar Found. (life Medal of Honor award 2004), Phi Delta Phi. Office: Sheppard White & Thomas PA 215 Washington St Jacksonville FL 32202 Office Phone: 904-356-9661. Office Fax: 904-356-9667. Business E-Mail: sheppardwhitethomas@worldnet.att.net, sheplaw@att.net.

**SHEPPE, JOSEPH ANDREW,** surgeon; b. Huntington, W.Va., Sept. 24, 1953; m. Kathy Chapman; children: Sheree Nicole, Natalee Marie, Brittany Lee. BS summa cum laude in Chemistry and Zoology, Marshall U., 1975; MD, W.Va. U., 1979. Diplomate Am. Bd. Surgery, Am. Bd. Colon and Rectal Surgery. Intern in gen. surgery Charleston (W.Va.) Area Med. Ctr., 1979-84; fellow in colon and rectal surgery William Beaumont Army Med. Ctr., Royal Oak, Mich., 1984-85; pvt. practice Columbia, SC, 1985—. Physician Bapt. Med. Ctr., Columbia, Providence Hosp., Columbia, Richland Meml. Hosp., Columbia, Lexington Med. Ctr., West Columbia, S.C.; clin. instr. in gen./colorectal surgery U. S.C. Med. Sch. Fellow ACS, Am. Soc. Colon and Rectal Surgery; mem. S.C. Med. Soc., Columbia Med. Soc. Home: 204 Leaning Tree Rd Columbia SC 29223-3009 Office: 1333 Taylor St Ste 4-a Columbia SC 29201-2949 Office Phone: 803-779-5600.

**SHEPPERD, THOMAS EUGENE,** accountant; b. Pekin, Ill., Aug. 19, 1941; s. William Thomas and Marguerite Louise (Meisinger) S.; m. Susan Abbott Belville, Oct. 7, 1960; children: Scott Thomas, Allison Marie Shepperd-Henry, Michele Lea. BS in Acctg., U. Ill., 1964. CPA, Ill., Mo., Iowa, Ind. From jr. acct. to mgr. Haskins & Sells, St. Louis, 1964-74, mgr. Washington, 1974-75, ptnr., 1975-77, Deloitte Haskins & Sells (formerly Haskins & Sells), St. Louis, 1977-89, Deloitte & Touche (merger Deloitte Haskins & Sells and Touche Ross & Co.), St. Louis, 1989—. Treas. Shepley concert com. Christ Ch. Cathedral, St. Louis, 1989; bd. dirs., treas. Care & Counseling, Inc., Howard Park Early Childhood Ctr.; trustee, chmn. bd. Diocesian of Mo. Investment Trust. Mem. AICPA (various coms., mem. exec. coun. 2003—), Mo. Soc. CPAs (adminstrv. v.p., bd. dirs. 1988-92, treas. 1992-95, v.p. 1996-97, pres.-elect 1997-98, pres., 1998-99, chair long range fin. planning com. and the office location com., terms on the tech. standards

peer review exec., profl. ethics coms., legislation com., acctg. and auditing procedures com., bd. dirs. 2003--), U. Ill. Press. Coun., David Kinley Assn., Noonday Club (treas., bd. dirs. 1977-81), Glen Echo Country Club. Republican. Episcopalian. Avocations: golf, travel, sports. Home: 15977 Chamfers Farm Rd Chesterfield MO 63005-4717 Office: Deloitte Touche 100 S 4th St Ste 200 Saint Louis MO 63102-1821

**SHER, SIR ANTONY,** actor, author; b. Cape Town, South Africa, June 14, 1949; LittD (hon.), U. Liverpool, U. Exeter. Performer (plays): Cloud Nine, Goosepimples, Torch Song Trilogy (Laurence Olivier Best Actor award), assoc. artist Royal Shakespeare Co., King Lear, Moliere, Tartuffe, Maydays, Red Noses, Richard III (London Critics Cir. Theatre award, best actor, 1984, London Evening Standard Theatre award, best actor. 1985), The Merchant of Venice, The Revenger's Tragedy, Hello and Goodbye, Singer, Tambulaine the Great, Travesties, Cyrano de Bergerac, The Winter's Tale, Macbeth, The Roman Actor, The Malcontent, Othello; (nat. theater) True West, The Trial, The Resistible Rise of Arturo Ui, Uncle Vanya, Titus Andronicus (TMA Best Actor award), Stanley (Laurence Olivier Best Actor award, 1997, Theatre World award, Tony award nominee 1997), Primo (Outer Critics' Cir. award, outstanding solo performance, 2006, Drama Desk award, outstanding solo performance, 2006); (TV movie) History Man, Mark Gertler, Moliere, Tartuffe, Collision Course, The Land of Dreams, Genghis Cohen, Macbeth, The Moonstone, Home; (film) Shadey, Erik the Viking, The Wind in the Willows, Alive and Kicking, Nrs. Brown, Churchill The Hollywood Years; author: Year of the King, Middlepost, Characters; The Indoor Boy, Cheap Lives; (with Gregory Doran) Woza Shakespeare!, The Feast, Beside Myself, I.D., Primo, Primo Time. Achievements include knighted for acting and writing. Mailing: c/o Paul Lyon-Maris ICM Oxford House 76 Oxford St London WIN OAX England

**SHER, GEORGE ALLEN,** philosophy educator; b. NYC, Nov. 10, 1942; s. Daniel and Clara (Landesberg) S.; m. Emily Fox Gordon, July 10, 1972; 1 child, Sarah Landesberg. BA, Brandeis U., 1964; PhD, Columbia U., 1972. Instr. philosophy Fairleigh Dickinson U., Teaneck, NJ, 1966—72, asst. prof. philosophy, 1972—74; assoc. prof. philosophy U. Vt., Burlington, 1974-80, prof., 1980-91; Herbert S. Autrey prof. philosophy Rice U., Houston, 1991—, chmn. dept. philosophy, 1993-2000. Mem. Inst. for Advanced Study, Princeton, N.J., 1987-88. Author: Desert, 1987, Beyond Neutrality: Perfectionism and Politics, 1997, Approximate Justice: Studies in Non-Ideal Theory, 1997, In Praise of Blame, 2005; editor: Moral Philosophy: Selected Readings, 1989, 2d edit., 1996; contbr. articles to profl. jours. Named fellow Nat. Humanities Ctr., Rsch. Triangle Park, N.C., 1980-81. Mem. Am. Philos. Assn. Home: 2425 Dryden Rd Houston TX 77030-1001 Office: Rice U Dept Philosophy MS 14 6100 Main St Houston TX 77251-1892 Office Phone: 713-348-2723. Business E-Mail: gsher@rice.edu.

**SHER, LEO,** psychiatrist; b. Kiev, Ukraine, June 13, 1961; s. Alexander and Ivetta (Iokhved) Sher. MD summa cum laude (hon.), Ukrainian Nat. Med. U., Kiev, 1985. Sr. staff fellow NIMH, Bethesda, Md., 1997—2000; asst. clin. prof. psychiatry and behavioral scis. The George Washington U., Washington, 2000—02; rsch. psychiatrist N.Y. State Psychiat. Inst., Columbia U. Med. Ctr., N.Y.C., 2000—; asst. clin. prof. psychiatry Columbia U. Coll. Physicians and Surgeons, 2001—06; assoc. clin. prof. psychiatry, 2006—; asst. attending physician The N.Y. Presbyn. Hosp., Columbia U. Med. Ctr., 2001—. Contbr. over 200 articles to profl. jours., chpts. to books. Recipient Charlotte Marker Zitrin, M.D. award, Albert Einstein Coll. of Medicine Psychiatry Residency Program at L.I. Jewish Med. Ctr., 1997, Internat. award for Excellence in Pub. Clin. Rsch. in Jour. Clin. Endocrinology and Metabolism, Endocrine Soc. and Pfizer, 2004. Mem.: Soc. Biol. Psychiatry. Jewish. Achievements include patents in field. Personal E-mail: drleosher@aol.com.

**SHERBELL, RHODA,** artist, sculptor; b. Bklyn. d. Alexander and Syd (Steinberg) S.; m. Mervin Honig, Apr. 28, 1956 (dec.); 1 child, Susan Honig. Student, Art Students League, 1950—53, Bklyn. Mus. Art Schs., 1959—61; pvt. study art, Italy, France, Eng. 1956. Cons., cour. mem. Emily Lowe Gallery, Hofstra U., Hempstead, N.Y., 1978, pres., 1989-81, instr., 1991—, life mem. bd. friends, pres. bd. trustees; tchr. instr. Mus. Modern Art, N.Y.C., 1959, NAD Art Sch., N.Y.C., 1985—, Art Students League, N.Y.C., 1980—; Nat. Portrait Gallery Mus. rep. to 150th anniversary Smithsonian Instn., Washington, 1996lectr. Nat. Arts Club, N.Y.C. One-woman shows include Huntington Township Art League, Embassy of U.S., Prague, 2002-03, Country Art Gallery, Locust Valley, N.Y., Bklyn. Mus. Art Sch., 1961, Adelphi Coll., A.C.A. Galleries, N.Y.C., 1960, Capricorn Galleries, Rehn Gallery, Washington, 1968, Huntington Hartford Mus., N.Y.C., 1969, N.Y. Cultural Ctr., 1970, Nat. Arts Collection, Washington, 1970, Montclair Mus. of Art, 1976, Nat. Art Mus. Sport, 1977, Jewish Mus. N.Y.C., 1980, Morris (N.J.) Mus. Arts and Scis., 1980, Black History Mus., 1981, Queens Mus., 1981-82, Nat. Portrait Gallery, Smithsonian Inst., Washington, 1981-82, Bergen Mus. Arts and Scis., N.J., 1984, William Benton Mus., Conn., 1985, Palace Theatre of the Arts, Stamford, Conn., Bronx Mus. Arts, 1986, Hofstra Mus. Art, L.I., N.Y., 1989-90, 97-98, County Art Gallery, N.Y.C., 1990, Hecksher Mus., 2000, Bronx Mus. N.Y., Bklyn. Mus., Mus. Modern Art, N.Y.C., Country Art Gallery, 1990, Port Washington Libr. Nat. Mus. Am. Art, Smithsonian Instn., 1982, NAD, N.Y.C., 1984, 89, Castle Gallery Mus. N.Y.C., 1987, Emily Lowe Mus., N.Y.C., 1987, Heckshire Mus., N.Y.C., 1989, Islip Art Mus., N.Y.C., 1989, Gallery Emanuel, N.Y.C., 1993, Sundance Gallery, Bridgehampton, N.Y., 1995, Artist Equity Exhbn., SoHo, 1995, NAD Exhbn., 1995, Main St. Petile Gallery, 2003, Huntington Arts Coun., 2003, 04, Huntington Twp. Art League, 2002-03, The Art Students League Instructors Exhbn., Salandes O'Reilly Gallery, N.Y.C., 2003; 2 person exhbn. Works on Paper, Hofstra Mus., Hofstra U., 1997-98, pastel exhbn., 2006; exhibited in numerous group shows including Portrait in bronze of Senator Norman J. Levy for Merrick Train Station, 2000, Aaron Copland's America, Hecksher Mus. Art, 2000, Nat. Art Mus., 2002; Huntington Arts Coun. Inc., 2003, Petite Gallery, Baseball Hall of Fame & Mus., Cooperstown, N.Y., 2004, Queens Mus., N.Y., 2004, Allied Arts of Am., 2003-04 (New Foundry award, 2004), Nat. TiesClub Show, 2004, Nat. Burlington Soc. Art Exhbn., 2004, Salamander OReily Gallery, N.Y., The Art Students League, 2004, Nat. Acad. Design Exhibitors, 2005, Nat. Portrait Gallery, 2005, 06; represented permanent collections, Stony Brook Hall of Fame, William Benton Mus. Art, Colby Coll. Mus., Oklahoma City Mus., Montclair (N.J.) Mus., Schonberg Libr. Black Studies, N.Y.C., Albany State Mus., Hofstra U., Bklyn. Mus. Colby Coll. Mus., Nat. Arts Collection, Nat. Portrait Gallery, Smithsonian Instn., Baseball Hall of Fame Cooperstown, N.Y., Nassau C.C., Hofstra U. Emily Lowe Gallery, Art Students League, Jewish Mus., "The Subway Series: The New York Mets Our National Pastime," Queens Mus., Black History Mus., Nassau County Mus., Stamford Mus. Art and Nature Ctr., Jericho Pub. Libr., N.Y., African-Am. Mus., Hempstead, N.Y., Stamford (Conn.) Mus. Art and Scis., (Monument Work) The Am. Baseball Family Story, The Sea Dogs, MTA, Pub. Monument for Senator Norman J. Levy Merrik R.R. Sta., N.Y., Yogi Berra Portrait, Nat. Gallery Smithsonian Inst., Mose Soyer painting, Smithsonian Am. Art Mus., Raphare Soyer Portrait, Dept. State, The Embassy Program, Prague, Czech Republic, 2002-04, Nat. Acad., 2005-06, Nat. Art Club, 2005-06, Nat. Portrait Gallery, 2006; also pvt. collections, TV shows, ABC, 1968, 81; ednl. TV spl. Rhoda Sherbell-Woman in Bronze, 1977; works include Seated Ballerina, portraits of Aaron Copland (Bruce Stevenson Meml. Best Portrait award Nat. Arts Club 1989), Eleanor Roosevelt, Variations on a Theme (36 works of collaged sculpture), 1982-86; appeared several TV shows; guest various radio programs; contbr. articles to newspapers, popular mags. and art jours.; mem. Conservation Art Group Coun. City of N.Y., 1994-97; exhbns. include: The Nat. Acad. Mus., 2003-04, Nat. Acad. Design, 2005—, Nat. Sculpture Soc., 2005—, Nat. Art Club, 2005—, Brookgreen Gardens, 2005-06, Nat. Portrait Gallery, 2006. Coun. mem: Nassau County Mus., 1978, trustee, 1st v.p. coun.; assoc. trustee Nat. Arts Mus. Sports, Inc., 1975—; cons., cmty. liaison WNET Channel 13, cultural coord., 1975-83; host radio show Not for Artists Only, 1978-79; commr. Women's Boxing Fedn., 1978; mem. Nat. Com. The City of NY, 1993; chmn. bd. Hofstra Mus., 1978-89; trustee Nat. Art Mus. of Sport, 1959—. Recipient Gold medal Allied Artists Am., 1989, Alfred G. B. Steel Meml. award Pa. Acad. Fine Arts, 1963-64; Jersey City Mus. prize for sculpture, 1961, 1st prize sculpture

Locust Valley Art Show, 1966, 67, Ann. Sculpture prize Jersey City Mus., Bank for Savs. 1st prize in sculpture, 1950, Ford Found. purchase award, 1964, 2 top sculpture awards Mainstreams 77, Cert. of Merit Salmagundi Club, 1978, prize for sculpture, 1980, 81, award for sculpture Knickerbocker Artists, 1980, 81, top prize for sculpture Hudson Valley Art Assn., 1981, Sawyer award NAD, 1985, Gold medal of honor Audubon Artists, 1985, Silvermine Exhbn. award, Gold medal Allied Artists Am., 1990, medal of honor for Bronze Queen Catherine, Nat. Arts Club, 2004, Pres.' award Nat Arts Club N.Y.C.; MacDowell Colony Fellow, 1976, AAAL and Nat. Arts and Letters grantee, 1960, Louis Comfort Tiffany Found. grantee, 1962, Ford Found. grantee, 1964, 67, also award, New Foundry award, Allied Artists Am., 2004; named one of top 5 finalist to do Monument of Queen Catherine of England, 1991; named to represent Nat. Portrait Gallery at Smithsonian Mus., 1996, sculpture selected to represent Nat. Portrait Gallery Mus., 1997; guest at Dept. of State Embassy Program, Prague, Czech Republic, 2003-04; Queen Catherine Bronze, Hofstra Mus. Sculpture Gardens, 2005. Fellow Nat. Sculpture Soc.; mem. NAD (Disegno exhbn. 2005), Sculpture Guild (dir.), Nat. Assn. Women Artists (Jeffery Childs Willis Meml. prize 1978), Allied Artists Soc. (dir. Gold medal 1990, The Pietro and Alfrieda Montana Meml. award 2000, award 2001), Audubon Artists (dir., Greta Kempton Walker prize 1965, Chaim Gross award, award for disting. contbr. to orgn. 1979, 80, Louis Weskeem award), Woman's Caucus for Art, Coll. Art Assn., Am. Inst. Conservation Hist. and Artistic Works, N.Y. Soc. Women Artists, Artists Equity Assn. N.Y., Nat. Sculpture Soc. (E.N. Richard Meml. prize 1989), Internat. Platform Assn., Profl. Artists Guild L.I., Painters and Sculptors Soc. N.J. (Bertrum R. Hulmes Meml. award), Am. Watercolor Soc. (award for disting. contbn. to orgn.), Catharine Lorillard Wolfe Club (hon. mention 1968), Nat. Arts Club (N.Y.C., Stevenson Meml. award 1989, Pres. award 1992, Robert Sayford award 2000, Bruce Stevenson Meml. award for Portrait 2000, Siegfort award 2000, ward for sculpture 2004), NAD (Helen F. Barnett prize 1965, Leila Gordon Sawyer prize 1989, The Dessle Green prize 1993, Charlotte Deenevidde award 2003, award for Am. baseball founding group, 2003).

**SHERBIN, DAVID M.,** lawyer; b. Detroit, Sept. 6, 1959; m. Abbe H. Sherbin. BA with honors, Oberlin College, 1981; JD, Cornell Law Sch., 1987. Assoc. Katten Muchin & Zavis, Chgo., 1987—91; sr. counsel Heller Fin. Inc., 1992—97; assoc. gen. counsel Fed. Mogul Corp., Southfield, Mich., 1997—2001; secs., 1999—, v.p., dep. gen. counsel, secs., 2001—04, sr. v.p., gen. counsel, sec., 2004—. Mem.: Chgo. Bar Assn., ABA. Office: Federal-Mogul Corp 26555 Northwestern Hwy Southfield MI 48034 Home: 4181 Southmoor Ln West Bloomfield MI 48323-3129 Office Phone: 248-354-7700. Office Fax: 248-354-8950. Business E-Mail: David_Sherbin@fmo.com.

**SHERBORNE, ROBERT,** editor; b. Fairborn, Ohio, Mar. 26, 1950; s. Henry Hall and Lauramay (Rider) S.; m. Pamela Saunders, Apr. 16, 1988; children: Laura, Sophie. BS in Comms., U. Tenn., 1976. Reporter Clarksville (Tenn.) Leaf Chronicle, 1976, Tullahoma (Tenn.) News, 1976-77, The Tennessean, Nashville, 1977-92, regional editor, 1993-94, spl. project editor, 1995—. Recipient Nat. Gold Mass Media award Nat. Conf. Christians & Jews, 1983; spl. citation Nat. Headliners award Press Club of Atlantic City, N.J., 1983. Office: The Tennessean 1100 Broadway Nashville TN 37203-3134 E-mail: sherborne@comcast.net.

**SHERBY, KATHLEEN REILLY,** lawyer; b. St. Louis, Apr. 5, 1947; d. John Victor and Florian Sylvia (Frederick) Reilly; m. James Wilson Sherby, May 17, 1975; children: Michael R.R., William J.R., David J.R. AB magna cum laude, St. Louis U., 1969, JD magna cum laude, 1973. Bar: Mo. 1976. Assoc. Bryan Cave, St. Louis, 1976-85; ptnr. Bryan Cave LLP, St. Louis, 1985—. Contbr. articles to profl. jours. Bd. dirs Jr. League, St. Louis, 1989-90, St. Louis Forum, 1992-99, pres., 1995-97; chmn. Bequest and Gift Coun. of St. Louis U., 1997-99; jr. warden Ch. of St. Michael and St. George, 1998-2000; bd. dirs. Bistate Chpt. ARC, 2000—, v.p. fin.; bd. trustees St. Louis Sci. Ctr., 2000—; officer Clayton Edn. Found., 2003—. Fellow Am. Coll. Trust and Estate Coun. (regent 1997-2004), Estate Planning Coun. of St. Louis (pres. 1986-87), Bar Assn. Met. St. Louis (chmn. probate sect. 1986-87), Mo. Bar Assn. (chmn. probate and trust com. 1996-98, chmn. probate law revision subcom. 1988-96); Phi Beta Kappa. Episcopalian. Home: 47 Crestwood Dr Saint Louis MO 63105-3032 Office: Bryan Cave LLP 1 Metropolitan Sq Ste 3600 Saint Louis MO 63102-2733 Office Phone: 314-259-2224. Business E-Mail: krsherby@bryancave.com.

**SHERE, DENNIS,** lawyer, writer, retired publishing executive; b. Cleve., Nov. 29, 1940; s. William and Susan (Luskay) S.; m. Maureen Jones, Sept. 4, 1965 (div. Aug. 23, 2005); children: Rebecca Lynn, David Matthew, Stephen Andrew. BS in Journalism, Ohio U., 1963, MS in Journalism, 1964; JD, DePaul U., 2003. Staff writer Dayton (Ohio) Daily News, 1966-69; asst. prof. Sch. Journalism Bowling Green (Ohio) State U., 1969-70; fin. editor Detroit News, 1970-72, city editor, 1973-75; editor Dayton Jour. Herald, 1975-80; pub. Springfield (Ohio) Newspapers Inc., 1980-83, Dayton Newspapers, Inc., 1983-88; gen. mgr. Media Group Moody Bible Inst., 1989—2001; with death penalty trial assistance divsn. Il. State Appellate Defender's Office, 2004—05; asst. pub. defender Kane County Pub. Defender's Office, Ill., 2005—. Author: Cain's Redemption - A Story of Hope & Transformation in America's Bloodiest Prison, 2005. Served with AUS, 1964-66. Mem. Sigma Delta Epsilon, Omicron Delta Kappa. Business E-Mail: Dennis.Shere@moody.edu.

**SHERER, SAMUEL AYERS,** lawyer, urban planner, consultant; b. Warwick, NY, June 17, 1944; s. Ernest Thompson and Helen (Ayers) S.; m. Dewi Sudewinahidah, June 28, 1980 (dec. Dec. 2000). AB magna cum laude, Oberlin Coll., 1966; JD, Harvard U., 1970; M in City Planning, MIT, 1970. Bar: DC 1972, U.S. Supreme Ct. 1979. Atty., advisor HUD, Boston, 1970; sr. atty. McCloughy Assoc., Washington, 1970-71, 71-761 bond. Urban Inst., Washington, 1971-72; atty., urban planner IBRD Jakarta (Indonesia) Urban Devel. Study, 1972-74; atty., advisor Office Minority Bus. U.S. Dept. Commerce, Washington, 1976-77; ptnr. Topping & Sherer, Washington, 1977-90; pres. Sherer-Axelrod-Monacelli, Inc., Cambridge, Mass., 1978-99; prin. The Washington Team, Inc., 1999—2000, Richardson & Sherer, LLC, 2000—04. Bd. dirs. The Urban Agr. Network; rep. Internat. Devel. Law Inst., Washington, 1983-90; sr. fellow Climate Inst., 1988—; cons. in field. Co-author: Urban Land Use in Egypt, 1977; editor: Important Laws and Regulations Regarding Land, Housing and Urban Development in the Arab Republic of Egypt, 1977, Important Laws and Regulations Regarding Land, Housing and Urban Development in the Hashemite Kingdom of Jordan, 1981. Bd. dirs. MIT Enterprise Forum of Washington-Balt., 1980-82; mem. DC Rep. Ctrl. Com., 1984-88; nat. governing bd. Ripon Soc., Washington, 1977-83. Urban Studies fellow HUD, 1969-70. Mem. DC Bar Assn., Phi Beta Kappa. Avocations: tennis, reading. Home and office: 3801 Connecticut Ave NW Apt 607 Washington DC 20008-4563 Office Phone: 202-363-1751. Personal E-mail: washteam@aol.com.

**SHERIDAN, JAMES EDWARD,** history professor; b. Wilmington, Del., July 15, 1922; s. Phillip Lambert and Ida Alverna (Green) S.; m. Sonia Landy, Sept. 27, 1947; 1 son, Jamy. BS, U. Ill., 1949, MA, 1950; PhD, U. Calif. at Berkeley, 1961. Lectr. Chinese history Stanford U., 1960; mem. faculty Northwestern U., 1961—, prof. history, 1968—, chmn. dept., 1969-74, assoc. dean Coll. Arts and Scis., 1985-89, prof. emeritus, 1992—. Author: Chinese Warlord: The Career of Feng Yu-hsiang, 1966, China: A Culture Area in Perspective, 1970, China in Disintegration: The Republican Era in Chinese History, 1912-1949, 1975, A Community of Caring: An Introduction to Kendal at Hanover, 1998; editor: The Transformation of Modern China series, 1975—. Served to ensign USN, 1941-46. Fulbright fellow, France, 1950-51; Ford Found. fellow, 1958-60; grantee Am. Coun. Learned Socs.-Social Sci. Rsch. Coun., 1966-67, 71-72 Home: 80 Lyme Rd Apt 438 Hanover NH 03755-1236 Office: Northwestern Univ Dept History Evanston IL 60201 E-mail: james.e.sheridan@valley.net.

**SHERIDAN, JIM,** film director, screenwriter; b. Dublin, 1949; Student, Univ. Coll., Dublin. Artistic dir. Project Arts Theatre, 1976—80, N.Y. Irish Arts Ctr., 1982—87; founder Children's Theatre Co., Dublin. Screenwriter:

Into the West, 1993; dir.: My Left Foot, 1989, The Field, 1990, In the Name of the Father, 1993, The Boxer, 1997, In America, 2001, Get Rich or Die Tryin, 2005; prodr., exec. prodr. Some Mother's Son, 1996, Agnes Browne, 1999, On the Edge, 2000, Borstal Boy, 2000, Bloody Sunday, 2001. Office: Hells Kitchen Ltd 21 Mespil Rd Dublin 4 Ireland also: Creative Artists Agy 9830 Wilshire Blvd Beverly Hills CA 90212-1804 E-mail: hellskit@iol.ie.

**SHERIDAN, JOHN J.,** musician, music educator; s. John J. and Martha S. Sheridan; m. Colleen M. Smith, May 5, 1989; children: Erin Colleen, Kelly Ann. AA, Bucks County C.C., 1985; MusB, Temple U., 1989; MA, NYU, 2000. Freelance performer, Langhorne, Pa., 1985—2003; adj. faculty jazz studies Bucks County C.C., Newtown, 1994—2003, assoc. prof. music, 2003—. Arts tech. com. Bucks County C.C., Newtown, Pa., 2002—03, music tech. coord., 1996—2003. Composer, studio musician: songs Another View Point, studio musician: rec. Purity, Is You Is. Office: Bucks County C C 275 Swamp Rd Newtown PA 18940-4106 Office Phone: 215-968-8126. Business E-Mail: sheridaj@bucks.edu.

**SHERIDAN, MARK WILLIAM,** mechanical engineer, financial planner; b. Bryn Mawr, Pa., July 9, 1959; s. Phillip Frederick and Shirley Frazer Sheridan; m. Deborah Sazdanoff Sheridan, Aug. 14, 1999; children: Kristina, Katrina, Marlena. BSME, Lafayette Coll., 1981; MBA, Cornell U., 1987, M. Engring. (Mech.), 1988. Registered profl. engr., Ohio. Project engr. Internat. Paper Co., Mobile, Ala., 1981-83, sr. process engr., 1983-85; assoc. Booz-Allen & Hamilton, Cleve., 1988-90; coord. long range planning appliance motor divsn. Emerson Electric Co., St. Louis, 1990-93, resident engr. Paragould Plant, 1993-96; dir. mfg. Thermodisc, Mansfield, Ohio, 1996—2002, dir. ops. devel., 2002—. Summer intern Saturn Corp., Troy, Mich., 1986, 87. Patentee in field. Bd. dirs. ABC Condominium Assn., St. Louis, 1992-94; chmn. JGSM Student Faculty Com./Quality of Life Com., Ithaca, N.Y., 1985-87; pres. Mobile Soap Box Derby, 1983-85; v.p. ways and means, bd. dirs. Mobile Jaycees, 1984-85; mem. Leadership Unltd., 2003-04; active YMCA; treas. First Presbyn. Ch. of Mansfield, 1998-03. Lester B. Knight scholar Cornell U., 1986-88, J. Stanford Smith scholar Cornell U., 1985-87; named Outstanding Young Man of Am., 1984, 85, 87. Mem. ASME, Inst. Indsl. Engrs., The Planning Forum, Soc. Indsl. Archaeology, World Future Soc., St. Louis Jaycees (bd. dirs. 1992-94), Am. Mensa. Republican. Avocations: golf, reading, computing, weightlifting. Home: 2403 Ranchwood Dr Mansfield OH 44903-9044 Office: Thermodisc 1320 S Main St Mansfield OH 44907-5500 Office Phone: 419-525-8295. Personal E-mail: sheridanmark@excite.com.

**SHERIDAN, NICOLETTE,** actress; b. Worthing, Sussex, Eng., Nov. 21, 1963; d. Sally Sheridan; m. Harry Hamlin, Sept. 7, 1991 (div. 1993). Actor: (films) The Sure Thing, 1985, Noises Off, 1992, Spy Hard, 1996, Beverly Hills Ninja, 1997, .com for Murder, 2002, Lost Treasure, 2003; (TV series) Knots Landing, 1986—93 (Soap Opera Digest award, 1990, 1991), Paper Dolls, 1984, Desperate Housewives, 2004— (co-recipient, Outstanding Performance by an Ensemble in a Comedy Series, Screen Actors Guild award, 2005, 2006); (TV films) Dead Man's Folly, 1986, Deceptions, 1990, Somebody's Daughter, 1992, A Time to Heal, 1994, Indictment: The McMartin Trial, 1995, Silver Strand, 1995, The People Next Door, 1996, Murder in My Mind, 1997, Dead Husbands, 1998, The Spiral Staircase, 2000, Haven't We Met Before?, 2002, Deadly Betrayal, 2003, Deadly Visions, 2004; (TV miniseries) Lucky/Chances, 1990, Knots Landing: Back to the Cul-de-Sac, 1997; TV appearances include Paradise, 1991, Will & Grace, 2003, Becker, 2003. Office: Desperate Housewives Touchtone Television 100 Universal City Plaza Bldg 212B Ste G Universal City CA 91608

**SHERIDAN, PATRICK MICHAEL,** retired finance company executive; b. Grosse Pointe, Mich., Apr. 13, 1940; s. Paul Phillip and Frances Mary (Rohan) S.; m. Diane Lorraine Tressler, Nov. 14, 1986; children: Mary, Patrick, Kelly, Kevin, James. BBA, U. Notre Dame, 1962; MBA, U. Detroit, 1975. Acct. Peat, Marwick, Mitchell & Co., Detroit, 1962-72, audit mgr., 1969-72; exec. v.p. fin. Alexander Hamilton Life Ins. Co., Farmington, Mich., 1973-76; sr. v.p. ops. Sun Life Ins. Co. Am., Balt., 1976-78, exec. v.p. 1978-79; pres. Sun Ins. Services, Inc., 1979-81; pres., chief exec. officer Am. Health & Life Ins. Co., Balt., 1981-85; chief exec. officer Gulf Ins. Co. 1985-86; sr. v.p., chief fin. officer Comml. Credit Co., 1985-86, sr. v.p. audit, 1987; exec. v.p., chief fin. officer Anthem, Inc, Indpls., 1987-99, ret., 1999. Rep. candidate for U.S. Congress, 1972; past pres. Charlesbrooke Cmty. Assn.; past. v.p. Jr. Achievement of Met. Balt., 1984-85; bd. dirs. Goodwill Industries of Balt., 1986, bd. govs. 1994; bd. dirs. Family Svcs. Assn., 1994, Goodwill Industries of Indpls., 1994; mem. adv. coun. Clowes Meml. Hall. Capt. AUS, 1963-65. Recipient various Jaycee awards. Fellow Life Mgmt. Inst.; mem. Am. Mgmt. Assn. (pres.'s assn.), AICPAs, Mich. Assn. CPAs, Md. Assn. CPAs, Am. Soc. CLUs, U.S. Jaycees (treas. 1973-74), Mich. Jaycees (pres. 1971-72), Detroit Jaycees (pres. 1968-69), Balt. C. of C. (bd. dirs.), Mensa, Notre Dame Club, Skyline Club.

**SHERIDAN, SONIA LANDY,** artist, retired art educator; b. Newark, Ohio, Apr. 10, 1925; d. Avrom Mendel and Goldie Cornelia (Hanon) Landy; m. James Edward Sheridan, Sept. 27, 1947; 1 child, Jamy. AB, Hunter Coll., 1945; postgrad., Columbia U., 1946-48; MFA with high honors, Calif. Coll. Arts and Crafts, 1961. Tchr. art public high schs., Calif., 1951-57; chmn. dept. art Taipei (Taiwan) Am. Sch., 1957-59; instr. Calif. Coll. Arts and Crafts, 1960-61; asst. prof. art Sch. Art Inst. Chgo., 1961-67, assoc. prof., 1968-75, prof., 1976-80, prof. emeritus, 1980—, founder, head generative sys. program, 1970-80. Artist-in-residence 3M Corp., 1970, 76, Xerox Corp., 1981; cons. French Ministry of Culture, 1988; lectr. univs., mus., art schs., workshops, Hungarian Acad. Scis. Symposium Collected Essays & Exhbn., Budapest, 1989, Internat. Soc. Electronic Arts, Liverpool, England; presenter in field. One-woman shows include Rosenberg Gallery, Chgo., 1966, Visual Studies Workshop, Rochester, N.Y., 1973, Iowa Mus. Art, Iowa City, 1976, Mus. Sci. Industry, Chgo., 1978, exhibited in group shows at Print Ann., Boston Mus., 1963, Software, Jewish Mus., N.Y.C., 1969—70 Photography into Art, London, 1972—73, Photokino, Cologne, Germany, 1974, Mus. Modern Art, N.Y.C., 1974, San Francisco Mus. Art, 1975, U. Mich. Mus. Art, 1978, Toledo Mus. Art, 1982—83, Mus. Modern Art, Paris, 1983, Siggraph, 1982, 1983, Reina Sofia Mus., Madrid, 1986, Smithsonian Instn., 1990, Tokyo Met. Mus. Photography, 1991, Madrid City Cultural Ctr., 1992, Karl Ernst Osthaus Mus., Hagen, Germany, 1992, Circulo des Belles Artes, Madrid, 1992, Yale U. Art Gallery, 1995, Tokyo Intercom. Ctr., 1995, U. Montreal, 1995, Internat. Soc. Electronic Arts, Liverpool, 1996, Hungarian Art Mus., 1996, Scirpton Mus., The Netherlands, 1997, Video Gallery, Hungary, 2000—02, Mus. Kommunikation, Frankfurt, Germany, 2001, 2d Biennial Museo Nacional de Belles Artes, Buenos Aires, 2002, Represented in permanent collections Hood Mus. Art, Dartmouth, Langlois Found., Montreal, Art Inst. Chgo., San Francisco Mus. Art, Mus. Sci. and Industry, Chgo., U. Iowa Mus. Art, Nat. Gallery Art, Ottawa, Can.; Visual Studies Workshop, Rochester, Tokyo Met. Mus. Photography, Fundacion Arte y Technologia, Madrid, Tweed Mus., U. Minn., Scrypton Mus., Tilburg, The Netherlands; author: Energized Artscience: Sonia Landy Sheridan, 1978; co-editor: Leonardo jour.; hon. editor:, 2000; contbr. articles, essays to profl. jours. Recipient citation, Nat. Assn. Schs. Art and Design, 2006; Guggenheim fellow, 1973, Workshop grantee, Nat. Endowment Arts, 1974, Pub. Media grantee, 1976, Artist grantee, 1981, Union Ind. Colls. Art grantee, 1975. Mem.: Internat. Soc. Electronic Arts, Internat. Soc. Interdisciplinary Study Symmetry, Coll. Art Assn. Personal E-mail: sonia.sheridan@valley.net.

**SHERIDAN, THOMAS BROWN,** mechanical engineering and applied psychology educator, researcher, consultant; b. Cin., Dec. 23, 1929; s. Mahlon Brinsley and Esther Anna (Brown) S.; m Rachel Briggs Rice, Aug. 1, 1953; children: Paul Rice, Richard Rice, David Rice, Margaret Lenore. BS, Purdue U., 1951; MS, UCLA, 1954; ScD, MIT, 1959; Dr. (hon.), Delft U. Tech., The Netherlands, 1991. Registered profl. engr., Mass. Asst. prof. mech. engring. MIT, Cambridge, 1959-65, assoc. prof., 1965-70, prof., 1970-78, prof. engring. and applied psychology, 1978—, prof. aeronautics and astronautics, 1994—, Ford prof., 1995—. Lectr. U. Calif., Berkeley, Stanford U., 1968; vis. prof. U. Delft, The Netherlands, 1972, Stanford U., 1989, Ben Gurion U.,

Israel, 1995; chmn. com. human factors, mem. com. aircrew-vehicle interaction, com. on commercially developed space facility, com. on human factors in air traffic control, mem. com. on nat. automated hwy. sys., com. on setting and enforceing speed limits, com. on intelligent vehicle initiative; chmn. com. on NASA aviation safety; mem. com. on electronic voting NRC; mem. adv. com. on applied phys., math. and biol. scis. NSF; mem. life scis. adv. com., study group on robotics, oversight com. flight telerobotic servicer NASA; mem. task force on appropriate tech. U.S. Congress Office Tech. Assessment; mem. study sect. accident prevention and injury control NIH; mem. Def. Sci. Bd. Task Force on Computers, Tng. and Gaming, Nuclear Regulatory Commn. on Nuclear Safety Rsch. Rev. Com. Author: Telerobotics, Automation and Human Supervisory Control, 1992, Humans and Automation, 2002; co-author: Man Machine Systems, 1974; editor: (with others) Monitoring Behavior and Supervisory Control, 1976, Perspectives on the Human Controller, 1997; assoc. editor Automatica, 1982-94; mem. edtl. adv. bd. Tech. Forecasting and Social Change, Computer Aided Design, Advanced Robotics, Robotics and Computer Integrated Mfg.; sr. editor Presence: Telerobots and Virtual Environments, 1991—. Served to 1st lt. USAF, 1951-53. Recipient Nat. Engring. award Am. Assn. Engring. Socs., 1997, Rufus Oldenburger medal ASME, 1997. Fellow IEEE (pres. Systems, Man and Cybernetics Soc. 1974-76, Centennial medal 1984, Norbert Wiener award 1993, Joseph G. Wohl award 1995, Millenium medal 2000), Human Factors Soc. (Paul M. Fitts award 1977, Arnold Small award 2000, pres. 1990-91, Pres. Disting. Svc. award 2000), Nat. Acad. Engring. Democrat. Mem. United Ch. of Christ. Home: 32 Sewall St Newton MA 02465 Personal E-mail: sheridan@mit.edu.

**SHERIDAN LABARGE, JOAN RUTH,** publishing executive; b. Forest Hills, NY, July 3, 1956; d. Thomas Patrick and Ruth B. (Stalzer) S.; 1 daughter. BS magna cum laude in Communication Arts, St. John's U., Jamaica, N.Y., 1978. Media planner BBDO, NYC, 1978-81; media supr. Ted Bates & Co., NYC, 1982-84; v.p., assoc. media dir. FCB Leber Katz Ptnrs., NYC, 1985-87; v.p., assoc. pub., Woman's Day Hachette Filipacchi Mags., NYC, 1987—95, v.p., pub. Family Life Mag., 1995—99; exec. v.p., group pub. dir. Weider Pub., 1999—2000; corp. pub., new bus. devel. G + J USA Publishing, 2001—, pub. Rosie, 2001—02, pub. YM Mag., 2003—04; pres. & pub. Working Mother mag., 2005—. Named Top Media Sales Rep, Mediaweek, 1992. Office: Working Mother 60 East 42nd St New York NY 10165 Office Phone: 212-351-6400. Office Fax: 212-351-6487. E-mail: joan.sheridan@workingmother.com.

**SHERIF, S. A.,** engineering educator; b. Alexandria, Egypt, June 25, 1952; came to US, 1978; s. Ahmed and Ietedal H. (Monib) S.; m. Azza A. Shamseldin, Feb. 6, 1977 (div.); children: Ahmed S., Mohammad S.; m. Vitrell Lynn McNair, May 30, 2003. BSME (hon.), Alexandria U., 1975, MSME, 1978; PhD in Mech. Engring., Iowa State U., 1985. Tchg. asst. mech. engring. Alexandria U., 1975-78; tchg. assoc. mech. and environtl. engring. U. Calif., Santa Barbara, 1978-79; rsch. asst. mech. engring. Iowa State U., Ames, 1979-84; asst. prof. No. Ill. U., Dekalb, 1984-87, U. Miami, Coral Gables, Fla., 1987—91; assoc. prof. mech. engring. U. Fla., Gainesville, 1991-2001, prof. mech. and aerospace engring., 2001—, mem. doctoral rsch. faculty, 1992—, founding dir. Wayne K. and Lyla L. Masur HVAC Lab., 1995—, asst. dir. Indsl. Assessment Ctr., 2001—, minority mentor, 2004—. ABET coord. for mech. engring., 1997—; coord. for mech. engring. So. Assn. Colls. and Schs., 2001—; affiliate Inst. for Sci. and Health Policy U. Fla., 2001—; cons. Solar Reactor Techs., Inc., Miami, 1988-91, Dade Power Corp., Miami, 1988-91, Ind. Energy Sys., Miami, 1988-91, Carey Dwyer Eckhart Mason Spring Beckham, P.A. Law Offices, Miami, 1988-89, Michael G. Widoff, P.A., Attys. at Law, Ft. Lauderdale, Fla., 1989-93, Law Offices Pomeroy and Betts, Ft. Lauderdale, 1991-92, Ctr. for Indoor Air Rsch., 1994-2000; cons. Fla. Power and Light Co., 1996-98; external examiner U. Roorkee, 1994-95, India—, Indian Inst. Tech., Delhi, 2002-, Alexandria U., Egypt, 2000-; adj. faculty cons. Kennedy Western U., Thousand Oaks, Calif., 1994-97; resident assoc. Argonne (Ill.) Nat. Lab., Tech. Transfer Ctr., summer 1992; faculty fellow NASA Kennedy Space Ctr., Cape Canaveral, Fla., summer 1993; rsch. assoc. summer faculty rsch. program USAF Office Sci. Rsch., Arnold Engring. Devel. Ctr., Arnold AFB, Tenn., 1994; faculty fellow NASA Marshall Space Flight Ctr., Huntsville, Ala., 1996, 97; ABET coord. for aerospace engring., 2002-; coord. for aerospace engring., So. Assn. Colls. and Schs., 2002-. Co-editor: Industrial and Agricultural Applications of Fluid Mechanics, 1989, The Heuristics of Thermal Anemometry, 1990, Heat and Mass Transfer in Frost and Ice, Packed Beds, and Environmental Discharges, 1990, Industrial Applications of Fluid Mechanics, 1990, rev. edit., 1991, Mixed Convection and Environmental Flows, 1990, Measurement and Modeling of Environmental Flows, 1992, Industrial and Environment Applications of Fluid Mechanics, 1992, rev. edit., 1998, Thermal Anemometry-1993, 1993, Developments in Electrorheological Flows and Measurement Uncertainty-1994, 1994, Heat, Mass and Momentum Transfer in Environmental Flows, 1995, Thermal Anemometry, 1996, Fluid Measurement Uncertainty Applications, 1996, Devices for Flow Measurement and Analysis, 1997, Heat and Mass Transfer in Environmental Flows, 1998, Industrial and Environmental Applications of Fluid Mechanics, 1999, rev. edit., 2001, Measurement and Modeling of Environmental Flows, 2002, Industrial and Environmental Applications of Fluid Mechanics, 2003, Fluid Measurement Uncertainty Applications, 2003; reviewer more than 45 internat. jours., more than 200 conf. procs.; mem. editl. com. SECTAM XXI, 2001-2002; book rev. editor ASME Applied Mech. Revs., 2001—; assoc. tech. editor Solar Energy jour., 2002—; guest editor Solar Energy Jour. Spl. Issue on Hydrogen Prodn., 2003-05; contbr. to 16 book chapters and numerous articles to profl. jours. NASA ambassador, 1996-98, lab. host student sci. tng. program Ctr. for Precollegiate Edn. and Tng., 1997—; mem. environ. awareness adv. com., Dade County Pub. Schs., 1989-91, lab. dir. cmty. lab. rsch. program, 1989-91, also faculty liaison design svcs. dept.; active Com. for Nat. Inst. for Environ., 1992—; mem. senate U. Fla., 1994-95, mem. OUTREACH Spkrs. program, 1996-98. Recipient cert. recognition for rsch. contributions, NASA, 1993, 1996, 1997, E.K. Campbell award of Merit for Outstanding Svc. and Achievement in Tchg., ASHRAE, 1997, Kuwait prize for applied scis., 2002. Fellow ASME (mem. energy resources bd. 2001-03, chmn steering com. internat. energy conversion engring. conf., 2002-03, coord. group fluid measurements, fluids engring. divsn. 1987-03, vice chmn. 1990-92, chmn. 1992-94, fluid measurements and instrumentation tech. com., 2003—, fluids engring. divsn. adv. bd. 1994—, fed. honors and awards com. 1995-01, mem. fluid mechs. tech. com. 1990—, fluid mech. com. 1987-90, K-19 com. on environ. heat transfer 1987—, fluid measurements and instrumentation tech. com., 2003—, chmn. 2003—, mem. K-6 com. on heat transfer in energy systems, 2001—, mem. fluid applications and systems tech. com. 1990—, systems analysis tech. com. advanced energy sys. divsn. 1989—, newsletter editor advanced energy sys. divsn. 1995-98, exec. com., 1999—, mem.-at-large honors awards 1999-00, sec., treas. 2000-01, vice chmn., 2001-02, chmn., 2002-03, sr. mem. and past chmn., 2003-04, fundamentals and theory tech. com. solar energy divsn. 1990-97, chmn. CGFM nominating com. 1992-94, mem. 1994-98, chmn. profl. devel. com. Rock River Valley sect. 1987, tech. activities operating com. Gator sect. 1994-96, MFFCC subcom. 1 on uncertainties in flow measurements 1995-00, certificate of appreciation, 1994, 97. 99, 03), ASHRAE (mem. heat transfer fluid flow com. 1988-92, 93-97, corr. mem 1992-93, 97—, mem. thermodynamics and psychrometrics com. 1988-92, 96-04, corr. mem. 1992-96, vice chmn. 1990-92, mem. liquid to refrigerant heat exchs. com. 1989-93, 96-97, sec. 1990-92, corr. mem. 1993-96, 97-01, corr. mem. air-to-refrigerant heat transfer com., 2000—, chmn. stds. project com. on measurement of moist air properties 1989-95, corr. mem. refrigeration load calculations com., 1999—, mem. tech. activities com. 2000—, head refrigeration sect., 2004-, E.K. Campbell award of merit for Outstanding Svc. and Achievement in Tchg., 1997, Disting. Svc. award, 2003, certificate of appreciation, 1995), AIAA (assoc., mem. terrestrial energy sys. tech. com. 2001—, certificate of appreciation, 2003); mem. AIChE, Internat. Assn. Hydrogen Energy, Internat. Solar Energy Soc., Am. Soc. for Engring. Edn., Internat. Energy Soc. (mem. sci. coun.), European Assn. Laser Anemometry (ASME/FED rep., mem. steering com.), Internat. Inst. Refrigeration (US nat. com., mem. commn. B1 on thermodynamics and transfer processes), Sigma Xi. Moslem. Achievements include co-inventor two US patents. Avocations: reading, soccer, basketball, history, astronomy. Office: U

Fla Dept Mech and Aerospace Engring 232 MAE B 720 Bldg PO Box 116300 Gainesville FL 32611-6300 Home: 3440 NE 41st Pl Ocala FL 34479 Office Phone: 352-392-7821. Office Fax: 352-392-1071. Business E-Mail: sasherif@ufl.edu.

**SHERIFF, SEYMOUR,** retired lawyer; b. Rye, NY, Aug. 22, 1917; s. Michael and Anna (Rosenfeld) S.; m. Selene Gloria Wolf, Oct. 15, 1950; children: Steven, Susan, Ellen, Carol. BSS cum laude, CCNY, 1935; JD cum laude, Yale U., 1938. Bar: D.C. 1938, N.Y. 1938, Md. 1957. Pvt. practice, Washington, 1938-58; sr. ptnr. Gardner, Morrison, Sheriff & Beddow, Washington, 1958-2000, ret., 2000. With AUS, 1942—45. Decorated Legion of Merit. Mem.: Phi Beta Kappa, Order of Coif.

**SHERIN, EDWIN,** theater director, film director, television director, actor; b. Danville, Pa., Jan. 15, 1930; s. Joseph and Ruth (Berger) S.; m. Jane Alexander, Mar. 29, 1975; children: Anthony J., Geoffrey B. (dec.), Jonathan E.; 1 stepchild, Jason E. AB in History and Polit. Sci., Brown U., 1952. Acting tchr. Am. Theatre Wing, N.Y.C., 1962-64; acting tchr. Am. Theatre Tng. Inst. Southeastern Mass. U., South Dartmouth, 1974; Lucille Lortel Disting. guest artist U. Bridgeport (Conn.), 1980; dir. Sch. Theatre Arts Boston U., 1981; acting tchr. Okla. Summer Arts Inst., 1985-86, One on One, L.A., 1989, 90; exec. v.p. Altion Prodns., L.A., 1985-93; pres. Pumpkin House Prodns., 1993—. Mem. nat. adv. for Mus. Am. Theatre; instr. Okla. Summer Arts Inst., guest dir. Calif. Inst. Arts; prof. dept. drama Fla. State U. Actor with Houseman's troupe Phoenix Theatre, N.Y.C., 1957-58, N.Y. Shakespeare Festival, 1956-60; appeared as: Octavius Caesar in, Anthony and Cleopatra, 1958; appeared in Broadway plays Come Blow Your Horn, 1960, Desert Incident, 1961, Romulus, 1962, Face of a Hero, 1963; TV films Playhouse 90, 1956-58, Studio One, 1956-58, Omnibus, 1957-60, East Side/West Side, 1960; dir. Broadway plays including The Great White Hope, 1968, Glory Hallelujah, 1969, 6 RMS RIV VU, 1973, Find Your Way Home, Of Mice and Men, 1974, Red Devil Battery Sign, 1975, Sweet Bird of Youth, 1976, Eccentricities of a Nightingale, 1976, The First Monday in October, 1978, Goodbye Fidel, 1980, The Visit, 1992; assoc. producing dir. Washington's Arena Stage, 1964-68; dir. Cosi Fan Tutte, N.Y. City Opera Co., 1972, A Streetcar Named Desire, Piccadilly Theatre, London, 1973, Semmelweiss, Studio Arena Theatre, Buffalo, N.Y., 1978, Outrage, Kennedy Ctr., Washington, 1982; films including Valdez is Coming, 1970, My Old Man's Place, 1971; producing artistic dir. Showdown at Adobe Hotel, Semmelweiss, Hedda Gabler, Night Must Fall, A Streetcar Named Desire, Hartman Theatre, Stamford, Conn., 1980-85; dir. Chelsea Walls, Naked Angels, N.Y.C., 1990, Karla, Long Wharf Theater, 2002, Ghosts, Shakespeare Theater, Washington, 2002, Prymate, B'Way, 2004; TV programs Hill Street Blues, Moonlighting, WIOU, L.A. Law, Tour of Duty, MEN, Medium; co-exec. prodr. Law and Order, 1993-94, exec. prodr., 1994-00, (TV films) The Father Clements Story, Lena, My 100 Children, Daughter of the Streets, Getting Even, A Marriage: Georgia O'Keeffe and Alfred Stieglitz, 1991. With USN, 1952-56, Korea. Recipient Outer Circle award, 1969; New Eng. Theatre award, 1969, N.Y. Drama Critics award, 1969, Drama Desk award, 1969, L.A. Drama Cir. award, 1971, Recipient Tony nomination, 1974, London Evening Std. citation, 1973, Joseph Jefferson award, 1976, Buffalo drama award, 1978, Emmy award, 1997; New Eng. Theatre Conf. award; Ford Found. grantee, 1965-66; Am. Theatre fellow Coll. of Am. Theatre. Mem. AFTRA, SAG, Actors Equity Assn., Dirs. Guild Am. (nat. v.p. 1997—), Dramatists Guild, Soc. Stage Dirs. and Choreographers (v.p. 1970-80), Lincoln' Soc., Phi Gamma Delta. Home: 32 Bellair Dr Dobbs Ferry NY 10522 Office Phone: 845-661-4889. Personal E-mail: edsherin@whalerock.us.

**SHERIN, KEITH S.,** electrical manufacturing company executive; BA, U. Notre Dame, 1981; MBA, Columbia U., 1991. With fin. mgmt. prgram GE, 1981-84, mem. corp. audit staff, 1984, exec. audit mgr., mgr. programs and planning; mgr. fin. commml. engine ops. GE Aircraft Engines, 1992-93; dir. fin. GE Plastics Europe, 1993-95; mgr. global fin. and fin. svcs. GE Med. Sys., 1995-96, v.p. fin. and fin. svcs. ops., 1996-98; sr. v.p., CFO General Electric Co., Fairfield, Conn., 1998—. Office: GE 3135 Easton Tpke Fairfield CT 06431-0002*

**SHERK, KENNETH JOHN,** lawyer; b. Ida Grove, Iowa, Feb. 27, 1933; s. John and Dorothy (Myers) Sherk; children: Karin Fulton, Katrina, Keith, Kyle. BSc, U. Iowa, 1955; JD, George Washington U., 1961. Bar: Ariz. 1962, U.S. Dist. Ct. Ariz. 1962, U.S. Ct. Appeals (9th cir.) 1966, U.S. Supreme Ct. 1974. Assoc. Moore & Romley, Phoenix, 1962-67, ptnr., 1967-79, Romley & Sherk, Phoenix, 1979-85; dir. Fennemore Craig, Phoenix, 1985—. 1st lt. U.S. Army, 1955-58, Korea. Recipient Profl. Achievement Svcs. award George Washington Law Assn., 1986, Ariz. Judges Assn., 1989, Disting. Svc. award Phoenix Assn. Def. Counsel, 1990; named Mem. of Yr. State Bar of Ariz., 1994. Fellow Am. Coll. Trial Lawyers, Am. Acad. Appellate Lawyers, Am. Bar Found., Ariz. Bar Found. (Walter E. Craig award 1999); mem. ABA (ho. of dels. 1990-93), Ariz. Bar Assn. (pres. 1985-86), Maricopa County Bar Assn. (pres. 1978-79). Republican. Congregationalist. Avocations: fishing, hiking, bicycling. Home: 1554 W Las Palmaritas Dr Phoenix AZ 85021-5429 Office: Fennemore Craig 3003 N Central Ave Ste 2600 Phoenix AZ 85012-2913 Office Phone: 602-916-5383. Business E-Mail: ksherk@fclaw.com. E-mail: ksherk@cox.net.

**SHERLING, FRED W.,** lawyer; b. Dec. 22, 1933; s. Weaver V. and Ruth M. (Bowen) S.; m. Camille Margaret Brochetto, Nov. 29, 1969; children: Charlotte, Sharon, Cheryl. BSchE, U. Tenn., 1957; LLB, George Washington U., 1961. Bar: U.S. Ct. Appeals (D.C. cir.) 1963, U.S. Ct. Customs and Patent Appeals 1963, U.S. Ct. Appeals (fed. cir.), 1982, U.S. Supreme Ct. 1982. Patent examiner U.S. Patent Office, Washington, 1957—63; assoc. solicitor, 1963—86; sole practice, 1986—. Mem. Patent Office Soc. Baptist. Office Phone: 703-370-2445. Personal E-mail: camila88@aol.com.

**SHERLOCK, PHYLLIS KRAFFT,** psychologist; b. Chgo., Dec. 22, 1936; d. Lee M. and Beatrice Elliott Krafft; m. Hugh Paul Sherlock, June 4, 1960 (dec. Oct. 1991); children: William, John, James BA in Philosophy and Religious Studies, U. N.C., 1958; postgrad., Boston U., 1959—60; PhD in Clin. Psychology, Pacific Grad. Sch. Psychology, 1980. Lic. Psychologist, Marriage, Family and Child Counselor. Social work trainee ARC, Chgo., 1959—60; child welfare worker Santa Clara County Social Svcs., San Jose, Calif., 1961—62; counselor Diabesis, San Francisco 1973—75; counselor chaplaincy svc. Stanford U. Med. Ctr., Calif., 1977—79; intern North County Cmty. Mental Health Clinic, Palo Alto, Calif., 1977—78; postdoctoral intern counseling and psychol. svcs. Cowell Health Svcs., Stanford U., 1980—81; faculty Pacific Grad. Sch. Psychology, 1989—92; pvt. practice, 1979—; supr. clin. dir. The Transitional Program, 1990—2001. Co-founder Pacific Grad. Sch. Psychology, Palo Alto, 1975-76; group facilitator Grad. Sch. Bus., Stanford U., 1980-82; supr. psychol. assts., 1988-2005, clin. dir. The Transitional Program, 1995-2002; adj. clin. faculty Sch. Edn., U. San Francisco, 1990-97 Author: The Feminine Q Set - Research on Wolf's Feminine Image and Theories, 1980; contbr. articles to profl. jours. Vol. Agnew State Hosp., 1971. Mem. Assn. Psychol. Type, Santa Clara County Psychol. Assn. Democrat. Avocations: reading, gardening, art, travel. Office: 1275 Dana Ave Palo Alto CA 94301-3112 Personal E-mail: phyllisdec22@earthlink.net.

**SHERMAN, ALAN ROBERT,** psychologist, educator; b. NYC, Nov. 18, 1942; s. David R. and Goldie (Wax) S.; m. Llana Helene Tobias, Aug. 14, 1966 (div. 1989); children: Jonathan Colbert, Relissa Anne; m. Ann Marie Redington, Aug. 22, 2002. BA, Columbia U., 1964; MS, Yale U., 1966, PhD, 1969. Lic. psychologist, Calif. Faculty psychology U. Calif., Santa Barbara, 1969—; clin. psychologist in pvt. practice Santa Barbara, 1981—. Cons. in field. Author: Behavior Modification, 1973; contbr. articles to profl. jours. and chpts. in books. Pres. Santa Barbara Mental Health Assn., 1978, 84-85, 91, Mountain View Sch. Site Coun., Santa Barbara, 1978-84. Recipient Vol. of Yr. award Santa Barbara Mental Health Assn., 1979, Tchg. Excellence awards Delta Delta Delta, Alpha Chi Omega, Gamma Phi Beta, Santa Barbara; NIMH predoctoral rsch. fellow, 1964-69; grantee in field. Fellow Behavior Therapy and Rsch. Soc.; mem. APA, AAUP (chpt. pres. 1978-79), Calif.

Psychol. Assn., Assn. for Advancement of Behavior Therapy, Santa Barbara County Psychol. Assn. (pres. 1985), Phi Beta Kappa (chpt. pres. 1977-78), Sigma Xi, Psi Chi (chpt. faculty advisor, 1979-2005). Office: Univ Calif Dept Psychology Santa Barbara CA 93106-9660 Office Phone: 805-893-3534. E-mail: sherman@psych.ucsb.edu. *Pursuing a creative profession which allows one to help improve the condition of others, provides intrinsic rewards that make the work process satisfying in itself. I am fortunate to be involved in two such professions, college teaching and psychotherapy. When you genuinely enjoy what you are doing, you are likely to be successful at it.*

**SHERMAN, ARTHUR,** theater educator, writer, actor, composer, sculptor; b. Dec. 5, 1920; s. Herman and Fay (Epstein) S.; m. Margery Frost Sherman, Apr. 15, 1974 (div. Sept. 1989); children: Claudia, Andrew Jay. MusB, Juilliard Sch. Music, N.Y.C., 1955; M in Music Edn., Manhattan Sch. Music, 1957; Doctoral Equivalency, CUNY, 1969. Dir. performing arts N.Y.C. (N.Y.) Tech. Coll., 1964-72; prof. speech and theatre John Jay Coll., N.Y.C., 1990—, Borough Man C.C., N.Y.C., 1990—. Judge Film Award Com., Australia, 1972-89, Acad. Awards, 1990; cons. Min. for Edn., Tasmania, Australia, 1977; presenter in field. Author: (screenplays) Thistle and Thorn, 1982, Same Difference, 1983, (book and lyrics) Lenore and the Wonder House, 1964, Prisms in the Looking Glass, 1993, Once Upon a Crime, We the Common Earth; (short stories) Max the Messiah and Noah's Arc, 2005; (book) Paradise Lagoon, 1989, Picture Book for Young Adults Paintings, Music and Lyrics, 1998, Songwriting Is Easy and Fun, 1996, also short stories; (comedy theater) But Its Not Chekhov, 1999; (comic screenplay) Weaning, 1999; (7-book novel) The Pleiades, Burning in Heaven, Freezing in Hell, Bloody Mooring, Scoring in Limbo, Chasing the Phoenix, The Pleiades and Beyond, Betrayal of Self; (with Edward Mapp) The Road to Mainstream, 1999, Red Herrings No Fishing Allowed, 2005; (play) To Hell with Buffalo Wings-Anyone for Eagle Wings?, 1999, Warsaw Ghetto Uprising, 2001; (music drama) Prisms in the Looking Glass, Paul Rodeson Theatre, 2006; actor, dir. films, TV, theater in U.S. and Australia; actor: (films) The Punisher, 1979, Death of a Soldier, 1985, Les Patterson Saves the World, 1988, The Last Bastion, 1987; sculptures displayed YWCA, Hamilton, Ont., Can., 1967, Lincoln Ctr., N.Y.C., 1969, State Bank, Sydney, Australia, 1974; bust of Louis Armstrong Meml. Mus. and House, Dame Judith Anderson Australian Consulate N.Y.; contbr. design WTC 9/11 Meml., 2003. Pres. United Fedn. Coll. Tchrs., NYC, 1971. With USN, 1943—46. Grantee, Australian Film Commn., 1981. Mem. ASCAP, Australasian Performing Rights Assn., Actors' Equity U.S. and Australia. Home: 315 W 57th St New York NY 10019-3158 Office: John Jay Coll 58th St 10th Ave New York NY 10019 Office Phone: 212-237-8353. Personal E-mail: arturoprof@rcn.com. Business E-Mail: asherman@jjaycuny.edu.

**SHERMAN, BEATRICE ETTINGER,** hotel executive; b. N.Y.C., May 29, 1919; d. Max and Stella (Schrager) Ettinger; m. Herbert Jacob Howard, Feb. 15, 1942 (dec. 1971); children: Robert David Howard, Carolyn Howard Smith; m. Ernest John Sherman, Dec. 29, 1974 (dec. Oct. 2000). Student, Gulf Park Jr. Coll., Gulfport, Miss., 1934—35, Shimer Jr. Coll., Mt. Carroll, Ill., 1936—38; BA, U. Miami, 1940; postgrad., Harvard U., 1940, Paris-Am. Acad., 1972, Alliance Française, Paris, 1973. Corp. sec., dir. Save Electric Corp., Toledo, 1940—67, Verd-A-Ray Corp., Toledo, 1944—67, Penetray Corp., Toledo, 1962—67; ptnr. Stella Assocs., Newark, 1960—80, BHS Ptnrs., Miami, 1983—; pres. Besman Inc., Miami, 1976—, All Am. Mobile Tel. Co., Coral Gables, 1986—2000; pres., bus. exec. hotelier Besman Hospitality, Gainesville, Fla., 1997—. Vol. worker Jewish Welfare Fedn., Toledo, 1942-69; vol. nurse's aid ARC, 1942-45; nat. spkr. United Jewish Appeal; mem. womens divsn. Greater Miami Jewish Fedn., 1969—, trustee, 1986-95; adv. bd. Miami Bell South; active Miami advertiser adv. bd. Bell South Advt. and Pub. Co.; vol. Nat. Coun. Jewish Women, Toledo, 1946-67, v.p., 1964-67, v.p., Miami, 1970-73; active Toledo chpt. Hadassah, 1943-67. Recipient Lion of Judah award Greater Miami Jewish Fedn., 1986. Mem. Assn. Telemessaging Svcs. Internat., Pioneers of Miami Beach. Home: 5108 SW 72d Ave Miami FL 33155-5530 Office: PO Box 558446 Miami FL 33255

**SHERMAN, BRADLEY JAMES,** congressman; b. LA, Oct. 24, 1954; s. Maurice H. and Lane (Moss) S. BA summa cum laude, UCLA, 1974; JD magna cum laude, Harvard U., 1979. Bar: Calif. 1979; CPA, Calif. Pvt. practice, L.A., 1980-91; chmn. Calif. Bd. Equalization, Sacramento, 1991-95; mem. US Congress from 27th Calif. dist., 1997—; mem. banking and fin. svcs. com., internat. rels. com. Lectr. on tax law and policy; mem. Calif. Franchise Tax Bd., 1991-95. Contbr. articles to legal jours. Bd. dirs., rep. on tax issues Calif. Common Cause, 1984-89; mem. exec. com. Calif. Dem. Com., 1991—. Mem. Calif. State Bar. Democrat. Jewish. Office: US Ho Reps 1030 Longworth HOB Washington DC 20515-0527 E-mail: brad.sherman@mail.house.gov.

**SHERMAN, DANIEL JAMES,** history professor, director; b. Ann Arbor, Mich., May 20, 1958; s. Stanley Morton and Claire Richter Sherman; life ptnr. Eduardo deJesus Douglas. AB, MA, Harvard U., 1980, Yale U., 1981, MPhil, 1982, PhD, 1985. Lectr. history, lit., social studies Harvard U., Cambridge, Mass., 1985—88; vis. asst. prof. history U. Rochester, NY, 1989—90; asst. prof. French studies and history Rice U., Houston, 1990—94, assoc. prof. French studies and history, 1994—99, prof. French studies and history, 1999—2001; prof. history U. Wis., Milw., 2001—, dir. Ctr. 21st Century Studies, 2001—. Vis. asst. prof. Cath. U. Am., Washington, 1989. Author: The Constuction of Memory in Interwar France, Worthy Monuments: Art Museums and the Politics of Culture in Nineteenth-Century France; editor: Museum Culture: Histories, Discourses, Spectacles; co-editor: Terror Culture, Politics: Rethinking 9/11, 2006; contbr. articles to profl. jours. Recipient History and Lit. Jr. prize, Harvard Coll., 1978, Laurence Wylie prize, 2000, award, Assn. American Publishers, 2000; fellow, NEH, 1988, 1990—91, Inst. Advanced Study, 1993—94, John Simon Guggenheim Meml. Found., 2001—02; grantee, Am. Coun. Learned Socs., 1988; Florence Gould Found., fellow dir., Nat. Humanities Ctr., 1999—2000. Mem. Soc. French Hist. Studies (mem. editl. bd. 1998—2001), Am. Hist. Assn. (J. Russell Major prize 2000), Coll. Art Assn. (assoc.). Jewish. Avocations: travel, photography, cooking. Office: University of Wisconsin-Milwaukee Center for 21st Century Studies Milwaukee WI 53201-0413 Office Phone: 414-229-4141. Office Fax: 414-229-5964.

**SHERMAN, DEANE MURRAY,** culture organization administrator; b. Beulah, N.D. m. John F. Sherman, Feb. 8, 1944; children: Betsy Deane, Mary Ann. Student, N.D. State U., George Washington U. Emeritus Arts Coun. Montgomery County, Md., 2000—. Bd. trustees Internat. Conservatory of Music, 1981—; sponsor Phia Berghout Harp Series, 1996-97. Decorated chevalier Ordre des Palm Academiques;recipient Hornbook award Montgomery County Tchrs. Assn., 1967, Leadership award Am. Biog. Inst., 1995, Strathmore Hall Found. award, 1998; honored guest Fukui Harp Festival, 1982, Internat. Harp Contest, Israel, 1984-94, U.S., 1991-95, Perugia Classico IV, 1998, Russian Internat. Festival and Harp Competition, 2000. Mem.: Friends of Franklin (founding mem., bd. dirs. 2003—), Help and Resource Porject (mem. 1989—), World Harp Congress (founder, v.p. 1990—), Women's Com. for Nat. Symphony, Md. Congress PTA (life), Nat. Congress PTA (life), Western Club Glasgow, Elstophos Sci. Club Washington. Home: 11016 Ardwick Dr North Bethesda MD 20852-3204

**SHERMAN, DEMING ELIOT,** lawyer; b. Providence, July 22, 1943; s. Edwin Fisk and Martha Amy (Parkhurst) S.; m. Jane Catherine Bauer, Dec. 20, 1966; children: Melissa Jane, Nicholas Deming. BA, Amherst (Mass.) Coll., 1965; JD, U. Chgo., 1968. Bar: R.I. 1968, U.S. Dist. Ct. R.I. 1970, U.S. Supreme Ct. 1974, Mass. 1985, U.S. Dist. Ct. Mass. 1985. Mng. ptnr. Edwards Angell Palmer & Dodge LLP, Providence, 1986—, ptnr., 1969—. gen. counsel, 2005—. Trustee First Night Providence, 1988-93, 2001-04, pres., 1991-93; bd. dirs. R.I. Philharm. Orch., 1985-2003, 04-, pres., 1993-95; trustee Providence Preservation Soc., 1990-2004, pres. 1996-99; trustee Providence Athenaeum, 2004-, v.p., pres.-mem. R.I. Com. on Jud. Tenure and Discipline, 1992-2000; bd. dirs. Providence YMCA, 1975-85, Blackstone Pk. Improvement Assn., 1979-, Nope's Island Conservation Assn., 1992-98, New Eng. Legal Found., 1994-, R.I. Legal Edn. Partnership, 2000-03, Grow

Smart RI, 1998-, sec., 1998-, pres., 2006-; corporator R.I. Hosp., 1989-; bd. dirs. Friends of Blackstone Pk. and Blvd., 2001-, pres., 2001-; trustee Festival Ballet Providence, 2002-, v.p., 2003-05, pres., 2005-. Fellow R.I. Bar Found.; mem. ABA, R.I. Bar Assn., Amherst Alumni Assn. R.I. (pres. 1980-91), Greater Providence C. of C. (bd. dirs. 1991-94). Home: 254 Irving Ave Providence RI 02906-5544 Office: Edwards Angell Palmer & Dodge LLP 2800 Financial Plz Providence RI 02903 Office Phone: 401-274-9200. Business E-Mail: dsherman@eapdlaw.com.

**SHERMAN, EDWARD FRANCIS,** dean, law educator; b. El Paso, Tex., July 5, 1937; s. Raphael Eugene and Mary (Stedmond) S.; m. Alice Theresa Hammer, Feb. 23, 1963; children: Edward F. Jr., Paul. BA, Georgetown U., 1959; MA, U. Tex., El Paso 1962, 67; LLB, Harvard U., 1962, SJD, 1981. Bar: Tex. 1962, Ind. 1976. Aide to gov. Nev., state govt. fellow, Carson City, 1962; law clk. judge U.S. Dist. Ct. (we. dist.), El Paso, Tex., 1963; ptnr. Mayfield, Broaddus & Perrenot, El Paso, 1963-65; tchg. fellow Law Sch. Harvard U., Cambridge, Mass., 1967-69; prof. Sch. Law Ind. U., Bloomington, 1969-77; Edward Clark Centennial prof. U. Tex., Austin, 1977-96; prof., dean Tulane U. Law Sch., 1996—2001, prof., 2001—. Fulbright prof. Trinity Coll., Dublin, 1973-74; vis. prof. Stanford Law Sch., 1977, U. London, 1989, Sch. Pub. Adminstrn., Warsaw, Poland, 1995, Chuo U., Tokyo, 1995, U. New South Wales, Australia, 2002; counsel Tex. County Jail Litigation, 1980-85; bd. dirs., officer Travis County Dispute Resolution, 1993-96; mem. arbitrtor panel, course dir. Internat. Ctrs. Arbitration; mem. STAR Vietnam Project (USAID) on new code of civil pro., 2003-04 Co-author: The Military in American Society, 1979, Complex Litigation, 1985, 4th edit., 2004, Processes of Dispute Resolution, 1989, 4th edit., 2006, Civil Procedure: A Modern Approach, 1989, 4th edit., 2003, Rau, Sherman & Shannon's Texas ADR and Arbitration Statutes, 1994, 4th edit., 2006. Capt. U.S. Army, 1965-67, lt. col. Res., 1970-90. Fellow Tex. Bar Found.; mem. ABA (reporter civil justice improvements project 1993, offer of judgment task force 1995, com. pro bono and pub. svc. 1997-99, chmn. task force on class action legis. 2002-03, reporter ABA Task Force on Asbestos 2003-2005, Robert McKay award for advancement of justice by law prof. 2004), Am. Arbitration Assn. (arbitrator panel), AAUP (gen. counsel 1986-88), Am. Law Inst., Tex. State Bar Assn. (alternative dispute resolution com. 1985-96, chair pattern jury charge com. 1983-94, Evans Tex. Bar award for excellence in dispute resolution 1998), Tex. Civil Liberties Union (gen. counsel 1985-91), La. Law Inst., La. State Bar (bd. govs. 1997-99, com. codes of lawyer and jud. conduct 1999-2001, com. on multi-juris. practice 2000—); La. Bar Found. (jud. liason com. 1999-2001), Assn. Am. Law Schs. (chmn. Sect. Litigation 1999, chmn. Sect. ADR 1995, com. on clin. legal edn. 1999-2002) Home: 21 Newcomb Blvd New Orleans LA 70118 Office: Tulane Law School 6329 Freret St New Orleans LA 70118 Office Phone: 504-865-5979. Business E-Mail: esherman@law.tulane.edu.

**SHERMAN, ETHAN,** contractor, publisher; b. N.Y.C., June 23, 1941; s. Frank Issac and Jean (Abel) S.; m. Irene Linder, Oct. 31, 1965; children: Adam Howard, Rachael Suzanne. BS, Rider U., 1963. With Style-Master, Poughkeepsie, NY, 1971—, pres., 1979—. Author, pub.: How I Straightened My Spine, 1991. Trustee The Ethan Sherman Found., Poughkeepsie, N.Y., 1995—. With USAF, 1969-71. Mem. Knights of Pythias (chancellor comdr. 1989, 2000). Avocations: sailing, camping, gardening. Home: 37 Hornbeck Rd Poughkeepsie NY 12603-1121 Office: Style-Master Home Products Inc 37 Hornbeck Rd Poughkeepsie NY 12603 Office Phone: 845-452-5322. Personal E-mail: sherm62@juno.com.

**SHERMAN, EUGENE JAY,** retired marketing professional, retired economist; b. N.Y.C., Jan. 10, 1935; s. Samuel and Sarah (Lavinsky) S.; m. Mary Eileen Van, Apr. 22, 1966; 1 child, Rebecca. BA, CCNY, 1956; MBA, NYU, 1959, postgrad., 1959-63. Economist Fed. Res. Bank N.Y., 1959-62, Chase Manhattan Bank, N.Y.C., 1962-65; v.p. Bank of N.Y., N.Y.C., 1965-72; sr. v.p., exec. dir., dir. rsch. Merrill Lynch and Co., N.Y.C., 1972-78; v.p., chief economist, mgr.internat. investment Internat. Gold Corp., N.Y.C., 1980-86; sr. v.p., chief economist Fed. Home Loan Bank N.Y., 1986-93; sr. v.p., dir. rsch. M.A. Schapiro & Co., Inc., N.Y., 1993-96. Gold com., N.Y.C., 1986—; adj. prof. Touro Coll., N.Y.C., 1997-98; exec.-in-residence, adj. prof. Baruch Coll., N.Y.C., 1997—, mem. faculty senate, fellow Weissman Ctr. for Internat. Bus. Author: Gold Investment: Theory and Application, 1986; contbr. articles to profl. jours. Recipient Tchg. Excellence award, Zicklin Sch., 2003. Mem. Money Marketeers (pres. 1971-72, honored fellow 1987), Downtown Economist Club (chmn. 1988-89), Forecasters (winner 1986, 95), Treasury Securities Luncheon (pres. 1995-96), N.Y. Assn. Bus. Economists. Avocations: outdoor activities, performing arts. Home: 115 E 9th St New York NY 10003-5414

**SHERMAN, FLOYD F.,** construction executive; b. Kerhonkson, NY; B, NY State Coll. Forestry, Syracuse Univ.; MBA, Ga. State Univ. Chmn., CEO Triangle Pacific, 1992—2001; pres., CEO, dir. Builders FirstSource, Dallas, 2001—. Served U.S. Army. Office: Builders FirstSource Ste 1666 2001 Bryan St Dallas TX 75201*

**SHERMAN, FRED,** biochemist, educator; b. Mpls., May 21, 1932; s. Harry and Ann (Kaufman) Sherman; m. Revina Freeman, July 25, 1958 (div.); children: Aaron, Mark, Rhea; m. Elena Rustchenko Bulgac, May 5, 2001. BA, U. Minn., Mpls., 1953; PhD, U. Calif., Berkeley, 1958; PhD (hon.), U. Minn. 2002. Postdoctoral fellow U. Wash., Seattle, 1959—60; 60postdoctoral fellow 61Lab. Genetique Physiol., Gif-sur-Yvette, France, 1960-61; sr. instr. U. Rochester, NY, 1961—62, asst. prof. NY, 1962—66, assoc. prof. NY, 1966—71, prof. dept. biochemistry Sch. Medicine & Dentistry NY, 1971—, chmn. dept. biochemistry NY, 1987—. 99. Instr. Cold Spring Harbor Lab., NY, 1970—87; Wander Meml. lectr., 1975; Wilson prof. U. Rochester, 1982. Co-author: Cold Spring Harbor Manual on Yeast Genetics and Molecular Biology, 1970—87; assoc. editor: Genetics, 1975—82, Molecular Cell Biology, 1979—88. Fellow NIH, 1959—61; grantee, 1963. Mem.: Am. Soc. Microbiology, Genetic Soc. Am. (bd. dirs. 1983—85), NAS (chmn. genet. sec. 2000—03), AAAS. Home: 69 Westminster Rd Rochester NY 14607-2223 Business E-Mail: fred_sherman@URMC.Rochester.edu.

**SHERMAN, FREDERICK SCOTT,** pediatric cardiologist; b. Cambridge, Mass., Feb. 7, 1949; s. Henry Sherman and Doris Gimpelson; m. Kathryn Rich; children: Alexis, Nathaniel. AB, Harvard U., 1971; MD, Yale U., 1975; MBA, U. Pitts., 2002. Resident in pediatrics U. Va., Charlottesville, 1975-78; asst. surgeon U.S. Pub. Health Svc., New Canton, Va., 1978-80; fellow in cardiology Children's Hosp., Boston, 1981-84; asst. prof. in pediatrics U. Calif., San Diego, Calif., 1984-88; prof. of pediatrics U. Pitts., 1988—. Dir. perinatal cardiology Magee Women's Hosp., Pitts., 1988—. Bd. dirs. Children's Home, Pitts., 1990—, Opera Theater of Pitts., 1995—. Fellow Am. Coll. Cardiology, Am. Acad. Pediatrics; mem. The Pitts. Golf Club, Am. Heart Assn., Am. Soc. Echocardiology. Avocations: golf, squash, opera. Office: Magee Womens Hosp 300 Halket St Pittsburgh PA 15213-3180

**SHERMAN, GEORGE M.,** former food products executive; b. NYC, Aug. 6, 1941; s. Joseph B. and Fredericka (Hand) S.; m. Betsy Rae Bicknell, Nov. 26, 1966; children: Jonathan, David, Michael, Matthew. BS, L.I. U., 1963; MBA, U. Louisville, 1971. Product gen. mgr. Gen. Electric Co., Bridgeport, Conn., 1966-79; pres. Weed Eater div. Emersen Electric Co., Houston, 1979-80; pres. Skil Corp. div. Emerson Electric Co., Chgo., 1980-82; group v.p. U.S. power tools group Black & Decker Corp., Balt., 1985, sr. v.p., pres. power tools divsn., 1986—89, exec. v.p., pres. power tools & home improvement divsn., 1989—90; CEO Danaher Corp, Washington 1990—2001; chmn. Campbell Soup Co., Camden, NJ, 2001—04. Mem. adv. bd. Nat. Home Ctr. Show, Chgo., 1987; bd. dirs. D.I.Y. Research Inst., Lincolnshire, Ill., 1988. Bd. dirs. Ctr. Stage, Balt., 1988. Served with U.S. Army, 1964-66. Mem. Am. Mgmt. Assn. (mem. gen. mgmt. council 1988). Clubs: Center (Balt.); Hillendale Country (Phoenix, Md.). Avocations: flying, skiing, scuba diving, racquetball, golf.

**SHERMAN, GERALD HOWARD,** lawyer, educator; b. NYC, Aug. 29, 1932; s. Abraham and Jean (Rose) S.; m. Lola Barbara Kay, Mar. 19, 1961; children: Jonathan, Ann. BBA, CCNY, 1953; LLB, Harvard U., 1958. Bar: N.Y. 1959, D.C. 1960. Mem. firm Cooper & Silverstein, Washington, 1958-61; ptnr. Silverstein & Mullens, Washington, 1961-99; shareholder Buchanan Ingersoll, P.C., 2000—06, Buchanan Ingersoll and Roaney PC, 2006—; gen. counsel Assn. Advanced Life Underwriting, 1970—. Adj. prof. Georgetown U. Law Ctr., 1974-87, dep. tech. dir., adv. bd. Tax Mgmt. Portfolios, 1960—, BNA Pension Reporter, 1975-81. Bd. dirs., v.p. Jewish Found. for Group Homes, 1982-90; bd. dirs. Am. Digestive Disease Soc., 1983-87, Washington Conservatory Music, 1995-01. Mem. ABA, Bar Assn. D.C. Home: 3804 Klingle Pl NW Washington DC 20016-5433 Office: 1770 K St NW Washington DC 20006-2304

**SHERMAN, GREGORY ALBERT,** psychologist; b. Saginaw, Mich., Jan. 23, 1960; s. John William and Helen (Gold) Sherman; m. Kaija Dianne Goettsch, Sept. 14, 1985; children: Hannah Ruth, Nathan Andrew. B Psychology, U. Colo., 1988; MA in Psychology, Biola U., 1991, PhD in Psychology, 1995. Dir. clin. svcs. Christian Counseling Ctr., Grand Rapids, Mich., 1995—. Mem.: APA. Office: Christian Counseling Ctr 3355 Eagle Park Dr NE 106 Grand Rapids MI 49525 Office Phone: 616-956-9614. E-mail: gsherman@cccwmich.org.

**SHERMAN, HOWARD D.,** financial consultant; b. Tuscon, May 25, 1961; s. Donald J. and Elaine (Schwartz) S. BA, George Washington U., 1982; MBA, U. Pa., 1986. Rsch. asst. Fed. Res. Bd., Washington, 1982—84; sr. analyst Investor Responsibility Rsch. Ctr., Washington, 1986—88; sr. v.p., dir. Inst. Shareholder Svcs., Washington, 1988—97, pres., CEO, 1997—99; pres. Thomson Fin. Investor Rels., NYC, 1999—2000; COO Governance Metrics Internat. Inc., 2001—. Spkr. in field. Contbr. articles to profl. jours. Mem. Phi Beta Kappa.

**SHERMAN, IAN MATTHEW,** lawyer; b. Chgo., Apr. 30, 1953; s. George and Vivian K. (Soffran) S.; m. Barbara Jan Smiley, Aug. 6, 1978; children: Wendy Joyce, Wesley Jacob, David Scott. AB, U. Ill., 1975; JD, Boston U., 1978. Bar: Ill. 1978, U.S. Dist. Ct. (no. dist.) Ill. 1978, U.S. Dist. Ct. (ea. dist.) Wis. 1995, U.S. Dist. Ct. (no. dist.) Ind. 2000, U.S. Ct. Appeals (7th cir.) 1984. Ptnr. Dykema Gossett PLLC (formerly Rooks, Pitts & Poust), Chgo., 1978—. Lectr. in field. Contbr. articles to profl. jours. Participant Youth Motivation Program Chgo. Pub. H.S., 1982; pro bono Am. Jewish Congress, Chgo., 1992—; vol. Chgo. (Ill.) Vol. Legal Svcs. Inst., 1982—; commr. Winnetka (Ill.) Park Dist., 2001—, v.p., 2002—03; bd. dirs. The Vol. Ctr., 1986—90, chmn. fin. com., 1986—87, sec., 1987—88, pres., 1988—89. Recipient Disting. Svc. award, Chgo. (Ill.) Vol. Legal Svcs. Inst., 2003. Mem.: Am. Bd. Trial Advocates, Chgo. Bar Assn. (chmn. med.-legal rels. com. 2001—02, cert. appreciation 1983, 2003), Ill. State Bar Assn., Ill. Assn. Healthcare Attys., Ill. Soc. Trial Lawyers, Phi Kappa Phi, Phi Beta Kappa. Home: 923 Oak St Winnetka IL 60093-2440 Office: Dykema Gossett PLLC 10 S Wacker Dr Ste 2300 Chicago IL 60606-7407 Office Phone: 312-876-1700. Business E-Mail: isherman@dykema.com.

**SHERMAN, IRWIN WILLIAM,** biological sciences educator, academic administrator; b. NYC, Feb. 12, 1933; s. Morris and Anna (Ezaak) S.; m. Vilia Gay Turner, Aug. 25, 1966; children: Jonathan Turner, Alexa Joy. BS, CCNY, 1954; MS, Northwestern U., Evanston, Ill., 1959, PhD, 1960. Asst. prof. U. Calif., Riverside, 1962-67, assoc. prof., 1967-70, prof. biology, 1970—2005, chmn. biology dept., 1974-79, emeritus prof., dean Coll. Natural and Agrl. Scis., dir. agrl. expt. sta., 1981-88, exec. vice chancellor, 1993-94; vis. scientist Scripps Rsch. Inst., 2006—. Instr. marine biol. lab., Woods Hole, Mass., 1963-68; mem. study sect. tropical medicine NIH, 1970-73; cons. Agy. Internat. Devel., 1978-90; mem. ad hoc study group U.S. Army, 1975-78. Author: The Invertebrates: Function and Form, 1976, Biology: A Human Approach, 1989, Malaria: Parasite Biology, Pathogenesis, Protection, 1998, Molecular Approaches to Malaria, 2005, The Power of Plagues, 2006. Steering com. World Health Orgn., 1978-87. With U.S. Army, 1954-56. USPHS fellow Rockefeller Inst., 1960-62, Guggenheim fellow, 1967, NIH/Nat. Inst. Med. Rsch. fellow 1973-74, Walter and Eliza Hall Inst. for Med. Rsch. fellow, 1986; Wellcome Trust lectr. Brit. Soc. Parasitology, 1987, Scripps Rsch. Inst. fellow 1991, 2003-05. Mem. AAAS, Am. Soc. Tropical Medicine and Hygiene, Soc. Protozoology, Soc. Parasitology, Sigma Xi. Democrat. Jewish. Avocations: painting, reading. Office: Scripps Research Inst Dept Cell Biology ICND 202 10550 N Torrey Pines La Jolla CA 92037 Office Phone: 858-784-2302. E-mail: isherman@scripps.edu.

**SHERMAN, JANANN MARGARET,** history professor, writer; b. Mpls., Apr. 9, 1944; d. Melvin Albert and Jeanette Mary Stephenson; m. Charles Daniel Sherman, May 30, 1962. PhD, Rutgers U., 1993. Electronics technician Motorola Inc., Mesa, Ariz., 1965—73; assoc. prof. U. of Memphis, 1994—. Author: (biography) No Place for a Woman: A Life of Senator Margaret Chase Smith, (monograph) Interviews with Betty Friedan, The Perfect 36: Tennessee Delivers Woman Suffrage; dir.: (exhbn.) The Perfect 36. Bd. dirs. Women of Achievement, Memphis, 2001—03, Shelby County Hist. Commn., Memphis, 2002—03, Memphis Network, 1998—2003; Tenn. coord. Nat. History Day, Memphis, 1999—2003; pres. West Tenn. Hist. Soc., Memphis, 2002—. Named Woman of Achievement, Women of Achievement, 2001; recipient First Pl. award. for No Place for a Woman, Nat. Fedn. of Press Women, 2001, Excellence in Cmty. Svc. award, DAR, 1995. Avocations: travel, reading. Home: 3153 Dothan St Memphis TN 38118 Office: U Memphis Alumni St Memphis TN 38152 Personal E-mail: jsherman1@midsouth.rr.com. E-Mail: sherman@memphis.edu.

**SHERMAN, JEFFREY BARRY,** retail executive; b. Passaic, N.J., June 25, 1948; s. Maxwell and Elinor (Richman) S.; m. Karin Lynn Swann, May 1, 1971; children: Erik, Brett, Peter, Kristin BS in Econs., CCNY, 1971; MBA, NYU, 1975. With Bloomingdale's, N.Y.C., 1971—, v.p. merchandising, 1982-83, sr. v.p., 1983-85, exec. v.p., 1985—, now pres. Avocations: skiing, sailing. Office: Bloomingdale's 59th St & Lexington New York NY 10022

**SHERMAN, JENNIFER L.,** lawyer; BBA, U. Mich., 1986, JD, 1989. Bar: Ill. 1989. Assoc. Barack Ferrazzano Kirschbaum Perlman & Nagelberg LLC, 1989—93; corp. counsel Hook-SupeRx, Inc./Revco Drug Stores, 1993—94; dep. gen. counsel, asst. sec. Fed. Signal Corp., Oak Brook, Ill., 1994—2004, v.p., gen. counsel, sec., 2004—. Office: Fed Signal Corp 1415 W 22nd St Oak Brook IL 60521 Office Phone: 630-954-2000.

**SHERMAN, JEREMY P.,** lawyer; b. Chgo., Mar. 8, 1951; BA magna cum laude, Am. U., 1973; JD with honors, George Washington U., 1976. Bar: Ill. 1976. Mem. Seyfarth Shaw LLP, Chgo., 1976, ptnr. Nat. chairperson Labor and Employment Practice Group, Ill. Office: Seyfarth Shaw LLP Ste 2400 131 S Dearborn St Chicago IL 60603 Office Phone: 312-460-5901. Business E-Mail: jsherman@seyfarth.com.

**SHERMAN, JIMMIE LEE,** mathematician, educator; b. LA, Feb. 15, 1944; s. Harold and Lillie Lee (White) Sherman. Student, Compton Jr. Coll. Bus. mgr., reporter Watts (Calif.) Star Rev. Newspaper, 1965—66; publicity dir. Watts Happening Coffee House, 1965—67; screen writer Universal Studios, Universal City, Calif., 1967—68; creative dir., tchr. Watts Writers Workshop, 1987; cons., tchr. Compton (Calif.) Unified Sch. Dist., 1988—90, Nat. Coun. Negro Women, Pomona, Calif., 1997—98; tchr. math. Motivational Inst., LA, 2002—. Publ. Lesson Book Libr. Publ. Co., LA, 1979—; tchr., tutor Jimmie Shermans Literacy Campaign, LA, 1999—; cons. in field. Author: numerous poems, Principles of Immortality, 2003. With U.S. Army, 1961—64. Named Worlds' Best Tchr. award, God's Little Angels Pvt. Sch., 2000, Poet of Yr., Famous Poets Soc., 2003; named to Wall of Tolerance, by Rosa Parks and Morris Dees, Nat. Campaign for Tolerance, 2005; recipient Quality of Life award, Sigma Gamma Rho, 1994, Breaking Barriers award, KJLH and LA

Dodgers, 1997, Shakespeare Trophy of Excellence award, Famous Poets Soc., 2003. Mem.: Shermans Future Tchrs. Assn. (hon.). Avocations: painting, poetry, writing, reading. Office Phone: 323-294-3465. Personal E-mail: jimmysherman@dslextreme.com.

**SHERMAN, JOHN ERIC,** plastic surgeon; b. NYC, 1951; m. Emily Sherman; 2 children. MD, NY Med. Coll., 1975. Internship & residency Montefiore Hospital Med. Ctr., NYC, 1975—78; chief resident plastic surgery Cornell Med. Ctr., 1978—80; fellowship reconstructive plastic surgery Memorial Sloan Kettering Cancer Ctr., 1979—80; plastic surgeon priv. practice, NYC, 1980—; attending plastic surgeon NY Hospital, Lenox Hill Hospital; clinical assist. prof. surgery Cornell U. Med. Coll. Author: Surgery of Facial Bone Fractures, 1987. Fellow: Am. Coll. of Surgeons; mem.: Am. Soc. of Maxillofacial Surgeons, Am. Soc. of Aesthetic Plastic Surgeons, Am. Soc. of Plastic & Reconstructive Surgeons. Avocation: golf. Office: 1016 5th Ave New York NY 10028

**SHERMAN, JOHN FOORD,** biomedical consultant; b. Oneonta, NY, Sept. 4, 1919; s. Henry C. and Ruth (Foord) Sherman; m. Betsy Deane Murray, Feb. 8, 1944 (dec.); children: Betsy Deane, Mary Ann. BS, Union U., 1949, DSc, 1970; PhD, Yale U., 1953. With NIH, 1953—74; assoc. dir. extramural programs Nat. Neurol. Diseases and Blindness, 1961—62, Nat. Inst. Arthritis and Metabolic Disease, 1962—63; assoc. dir. for extramural programs Office Dir. NIH, 1964—68, dep. dir., 1968—74; v.p. Assn. Am. Med. Colls., Washington, 1974—91, exec. v.p., 1987—91, spl. cons., 1991—94. Bd. advisors Am. Bd. Internal Medicine, 1991—98; sr. advisor Rsch!Am., 1994—. Asst. surgeon gen. USPHS, 1964—68; spl. rsch. chemotherapy and neuropharmacology; panel on data and studies NRC, 1976—87; biomed. libr. rev. com. NIH, 1981—98; bd. dirs. Spinal Cord Injury Edn. and Tng. Found., 1986—92, Musculoskeletal Transplant Found., 1987—2003. With U.S. Army, 1941—46. Decorated Bronze Star; recipient Meritorious Svc. award, USPHS, 1965, Disting. Svc. award, HEW, 1971, Sec.'s Spl. Citation award, 1973, Nat. Civil Svc. League award, 1973, Disting. Alumnus award, Union U.-Pharmacy Coll. Coun., 1974, Lifetime Achievement award, Nat. Assn. for Biomed. Rsch., 1990, Spl. Recognition award, Assn. Am. Med. Colls., 1996. Fellow: AAAS; mem.: Inst. Medicine NAS, Cosmos Club, Sigma Xi. Congregationalist. Personal E-mail: johnfsherman@msn.com.

**SHERMAN, JONATHAN HENRY,** lawyer; b. Washington, Jan. 4, 1963; s. Gerald Howard and Lola (Kay) Sherman; m. Catherine Sara Foot, Nov. 4, 2000; children: Benjamin Ashton, Julia Jean. BA in History magna cum laude, U. Rochester, 1984; MA in History, Yale U., 1989; JD, Stanford U., 1991. Bar: N.Y. 1992, U.S. Dist. Ct. (so. dist.) N.Y. 1992, U.S. Supreme Ct. 1995, U.S. Dist. Ct. (ea. dist.) N.Y. 1996, U.S. Ct. Appeals (11th cir.) 1996, U.S. Dist. Ct. (we. dist.) N.Y. 1998, D.C. 2000. Assoc. Cahill Gordon & Reindel, N.Y.C., 1991-2000; ptnr. Boies, Schiller & Flexner LLP, Washington, 2001—. Lectr. Stanford U., Palo Alto, Calif., 1991, Yale Coll., New Haven, 1993; adj. assoc. prof. law Fordham Law Sch., N.Y.C., 1998-2001. Sponsor, mentor Student-Sponsor Partnership, N.Y.C., 1992-96; contbr. The Cornerstone Sch., Jersey City, 1994; bd. dirs. Greater D.C. chpt. Crohn's and Colitis Found. Am., 2004—. Mem. ABA, N.Y. State Bar Assn. (media law com. 1997-99), Phi Beta Kappa. Office: Boies Schiller & Flexner LLP Ste 800 5301 Wisconsin Ave NW Washington DC 20015-2061 Office Phone: 202-237-9605. E-mail: jsherman@bsfllp.com.

**SHERMAN, JOSEPH OWEN,** pediatric surgeon; b. Chgo., Aug. 15, 1936; s. Joseph Owen and Mary Elizabeth (Kelly) Sherman; m. June Marie Martin, Mar. 16, 1963; children: Brian William, Lee Ann. Student, U. Ill., 1955—58; BS, Northwestern U., 1959, MD, 1962. Diplomate Am. Bd. Surgery, Am. Bd. Pediatric Surgery, lic. physician Ill. Rotating intern Passavant Meml. Hosp., Chgo., 1963-64; resident in gen. surgery VA Rsch. Hosp., Chgo., 1964-65, 67-68; Am. Cancer Soc. clin. fellow Northwestern U. Med. Sch., Chgo., 1965-66, from instr. to assoc. prof. surgery, 1967—86, prof. clin. surgery, 1986—; resident in pediatric surgery Children's Meml. Hosp., Chgo., 1966, 68-69; resident in thoracic surgery Mcpl. Tb San., Chgo., 1967. Emeritus staff dept. surgery Children's Meml. Hosp., 1995—, Evanston (Ill.) Hosp., 1995—. Contbr. articles to profl. jours. With Ill. Army N.G., 1953—57, with Ill. Air N.G., 1966—67. Fellow: ACS; mem.: AMA, Ill. State Med. Soc., Ill. Pediat. Surg. Assn., Chgo. Surg. Soc., Chgo. Med. Soc., Assn. Acad. Surgery, Am. Pediat. Surg. Assn. Avocations: photography, computer programing, indoor and outdoor gardening. Personal E-mail: j.o.sherman@att.net.

**SHERMAN, JUDITH DOROTHY,** theater producer, engineer, recording industry executive; b. Cleve., Nov. 12, 1942; d. William Paul and Laverne (Spoerke) Luekens; m. Kenneth Sherman, Aug. 1, 1964 Idiv. Aug. 1972); m. Max Wilcox, Jan. 1, 1981 (div. Jan. 1988); m. Curtis Macomber, Apr. 29, 1988. BA, Valparaiso U., 1964; MFA, SUNY, Buffalo, 1971. Rec. engr. Edward at the Moog, N.Y.C., 1971-72; producer-music dir. WBAI-FM, N.Y.C., 1972-76; owner-producer Judith Sherman Prodns., N.Y.C., 1976—. Rec. engr. Marlboro (Vt.) Music Festival, 1976-94; adminstrv. dir. La Musica di Asolo, Sarasota, Fla., 1986-88; vocalist Steve Reich and Musicians, 1971-72. Recipient Corp. Pub. Broadcasting award, 1976, two Grammy award nominations, 1991, Grammy award, Classical Prod. of Yr., 1993, Grammy award nominations, 1994, 95, 97, 98. Mem. NAFE, Chamber Music Am. (bd. dirs. 2000). NARAS. Democrat. Home and Office: 645 W 239th St Apt 2A Bronx NY 10463-1236

**SHERMAN, LAWRENCE WILLIAM,** criminologist; b. Schenectady, Oct. 25, 1949; s. Donald Lester and Margaret (Heckman) Sherman; m. Eva Fass Fass; children: Eliot, Katharine. BA, Denison U., Granville, Ohio, 1970; MA, U. Chgo., 1970; Diploma in Criminology, Cambridge U., Eng., 1973; PhD, Yale U., 1976; MA, U. Pa., 1999. Program rsch. analyst N.Y.C. Police Dept., 1971—72; asst. to assoc. prof. criminal justice SUNY, Albany, 1976—82; dir. rsch., v.p. Police Found., Washington, 1979—85; pres. Crime Control Ins., Washington, 1985—95; assoc. prof. to Disting. univ. prof. and chair dept. criminology and criminal justice U. Md., College Park, Md., 1982—99; Albert M. Greenfield prof. human relations, dept. sociology, dir. Jerry Lee Ctr. of Criminology and dir. Fels Inst. of Govt. U. Pa., Phila., 1999—, chmn. dept. chemistry, 2003—. Pres. Crime Control Rsch. Corp., Phila., 1981—; mem. panel on rsch. policies NRC-NAS, Washington, 2000—; lectr. FBI Acad., Quantico, 1980—2000; adj. prof. law and sci. dir. reintegrative shaming experiments Rsch. Sch. Social Scis., Australian Nat. U., Canberra, ACT, Australia, 1993—; dir. Justice Rsch. Consortium, Oxford, 2000—. Editor: (Book) Police Corruption: A Sociological Perspective, 1974; author: (book) Scandal and Reform: Controlling Police Corruption, 1978, Policing Domestic Violence: Experiments and Dilemmas, 1992 (Am.Sociological Assn. Disting. Scholarship award in Crime, Law and Deviance, 1973); co-author: Evidence Based Crime Prevention, 2002; contbr. articles to profl. jours. Recipient Bruce Smith award for disting. contbn. to criminal justice, Acad. of Criminal Justice Scis., 1994; fellow N.Y.C. Urban fellow, Alfred P. Sloan Foun., 1970—71. Fellow: Am. Soc. Criminology (pres. 2001—02, E.H. Sutherland Award for Disting. Contbn. to Criminology 1999); mem.: Acad. of Exptl. Criminology (pres. 1999—2001), Internat. Soc. Criminology (pres. sci. commn. 1995—99, pres. 2000—), Am. Acad. Polit. and Social Sci. (pres. 2001—). Home: 3507 Baring St Philadelphia PA 19104 Office: University of Pennsylvania 3809 Walnut St Philadelphia PA 19104 Business E-Mail: lws@sas.upenn.edu.

**SHERMAN, LOUIS ALLEN,** biology professor, department chairman; b. Chgo., Dec. 16, 1943; s. Stanley E. and Sarah R. Sherman; m. Debra Meddoff, June 15, 1969; children: Daniel, Jeff. BS in Physics, U. Chgo., 1965, PhD in Biophysics, 1970. Postdoctoral fellow Cornell U., Ithaca, NY, 1970-72; asst. prof. U. Mo., Columbia, 1972-78, assoc. prof., 1978-83, prof., 1983-88, dir. biol. scis., 1988-89; prof., head dept. biol. scis. Purdue U., West Lafayette, Ind., 1989-2000, prof. biol. scis., 1989—. Vis. scholar Hebrew U., Jerusalem, 2004—05. Contbr. articles to profl. jours. NIH fellow, 1965-72; Fulbright Hayes scholar, The Netherlands, 1979-80; NSF travel grantee, Fed. Republic Germany, Japan; grantee NIH, USDA, Dept. Energy. Fellow: AAAS, Am. Acad. Microbiology; mem.: AAUP, Plant Molecular Biology Soc., Biophys. Soc., Am. Soc. Plant Biologists, Am. Soc. Microbiology. Office: Purdue U Dept Biol Scis Lilly Hall West Lafayette IN 47907

**SHERMAN, MARY ANGUS,** public library administrator; b. Lawton, Okla., Jan. 3, 1937; d. Donald Adelbert and Mabel (Felkner) Angus; m. Donald Neil Sherman, Feb. 8, 1958; children: Elizabeth, Donald Neil II. BS in Home Econs., U. Okla., 1958, MLS, 1969. Br. head Pioneer Libr. System, Purcell, Okla., 1966-76, regional libr. Norman, Okla., 1976-78, asst. dir., 1978-80, dir., 1987—. Bd. dirs. McClain Bank, chair audit com., 1997—. Mem. bd. visitors Coll. Arts and Scis. U. Okla., 1998—2005; bd. dirs. U. Okla. Found., 2004—, Women's Resource Ctr., Norman, 1998—2003, pres., 2002. Named one of Disting. Alumni, Sch. Home Econs. U. Okla., 1980; recipient award of merit, U. Okla. Sch. Libr. and Info. Sci., 2000. Mem.: AAUW (pres. Okla. chpt. 1975—77, SW Ctrl. region dir. 1983—85, nat. bd. dirs. 1983—87, v.p. nat. membership 1985—87, Woman of Yr. Purcell chpt. 1982), ALA (councilor 1988—96, internat. rels. round table 1989—, planning and budget assembly 1990—91, internat. rels. com. 1992—96, orientation com. 1998—99, membership com. 1999—2000, chair sister libr. com. 2000—02, exec. bd. 2000—02, internat. rels. com. 2001—05, 2001—05), Okla. Libr. Assn. (pres. 1982—83, interlibr. cooperation com. 1993—95, chair 1994—95, legis. com. 1998—, Disting. Svc. award 1986), Internat. Fedn. Libr. Assns. (standing com. on pub. librs. 1999—), Tech. in Pub. Librs. Com., Pub. Libr. Assn. (divsn. of ALA, pres. pub. policy for pub. librs. sect. 1995—96, chmn. internat. rels. com. 2002—04), Norman Sister City Com., Norman C. of C. (bd. dirs. 1988—96, pres. 1994—95), Norman Soc. Internat. Affairs (v.p. 1998—99, pres. 1999—2001), Norman Assistance League Club (cmty. assoc.), Rotary (program chair 1991—92, bd. dirs. 1993—97, pres. 1995—96, group study exch. leader to Iceland 1996, dist. literacy chair 1998—2000, program chair 1999—2001, dist. group study exch. chair 2001—06, dist. gov. nominee 2005—09, dist. gov.-elect 2006—, Paul Harris fellow), Phi Beta Kappa, Beta Phi Mu, Kappa Alpha Theta (pres. Alpha Omicron House Corp. 1984—87, nat. dir. ho. corps. 1987—88), Delta Gamma Mothers (pres. 1978—79). Democrat. Methodist. Office: Pioneer Libr System 225 N Webster Ave Norman OK 73069-7133 Office Phone: 405-701-2642. Business E-Mail: mary@pls.lib.ok.us.

**SHERMAN, MAX RAY,** lawyer, dean, former state senator; b. Viola, Ark., Jan. 19, 1935; s. Ernest and Eva (Davenport) S.; m. Gene Alice Wienbroer, July 29, 1961; children: Lynn Ray, Holly Ruth. BA in History, Baylor U., 1957, LLD (hon.), 1978; JD with honors, U. Tex., 1960. Ptnr. Gibson, Ochsner and Adkins, Amarillo, Tex., 1960-77; Tex. State Senator, 1971-77; pres. West Tex. State U., Canyon, 1977-82; spl. counsel Tex. gov. State of Tex., Austin, 1983; dean Lyndon B. Johnson Sch. Pub. Affairs, Austin, 1983—97, prof., 1998—2005, emeritus, 2005—. Mem. exec. com. So. Regional Edn. Bd., 1986-87; v.p. Harry S Truman Scholarship Found.; mem. Nat. Commn. on Innovations in State and Local Govt., 1985-98, Tax Bd. Human Svcs., 1994-99. Contbr. articles to law revs. Served to capt. USAR, 1960-64. Recipient Austinite of Yr. award Greater Austin C. of C., 1997, Texan of Yr. award Tex. Legis. Conf., 1999; named One of Ten Best Legislators, Tex. Monthly, 1973, 75, 77; named Public Adminster. Educator of the Year, Centex Chpt. Am. Soc. for Public Adminster., 2004. Mem. ABA, Tex. Bar Assn., Nat. Assn. Schs. of Pub. Affairs and Adminstrs. (exec. council 1983-87, 88—, pres., 1988-89), Nat. Acad. Pub. Adminstrn., Assn. for Pub. Policy Analysis and Mgmt. (exec. com. 1983-86). Democrat. Presbyterian. Avocations: racquetball, tennis. Office: Univ Tex LBJ Sch Pub Affairs PO Box Y Austin TX 78713-8925 E-mail: max.sherman@mail.utexas.edu.

**SHERMAN, MILDRED MOZELLE,** music educator, vocalist, actress, opera director; b. Mt. Grove, Mo., Nov. 21, 1932; d. William Husley and Jessie Claire (Faulkner) Clark; m. Louis Leroy Sherman, Aug. 14, 1954; children: Clark Michael, Gayla Dawn. MusB, Bethany Coll., 1953; MusM, Ind. U., 1955; PhD, U. Wis., 1971; postgrad., U. Wis., Stevens Point, Kans. U., Baylor U. Instr. music Kans. State U., Manhattan, 1962—66; prof. music Howard Payne U., Brownwood, Tex., 1973—80, Grand Canyon U., Phoenix, 1980—84; prof. ch. music, dir. ch. music, drama, theatre So. Bapt. Theol. Sem., Louisville, 1984—2001, founding dir. Ch. Music Drama Theatre, sr. prof. ch. music, 2001—. Instr., rep. Inst. Pan Americano, Panama City, 1955-56; vis. prof. Belem and Rio Bapt. Sems., Brazil; owner Sherman Svcs., 2000—, Ky. Opera Roster, 2001—; vis. lectr. Staley, Cambridge, Union, Furman, Stetson, and Fla. Bapt. univs., 1990-99. Performer, dir. over 1000 operas, musicals, and plays including Women of the Bible, 1986—; author: The Vocal Technician, 1991, also short stories; author: (with P. Landgrave) The Light!dramatic musical, 2006; translator Mozarts Obligation of the 1st Commandment, 1986, Debussy's Prodigal Son, 1987, Massenet's Herodiade, 1997, Two from Galilee prodn. kit, 1996, (with Ted Nichols) opera Word of Honor, 2005, The Light, 2006; also monologues; contbg. author: New Dictionary of Religious Arts, 2001 Recipient Orpheus award Phi Mu Alpha Sinfonia, 1978; Lily Found. grantee, 1988-90; Baylor Univ. fellow, 1990-91. Mem. Nat. Opera Assn., Nat. Assn. Tchrs. Singing, Met. Opera Guild, Ch. Music Conf., DAR, Ea. Star, Christian Opera Assn. Bd., Sigma Alpha Iota. Baptist. Avocations: genealogy, handwork, animals, travel. Home: 3602 Coronado Dr Louisville KY 40241-2611 Office: So Bapt Theol Sem 2825 Lexington Rd Louisville KY 40280-0001 Business E-Mail: msherman@sbts.edu.

**SHERMAN, NORMAN MARK,** advertising agency executive; b. NYC, June 19, 1948; s. Sol and Rhoda (Kaplan) S.; m. Michelle Petnov, Jan. 8, 1978; 1 child, Michael Isaac. BA, U. Buffalo, 1970; MBA, Columbia U., 1972. Cert. tchr., N.Y. Product mgr. RCA Records, N.Y.C., 1972-73; dir. mktg. Shelter Records, N.Y.C., 1973-74; account exec. Rosenfeld Sirowitz & Lawson, N.Y.C., 1974-76, Benton & Bowles, N.Y.C., 1976-78, v.p. account supr., 1978-81, sr. v.p., mgmt. supr., 1981-84; exec. v.p., dir. account mgmt. Avrett, Free & Ginsberg, N.Y.C., 1984-85; sr. v.p., group account dir. D'arcy, Masius, Benton & Bowles, 1985-93, mng. dir., bd. dirs., 1993-96, corp. exec. v.p., 1996-98; mng. dir. The Sr. Network, Stamford, Conn., 1998-99; pres. N.Am. Gundersen Ptnrs. LLC, N.Y.C., 1999—2001; exec. v.p., dir. healthcare Hill, Holliday, Connors, Cosmopulos, 2002—. Home: 330 W 72nd St New York NY 10023-2641 Office: Hill Holliday 622 Third Ave New York NY 10017 Office Phone: 212-905-7023. E-mail: nsherman@hhny.com, nmsherman@yahoo.com.

**SHERMAN, PATSY O'CONNELL,** retired manufacturing executive, chemist; b. Mpls., Sept. 15, 1930; d. James Patrick and Edna Fern (Stitzel) O'Connell m. Hubert Townsend Sherman, Aug. 15, 1953; children: Sharilyn Kay Sherman Loushin, Wendy Jane Sherman Heil. BA, Gustavus Adolphus Coll., 1952. Chemist 3M, St. Paul, 1952-67, rsch. specialist, 1967-73, tech. mgr., 1973-82, mgr. tech. devel., 1982—92, tech. 1992. Trustee Gustavus Adolphus Coll., 1989-92. Recipient Disting. Alumni award Gustavus Adolphus Coll., 1975, Spurgeon award Boy Scouts Am., 1980; named to Minn. Inventors Hall of Fame, 1989, Nat. Inventors Hall of Fame, 2001. Mem. Am. Chem. Soc., Am. Soc. Tng. and Devel., Am. Soc. Engring. Edn. (dir. continuing profl. devel. div. 1986-89, chair 1989-90). Achievements include invention of Scotchgard (with Samuel Smith) in 1956. Personal E-mail: patsherman@aol.com.

**SHERMAN, RANDOLPH,** plastic and reconstructive surgeon, educator; b. St. Louis, May 27, 1951; s. Leon and Pearl (Lichtenfeld) S.; 1 child, Max Lassen. BA, U. Rochester, 1973; MD, U. Mo., 1977. Diplomate Am. Bd. Surgery, Am. Bd. Plastic Surgery (cert. added qualification in hand surgery). Intern in gen. medicine U. Wis., Madison, 1978; intern in surgery U. Calif., San Francisco, 1978-79, resident in surgery, 1979-81, SUNY, Syracuse, 1981-83; fellow in plastic and reconstructive surgery U. So. Calif., 1983-85, asst. prof. surger and orthopedics L.A., 1985-89, assoc. prof. clin. surgery and orthopaedics, 1991-92, assoc. prof. clin. surgery, orthopaedics and neurol. surgery, 1992-96, chmn. divsn. plastic and reconstructive surgery, 1994—, prof. clin. surgery, orthopaedics and neurol. surgery, 1996—. Mem. cons. staff City of Hope Nat. Med. Ctr., Duarte, Calif., 1985-91, 94—, St. John's Hosp., Santa Monica, 1989—, USC Univ. Hosp., 1997—; mem. staff, med. dir. Microsurg. Ctr. Hosp. Good Samaritan, L.A., 1985-93; mem. plastic and reconstructive surgery staff Kenneth Norris Jr. Cancer Hosp., L.A., 1985—,

L.A. County/U. So. Calif. Med. Ctr., L.A., 1985—; mem. staff St. Vincent Med. Ctr., L.A., 1986-92, Orthop. Hosp., L.A., 1986—; Shriner's Hosp. for Crippled Children, L.A., 1987-92, Children's Hosp. L.A., 1987—, Cedars Sinai Med. Ctr., L.A., 1987—, Estelle Doheny Eye Hosp., L.A., 1994—, numerous others; chief plastic and reconstructive surgery divsn. U. So. Calif. U. Hosp., L.A., 1991—, mem. active staff; dir. Am. Bd. Plastic Surgery 2000—. Am. Bd. Surgery, 2004—; vice-chair dept. surgery Keck Sch. Medicine, 2004—; assoc. med. dir. surg. svcs. L.A. County/U. So. Calif. Med. Ctr., 2005; mem plastic reconstructive surgery staff U. So. Calif. Hosp., 1991—; vice chair dept. surgery Keck Sch. Medicine, U. So. Calif. lectr., 2005; rschr. in field. Editor: Orthopedic Clinics, 1993; assoc. editor Surg. Rounds, 1989—, Jour. Hand Surgery, 1992-96, Am. Jour. Reconstructive Microsurgery, 1995—; sect. editor PRS 2005—; contbr. articles to profl. jours., chpts. to books. Founder L.A. chpt. Operation Smile Internat., 1993—. Recipient L.A. Humanitarian award Calif. Hosp., 1994; Microsurg. Devel. grantee Hosp. Good Samaritan, 1987-92, U. So. Calif. U. Hosp., 1992—; grantee Searle R&D, 1995-97, Cohesion Corp., 1997. Fellow ACS, Am. Assn. Plastic Surgeons, Am. Assn. Hand Surgeons (bd. dirs. 1991-95), Am. Soc. Hand Surgery, Am. Soc. Reconstructive Microsurgery (past pres.), Calif. Soc. Plastic Surgery; mem. Am. Soc. Plastic and Reconstructive Surgery, Am. Soc. Peripheral Nerve, Internat. Soc. Reconstructive Microsurgery, Calif. Med. Assn., Calif. Soc. Plastic Surgery, Assn. Acad. Chmn. Plastic Surgery, Plastic Surgery Rsch. Coun., Musculoskeletal Infection Soc., Undersea Med. Soc., Flying Physicians Assn., Wound Healing Soc. Avocations: flying, mountain climbing, scuba diving, jazz piano, gardening. Office: 1450 San Pablo St Ste 2000 Los Angeles CA 90089-0106 Office Phone: 323-442-6470. Business E-Mail: rsherman@surgery.usc.edu.

**SHERMAN, RAY,** musician; b. Chgo., Apr. 15, 1923; s. Maurie and Rose Vitto Sherman; m. Jeanne Kanter, Sept. 28, 1947; children: Susan Youngs, Nancy Estrada, Wendy. Pianist Gordon's Restaurant, Beverly Hills, Calif., 1940; pianist, arranger Jan Savitt Orch., Calif., 1946—47, Ray Bauduc Jazz Group, Hollywood, Calif., 1947; pianist Abe Burrows Radio Show, Hollywood, Calif., 1948, Judy Canova Radio Show, Hollywood, Calif., 1949—53; pianist, arranger Ben Pollack Jazz Group, Hollywood, Calif., 1950—52; pianist Phil Harris-Alice Faye Radio Show, Hollywood, Calif., 1950—54, Bob Crosby TV Show, Los Angeles, Calif., 1955, Guy Mitchell TV Show, Hollywood, Calif., 1957, Billy May Orch., Hollywood, Calif., 1958—87, Henry Mancini Orch., Los Angeles, Calif., 1958—88, Lo-da-mar Bowl, Santa Monica, Calif., 1941, Nelson Riddle Orch., Los Angeles, Calif., 1959—78, Rt. 66 TV Series, Hollywood, Calif., 1960—63, Benny Goodman Orch., Anaheim, Calif., 1961—61, Jerry Lewis Live TV Series, Hollywood, Calif., 1963—63, Hollywood Palace TV Series, Hollywood, Calif., 1964—64, Les Brown Band Of Renown, Calif., 1964—66, The Munsters TV Series, Universal City, Calif., 1964—66, I Dream Of Jeannie TV Series, Hollywood, Calif., 1965—70, Bewitched TV Series, Hollywood, Calif., 1965—71, Adam 12 TV Series, Burbank, Calif., 1968—75, Casino Gardens Ballroom, Ocean Park, Calif., 1941—41, Emergency TV Series, Burbank, Calif., 1972—79, Happy Days TV Show, Hollywood, Calif., 1977—84, Jack Sheldon Jazz Group, 1987—91, Pete Fountain Jazz Group, New Orleans, 1994—94, Peanuts Hucko And His Allstars, Switzerland, 1989—89, Sacramento Jazz Jubilee, Sacramento, 1978—2002; pianist, composer, arranger Various Jazz Festivals And Jazz Partys, 1970—2002, Various Jazz Clubs And Concerts, 1950—91, Various Rec. Companies, 1942—2000, Various Film Studios, Calif.; pianist Hollywood Tropics, Hollywood, Calif., 1942—42; webmaster www.raysherman.net, Duarte, Calif., 2003—; internet disk jockey Ray Sherman Radio 1, Duarte, Calif., 2004—, Ray Sherman Radio 2, Duarte, Calif., 2004—; arranger Jan Savitt Orch., 1942—42; pianist, arranger 211th CAAA ARMY BAND, 1943—46; pianist Jan Savitt Orch., Ocean Park, Calif., 1946—46, Will Osborn Orch., 1946—46; pianist, arranger Jerry Wald Orch., Los Angeles, Calif., 1946—46. Pianist, composer (animated short film) The Oomphs, pianist (film) The Days Of Wine And Roses, Touch Of Evil, Breakfast At Tiffany's, The Front Page, The Water Dance, Pete Kelly's Blues, Pennies From Heaven, The Cheap Detective, Batteries Not Included, (record album series) The Swing Era, (film) Pete Kelly's Blues, (record album series) Sounds Of The Great Bands, (record album) Doris Day: Cuttin' Capers, (film) West Side Story, (record) Primrose Lane, The Big Hurt, (record album) Ray Sherman At The Keyboard, Piano Chicago Style (JAZZ Jour. Internat. 1999 CRITICS' CHOICE, 2000), Dan Barrett And Blue Swing, Hollywood Heroes, (stage production) Cornilia Otis Skinner: Paris '90, (record album) Andrews Sisters In Hi-fi, (jazz performance) The Tonight Show (12/6/90), (film) Li'l Abner, Bye Bye Birdie, The Great Gatsby, (record album) Ben Pollack's Pic-a-rib Boys; composer, pianist: Stan Kenton's Neophonic Orch., 1968—69. Cpl. U.S. Army, 1943—46. Recipient 1st Prize, Tommy Dorsey Amature Swing Contest, 1938. Avocation: writing poetry. Personal E-mail: ray@raysherman.net.

**SHERMAN, RICHARD ALLEN, SR.,** lawyer; b. Atlanta, Mar. 16, 1946; s. Robert Hiram and Olivia Mae (Latham) S.; m. Mary Margaret Sawyer, June 23, 1973 (div. June 1994); children: Richard A. Jr., Jill Mary, James Warren. BA, Tulane U., 1968, JD, 1972. Bar: Fla. 1974, La. 1973, U.S. Ct. Appeals (5th cir.) 1978, U.S. Ct. Appeals (11th cir.) 1981, U.S. Supreme Ct. 1981. Ptnr., head appellate divsn. Wicker, Smith, Blomqvist, Davant, Tutan, O'Hara, McCoy et al, Miami, 1973-83; pvt. practice Ft. Lauderdale, Fla., 1983—; practice limited to handling appeals in Fla. Mem. ABA (vice-chmn. U.S. Ct. Appeals 5th cir. com. 1981), Fla. Bar Assn. (appellate rules com. 1979-81), Dade County Bar Assn. (chmn. appellate cts. com. 1982-83), Mensa, Pres. Club, Lauderdale Yacht Club, Upper Keys Sailing Club (bd. dirs.). Avocations: yacht racing, boating, scuba diving, travel, theater. Office: 1777 S Andrews Ave Ste 302 Fort Lauderdale FL 33316-2517

**SHERMAN, RICHARD BEATTY,** historian, educator; b. Somerville, Mass., Nov. 16, 1929; s. James Beatty and Hilda Louise (Ford) S.; m. Hanni Fey, June 13, 1952; children: Linda Caroline, Alan Theodore. AB, Harvard U., 1951, PhD, 1959; MA, U. Pa., 1952. Instr. history Pa. State U., State College, 1957-60; asst. prof. Coll. of William and Mary, Williamsburg, Va., 1960-65, assoc. prof., 1965-70, prof., 1970-87, chancellor prof., 1987-92, Pullen prof., 1992-94, prof. emeritus, 1994—. Fulbright prof. Am. history U. Stockholm, 1966-67. Author: The Negro and the City, 1970, The Republican Party and Black America, 1973, The Case of Odell Waller, 1992; co-author: The College of William and Mary: A History, 1993; contbr. articles to profl. jours. Served with U.S. Army, 1952-54. Am. Philos. Soc. grantee, 1964, 66, faculty rsch. grantee Coll. William and Mary, 1962, 63, 65, 80, 87. Mem. ACLU, Phi Beta Kappa. Democrat. Home: 205 Matoaka Ct Williamsburg VA 23185-2810 Office: Coll William and Mary Dept History Williamsburg VA 23185 E-mail: richardsherman@cox.net.

**SHERMAN, ROBERT ALAN,** lawyer; b. Boston, Nov. 10, 1953; s. Samuel and Rose C. (Cutler) S.; children: Matthew, Stephanie. BA, U. Rochester, 1975; JD, Boston U., 1978. Bar: Mass. 1978, U.S. Dist. Ct. Mass. 1979, U.S. Ct. Appeals (1st cir.) 1979. Assoc. Featherston & Griffin, Boston, 1978-81; from assoc. to ptnr. Gaffin & Krattenmaker, Boston, 1981-91; chief consumer protection divsn. Office of Atty. Gen., Boston, 1991-93, spl. counsel for A.G., 1993; spl. counsel Eckert, Seamans, Cherin & Mellott, Boston, 1994-96, ptnr., 1996—; now co-mng. shareholder Greenberg Traurig LLP, Boston. Legal analyst Fox TV, Newton, Mass., 1994-95, New Eng. Cable News, Newton, 1994—, Ct. TV, 1997—, CNBC, 1997—. Contbr. articles to profl. jours. Bd. dirs. Greater Boston Legal Svcs., 1991-93, Jewish Cmty. Ctr., 1994—; trustee Cambridge Ctr. Behavioral Studies, 1989-94; bd. overseers Beth Israel Deconess Med. Ctr. Recipient Humanitarian award Assn. Behavior Analysis, 1987. Avocations: running, scuba diving, reading, travel, music. Office: Greenberg Traurig LLP Third Fl One International Pl Boston MA 02110 Office Phone: 617-310-6015. Office Fax: 617-310-6001. Business E-Mail: shermanr@gtlaw.com.

**SHERMAN, ROGER TALBOT,** surgeon, educator; b. Chgo., Sept. 30, 1923; s. Joseph Bright and Alice Elizabeth (Baur) S.; m. Ruth Kathryn Thieman, Aug. 23, 1952 (dec. 2002); children: Nann, Alice, Nina, John, Julie; m. Mary Ellen Hulsey, July 12, 2003. AB, Kenyon Coll., 1946; MD, U. Cin., 1948. Diplomate Am. Bd. Surgery (mem.). Intern, fellow in pathology

St. Luke's Hosp., Chgo., 1948-50; resident in surgery Cin. Gen. Hosp., 1950-56; chief dept. exptl. surgery Walter Reed Army Med. Ctr., 1956-59; asst. prof. to prof. surgery U. Tenn., Memphis, 1959-72; prof., chmn. dept. surgery U. South Fla., Tampa, 1972-82; prof. surgery Emory U. Sch. Medicine, Atlanta, 1983-93; chief surgery Grady Meml. Hosp., Atlanta, 1983-92; Whitaker prof. surgery Emory U. Sch. Medicine, Atlanta, 1993-97; prof. emeritus, 1997—; dir. surg. edn. Piedmont Hosp., Atlanta, 1993-97. Mem. editorial bd. Am. Surgeon, 1970-91, Jour. Trauma, 1970-93; contbr. articles to profl. jour., chpt. to books. Served to maj. M.C. AUS, 1956-59. Recipient Golden Apple Tchr. of the Yr. award, 1972, Williams Disting. Tchg. award Emory U., 1984, Curtis P. Artz award, 1988. Fellow ACS (gov.); mem. Am. Assn. Surgery of Trauma (pres. 1979), Am. Surg. Assn., So. Surgical Assn., Southeastern Surg. Congress (pres. 1985), Internat. Surg. Soc., Am. Soc. Surgery of Alimentary Tract, Am. Burn Assn., Shock Soc., Am. Trauma Soc., Ga. Surg. Soc. (pres. 1997), Sigma Xi, Psi Upsilon, Alpha Omega Alpha. Home: 3747 Peachtree Rd NE Apt 813-814 Atlanta GA 30319-1352 *Surgery. The opening, exploration and repair of the living human body is an awesome responsibility afforded to only a few. To be privileged to be counted among those is a high honor, surpassed only by being trusted to teach others this demanding, and marvelous craft.*

**SHERMAN, SANDRA BROWN,** lawyer; b. Galesburg, Ill., May 14, 1953; d. Charles Lewis and Lois Maria (Nelson) Brown; m. Robert Sherman, June 10, 1979; children: Michael Wesley, Stephen Averill, Alexander Joseph. B of Music Edn., Ind. U., 1975; JD, U. Ill., 1979, LLM, 1981. Bar: Ill. 1979, Tex. 1982, N.J. 1984, U.S. Tax Ct. 1988, N.Y. 1997. Instr. law U. Ill., Champaign, 1979-81; assoc. Law Offices of William E. Remy, San Antonio, 1984, Gutkin Miller Shapiro & Selesner, Millburn, NJ, 1985-88, ptnr., 1989-91; counsel Riker Danzig Scherer Hyland & Perretti LLP, Morristown, NJ, 1991-95; ptnr. Riker Danzig Scherer Hyland & Perretti, LLP, Morristown, NJ, 1996—. Contbr. articles to profl. jours. Trustee, sec. Found. U. Medicine and Dentistry N.J., 1998—; trustee Jersey Battered Women's Svc., 1999—. Scholar Ind. U., 1971-75, U. Ill., 1977-79. Mem. ABA (probate and trust law divsn.), N.J. Bar Assn., Estate Planning Coun. No. N.J., Estate Planning Coun. N.Y.C., Park Ave. Club. Avocation: music. Office: Riker Danzig Scherer Hyland & Perretti LLP Headquarters Plz 1 Speedwell Ave Morristown NJ 07961-1981 Office Phone: 973-538-0800. Business E-mail: ssherman@riker.com.

**SHERMAN, SARAI,** sculptor, painter; b. Phila., 1922; BFA, Temple Univ., BS in Edn.; student, Barnes Found.; MFA, Univ. Iowa. Exhibitions include Palazzo Acad., Tod, Italy, 1983, Forum Gallery, NYC, 1986, exhibitions include Galleria Oddon della Scuttura Contemporary, Verona, Italy, 1989, Il Bisonte, Florence, Italy, 1997, exhibitions include Premio Suzzara, Italy, 1998, Premio Biella, 1999, Whitney Am. Mus., 2006. Recipient Award for Painting, Nat. Inst. Arts & Letters, 1964, European Cmty. prize, Premio Marzotto, 1967, Ann. Painting award, Republic of San Marino, 1975, Proctor prize, NAD, 1976. Mem.: NAD (academician 1999—). Subject of "Camera Picta: Sarai Sherman" by Rolando Bellini, 1995. Office: Forum Gallery 745 Fifth Ave New York NY 10151

**SHERMAN, SIGNE LIDFELDT,** portfolio manager, former research chemist; b. Rochester, NY, Nov. 11, 1913; d. Carl Leonard Broström and Herta Elvira Maria (Tern) Lidfeldt; m. Joseph V. Sherman, Nov. 18, 1944 (dec. Oct. 1984). BA, U. Rochester, 1935, MS, 1937. Chief chemist Lab. Indsl. Medicine and Toxicology Eastman Kodak Co., Rochester, 1937-43; chief rsch. chemist Chesebrough-Pond's Inc., Clinton, Conn., 1943-44; ptnr. Joseph V. Sherman Cons., N.Y.C., 1944-84; portfolio strategist Sherman Holdings, Troy, Mont., 1984—. Author: The New Fibers, 1946. Fellow Am. Inst. Chemists; mem. AAAS, AAUW (life), Am. Chem. Soc., Am. Econ. Assn., Am. Assn. Ind. Investors (life), Fedn. Am. Scientists (life), Union Concerned Scientists (life), Earthquake Engring. Rsch. Soc., Ctr. for Earthquake Engring. Rsch., N.Y. Acad. Scis. (life), Cabinet View Country Club. Office: Sherman Holdings Angel Island 648 Halo Dr Troy MT 59935-9415 E-mail: creative@libby.org.

**SHERMAN, SPENCER E.,** ophthalmologist; AB cum laude, Princeton U., Sigma XI, 1958; MD, Columbia Coll. Physicians & Surgeons, 1962. Diplomate Am. Bd. Ophthalmology. Intern Mt. Sinai Hosp., N.Y.C., 1962-63, attending ophthalmologist, 1968—, resident in ophthalmology, 1965-68; asst. clin. prof. ophthalmology NYU Sch. Medicine, N.Y.C.; staff Mt. Sinai Hosp., 1998—. Attending ophthalmologist Manhattan Eye & Ear Hosp., NYC, 1968—, Lenox Hill Hosp., NYC, 1968—, NY Eye and Ear Infirmary, Mt. Sinai Hosp., 1970—. Capt. USAMC, 1963-65. Named one of Best Drs. in NY, Castle Connolly Group, 1980—, Top Drs. in US, Ctr. for Study of Svc. Fellow ACS, Internat. Coll. of Surgeons, Am. Acad. of Ophthalmology (Honor and Svc. award); mem. AMA, Nat. Soc. Prevention Blindness, Found. Children with Learning Disabilities, Am. Soc. Refractive Surgeons, NY Acad. Medicine, NY Ophthalmologic Soc., Internat. Soc. Refractive Surgery, Am. Soc. Cataract & Refractive Surgery, Harmonie Club, Sunningdale Country Club, Maidstone Gun Club, Peconic Sportsman Club, East Hampton Tennis Club. Office: 166 E 63rd St New York NY 10021-7636 Fax: (212) 752-4285. Office Phone: 212-753-8300. E-mail: sesmdpc@aol.com.

**SHERMAN, STUART,** internist, gastroenterologist; b. New York, N.Y., Feb. 21, 1955; s. Sol and Rhoda (Kaplan) S.; m. Leslie Jane Derus, Oct. 5, 1991; children: Matthew, Benjamin. BA, SUNY, Binghamton, 1977; MD, Washington U., St. Louis, 1982. Diplomate Am. Bd. Internal Medicine. Resident in internal medicine U. Pitts., 1982-85, rsch. fellow, 1985-86; gastroenterology fellow Sch. of Medicine UCLA, 1986-89; therapeutic endoscopy fellow Sch. Medicine Ind. U., 1989-90; asst. prof. medicine and pancreaticobiliary endoscopy UCLA, 1990-92; asst. prof. medicine Ind. U., 1992-95, assoc. prof., 1995—, assoc. prof. radiology, 1996—. Cons. Bard Interventional Products Adv. Panel, Tewksbury, Mass., 1994—. Contbr. articles to profl. jours. Recipient Glaxo Award for excellence in gastroenterology Midwest Am. Fedn. Clin. Rsch., 1993, Young Scholars Rsch. award World Congress of Gastroenterology, L.A., 1994. Fellow Am. Coll. Gastroenterology (mem. editl. bd. Gastrointestinal Endoscopy); mem. ACP, Am. Soc. for Gastrointestinal Endoscopy, Am. Gastroent. Assn. Avocations: travel, skiing, tennis, golf. Office: Ind U Med Ctr 550 University Blvd Ste 2300 Indianapolis IN 46202-5149 E-mail: ssherman@induni.edu.

**SHERMAN, VICTOR,** lawyer; b. Indpls., Aug. 28, 1941; s. Marshall and Sara Lee Sherman; m. Claudia Ann Cron, Oct. 8, 1988; children: Mark, Daniel, Miles, Oliver, Luke. BS, UCLA, 1962; LLB, U. Calif., Berkeley, 1965. Bar: Calif. 1966, Conn. 1996, U.S. Ct. Appeals (9th cir.) 1971, U.S. Supreme Ct. 1996, Washington D.C. 2000, N.Y. 2001. Ptnr. Nasatir, Sherman & Hirsch, L.A., 1970-83, Main St. Law Bldg., Santa Monica, Calif., 1984—; mng. ptnr. Sherman & Sherman, Santa Monica, 1984—. Speaker, founder Advanced Criminal Law Seminar, Aspen, Colo., 1981—. Pvt. 1st class U.S. Army, 1960-67. Mem. Nat. Assn. Criminal Def. Lawyers (life), Am. Bd. Criminal Lawyers. Office: Sherman & Sherman 2115 Main St Santa Monica CA 90405-2215

**SHERMAN, WILLIAM FARRAR,** lawyer, former state legislator; b. Little Rock, Sept. 12, 1937; s. Lincoln Farrar and Nancy (Lowe) S.; m. Carole Lynn Williams, Sept. 2, 1967; children: John, Anna, Lucy. BA in History, U. Ark., 1960; LLB, U. Va., 1964. Bar: Ark. 1964, U.S. Supreme Ct. 1970. Assoc. Smith, Williams, Friday & Bowen, Little Rock, 1964-66; asst. U.S. atty. Ea. Dist. Ark., Little Rock, 1966-69, Ark. Securities Commr., Little Rock, 1969-71; ptnr. Jacoway, Sherman & Pence, Little Rock, 1971—2004; pvt. practice William F. Sherman Law Office, Little Rock, 2005—. Legal counsel Voice of the Retarded, 1991-2006; mem. Ark. Ho. of Reps., 1974-84; spl. assoc. justice Supreme Ct., 1991; del. Constnl. Conv. Ark., 1979. With U.S. Army, 1960-61, now brig. gen. U.S. Army ret. Mem. ABA, Ark. Bar Assn., Pulaski County Bar Assn., Ark. Bar Found. Democrat. Methodist. Office: 809 North Palm St Little Rock AR 72205 Office Phone: 501-372-3148. Personal E-mail: wfsherman@sbcglobal.net.

**SHERMAN, ZACHARY,** civil engineer, aerospace engineer, consultant; b. NYC, Oct. 26, 1922; s. Harry and Minnie (Schulsinger) Sherman; m. Bertha Leikin, Mar. 23, 1947; children: Gene Victor, Carol Beth. BCE, CCNY, 1943; MCE, Polytech. U. N.Y., Bklyn., 1953, PhD in Civil Engring. & Mechanics, 1969; MME, Stevens Inst. Tech., 1968. Registered profl. engr. N.Y., N.J. Stress analyst Gen. Dynamics, San Diego, 1943-45; sr. stress analyst Republic Aviation, Farmingdale, NY, 1945-47, 59-62; prof. civil engring. U. Miss., Oxford, 1954-59; lectr. Stevens Inst. Tech., Hoboken, NJ, 1962-67, CUNY, 1967-69; assoc. prof. aerospace engring. Pa. State U., State College, 1969-73; prin. Dr. Zachary Sherman Cons. Engrs., Santa Monica, Calif., 1973—; aerospace engr. FAA, N.Y.C., 1980-86. Designated cons. engr. rep. FAA, 1986—. Contbr. articles to profl. jours. NSF grantee, 1972. Fellow: ASCE; mem.: AIAA (v.p. Western Conn. chpt. 1977—78), N.Y. Acad. Scis., Sigma Xi. Achievements include development of beam/beam-column deck suspension bridge; solutions to pothole problems; prestressed aircraft wing. Home and Office: 2021 California Ave Apt 7 Santa Monica CA 90403-4531 Fax: 310-264-5990. Office Phone: 310-264-5990. Personal E-mail: aerozach@earthlink.net.

**SHERN, STEPHANIE MARIE,** investment company executive, accountant; b. Taylor, Pa., Jan. 7, 1948; d. Joseph and Stephanie (Malodovitch) Andrews; m. George Emil Shern, Sept. 25, 1971. AA, Keystone Jr. Coll., 1967; BS, Pa. State U., 1969. CPA, N.Y. Staff acct. to ptnr., nat. dir. consumer products industry Ernst & Young, N.Y.C., 1969—, ptnr., vice chmn., global and U.S. dir. R&CP markets. Dir. Met. Retail Fin. Execs., N.Y.C. Contbr. articles to profl. jours. Named Keystonian of Yr., Keystone Jr. Coll., 1984. Mem. AICPA, N.Y. State Soc. CPAs (bd. dirs. 1985—), Women's Econ. Round Table, Panther Valley Golf (Allamuch, N.J.), Beta Alpha Psi (mem. adv. forum 1984—). Republican. Ukrainian Orthodox. Home: 11 Green Briar Ct Little Falls NJ 07424-2307

**SHERNOFF, DAVID JORDAN,** psychology professor; b. Pomona, Calif., July 9, 1967; s. William Martin and JoAnn Shernoff; m. Elisa Steele, June 28, 1997. BS, Cornell U., 1989; EdM, Harvard Grad. Sch. Edn., 1991; PhD, U. Chgo., 2001. Asst. prof. No. Ill. U., DeKalb, 2003—. Domestic and internat. rsch. cons.; reviewer jour. articles and conf. papers; presenter in field. Author: (book) The Individual-Maker; contbr. jour. articles and chapters to books. Recipient Susan Colver-Rosenberger Meritorious Achievement award, U. Chgo., Dept. Edn., 1997—98, Role Motivation Dem. Life award, John G. Nichols Trust, Motivation Edn. Spl. Interest Group, Am. Ednl. Rsch. Assn., 2000—01; fellow, U. Wis., Madison, 2001—03. Mem.: Soc. Rsch. Child Devel., Soc. Rsch. Adolescence, Am. Ednl. Rsch. Assn. Liberal. Jewish. Avocations: water-skiing, racquetball, bicycling. Home: 315 Bridgeview Cir Geneva IL 60134 Office: No Ill U LEPF Graham Hall Coll Edn Dekalb IL 60115-2854 Office Phone: 815-753-8435. Business E-Mail: dshernoff@niu.edu.

**SHERO, RAY (REJEAN SHERO),** professional sports team executive; b. St. Paul, Minn., July 28, 1962; s. Fred and Mariette Shero; m. Karen Shero; children: Christopher, Kyle. Grad. St. Lawrence U., 1984. Player agent NHL; sr. ptnr. Sports Consulting Group, 1986—93; asst. gen. mgr. Ottawa Senators, 1993—98, Nashville Predators, 1998—2006; gen. mgr. Pitts. Penguins, 2006—. Office: Pitts Penguins Mellon Arena 66 Mario Lemieux Dr Pittsburgh PA 15219*

**SHERPA, FRAN MAGRUDER,** geography educator; b. Midland, Tex., Aug. 20, 1952; d. Edwin Howard Magruder and Barbara June Cowden; m. Ang Kazi Sherpa; children: Sarah, Susie, Sonia, Tsowang. BS Geography, Tex. State U., 1995, M Applied Geography, 1998. Registered massage therapist. Owner, operator Himalayan Excursions, Kathmandu, Nepal, 1983—85; investor, mgr. office Nepal Internat. Clinic, Kathmandu, Nepal, 1989—91; adj. prof. geography U. Tex. Permian Basin, Odessa, Tex., 2000—. Mem.: Am. Assn. Geographers. Avocations: photography, travel. Home: 2201 Neely Midland TX 79705 E-mail: fransherpa@cox.net.

**SHERR, ELLIOTT HAROLD,** neurologist, researcher; s. Walter R. and Karen Sherr; m. Linda M. Rubinstein, July 2, 1989; children: Rachel J., David A., Jessica J. BAS in Biology and Philosophy, Stanford U., Calif., 1984; MD, PhD, Columbia U., NYC, 1995. Diplomate Am. Bd. of Psychiatry and Neurology. Vis. scientist La Catolica U., Santiago, Chile, 1995—96; resident in pediats. U. Calif., San Francisco, 1996—2000, instr. neurology and pediats., 2000—02, asst. prof., 2002—. Mem. exec. com. Nat. Orgn. Dosirders of Corpus Callosum, Calif., 2003—06. Recipient Sci. Award, Child Neurology Found., 2004—06, Philip Dodge Young Investigator award, Child Neurology Soc., 2006. Mem.: Am. Acad. Neurology. Independent. Avocations: travel, cooking, cycling. Office: U Calif San Francisco Dept Neurology 350 Parnassus Ave San Francisco CA 94143-0137 Office Phone: 415-353-2525.

**SHERR, LAURENCE E.,** music educator, composer; s. Saul and Alice Sherr. Student, Vienna Internat. Music Ctr., 1975; BA magna cum laude, Duke U., 1978; MusM, U. Ill., 1981, D in Musical Arts, 1988; student, Banff Ctr., Can., 1981—82. Instr./tchg. asst. U. Ill., Urbana-Champaign, 1979—81, 1985—86; freelance artist and tchr. Atlanta, 1988—97; vis. asst. prof. New Coll., U. South Fla., Sarasota, 1989; instr. Clayton State U., Atlanta, 1994—95; part-time assoc. prof. Kennesaw State U., Atlanta, 1996—97, full time assoc. prof., 1997—, composer-in-residence, 1999—. Ednl. cons. Ga. Assessment Project Ga. State U., Atlanta, 1989—93; reviewer Ga. Coun. for the Arts, 1994, 95, N.C. Arts Coun., 1995. Composer: Brook by the Pagoda for piano, 1975, Trio in Baroque Style, 1975, Lamond House Suite for two clarinets, horn and bassoon, 1977, revised, 2004, Brass Quintet No. 1, 1978, Waves (5,3,4) for Percussion Ensemble, 1979, Choreopoem I: Movements for clarinet, trombone, vibraphone, percussion, double bass, and dancers, 1980, Interplay: Duo for Vibraphone and Marimba, 1981, Three Movements for Stoney for flute, clarinet, and trombone, with or without dancers, 1981, Isolated (within) for narrator, piano, and dancer(s), 1981, Emergence for classical guitar, 1981, String Trio for violin, viola, and cello, 1982, Four Short Pieces for solo violin, 1982 (finalist Old Dominion U. Diehn Composers Room Southeastern Regional Competition, 2000), Canon for a Couple, four-part canon, 1985, ...of a time when...for orchestra, 1987, Five Aphorisms: Solo for Marimba and Assorted Percussion, 1983, 1988, One (plus) for cello and percussion, with or without dancer(s), 1988, Debussy's Arabesque No. 1, transcribed for orch., 1990, Illuminations for orchestra, 1997, 1999, Elegy and Vision, version for solo viola, 2000, Fugitive Footsteps for baritone solo and mixed chorus, 2002, (commn.) Dhammapada Verses for soprano, flute, percussion, and piano, 1990, 2001 (finalist Susquehana U. New Music Ensemble Composers Competition competition, 2001), Soprano for soprano, flute, clarinet, piano and percussion, 1991, The Fiber Sculptures of a Celestial Vision for violin, viola, cello, and piano, 1991, Blue Ridge Frescos for classical guitar, 1991, 1995, Three Haiku for treble voices and piano, 1992, Elegy and Vision for solo cello, 1993, Journeys Within: Concerto for Flute and Chamber Ensemble, 1994 (Grand prize Delius Composition Contest, 1995), Nocturne for piano, 1999, Duo Concertante for flute and percussion, 2003, Capriccioso for flute or clarinet and marimba or piano, 2005. Grantee, Ill. Arts Coun., 1984, City Atlanta Bur. Cultural Affairs, 1990, Ga. Coun. for the Arts, 1990, 1993, Alliance Francaise d'Atlanta, Inc., 1992, Meet the Composer, Inc., 1997, Am. Composers Forum, 1998; residency Composers/Choreographers Workshop, Am. Dance Festival, 1981, residency Am. Music for Percussion Program, Charles Ives Ctr. for Am. Music, 1988, artist residency, Seaside Inst., 1994, Hambidge Ctr. for the Creative Arts and Scis., 1999, 2001, 2005, Va. Ctr. for the Creative Arts, 2000, 2002, 2004, MacDowell Colony, 2002. Mem.: ASCAP, Music Tchrs. Nat. Assn., Tampa Bay Composers' Forum, Soc. Composers, Coll. Music Soc., Am. Music Ctr., Am. Composers Forum, Pi Kappa Lambda. Office: Kennesaw State Univ Dept Music #3201 1000 Chastain Rd Kennesaw GA 30144

**SHERR, RONALD NORMAN,** artist; b. Plainfield, N.J., 1952; Student, Du Cret Sch. of Art, Nat. Acad. of Design; pvt. studies with Burton Silverman. Instr. Nat. Acad. Sch. of Fine Art, F.I.T., Art Students League. Exhibited in group shows at Allied Artists, Audubon Artists, Salmagundi Club, Nat. Acad.

of Design, N.Y.C., Gibbes Art Gallery, Charleston, S.C., Inst. of Arts and Letters, Doll & Richards, Boston, Indpls. Art Mus., 1978, Phoenix Art Mus., Westmoreland county Mus. of Art, Greensburg, Pa., Soc. of Illustrators, N.Y.C., U. Art Mus., Santa Barbara, Okla. Art Ctr., Elvehjem Mus., U. Wis., U. N.H., 1979, Colo. Springs Fine Arts Ctr., 1992, Grand Ctrl. Art Galleries, N.Y.C., 1992, Portraits Inc. N.Y.C., 1992, others; represented in permanent collections at Phoenix (Ariz.) Art Mus., Smithsonian Instn. Nat. Portrait Gallery, Gibbes Art Gallery, Charleston, S.C., Portraits, Inc., N.Y.C., Princeton (N.J.) U., U.S. Dept. Treasury, Washington, various pvt. collections. Recipient Norman V. Headrick prize Salmagundi Club, 1975, Margaret M. Bower award, 1981, Julius Hallgarten prize, Nat. Acad. of Design, 1976, 77, Henry Ward Ranger Fund, 1976, Emily Lowe award Allied Artists Ann., N.Y.C., 1982, Award for Excellence, Internat. Editorial Design Competition, 1983, Gold Medal of Honor Allied Artists of Am., 1986, Hubbard Art award for Excellence, Ruidoso, N.M., 1991; grantee Greenshields Found., 1975, John F. and Anna Lee Stacey Found., 1976. Home: 584 Cafferty Rd Upper Black Eddy PA 18972-9511 Studio: 44 Stuyvesant St New York NY 10003-7506

**SHERRATT, HOLLY,** art appraiser; BA in Art History, UCLA; MA in Visual Studies, U. Calif., Irvine. Trainee Laguna Art Mus., Laguna Beach, Calif.; intern Nat. Mus. Am. Art., Smithsonian Inst., Washington; curatorial staff Huntington Beach Fine Art Ctr., Calif.; modern, contemporary and Latin Am. art specialist Bonhams & Butterfields, San Francisco, 2000—, and cataloguer, prints and photographs dept. Exec. bd. Nat. Francisco Mus. Modern Art contemporary ext. Lectr. in field. Mem.: Phi Beta Kappa. Office: Bonhams & Butterfields 220 San Bruno Ave San Francisco CA 94103 Office Phone: 415-503-3311. Office Fax: 415-503-3274. Business E-Mail: holly.sherratt@bonhams.com.

**SHERRELL, JOHN BRADFORD,** lawyer; b. Indpls., Jan. 27, 1951; s. Carl and Mary Jean (Bell) S.; m. Sherry Naomi Calhoun, Apr. 28, 1977; children: David Alan, Corinne Elizabeth. BA, Yale U., 1973; JD, U. Mich., 1977. Bar: Calif. 1977. Ptnr. Latham & Watkins, Los Angeles, 1977—. Dep. gen. counsel to Ind. Commn. on L.A. Police Dept. Named an Am.'s Top Black Lawyers, Black Enterprise Mag., 2003. Mem. ABA, Calif. Bar Assn. (co-chair real estate fin. subsect. of real property sec. 1990-92), L.A. County Bar Assn. (barrister's exec. com. 1978-80, bd. trustees 1991-93). Office: Latham & Watkins 633 W 5th St Ste 4000 Los Angeles CA 90071-2005 Office Phone: 213-891-8174. E-mail: john.sherrell@lw.com.

**SHERRER, CHARLES DAVID,** dean, clergyman; b. Marion, Ohio, Sept. 21, 1935; s. Harold D. and Catherine E. (Fye) S. AB, U. Notre Dame, 1958, MA, 1965; S.T.L., Gregorian U., 1962; PhD, U. N.C., 1969; HHD, King's Coll., 1997. Ordained priest Roman Cath. Ch., 1961. Instr. English U. Portland, Oreg., 1963-64, asst. prof. Oreg., 1969-74, prof. Oreg., 1990—2005, prof. emeritus Oreg., 2005—, chmn. dept. Oreg., 1970-74, dean Grad. Sch. Oreg., 1982-87, mem. Bd. Regents Oreg., 1986-87, acad. v.p. Oreg., 1987-96; pres. King's Coll., Wilkes Barre, Pa., 1974-81. Bd. trustees Stonehill Coll., 1992-98; dir. studies Holy Cross Fathers, Ind. Province, 1979-88. Office Phone: 503-943-7596. Business E-Mail: sherrer@up.edu.

**SHERRER, GARY,** former state lieutenant governor, bank executive; m. Judy (Waller), 1965; children: Stuart and Nancy. Grad., Emporia State U. Sec. Kans. Dept. Commerce and Housing, 1995—2002; lt. gov. State of Kans., 1996—2003; exec. v.p. Gold Banc, Leawood, Kans., 2002—. Vice chmn. Governor's Cabinet. Recipient Disting. Alumni Award Emporia State U., 1994, Award of Excellence, 1995; Carl Perkins Humanitarian Award, 2000; Toll fellow, 1999. Mem. Nat. Conf. Lt. Govs. (chmn.). Republican.

**SHERRICK, DANIEL NOAH,** real estate broker; b. Greenup, Ill., Mar. 28, 1929; s. Conrad Donovan and Helen Lorene (Neeley) S.; m. Dora Ann Moore, Aug. 11, 1957; children: Renata Ann Sherrick McBride, Sherrie Dee Sherrick Sierra. BS in Edn., Eastern Ill. U., Charleston, 1956. Owner Midwest Ins. Agy., Greenup, 1956-60; supt. agys. Midwest Life Ins. Co., Lincoln, Nebr., 1960-62; asst. v.p. Gulf Life Ins. Co., Jacksonville, Fla., 1962-71; pres. Bank of Carbondale, Ill., 1971-74, Prescription Learning Corp., Springfield, Ill., 1974-76; exec. v.p. Imperial Industries, Inc., Miami Lakes, Fla., 1976-88, pres., chief exec. officer, 1988-90; broker, salesman Coldwell Banker Residential Real Estate, 1990-91, 93—; pres., bd. dirs. Palmer State Bank, Taylorville, Ill., 1991-93; broker-salesman Coldwell Banker Highlands Properties, 1993—. Pres. Alderman Park Civic Assn. Jacksonville, Ill., 1968, Heritage Hills Home Owners Assn., Carbondale, Ill., 1973. With USAF, 1948—52. Mem.: VFW, Greater Sebring C. of C., Am. Legion, Elks, Masons. Presbyterian. Home: 6228 Aquavista Dr Sebring FL 33876 Office: Coldwell Banker Highlands Properties 2521 US Hwy 27 S Sebring FL 33870-2127 Office Phone: 863-382-3157. Personal E-mail: dandora@strato.net.

**SHERRICK, REBECCA LOUISE,** academic administrator; b. Carthage, Ill., May 28, 1953; d. Otho Downing and Elizabeth (Potter) S. BA, Ill. Wesleyan U., Bloomington, 1975; doctorate (hon.), Ill. Wesleyan U., 2001; PhD, Northwestern U., 1980. Asst. prof. Carroll Coll., Waukesha, Wis., 1980-85, assoc. prof., 1987—, v.p. planning, 1990-91, v.p. enrollment and planning, 1991-92, v.p. enrollment and student svcs., 1992-93, v.p. administrn., 1993—, provost, 1998—2000; pres. Aurora U., Ill., 2000—. Recipient Woman of Distinction award Waukesha YWCA, 1991; Lincoln Acad. of Scholars awardee State of Ill., 1975; William Randolph Hearst fellow, 1976, 77. Mem. Alpha Lambda Delta, Phi Alpha Theta, Kappa Delta Pi, Phi Kappa Phi. Methodist. Avocations: swimming, gardening. Office Phone: 630-844-5476. Business E-Mail: rsherrick@aurora.edu.

**SHERRILL, MILTON LEWIS,** sculptor, painter; b. NYC, May 30, 1949; s. Ruth M. Sherrill. Student, Cooper Union, 1971; BA, SUNY, Old Westbury, 1974; MFA, Pratt Inst., 1976. Fine artist M.L. Sherrill Creative Concepts, Ltd., Mt. Vernon, NY, 1976—. Works commissioned by, Lcor Inc., NYC, Westchester County, NY, City of Mt. Vernon; contbr. art to newspapers, mags., jours; designer Florence Griffith Joyner Sports Award, Harriet Tubman The Freedom Corridor. sculpture. Grantee, Westchester Arts Coun., Abdoh & Ester Gottlieb Found.; Westchester Arts Alive grantee, 2000, 2001, 2002. Mem.: NY Artist Equity Assn., Nat. Sculpture Gallery, Internat. Sculpture Ctr. Avocation: antiques. Office: ML Sherrill Creative Concepts Ltd PO Box 2421 Mount Vernon NY 10551-2421 Office Phone: 800-650-6394. E-mail: mlsherrill3@yahoo.com.

**SHERRILL, THOMAS BOYKIN, III,** retired newspaper publishing executive; b. Tampa, Fla., Nov. 19, 1930; s. Thomas Boykin Jr. and Mary Emma (Addison) S.; m. Sandra Louise Evans, Dec. 27, 1969; children: Thomas Glenn, Stephen Addison. Circulation dir. Tampa (Fla.) Tribune, 1962—67, Sarasota (Fla.) Herald-Tribune, 1967—75; v.p. circulation The Dispatch Printing Co., Columbus, Ohio, 1975—78, v.p. mktg., 1978—97, bd. dirs., 1977—97; v.p. bd. dirs. Ohio Mag., Inc., Columbus, 1979—97; ret., 1997. Bd. dirs., past chmn. bd. dirs. Salvation Army; trustee, past chmn. bd. dirs. Better Bus. Bur. Ctrl. Ohio, Inc.; bd. dirs. Ctrl. Ohio Ctr. Econ. Edn.; v.p. trustee Columbus Dispatch Charities; past pres. Wesley Glen United Meth. Retirement Ctr.; pres.'s adv. bd. Meth. Theol. Sch. With USN, 1951-56. Recipient Disting. Svc. award Editor and Pub. Mag., 1978; named hon. mem. Troy State U., 1979, hon. Ky. Col., 1980, hon. lt. col. aide-to-camp to Gov. State of Ala., 1984. Mem. Internat. Circulation Mgrs. Assn. (pres. 1975, Pres's. award 1989), Internat. Newspaper Mktg. Assn., Ohio Newspaper Assn. (bd. dirs. 1984-97, pres. Hidden 48, Pres.'s award 1990), So. Circulation Mgrs. Assn. (life; pres. 1967-68, sec. and treas., 1968-75, C.W. Bevinger Meml. award 1972), Audit Bur. Circulations (bd. dirs. 1980-90), Am. Advt. Fedn., Navy League, Ohio Newspapers Found., Ohio Circulation Mgrs. Assn. (life; Pres.' award 1989), Columbus Area C. of C., SAR, Internat. Platform Assn., Athletic Club of Columbus, Muirfield Village Country Club, Kiwanis Club of Columbus (life, pres. 1982, George F. Hixon fellow). Republican. Home: 5215 Hampton Ln Columbus OH 43220-2270

**SHERRIS, DAVID ALLAN,** surgeon, researcher, educator; b. Buffalo, Feb. 1, 1961; s. Donald Allan Sherris and Doris Mary Jones; m. Lisa Ellen Dubiel, Apr. 11, 1993; children: David Jr., Matthew, Lara. BA, Middlebury Coll., 1984; MD, U. Rochester, 1988. Diplomate Am. Bd. Otolaryngology, Am. Bd. Facial Plastic and Reconstructive Surgery. Resident otolaryngology U. Rochester, NY, 1989—93; fellow facial plastic surgery, clin. instr. U. Wash., Seattle, 1993—94; asst. prof. otolaryngology Mayo Med. Sch., Rochester, Minn., 1994—2000, assoc. prof., 2000—03; cons. surgeon Mayo Clinic, Rochester, 1994—2003, chair facial plastic surgery, 2002—03; chief oto-laryngology SUNY, Buffalo, 2003—; chief of svc. otolaryngology Kaleida Health, 2003—; prof. otolaryngology U. Buffalo, 2005—. Author: Basic Surgical Skills, 1999, Essential Surgical Skills, 2004; author, editor: The Principles of Facial Reconstruction, 1995, reviewer: Archives of Facial Plastic Surgery, 2000—, mem. editl. bd.: Rhinology Jour., 2002—; contbr. 70 articles to profl. jours. Fellow: Am. Rhinologic Soc., Am. Acad. Otolaryn-gology Head and Neck Surgery (home study course faculty 2001—), Am. Acad. Facial Plastic and Reconstructive Surgery (active surgeon Face to Face Domestic Violence Program 1994—, Sir Harold Delf Gilles award 1994); mem.: Am. Bd. Otolaryngology (examiner 1999—). Avocations: running, skiing. Office: Millard Gates Hosp 3 Gates Cir Buffalo NY 14209 Office Phone: 716-887-5101. E-mail: dsherris@buffalo.edu.

**SHERROD, DANNY TROY,** writer, educator; b. North Richland Hills, Tex., Apr. 27, 1963; s. Yvonne Boatman and Dan Sherrod. AA and Sci., El Centro Coll., 1983—86; B of Humanities, So. Meth. U., 1997—2002. Caseworker Tex. Dept. of Human Services, Dallas, 1991—95; libr. specialist So. Meth. U., 1996—2003; tchr. writing, history L.P. Cowart Sch., 2003—. Author: (short story) Div. When it Rains - pub. in Primavera; editor: (newsletter) Theatre Hist. Soc. of Am.; contbr. jour. Legacies. Mem.: Humane Soc. of the U.S., People for the Ethical Treatment of Animals, SPCA of Tex., Golden Key Nat. Honor Soc. (life). Democrat. Home: 1119 Newport Ave Dallas TX 75224-1248

**SHERROD, LLOYD BRUCE,** retired nutritionist; b. Goodland, Kans., Mar. 5, 1931; s. Charles and Helen S.; m. Judith Harms Sherrod, Dec. 21, 1963; children: Donna J., Barbara E. BS, S.D. State U., Brookings, 1958; MS, U. Ark., Fayetteville, 1960; PhD, Okla. State U., Stillwater, 1964. Rsch. assoc. Okla. State U., Stillwater, 1963; asst. prof. U. Hawaii, Hilo, 1964-67; from assoc. prof to prof. Tex. Tech. U. Coll., Pantex, 1967-79; nutrition-chemistry instr. Frank Phillips Coll., Borger, Tex., 1979-88; part-time nutrition instr. Amarillo (Tex.) Coll., 1989-95; ret., 1995. Rschr. in field. Contbr. articles to sci. jours. Served with U.S. Army, 1951-53. Mem. AAAS, Am. Soc. Animal Science, Am. Dairy Science Assn., Am. Soc. Agronomy, Am. Inst. Biol. Scis., Tex. Jr. Coll. Tchrs. Assn., Am. Men and Women of Sci., Plains Nutrition Coun., Sigma Xi, Phi Kappa Phi, Gamma Sigma Delta. Home: PO Box 1017 Panhandle TX 79068-1017

**SHERROD, PHILIP LAWRENCE,** artist, composer, painter, poet; b. Pauls Valley, Okla., Oct. 12, 1935; s. Jesse Lawrence and Edrie Mae (Shumate) S.; m. Peggy Anne Elledge, Jan. 19, 1959 (div. 1959); m. Helena Alicia Decastro, Nov. 18, 1961 (div.); 1 child, Sandro Arentino Mateos. BS, Okla. State U., 1957, BA, 1959; postgrad., Art Students League, N.Y.C., 1961-63; Jacques Seligman Coll., 1968, Carroll Reese Mus., 1968. Tchr. Morristown Art Assn., NJ, 1973-74, NJ Ctr. for Visual Arts, 1977—2005, Art Students League, NYC, 1984—2006, Nat. Acad. Design Sch. of Fine Arts, 1994, 1996, 1998, 2005; master tchr. Bd. Cmty. Ctr., South Orange, NJ, 2004—06. Founding mem. Street Painters, NYC, 1977—. One-man shows include Leonard Hutton Hutschnecker Galleries, 1966, Gallery 9, Chatham, NJ, 1967, Jacques Seligmann Gallery, 1968, Selected Artists Gallery, 1968, East Rockaway Art Exhibition, 1969, Sonraed Gallery, 1971, Artemis East Gallery, 1972, Pace U., NYC, 1972, The Humanist Ctr., 1973, 74, Grace Gallery, 1973, Alan Stone Gallery, 1973, 75, 76, 83, 96-97, Tower Art Gallery, Highland Falls, NY, 1975, Gallery 100, Princeton, NJ, 1975, Monique Knowlton Gallery, 1976, Cone Gallery, 1976, Bridgeport U., Conn., 1976 Bayonne Jewish Cmty. Ctr., NJ, 1977, 47 Bond St. Gallery, NYC, 1979, Art Awareness Gallery, Lexington, NY, 1980, Artists Choice Mus., NYC, 1983; exhibited in group shows at Allan Frumkin Gallery, 1973, 75, Boston U. Gallery, 1979, SUNY, 1979, Cork Gallery, Lincoln Ctr., NYC, 1984-2000, Nat. Acad. of Design, NYC, 1966, 75, 76, 78, 82, 88-90, 93-95, 97-99, 2001—; NJ Ctr. for the Arts, 1977-2003, Mus. and Sculpture Garden, Smithsonian Inst., Washington, 1989, New England Fine Arts Inst., Boston, 1993, Rita Dean Gallery, Dan Diego, 1993, Gallerie des Hamptons, Westhampton Beach, 1994, Fordham U., 1996; represented in permanent collections Tulane U. Mus., New Orleans, Mus. of Fine Art, Springfield, Mass., Everhart Mus., Scranton, Pa., Rose Art Mus., Brandeis U., Waltham, Mass., Almsford House, Fine Arts Ctr., Anderson, Ind., Mus. City NY, Hirshorn Mus. & Sculpture Garden, Smith-sonian Inst. Mus.& Sculpture Garden, The Phillips Exeter Acad., NH, Worcester Fine Arts Mus., Herbert Johnson Mus., Ithica, NY, RI Sch. Design/Newark Mus., NJ, Nat. Acad. Mus., NYC, Am. Broadcasting Corp., Paramount Pictures Prodns., INA Corp., Montgomery Securities, San Fran-cisco, Boston, NYC, Allan Stone, Steven Paine, Richard Brown Baker, others; author: (poems) 30 Mental-Talia, 1980, Black Truck, 1981, Mr. Wigley Cums, 1983, Images Below the Belt, 1984, Sex (I) Con, 1985. Grantee Creative Artists Pub. Svc., 1980, Adolphe/Esther Gottlieb Found., 1981, 88, 96, 06, NEA, 1982, Am. Acad. in Rome, 1985-86, The Pollack-Krasner Found., Inc., 1989; recipient Purchase award Am. Acad. Arts and Letters, 1967, 69, 74, Childe Hassam Purchase award Prixe de Roma, 1985-86. Fellow Am. Acad. in Rome. Home: 41 W 24th St New York NY 10010-3210 Office Phone: 212-989-3174. Personal E-mail: bigdaddiehotssherrod@spaceboy.com.

**SHERRY, GEORGE LEON,** political science professor; b. Lodz, Poland, Jan. 5, 1924; came to US, 1939, naturalized 1945; s. Leon G. and Henrietta (Mess) S.; m. Doris H. Harf, Mar. 6, 1947; 1 child, Vivien Gail Sherry Greenberg. BA summa cum laude, CCNY, 1944; MA, Columbia U., 1951, MA, cert. Russian Inst., 1955, PhM, 1959; DHL (hon.), Occidental Coll., LA, 2005. Reporter, radio news writer The NY Times, NYC, 1944-46; editor, interpreter, then sr. interpreter UN, NYC, 1946-59, from polit. officer to dir. and dep. to under sec.-gen. for spl. polit. affairs, 1959-84; polit. advisor to missions Congo, Cyprus, India and Pakistan, 1962-66; asst. sec.-gen. for spl. polit. affairs UN (office in charge peacekeeping forces which won Nobel Peace Prize, 1988), NYC, 1984-85; Stuart Chevalier prof. diplomacy and world affairs Occidental Coll., LA, 1985—2004. Dir. Occidental at-the-UN program, NYC, 1986-2002; US del. staff Dartmouth Soviet-Am. confs., 1961-94; assoc. seminar on problem of peace Columbia U., NYC; cons. UN dept. peacekeeping ops., 1992, 93; UN envoy to follow Russian elections, 1993; cons. Internat. Peace Acad., 1993-97. Author: The United Nations Reborn: Conflict Control in the Post-Cold War World, 1990; editorial adv. bd. Polit. Sci. Quar., NYC, 1973-89; contbr. articles and revs. to profl. jours. Recipient Townsend Harris medal CCNY, 1993; UN Inst. for Tng. and Rsch. sr. fellow, 1985-93. Mem. Coun. on Fgn. Rels., UN Assn.-USA. Democrat. Avocations: piano playing, skiing, sailing.

**SHERRY, JOHN SEBASTIAN,** lawyer; b. Homestead, Pa., Apr. 18, 1946; s. Sebastian John and Margaret Josephine (Coyne) Sherry; m. Joan Carol Paulsen, Aug. 9, 1969; children: Brendan P., Michael S., Conor J. BA, U. Dayton, 1968; JD, Duquesne U., 1971. Bar: Pa. 1971, U.S. Dist. Ct. (we. dist.) Pa. 1971, U.S. Supreme Ct. 1975, U.S. Ct. Appeals (3d cir.) 1976, U.S. Claims Ct. 1977, U.S. Ct. Internat. Trade 1977, U.S. Tax Ct. 1977, U.S. Ct. Mil. Appeals 1977. Pvt. practice law, Pitts., 1971—; mng. atty. Travlers Ins. Co., Pitts., 1972-78; mng. trial atty. CNA Ins. Cos., Pitts., 1978-88, sr. mgr. staff counsel, 1988-94, mng. trial atty., 1994-96, asst. v.p. claims litigation, 1996-98; pvt. practice John S. Sherry & Assocs., Pitts., 1999—; prin. Sherry Dispute Resolution Svcs., Pitts., 2001—. Lectr. Trial Advocacy Found., Pitts., 1984, Nat. Inst. Trial Advocacy 1997, 98. Assoc. opinion editor: Pitts. Legal Jour., 1977—78; editor: YLS newsletter, 1980. Chmn. bd. auditors, South Park, Pa., 1977—85. Fellow: Acad. Trial Lawyers Allegheny County (bd. govs. 1997—98); mem.: ABA, Western Pa. Trial Lawyers Assn., Pa. Bar Assn. (jud. administrn. com. 1992—, ADR com. 2001—), Pa. Trial Lawyers Assn., Allegheny County Bar Assn. (CLE com. 1978—, coun. civil litigation sect. 1985—87, treas. 1988—2001, vice chmn. 1989, chmn. civil litigation

sect. 1990, civil procedure rules com. 1999—, ADR com. 2001—), South Park C. of C. (past pres.), Pine Lake Trout Club, Rivers Club, Lions. Democrat. Roman Catholic. Avocations: fishing, hunting, literature. Home and Office: 113 Stonegate Dr Mc Murray PA 15317-2766 Office Phone: 412-281-6557, 412-418-8935. E-mail: jsherryesq@msn.com.

**SHERRY, KRYSTAL A.,** real estate broker; b. Bayonne, N.J., July 26, 1975; d. Joseph James and Elaine M. Sherry. Grad. h.s., West Covina, Calif. Lic. real estate Nev. Realtor, Nev., 1993—2001; broker, owner Realty Success Sys., Ltd., Las Vegas, 2002—. Mem.: Nat. Assn. Realtors. Office: Realty Success Sys Ltd # 100 8064 W Sahara Las Vegas NV 89117 Office Phone: 702-968-6400.

**SHERRY, PAUL HENRY,** minister, religious organization administrator; b. Tamaqua, Pa., Dec. 25, 1933; s. Paul Edward and Mary Elizabeth (Stein) Sherry; m. Mary Louise Thornburg, June 4, 1957; children: Mary Elizabeth, Paul David. BA, Franklin and Marshall Coll., 1955; ThM, Union Theol. Sem., N.Y.C., 1958, PhD, 1969; D (hon.), Ursinus Coll., 1981, Elmhurst Coll., 1990, Defiance Coll., 1991, Lakeland Coll., Sheboygan, Wis., 1991, Re-formed Theological Acad., Debrecen, Hungary, 1994, United Theol. Sem. Twin Cities, 1995, Eden Theol. Sem., St. Louis, 2000, Chgo. Theol. Sem., 2000. Ordained to ministry United Ch. Christ, 1958. Pastor St. Matthew United Ch. of Christ, Kenhorst, Pa., 1958—61, Community United Ch. of Christ, Hasbrouck Heights, NJ, 1961—65; mem. staff United Ch. Bd. Homeland Ministry, N.Y.C., 1965—82; exec. dir. Community Renewal Soc., Chgo., 1983—89; pres. United Ch. of Christ, Cleve., 1989—99, pub. policy cons., 2000—02. Mem. gen. bd. Nat. Coun. Chs., N.Y.C., 1989—99, coord. anti-poverty program; cons. Ctr. for Cmty. Change, 2001—; mem. ctrl. com. World Coun. Chs., 1990—99; del. 8th Assembly, Harare, Zimbabwe, 1998, 7th Assembly, Canberra, Australia, 1991. Editor: The Riverside Preachers, Jour. Current Social Issues, 1968—80; contbr. articles to religious jours.; host (weekly programs local sta.), 1974—78, 1984—85, 1993—97. Bd. dirs. Nat. Interfaith Com. Worker Justice, 2000—; coord. anti-poverty program Nat. Coun. Chs., 2002—. Democrat. Mem. United Ch. Of Christ. Avocations: reading, hiking, cultural events. Home: 12700 Lake Ave # 1612 Lakewood OH 44107 Office: United Ch of Christ 700 Prospect Ave Cleveland OH 44115 Office Phone: 216-736-3710. E-mail: psher973@aol.com.

**SHERTZER, BRUCE ELDON,** education educator; b. Bloomfield, Ind., Jan. 11, 1928; s. Edwin Franklin and Lois Belle S.; m. Carol Mae Rice, Nov. 24, 1948; children: Sarah Ann, Mark Eldon. BS, Ind. U., 1952, MS, 1953, EdD, 1958. Tchr., counselor Martinsville (Ind.) High Sch., 1952-56; dir. div. guidance Ind. Dept. Pub. Instrn., 1956-58; assoc. dir. project guidance of superior students North Central Assn. Coll. and Secondary Sch., 1958-60; asst. prof. Purdue U., 1960—, assoc. prof., 1962-65, prof., 1965-95, head dept. ednl. studies, 1989-95, prof. emeritus of counseling, 1995—. Vis. prof. ednl. psychology U. Hawaii, 1967; Fulbright sr. lectr., Reading, Eng., 1967-68; vis. prof. U. So. Calif. Overseas Grad. Program, 1975, 82; chmn. Nat. Adv. Council for Career Edn., 1976 Author: Career Exploration and Planning 1973, 2d edit., 1976, Fundamentals of Counseling, 3d edit., 1980, Fundamentals of Guidance, 4th edit., 1981, Individual Appraisal, 1979, Career Planning, 3d edit., 1985, also articles. Chmn. bd. trustees Found. Am. Assn. of Counseling and Devel., 1986-87. With AUS, 1946-47. Mem. Am. Counseling Assn. (pres. 1973-74, Disting. Profl. Svc. award 1986). Home: 1620 Western Dr West Lafayette IN 47906-2236 Office: Beering Hall Purdue University West Lafayette IN 47907

**SHERVA, DENNIS G.,** retired investment company executive; b. Mpls., Dec. 3, 1942; s. Garfield Theodore and Dorothy Genevive (Oberlander) S.; m. Cathleen Marybeth Tischer, Oct. 15, 1965 (dec. July 31, 2004). BA, U. Minn., 1964; MA, Wayne State U., 1965. Chartered fin. analyst. Fin. analyst 1st Nat. Bank, Mpls., 1965-67; fin. analyst Honeywell, Inc., Mpls., 1967; v.p. Smith, Barney & Co., N.Y.C., 1967-71, Baker, Weeks & Co., N.Y.C., 1971-77; mng. dir. Morgan Stanley & Co., Inc., N.Y.C., 1977—2000. Bd. dirs. Morgan Stanley Ventures, San Francisco, Morgan Stanley Venture Capital, N.Y.C., Morgan Stanley Asset Mgmt. Inc., N.Y.C. Recipient All-Am. Research Team 1st place award Instl. Investor Mag., 1979, 81, 83, 84, 85, 87 Mem.: Nat. Assn. Securities Dealers (instl. com. 1985—90), PGA West Club, Torrington Country Club. Home: 42 Old South Rd PO Box 30 Litchfield CT 06759-0030 Home (Winter): 80715 Weiskopf Way La Quinta CA 92253

**SHERWIN, JAMES TERRY,** lawyer; b. NYC, Oct. 25, 1933; s. Oscar and Stella (Zins) S.; m. Judith Johnson, June 21, 1955 (div. Apr. 1984); children—Miranda, Alison, Galen; m. Hiroko Inouye, June 15, 1985. BA, Columbia U., 1953, LLB (Stone scholar), 1956. Bar: N.Y. 1956, U.S. Supreme Ct. 1963. Assoc. Kaye, Scholer, Fierman, Hays & Handler, N.Y.C., 1957-60; with GAF Corp., N.Y.C., 1960-83, 84-90, assoc. counsel, gen. mgr. European ops., 1969-71, group v.p. photography, 1971-74, exec. v.p. fin. and adminstrn., legal and investment svcs., 1974-83, vice chmn., chief adminstrv. officer Wayne, NJ, 1984-90; exec. v.p., CFO Triangle Industries, Inc., 1983-84; v.p., CFO Hunter-Douglas N.V., 1991-99, bd. dirs., 1999—. Bd. dirs. Internat. Rescue Com., chmn. exec. com., exec. v.p. to 1990; mem. coun. U. Bath, 2001—. Lt. comdr. USCGR, 1956-57. U.S. intercollegiate chess champion, 1951-53, N.Y. State champion, 1951, U.S. speed champion, 1956-57, 59-60, internat. master., 2001. Am. Chess Found. (pres., bd. dirs. to 1990), Marshall (NY) Chess Club (pres. 1967-69, gov. to 1990), Phi Beta Kappa. Home: The Chase Winsley Nr Bradford-on-Avon Wiltshire BA15 2LX England Office Phone: 44 1225 722113. Personal E-mail: jamestsherwin@btconnect.com.

**SHERWIN, MARTIN J.,** history professor; married. AB, Dartmouth Coll., 1959; PhD, UCLA, 1971. Walter S. Dickson prof. English and Am. History Tufts Univ. Founding dir. Nuclear Age History and Humanities Ctr., Tufts Univ. Author: A World Destroyed: Hiroshima and Its Legacies, 2003 (Stuart L. Bernath prize, Am. History Book prize); co-author (with Kai Bird): American Prometheus: The Triumph and Tragedy of J. Robert Oppenheimer, 2005 (Nat. Book Critics Cir. award for biography, 2005, Pulitzer Prize for biography, 2006); adv. (documentaries) The Day After Trinity, A History of Nuclear Strategy, War and Peace in the Nuclear Age, PBS, gen. editor Stanford Nuclear Age Series. Office: History Dept Tufts Univ Medford MA 02155 Office Phone: 617-627-5583. Business E-Mail: martin.sherwin@tufts.edu.*

**SHERWIN, STEPHEN A.,** health products executive; BA in Biology, Yale U.; MD, Harvard U. Diplomate Am. Bd. Medicine, Am. Bd. Med. Oncology. Former mem. staff Nat. Cancer Inst.; with Genentech, Inc., 1983—90; CEO, bd. dirs. Cell Genesys, Inc., Foster City, Calif., 1990—, pres., 1990—2001, chmn. bd. dirs., 1994—. Chmn. bd. dirs. Ceregene, Inc.; bd. dirs. Abgenix, Inc., Neurocrine Bioscis., Inc., Rigel Pharms, Inc., Calyx Therapeutics.

**SHERWOOD, ALLEN JOSEPH,** retired lawyer; b. Salt Lake City, Sept. 26, 1909; s. Charles Samuel and Sarah (Abramson) Shapiro; m. Edith Ziff, Jan. 19, 1941; children— Mary (Mrs. John Marshall), Arthur Lawrence Student, UCLA, 1927-30; AB, LLB, U. So. Calif., 1933. Bar: Calif. 1933, U.S. Supreme Ct. 1944. Pvt. practice law, L.A., 1933-54, Beverly Hills, 1954-95; ret. Legal counsel Internat. Family Planning Rsch. Assn., Inc., 1970-76; bd. dirs. Family Planning Ctrs. Greater L.A., Inc., 1968-84, pres., 1973-76 Mem. editorial bd. So. Calif. Law Rev., 1932-33. Contbr. articles to profl. jours. Mem. Calif. Atty. Gen.'s Vol. Adv. Coun. and its legis. subcom., 1972-78 Mem. Med.-Legal Soc. So. Calif. (bd. dirs. 1966-74), ABA, L.A. County Bar Assn., Beverly Hills Bar Assn., State Bar of Calif., Am. Arbitration Assn. (nat. panel arbitrators 1965—), Order of Coif, Tau Delta Phi, Brentwood Country Club (L.A.), Masons. Home: 575 Moreno Ave Los Angeles CA 90049-4840

**SHERWOOD, ARTHUR LAWRENCE,** lawyer; b. LA, Jan. 25, 1943; s. Allen Joseph and Edith S. Sherwood; m. Frances Merele, May 1, 1970; children: David, Chet. BA magna cum laude, U. Calif., Berkeley, 1964; MS, U. Chgo., 1965; JD cum laude, Harvard U., 1968. Bar: Calif. 1969, U.S. Dist. Ct. (cen. dist.) Calif. 1968, U.S. Dist. Ct. (no. dist.) Calif. 1971, Calif. 1971, U.S. Dist. Ct. (so. and ea. dists.) Calif. 1973, U.S. Ct. Appeals (9th cir.) 1973,

U.S. Ct. Appeals (D.C. cir.) 1991, U.S. Supreme Ct. 1980. Instr. UCLA Law Sch., 1968—69; assoc. Gibson, Dunn & Crutcher, L.A., 1968—75, ptnr., 1975—98, of counsel, 1998—. Judge pro tem L.A. Mcpl. and Superior Ct., 1980—98; instr. law UCLA, 1968—82; arbitrator N.Y. Stock Exch., Nat. Futures Assn. Co-author: Civil Procedure During Trial, 1995, Civil Procedure Before Trial. 1990; contbr. articles to profl. jours. Chmn. East Asian Art Coun., L.A. County Mus. Art, 1992—97, 2005—06. NASA fellow, U. Chgo., 1964—65. Mem.: Calif. Bar Assn., Phi Beta Kappa. Republican. Avocations: art, history. Office: 11828 Huntington Ridge Ct Potomac MD 20854

**SHERWOOD, DONALD LEWIS,** congressman; b. Nicholson, Pa., Mar. 5, 1941; s. Walter A. and Doris (Williams) Sherwood; m. Carol Evans, 1973; children: Jesse, Dana, Maria. BA in Econs., Dartmouth Coll., Hanover, NH, 1963. Founder, pres. Sherwood Chevrolet, Tunkhannock, Pa., 1967—; mem. US Congress from 10th Pa. dist., 1999—, mem. appropriations com., vice chmn. fgn. ops. subcommittee, 2005—. Ptnr. Sun Auto Grp., Clarks Summit, Sun Buick/Pontiac/GMC, Moosic. Appointed to Tunkhannock Area Sch. Bd., 1975-98, pres., 1992-98; pres. Wyo. County Indsl. Found., Wyo. County United Fund; bd. dirs. Triton Hose Fire Co. Fireman's Relief Assn., Wyo. County C. of C. With U.S. Army, 1963—66. Mem. Pa. Chevrolet Dealers Area Mktg. Grp. (dir.), Pa. Hardwood Lumber Mfrs. Assn., Pa. Farmers Assn.; v.p. N.E. Pa. Chevrolet Dealers Assn. Republican. Avocation: raises and shows belgian horses. Office: US Ho Reps 1131 Longworth Ho Office Bldg Washington DC 20515 Office Phone: 202-225-3731.*

**SHERWOOD, GLORIA N.,** graphics designer, genealogist, small business owner; b. Winfield, Kans. d. Edwin E. Schroeder and Anna Y. McCluer; stepmother Vivian J. Schroeder; children: Christina Knueven, J.E. Jurey, Jeannette Thornhill. B CMT cert., foster parent cert. Pvt. home health care nurse, Eufaula, Okla., 1996—2006; ret.; bus. owner Angelic Prints, Inc. Author: The Poetic Works of Gloria Sherwood Book 1 vol. 1, 2000, Poetic Work Book 1, vol. 2, 2002, Just Be 2000, Remember Me, 1999, Spiritual Wings, 2001, Awaited Healing, 2001; visual artist: New Trails, 1998, Deep Is the Soul, 2000, Out of Bondage, 2001. Recipient Award of Excellence in Christian Web sites Joyful Mom's Web site. Mem. NAFE, Nat. Home Gardening Club, Nat. Arbor Day Found., Angelwing Sisters, Nat. Audubon Soc., Nat. Wildlife Fedn., World Wildlife Fedn., Enfaula Arts Coun. Democrat. Avocations: performing arts, gardening, playing guitar, writing music, crafts.

**SHERWOOD, JACK ROBERT,** quality engineer, logistics consultant; b. LA, Mar. 29, 1931; s. William Jay and Evelyn Virginia (Easton) S.; m. Mary Jeannette Nicoloff, Dec. 27, 1957 (dec. Aug. 15, 1995); children: Lesley, John, Jeffrey, Whitney, Robin. Grad., Air Command and Staff Coll., USAF, 1975; BS in Indsl. Engrng., Pacific Western U., Santa Monica, Calif., 1978; Master's in Internat. Rels., Indsl. Coll. Armed Forces, 1982; PhD in Logistic Mgmt., Pacific Western U., Santa Monica, Calif., 1983. Cert. exec. logistics mgmt. US Army, advanced profl. designation in logistics mgmt. USAF. Asst. tech. mgr. logistic Naval Weapons Ctr., China Lake, Calif., 1976-78; cons./advisor Naval Civil Engring. Lab., Port Hueneme, Calif., 1978-79; asst. project mgr. logistics (exec. ILS mgr.) undersea surveillance project NA-VELEXSYSCOM, Washington, 1979—83; sr. ILS mgr. U.S. Space Command/NORAD/ADC, Colorado Springs, Colo., 1983-84; dep. dir. logis-tics Nat. Tng. Ctr., Ft. Irwin, Calif., 1985-86; supr. indsl. engring. Marine Corps Depot-West, Barstow, Calif., 1986-87; sr. logistics engr. McDonnell Douglas Astronautics, Huntington, Calif., 1987-89; quality engr. EG&G/REECo, Las Vegas, Nev., 1990-91. Exec. officer U.S. Naval Sea Cadet Corps, China Lake, 1977-78, tng. officer, Ventura, Calif., 1978-79; mem. San Diego Sch. Adv. Bd., 1976. Author: Project Management/Logistic Support, 1978-79, Material Review and Corrective Action Systems (Presdl. Mgmt. Improvement award & citation, USAF Mgmt. Improvement award). Mem. Rep. Presidential Task Force, 1982-; permanent mem. Nat. Rep. Senate Com., 1985—. Mem.: Elks (trustee Winter Haven chpt. 2001—02), Moose, Am. Legion (life). Address: 4179 Wales St 15 Kissimmee FL 34746 E-mail: robinhoodresearch@yahoo.com.

**SHERWOOD, JAMES WEBSTER, III,** writer; b. Hollywood, Calif., May 18, 1936; s. James Webster Sherwood Jr. and Versa Graybeal Hughes; m. Valdi Hiesinger, Apr. 17, 1964 (div. 1972); m. Marylou Coddington Lemke, July 4, 1972 (div. 1989); m. Karyn Virginia Lindig, Mar. 18, 1990; children: Veronica E.C. Sherwood, Alexandra C.E. Sherwood Patterson, Roxanna Z.S.R., Christopher Michael De Santis, James Webster IV, George Marshall De Santis. Student, Choate Sch., U. Chgo., 1954—55; BL, U. Paris, 1963. Reporter, columnist San Mateo (Calif.) Times, Burlingame Advance, 1951-52; mng. editor Chgo. Rev. Mag., 1954-55; prodr. Myers-Sherwood Pictures, Inc., Chgo., 1955; editor Trans World Pictures, Inc., Chgo., 1955; editor, columnist Westchester News-Advertiser, LA, 1956-57; prodn. asst. Cecil B. DeMille-Paramount Pictures, Hollywood, 1957-59; v.p., gen. mgr. Smith Limousine, NYC, 1977-85; pres., owner Sherwood Justice & Barton Limou-sine Corp., NYC, 1985—2005; dir. Hamilton Mfg. Corp., Holland, Ohio. Prodr., dir. Sherwood Films, Hollywood, 1958-60; cons. on Tom Jones, 1961; adaptor The Sicilian Clan, 1966; producer After Laughter, 1968, others; founder, pub. Opus Books. Author: Dining on Thorns, 1996, Some Sonnets of Flame & Flower, 1998; syndicated columnist 11 western states for Christian Sci. Monitor, Hungry Horse (Mont.) News, Hellenic Rev., 1956-58; editor Popular Libr., 1970-72; biographic researcher Holt, Rinehart & Winston, 1970-72; journalist Ladies Home Jour., Village Voice, N.Y., 1972-73; author: (verse play) The Wooed Wife, 1957; author: 101 Sonnets of Sex, God, The Circus and Love, 2d edit., 1959, (novels) Stradella, 1961, Shakespeare's Ghost, 2001, Sun of Another Sky, 2003. Pres. Shakespeare Oxford Soc. Recipient Nat. Book award for best translation preface to (with Ralph Manheim) Castle to Castle, 1970, John Dos Passos award for Creative Writing, 1987. Republican. Episcopalian. Avocation: walking. Home and Office: Grand Central Five Central Dr Plandome NY 11030-1408 Office Phone: 516-365-8890. E-mail: jazsherwood@aol.com.

**SHERWOOD, KEHELA (KAREN KEHELA SHERWOOD),** broadcast executive; Grad., UCLA. Asst. prodr. to Brian Grazer Imagine Entertainment, 1986—87, story editor, 1987, dir. devel., v.p., sr. v.p., pres. prodn., co-chair Imagine Films, 1997—. Mailing: Imagine Entertainment 7th Floor 9465 Wilshire Blvd Beverly Hills CA 90212*

**SHERWOOD, LOUIS MAIER,** endocrinologist, pharmaceutical executive; b. N.Y.C., Mar. 1, 1937; s. Arthur Joseph and Blanche (Burger) S.; m. Judith Brimberg, Mar. 27, 1966; children: Jennifer Beth, Arieh David. AB with honors, Johns Hopkins U., 1957; MD with honors, Columbia U., 1961. Diplomate Am. Bd. Internal Medicine, Subsplty. Bd. in Endocrinology and Metabolism. Intern Presbyn. Hosp., N.Y.C., 1961-62, asst. resident in medicine, 1962-63; clin. assoc. research fellow Nat. Heart Inst., NIH, Bethesda, Md., 1963-66; NIH trainee endocrinology and metabolism Coll. Physicians and Surgeons, Columbia U., N.Y.C., 1966-68; assoc. medicine Beth Israel Hosp. and Harvard Med. Sch., Boston, 1968-69; chief endocri-nology Beth Israel Hosp., 1968-72; asst. prof. medicine Harvard U., 1969-71, assoc. prof., 1971-72; physician-in-chief, chmn. dept. medicine Michael Reese Hosp. and Med. Ctr., Chgo., 1972-80; prof. medicine, div. biol. scis. Pritzker Sch. Medicine, U. Chgo., 1972-80; Ted and Florence Baumritter prof. medicine and biochemistry Albert Einstein Coll. Medicine, 1980-88, vis. prof. medicine, 1989—, chmn. dept. medicine, 1980-87; physician-in-chief Montefiore Hosp. and Med. Ctr., N.Y.C., 1980-87; adj. prof. medicine U. Pa., 1993—. Sr. v.p. med. and sci. affairs Merck, Sharp & Dohme Internat., 1987-89; exec. v.p. worldwide devel. Merck, Sharp & Dohme Rsch. Labs., 1989-92, sr. v.p. U.S. Med. and Sci. Affairs Merck Human Health, 1992-2002; pres. MEDSA, LLC, 2002—; Josiah Macy Jr. Found. fellow and vis. scientist Weizmann Inst., Israel, 1978-79; assoc. mem. subcom. endocrinology and metabolism Am. Bd. Internal Medicine, 1977-83; med. adv. bd. HPR, 1996-99; pres., chief med. officer Bone Measurement Inst., 1996-2002; mem. nat. rsch. adv. com. Dept. Vets. Affairs, 2000—, clin. rsch. roundtable Inst. Medicine, 2000-04. Editor: Beth Israel seminars New Eng. Jour. Medicine, 1968-71; mem. editorial bd. Endocrinology, 1969-73; assoc. editor Metabo-lism, 1970-85, Gen. Medicine B Study Sect., NIH, 1975-79; mem. editorial bd. Yr. in Endocrinology, 1976-86, Calcified Tissue Internat., 1978-80,

Internal Medicine Alert, 1979-89; contbr. numerous articles on endocrinology, protein hormones, calcium metabolism and ectopic proteins to jours. Trustee Michael Reese Med. Ctr., 1974-77; vis. council CUNY Med. Sch., 1986-95; alumni council Columbia Coll. Physicians and Surgeons, 1986—; bd. dirs. Jewish Fedn. Phila., 1997—, Alliance on Aging Rsch., 1997-2002. Served as surgeon USPHS, 1963-66. Recipient Joseph Mather Smith prize for outstanding alumni rsch. Coll. Physicians and Surgeons, Columbia U., 1972, Sr. Class Tchg. award U. Chgo., 1976, 77, Spl. Achievement award Alumni Assn. Profs. Medicine, 2002; grantee USPHS, 1968-88. Master: ACP (Outstanding Contbn. to Internal Medicine award 1987); mem.: AAAS, Acad. Pharm. Physicians and Investigators, Chgo. Soc. Internal Medicine, Assn. Program Dirs. Internal Medicine (coun. 1979—85, pres. 1983—84), Ctrl. Soc. Clin. Rsch., Mass. Med. Soc., Am. Soc. Hypertension (bd. dirs. 1992—97), N.Y. Acad. Medicine (bd. dirs. 1991—95), Am. Acad. Pharm. Physicians (trustee 2000—02, v.p. strategic alliances and planning 2000—03, sec. 2003—04, pres., chmn. bd. 2005—06, Lifetime Achievement award in Pharm. Medicine 2001), Am. Physicians Fellowship for Medicine in Israel (pres. 1993—97, Disting. Med. Svc. award 1998), Endocrine Soc. (bd. dirs. Hormone Found. 2002—05), Assn. Am. Physicians, Am. Soc. Clin. Investigation (pres. 1982—83), Am. Soc. Biol. Chemists, Am. Inst. Chemists, Am. Fedn. Clin. Rsch. (bd. dirs. Found. 1989—92, Spl. Recognition award 1992), Interurban Clin. Club, Alpha Omega Alpha, Phi Beta Kappa. Achievements include research in protein and polypeptide hormones: structure, function and regulation of secretion; molecular studies of hormone biosynthesis; clinical pharmacology, new drug development, outcomes research and disease; quality of care. Office: MEDSA 7598 Playa Rienta Way Delray Beach FL 33446 Office Phone: 561-865-4495. Personal E-mail: sherwool@earthlink.net. Business E-mail: lou@medsa.org. *To be a highly successful leader, you must be willing to surround yourself with outstanding individuals, give them your full support and enjoy their growth and accomplishments.*

**SHERWOOD, MIDGE,** author; b. Ironton, Ohio; d. Roy and Addie (Brace) Winters; m. Jack E. Sherwood, Jan. 19, 1946; children: Margaret Sherwood Simms, Melanie Sherwood. BJ, U. Mo., 1938. Women's editor Ironton Daily Tribune, 1933-38; city editor Ironton Daily News, 1938-40; asst. mgr. West coast news bur. TWA, Los Angeles, 1940-42; pub. relations dir. Western Air Lines, 1942-45; aviation columnist, corr. Skyways, So. Flight, 1945-48; owner, operator Midge Winters Agy., 1945-48; assoc. editor Matrix Mag., Women in Communications, 1950-55; book reviewer LA Times, 1963, Western Hist. Quarterly; free-lance writer, 1958—; columnist Pasadena Star-News, Calif., 1987; lectr. on Gen. George Smith Patton and pioneers of Western frontier. Author: And How it Grew, 1965; San Marino Ranch to City, 1977; Days of Vintage, Years of Vision, Vol. 1, 1982, Vol. II, 1987, Fremont: Eagle of the West, 2002, Days of Vintage, Years of Vision, vol. III, 2006, Western Journal Collection (1900-1995), Western Journal Collection (1995-2000); author (plays): Peace at Last; editor Western Jour.; contbr. columns newspapers. Chmn. Hertrich Meml., 1967; Paul Harris fellow Rotary; recipient Commendation award Gov. Pete Wilson, Calif., 1996. Mem. Soc. Fellows of Huntington Library, 1967; founder, archivist San Marino Hist. Soc. Recipient double award Conf. Calif. Hist. Socs., 1987; named Outstanding Citizen of San Marino, 1988. chmn. Annual Fremont's Day, 2005. Mem. Huntington Westerners (founder), Live Poet's Soc. Huntington Libr. (founder), Westerners Internat. (bd. dirs.), Phi Mu. Home: PO Box 80241 San Marino CA 91118

**SHERWOOD, ROBERT PETERSEN,** retired social sciences educator; b. Black Diamond, Wash., May 17, 1932; s. James Brazier and Zina (Petersen) S.; m. Merlene Burningham, Nov. 21, 1951; children: Robert Lawrence, Richard William, Rolene, RaNae. BS, U. Utah, 1956, MS, 1957; EdD, U. Calif., Berkeley, 1966. Tchr. Arden-Carmichael Sch. Dist., Carmichael, Calif., 1957-59, vice prin. jr. high, 1960-61, prin. jr. high, 1962-65; v.p., prin. San Juan Unified Sch. Dist., Sacramento, 1966-70; assoc. prof. Calif. State U., Sacramento, 1966-71; dir. outreach progs. Am. River Coll., Sacramento, 1971-73, acting assoc. dean of instrn., 1973-74, prof. sociology, 1970-92, chmn. sociology/anthropology dept., 1980-86; ret., 1992. Pres. acad. senate Am. River Coll., 1990-91. With USN, 1953-55. Recipient Merit Recognition award, Boy Scouts Am., 1989. Mem. NEA, Calif. Tchrs. Assn., Faculty Assn. Calif. Community Colls., Western Assn. Schs. and Colls., Calif. Fedn. Coll. Profs., Phi Delta Kappa (life). Mem. Lds Ch. Avocations: reading, writing, woodworking, travel. Home: 4053 Esperanza Dr Sacramento CA 95864-3069

**SHERWOOD, ROD(ERICK), III,** computer company executive; BA with hons. in Econs., Stanford U.; MBA, Harvard U. With Chrysler Corp., 1981—95; from corp. v.p., treas. to pres. Spaceway Broadband Svcs. Hughes Electronics, 1995—98, pres. Spaceway Broadband Svcs., 1998—99; sr. v.p., CFO BroadStream Corp., 1999—2000, Loudcloud Inc. 2000—02, Gateway Inc., Poway, Calif., 2002—03, exec. v.p., CFO, 2003—. Office: Gateway Inc 7565 Irvine Ctr Dr Irvine CA 92618-2930

**SHERZER, HARVEY GERALD,** lawyer; b. Phila., May 19, 1944; s. Leon and Rose (Levin) S.; m. Susan Bell, Mar. 28, 1971; children: Sheri Ann, David Lloyd. BA, Temple U., 1965; JD with honors, George Washington U., 1968. Bar: DC 1970, U.S. Ct. Appeals (DC cir.) 1970, U.S. Ct. Fed. Claims 1970, U.S. Ct. Appeals (fed. cir.) 1970, U.S. Supreme Ct. 1974. Law clk. to trial judges U.S. Ct. Fed. Claims, Washington, 1968-69; law clk. to chief judge U.S. Ct. Appeals for Fed. Cir., Washington, 1969-70; assoc. Sellers, Conner & Cuneo, Washington, 1970-75, ptnr., 1975-80; McKenna, Conner & Cuneo, Washington, 1980-82, Pettit & Martin, Washington, 1982-85, Howrey & Simon, Washington, 1985-2000, Howrey Simon Arnold & White, Washington, 2000—01, Greenberg Traurig, McLean, Va., 2001—03, Dickstein Shapiro LLP, Washington, 2003—. Adv. bd. The Govt. Contractor, 1996-99. Author: (with others) A Complete Guide to the Department of Defense Voluntary Disclosure Program 1996; contbr. articles to profl. jours. Office: Dickstein Shapiro 1825 Eye St NW Washington DC 20006 Office Phone: 202-775-4745. Business E-mail: sherzerh@dicksteinsharpiro.com.

**SHESKEY, SUSAN E.,** computer company executive; b. Oct. 13, 1947; Grad., Miami U., Oxford, Ohio. With Ameritech, Ohio Bell, Dell, Inc., Round Rock, Tex., 1993—, v.p. for global sales, svcs., mfg. and fulfillment IT, interim chief info. officer, 2005, v.p., chief info. officer, 2005—. Office: Dell Inc One Dell Way Round Rock TX 78682*

**SHESTACK, ALAN,** museum administrator; b. NYC, June 23, 1938; s. David and Sylvia P. (Saffran) S.; m. Nancy Jane Davidson, Sept. 24, 1967. BA, Wesleyan U., 1961, DFA (hon.), 1978; MA, Harvard U., 1963. Mus. curator graphic art Nat. Gallery Art, Washington, 1965-67; assoc. curator prints and drawings Yale Art Gallery, New Haven, 1967-68, curator prints and drawings, 1968-71, dir., 1971-85; adj. history of art Yale U., 1971-85; dir. Mpls. Inst. Art, 1985-87, Boston Mus. Fine Arts, 1987-93; dep. dir. Nat. Gallery of Art, Washington, 1993—. Mem. adv. com. Art Mus., Princeton, 1972-75; mem. vis. com. Harvard U. Art Mus., 1990-95, Davis Mus. Wellesley Coll., 1997—; mem. mus. panel Nat. Endowment for the Arts, 1974-77; mem. com. prints and illustrated books Mus. Modern Art, N.Y., 1972—; mem. Fed. Arts and Artifacts Indemnification Panel, 1979-83. Author: Fifteenth Century Engravings of Northern Europe, 1967, The Engravings of Martin Schongauer, 1968, Master LCZ and Master WB, 1971, Exhibitions Organized and Catalogued: Master E.S., 1967, The Danube School, 1969, Hans Baldung Grien, Prints and Drawings, 1981, (exhbn. catalog) Art for the Nation, 2000; contbr. articles to profl. jours. Woodrow Wilson fellow Harvard U., 1963, David E. Finley fellow, 1963-65. Mem. Print Coun. Am. (bd. dirs., v.p. 1970-71), Coll. Art Assn. (bd. dirs. 1972-76), Am. Assn. Mus., Am Fedn Arts (trustee 1981-94), Alpha Delta Phi, Phi Beta Kappa. Office: Nat Gallery Art 2000-B S Club Dr Hyattsville MD 20785 Office Phone: 202-842-6012. Business E-mail: A_Shestack@nga.gov.

**SHESTACK, JEROME JOSEPH,** lawyer; b. Atlantic City, Feb. 11, 1925; s. Isidore and Olga (Shankman) Shestack; m. Marciarose Schleifer, Jan. 28, 1951; children: Jonathan Michael, Jennifer. AB, U. Pa., 1944; LLB, Harvard U., 1949; LLD (hon.), Dickinson Coll. Law, 1997, Stetson Sch. of Law, 1998,

Whittier Coll. Law, 1998. Bar: Ill. 1950, Pa. 1952. Tchg. fellow Northwestern U. Law Sch., Chgo., 1949—50; asst. prof. law, faculty editor La. State Law Sch., Baton Rouge, 1950—52; dep. city solicitor City of Phila., 1952, 1st dep. solicitor, 1952—55; ptnr. Schnader, Harrison, Segal & Lewis, Phila. and Washington, 1956—91, Wolf, Block, Schorr & Solis-Cohen, Phila., 1991—. Adj. prof. law U. Pa., 1956; U.S. amb. to UN Human Rights Commn., 1979—80; U.S. del. to ECOSOC, UN, 1980; sr. U.S. del. to Helsinki Accords Conf., 1979—80; mem. U.S. Commn. on Improving Effectiveness of UN, 1989—; chmn. Internat. League Human Rights, 1973—94, hon. chmn., 1994—; U.S. del. to CSCE Conf., Moscow, 1991; founder, chmn. Lawyers Com. Internat. Human Rights, 1978—80, Jacob Blaustein Inst. Human Rights, 1988—92; mem. nat. adv. com. legal svcs. OEO, 1965—72; bd. dirs., exec. com. Lawyers Com. Civil Rights; mem. coun. Holocaust Mus., 1999—2004, exec. com., chair com. on conscience. Editor (with others): (monographs) Rights of Americans, 1971, Human Rights, 1979, International Human Rights, 1985, Bill of Rights: A Bicentennial View, 1991, Understanding Human Rights, 1992, Thomas Jefferson: Lawyer, 1993, Francis Scott Key, 1994, Abraham Lincoln, Circuit Lawyer, 1994, The Holocaust, 1997, Moral Foundations of Human Rights, 1997, The Philosophy of Human Rights, 1997, W.B. Yeats, Poet of Passionate Intensity, 1997, Corporate Social Responsibility, 2004. Mem. exec. com. Nat. Legal Aid and Defender Assn., 1970—80; trustee Eleanor and Franklin Roosevelt Inst., 1986—; bd. govs. Tel Aviv U., 1983—, Hebrew U., 1969—; chmn. bd. dirs. Am. Poetry Ctr., 1976—91; trustee Free Libr. Phila., vice chmn., 1989—96; v.p. Am. Jewish Com., 1984—89. With USNR, 1943—46. Recipient ABA medal, 2006; fellow Rubin, Columbia U. Law Sch., 1984, hon., U. Pa. Law Sch., 1980. Mem.: ABA Ctr. for Human Rights (chair 2003—05), ABA (ho. of dels. 1971—73, 1977—, jud. com. 1985—90, bd. govs. 1992—95, exec. com. 1994—95, pres.-elect 1996, pres. 1997—98, pres. ALI-ABA 1997—98), Nat. Conf. Bar Found. (bd. dirs. 1998—, pres. 2004), Internat. Assn. Jewish Lawyers and Jurists (Am. Soc. pres. 2000—02), Am. Acad. Appellate Lawyers, Am. Coll. Trial Lawyers, Am. Arbitration Assn. (bd. dirs. 1999—2003, highest medal 2005), Am. Law Inst., Am. Soc. Internat. Law (exec. com. 1993—, internat. com. jurists exec. com. 1998—2001, commr. 1999—), Internat. Acad. Trial Lawyers, Internat. Bar Assn. (chmn. com. on human rights 1990—94, chmn com. profl. ethics 2000—04), Order of Coif. Home: Parkway House 2201 Pennsylvania Ave Philadelphia PA 19130-3513 Office: Wolf Block Schorr & Solis-Cohen 1650 Arch St Fl 25 Philadelphia PA 19103-2029 Office Phone: 215-977-2290. Business E-mail: jshestack@wolfblock.com.

**SHETLAR, JAMES FRANCIS,** physician; b. Wichita, Dec. 26, 1944; MD, U. Kans., 1970. Resident in family practice Saginaw Cooperative Hosp., 1970-72; staff Covenant Hosp.; asst. clin. prof. Mich. State U. Mem. AMA, Am. Acad. Family Physicians, Mich. Acad. Family Physicians. Office: 163 Churchgrove Rd Frankenmuth MI 48734-1025 Office Phone: 989-652-9969.

**SHETTY, GUNAPALA,** biologist, researcher, educator; m. Shilpa Shetty, June 19, 1997. PhD, U. Mysore, India, 1993. Rsch. assoc. Indian Inst. Sci., Bangalore, Karnataka, India, 1993—96; post doctoral fellow U. Tex. MD Anderson Cancer Ctr., Houston, 1997—2002, instr., 2002—06. Contbr. articles to profl. jours. Recipient Rodney Withers Lecture award, U. Tex. MD Anderson Cancer Ctr., 2002; Sr. Rsch. fellow, Coun. Sci. and Indsl. Rsch., India, 1984—87, Postdoctoral fellow, Lalor Found., Inc., 2000—02, Instl. Rsch. grantee, U. Tex. MD Anderson Cancer Ctr., 2004—05. Mem.: Endocrine Soc., Am. Soc. Andrology, Soc. Study Reproduction. Achievements include the discovery that testosterone, the male hormone, can inhibit the early stage of spermatogenesis in pathological situations. Office: Univ Texas MD Anderson Cancer 1515 Holcombe Blvd Box 66 Houston TX 77030

**SHETTY, KAUP RAJMOHAN,** endocrinologist, educator; came to U.S., 1966; s. Muddanna and Girija M. Shetty; m. Vasanthi R. Shetty; children: Sandeep, Suparna. MB BChir, Mysore Med. Coll., Karnataka, 1965. Diplomate Am. Bd. Internal Medicine, cert. in internal medicine, endocrinology and metabolism, geriatric medicine. Resident in internal medicine VA Med. Ctr., Chgo. and Milw., 1967-70; fellow in endocrinology and metabolism Med. Coll. Wis. and Affiliated Hosps., Milw., 1970-72, attending physician in endocrinology and metabolism, 1972—; attending physician in geriatrics and gerontology VA Med. Coll., Milw., 1991—; assoc. prof. medicine Med. Coll. Wis., Milw., 1991-95, prof. medicine, 1995-2000, prof. medicine emeritus, 2000—. Contbr. articles to profl. jours., chapters to books. Fellow ACP, Royal Coll. Physicians Can., Am. Coll. Endocrinology; mem. Endocrine Soc., Am. Geriatric Soc., N.Y. Acad. Scis. Achievements include research in hormones and aging, post-polio syndrome, metabolic accompaniments of inactivity. Avocation: tennis. Office: VA Med Ctr 5000 W National Ave Milwaukee WI 53295-0001

**SHETTY, KISHORE V.,** dentist, director; DDS, MS, U. London, England, 1995. Lic. Am. Coll. Oral Implantology, 2004, Am. Bd. Spl. Care Dentistry, 2004, Nat. Dental Bd. Anesthesiology, 2005. Cons. oral medicine U. London, 1995—96, U. Tex. Health Sci. Ctr., San Antonio, 1996—98, Ohio State U. Med. Ctr., 1998—99; dir., cons. spl. needs dentistry La. State U. Health Sci. Ctr., 1999—2005; dir. medically complex patient clinic Health Sci. Ctr. U. Tex., Houston, 2004—. Contbr. articles to profl. jours. Bd. dirs. Acad. Dentistry for People with Disabilities, Chgo., 2001—06. Fellow, Acad. Dentistry for People with Disabilities, 2005. Mem.: Acad. Gen. Dentistry (licentiate), Royal Coll. Surgeons (hon.). Achievements include research in oral medicine. Home: 6516 MD Anderson Blvd Ste 475 Houston TX 77030 Home Fax: 713-500-4108.

**SHETTY, MULKI RADHAKRISHNA,** retired oncologist; b. Hiriadka, Karnataka, India, July 10, 1940; arrived in U.S., 1974; s. Sunderram and Kusumavati Shetty. MBBS, Stanley Med. Coll., Madras, 1964; DTM, U. Liverpool, Eng., 1968; LMCC, Med. Coun., Can., 1975. House surgeon and physician Bombay Hosp., 1965-66; sr. house officer Manor Pk. Hosp., Bristol, Eng., 1966-67, Torbay Hosp., 1967-68, St. Lukes Hosp., Huddersfield, 1969-70; sr. resident Gen. Hosp. Meml. U., New Foundland, 1971-72; intern Ottawa Gen. Hosp., 1972-73; fellow in chemotherapy Ont. Cancer Found., Ottawa, Can., 1973-74; fellow in clin. oncology U. Fla., Gainesville, 1974-75; attending oncologist N.W. Community Hosp., Arlington Heights, Ill., 1975-2000; ret., 2000. Cons. N.W. Cmty. Hosp., Arlington Heights, Ill., 1975—2000. Author: (book) Lung Cancer, 1980, Recent Advances in Chemotherapy, 1985, Wildlife Adventures, 1997, Chicago, 1997, Quotes and Notes, 2003, The Itinerant Indian, 2005, Encyclopaedia of Quotable Couplets, 2005; contbr. chapters to books, articles to profl. jours.; coined new word calcifectomy. Recipient Cert. for Oustanding Svc., Am. Cancer Soc., 1982. Hindu. Achievements include Reached the North Pole by icebreaker YA-MAL, Aug. 5, 2001.

**SHETTY, UMESHA,** chemist, researcher; s. Anantha and Thunga Shetty; m. Jyoti U. Shetty, Dec. 24, 1987; 1 child, Impana U. Shetty. PhD, U. of Sask., Can., 1983. Sr. staff fellow NIH, Bethesda, Md., 1989—99, chemist, 2002—. Contbr. scientific papers to profl. jours. (NIH Staff Recognition award, 1998). Recipient Gold medal, Bangalore U., 1973, State award, Karnataka State Govt., 1973, G.P. Nair award, Indian Drug Mfr.'s Assn., 1973, grad. fellowship, U. of Sask., 1979—83. Mem.: AAAS, Am. Chem. Soc. Achievements include discovery of excessive accumulation of myo-inositol in Down syndrome brain.

**SHEU, CHWEN,** finance educator; b. Tainan, Taiwan, Dec. 21, 1956; arrived in U.S., 1983, naturalized, 2001; s. Hsing-ming Sheu and Su-jen Chen; m. Litzang Hsu; children: Scott, Shawn. PhD, Ohio State U., 1990. Prof. Kans. State U., Manhattan, 1990—. Author: (rsch. and tchg. materials) Introduction to Operations Management, 1999, (video course) Theory of Constraints - Introduction, 2000. Recipient Best Paper award, Acad. Mgmt. Ops. Divsn., 2001; fellow, Kans. State U., 1999. Mem.: Decision Scis. Inst. (Instrnl. Innovation award 2001), Alpha Delta (hon.). Office: Kans State U 101 Calvin Hall Manhattan KS 66506 Business E-mail: csheu@ksu.edu.

**SHEVEREV, VALERY A.,** physics professor, consultant; b. Leningrad, Russia, Feb. 20, 1956; arrived in U.S., 1994; s. Alexander Sheverev and Tatyana Shevereva; m. Tatyana Z. Kovtun, Oct. 1, 1990; 1 child, Maria V. Tsabrova. MS in Physics, Leningrad State U., 1979, PhD in Physics (hon.), 1984. Scientist Leningrad State U., Russia, 1985—94; industry prof. industry Poly. U., Bklyn., 1994—. Owner Lenterra Inc. Grantee, NASA, 2004—, NSF, 2006. Mem.: Am. Chem.Soc., Am. Phys. Soc. Achievements include development of novel method for detection and identification of gases. Office: Poly Univ 6 Metrotech Ctr Brooklyn NY 11201 Office Phone: 718-260-3576. Office Fax: 718-260-3139. Business E-Mail: vshevere@poly.edu.

**SHEVITZ, MARK H.,** sales promotion and marketing executive; b. Dioles, France, July 10, 1955; came to U.S., 1956; s. Arthur E. and Marilyn (Sigoloff) S. Student, U. Mo., 1973-75. Rockhurst Coll., 1983-84; MBA, Washington U., St. Louis, 1988. Program dir. KFMZ-FM, Columbia, Mo., 1974-81; mgmt. supr. Bernstein-Rein Advt., Kansas City, Mo., 1981-84; account supr. The Hermann Group, St. Louis, 1984-86; dir. promotions, food svc. products divsns. Seven-Up Co., St. Louis, 1986-87; pres. Landing Assocs., St. Louis 1987-88, SJI, Inc., St. Louis, 1988-98, SJI Fulfillment, Inc., St. Louis, 1991—; CEO SJI Inc., St. Louis. Lectr. Washington U., St. Louis, 1988—, Bowling Green (Ohio) State U., 1977-89, Stephens Coll., Columbia, Mo., 1976-89, U. Mo., Columbia, 1975-81. Contbr. articles to profl. jours. Chpt. chmn. March of Dimes, mid.-Mo., 1978-81; mem. devel. bd. Cardinal Glennon Children's Hosp., St. Louis, 1984-88; event chmn. March of Dimes, St. Louis, 1990. Named Entrepreneur of Yr. St. Louis region, 1993. Mem. Assn. Promotion Mktg. Agys. Worldwide (sec./treas. 1998 2000), Porsche Club Am. (pres. St. Louis region 1986).

**SHEWARD, RICHARD S.,** judge; b. Jackson, Ohio, May 21, 1944; s. D.J. and M.A. (Rapp) S.; children: Carrin E., Alison M. BBA, Ohio U., 1967; JD, Capital U., 1974. Bar: Ohio 1974, U.S. Dist. Ct. (so. dist.) Ohio 1975, U.S. Supreme Ct. 1978. Asst. pros. atty. Franklin County (Ohio), 1974-76; ptnr. Sheward & Weiner, Columbus, Ohio, 1976-87; judge Franklin County Mcpl. Ct., 1987-91, Franklin County Ct. Common Pleas, 1991—, presiding judge, 1993—; instr. real estate law Columbus Tech. Inst., 1977-80. Mem. Upper Arlington (Ohio) Civic Assn.; mem. Franklin County Republican Central Com., 1978-87; bd. dirs. Easter Seal Soc. Columbus, 1990-93. Served with U.S. Army, 1968-71. Decorated Bronze Star, Air medal. Mem. ABA, Ohio Bar Assn., Columbus Bar Assn. (common pleas ct., chmn. criminal law com. 1985-86, 86-87), Franklin County Trial Lawyers Assn. (pres. 1984-85), Am. Arbitration Assn. (labor panel), Franklin County Pros. Atty. Alumni Assn. (chmn. 1979-87), Buckeye Rep. Club (pres. 1981), Touchdown Club, Agonis Club, Charity Newsies, Am. Inns Ct. (pres. Robert Duncan chpt. 1994-95), Masons (32 deg.). Office: Franklin County Common Pleas Ct 369 S High St Fl 9-c Columbus OH 43215-4516 Home: 7540 James River Close New Albany OH 43054-9026 Office Phone: 614-462-3770. E-mail: richard_sheward@fccents.org.

**SHEWMAKE, BRIDGETT LOREE,** project specialist; d. James Warren and Mildred Shewmake. MusB, U. Ala., Tuscaloosa, 1998. Cert. Music Therapist Cert. Bd. for Music Therapists, 1998. Music therapist Riverside Acad. of Music, Cleve., 1998—2000, Brook Mays Music, Ft. Worth, 2000—01; project specialist Ala. So., Thomasville, 2001—. Com. mem. Thomasville (Ala.) High At Risk Planning, 2001—; adv. bd. mem. Wilson Hall Mid. Sch. PAWS, Grove Hill, Ala., 2004—; bd. mem. Leadership Clarke County, Grove Hill, Ala., 2006—. Actor: (plays) Plaza Suite, (musical) You're a Good Man, Charlie Brown. Grad. Ala. CC Leadership Acad., Tuscaloosa, 2004—05, Leadership Clarke County, Grove Hill, Ala., 2005—06. Mem.: Nat. Orientation Dir's. Assn., SAEOPP. Office: Alabama Southern PO Box 2000 Thomasville AL 36784 Office Phone: 334-636-9642. Office Fax: 334-636-1380. Personal E-mail: bridgettmtbc@yahoo.com. Business E-Mail: bshewmake@ascc.edu.

**SHEWMAKER, KENNETH EARL,** history professor; b. LA, June 26, 1936; s. James Virgil and Jeanette M. (Greenberg) Shewmaker; m. Elisabeth L. Spalteholz, June 12, 1960; children: Richard Glenn, Nancy Jeanette. BS, Concordia Tchrs. Coll., 1960; MA, U. Calif., Berkeley, 1961; PhD, Northwestern U., 1966. Instr. Northwestern U., Evanston, Ill., 1965-66; asst. prof. Coll. William and Mary, Williamsburg, Va., 1966-67; from asst. prof. to assoc. prof. Dartmouth Coll., Hanover, NH, 1967-78, prof. history, 1978—2005, acting chair dept. history, 1985-86, chmn. dept. history, 1986-89, prof. emeritus, 2005—. Author: Americans and Chinese Communists, 1927-45: A Persuading Encounter, 1971 (Stuart L. Bernath prize, 1972); editor: Papers of Daniel Webster, Diplomatic Papers, Vol. 1, 1841-1843, 1983, Vol. 2, 1850-1852, 1987, Daniel Webster, The Completest Man, 1990; contbr. articles to profl. jours. Recipient Disting. Tchg. awards, Dartmouth Coll., 1986, 1996, 2004. Mem.: Soc. Historians Am. Fgn. Rels., Orgn. Am. Historians, N.H. Hist. Soc. Lutheran. Avocations: fly fishing, fly tying. Office: Dept History Dartmouth Coll Hanover NH 03755 Business E-Mail: shewmaker@dartmouth.edu.

**SHI, DAVID E.,** academic administrator, historian; s. Joseph and Evelyn Shi; m. Susan Thomson, June 1974; children: Jason, Jessica. BA magna cum laude, Furman U., 1973; MA, U. Va., 1975, PhD, 1976; HHD (hon.), Ctr. Coll., 2002. From asst. prof. to Frontis W. Johnston prof., chmn. history dept. Davidson (N.C.) Coll., 1976—93; v.p. acad. affairs Furman U., Greenville, SC, 1993—94, pres., 1994—. Bd. dirs. Nat. Commerce Fin. Corp., Memphis. Author: Facing Facts: Realism in American Thought and Culture 1850-1920, 1995, In Search of the Simple Life: American Voices, Past and Present, 1996, The Simple Life: Plain Living and High Thinking in American Culture, 1985 (Editors Choice award), Matthew Josephson, Bourgeois Bohemian, 1981; author: (with George Tindall) America: A Narrative History, 4th edit., 1996; contbr. articles to profl. jours. Bd. dirs. Urban League, Greenville. Capt. USAR. Recipient Presdl. Leadership award, James L. Knight Found., 1998, Presdl. award, John Templeton Found., 1999; fellow, Nat. Humanities Ctr., 1982—83, NEH, 1982—83, 1991—92, Huntington Libr., 1986—87; grantee, NEH, 1980, 1986; Andrew Mellon Faculty fellow, 1978, Travel grant, NEH, 1988. Mem.: Greenville C. of C. (bd. dirs.), Commerce Club (bd. dirs.), Omicron Delta Kappa, Phi Beta Kappa. Home: 1209 Roe Ford Rd Greenville SC 29617 Office: Furman U 3300 Poinsett Hwy Greenville SC 29613 Office Phone: 864-294-2100. Office Fax: 864-294-3939. E-mail: david.shi@furman.edu.

**SHI, JIAQI,** medical educator; MD, Hunan Med. U., China, 1995, PhD, 1999. Rsch. asst. prof. U. Ariz., Tucson, 2003—. Mem.: AACR (Bristol-Myers Squibb Oncology Scholar-in-Tng. award 2003).

**SHI, LIN,** marriage and family therapist, educator; d. Songshan Shi and Shufang Wang; m. Haibo Hu, Oct. 15, 1992. PhD, Tex. Tech U., Lubbock, 1999. Lic. marriage and family therapist U., 2002. Asst. prof. Sch. Family, Consumer, and Nutrition Sci., No. Ill. U., DeKalb, 2001—, program dir., 2005—. Marriage and family therapist Family Ctr., No., Ill. U., 2001—. Contbr. articles to profl. jours. Mem.: Internat. Family Therapy Assn., Am. Assn. Marriage and Family Therapy (cert. supr.). Office: Sch FCNS No Ill Univ 1425 W Lincoln Hwy Dekalb IL 60115 Office Phone: 815-753-6349.

**SHI, LIZHENG,** health economist; s. Risheng Shi and Zeer Li; m. Huahong Qiang, May 0, 1995. BS, Shanghai Med. U., 1987—92; MSc, Peking Union Med. Coll., 1992—94; MA, U. of Southen Calif., 1996—98; PhD, U. of So. Calif., 1995—2001. Rsch. assoc. Chinese Acad. of Med. Sciences, Beijing, 1994—95; rsch. asst. U. of So. Calif., 1995—2000; sr. health outcomes scientist Eli Lilly and Co., Indpls., 2000—. Contbr. articles to profl. jours. Summer fellowship, U. of So. Calif., 1998; U. of So. Calif., Sch. of Pharmacy, 1997, Best Grad. of the Yr., Peking Union Med. Coll., 1994, RongLing fellow, Shanghai Med. U., 1992. Mem.: Internat. Soc. for Pharmacoeconomics and Outcomes Rsch. (assoc.), Drug Info. Assn. (assoc.), Internat. Soc. for Bipolar Disorders (ISBD) (assoc.). Independent. Achievements include research in development of dual-selection method in the evaluation of pharmacy formulary evaluation. Office: Eli Lilly and Company Lilly Corp Ctr DC 6314 Indianapolis IN 46285 E-mail: lshi@lilly.com.

**SHI, QIN,** lawyer, technologist; m. Richard Bone. BSc in Biochemistry, Wuhan U., China, 1989; MSc in Math. and Computer Scis., Loyola U., Chgo., 1997; PhD in Molecular and Cellular Biology, Loyola U., Maywood, Ill., 1997; JD, Georgetown U. Law Ctr., Washington, 2002. Bar: Calif. 2003, D.C. 2004, U.S. Ct. Appeals (9th cir.) Fed. Cir. D.C. Biotech. engr. Wuhan Biotech R&D Ctr., China; bioinformatics specialist Gene Logic, Montgomery County, Md., Foley & Lardner LLP, Washington; informatics sci. advisor Heller Ehrman LLP; attorney Fenwick & West LLP, Mountain View, Calif., Latham & Watkins LLP, Menlo Park, Howrey LLP, Palo Alto. Spkr. ann. meetings intelligent Sys. Molecular Biology, 2000, 01. Contbr. legal and business analysis and scientific papers to profl. jours. and law revs. Mem.: IEEE, AAAS, ABA, Endocrine Soc., Internat. Soc. Computational Biology, Am. Intellectual Property Law Assn. Avocations: hiking, bicycling, running, travel. Office: Howrey LLP 1950 Univ Ave Palo Alto CA 94303 Office Phone: 650-798-3522.

**SHI, STONE D. H.,** research scientist; permanent resident, US; s. Ji-Liang Shi and San-Chun Jiang; m. Cathie D. Xiang, May 5, 1995; children: Constance K. X., Alan K. W. BS, Tsinghua U., Beijing, 1992, MS, 1995; PhD, Fla. State U., Tallahassee, 1999. Prin. scientist GlaxoSmithKline, King of Prussia, Pa., 1999—2003, Pfizer Global R&D, San Diego, 2003—. Recipient First award, Chinese Nat. Chemistry Olympic, 1987, Student award, Soc. Applied Spectroscopy, 1998. Mem.: Am. Soc. Mass Spectrometry. Achievements include first to apply electron capture dissociation to phosphopeptide mapping. Avocation: photography. Personal E-mail: stone.shi@homemail.com.

**SHI, YUN QING,** electrical engineer; b. Chong Qing, Sichuan, China; s. Kong Wai and Wen (Su) S. MS, Shanghai Jiao Tong U., 1980, U. Pitts., 1983, PhD, 1987. Lectr. Shanghai Jiao Tong U., 1980—82; tchg. fellow U. Pitts., 1984—87; asst. prof. N.J. Inst. Tech., Newark, 1987—95, assoc. prof., 1995—2002, prof., 2002—. Reviewer Maths. Rev., 1987—; co-gen. chair IEEE Internat. Workshop on Multimedia Signal Processing, 2002, co-tech chair, 05. Author: Image and Video Compression for Multimedia, 1999; contbr. chpts. to books; contbg. author: CRC Press Comprehensive Dictionary of Electrical Engineering, 1998; guest editor: (spl. issue on image sequence processing) Internat. Jour. Imaging Sys. and Tech., 1998, guest editor spl. issues, 2004, 05; mem. editl. bd. Internat. Jour. Images and Graphics, 1999—, Mutlidimensional Sys. and Signal Processing, 2006—; founding editor-in-chief Springer LNCS Transactions on Data Hiding and Multimedia Security, 2005—. Fellow: IEEE (fellow chair signal processing chpt., No. Jersey sect. 1996—, Circuits & Sys. Soc (CASS) tech. com. visual signal processing & comm. 2001—, CASS tech. com. multimedia systems and application 2001—, CASS disting. lectr. 2002—03, Signal Processing Soc.(SPS) tech. com. multimedia signal processing 2003—, CASS tech. life sci., sys. and apps. 2004—, co-chmn. workshop 2005, assoc. editor various transactions). Achievements include research in robust stability of 1-D and M-D Systems, spectral factorization, M-D interleaving schemes, unified optical flow field theory and algorithms, optical flow determination, video compression and transmission, image processing and pattern recognition, and digital multimedia data hiding, forensics and steganalysis. Business E-Mail: shi@njit.edu.

**SHIAO, SHYANG-YUN PAMELA K.,** nursing educator; d. Fan-Mo Kung and Kuang-Mei Kung-Sun; m. Jeansong Gene Shiao, Dec. 17, 1986; 1 child, Jacqueline Nina. PhD, Case Western Res. U., 1993. RN Bd. of Nursing, Tex., 1999. Regional RN, U. of Ala. Hosp., Birmingham, 1987—88; staff devel. instr. MetroHealth Med. Ctr., Cleve., 1988—90; project dir. Case Western Res. U., Cleve., 1991—93, asst. prof., 1993—98; assoc. prof. Oreg. Health Sci. U., Portland, 1998—99, U. of Tex. HSC, Houston, 1999—. ANCC magnet fellow-appraiser for nursing excellence ANA, Washington, 2006—. Leader: rsch. Meta-analysis of acupressure (Shannon Dir.'s award NIH, 1997), prin. program investigator: rsch. Oxygen Saturation Monitoring in Neonates, Vagal tone and Validation of Oxygen Saturation Monitoring in Neonates, Validation of Oxygen Saturation Measurements in Neonates (Rsch. award Am. Assn. Critical Care Nurses, 1995). Mem. award com. AACN, Calif., 2005—06; rsch. award com. Sigma Theta Tau Internat. Honor Soc. of Nursing, Ind., 2002—06. Fellow: Am. Acad. of Nursing (life). Office Phone: 713-927-7977. Personal E-mail: pshiao@eathlink.net.

**SHIARI, BEHROUZ,** mechanical engineer, researcher; s. Bahman Shiari and Mahvash N. Sharif; m. Flora Gilanpour; 1 child, Aryan. BSc, AmirKabir U. Tech., Tehran, Iran, 1986, MSc, 1988, PhD, 1999. Cert. profl. engr., Ont., Can. Instr. U. Guilan, Rasht, 1988—2000; rsch. assoc. Queen's U., Kingston, Ont., Canada, 2000—02, Carleton U., Ottawa, Ont., Canada, 2002—04, NRC of Can., Ottawa, 2004—. Head mech. engring. dept. Guilan U., Rasht, 1993—95, asst. dean grad. office faculty engring., 1998—2000. Author: Analytical Dynamics of Discrete Systems Vol.1; contbr. articles to profl. jours. Rsch. fellow, NSERC, 2004. Achievements include patents for Pulp Refiner Sensor. Home: 6886 Edgar Brault St Ottawa ON Canada K1C 1L7 Office: Nat Rsch Coun Can 100 Sussex Ottawa ON Canada K1A 0R6 Office Phone: 613 990 0981. Office Fax: 613 947 2838. Personal E-mail: shiari@yahoo.ca. Business E-Mail: behrouz.shiari@nrc-cnrc.gc.ca.

**SHIBASAKI, YOSHIO,** chemistry professor, researcher; b. Gyoda, Japan, Mar. 21, 1934; s. Reiji and Shige (Kobayashi) S.; m. Teiko Shizuka Shibasaki, Apr. 15, 1967; children: Hideaki, Miki. BS, Saitama U., Japan, 1959; DSc, U. Tokyo, 1980. Tech. official U. Tokyo, Japan, 1960-63, asst., 1963-67; lectr. Saitama U., Urawa, Japan, 1967-70, assoc. prof., 1970-92, prof., 1992-99, ret., 1999. Inventor: Kobunshi Kagaku, 1964, J. Polymer Science, 1967, 80, 98, 99. Internat. Conf. Thermal Analysis & Calorimetry, Japan Soc. Calorimetry & Thermal Analysis. Mem. AAAS, Am. Chem. Soc., N.Y. Acad. Sci. Avocation: photography. Home: 1642 Tsutsumine Gyoda 361-0035 Japan

**SHIBER, JOSEPH R.,** emergency physician; b. Balt., Oct. 29, 1968; s. William E. and Stella M. Shiber; m. Emily Fontane, May 27, 2002. MD, U. Md., Balt., 1996. Diplomate Am. Coll. Physicians Soc. of Internal Medicine, 2002; 2d degree Black Belt Aikido Schs. of Ueshiba, 2000, Black Belt Wadokai Roy Sunaka, Shihan, 2006. Chief resident U. Md., Balt., 2000—01; asst. prof. East Carolina U., Greenville, 2001—. Dir. Combined Residency Emergency-Internal Medicine, Greenville, NC, 2003—. Contbr. articles to profl. jours. Recipient Mitchell award, Jour. Emergency Medicine, 2005, Extreme Submission Fighting Tournament winner, Royce Gracie Alliance All Am. Martial Arts Acad., 2005. Fellow: Am. Coll. Emergency Physicians; mem.: AMA, Alpha Omega Alpha. Avocations: Aikido, grappling, Ju Jitsu. Office: E Carolina Univ 600 Moye Blvd Greenville NC 27834 Office Phone: 252-744-2954.

**SHICK, RICHARD ARLON,** finance educator; b. DuBois, Pa., July 17, 1943; s. Arlon Elmer and Melva Elizabeth (Bartell) S.; m. Linda B. Shick; children: Richard Arlon, Charles, Elizabeth. BS, SUNY, Buffalo, 1966, MBA, 1968, PhD, 1972. Asst. prof. banking and fin. U. Ga., Athens, 1970-75; assoc. prof. fin. St. Bonaventure (N.Y.) U., 1975-78, chmn. fin. dept., 1975-78, acting chmn. mktg. dept., 1976-99; assoc. prof. fin. Canisius Coll., Buffalo, 1978-99, prof. fin., 1999—, dean Richard J. Wehle Sch. Bus., 1979—2002. Bd. dirs. Better Bus. Bur., 1990-95, Statler Culinary program Emerson H.S., buffalo, 1992-98; sec., treas., bd. dirs. Chautauqua Brick Co., 1995—. Mem. editl. bd. Jour. Bus. Rsch., 1973-76, Jour. Fin. Rsch., 1977-81, Jour. Econs. and Bus., 1984-88, Fin. Rev., 1976-87, editor, 1981-82; contbr. articles to profl. jours. Chmn. mayor's rev. com. Buffalo Bd. Edn.; bd. dirs, chmn. devel. com. Buffalo Alliance Edn., Old Ft. Niagara, chmn. bd. dirs., chmn. devel. com., bd. dirs Buffalo Philharm. Orch., 1995-97, treas., 1996-97; mem. N.Y. State Com. to Promote Pub. Trust and Confidence in the Legal System, 1999; bd. dirs. Studio Arena Theatre, 2001-2005, v.p. bd., pres., chmn. NDEA fellow, 1966-68; U.S. Savs. and Loan League grantee, 1974, St. Bonaventure

---

U. grantee, 1976, US Govt. Title III grantee, 1999 Mem. Am. Fin. Assn., Jesuit Colls. and Univs. Deans of Bus. Schs. (treas. 1983-84, v.p. 1985-89, pres. 1987-88), Middle Atlantic Assn. Colls. and Schs. Bus. Adminstrn. (v.p. 1985-86, pres. 1986-87), Country Club Buffalo, Automobile Club Western N.Y. (bd. dirs. 1995-99, exec. com. 1998-99, 2001), Beta Gamma Sigma, Alpha Kappa Psi, Di Gamma, Alpha Sigma Lambda, Alpha Signa Nu. Republican. Home: 157 Crestwood Ln Buffalo NY 14221-1508 Office: Canisius Coll 2001 Main St Buffalo NY 14208-1035 Office Phone: 716-888-2660. E-mail: shick@canisius.edu.

**SHICKLEY, MARGARET S.,** librarian; b. Armstrong County, Pa., Mar. 11, 1938; d. Oscar Henry and Ella Margaret (Titus) Fry; m. Roger Clair Storms, Aug. 24, 1963 (dec. 1980); children: Ethel Charis, Eric Malcolm; m. Nelson W. Shickley Sr., June 23, 1996. BA in Christian Edn., Eastern Coll., 1961; MSLS, Clarion U., 1991. Organist, pianist Lee Bapt. Ch., Maine, 1965-78; tchr. sewing Beth Eden Bapt. Sch., Wheatridge, Colo., 1978-81; organist, pianist Evang. Meth. Ch., Altoona, Pa., 1984-91; libr. Manahath Sch. Theol., Hollidaysburg, Pa., 1984-90; piano tchr. Altoona, Pa., 1986-90; cataloging libr. Lancaster (Pa.) Bible Coll., 1991—. Music libr. Blair Concert Chorale, Altoona, 1987-90; choir dir. Bapt. Ch., New Bethlehem, Pa., 1990-91. Nat. sec. Nat. Temperance and Prohibition Coun., 1983-89, del., sec. Prohibition Nat. Com., Denver, 1979-95; trustee Prohibition Trust, 1992-2002. Mem. Am. Theol. Libr. Assn., Harmony Club (pres. 1977), Lee Lit Club (cmty. project chmn. 1976-77). Avocations: music, needlecrafts, sewing, knitting, reading. *The building of today is not finished. Each day influences the next. Yesterday was the foundation that set the general outline for today's framework of living—built with solid materials of learning, experiences, relationships and memories. The life materials of today include a possibility of change and involvement with others as essential to our life building. Today's building influences the interior decorating of Tomorrow and its beauty to be revealed. Thus God's blueprint will be made visible.*

**SHIDELER, ROSS PATRICK,** literature and language educator, writer, translator, poet; b. Denver, Apr. 12, 1936; BA, San Francisco State U., 1958; MA, U. Stockholm, 1963; PhD, U. Calif., Berkeley, 1968. Instr. in comparative lit. U. Calif., Berkeley, 1967-68; asst. prof. English Hunter Coll., NYC, 1968-69; asst. prof. Scandinavian lang. and comparative lit. UCLA, 1969-73, assoc. prof., 1973-79, prof., 1979—, chmn. program in comparative lit., 1979-86, 92-96, assoc. dean Grad. Divsn., 2003—. Author: (monograph) Voices Under the Ground: Themes and Images in the Poetry of Gunnar Ekelof, 1973, Per Olov Enquist-A Critical Study, 1984, Questioning the Father: From Darwin to Zola, Ibsen, Strindberg and Hardy, 1999; translator: (plays) The Night of the Tribades (Per Olov Enquist), 1977, The Hour of the Lynx (Per Olov Enquist), 1990; co-editor (with Kathleen L. Komar): Lyrical Symbols and Narrative Transformations, Essays in Honor of Ralph Freedman, 1998; U.S. assoc. editor Swedish Book Rev., 1984—. Fellow, Nat. Defense Fgn. Language, 1964—65; Fulbright-Hays fellow, 1966—67. Mem. MLA (exec. com. divsn. Scandinavian Langs. and Lits. 1993-97), Soc. Advancement Scandinavian Studies (exec. coun. 1985-89, v.p. 1997-99, pres. 1999-2001), Internat. Comparative Lit. Assn. (treas. 2004-). Office: UCLA Dept Comparative Lit Los Angeles CA 90024

**SHIDLER, JAY H.,** real estate company executive; BBA, U. Hawaii. Founder, mng. ptnr. The Shidler Group (predecessor co. to First Indsl.); chmn. bd. dirs. First Indsl. Realty Trust, Inc., Chgo., 1993—. Bd. dirs. Primus Guaranty, Ltd.; chmn. bd. dirs. Corp. Office Properties Trust; mem. investment and spl. coms. First Indsl. Realty Trust. Office: First Indsl Realty Trust Inc Ste 4000 311 S Wacker Dr Chicago IL 60606

**SHIEH, ERIC Y.,** music educator; b. St. Louis, June 26, 1981; s. Huey-Sheng and Min-Tsung Shieh. B in Music Edn., U. Mich., Ann Arbor, 2004, BA in English, 2004. Lic. tchr. Mo., 1999. Cmty. coord. Miniwanca Outdoor Leadership Camp, Shelby, Mich., 2004; orch. dir. Hazelwood Sch. Dist., St. Louis, 2004—. Assoc. Prison Creative Arts Project, Ann Arbor, Mich., 2002. Named Rookie of Yr. award, Hazelwood Sch. Dist., 2005; recipient Earl V. Moore award, U. Mich., Sch. Music, 2004, Arthur Miller award, U. Mich., Honors Coll., 2004.

**SHIEKMAN, LAURENCE ZEID,** lawyer; b. Phila., Feb. 13, 1947; s. Morton and Roberta (Zeid) S.; m. Marjorie Kershbaum, Dec. 25, 1970; children: Wendy K., Thomas K. BS in Econs., U. Pa., 1968, JD, 1971. Bar: Pa. 1971. Law clk. to Hon. A. Leon Higginbotham, Jr. U.S. Dist. Ct. (ea. dist.) Pa., 1971-73; asst. prof. Fla. State U. Coll. Law, Tallahassee, 1973-75; assoc. Pepper, Hamilton & Scheetz, Phila., 1975-78, ptnr., 1978—. Mem. ABA, Pa. Bar Assn., Phila. Bar Assn. Office: Pepper Hamilton LLP 3000 Two Logan Sq 18th & Arch Sts Philadelphia PA 19103-2799 Office Phone: 215-981-4347. Business E-Mail: shiekmanl@pepperlaw.com.

**SHIEKMAN, PHILIP MINER,** lawyer; b. Phila., Mar. 19, 1925; s. Samuel L. and Sarah R. (Miner) S.; m. Judith L. Gruberg, June 26, 1949 (dec. Oct. 2003); children: Stephen J., Carol S., Sally A.; m. Rena Wattenberg, June 5, 2005. BSE, U. Pa., 1948; JD, Harvard U., 1951. Bar: N.Y. 1951, Pa. 1956, U.S. Dist. Ct. (ea. dist.) Pa. 1956, U.S. Dist. Ct. N.Y. Assoc. Carter, Ledyard and Milburn, N.Y.C., 1951-53, Stroock and Stroock and Lavan, N.Y.C., 1953-56; ptnr. Cohen, Shapiro, Polisher, Shiekman and Cohen, Phila., 1956-95, chmn. exec. com., mng. ptnr., 1986-93; sr. counsel Fox Rothschild LLP, Phila., 1995—. Contbr. articles to profl. jours. Pres. endowments corp. Jewish Fedn. Phila., v.p., 1987-91; v.p. Jewish Cmty. Ctrs. Assn., N.Y.C., 1986-94; pres. YM and YWHA, Phila., 1982-84; pres. Jewish Cmty. Ctrs. Phila., 1989-1991. Ensign USN, 1944-46, ETO. Mem. ABA, Pa. Bar Assn., Phila. Bar Assn. (chmn. tax sect. 1979-81, bd. dirs. 1980-81). Avocations: long distance running, skiing, golf, bicycling. Home: Trianon Apt 612 20 Conshohocken State Rd Bala Cynwyd PA 19004 Office Phone: 215-299-2764.

**SHIELD, GENE,** health products executive; BSBA, The Citadel; MS in Systems Mgmt., U. So. Calif.; M in Health Care Adminstrn., Med. Coll. Va.; grad., USAF Squadron Officers Sch., Indsl. Coll. of the Armed Forces. Former chief managed care divsn. Office of Air Force Surgeon Gen.; former cons. to Surgeon Gen. on managed care, advisor for legis. and CHAMPUS benefits and policy issues; pres., CEO Humana Mil. Healthcare Svcs. Humana Inc., Louisville, 1994—2000, sr. v.p. govt. programs, pres./CEO Emphesys, 2000—. Office: Humana Inc 500 W Main St Louisville KY 40202

**SHIELD, JULIE MARIE KARST,** artist, educator; b. St. Louis, Mar. 28, 1933; d. Lansing Peter and Margaret Mary Shield. A, Briarcliff Jr. Coll., NY, 1953; studied at. Nat. Acad. Design, N.Y.C., Art Students League. Oil painting art tchr. Buckingham Coun. Arts, Va., 1995—96, Va., 1999; owner and dir. Wooden Boat Art Gallery, River John, Canada, 1997—99; oil and still life art tchr. Longwood Ctr. for the Visual Arts, 1997-1998, 2000—01; oil and still life art tchr. Julie Shield Workshop, Farmville, Va., 1998—99, oil painting, landscape and still life art tchr., 2000—02; multi-media art tchr. Holly Manor Nursing Home, Farmville, 2001—04. Mem. coun. Longwood Ctr. for Visual Arts, Farmville, Va., 2001—06. Set design, Ring Around the Moon, 1981, brush and ink drawings on wall panels, ARC, Palm Beach County Chpt., 1982, 11 oil paintings for movie set design, Illegally Yours, 1987, one-woman shows include First Nat. Bank of Palm Beach, Fla., 1984—85, Buckingham Coun. Arts, 1996, 1998, Cumberland Courthouse, Va., 1999, Cheese & Co., Farmville, Va., 2000, Cafe Roglia, 2002, Va. Southside C.C., 2002, exhibited in group shows at Va. Mus. Fine Arts, Warrenton, 1988, Hampden Sydney Music Festival, 1998—2006 Longwood Ctr. for Visual Arts, Farmville, Va., juried exhbn., Best of Show, Buckingham Arts Coun., 1995—2006. V.p. ctrl. Va. arts affiliate Va. Mus. Fine Arts, Richmond, 2004—05, pres., 2006—. Mem.: DAR (bd. mem., corr. sec. 1971—75), Buckingham Artists Guild (planning com. 1995—), Curdsville Cmty. Ctr. (sec. 2006—), English Speaking Union, Friends of the Libr., Hist.

---

Buckingham Inc., Audubon Artists Inc. (assoc.), Art Students League N.Y.C. (life; corr. sec.). Buckingham-Dillwyn Garden Club (sec. 1996—2006). Episcopalian. Avocations: museums, gardening, miniature horse. Home: 843 Simpson Rd Prospect VA 23960

**SHIELD, PAUL HAROLD,** psychiatrist, educator; b. N.Y.C., Oct. 1, 1942; m. Renee R. Shield; children: Sonja, Aaron, David, Lily. BA, Swarthmore Coll., 1963; Dr.med., U. Pa., 1967; grad., Boston Psychoanalytic Inst. Diplomate Am. Bd. Psychiatry. Intern Harbor Gen. Hosp., Torrance, Calif., 1967-68; resident dept. psychiatry Yale U., New Haven, 1968-71; asst. prof. psychiatry U. Pitts., 1973-74; asst. clin. prof. psychiatry Brown U., Providence, 1975—2005. Contbr. articles to profl. jours. Maj. USAF, 1971-73. Mem. Am. Psychoanalytic Assn. Office Phone: 401-272-1415. Personal E-mail: pshield1@aol.com.

**SHIELDS, ALLAN EDWIN,** writer, photographer; b. Columbus, Ohio, July 3, 1919; s. Richard Edwin and Eloessa (Smith) S.; m. Bernice Clark, Aug. 2, 1941; children— Allan Oakley, Richard Minter, Larry Michael, Catherine Marie AB, U. Calif.-Berkeley, 1941; MA, U. So. Calif., 1947, PhD, 1951. Prof. philosophy San Diego State U., 1949-68, 70-78; emeritus prof. San Diego State Coll., 1978—; dean Coll. Humanities and Fine Arts U. No. Iowa, 1968-70; owner, pub. Jerseydale Ranch Press, 1992-98. Seasonal ranger naturalist Nat. Park Service, Yosemite Nat. Park, 1955-60; freelance writer, photographer, 1978—; violinist-violist, frequent recitalist; mem., sometime concertmaster Merced Symphony Orch., Calif., 1979-91; founder, with wife, Jerseydale Ranch Press, 1992. Author: Guide to Tuolumne Meadows Trails, 1960, rev. edit., 1973, (with Herbert Searles) A Bibliography of the Works of F.C.S. Schiller, 1969, (with Richard Shields) Tuolumne Profile: Yosemite, 1967, (novella) The Tragedy of Tenaya, 1974, new version 1992, A Bibliography of Bibliographies in Aesthetics, 1974, (poetry) A Horse in the House, 1985, Mariposa Now and Then, 1993, Tuffy, an Angel Hid in a Cloud, 1994, What Animals Taught Me, 1995, (with Bernice Shields) Into the Valley: A Brief History of Jerseydale Ranch, 1995, (with John Sharsmith) Climb Every Mountain: A Portrait of Carl Sharsmith, 1996, The Spirit of Rin-Tin-Tin, 2001, also numerous poems and articles; editor: A Yosemite Adventure in 1863, 1992, Wild Bill Neely and the Pagan Brothers' Golden Goat Winery, 1993, The Song of Sonora, 1993, O.S.S.: One Sad Sack—Pvt. Neely Disciplines the Military, 1994, A Yosemite Naturalist's Odyssey, 1994, Wilderness Treks by Foot, Canoe, and Adobe Rocket, and Father's Far-Flung Fables, 1995, Dream Temple and Other Visions, 1997; pub. various profl. jours. Bd. dirs. San Diego Symphony. Served with USAAF, 1942-45 Mudd fellow in philosophy U. So. Calif., 1948-49 Mem. Am. Soc. for Aesthetics (trustee), Phi Beta Kappa, Phi Kappa Phi, Phi Mu Alpha Sinfonia (hon.). Home: 2444 Beverly Ave Clovis CA 93611-5927 Personal E-mail: ashields@csufresno.edu. *My greatest satisfactions have come with tasks completed to the best of my abilities. Whether raising children, building a building, nurturing a marriage, learning the violin, or writing, all have inherent standards demanding recognition. Though there is always joy in the process of doing, joy can be transformed into satisfaction only in completion evaluated against the standards of worth for that kind of undertaking.*

**SHIELDS, ANTHONY FRANK,** oncologist, hematologist; b. Highland Park, Mich., 1952; MD, Harvard U., 1979; PhD, MIT, 1979. Diplomate Am. Bd. Internal Medicine, Am. Bd. Oncology, Am. Bd. Hematology. Intern U. Wash. Hosp., 1979-80, resident internal medicine, 1980-81; fellow hematology/oncology U. Wash., 1981-84; mem. staff VA Med. Ctr., Seattle, 1987-95, Harper Hosp., Detroit, 1995—, Karmanos Cancer Inst., Mich., 1995—; asst. prof. U. Wash., 1987-93, assoc. prof., 1993-95, Wayne State U., 1995-99, prof. medicine and oncology, 1999—. Mem. Am. Assn. Cancer Rsch., Am. Soc. Clin. Oncology, Am. Soc. Hematology, Soc. Nuc. Medicine. Office: Karmanos Cancer Inst 4100 John R St 4th Fl Detroit MI 48201-2097 E-mail: shieldsa@karmanos.org.

**SHIELDS, BROOKE CHRISTA CAMILLE,** actress, model; m. Andre Agassi, Apr. 19, 1997 (annulled 1999); m. Chris Henchy, Apr. 4, 2001; children: Rowan Francis Henchy, Grier Hammond Henchy. BA, Princeton U., 1987. Model for Ivory Soap commls. starting in 1966, later for Calvin Klein jeans and Colgate toothpaste commls.; Actor (films) Alice, Sweet Alice, 1975, Pretty Baby, 1977, King of the Gypsies, 1978, Wanda Nevada, 1978, Just You and Me Kid, 1978, Blue Lagoon, 1979, Endless Love, 1980, Sahara, 1983, Backstreet Strays, 1989, Brenda Starr, 1992, Seventh Floor, 1993, Running Wild, 1993, Freaked, 1993, Freeway, 1996, The Misadventures of Margaret, 1998, The Weekend, 1999, The Bachelor, 1999, Black & White, 1999. After Sex, 2000, Rent-A-Husband, 2004; (TV movies) The Prince of Central Park, 1977, After the Fall, Wet Gold, I Can Make You Love Me: The Stalking of Laura Black, 1993, Nothing Lasts Forever, 1995, What Makes a Family, 2001, Miss Spider's Sunny Patch Kids, 2003; (TV mini-series) Widows, 2002; (TV series) Suddenly Susan, 1996-99 (People's Choice award Favorite Female in New Series 1997); TV Films Bob the Butler, 2005; TV appearances include: The Tonight Show, Bob Hope spls., The Diamond Trap, 1988, Friends, 1996, Just Shoot Me, 1997, I'm With Her, 2004, That 70's Show, 2004, Niptuck 2006-; appeared on Broadway in Grease, 1994-95 (Theatre World award 1995), Wonderful Town, 2004, Chicago, 2005; Author: Down Came the Rain: My Journey Through Postpartum Depression, 2005 (NY Times Bestseller list, 2005). Named Time Mag. Face of the '80s; recipient People's Choice award Favorite Young Picture Performer, 1981—84.

**SHIELDS, CHRISTOPHER ANDREW,** website director; b. Oneonta, N.Y., Aug. 8, 1968; s. Alexander J. Shields and Grace Marie Kathmann. BS, SUNY, New Paltz, 1991; MS, U. Md., Adelphi, 1997. Dir. nasdaq.com The Nasdaq Stock Market, Inc., Rockville, Md., 1996—. Prodr.(on-air personality): (podcast) cIndyCenter.com. Home: 282 M St SW Washington DC 20024 Office Phone: 301-978-5286. Personal E-mail: ifwagba@hotmail.com.

**SHIELDS, CYNTHIA ROSE,** college administrator; b. Monterey, Calif., June 1, 1954; d. William Lawrence and Rose Virdell Jackson; m. Franklin Shields, Sept. 19, 1981; 1 child, Brett. AA, San Francisco City Coll., 1980; BS, U. San Francisco, 1986; MPA, Golden Gate U., 1988; MS, Nat. U., 1994; EdD in Ednl. Leadership, U. Calif., Davis, 1997; cert. in conflict mgmt., U. Calif., Irvine, 2003. Cert. community coll. instr., supr., Calif. Acct. exec. KFSN-TV, Fresno, Calif., 1982-85; instr. Merced County Schs., Calif., 1985-89; gen. mgr., owner Ad Line Advt., Merced, 1991; re-entry coord. Merced Coll., 1989-90; youth outreach specialist, 1990-91; re-entry coord., 1991-98; counselor Long Beach City Coll., Calif., 2000—03, dir. outreach and pub. rels., 2003—. Sr. assoc. Sch. Leadership Ctr., Calif. Sch. Leadership Acad., 1989-92; ednl. cons. 1998-. Author curriculum materials. Bd. dirs. Merced Cmty. Med. Ctr. Found., 1991, MUHSD Found., 1992-94; mem. citizens adv. bd. Merced City Sch. Dist., 1985-87; chmn. Merced Conv. and Vis. Bur., 1991; coord. Merced Cmty. Housing Resource Bd., 1988-90; mem. Leaders program Nat. Inst. for Leadership Devel., 1996. Mem. AAUW, Merced City C. of C. (bd. dirs. 1991-93, v.p. fin. and ops. 1993-94), Phi Delta Kappa. Democrat. Avocations: community volunteer, reading, golf, bicycling.

**SHIELDS, JAMES JOSEPH,** academic administrator, educator, writer; b. Phila., Feb. 18, 1935; s. James Joseph and Lena Josephine (Dyer) Shields. BS in Polit. Sci., Saint Joseph's U., 1956; EdM, Temple U., 1959; EdD, Columbia U., 1963. Asst. dir. internat. studies Tchrs. Coll., Columbia U., N.Y.C., 1961, field rschr.; Tchrs. East Africa Program N.Y.C., Kampala, Uganda, 1961-62; asst. prof. history and philosophy edn. SUNY, New Paltz, 1962-64; asst. prof. comparative and internat. edn. CUNY, N.Y.C., 1964-69, assoc. prof., 1969-75, prof., 1975-98, prof. emeritus, 1999, head Sch. Adminstrn. Program, 1983-85, dir. Japan Initiative, 1986—98, chair dept. social and psychol. founds., 1988-90; dir. projects Ctr. Edn. Outreach and Innovation Tchrs. Coll. Columbia U., 1998—2004. Vis. prof. Tchrs. Coll., Columbia U., 1965—67, 1993—95, 1998—2002—03, Yale U., 1997; cons. Inst. Ednl. Devel., N.Y.C., 1964-71, Equitable Life Ins. Co., N.Y.C., 1981, N.Y.C. Bd. Edn. Dist. 4, 1996—97, Time Mag., 1998, Inst. Internat. Edn., 1998—99; evaluation bd. Nat. Coun. Accreditation Tchr. Edn., Washington, 1970—75; vis. rsch. prof. Tokyo Met. U., 1986—95; assoc. univ. seminar modern Japan Columbia U., N.Y.C., 1987—2004, chair, 1990—91. Author:

Education in Community Development: Its Function in Technical Assistance, 1967, Problems and Prospects in International Education, 1968, Foundations of Education: Dissenting Views, 1974, Japanese Schooling: Patterns of Socialization Equality and Political Control, 1989, rev. edit., 1993; contbr. chapters to books, articles to profl. jours. Mem. task force reconstructed ednl. sys. Pub. Edn. Assn., N.Y.C., 1977—78, mem. lifelong learning com. Tchrs. Coll., Columbia U., 2005—, mem. alumni coun., 1993—98, 1999—. With USAR, 1959—65. Recipient Youth Coun. award, Wyo. Gov., 1974, Higher Edn. award, Holy Family Coll., Phila., 1990, Ann. Gertrude Langsam Ednl. Reconstrn. award, Adelphi U., 1992; grantee, N.Y. State Edn. Dept., 1969—72, Japan-U.S. Friendship Commn., 1986—88, Japan Found. Ctr. Global Partnership, 1994, U.S.-Japan Found., 1994—96, Tokyo Found., 1998—2000; Rsch. Found. grantee, SUNY, 1964, Fulbright Travel grantee, 1964, Rsch. Found. grantee, CUNY, 1980—81, City Coll. Provost Fund grantee, 1988—90, postdoctoral fellow, Yale U., 1967—68. Fellow: Comparative and Internat. Edn. Soc. (hon.; N.E. region conf. coord. 1984, bd. dirs. 1992—95); mem.: Soc. Ednl. Reconstruction (exec. com. 1973—), Carnegie Coun. Ethics and Internat. Affairs (trustee 1998—2003, vice-chmn. 2001—03), Am. Ednl. Studies Assn. (exec. coun. 1970—75, pres. 1973—74, founder), Beaux Arts Alliance, Japan Soc. N.Y., N.Y. Athletic Club (N.Y.C.). Avocations: collecting long island painters (1850-1950), travel, gardening. Address: Trump Pl 200 Riverside Blvd Apt 11N New York NY 10069-0911 also: 42 Old Town Xing Southampton NY 11968-5015 Office Phone: 212-787-3326. E-mail: jshields11@juno.com.

**SHIELDS, JERRY ALLEN,** ophthalmologist, educator; b. Pride Station, Ky., June 9, 1937; s. Fendell Harris and Beulah Etta (Williams) S.; m. Carol Lally, Oct. 26, 1985; children: Jerry, Patrick, William, Margaret, John. BA, Murray State U., 1960; MD, U. Mich., 1964. Diplomate Am. Bd. Ophthalmology. Intern Denver Gen. Hosp., 1964-65; resident in ophthalmology Wills Eye Hosp., Phila., 1967-70, fellowship in retina, 1970, fellowship in pathology, 1971, dir. ocular oncology svc., 1973—; prof. ophthalmology Thomas Jefferson U. Hosp., Phila., 1980—. Author: Diagnosis and Management of Intraocular Tumors, 1983, Diagnosis and Management of Orbital Tumors, 1989, Intraocular Tumors: A Text and Atlas, 1991; contbr. articles to jours., chpts. to textbooks. Lt. MC, USN, 1965-67, Vietnam. Recipient Golden Apple award Sr. Residents Wills Eye Hosp., 1990; co-recipient award Brady Cancer Rsch. Inst., 1986. Mem. AMA, Am. Acad. Ophthalmology, Am. Assn. Rsch. Ophthalmology, Phila. Ophthalmic Club, Pa. Acad. Ophthalmology and Otolaryngology. Home: 617 Williamson Rd Bryn Mawr PA 19010-1932 Office: Wills Eye Hosp Dept Oncology 9th And Walnut St Philadelphia PA 19107-5599

**SHIELDS, JOHN CHARLES,** literature educator; b. Phoenix, Oct. 29, 1944; s. Granville Blaine and Elizabeth Merle (Hartgraves) S. BA, U. Tenn., Knoxville, 1967, MA in Coll. Teaching, 1969, PhD, 1978; EdS, George Peabody Coll., 1975. Tchr. English Sevier County High Sch., Sevierville, Tenn., 1967-68; head dept. English Battle Ground Acad., Franklin, Tenn., 1969-71; dir. academics Brentwood Acad., Nashville, 1971-73, Columbia (Tenn.) Mil. Acad., 1973-74; instr. U. Tenn., Knoxville, 1978-79; asst. prof. Ill. State U., Normal, 1979-86, assoc. prof. English, 1986-93, prof. English, 1993—. Cons. Ency. Britannica, Oxford Companion to African Am. Lit., Norton Anthology African Am. Lit., others; project dir. conf. on Phillis Wheatley NEH, 1983-85; faculty advisor Native Am. Student Soc. Ill. State U., 1990; Coll. of Arts and Sci. Lectr., Ill. State U., 2003—; mem. doctoral dissertation com. Assoc. editor Style, DeKalb, Ill., 1988-90, guest editor, 1990—; editor: The Collected Works of Phillis Wheatley, 1988, paperback, 1989; selected to be a mem. of the Adv. Bd. of The Greenwood Ency. of Am. Poetry, (7 vol.) contbr., adv. editor, contbr Oxford Companion to African Am. Lit., 1997—, Am. Nat. Biography, 24 vol., 1994—; contbr. New Dictionary of Nat. Biography, Great Britain, 1995—; author: The Am. Aeneas: Classical Origins of the American Self, Univ. of Tenn. Press, 2001 (nominated for Ralph Waldo Emerson prize, John Hope Franklin award, Susan M. Glasscoch Interdisciplinary Book prize and Lora Romero First Book prize); contbr. articles to lit. jour. and chpt. to books; manuscript reviewer various presses and jour. Spokesperson for Native Am. citizens, 1970—. Ford Found. fellow, 1968-69, Soc. for Humanities fellow Cornell U., 1984-85, NEH fellow, 1983, 84, 89, 93, John. C. Hodges Teaching Excellence award, 1969. Mem. MLA, Soc. Early Americanists, Internat. Soc. for 18th-Century Studies, Am. Studies Assn., Melville Soc., Coll. Lang. Assn., Phi Mu Alpha Sinfonia, Alpha Phi Omega, Sigma Nu. Unitarian Universalist. Avocations: piano, singing, native american culture, archaeology, rare book collecting. Home: 1412 Donegal Dr Normal IL 61761-5416

**SHIELDS, LAWRENCE THORNTON,** orthopaedic surgeon, educator; b. Boston, Oct. 2, 1935; s. George Leo and Catherine Elizabeth (Thornton) S.; m. Karen S. Knaus, Sept. 21, 1968; children: Elizabeth Coulter, Laura Thornton, Sarah Daley, Michael Lawrence. *Daughter Laura Thornton Shields married Craig Edward Griffith in July of 2000. They have two sons, Connor Shields Griffith and Charles William Griffith and one daughter, Claire Coulter Griffith. Elizabeth Coulter Shields married Yuri Vladimirovich Sobol in August of 2001. She is currently deputy director of the Sabit program at the U.S. Departments of State and Commerce. Sarah Daley Shields is program director of IREX in Washington DC. Son Michael Lawrence Shields, graphic artist, married Beth Colgan in June 2003. They have two sons, Collin Michael Shields and Brody Edward Shields.* AB, Harvard U., 1957; MD, Johns Hopkins U., 1961. Diplomate Am. Bd. Orthop. Surgery. Intern Barnes Hosp., Washington U., St. Louis, 1961—62, resident, 1962—63; resident orthop. surgeon Children's Hosp. Med. Ctr., Boston, 1966—67, Mass. Gen. Hosp., Boston, 1967—68, Peter Bent Brigham, Robert Breck Brigham Hosps., Boston, 1968—69, Harvard Med. Sch., Boston, 1965—69, instr., 1969—; orthop. surgeon Peter Bent Brigham & Women's Hosp., Children's hosps., 1969—, Waltham (Mass.)-Weston Hosp. and Med. Ctr., 1969—, also chief orthop. surgery pres. med. staff. Mem. Waltham Weston Orthop. Assocs.; proprietor Boston Athenaeum; mem. staff Hahnemann Hosp., Boston, Newton-Wellesley (Mass.) Hosp.; cons. orthop. surgeon VA Hosp., Boston; mem. faculty Harvard Med. Sch.; vis. scholar Trinity Hall Cambridge U., 1985; hon. prof. New Eng. Coll., Henniker, NH, Sussex, England, 1995; bd. dirs. Wal-West Health Sys., 1986—; pres. Mass. Bay Investment Trust; dir. Waltham Investment Group. Contbr. articles to med. jours. Bd. dirs. Mass. Acad. Emergency Med. Technicians, Waltham Boys' Club; bd. of overseers Boston Lyric Opera, 1993—; trustee, exec. com. Waltham-Weston Hosp. and Med. Ctr. Lt. M.C. USNR, 1963-65. Fellow: ACS, Mass. Hist. Soc. Libr., Am. Acad. Orthop. Surgeons, Mass. Hist. Soc.; mem.: Thomas B. Quigley Sports Medicine Soc. (v.p., pres. 2001—), R. Austen Freeman Soc. (v.p.), Mass. Med. Soc. (v.p. 1982-83, councillor), Mass. Orthop. Assn. (sec. 1986—), bd. dirs.), Royal Soc. Medicine, N.Y. Acad. Scis., Cox & Co., Boston Lyric Opera (bd. overseers 1993), English Speaking Union (bd. dirs.), Academie Brillat-Savarin, Confrerie de La Chaine des Rotisseurs (elected 1996), Waltham Hist. Soc., Trollope Soc. (founding mem., bd. dirs., London), Thoreau Soc., Internat. Consular Corps (hon.), Charles River Dist. (pres. 1982—83, treas., exec. com.), Titanic Hist. Soc., Boston Opera Assn. (bd. dirs.), Harvard Mus. Assn., Emerson Soc., Handel and Hayden Soc. (bd. overseers), Les Amis d'Escoffier Soc., L'Ordre Mondial (elected 1999), St. Crisplin's Soc. Boston (pres. 1991—, founding mem.), USS Wasp CV-19 Assn., Theodore Roosevelt Assn. New Eng. (founding), 33 Touchdown Club/Found. (founding), New Eng. Orthop. Club, Boston Orthop. Club, St. Botolph Club (Boston), Harvard Club, Rotary, Bull Dog Terries, Clover Club Boston, Algonquin Club Boston (pres. 1990—, bd. dirs.), Union Club Boston, East India, Devonshire Sports and Pub. Schs. Club (London), Pi Eta (Harvard). Home: 9 Beverly Rd Newton MA 02461-1112 Office: 721 Huntington Ave Boston MA 02115-6010 also: 20 Hope Ave Ste 314 Waltham MA 02453-2717 Office Phone: 781-893-0700. Business E-Mail: ltshields@mcb.harvard.edu.

**SHIELDS, MARLENE SUE,** elementary school educator; b. Denver, Apr. 7, 1939; d. Morris and Rose (Sniderman) Goldberg; m. Charles H. Cohen, Dec. 22, 1957 (dec.); children: Lee, Richard, Monica; m. Harlan Shields. BA magna cum laude, Met. State Coll., 1980; MA, U. No. Colo., 1986. Preschool tchr. Temple Emanuel, Denver, 1970-75; tchr. Kindergarten Temple Sinai,

Denver, 1975-80; tchr. pre-Kindergarten St. Mary's Acad., Englewood, Colo., 1980-83; tchr. Beach Court Elem., Denver, 1983-86, Valverde Sch., Denver, 1984-85; tchr. third grade Brown Elem., Denver, 1985-86; tchr. learning disabilities Cowell Elem. Sch., Denver, 1986-87, Sabin Elem. Sch., Denver, 1986; tchr. second grade Sabin Elem., Denver, 2006—. Mem. curriculum com. Denver Pub. Sch., 1989—, pers. subcom., 2000-02; citizen amb. Spain joint tchr. conf., 1995. Mem. personal subcom. Sabin Elementary Sch., 2000. Mem. Colo. Coun. Internat. Reading Assn., Nat. Assn. for Young Children, Nat. Tchrs. Colo. Math., Internat. Reading Assn., Carousel of Intervention, Delta Kappa Gamma (sec., v.p. grade level chair), PRIDE (lang. curriculum com., math. curriculum com., impact com., CDM rep. 1994-95), Delta Kappa Gamma (state 1st v.p., pres. Omega state chpt. 2005—, mem. coord. coun. women 2005—). Home: 5800 Big Canon Dr Englewood CO 80111-3516

**SHIELDS, PATRICK M.,** lawyer; b. Santa Monica, Calif., Apr. 7, 1974; AB with distinction, Stanford U., 1996; JD magna cum laude, Harvard Law Sch., 1999. Bar: Calif. 1999. Assoc. Quinn Emanuel Urquhart Oliver & Hedges, LLP, LA, ptnr., 2005—. Sr. editor Harvard Jour. of Law and Pub. Policy, 1996—98; editor: Harvard Law Rev., 1997—99; articles editor Harvard Law Rev., 1998—99. Mem.: State Bar Calif., Phi Beta Kappa. Office: Quinn Emanuel Urquhart Oliver & Hedges LLP 865 S Figueroa St 10th Floor Los Angeles CA 90017 Office Phone: 213-443-3000. E-mail: patrickshields@quinnemanuel.com.*

**SHIELDS, PORTIA HOLMES,** academic administrator; m. William H. Lewis. BS in Edn., D.C. Tchrs. Coll.; MA in Edn., George Washington U.; PhD in Early Childhood and Elem. Edn., U. Md. Various tchg. positions primary and secondary edn.; dir. med. and biomed. comm. Howard U. Coll. Medicine, Washington, 1989-93, dean Sch. of Edn., 1993-96; pres. Albany (Ga.) State U., 1996—. Presenter and cons. in field. Active Albany Mus. Art, Albany Tomorrow, Inc., Albany/Dougherty Cmty. Partnership for Edn. and Dougherty, 2000; chair steering com. Am. Reads Program; mem. bd. regents U. Sys. Ga., 1997; bd. dirs. Cmtys. in Schs. Mem.: Albany C. of C. (bd. dirs.), Nat. Coun. for Accreditation Tchr. Edn. (bd. dirs.), Am. Coun. on Edn. (bd. dirs., mem. appeals com.), Orgn. Instnl. Affiliates (bd. dirs.), Am. Assn. Colls. for Tchr. Edn. (bd. dirs.), Am. Assn. State Colls. and Univs. (com. on cultural diversity and social change). Office: Albany State U 504 College Dr Albany GA 31705 E-mail: pshields@asurams.edu.

**SHIELDS, ROBERT EMMET,** merchant banker, lawyer; b. Ridley Park, Pa., May 18, 1942; s. Joseph Leonard and Kathryn J. (Walsh) S.; m. Mary Katherine Reid, July 22, 1967; children: Christopher D., David R., Kevin M., Kathleen. AB, Coll. Holy Cross, 1964; LLB cum laude, NYU, 1967. Bar: Pa. 1968. Mem. faculty Boalt Hall Sch. Law U. Calif., Berkeley, 1967-68; assoc. Drinker Biddle & Reath, Phila., 1968-74, ptnr., 1974-94, mng. ptnr., 1979-83, 85-94, head corp. and securities group, 1983-93, CFO, 1993-94; mng. dir., prin., ptnr., COO Questor Gen. Ptnr., L.P., 1995—2003, Questor Ptnrs. Funds, L.P. and Questor Mgmt. Co., 1995—2003; vice chmn. AlixPartners Holdings, Inc., Southfield, Mich., 2003—, Questor Ptnrs. Holdings, Inc., Southfield, 2003—, TK Aluminum, Ltd., Hamilton, Bermuda 2003—. Sec. Wallquest Inc. Author: (with Eliot B. Thomas) Federal Securities Act Handbook, 4th edit, 1977; (with Robert H. Strouse) Securities Practice Handbook, 1987. Mem.: ABA, Archmere Acad. (mem. bd. trustees), Turnaround Mgmt. Assn., Phila. Bar Assn., Pa. Bar Assn., Am. Law Inst. (life), Skyline Club (Southfield, Mich.). Office: AlixPartners Holdings Inc 2000 Town Ctr Ste 2400 Southfield MI 48075-1406 Office Phone: 248-213-2200. E-mail: rshields@alixpartners.com.

**SHIELDS, THOMAS CHARLES,** lawyer; b. Evergreen Park, Ill., Apr. 26, 1941; s. Thomas James and Adelaide (McElligott) Shields; m. Nicoline M. Murphy, Sept. 14, 1974; children: Thomas James II, Nicoline M. E., Suzanne Adelaide, Kerry Anne. AB, Georgetown U., 1963; JD cum laude, Northwestern U., 1966. Bar: Ill. 1966, U.S. Dist. Ct. (no. dist.) Ill. 1966, U.S. Ct. Appeals (7th cir.) 1966, U.S. Tax Ct. 1968, U.S. Supreme Ct. 1977. Assoc. Hopkins & Sutter, Chgo., 1966-73, ptnr., 1973-93; mem., chair health law dept. Bell, Boyd & Lloyd, Chgo., 1994—; chief counsel Cath. Health Assn. U.S., St. Louis, 1994—2005. Lectr. Ill. Inst. Continuing Legal Edn., 1973; mem. adv. bd. Health Law Inst. Loyola U. Sch. Law, Chgo., 1984—89, Health Law Inst. DePaul U. Sch. Law, Chgo., 1985—96. Contbr. articles to profl. jours. Trustee Village of Riverside, Ill., 2001—; mem. Ill. Health Facilities Authority, 2000—03; governing mem. Chgo. Zool. Soc., Chgo., Cath. Charities Chgo.; bd. dirs. Cancer Rsch. Found., Chgo., 1987—, Brother Louie and Fannie Roncoli Found., 1994—. Mem.: Chgo. Bar Assn., Ill. Assn. Healthcare Attys. (bd. dir. 1983—89, pres. 1987—88), Ill. Bar Assn., Am. Hosp. Assn. (tax adv. group 1987—90), Am. Health Lawyers Assn. (bd. dir. 1983—91, pres. 1989—90), Chgo. Power Squadron, U.S. Power Squadron (legal officer 2005—), Mid-Am. Club Chgo. (bd. govs. 2001—, sec. 2004—), Order of Coif. Avocations: skiing, bicycling, golf, boating. Office: Bell Boyd & Lloyd 3 First Nat Plz Ste 3100 Chicago IL 60602 Office Phone: 312-807-4232. Business E-Mail: tshields@bellboyd.com.

**SHIELDS, THOMAS WILLIAM,** surgeon, educator; b. Ambridge, Pa., Aug. 17, 1922; s. John Jr. and Elizabeth (Flanagan) S.; m. Dorothea Ann Thomas, June 12, 1948; children: Thomas William, John Leland, Carol Ann. BA, Kenyon Coll., 1943, DSc (hon.), 1978; MD, Temple U., 1947. Resident surgery Northwestern U. Med. Sch., Chgo., 1949-55, prof. surgery, 1968-92, prof. Emeritus of surgery, 1992—; practice medicine specializing in surgery Chgo., 1956—; chief of surgery VA Lakeside Hosp., Chgo., 1968-87; chief thoracic surgery VA Lakeside Med. Ctr., Chgo., 1987-90. Editor: General Thoracic Surgery, 1972, 5th edit., 2000, 6th edit 2004, Bronchial Carcinoma, 1974, Mediastinal Surgery, 1991; assoc. editor Surgery, Gynecology and Obstetrics, Annals of Thoracic Surgery, 1993-2002; mem. editl. bd. Annals of Thoracic Surgery, Lung Cancer; contbr. articles to profl. jours. Served with U.S. Army 1951-53 Mem. ACS, AMA, Am. Assn. for Thoracic Surgery, Soc. Thoracic Surgery, Central, Western Surg. Assns., Société Internationale de Chirurgie, Soc. for Surgery of Alimentary Tract, Internat. Assn. for Study Lung Cancer, Japanese Assn. Thoracic Surgery (hon.), Pa. Assn. Thoracic Surgery (hon.), Pan Pacific Surg. Assn., Phi Beta Kappa, Sigma Xi, Alpha Omega Alpha. Home: 10513 E Cinnabar Ave Scottsdale AZ 85258-4908 Office: Northwestern U Feinberg Sch Medicine Galter 3-150 201 E Huron St Chicago IL 60611

**SHIELDS, WILL HERTHIE,** professional football player; b. Fort Riley, Kans., Sept. 15, 1971; m. Senia Shields; 2 children. Degree in comm., U. Nebr. Guard Kansas City Chiefs, 1993—. Named to Pro Bowl, 1996-1999, 2001-2005 Office: Kansas City Chiefs 1 Arrowhead Dr Kansas City MO 64129-1651*

**SHIELDS, WILLIAM DONALD,** physician, educator; b. Salt Lake City, Oct. 29, 1941; s. F. Alburn and Ruth (Clawson) Shields; m. Virginia Mary Howell, May 19, 1970; children: Stephen Christopher, Justin Michael, Christine Rebecca. BA in chemistry, U. Utah, 1967; MD, U. Utah Sch. Medicine, Salt Lake City, 1967—71. Cert. in neurology with special competence in child neurology Am. Bd. Psychiatry and Neurology, 1977, diplomate Am. Bd. Pediat., 1978. Resident U. So. Calif., L.A., 1971—73; fellow U. Utah, Salt Lake City, 1973—76; asst. prof. UCLA Sch. Medicine, 1976—83, assoc. prof., 1983—90, prof., 1990—, Rubin Brown prof., 1999. Chief, divsn. pediatric neurology UCLA Sch. Medicine, 1980—2005. Contbr. chapters to books, articles to profl. jours. Pres., bd. mem. Epilepsy Found. L.A., 1981—88; mem. profl. adv. bd. Epilepsy Found. Am., Landover, Md. Named a Top Dr., Am.'s Top Doctors, 2001—04; recipient Maxwell J. Schleifer Disting. Svc. Award, Exceptional Parent Found., 2004; grantee, Milken Family Found., 1986—2004, NIH, 1992—98. Fellow: Am. Acad. Pediat.; mem.: Nat. Inst. Neurologic Disease and Stroke, L.A. County Epilepsy Soc. (chmn. profl. adv. bd. 1981—86, pres. 1986—89), Am. Acad. Neurology, Profs. Child Neurology, Am. Epilepsy Soc. (Svc. Award 1996), Child Neurology Soc. (counselor 1994—96). Office: David Geffen Sch Medicine UCLA 10833 LeConte Ave Los Angeles CA 90095-1752 Office Phone: 310-825-6196. Office Fax: 310-825-5834. Business E-Mail: wshields@mednet.ucla.edu.

**SHIELY, JOHN STEPHEN,** manufacturing executive, lawyer; b. June 19, 1952; s. Vincent Robert and Mary Elizabeth (Hope) Shiely; m. Helen Jane Pauly, Aug. 29, 1981; children: Michael, Erin, Megan. BBA, U. Notre Dame, 1974; JD, Marquette U., 1977; M in Mgmt., Northwestern U., 1990. With Arthur Andersen & Co., Milw., 1977-79, Hughes Hubbard & Reed, Milw., 1979-83, Allen-Bradley Co., Milw., 1983-86, Rockwell Internat. Corp., Milw., 1985-86, Briggs & Stratton Corp., Milw., 1986—, gen. counsel, 1986-90, v.p., gen. counsel, 1990-91, COO, 1994-2001, CEO, 2001—03, chmn., pres., CEO, 2003—. Bd. dirs. Briggs & Stratton Corp., Quad/ Graphics, Inc., Pewaukee, Wis., 1996—, Marshall & Ilsley Corp., Milw., 1999—. Mem. Greater Milw. Com., 2000—; chmn. bd. Children's Hosp. and Health Sys., 2003—; mem. bd. regents Milw. Sch. Engring., 1995—; trustee Med. Coll. Wis., 2003—; mem. corp. bd. dirs. Rock and Roll Hall of Fame and Mus.; bd. dirs. Outdoor Power Equipment Inst. Mem.: Assn. Corp. Growth (past pres. Wis. chpt. 1988—). Office: Briggs & Stratton Corp PO Box 702 Milwaukee WI 53201-0702

**SHIEMBOB, MARK S.,** lawyer; b. Hartford, Conn., 1956; BA with distinction, Univ. Va., 1978, JD, 1982. Bar: Va. 1982. Ptnr., sect. chief, fin. Troutman Sanders LLP, Richmond, Va., mem. exec. com. Mem.: ABA, Va. Bar Assn., Am. Coll. Real Estate Lawyers, Mortgage Bankers Assn. Am., Internat. Coun. Shopping Ctrs. Office: Troutman Sanders LLP PO Box 1122 Richmond VA 23218-1122 also: Troutman Sanders LLP Troutman Sanders Bldg 1001 Haxall Point Richmond VA 23219 Office Fax: 804-697-1455, 804-698-6004. Business E-Mail: mark.shiembob@troutmansanders.com.

**SHIENTAG, FLORENCE PERLOW,** lawyer; b. NYC; d. David and Ester (Germane) Perlow; m. Bernard L. Shientag, June 8, 1938. BS, NYU, 1940, LLB, 1933, JD, 1940. Bar: Fla. 1976, N.Y. Law aide Thomas E. Dewey, 1937; law sec. Mayor La Guardia, 1939-42; justice Domestic Relations Ct., 1941-42; mem. Tchrs. Retirement Sys., N.Y.C., 1942-46; asst. U.S. atty. So. dist. N.Y., 1943-53; cir. ct. mediator Fla. Supreme Ct., 1992; pvt. practice N.Y.C., 1960—, Palm Beach, Fla., 1976—. Lectr. on internat. divorce; mem. Nat. Commn. on Wiretapping and Electronic Surveillance, 1973—, Task Force on Women in Cts., 1985-86. Contbr. articles to profl. jours. Candidate N.Y. State Senate, 1954; bd. dirs. UN Devel. Corp., 1972-95, Franklin and Eleanor Roosevelt Inst., 1985—; bd. dirs., assoc. treas. YM and YWHA; hon. commr. commerce, N.Y.C. Mem. ABA, Fed. Bar Assn. (exec. com.), Internat. Bar Assn., N.Y. Women's Bar Assn. (pres., dir., Life Time Achievement award 1994, special award 2002), N.Y. State Bar Assn., N.Y.C. Bar Assn. (chmn. law and art sect.), N.Y. County Lawyers Assn. (dir.), Nat. Assn. Women LAwyers (sec). Home: 737 Park Ave New York NY 10021-4256 Address: 44 Cocoanut Row Palm Beach FL 33480 Office Phone: 212-861-8800. *Success is a product of self respect and hard work at what you do well.*

**SHIER, ELIZABETH M.,** music educator; b. Woodbury, N.J., Apr. 29, 1963; d. Nick T. and Virginia (Vance) Macchiarolo; m. Wes Shier; children: Brittany, Erin, Jonathan, Nicolas. MusB in Edn. and Music Therapy, Henderson State U., 1985; MEd in Elem. Edn., U. North Tex., 1996. Cert. music tchr. preK-12 Tex., gen. elem. tchr. grades 1-8 Tex. Elem. music specialist North Little Rock (Ark.) Sch. Dist., 1986—87, Grapevine-Colleyville Ind. Sch. Dist., Euless, Tex., 1987—97, Birdville Ind. Sch. Dist., North Richland Hills, Tex., 1997—. Staff devel. trainer Birdville Ind. Sch. Dist., North Richland Hills, Tex., 2002—; cons./trainer Ctr. for Educator Devel. in Fine Arts, San Antonio, 2001—; workshop presenter Tex. Music Educators Assn., San Antonio, 1997—2003. Author: (musical play) The Wacky Wound-Up Watch; contbr. articles to ednl. jours. Vol. usher Bass Performance Hall, Fort Worth, Tex., 1998—99; team in tng. mentor Leukemia/Lymphoma Soc., Dallas, 2001—03; exec. bd. mem. Bear Creek and ACFT PTA's, Euless and North Richland Hills, Tex., 1991—2003. Mem.: Ctr. for Educator Devel. in Fine Arts, Music Educators Nat. Conf., Assn. of Tex. Profl. Educators, Tex. Music Educators Assn. (workshop presenter 1997—), Delta Omicron (life). Avocations: marathon running, triathlons and duathlons, travel, tap dancing. Office: Acad at Carrie F Thomas Elem 8200 O'Brian Way North Richland Hills TX 76180 Personal E-mail: macch1@sbcglobal.net.

**SHIER, GLORIA BULAN,** mathematics professor; b. The Philippines; came to U.S., 1966. d. Melecio Cauilan and Florentina (Cumagun) Bulan; m. Wayne Thomas Shier; children: John Thomas, Marie Teresita, Anna Christina. BS, U. Santo Tomas; MA, U. Ill., 1968; PhD, U. Minn., 1986. Tchr. Cagayan Valley Coll., Cagayan, Philippines, St. Paul Coll., Manila, Manila Div. City Schs.; asst. prof. U. of East, Manila; rsch. asst. U. Ill., Urbana, 1968—69; instr. Miramar C.C., San Diego, 1974—75, Mesa C.C., San Diego, 1975—80, Lakewood C.C., St. Paul, 1984, U. Minn., Mpls., 1986—87, North Hennepin C.C., Brooklyn Park, Minn., 1987—. Cons. PWS Kent Pub. Co., Boston, 1989—. Chairperson Filipino Am. Edn. Assn., San Diego, 1978-79. Fulbright scholar U.S. State Dept., U. Ill., 1966-70; fellow Nat. Sci. Found., Oberlin Coll., 1967; recipient Excellence in Teaching award UN Ednl. Scientific Cultural Organ., U. Philippines, Cert. Commendation award The Gov. of Minn., 1990, Outstanding Filipino in the Midwest Edn. Cat. award 1992, Cavite assn., 1998, Gintong Pamana Found.; Outstanding Filipino-Am. in Edn. Mem.: Am. Statis. Assn., Minn. Math. Assn. of Two Yr. Colls., Minn. Coun. Tchrs. Math., Internat. Group for Psychology of Math. Edn., Am. Math. Assn. for Two Yr. Colls., Nat. Coun. Tchrs. Math., Philippine-Am. Acad. Sci. and Engring., Math. Assn. Am., Am. Math. Soc., Fil-Minnesotan Assn. (bd. dirs. 1991—2004, v.p. 2004—), Cultural Soc. Filipino-Ams. (pres. 2001—), Sigma Xi, Phi Kappa Phi. Roman Catholic. Avocation: piano. Office Phone: 763-424-0834. Business E-Mail: gshier@nhcc.edu.

**SHIER, SHELLEY M.,** production company executive; b. Toronto, Mar. 15, 1957; d. Harry Shier and Rosaline (Cutler) Sonshine; m. Hank O'Neal, May 14, 1985. Student, H.B. Studio, NYC, 1975—76, Stella Adler Conservatory, 1976—80. Company mem., actor Soho Artists Theater, NYC, 1976-81; casting dir. Lawrence Price Prodns., NYC, 1981-82; pres. Hoss, Inc., NYC, 1983—; v.p. Chiaroscuro Records, NYC, 1987—; pres. Broadway Bound, Inc., NYC, 1998—. Cons. Peter Martin Assocs., NYC, 1983, Norwegian Cruise Line, Miami, Fla., 1983-98, Floating Jazz Festival, 1983—, Oslo (Norway) Jazz Festival, 1986—, New Sch. Social Rsch., NYC, 1989—, Big Bands Sea, Rhythm & Blues Cruise, Dixieland Sea, 1991—, Blues Cruise, 1991—, Beacons Jazz Awards Ceremony, Tribute Music Bob Wills Texas Playboys, Mardi Gras Sea. Talent acquisition agt. Save Children, NYC, 1986, Tomorrow's Children, NYC, 1990, Barcelona Olympics, NBC, 1992, Royal Caribbean Internat., Miami, 1994-96, Ultimate Caribbean Jazz Spectacular, Country Music Festival Caribbean, CUNARD NYC, 1997—, Broadway Sea, 1996, Millennium Sea, 1999—, Broadway Bound, 1999—, others. Avocations: Karate, photography, riding, fishing, weightlifting. Office: HOSS Inc 830 Broadway New York NY 10003-4827 Office Phone: 212-674-8631, 212-674-8631. Personal E-Mail: shelleymshier@aol.com. Business E-Mail: broadwaybound.inc@aol.com.

**SHIFFER, JAMES DAVID,** retired utilities executive; b. San Diego, Mar. 24, 1938; s. Kenneth Frederick and Thelma Lucille (Good) S.; m. Margaret Edith Rightmyer, Sept. 5, 1959 (div. July 1986); children: James II, Elizabeth, Russell; m. Esther Zamora, Sept. 13, 1986; stepchildren: Bryan Boots, Jeremy Hellier, Marisol Loughead. BS in Chem. Engring., Stanford U., 1960, MS in Chem. Engring., 1962. Registered profl. engr., Calif. Nuc. engr. Pacific Gas & Electric Co., Humboldt Bay Power Plant, Eureka, Calif., 1961-71; tech. mgr. Pacific Gas & Electric Co., Diablo Canyon Power Plant, Avila Beach, Calif., 1971-80; mgr. nuc. ops. Pacific Gas & Electric Co., San Francisco, 1980-84, v.p. nuc. power generation 1984-90, sr. v.p., gen. mgr. nuc. power generation bus. unit, 1990-91; exec. v.p. Pacific Gas & Electric Co., San Francisco, 1991-97; ret., 1997; pres., CEO PG&E Enterprises, San Francisco, 1994-95, also bd. dirs. Bd. dirs. Math., Engring. Sci. Achievement, 1992-2002. Mem. AIChE, Am. Nuc. Soc., Commonwealth Club of Calif. (bd. govs. 1992-97). Republican. Episcopalian. Avocations: golf, music. Home: 2550 Royal Oaks Dr Alamo CA 94507-2227 E-mail: jshiffer@msn.com.

SHIFFMAN, BERNARD, mathematician, educator; b. NYC, 1942; s. Max and Bella S.; m. Doris Judith Yaffe, July 11, 1965; children: Jonathan, Daniel. BS, MIT, 1964; PhD, U. Calif., Berkeley, 1968. C.L.E. Moore instr. MIT, 1968-70; asst. prof. math. Yale U., 1970-73; assoc. prof. Johns Hopkins U., Balt., 1973-77, prof., 1977—, chair dept. math., 1990-93. Mem. Inst. Advanced Study, Princeton, NJ, 1975, Math. Scis. Rsch. Inst., Berkeley, Calif., 1996, 99; series lectr. U. Kaiserslautern, West Germany, 1977, Inst. Math., Academia Sinica, Beijing, 1978, U. Paris VI, 1979, Nordic Summer Sch., Joensuu, Finland, 1981, U. Tokyo, 2000; mem. Inst. des Hautes Etudes Scientifiques, Bures-sur-Yvette, France, 1979; vis. prof. U. Paris VI, 1981, 85, U. Grenoble, 1992, 95, 2001, 03. Editor Forum Mathematicum, 1989-95; assoc. editor Am. Jour. Math., 1990-92, 2005—, editor, 1992-93, editor-in-chief, 1993-2005; rschr. publs. in complex analysis. Hon. Woodrow Wilson fellow, 1964, NSF fellow, 1965-68, Alfred P. Sloan rsch. fellow, 1973-75; recipient Woodrow Wilson Faculty Devel. award, 1979. Mem. Am. Math. Soc. Office: Johns Hopkins U Dept Math Baltimore MD 21218

SHIFFMAN, MICHAEL A., lawyer; b. Newark, July 23, 1941; LLB magna cum laude, Lincoln U., 1973. Bar: Calif. 1973, U.S. Dist. Ct. (no. dist.) Calif. 1973; lic. real estate broker. Atty. Lanahan & Reilley, San Francisco. Editor: Lincoln U. Law Rev., 1972-73. Mem. ABA, Internat. Bar Assn., State Bar Calif. Office: Lanahan and Reilley LLP 1 Market St San Francisco CA 94105-1521 E-mail: shifflaw@aol.com.

SHIFFRAR, MARGARET MARY, education educator; b. Fremont, Calif., Dec. 15, 1962; d. Arthur Louis and Ruth Margaret Shiffrar; m. Angela Thompson, July 2005. BA in Psychology, U. Calif., Santa Cruz, 1985; PhD, Stanford U., 1990. Post doctoral rschr. U. de Paris V, France, 1989—90; rsch. assoc. NASA Ames Rsch. Ctr., Moffet Field, Calif., 1990—91; psychology prof. Rutgers U., Newark, 1991—. Contbr. articles to profl. jours. Recipient Lansdoune scholar award, U. Victoria, 2003. Fellow: Am. Psychol. Soc., Am. Psychol. Assn.; mem.: Cognitive Neuroscience Soc, Psychonomic Soc., Vision Sciences Soc. Office: Rutgers U Psychology Dept 101 Warren St Newark NJ 07102

SHIFFRIN, NANCY, writer, educator; d. Martin and Minna Shiffrin. BA, Calif. State U., 1972; PhD, Union Inst., 1994. Adj. prof. LA Cmty. Coll. Dist., 1990—. Author: What She Could Not Name, 1987, The Holy Letters, 2000, My Jewish Name, 2002. Recipient 1st prize, Acad. Am. Poets Coll. Competition, 1972. Jewish. Avocations: yoga, hiking, Jewish culture. Office: PO Box 1506 Santa Monica CA 90406-1506 Personal E-mail: nshiffrin@earthlink.net.

SHIFLETT, CHRIS, musician; Band mem. Lost Kittenz; guitarist Me First & the Gimme Gimmes, 1995—; lead guitarist No Use For A Name, 1995—99; guitarist Foo Fighters, 1999—; band mem. Viva Death, 2002—, Jackson United, 2005—. With Me First & the Gimme Gimmes (albums) Have a Ball, 1997, Are a Drag, 1999, Blow in the Wind, 2001, Take a Break, 2002, Ruin Jonny's Bar Mitzvah, 2004, with No Use For A Name Leche Con Carne, 1995, Making Friends, 1997, More Betterness!, 1999, with Foo Fighters One by One, 2002 (Grammy Award, Best Rock Album, 2004), In Your Honor, 2005, (songs) All My Life, 2002 (Grammy Award, Best Hard Rock Performance, 2003), Darling Nikki, 2004, Best of You, 2005, DOA, 2005, Resolve, 2005, with Viva Death (albums) Viva Death, 2002, with Jackson United Jackson United, 2005. Office: RCA Records 1133 Ave of the Americas New York NY 10036 Office Phone: 212-930-4000.*

SHIFMAN, MIKHAIL, physicist; b. Riga, Latvia, Apr. 4, 1949; came to U.S., 1990; s. Arkady and Raisa (Yakovich) S.; m. Margarita Pusynya, Apr. 21, 1971; children: Julia, Anya. MA in Theoretical Physics, Moscow Inst. Physics & Tech., Dolgoprudny, Russia, 1972; PhD, Inst. Theoretical Exptl. Phys., Moscow, 1976. From jr. rsch. fellow to sr. rschr. Inst. Theoretical & Exptl. Physics, Moscow, 1976-89; prof. theoretical physics U. Minn., Mpls., 1990—. Lectr. on particle physics and field theory. Author: Vacuum Structure and QCD Sum Rules, 1992, Instantons in Gauge Theories, 1994, ITEP Lectures on Particle Physics and Field Theory, 2 vols., 1999, The Many Faces of the Superworld, 2000, The Supersymmetric World, 2000; At the rfrontiers of Particle Physics, 4 Vol., 2001 Recipient Humboldt Rsch. award Alexander-von-Humboldt Stiftung, Bonn, Germany, 1993, Rsch. award Japan Soc. for Promotion Sci., 1993, 96. Fellow Am. Phys. Soc. (Sakurai prize 1999). Achievements include invention (with others) invisible axion; rsch. in hadronic physics/quantum chromodynamics, SVZ sum rules, heavy-flavor hadrons based on the heavy quark expansions, supersymmetric guage theories in the strong coupling regime. Office: Theoretical Phys Inst Univ Minn 116 Church St SE Minneapolis MN 55455-0149 E-mail: shifman@physics.spa.umn.edu.

SHIFMAN, RUTH MIRI, dentist; b. Aug. 9, 1977; d. Sandra Lynn Shifman; m. John Charles Boone II, Oct. 12, 2002. Degree in Biochemistry, UCLA, 1999; DDS, U. Pacific, Stockton, Calif., 2002. Cert. dentist Calif., 2002. Dentist Northbank Dental Ctr., Ventura, Calif., 2003—, Long Beach (Calif.) Meml.- Children's Dental Health Clinic, 2003—. Vol. to underserved communities and dental health in the classroom Children's Dental Health Clinic, Long Beach & Catalina, Calif., 2004—. Mem.: ADA. Office: Northbank Dental Ctr 2772 Johnson Dr Ste 101 Ventura CA 93003 Office Phone: 805-658-1577. Office Fax: 805-658-7049. Personal E-mail: ruth_shifman@excite.com. Business E-mail: drshifman@northbankdental.com.

SHIFRIN, DONALD LEE, pediatrician; b. Portland, Oreg., Jan. 10, 1949; m. Barbara Sue Chamberlin, Nov. 3, 2002; children: Max Burton, Alexis Chamberlin. MD, Georgetown U., Washington, 1970. Cert. Am. Bd. Pediatrics, 1981. Physician Pediatric Assocs., Bellevue, Wash., 1978—. Clin. prof. pediat. U. Wash. Sch. Medicine, Seattle. Chair Maimonides Soc. Jewish Fedn. Greater Seattle, 2000—. Fellow: Am. Acad. Pediat. Office: Pedatric Associates 2700 Northup way Bellevue WA 98004 Office Phone: 425-827-4600. Home Fax: 425-828-2256; Office Fax: 324-828-2256. Business E-mail: dshifrin@peds-associates.com.

SHIGEMITSU, TOSHIRO, ophthalmologist, researcher; b. Kyoto, Feb. 7, 1953; s. Yoshito and Eiko (Yoshioka) S.; m. Kumiko Nakahori, Oct. 27, 1990. MD, Fujita Health U., Toyoake, Japan, 1982, DMS, 1987. Asst. prof. ophthalmology Fujita Health U., Toyoake, 1988-91, assoc. prof. ophthalmology, 1991—2001, vis. assoc. prof. ophthalmology, 2002—. Dir. ophthalmology Hojinkai Med. Found., Kawade Hosp., Toyota, 1984—99. Patentee in field; contbr. articles to profl. jours. Mem. judging com. Fund Med. Security Sys., Aichi, 1996—2002. Recipient Japan Soc. Clin. Ophthalmology poster prize, 1998, Silver medal, Japan Ophthalmol. Soc., 1990; grantee Eye Bank Assn. Aichi, 1993, 94, 95. Mem.: Am. Acad. Opthalmology, Toikai Med. Assn. (bd. dirs. 1999—2005), Japanese Soc. Pathology (sci. councillor 2001—), Toukai Soc. Glaucoma (bd. dirs. 1998—2002), Asia Pacific Intraocular Implant Assn. (faculty 1997—98), Japanese Ophthalmic Pathology Soc. (councillor 1997—), Am. Aging Assn., European Soc. Cataract and Refractive Surgeons, Am. Soc. Cataract and Refractive Surgery. Avocations: travel, movies, golf, art. Office: Shigemitsu Eye Clin & Rsch Fdn Inc 3-6-23 Kuzuha-Asahi Hirakata 573-1111 Japan Office Phone: 81 72 866 2238.

SHIH, CHUAN-KANG, anthropologist; arrived in U.S., 1983, naturalized, 2002; m. Liping Wang; 1 child, Gerry Chia-hsi. PhD, Stanford U., 1993; BA in History, Yunnan U., China, 1982; MA in Anthropology, Stanford U., 1986. Post-doctoral fellow Ctr. for Chinese Studies U. Mich., Ann Arbor, 1993—94; vis. assoc. prof. dept. anthropology U. Ill., Urbana-Champaign, 1994—95, asst. prof. dept. anthropology Urbana, 1995—2002, assoc. prof. dept. East Asian Langs. and Cultures, 1997—2002, rsch. fellow Ctr. for East Asian and Pacific Studies Champaign, 2002—03; asst. prof. dept. anthropology and Asian studies program U. Fla., Gainesville, 2003—. Univ. hon. prof. Yunnan U., Kunming, 2000—; vis. scholar dept. demography U. Calif., Berkeley, Calif., 2001—02. Contbr. articles to profl. jours. Recipient Career award, NSF, 2000—03, 2004—; fellow, Stanford U., 1983—87, Inst. for Women and

Gender Studies, Stanford U., 1989—90, Ctr. for Chinese Studies, U. Mich., 1993—94; grantee, Ctr. for East Asian Studies, Stanford U., 1985, 1987, Wenner-Gren Found. for Anthrop. Rsch., 1988, William and Flora Found., 1996, U. Ill. at Urbana-Champaign, 1997, 1998; Gen. Edn. Bd. Cultural Studies Course Devel. Grant, 1997. Mem.: Assn. for Asian Studies, Am. Anthrop. Assn. Office: U Fla Dept Anthropology PO Box 117305 Gainesville FL 32611 Office Phone: 352-392-2253 ext. 253. E-mail: ckshih@ufl.edu.

SHIH, J. CHUNG-WEN, Chinese language educator; b. Nanking, China; came to U.S., 1948, naturalized, 1960; d. Cho-kiang and Chia-pu (Fang) S. BA, St. John's U., Shanghai, 1945; MA, Duke U., 1949, PhD, 1955. Asst. prof. English Kings Coll. N.Y., 1955-56; asst. prof. U. Bridgeport, Conn., 1956-60; postdoctoral fellow East Asian Studies Harvard, 1960-61; asst. prof. Chinese Stanford, 1961-64; asso. prof. Chinese Pomona Coll., 1965-66; asso. prof. George Washington U., Washington, 1966-71, prof., chmn. dept. East Asian langs. and lit., 1971-93, prof. emeritus, 1993—, rsch. prof., 1994—. Author: Injustice to Tou O, 1972, the Golden Age of Chinese Drama: Yuan Tsa-chu, 1976, Return from Silence: China's Writers of the May Fourth Tradition, 1983, (interactive CD and book) Learn Chinese from Modern Writers, 2002. Bd. dirs. Sino-Am. Cultural Soc., Washington, 1971-80, 95—. AAUW fellow, 1964-65; Social Sci. Rsch. Coun. fellow, 1976-77; grantee NEH, 1979-80, 89-91, 95-97, Annenberg/CPB Project, 1989-92; Sr. scholars exchange program NAS, China, 1980. Mem. Assn. Asian Studies, Am. Council Fgn. Lang. Tchrs., Chinese Lang. Tchrs. Assn. (chmn. exec. bd. 1976-78) Home: 2500 Virginia Ave NW Washington DC 20037-1901 Office: George Washington U Dept East Asian Langs Washington DC 20052-0001 Business E-Mail: cwshih@gwu.edu.

SHIH, MARGARET, epidemiologist; BS, U. Calif. Berkeley, 1993; MD, PhD, Va. Commonwealth U., Richmond, 2002. Diplomate Am. Bd. Preventive Medicine, 2005. Fellow preventive medicine Assn. Tchrs. Preventive Medicine Ctr. Disease Control, Atlanta, 2004—05; chief, epidemiology unit Office Health Assessment and Epidemiology L.A. County Dept. Pub. Health, 2005—. Mem.: AMA, Am. Statis. Assn., Am. Coll. Preventive Medicine.

SHIHAB, FUAD SAID, medical educator, researcher; s. Said Mohamed Shihab and Sania Atef Olabi; m. Samar Foud Jammal, Sept. 2, 1994; children: Saeed, Omar, Tala. BS in Chemistry, Am. U., Beirut, 1981; MD, Am. U., 1985. Diplomate Am. Bd. Internal Medicine, 1989, Nephrology Am. Bd. Internal Medicine, 1992. Resident/intern Md. Gen. Hosp., Balt., 1986—89, chief resident, 1988; fellow nephrology U. Pa., Phila., 1989—91; fellow transplantation medicine Oreg. Health Scis. U., Portland, 1991—92; asst. prof. medicine U. Utah, Salt Lake City, 1992—97, prof. medicine, 2002—. Med. dir. kidney transplant U. Utah, 1994—. Contbr. scientific papers numerous to profl jour., articles. Fellow: ACP, Am. Soc. Nephrology; mem.: Nat. Kidney Found., Am. Soc. Transplantation (chairperson fellowship tng. com. 2002—).

SHIH-CARDUCCI, JOAN CHIA-MO, food service executive, educator, medical technologist, writer, biochemist; b. Rukuan, Chunghua, Taiwan, Dec. 21, 1933; came to U.S., 1955; d. Luke Chiang-hsi and Lien-chin Shih; m. Kenneth M. Carducci, Sept. 30, 1960 (dec. July 1988); children: Suzanne R., Elizabeth M. BS in Chemistry, St. Mary Coll., Xavier, Kans., 1959; intern in med. tech., St. Mary's Hosp., Rochester, N.Y., 1960. Med. rschr. Strong Meml. Hosp. U. Rochester, 1960-61; pharm. chemist quality control Strasenburgh Labs., Rochester, 1961-62; cooking tchr. adult edn. Montgomery County Pub. Schs., Rockville, Md., 1973-79; tchr. The Chinese Cookery Inc., Rockville, 1975-86, Silver Spring, Md., 1986—, pres. bd. dirs., 1975—; chemist NIH, Bethesda, 1987-2000; analytical chemist NIH/WRAIR, Rockville, Md., 1994-96. Author: The Chinese Cookery, 1981, Hunan Cuisine, 1984, Vegetarian Cuisine, 2000, The Art of The Chinese Cookery, 2001 (Pinnacle Book award 2005). Mem. Am. Chem. Soc., Internat. Assn. Cooking Profls. (Woman of Yr. 1994-2004). Republican. Roman Catholic. Avocations: piano, music, dance, gardening. Home and Office: The Chinese Cookery Inc 14209 Sturtevant Rd Silver Spring MD 20905-4448 Office Phone: 301-236-5311.

SHIKLER, AARON A., artist; b. Bklyn., Mar. 18, 1922; s. Frank and Annie (Blai) S.; m. Barbara Lurie, Oct. 4, 1947; children: Cathy M., Clifford M. B.F.A., BS in Edn.; M.F.A., Tyler Sch. Fine Arts, Temple U., 1948; student, Barnes Found., Merion, Pa., 1941-43, Hans Hoffmann Sch., N.Y.C., 1949-51. One man shows, Davis Galleries, N.Y.C., 1953, 54, 56, 58, 60, 62, 64, 67, 71, 83, 84, Bklyn. Museum, 1971, Palace of Legion of Honor, San Francisco, 1971, Long Gallery, Houston, 1972, 76, 82, 85, Davis & Long Co., 1975, 79, Temple U., 1985, Claude Bernard Gallery, Paris, 1988, Davis & Langdale Co., 1987, 90, 93, 2000, 03, Kunsthaus Bühler, Stuttgart, Germany, 2002; represented in permanent collections, Montclair (N.J.) Mus., Hofstra Mus. Art, L.I., Carnegie Inst., Pitts., Met. Mus. Art, Mint Mus. Art, Charlotte, N.C., Parrish Mus. Art, Southampton, L.I., N.A.D., Bklyn. Mus., Hirshorn Mus., Washington, Nat. Art Gallery, Wellington, N.Z., Nat. Gallery, Singapore, New Britain Mus. Am. Art, Sun Rise Mus., Charleston, W.Va., Sheldon Meml. Art Gallery, Lincoln, Nebr., Pa. State U. Gallery, Davis Galleries, 1987, Lyme Acad., 1986; executed: portraits Pres. and Mrs. John F. Kennedy for White House, Robert Lehman Pavilion at Met. Mus. Art, Henry F. duPont for Winterthur (Del.) Mus., Robert F. Kennedy for Dept. Justice, Washington, Sec. Carla Hills for HUD, Sec. Carla Hills for Yale Law Sch., Mrs. Lyndon B. Johnson for Johnson Library, Austin, Tex., Senator Mike Mansfield for U.S. Senate, Washington, Dr. Michael DeBakey for Baylor U., Pres.-Elect Ronald Reagan as Man of Yr. for Time mag., James M. Walton for Carnegie Inst., Pitts., Pres. Ronald Reagan and Mrs. Reagan for The White House, Andrew Heiskell for N.Y. Pub. Libr., William S. Paley for Mus. Broadcasting, Dr. Vartan Gregorian, N.Y. Pub. Libr., Dr. Manuel Koehane, Wesley Coll., Mass., Hillary R. Clinton for Time mag., 1999. Served with inf. AUS, 1943-46. Recipient Tiffany award, 1958; Dept. State grantee S.E. Asia and South Pacific, 1976; Temple U. Centennial fellow, 1985. Mem. NAD (Ranger award 1959, Proctor prize 1959, 60, Clarke prize 1961, Altman prize 1976). Clubs: Century Assn.

SHIKUMA, EUGENE YUJIN, travel company executive; b. Tokyo, Nov. 18, 1948; arrived in U.S., 1957; s. Mitsuo and Yukiko (Kanaoka) Shikuma. BSEE, U. Hawaii at Manoa, Honolulu, 1971, MS in Computer Sci., 1975. Lab. test engr. and scientist McDonnell Douglas Astronautics, Inc., 1971-72; systems engr. Lear Siegler Astronics, 1972-73; jr. coord. Japan Travel Bur. Hawaii, Inc., Honolulu, 1978-83, sr. coord., 1983-84, supr., 1984-89, mgr., 1989—. Bd. dir. Maui United Way, Kahului, Hawaii, 1988—89, Maui Hui Malama, Waiuku, 1989—90; mem. Maui County Visitor Task Force, 1995—; adv. bd. mem. Maui Acad. Travel and Tourism; bd. dir. Maui Visitors Bur., 2003—; mem. Maui Sister Cities Internat. Festival, 2005; com. mem. Maui County Sister Cities Festival, 2005, Maui Tourism Strategic Plan Com., 2005—; hon. chmn. bus. adv. coun. Hawaii Nat. Rep. Congl. Com., 2003; bd. dir., sec. Kamoa Views Apt. Owners Assn., 1991—96. Named Businessman of Yr., Nat. Rep. Congl. Com., 2004, Rep. of Yr., 2006; recipient Ronald Reagan Rep. Hawaii Gold medal, 2004, 2005, Congl. medal of distinction, 2006. Mem.: Maui Japanese C. of C., Maui C. of C. Avocations: swimming, coin collecting/numismatics, art, antique prints. Office Phone: 808-871-6600. Business E-Mail: eshikuma@jtb-hawaii.com.

SHILARO, PRISCILLA MURONJI, history professor; arrived in US, 1994; d. Justmore Shilaro Mbasu and Ruth Wekaya; 1 child, Anne Rebecca Mutashi. BE in Arts with honors, Kenyatta U., Kenya, 1987, MA in History, 1993; PhD, W.Va. U., Morgantown, 2000. Grad. tchg. asst. Maseno U. Coll. Maseno, Kenya, 1991—93; lectr. Maseno U., 1993—94; grad. instr. W.Va. U., 1994—97; asst. prof. history Stonehill Coll., North Easton, Mass., 2001—02; coord. africana studies program, asst. prof. history W.Va. U., 2002—05, asst. prof. history, 2002—. DuPont minority scholar Lynchburg Coll., Va., 1999; vis. lectr. Wash. U., St. Louis, 2000—01; coord. Africana studies program W.Va. U., 2002—05. Author: (book) A Failed Eldorado: Colonial Capitalism, Rural Industrialization, and the Kakamega Gold Rush, 1930-1952; contbr. articles to profl. jours. and books. Patron Kakamega Self-help Women's Group, Kakamega, Kenya, 1998—98; motivational spkr. Girls' High Schs.,

1991—94; mem. W.Va. U. Social Justice Com., 2003—05, W.Va. U. Coun. African & African-American Affairs, 2002—06, Stonehill Coll. History Dept. Early Modern Europe Search Com., North Easton, Mass., 2001; mem. dean's adminstrv. com. W.Va. U., Morgantown, 2002—05, mem. history dept. faculty rsch. and grad. studies com., 2004—05, mem. curiculum and instn. com., 2005; faculty advisor & mentor Stonehill Coll., North Easton, Mass., 2001—02. Recipient African Dissertation Internship award, Rockefeller Found., 1997—98; fellow, Assn. Am. U. Women, 1999—2000, W.Va. U., 2006; grantee, 2002—03, 2005; scholar, Lynchburg Coll., 1999. Mem.: Orgn. Am. Historians, Third World Studies, Hist. Assn. Kenya, African Studies Assn. Avocations: shopping, cooking, exercise, reading, films. Office: West Virginia University 220 Woodburn Hall P O BOX 6303 Morgantown WV 26506 Office Phone: 304-293-2421 ext. 5238. Office Fax: 304-293-3616. Business E-Mail: priscilla.shilaro@mail.wvu.edu.

SHILEPSKY, NANCY SUE, lawyer; b. Westport, Conn., Apr. 25, 1952; d. Morris Jacob and Rose (Pfeffer) S. BA magna cum laude, Tufts U., 1974; JD, Boston U., 1978. Bar: Mass. 1978, U.S. Dist. Ct. Mass. 1978. Dir. Legal Info. Ctr. Bklyn. Coll., 1978-79; staff atty. Western Mass. Legal Svcs., Springfield, 1980-81; ptnr. Northampton (Mass.) Law Collective, 1982-84; assoc. Schreiber & Assocs., Boston, 1984-87, McDonald, Noonan & Kaplan, Newton, Mass., 1987-88; ptnr. Rudavsky & Shilepsky, Boston, 1988, Shilepsky, Messing & Rudavsky, Boston, 1988—2005, Perkins Smith& Cohen, Boston, Shilepsky O'Connell, Boston, 2005—. Speaker Mass. Continuing Legal Edn., Inc., Boston, 1988—. Named one of top Boston lawyers, Boston Mag., 2004. Mem.: Boston Bar Assn. (treas. 2004—05), Mass. Bar Assn.-Labor & Employment Law Sect. (chmn. employee rights & responsibilities com. 1990—91, 1993—94, sect. coun. 1993—96), Boston Bar Assn.-Labor & Employment Law Sect. (co-chmn. 1996—99, sect. coun. 1996—). Office: Shilepsky O'Connell 225 Franklin St Boston MA 02110 Office Phone: 617-854-4275, 617-447-2806. Office Fax: 617-854-4040. Business E-Mail: nshilepsky@sholaw.com.

SHILLER, ROBERT JAMES, economist, educator; b. Detroit, Mar. 29, 1946; s. Benjamin P. and Ruth R. (Radzville) S.; m. Virginia M. Faulstich, June 13, 1976; 2 sons. BA, U. Mich., 1967; SM, MIT, 1968, PhD, 1972. Asst. prof. U. Minn., 1972-74; rsch. fellow Nat. Bur. Econ. Rsch., Cambridge, Mass., 1974-75; vis. scholar dept. econs. MIT, Cambridge, 1974-75, vis. prof., 1981-82; assoc. prof. dept. econs. U. Pa., Phila., 1974-81, prof. econs., 1981-82; prof. fin. Wharton Sch., 1981-82; prof. econs. Yale U., New Haven, 1982—. Co-founder Case, Shiller, Weiss Inc., MacroMarkets, LLC; vis. scholar dept. econs. Harvard U., 1980. Fgn. editor Rev. Econ. Studies, 1981-84; assoc. editor Jour. Econometrics, 1980-83; author: Market Volatility, 1989, Macro Markets, 1993, Irrational Exuberance, 2000, 2d edit., 2005, New Financial Order, 2003. Grantee NSF, 1976—; Guggenheim fellow. Fellow Econometric Soc., Am. Acad. Arts and Scis., Am. Philos. Soc., Am. Econ. Assn. (v.p. 2005), Eastern Econ. Assn. (pres. 2005). Office: Yale U Cowles Found New Haven CT 06520-8281 Office Phone: 203-432-3708. Business E-Mail: robert.shiller@yale.edu.

SHILLESTAD, JOHN GARDNER, diversified financial services company executive; b. Oak Park, Ill., Oct. 31, 1934; s. John Nelson and Isabel Blanche (Gardner) Shillestad; m. Astri Cedervall; children: Christine C, Annette. BBA, Northwestern U., 1964, MBA, 1967. CLU, CPCU; ChFC. Mktg. dir. spl. plans CNA Ins., Chgo., 1958-66; asst. v.p. Montgomery Ward Life, Chgo., 1966-69; pres., CEO Fort Dearborn Life Ins. Co., Chgo., 1969-79; sr. v.p. Hartford Life Cos., Conn., 1979-85, also bd. dirs. Conn., 1985-87; pres. JGS Fin. Svcs., Inc., 1987—, Columbian Mut. Life Ins. Co., Binghamton, NY, 1987—. Chmn. Columbian Life Ins Co, Washington Nat. Life NY; with Golden Eagles Sales Corp., 1997—2005; bd. dirs. Reassure Am, Valley Forge Life Ins. Co., 2004. Mem Bd Educ, Dist 30, Northbrook, Ill., 1976—79; mem adv bd SUNY Sch Mgt, Binghamton, Kellogg Sch Bus, Northwestern Univ; bd dirs Salvation Army, Binghamton, Partnership 2000, Southern Tier Equity Fund. With U.S. Army, 1954—56. Mem.: Broome County CofC (bd dirs), Pelican Marsh Golf Club (Naples, Fla), Sunset Ridge Club (Northfield, Ill). Republican. Congregationalist. Home: 3 Regentwood Rd Northfield IL 60093-2728 also: Unit 304 1600 Clermont Dr Naples FL 34109 E-mail: sjackshil@aol.com.

SHILLING, A. GARY, economist, consultant; b. Fremont, Ohio, May 25, 1937; s. A. Vaughn and Lettie E. (O'Harrow) S.; m. Margaret E. Bloete, Dec. 22, 1962; children: Geoffrey B., Andrew J., Stephen E., Jennifer E. AB in Physics magna cum laude, Amherst (Mass.) Coll., 1960; MA in Econs., Stanford (Calif.) U., 1962, PhD in Econs., 1965; LLD (hon.), Tiffin U., 1999; DHL (hon.), Ch. Divinity Sch. Pacific, 2006. Economist Standard Oil Co. (N.J.), N.Y.C., 1963-67; chief economist Merrill Lynch, Pierce, Fenner & Smith, N.Y.C., 1967-71; rsch. dir. Estabrook & Co., N.Y.C., 1971-72; sr. v.p., chief economist White, Weld & Co., N.Y.C., 1972-78; chmn., pres., dir. A. Gary Shilling & Co., Inc., Springfield, NJ, 1978—; pres. Lakeview Econ. Svcs., Inc., Springfield, 1979—; owner Lakeview Svcs., Inc., Springfield, 1993—. Bd. dirs. Nat. Life Vt., Montpelier, Palm Harbor Homes, Am. Productivity and Quality Ctr., Houston; adv. dir. Austin (Tex.) Trust Co., 1988—; informal econ. advisor Former Pres. George Bush, 1988—; mem. Nat. Com. on Jobs and Small Bus., 1986-87. Author: Is Inflation Ending? Are You Ready?, 1983, The World Has Definitely Changed: New Economic Forces and Their Implications for the Next Decade, 1986, After the Crash: Recession or Depression? Investment and Business Strategies for a Deflationary World, 1988, Deflation: Why it's coming, whether it's good or bad, and how it will affect your investments, business, and personal affairs, 1998, Korean and Chinese edits., 2000, Deflation: How to Survive and Thrive in the Coming Wave of Deflation, 1999, Chinese edit., 2000, Letting Off Steam, 2003; creator bd. game The Deflation Game, 1999; columnist Forbes, 1983—; Nihon Keizai Shimbun Jour. Bd. dirs. Aim Packaging Inc., 1986-89, Episcopal Ch. Found., N.Y.C., N.Y., 1989-97; chmn. Episcopal Preaching Found., Springfield, N.J., 1988—; trustee Bates Coll., Lewiston, Maine, 1988-91, Kent Pl. Sch., Summit, N.J., 1983-89, Henry J. Kessler Found., 1987-95; bd. dirs. The Gen. Theol. Episcopal Sem., N.Y.C., 1988-2001, treas., 1994-2001; chmn. N.J. State Revenue Forecasting Adv. Commn., 1995-2005; bd. dirs. Am. Rep. Ins. Co. N.Y., 1978-81, N.J. Shakespeare Festival, 1987-96, chmn., 1994-96. Named Wall St. Top Econs., Instl. Investor Mag., 1975, 76, Top Commodity Trading Advisor, Futures Mag., 1993, Third best Stockmarket Forecaster in the World, Money Sense Mag., 2003. Mem. Nat. Assn. Bus. Economists, N.Y. Soc. Security Analysts, Short Hills Club, Phi Beta Kappa, Sigma Xi. Republican. Episcopalian. Avocations: tennis, travel, gardening, hunting, fishing. Home: 33 Lakeview Ave Short Hills NJ 07078-2264 Office: A Gary Shilling & Co Inc 500 Morris Ave Springfield NJ 07081-1020 Office Phone: 973-467-0070. Business E-Mail: gary@agaryshilling.com.

SHILLING, ROY BRYANT, JR., academic administrator; b. Enville, Okla., Apr. 7, 1931; s. Roy Bryant and Lila M. (Prestage) S.; m. Margaret Riddle, Oct. 16, 1952; children: Roy Bryant III, Nancy Gale. BA, McMurry U., 1951, HHD, 1982; BD, So. Meth. U., 1957; MS, Ind. U., 1966, PhD, 1967. Presdl. asst. McMurry U., Abilene, Tex., 1959-61; asst. to pres. Tenn. Wesleyan Coll., 1961-64; asst. in devel. Ball State U., 1964-65; rsch. assoc. Ind. U., 1965-67; dir. planning and rsch. Baldwin Wallace Coll., 1967-68; exec. v.p. Southwestern U., 1968-69, pres., 1981-2000, pres. emeritus, 2000—; pres. Hendrix Coll., 1969-81; interim pres. McMurry Univ., 2002. Mem. Nat. Commn. on United Meth. Higher Edn., 1975-77. Mem. Ark. Arts and Humanities Coun., 1970-76, chmn., 1974-75; bd. dirs. Ark. Children's Hosp., 1981; mem. bd. higher edn. and ministry United Meth. Ch., 1972-80, mem. univ. senate, 1980-88, v.p. 1983-84, pres., 1984-88; chmn. Gulf dist. Rhodes Scholarship Selection Com., 1992, Ark. chmn., 1973-74, Tex. chmn., 1985-91; mem. Young Pres. Orgn., 1975-81; mem. bd. visitors Air U., 1991-94. With U.S. Army, 1952-54. Recipient Disting. Alumnus award McMurry U., 1980, Perkins Disting. Alumnus award So. Meth. U., 1987, Owen B. Sherrill award for leadership in econ. devel. Georgetown, 1988; named one of Top 100 Most Effective Coll. Pres. in Nation, Bowling Green State U./Exxon Edn. Found. 1986. Mem. North Ctrl. Assn. Colls. and Schs. (vice chmn., chmn. elect 1980-81), Nat. Assn Schs. and Colls. of United Meth. Ch. (v.p. 1975-76, pres.

1976-77), Nat. Coun. Ind. Colls. and Univs. (bd. dirs. 1984-88), So. U. Conf. (exec. com. 1974-78), 79-86, sec.-treas. 1979-86, v.p. 1991-92, pres. 1992-93), Am. Coun. Edn. (bd. dirs. 1989-91; mem. commn. on govt. and pub. rels. 1999-2000, spl. counselor to the pres. 2000-01), Inst. for Humanities (bd. dirs. Salado, Tex. chpt. 1985-91, mem. internat. coun. advs. 1994), NCAA Divsn. III Pres.'s Coun., 1998-2000, Philos Soc. Tex., Rotary, Masons, Alpha Chi, Phi Delta Kappa. Office: 1405 Mesa Ridge Ln Austin TX 78735-1639 E-mail: shilling@southwestern.edu.

**SHILLINGBURG, HERBERT THOMPSON, JR.,** dental educator; b. Mar. 21, 1938; s. Herbert Thompson and Stefi Marie (Schuster) Shillingburg; m. Constance Joanne Murphy, June 11, 1960; children: Lisa Grace, Leslie Susan, Lara Stephanie. Student, U. N.Mex., 1955-58, 65-66; DDS, U. So. Calif., 1962; DDS (hon.), U. Medicine and Pharmacy Targu Mures, Romania, 2006. Gen. practice dentistry, Albuquerque, 1964-67; asst. prof. fixed prosthodontics sect. UCLA Sch. Dentistry, 1967-70, chmn., 1970-72; chmn. dept. fixed prosthodontics U. Okla. Coll. Dentistry, Okla. City, 1972—2003, David Ross Boyd Disting. prof., 1983, prof. emeritus, 2003—. Cons. VA Hosp., Muskogee, Okla., 1975—84, Oklahoma City, 1977—93, U.S. Army Dental Activity, Ft. Knox, Ky., 1980—94. Author: (also in Japanese, German, Greek, Spanish, Italian, French, Portuguese, Polish, Korean, Chinese and Russian) Preparations for Cast Gold Restorations, 1974, Fundamentals of Fixed Prosthodontics, 1976, Fundamentals of Fixed Prosthodontics, 2d edit., 1981, Fundamentals of Fixed Prosthodontics, 3d edit., 1997, Guide to Occlusal Waxing, 1979, Guide to Occlusal Waxing, 2d edit., 1984, Guide to Occlusal Waxing, 3d edit., 2000, Restoration of the Endodontically Treated Tooth, 1984, Fundamentals of Tooth Preparations for Cast Metal and Porcelain Restorations, 1987; co-editor: Quintessence of Dental Technology, 1984—88; sect. editor: Quintessence Internat., 1988—2001, mem. editl. coun.: Jour. Prosthetic Dentistry, 1996—99. Capt. U.S. Army, 1962—64. Named Disting. Lectr., O U Assoc., 1989; recipient Award for tchg. excellence, UCLA Sch. Dentistry, 1969, 1972, 1973, Okla. Coll. Dentistry, 1976, 1978, 1982, 1987, 1993, 1994, 1st prize, Am. Med. Writers Assn., 1988, Award for tchg. excellence, Okla. Coll. Dentistry, 1997, La Mèdaille de la Ville de Paris (èchelon Argent), 1990, Outstanding Profl. Achievement award, O U Coll. Dentistry, 2003, Prof. of Hon., U. Medicine and Pharmaxy Targu-Mures, 2004, Herbert T. Shillingburg Endowed Prof. Prosthodontics, Coll. Dentistry, 2006. Fellow: Am. Coll. Dentists; mem.: ADA, Okla. State Dental Assn., Internat. Assn. Dental Rsch., Am. Coll. Prosthodontists (hon.), Am. Acad. Restorative Dentistry, Am. Acad. Fixed Prosthodontics (George H. Moulton award 1998), Acad. Operative Dentistry, Phi Kappa Phi, Omicron Kappa Upsilon (Stephen H. Leeper award for Tchg. Excellence Supreme Ch. 2000). Independent. Episcopalian. Avocations: travel, photography. Home: 1312 Brixton Rd Edmond OK 73034-3314 Office: U Okla Coll Dentistry PO Box 26901 Oklahoma City OK 73190-0001

**SHILLINGLAW, GORDON,** retired finance educator; b. Albany, N.Y., July 26, 1925; s. James McCombe and margaret Blanche (Stephens) Shillinglaw; m. Barbara Ann Cross, June 24, 1950; children: James McCombe, Laura Cross. AB magna cum laude, Brown U., 1945; MS, U. Rochester, 1948; PhD, Harvard U., 1952. Asst. prof. Hamilton Coll., Clinton, NY, 1951-52; cons. assoc. Joel Dean Assocs., Yonkers, NY, 1952-55; asst. prof. MIT, Cambridge, 1955-61; assoc. prof. Columbia U., N.Y.C., 1961-66, prof. acctg., 1966-90, prof. emeritus, 1991—. Vis. prof. Mgmt. Devel. Inst., Lausanne, Switzerland, 1964—65; mem. U.S. Cost Acctg. Stds. Bd., 1978—80, U.S. R.R. Acctg. Prin. Bd., 1985—87; dir. trustee Scudder Funds, AARP Investment Program Funds, 1979—2000; cons. in field. Author: Managerial Cost Accounting, 1961, 5th edit., 1982, Accounting: A Management Approach, 1964, 9th edit., 1993, Financial Accounting: Concepts and Applications, 1989; contbr. articles to profl. jours. Bd. dirs., treas. Feris Found. Am., Stamford, Conn., 1970—94; mem. bd. advisors Fund Directions, 1990—96. With USN, 1943—46. Recipient Disting. Tchr. award, Columbia U., 1970, Lifetime Achievement award, Instnl. Investor Newsletter, 2002. Mem.: Am. Acctg. Assn. (v.p. 1966—67), Beta Gamma Sigma, Phi Beta Kappa. Avocations: golf, genealogy. Home: 1150 8th Ave SW Apt 401 Largo FL 33770-3175 Personal E-mail: gshillinglaw@tampabay.rr.com.

**SHILLINGSBURG, CYNTHIA LYNN,** medical technician, educator; b. Reading, Pa., Aug. 20, 1956; d. Louis Fudeman and Eleanor Ruth Knowles-Fudeman; m. Richard Charles Shillingsburg, June 30, 1979; children: Ashley, Britta. BA, Alvernia Coll., Reading, PA, 1977—79. Faculty Thomas Jefferson U., Philadelphia, Pa., 1999—; icavl vascular lab. dir. The Glover Clinic, Drexel Hill, Pa., 1982—2001; assoc. degree instr. Ea. Coll., St. Davids, Pa., 1994—97; vascular technologist/cardiac sonographer Christiana Care Health Ctr., Newark, Del., 1999—2000. Chair Del. Valley Regional Vascular Curriculum Com. Adv. Bd., Bryn Mawr, Pa., 1994—97. Contbr. national institute of health grant Identification of Needs of Novice Allied Health Researchers, 2001. Girl scout leader Freedom Valley Girl Scout Coun., Valley Forge, Pa., 1991—2001; judge Pa, Jr. Acad. of Sci., Pa., 1997—2002. Mem.: Americal Soc. of Echocardiography, Soc. of Diagnostic Med. Sonographers, Soc. of Vascular Tech. (continuing edn. com. 2001—02). R-Liberal. United Methodist. Avocation: swimming, scuba diving, travel, camping, hiking, reading, parenting, cardiovascular training, musicals. Office: Thomas Jefferson University 130 South 9th Street Suite 1007 Philadelphia PA 19107-5233 Home: 2017 Harbour Gates Dr Apt# 203 Annapolis MD 21401-5377 Office Phone: 215-503-2507. Personal E-mail: lfclf@aol.com. Business E-mail: cynthia.shillingsburg@jefferson.edu.

**SHILLINGSBURG, MIRIAM JONES,** literature educator, academic administrator; b. Balt., Oct. 5, 1943; d. W. Elvin and Miriam R. Jones; m. Peter L. Shillingsburg, Nov. 21, 1967; children: Robert, George, John, Alice, Anne Carol. BA, Mars Hill Coll., 1964; MA, U. S.C., 1966, PhD, 1969; BGS, Miss. State U., 1994. Asst. prof. Limestone Coll., Gaffney, SC, 1969, Miss. State U., 1970—75, assoc. prof., 1975—80, prof. English, 1980—96, assoc. v.p. for acad. affairs, 1988—94; dean arts and scis. Lamar U., Tex. 1994—99; dean liberal arts and scis. Ind. U., South Bend, 2000—04, dean sch. edn., 2005—. Disting. acad. visitor Mark Twain U., 1993, 2001; Simms rsch. prof. U. S.C., 1998; vis. fellow Australian Def. Force Acad., 1989; Fulbright lectr. U. New South Wales, Duntroon, Australia, 1984-85. NEH fellow in residence, Columbia U., 1976-77. Author: Mark Twain in Australasia, 1988; editor: Conquest of Granada, 1988, The Cub of the Panther, 1997; mem. editl. bd. Works of W.M. Thackeray, Miss. Quar., So. Quar.; contbr. articles to profl. jours. and mags. Mem. South Cent. 18th Century Soc., Am. Lit. Assn., Pop Culture Assn., Sigma Tau Delta, Phi Kappa Phi, Simms Soc. (pres. 1996-97). Business E-Mail: mshillin@iusb.edu.

**SHILOH, ALLEN,** writer; b. Bastrop, La., May 24, 1947; s. Al and Rosia B (Davis) S.; children: Datoya Moneake Penn. Grad. high sch., Bastrop; student, Cal/Arts, 1966-68. Mail handler U.S. Postal Svc., Bell, Calif., 1972—. Author: (novels) The Brotherhood, Terror, 1973, Bayou Girl, 1990, (paperback) The Real First United States President, 1983, (short stories pub.) New Cosmic Star, 1968. Sgt. USAF, 1968-72, Vietnam. Avocations: photography, drawing. Home: 305 S Essey Ave Compton CA 90221-3417 Office Phone: 323-729-4121.

**SHILS, MAURICE EDWARD,** physician, educator, research scientist; b. Atlantic City, Dec. 31, 1914; s. Samuel L. and Sarah (Harris) S.; m. Cylia Finkiel, Feb. 19, 1939 (dec. Sept. 1987); children: Loraine J., Jonathan R.; m. Betty Ann Bell, Sept. 24, 1988. BA, Johns Hopkins U., 1937, ScD, 1940; MD, NYU, 1958. Intern joint program Cornell divsn. Bellevue Hosp. and Meml. Hosp., N.Y.C., 1958-59; fellow in physiology Meml. Hosp., 1959-60; instr., asst. prof. nutrition Sch. Pub. Health Columbia U., N.Y.C., 1946-54; instr. biochemistry Sch. Hygiene Johns Hopkins U., Balt., 1940-42; head Ctrl. Metabolic Lab. Sloan Kettering Inst., N.Y.C., 1960-72; from asst. to assoc. attending physician Meml. Hosp., N.Y.C., 1962-72, attending physician, 1972-85; assoc. prof. biochem. Sloan-Kettering divsn. Med. Coll. Cornell U., N.Y.C., 1959-62, from asst. prof. to prof. medicine Med. Coll., 1962-85, prof. emeritus, 1985—. Adj. prof. nutrition dept. pub. health scis. Wake Forest U. Sch. Medicine, Winston-Salem, N.C., 1989-94, cons., 1994-97. Author, sr. editor: Modern Nutrition in Health and Disease, 10th edit., 2005; contbr. more

than 200 rsch. and review articles to profl. jours. Fellow Am. Coll. Physicians, N.Y. Acad. Medicine (Acad. Plaque award 1987), Soc. Nutritional Scis.; mem. AMA (chmn. nutrition adv. group 1974-77, Goldberger award 1983), Am. Soc. Clin. Nutrition (pres. 1985-86, Excellence in Med. Sch. award 1994), Am. Bd. Physician Nutrition Specialists, Phi Beta Kappa, Alpha Omega Alpha. E-mail: mshils@triad.rr.com.

**SHIM, ELISABETH K.,** dermatologist; b. Chgo. BS, Northwestern U., 1990, MD, 1994. Assoc. clin. prof. U. So. Calif. Med. Ctr., L.A. Fellow: Am. Soc. for Dermatologic Surgery, Am. Coll. Mohs Micrographic Surgery, Am. Acad. Dermatology. Office: Ste 570 1301 20th St Santa Monica CA 90404

**SHIM, LEEM SEOP,** computer scientist, educator, researcher; b. Seoul, Korea (South), Aug. 23, 1954; s. Sang Don Shim and Jung Hee Park; m. Jong Sook Kim, Dec. 15, 1957; children: David Jaewoo, Mijung. BSEE, Seoul Nat. U., 1978; MS in Computer Sci., Ill. Inst. Tech., 1987, PhD in Computer Sci., 1991. Engr. Hyundai Engring. & Constrn. Co., Ltd., Seoul, 1980—82; adj. prof. Govs. State U., University Park, Ill., 1990—91; asst. to assoc. prof. Hanshin U., Osan-si, Kyunggi-do, Republic of Korea, 1994—2000; assoc. prof. Trinity Christian Coll., Palos Heights, 2000—02, Ind. U. Pa., Indiana, 2002—. Com. mem. UNB Internat. Symposium Artificial Intelligence, Frederickton, New Brunswick, Canada, 1991, Joint Conf. Artificial Intelligence, Expert Sys., Neural Networks and Fuzzy, Seoul, 1992; dept. chairperson Info. Sci. and Telecom., Hanshin U., Osan-si, Kyunggi-do, 1994—97; v.p. faculty union Hanshin U., Osan-si, Kyunggi-do, 1996—98, dean student affairs, 1998—99. Contbr. articles to profl. jours. 1st lt. Army of Republic of Korea, 1978—80, Seoul. Mem.: Korea Elec. and Electronic Assn., Korea Info. Sci. Soc., Internat. Soc. Tech.n Edn., IEEE Computer Soc., Assn. Computing Machinery. Achievements include research in rehabilitation training system for developmental disable people using multimedia data; English tutoring system using multimedia data; intelligent tutoring system for cardiovascular system; intelligent traffic information system; satellite mobile communication system analysis. Office: Ind Univ of Pa 210 S Tenth St Indiana PA 15705-1087 Home: 3908 Oleander Ct Apt H Calabasas CA 91302-2924 Personal E-mail: lshim@hanmail.net. E-mail: shim@iup.edu.

**SHIM, SANG KOO,** mental health services professional; b. Tokyo, Oct. 1, 1942; arrived in U.S., 1968; s. Sang Taek and Kum Ryon (Bae) Shim; m. Jae Hee Lee, July 12, 1972; children: Tammy, David. BS, Seoul Nat. U., Republic of Korea, 1967; MBA, No. III. U., 1970; MS, U. Wis., Madison, 1975. CPA Ill., cert. valuation analyst. Acct. Vaughn Mfg. Co., Chgo., 1970-72, Stewart-Warner Corp., Chgo., 1972-73; fin. cons. Cen. Acctg. Assn., News Bank, Ill., 1977-79; auditor Ill. Dept. Mental Health, Springfield, 1980-82, CFO, 1983-97; chief bur. app. acctg. Ill. Dept. Human Svcs., Springfield, 1997—2002. Bd. dirs. Metro City Bank, Doraville, Ga. Treas. Korean Assn. Greater St. Louis, 1982. Mem.: Nat. Assn. Cert. Valuation Analysts, Assn. Govt. Accts. (cert. govt. fin. mgr.), Ill. CPA Soc., Korean-Am. C. of C. (v.p. Greater St. Louis chpt. 1994—95). Office: Shim & Co CPA 1630 Lebanon Ave Belleville IL 62221 Home: PO Box 4187 Fairview Heights IL 62208-4187 Office Phone: 618-257-1788. Personal E-mail: skshim@aol.com

**SHIM, TAEHYUN,** mechanical engineer; s. Shim; children: Justin, Jennifer. PhD, U. Calif., Davis, Calif., 2001. Asst. prof. U. Mich., Dearborn, Mich., 2001—. Faculty advisor U. Mich.; cons. in field. Contbr. articles to profl. jours. Mem.: ASME (assoc.), Soc. Automotive Engrs. (assoc.; student advisor 2001—). Office: University of Michigan-Dearborn 4901 Evergreen Road Dearborn MI 48128 Office Phone: 313-593-5127. Office Fax: 313-593-3851. E-mail: tshim@umich.edu.

**SHIMADA, HARUO,** physical chemistry educator; b. Himeji, Hyōgo, Japan, Mar. 27, 1935; s. Shigeyoshi and Shige (Okamoto) S.; m. Ikuko Tanaka, Sept. 21, 1968; children: Yōko, Kenichiro. Grad., U. Tokyo, 1958, doctorate, 1968. Rschr. Yawata (Japan) Iron & Steel Co., 1958-72; sr. rschr. Nippon Steel Corp., Kawasaki, Japan, 1973-80, chief rschr., 1980-90; prof. Sci. U. Tokyo, Shinjuku, Japan, 1990—. Editorial mem.: (monthly jour.) Chem. Industry, 1972—; contbr. articles to profl. jours. Mem. AAAS, Nat. Assn. Corrosion Engrs., Internat. Tech. Inst. (life mem.). Avocations: jogging, swimming. Home: Chuō 5-3-5 Tokyo Ota 143-0024 Japan Office: Sci Univ Tokyo 1-3 Kagurazaka Shinjuku 1628601 Japan

**SHIMADA, KATSUNORI,** retired electrical engineer; b. Tokyo, Mar. 12, 1922; arrived in U.S., 1950; s. Katsujiro and Mume Shimada; m. Ikuko Ueno, Oct. 30, 1975; m. Kazuko Matsumoto; children: Karl, Keiko Shimada Stearns. BSEE, U. Tokyo, 1945; MSEE, U. Minn., 1954, PhD, 1958. Engr. Toshiba Japan, Kawasaki, Japan, 1945—50; instr. U. Minn., Mpls., 1950—58; asst. prof. engring. U. Wash., Seattle, 1958—64; supr. JPL, G&C Rsch. Group, Pasadena, Calif., 1964—80; mgr., Field Ctr. Integration JPL, Pasadena, 1980—85, supr. Celestrial Sensors, 1985—89; ret., 1989. Cons. Boeing Co., Seattle, 1960—63, NASDA of Japan, L.A., 1987—91; invited prof. engring. U. Tokyo, 1973; invited lectr. NEDO of Japan, Tokyo, 1983. Contbr. articles to profl. jours., tech. reports and memoranda. Com. mem. Nat. Parents Day Coalition, L.A., 1996—99, RSVP of Pasadena, 1993—95, Assoc. Retirees of Caltech/JPL, Pasadena, 1989. Resident rsch. fellow, JPL, 1963—64. Mem.: AIAA, IEEE (sr.), Sigma Xi, Eta Kappa Nu. Achievements include patents for cavity emitter for thermionics; thermionic diode switch; solid state power converter. Avocations: photography, computers, golf, travel. Home: 3840 Edgeview Dr Pasadena CA 91107 Personal E-mail: kshimmitzy@aol.com.

**SHIMCHICK, MARIE,** music educator; d. John George and Mary Shimchick. MusB magna cum laude, Ithaca Coll., 1981—85; M in reading, U. of Hartford, 1989—90. Teaching Cert., Music K-12 Conn., Teaching Cert., Reading Cons. K-12 CT, Coaching Cert. Conn., Conn. Writing Project Conn., 1996. Music tchr. New Lebanon Elem. Sch., Byram, Conn., 1985—89, Western and Ctrl. Jr. High Schools, Greenwich, Conn., 1985—87, Ea. Mid. Sch., Riverside, Conn., 1987—2003, Greenwich H.S., Conn., 2003—. Softball coach Western Jr. H.S., Greenwich, Conn., 1986—87, Ea. Jr. H.S., Riverside, Conn., 1988—89; asst. varsity softball coach Greenwich HS, 1992—94, varsity girls' golf coach, 2005—; softball coach Ea. Mid. Sch., Riverside, Conn., 1997—2004. Conductor, artistic director (choral) Eastmen; singer: Greenwich Choral Soc. Recipient Tchr. of the Yr., Phi Delta Kappa, 1999. Mem.: Internat. Reading Assn., Orgn. of Am. Kodaly Educators, Am. Orff-Schulwerk Assn., Nat. Assn. of Teachers of English, Music Educators Nat. Conf., Am. Choral Directors Assn. (life), U.S. Golf Tchrs. Fed. (level II instr.), Phi Delta Kappa, Sigma Alpha Iota (v.p. 1983—85, Scholastic Honor award 1985). Liberal. Eastern Orthodox Christian. Avocations: skiing, racquet sports, fine dining and wines, golf. Office: Greenwich H S 10 Hillside Rd Greenwich CT 06830 Personal E-mail: mshick@hotmail.com. Business E-Mail: marie_shimchick@greenwich.k12.ct.us.

**SHIMELMAN, SUSAN FROMM,** state agency administrator; b. NYC, May 5, 1942; BA, McGill U., Montreal, 1964; MS, Columbia U., 1970. Fellow Harvard U., Cambridge, Mass., 1964-65; Can. coun. fellow McGill U., Montreal, 1965-68; asst. dir. Yale-New Haven Hosp., 1970-80; exec. dir. New Haven Jewish Fedn., 1980-90; undersec. Office Policy and Mgmt., State of Conn., Hartford, 1991-94; sec., 1994—95, dir. presdl. debates, 1995; dir. spl. cts. jud. br. State of Conn., 1995—2001; dir. Office Fiscal Analysis, 2001—. Chair Prison and Jail Overcrowding Commn., Hartford, 1990—, Health Care State Commn., Hartford, 1992—, Econ. Info. and Tech., Hartford, 1994; vice chair Cmty. Econ. Devel. Found., Hartford, 1994. Bd. dirs. Fedn. United Way, New Haven, 1970-94; alt. N.E. Regional Compact, N.J. and Conn., 1991-94; active A Conn. Party, Hartford, 1990-94. Recipient Pres. award New Haven Jewish Fedn., 1990; named Powerful Woman of Vision, YWCA, 1988. Democrat. Home: 4 Kensington Park Bloomfield CT 06002-2146 Office Phone: 860-240-0211. Personal E-mail: sueshimelman@msn.com.

**SHIMER, DANIEL LEWIS,** finance company executive; b. San Angelo, Tex., July 30, 1944; s. Lewis V. and Mary A. (Slick) S.; married. BS in Acctg. and Mktg., Ind. U., 1972; postgrad. Loyola U., New Orleans, 1977. CPA. Sr. acct. Peat, Marwick, Mitchell & Co., Indpls., 1973—75; asst. treas. LTV Corp., Dallas, 1975—79; v.p. fin. Stoller Chem. Co., Houston, 1979—81; v.p., CFO Petro-Silver, Inc., Denver, 1981—83; v.p., treas. FoxMeyer Corp., Denver, 1983—86; v.p., treas., sec. CoastAmerica Corp., Denver, 1986—88; exec. v.p. Bard & Co., Denver, 1989—90; pres. nat accounts divsn. I Can't Believe It's Yogurt/ Brice Foods, Inc., Dallas, 1991—93; exec. v.p., CFO COREStaff Inc., Houston, 1994—96; venture ptnr. Austin Ventures, Dallas, 1996—2004; pres. Shimer Capital Ptnrs., Inc., Dallas, 1996—2004; gen. ptnr. Teakwood Capital, 2005—. Methodist. Avocations: carpentry, fishing. Home: 7436 Glenshannon Cir Dallas TX 75225-2048

**SHIMIZU, KAZUHIKO,** education educator; b. Akeno, Japan, Jan. 20, 1952; s. Kazuyoshi and Toyoko S.; m. Tsurumi Tamagawa, March 30, 1979; children: Kazutaka, Kazuma, Kazuki. BA, Tokyo U. Edn., 1974, MA, 1976; PhD, U. Tsukuba, Japan, 1997. Rsch. fellow Japan Soc. for the Promotion of Sci., Tokyo, 1980-81; asst. prof. Seisen Women's Jr. Coll., Nagano, Japan, 1983-86, assoc. prof., 1986-88; asst. prof. U. Tsukuba, 1988-91, assoc. prof., 1991-99, prof., 1999—, asst. pres., 2004—, vice provost grad. sch., 2004—, chmn. faculty edn., 2006—. Vis. assoc. prof. U. Hiroshima, 1992-96; vis. scholar U. Pa., Phila., 1995-96, U. Minn., Mpls., 2002, U. Mo., 2005; spl. lectr. Yonsei U., Seoul, Korea, 1996; guest lectr. Nat. Edn. Commn., Beijing, 1998, East China Normal U., Shanghai, 2001, Beijing Normal U., 2005. Author: Comparative and Hist. Study of Univ. Credit Sys. Between USA and Japan, 1998, Univ. Reform in Japan, 1999; author and editor: Development of University Evaluation, 2004, A Databook of Edn. Statistics, 2006. Mem. Coun. for Univ. Chartering and Sch. Judicial Person (Monbusho), 2000-02; mem. Japanese Univ. Accreditation Assn., 1994-2000, 2004—; trustee Assn. for the Advancement of Colls. in Japan, 1994—; mem. Inter-Univ. Seminar House, Tokyo, 1997-2002. Recipient rsch. fund Assn. Internat. Edn., Japan, 1990, grant-in-aid for sci. rsch. Ministry of Edn., Sci., Sport and Culture (Monbusho), Tokyo, 1998, 2000, 01, 03-06. Mem.: Japanese Assn. Higher Edn. Rsch. (editor 2000—02, trustee 2003—), Japan Soc. Edu. Sys. and Orgn. (office dir. 1999—), Japan Assn. Lifelong Edn. (office dir. 1998—2000), Comparative and Internat. Edn. Soc. Avocation: gardening. Home: 9015 Uede 407-0204 Yamanashi Japan Office: Faculty of Edn U Tsukuba 1-1-1 Tennodai 305-8572 Tsukuba Japan Business E-Mail: shimizuk@sakura.cc.tsukuba.ac.jp.

**SHIMIZU, YOSHIAKI,** art historian, department chairman; b. Tokyo, Feb. 27, 1936; came to U.S., 1953, naturalized, 1999; s. Mamoru and Michiko (Hayasaka) S.; children: Karen Akiko Marie, Kenneth Cuyler Norio, Katherine Kimie, Kei Robert. BA, Harvard U., 1963; MA, U. Kans., 1968; MFA, Princeton U., 1971, PhD, 1974. Asst. prof. dept. art and archaeology Princeton (N.J.) U., 1973-75, prof., 1984—, chmn. dept. art and archaeology, 1990-92, Marquand prof. art and archaeology, 1992—; dir. program in Asian art and archaeology, 1992—; asst. prof. U. Calif., Berkeley, 1975-78, assoc. prof., 1978-79; curator Japanese art Freer Gallery, Smithsonian Instn., Washington, 1979-84; guest curator Nat. Gallery Art, Washington, 1982-89; guest prof. U. Heidelberg, 1993. Guest prof. Ritsumeikan U., 1996; vis. fellow dept. art history U. Tokyo, 1996; mem. art adv. com. Japan Soc. Gallery, 1984—, adv. com. Asia Soc. Galleries, N.Y.C., 1992—, chmn. adv. com., 1999—; vis. scholar dept. comparative culture Sophia U., Tokyo, 1993. Author: (with John M. Rosenfield) Masters of Japanese Calligraphy, 1984; editor: (with Carolyn Wheelwright) Japanese Ink Paintings, 1976; author, editor: Japan: The Shaping of Daimyo Culture 1185-1858, 1988; mem. editorial bd. Archives of Asian Art, 1979-89. Asian Art, Smithsonian Inst., 1985-93; mem. vis. com. Arthur M. Sackler Gallery, Washington, 1984-94. Smithsonian Inst. fellow, 1967, Social Sci. Rsch. Coun./Am. Coun. Learned Socs. fellow, 1977-78, Asian Cultural Coun. fellow, 1995; J.D. Rockefeller III fellow, 1969-70. Mem. Coll. Art Assn. (bd. dirs. 1987-91), Japan Art History Assn., Japan Soc. N.Y., Ctr. for the Study of Japanese Woodblock Prints (mem. internat. adv. bd. 1983—) Home: 2 College Rd Princeton NJ 08540 Office: Princeton U Dept Art and Archaeology Princeton NJ 08540 E-mail: shimizu@princeton.edu.

**SHIMKHADA, DEEPAK,** art historian; b. Darkha, Nepal, Sept. 5, 1945; s. Ratna Prasad and Kausalya Shimkhada; m. Kanti Koirala, July 7, 1970; children: Leepi, Riti. BFA, U. Of Baroda, 1968; MFA, U. Of Baroda, Baroda, India, 1970; MA, U. Of So. Calif., 1974; PhD, Claremont u., 2001. Prof. Rio Hondo Coll., Whittier, Calif., 1995—96, Mt. San Antonio Coll., Walnut, Calif., 1997—98; asst. prof. Claremont Mckenna Coll., Claremont, California, Calif., 1999—. Pres. Found. For Indic Philosophy & Culture, Claremont, 2001—; vis. prof. Scripps Coll., Claremont, 1981—82. Contbr. exhibition catalog Usc Collects: A Sampling Of Taste, 1973; author: (exhibition catalog) NEPALI ART; Author, Man, Woman, and Nature in Asian Art, exhibition catalog, 1982, 1973; editor: (compilation) Original Buddhist Mantras In Sanskrit, 1985 (grantee N.Am. Buddhist Found., 1984), Himalayas At A Crossroads: The Portrait Of A Changing World, 1988; contbr. Woven Jewels, 1992. Founder Himalayan Arts Coun. of Pacific Asia Mus., Pasadena, Calif., 1986—94; v.p. Asian studies on the Pacific Coast, 2005—. Recipient Cert. award, Nepal Assn. of Fine Arts, 1966, 1969, Grad. Students Alumni Rsch. award, Ohio State U., 1980; fellow Fulbright fellow, U.S. Dept. Of State, 1972—74, Tuition fellowship, U. Of Chgo., 1974—77; grantee Sr. Cultural fellow, Govt. Of India, 1968—70, Jr. Rsch. fellow, Am. Inst. Of Indian Studies, 1978—79. Mem.: Am. Nepal Soc. Calif. (pres. 1998—2000), Art Hist. of So. Calif., South Asia Soc., Assn. For Asian Studies (v.p. Pacific coast 2005—07, grantee 1989). Home: 1682 Lowell Avenue Claremont CA 91711

**SHIMKUS, JOHN MONDY,** congressman; b. Collinsville, Ill., Feb. 21, 1958; s. Gene Louis and Kathleen (Mondy) S.; m. Karen Kay Muth; children: David, Joshua, Daniel. BS, U.S. Mil. Acad., 1980; MBA, So. Ill. U., Edwardsville, 1997. Advanced through grades to capt. U.S. Army, 1980-86; stationed at U.S. Army Base, Columbus, Ga., 1980-81, 85, served at Bamberg, Germany, 1981-84, stationed at Monterey, Calif, 1985-86; tchr. Metro East Luth. H.S., Edwardsville, Ill., 1986-90; treas. Madison County, Edwardsville, 1990-96; mem. U.S. Congress from 19th Ill. dist., 1997—, mem. energy and commerce com. Liaison officer U.S. Mil. Acad., 1987-96; treas. So. Ill. Law Enforcement Commn., 1990-96. Bd. dirs. Sr. Citizen Companion Program, Belleville, Ill., 1991; trustee Collinsville Twp., Ill., 1989-93; Rep. precinct committeeman, Collinsville, 1988—. Lt. col. USAR, 1985—. Mem. Nat. Assn. Counties, Ill. Treas. and Fin. Officers (bd. dirs.), Ill. County Treas. Assn., Am. Legion Post 365. Republican. Lutheran. Home: 504 Sumner Blvd Collinsville IL 62234-1934 Office: US Ho Reps 513 Cannon Ho Office Bldg Washington DC 20515-1319 also: Springfield Dist Office Ste C 3130 Chatham Rd Springfield IL 62704

**SHIMM, MELVIN GERALD,** law educator; b. N.Y.C., Jan. 30, 1926; s. Joseph George and Sadie Rosalie (Rosenblatt) Shimm; m. Cynia Brown, Aug. 15, 1948; children: David Stuart, Jonathan Evan. AB, Columbia U., 1947; LLB, Yale U., 1950. Bar: NY 50. Assoc. Cahill, Gordon, Zachry & Reindel, N.Y.C., 1950—51; atty. Wage Stblzn. Bd., Washington, 1951—52; Bigelow fellow U. Chgo., 1952—53; asst. prof. Duke U. Law Sch., Durham, NC, 1953—56, assoc. prof., 1956—59, prof., 1959—96, prof. emeritus, 1996—, assoc. dean, 1978—83. Vis. prof. NYU, 1957, U. So. Calif., 1965, U. Mich. Ann Arbor, 1973, U. Tex., Austin, 1976; chmn. Durham (NC) Bd. Adjustment, 1966—70; dir. dean. Am. Law Schs. Orientation Program in Am. Law, 1968—70, Duke Inst. in Transnat. Law, 1987—92; cons. The Brookings Instn., 1965—67; mem. NC Gen. Statutes Commn., 1984—88. Editor-inchief: Law & Contemporary Problems, Jour. Legal Eds., Am. editor: Jour. Bus. Law; editor: Yale Law Jour. Vice-chmn. Lucy Daniels Found., 1989—2003; bd. advisors Ctr. for Law, Ethics and Nat. Security, 1993—; pres. Beth El Congregation, Durham, NC, 1967—70, 1975—78; chmn. Jewish Fedn. Durham/Chapel Hill, 1973—75; trustee Jewish Cmty. Found., Durham/Chapel Hill, 2001—04. Lt. U.S. Army, 1943—46. Mem.: Order of Coif, Phi Beta Kappa. Office: Duke U Sch Law PO Box 90360 Durham NC 27708-0360 E-mail: shimm@law.duke.edu.

**SHIMMIN, MARGARET ANN,** women's health nurse; b. Forbes, ND, Oct. 26, 1941; d. George and Reba S. Diploma in Nursing, St. Luke's Hosp. Sch. Nursing, Fargo, N.D., 1962; BSW, U. West Fla., 1978; cert. ob-gyn nurse practitioner, U. Ala., Birmingham, 1983, MPH, 1986. Lic. nurse, Fla., N.D., Ala. Head nurse, emergency room St. Luke's Hosps., Fargo, 1962-67; charge nurse, labor and delivery, perinatal nurse educator Sacred Heart Hosp., Pensacola, Fla., 1970-82; ARNP Escambia County Pub. Health Unit, Pensacola, 1983-89; cmty. health nursing cons. Dist. 1 Health and Rehab. Svcs., Pensacola, 1989-96; sr. cmty. health nursing supr. Escambia County Health Dept., Pensacola, 1996—, nurse program specialist OSHA staff tng. and quality assurance, 2002—05, nurse program specialist diabetes intervention program, 2005—. Capt. nurse corps U.S. Army, 1967-70, Japan. Mem. NAACOG (cert. maternal-gynecol.-neonatal nursing, ob-gyn nurse practitioner), Fla. Nurses' Assn., ANA, N.W. Fla. ARNP (past sec./treas.), Fla. Perinatal Assn., Nat. Perinatal Assn., Healthy Mothers/Healthy Babies Coalition, Fla. Pub. Health Assn., U. West Fla. Alumni Assn., U. Ala. at Birmingham Sch. of Public Health Alumni Assn., Phi Alpha Republican. Presbyterian. Avocations: cooking, music, travel, photography, reading. Home: 8570 Olympia Rd Pensacola FL 32514-8029 Office: Escambia County Health Dept 1295 W Fairfield Dr Pensacola FL 32501-1107 Office Phone: 850-595-6048.

**SHIMODA, JERRY YASUTAKA,** retired national historic park manager; b. Haleiwa, Hawaii, Mar. 21, 1930; s. Tamotsu and Sasai Shimoda; m. Clara H. Segawa, Aug. 7, 1954; children: Karen Marie K., Randall T., Shaun T., Teri Ellen H., Jacqueline Y., David Y. BA in Govt., U. Hawaii, 1952, MA in Far Ea. Area Studies, 1957; postgrad., St. Louis U., 1957-59; PhD in Pub. Adminstrn., Kennedy-Western U., 2004. Historian Jefferson Nat. Expansion Meml. Nat. Hist. Site, St. Louis, 1957-60; chief historian, in charge hist. rsch. and visitor svcs. Saratoga Nat. Hist. Park, Stillwater, NY, 1960-66; chief historian Home of Franklin D. Roosevelt Nat. Hist. Site and, Frederick Vanderbilt Nat. Hist. Site, Hyde Park, NY, 1966-69; instr. Nat. Park Svc. Stephen T. Mather Tng. Ctr., Harpers Ferry, W.Va., 1969-72; supt. Pu'uhonua o Honaunau Nat. Hist. Park, 1972-96, Puukohola Heiau Nat. Hist. Site, Kawaihae, 1972-96; ret., 1996. Lectr. environ. edn. Pa. State U., U. W.Va., Shepard Coll., 1969—72; acting supr. Kaloko-Honokohau Nat. Hist. Pk., 1988—90; instr. environ. edn., interpretive and basic instructing techniques U. Hawaii, Hilo, Kapiolani C.C.; instr. Japanese culture U. Hawaii, Hilo, 1994; U.S. del. and translator U.S.-Japan Panel on Nat. Parks and Equivalent Res., 1968—97, World Conf. on Marine Parks, Tokyo, 1975; mem. internat. bd. dirs. Heritage Interpretation Internat., 1989—98; presenter in field. Author booklets on nat. parks, mgmt. and history; contbr. numerous articles to profl. publs., mags. and newspapers. Bd. dirs. Volcano Art Ctr.; mem. adv. com. Wailoa State Ctr.; mem. Hawaii Gov.'s Task Force on Ocean and Recreation; chmn. restoration com. St. Benedict's Ch., Honaunau, 1982-95; chmn. bd. dirs. Kahua Na'au 'Ao, 1996-97; vol. training cons. to Nat. Pk. Svc., 1996-2001; cons. Nat. Park Svc., 2001-. Recipient Spl. Achievement award Nat. Park Svc., 1964, 68, 70, resolution W.Va. Senate, 1971, Hawaii Ho. of Reps., 1982, sec.'s cert. Dept. Interior, 1971, Exec. of Yr. award West Hawaii chpt. Profl. Secs. Internat., 1981, cert. Govt. of Japan, 1981, staff plaque Pu'uhonua o Honaunau Nat. Hist. Park, Puukohola Heiau Nat. Hist. Site and Kaloko-Honokohau Nat. Hist. Park, 1988, cert. Japan Nat. Parks Assn., 1989, cert. of appreciation South Kona Aloha Lions Club, 1990, Meritorious Svc. award Sec. Interior, 1996, others. Mem. Hawaii Mus. Assn. (bd. dirs. 1988-92), Kona Hist. Soc. (bd. dirs. 1988-92), Big Island Ocean Recreation and Tourism Assn. (exec. com.), Kona Judo Club (pres. 1977-96), Rotary (pres. Kona Mauka 1978-79, co-founder Volcano chpt. 2001, Paul Harris fellow 1991, Disting. Svc. award 1992). Avocations: writing, reading, travel, teaching.

**SHIMP, KAREN ANN,** accountant, corporate financial executive; b. Atlantic, Iowa, July 17, 1959; d. Emerson Arnold and Verna Louise (Schmeling) Fett; m. Philip Kenneth Shimp, Jan. 30, 1988 (div.); 1 child, Keith Emerson. BSBA, Drake U., 1981. Acct. Midwest Mut. Ins. Co., West Des Moines, Iowa, 1981-84; staff acct. Deborah J. Kent, CPA, Palm Desert, Calif., 1985; fin. analyst Massey Sand & Rock Co., Indio, Calif., 1986-88; supr. interline Greyhound Lines, Inc., West Des Moines, 1989-93; fin. dir. City of Pella, Iowa, 1994-2000; dir. fin. orgnl. svcs. Cedar Falls (Iowa) Utilities, 2000—. Coord. Drake U. Bus. Aid Soc., 1980; mem. Inland Soc. Tax Consultants, 1987-91. Treas. Luth. Women's Missionary League, Indio, 1986-88, sec., 1988-89; v.p. Aid Assn. for Lutherans, Indio, 1988-89; bd. dirs. After School Kid's Klub, 1995-97, treas., Cedar Falls and Culture Bd., 2004-, treas., Family Svc. League Bd., 2001-. State of Iowa scholar, 1977. Mem. Inst. Mgmt. Accts., Kiwanis Internat (treas. 1996-97). Democrat. Avocations: sewing, reading, aerobics, taxes. Office: CVU Utility Pkwy PO Box 769 Cedar Falls IA 50613 Home: 915 W 10th St Cedar Falls IA 50613-2401 Office Phone: 319-268-5205. E-mail: kshimp@cfunet.net.

**SHIN, DONG HEE,** technology educator; b. Seoul, Korea, Oct. 30, 1970; arrived in US, 1997; s. Hong-Sik Shin and Young-Ja Seo; m. Youn Joo Shin, Jan. 7, 2003. BA in Comm., Sung Kun Kwan U., Seoul, 1996; MA in Telecomm., So. Ill. U., 1998; MS in Info. Mgmt., PhD in Telecomm., Syracuse U., 2004. Rschr. Korea Info. Soc. Rsch., Seoul, 1997; reporter Korea Ctrl. Daily, LA, 1999; lectr. Syracuse (NY) U., 2002—04; asst. prof. Pa. State U., Reading, 2004—. Cons. SK Club, Seoul, 2000; rschr. SK Telecomm., Seoul, 2001; project mgr. Verizon and NY State, Syracuse, NY, 2000—03; spkr. in field. Activist Assn. for Cmty. Networking, Chgo., 2002; advisor NY State Pub. Svc. Commn., Albany, 2003; adv. cons. Consortium of Seoul Digital City, 2004. Fellow, Syracuse U., 2002; scholar, So. Ill. U., 1997; rsch. grantee, Pa. State U., 2004. Mem. Am. Info. Sci. Assn., Internat. Comm. Assn., Internat. Telecomm. Soc. Presbyterian. Avocations: tennis, fishing, touring. Office: Pa State U PO Box 7009 Reading PA 19610 Home: 114 Bainbridge Cir Reading PA 19608 Office Phone: 610-396-6135. Office Fax: 610-396-6024. E-mail: dxs75@psu.edu.

**SHIN, ERNEST EUN-HO,** physicist, educator, researcher; b. Chin-do, Republic of Korea, Dec. 31, 1935; came to U.S., 1953; s. Hyung Sik and Ok Bin (Lim) S.; m. Shin-Ai Park, July 27, 1963; children: Irene, Juliet, Mariette, Michelle. BS in Physics, Carnegie Inst. Tech., 1957; AM in Physics, Harvard U., 1959, PhD in Physics, 1961. Rsch. fellow Cyclotron Lab., Harvard U., Cambridge, Mass., 1957-58, tchg. fellow physics dept., 1958-59; rsch. assoc. Arthur D. Little, Inc., Cambridge, 1960-62; prof. physics U. Miami, Coral Gables, Fla., 1966-72, founder, dir. Solid State Physics Lab., 1969-72; dir. Nieman Inst., Dallas, 1972-73; vis. scientist Korea Atomic Energy Rsch. Inst., Seoul, 1973-74; chmn., chief exec. officer Yulsan Am., Inc., San Francisco, 1974-89; dir. Chestnut Hill Inst., Napa, Calif., 1984—. Co-founder Yulsan Group Cos., Seoul, 1974; prof. Intercultural Inst. Calif., San Francisco, 1996—; chmn. Shinergy, LLC, San Francisco, 2001—. Contbr. over 100 articles on biophysics, math. physics and elem. particle physics, superconductivity, optical properties of metals to profl. jours.; patentee in field. Woodrow Wilson fellow Harvard U., 1959. Mem. AAAS, Am. Phys. Soc. (life), N.Y. Acad. Scis. Achievements include patent for bouyancy-driven electric power generator, 2005; development of space-time theory of fundamental particles, 2005. Avocations: ranching, gardening, painting, fishing. Office: Chestnut Hill Inst PO Box 3510 Napa CA 94558-0350 Home: 31 Skipping Rock Way Napa CA 94558-7006 Personal E-mail: eunho@aol.com. Business E-Mail: ernestshin@shinergyusa.com.

**SHIN, HYUN JOON,** industrial engineer; b. Seoul, Oct. 3, 1971; arrived in US, 2002; s. Seun Kyun Shin and Chung Mi Chang; m. Ji Youn Jung, Jan. 9, 1999; 1 child, Mina J. BS in indsl. engring., Korea U., Republic of Korea, 1995; MS in indsl. engring., Korea U., 1999; PhD, Korea U., Seoul, 2002. Postdoctoral rschr. Tex. A&M U., College Station, 2002—04; sr. engr. Samsung Electronics Co., Ltd., Asan, Choongnam, Republic of Korea, 2004—05; asst. prof. dept. indsl. info and sys. engring. Sungmyung U., 2005—. Sr. rschr. Korea U., Seoul, 1997—2002. Fellow, Korea Sci. and Engring. Found., 2003. Home: Dujeongdong Daelim Apt 101-1101 Choong-

nam Cheonan 330-210 Republic of Korea Office: Sangmyung Univ Anseodong 98-20 Choongnam Cheonan 330-720 Republic of Korea Fax: +82-41-550-5185. Office Phone: +82-41-550-5374. Personal E-mail: hjshin@smu.ac.kr.

**SHIN, JAE-HWA,** educator; PhD, Mo. Schf Journalism, Columbia, 2003. Dir. Fedn. Korea Industries, Seoul, 1994—98; asst. prof. U. So. Miss., Hattiesburg, 2003—. Mem.: Assn. Edn. Journalism and Mass Comm. Office: U So Miss Box 5121 Hattiesburg MS 39406 Office Phone: 601-266-4282.

**SHIN, MYUNG-KI,** computer scientist, researcher; b. Seoul, Republic of Korea, Feb. 27, 1970; s. Jung-Hwan Shin and Hee-Hyoung Kim; m. Hyun-Joo Park, Mar. 24, 1996; children: Ah-Young Judy, Tai-Yon Tony. BS in Computer Sci., Hongik U., Seoul, 1992, MS in Computer Sci., 1994; PhD in Computer Engring., Chungnam Nat. U., Daejeon, Republic of Korea, 2003. Rschr. Electronics and Telecomm. Rsch. Inst., Deajeon, Republic of Korea, 1994—2000, sr. rschr., 2000—03; guest rschr. Nat. Inst. Stds. and Tech., Gaithersburg, Md., 2004—. Chmn. tech. group Open Sys. Interconnection Association, Seoul, 1997—2000; rapporteur Asia—Pacific Telecommunity Standardization Program, Bangkok, 1999; working group chair IPv6 Forum Korea, Daejeon, 2000—03; program com. Global IPv6 Summit, Luxembourg, 2001—03; editor Internet Engring. Task Force, Reston, 2003—. Author: (internat. std.) Dual Stack Hosts Using Bump-in-the-API (Min. Award of Info. and Communication (South Korea), 2003); editor: Application Aspects of IPv6 Transition; author: (book) Next-Generation Protocol. Named This Year's Netizen, Nat. Computerization Agy., 1996; recipient Superior Rschr. award, Electronics and Telecom. Rsch. Inst., 2001. Mem.: Inst. Electronics, Info. and Comm. Engrs. Achievements include development of eXplicit Multicast Extension (Xcast+); IPv6 network and application deployment. Avocations: travel, golf, movies. Office: Natl Inst Stds and Tech 100 Bureau Dr Gaithersburg MD 20899 Office Phone: 301-975-3613. E-mail: mshin@nist.gov.

**SHIN, SUNGJAE,** nutritionist; b. Busan, South Korea, Dec. 15, 1968; s. Yonggoo Shin and Boonnam Lee; m. Kyungil Choi, Mar. 9, 1996; children: Minsuk children: Chewon, Cheyoung. Doctorate, Tokyo U. Fisheries, 1998. Cert. food processing Korea Certifying Orgn. Investigator Nat. Inst. Health and Nutrition, Tokyo, 2001—03; rsch. scholar U. Pitts., Pitts., 2003—. Contbr. scientific papers to profl. publs. Recipient Japanese Inviting Ednl. scholarship, Ministry Edn. In Japan, 1994—98, univ. scholarship, Pukyong U., 1987—94, rsch. grant, Jst Co., 2001. Mem.: JSBBA (assoc.). Achievements include research in Influence of the origin and level of dietary protein on TBI-induced oxidative damage in mice; Different onsets of oxidative damage to DNA and lipids in bone marrow and liver in rats given total body irradiation; Prostaglandin E2 reinforces the activation of Ras signal pathway in lung adenocarcinoma cells via EP3; Relation between oxidative damage and dietary protein: marginal protein level which modulates oxidative damage in mice with total body irradiation; Adequate intakes of vitamin E and protein prevent increases of oxidative damage to DNA, lipids, and protein induced by total body irradiation in mice; Vitamin E modulates radiation-induced oxidative damage in mice fed a high-lipid diet; Severe DNA damage in K-ras gene patterns of PCR products in mice fed a 1% protein diet and exposed to a high dose of radiation; High levels of apoptosis induced by total body irradiation in mice fed a low protein-low vitamin E diet; High levels of apoptosis induced by total body irradiation in mice fed a low protein-low vitamin E diet; High oleic acid oil suppresses lung tumorigenesis in mice through the modulation of extracellular signal-regulated kinase cascade; Induction of apoptosis in a human breast cancer cell overexpressing ErbB-2 receptor by alpha-tocopheryloxybutyric acid; Enhanced oxidative damage induced by total body irradiation in mice fed a low protein diet. Office: U Pitts Pittsburgh PA 15219 Home: 6 Resident Dr Apt C Killeen TX 76549-4136 Personal E-mail: ssjkfrihan@hanmail.net.

**SHIN, SUNNY HYUCKSUN,** social worker, educator; s. Jae-yeol Shin and Eu-Ja Chung; m. Eunice Eunkyung Lee. MSW, U. Wis., Madison, 1998; PhD, U. Ill., Urbana-Champaign, 2002. Lic. sch. social worker Wis., 1998. Asst. prof. Boston U. Sch. Social Work, 2002—. Consulting editor Families in Soc. Alliance for Children and Families, Washington, 2003—; consulting editor Children and Sch. NASW, Washington. Co-dir. Fishes and Loaves, Cambridge, Mass., 2002—05. Grantee Youth Alcohol Prevention Rsch., Nat. Inst. Alcohol Abuse and Alcoholism, 2006—; CHIPS fellow, NIMH, 2005. Office: Boston University School Social Work 264 Bay State Rd Boston MA 02215 Office Phone: 617-353-7912. Business E-Mail: hshin@bu.edu.

**SHIN, YONGSOON,** research scientist; b. Checheon, Chungcheong buk-do, Republic of Korea, Mar. 1, 1965; s. Hyeonpill Shin and Hwawall Jeong; m. Sookyoung Kim, Dec. 24, 1994; children: Mickey K., Michelle K. PhD, U. Tenn., Knoxville, 1999. Postdoctoral Pacific NW Nat. Lab., Richland, Wash., 1999—2001; sr. rsch. scientist, 2002—. Worship preparation Korean Presbyn. Ch. of Ctrl. Wash., Richland, 2005—. Recipient Korean Leadership scholarship, 1985—88, Rsch. Merit award, U. Tenn., 1998, Outstanding Performance awards, Pacific NW Nat. Lab., 2002—06. Mem.: Materials Rsch. Soc. (life), Am. Chem. Soc. (life). Achievements include discovery of 5 Syntheses of SiC ceramics by the carbothermal reduction of mineralized wood with silica; research in Bicontinuous, thermoresponsive, L3-phase silica nanocomposites and their smart drug delivery applications; Hygroscopic growth of self-assembled layered surfactant molecules at the interface of air/organic salts; Synthesis of supported carbon nanotubes in mineralized silica/wood composites; Synthesis of SiC ceramics by the carbothermal reduction of mineralized wood with silica; Synthesis of hierarchical titanium carbide from titania-coated cellulose paper; Morphology control of hierarchically ordered cellular ceramic materilas prepared by surfactant-directed sol-gel mineralization of wood cellular structures; Nuclear magnetic resonance investigation of hierarchically ordered positive and negative replica of wood cellular structures prepared by sol-gel mineralization; pH-controlled synthesis of hierarchically ordered ceramic materials with wood cellular structures by surfactant-directed sol-gel mineralization; Entraping enzyme in a functionalized nanoporous support; Sustained drug release on temperature-responsive poly(N-isopropylacrylamide)-integrated hydroxylapatite; A 129Xe NMR study of functionalized ordered mesoporous silica; The core-shell approach to formation of ordered nanoporous materials; Hierarchically ordered ceramics through surfactant-templated sol-gel mineralization of biological cellular structures; Hybrid nanogels for sustainable positive thermosensitive drug release; Molecular assembly in mesoporosity: A class of highly functional nanosclae materials; Ordered hierarchical porous materials: Towards tunable size- and shape-selective microcavities in nanoporous channels; Synthesis and applications of functionalized nanoporous materials for specific adsorption; Supercritical processing of functionalized size-selective microporous materials; EXAFS study of uranyl nitrate dimer at high and low temperature; A new methodology to functionalize surfaces of ordered mesoporous materilas based on ion exchange reactions; patents for Self-assembled monolayer and method of making; research in Imprinted coating: A novel synthesis of selective functionalized ordered mesoporous sorbents; Enhancement of uranyl adsorption on mesoporous titanium-based sorbents; Investigation of uranyl adsorption capacity and selectivity on silica sol-gel glasses vis molecular imprinting; Comparative UV-Vis studies of uranyl chloride complex in two basic ambient temperature melt systems: the observation of spectral and thermodynamic variation induced via hydrogen bonding; Spectroscopic probing of adsorption of uranyl to uranyl-imprinted silica sol-gel glass via steady-state and time-resolved fluorescence measurement; Synthesis of Naproxen via regioselective ring-opening of (2S, 3S)-epoxy-1-butanol; Regioselective oxirane ring opening of trans-2, 3-epoxy alcohols with arylaluminum complexes; Nanostructural control of hydrogen release and reactivity of ammonia borane; The structural feature of S1' subsite of Carboxypeptidase A; patents for Self-assembled monolayers and method of making; Imprinted coating synthesis of selective functionalized ordered mesoporous sorbents for separation and sensors. US 6, 251, 280; Self-assembled monolayers and method of making; patents pending for Materials for hydrogen storage and methods for preparing and using same; Method of Making Monolayers; patents for Self-assembled monolayer and method of making. Home: 1043

Sunstone Court Richland WA 99352 Office: Pacific Northwest Nat Lab 902 Battele Blvd POBox 999 MSIN K2-44 Richland WA 99354 Office Phone: 509-375-2693. Office Fax: 509-375-2186. Business E-Mail: yongsoon@pnl.gov.

**SHINAGEL, MICHAEL,** dean, English literature educator; b. Vienna, Apr. 21, 1934; came to U.S., 1941; s. Emanuel and Lilly (Hillel) S.; m. Ann Birdsey Mitchell, Sept. 1, 1956 (div. 1970); children: Mark Mitchell, Victoria Stuart; m. Rosa Joanne Bonanno, Dec. 6, 1973 (div. 1993); m. Marjorie Lee North, May 26, 1995. AB, Oberlin Coll., 1957; A.M., Harvard U., 1959, PhD, 1964; Doctorate (hon.), Internat. U. Ecuador, 1997; Doctorate (hon.), U. Argentina Empresa, 2003. Teaching fellow Harvard U., Cambridge, Mass., 1958-59, tutor in English, 1962-64, assoc. dir. career office, 1959-64, dean continuing edn., 1975—, lectr. extension, 1976—, sr. lectr. English, 1983—, master Quincy House, 1986—2001, univ. dean of continuing edn.; asst. prof. English, Cornell U., Ithaca, NY, 1964-67; prof., chmn. dept. English, Union Coll., Schenectady, NY, 1967-75. Bd. dirs. Harvard Coop. Soc., publ. Harvard Rev.; pres. bd. dirs. Ednl. Exch. Boston, 1982-87; editor Continuing Higher Edn. Rev., 1997—. Author: Defoe and Middle-Class Gentility, 1968; co-author: (handbook) Summer Institutes in English, 1965; editor: Concordance to Poems of Swift, 1972, Critical Edition of Robinson Crusoe, 1975 (revised 1993); co-editor: Harvard Scholars in English (1890-1990), 1991. With U.S. Army, 1952—54, Korea. Woodrow Wilson fellow, 1957; NEH grantee, 1965 Mem. Univ. Continuing Edn. Assn., Assn. Continuing Higher Edn., Mass. Hist. Soc., Old South Meeting House, The Johnsonians, The Saturday Club, Harvard Faculty Club (pres. 1985-87), Phi Beta Kappa. Avocations: reading, cooking, music, tennis. Home: 22 Grozier Rd Cambridge MA 02138 Office: Harvard U Divsn Continuing Edn 51 Brattle St Cambridge MA 02138-3701 Office Phone: 617-495-2930. Business E-Mail: michael_shinagel@harvard.edu.

**SHINAVER, ALAN L.,** educator; b. AuGres, Mich., Oct. 8, 1955; BS, Ctrl. Mich. U., Mt. Pleasant, 1978. Tchr. Saginaw Pub. Schs., Mich., 1978—, Arthur Hill HS, Saginaw, 2005—. Office: Arthur Hill HS 3115 Mackinaw St Saginaw MI 48602 Personal E-mail: ashinaver@spsd.net.

**SHINDLER, DONALD A.,** lawyer; b. New Orleans, Oct. 15, 1946; s. Alan and Isolene (Levy) S.; m. Laura Epstein, 1969; children: Jay, Susan. BSBA, Washington U., St. Louis, 1968; JD, Tulane U., 1971. Bar: La. 1971, U.S. Dist. Ct. (ea. dist.) La. 1971, U.S. Tax Ct. 1974, Ill. 1975, U.S. Dist. Ct. (no. dist.) Ill. 1975; CPA, La.; lic. real estate broker, Ill. Assoc. Pope, Ballard, Shepard & Fowle, Chgo., 1975-78, Rudnick & Wolfe, Chgo., 1978-81, ptnr., 1981-99; gen. counsel America's Second Harvest Nat. Food Bank Network, 1998-2000; ptnr. Piper Marbury Rudnick & Wolfe, Chgo., 1999—2002, Piper Rudnick LLP, Chgo., 2002—05, DLA Piper Rudnick Gray Cary US LLP, Chgo., 2005—. Lectr. in field. Contbr. articles on real estate to legal jours. Trustee Glencoe (Ill.) Pub. Libr., 1981-87, pres., 1986-87; alumni bd. govs. Washington U., 1992-93; mem. Glencoe Zoning Commn./Bd. Appeals, 1994-2000; Glencoe Plan Commn., 1986-87. Lt. JAGC, USNR, 1971-75. Fellow Am. Coll. Mortgage Attys.; mem. ABA, Ill. Leading Lawyers, La. State Bar Assn., Chgo. Bar Assn. (com. chmn. 1979-80, 83-84, 90-94, 96-99, editor land trust seminars 1984-96), Ill. Super Lawyers, Urban Land Inst. (mem. steering com. Chgo. dist. coun.), Ill. Super Lawyers (R/E), CoreNet Global (pres. Chgo. chpt. 1997-98, dir. 1991-2003), Internat. Assn. Attys. and Execs. in Corp. Real Estate (fall forum co-chair 2002, spring conf. co-chair, 2003, bd. dirs. 2003—), Union League Club (chair real estate group 1993-96), Order of Coif, Beta Gamma Sigma, Omicron Delta Kappa. Office: DLA Piper Rudnick Gray Cary US LLP Ste 1900 203 N La Salle St Chicago IL 60601-1210 Office Phone: 312-368-2175. Business E-Mail: donald.shindler@dlapiper.com.

**SHINDLER, STEVEN,** telecommunications industry executive; m. Mary Kay Shindler; 3 children. BA, Univ. Mich.; MBA, Cornell Univ. Positions through mng. dir. comm. fin. group Toronto Dominion Bank, 1987—96; exec. v.p., CFO Nextel Comm., 1996—2000; CEO Nextel Comm. (now NII Holdings Inc.), 2000—02; chmn., CEO NII Holdings Inc., Reston, Va., 2002—. Named Greater Washington area Entrepreneur of the Yr., Ernst & Young; recipient Bravo Bus. award as Internat. CEO of the Yr., Latin Trade mag. Office: NII Holdings Inc Ste 600 10700 Parkridge Blvd Reston VA 20191*

**SHINDURLING, JON J.,** judge; b. Idaho Falls, Idaho, Apr. 13, 1947; s. Boyd Thomas and Donna Marie (Fullmer) S.; m. Christine Moss, May 24, 1974; children: Melissa, Marianne, Amanda, Alison. BA in English, Ariz. State U., 1972; JD, U. Idaho, 1977. Bar: Idaho. Ptnr. May & May Law Offices, Twin Falls, Idaho, 1977-88, Wright Law Offices, Idaho Falls, 1990-93; field dir. Sch. of Urban and Wilderness Survival, Shoshone, Idaho, 1988-90; dep. prosecuting atty. Bonneville County, Idaho Falls, 1994-2000, chief dep., 1995-2000; dist. judge 7th Jud. Dist., 2000—. Mem. continuing legal edn. com. Idaho Law Found., Boise, 1985-88; mem. civil jury instns. com. Idaho Supreme Ct., Boise, 1987-89, 96—. Mem. coun. exec. bd. Boy Scouts Am.-Snake River Area, Twin Falls, 1979-90; bd. dirs. Magic Valley YFCA, Twin Falls, 1988-90, Idaho Falls Opera Theatre, 1993-99. Mem. Idaho State Bar (mem. bar examination com. 1979-82, chmn. com. 1980-82, mem. fee disputes resolution com. 1991—, bar examination grading com., 2003—). Mem. Lds Ch Associations. Avocations: reading, fishing, scouting. Office: Office Dist Ct 605 N Capital Ave Idaho Falls ID 83402-3582 Office Phone: 208-529-1350 ext. 1378. Business E-Mail: jshindurling@co.bonneville.id.us.

**SHINE, KATINA LYNNIECE WILBON,** neuropsychologist, consultant; d. Alma Armstead. Diploma in practical nursing, Bapt. Sch. Nursing, Little Rock, 1991; ASN, AA, U. Ark., Little Rock, 1996; BS in Liberal Arts, SUNY, Albany, 1998; MS in Counseling Psychology, U. Ctl. Tex., 1999; PhD in Psychology, U. Louisville, 2002. RN Mo.; lic. psychologist Mo. Staff nurse Ark. Easter Seal Soc., Little Rock, 1993—96; primary care nurse, mgr. Hospice of Ctrl. Ark., North Little Rock, 1996—97; intake coord., psychiat. nurse Metroplex Health Sys., Killeen, Tex., 1997—99; grad. assist., neuropsychology trainee U. Louisville, 2000—01; psychology intern St. Louis VA Med. Ctr., 2001—02; clin. psychologist, neuropsychology clin. mgr., 2002—. Rschr., lectr. in field. Contbr. articles to profl. jours. Vol. ARC Disaster Mental Health Team, St. Louis, 2004, Mental Health Assn. of St. Louis, 2004. Recipient Grad. Dean's citation, U. Louisville, 2002; fellow Acad. fellow, 1999—2001; scholar Edn. Alumni Assn. scholar, 1999—2000, Marie Erma Fust Fund scholar, Truman L. Scott scholar, U. Ark.-Little Rock, 1995, L.A. Horn Meml. scholar, 1995. Mem.: APA (divsn. clin. neuropsychology, divsn. of psychologists in pub. svc.), Nat. Register of Health Svc. Providers, Mo. Psychol. Assn. Office: #1 Jefferson Barracks Dr 116A/JB Saint Louis MO 63026

**SHINEFIELD, HENRY ROBERT,** pediatrician; b. Paterson, NJ, Oct. 11, 1925; s. Louis and Sarah (Kaplan) Shinefield; m. Jacqueline Marilyn Walker; children: Jill, Michael, Kimberley Putzer, Melissa Strome. BA, Columbia U., 1945, MD, 1948. Diplomate Diplomate: Am. Bd. Pediat. (examiner, 1975—, bd. dirs., 1979-84, v.p., 1981-84). 1949Rotating intern Mt. Sinai Hosp., N.Y.C., 1948; pediatric intern Duke Hosp., Durham, NC, 1949-50; asst. resident pediatrician N.Y. Hosp. (Cornell), 1950-51, pediatrician to outpatients, 1953-59, instr. in pediatrics, 1959-60, asst. prof., 1960-64, assn. prof., 1964-65, asst. attending pediatrician, 1959-63, asso. attending pediatrician, 1963-65; pediatrician to outpatients Children's Hosp., Oakland, Calif., 1951-53; chief of pediatrics Kaiser-Permanente Med. Center, San Francisco, 1965-89, chief emeritus, 1989—; co-dir. Kaiser-Permanente Vaccine Study Ctr., San Francisco, 1984—2005; assoc. clin. prof. pediatrics Sch. Medicine U. Calif., 1964-68, clin. prof. pediatrics, 1968—, clin. prof. dermatology, 1970—; asso. attending pediatrician Paterson (N.J.) Gen. Hosp., 1955-59; chief of pediatrics Kaiser Found. Hosp., San Francisco, 1965-86; attending Moffitt Hosp., San Francisco, 1967-88; practice medicine specializing in pediatrics Paterson, 1953-59. Cons. San Francisco Gen. Hosp., 1967—88, Children's Hosp., San Francisco, 1970—88, Mt. Zion Hosp., San Francisco, 1970—88; mem. rsch. grants rev. br. NIH, HEW, 1970—74; med. dir. USPHSR, 1969—; bd. dirs. San Francisco Peer Rev. Orgn., 1975—81, sec., exec. com., 1976—81; chmn. Calif. State Child Health Disability Bd., 1973—82; mem. Inst. Medicine NAS, 1980—; cons. Bur. Drugs FDA, 1970, NIH, HEW, 1974—85. Editl. bd. We. Jour. Medicine, 1968—80, Am. Jour. Diseases of Children, 1970—82; contbr. articles to profl. publs. Office. San Francisco Med. Adv. Com. Nat. Found. March of Dimes, 1969—80. Served USPHS, 1951—53. Fellow: Am. Acad. Pediat. (com. fetus and newborn 1969—76, com. on drugs 1978—82); mem.: AMA, Am. Pediatric Soc., We. Soc. Clin. Rsch., We. Pediatric Soc., Infectious Diseases Soc. Am., Soc. Pediatric Rsch., Phi Beta Kappa. Home: 2240 Hyde St 2 San Francisco CA 94109-1509 Office Phone: 415-519-8613. Personal E-mail: henryshinefield@aol.com.

**SHINEMAN, EDWARD WILLIAM, JR.,** retired pharmaceutical executive; b. Canajoharie, N.Y., Apr. 9, 1915; s. Edward W. and Bertelle H. (Shubert) S.; m. H. Doris Thompson, Apr. 15, 1939; children: Edward T., Alan B. AB, Cornell U., 1937. With apparatus dept., acctg. dept. Gen. Electric Co., 1938-46, line auditor, 1942-46; with Beech-Nut, Inc. and predecessor cos., 1946-68, asst. treas., 1948-63, contr., 1959-63, treas., 1963-68; asst. sec.-treas. Squibb Corp., 1968-81. Bd. dirs. Taconic Farms, Inc. Trustee Arkell Hall Found.; mem. emeritus coun. Cornell U. Mem. Fin. Execs. Inst., Inst. Mgmt. Accts. Republican. Home: 455 N End Ave Apt 411 New York NY 10282

**SHINER, JOSETTE SHEERAN,** federal agency administrator; b. Orange, N.J., June 12, 1954; d. James Joseph and Sarah Ann (Gallagher) Sheeran; children: Nicole Munier, Daniel John, Gabrielle. BA, U. Colo., 1976. Nat. desk editor N.Y. News World, 1976-77, Washington bur. chief, 1977-80; corr. The White House, 1980-82; Capital Life and mag. editor Washington Times, 1982-84, asst. mng. editor, 1984-85, dep. mng. editor, 1985-92, mng. editor, 1992-97; pres., CEO Empower Am., 1997-2000; mng. dir. Starpoint Solutions, Reston, Va., 2000—03, dep. U.S. Trade Rep. The White House, Washington, 2001—03, dep. U.S. Trade Repr., 2003—05; under sec. for econ. bus. & agrl. affairs US Dept. State, Washington, 2005—, US alt. gov. to The World Bank, Inter-Am. Bank, African Devel. Bank, Asian Devel. Bank, European Bank for Reconstruction & Devel., 2005—. Mem. Leadership Washington Alumni Assn., 1987-88, v.p., 1988-89, alumni chmn., 1989-90. Recipient Atrium award U. Ga., 1984, 100 Most Powerful Women in Washington award Washington Mag., 1998. Mem. White House Corrs. Assn., Am. News Womens Club, Nat. Press Club (newsmaker chmn. 1980-82, Meritorious Svc. award 1981, Vivian award 1981), Am. Soc. Newspaper Editors, Coun. Fgn. Rels. (Washington adv. bd. 1999-2001), Sigma Delta Chi. Office: US Dept State 2201 C St NW Rm 7256 Washington DC 20520

**SHINKLE, JOHN THOMAS,** lawyer; b. Albany, N.Y., May 9, 1946; s. Robert Thomas and Margery Joan (Kneip) S.; m. Csilla Elizabeth Bekasy, Sept. 2, 1967; children: Reka, Ildiko. BA, Yale U., 1967; JD, Harvard U., 1970. Bar: D.C. 1971, N.Y. 1983, U.S. Supreme Ct. 1974. Law clk. U.S. Ct. Appeals for D.C. Cir., Washington, 1970—71; assoc. Caplin & Drysdale, Washington, 1971—77, ptnr., 1977—80; assoc. dir. divsn. corp. fin. SEC, Washington, 1980—81, dep. gen. counsel, 1981—82; gen. counsel Salomon Bros. Inc., N.Y., 1982—94, v.p., 1982—87, dir., 1988—94, head Asia Pacific legal and compliance, 1995—2003; mng. dir. Salomon Bros. Hong Kong, 1996—97, Salomon Smith Barney Hong Kong, 1998—2003; gen. counsel global transaction svcs. Citigroup, NY, 2003; v.p., dep. gen. counsel Bristol-Myers Squibb Co., NY, 2003—04; mng. dir., sr. dep. gen. counsel, global corp. & investment bank Citigroup, Inc., NY, 2004—. Contbr. articles to profl. jours. Mem. ABA, Assn. Bar City N.Y., Securities Industry Assn. (chmn. fed. regulation com. 1989-91), Futures Industry Assn. (dir. 1989-97). Home: 220 Riverside Blvd Apt 30-G New York NY 10069 Office: Citigroup 388 Greenwich St New York NY 10013

**SHINN, CLINTON WESLEY,** lawyer; b. Haworth, Okla., Mar. 7, 1947; s. Clinton Elmo and Mary Lucille (Dowdy) Shinn; m. Catherine Borne; children: Laura Kathryn, Clinton Wesley, Timothy Daniel. BS, McNeese State U., 1969; JD, Tulane U., 1972; LLM, Harvard U., 1973. Bar: La. 1972, U.S. Dist. Ct. (ea. dist.) La. 1975, U.S. Dist. Ct. (we. dist.) La. 1980, U.S. Ct. Appeals (5th cir.) 1981, U.S. Ct. Appeals (11th cir.) 1982, U.S. Tax Ct. 1982. Asst. prof. law Tulane U., New Orleans, 1973—75; assoc. Stone, Pigman et al, New Orleans, 1975—78, ptnr., 1979—97, Gill & Shinn, LLC, Covington, La., 1998—2000, of counsel, 2000—; assoc. prof. law Appalachian Sch. Law, 1999—2002, prof. law, 2006—; assoc. prof. law Miss. Coll. Sch. Law, Jackson, 2002—05. Co-founder, bd. dirs. Childhood Ctr. Families Network, 1987—90; co-founder Camp Challenge, 1988; team leader Campaign for Caring, Children's Hosp., New Orleans, 1989—91; bd. dirs. Greater New Orleans YMCA, 1989—98, 1999—2000, exec. com., 1991—98, asst. sec., 1994—95, sec., 1996—98, mem. fin. com., 1994—98, exec. dir. search com., 1996, 2d vice-chair, 1998; mem. Leadership Coun., 1997—98; active Indian Guides/Princesses; bd. dirs. West St. Tammany YMCA, 1987—95, exec. com., 1988—95, chmn. bd. dirs., 1989—90, 1992—93; bd. dirs. La. Air & Waste Mgmt. Assn., 1993—99, chmn. corp. rels. com., 1992—93, vice chmn., 1996—97, chair, 1997—98, past chair, 1998—99; bd. dirs. Christ Episcopal Sch., Covington, 1988—91, chmn. long-range planning, 1990—91, mem. exec. com., 1989—91, chmn. legal com., 1989—91, chmn. admissions/recruitment com., 1988—90, mem. headmaster search com., 1993; bd. dirs. Christwood, 1992—2001, v.p. bd. dirs., 1997—99; bd. dirs. St. Catherine's Village Found., 2004—. Co-recipient Pals of the Yr. award, Greater New Orleans YMCA Indian Guides/Princesses, 1987—88; named Vol. of the Yr., West St. Tammany YMCA, 1992. Fellow: La. Bar Found., Am. Coll. Trust and Estate Counsel; mem.: ABA, Air and Waste Mgmt. Assn., New Orleans Estate Planning Coun., Nat. Wildlife Fedn. (life), La. Forestry Assn., La. Bar Assn., Nat. Assn. Securities Dealers (bd. arbitrators), Charles Clark Inn of Ct., Order Coif. Avocations: backpacking, gardening. Home: 101 Aspen Dr Madison MS 39110 Office: Appalachian Sch Law One Slate Creek Rd Grundy VA 24614 Business E-mail: shinn@mc.edu. *In all things be firm but fair.*

**SHINN, DAVID HAMILTON,** former diplomat, educator, writer; b. Yakima, Wash., June 9, 1940; s. Guy Wilson and Ada Louise (Gelvin) S.; m. Judy Karen Rolfe, Sept. 9, 1961; children: Steven Hamilton, Christopher Rolfe. AA, Yakima Valley Coll., 1960; BA, George Washington U., 1963, MA, 1964, PhD, 1980; cert. African studies, Northwestern U., Evanston, Ill., 1969. With U.S. State Dept., 1964-2000; rotational officer U.S. Embassy, Beirut, Lebanon, 1964-66; polit. officer Nairobi, Kenya, 1967-68; desk officer East African affairs Washington, 1969-72; polit. officer Dar es Salaam, Tanzania, 1972-74; dep. chief of mission Nouakchott, Mauritania, 1974-76, Office of Mayor, City of Seattle, 1977-78; dep. coord. state and local govt. U.S. Dept. State, Washington, 1978-81; dep. chief of mission Yaounde, Cameroon, 1981-83, Khartoum, Sudan, 1983-86; U.S. ambassador Ouagadougou, Burkina Faso, 1987-90; diplomat-in-residence Southern U., Baton Rouge, La., 1990-91; diplomat State Dept., Washington, 1991-96; U.S. Amb. Addis Ababa, Ethiopia, 1996-99; diplomat-in-residence UCLA, 1999-2000. Adj. prof. George Washington U., 2001—. Co-author: Historical Dictionary of Ethiopia, 2004. Pres. Am. Friends for Inst. Ethiopian Studies; trustee forum internat. Ethiopians Living in Diaspora; adv. People to People, Inc.; bd. dirs. Horn Relief, Ethiopian Christian Relief and Devel. Assn.; bd. dirs. African Ctr. Health and Human Security George Washington U. Recipient Superior Honor award State Dept., 1980, 85, 94, Alumnus of Yr. award Am. Assn. Cmty. Colls., 1994, Phi Theta Kappa, 1995. Mem. Internat. Studies Assn., Ethiopian Studies Assn., Am. Fgn. Svc. Assn., Sudan Studies Assn., Mid. East Inst., African Studies Assn., Am. Philatelic Soc., Rotary Internat. Methodist. Avocations: philately, skiing, physical fitness, antiques. Address: 23 8th St SE Washington DC 20003 Personal E-mail: dhshinn@earthlink.net.

**SHINN, GEORGE LATIMER,** investment banker, consultant, finance educator; b. Newark, Ohio, Mar. 12, 1923; s. Leon Powell and Bertha Florence (Latimer) S.; m. Clara LeBaron Sampson, May 21, 1949; children: Deborah, Amy, Martha, Sarah, Andrew. AB, Amherst Coll., 1948; LLD (hon.), Denison U., 1975, Amherst Coll., 1982; MA, Drew U., 1990, PhD, 1992. Trainee Merrill Lynch, Pierce, Fenner & Beane, 1948-49; various exec. positions, 1949-75; pres. Merrill Lynch & Co., Inc., 1973-75; chmn. bd., chief

exec. officer 1st Boston Corp., 1975-83; investment banking cons., 1983—2002. Adj. prof. history Drew U., Madison, N.J., 1992—2002; mem. exec. com. President's Pvt. Sector Survey on Cost Control, 1982-84; exec.-in-residence Columbia U. Grad. Sch. Bus., 1983-85; bd. govs. Am. Stock Exch., 1970-74; bd. dirs. trustee Colonial Group Mut. Funds, 1983-98; bd. dirs. Kelso & Co., 1992—, N.Y. Stock Exch., 1975-83, vice chmn., 1979-83; bd. dirs. N.Y. Times Co., 1978-99, Phelps, Dodge Corp., 1983-95, N.Y. Life Ins. Co., 1983-94, Lehigh Press, 1983-91, Superior Oil Co., 1984-87, Congoleum Corp. Gen. chmn. United Hosp. Fund, N.Y.C., 1973-74; trustee Kent Pl. Sch., Summit, N.J., 1966-73, Carnegie Found. for Advancement Teaching, 1976-85, Pingry Sch., 1977-79, Lucille P. Markey Charitable Trust, 1985-97, Rockefeller Family Office Trust, 1989-97, N.J. Coun. for the Humanities, 1994-2000, Arts Coun. Morris Area, 1978-91, Philharmonic Symphony Soc. N.Y., 1983-91, Nat. Humanities Ctr., 1988-94; trustee emeritus Amherst Coll., 1968-82, chmn. bd. trustees, 1973-80; bd. dirs. Rsch. Corp., 1975-86. Capt. USMCR, 1943-52. Fellow Am. Acad. Arts and Scis. N.Y. Acad. Medicine, River Club, Century Assn. Personal E-mail: gshinn1059@aol.com.

**SHINN, RONALD THEODORE,** lawyer; b. Ravenna, Ohio, Dec. 29, 1974; s. Ronald Theodore and Shirley Ann Shinn; m. Elizabeth Benham Benham, Oct. 3, 1998; children: Theodore Robert, Benham BA (hon.), Miami U., 1996; JD (hon.), U. Okla., 2002. Press sec. U.S. Rep. Wally Herger, Washington, 1996—99; atty. McAfee & Taft PC, Oklahoma City, 2002—. Contbr. articles to profl. jours. Home: 3360 Stonybrook Rd Oklahoma City OK 73120 Office: McAfee & Taft PC 211 N Robinson Oklahoma City OK 73102 Office Phone: 405-235-9621. Office Fax: 405-228-7323. Personal E-mail: ron.shinn@gmail.com. E-mail: ron.shinn@mcafeetaft.com.

**SHINNAR, REUEL,** engineering educator, consultant; b. Vienna, Sept. 15, 1923; came to US, 1962; s. Abraham Emil and Rosa (Storch) Bardfeld; m. Miryam Halpern, June 22, 1948; children: Shlomo, Meir Diploma in Chem. Engring., Technion, Haifa, Israel, 1945, M.Sc. in Chem. Engring., 1954; Dr. Engring. Sci., Columbia U., 1957. Various positions in chem. engring., Israel, 1945-58; adj. assoc. prof. Technion, Haifa, Israel, 1958-62; visiting research fellow Guggenheim Labs., Princeton (N.J.) U., 1962-64; prof. chem. engring. CCNY, 1964—, disting. prof., 1979—. Pinhas Naor lectr. Technion U., 1974; Wilhelm Meml. lectr. Princeton U., 1985, Kelly lectr. Purdue U., 1991; cons. to various oil and chem. cos. Contbr. numerous articles to profl. jours.; patentee in field. Fellow AICE (Founders award 1992, Alpha Chi Sigma award 1979), N.Y. Acad. Scis.; mem. AIAA, Am. Chem. Soc., Nat. Acad. Engring. Office: City Coll NY Dept Chem Engring 140th St and Convent Ave New York NY 10031 Office Phone: 212-650-6679. Business E-Mail: shinnar@ccny.cuny.edu.

**SHINNERS, STANLEY MARVIN,** electrical engineer; b. NYC, May 9, 1933; s. Earl and Molly (Planter) Shinners; m. Doris Shinners, Aug. 4, 1956; children: Sharon Rose Cooper, Walter Jay, Daniel Lawrence. BEE, CCNY, 1954; MSEE, Columbia U., 1959. Equipment engr. Western Electric Co., NYC, 1953-54; staff engr. electronics divsn. Otis Elevator Co., Bklyn., 1954-56; project engr. Consol. Avionics Corp., Westbury, NY, 1956-58; program mgr., fed. sys. Lockheed Martin Corp. (formerly Loral Corp., Unisys Corp.), Mitchel Field, NY, 1958-99. Adj. prof. engring. The Cooper Union, NYC, 1966—, NY Inst. Tech., Old Westbury, NY, 1972-92, Poly. Inst. Bklyn., 1959-72. Author: Control System Design, 1964, Techniques of Systems Engineering, 1967, A Guide to Systems Engineering and Management, 1976, Modern Control System Theory and Application, 1978, Modern Control System Theory and Design, 1992, 2d edit., 1998, Advanced Modern Control System Theory and Design, 1998. Recipient Career Achievement medal CCNY Alumni Assn., 1980. Fellow IEEE; mem. Am. Soc. for Engring. Edn., Eta Kappa Nu, Tau Beta Pi. Home: 28 Sagamore Way N Jericho NY 11753-2358 Personal E-mail: shinnerssm@optonline.net. *I was very poor financially as a child, but I received an abundance of love and encouragement from parents and family. I have always tried to succeed and to help others succeed. Above all, I have always tried to do what is right whether the decision had to be made in the business world or in private and family matters.*

**SHINOHARA, KATSUTO,** medical educator; b. Nagano, Japan, Apr. 26, 1954; s. Mitsuo and Fukue Shinohara; m. Beni Shinohara, Jan. 22, 1983; children: Yuma S., Reina M. MD, Yokohama City U., Japan, 1979. Prof. U. Calif., San Francisco, 2004—. Office: University of California San Francisco 1600 Divisadero St San Francisco CA 94143-1695 Office Phone: 415-353-7101.

**SHINOLT, EILEEN THELMA,** artist; b. Washington, May 18, 1919; d. Edward Lee and Blanche Addie (Marsh) Bennett; m. John Francis Shinolt, June 14, 1956 (dec. Aug. 1969). Student, Hans Hoffman Sch Art, 1949, Pa. Acad. Arts, 1950, Corcoran Sch. Art, 1945-51, Am. U., 1973-77. Sect. chief Dept. Army, Washington, 1940-73, retired, 1973. One-woman shows include various locations, 1982, 83, 85, 90, 94, 96; group shows include Perlmutter & Co., 1981, Fitch Fox and Brown, 1986, Foundry Gallery, 1987, Ann. Add Arts, 1986, Westminster Gallery, London, 1995; represented in permanent collections Women's Nat. Mus., Washington, Cameo Gallery, Columbia, S.C., Strathmore Hall Arts Ctr., North Bethesda, Md., 1997, 98, 99, 2000, 01, 02, 03, 04. Mem. Woman's Nat. Dem. Club, Washington, 1980—. Mem. Am. Art League (editor newsletter 1985-86, 1st pl. 1987, 2d pl. 1986), Arts Club Washington (exhbn. com. 1985—, admissions com. 1987-88), Miniature Painters, Sculptors & Gravers Soc. (historian 1989-2003, editor newsletter 1986-89), Fine Arts in Miniature. Roman Catholic. Avocations: reading, studying art periodicals, art galleries. Home: 5821 Queens Chapel Rd 232 Hyattsville MD 20782-3867

**SHINOZAKI, TAMOTSU,** retired physician, retired anesthesiologist; b. Dairen, Japan, Mar. 18, 1934; s. Yuichi and Shizue Shniozaki; m. Kazuko Sakanaka Shinozaki, Feb. 14, 1940; children: Aritomo, Yuji, Emiko. MD, Okayama U., 1958, D in Med. Scis., 1963. Diplomate Am. Bd. Anesthesiology; cert. spl. qualifications in critical care medicine. Intern St. Luke's Internat. Hosp., Tokyo, 1958—59; resident in anesthesiology Mary Fletcher Hosp., 1964—67; attending anesthesiologist Med. Ctr. Hosp. of Vt., Burlington, 1967—99; asst. prof. Med. Sch. U. Vt., Burlington, 1967—72, assoc. prof., 1972—90, clin. prof., 1990—99, med. co-dir. surg. ICU, 1985—99, prof. emeritus, 2000—; adminstrv. dir. surg. ICU Fletcher Allen Healthcare, Burlington, 1997—99, attending emeritus, 2000—. Cons. med. divsn. Hewlett Packard Co., Waltham, Mass., 1972-77, Intelligent Med. Sys., Carlsbad, Calif., 1987. Recipient Quality Cup award, Excellance in the Quality Movement, 1994. Fellow Am. Coll. Critical Care Medicine; mem. Sigma Xi. Home: 335 Dorset Hts South Burlington VT 05403 Business E-Mail: tshinoza@zoo.uvm.edu.

**SHINSEKI, ERIC KEN,** retired military officer; b. Lihue, Hawaii, Nov. 28, 1942; BS, U.S. Mil. Acad., 1965; MA in English, Duke U., 1976; student, U.S. Army Armor Sch., Ft. Knox, Ky., 1968-69, Army Command and Staff Coll., Ft. Leavenworth, Kans., 1978-79, Nat. War Coll., Ft. Lesley McNair, Washington, 1985-86. Commd. 2d lt. U.S. Army, 1965, advanced through grades to gen., 1997; forward observer B battery 2d battalion, 9th artillery, 3d brigade, 25th Infantry Divsn., U.S. Army, Vietnam, 1965-66; asst. S1 (pers.) base defense command XXIV Corps U.S. Army, Vietnam, 1969-70; comdr. A Troop, 3d squadron, 5th cavalry, 9th infantry divsn attached to 1st brigade, Du Pacific, Fort Shafter, Hawaii, 1971-74; instr. dept. English U.S. Mil. Acad., West Point, N.Y., 1976-78; comdr. 3d squadron 7th cavalry, 3d infantry divsn. then asst chief of staff, G-3, U.S. Army Europe and 7th Army, Germany, 1982-85; comdr. 2d brigade, 3d infantry divsn., to asst chief staff G3 VII Corps, U.S. Army Europe and 7th Army, 1987-90; dep. chief of staff adminstrn./logistics Allied Land Forces So. Europe, Germany, 1990-92; asst. divsn. comdr., 3d infantry divsn. U.S. Army and 7th Army Europe, Germany, 1992-93; commanding gen. 1st Cav. Divsn., Ft. Hood, Tex., 1994-95; asst. dep. chief of staff (ops. and plans) to dep. chief of staff (ops. and plans) U.S. Army, Washington, 1995-97; comdr. in chief, comdr. Stblzn. Force, U.S.

Army Europe and 7th Army, Bosnia, 1997-98; vice chief of staff U.S. Army, Washington, 1998-99, chief of staff, 1999—2003. Decorated Defense Disting. Svc. medal, Disting. Svc. medal, Legion of Merit with oak leaf cluster, Bronze Star medal with V device with 3 oak leaf clusters, Purple Heart with oak leaf cluster, Meritorious Svc. medal with 2 oak leaf clusters, Air medal, Army Commendation medal with oak leaf cluster, Army Achievement medal.

**SHIPKO, JANET M.,** human resources manager; b. Schenectady, NY, Nov. 3, 1953; d. Frederick J. and Elizabeth Shipko. MSc in Health Care Mgmt., U. Md., 1996. Assoc. chief of staff, res. affairs Tripler Army Med. Ctr., Honolulu, 2003—06; chief res. policy Office of Surgeon Gen., Falls Church, Va., 2006—, with, 2006—. Lt. col. USAR, 1982. Decorated Meritorious Svc. medal (3), Army Commendation medal (3), Army Superior Unit award (1), Armed Forces Res. medal (2), Army Achievement medal (2), Nat. Def. Svc. medal (3), Global War on Terrorism medal (1). Home: 3709 S George Mason Drive Apt 1705E Falls Church VA 22041 Office Phone: 703-681-3187. Office Fax: 703-681-3194. Business E-Mail: janet.m.shipko@us.army.mil.

**SHIPKO, RENEE,** marketing executive; d. Connie Spruill Boyd; m. Michael Louis Shipko, Apr. 9, 2005. BA in Broadcasting, U. NC, Greensboro, 1998. Radio news reporter 88.5 WFDD Pub. Radio, Winston-Salem, NC, 1999—2001; mktg. dir. Old Salem Mus. & Gardens, Winston-Salem, 2001—. Vol. Big Bros. Big Sisters Forsyth County, Winston-Salem, 1999—2003; co-founder, mem. Coalition Young Leaders, Winston-Salem, 2002—04; media program mgr. NC Jaycees, Asheboro, 2005—; pres. Winston-Salem Jaycees, 2006—. Recipient Best Feature Newspaper Story award, NC Assn. Pub. Health, Dance, Phys. Edn. & Recreation, 1999, William Brownfield award for most outstanding first-yr. Jaycee in NC, NC Jaycees, 2003. Mem.: SE Tourism Soc. (assoc.), Assn. State & Local History (AASLH) (assoc.), Winston-Salem Ski & Outing Club (v.p. 2002—04). Avocations: painting and art, hiking, swimming, travel. Office: Old Salem Mus & Gardens PO Box F Salem Sta Winston Salem NC 27108 Office Phone: 336-721-7329. Business E-Mail: rboyd@oldsalem.org.

**SHIPLER, DAVID KARR,** journalist, writer; b. Orange, NJ, Dec. 3, 1942; s. Guy Emery Jr. and Eleanor (Karr) Shipler; m. Deborah S. Isaacs, Sept. 17, 1966; children: Jonathan Robert, Laura Karr, Michael Edmund. AB, Dartmouth Coll., 1964; LittD (hon.), Middlebury Coll., 1988, Glassboro State Coll., NJ, 1988; AM (hon.), Dartmouth Coll., 1994; LittD (hon.), Birmingham Southern Coll., 2006. News clk. N.Y. Times, 1966—67, news summary writer, 1968, reporter met. staff, 1968—73, fgn. corr. Saigon bur., 1973—75, fgn. corr. Moscow Bur., 1975—, bur. chief Moscow Bur., 1977—79, chief Jerusalem bur., 1979—84, corr. Washington bur., 1985—87, chief diplomatic corr., 1987—88; sr. assoc. Carnegie Endowment for Internat. Peace, Washington, 1988—90. Guest scholar Brookings Instn., 1984—85; adj. prof. Am. U. Sch. Internat. Svc., Washington, 1990; Ferris prof. journalism and pub. affairs Princeton U., 1990—91; Woodrow Wilson vis. fellow, 1990—; writer-in-residence U. So. Calif., 1998; Montgomery fellow, vis. prof. gov. Dartmouth Coll., 2003. Author: Russia: Broken Idols, Solemn Dreams, 1983 (Overseas Press Club award), revised, 1989, Arab and Jew: Wounded Spirits in a Promised Land, 1986 (Pulitzer prize for Gen. Nonfiction, 1987), revised, 2002, A Country of Strangers: Blacks and Whites in America, 1997, The Working Poor: Invisible in America, 2004 (Myers Outstanding Book award Simmons Coll., finalist Nat. Book Critics Cir. award, finalist Helen Bernstein N.Y. Pub. Lib. award); exec. prod.: (documentaries) from Arab and Jew: Wounded Spirits in a Promised Land, 1989 (Alfred DuPont-Columbia U. award for Broadcast Journalism, 1990), Arab and Jew: Return to the Promised Land, 2002; contbr. articles to nat. mags. Trustee Dartmouth Coll., 1993—2003. With USNR, 1964—66. Co-recipient George Polk award, 1982; recipient award for disting. reporting, Soc. Silurians, 1971, award for disting. pub. affairs reporting, Am. Polit. Sci. Assn., 1971, award, N.Y. chpt. Sigma Delta Chi, 1973, Vento award, Nat. Law Ctr. on Homelessness and Poverty, 2004, Martin Luther King, Jr. Social Justice award, Dartmouth Coll., 2005, Labor Communicator of Yr. award, NY Labor Comms. Coun., 2005, award, DC Employment Justice Ctr., 2005. Office: 4005 Thornapple St Chevy Chase MD 20815-5037 *I have always been governed professionally by the conviction that an open society needs open examination of itself to survive. Defining problems, inspecting blemishes, probing wounds, and exposing injustice are the required pastimes of a free people. Nothing intelligent can come from ignorance. If information does not guarantee wisdom, it is at least a prerequisite, for the only wise course is through knowledge. To write about current affairs, then, is to play a small role in a great endeavor. It is to measure one's own performance continually against the highest standards of honesty, fairness, thoroughness, intelligence, to search every day for a bit of truth, then share it. These are the ingredients of happiness, for such a job involves a life of constant learning, perpetual self-education. It keeps a man whole.*

**SHIPLEY, DAVID,** editor; BA, Williams Coll., 1985. Exec. editor The New Republic Mag., 1993—95; splty. asst. to Pres., sr. presdl. speechwriter The White House, 1995—97; dep. editor, Millenium Project NY Times Mag., 1998—99, sr. editor, 1999—2001; assigning editor. Op-Ed page NY Times, 1990, nat. enterprise editor, 2001—02, dep. editor, Op-Ed page, 2002—03, editor, Op-Ed page, 2003—. Office: Op-Ed Page NY Times 229 W 43rd St New York NY 10036 Office Phone: 212-556-3652. Office Fax: 212-556-4100, 212-556-3690. Business E-Mail: shipley@nytimes.com.

**SHIPLEY, DAVID ELLIOTT,** lawyer, educator; b. Urbana, Ill., Oct. 3, 1950; s. James Ross and Dorothy Jean (Elliott) S.; m. Virginia Florence Coleman, May 24, 1980; 1 child, Shannon C. BA, Oberlin Coll., 1972; JD, U. Chgo., 1975. Bar: Ill. 1975. Assoc. Tillinghast, Collins & Graham, Providence, 1975-77; asst. prof. U. S.C. Sch. Law, Columbia, 1977-81, assoc. prof., 1981-85, prof., 1985-90, assoc. dean, 1989-90; dean U. Miss. Sch. Law, University, 1990-93, U. Ky. Coll. Law, Lexington, 1993-98; prof., dean Sch. Law U. Ga., Athens, 1998—2003, Thomas R. R. Cobb prof., 2003—. Vis. prof. Coll. William and Mary, Williamsburg, Va., 1983-84, Ohio State U. Coll. Law, Columbus, 1986-87. Author: South Carolina Administrative Law, 1983, 2d edit., 1989; co-author Copyright Law, 1992. Pres. Shandon Neighborhood Assn., Columbia, 1988-90, Athens Justice Project, Ga., 2003-05, minority affairs com. law sch. admissions coun., 2001-05, fin. and legal affairs coun., 2005—. Named Prof. of Yr., U. S.C. Sch. Law, 1990, faculty scholar, 1989-90, O'Byrne award for Student Faculty Rels., 2003-04, 04-05. Mem. ABA, R.I. Bar Assn., S.C. Bar Assn. (assoc.), Ga. Bar Assn. (assoc.). Methodist. Avocations: running, golf, yardwork, gardening, reading. Home: 475 River Bottom Rd Athens GA 30606-6430 Office: U Ga Sch Law 323 Rusk Hall Athens GA 30602-6012 Office Phone: 706-542-5184. Business E-Mail: shipley@uga.edu.

**SHIPLEY, SAM,** apparel designer; Grad., U. Colo., Boulder. Co-founder, designer (with Josia Lamberto-Egan, John Whitledge, and Jeff Halmos) Trovata, 2002—; launched women's collection, 2005—. Recipient Recipient CFDA/Vogue Fashion Fund award. Office: Trovata 505 31st St Newport Beach CA 92663*

**SHIPLEY, SAMUEL LYNN,** advertising executive, public relations executive; b. Marlborough, Mass., Nov. 14, 1929; s. Clifford Lynn and Esther (Jacobs) S.; m. Sue Finucan, Sept. 5, 1955; children: Jeffrey Lynn, Beth Ann, Amy. Student, Charles Morris Price Sch. Advt. and Journalism, U. N.H., 1948-50. Exec. dir. Democratic Party N.H., 1953-56; press. chmn. Shipley Assos., Inc., Wilmington, Del., 1962—; pres. Cable TV Advt. Inc., 1982—. Dir. Del. Devel. Dept., Dover, 1965-69; mem. bd. overseers Del. Coll. Art and Design. Nominee for Gov. Congress, 1976; pub. relations dir. Del. Democratic Com., 1964-68; chmn. Del. Dem. Com., 1982-90; bd. dirs. Blood Bank of Del., Jobs for Del. Grads., For Children; mem. Del. Heritage Comm.; trustee Grand Opera House; former chair Dem. State Com. With U.S. Army, 1951-53. Recipient Freedoms Found. Honor medal, 1966, Outstanding Grad. award Charles Morris Price Sch., 1974 Mem. Am. Advt. Fedn., Nat. Press Club, Wilmington Advt. Club, Masons. Home: 1196 Paper Mill Rd Newark DE 19711-2924 Office: 1300 Pennsylvania Ave Wilmington DE 19806-4311

Office Phone: 302-731-9696. Business E-Mail: samshipley@comcast.net. *The ingredients for success are good health, average intelligence, a giving spirit, positive thinking, good imagination, self-discipline, hard work, and persistence.*

**SHIPLEY, TONY L(EE),** software company executive; b. Elizabethton, Tenn., July 19, 1946; s. James A. and Edith J. (Crowder) S.; m. Lynda Anne Jenkins, Nov. 19, 1971; children: Blake Alan, Sarah Robyn. BS in Indsl. Engring., U. Tenn., 1969; MBA, U. Cin., 1975. Indsl. engr. Monsanto Co., Pensacola, Fla., 1969—72; mktg. mgr. SDRC, Cin., 1972—76; v.p. sales and mktg. Anatrol Corp., Cin., 1977—81; pres. Entek Sci. Corp., Cin., 1981—96; pres., CEO Entek IRD Internat. Corp., 1996—2000; founding mem. Queen City Angels. Bd. dirs. Ohio IT Alliance, CHMack, The Circuit, The Grid. Named Small Bus. Person of Yr., Greater Cin. C. of C., 1994, Entrepreneur of Yr. in Cin., No. Ky. Region, 1996; recipient Entrepreneurial Excellence award U. Cin., 2001, C.H. Lindner Outstanding Bus. Achievement award U. Cin., 2004 Mem. ASME, Soc. Automotive Engrs., Greater Cin. Software Assn. (pres. 1996-97, chmn. 1997-99, bd. dirs.), Greater Cin. C. of C., Leadership Class XVIII, Terrace Park (Ohio) Country Club (past pres.). Republican. Avocations: golf, fishing. Home: 7825 Calderwood Ln Cincinnati OH 45243-1319 Personal E-mail: tshipley@fuse.net.

**SHIPLEY, WALTER VINCENT,** retired bank executive; b. Newark, Nov. 2, 1935; s. L. Parks and Emily (Herzog) S.; m. Judith Ann Lyman, Sept. 14, 1957; children: Barbara, Allison, Pamela, Dorothy, John. Student, Williams Coll., 1954-56; BS, NYU, 1961. With Chem. Bank, N.Y.C., 1956-96; chmn., CEO, chmn. bd. dirs. Chase Manhattan Corp., N.Y.C., 1996-99; ret., 1999. Bd. dirs. Exxon Mobil Corp., Verizon Comms., Wyeth. Mem. The Bus. Coun., Coun. Fgn. Rels., Links, Augusta Nat. Golf Club, Baltusrol Golf Club (Springfield, N.J.). Office: JPMorgan Chase & Co 270 Park Ave New York NY 10017-2070

**SHIPMAN, DONALD GEORGE,** academic administrator; b. Wurzburg, Germany, June 12, 1959; s. Donald Ray and Melva Lee Shipman; m. Diane Lea Carven, Dec. 26, 1980; children: Donall Isaac, Samantha Diane. BS, U. Okla., 1995; M of Physician Asst. Studies, U. Nebr., 1998; EdD, W.Va. U., 2004. Commd. 2d ltr. US Army, 1977, advanced through grades to maj., ret., 2005; adminstr. St. Francis U., Loretto, Pa., 2006—. Decorated Bronze Star US Army. Mem.: W.Va. Assn. Physician Asst. (corr.), Order Mil. Med. Merit (life), Nat. Soccer Coaches Assn. Am. (licentiate). Independent. Avocations: coaching soccer, travel, humanitarian assistance. Office: St Francis U 117 Evergreen Dr Loretto PA 15940 Office Phone: 814-472-3131. E-mail: dshipman@francis.edu.

**SHIPMAN, JEAN PUGH,** medical librarian; b. Chambersburg, Pa., Aug. 6, 1957; d. Andrew Richard and Sara Elizabeth (Bert) Pugh; m. Mark James Shipman, Oct. 8, l988. BA, Gettysburg Coll., 1979; MSLS, Case Western Res. U., 1980. Reference libr. Johns Hopkins Sch. Medicine, Balt., 1980-81, sr. reference libr., 1981-82, access libr., 1982-84, psychiatry-neuroscis. librarian, 1984-88; mgr. libr. and audiovisual svcs. Greater Balt. Med. Ctr., 1988-90, NN/LM southeastern/atlantic regional coord., 1990—93; outreach info. svcs. libr. Health Scis. Libr., U. Wash., 1993—95, acting head access svcs., 1993—95, assoc. dir. info. resources mgmt., 1995—2000; dir. Tompkins-McCaw Libr. for Health Scis., assoc. Univ. Libr. Va. Commonwealth Univ. Librs., Richmond, Va., 2000—. Contbr. articles to profl. jours. Mem. Med. Libr. Assn. (Mid-Atlantic chpt. sec. 1991-92, pres.-elect 2005-06, pres. 2006—), Beta Phi Mu, Beta Beta Beta. Republican. Lutheran. Avocations: tennis, reading, cooking. Office: Tompkins-McCaw Libr for Health Scis 509 N 12th St PO Box 980582 Richmond VA 23298-0582 Office Phone: 804-828-0634. E-mail: jpshimpa@vcu.edu.

**SHIPPEY, SANDRA LEE,** lawyer; b. Casper, Wyo., June 24, 1957; d. Virgil Carr and Doris Louise (Conklin) McClintock; m. Ojars Herberts Ozols, Sept. 2, 1978 (div.); children: Michael Ojars, Sara Ann, Brian Christopher; m. James Robert Shippey, Jan. 13, 1991; 1 child, Matthew James. BA with distinction, U. Colo., 1978; JD magna cum laude, Boston U., 1982. Bar: Colo. 1982, U.S. Dist. Ct. Colo. 1985. Assoc. Cohen, Brame & Smith, Denver, 1983-84, Parcel, Meyer, Schwartz, Ruttum & Mauro, Denver, 1984-85, Mayer, Brown & Platt, Denver, 1985-87; counsel western ops. GE Capital Corp., San Diego, 1987-94; assoc. Page, Polin, Busch & Boatwright, San Diego, 1994-95; v.p., gen. counsel First Comml. Corp., San Diego, 1995-96; legal counsel NextWave Telecom Inc., San Diego, 1996-98; ptnr. Procopio, Cory, Hargreaves and Savitch, LLP, 1998—. Spkr. in field. Contbr. articles to profl. jours. Active Pop Warner football and cheerleading; bd. dirs. Southwestern Christian Schs., Inc., 2002—, San Diego Christian Found., 2001—05. Mem. Calif. State Bar (co-chair uniform comml. code com.), Phi Beta Kappa, Phi Delta Phi. Republican. Mem. Ch. of Christ. Avocations: tennis, golf, photography. Home: 15839 Big Springs Way San Diego CA 92127-2034 Office: Procopio Cory El Al 530 B St Ste 2100 San Diego CA 92101-4496    Office    Phone:    619-515-3226.    Business    E-Mail: sls@procopio.com.

**SHIPWAY, JOHN FRANCIS,** retired career officer; b. Cherry Valley, N.Y. m. Lynn Doe. MS in Chem. Engring., U. Louisville, 1965; attended, Basic Officer Nuclear Power, Bainbridger, Md., Naval Nuclear Power Tng. Unit, West Milton, N.Y., Naval Sub. Sch., Groton, Conn., Def. Syss. Mgmt. Coll., Ft. Belvoir, Va., 1988; grad., Navy War Coll., Newport, R.I. Commd. ensign USN, 1965; advanced through grades to rear admiral, 1994; communicator USS Cubera (SS 347), 1967; asst. damage control, main propulsion USS Von Steuben; exec. officer nuclear sub. NR-1, 1971-75; exec. officer USS Swordfish (SSN 579), 1977-78; asst. to program mgr. MK 48 torpedo acquisition program Naval Sea Sys. Cmd., 1978-81; comdr. USS Los Angeles (SSN 688), 1981-85; comdg. officer nuclear power tng. unit West Hamilton, N.Y., 1985-87; acquisition profl., 1985; program mgr. SSN 688 attack sub. acquisition program, 1988-91; program mgr. Seawolf, 1991-92; program exec. officer Dept. of Navy, 1992-95; dep. comdr. subs. naval sea sys. cmd., 1995-98; comdr. Naval Undersea Warfare Ctr., 1995-98; dir. strategic system programs Arlington, VA, 1998-2000. Decorated 4 Legion of Merit awards. Mem. Am. Soc. Naval Engrs., Assn. Scientists and Engrs., U.S. Naval Inst., Naval Sub. League.

**SHIRAI, SHUN,** law educator; b. Tokyo, June 18, 1942; s. Kyo and Tomi Shirai; m. Junko Matsushita, Apr. 10, 1969; children: Akiko, Yuko, Jin. LLB, Hitotsubashi U., Tokyo, 1966, LLM, 1969. Asst. prof. criminal law Kokugakuin U., Tokyo, 1974-81, prof., 1981—, dean Grad. Sch., 1999-2001. Atty. Tokyo 2nd Bar Assn., 1992—. Author: Phenomenology of Crime, 1984, rev. edit., 1998, Thought on Criminal Law of Ancient India, 1985, Legal History on Criminal Law of Ancient India, 1990, Philosophy of Criminal Law in Ancient India, 1995, Phenomenology and Indian Philosophy for the Study on Ancient Indian Criminal Law, 1997, Prof. Shirai's Lectures on the Law of Criminal Procedure, 1998, Philosophy of Criminal Law in Bhagavad-gita at Ancient India, 1998, Crime and Sorrowness of Human Being, 1999, Defence Lawyer's Statements in Criminal Court, 2000, Thoughts on Death Penalty in Ancient India, 2000, The Sanskrit, as a Legal Language, appearing in Judicial Documents of British India and Non-Violent Theory of Punishment, originated in Ancient India, 2000, Thought on Righteousness in Criminal Law, handed down by Tradition from Ancient India, 2002, On Basic Principles of Hindu Criminology, derived from Ancient Indian Criminal Law, 2002, Introduction to Study on Practice of Japanese Criminal Jurisdiction, 2003, Philosophy of Crime of Contemporary Indian Thought on Human Being, 2003, Peculiarity in Research Method on Hindu Criminology, 2004, On the Legal Meaning of Yajñavalkyasmrti, Ancient Indian Legal Script, Book II, Section 1, 2005, Phenomenological Criminology and Transcendental Intersubjectivity, 2006; contbr. chpts. to books. Mem. Indian History Congress. Buddhist. Home: 703 Ninen Bldg 2-16-1 Hanakawado Taito-ku Tokyo 111-0033 Japan Office: Kokugakuin U 4-10-28 Higashi Shibuya-Ku Tokyo 150-8440 Japan Office Phone: 03-5466-0111.

**SHIRE, DAVID LEE,** composer; b. Buffalo, July 3, 1937; s. Irving Daniel and Esther Miriam (Sheinberg) S.; m. Talia Rose Coppola, Mar. 29, 1970 (div.); 1 child, Matthew Orlando; m. Didi Conn. Feb. 11, 1984; 1 child, Daniel Joshua. BA, Yale U., 1959. Film scores include The Conversation, 1974, The Taking of Pelham 1-2-3, 1974, Farewell, My Lovely, 1975, The Hindenburg, 1975, All the President's Men, 1977, Saturday Night Fever (adaptation and additional music), 1977, Norma Rae, 1979 (Acad. award for best original song It Goes Like It Goes), Only When I Laugh, 1981, The World According to Garp, 1982, Max Dugan Returns, 1983, 2010, 1984, Return to Oz, 1985, Short Circuit, 1986, 'Night, Mother, 1986, Vice Versa, 1988, Monkey Shines, 1988, Paris Trout, 1991, Bed and Breakfast, 1992, The Journey Inside (IMAX), 1993, One Night Stand, 1994, Ash Wednesday, 2002, The Tollbooth, 2004; TV scores include Raid on Entebbe, 1977 (Emmy nomination), The Defection of Simas Kudirka, 1978 (Emmy nomination), Do You Remember Love?, 1985 (Emmy nomination), Promise, 1986, Echoes in the Darkness, 1987, The Women of Brewster Place, 1989, The Kennedys of Massachusetts, 1990 (Emmy nomination), Common Ground, 1990, Sarah Plain & Tall, 1991, Last Wish, 1992, Broadway Bound, 1992, Skylark, 1993, Remember, 1993, The Companion, 1994, My Brother's Keeper, 1995, Serving in Silence, 1995, The Heidi Chronicles, 1995, My Antonia, 1995, The Streets of Laredo, 1995, Last Stand at Saber River, 1997, Rear Window, 1998 (Emmy nomination), Double Platinum, 1999, Small Vices, 1999, These Old Broads, 2001, Two Against Time, 2001; theatre scores include The Sap of Life, 1961, Graham Crackers, 1962, The Unknown Soldier and His Wife, 1967, How Do You Do, I Love You, 1968, Love Match, 1970, Starting Here, Starting Now, 1977, Baby, 1983 (Tony nominee best mus. and best original score), Urban Blight, 1988, Closer Than Ever, 1989 (Outer Critics Circle award best off-Broadway musical and best score), Big, 1996 (Tony nominee best score), Take Flight, 2004; composer Sonata for Cocktail Piano, 1965; recorded songs include Autumn, 1959, Starting Here, Starting Now, 1965, What About Today?, 1969, Manhattan Skyline, 1977, The Promise, 1978 (Acad. award nomination), It Goes Like It Goes, 1979 (Acad. award), With You I'm Born Again, 1979; albums include Saturday Night Fever, 1977 (Grammy award 1978), Starting Here, Starting Now, 1977 (Grammy nomination 1977), Baby, 1984, Return to Oz, 1985, Closer Than Ever, 1990, David Shire at The Movies, 1991, Big, 1996. With Arnex N.G., 1960-66. Mem. Composers and Lyricists Guild Am., Am. Fedn. Musicians, Broadcast Music Inc., Acad. Motion Picture Arts and Scis., Nat. Acad. Rec. Arts and Scis., Nat. Acad. TV Arts and Scis., Dramatists Guild Am. (coun. mem.). Jewish. Office: Ste 304 16501 Ventura Blvd Encino CA 91436-2067 Office Phone: 818-971-7300. Personal E-mail: dshire@aol.com.

**SHIRE, DONALD THOMAS,** retired chemicals executive, lawyer; b. Boston, Jan. 13, 1930; s. Thomas J. and Nellie M. S.; m. Anne Court Bither, Nov 21, 1953; children: Jennifer Anne, Andrew Carter, Daniel Orchard. BS in Bus. Adminstrn, Boston U., 1951, LL.B., 1953; postgrad., Harvard Bus. Sch., 1985; LLD (hon.), Muhlenberg Coll., 1997. Atty. Air Products and Chems., Inc., 1957-64, atty., 1964-75, sec., asst. gen. counsel, 1975-78, v.p. energy and materials, 1978-85, v.p. human resources, 1986-90, sr. v.p. human resources and adminstrn., 1990-91, sr. v.p. adminstrn., 1991-93; ret., 1993; also bd. dirs. Air Products and Chems., Inc. Chmn. Air Products Found., 1991-93; bd. dirs. Lehigh Valley Bus./Edn. Partnership. Trustee Muhlenberg Coll. (life), 1976-95, Lehigh Valley Health Network., 1983-99, Lt. USNR, 1954-57. Mem. Am. Arbitration Assn. Home: 27 Drake Ln Scarborough ME 04074

**SHIRE, TALIA ROSE (TALIA ROSE COPPOLA),** actress; b. Jamaica, N.Y., Apr. 25, 1946; d. Carmine and Italia (Pennino) Coppola; m. David Lee Shire, Mar. 29, 1970 (div.); 1 son, Matthew Orlando; m. Jack Schwartzman, Aug. 23, 1979; children: Jason Francesco, Robert Carmine Coppola. Films include The Wild Racers, 1968, The Dunwich Horrors, 1970, Gas-s-s-s, 1971, The Christian Licorice Store, 1971, Godfather, 1972, The Outside Man, 1972, Godfather II, 1974 (Oscar nominee for Best Supporting Actress), Rocky, 1976 (Oscar nominee for best actress, N.Y. Film Critics award for Best Supporting Actress), Old Boyfriends, 1979, Rocky II, 1979, Prophecy, 1979, Windows, 1980, Rocky III, 1982, Rocky IV, 1985, Rad, 1986, New York Stories, 1989, Cold Heaven, 1991, Godfather Part III, 1990, Rocky V, 1990, Bed and Breakfast, 1992, Deadfall, 1993, (Disney channel movie) Mark Twain, 1990, (HBO movie) Getting There, 1991, A River Made to Drown In, 1997, Divorce: A Contemporary Western, 1998, Can I Play?, 1998, Palmer's Pick Up, 1999, Caminho dos Sonhos, 1999, Lured Innocence, 1999, The Visit, 2000, The Whole Shebang, 2001, Kiss the Bride, 2002, Family Tree, 2003, Dunsmore, 2003, I Heart Huckabees, 2004, Pomegranate, 2005, Homo Erectus, 2006; TV appearances include Foster & Laurie, 1975, (TV mini series) Rich Man, Poor Man, 1976, Kill Me If You Can, 1977, Daddy, I Don't Like It Like This, 1978, Blood Vows: The Story of a Mafia Wife, 1987, Murderer's Keep, 1988, Mark Twain and Me, 1991, For Richer, For Poorer, 1992, Please, God, I'm Only Seventeen, 1992, Chatilly Lace, 1993, Born into Exile, 1997; prodr. Hyper Sapien: People from Another Star, 1986, Lionheart, 1987; assoc. prodr.: The Landlady, 1998; dir. One Night Stand, 1995.*

**SHIREK, JOHN RICHARD,** retired savings and loan executive; b. Bismarck, N.D., Feb. 5, 1926; s. James Max and Anna Agatha (Lala) S.; m. Ruth Martha Lietz, Sept. 22, 1950; children: Barbara Jo (Mrs. James A. Fowler), Jon Richard, Kenneth Edward. Student, U. Minn., 1944-46; BS with honors, Rollins Coll., 1978. Sports editor Bismarck (N.D.) Tribune, 1943-44; with Gate City Savs. and Loan Assn., Fargo, ND, 1947-65, v.p., dir., 1960-65; exec. v.p., dir. 1st Fed. Savs. and Loan Assn., Melbourne, Fla., 1966-70; pres. dir. 1st Fed. Savs. and Loan Assn., Cocoa, Fla., 1970-82; exec. v.p., dir. The First F.A. (formerly 1st Fed. Savs. and Loan Assn. of Orlando), 1982-91 Interim pres. Freedom Savs. and Loan Assn., Tampa, Fla., 1987-88; trustee Savs. & Loan Found., Inc., 1980-84; dir. Fin. Trans. Syss., Inc., Magnolia Svcs. Corp., 1st Cocoa Corp., Magnolia Realty Co., 1982-91. Chmn., dir. United Fund, Fargo, N.D., 1962-65; dir., exec. bd. mem. Boy Scouts Am., 1960-70, mem. adv. bd. cen. Fla. coun., 1983-85, 91-95, exec. bd., 1985-91, v.p. long-range planning, 1989-91; bd. assocs. Fla. Inst. Tech., founding pres. 1968; moderator St. Johns Presbytery, 1979, chmn. adv. coun., 1980-81; chair local arrangements com. 1993 Gen. Assembly Presbyn. Ch.; moderator Synod of Fla., 1983, Ctrl. Fla. Presbytery, 1991, coordinating coun., 1992; coun. mem. Synod of South Atlantic, 2002-2003; mem. adv. bd. Brevard Art Ctr. and Mus., 1980-82; bd. dirs., founding chmn. devel. coun. Holmes Regional Med. Ctr., Melbourne, 1981-84; bd. dirs. Orlando Regional Med. Ctr. Found., 1982-85, Jr. Achievement Cen. Fla., 1989-91; mem. fin. com. Mayor's Task Force on Housing, 1983-84; chmn. spl. com. on Nat. Coun. Chs./World Coun. Chs. rels. Presbyn. Ch. in U.S.A., 1983-86; pres. Ecumenical Ctr. Inc., Orlando, 1985-91, bd. dirs., 2001—; chmn. Fla. coord. com. Nat. Found. Studies Columbia Theol. Sem., 1991-95. Lt. (j.g.) USNR, World War II. Mem. Fla. Savs. and Loan League (past dir.), Fla. Savs. and Loan Svcs. (past dir.), Savs. and Loan Found. (state membership chmn. 1976), Fla. Savs. and Loan Polit. Action Com. (dir. 1976-82), U.S. Savs. and Loan League (chmn. advt. and pub. rels. com. 1969-70, dir. S.E. conf. 1975-80), Downtown Melbourne Assn. (past pres.), Cocoa Rotary (pres. 1979), Masons, Shriners, Elks, Beta Theta Pi, Omicron Delta Epsilon. Republican. Home: PO Box 568831 Orlando FL 32856-8831

**SHIREMAN, JOAN FOSTER,** social work educator; b. Cleve., Oct. 28, 1933; d. Louis Omar and Genevieve (Duguid) Foster; m. Charles Howard Shireman, Mar. 18, 1967; 1 child, David Louis. BA, Radcliffe Coll., 1956; MA, U. Chgo., 1959, PhD, 1968. Caseworker N.H. Children's Aid Soc., Manchester, 1959-61; dir. research Chgo. Child Care Soc., 1968-72; assoc. prof. U. Ill., Chgo., 1972-85; prof. Portland State U., Oreg., 1985—2003, dir. PhD program, 1992-99; interim exec. dir. Partnership for Rsch., Tng. and Grad. Edn. in Child Welfare, 1994; prof. emerita Portland State U., Oreg., 2003—. Research cons. child welfare projects, Ill., 1968-85, Oreg. 1985—; lectr. U. Chgo., 1968-72. Author: Critical Issues in Child Welfare, 2003; co-author: Care and Commitment: Foster Parent Adoption Disclosure, 1985, Adoption: Theory, Policy and Practice, 1997; mem. editl. bd. Jour. Sch. Social Work, 1978-81, Social Work Rsch. and Abstracts, 1990-93, Children and Youth Svcs. Rev., 1990—, Jour. Social Work Edn., 1990—; contbr. articles to profl. jours., chpts. to books. Bd. dirs. Oreg. chpt. Nat. Assn. for Prevention Child Abuse, 1985-87, Friendly House, Portland, 1991-97, 2002-03, Camp

Fire U.S.A. Portland Metro Coun., 2002-04; mem. adv. com. Children's Svcs. divsn. State of Oreg., 1985-95. Grantee HEW, 1980-82, Chgo. Community Trust, 1982-86, Oreg. Children's Trust Fund, 1991-96. Mem. NASW, AAUP, Acad. Cert. Social Workers, Coun. on Social Work Edn., Phi Beta Kappa. Home: 13584 SW Snowfire Dr Portland OR 97236 Office: Portland State U Grad Sch Social Work PO Box 751 Portland OR 97207-0751 Office Phone: 503-725-5005. Business E-Mail: shiremanj@pdx.edu.

**SHIRES, GEORGE THOMAS,** surgeon, educator; b. Waco, Tex., Nov. 22, 1925; s. George Thomas and Donna Mae (Smith) S.; m. Robbie Jo Martin, Nov. 27, 1948; children: Donna Blain, George Thomas III, Jo Ellen. MD, U. Tex., Dallas, 1948. Intern Mass. Meml. Hosp., Boston, 1948—49; resident in surgery Parkland Meml. Hosp., Dallas, 1950—53; faculty U. Tex. Southwestern Med. Sch., Dallas, 1953—60, assoc. prof. surgery, acting chmn. dept., 1960—61, prof., chmn. dept. 1961—74; surgeon in chief surg. svcs. Parkland Meml. Hosp., 1960—74; prof., chmn. dept. surgery U. Wash. Sch. Medicine, Seattle, 1974—75; chief of svc. Harborview Med. Ctr., Seattle, Univ. Hosp., Seattle, 1974—75; chmn. dept. surgery N.Y. Hosp.-Cornell U. Med. Coll., 1975—91; dean, provost for med. affairs Cornell U. Med. Coll., 1987—91, prof. emeritus, 1996—; prof., chmn. surgery Tex. Tech. U., Lubbock, 1991—95, Canizaro disting. prof. surgery, 1995—97; prof. surgery U. Nev. Sch. Medicine, Las Vegas, 1997—. Cons. Surgeon Gen., U.S. Army, 1965—75, Jamaica Hosp., 1978—91, Inst. Medicine NAS, 1975—; metabolism and trauma com. NAS-NRC, 1964—71, com. trauma, 1964—71; rsch. program evaluation com., reviewer clin. investigation applications career devel. program VA, 1972—76; gen. med. rsch. program projects com. NIH NIH, 1965—69; mem. Surgery A study sect., 1970—74, chmn., 1976—78; mem. Nat. Adv. Gen. Med. Scis. Coun., 1980—84; cons. editl. bd. Jour. Trauma, 1968—88. Mem. editl. bd.: Year Book Med. Publs., 1970—92, Annals of Surgery, 1972—, Surg. Techniques Illustrated: An International Comparative Text, 1974—75, Am. Jour. Surgery, 1968—, Contemporary Surgery, 1973—89, assoc. editor-in-chief: Infections in Surgery, 1981, mem. editl. bd.: Jour. Clin. Surgery, 1980—82; editor: Surgery, Gynecology and Obstetrics, 1982—93. Lt. M.C. USNR, 1949—50, Lt. M.C. USNR, 1953—55. Fellow: Coll. Medicine South Africa (hon.); mem.: AMA, ACS (bd. regents 1971—82, chmn. bd. regents 1978—80, pres. 1981—82), James IV Assn. Surgeons (bd. dirs. 1980—81, sec. 1981—87, pres. 1987—91), Allen O. Whipple Surg. Soc., Western Surg. Assn., N.Y. Surg. Soc. (pres. 1981—82), So. Surg. Assn., Soc. Univ. Surgeons (chmn. publs. com. 1969—71), Soc. Surg. Chairmen (pres. 1972—74), Soc. Clin. Surgery, Soc. Surgery Alimentary Tract, Pan Pacific Surg. Assn., Pan-Am. Med. Assn. (surgery coun. 1971), Am. Burn Assn., Internat. Surg. Soc. (sec. 1978—81, v.p. 1982—83, pres. U.S. chpt. 1984—85), Internat. Soc. Burn Injuries, Halsted Soc., Digestive Disease Found. (founding mem.), Am. Surg. Assn. (sec. 1969—74, pres. 1980), Am. Burn Assn., Am. Assn. Surgery Trauma, Dallas Soc. Gen. Surgeons (pres. 1972—74, pres.-elect), Am. Bd. Surgery (dir. 1968—74, chmn. 1972—74, diplomate), Surg. Biology Club (sec. 1968—70), Phi Beta Pi, Alpha Pi Alpha, Alpha Omega Alpha. Office: U Nev Sch Medicine 2040 W Charleston Blvd Ste 501 Las Vegas NV 89102-2207 Office Phone: 702-671-2297. Business E-Mail: gtshires@nvtrauma.com, tshires@med.unr.edu.

**SHIRILAU, MARK STEVEN,** utilities executive; b. Long Beach, Calif., Dec. 13, 1955; s. Kenneth Eugene and Marrjorie Irene (Thorvick) Shirey; m. Jeffery Michael Lau, Nov. 25, 1984 (dec. Aug. 9, 1993). BSEE, U. Calif., Irvine, 1977, MS in Bus. Adminstrn., 1980, PhD, 1988; M in Engring., Calif. Poly. State U., 1978; diploma in theology, Episc. Theol. Sch., Claremont Calif., 1984; MA in Religion, Sch. Theology at Claremont, 1985. Ordained priest Ecumenical Cath. Ch., 1987, consecrated bishop, 1991; registered profl. engr., Calif., N.Y., Tex.; lic. contractor, Calif. Grad. asst. Electric Power Inst., 1977-78; pres., CEO M.S.E., Santa Ana, Calif., 1977-87; adminstrv. mgr. EECO Inc., Santa Ana, 1979-83; fin. engr. So. Calif. Edison Co., Rosemead, 1983-84, conservation engr., 1984-85, conservation supr., 1985-89; exec. v.p. Aloha Sys., Inc., Villa Grande, Calif., 1989-93, pres., 1993—, also bd. dirs.; lectr. engring. Citrus Coll., Glendora, Calif., 2000—. Bd. dirs. Ewing Consol. Corp., Outrider Trucking, Inc.; part-time instr. Santa Ana Coll., 1982-84, Citrus Coll., Glendora, Calif., 2000-; lectr. engring. West Coast U., Orange, Calif., 1984-91; bd. dirs. Am. Electronics Assn. Credit Union, Sweetwater Springs Water Dist., Heat Pump Coun. So. Calif., AIDS Interfaith Network Sonoma County, Stampede Svcs. Inc., Ewmark Corp. Author: Triune Love: An Insight into God, Creation, and Humanity, 1983, Salvation, Scripture and Sexuality, 1992, History and Overview of the Ecumenical Catholic Church, 1993, Power 101, A Basic Introduction to Electric Utility Power, 1998, The Five Fatal Fears, 2002, (screenplay) Blackout!, 2005. Archbishop, primate Ecumenical Cath. Ch.; chief chaplain svcs. Nolanville (Tex.) Police Dept., 1998-2000; chaplain Jonestown (Tex.) Police Dept., 2001—. Mem. IEEE (sr.), ASHRAE, Internat. Assn. Chiefs Police, Assn. Energy Mgrs. (sr.), Assn. Profl. Energy Mgrs. (bd. dirs.), Am. Soc. Nondestructive Testing, Assn. Energy Svcs. Profls. (bd. dirs., charter mem., exec. v.p.), Am. Soc. Safety Engrs., Nat. Assn. Chiefs Police, Pacific Bears Club (v.p.), Dignity Integrity (life), Eta Kappa Nu. Democrat. Home: 20 Lincoln Irvine CA 92604-1947 Office: 14801 Comet St Irvine CA 92604-2464 Office Phone: 949-851-2221. E-mail: archbishop@ecchurch.org, MarkS@alohasys.com.

**SHIRK, CHRISTINE LOUISE,** music educator; b. Des Moines, Aug. 26, 1951; d. Neil Condra and Eva Louise Adamson; children: Catherine Louise, Steven Ross. BS in edn., Drake U., 1973; MA, U. Ctrl. Fla., 2002. Special Education, Music Fla. Dept. of Edn., Pace Piano Instructor Internat. Piano Teachers Found. Substitute tchr. Smouse Spl. Edn. Sch., Des Moines, 1974—77, Arlington Country Day Montessori Sch., Tex., 1981—87; piano tchr. Pvt. Studio, Orlando, Fla., 1993—; spl. edn. music tchr. Orange County Pub. Schs., Orlando, Fla., 1999—. Spkr. in field. Leader and adult trainer Girl Scouts of Am., 1990. Grantee, Darden Found., 2000, 2001, 2003, 2005; Supts. grantee, Orange County Pub. Schs., 1999. Mem.: Music Educators Nat. Conf., Fla. Music Educators Assn. (spl. learner chair 2000), Fla. Elem. Music Educators Assn., Coun. for Exceptional Children, Ctrl. Fla. Orff. Avocations: reading, tennis, crafts. Home: 2614 Raccoon Run Lane Orlando FL 32837 Office: Cherokee School Orange County Public Sc 551 South Eola Orlando FL 32801 Office Phone: 407-897-6440. Personal E-mail: teachaut@aol.com. E-mail: shirkc@ocps.net.

**SHIRK, JACK ANDREW,** executive recruiter; b. Lancaster, Pa., Apr. 10, 1967; s. Gerald Stauffer and Carole Nellie Shirk; m. Mildred Lorenzana Lumbao, Jan. 19, 2001; 1 child, Madison Krystal. Degree in Music, Grove Sch. Music, 1990. Exec. recruiter Brelad-Pager Assoc., Woodland Hills, Calif., 1990—91, Taylor Bruce & Assoc., Beverly Hills, Calif., 1991—92; physician recruiter Akron Kenny & Assoc., Encino, Calif., 1992—94, Baker Ellord & Assoc., Encino, Calif., 1994—97; president The Nephrology Physician Network, West Hills, Calif., 1997—. Edn. com. mem. Nat. Assn. Physician Recruiters, Winter Pk., Fla., 2004—06. Sgt. USAF, 1980—86. Decorated Honoray award for spl. achieve. and unit adv. coun. USAF; named Hardest Working Man award, Taylor Bryce & Assoc., 1992. Avocations: music, travel, songwriting, real estate investing. Home: 6735 Julie Ln West Hills CA 91307

**SHIRLEY, BONNIE J.,** retired elementary school educator; d. John R. and Catherine G. Bartholomew; m. Alan D. Shirley, Nov. 26, 1966 (dec. Jan. 2003); 1 child, Scott A. BS in Sci., SUNY, Brockport, 1969, postgrad., 1974. Cert. tchr. N.Y. Tchr. Rochester (N.Y.) City Sch. Dist., 1967—2003, lead tchr., mentor, 1991—2003; tchr. Greece (N.Y.) Continuing Edn.; cons. Renaissance Learning, Madison, 2003—; asst. prof. Roberts Wesleyan Coll., Rochester, 1995—97. Mem. adv. bd. dept. edn. and human devel. SUNY, Brockport. Named Sector 3 Tchr. of Yr., Rochester, N.Y., 1999. Avocation: freelance writing. Home: 87 Ayer St Rochester NY 14615 Personal E-mail: bshirle1@rochester.rr.com.

**SHIRLEY, DAVID ARTHUR,** chemistry professor, science administrator; b. North Conway, NH, Mar. 30, 1934; m. Virginia Schultz, June 23, 1956 (dec. Mar 1995); children: David N., Diane, Michael, Eric, Gail; m. Barbara Cerny, Dec. 26, 1995. BS, U. Maine, 1955, ScD (hon.), 1978; PhD in

Chemistry, U. Calif.-Berkeley, 1858; D honoris causa, Free U. Berlin, 1987. With Lawrence Radiation Lab. (now Lawrence Berkeley Lab.), U. Calif., Berkeley, 1958-92, assoc. dir., head materials and molecular research div., 1975-80, dir., 1980-89, lectr. chemistry, 1959-60, asst. prof., 1960-64, assoc. prof., 1964-67, prof., 1967-92, vice chmn. dept. chemistry, 1968-71, chmn. dept. chemistry, 1971-75; sr. v.p. rsch., dean grad. sch. Pa. State U., University Park, 1992-96; dir. emeritus Lawrence Berkeley Nat. Lab., 1997—. Chair bd. overseers Fermilab. Contbr. over 400 rsch. articles. NSF fellow, 1955-58, 66-67, 70; recipient Ernest O. Lawrence award AEC, 1972, Humboldt award (sr. U.S. scientist); listed by Sci. Citation Index as one of the world's 300 most cited scientists for work published during 1965-78. Fellow Am. Phys. Soc.; mem. Nat. Acad. Scis., Am. Chem. Soc., AAAS, Am. Acad. Arts and Scis., Bohemian Club, Explorers Club, Sigma Xi, Tau Beta Pi, Sigma Pi Sigma, Phi Kappa Phi.

**SHIRLEY, DONNA,** museum director, former aerospace engineer; b. Wynnewood, Okla. 1 child, Laura. BS in Aerospace Engring., U. Okla., BA in Journalism; MS in Aerospace Engring., U. So. Calif. With Jet Propulsion Lab., Pasadena, Calif., 1966—, Cassini project engr., mgr. exploration initiative studies, mgr. automation and robotics, mgr. Space Sta. program, mgr. mission design sect., project engr. for Mariner 10, mgr. Mars Pathfinder microrover Flight Experiment team, mgr. Mars exploration program; ret., 1998; pres. Managing Creativity, Norman, Okla.; assist. dean aerospace mechanical engring. U. Oklahoma, 1999—2003; dir. Science Fiction Museum and Hall of Fame, Seattle, 2004—. Leader NASA-wide Sys. Engring. Working Group, 1990-93; leader NASA-wide team on program/project mgmt. NASA, 1991. Author: Managing Martians, 1998. Office: Science Fiction Museum and Hall of Fame 325 5th Ave N Seattle WA 98109

**SHIRLEY, JOE, JR.,** Native American tribal leader; b. Chinle, Ariz., Dec. 4, 1947; m. Vikki Shirley; 6 children. AA, Magic Valley Christian Coll., Albion, Idaho, 1968; BS in bus., Abilene Christian U., Abilene, Tex., 1973; MSW, Ariz. State U., Tempe, 1978. Various social work positions; exec. dir. Navajo Divsn. Social Services, 1983—84; supervisor Apache County, 1984—2003; pres. Navajo Nation, 2003—. Office: Navajo Nation PO Box 9000 Window Rock AZ 86515 Office Phone: 928-871-6352. Office Fax: 928-871-4025. E-mail: joeshirleyjr@yahoo.com.*

**SHIRLEY, JON ANTHONY,** software company executive; b. San Diego, Apr. 12, 1938; s. Joseph Roy and Mercedes (Miller) S.; m. Gail Grieg (div. June 1964); 1 child, Erickson; m. E. Mary L. Johanson, July 7, 1964; children: Peter, Mary. Grad., Hill. High Sch., Pottstown, Pa., 1956; student, MIT, 1956-57. Several Radio Shack div. Tandy Corp., Ft. Worth, 1963-72, v.p., 1972-83; pres., chief operating officer Microsoft Corp., Redmond, Wash., 1983—90, bd. dir., 1983—. Dir. Manzanita Capital, Seattle. Chmn. bd. trustees Seattle Art Mus.; trustee Mus. Flight, Seattle, Hill Sch., Pottstown, Pa.; mem. chmn. council Mus. Modern Art, N.Y.C. Named one of Top 200 Collectors, ARTnews Mag., 2004, 2005, 2006. Mem. Assn. Data Processing Service Orgns. (bd. dirs. 1986—). Clubs: Seattle Yacht. Democrat. Avocations: Collector of Modern & Contemporary Art, Collecting, restoring, showing and racing of Vintage Ferrari Motor Cars. Office: Microsoft Corp One Microsoft Way Redmond WA 98052*

**SHIRLEY-QUIRK, JOHN,** singer, educator; b. Liverpool, Eng., Aug. 28, 1931; arrived in US, 1990, naturalized, 2002; s. Joseph Stanley and Amelia (Griffiths) S.-Q.; m. Patricia May Hastie, July 1955 (dec. Feb. 1981); children: Kate, Peter; m. Sara Van Horn Watkins, Dec. 29, 1981 (dec. Dec. 1997); children: Benjamin, Emily (dec.), Julia. BSc, Liverpool U., 1953, MusD (hon.), 1977; D Univ., Brunel U., 1981. Asst. lectr. Acton Tech. Coll. London, 1956-60; vicar choral St. Paul's Cathedral, London, 1960-61; profl. singer, 1960—; joint artistic dir. Aldeburgh Festival, 1981-84. Mem. voice faculty Peabody Conservatory, Balt., 1991—; vis. artist Carnegie-Mellon U., Pitts., 1994-98. Numerous recs. and 1st performances, especially works of Benjamin Britten. Mem. ct. Brunel U., 1977-81. Flying officer RAF, 1952-55. Decorated comdr. Order of Brit. Empire. Mem. Royal Acad. Music (hon.), Royal Philharmonic Soc. Personal E-mail: jssq@peabody.jhu.edu.

**SHIRTLIFF, BRYAN,** retail executive; m. Eve Shirtliff; 4 children. B. U. Montana. Various positions Am. Stores Co., 1983—96; v.p., health and beauty care and gen. merchandise Bruno's Inc.; dir. health care Rite Aid Corp., Camp Hill, Pa., 1998—99, dir., health care and seasonal, 1999—2000, v.p., seasonal and hardlines, 2000—03, sr. v.p., category mgmt., 2003—. Home: Rite Aid Corporation 30 Hunter Lane Camp Hill PA 17011

**SHIRTUM, EARL EDWARD,** retired civil engineer; b. Montague, Mich., Feb. 20, 1927; s. Earl Willard and Elizabeth Caroline (Boelke) S.; m. Martha Louise Wright, June 19, 1953. BS in Civil Engring., Ind. Tech. Coll., Ft. Wayne, 1950. Bridge design squad leader Mich. Dept. Transp., Lansing, 1952-63, transp. planning engr., 1963-96. Mem. Bridge Replacement and Rehab. Com., Lansing, 1967-94. With U.S. Army, 1945-46, ETO. Mem. Mich. Profl. Engring. Soc. (rep. engr. in govt. 1974-77), Lansing Engr. Club (bd. mem. 1980-84). Republican. Methodist. Avocations: fishing, bridge. Home: 1617 Victor Ave Lansing MI 48910-6511

**SHIRVANI, SIR HAMID,** architect, educator, philosopher, writer, university president; b. Tehran, Iran, Oct. 20, 1950; arrived in US, 1974, naturalized, 1986; s. Majid and Taji (Granpisheh) Shirvani; m. Fatemeh Shokrollahi, Oct. 4, 2002. Diploma in architecture, Poly. of Cen. London, 1974; MArch, Pratt Inst., 1975; MS, Rensselaer Poly. Inst., 1977; MLA, Harvard U., 1978; MA, Princeton U., 1979, PhD, 1980; LHD (hon.), Soka U., Japan, 2003. Project designer London Borough of Barnet, 1973-74; asst. prof. architecture Pa. State U., 1979-82; prof., dir. grad. studies SUNY, Syracuse, 1982-85; prof., dir. Sch. Urban Planning and Devel., U. Louisville, 1985-86; prof. architecture and urban design U, Colo. Denver, 1986-91, dean Sch. of Architecture and Planning, 1986-91; prof. philosophy, dean Coll. Arts and Scis. U. Mass., Lowell, 1992-95; v.p. grad. studies and rsch., prof. urban studies CUNY Queens Coll., Flushing, 1995-2000; provost, exec. v.p., Martha Masters prof. art/architecture Chapman U., Orange, Calif., 2000—05; pres., prof. art and architecture Calif. State U., Stanislaus, 2005—. Vis. faculty So. Calif. Inst. Architecutre, U. So. Calif.; lectr. in field, including U. Tex., San Antonio, Lehigh U., U. Waterloo (Can.), U. Sydney (Australia), Mo. State U., Columbia U., NYC, Amsterdam Acad. Art, U. Venice (Italy), Chinese U. Hong Kong, So. China Inst. U., U. Calif., Irvine, Villanova U., Rutgers U., Ariz. State U., Duke U., U. Pa., Yale U., U. Colo., U. NC Author: Urban Design: A Comprehensive Reference, 1981, Urban Design Review, 1981, Urban Design Process, 1985, Beyond Public Architecture, 1990; editor Urban Design Rev., 1982-85, Urban Design and Preservation Quar., 1985-88; mem. editorial bd. Jour. Archtl. Edn., 1988-94, Avant Garde, 1988-93, Jour. Planning Edn., and Rsch. 1987-93, Art and Architecture, 1974-78, Jour. Am. Planning Assn., 1982-88. Recipient Gold medal in Architecture and Urbanism, Faculty Honor award, Acad. Leadership award, Faculty Rsch. award, Commendation award AIA, 2003, Justice award SGI, 2003; Knight of Holy Sepulchre, 2004. Fellow World Acad. Arts and Scis., Am. Soc. Landscape Archs. (recognition award), Royal Geog. Soc., Royal Soc. Arts, World Acad. Arts and Scis.; mem. Am. Inst. Cert. Planners, Am. Planning Assn. Democrat. Avocations: urban design divsn. 1987-89, Disting. award 1984, Urban Design award 1985), Sigma Xi, Omicron Delta Epsilon, Tau Sigma Delta (Silver medal in archtl. edn. 1988), Tau Beta Pi, Sigma Lambda Alpha. Office: Calif State U 801 W Monte Vista Ave Turlock CA 95382 Office Phone: 209-667-3201. Office Fax: 209-667-3206. E-mail: president@csustan.edu.

**SHIRVINSKI, ADAM JOHN,** management consultant; b. Mahanoy, Pa., Oct. 25, 1939; s. Adam F. and Louise Shirvinski; m. Jean Shirvinski, June 25, 1966; children: Adam Albert, Lisa Ellen, Lara Jean. BS in Engring., USCG Acad., 1961; MS in Quantitative Analysis, U.S. Naval Postgrad. Sch., Monterey, Calif., 1970; MS in Fin., Am. U, 1987. Group mgr.-product assurance EER Systems, Chantilly, Va., 1988—95; quality assurance mgr., air and space divsn. Sentel Corp., Alexandria, Va., 1995—98; sr. quality assurance specialist EDS Corp., Herndon, Va., 1998—2001; quality assurance

mgr. Intelli Dyne, LLC, Falls Church, Va., 1995—. Pres., CEO Adams' Quality, Inc., Potomac, Md. Capt. U.S. Coast Guard, 1961—88. Mem.: AFCEA (assoc.), IEEE (assoc.), Informs (assoc.), US Naval Inst. (assoc.), Am. Soc. for Quality (sr.), Army Navy Club (assoc.). Republican. Roman Catholic. Avocations: tennis, hunting, fishing. Home: L26-B3-S2 Lake Shore Dr HC88 Box 386 Pocono Lake PA 18347 Office: Adams' Quality, Inc 1897 Milboro Dr Potomac MD 20854 Office Phone: 301-279-7336.

**SHIRZAD, FARYAR,** federal official; married; 1 child. BS summa cum laude, U. Md.; JD, U. Va.; M in Pub. Policy, Harvard U. With Robins, Kaplan, Miller & Ciresi, Washington; internat. trade atty. Skadden, Arps, Slate Meagher & Flom, Washington; internat. trade counsel Senate Com. on Fin., 1997—2001; lead internat. trade policy coord. Bush-Cheney Transition Offices; asst. sec. for import adminstrn. U.S. Dept. Commerce, Washington, 2001—03; asst. to the Pres. for internat. econ. affairs The White House, Washington, 2004—; dep. nat. security advisor NSC, Washington, 2005—. Office: The White House 1600 Pennsylvania Ave Washington DC 20500

**SHISLER, ARDEN L.,** insurance and transportation company executive; b. Massillon, Ohio, 1941; COO K&B Transport, Dalton, Ohio, 1986—92, pres., CEO, 1992—2003; chmn. Nationwide Mut. Ins. Co., Columbus, Ohio, 2003—. Mem. Wayne County Farm Bureau; bd. mem. Ohio 4-H Found.; v.p. Ohio Farm Bur., 1974-84; pres. Ohio Agriculture Mktg. Assn., 1982-84. Office: Nationwide Mut Ins Co 1 Nationwide Plz Columbus OH 43215-2220*

**SHITABATA, PAUL KENT,** pathologist; b. Fukuoka, Japan, Sept. 20, 1962; s. George Joji and Janet Aiko (Ikeda) S.; m. Evangeline Chan Uy, Aug. 30, 1997. BA, Pomona Coll., 1984; MD, U. Hawaii, 1988. Diplomate Am. Bd. Pathology, Am. Bd. Dermatopathology. Med. dir. South Bay Surgicenter, Torrance, Calif., 1994—99, Long Beach Doctor's Hosp., Calif., 1996—99; with Affiliated Pathologists Med. Group, Torrance, 1994—. Med. dir. Pathology Inc., 2003—; CEO, pres. The Doctor's Dr., 1999—; bd. dirs. Logical Images; assoc. clin. prof. UCLA. Contbr. articles to profl. jours. Mem.: Asian Am. Physicians Assn. (bd. dirs. 1999—2004), Coll. Am. Pathologists (coun. plastic affairs 2003, mem. leadership devel. com. 2005), Alpha Omega Alpha. Avocation: jazz. Office: Pathology Inc 19951 Mariner Ave Ste 150 Torrance CA 90503 Office Phone: 310-225-3176. Business E-Mail: pshitabata@pathologyinc.com.

**SHIUE, WEN-TSONG,** electrical and computer scientist, educator; b. Tounan, Yunlin, Taiwan, Feb. 18, 1965; s. Chun-Ming Hsueh and Jui-Jung Shen; m. Shu-Ching Tu; children: Vivian, Stephen. MS, Western Mich. U., 1991; PhD, Ariz. State U., 2000. Adj. prof. Tamkang U., Taipei, Taiwan, 1991—96; chief electronics officer China Airlines, Taoyuan, Taiwan, 1991—96; rsch. assoc. Ariz. State U., Tempe, 1997—2000; sr. staff scientist Motorola Inc., Austin, Tex., 1999—2000; lead software scientist Silicon Metrics Corp., Austin, 2000—01; prof. Oreg. State U., Corvallis, 2001—. Contbr. articles to profl. jours. Recipient Travel Grant award, Ariz. State U., 1999; grantee, IEEE/ACM 36th Design Automation Conf., 1999; scholar, Motorola Inc., 1999, 2000. Mem.: IEEE Computer Soc., Assn. Computing Machinery, IEEE Circuits and Sys. Soc., Am. Soc. Engring Edn., Gamma Beta Phi. Avocations: swimming, travel. Office: Oreg State Univ Dept ECE Corvallis OR 97331 Home: 11608 Spicewood Pkwy Unit 5 Austin TX Office Phone: 541-737-6781. Personal E-mail: shiue@ieee.org. Business E-Mail: shiue@ece.orst.edu.

**SHIV, KUMAR,** bioscientist; s. Shyam and Daya Agarwal; m. Durgesh Kumar Agarwal; children: Sharad Kumar Agarwal, Sumit Kumar Agarwal. PhD, Ctrl. Drug Rsch. Inst., Lucknow, India, 1983. Dir. Amersham Bioscis., Piscataway, NJ, 1999—2002; prin. scientist GE Healthcare/Amesham Bioscis., Piscataway, NJ, 2002—04. Cons., Belle Mead, NJ, 2005—06. Contbr. over 75 articles to profl. jours. Fellow, CSIR, New Delhi, 1979-1983. Mem.: ACS. Achievements include over 25 patents. Home: 21 Muirhead Ct Belle Mead NJ 08502 Personal E-mail: skumar_08855@yahoo.com.

**SHIVAKUMAR, SUJAI,** political economist, policy advisor; b. Chennai, Tamil Nadu, India, Dec. 6, 1965; s. Jayasankar and Charu Shivakumar; m. Rama Shivakumar, June 24, 1999; 1 child, Tara. PhD, George Mason U., Fairfax, Va., 1996. Vis. scholar Ind. U., Bloomington, 1997—2001; policy advisor NAS, Washington, 2001—. Cons. Action Aid, Somalia, 1998—2001. Author: The Constitution of Development: Crafting Capabilities for Self-Governance, The Samaritan's Dilemma: The Political Economy of Development Aid. Office: NAS 500 Fifth St NW Washington DC 20001 Business E-Mail: sshivaku@nas.edu.

**SHIVCHARRAN, JAIGOBIN,** secondary school educator, consultant; b. Rose Hall, Guyana, Apr. 23, 1941; arrived in U.S., 1980; s. Moochoon and Yawa Shivcharran; m. Kawa Sakhichand-Bracelly (div.); children: Sharmila, Rajesh, Ormila; m. Ruby Singh, July 11, 1983. BA in Humanities, Thomas Edison State Coll., 1989; MA in ESL, CUNY, NYC, 1993; BS in Psychology and Sociology, Regents Coll., 1996; PhD in Linguistics, Summit U., 1998. Cert. tchr. N.Y., 1997. Tchr. Dept. Edn., Guyana, 1961—80, 1995—; figure clk. Feature Enterprise, NYC, 1989; case mgr. Dept. Social Svcs., NYC, 1989—95. Instr. Coll. St. Rose, NYC, Albany, 2000—, Adelphi U., Garden City, NY, 2001—; staff developer United Fedn. TRS, NYC, 2000—; cons. NY State United Tchrs., NYC, 2000—. Author: Native Language Transfer in Second Language Learning, 1997, Anthology of Short Stories, 2005. Mem.: Acad. Polit. Sci., Nat. Assn. Scholars, NY State Assn. Scholars. Avocations: reading, walking, dance, writing. Home: 132 Freeman St #2D Brooklyn NY 11222-5853 Office: Automotive High Sch 50 Bedford Ave Brooklyn NY 11222 Personal E-mail: jayshivcharran@aol.com.

**SHIVE, RICHARD BYRON,** architect; b. Cleve., Jan. 16, 1933; s. Roy Allen and Mary Elizabeth (Thompson) S.; m. Patricia Butler, Aug. 28, 1954; children: Lisa Ann, Laura Mary, John Thompson, Nancy Butler. BS, Rensselaer Poly. Inst., Troy, N.Y., 1954; postgrad., Newark (N.J.) Coll. Engring., 1957, Rutgers U., 1960-63. Registered architect, N.J., N.Y., Pa., Vt.; lic. profl. planner, N.J. Field engr. Wigton-Abbott Corp., Plainfield, NJ, 1954-55, The Glenwal Co., Rochelle Park, NJ, 1955; asst. supt. Wigton-Abbott Corp., Plainfield, 1955-57; archtl. draftsman Raymond B. Flatt, Architect, Bloomfield, NJ, 1957-58, chief draftsman, 1958-60; project architect Scrimenti/Swackhamer/Perantoni Architects, Somerville, NJ, 1960-66, assoc., 1966-69; ptnr. Scrimenti, Shive, Spinelli, Perantoni Architects, Somerville, 1969-86, Shive/Spinelli/Perantoni & Assocs., Architects & Planners, Somerville, 1986-97; prin. emeritus SSP Archtl. Group, 1998—2002; pvt. practice Richard B. Shive, AIA, Architect, 2003—. Adv. com. First Fidelity Bank, Bound Brook, N.J., 1989-91; chmn. bd. Somerset Health Care Corp., 1987-91. Contbr. articles to profl. jours. Bd. dirs., exec. com. N.J. Hosp. Assn., Princeton, 1986-92, 93-95; chmn. bd. trustees Somerset Med. Ctr., Somerville, 1973-96; mem. Nat. Trust for Hist. Preservation; bd. dirs. Ctr. for Health Affairs, Inc., 1992-93; mem. Borough of Bound Brook Planning Bd., 2000—; chmn. Borough of Bound Brook Redevel. Adv. Com., 2000—; mem. Somerset County Econ. Devel. Incentive Adv. Com., 1997—. Recipient award James F. Lincoln Arc Welding Found., 1973, President's award for outstanding svc. Rolling Hills coun. Girl Scouts U.S.A., 1988, Trustee of Yr. award N.J. Hosp. Assn., 1993, Outstanding Citizen of Yr. award Somerset County C. of C., 1993, Spirit of Somerset award, 2000; Paul Harris fellow Bound Brook-Middlesex Rotary Club, 1993. Mem. AIA, ASTM, ASHRAE, ACI (chpt. bd. dirs. 1978-83), N.J. Soc. Architects, Illuminating Engring. Soc., Nat. Fire Protection Assn., Greater Somerset County C. of C. (v.p. 1985-86, 92-93, Outstanding Citizen of Yr. award 1993), Rotary (pres. 1969-70, Paul Harris fellow 1993), Wash. Campground Assn. (pres. 1975-76, v.p. 1977-78, sec. 1978-97), Chi Phi (sec. 1973). Republican. Congregationalist. Avocations: fishing, photography, skiing, canoeing, backpacking. Home and Office: 1786 Middlebrook Rd Bound Brook NJ 08805-1432 Office Phone: 732-469-2682. Personal E-mail: rshive@verizon.net.

**SHIVELY, DANIEL JEROME,** retired transportation executive; b. Akron, Ohio, Sept. 2, 1924; s. Richard Miles and Josephine (Pellicer) S.; m. Pamela Marion Kurfess, July 31, 1954; children: Jennifer, Laurie, Thomas. Grad., U.S. Mcht. Marine Acad., King's Point, N.Y., 1945. Chief officer (tanker) Trinidad Corp., N.Y.C., 1946-51; co-owner, mgr. Shively Bros. Jersey Farm, Quaker City, Ohio, 1952-54; staff asst. Gulf Oil Corp., Phila., 1955-57; distbn. coord. Standard Oil Co., Cleve., 1957-73; budget coord. BP Oil Co., Wilmington, Del., 1973-79; mgr. mktg. budget and planning Standard Oil Co., Cleve., 1979-85; owner, mgr. Shively & Assocs., Cleve., 1985-88. Served to lt. (j.g.) USNR, 1945-61. Mem. Transp. Practitioners Assn. (exec. com. 1984-90, pres. local chpt. 1984-85), King's Point Club (treas. N.E. Ohio chpt. 1989-94, sec. 1999-2003), KC (chancellor 1986, dep. grand knight 1987-91). Republican. Roman Catholic. Avocations: farming, sailing. Home: 21347 Erie Rd Rocky River OH 44116-2133

**SHIVELY, GERALD E.,** economist, educator; b. Dayton, Ohio, Oct. 18, 1962; BA, Boston U., 1984, MA, 1985; PhD, U. Wis., Madison, 1996. Hon. fellow Dept. Econs. and Asian Econs., U. Melbourne, Victoria, Australia, 2003—04; prof. Purdue U., West Lafayette, Ind., 1996—. Co-editor-in-chief Agrl. Economics, 2006—; assoc. editor Environment and Devel. Economics, 2006—. Author: (book) Land Use Change in Tropical Watersheds: Evidence Causes and Remedies; contbr. articles to profl. jours. Named Outstanding Instr., Dept. of Agrl. Econs., Purdue U., 2003; recipient Alumni award in Economics, Boston U., 1984, Tchg. for Tomorrow award, Purdue U., 1998, Usha Mahajani prize, S.E. Asia Coun. of the Assn. for Asian Studies, 1994, Taylor award, Agrl. and Applied Econs., U. Wis.-Madison, 1996; fellow Nat. Security Edn. Program Grad. fellow, U.S. Govt., 1994, Grad. fellow, John H and Catherine T. MacArthur Found., 1993—96; grantee Fgn. Lang. Area Studies grantee, U.S. Govt., 1994, Fulbright grantee, Fulbright Program of U.S., 1994—95. Mem.: Assn. of Environ. and Resource Economists, Am. Agrl. Econs. Assn. Office: Purdue University 403 W State St West Lafayette IN 47907 Office Phone: 765-494-4218. Office Fax: 765-494-9176. E-mail: shivelyg@purdue.edu.

**SHIVELY, JOHN TERRY,** cruise line executive; b. Middletown, N.Y., July 1, 1943; s. Marvin Rathfelder and Esther (Manning) Westervelt; adopted child, Harold Eugene Shively. BA, U. N.C., 1965. Vol. worker VISTA, Bethel and Fairbanks, Alaska, 1965-68; health planner Greater Anchorage Area Cmty. Action Agy., 1968-69; health cons. Alaska Fed. Natives, Anchorage, 1969; dep. dir. Rural Alaska Cmty. Action Program, Anchorage, 1971-72; exec. v.p. Alaska Fedn. Natives, Anchorage, 1972-75; v.p. ops. NANA Regional Corp., Kotzebue, Alaska, 1975-77, NANA Devel. Corp., Anchorage, 1977-82; sr. v.p. NANA Regional Corp. Inc., 1986-92; pres. NANA Devel. Corp., 1992-94; commr. DNR, 1995-2000; chmn., CEO United Bar Corp., United Bank Alaska, 1987-88; sr. ptnr. Jade North, 2000—02; v.p. govt. and cmty. rels. Holland Am., 2002—. Dir. Unicorp. Inc., United Bank of Alaska, Resource Devel. Coun., exec. com., 2001—, pres, 2003—; dir. Alaska State C. of C., exec. com., 2003—. Mem. Greater Anchorage Area Comprehensive Health Plan Coun., 1969-75, chmn., 1969-75; founding mem. bd. dirs. Alaska Pub. Interest Rsch. Group, 1974-75, 86-90, chmn. 1987-90; mem. Gov.'s Rural Affairs Coun., 1971-76, Gov.'s Manpower Commn., 1971, Greater Anchorage Health Bd., 1969-75, Alaska Pipeline Edn. Com., 1973-74; bd. regents U. Alaska, 1979-83; bd. trustees Alaska Permanent Fund Bd., 1999-2000. Democrat. Episcopalian. Home and Office: 2301 Loren Cir Anchorage AK 99516 Personal E-mail: jtshively@att.net.

**SHIVELY, JUDITH CAROLYN (JUDY SHIVELY),** administrative assistant; b. Wilkinsburg, Pa., Jan. 30, 1962; d. John Allen and Edith (Crowell) S. BA in English, U. Nev., Las Vegas, 1984. Circulation aide Charleston Heights Libr., Las Vegas, 1979—86; asst. food editor Las Vegas Sun Newspaper, 1985—88, asst. horse racing editor, 1985—90, features writer, page editor, 1988—89, editor youth activities sect., 1989—90; racebook ticket writer, cashier Palace Sta. Hotel Racebook, Las Vegas, 1989—92; contract adminstr. nat. accts. Loomis, Fargo & Co., Las Vegas, 1992—2000; propr. Creative Computing, Las Vegas, 1996—; content prodn. Preference Techs., Inc., Las Vegas, 2000; data rsch. and processing PurchasePro.com, Las Vegas, 2000; adminstrv. asst. Uinta Bus. Systems, Las Vegas, 2001—02, Law Office of Frank Sorrentino, Las Vegas, 2003—; legal asst. Lee A. Drizin, 2006, Crosby & Assocs., 2006—. Horse racing historian, rschr., Las Vegas, 1985—; vol. rsch. asst. Dictionary of Gambling and Gaming, 1982-84; clk. Hometown News, Las Vegas, 1994-96. Staff writer horse race handicaps, columns, articles, feature stories Las Vegas Sun Newspaper, 1985-90; freelance writer for monthly horse racing publ. Inside Track, 1992-94. Mem. Phi Beta Kappa. Republican. Avocations: collecting horse racing books, clippings, materials for personal library of horse racing, computers. Home: PO Box 26426 Las Vegas NV 89126-0426 Personal E-mail: racehors1@aol.com.

**SHIVELY, MERRICK LEE,** pharmaceutical scientist, consultant; b. Alamogordo, N.Mex., Dec. 12, 1958; s. Milton Lee and Dorothy Jean (Garlock) S.; m. Maureen Lynch, Dec. 28, 1985; 1 child, Sierra Lange. BS in Pharmacy, U. Conn., 1982, PhD in Pharmaceutics, 1986. Registered pharmacist, Colo., Mass. Sr. rsch. assoc. Baxter Healthcare, Morton Grove, Ill., 1985-87; asst. prof. U. Colo., Boulder, 1987-93; sr. rsch. scientist Atrix Labs., Inc., Ft. Collins, Colo., 1993-94; sr. scientist Nexagen, Inc., Boulder, 1994-96; founder, mng. ptnr. Drug Delivery Solutions LLC, Louisville, Colo., 1996—. Pharm. cons. Glaxo, Synergen, Chemex, Cell Tech., Lilly; del. U.S. Pharmacopeia, 1988-94. Contbr. articles to Pharm. Rsch., Jour. Colloid Interface Sci., Drug Devel. and Indsl. Pharmacy, Internat. Jour. Pharmaceutics, others. Mem. Denver Econ. Com., 1989. Richardson-Vicks fellow, 1982-85. Mem. Am. Assn. Pharm. Scientists, Soc. of Controlled Release, Am. Chem. Soc., Rocky Mountain Pharm. Forum (treas. 1989—), Phi Kappa Phi, Rho Chi. Achievements include patents in field; discovery and method of manufacture of solid state emulsions, findings that the formation of multi-molecular inclusion compounds are responsible for unique properties. Home and Office: 10ll Turnberry Cir Louisville CO 80027-9594

**SHIVELY, WILLIAM PHILLIPS,** political scientist, educator; b. Altoona, Pa., Mar. 31, 1942; s. Arthur and Ruth Shively; m. Barbara Louise Shank, Aug. 29, 1964; children: Helen, David. BA, Franklin and Marshall Coll., 1963; PhD, U. N.C., 1968. Mem. faculty U. Oreg., Eugene, 1967-68, Yale U., 1968-71; mem. faculty U. Minn., Mpls., 1971—, prof. polit. sci., 1979—; provost arts, scis. & engring., 1995-97. Author: Craft of Political Research, 1974, 6th edit., 2004, Research Process in Political Science, 1985, Power and Choice, 1986, rev. edit., 1989, 10th edit., 2006, Comparative Governance, 1995, (with Christopher Achen) Cross-Level Inference, 1995; editor Am. Jour. Polit. Sci., 1977-79; contbr. articles on elections and voting to profl. jours. Home: 1572 Northrop St Saint Paul MN 55108-1322 Office: U Minn Dept Polit Sci 1414 Social Scis Tower Minneapolis MN 55455 Office Phone: 612-624-4395. Business E-Mail: shively@polisci.umn.edu.

**SHIVERS, MITCHELL EVERETT,** diplomat; b. NY, Nov. 19, 1947; s. Carl Everett and Mary Allison (Young) S.; m. Nancy Jane Shorsher; children: Mitchell Jr and Jane B. BS, Monmouth U., 1970; postgrad., New York U., 1975-77. Mgmt. exec. Merrill Lynch, NYC, Singapore, 1973—81; exec. dir. Samuel Montagu & Co., London, 1981—84; pvt. practice, 1984—85, 1992—93, Bay Head, NJ, 2003—; pres. Kleinwort Benson Inc., NYC, 1985—89, Fuji Securities, NYC, Chgo., 1989—92; mng. dir. Merrill Lynch, NYC, 1993—2001; ret., 2001; diplomat, sr. advisor, econ. sector chief Afghanistan Reconstrn. Group, U.S. State Dept., Kabul, 2004—05; bus. cons., 2001—. Vice-chmn. Cultural Trust of NJ; founder, chmn. Barnegat Bay Charities Inc., 2001—04. Recipient Anniversary Cup, Am.'s Cup Jubilee, 2001, N.J. Disting. Svc. medal, State of NJ, 2002. Mem.: Internat. Guild Bankers, Internat. Securities Markets Assn. (bd. dirs. 2000—). Avocations: competitive sailing, jogging, skiing, travel. Personal E-mail: mitchell_shivers@hotmail.com. E-mail: shiversm@gmail.com.

**SHIVERY, CHARLES W.,** utilities executive; BA, BS, Johns Hopkins U.; MBA, U. Balt. With Balt. Gas & Electric Co., 1972—80, asst. treas., 1980—88, treas., asst. sec., 1988—89, v.p. corp. fin., 1989—93, v.p., CFO, 1993—97; chmn., pres., CEO Constellation Power Source, Inc., 1997—2002;

CEO, pres. Constellation Enterprises, Inc., 1998—2002; pres., CEO Constellation Power Source Holdings, Inc., 2000—02; co-pres. Constellation Energy Group, Inc., 2000—02, 2000—02; pres., CEO NU Enterprises, Inc., 2002—04; interim pres. N.E. Utilities, Berlin, Conn., 2004, chmn., pres., CEO, 2004—. Office: Northeast Utilities PO Box 270 Hartford CT 06141-0270*

SHIVES, PAULA J., lawyer; b. Monongahela, Pa., Sept. 28, 1950; m. William Sutton. BA, Western Ky. U., 1973; JD, U. Ky., 1979. Bar: Ky. 1979. Assoc. gen. counsel Long John Silver Restaurants, Inc., Lexington, Ky., 1985—95, sr. v.p., gen. counsel, sec., 1995—99, Darden Restaurants, Inc., Orlando, Fla., 1999—. Mem.: ABA, Ky. Bar Assn., Fayette County Bar Assn. Office: 5900 Lake Ellenor Dr Orlando FL 32809 Home: 2011 Via Tuscany Winter Park FL 32789-1557 Office Phone: 407-245-6566.

SHKEL, YURI M., education educator, researcher; PhD, Moscow State U., 1988. Asst. prof. U. Wis.-Madison, 2000—. Office: Univ Wisconsin Madison 1415 Engineering Dr Madison WI 53706 Office Phone: 608-263-2479.

SHKLAR, GERALD, pathologist, periodontist, educator; b. Montreal, Que., Can., Dec. 2, 1924; came to U.S., 1950, naturalized, 1955; s. Louis and Ann (Schleifstein) S.; m. Judith Nisse, June 16, 1948 (dec. Sept. 18, 1992); children: David, Michael, Ruth; m. Se-Kyung Oh, July 13, 1997. BS, McGill U., 1947, DDS, 1949; MS, Tufts U., 1952; MA (hon.), Harvard U., 1971; D (hon.), U. Athens. Diplomate Am. Bd. Oral Pathology, Am. Bd. Periodontology. Asst. prof. oral pathology Sch. Dental Medicine Tufts U., Boston, 1953—59, assoc. prof. Sch. Dental Medicine, 1960—61, rsch. prof. peridontology Sch. Dental Medicine, 1961—71, lectr. oral pathology Sch. Dental Medicine, 1971—. Head dept. oral medicine and oral pathology Sch. Dental Medicine Harvard U., Boston, 1971-93, Charles A. Brackett prof. oral pathology, 1971-2000, Charles A. Brackett prof. oral pathology emeritus, 2000—; sr. clin. investagator Forsyth Inst., Boston, 1994—; cons. oral pathology Children's Hosp. Med. Ctr., Brigham and Women's Hosp., Mass. Gen. Hosp. Author: Oral Cancer, 1984; co-author (with Edmund Cataldo and Henry Goldman): Oral Pathology: An Atlas of Microscopic Pathology, 1975; co-author: (with Philip L. McCarthy) The Oral Manifestations of Systemic Disease, 1976, Diseases of the Oral Mucosa, 2d edit., 1982; co-author: (with David Chernin) Libellus De Dentibus, 1563, of Bartholomaei Eustachii, 1999, A Sourcebook of Dental Medicine, 2002; co-author: (with Fermin Carranza) History of Periodontology, 2003; contbr. over 350 articles to profl. jours., chapters to books. Fellow AAAS, Am. Acad. Dental Sci., Am. Acad. Oral Medicine, Am. Acad. Oral Pathology, Am. Coll. Dentists, Internat. Coll. Dentists; mem. ADA, Internat. Assn. Dental Rsch., Am. Acad. Periodontology, Am. Cancer Soc., Am. Assn. Cancer Rsch., Am. Assn. Cancer Edn., Am. Acad. History Dentistry, History of Sci. Soc., Sigma Xi, Omicron Kappa Upsilon. Avocations: harpsichord, flute. Home: 154 Evelyn Rd Waban MA 02468-1042 Office: 188 Longwood Ave Boston MA 02115-5819 Business E-Mail: gerald_shklar@hms.harvard.edu.

SHLADOVER, STEVEN ELLIOT, transportation research professional; b. N.Y.C., Feb. 15, 1950; s. Joel and Ida Shladover. SB, MIT, 1972, SM, 1974, ScD, 1978. Research asst. MIT, Cambridge, Mass., 1976-78, lectr., 1978; staff engr. Systems Control, Inc., Palo Alto, Calif., 1978-81; sr. engr. Systems Control Tech., Inc., Palo Alto, 1981-84, program mgr., 1984-86, dir. CAE systems, 1986-89, mgr., transp. systems engr., 1987-89; tech. dir. PATH Program, dep. dir. U. Calif., Berkeley, 1989—. U.S. Expert to Internat. Standards Orgn. (tech. com. 204, working group 14). Assoc. editor Jour. of Dynamic Systems, Measurement and Control, 1980-85; contbr. articles to profl. jours. Nat. mem. Met. Opera Guild, N.Y.C., 1973—; mem. San Francisco Opera Guild, 1979—, Mus. Soc., San Francisco, 1979—, Common Cause, Washington, 1983—. Named one of the Outstanding Young Men of Am., U.S. Jaycees, 1983; fellow NSF, 1972-75. Mem. SAE (ITS divsn. 1992—), Intelligent Transp. Soc. Am. (chmn. AVCS com. 1990-97), ASME (assoc. editor 1980-85, program chmn. dynamic systems and control div. 1986, honors com. 1988-91, sec. 1989-92, exec. com. 1992-97, chmn. 1996), Transp. Rsch. Bd. (com. new transp. systems and tech. 1988, com. on study advanced vehicle and hwy. techs. 1990-91, com. intelligent transp. systems 1992—, chmn., 2004—, com. on vehicle hwy. automation 1997—), MIT Alumni Assn., Calif. Alliance for Adv. Transp. Sys. (bd. dirs. 1994-2005). Democrat. Avocations: opera critic, tennis, international travel. Office: U Calif PATH Program 1301 S 46th St Bldg 452 Richmond CA 94804-4600 Business E-Mail: steve@path.berkeley.edu.

SHLAPAK, FRED, electronics executive; b. Canada; BSEE, MS, U. Waterloo, Can. Joined Motorola, Inc., 1970, applications engr. Canada, 1970, leader Can. semiconductor ops., 1976, head microsystems and digital divsn. Munich, 1982, leader European Semiconductor Group, asst. to pres. Semiconductor Products Sector, 1998—2000, exec. v.p. Semiconductor Products Sector, 2000, pres. Semiconductor Products Sector, exec. v.p., cons. to the office of the chmn. Schaumburg, Ill., 2003—. Mem.: Semiconductor Industry Assn. (bd. dirs.).

SHLAUDEMAN, HARRY WALTER, retired diplomat; b. L.A., May 17, 1926; s. Karl Whitman and Florence (Pixley) S.; m. Carol Jean Dickey, Aug. 7, 1948; children: Karl Frederick, Katherine Estelle, Harry Richard. BA, Stanford U., 1952. Joined U.S. Fgn. Svc., 1955; vice consul Barranquilla, Colombia, 1955-56; polit. officer Bogotá, Colombia, 1956-58; assigned lang. tng. Washington, 1958-59; consul Sofia, Bulgaria, 1960-62; chief polit. sect. Santo Domingo, Dominican Republic, 1962-64; officer charge Dominican Affairs State Dept., 1964-66; asst. dir. Office Caribbean Affairs, 1965-66; sr. seminar fgn. policy State Dept., 1966-67, spl. asst. to sec. state, 1967-69; dep. chief of mission Santiago, Chile, 1969-73; dep. asst. sec. state for Inter-Am. affairs Washington, 1973-75; amb. to Venezuela, 1975-76; asst. sec. state for Inter-Am. affairs, 1976-77; amb. to Peru, 1977-80; amb. to Argentina, 1980-83; exec. dir. Nat. Bipartisan Commn. on Central Am., 1983-84; spl. amb. to Cen. Am., 1984-86; amb. to Brazil Brasilia, 1986-89; amb. to Nicaragua, 1990-92; ret., 1992. Served with USMCR, 1944-46. Recipient Disting. Honor award Dept. State, 1966, Pres. Disting. Svc. award, 1988, Brazil's Order of Cruzeiro Benementium, 1989, Pres. Medal Freedom, 1992. Mem. Am. Acad. Diplomacy, San Luis Obispo Golf and Country Club, Phi Gamma Delta. Home: 7006 Pebble Beach Way San Luis Obispo CA 93401-8916 Office Phone: 805-544-7539. Personal E-mail: harrywal@aol.com.

SHLOSBERG, STUART R., prosthodontist; 3 children. BS, U. Manchester; M, U. Ind. Founder Beverly Hills Aesthetic Dentistry. Former prof. Harvard U., U. So. Calif. Mem.: Calif. Dental Assn., Am. Dental Assn., Am. Coll. Prosthodontists. Office: 414 Camden Dr #925 Beverly Hills CA 90210 Office Phone: 310-278-6630.

SHMAVONIAN, GERALD S., political organization administrator; b. LA, June 26, 1945; s. Sergius Neshan and Berje-Lucia (der Hareutunyan) Shmavonian. Student, U. Calif., Berkeley, 1964-70. Leader archaeol. excavation team, Guatemala, Turkey, 1970-75; pub. City Mags., 1975-80; special advisor Bicentennial Commission, Washington, D.C., 1987; chmn. Am. Nationalities Coun., Stanford U., 1983-86; pres. Am. Talent, 1986—2000, Am. Documentary Film Acad., 2001—02; ptnr. Assembly Plant Ptnrs., 2001—. Founder Tommrow Party, 2000—. Recipient Intercollegiate Boxing Championship, 1965. Mem. Calif. Scholarship Fedn. (life, pres. 1963), Nat. Forensic League (pres. 1963, degree of honor). Avocation: art. Home: 6219 N Prospect Ave Fresno CA 93711-1658

SHMUGER, MARC, film company executive; Grad., Wesleyan U. Sr. v.p. creative advt. Columbia Pictures, Sony Pictures Entertainment, 1991—92, v.p., creative dir., 1992—94, exec. v.p. worldwide mktg. Columbia TriStar, 1994—2000; pres. mktg. Universal Pictures, Universal City, Calif., 1998—2000, vice chmn., 2000—06, chmn., 2006—. Founder Art of War Prodn. Co., 1996. Prodr., writer (films) Dead of Winter, 1987. Named Entertainment Marketer of Yr., Advt. Age, 1999, 2000; named one of 50 Most Powerful People in Mktg., 1999, 2000, 50 Most Powerful People in Hollywood, Premiere mag., 2006. Mem.: Phi Beta Kappa. Office: Universal Pictures 100 Universal City Plz Universal City CA 91608*

SHMUNES, EDWARD, dermatologist; b. Jacksonville, Fla., July 24, 1940; s. Nathan and Anne Lillian (Berg) S.; m. Sue Shmunes, Apr. 17, 1996; children: Stephanie, Marjorie, Jenifer. MD, U. Fla., 1965. Diplomate Am. Bd. Dermatology. Intern U. Pub. Health Hosp., New Orleans, 1965-66; epidemic intelligence officer svc. Ctr. for Disease Control, Atlanta, 1966-68; resident in dermatology U. Pa., Phila., 1968-71; ptnr. Columbia (S.C.) Skin Clinic, 1973—, pres., 1991—2000. Grantee NIH, 2 yrs., U.S.C., 1985. Mem. Greek Orthodox Ch. Office: Columbia Skin Clinic 3 Medical Park Rd Ste 500 Columbia SC 29203-6873 Office Phone: 803-779-7316. Personal E-mail: edart777@aol.com

SHNAYERSON, ROBERT BEAHAN, editor, consultant; b. N.Y.C., Dec. 8, 1925; s. Charles and Madalene (Griffin) Beahan; m. Lydia Conde Todd, Dec. 23, 1950 (dec. Sept. 1973); children: Michael, Kate; m. Laurie Platt Winfrey, June 9, 1980; children: Maggie, Bonnie. AB, Dartmouth, 1950. Reporter N.Y. Daily News, 1946; reporter Life mag., N.Y.C., 1950-54; corr. Time-Life News Svc., 1954-56; contbg. editor Time mag., 1957-59, edn. editor, 1959-64, law editor, 1964-67, sr. editor, 1967-71; editor-in-chief Harper's Mag., N.Y.C., 1971-76; editor, pub. Quest mag., N.Y.C., 1976-81, Technology mag., N.Y.C., 1981-82; editorial dir. Sci. Digest mag., 1986-87. Editl. cons. Lear's mag., 1987-90; cons. in mag. field; sr. advisor Travel Holiday mag., 1989-95. Author: Illustrated History of the Supreme Court, 1986; author, editor: Wordworks, 1995—; contbr. articles to various mags. With USNR, 1943-46. Home: 118 Riverside Dr New York NY 10024-3708 Office Phone: 212-787-4590. E-mail: shnay@aol.com.

SHNEIDMAN, EDWIN S., psychologist, thanatologist; b. York, Pa., May 13, 1918; s. Louis and Manya (Zukin) S.; m. Jeanne E. Keplinger, Oct. 1, 1944; children: David William, Jonathan Aaron, Paul Samuel, Robert James. AB, UCLA, 1938, MA, 1940; MS, U. So. Calif., 1947, PhD, 1948. Diplomate: Am. Bd. Examiners Profl. Psychology (past v.p.). Clin. psychologist VA Center, Los Angeles, 1947-50, chief research, 1950-53; co-dir. Central Research Unit for Study Unpredicted Deaths, 1953-58; co-dir. Suicide Prevention Center, Los Angeles, 1958-66; chief Center Studies Suicide Prevention NIMH, Bethesda, Md., 1966-69; vis. prof. Harvard U., 1969; fellow Ctr. Advanced Study in Behavioral Scis., 1969-70; clin. assoc. Mass. Gen. Hosp., 1969, Karolinska Hosp., Stockholm, 1978; prof. med. psychology UCLA, 1970-75, prof. thanatology, 1975-88, emeritus, 1988—. Vis. prof. Ben Gurion U. of Negev, Beersheva, 1983 Author: Deaths of Man, 1973, Voices of Death, 1980; Definition of Suicide, 1985, Suicide as Psychache, 1993, The Suicidal Mind, 1996, Comprehending Suicide, 2001, Autopsy of a Suicidal Mind, 2004; editor: Thematic Test Analysis, 1951; editor: (with N.L. Farberow) Clues to Suicide, 1957, The Cry for Help, 1961, Essays in Self-Destruction, 1967, (with M. Ortega) Aspects of Depression, 1969, On the Nature of Suicide, 1969, (with N.L. Farberow, L.E. Litman) Psychology of Suicide, 1970, Death and the College Student, 1972, Death: Current Perspectives, 1976, 80, 84, Suicidology: Contemporary Developments, 1976, Endeavors in Psychology: Selections From The Personology of Henry A. Murray, 1981, Suicide Thoughts and Reflections, 1981 Served to capt. USAAF, 1942-45. Recipient Harold M. Hildreth award Psychologists in Pub. Service, 1966; Louis I. Dublin award Am. Suicidology, 1969. Mem. Am. Assoc. Suicidology (founder, past pres.), Am. Psychol. Assn. (past div. pres., Disting. Profl. Contbn. to Pub. Svc. award 1987, Henry A. Murray award 1997), Melville Soc. Address: 11431 Kingsland St Los Angeles CA 90066-1329 Office Phone: 310-397-5640.

SHNEIDMAN, J. LEE, historian, educator; b. N.Y.C., June 20, 1929; s. Bernard Wolf and Fannia Abramova (Raskin) S.; m. Conalee Levine, Sept. 3, 1961; children: Philip, Jack. BA, NYU, 1951, MA, 1952; PhD, U. Wis., 1957. Lectr. CCNY, 1956-57, U. Md. Overseas, 1957-58; asst. prof. Fairleigh Dickinson U., 1958-62; prof. history Adelphi U., 1963—2001, emeritus prof., 2001—. Chmn. seminar on hist., legal, and polit. thought Columbia U., 1985-2002. Author: Rise of the Aragonese-Catalan Empire, 2 vols, 1970, Spain and Franco, 1949-59, 1973, John F Kennedy, 1974. Dem. N.Y. County committeeman, 1970—. Mem. Am. Hist. Assn., Medieval Acad. Am., Am. Philatel. Soc., Internat. Psychohist. Assn., Rossica Soc., China Soc. Jewish. Home: 161 W 86th St New York NY 10024-3411 *Only by understanding from where we came can we understand where we are and where we are going.*

SHNEOUR, ELIE ALEXIS, biophysicist, researcher, historian; b. Neuilly-sur-Seine, France, Dec. 11, 1925; came to U.S., 1941, naturalized, 1944; s. Zalman and Salomea (Landau) S.; m. Polly M. Henderson, Sept. 7, 1990; children from previous marriage: Mark Zalman, Alan Brewster. BA, Columbia U., 1947; DSc (hon.), Bard Coll., 1969; MA, U. Calif., Berkeley, 1955; PhD, UCLA, 1958. Tchr. and rsch. fellow U. Calif., Berkeley, 1953-55, Am. Heart Assn. rsch. fellow, 1958-62, tchg. and rsch. fellow L.A., 1958; rsch. fellow Nat. Cancer Inst., 1956-57; Am. Heart Assn. rsch. fellow NYU, 1958-59; rsch. assoc. genetics Stanford U., 1962-65; assoc. prof. biology and neuroscis. U. Utah, 1965-69; rsch. neurochemist City of Hope Nat. Med. Ctr., Duarte, Calif., 1969-71. Dir. rsch. Calbiochem., 1971-75; pres. Biosystems Insts., Inc., 1975—; dir. Biosystems Rsch. Inst., 1979—; steering com. Nat. Acad. Sci. Study Group on Biology and the Exploration of Mars, 1964; chmn. Western Regional coun. Rsch. in Basic Bioscis. for Manned Orbiting Missions, Am. Inst. Biol. Scis., NASA, 1966-69; fellow Com. Sci. Investigation Claims of Paranormal, 1996—. Author: Extraterrestrial Life, 1965, (with Eric A. Ottesen) National Academy of Sciences, National Rsch. Coun., 1966, (with S. Moffat) Life Beyond the Earth, 1966, The Malnourished Mind, 1974; contbr. articles to profl. jours. Chmn. citizens adv. coun. San Diego Pub. Schs., 1971-72; adv. coun. Cousteau Soc., 1977-98; bd. dirs. Lunar Power System Coalition, 1993-2002; internat. v.p. Transinnova S.A. France, 1990—; chmn. sci. adv. bd. County of San Diego, 1995-2002, mem., 2002-. With U.S. Army, 1944-45. Recipient William Lockwood prize, Bard Coll. of Columbia U., 1947. Mem. IEEE, AAAS (chmn. So. Calif. Skeptics soc. Pacific divsn. 1988-90), Am. Chem. Soc., N.Y. Acad. Scis., Am. Inst. Biol. Scis., Am. Soc. for Biochemistry and Molecular Biology (chmn. sci. advisors program 1973-75, mem. com. on pub. policy 1974-76, congl. liaison 1992—), Am. Soc. Neurochemistry (mem. coun. 1971-73), Soc. Neurosci., Internat. Soc. Neurochemistry, U.S.C. of C. (bd. dirs. 1993-98), La Jolla Chamber Music Soc. (bd. dirs. 1994-97), Internat. Coun. for Global Health Progress (N.Am. adv. bd. 1996—), Sigma Xi, Phi Sigma. Office: Biosystems Rsch Inst 700 Front St M/S CDM 608 San Diego CA 92101-6000

SHNIDER, BRUCE JAY, lawyer; b. Lansing, Mich., Oct. 16, 1950; s. Harold A. and Raynor (Seidner) Shnider; m. Patricia Lynn Strandness, Dec. 28, 1973; 1 child, Ruth Strandness. AB magna cum laude, Dartmouth Coll., 1972; MPP, JD magna cum laude, Harvard U., 1977. Bar: Minn. 1977, U.S. Dist. Ct. Minn. 1977, U.S. Tax Ct. 1978, U.S. Ct. Appeals (8th cir.) 1980, U.S. Supreme Ct. 1981. Asst. to dir. Mich. Dept. Commerce, Lansing, 1972-73; law clk. United Mineworkers Am. Health/Retirement Funds, 1975; summer assoc. Robins, Davis & Lyon, Mpls., 1976; assoc. Dorsey & Whitney, Mpls., 1977-82, ptnr., 1983—, chmn. diversity com., 1990-93, chmn. tax practice group, 1994-98; practioner in resident Law Sch. U. Minn., 2006—. Bd. dirs. Minn. Justice Found., Mpls., 1989—91; v.p. Emergency Food Shelf Network, 2003—05, pres., 2005—. Mem.: ABA, Hennepin County Bar Assn., Minn. State Bar Assn. Home: 1908 James Ave S Minneapolis MN 55403-2831 Office: Dorsey & Whitney 50 S 6th St Ste 1500 Minneapolis MN 55402-1498 Office Phone: 612-340-2862. Business E-Mail: shnider.bruce@dorsey.com.

SHOAF, R. WAYNE, librarian; b. Boulder, Colo., Oct. 24, 1955; s. John Henry and Sue Chestnut Shoaf; m. Melinda Kaye Hayes, July 13, 1991. BA, Oberlin Coll., Ohio, 1979; MusB, Oberlin Conservatory, Ohio, 1979; MS, Columbia U., NYC, 1984. Tchg. asst. U. Colo., Engring. Ctr., Boulder, 1981—83; grad. asst. Columbia U., Serials Cataloging, Butler Libr., NYC, 1983—84; libr. NY Pub. Libr., Rodgers and Hammerstein Archives of Recorded Sound, Lincoln Ctr., 1984—85; cataloger, 1984—85; asst. archivist Arnold Schoenberg Inst., LA, 1985—86, acting archivist, 1986—87, archivist, 1987—98; mitarbeiter Arnold Schönberg Ctr., Vienna, 1998—98; co-team leader, music cataloging team and digital resources cataloging team, tech. svcs. U. So. Calif., LA, 1999—2004, metadata specialist, digital info. mgmt., 1999—2005, dir., info. delivery, orgn. and retrieval, 2005—. Author: (book) The Horn at the University of Colorado at Boulder: A Retrospective With an Emphasis on Recorded History. Boulder, CO, 1983; author: (with K. Glennan and J. McBride) Preliminary Catalog of the Archives of the Arnold Schoenberg Inst., 1986; author: (discography) The Schoenberg Discography, 1987, The Schoenberg Discography, 2nd ed., 1994; contbr. articles to profl. jours. Mem.: Soc. Calif. Archivists, Music Libr. Assn., Assn. For Recorded Sound Collections, Am. Soc. for Info. Scientists, Hist. Brass Soc., Internat. Horn Soc. Avocations: horn playing, book collecting, comic book historian. Office: U So Calif 651 West 35th St Los Angeles CA 90089-2571 Office Phone: 213-740-4090. Office Fax: 213-821-1617. E-mail: shoaf@usc.edu.

SHOAFF, THOMAS MITCHELL, lawyer; b. Ft. Wayne, Ind., Aug. 21, 1941; s. John D. and Agnes H. (Hanna) S.; m. Eunice Swedberg, Feb. 7, 1970; children: Andrew, Nathaniel, Matthew-John. BA, Williams Coll., 1964; JD, Vanderbilt U., 1967. Bar: Ind. 1968. Assoc. Isham, Lincoln & Beale, Chgo., 1967-68; ptnr. Baker & Daniels, Ft. Wayne, Ind., 1968—. Bd. dirs. Weaver Popcorn Co., Inc., Ft. Wayne, Dreibelbiss Title Co., Inc., Ft. Wayne, Am. Steel Investment Corp., Ft. Wayne. Bd. dirs. McMillen Found., Ft. Wayne, Wilson Found., Ft. Wayne. Mem. ABA, Allen County Bar Assn., Ind. State Bar Assn. Presbyterian. Avocations: golf, sailing. Office: Baker & Daniels 111 E Wayne St Ste 800 Fort Wayne IN 46802-2603 Office Phone: 260-460-1618. Business E-Mail: thomas.shoaff@bakerd.com.

SHOBE, DAVID SOREN, librarian, director; b. Kansas City, Mo., Mar. 27, 1967; AB, Washington U., St. Louis, 1989; MS, U. Ill., 1999; PhD, Yale U., 1994. Lic. patent agent: U.S. Patent & Trademark Office 2005. Postdoc. rsch. assoc. Wayne State U., 1994—95, U. Nebr., Lincoln, 1996—97; dir. Sud-Chemie Corp. Libr., Louisville, 1999—. Mem.: Am. Intellectual Property Law Assn., Spl. Librs. Assn., Am. Chem. Soc., Phi Beta Kappa. Home: 425 S Hubbards Lane 59 Louisville KY 40207 Office: Sud-Chemie Inc 1600 W Hill St Louisville KY 40210 Office Phone: 502-634-7409.

SHOBE, FRANKLIN DALE, mathematician, educator; b. Great Bend, Kans., Jan. 16, 1942; s. Chester Leslie and Dorothy Minerva Shobe; m. Carolyn Jean Caine, June 8, 1996; children: David, Martin, Nora. BA in Math., U. Kansas, Lawrence, 1964, MBA in Bus., 1977; MA in Math., U. Mo., Kansas City, 1967; PhD in Math. Scis., Clemson U., SC, 1997. Environ. analyst Franklin Assocs., Ltd., Prairie Village, Kans., 1977—79; assoc. environ. analyst Midwest Rsch. Inst., Kansas City, 1979—84; asst. prof. Tarkio Coll., Mo., 1984—85, St. Andrew's Pres. Coll., Laurinburg, NC, 1985—89; instr. math Ind. Acad., Muncie, 1995—, chair, math. and computer sci. divsn., 2005—. Capt. USAF, 1967—75. Mem.: Nat. Coun. Tchrs. Math., Soc. Indsl. and Applied Math., Am. Math. Soc., Math. Assn. Am., Ind. Assn. for Gifted, Nat. Assn. Gifted Children. Office: Ind Acad Ball State Univ Muncie IN 47306

SHOBER, AMY, education educator; d. Lynn E. Murphy and Philip E. Shober. BA, BS, Va. Poly. Inst. and State U., Blacksburg, 1998; MS, Pa. State U., 2002; PhD, U. Del., Newark, 2006. Lab. assessor Am. Assn. of State Hwy. and Transp. Officials, Gaithersburg, Md., 1998—99; grad. rsch. asst. Pa. State U., University Park, 1999—2002; grad. rsch. fellow U. Del., Newark, 2002—06; asst. prof. U. Fla., Wimauma, 2006—. Recipient Hazel Burgett Endowed PEO Scholar award, P.E.O., 2005; Grad. Rsch. Fellowship, Inst. of Soil and Environ. Quality at U. Del., 2002—06, J. Fielding Reed PPI Fellowship, Potash and Phosphate Inst., 2005. Mem.: Am. Soc. Agronomy, Soil Sci. Soc. of Am., Golden Key Nat. Honor Soc., Alpha Zeta, Phi Beta Kappa. Avocations: swimming, weightlifting, crocheting. Office: Univ of Fla Gulf Coast REC 14625 Cr 672 Wimauma FL 33598 Office Phone: 813-634-0000. Office Fax: 813-634-0001. Personal E-mail: ashober@gmail.com.

SHOCHAT, STEPHEN JAY, pediatrician, surgeon; b. Balt., Dec. 17, 1938; s. Albert J. and Rose (Blechman) S.; m. Sheila Floam, July 1960 (div. July 1979); children: Francine Lynne, Alisa Joy; m. Carla Ann Centi, Jan. 26, 1980; children: David Robert, Sarah Elizabeth. BS, Randolph Mason Coll., 1959; MD, Med. Coll. Va., 1963. Surg. resident Washington U. Med. Ctr., St. Louis, 1963-68; pediatric surg. resident Boston Children's Hosp., 1968-70; thoracic surg. resident Queen Elizabeth Hosp., Birmingham, Eng., 1970, George Washington Hosp., Washington, 1972; chief pediatric surgery Hershey (Pa.) Med. Ctr., 1973-77, Stanford (Calif.) Med. Ctr., 1977-94; sr. surgeon Children's Hosp. Phila., 1994-96; surgeon-in-chief, chmn. dept. surgery St. Jude Children Rsch. Hosp., Memphis, 1996—; prof. pediats. and surgery U. Tenn., Memphis, 1996-98. Lt. col. USAF, 1970-72. Office: St Jude Children Rsch Hosp Dept Surgery Memphis TN 38105 Office Phone: 901-495-2911. Business E-Mail: stephen.shochat@stjude.org.

SHOCKEY, JEREMY CHARLES, professional football player; b. Ada, OK, Aug. 18, 1980; s. Lucinda. Student, Northeast Oklahoma A&M Jr. College, 1999, Univ. of Miami, 2000—02. Tight end New York Giants, 2002—. Vol. United Way Found. Named NFL Rookie of the Yr., 2002; named to NFC Pro-Bowl team, 2002—03, 2005. Achievements include being a member of NCAA Champion Miami Hurricanes, 2001. Office: c/o New York Giants Giants Stadium East Rutherford NJ 07073*

SHOCKLEY, ALONZO HILTON, JR., school system administrator; b. Milford, Del., Sept. 30, 1920; s. Alonzo Hilton Sr. and Elizabeth (Hilton) S.; m. Kay Marilyn Falke, Aug. 13, 1979; children: Novella Lela Shockley Randolph, Cheryl Emmerly Shockley Durant, Alonzo Hilton III. BS, Del. State Coll., 1943; MA, Mich. State U., 1947; cert., NYU, 1956, postgrad., 1980, Queens Coll., 1961-62, U. Maine, 1963. Cert. tchr., N.Y., Pa., Del. Tchr. sci. Brooks HS, Prince Frederick, Md., 1948; prin. elem., jr. high schs. dept. public instrn., Dover, Del., 1948-58; rsch. assoc. Del. State Coll., Dover, 1958-60; elem. sch. tchr. Cen. Sch. Dist. 4, Plainview, NY, 1960-62; asst. elem. prin. Union Free Sch. Dist., Wyandanch, NY, 1962-64; assoc. adminstrn. official NY State Edn. Dept., Albany, 1964-65; edn. coord. Nassau County Commn. Econ. Opportunity, Garden City, LI, NY, 1965-66; dir. state and fed. programs Freeport Pub. Schs., NY, 1966-85; coord. state and fed. programs Amityville Pub. Schs., LI, NY, 1985-91, edinl. cons., 1988—. V.p. Internat. Rotary, Ronkonkoma, N.Y., 1997; v.p. Phi Delta Kappa of L.I. #1020. Contbr. articles in field of ednl. adminstrn. to profl. jours. Pres. mid L.I. chpt. UN Assn. of U.S., bd. dir. so. N.Y. divsn., mem. coun. pres. steeringcom., pres. Suffolk County chpt., 1995—; organizer of 1997 Mcpl. Elections Bill contbg. to the implementation of the Dayton Peace Accord, 1987; 6 time supr. for Bosnia/Herzegovia elections. Served with U.S. Army, 1942-45, NATOUSA; mem. NYU Alumni Chorus, 1980—, Huntington Men's Chorus, L.I., 1985—. Recipient Cert. of Merit for supervising registration in Bosnia and Herzegovina, Ctrl. Bosnia Canton 6, 1997. Mem. Am. Assn. Sch. Adminstrs., NEA, N.Y. State Tchrs. Edn., Assn. Childhood Edn. Internat., Assn. Supervision and Curriculum Devel., Nat. Assn. Elem. Prins., Amityville Sch. Dist. Adminstrs., Am. Acad. Polit. and Social Sci., NYU Alumni Assn. (bd. dirs., v.p.), Sch. Health, Edn. and Nursing Arts Professionals (pres.), Rotary (pres. Ronkonkomas, L.I.), Phi Delta (v.p. Long Island N.Y. chpt. 1994—). Home: 49 Gaymore Rd Port Jefferson Station NY 11776-1354

SHOCKLEY, CAROL FRANCES, psychologist, psychotherapist; b. Atlanta, Nov. 24, 1948; d. Robert Thomas and Frances Lavada (Scrivner) Shockley. BA, Ga. State U., Atlanta, 1974, MEd, 1976; PhD, U. Ga., Athens, 1990. Cert. in gerontology, diplomate Am. Bd. Forensic Examiners. Counselor Rape Crisis Ctr., Atlanta, 1979-80; emergency mental health clinician Gwinnett Med. Ctr., Lawrenceville, Ga., 1980-86; psychotherapist Fla. Mental Health Inst., Tampa, 1987-89, Tampa Bay Acad., Riverview, Fla., 1990-91; sr. psychologist State of Fla. Dept. of Corrections, Bushnell, 1991-92; pvt. practice psychologist Brunswick, Ga., 1992—2000, Griffin, Ga., 2002—. Mem. adv. bd. Mental Health/Mental Retardation, 1992—94. Author (with others): (book) Relapse Prevention with Sex Offenders, 1989.

Vol. Ga. Mental Health Inst., Atlanta, 1972; leader Alzheimer's Disease Support Group, Athens, Ga., 1984; vol. therapist Reminiscence Group Elderly, Athens, 1984—85. Recipient Meritorious Svc. award, Beta Gamma Sigma, 1975. Mem.: APA, Ga. Psychol. Assn., Psi Chi, Sigma Phi Omega. Avocations: astronomy, archaeology, music, travel. Office: 231B S 10th St Ste B Griffin GA 30223

**SHOCKLEY, EDWARD JULIAN,** retired air transportation executive; b. Augusta, Ga., Oct. 31, 1924; s. Julian P. and Margaret (Epps) S.; m. Dorothy Elizabeth Holley, Nov. 24, 1945; children: Edward J., Steven Holley. B.Aero. Engring., Ga. Inst. Tech., 1950; postgrad. (Sloan fellow), Stanford U. Grad. Sch. Bus., 1962-63. Flight test engr. Douglas Aircraft Co., 1950-53; with Lockheed-Ga. Co., 1953-80, dir. quality and safety, 1965-74, dir. mktg., 1974-78, v.p., 1978-80; pres. Lockheed Aircraft Service Co. div. Lockheed Corp., Burbank, Calif., 1980-86, sr. advisor to pres., 1986-87, ret., 1987; pres. Millimeter Wave Tech., Inc., Marietta, Ga., 1988-90, vice chmn. bd. dirs., 1991-92; ret., 1992. Dir. Aerosurge Mgmt. Cons., 1991-92; pres. Lockheed-Ga. Fed. Credit Union, 1971-74 Mem. bus. adv. coun. Ga. So. U.; mem. adv. coun. Sch. Bus. and Econs., Coll. of Charleston. Served with USN, 1941-46. Mem. Cherokee Town and Country Club. Republican. Methodist. Personal E-mail: eshock@charter.net.

**SHOCKLEY, FLOYD WAYNE,** entomologist; b. Richmond, Mo., Sept. 13, 1974; s. Daniel Paul and Deanna Kay Shockley; m. Shannon Elaine Myers, June 28, 1997. BA in Biology, Westminster Coll., 1996; MS in Entomology, Univ. Mo.-Columbia, 2000; PhD in Entomology, Univ. Ga.-Athens, 2002—. Lab tech. Westminister Coll., 1994—95, rsch. specialist, 1995—96; lab mgr. Univ. Mo. 1997—98, grad. rsch. asst., 1998—2000, rsch. specialist, 2000—02; grad. rsch. asst. U. Ga., 2002—05. Mem.: Coleop. Soc., Soc. Sys. Biology, Orgn. Trop. Studies (Mellon Rsch. Exploration Award), US Achievement Acad., Soc. Study Evolution, Ga. Acad. Sci., Fla. Entomol. Soc., Entomol. Soc. Am. (Plant Resistance to Insects Award), Mo. Acad. Sci., Ga. Entomol. Soc., Ctrl. States Entomol. Soc., Ctr. Sys. Entomol., SC Entomol. Soc., Willi Hennig Soc., Assn. Trop. Biology and Cons., Am. Mus. Nat. History, Am. Assn. for the Advancement of Sci., Am. Entomol. Soc., Sigma Xi, Pi Mu Epsilon, Beta Beta Beta. Avocation: Office: Dept Entomol Univ Ga 413 Biological Sci Bldg Athens GA 30602-2603 Home: 165 Warren Way Athens GA 30605 Office Phone: 706-542-6187.

**SHOCKLEY-ZALABAK, PAMELA SUE,** academic administrator; b. May 25, 1944; d. James William and Leatha Pearl (Cartwright) Shockley; m. Charles Zalabak, Dec. 30, 1975. BA in Comm., Okla. State U., 1965, MA in Comm., 1972; PhD in Orgnl. Comm., U. Colo., 1980. Instr. comm. Coll. Letters, Arts and Scis. U. Colo., 1976, from asst. to full prof., 1992, prof. comm. Colorado Springs, 1992—, dir., net and media ctr., 1992, spl. asst. to chancellor, 1994, vice chancellor for student success Colorado Springs, 1998—2001, interim chancellor, 2001—02, chancellor, 2002—. Cons. in field. Author six books; prodr.: (six video documentaries); contbr. articles to profl. jours. Recipient Disting. Svc. award, Colo. Speech Comm. Assn., Telly award; Lew Wentz Tri Delt scholar, 1961—65. Mem.: Internat. Comm. Assn., Speech Comm. Assn., Phi Kappa Phi. Democrat. Avocations: skiing, hiking, fly fishing. Office: Univ Colorado Chancellor's Office 1420 Austin Bluffs Pkwy Colorado Springs CO 80918

**SHOEMAKER, ALLEN L.,** psychology professor, consultant; b. Grand Rapids, Mich., Dec. 26, 1952; s. Leslie and Geraldine Shoemaker; children: James, Benjamin, Rebecca. PhD, U. Ill., Champaign-Urbana, 1980. Prof. psychology Calvin Coll., Grand Rapids, Mich., 1980—. Cons. in field. Contbr. articles to profl. jours. Mentor Kids Hope USA, Grand Rapids. Office: Calvin College 3201 Burton St SE Grand Rapids MI 49546 Office Phone: 616-526-8536. Business E-Mail: shoe@calvin.edu.

**SHOEMAKER, BOBBY JEAN (B.J. FOSTER),** writer; d. Farris Lee and Grace Helen Foster; m. Leonard Wiley Shoemaker, June 1, 1958; children: Sharon Dawn, Walker. BA, Va. Intermont Coll., 1981. Cert. paralegal Nat. Ctr. for Paralegal Tng., Atlanta, 1985. Exec. v.p. Leonard W. Shoemaker & Assoc. Consulting Engrs., Houston, 1970—90; author Houston, 1990—. Author: Bayou Shadows, 2000 (named Book of Yr., High Country Writers, 2001). Mem.: Elk River Club. Presbyterian. Avocations: horseback riding, golf, skiing, tennis, hiking.

**SHOEMAKER, CAMERON DAVID JAMES,** retired dean; b. Honolulu, Dec. 15, 1940; s. John James and Belle Bird (Kellogg) S.; m. Catherine LaMoyne Prevost, May 23, 1966 (div. 1969); 1 child, David James; m. Leona Martha Wohlwend, May 18, 1972; 1 child, Jennifer Lee. BA in Polit. Sci., The Citadel, 1963; MA in History, San Jose State U., 1973; EdD, U. San Francisco, 1990. Cert. flight instr. Commd. 2d lt. U.S. Army, 1963, advanced through grades to maj., 1971, fgn. area officer U.S., Korea, Germany and Vietnam, 1972-84, ret., 1984; fin. cons. Merrill Lynch, Carmel, Calif., 1984-85; mgmt. analyst Def. Lang. Inst., Monterey, Calif., 1985, ednl. tech. project mgr., 1985-86, dir. info. resources mgmt., 1986-90; evening coll. adminstr., instnl. researcher Monterey Peninsula Coll., 1990-92; dean of bus. Sacramento (Calif.) City Coll., 1992-98; dean Vista Coll., Berkeley, Calif., 1999-2000; dir. ednl. svcs. Heald Coll., Roseville, Calif., 2000—01; project mgr. Little Hoover Commn. on Calif. State Govt. and Economy, 2002—04, Calif. Dept. Alcohol & Drug Programs, 2004—05, ret., 2005. Instr. Chapman Coll., Monterey, 1982-84, Monterey Inst., 1987; chmn. Asian Employment Program Com., Monterey, 1983-84; guest lectr., Naval Postgrad. Sch., Monterey, 1986-87; mem. Handicapped Individual Program Com., Monterey, 1986-90, treas., 1989-90; adj. asst. prof. Embry Riddle Aeronautical U., 2006—. Contbr. articles to various publs. Pres., Creekside Cmty. Assn., Salinas, Calif. 1985-86; mem. County Svc. Area Adv. Bd., Salinas, 1985 87; Flood Control Dist. Planning Com., Salinas, 1986-87; active Leadership Monterey Peninsula, grad., 1992; pres. Forest View Homeowner's Assn., 2005—. Decorated Silver Star; recipient Comdrs. award for Civilian Svc. Dept. of Army, 1990; Carl D. Perkins fellow, 1993. Mem. Royal Asiatic Soc. Monterey Peninsula Scottish Soc. (treas. 1986-92), Los Rios Mgmt. Assn. (pres. 1995-96), Forest View Homeowners Assn. (pres. 2005—), Caledonian Club of Sacramento (treas. 1994-97, chief 1997-99). Republican. Roman Catholic. Home: 4029 Forest View Dr Washougal WA 98671 Office Phone: 360-991-5633. Personal E-mail: docshoe@comcast.net. *Personal philosophy: Always do what is right, regardless of the personal cost.*

**SHOEMAKER, CAROLYN SPELLMAN,** planetary astronomer; b. Gallup, N.Mex., June 24, 1929; d. Leonard Robert and Hazel Adele (Arthur) Spellmann; m. Eugene Merle Shoemaker, Aug. 18, 1951 (dec. July 1997); children: Christine Shoemaker Abanto, Patrick Gene, Linda Shoemaker Salazar. BA cum laude, Chico State Coll., 1949, MA, 1950; ScD, No. Ariz. U., 1990, St. Mary's U., N.S., Can., 2003. Vis. scientist Br. astrogeology U.S. Geol. Survey, Flagstaff, Ariz., 1980—; rsch. asst. Calif. Inst. Tech., Pasadena, 1981-85; rsch. prof. astronomy No. Ariz. U., Flagstaff, 1989—; mem. staff Lowell Obs., Flagstaff, 1993—. Guest observer Palomar Obs., Palomar Mountain, Calif., 1982-94; Ruth Northcott Meml. lectr. R.A.S.C., 1995; co-McGovern lectr. Cosmos Club Found., 1995. Co-recipient Rittenhouse medal Rittenhouse Astron. Soc., 1988, Scientist of Yr. award ARCS Found., 1995, James C. Watson medal NAS, 1998; recipient Woman of Distinction award Soroptimist, 1994, 20th Anniversary Internat. Women's Yr. award Zonta and 99s, 1995, NASA Exceptional Scientific Achievement medal, 1996, Woman of Distinction award Nat. Assn. Women in Edn., 1996, Shoemaker award Am. Inst. Profl. Geologists, 1997, plaque Internat. Forest Friendship, Atchison, Kans., 1997, Robert Burnham Jr. award Western Regional Astron. League, 2000, Ariz. Woman of Distinction award Alpha Delta Kappa, 2004; named Disting. Alumna of the Calif. State U., Chico, 1996. Fellow AAAS, Am. Acad. Arts and Scis.; mem. Astron. Soc. of Pacific, Am. Geophys. Union, Meteoritical Soc., Sigma Xi. Achievements include discovery of 32 comets including Periodic Comet Shoemaker-Levy 9 which impacted Jupiter in July 1994, more than 500 asteroids including 44 Earth approachers and approximately 68 Mars crossers, meteorites at Veevers

Crater, Australia and impactites at Wolfe Creek Crater, Australia. Home: 5231 Hidden Hollow Rd Flagstaff AZ 86001-3821 Office: Lowell Obs 1400 W Mars Hill Rd Flagstaff AZ 86001-4499 E-mail: cshoemaker@usgs.gov.

**SHOEMAKER, ELEANOR BOGGS,** television production company executive; b. Gulfport, Miss., Jan. 20, 1935; d. William Robertson and Bessie Eleanor (Ware) Boggs; m. D. Shoemaker, April 9, 1955 (div. 1987); children: Daniel W. III, William Boggs. Student in protocol, Southeastern U., 1952-53; student, George Washington U., Washington, 1953-56; BA in Communications and Polit. Sci. with honrs, Goucher Coll., 1981; postgrad., Villanova U. Feature writer Washington Times Herald, 1951-54; dir. Patricia Stevens Modeling Agy., Washington, 1955-56; free-lance model Julius Garfinkel, Woodward & Lothrop, Washington, 1951-56; research analyst Balt. County Council, Towson, Md., 1980-81; feature news reporter Sta. WGCB-TV, Red Lion, Pa., 1980-99; pub. speaker, protocol The Reliable Corp., Columbia, Md., 1982-86; media cons. The Enterprise Found., Columbia, Md., 1985-86; faculty, TV prodn. and communication St. Francis Prep Sch., Spring Grove, Pa., 1985-88; owner Windswept Prodns. Co., Felton, Pa., 1984—; mktg. svcs. coord. Yorktowne, Inc., Red Lion, Pa., 1993-95. Mem. conservation bd. Pa. Parks and Recreation Soc., 1984—; prodr. The Pa. County TV Prodn., 1981; prodr., host Westar 4 Channel 9 half hour weekly news program Keystone Report. Prodr. The Pa. County TV Prodn., 1981, The Pa. County TV Prodn. 1981, documentary Human Rights: A Special Report, Sta. WGCB-TV, 1989; prodr., host Westar 4 Channel 9 half hour weekly news program Keystone Report, 1990. Bd. dirs. York (Pa.) County Parks and Recreation, 1972-87, YWCA, York, 1957-82, Hist. York, 1990—; mem. exec. com. York County Reps., 1972-82; accreditation adv. com. York Coll. of Pa.; instr. YWCA Women in Politics; founder, mem. Child Abuse Task Force, York, 1983—; mem. select com. Pa. Agrl. Zoning, 1988; mem. steering com. York Forum, 1989-96; co-chmn. Cross Mill Restoration, 1987—; mem. Displaced Homemaker's Bd., 1989—, pres., 1993—; bd. dirs. Hist. York, 1990-95; founder, host Old Rose Tree Pony Club, 1967—; chmn. camp com. U.S. Pony Club Inc., 1973-75; chair Spring Valley County Pk. Task Force, 1972; master of fox hounds Mrs. Shoemaker's Hounds, 1969—; master of beagles Mrs. Shoemaker's Weybright Beagles, 1988-96; edn. chair Jr. League of York, 1962-70. Recipient pro bono child legal representation grant Pa. Bar Assn., 1983, Pa. Tree Farmer of Yr. award, 1987, Outstanding Achievement in Broadcasting award Am. Women in Radio and TV, 1992, Lay Person of Yr. award Pa. Recreation and Parks Assn. and Gov. Thornburg, 1982, Jefferson award nominee, 1992, Matrix award Ctrl. Pa. Women in Comm., 1993, First pl. corp. video prodn. Ctrl. Pa. Women in Comm., 1993, Agrl. award C. of C., Cross Mill Restoration, 1999, Albright Care Found. Outstanding Vol. award, Ridge, Normandie, 1999, Daughters of Am. Revolution Outstanding Achievement award in preservation Nat. Resources, 2000, Game Commn. Recognition award farm game program, 2000, Albright Care Founders award; selected journalist for Novosti Press USSR-U.S. Press Exch. program, 1989. Mem. Am. Polled Hereford Assn., York Area C. of C., York County C. of C. (publicity com. 1985-90, agri. bus. com.), Masters of Foxhounds Assn. Episcopalian. Avocations: foxhunting, beagling. Home and Office: PO Box 167 Felton PA 17322-0167

**SHOEMAKER, FRANK CRAWFORD,** retired physicist; b. Ogden, Utah, Mar. 26, 1922; s. Roy Hopkins and Sarah Parker (Anderson) Shoemaker; m. Ruth Elizabeth Nelson, July 11, 1944; children: Barbara Elaine, Mary Frances. AB, Whitman Coll., 1943, DSc (hon.), 1978; PhD, U. Wis., 1949. Staff mem. Radiation Lab. MIT, 1943-45; instr. physics U. Wis., 1949-50; mem. faculty Princeton (N.J.) U., 1950-89, prof. physics, 1962—89, prof. emeritus, 1989—, dir. undergrad. physics dept., 1981—89; assoc. dir. Princeton U. Pa. Accelerator, 1962-66; ret., 1989. Vis. scientist Rutherford High Energy Lab., 1965—66; main accelerator sci. head Nat. Accelerator Lab., 1968—69; prin. investigator Dept. of Energy High Energy Physics Contract, 1972—85. Fellow: Am. Phys. Soc.; mem.: Sigma Xi, Phi Beta Kappa. Home: 49 Meadow Lakes 03 East Windsor NJ 08520-3351 Office Phone: 609-258-6602. Business E-Mail: frankcs@princeton.edu.

**SHOEMAKER, HAROLD LLOYD,** information scientist; b. Danville, Ky., Jan. 3, 1923; s. Eugene Clay and Amy (Wilson) S.; m. Dorothy M. Maddox, May 11, 1947 (dec. Feb. 1991). AB, Berea Coll., 1944; postgrad., State U. Ia., 1943-44, George Washington U., 1949-50, NYU, 1950-52. Rsch. physicist State U. Iowa, 1944-45; Frankford Arsenal, Pa., 1945-47; rsch. engr. N.Am. Aviation, L.A., 1947-49, Jacobs Instrument Co., Bethesda, 1949-50; assoc. head systems devel. group The Teleregister Corp., N.Y.C., 1950-53; mgr. electronic equipment devel. sect., head planning Hughes Aircraft Co., L.A., 1953-58; dir. command and control systems lab. Bunker-Ramo Corp., L.A., 1958-68; v.p. Data Systems, 1968-69, corp. dir. data processing, 1969-75; tech. staff R & D Assocs., Marina Del Rey, Calif., 1975-85; info. systems cons., 1985—. Patentee elec. digital computer. Served with AUS, 1945-46. Mem. IEEE, Ky. Cols. Home: PO Box 3385 Granada Hills CA 91394-0385 E-mail: haroldshoe@cs.com.

**SHOEMAKER, INNIS HOWE,** art museum curator; b. Reading, Pa. d. William Erety and Jean (Miller) S. AB, Vassar Coll., 1964; MA, Columbia U., 1968, PhD, 1975. Curator Vassar Coll. Art. Gallery, Poughkeepsie, NY, 1965-68, 73-76; asst. dir. Ackland Art Mus., U. N.C., Chapel Hill, 1976-82, dir., 1983-86; Audrey and William H. Helfand sr. curator prints, drawings and photographs Phila. Mus. Art, 1986—; adj. prof. U. Pa., 2001—. Fellow in art history Am. Acad. in Rome, 1971-73; adj. prof. U. N.C., Chapel Hill, 1983-86. Co-author: The Engravings of Marcantonio Raimondi, 1981, Paul Cézanne: Two Sketchbooks, 1989; author: Model for Modernism: Earl Horter and His Collection, 1999; Jacques Villon and his Cubist Prints, 2001. Mem. vis. com. Lehman Loeb Art Ctr., Vassar Coll., 1993-. Mem. Coll. Art Assn. Am., Am. Assn. Mus., Print Coun. Am. (bd. dirs. 1986-89). Office: Phila Mus Art PO Box 7646 Philadelphia PA 19101-7646

**SHOEMAKER, RENE DENISE,** librarian, artist; b. Staten Island, N.Y., June 4, 1952; d. William Aaron Shoemaker and Gloria Pearl Heley; m. Harvey Sutlive; children: Katherine Shoemaker Sutlive, Samuel Aaron Shoemaker Sutlive. BFA, U. Ga., 1985; M in Libr. and Info. Sci., U. S.C. 1993. Libr. asst. U. Ga., Athens, 1981—93, libr. IV Coll. Environment & Design, 1993—, dir. Owens Libr. and Cir. Gallery, 1995—. Cons. libr. Studies Abroad program U. Ga., Italy, 1998. Fiber art, The Neighborhood, N.Y.C., 2004, The Other Side of Athens, Ga., 2004, Represented in permanent collections U. Ga., Toyota, Athens, Ga. Bd. dirs. Bike Athens, 2004. Grantee USDA, 1996. Mem.: Spl. Librs. Assn., Spl. Librs. Assn. (archivist 2003—, chair-elect solo divsn.), Internat. Coun. Monuments and Sites, Am. Craft Coun., Beta Phi Mu, Pi Delta Phi. Home: 148 Tribble Bottom Rd Arnoldsville GA 30619 Office: Coll Environment & Design U Ga 609 Caldwell Hall Athens GA 30602 Office Phone: 706-542-8292. Business E-Mail: rds@uga.edu.

**SHOEMAKER, ROBERT MORIN,** retired military officer, commissioner; b. Almont, Mich., Feb. 18, 1924; s. Uriah Beebe and Pomala (Morin) S.; m. Mary Alice Rickard, July 17, 1948. BS, U.S. Mil. Acad., 1946; postgrad., U.S. Army Command and Gen. Staff Coll., 1959, Army War Coll., 1967. Commd. 2d lt. U.S. Army, 1946, advanced through grades to gen., 1978, platoon leader, bn. staff officer, co. comdr. 18th Inf., Fed. Republic Germany, 1947-50, co. comdr., regtl. S2, S3, 23d Inf. Republic of Korea, 1953-54, staff officer inf. br. DA, 1954-56, student, faculty officer U.S. Army Aviation Sch. Ft. Rucker, Ala., 1959-62, project officer Army Concept Team Vietnam, 1962-63, bn. comdr., asst. chief of staff, G-3, 11th Air Assault Div. Ft. Benning, Ga., 1963-65, bn. comdr., squadron comdr. 1st Cav. Div., Vietnam, 1965-66, chief plans and programs Army Aviation DA, 1967-69, chief of staff, asst. div. comdr. 1st Cav. Vietnam, 1969-70, dep. comdr., chief. of staff III Corps and Ft. Hood, Tex., 1970, dept. comdr. MASSTER Ft. Hood, Tex., 1971-72, comdr. 1st Cav., 1973-75, comdr. III Corps Ft. Hood, 1975-77, dep. comdr. FORSCOM Ft. McPherson, Ga., 1977-78; comdr. U.S. Army Forces Command, 1978-82; ret., 1982; county commr. Bell County, Tex., 1987-94. Decorated D.S.M., Silver Star medal with oak leaf cluster, Legion of Merit, D.F.C., Bronze Star, Air medal with 48 oak leaf clusters, Army Commendation medal with oak leaf cluster, Croix de Guerre (France), Gallantry Cross

with palm (Republic of Vietnam), RVN Honor medal 1st class; Robert M. Shoemaker H.S., Killeen, Tex. named in his honor, Aug. 2001; named Disting. Grad., West Point, 2004. Home: 111 Bluff Ln Belton TX 76513-9804

**SHOEMAKER, WILLIAM C.,** journalist; b. Simpson County, Miss., Nov. 19, 1931; s. William Ezra and Saleta (Roach) S.; m. Nell Slade, Apr. 12, 1957. Grad. high sch., Miss. Reporter Jackson (Miss.) Daily News, 1949-51, 54-65; editor, pub. The Star-Herald, Koscivsko, Miss., 1965-89; pres. Shoemaker Offset Inc., Koscivsko, Miss., 1989—, Scott County Times, Miss., 1983-89, Simpson County News, 1983-87, Pontotoc Progress, 1985-89, Bulldog Pubs., 1983-90. Bd. dirs. Merchants and Farmers Bank. Chmn. Miss. Econ. Coun., 1996-97; chmn. Miss. svc. delivery area U.S. Job Tng. Partnership Act, 1983-95. With U.S. Army, 1951-54. Mem. Rotary. Independent. Office: PO Box 457 Kosciusko MS 39090-0457

**SHOEMAKER, WILLIAM EDWARD,** corporate financial executive; b. Charleston, W.Va., Sept. 17, 1945; s. Robert Edward and Janet Elizabeth (Hoglund) S.; 1 child, Marcus. BBA, U. Notre Dame, 1967. Assoc. buyer Proctor & Gamble, Cin., 1971; gen. mgr. Eastwind Inc., Anchorage, 1972-73; pres., operator Golden Horn Lodge, Inc., Bristol Bay, Alaska, 1973-79; treas. Hawley Resource Group, Inc., Anchorage, 1979-88; treas., chief fin. officer Golden Zone Resources, Inc., Campbell, Calif., 1988-90; ptnr. Resort Mgmt. Corp., Anchorage, 1987-90; pres. Discovery Holdings, Inc., Ft. Lauderdale, Fla., 1991—2005; pres., CEO Foresight Digital Co., 2005—. Bd. dirs. Pacific Art & Design Cons., Inc. Bd. dirs. Anchorage Econ. Devel. Corp., 1988-90, 4 Children's Sake, 1997—; mem. exec. com. Broward Child Welfare Initiative, 2002—; dir. Lovewell Inst. for Creative Arts, 2004-. Served to lt. USN, 1967—71. Republican. Avocations: boating, skiing, fishing. Office: Discovery Holdings Inc Ste 120 2400 E Las Olas Blvd Fort Lauderdale FL 33301-1529 Home: 1733 NE 8TH St Fort Lauderdale FL 33304-3474 Office Phone: 954-761-9111. Personal E-mail: weshoemaker@bellsouth.net.

**SHOEMATE, STEVEN R.,** lawyer; b. May 6, 1963; BS in Acctg., Lehigh Univ., 1985; JD with high honors, Duke Univ., 1988. Bar: NY 1989. Assoc. Gibson Dunn & Crutcher LLP, NYC, 1988—96, ptnr. corp. transactions and securities, 1996—, and co-ptnr.-in-charge NYC office. Mem. exec. and mgmt. committees Gibson Dunn and Crutcher LLP. Mem. Duke Univ. Law Rev., 1987—88. Mem.: Order of Coif. Avocation: helicopter skiing. Office: Gibson Dunn & Crutcher LLP 47th Fl 200 Park Ave New York NY 10166-0193 Office Phone: 212-351-3879. Office Fax: 212-351-5316. Business E-Mail: sshoemate@gibsondunn.com.

**SHOEN, EDWARD JOSEPH,** transportation and insurance companies executive; s. Leonard and Anna (Carty) S. BA, Coll. Holy Cross, 1971; MBA, Harvard U., 1973; JD, Ariz. State Univ., 1981. With Amerco Corp, 1971—; pres. U-Haul Internat., Inc., 1990—; pres., chmn. Amerco Corp., Reno, 1986—. Office: Amerco 1325 Airmotive Way Reno NV 89502*

**SHOENBERGER, BARBARA FRANCES,** artist, educator; b. Cin., Jan. 16, 1938; m. Charles Edward Shoenberger, Jan. 3, 1959 (div.); 1 child, Susan. BS in Design, U. Cin., 1961, postgrad., 1961-83, 86-88, Art Acad. Cin., 1974. Art instr. Operation Head Start, Cin., 1964-66; grad. teaching asst. U. Cin., 1977-79; substitute tchr. Cin. Pub. Schs., 1979-80; instr. in art history and fine art Thomas More Coll., Ft. Thomas, Ky., 1980-81, 83-84; art instr. Arts Consortium of Cin., 1983-86; art instr. studio art classes Artist's Studio, Cin., 1983—; painting instr. Cin. Women's Club, 1987, 88. Tutor U. Cin., 1979-81, part-time instr. in fine arts, 1983-2003, lectr. in fine art, evening coll., 1980-81; instr. Ind. Artists, 1984—, Artist's Studio, Cin.; cons. Ohio Arts Coun., Columbus, 1980; mem. com. Cin. Zoo Arts; tour guide Cin. Art Mus. One-woman shows include U. Cin. Coll. Medicine, 1985, 1992, numerous others, exhibited in group shows at Conf. Cin. Women, 1986, 1987, 1988, 1989, Nantucket (Mass.) juried group show, 1987, U. Cin. Coll. Medicine, 1994, 2001, U. Cin. Coll. Law, 1995—96, S.S. Mockbee, 2003, Habanero, Cin., 2006, Galleries on Sycamore, 2006, Habanero, 2006, U. Cin. Galleries on Sycamore, 2006; contbr. photographs to MacDowell Colony Newsletter, drawing to Cin. Mag. Recipient Cert. of Merit, Pres. Lyndon B. Johnson, 1966, 1st award for art Conf. Cin. Women, 1987; grantee U. Cin., 1980; MacDowell Colony fellow, 1986. Avocations: hiking, camping, poetry, photography. Home: 552 Lowell Ave Cincinnati OH 45220-2304

**SHOGAN, ROBERT,** news correspondent; b. NYC, Sept. 12, 1930; s. Albert and Millie (Jacobs) S.; m. Ellen Shrewsbury, May 26, 1959; children: Cynthia Diane, Amelia Ford. BA, Syracuse U., 1951; postgrad., U. Mich. Inst. Pub. Adminstrn., 1951, Columbia U., 1952. Reporter Detroit Free Press, 1956-59; telegraph editor Miami (Fla.) News, 1959-61; asst. editor Wall St. Jour., N.Y.C., 1961-65; evaluation officer Peace Corps, Washington, 1965-66; corr. Newsweek, Washington, 1966-73; nation polit. corr. Los Angeles Times, Washington, 1973-99. Profl.-in-residence Annenberg Sch. Communication, U. Pa., 1993; adj. prof. Johns Hopkins U., Ctr. for Study of Am. Govt., Washington, 1999—. Author: Question of Judgement, 1972, Promises to Keep, 1977, None of the Above, 1982, The Riddle of Power, 1991, Hard Bargain, 1995, Fate of the Union, 1998, The Double-Edged Sword, 1998, Bad News, 2001, War Without End, 2002, The Battle of Blair Mountain, 2004, Backlash, 2006; co-author: (with Tom Craig) The Detroit Race Riot, 1964. Served with U.S. Army, 1952-54. Recipient 1st prize Feature Writing, Mich. AP, 1959, Disting. Reporting Pub. Affairs award Am. Polit. Sci. Assn., 1969, Scribes Book award, 1972; rsch. grantee Harry S Truman Presdl. Libr., 1989, Lyndon B. Johnson Presdl. Libr., 1989, Gerald R. Ford Presdl. Libr., 1989; McCormick fellow Hoover Presdl. Libr., 1993; fellow Media Studies Ctr., 1998. Mem. Phi Beta Kappa Home: 3513 Raymond St Chevy Chase MD 20815-3227

**SHOGREN, JASON FREDRICK,** economics professor; b. Cloquet, Minn., Sept. 29, 1958; s. Travis L. and Lou Ann (Prevost) S.; m. Deborah Riley, June 16, 1984; children: Maija Liisa, Riley Travis. BA, U. Minn., Duluth, 1980; PhD, U. Wyo., 1986. Asst. prof. Appalachian State U., Boone, NC, 1986—90; assoc. prof. econs. Iowa State U., Ames, 1990—95; mem. coun. econ. adviser Exec. Office of Pres. of U.S., 1997; Stroock Disting. prof. natural resource conservation/mgmt. U. Wyo., Laramie, 1995—. Head resource environ. policy Ctr. for Agrl. and Rural Devel. Iowa State U., Ames, 1990-92; vis. prof. Yale U., 1993. Author/editor 10 books on environ. econs.; contbr. articles to profl. jours. Trustee Albany County Sch. Dist. 1, Laramie, 1997—. Mem. Assn. Environ. Resource Econs. (editor newsletter 1992-97). Office: U Wyo Dept Econs Laramie WY 82071

**SHOHET, STEPHEN BYRON,** medical educator; b. Boston, Nov. 29, 1934; s. Harmon Abraham and Grace (Cohen) S.; m. Geraldine Poplack, July 22, 1956; children: Ralph, Grace, Jason, Juliet. BA, Harvard U., 1956, MD, 1960. Diplomate: Am. Bd. Internal Medicine. Intern, resident in medicine Beth Israel Hosp., Boston, 1960—62; clin. assoc. NIH, 1962—64, sr. staff assoc., 1965; fellow in hematology, instr. medicine Peter Bent Brigham Hosp., 1965—69; asst. prof. Harvard U., 1969—71; assoc. prof. U. Calif., San Francisco, 1971—76, prof. medicine and lab. medicine, 1976—2003, prof. emeritus, 2003—; chief hematology, 1974—84, dir. Cancer Rsch. Inst., 1974—80, dir. MacMillan-Cargill Hematology Rsch. Lab., 1980—2003. Contbr. articles to med. jours., also chpts. on hematology and biology of blood cell membranes to books. Recipient various research and tng. grants NIH. Mem. Am. Soc. Clin. Investigation, Am. Soc. Hematology, Biophys. Soc., Am. Assn. Physicians, Red Cell Club, Western Assn. Physicians. Office Phone: 415-922-3070. E-mail: sbshohet@aol.com.

**SHOMAKER, GORDON ALEXANDER, JR.,** poet, writer; b. Denver, Colo., Mar. 21, 1926; s. Gordon Alexander and Laura Louise Shomaker. BA, U.S.C., 1947; MA, U. Colo., 1952; postgrad. U. Paris/Sorvonne, 1948. Steel mill worker, Pueblo, Colo., 1951; instr. of various U. Theatres, 1957—67; instr. speech, English various univs., 1966—67; instr. Quinnipiac Coll., Hamden, Conn., 1953—57; appliance repair clerk Shomaker Electric Co., Pueblo, Colo., 1950—51; instr. Steel Mill, Pueblo, Colo., 1947. Treas., playwright Theatre Original Plays, Pueblo, Colo., 1980—85; bd. dirs. Colo.

Outdoor, 2000—; summer stock stage mgr. NY Shakespeare, 1957. Playwright: plays Joshua, 1962, Literary Defectives, 1984, author poetry, short stories, one and two-act plays. Rschr. Conn. Pub., Hartford, 1952, Expenditure Coun., Inc., Conn. With U.S. armed forces, 1944—45, WWII. Mem.: Nature Conservancy, NAACP, Native Am. Rights Fund., Acad. Am. Poets. Avocations: walking, music. Home: 900 W Abriendo Apt # 1020C Pueblo CO 81004-1158

SHONK, ALBERT DAVENPORT, JR., advertising executive; b. LA, May 23, 1932; s. Albert Davenport and Jean Spence (Stannard) S. BS in Bus. Adminstrn., U. So. Calif., 1954. Field rep. mktg. divsn. LA Examiner, 1954-55, asst. mgr. mktg. and field supr. mktg. divsn., 1955-56, mgr. mktg. divsn., 1956-57; account exec. Hearst Advt. Svc., LA, 1957-59; account exec., mgr. Keith H. Evans & Assocs., San Francisco and Los Angeles, 1959-65; owner, pres. Albert D. Shonk Co., LA, 1965-97; gen. ptnr. Shonk Land Co. Ltd., Charleston, W.va., 1989-00; dir. Shonk, LLC, Del., 2001—. Pres. Signet Cir. Corp., Inc., 1977-81, dir., 1962-81, hon. life dir., 1981—, treas., 1989-2002, pres., 2002—. Founding chmn. Crittenton Assocs.; bd. dirs. Balboa Island Improvement Assn., 2000—, pres., 2005—; bd. dirs. Balboa Island Mus. & Hist. Soc., 1999—, treas.; co-chair Centennial com. Florence Crittenton Ctr., 1992, bd. dirs., sec., 1978, 1st v.p., 1978—79, exec. v.p., 1979—81, pres., 1981—83, chmn. bd., 1983—85, hon. life dir., 1986—, treas., 1997, pres., 1997—2001, chmn. bd. dirs., 2002—03, pres., 2004—05, pres. emeritus, 2006—. Recipient Medallion of Merit Phi Sigma Kappa, 1976, Founders award, 1961, NIC Interfraternal award, 1989. Mem.: Jr. Advt. Club LA (hon. life, dir., treas., 1st v.p.), Nat. Assn. Pubs. Reps. (past v.p. West Coast 1981—83), Pubs. Rep. Assn. of So. Calif., Advt. Club LA, Town Hall, U. So. Calif. Alumni Assn. (bd. govs. 2000—03), U. So. Calif. Marshall Sch. Bus. Alumni Assn. (nat. bd. 1991—99, treas. 1995—99), World Affairs Coun., U. So. Calif. Assocs., Marshall Assocs. (bd. dirs. 1999—), U. So. Calif. Half Century Trojans (co-chair 50 yr. reunion 2004, bd. dirs. 2004—), Rotary (bd. mem. L.A. Rotary Found. 2006—, Paul Harris fellow), Trojan Club, Skull and Dagger, U. So. Calif. Cardinal and Gold, Alpha Kappa Psi, Phi Sigma Kappa (dir. grand coun. 1962—70, 1977—79, grand pres. 1979—83, v.p. meml. found. 1979—84, chancellor 1983—87, pres. meml. found. 1984, found. trustee pres. 1984—95, chancellor 1990—91, recorder 1995—, found. trustee emeritus 1995—), Inter-Greek Soc. (v.p. 1976—79, pres. 1984—86, co-founder, hon. life, dir.). Home and Office: 225 Sapphire Ave Newport Beach CA 92662-1148 E-mail: adshonk@msn.com.

SHONS, ALAN RANCE, plastic surgeon, surgical oncologist, educator; b. Freeport, Ill., Jan. 10, 1938; s. Ferral Caldwell and Margaret (Zimmerman) S.; children: Lesley, Susan. AB, Dartmouth Coll., 1960; MD, Case Western Res. U., 1965; PhD in Surgery, U. Minn., 1976. Diplomate Am. Bd. Surgery, Am. Bd. Plastic Surgery. Intern U. Hosp., Cleve., 1965-66, resident in surgery, 1966-67; rsch. fellow transplantation immunology U. Minn., Mpls., 1969-72, asst. prof. plastic surgery, 1976-79, assoc. prof., 1979-84, prof., 1984; resident in surgery U. Minn. Hosp., 1972-74; resident plastic surgery NYU, 1974-76; dir. divsn. plastic and reconstructive surgery U. Minn. Hosp., St. Paul Ramsey Hosp., Mpls. VA Hosp., 1976-84; cons. plastic surgery St. Louis Park Med. Ctr., 1980-84; prof. surgery Case Western Res. U., Cleve., 1984-93, dir. divsn. plastic and reconstructive surgery, 1984-92; prof. surgery, assoc. dir. comprehensive breast program, H. Lee Moffitt Cancer Ctr. and Rsch. Inst. U. South Fla., Tampa, 1992—2003; surgeon pvt. practice, Great Neck, NY, 2004—. Examiner Am. Bd. Plastic Surgery, 1987-2000. Author: (with G.L. Adams and D. McQuarrie) Head and Neck Cancer, 1986; (with R. Jensen) Plastic Surgery Review, 1993. Capt. USAF, 1967-69. Fellow ACS (chmn. Minn. com. on trauma 1978-84); mem. AMA, Am. Soc. Plastic and Reconstructive Surgeons, Am. Assn. Plastic Surgeons, Minn. Acad. Plastic Surgeons (pres. 1981-82), Soc. Head and Neck Surgeons, Transplantation Soc., Plastic Surgery Rsch. Coun., Am. Soc. Aesthetic Plastic Surgery, Am. Soc. Maxillofacial Surgeons, Am. Assn. Immunologists, Am. Soc. Exptl. Pathology, Am. Cleft Palate Assn., Am. Soc. Craniofacial Surg. Assn., Fla. Soc. Plastic and Reconstructive Surgeons, Sigma Xi. Office: 935 Northern Blvd Great Neck NY 11021 Office Phone: 516-482-6893.

SHOOK, ANN JONES, lawyer; b. Canton, Ohio, Apr. 18, 1925; d. William M. and Lura (Pontius) Jones; m. Gene E. Shook Sr., Nov. 30, 1956; children: Scott, William, Gene Edwin Jr. AB, Wittenberg U., 1947; LLB, William McKinley Law Sch., 1955. Bar: Ohio 1956, U.S. Dist. Ct. (no. dist.) Ohio 1961, U.S. Ct. Appeals (6th cir.) 1981. Cost acct. Hoover Co., North Canton, Ohio, 1947-51; asst. sec. Stark County Prosecutor's Office, Canton, Ohio, 1951-53; ins. adjuster Traveler's Ins. Co., Canton, 1953-56; ptnr. Shook & Shook, Toledo, 1958-62, North Olmsted, Ohio, 1962—. Mem. at large coun. Olmsted Community Ch., Olmsted Falls, Ohio, 1987-90; chmn. ways and means com. North Olmsted PTA, 1968; area chmn. United Way Appeal, North Olmsted, 1963; v.p. LWV, Toledo, 1960-62. Mem. Cleve. Bar Assn. Avocations: reading, boating, dance, exercise. E-mail: shooklaw@worldnet.att.net.

SHOOK, JOHN ROBERT, philosopher; b. Buffalo, June 16, 1966; s. Robert Harold and Joan Shook; m. Karen Kazmierczak, Aug. 13, 1994; children: Adrienne, Eliza. BA in Philosophy, Case Western Res. U., Cleve., 1988; MA in Philosophy, U. Fla., Gainesville, 1990; PhD in Philosophy, U. Buffalo, 1994. Asst. prof. of philosophy Corning C.C., NY, 1995—99, assoc. prof. of philosophy, 1999—2000; asst. prof. of philosophy Okla. State U., Stillwater, 2000—03, assoc. prof. of philosophy, 2003—06; provost and sr. rsch. fellow Ctr. for Inquiry Transnational, Amherst, NY, 2006—. Author: (book) Pragmatism: An Annotated Bibliography, 1898-1940, Dewey's Empirical Theory of Knowledge and Reality; editor: Dictionary of Modern American Philosophers, Blackwell Companion to Pragmatism, (acad. jours.) Contemporary Pragmatism. Mem.: Soc. for the Advancement of Am. Philosophy (exec. com. 2006—), Am. Philos. Assn. Office: Center for Inquiry Transnational 3965 Rensch Rd Amherst NY 14228 Office Phone: 716-636-4869. Office Fax: 716-636-1733. Business E-mail: jshook@centerforinquiry.net.

SHOOP, GLENN POWELL, investment consultant; b. Gracemont, Okla., Sept. 1, 1920; s. Roy Alonzo and Myrtle Nancy (Goodfellow) S.; m. Louise Wilhelmina Vollmer, Mar. 19, 1943; children: Merilou Love, Paul, Nancy Jeffery. Student, U. Okla., 1938-42. Pilot Braniff Internat. Airways, Dallas, 1946-80. Cons. bd. dirs. Braniff Inc., 1984—88. Bd. dirs. 1st Bapt. Ch. Dallas, 1950-2000. Maj. USAF, 1942-46, WWII Republican. Achievements include first U.S. pilot to fly Concorde in U.S. scheduled service.

SHOOTER, ERIC MANVERS, retired neurobiology professor, consultant; b. Mansfield, Eng., Apr. 18, 1924; arrived in U.S., 1946; s. Fred and Martha (Johnson) Shooter; m. Elaine Staley Arnold, May 28, 1949; 1 child, Annette Elizabeth. BA, Cambridge (Eng.) U., 1945, MA, 1949, PhD, 1950, ScD, 1986; DSc, U. London, 1964. Sr. scientist biochemistry Brewing Industry Rsch. Found., 1950—53; biochemistry lectr. Univ. Coll., London, 1953—63; assoc. prof. genetics Stanford U., 1963—68, prof. genetics and biochemistry, 1968—75, prof., chmn. neurobiology dept., 1975—87, prof. neurobiology 1987—2004, prof. neurobiology emeritus, 2004—, chmn. Neurosci. PhD Program, 1972—82. Member Neurosci. Rsch. Program, N.Y.C., 1979—89; mem. tchg. staff Internat. Sch. Neurosci., Praglia, Italy, 1987—93; sr. cons. Markey Charitable Trust, Miami, Fla., 1985—97; bd. dirs. Regeneron Pharm., Inc., Tarrytown, N.Y. Assoc. editor (book series) Ann. Rev. Neurosci., 1984—2001; contbr. articles to profl. jours. Recipient Wakeman award, Duke U., 1988, Award for Disting. Achievement in Neurosci. Rsch., Bristol-Myers-Squibb, 1997; scholar, Josiah Macy Jr. Found., N.Y.C., 1974—75. Fellow: AAAS, Am. Acad. Arts and Scis., Royal Soc. (London); mem.: NAS, Am. Philos. Soc., Internat. Brain Rsch. Orgn., Internat. Soc. Neurochemistry, Am. Soc. Neurochemistry, Am. Assn. Biol. Chemists, Soc. for Neurosci. (Ralph W. Gerard prize 1995), Inst. Medicine of NAS, Alpha Omega Alpha (hon.). Avocation: travel. Home: 370 Golden Oak Dr Portola Valley CA 94028-7757 Office: Stanford U Sch Medicine Dept Neurobiology 299 Campus Dr Stanford CA 94305-5125 Office Phone: 650-723-7559. Business E-mail: eshooter@stanford.edu.

SHOPTAUGH, TERRY LEE, historian, archivist; b. St. Louis, Feb. 9, 1952; s. Don C. and Virgalee Shoptaugh; m. Deborah K. Janzen, May 13, 1952; 1 child, Amelia J. BA, Ctrl. Meth. Coll., 1974; PhD in Am. History, U. NH, 1984. Archivist S.E. Mo. State U., Cape Girardeau, 1982—86; prof. history, archivist Minn. State U., Moorhead, 1986—. Author: Roots of Success, 1997 (Red River Valley Heritage award, 1997), Moorhead, 2004. Mem.: Soc. Am. Archivists (life; cert. archivist). Office: Minn State Univ 1104 S Seventh Ave Moorhead MN 56563 Office Phone: 218-477-2343. Office Fax: 218-477-5924. Business E-mail: shoptaug@mnstate.edu.

SHOR, GEORGE G., JR., geophysicist, oceanographic administrator, engineer; b. N.Y.C., N.Y., June 8, 1923; s. George Gershon and Dorothy (Williston); m. Elizabeth Louise Noble, June 11, 1950; children: Alexander Noble, Carolyn Elizabeth, Donald Williston. BS, Calif. Inst. Tech., 1944, MS, 1948, PhD, 1954. Joined Seismic Explorations, Inc., Houston, 1948, party chief, 1949-50; asst. research geophysicist to research geophysicist Scripps Inst. Oceanography, La Jolla, Calif., 1953-69, prof. marine geophysics, 1969-90, prof. emeritus, 1990—, assoc. dir., 1968-91; mgr. Calif. Sea Grant program, 1969-73. Mem. NAS-NRC panel on Mohole site selection, 1959; com. on underwater telecommunications, 1968, USN Marine Geophys. Survey Liaison Council, 1965-67; spl. adv. to Com. for Coordination of Joint Prospecting for Mineral Resources in Asian Offshore Areas, 1976-91; chmn. ship scheduling panel Univ. Nat. Oceanographic Lab. Systems, 1987-89; sci. leader oceanographic expdns. to various parts of Pacific and Indian oceans, 1955-82. Served to lt. (j.g.) USNR, 1943-46; now comdr. USNR Ret. Fellow Geol. Soc. Am., Am. Geophys. Union, Am. Bamboo Soc. (pres. 1994-96); mem. Soc. Exploration Geophysicists, Scholia Club Home: 2655 Ellentown Rd La Jolla CA 92037-1147

SHORE, BILL, nonprofit organization executive; b. Pitts., Feb. 3, 1955; 3 children. BA, U. Pa.; JD, George Washington U. With senatorial and presdl. campaign staff to Sen. Gary Hart, 1978—87; chief of staff to Sen. Robert Kerrey US Senate, 1988—91; founder, exec. dir. Share Our Strength, Washington, 1987—; founder, chmn. Cmty. Wealth Ventures, Inc., 1997—. Bd. dirs. Timberland Co., 2001—; adj. prof. NYU; guest lectr. Harvard U., Stanford U. Author: (books) Revolution of the Heart, 1995, The Cathedral Within, 1999, The Light of Conscience, 2004. Office: Share Our Strength 1730 M St NW Ste 700 Washington DC 20036 Office Phone: 800-969-4767.*

SHORE, ELEANOR GOSSARD, retired medical school dean; b. Ottawa, Ill., Aug. 11, 1930; d. Arthur Paul and Mary Catherine (Lineberger) Gossard; m. Miles Frederick Shore, July 4, 1953; children: Miles Paul, Rebecca Shore Lewin, Susanna Shore LeBoutillier. BA magna cum laude, Radcliffe Coll., 1951; MD, Harvard U., 1955, MPH, 1970. Diplomate Am. Bd. Preventive Medicine. Med. intern New Eng. Med. Ctr. Hosp., Boston, 1955-56; resident in occup. medicine Harvard U. Health Svcs., Cambridge, Mass., 1966-68; Macy scholar Radcliffe Inst., Radcliffe Coll., Cambridge, 1966-68; resident in preventive medicine Harvard Sch. Pub. Health, Boston, 1970-71; asst. physician Radcliffe Coll., 1959-61, Harvard U. Health Svcs., 1961-73; rsch. assoc. dept. microbiology Harvard U. Sch. Pub. Health, 1971-76; asst. to pres. Harvard U., 1972-81; assoc. dean for faculty affairs Harvard Med. Sch., 1978-89, mem. faculty, 1978—2004, dean for faculty affairs, 1989—2004, sr. cons. to office acad. and clin. programs, 2005—. Mem. editl. bd. Harvard Med. Alumni Bull., 1976—. Bd. dirs. Mass.-Ukraine Citizens Bridge, Brockton, Mass., 1989-94, pres., 1991-92; bd. dirs. Needham (Mass.) Found. for Pub. Sch. Edn., 1990-94; bd. dirs. Mass. Health Rsch. Inst., 1990—99, sec., 1995-99; overseer Boston Mus. Sci., 1981—; trustee Schepens Eye Rsch. Inst., Boston, 1993—; mem. acad. coun. Real Colegio Complutense, Harvard U., 1995—; dep. dir. Harvard Med. Sch. Ctr. for Excellence in Women's Health, 1998-2004. Recipient Pres.'s Recognition award Am. Med. Women's Assn., 1996. Fellow Am. Acad. Preventive Medicine; mem. AAAS, APHA, Mass. Pub. Health Assn., Assn. Am. Med. Colls., Mass. Med. Soc., Aesculapian Club (treas. 1986-89, pres. 1990-91), E-mail: eleanor_shore@hms.harvard.edu.

SHORE, ERIC EUGENE, internist, consultant, lawyer; b. Phila., Feb. 12, 1948; s. Reuben and Mary (Osinoff) S.; m. Mona Diane Cherry, Oct. 23, 1977 (div. Dec. 1991); children: Brett Ian, Matthew Adam. Student, Temple U., 1965—67; BS in Biology, Chemistry, Widener U., 1969; DO, Phila. Coll. Osteo. Med., 1973; MBA in Med., Healthcare Mgmt., St. Joseph's U., 1997; postgrad in law, Widener U., 1999—2000; JD, Rutgers U., 2003. Med. diplomate Nat. Bd. Examiners, diplomate Am. Bd. Utilization Rev. and Quality Assurance. Intern Botsford Gen. Hosp., Farmington, Mich., 1973-74; resident Phila. Gen. Hosp., 1974—75; instr. in medicine Hahnemann Med. Coll., Phila., 1975-78; treas. med. staff West Park Hosp., Phila., 1986-87, chief of geriatrics, 1986-88; sec. of med. staff Jefferson Park Hosp., Phila., 1987-91, chief of family medicine, 1988-96; pres. Gen. Medicine Assocs. Ltd., Phila., 1987—, Bala Clin. Assocs., P.C., Phila., 1989; asst. prof. medicine Phila. Coll. Osteopathic Medicine, Phila., 1987—; clin. asst. prof. medicine Med. Coll. Pa., Phila., 1991—2001, Drexel Coll. Medicine, Phila., 2002—; mng. ptnr. Shore Law Offices, Phila., 2003—05, Shore and Dicks, LLC, Phila., 2005—. Med. dir. Fairmount Geriatric Ctr., Phila., 1985-88, Bala Nursing & Retirement Ctr., Phila., 1990-95; chmn. bd. UniMed Systems, Inc., Phila., 1989—, Am. Medigroup, Inc., 1997—; CEO, Am. MediGroup, Inc., 1996—; cons. medicine and geriatrics Phila. Psychiat. Ctr., Phila., 1987—. Author: (novel) The Nostradamus Conspiracy, 2000. Med. officer Civil Air Patrol, Phila., 1976-78. Recipient Legion of Honor, Chapel of Four Chaplains, Phila., 1981. Fellow: Am. Coll. Legal Medicine, Am. Coll. Utilization Rev. Physicians, Am. Acad. Family Physicians; mem.: ATLA, AMA (physician's recognition award 1990, 1994, 1997, 1999, 2003), ABA, AAAS, Pa. Bar Assn. (Mont. chpt.), N.Y. Acad. Scis., Am. Coll. Physician Execs., Am. Health Lawyers Assn., Am. Geriatrics Soc., Royal Soc. Medicine. Avocations: music, flying, computers, sculpting, tennis. Office: Shore and Dicks LLC 2 Bula Plz Ste 300 PO Box 2771 Bala Cynwyd PA 19004 Office Phone: 610-854-6413. Business E-mail: eshore@shoremedlaw.com.

SHORE, HOWARD LESLIE, composer; b. Toronto, Ontario, Canada, Oct. 18, 1946; s. Mac and Bernice (Ash) S.; m. Elizabeth Ann Cotnoir, Aug. 3, 1990; 1 child, Mae. Student, Berklee Sch. Music, 1965-67, Forest Hill Collegiate, Toronto, Ont., Can., 1961-64. Composer The Gorfaine/Schwartz Agy., Sherman Oaks, Calif. Composer films scores including I Miss You, Hugs and Kisses, 1978, The Brood, 1979, Scanners, 1981, Videodrome, 1983, Nothing Lasts Forever, 1984, After Hours, 1985, Belizaire the Cajun, 1987, Fire with Fire, 1986, The Fly, 1986, Nadine, 1987, The Local Stigmatic, 1987, Heaven, 1987, Moving, 1988, Dead Ringers, 1988 (Genie award), Big, 1988, She-Devil, 1989, An Innocent Man, 1989, Signs of Life, 1989, The Silence of the Lambs, 1991, A Kiss Before Dying, 1989, Naked Lunch, 1990, Prelude to a Kiss, 1992, Single White Female, 1992, (TV score) Scales of Justice, 1990, Guilty as Sin, 1993, Sliver, 1993, M. Butterfly, 1993, Mrs. Doubtfire, 1993, Philadelphia, 1993, The Client, 1994, Ed Wood, 1994, Nobody's Fool, 1994, Moonlight and Valentino, 1995, White Man's Burden, 1995, Seven, 1995, Before and After, 1996, The Truth About Cats and Dogs, 1996, Looking for Richard, 1996, Crash, 1996, Looking For Richard, 1996, That Thing You Do, 1996, The Game, 1997, Cop Land, 1997, Last Night, 1998, Silver, 1998, Analyze This, 1999, Dogma, 1999, High Fidelity, 2000, The Yards, 2000, The Cell, 2000, The Score, 2001, Jay and Silent Bob Strike Back, 2001, The Lord of the Rings: The Fellowship of the Ring, 2001, Panic Room, 2002, Spider, 2002, The Lord of the Rings: The Two Towers, 2002, Gangs of New York, 2002, The Lord of the Rings: the Return of the King, 2003 (Grammy award for Best Score Soundtrack Album, 2005), The Aviator, 2004 (Golden Globe award for Best Original Score 2005), others; music supr. Places in the Heart, 1984, Postcards From the Edge, 1990; music dir. The Hart & Lorne Terrific Hour, 1970, Saturday Night Live, 1975-80, 85-86. Recipient Career Achievement award for Film Music Composition, Nat. Bd. Review, 2005. Mem. ASCAP, SOCAN (founding mem.). Home: Wee Wah Lodge Tuxedo Park NY 10987 Office: The Gorfaine Schwartz Agency Inc 4111 W Alameda Ave Ste 509 Burbank CA 91505-4171

SHORE, JAMES H(ENRY), psychiatrist; b. Winston-Salem, NC, Apr. 6, 1940; s. James Henry and Ellen Elizabeth (Hayes) S.; m. Christine Lowenbach, Aug. 24, 1963; children— Ellen Ottilie, James Henry. MD, Duke U., 1965. Diplomate Am. Bd. Psychiatry and Neurology. Intern U. Utah Med. Ctr., 1965-66; resident in psychiatry U. Wash., 1966-69; chief mental health office Portland Area Indian Health Svc., Oreg., 1969-73; assoc. prof. psychiatry, dir. cmty. psychiatry tng. program U. Oreg. Health Sci. Ctr., 1973-75, prof., chmn. dept. psychiatry, 1975-85; from chmn. dept. psychiatry Health Sci. Ctr. to chancellor U. Colo., Aurora, 1985—2004, chancellor Health Scis. Ctr., 2004—05, chancellor emeritus Health Scis. Ctr., 2006—. Dir. Colo. Psychiatry Hosp., 1985-99; interim dir. U. Colo. Hosp., Denver, 1987-88, interim exec. vice chancellor, 1995-97, chancellor, 1998—; mem. exptl. and spl. edn. com. NIMH-Internal Rev. Group, 1976-80; cons. in field. Contbr. numerous articles to profl. publs. Mem. Various community bds. Served with USPHS, 1969-73. Decorated USPHS Commendation medal; various grants. Fellow Am. Psychiat. Assn., Am. Coll. Psychiatry (pres. 2003-04); mem. Am. Assn. Chmn. Depts. Psychiatry (pres. 1989), Am. Bd. Psychiatry and Neurology (dir. 1987—, pres. 1994), Residency Rev. Com. for Psychiatry (chmn. 1991-92). Office: U Colo Health Scis Ctr Mail Stop F800 PO Box 6508 Aurora CO 80045

SHORE, MILES FREDERICK, psychiatrist, educator; b. Chgo., May 26, 1929; s. Miles Victor and Margaret Elizabeth S.; m. Eleanor M. Gossard, July 4, 1953; children: Miles Paul, Rebecca M. Lewin, Susanna G. LeBoutillier. BA, U. Chgo., 1948; AB, Harvard U., 1950, MD, 1954. Intern U. Ill. Research and Edn. Hosp., Chgo., 1954-55; resident in psychiatry Mass. Mental Health Center, Beth Israel Hosp., Boston, 1956-61; asst. prof. psychiatry Tufts U. Sch. Medicine, Boston, 1964-68, assoc. prof., 1968-71, prof., 1971-75, prof. community health, 1972-75; founder, dir. Tufts Community Mental Health Center, 1968-74, asso. dean community affairs, 1972-75; mem. faculty Boston Psychoanalytic Inst., 1973—; Bullard prof. psychiatry Harvard Med. Sch., Boston, 1975—; supt. Mass. Mental Health Ctr., 1975-93; vis. scholar John F. Kennedy Sch. Govt. Harvard U., 1993—; cons. exec. edn. Harvard Med. Internat., 1999—, sr. cons., 2000—. Dir. program for chronic mental illness Robert Wood Johnson Found., 1985-92. Editl. bd. Psychat. Svcs. Jour., 1990; bd. editors Jour. Interdisciplinary History, 1975, Psycho History Rev., 1978; column editor Harvard Rev. Psychiatry, 1993; contbr. articles to profl. jours. Bd. dirs. Federated Dorchester Neighborhood Houses, Boston, 1975-78, tr. House, Boston, 1995—; bd. dirs. Mental Found., Boston, 1987—, chmn., 1999-2001; mem. Blue Ribbon Commn., Mass. Dept. Mental Health, 1979-80. Capt. U.S. Army, 1956-58. Community Mental Health Center grantee, 1954-75. Fellow Am. Psychiat. Assn. (life, joint chmn. on pub. affairs, adminstrv. psychiatry award 1987), Am. Coll. Psychiatrists (chmn. fin. com. 1983-89, bd. regents 1988-90, 1st v.p. 1994, pres. 1996-97, Bowis award for svc. 1990, Arthur P. Noyes award 1994); mem. Assn. Am. Med. Colls. (coun. acad. socs. 1992—), Boston Psychoanalytic Soc. and Inst. (chmn. bd. trustees 1970-73), Mass. Psychiat. Soc. (pres. 1970-71), Mass. Hosp. Assn. (trustee 1980-85), Am. Hosp. Assn. (chmn. governing coun. for psychiat. and substance abuse svcs. 1992-93, ho. of dels. 1996—02, region I policy bd. 1997—2000), Roxbury Clinic Record Club, Aesculapian Club, Mass. Hist. Soc. Office: Harvard Med Internat Ste 902 1135 Trumont St Boston MA 02120 E-mail: miles-shore@harvard.edu.

SHORE, RANDY, secondary school educator; b. New Castle, Ind., Dec. 23, 1954; s. Eugene Shore and Marcella McCord, Charles McCord (Stepfather) and Joan Shore (Stepmother); m. Toni Lynn Smith, June 4, 1977; children: Braden, Danielle Beard, Michelle Patterson, Brian, Janelle. BS, Ball State U., Muncie, Ind., 1979; MA, Ball State U., 1988. Tchr., coach Union Sch. Corp., Modoc, Ind., 1979—. Sponsor student coun., Modoc, 2001—; sponsor sr. class, 2003—; pres. Union Booster League, Modoc, 1974—83, 1990—94. Sunday sch. tchr. Separate Bapt. Ch., Losantville, Ind., 1977—81, Antioch Christian Ch., Losantville 1985—90, jr. ch. leader, 1990—95. Sgt. US Army NG, 1984—90. Decorated Army Commendation medal US Army; named Outstanding Life Sci. Tchr., Ball State U., 1983, Basketball Coach of Yr., Mid-Ea. Conf. Coaches Assn., 1986—87, Star Tchr., Mid Ea. Conf. Adminstrs. Assn., 1995, 1997, 1999, 2002, 2004, 2006, Tchr. of Month, Union HS Student Coun., 1996, Outstanding Am. Tchr., Nat. Honor Roll, 2006; recipient Cmty. Advancement award, Farmers' Achievement Orgn., 1979. Mem.: Ind. State Tchrs. Assn. (1983—84), Ind. Basketball Coaches Assn., Ind. Coaches of Girls Sports Assn. (20 Yr. Svc. award 2002), Hoosier Assn. Sci. Tchrs. Avocations: softball, horseback riding, travel. Home: 8730 N Wilbur Wright Rd Mooreland IN 47360 Office: Union School Corp 8707 W US 36 Modoc IN 47358 Office Phone: 765-853-5421. Office Fax: 765-853-6057. E-mail: rshore@usc.k12.in.us.

SHORE, RICHARD ARNOLD, mathematics professor; b. Boston, Aug. 18, 1946; s. Philip M. and Miriam (Krensky) S.; m. Naomi J. Spiller, Aug. 3, 1969; children: Deena A., Aviva R. B in Jewish Edn., Hebrew Coll., 1966; AB, Harvard U., 1968; PhD, MIT, 1972. Instr. U. Chgo., 1972-74; asst. prof. Cornell U., Ithaca, NY, 1974-78, assoc. prof., 1978-83; asst. prof. U. Ill.-Chgo., 1977; vis. assoc. prof. MIT, Cambridge, 1980; vis. prof. Hebrew U., Jerusalem, 1982-83; prof. math. Cornell U., Ithaca, 1983—. Organizing com. Logic Yr. at MSRI, 1989-90, other internat. meetings. Author: (with A. Nerode) Logic for Applications; editor North-Holland, Studies in Logic and the Foundations of Mathematics, 1996—; cons. editor Jour. Symbolic Logic, 1980-83, editor, 1984-93, coord. editor, 1989-91; mng. editor: Bull. Symbolic Logic, 1993-2000; contbr. articles to profl. jours. V.p. for edn. Hillel Acad. Broome County, Binghamton, N.Y., 1985-89; treas. Beth David Synagogue, 1993-96; pres. Jewish Fedn. of Broome County, 1998-2000; bd. dirs. Project Euclid, 2002—. NSF grantee, 1973-. Mem. Am. Math. Soc., Spl. Interest Group in Algorithms and Computation Theory, Assn. for Computing Machinery, Assn. for Symbolic Logic (coun. 1984—, pres. 2001-2004. Jewish. Home: 14 Kenwood Ave Newton MA 02459 Office: Cornell U Dept Math Malott Hall Ithaca NY 14853 Office Phone: 607-255-4081. Business E-Mail: shore@math.cornell.edu.

SHORE, ROBERT, artist, educator; b. Manhattan, N.Y., Feb. 27, 1924; s. Arthur and Ruth Shore; m. Marietta Saravia, May 31, 1964; children: Gigi Broide, Evan Arthur. Student, Cranbrook Acad. of Art, 1948—51, Boro Polytecnic Inst., London, England 1945—46, Art Students League, 1947—48. Staff artist Stars and Stripes U.S. Army, Paris, 1946—46; artist self-employed, New York, NY, 1946—; art tchr. Cooper Union, N.Y., 1952—55, Sch. Visual Arts, N.Y.C., 1957—80; art tchr. Parson's Sch. of Design New Sch. U., N.Y.C., 1979—96. Creative artist NASA, Washington, D.C., DC, 1963—70; tchr. art master class Syracuse (N.Y.) U., 1987—88; adj. assoc. prof. C.W. Post Coll., L.I., NY, 1971. Captain Vere (Gold Medal award Soc. Illustrators, 1965), Melville's Moby Dick, 1962, Melville's Billy Budd and Benito Cereno, 1965, Conrad's Heart of Darkness, 1969, Verne's From the Earth to the Moon and Around the Moon, 1970, Conrad's Three Tales of the Sea, 1972, Conrad's An Outcast of the Islands, 1975, exhibitions include Detroit (Mich.) Inst. Fine Arts, 1951, Cooper Union, N.Y., N.Y., 1953, Nat. Gallery, Washington, D.C., 1966, Artrain Inc., Ann Arbor, Mich., 2001—03. Technician 5th grade U.S. Army, 1943—46, European Theater (ETO). Recipient First prize, Am. Ho., 1952; fellow, Fulbright Found., 1952. Avocations: reading, films, art museums. Personal E-mail: robertshore1@mac.com.

SHORE, STEPHEN, photographer; b. N.Y.C., Oct. 8, 1947; m. Ginger Cramer Seippel, 1980; 1 child, Nicholas; 1 stepchild, Alex Seippel. Student, Minor White, Workshop, 1970. Photographer, 1953—. One-man shows, Met. Mus. Art, N.Y.C., 1971, Light Gallery, N.Y.C., 1972, 73, 75, 77, 78, 80, Phoenix Gallery, San Francisco, 1975, Mus. Modern Art, N.Y.C., 1976, Kunshalle, Dusseldorf, Germany, 1976, U. Akron, Ohio, 1978, Vision Gallery, Boston, 1978, La Photogaleria, Madrid, 1979, Ewing Gallery, Washington, 1979, Catskill Ctr. Photography, Woodstock, N.Y., 1980, Fraenkel Gallery, San Francisco, 1982, Mus. Arts and Scis., Daytona Beach, Fla., 1981, Polk Pub. Mus., 1982, ARCO Ctr. Visual Arts, L.A., 1982, N. Mex. State U. Art Gallery, Las Cruces, 1982, Art Inst. Chgo., 1984, Pace Wildenstein MacGill, N.Y.C., 1989, 95, Sprengel Mus., Hannover, 1995, Würt. Kunstverein, Stuttgart, 1995, Amerika Haus, Berlin, 1995, George

Eastman House, Rochester, N.Y., 1996, Skstiftung Kultur, Koln, Germany, 1999, Spazio Oberdan, Milan, Italy, 1999, 303 Gallery, N.Y.C., 2000, 03, Galerie Conrads, Düsseldorf, 2001, 02, Sprueth Magers Lee, London, 2003, Jeu de Paume, Paris, 2005, Hammer Mus., L.A., 2005, Photoespaña, Madrid, 2005, P.S. 1, N.Y.C., 2005; group shows include: Met. Mus. Art, N.Y.C., 1973, 82, 97, Internat. Mus. Photography, George Eastman House, 1975, Documenta 6, Kassel, W. Ger., 1977, Art Inst. Chgo., 1977, 79, 89, Mus. Modern Art, N.Y.C., 1978, 91, 2000, Corcoran Gallery, Washington, 1979, Kunsthaus, Zurich, Switzerland, 1980, U. Ariz. Mus. Art, Tucson, 1981, Nat. Gallery, Washington, 1989, Getty Mus., 1992, 97, Whitney Mus., N.Y.C., 1999, P.S. 1, N.Y.C., 1999, Victoria & Albert Mus., London, 1999, Sprenger Mus., Hannover, Germany, Uffizi Gallery, Florence, 2000, Tate Modern, London, 2003, Mus. Ludwig, Cologne, 2003; represented in permanent collections, Met. Mus. Art, N.Y.C., Mus. Modern Art, N.Y.C., Internat. Mus. Photography, George Eastman House, Rochester, N.Y., Mus. Fine Arts, Boston, Library of Congress, Washington, Art Inst. Chgo., Ctr. Creative Photography, U. Ariz., Tucson, Stedelijk Mus., Amsterdam, Netherlands, Neue Sammlung, Munich, W.Ger., Australian Nat. Gallery, Canberra; author: Andy Warhol, 1968, Uncommon Places, 1982, The Gardens at Giverny, 1983, Stephen Shore: Luzzara, 1993, Stephen Shore: Photographs 1973-1993, 1995, The Velvet Years, 1995, The Nature of Photographs, 1998, American Surfaces, 1999, Essex County, 2003, Uncommon Places: 50 Unpublished Photographs, 1973-1978, 2003, Uncommon Places: The Complete Work, 2004, American Surfaces Phaidon, 2005; portfolio 12 Photographs, 1976; contbr. articles to profl. jours. Nat. Endowment Arts grantee, 1974, 79; Guggenheim fellow, 1975, Am. Acad. (Rome) Spl. fellow, 1980, MacDowell Colony fellow, 1993. Mem. Century Assn.

**SHORE, THOMAS SPENCER, JR.,** retired lawyer; b. Akron, Ohio, Jan. 1, 1939; s. T. Spencer and Harriet G. (Delicate) S.; m. Margaret F. Kudzma, Aug. 12, 1961; children— Thomas Spencer III, John Christopher, Daniel Andrew, Mary Margaret. BA, Brown U., 1961; JD, Northwestern U., 1964. Bar: Ohio 1964. Assoc. Taft, Stettinius and Hollister, Cin., 1964-69, Rendigs, Fry, Kiely & Dennis, Cin., 1969-71, ptnr., 1972—2003; ret., 2003. Adj. asst. prof. Chase Law Sch., U. No. Ky. Bd. dirs. United Cerebral Palsy of Cin., 1978—; bd. dirs., sec. Boys Club Am., Cin.; trustee emeritus Family Svc. of Cin. Area; past pres. Vis. Nurse Assn. of Cin., hon. trustee; mem. Kennebunkport Zoning Bd. Appeals. Mem. Ohio Bar Assn., Cin. Country Club, Queen City Club, Webhanet Club, Edgcomb Tennis Club. Office: 900 4th and Vine Tower 1 W 4th St Cincinnati OH 45202 Home: PO Box 629 Kennebunkport ME 04046 E-mail: t.shore@rendigs.com.

**SHORENSTEIN, ROSALIND GREENBERG,** internist; b. NYC, Jan. 14, 1947; d. Albert Samuel and Natalie Miriam (Sherman) Greenberg; m. Michael Lewis Shorenstein, June 18, 1967; children: Anna Irene, Claire Beth. BA in Chemistry, Wellesley Coll., 1968; MA in Biochemistry and Molecular Biology, Harvard U., 1970, PhD in Biochemistry and Molecular Biology, 1973; MD, Stanford U., 1976. Diplomate Am. Bd. Internal Medicine. Resident in internal medicine UCLA Med. Ctr., 1976-79; pvt. practice internal medicine Santa Cruz, Calif., 1979—. Mem. dept. internal medicine Dominican Hosp., Santa Cruz, 1979—; co-dir. med. svcs. Health Enhancement & Lifestyle Planning Systems, Santa Cruz, 1983—. Contbr. articles to profl. journals. Dir. Santa Cruz Chamber Players, 1993-94, pres., bd. dirs., 1994—. Recipient Charlie Parkhurst award Santa Cruz Women's Commn., 1989; NSF fellow, 1968-72, Sarah Perry Wood Med. fellow Wellesley Coll., 1972-76. Mem. Am. Soc. Internal Medicine (del. 1994, 95), Calif. Soc. Internal Medicine (trustee 1994—, sec.-treas. 1996-2000), Am. Med. Women's Assn. (Outstanding Svc. award 1987, br. #59 pres. 1986—), Calif. Med. Assn. (com. on women 1987-93), Santa Cruz County Med. Soc. (mem. bd. govs. 1993—, sec. 1997-99, pres. 2000-01, sec. 2002-), Phi Beta Kappa, Sigma Xi. Jewish. Office: 700 Frederick St Ste 103 Santa Cruz CA 95062-2239 Office Phone: 831-458-1002.

**SHORENSTEIN, WALTER HERBERT,** commercial real estate development company executive; b. Glen Cove, NY, Feb. 23, 1915; m. Phyllis J. Finley, Aug. 8, 1945 (dec.); children: Joan (Dec.), Carole, Douglas. Student, Pa. State U., 1933-34, U. Pa., 1934-36; D in Econs. (hon.), HanYang U., Seoul, Republic of Korea, l988. With property sales mgmt. depts. Milton Meyer & Co., San Francisco, 1946-51, ptnr., 1951-60, owner, chmn. bd. dirs., 1960—, Shorenstein Group, San Francisco, Shorenstein Co., San Francisco, 1960—. Appt. by Pres. Johnson adv. del. UN Econ. Commn. for Asia and Far East, 1967, Pub. Advisory Com. U.S. Trade Policy; apptd. Pres. Carter Com. for Preservation fo White House; appt. by Pres. Clinton bd. dirs. Corp. Nat. Svc., 1994-96, active mem. U.S. Commerce Dept. Industry, 1995-96. Past chmn. bd. trustees Hastings Law Ctr., U. Calif., San Francisco; founding mem. exec. adv. com. Hubert H. Humphrey Inst. Pub. Affairs, U. Minn.; bd. visitors; past pres., hon. life bd. dirs. San Francisco Park and Recreation Commn.; chmn. Vietnam Orphans Airlift; bd. dirs. San Francisco Performing Arts Ctr.; trustee Asia Found.; fit. chmn. Dem. Nat. Conv., 1984; founder Joan Shorenstein Ctr. on Press, Politics and Public Policy, Harvard U., 1986; apptd. by Pres. Clinton to Nat. Svc. Commn., 1994, Bd. of Americorp, founding mem. WWII Nat. Monument com., Nat. Endowment Arts, White House Endowment Fund; apptd. by Pres. Carter chair White House Preservation Fund; apptd. by Mayor Frank Jordon chair Save the San Francisco Giants com.; personal advisor Pres. Johnson, Carter, Clinton; chmn. Pacific Rim Econ. Coun., San Francisco; bd. visitors Internat. Studies Bd. Stanford U.; co-founder Orpheum, Curran and Golden Gate Theatres, San Francsico; founder Johnson Presdl. Libr., Carter Ctr.; chmn. San Francisco U. N50 nat. com., 1995, also numerous polit. activities. Maj. USAF, 1940-45. Named Leader of Tomorrow, Time mag., l953, Calif. Dem. of Yr., 1985; recipient Nat. Brotherhood award NCCJ, 1982, Disting. Svc. award Dem. Nat. Com., 1983, Golden Plate award Am. Acad. Achievement, 1991, Svc. to Youth award Calif. Youth Orgn., 1994, Lifetime Achievement award Dem. Party, 1997; inducted Real Estate Legends Hall of Fame, 1997. Bay Area Coun. Bay Area Bus. Hall of Fame, 1991; Shorenstein award named in his honor Bay Area Coun. Mem. Calif. C. of C. (past bd. dirs.), San Francisco C. of C. (past chmn. bd. dirs., life bd. dirs.). Office: Shorenstein Co 555 California St Ste 4900 San Francisco CA 94104-1714

**SHORENSTEIN HAYS, CAROLE,** theater producer; m. Jeffrey Hays; 2 children. Co-owner Curran Theatre, Golden Gate Theatre, Orpheum Theatre, San Francisco. Prodr.: (Broadway plays) Can-Can, 1981, Woman of the Year, 1981—83 (Tony nom. best musical, 1981), Oliver!, 1984, Fences, 1987 (Tony award best play, 1987), A Midsummer Night's Dream, 1996 (Tony nom. best revival of a play, 1996), The Old Neighborhood, 1997—98, The Chairs, 1998 (Tony nom. best revival of a play, 1996), Not About Nightingales, 1999 (Tony nom. best play, 1999), Closer, 1999 (Tony nom. best play, 1999), The Tale of the Allergist's Wife, 2000—02 (Tony nom. best play, 2001), Proof, 2000—03 (Tony award best play, 2001), The Goat, or Who Is Sylvia?, 2002 (Tony award best play, 2002), Topdog / Underdog, 2002 (Tony nom. best play, 2002), Take Me Out, 2003—04 (Tony award best play, 2003), Caroline, or Change, 2004— (Tony nom. best musical, 2004). Office: Curran Theatre 445 Geary St San Francisco CA 94102 also: Golden Gate Theatre P O Box 7110 San Francisco CA 94102

**SHORR, HARRIET,** artist; b. NYC, May 14, 1939; BA, Swarthmore, 1960; BFA, Yale Sch. Art and Arch., 1962. One-woman shows include Gross McCleaf Gallery, Phila., 1970, Green Mountain Gallery, NYC, 1972, 1973, 1975, Fischbach Gallery, 1979, 1980, 1983, 1984, J. Rosenthal Fine Arts, Chgo., 1988, Galveston Art Ctr., Tex., 1989, Rahr West Mus., Manitowac, Wis., 1991, Neuberger Mus., Purchase, NY, 1992, Gallery Camino Real, Boca Raton, Fla., 1994, Cheryl Pelavin Fine Art, NYC, 2001, 2002, exhibited in group shows at Am. Fedn. of Arts, 1971, Hobart Coll., Geneva, NY, 1975, at Goddard Riverside Arts Ctr., NYC, 1980, at Marion Koogler McNay Art Mus., San Antonio, Tex., 1981, Mus. of Art, Carnegie Inst., Pitts., 1986, Am. Acad. Arts and Letters, NYC, 1990, Levinson-Kane Gallery, Boston, 1992, NY Studio Sch., NYC, 1996, Fischbach Gallery, 1997, Del. Ctr. Contemporary Arts, Wilmington, 2002, others, Represented in permanent collections Chgo. Art Inst., Bklyn. Mus., Chemical Bank, NYC, Milbank, Tweed, Hadley and McCloy, Lehman Bros., Estee Lauder Corp., Champion Internat.,

Stamford, Conn., one-woman shows include Clarion (Pa.) Coll., 2005, Cheryl Pelavin, N.Y.C., exhibited in group shows at Armory Arts Ctr., West Palm Beach, Fla., 2004, 2005. Recipient Nat. Endowment of Arts award, 1980, Am. Artist Achievement award, 1994, Purchase award, Am. Acad. Arts & Letters, 1999, Pollock-Krasner award, 2000. Mem.: NAD (academician 1994—).

**SHORS, CLAYTON MARION,** retired cardiologist; b. Beemer, Nebr., June 10, 1925; s. Joseph Albert and Morva Edith (Clayton) S.; m. Arlene Towle, June 6, 1948; children: Susan Debra, Clayton Robert, Scott Towle BS, U. Nebr., 1950, MD, 1952. Diplomate Am. Bd. Internal Medicine (subspecialty cardiovascular disease). Intern Detroit Receiving Hosp., 1952-53, resident, 1953-56; practice medicine specializing in cardiology Detroit; chief cardiology St. John Hosp., Detroit; ret., 2005. Bd. dirs. Sedona Acad.; mem. Sedona 30. Served with U.S. Army, 1943-46 Fellow Am. Coll. Cardiology, Internat. Coll. Angiology, Am. Heart Assn. Council on Clin. Cardiology; mem. Alpha Omega Alpha Home and Office: 6562 E Crested Saguaro Ln Scottsdale AZ 85262-7373

**SHORS, JOHN DENNIS,** lawyer; b. Ft. Dodge, Iowa, July 21, 1937; s. George A. and Catherine (Shaw) S.; m. Patricia Ann Percival, Oct. 7, 1967; children: John, Tom, Matt, Luke. BSEE, Iowa State U., 1959; JD, U. Iowa, 1964. Bar: Iowa, U.S. Supreme Ct. Assoc. then shareholder Davis, Brown, Koehn, Shors & Roberts, P.C., Des Moines, 1964—. Co-author: Closely Held Corporations in Business and Estate Planning, 1982. Pres. Mercy Hosp. Found., Des Moines, 1981-84; chair Iowa State U. Found., Ames, 1989-92; bd. dirs. Mercy Housing, Denver, 1992—. Cpl. U.S. Army, 1960-61. Recipient Iowa State U. Alumni medal, YLS Merit award Iowa State Bar Assn. Mem. Iowa State Bar Assn. (pres. 1992) Iowa Women Profl. Corp. (Good Guy award 1987), Iowa Rsch. Coun. (bd. dirs. 1994—), Am. Judicature Soc. (bd. dirs. 1974-79), Polk County Bar Assn. (pres. 1986), Rotary (Des Moines chpt.), DM Club. Republican. Roman Catholic. Office: Davis Brown Koehn Shors & Roberts PC 666 Walnut St Ste 2500 Des Moines IA 50309-3904 Business E-mail: johnshors@lawiowa.com.

**SHORT, ALEXANDER CAMPBELL,** lawyer; b. Washington, July 26, 1940; s. Joseph Hudson and Beth (Campbell) S.; m. Patricia Graves Thompson, Aug. 24, 1968; children: Joseph Graves, Ashley Campbell, Justin Owen. BA, Amherst Coll., 1963; MA, U. Pa., 1968; JD, U. Va., 1972. Bar: Conn. 1972, Md. 1973. Field and site rep. U.S. Dept. of HUD, Phila., 1963-69; assoc. Reid & Riege P.C., Hartford, Conn., 1972-73, Piper & Marbury, Balt., 1973-79, Miles & Stockbridge, Balt., 1979-81, ptnr., 1981-94; pvt. practice Balt., 1994-95; ptnr. Hooper, Kiefer & Cornell, LLP, Balt., 1995-96, Eastman & Short, LLP, Balt., 1996-2000; asst. atty. gen. State of Md., 2000—. Pres. Handel Soc. adv. bd. to Handel Choir, Balt., 1983-87; bd. dirs. Handel Choir, Balt., 1987-88, 2002-03, pres., 1987-88. Pres. North Balt. Neighborhood Coalition, 1996—2000; bd. dirs. Homeland Assn., Balt., 1984—85, Kernewood Assn., Balt., 1995—, Greater Homewood Cmty. Corp., 1997—2001; mem. bd. mgrs. Camp Dudley YMCA, 1991—96, 1998—2001, 2004—. Mem. Md. Bar Assn. (real property planning and zoning sect., 2004-, coun. 1981-88, 96-98, sec. 1982-84, chmn. elect 1984-86, chmn. 1986-88). Balt. Rotary Found. (bd. dirs. 2004-), Rotary Club Balt. (bd. dirs. 2004-). Democrat. Presbyterian. Avocations: choral singing, scouting, gardening. Office: Office of Atty Gen Ednl Affairs Divsn 200 St Paul Pl Baltimore MD 21202 Office Phone: 410-576-6967. E-mail: ashort@oag.state.md.us.

**SHORT, ELIZABETH M.,** internist, educator, retired federal agency administrator; b. Boston, June 2, 1942; d. James Edward and Arlene Elizabeth (Mitchell) Meehan; m. Michael Allen Friedman, June 21, 1976; children: Lia Gabrielle, Hannah Ariel, Eleanor Elana. BA in Philosophy magna cum laude, Mt. Holyoke Coll., 1963; MD cum laude, Yale U., 1968. Diplomate Am. Bd. Internal Medicine, Am. Bd. Med. Genetics. Resident in internal medicine Yale New Haven Hosp., 1968-70; postdoctoral fellow in human genetics Yale Med. Sch., 1970-72; resident U. Calif., San Francisco, 1972-73; sr. chief resident Stanford (Calif.) Med. Sch., 1973-75, asst. prof. medicine, 1975-83, assoc. dean student affairs, med. edn., 1978-83; dep. dir. acad. affairs, dir. biomed. rsch.-assn. Am. Med. Colls., Washington, 1983-88; dep. assoc. chief med. dir. for acad. affairs VA, Washington, 1988-92, assoc. chief med. dir. for acad. affairs, 1992-96; health policy cons. HHS, 1996—2001; ret., 2001. Vis. prof. human biology Stanford U., 1983-86; mem. Accreditation Coun. Grad. Med. Edn., 1988-97; mem. White House Task Force on Health Care Reform, 1993. Assoc. editor Clin. Rsch. Jour., 1976-79, editor 1980-84; contbr. articles to profl. jours. Mem. Nat. Child Health Adv. Coun., NIH, 1991-97; mem. com. edn. and tng. Office Sci. and Tech. Policy, White House, Washington, 1991-96, bd. dirs. Calif. Philharm., 2003-, vice chair exec. com., 2003-, treas., 2003-; exec. com. bd. dirs. Hillsides, 2003-, chair program assessment com., 2003-. Recipient Maclean Zoology award; Munger scholar, Markle scholar, Sara Williston scholar Mt. Holyoke Coll., 1959-63; Yale Men in Medicine scholar, 1964-68; Bardwell Meml. Med. fellow, 1963. Mem. AAAS, Am. Soc. Human Genetics (pub. policy com. 1984-95, chmn. 1986-94), Am. Fedn. Clin. Rsch. (bd. dirs. 1973-83, co-chmn. com. status women 1975-77, editor Clin. Rsch. Jour., 1978-83, nat. coun., exec. com., pub. policy com. 1977-87), Western Soc. Clin. Investigation, Calif. Acad. Medicine, Phi Beta Kappa, Alpha Omega Alpha. Home and Office: 3535 Ranch Top Rd Pasadena CA 91107 Personal E-mail: elizshort@aol.com.

**SHORT, JAMES F.,** investment company executive; b. Norfolk, Va., Feb. 23, 1968; s. Richard Turner IV and Florence King (Timolat) S. Grad., Woodberry Forest Sch., 1986; BA, Coll. William and Mary, Williamsburg, Va., 1990; MBA, U. Ga., Athens, 1996. CFA, CFP, CIMA, CIMC, ChFC. V.p., sr. portfolio mgr. Kempner Capital Mgmt., Galveston, Tex., 1998-2001; v.p., portfolio mgr. Bank of Am., 2001—02; chief investment officer Waypoint Advisors, Norfolk, Va., 2002—03; v.p. Invl. Engh Asset Mgmt., St. Petersburg, Fla., 2004—. Arbitrator NASD, 2003—. Mem. Gubernatorial Adv. Com., 1992-93; vol. Am. Health Assn., Am. Cancer Soc., Westminster Canterbury Retirement Home, Surfrider Found.; bd. dirs. Bridgers-Short Found.; mem. endowment com. All Saints' Episcopal Ch.; del. to congl. and state convs. Mem. CFA Inst., Fin. Planning Assn. (former Hampton Rds. chpt. bd. dirs.), Investment Mgmt. Cons. Assn., CFA Tampa Bay, Princess Anne Country Club, The Revelers (former bd. govs., v.p.), Theta Delta Chi, Sigma Iota Epsilon. Republican. Episcopalian. Avocations: collecting sports cards, surfing, baseball, volunteering, travel, politics. Office: Eagle Asset Mgmt PO Box 10520 Saint Petersburg FL 33733-0520 Home (Summer): 507 W Holly Rd Virginia Beach VA 23451-2829 Home: 2218 Cypress Hollow Ct Safety Harbor FL 34695-5517 Office Phone: 727-567-1059. Personal E-mail: brockturnershort@aol.com. Business E-mail: jas.short@eagleasset.com.

**SHORT, JAY MILTON,** biotechnology company executive; b. Lebanon, Ind., Mar. 5, 1958; s. Roy Milton and Patricia Ann (Brewer) S.; m. Heidi Patrice Messinger, July 26, 1980; children: Ryan Milton, Cole Evan. BA in Chemistry with honors, Taylor U., Upland, Ind., 1980; PhD in Biochemistry, Case Western Res. U., 1985. Tchg. asst. Taylor U., 1978-80, Kent (Ohio) State U., 1981, Case Western Res. U., Cleve., 1981-85; staff scientist R & D, Stratagene Cloning Systems, La Jolla, Calif., 1985-88, sr. staff scientist, 1988-89, v.p. long term rsch. and biol. ops., 1989-92, v.p. long term rsch. and ops., 1992-94; pres. Stratcyte, Inc., La Jolla, 1992-94, Diversa Corp., San Diego, 1994—, CEO, 1994—, chief tech. officer, 1994—, bd. dir. Bd. dirs. Stressgen, Inc., Invitrogen, Synomyx, Chem. Engring. News, BioCom, Innovase, Zymetrics; reviewer human genome project and patenting DNA sequences U.S. Congl. Office Tech. Assessment; chmn., ofcl. Instnl. Animal Care and Use Com.; mem. peer rev. com. Nat. Inst. Environ. Health Scis., Molecular Biology, Microbiology, NAS, Genetic Analysis Techniques, Analytical Biochemistry, Nucleic Acids Rsch.; com. on transgenic toxicology testing EEC 1991-94; lectr. in field; mem. adj. faculty U. Calif., San Diego, 1991; lectr. Ctr. for Drug Evaluation and Rsch., FDA, 1992, others. Editor Mutation Rsch.; contbr. numerous articles and abstracts to sci. jours Recipient 1st place award for innovation and entrepreneurship in biotech. U. Calif., 1990, 91; named Entrepreneur of Yr., Ernst and Young, 2001; numerous grants including Nat. Inst. Environ. Health Scis., 1989-94, NIH, 1990-94, Nat. Cancer Inst., 1992-95. Mem. AAAS, Am. Soc. Biochemistry and

Molecular Biology, Am. Soc. Microbiology, Environ. Mutagenesis Soc., Soc. Toxicology (chmn. conf. discussion group 1993), Japanese Environ. Mutagen Soc., N.Y. Acad. Scis. Achievements include patents in field. Avocations: flying, photography, collecting fossils, scuba diving. Office: Recombinant BioCatalysis Inc 10665 Sorrento Valley Rd San Diego CA 92121-1609

**SHORT, JOEL BARTON,** secondary school educator, department chairman; b. Joplin, Mo., Jan. 29, 1955; s. Joel William and Bobbie Zoe Short; m. Dawn Lea Schnedler, May 26, 1978; 1 child, Aaron Barton. BFA, S.W. Mo. State U., Springfield, 1980; MA in Theatre, Ctrl. Mo. State U., Warrensburg, 1986. Lifetime cert. 7-12 grades speech and theatre Mo. Tchr., dept. chmn. speech & theatre Belton (Mo.) HS, 1981—. Mem. tchrs. adv. coun. Sta.-KCPT Pub. TV, Kansas City, Mo., 1983—90; chmn. curriculum com. Belton HS, 1999—; bd. dirs. Teacher's Adv. Coun. Kansas City Rep., 2001—05, Jellybean Conspiracy Bd., Kansas City, Mo., 2004—. Dir.: over 60 plays. Bd. dirs. Leawood (Kans.) Stage Co., 2003—; elder First Christian Ch. of Olathe, Kans., 2001—06, Raymore (Mo.) Christian Ch., 1993—2001. Named Thespian Outstanding Tchr. of the Yr., 1990. Mem.: NEA, Mo. State Thespians (state bd. dirs. 1987—92), Speech and Theatre Assn. Mo. (bd. govs. 1992—, state bd. treas. 2002—05, historian 1998—, Loren Ried Svc. award), Ednl. Theatre Assn., Internat. Thespians Soc., Nat. Forensics League. Disciples Of Christ. Avocations: golf, cooking, acting, travel. Home: 19001 W 160th Ct Olathe KS 66062 Office: Belton HS 107 Pirate Pky Belton MO 64012 Office Phone: 816-348-2721. Office Fax: 816-348-1516. Business E-Mail: jshort@bsd124.org.

**SHORT, MARIANNE DOLORES,** lawyer; b. Mpls., Mar. 12, 1951; d. Robert Earl and Marion (McCann) S.; m. Raymond Louis Skowyra Jr., Nov. 1, 1980; 2 children. R. Louis Skowyra III & Nicholas Skowyra. BA in Philosophy and Polit. Sci., Newton Coll. of Sacred Heart, 1973; JD, Boston Coll., 1976. Bar: Minn. 1976, Mass. 1977, U.S. Dist. Ct. Minn. 1976, U.S. Dist. Ct. Mass. 1980, U.S. Dis. Ct. ND 2000, U.S. Ct. Appeals (8th cir.) 1980, U.S. Supreme Ct. 1988; civil trial specialist, Minn. State Bar Assn. Spl. asst. atty. gen., St. Paul, 1976-77; assoc. Dorsey & Whitney LLP, Mpls., 1977-82, ptnr., litig. practice, 1983—88, mem. policy com., 1987—88, 2000—; judge Minn. Ct. Appeals, 1988—2000. Chmn. recruiting com. Dorsey & Whitney, Mpls., 1985-87. Trustee Boston Coll., 1985—, Visitation Convent, St. Paul, 1985-91, St. Thomas Acad., 2000—; bd. overseers Boston Coll. Law Sch., 1998—, U. Minn. Law Sch., 2001—. Named Minn. Super Lawyer, Minn. Law & Politics Mag., 2000—06, Women to Watch, Bus. Jour., 2005, Atty. of Yr., Minn. Lawyer, 2005; named one of 15 Top Attys. in Minn., Minn. Lawyers, 2005; recipient Corp. Woman of Achievement award, Nat. Assn. Women Bus. Owners, 2004. Mem. ABA, Mass. Bar Assn., Minn. Bar Assn., Hennepin County Bar Assn. (ethics com.), Ramsey County Bar Assn., Am. Arbitration Assn. (arbitrator). Club: Town and Country (St. paul), Mpls. Club (bd. govs.) Avocations: running, skiing. Office: Dorsey & Whitney LLP Ste 1500 50 S Sixth St Minneapolis MN 55402-1498 Office Phone: 612-340-2833. Office Fax: 612-340-2807. Business E-Mail: short.marianne@dorsey.com.

**SHORT, MARION PRISCILLA,** neurogenetics educator; b. Milford, Del., June 12, 1951; d. Raymond Calistus and Barbara Anne (Ferguson) S.; m. Michael Peter Klein; 1 child, Asher Calistus Klein. BA, Bryn Mawr Coll., 1973; diploma, U. Edinburgh, Scotland, 1975; MD, Med. Coll. Pa., 1978. Diplomate Am. Bd. Psychiatry and Neurology, Am. Bd. Internal Medicine. Intern in internal medicine Hahnemann Med. Coll. Hosp., Phila., 1978-79; med. resident in internal medicine St. Lukes-Roosevelt Hosp., N.Y.C., 1979-81; neurology resident U. Pitts. Health Ctr., 1981-84; fellow in med. genetics Mt. Sinai Med. Ctr., N.Y.C., 1984-86; fellow in neurology Mass. Gen. Hosp., Boston, 1986-90, asst. neurologist, 1990-95; asst. prof. dept. neurology Harvard Med. Sch., Boston, 1990-95; asst. prof. dept. neurology, pediat. and pathology U. Chgo., 1995—97; program dir. genetics, transplantation and clin. rsch. AMA, Chgo., 2002—; fellow McLean Ctr. for Clin. Med. Ethics U. Chgo., 2002—03, sr. fellow McLean Ctr. for Clin. Med. Ethics, 2003—04. Recipient Clin. Investigator Devel. award, NIH, 1988—93; fellow, Inst. Medicine, Chgo., 1999. Mem. AMA, Am. Acad. Neurology, Am. Soc. for Human Genetics, Am. Coll. Med. Genetics. Office: Pediat Neurosurgery U Chgo MC 4066 5481 S Maryland Ave Chicago IL 60637-4325 Office Phone: 773-702-2475. Business E-Mail: mpshort@surgery.bsd.uchicago.edu.

**SHORT, MARTIN,** actor, comedian, film critic; b. Hamilton, Ont, Canada, Mar. 26, 1950; s. Charles Patrick and Olive Short; m. Nancy Dolman, 1980; children: Katherine, Oliver, Henry. Degree in social work, McMaster U., 1972. Actor: (films) Three Amigos, 1986, Innerspace, 1987, Cross My Heart, 1987, Three Fugitives, 1989, The Big Picture, 1989, Pure Luck, 1991, Father of the Bride, 1991, Captain Ron, 1992, (voice) We're Back! A Dinosaur's Story, 1993, Clifford, 1994, (voice) The Pebble and the Penguin, 1995, Father of the Bride 2, 1995, Mars Attacks!, 1996, Jungle 2 Jungle, 1997, The Fairy Godmother, 1997, A Simple Wish, 1997, Mumford, 1998, Akbar's Adventure Tours, 1998, (voice) Prince of Egypt, 1998, Get Over It, 2001, (voice) Jimmy Neutron: Boy Genius, 2001, (voice) Treasure Planet, 2001, Cinemagique, 2002, (voice) Treasure Planet, 2002; (TV series) The Associates, 1979, I'm a Big Girl Now, 1980-81, SCTV Network 90, 1982-84 (Emmy award for Outstanding Writing 1983), Saturday Night Live, 1985-86, (voice) The Completely Mental Misadventures of Ed Grimley, 1988-89, The Martin Short Show, 1994, (miniseries) Merlin, 1998; (TV films) The Family Man, 1979, Sunset Limousine, 1983, Alice in Wonderland, 1999, Prince Charming, 2001; writer (TV films) Martin Short's Concert for the North Americas, 1985, I, Martin Short Goes Hollywood, 1989, (TV series) Second City TV, 1981, SCTV Network 90, 1981-82, SCTV Channel, 1983, Saturday Night Live, 1984-85; exec. prodr. (TV series) The Martin Short Show, 1994, 99 Primetime Glick, 2001-03; writer, prodr. (TV films) Martin Short Shorts, 2003; dir. (TV films) Friends of Gilda, 1993; actor, writer, prodr. (films) Jiminy Glick in La La Wood, 2004; also numerous revues and cabaret appearances with Second City comedy troupe; 1977-78, Broadway appearances include The Goodbye Girl, 1993, Little Me, 1999 (Tony award for Best Actor in a Musical); stage appearances Martin Short: Fame Becomes Me, 2006. Office: William Morris Agency care Ames Cushing 1 William Morris Pl Beverly Hills CA 90212-2775*

**SHORT, RAY EVERETT,** minister, sociologist, educator, writer; b. Coffeyville, Kans., Jan. 5, 1919; s. Franklin Marion and Jennie (Messersmith) S.; m. Jeannette Louise Stephens, June 12, 1954 (dec. Jan. 2000); children: Glenn Alan, Linda Louise, Kenneth Ray, Timothy Wesley, Karen Amy; 1 stepdau., Mary Jennings. AB, Willamette U., 1944; postgrad., U. Chgo., 1946; BD, Duke, 1948, PhD, 1961; postgrad., U. Idaho, 1950-51. Ordained to ministry Meth. Ch., 1946. Dir. Westminster Found., Duke, 1944-46; co-pastor Interracial Meth. Ch., Durham, NC, 1947; asst. prof. religion, dir. chapel programs Fla. So. Coll., Lakeland, 1947-48; exec. dir. Fla. br. United World Federalists, 1948-51; dir. Intermountain Region, 1953-54, Wesley Found., U. Idaho, 1950-51; exec. dir. Student YMCA-YWCA, U. Denver, 1951-53; pastor Fairmont Meth. Ch., Lockport, Ill., 1954-56; grad. asst. sociology Duke, 1956-57; assoc. prof. religion, head divsn. religion and philosophy, chaplain Tenn. Wesleyan Coll., 1957-60; assoc. prof. sociology and religion, head dept. sociology U. Dubuque, Iowa, 1960-65, acting chmn. div. social sci. Iowa, 1962-65; assoc. prof. sociology, head dept. sociology and anthropology U. Wis., Platteville, 1965-70, prof. sociology, 1966-87, prof. emeritus, 1987—; prof. sociology and anthropology Copenhagen Study Ctr. U. Wis., spring 1974, nat. lectr., 1975—. Chmn. Peace and World Order divsn. North Iowa Meth. Conf., 1963-69; rep. U.S. Jr. C. of C. in testimony before U.S. Senate Com. on Fgn. Rels., 1950, Advocating Ltd., Dem. Fed. World Govt.; Midwest region rep. Nat. Coun. World Federalist Assn., 1964-73, pres. Midwest region, 1967-69, chmn. nat. coun., 1971-72, nat. v.p., 1991—; (with wife) WFA dels. to NGO Forum and 4th UN Conf. on Women, Beijing, 1995; D.C. hdqrs. WFA property named Ray and Jennette Short Peacemakers Bldg., 1997 (Presdl. WFA award 1998, Nat. World Federalist of Month, June 2004); co-chmn. Grenville Clark Club; mem. spl. Wis. Conf. called with Pres.'s Comn. for Observance of 25th Anniversary of UN, 1970-87; mem. Wis. U. Meth. Bd. on Ch. and Soc., 1973-80, chmn. World Peace divsn., mem. exec.

com., 1975-80. Author: Sex, Love or Infatuation: How Can I Really Know?, 1978, on videocassette, 1987, 2d edit. (Augsburg Bestseller); 11 fgn. edits., Sex, Dating and Love: Questions Most Often Asked, 1984, 2d edit., 1994, Sex, Love or Romance: You Can't Really Trust Your Heart?, 2004; contbr. articles to profl. jours. Nat. bd. Am. Freedom Assn.; nat. v.p. Campaign for UN Reform, 1983—87, 1st v.p., 1989—2004, exec. com., 1997—; bd. dirs. Dubuque Salvation Army, 1961—65; dir., founder Wis. Ann. World Peace Study Program, 1975—; Dem. candidate for Wis. 3d Dist. Congl. Seat, 1970, 1972; del. Dist. and State Convs., 1969—87, state platform com., 1975—87. Recipient Pick a Profl. award, 2003; NSF grantee Anthropology Inst., Fairmont State Coll., W.Va., 1962 Fellow Am. Sociol. Assn.; mem. AAUP, Nat. Coun. on Family Rels., Fedn. Am. Scientists, Nat. United Meth. Men (mem. peace adv. task force 1990—). Home: 505 S Miller Ave Lafayette CO 80026-1545 Office Phone: 303-666-5025. Personal E-mail: rayjshort@aol.com. *Nuclear and chemical weapons, crises of environments. While my life has largely been spent helping others have a better future, I now know we have to help assure that they have a future at all by establishing limited democratic enforcible world law.*

**SHORTAL, TERENCE MICHAEL,** systems company executive; b. St. Louis, Oct. 13, 1937; s. Harold Leo and Catherine Margaret S.; m. Linda Margaret Elias, May 29, 1965; children: Jennifer, Bradley Alexander. BSEE, U. Mo., 1961; MS, U.S. Naval Postgrad. Sch., 1966; grad. program execs., Carnegie Mellon U., 1979. Commd. ensign USN, 1961; advanced through grades to capt., 1980; ret., 1981; asst. officer in charge Engring. Duty Officer Sch. Vallejo, Calif., 1974-77; ship engring. mgr. AEGIS shipbldg. project Naval Ea Sys. Command, Washington, 1977-79; tech. dir. DDGX project, 1979-81; sr. v.p., dir. Kastle Sys., LLC, 1981—. Trustee Cathedral Choral Soc., Washington, 1983-95, 97—, pres., 1986-88, 2000-2002; mem. vestry St. John's Episcopal Ch., McLean, Va., 1982-85; bd. dirs. Langley Sch., McLean, 1984-94, pres. 1986-88. Decorated Meritorious Svc. medal (2), Navy Commendation medal (2); recipient award of merit Cathedral Choral Soc., 1996. Mem. IEEE (br. award 1961), Am. Soc. Naval Engrs. (Flagship Sect. award 1979), Nat. Press Club (Washington), City Club, Gridiron Club (Washington), Sigma Xi, Phi Kappa Theta. Home: 858 Canal Dr Mc Lean VA 22102-1408 Office: 1501 Wilson Blvd Arlington VA 22209-2403 Personal E-mail: mshortal@cox.net. Business E-Mail: mike@kastle.com.

**SHORTELL, STEPHEN MICHAEL,** dean, health services researcher; b. New London, Wis., Nov. 9, 1944; BBA, U. Notre Dame, 1966; MPH, UCLA, 1968; MBA, U. Chgo., 1970, PhD in Behavioral Sci., 1972. Rsch. asst. Nat. Opinion Rsch. Ctr., 1969; instr., rsch. assoc. Ctr. Health Adminstrv. Studies, 1970—72; acting dir. grad. program hosp. adminstrn. U. Chgo., 1973—74, from asst. prof. to assoc. prof., 1974—79; prof. dept. health svc. Sch. Pub. Health and Cmty. Medicine, U. Wash., 1979—82; A.C. Buehler Disting. prof. health svc. mgmt. Northwestern U., Evanston, Ill., 1982—98; Blue Cross disting. prof. health policy and mgmt Sch. Pub. Health, U. Calif., Berkeley, 1998—; dean Sch. Pub. Health, U. Calif, Berkeley, 2002—. Cons. VA, Robert Wood Found., Henry Kaiser Found.; asst. prof. Health Svcs. Orgn. U. Chgo., 1972—74; adj. asst. prof. dept. sociology U. Wash., 1975—76, dir. doctoral program dept. health svcs. Sch. Pub. Health and Cmty. Medicine, 1976—78; prof. sociology dept. sociology Northwestern U., 1982, prof. preventive medicine Sch. Medicine. Contbr. numerous articles to profl. jours. Recipient Baxter prize, Baxter-Allegiance Found., 1995, Honorary AHA Lifetime Mem. award, Gold Medal award, Amer. Coll. of Healthcare Exec., 1998, Dist. Investigator award, Assoc. for Health Services Research, 1998, Best Paper award, Acad. of Mgmmt., 1996, George R. Terry Book of the Year award, 1990. Fellow: Am. Coll. Healthcare Execs. (Gold medal 1998); mem.: Inst. Med.-NAS. Office: Univ Calif Berkeley Sch Pub Health 407 Warren Hl Berkeley CA 94720-0001

**SHORTER, JAMES RUSSELL, JR.,** lawyer; b. NYC, June 10, 1946; s. James Russell and Helen (Ibert) S. AB, Columbia Coll., 1968; JD, Harvard U., 1975; LLM in Taxation, NYU, 1979. Bar: NY 1976, US Dist. Ct. (so. and ea. dists.) NY 1976, US Tax Ct. 1987. Assoc. Thacher Proffitt & Wood, NYC, 1975-84, ptnr., 1984—. Capt. USNR, 1968-98. Mem. ABA (tax, bus. law sect.), N.Y. State Bar Assn. (internat. law and practice sect.), Assn. Bar City N.Y., Internat. Fiscal Assn., Harvard Club (N.Y.C.), Down Town Assn. (N.Y.C.). Republican. Home: 345 E 80th St Apt 26C New York NY 10021-0671 Office: Thacher Proffitt & Wood LLP Two World Financial Ctr 28th Fl New York NY 10281 Office Phone: 212-912-7628. Business E-Mail: jshorter@tpwlaw.com.

**SHORTESS, EDWIN STEEVIN,** marketing consultant; b. Cedar Rapids, Iowa, Oct. 31, 1920; s. Edwin Stephen and Rita (Clemente) S.; m. Jane Elizabeth Gallagher, Dec. 27, 1941 (div. Apr. 1970); children: E. Stephen, Richard J., Mark Andrew, Cathy Shortess Pool; m. Mary Francis Kerns, May 28, 1970; children: Dana Menshing, Emil Bartsche, Roger Bartsche, Lisa Bartsche Coccia, Vincent Bartsche, Kirsten Bartsche Chirico. Student, North Iowa U., 1938-39; BSEE, Chgo. Tech. Coll., 1942. Engring. rsch. analyst Douglas Aircraft Corp., El segundo, Calif., 1942-44; liaison engr. Martin Aircraft Corp., Omaha, 1944-45; chief engr., dir. Burlington (Iowa) Instrument co., 1945-53; adminstrv. engr., dir. Hickok Elec. Instrument Co., Cleve., 1953-59, ea. sales mgr. Paramus, N.J., 1960-65; v.p., gen. mgr., dir. Wacline, Dayton, Ohio, 1959-60; v.p., gen. mgr. Colo. Hickok, Grand Junction, 1965-69; pres. Shortess Rawson & Assocs., Kenilworth, N.J., 1969-86, mktg. cons. Allenwood, NJ, 1986—2004. Bd. dirs. Federated Purchasers Inc., Kenilworth, N.J. Author: Design and Application of Electrical Industrial Instruments, l964. Mem.: Instrument Soc. Engrs. (sr.). Republican. Methodist. Avocations: golf, bridge. Home and Office: 123 Everest Dr S Brick NJ 08724-2027 E-mail: edwin.shortes@verizon.net.

**SHORTLIFFE, EDWARD HANCE,** internist, medical educator, computer scientist; b. Edmonton, Alta., Can., Aug. 28, 1947; s. Ernest Carl and Elizabeth Joan Shortliffe. AB, Harvard U., 1970; PhD, Stanford U., 1975, MD, 1976. Diplomate Am. Bd. Internal Medicine. Trainee NIH, 1971—76; intern Mass. Gen. Hosp., Boston, 1976—77; resident Stanford Hosp., Palo Alto, Calif., 1977—79; asst. prof. medicine Stanford U. Sch. Medicine, Palo Alto, 1979—85, assoc. prof., 1985—90, chief divsn. gen. internal medicine, 1988—95, prof., 1990—2000; assoc. chair medicine Primary Care, 1993—95; assoc. dean info. resources and tech. Stanford U. Sch. Medicine, 1995—2000; prof., chair dept. biomed. informatics Columbia U. Coll. Physicians and Surgeons, N.Y.C., 2000—, Rolf H. Scholdager prof. biomed. informatics, 2005—; deputy v.p. Info. Tech., Health Scis., Columbia U., N.Y.C., 2002—; bd. dirs. Medco Health Solutions, Inc. Advisor Nat. Bd. Med. Examiners, Phila., 1987—93; pres. Symposium on Computer Applications in Med. Care, Washington, 1988—89; mem. Nat. Fed. Networking Adv. Coun., NSF, 1991—93; mem. computer sci. and telecomm. bd. NRC, 1991—96; bd. regents ACP-Am. Soc. Internal Medicine, 1996—2002; mem. Pres.'s Info. Tech. Adv. Com., 1997—2002; chmn. com. on healthcare and next generation internet NRC, 1998—2000; mem. Nat. Com. on Vital Health Stats., 2000—03; trustee N.Y. Acad. Medicine, 2005—. Editor: Rule-Based Expert Systems, 1984, Readings in Medical Artificial Intelligence, 1984, Medical Informatics: Computer Applications in Health Care, 1990, Medical Informatics: Computer Applications in Health Care and Biomedicine, 2d edit., 2000, Biomedical Informatics, 2006. Mem. com. Soc. and Engring. Pub. Policy NAS, 2001—03, 2005—. Recipient Grace M. Hopper award, Assn. Computing Machinery, 1976, Young Investigator award, Western Soc. Clin. Investigation, 1987, Rsch. Career award, Nat. Libr. of Medicine, 1979—84; scholar, Kaiser Family Found., 1983—88. Fellow: Am. Coll. Med. Informatics (pres. 1992—94), Am. Assn. Artificial Intelligence; mem.: Am. Clin. and Climatol. Assn., Am. Assn. Physicians, Am. Med. Informatics Assn., Am. Soc. for Med. Decisionmaking (pres. 1989—90). Achievements include development of several medical computer programs including MYCIN and ONCOCIN. Avocations: skiing, jazz. Office: 180 Ft Washington Ave Hrkness Pavilion Ste 550 622 W 168th St New York NY 10032-3720 Office Phone: 212-305-6896. Business E-mail: shortliffe@dbmi.columbia.edu.

**SHORT-MAYFIELD, PATRICIA AHLENE,** business owner; b. Ft. Benning, Ga., Oct. 12, 1955; d. William Pressley and Ilse Marie (Hofmann) Short; m. Thomas Hicks Fort, June 2, 1973 (div. Jan. 1981); m. Michael Patrick Mayfield, Aug. 11, 1984; 1 child, William Zachary. Grad. HS, Butler, Ga. Notary pub., Ga. Staff mem. Fairyland Day Care, Canton, Ga., 1973-74, Small World Child Care, Thomaston, Ga., 1974-77; nurses aide Kenneston Hosp., Marietta, Ga., 1977-80; staff worker Mental Health Ctr., Smyrna, Ga., 1980-81; dir. Kiddie Kollege, Marietta, 1981-85; bus. owner, mgr. Spiffy Clean by Mayfield, Marietta, 1985—95; lead cashier Petsmart, Kennesaw, Ga., 1994—. Choir staff Eastside Bapt. Ch., Marietta, 1988-89; vol. East Valley Elem. Sch., 1989-95, chorus vol., 1994-95; vol. East Cobb Middle Sch., 1995-98; active Nat. Congress Parents and Tchrs., Cobb County Humane Soc., 1991—. Mem. NAFE, Cobb County C. of C., Atlanta Hith Mus. Art, Dog Lovers Am. Republican. Baptist. Avocations: reading, walking, symphony, art, bicycling. Office: Spiffy Clean By Mayfield 2791 Georgian Ter Marietta GA 30068-3625 Office Phone: 770-424-5226. Personal E-mail: pshortm7@comcast.net.

**SHORTZ, RICHARD ALAN,** lawyer; b. Chgo., Mar. 11, 1945; s. Lyle A. and Wilma Warner (Wildes) S.; m. Jennifer A. Harrell; children: Eric, Heidi. BS, Ind. U., 1967; JD, Harvard U., 1970. Bar: Calif. 1971, U.S. Supreme Ct. 1980. Assoc. Gibson, Dunn & Crutcher, L.A., 1970-73; sr. v.p., gen. counsel, sec. Tosco Corp., L.A., 1973-83; ptnr. Jones, Day, Reavis & Pogue, L.A., 1983-95, Rogers & Wells, L.A., 1995-97, Morgan Lewis & Bockius, L.A., 1997—. Mem. L.A. World Affairs Inst., 1983—, Town Hall L.A., 1983—. 2nd lt. U.S. Army, 1970—71. Mem.: Calif. Bar Assn., L.A. Bar Assn., ABA, Merion Golf Club (Ardmore, Pa.), Loch Lomond Golf Club (Scotland), L.A. Country Club, Beach Club (Santa Monica, Calif.), Calif. Club. Republican. Episcopalian. Home: 1343 Pavia Pl Pacific Palisades CA 90272-4047 Office: Morgan Lewis & Bockius 300 S Grand Ave Ste 2200 Los Angeles CA 90071-3132 Office Phone: 213-612-2526. Office Fax: 213-612-2501. Business E-Mail: rshortz@morganlewis.com.

**SHORTZ, WILL,** puzzle editor; b. Crawfordsville, Ind., Aug. 26, 1952; s. Lyle A. and Wilma Warner (Wildes) S. AB, Ind. U., 1974; JD, U. Va., 1977. Editor Penny Press, Stamford, Conn., 1977-78; assoc. editor Games Mag., N.Y.C., 1978-82, sr. editor, 1982-89, editor, 1989-93; crossword editor N.Y. Times, N.Y.C., 1993—. Founder, dir. Am. Crossword Puzzle Tournament, Stamford, Conn., 1978—, World Puzzle Championship, N.Y.C., 1992, Stamford, 2000; puzzlemaster Weekend Edit. Sunday, NPR, Washington, 1987—; U.S. team capt. Internat. Crossword Marathon, 1989-90, World Puzzle Championship, 1993-99; riddle writer Batman Forever, 1995; co-founder, chmn. World Puzzle Fedn., 1999-2004, treas. 2004-; puzzle contb. Reader's Digest, 2002-. Author: Brain Games, 1979, The American Quiz Book, 1979, Brain Games 2, 1980, The Bantam Great Masters Winning Crossword Puzzles, vol. 1-3, 1980, World Class Championship Crosswords, 1982, Brain Games 3, 1983, Games Mag. Book of Crossword Puzzles, 1985, American Championship Crosswords, 1990, Games Mag. Giant Book of Games, 1991, Will Shortz's Best Brain Busters, 1991, Games Mag. Best Pencil Puzzles, 1992, Brain Twisters from the First World Puzzle Championships, 1993, N.Y. Times Daily Crossword Puzzles, vol. 40-71, 1995—, The Puzzlemaster Presents, 1996, Will Shortz's Tournament Crosswords, 1997; NY Times Sunday Crossword Puzzles, vol. 24-29, 1998—, Will Shortz's Favorite Crossword Puzzles, 2002, The Puzzlemaster Presents, vol. 2, 2004, Will Shortz's Tournament Crosswords, vol. 2, 2005, Sudoku-100 Wordless Crossword Puzzles, vol. 1-3, 2005. Named Wordplay documentary subject, 2006. Mem. Am. Antiquarian Soc., Am. Cryptogram Assn., Authors Guild, Nat. Puzzlers' League (pres. 1977, 81, historian 1992—). Avocations: ping pong/table tennis, book collecting. Office: NY Times 229 W 43rd St New York NY 10036-3959 Office Phone: 212-556-7435.

**SHOSKY, JOHN EDWIN,** media consultant, speechwriter; b. Colorado Springs, Colo., Nov. 1, 1955; s. Alexander Matthew and Barbara Marie (Middlekamp) Shosky. BA in Polit. Sci., Colo. Coll., 1979; MA in Philosophy, U. Wyo., 1987; PhD in Philosophy, Am. U., 1992. Dep. dir. media and sports commns. White House Conf. for Drug Free Am., Washington, 1987—88; sr. policy analyst White House Office Pub. Affairs, 1988; cons. to sec. HHS, Washington, 1984—91, cons. to Surgeon Gen., 1991—92; cons. to office of nat. drug control policy Exec. Office of the Pres., Washington, 1992—93, cons. to sec. of edn., 2003—05; pres., sr. writer Roncalli Comm., 1991—. Speech writer for govt. ofcls., corp. execs., profl. athletes, congressmen, senators; lectr. in philosophy and internat. studies Am. U., 1987—, asst. prof. philosophy, 1996—97, asst. dir. honors program, 1999—2003; adj. prof. philosophy George Mason U., 1990—94; vis. sr. mem. Linacre Coll., Oxford, England, 1997—; vis. prof. Charles U., Prague, 1998; vis. scholar Ins. of Logic, Acad. Scis., Czech Republic, 1998; vis. fellow Acad. Scis., Czech Republic, 2002—04. Contbr. articles to profl. jours. and publs. Mem.: Mind Assn., Hume Soc., Am. Philos. Assn., Austrian Wittgenstein Soc., U. Wyo. Alumni Assn. Republican. Roman Catholic. Home: 1806 Rollins Dr Alexandria VA 22307-1613

**SHOSS, CYNTHIA RENÉE,** lawyer; b. Cape Girardeau, Mo., Nov. 29, 1950; d. Milton and Carol Jane (Duncan) S.; m. David Goodwin Watson, Apr. 13, 1986; 1 child, Lucy J. Watson. BA cum laude, Newcomb Coll., 1971; JD, Tulane U., 1974; LLM in Taxation, NYU, 1980. Bar: La. 1974, Mo. 1977, Ill. 1978, N.Y. 1990. Law clk. to assoc. and chief justices La. Supreme Ct., New Orleans, 1974-76; assoc. Stone, Pigman et al, New Orleans, 1976-77, Lewis & Rice, St. Louis, 1977-79, Curtis, Mallet-Prevost, et al, N.Y.C., 1980-82; ptnr. LeBoeuf, Lamb, Greene & MacRae, L.L.P., N.Y.C., 1982—; mng. ptnr. London office LeBoeuf, Lamb, Leiby & MacRae, 1987-89. Assoc. editor Tulane Law Rev., 1972-74; frequent speaker before profl. orgns. and assns. Contbr. articles to profl. jours. Mem. bd. overseers Sch. Risk Mgmt., Ins. and Actuarial Sci., St. John's U. Mem.: ABA, The Risk Found., Assn. Life Ins. Counsel (bd. govs.). Office: LeBoeuf Lamb Greene Et Al 125 W 55th St New York NY 10019-5369 Office Phone: 212-424-8129. Business E-Mail: cshoss@llgm.com.

**SHOSTAK, G. SETH,** astronomer, writer; b. Norfolk, Kans., July 20, 1943; s. Arnold A. and Bertha Shostak; m. Karen A. Claffey, Apr. 28, 1984. BA, Princeton U., NJ, 1965; PhD, Calif. Inst. of Tech., Pasadena, 1971. Sr. astronomer SETI Inst., Mountain View, Calif., 1991—. Chair SETI permanent study group Internat. Acad. of Astronautics, Paris, 2002—. Author: (book) Sharing the Universe, (textbook) Life in the Universe, (book) Cosmic Company. Mem. SpaceWorld, Mountain View, 2002—06. Recipient Klumpke-Roberts award, Astron. Soc. of the Pacific, 2004. Jewish. Home: 1372 Cuernavaca Cr Mountain View CA 94040 Office: SETI Institute 515 N Whisman Road Mountain View CA 94043 Office Phone: 650-960-4530. Office Fax: 650-961-7099. E-mail: seth@seti.org.

**SHOTTS, WAYNE J.,** nuclear scientist, federal agency administrator; b. Des Plaines, Ill., Mar. 20, 1945; s. Norman Russell Shotts and Winnifred Mae (Averill) Shotts Goeppinger; m. Melinda Maureen Antilla, June 24, 1967 (dec. Feb. 1975); children: Kenneth Wayne Shotts, Jeffrey Alan Shotts; m. Jacquelyn Francyle Willis, Aug. 11, 1979. BA in Physics, U. Calif., Santa Barbara, 1967; PhD, Cornell U., 1973. Rsch. physicist E.I. duPont deNemours & Co., Wilmington, Del., 1973-74; physicist U. Calif., Livermore, Calif., 1974—, Lawrence Livermore Nat. Lab., Livermore, 1974-79, group leader, thermonuclear design divsn., 1979-85, divsn leader, nuc. chemistry, 1985-86, divsn. leader, prompt diagnostics, 1986-88, prin. dep. assoc. dir., military applications, 1988-92, prin. dep. assoc. dir. def. and nuc. techs., 1992-95, assoc. dir. nonproliferation arms control/internat. security, 1995—2004, dep. dir. ops., 2004—06; ret., 2006. Sci. advisor Dept. Energy Office of Det. Programs; tech. advisor Nuclear Weapons Council Standing and Safety Com.; mem. Navy Steering Task Group. Recipient Ernest Orlando Lawrence Meml. award U.S. Dept. Energy, Washington, 1990. Mem. Am. Phys. Soc., Am. Assn. Advancement Sci. Office: Lawrence Livermore Nat Lab PO Box 808 Livermore CA 94551-0808

**SHOTWELL, MALCOLM GREEN,** minister; b. Brookneal, Va., Aug. 14, 1932; s. John Henry and Ada Mildred (Puckett) S.; m. LaVerne Brown, June 19, 1954; children: Donna (dec.), Paula. BA in Sociology, U. Richmond, 1954; MDiv, Colgate Rochester Div. Sch., 1957; D Ministry, Ea. Bapt. Theol. Sem., 1990; DD (hon.), Judson Coll., 1990. Ordained to ministry Am. Bapt. Ch. in U.S.A., 1957. Student asst. Greece Bapt. Ch., Rochester, NY, 1954-57; pastor 1st Bapt. Ch., Cuba, NY, 1957-62, sr. pastor Galesburg, Ill., 1962-71, Olean, NY, 1971-81; area minister Am. Bapt. Chs. of Pa. and Del., 1981-90; regional exec. minister Am. Bapt. Chs. of Great Rivers Region, Ill. and Mo., 1990-96; interim pastor First Bapt. Ch., Jacksonville, Ill., 2002, Galesburg, Ill., 2003, Decatur, Ill., 2005—06. Mem. Midwest Commn. on Ministry Am. Bapt. Chs. U.S.A., 1990—96, mem. task force for So. Bapt. Am. Bapt. Chs. Relationships, 1990—96; cons. for ch. growth and planning. Author: Creative Programs for the Church Year, 1986, Renewing the Baptist Principle of Associations, 1990; contbg. writer Baptists in the Balance, 1997; rschr., writer, performer: (dramatic monologue) Our Neighbors, the Lincolns: A Clergyman Remembers, 1999—. Trustee No. Bapt. Theol. Sem., Lombard, Ill., 1993-96; mem. gen. exec. coun., 1990-96, regional exec. ministers coun., 1997-00, chmn. presdl. search com., 1997-98; bd. dirs. Ctrl. Bapt. Theol. Sem., Kansas City, Kans., 1990-96, Old State Capitol Found., 2004-; sec. bd. dirs. Shurtleff Fund, Springfield, Ill., 1990-96; tchr., libr. Ctrl. Bapt. Ch., Springfield, 1997-05; mem. Hist. Commn. Am. Bapts. Ill. and Mo., 1998-02; retreat leader in stress mgmt., 1985—; conf., spkr., pulpit supply preacher Bapt. Ch.; mentor ILCS Elem. Sch., Old State Capital Reenactment of Lincoln-Douglas Debates, 1999-01, 03-05; tour guide Old State Capital, Springfield, 2003—, Abraham Lincoln Presdl. Libr. and Mus., 2005-. Recipient George Younge Biennal award The Am. Bapt. Hist. Soc., 2006; Walter Pope Binns fellow William Jewell Coll., 1995. Mem. Ministers Coun. Ill. and Mo., Coun. Ret. Execs., Abraham Lincoln Assn., Am. Bapt. Men of Ill. and Mo. (v.p., coord. disaster relief ministries).

**SHOUL, MELVIN I.,** retired surgeon; b. Newburyport, Mass., 1922; MD, Tufts U., 1947. Diplomate Am. Bd. Surgery. Intern Boston City Hosp., 1947-49, resident in surgery, 1949-52; chief gen. surgery Murphy Army Hosp., 1954—; pvt. practice surgery, 1954—94; clin. instr. surgery Harvard Med. Sch., 1954—94; ret., 1994. Contbr. articles to profl. jours. With U.S. Army, 1953—54, Korea. Fellow ACS; mem. AMA, Boston Surg. Soc. Personal E-mail: melvins@aol.com.

**SHOUN, ELLEN LLEWELLYN,** retired secondary school educator; b. Germantown, Pa., Sept. 8, 1925; d. William Thomas and Ella (Hall) Llewellyn; m. Glenn Harte Shoun, June 25, 1949; children: Mary Deborah, Paul L., Eleanor C., Peter G., Elizabeth A. AB in Chemistry, Oberlin Coll., 1947; MA in Sci. Edn., Western Mich. U., 1972. Cert. libr. (ltd. profl.) Mich., secondary sch. tchr. Mich. Jr. chemist Am. Cyanamid, Stamford, Conn., 1947-49; Charles M. Hall Chem. instr. Oberlin (Ohio) Coll., 1949-51; br. libr. Bronson (Mich.) Pub. Libr., 1966-67; math. and sci. tchr. Bronson H.S., 1967-79; crew leader 1980 U.S. Census, Branch County, Mich., 1980; bus. mgr. Dr. C.F. Cole's Dental Office, Sturgis, Mich., 1982; reference aide Br. Dist. Libr., Coldwater, Mich., 1982-99; ret., 1999. Co-founder Bronson HS Cmty. Recycling Group, 1972—79. Trustee Bronson Pub. Libr., 1968—82, Housing Commn., 1975—, Bronson Cmty. Found., 2003—; instr. CPR Cmty. health Ctr., Coldwater, Mich., 1978—80; cmty. chorus Cmty. Found., 1987—; chair refugee family com. Bronson United Meth. Ch., 1974—82, ch. choir, 1967—, sec. adminstrv. bd., 1984—86; bd. dirs., treas., mgr. Food Pantry, 5 Ch. Coop., Bronson, 1993—. Named Hon. Grand Marshal, Polish Festival Parade, Bronson, 2002; recipient Cmty. Vol. of Yr. award, Gleaner Life Ins. Soc., 2001. Mem.: Phi Beta Kappa. Democrat. Avocations: photography, knitting, Scrabble.

**SHOUP, CHARLES SAMUEL, JR.,** chemicals and materials executive; b. Nashville, Dec. 10, 1935; s. Charles Samuel and Leola Ruth (Turner) S.; m. Frances Carolyn DiCarlo, June 7, 1958 (dec. Apr. 1999); children: Mark Steven, Elizabeth Ann Shoup Kehoe, Margaret Carol Shoup Meyer; m. Sara Jo Denkmann, May 5, 2001. AB, Princeton U., 1957; MS, U. Tenn., 1961, PhD, 1962. Rsch. chemist Oak Ridge (Tenn.) Natl. Lab., 1962-67; mgr. special projects Union Carbide Corp., N.Y.C., 1967-68; mgr. planning and controls Bell and Howell Co., Lincolnwood, Ill., 1968; v.p. Bell and Howell Sch. Inc., Chgo., 1968-69; mgr. tech. planning Cabot Corp., Boston and Cambridge, Mass., 1969-70, dir. corp. rsch., Mass., 1970-73; gen. mgr. Aearo Corp., Boston and Cambridge, Mass., 1973-87; v.p., Indpls. Cabot Corp., Boston and Cambridge, Mass., 1984-87; pres. Alphaflex Ind. Inc., Indpls. 1987-88, bd. dirs., 1988, Cemkote Corp., Indpls., 1988-91. Chmn. bd. dirs. Blasterz Corp., Carmel, Ind., 1992-2001; mem. adv. bd. Technalysis, Inc., Indpls., 1996-99; bd. dirs. Exec. Svc. Corps, Indpls., 1993—2004, mem. exec. com., 1994-2003, vice chmn., sec., 1997-99, chmn. bd. dirs., 2001-03; mem. bd. visitors Coll. Arts and Scis., U. Tenn., Knoxville, 1994-2000, assoc. bd. visitors, 2000—; bd. dirs Nat. Exec. Svc. Corps, Inc., 2001-04. Contbr. articles to profl. jours. Treas. Oak Ridge Arts Ctr., 1965-67; pres. Sherborn Edn. Found., 1974-76; chmn. Met. Div. United Way, 1982; bd. trustees, Ind. Safety Equipment Assn. 1978-81. Fellow Am. Inst. Chemists; mem. AAAS, Am. Chem. Soc., Noise Control Products and Materials Assn. (trustee 1977-87, pres. 1982-84), Sigma Xi. Presbyterian. Home: 13045 Abraham Run Carmel IN 46033-8618

**SHOWALTER, BUCK (WILLIAM NATHANIEL SHOWALTER III),** major league baseball team manager; b. DeFuniak Springs, Fla., May 23, 1956; Student, Chipola Jr. Coll., Fla., Miss. State U. Player various minor league teams N.Y. Yankee orgn., 1977-83, minor league coach, 1984, minor league mgr., 1985-89; coach N.Y. Yankees, 1989—92, mgr., 1992-95, Ariz. Diamondbacks, 1998—2000, Texas Rangers, 2002—. Named N.Y.-Pa. League Mgr. of Yr., 1985, Eastern League Mgr. of Yr., 1989, Am. League Mgr. of Yr., 1994, Nat. League Mgr. of Yr., 2004 Office: Texas Rangers 1000 Ballpark Way #400 Arlington TX 76011

**SHOWALTER, DAVID SCOTT,** accounting executive; b. Harrisonburg, Va., May 23, 1953; s. Harold Marvin and Martha (Myers) Showalter; m. Elizabeth Allison, June 1, 1974; children: Braxton, Allison, Mason. AS, Ferrum Coll., 1973; BSBA, U. Richmond, 1975. CPA Ill., 1994, Mo., 1997, Wis., 1995, Ind., 1988, NJ, 2003, NY, 2004; cert. govt. fin. mgr. 1994. Asst. to nat. industry dir. KPMG, N.Y., 1981-84, asst. to vice-chmn., 1986-88, ptnr., 1986—, area ptnr. in charge, Indpls., 1993-96; nat. industry dir. state, local govts., Chgo., 1996-98; global mng. ptnr. Assurance & Adv. Svcs. Ctr., Montvale, NJ, 1998—2002, industry sector leader pub. sector, 2002—04, dept. profl. practice, risk mgmt., 2004—. Vis. prof. U. Ill.; vis. scholar Ind. U.; trustee KPMG Found., N.Y.C., co-founder Audit Com. Inst., co-founder Assurance Rsch. Inst.; spkr. in field. Editor: (newsletter) Govt Acct and Auditing Update. Pres, Indpls. Youth Hockey Assn., 1990—93; pres. coun. Boy Scouts Am., St. Charles, Ill., 1995—97, chmn. bd. dirs., 1997—98, bd. dirs., 1998—; mem. U.S. C. of C. Homeland Security Task Force; bd. dirs. Greater Indpls. Rep. Fin. Com., 1990—94; elder 1st Presbyn. Ch., Ramsey. Named Ky Col. State of Ky, 1986, Sagamore of Wabash for Serv to State of Ind 1990, D Scott Showalter Day named in his honor, City of Indianapolis, 1994; named one of Top 100 Most Influential in Acctg., Acctg. Today, 2001; recipient Silver Beaver Award, Boy Scouts Am. 1994, Dist Eagle Scout Award, 1998. Mem.: AICPA (mem. com.), Assn. Sch. Bus. Ofcls., Ill. CPA Soc., NJ CPA Soc., Am. Acctg. Assn (v.p. practice, auditing sect., vice chmn. profl. rels. com). Govt. Fin. Officers Assn. (mem. com.). Presbyterian. Avocations: camping, jogging, backpacking, stamps. Home: 14 Forest Ridge Rd Upper Saddle River NJ 07458 Office: KPMG LLP 757 Third Ave New York NY 10017 Office Phone: 212-909-5905. Business E-Mail: dsshowalter@kpmg.com.

**SHOWALTER, ELAINE,** humanities educator; b. Cambridge, Mass., Jan. 21, 1941; d. Paul and Violet (Rottenberg) Cottler; m. English Showalter, June 8, 1963; children: Vinca, Michael. BA, Bryn Mawr Coll., 1962; MA, Brandeis U., 1964; PhD in English, U. Calif., Davis, 1970; LittD (hon.), Rutgers U., 2001. Teaching asst. English U. Calif., 1964-66, from instr. to assoc. prof., 1967-78; prof. English Rutgers U., from 1978, Princeton (N.J.) U.,

1984—2003; Avalon Found. prof. humanities Princeton (N.J.) U., 1987—, prof. emeritus, 2003—. Vis. prof. English and women's studies U. Del., 1976-77; vis. prof. Sch. Criticism and Theory, Dartmouth Coll.; 1986; prof. Salzburg (Austria) Seminars, 1988; Clarendon lectr. Oxford (Eng.) U., 1989; vis. scholar Phi Beta Kappa, 1993-94; numerous radio and TV appearances. Author: A Literature of Their Own, 1977, The Female Malady, 1985, Sexual Anarchy, 1990, Sister's Choice, 1991, Hystories, 1997, Inventing Herself, 2001, Teaching Literature, 2002; co-author: Hysteria Beyond Freud, 1993; editor: These Modern Women, 1978, The New Feminist Criticism, 1985, Alternative Alcott, 1987, Speaking of Gender, 1989, Modern American Women Writers, 1991, Daughters of Decadence, 1993, Scribbling Women, 1997; also articles and revs. Recipient Howard Behrman humanities award Princeton U., 1989; faculty rsch. coun. fellow Rutgers U., 1972-73, Guggenheim fellow, 1977-78, Rockefeller humanities fellow, 1981-82, fellow NEH, 1988-89; Cotsen fellow Princeton U., 1998-2001; Mellon fellow, 2003—; Huntington fellow, 2004—. Mem. MLA (v.p. 1996-97, pres. 1998). Office: Princeton U Dept Of English Princeton NJ 08544-0001

**SHOWALTER, MARILYN GRACE**, trade association administrator, director; AB, Harvard U., 1972, JD, 1975. Bar: Wash. 1975. Dep. pros. atty. King County, Wash., 1975—81, counsel to gov., 1981—83; pvt. practice, 1985—89; counsel house appropriations com. Wash. State House of Reps., 1989—92, dep. chief clk., house counsel, 1992—93, chief clk., 1994—95; advisor to Gov. Gary Locke, 1997—99; chair Utilities and Transp. Com., Portland, Oreg., 1999—2005, exec. dir., 2005—. Office: Pub Power Coun 1500 NE Irving Ste 200 Portland OR 97232 Business E-Mail: mshowalter@ppcpdx.org.

**SHOWALTER, MARK ROBERT**, astronomer; b. Abington, Pa., Dec. 5, 1957; s. James Grove Showalter and Sandra Khuen-Kryk; life ptnr. Frank Yellin, June 10, 1990. PhD, Cornell U., Ithaca, N.Y., 1984. Prin. investigator SETI Inst., Mountain View, Calif., 2005—. Mgr. Rings Node, NASA's Planetary Data Sys., Mountain View, 1989—2006. Mem.: Am. Astron. Soc., Phi Beta Kappa. Achievements include discovery of outer gossamer ring of Jupiter; Pan, 18th moon of Saturn; Mab, 26th moon of Uranus; Cupid, 27th moon of Uranus; R/2003 U 1 and R/2003 U 2, outer rings of Uranus. Office: SETI Inst 515 N Whisman Rd Mountain View CA 94043 Office Phone: 650-810-0234. Business E-Mail: mshowalter@seti.org.

**SHOWALTER, SHIRLEY H.**, academic administrator; b. July 30, 1948; BA cum laude in English, Ea. Mennonite U., Harrisonburg, Va., 1970; MA in Am. civilization, U. Tex., Austin, 1974, PhD in Am. civilization, 1981. Tchr. English Harrisonburg (Va.) H.S., 1970—72; tchg. asst. English and Am. Studies depts. U. Tex., Austin, 1973—75, asst. instr. Am. Studies dept., 1976; dir. continuing edn. Goshen Coll., Ind., 1979—82, project dir. Title II tech. and liberal arts devel. grant, 1982—85, project dir. Consortium Advancement of Pvt. Higher Edn. grant, 1985—86, asst. to prof. English, 1967—, pres., 1997—. Coord. Humanities program Harrisonburg (Va.) H.S., 1970—72; co-dir. Study-Svc. Term in Haiti Goshen Coll., 1981—82; rsch. asst. Consortium Advancement of Pvt. Higher Edn., Washington, 1986—87, interim v.p., 1987; chair English dept. Goshen Coll., 1990—93; sr. fellow Lilly Fellows program in Humanities and Arts Valparaiso U., Ind., 1993—94; co-dir. Study-Svc. Term in Ivory Coast Goshen Coll., 1993; lectr. and spkr. in humanities. Contbr. chapters to books, articles to profl. jours. Bd. mem. South Bend Symphony Assn.; mem. blue ribbon adv. group Boys and Girls Club; vice chair and mem. Hist. Com. of Mennonite Ch., 1984—88; co-sponsor Kid's Club No. Va. Mennonite Ch., 1987—88; chair curriculum com. Sojourner's Sunday Sch. class Coll. Mennonite Ch., 1987—88, mem. constn. revision com., 1988—92, tchr. H.S. age class, 1988—91, mem. worship commn., 1994—96; bd. mem. Coun. Christian Coll. and U., 2000—, Ind. Colls. of Ind., 1999—, Lantz Ctr. Christian Vocations, Indpls., 1998—; dir. Coun. Ind. Colls., 1999—; bd. dir. Mennonite Mutual Aid Trust; dir. Elkhart County Cmty. Found. Recipient Tchg. Excellence and Campus Leadership award, Sears Roebuck Found., 1990, Faculty Rsch., Goshen Coll., 1990, Knight Presdl. Leadership award, John S. and James L. Knight Found., 1999, 1999; fellow, George H. Gallup Rsch. Inst., 1999—2000, Coolidge Fellow, Yale U., Assn. Religion in Intellectual Life, 1996; grantee Faculty Rsch., Goshen Coll., 1977, 1982, Summer Stipend, Lilly Endowment, 1991. Mem.: AAUW, Am. Studies Assn., Am. Assn. Higher Edn. (Goshen Coll. rep. Forum on Exemplary Tchg. 1992, bd. dir. 1992—96), No. Ind. Partnership for the Arts, Willa Cather Pioneer Mem., Ind. Hist. Soc., Ellen Glasgow Soc., Blue Sky Assoc. Office: VP Programs Fetzer Inst 9292 West KL Ave Kalamazoo MI 49004-9398

**SHOWEN, DONALD EUGENE, JR.**, music educator; b. Charles Town, W.Va., Oct. 22, 1974; s. Donald Eugene and Carrie Alberta Showen; m. Tara Jenea Penick-Showen, Dec. 15, 2001. BA, Shepherd Coll., Shepherdstown, 1997. Coord. percussion studies Hancock H.S., Hancock, Md., 1993—94, Williamsport H.S., Williamsport, Md., 1994—98; asst. band dir. Jefferson H.S., Shenandoah Junction, W.Va., 1998—99; grad. asst. U. Fla. Sch. of Music, Gainesville, Fla., 1999—2000; dir. bands Jefferson H.S., Shenandoah Junction, W.Va., 2000—. Bd. directors New Hopewell Dance Studio, Shenandoah Junction, W.Va., 2001—. Mem.: Music Educators Nat. Conf., Phi Mu Alpha Sinfonia Frat. (pres. 1993—95). D-Liberal. Achievements include Jefferson High Jazz band won National Championship in 1999 and was named best jazz band in the state in 1999, 2001 and 2002; Symphonic and jazz bands received first place in a national competition in Orlando, Florida. Avocations: golf, golf, golf. Office: Jefferson High School Band R1 1 Box 83 Shenandoah Junction WV 25442

**SHOWER, ROBERT WESLEY**, corporate financial executive; b. Harvey, Ill., Sept. 5, 1937; s. Glenn Wesley and Chrissle Irene (Ford) S.; m. D. Elaine Crawford, March 25, 2006; children from previous marriage: David Wesley, Lynece Marie. BS, U. Tulsa, 1960; P.MD, Harvard Business Sch., 1972. Sr. auditor Arthur Andersen & Co., Tulsa, 1960-64; with The Williams Cos., Tulsa, 1964-86, asst. v.p., 1968-69, v.p. adminstrn., 1969-71, v.p., treas., 1971, v.p. fin., 1971-73, sr. v.p. fin., 1973-77, exec. v.p. fin. and adminstrn., dir., 1977-86; mng. dir. Shearson, Lehman, Hutton, Dallas, 1986-90; v.p. fin. Ameriserv Food Co., Dallas, 1990-91; sr. v.p. fin., CFO Seagull Energy Co., Houston, 1992-94, exec. v.p., CFO, 1994-96. Mem. Okla. Soc. CPAs, Lambda Chi Alpha, Delta Sigma Pi. Home: 33641 N 79th Way Scottsdale AZ 85262 Fax: 480-575-1286. E-mail: roshower@aol.com.

**SHPYRKO, OLEG G.**, physicist; b. Kiev, Ukraine, Apr. 30, 1976; PhD, Harvard U., Cambridge, Mass., 1998—2004. Postdoctoral fellow Harvard U., 2004—05; disting. postdoctoral fellow Argonne Nat. Lab., Ill., 2005—. Contbr. articles to profl. jours. Mem.: Am. Phys. Soc. Office: Argonne Nat Lab 9700 Cass Ave Argonne IL 60559

**SHRACK, CHRISTOPHER GEORGE**, curator, educator; b. Wichita, Kans., June 17, 1949; s. George William and Phyllis Star Shrack; m. Marsha Carol Gates, Mar. 20, 1986; children: Samuel Cody, Chelsea Christine, Emma Leigh, Gates Kipp. BFA with hons., Wichita State U., Wichita, Kans., 1973; AS, Pratt C.C., Pratt, Kans., 1987; cert. in Tchg., Sterling Coll., Sterling, Kans., 1990. Cert. tchr. Kans. Bd. Edn., 2006, arborist Kans., 1978, housing inspector Kans., 1995, wastewater operator Kans. Dept. Health and Environ., 2004, potable water operator Kans. Dept. Health and Environ., 2004. Graphic design artist Pennypower Shopping News Mag., Wichita, Kans., 1971—74, CGI Assoc. of Local Gov't., Pratt, Kans., 1976—80; instr. art Pratt C.C., 1980—88, Stafford Pub. Schs., Kans., 1991—94; housing insp./crew leader Kans. Weatherization Program, Pratt, 1994—98; instr. art St. John and Hudson Pub. Schs., Kans., 2000—02; curator mus., educator Kans. Dept. Wildlife and Pks., 2003—. Presenter in field; spkr. in field. Photo exhibition, Kans. Dept. Wildlife and Pks., 2006; contbr. Active Pratt Tree Ctr., 2003—; leader Stephen Ministry, Pratt, 2006—. Sgt. nat. guard USAF, 1967—72. Named Tchr. of Yr., Stafford County Soil Conservation, 1992, 1994; recipient Outstanding Svc. award, Pratt C.C., 1990. Mem.: Kans. Dept.

Wildlife and Parks Employees Group. Meth. Avocations: photography, art. Home: 226 NE 90th St Iuka KS 67066-9541 Office: Kansas Department of Wildlife and Parks 512 SE 25th Ave Pratt KS 67124-8174 Business E-Mail: chriss@wp.state.ks.us.

**SHRADER, CHARLES REGINALD**, historian; b. Nashville, July 3, 1943; s. Reginald Woodrow and Freda Olene (Presley) S.; m. Carole Anne Analore, Aug. 17, 1963; children: Peter Reginald, Sheila Lynne Shrader Bixby. BA cum laude, Vanderbilt U., 1964; MA History, Columbia U., 1970, M Phil, 1974, PhD History, 1976; Grad., U.S. Army Command/Gen. Staff, Coll., 1978, U.S. Army War Coll., 1982, NATO Def. Coll., 1984. Commd. 2d lt. U.S. Army, 1964, advanced through grades to lt. col., ret., 1987; asst. prof. history U.S. Mil. Acad., 1971-74; instr. European Divsn. U. Md., Pirmasens and Landstuhl, Germany, 1974-77; instr. U.S. Army Command and Gen. Staff Coll., 1977-80, U.S. Army War Coll., 1980-84; mem. staff NATO Def. Coll., Rome, 1984-85; independent historian, 1987—; exec. dir. Soc. for Mil. History, Carlisle, Pa., 1992-2000. Pres. Nat. Coalition Ind. Scholars, 2000-2002; adj. instr. Elizabethtown Coll., 1988-89, Penn State U.-Harrisburg, 1988-90; lectr. various Army vet. schs., CIA, U. Kans., U. Victoria/B.C., NATO Def. Coll. Mem. Carlisle Mcpl. Authority, 1993-2003, Carlisle Zoning Hearing Bd, 2005-. Mem. Army and Navy Club, Phi Kappa Psi, Phi Beta Kappa. Roman Catholic. Home and Office: 910 Forbes Rd Carlisle PA 17013-1721 Office Phone: 717-249-5625. E-mail: heriger@earthlink.net.

**SHRADER, RALPH W.**, management consultant; BEE, U. Pa.; MSEE minor in Math. and Nuc. Physics, U. Ill., PhD in Elec. Engring. Former pres. worldwide tech. divsn. Booz Allen & Hamilton, Mc Lean, Va., chmn., chmn., CEO, 1999—. Former chmn. bd. Armed Forces Comms. and Electronics Assn., mem. exec. com. Bd. dir. Wolf Trap Found. Nat. Park for Performing Arts, Abilities, Inc.; adv. coun. Character Edn. Partnership; chmn. bd. The Neediest Kids, Inc.; corp. chmn. Light the Night Walks, Washington, 2004; bd. dir. Abilities, Inc., ServiceSource, Va. Recipient David Sarnoff award, Armed Forces Comms. and Electronics Assn., Cmty. Leadership award, Northern Va. Cmty. Found., 2001. Office: Booz Allen & Hamilton Inc 8283 Greensboro Dr Mc Lean VA 22102

**SHRADER-FRECHETTE, KRISTIN**, science educator; m. Maurice Frechette; 2 children. B in Math. summa cum laude, Xavier U., 1967; PhD in Philosophy, U. Notre Dame, 1972. O'Neill Family prof. philosophy, concurrent prof. biol. sci. U. Notre Dame. Mem. exec. com. adv. bd. EPA, chair com. bioethics; prin. investigator grants NSF, Nat. Endowment for the Humanities, Coun. Philosophical Studies, U.S. Dept. Energy. Author: (books) Nuclear Power and Public Policy, 1983, Environmental Ethics, 1991, Four Methodological Assumptions in Cost Benefit Analysis, 1983, Science, Policy, Ethics, and Economic Methodology, 1984, Risk Analysis and Scientific Method, 1985, Nuclear Energy and Ethics, 1991, Risk and Rationality, 1991, Policy for Land: Law and Ethics, 1992, Burying Uncertainty: Risk and the Case Against Geological Disposal of Nuclear Waste, 1993, Method in Ecology, 1993, The Ethics of Scientific Research, 1994, Technology and Human Values, 1996, Environmental Justice: Creating Equality, Reclaiming Democracy, 2002; assoc. editor: Bioscience, editor-in-chief: Oxford U. Press monograph series Environ. Ethics and Sci. Policy, mem. editl. bd.: 18 profl. jours.; contbr. over 300 articles to profl jours. including Ethics, Jour. Philosophy, Philosophy of Sci., Synthese, Trends in Ecology Revolution, others. Fellow, Woodrow Wilson Found., NSF, Carnegie Found. Mem.: NAS (bd. dirs. environ. studies and toxicology, com. risk characterization, com. zinc-cadmium-sulfide dispersions), Internat. Soc. Environ. Ethics (past pres.), Risk Assessment and Policy Assn. (past pres.), Soc. Philosophy and Tech. (past pres.), Philosophy Sci. Assn., Am. Philosophical Assn. Office: Dept Philosophy and Dept Biol Scis 100 Malloy Hall Univ Notre Dame Notre Dame IN 46556 Business E-Mail: kristin.shrader-frechette.1@nd.edu.

**SHRANK, WILLIAM H.**, physician, researcher; b. N.Y. Md. Cornell U., N.Y., N.Y., 1998. Assoc. physician Med. Sch. Harvard U., Boston, 2005—; assoc. physician Brigham and Women's Hosp., Boston, 2005—.

**SHRAUNER, BARBARA WAYNE ABRAHAM**, electrical engineer, educator; b. Morristown, N.J., June 21, 1934; d. Leonard Gladstone and Ruth Elizabeth (Thrasher) Abraham; m. James Ely Shrauner, 1965; children: Elizabeth Ann, Jay Arthur. BA cum laude, U. Colo., 1956; AM, Harvard U., 1957, PhD, 1962. Postdoc. mrschr. Free U. Brussels, 1962-64, NASA-Ames Rsch. Ctr., Moffett Field, Calif., 1964-65; asst. prof. Washington U., St. Louis, 1966-69, assoc. prof., 1969-77, prof., 1977—2003, sr. prof., 2003—. Sabbatical Los Alamos (N.Mex.) Sci. Lab., 1975-76, Lawrence Berkeley Lab., Berkeley, Calif., 1985-86; cons. Los Alamos Nat. Lab., 1979, 84, NASA, Washington, 1980, Naval Surface Weapons Lab., Silver Spring, Md., 1984. Contbr. articles on transport in semiconductors, hidden symmetries of differential equations, plasma physics to profl. jours. Fellow Am. Phys. Soc. (sr. divsn. plasma physics, exec. com. 1980-82, 96-98); mem. IEEE (sr.; sr. exec. com. of standing tech. com. on plasma sci. and applications 1996-98), AAUP (local sec.-treas. 1980-82), Am. Geophys. Union, Phi Beta Kappa, Sigma Xi, Eta Kappa Nu, Sigma Pi Sigma. Home: 7452 Stratford Ave Saint Louis MO 63130-4044 Office: Washington U Dept Elec and Systems Engring 1 Brookings Dr Saint Louis MO 63130-4899 Office Phone: 314-935-6134. Business E-Mail: bas@wustl.edu.

**SHREEVE, JEAN'NE MARIE**, chemist, educator; b. Deer Lodge, Mont., July 2, 1933; d. Charles William and Maryfrances (Briggeman) Shreeve. BA in Chemistry, U. Mont., 1953, DSc (hon.), 1982; MS in Analytical Chemistry, U. Minn., 1956; PhD in Inorganic Chemistry, U. Wash., 1961. From asst. prof. to assoc. prof. chemistry U. Idaho, Moscow, 1961—67, prof., 1967—73, 2000—, acting chmn. dept. chemistry, 1969-70, 1973, head dept. and prof., 1973-87, v.p. rsch. and grad. studies, prof. chemistry, 1987-99, Jean'ne M. Shreeve chemistry prof., 2004—. Mem. nat. com. Stds. Higher Edn., 1965—67, 1969—73; Lucy W. Pickett lectr. Mt. Holyoke Coll., 1976; George H. Cady lectr. U. Wash., 1993; chmn. com. nat. medal sci. Pres. U.S., 2003—. Mem. editl. bd. Jour. Fluorine Chemistry, 1970—, Jour. Heteroatom Chemistry, 1988—95, Accounts Chem. Rsch., 1973—75, Inorganic Synthesis, 1976—; contbr. articles to sci. jours. Mem. bd. govs. Argonne (Ill.) Nat. Lab., 1992—98. Named Hon. Alumnus, U. Idaho, 1972; named to Idaho Hall of Fame, 2001; recipient Disting. Alumni award, U. Mont., 1970, Outstanding Achievement award, U. Minn., 1975, Sr. U.S. Scientist award, Alexander Von Humboldt Found., 1978, Excellence in Tchg. award, Chem. Mfrs. Assn., 1980; NSF Postdoctoral fellow, U. Cambridge, Eng., 1967—68, U.S. Hon. Ramsay fellow, 1967—68, Alfred P. Sloan fellow, 1970—72. Mem.: AAUW (officer Moscow chpt. 1962—69), AAAS (bd. dirs. 1991—95), Idaho Acad. Sci. (Disting. Scientist 2001), Am. Chem. Soc. (bd. dirs. 1985—93, chmn. fluorine divsn. 1979—81, mem. nat. bd. Petroleum Rsch. Fund 1975—77, mem. women chemists com. 1972—77, Harry and Carol Mosher award Santa Clara Valley sect. 1992, Shirley B. Radding award Santa Clara Valley sect. 2003, Garvan medal 1972, award for creative work in fluorine chemistry 1978), Göttingen (Germany) Acad. Scis. (corr.), Phi Beta Kappa. Avocations: fishing, gardening. Office: U Idaho Dept Chemistry Moscow ID 83844-2343 Fax: 208-885-9146. Office Phone: 208-885-6215. Business E-Mail: jshreeve@uidaho.edu.

**SHREM, CHARLES JOSEPH**, metals corporation executive; b. Cairo, May 9, 1930; arrived in U.S., 1959; s. Joseph C. and Paula (Cadranel) S.; m. Vivian L. Chalom, Jan. 30, 1955; children: Jeff, Leslie Allen. Degree in bus. and economy, Coll. Français, Cairo, 1951. Export mgr. Stanton Ironworks U.K., Middle East, 1950-57; comml. mgr. Soc. Sovibor, Paris, 1957-59; purchasing dir. Montanore, Inc., N.Y.C., 1959-65; exec. v.p. Commonwealth Metal Corp., Englewood Cliffs, NJ, 1965-85, pres., CEO, 1985-2000, chmn., 2000—02; bus. cons. Pompton Plains, NJ, 2002—. Bd. dirs. Adult Edn., Pequannock, N.J., 1970-80; chmn. bd. govs. Internat. Grad. U. Washington. Mem. U.S.C. of C. (econ. coun., exec. com. U.S. Polish Coun./U.S. C. of C.). Office: 933 Rte 23 Pompton Plains NJ 07444 Office Phone: 973-831-0111. E-mail: charles.shrem@verizon.net.

**SHREMBEK, CAROL ROSE**, claims consultant; b. Cleve., Oct. 27, 1957; d. Richard and Mary Rita Elchesen; m. David Edward Shrembek; 1 child, Nicole. BA, Kent State U., 1981; diploma in nursing, MetroHealth Sch. Nursing, Cleve., 1986. Cert. ACLS, legal nurse cons.; RN. Staff nurse Rainbow Babies and Childrens Hosp., Cleve., 1987—91, MetroHealth Med. Ctr., Cleve., 1986—87, 1991—93; asst. clin. mgr. Fairview Gen. Hosp., Fairview Park, Ohio, 1992—93; staff nurse S.W. Gen. Health Ctr., Middleburg Heights, 1993—96, StarMed Staffing Svcs., Independence, Ohio, 1996—98, Initial Health Care Svcs., Beachwood, Ohio, 1996—98; clin. nurse MetroHealth Med. Ctr., Cleve., 1998—2002; staff nurse MedSearch Staffing Svcs., Inc., Middleburg Heights, Ohio, 2002—04; St. John Westshore Hosp., Westlake, Ohio, 2003—; injury claim trainer State Farm, 2004—. Tchr. orientation classes Rainbow Babies and Childrens Hosp., Cleve., 1987—91, clin. preceptor, 1988—91; flight team MetroHealth Med. Ctr. Neonatal ICU, Cleve., 1991—93, clin. preceptor; workshop leader, spkr., cons. in field. Author: (novels) Cheri's Crossing, 2000, A Love Through Time, 2001. Roman Catholic. Avocations: gardening, reading, weightlifting. Personal E-mail: cshrembek@alltel.net.

**SHRENSKY, DON STEVEN**, accountant, consultant; b. Jersey City, N.J., Jan. 30, 1944; arrived in Israel, 1981; m. Joan L. Berman, Nov. 25, 1967; 2 children. BA, Rutgers State U., 1967; JD, Seton Hall U. Law Sch., 1971. Bar: N.J. 1972; CPA, N.Y., Israel. Ptnr. Gross, Manford & Reinschreiber, N.Y.C., 1970-81; chief acct. Mennen Medical Ltd., Rohovot, Israel, 1982-88; ptnr. Feldman Shrensky Brody & Co., Jerusalem, Israel, 1988-96; propr. Don Shrensky & Co., Jerusalem, 1997—. Speaker at conf., local groups and radio/TV. Treas. Assn. of Americans and Canadians in Israel, 1994-98, v.p., 1998-99; chmn. bd. Mercaz Harmony, 1985-95. Mem. AICPA, Inst. of CPAs in Israel, N.Y. Soc. CPAs, Assn. Ams. and Canadians in Israel, Jerusalem Rotary Club (bd. dirs. pres. 2003-2004), Jerusalem Rotary Found. (bd. dirs.). Office: Don Shrensky & Co PO Box 31570 Jerusalem 91001 Israel Office Phone: 972-2-6294272. E-mail: don@dscpa-israel.com.

**SHRESTHA, ANIL**, ecologist; s. Chain Krishna and Anjali Devi Shrestha; m. Reeta Shrestha, Nov. 25, 1987; 1 child, Arwin. MS, Cornell U., Ithaca, NY, 1993; PhD, Mich. State U., East Lansing, 1996. Rsch. assoc. U. Guelph, Ontario, Canada, 1997—2002; weed ecologist U. Calif., IPM Program, Parlier, 2002—. Editor: Cropping Systems: Trends and Advances. Fellow, Fulbright-Hays, 1991—93, C. S. Mott Found., 1993—96. Mem.: Am. Soc. Agronomy (assoc.), Weed Sci. Soc. Am. (assoc.). Office Phone: 559-646-6534.

**SHREVE, GENE RUSSELL**, law educator; b. San Diego, Aug. 6, 1943; s. Ronald D. and Hazel (Shepherd) S.; m. Marguerite Russell, May 26, 1973. AB with honors, U. Okla., 1965; LLB, Harvard U., 1968, LLM, 1975. Bar: Mass. 1969, Vt. 1981. Appellate atty. and state extradition hearing examiner Office of Mass. Atty Gen., 1968-69; law clk. U.S. Dist. Ct., Dallas, 1969-70; staff and supervising atty. Boston Legal Assistance Project, 1970-73; assoc. prof. Vt. Law Sch., Royalton, 1975-81; vis. assoc. prof. George Washington U., Washington, 1983-83; assoc. prof. law N.Y. Law Sch., N.Y.C., 1983-84, prof., 1984-87; vis. prof. law Ind. U., Bloomington, 1986, prof., 1987-94, Richard S. Melvin Prof. Law, 1994—. Author: A Conflict of Laws Anthology, 1997; co-author: Understanding Civil Procedure, 2d edit., 1994; mem. editl. bd. Am. Jour. Comparative Law, 1994-2003, Jour. Legal Edn., 1998-2001; contbr. numerous articles to legal jours. Mem. Am. Law Inst., Am. Soc. for Pol. and Legal Phil., Assn. Am. Law Schs. (civil procedure sect. chair 1997, conflict of laws sect. chair 1998). Democrat. Episcopalian. Office: Ind U Sch Law Bloomington IN 47405 Office Phone: 812-855-4230.

**SHREVE, SUSAN RICHARDS**, writer, educator; b. Toledo, May 2, 1939; d. Robert Kenneth and Helen (Greene) Richards; children— Porter, Elizabeth, Caleb, Kate. BA, U. Pa., 1961; MA, U. Va., 1969. Prof. English lit. George Mason U., Fairfax, Va., 1976—. Vis. prof. Columbia U., NYC, 1982—, Princeton U., 1991-93 Author: (novels) A Fortunate Madness, 1974, A Woman Like That, 1977, Children of Power, 1979, Miracle Play, 1981, Dreaming of Heroes, 1984, Queen of Hearts, 1986, A Country of Strangers, 1989, Daughters of the New World, 1992, The Train Home, 1993, Skin Deep: Women & Race, 1995, The Visiting Physician, 1995; (pseudonym Annie Waters) Glimmer, 1997, Plum & Jaggers, 2000, A Student of Living Things, 2006; (children's books) The Nightmares of Geranium Street, 1977, Family Secrets, 1979, Loveletters, 1979, The Masquerade, 1980, The Bad Dreams of a Good Girl, 1981, The Revolution of Mary Leary, 1982, The Flunking of Joshua T. Bates, 1984, How I Saved the World on Purpose, 1985, Lucy Forever and Miss Rosetree, Shrinks, Inc., 1985, Joshua T. Bates In Charge, 1992, The Gift of the Girl Who Couldn't Hear, 1991, Wait for Me, 1992, Amy Dunn Quits School, 1993, Lucy Forever & the Stolen Baby, 1994, The Formerly Great Alexander Family, 1995, Zoe and Columbo, 1995, Warts, 1996, A Goalie, 1996, Joshua Bates in Trouble Again, 1997, Jonah, The Whale, 1997, Ghost Cats, 1999, The End of Amanda, The Good, 2000, Blister, 2002, Trout & Me, 2003, Under the Watson's Porch, 2004; editor: Dream Me Home Safely, 2003; co-editor: How We Want to Live: Narratives on Progress, 1996, (with Porter Shreve) Outside the Law: Narratives on Justice, 1997, How We Want to Live: Narratives on Progress, 1998, Tales Out of School: Narratives on Education, 1999, Blister, 2001, Trout & Me, 2002, Under the Watson's Porch, 2003. Recipient Jenny Moore award George Washington U., 1978; John Simon Guggenheim award in fiction, 1980, Nat. Endowment Arts fiction award, 1982 Mem. PEN/Faulkner Found. (pres.), Phi Beta Kappa. Office Phone: 703-993-1338. Personal E-mail: srshreve@aol.com.

**SHRIBMAN, DAVID MARKS**, editor; b. Salem, Mass., Mar. 2, 1954; m. Cindy Skrzycki, Sept. 9, 1978; children: Elizabeth, Natalie. AB summa cum laude, Dartmouth Coll., 1976; AM, 1993; LHD, Salem State Coll., 1995. Mem. city staff and Washington bur. Buffalo Evening News, 1977-80; mem. feature and nat. staff The Washington Star, 1980-81; with Washington bur. N.Y. Times, 1981-84; congl. reporter, nat. polit. corr. The Wall St. Jour., 1984-93; chief Washington bur., asst. mng. editor The Boston Globe, 1993—2003; exec. editor, v.p. Pitts. Post-Gazette, 2003—. Bd. visitors Nelson A. Rockefeller Ctr. for Social Scis. Dartmouth Coll.; panelist Washington Week in Rev. PBS; analyst BBC radio; lectr. in field. Trustee Dartmouth Coll. James B. Reynolds scholar Jesus Coll.; recipient Pulitzer Prize for beat reporting, 1995. Mem. Phi Beta Kappa. Office: Pittsburgh Post Gazette 34 Blvd of the Allies Pittsburgh PA 15222

**SHRIER, ADAM LOUIS**, investment company executive, consultant; b. Warsaw, Mar. 26, 1938; came to U.S., 1943, naturalized, 1949; s. Henry Leon and Mathilda June (Czamanska) S.; m. Diane Kesler, June 10, 1961; children: Jonathan, Lydia, Catherine, David. BS, Columbia U., 1959; MS (Whitney fellow), MIT, 1960; D. Engr. and Applied Sci. NSF fellow, Yale U., 1965; postdoctoral fellow U. Cambridge, Eng., 1965—66; JD, Fordham U., 1976. With Esso Rsch. & Engring. Co., Florham Park and Linden, NJ, 1963—65, 1966—72, head. environ. scis. rsch. area, 1969—72; coord. pollution abatement activities, tanker dept. Exxon Internat. Co., N.Y.C., 1972—74; project mgr., energy sys. Exxon Enterprises Inc., N.Y.C., 1974—75, gen. mgr. solar energy projects, 1975—77, pres. solar thermal sys. divsn., 1977—81; corp. planning cons., sec. new bus. investments Exxon Corp., N.Y.C., 1981—82; divsn. mgr. supply and transp. Exxon Internat. Co., N.Y.C., 1983—86, mgr. policy and planning, 1986—88; mng. dir. Spltty. Tech. Assocs., Washington, 1988—97; pres. Global Devel. Opportunities, LLC, Washington, 1997—. Adj. lectr. chem. engring. Columbia U., NYC, 1967-69, adj. prof. internat. and pub. affairs, 2005—; industry adv. bd. Internat. Energy Agy., 1984-88, Energy and Environ. Policy Ctr., Harvard U., 1986-88, Internat. Energy Program, Johns Hopkins U., 1987-88; sr. assoc. Global Bus. Forum, 1988—, Cambridge Energy Rsch. Assocs., 1988—. Internat. Exec. Svc. Corps, 2001—, Citizens Devel. Corps, 2001—; adj. prof. internat. bus. U. Washington, 2000—. Contbr. articles to profl. jours. Mem. AIChE, Internat. Assn. Energy Econs., Am. Chem. Soc., U.S. Energy Assn., Mid. East Inst., Acad. Internat. Bus., Cosmos Club, Sigma Xi, Tau Beta Pi, Phi Lambda Upsilon. Achievements include patents in field. Office: 4000 Cathedral Ave NW Washington DC 20016-5249 Personal E-mail: alshrier@verizon.net.

**SHRIER, STEFAN,** mathematician, educator; b. Mexico City, Nov. 7, 1942; s. Henry Leon Shrier and Mathilda June Czamanska; m. Helaine G. Elderkin, 1985. BS in Engring., Columbia U., 1964, MS in Ops. Rsch., 1966; PhD in Applied Math., Brown U., 1977. Chmn. computer sci. program Wellesley (Mass.) Coll., 1972-75; sr. engr. Booz, Allen and Hamilton, Bethesda, Md., 1977-79; dir. Latin Am. ops. SofTech, Inc., Springfield, Va., 1979-80; mem. rsch. staff Systems Planning Corp., Arlington, Va., 1980-83; tech. dir. Grumman-CTEC, Inc. subs. Grumman Data Systems, Inc. (absorbed by Grumman Data Systems, Inc. Jan. 1988), McLean, Va., 1983-85, dir. Lab. Machine Intelligence and Correlation, 1984-87, dir. R & D, 1985-87; asst. dir. tech. dept. Grumman Data Systems, Inc., McLean, Va., 1988-90, dep. dir. tech. dept. Washington ops., 1990-91; mem. tech. staff MRJ, Inc., Fairfax, Va., 1991-95, program mgr., 1995-96; program dir. Crystal City Ops., 1997; chief scientist SeiCorp, Inc., Springfield, Va., 1997-98; mgr. Informatics ERIM Internat., Inc., Arlington, 1998; mgr. informatics ERIM Internat., Inc. subs. Veridian, Chantilly, Va., 1998—2000; founder, CEO Informetrics LLC, Alexandria, Va., 2000—. Professorial lectr. statistics George Washington U., 1981-84, adj. prof. stats., 1984-85; adj. prof. computer sci. George Mason U., 1985-87; sec. New Eng. Regional Computing Program, Cambridge, Mass., 1973-75. Contbr. articles to profl. jours. Fellow Washington Acad. Sci.; mem. Sigma Xi, Tau Beta Pi. Office: Informetrics LLC PO Box 19139 Alexandria VA 22320-0139

**SHRINER, THOMAS L., JR.,** lawyer; b. Lafayette, Ind., Dec. 15, 1947; s. Thomas L. Sr. and Margaret (Kamstra); m. Donna L. Galchick, June 5, 1971; children: Thomas L. III, John H., Joseph P., James A. AB, Ind. U., 1969, JD, 1972. Bar: Wis. 1972, U.S. Dist. Ct. (ea. dist.) Wis. 1973, U.S. Dist. Ct. (we. dist.) Wis. 1977, U.S. Dist. Ct. Colo. 2005, U.S. Ct. Appeals (7th cir.) 1972, U.S. Ct. Appeals (8th cir.) 1989, U.S. Ct. Appeals (fed. cir.) 1990, U.S. Supreme Ct. 1978. Law clk to Hon. John S. Hastings U.S. Ct. Appeals (7th cir.), Chgo., 1972-73; assoc. Foley & Lardner, Milw., 1973-79, ptnr., 1979—. Adj. prof. Law Sch. Marquette U., Milw., 2005—. Chmn. bd. trustees Cath. Charities of Archdiocese of Milw., 2001—02. Fellow Am. Coll. Trial Lawyers; mem. 7th Cir. Bar Assn. (pres. 1993-94), Phi Beta Kappa. Republican. Roman Catholic. Office: Foley & Lardner LLP 777 E Wisconsin Ave Ste 3800 Milwaukee WI 53202-5306 Office Phone: 414-297-5601. Business E-Mail: tshriner@foley.com.

**SHRINSKY, JASON LEE,** lawyer; b. Pitts., June 15, 1937; s. Abe and Sylvia S.; children: Jeffrey, Steven, Stacy. BA, U. Pitts., 1959; JD, George Washington U., 1962. Sr. ptnr. Shrinsky, Weitzman & Eisen, Washington, DC, 1971-87; ptnr., chair Telecom. Dept. Kaye, Scholer LLP, Washington, DC, 1987—, mem. exec. com., 1998. Panelist Paul Kagan Seminars on Radio and TV Acquisitions, Inst. Soc. Internat. Rsch.; atty.-advisor Complaints and Compliance Div. Broadcast Bur. FCC, Washington, 1961-64; bd. dirs. U.S. Com. Sports for Israel, Phila., FCC Bar Assn. Contbr. articles to Radio and Records mag., Broadcast Cable Fin. Jour. Prsdl. Presdl. del. Mt. Sinai transfer ceremonies, 1978; U.S. basketball chmn. 12th, 13th and 14th Maccabiah games, Israel; bd. dirs. Washington Hebrew Congregation, 1978-85, Spanish Broadcasting Sys., Inc.; mem. adv. bd. Bi-Wak Digital Music, Inc. Mem. Internat. Radio and TV Soc., Nat. Broadcaster's Club (past pres.), U. Pitts. Alumni Assn. (bd. dirs.). Jewish. Office: Kaye Scholer LLP McPherson Building 901 15th St NW, Ste 1100 Washington DC 20005-2327 Office Phone: 202-682-3500. E-mail: jshrinsky@kayescholer.com.

**SHRIRAM, K. RAM,** investment company executive; married; 2 children. BS, U. Madras, India. Mem. exec. team Netscape; pres. Junglee; v.p. bus. devel. Amazon.com, 1998—99; mng. ptnr. Sherpalo Ventures, 2000—. Bd. mem. Google, Inc., 1998—, 247customer.com, Plaxo, Zazzle.com, PodShow, Bus. Signatures. Named one of 400 Richest Americans, Forbes, 2006.*

**SHRIVASTAVA, AJAY,** biologist, researcher; s. Manmohan Shrivastava and Rama; m. Anju Bhatnagar, June 10, 1994; 1 child, Rachel. PhD, Columbia U., 1994. Assoc. rsch. scientist Yale U., New Haven, 1998—2000; rsch. investigator Bracco Rsch. USA, Princeton, NJ, 2000—. Project mgr. Bracco Rsch. USA, 2003—06. Contbr. papers to profl. jours. and pubs. Fellowship, Columbia U., 1989. Achievements include patents for HAPs against receptor tyrosine kinase; new assay to screen target for tyrosine kinase receptors; research in c-Myc binds YY-1. Home: 58 Magnolia Ln Princeton NJ 08540 Office: Bracco Rsch USA 305 College Rd E Princeton NJ 08540 Office Phone: 609-514-2508. Home Fax: 609-514-2588; Office Fax: 609-514-2588. Personal E-mail: biopro2@yahoo.com. Business E-Mail: ajay.shrivastava@bru.bracco.com.

**SHRIVER, DONALD WOODS, JR.,** theologian, educator; b. Norfolk, Va., Dec. 20, 1927; s. Donald Woods and Gladys (Roberts) S.; m. Peggy Ann Leu, Aug. 9, 1953; children: Gregory Bruce, Lionel, Timothy Donald. BA, Davidson Coll., 1951; BD, Union Theol. Sem. Va., 1955; MST, Yale U., 1957; PhD, Harvard U., 1963; LHD (hon.), Curtis Coll., 1970; DD (hon.), Wagner Coll., 1978, Southwestern Coll., Memphis, 1983; LHD (hon.), Davidson Coll., 1984, Union Theol. Sem. Am., 1991, Jewish Theol. Sem., 1993; DD, DD, Colgate U., 1996. Ordained to ministry Presbyn. Ch., 1955. Pastor Linwood Presbyn. Ch., Gastonia, NC, 1956-59; univ. min., prof. religion NC State U., Raleigh, 1963-72, dir. univ. program on sci. and soc., 1968-72; prof. ethics and soc. Emory U., Atlanta, 1972-75; William E. Dodge prof. applied Christianity Union Theol. Sem., NYC, 1975-96, pres. faculty, 1975-96. Adj. prof. bus. ethics Sch. Bus. Adminstrn., Columbia U., prof. ethics Sch. Internat. Affairs, 1995-98; sr. fellow freedom forum Sch. Journalism, Columbia U., 1992-93; adj. prof. ethics, 1994—; lectr. Duke U., Va. State U., Ga. State U., numerous colls. and univs. in Can., Kenya, India, Japan and Korea. Author: How Do You Do and Why: An Introduction of Christian Ethics for Young People, 1966, Rich Man Poor Man: Christian Ethics for Modern Man Series, 1972, (with Dean D. Knudsen and John R. Earle) Spindles and Spires: A Restudy of Religion and Social Change in Gastonia, 1976, (with Karl A. Ostrom) Is There Hope for the City?, 1977, The Social Ethics of the City's Prayer, 1980, The Gospel, The Church, and Social Change, 1980, The Lord's Prayer: A Way of Life, 1983, An Ethic for Enemies: Forgiveness in Politics, 1995; co-author: Redeeming the City, 1982, Beyond Success: Corporations and Their Critics in the Nineties, 1991; editor: The Unsilent South, 1965, Medicine and Religion: Strategies of Care, 1979, Honest Patriots: Loving a Country Enough to Remember Its Misdeeds, 2005. Dir. Urban Policy Study NC State U., 1971-73; precinct chmn. Dem. Party, Raleigh, del. to nat. conv., 1968; mem. Mayor's Com. on Human Rels., Raleigh, 1967-71; chmn. Urban Policy Seminar, Ctr. for Theology and Pub. Policy, 1978-82. Served with Signal Corps U.S. Army, 1946-47. Recipient The Union medal, Union Theol. Sem., 1991; Rockefeller Doctoral fellow Harvard U., 1963; Kent fellow in religion, 1959; fellow Am. Acad. in Berlin, 1999. Mem. Am. Soc. Christian Ethics (pres. 1979-80), Soc. for Values in Higher Edn., Soc. for Health and Human Values, Soc. for Sci. Study of Religion, AAAS, Am. Sociol. Assn., Am. Soc. Engring. Edn. (chmn. liberal arts divsn. 1972-73), United Christian Youth Movement of Nat. Coun. of Chs. (nat. chmn. 1951-53), Coun. on Fgn. Rels. Home and Office: 440 Riverside Dr Apt 58 New York NY 10027-6830 Office Phone: 212-222-5112. Personal E-mail: dwshriver@aol.com. *Modern people need to recover connections between memory and hope. The past we applaud pre-enacts the future we hope for, and the past we deplore forms our obligation, in the present, to make a different future. In a time when young people find it hard to envision a long human future, the connections of history and ethics are indispensable. The forging of such connections is my vocation as an educator.*

**SHRIVER, EUNICE MARY KENNEDY (MRS. ROBERT SARGENT SHRIVER JR.),** foundation administrator, volunteer, social worker; b. Brookline, Mass., July 10, 1920; d. Joseph P. and Rose (Fitzgerald) Kennedy; m. Robert Sargent Shriver, Jr., May 23, 1953; children: Robert Sargent III, Maria Owings Shriver Schwarzenegger, Timothy Perry, Mark Kennedy, Anthony Paul Kennedy. BS in Sociology, Stanford U., Palo Alto, Calif., 1943; student, Manhattanville Coll. of Sacred Heart, LHD (hon.), 1963, D'Youville Coll., 1962, Regis Coll., 1963, Newton Coll., 1973, Brescia Coll., 1974, Holy Cross Coll., 1979, Princeton U., 1979, Boston Coll., 1990; LittD (hon.), U. Santa Clara, 1962, Yale U., 1996, Cardinal Stritch U., 2002. With spl. war problems div. State Dept. Washington, 1943—46; sec. Nat. Conf. on Prevention and Control juvenile Delinquency, Dept. of Justice, Washington, 1947-48; social worker Fed. Penitentiary for Women, Alderson, W.Va., 1950, House of Good Shepherd & Juvenile Court, Chgo., 1951-54; exec. v.p. Joseph P. Kennedy, Jr. Found., 1956—; regional chmn. women's div. Community Fund-Red Cross Joint Appeal, Chgo., 1958; founder, CEO Spl. Olympics, 1968—90, founder, hon. chmn., 1990—. Cons. to Pres. John F. Kennedy's Panel on Mental Retardation, 1961; founder Community & Caring, Inc., 1981; mem. Chgo. Common. on Youth Welfare, 1959-62; mem. bd. Special Olympics Internat. Editor: A Community of Caring, 1982, 85, Growing Up Caring, 1990. Co-chmn. women's com. Dem. Nat. Conv., Chgo., 1956. Decorated Legion of Honor; recipient Albert Lasker Pub. Svc. award, Lasker Found., 1966, Philip Murray-William Green award (with Sargent Shriver), AFL-CIO, 1966, Humanitarian award A.A.M.D., 1973, Nat. Svc. Service award, 1973, Phila. Civic Ballet award, 1973, Prix de la Couronne Française, 1974, Presdl. Medal of Freedom, 1984, Freedom From Want medal, Roosevelt Inst., 1993, Jewish Sports Hall of Fame Humanitarium award, 2000, Champion of Children award, Phoenix Found. for Children, 2000, Aetna Voice of Conscience award, 2002, Juanita Kreps award, 2002, Life award, Noel Found., 2002, Theodore Roosevelt award, NCAA, 2002; inducted into Nat. Women's Hall of Fame, 2002; appeared on Special Olympics World Summer Games silver commemorative coin, 1995.

**SHRIVER, LIONEL (MARGARET ANN SHRIVER),** writer; b. Gastonia, NC, May 18, 1957; married. BA, Barnard Coll., 1978; MFA in Fiction Writing, Columbia Univ., 1982. Author: (novels) The Female of the Species, 1987, Checker & the Derailleurs, 1988, The Bleeding Heart, 1990, Game Control, 1995, A Perfectly Good Family, 1996, Double Fault, 1997, We Need to Talk about Kevin, 2003 (Orange Prize for fiction, Great Britain, 2005); contbr. articles Wall St. Jour., Economist, Phila. Enquirer. Mailing: c/o Author Mail Counterpoint Press 387 Park Ave S New York NY 10016*

**SHRIVER, MARIA OWINGS,** news correspondent; b. Chgo., Nov. 6, 1955; d. Robert Sargent and Eunice Mary (Kennedy) S.; m. Arnold Schwarzenegger, Apr. 26, 1986; children: Katherine, Christina, Patrick & Christopher. BA, Georgetown U. Coll. Am. Studies, Washington, 1977. News producer Sta. KYW-TV, 1977-78; producer Sta. WJZ-TV, 1978-80; nat. reporter PM Mag., 1981-83; news reporter CBS News, Los Angeles, 1983-85; news correspondent, co-anchor CBS Morning News, N.Y.C., 1985-86; co-host Sunday Today, NBC, 1987-90; anchor Main Street, NBC, 1987; co-anchor Yesterday, Today, and Tomorrow, NBC, 1989; anchor NBC Nightly News Weekend Edition, 1989-90, Cutting Edge with Maria Shriver, NBC, 1990, First Person with Maria Shriver, NBC, 1990—2004; First Lady of Calif., 2003—. Co-anchor summer olympics, Seoul, Korea, 1988; substitute anchor NBC News at Sunrise, Today, NBC Nightly News with Tom Brokaw; contbg. anchor Dateline, NBC, 1995-2004. Appeared in Last Action Hero, 1993; correspondent TV series The American Parade, 1984; prod: (TV Series) Portrait of a Legend, 1981; author What's Heaven, 1999, Ten Things I Wish I'd Known Before I Went Into the Real World, 2000, What's Wrong With Timmy, 2001, What's Happening to Grandpa?, 2003, And One More Thing Before You Go..., 2005 (Publishers Weekly bestseller list). Recipient Christopher award for "Fatal Addictions", 1990, Exceptional Merit Media award Nat. Women's Political Caucus, first-place Commendation award Am. Women in Radio and TV, 1991, Emmy nomination, George Peabody Award, 1998. Democrat. Roman Catholic. Office: First Lady Maria Shriver State Capitol Bldg Sacramento CA 95814-4906

**SHRIVER, PAMELA H.,** retired professional tennis player, sports analyst; b. Balt., July 4, 1962; m. Joseph Shapiro, 1998. Profl. tennis player, 1979—; winner 21 career singles, 112 career doubles titles 21 career singles, 92 career doubles titles; winner 7 Australian Opens (with Martina Navratilova), 4 French Opens (with Navratilova), 5 Wimbledons (with Navratilova), 6 U.S. Opens, French Open mixed doubles (with Emilio Sanchez); analyst, commentator HBO, NBC, CBS, ABC, BBC, ESPN; part-owner Balt. Orioles baseball team; pres. Women's Sports Legends. Mem. U.S. Fedn. Cup Team, 1986, 87, 89, U.S. Wightman Cup Team, 1978-81, 83, 85, 87; co-winner 1998 Wimbledon 35 and Over Doubles title; mem. President's Coun. on Phys. Fitness and Sports, 1986-92; mem. Md. Fitness Commn.; v.p. Internat. Tennis Hall of Fame. Active ann. charity tennis exhbn. through Balt. Cmty. Found., also trustee; trustee McDonogh Sch.; hon. chmn. Balt. Tennis Patrons. Recipient Gold medal 1988 Olympic Games in doubles (with Zina Garrison), Player Who Makes a Difference award Family Circle mag., 1996. Mem. U.S. Tennis Assn. (bd. dirs. 1997—), Women's Tennis Assn. (pres. 1991-94, Corel Trou David Gray Svc. award 1998), Tour Players Assn.

**SHRIVER, PHILLIP RAYMOND,** academic administrator; b. Cleve., Aug. 16, 1922; s. Raymond Scott and Corinna Ruth (Smith) S.; m. Martha Damaris Nye, Apr. 15, 1944; children: Carolyn (Mrs. William Shaul), Susan (Mrs. Lester LaVine), Melinda (Mrs. David Williams), Darcy, Raymond Scott II. BA, Yale U., 1943; MA, Harvard U., 1946; PhD, Columbia U., 1954; LittD, U. Cin., 1966; LLD, Heidelberg Coll., 1966, Eastern Mich., 1972, Ohio State U., 1973; DH, McKendree Coll., 1973; DPS, Albion Coll., 1974; LHD, Central State U., 1976, No. Ky. State U., 1980, Miami U., 1984, U. Akron, 1988. Mem. faculty Kent (Ohio) State U., 1947-65, prof. Am. history, 1960-65; dean Coll. Arts and Scis., 1963-65; pres. Miami U., Oxford, Ohio, 1965-81, pres. emeritus, prof. Am. history, 1981-94. Pres. Ohio Coll. Assn., 1974-75; chmn. coun. pres.'s Mid-Am. Conf., 1971-77; chmn. Ohio Bicentennial Commn. for NW Ordinance and U.S. Constn., 1985-89, Ohio Tuition Trust Authority, 1989-92; chmn. coun. pres.'s Nat. Assn. State Univs. and Land Grant Colls., 1975-76, mem. exec. coun., 1976-78. Author: The Years of Youth, 1960, George A. Bowman: The Biography of an Educator, 1963, (with D.J. Breen) Ohio's Military Prisons of the Civil War, 1964, A Tour to New Connecticut in 1811: The Narrative of Henry Leavitt Ellsworth, 1985, Miami University: A Personal History, 1998, (with C.E. Wunderlin Jr.) The Documentary Heritage of Ohio, 2000, (with E.F. Puff) The History of Presbyterianism in Oxford, Ohio, 2000. Bd. dirs. Cin. Ctr. Sci. and Industry, 1965-70; trustee Ohio Coll. Library Center, 1968-74; chmn. bd. Univ. Regional Broadcasting, 1975-76, 78-79. Served to lt. (j.g.) USNR, 1943-46, PTO. Decorated Order of Merit (Grand Duchy of Luxembourg); recipient Disting. Acad. Svc. award AAUP, 1965, Gov.'s award 1969, A.K. Morris award, 1974, Ohioana Career medal, 1987, Converse award, 1990, award of merit Am. Assn. for State and Local History, 1993, Bjornson award Ohio Humanities Coun., 2001, John E. Dolibois History prize, 2003, Statesman award Cin. (Ohio) Soc. Assn. Execs., 2004. Mem. Orgn. Am. Historians, Ohio Acad. History (pres. 1983-84, Disting. Svc. award 1991), Archaeol. Inst. Am., Ohio Hist. Soc. (trustee 1982-91, v.p. 1983-84, pres. 1984-86), Ohio Humanities Council (Bjornson award 2001), Am. Studies Assn., Mortar Board, Phi Beta Kappa, Omicron Delta Kappa, Phi Alpha Theta, Alpha Kappa Psi, Kappa Delta Pi, Phi Eta Sigma, Phi Kappa Phi, Kappa Kappa Psi, Alpha Lambda Delta, Beta Gamma Sigma, Sigma Delta Pi, Alpha Phi Omega, Delta Upsilon (Disting. Alumni Achievement award 1985) Clubs: Rotary. Presbyterian. Home: 5115 Bonham Rd Oxford OH 45056-1428 Office: Miami U Oxford OH 45056 E-mail: shriverp@muohio.edu.

**SHRIVER, SARGENT (ROBERT SARGENT SHRIVER JR.),** lawyer; b. Westminster, Md., Nov. 9, 1915; s. Robert Sargent and Hilda Shriver; m. Eunice Mary Kennedy, May 23, 1953; children: Robert Sargent III, Maria Owings, Timothy Perry, Mark Kennedy, Anthony Paul Kennedy. Student, Canterbury Sch.; BA cum laude, Yale U., 1938, LLB, 1941; LLD, St. Procopius Coll., 1959, Notre Dame U., DePaul U., Seton Hall Coll., 1961, St. Louis U., Kansas State U., Brandeis U., 1962, St. Michael's Coll., Vt., Fordham U., Boston Coll., Yale U., Duquesne U., N.Y.U., Wesleyan U.; DCL, U. Liberia, 1963; HHD, Salem Coll., 1963, Bowling Green State U.; LHD, Springfield Coll., Mass., 1963, U. Scranton, Providence Coll.; D in Polit. Sci., Chulalongkorn U., Bangkok, Thailand, The Am. U. of Paris, 2002. Bar: N.Y. 1941, Ill. 1959, U.S. Supreme Ct. 1969, D.C. 1971. With Winthrop, Stimson, Putnam & Roberts, 1940—41; asst. editor Newsweek, 1945—46; assoc. Joseph P. Kennedy Enterprises, 1947—48; asst. gen. mgr. Merchandise Mart, Chgo., 1948—61; dir. Peace Corps, Washington, 1961—66, Office Econ. Opportunity, Washington, 1964—68; spl. asst. to the Pres. The White House, Washington, 1965—68; U.S. amb. to France US Dept. State, Paris, 1968—70; sr. ptnr. Fried, Frank, Harris, Shriver & Jacobson, N.Y.C., Washington, L.A., London, Eng., 1971—86, of counsel, 1986—; pres. Spl. Olympics, Washington, 1986—90, CEO, 1990—96, chmn. bd. dirs., 1990—2003, chmn. emeritus, 2003—. Mem. Am. Com. on East-West Accord, 1978—, Ams. for SALT, 1979—. Author: Point of the Lance, 1964. Pres. Chgo. Bd. Edn., 1955—60; mem.-at-large Nat. Coun. Boy Scouts Am.; chmn. Internat. Orgn. Patrons on Israel Mus., 1972—75; bd. dirs. The Arms Control Assn., 1983—; Dem. candidate for v.p., 1972; ran for Dem. presdl. election, 1976; pres. Cath. Interracial Coun. Chgo., 1955—60. Lt. comdr. USNR, 1940—45. Named Lay Churchman of Yr. Religious Heritage Am., 1963; named to the Order of the Smile, 1989; recipient Vet. of the Year award, 1956, Yale U. medal, 1957, Chgo. medal of merit, 1957, James H. Hooey award, Cath. Conf. for Interracial Justice Coun. N.Y., 1958, Golden Heart Presdl. award, Philippines, 1964, Nat. Father of the Year award, 1964, Notre Dame Patriotism award, 1965, Nat. Brotherhood award, 1966, Laetare medal, U. Notre Dame, 1968, Hannah G. Solomon award, Nat. Coun. of Jewish Woman, 1972, Franklin D. Roosevelt Freedom from Want award, 1993, Presdl. Medal of Freedom, 1994, Equal Justice award, Nat. Ctr. on Poverty Law, 1999, William O. Douglas award, Pub. Counsel Law Ctr., 1999, Disting. Am. award, John F. Kennedy Library & Found., 2001, Lifetime Achievement award, Am. Law mag., 2005. Mem.: Chgo. Coun. Fgn. Rels. (dir.), Yale U. Law Sch. Assn. (exec. com., James J. Hooey award N.Y. chpt. 1958), Navy League (life), Yale Club (N.Y.C.), Onwentsia Club (Lake Forest, Ill.), Execs. Club (Chgo.), Econ. Club, Serra Club, Racquet Club, Delta Kappa Epsilon. Roman Catholic. Achievements include extensive world travel to visit Peace Corps projects, 1961-1966.

**SHRIVER, TIMOTHY PERRY,** sports association executive; b. Aug. 29, 1959; s. Robert Sargent Shriver and Eunice Mary Kennedy; m. Linda Potter Shriver; 5 children. BS, Yale U.; M in Religion and Religious Edn., Cath. U.; DEd, U. Conn.; D (hon.), New Eng. Coll, Albertus Magnus Coll., Loyola U. Balt. Tchr. New Haven Pub. Schs., New Haven; supr. Pub. Schs. Social Devel. Project, New Haven, 1987—96; pres. Spl. Olympics, Inc., Washington, DC, 1996—2003, pres., CEO, chmn., 2003—05, chmn., 2005—. Co-prodr.(film): Amistad, 1997, The Loretta Claiborne Story, 2000. Bd. dirs. Compact for Learning and Citizenship, Frank Porter Child Devel. Ctr. at U. N.C.; co-chair Am.'s Promise Task Force on Youth Svcs., 1997—; chmn. Collaborative for Advancement of Social and Emotional Learning at U. Ill., 1994—; bd. dirs. John F. Kennedy Libr. Found., Boston. Recipient Medal of City of Athens, Order de Manuel Amador Guerrera, Pres. of Panama, Conn. Citizen of Yr.; fellow Yale Child Study Ctrs. Sch. Devel. Program, 1984. Mem.: Am. Assn. on Mental Retardation (bd. mem.). Office: Special Olympics 1133 19th St, NW Washington DC 20036 Office Phone: 202-628-3630. Office Fax: 202-824-0200.

**SHRIVER, WILLIAM RUSSELL,** secondary school educator; b. Garfield Heights, Ohio, Aug. 15, 1950; s. William Washington and Olive Elizabeth (Doutt) S.; m. Karen Ann Wolfe, June 20, 1987; children: Lauren, Matthew. BA, Coll. of Wooster, 1972; MA, U. Chgo., 1973; postgrad., Cleve. State U., 1973-74. Nat. bd. cert. tchr. soc. studies 2002. Summer staff Philmont Scout Ranch, Cimarron, N.Mex., 1968-76; tchr. Mt. Vernon (Ohio) Sr. H.S., 1974—; tchr. Kenyon Acad. Partnership Kenyon Coll./Mt. Vernon Sr. H.S., 1983—; vice chair state tchr. edn. cert. adv. commn. Ohio Bd. Edn., Columbus, 1991-99, state tchr. cert. standards revision com., 1992-95; bd. examiners Nat. Coun. Accreditation of Tchr. Edn., Washington, 1993-02; mem. Ohio Gov.'s Commn. on Tchg. Success, 2001-03; mem. Ohio Educators Stds. Bd., 2004-2008, chair, 2004-2006. Bd. of session First Presbyn. Ch., Mt. Vernon, 1980-87, 89-95, 2001—2007. Mem. NEA (assembly del. 1983-99), Ohio Edn. Assn. (exec. com. 1987-93, 96-2002), North Ctrl. Ohio Edn. Assn. (pres. 1984-85, exec. sec. 1993-2004), Mt. Vernon Edn. Assn. (pres. 1976-78). Avocations: photography, genealogy. Office: Mt Vernon HS 300 Martinsburg Rd Mount Vernon OH 43050-4246 Business E-Mail: wshriver@mt-vernon.k12.oh.us.

**SHROPSHIRE, DONALD GRAY,** hospital executive; b. Winston-Salem, NC, Aug. 6, 1927; s. John Lee and Bess L. (Shouse) S.; m. Mary Ruth Bodenheimer, Aug. 19, 1950; children: Melanie Shropshire David, John Devin. BS, U. N.C., 1950; Erickson fellow postgrad., U. Chgo., 1958-59; LLD (hon.), U. Ariz., 1992; EdD (hon.), Tucson U., 1994. Personnel asst. Nat. Biscuit Co., Atlanta, 1950-52, asst. personnel mgr. Chgo., 1952-54; adminstr. Eastern State Hosp., Lexington, Ky., 1954-62; assoc. dir. U. Md. Hosp., Balt., 1962-67; adminstr. Tucson Med. Ctr., 1967-82, pres., 1982-92, pres. emeritus, 1992—; pres. Tucson Hosps. Med. Edn. Program, 1970-71, sec., 1971-86; pres. So. Ariz. Hosp. Council, 1968-69; bd. dirs. Blue Cross, 1967-76, chmn. provider standards com., 1972-76; chmn. Healthways Inc., 1985-92. Mem. bd. La Posada at Park Centre, Inc., Green Valley, Ariz., 1996-2000, chmn. bd., 1996-99, mem. emeritus, 2000—. Bd. dirs. Health Planning Coun. Tucson, mem. exec. com., 1969-74; chmn. profl. divsn. United Way, Tucson, 1969-70, vice chmn. campaign, 1988, Ariz. Health Facilities Authority, bd. dirs., 1992-2005; chmn. dietary svcs. com., vice chmn., 1988, Md. Hosp. Coun., 1966-67; bd. dirs. Ky. Hosp. Assn., 1961-62, chmn. coun. profl. practice, 1960-61; past pres. Blue Grass Hosp. Coun.; trustee Assn. Western Hosps., 1974-81, pres., 1979-80; mem. accreditation coun. for Continuing Med. Edn., 1982-87, chair, 1986; bd. govs. Pima C.C., 1970-76, sec., 1973-74, chmn., 1975-76, bd. dirs. Found., 1978-82, Ariz. Bd. Regents, 1982-90, sec., 1983-86, pres., 1987-88; mem. Tucson Airport Authority, 1987—, bd. dirs., 1990-95, pres., 1995; v.p. Tucson Econ. Devel. Corp., 1977-82; founder, dir., bd. dirs. Vol. Hosps. Am., 1977-88, treas., 1979-82; mem. Ariz. Adv. Health Coun. Dirs., 1976-78; bd. dirs. Tucson Tomorrow, 1983-87, Tucson Downtown Devel. Corp., 1988-95, Rincon Inst., 1992-97, Sonoran Inst., 1992-97, Pima County Med. Res. Corps, 2006—; dir. Mus. No. Ariz., 1988-2002, dir. emeritus, 2002—; nat. bd. advisors Eller Coll. Mgmt. U. Ariz., 1990—, mem. Dean's Bd. Coll. Fine Arts, 1992—, chmn., 1992-96. pres. Ariz. Coun. Econ. Edn., 1993-95; vis. panel Sch. Health Adminstrn. and Policy Ariz. State U., 1990-92; bd. dirs. Cmty. Found. So. Ariz., 1996-2001; mem. adv. bd. Steele Meml. Rsch. Ctr., U. Ariz. Coll. Medicine, 1996-2004. Named to Hon. Order Ky. Cols.; named Tucson Man of Yr. 1987, Tucson Father of Yr. 1997; recipient Disting. Svc. award Anti-Defamation League B'nai B'rith, 1989, Humanitarian award Arthritis Found. S.Am., 2001, Crystal Apple Lifetime Achievement award Tucson Metro Edn. Commn., 2004, Pima Med. Found. award, 2005, Humanitarian Achievement award, Ednl. Enrichment Found., 2005; co-recipient Paloma Family Svcs. Commitment to Children award, 2005; Pima CC Dinner honoree, 1986, 92. Mem. Am. Hosp. Assn. (nominating com. 1983-86, trustee 1975-78, ho. dels. 1972-78, chmn. coun. profl. svc. 1973-74, regional adv. bd. 1969-78, chmn. joint com. with NASW 1963-64, Disting. Svc. award 1989), Ariz. Hosp. Assn. (Salisbury award 1982, bd. dirs. 1967-72, pres. 1970-71), Ariz. C. of C. (bd. dirs. 1988-93), Assn. Am. Med. Colls. (mem. assembly 1974-77), Tucson C. of C. (bd. dirs. 1968-69), Nat. League for Nursing, Ariz. Town Hall (bd. dirs. 1982-92, chmn. 1990-92, treas. 1985, Circle of Disting. Svc. award 2002), Pima County Acad. Decathlon Assn. (dir. 1983-85), The Rotary Club of Tucson (pres. 1993-94), U. Ariz. Alumni Assn. Coll. Nursing (hon. alumnus 1998). Baptist/Presbyterian (ch. moderator, chmn. finance com., deacon, ch. sch. supt., trustee, bd. dirs. ch. found.) Office: Tucson Med Ctr 5301 E Grant Rd Tucson AZ 85712-2805 *It seems important to put something back into life - for all we take from it.*

**SHROPSHIRE, KENNETH L.,** law educator; b. LA, 1955; m. Diane Shropshire; children: Theresa, Samuel. BS in econ., Stanford U., 1977; JD, Columbia U., 1980. Bar: 1982. Assoc. Manatt, Phelps, Rothenberg & Tunney, LA, 1980—82; asst. v.p. (in charge of Olympic Boxing competition and facility during 1984 games) LA Olympic Organizing Com., 1982—85; atty. Gen. Bus., Sports and Entertainment Practice, 1982—86; atty. pvt. practice LA; David W. Hauck prof. legal studies Wharton Sch., U. Pa., 1986—, chmn. legal studies dept., 2000—; acting dir. Afro-Am. Studies Program U. Pa., 1997—98. Mem. US Olympic Com. Budget Com.; chair Mayor's Site Selection Com. New Sports Facilities, Phila. Author: (sports column) Africana.com, Agents of Opportunity: Sports Agents and Corruption in Collegiate Sports (Outstanding Acad. Book award, Choice mag.), The Sports Franchise

Game: Cities in Pursuit of Sports Franchises, Events, Stadiums, and Arenas, In Black and White: Race and Sports in America (Outstanding Acad. Book award, Choice mag., 1996, Gustavus Myers Ctr. Study Human Rights in N. Am. Outstanding Book award, 1997), Basketball Jones; co-author: The Sound of Philadelphia. Mem.: Sports Lawyers Assn. (pres. 2004), Phila. Sports Congress, ABA (program chmn. section on sports law), Sports Law Assn. (pres. elect 2003—). Office: Wharton Sch Univ Pa 3730 Walnut St Philadelphia PA 19104-6340 Office Phone: 215-898-3017. Business E-Mail: shropshk@wharton.upenn.edu.

**SHROPSHIRE, WALTER, JR.,** biophysicist, pastor; b. Washington, Sept. 4, 1932; s. Walter and Mary Virginia (Anderson) S.; m. Audrey Marie McConkey, June 28, 1958; children— Janet Marie, Susan Lynn, Edward Allen. BS in Physics, George Washington U., 1954, MS in Botany, 1956, PhD in Plant Physiology, 1958; MDiv summa cum laude, Wesley Theol. Sem., 1990; postdoctoral fellow biophysics, Calif. Inst. Tech., 1957-59. Ordained to ministry United Meth. Ch., 1977. Physicist Smithsonian Instn., Washington, 1954—63; asst. dir. Smithsonian Environ. Rsch. Ctr., Washington, 1963-86; Gast prof. U. Freiburg, Germany, 1968-69; biophysicist, dir. Omega Lab., Cabin John, Md., 1986—. Professorial lectr. botany George Washington U., 1960-85; Gast prof. U. Zurich, Switzerland, 1985-86; part-time adj. prof. Practice Min. and Mission Wesley Theol. Sem., 1990—. Editor: Phytochrome, 1972, Joys of Research, 1981, Photomorphogenesis, Vol 16A, 16B, 1983, Photobiology, 1984-85; Contbr. 50 articles to profl. jours. Pastor, Foundry United Meth. Ch., Washington, 1991-2003. Recipient Smithsonian Outstanding Performance award, 1967, Smithsonian Research award, 1968, Merit award Soc. John Wesley, 1997, Templeton Sci. and Religion Course prize, 1999, 2002; NSF grantee, 1960-66. Fellow Explorers Club, Am. Solar Energy Soc. Office: Omega Lab PO Box 189 Cabin John MD 20818-0189 Office Phone: 301-929-3150. E-mail: wshrop@erols.com. *The world is an incredible place, rich with unexplored and unexplained interconnections between the biological and physical domains. I am fortunate to have been born when science has begun to unravel some of the mysteries of these interconnections and especially fortunate to have had teachers who shared their enthusiasm for learning. I also have benefited from mystical religious experiences of others and my own that enable me to work at the interface between science and religion. My belief is that the pursuit of both subjective and objective knowledge of ourselves and the universe we live in is necessary to enable humanity to develop to its fullest potential. This is an exciting pursuit I hope to continue to participate in a long time.*

**SHROTRIYA, VISHAL,** research scientist; b. Mathura, Uttar Pradesh, India, July 10, 1979; s. Satish Vijay and Manjesh Shrotriya. B of Tech., Indian Inst. Tech., Mumbai, 2002; MS, postgrad., UCLA, 2004—. Rschr. UCLA, 2002—. Fellow, Henry Samueli Sch. Engring. and Applied Sci. Mem.: Am. Phys. Soc., Materials Rsch. Soc. Hindu. Achievements include invention of very efficient plastic solar cells. Office Phone: 310-794-1820.

**SHROYER-KENO, JOAN ELANE,** information analyst; b. Dover, Ohio, Feb. 14, 1958; d. Alta Ethilda and George Victor Shroyer; m. Jeffery Bruce Keno, Nov. 4, 1988. BS in Journalism, Kent State U., Ohio, 1980; M in Info. Mgmt., Syracuse U., 2004. Cert. Info. Sys. and Telecoms. Mgmt. Syracuse U., 2002. Cons. Alchoholism Coun. of Tompkins County, Ithaca, NY; info. project mgr. CBORD, Ithaca, NY, 1997—2000; database adminstr. enterprise sys. Lockheed Martin, Syracuse, NY, 2000—05, database adminstr., sr. enterprise sys., 2005—. Guest spkr. Syracuse U., 2003—06, instr. master's level info. sys. analysis and design, 2004. Author: (poetry composition) After Church, Guilty Little Conscience, Over 75 titles published in various college and university publs. Info. cons. Alchoholism Coun. of Tompkins County, Ithaca, NY, 1995. Achievements include Presentor Representing Lockheed Martin MRO World International Conference; Electronic work flow design reduced company turnaround time 47% in 12 months with no labor reductions; Electronic work flow design increased company volume 27% in 12 months with no additional labor resources. Avocations: writing poetry, automobile restoration, gardening, percussion/drumming troupe, ancient religions. Office: Lockheed Martin Syracuse NY 13290 Office Phone: 315-456-1243.

**SHRUM, JOHN,** equal rights officer; b. Flora, Ill., Apr. 13, 1953; s. William E. and Agnes M. Shrum; children: Jason E., Jarred W. Grad., Flora (Ill.) HS, 1972. Laborer Labor Union Local 1375, Flora, 1976—2003, bus. agt., 1981—83; asst. employee Fed. Emergency Mgmt. Agy., Chgo., 1993—; equal rights officer Ill. Dept. Transp., Effingham, 2003—. Mem. Clay County Bd., 2004—; precinct committeeman, vice chmn. Dem. Party Clay County, Ill., 1978—; trustee Faith Luth. Ch., 1990—. Named to Wall of Tolerance, So. Poverty Law Ctr., Montgomery, Ala., 2004. Home: 641 W North Ave Flora IL 62839 Personal E-mail: jwshrum@hotmail.com.

**SHRUM, ROBERT MATTHEW,** political strategist, educator, journalist; b. Connellsville, Pa., 1943; BA, Georgetown U.; JD, Harvard U. Prin. speechwriter to Senator George McGovern, 1972; staff dir., chief counsel US Senate Select Com. on Nutrition and Human Needs; press. sec. to Senator Edward M. Kennedy, 1980—84, speechwriter, 1980; polit. advt. prodr., 1985—2005; sr. advisor Gore-Lieberman campaign, 2000, Kerry-Edwards campaign, 2004; sr. fellow, prof. Robert F. Wagner Grad. Sch. Pub. Svc., NYU, 2005—; polit. analyst MSNBC, 2005—. Tchr: Yale U., Boston Coll. Columnist Slate. Mem.: Am. Assn. of Polit. Cons. (Pollie Award 1986, 1994, 1998). Democrat. Office: NYU Wagner The Puck Bldg 2nd Fl 295 Lafayette St New York NY 10012-9604 Business E-Mail: robert.shrum@nyu.edu.

**SHRUT, ARLENE R.,** entrepreneur, director; b. May 24, 1953; d. Martin Miles Shrut and Shirley Anstandig; m. Gary Kendall, Sept. 4, 1998. MusB, Eastman Sch. Music, N.J., 1975, MusM, 1977; DMA, U. So. Calif., 1981, Chmn geocampaning dept Fyramme U. School of Music, 1989—91, faculty The Juilliard Sch., N.Y.C., 1993—; co-founder Seoul Bay Festival, Vinalhaven, NY, 1994—96; music faculty Manhattan Sch., N.Y.C., 1996—; French artistic dir. New Triad for Collaborative Arts, N.Y.C., 2002—. Recorded for: Orion, Darian, Summit, Albany. Koldapsky Scholarship, U. So. Calif., 1979, Fulbright Scholar, IIE, 1981. Avocations: avlinary arts, gardening. Office: New Triad 350 Fifth Ave Ste 3704 New York NY 10118 Personal E-mail: arshrut@aol.com.

**SHTERN, VICTOR,** computer scientist, educator; b. St Petersburg, Russia, Aug. 5, 1933; arrived in U.S., 1976, naturalized, 1981; s. Yechiel Shtern and Gitta Foynitsky; m. Ludmila Davidovich, June 1, 1956; 1 child, Katerina Simons. MSEE with highest honors, Leningrad Mining Inst., Russia, 1957; PhD in Control Systems, Nat. Aluminium Inst., Leningrad, Russia, 1967; MBA with high honors, Boston U., 1985. Elec. engr. Power Industry Design Ctr., Leningrad, Russia, 1958—59; sr. scientist Nat. Aluminum Inst., Leningrad, 1959—75; sys. analyst Eye Rsch. Inst. Retina Found., Boston, 1976—78; mgr. software verification Incoterm Inc., Wellesley, 1978—80; software engr. Atex Systems, Bedford, 1980; assoc. prof. Boston U. Met. Coll., 1980—. Adj. assoc. prof. Leningrad Mining Inst., 1967—75; cons. Prime Computer, Framingham, Mass., 1983, Boston U. Sch. of Edn., 1984, Boston U. Coll. Comm., 1985, Keane Inc, Charlestown, 1987—89, Mitre Inc, Bedford, Mat. Tech. U., NYC, 1992—2003, Boston U. Corp. Edn. Ctr., Boston, 1992—2000, Oasys Inc, Lexington, 1992, Sanders Inc, Nasua, NH, 1993—93, Siemens Corp., Danvers, 1998, Quantum Corp., Shrewsberry, 1998—99, Torto Wheaton Rsch., Boston, 2003; panelist Nat. Sci. Found., 2000; book rvr. Author: (book) Core C+: A Software Engineering Approach, 2001, Core C+, in Chinese, 2002, Core C+, in Russian, 2003, Core C+, Inzynieria Programowania, in Polish, 2004, Industrial Experience with the Control System "Aluminum", 1971; co-author: Production of Aluminum, 1971; contbr. articles to profl. jours. Mem. adv. bd. Leningrad Chess Club, 1965—72; mem. resettlement com. absorbtion immigrants from USSR Combined Jewish Philanthropies, Boston, 1978—88. Fellow, Nat. Aluminium Inst., Leningrad, 1959—75, Nat. Aeronautics and Space Adminstrn., Am. Soc. Engring. Edn., 1982, 1983; grantee, Wang Labs., 1984. Jewish. Achievements include development of electrical and pneumatic instrumentation control systems for pulp and paper mills; training courses on

advanced Ada and software testing; training seminars on C, C+, Java, object-oriented design; live satellite broadcasts on Java, C, C+, object-oriented programming; undergraduate and graduate courses on Computer Simulation, Software Testing, Ada, C+, Java, Software Design, Design Patterns; process control systems for production of alumina and aluminium; development of on-line menu-driven programs for Patient Database Management; design of remote communication controller for a programmed airline reservation system; design of newspaper classified ad system; computer-based instruction software for high school introductory physical science course; development of interactive computer troubleshooting simulator with a computer-controlled videodisc player; software for studying subjects' reaction to iconic and textual menus; training courses on advance COBOL and SQL programming. Home: 65 Babcock St Apt 6 Brookline MA 02446 Office: Boston U 808 Commonwealth Ave Rm 250 Boston MA 02215 Office Phone: 617-358-0003. Personal E-mail: vshtern@bu.edu.

**SHTEYNGART, GARY,** writer; b. Leningrad, USSR, July 5, 1972; Diploma in Politics, Oberlin Coll., 1995. Writer various non-profit orgns., The New Yorker, Granta, GQ, Esquire, The NY Times mag. Author: The Russian Debutante's Handbook, 2002 (Stephen Crane award for First Fiction, Nat. Jewish Book award for Fiction, named Best Book of Yr. The Washington Post, Entertainment Weekly, named one of Best Debuts of Yr. The Guardian, named NY Times Notable Book), Absurdistan, 2006.\*

**SHU, CHI-WANG,** mathematics professor, researcher; b. Beijing, Jan. 2, 1957; arrived in U.S., 1982, naturalized, 1993; s. Kuang-Yao and Ding-Zhen (Shi) Shu; m. Din-Sui Loh, May 1, 1984, 1 child, Hai-Shuo. BS, U. Sci. and Tech. of China, 1982; PhD, UCLA, 1986. Rsch. assoc. U. Minn., Mpls., 1986—87; asst. prof. applied math. Brown U., Providence, 1987—91, assoc. prof., 1992—96, prof., 1996—, chmn., 1999—2005. Mng. editor Math. of Computation, 2002—, mem. editl. bd. SIAM Jour. Numerical Analysis, 1993—2001, Jour. Computational Math., 1993—, Comm. in Applied Analysis, 1996—, Acta Mathematicae Applicatae Sinica, —, Jour. Dynamics of Continuous Discrete and Impulsive Sys., Series B., Methods of Analysis, 2000—; contbr. Recipient Pub. Svc. Group Achievement award for pioneer work in computational fluid dynamics, NASA, 1992, First Feng Kang prize of Sci. Computing, Chinese Acad. Sci., 1995, Highly Cited Author in Math., Inst. Scientific Info. Web Sci., 2004—; grantee, NSF, NASA, Army Rsch. Office. Mem.: Soc. for Indsl. and Applied Math., Am. Math. Soc. Achievements include research in numerical solutions for discontinuous problems. Home: 135 Woodbury St Providence RI 02906-3511 Office: Brown U Div Applied Maths 182 George St Providence RI 02912-9056

**SHUART, CAREY CHENOWETH,** farmer, volunteer; b. Houston, June 1, 1944; d. Robert Carey Chenoweth and Elizabeth Dorothy Smith; m. Willard Warren Shuart, Apr. 17, 1965 (dec. Mar. 1996); children: Nora Wellington Shuart-Faris, Sarah Espy Shuart Szymanski. Student, U. Tex., 1962—66, U. Houston, 1991—93, Glassell Sch. Mus. of Fine Arts, Houston, 1990—2005. Owner, cons. Bien Trouvé Art Gallery, Houston, 1979—85; rice farmer Shuart Farms, Houston. Mem. adv. bd. Blaffer Gallery U. Houston, 2002—. Editor: (newsletter) U Friends, 1992—98. Mem. alumni bd. St. John's Sch., Houston, 1973—75; sustainer Jr. League of Houston, 1975—2004; founder, pres. Pink Ladies-Eagle Lake Cmty. Hosp., 1967—72, Civic Garden Club, Eagle Lake, Tex., 1983—85; chmn. adv. bd. Friends of Women's Studies U. Houston, 2001—; founder, patron Women's Archive and Rsch. Ctr. U. Houston; mem. photo subcom. Mus. Fine Arts, Houston, 2000—; bd. dirs. Friends of Women's Studies U. Houston, 1992—2004, Honors Coll., U. Houston, 1992—95. Named Vol. of Yr., U. Houston U. Rels. Divsn., 1992, 1995, U. Houston, 1995, 1996; recipient Nat. CASE award, St. Johns Sch., Houston, 1982, Outstanding Alumni award, 1991. Mem.: Nat. Soc. Colonial Dames in State of Tex. (chmn. 1982—86, 2003—05). Episcopalian. Avocations: photography, golf, social work. Office: Shuart Farms 2121 San Felipe #118 Houston TX 77019

**SHUART, JAMES MARTIN,** retired academic administrator; b. College Point, N.Y., May 9, 1931; s. John and Barbara (Schmidt) Shuart; m. Marjorie Strunk, Apr. 5, 1953; children: James Raymond, William Arthur. BA, Hofstra U., 1953, MA, 1962; PhD, NYU, 1966; D (hon.), L.I. U., 2000. Group rep. Home Life Ins. Co., 1955—57, N.Y. Life Ins. Co., 1957—59; adminstr. Hofstra U., Hempstead, NY, 1959—70, asst. dir. admissions, asst. dean faculty, asst. pres., exec. dean student svcs., assoc. dean liberal arts scis., trustee, 1973—75, v.p. adminstrv. svcs., 1975—76, pres., 1976—2001, pres. emeritus, 2001—. Mem. higher edn. adv. com. N.Y. State Senate, 1979-95; trustee Commn. on Ind. Colls. and Univs. N.Y. State, 1982-89, 92-95, chmn. 1988-89; mem. Am. Coun. on Edn.'s Labor/Higher Edn. Coun., 1983-88, Am. Coun. on Edns. Commn. on Leadership Devel., 1987-89, Peat Marwick Higher Edn. Pres.'s Adv. Com., 1988-96; bd. dirs. European Am. Bank, 1990-2001, Travelers-Solomon, Smith Barney World Funds, 1995-2000; chair Nassau County Property Tax Relief Commn., 1990-92; co-chair N.Y. State Temporary Commn. for L.I. Tax Relief, 1990-93; mem. nominating com. NASDQ, 2000— Trustee Molloy Coll., 1973-77, L.I. Power Authority, 2004—, Uniondale (N.Y.) Pub. Libr., 1966-68, L.I. Hosp. Planning Coun., 1971-75; mem. adv. bd. Adelphi U. Sch. Social Work, 1973-84; dep. county exec. Nassau County, 1973-75, commr. social svcs., 1971-73, commr. L.I. Reg. Planning Bd., 1978-83, chmn. 1981-83; bd. dirs L.I. Assn., 1986-90; pres., bd. dirs. Health Welfare Coun. Nassau County, 1971-80; chmn. Nassau Bd. Social Svcs., 1971-73; bd. dirs. Winthrop U. Hosp., 1979-86; mem. Nassau County Charter Revision Comm., 1993-96. Decorated officer Order of Orange Nassau (Netherlands); recipient Founders Day award NYU, 1967, Alumnus of Yr. award Hofstra U., 1973, George M. Estabrook Disting. svc. award Alumni Assn., 1974, Leadship in Govt. award U.W. Post Coll., L.I. U., 1978, Man of Yr. award Hempstead C. of C., 1978, award L.I. Pers. and Guidance Assn., 1977, Lincoln Day award Syosset-Woodbury Rep. Club, 1981, Disting. Leadership award L.I. Bus., 1982, 96, Joseph Giacalone award 1986, Medal of Honor L.I. Assn., 1988, Achievement award Pub. Rels. Profls. of L.I., 1995, Award L.I. Bus. Devel. Coun., 1994, 98, Educator of Yr. award WLIW Ch 21, 1999, Lifetime Achievement award L.I. Assn., 2001, award L.I. Software and Tech. Network, 2001; others; named to L.I. Hall of Fame, 1985, Lifetime Achievement award Met. Lacrosse Found., 2001. Home: 111 Cherry Valley Ave # M35 Garden City NY 11530-1570

**SHUB, HARVEY ALLEN,** surgeon; b. Bklyn., Oct. 28, 1942; s. Irving and Sara (Levin) S.; m. Susan Jayne Smith, Dec. 26, 1970; children: Carolyn, Todd. Student, NYU, 1960-61, 64-65; BS in Zoology, Physics, U. Miami, 1964; MD, U. Rome, Italy, 1971. Diplomate Am. Bd. Colon and Rectal Surgery. Intern Beth Israel Med. Ctr., N.Y.C., 1971-72, resident in surgery, 1972-76; fellow in colon and rectal surgery Muhlenberg Hosp., Plainfield, NJ, 1976-77; practice medicine specializing in colon and rectal surgery Orlando, Fla., 1977—; clin. dept. surgery Fla. Hosp., 1988-89, colon and rectal surgery, 1999—2001. Pres. med. staff Fla. Hosp., 1992-93; asst. cons. prof. dept. surgery Duke U., 1995; mem. staff Winter Park Meml. Hosp., South Seminole Cmty. Hosp., Fla. Hosp. and Med. Ctr., Orlando Regional Healthcare Sys.; clin. asst. prof. dept. family medicine U. South Fla., Tampa, 1982—; med. dir. Brevard Profl. Network, 2002-2004. Consulting editor Jour. Fla. Med. Assn.; contbr. articles to profl. jours. Chmn. pub. edn. com. Am. Cancer Soc. Orange County, 1982—86. Capt. M.C., USAR, 1971-77. Recipient Physician's Recognition awards AMA. Fellow ACS, Am. Soc. Colon and Rectal Surgeons, Internat. Coll. Surgeons, Southeastern Surg. Congress, Internat. Soc. Univ. Colon and Rectal Surgeons; mem. AMA, So. Med. Assn., Fla. Med. Assn. (sect. splty. medicine), Orange County Med. Assn., Piedmont Soc. Colon and Rectal Surgeons (pres. elect 1997, pres. 1998-2000), Orange County Ostomy Assn. (med. adviser), Fla. Soc. Colon and Rectal Surgeons (sec.-treas. 1980-82, pres. 1983-84, sec.-treas. 1986-98, pres. 1998-2000, treas. 2005—), Am. Soc. Gastrointestinal Endoscopy, Am. Soc. Laser Medicine and Surgery, Soc. Am. Gastrointestinal Endoscopic Surgeons. Office: 308 Groveland St Orlando FL 32804-4019 Home: 5252 Vista Club Run Sanford FL 32771-7153 Office Phone: 407-894-0481. Personal E-mail: tushmd4@aol.com.

**SHUBB, WILLIAM BARNET,** judge; b. Oakland, Calif., May 28, 1938; s. Ben and Nellie Bernice (Fruechtenicht) S.; m. Sandra Ann Talarico, July 29, 1962; children: Alisa Marie, Carissa Ann, Victoria Ann. AB, U. Calif., Berkeley, 1960, JD, 1963. Bar: Calif. 1964, U.S. Ct. Internat. Trade 1981, U.S. Customs Ct. 1980, U.S. Ct. Appeals (9th cir.) 1964, U.S. Supreme Ct. 1972. Law clk. U.S. Dist. Ct., Sacramento, 1963-65; asst. U.S. atty., Sacramento, 1965-71; chief asst. U.S. atty. (ea. dist.) Calif., 1971-74; assoc. Diepenbrock, Wulff, Plant & Hannegan, Sacramento, 1974-77, ptnr., 1977-80, 81-90; U.S. atty. Eastern Dist. Calif., 1980-81; judge U.S. Dist. Ct. (ea. dist.) Calif., 1990—, chief judge, 1996-2003; chmn. com. drafting of local criminal rules U.S. Dist. Ct. (ea. dist.) Calif., 1974, mem. speedy trial planning com., 1974-80; lawyer rep. 9th Cir. U.S. Jud. Conf., 1975-78; mem. faculty Fed. Practice Inst., 1978-80; instr. McGeorge Sch. Law, U. Pacific, 1964-66. Mem. ABA, Fed. Bar Assn. (pres. Sacramento chpt. 1977), Calif. Bar Assn., Assn. Def. Counsel, Am. Bd. Trial Advs., Sacramento County Bar Coun., Sacramento Rotary Club.

**SHUBERT, JOSEPH FRANCIS,** librarian; b. Buffalo, Sept. 17, 1928; s. Joseph Francis and Lena M. (Kohn) Shubert; m. Dorothy Jean Whearty, Feb. 5, 1955 (div. Feb. 1980); children: Julia Ellen, Susan, Alan Joseph. BS, State U. Tchrs. Coll., Geneseo, N.Y., 1951; MA, U. Denver, 1957. Reference and ext. libr. Nev. State Libr., Carson City, 1951-57, libr. cons., 1957-59, state libr., 1959-61; asst. dir. internat. rels. office ALA, 1962-66; state libr. Ohio, 1966-77; sec., treas. chief officer state Libr. Agys. N.Y. State Edn. Dept., 1973-76, chmn., 1976-78, state libr., asst. commr. librs., 1977-96, state libr. emeritus, 1996—; mem. adv. coun. U.S. Pub. Printer, 1974-77; mem. adv. com. White House Conf. Libr. and Info. Svcs., 1977-79; chmn. steering com. survey state libr. agys. U.S. Nat. Ctr. Edn. Stats., 1992—2003. Trustee Ohio Coll. Libr. Ctr., 1976—78; Disting. Alumnus lectr. U. Denver, 1979; mem. adv. com. Ctr. for Book Libr. of Congress, 1979—82, mem. network adv. coun., 1981—96; mem. adv. coun. Sch. Libr. and Info. Sci., Pratt Inst., 1980—2000; bd. dirs. N.E. Document Conservation Ctr., 1980—82, treas., 1986—89; mem. design task force White House Conf. Libr. and Info. Svcs., 1985; chmn. chief officers State Librs. in N.E., 1987—89; bd. dirs. Internat. Dist. Regional Info. Svc. Network State U. Albany, NY, 1994—97. Editor: The Bookmark, 1987—96; contbr. articles to periodicals. Dir. Friends N.Y. State Libr., Inc., 1998—; mem. adv. com. U. Wis. Inst. Edn., Federally Funded Literacy Program, 1992—94; co-chair 50th anniversary com. Coll. Geneseo, 2001. Named Disting. Alumnus, SUNY-Geneseo, 1985; named to Alumni Honor Roll, 1997; recipient Exceptional Achievement award, ALA Assn. Specialized and Coop. Libr. Agy. Assn., 1985, Disting. Pub. Svc. award, SUNY-Albany, Nelson A. Rockefeller Coll. Pub. Affairs and Policy, 1987, Hall of Fame award, Ohio Libr. Assn., 1991, Velma K. Moore award, N.Y. State Assn. Libr. Bds., 1996. Mem.: ALA (grass roots adv. 1996), Chief Officers State Libr. Agys. (chmn. 1977—78), N.Y. Libr. Assn. (hon. chair capital campaign 1999—2000, Outstanding Svc. award 1996), Meml. Libr. Assn., North Collins Libr. Assn., Nev. Libr. Assn. (pres.), Assn. Specialized and Coop. Lit. Agys. (pres. 1988—89), Task Force Pub. Libr. Stats. (mem. adv. com. 1990—96, chair steering com. NCES Survey State Libr. Agys. 1993—2003), Nat. Commn. Librs. and Info. Svcs., Nat. Ctr. Ednl. Stats., Nev. Congress Parents and Tchrs., Torch Club Albany. Roman Catholic. Home: 494 Madison Ave Albany NY 12208-3601 also: PO Box 1064 36 Lake Dr South Dennis MA 02660-2838 Business E-Mail: jshubert@nycap.rr.com, shubert@nycap.rr.com.

**SHUBIK, MARTIN,** economics professor; b. NYC, Mar. 24, 1926; s. Joseph Louis and Sara S.; m. Julia Kahn, Aug. 11, 1970; 1 child, Claire Louise. BA, U. Toronto, 1947, MA, 1949; PhD, Princeton U., 1953. Rsch. asst. Princeton U., 1950—53, rsch. assoc., 1953-55; fellow Ctr. for Advanced Study in Behavioral Scis., Palo Alto, Calif., 1955-56; cons. mgmt. consultation svcs. Gen. Electric Co., 1956-60; adj. rsch. prof. Pa. State U., 1957-59; vis. prof. econs. Yale U., New Haven, 1960-61, prof. econs. of orgn., dept. adminstrv. sci., 1963-75, Seymour H. Knox prof. math instl. econs., 1975—. Bd. dirs. Equity Strategies, 1965-90, Third Avenue Funds, 1990-, Perini Corp., 2004-; mem. staff T.J. Watson Rsch. Labs., IBM Corp., 1961-63; vis. prof. Escuela de Estudios Económicos U. Chile, Santiago, 1965, Inst. Advanced Studies, Vienna, Austria, 1968, 70, U. Melbourne, Australia, 1973; cons. Rand Corp., Santa Monica, Calif., 1963; dir. Cowles Found. for Rsch. In Econs., Yale U., 1973-76; external faculty Santa Fe Inst., 1994—, sci. bd. 1996—; cons. in field. Author or co-author: numerous books, including The War Game, 1979, (with G. Brewer) The Aggressive Conservative Investor, 1979, 2d edit., 2005, (with M.J. Whitman) Market Structure and Behavior, 1980, (with R.E. Levitan) Game Theory in the Social Sciences, vol. 1, 1982, vol. 2, 1984, The Theory of Money and Financial Institutions, vols. 1 and 2, 1999; mem. editorial bd. Conflict Resolution; mem. editl. adv. bd. Internat. Studies Series; assoc. editor Mgmt. Sci, 1965-81; contbr. articles to profl. jours. Served to lt. Royal Can. Navy. Recipient Lanchester prize, 1983, Koopman prize mil. ops. rsch., 1996; named hon. prof. U. Vienna Fellow Econometric Soc., World Acad. Arts and Scis.; mem. Am. Acad. Arts and Scis., Conn. Acad. Arts and Scis. Home: 18 Rockland Park Branford CT 06405 Office: PO Box 208281 30 Hillhouse Ave New Haven CT 06520-8281 Office Phone: 203-432-3694. Business E-Mail: martin.shubik@yale.edu.

**SHUCHART, EUGENE JOSEPH,** retired accountant; b. New Freedom, Pa., May 22, 1924; s. Albert Alan Shuchart and Victoria Ann Ryer-Shuchart; m. Angelita Rodriguez Shuchart, Nov. 24, 1956; children: Eugene Joseph Jr., Michael Albert, Larry Francis, Lisa Marie, David Alan. BS in Econs., Villanova U., Pa., 1950; MBA, U. Pa., 1951. CPA Dept. Energy State Va., Richmond, Va., 1956—80, ret., 1980. Acct. prof. George Washington U., 1968—79; instr. Edison Coll., 1981—97. With U.S. Army, 1943—46, Pacific. Decorated Purple Heart U.S. Army. Mem.: Nat. Assn. Ret. Fed. Employees (Disting. Career Svc. award 1980), Disabled Am. Vets (treas. 1996—97). Avocations: organ, piano, swimming, walking. Personal E-mail: eshuchart@aol.com.

**SHUCK, EDWIN HAYWOOD, III,** surgeon; b. Chattanooga, Tenn., 1948; MD, Washington U., St. Louis, 1973. Diplomate Am. Bd. Surgery, Am. Bd. Colon and Rectal Surgery. Intern Tulane U. Hosps., New Orleans, 1973-74, resident, 1974-78; fellow in colon and rectal surgery Carle Clinic, Urbana, Ill., 1978-79; privileges Meml. Hosp., Chattanooga, Tenn.; pvt. practice Colon & Rectal Surg. Assocs. Asst. prof. clin. surgery U. Tenn. Fellow ACS, Am. Soc. Colon and Rectal Surgery. Office: Colon & Rectal Surg 2341 McCallie Ave #305 Plz Chattanooga TN 37404

**SHUCK, JERRY MARK,** surgeon, educator; b. Bucyrus, Ohio, Apr. 23, 1934; s. James Edwin and Pearl (Mark) S.; m. Linda Wayne, May 28, 1974; children: Jay Steven, Gail Ellen, Kimberly Ann, Lynn Meredith, Steven James. BS in Pharmacy, U. Cin., 1955, MD, 1959, DSc, 1966. Intern Colo. Gen. Hosp., Denver, 1959-60; resident in surgery U. Cin. Integrated Program, 1960-66; mem. faculty dept. surgery U. N.Mex., Albuquerque, 1968-80, prof., 1974-80; prof. surgery Case-Western Res. U., Cleve., 1980—, Oliver H. Payne prof. dept. surgery, 1980—2005, chmn. dept., 1980-2000, prof. anatomy, 1991—, interim v.p. for med. affairs, 1993-95, dir., assoc. dean grad. med. edn., 2002—. Cons. FDA, 1972-77 Contbr. articles to profl. jours. Served to capt. U.S. Army, 1966-68. Mem. ACS, Am. Surg. Assn., Am. Bd. Surgery (bd. dirs., chmn. 1993-94, residency rev. com. for surgery 1994-2000, vice chmn. 1997-2000), Soc. Univ. Surgeons, Am. Ass n S urgery Trauma, Am. Trauma Soc. (founding mem.), Univ. Assn. Emergency Medicine (founding mem.), Am. Burn Assn. (founding mem.), We. Surg. Assn., Ctrl. Surg. Assn. (pres. 1996-97), Assn. Acad. Surgery, S.W. Surg. Assn., Cleve. Surg. Soc. (pres. 1988-89), Ohio Med. Assn., Acad. Medicine Cleve., Halsted Soc., Surg. Infection Soc. (founding mem.), B'nai B'rith, Jewish Cmty. Ctr. Club, The Temple Club. Democrat. Jewish. Office: Case Western Reserve U Dept Surgery 11100 Euclid Ave Cleveland OH 44106-2602

**SHUCK, ROBERT F.,** financial executive; s. Robert F. II and Gertrude (Lehr) S.; m. Page Downe, May 30, 1969; children: Robert F. IV, Hollister A. BA in Acctg. with honors, S.E. Mo. Coll., 1959; MBA, Northwestern U., 1961. CPA, Ill.; cert. fin. planner. With Raymond James Fin., Inc., St. Petersburg, Fla., 1969—, vice chmn., 1991—. Bd. dirs. RJ Comm., Inc. Bd.

dirs. Southeast Mo. Univ. Found.; trustee All Children's Hosp.; mem. long range devel. com. Fla. Coun. Econ. Edn.; mem. policy bd. Tampa Bay Partnership for Regional Econ. Devel.; mem. devel. found. St. Petersburg Jr. Coll.; stewardship chmn. Our Savior Luth. Ch., St. Petersburg. Mem. Securities Industry Assn. (sales and mktg. com.), Internat. Assn. for Fin. Planning (past bd. dirs.), Nat. Endowment for Fin. Edn. (trustee, mem. exec. com.). Office: Raymond James Fin 880 Carillon Pkwy Saint Petersburg FL 33716-1100 Office Phone: 727-567-5300.

**SHUE, ELISABETH,** actress; b. Wilmington, Del., Oct. 6, 1963; m. Davis Guggenheim, 1994; children: William, Stella Street, Agnes Charles Student, Wellesley Coll.; BA in Govt., Harvard U., 2000; studied with Sylvie Leigh, Showcase Theater. Appeared in Broadway plays including Some Americans Abroad, Birth and After Birth; Actor (films) The Karate Kid, 1984 (Young Artist award 1984), Link, 1986, Adventures in Babysitting, 1987, Cocktail, 1988, Body Wars, 1989, Back to the Future Part II, 1989, Back to the Future Part III, 1990, Soapdish, 1991, The Marrying Man, 1991, Twenty Bucks, 1993, Heart and Souls, 1993, Radio Inside, 1994, Blind Justice, 1994, The Underneath, 1995, Leaving Las Vegas, 1995 (Oscar nominee for Best Actress), The Trigger Effect, 1996, The .Saint, 1996, Palmetto, 1997, Deconstructing Harry, 1997, Cousin Bette, 1997, Molly, 1998, Hollow Man, 2000, Tuck Everlasting, 2002, Leo, 2002, Mysterious Skin, 2004, Hide and Seek, 2005, Dreamer: Inspired by a True Story, 2005; (TV movies) Charles and Diana, Double Switch, 1987, Hale the Hero, 1992, Blind Justice; (TV series) Call to Glory, 1984, Amy & Isabelle, 2001. Office: Creative Arts Agy 9830 Wilshire Blvd Beverly Hills CA 90212-1804*

**SHUE, ROBERT A.,** social studies educator; b. York, Pa., Nov. 17, 1954; s. Howard Curvin and Daisy May Shue. BS, Millersville State Coll., Pa., 1976, MEd, Western Md. Coll., Westminster, 1981. Tchr., asst. football coach Southwestern HS, Hanover, Pa., 1976—, coach boys track & field, 1984—. Avocations: sports, travel, history, politics. Office: Southwestern HS 200 Bowman Rd Hanover PA 17331

**SHUER, LAWRENCE MENDEL,** neurosurgery educator; b. Toledo, Apr. 12, 1954; s. Bernard Benjamin and Estelle Rose (Drukker) S.; m. Paula Ann Elliott, Sept. 4, 1976; children: Jenna, Tammy, Nichole. BA with high distinction, U. Mich., 1975, MD cum laude, 1978. Diplomate Am. Bd. Neurol. Surgery, Nat. Bd. Med. Examiners. Fellow in neurology Inst. Neurology, London, 1979; intern in surgery Stanford (Calif.) U. Sch. Medicine, 1978-79, resident in neuropathology, 1980, resident in neurosurgery, 1980-84, clin. asst. prof. surgery and neurosurgery, 1984-90, assoc. prof., 1990—2002, acting chmn. dept. neurosurgery, 1992-95, 96—, assoc. dean, 1996—, chief of staff Stanford Health Svs., 1996—; chief of staff Stanford U. Hosp. and Clinics, 1999—, prof., 2002—. Numerous presentations in field. Contbr. articles and abstracts to med. jours., chpts. to books. Recipient Kaiser tchr. award Stanford U., 1993; James B. Angell scholar. Mem. AMA, Am. Assn. Neurol. Surgeons, Congress Neurol. Surgeons, Western Neurosurg. Soc., Calif. Assn. Neurol. Surgeons (bd. dirs., treas. 1995—98, 2nd v.p. 1998—99, 1st v.p. 1999-2000, pres.-elect 2000-01, pres. 2002-03), Calif. Med. Assn., Am. Heart Assn. (fellow stroke coun.), Santa Clara County Med. Assn., San Francisco Neurol. Soc., Alpha Omega Alpha. Conservative. Jewish. Avocations: skiing, swimming, travel. Office: Stanford U Med Ctr 300 Pasteur Dr R229 Palo Alto CA 94304-5327 Office Phone: 650-723-6093. Business E-mail: lshuer@stanford.edu.

**SHUEY, JOHN HENRY,** manufacturing executive; b. Monroe, Mich., Mar. 14, 1946; s. John Henry and Bertha (Thomas) S.; children: Katherine, John Henry, John Joseph Satory. BS in Indsl. Engring., U. Mich., 1968, MBA, 1970. With Tex. Instruments Co., Dallas, 1970-74; asst. treas. The Trane Co., La Crosse, Wis., 1974-78, treas., 1978-81, v.p., treas., 1981-83, v.p. fin., chief fin. officer, 1983-86; also v.p., group exec. Am Standard; sr. v.p. and chief fin. officer AM Internat. Inc., Chgo., 1986-91; exec. v.p. Amcast Indsl. Corp., Dayton, Ohio, 1991-93, pres., COO, 1993-95, pres., CEO, 1995—, also chmn. bd. dirs., chmn. bd., pres., CEO, 1997—. Bd. dirs. Cooper Tire and Rubber Co., Findlay, Ohio, EMTEC. Bd. dirs. Wright State Univ. Found., 1996—; bd. trustees Dayton Ballet, 1996—, Ohio Found. of Ind. Colleges, 1994—. Mem. Fin. Execs. Inst. Congregationalist. also: Elkhart Products Corp 1255 Oak St Elkhart IN 46514-2277

**SHUEY, RICHARD LYMAN,** engineering educator, consultant; b. Chgo., May 7, 1920; s. Ralph Clement and Abbie Miriam (Strong) S.; m. Frances Barbara Fortier, Sept. 22, 1944; children: Roy Fortier, Marie Frances. BS in Engring., U. Mich., 1942, BSE in Math., 1942; PhD in Elec. Engring., U. Calif., Berkeley, 1950. Registered profl. engr., NY, Calif. Engr. U. Calif. Radiation Lab., Berkeley, 1946-50; rsch. staff, br. mgr. GE Rsch. Lab., Schenectady, N.Y., 1950-84; adj. prof. Rensselaer Polytech. Inst., Troy, N.Y., 1985—; cons. Schenectady, 1985—. Author: The Architecture of Distributed Computer Systems, 1997; contbr. articles to profl. jours. Bd. dirs. Self Help for Hard of Hearing N.Y. Assn., 1996-2001. Sr. mem. IEEE (various coms., offices 1952-87, Donald McLellan Cmty. Svc. award, 3d Millennium medal), AAAS, Am. Auditory Soc., Soc. Mfg. Engrs., Assn. Computing Machines, Sigma Xi, Tau Beta Pi. Avocations: golf, bridge, photography. Office: Computer Sci Dept RPI Troy NY 12180 Home: 242 Glen Eddy Dr Schenectady NY 12309-4967 Personal E-mail: shueyrl@juno.com.

**SHUFF, RONALD F.,** lawyer; BA in History, Kenyon Coll., Gambier, Ohio, 1974; JD, Capital U., Columbus, Ohio, 1977; MS, MIT Sloan Sch. Atty. Columbus & So. Electric Co., 1977-81; sec., gen. counsel Accuray Corp., Columbus, 1981—88; gen. counsel, asst. sec. Duriron Co., 1988—89, gen. counsel, sec., 1989—90; v.p., sec., gen. counsel Durco Internat. (formerly Duriron Co.), 1990—97, Flowserve Corp., Irving, Tex., 1997—. Sloan fellow, MIT, 1987-88. Office: Flowserve 5215 N OConnor Blvd Ste 2300 Irving TX 75039

**SHUFORD, JACOB L.,** academic administrator, career military officer; BA, Univ. SC, 1974; MPA, Harvard Univ.; M in nat. security studies & strategy, Naval War Coll.; Olmsted Scholar, Paris Inst. Pol. Sci., France. Commd. ensign USN, advanced through grades to rear adm.; served ops. dept. USS Blakely (FF 1072); ops. & plans officer Comdr. Naval Forces Korea; ops. officer USS Deyo (DD 989), USS Mahan (DDG 42); commande. officer USS Aries (PHM 5); mem. staff of CNO, Washington; spl. asst., personal aide to Sec. Office of Sec. of the Navy, Washington; commdg. officer USS Rodney M. Davis (FFG 60), USS Gettysburg (CG 64); air warfare comdr. USS Enterprise Battle Group, USS Carl Vinson & USS Enterprise Battle Groups, Operation Desert Fox; dir. Surface Combatant Force Level Study, Washington; chief of staff Roles & Missions organization, Washington; div. chief Force Structure, Resources & Assessment Directorate, Washington; dir. Senate liaison Office of Legis. Affairs, Washington; asst. comdr. Navy Personnel Command; commdg. officer Cruiser Destroyer Group Three, 2003—04; pres. Naval War Coll., Newport, RI, 2004—. Decorated Def. Superior Svc. medal, Legion of Merit (4 awards), Bronze Star, Meritorious Svc. medal (3 awards), Navy Commendation medal (3 awards), Navy Achievement medal. Office: Naval War College Office of President 686 Cushing Rd Newport RI 02841

**SHUGART, HOWARD ALAN,** physicist, researcher; b. Orange, Calif., Sept. 21, 1931; s. Howard Ancil and Bertha Elizabeth (Henderson) S.; m. Elizabeth L. Hanson, Feb. 6, 1971. BS, Calif. Inst. Tech., 1953; MA, U. Calif., Berkeley, 1955, PhD, 1957. Tchg. asst. physics U. Calif., Berkeley, 1953-56, assoc., 1957, lectr., 1957-58, acting asst. prof., 1958-59, asst. prof., 1959-63, assoc. prof., 1963-67, prof., 1967-93, prof. emeritus, 1993—, vice chmn., 1968—70, 1979—87, 1989—2001, acting chmn., 1979—81, 1983—84, 1987. Cons. Convair divsn. Gen. Dynamics Corp., 1960-61; mem. com. nuc. constants NRC, 1960-63; atomic beam group leader Lawrence Berkeley (Calif.) Nat. Lab., 1965-79, guest rschr., 1999—. Fellow Am. Phys. Soc. (acting sec. Pacific Coast 1961-64, exec. com. divsn. electron and atomic physics 1972-74), Nat. Speleological Soc. (gov. 1954-56); mem. Sigma Xi. Office: U Calif Dept Physics Berkeley CA 94720-7300

**SHUGART, JILL,** academic administrator; b. Dallas, July 15, 1940; d. Claude Ernest and Allie Merle (Hamilton) S. BA, Baylor U., 1962; MA, Tex. Woman's U., 1972, PhD, 1980. Middle sch. English tchr. Garland (Tex.) Ind. Sch. Dist., 1962-63, high sch. social studies tchr., 1963-76, high sch. asst. prin., 1976-79, dir. communications, 1979-82, asst. supt., 1982-85, supt., 1985—99, ret., 1999—; exec. dir. Region X Edn. Svc. Ctr., 2004—. Mem. legis. coun. U. Interscholastic League Tex., 1989-99; chmn. Dist. III music com., Tex., 1989-99; adj. prof. Tex. Women's U., Denton, 1983; chmn. Region X ESC Adv. Coun., rep. to commr.'s supt.'s com., 1993-95; cons. Richardson and Carrollton-Farmers Br. Sch. Dists., 2000-04; coord. Region 10 ESC Supr.'s Acad., 2000-04. Gen. chmn. Boy Scouts Am. Scouting Night, Dallas, 1988-89; chmn. City of Garland Comty. Action Com., 1995-99; sec. Tex. Sch. Alliance, 1995-96, chmn., 1998-99; life mem. Tex. and nat. PTA; pres. Garland br. Am. Heart Assn., 1990-91; co-chmn. sustaining dr. Garland YMCA, 1995-96; mem. Adv. Com. to Gov. and State Legisture, 1998; mem. steering com. Garland Econ. Devel. Partnership, 1994-99, Tex. Fast Growth Sch. Coalition; chair Tex. Sch. Alliance, 1998—. Recipient Lamar award for excellence Masons, Award of Distinction, Tex. Ret. Tchrs. Assn.; named Top 100 Educators to Watch, Executive Educator mag., 1985, Finalist as Outstanding Tex. Sch. Supt., 1990, Woman of Distinction, Soroptomist Club, Disting. Alumnus, Garland H.S., 2005; Paul Harris fellow. Mem. Quality Tex. Bd. Examiners, Garland Edn. Found. (bd. dirs. 1999-2006), Baylor Med. Ctr. Garland (bd. dirs. 2001-2006). Republican. Baptist. Avocations: travel, lake activities. Business E-Mail: jill.shugart@region10.org.

**SHUGHART, DONALD LOUIS,** retired lawyer; b. Kansas City, Mo., Aug. 12, 1926; s. Henry M. and Dora M. (O'Leary) Shughart; m. Mary I. Shughart, July 25, 1953; children: Susan O. Hogsett, Nancy J. Goede. AB, U. Mo., Columbia, 1949, JD, 1951. Bar: Mo. 1951, U.S. Dist. Ct. (we. dist.) Mo. 1951, U.S. Tax Ct. 1979. With Shughart, Thompson & Kilroy, PC, Kansas City, Mo., 1951—2002, ret., 2002. With AC, U.S. Army, 1944-47. Mem. Kansas City Bar Assn. (chmn. bus. orgns. com. 1990-91), Mo. Bar Assn. (chmn. corp. com. 1980-81, 82-83), Lawyers Assn. Kansas City, Am. Judicature Soc., Am. Orgn. Def. Lawyers (pres. 1971-72), U. Mo. Law Soc., Phi Delta Phi, Sigma Chi. Republican. Roman Catholic. Home: 1242 W 67th Ter Kansas City MO 64113-1941 Office Phone: 816-333-3819.

**SHUGHART, WILLIAM FRANKLIN, II,** economics professor, consultant; b. Harrisburg, Pa., Dec. 3, 1947; s. William Franklin and Mary Lucille Shughart; m. Hilary Celia Kauffman, Dec. 29, 1986; children: William Franklin III, Frank Jefferson. BA, Tex. A&M U., College Station, 1969, MS, 1970, PhD, 1978. Economist FTC, Washington, 1978—83; asst. prof. econs. Clemson (S.C.) U., 1984—85; assoc. prof. econs. George Mason U., Fairfax, Va., 1985—88; prof. econs. U. Miss., University, 1988—. Pres. Oxford (Miss.) Economics, Inc., 2004—. Author: Antitrust Policy and Interest-Group Politics, 1990, The Organization of Industry, 1990, Modern Managerial Economics, 1994, The Organization of Industry, 2nd ed., 1997, The Political Economy of the New Deal, 1998; editor: The Causes and Consequences of Antitrust, 1995, Taxing Choice, 1997, The Elgar Companion to Public Choice, 2001, The Economics of Budget Deficits, 2002, Policy Challenges and Political Responses, 2005. Petty officer 3rd class USN, 1971—74. Named F.A.P. Barnard Disting. prof., U. Miss., 1998—; recipient Sir Anthony Fisher Internat. Meml. award, Atlas Econ. Rsch. Found., 1998. Mem.: Pub. Choice Soc., Western Econ. Assn., Am. Econ. Assn., So. Econ. Assn. (trustee 1996—98). Home: 21 County Rd 3024 Oxford MS 38655 Office: Univ Miss Dept of Economics University MS 38677 Office Phone: 662-915-7579. Office Fax: 662-915-6943. Business E-Mail: shughart@olemiss.edu.

**SHUHAN, JANICE-LYNN NAZZIOLA,** secondary school educator; b. Passaic, N.J., Sept. 11, 1959; d. Gabriel Anthony and Camille Mary (Monisera) Nazziola. BS in Math., Montclair State U., 1981, MA in Adminstrn. and Supervision, 1999. Cert. tchr. Substitute tchr. Belleville (N.J.) High Sch., 1977-81, long-term substitute tchr., 1981—, secondary math. tchr., 1986—. Sch. choreographer Belleville Mid. and High Schs., 1978—; dir. mus. Belleville H.S., 1991—; performer nat. tour U.S. Coast, 1979-80; performer off-Broadway and dinner theatres, N.Y. and N.J., 1977-86; presenter N.J. Sch. Bds. Curriculum Fair at Conv. Hall, 1989, 90, 91, 92; profl. performer, actress, singer, dancer. Author (poem): Selections of the Heart and Soul, 2000, External Songs, 2000, Between Darkness and Light, 2000; co-author: The Peace to Come, 2001, Secret Hiding Places, 2001, 2001, Math Essentials, Selected Strategies of Teaching Math Essentials, 1992, 93; contbr. articles to profl. jours.; appeared in motion pictures Other People's Money, A Fire in the Dark, Carlito's Way, and nat. commls. Campaign mgr. Belleville B.O.E., 1989; judge Bell/Nutley Columbus Day Parade Bella Signorina, 1988-91; dance class instructor Nutley Italian Am. Club, 1988; bd. dirs. Cranford Dramatic Club Theatre, mem. bd. govs. Recipient Steven's Leadership award Steven's Inst., Hoboken, N.J., 1990, Outstanding Math Nat. Educator award Tandy Corp., 1991, Alumni Citation, Montclair State U., 2003; named Mrs. West Paterson N.J. America, Essex County Tchr. of Yr. 1999-00. Mem. NEA, ASCD, Nat. Coun. Tchrs. Math., Assn. Math. Tchrs. N.J., Belleville Edn. Assn., N.J. Edn. Assn. Republican. Roman Catholic. Avocations: acting, singing, dance, poetry. Office: Belleville High Sch 100 Passaic Ave Belleville NJ 07109-1898 E-mail: janicelyn1@aol.com.

**SHUHLER, PHYLLIS MARIE,** physician; b. Sellersville, Pa., Sept. 25, 1947; d. Raymond Harold and Catherine Cecilia (Virus) S.; m. John Howard Schwarz, Sept. 17, 1983; 1 child, Luke Alexander. BS in Chemistry, Chestnut Hill Coll., 1971; MD, Mich. State U., 1976; diploma of Tropical Medicine and Hygiene, U. London, 1980. Diplomate Am. Bd. Family Medicine. With Soc. Cath. Med. Missionaries, Phila., 1966-82; ward clk., nursing asst. Holy Family Hosp., Atlanta, 1971-72; resident in family practice Somerset Family Med. Residency Program, Somerville, NJ, 1976-79; physician East Coast Migrant Health Project, Newton Grove, NC, 1980; physician, missionary SCMM, Diocese of Sunyani, Berekum, Ghana, 1980-81; emergency rm. physician Northeast Emergency Med. Assn., Quakertown, Pa., 1981-82; founder, physician Family Health Care Ctr., Inc., Pennsburg, Pa., 1982-90; physician Lifequest Med. Group, Pennsburg, 1990-93; pvt. practice Pennsburg, 1993-99; physician Tri-Valley Primary Care Group, 1999—. Fellow Royal Soc. Tropical Medicine and Hygiene; mem. Am. Acad. Family Practice, Am. Bd. Family Practice, Am. Med. Women Assn. Pa. Acad. Family Practice, Lehigh Valley Women Med. Assn. Roman Catholic. Avocations: guitar, reading, bicycling, hiking. Office: 101 W 7th St Ste 2C Pennsburg PA 18073-1512

**SHUKLA, MANOJ K.,** soil physicist; s. Ravi and Shobha Shukla; m. Neeta Shukla, May 23, 1991; children: Utkarsh, Amogh. PhD, U. Agrl. Sciences, Vienna, Austria, 1998. Post doctoral rsch. assoc. U. of Ill., Urbana, Ill., 2000—01; rsch. scientist Ohio State U., Columbus, 2001—05. Asst. prof. N. Mex State U., Las Cruces, N.Mex., 2005—. Author: (text book) Principles of Soil Physics. Recipient Certficate of Appreciation, Ohio State U., 2005, Rsch. grant, RGBI, 2006, SCERP, 2006—;, Dept. Of Energy-netl, 2003—. Mem.: Soil Sci. Soc. of Am. (assoc. editor 2003). Office: Plant and Environmental Sci NMSU Corner of Knox and Coll Las Cruces NM 88003 Office Phone: 505-646-2324. E-mail: shuklamk@nmsu.edu.

**SHULA, DON FRANCIS,** retired professional football coach, professional sports team executive; b. Painesville, Ohio, Jan. 4, 1930; s. Dan and Mary (Miller) S.; children: David, Donna, Sharon, Anne, Michael; m. Mary Anne Shula. BS, John Carroll U., Cleve., 1951, H.H.D. (hon.), 1972; MA, Case Western Res. U., 1953; Sc.D. (hon.), Biscayne Coll., 1974, St. Thomas U., 1976, U. Miami, 1992, Fla. Atlantic U., 1999. Profl. football player Cleve. Browns, 1951-52, Balt. Colts, 1953-56, Washington Redskins, 1957; asst. coach U. Va., 1958, U. Ky., 1959, Detroit Lions, 1960-62; head coach Baltimore Colts, 1963-69, Miami (Fla.) Dolphins, 1970-96; vice chmn. Miami Dolphins, 1996—; owner, pres. Shula Enterprises. Author: The Winning Edge, 1972, (with Ken Blanchard) Everyone's A Coach, 1995. Fla. crusade chmn. Nat. Cancer Soc., 1975; co-chmn. Jerry Lewis March Against Dystrophy, 1975; nat. bd. dirs. Boy's Hope; mem. nat. sports com. Multiple Schlerosis Soc., Muscular Dystrophy Assn.; bd. dirs. Heart Assn. Greater Miami; established Don Shula Found., breast cancer rsch., 1991—; sponsor Don Shula Scholarship, 1978—. Coached 6 Superbowl teams, winning teams 1972, 73; recipient Coach of Yr. awards 1964, 66, 70, 71, 72, Coach of decade Profl. Football Hall of Fame, 1980, Pro Football's All-Time Winningest Coach, 1994, Brotherhood award Fla. region NCCJ, 1977, Light of Flames Leadership award Barry Coll., 1977, Concern award Cedars Med. Ctr., 1992, Solheim Lifetime Achievement award, 1992, Jim Thorpe award, 1993,Sportsman of Yr. Sports Illustrated, 1993, Horrigan award Pro Football Writers,1994, Horatio Alger award, 1995, Vince Lombardi Award of Excellence, 1999; named Balt. Colts Silver Anniversary Coach, 1977, elected to Pro Football Hall of Fame, 1997. Roman Catholic. Office: Shula Enterprises Inc 16 Indian Creek Is Miami Beach FL 33154-2904 *Success is never final; defeat is never fatal.*

**SHULA, MIKE,** college football coach; b. Balt., June 3, 1965; BA in Labor Relations, Univ. Ala., 1987. Offensive asst. Tampa Bay Buccaneers, 1988—90, quarterbacks coach, 1990—91, offensive coord., 1996—99; coaches asst. Miami Dolphins, 1991—92, quarterbacks coach, 2001—02; asst. coach Chgo. Bears, 1993—95; head coach Univ. Ala., 2003—. Office: Bryant Denny Stadium 100 Bryant Dr Tuscaloosa AL 35487*

**SHULA, ROBERT JOSEPH,** lawyer; b. South Bend, Ind., Dec. 10, 1936; s. Joseph Edward and Bertha Mona (Buckner) S.; m. Gaye Ann Martin, Oct. 8, 1978; children: Deirdre Regina, Robert Joseph II, Elizabeth Martin. BS in Mktg., Ind. U., 1958, JD, 1961. Bar: Ind. 1961. Ptnr. Bingham Summers Welsh & Spilman, Indpls., 1965-82, sr. ptnr., 1982-89; ptnr. Price & Shula, Indpls., 1989-91, Lowe Gray Steele & Darko, Indpls., 1991—2003; of counsel Norris Choplin and Schroeder, Indpls., 2003—05; pvt. practice Indpls., 2005—. Mem. faculty Nat. Inst. Trial Advocacy; guest lectr. Brit. Medicine and Law Soc., 1979, Ind. U. Sch. Law; medico-legal lectr. Ind. U. Schs. Medicine, Dentistry, and Nursing. Bd. dirs Ind. Indpls., 1995-99; founding pres. Oriental Arts Soc., Indpls., 1975-79, Meridian Women's Clinic, Inc., Indpls.; trustee Indpls. Mus. Art, 1975-78, life trustee, 1984—; bd. dirs. Ind. Repertory Theatre, Indpls., 1982-92, chmn. bd. dirs., pres., 1985-89; pres. Repertory Soc., 1993-96; v.p., bd. dirs. Flanner House of Indpls., Inc., 1977-88, chmn., 1988-99; pres. Internat. Ctr. of Indpls., Inc., 1993-96; commr. Indpls. Met. Devel. Commn., 2005—. Maj. JAGC, USAFR, 1961—65. Recipient Gov.'s award of Sagamore of the Wabash. 1998. Master Am. Inns of Ct.; fellow Internat. Soc. Barristers; mem. ABA, FBA, Ind. Bar Assn., Indpls. Bar Assn. (diplomate), Am. Bd. Trial Advs. (pres. 2000), Am. Law Inst., Am. Coll. Legal Medicine, Def. Trial Counsel Ind. (diplomate), Confrerie Chevaliers du Tastevin, Woodstock Country Club. Democrat. Episcopalian. Home: 7924 Beaumont Green Pl Indianapolis IN 46250-1663 Office: 3815 River Crossing Pky Indianapolis IN 46240 Office Phone: 317-848-7804. Business E-Mail: shulalaw@sprynet.com.

**SHULDINER, REED,** law educator; BSE, Princeton U., 1977; JD, Harvard U., 1983; PhD in Econs., MIT, 1985. Assoc. Wilmer Cutler, & Pickering, 1984—86; atty./adv. to Asst. Sec. for Tax Policy Tax Legis. Counsel, US Treasury Dept., 1986—89; counsel Cadwalader, Wickersham & Taft, 1989—90; asst. prof. U. Pa. Law Sch., Phila., 1990—94, prof., 1995—2004, assoc. dean, 2000—02, Alvin Snowiss prof. law, 2004—. Vis. prof. Yale U., 1994—95; William K. Jacobs, Jr. vis. prof. law Harvard U., 2005. Contbr. articles to law jours. Office: U Pa Law Sch 3400 Chestnut St Philadelphia PA 19104 E-mail: RShuldiner@law.upenn.edu.

**SHULENBURGER, DAVID EDWIN,** educational association administrator, economics educator, former academic administrator; b. Salisbury, N.C., Sept. 19, 1945; s. Hubert Ray and Allie (Goodnight) S.; m. Carol Prentice, Aug. 10, 1994; children: Adam Anthony, Neal Gordon, Luke Nathan. BA, Lenoir-Rhyne Coll., 1967; MA, U. Ill., 1968, PhD, 1974. Instr. Clemson U., SC, 1968-71; rsch. asst. U. Ill., Champaign, 1971-72, teaching asst., 1972, 74; staff labor economist U.S. Dept. Labor, Washington, 1973; asst. prof. bus. adminstrn. U. Kans., Lawrence, 1974-77, assoc. prof. bus. adminstrn., 1977-83, prof. bus. adminstrn., 1983—, undergrad. dir., 1982-85, assoc. dean, 1985-88, assoc. vice chancellor, 1989-92, vice chancellor, 1993-96, provost, exec. vice chancellor, 1996—2002, exec. v.p., provost, 2002—06; v.p. academic affairs Nat. Assn. State Univs. and Land-Grant Colls., Washington, 2006—. Cons. Kans. Dept. Human Resources, Topeka, 1975-77, fact-finder, 1979—; panel arbitrator United Mine Workers & P&M Coal Co., Pitts., 1982—; earnings expert for numerous law firms, Kans., Mo., 1979-89. Contbr. articles to profl. jours. Chmn. troop com. Boy Scouts Am., Lawrence, 1984, asst. scoutmaster, 1985—; mem. Kansas City City Coun.; pres. Lawrence Bus./Edn. Partnership, 1995-96. Internat. Curriculum grantee U.S. Dept. Edn., 1987. Mem. AAUP (chpt. pres. 1981-82), Indsl. Rels. Rsch. Assn., Am. Econ. Assn., So. Econ. Assn., Swarthout Soc. (bd. dirs. 1989—). Avocations: travel, camping, gardening. Office: NASULGC Ste 400 1307 New York Ave, NW Washington DC 20005-4722 Office Phone: 202-478-6040. Office Fax: 202-478-6046. E-mail: dshulenburger@nasulgc.org.*

**SHULER, ELLIE GIVAN, JR.,** retired military officer, museum administrator; b. Raleigh, N.C., Dec. 6, 1936; s. Ellie Givan and Berta (Williams) S.; m. Annette Fontaine Maury, Mar. 22, 1961; children: Ellie Givan III, Franklin Maury, Gray Hays. BSCE, The Citadel, 1959; MS in Mgmt., Rensselaer Poly. Inst., 1967; grad., Squadron Officer Sch., Maxwell AFB, Ala., 1964; postgrad., Naval War Coll.; grad. command and staff course, Nat. War Coll., 1976; grad. cen. flight instr. course, Castle AFB, Calif. Engr. in ing., S.C. Commd. 2d lt. U.S. Air Force, 1959, advanced through grades to lt. gen., 1988, various positions and locations, 1959-84, F-4C pilot, asst. flight comdr. 558th Tactical Fighter Squadron Cam Ranh Bay AFB, Republic of Vietnam, 1968-69, indsl. engr., then asst. dep. chief Engring. Mgmt. Div., Hdqrs. 2d Air Force Barksdale AFB, La., 1969-71; asst. exec. officer to comdr. in chief U.S. Air Force in Europe, Lindsey Air Sta., West Germany, 1972-73, base civil engr., comdr. 86th Civil Engring. Squadron Ramstein Air Base, Fed. Republic Germany, 1973-75; dir. ops. 3902d Air Base Wing, comdr. 3902d Ops. Squadron Offutt AFB, Nebr., 1976; dir. programs Office Dep. Chief of Staff for Engring. and Services SAC, Offutt AFB, Nebr., 1976-77, exec. to comdr. in chief, 1977-79; vice comdr., then comdr. 19th Bombardment Wing Robins AFB, Ga., 1979-80; comdr. 42d Bombardment Wing Loring AFB, Maine, 1980-81; comdr. 4th Air Div. F.E. Warren AFB, Wyo., 1981-84; comdr. 3rd Air Div. SAC, Andersen AFB, Guam, 1984-86; asst. dep. then dep. chief of staff, ops. SAC Hqrs., Offutt AFB, Nebr., 1986-88; comdr. 8th Air Force SAC, Barksdale AFB, 1988-91; retired, 1991; chmn. bd., CEO 8th Air Force Heritage Mus., 1992—98. Trustee, Longs Peak coun. Boy Scouts Am., 1983-84, chair bd. trustees, 1992-2004; trustee Falcon Found., USAF Acad., 8th Air Force Heritage Mus., 1992—. Decorated D.S.M. with oak leaf cluster, Legion of Merit with oak leaf cluster, D.F.C., Air medal with five oak leaf clusters, Air Force Commendation medal with oak leaf cluster. Mem. Soc. Am. Mil. Engrs. (chpt. pres. 1971), Am. Def. Preparedness Assn. (regional bd. dirs. 1981-84), Order of Dadealians (hon. flight capt. 1981-85), Council on Am.'s Mil. Past, Mil. Order of World Wars, Kiwanis, Tau Beta Pi. Republican. Episcopalian. Avocations: numismatics, golf, hunting, fishing, military. Office: 675 Willow Way W Alexander City AL 35010-6253 Office Phone: 256-215-5327. E-mail: egshuler@mindspring.com.

**SHULER, JON EMMETT,** securities industry professional; b. Aiken, SC, Sept. 21, 1946; s. Cyril Ovierre and Elizabeth Carolina (Smith) S.; m. Virginia Rose Harris, Aug. 1, 1981; children: Jon Emmett Jr., Kline Martin. BA in Econs., Clemson U., 1968; MBA, U.S.C., 1970. CFP, cert. investment mgmt. cons. Investment Mgmt. Cons. Assn., cert. investment mgmt. analyst Investment Mgmt. Cons. Assn. Broker J.C. Bradford & Co., Spartanburg, S.C., 1972-81, br. mgr., 1981-88, Raymond James & Assocs., Spartanburg, S.C., 1988-94; owner, pres., reg. investment adv. Wealth Mgmt. Assocs., Inc., 1994—. Co-author: Getting to the Heart of the Matter, 1999. Bd. dirs. Habitat for Humanity, Spartanburg, 1990; mem. ARC State Pub. Support Com., Columbia, S.C., 1993; trustee Spartanburg Day Sch., 1997—; v.p. endowments Boy Scouts Am., Palmetto, 1999-2002, mem. exec. bd., 2004-06. Mem. Rotary (pres. North Spartanburg chpt. 1990, chpt. sec., 2006—, Paul Harris fellow 1989), Soc. Mayflower Descendants. Republican. Presbyterian. Avocations: skiing, antiques, woodworking. Personal E-mail: jeshuler@hotmail.com.

**SHULER, KAREN BULL,** elementary school educator; b. Orangeburg, SC, Feb. 23, 1967; d. James Porter and Newell (Jeffords) Bull; m. Dahl Carlisle Shuler, Apr. 1, 1989; children: Sara Ruth, James Porter. BA in Early Childhood, Columbia Coll., 1988; MEd in Early Childhood, SC State U., 1992. Cert. tchg. SC. Elem. tchr. Orangeburg Sch. Dist. #3, Holly Hill, SC, 1988—. Mem. academic com. Holly Hill (SC) Acad., 2005—. Named Tchr. of Yr., Orangeburg Sch. Dist. #3, 1996—97. Mem.: Assn. Supr. and Curriculum Devel., Palmetto State Tchrs. Assn. Avocations: baking, reading, piano, walking, boating. Home: 1028 Planters Trace Rd Santee SC 29142 Office: Holly Hill Elem 1490 Brant Ave Holly Hill SC 29059

**SHULER, KURT EGON,** chemist, educator; b. Nuremberg, Germany, July 10, 1922; came to U.S., 1937, naturalized, 1944; s. Louis and Donie (Wald) Schulherr; m. Beatrice Gwyn London, Nov. 11, 1944. BS, Ga. Inst. Tech., 1942; PhD, Cath. U. Am., 1949. Fellow Johns Hopkins U., 1949-51; sr. staff mem., asst. group supr., chem. physics group Applied Physics Lab., Johns Hopkins, 1951-55; supervisory phys. chemist Nat. Bur. Standards, 1955-58, cons. to dir., 1958-61, asst. dir., sr. research fellow, 1963-68; rsch. staff, sci. adviser to v.p. rsch. Gen. Motors Corp., 1958; spl. asst. to dir. rsch. Inst. Def. Analyses, 1961-63; vis. prof. chemistry U. Calif., San Diego, 1966-67, prof. chemistry, 1968-91, prof. emeritus, 1991—, chmn. dept., 1968-70, 84-87. Cons. in field; mem. Solvay Conf., 1962, 78; mem. adv. panel, chemistry div. NSF, 1963-66; bd. editors: Jour. Statis. Physics, 1968-80; mem. adv. bd.: Chem. Engring. News, 1967-70; contbr. articles to profl. jours. Served with U.S. Army, 1944-46. Recipient Distinguished Service award Nat. Bur. Standards, 1959, Gold medal award Dept. Commerce, 1968; Solvay Found. fellow, 1975 Fellow Am. Inst. Chemists, AAAS, Am. Phys. Soc., Washington Acad. Sci.; mem. Am. Chem. Soc., Washington Philos. Soc. Clubs: Rancho Santa Fe Golf. Home: PO Box 1504 Rancho Santa Fe CA 92067-1504 Office: Univ Calif San Diego Dept Chemistry La Jolla CA 92093 E-mail: kshuler@ucsd.edu.

**SHULER DONNER, LAUREN,** film producer; BS in Film and Broadcasting, Boston U. Assoc. prodr.: (films) Thank God It's Friday, 1978; Mr. Mom, 1983; Ladyhawke, 1985; St. Elmo's Fire, 1985; Pretty in Pink, 1986; Three Fugitives, 1989; Radio Flyer, 1992; Dave, 1993; Free Willy, 1993; prodr.: (TV films) Amateur Night at the Dixie Bar and Grill, 1979; (films) Free Willy 2: The Adventure Home, 1995, You've Got Mail, 1998, Any Given Sunday, 1999, X-Men, 2000, X2: X-Men United, 2003, Timeline, 2003, Constantine, 2005; exec. prodr.: Assassins, 1995; Free Willy 3, 1997; Volcano, 1997; Out Cold, 2001; Just Married, 2003; prodr.: She's The Man, 2006, X-3, 2006, Unaccompanied Minors, 2006. Office: The Donners' Co 9465 Wilshire Blvd Ste 430 Beverly Hills CA 90212

**SHULEVITZ, URI,** writer, illustrator; b. Warsaw, Feb. 27, 1935; came to U.S., 1959, naturalized, 1969; Student, Tel-Aviv Art Inst., 1953-55; Tchrs. Cert., Tchrs. Coll. Israel, 1956; student, Bklyn. Museum Art Sch., 1959-61. Instr. illustrating and writing children's books The New Sch., 1970-86; dir. illustrating and writing children's books Hartwick Coll., 1974-92. Author, illustrator: The Moon In My Room, 1963, One Monday Morning, 1967, Rain Rain Rivers, 1969, Oh What a Noise, 1971, The Magician, 1973, Dawn, 1974, The Treasure, 1978, (Caldecott honor Book 1979) The Strange and Exciting Adventures of Jeremiah Hush, 1986, Toddlecreek Post Office, 1990, The Secret Room, 1993, Snow, 1998 (Caldecott Honor book 1999), What is a Wise Bird like you Doing in a silly tale like this?, 2000, The Travels of Benjamin of Tudela, through three Continents in the Twelfth Century, 2005, So Sleepy Story, 2006; author: Writing with Pictures: How to Write and Illustrate Children's books, 1985; illustrator: The Mystery of the Woods, 1964, Charley Sang a Song, 1964, A Rose, A Bridge and A Wild Black Horse, 1964, The Second Witch, 1965, The Carpet of Solomon, 1966, Maximilian's World, 1966, The Silk Spinners, 1967, The Fool of the World and the Flying Ship, 1968 (Caldecott medal 1969), Runaway Jonah and Other Tales, 1968, The Twelve Dancing Princesses, 1966, Oh What A Noise!, 1971, Soldier and Tsar in the Forest, 1972, The Fools of Chelm, 1973, The Touchstone, 1976, Hanukah Money, 1978, The Lost Kingdom of Karnica, 1979, The Golem, 1982, Lilith's Cave: Jewish Tales of the Supernatural, 1988, The Diamond Tree, 1991, The Golden Goose, 1995, Hosni The Dreamer, 1997, others. Served with Israeli Army, 1956-59. Guggenheim fellow, 1999. Mem Authors Guild. Office: care Farrar Straus & Giroux Inc 19 Union Sq W New York NY 10003-3304

**SHULGASSER-PARKER, BARBARA,** critic, writer; b. Manhasset, N.Y., Apr. 10, 1954; d. Lew and Luba (Golante) S.; m. Norman Parker, Sept. 1999; 1 child: Atticus. Student, Sarah Lawrence Coll., 1973-74; BA magna cum laude, CUNY, 1977; MS, Columbia U., 1978. Feature writer Waterbury (Conn.) Rep., 1978-81; reporter, feature writer Chgo. Sun Times, 1981-84; film critic San Francisco Examiner, 1984-98; freelance book critic N.Y. Times Book Rev., N.Y.C., 1983—; film critic Chgo. Tribune, 1999—2001. Author: Funny Accent, 2001; co-author: (screenplay, with Robert Altman) Ready to Wear, 1994; freelance video columnist N.Y. Times Sunday Arts & Leisure, 1989, features for Vanity Fair, Glamour and Mirabella mags.

**SHULKIN, BARRY,** health facility administrator; b. Amarillo, Tex., Apr. 2, 1952; s. Stanley and Harriet Shulkin; m. Patricia Ann Mandel, June 17, 1990; children: Zachary David, Jeffrey Daniel. BA, U. Tex., Austin, 1974; MD, U. Tex., Dallas, 1978; MBA, U. Mich., Ann Arbor, 2002. Prof. radiology U. Mich., Ann Arbor, 1999—2004; dir. nuc. medicine St. Jude Children's Rsch. Hosp., Memphis, 2004—. Chair fin. com. Am. Bd. Nuc. Medicine, St. Louis, 2004. Grantee, NIH, 1991—2001. Fellow: ACP Avocation: running. Office: St Jude Children's Research Hospital 332 North Lauderdale MS 752 Memphis TN 38105 Office Phone: 901-495-3347.

**SHULKIN, MARTIN B.,** lawyer; b. Cambridge, Mass., Apr. 24, 1944; BA, Williams Coll., 1966; JD, Boston Coll., 1969. Bar: Mass. 1969, Fla., US Ct. Appeals 1st Cir., US Dist. Ct. Dist. Mass. Jud. clk. to Hon. G. Joseph Tauro Superior Ct. Mass., 1969-70; assoc. Burns & Levinson LLP, Boston, 1970—71, ptnr., 1980—99, mng. ptnr., 1992—96; founding ptnr. Soble, Soble & Shulkin, Boston, 1972—79; ptnr. Sweeney & Franklin, Boston, 1979—80, Duane Morris LLP, Boston, 1999—, mng. ptnr. Boston office, 1999—. Editor Boston Coll. Law Rev., 1968-69. Mem. ABA, Boston Bar Assn., Order of Coif. Office: Duane Morris LLP Ste 500 470 Atlantic Ave Boston MA 02210 Office Phone: 617-289-9210. Office Fax: 617-289-9201. Business E-Mail: mbshulkin@duanemorris.com.

**SHULL, CLAIRE,** documentary film producer, casting director; b. NYC, Oct. 26, 1925; d. Barnet Joseph and Fannie (Florea) Klar; m. Leo Shull, Aug. 8, 1948; children: Lee Shull Pearlstein, David. Student, Am. Acad. Dramatic Arts, NYC, 1943—44, NYU, 1973—74. Editor, assoc. pub. Show Bus. Publs., NYC, 1957-85; owner, founder Claire/Casting, NYC and Miami, Fla., 1972—, Claire/Casting Film Prodns., NYC and Miami, 1978—; cons. dir., prodr., dir. film and TV The Bass Mus., Miami Beach, Fla., 1992—. Miami corr. film, TV, theatre Show Bus. Weekly, 1999—; curator archives Show Bus. Pubs. Performing Arts Theatre Collection, N.Y. Pub. Libr., 2005—. Actress in The Front Page, USO European tour, 1945-46, on (Broadway) Tenting Tonight, 1947; prodr., dir. HBO TV series How To Break into Show Business, 1980-81, Cable-TV series, Join Us at the Bass, 1993-97. Recipient gold award and distinctive merit TV award Advt. Club. Hartford, Conn., 1984, Clio award, 1989. Mem.: Drama Desk, Actors Equity Assn., Ind. Casting Dirs. Assn. NY, South Fla. Internat. Press Club, Miami Internat. Press Club.

**SHULL, JOE A.,** lawyer; b. Houston, Sept. 8, 1945; BBA, U. Tex., 1967, JD, 1969; LLM in Taxation, George Washington U., 1976. Bar: Tex. 1969, D.C. 1973, Va. 1976. Law clerk to trial judges U.S. Ct. Claims; ptnr., Bus. Transactions, Mergers & Acquisitions practices Venable LLP, Washington.

Served to capt. U.S. Army, 1970—72. Mem. ABA, D.C. Bar, Va. State Bar. Office: Venable LLP 575 7th St NW Washington DC 20004 Office Phone: 202-344-4821. Office Fax: 202-344-8300. Business E-Mail: jashull@venable.com.

**SHULMAN, ABRAHAM,** otolaryngology educator, hospital administrator; b. N.Y.C., Feb. 24, 1929; s. Ben and Libby (Sarnoff) S.; m. Arlene P., Sept. 8, 1957; children: Rachel, Melanie. BS, CCNY, 1950; MD, U. Berne, 1955. Bar:; diplomate Am. Bd. Otolaryngology., 1962. Rotating surg. intern Queens County Gen. Hosp., 1955—56; resident in otolaryngology Kings County Hosp., Bklyn., 1957—60; clin. instr. Downstate Med. Ctr. SUNY, 1962—64, assoc. prof. Downstate Med. Ctr., 1975—89; prof. clin. otolaryngology SUNY Health Sci. Ctr., Bklyn., 1989—92, prof. emeritus clin. otolaryngology, 1992—; clin. instr. Albert Einstein Coll. Medicine, 1966—68, asst. clin. prof. otolaryn. surgery, 1968—75. Asst. surgeon Bklyn. Eye & Ear Hosp., 1966-69; otology cons. College Point chief of otolaryngology Lincoln Hosp., 1967-70, Bklyn. VA Med. Ctr., 1977-85, chief otolaryngology, staff attending otolaryngologist, 1985—, acting chief of otolaryngology, 1990-91; lectr., asst. attending otolaryngologist Mt. Sinai Hosp., 1974; chief otolaryngology Lincoln Hosp., 1967-1970; asst. attending otolaryngology Bronx Mcpl. Hosp., 1967-75; chief Otolaryngologist, asst. attending otolaryngologist, Kings County Hosp., 1962-64, dir. otolaryngology, 1975-92, attending otolaryngologist, 1975—, Brookdale Med. Ctr., 1982-86; chief otolaryngology Cath. Med. Ctr., Bklyn. and Queens, 1969-94, attending otolaryngologist St. John's Queens Hosp., 1969-94; chmn. Internat. Tinnitus Forum, 1982—; Martha Entenmann Tinnitus Rsch. Ctr., Inc., dir. otology neurotology 1994—. Editor (co-chief): Internat. Tinnitus Jour., 1994—; editor: (text) Tinnitus Diagnosis and Treatment, 1991—. Cons. Children's Devel. Ctr., 1975; med. cons. Office Vocat. Rehab., 1974; dir. med. svc. Lexington Sch. of the Deaf, 1972-74. Lt. comdr. USNR, 1960-62. Recipient Cert. of Appreciation, Am. Speech and Hearing Assn., 1989—, Hocks award, Am. Tinnitus Assn., 1990, Honor award, Am. Acad. Otolaryngology, 1994, Myrtle Reed award, Hadassah Zionist Orgn. Am., honoree, Neuro Equilibrimetric Soc., 1998. Fellow ACS, AMA, Am. Acad. Ophthalmology and Otolaryngology, Am. Neurotology Soc., Am. Audiology Soc., Am. Soc. Ophthalmologic and Otolaryngology Allergy, Am. Soc. Facial Plastic Surgery, Internat. Coll. Surgeons, Adam Politzer Soc.; mem. Am. Coun. Otolaryngology, Am. Soc. Contemporary Medicine and Surgery, Pan-Am. Assn. Otorhinolaryngology and Bronchoesophagology, N.Y. Acad. Sci., Soc. for Cryosurgery, Queens County Med. Soc., Soc. Univ. Otolaryngologists, Bklyn. Oncology Soc., Assn. for Rsch. in Otolaryngology, Neuroequilibrimetric Soc., Harvey Soc., Centurion Club, Sigma Xi. Office: SUNY Health Sci Ctr Bklyn Div Otolaryngology 450 Clarkson Ave Brooklyn NY 11203-2056 Office Phone: 718-773-8888. Personal E-Mail: metrc@inch.com.

**SHULMAN, ARTHUR,** communications executive; b. NYC, Mar. 4, 1927; s. Jacob and Sarah (Hochman) S.; m. Jan. 30, 1958; children: James, Karen. BA, Syracuse U., 1950. Asst. to pub. TV Guide Mag., Radnor, Pa., 1958-72; pub. Seventeen Mag., N.Y.C., 1972-73; dir. regional ops. TV Guide, 1974-82; dir. comm. B'nai B'rith Internat., Washington, 1983-93. Author: How Sweet It Was, 1966, The Television Years, 1972. Dir. Penn Wynne (Pa.) Civic Assn., 1965-66. S/Sgt. US Army, 1945-46, Japan. Mem. Radio & TV Execs. Soc., Nat. Press Club, Overseas Press Club, Nat. Acad. TV Arts & Scis. Jewish. Address: 4017 Jardin Ln Sarasota FL 34238-4504 Personal E-Mail: artshulman@comcast.net.

**SHULMAN, GERALD I.,** physician, scientist, endocrinologist, educator; b. Detroit, Feb. 8, 1953; BS with high honors and distinction, U. Mich., 1974; MD, PhD, Wayne State U., 1979; MA, privatim (hon.), Yale Univ., 1997. Intern Duke U., Durham, NC, 1979-80, residency, 1980-81; fellowship in endocrinology and metabolism Mass. Gen. Hosp., Boston, 1981-84; asst. prof. medicine Harvard U., Boston, 1985-87; assoc. prof. Sch. Medicine Yale U., New Haven, 1989-96; assoc. dir. Yale MD-PhD Program Sch. Medicine Yale U., New Haven, 1993—, prof. medicine, cellular and molecular physiology, 1996—. Vis. prof. Vanderbilt U., 1994, Albert Einstein Coll. Medicine, 1999, Washington U. Sch. Medicine, 2001, Cambridge U., 2002, U. Md., 2004; assoc. dir. Yale Diabetes Endocrine Rsch. Ctr., 1996—; investigator Howard Hughes Med. Inst., 1997—; Sipersten lectr. U. Calif., San Francisco, 2006; program dir. Yale/New Haven Hosp. Gen. Clin. Rsch. Ctr.; Pfizer prof. U. Colo.; mem. NIH study sects.; lectr. in field. Mem. editl. bd. Diabetes, Am. Jour. Physiology; assoc. editor: Diabetic Medicine, Jour. Clin. Investigation, Am. Jour. Medicine, Diabetologia, Internat. Jour. Molecular Medicine, Am. Jour. Physiology, Jour. Biol. Chemistry, Cell Metabolism, 2004—, PLoS Medicine, 2004—; contbr. articles to profl. jours. Recipient Outstanding Investigator award for Clinical Rsch., 1994, Am. Fed. Med. Rsch., 1997, Diabetes Care Rsch. award, Boehriger Mannheim/Juvenile Diabetes Found. Internat., 1997, Young Investigator award in diabetes, Novartis, 1999, Mary June Kugel award, Juvenile Diabetes Rsch. Found. Internat., 1999, E.H. Ahrens Jr. award, Assn. for Patient-Oriented Rsch., 2001, Josiah Brown award in Diabetes, UCLA, 2002, Disting. Clin. Scientist award, Am. Diabetes Assn., 2004, John Shaw Lectureship, ASEAN2, 2006, Sipersten Lectureship, U. Calif. San Francisco, 2006. Fellow ACP, Internat. Soc. Magnetic Resonance in Medicine, Am. Coll. Endocrinologists; mem. Am. Diabetes Assn. (clin. rsch. grantee 1996, Outstanding Sci. Achievement Lilly Lectr. award 1997, Mentor award 1997, 99, Disting. Clin. Scientist award 2004); mem. Am. Physicians, Am. Soc. Clin. Investigation, Endocrine Soc., Inst. Medicine of Nat. Acad. Scis., Am. Physiol. Soc., European Assn. Study of Diabetes, Interurban Clin. Office: Howard Hughes Med Inst Yale U Sch Medicine PO Box 9812 New Haven CT 06536-0812 Fax: 203-737-4059. Business E-Mail: gerald.shulman@yale.edu.

**SHULMAN, LAWRENCE EDWARD,** biomedical researcher, rheumatologist; b. Boston, July 25, 1919; s. David Herman and Belle (Tishler) S.; m. Pauline K. Flint, July 19, 1946; m. Reni Trudinger, Mar. 20, 1959; children: Kathryn Verena, Barbara Corina. AB, Harvard U., 1941, postgrad., 1941-42; PhD, Yale U., 1945, MD, 1949. Diplomate Nat. Bd. Med. Examiners. Intern Johns Hopkins Hosp., 1949-50, resident and fellow in internal medicine, 1950-53; dir. connective tissue div. Johns Hopkins U., 1955-75, assoc. prof. medicine, 1964—; assoc. dir. div. arthritis, musculoskeletal and skin diseases NIH, Bethesda, Md., 1976-86, dir., 1982-86, dir. Nat. Inst. Arthritis, Musculoskeletal and Skin Diseases, 1986-94, dir. emeritus, 1994—, emissary for clin. rsch., 1995—. Chmn. med. adminstrn. com. Arthritis Found., Atlanta, 1974-75, exec. com., 1972-77; dir. Lupus Found. Am.; med. adv. bd. United. Scleroderma Found., Watsonville, Calif., 1977-88; chmn. sci. group rheumatic diseases WHO, 1989; W.R. Graham meml. lectr., 1973; Cochrane disting. lectr., 1993; vice. chmn. Imperial Coll., London, 2002. Discoverer: Eosinophilic Fasciitis, 1974, new med. sign friction rubs in scleroderma, 1961. Recipient Sr. Investigator award Arthritis Found., 1957-62, Disting. Svc. award, 1979, Heberden medal for rsch., London, 1975, Superior Svc. award USPHS, 1985, master Am. Rheumatism Assn., 1986, Spl. Recognition award Nat. Osteoprosis Found., 1991, Spl. award Am. Acad. Orthop. Surgeons, 1992, Presdl. citation for leadership Am. Acad. Dermatology, 1993, Leadership award Lupus Found. Am., 1994, Career Achievement Award Am. Coll. Rheumatology, 1994, Outstanding Support Rsch. award Am. Soc. Bone Mineral Rsch., 1994, Gold medal Am. Coll. Rheumatology, 1995, award of Merit, NASA, 1995, Dean's Spl. Recognition award Johns Hopkins Medicine, 2004. Fellow ACP, AAAS; mem. Am. Rheumatism Assn. (pres. 1974-75), Pan-Am. League Against Rheumatism (pres. 1982-86, Morino Gold medal award 2002), Soc. Investigative Dermatology, Am. Soc. Bone Mineral Rsch. Home: Apt 7BC 3900 Watson Pl B NW Washington DC 20016 Office: NIH 9000 Rockville Pike Bethesda MD 20892-0003 Office Phone: 301-496-4574. Business E-Mail: lcshulman@comcast.net.

**SHULMAN, MAX REES,** lawyer; b. Winston Salem, NC, July 11, 1945; AB, Harvard U., 1967; JD, Columbia U., 1970. Bar: N.Y. 1972, U.S. Dist. Ct. (so. and ea. dists.) N.Y., 1974, U.S. Ct. Appeals (2nd cir.) 1982, U.S. Ct. Internat. Trade, 1982, U.S. Supreme Ct. 1987, U.S. Ct. Appeals (9th cir.) 1987, U.S. Ct. Appeals (fed. cir.) 1988, U.S. Ct. Appeals (5th cir.) 1989.

Lawyer Cravath, Swaine & Moore, N.Y.C., ptnr., litig. Office: Cravath Swaine & Moore Worldwide Plz 825 8th Ave Fl 38 New York NY 10019-7475 Office Phone: 212-474-1890. Office Fax: 212-474-3700. Business E-Mail: mshulman@cravath.com.

**SHULMAN, MILDRED,** artist; b. Perth Amboy, N.J., Aug. 13, 1927; d. Abraham and Estelle Shulman; m. Ben Spina, Feb. 20, 1947 (div. Aug. 1954). Student, Sch. Indsl. Arts, N.Y.C., 1942—45, McDowell Sch. Art, 1946—47, NYU, 1961—62, Art Student's League, 1991—95. Contr. Continental Mdse. Co., Inc., N.Y.C., 1959-65, Famous Fashion Shops, N.Y.C., 1966-69; owner, pres. Luminere Creations, Inc., N.Y.C., 1969-91; self-employed artist N.Y.C., 1991—. Author: Barter "The Silent Giant", 1985. Mem.: Midtown West Art Assn., Am. Soc. Portrait Artists, Nat. Mus. Women in Arts, Art Students League, New Art Ctr., Salmagundi Club. Achievements include 3 patents flexible screen partitions, electrical lighting design, sculpting method. Avocations: hiking, swimming. Office Phone: 212-242-2846.

**SHULMAN, ROBERT GERSON,** biophysics professor; b. NYC, Mar. 3, 1924; s. Joshua S. and Freda (Lipshay) S.; m. Saralee Deutsch, Aug., 1952 (dec. Oct. 1983); children: Joel, Mark, James; m. Stephanie S. Spangler, May 11, 1986. AB, Columbia U., 1943, MA, 1947, PhD, 1949. Rsch. assoc. Columbia U. Radiation Lab., N.Y.C., 1949; AEC fellow in chemistry Calif. Inst. Tech., Pasadena, 1949-50; head semicondr. research sect. Hughes Aircraft Co., Culver City, Calif., 1950-53; mem. tech. staff Bell Labs., Murray Hill, NJ, 1953-66, head biophysics rsch. dept., 1966-79; prof. molecular biophysics and biochemistry Yale U., 1979-94, dir. divsn. biol. scis., 1981-87, Sterling prof. molecular biophysics and biochemistry, 1994—2002, Sterling prof. emeritus molecular biophysics and biochemistry, 2002—, sr. rsch. scientist dept. diagnostic radiology, 2002—. Rask Oersted lectr. U. Copenhagen, 1959; vis. prof. Ecole Normale Superieur, Paris, 1962; Appleton lectr. Brown U., 1965; vis. prof. U. Tokyo, 1965; Reilly lectr. U. Notre Dame, Ind., 1969; vis. prof. biophysics Princeton U., 1971-72; Regents lectr. UCLA, 1978 Lt. (j.g.) USNR, 1944-46. Guggenheim fellow in lab. molecular biology MRC Cambridge (Eng.) U., 1961-62; recipient Havinga medal Leiden U., 1983, Gold medal Soc. Magnetic Resonance in Medicine, 1984, Mem. Nat. Acad. Scis., Inst. Medicine. Achievements include research in spectroscopic techniques applied to physics, chemistry and biology. Office: Dept Diagnostic Radiology MRRC Yale U PO Box New Haven CT 06520-8043 Office Phone: 203-785-6201. Business E-Mail: Robert.Shulman@Yale.edu.

**SHULMAN, ROBERT JAY,** pediatrician, educator, nutritionist, gastroenterologist; b. Newark; s. Irving Jack and Shirley Shulman; children: David Ian, Hannah Rachel. BA, Emory U., 1972; MD, Chgo. Med. Sch., 1976. Diplomate in pediatrics and pediatric gastroenterology Am. Bd. Pediatrics. Asst. prof. pediat. Baylor Coll. Medicine, Houston, 1982-89, assoc. prof., 1989—96, prof., 1996—; dir. nutritional support team Tex. Children's Hosp., Houston, 1982—; chair pediatric gastroenterology Tex. Children's Hosp. Found., 2003. Chmn. sub-bd. in pediatric gastroenterology Am. Bd. Pediatrics, 2003—06. Author: Young Chef's Nutrition Guide and Cookbook, 1990, Keys to Child Nutrition, 1991; author: (with others) Pediatric Parenteral Nutrition, 1997, Principles and Practice of Pediatrics, 1998, Pediatric Gastroenterology and Nutrition in Clinical Practice, 2001; co-editor: Nutrition in Your Pocket, 2002; mem. editl. bd. Jour. Pediat. Gastroenterology and Nutrition, 1994—96. Fellow: Am. Acad. Pediat.; mem.: Soc. Pediat. Rsch., N.Am. Soc. Pediat. Gastoenterology and Nutrition (exec. coun. 1997—99), Am. Inst. Nutrition sect. 1997—99, pres. 1997—99), Am. Gastroent. Assn. Avocation: guitar. Office: Baylor Coll Medicine 1100 Bates Ave Houston TX 77030-2600

**SHULMAN, RON E.,** lawyer; b. Boston, 1955; BA, Amherst Coll., Mass., 1977; JD, Rutgers U., 1981. Bar: N.Y. 1982, Calif. 1995. Ptnr. Fish & Neave, N.Y.C., 1981—95, Wilson Sonsini Goodrich & Rosati, Palo Alto, Calif., 1995—. Named one of Top Ten Jury Trial Lawyers in Country, The Nat. Law Jour., 2002. Office: Wilson Sonsini Goodrich & Rosati PC 650 Page Mill Rd Palo Alto CA 94304-1050 Office Phone: 650-493-9300. Office Fax: 650-493-6811. Business E-Mail: rshulman@wsgr.com.

**SHULMAN, STEPHEN NEAL,** lawyer; b. New Haven, Apr. 6, 1933; s. Harry and Rea (Karrel) S.; m. Sandra Paula Still, Aug. 14, 1954; children: Harry, Dean, John. BA, Harvard, 1954; LL.B. cum laude, Yale, 1958. Bar: Conn. 1958, D.C. 1960. Indsl. relations Bendix Aviation Corp., 1954-55; law clk. to Justice Harlan, U.S. Supreme Ct., 1958-59; vis. asst. prof. U. Mich. Law Sch., 1959; asso. firm Covington & Burling, Washington, 1959-60; asst. U.S. atty. Washington, 1960-61; exec. asst. to sec. labor, 1961-62; dept asst. sec. of def., 1962-65; gen. counsel U.S. Air Force, 1965-66; chmn. Equal Employment Opportunity Commn., 1966-67; mem. Kane, Shulman & Schlei, Washington, 1967-70; mem. firm Cadwalader, Wickersham & Taft, N.Y.C., also Washington, 1971-95, Freedman, Levy, Kroll & Simonds, Washington, 1995-99, O'Connnor & Hannan, L.L.P., Washington, 1999—2005; counsel Ivins, Phillips & Barker, Chartered, Washington, 2005—. Vis. prof. mgmt. U. Okla., 1965-66. Co-author: The Law of Equal Employment Opportunity, 1990; editor in chief Yale Law Jour., 1957-58. Mem. Book and Gavel, Order of Coif, Cum Laude Soc., Phi Alpha Delta. Home: 1332 Skipwith Rd Mc Lean VA 22101-1841 Office: Ivins Phillips & Barker Chartered 1700 Pennsylvania Ave Washington DC 20006-4723 Office Phone: 202-662-3455. E-mail: sshulman@ipbtax.com.

**SHULMAN, STEVEN J.,** health services company executive; Dir. of medical econ. Kaiser Permanente, 1974—82; pres., east ctrl. divsn. CIGNA Healthplans, 1983—86; co-founder Value Health Inc., pres., pharmacy divsn. mgmt group, 1987—91; chmn., pres., CEO Prudential Healthcare Inc., 1997—99; founder Internet HealthCare Group, chmn., CEO, 2000—02; CEO Magellan Health Svcs., Avon, Conn., 2002—, chmn., 2003—. Bd. dir. Lumenos, Digital Ins., RealMed, BenefitPoint Inc., NDCHealth Corp., Internet Health Care Group, HealthMarkets Inc. Office: Magellan Health Svcs 55 Nod Rd Avon CT 06001 Office Phone: 860-507-1900.*

**SHULMAN, YECHIEL,** engineering educator; b. Tel Aviv, Jan. 28, 1930; came to the U.S., 1950; s. David and Rachel (Chonowski) S.; m. Ruth Danzig, June 29, 1950; children: Elinor D., Ron E., Orna L. BS in Aero. Engring., MIT, 1954, BS in Bus. and Engring. Adminstrn., 1954, MS in Aero. Engring., 1954, DSc Aero. and Astro., 1959; MBA, U. Chgo., 1973. Assoc. prof. mech. engring. Northwestern U., Evanston, Ill., 1959-67; v.p. adv. engring. Anocut, Inc., Elk Grove Vill., Ill., 1967-72; v.p. corp. devel. Alden Press, Elk Grove Vill., Ill., 1973-84; pres. MMT Environ., Inc., Shoreview, Minn., 1984-87; cons. Shulman Assocs., Mpls., 1987-89; prof. mech. engring. dept. U. Minn., Mpls., 1989-2000, H. W. Sweatt chair in technol. leadership and dir. ctr. for devel. technol. leadership, 1989-2000, dir. grad. studies mgmt. of tech. program, 1990-2000, prof. emeritus mech. engring. dept., 2000—. Mem. ASME, Internat. Assn. for Mgmt. of Tech. Business E-Mail: shulman@umn.edu.

**SHULRUFF, STUART P.,** lawyer; b. Chgo., Apr. 28, 1959; BS, U. Ill., 1981; JD cum laude, Loyola U., 1984. CPA Ill., 1981; bar: Ill. 1984. Ptnr. Katten Muchin Zavis Rosenman, Chgo. Mem.: Ill. Bar Assn., Chgo. Bar Assn. Office: Katten Muchin Zavis Rosenman 525 W Monroe St Chicago IL 60661 Office Phone: 312-902-5694, 312-577-8680. E-mail: stuart.shulruff@kmzr.com.

**SHULTIS, ROBERT LYNN,** finance educator, consultant, retired professional society administrator; b. Kingston, NY, June 30, 1924; s. Albert H. and Dorothy Elizabeth (Jenkins) S.; m. Bernice Elizabeth Johnson, Jan. 20, 1946; 1 son, Robert Lee. BS, Columbia Univ. Sch. Bus., 1949, postgrad., 1949-51. Staff acct. Price Waterhouse, N.Y.C., 1949-52; credit mgr., controller Organon, Inc., West Orange, NJ, 1952-68; v.p., treas., chief fin. officer Arwood Corp., Rockleigh, NJ, 1968-72; v.p., controller Technicon, Tarrytown, NY, 1972-80; exec. dir. Inst. of Mgmt. Accts., Montvale, NJ, 1980-86; faculty, exec. dir. Ctr. for Exec. Devel. Coll. William & Mary, Williamsburg, Va.,

1987-91. Instr. Rutgers U., 1964-74, Fairleigh Dickinson U., 1967-68; mem. Fin. Acctg. Standards Adv. Coun., 1981-86; lectr., seminar leader, cons. on controllership, activity-based costing, cost mgmt.; cost sys. design Boston U., U. Calif., Berkeley, U. Minn., Michigan State U., So. Meth. U., Baldwin Wallace Coll., George Mason U., James Madison U., U.N.C., Colo. State U., others, 1990—. Editor: Management Accountants' Handbook, and supplements, 1991-94; contbr. feature articles to Va. Gazette, 2001—; contbr. articles to profl. jours. Bd. advs. U. Fla. Sch. Accountancy, James Madison U. Sch. Accountancy; fin. and budget com. Kingsmill Cmty. Svcs. Assn.; interpreter Historic Jamestowne Island, 1997—. With USAF, 1943-45 Decorated Presdl. Unit Citation, ETO Ribbon, eight battle stars. Mem. AAUP, VFW, Am. Legion, Fin. Execs. Internat. (editl. adv. bd.), Inst. Mgmt. Accts., Assn. for Preservation of Va. Antiquities, Kingsmill Club, Beta Alpha Psi (adv. forum).

**SHULTZ, DELRAY FRANKLIN (LUCKY SHULTZ),** business coach, consultant; b. South Bend, Ind., Apr. 4, 1948; s. Jack Raymond and Georgina Martha (Johnston) Shultz; m. Catherine Elizabeth Yontz, June 6, 1970; children: Jeremy Frank, Eric Bruce, Jon Karl. BS, USAF Acad., 1970; MS, Air U., 1978. Commd. 2d lt. USAF, 1970, advanced through grades to capt., 1973, navigator Anchorage, 1972—77, adminstrv. contracting officer LA, 1978—81; mgr. purchasing, contracts supr. BP Exploration, Anchorage, 1981—92, internal cons. Bogotá, Colombia, 1992—93; mgr. contracts, internal cons. Alaska Petroleum Contractors, Anchorage, 1994—97; mgr. assurance and devel., internal cons. Natchiq Inc., Anchorage, 1997—2000; owner Pathways to Leadership, Seattle, 1999—2003, Entrepreneur's Source, Seattle, 2002—03, Lucky Shultz & Assocs., 2003—; pres. IGC Assocs., Inc. 2003; fin. aide Alaska State Senate Senator Fred Dyson, 2004—. Adj. prof. U. Alaska, Anchorage, 1989—96; edn. coord. Bus. Network Internat. (Mill Creek, Wash. chpt.), 2001—03. Bd. dirs., vice chair bd. dirs. Family Connection, Inc., Anchorage, 1981—84; del. Alaska Reps., Anchorage, 1988, 1996; dir., bd. elders Bethany Christian Cmty., Anchorage, 1982—93. Named Outstanding Young Men Am., U.S. Jr. C. of C., 1978; recipient Silver medal, Buckley Sch. Pub. Speaking, 1997. Mem.: Nat. Assn. Purchasing Mgrs., Nat. Contract Mgmt. Assn. Avocations: commercial pilot, public speaker, personal development teacher/coach, musician. Office Phone: 907-694-6683. Personal E-mail: akluck@yahoo.com.

**SHULTZ, GEORGE PRATT,** economics professor, former secretary of state; b. NYC, Dec. 13, 1920; s. Birl E. and Margaret Lennox (Pratt) S.; children: Margaret Ann Shultz Tilsworth, Kathleen Pratt Shultz Jorgensen, Peter Milton, Barbara Lennox Shultz White, Alexander George; m. Charlotte Mailliard, Aug. 15, 1997. BA in Econs., Princeton U., 1942; PhD in Indsl. Econs., MIT, 1949; Hon. degree, Yeshiva U., U. Tel Aviv, Technion-Israel Inst. Tech., Keio U., Tokyo, Brandeis U., U. Notre Dame, Princeton U., Loyola U., U. Rochester, Carnegie-Mellon U., Baruch Coll., Northwestern U., Tblisi State U.; Hon. degree (hon.), Columbia U. Mem. faculty MIT, 1949-57, assoc. prof. indsl. relations, 1955-57; prof. indsl. relations Grad. Sch. Bus., U. Chgo., 1957-68; dean sch. Grad. Sch. Bus. U. Chgo., 1962-68, fellow Ctr. for Advanced Study in Behavioral Scis., 1968-69; sec. US Dept. Labor, 1969-70; dir. Office Mgmt. & Budget Exec. Office of the Pres., 1970-72; sec. US Dept. Treasury, 1972-74; asst. to the Pres. The White House, 1972—74; chmn. Council on Econ. Policy, East-West Trade Policy com.; exec. v.p. Bechtel Corp., San Francisco, 1974-75, pres., 1975-81, vice chmn., 1977-81; also dir.; pres. Bechtel Group, Inc., 1981-82; prof. mgmt. and pub. policy Stanford U., 1974-82, prof. internat. econs., 1989-91, prof. emeritus, 1991—; chmn. Pres. Reagan's Econ. Policy Adv. Bd., 1981-82; sec. US Dept. State, 1982-89; Thomas W. and Susan B. Ford disting. fellow Hoover Instn., Stanford, 1989—. Bd. dirs. Accretive Health, Fremont Group; mem. adv. coun. Bechtel Inc.; chmn. J.P. Morgan Chase Internat. Coun., Accenture Energy adv. bd.; chmn. adv. coun. Inst. Internat. Studies, 1990—98; mem. Calif. Gov.'s Econ. Policy Adv. Bd., 1995—98, 2003—; chmn. Govs. Coun. Econ. Advisors, 2004—. Author: Pressures on Wage Decisions, 1950, (with Charles A. Myers) The Dynamics of a Labor Market, 1951, (with John R. Coleman) Labor Problems: Cases and Readings, 1953, (with T.L. Whisler) Management Organization and the Computer, 1960, (with Arnold R. Weber) Strategies for the Displaced Worker, 1966, (with Robert Z. Aliber) Guidelines, Informal Controls and the Marketplace, 1966, (with Albert Rees) Workers and Wages in the Urban Labor Market, 1970, Leaders and Followers in an Age of Ambiguity, 1975, (with Kenneth W. Dam) Economic Policy Beyond the Headlines, 1977, 2d edition, 1998, Turmoil and Triumph: My Years as Secretary of State, 1993; also articles, chpts. in books, reports, and essays. Served to maj. USMCR, 1942—45. Recipient Medal of Freedom, 1989, Seoul Peace prize, 1992, Eisenhower medal for Leadership and Svc., 2001, Reagan Disting. Am. award, 2002, Ralph Bunche award for diplomatic excellence, 2002; Disting. fellow, Am. Econ. Assn., 2005. Fellow Am. Econ. Assn. (disting.); mem. Indsl. Relations Research Assn. (pres. 1968), Nat. Acad. Arbitrators. Republican. Office: Stanford U Hoover Instn Stanford CA 94305-6010 Business E-Mail: shultz@hoover.stanford.edu.

**SHULTZ, JACK ELLSWORTH,** education educator; b. Dec. 31, 1955; s. Emlyn Leslie Shultz and Florence Louise Schalles; m. Wendy Ellen Miller, June 21, 1986. BS, Bloomsburg U., Pa., 1979, MEd, 1983. Cert. instructional II-comm. & reading PA, 1987. Title I reading tchr. Del. Valley Sch. Dist., Matamoras, Pa., 1983—86, Warwick Sch. Dist., Lititz, Pa., 1986—89; reading & social studies tchr. Keystone Job Corps, Drums, Pa., 1990—2002; title I reading tchr. N.W. area sch. dist., Shickshinny, Pa., 2002—. Logo and cachet, Nescopeck Centennial, 1996; author: An Early History of Nescopeck, 1996. Mem. Friends of Gettysburg, Gettysburg, Pa., 2004, Civil War Preservation Trust, Hagertown, Md., 2000—, Colonial Williamsburg Found., Williamsburg, Va., 2000—. Mem.: FCC (life restricted radiotelephone operator permit issued), Smithsonian Nat. Mus. of the Am. Indian (charter), Nat. Rifle Assn. (life), Nat. Muzzleloading Assn. Republican. Meth. Avocations: history, woodworking, hunting, fishing, drawing. Home: 834 First St Nescopeck PA 18635 Office Phone: 570-542-4126. Business E-Mail: shultzj@northwest.k12.pa.us.

**SHULTZ, JOHN DAVID,** lawyer; b. LA, Oct. 9, 1939; Student, Harvard Coll., 1960—61; BA, U. Ariz., 1964; JD, Boalt Hall, U. Calif., Berkeley, 1967. Bar: N.Y. 1968, Calif. 1978. Assoc Cadwalader, Wickersham & Taft, N.Y.C., 1968—77; ptnr. Lawler, Felix & Hall, L.A., 1977—83, mem. exec. com., chmn. planning com., co-chmn. recruiting and hiring com.; ptnr. Morgan, Lewis & Bockius, L.A., 1983—, chmn. mgmt. com., mem. lateral entry com., chmn. profl. evaluation com., chmn. practice devel. com., chmn. recruiting com. Mem. adv. bd. Internat. and Comparative Law Ctr., Southwestern Legal Found., 1981—; active Practicing Law Inst. Adv. Bd., Corp. and Securities Law, 1992—; Trustee St. Thomas Ch., N.Y.C., 1969—72, Shore Acres Point Corp., Mamaroneck, NY, 1975—77. Mem.: N.Y. State Bar Assn., State Bar Calif., Assn. Bar City of N.Y., ABA. Office: Morgan Lewis & Bockius LLP 300 S Grand Ave Ste 22 Los Angeles CA 90071-3109

**SHULTZ, LOIS FRANCES CASHO,** nursing supervisor; b. Phila., Apr. 29, 1936; d. Ellwood Francis Casho and Beatrice Mae Gunther Casho; m. Thomas Eugene Shultz, Aug. 15, 1959 (div. June 1983); children: David T., Patricia Shultz Bichefsky, Jeffrey A. Nursing diploma, Temple U. Hosp., 1957; BSN, U. Pa., 1961. RN Pa., 2003, bd. cert. gerontol. nursing, ANCC, 2001. Staff nurse Temple U. Hosp., Phila., 1957, pvt. duty nurse, 1958-59; nursing instr. St. Luke's Hosp. Sch. Nursing, Bethlehem, Pa., 1959-61, Reading (Pa.) Area C.C., 1985-88; asst. DON Reading Nursing Ctr., West Reading, 1988-89; night supr. Berks County Home-BerksHeim, Leesport, Pa., 1989—2004; ret., 2004. Mem. Berks County Bd. Assistance, Reading, 1980—, chmn., 1988-2001, chmn. cmty. rels. com., 2001—; pres., dir. Berks County Med. Soc. Aux.; bd. dirs., chmn., mem. children and youth com. Berks County Mental Health Assn.; bd. dirs., past bd. dirs., chmn., mem. Berks County Children and Youth Svcs.; organizer, past dir. Reading Is Fun-damental for Berks County; past mem., chmn., mem. programs and svcs. sub-com. United Way Home Health Care Study Com.; bd. dirs. Berks-Schuylkill unit Arthritis Found., 2005—, sec., 2006—. Mem. Nat. Soc. DAR (1st vice regent br. Berks County chpt. 1977-80). Republican. Presbyterian. Home: 5 Wendy Rd Reading PA 19601-1031 Personal E-mail: templenurse@1usa.com.

**SHULTZ, MARY JANE,** chemist, educator; b. Cosmos, Minn., Feb. 23, 1948; d. John Thomas and Lorraine Mary (Derhaag) Merritt; m. Frederic W. Shultz, June 9, 1970; children: Christopher, Kimberly, Ryan. BS, U. Wis., 1970; PhD, MIT, 1975. Rsch. fellow Harvard U., Cambridge, Mass., 1976-77; rsch. assoc. Boston Coll., Chestnut Hill, Mass., 1977-78; asst. prof. U. Mass., Boston, 1978-79; rsch. fellow Brandeis U., Waltham, Mass., 1979-85; asst. prof. Tufts U., Medford, Mass., 1979-85, assoc. prof., 1985—, vis. prof. MIT, Cambridge, 1985-87; mem. adv. bd. Dudley Wright Ctr., Medford, 1994—. Contbr. articles to profl. jours. Mem. Am. Chem. Soc., Am. Phys. Soc., Sigma Xi. Avocations: skiing, gardening, travel. Office: Tufts U 62 Talbot Ave Medford MA 02155-5813

**SHULTZ, STEPHEN A.,** secondary school educator; BS, NYU, N.Y.C., 1972; MA, NYU, 1976; postgrad., Bklyn. Coll., 1992. Social studies tchr. N.Y.C. Schs., 1972—88; asst. prin. social studies Boys and Girls H.S., Bklyn., 1988—2001; dir. social studies, art in edn. Rocky Point Pub. Schs., Rocky Point, NY, 2001—. Author: Teachers Manual - Global History and Geography, Teachers Manual - U.S. History and Government. Named Tchr. of the Yr., Assn. of Tchrs. Social Studies/United Fedn. Tchrs., 1987—88; fellow, Rockefeller Found., 1986, Gilder Lehrman fellow. Mem.: Nat. Coun. for the Social Studies, L.I. Coun. for the Social Studies. Avocations: race walking, tropical fish, reading.

**SHUMACKER, HARRIS B., JR.,** retired surgeon, educator, author; b. Laurel, Miss., May 20, 1908; s. Harris B. and Corinne (Teller) S.; m. Myrtle E. Landau, Dec. 1, 1933 (dec.); children: Peter D., James N.; m. Grace McConnel, Nov. 9, 1998. BS, U. Tenn., Chattanooga, 1927; A.M., Vanderbilt U., 1928; MD, Johns Hopkins U., 1932; D.Sc. (hon.), Ind. U., 1985. Diplomate Am. Bd. Surgery, Am. Bd. Thoracic Surgery. Asst. in surgery Johns Hopkins U., 1932-35, instr., 1938-41, asst. prof., 1941-46; asst. in surgery Yale U., 1936-37, instr., 1937-38, assoc. prof., 1946-48; prof. surgery Ind U., 1948-70, chmn. dept., 1948-68, Disting. prof., 1970-78, Disting. prof. emeritus, 1978—. Prof., sr. advisor Uniformed Svcs. U. of Health Scis., Bethesda, Md., 1981-87, Disting. prof. surgery, 1988—; pres. Uniformed Svcs U. Assocs., 1987-88; hon. mem. surg. faculties in Peoples Republic of China, 1979-; dir. cardiovascular-thoracic surgery St. Vincent Hosp., 1973-78, sr. surg. cons., 1978-81. Served from capt. to lt. col. M.C., U.S. Army, 1942-46; cons. surgeon gen., 1949-60 Recipient Roswell Park award, 1968, Medal of Honor, Evansville U., 1970, Disting. Alumus award U. Tenn. at Chattanooga, Curtis medal, 1970, Spl. Alumnus award Johns Hopkins U., 1973, Disting. Svc. award Am. Soc. Abdominal Surgery, letter of commendation Surgeon-Gen. USN, 1987, Disting. Svc. medal Uniformed Svc. U. Health Scis., 1988, René Leriche prize Soc. Internat. de Chir., 1993. Fellow Royal Coll. Surgeons Eng. (hon.); mem. Am. Assn. Surgery of Trauma, Am. Surg. Assn. (1st v.p. 1961, sec. 1964-68), Soc. Surg. Assn., Ctrl. Surg. Assn., Pan-Pacific Surg. Assn. (trustee 1961-64, v.p., 1964-75, pres. 1975-78), AMA (chmn. sect. gen. surgery), Internat. Surg. Soc., Internat. Soc. Cardiovasc. Surgeons (v.p. 1957-59, pres. N.Am. chpt. 1956-58), Soc. Clin. Surgery (pres. 1961-63), ACS (chmn. forum com. 1955-60, chmn. nat. TV com. 1964-68, Disting. Service award 1968), Soc. U. Surgeons (pres. 1951), Soc. for Vascular Surgery (pres. 1958-59, disting. fellow 2003), Am. Thoracic Surg. Assn., Soc. Thoracic Surgeons (hon.), Internat. Surg. Group (v.p 1974-75, pres. 1975-76), Polish Surg. Assn. (hon.), Sociedad Cubana de Angiologia (hon.), Societa Italiana di Chirurgia (hon.), Internat. Surg. Group (hon.), Phi Beta Kappa, Sigma Xi, Alpha Omega Alpha.

**SHUMAKER, GREGORY M.,** lawyer; b. Reading, Pa., 1962; ScB, Brown Univ., 1984; JD, Univ. Notre Dame, 1987. Bar: Pa. 1987, DC 1988, admitted to practice: US Dist. Ct., DC. Adminstrv. ptnr. Jones Day, Washington. Mem.: DC Bar Assn. Office: Jones Day 51 Louisiana Ave NW Washington DC 20001-2113 Office Phone: 202-879-3679. Office Fax: 202-626-1700. Business E-Mail: gshumaker@jonesday.com.

**SHUMAKER, TARA L.,** performing arts educator; b. N. Wildesboro, N.C., Nov. 11, 1973; d. Bobby Lee and Shirley Ann (Pipes) Shumaker. BFA in Dance, E. Carolina U., 1997; MFA in Dance, U. N.C., 2001. Tchg. asst. U. N.C., Greensboro, 1998—2001; tchr., choreographer J.H. Rose H.S., 2001—05. Guest lectr. U. N.C., Greensboro, 1998—2001. Dancer Wilkes Cmty. Coll. Theatre, Powder Horn Theater, High County Youth Ballet, Burklyn Ballet Theatre, Horn In The West, 1996, 1998, Dancing for Friends, 1999, Internat. Dance Conf., 1999, N.C. Dance Festival, 1999, John Gamble Dance Theater, 2000, Dance Nova Dance Co., 2000, Am. Dance Festival, 2001, Dance Collective, 2002. Artistic dir. Pitt County Contemporary Dance Co. Avocations: martial arts, yoga, pilates. Home: PO Box 99 North Wilkesboro NC 28659

**SHUMAN, ANN,** investment company executive; b. 1968; BA in Eng. Trinity Univ., San Antonio, Tex.; JD, Univ. Chgo. Atty., derivatives, investments products group Sidley & Austin, Chgo.; with Chgo. Merc. Exch. Holdings, Inc., Chgo., 2000—, dir., co-head copr. devel., 2005—. Named one of 40 Under Forty, Crain's Bus. News, 2005. Office: Chgo Merc Exch Holdings Inc 20 Wacker Dr Chicago IL 60606 Office Phone: 312-930-1000.*

**SHUMAN, CAROLYN RAE (THORBURN),** psychologist, columnist, writer, nurse; d. Donald Spencer and Eileen Mary Thorburn; m. Gary H. Shuman, Nov. 22, 1975; m. Dennis Lee Atkin, June 15, 1963 (div. July 20, 1968); 1 child, Dennis Lee Atkin, Jr. PhD, Tex. A&M U., Commerce, 1985—96; MS, East Tex. State U., Commerce, 1985—90; BS, Bapt. Coll. of Charleston, SC, 1977—78; AA, Armstrong State Coll., Savannah, Ga., 1972—76. RN 1975. Owner Ctr. for Cognitive Therapy, Hamilton, Bermuda, 1999—2003; dir. family svc. ctr. USNAS-Bermuda, St David's, 1992—95; psychotherapist/psychologist Ashton Associates, Hamilton, 1994—99; clin. supr. USNAS-Bermuda, St. David's, 1991—94; adj. prof. Webster U., U. of Md., City Colleges of Chgo., USNAS-Bermuda, 1991—97. Cons. King Edward Hosp. VII EAP, Hamilton, 2001—03, Family Learning Ctr., Hamilton, 1994—96. Author: (book) Jenny Is Scared: When Sad Things Happen in the World (Psychology Grad. Faculty Scholarship, Tex. A&M-Commerce, 1987). Mem., spkr. Bermuda Chamber of Commerce, Hamilton, 2000—03; mem. Fairhaven Christian Care/ Nat. Drug Strategy/, Hamilton, 1998—2001. Recipient Journalism Enterprise, Ga. AP, 1972; scholar Honors Scholarship, Armstrong State Coll., 1973-1975, Grad. Faculty Honors, Tex. A&M Psychology Dept., 1987. Mem.: Nat. Writer Assn., Bermuda Psychol. Assn. (assoc.; pub. info. officer 2003—04), APA (life). Achievements include research in cross culture, health, cognitive behavior therapy, hardiness; death studies (Psychology Journal, 1992); presentations, Death & Dying, SWPA, 1993-1997. Avocations: writing, swimming, travel, music. Home: 1941 SE 26th Terrace Cape Coral FL 33904-3248 Office: Family and Children First DelPrado Boulevard Cape Coral FL 33904 Office Phone: 441-505-5792. E-mail: drcshuman@datkin.net.

**SHUMAN, CHARLES R.,** medical educator, internist; b. Harrisburg, Pa., Sept. 18, 1918; s. Charles R. and Esther G. Shuman; m. Mary M. Shuman; children: Charles R., Sandra J. DeSante. BA, Gettysburg Coll., Pa., a 1940, DS (hon.), 1973; MD, Temple U., Phila., 1943, MS, 1944. Diplomate Am. Bd. Internal Medine. Intern Temple U. Hosp., Phila., 1943—44, resident in internal medicine, 1944—46, 1948—49, instr., 1949—52, asst. prof. medicine, 1952—58, assoc. prof. medicine, 1958—63, prof. medicine, 1966—89, prof. emeritus, 1989—, chief metabolic svcs., 1952—78. Cons. metabolic diseases Phila. Gen. Hosp., 1957—66, VA Hosp., 1957—66, Doylestown Hosp., 1965—80; mem. various editl. bds. Capt. U.S. Army, 1946—48. Recipient Golden Apple awrd, Temple U. Sch. Medicine, 1963. Fellow: ACP, Phila. Coll. Physicians; mem.: AMA, Profl. Diabetes Acad. (bd. dirs.), Endocrine Soc. Phila., J. Aitken Miegs Med. Assn., Am. Geriatric Soc., Am. Diabetes Assn. (coord. Ea. Pa. 1965—74, dir. 5th allied health postgrad. course 1973, co-dir. 21st postgrad. course 1974, chmn. com. on use of therapeutic agts. 1974—75, bd. dirs. 1976—, vice chmn. com. on stats. 1978—80, coord. com. sci. activities 1978—80, ad hoc com. gestational diabetes 1979, Ann. Tchg. award 1978, lifetime achievement award), Am. Fedn. Clin. Rsch., Pa. Med. Soc. (com. on med. ecion. 1978—80, nominating com. 1979—80), Phila. County Med. Soc. (dir. postgrad. inst. 1966—67, bd.

dirs. 1972—78, pres. 1977). Temple U. Med. Alumni Assn. (trustee, mem. exec. com. 1977—, chmn. awards com. 1992—93, Man of Yr. awrd 1978), Alpha Omega Alpha, Sigma Xi. Republican. Presbyterian. Avocations: travel, music, gardening. Home: 111 Delene Rd Jenkintown PA 19046 Office: Temple U Hosp 3401 N Broad St Philadelphia PA 19140

**SHUMAN, EARL STANLEY,** songwriter, music publisher; b. Boston, Aug. 2, 1923; s. Benjamin Morris and Mildred Judith (Kaplan) S.; m. Margaret Stein, Nov. 25, 1956; children: Cathy Elizabeth, Daniel James, Steven Lewis. BA, Yale U., 1947. Owner, pres. Earl/Peg Music Cos., N.Y.C., 1957—; pub. BMI, ASCAP, N.Y.C., 1977—. Composer (lyric writer) popular songs including Seven Lonely Days, 1953 (Country and Western award 1970), Hey There Lonely Girl, 1970 (Gold record), Banjo's Back in Town, Caterina, Clinging Vine, Close to Cathy, Hotel Happiness, Left Right Out of Your Heart, Most People Get Married, My Shy Violet, The River, Starry-Eyed, Theme For a Dream, Time, Time, Young New Mexican Puppeteer; lyricist (musicals) Secret Life of Walter Mitty, 1964 (award 1965), (country song) Leaves are the Tears of Autumn, 1968 (Country and Western award 1969), (TV themes) Coronet Blue, ABC TV, 1967, Confidence/NFL-CBS, 1967-76, (Movie Title Songs) The Disorderly Orderly, Judith, Situation Hopeless But Not Serious, Robinson Crusoe on Mars, Barrabas, Monica (love theme from The Carpetbaggers), Love Me Longer (love theme from Arrivederci Baby); pub. Bat Out of Hell album, 1977 (platinum award 1979). Capt. USMCR, 1943-46, 50-51. Mem.: ASCAP. Avocations: music, baseball. Home and Office: 111 E 88th St Apt 3B New York NY 10128-1158 Office Fax: 212-722-3698. Personal E-mail: earlmusic@earthlink.net.

**SHUMAN, JOSEPH DUFF,** lawyer; b. Pitts., Dec. 27, 1942; s. Joseph and Anna Jane (Phillips) D.; m. Ann Stewart McMillan, Nov. 9, 1969; children: David Stewart, Lauren Forbes. BA, Yale U., 1964; LLB, Harvard U., 1967. Bar: Pa. 1968, U.S. Dist. Ct. (we. dist.) Pa. 1968. Assoc. Thorp, Reed & Armstrong, LLP, Pitts., 1967-73, ptnr., 1974—2004, co-chmn., corp. and bus. law dept., 1990-94, chmn., 1994-97, sr. counsel, 2004—. Republican. Presbyterian. Office: Thorp Reed & Armstrong LLP One Oxford Ctr 301 Grant St 14th Fl Pittsburgh PA 15219-1425 Business E-Mail: jshuman@thorpreed.com.

**SHUMAN, R. BAIRD,** academic administrator, consultant, language educator, writer; b. Paterson, NJ, June 20, 1929; s. George William and Elizabeth (Evans) Shuman. AB (Trustees scholar), Lehigh U., 1951; M.Ed., Temple U., 1953; PhD (Univ. scholar), U. Pa., 1961; cert. in philology, U. Vienna, Austria, 1954. Tchr. Phila. Pub. Schs., 1953-55; asst. instr. English U. Pa., 1955-57; instr. humanities Drexel U., Phila., 1957-59; asst. prof. English San José (Calif.) State U., 1959-62; asst. prof. English, edn. Duke U., 1962-63, assoc. prof., 1963-66, prof. edn., 1966-77; prof. English, 1977-93, dir. English edn. U. Ill., Urbana-Champaign, 1977-85, dir. freshman rhetoric, 1979-84, coord. Univ. Associates in Rhetoric Program, 1978-84, dir. devel., 1988-93, acting dir. Ctr. for Study of Writing, 1989-90, prof. emeritus, 1993—. Vis. prof. Moore Inst. Art, 1958, Phila. Conservatory Music, 1958—59, Lynchburg Coll., 1965, King Faisal U., Saudi Arabia, 1978, Saudi Arabia, 81, Bread Loaf Sch. English, Middlebury Coll., 1980, E. Tenn. State U., Johnson City, 1980, Olivet Nazarene Coll., 1984, 86, 88, U. Tenn., Knoxville, 1987; com. mem. William Inge Nat. Festival, 1989—95; contbg. cons. Lit. Rsch. Ctr.; cons. in field. Author: Clifford Odets, 1962, Robert E. Sherwood, 1964, William Inge, 1965, Strategies in Teaching Reading: Secondary, 1978, Elements of Early Reading Instruction, 1979, The First R: Strategies in Early Reading Instruction, 1987:; rev. edit., 1989, Classroom Encounters: Problems, Case Studies, Solutions, 1989, Resources for Writers, 1992, American Drama 1918-1960, 1992, Georgia O'Keeffe, 1993; author: (with Robert J. Krajewski) The Beginning Teacher: A Guide to Problem Solving, 1979; author: (with Eric Hobson) Reading and Writing in High School; author: (with Denny T. Wolfe Jr.) Teaching English Through the Arts, 1990; editor: Nine Black Poets, 1968, An Eye for an Eye, 1969, A Galaxy of Black Writing, 1970, Creative Approaches to the Teaching of English: Secondary, 1974, Questions English Teachers Ask, 1977, Educational Drama for Today's Schools, 1978, Education in the 80's-English, 1980, The Clearing House: A Closer Look, 1984, 70th anniversary issue Clearing House, 1995, Great American Writers: 20th Century, 13 vols., 2002, Cyclopedia of Literary Places, 3 vols., 2003, The Clearing House: A Retrospective, 2004, Ednl. Leadership, 1989—96; exec. editor: Clearing House Jour., 1976—2006, cons. editor: Poet Lore, 1977—90, Cygnus, 1978—2001, Jour. Aesthetic Edn., 1978—82, contbg. editor: Reading Horizons, 1975—85. Active Nat. Trust Hist. Preservation. NEH grantee, Trinity Coll., Dublin, Ireland, 1985. Mem.: MLA, Union Profl. Employees (editor newsletter, mem. exec. com. 1988—92, mem. editl. bd. Poeteka 2005—), Am. Fedn. Tchrs., Nat. Soc. Study Edn., Internat. Assn. Univ. Profs. English, Internat. Reading Assn. (coord. symposium cultural literacy Queensland, Australia 1988), Conf. English Edn. (mem. exec. com. 1976—79), Internat. Fedn. Tchrs. English, Nat. Coun. Tchrs. English (evaluator ERIC Clearing House, mem. com. alt. careers English profs.). Democrat. Home: PO Box 27647 Las Vegas NV 89126-1647 E-mail: rbaird@intermind.net. *An education that does not produce people who are vibrantly alive, intoxicated with the wonder of existence, has fallen short. Joy of learning is the fulcrum upon which the human equation is balanced. I have always believed that emotion prevails over intellect and have led my life accordingly with the inevitable result of being extraordinarily happy for most of my days.*

**SHUMAN, SAMUEL IRVING,** lawyer, educator; b. Fall River, Mass., Aug. 7, 1925; s. Max and Fannie S.; children: Maxim Erric, Michael A. AB, U. Pa., 1947, MA, 1948, PhD, 1951; JD, U. Mich., 1954; SJD, Harvard U., 1959. Bar: Mich. 1954, Tex. 1959. Research asst. Legis. Research Center, U. Mich., Ann Arbor, 1953-54, vis. prof. law, 1961; vis. prof. U. Rome, 1963-64; asst. prof. law Wayne State U., Detroit, 1954-55, assoc. prof., 1955-56, prof., 1957-80; prof. dept. psychiatry Wayne State U. Med. Sch. Lectr. Internat. Faculty Comparative Law, Luxembourg, 1964; prof. forensic psychiatry, spl. counsel Lafayette Clinic, Mich. Dept. Mental Health; gen. counsel Mich. Psychiat. Assn., Epilepsy Center Mich. Author: Legal Positivism: Its Scope and Limitations, 1963, (with N.D. West) Introduction to American Law: Cases and Materials, 1971, Psychosurgery and the Medical Control of Violence: Autonomy and Deviance, 1977; editorial bd.: Am. Jour. Jurisprudence, 1969-79. Bd. dirs. Tex. Modern Art Found. Recipient Wayne State U. Bd. Govs. Faculty Recognition award, 1978; Probus Club award Disting. Acad. Achievement in Humanities, 1963; Fulbright fellow Italy, 1961; Rockefeller Found. grantee, 1959, 61; Fulbright travel grantee Germany, 1961; Wayne State U. research grantee, 1960-64; Internat. Research & Exchanges Bd. grantee, 1973 Mem. Am. Law Inst. (life). E-mail: sishuman@mail.ev1.net.

**SHUMAN, STANLEY S.,** investment banker; b. Cambridge, Mass., June 22, 1935; s. Saul A. and Sarah L. (Saxe) S.; m. Ruth H. Lande, 1967 (div. 1979); children: David Lande, Michael Adam; m. Sydney Roberts Gould, 1992. BA, Harvard U., Cambridge, 1956, JD, 1959, MBA, 1962. Bar: Mass. 1959, N.Y. 1991. Mng. dir. Allen & Co., LLC, NYC, 1961—. Bd. dirs. News Corp., 1982-2005, News Am. Holdings Inc., Sesac Inc., Six Flags, Inc.; mem. Pres.'s Fgn. Intelligence Adv. Bd., 1995—2001. Mem. Fin. Control Bd., NYC, 1977-97; trustee Channel 13 WNET, 1990—, Carnegie Hall, 1990—, Mus. TV and Radio, 1996—, NY Law Sch., 1990-96, The Markle Found., 1992-03, Nat. Pub. Radio Found., 1992—; chmn. Nat. Econ. Devel. and Law Ctr., 1978-83; chmn. adv. bd. Inst. Policy Scis. and Pub. Affairs Duke U., 1992-96, Palamon Capital Ptnrs. Harvard U. and Dept. Bd. Overseers Com. U. Resources, 1995—; bd. advisors; hon. trustee The Dalton Sch., 1977-84, 84-, Phillips Acad., Andover, Mass., 1972-80; pres. Wiliwyck Sch., 1971-78; v.p. exec. com. Jewish Guild for the Blind, 1973-80; trustee Jewish Publ. Soc., 1986-90, Vail Valley Found.; mem. Coun. on Fgn. Rels.; dir. Lower Manhattan Devl. Corp. Clubs: Harvard (Boston), Harvard (NYC), Econ. Club NY, Deepdale Golf Club, Atlantic Golf Club, Eagle Rock Golf Club, Quaker Ridge Golf Club, East Hampton Tennis.

**SHUMATE, ALEX,** lawyer; b. DeKalb, Miss., June 14, 1950; m. Sharon Louise Holley, Aug. 3, 1974; children: John Alexander, Aaron Michael. BA in Polit. Sci., Ohio Wesleyan U., 1972; JD, U. Akron, 1975. Bar: Ohio 1975,

U.S. Dist. Ct. (no. and so. dists.) Ohio 1976, U.S. Supreme Ct. 1980. Asst. atty. gen. State of Ohio, Columbus, 1975-83; atty. Brownfield, Bally & Goodman, Columbus, 1983-85; chief counsel, dep. chief of staff Gov., State of Ohio, Columbus, 1985-88; mng. ptnr.- Columbus, Ohio Office Squire, Sanders & Dempsey L.L.P., Columbus, 1988—. Bd. dirs. Bank One Corp., Chgo, Bank One, N.A., Columbus, Intimate Brands, Inc., Columbus, William Wrigley Jr. Co., Chgo. Bd. trustees Ohio State U., Ohio Wesleyan U., Columbus Mus. of Art; governing com. The Columbus Found.; 1st vice chmn. Columbus Urban League; bd. trustees, exec. com. BalletMet; bd. govs. Pub. Policy Com., United Way of Franklin County; exec. com. 29th Dist. Citizens Caucus, 1992 Commn., Christopher Columbus Quincentennial Jubilee Commn.; founding trustee Participation 2000, Berwick Civic Assn. Recipient Jewish Nat. Fund Tree of Life award 1996, Robert S. Crane Trusteeshp award Leadership Columbus, 1995, Spl. Achievement award NAACP, 1989, Disting. cmty. Svc. award Columbus Urban League, 1987, Cert. of Outstanding Achievement 116th Ohio Gen. Assembly 1985, Polit. Leadership award 29th Dist. Citizens Caucus, 1984, Outstanding Legal Cmty. Svc. award Captial U. Sch. of Law, 1982, Superior Achievement award United Negro Coll. Fund, 1982; named Outstanding Alumni U. Akron Law Sch., 1994, Disting. Alumnus Ohio Wesleyan U., 1992. Fellow Columbus Bar Assn. (governing bd., Cmty. Svc. award 1986), Ohio State Bar Assn. (coun. of dels.); mem. Lambda Boule, John Mercer Langston Bar Assn., Greater Columbus C. of C. (1st vice chair), The Capital Club (bd. govs.). Office: Squire Sanders & Dempsey LLP 41 S High St Ste 1300 Columbus OH 43215-6197 Office Phone: 614-365-2739. Office Fax: 614-365-2499. Business E-Mail: ashumate@ssd.com.

**SHUMWAY, ERIC,** academic administrator; BA, Brigham Young U., 1964, MA, 1966; PhD, U. Va., 1973. Prof. English and modern languages Brigham Young U.-Hawaii, 1966—, pres., 1994—. Office: Brigham Young U-Hawaii 55-220 Kulanui St Laie HI 96762 Business E-Mail: shumwaye@byuh.edu.

**SHUMWAY, JAMES M.,** dean, medical educator; b. San Francisco, Dec. 16, 1947; s. Berte A. Olson; m. Lizbeth A. Pyle, Mar. 24, 1984; 1 child, Wesley A. BA, U. Pacific, Stockton, Calif., 1970; MEd, U. NC, 1976, PhD, 1981. Dir. faculty devel. U. Ky. Coll. Medicine, Lexington, Ky., 1980—83; project dir. Aramco dental auxillary tng. project U. Ky. Coll. Dentistry, Lexington, Ky., 1983—85; from asst. to assoc. prof. medicine and pediat. W.Va. U. Sch. Medicine, Morgantown, 1985—91, assoc. dean med. edn., 1991—, prof. medicine and pediat., 1996—; interim dean W.Va. U. Sch. Pharmacy, Morgantown, 1994—95. Mem. med. sch. site rev. teams Liaison Com. on Med. Edn., Chgo., 1988—; chair Faculty Senate W.Va. U., Morgantown, 1998—99, chair Ext. Divsn. Vis. Com., 2003—; vis. prof. U. Dundee Sch. Medicine, Dundee, Scotland, 2000; cons. Fla. Atlantic U., Boca Raton, 2004—. Mem. editl. adv. bd. Dominion Post Newspaper, Morgantown, 2005—05; chmn. bd. dirs. W.Va. Rivers Coalition, Elkins, 1989—2001. Recipient Innovation of Pharmacy Edn. award, Am. Assn. Colls. Pharmacy, 1993; grantee, Nat. Libr. Medicine, 1990—93, Fund for the Improvement of Post-Secondary Edn. HHS, 1991—94, Astra-Merck Found., 1995—96; Faculty fellow, Liaison Com. on Med. Edn., 1988, Harvard-Macy scholar, Harvard U. Macy Inst., Boston, 1995. Mem.: Assn. Med. Edn. in Europe, Am. Ednl. Rsch. Assn., Assn. Am. Med. Colleges (nat. chmn. undergrad. med. edn. 2003—04, group on ednl. affairs), Generalists in Med. Edn. Avocations: telemark skiing, whitewater kayaking/canoeing, piano playing, fly fishing, youth soccer. Office: WVa Univ Sch Medicine PO Box 9007 Morgantown WV 26506 Office Phone: 304-293-1829. Office Fax: 304-293-7814. Business E-Mail: jshumway@hsc.wvu.edu.

**SHUPE, SCOTT MARSHALL,** engineering educator, consultant; s. Keith L. and Marita W. Shupe; m. Mayumi-Mae Lacaya Santiago, Sept. 27, 1997; children: Marshall, Catalina. BS, Dalhousie U., Halifax, NS, Can., 1986; M of Engring., U. NB, Fredericton, NB, Can., 1991; PhD, U. Ariz., Tucson, 2000. Rsch. assoc. NRC, Denver, 2000—02; project leader, sr. analyst Space Imaging, Sacramento, 2002—04; cons. Shupe Geomapping, 2004—; adj. prof. Cosumnes River Coll., 2005—06; faculty mem. U. Coll. Fraser Valley, Abbotsford, British Columbia, Canada, 2006—. Scholar, Swiss Fed. Inst. Tech., 1991. Mem.: Can. Remote Sensing Soc., Am. Assn. Geographers, Am. Soc. Photogrammetry and Remote Sensing.

**SHUPP, MATTHEW RYAN,** director, educator; b. Kingston, Pa., Aug. 22, 1977; s. Lester Russell, Jr. and Sally Ann Shupp; life ptnr. Cara Lee Shupp. BA, Shippensburg U., 2000, MS, 2003. Nat. cert. counselor Nat. Bd. Cert. Counselors. Residence dir. Shippensburg U., Shippensburg, Pa., 2000—03; coord. student life The Restaurant Sch. at Walnut Hill Coll., Philadelphia, Pa., 2003—04; asst. dir. student life CC of Phila., 2004—. Adj. instr. Delaware County CC, Media, Pa., 2004—. Contbr. articles to profl. jours. Mem.: Am. Coll. Pers. Assn., Pa. Coll. Pers. Assn., Nat. Orientation Dirs. Assn. Democrat. Office: CC of Phila 1700 Spring Garden St Rm S1 19 Philadelphia PA 19130 Office Phone: 215-751-8882. Office Fax: 215-972-6324. Business E-Mail: mshupp@ccp.edu.

**SHUR, MICHAEL,** electrical engineer, educator, consultant; b. Kamensk-Uralski, Sverdlovsk, USSR, Nov. 13, 1942; came to U.S., 1976. s. Saul and Anna (Katz) S.; m. Paulina Gimmelfarb, Sept. 25, 1966; children: Luba, Natasha. MS, Leningrad Elec. Tech. Inst., 1965; PhD, Ioffe Inst., Leningrad, 1967; DSc, Ioffe Inst. St. Petersburg, 1992; Hon. Doctorate, St. Petersburg State Tech. U., 1994. Scientist Ioffe Inst., 1965-75; asst. prof. Wayne State U., Detroit, 1976-77, Oakland U., Rochester, Mich., 1978; prof. U. Minn., Mpls., 1979-92; John Marshall Money prof. U. Va., Charlottesville, Va., 1989-96; Patricia W. and C. Sheldon Roberts prof. Rennselaer Poly. Inst., 1996—; assoc. dir., prof. physics and info. tech. Ctr. Integrated Electronics and Electronics Mfg., 1997—; dir. Ctr. for Broadband Data Transport Sci. and Tech., 2002—; co-dir. NSF Industry/Univ. Coop. Rsch. Ctr. Connection One, 2004—; co-founder, v.p. Sensor Electronic Tech., Inc. 1999 Editor-in chief Internat. Jour. High Speed Electronics and Systems, mem. hon. editl. bd. Solid State Electronics, Internat. Semiconductor Device Rsch. Symposium; contbr. over 1000 articles to profl. jours., chapters to books; author: Gunn Effect, 1971, Physics of Semiconductor Devices, 1990, GaAs Devices and Circuits, 1991, Introduction to Electronic Devices, 1996, many others; co-author: Ferroelectrics and Antiferroelectrics, 1971, Gunn Effect, 1975, Semiconductor Device Modeling for VLSI, 1993, Introduction to Device Modeling and Circuit Simulation, 1998, Introduction to Solid State Lighting, 2002; co-editor: Semiconductor Technology: Processing and Novel Fabrication Techniques, 1997, Sensitive Skin, 2000, others; regional editor (USA): physicia status solidi. Recipient Van Der Ziel award, Internat. Semiconductor Device Rsch. Symposium, 1999, Humboldt Sr. Rsch. award, 2002, SOE Rsch. award, Rensselaer Poly. Inst., 2003, Compound SEMI Pioneer award, 2003. Fellow: AAAS, IEEE (v.p. pubs. IEEE Sensor Coun., assoc. editor IEEE Trans. 1990—93, MTT Disting. Microwave lectr., EDS Disting. lectr., Leon Kirchmaeyer award 2007), World Innovation Found., Electrochem. Soc., Am. Phys. Soc.; mem.: ASEE, Humboldt Soc. Am., Materials Rsch. Soc., Sigma Xi, Tau Beta Pi, Eta Kappa Nu. Achievements include more than 30 patents on solid-state devices. Business E-Mail: shurm@rpi.edu. *When we were penniless refugees, the United States adopted me and my family with compassion and friendship, gave us work and citizenship. Our debt of gratitude to the American people who accepted us as their own we will never be able to repay.*

**SHURE, MYRNA BETH,** psychologist, educator; b. Chgo., Sept. 11, 1937; d. Sidney Natkin and Frances (Laufman) Shure. Student, U. Colo., 1955; BS, U. Ill., 1959; MS, Cornell U., 1961, PhD, 1966. Lic. psychologist Pa. Asst. prof. U. R.I.; head tchr. Nursery Sch., Kingston, 1961-62; asst. prof. Temple U., Phila., 1966-67, assoc. prof., 1967-68; instr. Hahnemann Med. Coll., Phila., 1968-69, sr. instr. psychology, 1969-70, asst. prof., 1970—73, assoc. prof., 1973—80, prof., 1980—2002, Drexel U., Phila.—2002. Spl. cons. PBS Children's TV Show The Puzzle Place; adv. bd. Parents Mag., 2004—. Author (with George Spivack): Social Adjustment of Young Children, 1974; author: (with George Spivack and Jerome Platt) The Problem Solving Approach to Adjustment, 1976; author: (with George Spivack) Problem Solving in Childrearing, 1978; author: (child curricula manual) I

Can Problem Solve, 1992; author: (trade book) Raising a Thinking Child, 1994; author: (audiotape, workbook, paperback) Raising a Thinking Preteen, 2000 (Parents' Choice award, 2001, Parent's Guide Classic award, 2001); author: Thinking Parent, Thinking Child, 2004; mem. editl. bd. Jour. Applied Devel. Psychology. Recipient Lela Rowland Prevention award, Nat. Mental Health Assn., 1982, Sarah award, Women in Comm. (Phila. chpt., 1998, Psychology in the Media award, Pa. Psychol. Assn., 1999, award, Ctr. for Substance Abuse Prevention, 2001; rsch. grantee, NIMH, 1971—75, 1977—79, 1982—85, 1987, 1988—93, NJ Gov.'s Juvenile Justice and Delinquency Prevention grantee. Fellow: APA (divsn. clin. psychology, child sect. 1994, Disting. Contbn. award divsn. cmty. psychology 1984, Task Force on Prevention award 1987, Task Force on Model Programs award 1994, U. Utah and Juvenile Justice Dept. of Delinquency Prevention award 1996, U.S. Dept. Edn. award 2001; mem.: Phila. Soc. Clin. Psychologists, Soc. Rsch. in Child Devel., Nat. Assn. Edn. Young Children, Nat. Assn. Sch. Psychologists. Home: 1500 Locust St Apt 3311 Philadelphia PA 19102-4323 Office: Drexel U Dept Psychology 245 N 15th St MS 626 Philadelphia PA 19102 Office Phone: 215-762-7205. Business E-Mail: mshure@drexel.edu.

**SHURN, PETER JOSEPH, III,** lawyer; b. Queens, N.Y., Aug. 30, 1946; s. Peter J. Jr. and Vivienne M. (Tagliarino) Shurn; m. Ingrid Kelbert; children: Steven Douglas, Vanessa Leigh, David Michael. BSEE magna cum laude, Poly. Inst. Bklyn., 1974; JD magna cum laude, New Eng. Sch. Law, 1977; LLM in Patent and Trade Regulation Law, George Washington U., 1981. Bar: N.C. 1977, Va. 1979, Tex. 1982. Rsch. scientist GTE Labs., 1965—77; pvt. practice Raleigh, NC, 1977—78; assoc. Burns, Doane, Swecker & Mathis, Alexandria, Va., 1978—80; ptnr. Arnold, White & Durkee. Houston, 1981—2000, Howrey, Simon, Arnold and White LLP, Houston, 2000—01; pvt. practice Houston, 2001—. Adj. prof. S. Tex. Coll. Law, 1984—88, 2000—; invited mem. nat. panel neutrals Am. Arbitration Assn., 1993—. Contbr. articles to profl. jours. With U.S. Army, 1966—68. Fellow: Coll. State Bar Tex., Houston Bar Found. (life); mem.: IEEE, ABA, ATLA, Houston Patent Law Assn., Am. Patent Law Assn. (Robert C. Watson award 1981), Houston Patent Law Assn., Sigma Xi. Office: 14138 Heatherfield Dr Houston TX 77079-6805 Office Phone: 281-496-0865. Business E-Mail: pjshurn@ieee.org.

**SHURR, GEORGE W.,** geologist, consultant; b. Rock Rapids, Iowa, June 22, 1943; s. John B. and Bernita Shurr; m. Margaret A. Siemer, Aug. 15, 1965; children: Sharla Kathryn Krell, Robert James. BA, U. S.D., 1965; MS, Northwestern U., 1967; PhD, U. Mont., 1975. Cert. geologist Wyo., Minn. Field geologist S.D. Geol. Survey, Vermillion, 1962—72; prof. St. Cloud (Minn.) State U., 1967—98; rsch. geologist U.S. Geol. Survey, Denver, 1975—85; exploration geologist GeoShurr Resources, LLC, Ellsworth, Minn., 1998—. Contbr. articles to profl. jours. Bd. suprs. Haven Twp., St. Cloud, 1980—90, Sherburne County Soil and Water Dist., St. Cloud, 1986—90; precinct chairperson Dem. Farmer Labor Party, St. Cloud, 1984—88. Faculty fellow, NSF, 1971—72. Mem.: Rocky Mountain Assn. Geologists, Geol. Soc. Am., Am. Assn. Petroleum Geologists. Methodist. Avocations: hiking, reading, travel, history, ecology. Office: GeoShurr Resources LLC 1803 11th St Ellsworth MN 56129 Office Phone: 507-967-2156. Office Fax: 507-967-2156. E-mail: geoshurr@frontiernet.net.

**SHURTLEFF, AKIKO AOYAGI,** artist, consultant; b. Tokyo, Jan. 24, 1950; d. Kinjiro and Fumiyo (Sugata) Aoyagi; m. William Roy Shurtleff, Mar. 10, 1977 (div. Jan. 1995); 1 child, Joseph Aoyagi. Grad., Women's Coll. Art, Tokyo, 1971; student, Acad. Art, San Francisco, 1991—92. Fashion designer, illustrator Marimura Co. and Hayakawa Shoji, Inc., Tokyo, 1970-72; co-founder, art dir. Soyfoods Ctr. consulting svcs., Lafayette, Calif., 1976-94; freelance illustrator, graphic designer. Lectr. U.S. Internat. Christian U., Tokyo, 1977, Japanese Tofu Mfrs. Conv., Osaka, 1978; presenter cooking demonstrations; tchr. cooking classes. Co-author, illustrator: The Book of Tempeh, 1979, Tofu and Soymilk Production, 1979, Miso Production, 1979, Tempeh Production, 1980, The Book of Tofu and Miso, 2001, The Book of Tofu, 2005, The Book of Miso, 2005, co-author, illustrator: Chinese edit., 2005, illustrator: Spirulina, 1982, The Book of Shiatsu-The Healing Art of Finger Pressure, 1990, Staying Healthy with Nutrition, 1992, Culinary Treasures of Japan, 1992, Yookoso, An Invitation to Contemporary Japanese, vols. 1 and 2, 1994—95, Blue Collar and Beyond, 1995, Damn Good Ready to Go Resumes, 1995, Homework, 1995, Vegetarian's A to Z Guide to Fruits and Vegetables, 1996, Hubert Keller's Cuisine, 1996, Doctor Generic Will See You Now, 1996, Everyday Pediatrics for Parents, 1996, Angels in My Kitchen-Devine Desserts Recipes, 1997; The Shurtleff and Lawton Families: Genealogy and History, 2005; designer co. logos, greeting cards:. Office: PO Box 443 Lafayette CA 94549-0443

**SHURTLEFF, MALCOLM C.,** plant pathologist, consultant; b. Fall River, Mass., June 24, 1922; s. Malcolm C. and Florence L. (Jewell) S.; m. Margaret E. Johnson, June 14, 1950; m. Freda L. Nothnagel, Aug. 1, 1990; children: Robert Glen, Janet Lee, Mark Steven. BS in Biology, U. R.I., 1943; MS in Plant Pathology, U. Minn., 1950, PhD in Plant Pathology, 1953. Asst. plant pathologist Conn. Agrl. Expt. Sta., New Haven, 1942, R.I. Agrl. Expt. Sta., Kingston, 1943; asst. extension prof. U. R.I., Kingston, 1950-54; assoc. extension prof. Iowa State U., Ames, 1954-61; prof. plant pathology U. Ill., Champaign-Urbana, 1961-92, prof. emeritus, 1992—; cons., writer Urbana, 1992-98. Adj. prof. Tex. A&M U., College Station, 1998—. Author: How To Control Plant Diseases, 1962, 66 (award Am. Garden Guild 1962, 66), How To Control Lawn Diseases and Pests, 1973, How To Control Tree Diseases and Pests, 1975, Controlling Turfgrass Pests, 1987, 97, 2002, A Glossary of Plant Pathological Terms, 1997, The Plant Disease Clinic and Field Diagnosis of Abiotic Diseases, 1997, Diagnosing Plant Diseases Caused by Nematodes, 2000; editor-in-chief Phytopathology News, 1966-69, Plant Disease, 1969-72; contbr. numerous articles to encys., profl. publs. and mags. Lt. (j.g.) USN, 1943-46. PTO Recipient Disting. Svc. award USDA, Washington, 1986, E.C. Stakman award U. Minn., 2000. Fellow Am. Phytopathological Soc. (councilor at large 1970-71, Excellence in Extension Plant Pathology award 1991); mem. Internat. Soc. Plant Pathology (chmn. extension com. 1975-80), Am. Phytopathological Soc. (mem. various coms.). Avocation: photography. Home: 6730 Heron Ln Pearland TX 77584-6618 Personal E-mail: lmshurt@att.net.

**SHURTLEFF, MARK L.,** state attorney general; BA, Brigham Young U.; JD, U. Utah. Officer, atty. JAG USN, 1985—90; pvt. practice in law Calif., 1990—93; asst. atty. gen. State of Utah, 1993—97; dep. county atty. Salt Lake County, 1997—98; commr. Salt Lake County Commn., 1999—2000, chmn., 2000; atty. gen. State of Utah, 2001—. Leader Boy Scout troops, 1980—; anti-drug lectr., at-risk youth mentor. Republican. Office: Office of Atty General State Capitol East Office Bldg Ste 320 Salt Lake City UT 84114-0810

**SHURTLIFF, MARVIN KARL,** lawyer; b. Idaho Falls, Idaho, Nov. 6, 1939; s. Noah Leon and Melba Dorothy (Hunting) S.; m. Peggy J. Griffin, Nov. 23, 1963; 1 dau., Jennifer Karyl. BA, Idaho State Coll., 1962; JD, U. Idaho, 1968. Bar: Idaho 1968. Tchr. pub. schs. Jefferson County, Idaho, 1964-65; atty. U.S. Dept. Justice, Washington, 1968-74; commr. Idaho Pub. Utilities Commn., 1974-75, pres., 1975-76; spl. asst., legal counsel Gov. of Idaho, Boise, 1977; U.S. atty. for Dist. of Idaho, Boise, 1977-81; practice law Boise, 1981—. Mem. Idaho Ho. of Reps., 1962-64 Mem. Idaho State Bd. Edn., 1990—95. Idaho Commn. on Redistricting, 2001. Mem. Idaho Bar Assn. Democrat. Home: 62 Horizon Dr Boise ID 83702-4419 Office: PO Box 1652 Boise ID 83701-1652

**SHUSHKEWICH, KENNETH WAYNE,** structural engineer; b. Winnipeg, Man., Can., Sept. 22, 1952; m. Valdine Cuffe, Sept. 28, 1980. BSCE, U. Man., Winnipeg, 1974; MS in Structural Engring., U. Calif., Berkeley, 1975; PhD in Structural Engring., U. Alta., Edmonton, Can., 1985. Engr. Wardrop and Assocs., Winnipeg, 1974—78, Preconsult Can., Montreal, Que., 1978—80; prof. U. Alta., 1981—85, U. Man., 1985—87; engr. T.Y. Lin Internat., San Francisco, 1988—90, H.J. Degenkolb Assocs., San Francisco, 1990—92, Ben C. Gerwick, Inc., San Francisco, 1993—94, J. Muller Internat., Chgo., 1994—95, T.Y. Lin Internat., San Francisco, 1995—99, KSI Bridge Engrs.,

San Francisco, 1999—. Prin. works include design of prestressed concrete segmental bridges; design mgr. for long-span west approach bridge of Northumberland Strait Crossing in Can.; contbr. articles to profl. jours. Recipient award for design of Vierendeel truss bridge, Man. Design Inst., 1977. Fellow ASCE; mem. Am. Concrete Inst., Prestressed Concrete Inst., Internat. Assn. Bridge and Structural Engrs. Achievements include invention of strutted box widening method for long-span bridge widening. Office: PO Box 2590 San Francisco CA 94126-2590

**SHUSTER, ALVIN,** journalist, reporter; b. Washington, Jan. 25, 1930; s. Fred and Dora (Levy) S.; m. Miriam Schwartz, June 22, 1952; children: Fred, Jessica, Beth. AB, George Washington U., 1951. Reporter Washington Bur. N.Y. Times, 1952-61, asst. news editor, 1961-66, reporter London Bur., 1967-70; bur. chief Saigon, Vietnam, 1970-71, London, 1971-75, Rome, 1975-77; dep. editor editorial pages L.A. Times, 1977-83, fgn. editor, 1983-95, sr. consulting editor, 1995—. Pres. Fgn. Corrs. Assn., London, 1973-74; trustee Monterey (Calif.) Inst. Internat. Studies, 1983-99; chmn. Pulitzer Prize Jury Internat. Reporting, 1999. Editor: The Witnesses, 1964, Washington: The New York Times Guide to the Nations' Capital, 1967, International Press Institute Report, 1995-99; assc. editor Global Journalist, 1999-2004; contbg. author: The Kennedy Years, 1964; contbg. editor Columbia Journalism Rev., 1999-2004. Nieman fellow Harvard U., 1966-67. Mem. Reform Club (London). Office: Los Angeles Times 202 W 1st St Los Angeles CA 90012

**SHUSTER, BETH,** editor; b. Washington; BA in Eng. Lit., Univ. Calif., Santa Cruz. Reporter State News Svc., Wash., Riverside (Calif.) Press-Enterprise; ditr. writer LA Daily News, 1987—93; police reporter, edn. writer to state desk LA Times, 1994—2004, edn. editor, 2004—. Office: Edn Editor LA Times 202 W First St Los Angeles CA 90012 Office Phone: 213-237-7847. Office Fax: 213-237-4712.*

**SHUSTER, BUD,** business executive, former congressman; b. Glassport, Pa., Jan. 23, 1932; s. Prather and Grace (Greinert) S.; m. Patricia Rommell, Aug. 27, 1955; children: Peg, Bill, Debbie, Bobby, Gia. BS, U. Pitts., 1954; MBA, Duquesne U., 1960; PhD in Econs. and Mgmt., Am. U., 1967. Nat. account mgr. Univac divsn. Sperry Rand, 1956, Univac divsn. Remington Rand Co. (now Sperry Rand), 1956-60; dist. mgr. Western Pa. RCA, 1960-62, mgr. ops. Washington, 1962-65, v.p. EPD divsn., 1965-68; pres. computer terminal co., 1968-72; mem. 93rd-106th Congresses from 9th Pa. dist., Washington, 1973-2001, former chmn. U.S. House Transp. Com., former ranking mem. U.S. House Select Com. on Intelligence; pres. Strategic Advisors, Everett, Pa., 2001—; chmn. Safe Extensions, Inc. Vis. prof. St. Francis U., Loretto, Pa., 2001. Author: Believing in America, 1983. Del. Rep. Nat. Conv., 1976, 80, 84, 88, 92, 96; co-chair Energy, Environment & Transp. Platform Subcom.; sr. transp. advisor Bush-Quayle Campaign; also mem. platform com.; chmn. Reagan-Bush Campaign in Western Pa.; sr. advisor to transition team for Dept. Transp., 1980-81; trustee J.F. Kennedy Ctr. for Performing Arts. With Counter-Intelligence U.S. Army, 1954—56. Recipient Watchdog of Treasury award, Guardian of Small Bus. award, Golden Age Hall of Fame award. Mem. Pa. Soc., Chowder and Marching Soc., Capitol Hill Club, Phi Beta Kappa, Omicron Delta Kappa, Sigma Chi (Significant Sig award).

**SHUSTER, CARL,** food products executive; b. Minnesota; m. Laura Shuster; children: Alexandra, Jake. Employee Kimpton Grp., San Francisco; gen. mgr. Restaurant Associates, NYC; pres.,CEO Wolfgang Puck Catering, Las Vegas, 1998—. Office: Wolfgang Puck Private Dining and Catering 6430 S Arville Las Vegas NV 89118 Office Phone: 702-369-0558. Office Fax: 702-369-5490.*

**SHUSTER, FREDERICK,** retired internist, gastroenterologist; b. Newark, Sept. 12, 1933; s. Ralph and Anne (Weinstein) S.; m. Jane A. Block, June 11, 1958; children: Alan R., Robert G. BS, Rutgers U., 1955; MD, U. Chgo., 1959. Diplomate Am. Bd. Internal Medicine, Am. Bd. Gastroenterology. Intern U. Mich. Hosp., Ann Arbor, 1959-60, resident internal medicine, 1960-62; resident gastroenterology VA Hosp. U. Miami, Fla., 1962-63; pvt. practice N. Miami Beach, Fla., 1963-97; from clin. instr. to assoc. prof. medicine U. Miami, Fla., 1963—; pvt. practice Aventura, Fla., 1997-98; ret., 1998. Chmn. dept. medicine Parkway Regional Med. Ctr., N. Miami Beach, 1967, 70, chief of staff, 1974-75, chief divsn. gastroenterology, 1976-77, chmn. pharmacy and therapeutics com., 1978-98. Chmn. med. advisory com. Crohn's and Colitis Found., S. Fla. chpt., Miami, 1979-81. Major U.S. Army, 1967-69. Recipient Physician's Recognition award in Continung Edn., AMA, Chgo., 1970—. Fellow Am. Coll. Physicians, Am. Coll. Gastroenterology, Alpha Omega Alpha. Jewish. Avocations: bowling, ballroom dancing, stock market research and investing. E-mail: fred991@att.net.

**SHUSTER, MARGUERITE,** minister, educator; b. Oxnard, Calif., Sept. 10, 1947; d. Carroll Lloyd and Grace Margaret (Hornbeck) S. BA with great distinction, Stanford U., 1968; MDiv, Fuller Sem., Pasadena, Calif., 1975; PhD, Fuller Grad. Sch. Psychology, Pasadena, 1977. Ordained to ministry Presbyn. Ch. (U.S.A.), 1980. From asst. to assoc. pastor Arcadia (Calif.) Presbyn. Ch., 1980-86; pastor Knox Presbyn. Ch., Pasadena, Calif., 1987-92; adj. asst. prof. preaching Fuller Sem., Pasadena, 1988-90; assoc. prof. preaching Fuller Theol. Sem., Pasadena, 1992—2001; prof. preaching, 2001. Del. gen. Assembly Mission Consultation Planning Team, 1984—85, Inst. Ecumenical and Cultural Rsch., Collegeville, Minn., 1985, Collegeville, 86; com. chair Gen. Assembly, 1988; Staley lectr. Sterling Coll., 2001; Harp lectr. Anderson Sch. Theology, 2004. Author: Power Pathology, Paradox, 1987 The Fall and Sin: What We Have Become as Sinners, 2004; mem. editl. bd.: Theology, News and Notes, 1986—2005; contbr. articles sermons, and revs. in religious jours. and books; editor (contbr.): Perspectives on Christology, 1991, Who We Are: Our Dignity as Human, 1996. Bd. dirs. Sierra Madre Mountain Conservancy, 2002—. Named one of Outstanding Young Women in Am., 1979, 1983. Mem. Presbytery of San Gabriel (chair, com. on ministry 1991, moderator, permanent jud. commn. 1993-95, moderator Presbytery 1996), Phi Beta Kappa. Home: 675 Mount Wilson Trl Sierra Madre CA 91024-1232 Office: Fuller Theol Sem 135 N Oakland Ave Pasadena CA 91182-0001 Office Phone: 626-584-5248. Business E-Mail: shuster@fuller.edu. *A goal: so to trust in Jesus Christ, especially in times of sorrow and disappointment, that others might find it easier rather than more difficult to believe in a loving, omnipotent God.*

**SHUSTER, ROBERT G.,** electronics executive, consultant; b. N.Y.C., June 1, 1927; s. Reuben Chandler and Therese G. (Giraud); m. Marianne B. Lynski, Apr. 20, 1970 (div. Jan. 1987); m. H. Elizabeth Young, May 20, 1989 (div. Dec. 1995); m. Erika Megas, May 5, 2002. BSEE, CCNY, 1948; MSEE, Columbia U., 1955, postgrad., 1959-64. Test engr. Elec. Testing Labs., N.Y.C., 1948-50; project leader Sperry Gyroscope Co., Great Neck, NY, 1950-59; project mgr. RCA Advanced Communications Lab., N.Y.C., 1959-67; prin. scientist Tracor, Inc., Rockville, Md., 1967-75, v.p. electronics systems div., 1975-87; pres. Tracor Tech. Resources, Inc., Rockville, Md., 1984-90, RGS Assocs., McLean, Va., 1990—; v.p. C-Cubed Corp., Alexandria, Va., 1990-93, pres., 1993-95; sr. cons., 1996—. Mem. IEEE (sr.), N.Y. Acad. Scis. Avocations: photography, hiking.

**SHUSTER, WILLIAM (BILL SHUSTER),** congressman; b. McKeesport, Pa., Jan. 10, 1961; s. E.G. "Bud" Shuster; m. Rebecca Shuster; children: Ali, Garrett. BA in Polit. Sci. and Hist., Dickinson Coll., Carlisle, Pa., 1983; MBA, American U., Washington. Mgr. retail stores Goodyear Tire and Rubber Corpn.; dist. mgr. Bandag Inc.; mem. US Congress from 9th Pa. dist., 2001—. Mem. small. bus. com. US Congress, mem. armed svcs. com., mem. transp. and infrastructure com., chmn. econ. devel., pub. bldgs. and emergency mgmt. subcommittee. Mem.: Rural Health Care Coalition, Nat. Fedn. Ind. Bus., NRA, Masons. Republican. Lutheran. Office: US Ho Reps 1108 Longworth Ho Office Bldg Washington DC 20515-3809 Office Phone: 202-225-2431.*

**SHUSTERMAN, NATHAN,** underwriter, financial consultant; b. Montreal, Que., Aug. 27, 1927; arrived in US, 1950; s. Aaron and Annie (Nulman) S.; m. Norma Thalblum, Jan. 1950; children: Mark D., Claudia S. Student, Sir George Williams Coll., Montreal, 1944-47; grad., N.Y. Inst. Fin. CLU, chartered fin. cons. Retailing mgr. Jefferson Stores, Miami, Fla., 1950-65; gen. agt. Protective Life Ins. Co., Miami, 1965—. Chmn. emeritus field adv. coun., past pres. Protective Club; pres. Am. Fin. Counseling Corp., Miami; instr. estate and tax planning Am. Coll., Bryn Mawr, Pa., 1972—, U. Miami, Coral Gables, Fla., 1972—; registered rep. Pro Equity Services Inc.; cons. in field. Named Man of Yr., Gen. Agts. and Mgrs. Assn., Miami, 1965-67. Mem. North Dade-South Broward Estate Planning Coun., Million Dollar Round Table (life), Top of Table, Assn. Advanced Life Underwriting, Soc. Fin. Svc. Profls. (past pres. Miami chpt.), Nat. Assn. Ins. and Fin. Advisors (Nat. Sales Achievement award, Nat. Quality award), Fla. Assn. Ins. and Fin. Advisors, Miami Assn. Ins. and Fin. Advisors, Internat. Assn. Fin. Planners, Am. Soc. Pension Actuaries (assoc.), Optimists (pres. North Miami Beach, Fla. chpt. 1971), Masons, Shriners, B'nai B'rith (pres. Miami chpt 1950). Office: Am Fin Counseling Corp 16121 NE 18th Ave Miami FL 33162-4749 Home: 21050 NE 38th Ave Apt 1701 Miami FL 33180-4078 Office Phone: 305-949-0906.

**SHUSTERMAN, NEAL DOUGLAS,** writer, scriptwriter; b. NYC, Nov. 12, 1962; s. Milton and Charlotte Ruth (Altman) S.; m. Elaine Gale Jones, Jan. 31, 1987; children: Brendan, Jarrod, Joelle, Erin. BA in Psychology and Drama, U. Calif., Irvine, 1985. Author, screenwriter, 1987—. Author: Guy Talk, 1987, The Shadow Club, 1988 (Children's CHoice award Internat. Reading Assn. 1989), Dissidents, 1989, Speeding Bullet, 1991 (Best Book for Teens award N.Y. Pub. Libr., nominated Calif. Young Reader Medal 1995-96), Kid Heroes, 1991, What Daddy Did, 1991 (Best Book for Young Adults award ALA, Outstanding Work of Fiction award So. Calif. Coun. Lit. for Children and Young People, Children's Choice award and Young Adult Choice award Internat. Reading Assn., Pick of the List award ABA, Best Book for Teens award N.Y. Pub. Libr., Okla. Sequoyah award 1994), The Eyes of Kid Midas, 1992 (ALA Best Book for Reluctant Readers), Darkness Creeping, 1993, Piggyback Ninja, 1994, Scorpion Shards, 1995 (N.Y. Pub. Libr. Best Book for the Teenaged), Darkness Creeping II, 1995, Mindquakes, 1996 (ALA YALSA Quick Pick), Mindstorms, 1996, Mindtwisters, 1997, The Dark Side of Nowhere, 1997 (ALA Best Book, ALA Quick Pick--Top 10 Book), Thief of Souls, 1999, Downsiders, 1999 (ALA Best Book, ALA Quick Pick), MindBenders, 2000, The Shadow Club Rising, 2002, Shattered Sky, 2002, Full Tilt, 2003 (Tex. Lonestar award), The Schwa Was Here, 2004 (Boston Globe Horn Book award, ALA Best Book, ALA Notable), Dread Locks, 2005 (ALA Quick Pick), Red Rider's Hood, 2005 (ALA Quick Pick), Duckling Ugly, 2006, Everlast, 2006; screenwriter: Double Dragon, 1992, Evolver, 1993; dir. Heart on a Chain, 1991 (Golden Eagle award CINE), What About the Sisters, 1993 (Golden Eagle award CINE), Games: How to Host a Teen Mystery, Hot Times at Hollywood High, 1994, Barbecue with the Vampire, 1997, Roswell that Ends Well, 1999, How to Host a Murder: Roman Ruins, 1996, The Good, the Bad and the Guilty, 1997, The Tragical Mystery Tour, 1998, The Maiming of the Shrew, 2000, Saturday Night Cleaver, 2000, An Affair to Dismember, 2003, (TV) Goosebumps: The Werewolf of Fever Swamp, 1996, Goosebumps: Night of the Living Dummy III, 1997, Animorphs (staff writer), 1998, Pixel Perfect, 2004. Mem. PEN, Writers Guild Am. West, Soc. Children's Book Writers and Illustrators. Avocations: swimming, tennis, storytelling. Home: P O Box 80093 Rancho Santa Margarita CA 92688 E-mail: NStoryman@aol.com.

**SHUTE, RICHARD EMIL,** federal agency administrator, engineer; b. Bklyn., May 1, 1938; s. William Leonard and Doris S.; m. Linda Janan McElhiney, Mar. 7, 1960. BS in Mech. Engring., U. Miami, 1960; MBA, Fla. State U., 1970. Registered profl. engr., Fla. Engr. Pratt and Whitney Aircraft, West Palm Beach, Fla., 1962-65; Gen. Dynamics Corp., San Diego, 1962-64; aerospace engr. NASA/Kennedy Space Ctr., Fla., 1964-71; dir. planning and evaluation Fla. Dept. Health and Human Services, Tallahassee, 1971-76; dir. office program devel. Office Human Devel., HHS, Washington, 1976-87; dir. office of mgmt. and info. systems U.S. Dept. Commerce, Washington, 1987-90; pres. Richard E. Shute and Assocs. Mgmt. Cons., 1990—. Mem. Nat. Assn. Security Dealers (bd. arbitrators).

**SHUTLER, MARY ELIZABETH,** academic administrator; b. Oakland, Calif., Nov. 14, 1929; d. Hal Wilfred and Elizabeth Frances (Gimbel) Hall; m. Richard Shutler Jr., Sept. 8, 1951 (div. 1975); children: Kathryn Allice (dec.), John Hall, Richard Burnett. BA, U. Calif., Berkeley, 1951; MA, U. Ariz., 1958, PhD, 1967. Asst., assoc., full prof. anthropology, chmn. dept. San Diego State U., 1967-75; prof. anthropology, dept. chmn. Wash. State U., Pullman, 1975-80; dean Coll. Arts and Scis., prof. anthropology U. Alaska, Fairbanks, 1980-84; vice chancellor, dean of faculty, prof. anthropology U. Wis. Parkside, Kenosha, 1984-88; provost, v.p. for acad. affairs, prof. anthropology Calif. State U., L.A., 1988-94; provost West Coast U., L.A., 1994-97; dean Sch. of Arts and Scis. Nat. U., La Jolla, Calif., 1997—2004, dean emeritus, 2004—. Mem. core staff Lahav Rsch. Project, Miss. State U. 1975-92. Co-author: Oceanic Prehistory, 1975, Deer Creek Cave, 1964, Archaeological Survey of Southern Nevada, 1963, Stuart Rockshelter, 1962; contbr. articles to jours. in field. Mem. coun. Gamble House. Fellow Am. Anthropol. Assn.; mem. Soc. for Am. Archaeology, Am. Schs. for Oriental Rsch., Am. Coun. Edn., Am. Assn. for Higher Edn., Am. Assn. State Colls. and Univs., Delta Zeta. Republican. Roman Catholic. Avocations: travel, gardening. E-mail: bullet18@netzero.com.

**SHUTRAN, RICHARD,** lawyer; b. New Britain, Conn., Mar. 27, 1952; BA, Trinity Coll., 1974; JD cum laude, NYU, 1978. Bar: N.Y. 1979, US Dist. Ct. (ea. & so. dist. N.Y.). Co-mng. ptnr. & chmn. project fin. group Dewey Ballantine LLP, N.Y.C. Mem.: N.Y. State Bar Assn. Office: Dewey Ballantine LLP 1301 Ave of the Americas New York NY 10019-6092 Office Phone: 212-259-6710. Office Fax: 212-259-6333. Business E-mail: rshutran@dbllp.com.

**SHUTTLEWORTH, ANNE MARGARET,** psychiatrist; b. Detroit, Jan. 17, 1931; d. Cornelius Joseph and Alice Catherine (Rice) S.; m. Joel R. Siegel, Apr. 19, 1959; children: Erika, Peter. AB, Cornell U., 1953, MD, 1956. Intern Lenox Hill Hosp., N.Y.C., 1956-57; resident Payne Whitney Clinic-N.Y. Hosp., 1957-60; practice medicine specializing in psychiatry Maplewood, NJ, 1960—. Cons. Maplewood Sch. System, 1960-62; instr. psychiatry Cornell U. Med. Sch., 1960; mem. Com. to Organize New Sch. Psychology, 1970. Mem. AMA (Physicians Recognition award 1975, 78, 81, 84, 87, 90, 93, 96, 99, 02, 05), Am. Psychiat. Assn., Am. Med. Women's Assn., NY Acad. Scis., Acad. Medicine NJ, Phi Beta Kappa, Phi Kappa Phi. Office: 2066 Millburn Ave Maplewood NJ 07040-3715

**SHUTZ, BYRON CHRISTOPHER,** real estate company officer; b. Kansas City, Mo., Feb. 16, 1928; s. Byron Theodore and Maxine (Christopher) S.; m. Marilyn Ann Tweedie, Mar. 30, 1957; children: Eleanor S. Gaines, Byron Christopher, Collin Reid, William S. Moskow, Lindley Anne Baile. AB in Econs., U. Kans., 1949. Ptnr. Herbert V. Jones & Co., Kansas City, Mo., 1953-72; pres. Herbert V. Jones Mortgage Corp., Kansas City, 1967-72, The Byron Shutz Co., Kansas City, 1973—. Dir. 1st Am. Financial Corp., Rothschild's, Inc., Bus. Men's Assurance Co., Faultless Starch, Bon Ami Co. Chmn. bd. trustees U. Kansas City, 1979-81; trustee Pembroke-Country Day Sch., 1974-77, Midwest Rsch. Inst., 1980-89; chmn., bd. govs. Kansas City Art Inst., 1960-62; chmn. bd. dirs. Ctr. for Bus. Innovation, Inc., 1985-87; bd. dirs. Kansas City Crime Commn. 1st lt. USAF, 1951-53. Mem. Mortgage Bankers Assn. Am. (bd. govs. 1966-74), Am. Inst. Real Estate Appraisers. Clubs: Kansas City Country, University, Mercury (pres. 1978-79); Fla. Yacht (Jacksonville), Ocean Reef (Key Largo, Fla.). Home: 1001 W 58th Ter Kansas City MO 64113-1159 Office: 800 W 47th St Kansas City MO 64112-1251 E-mail: arrowrock3@sbcglobal.net.

**SHVO, MICHAEL,** real estate broker; b. Tel Aviv, Dec. 29, 1972; s. Hannah Shvo. With Prudential Douglas Elliman, NYC, 1998—2005, v.p., 2002—05; founder, pres. Shvo Group, 2005—. Mem.: Real Estate Bd. NY. Office Phone: 212-380-2100. E-mail: mshvo@shvo.com.

**SHWARTZ, SIMA M.,** music educator; arrived in U.S., 1995; d. Michael Shwartz and Sophia Leshchiner; m. Vladimir A. Shpachenko, June 7, 1975 (div. Oct. 1978); 1 child, Nadia Shpachenko. Grad., Music Sch. for Gifted Youth, Kharkov, 1964; MusM in Tchg. Piano, Accompanist, Performer, State Inst. Arts, Kharkov, 1969. Piano faculty Kharkov Music Schs., 1964—91; accompanist Kharkov State Philharm., 1964—91, Kharkov Inst. Arts, 1964—65; piano faculty Severodonetsk State Music Coll., 1969—72; founder, condr. Kharkov Children Orch., Kharkov, 1990—91; piano tchr. Gilloh Dalled Sch. Jerusalem, 1992—95; founder, piano tchr. Sima's Music Club, Cambridge, Mass., 1996—2000; piano faculty The Music Sch., Providence, 1999—2000; founder, piano tchr. Shwartz Piano Sch., Marlborough, Mass., 2000—02; piano faculty Performing Arts Sch., Worcester, Mass., 2003—04. Mem.: Mass. Music Tchrs. Assn. (v.p. membership), Music Tchrs. Nat. Assn. Avocations: walking, ping pong/table tennis, reading, theater.

**SHWAYDER, ELIZABETH YANISH,** sculptor; b. St. Louis; d. Sam and Fannie May (Weil) Yaffe; m. Nathan Yanish, July 5, 1944 (dec.); children: Ronald, Marilyn Ginsburg, Mindy; m. M.C. Shwayder, 1988 (dec.). Student, Washington U., 1941, Denver U., 1961; pvt. studies. One-woman shows include Woodstock Gallery, London, 1973, Internat. House, Denver, 1963, Colo. Women's Coll., Denver, 1975, Contemporaries Gallery, Santa Fe, 1963, So. Colo. State Coll. Pueblo, 1967, others; group shows include Salt Lake City Mus., 1964, 71, Denver Art Mus., 1961-75, Oklahoma City Mus., 1969, Joslyn Mus., Omaha, 1964-68, Lucca (Italy) Invitational, 1971, Denver Art Mus., Mus. Natural History, Mizel Mus., Eden Theatrical Workshop, Rose Hosp. Aux., Nat. Mus. Women in the Arts, Colo. Chpt. 8th Air Force Aux., Women's Art Ctr., others; represented in permanent collections Colo. State Bank, Bmh Synagogue, Denver., Colo. Women's Coll., Har Ha Shem Congregation, Boulder, Colo., Faith Bible Chapel, Denver, others. Chmn. visual arts Colo. Centennial-Bicentennial, 1974-75; pres. Denver Coun. Arts and Humanities, 1973-75; co-chmn. visual arts spree Denver Pub. Schs., 1975; trustee Denver Ctr. Performing Arts, 1973-75; chmn. Concerned Citizens for the Arts, 1976; pres. Beth Israel Hosp. Aux., 1985-87; organizer Coat Drive for the Needy, Denver, N.Y.C., 1982-87, Common Cents penny drive for homeless, 1991-93; bd. dirs. Mizel Mus., Srs., Inc.; active Mayor's Com. on Cultural Affairs, Denver Art Mus., Mus. Natural History, Freedom Found. at Valley Forge, Hospice of Metro. Denver; bd. dirs. Rainbow Bridge; bd. dirs. Diabetes Found., Asian Arts Assn. Denver Art Mus., also pres.; historian Childrens Diabetes Found., Univ. Colo. Found. Inc. Humanities scholar Auraria Librs.-U. Colo.; recipient McCormick award Ball State U., Muncie, Ind., 1964, purchase award color Women's Coll., Denver, 1963, Tyler (Tex.) Mus., 1963, 1st prize in sculpture 1st Nat. Space Art Show, 1971, humanitarian award Milehi Denver Sertoma, 1994, The Gleitsman Found., 1994, svc. to mankind awards Freedom Found. at Valley Forge, Mile Hi Sertoma Club, Minoruyasui Found., Gleitsman Found. Mem. Denver Art Mus., Asian Arts Assn. (pres.). Home: Unit 503 2400 Cherry Creek South Dr Denver CO 80209-3259

**SHYAMALAN, M. NIGHT (MANOJ NELLIYATTU SHYAMALAN),** film director; b. Pondicherry, Tamil-Nadu, India, Aug. 6, 1970; s. Jayalakshmi Shyamalan and Nelliate C; m. Bhavna Vaswani, 1993; 2 children. Grad., NYU, 1992. Actor, dir., prodr., writer: (films) Praying with Anger, 1992, Unbreakable, 2000, Signs, 2002, The Village, 2004, Lady in the Water, 2006; actor, dir., writer: The Sixth Sense, 1999 (Bram Stoker Award for Best Screenplay, 1999, Golden Satellite Award for Best Original Screenplay, 1999, Visionary Award, Palm Springs Internat. Film Festival, 2000, Nebula Award for Best Script, Sci. Fiction and Fantasy Writers Am., 1999, nominated for Best Dir. and Best Original Screenplay, Acad. Awards 2000, Nominated for Best Screenplay, Golden Globes, 2000); dir., writer: Praying Wide Awake, 1998; writer screenplay Stuart Little, 1999. Named one of 50 Most Powerful People in Hollywood, Premiere mag., 2003—05; recipient Samman award, Pravasi Bharatiya Divas, 2005. Office: United Talent Agy Inc c/o Peter Benedek 9560 Wilshire Blvd Fl 5 Beverly Hills CA 90212-2400*

**SHYER, JOHN D.,** lawyer; b. Nashville, May 4, 1956; s. Michael and Hilda (Wertheim) S.; m. Marsha Anne Gisser, May 7, 1989; children: Allison Parcell, Michael Wertheim. AB, Princeton U., 1978; JD, Stanford U., 1981. Bar: N.Y. 1982, U.S. Ct. Appeals (2d cir.) 1983, U.S. Ct. Appeals (3d cir.) 1992. Assoc. Donovan, Leisure, Newton & Irvine, N.Y.C., 1981-85, Latham & Watkins LLP, N.Y.C., 1985-89, ptnr., 1989—. Trustee Princeton (N.J.) Broadcasting Svc., 1985—. Mem. Assn. Bar City N.Y., Employment and Labor Lawcast (bd. editl. advisors 1994—). Avocations: travel, hiking, reading. Office: Latham & Watkins LLP 885 3rd Ave Ste 1000 New York NY 10022-4834 Office Phone: 212-906-1200. Business E-Mail: john.shyer@lw.com.

**SHYU, MEI-LING,** information scientist, educator; d. Chun-Jou Shyu and Yu-Hwa Chao; m. Shu-Ching Chen, May 20, 1990; children: Winnie Chen, Tiffany Chen, Jonathan Chen. MS in Restaurant, Hotel, Instl. and Tourism, Purdue U., West Lafayette, Ind., 1997; MS in Computer Sci., Purdue U., 1992, MSEE, 1995, PhD in Electrical and Computer Engring., 1999. Asst. prof. dept. elec. and computer engring. U. Miami, Fla., 2000—05, assoc. prof. dept. elec. and computer engring., 2005—. Grad. student supr. U. Miami, Coral Gables, Fla.; internat. conf. organizer. Contbr. scientific papers. Recipient Metadata Mgmt. award, NOAA, 2004; grantee, NSF, NOAA, FDOI. Mem.: ACM, IEEE (sr. Svc. award 2005). Achievements include design and development of Fishery and Coral Reef databases for NOAA researchers. Office: Univ Miami Dept Elec and Computer Engring Coral Gables FL 33124 Office Phone: 305-284-5566. Office Fax: 305-284-4044. Business E-Mail: shyu@miami.edu.

**SHYY, WEI,** aerospace and mechanical engineering researcher, educator; b. Tainan, Taiwan, China, July 19, 1955; arrived in U.S., 1979; s. Chiang-Chen and June-Hua (Chao) S.; m. Yuchen Shih; children: Albert, Alice, Andrew Chang, Kevin Chang. BS, Tsin-Hua U., Taiwan, 1977; MSE, U. Mich., 1981, PhD, 1982. Postdoctoral rsch. scholar U. Mich., Ann Arbor, 1982-83; rsch. scientist GE Corp. Rsch. and Devel. Ctr., Schenectady, NY, 1983-88; faculty mem. of aeronautics and astronautics Nat. Cheng-Kung U., Taiwan, 1987; assoc. prof. aerospace engring., mechanics and engring. sci. U. Fla., Gainesville, 1988-92, prof. aerospace engring., mechanics and engring. sci., 1992—, chmn. dept. aerospace engring, mechs. and engring. sci., 1996—2002, chmn. dept. mech. and aerospace engring., 2002—; dir. NASA URETI: Inst. for Future Space Flight, Gainesville, 2002—05; Clarence L. "Kelly" Johnson prof., chmn. dept. aerospace engring. U. Mich., Ann Arbor, 2005—. Dir. Space Grant Consortium NASA, Fla., 1998—2000, dir. Univ. Rsch. Engring. and Tech. Inst. on 3rd Generation Reusable Launch Vehicle; cons. in field; lectr. in field. Editor: Recent Advances in Computational Fluid Dynamics, 1989; author: Computational Modeling for Fluid Flow and Interfacial Transport, 1994; co-author: Computational Fluid Dynamics with Moving Boundaries, 1996, Computational Techniques for Complex Transport Phenomena, 1997; editor: Fluid Dynamics at Interface, 1999; assoc. editor Jour. Applied Mechanis Rev., Computer Modeling in Engineering and Sciences, mng. editor Cambridge U. Press.: Aerospace Book Series, mem. editl. adv. bd. Numerical Heat Transfer Jour., Progress in Computational Fluid Dynamics, Internat. Jour. Numerical Methods for Heat and Fluid Flow; contbr. articles. Fellow AIAA (Pendray Aerospace Lit. award 2003), ASME; mem. Minerals, Metals and Materials Soc., Am. Phys. Soc., Combustion Inst. (Heat Transfer Meml. award, 2005). Office: U Mich Dept Aerospace Engring 3064 FXB Bldg 1320 Beal Ave Ann Arbor MI 48109 Business E-Mail: weishyy@umich.edu.

**SIAHPOOSH, FARIDEH TAMADDON,** librarian; b. Eshghabad, Turkestan, Russia, Nov. 15, 1928; came to U.S., 1964; d. Hosane and Ghamar (Ramzi) Tamaddon; m. Ismail Siahpoosh, Nov. 30, 1952. BA, Tehran U., Iran, 1962; student, Columbia U., 1967; MLS, Queens Coll., Flushing, N.Y., 1972.

Cert. librarian, N.Y. Reference libr. Queens Borough-Pub. Libr. Brs., N.Y.C., 1974-85, asst. br. mgr., 1985—94; part-time libr. Baha'i Internat. Cmty., N.Y.C., 1994—. Intern Baha'i World Ctr. Libr., Haifa, Israel, 1998; mem. L.I. Multi-Faith Forum; part-time ref. libr. Shelter Rock Pub. Libr., 1998—. Mem. ALA. Mem. Baha'i Faith. Home and Office: 19 Ridge Dr E Roslyn NY 11576-1443 Office Phone: 516-627-1919. Personal E-mail: fsiahpoosh@hotmail.com.

**SIAMIS, JANET NEAL,** painter; b. Cleve., July 31, 1938; m. John M. Siamis, Jan. 8, 1965. Student, Rollins Coll., 1956—57, Antelope Valley Coll., 1978—81; studied with Ralph Love. Prin. works include Home Savings Am, Flour Corp., Irvine Calif., Kaiser Permanente, Represented in permanent collections Security Pac Bank, Embassy Suites Hotel, Marriott Hotel, Presidential Suites, various locations, exhibitions include Lancaster Mus., 1985, Tallahassee City Hall, 1988—89, Fla. Watercolor Ann, St. Petersburg, 1991 (Judge's Choice award, 1991), 1996. Home: POBox 1383 4308 Coastal Hwy Crawfordville FL 32326

**SIART, WILLIAM ERIC BAXTER,** non-profit education organization administrator; b. LA, Dec. 25, 1946; s. William Ernest and Barbara Vesta (McPherson) Baxter; m. Noelle Ellen Reid, Sept. 17, 1966; children—Shayne Allison, Tiffany Ann BS in economics, Santa Clara U., 1968; MBA in fin., U. Calif., Berkeley, 1969. With Bank of Am., 1969-78, v.p. corp. banking Brussels, 1977-78; sr. v.p. charge mktg. Western Bancorp, Los Angeles, 1978-81; pres., COO First Interstate Bank of Nev. N.A., Reno, 1981-82, pres., CEO, 1982-84, chmn. bd., pres., CEO 1984; formerly chmn., pres., CEO First Interstate Bank Calif., LA, also bd. dirs.; pres. First Interstate Bancorp, LA, 1990-96, CEO, 1994-96; founder, chmn. bd. Excellent Edn. Devel. (ExED), Santa Monica, Calif., 1998—. Bd. trustees J. Paul Getty Trust, 2005—; bd. dirs. Calif. Cmty. Found., 2005—. Mem. Am. Bankers Assn. (mem. govt. relations council), Reno-Sparks C. of C. (dir.). Republican. Roman Catholic. Office: ExED 429 Santa Monica Blvd Santa Monica CA 90401 Office Phone: 310-394-1152. Office Fax: 310-394-7380. E-mail: wsiart@exed.net.*

**SIAS, MARY,** university president; b. Jackson, Miss., July 2, 1950; d. Augusta and Ada Lee (Hill) Evans; m. Shadrach Sherman Sias III, Mar. 20, 1976; 1 child, Adrienne Marie. BA, Tougaloo Coll., 1972; MS, U. Wis., 1974, PhD, 1980; MBA, Abilene Christian U., 1983. Instr. sociology Grambling (La.) State U., 1977-79; asst. prof. sociology U. Tex. at Dallas, Richardson, 1980-81, So. Meth. U., Highland Park, Tex., 1981-82; dir. women's resource ctr. YWCA Met. Dallas, 1982-83, asst. mgr. ctrl. br., 1983-84, exec. dir., 1984-95; sr. v.p. U. Tex., Dallas, 1995—2004; pres. Ky. State U., Frankfort, 2004—. Bd. dirs. Oaks Bank & Trust, Dallas Co-author: Planned Resettlement in Nepal's Terrain, 1976. Bd. dirs. King Found. Doctoral fellow Ford Found., 1972; recipient Maura award Women's Ctr., 1988, Trailblazer award South Dallas Bus. and Profl. Club, 1989, Outstanding Texan award State of Tex., 1989, She Knows Where She's Going award Girls, Inc., 1994, award of distinction Girl Scouts U.S.A., 1997, Women of Excellence award Women's Enterprise mag., 1998, Lance of Champions award Women of Enterprise mag., 2004, Profiles in Leadership award So. Meth. U., 2004. Mem. Nat. Assn. YWCA Execs., Greater Dallas C. of C., State Bar Tex. Avocations: reading, upholstering, refinishing furniture. Home: 201 Cold Harbor Dr Frankfort KY 40601-3009 Office: Ky State U Hume Hall 400 E Main St Frankfort KY 40601 Office Phone: 502-597-6260. Business E-Mail: msias@kysu.edu.

**SIBBALD, JOHN RISTOW,** management consultant; b. Lincoln, Nebr., June 20, 1936; s. Garth E.W. and Rachel (Wright) S.; div.: children: Allison, John, Wright. BA, U. Nev., 1958; MA, U. Ill., 1964. Office mgr. Hewitt Assocs., Libertyville, Ill., 1964-66; coll. rels. mgr. Pfizer Inc., N.Y.C., 1966-69; pres., CEO Re-Con Systems, N.Y.C., 1969-70; v.p. Booz, Allen & Hamilton, N.Y.C., 1970-73, Chgo., 1973-75; pres., founder John Sibbald Assocs., Inc., Chgo., 1975. Mem. Nat. Advisory Coun., Nat. Club Assn. Author: The Career Makers, 1990, 92, The New Career Makers, 1995; pub. Club Leaders Forum; contbr. articles to profl. jours. Capt. AUS, 1958-64. Mem. St. Louis Club. Episcopalian. Office: 7733 Forsyth Blvd Saint Louis MO 63105-1817 Office Phone: 314-727-0227. E-mail: jsibbald@sibbaldassociates.com.

**SIBBERNSEN, RICHARD,** telecommunications industry executive; b. Omaha; BA, Marquette U., 1971; grad., Creighton U., 1974. Various human resources positions Tenneco, Inc.; head corp. human resources TNT Ltd., Sydney, 1993—97; v.p. human resources Bellsouth Corp., Atlanta, 1997—. Office: Bellsouth Corp 1155 Peachtree St NW Atlanta GA 30309-3610 Office Phone: 404-249-2000. Office Fax: 404-249-2071. E-mail: rsibb@bellsouth.net.

**SIBELMAN, SIMON PHILIP,** language educator; b. Richmond, Va., June 21, 1948; s. Morris Leon and Rose Leah Sibelman. BA summa cum laude, U. Richmond, 1970; PhD, Kings Coll., U. London, 1985. Lang. tchr. St. Christopher's Sch. for Boys, Richmond, Va., 1972—82; dir. adult edn., reader in lit. Spiro Inst. for the Study of Jewish His. and Culture, London, 1984—90; asst. prof. U. Wis. Oshkosh, Oshkosh, Wis., 1990—2000, assoc. prof., 2000—05, prof., 2005—. Ednl. advr. bd. London Jewish Cultural Ctr., London, 2003—; panelist evaluator Nat. Endowment for the Humanities, Wash., DC, 2002—; com. mem. Am. Assn. of Tchrs. of French. Author: Silence in the Novels of Else Wisel, 1995; editor: Teaching the Shoah in the 21st Century, 2004; contbg. editor (assoc.): Encyclopedia of Modern Jewish Culture, 2004; author: The Legacy of the Holocaust Nat. Perspectives, 2004; contbr. chapters to books, articles various prof. jour. named to John Rosebush Disting. Professorship, U. Wis., 2006; recipient TRISS Endowed Professorship, 2003, Dist. Tchg. award, 1995; NEH, 2003, Rsch. grant, Ashdown Trust, 2003, U. Wis., 2002, 2001, Vander Putten Internat. Fund grant, 2001, Rsch. grant, 1997, Assoc. Rsch. fellow, Inst. for Rsch. in Humanities, U. Wis. 1994—95. Mem.: Am. Assn. of Tchrs. of French, Am. Assn. of Jewish Studies, Modern Lang. Assn., Am. Coun. of Christian and Jews, Brai Brith, US Holocaust Meml. Mus. Independent. Avocations: hiking, gardening, travel, gourmet cuisine. Home: 686 Bowen St Oshkosh WI 54901 Office: U Wis Oshkosh DFLL 800 Algoma Blvd Oshkosh WI 54901 Office Phone: 920-424-2375. Office Fax: 920-424-7289. E-mail: sibelman@uwosh.edu.

**SIBERT, POLLY LOU,** conductor, music educator; b. Washington, Pa., Sept. 22, 1962; d. Earl Richard and Virginia Gray Sibert. B in Music Edn., James Madison U., Harrisonburg, Va., 1984, MusM in Orchestral Conducting, 1996; D in Music Edn., Shenandoah Conservatory of Shenandoah U., Winchester, Va., 1999. Orch. dir. Chesterfield (Va.) County Schs., 1985—92; violin maker, restorer self-employed, Chester, Va., 1989—92, Charlottesville, Va., 1992—; orch. dir. Charlottesville (Va.) City Schs., 1992—; first violinist Lynchburg (Va.) Symphony, 2002—. Expert panelist mid. sch. music AECT Project Pa. State U. Edn. Sch., 2002—; cons. music pupil. Frank J. Hackinson Music Co., Inc., Ft. Lauderdale, 2003—. Bowing editor (music) Nancy's Waltz, 1997; author: (dissertation) A Study of the Violin Bow: Identification and Application of Criteria and Tchg. Strategies, 1999; contbr. author (book) Strategies for Teaching: Technology, 2001; author: (jour. article) The Am. String Tchr., 2001. Mem.: NEA, Nat. Sch. Orch. Assn., Am. String Tchrs. Assn., Va. Music Educators Assn. Methodist. Achievements include Built two stringed instruments: a violin and a viola. Avocations: golf, antiques, crocheting. Home: 3003 Colonial Dr Charlottesville VA 22911-9109 Office: Charlottesville City Schs 1564 Dairy Rd Charlottesville VA 22903 E-mail: PLSibert@aol.com.

**SIBILLA, SUZANNE ROSE,** training and organizational development consultant; b. San Jose, Calif., Oct. 15, 1961; d. Susan Pilar Asuzano; m. Michael E. Coutches. BA, Westmont Coll., 1983; MA, Antioch U., 1989. Registered drama therapist Nat. Assn. Drama Therapists, lic. marriage, family, child counselor. Cons. tng. and orgnl. devel. Assn. Psychol. and Ednl. Counselors Asia, Thailand, Malaysia, Singapore; program dir. State of Oreg., Salem, 1988-93; cons. Hewlett Packard, Sun, Raychem, FEMA, CPC Hosps.,

San Jose, Fremont, Palo Alto, Calif., 1993-95; mgr. tng. and orgnl. devel. Tencor Instruments-KLA and TENCOR, Milpitas, Calif., 1995-97; mng. cons., tng. Sibilla & Assocs., Fremont, Calif., 1997—; orgnl. change specialist NEOPOST, 1998—; corp. tng. mgr. WebMD, 1999—2001; ind. cons. Hewlett Packard, 2001—, Compaq, 2001—, Right Mgmt. Cons., 2001—; cons. Sibilla and Assocs., 2001—. Initiator memtorship program Tencor, Palo Alto, 1997. Guest (film and TV program) People Are Talking, 1993, (TV series) Mornings on Two, 1994. Dir. mentorship program for girls YWCA, Daly City, 1993—95. Mem.: ASTD, NAFE, Women in Tech. Internat., Calif. Assn. Marriage, Family and Child Counselors (cert.), Assn. Psychol. and Ednl. Counselors Asia (cons. tng. and orgnl. devel. 1988—92, Key Presenter award 1992), Toastmasters, Mentium 100 (chairperson steering com. 1996—97). Avocations: acting, waterskiing, sailing, swimming, travel. E-mail: srsibilla@aol.com.

**SIBLEY, DAVID ALLEN,** illustrator, writer, ornithologist; b. 1962; s. Fred Sibley; m. Joan Walsh; 2 children. Illustrator (books) Wind Masters: The Lives of N.Am. Birds of Prey, 1995, author & illustrator Sibley Guide to Birds, Nat. Audubon Soc., 2000, Sibley Guide to Bird Life & Behavior, 2001, Sibley's Birding Basics, 2002, Sibley Field Guide to Birds of Eastern N Am., Birds of Western N.Am., 2003, co-author, illustrator (NY Times Syndicated Column) Sibley on Birds, 2002—. Recipient Roger Tory Peterson award, Am. Birding Assn., 2002. Office: Russell Galen at Scovill Chichak Galen Inc Rm 1020 381 Park Ave S New York NY 10016 also: NY Times Syndication Sales Corp 14th Fl 122 E 42nd St New York NY 10168 Office Phone: 212-679-8686.*

**SIBLEY, JAMES MALCOLM,** retired lawyer; b. Atlanta, Aug. 5, 1919; s. John Adams and Nettie Whitaker (Cone) S.; m. Karen Norris, Apr. 6, 1942; children: Karen Mariea, James Malcolm Jr., Jack Norris, Elsa Alexandria Victoria, Quintus Whitaker. AB, Princeton U., 1941; student, Woodrow Wilson Sch. Law, 1942, Harvard Law Sch., 1945—46. Bar: Ga. 1942. Assoc. King & Spalding, Atlanta, 1942-47, ptnr., 1947-91. Bd. dirs. Summit Industries, Inc.; exec. com., mem. pub. affairs com. Coca-Cola Co., 1979-91; chmn. exec. com. John H. Harland Co., 1963-91; chmn. exec. com., mem. compensation com. Trust Co. of Ga., 1975-92; mem. exec. com., mem. compensation com. SunTrust Banks, Inc., 1985-92. Trustee Joseph B. Whitehead Found., Lettie Pate Evans Found., A.G. Rhodes Home, Inc., Robert W. Woodruff Found., Inc. (formerly Trebor Found.), John H. and Wilhelmina D. Harland Charitable Found., Inc.; trustee emeritus Berry Coll., The Lovett Sch., Callaway Gardens Found., Emory U. With USAF, 1942—45. Mem. ABA, Ga. Bar Assn., Atlanta Bar Assn., Am. Coll. Probate Counsel, Am. Bar Found., Am. Law Inst., Piedmont Driving Club, Commerce Club. Episcopalian. also: King & Spalding 191 Peachtree St NE Ste 40 Atlanta GA 30303-1740 Home: 3045 Slaton Dr NW Atlanta GA 30305-2006*

**SIBLEY, LYNN M.,** anthropologist, educator; b. Nashville, Tenn., Mar. 4, 1949; d. James G. and Peggy L. Middleton; m. George J. Armelagos, June 21, 1991; 1 child, Gabriel. PhD (Anthropology), U. of Colo., Boulder, Colorado, 1988—93; MS (Nursing), U. of Utah, Salt Lake City, Utah, 1978—80; BS (Nursing), U. of Colo., Denver, Colorado Health Sciences Center, 1970—73; MA (Anthropology), U. of Colo., Boulder, Colorado, 1986—87. Registered Nurse, Colo. State Bd. of Nursing, 1974, Certified Nurse Midwife, Am. Coll. of Nurse Midwives, 1980. Faculty U. of Colo. Sch. of Nursing, Denver, Colo., 1980—85; sr. tech. advisor Am. Coll. of Nurse-Midwives, Washington, 1995—; adj. asst. prof. of anthropology Emory U., Atlanta, Ga., 1995—; vis. clin. instr. Med. Coll. of Va., Richmond, Va. Cons. People's Clinic, Boulder, Colo., 1983—83; co-organizer, nsf nasa conf. on remote sensing U. of Colo., Boulder, Colo.; cons., tech. consultation on attendance at birth: cmty. birth attendants UNICEF and World Bank, New York City, NY, 1997; consultant-,global tech. consultation on safe motherhood Global Safe Motherhood Inter-Agency Working Group, Colombo, Sri Lanka, 1997; cons. Nat. Summit on Safe Motherhood, Centers for Disease Control and others, Atlanta, 2001; co-chair, workshop on home based life saving skills Am. Coll. of Nurse Midwives, Tucson; cons. Johns Hopkins Sch. of Pub. Health, Baltimore, Md., 2002—. Author: (journal article) Journal of Nurse-Midwifery; co-author (journal article) Current Anthropology, Obstetrics and Gynecology, Medical Anthropology; author: (journal article) American Journal of Physical Anthropology, Journal of Nurse Midwifery, Quickening, Journal of Women's Health and Midwifery; co-author (training manual) Home Based Life Saving Skills. Recipient Sigma Theta Tau,, Gamma Rho Chpt., 1980, Phi Kappa Phi, U. of Utah Chpt., 1980, Nat. Dean's List, A Nat. Honor Soc., 1980; fellow Grad. Tchg./Rsch. Asst., U. of Colo., 1986-1988, Fulbright Dissertation Fellowship, Belize, US Fulbright Program, 1989-1990; grantee Nurse Traineeship, US HHS, 1978-1980, NSF Doctoral Grant for Improving Dissertation Rsch., NSF, 1989-1990. Mem.: Am. Assn. of Phys. Anthropologists, Am. Anthrop. Assn., APHA, Am. Coll. of Nurse Midwives. Achievements include development of Co-team leader for development of Home Based Life Saving Skills, an innovative community based stragety to reduce maternal and neonatal mortality in developing countries; research in Traditional Birth Attendant Training Effectiveness, a meta-analysis of global TBA training programs spanning 30 years of publications; Analysis of paleo-obstetrics in ancient Sudanese Nubia. Avocations: sea kayaking, sea kayaking, sea kayaking. Home: 1327 Peachtree St NE #504 Atlanta GA 30309 Office: American College of Nurse Midwives 8403 Colesville Rd Ste 1550 Silver Spring MD 20910-6374 Personal E-mail: antls#learnlink.emory.edu. E-mail: antls@learnlink.emory.edu.

**SIBLEY, WILLIAM ARTHUR,** academic administrator, physics professor, consultant; b. Ft. Worth, Nov. 22, 1932; s. William Franklin and Sada (Rasor) S.; m. Margie Elaine Gregory, Dec. 21, 1957; children: William Timothy, Lauren Shawn, Stephen Marshall. BS, U. Okla., 1956, MS, 1958, PhD, 1960. Tchg., rsch. asst. U. Okla., 1956-60; postdoctoral rsch. in defect solid state Kernforschungsanlage Julich and Tech. U. Aachen, Germany, 1960-61; rsch. solid state divsn. Oak Ridge Nat. Lab., 1961-70; prof., head physics Okla. State U., Stillwater, 1970-76, dir. Sch. Phys. and Earth Scis., 1976-78, asst. v.p. rsch., 1978-88; v.p. acad. affairs U. Ala., Birmingham, 1990-96; program dir. NSF, Washington, 1988-89, acting dir. divsn. materials rsch., 1990, program dir., 1996-99, acting divsn. dir. rsch., evaluation and comm. divsn., 1998-99; pres. Okla. Ctr. for Advancement of Sci. and Tech., 2000—02; CEO dir. Okla. Sci. and Tech. R & D, 2002—04; ret., 2004; cons. univs. and businesses, 2004—. Mem. solid state sci. com. NAS, 1977-83; bd. dirs. Oak Ridge Assoc. Univs., 1982-88, Coun. on Govt. Rels., 1987-93, Okla. Ctr. for Advancement Sci. and Tech., 1987-88; trustee, chmn. materials rsch. counsel Southeastern Univ. Rsch. Assn., 1992-95; cons. univ. edn. and rsch. counsel University Management 2010, 1998; contbr. articles to profl. jours. Pres. Stillwater Indsl. Found., 1985-86. Served to lt. AUS, 1951-53. Maj. USAR, 1953-60, Korea. Fellow Am. Phys. Soc.; mem. Omicron Delta Kappa, Sigma Xi, Sigma Pi Sigma, Pi Mu Epsilon. Baptist. Home: 2517 Thunderwind Cir Edmond OK 73034-6880 Personal E-mail: sibleybill@aol.com

**SIBLEY, WILLIAM AUSTIN,** neurologist, educator; b. Miami, Okla., Jan. 25, 1925; s. William Austin and Erna Johanna (Quickert) S.; m. Joanne Shaw, Sept. 4, 1954; children: John, Mary Jane, Peter, Andrew. BS, Yale U., 1945, MD, 1948. Intern Univ. Hosp., Cleve., 1948-50; asst. resident neurologist Neurol. Inst. Presbyn. Hosp., N.Y.C., 1953-55, chief resident neurologist 1955-56; asst. prof. neurology Western Res. U., Cleve., 1956-63, assoc. prof., 1963-67; prof. U. Ariz. Coll. Medicine, Tucson, 1967—, head dept. neurology, 1967-82. Chmn. therapy com. Internat. Fedn. Multiple Sclerosis Socs., 1986-92, 96-98. Served to capt. M.C. USAF, 1951-53. Recipient LaFayette B. Mendel prize in physiol. chemistry, Yale U., 1945, John Dystel award, Am. Acad. Neurolgy and Nat. Multiple Scerosis Soc., 2006. Mem. Am. Neurol. Assn. (v.p. 1979-80), Am. Acad. Neurology (v.p. 1985-87), Central Soc. for Neurol. Research (pres. 1968) Achievements include helping establish effectiveness of beta-interferon therapy in multiple sclerosis. Home: 2150 E Hampton St Tucson AZ 85719-3810 Office: 1501 N Campbell Ave Tucson AZ 85724-0001

---

**SIBLEY, WILLIS ELBRIDGE,** anthropology educator, consultant; b. Nashville, Feb. 22, 1930; s. Elbridge and Elizabeth Reynolds (LaBarre) S.; m. Barbara Jean Grant, June 9, 1956; children: Sheila Katherine, Anthony Grant, Michael David. BA, Reed Coll., 1951; MA, U. Chgo., 1953, PhD, 1958. Instr. sociology and anthropology Miami (Ohio) U., 1956-58; asst. prof. anthropology U. Utah, 1958-60; from asst. prof. to prof. anthropology Wash. State U., 1960-71; prof. anthropology Cleve. State U., 1971—, chmn. dept., 1971-77, Cleve. (City) faculty fellow, 1987, interim chmn., 1989-90, prof. emeritus, 1990—; sr. program analyst EPA, Washington, 1977-78; Govtl. fellow Am. Coun. on Edn., 1978; Rockefeller Found. vis. prof. anthropology U. Philippines, Quezon City, 1968-69; postdoctoral fellow in society and tech. Carnegie-Mellon U., 1981-82. Fulbright grantee, 1954-55, 64; NIMH grantee, 1959-61; NSF grantee, 1964-71; Nat. Acad. Scis.-NRC travel grantee, 1966; Office Edn., HEW research grantee, 1967 Fellow AAAS, Assn. Profl. Anthropologists (pres. Washington chpt. 1999—), Am. Anthropol. Assn. (treas. 1989-91, com. on pub. policy 2000-2002), Soc. Applied Anthropology (sec. 1977-80, pres. 1981-82); mem. AAUP (treas. Wash. State U. chpt. 1962-63, v.p. 1963-64, pres. 1965-66, pres. Cleve. State U. chpt. 1979-80, treas. 1980-81, interim pres. 1989-90), ACLU (pres. Pullman chpt. 1963, 66), Ctrl. States Anthropol. Soc. (past mem. exec. bd., treas. 1986-89), Wash. Assn. Profl. Anthropologists, Edgewater Yacht Club (Cleve., commodore 1991), Chesapeake Yacht Club (Shady Side, Md.) (gov. 1999, 2000). Home: 1190 Cedar Ave Shady Side MD 20764 Office: Cleve State U Dept Anthropology Cleveland OH 44115 Office Phone: 301-261-9404. Personal E-mail: shadyside1190@comcast.net.

**SIBO, ELSA LYNETTE,** secondary school educator; d. Lawrence E. and V. Azalee Chapman; m. Richard J. Sibo, Feb. 8, 1964 (dec. Mar. 1, 1986). BA, Blue Mountain Coll., 1962; MEd, U. Nev., 1978. Tchg. cert. Miss., 1962, Tex., 1972, Ga., 1973, Nev., 2002. Tchr. English Greenville H.S., Miss., 1962—64, Schertz-Cibolo Ind. Sch. Dist., Schertz, Tex., 1964—65; tchr. English, speech Randolph Field Ind. Sch. Dist., Universal City, Tex., 1965—72, Clayton County Sch. Dist., Jonesboro, Ga., 1973—74; tchr. English St. Yves H.S., Las Vegas, 1975—76; grad. asst. reading ctr. part time staff U. Nev., 1976—78; tchr. English Clark County Sch. Dist., 1978—2002, CC of So. Nev., Henderson, 2003—. Mem., pres., sec., treas., com. mem. Gamma Chpt., Delta Kappa Gamma, Las Vegas, 1972—2005. Fellow Study Stipend, Delta Kappa Gamma, 1982. Mem.: NEA (life), Delta Kappa Gamma (Rose of Recognition 1983), Kappa Delta Pi (assoc.). Independent. Methodist. Avocations: travel, hiking, ballroom dancing. Personal E-mail: lsibo@earthlink.net.

**SIBOLSKI, ELIZABETH HAWLEY,** academic administrator; b. Gt. Barrington, Mass., Aug. 18, 1950; d. William Snyder and Frances Harrington (Smith) Gallup; m. John Alfred Sibolski Jr., Aug. 15, 1970. BA, The Am. U., 1973, MPA, 1975, PhD, 1984. Acting dir. acad. adminstrn. Am. U., Washington, 1974, planning analyst 1974—79, asst. dir. budget and planning, 1980—83, dir. instl. rsch., 1984—85, exec. dir. univ. planning and rsch., 1985—2000; exec. assoc. dir. Middle States Commn. on Higher Edn., Phila., 2000—. Trustee Mortar Bd. Nat. Found., 1989—95. Recipient Commencement award, Am. U. Women's Club, 1973. Mem. Soc. Coll. and Univ. Planning (bd. dirs. 1995-2000, pres. 1998-99), Mortar Bd. (sect. coord. 1975-82), Pi Alpha Alpha, Phi Kappa Phi (chpt. officer 1986-92), Pi Sigma Alpha, Omicron Delta Kappa. Avocations: breed, raise and show morgan horses. Home: 565 Wayward Dr Annapolis MD 21401-6747 Office: Middle States Commn on Higher Edn 3624 Market St Philadelphia PA 19104-2614 Business E-Mail: esibolski@msche.org.

**SIBOLSKI, JOHN ALFRED, JR.,** educational association executive; b. Nov. 4, 1946; s. John A. and Isabelle Barcaster S.; m. Elizabeth Gallup, Aug. 15, 1970. AA in Data Processing, Andover Inst. Bus., 1966; BS in Tech. of Mgmt., Am. U., 1967; cert. in data processing, 1974, grad. cert. in data processing, 1978. With Automated Systems Corp., Washington, 1969-71, KMS Tech. Ctr., Arlington, Va., 1971-72; ind. cons., 1972-73, 74-76; with Law Enforcement Asst. Adminstrn., Dept. Justice, Washington, 1973-74; D.A. Lewis, Assocs., Clinton, Md., 1974; with Bur. Nat. Affairs Inc., Washington, 1976-80; mgr. systems. devel. NEA, Washington, 1980-90, Saturn Corp., Cheverly, Md., 1990-91, FBI, Washington, 1991—. Recipient spl. achievement award Dept. Justice, 1974. Mem. Fata Processing Mgmt. Assn., Am. Soc. for Info. Sci. Home: 565 Wayward Dr Annapolis MD 21401-6747 Office: FBI 10th St And Pa Ave Washington DC 20535-0001 E-mail: jsibolski@comcast.net.

**SIBONY, GEDI,** sculptor; b. NYC, 1973; BA, Brown U., Providence, 1995; student, Skowhegan Sch. Painting and Sculpture, Maine, 1999; MFA, Columbia U., NYC, 2000. Exhibited in group shows at Two Person Show, Gallery 16, San Francisco, 1998, Superimposition, Caren Golden Fine Art, NYC, 2001, Silent Takeover, Staedtische Galerie, Baden, Switzerland, 2002, One Fine Day, Block Gallery, Sydney, Australia, 2003, Breaking Ground, White Columns, NYC, 2003, Playpen: Selections Summer, The Drawing Ctr, NYC, 2004, Slouching Towards Bethlehem, The Project, NYC, 2004, Floorplay, Bklyn. War Meml., 2004, Greener Pastures Contemporary Art, Toronto, Can., 2005, Art Rev. 25, Philips De Pury, NYC, 2005, Make It Now, The Sculpture Ctr., NY, 2005, Walls 'n Things, Nicole Klagsbrun Gallery, NYC, 2005, Poetry in the Backyard, Galerie Art: Concept, Paris, 2006, Whitney Biennial: Day for Night, Whitney Mus. Am. Art, 2006, exhibitions include The Qualities Depend Upon Other Qualities, 2004, Some Places Exist, London, 2005, The Wrong Gallery, NYC, 2005. Grantee, Rema Hort Mann Found., 2004. Mailing: c/o CANADA Gallery 55 Chrystie St New York NY 10002*

**SIBUMA, BERNADETTE,** educational consultant; b. Olongapo, Philippines, Jan. 20, 1975; arrived in U.S., 1980; d. Bernardo and Bibiana Espiritu Sibuma. BS in Ednl. Psychology, Cornell U., Ithaca, N.Y., 1997; MA Instrnl. Tech. and Media, Columbia U., N.Y.C., 2002, postgrad. in Instrnl. Tech. and Media, 2002—. Rsch. asst. II Harvard Med. Sch., Boston, 1997—99; rsch. asst. III Harvard Project Zero, Cambridge, Mass., 1999—2000; dir. of volunteers Media and Tech. Charter H.S., Boston, 2000—01; rsch. assoc. Inst. for Learning Technologies, Columbia U., NYC, 2002—04, 2005—. Usability cons. Teachers Coll., Columbia U., New York, NY, 2003—04. Scholar, Teachers Coll., Columbia U., 2003—05. Mem.: Cognitive Neurosci. Soc., Assn. Psychol. Sci., Assn. for the Advancement of Computing in Edn., Am. Ednl. Rsch. Assn., Kappa Delta Pi. Personal E-mail: bes2004@columbia.edu.

**SICART, PIERRE-ALEXANDRE SERGE HENRY,** writer; b. Toulouse, France, Jan. 27, 1975; s. Pierre Alain Thierry Sicart and Micheline Marie Mauricette Ory. DEUG in English, U. Toulouse II, France, 1997; Licentiate Integrated European Studies, U. St. Andrews, Scotland, 1998; PhD in French Lit. with honors, NYU, N.Y.C., 2005; Doctorat es Lettres with highest honors, U. Toulouse II, France, 2005. Computer expert trainee Tocquevile Asset Mgmt., N.Y.C., 1996; web designer, asst. forum mgr. and interpreter Leisure On Line, Saint-Orens, France, 1996—98; tchg. asst. elem. and intermediate French N.Y. U., N.Y.C., NY, 2001—02, tchg. asst. French lang. and lit., 2002—03; freelance voice actor N.Y. Audio Prodns., 2006—. Co-author: Le Web pas cher, 1999; co-editor: Amberzine 12-15, 2005; co-editor and translator: Maîtriser Office 2000 visuel, 1999, Moteurs de recherche pour le WEB, 1999; co-translator Trésors cachés Office 2000, 1999; author: (short stories) État de crise, 1999, Le Crabe et la Fée, 2000, Comment j'ai sauvé la Terre des Martiens, 2000, Sur la digue, 2001 (first text in prose awarded poetry prize Acad. des Jeux Floraux, 2001), 25¢, 2001, Le Temple sous la lune, 2002, L'Adieu aux légendes, 2003, Le Mauvais choix, 2005, Fors l'Honneur, 2005; designer: French phonetic game, 2004; contbr. articles to profl. jours. Capt. N.Y. U. Taekwondo Club, N.Y.C., 2003—04. Named Most Valuable Player Taekwondo, NYU Athletics, 2001—02, Graduation Std. Bearer, Grad. Sch. Arts and Scis., NYU, 2005; recipient Press's Svc. award, NYU, 2003; grantee Grad. Sch. Arts and Scis. NYU, 2003—04, 2004—05, Tech. and Tchg. Mentoring Program NYU, 2003—04; Socrates-Erasmus scholar, European Union, 1997—98, Merit scholar, French govt., 1998—99, MacCracken fellow, Grad. Sch. Arts and Scis. NYU, 1999—2003, Dean's

---

Dissertation fellow, Grad. Sch. Arts and Scis. NYU, 2003—04. Mem.: MLA, Poetic Genius Soc., Mensa. Office Phone: 917-406-8567. Personal E-mail: sicart@gmail.com. E-mail: french@nyu.edu.

**SICES, DAVID,** language educator, translator; b. NYC, June 10, 1933; s. Harry and Henrietta (Finger) S.; m. Joan Picker, May 25, 1956 (div. 1961); children: Andrew M., Anne; m. Jacqueline Boulon, July 25, 1963; children: Laura, Harry J. AB, Dartmouth Coll., 1954, MA (hon.), 1971; PhD, Yale U., 1962. Instr. Dartmouth Coll., Hanover, NH, 1957-62, asst. prof., 1962-67, assoc. prof., 1967-71, prof. French and Italian, 1971-75; prof. emeritus, 1995—. Cons. NEH, Washington, 1986—, Can. Arts Council, Ottawa, 1997; mem. screening com. French Govt. Assistantships, NYC, 1978-83. Author: Harmony of Contrasts, 1968, Theater of Solitude, 1974; co-author: French Idioms, 1996; co-author: 2001 French Idioms, 1996; translator: Comedies and Proverbs of Musset, 1994, Michel Zink, Historical Dramas of Musset, 1997, The Invention of Literary Subjectivity, 1998; co-translator: Machiavelli's Discourses, 2002; co-editor, translator: Comedies of Machiavelli, 1985, Machiavelli and His Friends, 1996, The Sweetness of Power, 2002. Fulbright-Hays fellow, Paris, 1956-57, Fulbright-Hays summer seminar, Rome, 1966; fellow Am. Council Learned Socs., 1969-70; humanities devel. grant Dartmouth Coll., Hanover, 1976. Mem. AAUP, Am. Assn. Tchrs. French, Am. Assn. Tchrs. Italian, Dante Soc. Am. Avocations: music, travel, photography. Home: 750 Weaver Dairy Rd Apt 140 Chapel Hill NC 27514-1440 E-mail: david.sices@dartmouth.edu.*

**SICHERMAN, HARVEY,** think-tank executive; BS in History, U. Scranton, 1966; PhD in Polit. Sci., U. Pa., 1971. Assoc. dir. for rsch. Fgn. Policy Rsch. Inst., Phila., 1978—80; spl. asst. Sec. of State Alexander M. Haig Jr., 1981—82; mem. policy planning staff Sec. of State James A. Baker III; cons. Sec. of the Navy John F. Lehman, Jr., 1982—87, Sec. of State George Schultz, 1988; pres., dir. Fgn. Policy Rsch. Inst., Phila., 1994—. Author: The Three Percent Solution and the Future of NATO, 1982, Palestinian Autonomy, Self-Government and Peace, 1993; co-author (with Alexander M. Haig Jr.): New Directions in U.S.-Chinese Relations, 1997; co-editor (with Murray Weidenbaum): The Chinese Economy: A New Scenario, 1999; co-editor: (with John Lehman) America the Vulnerable: Our Military Problems and How To Fix Them, 2002; contbr. articles to profl. jours. Office: Fgn Policy Rsch Inst Ste 610 1528 Walnut St Philadelphia PA 19102

**SICHERMAN, MARVIN ALLEN,** lawyer; b. Cleve., Dec. 27, 1934; s. Harry and Malvina (Friedman) S.; m. Sue Kovacs, Aug. 18, 1957; children: Heidi Joyce, Steven Eric. BA, Case Western Res. U., 1957, LLB, 1960, JD, 1968. Bar: Ohio 1960. Mng. prin. Dettelbach, Sicherman & Baumgart, Cleve., 1971—. Mem. editl. bd.: Case-Western Res. Law Rev, 1958-60; contbr. articles to legal jours. Mem. Beachwood (Ohio) Civic League, 1972-92; mem. Beachwood Bd. Edn., 1978-86, pres., 1981, 85, v.p., 1984; trustee Beachwood Arts Coun., 1977-84. Mem. Ohio Bar Assn. (lectr. truth in lending 1969, lectr. bankruptcy 1972, 81, 84, 99, 2000-05, Meritorious Service awards 1971, 77, 78, 79, 83, 84, 85, 86, 87), Cleve. Bar Assn. (lectr. practice and procedure clinic 1960-80, 82-87, chmn. bankruptcy ct. com. 1971-73), Jewish Chautauqua Soc., Tau Epsilon Rho, Zeta Beta Tau. Jewish (trustee Temple brotherhood 1968-76, sec. 1971-73). Jewish. Home: 24500 Albert Ln Cleveland OH 44122-2302 Office: Dettelbach Sicherman & Baumgart 1100 Ohio Savings Plz Cleveland OH 44114 Office Phone: 216-696-6000. Business E-Mail: msicherman@dsb-law.com.

**SICHUK, GEORGE,** entrepreneur, quantum biochemist, educator; b. Butler Twp., Pa., May 10, 1933; s. Stephan Nicholas and Eva (Hawranick) Sichuk; m. Georgiana Nadya Stroyen, July 27, 1968. BA, Drew U., 1954; ScD, Rutgers U., 1962. Rsch. assoc. Sloan-Kettering Inst. Cancer Rsch., N.Y.C., 1961—71; asst. prof. biology Montclair State Coll., Upper Montclair, NJ, 1972—75, William Paterson Coll., Wayne, NJ, 1975; lectr. interdisciplinary studies Bloomfield (N.J.) Coll., 1976; sci. tchr. Eastside H.S., Paterson, NJ, 1988—93; entrepreneur author Lincoln Park, NJ, 1993—. Author: Gabriel's Voice, 1996, Uriel's Light, 1997, One Man's Testament, 1998, Constitutional Imperatives for Rational Government, 2003, Common Sense Plus, 2004, The Pentian Truth: Thomas Paine, the Mozart of Reason, 2004; contbr. articles to profl. med. jours. Good will amb. U.S. Govt., Cuba, 1960; coach Police Athletic League, Lincoln Park, 1977—79; CEO NJ Citizens Orgn., 1967—68; exec. and coach Orthodox Citizens' Club, NJ, 1980—90. Achievements include clarification of relationship of the endocrine and immune systems to cancer to direct attention to the nucleic acids (DNA and RNA); clarification of transplantation immunology; proof that "butter yellow" a dibenzanthracene used to give margarine a yellow color is a carcinogen; research in the role of sex hormones in thrombotic disease; dynamic relationship between dietary protein quality and function of adrenal cortex in mammals; harmonic function of the human brain, denial of monotheism; and proof of origin of viruses, identifying vectors of disease; proof that DES can cause thromboembolic disease. Avocations: geo-politics, house maintenance engineering, golf, flying, music. Home: 18 Sewanois Ave Lincoln Park NJ 07035-1710

**SICILIANI, ALESSANDRO DOMENICO,** conductor; b. Florence, Italy; s. Francesco and Ambra Siciliani; 1 child, Giacomo Francesco. Student, Giuseppe Verdi Milano Cons., Rome, Santa Cecilia; studied with Franco Ferrara. Music advisor Columbus Symphony Orch., 1991—2006, music dir., 1992—2006. Condr. Nat. Radio Orchs. of Rome and Naples, Symphony of Abruzzi, Palermo Symphony Orch., Cagliari Symphony Orch., Bari Symphony Orch., N.Y. City Opera, Opera Co. of Phila., New Orleans Opera, Ky. Opera, Teatro San Carlo, Naples, Italy, Teatro dell'Opera, Rome, Teatro Massimo, Palermo, Italy, Verdi, Pisa, Italy, also Barcelona, Spain, Marseille, France, Avignon, and Liege, France; condr. revivals Cavalleria Rusticana. Pagliacci, N.Y. City Opera a revival La Rondine, Am. premiere Schubert's Fierrabras; appeared with Pitts. Symphony, Nat. Symphony, Washington, D.C., Munich Symphony Orch., Cologne Symphony Orch., Dresden Symphony Orch., Stockholm Symphony Orch., Goteborg Symphony Orch., Hong Kong Symphony Orch., Nat. Arts Ctr. Orch. of Ottawa, English Chamber Orch., Symphonia Varsovia, Perugia Chamber Orch., Padova Chamber Orch.; participant festivals including Schleswig-Holstein, Panatenee Pompeiane, Printemps Festival of Praha, Spring Festival in Saratoga Springs, Sagra Musicale Umbra; prin. guest condr. Orch. Teatro Colon, Buenos Aires, Teatro Mcpl. Sao Paulo. Recipient Amerigo Vespucci award, 1992.*

**SICILIANO, ROCCO CARMINE,** cultural institute executive; b. Salt Lake City, Mar. 4, 1922; s. Joseph Vincent and Mary (Arnone) S.; m. Marion Stiebel, Nov. 8, 1947; children: Loretta, A. Vincent, Fred R., John C., Maria. BA with honors, U. Utah, 1944; LL.B., Georgetown U., 1948; LHD, Hebrew Union Coll., Gettysburg Coll., 2000, U. Utah, 2001. Bar: D.C. bar 1949. Legal asst. to bd. mem. NLRB, Washington, 1948-50; asst. sec.-treas. Procon Inc., Des Plaines, Ill., 1950-53; asst. sec. labor charge employment and manpower Dept. Labor, Washington, 1953-57; spl. asst. to Eisenhower for personnel mgmt., 1957-59; prin. Wilkinson, Cragun & Barker, 1959-69; pres. Pacific Maritime Assn., San Francisco, 1965-69; undersec. of commerce Washington, 1969-71; pres., chmn. bd., chief exec. officer Ticor, Los Angeles, 1971-84, chmn., exec. com., 1984-85; of counsel Jones, Day, Reavis & Pogue, 1984-87; chmn. bd., chief exec. officer Am. Health Properties, Inc., 1987-88; chmn. Dwight D. Eisenhower World Affairs Inst., Washington, 1991-2001; apptd. mem. Eisenhower Meml. Commn., 2000, chmn., 2001—. Chmn. Ctr. for Govtl. Studies, 1992—; contbr. Calif. Citizens Budget Commn.; mem. Fed. Pay Bd., 1971-73; trustee emeritus J. Paul Getty Trust. Author: Walking on Sand, 2004. Past chmn. Calif. Bus. Roundtable; trustee Com. for Econ. Devel.; co-chmn. Calif. Commn. on Campaign Financing. 1st lt. AUS, 1943-46, MTO, ETO. Decorated Bronze Star for Valor, Combat Infantryman's badge; Order of Merit (Italy). Mem. Nat. Acad. Pub. Adminstrn., Met. Club (Washington), L.A. Philharm. Assn. (life dir.), Calif. Club (L.A.). Home: 612 N Rodeo Dr Beverly Hills CA 90210-3208

**SICK, WILLIAM NORMAN, JR.,** technology company executive; b. Houston, Apr. 20, 1935; s. William Norman and Gladys Phylena (Armstrong) S.; m. Stephanie Anne Williams, Sept. 14, 1963; children: Jill Melanie, David

Louis. BA, Rice U., 1957, BSEE, 1958. With Tex. Instruments Inc., various locations, 1958-87; exec. v.p. Tex. Instruments, Inc., Dallas, 1982-87; pres. semicondr. products group Tex. Instruments Inc., Dallas, 1982-86; bd. dirs. Tex. Instruments, Inc., 1985-87; CEO Am. Nat. Can Co., Chgo., 1988-89; also bd. dirs. Am. Nat. Can. Co., Chgo., 1988-89; mem. exec. com. Pechiney, Paris, 1989; bd. dirs. Pechiney Internat., 1989; vice chmn., bd. dirs. Triangle Industries, N.Y.C., 1988—89; chmn., CEO, Bus. Resources Internat., Winnetka, Ill., 1989—; co-founder, mng. dir. Signature Capital Mgmt., LLC, Northfield, Ill., 1997—2003. Bd. dirs., former chmn. Acoustic Tech., Mesa, Ariz.; co-founder Metasolv, Dallas; bd. dir., co-founder VIRxSYS, Gaithersburg, Md.; former chmn. Aware, Bedford, Mass., Power Trends, Warrenville, Ill.; guest lectr. Sophia U., Tokyo, 1973. Trustee, past chmn. Shedd Aquarium, Chgo., 1990—; trustee Rice U., 1996-2006, Santa Fe Inst., 2000—; bd. dirs. Millennium Park Inc., 2004—; mem. Chgo. Coun. Fgn. Rels. Mem. Exec. Club Chgo., Glen View Club, Sigma Xi, Tau Beta Pi, Sigma Tau. Episcopalian. Office: Bus Resources Internat 565 Sheridan Rd Winnetka IL 60093-0500

**SICKLER, JOHN J.,** manufacturing executive; Former head corp. devel. Teleflex, Plymouth Meeting, Pa., pres. aerospace segment, 1986—90, vice chmn., 2000—, interim CFO, 2003—04. Bd. dirs. PennEngring. Office: Teleflex 155 South Limerick Rd Limerick PA 19468

**SICKLES, EDWARD,** radiologist; b. N.Y.C., Apr. 17, 1945; s. Leon R. and Mildred (Spector) S.; m. Dale Gottdiener, Dec. 25, 1966; 1 child, Ellen. BA, Columbia U., 1965; MD, Cornell U., 1969. Diplomate Am. Bd. Radiology, Am. Bd. Internal Medicine. Asst. prof. radiology U. Calif., San Francisco, 1977-82, assoc. prof. radiology, 1982-87, prof. radiology, 1987—2005, prof. emeritus radiology, 2005—. Chief breast imaging svc. U. Calif. Med. Ctr., San Francisco, 1977—2005; com. mem. nat. mammography quality assurance adv. com., U.S. FDA, Rockville, Md., 1997-2000; lectr. in field. Contbr. articles to profl. jours.; books. Bd. dirs. San Francisco chpt. Susan G. Komen Breast Cancer Found., San Francisco, 1993—96. Surgeon USPHS, 1971-73. Recipient Comm. Svc. award Susan G. Komen Breast Cancer Found., San Francisco, 1991. Fellow Am. Coll. Radiology (chair COMISA 1992—); mem. Soc. Breast Imaging (past pres. 1985, Gold medalist 1999), Soc. for the Study of Breast Disease (past pres. 1986), Soc. Latinoamericana de Imagenolgia Mamaria, Soc. Gaucha de Radiologia, La Soc. Canadienne Francaise de Radiologie. Office: UCSF Dept Radiology 1600 Divisadero St #H-2801 San Francisco CA 94115

**SICKLES, ROBIN C.,** economics and statistics professor, consultant; b. Pitts., Dec. 24, 1949; s. Walter E. and Georgene N. Sickles; m. Janet C. Meininger, July 3, 1981; children: Danielle L., David C. BS in Econs., Ga. Inst. of Tech., 1972; PhD in Econs., U. of N.C., 1976. Asst. prof. dept. of econs. George Wash. U., Washington, 1976—79; vis. prof. dept. of econs. U. of Pa., Phila., 1979—80, asst. prof. dept. of econs., 1980—85; faculty rsch. fellow Nat. Bur. of Econ. Rsch., Cambridge, 1984—92; assoc. prof. dept. of econs. Rice U., Houston, 1985—87, prof. dept. of econs., 1987—; vis. scholar dept. of econs. U. of Mich., Ann Arbor, 1992; vis. adj. prof. European Inst. of Bus. Adminstrn., Fontainebleau, France, 1992—94; vis. scholar Bd. Govs. Fed. Res. Sys., Washington, 1993; vis. prof. pure and applied math. Inst. of Stats. Univ. Catholique de Louvain, Louvain-la-Neuve, Belgium, 1999. Dir. Rice U. Ctr. for the Study of Institutions and Values, Houston, 1999—2002; dir. grad. program in econs. Rice U., Houston, 2000—; dir. Law and Econ. Cons. Group, Houston, 2002—. Author: (book) The Causes, Correlates and Consequences of Death Among Older Adults: Some Methodological Approaches and Substantive Analysis-Kluwer, Unlocking the Assets: Energy and the Future of Central Asia and the Caucasus: A Political, Economic, and Cultural Analysis-Palgrave, (book chpt.) Handbook of Population and Family Economics-North Holland, Handbook of Applied Economics, Volume II-Microeconometrics-Basil Blackwell, (jour. articles) Internat. Econ. Rev., Rev. of Econs. and Stats., Jour. of Econs., Jour. of Bus. and Econ. Stats., Jour. of Applied Econometrics, Am. Econ. Rev., Jour. of Productivity Analysis, Internat. Jour. of Indsl. Orgn., Econ. Jour.; editor (in chief): (profl. jour.) Jour. of Productivity Analysis; assoc. editor (profl. jour.) Jour. of Applied Econometrics, Comms. in Stats., So. Econ. Jour., Jour. of Bus. and Econ. Stats., Jour. of Econometrics, Empirical Econs., editl. bd. Jour. of Productivity Analysis. Mem. bd. dirs. Afton Oaks Civic Assn., Houston, 1988—94; coach Southwestern YMCA, Houston. Grantee, NSF, 1978—80, 1980—83, 1984—87, Nat. Bur. of Econ. Rsch., 1982, NIH, 1986—89, Baker Inst. for Pub. Policy, 1996—2002. Mem.: Am. Econ. Assn., Econometric Soc. Office: Dept of Econs Rice Univ 6100 S Main St MS-22 Houston TX 77005-1892 Office Phone: 713-348-4875.

**SICO, JASON JONATHON,** neurologist, internist, consultant; b. Scranton, Pa., Dec. 2, 1977; s. Michael Anthony and Kathie Anne Sico. MD, Temple U., Phila., 2003. Resident Yale New Haven Hosp., 2003—. Dir. broadcast prodn. Channel 78, Scranton Today, Pa., 1998—99. Mem.: Am. Acad. Neurology (assoc.). Home: 78 Cove Street Unit 1 New Haven CT 06512 Office: Yale New Haven Hospital 20 York Street New Haven CT 06510 Office Phone: 203-688-2342. Office Fax: 203-688-1322. Personal E-mail: jason.sico@yale.edu.

**SICOLI, MARY LOUISE CORBIN,** psychologist, educator; b. Delaware County, Pa., Nov. 15, 1944; d. C.M. Lewis and Lucille (Weber) Corbin; m. Thomas Sicoli, Aug. 27, 1967; children: Michael, Kathryn Francesca. BS, West Chester U., Pa., 1966, MS, 1974, U. Wis., Madison, 1967; PhD, Bryn Mawr Coll., Pa., 1977. Tchr. music, supr. Unionville-Chadds Ford (Pa.) Sch. Dist., 1967-70; supr. student tchrs. Rosemont (Pa.) Coll., 1976-78; prof. psychology, campus psychologist, coord. psychol. svcs. Cabrini Coll., Radnor, Pa., 1974—. Cons. Children's Svcs. Southea. Pa., 1974-80; supr. doctoral interns in psychology Bryn Mawr Coll., 1979-86; presenter in field. Contbr. articles to profl. jours., scientific papers at profl. Confs. Founding mem. bd. dirs. Maternal Support Sys. Chester County, 1981—; mem. Citizens Action for Better TV, 1981—; founder, chair Psychol. Aspects Popular Culture, Popular Culture Assn. Recipient Legion of Honor award Chapel of the Four Chaplains, 1980, Christian and Mary Lindback award for Disting. Coll. Teaching, 1984; named hon. alumnus Cabrini Coll., 2005. Fellow Pa. Psychol. Assn. (founder campus psychologist network); mem. AAUP, Am. Psychol. Assn., Ea. Psychol. Assn., Jean Piaget Soc., Assn. Moral Devel., Kappa Delta Pi, Psi Chi (founding adv., Ea. Region Chpter. award 2005), Delta Epsilon Sigma. Home: 404 Darlington Dr West Chester PA 19382-2139 Office: Cabrini Coll Dept Psychology Radnor PA 19087 Office Phone: 610-902-8310. Business E-Mail: mlsicoli@cabrini.edu.

**SICONOLFI, MICHAEL,** editor; b. NYC; m. Lisa Siconolfi; children: Nicholas, Jessica. BA in English, Queens Coll.; MA in Journalism, NYU. Regional copyreader The Wall Street Jour., NYC, 1984—85, reporter, 1985, sr. writer, 1994, news editor Money & Investing sect., 1999, dep. editor, Money & Investing sect., 1999, sr. editor, 2003—. Co-recipient Gerald Loeb award, disting. bus. and fin. journalism, 1995, Deadline Club award, NY Soc. of Profl. Journalists, 1995, NY Press Club award, bus. category, 1999; recipient Loeb award, UCLA Anderson Sch. of Mgmt., 1998, Minard Editor award, 2004. Office: The Wall Street Journal 200 Liberty St New York NY 10281*

**SICURO, NATALE ANTHONY,** academic and financial administrator, consultant; b. Warren, Ohio, July 19, 1934; s. Gaetano and Antonette (Montecalvo) S.; m. Linda Lou Rockman, Aug. 3, 1957; children: Michael, Christine, Paul. BS, Kent State U., 1957, PhD, 1964; MS in Pub. Health, U. N.C., Chapel Hill, 1958. Tchr., coach, recreation adminstr. schs. in N.E. Ohio, 1958-62; instr., grad. asst., teaching fellow Kent State U., 1962-64; asst. supt. Geauga (Ohio) County schs., 1964-65; dir. program planning, asst. dean regional campuses Kent State U., 1965-68, 70-72, dean continuing edn., assoc. provost med. affairs, 1972-78; sr. cons., mgr. Peat, Marwick, Mitchell Washington and U.S.A., 1968-70; pres. So. Oreg. State Coll., Ashland, 1979-86, Portland State U., 1986-88, Roger Williams U., Bristol, R.I., 1989-93, Roger Williams U. Sch. Law, Bristol, 1992-93; Jones Disting. Univ. prof. Jones Inst. for Ednl. Excellence Tchrs. Coll., Emporia (Kans.) State U., 1993-94; pres.

SICURO Ednl. Cons., 1994-96; investment mgmt. cons. Paine Webber Princeton Portfolio Mgmt. Group, Princeton, N.J., 1996-97; retired, 1997. Pres. Ohio Council Continuing Edn., 1975-76; bd. dirs. So. Oreg. Coll. Found., 1979-86; state rep., chmn. fed. relations com. Am. Assn. State Colls. and Univs., 1979-86, bd. dirs. 1987-88, chmn.-elect, 1988; chmn. Govtl. Relations Commn., Am. Council on Edn., 1983-86; mem. council of presidents Nat. Assn. Intercollegiate Athletics; chmn. council of presidents Evergreen Conf.; co-chmn. council of presidents Columbia Football League; dir. Rogue Valley Physicians Service. Pres. United Way of Jackson County, Oreg., 1982; bd. dirs. Ashland YMCA, 1980-81, Ashland Indsl. Devel. Corp., 1982-85; mem. Jackson County Econ. Devel. Com., 1981-86, Am. Council on Edn., 1986-87. Mem. Nat. Challenges Commn. Higher Edn., Ashland Rotary, Bristol Rotary, Phi Delta Kappa, Phi Kappa Phi. Roman Catholic.

**SIDAMON-ERISTOFF, ANNE PHIPPS,** not-for-profit developer; b. N.Y.C., Sept. 12, 1932; d. Howard and Harriet Dyer (Price) Phipps; m. Constantine Sidamon-Eristoff, June 29, 1957; children: Simon, Elizabeth, Andrew. BA, Bryn Mawr Coll., 1954. Chairwoman emerita Am. Mus. Natural History, N.Y.C.; dir.-at-large Black Rock Forest Consortium; mem. distbn. com. N.Y. Cmty. Trust. Trustee God Bless Am. Fund, Storm King Art Ctr., Mountainville, NY; hon. trustee World Wildlife Fund; bd. dirs. Greenacre Found., Highland Falls (N.Y.) Libr.; past bd. dirs. Scenic Hudson, St. Bernard's Sch., N.Y.C., Mus. Modern Art, N.Y.C., Mus. Hudson Highlands, Hudson River Found. Address: 120 E End Ave New York NY 10028-7552

**SIDAMON-ERISTOFF, CONSTANTINE,** lawyer; b. NYC, June 28, 1930; s. Simon C. and Anne Huntington (Tracy) Sidamon-E.; m. Anne Phipps, June 29, 1957; children: Simon, Elizabeth, Andrew. BSE in Geol. Engring, Princeton U., 1952; LLB, Columbia U., 1957. Clk., then assoc. firm Kelley Drye Newhall Maginnes & Warren, NYC, 1957-64; individual practice law NYC, 1964-65, 74-77; exec. asst. to Congressman John V. Lindsay, 1964-65; city coord. Lindsay Mayoral Campaign, NYC, 1965; asst. to mayor City of NY, 1966, commr. hwys., 1967-68, transp. adminstr., 1968-73; ptnr. Sidamon-Eristoff, Morrison, Warren, & Ecker, NYC, 1978-83; counsel Morrison & de Roos, 1984-88; pvt. practice NYC, 1988-89; regional adminstr. Region II EPA, NYC, 1989-93; of counsel Patterson, Belknap, Webb & Tyler, NYC, 1993-99, Lacher & Lovell-Taylor, NYC, 1999—. Mem. NY State Met. Transp. Authority Bd., 1974—89; commr. NY State Jud. Commn. on Minorities, 1987—91; mem. Gov.'s Coun. on Hudson River Valley Greenway, 1989; trustee United Mut. Savs. Bank, NYC, 1979—82, Phipps Houses, NYC, 1974—, chmn., 1986—2001, chmn. emeritus 2001—. Trustee Am. Beautiful Fund, Washington, 1985—97, Allaverdy Found., NYC, 1962—, Carnegie Hall, NYC, 1967—92, Millbrook (NY) Sch., 1971—89, hon. trustee, 1989—; trustee Am. Farm Sch., Thessaloniki, Greece, 1973—79, Orange County (NY) Citizens Found., 1974—81, Coun. Mcpl. Performance, 1981—85, vice chmn., 1986—87; bd. dirs. Mid-Hudson Pattern for Progress, Poughkeepsie, NY, 1975—89, chmn., 1981—85, Am. Friends of Ga., Inc., 1995—, Audubon NY, 1999—; dir. Nat. Audubon Soc., 2005, Citizens Union Found., 1997—; NY State Rep. committeeman, 1980—89; mem. Orange County (NY) Planning Bd., 1997—; bd. dirs. Tolstoy Found., NYC, 1975—2002, chmn. bd. dirs., 1979—89, 1994—2001; bd. dirs. Caramoor Ctr. Music and Arts, Katonah, NY, 1961—80, Boyce Thompson Inst. for Plant Rsch., Ithaca, NY, 1994—2006. 1st lt. arty. AUS, 1952—54, Korea. Decorated Bronze Star; co-recipient Civic Leadership award (with wife), Citizens Union, 1997, Force for Nature award (with wife), Natural Resources Def. Coun., 1999, Environ. Leadership award (with wife), Nat. Audubon Soc., 2001; recipient Honor award, Kings County chpt. NY State Soc. Profl. Engrs., 1969, Greater NY Coun. Girls Scouts US, 1973, Nat. and NY Parks and Conservation Assn., 1992, Bd. Leadership award, Coun. Mcpl. Performance, 1984, Transp. Man of Yr. award, Greater NY March of Dimes, 1985, award of excellence, Mid-Hudson Pattern for Progress, 1990, Bronze medal, USEPA, 1993. Mem. ABA, NY State Bar Assn., Assn. Bar of City of NY, NY County Lawyers Assn., Kent Moot Ct., AIME, Phi Delta Phi, Delta Psi, Century Assn. (NYC), Knickerbocker Club (NYC), Racquet and Tennis Club (NYC). Republican. Eastern Orthodox. Office: Lacher & Lovell-Taylor 4th Fl 750 Lexington Ave New York NY 10022-8165 Office Phone: 212-872-1500. E-mail: cseristoff@lttlaw.com, ananouri@aol.com.

**SIDBURY, ROBERT,** pediatrician; b. Durham, NC, Sept. 23, 1963; s. James Buren Jr. and Alice Rayle Sidbury; 1 child, Claire Winnie. BS in Psychology, Duke U., 1985, MD, 1993. Diplomate Am. Bd. Dermatology, Am. Bd. Pediat. Dermatology. Intern U. Calif., San Francisco, 1993—94, rsch. fellow, 1994—95; resident in dermatology Oreg. Health & Sci. U., Portland, Oreg., 1995—98; fellow pediat. dermatology Childrens Meml. Hosp., Chgo., 1998—2000; asst. prof. pediat. Childrens Hosp., Seattle, 2000—. Faculty U. Wash. Sch. Medicine, 2004—05; instr. dermatology Bastyr U.; presenter, lectr. in field. Mem. editl. bd.: On The Surface; contbr. articles to profl. jours., chapters to books. Named Tchr. of Yr., Providence Family Practice, 2003, Top Doctor, Seattle Mag., 2004; recipient Dermatology Investigator award, Dermatology Found., 1998. Fellow: Am. Acad. Pediatrics, Am. Acad. Dermatology (edn. slide series task force 2004); mem.: Soc. for Pediat. Dermatology. Democrat. Office: Childrens Hosp Univ Wash Sch Med 4800 Sand Point Way NE Seattle WA 98105 Office Phone: 206-987-2158. Office Fax: 206-987-2217. Business E-Mail: robert.sidbury@seattlechildrens.org.

**SIDDAYAO, CORAZÓN MORALES,** economist, educator, consultant; b. Manila, July 26, 1932; came to U.S., 1968; d. Crispulo S. and Catalina T. (Morales) S. Cert. in elem. teaching, Philippine Normal Coll., 1951; BBA, U. East, Manila, 1962; MA in Econs., George Washington U., 1971, MPhil, PhD, 1975. Cert. Inst. de Francais, France. Tchr. pub. schs., Manila, 1951-53; exec. asst. multinational oil corps., 1953-68; asst. pensions officer IMF, Washington, 1968-71; cons. economist Washington, 1971-75; rsch. assoc. Policy Studies in Sci. and Tech. George Washington U., Washington, 1971-72, teaching fellow dept. econs., 1972-75; natural gas specialist U.S. Fed. Energy Adminstrn., Washington, 1974-75; sr. rsch. economist, assoc. prof. Inst. S.E.A. Studies, Singapore, 1975-78; sr. rsch. fellow energy/economist East-West Ctr., 1978-81, project dir. energy and industrialization, 1981-86; vis. fellow London Sch. Econs., 1984-85; sr. energy economist in charge energy program Econ. Devel. Inst., World Bank, Washington, 1986-94; ret., 1994. Affiliate prof. econs. U. Hawaii, 1979—94; co-dir. UPecon Inst. Resource Studies, 1995—; vis. prof. econs. U. Montpellier, France, 1992, France, 1995—96, France, 1997—; vis. prof. pub. policy Miami U., 1997; lectr. pub. policy George Mason U., 2000; tchr. coord. English for Hispanic program Parish, 2002; cons., spkr. in field. Author or co-author: Increasing the Supply of Medical Personnel, 1973, The Offshore Petroleum Resources of Southeast Asia: Some Potential Conflicts and Related Economic Factors, 1978, Round Table Discussion on Asian and Multinational Corporations, 1978, The Supply of Petroleum Resources in Southeast Asia: Economic Implications of Evolving Property Rights Arrangements, 1980, Critical Energy Issues in Asia and the Pacific: The Next Twenty Years, 1982, Criteria for Energy Pricing Policy, 1985, Energy Demand and Economic Growth, 1986; editor, co-author: Energy Policy and Planning series, 1990-92, Energy Investments and the Environment, 1993; co-editor: Investissements Energetiques et Environnement, 1993; co-editor: (series) Energy Project Analysis for the CIS Countries (Russian), 1993, Politique d'Efficacité de l'Énergie et Environnement, Expérience pratiques, 1994, Matériel Pedagogical sur la Politique d'Efficacité de l'Energie et Environnement, 1994; contbr. chpts. to books, articles to profl. jours. Grantee in field; recipient Outstanding Alumni award Arellano Pub. H.S., 1998, Philippine Normal U., 2003 Mem.: Alliance Francaise, Internat. Assn. Energy Economists (charter 1986—2003), Am. Econ. Assn., Les Amis de l'Abbaye de Chancelade, Eucharistic Frat. 3d Order of St. P.J. Eymard, World Bank 1818 Soc. (bd. dirs. 1999—2000), John Carroll Soc., Chorale de St. Louis de France, Perpetual Adoration Soc. of St. Agnes (Arlington), Omicron Delta Epsilon. Roman Catholic. Office: 1201 S Eads St Ste 1712 Arlington VA 22202-2845 *Power and money were never the stimuli to my endeavors. Spiritual and intellectual challenges are what drive me. In the end, all our achievements mean nothing if we have not learned to appreciate them as gifts and share what we can with others.*

**SIDDEEK, MOHAMED SHAREEF MOHAMED,** marine biologist, educator; arrived in U.S., 2000; s. Mohamed Lebbe Marikkar M. Shareef and Ismail Lebbe Marikkar Zulaiha; m. Fathima Zeena Ishie, May 21, 1985; children: Hani, Esra Fathima. PhD, U. of East Anglia, Norwich, Eng., 1981; BSc in Math. with honors, U. of Colombo, Sri Lanka, 1972. Med. lab. tech. Med. Rsch. Inst. Med. lab. technologist Gen. Hosp., Colombo, 1967—74; rsch. officer (biometrics) Nat. Aquatic Resources Agy., Colombo, 1974—85; assoc. rsch. scientist Kuwait Inst. for Sci. Rsch., Kuwait, 1985—90; assoc. prof. fisheries Sultan Qaboos U., Muscat, Oman, 1990—2000; shellfish biometrician Alaska Dept. Fish and Game, Juneau, Alaska, 2000—. Vis. lectr. fisheries U. of Colombo, 1983—85; guest grad. lectr. in fisheries Juneau Fisheries Ctr., U. Alaska-Fairbanks, Juneau, 2004; keynote spkr. Sultan Qaboos U., 2001, 05; invited spkr. Halifax, Canada, 02; invited reviewer internat. jour. articles and tech. reports in fisheries. Contbr. articles and tech. reports to profl. publs. Named Outstanding Rschr., Sultan Qaboos U., 1997; recipient Assessment and Mgmt. grant, Kuwait Inst. Sci. Rsch., 1986—89, Shrimp Ecology and Assessment grant, Ministry of Fisheries, Muscat, 1995, Kingfish Stock Assessment and Mgmt. grant, 1998, scholarship for PhD study, Colombo Plan, 1978, Crab Biometrics grant, NOAA, 2000—06. Mem.: Sri Lanka Assn. for Advancement of Scis., Am. Fisheries Soc. Office: Alaska Dept Fish and Game 1255 W 8th St Juneau AK 99811-5526 Office Phone: 907-465-6107. Office Fax: 907-465-2604. Personal E-mail: shareef_siddeek@fishgame.state.ak.us.

**SIDDEEQ, BAIYINAH NAWAL RUBYE,** secondary school educator; AA, Emory U., 1995, BA in Elem. Edn., 1997. Asst. tchr. Sister Clara Muhammad Sch., Indpls., 1993; co-founder, jr. counselor A Step Up! Summer Enrichment Program, Stone Mountain, Ga., 1995; tutor for academically challenged Cook Elem., Atlanta, 1995; math specialist Medlock Elem., Decatur, Ga., 1996; tchr. Fernbank Elem., Decatur, Ga., 1997; instr. essay, creative writing Md. Homeschoolers, Gaithersburg, Md., 1999—2000; tchr. English Washington Homeschoolers, College Park, Md., 1999—2002; prep instr. English, SAT Muslimah's Alt. to Pub. H.S. (MAPHS), Beltsville, Md., 2001—02; tchr. English Sch. Knowledge, Indpls., 2003; lit./social studies tchr., grades 6-8 Al-Hada Sch., College Park, Md., 2003—. Author: (novels) If I Should Speak, 2001, (children's book) Amir's Cap is Green, 1999, The Show and Tell, 1997, (novels) A Voice, 2003. Recipient Academic Excellence award, Delta Sigma Theta, 1996—97; scholar Phi Theta Kappa scholar, 1993—94. Personal E-mail: baiyinah@hotmail.com.

**SIDDIQEE, MUHAMMAD WAHEEDUDDIN,** electrical engineer; b. Lahore, Pakistan, Aug. 23, 1931; s. Muhammad Nazeeruddin and Ayesha Humaira Siddiqee; m. Sabiha Sultana Siddiqee, Dec. 24, 1961; 2 children. BA in Physics, Forman Christian Coll., Lahore, Pakistan, 1951; BSEE, Engring. Univ., Lahore, 1955; MSEE, U. Tenn., 1960; PhD in Control Sci., U. Minn., 1967. Elec. engr. Siemens Pakistan, Lahore, 1955—56, Siemens Germany, Erlangen, 1956—58; sr. elec. engr. Siemens Pakistan, Karachi, 1958—61; staff scientist Stanford Rsch. Inst., Menlo Park, Calif., 1967—82; info. systems specialist Lockheed Missiles and Space Co., Sunnyvale, Calif., 1982—93; tchr. Sunnyvale Sch. Dist., 1995—. Project leader Stanford Rsch. Inst., Menlo Park, Calif., 1976—82. Contbr. articles to profl. jours. Pres. United Muslims of Am., Calif., 1991—93, San Francisco Islamic Ctr., Calif., 1981—83, Pakistan Assn., San Francisco, 1975—77. Recipient Lockheed Pub. award, Lockheed Missiles and Space Co., Calif., 1988. Mem.: Assn. Ret. Am. Muslims (pres., founder 1996—). Avocations: sitar, cmty. activism in human rights and interfaith dialogue. Home: 1733 Banff Dr Sunnyvale CA 94087

**SIDDIQI, JAVED,** neurosurgeon; HBSc, U. Western Ont., London, Can., 1983, MD, 1991; DPhil, Oxford U., Eng., 1987. Diplomate Am. Bd. Neurol. Surgery. Chief neurosurgery Arrowhead Regional Med. Ctr., Colton, Calif., 1999—, residency program dir., 1999—; chmn. dept. of clin. neurol. scis. Riverside County Regional Med. Ctr., Moreno Valley, Calif., 2001—. Temp. advisor WHO, Geneva, 1986; asst. prof. in polit. sci. U. Western Ont., 1991—95, asst. prof. in history of medicine, 1992—97; asst. prof. anatomy and surgery Western U. Health Sciences, Pomona, Calif., 1999—; presenter in field. Author: World Health & World Politics, (photography book) In Their Hands; editor: (book) Multidisciplinary Critique of Phillip Rushton's Theory on Racial Ranking; photography exhibit, In Their Hands; contbr. book, articles to profl. publs. Scholar, Rhodes Trust, 1984—87, Med. Rsch. Coun. of Can., 1983; vis. scholar History of Medicine scholar, Hannah Inst. for the History of Medicine, 1988; Rsch. scholar, Natural Sciences and Engring. Rsch. Coun. of Can., 1982, Rhodes scholar, 1984—87, Logan Clendening Travelling fellow, U. Kans., 1988, Arts & Sciences Rsch. scholar, U. of Western Ont., 1989, Travel scholar, Couchiching Conf., 1990, CNS scholar, U. of Western Ont., 1994. Fellow: Royal Coll. Surgeons Can.; mem.: Am. Assn. Rhodes Scholars.

**SIDDIQUE, MUHAMMAD,** poultry pathobiologist; b. Faisalabad, Punjab, Pakistan, Jan. 1, 1950; s. Ghulam Ahmad and Naziran Begum; m. Farkhanda Jamil, Oct. 17, 1976; children: Amir, Imran, Hina. DVM, West Pakistan Agrl. U., Faisalabad, 1972; MSc with honors, U. Agr., Faisalabad, 1978; PhD, Inst. Agron. N.B., Bucharest, Romania, 1984; postgrad., U. Ga. Vet. officer L&DD, Lahore, Pakistan, 1973-74; lectr. in vet. pathology U. Agr., Faisalabad, 1975-86, asst. prof. vet. pathology, 1986-89, asst. prof. vet. microbiology, 1989-90, assoc. prof. vet. microbiology, 1990-99, chmn. dept. vet. microbiology, 1990-93, 96-98, prof. vet. microbiology, 1999—. Author: Current Situation of Poultry Industry in Pakistan, 1979; contbr. articles to profl. jours. Mem. Pakistan Vet. Med. Assn. (life, pres. 1987-89, mem. coun., Spl. award 1995), Pakistan Sci. Forum. Avocations: reading scientific treatises, quiz and mentor challanges. Home: 62 Rachna Town Faisalabad Punjab Pakistan Office: U Agr Vet Microbiology Faisalabad Punjab 38040 Pakistan

**SIDDIQUI, AFZAL A.,** medical educator; b. Aligarh, U.P., India, 1958; arrived in U.S., 1986, naturalized, 2004; s. Iqbal Siddiqui and Jamal Nizami; m. Shahana Siddiqui; children: Bilal, Sabrina. MS, Aligarh U., India, 1978, MPhil, 1982; PhD, U. Westen Ont., 1986. Post-doctoral rsch. assoc. Morehouse Coll. and Ctrs. Disease Control, Atlanta, 1986—87, U. Ill., Rockford, Ill., 1987—88; rsch. scientist and co-ordinator vaccine program U. We. Ont., London, Ontario, Canada, 1988—95; rsch. fellow Sch. Pub. Health Harvard U., Boston, 1995—97; asst. prof., health rsch. scientist East Tenn. State U., Johnson City, Tenn., 1997—2000, Veterans Affairs Med. Ctr., Johnson City, 1997—2000; assoc. prof. medicine Health Scis. Ctr. Tex. Tech U., Amarillo, Tex., 2000—. Grant reviewer in field; paper reviewer in field. Contbr. chapters to books, articles to profl. jours. Grantee, NIH, 2001—. Mem.: Am. Soc. Microbiology, Infectious Diseases Soc. Am., Am. Soc. Tropical Medicine and Hygiene, Am. Soc. Parasitologists, Sigma Xi. Achievements include research in vaccines and new therapies for parasitic infections. Office: Texas Tech Univ Health Sciences Center 1400 Wallace Blvd Amarillo TX 79106 Office Phone: 806-354-5524. E-mail: afzal.siddiqui@ttuhsc.edu.

**SIDDONS, ANNE RIVERS (SYBIL ANNE RIVERS SIDDONS),** writer; b. Fairburn, Ga., Jan. 9, 1936; m. Heyward Siddons, 1966; 4 stepchildren. BA Auburn U., 1958, student Atlanta Sch. Art, 1958. Mem. advt. dept. bank; sr. editor Atlanta mag., 1960. Author: (novels) John Chancellor Makes Me Cry, 1975, Heartbreak Hotel, 1976, The House Next Door, 1978, Fox's Earth, 1981, Homeplace, 1987, Peachtree Road, 1988, Kings Oak, 1990, Outer Banks, 1991, Colony, 1992, Hill Towns, 1993, Downtown, 1994, Fault Lines, 1995, Up Island, 1997, Low Country, 1998, Nora, Nora, 2000, Islands, 2003, Sweetwater Creek, 2005.

**SIDDONS, JOY AGNES GARBEE,** music educator; b. Lynchburg, Va., July 18, 1952; d. Clyde Lewis and Julia Schmitt Garbee; m. James Siddons, July 2, 1977. BS, Liberty U., 1984; MEd, Lynchburg Coll., 1996; MusEdM, Shenandoah U., 1998. Music educator Bedford County Pub. Schools, Bedford, Va., 1984—2003, Fairfax County Pub. Schools, Springfield, Va., 2003—. Dir. of music United Meth. churches, 1988—. Dir.: children's choirs and musical theater prodns. Mem.: Music Educators Nat. Conf., Phi Delta Kappa. United Methodist. Home: 6020 Woodland Ter Mc Lean VA 22101 Office: Fairhill Elem Sch 3001 Chichester Ln Fairfax VA 22116 Office Phone: 703-208-8100.

**SIDDOWAY, CHRISTINE HELEN SMITH**, geology educator; b. Savanna, Ill., 1961; d. Donald Eugene and Susan Margaret Finn Smith; m. Michael Frank Siddoway, 1996. BA, Carleton Coll., 1984; MSc, U. Ariz., 1987; PhD, U. Calif., Santa Barbara, 1995. Postdoctoral rsch. fellow Fulbright Program, Coun. for Internat. Exch. of Scholars, Siena, Italy, 1995—96; asst. prof. Colo. Coll., Colorado Springs, 1996—2001, assoc. prof., 2001—; vis. prof. U. Minn., Mpls., 2002—03. Cons. Colo. Geol. Survey, Denver, 2002—03. Contbr. sci. articles in geology jours. and spl. publs. Grantee, NSF, 1996, 2001, 2004. Mem.: Geol. Soc. Am., Am. Geophys. Union. Achievements include research in US Antarctic research program. Office: Colorado Coll Dept Geology 14 E Cache la Poudre Colorado Springs CO 80903 Office Phone: 719-389-6621. Office Fax: 719-389-6910.

**SIDEBOTTOM, WILLIAM GEORGE**, communications executive; b. Greeley, Colo., July 21, 1948; s. William Carroll and Florence Elaine (Krusenstjerna) S.; m. Rosemary Russell, May 16, 1981; children: Faith Ann, William Jeremiah. BS in Mgmt. cum laude, U. West Fla., 1975; MA in Pub. Policy magna cum laude, Regent U., 1985. Mgr. Mgmt. Recruiters, Internat., Pensacola, Fla., 1976—79, divsn. mgr. Virginia Beach, Va., 1979—81; dir. comm. Rock Ch., Virginia Beach, 1981—83; dir. devel., v.p. comm. Nat. Freedom Inst., Chesapeake, Va., 1983; pres. William G. Sidebottom & Assocs., 1986—, InterAct Response Comm., 1997—2004; founder and mng. dir. X'el Commn., 2004—. Co-founder, pres. Common Good, Inc., 2001—; pres. Sr.'s Alliance, 2003—. Author: Who Owns the Children, 1985; sr. editor: The Perspective Papers, 1985, Essential Lectures, 1985. Cons. Am. Ctr. for Law and Justice, 1990-2002, Christian Advocates Serving Evangelism, 1995-2002, Christian Coalition, 1999-2003; v.p. Liberty Coun., 2005—; sr. flight instr. U.S. Navy Aviation Tng. Ctr. Capt. USMC, 1970-76. Mem.: Pi Kappa Delta, Phi Kappa Phi. Mem. Charismatic Episcopal Ch. E-mail: xelcomm@comcast.net.

**SIDER, RONALD J.**, theology educator, author; b. Stevensville, Ont., Can., Sept. 17, 1939; m. Arbutus Lichti Sider, Aug. 19, 1961; children: Theodore Ronald, Michael Jay, Sonya Maria. BA with honors, Waterloo Luth. U., 1962; MA in History, Yale U., 1963, BD, 1967, PhD in History, 1969; D (hon.), Westminster Coll., 1998; DHL (hon.), Malone Coll., 2005. Lectr., asst. prof., then assoc. prof. Messiah Coll., 1968-78, acting dir., dean, 1971-75; assoc. prof. theology Ea. Bapt. Theol. Sem., Wynnewood, Pa., 1978-84, prof. theology and culture, 1984—2002, Ronald J. Sider prof. theology, holistic ministry and pub. policy, 2002—; dir. Sider Ctr. on Ministry and Pub. Policy Eastern U., 2002—. Coord., chair, convenor workshops in field; coord. Internat. Consultation on Simple Lifestyle, London, 1980; lectr. in field. Editor: Preaching on Peace, 1982, Lifestyle in the Eighties: An Evangelical Commitment to Simple Life-Style, 1982, Evangelicals and Development: Toward a Theology of Social Change, 1982, Living More Simply, 1980, Cry Justice: The Bible on Hunger and Poverty, 1988, 91, For They Shall Be Fed, 1997, (with Diane Knippers) Toward an Evangelical Public Policy, 2005; author: Christ and Violence, 1979, Karlstadt's Battle with Luther: Documents in a Liberal-Radical Debate, 1978, 82, Evangelism, 1985, Rich Christians in an Age of Hunger: A Biblical Study, 1977, rev. edit., 1984, 90, 97, 2005, German edit., 1979, Dutch edit., 1980, Portuguese edit., 1984, Japanese edit., 1989, Chinese edit., 1998, Korean edit., 1998, Andreas Bodenstein Von Karlstadt, 1974, Genuine Christianity, 1996, (with Richard K. Taylor) Nuclear Holocaust and Christian Hope, 1982, English edit., 1984, (with Oliver O'Donovan) Peace and War: A Debate About Pacifism, 1985, (in Chinese) Evangelical Faith and Social Ethics, 1986, Completely Pro-Life, 1987, (with Michael A. King) Preaching About Life in Threatening World, 1988, (with Kathleen Hayes), JustLife/88: A 1988 Election Study Guide for Justice, Life and Peace, 1988, Testing the Limits of Nonviolence, 1988, One-Sided Christianity? Uniting the Church to Heal a Lost and Broken World, 1993, Cup of Water, Bread of Life: Inspiring Stories About Overcoming Lopsided Christianity, 1994, Korean edit., 1999, Good News and Good Works: A Theology for the Whole Gospel, 1999, Living Like Jesus, 1999, Just Generosity: A New Vision for Overcoming Poverty in America, 1999, 2d edit., 2006, (with Philip N. Olson and Heidi Rolland Unruh) Churches That Make a Difference: Reaching Your Community with Good News and Good Works, 2002, Doing Evangelism Jesus' Way, 2003, The Scandal of the Evangelical Conscience, 2005, (with Heidi Rolland Unruh) Saving Souls, Serving Society: Understanding The Faith Factor in Church Based Social Ministry, 2005; co-editor: Transformation mag., 1984-99; editor, contbr.: The Chicago Declaration, 1974; pub. Prism mag., 1993—, Green Cross, 1994-98, Creation Care, 1998-2002; contbr. numerous articles to profl. publs., chpts. to books. Head voter registration drive, New Haven, 1967; pres. Diamond St. Cmty. Ctr., 1986-91; exec. dir. Evangelicals for Social Action, 1987-92, pres., 1992—; exec. dir. Just Life, 1987-91, pres., 1991-94; bd. dirs. Bread for the World, 1978-84, Mennonite Ctrl. Com., 1978-80, Call to Renewal, 1996-2005 Evangel. Environ. Network, 2005—; co-chair Nat. Workshop on Race and Reconciliation, Atlanta, 1975. Malcolm Chase fellow, 1962-63, R.E. Darling fellow, 1963-64, fellow Yale U., 1967-68, Inst. for Advanced Christian Studies, 1976; co-chair Working Group on Human Needs and Faith-Based and Cmty. Initiatives II, 2002-03. Mem. Nat. Assn. Evangelicals (mem. social action commn. 1975—). Mennonite. Home: 312 W Logan St Philadelphia PA 19144-4120 Office: Palmer Sem 6 E Lancaster Ave Wynnewood PA 19096-3430 Office Phone: 610-645-9354. Business E-Mail: rsider@eastern.edu.

**SIDEROW, NEIL**, real estate company executive; BA, NYU; MBA, Pace U. Founding ptnr., COO Murray Hill Properties; vice chmn. TCN Worldwide, 2003— also bd. dirs. Offices Murray Hill Properties LLC 1140 Ave of the Americas New York NY 10036

**SIDERYS, HARRY**, surgeon, educator; b. N.Y.C., Mar. 2, 1927; s. George and Helen Siderys; m. Cathy Luan Ruby, Apr. 18, 1970; children: George, Robert, William, Christopher. BA, Amherst Coll., 1948; MD, SUNY, 1952. Diplomate Am. Bd Surgery, Am. Bd. Thoracic Surgery, Am. Bd. Vascular Surgery. Asst. prof. surgery Ind. U. Sch. Medicine, Indpls., 1962—; chief surgery St. Francis Hosp., Beech Grove, Ind., 1964—66; chmn. cardiovascular surgery Meth. Hosp., Indpls., 1980—90; chief cardiothoracic surgery Marion County Gen. Hosp., Indpls., 1967—69; sr. surgeon Corvasc, Indpls., 2000—. Founder cardiovascular surgical svcs. Meth. Hosp., Indpls., 1965—, dir. residency thoracic and cardiovascular surgery, 1973—76; examiner grad. program surgery Grad. Edn. Surgery, 1962—80. Contbr. articles various profl. jours. Chmn. Quality Assurance Cardiovascular Med. and Surgical, 1993—. With USN, 1945—46. Mem.: ACS, AMA, Soc. Clin. Vascular Surgery, Internat. Soc. Heart Transplantation, Am. Soc. Artificial Internal Organ, Midwest Vascular Surgical Soc., Am. Coll. Cardiology, Am. Assn. Thoracic and Cardiovascular Surgery, Soc. Thoracic Surgeons, Internat. Cardiovascular Soc., Marion County Med. Assn., Ind. State Med. Assn., Am. Assn. Thoracic and Cardiovascular Surgery, Midwest Chest Club. Achievements include first coronary bypass in Ind., 1973; first ventricular asst. device in Ind., 1973. Home: 9015 Kirkham Ct Indianapolis IN 46260 Office: Corvasc 1801 N Senate Blvd Indianapolis IN 46202 Personal E-mail: hsiderys@aol.com.

**SIDES, I. RUTH S.**, retired music educator; d. John Daniel Donald and I. Ruth Schulmeyer; m. Anthony Fred Sides, May 25, 1972 (dec. Sept. 7, 1997); children: Rebecca Ruth Desenti, Connie Susanne Moore. BA, Baldwin Wallace Coll., 1968. Cert. tchg. Ohio, 1968. Dir. band and choruses Ridgemont Local Schs., Ridgeway, Ohio, 1967—71; dir. choral music Groveland H.S., Fla., 1972—93, South Lake H.S., 1993—2005, chair dept. fine arts and fgn. langs., 2002—05. Cert. judge Fla. BBQ Assn., Fla., 2002—. Nominee Disney's Am. Tchr., Walt Disney World, 2001; recipient Tchr. Of The Yr., Hardin County Schools, 1969-1970, Outstanding Young Women Am., 1973, Teacherific - Judge's Choice, Walt Disney World, 2000. Mem.: Fla. Vocal Assn., Fla. Music Educators Assn. Avocations: cooking, sewing, travel. Home: 11844 Lake Minneola Shores Clermont FL 34715

**SIDES, JACK DAVIS, JR.**, lawyer; b. Dallas, Sept. 18, 1939; s. Jack Davis Sr. and Edith Eugenia (Lowrie) S.; m. Nancy Pauline Cantwell, July 22, 1967 (div. Sept. 1976); children: Mary Katharine, Jack Davis III; m. Laura Gail Miller, Aug. 2, 1979; children: Susan Ashley, Stacy Anne. BBA, U. Tex., 1962, JD with honors, 1963. Bar: Tex. 1963. Assoc. Jackson, Walker, et al, Dallas, 1963-67, White, McElroy, White, Sides & Rector, Dallas, 1968-78; sole practice Dallas, 1978—. Editor: U. Tex. Law Review, 1963. Trustee Highland Park Sch. Dist., 1996-2002; With USAFNG, 1963-69. Fellow Dallas Bar Found., Tex. Bar Found. (life); mem. ABA, Tex. Bar Assn. (grievance subcom. 1979-86), Dallas Bar Assn. (ethics com. 1973-77, jud. com. 1988—), Tex. Assn. Def. Counsel, Dallas Assn. Def. Counsel (sec. 1973-74). Clubs: Brook Hollow Golf (Dallas). Republican. Methodist. Avocations: reading, tennis, exercise.

**SIDES, LARRY EUGENE**, advertising executive; b. Albany, Ga., Nov. 14, 1946; s. Robert N. and Florine (Stewart) Sides; m. Kathy Ashworth, Aug. 13, 1950. BA in Radio and TV, U. La., 1970, MS in Communications, 1975. News reporter Sta. KATC-TV, Lafayette, La., 1970-71; account exec. Herbert S. Benjamin Assocs., Lafayette, La., 1971-76; pres. Sides & Assocs., Lafayette, La., 1976—. Vice-chmn. Crimestoppers, Lafayette, 1985; pres. Gateway Found., 1990; active Leadership La., 1989, 1990; mem. Coun. for Better La., 1991—94; bd. dirs. La. Coun. on Child Abuse, 1992—96; active Leadership Lafayette, 1995; mem. exec. com. Cristo en Cuba Coord. Coun.; bd. dirs. Episcopal Sch. Acadiana, Lafayette, 1987; mem. vestry Episcopal Ch. of Ascension, 2002—04, coord. Cuba project, 2001—, jr. warden, 2002; sr. warden Episcopal Diocese of We. La., 2003, chmn. Commn. on Internat. Missions, 2003—; mem. Global Episcopal Mission Network, 2004; bd. dirs. Nat. Cristo En Cuba Coordinating Coun. Named Outstanding Young Men of Am., Lafayette Jaycees, 1976; recipient Disting. Alumni award dept. comms., U. La., 1995. Mem.: Acadiana Advt. Fedn., Pub. Rels. Soc. Am., Am. Soc. Hosp. Pub. Rels., Am. Assn. Advt. Agys. (pres. La. coun. 1989—90), Lafayette C. of C. (pres. 1989, bd. dirs. 2003, Entrepreneur of Yr. 1983), Beaver Club (pres. 1986, Outstanding Club Mem. award 1976), Sigma Nu (alumni pres. Lafayette chpt. 1977). Home: 1015 W Saint Mary Blvd Lafayette LA 70506-3420 Office: 404 Eraste Landry Rd Lafayette LA 70506-2324

**SIDHU, JAY S.**, bank executive; b. India, Aug. 8, 1951; arrived in U.S. at age 18; BA, Banaras Hindu U.; MBA, Wilkes U., 1973. Vice chmn., COO Penn Savings Bank, 1986—89; treas., CEO Sovereign Bank, 1987—89; pres., CEO Sovereign Bancorp Inc. (formerly Penn Savings Bank), Wyomissing, Pa., 1989—2002, chmn., pres., CEO, 2002—. Office: Sovereign Bancorp Inc PO Box 12646 1130 Berkshire Blvd Reading PA 19612 E-mail: jsidhu@sovereignbank.com.

**SIDJANSKI, DUSAN**, economist, educator; b. Belgrade, Yugoslavia, Oct. 23, 1926; arrived in Switzerland, 1943; s. Vlastimir and Mara (Yankovitch-Petrovich) Sidjanski; 1 child, Sacha; life ptnr. Clarina Firmenich. D. in Polit. Sci., U. Lausanne, Switzerland, 1954. From collaborator to asst. prof. Ctrl. U. Venezuela, 1950-53; head rsch. Intergovernmental Com. European Migrations, Geneva, 1956—57; head rsch., dir. Denis de Rougemont European Centre Culture, 1957—80; pvt. tchr. U. Geneva, 1959, from lectr. to prof. polit. sci. Inst. European Studies, 1963—68, prof., 1968—98, emeritus prof., 1995—, past founder, dir. dept. polit sci. faculty econ. and social scis., former vice-dean faculty social and econ. scis. Former hon. advisor permanent del. Venezuela, Geneva. Author: (book) Fédéralisme amphictyonique, 1956, Partis politiques face à l'intégration européenne, 1961, Dimensions européennes de la science politique, 1963, Federative Aspects of the European-Community in Studies, in Conjecture, 1965, Décisions closes et décisions ouvertes, 1965, Dimensiones institucionales de la integracion latinamericano, 1967, Verso l'Europa Unita Gruppi di Promozione, 1968, The Federal Future of Europe, 2000, The Federal Approach to the European Union, 2001, others; contbr. articles to profl. jours. Bd. dirs. Latsis Found., 2003—. Mem.: EUSA, ECPR, Assn. Inst. Europe (gen. sec.), Hellenic Inst. Internat. Law (collaborator-corr.), French and Swiss Assn. Polit. Sci. (former pres.), European Cultural Ctr. (pres. 2003—), Internat. Assn. Polit. Sci. Avocations: music, sports, skiing, tennis, swimming. Home: 16 chemin de La Rippaz 1223 Cologny Geneva Switzerland Office: Latsis Foundation 33 ch de l'Avanchet 1216 Geneva Switzerland E-mail: dusan.sidjanski@politic.unige.ch.

**SIDLIK, THOMAS W.**, automotive executive; b. New Britain, Conn., Nov. 14, 1949; BS with hon. in Econ. & Fin., N.Y.U., 1971; MBA in Fin., U. Chgo., 1973. With controller's office car product devel. Ford Motor Co., 1973—80; mgr., car product fin. analysis Chrysler Corp., 1980, mgr., advanced product analysis, 1981, mgr., engring. and product devel. fin. control, 1982, controller, svc. and parts org., 1984, mgr., corp. fin. analysis, 1984, dir., engring. ops., 1987, gen. mgr. special projects engring., 1989, controller, product devel. group, 1989, group controller, product devel. & procurement, 1990, gen. mgr., sales & mktg. ops. planning, 1991, exec. dir., sales & mktg, planning and warranty programs, 1992, v.p., customer satisfaction and vehicle quality, 1992, v.p., chmn., Chrysler Fin. Corp., 1994, 1996, gen. mgr., small car ops., 1996; mem., bd. of mgmt. procurement & supply Chrysler Group DaimlerChrysler AG, 1998—, gen. mgr. Jeep Ops., 1998—. Mgmt. bd. Daimler Chrysler, 1998—; exec. sponsor Automotive Industry Action Group (AIAG). Vice-chmn. Nat. Minority Supplier Devel. Coun. (NMSDC); chmn. Coun. Exec. Com.; bd. overseers Leonard N. Stern Sch. of Bus., NYU. Office: Daimler Chrysler Corp 1000 Chrysler Drive Auburn Hills MI 48326-2766

**SIDMAN, RICHARD LEON**, neuroscientist, educator; b. Boston, Sept. 19, 1928; s. Manuel and Annabelle (Seltzer) Sidman; m. Ljiljana Lekic, 1974. AB, Harvard U., 1949, MD (Jeffries Wyman scholar), 1953. Intern in medicine Boston City Hosp., 1953_54, asst. resident in neurology Mass. Gen. Hosp., Boston, 1955—56; staff scientist NIH, Bethesda, Md., 1956—58; instr. to prof. neuropathology Harvard U. Med. Sch., Boston, 1959—69, Bullard prof., 1969—99, prof. emeritus, 1999—; chief div. neurogenetics New Eng. Regional Primate Rsch. Ctr. Harvard Med. Sch., Southborough, Mass., 1991—99; prof. neuropathology emeritus dir. neurosurgery Brigham and Womens Hosp., Boston, 1999—; sr. rsch. assoc. dept. neurology Beth Israel Deaconess Med. Ctr., Boston, 2001—. Chief dept. neuropath. Children's Hosp., Boston, 1972—88; 1st Richard Stearns Meml.ml. lectr. Albert Einstein Coll. Medicine, 1958; Bailey Meml. lectr. U. Sask., Canada, 1978; Waisman Meml. lectr. U. Wis. Author: (with M. Sidman): Neuroanatomy - A Programmed Text, vol. 1, 1965; author: (with others) Catalog of the Neurological Mutants of the Mouse, 1965; author: (with R.D. Adams) Introduction to Neuropathology, 1968; author: (with others) Atlas of the Mouse Brain and Spinal Cord, 1971; contbr. numerous articles, book chpts., revs. on neuroembryology pathology and genetics to profl. publs. Mem. sci. adv. coun. Retinitis Pigmentosa Found.; bd. sci. overseers Jackson Lab., Bar Harbor, Maine. With USPHS, 1956—58. Recipient Soma Weiss student rsch. prizes, Harvard U. Med. Sch., 1951—53, Boylston Soc. Essay prize, 1953; fellow Neuroscis. Rsch. Program fellow, 1971—79; Harvard U. Mosley Travelling fellow, 1954—55. Fellow: Nat. Acad. Sci., Am. Acad. Arts and Scis.; mem.: AAAS, Tissue Culture Assn., Soc. Neurosci., Soc. Devel. Neurosci., Internat. Soc. Devel. Neurobiology, Soc. Devel. Biology, Internat. Brain Rsch. Orgn., Histochem. Soc., Am. Soc. Cell Biology, Am. Assn. Neuropathologists, Am. Assn. Anatomists, Am. Acad. Neurology. Office: Harvard Inst Medicine 855 77 Ave Louis Pasteur Boston MA 02115 Office Phone: 508-341-6552. Business E-Mail: richard_sidman@hms.harvard.edu.

**SIDMAN, ROBERT JOHN**, lawyer; b. Cleve., Aug. 4, 1943; s. Charles Frances and Louise (Eckert) S.; m. Mary Mato, July 29, 1967; children: Christa Mary, Alicia Mary. BA, Benedictine Coll., 1965; JD, U. Notre Dame, 1968. Bar: Ohio 1968, U.S. Dist. Ct. (so. dist.) Ohio 1970, U.S. Ct. Appeals (6th cir.) 1971, U.S. Supreme Ct. 1971. Law clk. U.S. Dist. Ct. (so. dist.) Ohio, Columbus, 1968-70; assoc. Mayer, Tingley & Hurd, Columbus, 1970-75; judge Bankruptcy Ct. U.S. Dist. Ct. (so. dist.) Ohio, Columbus, 1975-82; ptnr. Vorys, Sater, Seymour & Pease, Columbus, 1982—. Prof. Ohio State U. Law Sch., Columbus, 1984, 85, 86. Mem. Nat. Conf. Bankruptcy Judges (bd. dirs. 1981-82), Assn. Former Bankruptcy Judges (bd. dirs.

1983-89, treas. 1986-87, pres. 1988-89). Office: Vorys Sater Seymour & Pease PO Box 1008 52 E Gay St Columbus OH 43215-3161 E-mail: rjsidman@vssp.com, rsidman843@aol.com.

**SIDRAN, MIRIAM**, retired physicist; b. Washington, May 25, 1920; d. Morris Samson and Theresa Rena (Gottlieb) S. BA, Bklyn. Coll., 1942; MA, Columbia U., N.Y.C., 1949; PhD, NYU, 1956. Rsch. assoc. dept. physics NYU, N.Y.C., 1950-55, postdoctoral fellow, 1955-57; asst. prof. Staten Island Community Coll., Richmond, NY, 1957-59; rsch. scientist Grumman Aerospace Corp., Bethpage, NY, 1959-67; prof. N.Y. Inst. Tech., N.Y.C., 1967-72; NSF rsch. fellow Nat. Marine Fisheries Svc., Miami, Fla., 1971-72; assoc. prof. then prof. physics Baruch Coll., N.Y.C., 1972-89, chmn. dept. natural scis., 1983-89, prof. emerita, 1990—. V.p. Baruch chpt. Profl. Staff Congress, 1983-89. Contbr. numerous articles to profl. and govtl. publs., chpts. to books. N.Y. State Regents scholar, 1937-41; NSF summer fellow, Miami, 1970. Mem. N.Y. Acad. Scis., Am. Assn. Physics Tchrs., Physics Club N.Y., N.Y. Gilbert and Sullivan Soc., Wynmoor Computer Club, Friends of Mozart, Sigma Xi, Sigma Pi Sigma. Avocations: french and hebrew languages, music, bicycling, poetry, opera. Home: 210 W 19th St Apt 5G New York NY 10011-4009

**SIDRANSKY, DAVID**, molecular biologist; b. El Paso, Tex., June 21, 1960; s. Julia and Amalia Sidransky; m. Lynn R. Clahr, Sept. 26, 1990; children: Elie M., Anina Libi, Yair S. BS in Chemistry, magna cum laude, with highest honors, Brandeis U., 1981; MD, Baylor U., 1984. Diplomate Am. Bd. Internal Medicine, Am. Bd. Med. Oncology. Intern in internal medicine Baylor Coll. Medicine, Houston, 1984-85, resident in internal medicine, 1985-87, clin. investigator Inst. Molecular Genetics, 1986-87, chief resident in internal medicine, 1987-88; sr. clin. fellow in oncology Johns Hopkins Hosp., Balt., 1988-89, rsch. fellow in oncology, 1989-92, asst. prof. oncology, 1992-94, asst. prof. otolaryngology, head and neck surgery, 1992-94, assoc. prof. oncology, 1994-98, dir. head and neck cancer rsch. divsn., 1994—, prof. otolaryngology, head and neck surgery, 1998—, prof. pathology, 1998—, prof. cellular and molecular medicine, 1998—, prof. urology, 1999—. Mem. external adv. bd. U. Calif., San Diego Cancer Ctr., U. Tex. M.D. Anderson Cancer Ctr., Houston; mem. sci. adv. coun. Israel Cancer Sch. Fund; mem. med. adv. coun. Israel Children's Cancer Found.; mem. devel. diagnostics com. Nat. Cancer Inst., 1996—, mem. cancer prevention and control com., 1996—; bd. sci. counselors, chmn. early detectin rsch. network; bd. dirs. ImClone, 2004-, Alfacell Corp., 2004-; sr. editor Clinical Cancer Research. Contbr. articles to profl. jours. including Sci., Cancer Rsch., Sci., Nature Medicine; chmn., editl. bd. Internat. Jour. Cancer-Predictive Oncology; sr. editor Clin. Cancer Rsch.; assoc. editor Cancer Rsch., Jour. Nat. Cancer Inst., Oral Oncology. Recipient award Found. for the Promotion of Cancer Rsch., Japan, 1995, Sarstedt Internat. Rsch. prize German Soc. Clin. Chemistry, 1997, Cheng Suen Man Shook Found. award Hong Kong Cancer Inst., 1998, Walter Hubert award Brit. Assn. Cancer Rsch., 1998, Alton Ochsner award Relating Smoking and Health Am. Coll. Chest Physicians, 1998, award Internat. Union Against Cancer Role, 1999, Richard and Hinda Rosenthal Found. award, Am. Assn. Cancer Rsch., 2004. Mem. AAAS, Am. Soc. for Head and Neck Surgery, Am. Assn. for Cancer Rsch., N.Y. Acad. Scis. Jewish. Avocation: racquetball. Office: Johns Hopkins U 720 Rutland Ave Ste 818 Baltimore MD 21205-2109

**SIDWELL, DAVID H.**, bank executive; BA, Cambridge U., Eng., 1975. Chartered acct. With PricewaterhouseCoopers, 1975—84; from controller to CFO J.P. Morgan Chase & Co., N.Y., 1984—2004; CFO Morgan Stanley, 2004—. Office: c/o Morgan Stanley 1585 Broadway New York NY 10036*

**SIEBE, CAROL ANN**, retired elementary school educator; b. Petaluma, California, Aug. 30, 1946; d. Ernest Henry and Minnie Corda; m. Norman Thomas, Mar. 21, 1970; children: David Henry, and Meredith Ann. BA, U. San Francisco, 1968; tchg. credential, Calif., 1970; MA edn. leadership, St. Mary's Coll., 1996. Elem. tchr. Two Rock Sch., Petaluma, Calif., 1970—72, supr. primary curriculum, 1986-92, lead tchr., 1994—2004; ret., 2004. Leader Wilson 4-H Club, Petaluma, 1981; softball coach Petaluma Girl's Softball Assn., 1984-85; active Children's Home Soc., Petaluma. Mem. Delta Kappa Gamma (2d v.p. Gamma Tau chpt. 1988—, pres. 1995-97). Republican. Roman Catholic. Avocations: reading, cooking, aerobic walking, gardening.

**SIEBEL, KENNETH**, investment advisor; BBA in Fin., MBA, U. Wisconsin. With Smith, Barney & Co., NYC, San Francisco; co-founder, ptnr. Robertson, Colman & Siebel (now Bank of Am. Securities and Bank of Boston Robertson Stephens), 1969—77; chmn., CEO Wood Island Associates, 1977—98; chief investment officer US Trust Co., 1998—; chmn. Private Wealth Partners, LLC, Larkspur, Calif. Mem. fin. and investment comm., corp. partnerships comm., and resources commitment comm. Conservation Internat. Trustee San Francisco Museum of Modern Art, Gordon & Betty Moore Found. Office: US Trust Co Ste 2300 101 California St San Francisco CA 94111

**SIEBEL, THOMAS M.**, software company executive; BA, U. Ill., Urbana-Champaign, MS in Computer Sci., MBA. Various positions including group v.p., gen. mgr. Oracle Corp.; CEO Gain Tech., until 1992, Siebel Systems, San Mateo, Calif., 1993—2004, chmn., 1993—. Author: Virtual Selling, Cyber Rules, Taking Care of eBusiness. Bd. advisors U. Ill., Coll. Engring., Stanford U. Grad. Sch. Bus.; Stanford U. Law Sch. Named one of top 25 managers in the world, Business Week mag., 2000, 2001, 400 Richest Americans, Forbes, 2000; recipient David Packard Award, Bus. Executives for Nat. Security, 2002, CEO of the Year, Industry Week mag., 2002. Office: Siebel Systems 2207 Bridgepointe Pkwy San Mateo CA 94404*

**SIEBERT, CALVIN D.**, economist, educator; b. Hillsboro, Kans., Feb. 11, 1934; s. Ira and Margaret (Everett) S.; m. Valerie Dawn Nanninga, Feb. 18, 1960; children— Douglas Erik, Derek Christopher. BA, U. Kans., 1958, MA, 1960; PhD in Econs., U. Calif., Berkeley, 1966. Asst. prof. econs. U. Iowa, 1965-68, assoc. prof., 1968-75, prof., 1975—, chmn. dept., 1969-71, 75-79. Rockefeller Found. vis. assoc. prof. U. Philippines, 1971-72 Contbr. articles to profl. jours. With U.S. Army, 1954-56. Ford Found. grantee, 1964-65 Mem. Am. Econ. Assn., Phi Beta Kappa. Home: 341 N 7th Ave Iowa City IA 52245-6003 Office: U Iowa Dept Econs S318 Pbb Iowa City IA 52242 Business E-Mail: calvin_siebert@uiowa.edu.

**SIEBERT, DIANE DOLORES**, author, poet; b. Chgo., Mar. 18, 1948; m. Robert William Siebert, Sept. 21, 1969. RN. Author: Truck Song, 1984 (Notable Childrens Book award ALA 1984, Sch. Libr. Jour. one of Best Books 1984, Outstanding Childrens Book award NY Times Book Rev. 1984, Reading Rainbow Selection book 1991), Mojave, 1988 (Childrens Editors Choice 1988, Internat. Reading Assn. Tchr. Choice award 1989, others), Heartland, 1989 (award Nat. Coun. for Social Studies/Childrens Book Coun. 1989, on John Burroughs List Nature Book for Young Readers 1989, Ohio Farm Bur. Women award 1991), Train Song, 1990 (Notable Childrens Book award ALA, 1990, Redbook Mag. one of Top Ten Picture Books 1990, one of Best Books award Sch. Libr. Jour. 1990, others), Sierra, 1991 (Outstanding Sci. Trade Book for Children award NSTA 1991, Notable Childrens Trade Book in Field Social Studies award Nat. Coun. Social Studies 1991, Beatty award Calif. Libr. Assn. 1992), Plane Song, 1993 (Outstanding Sci. Trade Book for Children 1994, Reading Rainbow Selection book, Platinum award Oppenheim Toy Portfolio, Tchrs. Choice award Internat. Reading Assn. 1994), Cave, 2000 (Notable Childrens's Book in the english Language Arts, 2001, Nat. Coun. of English Tchr., named to John Burroughs List of Nature Books for Young Readers 2000), Mississippi (named to John Burroughs List 2001), 2001, Motorcycle Song, 2002, Rhyolite, 2003, Tour America, 2006. Avocations: environmental affairs, running, classical guitar, motorcycle, animals. Home: 9676 SW Jordan Rd Culver OR 97734-9567 Personal E-Mail: dsiebert48@msn.com.

**SIEBERT, KARL JOSEPH,** food science educator, consultant; b. Harrisburg, Pa., Oct. 29, 1945; s. Christian Ludwig and Katharine (Springer) S.; m. Sui Ti Atienza, Mar. 14, 1970; children: Trina, Sabrina. BS in Biochemistry, Pa. State U., 1967, MS in Biochemistry, 1968, PhD in Biochemistry, 1970. Chemist Applied Sci. Labs., State College, Pa., 1968—70, assoc. Stroh Brewery Co., Detroit, 1971, head R & D sect., 1971-73, mgr. R & D lab., 1973-82, dir. rsch., 1982-90; v.p. Strohtech, Detroit, 1986-90; prof. Cornell U., Geneva, NY, 1990—, chmn. dept. food sci. and tech., 1990-95, also assoc. dir. Cornell Inst. Food Sci. Ithaca, NY, 1990-95. Contbr. articles to profl. jours. Bd. visitors Oakland U. Biology Dept., Rochester, Mich., 1985-89; bd. dirs. Cornell Rsch. Found., 1990-96, Geneva Concerts Inc., 1991-98. Capt. USAR, 1967-75. Recipient Presdl. award Master Brewers Assn., 1986, 90; named hon. prof. Moscow State Acad. Food Prodn., 1996. Fellow NSF; mem. Am. Chem. Soc. (divsn. agrl. and food chemistry, computers in chemistry divsn.), Master Brewer Assn., Am. Soc. Brewing Chemists (chmn. tech. com. 1988-88, mem. editl. bd. 1983-91, 96—, Eric Kneen Meml. award 1998, 99, 2004, award of distinction 1999), Inst. Food Technologists (divsn. fruit and vegetable tech., food chemistry, food microbiology, sensory analysis), Internat. Chemometrics Soc. (N.Am. chpt.), Sigma Xi (pres. Geneva chpt. 2005-06). Avocations: computers, electronics. Home: 9 Parkway St Geneva NY 14456-9765 Office Phone: 315-787-2299. E-mail: kjs3@cornell.edu.

**SIEBERT, MURIEL (MICKIE),** brokerage house executive, retired bank executive; b. Cleve., 1932; d. Irwin J. and Margaret Eunice (Roseman) Siebert. Student, Western Res. U., 1949-52; DCS (hon.), St. John's U., St. Bonaventure U., Molloy Coll., Adelphi U., St. Francis Coll., Mercy Coll., Coll. New Rochelle, St. Lawrence U., Manhattan Coll., Seton Hall Coll., Case Western Res. U., Marymount Manhattan Coll., Hofstra U., U. Rochester, U. NC, Asheville, 2004, U. NC, Greensboro, 2005. Security analyst Bache & Co., 1954-57; analyst Utilities & Industries Mgmt. Corp., 1958, Shields & Co., 1959-60; ptnr. Stearns & Co., 1961, Finkle & Co., 1962-65, Brimberg & Co., NYC, 1965-67; individual mem. (first woman mem.) NY Stock Exch., 1967; chmn., pres. Muriel Siebert & Co., Inc., 1969-77; trustee Manhattan Savs. Bank, 1975-77; supt. banks, dept. banking State of NY, 1977-82, dir. Urban Devel. Corp., NYC, 1977-82, Job Devel. Authority, NYC, 1977-82, State of NY Mortgage Agy., 1977-82; chmn., pres. Muriel Siebert & Co., Inc., NYC, 1983—. Former assoc. in mgmt. Simmons Coll.; former mem. adv. com. Fin. Acctg. Stds. Bd., 1981-84; former mem. adv. bd. Minority and Women-Owned Bus. Enterprise; guest lectr. numerous colls. Author: Changing the Rules - Adventures of a Wall Street Maverick, 2002. Ran for Rep. nomination, U.S. Senate, 1982; former mem. women's adv. com. Econ. Devel. Adminstrn., NYC; former trustee Manhattan Coll.; former v.p., current mem. exec. com. Greater NY Area coun. Boy Scouts Am.; former mem. NY State Econ. Devel. Bd., NY Coun. Economy; bd. overseers NYU Sch. Bus., 1984-88; former bd. dirs. United Way of NYC; former trustee Citizens Budget Commn., LI U.; mem. bus. com. Met. Mus., bus. com. of NY State Bus. Coun.; adv. coun. Women's Campaign Fund; bd. dirs., past pres. NY Women's Agenda; trustee Guild Hall Mus. EH; current appointee Commn. Jud. Nomination; founding mem. The Mus. Women-The Leadership Coun; founder, bd. dirs. The WISH List; bd. dirs. Breast Cancer Rsch. Found., Animal Rescue Fund of the Hamptons; mem. Bretton Woods Com.; former Tokyo adv. com. Sister City Program NYC Recipient Spirit of Achievement award Albert Einstein Coll. Medicine, 1977, Women's Equity Action League award, 1978, Outstanding Contbns. to Equal Oppty. for Women award Bus. Coun. UN Decade for Women, 1979, Silver Beaver award Boy Scouts Am., 1981, Elizabeth Cutter Morrow award YWCA, 1983, Emily Roebling award Nat. Women's Hall of Fame, 1984, Entrepreneurial Excellence award White House Conf. on Small Bus., 1986, NOW Legal Def. and Edn. Fund award, 1981, Brotherhood award NCCJ. 1989, Women on the Move award Anti-Defamation League, 1990, Bus. Philanthropist of Yr. award So. Calif. Conf. for Women Bus. Owner's, 1990, award Borough of Manhattan, 1991, Benjamin Botwinick prize Columbia Bus. Sch., 1992, Women in Bus. Making History award Women's Bus. Coun. NY C. of C., 1993, Disting. Woman of Yr. award Greater NY Boy Scouts of Am., 1993, Corning Excellence award NYC Bus. Coun., 1993, Woman of Yr. award Fin. Women's Assn. NY, 1994, Medal of Honor award Ellis Island, 1994, Star award N.Y. Women's Agenda, 1994, NY Urban Coalition's Achievement award, 1994, Women of Distinction award Crohn's and Colitis Found., 1994, Entrepreneurial Leadership award Nat. Found. Tchg. Entrepreneurship, 1994, Athena award, 1997, USO Women of Yr. award, 1998, Sara Lee Frontrunner award, 1998, Mattel/Barbie Ambassador of Dreams award, 1999, Town Hall Friend of Arts award, 2000, Pride of NY (PONY) award, 2001, I.O. Salzberger award, 2001, Friars Found. Applause award, 2003, numerous others; honoree Am Bankers Assn., 2003, Enterprising Women's Mag. Lifetime Achiev. award, 2003, Lifetime Achievement award US China Women Bus. Leaders, 2005; inductee Nat. Woman's Hall of Fame, Seneca Falls, NY, 1994, Internat. Women's Forum Hall of Fame, 1994, Ohio Women's Hall Fame, 1994; NY Univ.'s Stern Sch. Bus. 1st Woman Stovall fellow, 1992; established Siebert Entrepreneurial Philanthropic Program, 1990. Mem. Women's Forum (founding mem., pres.), Com. 200, Fin. Women's Assn. (Cmty. Svc. award 1993), Coun. on Fgn. Rels., Nat. Assn. Women Bus. Owners (NAWBO's Veuve Clicquot Bus. Women of Yr. award 1992, Mayor's Lifetime Achievement award for Women Bus. Owners 1993), Econ. Club (exec. com.), Southampton Bath and Tennis Club (founding mem., bd. dirs.), Women's Campaign Fund, Fashion Group Internat., Friars Club, River Club, Doubles Club, Westchester Country Club, Breakers Country Club of Palm Beach. Office: Muriel Siebert Co Inc 885 3rd Ave Ste 1720 New York NY 10022-4834 Personal E-mail: MSiebert@siebertnet.com.

**SIEBERT, THOMAS L.,** lawyer, former ambassador; b. Cleve., May 2, 1946; m. Deborah Simpson; 4 children. BA, JD, Georgetown U. Intern Rep. Robert E. Sweeney, 1965—66; vol. Senator Robert F. Kennedy, 1966—68; aide Senator Carl Hayden, 1968—70; assoc. Pittman, Lovett, Ford & Hennessey, Washington, 1971—78; ptnr. Lovett, Ford, Hennessey, Stambler & Siebert, 1978—87; of counsel Besozzi & Gavin, 1987—93, Besozzi, Gavin & Craven, Washington, 1993; U.S. amb. to Sweden U.S. Embassy, Stockholm, 1994—96; mem. Patton Boggs LLP, Washington. Chmn. Plenipotentiary Conf., Internat. Telecom. Union, 1998; chmn., pres. U.S. Telemetry Corp., 1999—. Bd. regents Cath. U.; bd. visitors St. John's Coll., Georgetown U. Law Ctr.; mem. bd. visitors and govs Washington Coll.; active U.S. Naval Acad. Midshipmen Program, Md. Hall for the Creative Arts. Mem.: ABA, Annapolis Assn., Fed. Comm. Bar Assn., D.C. Bar.

**SIECKERT, KRISTINE ELLEN,** school psychologist, consultant; b. Milw., Oct. 25, 1948; d. Jacob George and Leopoldine Christina Schweitzer; m. Dana Jeffery Sieckert, Nov. 11, 1971 (div. June 3, 1992); 1 child, Christopher Jacob. BS, U. Wis., Milw., 1970, MS, 1979; EdS, Pitts. State U., Kansas, 1980. Cert. sch. psychologist NASP, 1986. Sch. psychologist Miami Pub. Schs., Okla., 1980—85, acting dir. spl. edn., 1984—85; sch. psychologist Oconomowoc Area Pub. Schs., Wis., 1986—; coord. English lang. learner svcs. Oconomowoc Area Sch. Dist., 1999—. Crisis response leader Nat. Orgn. Victims Assistance, 1997—; nat. emergency assistance team NASP, 1997—; cons. Wis. Governors Task Force Sch. Safety, Madison, 1999, Wis. Atty. Gen. Task Force Sch. Safety, Madison, 2000, ARC, Milw., 2001—02. Crisis response leader NASP, 1997—. Victims Assistance, Washington, 1997—. Nominee Woman of Distinction award, YWCA, 2001; recipient Educator of Yr. award, Miami Pub. Schs., 1984, Wis. Suicide Prevention Program award, 1992, Wis. Sch. Psychologist of Yr., Wis. Sch. Psychologist Assn., 1999, Nat. Sch. Psychologist of Yr., Nat. Sch. Psychologist Assn., 2000. Mem.: NASP (nat. emergency assistance team charter mem. 1997—, Nat. Sch. Psychologist of Yr. 2000), Suburban Sch. Psychologist Assn. (pres. 1993—95), Wis. Sch. Psychologist Assn. (pres. 2001—03, Wis. Sch. Psychologist of Yr. 1999). Roman Catholic. Avocations: walking, swimming, reading, travel. Office: Oconomowoc Area Sch Dist 7077 Brown St Oconomowoc WI 53066

**SIEDLE, ROBERT DOUGLAS,** management consultant; b. Canton, Ohio, Aug. 08; BA in Econs., Hiram Coll., 1956; profl. cert. in mgmt., Kent State U. Western Res. U., 1963. Tchr., prin. Ohio secondary schs., 1957-65; salesman, area rep. visual products divsn. 3M Co., 1966-68; mgr. market devel. and tng.

AV divsn. Bell & Howell, 1968-69; Chgo. br. mgr. info. systems divsn. Am. Std., 1969-72; mgr. edn. systems divsn. Audiotronics Corp., 1972-76; gen. mgr. Niles Entertainment/Wardway Films, 1977-80; pres. The Ultimate Image, Lakeland, Fla., 1985—. Prodr.: (films) New Dimensions in Learning II, 1969, District 65: The Exceptional Child, 1969, Career Exploration: Health, 1976, The Wide World of Work, 1976; author: Multisensory Learning: A Training Guide, 1973, Alphabet Zoo, 1973, City of Boston Young Adult Alternate Career Program, 1974, The Quick Job Hunt Guide, 1991; author, prodr., dir.: (multimedia rd. show) "Rap" With Students, 1975; prodr., editor: (film) Stampin' Ground, 1977; author poetry appearing in books and mags., 1991—; appeared on nat. radio and TV programs in U.S. and Can. Mem. task force Founder Wall Ronald Reagan Ctr., Washington, 2005—. Recipient Internat. Peace prize United Cultural Conv., 2002; named to Nat. Aviation and Space Exploration Wall of Honor Smithsonian Nat. Air and Space Mus. Dulles Ctr., 2000, Roll of Honor Eisenhower Ctr., DC, 2005, Honors Courtyard Ronald Reagan Ctr., Capitol Hill, 2005; VFW Patriot Corps award, 2004; Congl. Order of Merit award, 2005. Mem.: Smithsonian Instn., Profl. Football Rschrs. Assn., Nat. Space Soc., Aerospace Edn. Found., Smithsonian Air and Space Soc., Hat in the Ring Soc. (Bronze Membership award 2005), Am. Air Mus. (Britain) (founding mem.), Exptl. Aircraft Assn. (life), World Nations Congress (life; senator), Navy League U.S. (life), U.S. Naval Inst. (life), Fla. Air Mus. Sun 'n Fun (life), Aircraft Owners and Pilots Assn. Safety Found. (life), Air Force Assn. (life), Aircraft Owners and Pilots Assn. (life), Naval Aviation Mus. Found. (life), Am. Assn. Individual Investors, Smithsonian Inst., Internat. Honour Soc. (charter mem.), Popular Rotorcraft Assn., Inc., Helper Soc. (St. Labre Indian Sch. Edn. Assn.), Century Soc. (St. Labre Indian Sch. Edn. Assn.), Soc. Prevention Cruelty to Animals, Inc., Living Planet Soc. (world wildlife fund, Humanitarian award 2002), Defenders of Wildlife (pres.' coun.), Airship Assn. Ltd., Air Force Meml. Found. (charter sponsor), WW II Meml. Soc. (charter), Lighter-than-Air Soc. (life), Pituitary Network Assn. (life), Steamship Hist. Soc. (life), Great Lakes Hist. Soc. (life). Baptist. Office: The Ultimate Image PO Box 91388 Lakeland FL 33804-1388 E-mail: Office22@webtv.net, metalogenman@aol.com.

**SIEDLECKI, NANCY THERESE,** lawyer, funeral director; b. Chgo., May 30, 1954; d. LeRoy John and Dorothy Josephine (Wilczynski) Schielka; m. Jonathan Francis Siedlecki, June 18, 1977; children: Samantha Ann, Abigail Marie. Grad. funeral dir., Worsham Coll., 1974; student, Loyola U., Chgo., 1974—76, U. Ill., 1976—77; JD with honors, Chgo.-Kent Coll. Law, 1980. Bar: Ill. 1980. Paralegal in real estate Rosenberg, Savner & Unikel, Chgo., 1974—77; pvt. practice law Burr Ridge, Ill., 1980—; cons. wills, trusts, probate and small bus. corps., Chgo., 1980—. Mem.: ABA, DuPage Bar Assn., DuPage County Bar Assn., Chgo. Bar Assn., Ill. State Bar Assn., NFDA, Ill. Funeral Dirs. Assn., Union League Club of Chgo., Lyric Opera Chgo. Roman Catholic. Office: Village Law Bldg 5300 Main St Downers Grove IL 60515-4846 Office Phone: 630-969-1009. Business E-Mail: nsvillagelaw@aol.com.

**SIEDLECKI, PETER ANTHONY,** English language and literature educator; b. North Tonawanda, N.Y., May 19, 1938; s. Anthony Paul and Mary Barbara (Litwin) S.; m. Rose Mary Murphy, June 25, 1960 (div. 1978); children: Christopher, Gregory, Jeffrey, William; m. Lynnette Noreen Mende, Apr. 26, 1980; children: Peter Emmanuel Mende-Siedlecki. BA, Niagara U., 1960, MA, 1966; PhD, SUNY, Buffalo, 1982. Tchr. English Lewiston-Porter Sr. H.S., Youngstown, NY, 1960—64, Grand Island (N.Y.) Sr. H.S., 1964—65; prof. English Rosary Hill Coll., Amherst, NY, 1965—74, Daemen Coll., Amherst, NY, 1974—, dean, divsn. arts and scis., 2001—, chair divsn. humanities and social scis., 1998—2001; prof. Am. Lit. Jagiellonian U., Krakow, Poland, 1982-84, Friedrich-Schiller U., Jena, 1988-89. Commentator pub. radio, 1995—. Author (poetry) Voyeur; contbr. articles to profl. jours. Bd. dirs. Freudig Singers. Fulbright Sr. lectr., Council for Internat. Exchange of Scholars, 1982-84, 88-89. Mem. MLA, Assn. Am. Colls. and Univs., Coll. English Assn., Fulbright Alumni Assn. Democrat. Home: 249 Winspear Ave Buffalo NY 14215-1035 Office: Daemen College 4380 Main St Buffalo NY 14226-3592 Office Phone: 716-839-8304. E-mail: psiedlec@daemen.edu.

**SIEFERS, ROBERT GEORGE,** banker; b. Pitts., Aug. 28, 1945; s. George Francis and Idella Alice (Eiler) S.; m. Janice Lynn Kirkpatrick, Mar. 25, 1970; children: Robert Scott, Jillian Stewart BA, Mt. Union Coll., 1967; MBA, Kent State U., 1971; JD, Cleveland Marshall Law Sch., 1976. Security analyst Nat. City Bank, Cleve., 1971-76, v.p., investment rsch. dir., 1976-80, v.p. adminstrn. and rsch., 1980-82; sr. v.p. corp. planning Nat. City Bank, Cleve., 1982-85; sr. v.p. corp. banking Nat. City Bank, Cleve., 1985-86; pres., chief exec. officer Ohio Citizens Bank (affiliate Nat. City Corp.), Toledo, 1986-90; vice chmn., CFO Nat. City Corp., Cleve., 1997—. Bd. dirs. HCR Corp. Bd. trustees Mt. Union Coll. Republican. Presbyterian Club: Chagrin Valley Country. Office: Nat City Corp 1900 E 9th St Cleveland OH 44114-3401

**SIEFERT-KAZANJIAN, DONNA,** corporate librarian; b. N.Y.C. d. Merrill Emil and Esther (Levins) Siefert; m. George John Kazanjian June 15, 1974; 1 child, Merrill George. BA, NYU, 1969; MSLS, Columbia U., 1973; MBA, Fordham U., 1977. Asst. librarian Dun & Bradstreet, N.Y.C., 1969-73; research assoc. William E. Hill & Co., N.Y.C., 1973-76; sr. info. analyst Info. for Bus., N.Y.C., 1976-77; librarian Handy Assocs., N.Y.C., 1979-90; mgr. Infoserve Fuchs Cuthrell & Co., Inc., N.Y.C., 1991-94; info. specialist Heidrick & Struggles, Inc., N.Y.C., 1994-2001; learning media specialist St. Mary's Elem. Sch., Manhasset, NY, 2002—03; libr. I Manhasset Pub. Libr., 2003—. Mem.: Rsch. Roundtable, Spl. Librs. Assn., Mensa, Am. Mensa Ltd. Roman Catholic.

**SIEG, ALBERT LOUIS,** photographic company executive; b. Chgo., Mar. 25, 1930; s. Albert Fredrick and Louise Augusta (Strege) S.; m. Irma Alice Spencer, Sept. 3, 1955; children: Karen, Diane, Susan BS in Chemistry, U. Ill., 1951; PhD in Organic Chemistry, U. Rochester, 1954; P.MD, Harvard Bus. Sch., 1971. Supr. emulsion Eastman Kodak Co., Rochester, NY, 1970-72, corp. mgr. instant, 1972-76, mgr. paper mgmt., 1976-81, v.p., dir. 1981-84; pres. Kodak Japan K.K., Tokyo, 1984-89; pres., rep. dir. Eastman Kodak Japan, Tokyo, 1989-91, also bd. dirs.; pres., rep. dir. Eastman Chems. Japan Ltd., Tokyo, 1989-91; v.p., dir. strategic resources, sec. imaging bd. Eastman Kodak Co., Rochester, 1991-92, ret., 1992; prin., cons. Albert L. Sieg Assocs., Rochester, 1992—. Bd. dirs. Kodak Japan Industries, Ltd., XM Corp.; sr. lectr. U. Rochester, 1960-69; mem. adv. bd. Worldscape, Inc., 2001-. Co-author: 8th Here's How, 1972; co-author (with S. Bennett, Oliver Wight) Tokyo Chronicles, 1994; inventor in field. Bd. dirs. St. John's Home Found., 2000—; chmn. corp. gifts Rochester Philharm. Orch., 1982-88. Corp. gifts Internat. Mus. Photography at George Eastman House, 1993, 94; pres. Reformation Luth. Ch., Rochester, 1978-83; bd. dirs. St. John's Home for the Aging, 1994-99, vice chmn. bd. dirs., 1997-99; bd. dirs. St. John's Nursing Home, 1994-99, vice chmn. bd. dirs., 1997-99, chmn., 1999-2001; bd. dirs. St. John's Sr. Svcs., 1997-2001, chair elect, 1997-99, chair, 1999-01, pres., 1997-01; bd. dirs. St. John's Found., 2001—, sec., 2005-06, chmn.-elect, 2006—. Served with Med. Svc. Corps, U.S. Army, 1955-57. Recipient George Eastman Medal Kodak Camera Clubs, 1980; Kiwanis Club Chgo. fellow, U. Ill., 1947-51; Am. Cyanamide fellow, 1953-54 Fellow Am. Inst. Chemists, Photog. Soc. Am. (v.p. 1969-84, bd. dirs. 1992—, exec. v.p. 1995-99, pres. 1999-2003, Harold Lloyd award 1978, Progress medal 1995); mem. AAAS, N.Am. Nature Photography Assn. (bd. dirs. 2005-06, pres. 2006—), Am. Chem. Soc., Soc. Photog. Scientists and Engrs., Rochester C. of C., Am. C. of C. in Japan (bd. govs. 1988-91, v.p. 1989-91), Internat. Stereoscopic Union (pres. 1993, 94), Am. Club Tokyo, Fgn. Corrs Club. Republican. Avocations: skiing, photography, gardening. Home and Office: 159 Hillhurst Ln Rochester NY 14617-1938 Personal E-Mail: albert4182@aol.com.

**SIEG, KENT G.,** historian; b. Oklahoma City, July 20, 1964; s. Marianne Sieg. PhD, U. Colo., Boulder, 1993. Historian U.S. Dept. of State, Washington, 1995—2001, U.S. Army Corps of Engrs., Ft. Belvoir, Va., 2001—05, Dept. of Def., Ft. Meade, Md., 2005—. Mem.: Coun. on Am.'s Mil. Past, Soc. Historians of Am. Fgn. Rels.

**SIEGAL, ALLAN MARSHALL,** journalist, consultant; b. NYC, May 1, 1940; s. Irving and Sylvia Norma (Wrubel) S.; m. Gretchen M-P. Leefmans, May 31, 1977; children— Anna Marianita, Peter Bert Grad., NYU, 1962. With New York Times, 1960—2006, editor Pentagon Papers, 1971, asst. fgn. editor, 1971-76, asst. to exec. editor, 1976-77, news editor, 1977-87, asst. mng. editor, 1987—2006, standards editor, 2003—06, founding editor nat. edit., 1980; tchr. journalism NYU, 1966, Columbia U., 1967-69. Juror Pulitzer Prizes, 1987-89. Co-author: The New York Times Manual of Style and Usage, 1999. Named Shorenstein fellow in press, politics, and public policy, John F. Kennedy Sch. Govt., Harvard U., 2006; recipient Ethics in Journalism award, Soc. of Profl. Journalists, 2006. Mem. Century Assn., Am. Soc. Newspaper Editors.

**SIEGAL, BURTON LEE,** product designer, consultant, inventor; b. Chgo., Sept. 27, 1931; s. Norman A. and Sylvia (Vitz) S.; m. Rita Goran, Apr. 11, 1954; children: Norman, Laurence Scott BS in Mech. Engring., U. Ill., 1953. Torpedo designer U.S. Naval Ordnance, Forest Park, Ill., 1953-54; chief engr. Gen. Aluminum Corp., Chgo., 1954-55; product designer Chgo. Aerial Industries, Melrose Park, Ill., 1955-58; chief designer Emil J. Paidar Co., Chgo., 1958-59; founder, pres. Budd Engring. Corp., Chgo., 1959—. Dir. Dur-A-Case Corp., Chgo.; design cons. to numerous corps. Holder more than 127 patents in more than 40 fields including multimemory for power seats and electrified office panel sys., Piezo ink jet valves; contbr. articles to tech. publs. Mem. math., sci. and English adv. bds. Niles Twp. High Schs., Skokie, Ill., 1975-79; electronic cons. Chgo. Police Dept., 1964. Nominee Presdl. medal Tech., Sen. Paul Simon and Rep. Dan Rostenkowski, 1986; named Winner, Internat. Extrusion Design Competition, 1975, Inventor of Yr., Patent Law Assn. Chgo., 1986, Disting. Alumni, Coll. Engring., U. Ill., 2005. Mem. ASME, Soc. Plastics Engrs., Soc. Mfg. Engrs., Inventors Coun., Soc. Automotive Engrs., Pres.'s Assn. Ill. Office: Skokie IL 60076 *A true professional can perform any time, any place, independent of his mood.*

**SIEGAL, JACOB J.,** management and financial consultant; b. Phila., Apr. 4, 1929; s. Louis and Henrietta (Greenberg) S.; m. Dolores Berg, June 8, 1952; children: Marla, Karen, Leslie. BS, Temple U., 1951, LLB, 1954; postgrad., U. Chgo., 1973. Bar: Pa. 1955, Ill. 1973. With City of Phila., 1954-61, chief counselor, 1959-61, dep. city solicitor, 1958-61; pvt. practice law, partner firm Meltzer & Schiffrin, Phila., 1961-72; v.p., gen. counsel, dir. Bluebird Inc., Phila., 1972-74, exec. v.p., 1974-78, pres., 1978-79, chmn., chief exec. officer, 1979. Chmn. bd. Armen Cadillac-Osmobile, Inc. Mem. Am. Meat Inst. (dir., conv. speaker 1978) Home: 101 Cheswold Ln Haverford PA 19041-1865 Office: PO Box 193 Plymouth Meeting PA 19462-0193

**SIEGAL, JOEL DAVIS,** lawyer; b. Plainfield, NJ, Feb. 9, 1937; s. Samuel and Florence (Ravitz) Siegal; 2 children. BA in Polit. Sci., U. Wis., 1958; JD, Yale U., 1961; MA in Internat. Rels., U. Stockholm, 1963. Bar: NJ 1962, US Dist. Ct. NJ 1962, US Ct. Appeals (3d cir.) 1963, NY 1965, US Supreme Ct. 1969, US Dist. Ct. (so. and ea. dists.) NY 1975. Law clk. to Hon. Arthur S. Lane US Dist. Ct., Newark, 1961—62; law clk. to Hon. Phillip Forman US Ct. Appeals (3d cir.), 1963-64; assoc. Hellring Lindeman Goldstein & Siegal, Newark, 1967-70, ptnr., 1970—. Commr. Nat. Conf. Commrs. Uniform Laws, 1991—98; mem. US Dist. Ct. Adv. Bd., Newark, 1991—92. Contbr. articles to profl. jours. Mcpl. chmn. Borough of Alpine Dems., NJ, 1983—86. Fellow: Am. Bar Found.; mem.: ABA, Assn. Fed. Bar NJ (nat. del. NJ 1974, pres. 1990—92, adv. bd. 1993—), Bergen Bar Assn., Essex County Bar Assn., NJ Bar Assn., Harmonie Club NYC. Office: Hellring Lindeman Goldstein Siegal 1 Gateway Ctr Fl 8 Newark NJ 07102-5386 also: 32-40 N Dean St Englewood NJ 07631 Office Phone: 973-621-9020. Business E-Mail: jdsiegal@hlgslaw.com.

**SIEGAL, JUDY A.,** social services administrator; b. Chgo., July 28, 1947; d. Sidney and Carolyn Hedish Axelrod; m. Barry Preston Siegal, Dec. 29, 1968; children: Joshua, Kimberly, Marni. BA, U. Mich., 1969. Dir. coop. edn. Roosevelt U., Chgo., 1970—74; vol. coord. Resource Ctr. for Elderly, Arlington Heights, Ill., 1988—92; cmty. affairs coord. Sportmart, Inc., Wheeling, Ill., 1992—98; region dir. Women's Am. Ort, Northbrook, Ill., 1998—2000, Midwest dir. major gifts, 2000—02, Midwest dir. devel., 2002—. Mem. Chgo. Coun. on Planned Giving; bd. dirs. Congregation Bnai Tikvah, Deerfield, Ill. Recipient Pres.' award, Internat. Mass Retail Assn., Washington, 1996. Mem.: Women in Devel. North, Miriam's Path. Jewish. Avocations: reading, needlecrafts, singing. Office: Women's Am Ort 3701 Commercial Northbrook IL 60062 E-mail: jsiegal@waort.org.

**SIEGAL, RITA GORAN,** engineering company executive; b. Chgo., July 16, 1934; d. Leonard and Anabelle (Soloway) Goran; m. Burton L. Siegal, Apr. 11, 1954; children: Norman, Laurence Scott Student, U. Ill., 1951-53; BA, DePaul U., 1956. Cert. elem. tchr., Ill. Tchr. Chgo. Public Schs., 1956-58; founder, chief exec. officer Budd Engring. Corp., Skokie, Ill., 1959—; founder, pres. Easy Living Products Co., Skokie, 1960—; pvt. practice in interior design, Chgo., 1968-73; dist. sales mgr. Super Girls, Skokie, 1976. Lectr. Northwestern U., 1983; guest speaker nat. radio and TV. 1979—. Contbr. to profl. jours. Mem. adv. bd. Skokie High Schs., 1975-79; advisor Cub Scouts Skokie coun. Boy Scouts Am., 1975; bus. mgr. Nutrition for Optimal Health Assn., Winnetka, Ill., 1980-82, pres., 1982-84, v.p. med./profl., 1985-93; leader Great Books Found., 1972; founder Profit Plus Investment, 1970; bd. dirs. Noha, Internat. Named Prominent Alumni, Sullivan HS, 2001; recipient Cub Scout awards, Boy Scouts Am., 1971—72, Nat. Charlotte Danstrom award, Nat. Women of Achievement, 1988, Corp. Achievement award, 1988, Frannie Award, U. Ill., 1998. Mem. North Shore Women in Mgmt. (pres. 1987-88), Presidents Assn. Ill. (bd. dirs 1990-94, membership chair 1991-93), Inventors Coun., Oriental Art Soc. Chgo. (publicity chair) *Believe in yourself, if others can do it so can you. Prioritize so you are not overwhelmed by your responsibilities.*

**SIEGEL, ABRAHAM J.,** economics professor, academic administrator; b. N.Y.C., Nov. 6, 1922; s. Samuel J. and Dora (Drach) S.; m. Lillian Wakshull, Dec. 22, 1946; children: Emily Jean Siegel Stangle, Paul Howard, Barbara Ann Pugliese. BA summa cum laude, CCNY, 1943; MA, Columbia U., 1949; PhD, U. Calif., Berkeley, 1961. Instr. dept. econs. CCNY, 1947-49; research economist Inst. Indsl. Relations, U. Calif., Berkeley, 1952-54; instr. dept. econs. M.I.T., Cambridge, 1954-56, asst. prof., 1956-59, assoc. prof., 1959-64, prof. dept. econs. Sloan Sch. Mgmt., 1964-93, assoc. dean Sloan Sch. Mgmt., 1967-80, dean, 1980-87, prof. emeritus, sr. lectr., 1993—. Spl. lectr. Trade Union Program, Harvard U., 1961-64; vis. prof. Brandeis U., 1956-60; vis. prin. mem. div. Internat. Inst. Labour Studies, Internat. Labour Office, Geneva, 1964-65; assoc. staff dir. Com. Econ. Devel., Study Group on Nat. Labor Policy, 1960-61; trustee, chmn. adminstrv. com. M.I.T. Retirement Plan for Staff Mems., 1970-91. Co-author: Industrial Relations in the Pacific Coast Longshore Industry, 1956, The Public Interest in National Labor Policy, 1961, The Impact of Computers on Collective Bargaining, 1969, Unfinished Business: An Agenda for Labor, Management and the Public, 1978. Bd. dirs. Whitehead Inst. Biomed. Rsch., Analysis Group, Inc., Internat. Data Group; mem. Framingham Sch. Com., South Middlesex Regional Dist. Vocat. Sch. Com., 1968-71. With USAF, 1943-46. Mem. Am. Econ. Assn., Indsl. Relations Research Assn., Nat. Acad. Arbitrators, Am. Arbitration Assn. (mem. various panels), Inst. Mgmt. Scis. Bus. Roundtable (exec. com.), Phi Beta Kappa. Office: MIT Sloan Sch Mgmt 50 Memorial Dr Cambridge MA 02142-1347 Home: 217 Del Pond Dr Canton MA 02021-2754

**SIEGEL, ARTHUR HERBERT,** finance company executive; b. NYC, Jan. 5, 1938; s. Joseph Kenneth and Gertrude Sylvia (Hecker) Siegel; m. Eleanor Novick, June 5, 1960; children: Joan Aileen, Linda Beth, Mark Eric. AB, Columbia U., 1958, MBA, 1960. With Price Waterhouse, N.Y.C., 1960-97, mgr. L.I., 1961-72, ptnr. Boston, 1972-83, nat. dir. acctg. svcs. N.Y.C., 1984-88, vice chmn. bus. adv. and auditing svcs., 1988-95; mem. Fin. Acctg. Stds. Bd. Emerging Issues Task Force, 1985-88, Fin Acctg. Stds. Adv. Coun., 1985-90; mem. adv. coun. Sch. Acctg., U. So. Calif., 1987-89. Exec. dir. Independence Stds. Bd., 1997—2001; bd. dirs., chmn. audit com. Rotech Healthcare, Inc., 2002—; bd. dirs. Solomon Schechtar Sch., North Jersey, NJ. Bd. dirs. Nat. Multiple Sclerosis Soc., treas., exec. com., chmn. fin. com.,

1990—98. Mem.: AICPA (chmn. task force risks and uncertainties 1985—87, chmn. SEC practice exec. com. 1994—97), Mass. Soc. CPAs (pres.-elect 1983), N.Y. Soc. CPAs (Silver Medal award), World Union Progressive Judaism, Assn. Reform Zionists Am. (bd. dirs. 2004—), Beta Gamma Sigma. Home and Office: Apt 3A 179 E 70th St New York NY 10021-5109 Office Phone: 212-327-0794. Personal E-mail: ASiegs@ix.netcom.com.

**SIEGEL, BARRY,** journalist, writer, literature educator; b. St. Louis, Sept. 7, 1949; m. Marti Devore; 1 child, Alexandra Nicole. BA magna cum laude, Pomona Coll., 1971; MS in Journalism, Columbia U., 1972. Stringer LA bur. Newsweek, 1973; news editor West Coast Women's Wear Daily, 1973—76; writer View sect. LA Times, 1976—78, writer spl. assignment, 1979, corr. Nat., 1980—83, corr./sr. writer, 1983—2003, spl. corr., 2003—; prof. English & comparative lit., dir. Literary Journalism Prog. U. Calif., Irvine, 2003—. Vis. lectr. U. So. Calif., 1988. Author: A Death in White Bear Lake, 1990, Shades of Gray, 1992, The Perfect Witness, 1998, Actual Innocence, 1999, Lines of Defense, 2002; contbr. articles to profl. jours. Recipient USA West Journalism award, PEN Ctr., 1987, USA West Lit. award in Journalism, 2000, Golden Medallion Media award, State Bar Calif., 1984, Silver Gavel award, ABA, 1985, Paul Tobenkin Meml. award, 1997, Pulitzer Prize for Feature Writing, 2002. Office: U Calif Mail Code: 2650 408 Humanities Instructional Bldg Irvine CA 92697 Office Phone: 949-824-3023. Office Fax: 949-824-2916. E-mail: bsiegel@uci.edu, barry@barry-siegel.com.

**SIEGEL, BARRY ALAN,** radiologist; b. Nashville, Dec. 30, 1944; s. Walter G. Siegel and Lillian B. Ivener; m. Pamela M. Mandel, Aug. 18, 1968 (div. Mar. 1981); children: Peter A., William A.; m. Marilyn J. Siegel, Jan. 29, 1983 AB, Washington U., St. Louis, 1966, MD, 1969. Diplomate Am. Bd. Nuc. Medicine, Am. Bd. Radiology. Intern Barnes Hosp., St. Louis, 1969-70; from resident in radiology to prof. Mallinckrodt Inst. Radiology Washington U., 1970—79, prof. radiology Mallinckrodt Inst. Radiology, 1979—, dir. divsn. nuc. medicine Mallinckrodt Inst. Radiology, 1973—, mem. Siteman Cancer Ctr., 1996—. Dir. Am. Bd. Nuc. Medicine, L.A., 1985—90, sec., 1990; chmn. adv. com. on med. uses of isotopes NRC, Washington, 1990—96; chmn. radiopharm. drugs adv. com. FDA, Rockville, Md., 1982—85, radiol. devices panel, 1992—95; mem. U.S. Pharmacopeia Adv. Panel on Radiopharms., 1975—2000, Armed Forces Radiobiol. Rsch. Inst. Bethesda; coun. experts, chair radiopharm. expert com. U.S. Pharmacopoeial Conv., 2000—05; co-chair working group Nat. Oncologic PET Registry, 2005—; cons. in field. Author, editor 33 books; contbr. articles to profl. jours., chpts. in books. Maj. USAF, 1974—76. Recipient Conmer.'s Spl. citation U.S. FDA, 1988, Honor citation U.S. Pharmacopeial Conv., 1995, 2000. Fellow: ACP, ACR, Coll. Nuc. Physicians, Am. Coll. Radiology (vice chmn. commn. on nuc. medicine 1981—93, editor-in-chief profl. self evaln. program 1988—2002, chmn. nuc. medicine com. imaging network 1998—); mem.: ACS (chmn. diagnostic imaging com. oncology group 1998—, mem. exec. com. 2000—), AMA, Acad. Molecular Imaging (chair inst. Clin. PET com. 2001—02, bd. dirs. 2004—), Soc. Nuc. Medicine (trustee 1981—85, 1987—91, Georg Charles de Hevesy Nuclear Pioneer award 2003), Radiol. Soc. N.Am., Am. Univ. Radiologists, Am. Roentgen Ray Soc. Office: Washington U Mallinckrodt Inst Radiology 510 S Kingshighway Blvd Saint Louis MO 63110-1016 Office Phone: 314-362-2809. Business E-Mail: siegelb@mir.wustl.edu.

**SIEGEL, BERNARD LOUIS,** lawyer; b. Pitts., Sept. 15, 1938; s. Ralph Robert and Frieda Sara (Stein) S.; m. Marcia Margolis, Sept. 3, 1961 (div. Aug. 1983); children: Jonathan, Sharon; m. Susan Erickson, Aug. 31, 1997 (div. June 2001). BA, Brandeis U., 1960; JD, Harvard U., 1963. Bar: Pa. 1964, U.S. Dist. Ct. (we. dist.) Pa. 1964, U.S. Dist. Ct. (ea. dist.) Pa. 1985, U.S. Ct. Appeals (3d cir.) 1985, U.S. Supreme Ct. 1985. Assoc. Silin, Eckert & Burke, Erie, Pa., 1963-66; ptnr. Silin, Eckert, Burke & Siegel, Erie, 1966-73; 1st asst. dist. atty. Erie County, 1972-76; dep. atty. gen. Pa. Dept. Justice, Phila., 1976-78; dep. dist. atty. Dist. Atty. of Phila., 1978-86; pvt. practice Phila., 1986—. Adj. prof. La Salle U., Phila., 1986—95, Phila., 2006; lectr. Fed. Law Enforcement Tng. Ctr., Glynco, Ga., 1986—97, Mercyhurst Coll., Erie, 1974—76, Nat. Coll. Dist. Attys., Houston, 1978—85; adj. prof. Temple U. Law Sch., 1986—95, 2006; mem. criminal rules com. Pa. Supreme Ct., Phila., 1976—85; commr. Pa. Crime Commn., Harrisburg, 1976—79. Author: (with others) Pennsylvania Grand Jury Practice, 1983, By No Extraordinary Means, 1986. Mem.: ABA, Phila. Bar Assn. (chmn. criminal justice sect. 1990—91, Justice Thurgood Marshall award 2004), Pa. Bar Assn. (chmn. criminal law sect. 1988—91), Pa. Assn. Criminal Def. Lawyers (bd. dirs. 1988—, treas. 2002—04, v.p. 2004—, Josel Advocacy award 2005), Nat. Assn. Criminal Def. Lawyers. Democrat. Jewish. Avocations: bicycling, reading, hiking. Office: 1515 Market St Ste 1915 Philadelphia PA 19102-1920 Office Phone: 215-751-9830. E-mail: bernardlsiegel@comcast.net.

**SIEGEL, BETTY LENTZ,** university president; b. Cumberland, Ky., Jan. 24, 1931; d. Carl N. and Vera (Hogg) Lentz; m. Joel H. Siegel, June 6; children: David Jonathan, Michael Jeremy. BA, Wake Forest U., 1952; M in Edn., U. NC, 1953; PhD, Fla. State U., 1961; postgrad., Ind. U., 1964-66; doctorate (hon.), Miami U., 1985, Cumberland Coll., 1985, Ea. Ky. U., 1992, Morehead State U., 2002; degree (hon.), Lynchburg Coll., Jane Coll. State U. Asst. prof. Lenoir Rhyne Coll., Hickory, N.C., 1956-59; assoc. prof., 1961-64; asst. prof. U. Fla., Gainesville, 1967-70, assoc. prof., 1970-72, prof., 1973-76, dean acad. affairs for continuing edn., 1972-76; dean Sch. Edn. and Psychology Western Carolina U., Cullowhee, N.C., 1976-81; pres. Kennesaw State U., Marietta, Ga., 1981—. Bd. dirs. Nat. Services Industries; cons. numerous sch. systems. Author: Problem Situations in Teaching, 1971, Becoming An Invitational Leader, 2002; contbr. articles to profl. jours. Bd. dirs. United Way Atlanta, Ga. Partnership for Excellence in Edn., Ga. Coun. Econ. Edn., Northside Hosp. Found., Atlanta Ballet; Ga. rep. so. growth policy bd. Commn. on Future of South 1998. Recipient Disting Tchr. of Yr. award U. Fla., 1969, Mortar Bd. Woman of Yr. award U. Fla., 1973, Mortar Bd. Educator of Yr., Ga. State U., 1983, CASE award, 1986, Alumna of Yr. award Wake Forest U., 1987, "Grad Made Good" award Fla. State U. Alumni Assn, Omicron Delta Kappa, 1991, Spirit of Life award City of Hope, 1992, Woman of Achievement award Cobb Chamber YWCA, 1992, First Lifetime Achievement award YWCA, N.W. Ga., Oak award outstanding Alumni Ky., 1998, Adminstrv. Leadership award Assn. Gerontology in Higher Edn., 2001, Women in Bus. Lifetime Achievement award, 2001, Peabody award UNC-Chapel Hill Sch. Edn., 2003, Justice Robert Benham award outstanding leadership, svc. and commitment equality of all citizens Black's United for Youth of Cobb County, 2004, Howard Washington Thurman Ecumenical award Morehouse Coll.'s Martin Luther King, Jr. Internat. Chapel, 2005, Leita Thompson Lifetime Achievement award; named 50 Most Influential Women in Ga., One of 100 Most Influential People in State of Ga., Ga. Trend Mag., Outstanding Alumni, Fla. State U. 1, Justice Robert Benham, 2001, Cobb Citizen of Yr., 1996, Ga. Woman of Yr. Ga. Commn. Women, 1997, Divas for Life Bus. to Bus. Mag., 2001, 100 Most Disting. Alumni Cumberland Coll.; named to Jr. Achievement Hall of Fame, 1999, 20 Women Making a Mark on Atlanta Atlanta mag., 20 Yrs., 20 Leaders Ga. Trend mag. Mem. Am. Psychol. Assn., Am. Assn. State Colls. and Univs. (bd. dirs., chmn. 1990), Am. Coun. Edn. (bd. dirs., bd. advisors), Am. Inst. Mng. Diversity (bd. dis.), Soc. Internat. Bus. Fellows, Commn. on Women in Higher Edn. Internat. Alliance Invitational Edn. (co-founder, co-dir.), Nat. Ctr. Study of Freshman Yr. Experience, So. Inst. Bus. and Profl. Ethics (mem. gov. bd.), Am. Cancer Soc. (Cobb chpt.), Cobb Exec. Women (founder) Ga. Exec. Women's Network, Internat. Bus. Forum, State Bar Ga., Found. Freedom, Bus./Higher Edn. Forum, mem. exec. com.), Cobb C. of C. (chair 1996), Kiwanis (Atlanta chpt.), Am. Humanics, Inc., Phi Alpha Theta, Pi Kappa Delta, Alpha Psi Omega, Kappa Delta Pi, Pi Lambda Theta, Phi Delta Kappa, Delta Kappa Gamma. Office: Kennesaw State Univ Office of the President 1000 Chastain Rd NW Kennesaw GA 30144-5591

**SIEGEL, CAROLYN AUGUSTA,** judge, lawyer, social worker; b. Buffalo, Dec. 29, 1943; d. Joseph Frederick and Louise Augusta (Knecht) S.; m. Roger John Walsh, Feb. 15, 1969 (div. Nov. 1, 1989); children: Kristin N. Jaeger, Jocelyn N. Walsh. BA, St. Bonaventure U., 1965; MS, SUNY, Buffalo, 1973, MSW, JD, SUNY, Buffalo, 1999. Bar: N.Y. 2000; cert. elem. and exceptional tchr., lic. Master Social Worker N.Y. Indsl. investigator N.Y. Dept. Labor, Buffalo, 1966-67; tchr. St. Bonaventure Grammar Sch., Buffalo, 1967; adminstrv. analyst N.Y. State Dept. Law, Albany, 1967-68; caseworker N.Y. State Dept. Social Svcs., Buffalo, 1968-72; resource agent N.Y. State Dept. Mental Hygiene, Buffalo, 1972-73; resource and reimbursement agt. N.Y. State Office Mental Retardation and Developmental Disabilities, Buffalo, 1982—2001; coord. policy svcs. Erie 1 BOCES, West Seneca, NY, 2001—; town justice Town of Colden, 2004—. Mem. surrogate decision-making panel N.Y. State Commn. on Quality of Care; adj. instr. SUNY, Buffalo, 2004—; cert. instr. Mandated Child Abuse Reporters, 2005—. Contbr. articles to profl. jours. Pres. Bd. Edn. Springville (N.Y.)-Griffith Inst. Ctrl. Sch. Dist., 1980-95; bd. visitors Buffalo Psychiat. Ctr., 1994—, pres., 1998—; bd. dirs. Erie County Mental Health Assn., Buffalo; 4H Group Leader Erie County Coop. Extension, East Aurora, N.Y., 1974-92; town chmn. Am. Cancer Soc., Buffalo. Mem.: ABA, Erie County Magistrates Assn., N.Y. Magistrates Assn., Erie County Bar Assn., Women's Bar Assn., N.Y. State Bar Assn. Home: PO Box 360 West Falls NY 14170-9624 Office: Erie 1 BOCES 355 Harlem Rd West Seneca NY 14224 Business E-Mail: csiegel@e1b.org.

**SIEGEL, DANIEL JOEL,** lawyer; b. Phila., July 9, 1959; s. Bertram and Rita (Starr) S.; m. Eileen H. Watts, June 22, 1986; children: Bradley Eric, Douglas Steven AB, Franklin & Marshall Coll., 1981; JD, Temple U., 1984. Bar: Pa. 1984, N.J. 1984, U.S. Dist. Ct. (ea. dist.) Pa. 1984, U.S. Dist. Ct. N.J. 1984, U.S. Ct. Appeals (3d cir.) 1985. Assoc. Ronald A. Blumfield, Phila., 1983—86; ptnr. Gay & Chacker, Phila., 1986—2001; with Anapol, Schwartz, Weiss, Cohan, Feldman & Smalley PC, 2001—04, ptnr., 2004—05; counsel Law Offices Daniel J. Siegel, LLC, Havertown, Pa., 2005—. Lectr in field Author: Is There an Automatic Supersedeas - Or - Is the Automatic Supersedeas Constitutional?, 1994; co-author: (chpts.) The Bill of Rights: A Bicentennial View, 1991, Tort and Insurance Law Update, 1993, The New Workers' Compensation Act: Comp in the Nineties and Beyond, 1993, Workers' Compensation - Tips From Local Practitioners, 1994, Workers' Compensation - Winning Strategies in Workers' Compensation Cases, 1995, Hot Tips in Auto Law, 1995; contbr. articles to profl. jours Bd. govs. Handgun Control, Inc., Washington, 1995-2000, trustee, 1995-97 Phila. area spokesman, 1982-2000; mem., spokesperson Pa.'s Against Handgun Violence, 1993-2000, founding pres., 1995-2000, Phila. chpt., 1996-2000, pres., 1994-96; vol. alumni admissions program Franklin and Marshall Coll., Lancaster, Pa., 1986—, student-alumni ptnr. program, 1996—; vol. People for the Am. Way, Washington, 1988—; founding mem. young mems. group Temple Beth Israel, 1990; counsel, bd. dirs. Found. Ichtyosis & Related Skin Types, 2000— Recipient Increase the Peace Hero, WUSL-FM, 1994. Mem. ABA, ATLA, Am. Philatelic Soc. (bd. v.p. 1993-95, gen. chmn. 1991, youth activities com. 1977-79, 84-92, spkrs. bur. 1979—), Pa. Bar Assn., Pa. Trial Lawyers Assn., Phila. Bar Assn., Phila. Trial Lawyers Assn., Collectors Club Phila. (editor 1992-96, treas. 1993-96, corr. sec. 1992, founding pres. 1990-91), Phila. Nat. Stamp Exhbn. (formerly Associated Stamp Clubs SE Pa. and Del., pres. 1989-95, legal coun. 1985-89, dir. 1986-89, 95-96) Democrat. Home: 1705 Marilyn Dr Havertown PA 19083-1226 Office: 66 West Eagle Rd Ste 1 Havertown PA 19083-1425 Office Phone: 610-446-3457. Business E-Mail: dan@danieljsiegel.com.

**SIEGEL, DAVID B.,** lawyer; b. 1953; BA summa cum laude, U. Pa., MA, 1975; JD, U. Penn., 1979. Bar: DC 1979. Law clk. to Judge Clarence C. Newcomer U.S. Dist. Ct. Pa. (ea. dist.), 1979—81; with Crowell & Moring LLP, Washington, 1981—, ptnr., mng. ptnr., chmn., 2006—. Contbr. articles to profl. jours. Office: Crowell & Moring LLP 1001 Pennsylvania Ave NW Ste 1100 Washington DC 20004-2595 Office Phone: 202-624-2662. Office Fax: 202-658-5116. E-mail: dsiegel@crowell.com.*

**SIEGEL, DAVID BURTON,** lawyer; b. NYC, Mar. 22, 1949; s. Henry and Ruth (Rosenzweig) S.; m. Barbara Joan Brown, Aug. 6, 1972; children: Jeffrey Spencer, Carolyn Rose, Laura Ellen. AB, Columbia Coll., 1971; JD, NYU, 1974. Assoc. atty. Kelley Drye & Warren, NYC, 1974-77; corp. counsel W.R. Grace & Co, NYC, 1977-87, asst. gen. counsel, 1987-91, assoc. gen. counsel Boca Raton, Fla., 1991-93, v.p., dep. gen. counsel, 1993-98, sr. v.p., gen. counsel and sec., 1998-2001, sr. v.p., gen. counsel, chief restructuring officer, 2001—05. Mem. Econ. Coun. Palm Beach County, Fla., 1993-99; mem. bd. dirs. Edn. Partnership of Palm Beach County, 1994-96, treas., 1995-96. Home and Office: 446 Putnam Forest Rd Stowe VT 05672 Office Phone: 802-253-9264. Business E-Mail: david.siegel@grace.com.

**SIEGEL, EDWARD M.,** lawyer; b. N.Y.C., Apr. 14, 1934; s. Charles and Rose (Fritzhand) S.; m. Elyse R. Roth, Mar. 9, 1969; children: Eric, Eve-Lynn. BA, Columbia Coll., 1955; MA, Columbia U., 1957, JD, 1960. Bar: NY 1961. Legal asst. to dean Columbia U. Law Sch., N.Y.C., 1960-65; gen. counsel Transp. Displays, Inc., N.Y.C., 1965-75, corp. sec., 1968-75, v.p., 1972-73, sr. v.p., 1973-75; pub. affairs mgr. J.C. Penney Co., N.Y.C., 1975-77; gen. counsel, corp. sec. Electro Audio Dynamics, Inc., Great Neck, N.Y., 1977-85, v.p., 1981-85; v.p. legal affairs East View Co., N.Y.C., 1985-87; ptnr. Bangser Klein Rocca & Blum (formerly Bangser & Weiss), N.Y.C., 1988-92; sr. v.p., gen. coun., corp. sec. Nat. Med. Funding Corp., N.Y.C., 1992-94; atty pvt. practice N.Y.C., 1994—. Mem. N.Y. State Bar Assn., Columbia Law Sch. Alumni Assn. (dir. 1966-70). Home: 1036 Park Ave Apt 6D New York NY 10028-0971

**SIEGEL, FREDERIC RICHARD,** geology educator; b. Chelsea, Mass., Feb. 8, 1932; s. Louis and Eva (Minsky) S.; m. Felisa Matilde Puszkin, Mar. 3, 1962; children: Gabriela Davina, Galia Dinah. BA, Harvard U., 1954; MS, U. Kans., 1958, PhD, 1961. Prof. titular Universidad Nacional de Tucuman, Argentina, 1961-63; head geochemistry divsn. Kans. Geol. Survey, Lawrence, 1963-65; assoc. prof. geochemistry George Washington U., Washington, 1965-69, prof., 1969-99, prof. emeritus geology, 1999—; dir. geochemistry program, 1965-99, chmn. dept. geology, 1976-86. Tech. cons. UN Devel. program, Havana, Cuba, 1980. Author: Applied Geochemistry, 1974, Geoquimica Aplicada, 1992, Natural and Anthropogenic Hazards in Development Planning, 1996, Environmental Geochemistry of Potentially Toxic Metals, 2001; co-author: Geochimica Ambientale, 2004; editor: Review of Research on Modern Problems in Geochemistry, 1979. With U.S. Army, 1954-56; ETO. Recipient Erasmus Haworth award Dept. Geology, U. Kans., 1958; Fulbright prof., 1970, Best Paper award Energy Minerals divsn. Am. Assn. Petroleum Geologists, 1989. Mem. Assn. Exploration Geochemists (councillor 1988-95), Geochem. Soc., Internat. Assn. Geochemists and Cosmochemists, Soc. Environ. Geochemistry and Health. Jewish. Home and Office: 4353 Yuma St NW Washington DC 20016-2027 Business E-Mail: nzkara@gwu.edu.

**SIEGEL, GEORGE HENRY,** management consultant; b. Bklyn., Oct. 8, 1926; s. Samuel S. and Sara Siegel; m. Lenore D. Greenberg, Oct. 28, 1951; children: Arthur B., Ellen S. BEE, CCNY, 1948; MS Indsl. Engring. NYU, 1951. Registered profl. engr., N.Y. From engr. to gen. mgr. Gen. Electric Corp., Syracuse, Utica and Binghamton, NY, 1951-74; v.p., gen. mgr. flight systems div. Bendix Corp., 1974-77, chief tech. officer, 1977-79, v.p., gen. mgr. diesel engine controls 1979-82; v.p. group exec. Bendix Automation Co., Cleve., 1983-84; v.p. tech. Allied-Signal Internat., Morristown, NJ, 1984-90; v.p. Volt Tech. Svcs. Co., N.Y.C., 1991-93; pres. Point North Assocs., Inc., Madison, NJ, 1990—. Invited guest lectr. UCLA, 1960-63. Bd. visitors Oakland U., Rochester, Mich., 1977-83. Served with AUS, 1944-46. Mem. IEEE (sr., life, assn. chmn. 1965), Soc. Automotive Engrs. E-mail: siegelgh@att.net.

**SIEGEL, HERBERT BERNARD,** management consultant; b. NYC, Mar. 10, 1934; s. Jacob and Clara Dora (Goldgeier) S.; m. Joan Miriam Goodkin, Nov. 6, 1965; children: Jeffrey Roy, Lori Robin, Amy Hope, Jonathan Stuart. Degree, NYU, 1959, postgrad., 1960-63, Harvard U., Cambridge, Mass., 1975; PhD in Internat. Law, Columbia U., N.Y.C., 1999; postgrad., Coll. of Law of Eng. and Wales, 2003—05. Diplomate Am. Acad. Profl. Cons. and Legal Experts; cert. profl. mgmt. cons.; chartered cons., U.K.; accredited profl. cons. Pres. Emle Industries, Inc., N.Y.C., 1968-72; fed. pres. trustee Toys R Us, N.Y.C., 1973-78; pres. Nat. Silver Co., N.Y.C., 1973-78, F.B. Rogers Silver Co., N.Y.C., 1979-82; pres., chief exec. officer Quaker City Steel Co., 1980-86, Seal-Kap Packaging Co., N.Y.C., 1980-90, J. Ramsey Reese, Inc., Tarrytown, N.Y., 1980-87; pres. Deerhill Devel. Corp., 1980-87, Columbia Profl. Baseball Club, Inc., 1980-87; pres., CEO J.R. Reese Enterprises, Ltd. et al, 1989—91; prin. officer Whitestone Cons. Group, Ltd., 1991—; cons.-in-residence Magrill Bros., Inc. Thesis examiner Grad. Sch. Banking, Rutgers U., 1963-64; chmn. Fin-Tec Corp.; lectr. Grad. Sch. Mgmt. and Orgn., Yale U.; bd. dirs. Swissco Industries, Inc.-Fin-Tec Svc. Corp., Nat. Coin Entertainment Co. Inc., Motorcycle Malls of Am., Inc., Advanced Rehab. Ctrs., Inc., N.Y. Pacific Exch. Ltd., Silvergull Industries Inc., Havemeyer Equities, Inc., Lionville Packing Co., Coast-to-Coast Mktg. Am., Inc., Tritium Card Svcs., Inc., Topps Discount Stores, Inc., White Front Stores, Inc., Magrill Bros., Inc., Interstate Stores, Inc.; trustee Dime Savs. Bank of Williamsburg, N.Y.C., Neisner Bros. Dept. Stores, United Cerebral Palsey, Nassau; expert witness. Author: A Trustee's View of Chapter Ten, 1981, Tomorrow's America, Made Today in the U.S.A., 1993, The Entropy of Government Deficits, 1995, Corporate Rehabilitation After Bankruptcy, 1995, The Masquerade of Cost Cutting, 1996, Market Economics for Multinational Corporations, 1997, International Trade and the Competitive Environment, 1997, Accounting Strategies for Multinational Corporations, 1998, Statistics That Measure the Wealth of Multinational Companies, 1998, Developments and Organizational Behavior in International Business Environments, 1998, Privatization: A Social Milestone or Millstone?, 1999. Served security agy. U.S. Army, 1955—57. Mem.: ABA, Inst. Bus. Appraisers, Prime Raters Fin. Club (pres.), Soc. Profls. in Dispute Resolutions, Turnaround Mgmt. Assn., Am. Soc. Appraisers, N.Y. Acad. Sci., Nat. Assn. Corp. Dirs., Am. Acad. Profl. Consultants and Experts, Am. Bankruptcy Inst., Am. Mgmt. Assn., Internat. Studies Assn., Am. Lawyers Expert Network, Internat. Bar Assn., Am. Cons. League, Mensa, NYU Alumni Club. Office Phone: 516-431-7300. E-mail: herb.whitestone@verizon.net.

**SIEGEL, HERBERT JAY,** communications executive, director; b. Phila., May 7, 1928; s. Jacob and Fritzi (Stern) S.; m. Ann F. Levy, June 29, 1950; children: John C., William D. BA in Journalism, Lehigh U., 1950. Sec., dir. Official Films, Inc., N.Y.C., 1951-54; v.p., dir. Bev-Rich Products, Inc., Phila., 1955-56; chmn. bd. Westley Industries, Inc., Cleve., 1955-58; v.p. Phila. Ice Hockey Club, Inc., 1955-60; chmn. bd. Fort Pitt Industries, Inc., Pitts., 1956-58, Seeburg Corp., 1958-60, Centlivre Brewing Corp., Ft. Wayne, Ind., 1959-61; dir. Baldwin Rubber Co., Pontiac, Mich., Mono-Sol Corp., Gary, Inc., 1959-62; chmn. bd. Baldwin-Montrose Chem. Co., 1960-67; pres., chmn. bd. Gen. Artists Corp., 1960-64, chmn., 1960-62; chmn. bd. pres. Chris-Craft Industries, Inc., 1968—2001; chmn. bd. BHC Comm. Inc., 1977—2001, pres., 1977-96; chmn. bd. dirs. United TV, Inc. 1982—2001, chmn. bd., 1982-96, CEO, 1983-90; bd. dirs. Warner Communications, Inc., 1984-89. Bd. dirs. Piper Aircraft Corp., 1971-77, Paramount Pictures, 1963-64, Harvard-Mahoney Neurosci. Inst., 2000. Bd. dirs. Friends of Israel Defense Forces, 1996—, Research to Prevent Blindness, 2000—, Phoenix House, 1978-81; bd. advisors Vets. Bedside Network, 1980-90; v.p. Friars Nat. Assn. Found., 1980—, Chas. A. Dana Found., Inc., 1996—; trustee Lehigh U., 1989-92, Blair Acad., 1985-92. Named one of Forbes Richest Americans, 2006. Office: News America Inc 767 5th Ave 46th Flr New York NY 10153-0023

**SIEGEL, HERRICK JOVE,** orthopedic surgeon; s. Michael Elliot and Marsha Rose Siegel; m. Joanna Leigh Fein, Jan. 9, 1999; children: Nicholas Ryan, Dylan Andrew. MD, NY U., 1995. Orthopaedic Surgeon Am. Bd. of Orthopedic Surgery, 2005. Asst. prof. surgery U. of Ala., Ala., 2002—, chief, orthopedic oncology, 2002—06. Orthopaedic Oncology fellow, Mayo Clinic, 2000—02. Mem.: Mid-Am. Orthopedic Soc., Musculoskeletal Tumor Soc., Am. Acad. of Orthopedic Surgeons, Am. Acad. of Orthopedic Surgeons (assoc.). Office: Univ of Ala at Birmingham 1530 3rd Ave South Birmingham AL 35294 Office Phone: 205-934-4667. Home Fax: 205-975-5953. Business E-Mail: herrick.siegel@ortho.uab.edu.

**SIEGEL, HOWARD JEROME,** lawyer; b. Chgo., July 29, 1942; s. Leonard and Idele (Lehrner) S.; m. Diane L. Gerber; children: Sari D., Allison J., James G. BS, U. Ill., 1963; JD, Northwestern U., 1966. Bar: Ill. 1966, U.S. Dist. Ct. (no. dist.) Ill. 1967. Assoc. Ancel, Stonesifer & Glink, Chgo., 1966-70; ptnr. Goldstine & Siegel, Summit, Ill., 1970-75; sole practice Chgo., 1975-77; pres. Wexler, Siegel & Shaw, Ltd., Chgo., 1978-82; ptnr. Keck, Mahin & Cate, Chgo., 1982-95, Neal Gerber & Eisenberg, Chgo., 1995-99; counsel Fagel & Haber, Chgo., 1999—. Bd. dirs. various corps. Mem.: ABA, Chgo. Bar Assn., Ill. Bar Assn., Twin Orchard Country Club (Long Grove, Ill.). Office: FabelHaberLLC 55 E Monroe 40th Fl Chicago IL 60603 Office Phone: 312-580-2248. Business E-Mail: hsiegel@fagelhaber.com.

**SIEGEL, IRA T.,** publishing executive; b. N.Y.C., Sept. 23, 1944; s. David Aaron and Rose (Minsky) S.; m. Sharon Ruth Sacks, Sept. 5, 1965. BS, NYU, 1965; MBA, L.I. U., 1968. Bus. mgr. Buttenheim Pub. Co., N.Y.C., 1965-72; corp. v.p. rsch. Cahners Pub. Co. div. Reed Pub. USA, Boston, 1972-86; pres., COO, R.R. Bowker Pub. Co. div. Reed Pub. USA, New Providence, N.J., 1986-91; pres. Martindale-Hubbell div. Reed Pub. USA, New Providence, N.J., 1990-91; pres., CEO Reed Reference Pub. (includes R.R. Bowker Co., Martindale-Hubbell, Nat. Register Pub. Co., The Salesman's Guide, Marquis Who's Who), New Providence, N.J., 1991-95, Lexis-Nexis, Dayton, Ohio, 1995-97. Bd. dirs. Seisint (formerly eData.com), Boca Raton, Fla., 1999-2004.

**SIEGEL, JACK MORTON,** retired pharmaceutical executive; b. Sioux City, Iowa, June 11, 1922; s. Harry and Rose (Perlman) S.; m. Betty Virginia Collins, Feb. 22, 1946 (dec. Feb. 1986); children: Jennifer L. Mastricola, Marjorie G., Thomas A.; m. Dolores E. Williams Kinert, Dec. 20, 1991 BS in Chemistry, UCLA, 1944, PhD in Chemistry, Washington U., St. Louis, 1950. Chemist The Clinton Labs., Oak Ridge, Tenn., 1944-46; asst. prof. chemistry U. Ark. Sch. Medicine, Little Rock, 1950-55; chemist, v.p. P-L Biochems. Inc., Milw., 1955-82; v.p., gen. mgr. Pharmacia P-L Biochems. Inc., Milw., 1982-87, pres., 1987-89. Contbr. articles to profl. jours. Mem. AAAS, Am. Chem. Soc. Democrat. Jewish.

**SIEGEL, JAY STEVEN,** chemistry educator; b. Inglewood, Calif., Aug. 16, 1959; s. Erwin and Jeanne (Strzesak) S. BS, Calif. State U., Northridge, 1980; MA, Princeton U., 1982, PhD, 1985. Researcher Princeton (N.J.) U., 1981-83, 84-85, Eidgenossische Technishche Hochschule, Zürich, Switzerland, 1983-84, U. Louis Pasteur, Strasbourg, France, 1985-86; asst. prof. U. Calif., San Diego, 1986—, Observer, mem. com. on stereochemistry Internat. Union of Pure and Applied Chemists, 1985—. Contbr. articles to sci. jours. Calif. State scholar, 1977-70; Swiss U. grantee, 1983-84, NSF-CNRS Sci. Exchange grantee, 1985-86; named Presdl. Young Investigator NSF 1988—. Mem. Am. Chem. Soc., N.Y. Acad. Sci., Sigma Xi. Office: U Calif San Diego Dept Chemistry B-014 La Jolla CA 92093

**SIEGEL, JEFFREY NORTON,** lawyer; b. NYC, Nov. 27, 1942; s. George Siegel and Rose (Friedman) Gerber; m. Judith Sharon Chused, June 11, 1966; children: Daniel, Linda. AB, Brown U., 1964; LLB, Harvard U., 1967. Bar: N.Y. 1968. Assoc., ptnr. Golenbock & Barell, N.Y.C., 1967—89; ptnr. Whitman & Ransom, N.Y.C., 1990—93, Shack Siegel Katz & Flaherty, P.C., N.Y.C., 1993—2005; with Blank Rome LLP, N.Y.C., 2005—. Mem. bus. com. The Jewish Mus. Mem. ABA, Assn. Bar City N.Y. (com. securities regulation 1987-90, com. profl. responsibility 1979-84), Phi Beta Kappa. Home: 975 Park Ave New York NY 10028-0323 Office: Blank Rome LLP 405 Lexington Ave New York NY 10174-0002 Business E-Mail: jsiegel@blankrome.com.

**SIEGEL, JEREMY JAMES,** financial analyst, educator; b. Chgo., Nov. 14, 1945; s. Bernard G. and Gertrude (Levite) S.; m. Ellen Ruth Schwartz, Jan. 14, 1980; children: Andrew M., Jeffrey Eric. BA, Columbia U., 1967; PhD, MIT, 1971. Asst. prof. bus. econs. Grad. Sch. Bus. U. Chgo., 1972-76; assoc. prof. fin. Wharton Sch. Bus. U. Pa., Phila., 1976—86, prof. fin. Wharton Sch. Bus., 1986—98, Russell E. Palmer Prof. Fin. Wharton Sch. Bus., 1998—. Macroecons. coord. The Morgan Bank, (Now J.P. Morgan) N.Y.C., 1984-99;

acad. dir. Securities Industry Inst., 1987- Author: Revolution on Wall Street, 1993, Stocks for the Long Run, 1994, 98, 02, Future for Investors, 2005; contbr. numerous articles to profl. jours NSF fellow, 1971-72; recipient Graham and Dodd award Assn. Investment Mgmt., 1992, Nicolas Molodovsky award CFI Inst., 2005; voted best bus. sch. prof. Bus. Week mag., 1994. Office: U Pa Wharton Sch Dept Fin Philadelphia PA 19104

SIEGEL, KENNETH S., lawyer, director; BA Cornell U., 1977; JD, NYU, 1980. Assoc. Cravath Swaine & Moore, NYC, 1980—85, O'Sullivan Graev & Karabell LLP, NYC, 1985—87, ptnr., 1987—94, Baker & Botts LLP, NYC, 1994—97; sr. v.p., gen. counsel Cognizant Corp., Westport, Conn., 1997—98, IMS Health, Westport, Conn., 1998—2000, Gartner Group, Stamford, Conn., 2000; exec. v.p., gen. counsel Starwood Hotels and Resorts Worldwide Inc., White Plains, NY, 2000—, sec., 2001—, chief administrv. officer, gen. counsel, 2006—. Office: Starwood Hotels & Resorts Worldwide Inc 1111 Westchester Ave White Plains NY 10604

SIEGEL, KRISTI ELLEN, language educator; b. Breckenridge, Minn., Jan. 2, 1951; d. Dennis Elton and Cleo Ardell Hjalmer; m. Ronald Siegel, Sept. 30, 1978; children: Aaron, Adam, Ross, Elizabeth. PhD, U. Wis., Milw., 1991. Lectr. Mt. Mary Coll., Milw., 1992-99, asst. prof., 1999—2002, assoc. prof., 2002—, chair dept. English, 2003—, chair divsn. langs., lit. and comm. Author: Word 97 Fundamentals for the Workplace, 1998, Women's Autobiographies, Culture, Feminism, 1999, 2d edit., 2001, Excel 97/Power Point 97 for the Workplace, 1999; editor: Issues in Travel Writing: Empire, Spectacle, and Displacement, 2002, Gender, Genre and Identity in Women's Travel Writing, 2004; contbg. author: Special Needs Adoption Network: A Series on Adoption and Foster Care Issues, 2000. Mem.: MLA, AAUW (bd. dirs.), Internat. Soc. Travel Writing (steering com.), Soc. Tech. Comm., Autobiography Assn., Nat. Coun. Tchrs. English. Avocations: writing, music, tennis. Office: Mt Mary Coll 2900 N Menomonee River Pky Milwaukee WI 53222 Home: W223 N2257 Meadowood Ln Waukesha WI 53186-1182 Office Phone: 414-258-4810 ext 395. E-mail: siegelkr@mtmary.edu.

SIEGEL, LAURIE, human resources specialist; married; 2 children. B of Gen. Studies, U. Mich.; MBA, Harvard U. Dir. global compensation Avon Products; prin. Strategic Compensation Assocs.; various positions in human resources Honeywell Internat., 1995—2003; sr. v.p. human resources Tyco Internat. Ltd., Princeton, NJ, 2003—. Bd. dirs. Hayes Lemmerz Internat., Inc. Office: Tyco International PO Box 5260 Princeton NJ 08543-5260 Office Phone: 609-720-4200. Office Fax: 603-720-4208.

SIEGEL, LLOYD HARVEY, architect, real estate developer, consultant; b. NYC, Nov. 27, 1928; s. Saul M. and Lillian (Bell) Siegel; m. Margot Kopsidas Phillips, Oct. 25, 1987. BArch, Princeton U., 1949; MArch, MIT, 1953. Registered architect, N.Y., N.J., Conn., Ohio, Ill., Mich., cert. Nat. Coun. Archtl. Registration Bds. Designer Skidmore, Owings & Merrill, then I. M. Pei & Assocs., then Antonin Raymond, N.Y.C., 1955-60; assoc. Kelly & Gruzen, N.Y.C., 1960-66; dep. health svcs. adminstr. City of N.Y., 1966-70; dep. exec. dir. health and hosps. governing commn. Cook County, Chgo., 1970-76; prin. L.H.S. Cons. in Health Planning, Facility Design & Mgmt., Washington, 1976—, Siegel & Schroeder, P.C., Chgo., 1983-87; dir. Office Architecture & Engring. VA, Washington, 1987-94, dir. Facilities Quality Office, 1994-98, dir. Facilities Mgmt. Svc. Delivery Office, 1999-2001; dir. Facilities Strategic Mgmt. Office, 2001—. Prin. Yacht Harbor Devel. Co., South Haven, Mich., 1983—88, Siegel & Schroeder Developers Inc., Chgo., 1983—88; mem. adv. coms. HEW; mem. pub. adv. panels GSA; mem. adv. com. Legislature State of Ill.; mem. fellowship evaluation com. AIA-Am. Hosp. Assn.; mem. tech. adv. com. Northeastern Ill. Planning Commn.; chmn. Com. Architecture for Health, 1984. Author: (book) Hidden Asset? Interstitial Space, A Critical Evaluation, 1987; photography (permanent collections) Met. Mus. Art, N.Y.C., Mus. Modern Art, others; prin. works include N.Y. World's Fair Spanish Pavillion, N.Y.C. (N.Y. chpt. AIA award, 1964), Williams Meml. Residence, Flushing, N.Y. (Queens C. of C. award, 1964), Hebrew Home for Aged, Riverdale, N.Y. (Bronx C. of C. award, 1966). Recipient Presdl. Fed. Design Achievement award, Pres.'s award, Nat. Inst. Bldg. Scis., 2002; Fulbright fellow, Università di Roma, 1954, Politecnico di Milano, 1955. Fellow: AIA; mem.: Urban Land Inst., Univ. Club, Cosmos Club, Arts Club. Avocations: micology, micophagy, oenology. Home: 3133 Connecticut Ave NW Washington DC 20008-5147 Office: VA 810 Vermont Ave NW Washington DC 20420-0001

SIEGEL, LOUIS PENDLETON, forest products executive; b. Richmond, Va., Nov. 6, 1942; s. John Boschen Jr. and Francis Beale (Tyler) S.; m. Nancy Dicks Blanton, Apr. 10, 1974 (dec. July 1976); m. Nancy Northon, June 26, 1982; children: Kathryn Tyler. AB in Econs., Dartmouth Coll., 1967. Asst. cashier, security researcher First Nat. Citibank, N.Y.C., 1967-71; v.p. security rsch. Drexel Burnham Lambert, N.Y.C., 1971-79; with Potlatch Corp., San Francisco and Spokane, Wash., 1979—, sr. v.p. fin. and adminstrn. San Francisco, 1989, group v.p. wood products and corp. planning, 1989-92, group v.p. pulp and paperboard and corp. planning, 1992-93, exec. v.p. pulp-based ops. and corp. planning, 1993-94, pres., COO San Francisco and Spokane, Wash., 1994-99, also bd. dirs. Spokane, CEO, 1999—2006, chmn., 1999—. Bd. dirs. San Francisco Fed. Corp., 1985-96. Pres., bd. dirs. Bay Area Sci. Fair, San Francisco, 1989-90; trustee Am. Forest Found., 1999-, chmn. trustees, 2000-; bd. dirs. Nat. Coun. for Air and Stream Improvement, 1999-, chmn. bd., 2003-06; pres. Area One, Boy Scouts Am., 2003-05. With USCG, 1964-65. Mem.: Am. Forest and Paper Assn. (bd. dirs. 1999—). Republican. Episcopalian. Avocations: golf, fishing. Office: Potlatch Corp 601 W Riverside Ave Ste 1100 Spokane WA 99201-0603 Office Phone: 509-835-1565.

SIEGEL, LUCY BOSWELL, public relations executive; b. NYC, July 5, 1950; d. Werner Leiser and Carol (Fleisher) Boswell; m. Henry Winter Siegel, Nov. 11, 1979 (div.); children: David Alan Siegel, Joshua Adam Siegel. BA, Conn. Coll., 1972. Assoc. editor Conn. Western, Litchfield, Conn., 1972-73; assoc. editor, editor United Bus. Publ., NYC, 1974—78; mgr. external communications Equitable Life Assurance Soc., NYC, 1978—86; mgr. internat. affairs Cosmo Pub. Rels. Corp., Tokyo, 1986-87, dir. internat. affairs, 1987-88, pres. NYC, 1988—90, Siegel Assocs. Internat., NYC, 1990—97; sr. v.p. Lobsenz Stevens, NYC, 1997—99; sr. prin., mng. dir. Publicis Dialog, NYC, 1999—2000, exec. v.p., group mng. dir., 2000—04; pres., CEO Bridge Global Strategies LLC, NYC, 2004—. Contbr. articles to jours. and mags. Bd. dirs. NYC chpt. Am. Jewish Com., 1993—, sec. 1993-05. Mem. Pub. Rels. Soc. Am. (treas., dir. NYC, v.p. NYC chpt. 2004—, exec. bd. internat. sect. 2004) Women Execs. in Pub. Rels. (bd. dirs. 1997-99), Inst. Pub. Rels. (mktg. com. mem., 2004-). Democrat. Jewish. Home: 41 W 96th St Apt 12B New York NY 10025-6519 Office: 15th Fl 575 Lexington Ave New York NY 10022

SIEGEL, MARC MONROE, television producer, scriptwriter, director; b. N.Y.C., Dec. 8, 1916; s. Isaac and Annie N. (Natelson) S.; m. Anne Dorothy Fishman, Sept. 8, 1940; 1 son, Peter Kieve. BA, Washington Sq. Coll., 1936; MA, N.Y. U. Sch. Edn., 1938. Free-lance mag. writer, especially for New Yorker mag. 1948-50; writer: Eternal Light radio series, NBC, N.Y.C., 1950-60; writer-dir-producer: Directions, ABC-TV, N.Y.C., 1961-78; exec. producer chief writer: Heritage: Civilization and the Jews, WNET, N.Y.C., 1978-84; author: feature screenplays A Child is Crying, 1961, The Young Adventurers, 1963; ABC News Bicentennial spls. Rendezvous With Freedom, 1973, The Right to Believe, 1975, The Will to Be Free, 1976; ABC News feature The Panama Canal, 1977 (Writers Guild award); (Recipient numerous awards, including: Edinburgh Film Festival award 1948, Venice Film Festival award 1962, Cannes Film Festival award 1964, Eternal Light award Jewish Theol. Sem. award 1969). Served with USAAF, 1943-45. Peabody award, 1979, 84; Gabriel award Nat. Assn. Catholic Broadcasters, 1979; Emmy award, 1984, Christopher award, 1984; also several awards Freedoms Found. Mem. Nat. Acad. TV Arts and Scis., Writers Guild Am. East (council 1972-73, 78-79, 84-88, awards 1959, 73, 78, 85, Jablow Meml. award 1984, advisor on Writing Jour. 1993—), Dirs. Guild Am. Democrat. Home: 75 Central Park W New York NY 10023-6011 Office Phone: 212-787-7326.

SIEGEL, MARK S., energy executive; b. 1951; BA magna cum laude, Colgate U.; JD, U. Calif., Berkeley. Exec. v.p. Shamrock Holdings, Inc., 1988—92; pres. music divsn. Blockbuster Entertainment Corp., 1992—93; founder, pres. Remy Investors and Consultants, Inc, LA, 1993—; chmn. bd., dir. UTI Energy Corp., 1995—2001, Patterson-UTI Energy Inc., Snyder, Tex., 2001—. Mem. bd. trustees J. Paul Getty Trusy, 2005—. Office: Patterson-UTI Energy Inc 4510 Lamesa Hwy Snyder TX 79549 Office Phone: 325-574-6300. Office Fax: 325-574-6390.*

SIEGEL, MARVIN, newspaper editor; b. NYC, June 23, 1935; s. Murray and Belle (Diamond) S.; 1 child, Joshua Murray. BA, U. Mich., 1957. Reporter The Record, Hackensack, NJ, 1957-59; free-lance writer Western Europe, 1960-62; reporter Fairchild Publs., N.Y.C., 1962-63; editor The World Telegram, N.Y.C., 1963-66; copy editor The N.Y. Times, 1966-67, asst. met. editor, 1967-76, founding editor Weekend sect., 1976-82; founding editor World of N.Y., 1982-86; founding editor Edn. Life The N.Y. Times, 1986, dep. editor Week in Rev., 1987, culture news editor, 1988-92, dep. editor Book Rev., 1992-95; asst. to mng. editor, 1995—. Co-author: The World of New York, 1985, The New York Times Great Lives of the 20th Century, 1988; editor: Deadly Sins, 1994, The Last Word: The New York Times Book of Obituaries and Farewells, 1997; Judge Turks and Caicos Internat. Film Festival, 2004, Dubrovnik Internat. Film Festival, 2005. Pfc. U.S. Army. Jewish. Office: NY Times Co 229 W 43d St New York NY 10036-3913 Business E-Mail: marvins@nytimes.com.

SIEGEL, MARY ANN GARVIN, writer; b. Louisville, Apr. 3, 1944; d. Samuel Hughes and Ann Wendell (Smith) Garvin; m. Charles Holladay Siegel, Sept. 2, 1967 (div.); children: Emily Hughes, Charles Holladay, Jr., Margaret Shafer. BA, Conn. Coll., 1966. Photog. rschr. Time Inc., NYC, 1966—67, Nat. Geog. Soc., Washington, 1967—68; content author and editor FundraisingINFO.com, 2000—01. Leadership Atlanta, 1993-94, exec. com., 1995-96. Trustee Conn. Coll., New London, 1985-90; chair Friends of Spelman Coll., Atlanta, 1990-92; active Atlanta/Fulton County adv. bd. United Way Met. Atlanta, 1994-96; Olympic Envoy to Republic of Nauru, Atlanta Com. Olympic Games, 1994-96; formerly active adv. bd. N.C. Outward Bound Sch., Asheville. Recipient Agnes Berkeley Leahy award Conn. Coll. Alumni Assn., 1991. Personal E-mail: seagullwrite@yahoo.com.

SIEGEL, MICHAEL ALAN, dental educator; b. Balt., Feb. 6, 1953; s. Harold W. and Ellen Rosenbach Siegel; m. Sharon Crane, July 22, 1979; 1 child, Sarah Emily. BS, U. Md., College Park, 1975; DDS, Balt. Coll. of Dental Surgery, 1979; MS, U. Md., Balt., 1986. Diplomate Am. Bd. of Oral Medicine, 1988. Resident Walter Reed Army Hosp., 1980—82, intern in dentistry and gen. practice, 1982; assoc. prof. oral medicine Balt. Coll. of Dental Sugery, Balt., 1982—2002; assoc. prof. dermatology U. Md. Med. Sch., Balt., 1991—2002; assoc. faculty mem. Grad. Sch., U. Md., Balt., 2002; prof. and chmn. dept. of diagnostic scis. Nova Southeastern U. Coll. of Dental Medicine, Ft. Lauderdale, Fla., 2003—. Cons. Balt. VA Hosp., 1982—2002; mem. editl. bd. Oral Surgery, Oral Medicine, Oral Pathology, Oral Radiology and Endodontics, 1992—. Presenter (400+ continuing dental education courses) Current Concepts in Oral Medicine; author: (100+ articles, chapters and abstracts) Oral Medicine. Capt. U.S. Army Dental Corps, 1979—82, Washington, D.C. Fellowship, Acad. Gen. Dentistry, 1986. Fellow: Acad. Gen. Dentistry, Am. Acad. Oral Medicine (bd. trustees 1990—2003, pres. 2000—02); mem.: ADA (chmn. coun. sci. affairs 2002—03), Internat. Assn. for Dental Rsch., Omicron Kappa Upsilon (pres. 1999—2000). Achievements include research in over $3,000,000 in research funding. Office: Nova Southeastern Univ 3200 S University Dr Fort Lauderdale FL 33328-2018 Office Phone: 954-262-4309. Business E-Mail: masiegel@nova.edu.

SIEGEL, MICHAEL ELLIOT, nuclear medicine physician, educator; b. NYC, May 13, 1942; s. Benjamin and Rose (Gilbert) S.; m. Marsha Rose Snower, Mar. 20, 1966; children: Herrick Jove, Meridith Ann. AB, Cornell U., 1964; MD, Chgo. Med. Sch., 1968. Diplomate Nat. Bd. Med. Examiners. Intern Cedars-Sinai Med. Ctr., L.A., 1968-69, resident in radiology, 1969-70; NIH fellow in radiology Temple U. Med. Ctr., Phila., 1970-71; NIH fellow in nuclear medicine Johns Hopkins U. Sch. Medicine, Balt., 1971-73, asst. prof. radiology, 1972-76; assoc. prof. radiology and medicine U. So. Calif., L.A., 1976—, prof. radiology, 1989—, dir. divsn. nuclear medicine, 1982-99. Dir. Sch. Nuclear Medicine, Los Angeles County-U. So. Calif. Med. Ctr., 1976-99; dir. divsn. nuclear medicine Kenneth Norris Cancer Hosp. and Rsch. Ctr., L.A., 1983-99; dir. dept. nuclear medicine Orthopaedic Hosp., L.A., 1981-2006, Intercmty. Hosp., Covina, Calif., 1981-2006, U. So. Calif. Univ. Hosp., L.A., 1993—; clin. prof. radiology U. Calif., San Diego, 2000—. Author: Textbook of Nuclear Medicine, 1978, Vascular Surgery, 1983, 88, numerous other textbooks; editor: Nuclear Cardiology, 1981, Vascular Disease: Nuclear Medicine, 1983. Mem. Maple Ctr., Beverly Hills. Served as maj. USAF, 1974-76. Recipient Outstanding Alumnus award Chgo. Med. Sch., 1991. Fellow Am. Coll. Nuclear Medicine (sci. investigator 1974, 76, nominations com. 1980, program com. 1983, trustee 1993, disting. fellow 1993, bd. reps. 1993—, bd. dirs. 1994—, treas. 1996—, chmn. ann. sci. program 1996—, pres.'s award 1997, v.p. 1997-98, pres. 1999—, CEO 2005—); mem. Nuclear Medicine (sci. exhbn. com. 1978-79, program com. 1979-80, Silver medal 1975), Calif. Med. Assn. (sci. adv. bd. 1987—), Radiol. Soc. N.Am., Soc. Nuclear Magnetic Resonance Imaging, Friars So. Calif., Alpha Omega Alpha. Achievements include research on development of nuclear medicine techniques to treat recurrent joint effussions, evaluate cardiovascular disease and diagnose and treat cancer; clinical utilization of video digital displays in nuclear medicine development; invention of pneumatic radiologic pressure system. Office: U So Calif Med Ctr Rm 5250 1200 N State St Los Angeles CA 90033-1029 Business E-Mail: mesiegel@usc.edu.

SIEGEL, NATHANIEL HAROLD, sociology educator; b. Bklyn., May 17, 1929; s. Victor and Yetta (Kogel) S.; m. Annabelle Replansky, Mar. 3, 1958; children— Anthony, Jennifer. AB, Bklyn. Coll., 1950; A.M., N.Y.U., 1952, PhD, 1956. Asst. prof. sociology Columbia, 1956-59; sociologist Hillside Hosp., Queens, NY, 1958-63; assoc. dir. behavioral research N.Y.C. Dept. Health, 1963-64; chief social sci. tng. sect. NIMH, 1964-67, cons., 1970-79; prof. sociology Queens Coll., 1967-79, chmn. dept., 1973-77, v.p., dean faculty, 1970-74, provost, 1974-77, acting pres., 1977-78; sr. v.p. acad. affairs SUNY Purchase, 1979-94; prof. sociology SUNY, 1979-2000, prof. emeritus, 2000—. Served with M.C. AUS, 1950-51. Home: 8 Birchfield Rd Larchmont NY 10538-1505

SIEGEL, PAUL, judge; b. Troy, NY, May 7, 1938; s. Benjamin and Mary (Silverman) S.; 1 child, Mark Aron; m. Janique Auvertin, Apr. 30, 1994. BS in Physics magna cum laude, U. Miami, 1958, LLB cum laude, 1962. Bar: Fla. 1963, DC 1964, U.S. Supreme Ct. 1967, U.S. Ct. Appeals (5th cir.) 1967, U.S. Ct. Appeals (11th cir.) 1982; cert. civil trial lawyer Fla. Bar. Mem. gen. counsel's office AEC, Washington, 1962-65; ptnr. Sinclair, Louis, Siegel, Heath, Nussbaum & Zavertnik, P.A., Miami, Fla., 1972-91; judge Dade County (Fla.) Cir. Ct., 1991—. Author: Florida Trial Objections, 2004; editor-in-chief, exec. editor: U. Miami Law Rev. Chmn. bd. dirs. Alliance Francaise of Dade County, 1983-87, pres., 1990-92; pres. Pro-Mozart Soc. Greater Miami, 1984-92. Home: 235 E San Marino Dr Miami FL 33139-1151 Office: Lawson E Thomas Courthouse Ctr 175 NW 1st Ave Ste 2019 Miami FL 33128 Office Phone: 305-349-5726. E-mail: psiegel@jud11.flcourts.org.

SIEGEL, RANDY, publishing executive; BA with honors, Wesleyan U.; MBA, Yale U., 1988. Pub., editor Cleveland Free Times; mktg. mgr. Washington Post; mktg. dir. Newsweek; pres. Venturion, Ltd; cons. Parade, 1999—2001, sr. v.p., 2001—03, assoc. publ., 2003, exec. v.p., pub., 2003—04, pres., pub., 2004—. Siegel's bus. experience includes the launches of Newsweek Interactive, HearSay mag. (a nat. coll. music publ.) and BrassRing.com, a joint venture among The Washington Post, Tribune Co. and Accel Ptnrs.; a major contbr. to Parade's strong positioning in the marketplace; led the sales, mktg. and comm. efforts for The Great Am. Bake Sale, a new program presented jointly by Parade and Share Our Strength, a leading nat. anti-hunger orgn.; he cemented a partnership with ESPN.com to create a program including sales, mktg. opportunities, and the All-Am. HS Sports program; mem. exec. com. The Quills. Office: Parade Publ Inc 711 3rd Ave New York NY 10017-4014 Office Phone: 212-450-0980. Office Fax: 212-450-7091. Business E-Mail: randolph_siegel@parade.com.*

SIEGEL, REVA, law educator; BA, Yale U., 1978, MPhil, 1982, JD, 1986. Law clk. for Hon. Spottswood W. Robinson, III, US Ct. Appeals, Washington, DC, 1986—87; acting prof. U. Calif., Berkeley, 1988—94; vis. prof. Yale U., New Haven, 1993—94, prof. law, 1994—99, Nicholas deB. Katzenbach prof., 1999—. Vis. prof. Harvard Law Sch., 1998—99, Columbia U., 2001—02. Co-editor: Directions in Sexual Harassment Law, 2004; contbr. articles to law jours. Office: Yale Law Sch PO Box 208215 New Haven CT 06520 E-mail: reva.siegel@yale.edu.

SIEGEL, RICHARD DAVID, lawyer, former government official; b. Lewistown, Pa., Oct. 13, 1939; s. Robert and Pearl Eleanor (Nieman) S.; m. Marjorie Esther Greenwald, Mar. 13, 1966; children— Andrew, Jonathan, Michele. BA, U. Pa., 1960; JD, Harvard U., 1963. Bar: Pa., D.C., U.S. Supreme Ct. Staff writer Phila. Inquirer, 1964-66; spl. asst. U.S. Rep. Richard Schweiker, Washington, 1966-69; legis. counsel U.S. Senator Richard Schweiker, Washington, 1969-71; assoc. minority counsel Senate Com. on Labor and Human Resources, Washington, 1971-73; sole practice Washington, 1978-79; mem. various firms, 1973-78, 80-81; dep. asst. sec. for natural resources and environment USDA, Washington, 1981-87; pvt. practice, Washington, 1987—. Contbr. articles to profl. jours. Treas. Com. for Senator Schweiker, Washington, 1974-77; v.p. Tifereth Israel Congregation, Washington, 1980-82, 93-99, 2004-05; sec.-treas. North Am.-Israel Hort. Found., 1987-95. With USCGR, 1963-64. Mem. ABA, FBA, Pa. Bar Assn., Assn. Former Senate Aides. Republican. Jewish. Home: 3141 Aberfoyle Pl NW Washington DC 20015-2325 Office: 1400 16th St NW Washington DC 20036-2220 Office Phone: 202-518-6364. E-mail: rsiegel@ofwlaw.com

SIEGEL, RICHARD LAWRENCE, immunologist, allergist; b. Miami, Fla., Jan. 22, 1949; MD, Washington U., St. Louis, 1977; also PhD. Diplomate Am. Bd. Allergy and Immunology, Am. Bd. Diagnostic Lab. Immunology, Am. Bd. Pediats. Resident in pediats. Children's Hosp. Med. Ctr., Boston, 1977-79, fellow in allergy and immunology, 1979-81; allergist U. Comm. Hosp., Tampa, Fla. Fellow AIS, Am. Coll. Allergy, Asthma and Immunology; mem. Am. Acad. Pediats., Am. Acad. Allergy and Immunology. Office: 3450 E Fletcher Ave Ste 210 Tampa FL 33613-4600 Office Phone: 813-972-3131.

SIEGEL, ROBERT, heat transfer engineer; b. Cleve., July 10, 1927; s. Morris and Mollie (Binder) S.; m. Elaine Jane Jaffe, July 19, 1951; children: Stephen, Lawrence. BS, Case Inst. Tech., 1950, MS, 1951; ScD, MIT, 1953. Heat transfer engr. GE, Schenectady, NY, 1953-54; heat transfer analyst Knolls Atomic Power Lab., Schenectady, 1954-55; rsch. scientist NASA Lewis Rsch. Ctr., Cleve., 1955-99; tech. cons., 1999—. Adj. prof. U. Toledo, 1981, 85, 95, adj. prof. mech. engring. U. Akron (Ohio), 1987, adj. prof. mech. engring. Cleve. State U., 1989, 91; mem. adv. coun. U. Akron, 1989-96. Author: Thermal Radiation Heat Transfer, 1972, 4th edit., 2002; tech. editor ASME, 1973-83, AIAA, 1986-98; author numerous sci. papers. With U.S. Army, 1945-47. Recipient Exceptional Sci. Achievement medal NASA, 1986, Space Act award, 1993, ASME-AIChE Max Jakob Meml. award, 1996. Fellow ASME (Heat Transfer Meml. award 1970, Max Jakob Bd. of award 1999-2002), AIAA (Thermophysics award 1993); mem. Sigma Xi, Tau Beta Pi. Avocations: ballroom dancing, piano. Home and Office: 3052 Warrington Rd Shaker Heights OH 44120-2425

SIEGEL, ROBERT (BOB) A., lawyer; AB with great distinction, U. Calif., Berkeley, 1971; JD magna cum laude, U. Mich. Bar: Calif. Ptnr. O'Melveny & Myers LLP, LA, vice-chair, head, chair labor and employment law dept., mem. policy com. Tchr., lectr. ALI-ABA, Am. Arbitration Assn., Practising Law Inst. Sr. editor The Railway Labor Act (BNA). Mem.: ABA (labor and employment law sect., equal opportunity com., railway and airline labor law com. (past co-chmn.)), Order of the Coif, Phi Beta Kappa. Office: O'Melveny & Myers LLP 400 S Hope St Los Angeles CA 90071 Office Phone: 213-430-6005. Office Fax: 213-430-6407. Business E-Mail: rsiegel@omm.com.

SIEGEL, ROBERT CHARLES, broadcast journalist; b. NYC, June 26, 1947; s. Joseph and Edith Ruth (Joffe) S.; m. Jane Claudia Schwartz, June 17, 1973; children: Erica Anne, Leah Harriet. BA, Columbia U., 1968, postgrad. sch. journalism, 1969-70. Newscaster Sta. WGLI, Babylon, N.Y., 1968-69; reporter, news dir. Sta. WRVR-FM, N.Y., 1971-76; assoc. producer, editor Nat. Pub. Radio, Washington, 1976-78, sr. editor, 1976-79, dir. news and info., 1983-87, host All Things Considered, 1987—, sr. editor London, 1979-83. Host Ea. Europe: Breaking with the Past, The Learning Channel, Washington, 1990, Earth Scope, Arlington, Va., 1990-91. Editor: The NPR Interviews. Recipient DuPont-Columbia award Columbia U., 1984. Jewish. Avocations: reading, golf, baseball. Home: 1340 19th Rd S Arlington VA 22202-1637 Office: Nat Pub Radio All Things Considered 635 Massachusetts Ave NW Washington DC 20001-3753 E-mail: rsiegel@npr.org.

SIEGEL, ROBERT HAROLD, English literature educator, writer; b. Aug. 18, 1939; married; 3 children. Student, Denison U., 1957-59; BA in English, Wheaton Coll., 1961; MA, Johns Hopkins U., 1962; PhD in English, Harvard U., 1968. Instr. Dartmouth Coll., 1967-68, asst. prof., 1968-75; vis. lectr. Princeton (N.J.) U., 1975-76; poet-in-residence, McManes vis. prof. Wheaton (Ill.) Coll., 1976; asst. prof. U. Wis., Milw., 1976-79, assoc. prof. English, 1979-83, prof. 1983—, prof. emeritus, 1999—. Poet on faculty Summer Writers' Inst., Wheaton Coll., 1980, Wesleyan U., 1982, 83, New Eng. Young Writers Conf., 2002-2006; vis. prof. J. W. v. Goethe U., Frankfurt, Fed. Republic Germany, 1985; lectr., reader various univs. Author: (fiction) Alpha Centauri, 1980, Whalesong, 1981, The Kingdom of Wundle, 1982, White Whale, 1991, The Ice at the End of the World, 1994; (poetry) The Beasts and the Elders, 1973, In A Pig's Eye, 1980, The Waters Under the Earth, 2005, A Pentecost of Finches: New and Selected Poems, 2006; contbr. poems to Atlantic Monthly, Sewanee Rev., other jours. Recipient Margaret O'Loughlin Foley award Am. mag., 1970, award Cliff Dwellers' Arts Found., 1974, Chgo. Poetry prize Soc. Midland Authors, 1974, Poetry prize Prairie Schooner, 1977, Jacob Glatstein Meml. prize Poetry mag., 1977, award Ingram Merrill Found., 1979, Gold medallion ECPA, 1981, Book of Yr. award Campus Life mag., 1981, 1st Pl. prize for juvenile fiction Coun. for Wis. Writers, 1981, 1st Pl. prize poetry Soc. Midland Authors, 1981, Matson award Friends of Lit., 1982, Golden Archer award Sch. Libr. Assn., U. Wis., Oshkosh, 1986, 1st prize Milton Ctr. Poetry Contest, 1994, ERA 1st place in poetry, 2003; Dartmouth Coll. faculty fellow, 1971; Gilman fellow Johns Hopkins U., 1961-62; tchg. fellow Harvard U., 1965-67, Yaddo Artists' Colony, 1974, 75, Transatlantic Rev. fellow Bread Loaf Writers Conf., 1974, Nat. Endowment for Arts, 1980; grantee U. Wis., 1978, 84, 88-89, 96-97. Office: U Wis English Dept Milwaukee WI 53201 Business E-Mail: grindel@msn.com, siegelrh@uwm.edu.

SIEGEL, SAMUEL, metals company executive; b. Elizabeth, N.J., Oct. 30, 1930; s. Morris and Anna (Fader) S.; m. Raenea Kershenbaum, Mar. 29, 1953; children: Daryl Lynn, Annie Roslyn. BBA, CUNY, 1952. CPA, N.Y. Cost accountant Seaporcel Metals, Inc., Long Island City, NY, 1955-56; asst. to controller Deltown Foods, Inc., Yonkers, NY, 1956-57; sr. accountant Touche Ross, N.Y.C., 1957-61; corp. treas. chmn., chief fin. officer, treas., sec., dir. Nucor Corp., Charlotte, NC, 1961-99; ret., 2000. Mem. AICPA, Am. Soc. Corp. Secs., Fin. Execs. Inst. Office: 3421 Windbluff Dr Charlotte NC 28277-9850 Office Phone: 704-542-8000.

SIEGEL, SHELDON C., pediatrician, immunologist, allergist; b. Mpls., Jan. 30, 1922; s. Carl S.; m. Priscilla Rikess, Mar. 3, 1946; children— Linda, Nancy. AA, Va. Jr. Coll., 1940; BA, BS, U. Minn., 1942, MD, 1945. Intern U. Minn. Hosp., 1946, resident in pediatrics, 1947-48; fellow in pediatric allergy Rochester, NY, 1949-50; practice medicine specializing in pediatric allergy and pediatrics St. Paul, 1950-52, San Antonio, 1952-54, Los Angeles, 1954—; clin. instr. pediatrics U. Rochester, 1949-50, U. Minn., 1950-51; asst. prof. pediatrics U. Tex., 1952-54; asst. clin. prof. U. Calif. at Los Angeles Med. Sch., 1955, clin. assoc. prof., 1957-62, clin. prof., 1963—, co-chief pediatric allergy clinic, 1957—. Editorial bd.: Jour. Allergy, 1973-75; contbr. articles to med. jours. Fellow Am. Acad. Allergy (pres. 1974), Am. Coll. Allergists, Am. Acad. Pediatrics; mem. AMA, Allergy Found. Am. (pres. 1976), Calif. Med. Assn., Los Angeles County Med. Assn., L.A. Pediatric Soc., Calif. Soc. Allergy, L.A. Soc. Allergy, Western Pediatric Rsch. Soc., Am. Bd. Med. Specialists, Sigma Xi. Office: 11620 Wilshire Blvd Los Angeles CA 90025-1706 Office Phone: 310-312-5050.

**SIEGEL, STANLEY,** lawyer, educator; b. NYC, Mar. 2, 1941; s. David Aaron and Rose (Minsky) S. BS summa cum laude, NYU, 1960; JD magna cum laude, Harvard U., 1963. Bar: N.Y. 1963, D.C. 1964, Mich. 1970, Calif. 1976; CPA, Md. Atty. Office Sec. of Air Force 1963-66; asst. prof. law U. Mich., Ann Arbor, 1966-69, assoc. prof., 1969-71, prof., 1971-74; ptnr. Honigman, Miller, Schwartz & Cohn, Detroit, 1974-76; prof. law UCLA, 1976-86, NYU, 1986—; assoc. dean, 1987-89. Vis. prof. Stanford Law Sch., 1973, Ctrl. European U., Budapest, 1993—2001, U. Konstanz, Germany, 1996, Tel Aviv U., 1998; fellow Max-Planck Inst., Hamburg, 1988; cons. reorgn. U.S. Postal Svc., 1969—71; exec. sec. Mich. Law Revision Commn., 1973; mem. bd. examiners AICPA, 1980—83. Author: (with Schulman and Moscow) Michigan Business Corporations, 1979, (with Conard and Knauss) Enterprise Organization, 4th edit., 1987, (with D. Siegel) Accounting and Financial Disclosure: A Guide to Basic Concepts, 1983, (with others) Swiss Company Law, 1996; mem. editl. bd. Lexis Electronic Author's Press, 1996-98. Served to capt. USAF, 1963-66. Mem. ABA, D.C. Bar Assn., Calif. Bar Assn., Assn. of Bar of City of N.Y., Am. Law Inst., AICPA. Office: NYU Law Sch 40 Washington Sq S New York NY 10012-1099

**SIEGEL, STEPHEN,** real estate company executive; Doctorate (hon.), Monmouth U., 2003, Baruch Coll., 2003. Chmn., CEO Insignia; global chmn. CB Richard Ellis, N.Y.C., 2003—. Named one of 100 Most Influential Bus. Leaders in N.Y.C., Crain's N.Y., 2003; recipient Humanitarian award, Found. Fighting Blindness, 1999, Urban Leadership award, NYU Real Estate Inst., 2000, Leadership Excellence award, Monmouth U. Real Estate Inst., 2001, Ellis Island Medal of Honor, Nat. Ethnic Coalition Orgn., 2002, Man of Yr. award, Crohns & Colitis Found., 2002. Office: CB Richard Ellis 16-19 Fls 200 Park Ave New York NY 10166

**SIEGEL, STEVEN L.,** finance company executive, consultant; b. New Rochelle, NY, Feb. 21, 1962; s. Stuart A. Siegel and Stephanie (Kaplita) m. Elizabeth Ellen Starr, Dec. 12, 1987 (div. Jan. 1993). BS in Fin., Calif. Coast U., MBA in Internat. Fin.; D in Internat. Fin. magna cum laude, So. Calif. U., Santa Ana. Fin. analyst Am. Express, Plantation, Fla., 1982-84; investment banker Kidder Peabody & Co., Ft. Lauderdale, Fla., 1985-87, Shearson Lehman Hutton, Boca Raton, Fla., 1987-89; pres. internat. divsn. Cabe Internat. Cons., Inc., Boca Raton, 1989-92; fin. and adminstv. dir. Ensec, Inc., Boca Raton, 1994-95, Art Collectors Internat., Miami, Fla., 1995-96; CFO, COO Enternet Communications Group, Inc., Ft. Lauderdale, 1996—97, S.L. Siegel and Assoc. Consulting Group, 1997—2004, Pan Am., 2004—05, Acad. Fire Protection, 2006—. Mng. dir. Fed. Group Ltd., 2001—02, bd. dir., Bought Deal, Inc.; bd. advisors Howa Telco, 1997—2002; pres., CEO Champion Accessories, 2002—03. Mem. Lambda Epsilon. Avocations: golf, sailing. Address: 2460 Deercreek CC Blvd Deerfield Beach FL 33442 Office Phone: 917-325-0114. Personal E-mail: drsls@earthlink.net.

**SIEGEL, STUART ELLIOTT,** pediatric oncologist, educator; b. Plainfield, NJ, July 16, 1943; s. Hyman and Charlotte Pearl (Freinberg) S.; m. Linda Wertkin, Jan. 20, 1968 (dec. 2003); 1 child, Joshua; m. Barbara Frankel, May 29, 2005. BA, MD, Boston U., 1967. Diplomate Am. Bd. Pediatrics, Am. Bd. Pediatric Oncology. Intern U. Minn. Hosp., Mpls., 1967-68, resident, 1968-69; clin. assoc. NIH, Bethesda, Md., 1969-72; asst. prof. pediatrics U. So. Calif. Sch. Medicine, L.A., 1972-76, assoc. prof., 1976-81, prof., 1981—, vice chmn. dept. pediat., 1994—; head div. hematology-oncology Childrens Hosp. L.A., 1976—, dep. physician-in-chief, 1987-90; dir. Childrens Ctr. for Cancer and Blood Diseases, L.A., 1996—. Mem. clin. cancer program project com. NIH, Nat. Cancer Inst., HEW, Bethesda, Md., 1978-82; pres. So. Calif. Children's Cancer Services, L.A., 1977-95. Bd. dirs. Nat. Leukemia Broadcast Coun., 1987—, Ronald McDonald Children's Charities, 1988-95, Make-A-Wish Found., 1987-95, Children's Hosp. L.A. Found., 1994-2000, Ronald McDonald House Charities, 1995—, L.A. Regional Coun. Am. Cancer Soc., 1996—, Nat. Childhood Cancer Found., 1995-2003, 2005—; pres. Ronald McDonald House Charities So. Calif., 1996—; bd. trustees, Children's Hosp., L.A., 2000—; treas. Padres Contra El Cancer, 2003-04; mem. organizing com. Live Strong Young Adult Alliance, 2005—. Surgeon USPHS, 1969-72. Named to NAt. Caring Hall of Fame, 2001. Fellow Am. Acad. Pediatrics. Office: Childrens Hosp LA Divsn Hematology Oncology MS#54 PO Box 54700 Los Angeles CA 90054-0700 Office Phone: 323-669-2205. Business E-Mail: ssiegel@chla.usc.edu.

**SIEGEL, VIVIAN,** biology editor; b. L.A., Aug. 24, 1960; d. Edward and Harriet (Greenberg) S. AB in Biochemistry and Math., Bowdoin Coll., Brunswick, Maine, 1977-81; PhD in Genetics, U. Calif., San Francisco, 1981-87. Postdoctoral fellow U. Calif., San Francisco, 1987-88, 89-93, postgrad. rschr., 1993-94; postdoctoral fellow Max Planck Inst. Devel. Biology, Tubingen, Germany, 1988-89; sr. editor Cell, Cambridge, Mass., 1994—98; dep. editor Cell, Molecular Cell, Cambridge, 1998—99, editor, 1999—2003, Developmental Cell, Cambridge, 2001—03; exec. editor Pub. Libr. of Sci., San Francisco, 2003—05; editor PLOS Biology, San Francisco, 2003—05; dir. editor U. Calif., San Diego, 2006—. Contbr. articles to profl. jours. Postdoctoral fellow Jane Coffin Childs Found. Biomed. Rsch., 1988-91, sr. postdoctoral fellow Am. Cancer Soc., Calif. divsn., 1991-93. Mem. Am. Soc. Cell Biology, Genetics Soc. Am. Achievements include functional dissection of signal recognition particle; definition of a translocation-competent state for secretory proteins; demonstration of the existence of a signal recognition particle in ciliates and fungi; demonstration that the bicoid protein of Drosophila is an anterior morphogen; identification of the pipsqueak gene and definition of its role in Drosophila oogenesis and eye development. E-mail: viviansiegel@gmail.com.

**SIEGER, DIANA R.,** foundation administrator; b. Detroit, Oct. 15, 1951; d. Robert R. and Rosemary F. Sieger; m. Thomas A VanTol, July 21, 1973 (div. Apr. 2, 1982). BA, Western Mich. U., 1973, MSW, 1978; DHL (hon.), Aquinas Coll., 1998, Grand Valley State U., 2000. Asst. program dir., svc. mil. families, vets. and disaster svcs. ARC, Kent County Chpt., Grand Rapids, Mich., 1974—77; student asst. State of Mich., Dept. Labor and Governor's Office, Lansing, 1977—78; assoc. exec. United Way Kent County, 1978—87; pres. Grand Rapids Cmty. Found., 1987—. V.p., cmty. found. Coun. Mich. Founds., Grand Haven, 1999—, mem.com. cmty. founds., 1988—; bd. dirs. Mich. Cmty. Founds. Venture Funds; chairperson, com. cmty. founds. Coun. Founds., Washington, 1999—2000. Com. mem. maj. corridor task force ITP, Grand Rapids, 2001—02; bd. chairperson, bd. mem. Leadership Grand Rapids, 1991—97; bd. mem. Butterworth Hosp., 1994—97; mem., regional issues com. Grand Rapids Area C. of C., 1990—2002; v.p. cmty. founds. Coun. Mich. Founds., 1999—2002; bd. mem. Mich. Cmty. Founds. Venture Funds, 1994—2002; mem. Kent County Family and Children's Coordinating Coun., 1995—, chairperson, 2001—03; mem., fellowship selection com. Transatlantic Cmty. Found. Fellowship German Marshall Fund, Washington, 2000—; chairperson, com. cmty. founds. Coun. Founds., 1995—2000, mem. stds. implementation com., 2001—; chmn. Mich. Cmty. Founds. Venture Funds, 1994—. Named Grantmaker of Yr., Nat. Soc. Fund Raising Profls., 1996, Disting. Cmty. Trustee, Leadership Grand Rapids, 2001, Outstanding Alumni Acad., Western Mich. U., 2002; named one of Most Influential Women in West Mich., Grand Rapids Bus. Jour., 2004, 2006; named to Nat. Honor Soc. Pub. Affairs and Adminstrn., Pi Alpha Alpha Soc., 1998; recipient Tribute award, YWCA, 1995, Galaxy award, Nat. Kidney Found. Mich., 1999; fellow Transatlantic Cmty. Found. fellow, German Marshall Fund, C.S.

Mott Found., King Baudoin Found., 2000. Mem.: Grand Rapids C. of C. Avocations: travel, art collecting, running, dancing - tap. Office: Grand Rapids Cmty Found 161 Ottawa NW #209-C Grand Rapids MI 49503 E-mail: dsieger@grfoundation.org.

**SIEGERT, BARBARA (BARBARA MARIE SIEGERT),** health care administrator; b. Boston, May 22, 1953; d. Salvatore Mario and Mary Kathleen (Wagner) Tartaglia; m. Herbert C. Siegert (dec. Apr. 1974); children: Carolyn Marie, Herbert Christian Jr. Diploma, Newton-Wellesley (Mass.) Hosp. Sch. Nursing, 1956; MEd, Antioch U., 1980. Diplomate Am. Bd. Med. Psychotherapists. Supr. nursing Hogan Regional Ctr., Hathorne, Mass., 1974-78; community mental health nursing advisor Cape Ann area office Dept. Mental Health, Beverly, Mass., 1978-79, dir. case mgmt., 1979-87, dir. case mgmt. north shore area office, 1988-91; dir. case mgmt. Dept. Mental Health-north shore area-Lynn (Mass.) site, Lynn, Mass., 1991-92. Mem. interdisciplinary faculty, profl. cons. com., lecture staff clin. pastoral counseling program Danvers State Hosp./Hogan/Berry Regional Ctrs., Hathorne, Mass., 1982-86; nursing edn. adv. com. North Shore Community Coll., Beverly, 1983-91; tchg. staff Balter Inst., Ipswich, Mass., 1987-88. Mem. Internat. Cultural Diploma Honor, 1989—. Recipient Spl. Recognition award Lexington (Mass.) Pub. Schs., 1973, Peter Torci award Lexington Friends of Children in Spl. Edn., 1974. Home: 63 Willow Rd # B Boxford MA 01921-1218

**SIEGFRIED, DAVID CHARLES,** retired lawyer; b. NYC, Feb. 15, 1942; s. Charles Albert and Marjorie Claire (Young) S.; m. Meri Stephanie (Smith); children: Karin Elisabeth, Christine Elise. BA, Princeton U., 1964; JD, Harvard U., 1967. Bar: N.Y., 1970. Assoc. Milbank, Tweed, Hadley, and McCloy, N.Y.C., 1968-76, ptnr., 1977—98, resident ptnr. Hong Kong and Singapore, 1979-83, 85-88. Bd. dirs. Princeton Alumni Weekly; spkr. in field. Bd. dirs. Cmty. Agy. Corp. N.J., Inc., v.p. alumni assn.; vice chmn. Princeton U. Alumni Coun.; vice chmn. Millburn Hist. Preservation Commn. 1st lt. USAR, 1967-74. Mem.: Millburn Short Hills Hist. Soc. (bd. dir., past pres.), Assn. Bar City of N.Y., N.Y. State Bar Assn., Cricket Club, Princeton Club (Singapore), Am. Club (Hong Kong and Singapore), Baltusrol Golf Club, Short Hills (NJ) Club, Princeton Club. Congregationalist. Avocations: running, tennis, historic reading. Home: 30 Western Dr Short Hills NJ 07078-3230

**SIEGFRIED, JONATHAN D.,** lawyer; b. N.Y.C., Dec. 12, 1948; BA cum laude, Yale U., 1970; JD cum laude, Harvard U., 1970. Bar: NY 1976, US Dist. Ct. (So. Dist.) NY 1976, US Dist. Ct. (Ea. Dist.) NY 1976, US Supreme Ct. 1978, US Ct. Appeals (2nd Cir.) 1980. Former exec. asst. City of NY, Hon. John V. Lindsay; counsel US Dist. Ct., So. Dist. NY; mng. ptnr. Thelen Rein & Priest LLP. Bd. dirs. Legal Aid Soc., NYC, 2004—. Mem.: Assn. Bar of City of NY (com. fed. legis.), NY State Bar Assn. (com. fed. cts.), Fed. Bar Coun. Office: Thelen Reid & Priest LLP 875 Third Ave New York NY 10022-6225 Office Phone: 212-603-2198. Office Fax: 212-603-2001. E-mail: jsiegfried@thelenreid.com.

**SIEGLER, KELLY R.,** lawyer; b. Oct. 1962; m. Sam Siegler. Degree in internat. bus. Asst. dist. atty. Harris County, Houston, 1987—. Named America's Top 50 Women Litigators, Nat. Law Jour., 2002, Named to Winners of Spl. Reports, 2003, 2004; named one of Top 10 Litigators, 2003. Mem.: Tex. Dist. and County Atty. Assn. Office: Harris County District Attorney's Office Ste 600 1201 Franklin St Houston TX 77002-1923 Office Phone: 713-755-5800.

**SIEGLER, MARK,** internist, educator; b. N.Y.C., June 20, 1941; s. Abraham J. and Florence (Sternlieb) S.; m. Anna Elizabeth Hollinger, June 4, 1967; children:Dillan, Alison, Richard, Jessica. AB with honors, Princeton U., 1963; MD, U. Chgo., 1967. Diplomate Am. Bd. Internal Medicine. Resident, chief resident internal medicine U. Chgo., 1967-71; hon. sr. registrar in medicine Royal Postgrad. Med. Sch., London, 1971-72; asst. prof. medicine U. Chgo., 1972-78, assoc. prof. medicine, 1979-85, acting dir. div. gen. internal medicine, 1983-85, dir. MacLean Ctr. Clin. Med. Ethics, 1984—, prof. medicine, 1985—, Lindy Bergman prof., 1997-2000, Lindy Bergman Disting. Svc. prof., 2000—, dir. fellowship tng. program in clin. med. ethics, 1986—. Vis. asst. prof. medicine U. Wis., Madison, 1977; vis. assoc. prof. medicine U. Va., Charlottesville, 1981-82. Co-author: Clinical Ethics, 1981, 2d edit., 1986, 3d edit., 1992, 4th edit., 1998, 5th edit., 2002, An Annotated Bibliography of Medical Ethics, 1988, Institutional Protocols for Decisions About Life-Sustaining Treatment, 1988; co-editor: Changing Values in Medicine, 1985, Medical Innovations and Bad Outcomes, 1987; editl. bd.: Am. Jour. Medicine, 1979—94, 1997—, Archives Internal Medicine, 1979—90, Bibliography of Bioethics, Jour. Med. Philosophy, 1978—89, Jour. Med. Philosophy, 1978—89, Jour. Clin. Ethics, 1989—, Jour. Med. Ethics (London), 2002—; contbr. articles to profl. jours. Mem. adv. bd. Bioethics Inst., Madrid, Notre Dame Ctr. for Ethics and Culture. Grantee Andrew W. Mellon Found., Henry J. Kaiser Family Found., Pew Charitable Trusts, Field Found. Ill., Ira De Camp Found., Gaylord & Dorothy Donnelley Found.; Phi Beta Kappa vis. scholar, 1991-92, Chirone prize Italian Nat. Acad. Medicine, 1996; mem. NAS Cloning Panel, 2001-02, others. Fellow ACP (human rights com., ethics com. 1985-90), Hastings Ctr.; mem. ACS (ethics com. 1992—), Assn. Am. Physicians, Chgo. Clin. Ethics Program (pres. 1989-90). Office: Univ Chgo MC 6098 MacLean Ctr Clin Med Ethics 5841 S Maryland Ave Chicago IL 60637-1463

**SIEJKA, GEORGE JOHN,** artist; b. Vienna, June 24, 1946; came to U.S., 1950; Cert. Fine Arts, Sch. Visual Arts, N.Y.C., 1969; BS in Art Edn. cum laude, NYU, 1974, MA in Fine Arts, 1975. Represented by Nancy Hoffman Gallery, N.Y.C. Group exhbns. include Fitchburg (Mass.) Art Mus., Anchorage (Alaska) Mus. Art, Rockford (Ill.) Coll. Art Gallery, Chgo. Internat. Exposition, Nancy Hoffman Gallery, NY. Recipient Founders Day award NYU, 1974. Mem. N.Y. Artists Equity Assn. Home: 534 Main St Apt 2 Beacon NY 12508

**SIEKERT, ROBERT GEORGE,** retired neurologist, retired educator; b. Milw., July 23, 1924; s. Hugo Paul and Elisa (Kraus) S.; m. Mary Jane Evans, Feb. 17, 1951; children: Robert G. Jr., John E., Friedrich A.P. BS, Northwestern U., 1945, MS, 1947, MD, 1948. Diplomate Am. Bd. Psychiatry and Neurology. Instr. anatomy U. Pa., Phila., 1948-49; fellow neurology Mayo Found., Rochester, Minn., 1950-54; cons. Mayo Clinic, Rochester, 1954-91, head neurology sect., 1966-76, bd. govs., 1973-80, prof. neurology med. sch., 1969-91, prof. emeritus neurology, 1991—. Chmn. Internat. Stroke Conf. Am. Heart Assn., 1976-93. Editor Mayo Clinic Procs., 1982-86; cons. editor Jour. Stroke, 1992-2001; contbr. articles to profl. jours.; described transient cerebral ischemic attacks. Trustee Mayo Found., Rochester, 1973-81, chmn. emeritus com., 1997-98. Served to lt. j.g. M.C., USNR, 1950-52. Recipient Disting. Achievement award, Am. Heart Assn., 1984, Merit award, 1989, Robert G. Siekert Young Investigator award Am. Heart Assn., 1986. Fellow Am. Coll. Physicians; mem. Am. Neurol. Assn., Northwestern U. Med. Sch. Alumni Assn. (Service award 1983), Swiss Neurol. Soc. (corr.), Alpha Omega Alpha. Avocation: stamp collecting/philately. Office: Mayo Clinic 200 1st St SW N-10 Rochester MN 55905-0002 Office Phone: 507-284-2691.

**SIEKIERSKI, MACIEJ M.,** curator; b. Poznan, Poland; s. Konrad Siekierski and Helena Buczak-Siekierski; m. Anna Bendisz-Siekierski, Mar. 24, 1979; children: Nicholas, Victoria, Maximilian. BA in History and Russian, San Jose State Coll., 1970; MLS, San Jose State U., 1986; MA in History, U. Calif., Berkeley, 1971, PhD in History, 1984. Curator Hoover Inst., Stanford U., Calif., 1984—. Contbr. articles to profl. jours.; mem.: Polish Inst. Arts and Scis. Am., Am. Assn. Advancement Slavic Studies, Am. Hist. Assn. Home: 1752 Hull Ave Redwood City CA 94061 Office: Hoover Inst Stanford CA Office Phone: 650-725-6955.

**SIEKMAN, THOMAS CLEMENT,** lawyer; b. Somerville, Mass., Sept. 22, 1941; s. Aloysius C. and Estelle M. (Forte) S.; children: Michael T., James T., Amy K. BS in Engring., Merrimack Coll., 1963; JD, Villanova U., 1966. Bar:

Mass. 1966, U.S. Dist. Ct. Mass. 1969. Patent atty. Bethlehem (Pa.) Steel, 1966-68, Mohawk Data Scis., Herkimer, Mass., 1968-72, Chittick, Thompson & Pfund, Boston, 1972-73; from patent atty. to v.p. and gen. counsel Digital Equipment Corp., Maynard, Mass., 1973-98; Sr. v.p., gen. coun., sec. Compaq Computer Corp., 1998—2002; of counsel Skadden, Arps, Slate, Meagher & Flom LLP; chmn. Martha Stewart Living Omnimedia, Inc., 2004—05, lead dir., 2005—. Bd. dirs., chmn. N.E. Legal Found; bd. dirs. Martha Stewart Living Omnimedia, Inc., 2003- Trustee Mass. Taxpayers Found., Merrimack Coll.; mem. New Eng. Legal Found.; mem. Houston cmty. adv. bd. Teach Am.; bd. dirs. Houston African-Am. Mus. Mem. ABA, Am. Corp. Counsel Assn., Assn. Gen. Counsel. Avocations: squash, skiing. Office: Skadden, Arps, Meagher & Flom LLP 1440 New York Ave, NW Washington DC 20005

**SIEKMANN, DONALD CHARLES,** accountant; b. St. Louis, July 2, 1938; s. Elmer Charles and Mabel Louise (Blue) S.; m. Linda Lee Knowles, Sept. 10, 1966; 1 child, Brian Charles. BS, Washington U., St. Louis, 1960. CPA, Ohio, Ga. Regional mng. ptnr. Arthur Andersen & Co., Cin., 1960-98. Trustee Touchstone Group Mut. Funds, Riverfront Group Mut. Funds, Constellation Group Mutual Funds; exec. Duro Bag Mfg. Co. Columnist Cin. Enquirer, 1983-86, Gannett News Services, 1983-86; editor "Tax Clinic" column Tax Advisor mag., 1974-75. Mem. bd. Cin. Zool. Soc., 1985-88; officer, bd. dirs. Cin. Found. for Pub. TV, 1984-88, Cin. Symphony Orch., 1973-85, Cin. Ballet Co., 1973-88, Atlanta Symphony Orch., 1988-91, The Atlanta Opera, 1988-91, Cin. Theatrical Assn., Jewish Hosp., 1993—, Cin. Assn. for Performing Arts, 1992—, Cin. United Way, 1992-99, Cin. Pk. Bd. Found., 1995-98; pres. Greater Cin. Arts and Edn. Ctr., 1996-99; mem. Friends of Sch. for Creative and Performing Arts, 1996-99, Cin. Arts Festival, 1992-96, Ronald McDonald House, 1998—. Mem. AICPA, Ohio Soc. CPAs, Cin. Country Club (trustee 1983-88), Optimists Club (pres. Queen City chpt. 1986). Clubs: Cin. Country (trustee 1983-88). Lutheran. Home: 5495 Waring Dr Cincinnati OH 45243-3933 E-mail: dsiekmann@aol.com.

**SIELICKI-KORCZAK, BORIS ZDZISLAW,** political educator, investigative consultant; b. Wilno, Lithuania, Poland, Feb. 11, 1939; came to U.S., 1980; s. Witold and Antonina (Arciszewski) Sielicki-Korczak; m. Barbara Maria Kaniewski, May 29, 1971; children: Robert, Sandra. MSC, Warsaw U., 1964, Kunstindustriskole, Copenhagen, 1971; PhD, Basel (Switzerland) U., 1973. Pres. Impolex Ltd., Copenhagen, 1970-79; field operative Europe CIA, 1983-90; pres., educator Anti-Soviet Rsch. Ctr., McLean, Va., 1984; export dir. Worldwide Investment Ltd., Arlington, Va., 1985-87; pres. Amexim Internat. Co. Ltd., Arlington, 1986-89, BK & Assocs., Arlington, 1990—, Boris S. de Korczak, Inc., Fairfax Station, Va., 1986—. Pres. R.R. Internat. Ltd., Copenhagen, 1983-89; mng. dir. Securitas Inc., Arlington, 1986-87; multiple appearance on U.S. and fgn. TV shows as expert on terrorism, USSR and Russian intelligence and its ops.; crime scene analyst, 1986—. Author: A Man From Atlantis, 1976; designer anti-drug poster. Dir. Nat. Lyric Opera Co., Washington, 1981-91; chief investigator Nat. Police Def. Found., 1995-98; legis. asst. to Congl. James A. Traficant, U.S. Congress, 2001-2003; sr. analyst 17th Dist. Ohio Congl. Office, Washington. Independent. Avocations: chess, classic music, travel, art, history. Business E-Mail: bkorczak@cox.net.

**SIEM, PAULINE M.,** library director; b. Blue Earth, Minn., Nov. 24, 1954; d. Richard Ralph and Neva Theresa (Fischer) Quaday; m. Merlyn Richard Siem, June 30, 1983; 1 child, Steven Richard; m. Patrick Alois Malone, Sept. 20, 1975 (div. May 1981); 1 child, Jason Michael Malone. AA in Liberal Studies, Minn. State U., Mankato, 1991, BSBA (hon.) in Mgmt., 1996; MA in Libr. & Info. Sci. with honors, U. Wis., Milw., 2006. Cert. Libr. Minn., 2000. Libr. circulation clk. Blue Earth Cmty. Libr., Minn., 1996—97, libr. adminstrv. aid, 1997—99; interim office mgr. Blue Earth C. of C., 1998; county libr. dir., rotation libr. Faribault County Libr., Blue Earth, 1999—2005; interim city libr. dir. Blue Earth Cmty. Libr., 2000; libr. dir. Faribault County, Blue Earth, 2005—. Children's program dir. Faribault County Libr., Blue Earth, 2000—, children's program craft instr., Bricelyn, Easton, Minn. Lake, 2003; team leader edn. com. Faribault County Local Redevelopment Agy., Blue Earth, 2001—03, strategic planner edn. com., 2001—03; fund raiser Libr. Friend, Bricelyn, Minn., 2004—05. Philanthropist Am. Liver Found., Mpls., 2001—04; philanthropist Mary V. Garver Scholarship, Chgo., 2004; philanthropist Miriam L. Hornback Scholarship, Chgo., 2004; educator MADD, Irving, Tex., 2003—05; philanthropist Faribault County Food Shelf, Blue Earth, 1983—2004, Blue Earth Cmty. Libr., Blue Earth, 1999, Faribault County Libr. Svc., Blue Earth, 2000—05, Faribault County Children's Toy Drive, Blue Earth, 2002—04, Faribault County Veterans Adminstrn., Blue Earth, 2003, KJLY Radio Sta., Blue Earth, 2003, Libr. Friend, Bricelyn, 2004, 700 Club, Va. Beach, 1998, Samaritan's Purse, Operation Christmas Child, Boone, NC, 2002—04, Living Word Christian Ctr., Brooklyn Park, Minn., 2003—; choir mem. ladies trio, ensemble, and mixed ensemble First Bapt. Ch., Minn., 2002—, asst. dir. youth club, 2002—03, deaconess bd., 2003—05, ch. bd. clk., 2005. Pvt. e2 U.S. Army, 1974—75, Texas. Recipient Merit award, Minn. State U., 1992. Mem.: ALA (assoc.), Aid Assn. Luth. Fraternal Ins. Orgn. (treas. 1988—92, v.p. 1987—88), Soc. Am. Archivist (assoc.), Minn. Libr. Assn. (assoc.). Avocations: art museums, antiques. Home: 319 W 1st St Blue Earth MN 56013 Office: Faribault County Libr 120 S Main St Blue Earth MN 56013 Office Phone: 507-526-7182.

**SIEMER, DEANNE CLEMENCE,** lawyer; d. Edward D. and Dorothy E. (Helsdon) S.; m. Howard P. Willens; 1 child, Jason L. BA, George Washington U., 1962; LLB, Harvard U., 1968. Bar: N.Y. 1968, D.C. 1969, Md 1972, Commonwealth of No. Mariana Islands 1976. Economist Office of Mgmt. and Budget, Washington, 1964-67; assoc., then ptnr. Wilmer, Cutler & Pickering, Washington, 1968-77, 80-90; ptnr. Pillsbury, Madison & Sutro, Washington, 1990-95; mng. dir. Wilsie Co., Washington and Saipan, 1995—. Gen. counsel U.S. Dept. of Def., Washington, 1977—79; spl. asst. to sec. U.S. Dept. of Energy, Washington, 1979—80. Author: Tangible Evidence, 3d edit., 1996, National Security and Self-Determination: United States Policy in Micronesia, 1999, Corel Presentations for Litigators, 2000, PowerPoint for Litigators, 2000, Effective Use of Courtroom Technology: A Judge's Guide to Pretrial and Trial, 2001, An Honorable Accord: The Covenant Between the Northern Mariana Islands and the United States, 2001, Effective Use of Courtroom Technology: A Lawyer's Guide to Pretrial and Trial, 2002, Easy Tech: Cases and Materials on Courtroom Technology, 2002, The Patronus Technique: A Practical Proposal In Asbestos-Driven Bankruptcies, 2002, Power Point 2002 for Litigators, 2002, Basic Power Point Slides, 2003, Argument Slides, 2003, The Evidence Camera, 2004, Oral Histories of the Northern Mariana Islands: Political Life and Developments 1945-1995, 2004, The Digital Projector and Laptop Computer, 2005, PowerPoint 2003: 50 Great Tips for Better, Easier Slides, 2005, From the White House: Documents on the Northern Mariana Islands and Micronesia (1945-1995) Collected from the Presidential Libraries, 2005, The Secret Guam Study: The Documents, 2005, Asbestos Prepackaged Bankruptcies: Apply the Brakes But Retain Flexibility for Debtors, 2005. Mem. Lawyers Com. Civil Rights, Washington, 1973—; mediator U.S. Ct. Appeals, Washington, ; trustee Nat. Inst. Trial Advocacy, 1989—, Am. Law Inst., 1988—; arbitrator Atty. Client Arbitration Bd., 1990—, NASD, 2001-; mem. com. sci. and nat. security NAS, 2002-. Recipient citation Air Force Assn., 1977, Dist. Pub. Svc. Medal Sec. of Def., 1979, Commendation Pres. of U.S. 1981; grantee Nat. Endowment Humanities, Commonwealth of No. Mariana Islands Divsn. Hist. Preservation, No. Mariana Islands Coun. Humanities. Mem. D.C. Bar Assn. (Disting. Svc. award 2006), No. Marianas Bar Assn. Episcopalian. Business E-Mail: wilsieco@aol.com.

**SIEMER, PAUL JENNINGS,** public relations executive; b. St. Louis, Jan. 24, 1946; s. Robert Vincent and Pauline Mary (Nece) S.; m. Susan MacDonald Arnott, Aug. 26, 1967 Student, U. Notre Dame, 1964-67. Reporter South Bend Tribune, Ind., 1967-69; reporter St. Louis Globe-Democrat, 1969-76; account exec. Fleishman-Hillard Inc., St. Louis, 1976-79, v.p., sr. ptnr., 1979-84, exec. v.p., sr. ptnr., 1984-95; ptnr. Stolberg &

Siemer Inc., St. Louis, 1995—. Mem. Pub. Relations Soc. Am. Roman Catholic. Home: 2961 Hatherly Dr Saint Louis MO 63121-4551 Office: Stolberg & Siemer Inc 818 Lafayette Ave Saint Louis MO 63104-3702 Office Phone: 314-436-6577.

**SIEMON-BURGESON, MARILYN M.,** education administrator; b. Whittier, Calif., Nov. 15, 1934; d. John Roscoe and Louise Christina (Secoy) Mason; m. Carl J. Siemon, Aug. 18, 1956 (div. Oct. 1984); children: Timothy G., Melanie A. Siemon tms; Troy M.; m James K. Burgeson, Jan. 24, 1987. BA, U. Redlands, 1956; MA, Pacific Oaks Coll., 1975; postgrad., Point Loma Coll., 1979—80. Cert. adminstr., elem. and early childhood tchr. Tchr. Sierra Madre Cmty. Nursery Sch., Calif., 1970—77; tchr. parent edn. and music Pasadena Unified Schs., 1977—79, project coord., 1980—82, tchr. curriculum resource dept., 1982—83, adminstr. Washington Children's Ctr., 1983—99; endorsed trainer High Scope Found. Register, 1990—; cons. staff devel. and tng. Pasadena. Trainer Program for Infant/Toddler Caregivers; instr. Citrus Coll., 1996-98; conf. chair Calif. High Scope Educators, 1995—. Active Arcadia (Calif.) Bicentennial Commn., 1974-76; mem. policy coun. for cmty. housing svcs. Pasadena Head Start, 1992-95; life mem. Sierra Madre Sch. PTA; mem. Child Care Coalition, Pasadena; Altar Guild, lay Eucharistic minister St. Edmunds, San Marino, Calif., vestry mem., 2003-06. Ednl. Professions Devel. fellow Pacific Oaks Coll., Pasadena, 1969. Mem.: AAUW (co-chair Math.-Sci. Conf. 1983, chair coll./univ. rels. 1988—, v.p. ednl. found. 1996—98, Calif. state divsn. program v.p. 2002—04, leadership devel. com. 2005—, chmn. L.A. interbr. coun. program 2006—, past pres., chmn. 2006—), grantee 1982—83, Woman of Achievement award 2006), Calif. Child Devel. Adminstrs. Assn. (bd. dirs.), Women's Ednl. Leadership (asst. program v.p.), Child Care Info. Svc. (chair parent edn. and family affairs 1986—, bd. dirs.), Nat. Assn. Edn. Young Children (grantee 1970), Pasadena Women's City Club (dir. membership 2000—02, chmn.), Coun. Women's Clubs (pres. 1995—98), Pasadena Coll. Women's Club (pres. 2000—02, pres. Scholarship Found. 2002—04), Delta Kappa Gamma (pres. Omicron chpt. 1986—88, 1992—94, legis. chmn. Chi state area XIII 2005—). Republican. Episcopalian. Avocation: music. Home: 2266 Kinclair Dr Pasadena CA 91107-1022 Personal E-mail: mburgeson@earthlink.net.

**SIEMS, BENNETT A.,** performing company executive; s. William R. and Mary Louise Siems. BA, Brown U., 1990. Tchr. Princeton (N.J.) Day Sch., 1990—93; prin., owner Bennett Siems Tutoring, Ednl. Svcs., Mpls., 1993—; Willie Aug. Project, Mpls., 1998—. Composer (musician): Surrender to the Wind (named #1 new addition, XM Radio Real Jazz 70, 2006, Hon. Mention award City Pages Top 10 Minn. CDs, 2004), Twin Cities Jazz Society Jazz from J to Z, Shadow Chasers; composer: (co-choreographer, musician) Empire at Twilight (Meet the Composer, Inc. Creative Connections grant, 2005); composer: Dare to Dream (Am. Composers Forum, Harriet Tubman Ctr. Composer fellowship, 2001); Timescape; musician: Grand Marais Jazz Festival, Mainstage All-Star Guitar Summit; author: (scholarly essay) Brer Robert: The Bluesman and the African American Trickster Tale Tradition, in Southern Folklore. Nominee Six Minn. Music awards, Minn. Music Acad., 2000-2005; recipient Tchr. Recognition award for Outstanding Letter of Recommendation, Duke U., 1997, Oustanding Vol. Achieve. award, Sierra Club North Star Chpt., 2004, All-Time Top Fifty Daily Downloads award, AllAboutJazz.com, 2005; grantee, Meet the Composer, Inc., N.Y.C., NY, 2001, 2002, 2006, Am. Composers Forum, 2002. Mem.: ASCAP (ASCAPlus Awards 2000-2005), Am. Composers Forum, Nature Conservancy, Phi Beta Kappa. Avocations: hiking, wilderness advocacy, canoeing, volleyball. Office Phone: 612-825-9952. Business E-Mail: willieaugust@hotmail.com.

**SIENA, JAMES,** artist; b. Oct. 28, 1957; BFA, Cornell U., 1979. One-man shows include Pierogi 2000, Bklyn., 1996, Cristinerose Gallery, N.Y.C., 1997, Daniel Weinberg Gallery, San Francisco, 1998, L.A. 2000, 2002, Gorney Bravin & Lee, N.Y.C., 2000, 2001, 2003, San Francisco Art Inst., 2003, exhibited in group shows at Nova Zembla, Hertogenbosch, Holland, 1993, Drawing Ctr., N.Y.C., 1993, Kunstverein Munich, Germany, 1994, Geoffrey Young Gallery, Great Barrington, Mass., 1994, Lombard/Fried Fine Arts, N.Y.C., 1995, Chassie Post Gallery, 1995, Bklyn. Mus. Art, 1997, Phyllis Kind Gallery, N.Y.C., 1998, Nicholas Davies Gallery, 1998, San Francisco Mus. Modern Art, 1999, Am. Acad. Arts and Letters, N.Y., 1999, 2000 (award in art, 2000), Galerie Anne de Villepoix, Paris, 2000, Greater N.Y. PS1, L.I. 2000, New Editions Monoprints Pace/Prints, N.Y.C., 2002, 177th Ann. Nat. Acad. Design Mus., 2002, OSP Gallery, Boston, 2002—03, Whitney Biennial, Whitney Mus. Am. Art, 2004, Represented in permanent collections Mus. Modern Art, N.Y.C., San Francisco Mus. Modern Art, Whitney Mus. Am. Art, N.Y., Met. Mus. Art. Named invited exhibitor, Whitney Mus. Am. Art, N.Y., 2004; recipient Biennal Competition award, Louis Comfort Tiffany Found., 1999; fellow in painting, N.Y. Found. for the Arts, 1994.

**SIEPI, CESARE,** opera singer; b. Milan, Feb. 10, 1923; Operatic debut in Rigoletto, Schio, Calif., 1941, Il Nabucco, LaScala Opera, Milan, 1946, Don Carlo, Met. Opera, N.Y.C., 1950; soloist debut in Carnegie Hall, N.Y.C., 1951; sang in Mozart and Verdi requiems, Edinburgh Festival, Albert Hall, London; leading bass at, Salzburg Festival, LaScala, Milan; appeared in: play Bravo Giovanni, 1962; appeared: play Vienna Staatsoper; made many opera recordings for, London Records. (Winner Nat. Singing Competition, Florence 1941, recipient Italy's Orfeo award 1956). Achievements include making operatic debut, Rigoletto, Schio, at age of 18. Home: 12095 Brookfield Club Dr Roswell GA 30075-1261

**SIEPMANN, JAMES PATRICK,** research and development company executive, retired physician; b. Rochester, Minn., Jan. 16, 1960; s. Richard James and Mary Margaret Siepmann; m. Victoria Lynn Ewert, Sept. 4, 1982; children: Jeffrey Michael (dec.), Justine Nicole, Jennifer Ashley, Jessica Raquel, Joelle Kristina, Jarett James. BA, U. St. Thomas, St. Paul, 1982; MD, Mayo Med. Sch., Rochester, Minn., 1986. Diplomate Am. Bd. Family Practice. Resident in family practice Mayo Grad. Sch. Medicine, Rochester, 1986—89; pvt. practice Oshkosh, Wis., 1989—2000; founder, chmn. Light-Time, Winnebago, Wis., 2000—. Med. dir. United Health Wis., Appleton, 1993-95; chmn. dept. family practice Mercy Med. Ctr., Oshkosh, 1992-94; team physician Lourdes H.S., Oshkosh, 1993-99. Editor Jour. Theoretics, 1999-2004. Founding pres. sch. bd. Oshkosh Area Cath. Sch. Sys. (now consol.), 1991-93 Mem. IEEE, AMA, Optical Soc. Am., Internat. Soc. Optical Engring., Wis. Med. Soc. (del. 1994-98, bd. dirs. polit. action com. 1994—99, Wis. Physician-Citizen of Yr. award 1993). Roman Catholic. Achievements include patents for humidifier and in the optoelectronic field. Avocations: inventing, theoretics, writing, computer science, collecting fine wines. Home: 2941 Prairie Wood Dr Oshkosh WI 54904-8478 Office: 3555 Moser St Oshkosh WI 54904 E-mail: siepmann@lighttime.com.

**SIER, RUTH ELAINE,** music educator; b. York, Pa., May 11, 1954; d. Gilbert William and Phyllis Elaine (Storms) S. BS in Music Edn., West Chester U., 1976, MMus in Music Edn., 1985; postgrad., King's Coll., Cambridge, Eng., 1987. Cert. music specialist, Pa., Del. Music specialist Pennsbury Sch. Dist., Yardley, Pa., 1977-83, Cen. Dauphin Sch. Dist., Harrisburg, Pa., 1985-87, Dept. Def. Dependents Schs., Lakenheath, Eng., 1987-89, Maine Sch. Adminstrv. Dist. # 3, Unity, 1990—91; elem. music substitute Eastern Lebanon County Sch. Dist., Myerstown, Pa., 1994; elem. and mid. sch. music substitute York City Sch. Dist., York, Pa., 1995—96; strings specialist K-8 Ctrl. York Sch. Dist., York, Pa., 2000, Red Clay Cons. Sch. Dist., Wilmington, Del., 2000—. Dir. Exodus Summer Arts Program, York, Pa., 1989-92; musicals/drama instr. York Little Theatre; guest instr., ESTA String Conf., Italy; asst. dir. Lawrenceville (N.J.) Youth Symphony; handbell and yough program dir.; ch. choir, York; pvt. studio tchr.; York. Am. Women of Today scholar Am. Bus. Women's Assn., 1973, 74. Mem. Folio Soc. Home: 21 Williamstown Cir York PA 17404

**SIERA, STEVEN G.,** career planning administrator, educator; b. Detroit, Apr. 19, 1949; s. Lucian F. and Ethel M. Siera; m. Maureen Stern, July 24, 1971; 1 child, Scott G. BS, Maryville Coll., 1970; MS, U. Tenn., 1974; PhD, N.Mex State U., 1984. Dir., career planning and placement No. State Coll., Aberdeen, SD, 1980—83; dir., student svcs. U. Sci. and Arts of Okla.,

---

Chickasha, 1984—86; assoc., asst. prof. Northeastern State U., Tahlequah, Okla., 1986—92; assoc. prof. U. of Pacific, Stockton, Calif., 1992—94; dir., rsch. and assessment Kent Sch. Dist., Wash., 1994—2003; dir. of grad. programs in edn., assoc. prof. St. Martin's U., Lacey, Wash., 2003—. Mem. Wolf Haven Internat., Tenino, Wash., 2005—. Recipient Contributions to Survey Rsch. in Edn. award, Am. Ednl. Rsch. Assn., 2005, President's award, Wash. Orgn. for Reading Devel., 2005. Mem.: ASCD, Wash. Ednl. Rsch. Assn., NW Assn. Colleges Tchr. Edn., Am. Assn. Colleges Tchr. Edn., Am. Ednl. Rsch. Assn. (chair 1995—97, program chair 2004—). Achievements include research in Teacher participation in scoring sessions: Effects on teacher practices and student writing performance; Relationship of Miller Analogies Test score and undergraduate GPA's to graduate GPA and Oklahoma Certification Test score of school administration candidates; Four methods of following up mailed questionnaires; Relationship of selected factors to performance on Oklahoma Teacher Competency Examinations; Supervisor and student leader perceptions of CSAO performance; Employer preferences and practices in teacher hiring; Elementary teachers' use of nonfiction literature in the classroom; Comparability of prediction of first grade reading achievement for the Peabody Picture Vocabulary Test and the Test de Vocabulario en Imagenes Peabody; Dental school and undergraduate school performance, aptitude examination, and demographic data as predictors of performance on the California Dental Licensure Examination; Instruction does make a difference: Attitudes and perceptions of young readers in whole language and traditional classrooms; Vocabulary generated by students in whole language and basal first grade classrooms; Emergent literacy, preschool through first grade: Three studies; Validity of a state certification examination with respect to principals' ratings after three years; Reading perceptions and attitudes of kindergarten students. Avocations: travel, golf, gardening. Office: St Martin's U 5300 Pacific Ave SE Lacey WA 98503 Office Phone: 360-438-4589. E-mail: ssiera@stmartin.edu.

**SIERACKI, ERIC P.,** diversified financial services company executive; BS in Econs., U. Pa. Mgr. Grant Thornton; sr. v.p. Countrywide Asset Mgmt. Corp., 1988—89; exec. v.p. corp. fin. Countrywide Fin. Corp., Calabasas, Calif., 1989—94, mng. dir., 1994—2002, sr. mng. dir. corp. fin., treas., & corp. develop., investor rels., 2002—05, exec. mng. dir., CFO, 2005—. Office: Countrywide Fin Corp 4500 Park Granada Calabasas CA 91302-1613*

**SIERLES, FREDERICK STEPHEN,** psychiatrist, educator; b. Bklyn., Nov. 9, 1942; s. Samuel and Elizabeth (Meiselman) S.; m. Laurene Harriet Cohn, Oct. 25, 1970 (div. Aug. 1990); children: Hannah Beth Alterson, Joshua Caleb. AB, Columbia U., 1963; MD, Rosalind Franklin U., 1967. Diplomate Am. Bd. Psychiatry and Neurology. Intern Cook County Hosp., Chgo., 1967-68; resident in psychiatry Mt. Sinai Hosp., N.Y.C., 1968-69, assoc. attending psychiatrist Chgo., 1973-74; resident in psychiatry Rosalind Franklin U., North Chgo., Ill., 1969-71, chief resident, 1970-71, asst. prof., 1974-78, assoc. prof., 1978-88, dir. med. student edn., 1974—94, instr. psychiatry, 1973—; staff psychiatrist U.S. Reynolds Army Hosp., Ft. Sill, Okla., 1971-73. Cons. psychiatry Cook County Hosp., 1974-79, St. Mary of Nazareth Hosp., 1979-84, Gt. Lakes Naval Hosp., 1987-90, Jackson Park Hosp., 1987-89, Mt. Sinai Hosp., 1988—, Elgin Mental Health Ctr., 1997—; chief mental health clinic, North Chicago VA Hosp., 1982-85, chief psychiatry svc., 1983-85. Author: (wth others) General Hospital Psychiatry, 1985, Behavioral Science for the Boreds, 1987, rev. 2d edit., 1989, rev. 3d edit., 1993, USMLE Behavioral Science Made Ridiculously Simple, 1998; editor: Clinical Behavioral Science, 1982, Behavioral Science for Medical Students, 1993; mem. editl. bd. Acad. Psychiatry, 2000—; contbr. articles to profl. jours. Coach Glenview (Ill.) Youth Baseball, 1987-89, mgr. 1990 (age 10-12 Glenview World Series winner 1990), Glenview Tennis Club, 1986-90 (3.5 Men's Doubles League winner 1989-90). Maj. M.C., U.S. Army, 1971-73. N.Y.State Regents scholar, 1959-63; NIMH grantee, 1974-83, Chgo. Med. Sch. grantee, 1974-83; recipient Seymour Vestermark award NIMH/Am. Psychiat. Assn., 2003. Fellow Am. Psychiat. Assn. (disting. life fellow, coun. edn. and career devel. 1993-95); mem. Ill. Psychiat. Soc. (fellowship com. 1985-99), Columbia Coll. Alumni Secondary Sch. Com., Assn. Dirs. Med. Student Edn. in Psychiatry (exec. coun. 1985-99, chmn. program com. 1987-88, treas. 1989-91, pres-elect 1991-93, pres. 1993-95, immediate past pres. 1995-99), Alliance for Clin. Edn., Am. Assn. Dirs. Psychiat. Residency Tng. (exec. coun. 2000-03, chair workforce coalition 2000-03), Sigma Xi, Alpha Omega Alpha, Phi Epsilon Pi. Office: Rosalind Franklin Univ Chgo Med Sch 3333 Green Bay Rd North Chicago IL 60064-3037 Business E-Mail: frederick.sierles@rosalindfranklin.edu.

**SIEROCKI, JOHN STANLEY,** oncologist; b. New Haven, Conn., 1947; MD, Hahnemann U., 1973. Diplomate Am. Bd. Internal Medicine, Am. Bd. Med. Oncology. Intern Hahnemann U., Phila., 1973—74, resident in medicine, 1974—76; fellow in med. oncology Meml. Sloan-Kettering Cancer Ctr., N.Y.C., 1976—78; attending physician in medicine, hematology and med. oncology Med. Ctr. at Princeton, NJ, 1983—. Assoc. clin. prof. medicine U. Medicine and Dentistry N.J.-R.W. Johnson, 1985—. Named one of Top Drs. in N.Y. Metro Area, Castle Connolly, Top Drs. 2003, N.J. Monthly Mag. Office: Princeton Med Group 419 N Harrison St Princeton NJ 08540-3521 Office Phone: 609-924-9300. E-mail: jsierocki@princetonhcs.org.

**SIES, TIMOTHY RAY,** music educator; s. Terry R. and Marian D. Sies. MusB Edn., Wright State U., 2001; postgrad., Ohio State U. Cert. K-12 music tchr. Ohio. Student tchr. Huber Heights (Ohio) City Schs.; lead music educator Marburn Acad., Columbus, 2002—04; music dir. Bishop Ready HS, Columbus, 2004; dir. vocal studies North Coll. Hill City Schs., Cin., 2004—. Asst. tchr. Gospel Music Workshop of Am., New Orleans; musical instrument digital interface lab instr. Wright State U., Dayton, Ohio, 1999—2001; pvt. practice music theory tutor, voice tutor, trumpet tchr.; head coach jr. high wrestling North Coll. Hill City Schools, 2004—05, varsity wrestling head coach. Recipient Outstanding Service in Music award, Aley Meth. Ch., Music Edn. award, Wright State U., 1999; Juanita C. Burns scholar. Mem.: SW Ohio Wrestling Coaches Assn., Ohio Wrestling Coaches Assn., North Coll. Hill Edn. Assn., Ohio Edn. Assn., Ohio Music Edn. Assn., Music Educators Nat. Conf., Golden Key Internat. Honor Soc. (life), Kappa Delta Pi. Office: North Coll Hill City Schs 1620 W Galbraith Rd Cincinnati OH 45239 Office Phone: 513-931-8181.

**SIESS, ALFRED ALBERT, JR.,** engineering executive, management consultant; b. Bklyn., Aug. 16, 1935; s. Alfred Albert and Matilda Helen (Suttmeier) S.; m. Gale Murray Scholes, Dec. 17, 1966; children: Matthew Alan, Daniel Adam. BCE, Ga. Inst. Tech., 1956; postgrad. in bus., Boston Coll., 1968; MBA, Lehigh U., 1972. With fabricated steel constrn. divsn. Bethlehem (Pa.) Steel Corp., 1958-76, project mgr., 1969-76, engr. projects and mining divsn., 1976-86; sr. cons. T.J. Trauner Assocs., Phila., 1986-87; assoc. S.T. Hudson Internat., Phila., 1987-89; mng. dir. mktg. SWIN Resource Sys., Inc., Bloomsburg, Pa., 1989-90; mem. adj. faculty Drexel U., 1976-96. Weekly columnist Economic and Environmental Issues, East Pa. edit. The Free Press, 1981-86; co-patentee suspension bridge erection equipment. Founder S.A.V.E. Inc., Coopersburg, Pa., 1969, pres., 1970, 75, 81, bd. dirs. 1970—. Served with C.E., USN, 1956-58. Recipient Environ. Action award, S.A.V.E., Inc., 1975. Mem. ASCE (chmn. environ. tech. com. Lehigh Valley sect. 1971-83, life), Lions, Chi Epsilon. Republican. Mem. United Church of Christ. Home: 6460 Blue Church Rd Coopersburg PA 18036-9371 Office: C E Resource Group PO Box 39 Coopersburg PA 18036-0039 Office Phone: 610-965-3263. Business E-Mail: newmill05@earthlink.net.

**SIEVERS, SALLY RIEDEL,** mathematics professor; b. Butte, Mont., Dec. 23, 1941; d. Caroline S.; m. Anil Nerode, May 16, 1970; 1 child, Nathanael Caldwell Nerode. BS, Stanford U., 1963; MS, Cornell U., 1965, PhD, 1972. Lectr. math. Ithaca (N.Y.) Coll., 1970-72; dir. calculus exam.-tutorial program Cornell U., Ithaca, 1972-75; lectr. math. and computer sci. Wells Coll., Aurora, N.Y., 1977—. Cons. U.S. EPA Health Effects Lab., 1979-81. NSF fellow, 1963-67. Mem. Am. Math. Assn., Assn. for Women in Math., AAUP (sec. Wells Coll. chpt. 1997-98), Phi Beta Kappa. Office: Wells Coll Dept Math Aurora NY 13026

---

**SIEVERT, FREDERICK J.,** insurance company executive; b. 1948; Sr. v.p., CFO N.Y. Life Ins. Co., N.Y.C., 1992-95, exec. v.p., 1995-97, vice chmn., 1997—, pres., 2000—. Pres. Life Ins. Council NY, 2003. Office: NY Life Ins Co 51 Madison Ave New York NY 10010*

**SIEVERT, MARY ELIZABETH,** small business owner, retired secondary school educator; b. Sioux City, Iowa, Sept. 28, 1939; d. Arthur Harry and Bertha Busboom Sievert. BS, Morningside Coll., 1960; MA, U. Nebr., 1962; postgrad., U. Iowa, Hope Coll., U. Calif., Irvine. Scir. chemistry lab. Morningside Coll., Sioux City, Iowa, 1959—60; tchr. chemistry Davenport Schs., Iowa, 1962—86, Blackhawk Coll., Moline, Ill.; admissions officer St. Luke's Hosp., Davenport; SSTP counselor U. Iowa, Iowa City; computer instr. Grinnell Coll., Iowa, 1983; P/K-12/A sci. coord. Davenport Schs., 1986—96, AGATE dept. chair, 1995—99; pres., CEO Memorabilia ExtraOrdinaire, Davenport, 1996—. Exchange tchr. Rowley Regis Coll., Birmingham, England, 1975; pres., CEO Quad Cities Sci. and Engring. Fair, Davenport, 1962—99; adv. evaluation coun. Antique Am., Davenport, 2000—01; antiques and collectibles lectr. Ea. Iowa C.C., Davenport, 2001—, Blackhawk Coll., Moline, Ill., 2002—. Contbr. articles to profl. jours. Fundraising v.p. Miss Iowa Bd., Davenport, 1999—2001; mem. plan and zone commn. City of Davenport, 1988—94; WelcomeAires mem. QC vol. bur. QC Internat. Airport, 2000—; charter mem. 1st in the Nation in Edn. Rschr. Found., 1986—97; 63 com. woman Scott County Rep. Party; handbell ringer, former dir. vacation Bible sch. Holy Cross Luth. Ch., Davenport; mem. bd. Christ Lutheran Ch., 2002—. Named Outstanding H.S. Chemistry Tchr. of Yr. in Iowa, Iowa Acad. Scis., 1969, Outstanding Young Educator, Davenport Jaycees, Centennial Tchr. of Yr. in Iowa, NIH, 1987; named to Iowa Sci. Tchrs. Hall of Fame, 2002; recipient Regional Catalyst award for outstanding chemistry tchr., Chem. Mfg. Assn., 1985, Golden Apple award for top educator, Scott County Edn. Orgn., 1998; fellow Woodrow Wilson fellow for outstanding H.S. chemistry tchrs., Princeton U., 1982; scholar NSF. Mem.: AAUW (past pres. local br. and Iowa State), NEA (life), U. Nebr. Alumni Assn. (life), Morningside Alumni Assn. (life), Delta Kappa Gamma (former local and state parliamentarian, mem. Hapke scholarship com.), Pi Lambda Theta (life; mem. charter alumni chpt.), Sigma Kappa (life). Avocations: bridge, gardening, travel, theater, symphony. Office: Memorabilia ExtraOrdinaire Inc 2707 East Hayes St Davenport IA 52803

**SIEVERT, VICKI LEE,** retired music educator; d. Joe Sproul and Ruby Baughman-Sproul; m. Richard Paul Sievert, Mar. 16, 1974; children: Michael William, Cassandra Ruth. MusB, Bowling Green State U., 1970. Profl. tchg. cert. Ohio, cert. Level 1 Am. Orff Schulwerk Assn., cert. Level II Am. Orff Schulwerk Assn. Music specialist pub. sch. Benton/Carroll/Salem Sch. Dist., Oak Harbor, Ohio, 1970–2003; elem. music specialist Genoa (Ohio) Local Sch. Dist., 2003—04; music dir. Oak Harbor United Meth. Ch., 2002—. Music dept. chair Benton/Carroll/Salem Sch. Dist., Oak Harbor, Ohio, 1989—98, co-chair curriculum update com. dept. music, 2001—03, chair curriculum and nat. standards com. music strategic plan, 2002—04. Com. chair Oak Harbor (Ohio) United Meth. Ch., choir dir., 2000—, bd. mem. Mem.: Music Educators Nat. Conf. (assoc.), Ohio Educators Assn. (assoc.; sec. 1996—98), Ohio Music Educators Assn. (life; mentor). Avocations: handcrafts, playing piano. Home: 8845 W State Rt 163 Oak Harbor OH 43449

**SIEVING, PAUL A.,** federal agency administrator, ophthalmologist, educator; BS in Physics and History with honors, Valparaiso U., 1970, DS (hon.), 2003; MS in Physics, Yale U., 1973; postgrad., Yale Law Sch., 1974; MD, U. Ill. Med. Sch., 1978; PhD in Bioengring., U. Ill. Grad. Sch., 1980. Diplomate Nat. Bd. Med. Examiners, 1978, Am. Bd. Ophthalmology, 1983. Med. resident in ophthalmology U. Ill. Eye and Ear Infirmary, 1978—82; postdoctoral fellow in retinal physiology U. Calif., San Francisco, 1982—84; clin. fellow in retinal degenerations Harvard, Berman-Gund Lab, Mass. Eye and Ear Infirmary, 1984—85; asst. prof. ophthalmology U. Mich., Ann Arbor, 1985—89, assoc. prof., 1989—94, prof., 1994—2001, Paul R. Lichter prof. of ophthalmic genetics, 1990—2001; dir. Nat. Eye Inst., NIH, Bethesda, Md., 2001—. Chair Retinal Diseases NEI, Vision Rsch.: A Nat. Plan, 2000—2003. Named one of Best Doctors in Am., 1996, 1998, 2001; recipient Olga Keith Weiss scholar, 1989, Disting. Alumnus, Valparaiso U., 1991, Sr. Sci. Investigator award, 1998, Alcon Rsch. award, Alcon Rsch. Inst., 2000; James scholar, U. Ill. Med. Sch., 1978. Mem.: RP Found. Fighting Blindness (Sci. Adv. Bd. 1989—2001, vice-chair rsch. 1995—2001), Internat. Soc. Clinical Electrophysiology of Vision (tres. 1986—94), Am. Ophthal. Soc., Sigma Xi. Achievements include specializing in the treatment of human genetic retinal and macular degenerations and research to prevent blindness. Office: Nat Eye Inst NIH Bldg 31 6A03 31 Center Dr Bethesda MD 20892-2510

**SIEVWRIGHT, JULIA ANN,** elementary school educator; d. Ronald Irvin and Ann Julia Budd; m. Curtis James Sievwright, Mar. 31, 1982; children: Dane Wyatt, Drew Tanner. BS in Elem. Edn., U. Minn., 1992; MEd, St. Mary's U. Minn., 1999. Cert. tchr. Nat. Bd. Profl. Tchg. Standards, 2001. Tchr. elem. sch. Dist. 196, Eagan, Minn., 1992—. Founder, prin. PaW Print Pub., Eagan, 2002—. Fundraiser Shrine Children's Hosp., Minn., 1993—95. Mem.: ASCD. Office: Pinewood Community School 4300 Dodd Road Eagan MN 55123

**SIFF, MARLENE IDA,** artist, space designer; b. N.Y.C. d. Irving Louis and Dorothy Gertrude (Lahn) Marmer; m. Elliott Justin Siff, July 11, 1959; children: Bradford Evan, Brian Douglas. BA, Hunter Coll., 1957. Cert. tchr. elem. edn., N.Y., N.J. Tchr. Stewart Manor (N.Y.) Sch. Sys., 1957-59, Teaneck (N.J.) Sch. Sys., 1959-60; freelance interior designer Westport, Conn., 1966-70; designer Varo Inertial Products, Trumbull, Conn., 1970; designer signature collections J.P. Stevens & Co. Inc., N.Y., 1974-78, J.C. Penney Co., N.Y., 1978, C.R. Gibson Co., Norwalk, Conn., 1980. Corp. sec., treas., bd. dirs. Belmar Corp., Westport, 1972—; chmn. bd. Marlene Designs Inc., Westport, 1973-77; owner Marlene Siff Design Studio, Westport, 1978—; aesthetic cons. Alcide Corp., Norwalk, 1980-88. One-person shows include David Segal Gallery, N.Y.C., 1987, Conn. Pub. TV Gallery, Hartford, 1987, Paul Mellon Art Ctr., Choate Rosemary Hall, Wallingford, Conn., 1989, Conn. Nat. Bank Hdqs., Norwalk, 1990, Michael Stone Collection, Washington, 1992, Bergdorf Goodman Men, N.Y.C., 1993, Joel Kessler Fine Art, Miami Beach, Fla., 1994, Park Pl., Stamford, Conn., 1995, Westport Arts Ctr., 1995, Mitchells, Westport, 1998, NIH, Bethesda, Md., 1999, Durst Lobby Gallery, N.Y.C., 1999, Rosenthal Gallery at Rich Forum, Stamford, Conn., 2005; represented in permanent collections B'nai Brith Klutznick Nat. Jewish Mus., Washington, 1997. Decorator Easter Seal Home Svc. Charity Ball, 1976; bd. dirs. United Jewish Appeal, Westport, 1982-86; com. mem. Levitt Pavillion of the Performing Arts, Westport, 1982-89. Recipient award for creating the most beautiful working environment in an indsl. facility in lower Conn., Lower Conn. Mfrs. Assn., 1970. Mem.: LVW, Art Adv. Coun. Herbert F. Johnson Mus. Art at Cornell U. NY, Anti Defamation League, Nat. Coun. Jewish Women, Kappa Pi. Jewish. Avocations: tennis, swimming, race walking, gardening. Home: 15 Broadview Rd Westport CT 06880-2303 Office Phone: 203-226-8557. Business E-Mail: marlene@marlenesiff.com.

**SIFFERT, JOHN SAND,** lawyer, educator, writer; b. NYC, Mar. 26, 1947; s. Robert Spencer and Miriam (Sand) S.; m. Goldie Alfasi-Siffert, June 1, 1975; children: David Alfasi, Matthew Alfasi. BA, Amherst Coll., 1969; JD, Columbia U., 1972. Bar: N.Y. 1973, U.S. Dist. Ct. (so. dist.) N.Y. 1974, (ea. dist.) N.Y. 1974, U.S. Ct. Appeals (2d cir.) 1974, U.S. Supreme Ct. 1979. Law clk. to Hon. Murray I. Gurfein US Dist. Ct. (so. dist.) N.Y., 1972-74; asst. U.S. atty. (so. dist.) N.Y., 1974-79; ptnr. Fulop & Hardee and predecessor firm Barovick, Konecky et al N.Y.C., 1979-83, Lankler & Siffert, N.Y.C., 1983-84, Lankler Siffert & Wohl LLP, N.Y.C., 1984—. Adj. prof. N.Y.U., 1979—; adv. coun. procurement policy bd. City of N.Y., 1991-95; mem. adv. bd. N.Y. Civil Rights Coalition, 1995—; bd. dirs. N.Y.C. Off-Track-Betting, 1996-2004; spl. master First Dept. Appellate Divsn., 1999—; mem. divsn. first dept. Indigent Def. Orgn. Oversight Com., 2003-2004; mem. appellate divsn. Dept. Disciplinary Com. 1st Jud. Dept., 2005—. Co-author: Business Crime, 1981, Modern Federal Jury Instructions-Criminal, Modern Federal Jury Instructions-Civil. Mem. adv. bd. N.Y. Civil Rights Coalition, 1995—;

bd. dirs. N.Y. Lawyers for Pub. Interest, 1998—, sec., 2003—06, chair, 2006—. Fellow: Am. Coll. Trial Lawyers (chmn. com. on admission to fellowship 2001—04, chmn. N.Y. downstate com. 2004—06, bd. regents 2006—); mem.: ABA, N.Y. Coun. Def. Lawyers (bd. mem. 2004—), Fed. Bar Coun. (pres. Inns of Ct. 2001—02), Assn. Bar City N.Y. (chmn. fed. legis. com. 2003—06, exec. bd. 2006—), N.Y. State Bar Assn. Democrat. Jewish. Office: Lankler Siffert & Wohl 500 5th Ave Fl 33 New York NY 10110-3398 Business E-Mail: jsiffert@lswlaw.com.

**SIFFERT, ROBERT SPENCER,** orthopedic surgeon; b. NYC, June 16, 1918; s. Oscar and Sadye (Rusoff) Siffert; m. Miriam Sand, June 29, 1941; children: Joan, John. AB in Biology with honors, NYU, 1939, MD, 1943. Diplomate Am. Bd. Orthrop. Surgery, Nat. Bd. Med. Examiners. Intern Kings County Hosp., Bklyn., 1943; resident in surgery Mt. Sinai Hosp., N.Y.C., 1946-49, fellow in pathology, 1949-52, mem. staff, 1949—, dir. orthor. surgery, orthop. surgeon in chief, 1960-86, Lasker/Siffert Disting. Svc. prof., 1986—; pvt. practice N.Y.C., 1949—. Sr. orthop. cons. N.Y.C Dept. Health, 1952—60; attending orthop. surgeon Blythedale Children's Hosp., Valhalla, 1960—86, cons., 1986—90; dir. dept. orthops. City Hosp., Elmhurst, 1965—86; prof., chmn. dept. orthrops. Mt. Sinai Sch. Medicine, 1966—86, Dr. Robert K. Lippman prof., 1983—86, acting chmn., 1993—94. Author (with J. F. Katz): (book) Management of Hip Disorders in Children, 1983; author: See How They Grow, 1985; contbr. articles to profl. jours. Bd. dirs., mem. profl. adv. com. Easter Seal Soc. Crippled Children and Adults, 1st v.p., 1977—79; mem. adv. bd. CARE-MEDICO, 1972—83, bd. dirs., chmn., 1981—83; bd. dirs. CARE, 1983—90; mem. adv. bd. Orthopaedics Overseas, 1981—93. Capt. USAAF, 1944—46, CBI. Decorated 4 Battle Stars; recipient Ann. award in medicine, N.Y. Pub. Health Assn., 1956, N.Y. Philanthropic League, 1959, Richman award for humanism in medicine, Mt. Sinai Sch. Medicine, 1989, Lifetime Achievement award, NY Arthritis Found., 2004. Fellow: APHA, ACS; mem.: N.Y. State Med. Soc. (chmn. orthrop. sect. 1967—68), N.Y. Acad. Medicine (fellow orthop. sect. 1952, sec. 1962—63, chmn. 1963—64), Orthop. Rsch. Soc., Internat. Skeletal Soc., Internat. Soc. Orthop. Surgery and Traumatology, Assn. Bone and Joint Surgeons, Am. Acad. Orthop. Surgery (chmn. com. care handicapped child), Am. Orthop. Assn., Century Assn. (N.Y.C.), Phi Beta Kappa, Alpha Omega Alpha. Office Phone: 212-288-2566. Personal E-mail: rssiffert@aol.com.

**SIFNEOS, PETER EMANUEL,** psychiatrist, educator; b. Greece, Oct. 22, 1920; came to U.S., 1941, naturalized, 1944; s. Demitrios Z. and Mary E. (Lucas) S.; divorced; children: Ann Lucas Callahan, Peter Gray, Jean Coit Sifneos Schafer. B.Sc., Sorbonne, 1940; MD, Harvard U., 1946; PhD (hon.), U. Athens, Greece, 1998. Diplomate: Am. Bd. Psychiatry. Intern Boston City Hosp. and Harvard Med. Svc., 1946-47; resident in psychiatry McLean Hosp., Belmont, Mass., 1950-52; chief resident Mass. Gen. Hosp., Boston, 1952-53, mem. staff, chief psychiat. clinic, 1954-68; fellow Harvard U. Sch. Public Health, 1953-54; mem. faculty Harvard U. Med. Sch., 1952—, prof. psychiatry, 1973-91, prof. emeritus, 1991—; staff, assoc. dir. psychiatry dept. Beth Israel Hosp., Boston, 1968-94. Author: Ascent from Chaos, 1964, Short-Term Psychotherapy and Emotional Crisis, 1972, Short-Term Dynamic Psychotherapy Evaluation and Technique, 1979, 2d edit.. 1987, Short-Term Anxiety Provking Psychotherapy, 1992, Escape?, 1998, 2d edit., 2002; editor-in-chief Psychotherapy and Psychosomatics, 1974-91; contbr. over 125 articles to profl. jours. Served with AUS, 1944-46, U.S. Army Med. Corp., Germany, 1947-50. Fellow: Am. Psychiat. Assn. (disting. life 2003); mem.: AMA, Am. Psychosomatic Soc., Italian Psychosomatic Soc. (hon.), Boston Psychoanalytic Soc. (life), Hellenic Psychosomatic Soc. (hon.), Internat. Fedn. Med. Psychotherapy (v.p. 1976—88, bd. dirs. 1988—94). Democrat. Home and Office: 59 Common St Belmont MA 02478-3022 E-mail: pesifneos@aol.com. *The principles which helped me most have been a belief in good education, a fierce sense of non-conformity, a strong sense of independence, an admiration of creativity and new ideas, a love of writing, teaching, reading, classic music, traveling, lecturing and conducting workshops, seminars all over North and South America and Europe, swimming, and luck in being healthy.*

**SIFTON, CHARLES PROCTOR,** federal judge; b. NYC, Mar. 18, 1935; s. Paul F. and Claire G. S.; m. Susan Scott Rowland, May 20, 1986; children: Samuel, Tobias, John. AB, Harvard U., 1957; LL.B., Columbia U., 1961. Bar: N.Y. 1961. Assoc Cadwalader, Wickersham & Taft, 1961-62, 64-66; staff atty. U.S. Senate Fgn. Rels. Com., 1962-63; asst. U.S. atty. N.Y.C., 1966-69; ptnr. LeBoeuf, Lamb, Leiby and MacRae, 1969-77; judge U.S. Dist. Ct. (ea. dist.) N.Y., Bklyn., 1977—, chief judge, 1995-2000, sr. judge, 2000—. Mem.: Bar Assn. City of N.Y. Office: US Dist Ct US Courthouse 225 Cadman Plz E Rm 244 Brooklyn NY 11201-1818

**SIFTON, DAVID WHITTIER,** retired magazine editor; b. NYC, Sept. 12, 1940; s. David William and Dorothy (Whittier) S. BA, Trinity Coll., Hartford, Conn., 1962; MA, Stanford U., 1967. Editor Inside Edn., N.Y. State Edn. Dept., 1968-70; adminstrv. editor Med. Econs., Oradell, NJ, 1970-72; editor Drug Topics, Oradell, 1972-75; editor in chief Current Prescribing, Oradell, 1975-78, RN mag., Oradell, 1978-83; dir. spl. editorial projects Med. Econs. Co., 1983-90 editor PDR Publs., Montvale, 1990—2003; ret., 2003. Founder Physicians' Desk Reference on CD-ROM, PDR's Drug Interactions and Side Effects Index, PDR's Indications Index, Pocket PDR (handheld electronic database), The PDR Family Guide to Prescription Drugs, The PDR Family Guide to Women's Health, The PDR Family Guide to Nutrition and Health, The PDR Family Guide to Lifelong Health, The PDR Family Guide Encyclopedia of Medical Care, The PDR Family Guide to Over-the-Counter Drugs, The PDR Family Guide to Natural Medicines and Healing Therapies, The PDR Family Guide to Common Ailments, The PDR Family Guide to Nutritional Supplements, The PDR Guide to Biological and Chemical Warfare Response, The PDR Drug Guide for Mental Health Professionals. Served to 1st lt. USAF, 1963-66. Decorated Air Force Commendation medal; grantee Ford Found., 1967 Mem. Am. Bus. Press (chmn. editorial com. 1975-76) Republican. Episcopalian. Personal E-mail: david.sifton@verizon.net.

**SIFTON, SAM,** editor; AB, Harvard U., 1988. Asst. editor Am. Heritage, 1988—90; media critic NY Press, restaurant critic, mng. editor; founding editor Talk Mag.; dep. dining editor NY Times, NYC, 2001, dep. culture editor, 2004—05, culture editor, 2005—. Tchr. NYC Pub. Schs., 1990—94. Office: Culture Editor NY Times 229 W 43rd St New York NY 10036 Office Phone: 212-556-7411. Office Fax: 212-556-1516.*

**SIGAFOOS, THOMAS W., JR.,** principal; b. Easton, Pa., Feb. 19, 1967; s. Thomas W. Sigafoos Sr. and Darlene F. Webber. BA, Moravian Coll., 1989; MEd, East Stroudsburg U., 1994. Cert. elem. and secondary sch. prin. Pa., 1996, supt. Pa. Elem. tchr. Stroudsburg (Pa.) Area Sch. Dist., 1989—96; prin. Colonial Elem. Sch., Plymouth Meeting, Pa., 1996—2000; prin., dir. of fed. programs Ridge Pk. Elem. Sch., Conshohocken, Pa., 2000—. Regional rep. PA Assoc. of Elem. Sch. Principals, Summerdale, Pa., 2001—07; pa rep. to naesp PAESSP, Summerdale, Pa., 2001—05; zone 2 dir. NAESP, Alexandria, VA, 2005—. Actor: Moravian College Theatre Company. Mem.: Pa. Assn. Elem. Sch. Prins. (rep. to Nat. Assn. Elem. Sch. Prins. 2001—05, regional rep. 1997—2001, zone dir. 2005—). Democrat. Avocations: travel, reading, gardening. Home: 109 Kings Rd Plymouth Meeting PA 19462-1816 Office: Ridge Park Elem Sch 200 Karrs Lane Conshohocken PA 19428 Office Fax: 610-825-7983. Personal E-mail: tomsigafoos@aol.com. Business E-Mail: tsigafoos@colonialsd.org.

**SIGAL, JILL L.,** federal agency administrator; BA, Vermont U.; JD, George Washington U. Advisor office of gen. counsel Dept. of Energy; pres. Jill Sigal Assocs.; dep. asst. sec. for environ. and sci. Office Congl. and Intergovernmental Affairs US Dept. Energy, 2003—04, prin. dep. asst. sec., 2004—05, acting asst. sec., 2005, asst. sec., 2005—. Office: US Dept Energy Forrestal Bldg 1000 Independence Ave SW Rm 7B-138 Washington DC 20585 Office Phone: 202-586-5450.

**SIGAL, LEONARD H.,** physician; b. N.Y.C., Aug. 26, 1951; s. Morris Lloyd and Theresa (Green) S.; m. Judith Halden, June 6, 1976 (div. May 31, 1981); m. Barbara K. Snyder, June 15, 1986; children: Merissa, Caroline SB, MIT, 1972; MD, Stanford U., 1976. Intern, resident Mt. Sinai Hosp., N.Y.C., 1976-79; chief internal medicine Westchester Community Health Plan, White Plains, NY, 1979-81; fellow rheumatology Yale U. Sch. Medicine, New Haven, 1981-84, fellow immunology, 1982-84; chief rheumatology Syracuse (N.Y.) VA Med. Ctr., 1984-88; asst. prof. medicine and immunology SUNY Health Sci. Ctr., Syracuse, 1984-88; asst. prof. medicine UMDNJ - R.W. Johnson Med. Sch., New Brunswick, NJ, 1988—, asst. prof. molecular genetics and microbiology, 1988—91, prof., chief divsn. rheumatology, dept. medicine, 1991—2003; dir. Immunology Pharm. Rsch. Inst Bristol-Myers Squibb, Princeton, NJ, 2003—. Speaker in field. Author (editor): Immunology to Inflammation: Basic Mechanisms and Clinical Consequences, 1990. Recipient Research Grant Arthritis Found., 1988, Research Grant Am. Heart Assn., 1989. Fellow ACP, Am. Coll. Rheumatology; mem. Am. Assn. Immunologists, Clin. Immunology Soc., Soc. Exptl. Biology and Medicine, MIT Club. Democrat. Jewish. Avocations: reading, tennis, sailing, photography, kayaking. Home: 26 Hastings Rd Belle Mead NJ 08502 Office: J3100 Pharm Rsch Inst Bristol Myers Squibb Rte 206 and Provinceline Rd PO Box 4000 Princeton NJ 08543-4000 Office phone: 609-252-6050. Business E-Mail: leonard.sigal@bms.com.

**SIGAL-IBSEN, ROSE,** artist; b. Bucharest, Romania, Aug. 22; arrived in U.S., 1957; d. Joseph and Tilly (Eckstein) Cohen; m. Albert D. Sigal, Dec. 25, 1941 (dec. May 1970); 1 child, Daniel M.; m. Joseph Ibsen, Oct. 1973 Diploma, Fashion Inst. Technology, N.Y.C., 1978; Parson, Sch. of Design, N.Y.C., 1985—86; student, Koho Sch. of Sumi-E, N.Y.C., 1979—90, Zhejiang Acad. Fine Arts, China, 1990. Curator Metro N.Y. Chpt. of Sumi-E Soc., 1990—, v.p., 1990—. One-woman shows include China-Gallery Weizhi Schubert, Hanover, Germany, 1991, Manhattan Savs. Bank, N.Y.C., 1993—94, Chem. Bank, 1993—95, N.Y. Pub. Libr., 1996, Bankers Fed., N.Y.C., 1996, Rep. Bank for Savs., 1996, Roumanian Cultural Found., Bucharest, 1998, World Fine Art Gallery, N.Y.C., 1998, Romanian Embassy, Washington, 2000, Berkeley Coll. Gallery, 2006, others, numerous group shows including most recently, exhibited in group shows at Broome St. Gallery, NYC, 2001—02, 2005—06, Sumi-e Soc. Am. Inc. at Courthouse Galleries of Portsmouth Va., 2001 (Hallie Hazen Meml. award, 2001), Pen and Brush Ann. Mixed Media, 2002, Korean Cultural Ctr., L.A., 2002, Japanese-Artists Assn. N.Y., 2002, Mobile Mus. Art, 2004, NY Hall of Sci., 2005, Hammond Mus., 2005, Keith and Janet Kelly U. Art Gallery, Calif. State Poly. U., Pomona, 2005, Courage Card design, 1998. Recipient Manhattan Arts award Cover Art Competition, N.Y.C., 1992, 94, 95, 97, King Point award, Fla., 1991, Tenth Japanese Internat. Calligraphy Exhbn. award, N.Y.C., 1996, Manhattan Arts Internat. Showcase award, Emily N. Hatch Meml. award Pen and Brush, Inc., Spring Watercolor Exhbn., 1998, Hallie Hazen Meml. award Sumi-e Soc. Am., 2001. Mem. Nat. Mus. of Women in the Arts, Artist Equity of N.Y., Am. Soc. Contemporary Artists, Art of Ink in Am., The Oriental Brushwork Soc. of Am.—Sumi-e Soc. Found. Avocations: sculptor in clay, dance. Home: One Irving Pl Apt 2-22B New York NY 10003-9741

**SIGALL, HAROLD FRED,** psychology professor; b. NYC, June 29, 1943; s. Walter and Regine (Goldenberg) S.; m. Brenda Ann Alpert, Aug. 8, 1965; children: Elana, Jennifer, Emily. BS, CUNY, 1964; PhD, U. Tex., 1968. Asst. prof. psychology U. Rochester, NY, 1968-72; assoc. prof. U. Md., College Park, 1972-78, prof., 1978—, dir. grad. program in social psychology, dir. grad. studies dept. psychology, 2000—, chair dept. psychology, 2006—; cons. editor Jour. Applied Social Psychology, 1992—. Cons. social rsch. and decision making to numerous orgns., lectr. Smithsonian Inst., Washington, 1984, 85; vis. prof. U. Bologna, 1997, 2002. Editor Personality and Social Psychology Bull., 1977-81. Bd. dirs. Columbia (Md.) Jewish Congregation, 1985-87, Howard County (Md.) Jewish Cmty. Sch., Columbia, 1986-87; mem. Human Rights Commn., Howard County, 1994-99. NDEA fellow, 1967-68, Danforth Found. fellow, 1970-71. Fellow APA, Am. Psychol. Soc.; mem. Soc. Exptl. Social Psychology. Home: 5060 Castle Moor Dr Columbia MD 21044-1871 Office: U of Md Dept Psychology College Park MD 20742-0001 Office Phone: 301-405-0424. Business E-Mail: hsigall@psyc.umd.edu.

**SIGBAND, NORMAN BRUCE,** communications educator; b. Chgo., June 27, 1920; s. Max and Bessie S.; m. Joan C. Lyons, Aug. 3, 1944; children: Robin, Shelley, Betsy. BA, U. Chgo., 1940, MA, 1941, PhD, 1954; LHD (hon.), DePaul U., 1986. Assoc. prof. bus. communication DePaul U., 1946-50, assoc. prof., 1950-54, prof., 1954-65; prof. mgmt. communication U. So. Calif., 1965—, chmn. dept. mktg., 1970-72, assoc. dean Sch. Bus., 1973-80, Disting. prof. emeritus, 1989—. Disting. Centennial lectr. U. Tex., Austin, 1986; cons. to industry; spkr., condr. workshops, seminars in field; scholar-in-residence Va. Commonwealth U., 1987, DePaul U., 1988; Borchard lectr., 2003. Author books including: Practical Communication for Everyday Use, 25th edit., 1954, Effective Report Writing for Business, Industry and Government, 1960, Communication for Management, 1970, Communicacion Para Directivos, 1972, Management Communication for Decision Making, 1972, Communication for Management and Business, 1976, Communication for Managers, 6th edit., 2001, Communicating in Business, 1987, 3d edit., 1989, in Spanish, 1993, in Chinese, 2001, Patient-Pharmacist Consultation: A Communication Skills Approach, 1993, Communication for Pharmacists and Other Health Professionals, 1995, 2d edit., 1996, (with J. Biles) The Status of American Universities: Challenges and Opportunities, 2003; movies include: Communication Barriers and Gateways, 2d edit., 1993, Listening: A Key to Problem Solving (award winner), 2d edit., 1993, The Grapevine, The Power of a Minute, 1992; gen. editor books including: Harcourt Brace Jovanovich Bus. series; contbr. numerous articles to profl. jours., mags. Served to capt AUS 1942-46, ETO. Decorated Bronze Star; recipient recognition award City of L.A., 1985, hon. alumnus award U. So. Calif., 1991. Fellow Am. Bus. Communication Assn. (pres. 1964-65); mem. Internat. Communication Assn., Acad. Mgmt., Anti-Defamation League, Hadassah Assocs., Blue Key, Phi Kappa Phi, Alpha Kappa Psi, Beta Gamma Sigma. Democrat. Jewish. Home: 3109 Dona Susana Dr Studio City CA 91604-4355 Office: 1985 Zonal Ave Los Angeles CA 90089-0105

**SIGEL, ANTHONY B.,** art conservator; Assoc. conservator objects Straus Ctr. Conservation, Harvard Art Museums, Cambridge, Mass. NEA Rome Prize Fellowship for Historic Preservation and Conservation, 2004—05. Office: Straus Ctr Conservation Harvard Art Museums 32 Quincy St Cambridge MA 02138

**SIGEL, JOHN D.,** lawyer; b. 1953; BA, Middlebury Coll., 1975; JD, Cornell Univ., 1980. Bar: Mass. 1980. Ptnr., vice chmn. Bankruptcy & Comml. dept. Wilmer Cutler Pickering Hale & Dorr, Boston. Editor (mng.): Cornell Law Rev.; contbr. articles to profl. jours. Named a Mass. Super Lawyer, Boston Mag., 2004. Fellow: Am. Coll. of Bankruptcy; mem.: Mass. Bar Assn., Boston Bar Assn. Office: Wilmer Cutler Pickering Hale & Dorr 60 State St Boston MA 02109 Office Phone: 617-526-6728. Office Fax: 617-526-5000. Business E-Mail: john.sigel@wilmerhale.com.

**SIGEL, MARSHALL ELLIOT,** financial consultant; b. Hartford, Conn., Nov. 25, 1941; s. Paul and Bessie (Somer) Sigel; m. Sybil R. Miller, Nov. 23, 1995. BS in Econs., U. Pa., 1963; JD, U. Miami, 1982, LLM in Taxation, 1983. Exec. v.p. Advo-Sys. divsn. KMS Industries, Inc., Hartford, 1963—69, pres., 1969—72, Ad-Type Corp., Hartford, 1963—69, Ad-Lists, Inc., Hartford, 1963—69; fin. cons. Hartford, 1972—83, Boca Raton, Fla., 1987—; pvt. practice law, 1983—87. Bd. dirs. Wharton Sch. Club S. Fla. Mem.: World Pres. Orgn., Fraternal Order Police Assocs., Boca Grove Club, 100 Club So. Palm Beach County. Home and Office: PO Box 273408 Boca Raton FL 33427-3408

**SIGELL, LEONARD TRITTACK,** pharmacologist, educator; b. Portland, Oreg., Dec. 28, 1938; s. Edward Trittack and Rose (Lichtgarn) S. BS (RPh) Pharmacy, Oreg. State U., 1961; PhD in Pharmacology, U. Oreg., 1964. Reg. pharmacist, Oreg.; cert. prevention specialist. Registered pharmacist Fred Meyer Pharmacy, Portland, 1962-64; staff Oreg. Poison Ctr., Portland, 1962-64; mem. faculty dept. pharmacology, dept. medicine U. Cin., 1964-97; dir. Drug and Poison Info. Ctr., Cin., 1966-97, dir. emeritus Dept. Pharmacology & Cell Biophysics, 1997—, dir. emeritus, 1997—. Former evaluator Law Enforcement Assistance Adminstrn., Open House Counseling Svc., Inc., Charlotte, N.C.; former mem. Nat. Adv. Panel to HEW Model Health Care Tech. Ctr. U. Mo., student rsch. awards com. Am. Assn. Poison Control Ctrs.; mem. profl. effectiveness program com. U. Cin., adv. com. Med. Ctr. Librs., past mem. admissions com. U. Coll. Medicine, Univ. Hosp.; mem. Cin. Health Dept. Pharmacy and Therapeutics com., Hamilton County Drug Abuse Coordinating Com.; past mem. steering com. Hamilton County Comty. Mental Health Bd.; former cons. multi-purpose Arthritis Ctr. for Tri-State area. Contbr. articles to numerous profl. jours.; mem. edtl. bd. Poisindex, former mem. editors cons. panel Jour. Am. Med. Assn.; past book reviewer Archives Internal Medicine, past reviewer Am. Jour. Diseases of Children; reviewer Drug Intelligence and Clin. Pharmacy; past referee Am. Jour. Hosp. Pharmacy. Mem. Alcohol and Drug Abuse Prevention Assn. of Ohio, Assn. of Ohio Substance Abuse Programs; past mem. Citizens Against Substance Abuse; bd. dirs. Adolescent Clinic of Children's Hosp. Med. Ctr., U.S. Pharmacopoeia Conv. Recipient Oscar Schmidt Pub. Svc. award, U. Cin., 1990-91; grantee, Nat. Inst. Occupl. Safety and Health, Marion Merrell Dow, McNeil Consumer Products Co. Mem. Am. Assn. Poison Control Ctrs., Drug Info. Assn., Am. Soc. Hosp. Pharmacists (assoc.), Ohio Assn. Poison Control Ctrs. (pres.), Cin. Bar Assn./ Acad. Medicine Substance Abuse Task Force, Rho Chi, Kappa Psi. Office Phone: 760-360-9084. Personal E-mail: ltsnrjk@earthlink.net.

**SIGERSON, MARJORIE LORRAINE,** librarian; b. Pitts., June 11, 1923; d. Roy Allen and Myrtle Mae (Bering) Parke; m. David Kinley Sigerson, Apr. 9, 1943 (div. Dec. 1985); children: Diane Parke, David Kinley. Student, Carnegie Inst. Tech., 1941—42, U. Pitts., 1942—43. Libr. Mus. Arts and Scis., Daytona Beach, Fla., 1963—, trustee, 1978—81, pres. Guild, 1978—79. Mem. com. Halifax Art Festival, 1963—99; mem. coun. Garden Clubs of Halifax Dist., 1965—67; charter mem. Ormond Beach (Fla.) Meml. Hosp. Aux., 1967—76; pres. Street Sch. PTA, New City, NY, 1958—59; leader Girl Scouts U.S.A., 1956—58. Recipient award for disting. svc., Mus. Arts and Scis., 1977, 1979, 1996, 2003. Mem.: Guild Mus. of Arts and Sci. (pres. 1978—79), Friendship Force of Daytona Beach, Cherry Laurel Garden Club (pres. 1966—67), Harvard Dames Club (sec. 1946—47). Presbyterian. Home: 210 Royal Dunes Blvd Ormond Beach FL 32176-4769 Office: Mus Arts & Scis 1040 Museum Blvd Daytona Beach FL 32114-4510

**SIGETY, CHARLES BIRGE,** investment company executive; b. NYC, Sept. 30, 1952; s. Charles Edward and Katharine Kinne (Snell) S.; m. Elizabeth Ross Pennington, Nov. 27, 1976; children: Austin Douglas, Katharine Colyer, Alexander Birge. BA in English Lit., Bates Coll., 1975. Lic. nursing home adminstr. Adminstr. in tng. Florence Nightingale Nursing Home, NYC, 1972, asst. dir. facility ops., 1975, dir. facility ops., 1975-78, assoc. adminstr., 1978-81, exec. dir., 1981-82; pres., CEO Profl. Med. Products, Inc., Greenwood, SC, 1982-96; pres. Upper Savannah Internat. Trade Assn., Greenwood, 1993, Petersburg Landing Devel., Inc.; CEO Bison Investments, Inc., Tampa, Fla., 1996—, Aerial Machine & Tool Corp., Vesta, Va., 1998—2006, Polyten Plastics, LLC, Washington, 1998-2000, Coeur Acquisition, LLC, Washington, NC, 1999, Polyten, LLC, Washington, NC, 2000—03; mem. bd. advisors MD Internat., 2003—. Mem. adv. bd. Liberty Mut. Ins. Cos. S.C., 1986—96, NationsBank (Bank of Am.), Greenwood, SC, 1984—96; vice chmn. Upper Savannah Bus. Group on Health Care, 1981—87, S.C. Bus. Roundtable for the Initiative for Work Force Excellence, Columbia, 1988—92; dir. exec. com. Osteo Am., Inc., 1993—96; bd. advisors Capital South Ptnrs., 2004—; pres. Petersburg Landing Develop., Inc., 2005—; mem. bd. adv. MD Internat., 1992—2000, 2003—. Bd. visitors Med. U. S.C., 1988; treas. YPO HealthCare Focus Forum, 1997; active Soc. of Internat. Bus. Fellows, 1999—; bd. dirs. Stewards Found., 2003—, active Def. Orientation Conf. Assn., 2004—. Mem. Health Industry Mfrs. Assn. (ofcl. rep. 1982-96, 99-2002), Upper Savannah Internat. Trade Assn. (pres. 1993), Young Pres.'s Orgn., Chief Execs. Orgn., World Pres.' Orgn. Avocations: hunting, sailing. Office: Bison Investments Inc 3225 S Macdill Ave # 236 Tampa FL 33629-8171 Office Phone: 813-832-6359.

**SIGETY, CHARLES EDWARD,** lawyer, financial planner; b. NYC, Oct. 10, 1922; s. Charles and Anna (Toth) S.; m. Katharine K. Snell, July 17, 1948; children: Charles, Katharine, Robert, Cornelius, Elizabeth. BS, Columbia U., 1944; MBA, Harvard U., 1947; LLB, Yale U., 1951; LHD (hon.), Cazenovia Coll., 1984. Bar: NY 1952, DC 1958. With Bankers Trust Co., 1939-42; instr. adminstrv. engring. Pratt Inst., 1948; instr. econs. Yale U., 1948-50; vis. lectr. acctg. Sch. Gen. Studies Columbia U., NYC, 1948-50, 52; rapporteur com. fed. taxation for U.S. coun. Internat. C. of C., 1952-53; asst. to com. fed. taxation Am. Inst. Accts., 1950-53; with Compton Advt. Agy., NYC, 1954; vis. lectr. law Yale U., 1952; pvt. practice law NYC, 1952—67; pres., dir. Video Vittles, Inc., NYC, 1953—67; dep. commr. FHA, 1955-57; of counsel Javits and Javits, 1959-60; 1st asst. atty. gen. NY, 1958-59; dir., mem. exec. com. Gotham Bank, NYC, 1961—63; dir. NY State Housing Fin. Agy., 1962—63; chmn. Met. Ski Slopes, Inc., NYC, 1962—65; pres., exec. adminstr. Florence Nightingale Health Ctr., NYC, 1965—85; dir. Schaerer AG, Wabern, Switzerland, 1982-88; chmn. Kenbar Group, NYC, 1997—, Internat. Bioimmune Sys., Inc., Great Neck, NY, 1999—. Professorial lectr. Sch. Architecture, Pratt Inst., NYC, 1962-66; mem. Sigety Assocs., cons. in housing mortgage financing and urban renewal, 1957-67; ho. cons. Govt. of Peru, 1956; mem. missions to Hungary, Poland, Fed. Republic Germany, Malta, Czechoslovakia, Russia, Israel, Overseas Pvt. Investment Corp., 1990-92; owner, operator Peppermill Farms, Pipersville, Pa., 1956—. Bd. dirs., sec., v.p., treas. Nat. Coun. Health Ctrs, 1969 85; bd. dirs. Am. Hungarian Found., 1974-76, Pritikin Rsch. Found., 1991—, Stratford Arms Condo Assn., 1992-93, 2002-, Global Leadership Inst., 1993—, Hepatitis B Found., Doylestown, 2005—; founding mem., bd. dirs., Natl. Assn. for Continence, 1982, trustee Cazenovia Coll., NY, 1981-2002, Delaware Valley Coll. Sci. and Agr., Doylestown, Pa., 1998-2005; trustee, v.p. Woodmere Art Mus. Phila., 2000-05, Navy Supply Corps Found., Athens, Ga., 2000—; del. White House Conf. on Aging, 1971, White House Conf. on Mgmt. Tng. and Market Econs. Edn. in Ctrl. and Ea. Europe, 1991; bd. visitors Lander Coll., U. SC, Greenwood, 1982-84; mem. fin. com. World Games, Santa Clara, 1981, London, 1985, Karlsruhe, 1989, The Hague, 1993, Confrerie des Chevaliers du Tastevin, Confrerie de la Chaine des Rotisseurs, Wine and Food Soc., Wednesday 10 Club, chmn. Alumni Assn. Townsend Harris HS, NYC, 2005-. Lt. (j.g.) Supply Corps, USNR, 1942-46. Recipient President's medal Cazenovia Coll., 1990, George Washington laureate Am. Hungarian Found., 1996; named Prin. for Day, Townsend Harris HS NYC Bd. Edn., 1997-2001, 2005, Disting. Alumnus US Navy Supply Corps Assn., Athens, Ga., 1998; Baker scholar Harvard U., 1947. Mem. DCA (Defense Orientation Conf. Assn.). Presbyterian. Office Phone: 212-410-8787. Personal E-mail: sigety@msn.com.

**SIGETY, CORNELIUS EDWARD,** small business owner; b. N.Y.C., June 6, 1958; s. Charles Edward and Katharine (Snell) Sigety; m. Virginia Wong. Oct. 28, 1995; children: Charles Edgar, Bradford Earle, Cornelia Ring. BA, U. Rochester, N.Y., 1980; MBA, Harvard U., Boston, 1985. Asst. adminstr. Florence Nightingale Health Ctr. N.Y., 1980-83; v.p. Profl. Med. Products, Greenwood, SC, 1985-88; mng. dir. Kenbar Group, N.Y., 1988—. Bd. dirs. Heritage Conservancy. Mem. Union Club, Doylestown Country Club, Mantoloking Yacht Club. Presbyterian. Avocations: sailing, golf, skiing. Home: PO Box 369 Pipersville PA 18947-0369 E-mail: cesigety@hotmail.com.

**SIGFRIDSON, ANDREW CARL,** real estate broker, investor; b. Putnam, Conn., June 2, 1976; s. Kenneth Carl Sigfridson and Betsy Jean DiQuattro, Robert DiQuattro (Stepfather) and Laurie Sigfridson (Stepmother); m. April Lyn Wernig, Mar. 17, 2002; 1 child, Alyssa Kate. BA, Bowdoin Coll., 1998. Broker comml. real estate CB Richard Ellis The Boulos Co., Portland, Maine, 1998—. Cons. Gulf of Maine Rsch. Inst., Portland, 2004—05. Contbr. articles to mags. Dir. Realize!Maine, Portland, 2005—06. Named Broker of Yr. Maine, CBRE New Eng., 2004; named one of Realtors' 30 under 30, Realtor

Mag., 2005. Mem.: Maine Comml. Assn. Realtors (dir. 2003—, v.p. 2003—), Maine Real Estate Developers Assn. (dir. 2004—), Nat. Assn. of Realtors. Independent. Avocations: golf, sailing, skiing. Office: CB Richard Ellis The Boulos Company One Canal Plaza Portland ME 04101 Office Phone: 207-772-1333. Office Fax: 207-871-1288. Business E-Mail: dsigfridson@boulos.com.

**SIGLER, JAMIE-LYNN,** actress; b. Jericho, NY, May 15, 1981; m. A.J. DiScala (separated). Student, NYU. Actor: (films) A Brooklyn State of Mind, 1997, Campfire Stories, 2001, Death of a Dynasty, 2003; (TV films) Call Me: The Rise and Fall of Heidi Fleiss, 2004; (TV series) The Sopranos, 1999—; (Broadway plays) Beauty and the Beast, 2002—03; singer: (albums) Here to Heaven, 2001; author: (autobiography) Wise Girl, 2002. Achievements include started acting at NY regional theaters; starred in over two dozen theatrical prodns. including Annie, The Wizard of Oz, The Sound of Music, The Wiz, and Gypsy.

**SIGLER, THERESA JANE,** school system administrator; b. Marion, Ohio, Mar. 24, 1951; d. William Howard and Joanna Elizabeth Byrd; m. Timothy Joseph Sigler, July 11, 1981; 1 child, Andrew Joseph. BA summa cum laude, Walsh U., North Canton, Ohio, 1972; MA, U. Mo., Kansas City, 1979. Cert. elem. edn. K-8 Walsh U., 1972, reading edn. K-12 U. Mo., 1979, gifted edn. K-12 Ashland U., 1985, gen. supervision K-12 Ashland U., 1985, elem. prin. Ashland U., 1987, asst. supt. cert. Ashland U., 1988, supt. Ashland U., 1990. Tchr. grade 1 Sandy Valley Local Sch. Dist., Canton, Ohio, 1972—73; tchr. multiage 3/4 Ctr. City Sch., Dayton, Ohio, 1973—74; tchr. grade 6 St. Pius X, Reynoldsburg, Ohio, 1974—76; reading specialist Canton Local Sch. Dist., 1980—84; reading/lang. arts supr. Stark County Bd. Edn., Canton, 1984—86; dir. curriculum and staff devel. Barberton (Ohio) City Sch. Dist., 1986—2000, Woodridge Local Sch. Dist., Peninsula, Ohio, 2000—. Cons. Am. Book Co., N.Y.C., 1976—80; adj. prof. Ashland U., Mussillon, Ohio, 1984—; presenter in field. Designed/developed (how to teaching audio visual vhs tape) Implementing and Integrating a New Language Arts Program at Grades K-8. Com. mem. United Way, Barberton, Ohio; mem. Barberton Head Start, 1996—2000, Decker Family Devel. Ctr., Barberton, 1996—2000; sec. Magical Theatre Co., Barberton, 1996—2000. Recipient Title I Program of the Yr. - Barberton City Schools, Ohio Dept. Edn. - Fed. Programs, 1994, Star Partnership award - Decker Family Devel. Ctr., Summit Edn. Initiative Found., 2000; grantee, Ohio Dept. Edn., 1986—2004, Barberton Found., 1996—2000; scholar, Kiwanis, 1970—72. Mem.: ASCD (assoc.), Internat. Reading Assn. (assoc.), Nat. Staff Devel. Coun. (assoc.), Ednl. Rsch. Svc. (assoc.), Delta Kappa Gamma (assoc.), Phi Delta Kappa (assoc.). Avocations: golf, reading, theater, bicycling, music. Home: 6516 Shenandoah Ave NW Canton OH 44718 Office: Woodridge Local Schools 4411 Quick Rd Peninsula OH 44264

**SIGMAN, STANLEY T.,** telecommunications industry executive; b. Lubbock, Tex. m. Gerry Lynn Sigman; 2 children. BBA, W. Tex. State U., 1970. Stockman Southwestern Bell Telephone, Hereford, Tex., 1965; exec. v.p. Southwestern Bell Mobile Sys., 1986—91, mng. dir., cellular and paging, SBC Comm., Teléfonos de México Mexico City, 1991—93, v.p., gen. mgr. Okla., 1993—94, exec. v.p., 1994—95, pres., CEO, 1995—99, group pres., SBC opers., 1999; sr. exec. v.p., svcs. Southwestern Bell Telephone Co., CEO, pres.; group pres.; COO SBC Communications Inc., 2001—02; pres., CEO Cingular Wireless LLC, Atlanta, 2002—. Office: Cingular Wireless Glenridge Highlands Two 5565 Glenridge Connector Atlanta GA 30342*

**SIGMON, J. LEWIS, JR.,** medical educator; b. Newton, NC, July 8, 1940; MD, U. N.C., 1966. Intern David Grant USAF Hosp., 1966-67; resident Charlotte (N.C.) Meml. Hosp., 1969-71; chmn. dept. family medicine Carolinas Med. Ctr., Charlotte, 1984-95, clin. coord. Charlotte Ofcl Reg. Primary Care Edn., 1995—2001, sr. ind. cons. in grad. med. edn., family and ins. medicine, 2001—, dir. family medicine residency program Monroe, 1997—2001; prof. family medicine U. NC, 1993—2004, prof. emeritus, 2004—. Acad. coun. Nat. Inst. for Program Dir. Devel., Kansas City, Mo., 1999—2003; pres. Am. Bd. Family Medicine Found., 2000—06; residency rev. com. for family medicine ACGME, 1997—2003, specialist site visitor for residency rev. com., 2004—; step 3 test com. USMLE/NBME, 2005—. Recipient Disting. Svc. award, U. NC Sch. Medicine, 2005. Mem. AMA, N.C. Acad. Family Physicians, Am. Acad. Ins. Medicine. Personal E-mail: sigmonjr@aol.com

**SIGMON, JOYCE ELIZABETH,** professional society administrator; b. Stanley, NC, Oct. 4, 1935; d. Rome Alfred and Pearl Elizabeth (Beal) S. BS, U. N.C., 1971; MA, Loyola U., 1980. Cert. assn. exec. Dental asst. Dr. Paul A. Stroup, Jr., Charlotte, N.C., 1953-63; instr. Wayne Tech. Inst., Goldsboro, N.C., 1963-65, Ctrl. Piedmont CC, Charlotte, 1965—69; dir. Dental Assisting Edn. ADA, Chgo., 1971-85, asst. sec. Coun. Prosthetics Svcs., 1985-87, mgr. Office Quality Assurance, 1987—90, exec. dir. Aux., 1990-92; dir. adminstrv. activities Am. Acad. of Implant Dentistry, Chgo., 1993—; exec. sec. Am. Bd. of Oral Implantology/Implant Dentistry, 1993-99. Deacon 4th Presbyn. Ch., 1973-75, elder 1975-77, 88-91, 2002-05, trustee, 1991-94; moderator Presbyn. Women in 4th Ch., 1987-91, Stephen min., 1997-99 Mem. Am. Soc. Assn. Execs., Chgo. Soc. Assn. Execs. (chair CAE com. 1991-92), Am. Dental Assts. Assn., N.C. Dental Assn. (pres. 1968-69), Charlotte Dental Assts. Soc. Presbyterian. Home: 260 E Chestnut St Chicago IL 60611-2401 Office: Am Acad Implant Dentistry 211 E Chicago Ave Chicago IL 60611-2637 Personal E-mail: jesigmon@aol.com

**SIGMOND, CAROL ANN,** lawyer; b. Phila., Jan. 9, 1951; d. Irwin and Mary Florence (Vollmer) S. BA, Grinnell Coll., 1972; JD, Cath. U., 1975. Bar: Va. 1975, D.C. 1980, Md. 1988, N.Y. 1990, U.S. Dist. Ct. (ea. dist.) Va. 1975, U.S. Dist. Ct. (so. and ea. dist.) N.Y. 1991, U.S. Ct. Appeals (4th cir.) 1976, U.S. Ct. Appeals (fed. cir.) 1987, U.S. Ct. Appeals (2d cir.) 2000, Fed. Claims Ct. 2002, Ct. Internat. Trade 2006. Asst. gen. counsel Washington Met. Area Transit Authority, 1978-85; acting assoc. gen. counsel for appeals and gen. law, 1985-86; assoc. Patterson, Belknap, Webb & Tyler, Washington, 1986-89, Berman, Paley, Goldstein & Kannry, NYC, 1991—93; prin. Law Offices of Carol A. Sigmond, NYC, 1993—97; of counsel Pollack & Greene, LLP, NYC, 1998—2000; pvt. practice NYC, 2000—03; ptnr. Kehl, Katzive, & Sigmond, NYC, 2004—05, Dunnington, Bartholomew & Miller, LLP, NYC, 2005—. Mem. ABA, D.C. Bar Assn., Assn. Bar City N.Y., N.Y. County Lawyers Assn., Women's Nat. Dem. Club. Democrat. Mem. Lds Ch. Avocations: piano, singing. Office: Dunnington Bartholow & Miller LLP 477 Madison Ave 12th Fl New York NY 10022 Office Phone: 212-682-8811. Business E-Mail: csigmond@dunnington.com

**SIGMOND, RICHARD BRIAN,** lawyer; b. Phila., Dec. 7, 1944; s. Joseph and Jean (Nissman) S.; children: Michael, Catherine, Alina; m. Susan Helen Peteraf, Dec. 24, 1984. BS, Phila. Coll. Textiles & Sci., 1966; JD, Temple U., 1969. Bar: Pa. 1969, U.S. Supreme Ct. 1973, U.S. Dist. Ct. (ea. dist.) Pa. 1975, U.S. Ct. Appeals (3d cir.) 1975, N.Y. 1982, D.C. 1995. Atty. Pub. Defender Assn., Phila., 1969-70; ptnr. Meranze, Katz, Spear & Wilderman, Phila., 1970-84; sr. ptnr. Spear, Wilderman, Sigmond, Borish & Endy, Phila., 1985-89, Jennings Sigmond, Phila., 1989—; gen. counsel Internat. Brotherhood Painters and Allied Trades, 1997-2000. Chmn., bd. dirs. Gatehouse Phila., 1972-83; lectr. Pvt. Industry Coun., Phila., 1985—; labor studies div., Pa. State U., 1978-82, 85-86; gen. counsel Stabilization Agreement, Sheet Metal Industry Trust Fund, 1994—, Internat. Painters and Allied Trades Industry Pension Fund, 1997—. Mem. ABA (labor law com., litigation com.), AFL-CIO (lawyers coordinating com.), Pa. Bar Assn. (labor law com.), Phila. Bar Assn. (labor com.), Phi Alpha Delta. Avocations: sailing, writing. Office: Penn Mutual Towers 510 Walnut St Fl 16 Philadelphia PA 19106-3601 Office Phone: 215-922-6700. Business E-Mail: r.sigmond@jslex.com.

**SIGMUND, DIANE WEISS,** judge; b. NYC, Mar. 1, 1943; BS, Pa. State U., 1963; JD magna cum laude, Temple U., 1977. Bar: Pa. 1977. Law clk. Blank, Rome, Cominsky & McCauley, Phila.; judge U.S. Bankruptcy Ct. (Pa. ea. dist.), 3rd circuit, Phila., 1993—, chief judge 2004—. Mem. steering com.

Ea. Dist. Pa. Bankruptcy Conf., 1995—, 3d Cir. Task Force Equal Treatment in Cts., Gender Commn., 1995-97; chmn. endowment edn. Nat. Conf. Bankruptcy Judges, 1996—, bd. govs., 1998-2002; mem. com. on automation and tech. Jud. Conf. U.S., 1997-2004. Fellow Am. Coll. Bankruptcy. Office: Robert NC Nix Courthouse 900 Market St Rm 203 Philadelphia PA 19107-4237

**SIGMUND, PAUL EUGENE,** political science professor; b. Phila., Jan. 14, 1929; s. Paul Eugene and Marie (Ramsey) S.; m. Barbara Rowena Boggs, Jan. 25, 1964 (dec. 1990); children— Paul Eugene, David, Stephen. AB, Georgetown U., 1950; AB Fulbright scholar, U. Durham, Eng., 1950-51; MA, Harvard, 1954, PhD, 1959; postgrad., U. Paris, France, U. Heidelberg, U. Cologne, Germany, 1955-56. Teaching fellow Harvard, 1953-55, 58-59, instr., 1959-63; assoc. prof. politics Princeton, 1963-70, prof. politics, 1970—. Author: Nicholas of Cusa and Medieval Polit. Thought, 1963; author: (with Reinhold Niebuhr) The Democratic Experience, 1969; author: Natural Law in Political Thought, 1971, 2d edit., 1981, The Overthrow of Allende and the Politics of Chile, 1977, Multinationals in Latin Am.: The Politics of Nationalization, 1980, Liberation Theology at the Crossroads: Democracy or Revolution?, 1990, paperback, 1992, The U.S. and Democracy in Chile, 1993, The Ideologies of the Developing Nations, 1963; editor, 1967, 2d edit., 1972, Models of Polit. Change in Latin Am., 1970; co-editor (with Pedro Aspe): The Polit. Economy of Income Distbr. in Mex., 1983; editor: Poder, Sociedad y Estado en USA, 1985, Evangelization and Religious Freedom in Latin Am., 1999, The Selected Political Writings of John Locke, 2005; translator: The Mil. and the State in Latin Am. (A. Roquié), 1987, St. Thomas Aquinas, On Politics and Ethics, 1988, Nicholas Cusa, The Cath. Concordance, 1991, 2d edit., 1995; assoc. editor: World Politics. Served to 1st lt. USAF, 1956-57. Mem. Am. Polit. Sci. Assn., Latin Am. Studies Assn., Phi Beta Kappa. Home: 8 Evelyn Pl Princeton NJ 08540-3818

**SIGNO, REIS T.,** science educator; s. Joaquim Nicolau and Nair Olivia Reis; m. Marcia Maria Oliveira, Apr. 10, 2004; 1 child, Joana Oliveira Reis. PhD, U. of Sao Paulo, 1999. Postdoctorate U. Sao Paulo, 1999—2001; asst. prof. U. of Mo., Rolla, 2002—. Mem.: Am. Ceramic Soc. (assoc.). Achievements include patents for Glass and Glass-Ceramic Sealant Compositions. Office: U Mo 302 Straumanis Hall Rolla MO 65409 Office Phone: 573-341-7094. Office Fax: 573-341-2071. Personal E-mail: reis@umr.edu. E-mail: reis!@umr.edu.

**SIGNOROVITCH, DENNIS J.,** communications executive; b. Norristown, Pa., July 23, 1945; s. James and Regina S.; m. Susan M. McLaughlin, 1968; children: James Edward, Sarah Elizabeth. BS in Fgn. Svc., Georgetown U., 1967; MA, Old Dominion U., 1972. Instr. U. Toledo, 1972-77; writer/editor Doehler Jarvis div. NL Industries, Toledo, 1977-78; mgr. pub. rels. Eltra Corp., N.Y.C., 1979, mgr. planning, 1980; various assignments AlliedSignal Corp., Morristown, N.J., 1980-92; v.p. pub. affairs AlliedSignal Inc., Torrance, Calif., 1992-98; v.p. mktg. and comm. AlliedSignal Aerospace, Torrance, 1998-99; v.p. comms. Honeywell Aerospace, 1999—. Mem. Exec. Comm. Forum. With U.S. Army, 1967-70. Decorated Bronze Star with oak leaf cluster. Mem. The Conf. Bd. (corp. comm. coun. 1991), Arthur W. Page Soc., San Francisco Acad. (trustee), Aerospace Industries Assn. (chmn. comms. coun. 2001—). Office: Honeywell Aerospace 2525 W 190th St Torrance CA 90504-6002

**SIGULER, GEORGE WILLIAM,** diversified financial services company executive; b. Cleve., Apr. 26, 1947; s. John Frederick and Helen Alice (Popp) S.; m. Pamela Ann Mallon, Oct. 31, 1981; children: George William Jr., Emily Ann, Charles Arthur, Mary Elizabeth, Andrew Cooper. AB, Amherst Coll. 1970; MBA, Harvard U., 1972. Ptnr. Harvard Mgmt. Co., Boston, 1974-83; chief of staff HHS, Washington, 1983-84; exec. v.p. Monarch Capital Corp., Springfield, Mass., 1984-87, vice chmn. bd., 1987-91; pres. Associated Capital Investor, San Francisco, 1990-91; mng. dir. Mitchell Hutchins Instl. Investors, Inc., N.Y.C., 1991-95; founder Siguler Guff & Co., 1995—. Assoc. treas. Harvard U., 1973-88; bd. dirs. Venture Lending and Leasing, Inc., Russia Ptnrs., L.P.; dir. Emerging Mkt. Pvt. Equity Assn., Rand Corp., Siguler Guff Distressed Opportunities Fund, Siguler Guff B.R.I.C. Opportunities Fund; mem. Bus. Forum 1999—; mem. adv. bd. Rand Corp. Ctr. Asia Pacific Policy, 2004. Mem. vis. com. Harvard U. Med. Sch., Boston, 1986—; mem. nat. adv. com. on community health resources HHS, Washington, 1985-90; trustee Perkins Sch. Blind, Watertown, Mass., 1976-83, New Eng. Aquarium, 1989-91, Bement Sch., 1999-. Recipient Disting. Svc. award HHS, 1984. Republican. Presbyterian. Office: Siguler Guff & Co 825 Third Ave 29th Fl New York NY 10022

**SIGURDSON, MIKE JAMES,** visual art educator; b. Bismarck, N.D., Nov. 21, 1966; s. Roland Pete and Alyce Marie Sigurdson; m. Theresa Lynn Fernandez, June 18, 1999. BA Comml. Art, Southwestern Okla. State U., Weatherford, 1992, BA Art Edn., 1994; postgrad. studies Ednl. Adminstrn., U. North Tex., Denton, 2004—. Freelance artist Self Employed, Irving, Tex., 1994—; art tchr. Bowie Middle Sch., Irving, Tex., 1994—99, boys basketball coach, 1995—; mens basketball asst. coach North Lake Jr. Coll., Irving, 2000—01; art tchr. Acad. H.S., Irving, 2001—; men's basketball asst. coach North Lake Jr. Coll., Irving, 2005—. Book Cover Art, Just Give Me a Zero!, 1999, Poster, 40th Anniversary Irving Community Concert Association, 1995, exhibitions include Gulf Coast Power Boat Assn., 2005. Nominee Tchr. of Yr., Irving Tex. Sch. Dist., 2004. Mem.: Tex. Art Educators Assn. Democrat. Lutheran. Avocations: art, sports. Home: 546 Briaroaks Dr Lake Dallas TX 75065 Office: Acad High Sch 4601 N MacArthur Blvd Irving TX 75038 E-mail: msigurdson@irvingisd.net

**SHILLING, CALVIN S.,** warehousing company executive; B in applied math., Northrop Inst. Tech. Positions with PepsiCo, Dr. Pepper, Electronic Data Systems; v.p. info. services Alex Lee Inc.; v.p., CIO ea. region SuperValu (formerly Richfood), 1998—2001; exec. v.p., CIO AmeriCold Logistics LLC, 2001—. Named one of Premier 100 IT Leaders, Computerworld, 2005. Office: AmeriCold Logistics LLC Ste 800 10 Glenlake Pkwy S Atlanta GA 30328 Office Phone: 678-441-1544. E-mail: csihilling@amclog.com.*

**SIHLER, WILLIAM WOODING,** finance educator; b. Seattle, Nov. 17, 1937; s. William and Helen Alice (Wooding) S.; m. Mary Elizabeth Unwin, Aug. 21, 1963; children: Edward Wooding, Jennifer Sihler Zysman. AB summa cum laude in Govt. (Sheldon traveling fellow), Harvard U., 1959, MBA with high distinction, 1962, DBA, 1965. Instr., asst. prof. Harvard U. Bus. Sch., 1964-67; assoc. prof. Darden Grad. Bus. Sch., U. Va., Charlottesville, 1967-72, prof., 1972-76, A.J. Morris prof., 1976-84, Ronald E. Trzcinski prof., 1984—, assoc. dean acad. affairs, 1972-77; exec. dir. Bankers Assn. Fgn. Trade/Ctr. for Internat. Banking Studies, 1977-91; dir. Tayloe Murphy Ctr. U. Va. Bd. dirs. Curtiss-Wright Corp.; pres. Southeastern Cons. Group, Ltd. Co-author: Financial Management: Text and Cases, 2d edit. 1991, The Troubled Money Business, 1992, Financial Service Organizations: Cases in Strategic Management, 1993, Cases in Applied Corporate Finance, 1994, Building Value with Capital-Structure Strategies, 1998, Financial Turnarounds--Preserving Value, 2001, Smart Financial Management: The Essential Reference for the Successful Small Business, 2004; editor: Classics in Commercial Bank Lending, vol. 1, 1981, vol. 2, 1985; contbr. articles to profl. jours. Vis. com. Sch. Mgmt., Case Western Res. U., 1976-86, bd. overseers, 1980-86. Recipient DeL. K. Jay prize Harvard U., Disting. Prof. award U. Va. Alumni Assn., 1982; C.J. Bonaparte scholar Harvard U. Mem. Fin. Mgmt. Assn., Am. Econ. Assn., Am. Fin. Assn., Eastern Fin. Assn., Univ. Club (N.Y.C.), Harvard Club (N.Y.C.), Greencroft Club (Charlottesville), Phi Beta Kappa, Beta Gamma Sigma. Home: 3215 Heathcote Ln Keswick VA 22947-9160 Office: PO Box 6550 Charlottesville VA 22906-6550 Office Phone: 434-924-7489.

**SIIROLA, JEFFREY JOHN,** chemical engineer; b. Patuxent River, Md., July 17, 1945; s. Arthur Raymond and Nancy Ellen (Harris) S.; m. Sharon Ann Atwood, Apr. 24, 1971; childen: John Daniel, Jennifer Ann. BS in Chem.

Engring., U. Utah, 1967; PhD, U. Wis., 1970. Rsch. engr. Eastman Chem. Co., Kingsport, Tenn., 1972-74, sr. rsch. engr., 1974-80, rsch. assoc., 1980-88, sr. rsch. assoc., 1988-95, tech. fellow, 1995—. Trustee CACHE Corp., Austin, Tex., 1983—. Co-author: Process Synthesis, 1973. Appalachian tr. maintenance Eastman Hiking Club, Kingsport, 1973—. With U.S. Army, 1970-72. Fellow AIChE (A.E. Marshall award 1967, Computing Practice award 1991, bd. dirs. 1999-2001, pres.-elect 2004, pres. 2005); mem. Nat. Acad. Engring., Chem. Scis. Roundtable, Accreditation Bd. for Engring. and Tech., Am. Chem. Soc., Am. Soc. for Engring. Edn., Am. Assn. for Artificial Intelligence, Kingsport C. of C. Achievements include development of the AIDES chem. process flowsheet invention procedure. Home: 2517 Wildwood Dr Kingsport TN 37660-4748 Office: Eastman Chem Co 200 S Wilcox Dr PO Box 1972 Kingsport TN 37662-5150 Office Phone: 423-229-3069. E-mail: siirola@eastman.com.

**SIKANDER, SHAHZIA,** artist; b. Lahore, Pakistan, 1969; BFA, Nat. Coll. Arts, Lahore, Pakistan, 1992; MFA, RISD, Providence, 1995. Artist-in-residence Otis Coll. Art and Design, LA, 2005. Work represented in numerous newspapers and mags., represented in solo and group exhibitions at MoMA, NY, Hirshhorn Mus. and Sculpture Garden, Nat. Gallery Canada, Musée d'Art moderne de la Ville de Paris, one-woman shows include Barbara Davis Gallery, Houston, 1996, Hosfelt Gallery, San Francisco, 1997, Deitch Project, N.Y.C., 1997, Renaissance Soc. U. Chgo., 1998, Kemper Mus. Contemporary Art and Design, Kansas City, Mo., 1998—88, Hirshhorn Mus., Washington, 1999, exhibited in group shows at Rhotas Gallery, Islamabad, Pakistan, 1992, Pacific Asia Mus., Pasadena, Calif., 1994—95, Bradford (Eng.) City Mus., 1996, Glassell Sch. Art Mus. Fine Arts, 1996, 1997, Laing Gallery, New-castle, Eng., 1997, Whitney Mus. Am. Art, 1997, Queens Mus. Art, Flushing Meadows, N.Y., 1997, Yerba Buena Gardens Ctr. Arts, San Francisco, Forum for Contemporary Art, St. Louis, 1998, Bard Coll., Annandale-on-Hudson, N.Y., 1998, Ludwig (Austria) Mus., 1998, Aldrich Mus. Contemporary Art, Conn., 1998, also exhbns. in Portugal, Johannesburg, South Africa, Mexico City, Drawing to Drawing, Hosfelt Gallery, 2003, Vancouver Art Gallery, 2003, Venice Biennale, 2005, Queens Mus. Art, 2006. Recipient Haji Sharif award for miniature painting, Shakik Ali award and Kipling award, Nat. Coll. Art, Lahore, 1993; grad. fellow, RISD, 1993—95, core program fellow, Glassel Sch. Art Mus. Fine Arts, Houston, 1995—97, grantee, Louis Comfort Tiffany Found., 1997, Joan Mitchell grantee, 1998—99, MacArthur Fellow, John D. and Catherine T. MacArthur Found., 2006. Address: care Deitch Projects 76 Grand St New York NY 10013-2222*

**SIKER, EPHRAIM S.,** anesthesiologist; b. Port Chester, N.Y., Mar. 24, 1926; s. Samuel S. and Adele (Weiser) S.; m. Eileen Mary Bohnel, Aug. 5, 1951; children— Kathleen Ellen, Jeffrey Stephen, David Alan, Paul William, Richard Francis. Student, Duke U., 1943-45; MD, N.Y.U., 1949. Diplomate: Am. Bd. Anesthesiology (dir. 1971—, sec.-treas. 1974-82, pres. 1982-83) Nat. Bd. Med. Examiners. Intern Grasslands Hosp., Valhalla, N.Y., 1949-50, resident in anesthesia, 1950; resident dept. anesthesiology Mercy Hosp., Pitts., 1952-53, assoc. dir. dept., 1955-62, chmn., 1962-92; practice medicine, specializing in anesthesiology Pitts., 1954—; pres. Pitts. Anesthesia Assocs., Ltd., 1967-89; dir. anesthesia services Central Med. Ctr., Pitts., 1973-89. Courtesy staff St. Clair Meml. Hosp., Pitts., 1954—89; clin. prof. dept. anesthesiology U. Pitts. Sch. Medicine, 1968—; mem. exec. com. Am. Bd. Med. Spltys., 1978—81; Exch. cons. Welsh Nat. Sch. Medicine, Cardiff, 1955—56; mem. Pa. Gov.'s Commn. on Profl. Liability Ins., 1968—70; mem. adv. panel U.S. Pharmacopeia, 1970—76; mem. Am. Acupuncture Anesthesia Study Group NAS to Peoples Republic China, 1974; mem. adv. com. on splty. and geog. distbn. of physicians Inst. Medicine NAS, 1974—76; trustee Ednl. Coun. for Fgn. Med. Grads., 1980—82, Mercy Hosp. Found., 1983—95; bd. dirs., sec. Anesthesia Patient Safety Found., 1985—89, mem. exec. com., 1985—92, exec. dir., 1992—97. Author: (with F.F. Foldes) Narcotics and Narcotic Antagonists, 1964; sect. on narcotic: (with F.F. Foldes) numerous other publs. in med. lit. Ency. Brittanica. Served to lt. M.C. USNR, 1950-52. USPHS postdoctoral research fellow, 1954; hon. fellow faculty anaesthetists Royal Coll. Surgeons, Eng., 1974; hon. fellow faculty anesthetists Coll. Medicine South Africa, 1983; recipient Hippocratic award Mercy Hosp., 1982 Fellow Royal Coll. Surgeons Ireland, Faculty Anaesthetists (hon. 1988); mem. Am. Soc. Anesthesiologists (pres. 1973—, bd. dirs. Disting. Svc. award 1984), AMA (alt. del. 1962), Pa. Med. Soc., Allegheny County Med. Soc., Pa. Soc. Anesthesiologists (pres. 1965, Disting. Svc. award 1986), Royal Soc. Medicine (Eng.), Pitts. Acad. Medicine, Am. Coll. Anesthesiologists (bd. govs. 1969-71), World Fedn. Anesthesiologists (chmn. exec. com. 1980-84, v.p. 1984-88), Assn. Anesthesia Program Dirs. (pres. 1987-89), Japanese Soc. Anesthesiologists (hon.). Achievements include developing Siker Laryngoscope, 1956. Home: 185 Crestvue ManorDr Pittsburgh PA 15228-1814 E-mail: r.siker@msn.com. *If you have to tell someone who you are, then you probably aren't. People are measured by more than their deeds, and such estimations are frequently made on the basis of their inter-personal relationships. While achievement and effort usually bear a linear relationship to each other, the impact that the achiever has on society depends upon the impact he makes on individuals.*

**SIKES, CYNTHIA LEE,** actress, children's advocate, singer; b. Coffeyville, Kans., Jan. 2, 1954; d. Neil and Pat (Scott) S.; m. Alan Bud Yorkin, June 24, 1989. Student, Am. Conservatory Theater, San Francisco, 1977-79. Actor: (TV series) St. Elsewhere, 1981—83, L.A. Law, 1989, JAG, 2000—01, (TV movies) Oceans of Fire, 1986, His Mistress, 1990; prodr., actor: Sins of Silence, 1996; actor: (films) Man Who Loved Women, That's Life, Arthur on the Rocks, Love Hurts, 1988, Possums, 1998, Going Shopping, 2005, (Broadway musical) Into the Woods, 1988—89. Active Hollywood Women's Polit. Com.; apptd. Pres. Clinton's Adv. Com. on Arts John F. Kennedy Ctr. for Performing Arts, 1999; apptd. commr. Calif. Svc. Corps, 2005—. Recipient Gov.'s Medal of Merit, Kans., 1986. Democrat. Avocations: hiking, writing, reading.

**SIKLOS, RICHARD,** reporter; Corp. media reporter NY Times. Author: Shades of Black, 1995. Office: NY Times 229 West 43rd St New York NY 10036 Office Phone: 212-556-1474. Office Fax: 212-556-1448.*

**SIKORA, BARBARA JEAN,** library director; b. Passaic, N.J., Apr. 12, 1943; d. Stanley Francis and Jean (Sobczyk) S. BA in Edn., English, William Paterson Coll., 1969, MEd in Learning Disabilities, 1978; MLS, Rutgers U., 1978; Cert. in Fundraising Mgmt., Fairleigh Dickinson U., 1990. Profl. libr. N.J. Tchr. Clifton (N.J.) Pub. Schs., 1969-73; office mgr. Singer/TRW, Fairfield, NJ, 1974-76; prin. libr. Passaic Pub. Libr., 1978-88; asst. libr. dir. Pub. Libr. Livingston NJ, 1989-90, libr. dir., 1991—. Adj. faculty William Paterson Coll., 1977-90; trustee Wayne Pub. Libr., 1986-88; bd. dirs. Polish and Slavic Fed. Credit Union, 1999—. Mem. Polish Heritage Festival Com., Holmdel, N.J., 1987—, gen. chmn., 1999; trustee, bd. dirs. Livingston Area C. of C., 1998—; pres. Libr. Pub. Rels. Coun., 1997; West Essex br. YMCA of the Oranges, 1997—; mem. Polish Children's Heartline, Inc. Grantee U.S. Dept. Edn. libr. literacy program, 1987, N.J. State Libr. Leadership Inst., 1988, Christopher Leadership Inst., 1997; Paul Harris fellow Rotary Internat., 1999. Mem. ALA (ethics com. 1995-99), AAUW, N.J. Libr. Assn., Nat. Spkrs.' Assn., Rotary (pres. Livingston chpt. 1994-96, 2000), Rutgers Sch. Comm. and Info. Libr. Studies Alumni Assn. (pres. 1991-94), Beta Phi Mu. Avocation: writing. Home: The Mill 300 Main St Apt 314 Little Falls NJ 07424-1359 Office: Pub Libr Livingston 10 Robert Harp Dr Livingston NJ 07039 E-mail: sikora@bcols.org.

**SIKORA, CLIFFORD S.,** lawyer; b. Harrisburg, Pa., 1962; BS, Cornell Univ., 1984; MPA, Univ. Del, 1986; JD, Univ. Dayton, 1989. Bar: Pa. 1989, DC 1999. Adv. atty., office of gen. counsel, dept. elec. rates and corp. regulation Fed. Energy Regulatory Commn., 1989—91, supervising atty. Office of gen. counsel, dept. elec. rates and corp. regulation, 1991—93, legal adv. to Commr. Donald F. Santa, Jr., 1993—95; counsel, com. on energy and natural resources US Senate, 1995—96; of counsel Troutman Sanders LLP, Washington, 1996—99, ptnr. energy group, 1999—, energy practice group leader, 2001—. Named to BTI Client Service All-Star Team for Law Firms,

2005. Office: Troutman Sanders LLP Ste 1000 401 Ninth St NW Washington DC 20004-2134 Office Phone: 202-274-2966. Office Fax: 202-654-5627. Business E-Mail: clifford.sikora@troutmansanders.com.

**SIKORA, DARRYN MARIE,** pediatric psychologist; b. Glendale, Calif., Sept. 15, 1962; d. Richard Pack and Darlene Rae Tiffany, Theodore Wallace Tiffany (Stepfather) and Karen Pack (Stepmother); m. Thomas L. Sikora; children: Emily Marie, Elizabeth Grace. BA, U. Calif., Irvine, 1983; MA, W.Va. U., Morgantown, 1986, PhD, 1989. Lic. Psychologist Bd. of Psychologist Examiners, Oreg., 1991. Pediatric psychologist Oreg. Health & Sci. U., Portland, 1990—. Autism program dir. Oreg. Health & Sci. U., Portland, 2003—. Author several peer-reviewed jours. Grant, Cure Autism Now, 2005. Achievements include research in Role of Cholesterol Metabolism in Autism. Avocations: skiing, camping, martial arts. Office: Oregon Health & Science Univ 707 SW Gaines Rd Portland OR 97239 Office Phone: 503-494-2749.

**SIKOROVSKY, EUGENE FRANK,** retired lawyer; b. Jackson, Mich., Nov. 27, 1927; s. Frank Joseph and Betty Dorothy (Malik) S.; m. Patricia O'Byrne, July 11, 1953; children: Paul, Charles, Catherine, Elizabeth, Emily. BSEE, U. Mich., 1948; LLB, Harvard U., 1951. Bar: N.Y. 1952, Va. 1970, Ill. 1978. Assoc. predecessor firms Cahill, Gordon & Reindel, 1954-63, ptnr., 1964-68; v.p., gen. counsel, dir. Reynolds Metals Co., Richmond, Va., 1969-76; gen. counsel Gould Inc., Rolling Meadows, Ill., 1977-79, v.p., 1977-81; dep. gen. counsel Bell & Howell Co., Skokie, Ill., 1981-83, v.p., 1983-88, gen. counsel, 1983-92, sec., 1984-92, sr. v.p., dir., 1988-92. Lt. USNR, 1951-54. Mem. Ill. State Bar Assn., Tau Beta Pi, Eta Kappa Nu, Phi Eta Sigma, Phi Delta Theta. Episcopalian. Home: 720 Grandview Ln Lake Forest IL 60045-3953 E-mail: genesikor@earthlink.net.

**SIKORSKA, ELZBIETA MAGDALENA,** artist; b. Warsaw, Jan. 8, 1950; came to U.S., 1986; d. Eugeniusz Sikorski and Zofia Domanska Sikorska. Student, Acad. Fine Arts, Warsaw, 1969-74. Exhibited in one-person shows in Warsaw, West Berlin, and Nykoping, Denmark, Addison/Ripley Gallery, Washington, 1989, 90, 92, 96, Collins Pettit Gallery, Taos, N.Mex., 1992, Soc. for Arts, Chgo., 1997, Kordegarde Gallery, Warsaw, 1998, The Art Ctr., Waco, 2001, Gomez Gallery, Balt., 2001, Md. Art Place, 2003, Savannah Coll. of Art and Design, Savannah, Ga., 2004, Spheris Gallery, Bellows Falls, Vt., 2004, Polish Inst., Leipzig, Germany, 2004; group shows in Poland, Denmark, France, Germany, Can., also Barn Gallery, Ogunquit, Maine, 1988, Nat. Mus., Warsaw, 1991, Nat. Mus. Women in the Arts, Washington, 1992, Reeves Contemporary, NY, 2003, others; represented in collections at Nat. Mus., Krakow, Poland, St. Xavier Coll., Chgo., Nat. Mus. of Women in the Arts, Washington DC, others. Recipient awards for paintings, also travel and study grants, individual artist award, Visual Arts, Md. State Arts Council, 2002, fellowship for visual arts, Arts and Humanities Council of Montgomery County, 2002.

**SIKORSKI, GERRY,** congressman; b. Breckenridge, Minn., Apr. 26, 1948; s. Elroy and Helen S.; m. Susan Jane Erkel, Aug. 24, 1974; 1 dau., Anne. BA with highest honors, U. Minn., 1970; JD with high honors, U. Minn. Law Sch., 1973. Bar: Minn. 1973, DC 1997. Mem. Minn. Senate, 1976-82, majority whip, 1980-82; mem. 98th-102nd Congresses from 6th Minn. dist., 1983—93; freshman whip 98th-99th Congresses; ptnr. Holland & Knight LLP, Washington, gov. sect. leader, former chmn. dirs. com., former chair, pub. law dept. Mem. Energy and Commerce Com., Post Office and Civil Service Com., Select Com. on Children Youth and Families; served with Chmn. John D. Dingell, Subcommittee on Oversight and Investigations; vice chair to Henry Waxman, Health and Environment Subcommittee; sponsor Clean Air Act. Author: Community Right to Know Law, Acid Rain Control Act. Mem.: ABA, DC Bar, Phi Beta Kappa. Office: Holland & Knight LLP 2099 Pennsylvania Ave NW Ste 100 Washington DC 20006 Office Phone: 202-828-5007. Business E-Mail: gsikorsk@hklaw.com.

**SIKORSKI, JAMES ALAN,** research chemist; b. Stevens Point, Wis., Nov. 9, 1948; s. John Paul and Florence Lucille (Wierzba) S.; m. Jeanne Delaney, Apr. 15, 1968 (div. 1975); 1 child, Christine René; m. Georgina Weber, Nov. 19, 1977. BS, Northeast La. State Coll., 1970; MS, Purdue U., 1976, PhD, 1981. With Monsanto Agrl. Co., St. Louis, 1976-91, sci. fellow, 1987-91, Monsanto Corp. Rsch., St. Louis, 1991-93; sci. fellow med. chem. G.D. Searle R&D, St. Louis, 1994-2000; sci. fellow med. chemistry Pharmacia Discovery Rsch., St. Louis, 2000—. Instr. organic chemistry St. Louis C.C., 1977-78; adj. prof. biochemistry Coll. Meth. Coll., 1995-97; invited spkr. tech. presentations and seminars. Contbr. chpts. to books, rev. articles, symposia-in-print and articles to profl. jours.; patentee and co-patentee in field. Mem. AAAS, Am. Chem. Soc. (St. Louis ACS award St. Louis Mo. sect. 1994, Kenneth A. Spencer award Kansas City Mo. sect. 1999, Internat. Soc. Heterocyclic Chemistry. Avocations: hiking, canoeing, skiing, photography, snorkeling. E-mail: james.a.sikorski@pharmacia.com.

**SIKORSKI, LORENA L.,** secondary school educator; b. Sarasota, Fla., Nov. 28, 1951; d.Raymond J. and M. Louise (Fatjo) S. BA, Calif. State U., Fullerton, 1973, MS, 1984. Cert. educator. Tchr. music and sci. pub. schs., Garden Grove, Calif., 1974—. Administr., dir. Gay and Lesbian Educators So. Calif., Inc., Orange County, 1985-87; prof. Sikorski Music Studio, Huntington Beach, Calif., 1974-90; chair electives dept. Jordan Intermediate Sch. 2001, chair sci. dept. Lake Intermediate Sch., 2003-04. Composer: Just to Know Him, 1975, Happiest Christmas Ever, 1975, Epopee–Love's Quiet Song, 1991; co-author: Invisible Minority, 1988. Asst. condr. Oriental Chamber Orch., Bellflower, Calif., 1988, Gt. Am. Yankee Freedom Band, 1989; artistic dir. Pacific Coast Freedom Band, Long Beach, Calif., 1990 9st bass trombonist Huntington Beach Cmty. Concert Band, 1992-93; assoc. dir. Hollywood Wind Ensemble, 2005-06, Long Beach Cmty. Band, 2005-2006. Recipient Cmty. Svc. award Sunnyside Sch., 1984, Recognition award Calif. Assembly, 1989, Cmty. award So. Calif. Women for Understanding, 1989, Musicianship award Gt. Am. Yankee Freedom Band, LA, 1986, Gold Starr award Gay and Lesbian Educators So. Calif., 1989; Conducting Honors Pacific Coast Freedom Band, 1991; recognized for outstanding intermediate tchg. level Orange County Music & Arts Adminstrs. Assn., 2001. Mem.: NEA, Garden Grove Edn. Assn. (internat. segment dir. 1994—96, sch. site rep. 2003—), Calif. Tchrs. Assn. Democrat. Personal E-mail: scimastr@aol.com.

**SILAK, CATHY R.,** lawyer, former state supreme court justice; b. Astoria, NY, May 25, 1950; d. Michael John and Rose Marie (Janor) S.; m. Nicholas G. Miller, Aug. 9, 1980; 3 children. BA, NYU, 1971; M in City Planning, Harvard U., 1973; JD, U. Calif., 1976. Bar: Calif. 1977, U.S. Dist. Ct. (no. dist.) Calif. 1977, DC 1979, U.S. Ct. Appeals (D.C. cir.) 1979, U.S. Dist. Ct. (so. dist.) N.Y. 1980, Idaho 1983, U.S. Dist. Ct. Idaho 1983, U.S. Ct. Appeals (2nd cir.) 1983, U.S. Ct. Appeals (9th cir.) 1985. Law clk. to Hon. William W. Schwarzer U.S. Dist. Ct. (no. dist.), Calif., 1976-77; pvt. practice San Francisco, 1977-79, Washington, 1979-80; asst. U.S. atty. So. Dist. of N.Y., 1980-83; spl. asst. U.S. atty. Dist. of Idaho, 1983-84; pvt. practice Boise, Idaho, 1984-90; judge Idaho Ct. Appeals, 1990-93; justice Idaho Supreme Ct., Boise, 1993—2000; ptnr. Hawley, Troxell, Ennis, and Hawley, 2001—. Assoc. gen. counsel Morrison Knudsen Corp., 1989-90; mem. fairness com. Idaho Supreme Ct. and Gov.'s Task Force on Alternative Dispute Resolution; instr. and lectr. in field. Assoc. note and comment editor Calif. Law Rev., 1975-76. Land use planner Mass. Dept. Natural Resources, 1973; founder Idaho Coalition for Adult Literacy; bd. dirs. Literacy Lab., Inc.; mem. adv. bd. Boise State U. Legal Asst. Program. Recipient Jouce Stein award Boise YWCA, 1992, Women Helping Women award Soroptimist, Boise, 1993. Fellow Idaho Law Found (nat., lectr.); mem. ABA (nat. conf. state trial judges jud. adminstrn. divsn.), Nat. Assn. Women Judges, Idaho State Bar (corp./securities sect., instr.), Am. Law Inst., Fellows of the Am. Bar Found., Am. Judicature Soc. (bd. dirs.). Office: Hawley Troxell Ennis & Hawley PO Box 1617 Boise ID 83702-1617

**SILANO, LAWRENCE,** music educator; b. Orange, NJ, Sept. 19, 1944; s. Lawrence and Mildred Silano; m. Karen Ann Vaughn, Aug. 25, 1978; children: Christian, Jason, Jessica. BA, West Liberty State Coll., 1966; MusM, W.Va. U., 1968. Cert. tchr. NJ, 1968. Music tchr. Wayne Bd. Edn., NJ, 1968—. Named an Outstanding Educator, Coll. NJ, 2001. Mem.: NRA. Roman Catholic. Avocations: pistol shooting, high power rifle, golf, tennis. E-mail: lsilano44@aol.com.

**SILANTIEN, JOHN JOSEPH,** music educator; b. Pawtucket, R.I., Nov. 20, 1947; s. John and Lucy Helen Silantien; children: John Andrew, Ryan Danek. BA in Music Edn., Hartt Coll. Music, West Hartford, Conn., 1964—68; MusM, Cath. U., Washington, D.C., 1968—71; MusD, U. Ill., Urbana, 1975—80. Soloist The U. S. Army Band, Washington, DC, 1968—71; choral, gen. music tchr. Andrew Jackson Jr. H.S., Suitland, Md., 1971—72; dir. choral activities Northwood H.S., Silver Spring, Md., 1972—75; asst. prof. Eastman Sch. Music, Rochester, NY, 1977—80; editor The Choral Jour., Lawton, Okla., 1992—98; music dir. San Antonio Symphony Mastersingers, 1983—; dir. choral activities U. Tex., San Antonio, 1980—; dir. choral music U. Presbyn. Ch., San Antonio. Lectr. in field. Contbr. articles to profl. jours. Specialist five U.S. Army, 1968—71, Ft. Myer, Arlington, Va. Recipient, Fulbright-Hays Award, 1978—79; grantee, Rockefeller Found., 1973; scholar, Presser Found., 1964—65. Mem.: Tex. Choral Directors Assn., Tex. Music Educators Assn., Coll. Music Soc., Internat. Fedn. for Choral Music, Chorus Am., Am. Choral Directors Assn., Pi Kappa Lambda, Phi Mu Alpha Sinfonia. Office: Dept Music Univ Texas San Antonio TX 78249 Office Phone: 210-458-5328. Office Fax: 210-458-4381. Business E-Mail: john.silantien@utsa.edu.

**SILAS, CECIL JESSE,** retired petroleum company executive; b. Miami, Fla., Apr. 15, 1932; s. David Edward and Hilda Videll (Carver) S.; m. Theodosea Hejda, Nov. 2, 1965; children: Karla, Peter, Michael, James. BSChemE, Ga. Inst. Tech., Atlanta, 1953. With Phillips Petroleum Co., Bartlesville, Okla., 1953-94, pres. Europe-Africa, Brussels and London, 1968-74, mng. dir. natural resource group Europe/Africa London, 1974-76, v.p. gas and gas liquids div. natural resources group Bartlesville, 1976-78, sr. v.p. natural resources group, 1978-80, exec. v.p. exploration and prodn., minerals, gas and gas liquids, 1980-82, pres., chief operating officer, 1982-85, chmn., CEO, 1985-94. Bd. dirs. Boys/Girls Clubs Am., Atlanta, parton councillor Atlantic Coun. of the U.S.; bd. dirs. Okla. Found. for Excellence, Okla. Found.; trustee Frank Phillips Found. Served to 1st lt. Chem. Corps, AUS, 1954-56. Decorated comdr. Order St. Olaf (Norway); inducted into Ga. Inst. Tech. Athletic Hall of Fame, 1959, recipient Former Scholar-Athlete Total Person award, 1988; inducted into Okla. Bus. Hall of Fame, 1989; named CEO of Yr., Internat. TV Assn., 1987. Mem. Am. Petroleum Inst., U.S. C. of C. (past chmn. bd. dirs.), 25 Yr. Club, Phi Delta Theta. Avocations: fishing, golf, hunting. Office: PO Box 2127 Bartlesville OK 74005-2127

**SILAS, NANCY,** small business owner; b. Gainesville, Fla., Sept. 7, 1943; d. Joseph N Simmons and Roberta (Thompson) Walker Simmons. BS, Fla. A&M U., Tallahassee, 1965; postgrad., U. South Fla., Tampa, 1969—77, Fla. Internat. U., Miami, 1978. Tchr. jr. and sr. high sch. Hillsborough County, Tampa, Fla., 1965—82; interior decorator Interior Show Rm., Tampa, Fla., 1986—89; self employed clothes/accessories, Tampa, Fla., 1989—93; bus. owner Source Innova Concepts Intl Inc, Gainesville, Fla., 2000—04, Fragrance Boutique (Nancy's Fancy and Fine Things), Gainesville, 2003—. Bd. dirs. Source Innova, Gainesville, Fla., 1999—; pres. exec. dir. Concepts Internat., Inc., Gainesville, 1999—; advocacy cons. For Youth /Women, Gainesville, Fla., 1999—; spkr. in field, seminar presenter. Author: (poetry book) Shapes of Human Forms, 2003. Vol. youth Weed And Seed Program, Gainesville, Fla., 2000—02. Grantee Bus. Grant, Gainesville, Fla., 2000. Mem.: Partners Cmty. (assoc.; parliamentarian 2002). Avocations: interior design, community projects, fine arts/crafts. Office: Source Innova Concepts Itl Inc # 23 2114 NW 55th Blvd Gainesville FL 32653

**SILAS, PAUL,** former professional basketball coach; b. Prescott, Ariz. m. Carolyn Silas; children: Paula, Stephen. Student, Creighton U. Mem. St. Louis Hawks, 1964, Phoenix Suns, Boston Celtics, Denver Nuggets, Seattle Supersonics; head coach San Diego Clippers, 1980-83; asst. coach N.J. Nets, 1988-89, 92-95, N.Y. Knicks, 1989-92, Phoenix Suns, Charlotte Hornets, 1997-98, head coach, 1999—2003, Cleve. Cavaliers, 2003—05. Host ann. corp. basketball tournament for Spl. Olympics, N.Y. Named NBA All-Star, NBA All-Defensive first team, 1975, 76, NBA All-Defensive second team, 1971, 72, 73. Achievements include rank of 14th on the all-time list with 12,357 career boards.

**SILBER, JOHN ROBERT,** retired academic administrator, law educator, philosophy educator; b. San Antonio, Aug. 15, 1926; s. Paul G. and Jewell (Joslin) S.; m. Kathryn Underwood, July 12, 1947 (dec.); children: David Joslin (dec.), Mary Rachel, Judith Karen, Kathryn Alexandra, Martha Claire, Laura Ruth, Caroline Jocasta. Postgrad., Northwestern U., 1944; BA summa cum laude, Trinity U., 1947; postgrad., Yale Div. Sch., 1948, U. Tex. Sch. Law, 1949; MA, Yale, 1952, PhD, 1956; L.H.D., Kalamazoo Coll., 1970; many others. Instr. dept. philosophy Yale U., 1952—55; asst. prof. U. Tex., Austin, 1955—59, assoc. prof., 1959—62, prof. philosophy, 1962—70, chmn. dept. philosophy, 1962—67, Univ. prof. arts and letters, 1967—70, chmn. (Comparative Studies Program), 1967, dean Coll. Arts and Scis., 1967—70; Univ. prof., prof. philosophy and law Boston U., 1971—, pres., 1971-96, prof. internat. rels., 1996—2003, chancellor, 1996—2003, pres. emeritus, 2003—. Vis. prof. Bonn U., 1960; fellow Kings Coll. U. London, 1963-64; bd. dirs. Mut. Am. Inst. Funds, Inc. Author: The Ethical Significance of Kant's Religion, 1960, Straight Shooting: What's Wrong With America and How to Fix It, 1989, Ist Amerika zu retten?, 1992; editor: Kant's Religion Within the Limits of Reason Alone, 1960, Works in Continental Philosophy, 1967—; assoc. editor: Kant-Studien, 1968-; contbr. to profl. jours. Chmn. Tex. Soc. to Abolish Capital Punishment, 1960-69; mem. Nat. Commn. United Meth. Higher Edn., 1974-77; exec. bd. Nat. Humanities Inst., 1975-78; trustee Coll. St. Scholastica, 1973-85, U. Denver, 1985-89, WGBH Ednl. Found., 1971-96, Adelphi U., 1989-97; bd. visitors Air U., 1974-80; bd. dirs. Greater Boston coun. Boy Scouts Am., 1981-93, v.p. fin., 1981-93, Silver Beaver award, 1989, Disting. Eagle, 1997; mem. Nat. Humanities Faculty, 1968-73, Nat. Captioning Inst., 1985-94; bd. advisors Matchette Found., 1969-70; mem. Nat. Bipartisan Commn. on Ctrl. Am., 1983-84, U.S. Strategic Inst., 1983-2001; Presdl. Adv. Bd. Radio Broadcasting to Cuba, 1985-92, v.p. 1984-98, vice chmn., 1998-2001; bd. dir. US Strategic Inst., 1983-2001, v.p., 1984-98, vice chmn., 1998-2001; adv. bd. Schurman Libr. of Am. Hist., Ruprecht-Karl U., Heidelberg, 1996—; mem. def. policy bd. U.S. Dept. Def., 1987-90; mem. internat. coun.advisors Inst. for Humanities at Salado, 1988—; bd. dirs. New Eng. Holocaust Meml. Com., 1989-95, Brit. Inst. of U.S., 1989—, Bette Davis Found., 1997—, Boston Police Found., 1997—; Dem. gubernatorial candidate of Mass., 1990; bd. dirs. U.S. Strategic Inst., 1983-2001, vice chmn., 1998-2001; bd. dirs., vice chmn. Americans for Med. Progress, 1992—, chmn., 1994-95, mem. exec. com. 1995—; chmn. Mass. Bd. Edn., 1996-99; bd. advisors Nat. Assn. Scholars. Recipient E. Harris Harbison award for disting. tchg. Danforth Found., 1966, Wilbur Lucius Cross medal Yale Grad. Sch., 1971, Outstanding Civilian Svc. medal U.S. Army, 1985, Disting. Pub. Svc. award Anti-Defamation League of B'nai B'rith, 1989, Horatio Alger award, 1994, -Swiss Friendship award, 1991, Israel Peace medal, 1985, Ehrenmedaille U. Heidelberg, 1986, White House Small Bus. award for entrepreneurial excellence, 1986, Cross of Paideia, Greek Orthodox Archdiocese of North and South Am., 1988, Pro Bene Meritis award U. Tex., Austin, 1997; Fulbright rsch. fellow Germany, 1959-60; Guggenheim fellow Eng., 1963-64; decorated with Knight Comdr.'s Cross with Star of Order of Merit Fed. Republic of Germany, 1983; commandeur Nat. Order of Arts and Letters (France), 1985. Fellow Royal Soc. Arts; mem. Am. Philos. Assn., Am. Soc. Polit. and Legal Philosophy, Nat. Inst. Philosophy, Am. Assn. Higher Edn., Nat. Assn. Ind. Colls. and Univs. (dir. 1976-81), Phi Beta Kappa. Office: Boston Univ 73 Bay State Rd Boston MA 02215-1708 Office Phone: 617-353-2208.

**SILBER, STEVEN A.,** lab administrator, physician; MD, Johns Hopkins U. Sch. Medicine, 1976. Resident, internal medicine U. Pa. Hosp., fellow, gen. internal medicine, chief resident; med. and regulatory affairs, clin. rsch. and devel. SmithKline Beecham; faculty mem. U. Pa., Phila.; pres. Premier Rsch., 2000—02; chief med. officer SCP Comms., Inc., N.Y.C., 2002—. Founder Info. Cos. of Am., Med. Broadcasting Co. Office: SCP Communications 134 W 29th St New York NY 10001

**SILBERBERG, DONALD H.,** neurologist; b. Washington, Mar. 2, 1934; s. William Aaron and Leslie Frances (Stone) S.; m. Marilyn Alice Damsky, June 7, 1959; children: Mark, Alan. MD, U. Mich., 1958; MA (hon.), U. Pa., 1971. Intern Mt. Sinai Hosp., N.Y.C., 1958-59; clin. assoc. in neurology NIH, Bethesda, Md., 1959-61; Fulbright scholar Nat. Hosp., London, 1961-62; NINDB spl. fellow in neuro-ophthalmology Washington U., St. Louis, 1962-63; assoc. neurology U. Pa., 1963-65, asst. prof., 1965-67, assoc. prof., 1967-71, prof., 1971-73, acting chmn. dept., 1973-74, prof., vice chmn. neurology, 1974-82, chmn., 1982-94, sr. assoc. dean, dir. internat. programs, 1994—2004. Active staff U. Pa. Med. Ctr., Phila.; cons. Children's Hosp. Phila.; pres., CEO Betasteron Found., Inc., 1994—. Contbr. articles to profl. jours., abstracts, chpts. in books. Recipient grants in study of multiple sclerosis. Mem.: Global Network for Rsch. on Mental and Neurol. Health (founding v.p.), World Fedn. Neurology, Phila. Neurol. Soc. (pres. 1978—79), Assn. Univ. Profs. Neurology (pres.-elect 1993), Nat. Multiple Sclerosis Soc. (trustee 1997—99, 2001—03), Coll. Physicians Phila., Am. Soc. Neurochemistry, Am. Neurol. Assn., Am. Acad. Neurology, Alpha Omega Alpha. Office: U Pa Med Ctr Dept Neurology 3400 Spruce St Philadelphia PA 19104-4206

**SILBERBERG, RICHARD HOWARD,** lawyer; b. NYC, Feb. 20, 1951; BA, U. Wis., 1972; JD, NYU, 1975. Bar: NY 1976, US Dist. Ct. (so. and ea. dists.) NY, 1976, US Ct. Appeals (2d cir.) 1981, US Ct. Internat. Trade 1983, U.S. Ct. Appeals (fed. cir.) 1988, US Ct. Appeals (3d cir.) 1991, US Supreme Ct. 1994, US Ct. Appeals (11th cir.) 1996, US Ct. Appeals (1st cir.) 1997. Assoc. Delson & Gordon, N.Y.C., 1975-83, ptnr., 1983-87; ptnr., trial group Dorsey & Whitney, N.Y.C., 1988—, mng. ptnr., 1994-97, co-chair global trial group, 2004—. Mem. panel arbitrators U.S. Dist. Ct. for Ea. Dist. N.Y., 1987—; mem. panel mediators US Dist. Ct. So. Dist. NY, 1992—; trustee Lawyers Com. Civil Rights Under Law, 1992—; dir. Fund Modern Cts., 1999—, High 5 Tickets to the Arts, 1999—, NYU Law Alumni Assn., 2002. Mng. editor NYU Jour. Internat. Law and Politics, 1974-75. Mem.: Am. Arbitration Assn. (mem. panel neutrals 1992—). Office: Dorsey & Whitney LLP 250 Park Ave New York NY 10177-0001 Office Phone: 212-415-9231. Office Fax: 212-953-7201. Business E-Mail: silberberg.richard@dorsey.com.

**SILBERFARB, PETER MICHAEL,** psychiatrist, educator; b. Jersey City, Oct. 28, 1938; m. Anne Wagner, 1962; children: Benjamin, Leah S. BS, Bucknell U., 1960; postgrad., NYU, 1960-61; MD, Hahnemann Coll., 1965; MA (hon.), Dartmouth Coll., 1986. Diplomate Nat. Bd. Med. Examiners, Am. Bd. Psychiatry and Neurology (pres. 1998). Intern Hahnemann Med. Coll. Hosp., Phila., 1965-66; resident in internal medicine Dartmouth Affiliated Hosps., Hanover, NH, 1966-68, resident in internal medicine and psychiatry, 1968-69, psychiatry resident, 1971-72, chief resident in psychiatry, 1972-73; instr. in psychiatry Med. Sch., Dartmouth Coll., Hanover, 1972-73, asst. prof. of psychiatry, 1973-77, dir. tng. and edn., 1976-86, assoc. prof. clin. psychiatry, assoc. prof. clin. medicine, 1977-80, dir. grad. edn. and residency tng., 1978-86, assoc. prof. psychiatry, assoc. prof. medicine, 1980-82, dir. tng. and edn., 1984—2002, prof. psychiatry, prof. medicine, 1986—2002, chmn. dept. psychiatry, 1986—2002, Raymond Sobel prof. psychiatry, 1993, prof. emeritus. Cons. psychiatrist Mary Hitchcock Meml. Hosp., Hanover, 1973—; dir. psychiat. in-patient svc. Dartmouth-Hitchcock Med. Ctr., 1973-75, dir. cancer psychiatry program Norris Cotton Cancer Ctr., 1975-2002, acting dir. psychiatry consultation svc., 1977-79, assoc. dir. cancer control Norris Ctr., 1981-86; sec. psychiatry com. Cancer and Leukemia Group B, 1976-79, vice chmn., 1979-2000; mem. grant rev. com. for cancer control Nat. Cancer Inst., 1979, 80, mem. spl. grant rev. com., 1981, 82, 85, cons. to bd. sci. counselors, 1982, mem. cancer control grant rev. com., 1989-90; vice chmn. adv. com. for psychosocial and behavioral rsch. Am. Cancer Soc., 1982-88, chmn., 1988-89; cons. collaborative ctr. for cancer pain relief WHO, Milan, 1985; mem. accreditation coun. for grad. med. edn. Appeals Bd. for Psychiatry, Chgo., 1983, specialist site visitor, 1985-90, mem. residency rev. com. for psychiatry, 1991-96; dir. Am. Bd. Family Practice, 1996-2000; mem. exec. com. Am. Bd. Med. Specialties, 1996-99. Author chpts. to books; mem. editl. bd. Jour. Psychosocial Oncology, 1983-91, Internat. Jour. Psychiatry in Medicine, 1986-90, Contemporary Psychiatry, 1987-91, Psychoncology, 1991-96; referee numerous manuscripts; contbr. articles to profl. jours. Surgeon USPHS, 1969-71. Fellow Am. Psychiat. Assn. (cons. to task force on treatment if psychiat. disorders 1989), Am. Coll. Psychiatrists; mem. AMA, Am. Soc. Psychiat. Oncology/AIDS, Am. Soc. Clin. Oncology, Am. Assn. Dirs. Psychiat. Residency Tng. (mem. curriculum com. 1979-88, mem. task force on med. students and residents, chmn. com. regional dirs. 1984-88, mem. exec. com. 1984-88), Am. Psychosomatic Soc., N.H. Psychiat. Soc. (chmn. membership com. 1974-76, chmn. continuing edn. com. 1977-79), N.H. Med. Soc., Assn. Rsch. in Nervous and Mental Disease, Assn. Acad. Psychiatry, Benjamin Rush Soc. Home: Bragg Hill Norwich VT 05055 Office: Dartmouth Coll Med Sch Dept Psychiatry Lebanon NH 03756-0001

**SILBERG, JAY ELIOT,** lawyer; b. N.Y.C., Apr. 5, 1941; s. Arnold and Lillian (Liberman) S.; m. Ruth Vogel, June 22, 1975; children: Eric, Karen, Joanne. BA cum laude, Amherst Coll., 1963; LLB, Harvard U., 1966. Bar: N.J. 1966, US Dist. Ct. NJ 1966, US Ct. Appeals (DC cir.) 1970, US Ct. Appeals (7th cir.) 1982, US Supreme Ct. 1983, US Ct. Appeals (6th cir.) 1986, US Ct. Appeals (9th cir.), 1990, US Ct. Appeals (fed. cir.), 1997, US Ct. Appeals (11th cir.), 2000, US Ct. Appeals (2d cir), 2002. Atty. Office of Council AEC, Washington, 1966-69; assoc. Shaw, Pittman, Potts & Trowbridge, Washington, 1969-72, ptnr., 1973—2005, Pillsbury, Winthrop, Shaw and Pittman, 2005—. Republican. Jewish. Home: 6109 Neilwood Dr North Bethesda MD 20852-3706 Office: Pillsbury Winthrop Show and Pittman 2300 N St NW Washington DC 20037-1128

**SILBERGELD, ARTHUR F.,** lawyer; b. St. Louis, June 1, 1942; s. David and Sabina (Silbergeld) S.; m. Carol Ann Schwartz, May 1, 1970; children: Diana Lauren, Julia Kay. BA, U. Mich., 1968; M in City Planning, U. Pa., 1971; JD, Temple U., 1975. Bar: N.Y. 1976, Calif. 1978, D.C. 1983, U.S. Ct. Appeals (2nd cir.), U.S. Ct. Appeals (9th cir.), U.S. Ct. Appeals (D.C. cir.), U.S. Supreme Ct. 1999. Assoc. Vladeck, Elias, Vladeck & Lewis, N.Y.C., 1975-77; field atty. NLRB, L.A., 1977-78; ptnr., head employment law practice group McKenna, Conner & Cuneo, L.A., 1978-89; ptnr. Graham & James, L.A., 1990-96; labor ptnr. Sonnenschein Nath & Rosenthal, L.A., 1996-99; ptnr. Proskauer Rose LLP, L.A., 1999—. Instr. extension divsn. UCLA, 1981-89. Author: Doing Business in California: An Employment Law Handbook, 2nd edit., 1997, Advising California Employers, 1990-95 supplements; contbr. articles to profl. jours. Founding mem. L.A. Mus. Contemporary Art; bd. dirs. Bay Cities unit Am. Cancer Soc., Calif. 1981-85, Jewish Family Svc., L.A., 1981-85, So. Calif. Employers Roundtable, Leadership coun., So. Poverty Law Ctr., Leadership Task Force, Drs. Without Borders; pres. Mo. Valley Fedn. of Temple Youth, 1959-60, Exec. Com., Calif. Com. South Human Rights Watch, 2005—; treas. L.A. Child Devel. Ctr., 2001-. Mem. ABA (labor and employment law sect.), L.A. County Bar Assn. (mem. exec. com. 1984-, chmn. labor and employment law sect. 1999-2000, trustee 2000-01), Mus. Modern Art (N.Y.C.), Coll. of Labor and Employment Lawyers. Office: Proskauer Rose LLP 2049 Century Park E Fl 32 Los Angeles CA 90067-3101 Office Phone: 310-557-2900.

**SILBERGELD, ELLEN KOVNER,** epidemiologist, researcher, toxicologist; b. Washington, July 29, 1945; d. Joseph and Mary (Gion) Kovner; m. Alan Mark Silbergeld, 1969; children: Sophia, Nicholas. AB, Vassar Coll., 1967; PhD, Johns Hopkins U., 1972. Kennedy fellow Johns Hopkins Med. Sch., Balt., 1974—75; scientist NIH, Bethesda, Md., 1975—81; chief toxics scientist Environ. Def. Fund, Washington, 1982—90; prof. epidemiology, toxicology and pharmacology U.Md., Balt., 1990—2001, affil. prof. environ. law, 1990—2001, dir. program in human health and environ., 1996—2000, prof. dept. pathology, 1995—2000, adj. prof. dept. pharmacology and exptl. therapeutics, 1995—2000; prof. environ. health scis. epidemiology, and health policy and mgmt. Bloomberg School Public Health, Johns Hopkins U., Balt., 2001—. Mem. sci. adv. bd. EPA, 1983—89, 1993—99, Dept. Energy, 1994—95; mem. bd. on environ. sci. and toxicology NAS-NRC, 1983—89; mem. Com. Geosci. Environ. and Resources, 1994—98; mem. bd. biotech. and agr., 1999—2004; mem. bd. sci. councellors Nat. Inst. Environ. Health Scis., 1987—93; cons. Oil and Chem. Atomic Workers, 1970, NSF, 1974—75, OECD, 1987—90. Mem. editl. bd.: Neurobehavioral Toxicology, 1979—87, Am. Jour. Medicine, 1980—, Neurotoxicology, 1981—86, Environ. Rsch., 1983—, editor-in-chief:, 1994—. Mem. Homewood Friends Meeting. Recipient Wolman award, Md. Pub. Health Assn., 1991, Barsky award, APHA, 1992, Md. Gov. Excellence citation, 1990, 1993; Fulbright fellow, London, 1967, Woodrow Wilson and Danforth fellow, 1967, NAS Exch. fellow, Yugoslavia, 1976, MacArthur Found. fellow, 1993—98, Baldwin scholar, Coll. Notre Dame. Mem.: APHA, AAAS, Soc. for Neurosci., Soc. Toxicology, Soc. for Occupl. and Environ. Health (sec.-treas. 1983—85, pres. 1987—89), Am. Soc. Tropical Med. Hygiene, Collegium Ramazzini (councillor), Phi Beta Kappa. Office: Bloomberg Sch Pub Health 615 N Wolfe St Baltimore MD 21205

**SILBERLING, SHERRILL JEAN,** literature and language educator; b. Pottsville, Pa., Jan. 29, 1946; d. Allen and Florence Clara Silberling. BA, Muhlenberg Coll., Allentown, Pa., 1968; MA, Bucknell U., Lewisburg, Pa., 1973. Pa. secondary tchg. cert. Pa. Dept. Edn., 1968. Lit. and speech tchr. Pottsville Area HS, Pa., 1968—. Correspondent and feature writer Harrisburg Patriot Newspaper, Pa., 1980—85; English instr. Penn State U. Schuylkill Campus, Schuylkill Haven, Pa., 1992—94; lectr. Lehigh Carbon C.C., Schnecksville, Pa., 2003—. Contbr. articles and poems to various publ. Mem. Library Friends Pottsville Free Pub. Library, Pottsville, Pa., 2000—05. Recipient Dr. Alex Atty award, Pottsville Area HS Student Coun., 1980, 2003, U. Scholars Program Disting. Tchg. Award, Penn State U. State Coll. Mem.: NEA (life), Pa. State Edn. Assn. (life). Avocations: creative writing, reading, fitness walking, gardening. Home: 1935 W Norwegian St Pottsville PA 17901 Office: Pottsville Area HS 16th St & Elk Ave Pottsville PA 17901 Office Phone: 570-621-2960. E-mail: ssilberling@pottsville.k12.pa.us.

**SILBERMAN, ALAN HARVEY,** lawyer; b. Chgo., Oct. 22, 1940; s. Milton J. and Mollie E. (Hymanson) S.; m. Margaret Judith Auslander, Nov. 17, 1968; children: Elena, Mark. BA with distinction, Northwestern U., 1961; LLB, Yale U., 1964. Bar: Ill. 1964, U.S. Dist. Ct. (no. dist.) Ill. 1966, U.S. Ct. Appeals (7th cir.) 1970, (5th and 9th cir.) 1977, (D.C. cir.) 1979, (4th cir.) 1980, (11th cir.) 1981, (3rd cir.) 1982, (8th and 10th cir.) 1993, U.S. Supreme Ct. 1978. Law clk. U.S. Dist. Ct., Chgo., 1964-66; assoc. Sonneschein Nath & Rosenthal, Chgo., 1964-71, ptnr., 1972—. Mem. antitrust adv. bd. Bur. Nat. Affairs, Washington, 1985—; mem. Ill. Atty. Gen. Franchise Adv. Bd., 1996—; bd. dirs., mem. exec. com. Mercaz, USA. Contbr. articles to profl. jours. Bd. dirs., v.p., sec. Camp Ramah in Wis., Inc., Chgo., 1966-86, pres., 1986-94; bd. dirs. Nat. Ramah Commn., Inc. of Jewish Theol. Sem. Am., N.Y.C., 1970—, v.p., 1986-94, pres., 1994-99, sr. v.p., 1999-2003; mem. U.S. del. 33d World Zionist Congress, Jerusalem, 1997, 34th World Zionist Congress, Jerusalem, 2002; bd. dirs., mem. exec. com. Masorti Olami/World Coun. of Conservative Synagogues, 2002—, v.p. 2005, pres., 2005—; bd. govs. Northwestern U. Law., 2004—. Mem. ABA (chmn. antitrust sect. FTC com. 1981-83, chmn. nat. insts. 1983-85, mem. coun. antitrust sect. 1985-88, fin. officer 1988-90, sect. del. ho. of dels. 1990-92, chmn.-elect 1992-93, chmn. 1993-94), Ill. Bar Assn. (chmn. antitrust sect. 1975-76), Northwestern U. 1851 Soc. (chair 1994-97), Lex Mundi (bd. dirs. 2005—, vice chmn. com. antitrust competition and trade 1999-2003, internat. chair elect 2003-05, chair 2005—). Home: 430 Oakdale Ave Glencoe IL 60022-2113 Office: Sonnenschein Nath Ste 7800 233 S Wacker Dr Chicago IL 60606-6491 Office Phone: 312-876-8103. Business E-mail: ASilberman@sonnenschein.com.

**SILBERMAN, CHARLOTTE SCHATZBERG,** retired lawyer, artist; b. N.Y.C., Oct. 15, 1918; d. Louis and Annie (Hammerman) Schatzberg; m. Bernard Silberman, Sept. 24, 1942 (dec. Mar. 1991); children: Adela Wagman, Margery Miller Moores. BA, Hunter Coll., 1938; LLB, JD, Bklyn. Law Sch., 1940; postgrad., SUNY, Albany, 1977-84, Fla. Atlantic U., 1984—. Bar: N.Y. 1941. Pvt. practice law, N.Y.C., 1940-43, Albany, N.Y., 1947-57; atty. State N.Y., Albany, 1957-63; assoc. counsel SUNY, Albany, 1963-74; dir. paralegal studies, 1975-77. Works exhibited Soc. of Four Arts, 1990, Cornell Mus., Delray Beach, Fla., 1994, 95. Home: 7076 Huntington Ln Apt 401 Delray Beach FL 33446-2554

**SILBERMAN, ENRIQUE,** physicist, director; b. Buenos Aires, Dec. 9, 1921; came to U.S., 1966; m. 1949; 2 children. PhD in Engring., U. Buenos Aires, 1945. Investigator physics Argentina Atomic Energy Commn., Buenos Aires, 1953-58; head dept. Arg AEC, 1958-63; prof. U. Buenos Aires, 1963-66; prof. physics Fisk U., Nashville, 1966—; dir. photonic materials and devices NASA Ctr., 1992—. Guest prof. U. Notre Dame, 1963; cons. Arg Nat. Coun. Sci. Rsch., 1964; vis. prof. Vanderbilt U., 1967—. Mem. AAAS, Am. Assn. Physics Tchrs., Am. Phys. Soc., Arg Physics Assn. Office: Fisk U Dept Physics Nashville TN 37208-3051 Office Phone: 615-329-8620. Business E-Mail: esilber@fisk.edu.

**SILBERMAN, H. LEE,** public relations executive, consultant; b. Newark, Apr. 26, 1919; s. Louis and Anna (Horel) S.; m. Ruth Irene Rapp, June 5, 1948; children: Richard Lyle, Gregory Alan, Todd Walter. BA, U. Wis., 1940. Radio continuity writer Radio Sta. WTAQ, Green Bay, Wis., 1940-41; reporter Bayonne (N.J.) Times, 1941-42; sales exec. War Assets Adminstrn., Chgo., 1946-47; copy editor Acme Newspictures, Chgo., 1947; reporter, editl. writer Wichita (Kans.) Eagle, 1948-55; reporter Wall St. Jour., N.Y.C., 1955-57, banking editor, 1957-68; 1st v.p., dir. corp. rels. Shearson-Hamill & Co., N.Y.C., 1968-74; N.Y. corr. Economist of London, 1966-72; from contbg. editor to editor in chief Finance mag., 1970-76; from v.p., dir. to exec. v.p. Fin. Svcs. Group, Carl Boyir & Assos., Inc., N.Y.C., 1976-86, exec. v.p., 1981-86; sr. counselor Hill & Knowlton, Inc., N.Y.C., 1986-93, sr. v.p., 1993-96, sr. mng. dir., 1996; pres. LSA Media Cons., 1997—. Cons. in field. Contbr. articles to profl. jours. Capt. C.E. AUS, 1942-46. Recipient Loeb Mag. award U. Conn., 1965; Loeb Achievement award for disting. writing on fin. Gerald M. Loeb Found., 1968 Mem.: Soc. Profl. Journalists, Soc. Silurians, NY. Fin. Writers Assn., Deadline Club NY, Zeta Beta Tau. Republican. Home and Office: 475 E 2nd St Clayton NC 27520-2558

**SILBERMAN, JOHN ALAN,** lawyer; b. Balt., Sept. 20, 1951; s. Ronnie A. and Dovera (Gogel) S. BA, Northwestern U., 1972; JD, Harvard U., 1976. Bar: N.Y. 1977, U.S. Dist. Ct. (so. and ea. dists.) N.Y. 1977. Assoc. Paul, Weiss, Rifkind, Wharton & Garrison, N.Y.C., 1976-84, ptnr., 1985-96; prin. John Silberman Assocs., N.Y.C., 1996—. Bd. dirs., Pres.'s adv. coun. on the Arts John F. Kennedy Ctr., Washington, 1999—, Found. for Contemporary Performance Arts, N.Y.C., 1998—. Office: John Silberman Assocs PC 145 E 57th St New York NY 10022-2141

**SILBERMAN, LARRY (LAURENCE HIRSCH SILBERMAN),** federal judge; b. York, Pa., Oct. 12, 1935; s. William and Anna (Hirsch) S.; m. Rosalie G. Gaull, Apr. 18, 1957; children: Robert Stephen, Katherine DeBoer Balaban, Anne Gaull Otis. BA, Dartmouth Coll., 1957; LLB, Harvard U., 1961. Bar: Hawaii 1962, D.C. 1973. Assoc. Moore, Torkildson & Rice and Quinn & Moore, Honolulu, 1961-64; ptnr. Moore, Silberman & Schulze, Honolulu, 1964-67; atty. appellate divsn. gen. counsel's office NLRB, Washington, 1967-69; solicitor of labor U.S. Dept. Labor, Washington, 1969-70, undersec. labor, 1970-73; ptnr. Steptoe & Johnson, Washington, 1973-74; dep. atty. gen. U.S. Washington, 1974-75; amb. to Yugoslavia, 1975-77; mng. ptnr. Morrison & Foerster, Washington, 1978-79, 83-85; exec. v.p. Crocker Nat. Bank, San Francisco, 1979-83; judge U.S. Ct. Appeals (D.C. cir.), Washington, 1985—2000, sr. judge, 2000—. Lectr. labor law and legis. U. Hawaii, 1962—63; adj. prof. adminstrv. law Georgetown U., Washington, 1987—94, 1997, 1999—2001, NYU, 1995, 96, Harvard U., 1998; adj. prof. labor law Georgetown U., Washington, 2001, disting. visitor from the Judiciary tchr. adminstrv. law and labor law, 2002—; Pres.' spl. envoy on ILO

affairs, 1976; gen. adv. com. on Arms Control and Disarmament, 1981—85; mem. Def. Policy Bd., 1981—85; vice-chmn. State Dept.'s Commn. on Security and Econ. Assistance, 1983—84. Bd. dirs. Com. on Present Danger, 1978-85, Inst. for Ednl. Affairs, 1981-85; mem U.S. Fgn. Intelligence Surveillance Act Ct. of Rev., 1996-2003; co-chmn. Commn. on Intelligence Capabilities of the U.S. Regarding Weapons of Mass Destruction, 2004; vice chmn. adv. coun. on gen. govt. Rep. Nat. Com., 1977-80. With AUS, 1957-58. Am. Enterprise Inst. sr. fellow, 1977-78, vis. fellow 1978-85. Mem. Coun. on Fgn. Rels.*

**SILBERMAN, LINDA JOY,** law educator; b. 1944. BA, U. Mich., 1965, JD, 1968. Bar: Ill. 1969. Fulbright scholar U. London, 1968-69; assoc. Sonnenschein, Levinson, Carlin, Nath & Rosenthal, 1969-71; asst. prof. law NYU Sch. Law, 1971-74, assoc. prof., 1974-77, prof., 1977—, now Martin Lipton prof. law, assoc. dir. Inst. Jud. Adminstrn., 1991-95; vis. prof., U. Pa., 1981, 1984-85, Columbia U., 1982-83, prof.-in-residence appellate staff, Dept. Justice, 1985-86; cons. NY Law Revision Commn., 1983-85, Hague Conv. Civic Aspects Internat. Child Abduction. Mem. Am. Law Inst, Order of Coif. Author: Non-Attorney Justice in the United States, 1979; co-author: (with Foster & Freed) Family Law: Cases and Materials, 1977; contbr. articles to legal journals. Achievements: first woman to receive full-time tenure track appt. and first woman to be tenured a full professor at NYU Sch. Law. Office: NYU Sch Law Vanderbilt Hall Rm 339 40 Washington Sq S New York NY 10012-1099 Office Phone: 212-998-6204. E-mail: silberml@juris.law.nyu.edu.

**SILBERMAN, ROBERT A. S.,** lawyer; b. Lebanon, Pa., Mar. 4, 1945; s. Henry T. and Genevieve (Mensh) S.; m. Nancy D. Netzer, Nov. 10, 1974. BA magna cum laude, Yale U., 1967; JD, Harvard U., 1970. Bar: Mass. 1970, Pa. 1984. Assoc. Csaplar & Bok, Boston, 1970—78, ptnr., 1978—90, Gaston & Snow, Boston, 1990—91, Edwards & Angell, Boston, 1991—2000, Israel & Silberman PC, Wellesley, Mass., 2000—. Mem. editl. bd. Managed Care Law Strategist, Am. Lawyer Media newsletter, 1999-2001. Citizens rev. com. United Way Mass. Bay, Boston, 1981-89; bd. dirs. All Newton (Mass.) Music Sch., 1994-96, v.p., 1995-96; bd. overseers Boston Baroque, 1998-2000, bd. dirs., chmn. bd. overseers, 2000-02, chmn. bd. dirs., 2003—. Mem. ABA (vice chmn. health law com. sect. bus. law 1992-95, chmn., 1995-99), Internat. Bar Assn., Boston Bar Assn., Phi Beta Kappa. Office: Israel & Silberman PC 15 Walnut St Ste 100 Wellesley MA 02481 Office Phone: 781-235-1500. Business E-Mail: rsilberman@israelsilberman.com.

**SILBERSACK, BARBARA WYSPIANSKA,** law librarian; b. Plainfield, NJ, 1954; d. Franciszek and Jadwiga Wyspianski; m. Roger Alan Silbersack, July 13, 1985. B Music Edn., U. Cin., 1976; MLS, Ind. U., 1991. Law libr. Smith & Schnacke, Cin., 1984-89, Thompson Hine LLP, Cin., 1989—. Spkr., lectr. various confs. Clk. to the bd. Cin. Law Libr. Assn., 1997—; mem. adv. bd. Info. Innovators Inst., 1998-99. Mem. Spl. Librs. Assn. (chair chpt. pub. rels. com. 1990-91, chair chpt. mentoring com. 1992-93, pres. Cin. chpt. 1994-95, chair legal divsn. 1996-97, editor legal divsn. newsletter 1998—), Am. Assn. Law Librs., Ohio Regional Assn. Law Librs., Cin. Bar Assn. Roman Catholic. Avocations: classical music, cooking. Office: Thompson Hine LLP 312 Walnut St Ste 1400 Cincinnati OH 45202-4089

**SILBERSACK, JOHN WALTER,** literary agent; b. NYC, Dec. 8, 1954; s. Walter Roy and Joan Small Silbersack; m. Elionora van Tyen Wilking, June 29, 1985; children: Nichols Clay, Johanna van Tyen, Catryn Center. AB, Brown U., 1977. Pub. dir. Roc Books Penguin Pub. Group, NYC, 1986—92; editor in chief Warner Aspect, Warner Books, NYC, 1992—93; sr. vice pres./pub. dir. Harper Entertainment/Harper Children's Entertainment, Harper Collins Publishers, NYC, 1993—99; exec. v.p. Trident Media Group, 2001—; sr. v.p. Epicom Media, NY, 2001—. Author: No Frills Science Fiction, 1983, Rogers Rangers, 1983; editor: The Berkley Showcase: New Writings in Science Fiction and Fantasy, 1980—83, The Magic of Christmas, 1992; contbr. introductions, revs. and literary criticism. Mem.: Trap Door Spiders, Sci. Fiction Writers Am., Thurs. Evening Club, Manhasset Bay Yacht Club (trustee 2006—), Century Assn. Home: 5 Harbor Road Sands Point NY 11050 Office: Trident Media Group 41 Madison Avenue New York NY 11050 Office Phone: 212-333-1513. Office Fax: 212-262-4849. Personal E-mail: quidnetma@aol.com. E-mail: jsilbersack@tridentmediagroup.com.

**SILBERSACK, MARK LOUIS,** lawyer; b. Cin., Dec. 27, 1946; s. Joseph Leo and Rhoda Marie (Hinkler) S.; m. Ruth Ann Schwallie, Sept. 7, 1985. AB, Boston Coll., 1968; JD, U. Chgo., 1971. Bar: Ohio 1971, U.S. Dist. Ct. (so. dist.) Ohio 1973, U.S. Ct. Appeals (6th cir.) 1974, U.S. Supreme Ct. 1975. Atty. Dinsmore & Shohl LLP, Cin., 1971—. Lectr. Ohio CLE Inst., Columbus, 1981-91. Co-author: Managed Care: The PPO Experience, 1990, Information Sharing Among Health Care Providers, 1994. Bd. dirs. United Way, Cmty. Chest, 1985-89, 2001—, chmn. pub. policy com., 1998—; vice-chmn. Ohio United Way, Columbus, 1989-94, chmn. bd. dirs., 1994-96; pres. Hyde Park Neighborhood Coun., Cin., 1989-91, Hyde Park Ctr. for Older Adults, 1989-91; active Cin. Bd. Health, 1991-97, chmn., 1995-97; bd. dirs. Cath. Social Svc. of S.W. Ohio, 1998-2003; bd. dirs., Children, Inc., 2003-. Mem. ABA, FBA, Ohio State Bar Assn. (chmn. antitrust sect. 2005-), Cin. Bar Assn., Cin. Bar Assn., Hyde Park Golf and Country Club. Republican. Roman Catholic. Avocations: reading, travel, theater. Home: 3465 Forestoak Ct Cincinnati OH 45208-1842 Office: Dinsmore & Shohl LLP 1900 Chemed Ctr 255 E 5th St Cincinnati OH 45202-4700 Office Phone: 513-977-8243. Business E-Mail: mark.silbersack@dinslaw.com.

**SILBERSTEIN, ALAN MARK,** financial services executive; b. Munich, Dec. 22, 1947; came to U.S., 1949; s. Leon and Rose S.; m. Carol Krongold, Aug. 30, 1970; children: Eric, Adam, Meredith. BS in Engring., Columbia U., 1969; MBA, Harvard U., 1972. Design engr. Ford Motor Co., Dearborn, Mich., 1969-70; budget analyst N.Y.C. Bur. of Budget, 1972-74; various positions Chem. Bank, N.Y.C., 1974-88, exec. v.p., head Consumer Banking Group, 1990-92; exec. v.p. and dir. of retail banking Midlantic Corp., Edison, N.J., 1992-95; CEO claims divsn. Travelers Property Casualty Corp., Hartford, Conn., 1995-96, exec. v.p., 1997-98; pres. Silco Assocs., 1998—; pres., CEO Western Union Fin. Svcs., Inc., 2000—01. Bd. dirs. global Payments Inc., Capital Access Network, Debt Resolve, Inc. Trustee Tenafly Bd. Edn., N.J., 1983-86, Yeshiva U. Sy Syms Sch. Bus., 1989—; mem. consumer adv. coun. Fed. Res. Bd., 1989-91; bd. dirs. N.Y. State Tree Consortium Inc., 1990-92; mem. exec. No. N.J. Boy Scouts Am., 1992-2003; adv. coun. Columbia U. Sch. Engring., 1998-2004. Mem. Am. Bankers Assn. (chmn. retail banking exec. com. 1992—), Harvard Bus. Sch. Club N.Y. (sec. 1981-85, bd. dirs. 1982-83, 85-88), Coun. Fgn. Rels., Bus. Execs. for Nat. Security.

**SILBERSTEIN, EDWARD BERNARD,** nuclear medicine educator, oncologist, researcher; b. Cin., Sept. 3, 1936; s. Bernard Gumpert and Harriet Louise (Kahn) S.; m. Jacqueline Rose Mervis, Oct. 2, 1988; children: Scott, Lisa. BS magna cum laude, Yale U., 1958; MD, Harvard U., 1962; postgrad. in art history, U. Cin. Bd. cert. in Internal Medicine, Hematology, Nuclear Medicine, Med. Oncology Am. Bd. Internal Medicine. Intern Cin. Gen. Hosp., 1962—63, resident in internal medicine, 1963—64; resident Univ. Hosps. Cleve., 1966—67; NIH fellow in hematology New Eng. Med. Ctr., Boston, 1967—68; asst. prof. radiol. medicine U. Cin. Med. Ctr., 1968—72, assoc. prof. radiol. medicine, 1972—76, prof. radiol. medicine, 1976—; Eugene L. and Sue R. Saenger prof. radiol. scis., 1990—2000, prof. emeritus of radiology and medicine, 2000—. Assoc. dir. E.L. Saenger Radioisotope Lab., 1980—; chmn. Environ. Safety Health Com. Dept. Energy Fernald Facility, 1986-91; mem. U.S. Pharmacopeia Com. of Revision, 1990—; mem. Nat. Coun. on Radiation Protection and Measurement, 1997—; cons. Nuclear Regulatory Commn., 1989—; dir. divsn. nuclear medicine Jewish Hosp., 1976-95; cancer pain panel Agy. for Health Care Planning and Rsch., 1992-93; mem. Am. Nuclear Soc. Com. on Isotope Assurance, 2003-05; vis. prof. various lecturerships. Author: Differential Diagnosis in Nuclear Medicine, 1984, Bone Scintigraphy, 1984, Diagnostic Patterns in Nuclear Medicine, 1998; contbr. 230 abstracts and articles to profl. jours., 50 book chapters; reviewer 13 profl. jour. Active Race Rels. Commn. Greater Cin., 1995—2000;

trustee Cin. Opera Assn., 1993—, v.p., 2003—; active Jewish Cmty. Rels. Coun., 1992—; trustee Isaac M. Wise Temple, 1992—2000, treas., 1997—2000; bd. dirs. Talbert House, 1969—, Air Pollution Control League, Cin., 1980—95. Capt. US Army Med. Corps, 1964—66. Recipient Pearl S. Gantz award for Cmty. Svc., United Way of Cin., 2002, VIP Volunteerism award, Hamilton County Mental Health Bd., 2005; fellow, Am. Col. Nuc. Physicians. Mem.: Am. Bd. Nuclear Medicine (chmn. 1999), Soc. Nuc. Medicine (sec. 1989—92, 1989—92, bd. dirs. 1989—99, pres. S.E. chpt. 1990—91, chair sci. program 1992—94, spkr. Ho. of Dels. 2002—04, Speaker's award 2004, Marshall Brucer award 2002), Literary Club, Sigma Xi, Phi Beta Kappa. Jewish. Avocations: tennis, history of art, archaeology, travel. Office: U Cin Med Ctr Mont Reid Pavilion G026 234 Goodman St Cincinnati OH 45219-2364 Office Phone: 513-584-9032. Business E-Mail: silbereb@healthall.com.

**SILBERT, EARL J.,** lawyer; b. Boston, Mar. 8, 1936; s. Coleman and Lillian (Rosenberg) S.; m. Patricia Allott, Oct. 18, 1969; children: Sarah, Leslie. BA magna cum laude, Harvard U., 1957, LLB cum laude, 1960. Bar: Mass. 1960, D.C. 1963, U.S. Supreme Ct. 1975, U.S. Ct. Appeals (Fed. cir.) 1985. Lawyer tax divsn. U.S. Dept. Justice, Washington, 1960-64, asst. U.S. atty. for D.C., 1964-69, atty. advisor office criminal justice U. Dept. Atty. Gen., 1969-70, exec. asst. to U.S. atty. for D.C., 1972-73, U.S. atty. for D.C., 1974-79; prin. Schwalb, Donnenfeld, Bray & Silbert, Washington, 1979—98; ptnr. DLA Piper Rudnick Gray Cary, 1998—. Commr. Law Rev. Commn. of D.C., 1975-79; mem. com. on grievances U.S. Dist. Ct. D.C., 1980-87, chairperson, 1989—; master of bench Charles Fahy Am. Inn of Ct., 1984-87, Edward Bennett Williams Inn of Ct., 1989—; chairperson hearing com. Bd. on Profl. Responsibility, 1983-86; mem. adv. com. for rev. of admissions process D.C. Ct. Appeals, 1988; mem. adv. com. on rules criminal procedure Superior Ct. of D.C., 1985—; practicioners adv. bd., US Sentencing Commn.; DC Adv. Commn. on Sentencing. Contbr. articles to profl. jours. Pres. Nat. Assn. Former U.S. Attys., 1985-86, Asst. U.S. Attys. Assn. for D.C., 1985-86; former chmn. Hearing Com., Bd. of Profl. Responsibility, Dist. of Columbia; former chmn. Grievance Com., US District Ct., District of Columbia; master bench, Edward Bennett Williams Inn Ct. Named one of 75 Best Lawyers in Washington, Washingtonian survey mag., 2002. Fellow Am. Coll. Trial Lawyers (chairperson D.C. 1989, 90, regent 1993—; pres. 2000-2001); mem. ABA (chairperson Ethics in Govt. Act white collar crime com. 1989—, standing com. on assn. standards for criminal justice 1976-79, com. on law and nat. security, taxation and criminal justice), Nat. Assn. Criminal Def. Lawyers, Phi Beta Kappa. Jewish. Office: DLA Piper Rudnick Gray Cary 1200 19th St NW Washington DC 20036-2412 E-mail: earl.silbert@dlapiper.com.*

**SILBEY, JOEL HENRY,** history professor; b. Bklyn., Aug. 16, 1933; s. Sidney and Estelle (Mintzer) S.; m. Rosemary Johnson, Aug. 13, 1959; children: Victoria, David. BA, Bklyn. Coll., 1955; MA, U. Iowa, 1956, PhD, 1963. Asst. prof. San Francisco State Coll., 1960-64, U. Md., College Park, 1965-66; asst. prof. Am. History Cornell U., Ithaca, NY, 1966-67, assoc. prof., 1967-68, prof., 1968-86, Pres. White prof. history, 1986—2002, prof. emeritus, 2002—; Harold V. Harmsworthy prof. Am. history U. Oxford, 2004—05. Vis. assist. prof. history U. Pitts., 1964-65. Author: The Shrine of Party, 1967, The Transformation of American Politics, 1968, A Respectable Minority: The Democratic Party in the Civil War Era, 1977, The Partisan Imperative: The Dynamics of American Politics before the Civil War, 1985, The American Political Nation, 1838-1893, 1991, The American Party Battle, 1828-1876, 1999, Martin Van Buren and the Emergence of American Popular Politics, 2002, Storm Over Texas: The Annexation Controversy and the Road to Civil War, 2005; editor: (with others) Voters, Parties and Elections, 1972, American Political Behavior, 1984, The History of American Electoral Behavior, 1978; editor-in-chief: Encyclopedia of the American legislative System, 1993; editorial cons. numerous publs.; contbr. numerous articles to profl. jours Am. Philos. Soc. fellow, 1969-70; NSF fellow, 1970-74; NEH fellow, 1980-81; vis. fellow Ctr. for Advanced Study in the Behavioral Scis., 1985-86; vis. scholar Russell Sage Found., 1988-89; John Simon Guggenheim Meml. fellow, 1989-90. Mem. Am. Hist. Assn. (program com. 1977), Orgn. Am. Historians (chmn. program com. 1983), So. Hist. Assn., Social Sci. History Assn. (co-chmn. membership com., mem. exec. com). Home: 105 Judd Falls Rd Ithaca NY 14850-2715 Office: Cornell U 140 Mcgraw Hall Ithaca NY 14853-4601 Office Phone: 607-255-4966. Business E-Mail: jhs@cornell.edu.

**SILBEY, ROBERT JAMES,** chemistry professor, researcher, consultant; b. NYC, Oct. 19, 1940; s. Sidney Richard and Estelle (Mintzer) S.; m. Susan Sorkin, June 24, 1962; children: Jessica, Anna. BS, CUNY Bklyn. Coll., 1961; PhD, U. Chgo., 1965; PhD (hon.), Bklyn. Coll., 2004. From asst. prof. to assoc. prof. MIT, Cambridge, 1966-76, prof., 1976—, chmn. dept. chemistry, 1990-95, dir. ctr. for materials sci. and engring., 1998-2000, dean of sci., 2000—. Vis. prof. U. Utrecht, The Netherlands, 1972-73, 97, U. Grenoble, France, 1983; cons. Exxon Rsch., Clinton, N.J., 1984-98. Author: Physical Chemistry, 1991, 4th edit., 2004; editor: Conjugated Polymers, 1991; contbr. articles to profl. jours. Recipient Alexander von Humboldt Found. Sr. Scientist award, 1989, Max Planck award, 1992; Alfred P. Sloan fellow, 1968, John S. Guggenheim fellow, 1972; Dreyfus Found. Tchr.-Scholar grantee, 1969. Fellow AAAS, Am. Acad. Arts and Sci., Am. Phys. Soc.; mem. NAS. Avocations: sailing, swimming. Office: MIT Dept Chemistry 77 Mass Ave Cambridge MA 02139-4307 Office Phone: 617-253-8900. Business E-Mail: silbey@mit.edu.

**SILBIGER, MARTIN L.,** radiologist, educator, dean; b. Ravenna, Ohio, Mar. 17, 1938; s. Alfred James and Evelyn Norma (Cheswick) Silbiger; m. Ruth Hope Steele, June 4, 1957; children: Martin, Eve, Jonathan, Holly, Wendy. BA, U. Pa., 1958; MD, Western Reserve U., 1962; MBA, U. South Fla., 1989. Diplomate Am. Bd. Radiology, Am. Bd. Nuc. Medicine. Intern Univ. Hosps. Cleve., 1962—63; resident Johns Hopkins Hosp., 1963—66; with NIH, 1966—68; radiologist Tampa (Fla.) Gen. Hosp., 1968—; prof. U. South Fla., Tampa, 1982—; chief of staff Tampa Gen. Hosp., 1978—80; chmn. dept. radiology U. South Fla. Coll. Medicine, 1982—95; dean coll. medicine U. South Fla., 1995—2000, v.p. health scis., 1995—2000. Founder Hillsborough County Med. Assn. Found., Tampa, 1992; treas. Cmty. Found. Tampa, 1993—95; bd. dirs. Moffitt Cancer Ctr., Tampa, 1985—2000, Moffitt Cancer Ctr. Found., 1994—2000. Avocations: reading, rollerblading, golf, tennis. Home: 1827 Bayshore Blvd Tampa FL 33606-3210 Office: 3301 Alumni Dr Tampa FL 33612-9413 also: 1209 Bruce B Downs Blvd PO Box 66 Tampa FL 33601-0066

**SILCOX, GORDON BRUCE,** executive coach; b. Takoma Park, Md., May 11, 1938; s. Walter Bruce and Ruth May (Davis) S.; m. Judith Andrea Smith, Mar. 7, 1970 (div. Apr. 1998); children: Andrea Davis, Jessica Lyn. AB, Princeton U., 1960; MBA, U. Pa., 1965. Trust investment officer Am. Security Bank, Washington, 1967—69; v.p., trust investment officer, head trust investment divsn. First Am. Bank, N.A., 1969—77; prin. Paul Stafford Assocs., Ltd., Washington, 1977-83; v.p., mgr. MSL Internat. Ltd., Washington, 1983-86; v.p. Manchester, Inc., Washington, 1987-91, sr. v.p., 1991—2003; prin. Words on Purpose LLC, Fairfax, Va., 2003—. Pres. Wash. Human Resource Forum, 1993-95. Treas. Princeton U. Class of 1960, v.p., 1980-85. Lt. (j.g.) USN, 1962-63. Mem. Univ. Club, Princeton Club (treas. Washington 1972-74, N.Y.C.). Methodist. Home and Office: 3159 Colchester Brook Ln Fairfax VA 22031-2609 Office Phone: 703-280-1041. E-mail: gsilcox@wordsonpurpose.com.

**SILER, EUGENE EDWARD, JR.,** federal judge; b. Williamsburg, Ky., Oct. 19, 1936; s. Eugene Edward and Lowell (Jones) Siler; m. Christy Duane Minnich, Oct. 18, 1969; children: Eugene Edward, Adam Troy. BA cum laude, Vanderbilt U., 1958; LLB, U. Va., 1963; LLM, Georgetown U., 1964, U. Va., 1995. Bar: Ky. 1963, Va. 1963, D.C. 1963. Pvt. practice, Williamsburg, 1964—65; county atty. Whitley County, Ky., 1965—70; US atty. (ea. dist.) Ky. US Dept. Justice, Lexington, 1970—75; judge (ea. & west.) Ky. US Dist. Ct., 1975—91, chief judge (ea. dist.) Ky., 1984—91; judge US Ct. Appeals (6th Cir.), 1991—2001, sr. judge, 2001—. Trustee Cumberland Coll.,

Williamsburg, 1965—73, 1980—88; campaign co-chmn. Congressman Tim L. Carter, 1966, 5th Congl. Dist., U.S. Senator J.S. Cooper, 1966; 1st v.p. Ky. Bapt. Convention, 1986—87, 2002—03, pres., 2003—04; bd. dirs. Bapt. Healthcare System Inc., 1990—2004. With USN, 1958—60, with USNR, 1960—83. Recipient Freedom's Found. medal, 1968; E. Barrett Prettyman fellow, 1963—64. Mem.: Va. State Bar, D.C. Bar Assn., Ky. Bar Assn. (Judge of Yr. 1992), Fed. Bar Assn. Republican. Baptist. Home: PO Box 129 Williamsburg KY 40769-0129 Office: US Ct Appeals 310 S Main Street Room 333 London KY 40741*

**SILER, VIRGINIA CARLISLE,** retired elementary school educator; d. Stanley Gordon and Jane Carlisle Volbrecht; m. David Colin Beckman, July 31, 1990;; children: Scott Q., Christina Carlisle. BA, U. Pacific, 1975, cert. in Tchg., 1985. Tchr. Stockton (Calif.) Unified Sch. Dist., 1986—97, 2001—04, ret., 2004. Counselor gang determent City Lodi, Calif., 2000. Avocations: gardening, fishing, camping. Home: 215 Donner Dr Lodi CA 95240-0668

**SILETS, HARVEY MARVIN,** lawyer; b. Chgo., Aug. 25, 1931; s. Joseph Lazarus and Sylvia Silets; m. Elaine L. Gordon, June 25, 1961; children: Hayden Leigh, Jonathan Lazarus (dec.), Alexandra Rose. BS cum laude, DePaul U., 1952; JD (Frederick Leicke scholar), U. Mich., 1955. Bar: Ill. 1955, U.S. Dist. Ct. (no. dist.) Ill. 1955, N.Y. 1956, U.S. Tax Ct. 1957, U.S. Ct. Mil. Appeals 1957, U.S. Ct. Appeals (7th cir.) 1958, U.S. Supreme Ct. 1959, U.S. Ct. Appeals (6th cir.) 1965, U.S. Ct. Appeals (2d cir.) 1971, U.S. Ct. Appeals (5th cir.) 1972, U.S. Ct. Appeals (11th cir.). Assoc. Paul, Weiss, Rifkind, Wharton & Garrison, N.Y.C., 1955—56; asst. atty. U.S. Dist. Ct. (no. dist.) Ill., 1958—60; chief tax atty. U.S. Atty. No. Dist. Ill., Chgo., 1960—62; ptnr Harris, Burman & Silets, Chgo., 1962—79, Silets & Martin, Ltd., Chgo., 1979—92, Katten Muchin Zavis Rosenman, Chgo., 1992—. Asst. advance tng. program IRS, U. Mich., 1952-53; law lectr. advance fed. taxation John Marshall Law Sch., 1962-66; adj. prof. taxation Chgo.-Kent Coll. Law, 1985—; gen. counsel Nat. Treasury Employees Union, 1968-92; mem. adv. com. tax litigation U.S. Dept. Justice, 1979-82; mem. Tax Reform Com., State of Ill., 1982-83; mem. Speedy Trial Act Planning Group U.S. Dist. Ct. (no. dist.) Ill., 1976-79; mem. civil justice reform act adv. com. U.S. Dist. Ct. (no. dist.) Ill., 1991-94; lectr. in field. Contbr. articles to profl. jours. Trustee Latin Sch., Chgo., 1970-76; active Chgo. Crime Commn., 1975-93, Govv.'s Commn. Reform Tax Laws, Ill., 1982-83. With AUS, 1956-58. Fellow Am. Coll. Trial Lawyers (chmn. com. on fed. rules of criminal procedure 1982-91, fed. rules of evidence com. 1988-93, jud. com., fed. criminal procedures com., Upstate Ill. com. chmn. 1990-91), Am. Coll. Tax Counsel, Internat. Acad. Trial Lawyers, Soc. Advanced Legal Studies (London, lectr. internat. symposium on econ. crime, Cambridge U. 1999-05); mem. ABA (active various coms.), Bar Assn. 7th Fed. Cir. (chmn. com. criminal law and procedure 1972-82, bd. govs. 1983-86, sec. 1986-88, v.p. 1989-90, pres. 1990-91), NACDL, FBA (bd. dirs. 1971—, pres. 1977-78, v.p. 1976-77, sec. 1975-76, treas. 1974-75, active various coms.), Chgo. Bar Assn. (tax com. 1958-66, com. devel. law 1966-72, 78-88, com. fed. taxation 1968—, com. evaluation candidates 1978-80, exec. com. tax sect. 1994—), Am. Bd. Criminal Def. Lawyers, Decalogue Soc. Lawyers, Bar Assn. N.Y. City, Standard Club, Chgo. Club, Phi Alpha delta, Pi Gamma Mu. Office: Katten Muchin Rosenman LLP 525 W Monroe St Chicago IL 60661-3693 Office Phone: 312-902-5511. E-mail: harvey.silets@kattenlaw.com.

**SILIANOFF, DAVID,** secondary school educator, educator, mathematics educator; BS in Math., Westminster Coll., New Wilmington, Pa., 1986; MEd in Adult Edn., Pa. State U., U. Pk., Pa., 1994; MS in Ednl. Tech. Mgmt., Carnegie-Mellon U., Pitts., Pa., 2006; cert. in Tchg. Math., Westminster Coll., 2000; cert. in Prin., Saint Francis Coll., 2000. Tchr. math. Norwin Sch. Dist., North Huntingdon, Pa., 1995—. Recipient Outstanding Master's Paper award, Pa. State U., 1994, Norwin Groundbreaking Educator award, Norwin Sch. Dist., 1998, Tchr. of Yr. award, Wal-Mart and Sam's Club, 2002. Mem.: Nat. Coun. Tchrs. Math., Math. Assn. Am.

**SILICIANO, ROBERT F.,** immunologist, medical educator; b. Rochester, NY, 1952; BA in Chem., Princeton U., 1974; MD, Johns Hopkins U., 1978, PhD in Immunology, 1983. Fellow Johns Hopkins U., Dana-Farber Cancer Inst., Harvard U., 1983—86, pathology instr., 1986—88; asst. prof. Johns Hopkins U. Sch. Med., 1988—92, assoc. prof., 1992—98, prof. med. & molecular biology and genetics, 1998—. Investigator Howard Hughes Med. Inst., Chevy Chase, Md., 2002—. Recipient Disting. Clin. Sci. award, Doris Duke Charitable Found., 2001. Office: Johns Hopkins U Sch Med 725 N Wolfe St 1049 Ross Baltimore MD 21205

**SILJAK, DRAGOSLAV D.,** engineering educator, researcher; b. Belgrade, Serbia, Sept. 10, 1933; came to U.S. 1964, naturalized; s. Dobrilo T. and Ljubica Z. (Zivanovic) S.; m. Dragana T. Todorovic, Sept. 28, 1967; children— Ana, Matija. BSEE, U. Belgrade, 1958, MSEE, 1961, ScD, 1963. Docent prof. U. Belgrade, 1963-64; assoc. prof. U. Santa Clara, Calif., 1964-70, prof. engring., 1970-84, B. and M. Swig Univ. chair, 1984—. Author: Nonlinear Systems, 1969, Large Scale Systems, 1978, Decentralized Control of Complex Systems, 1991; mem. editl. bd. Difference Equations, Nonlinear World, Comm. in Applied Analysis, Internat. Jour. Computer Rsch., Nonlinear Analysis: Theory, Methods and Applications, Dynamics of Cont., Disc. and Impulsive Systems, Math. Problems in Engring., Stability and Control: Theory and Applications. Disting. prof. Fulbright Found., 1984. Life fellow IEEE; mem. Serbian Acad. Scis. and Arts (hon.). Mem. Christian Orthodox Ch. E-mail: dsiljak@scu.edu.

**SILK, FREDERICK C.Z.,** financial consultant; b. Pretoria, Transvaal, South Africa, Aug 29, 1934; arrived in Canada, 1964; s. Frederick Charles and Edythe D'Olier S.; m. Margaret Colbourne, May 12, 1962; children: Michael, Alison, Jennifer. BS, Rhoden U., Grahamstown, Republic South Africa, 1954, cert. acctg. theory, U. Witwatersrand, Johannesburg, Republic South Africa, 1957. Acct., cons. Deloitte, Plender, Haskins & Sells, Johannesburg, London and N.Y.C., 1954-64; mgmt. cons. P.S. Ross & Ptnrs., Montreal, Que., Canada, 1964-68; v.p. fin. and adminstrn. J&P Coats Ltd., Montreal, Que., Canada, 1968-74; treas. Standard Brands, Ltd., Montreal, Que., Canada, 1974-75; asst. treas. Standard Brands, Inc., N.Y.C., 1975-78; treas. Harlequin Enterprises, Ltd., Toronto, Ont., Canada, 1978-82; v.p., treas. Nabisco Brands, Ltd., Toronto, 1982-95; pvt. treas. cons. Toronto, 1995—. Fellow Inst. Chartered Accts. (Eng., Wales), Inst. Chartered Accts. (South Africa), Fin. Execs. Internat. Avocations: music, choral music, Gilbert and Sullivan operettas. Office: 80 Front St E Ste 602 Toronto ON Canada M5E 1T4 Personal E-mail: fczsilk@hotmail.com.

**SILK, JAMES J.,** law educator; AB, U. Mich., 1969; MA, U. Chgo., 1981; JD, Yale U., 1989. Bar: NY, Conn., DC, US Dist. Ct., DC. Atty. Arnold & Porter, 1989—93; dep. dir. Robert F. Kennedy Meml. Ctr. for Human Rights, 1993, dir., 1994—99; exec. dir. Orville H. Schell Jr. Ctr. for Internat. Human Rights Yale Law Sch., New Haven, 1999—, lectr. 1999—2004 clin. prof. law, 2004—. Adj. lectr. Am. U., 1996, 97. Office: Yale Law Sch PO Box 208215 New Haven CT 06520 E-mail: james.silk@yale.edu.

**SILK, KENNETH R.,** psychiatrist, medical educator; b. Fall River, Mass., May 27, 1944; m. Joan Margeson. BS, Brandeis U., 1966; MD, Albert Einstein Coll. Medicine, Bronx, N.Y., 1970. Cert. psychiatry Am. Bd. Psychiatry and Neurology, 1980. Pediat. intern Montefiore Hosp. and Med. Ctr., 1970—71; resident in psychiatry Yale U. Sch. Medicine, 1971—75; prof. psychiatry U. Mich., Ann Arbor, 1975—. Mem.: Internat. Soc. Personality Disorders (sec.-treas. 2005). Office: Univ Mich Psychiatry Dept 1500 E Med Ctr Dr Box 0295 Ann Arbor MI 48109-0295 Office Phone: 734-615-5276. Home Fax: 734-936-9761; Office Fax: 734-936-9761. Business E-Mail: ksilk@umich.edu.

**SILK, MARK REUEL,** religious studies educator, writer; b. Cambridge, Mass., May 12, 1950; s. Leonard and Bernice Silk; m. Tema Kaiser, June 25, 1978; children: Abraham, Ezra, Isaac. AB, Harvard U., Cambridge, Mass., 1972, PhD, 1982. Lectr. Harvard U., 1982—85; editor Boston Rev., Boston,

1985—86; staff writer, editl. writer, columnist Atlanta Jour. Constn., 1987—96; dir. The Leonard E. Greenberg Ctr. Study Religion in Pub. Life Trinity Coll., Hartford, Conn., 1996—, assoc. prof. religion in pub. life, 1996—, dir. Pub. Values Program, 2005—. Adv. bd. Inst. Advanced Study of Religion Yale U., New Haven, 1999—2002; adv. bd. Gralla Fellows Program for Religion Journalists Brandeis U., Waltham, Mass., 1999—; adv. bd. nat. program First Freedom Ctr., Richmond, Va., 2003—. Author: Spiritual Politics: Religion and America Since World War II, 1988, Unsecular Media: Making News of Religion in America, 1995; editor: Religion by Region, Religion in the News; contbg. editor: The Rev. Faith and Internat. Affairs, 2006—, mem. editl. bd.: Jour. Media and Religion, 2001—; contbr. articles to profl. jours. Mem. cmty. relations coun. Hartford Jewish Fed., Conn. Recipient Best article of Yr. award, editl. bd. Am. Quarterly, 1984; fellow, Harvard U., 1975—76. Mem.: Am. Acad. Religion, Phi Beta Kappa. Democrat. Jewish. Home: 63 Highland St West Hartford CT 06119 Office: Trinity Coll 300 Summit St Hartford CT 06106 Office Phone: 860-297-2352. Office Fax: 860-297-5125. Business E-Mail: mark.silk@trincoll.edu.

**SILK, THOMAS,** lawyer; b. Beaver, Pa., Dec. 12, 1937; s. Thomas and Alice Genevieve (Beck) S.; m. Arlene Schlaifer, 1959 (div.); 1 child, Nicole Amory; m. Susan Clark, 1979 (div.); m. Suzanne Vinson, 1996. AB, U. Calif., Berkeley, 1959, LLB, 1963. Bar: Calif. 1964, U.S. Dist. Ct. (no. dist.) Calif. 1964, U.S. Ct. Appeals (D.C., 2-10th cirs.) 1966-68, U.S. Tax Ct. 1966, U.S. Supreme Ct. 1967. Appellate atty. tax divsn. U.S. Dept. Justice, Washington, 1964-66, spl. asst. to asst. atty. gen. tax divsn., 1966-68; assoc. Brobeck, Phleger & Harrison, San Francisco, 1968-71; founder, chmn. Silk, Adler & Colvin, San Francisco, 1977—. Lectr., author, and advisor in field. Editor, co-author: Philanthropy and Law in Asia, 1999; author: Corporate Philanthropy and Law: A Guide to Tax Charities and An Introduction to Compliance with Anti-Terrorist Laws, 2003, Rational Exuberance: An Exploration of the Adaptation of California's Charitable Sector to Changing Governance Standards - Notes from the Field, Advisor ALI Project on the Principles of the Law of Nonprofit Organizations, 2004—. Trustee CompassPoint; trustee, sec. Hertz Found. Office: Silk Adler & Colvin Ste 1220 235 Montgomery St San Francisco CA 94104-2902 Office Phone: 415-421-7555. Business E-Mail: tom@silklaw.com.

**SILKENAT, JAMES ROBERT,** lawyer; b. Salina, Kans., Aug. 2, 1947; s. Ernest E. and Mildred R. (Iman) S.; children: David Andrew, Katherine Anne. BA, Drury Coll., 1969; JD, U. Chgo., 1972; LLM, NYU, 1978. Bar: N.Y. 1973, D.C. 1980. Assoc. Cravath, Swaine & Moore, N.Y.C., 1972-80; counsel Internat. Fin. Corp., Washington, 1980-86; ptnr. Morgan, Lewis & Bockius, N.Y.C., 1986-89, Morrison & Foerster, N.Y.C., 1989-92, Pillsbury, Winthrop, N.Y.C., 1992—2002, Arent Fox, N.Y.C., 2002—. Chmn. Council N.Y. Law Assocs., 1978-79, Lawyers Com. Internat. Human Rights, 1978-80. Editor ABA Guide to Fng. Law Firms, Moscow Conf. on Law Bilateral Econ. Rels., ABA Guide to Internat. Bus. Negotiations, The Law of International Insolvencies and Debt Restructurings; contbr. articles to profl. jours. Capt. U.S. Army, 1972-73. Fellow NEH, 1973, U.S. Dept. State, 1981. Fellow Am. Bar Found. (chmn. 2004-05); mem. ABA (chmn. internat. law and practice sect. 1989-90, chmn. sect. officer's conf. 1990-92, mem. ho. of dels. 1989—, bd. govs. 1994-97). Office: Arent Fox 1675 Broadway New York NY 10019 Office Phone: 212-492-3318. E-mail: silkenat.james@arentfox.com.

**SILKOV, ANTONINA,** research scientist; b. Simferopol, Ukraine, 1968; arrived in U.S., 2001; d. Viktor and Neli Grazhdan; m. Andrey Silkov, Nov. 26, 1994; 1 child, Ilay. MSc with honors, Simferopol State U., Ukraine, 1990; PhD, Weizmann Inst. Scis., Rehovot, Israel, 2001. Postdoctoral rsch. scientist Columbia U., N.Y.C., 2001—. Home: 647A Bruce St Ridgefield NJ 07657 Office: 1130 Nicholas Ave New York NY 10032 Office Phone: 212-851-4655. Business E-Mail: as2137@columbia.edu.

**SILLARS, MALCOLM OSGOOD,** communications educator; b. Union City, NJ, Feb. 12, 1928; s. Malcolm Osgood and Dorothy Edna (Browning) S.; m. Charlotte Jane Grimm, June 1, 1948; children— Paul Louis, Bruce Malcolm, Alan Leslie. BA, U. Redlands, 1948, MA, 1949; PhD, U. Iowa, 1955. Asst. prof. comm. Iowa State U., Ames, 1949-53; asst. prof. Calif. State U., L.A., 1954-56, prof., 1956—71; dean, 1970-71; pres. Calif. State U. Northridge, 1969-70; prof. U. Mass., Amherst, 1971-74; prof. communication U. Utah, Salt Lake City, 1974-97, dean humanities, 1974-81, ret., 1998. Author: Speech: Content and Communications, 6th edit., 1991, Argumentation and Critical Decision Making, 6th edit., 2005, Communication Criticism, 2d edit., 2001; contbr. articles to profl. jours. Recipient Silver Beaver award Boy Scouts Am. Mem. ACLU, Nat. Comm. Assn. (pres.), We. States Comm. Assn. (pres.). Democrat. Home: 3508 Eastoaks Dr Salt Lake City UT 84124-3811 E-mail: m.sillars@utah.edu.

**SILLERMAN, ROBERT F. X.,** communications executive, banker; b. N.Y.C., Apr. 12, 1948; s. Michael McKinley and Estelle (Levande) Sillerman; m. Jane Waxenberg, July 13, 1969 (div. Dec. 1970); m. Laura Baudo, Feb. 25, 1974. BS magna cum laude, Brandeis U., 1969. CEO, chmn. bd. Youth Markets Cons., Inc., Boston, 1966-74, Nat. Discount Mktg., Great Neck, NY, 1974-78, Sillerman-Morrow Broadcasting Group, Middletown, NY, 1978-85; co-chmn. bd. Legacy Broadcasting, L.A., 1985-89; CEO, chmn. bd. Sillerman-Magee Comm. Mgmt. Corp. (now Sillerman Comm. Mgmt. Corp.), N.Y.C., 1985, TV Programs of Am., Hollywood, Calif., 1985; founder, CEO, chmn. SFX Broadcasting, Inc.(acquired by Hicks, Muse, Tate & Furst), 1992—95, exec. chmn., 1995—98; founder, exec. chmn., mem. of the office of the chmn., dir. SFX Entertainment, Inc. (acquired by Clear Channel Communications), 1997—2000; chmn. FXM, Inc., 2000—05; founder, mng. mem. FXM Asset Mgmt. LLC, 2003—; mng. mem. MJX Asset Mgmt., 2003—; CEO, pres. chmn. bd CKX, Inc., Las Vegas, Nev. 2005—. Co-chmn. Legacy Broadcasting, Inc., 1986—; chmn. Met. Broadcasting, Inc., 1988-89. Recipient Bearer of the Torch award Anti-Defamation League, N.Y.C., 1982. Mem. Nat. Assn. Broadcasters, Nat. Radio Broadcasters Assn. Office: CKX Inc 6730 S Las Vegas Blvd Las Vegas NV 89119 Address: Southampton Coll LI Univ 239 Montauk Hwy Southampton NY 11968-4196 Office Phone: 702-798-7777, 631-283-4000. Office Fax: 702-798-6847, 631-283-4081.

**SILLERUD, ARLEN ROGER,** retired secondary school educator; b. Nov. 28, 1934; BS, Moorhead State U., 1958; postgrad., Bemidji State U., 1969-70, U. Minn., 1988-90. Tchr. Ada School Dist., Ada, Minn., 1958-90. Chmn. Norman County Reps., Ada, Minn., 1996—, county, dist., and state del., 1994-2000., 2000—, state ctrl. del., 1997-2001, alt., 2000—; elder Zion Luth. Ch., Ada, 1994-2005, Gideon spkr., 1971—. Achievements include rsch. in heart fibrillation, that the heart can be restarted by electric shock; creator five solutions to clean up oil spills; inventor wind deflector for trucks. Home: 807 3rd Ave E Ada MN 56510-1120

**SILLMAN, AMY,** painter, art educator; b. Oct. 1955; Student, Beloit Coll. NYU; BFA, Sch. Visual Arts, Manhattan; MFA, Bard Coll. Milton Avery prof. arts, faculty Milton Avery Grad. Sch. Arts, Bard Coll., 1996—. One-man shows include Brent Sikkema Gallery, 2000, exhibitions include Casey Kaplan Gallery, Manhattan, N.Y., 1996, 1998, White Columns, 1996, Postmasters Gallery, N.Y.C., 1997, Sixth@Prince Fine Art, 1999, Exit Art, 2000, Whitney Biennial, Whitney Mus. Am. Art, NY, 2004. Recipient Tiffany Found. award, 1999—2000; Guggenheim fellow, 2001—02. Personal E-mail: amyfelix@aol.com.

**SILLMAN, AMY,** cell biologist; AB in Biochemistry, Harvard Coll., Cambridge, Mass., 1989; PhD in Immunology, U. of Pa., Phila., 1999. Postdoctoral scholar U. of Calif. Davis, 2000—03; postdoctoral scholar-fellow U. of Calif. San Francisco, 2003—. Lectr., biology Rsch. Sci. Inst., Cambridge, Mass., 2005—, Cambridge, 1996, Shanghai, 2000—. Contbr. articles to profl. jours. Recipient Elizabeth Cary Agassiz Cert. of Merit, Harvard U., 1988—89; fellow Rsch. fellow, Dermatology Found., 2003. Mem.: Am. Soc. for Cell Biology. Achievements include research in Defined the interaction between the PLCgamma enzyme and one of its upstream

activatorsin B lymphocytes, the kinase Syk. Office: University of California San Francisco 513 Parnassus Ave San Francisco CA 94143 Personal E-mail: amy_sillman@post.harvard.edu. E-mail: amy.sillman@ucsf.edu.

**SILLMAN, ARNOLD JOEL,** physiologist, educator; b. NYC, Oct. 10, 1940; s. Philip and Anne L. (Pearlman) S.; m. Jean Fletcher Van Keuren, Sept. 26, 1969; children: Andrea Jose Calloway, Diana Van Keuren Taylor. AB, UCLA, 1963, MA, 1965, PhD, 1968. Asst. prof. UCLA, 1969-73, U. Calif., Davis, 1975-78, assoc. prof., 1978-85, prof., 1985—; asst. prof. U. Pitts., 1973-75, interim dir. aquaculture and fisheries program, 1994—95, vice chair sect. neurobiology, physiology and behavior, 1998—, acting chair, 2001. Contbr. articles to profl. jours. USPHS trainee, UCLA, 1966-67; fellow NSF, 1967-68, Fight for Sight, Inc., 1968-69. Recipient Acad. Senate Disting. Tchg. award, 1996. Mem.: Am. Physiol. Soc., Soc. Gen. Physiologists, Am. Soc. Zoologists, Assn. Rsch. in Vision and Ophthalmology, AAAS, N.Y. Acad. Sci. Jewish. Home: 1140 Los Robles St Davis CA 95616-4927 Office: U Calif Sect Neurobiology Physiology & Behavior Coll Biol Scis Davis CA 95616 Office Phone: 530-752-3207. E-mail: ajsillman@ucdavis.edu.

**SILLS, BEVERLY (MRS. PETER B. GREENOUGH),** performing company executive, singer; b. Bklyn., May 25, 1929; d. Morris and Sonia (Bahn) Silverman; m. Peter B. Greenough, 1956 (dec. Sept. 7, 2006); children: Meredith, Peter B.; stepchildren: Lindley, Nancy, Diana. Studied with Estelle Leibling, studied with Paolo Gallico, studied with Desire Defrere; doctorate (hon.), Harvard U., NYU, New Eng. Conservatory, Temple U.; degree (hon.), Harvard U., NYU, Calif. Inst. Arts. Gen dir. N.Y.C. Opera, 1979 1989; pres. N.Y.C. Opera Bd., 1989-90; mng. dir. Met. Opera, N.Y.C., 1991-94; chairwoman Lincoln Ctr. for Performing Arts, Inc., N.Y.C., 1994—2002, Met. Opera, N.Y.C., 2002—05. Bd. dirs. Met. Opera, 1991-2005; cons. Nat. Coun. on Arts. Radio debut as Bubbles Silverman on Uncle Bob's Rainbow House, 1932; appeared on Major Bowes Capitol Family Hour, 1934-41, on Our Gal Sunday; toured with Shubert Tours, Charles Wagner Opera Co., 1950, 51; operatic debut Phila. Civic Opera, 1947; debut, N.Y.C. Opera Co. as Rosalinda in Die Fledermaus, 1955; debut San Francisco Opera, 1953; debut La Scala, Milan as Pamira in Siege of Corinth, 1969, Royal Opera, Covent Garden in Lucia di Lammermoor, London, 1971, Met. Opera, N.Y.C., 1975, Vienna State Opera, 1967, Teatro Fenice in La Traviata, Venice; appeared Teatro Colon, Buenos Aires; recital debut Paris, 1971, London Symphony Orch., 1971; appeared throughout U.S., Europe, S. Am. including Boston Symphony, Tanglewood Festival, 1968, 69, Robin Hood Dell, Phila., 1969; title roles in: Don Pasquale, Norma, Ballad of Baby Doe, Thais, La Traviata, Anna Bolena, Maria Stuarda, Lucia de Lammermoor, Barber of Seville, Manon, Louise, Tales of Hoffmann, Daughter of the Regiment, The Magic Flute, Elizabeth in Roberto Devereaux, I Puritana, Julius Caesar, Suor Angelica, Il Tabarro, Gianni Schicchi, Faust, La Loca, Merry Widow, Turk in Italy, Rigoletto, I Capuleti e I Montecchi, Lucrezia Borgia, Ariodante, Le Coq D'Or, others; recordings include The Art of Beverly Sills, Welcome to Vienna, Great Scores (with Placido Domingo); ret. from opera and concert stage, 1980; numerous TV spls; author: Bubbles: A Self-Portrait, 1976, Bubbles: An Encore, Beverly: An Autobiography. Active with March of Dimes, 1971- (Past chmn. bd., past nat. chmn. Mothers' March on Birth Defects); bd. dirs. Apollo Theatre Found., 1999-2001. Recipient Handel medallion, 1973, Pearl S. Buck Women's award, 1979, Emmy award for Profiles in Music, 1976, Emmy award for Lifestyles with Beverly Sills, 1978, Presdl. Medal of Freedom, 1980, Kennedy Ctr. Honors award, 1980, Heinz award in Arts and Humanities, 1995, Grammy award for Best Classical Vocal Soloist Performance, 1976, Best Opera Recording, 1978, Bess Wallace Truman award, March of Dimes, 1994, Juanita Kreps award, JC Penny Co., 1996, MS Hope award, Nat. Multiple Sclerosis Soc., 1998, Medal of the Order of Arts and Letters, Min. French Culture, 2000. Office: Met Opera Lincoln Ctr Performing Arts 140 W 65th St New York NY 10023

**SILLS, RICHARD REYNOLDS,** scientist, educator; b. N.Y.C., Sept. 19, 1946; s. Leonard Harold and Carol (Rudin) S. BA, Boston U., 1968. Tchr. N.Y.C. Pub. Schs., 1968-70, 79-81; v.p. Plutronics, Inc., N.Y.C., 1981-85; pvt. practice N.Y.C., 1985—. Author: (children's book) Jonny the Jester, 1977; contbr. articles to profl. jours.; patentee method and apparatus for encoding and decoding signals, method and apparatus for modifying synthesized sound signals, analog processing system. Mem. Rep. Nat. Com., Washington, 1981—, Rep. Presdl. Task Force, Washington, 1982—, Rep. Senatorial Inner Cir., 1987—, Rep. Senatorial Trust, 1999—; founding mem. Chmn.'s Club, Ronald Reagan Presl. Found., 1997—. Named Educator of Decade, Found. for Universal Brotherhood Inc., 1978; recipient Rep. Senatorial Medal of Freedom, 1999. Mem. AAAS, N.Y. Acad. Scis., Union of Concerned Scientists. Avocations: running, weightlifting.

**SILSBY, PAULA D.,** prosecutor; b. Ellsworth, Maine, 1951; JD, U. Maine, 1976; BA, Mt. Holyoke Coll. Bar: Maine 1976. US atty. (dist. Maine) US Dept. Justice, Portland, 2001—. Fellow: Maine Bar Found. Office: US Attys Office 100 Middle St Ste 6 Portland ME 04101-4182*

**SILVA, A. R.,** surgeon, educator; MD, U. Para, Brazil, 1953. Intern Monmouth Med. Ctr., Long Branch, NJ, 1957, resident surgery, 1958—62; intern surgery UCLA, 1963—64; pvt. practice Gen. Surgery and Oncology Corona, Calif., 1965—. Rsch. surgeon, clin. investigator Surgery Dept. UCLA, 1962—65; assoc. clin. prof. U. Calif. Irvine, 1977—; staff mem. Corona Regional Med. Ctr., U. Calif. Irvine Med. Ctr., Orange; chmn. cancer com. Corona Regional Med. Ctr., mem. exec. com. Contbr. articles to profl. jours. Bd. dirs. Corona Regional Med. Ctr. Found.; pres. Inland Empire unit Am. Cancer Soc., bd. dirs. Inland Empire unit. Mem.: AMA, ACS (regional surveyor cancer dept.), Tri-County Surg. Soc, So. Calif. (bd. dirs.) N Y Acad. Scis., So. Calif. Acad. Clin. Oncology, Soc. Surg. Oncology, Soc. Lagaroendoscopic Surgeons, Royal Soc. Medicine Eng., Riverside County Med. Assn. (bd. councilors, past pres. 1988, mediation and med. care com., past chmn. credentials com.), Pan Pacific Surg. Assn., Pan Am. Med. Soc., Orange County Surg. Soc., John E. Connelly Surg. Soc., Internat. Coll. Surgeons, Calif. Med. Assn. (alt. del Dist. II), Assn. Clin. Faculty, Am. Soc. Colon and Rectal Surgeons, Am. Soc. Clin. Oncology, Am. Soc. Abdominal Surgeons, Am. Bd. Surgery, Am. Assn. Fgn. Med. Grads. Office: PO Box 515 Corona CA 92878

**SILVA, CLARENCE,** bishop; b. Honolulu, Aug. 6, 1949; Student, St. Joseph Sem., Mountain View, Calif., St. Patrick Sem., Menlo Pk. Ordained priest Diocese of Oakland, Calif., 1975; parochial vicar St. Bernard Parish, Oakland, St. Bede Parish, Hayward, Calif.; pastor St. Peter Martyr Parish, Pittsburgh, Pa.; St. Anthony Parish, Oakland, Calif., St. John the Baptist Parish, El Cerrito, Calif., St. Andrew-St. Joseph Parish, Oakland, Calif., St. Leonard-St. Paul Parish, Fremont, Calif.; vicar gen. & moderator of curia Diocese of Oakland, 2004—05; Bishop of Honolulu, 2005—. Roman Catholic. Office: Diocese of Honolulu 1184 Bishop St Honolulu HI 96813-2858 Office Phone: 801-533-1791.

**SILVA, DANIEL JOSEPH,** writer; b. Kalamazoo, Mich., Dec. 19, 1960; s. Richard and Carol Ann (Koerber) S.; m. Jamie Sue Gangel, Sept. 8, 1988; children: Lily Elizabeth, Nicholas Jacob (twins). BA, Calif. State U., Fresno, 1983. Fgn. news editor UPI, Washington, 1985-86; Mideast corr. Cairo, Egypt, 1986-87; exec. prodr. CNN, Washington, 1988—. Author: The Unlikely Spy, 1997 (NY Times bestseller list), Mark of the Assassin, 1998, Marching Season, 1999, Kill Artist, 2000, English Assassin, 2002, Confessor, 2003, Death in Vienna, 2004, Prince of Fire, 2005 (NY Times bestseller list), The Messenger, 2006. Office: c/o Marilyn Duckworth Putnam 375 Hudson St New York NY 10014*

**SILVA, EUGENE JOSEPH,** lawyer; b. Gloucester, Mass., May 23, 1942; s. Edward Joseph and Rose (Lebre) Silva; m. Nancy Blue-Pearson, Jan. 8, 1972; children: Eugene Joseph II, Michael Joseph. BS with honors, Maine Maritime Acad., 1964; JD, U. Notre Dame, 1972. Bar: Calif. 1972, US Dist. Ct. (so. and cen. dists.) Calif. 1972, Tex. 1977, US Dist. Ct. (so. and ea. dists.) Tex. 1978, US Ct. Appeals (5th, 9th, 2d and 11th cirs.) 1978, US Supreme Ct. 1981; lic.

Master Mariner. Assoc. Luce, Forward, Hamilton & Scripps, San Diego, 1972-77, Vinson & Elkins, Houston, 1977-79, ptnr., 1980—2003. Mem. adv. bd. Admiralty Law Inst. Tulane U., 1999—. Bd. dirs. Cabrillo Festival Inc., San Diego, 1974—77, San Jose Clinic, Inc., 1990—97, pres., 1993—95; bd. dirs. Portuguese Heritage Scholarship Found., 1995—, St. Joseph Hosp. Found., 1995—2000. Decorated Knight Grand Cross Equestrian Order Holy Sepulchre Jerusalem; named one of Best Lawyers in Am., 1991—2005; recipient Outstanding Alumni award, Maine Maritime Acad., 1990. Mem. Calif. Bar Assn., Tex. Bar Assn., Grays Inn U. Notre Dame Sch. Law (pres. 1970-72), Maritime Law Assn. US (proctor in admiralty 1974-2005), Portuguese Union Calif. (bd. dirs. 1973-74), Portuguese Am. League San Diego (pres. 1974-75), Portuguese Am. Leadership Coun. US, Notre Dame Club (pres. San Diego chpt. 1976-77). Roman Catholic. Home: 8 Smithdale Estates Dr Houston TX 77024-6600 Office: Vinson & Elkins 2300 First City Tower 1001 Fannin St Ste 3300 Houston TX 77002-6706 Personal E-mail: ejsilva@swbell.net.

**SILVA, JANA KAIDA,** obstetrician, maternal/fetal medicine specialist; b. Honolulu, Jan. 15, 1959; d. Edward M. and Alice I. Kaida; m. Marvin V. Silva, June 29, 1984; children: Natassia, Gavin, Colin, Alana. BSN cum laude, U. Wash., 1982, BA in Psychology, cum laude, 1982; MD, U. Hawaii, 1991. Diplomate Am. Bd. Ob-gyn., Am. Bd. Maternal Fetal Medicine, Nat. Bd. Med. Examiners; RN. Intern, resident in integrated ob-gyn. U. Hawaii, 1991—95; clin. fellow Cedars Sinai Med. Ctr., UCLA, 1995—97; maternal fetal medicine specialist Fetal Diagnostic Inst. Pacific Univ., Honolulu, 2005—; asst. prof. U. Hawaii, Honolulu, 1997—; rsch. fellow Native Hawaiian Ctr. of Excellence, Honolulu, 2002—04; asst. prof. rsch. divsn. dept. Native Hawaiian Health, John A. Burns Sch. Medicine U. Hawaii, 2004—. Contbr. chapters to books, articles. Fellow: ACOG; mem.: Soc. Maternal Fetal Medicine, Am. Inst. Ultrasound in Medicine. Avocations: cooking, fishing, travel. Office: 677 Ala Moana Blvd Ste 1016B Honolulu HI 96813 Office Phone: 808-587-8558. E-mail: jksilva@hawaii.edu.

**SILVA, JOSEPH, JR.,** dean, medical educator; BA in biol. scis., Rutgers U., 1962; MD, Northwestern U., 1966. Diplomate Am. Bd. Internal Medicine, 1972. Intern Johns Hopkins Hosp., Balt., 1962—66, asst. resident in medicine, 1967—68, sr. resident in medicine, 1968—69; fellow in infectious diseases U. Mich. Med. Ctr., Ann Arbor, 1969—70; asst. prof. internal medicine divsn. infectious diseases U. Mich., prof., 1980—82; prof. and chair. of internal med. U. Calif. Davis, 1982—97; dean U. Calif Davis Sch. Medicine, 1997—2005, sr. adv. to chancellor health sciences, 2005—, dean emeritus; CEO U. Calif. Davis Health Sys.1, 1997—. Served 2 yrs. in USAF. Fellow: Royal Soc. Medicine, London, Infectious Diseases Soc. Am., ACP (regent); mem.: Sociedad Medica de Santiago, Chile (assoc. mem.), Internat. Immunocompromised Host Soc., Sacramento/Sierra Med. Soc., Western Assn. Physicians, Western Assn. Clin. Investigation, Soc. Intestinal Microecology and Disease, Soc. Hosp. Epidemiologists of Am., Sacramento/El Dorado Med. Soc. (affiliate), Reticuloendothelial Soc., Mich. Soc. Med. Rsch., Mich. Soc. Infection Control, Ctrl. Soc. Clin. Rsch., Calif. Acad. Medicine, Am. Soc. Tropical Medicine and Hygiene, Am. Soc. Internal Medicine, Am. Fedn. Clin. Rsch., Calif. Med. Assn., AMA, AAAS, Alpha Omega Alpha. Office: U Calif SCh Medicine 2315 Stockton Blvd Rm 1501 Sacramento CA 95817 Office Phone: 530-752-0321. E-mail: josilva@ucdavis.edu.*

**SILVA, LUIS M.,** marketing professional; b. San Juan, PR, July 1, 1963; s. Armando Silva and Vivian Cabrera; m. Mayra Muniz, Sept. 1, 1995; children: Rafael J., Sebastian A., Andrea P. BS in Gen. Sci. (cum laude), Bethany Coll., Santa Cruz, 1984. Area sales specialist AstraZeneca, San Juan, PR, 1997—98, managed care liaison, 1997—99, oncolgy care specialist, 1998, regional tng. coord. Atlanta, 1999—2000, dist. sales mgr. Boston, 2000—02, mktg. mgr. Wilmington, Del., 2002—. Faculty Strategic Rsch. Inst., 2003. E-mail: luis.silva@astrazeneca.com.

**SILVA, MARY BARNES,** retired elementary school educator; d. Walter Howard and Rosalinda M. Barnes. BS Edn., Kent State U., 1964; M Edn., U. Hawaii, 1976. Provisional Ohio, profl. Hawaii. Tchr. St. Louis Sch., Louisville, Ohio, 1960—62, Elyria Pub. Schs., Ohio, 1962—68, Kailua Elem., Hawaii, 1968—78, tchr. academically gifted and talented, 1978—88; tech. coord. Royal Sch., Honolulu, 1988—2001; ret., 2001. Adviser student coun., newspaper, yearbook Kailua Elem., 1979—88, chair grade level, 1975—78, Royal Sch., Honolulu, 1993—2001, chair sch. cmty.-based mgmt., 1994—99, sch. facilitator, 1995—99, tech. trainer, 1996—2001. Pres., vp., sec., treas. Assn. of Apt. Owners, Honolulu, 1979—2004. Named Tchr. of Yr., Honolulu Dist., 1997. Mem.: NEA (life), Hawaii State Ret. Tchrs. Assn., Hawaii Edn. Assn. (life), Contemporary Mus., Bishop Mus., Acad. Arts. Avocations: travel, the arts. Home: 411 Magellan Ave 808 Honolulu HI 96813 Personal E-mail: malia.aloha@hawaiiantel.net.

**SILVA, MICHAEL ANTHONY,** biologist, educator; b. El Paso, June 19, 1966; s. Antonio and Yolanda Silva; m. Rebecca Silva; children: Cassandra, Mark, Hannah. BS, U. Tex. El Paso, 1990, MS, 1993. Prof. biology El Paso C.C., 1995—. Mem.: Sci. Rsch. Soc., Sigma Xi. Office: El Paso Cmty Coll PO Box 20500 El Paso TX 79998-0500

**SILVA, TONY,** education educator, editor; b. Bethlehem, Pa., Oct. 3, 1953; s. Anthony and Regina (DeSantis) Silva; m. Margie Berns. AA in Liberal Arts, Northampton County Area C.C., 1975; BA in Spanish, Kutztown State U., 1977; MA, U. of Ill., 1981; PhD in English, Purdue U., 1990. Prof. Auburn U., Ala., 1990—91, Purdue U., West Lafayette, Ind., 1991—. Consulting: jour. editing; profl. conf. planning. Mem.: Conf. on Coll. Composition and Comm., Tchrs. of English to Spkrs. of Other Languages, Nat. Coun. Tchrs. of English. Achievements include research in Second Language Writing. Home: 2315 Sycamore Lane West Lafayette IN 47906 Office: Purdue University English Dept 500 Oval Dr West Lafayette IN 47907-2038 Office Phone: 765-494-3769. Office Fax: 765-494-3780. Personal E-mail: tony@purdue.edu.

**SILVER, ADAM,** sports association executive; BA, Duke U.; JD, U. Chgo. Legis. aide Congressman Les AuCoin, Washington; law clk. Judge Kimba Wood Fed. Dist. Ct., N.Y.C.; litig. assoc. Cravath, Swaine & Moore, N.Y.; spl. asst. to commr. NBA, 1992—96; pres. NBA Entertainment, Secacus, NJ, 1997—2000, 2000—, COO, 2000—. Prodr.: Michael Jordan to the Max, 2000. Office: NBA Entertainment 450 Harmon Meadow Blvd Secaucus NJ 07904

**SILVER, ALAN IRVING,** lawyer; b. St. Paul, Sept. 17, 1949; s. Sherman J. Silver and Muriel (Bernstein) Brawerman; m. Janice Lynn Gleekel, July 8, 1973; children: Stephen, Amy. BA cum laude, U. Minn., 1971, JD cum laude, 1975. Bar: Minn. 1975, U.S. Dist. Ct. Minn. 1975, U.S. Dist. Ct. (ea. dist.) Wis. 1975, U.S. Ct. Appeals 8th and 10th cirs.) 1975. Assoc. Doherty, Rumble & Butler, P.A., St. Paul, 1975-80, ptnr. Mpls., 1980-99, Bassford, Remele (formerly called Bassford, Lockhart, Truesdell & Briggs, P.A.), Mpls., 1999—. Mem. 2d Jud. Dist. Ethics Com., St. Paul, 1985-88, 4th Jud. Dist. Ethics Com., Mpls., 1990-97. Author: Building a New Foundation: Torts, Contracts and the Economic Class Doctrine, 2000, other numerous continuing edn. seminar material. Vol. atty. Legal Assistance Ramsey County, St. Paul, 1975-82; mem. St. Louis Park (Minn.) Sch. Bd., 1993-99, chair, 1995-97; mem. St. Louis Park Human Rights Commn., 1987-91; chmn. site mgmt. coun. Susan Lindgren Sch., St. Louis Park, 1986-93; bd. dirs. Jewish Cmty. Rels. Coun., Anti-Defamation League Minn. and Dakotas, 1987-93, 97—, treas., 1992-93, v.p., 2003-06, pres. 2006-. Mem. ABA, Minn. Bar Assn. (exec. bd. antitrust sect. 1984, litigation chair probate and trust sect.), Hennepin County Bar Assn. Avocations: running, guitar, reading. Home: 4320 W 25th St Minneapolis MN 55416-3841 Office: Bassford Remele Ste 3800 33 S 6th St Minneapolis MN 55402-1501 Office Phone: 612-376-1634. Business E-Mail: alans@bassford.com.

**SILVER, BARNARD JOSEPH STEWART,** mechanical and chemical engineer, consultant, inventor; b. Salt Lake City, Mar. 9, 1933; s. Harold Farnes and Madelyn Cannon (Stewart) S.; m. Cherry Bushman, Aug. 12, 1963; children: Madelyn Stewart Palmer, Cannon Farnes. BSME, MIT, 1957; MS in Engring. Mechanics, Stanford U., 1958; grad. Advanced Mgmt. Program, Harvard Grad. Sch. Bus., 1977. Registered profl. engr. Colo. Engr. aircraft nuclear propulsion divsn. GE Co., Evandale, Ohio, 1957; engr. Silver Engring. Works, Denver, 1959-66, mgr. sales and tech. svcs., 1966-71, pres., 1998-99, chmn. bd., 1999—; chief engr. Union Sugar divsn. Consol. Foods Co., Santa Maria, Calif., 1971-74; directeur du complex SODESUCRE Abidjan, Cote d'Ivoire, 1974-76; supt. engring. and maintenance U and I Inc., Moses Lake, Wash., 1976-79; pres. Silver Enterprise Denver, Moses Lake, 1971—, Silver Energy Systems Corp., Moses Lake, 1980-98, chmn. bd., 1998—; pres., gen. mgr. Silver Chief Corp., 1983—; pres. Silver Corp., 1984—; chmn. bd. Silver Pubs., Inc., 1986-87, 90—; exec. v.p. Cascadian Inulin L.L.C., Sedro-Wooley, Wash., 1996—97; mgr. Silver Inulin LLC, Moses Lake, 1996-98; dir. processing rsch. Inuloa, Wyo., 1999—2001; bd. mgrs. Inula, Wyo., Lovell; v.p. Barnard J. Stewart Cousins Land Co., 1987—88, 1992—2003; chmn. Mid. East Peace Inst., 1998—; founder Life Energy Foods, L.L.C., Holladay, 2000—. Dir. Isle Piquant Sugar Found., 1993-94; mem. steering com. World Botanical Inst., 1993-99; instr. engring. Big Bend C.C., 1980-81. Patentee in field, including patent for novel inulin fractions extracting soluable substances from subdivided solids, 1995. Explorer adviser Boy Scouts Am., 1965-66, 89-90, chmn. cub pack com., 1968-74, 94-96, chmn. scout troop com., 1968-74, vice chmn. Columbia Basin Dist., 1986-87; pres. Silver Found., 1961-87, v.p., 1987-97, sec., treas. 1997—; edml. counselor MIT, 1971-89; pres. Chief Moses Jr. H.S. Parent Tchr. Student Assn., 1978-79; missionary Ch. of Jesus Christ of Latter-day Saints, Can., 1953-55, Hawaii, P.R., Ctrl. and South Am., Asia 1969, West Africa, 1988, Cote d'Ivoire, 1988-89, Zaire, 1989, Holladay North Stakes, 1991, 95,-97, Cheyenne, 1998-99, Salt Lake Inner-City Project Mission, 2000-03; Sunday Sch. 2d counselor Wasatch br. Utah Correctional Facility; dist. pres. No. B.C., No. Alberta, Yukon and N.W. Ters., 1955; stake high counselor, Santa Maria, Calif., 1971-72, Moses Lake Wash., 1977-79; presiding elder Cote d'Ivoire, 1974-76, 88; 2d counselor Moses Lake Stake Presidency, 1980-88; bd. dirs. Columbia Basin Allied Arts, 1986-88; mem. Health Sci. Coun. U. Utah, 1991—; mem. Sunday sch. gen. bd. Ch. of Jesus Christ of Latter-Day Saints, 1991-93, com. for mems. with Disabilities, 1992-93, CHOICE adv. bd., 1993-95; emergency preparedness dir. Holladay North Stake, 1993-95. Served with Ordnance Corps., U.S. Army, 1958-59. Decorated Chevalier Ordre National (Republic of Cote d'Ivoire). Mem. ASME (life), Assn. Energy Engrs., AAAS, Am. Soc. Sugar Beet Technologists, Internat. Soc. Sugar Cane Technologists, Am. Soc. Sugar Cane Technologists, Environ. Engrs. & Mgrs. Inst., Sugar Industry Technicians, Nat. Fedn. Ind. Bus., Utah State Hist. Soc. (life), Mormon Hist. Assn., G.P. Chowder and Marching Soc., Western Hist. Assn., Sons of Utah Pioneers (life), Univ. Archeol. Soc. (life), Kiwanis, Cannon-Hickley Study Group, Sigma Xi (life, sec., treas., Utah chpt. 1994-99), Pi Tau Sigma, Sigma Chi, Alpha Phi Omega. Republican. Mem. Lds Ch. also: Life Energy Foods LLC 4390 South 2300 East Holladay UT 84125-3651 also: Silver Pubs LLC 4390 S 2300 E Holladay UT 84124-3501 Office Phone: 801-278-9445. E-mail: bsilver@xmission.com.

**SILVER, BRIAN QUAYLE,** broadcast journalist, musician, educator; b. Denver, Sept. 8, 1942; s. Harold Farnes and Madelyn Cannon (Stewart) S.; m. Shubha Sankaran, Dec. 4, 1988; adopted children: Laila Benazir Robinson, Zain Ganapathi Ramdas Sankaran. BA, Harvard Coll., 1964; postgrad., Sch. Oriental and African Studies U. London, 1969-70; PhD., U. Chgo., 1980. Asst. prof. Urdu U. Minn., 1971-74; assoc. prof. Urdu & Indo-Muslim studies Harvard U., 1974-83; lectr. music U. Va., Charlottesville, 1995; dir. internat. house, asst. dean study abroad Duke U., 1983-86; exec. dir. Internat. Music Assocs., Washington, 1982—; chief, Urdu svc. Voice of Am., Washington, 1986—. Dir. internat. exchange programs Pan Orient Arts Found., Manchester, N.H., 1968—, exec. dir., 1994—; bd. dirs. Archive Rsch. Ctr. Ethnomusiclogy, New Delhi, India, 1983-98; South Asia coun. Assn. Asian Studies, Ann Arbor, Mich., 1983-86. Sitar performance in India, Pakistan, Bangladesh, Morocco, Rumania, England, Guatemala, Peru, Canada and U.S., 1966—; contbr. numerous publs. on South Asian Music and Urdu Lit. Dir. Durham Chpt. UNICEF, 1984-86. Named Khansahib, All-Pakistan Music Conf., Lahore, 1988; recipient Gold medal, 1989; grantee in aid D.C. Commn. for Arts and Humanities/Nat. Endowment for Arts, 1991-92, 96-97; Fulbright grantee Inst. Internat. Edn., India, 1964-66; Ford fellow Am. Coun. Learned Socs., England, Pakistan, India, 1969-71, Am. Inst. Indian Studies, India, 1982-83. Mem. Soc. Ethnomusicology (New England chpt. v.p. 1978-80), Assn. Asian Music, Internat. Coun. Tradition Mus., Asia Soc., Assn. Asian Studies, Folklore Soc. Greater Washington. Democrat. Avocations: cooking, gardening, films, travel. Home: 1730 C St NE Washington DC 20002-6661 Office: Internat Music Assocs PO Box 15526 Washington DC 20003-0526 E-mail: PanOrient@aol.com.

**SILVER, CHARLES MORTON,** communications company executive; b. New Haven, Sept. 22, 1929; s. Sam and Rose (Fischman) S.; m. Rose Charek, Mar. 27, 1960; children— Ronni Ellen, Suzanne Paula, Steven Mitchell. BS, U Conn., 1954. With Arthur Andersen & Co., N.Y.C., 1954-61, ITT, N.Y.C., 1961-88, ret. as v.p. and assoc. treas., 1988. Served with U.S. Army, 1947-48, 50-51. Mem. Roxbury Swim and Tennis Club. Home: 51 Akbar Rd Stamford CT 06902-1401 E-mail: rosecs50@aol.com.

**SILVER, DAVID,** lawyer; b. N.Y.C., Jan. 27, 1931; s. Sol and Fannie (Stein) S.; m. Meryl Young, Sept. 14, 1952 (dec.); children: Daniel, Matthew, Joshua; m. Ann Schwartz, June 4, 1993. BA, CCNY, 1953; LL.B. cum laude, Harvard U., 1958. Bar: N.Y. 1958, D.C. 1979. Pvt. practice law, N.Y.C., 1960-61; spl. counsel SEC, Washington, 1961-65; gen. counsel Investors Planning Corp., N.Y.C., 1965-66; asst. counsel Investment Co. Inst., Washington, 1966-69, gen. counsel, 1969-77, pres., 1977-91, ICI Mut. Ins. Co., Washington, 1987-2001. Cons. securities regulation Govt. of India, 1964; mutual fund regulation Govt. of China, 1999; lectr. Law Sch. Boston U., 1995—98; mem. individual investor adv. com. N.Y. Stock Exch., 1994—99; dir. PGAM, Milan, 2001—. Served with U.S. Army, 1953-55. Mem. Fed. Bar Assn. (exec. coun. securities com., past chmn. investment co. com.). Home and Office: 9410 Brooke Dr Bethesda MD 20817-2110 Business E-Mail: anndave@verizon.net.

**SILVER, DAVID MARTIN,** chemist; b. Chgo., Sept. 25, 1941; s. Edward A. and Beatrice E. (Rochwiak) S.; m. Sylvia Doktorsky, June 9, 1963; children: Deborah, Joel. BS, Ill. Inst. Tech., 1962; MA, Johns Hopkins U., 1964; PhD, Iowa State U., 1968. Fellow Harvard U., Cambridge, Mass., 1968-69; vis. scientist U. Paris, 1970; chemist Johns Hopkins U., Laurel, Md., 1970—; dir. Paradigm Med. Industries, Inc., Salt Lake City, 1995—98, 2000—, Biosign Technologies, Inc., Toronto, Canada, 2006—. Exec. com. Nat. Resource for Computation in Chemistry, Berkeley, Calif., 1979—82; Dunning prof. ophthalmology Wilmer Eye Inst. Johns Hopkins U., 1998—99; vis. prof. ophthalmology Debrecen U. Med. Ctr., Hungary, 2001; bd. dirs. Paradigm Med. Industries, Inc.; Dunning prof. ophthalmology Wilmer Eye Inst. Johns Hopkins U., Balt., 1998—99; vis. prof. ophthalmology Med. Ctr. Debrecen U., Hungary, 2001. Editor-in-chief: Johns Hopkins APL Tech. Digest, 2002—; contbr. articles to profl. jours. Recipient Postdoctoral fellowship, NSF, 1968-69; grantee Nat. Research Coun., 1975, NSF, 1976-81, NATO, 1979-85. Mem. AAAS, Am. Chem. Soc., Am. Geophys. Union, Wash. Acad. Sci., Assn. for Rsch. in Vision and Ophthalmology, Cosmos Club (Washington). Achievements include patents in field. Home: 17 Avalon Ct Bethesda MD 20816-1124

**SILVER, DEE EDWARD,** physician, neurologist; b. Keystone, Iowa, Dec. 8, 1939; s. Grant Mason and Cora Ann (Larson) S.; m. Penelope Neena Diumenti (div. May 1988); 1 child, Helen Diumenti Silver; m. Marilyn Janet Lyddy, Mar. 8, 1998. BA, Iowa State Tchrs. Coll., Cedar Falls, 1961; MD, U. Iowa, Iowa City, 1967. Diplomate Am. Bd. Neurology. Head dept. electro-encephalography and neurophysiology Balboa Naval Hosp., San Diego, 1971—73; physician, ptnr., head dept. neurology Coastal Neurol. Med.

Group, La Jolla, Calif., 1973—. Med. dir. San Diego Parkinsons Disease Info. Ctr., 1986—; bd. dirs. Ellen Browning Scripps Soc., San Diego, 1986-94, 1996-2005; mem. exec. cabinet Scripps Inst. Medicine and Sci., San Diego, 1994-2004; head neurology dept. Balboa Naval Hosp., 1972-73 Author and editor publs. in field Lt. comdr. USN, 1971-73 Mem. AMA, Calif. Med. Assn. (del. 1981-84), Am. Acad. Neurology, Movement Disorder Soc., Rotary Internat. (Paul Harris fellow 1986), Purple Key Soc Republican. Avocations: tennis, fly fishing, hunting, golf, trumpet. Home: PO Box 224 Rancho Santa Fe CA 92067-0224 Office: 9850 Genesee Ave Ste 740 La Jolla CA 92037-1218 Office Phone: 858-453-3842.

**SILVER, HARRY R.,** lawyer; b. Phila., Aug. 8, 1946; s. Jerome Benjamin Silver and Josephine Sandler (Steinberg) Furr; m. Jessica Dunsay, Nov. 23, 1972; children: Gregory, Alexander. BA, Temple U., 1968; JD, Columbia U., 1971. Bar: N.Y. 1972, D.C. 1973, U.S. Dist. Ct. D.C., U.S. Ct. Claims, U.S. Ct. Appeals (1st, 4th, 5th, 7th, 8th, 9th, 10th, fed. and D.C. cirs.), U.S. Supreme Ct. Law clk. to Hon. Harold R. Medina, U.S. Ct. Appeals (2d cir.), N.Y.C., 1971-72; assoc. Arent, Fox, Kintner, Plotkin & Kahn, Washington, 1972-74; atty. U.S. Dept. Justice, Washington, 1974-77, U.S. Dept. Energy, Washington, 1977-78; assoc. Akin, Gump, Strauss, Hauer & Feld, Washington, 1978-81, ptnr., 1981-88, Oppenheimer, Wolff & Donelly, Washington, 1988-91, Davis Wright Tremaine, Washington, 1991-94, Ober, Kaler, Grimes & Shriver, Washington, 1994—2004, Patton Boggs, Washington, 2004—. Mem.: ABA, Fed. Bar Assn. Avocations: running, music, travel. Home: 6829 Wilson Ln Bethesda MD 20817-4948 Office: Patton Boggs 2550 M St NW Washington DC 20037 Office Phone: 202-457-6453. E-mail: hsilver@pattonboggs.com.

**SILVER, HERBERT,** physician; b. Bklyn., N.Y., Feb. 18, 1932; s. Ben and Sylvia (Weinstock) S.; m. Judith Elaine Miller, Aug. 28, 1966; children: Rand Kenneth, David Jeffrey. BA, Adelphi U., 1953; MD, SUNY, Buffalo, 1957. Diplomate Am. Bd. Pathology. Intern Maimonides Med. Ctr., 1957-58; resident Nassau Univ. Med. Ctr., 1958-60, Hosp. of U. Pa., 1960-62; assoc. pathologist, dir. blood bank/hematology Barnes-Jewish Hosp., St. Louis, 1964-70; dir. transfusion medicine Hartford (Conn.) Hosp., 1970—2001; assoc. prof. U. Conn. Med. Ctr., Farmington, 1970-90, U. Conn. Sch. of Allied Health, Storrs, 1977—2002. Cons. St. Francis Med. Ctr., Hartford, Conn., 1978-2002, Conn. Children's Med. Ctr., 1980-2002; med. dir. Hartford Med. Lab, 1985-99. Author, editor: Probability of Inclusion in Paternity Testing, 1982, Problem Solving in Immunohematology, 1987; guest editor Transfusion Jour., 1992-96; contbr. articles to profl. jours. Bd. dirs. Emanuel Synagogue, West Hartford, Conn. Capt. U.S. Army Med. Corps, 1962-64. Mem.: ABA, Fed. Bar Assn. Avocations: running, music, travel. Mem.: AMA, Coll. Am. Pathologists, Am. Soc. Clin. Pathology, Am. Assn. Blood Banks (bd. dirs. 1987—92, Disting. Svc. award 1993, John Elliott Meml. award 2000). Democrat. Jewish. Avocations: bicycling, clarinet. Home: 32 Beacon Hill Dr West Hartford CT 06117-1003 Personal E-mail: herbsilver32@yahoo.com.

**SILVER, JOAN MICKLIN,** film director, screenwriter; b. Omaha, May 24, 1935; d. Maurice David and Doris (Shoshone) Micklin; m. Raphael D. Silver, June 28, 1956; children: Dina, Marisa, Claudia. BA, Sarah Lawrence Coll., 1956. Writer, dir. (movies) Hester Street, 1975 (Writers Guild best screenplay nomination), Chilly Scenes of Winter, 1981, (TV film PBS) Bernice Bobs Her Hair starring Shelly Du Vall, 1975; dir. (documentary) Only Faster: Six Legendary Jewish Comediennes, 2005; dir. (TV films HBO) Finnegan, Begin Again with Robert Preston and Mary Tyler Moore, Parole Board, A Private Matter with Sissy Spacek and Aidan Quinn, (TV film Showtime) In The Presence of Mine Enemies, 1997, (films) Between the Lines, 1976, Crossing Delancey with Amy Irving, 1988, Loverboy, 1989, Stepkids, 1991; dir. stage plays and musicals including Album, Maybe I'm Doing It Wrong, Off-Broaday prodn. A...My Name is Alice; prod. On The Yard, (radio) Great Jewish Stories from Eastern Europe and Beyond, 1995; dir. (feature film) A Fish in the Bathtub, 1998, (TV film Lifetime) Invisible Child, 1999, (TV film Showtime) Charms for the Easy Life, 2001, TV film LifeTime) Hunger Point, 2003. Office: Silverfilm Prodns Inc 510 Park Ave New York NY 10022-1105 Office Phone: 646-282-0312.

**SILVER, JOEL,** film producer; b. South Orange, N.J., July 14, 1952; m. Karyn Fields, July 10, 1999. Attended, Lafayette Coll. Owner Silver Pictures; co-owner (with Robert Zemenckis) Dark Castle Entertainment. Film producer: The Warriors, 1979, Xanadu, 1980, 48 Hours, 1982, Jekyll & Hyde...Together Again, 1982, Streets of Fire, 1984, Brewster's Millions, 1985, Weird Science, 1985, Commando, 1985, Jumpin' Jack Flash, 1986, Lethal Weapon, 1987, Predator, 1987, Action Jackson, 1988, Die Hard, 1988, Lethal Weapon 2, 1989, Roadhouse, 1989, The Adventures of Ford Fairlane, 1990, Die Hard 2, 1990, Predator 2, 1990, Hudson Hawk, 1991, Ricochet, 1991, The Last Boy Scout, 1991, Lethal Weapon 3, 1992, Demolition Man, 1993, Richie Rich, 1994, Demon Knight, 1995, Assassins, 1995, Fair Game, 1995, Executive Decision, 1996, Bordello of Blood, 1996, Father's Day, 1997, Conspiracy Theory, 1997, Lethal Weapon 4, 1998, Made Men, 1999, The Matrix, 1999, The House on Haunted Hill, 1999, Romeo Must Die, 2000, Dungeons and Dragons, 2000, Exit Wounds, 2001, Proximity, 2001, Swordfish, 2001, Thir13en Ghosts, 2001, Ghost Ship, 2001, Cradle 2 the Grave, 2003, The Matrix Reloaded, 2003, The Matrix Revolutions, 2003, Gothika, 2003, House of Wax, 2005, Kiss Kiss Bang Bang, 2005, V for Vendetta, 2005; TV prodr.: W.E.I.R.D. World, 1995, Action, 1999, The Strip, 1999, Freedom, 2000, Jane Doe, 2001, Newton, 2003, Next Action Star, 2004, Best Your Life, 2004, Veronica Mars, 2004, The Studio, 2005. Office: Silver Pictures care Warner Bros Pictures 4000 Warner Blvd Bldg 90 Burbank CA 91522-0001*

**SILVER, JONATHAN,** private school administrator; BA in Polit. Sci., U. Rochester, 1988, MSEd in Ednl. Thought and Policy, 1994; MS in History and Policy, Carnegie Mellon U., 1995, PhD in History, 2004. Asst. to the pres. for instl. planning and academic resources Shady Side Acad., Pitts., 1998—2001; head upper sch. Emery/Weiner Sch., Houston, 2004—05, asst. head sch., 2005—. Office: Emery/Weiner School 9825 Stella Link Houston TX 77025 Office Phone: 832-204-5900.

**SILVER, LAWRENCE ALAN,** retired marketing professional; b. Sept. 5, 1943; s. Marcia (Azersky) S.; m. Deena Rae Rosenberg, Feb. 26, 1967; children: Cheryl Ann Edwards, Elyse Stephanie, Marc Aaron. BJ, Boston U., 1965, MS, 1966. Reporter New Haven Register, 1958-66; dir. pub. rels. Spear & Staff, Inc., Babson Park, Mass., 1966-70; pres. Silver Assocs. Pub. Rels. & Advt., Holliston, Mass., 1971-82, RJ Comm., Inc., St. Petersburg, Fla., 1982—2003; sr. v.p., dir. mktg. Raymond James Fin., Inc., St. Petersburg, 1982—2003, v.p. investor rels., 1983—2003, coord. quality svcs., 1989—2003; mng. dir. You Deserve Better, 2005—. Instr. journalism Framingham (Mass.) State Coll., 1974-80. Assoc. editor Venture Capital Jour., 1978—82, columnist On Wall St. Mag., 2000—. Mem. Holliston Bylaw Study Com., 1978—82, U. Tampa Ctr. Quality Steering Com., 1993—95, 1996—99, Fla. Edn. and Industry Coalition, 1988—95, St. Petersburg Jr. Coll. Cmty. Outreach Program, 1988—89, Fla. Sch. Adv. Coun., 1993—99; trustee Am Stage Theater, St. Petersburg, 1994—96; founding bd. dirs. Jewish Cmty. Ctr. Greater Framingham, 1966-72; mem. adv. coun. Clearwater Jr. League, 1993—94; mem. sch. adv. coun. Tarpon Springs H.S., 1988—93; dir. You Deserve Better; bd. dirs. Greenhave Civic Assn., 2005—; founding pres. Temple Beth Torah, Holliston 1972—73; bd. dirs. men's club Temple Ahavat Shalom, Fla., 1983—84, trustee, 1985—86, pres. brotherhood, 1985—86; regional bd. dirs. Jewish Nat. Fund, 1998—, mktg. com., 2005—. Mem. Securities Industry Assn. (Pub. Rels. Advt. Roundtable 1986-90, Mktg. Roundtable 1987-96, sales and mktg. com. 1991—2003, editor Marketshare 1994-96), Boston U. Nat. Alumni Coun. Home: 90 Greenhaven Cir Oldsmar FL 34677-4842 Office: Raymond James & Assocs 880 Carillon Pkwy Saint Petersburg FL 33716-1100 Office Phone: 727-785-8943. E-mail: youdeservebetter@earthlink.net.

**SILVER, LYNN LESLIE,** research scientist, consultant; b. NYC, Sept. 12, 1946; d. Aaron Zack Silver and Shirley Silver Black. BA, Brandeis U., Waltham, Mass., 1968; PhD, Tufts U. Sch. Medicine, Boston, 1974. Rsch. fellow Merck & Co., Rahway, NJ, 1982—87, sr. rsch. fellow, 1987—95, sr.

investigator, 1995—2003; prin. LL Silver Consulting, LLC, Springfield, NJ, 2004—. Mem. editl. bd. Antimicrobial Agents and Chemotherapy, Washington, 1997—; mem. sci. adv. bd. Cumbre Pharms., Dallas, 2005—; invited spkr., leader, chmn. and co-chmn. numerous sci. meetings. Author (and co-author): (peer reviewed sci. papers) Jour. Biol. Chemistry; Nature; Science. Mem.: Am. Soc. Microbiology. Achievements include discovery of antibacterial agents; research in mechanism of action and resistance to antibacterial agents.

**SILVER, MALCOLM DAVID,** pathologist, educator; b. Adelaide, South Australia, Apr. 29, 1933; s. Eric Bertram and Stella Louisa (Riley) S.; m. Meredith May Galloway, Jan. 19, 1957; children: Stuart Faulkner, Claire Eleanor, Caryl Louise. MD, U. Adelaide; PhD, McGill U. Diplomate: Am. Bd. Pathology. Resident med. officer Royal Adelaide Hosp., 1957-58; resident in pathology Royal Victoria Hosp.-Pathol. Inst., McGill U., Montreal, Que., Canada, 1958-63; research fellow dept. exptl. pathology John Curtin Sch. Med. Research, Australian Nat. U., Canberra, 1963-65; asst. prof. pathology U. Toronto, 1965-68, assoc. prof., 1968-74, prof., 1974—79, chmn. dept. pathology, 1985-95, prof. dept. laboratory medicine and pathobiology, 1997-98; staff pathologist Toronto Gen. Hosp., 1965-72, sr. staff pathologist, 1972-79; prof., chmn. dept. pathology U. Western Ont., London, Ont., Canada, 1979-85; chief pathology Univ. Hosp., London, 1979-85; pathologist in chief Toronto Gen. Hosp., 1985-89, The Toronto Hosp. (Toronto Gen. and Toronto Western Divs.), 1989-91, sr. staff pathologist, 1991-98. Prof. emeritus U. Toronto, 1998—. Contbr. articles to profl. jours. Fellow Royal Coll. Pathologists Australasia, Royal Coll. Physicians and Surgeons Can.; mem. Can. Assn. Pathologists, Ont. Assn. Pathologists, Internat. Acad. Pathology, Can. Cardiovasc. Soc., Soc. for Cardiovasc. Pathology. E-mail: md.silver@utoronto.ca.

**SILVER, MELVYN DAVID,** lawyer, arbitrator; b. N.Y.C., June 2, 1938; s. Albert and Gloria Silver; m. Ruth Silver Taube, Feb. 29, 1988. BS in Metall., NYU, 1959, MS in Materials Sci., 1962; JD, Georgetown U., 1970. Bar: Calif. Assoc. IBM, San Jose, Calif., 1970-73, Morgan Beauzay & Hammer, San Jose, Calif., 1973-81; ptnr. Suden & Silver, San Jose, Calif., 1981-91, Silver & Taube, San Jose, Calif., 1991—. Labor arbitrator Am. Arbitration Assn., Calif. State Mediation Svc., Fed. Mediation and Conseiliation Svc., Calif. Pub. Employee Rels. Bd., L.A. City Employee Rels. Bd., 1988—. Patentee in field. With U.S. Army, 1955-62. Mem. Santa Clara Trial Lawyers Assn. (pres. 1995), Santa Clara County Pers. Bd. (chairperson 1990-94). Office: Silver & Taube # 205 300 S 1st St Ste 205 San Jose CA 95113-2837

**SILVER, MICHAEL,** education educator; b. Landsberg, Germany, Jan. 30, 1948; came to U.S., 1949; s. Norman and Esther Silver; m. Beverley Ann Moss, May 16, 1971; children: Sabina, Joseph. AB, Washington U., 1970, MEd, 1973, PhD, 1982. Cert. supt. Mo., Wash. Tchr. Normandy Sch. Dist., St. Louis, 1970-72, Parkway Sch. Dist., St. Louis, 1972-75, asst. prin., 1976-79, administrv. asst., 1979-83, asst. to supt., 1983-84, asst. supt., 1984-86; supt. Tukwila Sch. Dist., Seattle, 1986—2003; asst. prof. ednl. administrn. Seattle U. Bd. dirs. Cities in Schs., Seattle; mem. adv. bd. Sta. KCTS, Seattle, 1990-2003; vis. exec. Seattle U. Sch. Edn., 1995. Author: Values Education, 1976, Facing Issues of Life and Death, 1976. Pres. SeaTac Task Force, Seattle, 1989; bd. dirs. Anti-Defamation League, Seattle, 1987—; mem. City of Tukwila (Wash.) Coun., 1988-90. Recipient A Plus award Wash. Coun. Econ. Edn., 1992, Excellence in Ednl. Leadership award Univ. Coun. for Ednl. Administrn., 1998, Art Tribute award, Wash. Art Edn. Assn., 2001; named Exec. Educator, 100 Exec. Educator Mag., 1985, 1996 Assoc. for Inst. for Ednl. Inquiry Leadership Program; named to Homework Ctrl.; 100 Most Influential People in U.S. Pub. Edn.; I/D/E/A fellow Charles F. Kettering Found., 1978, 88, Title VI fellow Washington U., 1971-73; named Supt. of Yr. Wash. Libr. Media Assn., 2000. Mem. ASCD, Am. Assn. Sch. Administrs., Wash. Assn. Sch. Administrs. (met. chpt., pres. 1989-90), King County Supts. (chmn. adv. com. 1989-90, 95-96), Southcenter Rotary Club (Paul Harris fellow 1994), Southwest King County C. of C., Phi Delta Kappa. Home: 14127 SE 50th St Bellevue WA 98006-3409 Office: Seattle U Sch Edn PO Box 222000 901 12th Ave Seattle WA 98122 Office Phone: 206-296-5798. Personal E-mail: silver@eskimo.com. Business E-Mail: silverm@seattleu.edu.

**SILVER, MICHAEL JOEL,** lawyer; b. Balt., Feb. 8, 1955; s. Edgar P. and Ann W.S.; m. Abbe Rebecca Levitt, May 14, 1983; children: Rachel, Lucy. AB, Harvard U., 1977; JD, U. Chgo., 1980. Bar: Md. 1980. Assoc. Piper & Marbury, Balt., 1980-87, ptnr. Balt. & N.Y.C., 1987-92; now ptnr. Hogan & Hartson LLP, Balt. Office: Hogan & Hartson LLP 111 S Calvert St Fl 16 Baltimore MD 21202-6174 Office Phone: 410-659-2741. Business E-Mail: mjsilver@hhlaw.com.

**SILVER, MORRIS,** economist, educator; b. N.Y.C., July 9, 1931; s. Julius and Lilly Silver; m. Sondra P. Hartman, Jan. 26, 1958; children: Gerald David, Ronald Alan. BA, CCNY, 1958; PhD (Earhart Found. fellow, Ford Found. fellow), Columbia U., 1964. Mem. faculty City Coll. CUNY, 1964—, assoc. prof. econs., 1968—, prof., 1972—, chmn. dept., 1969-95. Rsch. assoc. Nat. Bur. Econ. Rsch., 1967—71; cons. crime deterrence and offender career Nat. Ctr. Health Svcs. Rsch., 1970—, Hudson Inst., 1974. Author (with r. D. Auster): The State as a Firm, 1979; author: Affluence, Altruism, and Atrophy: The Decline of Welfare States, 1980, Prophets and Markets: The Political Economy of Ancient Israel, 1983, Enterprise and the Scope of the Firm, 1984, Economic Structures of the Ancient Near East, 1985, Foundations of Economic Justice, 1989, Taking Ancient Mythology Economically, 1992, Economic Structures of Antiquity, 1995. With U.S. Army, 1953—55. Mem.: Am. Econ. Assn. Jewish. Office: Dept Econs City Coll 133 D St New York NY 10031 E mail mailver12@nyc.rr.com

**SILVER, N. CLAYTON,** psychology professor, consultant; s. Keith Sol Silver and Joanne Doris Friedlander; m. Susan Lynn Safire, June 26, 1999. BA, U. Cin., 1980; MS, PhD, Tulane U., 1988. Vis. lectr. Dillard U., New Orleans, 1987; asst. prof. So. U., New Orleans, 1987—88, Appalachian State U., Boone, NC, 1989—90, U. Ctrl. Fla., Orlando, 1990—93; vis. asst. prof. U. Richmond, Va., 1988—89; asst. prof. U. Nev., Las Vegas, 1993—96, assoc. prof., 1997—. Cons. Shook, Hardy & Bacon, Kansas City, Mo., 2004—05, RSK Assessments, Inc., Orlando, 2002—05; presenter in field. Author: A Guide Book of Statistical Software for the Social and Behavioral Sciences, 1998; mem. editl. bd. Ednl. and Psychol. Devel., 1994—; contbr. articles to profl. jours. Grantee, Office Naval Rsch., 1984, N.C. Bd. Sci. and Tech., 1990—91, Met. Alcoholism Coun., 1991—92. Mem.: Rocky Mountain Psychol. Assn., So. Psychol. Assn. Avocations: bowling, stamp collecting/philately. Office: U Nev Las Vegas 4505 Maryland Pky Las Vegas NV 89154-5030 Office Phone: 702-895-0191.

**SILVER, NEIL MARVIN,** manufacturing executive; b. Bklyn., June 2, 1928; s. Jack and Rose (Eisenberg) S.; m. Leah Rebecca Coffman Silver, Sept. 4, 1949; children: Pamela Sue, Carole Beth. Student, U. Mich., 1945-46, 48-49; BS, U. Ill., 1951. Asst. mgr. Wolverine Parking Co., Lansing, Mich., 1951-54; treas. Capitol Parking Co., Indpls., 1955-60; controller, asst. to pres. Eberhart Steel Products, Inc., Mishawaka Tool & Die, Inc., Ind., 1961-63; PRES. Allied Quality Products, Inc., Mishawaka, Ind., 1964-67; treas. Allied Screw Products, Inc., Mishawaka, Ind., 1968-88, chmn., sec., 1989—. Bd. dirs. Ind. State Anti-Defamation League, 1955-57; bd. dirs., treas., pres., chmn. Fin. Commn., Family and Children's Ctr., Inc., Mishawaka, Ind., 1957-77; bd. dirs., treas. Family Svc. Assn. St. Joseph County, Ind., 1955-57. With U.S. Army, 1946-48. Mem. AIAA, Soc. Mfg. Engrs., SAE Internat., Internat. Computing Soc., ASM Internat., B'nai B'rith. Avocations: photography, travel. Office: Allied Screw Products Inc PO Box 543 815 E Lowell Ave Mishawaka IN 46545-6480

**SILVER, R. PHILIP,** packaging products executive; b. 1942; Grad., U. Mo., 1967. With Amour & Co., Atlanta, 1967—68, Boise Cascade Corp., Idaho, 1968—75; exec. v.p. Fla. Gas Co., Orlando, Fla., 1975—80; pres. Continental

---

Can, Norwalk, Conn., 1980—86; pres. treas. Silgan Holdings Inc., Stamford, Conn., 1987—93, chmn., co-CEO, 1994—2004, co-chmn., co-CEO, 2004—. Office: Silgan Holdings Inc 4 Landmark Sq Stamford CT 06901

**SILVER, RICHARD TOBIAS,** oncologist, educator; b. Jan. 18, 1929; m. Barbara Silver; 1 son, Adam Bennett. BA, Cornell U., 1950, MD, 1953. Diplomate Nat. Bd. Med. Examiners, Am. Bd. Internal Medicine, Am. Bd. Clin. Oncology. Intern N.Y. Hosp.-Cornell Med. Ctr., N.Y.C., 1953-54, asst. resident in medicine, 1956-57, resident in hematology, 1957-58; clin. assoc. gen. medicine br. Nat. Cancer Inst., NIH, Bethesda, Md., 1954-56; asst. in medicine Cornell U. Med. Coll., N.Y.C., 1956-58, instr. medicine, 1958-62, clin. asst. prof., 1962-67, clin. assoc. prof., 1967-73, clin. prof., 1973—2002; pres. N.Y. State Soc. Med. Oncologists and Hematologists, 1991—; asst. attending physician N.Y. Hosp., 1964-67, assoc. attending physician, 1967-73, attending physician, 1973—; dir. clin. oncology and chemotherapy rsch. N.Y. Hosp. Divsn. Hematology & Med. Oncology, 2000; prof. medicine, med. dir. Leukemia and Myeloproliferative Ctr., Weill Med. Coll. of Cornell U., 2002—. Asst. vis. physician 2d Cornell Med. div. Bellevue Hosp., N.Y.C., 1963-66; vis. Fulbright prof. U. Bahia Sch. Medicine, Brazil, 1958-59; vis. prof. Hershey Hosp.-Pa. State Hosp., 1976, Mayo Clinic, 1977, Upstate Med. Ctr., Binghamton, N.Y., 1977, Med. Coll. Va., 1979, Med. Sch. Colubia U., 1982, N.J. Coll. Medicine, New Brunswick, 1983, Meml. Med. Ctr. U. Ga., 1984, 86; invited lectr. and presenter in field; chair 1st and 2d Internat. Congresses Myelproliferative and Myelodysplastic, 2001, 2003; vis. faculty curriculum devel. Annenberg Ctr. Rancho Mirage, Calif., 1994—; mem. rev. bd. NIH, Nat. Cancer Inst.; cons. Cancer Chemotherapy Investigative Rev. Bd., 1980, clin. trials com., 1979-81; mem. Cornell U. Coun., 1987—; spl. site visitor medicine A Roswell Park Meml. Inst., NIH-Nat. Cancer Inst., 1976, mem. combined modality com. divsn. cancer treatment, 1977-79, clin. trials com., 1979-81, cons. cancer chemotherapy rev. bd., 1980; vis. Fulbright lectr. Sch. Medicine U. Bahia, Brazil, 1958-59; lectr., presenter in field. Author: Morphology of the Blood and Marrow in Clinical Practice, 1970; co-author: (with R.D. Lauper, C.I. Jarowski) A Synopsis of Cancer Chemotherapy, 1977, 2ndedit., 1986, monographs; editor: Clinical Topics in Cancer: Diagnosis and Treatment, 1982; cons. editor Am. Jour. Medicine, 1974-84; mem. editl. adv. bd., 1984; editor, contbr.: Topics in Cancer, 1982; mem. editl. adv. bd. Cancer Investigation, 1983-94; ad-hoc rev. New Eng. Jour. Medicine, Annals of Internal Medicine, Mayo Clinic Procs., Blood, Cancer, Am. Jour. Hematology, Med. Rsch. Coun., Eng., others; contbr. chpts. to books and articles to profl. jours. Trustee Frances and Edwin Cummings Meml. Fund, 1985-92; med. dir. Rsch. for Blood Health, Inc., 1968-85, Arnold K. Krakower Hematology Found., 1966-75, Cancer Rsch. and Treatment Fund, 1985—. Recipient Pasmantier award, Timothy Gee award for outstanding tchr., clinician, inventor and humanist, 2001; N.Y. State scholar for profl. study of medicine. Fellow ACP; mem. N.Y. State Soc. Med. Hematologists and Oncologists (pres. 1991-2000), Cornell U. Med. Coll. Alumni Assn. (pres. 1973-76, sr. advisor 1976—), Am. Soc. Clin. Oncology (mem. com. clin. practice 1976, com. on pub. affairs 1981-83, chmn. program com. 1977), Internat. Soc. Hematology (chmn. bone marrow biopsy wokshop XV congress 1974, internat. adv. com. XX Congress 1984, lectr.), Am. Soc. Hematology (chmn., guidelines com.), Leukemia Soc. Am. (med. dir., v.p. N.Y.C. chpt. 1968-78), Chronic Myeloid Leukemia, Sass Found Hematologic Rsch. (bd. advs.), N.Y. Soc. Study of Blood, N.Y. County Med. Soc., N.Y. State Med. Soc. Oncologists and Hematologists (pres. 1991-93, mem. exec. com. 1991—), Harvey Soc., Am. Fedn. Clin. Rsch., Am. Assn. Cancer Rsch., Explorers Club (bd. dirs., chmn. sci. adv. com. 1987), Sigma Xi. Office: NY Presby Hosp Weill Cornell Med Ctr 525 E 68th St Box 581 New York NY 10021 Office Phone: 212-746-2098. Business E-Mail: rtsilve@med.cornell.edu.

**SILVER, RICK,** marketing professional; Grad. cum laude, U. S.C., 1974. Pvt. practice as vice chmn., 1976—. Office: 1411 Gervais St Columbia SC 29201 Office Phone: 803-254-8158. E-mail: rick.silver@cnsg.com.

**SILVER, ROSLYN OLSON,** federal judge; b. Phoenix, Feb. 28, 1946; BA, U. Calif. Santa Barbara, 1968; JD cum laude, Ariz. State U., 1971. Bar: Ariz. 1971, U.S. Ct. Appeals (9th cir.) 1980, U.S. Supreme Ct. 1984. Law clk. Hon. Lorna E. Lockwood Ariz. Supreme Ct., Phoenix, 1971-72; advisor, litigator Navajo Nation Native Am. Rights Fund, Phoenix, 1974-76; legal labor counsel Dial Corp., Phoenix, 1976-78; ptnr. Logan and Aguirre, Phoenix, 1978-79; legal counsel EEOC, Phoenix, 1979-80; asst. U.S. Atty. Dist. Ariz., Phoenix, 1980-84; asst. atty. gen. Ariz. Atty. Gen.'s Office, Phoenix, 1984-86; acting 1st asst., chief criminal divsn. Office, U.S. Atty. Office, Phoenix, 1986-94; judge Dist. Ariz. U.S. Dist. Ct., Phoenix, 1994—. Chair local rules com. Ariz. Dist. Ct.; mem. regional sect. panel Harry S Truman Scholarship Found. Contbg. editor: Rutter Group Practice Guide; contbr. articles to profl. jours. Mem. bd. visitors U. Ariz. Law Sch.; mem. adv. panel Lodestar Mediation Clinic, Ariz. State U. Law Sch. Named one of 100 Significant Women and Minorities in Ariz.'s Legal History, 2000. Mem. ABA, Fed. Bar Assn., Nat. Assn. Women Judges, Ariz. Bar Assn. (Pub. Lawyer of Yr. 1990), Ariz. Women Lawyers Assn. (outstanding legal practitioner award 1999), Ariz. State U. Alumni Assn. (outstanding alumnus award 1996). Office: US Dist Ct 401 W Washington SPC 59 Phoenix AZ 85003 Office Phone: 602-322-7520.

**SILVER, SALLY,** minister; b. Farmington, Maine, July 8, 1943; d. Edwin Raymond and Ethel Elizabeth Pearson; children: Gregory, Peter. Spiritual min., Fairfield Spiritual Ch., 1990—92. Tchr. Tangwala Healing Ctr., Oquossoc, Maine, 1973—80; founder, tchr. Western Maine Woman's Meditation Soc., Kingfield, Maine, 1979—85, Crystalmaineia, Eustis, Maine, 1992-98; reader, min. tchr. Light of the Moon, Portland, Maine, 1993—98; min., bd. mem. Ctr. of Eternal Light, Cape Coral, Fla., 1994—97; min., clairvoyant tchr. Planet Earth Book Ctr., Ft. Myers Fla. 1997—2005. Rd. mem. Ctr. of Eternal Light, Cape Coral, Fla., 1994—97. Min. Universal Brotherhood Movement, 1994—, Fla. Assn. of Spiritual Ministers, 1994. Avocations: reading, painting. Home: 99 W Kingfield Rd Kingfield ME 04947-4252 Office Phone: 239-272-9165.

**SILVER, SHELDON,** state legislator, lawyer; b. NYC, Feb. 13, 1944; s. Nathan and Frieda (Bearman) S.; m. Rosa Mandelkern, June 25, 1967; children: Edward, Janine, Michelle, Esther. BA, Yeshiva U., 1965; JD, Bklyn. Coll., l968. Bar: N.Y. 1969, U.S. Dist. Ct. (so. and ea. dists.) N.Y. 1970. Assoc. Schechter & Schwartz, N.Y.C., 1968-71; law sec. to Judge Francis Pecora N.Y.C., 1971-76; ptnr. Agri, Bilder & Silver, N.Y.C., 1976-81; pvt. practice N.Y.C., 1981—. Mem. N.Y. State Assembly, 1977—, chmn. ways and means com., 1992, speaker, 1994. Vice pres. Bialystoker Synagogue, Young Israel Synagogue. Named Man of Yr., Harry S. Truman Dem. Club, 1977, United Jewish Appeals, l983, also others. Democrat. Office: 250 Broadway Ste 2301 New York NY 10007

**SILVER, WARREN M.,** state supreme court justice; m. Evelyn Silver. Grad., Tufts U., 1970; JD, Am. U. Wash. Coll. of Law, 1973. Atty., priv. practice, Bangor, 1977—; justice Maine Supreme Ct., 2005—. Bd. dirs. Bangor Museum and Ctr. for History. Mem.: Maine Trial Lawyers Assn. (bd. of governors, pres. supreme judicial court's civil rules com.). Office: Maine Supreme Ct Penobscot Cty Courthouse 97 Hammond St Bangor ME 04401*

**SILVERBERG, CAROL EVE,** theater educator; b. Queens, N.Y., June 27, 1967; BA, Pace U., N.Y.C., 1989; MA, Binghamton U., N.Y., 1995; postgrad., Binghamton U. Box office mgr. Jean Cocteau Repertory, N.Y.C., 1987—89, Corning Summer Theatre, Corning, N.Y., 1989—92; asst. box office mgr. Glimmerglass Opera, Cooperstown, NY, 1996—2002; instr. Binghamton U., 1995—2001; instr. Hartwick Coll., Oneonta, NY, 2002—; adj. lectr. English Broome C.C., Binghamton, 2001—. Textbook reviewer McGraw Hill, N.Y.C., 2005—. Adminstrv. vol. Binghamton Philharmonic, 1997; treas. Grad. Student Orgn., Binghamton, 1993—95; bd. dirs. Corning Children's Theatre, 1992. Grantee Profl. Devel. grantee, Hartwick Coll., 2003—04, Broome C.C., 2004, Travel/Rsch. grantee, Binghamton U., 2004. Mem.: NEA, Broome C.C. Faculty Assn. Office: Broome Community College PO Box 1017 Binghamton NY 13902

---

**SILVERBERG, LEWIS HENRY,** lawyer, consultant; b. LA, Nov. 1, 1934; s. Milton Henry and Marjorie Vella (Coates) S.; children: Stephen, Richard, Donna; m. Alice Ellen Deakins, Mar. 9, 1979. BA, Pomona Coll., 1955; JD, UCLA, 1958. Bar: Calif. 1959, U.S. Supreme Ct. 1966. Pvt. practice, San Diego, 1959-89; bus. cons., 1993—. Active various pub., charitable and ednl. orgns. Office: 1515 Merritt Dr El Cajon CA 92020-7847 Office Phone: 619-588-8083. Personal E-mail: lew@the-silverbergs.net.

**SILVERBERG, MICHAEL JOEL,** lawyer; b. Rochester, N.Y., Aug. 12, 1932; s. Goodman and Minnie (Krovetz) S.; m. Charlotte Goldman, June 19, 1955; children: Mark (dec. 1999), Daniel. BA, U. Rochester, 1954; JD, Columbia U., 1957. Bar: N.Y. 1958, U.S. Dist. Ct. (so. dist.) N.Y. 1958, U.S. Dist. Ct. (ea. dist.) N.Y. 1990, U.S. Ct. Appeals (2d cir.) 1975, U.S. Supreme Ct. 1967. Instr. Columbia U. Law Sch., N.Y.C., 1957—58; assoc. Phillips Nizer LLP (formerly Phillips, Nizer, Benjamin, Krim & Ballon), NYC, 1960—67, ptnr., 1967—2006, counsel, 2006—. Vol. civil rights lawyer Miss. Lawyers Com. for Civil Rights Under Law, 1965; pres. Nat. Alliance Mentally Ill N.Y.C., Inc., 1997—2003; cons. sci. program com. Am. Psychiat. Assn., 2000—01. Bd. editors Columbia Law Rev., 1955—57. Bd. dirs. Nat. Alliance on Mentally Ill of NY State, 1998-2004, 2005-, pres. 1999-2004, 2005-; mem. adv. bd. dept. psychiatry Columbia U.; mem. adv. bd. NYC Vis. Nurse Svc.; mem. nat. adv. coun. Columbia Teen Screen Program; mem. bd. editors Columbia Law Rev., 1955-57. Fulbright scholar U. Strasbourg, France, 1958-59; named one of NY Super Lawyers Gen. Litig., 2006. Mem. ABA, N.Y. State Bar Assn. (com. on internat. litigation), Assn. Bar City N.Y., Am. Trial Lawyers Assn. Home: 205 W End Ave New York NY 10023-4804 Office Phone: 212-841-0533. Personal E-mail: msilverberg@phillipsnizer.com.

**SILVERBERG, ROBERT,** writer; b. NYC, 1935; s. Michael and Helen (Baim) S.; m. Barbara Brown, 1956; m. Karen Haber, 1987. BA, Columbia U., 1956. Author: (novels) Thorns, 1967, The Masks of Time, 1968, Hawksbill Station, 1968, Nightwings, 1969, To Live Again, 1969, Tower of Glass, 1970, The World Inside, 1971, Son of Man, 1971, A Time of Changes, 1971, Dying Inside, 1972, The Book of Skulls, 1972, Born with the Dead, 1974, Shadrach in the Furnace, 1976, Lord Valentine's Castle, 1980, Majipoor Chronicles, 1982, Lord of Darkness, 1983, Valentine Pontifex, 1983, Gilgamesh the King, 1984, Tom O'Bedlam, 1985, Star of Gypsies, 1986, At Winter's End, 1988, To the Land of the Living, 1989, The New Springtime, 1990, (with Isaac Asimov) Nightfall, 1990, The Face of the Waters, 1991, (with Isaac Asimov) The Ugly Little Boy, 1992, Kingdoms of the Wall, 1993, (with Isaac Asimov) The Positronic Man, 1993, Hot Sky at Midnight, 1994, Mountains of Majipoor, 1995, Starborne, 1996, Sorcerers of Majipoor, 1997, The Alien Years, 1998, Lord Prestimion, 1999, The King of Dreams, 2001, The Longest Way Home, 2002, Roma Eterna, 2003, Phases of the Moon, 2004, In the Beginning: Tales from the Pulp Era, 2006; (non-fiction) The Face of the Lost Cities and Vanished Civilizations, 1962, The Great Wall of China, 1965, The Old Ones: Indians of the American Southwest, 1965, Scientists and Scoundrels: A Book of Hoaxes, 1965, The Auk, the Dodo and the Oryx, 1966, The Morning of Mankind: Prehistoric Man in Europe, 1967, Mound Builders of Ancient America: The Archaeology of a Myth, 1968, If I Forget Thee, O Jerusalem: American Jews and the State of Israel, 1970, The Pueblo Revolt, 1970, The Realm of Prester John, 1971. Recipient Hugo award World Sci. Fiction Conv., 1956, 69, 87, 90; Nebula award Sci. Fiction Writers Am., 1970, 72, 75, 86, Grand Master Nebula award, 2004. Mem. Sci. Fiction Writers Am. (pres. 1967-68) Address: PO Box 13160 Oakland CA 94661-0160 E-mail: ragberg@attglobal.net.

**SILVERBERG, STEVEN GEORGE,** pathologist, educator; b. NYC, Nov. 30, 1938; s. Bertram P. and Esther (Weintraub) S.; m. Kiyoe Ono, Nov. 16, 1968. AB, Bklyn. Coll., 1958; MD, Johns Hopkins U., 1962. Diplomate Am. Bd. Pathology. Intern in medicine Bellevue/Meml. Hosp., NYC, 1962-63; resident in anatomic pathology Yale-New Haven Hosp., 1963-65; asst., assoc. prof. pathology Meml. Hosp. Cancer Allied Diseases, NYC, 1965-66; asst., assoc. prof. pathology Med. Coll. Va., Richmond, Va., 1968-72; assoc. prof. pathology U. Colo., Denver, 1972-81; prof., dir. anatomic pathology George Washington U., Washington, 1981-96, U. Md., Balt., 1996—2004, clin. prof., 2004—. Exec. dir. Colo. Regional Cancer Ctr., Denver, 1976-80. Co-author: Pathology in Gynecology and Obstetrics, 1969, 4th edit., 1993; editor: Principles and Practice of Surgical Pathology, 1983, 4th edit., 2005; editor-in-chief Internat. Jour. Gyn. Pathology, 1984-92, Pathology Case Revs., 1995—; contbr. 220 articles to profl. jours. Capt. USAF, Japan, 1966-68. Jonas Salk scholar CUNY, 1958. Fellow Am. Soc. Clin. Pathologists (life, coun. 1977—), Disting. Svc. award 1991, H.P. Smith Disting. Pathology Educator award 1997); mem. Internat. Soc. Gyn. Pathologists (pres. 1998-2001), Assn. Dirs. Anatomic and Surg. Pathology (pres. 1998-2000), Internat. Soc. Breast Pathol. (pres. 2003-2005), Alpha Omega Alpha. Avocations: reading history, travel, collecting japanese oriental illustrated books, wine. Office: Dept Pathology U Md Med Sys 22 S Greene St Baltimore MD 21201-1544 Office Phone: 410-328-5072.

**SILVERMAN, ALAN HENRY,** lawyer; b. NYC, Feb. 18, 1954; s. Melvin H. and Florence (Green) S.; m. Gretchen E. Freeman, May 25, 1986; children: Willa C.F., Gordon H.F. BA summa cum laude, Hamilton Coll., 1976; MBA, JD, U. Pa., 1980. Bar: N.Y. 1981, U.S. Dist. Ct. (so. and ea. dists.) N.Y. 1981, U.S. Ct. Internat. Trade 1981, D.C. 1986, U.S. Supreme Ct. 1990. Assoc. Hughes, Hubbard & Reed, N.Y.C., 1980-84; asst. counsel Newsweek, Inc., N.Y.C., 1984-86; v.p., gen. counsel, sec., dir. adminstrn. Cable One, Inc., Phoenix, 1986—. Contbr. articles to profl. jours. Mem. prevention adv. com. Gov. Pa. Justice Commn., 1975-79; bd. dirs. Lawyers' Alliance for N.Y., 1982-85, N.Y. Lawyers Pub. Interest, 1983-85, Nat. Assn. JD-MBA Profls., 1983-85, Bus. Vols. for Arts, Inc., Phoenix, 1989-93, Ariz. Vol. Lawyers for the Arts, Inc., 1994-97, First Amendment Coalition Ariz., Inc., 1991—, Phoenix Falcons Fencing Club, Inc., 2003-05; mem. Maricopa County Citizens Jud. Adv. Coun., 1990-93; mem. citizens' bond com. City of Phoenix, 2000. Mem. ABA, Bd. of Bar of City of N.Y., D.C. Bar Assn., Phi Beta Kappa. Home: 5833 N 30th St Phoenix AZ 85016-2401 Office: Cable One Inc 1314 N 3d St Phoenix AZ 85004 Office Phone: 602-364-6190. E-mail: alan.silverman@cableone.net.

**SILVERMAN, ARNOLD BARRY,** lawyer; b. Sept. 1, 1937; s. Frank and Lillian Lena (Linder) S.; m. Susan L. Levin, Aug. 7, 1960; children: Michael Eric, Lee Oren. B of Engring. Sci., Johns Hopkins U., 1959; JD cum laude, U. Pitts., 1962. Bar: U.S. Dist. Ct. (we. dist.) Pa. 1963, Pa. 1964, U.S. Patent and Trademark Office 1965, U.S. Supreme Ct. 1967, Can. Patent Office 1968, U.S. Ct. Claims 1975, U.S. Ct. Appeals (3d cir.) 1982, U.S. Ct. Appeals (fed. cir.) 1985, U.S. Ct. Appeals (4th cir.) 2000. Patent atty. Alcoa, New Kensington, Pa., 1962-67, 68-72, sr. patent atty., 1972-76; ptnr. Price and Silverman, Pitts., 1967-68; v.p., gen. patent counsel Joy Mfg. Co., Pitts., 1976-80; ptnr. Murray Silverman & Keck, Pitts., 1980-81, Buell, Blenko, Ziesenheim & Beck, Pitts., 1984; ptnr. intellectual property dept. Eckert, Seamans, Cherin & Mellott, Pitts., 1984—, chmn., 1992—2005, chmn. info. tech. practice group, 1992-97; spl. asst. atty. gen. State of W.Va., 1985—; spl. counsel patents U. Pitts., 1975—. Spkr. on patents, trademarks, copyright, trade secrets, computer law; nat. panel of arbiters Am. Arbitration Assn., 1987—. Contbr. more than 85 articles to profl. jours. Mem. Churchill CSC (Pa.), 1967-90, chmn., 1975-90; mem. Pitts. law com. Anti-Defamation League, 1981—, regional adv. bd., 1982—, ch-chmn. Pitts. region ann. dinner, 1983, mem. chmn. by-laws com., 1983; bd. govs. Slippery Rock U. Found., 1985-91; Pitts. steering com. MIT Enterprise Forum, 1986-87. With U.S. Army, 1963-64. Recipient Am. Spirit Honor medal, Ft. Knox, 1963; named Pa. Super Lawyer 2004, 05, 06. Fellow: Mensa (lawyers in Mensa 1978—, nat. assoc. counsel patents and trademarks copyrights 1980—82, inventors' spl. interest group 1980—86); mem.: ASME, ABA, Assn. Corp. Patent Counsel (emeritus mem.), Intertel (treas. Pitts. Forum 1983—), Stratford Cmty. Assn. (v.p. 1966—67, gov. 1966—70, pres. 1967—68), Golden Panthers, U. Pitts. Law Alumni Assn. (bd. dirs. 1992—2004, treas. 1997—99, v.p. 1998—99, pres.-elect 1999—2000, pres. 2001—02), Johns Hopkins Soc. Engring. Alumni, Johns Hopkins U. Alumni Assn. (chmn. publicity com. 1963—66, exec. com. 1966—87, v.p. 1969—70, pres. 1971—72, nat. alumni coun. 1989—92, 2003—), Brit. Inst. Chartered Patent

Agts. (fgn. mem.), Licensing Execs. Soc. (co-chmn. Pitts. chpt. 1994—96), Am. Chem. Soc. (chemistry and the law sect.), Nat. Assn. Coll. and Univ. Attys., Pa. Bar Assn. (co-chmn. sports/entertainment arts law com. 2001—03), D.C. Bar Assn., U.S. Trademark Assn. (chmn. task force on advt. agys. 1981, membership com. 1987—89), Am. Intellectual Property Law Assn. (membership com. 1985—88, pub. rels. com. 1994—), Pitts. Patent Law Assn. (chmn. pub. rels. com. 1968—69, chmn. patent laws com. 1970—72, chmn. legis. action com. 1972—75, chmn. nominating com. 1973, bd. mgrs., newsletter editor 1974—88, sec.-treas. 1976—84, v.p. 1984—85, pres. 1985—86, pub. rels. com. 1994—95, program com. 1995—96), Allegheny County Bar Assn. (chmn. pub. rels. com. 1978—80, vice-chmn. intellectual property sect. 1981—83, chmn. 1984—85), Robert Bruce Assn. Law Fellows (life), U. Pitts. Gen. Alumni Assn. (life; bd. dir. 2001—06, exec. com. 2002—06, sec. 2003—06, strategic planning com. 2003—06, leadership coun. 2006—), Duquesne Club, Order of Coif, Psi Chi, Tau Epsilon Rho. Republican. Jewish. Home: 2019 High Pointe Ct Murrysville PA 15668-8515 Office: 600 Grant St 44th Fl Pittsburgh PA 15219-2703 Office Phone: 412-566-2077. Business E-Mail: asilverman@eckertseamans.com. *Welcome challenge and perform all tasks with enthusiasm, in a moral manner and to the very best of your ability.*

**SILVERMAN, ARTHUR CHARLES,** lawyer; b. Lewiston, Maine, June 13, 1938; s. Louis A. and Frances Edith (Brownstone) S.; BS in Elec. Engring., BS in Indsl. Mgmt., MIT, 1961; JD, Columbia U., 1964; m. Donna Linda Zolov, June 18, 1961; children: Leonard Stephen, Daniel Edward. Bar: N.Y. 1965, U.S. Supreme Ct. 1971. Engr., engring. asst. Gen. Electric Co., Pittsfield, Mass. and Phila., 1958-62; assoc. Baer & Marks, N.Y.C., 1965-68; assoc. Golenbock and Barell, N.Y.C., 1968-72, ptnr., 1972-89; ptnr. Reid & Priest LLP, N.Y.C., 1989-98, dep. chair, 1996-98; ptnr. Thelen Reid & Priest LLP, N.Y.C., 1999—. Treas., trustee Ramaz Sch., 1977-84, vice chmn., 1984-85, 86-88, chmn., 1988-92, hon. chmn., 1992—; bd. govs. MIT Hillel Found., 1979-84; mem. Bd. Jewish Edn. of City of N.Y., 1981-84; mem. exec. com. Nat. Jewish Ctr. for Learning and Leadership, 1984-90. Mem. IEEE, ABA, NSPE, N.Y. State Bar Assn., Fed. Bar Council, Assn. Bar City N.Y., N.Y. Soc. Architects, Internat. Bar Assn., Inter-Pacific Bar Assn., Constrn. Mgmt. Inst., Constrn. Specifications Inst. Home: 200 E 74th St New York NY 10021-3618 Office: Thelen Reid & Priest LLP 875 Third Ave New York NY 10022 Office Phone: 212-603-2553.

**SILVERMAN, BARRY G.,** federal judge; b. NYC, Oct. 11, 1951; 1 child, Bagel Ann. BA summa cum laude, Ariz. State U., 1973, JD, 1976. Bar: Ariz. 1976, U.S. Dist. Ct. Ariz. 1976, U.S. Ct. Appeals (9th cir.) 1976, U.S. Supreme Ct. 1980. Asst. city prosecutor, Phoenix, 1976—77; dep. atty. Maricopa County, 1977—79; ct. commr., 1979—84; judge Superior Ct. Ariz. Maricopa County, 1984—95; apptd. magistrate judge U.S. Dist. Ct. Ariz., 1995—98; judge U.S. Ct. Appeals 9th cir., 1998—. Instr. constnl. law Coll. Law, Ariz. State U., 1983, adj. faculty. advanced criminal procedure, 89; lectr. cmty. property BAR/BRI Ariz., Idaho and Nev. Bar Rev. Courses, 1989—94. Recipient Excel award, Soc. Nat. Assn. Publs., 1992. Mem.: ABA, Maricopa County Bar Assn. (Henry Stevens award 1991), State Bar Ariz. Avocations: magic, beagles, baseball, wine tasting. Office: US Ct of Appeals 401 W Washington St SPC 78 Phoenix AZ 85003*

**SILVERMAN, BRUCE GARY,** advertising executive, consultant; b. NYC, Feb. 16, 1945; s. Edward E. and Lillian (Brill) S.; children: Jennifer, Matthew; m. Nancy Cole, 1996; children: Christen Cole, Larry Cole. BA, Adelphi U., 1965; JD, Albany Law Sch., 1967. Sr. v.p., exec. creative dir. Ogilvy & Mather Inc., NYC, 1967-80; exec. v.p., exec. creative dir. Bozell & Jacobs Inc., Dallas, 1981-83, Batten, Barton, Durstine & Osborn Inc., LA, 1984-85; exec. v.p., creative dir. Asher/Gould Advt. Inc., LA, 1986-89, pres., chief creative officer, 1989-95, pres., COO, 1996-97; pres. Western Internat. Advocacy Group, LA, 1997-98; exec. v.p., mng. dir. Initiative Media, LA, 1998—; pres., CEO Initiative Ptnrs., USA, 1999—2002; pres. WONG-DOODY Advt., L.A., 2003—05; pres., CEO Pocket Billboards, Inc., Studio City, Calif., 2005—. V.p., bd. dirs. L.A. Children's Mus., 1984-88; chmn. Resource Devel. com. Starbright Pavillion Found., 1993. Mem. Acad. TV Arts and Scis., Am. Assn. Advt. Agys. (bd. dirs., vice chmn. western region 2002). Home: 3168 Dona Mema Pl Studio City CA 91604-4264 Office: Pocket Billboards Inc 12750 Ventura Blvd Ste 202 Studio City CA 91604 Personal E-mail: bgsla@adelphia.net.

**SILVERMAN, BURTON PHILIP,** artist; b. Bklyn., June 11, 1928; s. Morris Daniel and Anne (Firstenberg) S.; m. Claire Guss, June 12, 1969; children: Robert Arthur, Karen Lila. BA, Columbia Coll., 1949. Freelance illustrator Life, Fortune, Esquire, Time, Newsweek, Sports Illus., New York, The New Yorkers mags., 1959—; instr. Sch. Visual Arts, N.Y.C., 1964-67. Co-author: Abel, 1968, A Portfolio of Drawings, 1968; author: Painting People, 1977, Breaking the Rules of Watercolor, 1983, Sight and Insight: The Art of Burton Silverman, 1999; contbr. articles and drawings to profl. jours.; one-man exhbns. include Davis Gallery, N.Y.C., 1956, 58, 62, Kenmore Galleries, Phila., 1963, 67, 70, FAR Gallery, N.Y.C., 1965, 70, 75, 77, Genesis Gallery, N.Y.C., 1979, Sindin Galleries, N.Y.C., 1983, Capricorn Galleries, Bethesda, Md., 1979, 91, Gallery 52, South Orange, N.J., 1967, 70, 77, Harbor Gallery, L.I., 1971, 74, U. Utah, 1967, Doll and Richards, Boston, 1980, Grand Ctrl. Galleries, N.Y.C., 1988, Cudahy's Gallery, N.Y.C., 1990, Joseph Keiffer, Inc., N.Y.C., 1993, Gerold Wunderlich & Co., N.Y.C., 1996, 97, Merrill Gallery, Denver, 1996, 98, Butler Inst. of Am. Art, 1999, Brigham Young Mus., Provo, 1999, Gallery Henoch, N.Y.C., 2001, 04; group exhbns. include Butler Inst. Am. Art, Youngstown, Ohio, 1954-71, 74, 76, 79, 88, 90, 93, 2002, Nat. Acad. Design, N.Y.C., 1958-96, 98, 2001, 03, Am. Watercolor Soc., N.Y.C., 1978-82, 84-87, 89-91, 95-96, 97, 99, 2002, Pa. Acad. Fine Art, 1949, New Britain (Conn.) Mus. Am. Art, 1964, Wadsworth Atheneum, Hartford, Conn., 1961, Am. Acad. Arts and Letters, 1967, 74, 76, 79, N.Y. Hist. Soc., 1976, Pa. State Mus. Art, Portsmouth (Va.) Mus. Art, 1976, 79-80, 82 (Purchase prize, 1979, 82), Mexico City Mus. Art, 1990, Nat. Portrait Gallery, Washington, 1993, Hofstra Mus., N.Y.C., 1993, South Bend (Ind.) Mus. Art, 1994, Old Forge (N.Y.) Mus. and Gallery, 1994, Ogunquit Mus., 1997, Del. Art Mus., Wilmington, 2004. With AUS, 1951-53. Named to Hall of Fame, Soc. of Illustrators, N.Y., 1990, Pastel Soc. Am., 1992; named Artist of Am., 1991, 94, 2000; recipient Gold medal Nat. Portrait Soc., 2004. Mem. NAD (numerous awards and prizes including Joseph Isidor Gold medal 1992, Ranger Purchase prize 1962, 84, Benjamin Altman figure prize 1969, academician, 1972-), Am. Watercolor Soc. (numerous awards and prizes including Gold medal 1979, Silver medal 1984, 95, annuals), Pastel Soc. Am. (hon.). E-mail: bpsart@aol.com. *In art I am wary of things too facile, or appealing. My painting is rooted in a realist tradition that is equally concerned with objective facts and subjective realities. It is a visual language that allows me to explore the tensions and ambiguities engendered by this dual aspect of human experience. Art is my life and my life is in my art.*

**SILVERMAN, DAN,** chef; BFA, French Culinary Inst., 1988. With Bouley, NYC, Le Bernardin, NYC, Chez Panisse, NYC, Zuni Café, Calif.; exec. chef Alison on Dominick, Union Sq. Cafe, NYC, 2001—03; owner, exec. chef Lever House Restaurant, NYC, 2003—. Office: Lever House Restaurant 390 Park Ave New York NY 10022*

**SILVERMAN, ERIC F.,** lawyer; b. Phila., Sept. 21, 1954; s. Robert L. and Marilyn L. S.; m. Joann B. Silverman, Oct. 7, 1979; children: Amy, Laura, Charlie. BA, Middlebury Coll., 1976; JD, Georgetown U., 1982. Bar: N.Y. 1982. Energy/environ. planner Henningson, Durham, Richardson, Washington, 1976-79; mgmt. cons. Booz Allen & Hamilton, Washington, 1980; ptnr. & chmn. global project fin. group Milbank Tweed Hadley & McCloy, N.Y.C., 1982—. Author: Resource Recovery - A Plan for Small Communities and Institutions, 1976; editor: Project Finance newsletter. Mem. Fed. Energy Bar Assn., ABA (energy/environ. natural resources div.), N.Y. State Bar Assn., Bar Assn. City N.Y. Office: Milbank Tweed Hadley McCloy 1 Chase Manhattan Plz Fl 54 New York NY 10005-1401 Office Fax: 212-530-5219. Business E-Mail: esilverman@milbank.com.

**SILVERMAN, GARY R.,** lawyer; b. 1961; BA, Brandeis U., 1983; JD, Northwestern U., 1986; MBA, U. Chgo., 1990. Bar: Ill. 1986, Colo. 1987, DC 1988, NY 1994. Ptnr. Corp. & Fin. Dept. Kaye Scholer LLP, Chgo., NYC. Mem.: ABA. Office: Kaye Scholer LLP Ste 4100 3 First Nat Plaza Chicago IL 60602 also: 425 Park Avenue New York NY 10022 Office Phone: 312-583-2330. E-mail: gsilverman@kayescholer.com.

**SILVERMAN, GILBERT B.,** retired real estate developer, art collector; b. May 1925; 3 children. B, U. Calif., Berkeley. Chmn, CEO Silverman Companies, Bingham Farms, Mich.; owner Amurcon. Named one of Top 200 Collectors, ARTnews Mag., 2004, 2005, 2006. Mem.: Bldg. Industry Assn. (pres. 1996). Avocation: collector of Fluxus-related materials & conceptual art. Office: Silverman Companies Ste 220 32100 Telegraph Rd Bingham Farms MI 48025*

**SILVERMAN, HENRY RICHARD,** travel services company executive; b. NYC, Aug. 2, 1940; s. Herbert Robert and Roslyn (Moskowitz) S.; m. Susan H. Herson, June 13, 1965 (div. Jan. 1977); children: Robin Lynn, Deborah Leigh; m. Nancy Ann Kraner, Jan. 22, 1978; 1 child, Catherine Anne Grad. cum laude, Hackley Sch., Tarrytown, N.Y., 1957; BA with honors, Williams Coll., 1961; LL.B., U. Pa., 1964; postgrad. in corp. fin. and taxation, NYU, 1965. Bar: N.Y. 1965, U.S. Tax Ct. 1965, U.S. Ct. Appeals (2d cir.) 1965. Practice law, 1965-66; with White, Weld & Co., beginning 1966; then gen. ptnr. Oppenheimer & Co., until 1970; pres., chief exec. officer ITI Corp., 1970-72; founder, pres. Trans-York Securities Corp., 1972; exec. v.p., chmn. exec. com. Ladenburg, Thalmann & Co., 1973; pres., CEO Vavasseur Am. Ltd., subs. U.K. mcht. bank, 1974-75; gen. ptnr. Brisbane Ptnrs., 1976-77; prin. various investment groups, 1977—, Silverman Energy Co., N.Y.C., 1977—, NBC Channel 20, Springfield, Ill., 1977-83, ABC Channel 9, Syracuse, NY, 1977-81; prin., dir. Delta Queen Steamboat Co., New Orleans, 1977-86; also prin. outdoor advt., music pub., motion picture prodn., radio broadcasting & hardware mfg. cos.; pres., CEO Reliance Capital Corp., subs. Reliance Group Holdings, Inc., N.Y.C., 1982—; sr. v.p. bus. devel. Reliance Group Holdings, Inc., N.Y.C., 1982-90; chmn., CEO Days Inns Am., Inc., Atlanta, 1984-89; also dir.; pres., CEO Telemundo Group, Inc., N.Y.C., 1986-90; gen. ptnr. Blackstone Group, N.Y.C., 1990-91; chmn., CEO, pres. HFS Inc., N.Y.C., 1990—; chmn., pres., CEO Cendant Corp., N.Y.C., 1996—2004, chmn., CEO, 2004—. Bd. dirs. NY Univ. Hosp., N.Y.C. 1987—. Served to lt. USNR, 1965-73 Recipient Am. Heritage Award, Anti-Defamation League, 1998. Mem.: Harmonie (N.Y.C.). Republican. Jewish. Avocation: tennis. Office: Cendant Corp 9 W 57th St Fl 37 New York NY 10019-2701*

**SILVERMAN, IRA NORTON,** news producer; b. Bklyn., May 17, 1935; s. Joseph and Mildred (Axelrod) S.; m. Elizabeth Parsons Aspray, June 16, 1979; children by previous marriage: Gary, Bruce; stepchildren: Elizabeth, Aime, Alison. AB, Columbia U., 1957. Newspaper, mag. and book editor, 1957—67; prodr., writer NBC News, 1967—79; sr. prodr. spl. projects NBC Nightly News, Washington, 1977—95; contbr. The New Yorker, N.Y.C., 1995—, editl. cons., 1995—96; cons. NBC News, 1998, PBS, 1999, 2002. Co-author: The Pleasant Avenue Connection, 1976. Recipient Nat. Headliner award, 1977, 78, 81, 87, Alfred I. DuPont-Columbia U. award, 1983-84, 85-86, Emmy award for news and documentary, 1985, 87, award Overseas Press Club Am., 1987, 90, George Polk award L.I. U., 1988, Excellence in TV award Channels mag., 1990, George Foster Peabody award U. Ga., 1991, Citation for Excellence Overseas Press Club, 1992.

**SILVERMAN, JANE ARESTY,** not-for-profit organizational consultant; b. NYC, Apr. 5, 1945; d. Julian Joseph and Esther Bradford Aresty; m. Ira David Silverman, June 16, 1968 (dec. June 23, 1991); children: Jacob Louis, Rachel Emma, Sarah Julia. BA magna cum laude, Radcliffe Coll., 1967; MCP, U. Pa., 1970. Dir. of tng. The Harlan Co., N.Y.C., 1982—85; pres. Tng. Mgmt. Corp., Princeton, NJ, 1985—98; exec. dir. Assn. of Jr. Leagues Internat., N.Y.C., 1998—2002; pres. Jane Silverman and Assocs., LLC, Princeton, 2003—. Adv. com. Ctr. for Civil Soc., UCLA Sch. of Pub. Policy and Social Rsch., L.A., 1998—; nonresident fellow UCLA Sch. of Pub. Policy and Social Rsch., L.A., Calif., 1998—; mem. John W. Gardner leadership award jury Ind. Sector, Washington, 1999—2001. Editor: Housing: Supply and Affordability, Management and Control of Growth, vol. IV, 1978, vol. V, 1980. Trustee Opera Festival of NJ, Princeton, 1989—94, Princeton (NJ) Libr. Found., 2003—, Planned Parenthood Assn. of the Mercer Area, Trenton, NJ, 2003—; trustee, exec. com. Radcliffe Coll., Cambridge, Mass., 1994—99, Young Audiences of NJ, Princeton, 1986—94; internat. adv. com. New Israel Fund, 2003—; trustee Jewish Found. for Christian Rescuers (Thanks to Scandinavia), N.Y.C., 1989—93; officer Am. Jewish Com., NYC, 1996—. Recipient Nat. Disting. Leadership award, Am. Jewish Com., 2003, Phillip Forman Human Rels. award, Cen. N.J. chpt. Am. Jewish Com., 1999, Alumni award, Princeton Day Sch., 1994. Mem.: ASTD, N.J. Ctr. for Nonprofits, N.J. Soc. of Assn. Execs. (assoc.). Jewish. Avocations: travel, music, reading. Home: 118 Winant Rd Princeton NJ 08540 Office: Jane Silverman and Assocs LLC 118 Winant Rd Princeton NJ 08540 E-mail: silvermanjane@msn.com.

**SILVERMAN, JONATHAN,** actor; b. L.A., Aug. 5, 1966; s. Hillel Emanuel and Devora (Halaban) S. Student, U. So. Calif. Appearances include (films) Girls Just Want to Have Fun, 1985, Brighton Beach Memoirs, 1986, Caddyshack II, 1988, Stealing Home, 1988, Weekend at Bernie's, 1989, Class Action, 1991, Little Sister, 1992, Age Isn't Everything, 1992, Weekend at Bernie's II, 1993, Little Big League, 1994, Teresa's Tattoo, 1994, Two Guys Talking About Two Girls, 1994, 12 Bucks, 1998, Freak City, 1999, Just a Little Harmless Sex, 1999, Men Named Milo, Women Named Greta, 2000, The Medicine Show, 2000, The Cookout, 2004; (TV movies) Traveling Man, 1989, For Richer, For Poorer, 1992, Broadway Bound, 1992, 12:01, 1993, Hands That See, 1994, London Suite, 1996, The Inspectors, 1998, Inspectors 2: A Shred of Evidence, 2000, Bobbie's Girl, 2002, Deacons for Defense, 2003, Crazy Love, 2003, DeMarco Affairs, 2004; (TV series) Gimme a Break!, 1985-87, The Single Guy, 1995-97, (voice) Free for All, 2003; (plays) Brighton Beach Memoirs, Biloxi Blues, Broadway Bound (Helen Hays award 1988), The Illusion (Drama Lounge award 1990), Pay or Play (Drama League award), Sticks and Stones, 1994, Denial, 1998, The Odd Couple II, 1998, Freak City, 1999, Dirk and Betty, 1999, Denial, 1999. Co-founder Artists for a Free South Africa, L.A., 1989—. Mem. Young Artists United (hon. N.Y. and L.A. chpt. 1990, 91). Address: United Talent Agy Ste 500 9560 Wilshire Blvd Beverly Hills CA 90212 also: William Morris Agy 151 El Camino Dr Beverly Hills CA 90212

**SILVERMAN, JOSEPH,** chemistry professor; b. NYC, Nov. 5, 1922; s. Jakob and Mary (Chechick) S.; m. Joan Aline Jacks, Jan. 14, 1951; children: Joshua Henry, David Avrom. BA, Bklyn. Coll., 1944; A.M., Columbia U., 1948, PhD, 1951. Head research dept. Walter Kidde (nuclear labs.), Garden City, N.Y., 1952-54; v.p., tech. dir. RAI Research Corp., L.I. City, N.Y., 1954-59; assoc. prof. chemistry State U. N.Y., Stony Brook, 1959-60; prof. dept. materials and nuclear engring. U. Md., College Park, 1960-92, prof. emeritus, 1992—. Cons. Danish AEC, Indsl. Research Inst., Japan, Boris Kidric Inst., Yugoslavia, Bechtel Co., GPU Nuclear Corp., GE, IAEA, Vienna; disting. vis. prof. Tokyo U., 1974; gen. chmn. 2d Internat. Meeting on Radiation Processing, Miami, Fla., 1978, 3d Tokyo, 1980, chmn. 6th, Ottawa, 1987; trustee Washington Inst. Values in Pub. Policy, 1981-87. Editor Internat. Jour. Applied Radiation and Isotopes, 1973-78, Trans. 1st Internat. Meetings on Radiation Processing, 1977, 3d edit., 1981; mem. editorial adv. bd. Radiation Physics and Chemistry, 1978-95. Served with AUS, 1944-46. Recipient Founders award 6th Internat. Meeting on Radiation Processing, 1987, Centennial medal U. Md. Coll. Engring., 1994; grad. rsch. fellow Brookhaven Nat. Lab., 1949-51; Guggenheim fellow, 1966-67. Fellow Nordic Soc. Radiation Chemistry and Tech., Am. Phys. Soc., Am. Nuclear Soc. (Radiation Industry award 1975); mem. Am. Chem. Soc., Sigma Xi. Home: 8101 Connecticut Ave Apt S407 Chevy Chase MD 20815-2839 Office: U Md Dept Materials Sci and Engring College Park MD 20742-2115 E-mail: jagman@umd.edu.

**SILVERMAN, JOSEPH HILLEL,** mathematics professor; b. N.Y.C., Mar. 27, 1955; s. Harry and Shirley (Seiner) S.; m. Susan Leslie Greenhaus, June 13, 1976; children: Deborah, Daniel, Jonathan. ScB, Brown U., 1977; MA, Harvard U., 1979, PhD, 1982. Moore instr. MIT, Cambridge, 1982-86; assoc. prof. Boston U., 1986-88; assoc. prof. math. Brown U., Providence, 1988-91, prof., 1991—, 2001—04. Programme devel. and v.p. rsch., NTRU Cryptosystems, Inc., 1997—. Author: Arithmetic of Elliptic Curves, 1986; editor: Arithmetic Geometry, 1987, Rational Points on Elliptic Curves, 1992, Advanced Topics in Arithmetic of Elliptic Curves, 1995, Diophantine Geometry (with M. Hindry), 2000. Fellow NSF, 1983-86, Sloan fellow Sloan Found., 1987, Guggenheim Found. fellow, 1998. Mem. Am. Math. Soc. Avocation: bridge. Office: Brown U Dept Math PO Box 1917 Providence RI 02912-1917

**SILVERMAN, KENNETH EUGENE,** language educator, writer; b. NYC, Feb. 5, 1936; s. Gustave and Anna (Goldberg) S.; children: Willa Zahava, Ethan Leigh. BA, Columbia U., 1956, MA, 1958, PhD, 1964. Instr. English U. Wyo., Laramie, 1958-59; preceptor in English Columbia U., NYC, 1962-64; prof. English, co-dir. The Biography Seminar NYU, NYC, 1964-2001. Adv. coun. Inst. Early Am. History and Culture, 1984-87. Author: Timothy Dwight, 1969, A Cultural History of the American Revolution, 1976, The Life and Times of Cotton Mather, 1984, Edgar A. Poe: Mournful and Never-ending Remembrance, 1991, Houdini!!! The Career of Ehrich Weiss, 1996, Lightning Man: The Accursed Life of Samuel F.B. Morse, 2003; editor: anthology Colonial American Poetry, 1968; compiler: Selected Letters of Cotton Mather, 1976; mem. editl. bd. Early Am Lit., 1969-72, 77-80, William and Mary Quar., 1984-87. Am. Lit. 1987-90. Recipient Bancroft prize in Am. history, 1985, Pulitzer Prize for biography, 1985, Edgar Allan Poe award Mystery Writers Am., 1992; grantee Bicentennial award NEH, 1972-74, Am. Philos. Soc., 1986, Am. Coun. Learned Socs., 1986; Guggenheim fellow, 1989-90. Mem. Am. Acad. Arts and Scis., Soc. Am. Historians, Am. Antiquarian Soc., Authors Guild, Soc. Am. Magicians. Jewish. Personal E-mail: ks2@nyu.edu.

**SILVERMAN, LEON,** lawyer; b. N.Y.C., June 9, 1921; BA, Bklyn. Coll., 1942; LL.B., Yale U., 1948; postgrad., London Sch. Econs., 1948-49. Bar: N.Y. 1949. Assoc. firm Riegelman, Strasser, Schwartz & Spiegelberg, N.Y., 1949-53; asst. U.S. atty. So. Dist. N.Y., 1953-55; asst. dep. atty. gen. Dept. Justice, Washington, 1958-59, spl. prosecutor, 1981-82, ind. counsel investigating Sec. Labor, 1987; co-chmn. firm Fried, Frank, Harris, Shriver & Jacobson, N.Y.C., 1960—80, counsel to, 1980—. Counsel N.Y. Gov.'s Com. to Rev. N.Y. Laws and Procedure in the Area of Human Rights, 1967-68, Com. to Rev. Legis. and Jud. Salaries, 1972-73; mem. adv. com. on criminal rules to com. to monitor N.Y. drug laws; pres. N.Y. Legal Aid Soc., 1970-72, dir., 1966—; pres U.S. Supreme Ct. Hist. Soc., 1980-92, chmn. 1992-; spl. master Appellate divsn. 1st dept. N.Y. Supreme Ct., 1984—. Trustee William Nelson Cromwell Found., 1983—; chmn. Legal Council for Soviet Jewery, 1987—. Recipient Judge Learned Hand Human Relations award, 1981, Emory Buckner Pub. Service medal, 1982, Judge Joseph M. Proskauer award, 1982. Mem. ABA, N.Y. State Bar Assn., Fed. Bar Assn., Am. Coll. Trial Lawyers (regent 1979—, pres. 1982-83), Am. Law Inst., Am. Judicature Soc., Practising Law Inst. (trustee), Assn. Bar City N.Y., Fed. Bar Council. Home: 16 Oak Dr Great Neck NY 11021-1810 Office: Fried Frank Harris Shriver & Jacobson 1 New York Plz 25th Fl New York NY 10004-1980

**SILVERMAN, LESLIE E.,** commissioner; b. Needham, Mass. Grad., U. Vt.; JD, Am. U.; M with distinction, Georgetown U. Bar: D.C., Mass. Law clk. U.S. Atty.'s Office; assoc. Keller & Heckman, 1990—97; labor counsel Senate Health, Edn., Labor and Pensions Com., 1997—2002; commr. US Equal Employment Opportunity Commn., Washington, 2002—. Office: US Equal Employment Opportunity Commn 1801 L St NW Washington DC 20507*

**SILVERMAN, MARTIN MORRIS BERNARD,** secondary school educator; b. Boston, May 27, 1936; s. Joseph Lazarus and Sonya Lillian (Feldman) S.; m. Joseph Harvey. BS in Chemistry, U. Mass., 1960, MEd, 1962; EdM, Columbia U., 1974, EdD, 1985. Math. and sci. tchr. Northampton (Mass.) Pub. Schs., 1960-62, U.S. Dept. of Def., Korea and Bermuda, 1963-66; tchr. math, sci. N.Y.C. Bd. Edn., 1966-91. Rsch. scholar biophysics NYU, 1986—; biochemistry rsch. asst. Harvard U. Med. Sch., Boston, 1960; supr., dir. sci. fairs and competitions; cons. in field. Writer, musician, composer and performer; photographer Explorers Jour., U. Mo. Archives Collection, Jour. Violin Soc. Am. Curator musical instrument collection, instrument restorer Abrons Arts Ctr., Henry Street Settlement, 2000—03; mem. Violin Craftsmanship Inst., U. NH., 1995, 1996, String Inst. Restoration Workshop, Oberlin Coll., 1995, 1996. Internat. Ctr. Photography scholar, N.Y.C., 1975. Mem. Violin Soc. Am., Jour. Violin Soc. Am., Nat. Assn. Watch Clock Collectors Assn., Musical Box Soc. Internat., Mensa, Explorers Club. Home: 25 Montgomery St New York NY 10002-6557

**SILVERMAN, MATTHEW ADAM,** school system administrator; Doctorate, Nat. Louis U., Evanston, Ill., 2006. Dir. of curriculum Beach Pk. Sch. Dist. 3, Ill., 1999—. Office Phone: 847-599-5029.

**SILVERMAN, MERVYN F.,** health science association administrator, consultant; BS cum laude, Washington and Lee U., 1960; MD, Tulane U., 1964; MPH, Harvard U., 1969. Cert. Am. Bd. Preventive Medicine. Physician Peace Corps, Thailand, 1965-67, regional med. dir. East Asia and the Pacific Washington, 1967-68; spl. asst. to commr. FDA, Washington, 1969-70, dir. Office of Consumer Affairs, 1970-72; dir. health Wichita (Kans.)-Sedgwick County Dept. Cmty. Health, 1972-77; med. dir. Planned Parenthood Kans., Wichita, 1976-77; dir. health Dept. Health, San Francisco, 1977-85; health care cons. Mervyn F. Silverman & Assocs., Inc., 1985—; dir. AIDS health svcs. program Robert Wood Johnson Found., 1986-92; nat. spokesperson Am. Found. for AIDS Rsch., 1986-96, pres., also bd. dirs. Resident physician Sta. KPIX-TV, San Francisco, 1979-83; dir., prodr., host weekly health program Sta. KMPX Radio, 1980-82; sr. tech. advisor Acad. Ednl. Devel.-AIDSCOM, 1990-92; former med. advisor to bd. dirs. Golden Gate chpt. ARC, San Francisco; past vice chmn. Adv. Health Coun., State of Calif.; former assoc. clin. prof. Wichita State U.; former assoc. clin. prof. U. Hawaii; former adj. assoc. prof. Sch. Pub. Health and Tropical Medicine Tulane U.; former adj. prof. Inst. Health Policy Studies, Sch. Medicine, U. Calif., San Francisco; former mem. nat. adv. coun. Harvard AIDS Inst.; spkr., presenter in field. Author: (with others) Humanistic Perspectives in Medical Ethics, 1972, What to Do About AIDS, 1986, AIDS and Patient Management: Legal, Ethical and Social Issues, 1986, AIDS: Facts and Issues, 1986, AIDS in Children, Adolescents and Heterosexual Adults: An Interdisciplinary Approach to Prevention, 1988, others; contbg. and consulting editor Modern Medicine Publs., Mpls., 1970-75; contbg. editor Healthline, 1983-85; contbr. articles to profl. jours. Bd. dirs., vice-chmn. U.S-China Ednl. Inst. Recipient Award for Courageous Leadership, San Francisco Found., Award of Excellence, KAIROS Support for Care Givers, Civic Achievement award Bay Area Non-Partisan Alliance, Heroes in Medicine award Internat. Assn. Physicians in AIDS Care, Pub. Health Hero award U. Calif., Berkeley, 2001; Wear Found. fellow Wichita State U.. scholar Kans. Newman Coll. Mem. APHA, AMA, Omicron Delta Kappa, Delta Omega. Address: 9 Crolona Heights Dr Crockett CA 94525

**SILVERMAN, MOSES,** lawyer; b. Bklyn., Mar. 3, 1948; s. Bernard and Anne Silverman; m. Betty B. Robbins, Jan. 19, 1980; children: Benjamin, Rachel. AB, Colby Coll., 1969; JD, NYU, 1973. Bar: N.Y. 1974, U.S. Dist. Ct. (so. and ea. dists.) N.Y. 1974, U.S. Ct. Appeals (2d cir.) 1974, U.S. Ct. Appeals (D.C. cir.) 1977, U.S. Supreme Ct. 1977, D.C. 1982, U.S. Ct. Appeals (fed. cir.) 1985, U.S. Ct. Appeals (11th cir.) 2001, U.S. Dist. Ct. (D.C.) 2001, U.S. Ct. Appeals (9th cir.) 2002. Assoc. Paul, Weiss, Rifkind, Wharton & Garrison, NYC, 1973-81, ptnr., 1981—. Vol. U.S. Peace Corps., Istanbul, Turkey, 1969-70; bd. dirs. Legal Aid Soc., 1998-05; overseer Colby Coll., 2002-. Mem. ABA, N.Y. State Bar Assn., Assn. Bar City N.Y. Home:

7 Gracie Sq New York NY 10028-8001 Office: Paul Weiss Rifkind Wharton & Garrison 1285 Ave of Americas New York NY 10019-6064 Office Phone: 212-373-3355. Business E-Mail: msilverman@paulweiss.com.

**SILVERMAN, NORMAN ALAN,** cardiac surgeon; b. Boston, Dec. 19, 1946; BA, Dartmouth Coll., 1968; MD, Boston U., 1971. Prof. surgery U. Ill., Chgo., 1980-89; divsn. head Henry Ford Hosp., Detroit, 1989—; prof. surgery Case-Western Res. U., Cleve., 1992—. Contbr. 200 scientific articles to profl. jours. Lt. comdr. USPHS, 1973-75. Fellow Am. Coll. Surgeons, Am. coll. Cardiology, Am. Coll. Chest Physicians. Avocation: sailing. Office: Henry Ford Hosp 2799 W Grand Blvd Detroit MI 48202-2689 Office Phone: 313-916-2695. Business E-Mail: nsilver1@hfhs.org.

**SILVERMAN, NORMAN HENRY,** cardiologist, educator; b. Johannesburg, Sept. 29, 1942; came to U.S., 1972; s. Simon Cecil and Jean (Krawitz) S.; m. Heather Silverman. DSc in Medicine, U. Witwatersrand, Johannesburg, 1985, postgrad. Diplomate Am. Bd. Pediatrics. Asst. prof. pediatrics Stanford U. Med. Ctr., Palo Alto, Calif., 1974—75, prof. pediat. cardiology, 2002—; asst. prof. pediatrics U. Calif., San Francisco, 1975—79, assoc. prof. radiology, 1979—85, prof. pediat. in residence, 1985—2002, prof. radiology in residence, 1985—2002. Co-author: Two Dimensional Echocardiography, 1982, Congenital Heart Disease, 1990; author: Pediatric Echocardiography, 1993; co-editor: Fetal Cardiology, 2003. Lt. South African Def. Force, 1968-69. Grantee March Dimes, 1977-79, Am. Heart Assn., 1978-80, 90-92; Roma and Marvin Auerback scholar pediat. cardiology Lucile Packard Children's Hosp. and Stanford U. Med. Ctr. Fellow Am. Coll. Cardiology, Coll. Physicians South Africa, Soc. Pediatric Rsch., Am. Pediatric Soc., Am. Heart Assn., Am. Soc. Echocardiography. Achievements include research in echocardiography of congenital heart disease in infants and children; fetal echocardiography and treatment. Office: Stanford U Med Ctr 750 Welch Rd #305 Palo Alto CA 94304 Office Phone: 650-723-7913. E-mail: norm.silverman@stanford.edu.

**SILVERMAN, OZZIE,** consulting strategist; b. Montreal, Que., Can., Jan. 30, 1939; s. Louis and Fanny (Black) S.; m. Sheela Marsha Zangwill, Aug. 22, 1962; children: Caroline, Marjorie. BSME, McGill U., 1963, diploma in mgmt., 1968, MBA, 1969. Cert. Que. Order of Engrs. Supr. quality control engring. Pratt and Whitney, Montreal, 1964-68; sr. mktg. rschr. United Aircraft, Montreal, 1969-70; asst. chief internat. Dept. Industry, Trade and Commerce, Ottawa, Ont., Canada, 1972-77; dir. industry projects Ministry of State for Sci. and Tech., Ottawa, 1977-86; dir. strategic techs. policy Industry, Sci. and Tech. Can., Ottawa, 1986-91; dir. gen. sci. strategy and innovation policy Industry Can., Ottawa, 1992-98; cons. ptnr. SECOR Cons., Inc., Ottawa, 1998—. Chmn. com. for sci. and tech. policy Orgn. for Econ. Coop. and Devel., Paris, 1995-98. Avocation: inuit and japanese graphic art. Home and Office: 112 Pigeon Terr Ottawa ON Canada K1V 9H7 Office Phone: 613-737-5596. E-mail: osilverman@secor.ca.

**SILVERMAN, RANDY H.,** conservator, consultant; b. Hollywood, Fla., June 16, 1953; s. Alvin Silverman and Phyllis Jo Crown; m. Eileen Hallet Stone, Nov. 30, 1999; 1 child, Daniel Ian Gittens Stone. MLS, Brigham Young U., 1986. Bookbinder Colonial Bookbindery, Ft. Lauderdale, Fla., 1978—80, Dobbs Bros. Restoration & Conservation Co., St. Augustine, 1980—82; asst. rare book conservator Brigham Young U. Lee Libr., Provo, Utah, 1983—85, collections conservator, 1985—87; preservation libr. U. Utah Marriott Libr., Salt Lake City, 1993—. Adj. instr. Sch. Libr. and Info. Scis., Brigham Young U., Provo, 1988—92; adj. instr. Sch. Libr. and Info. Mgmt., Emporia State U., Kans., 1998—; adj. instr. Sch. Info. Resources and Libr. Sci., Ariz. State U., Tucson, 2003—; lectr. Rhodes scholars program Utah Humanities Coun., Salt Lake City, 1999—; mem. program adv. com. preservation and conservation studies program U. Tex., Austin, 1999—; cons. LDS Ch. Geneal. Libr., Salt Lake City, 1986, Cath. Diocese Hist. Rsch. Ctr., Houma-Thibodaux, La., 1988, Grinnell Coll. Burling Libr., Idaho, 1990, U. B.C. Libr., Vancouver, 1990, U.S. Nat. Parks Svc. Timpanogos Cave Nat. Monument, Alpine, Utah, 1991, Buffalo Bill Hist. Soc., Cody, Wyo., 1993, Davis County Libr., Farmington, Utah, 1994, Minn. Hist. Soc. St. Paul, 1996, Archives Ont., Toronto, 1997, Colo. State U. Libr., Ft. Collins, 1997, Stanford U. Libr., Calif., 1998, Western Mining and R.R. Mus., Helper, Utah, 1999, Pk. City Mus., 1999, Gov.'s Office State of Utah, Salt Lake City, 2000, Carleton Coll. Libr., Northfield, Minn., 2000, U. N.Mex Zimmerman Libr., Albuquerque, 2001, Idaho State Hist. Soc. Libr. and Archives, Boise, 2001, Paul W. Bryant Mus. U. Ala., Tuscaloosa, 2002, So. Oreg. U. Libr., Ashland, 2002, Multnomah County Libr., Portland, Oreg., 2003, Nat. Libr. Trinidad and Tobago, Port of Spain, 2004—, U. Hawaii at Manoa Hamilton Libr., Honolulu, 2004—, U. Mont. Libr., Missoula, 2004—04, Nat. Coll. Naturopathic Medicine Libr., Portland, Oreg., 2004, Pratt Inst. Libr., Bklyn., 2004—, Ea. Oreg. U. Libr., La Grande, 2004, U. Tenn. Paul Meek Libr., Martin, Tenn., 2004, U. W.I. Libr., Kingston, Jamaica, 2004. Co-author: New book repair methods in research libraries; photographer (cover illustrations) Typographia Lascialfari, Sunflower, Courtyard of the Palazzo Vecchio, Florence, Italy; contbr. articles book revs., abstracts and monographs to profl. jours. Mem. U. of Utah Comprehensive Emergency Mgmt. Team, 2001; co-chair Friends of the Jewish, Muslim, and Inter-Faith Communities, Salt Lake City, 1989—2004; mem. adv. bd. Nicholson Baker's Am. Newspaper Repository, South Berwick, Maine, 1999—2003; pres. Utah Libr. Assn., Salt Lake City, 2000—01. Named dept. chr., Librs. U. Utah, 2004; grantee, Rsch. Librs. Group, 1989, Coun. Libr. Resources, 1987, NEH, 1994—98, Preservation Roadshow, Utah Humanities Coun., 1999, Utah Humanities Coun. and Utah Office Mus. Svcs., 2001, U. Utah Rsch. Com., 2001, Nat. Pk. Svc. Nat. Ctr. for Preservation Tech. and Tng., 2004—; Travel fellow, Kress Found., 1996. Mem.: Am. Inst. Conservation of Hist. and Artistic Works (assoc.; co-chair, collections conservation discussion group 1995—2000, Kress Conservation Publ. fellow 1994). Jewish. Achievements include advocated passage of Utah's Centennial Document Paper Law in 1996, principal consultant for Colorado State U. Libr. on the recovery of 425,000 books damaged by flooding in largest water-related library disaster in U.S. history, 1997. Avocation: travel. Office: Univ Utah Marriott Libr 295 S 1500 E Salt Lake City UT 84112-0860 Office Phone: 801-585-6782. Office Fax: 801-585-3464. E-mail: randy.silverman@utah.edu.

**SILVERMAN, RICHARD BRUCE,** chemist, educator, biochemist; b. Phila., May 12, 1946; s. Philip and S. Ruth (Simon) S.; m. Barbara Jean Kesner, Jan. 9, 1983; children: Matthew, Margaret, Philip. BS, Pa. State U., 1968; MA, Harvard U., 1972, PhD, 1974. From asst. prof. to prof. Northwestern U., Evanston, Ill., 1976—86, prof. Phila., mem. Inst. Neurosci., 1990—. Mem. adv. panel NIH, Bethesda, Md., 1981, 83, 85, 87-91, 2001; expert analyst CHEMTRACTS; scientific adv. bd. Influx, Inc., 1998-2003, Protez Pharml., 2004—, Synchem, 2003—. NIGMS adv. coun., 2002, 2005; cons. in field. Mem. editl. bd.: Jour. Enzyme Inhibition, 1988—2002, Archives Biochem. & Biophys., 1993—, Jour. Medicinal Chemistry, 1995—2000, Enzyme Inhibition and Medicinal Chemistry, 2002—, Letters in Drug Design & Discovery, 2003—, Bioorganic & Medicinal Chemistry, 2003—, Bioorganic & Medicinal Chemistry Letters, 2003—, Current Enzyme Inhibition, 2004—. Mem. adv. bd. Ill. Math. & Scis. Acad., 2003. With U.S. Army, 1969-71. Recipient Career Devel. award USPHS, 1982-87, E. LeRoy Hall award for tchg. excellence, 1999, Northwestern Alumni Tchg. award, 2000; postdoctoral fellow Brandeis U., Waltham, Mass., 1974-76, DuPont Young Faculty fellow, 1976, Alfred P. Sloan Found. fellow, 1981-85; grantee various govt. and pvt. insts., 1976—. Arthur C. Cope. Sr. scholar ACS, 2003. Fellow: AAAS; mem. Am. Chem. Soc. (nat. elected nominating com. divns. biol. chemistry 1993—96, long-range planning com. divsn. med. chem. 1999—2002), Am. Soc. Biochem. Molecular Biology, Am. Inst. Chemists. Avocation: travel. Office: Northwestern U Dept Chemistry 2145 Sheridan Rd Evanston IL 60208-3113 Office Phone: 847-491-5653. Business E-Mail: Agman@chem.northwestern.edu.

**SILVERMAN, ROBERT MARK,** education educator, researcher; m. Kelly L. Patterson, July 1, 1999. BSc, Ariz. State U., 1989, MPA, 1991; PhD, U. Wis., Milw., 1997. Asst. prof. Jackson State U., Miss., 1998—2000; assoc. prof. Wayne State U., Detroit, 2000—02, U. Buffalo, 2003—. Sr. rsch. assoc.

U. Buffalo, 2003—. Author: (book) Doing Business in Minority Markets: Black and Korean Entrepreneurs in Chicago's Ethnic Beauty Aids Industry, 2000; editor: Community-Based Organizations: The Intersection of Social Capital and Local Context in Contemporary Urban Society, 2004. Office: U at Buffalo 201k Hayes Hall; 3435 Main St Buffalo NY 14214 Office Phone: 716-829-2133. Business E-Mail: rms35@buffalo.edu.

**SILVERMAN, ROSS O.,** lawyer; b. Toledo, Ohio, Aug. 3, 1960; BA, Ohio State U., 1982; JD cum laude, U. Toledo, 1985. Bar: Ga. 1986, DC 1989, Ill. 1995, NY 2003, US Dist. Ct., So. and Ea. Dist. NY, No Dist. Ill., US Ct. Appeals, 7th Cir. Trial atty. Criminal Sect. Tax Div., US Dept. Justice, 1988—90; asst. US atty. No. Dist. Ill., 1990—94; ptnr. Katten Muchin Zavis Rosenman, Chgo. Mem.: DC Bar, State Bar Ga., Ill. State Bar Assn., Chgo. Bar Assn. Office: Katten Muchin Zavis Rosenman 525 W Monroe St Chicago IL 60661 Office Phone: 312-902-5240. Office Fax: 312-577-8989. E-mail: ross.silverman@kmzr.com.

**SILVERMAN, SAM MENDEL,** physicist, lawyer; b. NYC, Nov. 16, 1925; s. Moshe Aaron and Gitel (Korenbaum) S.; m. Jacqueline Greenberg, Sept. 12, 1948 (div. Apr. 1965); children: Ann, William, Nancy; m. Phyllis Rolfe, June 26, 1966; children: Gila, Aaron. BChE, CCNY, 1945; PhD, Ohio State U., 1952; JD, Suffolk U., 1982. Bar: Mass. 1982, U.S. Dist. Ct. Mass. 1982, U.S. Ct. Appeals (1st cir.) 1982, N.Y. 1983, U.S. Supreme Ct. 1986. Assoc. Ohio State U., Columbus, 1952-55; asst. prof. chem. physics U. Toledo, 1955-57; rsch. physicist Air Force Cambridge Rsch. Labs., Bedford, Mass., 1957-80, chief polar atmospheric processes br. and dir. geopole obs., 1963-74, cons., 1980—. Vis. rsch. assoc. Queens U., Belfast, 1963-64; vis. prof. Osmania U., Hyderabad, India, 1965-66; mem. adv. bd. Inst. Space and Atmospheric Studies, U. Sask. (Can.), 1965-69; sr. rsch. physicist Boston Coll., 1981-97; co-chmn. interdivisional comm. history Internat. Assn. Geomagnetism and Aeronomy, 1987-91; lectr. palliative care courses, Poland, 1993, 94, 2000. Contbr. articles to profl. jours. Mem. Town Meeting Lexington, Mass., 1973-79, 84—; elected mem. Lexington Dem. Town Com., 1996—; legal counsel Internat. Work Group on Death, Dying and Bereavement. With USAAF, 1945-46. Recipient Thurgood Marshall award, com. pub. counsel svcs. Mass. Pub. Defender's Agy., 2002. Fellow Am. Phys. Soc., Explorers Club; mem. Am. Geophys. Union (editor History of Geophysics newsletter 1983-91), Internat. Work Group on Death, Dying and Bereavement. Home: 18 Ingleside Rd Lexington MA 02420-2522 Office Phone: 781-861-0368. E-mail: smpr@rcn.com.

**SILVERMAN, SARAH,** actress, comedian, writer; b. Bedford, NH, Dec. 1, 1970; Actor: (TV series) Saturday Night Live, 1993—94, Mr. Show with Bob and David, 1995—97, Greg the Bunny, 2002, (voice) Crank Yankers, 2002,; (TV miniseries) Pilot Season, 2004; (TV films) Mr. Show and the Incredible, Fantastical News Report, 1998, Smog, 1999, Late Last Night, 1999, Rocky Times, 2000, (voice) Saddle Rush, 2002,: (films) Overnight Delivery, 1998, Bulworth, 1998, There's Something About Mary, 1998, The Bachelor, 1999, The Way of the Gun, 2000, Black Days, 2001, Say It Isn't So, 2001, Heartbreakers, 2001, Evolution, 2001, Run Ronnie Run, 2002, The School of Rock, 2003, Nobody's Perfect, 2004, (voice) Hair High, 2004, Rent, 2005; actor, co-prodr.: Who's the Caboose?, 1997; writer, actor: Sarah Silverman: Jesus is Magic, 2005; actor: (TV series, guest appearance) Star Trek: Voyager, 1996, The Larry Sanders Show, 1996, Seinfeld, 1997, Brotherly Love, 1997, JAG, 1997, The Naked Truth, 1997, Futurama, 2000, V.I.P., 2002, Frasier, 2003, Monk, 2004, Entourage, 2004, (voice) Aqua Teen Hunger Force, 2004, Drawn Together, 2004, American Dad, 2005. Office: Creative Artists Agy Inc 9830 Wilshire Blvd Beverly Hills CA 90212*

**SILVERMAN, STANLEY WAYNE,** chemical company executive; b. Phila., June 18, 1947; m. Ellen J. Seligsohn, June 7, 1970. BSChemE, Drexel U., 1969, MBA, 1974; AMP, Harvard U., 1989. Process engr. Atlantic Richfield Co., Phila., 1969-71, PQ Corp., Phila., 1971-74, mgr. oper. planning Valley Forge, Pa., 1974-76, product mgr., 1976-80, mktg. mgr., 1980-82, nat. sales mgr., 1982-84, pres. Nat. Silicates Ltd. subs. Toronto, Ont., Can., 1984-87, pres. indl. chem. group Valley Forge, 1987-90, exec. v.p., COO, 1990-99, pres., CEO, bd. dirs., 2000—05; dir. C&D Techs., 2003—. Chmn. adv. coun. Drexel U. Coll. Engring, 1991-93, alumni bd. govs., 1998, bd. trustees, 2000—; bd. dirs. Phila. Acad., Inc., 1999—2004. Named among 100 most accomplished grads. Drexel U., 1992; recipient Alumni Achievement award Drexel U., 1995. Mem. Soap and Detergent Assn. (bd. dirs. 2004—, chmn bd. 2004—), Am. Chemistry Coun. (bd. dirs. 2001—). E-mail: stan.silverman@comcast.net.

**SILVERMAN, VICTORIA LILLIAN,** consultant, fundraiser, cultural organization administrator; b. St. Louis, July 2, 1961; d. Thomas and Eva Alice (Hasko) Schiff; m. Lloyd Alan Silverman, Dec. 31, 1995; children: Anyu Isabella, Emmanuelle Snow. BA, Washington U., 1983; postgrad., St. Louis U., 1985-86. Assoc. dir. devel. Jewish Cmty. Ctr., St. Louis, 1983-85; assoc. dir. engring. Washington U., 1986-89; dir. engring. fund Stanford (Calif.) U., 1989-92; dir. major gifts and planned giving U. Calif., Santa Barbara, 1992-95; v.p. devel., exec. dir. found. St. Francis Med. Ctr., Santa Barbara, 1995; dir. devel. Am. Film Inst., L.A., 1995—2001; v.p. external affairs St. Louis Symphony Orch., 2001—03; ptnr. VLS Strategies, Inc., 2003—; v.p. Internat. Mus. of Women, 2004—. Cons. Stanford Engring. Sch., 1992, COCA, St. Louis, 2002—03, various orgns. Bd. dirs. Santa Barbara Ballet, 1990-92; vol. fundraiser Walter Capps for Congress, Santa Barbara, 1991. Mem. Coun. Advancement Support Edn. (presentor 1992—, conf. dir. 1995). Democrat. Jewish. Avocations: psychiatrist, dance and film enthusiast. Office: Ste 460 101 Howard St San Francisco CA 94119 Office Phone: 413 343 1669.

**SILVERMAN, WILLIAM A.,** lawyer; b. Phila., Mar. 1, 1945; BA, Univ. Pa., 1966; JD, Univ. Chgo., 1969. Bar: Ill. 1969, DC 1974, lic.: US Ct. Internat. Trade 1980, US Ct. Appeals, Fed. Cir. 1982. Asst. prof. Univ. Ill. Ctr. for Urban Studies, Coll. Edn., Chgo., 1969—71; ptnr., regulated industries, govtl. rels. Hunton & Williams LLP. Washington. Office: Hunton & Williams LLP 1900 K St NW Washington DC 20006-1109 Office Phone: 202-419-2013. Office Fax: 202-778-2201. Business E-Mail: wsilverman@hunton.com.

**SILVERS, GERALD THOMAS,** retired publishing executive; b. Cin., Aug. 26, 1937; s. Steve Allen and Tina Mae (Roberts) S.; m. Ann Gregory Woodward, July 25, 1964. BA, U. Ky., 1960. Asst. rsch. svcs. mgr. Cin. Enquirer, 1963-72, rsch. svcs. dir., 1972-74, rsch. dir., 1974-90, v.p. mktg. svcs., 1990-94, v.p. market devel., 1994—2003; ret., 2003. Active U. Ky. Devel. Coun., Lexington, 1986—; trustee Neediest Kids of All, 1991—; region 5 exec. com. (pres. 1985-86) bd. overseers Taft Mus. Art, 1999—, treas., bd. govs., 2002—. 1st lt. U.S. Army, 1960-62. Recipient Thomas H. Copeland award of merit, 1991. Mem. U. Ky. Alumni Assn. Cin. Chpt. (pres. 1985), Newspaper Rsch. Coun. (pres. 1985-86), Internat. Newspaper Market Assn., Am. Mktg. Assn., Am. Art Soc. Cin. (pres. 1999-2001). Presbyterian. Home: 229 Watch Hill Rd Fort Mitchell KY 41011-1822

**SILVERS, ROBERT B.,** editor; b. NY, Dec. 31, 1929; s. James J. and Rose (Roden) S. AB, U. Chgo., 1947; cert., Ecole de Sci. Politiques, Paris, 1956. Paris editor Paris Rev., 1954-59; asst. editor Harpers Mag., N.Y.C., 1959-63; co-editor N.Y. Rev. of Books, N.Y.C., 1963—. Editor: Writing in America, 1962, Hidden Histories of Science, 1995, Doing It: Five Performing Arts, 2001; co-editor: The Legacy of Isaiah Berlin, 2001, Striking Terror: America's New War, 2002, The Company Ady Kept: Writers in Unforgettable Friendships, 2006. Trustee NY Pub. Libr., 1996—; Ditchley Found., 1996—, Am. Acad. in Rome, 1998-, Paris Rev. Found., 2002-. With SHAPE U.S. Army, 1952. Decorated Legion d'Honneur, l'Ordre Nat. du Merite France. Mem. Am. Acad. Arts and Scis., Coun. Fgn. Rels., Century Assn., Knickerbocker Club. Office: NY Rev of Books 1755 Broadway New York NY 10019-3743 Office Phone: 212-757-8070.

**SILVERS, SALLY,** choreographer, performing company executive; b. Greeneville, Tenn., June 19, 1952; d. Herbert Ralston and Sara Elizabeth (Buchanan) S.; life ptnr. Bruce Erroll Andrews. BA in Dance and Polit. Sci., Antioch Coll., 1975. Artistic dir. Sally Silvers & Dancers, N.Y.C., 1980—. Mem. faculty Leicester Poly., 1986, 87, 89, summer choreography project Bennington Coll., 1988-92, Chisenhale Dance Space, London, 1989, 91, Am. Dance Festival, Durham, N.C., 1990, 92; guest lectr. European Dance Devel. Ctr., Arnhem, The Netherlands, 1992—. Choreographer (performances) Politics of the Body Microscope of Conduct, 1980, Social Movement, 1981, Connective Tissue, 1981, Less Time You Know Praxis, 1981, Don't No Do And This, 1981, Lack of Entrepreneurial Thrift, 1982, Celluoid Sally and Mr. E, 1982, Mutate, 1982, Being Red Enough, 1982, Disgusting, 1982, Bedtime at the Reformatory, 1982, Eat the Rich, 1982, They Can't Get It in the Shopping Cart, 1982, Blazing Forceps, 1982, And Find Out Why, 1983, Choose Your Weapons, 1984, Extend the Wish for Entire, 1985, No Best Better Way, 1985, Every All Which is Not Us, 1986, Swaps Ego Say So, 1986, Be Careful Now, You Know Sugar Melts in Water, 1987, Fact Confected, 1987, Both, Both, 1987, Tizzy boost, 1988, Moebius, 1988, Whatever Ever, 1989, Get Tough, Sports and Divertissement, 1989, Flap, 1989, Swan's Crayon, 1989, Fanfare Tripwire, 1990, Harry Meets Sally, 1990, Along the Skid Mark of Recorded History, 1990, Matinee Double-You, 1991, Grand Guignol, 1991, Dash Dash Slang Plural Plus, 1992, The Bubble Cut, 1992, Vigilant Corsage, 1992, Oops Fact, 1992, Small Room, 1993, Exwhyzee, 1993, Elegy, 1993, Now That It Is Now, 1994, Give Em Enough Rope, Swoon Noir, 1994, Radio Rouge, 1995, Braceletizing, 1995, Hush Comet, 1995, Bite the Pillow, 1995, Pandora's Cake Stain, 1996, Secrets Of, 1997, HUSHHUSH, Sugar Raised, 1998 Capture, Teddy Growl, 1999, Storming Heaven, 2000, Swaphot Trouble, 2001, Strike Me Lightning, 2002, Spaced Out, 2003, Dreams Do Come True, 2004, Dang Me, 2004; video and performance filmmaker: (films) Little Lieutenant, 1993 (Silver); N.Y. Dance on Camera Festival, Mechanics of the Brain, 1997; co-author: (book) Resurgant New Writings By Women, 1992; contbr. articles to profl. jours.; choreographer RUPT, Versus, Oven Rack Professionals, 2005. Grantee Nat. Endowment Arts, 1987, 89, 90, 91, 98, Jerome Found., 1993, 1996, Meet the Composer N.Y. Found. for the Arts, 1995; Guggenheim Found. fellow, 1988; Found. Contemporary Performance Arts, 2001. Mem. Segue Found. (bd. dirs. Segue Performance Space 1992-2002). Avocations: reading, writing, art events, costume design. Home: 303 E 8th St Apt 4F New York NY 10009-5212

**SILVERS, WILLYS KENT,** geneticist; b. NYC, Jan. 12, 1929; s. Lewis Julian and Miriam Elizabeth (Rosenzweig) Silvers; m. Abigail M. Adams, Sept. 29, 1956 (dec. June 18, 2005); children: Deborah Elizabeth, Willys Kent. BA, Johns Hopkins U., 1950; PhD, U. Chgo., 1954. Assoc. staff scientist Jackson Lab., Bar Harbor, Maine, 1956-57; assoc. mem. Wistar Inst., Phila., 1957-65; mem. faculty U. Pa. Med. Sch., 1965—, prof. genetics, 1967-98, prof. emeritus, 1998—. Mem. allergy and immunology study sect. NIH, 1962—66, adv. bd. primate rsch. ctrs., 1968—71; mem. com. cancer immunobiology Nat. Cancer Inst., 1974—78; bd. sci. overseers Jackson Lab., Bar Harbor, 1980—89. Author: The Immunobiology of Transplantation, 1971, The Coat Colors of Mice: A Model for Mammalian Gene Action and Interaction, 1979; mem. editl. bd. Transplantation, 1963—71, Jour. Exptl. Zoology, 1965—70, 1981—86, Jour. Immunology, 1973—77, Jour. Reticuloendothelial Soc., 1974—77; contbr. articles to profl. jours. Mem.: Am. Genetic Assn. (coun. 1980—83, pres. 1983). Home: 210 Millcreek Rd Ardmore PA 19003-1506 Office: U Pa Dept Genetics Sch Medicine Philadelphia PA 19104 Personal E-Mail: wsilvers@aol.com.

**SILVERSTEIN, BARBARA ANN,** conductor, artistic director; b. Phila., July 24, 1947; d. Charles and Selma (Brenner) S.; m. Bernard J. Taylor II, Aug. 19, 1978. Student, Bennington Coll., 1965-67; BMus, Phila. Coll. Performing Arts, 1970; MA, U. Del., 1997. Assoc. music dir. Suburban Opera Co., Chester, Pa., 1967-75; asst. condr. Toledo Opera Assn., 1975-76; asst. condr., coach Curtis Inst. Music, Phila., 1973-77; asst. condr. Phila. Lyric Opera, 1971-74, Des Moines Opera Festival, Indianola, Iowa, 1974-78; music dir., condr. Savoy Co., Phila., 1977-80, Miss. Opera, Jackson, 1979-82; artistic dir., condr. Pa. Opera Theater, Phila., 1976-93; guest condr. Anchorage Opera, 1982, Opera Del., Wilmington, 1981, 83, Utah Festival Opera Co., 1993-96, Lyric Opera Kansas City, 1995—, Opera Roanoke, Va., 1995, 98, Hollins U., 1999; mng. editor Epotec Inc., 1999-2000, dir. comm., 2000—01; prof. English U. Del., Ursinus, 1996—2004; asst. prof. Cecil Cmty. Coll., 2004—. Recipient alumni award U. of Arts. Mem. Am. Fedn. Musicians, Jusic Fund Soc., Pa. Coun. on the Arts (adv. panel 1987-90, OPERA Am. (bd. dirs. 1987-93, exec. com. 1988-93). Jewish. Avocations: scuba diving, reading.

**SILVERSTEIN, KEN,** journalist; Investigative reporter LA Times, Washington; contbg. editor Harper's, NYC, Washington editor, 2006—. Office: Harpers Mag 11th Fl 666 Broadway New York NY 10012 Office Phone: 212-420-5720. Office Fax: 212-228-5889. E-mail: letters@harpers.org.

**SILVERSTEIN, LARRY A.,** real estate developer; m. Klara Silverstein; children: Roger, Lisa, Sharon. BA, NYU, 1952; JD, Brooklyn Law Sch. Bar: N.Y. Pres. Silverstein Properties, Inc., N.Y.C.; owner 529 Fifth Ave., 570 Seventh Ave., One River Place, Two River Place, 120 Wall St., 120 Broadway, Seven World Trade Ctr.; 99 year leaseholder World Trade Ctr., 2001—. Gov., past chmn. Real Estate Bd. N.Y.; founder, chmn. emeritus NYU Real Estate Inst.; chmn. Realty Found. Trustee NYU, vice chmn. bd. trustees; trustee South St. Seaport Mus., Mus. Jewish Heritage; bd. chmn. United Jewish Appeal, Fedn. Jewish Philanthropies, NY. Avocations: classical music, yachting. Office: Silverstein Properties Inc 120 Broadway Suite 230 New York NY 10271

**SILVERSTEIN, LEONARD A.,** lawyer; b. Mobile, Ala., Apr. 18, 1958; s. Burton Howard and Fannye Mitchell Silverstein; m. Ellen Sue Frauenthal, May 25, 1986; children: Andrew, Laura, Anna. BA magna cum laude, Vanderbilt U., Nashville, 1980; JD, Vanderbilt U., 1983. Bar: Ga. 1983. Assoc./ptnr. Powell Goldstein Frazer & Murphy LLP, Atlanta, 1983—94; ptnr. McKenna Long & Aldridge LLP, Atlanta, 1994—. Mem. Ga. Biomed. Partnership, Atlanta, 2002—; mem., biosciences exec. com. Met. Atlanta C. of C., 2002—. Contbr. articles to profl. jours.; assoc. mng. editor, Vanderbilt Law Rev., 1982—83. Pres. Vanderbilt U. Alumni Club, Atlanta, 1991; co-pres. Bach n' Rollers, Divsn. of The Atlanta Symphony Assocs., 1992—93; bd. mem. and exec. com. mem. Zoo Atlanta, 1996—2001, bd. mem., 2003, Am.-Israel C. of C., S.E. Region, Atlanta, 1995—; bd. mem. and exec. com. mem. Am. Jewish Com., Atlanta, 1999—; bd. of trustees The Atlanta Symphony Assocs., 1992—93. Recipient IPO Rainmaker, IPO Counsel - The Corp. Fin. Inst., 1996. Mem.: Vanderbilt U. Alumni Assn. (bd. dirs. 1992—96), Ga. Bar Assn. (vice chair/chair elect of securities subcom. 2001—02), Atlanta Bar Assn. Achievements include patents pending for Reloaded Rights Plan for Preferred and Common Stock Rights Plans. Avocations: triathlons, golf. Office: McKenna Long & Aldridge LLP 303 Peachtree St Ste 5300 Atlanta GA 30308 Office Phone: 404-527-4390. Business E-Mail: lsilverstein@mckennalong.com.

**SILVERSTEIN, MARC,** TV host, reporter; m. Kathy Silverstein; children: Spencer, Lexy. BA in Broadcast Journalism, Am. U., Washington, DC. Consumer/investigative reporter WSYX-TV, Columbus, Ohio, WMAR-TV, Baltimore; broadcast journalist NBC, Washington. Spkr., emcee for various events. Co-host (TV series) The Best Of, Food Network, host (TV specials) Ballpark Cafe, Snacks Unwrapped, Ice Cream Unwrapped, Champagne Uncorked; co-author: Food Network Best Of The Best Of. Recipient Emmy award for special reporting. Pub. Svc. award, Nat. Highway Traffic Safety Adminstrn.*

**SILVERSTEIN, MARTIN J.,** lawyer, former ambassador; b. N.Y.C. married; 6 children. BA in Polit. Sci., Rutgers U., 1976; JD, Temple U., 1979. Bar: Pa., N.J., U.S. Ct. Internat. Trade, U.S. Ct. Customs and Patent Appeals. Founder Martin J. Silverstein and Assocs.; U.S. amb. to Uruguay US Dept. State, Montevideo, 2001—05; sr. counsel Greenberg Traurig LLP, Washington, 2005—. Mem. Fed. Jud. Nominating Commn., Pa. Active M.D. Anderson Cancer Ctr., Lower Merion Hist. Soc., U.S. Negro Coll. Fund, Phila. C. of C.; bd. mem. Vietnam Vets. Com. for Better Legislation. Recipient Citizens Commendation for Bravery, Phila. Police Dept. Mem.: Internat. Rep. Inst., Am. Payne Svc. Assn., Ctr. for Security Policy, Fgn. Policy Rsch. Inst., Am. Enterprise Inst., Heritage Found., World Affairs Coun. Office: Greenberg Traurig LLP 800 Connecticut Ave NW Ste 500 Washington DC 20006*

**SILVERSTEIN, PAUL ADAM,** education educator, researcher; PhD, U. Chgo., 1998; BA, Princeton U., N.J., 1992. Mellon fellow in humanities Barnard Coll., N.Y.C., 1998—2000; assoc. prof. anthropology Reed Coll., Portland, 2000—. Author: (book) Algeria in France: Transpolitics, Race, and Nation; editor: MERIP, 2002—. Fellow Faculty Rsch. Abroad grant, Fulbright-Hays, 2003. Office: Reed Coll 3203 SE Woodstock Blvd Portland OR 97202 Office Phone: 503-517-7606. Office Fax: 503-777-7776. Business E-Mail: paul.silverstein@reed.edu.

**SILVERSTEIN, PAUL N.,** lawyer; b. NYC, 1955; BFA, CUNY, 1977; JD, Bklyn. Law Sch., 1981. Bar: NY 1982. Ptnr., Bankruptcy Andrews Kurth LLP, NYC, mem. mgmt. com. Mem.: ABA, NY State Bar. Office: Andrews Kurth LLP 450 Lexington Ave New York NY 10017 Office Phone: 212-850-2819. Office Fax: 212-813-8158. Business E-Mail: paulsilverstein@andrewskurth.com.

**SILVERSTEIN, SAMUEL CHARLES,** cellular biology and physiology professor, researcher; b. NYC, Feb. 11, 1937; s. Paul Robert and Jeanette (Kamen) S.; m. Jo Ann Kleinman, Apr. 2, 1967; children: David Paul, Jennifer Kate. AB, Dartmouth Coll., 1958; MD, Albert Einstein Coll. Medicine, 1963. Intern in medicine U. Colo. Med. Center, 1963-64; postdoctoral fellow dept. cell biology Rockefeller U., 1964-67; resident in medicine Mass. Gen. Hosp., 1967—68; asst. prof. cellular physiology and immunology Rockefeller U., 1968-71, assoc. prof., physician, 1972—; John Dalton prof. physiology, prof. medicine Columbia U. Coll. Physicians and Surgeons, N.Y.C., 1983—, chmn. dept., 1983—2003. Founder, dir. Columbia U. Summer Rsch. Program for Secondary Sch. Sci. Tchrs., 1990—; prin. investigator, program dir. Pre and Post-doctoral Tng. Immunology, 1997—2005. Editor: Transport of Macromolecules in Cellular Systems, 1979; chmn. editl. bd. Jour. Cell Biology, 1979-82, editor, 1978-89. Bd. dirs. Arnold P. Gold Found., 1998-, Cancer Rsch. Fund, Damon Runyon Found., 1990-; bd. dirs. Rsch. Am., 1993-2005, mem. exec. com., 1996-2006. Recipient John Oliver LaGorce medal, Nat. Geog. Soc., 1967, Marie Bonazinga Rsch. award, Soc. Leukocyte Biology, 1984, Disting. Alumnus award, Albert Einstein Coll. Medicine, 1987, N.Y.C. Mayor's award Publ. Understanding of Sci. and Tech., 2003, Westy award Contbns. Sci. Edn. N.Y.C. Schs., 2004, Fountain Valley Sch. Trustees 75th Anniversary award, Colorado Springs, 2005; fellow Helen Hay Whitney, 1964—67, John Simon Guggenheim, 2005, Pres. Lasker/Funding First, 2001—04. Fellow: AAAS (chair sect. medicine 1998), N.Y. Acad. Sci. (edn. com.), Am. Soc. Microbiology; mem.: Am. Acad. Arts and Scis., Inst. Medicine Nat. Acad. Scis., Fedn. Am. Socs. for Exptl. Biology (bd. dirs. 1991—96, v.p. 1993—94, pres. 1994—95, chmn. pub. affairs adv. com. 1995—96), Practitioners Soc. N.Y., Assn. Am. Physicians, Am. Physiol. Soc., Am. Soc. Biol. Chemists, Infectious Diseases Soc. Am., Am. Assn. Immunologists, Am. Soc. Clin. Investigation, Am. Soc. Cell Biology (Bruce Alberts award for Excellence in Sci. Edn. 2005), Century Assn., Explorers Club, Am. Alpine Club (dir. 1963—64, 1969—74). Achievements include research and numerous publications in field of virology, cell biology, immunology, science policy and mountaineering. Office: Columbia U Coll Physicians & Surgeons 630 W 168th St New York NY 10032-3795 Office Phone: 212-305-3546. Business E-Mail: scs3@columbia.edu.

**SILVERSTEIN, SUZANNE,** art therapist; b. L.A., Jan. 14, 1948; d. Lita (Factor) Kilpatrick; m. Andrew Chiaramonte, July 4, 1988; 1 child, Jaysen Pascal. BFA, Calif. Inst. of the Arts, L.A., 1971; MA, Immaculate Heart Coll., L.A., 1975. Art therapy coord., supr. family and child program Thalians Mental Health Ctr., L.A., 1977—; art therapy coord., supr. famil and child program dept. psychiatry Cedars-Sinai Med. Ctr., L.A., 1977—; pres., co-founder Psychol. Trauma Ctr., L.A., 1981—. Faculty clin. art therapy dept. Immaculate Heart Coll., 1975-81, Loyola Marymount U., 1981-82, leader, group dynamics class, 1975-82; adminstr. Psychol. Trauma Ctr., 1981—, pres. 1981—. Author: (with others) Expanding Mental Health Interventions in Schools, 1988. Fellowship Thalians Mental Health Ctr./Cedars Sinai Med. Ctr., L.A., 1975-76. Mem. Am. Art Therapy Assn., So. Calif. Art Therapy Assn. Office: Psychol Trauma Ctr 8730 Alden Dr Rm C212 Los Angeles CA 90048-3811 Office Phone: 310-423-3541. Business E-Mail: suzanne.silverstein@cshs.org.

**SILVERSTONE, HARRIS J.,** chemistry professor; b. NYC, Sept. 18, 1939; s. Sidney M. and Estelle Silverstone; m. Ruth C. Federman, 1960; children: Robert, Aron, Nancy, Murray. AB, Harvard U., 1960; PhD, Calif. Inst. Tech., 1964. Asst. prof. Johns Hopkins U., Balt., 1965-68, assoc. prof., 1968-71, prof., 1971—. Contbr. articles to profl. jours. NSF Postdoctoral fellow Yale U., 1964. Mem. Am. Phys. Soc., Am. Chem. Soc. Theoretical Chem. Physics. Office: Johns Hopkins U 3400 N Charles St Baltimore MD 21218-2685

**SILVERTHORN, ANN,** writer; b. Erie, Pa., Sept. 7, 1957; d. Lee Burton and Mary Lou (Waldinger) Silverthorn; m. James Scott DeDad, July 30, 1982; children: Krista DeDad, Kasey DeDad, Michael DeDad. BA in English magna cum laude, Gannon U., 1996, MA in English, 1999. Web editor InfoStor, Tulsa. adj. prof. Gannon U. Author: Delaware County, 1998, Blinds, 1999, (audiotape) Truckin Tales, 1999. Pres. Gardnview PTA, Erie, 1995—98, legis. chmn.; sec. Erie County Coun. PTA, Erie, 1998—99; Erie County ct.-apptd. spl. advocate. Mem.: Phi Alpha Theta, Omicron Delta Kappa. Republican. Avocations: creative writing, art, music, golf. Home: 3023 Coleridge Dr Erie PA 16506 Office Phone: 814-838-1912. E-mail: silverthorn@adelphia.net.

**SILVERTHORN, DEE UNGLAUB,** physiologist, educator; d. Walter George and Saidee Parker Unglaub; m. Andrew Charles Silverthorn, July 27, 1972. BS in Biology with honors, Tulane U., 1970; PhD in Marine Sci., U. SC, 1973. Rsch. assoc. dept. biochemistry Med. U. SC, 1973—74, from instr. to asst. prof. dept. physiology, 1977—77; rsch. scientist dept. physiology and biophysics U. Tex. Med. Br., Galveston, 1978—80; faculty in biology and math. St. Stephens Sch., Austin, Tex., 1981—82; pvt. practice Austin, 1983—86; lectr. dept. zoology U. Tex., Austin, 1986—92; sr. lectr. biol. scis., 1992—. Vis. assoc. prof. biology U. Houston, 1977—78; adj. rsch. scientist Nat. Marine Fisheries Svc., Galveston, 1977—78; alumni adv. coun. for natural scis. U. SC, 2001—. Author: Human Physiology: An Integrated Approach, 1998 (Robert W. Hamilton Author award, 1998), 3d edit., 2004; editor: Laboratory Manual for Physiology: A Benjamin Cummings Custom Edition, 2005. Recipient Textbook Excellence award, Text and Acad. Authors Assn., 2001; Belle W. Baruch Predoctoral fellow, U. SC, 1970—73. Mem.: Nat. Assn. for Biology Tchrs., Soc. for Coll. Sci. Tchrs., Am. Assn. Anatomists, Assn. for Biology Lab. Edn., Coun. for Undergrad. Rsch., Soc. for Integrative and Comparative Biology, Human Anatomy and Physiology Soc. (liaison 1997—), Am. Physiol. Soc. (chair tchg. physiology sect. 1999—2002, editor Advances in Physiology Edn. 2001—, Arthur C. Guyton Physiology Tchr. of Yr. award 2001, Bernard Disting. lectr. 2005). Avocation: art. Office Phone: 512-471-6560.

**SILVERTHORN, ROBERT STERNER, JR.,** lawyer; b. Oklahoma City. Dec. 22, 1948; s. Robert Sterner and Marilyn I. Silverthorn; m. Mary Russell Cofer, June 26, 1982; children: Robert Sterner III, Christine Elizabeth. BA, Dickinson Coll., 1969; JD, U Louisville, 1974; postgrad., Nat. Def. U., 1988, U.S. Army War Coll., 1993. Bar: Ky. 1975, U.S. Dist. Ct. (we. dist.) Ky. 1975, U.S. Tax Ct. 1975, U.S. Dist. Ct. (ea. dist.) Ky. 1980, U.S. Dist. Ct. (so. dist.) Tex. 1981, U.S. Dist. Ct. (no. dist.) Ohio 1983, U.S. Dist. Ct. (so. dist.) Ind. 1993, U.S. Supreme Ct. 1983. Pvt. practice, Louisville, 1977-; assoc. Pallo White & O'Conner, Louisville, 1975-76, Hargadon Lenihan & Harbolt, Louisville, 1976-82; ptnr. White Diamond & Silverthorn, Louisville, 1982-

83; of counsel Nutt & Mayer, Louisville, 1983-91; mng. ptnr. Morris, Silverthorn & Dutton, Louisville, 1991-92, Silverhorn Law Offices, 1993—; commd. 2d lt. U.S. Army, 1970, advanced through grades to maj. gen., 2000, comdr. gen. 84th Divsn., 1998, comdr. gen. 95th divsn., 2000-04; bd. dirs. Maroco Leasing, Inc., Louisville, Akima Mgmt. Svcs., Charlotte, NC; repeat guest radio talk show Ask the Lawyers Sta. WHAS; mil. commentator WAVE-TV (NBC). Pres. Windhurst Acres Homeowners Assn., St. Matthews, Ky., 1981-85; chmn., pres. Hurstbourne Village Office Condo, Louisville, 2005—; bd. dirs. Am. Cherokee dist. Boy Scouts Am., dePaul Sch. Louisville, 1997-99. Decorated Disting. Svc. medal, Meritorious Svc. medal with 6 oak leaf clusters, Bronze Star with 1 oak leaf cluster, Air medal, Army Commendation medal with 3 oak leaf clusters, Army Achievement medal; recipient Constl. Book award U. Louisville, 1975. Mem. ABA (past vice chair real property sect.), Ky. Bar Assn. (chmn. civil litigation sect. 2001-02), Louisville Bar Assn., Ky. Acad. Trial Attys., Res. Officers Assn., Assn. of Century (pres. 1993-95), Assn. U.S. Army (chmn. Louisville Armed Forces Day com. 1986-88), Sr. Army Res. Comdrs. Assn. (pres. 2001-04), Louisville Area C. of C. (mil. affairs com.), Hurstbourne Country Club, Jefferson Club, Rotary Club of Jeffersontown, Ky. (pres. 1995-96, dist. 6710 asst. gov. 1997-2000), Masons, Delta Theta Phi (dean), Sigma Chi. Methodist. Office: Silverthorn Law Offices Ste 200 2305 Hustbourne Village Dr Louisville KY 40299-1861 Office Phone: 502-495-2300. Personal E-mail: RSilvertho@aol.com. Business E-Mail: silverthornlaw@bellsouth.net.

**SILVERTOOTH, CARL DENNIS,** artist; b. Kileen, Tex. s. Carl Edward and Sonja Olga Silvertooth; life ptnr. Mary Nell Clayton; 1 child, Ian Dayne. Studied with (hon.), M.Schmidt, A.Armstrong., C.C. Art Mus./, Corpus Christi, Texas, 1974. Entrepenuer Sonja's European Restaurant, Corpus Christi, 1990—2006. Exhibitions include American Cowboy (1st pl., Philbrook Mus., Tulsa, 1979), Once Upon A Time, Plains Indian, Prophet, Reawakening, Rising Sun, Sequoyeh, Time Expired, Timekeeper, White Horse, Shadow Woman, American Man, Tonk-a-Wond-A, Rainbow, Free No More, Greatest Loss, Beneath The Dream Robe, Bronco, Calls His Grandfather, Challenge, Flute Player/Piper, Mountain. Named Artist of Yr., Sante Fe Mag., 1980; recipient Best Sculpture, Art About Town, Dallas Crippled Children Soc., 1977. Independent. Achievements include Best Sculpture, Art About Town, Dallas Crippled Children Soc. 1977. Artist of the Year, Sante Fe Magazine, Aug. of 1980. Avocations: motorcycling, cooking. Office Phone: 361-884-7774. Office Fax: 361-884-7775. Personal E-mail: twoth_48@yahoo.com.

**SILVESTRI, ALAN ANTHONY,** film composer; b. NYC, Mar. 26, 1950; s. Louis and Elizabeth (Clarke) S.; m. Sandra Dee Shue; children: Alexandra, Joseph, James. PhD in Music (hon.), Berklee Coll. Music, Boston, 1995. Film scores include The Doberman Gang, 1972, The Amazing Dobermans, Las Vegas Lady, 1976, Romancing the Stone, 1984, Par ou t'es rentre? On t'as vu sortir, 1984, Fandango, 1984, Cat's Eye, 1984, Back to the Future, 1985 (Grammy award nominations best instrumental composition and best album of original score for a motion picture, 1985), Summer Rental, 1985, Clan of the Cave Bear, 1986, The Delta Force, 1986, American Anthem, 1986, Flight of the Navigator, 1986, No Mercy, 1986, Critical Condition, 1987, Outrageous Fortune, 1987, Predator, 1987, Overboard, 1987, Who Framed Roger Rabbit?, 1988 (Grammy award nominations best instrumental composition and best album of original score for a motion picture, 1988), My Stepmother Is an Alien, 1988, Mac and Me, 1988, She's Out of Control, 1989, Downtown, 1989, The Abyss, 1989, Back to the Future II, 1989, Back to the Future III, 1990, Young Guns II, 1990, Predator II, 1990, Soapdish, 1991, Dutch, 1991, Ricochet, 1991, Shattered, 1991, Father of the Bride, 1991, Ferngully: The Last Rainforest, 1992, Death Becomes Her, 1992, Stop! Or My Mom Will Shoot, 1992, The Bodyguard, 1992, Cop and a Half, 1993, Sidekicks, 1993, Super Mario Bros., 1993, Judgment Night, 1993, Grumpy Old Men, 1993, Clean Slate, 1994, Blown Away, 1994, Forrest Gump, 1994 (Academy award nomination best original score, Grammy award nomination best instrumental performance for "Feather Theme from Forrest Gump," Golden Globe award nomination best original score), Richie Rich, 1994, The Quick and the Dead, 1994, The Perez Family, 1995, Judge Dredd, 1995, Father of the Bride II, 1995, Sgt. Bilko, 1995, Grumpier Old Men, 1995, Eraser, 1996, Long Kiss Goodnight, 1996, Fools Rush In, 1996, Volcano, 1997, Contact, 1997, Mousehunt, 1997, Odd Couple II, 1998, Parent Trap, 1998, Holyman, 1998, Practical Magic, 1998, Siegfried & Roy, The Magic Box, 1999, Stuart Little, 1999, Reindeer Games, 2000, What Lies Beneath, 2000, What Women Want, 2000, Castaway, 2000 (Grammy award winner for best instrumental composition for "Theme from Castaway"), The Mexican, 2001, What Women Want, 2000, The Mummy Returns, 2001, Serendipity, 2001, Showtime, 2002, Lilo & Stitch, 2002, Stuart Little 2, 2002, Maid in Manhattan, 2002, Identity, 2003, Lara Croft Tomb Raider: The Cradle of Life, 2003, Two Soldiers, 2003, Van Helsing, 2004, The Polar Express, 2004; TV themes include CHiPs, 1978-83, Manimal, 1983. Recipient ACE award Nat. Acad. Cable Programming for Tales from the Crypt - All Through the House, 1990, Saturn award Acad. Arts and Sci. for fantasy and horror film, 1987, Grammy award for Best Song Written for Motion Picture for The Polar Express, 2006; Grammy nominations for Back to the Future, 1985, Who Framed Rger Rabbit?, 1988, Forrest Gump, 1994, Castaway, 2001; nominated for Golden Globe, Forrest Gump, 1994.

**SILVESTRI, GINA,** lawyer; b. NJ, Feb. 18, 1972; BA magna cum laude, Seton Hall U., NJ, 1994; JD, Thomas M. Cooley Law Sch., Mich., 1995. Bar: NY 1999, NJ 2001, U.S. Dist. Ct. of NJ (Dist. Ct. NJ) 2001. Atty. Gina Silvestri, Esq., Jackson, NJ, 2003—04; assoc. atty. Law Office Of Terence G. Van Dzura, Edison, NJ, 2001—03, William J. Leininger, PC, SI, 2000—01, Law Office Of Mahipal Singh, PC, Jackson Heights, NY, 1999—2000. Fla. notary pub., Fla., 2004—. Mem.: NJ Bar Assn., NY Bar Assn., Alpha Phi (life). Personal E-mail: gsilvst@prodigy.net.

**SILVESTRO, CLEMENT MARIO,** museum director, historian; b. New Haven, Sept. 7, 1924; s. Joseph and Rose (Griego) S.; m. Betty C. Mack, June 26, 1950; 1 dau., Elizabeth J. Silvestro Casner. BS, Central Conn. State Coll., 1949; MS, U. Wis., 1951; PhD, 1959. Asst. to dir. Wis. Hist. Soc., 1956-57; dir. Am. Assn. State and Local History, 1957-64; editor History News, 1957-64; assoc. dir. Chgo. Hist. Soc., 1964-65, dir., 1965-74, sec., 1970-74; dir. Mus. of Our Nat. Heritage, Lexington, Mass., 1974-92. Mem. exec. com. Am. Assn. Museums, 1965-71, v.p., 1966-71; vis. lectr. Northeastern U., 1983-85 Co-author: A Decade of Collecting: Maps, 1985 Mem. Chgo. Archtl. and Landmark Com., 1968-74; mem. Ill. Historic Sites Adv. Council, 1970-74, U.S. ICOM, Nat. Com., 1970-74; chmn. Pres.'s Adv. Council on Historic Preservation, 1974-77; mem. adv. bd. Eleutherian Mills-Hagley Found., 1973-76; U.S. rep. to UNESCO Internat. Adv. Com. to Safeguard City of Venice, 1975; trustee U.S. Capitol Hist. Soc.; trustee, pres. Fruitlands Mus., 1982-85. Served with USAAF, 1943-45. Decorated Air medal with oak leaf clusters. Mem. Am. Assn. Mus., Orgn. Am Historians (chmn. hist. sites com. 1973-78), Chgo. Hist. Soc., Colonial Soc. Mass., Bostonian Soc., Mass. Hist. Soc. (resident), Union Club Boston, Masons. Home: 200 West Shore Rd Hancock Point ME 04640-0119 E-mail: silvestro@adelphia.net.

**SILVEY, ANITA LYNNE,** editor; b. Bridgeport, Conn., Sept. 3, 1947; d. John Oscar and Juanita Lucille (McKitrick) Silvey. BS in Edn., Ind. U., 1969; MA in Comm. Arts, U. Wis., 1970. Editorial asst. children's book dept. Little Brown and Co., Boston, 1970-71; asst. editor Horn Book Mag., Boston, 1971-75; mng. editor, founder New Boston Rev., 1975-76; mktg. mgr. children's books, libr. svcs. mgr. trade divsn. Houghton Mifflin, Boston, 1976-84; editor-in-chief Horn Book Mag., Boston, 1985-95; v.p., pub. Children's Books Houghton Mifflin Co., Boston, 1995—2001. Editor: Children's Books and Their Creators, 1995, Help Wanted: Stories About Young People and Work, 1997, Essential Guide to Children's Books and their Creators, 2002, 100 Best Books for Children, 2004, 500 Great Books for Teens, 2006. Named one of 70 Women Who Have Made a Difference, Women's Nat. Book Assn., 1987. Mem.: ALA (chmn. children's librs., Laura Ingalls Wilder award 1987—89), Assn. Am. Pubs. (mem. libr. com.), Internat. Reading Assn. (mem. IRA Book award com. 1985—87), New Eng. Round Table (chmn. 1978—79). Personal E-mail: anitasilvey@aol.com.

**SILVIA, DAVID ALAN,** insurance broker; b. Taunton, Mass., Mar. 5, 1953; s. Edward J. and Loretta (Sousa) S.; m. Janet E. McMahon, Apr. 16, 1988 (div. Jan. 1996); 1 child, David. BA, Roger Williams U., 1975. Sales rep. New England Brass, Taunton, Mass., 1976-81; ins. agt. Prudential Ins., Raynham, Mass., 1981-82; owner, ptnr. CS Assocs., North Attleboro, Mass., 1982-86; asst. ice hockey coach New England Hockey Inst., 2002—. Independent. Office: 495 Somerset Ave North Dighton MA 02764-1809 Office Phone: 508-880-0650. Business E-Mail: dsilviabroker@aol.com.

**SIM, CRAIG STEPHEN,** retired investment banker; b. Bklyn., Apr. 23, 1942; s. William Henry Craig and Lenore (Overton) S.; m. Susan Hart; children: Brandon Craig William, Stephanie Brooke. BA, Gettysburg Coll., 1965. Account exec. Francis I. duPont & Co., N.Y.C., 1969-72; v.p. E.F. Hutton & Co., N.Y.C., 1972-75; sr. v.p. Donaldson, Lufkin & Jenrette, N.Y.C., 1975-83; exec. v.p. Shearson Am. Express, N.Y.C., 1983-84; mng. dir. Donaldson, Lufkin & Jenrette, N.Y.C., 1984-2001, Credit Suisse First Boston, 2001—. Trustee Gettysburg Coll., 1995-2001, Vt. Hist. Soc. Served to capt. USMC, 1965-69. Mem. Bond Club N.Y. (gov. 1979-80, 84-85, 90-93), Lawrence Beach Club (gov.), St. Andrew's Soc. (N.Y.C.), Burns Soc. City of N.Y. (trustee), L.I. Wyandanch Club, Seawanhaka Corinthian Yacht Club, Army and Navy Club (Washington), Union Club. Address: PO Box 57 Charlotte VT 05445

**SIM, FRANKLIN H.,** orthopedic surgery educator; children: Leslie, Sheridan. MD, Dalhousie U. Med. Sch., 1960—64. Med. dr. MN, 1972. Prof. orthop. surgery Mayo Clinic, Rochester, Minn., 1972—. Chair, divsn. orthop. oncology Mayo Clinic, 2000—. Second lt Black Watch Rgt., 1961, Germany. Office: Mayo Clinic 200 First St SW Rochester MN 55905

**SIMAAN, MARWAN,** electrical engineering educator; b. July 23, 1946; m. Rita Simaan. MSEE, U. Pitts., 1970; PhDEE, U. Ill., 1972. Registered profl. engr., Pa. Rsch. engr. Shell Devel. Co., Houston, 1974-76; assoc. prof. elec. engring. U. Pitts., 1976-85, prof., 1985-89, Bell of Pa./Bell Atlantic prof., 1989—, chmn. dept. elec. engring., 1991—. Cons. Gulf Rsch. and Tech., Pitts., 1979-85, ALCOA, Pitts., 1986-89. Editor: Vertical Seismic Profiles, 1984, Two-dimensional Transforms, 1985, Artificial Intelligence in Petroleum Exploration, 1989, Expert Systems in Exploration, 1991, (series) Advances in Geophysical Signal Processing; co-editor jour. Multidimensional Sys. and Signal Processing; mem. editl. bd. multiple jours., including IEEE Procs., IEEE Transactions on Cirs. and Sys., IEEE Transactions on Geosci. and Remote Sensing, Jour. Optimization Theory and Applications, Integrated Computer-aided Engring. Jour., Jour. Cirs., Sys. and Computers; contbr. over 300 articles on signal processing and control to profl. publs. Grantee NSF, NIH, ONR, Def. Advance Rsch. Project Adminstrs., Ben Franklin, Westinghouse, Gulf, ALCOA; recipient Outstanding ECE Alumnus U. Ill. Fellow: AAAS (sec. engring. sect. M 2003—), IEEE (Best Paper award 1985, 1999), Am. Soc. Engring. Edn.; mem.: NAE, Am. Assn. Artificial Intelligence, Soc. Exploration Geophysicists, Sigma Xi (Best Paper award Alcoa chpt. 1988), Eta Kappa Nu. Achievements include patent in application of signal processing technology in aluminum manufacturing. Office: Univ Pitts Dept Elec Engring Pittsburgh PA 15261-0001 Office Phone: 412-624-8099. E-mail: simaan@engr.pitt.edu.

**SIMANDLE, JEROME B.,** federal judge; b. Binghamton, N.Y., 1949; s. Paul R. Sr. and Mary F. Simandle; married; children: Roy C., Liza Jane. BSE magna cum laude, Princeton U., 1971; JD, U. Pa., 1976; diploma in Social Scis., U. Stockholm, 1974-75. Bar: Pa. 1977, N.J. 1978. Law clk. to Hon. John F. Gerry U.S. Dist. Ct., NJ, 1976-78; asst. U.S. atty. Dist. N.J., 1978-83; U.S. magistrate judge U.S. Dist. Ct., NJ, 1983-92, judge NJ, 1992—. Mem. lawyers adv. com. U.S. Dist. Ct., NJ, 1984—95; mem. ct. adminstrn. case mgmt. com. Jud. Conf. U.S., 1991—97; mem. joint adv. coun. of Adminstrv. Office of U.S. Cts., 2002—; mem. CPR Inst. for Dispute Resolution Commn. on Ethics and Stds. in Alternative Dispute Resolution, 1996—2002; chair Third Cir. Com. on Rules of Practice and Procedure, 2003—; mem. Third Cir. Model Civil Jury Instrns. Com., 2004—. Internat. grad. fellow Rotary Found., 1974-75. Master: Camden Inn of Ct. (program chmn. 1990—93, vice chmn. 1996—2004); fellow: Am. Bar Found.; mem.: Camden County Bar Assn., Am. Judicature Soc., Fed. Judges Assn. (bd. dirs. 1997—, treas. 2003—, co-editor In Camera 2004—). Office: Mitchell H Cohen US Courthouse Rm 6010 1 John F Gerry Pl Camden NJ 08101-0888

**SIMAO, PAUL,** news agency executive; Writer Reuters Am., Inc., Canada, bur. chief Atlanta, 2000—. Office: Reuters America 3340 Peachtree Rd NE Ste 200 Atlanta GA 30326-1028 Business E-Mail: paul.simao@reuters.com.

**SIMBERLOFF, DANIEL,** biologist, educator; b. Easton, Pa., Apr. 7, 1942; s. Isaac and Ruth (Koplowitz) S. A.B., Harvard U., 1964; Ph.D., 1969. Asst. prof. biology Fla. State U., Tallahassee, 1968-73, assoc. prof., 1973-78, prof., 1978—1997, Robert O. Lawton Disting. prof., 1986; Nancy Gore Hunger prof. environ. studies, dept. ecology and evolutionary biology, U. Tenn., 1997-; vis. prof. U. Mich., 1974, U. Minn., 1980, Hebrew U., Jerusalem, 1984, bd. dirs. Nat. Sci. Bd.; mem. species survival commn. Internat. Union Conservation Nature and Natural Resources; contbr. articles to sci. jours; editor Jour. Biogeography, 1974—, Biodiversity and Conservation; mem. editl. bd. Jour. Biogeography, Northeast Gulf Sci. Environ. and Ecological Statistics, Raffles Bulletin of Zoology, Ecologie, Oecologia, BioScience, Biological Invasions. Co-editor: Ecological Communities: Conceptual Issues and the Evidence, 1984, (with D. Schmitz and T. Brown) Strangers in Paradise: Impact and Management of Nonindigenous Species in Florida, 1997. Recipient Developing Scholar award Fla. State U., 1977, Rector's medal U. Helsinki, Finland, 1983, Disting. Statistical Ecologist award, Internat. Assn. Ecology, 1994. Mem. Am Acad. Arts and Scis., British Ecol. Soc., Soc. Conservation Biology, Nature Conservancy, Ecol. Soc. Am. (Mercer award 1971), Am. Soc. Naturalists, Soc. for Study Evolution, Brit. Ecol. Soc., Soc. for Systematic Zoology. Jewish. Home: 2145 Indian Hills Dr Knoxville TN 37919-8914 Office: Ecology and Evolutionary Biology Univ Tenn 480 Dabney Hall Knoxville TN 37996-1610 Office Phone: 865-974-0849. Office Fax: 865-974-3067. E-mail: dsimberloff@utk.edu.

**SIME, KAREN RACHEL,** entomologist; b. Sacramento, Calif., June 24, 1969; d. Rodney Jerome and Ruth Lewin Sime; m. M. McDonald. BS, U. Calif., Berkeley, 1991; PhD, Cornell U., Ithaca, NY, 2001. Rsch. specialist U. Calif., Berkeley, 2002—. Instr. Weill Cornell Med. Coll., Doha, Qatar, 2003, Calif. Poly. State U., San Luis Obispo, 2005. Contbr. articles to profl. jours. Fellow, NSF, 1994—97, Max Planck Inst., Chem. Ecology, 2001; grantee, NSF, 1996—99; Liberty Hyde Bailey fellow, Cornell U., 1992—99. Mem.: Pacific Coast Entomol. Soc., Internat. Soc. Hymenopterists, Entomol. Soc. Am., Sierra Club. Liberal. Avocations: skiing, travel, foreign language study. Home: 1237 1/2 Kains Ave Berkeley CA 94706 Office: University of California Dept Env'tl Science Policy & Mgmt Berkeley CA 94720-3114 Office Phone: 916-202-6437. Business E-Mail: krs1@cornell.edu.

**SIMECKA, BETTY JEAN,** marketing executive; b. Topeka, Apr. 15, 1935; d. William Bryan and Regina Marie (Rezac) S.; m. Alex Pappas, Jan. 15, 1956 (div. Apr. 1983); 1 child, Alex William. Student, Butler County C.C., 1983—85. Freelance writer and photographer, L.A., also St. Marys, Kans., 1969-77; co-owner Creative Enterprises, El Dorado, Kans., 1977-83; coord. excursions into history Butler County C.C., El Dorado, 1983-84; dir. Hutchinson (Kans.) Conv. & Visitors Bur., 1984-85; dir. mktg. divsn. Exec. Mgmt., Inc., Wichita, 1985-87; exec. dir. Topeka Conv. and Visitors Bur., 1987-91, pres., CEO, 1991-96; pres. Internat. Connections, Inc., 1996-97, Simecka and Assoc., 1996-99, Pinnacle Prodns., L.L.C., 1997-99; pres., CEO Cultural Exhbns. and Events, L.L.C., 1999—2003; organizer Czars: 400 Years of Imperial Grandeur exhbn., 2002—04; v.p. mktg. Sunflower Exhbns., L.L.C., 2003—04; mktg. cons., 2003—. Dir. promotion El Dorado Thunderboat Races, 1977-78. Contbr. articles to jours. and mags.; columnist St. Marys Star, 1973-79. Pres. St. Marys Summer Track Festival, 1973-81; chair spl. events Mulvane Art Mus., 1990, sec., 1991-92; membership chair,

1993-94, bd. dirs., 1995-96; bd. dirs. Topeka Civic Theater, 1991-96, co-chair spl. events, 1992; Kans. chair Russian Festival Com., 1992-93; vice-chair Kans. Film Commn., 1993-94, chair, 1994; bd. dirs. Kans. Expoctr. Adv. Bd., 1990-96, Brain Injury Assn. Greater Kansas City, Concerned Citizens Topeka, 1998-2000; pres. Kans. Internat. Mus., 1994-96. Recipient Kans. Gov.'s Outstanding Tourism award City of Topeka, 1993, Disting. Svc award City of Topeka, 1995, Hist. Ward Meade Disting. award Topeka Parks and Recreation Dept., 1995; named Kansan of Yr., Topeka Capitol-Jour., 1995, Sales and Mktg. Exec. of Yr., 1995, Internat. Soroptomists, Topeka chpt., Woman of Distinction, 1996. Mem. Nat. Tour Assn., Sales and Mktg. execs. (bd. dirs. 1991-92), Internat. Assn. Conv. and Visitors Burs. (co-chair rural tourism com. 1994), Am. Soc. Assn. Execs., Travel Industry Assn. Kans. (membership chair 1988-89, sec. 1990, pres. 1991-92, Outstanding Merit award 1994), St. Marys C. of C. (pres. 1975), I-70 Assn. (v.p. 1989, pres. 1990), Optimists (social sec. Topeka chpt. 1988-89). Republican. Methodist. Holder Nat. AAU record for 100-yard dash, 1974. Office Phone: 785-220-1606. Personal E-mail: bsimecka@giantcomm.net.

**SIMENDINGER, THEODORE JOHN,** writer, publishing executive; b. Phila., Oct. 6, 1954; s. Theodore John and Margaret Smith Simendinger; m. Bonita Ann Kolish; 1 child, Grace. BS, Jacksonville U., 1976. Founder, chmn. Pro Leisure Tour, Inc., Greenwood Village, Colo., 2000—; v.p., sales talent devel. First Data Corp., 2004—. Career devel. cons. Airplane Reader Pub., Greenwood Village, 2000—. Author: Critters, Fish & Other Troublemakers, 2001, Rich Without Money, 2002, 12 Miles to Paradise, 2003, Searching for Tendulkar, 2004, Jurassic Trout, 2004, Tuki Banjo, Superstar, 2005, How to Manage the Worry Circle, 2005, The Rise And Fall of Piggy Church, 2006, Maximum Horsepower: How to Strengthen Your Sales Force, 2006. Founder, chmn. No Bats Baseball Club, Global Ambassadors for the Good of the Game, Greenwood Village, Colo, 1991—. Named Alumnae of the Yr., Jacksonville U., 2003. Avocations: reading, writing, comedy, fishing. Office Phone: 720-332-5344.

**SIMEONOV, SIMEON,** computer scientist; BS in Computer sci., Economics, & Math., Macalester Coll.; MS in Computer sci., Boston U. V.p. Emerging Technologies; chief arch. Macromedia Corp.; prin. Polaris Ventures, 2002—. Author: Building Web Services with Java, 2001. Named one of Top 100 Young Innovators, MIT Tech. Review, 2004. Office: Polaris Ventures 1000 Winter St Waltham MA 02451

**SIMERAL, WILLIAM GOODRICH,** retired chemical company executive; b. Portland, Oreg., May 22, 1926; s. Claire Cornelius and Geneva G. Simeral; m. Elizabeth Louise Ross, June 25, 1949; children: Linda Simeral McGregor, Karen Simeral Schousen, William Goodrich Jr., John David; m. Marion Poore Anderson, Nov. 3, 2001. BS in Physics, Franklin and Marshall Coll., Lancaster, Pa., 1948; PhD in Physics, U. Mich., 1953. With E.I. duPont de Nemours and Co., Inc., 1953-87, v.p., gen. mgr. plastics dept. Wilmington, Del., 1974-76, v.p., gen. mgr. plastic products and resins dept., 1976-77, sr. v.p., dir., mem. exec. com., 1977-81, exec. v.p., dir., mem. exec. com., 1981-87; vice chmn. bd., chief operating officer Conoco Inc., 1984-85. Trustee Franklin and Marshall Coll., 1977—, chmn. bd., 1991-94; trustee, bd. dirs. Wilmington Med. Ctr., 1978-93, chmn. bd., 1982-86; bd. dirs. YMCA Wilmington and New Castle County, 1978-81. Mem. Chem. Mfrs. Assn. (vice chmn. bd. 1980-81, chmn. exec. com. 1981-82, chmn. bd. 1982-83), Am. Phys. Soc., Phi Beta Kappa, Sigma Xi, Wilmington Country Club.

**SIMES, MICHAEL LOUIS,** lawyer; s. Irwin M. and Ann L. Simes. BA, SUNY, Albany, 1988—91; JD, U. Ariz., Tuscon, 1991—94; MBA, Ariz. State U., Tempe, 2001—03. Bar: Ariz. 1994, Colo. 1996. Atty. Michael Simes, LLC, Tempe, 2000—. Author: (book) Technology Transfer: Path to a New Economy. Sec. Ariz. Coalition for Tomorrow, Phoenix, 1995—99. Recipient Pres. award, Ariz. Coalition for Tomorrow, 1998. Achievements include being a recognized expert in website and electronic services by the state bar of Arizona. Office: Michael Simes LLC 903 S Rural Rd #101-323 Tempe AZ 85281 Business E-Mail: info@michaelsimes.com

**SIMES, STEPHEN MARK,** pharmaceutical executive; b. N.Y.C., Nov. 23, 1951; s. Herbert H. and Mimi (Maurer) S.; m. Anita H. Herzog, Aug. 23, 1975. BS in Chemistry, Bklyn. Coll., 1973; MBA in Mktg., NYU, 1980. Sales rep. G.D. Searle and Co., N.Y.C., 1974-78, supr. sales tng. Chgo., 1978-79, dist. sales mgr. N.Y.C., 1979-81, product mgr. Chgo., 1981-82, sr. product mgr., 1982-83, dir. pub. affairs and communications, 1983-84; v.p. Gynex Inc., Chgo., 1984-88; dir. Gynex Pharms. Inc., Deerfield, 1985-93; pres., dir. Gynex Labs., Chgo., 1985-88; pres., CEO Contracap Inc., 1988-89, Gynex Pharms., Inc., Chgo., 1989-93, chmn., 1992-93; sr. v.p., dir. Bio-Technology Gen. Corp., 1993-94; pres., CEO, dir. Unimed Pharms., Inc., 1994-97; bd. dirs., CEO, pres. Simes Pharm. Cons., 1997-98. Vice chmn., CEO, pres., BioSante Pharms., Inc., Lincolnshire, Ill., 1998—. Mem.: Internat. Soc. For Study of Women's Sexual Health, Drug Info. Assn., iBio, Biotech. Industry Orgn., N.Am. Menopause Soc., Endocrine Soc., Licensing Exec. Soc., Chgo. Coun. Fgn. Rels. Office: 111 Barclay Blvd Lincolnshire IL 60069

**SIMIC, CHARLES,** language educator, poet; b. Beograd, Yugoslavia, May 9, 1938; arrived in U.S., 1954, naturalized, 1971; s. George and Helen (Matijevich) Simic; m. Helen Dubin, Oct. 1964; children: Anna, Philip. BA, NYU, 1967. Editl. asst. Aperture, Quar. of Photography, N.Y.C., 1966—69; prof. English Calif. State U., Hayward, Calif., 1970—73, U. N.H., Durham, NH, 1973—. Author: What the Grass Says, 1967, Somewhere Among us a Stone is Taking Notes, 1969, Dismantling the Silence, 1971, White, 1972, Return to a Place Lit by a Glass of Milk, 1974, Biography and a Lament, 1976, Charon's Cosmology, 1977, Classic Ballroom Dances, 1980, Austerities, 1982, Weather Forecast for Utopia and Vicinity, 1983, Selected Poems, 1985, rev. edit., 1990, Unending Blues, 1986, The World Doesn't End, 1989 (Pulitzer Prize for poetry, 1990), The Book of Gods and Devils, 1990, Hotel Insomnia, 1992, A Wedding in Hell, 1994, Frightening Toys, 1995, Walking the Black Cat, 1996, Looking for Trouble, 1997, Selected Early Poems, 1999, Jackstraws, 1999, rev. edit., 2000, Night Picnic, 2001, Voice at 3 A.M., 2003, My Noiseless Entourage, 2005, (essays) The Uncertain Certainty, 1985, (novels) Wonderful Words, Silent Truth, 1990, Dimestore Alchemy, 1992, The Unemployed Fortune Teller, 1994, Orphan Factory, 1998, A Fly in the Soup, 2000, Metaphysician in the Dark, 2003; translator (with C.W. Truesdale): Fire Gardens, 1970; translator: The Little Box, 1970; translator: (with Mark Strand) Another Republic, 1976; translator: Four Modern Yugoslav Poets, 1970, Homage to the Lame Wolf, 1979; translator: (with P. Kastmiler) Atlantis, 1987; translator: Roll Call of Mirrors, 1987, Some Other Wine and Light, 1989, Bandit Wind, 1991, The Horse Has Six Legs, 1992, Night Mail, 1992, Devil's Lunch, 1999, A Wake for the Living, 2002; contbr. Selected Poems of Tomaz Salamun, 1987, RollCall of Mirrors, 1987, poems to mags. and anthologies. With U.S. Army, 1961—63. Recipient PEN Internat. award for transl., 1970, 1980, Edgar Allan Poe award, Am. Acad. Poets, 1975, award, Nat. Inst. Arts and Letters, 1976, AAAL award, 1976, Harriet Monroe poetry award, U. Chgo., 1980, CiCastignola award, Poetry Soc. Am., 1980; fellow Guggenheim fellow, 1972—73, Nat. Endowment for the Arts, 1974—75, 1979—80, Fulbright Travelling fellow, 1982, Ingram Merrill fellow, 1983—84, Mac Arthur fellow, 1984—89. Mem.: Acad. Arts and Letters. Home: PO Box 192 Strafford NH 03884-0192 Office: U NH Dept English Durham NH 03824

**SIMIONESCU, PETRU-AURELIAN,** engineering educator, researcher; b. Deva, Hunedoara, Romania, Feb. 26, 1968; s. Aurelian and Elena Simionescu; m. Florentina Popa, Feb. 26, 2000. BS, Polytechnica U., Bucharest, Romania, 1992; PhD, Polytechnica U., 1999, Auburn U., Ala., 2004. Asst. prof. U. Tulsa, 2005—. Vis. scholar U. Newcastle, Newcastle upon Tyne, 1997, Auburn U., Ala., 1999—2001. Author various jour. articles. Tempus grant, European Union, 1995, Acad. Exch. grant, Romanian Min. Edn., 1996. Mem.: ASME (licentiate), Soc. Automotive Engrs. (licentiate), Soc. Indsl. and Applied Math. (licentiate). Office: U Tulsa 600 S College Ave Keplinger Hall L185 Tulsa OK 74104-3189 Office Fax: 918-631-2397. Business E-Mail: psimionescu@utulsa.edu.

**SIMIS, THEODORE LUCKEY,** investment banker, information technology executive; b. NYC, June 17, 1924; s. Theodore William Ernest and Helen (Luckey) S.; m. Laura Cushman Ingraham, Sept. 8, 1946; children—Nancy Simis Ricca, Theodore Steven, Karen Simis Woods, June Simis Sobocinski BS, NYU, 1950, MBA, 1952. With Bell System, 1941-79; various positions to officer level with N.Y. Telephone Co., N.J. Telephone Co., and AT&T; v.p. Warner Amex Cable Co., 1980-81; sr. v.p. E.F. Hutton, Sarasota, Fla., 1982-87; vice chmn., bd. dirs. XMX Corp., Burlington, Mass., 1986-2000, 2005—, OPIX Corp., Burlington, 2000—04; pres. Pvt. Transatlantic Telecommunication System Inc., McLean, Va., 1987-89; chmn. Value Added Network System, Inc., Sarasota, Fla., 1990-91. Dir. Liebenzell Mission, Schooleys Mountain, N.J.; vis. Nieman fellow Harvard U., 1977. Life mem. Republican Nat. Com., 1981—. 1st lt. USA Army, 1942-53, ETO Mem. N.Y. Acad. Scis., U.S. C. of C., NYU Club. Lutheran. Home: 6025 Manasota Key Rd Englewood FL 34223-9245 Fax: 941-475-1128. Office Phone: 941-474-8690. Personal E-mail: tlslns@cs.com.

**SIMITIS, SPIROS,** legal educator; b. Athens, Greece, Oct. 19, 1934; s. George and Fanny (Christopoulo) S.; m. Ilse Grubrich, Aug. 3, 1963. JD, U. Marburg, Fed. Republic Germany, 1956. Assoc. prof. U. Frankfurt, Fed. Republic Germany, 1963, prof., 1969, U. Giessen, Fed. Republic Germany, 1964-69; vis. prof. London Sch. Econs., U. Calif. - Berkeley, 1976, U. Pa., 1980, U. Strasbourg, France, 1987-88, Paris, 1990—2001, Yale U., New Haven, 1981—. Sec. gen. Internat. Civil Status Commn., 1966—80; chmn. Data Protection Experts Com. of the Coun. of Europe, Strasbourg, 1982—86; with Hesse Data protect commr., 1975—91; mem. rsch. coun. European Univ. Inst.; chmn. social rights com. European Commn., 1998; chmn. German Nat. Ethic Coun., 2000—05. Contbr. numerous articles to legal publs. Mem.: Athens Acad. Scis., German Coun. Pvt. Internat. Law, German Lawyers Assn. (bd. dirs. 1970—82). Office: Johann Wolfgang Goethe U Senckenberganlage 31 Postfach 111932 60054 Frankfurt Germany Office Phone: 0049-69-79822733. E-mail: simitis@jur.uni-frankfurt.de.

**SIMJEE, AISHA,** ophthalmologist, educator; b. Surat, India, Jan. 23, 1944; came to U.S., 1970; d. Yusuf Esmail Simjee and Amina Ahmed Badat; m. Sabbir A. Dadabhai, Apr. 28, 1978; children: Alia Dadabhai, Sufia Dadabhai. Intermediate Sci. degree, Rangoon (Burma) U., 1963; MB, BS, Inst. Medicine, Rangoon, 1968. Diplomate Am. Bd. Ophthalmology. Intern Rangoon Gen. Hosp., 1968-69, South Balt. Gen. Hosp., 1970-71; rschr. in ophthalmology Johns Hopkins Hosp., Balt., 1971-72; resident in ophthalmology Eye Dept. Howard U. Hosp., D.C. Gen. Hosp., Armed Forces Inst. Pathology, Washington, 1972-75; fellow in cornea external diseases Wills Eye Hosp., Phila., 1975-76; fellow in ophthalmic pathology and med. retina Scheie Eye Inst., Phila., 1976-77; asst. prof. ophthalmology Howard U., Washington, 1977-78; clin. assoc. prof. ophthalmology U. Calif., Irvine, 1978—; pvt. practice Orange, Calif. Mem. med. adv. bd. Orange County Eye & Tissue Bank, 1990—; attending physician St. Joseph Hosp., Orange, 1978—, U. Calif. Irvine Med. Ctr., 1978—. Contbr. articles to profl. jours. Vol. ophthalmologist La Amistad de Jose Clinic, Spanish Care Program of St. Joseph Hosp., 1988—, Testing 1-2-3 Screening Clinic St. Joseph Hosp., ann. eye screening for local sch. children, Project Orbis, S.E.E. Internat., Santa Barbara, Am. Eye Care Project, Hope World Wide, 2002—, Internat. Asst. Mission, 2002—. Named Woman of Achievement, Rancho Santiago Coll., Santa Ana, 1990; recipient certs. of recognition Calif. state senator John Seymour, Calif. congressman Christopher Cox, Calif., lt. gov. Leo McCarthy; recipient Pride in the Profession award AMA Found., 2005, Woman of Vision award We Give Thanks or Orange County, 2006. Fellow ACS, Am. Acad. Ophthalmology (Nat. Eye Care Project 1986—); mem. AMA (Pride in Profession award 2005), Calif. Med. Assn., Orange County Med. Assn. (bd. dirs. 1995-02), Orange County Soc. Ophthalmology (exec. com. 1992-02). Office: 1310 W Stewart Dr Ste 501 Orange CA 92868-3856 Office Phone: 714-771-2020. Personal E-mail: drsimjee@sbcglobal.net.

**SIMKANICH, JOHN JOSEPH,** lawyer, engineer; b. Clairton, Pa., 1941; BSEE, Drexel Inst. Tech., 1964; MSEE, Purdue U., 1966; JD, George Washington U., 1972. Bar: U.S. Patent Office 1970, Pa. 1973, U.S. dist. Ct. (ea. dist.) Pa. 1977, U.S. Supreme Ct. 1977, U.S. Ct. Appeals (Fed. cir.) 1982, U.S. Ct. Appeals (3d cir.) 1992. Elec. engr. U.S. Steel Co., 1963-65; engr. Westinghouse Aerospace, Balt., 1966-69; sys. developer TRW Sys. Inc., Washington, 1969-70; patent atty. Burroughs Corp., Paoli, Pa., 1970-74, Johnson & Johnson, New Brunswick, NJ, 1974-77; pvt. practice intellectual property law Phila., 1977—. Adv. Soup, Inc., Washington, 1970-72; introducted to FTC truth-in-advt. law; presenter in field. Patentee in field; product developer and licensing; analog and digital computer designer, programmer. Mem. IEEE (sr.), Pa. Bar Assn., Bucks County Bar Assn., Phila. Intellectual Property Law Assn., Am. Intellectual Property Law Assn., Delta Theta Phi, Eta Kappa Nu. Roman Catholic. Republican. Avocations: marathons, triathlons. Office: Paul & Paul 2900 Two-Thousand Market St Philadelphia PA 19103

**SIMKIN, STEVEN,** lawyer; b. NYC, Aug. 6, 1947; BS cum laude, U. Pa., 1969, MCP, JD cum laude, 1973. Bar: N.Y. 1974, U.S. Dist. Ct. (so. dist.) N.Y., U.S. Ct. Appeals (2nd cir.). Ptnr. Paul, Weiss, Rifkind, Wharton & Garrison, N.Y.C., 1982—, chair, Real Estate Dept. Assoc. editor U. Pa. Law Rev., 1972-73. Mem. N.Y. State Bar Assn. (exec. com. real property law sect. 1988-90), Order of Coif, Pi Gamma Nu, Beta Gamma Sigma. Office: Paul Weiss Rifkind Wharton & Garrison 1285 Avenue Of The Americas Fl 22 New York NY 10019-6064 Office Phone: 212-373-3073. Office Fax: 212-373-2058. Business E-Mail: ssimkin@paulweiss.com

**SIMKIN, TOBY JAMES,** theater producer, consultant; b. Chalfont, England, Apr. 21, 1964; s. Brigadier Byron and Irene Simkin; life ptnr. DJ Wizniak, May 11, 1988. Exec. prodr. Nederlander Worldwide Entertainment, NYC, 1999—. Cons. Music Theatre Internat., NYC, 1995—; bd. mem. Delphi Prodns., NYC, 2003—05. Prodr.: (broadway musicals and plays). Mem.: League Am. Theaters & Prodrs. (assoc.). Office: Nederlander Worldwide Entertainment 1450 Broadway 20th Fl New York NY 10018

**SIMKO, JAN,** English, foreign language and literature educator; b. Zlaté Moravce, Slovakia, Oct. 30, 1920; arrived in U.S., 1967; s. Simon Simko and Terezia Simkova; m. Libusa Safarikova, Dec. 20, 1950 (div. 1970, dec. 2004); children: Jan, Vladimir (dec.). Diploma in English, U. Bratislava, 1942, Diploma in German, 1943, PhD in English, 1944; MPhil in English, U. London, 1967. Tchr. English and German various bus. schs., 1942-45; asst. depts. English and German U. Bratislava, 1945-46; instr. English Econom U., 1946-47; faculty U. Bratislava, 1950-68, from asst. prof. to prof. English, 1957-68; prof. English Rio Grande Coll., Ohio, 1968-75. Instr. Shakespeare Georgetown U., 1984; vis. prof. English, scholar-in-residence W. Va. U., Parkersburg, 1989-90; instr. Slovak Fgn. Svc. Inst., Washington, 1974, 96, fed. govt., 1989, 91-93, IMF & World Bank, 1994-95; examiner critical langs. program Kent (Ohio) State U., 1974-91; feature writer Voice of Am., 1983-94; translator U.S. Dept. State, 1997—2005; dd. linguistics Slovak Acad. of Scis., 1957-67. Author: 3 English textbooks, 2 bilingual dictionaries, 1 linguistic monograph; editor: Lectures in the Circle of Modern Philology, 2 vols., 1965-66; chief consulting editor: textbooks of Slovak and Czech, 1993-96; contbg. writer: The Review, 1995-2002; Am./Can.-Slovak press; contbr. articles to profl. jours. With Czechoslovak infantry, 1946. Grantee Brit. Coun., 1947-49, Folger Shakespeare Libr./U.S. Dept. State, 1967-68; Internat. Rsch. and Exch. Bd., 1982, others; recipient awards W.Va. U., 1990, Bratislava U., 1995, medal Pres. of Slovakia, 2002. Mem. MLA (life), Slovak Studies Assn., Soc. for Slavic and Arts, Met. Opera Guild, Shakespeare Theatre Guild, Nat. Symphony Orch. Assn., English-Speaking Union. Roman Catholic. Avocations: classical music, opera, theater, fine arts, swimming. Home: Apt 511 725 24th St NW Washington DC 20037 Office Phone: 202-429-8899. Personal E-mail: jansimko@hotmail.com.

**SIMMAN, RICHARD,** plastic surgeon, researcher; arrived in U.S., 1993; BS, Louvain Cath. U., Brussels, MD, 1991. Asst. prof. surgery East Tenn. State U., Johnson City, 2001—03; dir. of rsch., program dept. of surgery, divsn. of plastic surgery Wright State U. Sch. of Medicine, Dayton, Ohio,

2003—. Cons. Pfizer, 2002—. Contbr. articles to profl. jours. Grantee, Wright State U. Sch. of Medicine, 2004. Mem.: Coll. of Cert. Wound Specialists (bd. dirs.), Am. Acad. Wound Mgmt. (life). Achievements include research in wound healing and tissue engineering using adult stem cells. Avocations: travel, music, fishing. Office: Wright State U Sch Medicine One Wyoming St Weber CHE 7000 Dayton OH 45409 Office Phone: 937-208-4955. Personal E-mail: richard.simman@wright.edu.

**SIMMONDS, RAE NICHOLS,** musician, composer, educator; b. Lynn, Mass., Feb. 25, 1919; d. Raymond Edward and Abbie Iola (Spinney) Nichols; m. Carter Fillebrown, Jr., June 27, 1941 (div. May 15, 1971); children: Douglas C. (dec.), Richard A., Mary L., Donald E.; m. Ronald John Simmonds, Oct. 9, 1971 (dec. Nov. 1995). AA, Westbrook Coll., Portland, Maine, 1981; B in Music Performance summa cum laude, U. Maine, 1984; MS in Edn., U. So. Maine, 1989; PhD, Walden U., 1994. Founder, dir. Studio of Music/Children's Studio of Composer, Portsmouth, NH, 1964-71, Studio of Music, Bromley, England, 1971-73, Bromley Children's Theatre, 1971-73, Oughterard Children's Theatre, County Galway, Ireland, 1973-74, Studio of Music, Portland, Maine, 1977-96, West Baldwin, Maine, 1997—; resident playwright Children's Theatre of Maine, Portland, 1979-81; organist, choir dir. Stevens Ave. Congl. Ch., Portland, 1987-95; field faculty advisor Norwich U., Montpelier, Vt., 1995. Field advisor grad. program U. Coll., Norwich U., 1995; cons./educator mus. tng. for disabled vets. VA, Portsmouth, N.H., 1966-69; show pianist and organist, mainland U.S.A., 1939-59, Hawaii, 1959-62, Rae Nichols Trio, 1962—; mus. dir. Theatre By the Sea, Portsmouth, N.H., 1969-70. Author/composer children's musical: Shamrock Road, 1980 (Blue Stocking award 1980), Glooscap, 1980; author/composer original scripts and music: Cinderella, If I Were a Princess, Beauty and the Beast, Baba Yaga - A Russian Folk Tale, The Journey - Musical Bible Story, The Perfect Gift - A Christmas Legend; original stories set to music include: Heidi, A Little Princess, Tom Sawyer, Jungle Book, Treasure Island; compositions include: London Jazz Suite, Bitter Suite, Jazz Suite for Trio, Sea Dream, Easter (chorale), Rae Simmonds Jazz Trio Songbook Series, (CD) Fascinatin' Gershwin Rae Simmonds Jazz Trio, 2000; contbr. Maine Women Writers Collection. Recipient Am. Theatre Wing Svc. award, 1944, Pease AFB Svc. Club award, 1967, Bumpus award Westbrook Coll., 1980; Nat. Endowment for Arts grantee, 1969-70; Women's Lit. scholar, 1980, Westbrook scholar, 1980-81, Nason scholar, 1983; Kelaniya U. (Colombo, Sri Lanka) rsch. fellow, 1985-86. Mem. ASCAP, Internat. Soc. Poets, Internat. League Women Composers, Music Tchrs. of Maine, Am. Guild of Organists, Music Tchrs. Nat. Assn., Internat. Alliance for Women in Music, Doctorate Assn. N.Y. Educators, Inc., Delta Omicron, Phi Kappa Phi. Democrat. Episcopalian. Avocations: travel, stamp collecting/philately. Home: 230 Douglas Hill Rd West Baldwin ME 04091-9715

**SIMMONDS, ROBERT MAURER,** education educator; b. Beaver Falls, Pa., Apr. 16, 1947; s. Harold Maurer and Mary Simmonds; m. Deborah Lynne Carawan, June 25, 1977; children: Stephen Maurer, Kent Hayes. BS, Youngstown State U., 1973, MS, 1975; advanced cert. edn., Coll. William and Mary, 1983, EdD, 1985; grad. sr. exec. fellows program JFK Sch. Govt., Harvard, 2004. Regional planner Southeastern Va. Planning Dist. Commn., Norfolk, 1977—78; statis. rsch. analyst Nat. Ctr. for State Cts., Williamsburg, Va., 1978—82; assoc. prof. St. Leo Coll., Ft. Eustis, Va., 1982—85; ops. rsch. analyst U.S. Army Transp. Sch., Ft. Eustis, 1985—88, assoc. prof. ops. rsch., 1988—2001; dept. chmn. sys. engring. dept. U.S. Army Logistics Mgmt. Coll., Ft. Lee, 2001—. Cons. Dep. Chief of Staff for Tng., Ft. Monroe, Va., 1992, Picatinny Arsenal, N.J., 1994-96, Concepts and Analysis Agy., Washington, 1999-2001. Contbr. articles to profl. jours. Bd. dirs. Terence M. Lyon Pediatric Arthritis and Other Related Diseases Assn., Inc. With USN, 1965—68. Avocations: walking, golf. Office: US Army Logistics Mgmt Coll 2401 Quarters Rd Fort Lee VA 23801-1705 Office Phone: 804-765-4607. Personal E-mail: orsased1@comcast.net. Business E-Mail: robert_simmonds@US.army.mil.

**SIMMONS, ADELE SMITH,** foundation executive, former educator; b. Lake Forest, Ill., June 21, 1941; d. Hermon Dunlap and Ellen T. (Thorne) Smith; m. John L. Simmons; children— Ian, Erica, Kevin BA in Social Studies with honors, Radcliffe Coll., 1963; PhD, Oxford U., Eng., 1969; LHD (hon.), Lake Forest Coll., 1976, Amherst Coll., 1977, Franklin Pierce Coll., 1978, U. Mass., 1978, Alverno Coll., 1982, Marlboro Coll., 1987, Smith Coll., 1988, Mt. Holyoke Coll., 1989, Am. U., 1992, Tufts U., 1994. Asst. prof. U. Boston, 1969-72; dean Jackson Coll., Medford, Mass., 1970-72; asst. prof. history, dean student affairs Princeton U., NJ, 1972-77; pres. Hampshire Coll., Amherst, Mass., 1977-89, John D. and Catherine T. MacArthur Found., Chgo., 1989—99; vice chair, sr. exec. Chgo. Metropolis 2020, 1999—; sr. assoc. Ctr. for Internat. Studies U. Chgo., 1999—2005. Bd. dirs. Marsh & McLennan Cos., N.Y.C., Shorebank Corp., Chgo., Union Concerned Scientists, Synergos Inst., Environ. Def., bd. mem., Am. Prospect; bd. dirs. Global Fund for Women, Field Mus., Chgo., Mexican Fine Arts Ctr. Mus., Chgo. Coun. on Fgn. Rels.; emeritus mem. bd. dirs. Rocky Mountain Inst.; former corr. in Mauritius and Tunisia for N.Y. Times, The Economist; high level adv. bd. UN, 1993—; mem. adv. com. World Bank Inst.; mem. bd. overseers Harvard U., 1972-78; chair Fair Labor Assn.; sr. advisor World Econ. Forum. Co-author: (with Freeman, Dunkle, Blau) Exploitation from 9 to 5: Twentieth Century Fund Task Force Report on Working Women, 1975; author: Modern Mauritius, 1982; contbr. articles on edn. and pub. policy in The N.Y. Times, Christian Sci. Monitor, The Bulletin of Atomic Scientist, Harper's, The Atlantic Monthly and others. Commr. Pres.'s Commn. on World Hunger, Washington, 1978-80, Pres.'s Commn. on Environ. Quality, 1991-92; mem. Commn. Global Governance; trustee Carnegie Found. for Advancement Teaching, 1978-86; chair Mayor Richard Daley's Youth Devel. Task Force, 1993-95. Named one of Chgo. 100 Most Influential Women, Crain's Chgo. Bus., 2004. Fellow Am. Acad. Arts and Scis.; mem. Phi Beta Kappa. Office: Chgo Metropolis 2020 30 W Monroe St Chicago IL 60603 Office Phone: 312-332-8161. Business E-Mail: adele.simmons@cm2020.org

**SIMMONS, ANNE L.,** federal official; b. Spencer, Iowa, Jan. 4, 1964; d. Donald Lewis and Lois Amber (Blass) S. B in Spl. Studies, Cornell Coll., 1986. Intern for Congressman Berkley Bedell, Washington, 1986; field staff Iowans for Clayton Hodgson, Sioux City, Iowa, 1986; exec. asst. Atomic Indsl. Forum, Bethesda, Md., 1986-87; staff asst. House Armed Svcs. Com., Washington, 1987; legis. asst. to Congressman Tim Johnson Washington, 1988-93; staff dir. gen. farms commodities subcom. House Agriculture Com., Washington, 1993, staff dir. environ., credit and rural devel. subcom., 1994, minority resource conservation rsch. and forestry subcom., 1995-96. Profl. Staff Ho. Com. on Agrl., 1997—. Music scholar Cornell Coll., 1982-86. Mem. Delta Phi Alpha. Democrat. Office: House Agriculture Com 1301 Longworth House Ofc Bldg Washington DC 20515-0001 E-mail: anne.simmons@mail.house.gov.

**SIMMONS, BILL,** sportswriter; b. Boston, Mass., 1969; m. Kari Simmons, Apr. 1, 1999. BA, Holy Cross Univ., Springfield, Mass., 1991. Free-lance website journalist, 1992—98; writer Jimmy Kimmel Live, 2003—04; Page 2 columnist ESPN.com, 1999—; columnist ESPN The Mag., 2003—. Appeared in (films) Doing Time on The Longest Yard, 2005, The Mean Machine, 2005; author: (sports book) Now I Can Die in Peace, 2005. Office: c/o ESPN 935 Middle St Bristol CT 06010*

**SIMMONS, CHARLES B., JR.,** lawyer; b. Wilmington, NC, Mar. 19, 1961; BA summa cum laude, Yale Univ., 1984; JD, Univ. Va., 1987. Bar: NC 1987. Ptnr., capital mkts group, ptnr.-in-charge, Charlotte Alston & Bird LLP, Charlotte, NC. Bd. dir. Junior Achievement Carolinas; adv. com. Queens Univ. Law Sch. Mem.: ABA, NC Bar Assn., Phi Beta Kappa. Office: Alston & Bird LLP Ste 4000 Bank of Am Plz 101 S Tryon St Charlotte NC 28280-4000 Office Phone: 704-444-1035. Office Fax: 704-444-1111. Business E-Mail: csimmons@alston.com.

**SIMMONS, CHARLES BEDFORD, JR.,** judge; b. Greenville, S.C., Dec. 4, 1956; s. Charles Bedford and Mary Margaret (Mason) S.; children: Charles B. III, Elizabeth S., Mason W. AA magna cum laude, Spartanburg Meth. Coll.,

1977; BS magna cum laude, E. Tenn. State U., 1979; JD, U. S.C., 1982. Bar: S.C. 1982, U.S. Dist. Ct. S.C. 1983, U.S. Ct. Appeals (4th cir.) 1986. Law clk. to presiding justice S.C. Cir. Ct., Greenville, 1982-83; with Carter Law Firm, Greenville, 1983-86; ptnr. Wilkins, Nelson, Kittredge & Simmons, Greenville, 1986-89; civil ct. judge Greenville, 1989—; presiding judge 13th Circuit Drug Ct. Mem. bench-bar com. S.C. Supreme Ct., 1992-97; presiding judge 13th cir. Drug Ct; bd. mem. Nat. Assn. Drug Ct. Profls Mem. adv. com. paralegal program Greenville Tech. Coll., 1989-97, chmn., 1990-91; mem. Friends of 200 Adv. Bd., 1991-99. Named Big Brother of Yr., Big Bros.-Big Sisters, 1988; recipient Svc. to Manking award Rotary Club, 1989, Outstanding Young Disting. Svc. award Greenville Jaycees, 1990-91. Mem. ATLA, S.C. Bar Assn. (young lawyer liason 1985-89, named Outstanding Young Lawyer of Yr. 1989), Nat. Assn. Drug Ct. Profls. (bd. dirs.), Greenville Bar Assn., S.C. Trial Lawyers Assn., Greenville Young Lawyers (pres. 1988—1990), Gamma Beta Phi, Pi Gamma Mu, Phi Delta Phi. Clubs: Greenville City, Textile (v.p. 1985-87), Revelers (Greenville). Presbyterian. Office: Ste 313 County Courthouse Greenville SC 29601 Office Phone: 864-467-8556. Business E-Mail: csimmons@greenvillecounty.org.

SIMMONS, CLINTON CRAIG, human resources executive; b. Cleve., Nov. 25, 1947; s. Benjamin F. and Catharin (Thornton) R.; m. Cheryl LeRoy, June 16, 1973; 1 child, Eric. BBA, Miami U., Oxford, Ohio, 1969; grad. quality mgmt. course, Winter Park, Fla., 1986. Cert. quality edn. system instr. Specialist employee, cmty. rels. Euclid Lamp Plant, GE, Cleve., 1970-75; employee, indsl. rels. rep. Bailey Controls Co., Wickliffe, Ohio, 1975-78; mgr., coll. recruiting Gen. Tire and Rubber, Akron, Ohio, 1978-81, profl. staffing coord., 1981-82; regional human resource mgr. Gilbane Bldg. Co., Cleve., 1982-86, human resource mgr. Western regions, 1987-88; asst. v.p., dir. human resources St. Alexis Hosp. Med. Ctr. CA Div. Sisters of St. Francis, 1988-90; corp. pers. mgr. MK-Ferguson Co., 1990-94, mgr. human resources, 1993-94; mgr. human resources engring., constrn. and environ. group Washington Group Internat., Cleve., 1994-2001, sr. mgr. human resources, 2001—; human resources cons. Key Source HCI, LLC, 2003—, Highbridge Assoc., 2003—; chmn. human resource consultors Health, Human Svcs. Secretariat Cath. Diocese Cleve., 2005—; pres. Diversity Leaders, LLC, 2005—. Author: (with w.J. McBurney Jr.) College Recruitment: Effective Programs and Practices, 1982. Past chmn. orgn. and extension com. Newton D. Baker Dist., Greater Cleve. coun. Boy Scouts Am., 1970-71; mem. Human Resource Com. for Greater Cleve. United Way, NAACP, Urban League of Cleve.; mem. pension and benefit coms. Greater Cleve. Hosp. Assn., 1988-90; Bd. Edn. commr. Villa Angela Acad. (pres., 1986-87, U.S. Edn. Dept. award 1987); founder, advisor Explorer Post, Gilbane Bldg. Co., Cleve., 1984-88; Cleve., 1988—; v.p. adv. bd. Cath. Social Svcs. Cuyahoga County, chmn. coun. advisors, 1992-93; mem. urban regional bd. Cath. Edn. Cleve., 1986; trustee Marotta Montessori Sch. of Cleve., 1993—, pres.-elect, 1993, chmn. coun. advisors Cath. Social Svcs. Cuyahoga County, 1992—; bd dirs CSA Health Sys., 2005-. Recipient commendation Nat. Alliance of Bus., Akron, 1979, Cmty. Svc. award WJW-Northwest Orient Airlines, 1975. Mem. Cleve. EEO Assn., Soc. Human Resources Mgmt., Soc. Am. Mil. Engrs., U.S. Naval Inst., Mid-West Coll. Placement Assn. (chmn. rubber industry com. 1979-81), Ctr. for Human Svcs. (v.p., trustee, vice chmn. bd. trustees), Internat. Human Resources Assn., Indsl. Rels. Rsch. Assn., Human Resources Systems Assn., Alpha Phi Alpha. Democrat. Roman Catholic. Home: 24400 Emery Rd Cleveland OH 44128-5614 E-mail: c.simmons@thekeysource.com, csimmons@highbridgeassociates.com.

SIMMONS, DANNY, JR., artist, poet, art gallery director, foundation administrator; Founder, pres. Rush Arts Gallery, NYC, Corridor Gallery, Bklyn.; co-founder Rush Philanthropic Arts Found., NYC; founder, dir. Def Poetry Jam, NYC. Exhibitions include NYC Groove, Noel Gallery, Charlotte, NC, 1999, Be Still & Listen, 2001, Represented in permanent collections Smithsonian Instn., Chase Manhattan Bank, March of Dimes, Schomberg Ctr. for Black Culture, UN Gen. Assembly, Warner Brothers/Black Pearl Entertainment. Bd. dir. Bklyn. Acad. Music. Brothers: Joseph Run Simmons of Run DMC and music producer Russell Simmons. Office: Rush Arts Gallery Ste 311 526 W 26th St New York NY 10001

SIMMONS, DEBORAH JO, pharmacist, director; b. Houston, July 31, 1953; d. Joe George Haskovec and Olga Norma (Clifton) Kirkland; m. Dennis Edwin Simmons, Mar. 24, 1979 (div. May 1988). BS, U. Tex., 1975. Registered pharmacist, Tex., Fla. Pharmacy intern Eckerd Drug Co., Dallas County, Tex., 1976, pharmacist, 1976-82, pharmacy area mgr. north Tex. Garland, 1982-86, pharmacy svcs. mgr. north Tex., 1986-90, pharmacy svcs. mgr. Largo, Fla., 1990-92; dir. pharmacy devel. Eckerd Corp., Largo, 1992—2002, sr. dir. pharmacy devel., 2002—05. Dir. Eckerd Credit Union, Largo, 1993, 96, 98, vice-chair, 1994-95, 97. Mem. Am. Pharmacy Assn. (administrv. practice mem.-at-large 1997-99, chair-elect 2000, chair 2001, nominating com. 1999, 2000, publs. com. 1997-98, awards com. 2000, pharmacy practice com. 2001), Tex. Pharmacy Assn. (pub. affairs com. 1988-91, vice-chair ho. dels. 1990-91, chair 1991-92), Fla. Pharmacy Assn. (orgnl. affairs coun. 1999-2001, profl. affairs coun. 2001-03), Dallas County Pharmacy Soc. (pres. 1989-90), Am. Heart Assn. (bd. dirs. Pinellas County, 1999-04, vice chmn. 2002-03, chmn. 2003-04). Avocations: travel, reading. Personal E-mail: dsimmons731@msn.com.

SIMMONS, DEBRA ADAMS, editor; m. Jonathan Simmons; children: Jacob, Jonathan. BA, Syracuse U., NY; diploma in Advanced Exec. Program, Northwestern U. Reporter Syracuse (N.Y.) Herald-Jour., The Hartford (Conn.) Courant; metro editor The Virginian Pilot; asst. metro editor and reporter Detroit (Mich.) Free Press; dep. mng. editor The Virginian-Pilot, Norfolk, Va., 2000—03; mng. editor Akron (Ohio) Beacon Jour., 2003, 2003—, v.p., 2003—. Office: Akron Beacon Journal 44 E Exchange St PO Box 640 Akron OH 44309-0640

SIMMONS, DEIDRE WARNER, retired performing company executive, arts consultant; b. Easton, Pa., May 11, 1955; d. Francis Joseph and Irene Carol (Burd) Mooney; m. Robert D. Jacobson, June 27, 1981 (div. Mar. 1989); m. William Richard Simmons, Aug. 18, 1990; children: Caitlin Dawn, Abigail Patricia, Samantha Irene. BA in Music, Montclair State Coll., 1978. Music tchr. Warren Hills Regional Sch., Washington, NJ, 1978-80; devel. dir. N.J. Shakespeare Festival, Madison, 1981-83; dir. contbns. Parent Found., Lancaster, Pa., 1983-86; exec. dir. Fulton Opera House, Lancaster, 1986—95, capital campaign counsel, 1995—2000, dir. theatre advancement, 2000—03; arts cons., 2003—. bd. dirs. WITF, vice chmn., 2005—; chmn. Lancaster Arts, 2005; bd. dirs Lancaster Country Day Sch. Vice chmn. bd. dirs. Ind. Eye, Lancaster, 1986—89; bd. dirs. Pa. Dutch Conv. and Visitors Bur., Lancaster Campaign; chair Destination Downtown. Recipient Exemplar award, Lancaster C. of C. and Industry, 2003. Mem.: League Hist. Theatres, Theatre Comm. Group. Avocations: piano, singing. E-mail: dwsimmons@comcast.net.

SIMMONS, DONNA MARIE, neuroscientist, histotechnologist, neuroendocrinologist, researcher; b. Hartford, Conn., Oct. 13, 1943; d. John Henry and Ellen Louise (Meehl) Strayer; m. Corvin Gale Simmons, Sept. 17, 1964. Student, U. Wash.. We. Wash. State U.; PhD, U. So. Calif., 2005. Histologic technician, instr. Tacoma Gen. Hosp. Sch. Med. Tech., Tacoma, 1963: lab. technician Med. Sch. U. Wash., 1964; histologic technician Northgate Med. Lab., Seattle, 1964—67; rsch. technologist in neuroanatomy Regional Primate Rsch. Ctr. U. Wash., 1967—82; rsch. asst. Devel. Neurobiology Lab. Salk Inst., La Jolla, Calif., 1982—85, sr. technician. lab. mgr. Neural Sys. Lab. Howard Hughes Med. Inst., 1985—90; vis. faculty neurosciences dept. Baylor U. Med. Sch., 1990; rsch. assoc. dept. biol. scis.-neurobiology U. So. Calif., L.A., 1990—. Cons., lectr. in field; judge Greater San Diego Sci. and Engring. Fair, 1987-89, Calif. Sci. Fair, 1992—; leader sci. del. to People's Rep. of China, 1986; chair China Scientist Exch. Fund, 1986-87; mem. Swiss Histology Meeting Exch., 1990. Author: tech. articles, revs. in field; mem.

editl. bd. Jour. Histotech, 1982-2002. Recipient Diamond Cover award Jour. Histotech., 1990; various svcs. awards; best non-clin. pub. in field, 1985; Hudson Hoagland USA-Australia Exch. Med. Rsch. fellow Prince Henry's Rsch. Inst. Monash U., 1996. Mem. AAAS, Am. Soc. Clin. Pathologists (affiliate), Wash. State Histology Soc. (past pres., histology liason Am. Soc. Med. Tech.), Nat. Soc. Histotech. (charter, regional dir. 1980-82, jud. chair 1983-86), Calif. Soc. Histotech. (San Diego dir. protem 1985-86), Assn. Women in Sci. (San Diego charter, bd. dirs. 1985-90), Soc. for Neurosci., Women in Neurosci., N.Y. Acad. Sci., J.B. Johnston Club, Cajal Club, Sierra Club, NOW, Am. Alpine Club, Sigma Xi. Office: U So Calif Mc 2520 Los Angeles CA 90089-0001

SIMMONS, EDWIN HOWARD, military officer, historian; b. Paulsboro, N.J., Aug. 25, 1921; s. Edwin Lonsdale and Nettie Emma (Vankirk) S.; m. Frances Bliss, Apr. 25, 1962; children: Edwin Howard, Clarke Vankirk, Bliss, Courtney. BA, Lehigh U., 1942; MA, Ohio State U., 1955; postgrad., Amphibious Warfare Sch., 1949—50, Nat. War Coll., 1966—67. Commd. 2d lt. USMC, 1942, advanced through grades to brig. gen., 1967; asst. prof. NROTC, Ohio State U., 1952-55; with Hdqrs. Marine Corps, 1955- 59; naval attache Dominican Republic, 1959-60; with Hdqrs. Marine Corps and Joint Staff, 1962-65, 3d Marine Divsn., 1965-66, 1st Marine Divsn., Vietnam, 1970-71; dep. fiscal dir. Marine Corps, 1967-70; dir. Marine Corps history and museums USMC Hdqrs., Arlington, Va., 1971-95, dir. emeritus, 1996—. Pres. Am. Mil. Inst., 1979; v.p. U.S. Commn. Mil. History, 1979-83; exec. v.p. Marine Corps Hist. Found., 1979-96; pres. Coun. Am. Mil. Past, 1991-95. Author: The United States Marines, 1974, 76, 98, 2002, Marines, 1987, Dog Company Six, 2000, Frozen Chosin, 2002; editor: The Marines, 1998; mng. editor: Marine Corps Gazette, 1946-49; sr. editor: Publs. Group, Marine Corps Schs., 1960-61; Contbr. to numerous books, encys., mags., jours. and annuals. Decorated D.S.M., Silver Star, Legion of Merit with two gold stars, Bronze Star with gold star, Meritorious Svc. medal, Navy Commendation medal, Purple Heart; knight Nat. Order of Vietnam, Vietnamese Cross of Gallantry with 2 palms and silver star; recipient Centennial Disting. Grad. medallion Ohio State U., 1970. Fellow Co. Mil. Historians; mem. Am. Soc. Mil. Comptrollers (nat. v.p. 1967-69, pres. 1969-70), Nat. War Coll. Alumni Assn. (v.p. 1969-70, 74-75), Phi Beta Kappa, Omicron Delta Kappa, Phi Sigma Kappa. Home: 9020 Charles Augustine Dr Alexandria VA 22308-2822

SIMMONS, GARY, artist; b. NYC, Apr. 14, 1964; BFA, Sch. Visual Arts, 1988; MFA, Calif. Inst. Arts, 1990. Exhibited in group shows at Am. Fine Arts Co., NYC, 1989, Espace de Dieu, Paris, 1990, Simon Watson Gallery, NYC, 1990, 1991, Mus. Fine Arts, Boston, 1991, Walker Arts Ctr., Mpls., 1991, Madison Art Ctr., Wis., 1991, U. Calif., Riverside, 1992, Whitney Mus. Art, NYC, 1993, 1994, 1999, Stedelijk Mus., Eindhoven, Netherlands, 1996, Inst. Contemporary Art, Boston, 1997, Royal Coll. Arts, London, 1998, Mus. Modern Art, NYC, 1999, Main Line Art Ctr., Haverford, Pa., 2000, Mus. Contemporary Photography, Chgo., 2001, San Francisco Mus. Modern Art, Calif., 2003, Krannert Art Mus., Champaign, Ill., 2004, Contemporary Arts Mus., Houston, 2005, others, one-man shows include Jason Rubell Gallery, Miami, 1992, Galerie Philippe Rizzo, Paris, 1993, Smithsonian Inst., Washington, 1994, Lannan Found., LA, 1995, Galeri Charlotte Lund, Stockholm, 1997, Mus. Contemporary Art, San Diego, 1997, St. Louis Art Mus., 1999, Musee D'Art Americain, Giverny, France, 2000, Phila. Mus. Art, 2001, CAIS Gallery, Seoul, Korea, 2002, Metro Pictures, NYC, 1993, 1995, 1996, 1996, 1998, 2001, 2004, Margo Leavin Gallery, LA, 1998, 2000, 2003, 2005, Bohen Found., NYC, 2006, others. Mailing: c/o Margo Leavin Gallery 812 N Robertson Blvd Los Angeles CA 90069 also: c/o Metro Pictures Gallery 519 W 24th St New York NY 10011*

SIMMONS, GENE (CHAIM WITZ, GENE KLEIN), musician; b. Haifa, Israel, Aug. 25, 1949; came to U.S., 1958, naturalized, 1963; s. Flora Witz; children Nicholas, Sophie (with Shannon Tweed). BE, SUNY, 1970; BA in Edn., Richmond Coll., CUNY, 1972. Tchr., Spanish Harlem, NY; asst. to editor Glamour and Vogue; asst. to dir. Puerto Rican InterAgency Coun.; member in bands called Bullfrog Beer, Coffee, Long Island Sounds, Cathedral, and Wicked Lester; co-founder Kiss, 1973—; founder Simmons Records; ptnr. Simmons Abramson Mktg., 2006—; chmn. NGTV (No Good TV), 2006—. Albums (with Kiss): Kiss, 1974, Hotter Than Hell, 1974, Dressed to Kill, 1975, Alive, 1975, Destroyer, 1976, Rock & Roll Over, 1976, Love Gun, 1977, Alive II, 1977, Double Platinum, 1978, Dynasty, 1979, Unmasked, 1980, Music From the Elder, 1981, Killers, 1982, Creatures of the Night, 1982, Lick It Up, 1983, Animalize, 1984, Asylum, 1985, Crazy Nights, 1987, Hot In The Shade, 1989, Smashes, Thrashes and Hits, 1989, Revenge, 1992, Alive III, 1993, Kiss My Ass, 1995, MTV: Kiss Unplugged, 1996, Carnival of Souls, 1997, You Wanted the Best You Got the Best!, 1997, Greatest Kiss, 1997, Psycho Circus, 1998, Kiss: The Box Set, 2001, The Very Best of Kiss, 2002, Kiss Symphony Alive VI, 20th Century Masters: Millenium Collection Vol. 1 and 2, Kiss Gold, Kiss Rock the Nation; (solo albums) Gene Simmons, 1978, ***Hole, 2004; actor (films) Runaway, 1984, Never Too Young To Die, 1986, Trick or Treat, 1986, Wanted: Dead or Alive, 1987, The Decline of Western Civilization Part II: The Metal Years, 1988, The Return of Bruno, 1988, Red Surf, 1990, Detroit Rock City, 1999, Wish You Were Dead, 2000, The New Guy, 2002; (TV series) My Dad the Rock Star, 2003 Gene Simmons' Rock School, 2005, Gene Simmons Family Jewels, 2005-; (TV appearances) The Paul Lynde Halloween Special, 1976, KISS Meets the Phantom of the Park, 1978, Miami Vice, 1985, Hitchhiker, 1986, Millennium, 1996, Talk to Me, 2000, (voice only) Family Guy, 2001, 2002, 2005, King of the Hill, 2003 Who Wants to Be a Millionaire, 2001, At Any Cost, 2002, (voice only) King of the Hill, 2003, Gene Simmons TV Special '24/7', 2004, Third Watch, 2004; creater (TV) Baby 101, Mr. Romance, The Apprentice 3, 2005; guest judge American Idol: The Search for a Superstar, 2005; composer (films) Reform School Girls, 1986, Less Than Zero, 1987, (TV) Kiss: The Last Kiss, 2000, Kiss: Beyond the Makeup, 2001, (video game) Underground, 2003; prodr. (TV series) Detroit Rock City, 1999, Smash, 2001; writer (video) KISS: eXposed, 1987; author: Kiss and Makeup, 2001, Sex Money Kiss (both NY Times Best Selling Books), 2005; founder Simmons Publishing; published(magazine) Gene Simmons Tongue, 2001- (Sterling/Macfadden); Gene Simmons Game mag.; released (audio visual, CD) Speaking in Tongues; launched fashion label, Gene Simmons-Dragonfly, 2002; performer, writer (song) I Am Indy, 2006; TV commericals, shows and advertising associated with KISS include Cannon Camera (Japan), NASCAR, Nat. Hot Rod Assn. (NHRA), Pepsi Cola, Coca Cola, Holiday Inn, VISA cards, KISS/Platinum online comics, KISS Girls; sponsor Worldwide Mktg. and Branding of Indy Racing League, 2006-. Winner 27 Gold Record Albums, 9 Platinum Record Albums, 7 Multi-Platimun Record Albums. Mem. Am. Fedn. Musicians, AFTRA, ASCAP. Discovered Van Halen in 1977 and produced 15 song demo album; inventor of Axe bass guitar in 1980; speaks several languages English, Hungarian, Hebrew, German, learning Japanese and Mandarin Chinese; Kiss has been America's Number One Gold Record award winning group of all time according to RIAA; in honor of Gene Simmons US Postage Stamp; self-titled debut from the group BAG to mark first release from Gene Simmons' Simmons Records in over a decade in 2005. Office: $immons Records PO Box 15097 Beverly Hills CA 90210 *Listen to everyone around you, but do only what you believe.*

SIMMONS, GEOFFREY STUART, physician, educator, writer; b. Camp Gordon, Ga., July 28, 1943; s. Ted R. and Jane A. (Lavander) Simmons; m. Sherry Simmons, Sept. 7, 1985; children: Bradley, Anais. BS, U. Ill., 1965, MD, 1969. Diplomate Am. Bd. Internal Medicine; cert. instr., ham operator, trainer Cmty. Emergency Response Team. Intern U. So. Calif., L.A., 1969-70, resident, 1971-74; pvt. practice Astoria, Oreg., 1974-77, Eugene, Oreg., 1977—; chmn. internal medicine dept. Peace Health Med. Group, 1996-98, 2000—. Med. corres. KUGN Radio, 1993—95; chair Med. Res. Corps Coun., 2002—; trainer Cmty. Emergency Response Team. Author: (book) The Z Papers, 1977, The Adam Experiment, 1978, Pandemic, 1980, Murdock, 1982, The Glue Factory, 1995, To Glue or Not to Glue, 1997, What Darwin Didn't Know, 2004; med. commentator KABC Radio, 1970. Mem.: Eugene Citizen Corps., Lane County Med. Soc. (chmn. task force for disaster preparedness

2001—02, trainer cmty. emergency response team 2004—, vol. mgr. cert. program 2004—, lead cert. trainer cmty. emergency response teams). Avocations: writing, teaching disaster preparedness.

SIMMONS, GEORGE FINLAY, retired mathematics professor; b. Austin, Tex., Mar. 3, 1925; s. George Finlay and Armede Victoria (Hatcher) S.; m. Hope Bridgeford, Sept. 11, 1954; 1 child, Nancy Bingham. BS, Caltech, 1946; MS, U. Chgo., 1948; PhD, Yale U., 1957. Instr. U. Chgo., 1947-50, U. Maine, Orono, 1950-52, Yale U., New Haven, 1952-56; asst. prof. U. R.I., Kingston, 1956-58, Williams College, Williamstown, Mass., 1958-62; assoc. prof.-math. Colo. Coll., Colorado Springs, 1962-65, prof., 1965-90, prof. emeritus, 1990—. Author: Introduction Topology and Modern Analysis, 1962, Differential Equations, 1972, 3d edit., 2006, Precalculus Mathematics in a Nutshell, 1981, Calculus with Analytic Geometry, 1985, 2nd edit., 1995, Calculus Gems: Brief Lives and Memorable Mathematics, 1992. Mem. Math. Assn. Am. Avocations: travel, cooking, fishing, billiards. Home: 1401 Wood Ave Colorado Springs CO 80907-7348 Office: Colorado College Dept Math Colorado Springs CO 80903

SIMMONS, HAROLD C., sugar company executive; b. 1931; BA, MA, U. Tex., 1952. Investigator U.S. Civil Service, Dallas, 1952-55; book examiner Fed. Deposit Ins. Corp., Dallas, 1955-56; loan officer Republican Nat. Bank, Dallas, 1956-61; with Amalgamated Sugar Corp., Dallas, 1961—, chmn., chief exec. officer, also bd. dirs. Ogden, Utah; pres., chief exec. officer, dir. Contran Corp., Dallas; chmn., dir. NL Industries Inc., Houston, 1961—; chmn. Nat. City Lines, Dallas; chmn. bd. dir. Valhi, Inc., Dallas. Named one of Forbes' Richest Americans, 2006. Office: Valhi Inc Three Lincoln Centre 5430 Lbj Fwy Ste 1700 Dallas TX 75240-2620 also: NL Industries Inc 300 N Sam Houston Pky E Houston TX 77060-3301 Office: The Amalgamated Sugar Company 3184 Elder St Boise ID 83705-4709

SIMMONS, HARRIS H., banker; b. Salt Lake City, June 25, 1954; s. Roy William and Elizabeth (Ellison) S. BA in Econs., U. Utah, 1977; MBA, Harvard U., 1980. Comml. loan officer Allied Bancshares, Houston, 1980-81; asst. v.p. Zions Bancorp, Salt Lake City, 1981, fin. v.p., 1981-82; sr. v.p. fin. Zions Utah Bancorp, Salt Lake City, 1982-83, exec. v.p., sec., treas., 1984-86, pres., 1986—90; pres., CEO Zions 1st Nat. Bank, Salt Lake City, 1990—98, chmn., 1990—; pres., CEO Zions Bancorporation, Salt Lake City, 1990—, chmn., 2002—. Bd. dirs. Questar, Inc., Salt Lake City, Entrada Industries, Inc., Salt Lake City, Keystone Comm., Salt Lake City, Simmons Family, Inc., Salt Lake City, Zions 1st Nat. Bank, Salt Lake City, Nat. Bank Ariz., Tucson, Nev. State Bank, Las Vegas. Bd. dirs. United Way, Salt Lake City, 1983-89; bd. dirs. Utah Symphony, 1986—, vice chmn., 1990-95, chmn., 1995—; trustee Salt Lake City C.C., 1993—; v.p. fin. Great Salt Lake coun. Boy Scouts Am., 1991-95; co-chair Greater Salt Lake Shelter-the-Homeless Com., 1986-89, v.p. 1989—. Pres., dir., past vice-chmn. ABA; mem. Utah Bankers Assn. (bd.dirs. 1987-92, chmn. 1990-91), Salt Lake Area C. of C. (bd. dirs. 1991-94), Phi Beta Kappa. Mem. Lds Ch. Office: Zions Bancorporation 1 S Main St Salt Lake City UT 84111*

SIMMONS, HOWARD L., education educator; b. Mobile, Ala. BS in Secondary Edn., Spring Hill Coll., 1960; MAT in Slavic Langs. and Lit., Ind. U., 1965; PhD in Design and Mgmt. of Postsecondary Edn., Fla. State U., 1975; LHD (hon.), Sojourner-Douglass Coll., 1995; HHD (hon.), King's Coll., 1998. Assoc. dir., asst. exec. sec. Commn. on Higher Edn. Middle States Assn. Colls. and Schs., Phila., 1974-95, exec. dir., 1988-95; prof. edn. leadership in higher edn. Ariz. State U., Tempe, 1996-2000, prof. emeritus, 2000—, assoc. dean, 1996-97; chair Dept. Adv. Studies, Leadership and Policy, 2003—; prof., coord. higher edn. doctoral program Morgan State U., Balt., 2001—. Vis. lectr. Russian Lafayette Coll., Easton, Pa., 1970—71; part-time Russian/Spanish instr. Clayton (Mo.) High Sch., 1965—67; dean instructional servs. Northampton C.C., Bethlehem, Pa., 1972—74; chmn. dept. fgn. lang. Forest Park C.C., Mo., 1964—69; sr. rsch. Ariz. State U., 1986—87, Nat. Ctr. Postsecondary Governance and Fin., 1986—87; cons. in field including cons./evaluator North Ctrl. Colls. and Schs., 1997—; prin. cons. Global Cons. in Higher Edn.; apptd. mem. Bd. Behavioral Health Examiners State of Ariz, 1999; mem. commn. accreditation Coun. Chiropractic Edn., 2000; apptd. mem. Accreditation Commn. for Acupuncture and Oriental Medicine, 2002—; chair Accreditation Com. on Acupuncture and Oriental Medicine, 2005; keynote speaker in field. Contbr. articles to profl. jours. Gov. apptd. mem. Bd. Behavioral Health Examiners. NDEA grantee Spring Hill Coll., 1958-60, grantee Japan-U.S. Friendship Commn., 1993-94; NDEA fellow Ind. U., 1963-64, Edn. Professions Devel. Act fellow Fla. State U., 1973-75, fellow Am. Coun. Edn., 1972-73; USIA Acad. Specialist grantee, Quito, Ecuador, 1996; ETS-HBCU rsch. scholar, 2003-04. Mem. Accrediting Commn. for Acupuncture and Oriental Medicine (elected chair 2005—), Am. Ednl. Rsch. Assn., Am. Assn. for Cmty. and Jr. Colls. (assoc.), Assn. for Study of Higher Edn., Assn. Tchrs. Slavic and East European Langs., Assn. Caribbean Tertiary Instn., Am. Assn. for Higher Edn. (exec. bd. black caucus, nat. cultural diversity award by caucuses 1992), Lang. Labs. and Faculty Assn. Pres. (dir.), Phi Delta Kappa, Kappa Delta Pi. Home: 218 N Charles St Apt 604 Baltimore MD 21201 Office: Morgan State U Jenkins Hall 301 1700 E Cold Spring Ln Baltimore MD 21251 Office Phone: 443-885-1969. Business E-Mail: hsimmons@moac.morgan.edu. E-mail: simmons421@aol.com.

SIMMONS, JANET BRYANT, writer, publishing executive; b. Oakland, Calif., Apr. 22, 1925; d. Howard Pelton and Janet Horn (McNab) Bryant; m. William Ellis Simmons, May 17, 1944 (div. 1979); children: William Howard, Janet Margaret Simmons McAlpine. BA, San Jose State U., Calif., 1965; MA, U. San Francisco, 1979. Social worker Santa Clara County Social Svcs., San Jose, Calif., 1965-91; editor, pub. Enlightenment Press, Santa Clara, 1991—. Author: The Mystical Child, 1996. Mem. AAUW, Am. Booksellers Assn., Pubs. Mktg. Assn., Bay Area Ind. Pubs. Assn., Audubon Soc., Jacques Cousteau Soc. Avocations: playing piano, swimming, tai chi, travel, gardening. Office: Enlightenment Press PO Box 3314 Santa Clara CA 95055-3314 Personal E-mail: simmonssj@aol.com.

SIMMONS, JEAN BYERS, academic administrator, director; b. Ft. Worth, July 29, 1956; d. James Clifford and Don Jean Carter; m. Jim Allen Simmons, Sept. 30, 1973; children: Jeffrey Brent, Joshua Allen. B of Arts History magna cum laude, Columbia Coll., Mo., 2002; M of History, Tarleton State U., 2004. DataTel Columbia Coll., Columbia Coll., 2002—03, acad. advisor, 2003—05; dir. Embry Riddle Aeronautical U., 2005—. Trainer Columbia Coll., Columbia, Mo., 2000—05. Fund raising Little League, White Settlement, Tex., 1984—90; mem. PTA, 1980—93; treas. Brewer Bear Athletic Booster Club, 1990—93. Mem.: Phi Alpha Theta (life), Alpha Sigma Lambda (life). Democrat-Npl. Baptist. Avocations: travel, reading, swimming, researching. Home: 508 Meadow Park Dr White Settlement TX 76108 Office: Embry-Riddle Aeronautical Univ NAS JRB Bldg 1525 Fort Worth TX 76127 Office Phone: 817-737-8180. Personal E-mail: js114729@sbcglobal.net. Business E-Mail: jean.simmons@erau.edu.

SIMMONS, JOHN DEREK, retired financial consultant; b. Essex, Eng., July 17, 1931; arrived in U.S., 1952; s. Simon Leonard and Eve (Smart) Simmons; m. Rosalind Wellish, Mar. 5, 1961; children: Peter Lawrence, Sharon Leslie. BS, Columbia U., 1956; MBA, Rutgers U., 1959; postgrad., NYU, 1959-62. Chief cost acct. Airborne Accessories, Hillside, NJ, 1952-57; sr. cost analyst Curtiss-Wright Corp., Wood Ridge, NJ, 1957; sr. fin. analyst internat. group Ford Motor Co., Jersey City, 1958-60; sr. rsch. assoc. Nat. Assn. Accts. (now Inst. Mgmt. Accts.), N.Y.C., 1960-64; asst. to v.p. fin. Air Reduction Co., Inc., 1965—67; mgr. corp. planning Anaconda Wire & Cable Co., N.Y.C., 1968; assoc. cons. Rogers, Slade & Hill, Inc., N.Y.C., 1969-71; v.p., security analyst, economist Moore & Schley, Cameron & Co. (name now Fourteen Rsch. Corp.), 1972-81; v.p.; security analyst Merrill Lynch Capital Markets, N.Y.C., 1981-88; security analyst Arnhold and S. Bleichroeder, Inc., 1988—89; v.p., security analyst, corp. fin. specialist Smith Barney, Harris Upham & Co., Inc. (now Salomon Smith Barney, Inc.), 1989—90; sr. cons. Carl Byoir & Assocs., 1991—94; assoc. mng. dir. Commonwealth Assocs., 1994—95; mng. dir. State St. Capital Markets Corp., 1996; v.p. GKN

Securities Corp., 1996—97; dir. instnl. sales Gabelli & Co., Rye, 1997; assoc. Manning, Selvage & Lee, N.Y.C., 1998—2001; ret., 2001. Lectr. fin. bus. Rutgers U., NJ, 1957—64; lectr. Marymount Manhattan Coll., NYC, 2002—. Contbr. articles to profl. jours. Docent Asia Soc. and Mus., NYC, 2002—05. 1st lt. Brit. Army, 1950—52. Grantee personal coat of Arms, by Queen Elizabeth II: manorial Lord of Ash, Suffolk, Eng. Mem.: Knight Templar Sovereign Mil. Order Temple of Jerusalem. Home: 360 E 72d St New York NY 10021-4753 Personal E-mail: johnlordash@aol.com.

**SIMMONS, JOSEPH (RUN SIMMONS, REVEREND RUN)**, musician; b. Hollis, Queens, NY, Nov. 24, 1964; s. Daniel and Mary Simmons; m. Justine Jones Simmons, June 25, 1994; children: Daniel, Russell II; children: Angela, Vanessa, Joseph Jr. Founding mem. Run-D.M.C., 1983—2002. Co-owner & pres. Phat Farm Footwear; co-owner & CEO Run Athletics. Musician: (albums) Run-D.M.C., 1984, King of Rock, 1985, Raising Hell, 1986, Tougher Than Leather, 1988, Back from Hell, 1990, Down With the King, 1993, Crown Royal, 1999, (solo albums) Distortion; actor: (films) Krush Groove, 1986, Tougher Than Leather, 1988, Who's the Man?, 1993, Red Dragon, 2002; co-exec. prodr., actor (TV series) Run's House, 2005—. Ordained min. Zoe Ministries, NYC. Office: Phat Farm Corp Office 512 Fashion Ave New York NY 10018 also: Zoe Ministries 310 Riverside Dr New York NY 10025*

**SIMMONS, KENNETH JOSEPH**, lawyer; b. Cambridge, Mass., Nov. 13, 1941; s. John Joseph and Inez Theresa (Baptiste) S.; m. Carolyn Estella Cleland, June 10, 1972; children: Kenneth J., Stacey L., Lesley A., Christine R. AB, Boston Col., 1963; LLB, Suffolk U., 1966. Bar: Mass. 1967, U.S. Dist. Ct. Mass. 1970, U.S. Supreme Ct. 1973. Mem. McCarthy & August, Cambridge, 1969-74; ptnr. August & Simmons, Cambridge, 1974—. Executive bd. Cambridge coun. Boy Scouts Am., 1970-2001; fin. comm. Town of Arlington, Mass., 1976—; mem. dist. com. Boston Minuteman Coun., 2001—. Capt. U.S. Army, 1967-69, Vietnam. Mem. Cambridge-Arlington-Belmont Bar Assn. (pres. 1988-89), Middlesex County Bar Assn., Arlington Rotary Club (pres. 1978-79), Touchdown Club of Arlington (pres. 2000-01). Office: August & Simmons 161 3rd St Cambridge MA 02141-1795 Office Phone: 617-491-2112.

**SIMMONS, KIMORA LEE**, apparel designer, television personality, model; b. St. Louis, May 3, 1975; d. Vernon Whitlock and Joanne Perkins; m. Russell Simmons, 1998; 2 children. Former model Chanel; founder, CEO, dir. Baby Phat Clothing. Appearances include (films) Unzipped, 1995, Catwalk, 1996, Brown Sugar, 2002, The Big Tease, 1999, Beauty Shop, 2005, Rebound, 2005, (TV series) America's Next Top Model, 2003, Life & Style, 2004—, Fashion Week Diaries, 2005; exec. prodr.: (Broadway plays) Def Poetry Jam, 2003 (Tony award). Established Kimora Lee Simmons Scholarship Fund, Kimora Lee Simmons Foundation. Named Vibe Vixen, Vibe mag., 2005, Outstanding Stylemaker, Asian Excellence Awards, 2006. Office: Sony Pictures Entertainment 10202 W Washington Blvd Culver City CA 90232*

**SIMMONS, LEE GUYTON, JR.**, zoological park director; b. Tucson, Feb. 20, 1938; s. Lee Guyton and Dorothy Esther (Taylor) S.; m. Marie Annette Geim, Sept. 6, 1959; children: Lee Guyton, Heather, Heidi. Student, Cen. State Coll.; DVM, Okla. State U. Resident veterinarian Columbus Zoo, Powell, Ohio, 1965-66, Henry Doorly Zoo, Omaha, 1966-70, dir., 1970—. Research cons. VA Hosp.; assoc. instr. U. Nebr. Med. Ctr., Omaha; assoc. clin. prof. Creighton U. Sch. Dentistry. Contbr. articles to profl. jours. Bd. dirs. Nebr. State Mus., Lincoln. Served with USAR. Recipient Nat. Idealism award City of Hope, 1979; named Man of Yr., Lions Club, 1978. Fellow AVMA, Am. Assn. Zool. Veterinarians (pres.), Am. Assn. Zool. Parks, Nebr. Vet. Med. Assn. (Veterinarian of Yr. 1979). Lodges: Rotary. Office: Henry Doorly Zoo Office of the Director 3701 S 10th St Omaha NE 68107-2200

**SIMMONS, LYNDA MERRILL MILLS**, retired principal; b. Salt Lake City, Aug. 31, 1940; d. Alanson Soper and Madeline Helene (Merrill) Mills; m. Mark Carl Simmons, Nov. 17, 1962; children: Lisa Lynn Simmons Morley, William Mark, Jennifer Louise, Robert Thomas. BS, U. Utah, Salt Lake City, 1961, MS, 1983. Cert. sch. adminstr., Utah. Tchr. Wasatch Jr. H.S./Granite Dist., Salt Lake City, 1961-64, Altamont (Utah) H.S./Duchesne Dist., 1964-66; tchr. spl. edn. Park City (Utah) H.S., 1971-73; resource tchr. Eisenhower Jr. H.S., Salt Lake City, 1979-88; tchr. specialist Granite Sch. Dist., Salt Lake City, 1985-90; asst. prin. Bennion Jr. H.S., Salt Lake City, 1990-93; prin. Hartvigsen Sch., Salt Lake City, 1993—2002; ret., 2002. Adj. prof. spl. edn. U. Utah, Salt Lake City, 1987—, Utah Prin. Acad., 1994-95, co-chair Utah Spl. Educators for Computer Tech., Salt Lake City, 1988-90; adv. com. on handicapped Utah State Office Edn., 1990-93; presenter in field; ednl. cons. 2006-. Author: Setting Up Effective Secondary Resource Program, 1985; contbr. articles to profl. jours. Dist. chmn. Heart Fund, Cancer Dr., Summit Park, Utah, 1970-82; pack leader Park City area Boy Scouts Am., 1976-80; bd. dirs. Jr. League Salt Lake City, 1977-80, cmty. bd., 1997—; cookie chmn. Park City area Girl Scouts U.S., 1981; dist. chmn. March of Dimes, 1982—. Recipient Amb. award Salt Lake Conv. and Vis. Bur., 1995; named Bus. Woman of Yr., South Salt Lake C. of C., 2001. Mem. Nat. Assn. Secondary Sch. Prins., Park City Young Women's Mut. (pres. 1989-93, family history coms. 1993-95), Women's Athanaeum (v.p. 1990-93, pres. 1994-2001), Gen. Fedn. Women's Clubs (pres. Salt Lake dist. 1998-2002, comty.-improvement chairperson Utah 1996-98, chairperson Woman of Yr., 1998—) Coun. for Exceptional Children (pres. Salt Lake chpt. 1989-90, pres. Utah Fedn. 1991-93, Spl. Educator of Yr. 1995), Granite Assn. Sch. Adminstrs. (sec.-treas. 1992-94); Mission for Ch. of Jesus Christ of Latter Day Saints, Blacksburg, Va. 2001-04 Mem. Lds Ch. Avocations: reading, cooking, writing, sports, handiwork.

**SIMMONS, LYNDA TEEL**, nurse, healthcare executive; d. A. Stokes. A in Nursing, Columbus Coll., 1969, BA in Psychology, 1973; BSN, Troy State U., 1984, MSN magna cum laude, 1986. RN State Med. Agy., Clin. Nurse Specialist. Head nurse emergency room Columbus Med. Ctr., Ga., 1972—75; hosp. supr. Drs. Hosp. Hosp. Corp. Am., 1975—80; dir. surgical nursing divsn. Columbus Med. Ctr., 1980—82; critical care instr. BSN Program Auburn U., Auburn, Ala., 1985; RN State Med. Agy., Columbus, Ga., 1988—93; CEO Simmons Healthcare Enterprises, 1996—. Lectr. seminars, 2004. Mem.: Am. Assn. Critical Care Nurses, Emergency Nurse Assn., Soc. Critical Care Medicine, Am. Assn. Legal Nurse Cons., Sigma Theta Tau. Avocations: horseback riding, fencing, tennis, swimming. Office: Simmons Healthcare Enterprises 1303 Pagoda Dr Columbus GA 31907

**SIMMONS, MARK PITKIN**, botanist, educator; b. Norfolk, Va., Apr. 6, 1972; s. Vernon Pitkin and Lida Swaney Simmons. BA, U. Richmond, 1994; PhD, Cornell U., 2000. Postdoctoral fellow Ohio State U., Columbus, 2000—01; asst. prof. Colo. State U., Ft. Collins, 2001—. Curator herbarium Colo. State U., 2001—. Contbr. articles to profl. jours., chapters to books. Bd. dirs. Colo. Native Plant Soc., Denver, 2002—04. Recipient Pub.'s award for excellence, Soc. Systematic Biologists, 2000; fellow Mellon Found., 1995—99; grantee NSF, 2003—. Fellow: Willi Hennig Soc. Avocations: rock and ice climbing, motorcycling, triathlons. Office: Dept Biology Colo State U Fort Collins CO 80523 Office Fax: 970-491-0649. Business E-mail: psimmons@lamar.colostate.edu.

**SIMMONS, MARTHA R.**, mortgage company executive; Grad., Am. Bankers Assn. Nat. Trust Sch., Northwestern U., Am. Bankers Assn. Nat. Commercial Lending Sch., U. Okla., Sch. for Exec. Develop., U. Ga. Former bus. mgr. SunTrust Bank; former pres. Gainesville, Ga. market SunTrust Mortgage, Inc. (subsidiary of SunTrust Bank), bus. mgr., central region Richmond, Va., 2002—04, exec. v.p., nat. retail production mgr., 2004—. Former vice chair of edu. Greater Hall Chamber of Commerce, former chmn., co-chair, HALLmark Initiative campaign, 2001. Named one of 25 Women to Watch, US Banker mag., 2005. Office: SunTrust Mortgage Inc 901 Semmes Ave Richmond VA 23224-2270*

**SIMMONS, MARVIN GENE**, retired geophysics educator; b. Dallas, May 15, 1929; s. Burt H. and Mable (Marshall) S.; m. Dorothy Richter; children by previous marriage: Debra Lynn, Sandra Kay, Pamela Jean. BS, Tex. Agrl. and Mech. Coll., 1949; MS, So. Methodist U., 1958; PhD, Harvard U., 1962. Registered profl. geologist, N.H., Ky. Petroleum engr. Humble Oil Co., 1949-51; propr. gravel business, 1953-58; asst. prof. So. Meth. U., 1962-65; prof. geophysics MIT, 1965-89, prof. emeritus, 1989—; ret., 1989; prin. Hager-Richter Geoscience Inc., 1989—. Cons. NASA, 1965-72; chief scientist NASA (Manned Spacecraft Center), Houston, 1969-71; cons. on siting of nuclear facilities; sec. Internat. Heat Flow Com., 1967-71; chmn. com. drilling for sci. purposes Nat. Acad. Scis., 1965; Mem. geophysics panel NSF. Served with USAF, 1951-53. NSF postdoctoral fellow, 1961-62 Fellow Geol. Soc. Am., Am. Geophys. Union; mem. ASTM (com. C-18 on dimension stone 1986—), Boston Geol. Soc. (pres. 1967-68), Soc. Exploration Geophysicists, Sigma Xi, Tau Beta Pi. Achievements include research on physical properties of materials, lunar exploration, marine geophysics, temperature of earth, regional geophysics, engineering geology and geophysics. Home: 140 Range Rd Windham NH 03087 Office: 8 Industrial Way Unit D10 Salem NH 03079-2837

**SIMMONS, MAYA TRANEMOSE**, painter; b. Paris, June 23, 1966; (parents Am. citizens); d. Arthur Eugene Simmons and Gitte Tranemose. Cert. in edn., St. Lawrence Coll., Athens, Greece, 1984; student, Sch. Arts, Crafts and Design, Copenhagen, 1986-88. One-woman shows include Carré d'Or, Paris, 1993; exhibited in group shows at IV Internat. Contest of Children's Art, Moscow, 1980 (I See the World award dedicated to XXII Olympiad), BP Gallery, Belgium, 1992 (Young European artist award), Nesles Gallery, Paris, 1993, Chim Gregg Art Gallery, Calif., 1994; represented in permanent collections BP Oil Europe, Brussels, Valeurs de l'Art mag, Lille, France. Recipient Critics' Picks award for artistic achievement in Manhattan Arts Internat. 1995 Cover Art Competition, N.Y.C., Open Studios Press award, 1996. Avocations: swimming, travel, reading. Personal E-mail: simmons84@aol.com.

**SIMMONS, MICHAEL ANTHONY**, pediatrician; m. Margaret Clare Martindale (div.); children: Kristen Ann, Jeffrey Michael, Jennifer Clare Roe, Jason Davis. AB cum laude, Harvard Coll., 1963, MD, 1967. Diplomate Am. Bd. Pediatrics, Am. Bd. Neonatal-Perinatal Medicine. Intern Harriet Lane Svc., Johns Hopkins Hosp., Balt., 1967—68, asst. resident, 1968—69, sr. asst. resident, 1969; chief resident Dept. Pediatrics, U. Colo. Med. Ctr., Denver, 1971—72, rsch. fellow in perinatal medicine, 1972—74; clin. instr. in pediatrics, 1974—77, assoc. prof. pediatrics, 1977; assoc. prof. pediatrics and obstetrics Johns Hopkins U. Sch. Medicine, Balt., 1977—83; prof., chmn. dept. pediatrics U. Utah Sch. of Medicine, Salt Lake City, 1983—94; dean U. N.C. at Chapel Hill Sch. Medicine, 1994—97, prof. pediatrics, 1994—, interim chief, 1997. Adj. prof. dept. obstetrics and gynecology U. Utah Sch. of Medicine, Salt Lake City, 1984-94; co-dir. newborn svcs. U. Colo. Med. Ctr., Denver, 1974-77, Johns Hopkins Hosp., 1977-83; mem. staff Denver Gen. Hosp., 1976-77, Denver Children's Hosp., 1976-77; vice chmn. clin. affairs dept. pediatrics Johns Hopkins Hosp., 1981-83; chief of pediatrics U. Utah Med. Ctr., Salt Lake, City, 1983-94; med. dir. Primary Children's Med. Ctr., 1983-94; bd. dirs. Triangle Univs. Licensing Consortium, U. N.C. Hosps. Contbr. numerous articles to profl. jours. Fellow Am. Acad. of Pediatrics (excellence in pediatric rsch. com. 1991—, coun. on govt. affairs 1992—); mem. Perinatal Rsch. Soc. (coun. 1982-84, pres.-elect 1985-87, pres. 1989), Western Soc. for Pediatric Rsch. (coun. 1985-86, pres.-elect 1987, pres. 1988), Soc. for Pediatric Rsch., Am. Bd. Pediatrics (sub-bd. of neonatal-perinatal medicine 1983-89, chmn. 1984-88). Office: UNC Health Care 101 Manning Dr Chapel Hill NC 27514 Office Phone: 336-832-6160. Personal E-mail: michael.simmons@mosescone.com.

**SIMMONS, MICHELLE HOLSCHUH**, school librarian, educator; b. Green Bay, Wis., Apr. 5, 1971; d. James and Rose Mary Holschuh; m. Robert Holschuh Simmons, Aug. 17, 1996; 1 child, Benedict Paul. BA, Coll. St. Benedict, St. Joseph, Minn., 1993; MA in Tchg., Minn. State U., Mankato, Minn., 1996; MA, student, U. Iowa, Iowa City, Iowa, 2000—. Tchr. English Omaha South H.S., 1996—99; libr. Cornell Coll., Mt. Vernon, Iowa, 2000—04. Contbr. articles to profl. jours. Recipient Libr. Instrn. Round Table Top 20 Instrn. Article, ALA Libr. Instrn. Round Table, 2006, Ilene F. Rockman Instrn. Publ. of Yr. award, 2006. Mem.: ALA (Libr. Instrn. Round Table Top 20 Instrn. Article award 2006), Assn. Coll. and Rsch. Librs. Democrat. Avocations: travel, cooking, reading. Home: 4006 Ardsley Court Greensboro NC 27407 Personal E-mail: michelle-h-simmons@uiowa.edu.

**SIMMONS, PETER**, lawyer, urban planner, educator; b. N.Y.C., July 19, 1931; s. Michael L. and Mary A. S.; m. Ruth J. Tanfield, Jan. 28, 1951; children: Sam, Lizzard. AB, U. Calif., Berkeley, 1953, LLB, 1956; postgrad., U. Wis., 1956—58. Prof. SUNY, Buffalo, 1963-67; mem. faculty Ohio State U., 1967-75, U. Ill., 1972, Case Western Res. U., 1974-75; prof. law and urban planning Rutgers U. Coll. Law, Newark, 1975—, dean, 1975-93; univ. prof. Rutgers U., Newark, 1993—. Contbr. articles to profl. jours. Mem. Ohio Housing Commn., 1972-74; commr. Ohio Reclamation Rev. Bd., 1974-75; chmn. N.J. Criminal Disposition Commn., 1983-84; mem. N.J. Law Revision Commn., 1987—. Alvord fellow, 1956—58. Mem. Am. Planning Assn., Urban Land Inst., Am. Law Inst., AAUP (nat. coun. 1973-75). Office: Rutgers U Law Sch 15 Washington St Newark NJ 07102-3192 E-mail: psimmons@andromeda.rutgers.edu.

**SIMMONS, PETER LAWRENCE**, lawyer; b. NYC, May 1, 1965; s. John Derek and Rosalind (Wellish) S.; m. Corinne Ryan, Apr 7, 2001; children: Mark R., Matthew S. AB magna cum laude, Columbia U., 1985, JD, 1987. Bar: N.Y. 1987, U.S. Dist. Ct. (so. and ea dists.) N.Y 1988, U.S. Ct. Internat. Trade 1991, U.S. Spreme Ct. 1991, U.S. Ct. Appeals (2d cir.) 1992, U.S. Ct. Appeals (1st cir.) 1993, U.S. Ct. Appeals (6th cir.) 2001. Law clk. to Hon. Lawrence W. Pierce U.S. Ct. Appeals (2d cir.), 1987-88; assoc. Fried, Frank, Harris, Shriver & Jacobson LLP, N.Y.C., 1988-94, ptnr., 1994—. Treas., sr. editor Columbia Law Rev., 1985-87. Harlan Fiske Stone scholar, 1985-87. Mem.: ABA, Assn. Bar City NY (profl. responsibility com. 1998—2001, civil rights com. 1989—92), NY Bar Assn., Fed. Bar Coun., Phi Beta Kappa. Home: 91 West Rd Short Hills NJ 07078 Office: Fried Frank Harris Shriver & Jacobson LLP 1 New York Plz 22 New York NY 10004-1980 Office Phone: 212-859-8455. Business E-mail: peter.simmons@friedfrank.com.

**SIMMONS, RICHARD DE LACEY**, mass media executive; b. Cambridge, Mass., Dec. 30, 1934; s. Ernest J. and Winifred (McNamara) S.; m. Mary DeWitt Bleecker, May 20, 1961; children: Christopher DeWitt, Robin Bleecker Turner. Grad., 1951; AB, Harvard Coll., 1955; LLB, Columbia U., 1958. Bar: N.Y. 1959. V.p., gen. counsel Dun & Bradstreet Corp., N.Y.C., 1969-73, exec. v.p., 1976-79, vice chmn., 1979-81; pres. Moody's Investors Svc., N.Y.C., 1973-75, Dun & Bradstreet, Inc., N.Y.C., 1975; pres., chief oper. officer Washington Post Co., Washington, 1981-91; pres. Internat. Herald Tribune, Paris, 1989-96. Bd. dirs. Washington Post Co. Office: 105 N Washington St Ste 202 Alexandria VA 22314-3022

**SIMMONS, RICHARD J.**, lawyer; b. Brockton, Mass., Nov. 26, 1951; BA summa cum laude, U. Mass., 1973; JD, U. Calif., Berkeley, 1976. Bar: Calif. 1976. Ptnr. Sheppard, Mullin, Richter & Hampton LLP, L.A., 1995—. Lectr. State of Calif., 1977-88; instr. UCLA, 1980-87; appointed to bd. Calif. Minimum Wage Bds. 1982, 84, 87; adv. bd. U. Calif. Boalt Hall Law Sch. Indsl. Relations Law Journal, 1985—. Reviews editor, editor in chief: Indsl. Relations Law Jour. 1975-76; Author: Wrongful Discharge and Employment Practices Manual, 2001, Employee Handbook and Personnel Policies Manual, 1983, 87, 92, 2004, Wage and Hour Manual for California Employers, 1982, 86, 88, 89, 91, 2001, 04, 05, Employment Discrimination and EEO Practice Manual for California Employers, 1982, 85, 91, 2000, 05, Employer's Guide to the American with Disabilities Act, 1990, 91, 92, The Employer's Guide to the California Family Rights Act of 1991, 92, 2000, Employer Obligations Under the Federal Plant Closing Law, 1989, 90, The New Federal Polygraph Law, 1989, The New Federal Immigration Law: The

Immigration Reform and Control Act of 1986, 1987, COBRA: The Federal Health Insurance Rules for the 1990's, 1987,90, 2001; contbr. articles to profl mags. and jours. Commonwealth scholar. Mem. ABA (labor, employment law, tax sect.), L.A. County Bar Assn. (tax, labor sect.), The State Bar Calif., Calif. Soc. Health Care Attys., Am. Soc. Health Care Attys., Phi Kappa Phi. Office: Sheppard Mullin Richter & Hampton 333 S Hope St Ste 4700 Los Angeles CA 90071-1448 Office Phone: 213-617-5518. Business E-mail: rsimmons@smrh.com.

**SIMMONS, RICHARD L.**, surgeon; b. Boston, Feb. 23, 1934; s. Nathanial J. and Anne Dorothy (Levenson) S.; widowed (Feb. 1993); children: Nicole, Janine. AB in Biochem. Scis. magna cum laude, Harvard U., 1955; MD summa cum laude, Boston U., 1959. Diplomate Am. Bd. Surgery. Intern, resident in surgery Columbia Presbyn. Med. Ctr., N.Y.C., 1959-66; clin. and rsch. fellow Mass. Gen. Hosp., Boston, 1965; rsch. fellow in surgery Harvard Med. Sch., Boston, 1965; instr. surgery Columbia U. Coll. P&S, N.Y.C., 1965-68; from asst. prof. to assoc. prof. surgery U. Minn., Mpls., 1968-72, prof. surgery and microbiology, 1972-87; George V. Foster prof. surgery U. Pitts., 1987—98; chmn. dept. surgery U. Pitts. Med. Ctr., 1987-98; prof. emeritus, 1998—; assoc. dean for clin. affairs Sch. Medicine U. Pitts., 1989-92, prof. molecular genetics and biochemistry, 1992—; med. dir. U. Pitts. Med. Ctr., 1996—. Chief of surgery Presbyn.-Univ. Hosp., Pitts., 1987—98. Author/co-author 15 books; contbr. more than 1200 articles to profl. jours. Recipient Disting. Svc. Prof. Surgery, 1994, other awards and grants. Mem. AMA, AAAS, ACS (pres. Southwestern Pa. chpt. 1992), NAS Inst. Medicine, Am. Soc. for Microbiology, Am. Soc. Transplant Physicians (pres. 1980-81), Am. Assn. Immunologists, Am. Assn. Pathologists, Am. Surg. Assn. (chmn. program com. 1990), Assn. for Acad. Surgery, Ctrl. Surg. Assn., Cell Transplant Soc., Halsted Soc., Infectious Diseases Soc. Am., Midwest Surg. Soc. (hon.), Reticuloendothelial Soc., Soc. for Leukocyte Biology, Soc. for Microbiology, Soc. Clin. Oncologists, Surg. Infection Soc. (pres. 1988), Soc. Surg. Chmn., Soc. Univ. Surgeons (exec. coun. 1973-81, pres. 1977-78), Allegheny County Med. Soc., Transplantation Soc. (councillor 1977-80, Peter Medawar prize 2004—), others. Office: Univ Pittsburgh Med Ctr 200 Lothrop St Pittsburgh PA 15213-2582 Business E-mail: simmonsrl@upmc.edu.

**SIMMONS, RICHARD MILTON TEAGLE**, physical fitness specialist, television personality; b. New Orleans, July 12, 1948; With Coty Cosmetics, beginning 1971; maitre d' Derrick's, Los Angeles; founder Ruffage and the Anatomy Asylum, Beverly Hills, Calif., from 1975; star The Richard Simmons Show, 1980-1984; owner nationwide chain of exercise salons, Simmons Richard Exercise Studio Simmons, Beverly Hills, Calif., 1974-; sponsor, creator, Cruise to Lose Program, Carnival Cruise Lines; lectr. and supportor in the field; author: (with Suzy Kalter) Never-Say-Diet Book, 1980, Never-Say-Diet Cookbook, 1982, Richard Simmons' Better Body Book, 1983, Reach for Fitness, 1986, Richard Simmons' Never Give Up: Inspirations, Reflections, Stories of Hope, 1993, Farewell to Fat Cookbook, 1996, (autobiography) Still Hungry- After All These Years!; column Simmons Says, Soap Opera Digest, from 1981; contbr. articles to various publs.; album Reach, 1982; producer (videos) Sweatin' to the Oldies, 1988, Sweatin' to the Oldies II, 1990, Sweatin' to the Oldies III, 1991, Sweatin' to the Oldies IV, Sweat & Shout: An Aerobic Workout, 1992, Disco Sweat, 1995, Dance Your Pants Off, Groovin' In the House, Blast Off, Platinum Sweat; creator Deal-A-Meal Food Plan and FoodMover; appeared numerous commls., infomercials and QVC; guest numerous talk shows including Merv Griffin, Mike Douglas, Phil Donahue, Charlie Rose, AM Los Angeles, Rosie O'Donnell Show, David Letterman; Real People; cameo appearances: General Hospital, 1979-1983, All Star Salute to Mother's Day, 1981; appearances on: CHiPs, 1977, Fame, 1982, Biography, 1987, Saturday Night Live, 1994, "Whose Line Is It Anyway?", 1998, Arrested Development, 2003 appeared in movies: Satyricon, 1969, The Crowns, 1970; actor (voice) Rudolph the Red-Nosed Reindeer: The Movie, 1998, (voice) Hercules: Zero to Hero, 1999, (TV series) DreamMaker, 1999. Office: Good Times Entertainment 16 E 40th St New York NY 10016-0113 also: Simmons Richard Exercise Studio Simmons 9306 Civic Center Dr Beverly Hills CA 90210

**SIMMONS, ROBERT J.**, treasurer; b. Provo, Utah, Aug. 5, 1962; BS magna cum laude, Brigham Young U., 1986; M in Mgmt., Northwestern U., 1989. Comml. banking offier Bank of Am., L.A., 1986-88; mgr. treasury ops. Oracle Corp., Redwood City, Calif., 1989-90, asst. treas., 1990—96; v.p., treas. Iomega Corp., Roy, Utah, 1996—99; exec. v.p., CFO Campus Pipeline, Salt Lake City, 1999—2001; CFO Consonus Inc., 2001; corp. treasurer E Trade Fin. Corp., 2001, CFO, 2004—. San Francisco Treasury Mgmt. Assn. (pres.). Avocations: golf, skiing, guitar. Office: E Trade 135 E 57th St New York NY 10022

**SIMMONS, ROBERT RANDOLPH**, principal; b. Phila., Aug. 27, 1935; s. Aaron J. Simmons and Lou (Randolph) Higgs; m. Patricia Ann Grace, June 26, 1975; children: Darris, William, Cynthia L., Tricia M., Robby R. BA in History, Mich. State U., 1958; MA in Community Sch. Leadership, Ea. Mich. U., 1967, Specialist of Arts, 1976; EdD, U. Mich., 1978. Cert. tchr., elem. sch. adminstr., Mich.; cert. primary and elem. sch. tchr., N.Y. Tchr. Flint (Mich) Community Schs., 1962-68, asst. prin., 1968-70, prin., 1970—, elem. liaison prin., 1992—. Adj. prof. edn. Ea. Mich. U., Ypsilanti, 1988—; NEA Mastery In Learning sch. renewal site-based cons., 1987—, cons. parent edn. Flint Community Schs., 1970—, cons. sch. improvement, Mich., 1989—; presenter Mich. Dept. Edn., MSU, 1987—; co-sponsor Mentor's for At-Risk Males Program, Flint, 1989. Contbr. to book: Parents and Schools: From Visitors to Partners, 1993; contbr. articles to profl. jours.; contbg. author in-dist. teaching materials Flint Cmty. Schs. Adv. bd. Cmty. Alliance Resource Environment, Flint, 1989—; bd. dirs., co-sponsor Stewart/Brennan Youth Clubs, Inc., 1987—; active Coalition for Positive Youth Devel., 1990—, Urban League Flint; Leonard Floyd scholarship com. New Jerusalem Full Gospel Bapt. Ch., pres. Inspirational Voice Choir, 1983-85, 90—; learning peer mentor Nat. Peer-Based Svc., 2003— Recipient Drum Maj. award Mayor Woodrow Stanley, City of Flint, 1992, 96, Staff Devel. Policy Bd. award Mich. State Bd. Edn., 1987, Chpt. 1 Excellence in Edn. scholarship award, 1986, Flint Tchr.'s Golf Championship award, 1974, 78-79, 81, 83-84, Golf award Greater Flint Olympian-CANUSA Assn., 1981, 84, Outstanding Achievement in Edn. cert. Ctrl. Flint Optimist, 1993, Gov. and Mich. Cmty. Svc. Commn. award, 1993, Pupil Pers. Golf trophy Flint Cmty. Sch., 2002 Mem. NAESP (Presenter award 1988), ASCD, NAACP, Nat. Community Edn. Assn. (Presenter award 1973), Mich. Elem. and Mid. Sch. Prin. Assn. (Presenter awards 1987-91), Flint Assn. Elem. Sch. Prins., Congress Flint Sch. Adminstrs. (pres. 1991—), Mich. Community Edn. Assn. (Presenter award 1973), Phi Delta Kappa (treas. Flint chpt. 1985-87, 25 Yr. Svc. award 1992), Alpha Phi Alpha. Democrat. Avocations: golf, jazz, reading, music. Home: PO Box 804 1235 Peashing St Flint MI 48501-0804 Office: 1950 Burr Blvd Flint MI 48503-4232 Office Phone: 810-760-1607. Personal E-mail: rsimm1002@aol.com.

**SIMMONS, ROBERT RUHL**, congressman; b. NYC, Feb. 11, 1943; s. Charles Herbert Jr. and Roxane Page (Ruhl) S.; m. Edith Heidi Paffard, June 22, 1974; children: Jane Adams, Robert Waldo Ruhl. BA, Haverford Coll., 1965; MPA, Harvard U., 1979; LLD (hon.), U. New Haven, 2003; DHL (hon.), U. Bridgeport, 2005. Ops. officer CIA, Washington, 1969-79; legis. asst. U.S. Senator John H. Chafee, Washington, 1979-81; staff dir. intelligence com. U.S. Senate, Washington, 1981-85; vis. lectr. Yale U., New Haven, 1986—95; tchg. asst. U. Conn., 1988—91; mem. Conn. Gen. Assembly, Hartford, 1991—2001, U.S. Congress from 2nd Conn. dist., Washington, 2001—; mem. armed svcs. com., homeland security com. and transp. and infrastructure com. Contbr. articles to profl. jours. Mem. Republican Nat. Com. Col. USAR, 1970-2003. Decorated Bronze Star with 1 oak leaf cluster, Meritorious Svc. medal, Army Commendation medal with 1 oak leaf cluster, Vietnam Svc. medal with four campaign stars, Nat. Def. medal, Army Res. Achievement medal, Vietnam Civilian Svc. medal; named to Infantry Officer

Candidate Sch. Hall of Fame, 2003. Republican. Episcopalian. Avocations: chinese art, forestry. Office: 215 Cannon House Office Bld Washington DC 20515-0702 also: 2 Courthouse Square, 5th Floor Norwich CT 06360 Office Phone: 202-225-2076.

**SIMMONS, RUSSELL,** recording industry executive; b. Queens, NY, Oct. 4, 1957; s. Daniel and Evelyn Simmons; m. Kimora Lee, Dec. 20, 1998 (separated 2006); children: Ming, Aoki Lee. Attended, CCNY. Co-founder, owner Def Jam Records, NYC, 1983—; chmn., CEO, pres. Rush Communications, 1990—; owner Rush Artist Mgmt., PHAT Fashion, Rush Prodr. Mgmt.; partner Rush Model Mgmt. Represents Public Enemy, LL Cool J, others. Co-prodr.: (films) Krush Groove, 1985, The Funeral, 1996; prodr.: Tougher Than Leather, 1988, The Nutty Professor, 1996, How to be a Player, 1997; exec. prodr.: The Addiction, 1995, Gridlock'd, 1997, Waist Deep, 2006; prodr.: (TV special) Def Comedy Jam Primetime, 1994; (TV series) Def Poetry Jam, 2002; author: (autobiography) Life and Def, 2001. Founder Rush Philanthropic Arts Found. 10 gold albums, 6 platinum albums, 2 multiplatinum albums; named one of 100 Most Influential Black Americans, Ebony mag., 2006. Achievements include bringing hip-hop culture into the American mainstream.*

**SIMMONS, RUTH J.,** academic administrator; b. Grapeland, Tex., July 3, 1945; d. Isaac and Fannie Stubblefield; m. Norbert Simmons, 1968 (div. 1989); children: Khari, Maya. Student, Universidad Internacional, Saltillo, Mex., 1965, Wellesley Coll., 1965—66; BA, Dillard U., 1967; postgrad., Universite de Lyon, 1967—68, George Washington U., 1968—69; AM, Harvard U., 1970, PhD in Romance Langs., 1973; LLD (hon.), Amherst Coll., 1995; LHD (hon.), Howard U., 1996, Dillard U., 1996; LLD (hon.), Princeton U., 1996, Lake Forest Coll., 1997; LHD (hon.), U. Mass., 1997; LLD (hon.), Dartmouth Coll., 1997, Mt. Holyoke Coll., 2001, U. Pa., 2001, Harvard U., 2002, George Washington U., 2002, Columbia U., 2002, Washington U., 2002, U. So. Calif., 2003, Boston U., Rensselaer Polytechnic Inst., N.Y. U., Northeastern; D of Women's Studies (hon.), Ewha Woman's U., Rep. of Korea, 2002; LittD (hon.), U. Toronto; LHD, Jewish Theol. Sem., 2004, Taugaloo Coll., 2004. Interpreter lang. svcs. divsn. U.S. Dept. State, Washington, 1968—69; instr. French George Washington U., 1968—69; admissions officer Radcliffe Coll., 1970—72; asst. prof. French U. New Orleans, 1973—75, asst. dean coll. liberal arts, asst. prof. French, 1975—79; adminstrv. coord. NEH liberal studies project Calif. State U., Northridge, 1977—78, acting dir. internat. programs, vis. assoc. prof. Pan-African studies, 1978—79; asst. dean grad. sch. U. So. Calif., 1979—82, assoc. dean grad. sch., 1982—83; dir. studies Butler Coll. Princeton U., NJ, 1983—85, acting dir. Afro-Am. studies, 1985—87, asst. dean faculty, 1986—87, assoc. dean faculty, 1986—90, vice provost, 1992—95; provost Spelman Coll., 1990—91; pres. Smith Coll., Northampton, Mass., 1995—2001; pres Brown U., Providence, 2001—. Peer reviewer higher edn. divsn. NEH, 1980—83, bd. cons., 1981; mem. grad. adv. bd. Calif. Student Aid Commn., 1981—83; chair com. to visit dept. African-Am. studies Harvard U., 1991; mem. strategic planning task force N.J. Dept. Higher Edn., 1992—93; mem. nat. adv. commn. EQUITY 2000 Coll. Bd., 1992—95; mem. adv. bd. ctrl. N.J. NAACP Legal Def. Fund, 1992—95; mem. Mid. States Assn. Accreditation Team, Johns Hopkins U., 1993; chmn. accreditation team Bryn Mawr Coll., 1999; chair rev. panel for model instns. planning grants NSF, 1993; mem. Conf. Bd., 1995; bd. dirs. MetLife, JSTOR, Pfizer Inc., 1997—, COFHE, Com. Econ. Devel.; Goldman Sachs, 1999—, Tex. Instruments, 1999—; mem. adv. coun. dept. Romance Langs. and Lit. Princeton U., 1996; trustee Carnegie Corp., 1999—; presenter, spkr. and panelist in field. Mem. editl. bd.: World Edn. series Am. Assn. Collegiate Registrars and Admissions Officers, 1984—86; contbr. articles to profl. jours. Named mem. Women's Progress Commemoration Commn. by Pres. Bill Clinton, 1999; chmn. Congl. Black Caucus Found. Washington, 2004; mem. adv. bd. N.J. Master Faculty Program Woodrow Wilson Nat. Fellowship Found., 1987—90, trustee, 1991—96, Inst. Advances Study, 1995—98, The Clarke Sch. for Deaf, 1995—; mem. bd. trustees Acad. Music, 1995—98; mem. bd. advisors 1st Internat. Conf. on AIDS, Ethiopia, 1998. Named Women of Yr., CBS, 1996, Glamour Mag., 1996, Disting. Fulbright Alumna, Inst. Internat. Edn., 1997, Woman of World, NASA, 1998, Am. Best Coll. Pres., Time mag., 2001, Woman Yr., Ms. mag., 2002; named one of Newsweek Person to Watch, 2002; recipient Disting. Svc. award, Assn. Black Princeton Alumni, 1989, Dillard U., 1992, Pres.'s Recognition award, Bloomfield Coll., 1993, TWIN award, Princeton Area YWCA, 1993, Women's ogm. Tribute award, Princeton U., 1994, Leadership award, Third World Ctr. Princeton U., 1995, Tex. Excellence award, Leap Program, 1995, Benjamin E. Mays award, A Better Chance, 1995, Centennial medal, Harvard U. Grad. Sch. Arts & Scis., 1997, Achievement award, Nat. Urban League, 1998, Tchr. Coll. Medal for Disting. Svc., Columbia U., 1999, Pres. award, United Negro Coll. Fund, 2001, "Drum Major for Justice" Edn. award, So. Christian Leadership Conf./W.O.M.E.N., 2002, Fulbright Lifetime Achievement Medal, 2002, R.I. History Makers award, 2002, Amelia Earhart award, 2002, ROBIE Humanitarian award, The Jackie Robinson Found., 2004, The Eleanor Roosevelt Val-Kill medal, 2004, fellowship, DAAD, Presdl. Medal of Honor, Dillard U., 2006; fellow, Danforth Found., 1967—73, Sr. Fulbright fellow, 1981; scholar, KYOK, 1963, Worthing Found., 1963—67, Fulbright scholar, U. de Lyon, 1967—68. Fellow: Am. Acad. Arts & Scis.; mem.: AAAS, Coun. Foreign Rels., Am. Philos. Soc. Office: Office of Pres Brown U One Prospect Street, Campus Box 1860 Providence RI 02912 Office Phone: 401-863-2234. Office Fax: 401-863-7737. E-mail: president@brown.edu.* ˙

**SIMMONS, SARAH R.,** lawyer; b. Ducktown, Tenn., Jan. 23, 1948; BA magna cum laude, U. Ariz., 1970, postgrad.; JD magna cum laude, U. Denver, 1973. Bar: Colo. 1974, Ariz. 1975. Mem. Molloy, Jones & Donahue, Tucson, Brown & Bain, P.A., Lewis & Roca LLP, 2002—05; judge Ariz. Supreme Ct. Pima County, 2006—. Mem. Davis Monthan 50, 1991—, pres., 1998-2000; trustee Tohono Club Park, 1995-2004, sec., 1997-99, v.p. 1999-2001, pres., 2001-03; trustee Tucson Airport Authority, 1996-2006, bd. dir., 2005-06; mem. Law Coll. Assn. Bd., 1996—, sec. 1998-99, pres. 2000-01; 4th R bd. Tucson Unified Sch., 1996-2003; bd. dir. United Way Tucson, 1995-2000, Family Advocacy Resource and Wellness Ctrs., Resources Women, 1995-2000; bd. dir. Ariz. Town Hall, 1998-2003; mem. adv. bd. Ariz. Drug Free Workplace, 1991-2002, So. Ariz. Sports Devel. Corp., U. Ariz. Social and Behavioral Scis., 1994-96; sec. So. Ariz. Minutemen, 1996-98; mem. bd. visitors Coll. Law, chair, 2002-06; v.p. Met. Tucson Conv. and Visitors Bur., 2003-05, pres. 2005-06. Recipient Outstanding Alumni award U. Ariz. Coll. of Law, 1993, Tucson Woman of Yr. C. of C., 1994, Women on the Move award YWCA, 1995, Alice Truman Leadership award, 2003; named one of 100 Women and Minorities in the Law, 2000, Women Who Lead, U. Ariz. Women's Studies Adv. Coun., 2003. Fellow ABA, Ariz. Bar Assn.; mem. Nat. Assn. Bond Lawyers, State Bar Ariz. (bd. govs. 1987-95, sec.-treas. 1989-90, 2d v.p. 1990-91, 1st v.p. 1991-92, pres.-elect 1992-93, pres. 1993-94, employment law sect., profl. conduct com., fee arbitration com., co- mem. of yr. 2004), Ariz. Women Lawyers Assn. (charter), Colo. Bar Assn., Pima County Bar Assn. (bd. dirs. 1985-94), Am. Judicature Soc., So. Ariz. Legal Aid (bd. dir. 1990-93), Lawyers against Hunger (v.p. D-M 50 1996-98, pres. 1998-2000), Order St. Ives, Phi Beta Kappa, Phi Kappa Phi, Phi Alpha Theta, Kappa Beta Pi. Office: Ariz Supreme Ct in Pima County 110 W Congress Tucson AZ 85701 Office Phone: 520-740-8441. E-mail: ssimmons@sc.pima.gov.

**SIMMONS, SHERWIN PALMER,** lawyer; b. Bowling Green, Ky., Jan. 19, 1931; AB, Columbia U., 1952, LLB, 1954, JD, 1969. Bar: Tenn. 1954, Fla. 1957. Assoc. Fowler, White, Collins, Gillen, Humkey & Trenam, Tampa, Fla., 1956-60, prnr., 1960-70, Trenam, Simmons, Kemker, Scharf & Barkin, Tampa, 1970-77; stockholder, pres. Trenam, Simmons, Kemker, Scharf, Barkin, Frye & O'Neill, PA, Tampa, 1977-94; ptnr., chair tax group Steel Hector & Davis, LLP, Miami, Fla., 1994—2005; shareholder, vice chair tax group, chair tax practice Buchanan Ingersoll PC, Miami, 2005—. Atty. adv. U.S. Tax Ct., Washington, 1954—56, mem. nominating commn., 1978—81; mem. adv. group Commr. of IRS, 1978—79, 1989—90, U.S. Dept. Justice,

1979—80; adj. prof. U. Miami, 1995—. Contbr. articles to profl. jours. Trustee Hillsborough County Soc. Crippled Children & Adults, 1956—85, pres., 1960—61; mem. adv. bd. Salvation Army, 1959—62, 1964—66, sec., 1960—61; treas., chmn. Hillsborough County Pub. Edn. Study Commn., 1965—66; chmn., bd. dirs. Fla. Orch., 1987—89; founding trustee, pres. Am. Tax Policy Inst., 1996—99; trustee Tampa Bay Performing Arts Ctr., Inc., 1984—93, mem. program adv. com., 1985—89, mem. investment com., 1986—91. Fellow: Am. Coll. Tax Counsel (regent 1987—93, vice chmn. 1989—91, chmn. 1991—93), Am. Bar Found. (mem. devel. com. 1992—94), Am. Coll. Trust and Estate Counsel (bd. regents 1982—88); mem.: ABA (vice chmn. adminstrn. taxation sect. 1972—75, chmn. 1975—76, ho. of dels. 1985—90, bd. govs. 1990—93, chmn. bd. govs. Com. 1992—93, chmn. commn. multidisciplinary practice 1998—2000), Am. Law Inst. (mem. coun. 1985—, mem. exec. com. 1994—97, 1999—, mem. com. 1994—97, 1999—), Internat. Fiscal Assn., Internat. Acad. Estate and Trust Law, So. Fed. Tax Inst. (trustee, pres. 1974, chmn. 1975, trustee emeritus 1999—), Am. Judicatrue Soc., Fla. Bar Assn. (chmn. taxation sect. 1964—65), Am. Law Network ABA-Am. Law Inst. (mem. com. continuing profl. edn. 1973—), Am. Bar Retirement Assn. (bd. dirs. 1984—90, v.p. 1987—88, pres. 1988—89). Office: Buchanan Ingersoll PC 34th Fl Bank Am Tower 100 SE 2d St Miami FL 33131 Office Phone: 305-347-4060. Business E-Mail: spstax@bipc.com.

**SIMMONS, SUE,** newscaster; b. NY, May 27, 1943; d. John Simmons. Corr. WTNH-TV, New Haven, 1973-74, WBAL-TV, Balt., 1974, anchor, host Balt. at One, 1975—76; corr./anchor. WRC-TV, Washington, 1976—80; co-anchor News Channel 4/Live at Five/News Channel 4 at 11 p.m WNBC News, NYC, 1980—; host Images: A Year in Review, WNBC, 2002—. Recipient four Emmy awards, award for Outstanding Performance by a News Commentator, Barnabus McHenry, Vice-Chmn. Pres.'s Task Force on Arts and Humanities, 1981; named to the NY State Broadcasters Assn. Hall of Fame, 2005 Office: WNBC-TV 30 Rockefeller Plz New York NY 10112-0002*

**SIMMONS, SUSAN ANNETTE,** management consultant and statistics educator; b. Pascagoula, Miss., Apr. 12, 1947; d. Emmitt Leroy and Margie Marie (Coker) S. BS, Miss. State Coll. for Women, 1969; MBA, Miss. State U., 1970; PhD, U. Miss., 1976. Asst. prof. Eastern Ky. U., 1976-78, U. Southwestern La., Lafayette, 1978-80; assoc. prof. U. Iowa, Iowa City, 1980-83; assoc. prof. Sam Houston State U., Huntsville, Tex., 1983-90; profl. The Citadel, Charleston, SC, 1990—, dir. bus. web site devel., 2001—. Editor Jour. Bus. Strategies, 1985-87; contbr. articles to profl. jours. Mem. Nat. Decision Scis. Inst., Am. Econs. Assn., SE Decision Scis. Inst. (v.p. student liaison 1978-79, sec. 1979-81, 91-92, coun. 1981-83, placement dir. 1989-90, v.p. pub. 1993-94, mem. coun. 1994-96), Phi Kappa Phi, Omicron Delta Epsilon, Kappa Epsilon (assoc.).Baptist. Office: The Citadel Sch Bus Administr Charleston SC 29409-0001

**SIMMONS, SUZAN,** psychologist; b. Helena, Mont., Nov. 26, 1951; d. Paul H. and R. Ellen (Berry) Cresap. BA in Elem. Edn., Jamestown Coll., 1976; MS in Student Pers. and Guidance, Okla. State U., 1980, PhD in Counseling Psychology, 1983. Cert. health svc. provider in psychology, psychologist, Iowa. Counselor II student counseling svc. Iowa State U., Ames, 1983-86; psychologist Ctrl. Iowa Psychiat. Svcs., Des Moines, 1987-90, Iowa Health Physicians (formerly Integra Health), Des Moines, 1991—2004; psychologist/clin. dir. Spectrum, Iowa Meth. Med. Ctr., Des Moines, 1990; psycholgist pvt. practice, 2004—. Mem. multicultural nonsexist adv. com. Ankeny (Iowa) Community Schs., 1992-94. Fellow Am. Coll. Advanced Practice Psychologists (founding mem.), Internat. Coll. Prescribing Psychologists and the Prescribing Psychology Registry; mem. APA, Iowa Psychol. Assn., Coun. Nat. Register Health Svc. Providers in Psychology, Iowa Pain Inst., Jour. Club. Methodist. Avocations: outdoors, music, pets. Office: Ste 5 1000 73rd St Des Moines IA 50311 Office Phone: 515-222-1175. E-mail: tsimmons3@aol.com.

**SIMMONS, SYLVIA JEANNE QUARLES (MRS. HERBERT G. SIMMONS JR.),** academic administrator, educator; b. Boston, May 8, 1935; d. Lorenzo Christopher and Margaret Mary (Thomas) Quarles; m. Herbert G. Simmons, Jr., Oct. 26, 1957; children: Stephen, Alison, Lisa. BA, Manhattanville Coll., 1957; MEd, Boston Coll., 1962, PhD, 1990; DHL (hon.), St. Joseph's Coll., 1994; EdD (hon.), Merrimack Coll., 1989. Montessori tchr. Charles River Park Nursery Sch., Boston, 1970-76; registrar Boston Coll. Sch. Mgmt., Chestnut Hill, 1966-70; dir. fin. aid Radcliffe Coll., Cambridge, Mass., 1970-75, assoc. dean admissions and fin. aid, 1972-75, assoc. dean admissions, fin. aid and women's edn., 1975; assoc. dean admissions and fin. aid Harvard and Radcliffe, from 1975; assoc. v.p. for acad. affairs ctrl. adminstrn. U. Mass., Boston, 1976-79, spl. asst. to chancellor, 1979; v.p. field svcs. Am. Student Assistance, 1982-84, sr. v.p., 1984-93, exec. v.p., 1993-95, pres., 1996; mem. faculty Harvard U., 1970-77, pres. faculty, 1995-96; lectr. Boston U., 1991—. Cons. Mass. Bd. Higher Edn., 1973—77. Co-editor: Student Loans Riches and Realities. Past bd. dirs. Rivers Country Day Sch., Weston, Mass., Simons's Rock Coll., Great Barrington, Mass., Wayland (Mass.) Fair Housing, Cambridge Mental Health Assn., Family Svcs. Greater Boston, Concerts in Black and White, Mass., Higher Edn. Assistance Corp.; chmn. bd. dirs. North Shore Cmty. Coll., 1986-88, mem. bd. dirs., 1985—; trustee and alumnae bd. dirs. Manhattanville Coll., 1986—; mem. adv. com. Upward Bound, Chestnut Hill Boston Coll., 1972-74, Women in Politics John McCormick Inst., 1994-2000; Camp Chimney Corners, Becket, Mass., 1971-77; bd. dirs. Am. Cancer Soc., Mass., 1987-89, Boston Coll., 1990-98, Merrimack Coll., 1992-2000, Mass. Found. for Humanities, 1990-92, Mass. Bay United Way, 1990-94, Grimes King Found., 1992—, St. Elizabeta's Hosp., 1991—, Anna Stearns Found., 1996—, Regis Coll., 1997—, Edn. Resources Inst., 1998—, Supreme Ct. Jud. Hist. Soc., 2001—, Newton Country Day Sch., 2002—, Shirley Eustes House, 2002—; overseer Mt. Ida Coll., 1990—, Exec. Svc. Corp., 1997—, Supreme Ct. Judicial Hist. Soc., 2001—, Newton County Day Sch., 2002—, Shirely Euestes House, 2002, The Edn. Resources Inst., 1998, Mus. Fine Arts, Boston, Mass., 2002—; chair Coll. Club Scholarship com., 1997. Recipient Educator of Yr. award Boston and Vicinity Club, 1989, Bicentennial medal Boston Coll., 1976, Achievement award Greater Boston YMCA, 1977, Human Rights awsard Mass. Tchrs. Assn., 1988, Pres'. award Mass. Ednl. Opportunity Assn., 1988, Archbishop Timothy Healy award, 1997, Outstanding Alumna award Girl's Latin Sch., 1998; named One of Ten Outstanding Yung Leaders, Boston Jr. C. of C., 1971, Sojourner's Daus.: 25 African women who have made a difference, 1991. Mem. Eastern Assns. Fin. Aid Officers (2st v.p. 1973), Coll. Scholarship Svc. Coun., Links (pres. local chpt. 1967-69), Nat. Assn. Fin. Aid Adminstrs. (dir. 1975-77), Jack and Jill Am. (pres. Newton chpt. 1972-74), Manhattanville Club (pres. Boston 1966-68), Delta Sigma Theta, Delta Kappa Gamma (pres. 1988-90). Home: 19 Clifford St Roxbury MA 02119-2120 Office: 330 Stuart St Boston MA 02116-5237 Personal E-mail: ssimm38414@aol.com.

**SIMMONS, WILLIAM,** retired aerospace engineer, research and development company executive; b. Chgo., Apr. 24, 1932; s. Walter Garfield and Edna Dean (Winch) S.; m. Barbara Millet Haury, Oct. 4, 1954; children: Sheryl Lee, Cynthia Jane, Shelly Jean. BA in Physics, Carleton Coll., 1953; MS in Physics, U. Ill., 1955, PhD in Physics, 1960. Mem. tech. staff Space Tech. Labs., Redondo Beach, Calif., 1960-62; sr. rsch. scientist Gen. Tech., Torrance, Calif., 1962, TRW, Redondo Beach, 1962-71, dir. rsch., 1984-89, chief engr. spl. projects assigned to Lawrence Livermore (Calif.) Labs., 1989-92; engring. mgr. Lawrence Livermore Labs., 1972-84, rsch. reviewer, 1985-89; prof. engring. UCLA, 1968-72. Tech. panel mem. U. Calif., Berkeley, 1985; tech. reviewer Dept. Energy, Washington, 1986—, mem. rev. com., 1987—; cons. in field, 1992-99. Editor, reviewer 2 books, 1982, 83; contbr. numerous articles to profl. jours.; 10 patents for electro-optics devices. Named Disting. Engring. Prof. of Yr. UCLA, 1972, one of Top 100 Innovators in U.S.A. Sci. Digest, 1986; George F. Baker Found. scholar Carleton Coll. 1949-53. Mem. IEEE (sr. life, gen. chmn. symposia 1988, 89, Simon Ramo Major medal 1987), Laser Engring. and Optical Soc., Am. Phys. Soc. (chmn. SE Photographic and Instrumentation Engrs., U.S. Chess Club, Phi Beta Kappa,

Sigma Xi. Republican. Avocations: chess, ping pong/table tennis, bridge. Office: Sys Solutions 1621 W 25th St Ste 231 San Pedro CA 90732-4300 Office Phone: 310-541-4140. E-mail: wwsimmons@cox.net.

**SIMMS, LEONARD JAY,** psychology professor; b. Cleve., Ohio, Mar. 12, 1971; s. Manly Ronald and Margaret Blema Simms; m. Ericka Ellen Nus, Sept. 3, 2000. BS in Psychology, Calif. Poly. State U., San Luis Obispo, 1995; MA in Psychology, U. of Iowa, Iowa City, 1998, PhD in Clin. Psychology, 2002. Postdoctoral rsch. scholar U. of Iowa, 2002—03; asst. prof. SUNY, Buffalo, 2003—. Contbr. articles to profl. jours. Mem.: APA, Assn. for Rsch. in Personality, Soc. for Personality and Social Psychology, Assn. for Behavioral and Cognitive Therapy, Soc. for Rsch. in Psychopathology, Assn. for Psychol. Sci. Office: SUNY Dept Psychology Park Hall 218 Buffalo NY 14260 Office Phone: 716-645-3650. E-mail: ljsimms@buffalo.edu.

**SIMMS, MARIA ESTER,** health facility administrator; b. Bahia Blanca, Argentina; arrived in U.S., 1963; d. Jose and Esther (Guays) Barberio Esandi; m. Michael Simms, July 15, 1973 (dec. Aug. 1993); children: Michelle Bonnie Lee Carla, Michael Londen Valentine, Matthew Brandon. MD, Facultad del Centenario, Rosario, Argentina, 1962; cert. physician asst. with honors, U. So. Calif., 1977. Diplomate. Pres. Midtown Svcs. Inc., LA, 1973—; dir. internat. affairs, speaker Gov. of Papua, New Guinea, 1996—; dir., CFO, pres. World Film Inst., 1996—; commr. Inmate Welfare Commn. Los Angeles County Sheriff's Dept., 1977—. Dir. internat. affairs, spkr. on humanitarian, cultural and econ. matters Govt. of Papua New Guinea; adv. internat. spkr. women, children and animal rights; bd. dirs. Kohtakt, Raduga. Chmn. bd. dirs. Am. Film Inst., Washington; chmn. bd. trustees World Film Inst., dir. internat. affairs; spkr.-humanitarian Econ. and Cultural Consulate of Papua New Guinea, LA; bd. dirs. Glendale Symphony Orch.; mem. Tumate Welfare Commn.; commr. Los Angeles County Sheriff Dept. Fellow: Am. Acad. Physician's Assts.; mem.: Physicians Social Responsibility, Bus. Law Enforcement (N.E. divsn.), So. Calif. Alliance Survival, Inst. Noetic Scis., Noetic Scis. Soc., Mercy Crusade Inc., Internat. Found. Survival Rsch., Supreme Emblem Club U.S., Shriners, Flying Samaritans, Order Eastern Star. Avocations: coin collecting/numismatics, designing, writing, painting, flying. Office Phone: 323-255-0734. Personal E-mail: msimms1234@aol.com.

**SIMMS, MARSHA E.,** lawyer; b. St. Louis, Sept. 15, 1952; AB, Barnard Coll., 1974; JD, Stanford U., 1977. Bar: NY 1978. Ptnr., corp. dept. Weil, Gotshal & Manges LLP, NYC. Bd. trustees Lawyers' Com. Civil Rights Under Law, Ednl. Broadcasting Corp. (Channel 13). Mem. editl. bd.: Bus. Lawyer. Former trustee Stanford Alumni Assn.; former mem. campaign steering com. Stanford Law Sch. Named one of Am. Top Black Atty., Black Enterprise, 2003. Mem.: ABA, Am. Law Inst., Met. Black Bar Assn., NY State Bar Assn., Am. Arbitration Assn. (past bd. dirs.). Office: Weil Gotshal & Manges LLP 767 Fifth Ave New York NY 10153 Office Phone: 212-310-8116. Office Fax: 212-310-3007. Business E-Mail: marsha.simms@weil.com.

**SIMMS, PHIL,** sports commentator, retired professional football player; b. Lebanon, Ky., Nov. 3, 1956; m. Diana Simms; children: Christopher, Matthew, Deirdre. Grad., Morehead State U., 1979. Quarterback N.Y. Giants, 1979-94; studio analyst ESPN, Prime Time Monday, 1994—95; game analyst NBC, 1995—98; lead analyst CBS Sports, 1998—. Co-author (with Rick Meier): Phil Simms on Passing: Fundamentals of Throwing the Football, 1996; (with Vic Carucci) Sunday Morning Quarterback: Going Deep on the Strategies, Myths, and Mayhem of Football, 2004. Named to Pro Bowl Team, 1985, 1993; Named All-Pro, 1986; recipient Pro Bowl Player of Game award, 1986, MVP award Super Bowl XXI, 1987. Mem. NFL Championship Teams, 1986, 1990. Office: CBS 51 W 52nd St New York NY 10019*

**SIMNJANOVSKI, RISTE,** counseling administrator; b. Escondido, Calif., Dec. 24, 1979; s. Djoko and Zorka Simnjanovski. BA, U. Redlands, Calif., 2002, MA, 2004. Cert. tchr. Calif., 2003. Resident dir. U. Redlands, Calif., 2002—04, asst. dir. cmty. svc., 2002, asst. dir. admissions leadership, 2003, admissions counselor, 2005—. Named to All-SCIAC Men's Soccer, 1999—2001; recipient Player of Yr., san Diego Soccer Club, 1998, Male Athlete of yr., 1998, Resident Advisor of yr., U. Redlands, 2001, MA Student of Yr., 2002; cummings Endowed scholarship, 1998—2002. Mem.: CCPA, National Assn. Student Pers. Admstrs., Am. Coll. Pers. Assn., Phi Alpha Theta. Avocations: soccer, computers, drums, linguistics, research. Office: U Redlands 1200 E Colton Redlands CA 92373

**SIMOKAITIS, FRANK JOSEPH,** military officer, lawyer; b. St. Louis, Dec. 12, 1922; s. Frank and Constance (Ladish) S.; m. Mary Jane Feeny; children: Peggy, Mary, Frank (dec.). Student, Washington U., St. Louis, 1945-47; LL.B., St. Louis U., 1950, JD, 1970. Bar: U.S. Supreme Ct. U.S 1950, Mo. 1950, also other fed. cts. 1950. Commd. 2d lt. USAAF, 1943; advanced through grades to maj. gen. USAF, 1973; plans and ops. officer Hdqrs. Pacific Air Force, 1960-63; staff officer Hdqrs. USAF, Washington, 1963-69, exec. asst. to sec. air force, 1969-73; comdt. Air Force Inst. Tech., 1973-78; dir. Dept. Def. affairs Hdqrs. NASA, Washington, 1978-83, cons., 1983—. Bd. dirs. Dayton chpt. ARC, Greater Miami chpt., arbitrator Better Bus. Bur. Decorated D.S.M. with oak leaf cluster, Legion of Merit, Air medal with 4 oak leaf clusters, Air Force Commendation medal. Mem. Miami Air Force Assn. (bd. dirs.), Navy League (v.p. U.S. Miami coun.), Univ. Club of Washington D.C., Patrick AFB Officers Club. Home: 1594 Frontier Dr Melbourne FL 32940

**SIMON, ALBERT,** retired physicist, retired engineer, retired educator; b. NYC, Dec. 27, 1924; s. Emanuel D. and Sarah (Leitner) S.; m. Harriet E. Rubinstein, Aug. 17, 1947 (dec. June 1970); children: Richard, Janet, David; m. Rita Shiffman, June 11, 1972. BS, CCNY, 1947; PhD, U. Rochester, 1950. Registered profl. engr., N.Y. State. Physicist Oak Ridge Nat. Lab., 1950-54, assoc. dir. neutron physics divsn., 1954-61; head plasma physics divsn. Gen. Atomic Co., San Diego, 1961-66; prof. dept. mech. engring. U. Rochester, NY, 1966—2005, prof. physics, 1968—2005, prof. emeritus, 2005; chmn. dept. mech. engring. U. Rochester, 1977-84. Mem. Inst. for Advanced Study, Princeton, 1974-75; sr. vis. fellow U.K. Sci. Rsch. Coun., Oxford U., 1975 Author: An Introduction to Thermonuclear Research, 1959; contbr. to: Ency. Americana, 1964, 74; editor Advances in Plasma Physics, 1967—. With USN, 1944—46. Recipient Univ. Mentor award, 1988-89; John Simon Guggenheim fellow, 1964-65. Fellow Am. Phys. Soc. (chmn. plasma physics divsn. 1963-64); mem. ASME, ASEE (chmn. nuc. engring. divsn. 1985-86). Home: 2470 East Ave Apt 314 Rochester NY 14610 Office Phone: 585-275-4431. Business E-Mail: simo@me.rochester.edu.

**SIMON, BARRY PHILIP,** lawyer, air transportation executive; b. Paterson, N.J., Nov. 22, 1942; s. Alfred Louis and Rhoda (Tapper) S.; m. Hinda Bookstaber, Feb. 9, 1964; children: Alan, John, Eric. BA, Princeton U., 1964; LLB, Yale U., 1967. Bar: N.Y. 1965, Tex. 1986. Assoc. atty. Hughes Hubbard & Reed, N.Y.C., 1967-69, Sullivan & Cromwell, N.Y., 1969-72, Shea & Gould, N.Y.C., 1972-73; v.p., gen. counsel Teleprompter Corp., N.Y.C., 1973-82; v.p., sec., gen. counsel Continental Airlines, L.A. and Houston, 1982-86, v.p. in-charge internat. div. Houston, 1987-90, sr. v.p. legal affairs, gen. counsel, sec., 1990-92; sr. v.p. Tex. Air Corp., 1986-87; sr. v.p. legal affairs, gen. counsel, sec. Ea. Airlines, Miami, 1987-90; exec. v.p., gen. counsel GAF Corp., Wayne, N.J., 1993-95; sr. v.p. for internat. ops. Continental Airlines, Houston, 1996—2000; exec. v.p., gen. counsel Northwest Airlines Corp., Eagan, Minn. Bd. dirs. Amadeus Reservations Sys. Mem. copyright com. Nat. Cable TV Assn., Washington, 1974-76, mem. utilities com., 1973-82; bd. dirs. Houston Grand Opera, Inprint, Alley Theatre. Recipient Class of 1888 Lit. prize Princeton U., 1961 Office: Northwest Airlines 2700 Lone Oak Pky Eagan MN 55121 Office Phone: 612-726-2111. Fax: 612-726-7123.

**SIMON, BERNECE KERN,** retired social worker; b. Denver, Nov. 27, 1914; d. Maurice Meyer and Jennie (Bloch) Kern; m. Marvin L. Simon, Feb. 26, 1939; 1 child, Anne Elizabeth. AM, U. Chgo., 1936, MA, 1942. Social worker Jewish Children's Bur. Chgo., 1938-40, U. Chgo. Hosps. and Clinics,

1940-44; mem. faculty U. Chgo., 1944-81, instr., 1944-48, asst. prof., 1948-60, prof. social casework, 1960—81, prof. emeritus, 1981—, Samuel Deutsch prof. Sch. Social Service Adminstrn., 1960-81. Mem. bd. editors 17th Edit. Ency. Social Work, 1975—77, Social Svc. Rev., 1975—99, Social Work, 1978—82; book rev. editor: Social Work, 1982—87, cons. editor: Jour. Social Work Edn., 1991—94; contbr. articles to profl. jours., chapters to books. Mem.: NASW, Nat. Acads. Practice Social Work, Acad. Cert. Social Workers, Coun. Social Work Edn. (mem. nat. bd. dirs., sec. 1972—74).

**SIMON, BRUCE HARVEY,** lawyer; b. N.Y.C., Dec. 27, 1934; s. Morris and Pearl (Mandelstein) S.; m. Arlene Bartfield, June 16, 1957; children: Douglas, Charles, Rachel. BA, Bklyn. Coll., 1956; LLB, Harvard U., 1959. Bar: N.Y. 1961, U.S. Ct. Appeals (2d, 3d, 4th and 5th cirs.) U.S. Dist. Ct. (so., ea. and no. dists.) N.Y. Assoc. Cohen & Weiss, N.Y.C., 1960-66; ptnr. Cohen, Weiss & Simon, N.Y.C., 1966—. Mem. N.Y.C. Bd. Collective Bargaining; bd. dirs. AFL-CIO Lawyers Coordinating Com., 1982—; disting. practitioner in residence Cornell Law Sch., 1995. Contbr. articles to legal publs. Served with U.S. Army, 1959-60. Mem. ABA, Fed. Bar Coun. Democrat. Jewish. Office: Cohen Weiss & Simon 330 W 42nd St Fl 25 New York NY 10036-6976 E-mail: bsimon@cwsny.com.*

**SIMON, CARLY,** singer, composer, author; b. NYC, June 25, 1945; d. Richard S.; m. James Taylor, 1972 (div. 1983); children: Sarah Maria, Benjamin Simon; m. James Hart, Dec. 23, 1987. Studied with Pete Seeger. Singer, composer, rec. artist, 1971—. Albums include Carly Simon, 1971, Anticipation, 1972, No Secrets, 1973, Hotcakes, 1974, Playing Possum, 1975, The Best of Carly Simon, 1975, Another Passenger, 1976, Boys in the Trees, 1978, Spy, 1979, Come Upstairs, 1980, Torch, 1981, Hello Big Man, 1983, Spoiled Girl, 1985, Coming Around Again, 1987, Greatest Hits Live, 1988, My Romance, 1990, Have You Seen Me Lately?, 1990, Carly Simon, This Is My Life, 1992, Carly Simon's Romulus Hunt: A Family Opera, 1993, Bells Bears & Fishermen, 1994, Letters Never Sent, 1994, Film Noir, 1997, Bedroom Tapes, 2000, Christmas Is Almost Here, 2002, Christmas Is Almost Here Again, 2003, Moonlight Serenade, 2005, Into White, 2006; single records: You're So Vain/Nobody Does It Better, 1977, Let the River Run, 1988 (Academy award best original song, 1989), (with Frank Sinatra) In the Wee Small Hours of the Morning, 1993, Clouds in My Coffee, 1995; TV appearance: Carly in Concert: My Romance, 1990; singer & composer(films) Torchlight, 1985, Postcards from the Edge, 1990, This Is My Life, 1992, Marvin's Room, 1996, Primary Colors, 1998, Madeline, 1998, Piglet's big Movie, 2003, Pooh's Heffalump Movie, 2005; actor No Nukes, 1980, In Our Hands, 1984, Perfect, 1985, Little Black Book, 2004; author: (children's books) Amy the Dancing Bear, The Boy of the Bells, Fisherman's Song, The Nighttime Chauffeur. Recipient Best New Artist award, Grammy Awards, 1971.*

**SIMON, DAVID,** real estate company officer; BS, Ind. U.; MBA, Columbia U. Assoc. First Boston Corp., N.Y.C.; CFO, COO Melvin Simon & Assocs., Inc.; v.p. Wasserstein Perella & Co., N.Y.C., til 1990; pres., CEO Simon Property Group, 1990-96, CEO, 1996—. 2d. vice-chmn. Nat. Assn. Real Estate Investment Trusts, Inc.; trustee Internat. Coun. Shopping Ctrs.; dir. 1st Health Corp. Mem. urban Land Inst. Office: Simon Property Group Inc 115 W Washington St Ste 1465 Indianapolis IN 46204-3464

**SIMON, DAVID FREDERICK,** lawyer; b. El Paso, Tex., Apr. 14, 1953; s. Maurice and Susan (Bendekovits) S.; m. Deborah Hart, Mar. 1, 1980; children: Stephen, Rebecca Elizabeth, Nathaniel Cody. BS magna cum laude, U. Buffalo, 1974; JD cum laude, U. Pa., 1977. Bar: Pa. 1977, N.J. 1978. Law clk. to presiding judge Phila. Ct. Common Pleas, 1977-79; assoc. Wolf, Block, Schorr & Solis-Cohen, Phila., 1979-85, ptnr., 1985-90; sr. v.p. U.S. Healthcare Inc., Blue Bell, Pa., 1990-96; chief legal officer Aetna U.S. Healthcare, Inc., Blue Bell, 1996—2000; chief counsel Pa. Ins. Dept., Harrisburg, 2001—03; sr. v.p. Jefferson Health Sys., Inc., Radnor, Pa., 2003—05. Adv. coun. Pa. Dept. Conservation and Natural Resources, 1996-97, Pa. MCare Commn., 2006; bd. mgrs. U. Pa. Law Sch. Alumni, 1997-2003; dean's adv. coun. SUNY Buffalo Sch. Mgmt., 1999—, chmn., 2003-2005. Mem. Phila. Bar Assn. (exec. com. young lawyers sect. 1983-85, chmn. computer and new com. 1984-85), Pa. Bar Assn. (chmn. in-house counsel com. 1993-94), Pa. Bar Inst. (bd. dirs. 1992-96). Avocations: photography, electronics. Home: PO Box 551 Gwynedd Valley PA 19437-0551 Office: Jefferson Health Sys Inc 259 N Radnor-Chester Rd Radnor PA 19087-5288 Personal E-mail: simond@jhsmail.org.

**SIMON, DAVID L.,** art historian; s. Abe M. and Thelma D. Simon; m. Sonia Chalif Simon, June 11, 1971; 1 child, David L. Jr. BA, Boston U., 1969, MA, 1971; PhD, U. London, 1977. Instr. Boston U., 1973—74; from asst. to assoc. prof. SUNY, Cortland, 1974—81; prof. Colby Coll., Waterville, Maine, 1981—. Author: La Condesa Dona Sancha, 1995; editor: (jour.) Gesta, 1998; co-author: Janson's History of Art, 2006. Recipient award, Am. Coun. Learned Societies, 1978, Basset Tchg. award, Colby Coll., 2005; Met. Mus. Art fellow, 1980—81. Mem.: Internat. Ctr. Medieval Art, Coll. Art Assn. Office: Colby Coll 5640 Mayflower Hill Waterville ME 04901 Business E-Mail: dlsimon@colby.edu.

**SIMON, DIANE ROSE,** music educator, writer, poet; b. Appleton, Wis., Oct. 19, 1945; d. Raymond George and Violet Beatrice (Behnke) Rippl; m. Ronald Philip Simon, Sept. 18, 1938; children: David Clarence, Mary Anne. Student, Stevens Point State Tchrs. Coll., 1966; BMus, Ariz. State U., Tempe, 1969, post grad., 1971—94; student, Paris Am. Acad., 1970, Union Coll., Shenectady, NY, 1970, Westminster Choir Coll., Princeton, NJ, 1979, Grand Canyon Coll., 1992, Inst. Children's Lit., 1998—2003, Poetry Laureate Program, Owings Mills, Md., 2002—04. Dir. band chorus gen music Wollton Elem. Dist., Ariz., 1969—70; saxophone instr. Ariz. We Coll., Yuma, 1969—70; woodwind specialist Yuma Sch. Dist., 1970—72; dir. band Balsz Sch. Dist., Phoenix, 1972—76. Paradise Valley Sch. Dist., Phoenix, 1976—77; dir. band, chorus, gen. music Mesa Pub. Schs., Ariz., 1978—94; ret., 1994; pvt. music lessons, 1965—. Mem. Yuma Symphony, 1969—72; dir. saxophone ensembles Yuma Sch. Dist. #1, 1970—72; saxophone clinician, adjudicator Ariz. Music Educators Assn., 1972—76, 2002. Author: Expressions of the Heart, 1997, Family Treasures, 1998, With a Giggle and a Tear, 1998, Butterflies in the Meadow, 1999, The Rat and The Hat, 1999, Into the Millennium, 2000, Sunrise Over the Desert, 1999; pub.: Beneath the Mesquite, 1999; poet (poetry) pub. numerous anthologies (Editors Choice Award cert., 1996, 1997, 1998, 1999, 2000, 2001, 2002, 2003); contbr. articles to profl. publs. Recipient The Muse of Fire trophy, medallion, The Famous Poets Soc., 2000, The Shakespeare Trophy of Excellence award, 2004. Mem.: Internat. Libr. Poetry, Internat. Soc. Poets (Disting. Membership 1996, Internat. Poet of Merit award Medallion and Commemorative Plaque 1996, 1998, Poet of Merit award medallion 2002, Silver award bowl trophy 2002, Poet of Merit award medallion 2004, Outstanding Achievement in Poetry Silver award cup 2004, Outstanding Achievement in Poetry Crystal award trophy 2006). Republican. Roman Catholic. Home: 732 W Curry St Chandler AZ 85225 Personal E-mail: rddmasimon@worldnet.att.net.

**SIMON, DOLORES DALY,** copy editor; b. San Francisco, Nov. 18, 1928; d. Francis Edward and Jeannette (Cooke) Daly; m. Sidney Blair Simon, Aug. 24, 1952 (div. Nov. 1955); children: John Roderick, Douglas Brian. BA in Journalism, Pa. State U., 1950. County editor Centre Daily Times, State College, Pa., 1950-51; soc. editor Bradford (Pa.) Era, 1951-52; copy editor Harper & Bros., Pubs., N.Y.C., 1955-60; copy chief Harper & Row, Pubs., N.Y.C., 1960-88; freelance editor, copy editor Warwick, NY, 1988—. Co-author: Recipes into Type, 1993 (Best Food Reference 1994). Mem. James Beard Found., Phi Mu. Democrat. Avocation: book collecting. Office: Editl Svcs 63 Blooms Corners Rd Warwick NY 10990-2403 Office Phone: 845-986-4442.

**SIMON, DONALD JOHN,** financial planner, small business owner; b. Chgo., July 16, 1947; s. Nicholas J. and Alice R. (Vaughn) S.; 1 child, Joshua K. BSBA, Oglethorpe U., 1969. CFP, CLU, ChFC. Sales rep. D. W. Shaw,

---

Inc., Berlin, NJ, 1969-74; owner Simon Fin. Co., Vero Beach, Fla., 1975—. Mem. Nat. Assn. Ins. and Fin. Advisors, Indian River C. of C., Indian River Estate Planning Coun. Avocations: music, bicycling, boating.

**SIMON, ECKEHARD (PETER),** foreign language educator; b. Schneidemühl, Germany, Jan. 5, 1939; came to U.S., 1955, naturalized, 1960; s. Herbert and Doris (Keiler) S.; m. Eileen Higginbottom, Dec. 19, 1959; children: Anders, Conrad (dec.), Matthew, Frederick. AB, Columbia U., 1960; A.M., Harvard U., 1961, PhD, 1964. Instr., German Harvard U., Cambridge, Mass., 1964-65, asst. prof., 1965-69, assoc. prof., 1969-71, prof., 1971—, Victor S. Thomas prof. Germanic langs. & lits., 1996—, head tutor and lang. coordinator, 1965-76, chmn. dept. German, 1976—82, 1996—99, chmn. com. on medieval studies, 1992—95, 2001—02. Author: Neidhart von Reuental: Geschichte der Forschung und Bibliographie, 1968, Neidhart von Reuental, 1975, The Türkenkalender (1454) Attributed to Gutenberg and the Strasbourg Lunation Tracts, 1988, Die Anfänge des weltlichen deutschen Schauspiels, 1370-1530, 2003; editor: The Theatre of Medieval Europe, New Research in Early Drama, 1991; mem. editl. bd.: Dictionary of the Middle Ages, 1982-89; contbr. articles to profl. jours. Woodrow Wilson fellow, 1960-61, NEH Younger Scholar fellow, 1968-69, Rsch fellow, 1977-78, Guggenheim fellow, 1968-69, Fulbright fellow U. Cologne, 1983, Sr. Exchange fellow Dumbarton Oaks, Washington, 2001. Mem. MLA, Am. Assn. Tchrs. German, Medieval Acad. Am. (asst. editor Speculum 1981-94, book review editor 1994-2000). Home: 11 Hayes Ave Lexington MA 02420-3521 Office: Harvard U Barker Ctr 345 Cambridge MA 02138-3879 Office Phone: 617-496-9359. Business E-Mail: simon2@fas.harvard.edu.

**SIMON, ERIC JACOB,** neuroscientist, educator; b. Wiesbaden, Germany, June 2, 1924; came to U.S., 1938, naturalized, 1945; s. Joseph and Paula (Meyer) S.; m. Irene M. Ronis, Aug. 9, 1947; children: Martin A., Faye Ruth, Lawrence D. BS, Case Inst. Tech., Cleve., 1944; MS, U. Chgo., 1947, PhD, 1951; doctorate (hon.), U. René Descartes Sorbonne, Paris, 1982. Postdoctoral trainee in biochemistry Columbia U. Coll. Physicians and Surgeons, 1951-53; lectr. in chemistry CCNY, 1952-59; research assoc. Cornell U. Med. Coll., 1953-59; asst. prof. medicine NYU Med. Center, 1959-64, assoc. prof. exptl. medicine, 1964-72, prof. exptl. medicine, 1972-80, prof. psychiatry and pharmacology, 1980—. Harry Williams Meml. lectr. Dept. Pharmacology Emory U., Atlanta, 1986; mem. initial rev. com. Nat. Inst. Drug Abuse, 1976-80, chmn. 1979-80, mem. Nat. Adv. Coun. on Drug Abuse, 1989-92; Sterling-Winthrop lectr. Albany Med. Coll., 1977; vis. prof. Coll. de France, Paris, 1990; vis. lectr. Shanghai and Beijing, 1985. Trustee Teaneck (N.J.) Bd. Edn., 1975-79. Served with U.S. Army, 1944-46. Recipient Rsch. Pace Setter award Nat. Inst. Drug Abuse, 1977, Louis and Bert Freedman Found. award N.Y. Acad. Scis., 1980, Nathan B. Eddy Meml. award Coll. on Problems of Drug Dependence, Lexington, Ky., 1983, Alumni Profl. Achievement award U. Chgo., 1986; Health Rsch. Coun. NYC career scientist, 1959-75. Fellow AAAS, N.Y. Acad. Scis. (trustee 1986-89); mem. Am. Soc. Biol. Chemists, Am. Soc. Neurochemistry, Am. Soc. Pharmacology, Internat. Soc. Neurochemistry, Am. Chem. Soc., Sigma Xi. Lodges: B'nai B'rith. Research, publs. on opiate receptors, endorphins, biochemistry of analgesic action, vitamin E metabolism, acyl-coenzyme A synthesis. Office: 550 1st Ave New York NY 10016-6402 Office Phone: 212-263-5637. Business E-Mail: eric.simon@nyu.edu.

**SIMON, EVELYN,** lawyer; b. N.Y.C., May 13, 1943; d. Joseph and Adele (Holzschlag) Berkman; m. Fredrick Simon, Aug. 18, 1963; children: Amy Jocelyn, Marcie Ann. AB in Physics, Barnard Coll., 1963; MS in Physics, U. Pitts., 1964; JD, Wayne State U., 1978; LLB, Monash U., Melbourne, Australia, 1980. Bar: Mich. 1980, Victoria (Australia) 1981. Supr. engring. Chrysler Corp., Detroit, 1964-72; edn. and profl. mgr. Engring. Soc. Detroit, 1972-78; solicitor Arthur Robinson & Co., Melbourne, 1980-81; sr. atty. Ford Motor Co., Detroit, 1981-89; assoc. gen. counsel Sheller-Globe Corp., Detroit, 1989-90; v.p. planning, gen. counsel United Techs. Automotive Inc., Dearborn, Mich., 1991-94, v.p. bus. devel. and legal affairs, 1995-96, v.p. Asian bus. devel., 1997-98; pvt. practice, 1999—. Cons. internat. bus. devel., 1998—. Mem.: Mich. Bar Assn. Office: 1787 Alexander Dr Bloomfield Hills MI 48302-1204 Office Phone: 248-539-0969. E-mail: evelynsimon@prodigy.net.

**SIMON, GARY LEONARD,** internist, educator; b. Bklyn., Dec. 18, 1946; s. Bernard and Dorothy (Ligeti) Simon; m. Vicki Thiessen, Aug. 29, 1970; children: Jason, Jessica. BS, U. Md., 1968, MD, 1975; PhD, U. Wis., 1972. Diplomate Am. Bd. Internal Medicine, Am. Bd. Infectious Diseases. Resident in internal medicine U. Md. Hosp., Balt., 1975—78; fellow infectious diseases Tufts-New Eng. Med. Ctr., Boston, 1978—80; asst. prof. dept. medicine George Washington U., Washington, 1980-84, assoc. prof., 1984-89, assoc. chmn. medicine, 1984-97, prof., 1989—, dir. divsn. infectious diseases, 1993—, vice chmn. medicine, 1997—; Cons. on AIDS Nat. Am. Med. Coll., Washington, 1990—. Contbr. articles to profl. jours. Fellow: ACP (Laureate award 2000), Infectious Disease Soc.; mem.: Internat. AIDS Soc., Assn. Subspecialty Profs., Am. Soc. Microbiology. Office: George Washington U 2150 Pennsylvania Ave NW Washington DC 20037-3201 Office Phone: 202-741-2234. Business E-Mail: gsimon@mfa.gwu.edu.

**SIMON, GEORGE T.,** lawyer; BA, Trinity Coll., 1969; JD, Harvard U. Law Sch., 1972. Bar: N.Y. 1973, Ill. 1982. Staff atty. SEC, Washington, 1976—81; ptnr. Foley & Lardner LLP, Chgo., 1991—, mem. mgmt. com. Mem.: SEC Hist. Soc. (chmn., market regulation com.), Trinity Coll. (bd. fellows 1998—2002), Securities Industry Assn., ABA, Northwestern U. Law Sch. Garrett Inst. (exec. com.). Office: Foley & Lardner LLP 321 N Clark St Ste 2800 Chicago IL 60610-4764 Office Phone: 312-832-4554. Business E-Mail: gsimon@foley.com

**SIMON, GREGORY,** lawyer; b. Blytheville, Ark., Nov. 18, 1951; s. Michael F. and Marcella (Kallile) S.; m. Jennifer Lee Marberg, Dec. 21, 1978 (div. Mar. 1982); m. Margo Lynn Reid, Sept. 5, 1988; children: Michael Reid Simon, Kallile Speice Simon. Student, U. Wien, Vienna, 1971-72; BA, U. Ark., 1973; JD, U. Wash., 1983. Bar: Wash. 1983. Press sec. Barry Commoner for Pres., Flushing, NY, 1980; law clk. Riddell, Williams et al, Seattle, 1982; atty. Roberts & Shefelman, Seattle, 1983-85; counsel, staff dir. Investigation and Oversight subcom. House Com. on Sci., Washington, 1985-91; legis. dir. Senator Al Gore, Washington, 1991-93; chief domestic policy advisor Vice Pres. Al Gore, Washington, 1993—2001; chair Infotech Strategies, 2002—03; pres. Fastercures/Ctr. Accelerating Med. Solutions, Washington, 2003—. Named Outstanding Oralist, N.W. Round, Jessup Internat. Law Competition, 1983; European Cmty. Visitors Program fellow, Brussels, Strasbourg, London, Rome, Madrid, 1989; Sharon Nelson Leadership award, Shidler Ctr. Law, Commerce, Tech., U. Wash. Law Sch., 2004. Office: FasterCures Ctr Accelerating Med Solutions 509 Seventh St NW Washington DC 20004 Office Phone: 202-654-7090. Office Fax: 202-654-7079.

**SIMON, HAROLD,** radiologist; b. Trenton, N.J., May 13, 1930; s. John and Rae B. Simon; m. Jane L. Ludwig, Feb. 25, 1956; children: Steven Gregg, John Gregory. MD, Duke U., 1955. Diplomate Am. Bd. Radiology, Am. Bd. Nuclear Medicine. Intern U.S. Naval Hosp., Chelsea, Mass., 1955-56; resident in radiology Mass. Gen. Hosp., Boston, 1958-61, Oak Ridge Inst. Nuc. Medicine, 1959; instr. radiology Med. Sch., Tufts U., Boston, 1961-63, clin. asst. prof., 1965, assoc. clin. prof., 1971-77, clin. prof., 1977-98; pvt. practice Newton Lower Falls, Mass., 1963-95; mem. staff Newton (Mass.) Wellesley Hosp., assoc. chief radiology, 1977—, radiologist-in-chief, 1987-95; cons. VA Med. Sys., 1997—. Dir. Sch. Nuc. Med. Tech.; bd. dirs., mem. CRC com., mem. audit com. Grove Bank, chmn. audit com., 1995—96; bd. dirs., treas. Newell Physicians, Inc., 1986—93; mem. staff Intracoastal Med. Sys., West Palm Beach, Fla., 1997—2001; bd. overseers Newell Health Corp.; cons. VA Hosp., Boston, 1996—, Charitas Norwood (Mass.) Hosp. Contbr. articles to profl. jours. With USNR, 1955—58, med. officer USN, 1956—58. Fellow: Am. Coll. Radiology; mem.: Mass. Radiology Soc., Mass. Med. Soc. (mem. ins. com. 1992—95), New Eng. Roentgen Ray Soc., Am.

---

Roentgen Ray Soc., Radiol. Soc. N.Am., Banyon Country Club, Belmont Country Club, Pinebrook Country Club (pres. 1982—85), Phi Beta Kappa, Phi Eta Sigma. Home: 252 Atlantic Ave Palm Beach FL 33480-3709

**SIMON, HERBERT,** real estate developer, professional basketball team executive; b. Bklyn., Oct. 23, 1934; s. Max and Mae Simon; m. Bui Simon; children: Jennifer, Stephen, Sarah, Rachel, Asher, Sean. Grad., CCNY. With Albert Frankel Co., Indpls., 1959; co-founder Melvin Simon and Associates, Inc., Indpls., 1959—; went pub. and became Simon Property Group, 1993; merged with DeBartolo Realty Corp. and became Simon DeBartolo Group, 1996; name changed back to Simon Property Group, 1998; now co-chmn. bd. Simon Property Group, Inc.; co-owner Ind. Pacers, NBA, Indpls., 1983—. Named one of Forbes' Richest Americans, 2006. Office: Simon Property Group Inc 115 W Washington St Indianapolis IN 46204 also: Ind Pacers 125 South Pennsylvania St Indianapolis IN 46204*

**SIMON, HORST D.,** computer scientist; b. Aug. 8, 1953; married; 2 children. Diploma in Math., Technische U. Berlin, 1978. PhD, U. Calif., 1982. Asst. prof. SUNY, Stony Brook, NY, 1982—83; with Boeing Computer Svcs., 1983—89, coord. engring. and tech. applications divsn., 1983—86, mgr. computational math. group, 1986—87; mgr. rsch. dept. computer sci. corp. NASA Ames Rsch. Ctr., Moffett Field, Calif., 1989—94; rsch. market devel. mgr. advanced sys. divsn. Silicon Graphics, 1994—96; dir. Nat. Energy Rsch. Sci. Computing Divsn., Computational Rsch. Divsn. Lawrence Berkeley Nat. Libr., 1996—. Spkr. in field; mem. indsl. adv. bd. dept. computer sci. U. Calif., Davis; mem. internat. adv. panel Inst. HPC, Singapore. Editor: (books) Scientific Applications of the Connection Machine, 1989, Parallel Computational Fluid Dynamics, 1992, Parallel Processing for Scientific Computing, 1995, Solving Irregularly Structured Problems in Parallel, 1998; contbr. articles to profl. jours., chapters to books; mng. editor: Internat. Jour. High Speed Computing, 1989—97, mem. editl. bd.: SIAM Jour. Sci. and Statistical Computing, 1989—95, Jour. Sci. Programming, NHSE Review, Advances in Engineering Software (formerly Computing Systems Engineering), others. Recipient (with NAS Parallel Benchmarks Team) H. Julian Allen award, 1995, (with group from Cray and Boeing) Gordon Bell Prize, 1988. Office: NERSC Divn Dir Berkeley Lab MS 50B4230 One Cyclotron Rd Berkeley CA 94720-8150*

**SIMON, H(UEY) PAUL,** lawyer; b. Lafayette, La., Oct. 19, 1923; s. Jules and Ida (Rogére) S.; m. Carolyn Perkins, Aug. 6, 1949 (dec. Dec. 1999); 1 child, John Clark. BS, U. Southwestern La., 1943; JD, Tulane U., 1947. CPA La., 1947; bar: La. 1947. Pvt. practice, New Orleans, 1947—; asst. prof. advanced acctg. and taxation U. Southwestern La., 1944-45; staff acct. Haskins & Sells (now Deloitte & Touche), New Orleans, 1945-53, prin., 1953-57; ptnr. Deutsch, Kerrigan & Stiles, 1957-79; sr. founding ptnr. Simon, Peragine, Smith & Redfearn, 1979—. Mem. New Orleans Bd. Trade. Author: Community Property and Liability for Funeral Expenses of Deceased Spouse, 1946, Income Tax Deductibility of Attorney's Fees in Action in Boundary, 1946, Fair Labor Standards Act and Employee's Waiver of Liquidated Damages, 1946, Louisiana Income Tax Law, 1956, Changes Effected by the Louisiana Trust Code, 1965, Gifts to Minors and the Parent's Obligation of Support, 1968; co-author: Deductions—Business or Hobby, 1975, Role of Attorney in IRS Tax Return Examination, 1978; assoc. editor: The Louisiana CPA, 1956-60; mem. bd. editors Tulane Law Rev., 1945-46, adv. bd. editors, 1992—; estates, gifts and trusts editor The Tax Times, 1986-87. Bd. dirs., mem. fin. com. World Trade Ctr., 1985-86; mem. New Orleans Met. Crime Commn., Coun. for a Better La., New Orleans Met. Area Com., Bur. Govtl. Rsch., Pub. Affairs Rsch. Coun.; co-chmn. NYU Tax Conf., New Orleans, 1976; mem. dean's coun. Tulane U. Law Sch. Fellow Am. Coll. Tax Counsel; mem. ABA (com. ct. procedure tax sect. 1958—), AICPA, La. Bar Assn. (com. on legis. and adminstrv. practice 1966-70, bd. cert. tax atty.), New Orleans Bar Assn., Internat. Bar Assn. (com. on securities issues and trading 1970-88), Am. Judicature Soc., Soc. La. CPAs, New Orleans Assn. Notaries, Tulane U. Alumni Assn., New Orleans C. of C. (coun. 1952-66), Tulane Tax Inst. (program com. 1960-96, emeritus 1997--), Internat. House (bd. dirs. 1976-79, 82-85), Internat. Platform Assn., City Energy Club, Press Club, New Orleans Country Club, Phi Delta Phi (past pres. New Orleans chpt.), Sigma Pi Alpha. Roman Catholic. Achievements include being listed annually in the best lawyers in Am. 1985-; becoming the 11th attorney-CPA in La. history. Office: 30th Fl Energy Ctr New Orleans LA 70163 Home: 71071 Riverside Dr Covington LA 70434 Mailing: PO Box 2759 Covington LA 70434 Office Phone: 504-258-9177. Personal E-mail: hpsimon@aol.com. Business E-Mail: hpsimon@spsr-law.com. *Developing and maintaining consistency and constancy in feeling and showing genuine respect towards others, nourish and stimulate an individual to day by day become a better person. Whether alone or in the presence of others, one who abides by the guidance and rules he would advocate to others invariably finds the greatest reward of all--true respect for one's self.*

**SIMON, J. RICHARD (JENNINGS RICHARD SIMON),** psychologist, educator; b. Marinette, Wis., Sept. 17, 1929; s. Leonard Robert and Sophie Sip (Cohn); m. Betty Ethel Pearl, Aug. 26, 1954; children: Alissa, Susan. BBA, U. Wis., 1951, MS, 1953, PhD, 1955. Fulbright rsch. fellow U. Cambridge, Eng., 1955-56; assoc. rsch. scientist Am. Inst. Rsch., Pitts., 1956-57; from asst. prof. to prof. psychology, indsl. engring. U. Iowa, Iowa City, 1957-99, prof. emeritus, 1999—. Vis. prof. U. Sheffield, Eng., 1971-72, U. Warwick, Eng., 1981; hon. rsch. fellow Univ. Coll. London, 1987, 93; vis. prof. Birkbeck Coll., U. London, 1997-99; reviewer for profl. jours., govt. agys. Cons. editor: Jour. Exptl. Psychology, 1970-74, Jour. Exptl. Psychology: Human Learning and Memory, 1975, Jour. Motor Behavior, 1976-88; contbr. articles to profl. jours. NIH fellow, 1971. Fellow APA, Am. Psychol. Soc. (charter); mem. Inst. Indsl. Engrs., Am. Soc. Engring Edn. Human Factors Soc., Psychonomic Soc., Midwestern Psychol. Assn., Sigma Xi, Phi Beta Kappa, Phi Kappa Phi, Phi Eta Sigma. Achievements include discovery of simon effect; research in human info. processing and performance changes accompanying aging. Home: 1620 College Court Pl Iowa City IA 52245-4416 Office: Univ Iowa Dept Psychology Seashore Hall Iowa City IA 52242 E-mail: j-simon@uiowa.edu.

**SIMON, J. STEPHEN,** oil industry executive; BS civil engring. Duke U.; MBA, Northwestern U., Evanston, Ill. With Exxon U.S.A., 1967, mgr. refinery Baton Rouge; supply and transp. mgr. Esso Europe, Esso U.S.A.; exec. asst. to the pres. Exxon Corp.; gen. mgr. Esso Caribbean and Ctrl. Am.; pres. Esso Italiana; exec. v.p. Exxon Co. Internat., 1997—99; pres. Exxon-Mobil Refining and Supply Co., 1999—2004; v.p. ExxonMobil Corp., 1999—2004, sr. v.p., 2004—. Bd. dir. ExxonMobil Corp., 2006—. Mem. governance com. Nat. Action Council for Minorities in Engring.; mem. bd. vis., mem. Pres. Council Duke Univ. Sch. Engring.; mem. Kellogg adv. bd. Northwestern Univ. Office: ExxonMobil Refining and Supply Co 3225 Gallows Rd Fairfax VA 22037*

**SIMON, JACQUELINE ALBERT,** political scientist, writer; d. Louis and Rose (Axelroad) Albert; m. Pierre Simon; children: Lisette, Orville. BA cum laude, NYU, MA, 1972, PhD, 1977. Adj. assoc. prof. Southampton Coll., 1977-79; mng. editor Point of Contact, NYC, 1975-76; assoc. editor, US bur. chief Politique Internationale, Paris, 1979—. Sr. fellow Inst. French Studies, NYU, 1980—; adj. assoc. prof., 1982-85; assoc. prof. govt. Southampton Coll., 1982-83; frequent appearances French TV and radio. Author: A Century of Artists' Letters: Delacroix to Leger, 2004; contbg. editor: Harper's mag., 1984—92; contbr. numerous articles to French mag., revs., books on internat. affairs. Bd. dirs. Fresh Air Fund, 1984—. Overseas Press Club Found. Mem. Overseas Press Club of Am. (bd. dirs., treas. 2000-04), Phi Beta Kappa. Home: 988 5th Ave New York NY 10021-0143 Personal E-mail: jasimon@verizon.net.

**SIMON, JAMES LOWELL,** lawyer; b. Nov. 8, 1944; s. K. Lowell and Elizabeth Ann (Unholz) S.; m. RuthAnn Beck, July 4, 1997; children: Heather Lyn Small, Brandon James; stepchildren: Gary G. Mower, Richard M. Nazareth II, Juliet A. Nazareth; student, U. Ill., 1962-63, JD with honors, 1975; BSEE magna cum laude, Bradley U., 1967. Bar: Fla. 1975, Utah 1999,

Calif. 2002, U.S. Dist. Ct. (mid. dist.) Fla. 1976, U.S. Dist. Ct. Utah 1999, U.S. Dist. Ct. (no. dist.) Calif. 2002, U.S. Ct. Appeals (11th cir.) 1981, U.S. Patent Office 1983. Engr. Pan Am. World Airways, Cape Kennedy, Fla., 1967-68; assoc. Akerman, Senterfitt & Eidson, Orlando, Fla., 1975-80; ptnr. Bogin, Munns, Munns & Simon, Orlando, 1980-87, Holland & Knight, LLP, 1987-99; corp. counsel Agilent Technologies Inc., Palo Alto, Calif., 2000—. With Seminole County Sch. Adv. Coun., Fla., 1981-88, chmn., 1982-83; with Forest City Local Sch. Adv. Com., Altamonte Springs, Fla., 1981-84, Code Enforcement Bd., Altamonte Springs, 1983-84, Cen. Bus. Dist. Study com., Altamonte Springs, 1983-85, Rep. Coun. of '76, Seminole County, 1982-87; mem. Seminole County Libr. Adv. Bd., 1989-92, sec., 1990, pres., 1991, Seminole County Citizens for Quality Edn., 1990-92; mem. Seminole County Sch. Dist. Strategic Planning Com., 1991-99, Leadership Orlando Alumni, 1992-99; bd. dirs. Found. for Seminole County Pub. Schs., 1992-95, chmn., 1993-94; bd. dirs. Greater Seminole C. of C., 1993; active Lake Brantley HS Band Boosters, 1995-2000, Lake Brantley HS PTSA, 1995-2000, Chorus Boosters, 1997, Leadership Club-Heart of Fla. United Way, 1997; sponsor concerts Orlando Philharm. Orch. for Boys and Girls Clubs. Cen. Fla., 1996-97; regional dir. region 5 Holocaust Remembrance Project, 1997-99. Capt. USAF, 1968-72. Mem. ABA, Am. Corp. Counsel Assn., Am. Intellectual Property Law Assn., Intellectual Property Owners Assn. (chmn. copyright law com. 2003-05), U. Ill. Alumni Club, Phi Kappa Phi, Tau Beta Pi, Sigma Tau, Eta Kappa Nu Republican. Home: 1675 Tupolo Dr San Jose CA 95124-4754 Office: M/S 54U PB 5301 Stevens Creek Blvd Santa Clara CA 95051 Office Phone: 650-485-5672. Personal E-mail: JimandRuthann@comcast.net. Business E-Mail: jim_simon@agilent.com

**SIMON, JEFFREY S.,** psychiatrist; b. Tomah, Wis., Oct. 21, 1955; m. Molly M. Sheedy, June 28, 2002; children: Sydney S., Alex J., Mikaela R. MD, Med. Coll. of Wis., 1981. Founder Northbrooke Rsch. Ctr., Brown Deer, Wis., 1989—. Recipient Rsch. award, Milw. Chpt. of the Alliance of the Mentally Ill, 1998, Wis. Chpt. of the Alliance of the Mentally Ill, 2001. Office: Northbrooke Rsch Ctr 9275 N 49th Ste 200 Brown Deer WI 53223 Office Phone: 414-357-9444.

**SIMON, JIMMY LOUIS,** pediatrician, educator; b. San Francisco, Dec. 27, 1930; s. Sylvain L. and Hilda H. (Netter) S.; m. Marilyn S. Wachter, June 21, 1953; children: Kent, Nancy. AB, U. Calif.-Berkeley, 1952; MD, U. Calif.-Berkeley, San Francisco, 1955. Diplomate Am. Bd. Pediats. Intern U. Calif., San Francisco, 1955-56; resident Grace-New Haven Hosp., 1956-57; sr. asst. resident Boston Children's Hosp., 1957-58; instr., asst. prof. pediats. U. Okla., Oklahoma City, 1960-64; asso. prof. U. Tex. Med. Br., Galveston, 1966-72; prof. pediatrics, 1972-74; prof., chmn. pediats. Bowman Gray Sch. Medicine, Wake Forest U., Winston-Salem, NC, 1974-96; prof., chmn. emeritus Wake Forest U. Sch. Medicine, Winston-Salem, NC, 1996—. With USAF, 1958-60. Mem. Am. Pediat. Soc., Am. Acad. Pediats., Am. Bd. Pediats., Ambulatory Pediat. Assn., Alpha Omega Alpha. Office: Wake Forest U Sch Medicine Dept Pediatrics Medical Center Blvd Winston Salem NC 27157-0001

**SIMON, JOHN A.,** investment company executive; Bachelor's degree, Princeton U.; M in Pub. Policy, Harvard U. Various positions including dep. dir. rsch. and devel. Exec. Office Adminstrn. Commonwealth of Mass.; dir. bus. info. and strategic planning Harvard Pilgrim Health Care; dep. asst. adminstr. U.S. Agy. Internat. Devel., 2002—03; spl. asst. to Pres., sr. dir. for relief, stabilization and devel. Nat. Security Coun. The White House, dir. devel. issues, 2003—05; exec. v.p. Overseas Pvt. Investment Corp. (OPIC), 2006—. Office: Overseas Pvt Investment Corp 1100 New York Ave NW Washington DC 20527*

**SIMON, JOHN BERN,** lawyer; b. Cleve., Aug. 8, 1942; s. Seymour Frank and Roslyn (Schultz) S.; children: Lindsey Helaine, Douglas Bernard. BS, U. Wis., 1964; JD, DePaul U., 1967. Bar: Ill. 1967. Asst. U.S. atty. U.S. Justice Dept., Chgo., 1967-70, dep. chief civil div., 1970-71, chief civil div., 1971-74; spl. counsel to the Ill. Dept. Pub. Aid, Chgo., 1976-77; legal cons. to Commn. on Rev. of Nat. Policy Toward Gambling, Chgo., 1975-76; ptnr. firm Friedman & Koven, 1975-85, mem. exec. com., 1983-85; ptnr. firm Jenner & Block, 1986—. Spl. cons. to adminstr. DEA Dept. Justice, 1976-77; counsel to Gov.'s Revenue Study Commn. on Legalized Gambling, 1977-78; spl. counsel Ill. Racing Bd., 1979-80; lectr. tng. seminars and confs.; instr. U.S. Atty. Gen.'s Advocacy Inst., Washington, 1974; lectr. Nat. Conf. Organized Crime, Washington, 1975, Dade County Inst. Organized Crime, Ft. Lauderdale, Fla., 1976; faculty Cornell Inst. Organized Crime, Ithaca, N.Y., 1976, judge Miner Moot Ct. competition Northwestern U., 1971-73; mem. law coun. DePaul U., 1974-83, mem. alumni assn., 1984-85, chmn., 1975-79; adj. prof. DePaul U. Coll. Law, 1977, 81; faculty Practising Law Inst., Chgo., 1984. Contbr. articles to profl. jours. Bd. dirs. Lawyer's Trust Fund Ill., 1998-2004, treas., 2000-01, v.p., 2002-03, pres., 2003-04, Cmty. Film Workshop of Chgo., 1977-90, Friends of Glencoe Parks, 1977-78, sec., 1978-79; mem. nominating com. Glencoe Sch. Bd., 1978-81, chmn. audit rules com., 1980-81; pres Glencoe Hist. Soc., 1979-82; mem. Glencoe Zoning Bd. Appeals, Zoning Commn., Sign Bd. Appeals, 1981-86, chmn., 1984-86; mem. Ill. Inaugural Com., 1979, 83, 87, 95; bd. dirs., mem. exec. com. Chgo. World's Fair 1992 Authority, 1983-85; mem. Chancery divsn. task force Spl. Commn. on Adminstrn. of Justice in Cook County, 1985-87; trustee De Paul U., 1990, chair phys. plant and property com., 1992-94, vice chair, 1995-2004, chair, 2004—; commr. Ill. Racing Bd., 1990—; gen. trustee Lincoln Acad. Ill., 1993—, regent, 1999—, chancellor, 2001—; mem. Ill. Supreme Ct. Planning and Oversight Com. for Jud. Performance Evaluation Program, 1997-98, 2000-05, Ill. Supreme Ct. Rules Com., 2004—. Recipient Bancroft-Whitney Am. Jurisprudence award, 1965, 66, Judge Learned Hand Human Rels. award Am. Jewish Com., 1994, award for outstanding svc. to legal profession DePaul U. Coll. Law, 1996, Am. ORT Jurisprudence award, 1999. Mem. ABA (com. on liaison with the judiciary 1983-95), Fed. Bar Assn., Chgo. Bar Assn. (fed. civil procedure com. 1979-85, chmn. 1985-86, bd. mgrs. 1987-89, chmn. house com. 1989-90, treas. 1990-91, 2d v.p. 1991-92, 1st v.p. 1992-93, pres. 1993-94), Ill. State Bar Assn., Women's Bar Assn., Ill. Police Assn., Ill. Sheriffs Assn., U.S. Treasury Agts. Assn., Chgo. Bar Assn., DePaul U. Alumni Assn. (pres. 1985-87, chmn. spl. gifts com. campaign, chmn. Simon Commn. 1989-91, nat. chair for ann. giving 1991-94), Std. Club. Office: Jenner & Block One IBM Plz 42nd Fl Chicago IL 60611

**SIMON, JOHN DOUGLAS,** chemistry educator; b. Cin., Feb. 11, 1957; s. Thomas Henry and Sally Sussler Simon; m. Diane Marie Szaflarski, Dec. 7, 1991; 1 child, Katherine Anne (dec.). BA, Williams Coll., 1979; MA, Harvard U., 1981, PhD, 1983. Postdoctoral rschr. UCLA, 1983-85; prof. chemistry U. Calif., San Diego, 1985—97; George B. Geller prof., dept. chemistry Duke Univ., 1997—, chmn. dept. chem., 1999—2004, vice provost academic affairs, 2005—. Mem. molecular and cellular biophysics study sect. NIH, Bethesda, Md., 1994-99. Author: Braving the Elements, 1985; contbr. articles to profl. jours. Recipient Fresenius award Nat. Chemistry Fraternity, 1993; Alfred P. Sloan fellow Sloan Found., 1988-90; Camille and Henry Dreyfus Tchr. scholar Dreyfus Found., 1990-95. Mem. AAAS, Am. Phys. Soc., Am. Chem. Soc.; fel. Am. Physical Soc.

**SIMON, KARLA W.,** law educator; b. New Haven, May 30, 1947; d. Frederick Tyler and Irene Marianne (Schoening) S.; m. Leon E. Irish. BA, Western Coll., Oxford, Ohio, 1969; JD, Duke U., 1972; LLM in Taxation, NYU, 1976. Bar: N.C. 1972, U.S. Dist. Ct. (mid. dist.) N.C. 1973, U.S. Ct. Appeals (4th cir.) 1974, U.S. Supreme Ct. 1991. Ptnr. Hobbet & Simon, Durham, NC, 1972-76; rsch. fellow Yale U. Law Sch., New Haven, 1976-78; asst. prof., assoc. prof. Seton Hall U. Sch. Law, Newark, 1978-84; prof. U. San Diego Sch. Law, 1984-89, coord. L.A. grad. tax program, 1984-88; prof. Cath. U. Am. Sch. Law, Washington, 1989—. Instr. U. Fla. Coll. Law, Gainesville, 1975; adj. asst. prof. Yeshiva U. Benjamin Cardozo Sch. Law, N.Y.C., 1977-78; vis. prof. UCLA Sch. Law, 1982-84, Ctrl. European U., 1997—, Peking Univ. Law Sch. 2005; vis. fellow Yale Law Sch., 1992-93; cons. O'Melveny & Myers, Washington, 1988-93; exec. dir. Am. Tax Policy Inst., Washington, 1990-92; pres., CEO Internat. Ctr. for Non-for-Profit Law, 1992-97, exec. v.p., 1997-2001; chair Internat. Ctr. Civil Soc. Law, 2002—. Editor in chief: Inter. Jour. Civil Soc. Law, 2003—. Mem. ABA (vice chmn.

spl. project com. sect. taxation 1994-95, tax procedure com. sect. adminstrv. law 1989-94 sect. internat. law 2003—), Am. Coll. Tax Counsel, Am. Law Inst. Democrat. Avocations: reading, collecting art and antiques. Office: Cath U Am Sch Law 3600 John Mccormack Rd NE Washington DC 20064-0001 Home: 304 Kyle Rd Crownsville MD 21032 Office Phone: 202-319-5140. Business E-Mail: simon@law.edu.

**SIMON, KEITH R.,** safety engineer, petroleum engineer, radio personality; b. Lafayette, La., July 2, 1955; s. Jean Raymond and Ranelle T. (Touchet) S.; m. Martha Simon, Oct. 16, 1976 (div. Oct. 1979); 1 child, Jamie. BSN, BS, postgrad., U. La., 1980, student, 1981. Cert. nurse, nursing instr.; crane operator, first aid, offshore orientation lead abatement 1991, API thread inspector 1985, safety profl. 1991. Ops. mgr. Boco of Lafayette, 1980-82, exec. v.p., 1982-84, sr. project supr. La., 1980—82, exec. v.p., 1982—84; safety dir., corp. security Petro-Drive, Inc., 1989—91; divsnl. mgr. Petro-Drive/Boco of Lafayette, Inc., La., 1984—86, v.p., 1991—; offshore internat. sector mgr. Sigma Coatings USA, 1998—; offshore internat. project mgr. Sigmakalon, Houston, 2000—03; v.p. ops. Chavez Svc. Cos., 2004—; pres. and owner Silver Bullet Prodns. Inc., 1983—, Silver Bullet Limousine, 1983—. Mem. ARC, 1986—. Named Coors Lite Nat. Disc Jockey, 1984, named in Men Achievement, 1991, 2000 Notable Am. Men, 1992, Personalities Am., 1993; recipient Silver Shield of Valor award, 1992, Lifetime Achievement award, 1993. Mem.: ARC, Assn. Gen. Contractors, Am. Bldg. Contractors, Ind. Am. Drilling Contractors, Nat. Safety Coun., Acadiana Safety Assn., Nat. Assn. of Corrosion Engrs., Steel Structure Painting Coun., Lafayette Soc. Tng. and Devel., Am. Soc. Safety Engrs. Achievements include engineered, developed new techs., methodologies for offshore oil drilling. Avocations: skiing, softball, football, disc jockey. Office: 1401 Destrehan Ave Harvey LA 70058-2436 Home: 104 Pomerol Pl Lafayette LA 70503-6527 E-mail: ksimon007@bellsouth.net.

**SIMON, KENNETH MARK,** lawyer; b. Pitts., Apr. 25, 1952; s. Harvey and Jean (Busis) S.; m. Janet Hahn, June 24, 1979; children: Eliza, Jessica, Zachary. BA magna cum laude, U. Pitts., 1974; JD, Georgetown U., 1977. Bar: DC 1977. Assoc. Dickstein, Shapiro & Morin, Washington, 1977-85; ptnr. Dickstein, Shapiro Morin & Oshinsky LLP, Washington, 1985—, co-head Corp. & Fin. Practice Group, 1999—2004, group leader, Energy Practice Group, 2004—. Sec. Ocean State Power, Burrillville, R.I., 1989-96 Gen. counsel Conservation Internat., Washington, 1988-93. Mem. Fed. Energy Bar (com. on cogeneration and ind. power, vice-chmn. 1989-90, chmn. 1990-91), D.C. Bar Assn. (sect. on environment, energy and natural resources energy com., chmn. energy com. 1988-90), Electric Generation Assn. (gen. counsel 1997-99). Democrat. Office: Dickstein Shapiro Morin Oshinsky LLC 2101 L St NW Washington DC 20037-1526 Office Phone: 202-828-2227. Office Fax: 202-887-0689. E-mail: simonk@dsmo.com.

**SIMON, LEONARD SAMUEL,** banker; b. NYC, Oct. 28, 1936; s. Nathaniel and Lena (Pasternack) S.; m. Marion Appel, Sept. 1, 1957; children: Andrew, Jonathan. BS, MIT, 1958; MS, Columbia U., 1959, PhD, 1963. Mem. faculty Grad. Sch. Mgmt., U. Rochester, 1962-79, prof., 1974-79; v.p. Community Savs. Bank, Rochester, NY, 1969-74, sr. v.p., 1974-77, exec. v.p., 1977-83, Rochester Community Sav. Bank, 1983-84, chmn., chief exec. officer, 1984-97; chmn., CEO, pres. RSCB Fin., Inc., 1995-97; chmn. Capital Internet Grp., 1997—2000; vice chmn. Charter One Fin. Inc., 1997—2001. Bd. dirs Integrated Nano Tech., Inc., Landmark Tech. Ptnrs., LLC; chmn. Telephone Computing Svc. Corp., 1974—79, Cmty. Preservation Corp., 2004—, pres. bd. effectiveness inst.; trustee Tchrs. Ins. Annuity Assn. Editor-in-chief, founding editor: Interfaces, 1970-76; Author books and articles in field. Past chmn. Rochester-Monroe County chpt. ARC, Rochester Area Ednl. TV Assn., Career Devel. Svcs. of Rochester; past trustee Ctr. for Govt. Rsch.; mem. Urban Policy Conf., Brookings Instn., 1972-73, 64th Am. Assembly; bd. dirs Cmty. Preservation. Ford Found. grantee, 1964; recipient MIT Corp. Leadership award, 1987. Mem. Genesee Valley Club, Beta Gamma Sigma.

**SIMON, LOTHAR,** publishing executive; b. Wuppertal, Germany, Sept. 17, 1938; arrived in U.S., 1961, naturalized, 1973; s. Fritz and Erna (Backhaus) S.; m. Jeannine Rechtman, Oct. 30, 1964; 1 child, Charles. Mgr. book dept. Franz Bader Book Shop and Globe Book Shop, Washington, 1961-66; sales mgr. Humanities Press Inc., N.Y.C., 1966-73; pres. Longman Inc., N.Y.C., 1973-81; pub. cons., 1981-82; pres., CEO Sheridan House, Inc., Dobbs Ferry, NY, 1982—. Mem. Assn. Am. Pubs., Town Club (Scarsdale, N.Y.). Democrat. Office: Sheridan House Inc 145 Palisade St Dobbs Ferry NY 10522-1617 Office Phone: 914-693-2410. Business E-Mail: lothars@sheridanhouse.com.

**SIMON, LOU ANNA KIMSEY,** academic administrator; BA in Math., Ind. State U., 1969, MS in Student Personnel and Counseling, 1970; PhD in Higher Edn., Mich. State U., 1974. Faculty mem. Mich. State U.; asst. dir. Office Instil. Rsch., 1974—78, asst. provost gen. academic administrn. 1981—87, assoc. provost, 1987—92, v.p. acad. affairs, 1993—2004, interim pres., 2003, pres., 2005—. Office: Mich State U 450 Administration Bldg East Lansing MI 48824-1046 Office Phone: 517-355-6560. Business E-Mail: presmail@msu.edu.

**SIMON, MARC,** communications executive; BS in Acctg., U. Ill., JD. CPA 1971. CFO, dir. APAC Customer Svcs. Inc. HA-LO Industries, Inc., Niles, Ill., 1995—98, vice chmn. APAC, 1998, exec. v.p., COO APAC Teleservices, Inc., 1998—2001, pres., CEO, 2001—.

**SIMON, MARTIN STANLEY,** economist, consultant; b. St. Louis, Sept. 6, 1926; s. Elmer Ellis and Bee Marion (Werner) S.; m. Rita Edith Scheinhorn, June 18, 1950; children: Deborah, Richard. BBA, CCNY, 1949; MA, NYU, 1953. Econ. statistician Indsl. Commodity Corp. N.Y.C., 1949-52; agrl. econ. statistician Dept. Agr., Washington, 1952-58; commodity analyst Connell Rice & Sugar Co., Inc., Westfield, NJ, 1958-62, asst. to pres., 1962-67, v.p., 1967-74; sr. v.p. Connell Rice & Sugar Co., Inc. (now The Connell Co.), Berkeley Heights, NJ, 1974-99; pres. Eureka Group, LLC, Westfield, NJ, 1999—, The Rice Econs. Group, LLC, Westfield, NJ, 1999—; cons. AID, Jamaica, 1963; mem. Rice Insp. Industry Adv. Com., Washington, 1971-72; adv. U.S. Del. to UN FAO Intergovtl. Meetings on Rice, 1981; export dir., bd. dirs Assn. Administrn. Rice Quotas, Inc., 1997-99. Served with U.S. Army, 1944-46, ETO. Recipient Class of 1920 award for merit in econ. stats. CCNY, 1949 Mem. Am. Econ. Assn., Am. Rice Millers Assn. (chmn. legis. options working group 1984-86, govt. programs com. 1984-86, PL480 subcom. 1988-90), Nat. Economists Club. Office: The Rice Econs Group LLC PO Box 2446 Westfield NJ 07091-2446 E-mail: rice.economics@prodigy.net.

**SIMON, MELVIN,** real estate developer, professional sports team executive; b. Oct. 21, 1926; s. Max and Mae Simon; m. Bren Burns, Sept. 14, 1972; children: Deborah, Cynthia, Tamme, David, Max. BS in Acctg., CCNY, 1949, M in Bus., Real Estate, 1983; PhD (hon.), Butler U., 1986, Ind. U., 1991. Leasing agt. Albert Frankel Co., Indpls., 1955-60; co-founder Melvin Simon & Associates, Indpls., 1959—, pres., 1960-73, co-chmn. bd., 1973—; went pub. becoming Simon Property Group, Inc.; merged with DeBartolo Realty Corp. to become Simon DeBartolo Group, 1996; reverted to Simon Property Group, 1998; now co-chmn. Simon Property Group, Inc.; co-owner Ind. Pacers, NBA, Indpls., 1983—. Adv. bd. Wharton's Real Estate, Phila., 1986—. Adv. bd. dean's council Ind. U., Bloomington; bd. dirs United Cerebral Palsy, Indpls., Muscular Dystrophy Assn., Indpls., Jewish Welfare Found., Indpls.; trustee Urban Land Inst., Internat. Council Shopping Ctrs. Served U.S. Army. Recipient Horatio Alger award Boy's Club Indpls., 1986; named Man of Yr., Jewish Welfare Fund, 1980; named one of Forbes' Richest Americans, 2006. Democrat. Jewish. Office: Indiana Pacers 125 S Penn St Indianapolis IN 46204*

**SIMON, MELVIN I.,** molecular biologist, educator; b. NYC, Feb. 8, 1937; s. Hyman and Sarah (Liebman) S.; m. Linda, Jan. 7, 1959; children—Joshua, David, Rachel BS, CCNY, 1959; PhD, Brandeis U., 1963. Postdoctoral fellow Princeton U., N.J., 1963-65; prof. biology U. Calif.-San Diego, La Jolla,

1965-82, Calif. Inst. Tech., Pasadena, 1982—, chmn., 1995-2000, prof., 2000—. Pres., dir. Agouron Inst., La Jolla, 1980— Contbr. articles to profl. jours. Mem. Nat. Acad. Scis. (Selman A. Waksman microbiology award 1991), Am. Soc. Microbiology

**SIMON, MELVON,** real estate company officer; married; 5 children. Leasing rep. Albert Frankel Co., Indpls.; co-founder Melvin Simon & Assocs., Indpls., 1960; co-chmn. bd. Simon Property Group, Inc., Indpls., 1993—; co-owner NBA Ind. Pacers. Prodr.: (films) Porky's. Office: Simon Property Group Inc National City Ctr 115 W Washington St Indianapolis IN 46204

**SIMON, NANCY LYNN,** performing arts educator, director; b. Chgo., June 20, 1942; d. Otis Benjamin Simon and Virginia Ruth Gilliland. BA, Whitman Coll., Walla Walla, Wash., 1959—63; MA, Tufts U., Somerville, Mass., 1963—65; PhD, U. Wash., Seattle, 1965—75. Paul Garrett prof. dramatic arts, dir. Harper Joy Theater Whitman Coll., 1967—; freelance theatre/opera dir., 1983—. Recipient George Ball Advising Excellence award, Whitman Coll., 1997, Thomas D. Howells award for disting. tchg. in humanities and arts, 2005, Paul Garrett Endowed Professorship award, 2006. Mem.: Artists Trust, Theatre Comm. Group, US Inst. Theater Tech., Actors' Equity Assn. Office: Whitman Coll 345 Boyer Ave Walla Walla WA 99362

**SIMON, NEIL,** playwright, screenwriter, television writer; b. Bronx, NY, July 4, 1927; s. Irving and Mamie Simon; m. Joan Baim, Sept. 30, 1953 (dec. 1973); children: Ellen, Nancy; m. Marsha Mason, 1973 (div. 1981); m. Diane Lander, 1987 (div. 1988); 1 child, Bryn; m. Diane Lander, 1990 (div. 1998); m. Elaine Joyce, 1999. Student, NYU, 1946; LLD (hon.), Hofstra U., 1981, Williams Coll., 1984. Sports editor Rev-Meter, Lowry Field, Colo., 1945—46; owner Eugene O'Neill Theatre, NYC. Author: materials for Tamiment (Pa.) revues, 1952—53, (Broadway plays) (with Danny Simon) Catch a Star, 1955, New Faces of 1956, 1956, (book for Broadway musical) Little Me, 1962 (Tony award nom. best book of a musical, 1963), Promises, Promises, 1970 (Tony award nom. best musical, 1969), They're Playing Our Song, 1980 (Tony award nom. best book of a musical, 1979), (Broadway plays) Come Blow Your Horn, 1961, Barefoot in the Park, 1964 (Tony award nom. best play, 1963), The Odd Couple, 1966 (Tony award best author, 1965, Writers Guild of Am. award best comedy, 1968), Sweet Charity, 1966 (Evening Standard Drama award, 1968, Tony award nom. best musical, 1966), The Star-Spangled Girl, 1967, Plaza Suite, 1969 (Tony award nom. best play, 1969), Last of the Red Hot Lovers, 1970 (Tony award nom. best play, 1970), The Gingerbread Lady, 1971, The Prisoner of Second Avenue, 1972 (Tony award nom. best play, 1972), The Sunshine Boys, 1973 (Tony award nom. best play, 1973), The Good Doctor, 1974 (Tony award nom. best score, 1974), God's Favorite, 1975, California Suite, 1977, Chapter Two, 1978 (Tony award nom. best play, 1978), I Ought to be in Pictures, 1981, Fools, 1982, Brighton Beach Memoirs, 1983 (NY Drama Critics Circle award best play, 1983), Biloxi Blues, 1986 (Tony award best play, 1986), The Odd Couple (female version), 1986, Broadway Bound, 1987 (Tony award nom. best play, 1987, Pulitzer prize nom. in drama, 1987), Rumors, 1990, Lost in Yonkers, 1991 (Tony award best play, 1991, Pulitzer prize in drama, 1991, Outer Critics Circle award outstanding play, 1991, Drama Desk award outstanding new play, 1991), Jake's Women, 1993, Laughter on the 23rd Floor, 1995, London Suite, 1995, Proposals, 1997, The Dinner Party, 2000, 45 Seconds From Broadway, 2001, (screenplay adaptations of plays) Come Blow Your Horn, 1963, Barefoot in the Park, 1967, The Odd Couple, 1968 (Acad. award nom. best adapted screenplay, 1969, Writers Guild of Am. award best comedy, 1969), Sweet Charity, 1969, Plaza Suite, 1971, The Star-Spangled Girl, 1971, Last of the Red Hot Lovers, 1972, The Prisoner of Second Avenue, 1975, The Sunshine Boys, 1975 (Writers Guild of Am. award best comedy adaptation, 1975, Acad. award nom. bext adapted screenplay, 1976, BAFTA award nom. best adapted screenplay, 1977, Golden Globe nom. best adapted screenplay, 1976), California Suite, 1978 (Acad. award nom. best adapted screenplay, 1979), Chapter Two, 1979, Brighton Beach Memoirs, 1986, Biloxi Blues, 1988, Broadway Bound, 1992, Lost in Yonkers, 1993; author & prodr. (screenplay adaptations of plays) Only When I Laugh (adapted from play The Gingerbread Lady), 1981, I Ought to be in Pictures, 1982; author: (screenplays) After the Fox, 1966, The Out-of-Towners, 1970 (Writers Guild of Am. award best comedy screenplay, 1970), The Heartbreak Kid, 1973 (Golden Globe nom. best screenplay, 1973), Murder by Death, 1976, The Goodbye Girl, 1977 (Golden Globe award best screenplay, 1977, Acad. award nom. best screenplay, 1978, BAFTA award nom. best screenplay, 1979), The Cheap Detective, 1978, Seems Like Old Times, 1980, The Lonely Guy (adaptation), 1984, The Sluggers Wife, 1984, The Marrying Man, 1991; author & prodr. (screenplays) Max Dugan Returns, 1983, The Odd Couple II, 1997; author: (TV series) Cavalcade of Stars, 1949—52, The Tallulah Bankhead Show, 1951, Stanley, 1956, The Sid Caesar Show, 1956—57 (Emmy award, 1956, 1957), The Phil Silvers Arrow Show, 1958—59 (Emmy award, 1958), The Garry Moore Show, 1959—60, The Odd Couple (based on play), 1970—75, also NBC spl. The Trouble with People, 1972, (TV films) Kibbe Hates Fitch, 1964, (teleplay) The Good Doctor, 1978, Sonny Boys, 1982, (teleplay) Jake's Women, 1996, London Suite, 1996, (autobiography) Rewrites: A Memoir, 1996. Cpl. USAF, 1945—46. Recipient Sam S. Shubert award, Shubert Found., 1968, Special Tony award for overall contribution to theater, 1975, Am. Comedy award for lifetime achievement, 1989, Drama League Unique Contribution to Theater award, 1991, Kennedy Ctr. Honors Lifetime Achievement award, 1995, Mark Twain prize, Kennedy Ctr., 2006. Mem.: Writers Guild Am. (Laurel award 1979), Dramatists Guild.*

**SIMON, NICHOLAS J., III,** medical products executive; BS in Microbiology, U. Md.; MBA, Loyola Coll. Dir. bus. devel. Genentech, 1989—95, v.p. bus. and corp. devel., 1995—2000; founder, CEO Collabra Pharma, Inc., 2000—, dir., 1998—. Dir. Intermune, Inc., Predict, Inc., Genitope, Inc., BioStreet, Collabra Pharms., Inc.

**SIMON, NORMA PLAVNICK,** psychologist; d. Mark and Mary Plavnick; m. Robert G. Simon, Dec. 18, 1949; children: Mark Allan, Susan. BA, NYU, 1952, cert. in psychoanalysis, 1977; MA, Columbia U., 1953, EdD, 1968. Diplomate Am. Bd. Profl. Psychology, Am. Bd. Counseling Psychology, Am. Bd. Psychoanalysis. Psychologist Queens Coll. Counseling Ctr., Flushing, NY, 1968-70, asst. dir., 1970-76, dir., 1976; gen. practice psychology N.Y.C., 1970—. Faculty, supr. New Hope Guild, Bklyn., 1976—, dir. child and adolescent tng. prog. 1988-98; adj. prof. clin. psychology Columbia U., N.Y.C., 1986-2002; supr. NYU Postdoctoral Prog. in Psychoanalysis, 1988—; mem. com. on profl. practice and ethics Nat. Register Health Svc. Providers, 1998-2003. Author: (with Robert G. Simon): Choosing a College Major: Social Science, 1981; co-author 3 book chpts. on licensure and ethics in psychology; mem. editl. bd. The Counseling Psychologist jour., 1986-89, Profl. Practice and Rsch. in Psychology, 1994-99, Jour. Infant, Child and Adolescent Psych Therapy, 1999—, vice chair N.Y. State Bd. for Psychology State Edn. Dept., Albany, 1978-82, chair, 1982-88; bd. dirs. Pelham (N.Y.) Guidance Coun., 1980-83; pres.-elect Assn. State and Provincial Psychology Bds., 1990, pres., 1991. Recipient Morton Berger award, Assn. State and Provincial Psychology Bds., 1998, Outstanding Psychologist award, Acad. Counseling Psychology, 2003. Fellow: APA (mem. bd. profl. affairs 1987—89, chair bd. profl. affairs 1988—89, policy and planning bd. 1991—93, mem. ethics com. 1995—97, vice chair ethics com. 1996—97, chair ethics com. 1997, workgroup on telehealth 1998—2000, mem. accreditation com. 2004—, NGO UN team assoc. 2006—, John Black award 1994, Disting. Psychologist of Yr., Divsn. Ind. Practice 2004, Karl Heiser award 1993), Am. Bd. Counseling Psychology (bd. dirs. 1992—2000, pres.-elect 1999, pres. 2001—03), Nat. Acads of Practice (elected disting. practitioner), Am. Bd. Profl. Psychology (trustee 1998—2001, pres.-elect 2001—, pres. 2004—05).

**SIMON, PAUL,** musician, composer; b. Newark, Oct. 13, 1941; s. Louis and Belle S.; m. Peggy Harper, 1970 (div. 1975); 1 son, Harper; m. Carrie Fisher, Aug. 16, 1983 (div. July 1984); m. Edie Brickell, May 30, 1992; children: Adrian Edward, Lulu, Gabriel. BA, Queens Coll.; postgrad., Bklyn. Law Sch. With mus. group Simon and Garfunkel, 1964-71; soloist, 1972—; songs recorded with Garfunkel include Mrs. Robinson (Grammy award for record of yr., 1969), The Boxer, Bridge Over Troubled Water; albums with Garfunkel include Wednesday Morning 3 A.M. 1964, Sounds of Silence, 1966, Parsley, Sage, Rosemary and Thyme, 1966, The Graduate (soundtrack), 1968 (Grammy award for instrumental composition written for film, 1969), Bookends, 1968, Bridge over Troubled Water, 1970 (4 Grammy awards: album of yr., best instrumental arrangement, pop contemporary award, song of yr., 1971), Simon and Garfunkel's Greatest Hits, 1972, Concert in the Park, 1982; solo albums include Paul Simon, 1972, There Goes Rhymin' Simon, 1973, Live Rhymin', 1975, Still Crazy After All These Years, 1975 (2 Grammy awards for album of yr. & male pop vocal performance, 1976), Greatest Hits, Etc., 1977, One-Trick Pony, 1980, Hearts and Bones, 1983, Graceland, 1986 (2 Grammy awards for album of yr. 1986, and record of yr., 1987), Negotiations and Love Songs 1971-86, 1989, Paul Simon: Solo, 1990, The Rhythm of the Saints, 1990, 1964-93, 1993, Born at the Right Time, 1991, Collection, 1991, Paul Simon & Friends, 1993, Songs from the Capeman, 1997, In Concert/Live Rhymin, 1998, You're the One, 2000, Surprise, 2006, Recorded as Jerry Landis, 2006; concerts include Central Park, 1991, Born at the Right Time tour, Johannesburg, South Africa, 1992, series with Art Garfunkel, Paramount, 1993; appeared in films Annie Hall, 1977, One-Trick Pony, 1980; appeared in Showtime prodn. Paul Simon's Graceland: The African Concert, 1987; author: (book) At the Zoo, 1991; (musical) The Capeman, 1998. Recipient Emmy award for Paul Simon Spl., NBC-TV, 1977; inducted into Rock & Roll Hall of Fame (as Simon & Garfunkel), 1990, inducted into Rock & Roll Hall of Fame (as solo artist), 2001; named one of 100 Most Influential People, Time mag., 2006 Mem.: Alpha Epsilon Pi (life).*

**SIMON, PETER E.**, publishing executive; b. Bklyn., July 29, 1953; BA in English, CCNY, 1971; MA in Libr. Sci., Columbia U., 1980. Database mgr. R.R. Bowker, N.Y., 1982-84; v.p. R.R. Bowker/Reed Reference Pubs., 1984-93; sr. v.p. Reed Reference Pub., New Providence, N.J., 1993-95, exec. v.p., 1995-97; v.p. bus. devel. Net. Info. Svcs./Lexis-Nexis, Horsham, Pa., 1997-98; v.p. new product planning and devel. The Gale Group, Farmington Hills, Mich., 1998-; v.p. product mgmt., 1999, v.p. bus. devel., 1999-2000; dir. content lic. The Deal, LLC, N.Y., 2000-2001; v.p. strategic devel. Digital Owl, Orlando, Fla., 2001—02; dir. new bus. devel. Nstein Techs. Corp., 2002—03; v.p. product mgmt. NewsBank, Inc., Naples, Fla., 2003—. Mem. Info. Industry Assn. (chmn. content divsn., bd. dirs.), Phi Beta Kappa.

**SIMON, RAYMOND JOSEPH**, federal agency administrator, former school system administrator; b. Conway, Ark. m. Phyllis Simon; 1 child, Sandy. BS math./acctg., U. Ctrl. Ark., MS math.; MSE, sch. adminstrn., U. Ark. Math tchr. North Little Rock H.S.; with sch. food svcs. and computer svcs.; asst. supt. for fin. Conway Sch. Dist., Ark., supt. Ark., 1991—97; dir. Ark. Dept. Edn., Little Rock, 1997—2003; asst. sec., elem. and secondary edn. US Dept. Edn., Washington, 2004—05, acting dep. sec., 2005, dep. sec., 2005—. Adj. prof. U. Ctrl. Ark. Grad. Sch., U. Ark. Little Rock, Ark. State U., Beebe. Mem. Conway Planning Commn.; exec. bd. Quapaw Area Coun.; Boy Scouts Am.; bd. dirs. Conway Civic Orch. Office: US Dept Edn 400 Maryland Ave SW Rm 7E308 Washington DC 20202

**SIMON, ROBERT G.**, lawyer; b. N.Y.C., Feb. 21, 1927; s. Monroe and Claire S. S.; m. Norma Plavnick, Dec. 18, 1949; children: Mark A., Susan. BA, Cornell U., 1947; LLB, JD, Georgetown U., 1950; LLM, NYU, 1961. Bar: D.C. 1950, N.Y. 1951, U.S. Supreme Ct. 1955. Assoc. firms in, N.Y., 1950-52; legal sec. to judge U.S. Dist. Ct. So. Dist. N.Y., 1953-58; assoc. Jaffe & Wachtell, N.Y.C., 1958-61; legal adv. TV series The Verdict Is Yours, 1958-60; successively dir. bus. affairs, v.p., sr. v.p. mgr. bus. affairs dept. McCann-Erickson, Inc., N.Y.C., 1961-80; sr. broadcast atty. The Interpublic Group of Cos., N.Y.C., 1980-95. Adj. faculty Manhattan Community Coll., 1967, Baruch Coll., 1968, CCNY, 1968, New Sch. Social Research, 1972-73; speaker in field. Author: (with Norma Simon) Choosing a College Major: The Social Sciences, 1981; contbr. articles to profl. jours. Dem.-Liberal candidate for county clk. Westchester County, N.Y., 1952; chmn. Narcotics Guidance Coun., Pelham, N.Y., 1973; mem. Nat. Media Coun. on Disability, 1986-90; bd. dirs., gen. counsel Nat. Challenge Com. on Disability, 1986-88; mem. adv. bd. The Caption Ctr. WGBH Found., 1987—; mem. state bd. for podiatry N.Y. State Dept. Edn., 2000—. With USAAF, 1944-46. Mem.: NATAS (chpt. gov. 1972—85; treas. 1976—81, 1st v.p. 1981—83, nat. trustee 1981—85, pres. 1983—85, chpt. gov. 1996—97, nat. trustee 1996—98), Am. Assn. Advt. Agy.s (com. on broadcast adminstrn. policy 1985—93), N.Y. County Lawyers Assn. (com. on comms. and entertainment law 1990—, not-for-profit orgns., alternate dispute resolution com. 1998—), Hemlock Soc. N.Y. (bd. dirs. 2000—02).

**SIMON, ROGER**, newspaper columnist; b. Chgo., Mar. 29, 1948; s. Sheldon and Pauline (Odess) S.; m. Marcia Kramer, May 15, 1977. BA, U. Ill., 1970. Reporter City News Bur. Chgo., 1970; columnist Waukegan News-Sun, Ill., 1970-72, Chgo. Sun-Times, 1972-84, Balt. Sun, 1984—96, nationally syndicated columnist Balt., 1984—95; columnist Regardie's mag., Washington, 1986-91, Chgo. Tribune, 1998—99; polit. editor, chief polit. corr. U.S. News and World Report, Washington, 1999—2005; work syndicated by Creators Syndicate; chief polit. corr. Bloomberg News, Washington, 2006—. Author: Simon Says: The Best of Roger Simon, 1985, Road Show: In America, Anyone Can Become President, It's One of the Risks We Take, 1990, Show Time: The American Political Circus and the Race for the White House, 1999, Divided We Stand: How Al Gore Beat George Bush and Lost the Presidency, 2001, contbr. freelance articles to Playboy mag., The New Republic, Washingtonian Mag., N.Y. Times Review of Books. Recipient Page One award Chgo. Newspaper Guild, 1972, 74, 75, 77, 78, 79, 82, 1st place award for public service UPI, 1974, 80, 82, 83, Silver Gavel award ABA, 1975, 76, 79, Nat. Merit award Assn. Trial Lawyers Am., 1975, 76, Disting. Reporter award Inland Daily Press Assn., 1973, 1st place award for column AP, 1976, 77, 78, 80, 95, Peter Lisagor award, 1980, 82, 83, Distinguished Writing award for commentary Am. Soc. Newspaper Editors, 1984, 86, 2nd place, 1993, Washington-Balt. Newspaper Guild award, 1986, 87, 92, Front Page award for commentary Washington-Balt. Newspaper Guild, 1986, 87, 92, Nat. Headliner award for outstanding column, 1987, 89, 2nd place, 1992, Best Column award Md. chpt. Soc. Profl. Journalists, 1991, 92, 95, 2nd Place Humor award Soc. Newspaper Columnists, 1995, Nat. Headliner award for polit. reporting, 2004; work included in Best Newspaper Writing 1984, 86, 93. Mem. U. Ill. Alumni Assn., Pres.' Council.*

**SIMON, RONALD CHARLES**, curator; b. Phila., Feb. 23, 1951; s. Samuel Charles and Emily (Luzenberg) Simon. BA, Dickinson Coll., 1973; postgrad., Brit. Film and TV Inst., Stirling, Scotland, 1973, Columbia U., 1973-75. Researcher NBC, N.Y.C., 1976—77; mgr. media prodn. 1st Boston Corp., N.Y.C., 1979; curator TV, Mus. TV and Radio, N.Y.C., 1979—. Adj. prof. Hunter Coll., CUNY, 1987—, Columbia U., N.Y.C., 1991—; cons., lectr. to mus. and colls. including Smithsonian Instn., Whitney Mus. Am. Art, NYU, Cooper Hewitt Mus., 1995—. Exhbns. curated include The Television of Dennis Potter, 1992, Witness to History, Jack Benny: The Radio and Television World, 1991, contbg. author Encyclopedia of TV, 1997, Encyclopedia of Radio, 2002, creative cons., host CD-ROM Total TV, 1997; author: Worlds Without End: The Art and History of Soap Opera, 1997; advisor, contbg. author St. James Ency. Popular Culture, 1999, Violence in America: An Encyclopedia, 1999; author: The Television of Dennis Potter, 1992. Mem. George Foster Peabody Awards Bd., 2003—; bd. dirs. United Action for Animals, 2004—. Decorated chevalier of Art and Sci. Ministry of French Culture; Metzger Conway Fellow, Dickinson Coll., 2002, Cogan Alumni fellow, 2006. Mem.: NATAS (panelist and juror for numerous awards 1985—; mem. editl. bd. TV Quar. 1987—), TV Ltd. (bd. dirs. 2000—). Home: 141 E 17th St New York NY 10003-3402 Office: Television & Radio 25 W 52nd St New York NY 10019-6104 Office Phone: 212-621-6680. Personal E-mail: ronsimonnyc@yahoo.com. Business E-Mail: rsimon@mtr.org.

**SIMON, RONALD ISAAC**, financial executive; b. Cairo, Nov. 4, 1938; came to U.S., 1942; s. David and Helene (Zilkha) S.; m. Anne Faith Hartman, June 19, 1960; children: Cheryl, Eric, Daniel. BA, Harvard U., 1960, MA,

Columbia U., 1962, PhD, 1968. V.p. Harpers Internat., N.Y.C., 1959-62; fin. analyst Amerace Corp., N.Y.C., 1965-66; v.p. Am. Foresight Inc., Phila., 1966-67; asst. to pres. Avco Corp., Greenwich, Conn., 1967-70; exec. v.p. Avco Community Developers Inc., La Jolla, Calif., 1970-73; pres. Ronald I. Simon Inc., La Jolla 1973—99; pres., CEO Delta Data Systems Corp., Phila., 1980-81; exec. v.p. Towner Petroleum Corp., Houston, 1983-85; mng. dir., chief fin. officer The Henley Group Inc., La Jolla, 1986-90; pvt. practice fin. cons. La Jolla, 1990—2000. Vice-chmn. bd. dirs. Softnet Corp., San Francisco, 1998—2002, acting chmn. and CEO, 2001; CFO WingCast LLC, San Diego, 2001—02; bd. dirs. Collateral Therapeutics, Inc., San Diego, 1999—2002; exec. v.p., CFO/bd. dirs. Western Water Co., San Diego, 1997—2000; bd. dirs. Am. Independence Corp., NY, 2002—, WFS Fin., Inc., Irvine, Calif., 2003—06, BDI Investments, San Diego, 2003—05, Cardium Therapeutics, 2006—. Bd. dirs. San Diego Opera Co., 1988-90, Univ. Art Gallery U. Calif., San Diego, 1991-95; bd. dirs., treas. Lyric Opera, San Diego, 2003-2005. Ford Found. fellow, 1963-65.

**SIMON, SCOTT JAMES**, computer scientist; b. Stillwater, Okla., Oct. 6, 1969; s. Marilyn Kay and Gary Michael Simon. BA in Philosophy, U. No. Tex., 2001, MS in Info. Techs., 2002, PhD in Interdisciplinary Info. Sci., 2005. Cert. Enterprise Portal adminstr. Oracle-PeopleSoft, CA, 2005, PeopleTools I Oracle-PeopleSoft, CA, 2005. Asst. prof. U. South Fla., Tampa, 2006—. Author: Preformations, 2001. Creuzot scholarship, U. North Tex., 2000, Doctoral Rsch. fellowship, Tex. Ctr. for Digital Knowledge, 2002. Mem.: Assn. of Libr. and Info. Sci. Educators, Inter-Soc. of Electronic Arts, Internat. Assn. of Music Info. Retrieval, Assn. of Info. Sci. and Tech. Office: Univ North Tex Denton TX 76203

**SIMON, SEYMOUR**, lawyer, former state supreme court justice; b. Chgo., Aug. 10, 1915; s. Ben and Gertrude (Rusky) S.; m. Roslyn Schultz Biel, May 26, 1954; children: John B., Nancy Simon Cooper, Anthony Biel. BS, Northwestern U., 1935, JD, 1938; LLD (hon.), John Marshall Law Sch., 1982, North Park Coll., 1986, Northwestern U., 1987. Bar: Ill. 1938. Spl. atty. Dept. Justice, 1938-42; practice law Chgo., 1946-74; judge Ill. Appellate Ct., Chgo., 1974-80; presiding justice Ill. Appellate Ct. (1st Dist., 3d Div.), 1977, 79; justice Ill. Supreme Ct., 1980-88; ptnr. DLA Piper Rudnick Gray Cary, Chgo., 1988—. Former chmn. Ill. Low-Level Radioactive Waste Disposal Facility Siting Commn.; former dir. Nat. Gen. Corp., Bantam Books, Grosset & Dunlap, Inc., Gt. Am. Ins. Corp. Contbr. articles to profl. jours. Mem. Cook County Bd. Commrs., 1961-66, pres., 1962-66; pres. Cook County Forest Preserve Dist., 1962-66; mem. Pub. Bldg. Commn., City Chgo., 1962-67; Alderman 40th ward, Chgo., 1955-61, 67-74; Democratic ward committeeman, 1960-74; bd. dirs. Schwab Rehab. Hosp., 1961-71, Swedish Covenant Hosp., 1969-75. With USNR, 1942-45. Decorated Legion of Merit; recipient Pub. Svc. award Tau Epsilon Rho, 1963, Northwestern U. Sch. of Law, 2006, Hubert L. Will award Am. Vets. Com., 1983, award of merit Decalogue Soc. Lawyers, 1986, Judge Learned Hand award Am. Jewish Com., 1994, Frances Feinberg Meml. Crown award Associated Talmud Torahs of Chgo., 1995, Bill of Rights in Action award Constl. Rights Found., 1997, Chgo. Coun. Lawyers and the Appleseed Fund Justice Commitment to Justice award, 1998, Civic Contbn. award LWV Chgo., 2000, Lifetime Achievement award Ill. Judges Assn., 2002, Justice award Jewish Judges Assn. Ill., 2003, John Peter Altgeld Freedom of Speech award Newberry Libr. Bughouse Sq. Debate Com., 2005; named to Sr. Citizen's Hall of Fame, City of Chgo., 1989, Hall of Fame Jewish Cmty. Ctrs. Chgo., 1989, Laureate Lincoln Acad. Ill., 1997. Mem. ABA, Ill. Bar Assn., Ill. Judges Assn., Chgo. Bar Assn. (Justice John Paul Stevens award 2004, Abraham Lincoln Marovitz Lena a Hand award 2006), Chgo. Hist. Soc., Decalogue Soc. Lawyers (Merit award 1986), Izaak Walton League, Am. Legion, VFW, Jewish War Vets., Chgo. Hort. Soc., Comml. Club Chgo., Std. Club, Variety Club, Order of Coif, Phi Beta Kappa, Phi Beta Kappa Assocs. Home: 1555 N Astor St Chicago IL 60610-1673 Office: DLA Piper Rudnick Gray Cary Suite 1900 203 N LaSalle St Chicago IL 60601-1293 Office Phone: 312-368-7070. Office Fax: 312-236-7516. Business E-Mail: seymour.simon@dlapiper.com.

**SIMON, SHELDON WEISS**, political science professor; b. St. Paul, Jan. 31, 1937; s. Blair S. and Jennie M. (Dim) S.; m. Charlann Lilwin Scheid, Apr. 27, 1962; 1 child, Alex Russell BA summa cum laude, U. Minn., 1958, PhD, 1964; MPA, Princeton U., 1960; postgrad., U. Geneva, 1962—63. Asst. prof., then prof. U. Ky., 1966-75; prof. polit. sci. Ariz. State U., 1975—, chmn. dept., 1975-79, dir. Ctr. Asian Studies, 1980-88. Vis. prof. George Washington U., 1965, U. B.C., Can., 1972-73, 79-80, Carleton U., 1976, Monterey Inst. Internat. Studies, 1991, 96, Am. Grad. Sch. Internat. Mgmt., 1991-92; cons. USIA Rsch. Analysis Corp., Am. Enterprise Inst. Pub. Policy Rsch., Hoover Instn., Orkand Corp.; cons., dir. S.E. Asian Projects, Nat. Bur. Asian Rsch., 1998—; Smithsonian Instn. lectr. on internat. politics for the Crystal and Radisson Cruise Lines, 2000—. Author: Asian Neutralism and U.S. Policy, 1975, The ASEAN States and Regional Security, 1982, The Future of Asian-Pacific Security Collaboration, 1988; editor: The Military and Security in the Third World, 1978, East Asian Security in the Post-Cold War Era, 1993, Southeast Asian Security in the New Millenium, 1996, The Many Faces of Asian Security, 2001, Disrupting Violence: Religion and Conflict in South and Southeast Asia, 2006, others; contbr. articles to profl. jours., chpts. to books. Mem. Com. Fgn. Relations, Phoenix, 1976—; bd. dirs. Phoenix Little Theater, 1976-79 Grantee Am. Enterprise Inst., 1974, Earhart Found., 1979, 81, 92, 84, 88, U.S. Inst. Peace, 1994-96, 2000-01, Nat. Bur. Asian Rsch., 1998, W. Alton Jones Found., 2000; U.S. Pacific Command, 2002-03, Hoover Instn. fellow, 1980, 85. Mem. Am. Polit. Sci. Assn., Assn. Asian Studies, Internat. Studies Assn. (profl. ethics com. 1987-91, v.p. 1991-93), Asia Soc. (contemporary affairs com. 1987-92), U.S. Coun. for Asia-Pacific Security (exec. bd. 1998-2003), Phi Beta Kappa. Democrat. Jewish. Avocations: acting, singing tennis. Home: 5630 S Rocky Point Rd Tempe AZ 85280-2124 Office: Ariz State U Polit Sci Dept Tempe AZ 85287-3902 Office Phone: 480-965-1317. Business E-Mail: shells@asu.edu.

**SIMON, TREVOR**, management consultant, educator, human resources specialist; s. Thelma Corrica and Patrick Simon; m. Julia Ruffins; 2 children. BS in Profl. Aeronautics, Embry-Riddle Aero. U., 1996; MBA in Human Resources Mgmt., Wayland Bapt. U., 2001; PhD, Capella U., Mpls., 2001—04. With USAF, 1986, dir. tng., 2003—; USAF tng. course developer 362nd Tng. Wing, Wichita Falls, Tex., 1990—98; dir., tng. Field Tng. Detachment, Clovis, N.Mex.; tchr. U. Phoenix, ITT Tech. Inst. Owner TS Consulting, Clovis, N.Mex., 1995—. Co-chair C. of C. Amb., Clovis, N.Mex., 2004. Decorated Global War on Terrorism Svc. medal, Korean Defense Svc. medal, NATO medal, Kuwait Liberation medal Kingdom of Saudi Arabia, Govt. Kuwait. Mem.: Nat. Bus. Edn. Assn., Toastmasters, Soc. Human Resource Mgmt., Acad. Mgmt. Achievements include development of a training program to eliminate backlogs in current training system. Avocations: reading, flying, travel. Home: 4208 Brians Way Clovis NM 88101 Office: Field Training Detachment 116 E Octagon Ave Clovis NM 88103 Office Phone: 505-784-4085. Personal E-mail: trevorsimon@email.uophx.edu.

**SIMON, WILLIAM**, retail executive; 2 children. B. in Economics, U. Conn., MBA. Various mktg. and devel. positions Cadbury-Schweppes, Pepsico, RJR-Nabisco; v.p. consumer mktg. Diageo PLC, 1998, pres. Southeast region; sec. Fl. Dept. Mgmt. Services, 2003—05; senior v.p. global bus. devel. Brinker Internat., Dallas, 2005—06; exec. v.p. specialty divsn. Wal-Mart Stores Inc., Bentonville, Ark., 2006—. Served USN, served USNR. Office: Wal-Mart Stores Inc 702 SW Eighth St Bentonville AR 72716*

**SIMON, WILLIAM H.**, law educator; b. 1947; AB, Princeton, 1969; JD, Harvard U., 1974. Bar: Mass. 1974. Assoc. Foley, Hoag & Eliot, Boston, 1974-77; staff atty. legal svcs. inst. Harvard U., 1979-81; asst. prof. Stanford U., 1981-84, assoc. prof., 1984-85, prof., 1985—2003, Montgomery prof., 1995—99, William W. and Gertrude H. Saunders prof. law, 1999—2003; Arthur Levitt prof. law Columbia U., NYC, 2003—. Vis. prof. law Harvard U., 1987—88, 1997—2001, 2002, U. Calif., Berkeley, 1997—98; vis. staff mem Nat. Ctr. for Econ. Develop. and Law, 1990. Contbr. articles to law

jours. Grantee Guggenheim fellow, 1994. Office: Columbia Sch Law 435 W 116th St, Rm 536 New York NY 10027 Office Phone: 212-854-9215. Office Fax: 212-854-7946. E-mail: wsimon@law.columbia.edu.

**SIMON, WILLIAM LEONARD**, scriptwriter, television producer, writer, film producer; b. Washington, Dec. 3, 1930; s. Isaac B. and Marjorie (Felsteiner) Simon; m. Arynne Lucy Abeles, Sept. 18, 1966; 1 child, Victoria Marie 1 stepchild, Sheldon M. Bermont. BEE, Cornell U., 1954; MA in Edni. Psychology, Golden State U., 1982, PhD in Comm., 1983. Writer features and TV movies, documentary and indsl. films, TV programs, 1958—; lectr. George Washington U., Washington, 1968-70. Juror Coun. Nontheatrical Events Film Festival, 1975—90, Cindy Festival Blue Ribbon Panel, 1985—; jury chmn., bd. dirs. CINE Film Festival, 1988—. Author: more than 600 produced works for motion pictures and TV; author: (screenplays) Fair Woman Without Discretion, Majorca, Swindle, A Touch of Love, In the Shadows of Her Life; author: (teleplays and documentaries) From Information to Wisdom, Flight of Freedom II, Missing You; author: (home video) Star of India, Combat Vietnam series; writer, prodr. The Star of India: Setting Sail; co-author: Profit from Experience-The Story of Transformation Management, 1995, Lasting Change, 1997; author: Beyond the Numbers, 1996; co-author: On the Firing Line, My 500 Days at Apple Computer, 1998, High Velocity Leadership--The Mars Pathfinder Approach to Faster, Better, Cheaper, 1999, Driving Digital--What Microsoft is Learning from its Customers about Thriving in the Digital Revolution, 2000, The Afterlife Experiments-- Breakthrough Scientific Evidence of Life After Death, 2002, The Art of Deception, 2002, In Search of Business Value, 2004, The Art of Intrusion: The Real Stories Behind the Exploits of Hackers, Intruders and Decievers, 2005, iCon: Steve Jobs - The Greatest Second Act in the History of Business, 2005, The Truth About Medium-Extraordinary Experiments with the Real Allison Du Bois of NBC's Medium, 2005, The G.O.D. Experiments, 2006, A Cat by the Tail, 2006, The Healing Energy Experiments -- Science Reveals Our Natural Power to Heal, 2006, Gorgeous Disaster--The Tragic Story of Debra LaFave, 2006. Pres. Foggy Bottom Citizens Assn., 1963—65, mem. exec. bd., 1965—69; v.p. Shakespeare Summer Festival, 1966—67, trustee, 1965—70; mem. interview com. Cornell U., 1987—88. Lt. USN, 1954—58. Named 30 Best Bus. Books of 1997, Exec. Book Summaries; recipient 12 Golden Eagle awards, Cine Film Festival, Gold medal, N.Y. Internat. Festival, Freedoms Found., Gold Cindy, IFPA, awards, Berlin, Belgrade and Venice Film Festivals, others. Mem.: NATAS (gov. DC chpt. 1970—73, gov. San Diego chpt. 1998—2002), Writers Guild Am., Silver Cir., Rotary (bd. dirs., program chmn.), Tau Beta Pi, Eta Kappa Nu (chpt. pres. 1953—54). Republican. Avocations: crew member square-rigged brig Pilgrim, San Diego Museum ship Star of India, tennis. E-mail: bill@simon1.com.

**SIMONDS, CHARLES FREDERICK**, artist; b. N.Y.C., Nov. 14, 1945; s. Robert and Anita I. (Bell) S. BA, U. Calif., Berkeley, 1967; MFA, Rutgers U., 1969. One man shows include Ctr. Nat. d'Art Contemporain, Paris, 1975, Mus. Modern Art, N.Y.C., 1976, Westfälischer Kunstverein, Munster, 1978, Mus. Ludwig, Cologne, 1979, Mus. Contemporary Art, Chgo., 1981, Phoenix (Ariz.) Mus. Art, 1982, Brooks Meml. Art Gallery, Memphis, 1982, Solomon R. Guggenheim Mus., N.Y., 1983, Leo Castelli Gallery, N.Y., 1984, Architekturmuseum, Bâle, 1985, Corcoran Gallery Art, Washington, 1988, Fundació "la Caixa," Barcelona, 1994, Galerie nat. Jeu Paume, Paris, 1994, retrospective IVAM, Valencia, Spain, 2003; exhibited in group shows Whitney Mus. Am. Art, N.Y., 1975, 77, Mus. d'Art moderne Ville de Paris, 1975, Stedelijk Mus., Amsterdam, 1978, Mus. Modern Art, N.Y., 1979, Hayward Gallery, London, 1980, Tate Gallery, London, 1983, Solomon R. Guggenheim Mus., N.Y., 1985, 87, 89; works included in publs. including Artforum, 1980, Art/Cahier, 1977, Sprache im Technischen Zeitalter, 1978, Art in America, 1983, Images and Issues, 1982, ARTnews, 1978, Beaux Arts, 1986. Fellow Am. Acad. Rome. Home: 26 E 22nd St New York NY 10010-6107 E-mail: simondsc@aol.com.

**SIMONDS, JOHN EDWARD**, retired newspaper editor; b. Boston, July 4, 1935; s. Alvin E. and Ruth Angeline (Rankin) S.; m. Rose B. Muller, Nov. 16, 1968; children— Maximillian P., Malia G.; children by previous marriage— Rachel F. Cobb, John B. BA, Bowdoin Coll., 1957. Reporter Daily Tribune, Seymour, Ind., 1957-58, UPI, Columbus, Ohio, 1958-60; reporter, asst. city editor Providence Jour. Bull., 1960-65, Washington Evening Star, 1965-66; corr. Gannett News Svc., Washington, 1966-75; mng. editor Honolulu Star Bull., 1975-80, exec. editor, 1980-87, sr. editor, editl. page editor, 1987-93; exec. Hawaii Newspaper Agy., Honolulu, 1993-99; reader rep. The Honolulu Advertiser, Honolulu, 1999—2002; ret. 2004. Served with U.S. Army, 1958. Mem. Am. Soc. Newspaper Editors, AP Mng. Editors, Soc. Profl. Journalists, Nat. Conf. Editl. Writers, Orgn. News Ombudsmen, Hawaii Lit. Arts Coun. Home: 5316 Nehu Pl Honolulu HI 96821-1941 Office: The Honolulu Advertiser 605 Kapiolani Blvd Honolulu HI 96813-5195 Office Phone: 808-383-7984. Personal E-mail: simondsj001@hawaii.rr.com.

**SIMONDS, MARSHALL**, retired lawyer; b. Boston, Sept. 17, 1930; s. Sidney Lawrence and Evelyn (Peterson) S.; m. Katharine Blewett, May 9, 1969; children: Robert Bradley, Joshua Lawrence. BA, Princeton U., 1952; LLB, Harvard U., 1955. Bar: Mass. 1955. Since practiced in Boston; ptnr. Goodwin, Procter & Hoar, Boston, 1965-2000; counsel Mass. Crime Commn., 1963-65; spl. asst. atty. gen. Commonwealth of Mass., 1967—2000; dir. Dynatech Corp., 1960-85, Data Packaging Corp., 1972-79; trustee Middlesex Instn. Savs., 1974-79 Moderator of Carlisle, Mass., 1967-2000; trustee Trustees for Reservations, 1972-78; bd. dirs. South Boston Neighborhood House, 1972-78. Served with USMCR, 1955. Fellow Am. Coll. Trial Lawyers, Am. Bar Found.; Mass. Bar Found.; mem. ABA, Mass. Bar Assn., Boston Bar Assn. (coun. 1980-82), New Eng. Legal Found. (dir.), Am. Kennel Club (dir.), Labrador Retriever Club (bd. dirs.), Orthopedic Found. for Animals (bd. dirs.), Harvard Club (Boston). Address: Bliss Hill Rd Morrisville VT 05661

**SIMONDS, ROBERT**, producer; b. Phoenix, 1964; Exec. prodr. Big Daddy, 1999, Taxi, 2004, The Shaggy Dog, 2006; prodr. Problem Child, 1990, Problem Child 2, 1991, Airheads, 1994, Billy Madison, 1995, Bulletproof, 1996, Happy Gilmore, 1996, Leave It to Beaver, 1997, That Darn Cat, 1997, The Waterboy, 1998, Dirty Work, 1998, The Wedding Singer, 1998, Half Baked, 1998, Screwed, 2000, Little Nicky, 2000, Head Over Heels, 2001, See Spot Run, 2001, Joe Dirt, 2001, Corky Romano, 2001, Just Married, 2003, Cheaper by the Dozen, 2003, Herbie: Fully Loaded, 2005, Rebound, 2005, Yours, Mine and Ours, 2005, The Pink Panther, 2006.*

**SIMONE, JOSEPH**, clergyman, educator; b. Bridgeport, Conn., Jan. 13, 1924; s. Dominic and Anna (Mastrianni) S.; B.A., Elon Coll., 1958; M.A., Andover Newton Theol. Sch., 1968; m. Viola Ruskay, June 27, 1953; children— J. Scott, Zachary D., Claudia A. Ordained to ministry Congl. Ch., 1960; pastor Congl. Ch., Chicopee Falls, Mass., 1958-61, 1st Congl. Ch., Farmington, N.H., 1961-63, Hope Congl. Ch., East Providence, R.I., 1963-65, All Souls Ch., Lowell, Mass., 1965-69; tchr. English, also guidance counselor, 1969-87. Chmn. ecumenical commn. Greater Lowell Council Chs., 1967-68; founder Ecumenical Dialogue with Clergymen and Laymen, Lowell, 1966, Radio Ministry on Ecumenism, Lowell, 1966-69; chaplain Roger Hall Sch. for Girls, Lowell, 1965-69. Bd. dirs. Jewish-Arab Ednl. Fund, Lowell Served with AUS, 1942-45. Mem. Andover Assn. Ministers United Ch. of Christ (adv. com. 1966-87), Assn. Clin. Pastoral Edn., Am., Mass. sch. counselors assns., N.E.A., Nat. Vocational Guidance Assn., Am. Personnel and Guidance Assn., Sigma Mu Sigma (v.p. 1957). Mason. Home: 117 Jenkins Rd Andover MA 01810-2303

**SIMONE, JOSEPH R.**, lawyer; b. NYC, Jan. 7, 1949; m. Virginia E. Simone, May 29, 1971; children: Jacquelyn, Robert. BA cum laude, Queens Coll., 1971; LLM in Taxation, NYU, 1977; JD cum laude, Fordham U., 1974. Bar: N.Y. 1975, U.S. Dist. Ct. (so. dist.) N.Y. 1975, U.S. Ct. Appeals (2d cir.) 1975. Ptnr. Patterson, Belknap, Webb & Tyler, NYC, 1982-88, Schulte, Roth & Zabel, NYC, 1988—2002; spl. prof. law Hofstra U. Sch. Law, 1998—; of counsel Pitney Hardin LLP, NYC, 2003—, ptnr., 2004—. Author: (textbooks) Pension Answer Book, 5th edit., 1990, Essential Facts: Pension and Profit-sharing Plans, 1999; editl. advisor Jour. of Pension Planning. Mem. Am. Arbitration Assn. (panel on multiemployer pension plans), Am. Coll. Employee Benefits (counsel 2003—), Phi Beta Kappa. Office: Pitney Hardin LLP 7 Times Sq New York NY 10036 Office Phone: 212-297-5859. E-mail: jsimone@pitneyhardin.com.

**SIMONEAU, CYNTHIA LAMBERT,** editor, educator; b. Central Falls, R.I., May 18, 1958; d. Roland and L. Jean Simoneau; m. Paul E. Lambert, Oct. 24, 1981; children: Thomas S. Lambert, Marc S. Lambert. BA, U. R.I. 1980. Asst. news editor Newtown (Conn.) Bee, 1980-82; reporter Bridgeport (Conn.) Post & Telegram, 1982-83, bur. chief, 1983-91; editor Woman Wise Conn. Post, Bridgeport, 1991-97, asst. mng. editor, 1997—2004, cons. editor, 2004—. Adj. prof. So. Conn. State U., New Haven, 1993—, Fairfield (Conn.) 2003—, Sacred Heart U., Fairfield, Conn., 2004, Quinnipiac U., Hamden, Conn., 2005— Eucharistic min., mem. parish adv. coun., former religious edn. tchr., St. Thomas Aquinas Ch., Fairfield, Conn. Mem. Soc. Profl. Journalists (bd. dirs. Conn. chpt. 1983-2003, treas. Conn. chpt. 1985-95, 2003—, pres. Conn. chpt. 1995-97, Journalism Excellence awards for news stories and columns, 2 Pres.'s award Conn. chpt., Women of Dist. award Girl Scout Coun.). Avocation: reading. Office: Conn Post 410 State St Bridgeport CT 06604 E-mail: csimonea@aol.com.

**SIMONEAU, DANIEL ROBERT,** accountant, educator, artist; b. Lewiston, Maine, Aug. 3, 1962; s. Robert Eugene and Rolande Muriel (Plante) S. BFA, U. So. Maine, 1984. Reconciling specialist Fleet/Norstar Bank of Maine, Lewiston, 1981—84, acct., 1984—88, Sterling Engineered Products, Auburn, Maine, 1988—89; fin. analyst Pioneer Plastics Corp., Auburn, Maine, 1989—91; acct. Aeroquip Corp., New Haven, Ind., 1992, coord. adminstrv. sys. Maumee, Ohio, 1992—93, acct., 1993—94, Trinova Corp., Maumee, 1994—96, chmn. employee activities com. ann. outing Toledo, 1995; fin. edn. specialist PeopleSoft, Inc., Westchester, Ill., 1996—98, instr. master tech., 2000—02; sr. cons. The Revere Group, Deerfield, Ill., 1998—2000, functional specialist, 2000; PeopleSoft developer Robert W. Baird, Milw., 2002—, asst. v.p., 2003—, leader Application Devel. Team, 2005—. Treas. Cream City Found., 2003—05. Contbr. article to mag. Chmn. award winners show Spectrum Friends of Fine Art, Toledo, 1995. Recipient Recognition award Spectrum Friends of Fine Art, 1994, com. award Spectrum Gallery, 1994, 3d pl. award Toledo Fedn. Art Socs., 1992, 3d Judge's award Lewiston Art Festival Com., 1988, 90, 91, Purchase award Portland Art Festival Com., 1981, 91. Mem. Northwestern Ohio Watercolor Soc., Coll. Art Assn., Friends of Arts Chgo., Transparent Watercolor Soc. Am. (life, membership chair 2003-05), Midwest Water Color Soc. (life), Wis. Watercolor Soc. Office: Robert W Baird 777 E Wisconsin Ave Milwaukee WI 53201-0672 Home: 9507 74th St Kenosha WI 53142-8194

**SIMONIAN, SIMON JOHN,** surgeon, scientist, educator, health science association administrator; b. Antioch, French Ter., Apr. 20, 1932; arrived in U.S., 1965, naturalized, 1974; s. John Simon and Marie (Tomboulian) Simonian; m. Arpi Ani Yeghiayan, July 11, 1965; children: Leonard Armen, Charles Haig, Andrew Hovig. MD, U. London, 1957; BA in Animal Physiology, St. Edmund Hall, U. Oxford, Eng., 1964; MSc in Nutrition, Immunology and Genetics, Harvard U., 1967, ScD in Nutrition, Immunology and Genetics, 1969; MA in Animal Physiology, U. Oxford, 1969; DSc (hon.), Nat. Acad. Scis., Armenia, 1998. Diplomate Am. Bd. Surgery, 1977. Rsch. team mem. smallpox vaccine lyophilization immunology unit Lister Inst. Preventive Medicine, Elstree, Essex, England, 1951—52; intern in medicine Univ. Coll. Hosp., London, 1957; intern in surgery Edinburgh (Scotland) Royal Infirmary, 1957-58, resident in surgery, 1961-62; clin. clk. Nat. Hosp. & Inst. of Neurology, 1958; resident Edinburgh Western Gen. Hosp., 1958-59, City Hosp., Edinburgh, Birmingham Accident and Burns Hosp., U. Birmingham, Eng., 1959-60; demonstrator dept. anatomy Edinburgh U., 1960-61; rsch. fellow in pathology Lab. Chem. Pathology Harvard U., Harvard Med. Sch., Boston, 1965-68; trainee NIH US Army Devel. Command Immunology Rsch. Harvard Med. Sch., 1967; instr. immunology Harvard Med. Sch., Boston, 1966-70, instr. in surgery and immunology, 1968—69, surg. dir. course on transplantation, biology and medicine, 1968-70, assoc. in surgery and immunology, 1969—70; vis. prof., invited spkr. Harvard Med. Sch., Mass. Gen. Hosp., Brigham and Womens Hosp., New Eng. Deaconess Hosp., 1982; dir. transplantation immunology unit, lab. asst. in surgery Brigham and Womens Hosp., Boston, 1968-70; resident in surgery Boston City Hosp., 1970-74; attending surgeon in transplantation and gen. surgery services U. Chgo. Med. Ctr., 1974-77; asst. prof. surgery, mem. com. immunology U. Chgo., 1974-77; dir., surgeon-in-chief divsn. renal transplantation Hahnemann U. Sch. Medicine and Hosp., 1978-88; prof. surgery, 1978-88, chmn. Transplantation Com., 1983-88, chmn. quality assurance of surgery com., 1986-88; dept. surgery coord. with joint commn. for accreditation of hosps. Hahnemann U. Sch. Medicine, 1986—88; chief and chmn. dept. surgery twelve divsns. St. John Hosp. and Med. Ctr., Detroit, 1988-89, chmn. credentials com. of surgery and oper. rm. com., 1988-89, assoc. v.p. for med. affairs, 1989-90; pres., CEO Vein Inst. Met. Washington, Inc., 1990—2006; assoc. attending staff Fairfax Hosp., Falls Church, Va., 1990-92, active attending faculty, 1992—; guest lectr., 1994, 99; clin. assoc. prof. surgery Georgetown U. Sch. Medicine, Washington, 1992-95, guest lectr., 1994—, clin. prof. surgery, 1995—. Vis. prof., invited spkr. Vanderbilt U., 1968, Cedars-Sinai Med. Ctr., UCLA, 1977, Addenbroke's Hosp., Cambridge U., 1977, Karolinska Inst., Stockholm, 1977, Huddinge Hosp., U. Stockholm, 1977, Med. Coll. Pa. and Hosp., 1980, 81, 85, Grad. Hosp., U. Pa., 1981, 85, U. Athens, 1981, U. Coll. Hosp., U. London, 1981, Western Gen. Hosp. Edinburg U., 1981, VA Hosp., Tufts U., 1982, John Radcliffe Hosp., U. Oxford, 1982, Nat. Acad. Scis., Yerevan, Armenia, 1995, St. Edmund Hall, U. Oxford, 1997, Christ Ch. Hosp., Chgo., 1974—77, South Chgo. Hosp., 1974—77, Del. Med. Ctr., Wilmington, 1977, Wilkes Barre (Pa.) Gen. Hosp., 1979, Robert Packer Hosp., Guthrie Clinic, Sayre, Pa., 1980, Abington Meml. Hosp., Phila., 1982, Crozer Chester Med. Ctr., Pa., 1982, St. Agnes Hosp. Med. Ctr., Phila., 1982, Sacred Heart Hosp., 1982, Riverview Hosp., Red Bank, NJ, 1983, Easton (Pa.) Hosp., Allentown, 1983, Newcombe Med. Ctr., Vineland, NJ, 1983, Cath. Med. Ctr., Manchester, NH, 1984, Burlington County Med. Ctr., Mount Holly, NJ, 1984; invited spkr. various locations; cons. Michael Reese Hosp., Chgo., 1976—77; cons. gen. surgery City of Phila., 1986—88; cons. vascular surgery Coll. Podiatry, Phila., 1986—88; cons. venous vascular surgery Podiatry Residence Program, No. Va. Med. Coll., Richmond, 1994—; cons. surgery John F. Kennedy Meml. Hosp., Stratford, NJ, 1982—86, St. Agnes Hosp. Med. Ctr., Phila., 1982—86; cons. Am.-Armenian Cultural Assn., 2001; surgeon in chief, med. team support U.S. Pres. Ronald W. Reagan, 1988, George H. W. Bush, 1989, U.S. Presdl. visits to Detroit; vis. surgeon inst. Vein Disease, Mich., 1989—90; vis. scientist Argonne Nat. Lab., Ill., 1969, vis. scientist, collaborator, 1974—77; founding mem. sci. bd. ctr. regenerative biology Ind. U., 2001—05; invited spkr., panelist 8th Internat. Congress of Nephrology, Athens, 1981; bd. dirs., invited spkr. 1st Internat. Soc. for Endo. and Surgery, San Diego, 1992; invited spkr., panelist 4th Internat. Dialogue Transition to Global Soc., U. Md., College Park, 1995; invited spkr. 3d Armenian Med. World Congress, Montreal, 1986, 4th Armenian Med. World Congress, LA, 1989; invited spkr., chairperson of session 5th Armenian Med. World Congress, Paris, 1992; invited spkr. 6th Armenian Med. World Congress, Boston, 1995, 7th Armenian Med. World Congress, Lyon, France, 1998, 8th Armenian Med. World Congress, Toronto, 2001; eminent scholar external assessor U. Zambia, Lusaka, 1994; mem. faculty internat. consensus panel The Investigation Chronic Venous Insufficiency, Paris, 1997; mem. internat. consensus panel Thromboembolism, Rhodes, Greece, 1999, Thrombophilia, Limasol, Cyprus, 2003, The Prevention, Investigation and Treatment of Venous Thromboembolism and Thrombophilia, Windsor, England, 2005; sci. advisor, invited spkr. 8th Pan-Am. Congress Phlebology and Lymphology, Campo Grande, Brazil, 1998; invited spkr., sci. advisor 9th Pan-Am. Congress Phlebology and Lymphology, Cordoba, Argentina, 2000; hon. mem. Internat. Forum Minisurgery of Varicose Veins, Frankfurt, Germany, 2000, Korean Soc. Phlebology, 2003; Guthrie lectr. Robert Packer Hosp.; Venus lectr., Rhodes, Greece, 1999, Internat. Union Angiolo European Chpt. Congress, 2003; Diomed. lectr., 03; Kwang Dong lectr. Phlebological Tech. Korea Ann. Congress, Seoul, 2003; BSN Jobst lectr. Internat. Union Phle-

bology USA Congress, San Diego, 2003; keynote spkr. 18th Internat. Union Angiolo World Congress, Tokyo; Jonathan E. Rhoads ann. orator Phila. Acad. Surgery. Co-author: (books) Manual of Vascular Access Procedures, 1987, Prevention of Venous Thromboembolism, 2002, Diagnosis and Treatment of Lymphedema, 2006; cons. to editl. bd. Dateline: Issues in Transplantation, 1985—87, mem. editl. bd. Phila. Medicine, 1988, Transplantation Procs., 1987—96, Jour. Transplantation Abstracts, 1969—70, Internat. Angiology, 1998—, assoc. editor Am. Coll. Phlebology Vein Line, 2000—06, reviewer Jour. Oncology and Dermatologic Surgery, 1993, Jour. Dermatologic Surgery, 1997, Jour. Vascular Surgery, 2000—, The Surgeon Journal Royal College of Surgeons Edinburgh and Ireland, Venous Digest, 2002; translator (in English): Short Saphenous Vein issue, Jour. de Phlebologie, 1999; contbr. articles to profl. jours. and books; appeared in med. movie Giving. Co-founder Armenian Youth Soc., London, Eng., 1953, pres. 1953-54; Armenian Studies Program U. Chgo., 1975; bd. govs. Friends Sch., London, 1964-65; Mass. del., co-founder Armenian Assembly of Am., Washington, 1970-74; fellowtrustee, co-founder Entry into Manhood of Armenian Youth at Age 13, 1981; co-founder Armenian Am. Health Assn. of Greater Washington, 1992, mem. pharms. com. 1992—, chmn. nominating com., 1993; sec., bd. dirs. Woodrock Inc., Potomac, Md., 1993-94; mem. Am. Friends of St. Edmund Hall, U. Oxford, 1992—, U.S. Campaign for St. Edmund Hall, 1995—, mem. bd. advisors, 1999-03, mem. campaign steering bd., 2000—; mem. St. Mary's Armenian Apostolic Ch., Washington, guest preacher, 1994, 95, 96; guest spkr. Armenian Ch. Youth Orgn. Am., Washington, 1998; mem. Am. Friends State U. Armenia, Yerevan, 1994-, bd. dirs. mammography unit and wellness ctr. State Med. U., Yerevan, Armenia, 1997-98; bd. dirs. Arlington (Va.) Symphony Orch., 1992-96, sci. com. Armenia-U.S.A., 1996—; mem. regional com. U.S. Campaign for Univ. Oxford, 1993; active amphitheatre endowment fund Boston City Hosp., 1994; dist. benefactor, fundraiser Eurasia Found., 1996; sci. advisor, chmn. session, invited spkr. Internat. Union Plebology, World Congress, 11th, Monreal, Can., 1992, 12th, London, Eng., 1995, 13th, Sydney, Australia, 1998, 14th, Rome, 2001; sci. advisor, chmn. session, invited spkr. Internat. Union Angiology World, Congress 17th, London, Eng., 1995, 18th, Tokyo, 1998, 19th, NYC, 2001, 20th, Rome, 2004, 15th, Brazil, 2005. H.J. Turtle scholar, 1943-46, R. Wright scholar, 1943-46, A. Koundakjian scholar, 1943-48, K. Clay scholar, 1946-48, Nairn scholar London U., 1949-52, Middlesex scholar London U., 1952-57; recipient N.K. Harris award, 1946, Leadership award, 1949, Suckling prize obstetric rsch. U. London, 1956, Brit. Med. Rsch. Coun. award Lab. Physiology Oxford U., 1962-64, NIH award transplantation and immunology rsch. Harvard Med. Sch. and Peter Bent Brigham Hosp., 1970, R. Alt prize surg. rsch. Boston City Hosp. and Beverly Hosp., 1973, Thompson award immunological rsch. U. Chgo., 1974-77, Johnson award immunological rsch. U. Chgo., 1975-77, Upjohn award, 1982, Presdl. Rep. Ronald Reagan Medal of Merit, 1982, U.S. Pres. Ronald W. Reagan Seal and Medal, 1988, Kabakjian award eradication of small pox Armenian Student Assn. Am., 1986, Disting. Alumni award Med. Soc. St. Edmund Hall, U. Oxford, 1997, Kaken award, 1998, STD award, 2000, Contbns. to Health Rsch. award; named Outstanding New Citizen of Citizenship Coun. Met. Chgo. and Dept. Justice, Washington, 1976; Businessman of Yr. Leadership award Nat. Rep. Congl. Com., 2003, Physician of Yr. Leadership award, 2003, Stanley N. Gershoff PhD prize Friedman Sch. Nutrition Tufts U., Boston, 2006; co-endowed The John and Marie J. Simonian award, St. Nerces Sem., 1981, John R. Pfeifer, MD Rsch. award, Providence Hosp., Southfield, Mich., 1992, Joseph E. Murray, MD prof. plastic surgery Harvard Brigham Women and Children's Hosps., Boston, 1999, John R. Pfeifer MD prof. vascular surgery U. Mich., Ann Arbor, 2006, David B. Skinner MD prof. thoracic surgery Weill Cornell Med. Coll. NY Presbyn. Hosp., 2006; endowed Marie J. Simonian Prize, Georgetown U. Hosp. Med. Ctr., 1991 (prize com. 1991—), The Thomas J. Gill III MD prize dept. pathology Brigham Women's Hosp., Boston, 2003, Simon J. and Arpi A. Simonian Prize for scholastic excellence for doctoral candidates, Harvard U., 2006; recognized for philanthropy to Hahnemann U. by placques in med. sch. and hosp. lobbies., 1980—, Simon and Arpi Simonian plasma physics room Sch. of Humanities and Scis. U. Yerevan, Armenia, 1994, plaque in Cyrus Vesuna Auditorium and Conf. Ctr., Fairfax Hosp., Falls Church, Va., 1995, name on wall Inova's Claude Moore Health Edn. Ctr., Fairfax, Va., 2006; grantee U.S. Govt., industry cos., founds. Fellow: ACS (Phila., Mich. and Washington chpts.), Am. Coll. Phlebology, Phila. Acad. Surgery (Jonathan E. Rhoads ann. orator 1984—, Samuel D. Gross prize com. 1988), Royal Coll. Surgeons Edinburgh; mem.: APHA, AAAS, AMA, AAUP, Leadership Coun., Harvard Sch. Pub. Health (founding mem. 2003—), Phlebological Surgery Sect., Am. Coll. Phlebology (founding chair, bd. dirs. 2002—03, past chair 2003—), Ambulatory Phlebectomy Sect., Am. Coll. Phlebology (chmn. program com. and sec. treas. 1999—2001, sect. chair elect 2000—01, chair, bd. dirs. 2001—02), European Acad. Scis. and Arts (pfg.), Northern Va. Med. Soc., North Am. Soc. Phlebology, Chgo. Soc. Gastroenterology, Transplantation Soc. (membership com. 1980—82), Pa. Med. Soc., Phila. County Med. Soc. (rep. ctr. city br. 1981—83, pres. 1984, bd. dirs. 1985—87, chairperson long range planning com. 1986—98), Greater Del. Valley Soc. Transplant Surgeons (councilor 1978—80, pres. elect 1980—82, pres. 1982—85, councilor 1985—88), Phila. Acad. Scis. (co-chmn. membership com. 1982—88, invited spkr. 1982), Chgo. Soc. Gastroenterology, Assn. of Ill. Transplant Surgeons, Am. Venous Forum (co-chair session, ofcl. disscussant 10th ann. meeting 1999, chair Internat. Rels. Com. 2001—02), Am. Soc. Transplant Surgeons (co-founding mem. 1974, chair immunosuppression studies com. 1974—77, membership com. 1980—82), NY Acad. Scis., Samuel Hahnemann Surg. Soc., Am. Coll. Phlebology (curriculum devel. projects com. 1992—2006, co-chmn. symposiums and session 1992—, faculty 1993—2006, panelist 10th ann. congress 1996, membership com. 1998—2006, chmn. sci. program com. 13th ann. congress 1999, program chair 14th ann. congress 2000), Internat. Cardiovasc. Soc. (chair session 22d world congress 1995, N.Am. chpt.), European Soc. Organ Transplant, Am. Soc. Artificial Internal Organs, Am. Technion Soc., Wayne County Med. Soc., Greater Washington Telecomm. Assn. (pres.' club 1994), Am. Soc. Lymphology (nat. adv. bd., chair sci. com. 1999—, pres.-elect 2000—01, pres. 2001—03, re-elected pres. 2003—06), Am. Fedn. Clin. Rsch., Transplantation Soc. Mich., Assn. Acad. Surgery, Armenian Med. and Dental Assn. Greater Phila. (co-founder 1983, pres. 1983—85, Outreach award 1986), Assn. for Study of Med. Edn., Physicians for Social Responsibility, Cancer Rsch. Assn. Boston, Am. Venous Found. (bd. dirs. 2000—06), Brit. Med. Assn., Am. Armenian Med. Assn. (co-founder 1972, 25th anniversary co-founder award 1997), Nat. Assn. Armenian Studies and Rsch. (rep. Midatlantic region 1994—2003, bd. dirs. 2004—), Royal Coll. Physicians of London Licentiates, Med. Soc. Va., Fairfax County Med. Soc., Mich. State Med. Soc., Chgo. Assn. Immunologists, Detroit Surgical Assn., Detroit Acad. Surgery, Am. Coll. Physician Execs., Am. Assn. Vascular Surgery, Royal Coll. Surgeons of Eng., Nat. Acad. Scis. Armenia (fgn.), Organ Procurement Agy. Mich. (adv. bd. 1988—89), Armenian Gen. Benevolent Union (invited spkr. 1982, pres.' club 1990—), End Stage Renal Disease Network 24 (med. rev. bd. 1980—82, 1986—87), Soc. Brigham Surg. Alumni, Immunology Club Boston, Med. Club (Phila.), Sigma Xi. Mem. Soc. Of Friends. Achievements include bilateral lung reimplantation resulting in normal function without vagus nerves; reversal of renal allograft rejection using IgG concentrate of antilymphocyte serum (ALS) and of antihymocyte globulin (ATG); prevention and treatment of massive gastroduodenal hemorrhage from hemorrhagic gastritis using pioneering antacids to neutralize gastric acid pH7; discovered essential amino acids phenylalanine and tryptophan that are essential for antibody formation; participated in the lyophilization of the smallpox vaccine which was used by the WHO in 1966; to vaccinate everybody resulting in eradication of smallpox in 1977 which was the first and only major disease eradicated in the history of medicine and public health; co-discoverer of immunogenetic control of antibody formation that will lead to design future drugs to treat patients as genetically unique; research advantages and disadvantages and prevention of splenectomy in renal transplant recipients; stage-enmasse cardiopulmonary reimplantation that resulted in normal function without vagus nerves; zinc deficiency depresses the action of zinc dependent enzymes, priming the recipient with donor antigen improves kidney transplant survival; discovery of stable bonding protein carriers and cytotoxic agents for treatment of organ transplant rejection and cancer; combined surgery and sclerotherapy corrects abnormal structure, function and aesthetics of leg varicose veins; pioneering conversion

of arteriovenous shunt to arteriovenous fistula for immediate long term hemodialysis; first to use needle phlebectomy in USA; first to use beaver microblade phlebectomy; first to use bupivacaine wound infiltration in venous surgery wounds to minimize post operative pain; abolition of concurrent deep and perforator vein incompetence by surgical correction of superficial vein incompetence; evolving concepts in management of accute superficial and deep thromboembolism, phlebolymphedema; first to develop the largest phlebology organization participating with insurance in the United States; first to use the name Vein Institute. Personal E-mail: sjsimonian@comcast.net.

**SIMONIN, HOWARD A.,** biologist; b. Ypsilanti, Mich., Mar. 13, 1949; s. Joe W. and Myrtle D. Simonin; m. Martha M. Cavanaugh, Feb. 19, 1983; children: Paul W., Mark A. BS, SUNY, Cortland, 1971; MS, Mich. State U., East Lansing, 1973. Aquatic biologist NY State Dept. Environ. Conservation, Rome, 1974—79, 1983—; fish pond specialist U. S. Peace Corps, Roseau, Dominica, 1979—81; biologist aid Nat. Park Svc., Ind., 1982—83. Contbr. articles to profl. jours. Scoutmaster, asst. scoutmaster Boy Scout Troop 55, Holland Patent, NY, 1995—2006; bldg. chmn. First United Meth. Ch., Rome, 2005—06. Mem.: Am. Chem. Soc., NY Chpt. Am. Fisheries Soc. (environ. concerns chmn. 1994—2000), Am. Fisheries Soc. (cert. fisheries profl. 1984). Achievements include research in effects of pesticides, acid rain, and mercury on aquatic life. Avocations: camping, fishing, canoeing. Office: New York State Dept Environmental Cons 8314 Fish Hatchery Rd Rome NY 13440 Office Phone: 315-337-0910. Office Fax: 315-337-0988. Business E-Mail: hasimoni@gw.dec.state.ny.us.

**SIMONS, ALBERT, III,** lawyer; b. Charleston, S.C., Nov. 22, 1950; s. Albert Jr. and Caroline Pinckney (Mitchell) S.; m. Theodora Bonnell Wilbur, Jan. 28, 1970; children: Albert IV, Charles A., Theodora B. BA, U. Va., 1972, JD, 1976. Bar: S.C. 1977, N.Y. 1978. Ptnr. Orrick, Herrington & Sutcliffe, N.Y.C., 1984—. Mem. S.C. Bar Assn., N.Y. State Bar Assn. Office: Orrick Herrington & Sutcliffe 666 5th Ave Rm 203 New York NY 10103-1798 Business E-Mail: asimons@orrick.com.

**SIMONS, ANNEKE PRINS,** artist, educator; b. Amsterdam, The Netherlands, Feb. 15, 1930; arrived in U.S., 1940; d. Raphael Hugo and Charlotte Prins. BA, Vassar Coll., Poughkeepsie, NY, 1952; MAT, Harvard-Radcliffe, Cambridge, Mass., 1953; PhD, Pa. State U., Univ. Park, Pa., 1968; MA in Social Sci., Jersey City State Coll., Jersey City, NJ, 1975. Tchr., originator adult art edn. South End House, Boston, 1953—54; part-time asst. tchr. Boston Mus. Children's Rm., Boston, 1954—56; with Met. Mus. Art, NYC, 1957—61; tchr., art dir. Twin Pines, Oakland, Calif., 1961—62; grad. rsch. asst. tchr. art edn. Pa. State U., Univ. Park, Pa., 1962—64; prof. N.J. City U., 1967—2000; prof. emeritus. Senator-at-large Jersey City State Coll., mem. personnel com. art dept., dir. art program gifted H.S. students. One-woman shows include The Courtney Gallery, Jersey City State Coll., 1979, The Gallery, Jersey City, NJ, 1981, Stevens Inst. Tech., Hoboken, NJ, 1984, Jersey City Mus., 1996, exhibited in group shows at Gallery Stendhal, NYC, 1991, Jersey City State Coll., 1992, juried show, C.A.S.E. Mus., Jersey City, NJ, 1982, exhibitions include Lemmerman Gallery, NJ City U., 1999, City Spirit Cultural Arts Festival, Jersey City, NJ, 1981 (Best in Show, 1981), Visceglia Art Ctr. Caldwell Coll., Caldwell, NJ, 1994, The Rotunda Gallery, City Hall, Jersey City, NJ, 1995, Viridian Gallery, NYC, 1997, numerous others; contbr. articles to profl. jours. Co-founder Genesis Project, Jersey City, 1986—2004. Recipient Martin Luther King, Jr. Cmty. Svc. award, Jersey City U., 1999; grantee Chinese Art Hist. Coll. Tchrs. summer seminar, Nat. Endowment Humanities, 1975; grad. sch. fellowship, Pa. State U., 1964—65. Mem.: Harvard Club NY, NJ.

**SIMONS, AUDREY KAY,** music educator; b. Allentown, Pa., Feb. 9, 1967; d. Edward Wilson and Claire Christine Buss; m. Anthony Russell Simons; 1 child, Luke Edward. MusM, Temple U., Philadelphia, Pa., 1989—92; MusB, Susquehanna U., Selinsgrove, Pa., 1985—89. Cello & piano instr. Susquehanna U. Cmity Music Program, Selinsgrove, Pa., 1986—89; instr. music history Temple U. Tchg. Assistantship, Philadelphia, Pa., 1989—91, Montgomery County Cmty. Coll., Blue Bell, Pa., 1993—98; artist/lectr. Moravian Coll., Bethlehem, Pa., 1993—; asst. music dir. Pocono Youth Orchestra, Stroudsburg, Pa., 1993—. Cellist Allentown Symphony Orchestra, Allentown, 1992—, Classical Attitude String Quartet, Bethlehem, 1993—, Chestnut Hill Chamber Players, Center Valley, 2003—, Pocono Chamber Music Soc., East Stroudsburg, Pa., 2005—. Recipient Presser Found. music scholarship, Susquehanna U., 1988, Elizabeth G. Eyster award music, 1987, music scholarship, 1985—89; scholar dean's list, 1985—89. Mem.: Internet Cello Soc., Violoncello Soc., Music Tchrs. Nat. Assn., Am. String Tchrs. Assn., Sigma Alpha Iota. Home: 4955 Chestnut Hill Rd Center Valley PA 18034 Office: Moravian Coll 1200 Main St Bethlehem PA 18018 Personal E-mail: asimons94@aol.com.

**SIMONS, BARBARA,** retired elementary school educator; b. N.Y.C., May 25, 1947; d. Abraham William and Gertrude (Monash) Cohn; m. Bernard Louis Simons, Dec. 23, 1972. BA, Bklyn. Coll., 1969; MS, Syracuse U., 1970. Lic. tchr., N.Y. Tchr. Pub. Sch. 209K, Bklyn., 1970-71, Pub. Sch. 177K, Bklyn., 1971-75, Pub. Sch. 95K, Bklyn., 1975-92, Pub. Sch. 215K, Bklyn., 1993—2002; ret. 2002. Mem. Am. Fedn. Tchrs., United Fedn. Tchrs. (del. 1976-90), N.Y. United Tchrs., N.Y. Edn. Guild. Avocations: tennis, travel, bowling, golf. Home: 2428 E 27th St Brooklyn NY 11235-2004

**SIMONS, DOLPH COLLINS, JR.,** publishing executive, editor; b. Lawrence, Kans., Mar. 11, 1930; s. Dolph Collins and Marie (Nelson) S.; m. Pamela Counseller, Feb. 7, 1952; children: Pamela, Linda, Dolph Collins, Dan. AB, U. Kans., 1951; LLD (hon.), Colby Coll., 1972. Reporter Lawrence Jour.-World, 1953, asso. pub., 1957, pub., 1962—2004, editor, 1978—, pres., 1969—2004; reporter The Times, London, 1956, Johannesburg (South Africa) Star, 1958; chmn. World Co. Mem. Pulitzer Awards Jury, 1977, 78, 80, 81. Trustee, past pres. William Allen White Found.; trustee Midwest Rsch. Inst.; former trustee Menninger Found.; Nat. Parks Conservation Assn.; former mem. governing bd. Children's Mercy Hosp., Kansas City, Mo.; former trustee, former chmn. U. Kans. Endowment Assn.; past bd. dirs. Greater Kansas City Cmty. Found., Commerce Bancshares, Kansas City, Mo.; former trustee The Freedom Forum, Kans. Nature Conservancy; mem. Kans. Biosci. Authority Bd. Served to capt. USMRC, 1951—53. Recipient Elijah Parish Lovejoy award, 1972; Fred Ellsworth award for significant service to U. Kans., 1976; Disting. Service citation, 1980 Mem. Newspaper Advt. Bur. (past dir.), Am. Soc. Newspaper Editors, Inland Daily Press Assn. (past dir.), Kans. Press Assn. (past pres., dir.), AP (past dir.), Am. Newspaper Pubs. Assn. (past dir., past nat. sec.), Lawrence C. of C. (past pres., dir.), U. Kans. Alumni Assn. (past pres., dir.), Lawrence Country Club, Kansas City Country Club, Kansas City River Club, Masons, Rotary, Sigma Delta Chi, Phi Delta Theta. Republican. Episcopalian. Home: 2425 Vermont St Lawrence KS 66046-4761 Office: 609 New Hampshire St Lawrence KS 66044-2243 Personal E-mail: dsimonsjr@ljworld.com.

**SIMONS, ELIZABETH R(EIMAN),** biochemist, educator; b. Vienna, Sept. 1, 1929; came to U.S., 1941, naturalized, 1948; d. William and Erna Engle (Weisselberg) Reiman; m. Harold Lee Simons, Aug. 12, 1951; children: Leslie Ann Mulert, Robert David. BChemE, Cooper Union, N.Y.C., 1950; MS, Yale U., 1951, PhD, 1954. Rsch. chemist Tech. Ops., Arlington, Mass., 1953-54; instr. chemistry Wellesley (Mass.) Coll., 1954-57; rsch. asst. Children's Hosp. Med. Ctr. and Cancer Rsch. Found., Boston, 1957-59, rsch. assoc. pathology, 1959-62, rsch. assoc. Harvard Med. Sch., 1962-66, lectr. biol. chemistry, 1966-72; tutor biochem. scis. Harvard Coll., 1971-94; assoc. prof. biochemistry Boston (Mass.) U., 1972-78, prof., 1978—, asst. dir. Office Med. Edn., 2000—. Contbr. articles to profl. jours. Grantee in field. Mem.: AAAS, Soc. for Neurosci., Biophys. Soc., Am. Soc. Hematology, Am. Soc. Cell Biology, Am. Soc. Biol. Chemists, Am. Chem. Soc. Office: Boston U Sch Medicine 80 E Concord St Roxbury MA 02118-2307 Office Phone: 617-638-4332. Business E-Mail: esimons@bu.edu.

**SIMONS, ELWYN LAVERNE,** physical anthropologist, primatologist, paleontologist, educator; b. Lawrence, Kans., July 14, 1930; s. Verne Franklin and Verna Irene (Cuddeback) S.; m. Friderun Annursel Ankel, Dec. 2, 1972; children: Cornelia Verna Mathilde, Verne Franklin Herbert; 1 child by previous marriage: David Brenton. BS in Biology, Rice U., 1953; MA, Princeton U., 1955, PhD in Paleobiology, 1956; D.Phil., Oxford U., Eng., 1959; MA (hon.), Yale U., 1967; DSc, Oxford U., 1995. Demonstrator, exhibitor Oxford U., 1956-58; lectr. geology Princeton (N.J.) U., 1958-59; asst. prof. zoology U. Pa., Phila., 1959-61; vis. assoc. prof. geology, curator vertebrate paleontology Yale U., New Haven, 1960-61, head divsn. vert. paleontology, 1961-77, prof. paleontology, 1967; prof. geology, curator charge div. vertebrate paleontology Peabody Mus., 1965-77; prof. biol. anthropology, anatomy Duke U., Durham, NC, 1977-82, 1982, prof. zoology, dir. Duke Primate Center, 1977-91, sci. dir., 1991—2001, head, div. fossil primates, 2001—. Dir. Paleontol. Expdns., Egypt, 1961—68, Egypt, 1977—99, India, 1968—69, India, 1996, India, 98, India, 1999—2000; rsch. expdns. for fossil mammals, Wyo., 1960—96, Wyo., 1998—99, Iran, 1970, Spain, 71, Madagascar, 1983—2004; Barbour-Schramm Meml. lectr. U. Nebr., 1974; David French lectr. Claremont Coll., 1974; traveling lectr. French Bur. Fgn. Affairs, 1976; bd. dirs. Ctr. Tropical Conservation, NC. Author: Primate Evolution: An Introduction To Man's Place In Nature, 1972; co-editor: Macmillan Series in Physical Anthropology; A Simons Family History in England and America, 1975, Candebec in France and England, 2005; contbr. numerous articles to profl. publs. Decorated chevalier Ordre Nat., Madagascar; named hon. citizen, Fayum Province of Egypt, 1981; recipient Annadale Meml. medal, Asiatic Soc. Bengal, 1973, Sr. U.S. Scientist award, Alexander von Humboldt Found., 1975. Mem. AAAS, Am. Philos. Soc., Nat. Acad. Scis., Soc. Vertebrate Paleontology, Inst. Human Paleontology, Am. Assn. Zool. Parks and Aquariums (primate specialist group, advisor prosimian taxon group), Assn. Phys. Anthropology (Charles R. Darwin award 2000), Madagascar Fauna Group (bd. dirs.), Internat. Assn. Human Biologists, Sigma Xi. Democratic. Achievements include research in the early mammals, prosimians and primate and human evolution, with special interest in living prosimians, higher primate and human origin and evolution; discovery of 1st tarsiers and 1st marsupials in Africa; naming of earliest known ape Aegyptopithecus in Oligocene of Africa; discovery of Gigantopithecus in India, 1968; naming of earliest anthropoids Oligopithecus, 1962, Qatrania, 1983, Serapia and Arsinoea, 1992; discovery of and naming of new species of Propithecus: Golden Crowned Sifaka in Madagascar, 1989; conservation of lemurs and rain forest of Madagascar. Office: Duke Primate Ctr Divsn Fossil Primates 1013 Broad St Durham NC 27705 Office Phone: 919-416-8420 x 27. Office Fax: 919-416-8584. Business E-Mail: esimons@duke.edu.

**SIMONS, GAIL S.,** artist, educator, librarian; b. Elgin, Ill., Aug. 13, 1963; d. James Philip and Vivian Faith (Ewalt) S. Cert. Christian edn., Lincoln Christian Coll., 1986; BFA, Judson Coll., 1991. Tchg. asst. Pub. Sch. Dist. 300, Dundee, Ill., 1986-89; illustrator computer clip art Media Mktg. Svcs., St. Charles, Ill., 1989; computer data plant op. Judson Coll., Elgin, Ill. 1990-91, watercolor painting instr., 1991—; libr. Dundee Twp. Pub. Libr., East Dundee, Ill., 1994—, staff artist, 1991—. Youth/adult choral dir. First Congl. Ch., Carpentersville, Ill., 1986-96; stop motion animator, Chgo., 1991. Exhibited works at Ruth M. Wendt Gallery, East Dundee, 1997-99, Agora Gallery, N.Y.C., 1999—, Incognito Gallery, Fox Lake, Ill., 2001, art-exchange.com, 2003; actress, asst. dir., set/prop designer various musicals and plays. Deaconess/Sunday sch. dir. Congl. Ch., Carpentersville, 1986-96; watercolor/craft tchr. Pub. Libr. East Dundee, 1997—; wildlife adv.; youth leader. Mem. Christians in the Visual Arts, N.W. Area Arts Coun., Dundee Twp. Fine Arts Coun., Alpha Chi Soc. Avocations: collecting, gardening, writing, entomology, old movies. Office: Dundee Twp Pub Libr Dist 555 Barrington Ave East Dundee IL 60118-1422 E-mail: gailmominsect@msn.com.

**SIMONS, GALE GENE,** nuclear and electrical engineer, educator; b. Kingman, Kans., Sept. 25, 1939; s. Robert Earl and Laura V. (Swartz) S.; m. Barbara Irene Rinkel, July 2, 1966; 1 child, Curtis Dean. BS, Kans. State U., 1962, MS, 1964, PhD, 1968. Engr. Argonne Nat. Lab., Idaho Falls, Idaho, 1968-77, mgr. fast source reactor, head exptl. support group, 1972-77; prof. nuc. engring. Kans. State U., Manhattan, 1977—2001, assoc. dean for rsch., dir. rsch. coun. Coll. Engring., 1988-97, emeritus prof., 2001—, bd. dirs. Rsch. Found., 1988-97, Presdl. lectr., 1983-96, career counselor, 1988-96. Bd. dirs. Kans. Tech. Enterprise Corp., Topeka; com. mem. Kans. Gov.'s Energy Policy Com., Topeka, 1992-97; presenter, cons. in field Contbr. over 100 articles to sci. jours.; patentee radiation dosimeter. Expert witness State of Kans., Topeka, 1986. Fellow AEC, 1964-67; recipient numerous rsch. grants Mem. AAAS, IEEE, Am. Nuclear Soc., Health Physics Soc., Assn. for Engring. Edn., Masons, Rotary, Phi Kappa Phi, Tau Beta Pi, Pi Mu Epsilon. Home: 2395 Grandview Ter Manhattan KS 66502-3729

**SIMONS, HELEN,** school psychologist, psychotherapist, educator; b. Chgo., Feb. 13, 1930; d. Leo and Sarah (Shrayer) Pomper; m. Broudy Simons, May 20, 1956 (div. May 1972); children: Larry, Sheri. BA in Biol., Lake Forest Coll., 1951; MA in Clin. Psychology, Roosevelt U., 1972; D of Psychology, Ill. Sch. Profl. Psychology, 1980. Intern Cook County Hosp., Chgo., 1979-80; pvt. practice psychotherapy Chgo., 1980—; sch. psychologist Chgo. Bd. Edn., 1974-79, 80—. Faculty Internat. Soc. for Prevention of Child Abuse and Neglect; lectr., presenter at workshops. Contbr. articles to profl. jours. Mem.: APA, Internat. Sch. Psychologists Assn., Internat. Assn. Applied Psychology, Internat. Soc. for Prevention of Child Abuse and Neglect, Internat. Coun. Psychologists, Chgo. Sch. Psychol. Assn., Chgo. Psychol. Assn., Ill. Sch. Psychologists Assn., Nat. Sch. Psychologists Assn. Avocations: music, dance, reading. Home: 6145 N Sheridan Rd Apt 29D Chicago IL 60660-6855 Office: Gladstone Sch 1231 S Damen Ave Chicago IL 60608 Personal E-mail: hpompers@aol.com.

**SIMONS, JAMES HARRIS,** technology company executive; b. Apr. 25, 1938; married; 5 children. BS, MIT, 1958; PhD in Math., U. Calif., Berkeley. Tchr. math. MIT and Harvard U., 1961—64; chmn. math. dept. SUNY, Stony Brook, 1968; res., founder Renaissance Techs. Corp., East Setauket, NY, 1982—. Chmn. Stony Brook Found., 1989—; chmn. bd. dirs. Franklin Electronic Pubs., Segue Software; bd. dirs. Brookhaven Sci. Assocs. Co-author (with Shiing-Shen Chern): Characteristic Forms and Geometric Invariants, 1974. Named one of Forbes' Richest Americans, 2006; recipient Oswald Veblen prize in Geometry, Am. Mathematical Society, 1976. Office: Renaissance Techs Corp 600 Route 25A East Setauket NY 11733-2841 also: 800 3rd Ave Fl 33 New York NY 10022-7604

**SIMONS, JOHN NELSON,** surgeon, consultant; b. Lawrence, Kans., Sept. 19, 1932; s. Dolph Collins and Marie Nelson Simons; m. Ann Marie Leyendecker, July 2, 2005; children: John Jr., Andrea, James, Suzanne, Melissa. BA, U. Kans., 1954; MD, U. Pa., 1958; M in Surgery, U. Minn., 1963. Cert. Am. Bd. Surgery, 1965, Am. Bd. Plastic Surgery, 1967. Cons. plastic surgery Mayo Clinic, Rochester, Minn., 1965—66, asst. prof. plastic surgery, 1965—72, assoc. prof. plastic surgery, 1972—73, head sect. plastic surgery. Founder, CEO Health Campus Internat. Consultants in Health Care Delivery, East Gulf Lake, Minn., 1995—. Republican.

**SIMONS, LAWRENCE BROOK,** lawyer; b. N.Y.C., Oct. 19, 1924; s. Harry A. and Marion B. (Brook) Simons; m. Annalou Kadin, Aug. 24, 1947; children: Barbara Flexner, Kenneth. Student, Duke U., 1941-43, 46-47; JD, Columbia U., 1949. Bar: N.Y. 1949, U.S. Dist. Ct. (so. dist.) N.Y. 1949, DC 1984, U.S. Supreme Ct. 1987. Assoc. Spring & Eastman, N.Y.C., 1949-53; v.p., gen. mgr. Carlie Knitting Mills, San Juan, PR, 1953-58; pres. ELS Constrn. Co. Inc., S.I., NY, 1958-77; asst. sec. housing FHA commn. HUD, Washington, 1977-81; ptnr. Powell, Goldstein, Frazier & Murphy, Washington, 1981—. Mem. task force quality life Dept. of Def., 1995. Chmn. bd. dirs. Nat. Housing Conf., 1981—; mem. Nat. Housing Task Force, 1988, Nat. Housing Trust, 1990—; trustee Bayley Seton Hosp., S.I., 1981—90, NHP Found., Inc., 1991—2003; chmn. bd. dirs. N.Y. State Urban Devel. Corp., 1975—77, Pa. Ave. Devel. Corp., 1981—87; trustee Affordable Housing

Found., 1990—92, Ctr. Democracy, 1990—96; pres. Ctr. Housing Policy, 1992—96, bd. dirs., 1996—; commr. Beaufort (S.C.) Housing Authority, 1997—, Affordable Housing Commn., Hilton Head, SC, 1997—99. With U.S. Army, 1943—46, ETO. Named Man of the Yr., Nat. Housing Conf., 1985. Mem.: ABA, Nat. Assn. Home Builders (named to Housing Hall of Fame 2002), Sea Pines Country Club, Lambda Alpha. Democrat. Jewish. Avocation: golf. Home: 40 Plantation Dr Hilton Head Island SC 29928-4402 Office: Powell Goldstein Frazier Murphy 1001 Pennsylvania Ave NW Washington DC 20004-2505 Personal E-mail: simonshhi@adelphia.net.

**SIMONS, LEWIS MARTIN,** journalist; b. Paterson, N.J., Jan. 9, 1939; s. Abram and Goldie (Fleisher) S.; m. Carol Lenore Seiderman, Feb. 7, 1965; children: Justine, Rebecca, Adam P.D. BA, NYU, 1962; MS, Columbia U., 1964. Corr. AP, Kuala Lumpur, Singapore, Saigon, Denver, 1965-70, Washington Post, Bangkok, New Delhi, Washington, 1971-82; bur. chief Knight-Ridder Newspapers, Tokyo and Beijing, 1982-95; fgn. policy corr. Time mag., 1996-97; freelance writer, 1997—. Author: Worth Dying For, 1987; contbg. author: Crimes of War, 1999, The World of Islam, 2001, Breach of Faith, 2002; contbr. to Nat. Geog. mag., Smithsonian mag., Atlantic Monthly, N.Y. Times, Washington Post. With USMC, 1962-64. Recipient Grand prize and Investigative Reporting award Am. Newspaper Guild, 1981, Citation for Excellence, Overseas Press Club Am., 1983, Jessie Meriton White award Friends World Coll., 1986, Investigative Reporters and Editors award U. Mo., 1986, Award of Excellence, World Affairs Coun., 1984, 86, 89, 92, Pulitzer Prize, 1986, George Polk award, 1985, Malcolm S. Forbes award Overseas Press Club Am., 1986, 92, Gerald Loeb award UCLA, 1993, Alumni award Columbia U. Grad. Sch. Journalism, 2004; Edward R. Murrow fellow Coun. of Fgn. Rels., 1970-71. Mem. Fgn. Corrs. Club Japan (bd. dirs. 1991-92, pres., 1993-94). E-mail: clsimons@ix.netcom.com.

**SIMONS, LYNN OSBORN,** educational consultant; b. Havre, Mont., June 1, 1934; d. Robert Blair and Dorothy (Briggs) Osborn; m. John Powell Simons, Jan. 19, 1957; children: Clayton Osborn, William Blair. BA, U. Colo., 1956. Tchr. Midvale (Utah) Jr. H.S., 1956-57, Sweetwater county Sch. Dist. 1, Rock Springs, Wyo., 1957-58, U. Wyo., 1959-61, Natrona County Sch. Dist. 1, Casper, Wyo., 1963-64; credit mgr. Gallery 323, Casper, 1972-77; Wyo. state supt. pub. instrn. Cheyenne, 1979-91; sec.'s regional rep. region VIII U.S. Dept. Edn., Denver, 1993—2001; mem. Denver Fed. Exec. Bd., 1995-2001; mem. exec. bd. combined Fed. campaign, 1994—2001; ednl. cons., 2001—03; state planning coord. Capitol Bldg., Cheyenne, Wyo., 2003. Mem. State Bds. Charities and Reform, Land Commrs., Farm Loan, 1979-91; mem. State Commns. Capitol Bldg., Liquor, 1979-91; Ex-officio mem. bd. trustees U. Wyo., 1979-91; ex-officio mem. Wyo. Community Coll. Commn., 1979-91; mem. steering com. Edn. Commn. of the States, 1988-90; mem. State Bd. Edn., 1971-77, chmn., 1976-77; advisor Nat. Trust for Hist. Preservation, 1980-86. Bd. dirs. Cheyenne Bot. Gardens Found., 2004—. Mem. LWV (pres. 1970-71). Democrat. Episcopalian.

**SIMONS, RICHARD DUNCAN,** lawyer, retired judge; b. Niagara Falls, NY, Mar. 23, 1927; s. William Taylor and Sybil Irene (Swick) S.; m. Muriel (Penny) E. Genung, June 9, 1951 (dec. 1992); m. Esther (Esi) Turkington Tremblay, May 21, 1994; children: Ross T., Scott R., Kathryn E., Linda A. AB, Colgate U., 1949; LLB, U. Mich., 1952; LLD (hon.), Albany Law Sch., 1983. Bar: N.Y. 1952. Pvt. practice, Rome, NY, 1952-63; asst. corp. counsel City of Rome, 1955-58, corp. counsel, 1960-63; justice 5th jud. dist. N.Y. Supreme Ct., 1964-83, assoc. justice appellate divsn. 3d dept., 1971-72, assoc. justice appellate divsn. 4th dept., 1973-82; assoc. judge N.Y. Ct. Appeals, 1983—97, acting chief judge, 1992-93; counsel McMahon & Grow, Rome, NY, 1997—; dir. N.Y. State Capital Defender Office, 1997-2000; chief judge Oneida Indian Nation, 1997—. Jurist in residence Syracuse U. Law Sch., 1998; mem. Law Sch. Admission Svcs., Bar Passage Study Com.; mem. chief judges commn. Future of NY Govts. Editorial staff: N.Y. Pattern Jury Instructions, 1979-83. Chmn. Republican City Com., 1958-62; vice chmn. Oneida County Rep. Com., 1958-62; bd. mgrs. Rome Hosp. and Murphy Meml. Hosp., 1953; trustee Rome Arts and Cmty. Ctr., 2003-2004, mem. chief judge's commn. fiduciary appointments, chief judge's com. promote trust and confidence in legal sys., N.Y. Fair Elections Project, Inc., Campaign for Effective Justice. Served with USN, World War II. NEH fellow U. Va. Law Sch., 1979. Fellow Am. Bar Found., N.Y. State Bar Found. (chmn. 1997-98); mem. ABA, N.Y. State Bar Assn. (chair task force on ct. reorgn. 1999-2003, chair spl. com. ct. structure and jud. selection 2004-05, Disting. Svc. award 2000), Oneida County Bar Assn., Rome Bar Assn., Am. Law Inst., Inst. Jud. Adminstrn. Home: 6520 Pillmore Cir Rome NY 13440-7337 Office: McMahon & Grow 301 N Washington St Ste 4 Rome NY 13440-5152

**SIMONS, ROBERT EDWARD,** mechanical engineer, consultant; s. Stanley and Mary Simons; m. Miriam Freda Andros, Apr. 23, 1940; children: Anthony Robert, Gina Marie DaLatri, Lisa Marie Luber, Mark Edward. AAS, Dutchess C.C., Poughkeepsie, 1960; BSME, Pa. Mil. Coll., Chester, 1962; MS in Ops. Rsch. and Applied Stats., Union Coll., Schenectady, NY, 1985. Engr. GE Corp., Phila., 1962—66, IBM Corp., Poughkleepsie, 1966—69, project/devel. engr. Poughkeepsie, 1969—79, sr. engr., 1979—87, sr. tech. staff mem., 1987—93; cons. Electronics Cooling Applications, Poughkeepsie, 1993—97, IBM Corp., Poughkeepsie, 1997—. Guest editor IEEE Transactions (CHMT/CPT), N.Y.C., 1992—2002. Co-author: (packaging handbook chpt.) Heat Transfer in Electronic Packages; author: (book chpt.) Bibliography of Heat Transfer in Electronic Equipment: 1990-1994, Bibliography of Heat Transfer in Electronic Equipment, 1989, 1987, 1986; co-author: Recent Development in Thermal Technology for Electronic Packaging; author: Bibliography of Heat Transfer in Electronic Equipment, 1988. Recipient Semi-Therm Significant Contbr. award, IEEE Semiconductor Thermal Measurement and Mgmt. Symposium, 1995, Best Paper award, 2000, Semiconductor Thermal and Temperature Measurement Symposium, 1994 EDN Award for Excellence, EDN Mag., 1969. Achievements include co-invention of Thermal Conduction Module concept used to cool 3 generations of IBM mainframe computers; patents for cooling electronic packages and equipment; research in liquid cooling techniques for electronic equipment. Home: 16 Shamrock Cir Poughkeepsie NY 12603

**SIMONS, RYAN WILLIAM,** urban planner; b. Twentynine Palms, Calif., Sept. 26, 1982; s. William Michael and Joan Ellen Simons; m. Debra Lee Wike, June 24, 2006. BS, East Carolina U., Greenville, NC, 2004. Planning cons. Wilson (NC) Downtown Devel. Corp., 2004—05; county planner County of Dare, NC, Manteo, 2005—. Master: Greenville Lodge #284, A.F.&A.M.; mem: Am. MENSA, Ltd. Achievements include research in Preservation of 19th Century Tobacco Warehouses in Eastern North Carolina. Avocations: golf, cigars, jogging.

**SIMONS, STEPHEN,** mathematics professor, researcher; b. London, Aug. 11, 1938; came to U.S., 1965; s. Jack Isidore Simons and Ethel Esther (Littman) Harris; m. Jacqueline Mania Berchadsky, Aug. 13, 1963; 1 son, Mark. BA, Cambridge U., Eng., 1959, PhD, 1962. Instr. U. B.C., Vancouver, Can., 1962-63; asst. prof. U. B.C., Vancouver, Can., 1964-65, U. Calif., Santa Barbara, 1965-67, assoc. prof., 1967-73, prof., 1973—2002, prof. emeritus, 2002—, chmn. dept., 1975-77, 88-89. Trustee Math. Scis. Rsch. Inst., Berkeley, Calif., 1988-94. Peterhouse rsch. fellow, Cambridge U., 1963-64. Mem. Am. Math. Soc. Office: Univ Calif Dept Math Santa Barbara CA 93106

**SIMONS, THOMAS W., JR.,** history professor; b. Crosby, Minn., Sept. 4, 1938; s. Thomas Winston and Mary Jo (Enochs) S.; m. Margaret Eleanor Quinn, Dec. 23, 1963; children: Suzanne Beatrix, Benjamin Thomas. BA, Yale U., 1958; MA, Harvard U., 1959, PhD, 1963. Joined Fgn. Svc., Dept. State, 1963; sec. del., tech. sec. U.S. Del. to 6th round trade negotiation in GATT, 1964-67; consular officer, polit. officer Am. Embassy, Warsaw, Poland, 1968-71; Coun. on Fgn. Rels. fellow Hoover Instn., Stanford, Calif., 1971-72; internat. rels. officer Bur. Politico-Mil. Affairs, 1972-74, mem. policy planning staff, 1974-75; chief external reporting unit, polit. sect. Am. Embassy, Moscow, 1975-77, dep. chief of mission Bucharest, Romania, 1977-79, counselor for polit. affairs London, 1979-81; dir. for Soviet Union affairs Dept. State, 1981-85; mem. Sr. Seminar in Fgn. Policy, 1985-86; dep. asst.

sec. for European and Can. affairs Dept. State, 1986-89; diplomat-in-residence, adj. prof. history Brown U., Providence, 1989-90; amb. extraordinary and plenipotentiary Poland, 1990-93. Coord. U.S. assistance to new ind. states of former Soviet Union, Washington, 1993-95; amb. extraordinary and plenipotentiary, Pakistan, 1995-98; cons. prof. history Stanford U., 1998-2002, Ctr. Internat. Security and Coop., Stanford U., 1998—; program dir. Davis Ctr. for Russian and Eurasian Studies, Harvard U., 2002—; vis. diplomat-scholar Wellesley Coll., 2002-2003. Author: The End of the Cold War?, 1990, Eastern Europe in the Postwar World, 2d edit., 1993.

**SIMONSEN, LORENCE B.,** director; b. Fairview, Mont., Aug. 22, 1939; s. Merrion Peter Raymond Simonsen and Florence Charlotte Pottenger / Simonsen; m. Vicki K. Klepper, Dec. 24, 1966; children: Lorence II B., Lisa Marie, Bradford Soren. BA, Concordia Coll., 1960; ME, U. Mont., 1967, EdD, 1972; student, Ea. Wash. U., 1992—93. Cert. tchr. N.D., Mont., Wash. Tchr. English Crosby (N.D.) Pub. Schs., 1960—61; tchr. English and social studies Chaska (Minn.) Pub. Schs., 1962—63; tchr. English Shelby (Mont.) Pub. Schs., 1963—65; tchr. English and speech Glagow (Mont.) Pub. Schs., 1965—66; asst. instr. speech U. Mont., Missoula, Mont., 1966; instr. English and speech Dawson Coll., Glendive, Mont., 1967—72; supt. Richey, Mont., 1973—76; supt. schs. Shelby (Mont.) Pub. Schs., 1976—78; dean adminstrv. svcs. Am. Samoa C.C., Pago Pago, 1978—80; supt. schs. Mary Walker Sch. Dist., Springdale, Wash., 1980—85, Granger (Wash.) Pub. Schs., 1985—91, Bonner County Schs., Sand Point, Idaho, 1991—92, Wolf Point (Mont.) Schs., 1993—96; dir. grant program CC Spokane, Wash., 1996—98. Presenter in field; mem. adv. bd. Heritage Coll., 1990—91; chmn. resolutions com. Newasa, 1982—83; chmn. curriculum evaluation com. Dawson Coll., 1972—74, pres. faculty senate, 1971—72. Author: Legends of the Rivers, 2006. Chmn. ctrl. commn. Dawson County Dem. Party, Glendive, Mont., 1967—69. Recipient Parent of Yr. award, Pacific Luth. U., 1988; fellow, Dept. of Edn., 1969. Avocations: poetry, songwriter, gardening, hunting, fishing.

**SIMONSON, DAVID C.,** retired newspaper association executive; b. N.Y.C., May 9, 1927; s. Simon and Rebecca (Coolman) S.; m. Lois E. Sneider, Nov. 1, 1952; children: Peter, Eric, John Frederick. BA, Hamilton Coll., 1948; postgrad., U. Vt., 1949, Art Student League of N.Y., 1949. Copywriter Forwell & Mart Advt., N.Y.C., 1949-50; reporter, editor Croton-Cortland News, Croton, N.Y., 1950-52; gen. mgr. Colony Publs., N.Y.C., 1952-54; editor, mgr. County Press Newspapers, Croton, 1955-59; promotion dir. Amcrete Corp., Peekskill, N.Y., 1959-60; various positions in mgmt. Patent Trader, Mt. Kisco, N.Y., 1960-72, pub., 1972-77; pres./pub. Pioneer Press Newspapers, Wilmette, Ill., 1977-86; exec. v.p.; chief exec. officer Nat. Newspaper Assn., Washington, 1987-92; retired, 1992. Bd. dirs. Christian Herald Assn., N.Y.C., NY; lectr. Medill Sch. Journalism, Meridian House, U.S.A., numerous state press assns.; media cons.; seminar leader Ea. Europe for World Pres Freedom Com.; cons. to Slovenian publs. for U.S. Info. Agy., 1993—94; cons. to Slovakian publs. for USIA, 1995; cons. to African publs. for UNESCO, 95; cons. to Bulgarian Publs. for USIA, 96, 97; cons. to U.S. State dept. World Freedom Com., 2002—; cons. to Bulgarian Publs. for USIA Croatian Publs., 1999; seminar leader Voice of Am. for Bulgarian Publs., 1997, Bosnian pubs., 2000, Albanian publs., 2000; U.S. rep. Media Conf., Prague, 2001; DVTV U.S. rep. with Chinese journalists, 01; participant Freedom Forum Roundtables; media panel cons. U.S. Dept. of State, 2003. Author: What a Free Press Means to Me, 2004, Global Issues, 2005. Chmn. planning bd. Town of Croton-on-Hudson, N.Y., 1962-67, trustee, 1967, mayor, 1969. With USNR, 1945-46. Recipient Lesher award Suburban Newspapers of Am., 1998. Mem. Suburban Newspapers Am. (pres. 1984-85, bd. dirs. 1980-84), Ill. Press Assn (bd. dirs. 1980-84, 1st v.p. 1986), N.Y. Press Assn. (bd. dirs. 1966-76, 1st v.p. 1976), Nat. Newspaper Assn. (bd. dirs. 1985-86), Cook County Pubs. Assn. (pres. 1983-84). Avocations: painting, cartooning. Home: 1805 28th St S Arlington VA 22202-1536 E-mail: simonsondc@aol.com.

**SIMONSON, JAMES S.,** lawyer; b. Madison, Wis. BA, Univ. Wis., 1956; LLB, Harvard Univ., 1959. Bar: Minn. 1959. Ptnr., comml. litigation, chmn. trial dept. Gray Plant Mooty, Mpls. Fellow: Am. Coll. Trial Lawyers; mem.: Fed. Bar Assn., Eighth Cir. Ct. Appeals Bar Assn., Minn. State Bar Assn. Office: Gray Plant Mooty 500 IDS Ctr 80 S 8th St Minneapolis MN 55402 Office Phone: 612-632-3300. Office Fax: 612-632-4300. Business E-Mail: james.simonson@gpmlaw.com.

**SIMONSON, LEE STUART,** broadcast executive; b. Balt., July 3, 1948; s. Theodore and Sara (Silver) S.; m. Nancy Paula Levin, Mar. 25, 1973; children: Laura Todd, Michael Theodore. BA, U. Md., 1970; postgrad., WGMS-AM-FM (subs. RKO Gen.), Washington, 1971-73, retail sales mgr., 1973-76; sales mgr. WFYR-FM (subs. RKO Gen.), Chgo., 1976-80; v.p. gen. mgr. WRKS-FM (subs. RKO Gen.), N.Y.C., 1980-84, WOR-AM (subs. RKO Gen.), N.Y.C., 1984-88; vice chmn., COO, owner radio stas. Broadcasting Ptnrs., Inc., N.Y.C., 1988-95; chmn., CEO Broadcasting Ptnrs. Holdings, LP, N.Y.C., 1997-2000; pres. Simonson Assocs., 2000—. Bd. dirs. TheaterMania.com, MIVA, Inc. Bd. dirs. N.Y.C. chpt. March of Dimes, 1982—. With U.S. Army, 1970—76. Jewish. Office: Home phone: 212-247-3077. Personal E-mail: SIMONSONLS@aol.com.

**SIMONSON, STEWART GERARD,** retired federal agency administrator; b. May 11, 1963; U. Wis., 1986, JD, 1994. Bar: Wis., DC. Legal counsel to gov. of Wis., 1995—99; corp. sec., counsel AMTRAK, 1999—2001; dep. gen. counsel U.S. Dept. Health & Human Svcs., 2001—03; spl. counsel to sec., 2003—04, asst. sec. pub. health emergency preparedness, 2004—; ret., 2006. Office: US Dept Health & Human Svcs 200 Independence Ave SW Washington DC 20201 Office Phone: 202-619-0257.

**SIMONSON, SUSAN KAY,** hospital clinical care coordinator; b. La Porte, Ind., Dec. 5, 1946; d. George Randolph and Myrtle Lucille (Opfel) Menkes; m. Richard Bruce Simonson, Aug. 25, 1973. BA with honors, Ind. U., 1969; MA, Washington U., St. Louis, 1972. Perinatal social worker Yakima Valley Meml. Hosp., Yakima, Wash., 1979-81, dir. patient support program, 1981—, dir. social svcs., 1982-98; instr. Spanish, ethnic studies, sociology Yakima Valley Coll., Yakima, Wash., 1981—. Pres. Yakima Child Abuse Council, 1983-85; developer nat. patient support program, 1981. Contbr. articles to profl. jours. Mem. adv. council Robert Wood Johnson Found. Rural Infant Health Care Project, Yakima, 1980, Pregnancy Loss and Compassionate Friends Support Groups, Yakima, 1982—, Teen Outreach Program, Yakima, 1984—. Recipient NSF award, 1967, discharge planning program of yr. regional award Nat. Glasrock Home Health Care Discharge Planning Program, 1987; research grantee Ind. U., 1968, Fulbright grantee U.S. Dept. State, 1969-70; Nat. Def. Edn. Act fellowship, 1970-73. Mem. NASW, Soc. Hosp. Social Work Dirs., Am. Hosp. Assn. (regional award 1989), Phi Beta Kappa. Office: Yakima Valley Meml Hosp 2811 Tieton Dr Yakima WA 98902-3799 Office Phone: 509-575-8151.

**SIMONT, MARC,** artist; b. Paris, Nov. 23, 1915; came to U.S., 1927, naturalized, 1936; s. Josep and Dolors (Basté) S.; m. Sara Dalton, Apr. 7, 1945; 1 son. Marc Dalton. Attended, Academie Julian, Academie Ranson, André Lhote Sch., all Paris, 1932-35, NAD, N.Y.C., 1936. Asst. to Ezra Winter on Jefferson Wing mural Library of Congress, 1940; author, illustrator 9 children's books, 1939—; illustrator 80 books; author, illustrator: Opera Soufflé, 1950, Polly's Oats, 1951, The Lovely Summer, 1952, (with Red Smith) How to Get to First Base, 1952, Mimi, 1955, The Plumber Out of the Sea, 1955, The Contest at Paca, 1959, How Come Elephants?, 1965, Afternoon in Spain, 1965, A Childs' Eye View of the World, 1972, The Goose That Almost Got Cooked, 1997; translator, illustrator The Lieutenant Colonel and The Gypsy, 1971, The Stray Dog, 2001 (Caldecott honor, NEBA award, 2005); translator Ibrahim, 1989. Recipient Caldecott honor, 1950, 2001, Caldecott award, 1957, citation merit Soc. Illustrators, 1965, Il-lustrad'Or Profl. Assn. Illustrators of Catalonia, 1997; Tiffany Found. fellow, 1937 Boston Globe-Horn Book Award 2001. Mem. Am. Vets. Com., Authors Guild Home: 336 Town St West Cornwall CT 06796-1304

**SIMONTON, DEAN KEITH,** psychology professor; b. Glendale, Calif., Jan. 27, 1948; s. Dean Clarence Simonton and Laverne (Merkobrad) Williams; m. Susan Youel, June 21, 1971 (div. 1982); m. Melody Boyer, Dec. 29, 1984 (div. 2004); m. Karen Horobin, Mar. 20, 2005. BA in Psychology magna cum laude, Occidental Coll., 1970; MA in Social Psychology, Harvard U., 1973, PhD with distinction, 1975. Asst. prof. psychology U. Ark., Fayetteville, 1974-76; from asst. prof. to prof. U. Calif., Davis, 1976—2004, disting. prof., 2004—. Cons. Wissenschaftzentrun, Berlin, 1979, Ctr. for Creative Leadership, Greensboro, N.C., 1983, NATO, Brussels, Belgium, 1980-81, Dept. Def., Washington, 1983, Creative Problem Solving Inst., 1984, Arvin Perlmutter, Inc., 1992, Milken Family Found., 1994, Templeton Found., 2002. Author: Genius, Creativity and Leadership, 1984, Why Presidents Succeed, 1987, Scientific Genius, 1988, Psychology, Science, and History, 1990, Greatness, 1994, Genius and Creativity, 1997, Origins of Genius, 1999, Great Psychologists and Their Times, 2002, Creativity in Science, 2004; editor Jour. Creative Behavior, 1993-99; contbr. numerous articles to profl. jours. Recipient Excellence award Mensa Adn. and Rsch. Found., 1986, Francis Galton award Internat. Assn. Empirical Aesthetics, 1996. Theatrical Innovation prize, Soc. Personality and Soc. Psychology, 2004. Fellow AAAS, Am. Psychol. Soc., Am. Assn. Applied and Preventive Psychology, Am. Psychol. Assn. (mem.-at-large 1979-82, pres. psychology and the arts divsn. 1985-86, Rudolf Arnheim award Outstanding Contbn. to Psychology and the Arts, 1996, George A. Miller award 1997, William James Book award, 2000, Robert S. Daniel Four Yr. Coll./Univ. Tchg. award, 2006); mem. Phi Beta Kappa, Sigma Xi. Home: 1331 Arena Dr Davis CA 95616-0274 Office: U Calif Dept Psychology Davis CA 95616 Office Phone: 530-752-1677. Business E-Mail: dksimonton@ucdavis.edu.

**SIMONYI, CHARLES,** software engineer; b. Budapest, Hungary; BS, U. Calif., Berkeley, 1972; PhD, Stanford U., 1976. Developer Xerox Rsch. Ctr., Palo Alto, Calif., 1972-80, mgr., 1981-91; chief architect Microsoft Rsch. Corp., Redmond, Wash., 1991—2002; pres., CEO Intentional Software Corp., 2002—. Named one of 400 Richest Ams., Forbes mag., 2006. Mem. NAE Achievements include development of new approaches in programming technology; program representation where new abstraction mechanisms can be introduced without invalidating legacy code. Office: Intentional Software Corp 500 108th Ave NE #1050 Bellevue WA 98004 Office Phone: 425-467-6600. Office Fax: 425-467-6601. E-mail: charles@intentsoft.com.*

**SIMPKINS, ANNELLEN,** author; b. Apr. 29, 1947; BA, Goucher Coll., Balt., 1969; MA, Goddard Coll., 1975; PhD, U.S. Internat. U., San Diego, 1983. Co-author: (with C.A. Simpkins) Principles of Self Hypnosis: Pathways to the Unconscious, 1990, Principles of Meditation: Eastern Wisdom for the Western Mind, 1996, Meditatie, Een Inleiding In Ontspanning, 1996, Living Meditation: From Principle to Practice, 1997, Zen Around the World: A 2500 Year Journey from the Buddha to You, 1997, Meditation From Thought to Action, 1998; Simple Zen: A Guide to Living Moment by Moment, 1999, Simple Taoism: A Guide to Living in Balance, 1999, Principios de Meditación, Meditatie Stap voor Stap, 1999, Le Petit Livre du Tao, 2000, Le Petit Livre du Zen, 2000, Simple Confucianism: A Guide to Living Virtuously, 2000, Simple Buddhism: A Guide to Enlightened Living, 2000, Effective Self Hypnosis, 2000, Timeless Teachings from the Therapy Masters, 2001, Chung DoKwan: The Power of Tae Kwan Do, 2002, A Perfect World: The Rom Files, 2002, Tao in Ten, 2003, Zen in Ten, 2003, Buddhism in Ten, 2003, Yoga Basics, 2003, Self-Hypnosis for Women, 2004, Taekwondo: Building on the Basics, 2005.

**SIMPKINS, NEIL P.,** investment company executive, automotive executive; Grad. with honors, Oxford U.; MBA, Harvard Bus. Sch. Consultant Bain & Co., London; principal Bain Capital, 1993—99; sr. mng. dir., private equity group Blackstone Group L.P., 1999—; chmn. TRW Automotive, Livonia, Mich., 2003—. Bd. dirs. Vanguard Health Systems Inc. Office: Blackstone Group 345 Park Ave New York NY 10154 also: TRW Automotive 12001 Tech Ctr Dr Livonia MI 48150*

**SIMPLOT, JOHN R.,** agribusiness executive; b. Dubuque, Iowa, Jan. 4, 1909; m. Esther Becker; children: Richard, Don, Scott, Gay Simplot Otter. Potato sorter during Great Depression; founder, chmn. J.R. Simplot Co., Boise, Idaho, 1941—. Bd. dir. Micron Tech., First Security Corp., Continental Life and Accident Co., Morrison-Knudsen, Inc.; former chmn. bd. trustees Coll. Idaho. Named one of Forbes' Richest Americans, 2006. Achievements include patents for commercial frozen french fries in 1950's. Avocations: skiing, horseback riding, hunting, fishing. Office: J R Simplot Co PO Box 27 1 Capitol Ctr Boise ID 83707*

**SIMPSON, ALAN K.,** former US senator, lawyer; b. Cody, Wyo., Sept. 2, 1931; s. Milward Lee and Lorna (Kooi) S.; m. Ann Schroll, June 21, 1954; children— William Lloyd, Colin Mackenzie, Susan Lorna. BS, U. Wyo., 1954, JD, 1958; LLD (hon.), Calif. Western Sch. of Law, San Diego, 1983, Colo. Coll., Colo. Springs, 1986, Notre Dame U., South Bend, Ind., 1987, Am. U., Washington, D.C., 1989, Rocky Mountain Coll., Billings, Mont., 1996, U. Wyo., Laramie, 1999. Bar: Wyo. 1958, U.S. Supreme Ct. 1964. Asst. atty. gen. State of Wyo., 1959; city atty. City of Cody, 1959-69; ptnr. Simpson, Kepler, and Simpson, Cody, Wyo., 1959-78; mem. Wyo. Ho. of Reps., 1964-77, majority whip, 1973-75, majority floor leader, 1975-77, speaker pro tem, 1977; mem. U.S. Senate from Wyo., 1978-96, asst. majority or minority leader, 1984-94, chmn. vets. affairs com., chmn. fin. subcom. on Social Security and Family Policy, chmn. subcom. on Immigration and Refugee Policy; mem. Spec. Com. on Aging; dir. Inst. Politics Kennedy Sch. Govt. Harvard U., 1999—2000; ptnr. and shareholder Burg Simpson Eldredge Hersh Jardine and Simpson Kepler & Edwards PC, Cody, Wyo. Guest lectr. London exchange program Regent's Coll., London, 1987; vis. lectr. Lombard chair Shorenstein Ctr. for Press, Politics and Pub. Policy, Kennedy Sch. Govt., Harvard U., 1997-2000; bd. dirs. Am. Express Funds; former dir. Biogen; mem. Presdl. Debate Commn.; co-chair Continuity in Govt. Commn. Chmn. bd. trustees Buffalo Bill Hist. Ctr., Cody; trustee emeritus, Grand Teton Music Festival; former mem Smithsonian Inst., Washington; adv. bd. Folger Shakespeare Libr., Washington; past mem. Am. Battle Monuments Commn.; past bd. mem. Kennedy Ctr. for Performing Arts, Washington. Recipient Nat. Assn. Land Grant Colls. Centennial Alumni award U. Wyo., 1987, Disting. Alumnus award, 1985, Lifetime Svc. award United Calif. Bank, L.A. 1969-73; asst. v.p. mktg. 1st Hawaiian Bank, Honolulu, 1973-78; v.p. corp. comms. Pacific Resources Inc., Honolulu, 1978-89, BHP Hawaii, Inc., 1989-98; v.p. corp. rels. Tesoro Petroleum Corp., San Antonio, 1998-2000; v.p. corp. comms. Edison Internat., Rosemead, Calif., 2000—01; pres. Simpson Comm., 2001—. Bd. dirs. Arts Coun., Hawaii, 1977-81, Hawaii Heart Assn., 1978-83, Coun. Pacific Girls Scouts USA, 1982-85, Child and Family Svcs., 1984-86, Honolulu Symphony Soc., 1985-91, Sta. KHPR Hawaii Pub. Radio, 1988-92, Kapiolani Found., 1990-95, Hanahauoli Sch., 1991-98, Hawaii Strategic Devel. Corp., 1991-98, Children's Discovery Ctr., 1994-98, Pacific Asian Affairs Coun., 1994-96, Hawaii MADD, 1992-96, Girl Scout Coun. Mt. Wilson Dist., 2005—; adv. dir. Hawaii Ads at Work, 1991-98; bd. dirs., 2d v.p. Girl Scout Coun. Hawaii, 1994-96, mem. adv. bd., 1996-98; trustee Hawaii Loa Coll., 1984-86, Kapiolani Women's and Children's Hosp., 1987-98, Hawaii Sch. for Girls at LaPietra, 1989-91, Kapiolani Med. Ctr. at Pali Momi, 1994-98; bd. dirs. Aloha coun. Boy Scouts Am., 1998, Alamo coun., 1998-2000; found. bd. dirs. Hawaii Pub. TV, 1998. Bd. dirs., San Pedro Playhouse, 1999-2000; bd. dirs. Red Cross of San Antonio, 1999-2000; commr. Hawaii State Commn. on Status of Women, 1985-87,

State Sesquecentennial of Pub. Schs. Commn., 1990-91; bd. dirs. Art Wilson coun. Girl Scouts Am., 2005—. Named Advt. Woman of Yr., Honolulu Advt. Fedn., 1982, Pub. Rels. Profl. of Yr., Honolulu Pub. Rels. Soc., 1993, Communicator of Yr., Utilities Communicators Internat., 1983; recipient Silver Anvil award Pub. Rels. Soc. Am., 1983, 97. Mem. Internat. Pub. Rels. Assn. (Golden World award 1997), Am. Mktg. Assn., Pub. Rels. Soc. Am. (bd. dirs. Honolulu chpt. 1984-86, Silver Anvil award 1984, Pub. Rels. Profl. Yr. 1991), U. So. Calif. Alumni Assn. (bd. dirs. Hawaii 1981-83), Outrigger Canoe Club, Rotary (pub. rels. chmn. 1988-97, Honolulu chpt., bd. dirs. 1998), Rotary Club of San Antonio, Alpha Phi (past pres., dir. Hawaii), Hawaii Jaycees (Outstanding Young Person of Hawaii 1978.

**SIMPSON, ASHLEE NICOLE,** vocalist, actress; b. Dallas, Oct. 3, 1984; d. Joe and Tina Simpson. Studied, Sch. of Am. Ballet. Singer: (albums) Autobiography, 2004, I Am Me, 2005; performer: (songs) "Just Let Me Cry", Freaky Friday Soundtrack, 2003; actor: (films) The Hot Chick, 2002, Raise Your Voice, 2004, Undiscovered, 2005; (TV series) 7th Heaven, 2002—04, The Ashlee Simpson Show, 2004—05; musical guest appearance Saturday Night Live, 2004, guest appearance Saved By the Bell: The New Class, 1993, The View, 1997, Malcom in the Middle, 2001, 60 Minutes, 2004, Newlyweds: Nick & Jessica, 2003, 2004; actor: (plays) Chicago, 2006. Recipient Female New Artist of Yr., Billboard Music Awards, 2004. Avocations: vintage shopping, writing and recording music, spending time with family and friends.*

**SIMPSON, A.W. BRIAN,** law educator; b. 1931; Degree (hon.), Dalhousie Law Sch., Can., 2003, U. Kent at Canterbury, Eng., 2003. Fellow Oxford U., Eng., 1955-72; prof. U. Kent, Canterbury, Eng., 1972-84, U. Chgo., 1984-87, U. Mich. Law Sch., Ann Arbor, 1987—, Charles F. and Edith J. Clyne Prof. of Law. Lectr. Centre for Human Rights, London Sch. Econs., 2003. Author: Human Rights and the End of Empire: Britain and the Genesis of the European Convention, History of the Common Law of Contract, Biographical Dictionary of the Common Law, Cannibalism and the Common Law, A History of the Land, Law, Legal Theory and Legal History, In the Highest Degree Odious: Detention Without Trial in Wartime Britain, Leading Cases in the Common Law; contbr. articles to law jours. Named Hon. Queen's Coun., 2001. Fellow: Am. Acad. Arts and Scis., Lincoln Coll., Oxford (hon.); mem.: British Acad. Office: U Mich Law Sch 409 Hutchins Hall 625 S State St Ann Arbor MI 48109-1215 Office Phone: 734-763-0413. Business E-Mail: bsimpson@umich.edu.

**SIMPSON, BENNETT,** art critic, art museum curator; BA, Univ. Virginia, 1994. Former editor ArtByte Mag., NYC, Purple Mag., NYC; Whitney Lauder curatorial fell. Inst. Contemporary Art, 2001—02, assoc. curator Phila., 2002—03, Boston, 2004—. Exhibitions include Apex Art, NYC, 1999, Elysian Fields, Centre Pompidou, Paris, 2000, Shoot the Singer: Music on Video, ICA, Phila., 2002, Make Your Own Life: Artists in and out of Cologne, 2004; contbr. articles to numerous profl. jours. Office: ICA Boston 955 Boylston St Boston MA 02115*

**SIMPSON, BERYL BRINTNALL,** botany educator; b. Dallas, Apr. 28, 1942; d. Edward Everett and Barbara Frances (Brintnall) S.; children: Jonathan, Meghan. AB, Radcliffe Coll., 1964; MA, PhD, Harvard U., 1968. Rsch. fellow Arnold Arboretum/Gray Herbarium, Cambridge, Mass., 1969-71; curator Smithsonian Instn., Washington, 1971-78; prof. U. Tex., Austin, 1978—. Chmn. U.S. Com. to IUBS, 1985-88; co-pres. Internat. Congress Systematic and Evolutionary Biology, 1980-85. Author: Economic Botany, 1994, 3d edit., 2001; editor: Mesquite, 1977; contbr. over 160 articles and notes to profl. jours. Recipient Greenman award Mo. Bot. Garden, 1970. Fellow AAAS, Am. Acad. Arts and Sci., Soc. for Study Evolution (coun. 1975-80, pres. 1985-86), Bot. Soc. Am. (pres. 1990-91, Merit award 1992), Bot. Soc. Washington (v.p. 1975), Am. Soc. Plant Taxonomists (pres. 1994, Cooley award, Asa Gray award), Am. Inst. Biol. Scis. (bd. dirs. 1993-95), U.S.-Mex. Found. for Sci. (bd. govs.), Soc. Econ. Botany (pres. 1999). Office: 1 University Station A6700 Univ Tex Sect Integrative Biology Austin TX 78712 Business E-Mail: beryl@mail.utexas.edu.

**SIMPSON, BOB R.,** energy executive; BS Acctg. with honors, Baylor U., MBA. Tax mgr. Southland Royalty Co., 1976—79, v.p. Fin. & Corp. Devel., 1979—86; co-founder, CEO XTO Energy Inc., Fort Worth, Tex., 1986—96, dir., 1990—, chmn., 1996—. Mem. Nat. Petroleum Council. Office: XTO Energy Inc 810 Houston St Fort Worth TX 76102-6298

**SIMPSON, CAM,** reporter; State Dept. corr. Chgo. Tribune, Washington. Recipient George Polk award for Internat. Reporting, 2006, Madeline Dane Ross award, Overseas Press Club, 2006. Office: Chicago Tribune Washington Bur Ste 700 1025 F St NW Washington DC 20004 Office Phone: 202-824-8237. Office Fax: 202-824-8302. E-mail: csimpson@tribune.com.*

**SIMPSON, CAROL LOUISE,** investment company executive; b. Phila., Jan. 30, 1937; d. William Huffington and Hilda Agnes (Johnston) S. Student, Phila. C.C., 1985—87, U. Minn., 1986—88. Cert. Nat. Assn. Securities Dealers, Inc., Washington; registered options, mcpl. securities, gen. securities, fin. and ops. prin.; lic. life, accident, health ins. Exec. asst. Germantown Fed. Savs., Phila., 1954-67; asst. sec. Am. Med. Investment Co., Inc. (formerly Cannon and Co., Inc.), Blue Bell, Pa., 1967-91; v.p., sec. AMA Investment Advisers, Inc. (formerly Pro Svcs., Inc.), Blue Bell, Pa., 1967-91; exec. v.p., sec. Rutherford Fin. Corp., Phila., 1991-2000, Rutherford, Brown & Catherwood Inc., Phila., 1991-2000, Walnut Asset Mgmt. Inc., Phila., 1991-98. Mem. Investment Co. Inst. (fed. legis. com. 1984-91, investment advisers com. 1988-2000, compliance com. 1990-2000), VNA Cmty. Svcs. Found. (bd. dirs. 1995-2001), Vis. Nurse Assn. Cmty. Svcs. (bd. dirs. 1997-2000), Whitemarsh Valley Country Club. Republican. Home: 7701 Lawnton St Philadelphia PA 19128-3105

**SIMPSON, CAROL MANN,** librarian, educator, editor; b. Aberdeen, Md., Nov. 28, 1949; d. Joey Mathew and Grace Winifred (Fielman) Pirrung; m. Robert Smith Mann, Jan. 4, 1969 (div. May 1986); children: Stephen, David (dec.), Sarah; m. Douglas Michael Simpson, Jan. 18, 1992; stepchildren: Brian, Kevin. BS in Edn., Southwestern U., 1971; MA, U. Tex., 1975, MLS, 1977; EdD, East Tex. State U., 1987. Cert. art and French tchr., libr., learning resources specialist, supr., Tex. Tchr. Round Rock (Tex.) Ind. Sch. Dist., 1970-74; libr. Mesquite (Tex.) Ind. Sch. Dist., 1977-90, coord. libr. and media svcs., 1990-92, facilitator libr. tech., 1992—98; assoc. prof. U. North Tex. Sch. Libr. and Info. Scis., Denton, 1998—2006; adj. prof. Tex. Women's U., 1992-93. Fellow Tex. Ctr. for Digital Knowledge, 2000—; cons. Orex Petroleum, Dallas, 1988, Mesquite Pub. Libr., 1989-90, HBW Assocs., Dallas, 1988-89; reviewer Booklist, 1984-95, Sch. Libr. Jour., 1984-95, Video Rating Guide for Librs., 1989-92. Author: Copyright for School Libraries, 1994, Internet for Library Media Specialists, 1995, Copyright for Schools, 1997, 2005, Copyright Catechism, 2005, Internet for Schools, 1997, 2003, Ethics for School Librarianship, 2003; editor: Technology Connection, 1995—99, The Book Report, 1999—2003, Library Talk, 1999—2003, Library Media Connection, 2003—; contbr. articles to profl. jours. Mem. ALA, Assn. for Ednl. Comms. and Tech., Tex. Libr. Assn., Am. Assn. Sch. Librs., Tex. Assn. Sch. Librs. Methodist. Avocations: genealogy, computers, gardening. Home: 1086 Holly Ln Lewisville TX 75067-5710 Office: U North Tex Sch Libr and Info Scis PO Box 311068 Denton TX 76203

**SIMPSON, CARTER B.,** lawyer; b. Pitts., July 19, 1950; s. John W. Simpson; m. Paulette Peters, May 1, 1982; children: Christina B., Carter B. Jr. BSE in Elec. Engring., Princeton U., 1972; JD, U. Mich., 1976. Assoc. Cadwalader, Wickersham & Taft, NYC, 1976—86, counsel, 1986—88; counsel, antitrust and litig. Mobil Corp., Fairfax, Va., 1988—91, sr. counsel, antitrust, 1991—96, sr. counsel, antitrust and trade regulation, 1996—99; downstream antitrust counsel Exxon Mobil Corp., Fairfax, 2000—06; sr. counsel antitrust and trade regulation Downstream Cos., 2006—. Adv. bd. mem.: Antitrust Counselor, Bus. Laws Inc., 1995—. Dir. Overlook Condo Assn., Wintergreen, Va., 2005. Mem.: ABA Antitrust Sect. (vice chair Clayton

Act com. 1995—99). Home: 10007 Thompson Ridge Ct Great Falls VA 22066 Office: Exxon Mobil Corp 3225 Gallows Rd Fairfax VA 22037 Office Phone: 703-846-2829. E-mail: carter.b.simpson@exxonmobil.com.

**SIMPSON, CHAD W.,** pharmacist, educator; s. David Henry Simpson and Sharon Janine Park, Robert Frank Park, Jr. (Stepfather); life ptnr. C. S. Corning. BS in Pharmacy, Southwestern Okla. State U., 1996. Registered pharmacist Tex. Pharmacist Eckerd, San Antonio, 1996, Wal-Mart, 1996—98; pharmacy edn. coord. Bapt. St. Anthony's Health Sys., Amarillo, Tex., 1998—; instr. Amarillo Coll., 1999—2003. Mem. tech. adv. com. Amarillo Coll. Pharmacy, 1999—; bd. dirs. Tex. Soc. Health Sys. Pharmacists; mem. taskforce technician registration Tex. State Bd. Pharmacy. Author: (poster with abstract) Texas Society of Health System Pharmacists 53rd Annual Seminar, 2001. Mem.: Panhandle Soc. Health Sys. Pharmacists (pres. 2002—03), Tex. Soc. Health Sys. Pharmacists (vice-chair comm. coun. 2003—04, chair comm. coun. 2004—). Avocations: writing, cooking, reading. Office: Bapt Saint Anthony's Health Sys 1600 Wallace Blvd Amarillo TX 79106

**SIMPSON, CHARLES R., III,** judge; married; 3 children. BA, U. Louisville, 1967, JD, 1970. Bar: Ky. 1970, U.S. Dist. Ct. (we. dist.) Ky. 1971, U.S. Cir. Ct. (6th cir.) 1985. With Rubin, Trautwein & Hays, Louisville, 1971-75, Levin, Yussman & Simpson, Louisville, 1975-77; judge U.S. Dist. Ct. (we. dist.) Ky., Louisville, 1986—, chief judge, 1994—2001; pvt. practice Louisville, 1977-86. Part-time staff counsel Jefferson County Judge/Exec., 1978-84; adminstr. Jefferson County Alcoholic Beverage Control, 1983-84. Roman Catholic. Office: We Dist Ct Ky 247 US Courthouse 601 W Broadway Louisville KY 40202-2238 E-mail: judgesimpson@kywd.uscourts.gov.

**SIMPSON, DANIEL H.,** ambassador; b. Wheeling, W.Va., July 9, 1939; married; 4 children. BA, Yale U., 1961; cert. in African studies, Northwestern U., 1973. Joined Fgn. Svc., U.S. Dept. State, Washington, 1966—, staff asst. Bur. Security and Consular Affairs, 1966-67, speech writer for asst. sec. state for African affairs, 1968, desk officer for Rhodesia, Botswana, Lesotho, and Swaziland, 1973-74; tng. officer USIA, Washington, 1967-68; polit., econ. and consular officer Am. Embassy, Bujumbura, Burundi, 1968-70, polit. officer Pretoria, Republic South Africa, 1970-72, dep. chief mission Beirut, until 1989; amb. to Cen. African Republic, Bangui, 1989-92; dep. comdr. Army War Coll., Carlisle, Pa., 1993-94; ambassador to Somalia Mogadishu, 1994-95; ambassador to Congo Kinshasa, 1995-98; v.p. Nat. Def. U., Washington, 1998-2000; regional dir. OSCE, Bosnia-Herzegovina, 2000—01; assoc. editor Pitts. Post-Gazette and Toledo Blade, 2001—. Address: Pitts Post-Gazette 34 Blvd of the Allies Pittsburgh PA 15222 Home: 112 Washington Pl #20A Pittsburgh PA 15219 Office Phone: 412-263-1976. E-mail: dsimpson@post-gazette.com.

**SIMPSON, DAVID MICHAEL,** financial planner, educator; s. Clarence Vincent and Joy Wanell Simpson; m. Sandra E. Sephton, Jan. 25, 1998; children: Jonathan David, Thomas Hunter, Melanie Kate. BA, Duke U., Durham, NC, 1987; M in Pub. Affairs, U. Tex., Austin, 1990; PhD, U. Calif., Berkeleu, 1996. Dir. U. Louisville Ctr. for Hazards Rsch., 2003—; assoc. prof. U. Louisville, 2005—. Mem.: Am. Inst. Cert. Planners. Office: U Louisville 426 West Bloom St Louisville KY 40208 Office Phone: 502-852-7906.

**SIMPSON, DAVID WILLIAM,** artist, educator; b. Pasadena, Calif., Jan. 20, 1928; s. Frederick and Mary Adeline (White) S.; m. Dolores D. Debus, July 30, 1954; 1 stepchild, Gregory C. Vose; 1 child, Lisa C. B.F.A., Calif. Sch. Fine Arts, 1956; MA, San Francisco State Coll., 1958. Instr. art Am. River Jr. Coll., Sacramento, 1958-60, Contra Costa Jr. Coll., San Pablo, Calif., 1960-65; prof. art U. Calif., Berkeley, 1967-91, prof. emeritus, 1991—. Exhibited in one-man shows including Robert Elkon Gallery, NYC, 1961, 63-64, San Francisco Mus. Art, 1967, Henri Gallery, Washington, 1968, Oakland Mus., 1978, Modernism, San Francisco, 1980-81, 84, 86, 2001, Sheldon Meml. Art Gallery, Lincoln, Nebr., 1990, Mincher/Wilcox Gallery, San Francisco, 1991-93, Angles Gallery, Santa Monica, Calif., 1991-92, 94, 99, Bemis Found., Omaha, 1991, Anthony Ralph Gallery, NYC, 1992, John Berggruen Gallery, San Francisco, 1994, Charlotte Jackson Fine Art, Santa Fe, 1995, Laguna Art Mus., Laguna Beach, Calif., 1995 Haines Gallery, San Francisco, 1997, 99, 2004, Studio La Citta, Verona, Italy, 1998, 2002, Renate Schröder Gallery, Cologne, Germany, 2000-02, Artothek, Cologne, 2002, James Kelly Contemporary, Santa Fe, 2003, Studio G-7, Bologna, Italy, Sonja Roesch Gallery, Houston, 2005; group shows include Mus. Modern Art, NYC, 1963, Carnegie Internat., Pitts., 1961-62, 66-67, LA Mus. Art, 1964, U. Ill., 1969, Expo '70, Osaka, Japan, 1970, Josly Art Mus., Omaha, 1970, John Berggruen Gallery, San Francisco, 1979, 93, Angles Gallery, Santa Monica, 1988, 90, John Good Gallery, NY, 1992, Cheryl Haines Gallery, San Francisco, 1996, Mus. di Arte Moderna e Contemporanea, Trento, Italy, 1996, Studio La Citta, Verona, Italy, 1996-2005, Llonja, Palma De Majorca, Spain, 1997, Mus. Cantonale d'Arte, Lugano, Switzerland, 1997, Haines Gallery, San Francisco, 1997, Palazzo Ducale, Gubbio, Italy, 1999, Palazzo Ducale, Panza Della Gran Guardia, Verona, 2002, Albright-Knox Gallery, Buffalo, NY, 2005, Fondazione Marenostrum Porto Venere, Italy, Kunstverein Lingen Kuntshauz, Germany, 2005; others; represented in permanent collections including Phila. Mus. Art, Nat. Collection Fine Arts, Wash., Seattle Art Mus., La Jolla (Calif.) Mus. Art, Mus. Modern Art, NYC, San Francisco Mus. Art, Oakland (Calif.) Mus., Panza Collection, Italy, Laguna Art Mus., Laguna Beach, Calif., U. Art Mus., Berkeley, Calif., Mus. Cantonale d'Arte Lugano, Switzerland, Mus. Di Arte Moderna e Contemporanea Di Trento e Roverato, Sassuolo, Panza Collection, Italy, Albright Knox Gallery, Buffalo, San Jose Mus., Calif. Home: 565 Vistamont Ave Berkeley CA 94708-1244 Office: U Calif Dept Art Berkeley CA 94720

**SIMPSON, DEBORAH,** medical educator; BA, U. Calif., Santa Barbara, 1974; MA, Ohio State U., Columbus, 1976; PhD, U. Minn., Mpls., 2003. Assoc. dean ednl. support and evaluation, dir. office ednl. svcs., prof. family and cmty. medicine Med. Coll. Wis., Milw., 1984—. Recipient Disting. Svc. award, Med. Coll. Wis., 2001, Excellence in Edn. award, Soc. Tchrs. Family Medicine, 2001; McCann Faculty scholar, Joy McCann Found., 2005. Mem.: Soc. Dirs. Rsch. Med. Edn., Assn. of Am. Med. Coll. (chair 1999—2001, ctrl. group ednl. affairs, chair 2003—04, Med. Edn. Laureate 1999). Avocations: hiking, recreational sports. Office: Med Coll Wis 8701 Watertown Plank Rd Milwaukee WI 53226 Office Phone: 414-456-4332. Office Fax: 414-456-6506.

**SIMPSON, DENNIS DWAYNE,** psychologist, educator; b. Lubbock, Tex., Nov. 9, 1943; s. Homer Arnold and Georgie Lee (Barrett) S.; m. Sherry Ann Johnson, Aug. 20, 1965; children: Jason Renn, Jeffrey Todd, Jennifer Lynn. BA, U. Tex., 1966; PhD, Tex. Christian U., 1970. Asst. prof. psychology Tex. Christian U., Ft. Worth, 1970-74, assoc. prof., 1974-79, prof. 1979-82, dir., prof., 1989—, S.B. Sells prof. psychology. Vis. prof. Tex. A&M U., College Station, 1982-89. Mem. sci. adv. bd. NICA Rsch. Ctrs., Washington, 1992—; mem. adv. bd. Nat. Drug Treatment Evaluation Studies, Washington, 1992—; cons. WHO, fgn. govts. regarding drug rsch. Mem. editl. bd. Am. Jour. Drug and Alcohol Abuse, Substance Abuse Treatment, Substance Use and Misuse; contbr. over 250 articles to profl. jours.; author: 9 books. Recipient Disting. Rsch. Achievement award Tex. Commn. on Alcohol and Drug Abuse, 1987; recipient numerous grants. Mem.: APA, Southwestern Psychol. Assn., Acad. for Health Svcs. Rsch. and Health Policy, The Coll. on Problems of Drug Dependence. Achievements include research emphasis on the process of treatment service delivery in relation to client attributes and how they related to retention rates, relapse and posttreatment outcomes; research in drug use in the workplace; organizational behavior and its role in transferring evidence-based innovations into practice in community-based treatment agencies as well as criminal justice settings; other areas. Office: Tex Christian U Inst Behavioral Rsch PO Box 298740 Fort Worth TX 76129-0001 Business E-Mail: ibr@tcu.edu.

**SIMPSON, DICK WELDON,** political science educator; b. Houston, Nov. 8, 1940; s. Warren Weldon and Ola Ela (Felts) S.; m. Sarajane Avidon, Mar. 22, 1987; children: Kate Donley, August Donley. BA, U. Tex., 1963; MA, Ind. U., 1964, PhD, 1968; MDiv, McCormick Theol. Sem., 1984. Ordained to ministry United Ch. of Christ, 1985. Rsch. asst. Ind. U., Bloomington, 1965; fgn. area fellow Ford Found., Africa, 1966-67; instr. U. Ill., Chgo., 1967-68, asst. prof., 1968-71, assoc. prof. polit. sci., 1972-96, prof., 1996—, head dept., 2006—. Exec. dir. Inst. on Ch., Chgo., 1984-86, Clergy and Laity Concerned, Chgo., 1987-89. Author: Winning Elections, 1972, 74, 81, 96, Strategies for Change, 1976, Politics of Compassion, 1989; editor: Chicago's Future, 1976, 80, 83, 88, 93, Rogues, Rebels, and Rubber Stamps, 2001, Inside Urban Politics, 2004; prodr., polit. advisor 8 documentary films including By the People, 1970, Teaching Politics, 2006. Alderman Chgo. City Coun., 1971-79; campaign mgr. McCarthy for Pres., Ill., 1967-68; transition team Mayors Washington and Byrne, 1979, 83, State's Atty. O'Malley and County Clk. Orr, 1990, 91, Ill. Atty. Gen. Lisa Madigan, 2003; congl. candidate, 1992, 94. Humanities Inst. fellow U. Ill., Chgo., 1985-86, Great Cities fellow, 1997-98, 2005-06; rsch grantee Joyce, Amoco, Woods, McArthur, Carnegie, Wieboldt Founds., 1972-2003; recipient award Clarence Darrow Cmty. Ctr., Clergy and Laity Concerned, IVI-IPO. Mem. Am. Polit. Sci. Assn. (Excellence in Tchg. award, 2002), Midwest Polit. Sci. Assn., Ill. Polit. Sci. Assn. (past pres.), City Club Chgo. (v.p., award). Office: Dept Polit Sci U Ill M/C 276 1007 W Harrison St Chicago IL 60607-7137 Office Phone: 312-413-3780. E-mail: simpson@uic.edu.

**SIMPSON, DOROTHY AUDREY,** retired speech educator; b. Las Vegas, N.Mex., Feb. 29, 1944; d. Clyde Joseph and Audrey Shirley (Clements) Simpson; m. Gary Alan Beimer, May 13, 1972 (div. Apr. 1986); children: Laura Lea Beimer Mitchell, Rose; m. Ian B. Croxton, Dec. 27, 1992 (div. Oct. 1993); m. Doyle W. Hauschulz, Feb. 23, 2001 (div. June 2003). BA, N.Mex. Highlands U., 1965; MS, U. Utah, 1968; EdD, U. N.Mex., 1989. Cert. secondary edn., N.Mex. Tchr. West Las Vegas (N.Mex.) H.S., 1966-67, Santa Rosa (N.Mex.) H.S., 1968-71, Questa (N.Mex.) Consol. Schs., 1972-73; prof. speech commn., assoc. dean coll. arts and scis. N.Mex. Highlands U., Las Vegas, 1975—2003, prof. emeritus, 2003—. Ednl. cons. Rancho Valmora, 2003—. Author: Hovels, Haciendas, and House Calls: The Life of Carl H. Gellenthien, M.D., 1986, Speaking for Life: A Speech Communication Guide for Adults, 1990, Wreck of the Destiny Train, 1993; From Pajarito to Lungchow, 2003. Active 1st Bapt. Ch., Las Vegas, 1959—. Recipient Educator of Yr. award Pub. Svc. Co. of N.Mex., Albuquerque, 1990. Mem. P.E.O. Republican. Avocation: writing. Home: PO Box 778 Las Vegas NM 87701-0778

**SIMPSON, EUGENE THAMON,** music educator, singer; b. North Wilkesboro, N.C., Apr. 10, 1932; s. Eugene Tyra and Roxie Johnson Simpson; m. Ingres La Verne Hill, June 9, 1973 (div.); children: Eugene Tyra II, Adrienne Adele. MusB, Howard U., 1951, Yale U., 1953, MusM, 1954; EdD, Columbia U., 1968. Tchr. music Chelsea High Sch., N.Y.C., 1956; asst. choral dir. Second Army Chorus, Ft. Meade, Md., 1956—58; tchr. music N.Y.C. High Schs., 1959—68; chmn. voice and choral Va. State U., Petersburg, 1968—70; chmn. music dept. Bowie State U., Md., 1970—75; prof. music Rowan U., Glassboro, NJ, 1980—2000, chmn. dept. music, 1980—2000. Author: Analysis and Performance of Schwanengesang of Schubert, 1968, Black Genius: The Life, Spirit and Music of Hall Johnson, 2005; composer: Hold On, 1973, Steal Away, Sinnah Please Don't Let Dis Harvest Pass, Nobody Knows De Trouble I've Seen, True Religion, Too Late Sinnuh, Sistuh Mary Had-a-But One Child, Let Us Break Bread Together; singer: (albums) Danse Calinda, Swing Low Sweet Chariot, Born to Sing the Blues, Life, I Love You Because, 18 Yellow Roses, St. Martin De Porres Mass, The Cascading Voices with Brass, I Hear America Singing, Just A Closer Walk, Melodies of the World, The Wonderful World of Folk, Belefonte at the Greek Theater, Special for Young Lovers, Great Movie Themes, James Brown Showtime, An Evening with Belafonte/Mouskouri, Belafonte, Ballads, Blues and Boasters, King of the Gospel Singers, Porgy and Bess, Mother Nature, Father Time, On the Country Side, Tell Me Why, It's Magic, The Dinah Washington Years, Simon Estes, Singin' Through the Storm, (TV series) The Night They Saved Christmas, The Ed Sullivan Show, Those Ragtime Years, Camera Three. Founding chair Nat. Com. Ethnic Com., 1976—86; mem. adv. bd. Nat. Choral Coun., 1980—85; choral panelist NEA, 1987—88. With U.S. Army, 1956—59. Fellow, Ford Found.; scholar, Howard U., Washington, 1947—51, Yale U., 1951—54; Tanglewood fellow. Mem.: SAG, Am. Coun. Edn., Am. Soc. Composers, Authors and Pubs., Am. Guild Musical Artists, Am. Fedn. Tchrs., Nat. Assn. Tchrs. Singing (gov. 1978—82, mem. com. 1982—87), N.J. Choral Dirs. Assn. (pres. 1977—79), Am. Choral Dirs. Assn. (life; chair ethic music com. 1977—79), Alpha Phi Alpha, Phi Mu Alpha, Pi Kappa Lambda, Kappa Delta Pi, Phi Delta Kappa, Pi Lambda Kappa. Home: 10 Aspen Rd Sicklerville NJ 08081 E-mail: thamspx1@verizon.net.

**SIMPSON, FREDERICK JAMES,** retired science administrator; b. Regina, Sask., Can., June 8, 1922; s. Ralph James and Lillian Mary (Anderson) S.; m. Margaret Christine Simpson, May 28, 1947 (dec. Apr. 2003); children: Christine Louise, Steven James, Leslie Coleen, Ralph Edwin, David Glen. B.Sc., U. Alta., Can., 1944, M.Sc. in Agr., 1946; PhD in Bacteriology, U. Wis., 1952. With Nat. Research Council Can., 1946-84; asst. dir. Atlantic Research Lab., Halifax, N.S., 1970-73, dir., 1973-84; sci. cons., 1985-90. Vis. scientist U. Ill., Urbana, 1955-56, vis. prof., 1964; mem. exec. council Atlantic Provinces Interuniv. Com. on Scis., 1976-79, chmn., 1981-84; pres. Fed. Inst. Mgmt., Halifax, 1981-82 Contbr. numerous articles to profl. jours. Treas. Lunburg Condominium Corp. No. 1, 1998—. Decorated Queen's Silver Anniversary medal. Fellow Royal Soc. of Arts (London); mem. Can. Soc. Microbiologists (hon., sec.-treas. 1969-70, v.p. 1971-72, pres. 1972-73), Nova Scotian Inst. Sci. (v.p. 1975-76, pres. 1977-78), Internat. Phycological [...] Aqua [...] Assn. Can., Sigma Xi. United Ch. of Canada.

**SIMPSON, H. RICHARD (DICK SIMPSON),** retail buyer; b. Oct. 10, 1928; s. Bert M. and Violet K. (Mathias) S.; m. Marion Welty, 1950; children: Carla Sue, Barry Nelson, Richard Drew, Catherine Irene; m. Joan Rose Marshall, March 22, 1970; m. Charlotte S. Fox, Dec. 12, 1999. Student, U. Akron, 1949-50; BS, U. Md., 1955. Mgr. Tex. GMC, Detroit, 1959-62. Pres. Friendly Pontiac, Friendly Toyota, Derrick Chrysler, Simpson Oil Corp., Corp. S., Dick Tiger Homes, Austin, 1955-86, Simpson Hill Country Realty and Builders, 1989-2003, 05. Served to lt. col. USAF, 1953-75; Korea. Decorated D.F.C., Air Medal. Mem. Soc. Automotive Engrs., Res. Officers Assn., Horseshoe Bay Yacht Club, Horseshoe Bay Country Club, Rotary Internat., Masons. Methodist. Office: PO Box 8186 Horseshoe Bay TX 78657-8186 Office Phone: 800-292-1545. Personal E-mail: dicksimpson_hsb@yahoo.com.

**SIMPSON, HUGH L.,** news correspondent, newswriter; b. Kingston, Jamaica, Jan. 17, 1942; s. Melville Herbert (Stepfather) and Aldina Poulton (Willis) Simpson; m. Stephanie Anna Harcken, Jan. 7, 1988; children: Star, Susan, Andrew(dec.). AA, Maui Cmty. Coll. Radio stringer WWRL, NYC, 1964; radio news reporter WMCA, NYC, 1964—68; press sec. for black media Robert F. Kennedy Presdl. Campaign, 1968; news writer WABC-TV, NYC, 1968; on-camera news reporter WCBS-TV, NYC, 1968—72; freelance Minn., SD and ND, 1973—. Mem.: Phi Theta Kappa.

**SIMPSON, INDIA.ARIE,** musician; b. Denver, Oct. 3, 1976; d. Ralph and Joyce Simpson, Gary Harris (Stepfather). Student, Savannah Coll. Art and Design. With Motown Records, 1999—. Musician: (recordings) Acoustic Soul, 1999 (Cert. Gold), (songs) Peaceful World (with John Mellencamp), Just Another Parade, Just Another Parade (with Cassandra Wilson), Good Man for film We Were Soldiers, (tour) Women in Hip-Hop and Soul, 2001, (recordings) Voyage to India (Gest R&B Album Grammy, 03); contbg. musician (compilation) Conceptions: Musical Tribute to Stevie Wonder, 2003. Nominee 7 Grammy awards, 2002; named Best New Artist, Vibe Mag., 2001, MTV2, 2001, Billboard Video Awards, 2001, Best R&B Female Artist, BET, 2002, Best Female R&B Artist, 2003; named one of Top 100 It Entertainers, Entertainment Weekly mag., 2001; recipient Essence award,

2002, Best Urban/Alternative Performance for Little Things, Grammy Awards, 2003. Office: Universal Music Enterprises Motown Records 2220 Colorado Ave Santa Monica CA 90404

**SIMPSON, JACK BENJAMIN,** medical technologist, business executive; b. Tompkinsville, Ky., Oct. 30, 1937; s. Benjamin Harrison and Verda Mae (Woods) S.; m. Winona Clara Walden, Mar. 21, 1957; children: Janet Lazann, Richard Benjamin, Randall Walden, Angela Elizabeth. Student, Western Ky. U., 1954-57; grad., Norton Infirmary Sch. Med. Tech., 1958. Asst. chief med. technologist Jackson County Hosp., Seymour, Ind., 1958-61; chief med. technologist, bus. mgr. Mershon Med. Labs., Indpls., 1962-66; founder, dir., officer Am. Monitor Corp., Indpls., 1966-77; founder, pres., dir. Global Data, Inc., Ft. Lauderdale, Fla., 1986—. Mng. ptnr. Astroland Enterprises, Indpls., 1968—, 106th St. Assocs., Indpls., 1969-72, Keystones Ltd., Indpls., 1970-82, Delray Rd. Assoc. Ltd., Indpls., 1970-71, Allisonville Assocs. Ltd., Indpls., 1970-82, Grandview Assocs. Ltd., 1977—, Rucker Assocs. Ltd., Indpls., 1974—; mng. ptnr. Raintree Assocs. Ltd., Indpls., 1978—, Westgate Assocs. Ltd., Indpls., 1978—; pres., dir. Topps Constrn. Co., Inc., Bradenton, Fla., 1973-91, Acrovest Corp., Asheville, N.C., 1980—; dir. Indpls. Broadcasting, Inc.; founder, bd. dirs. Bank of Bradenton, 1986-92; founder, CFO Biomass Processing Tech., Inc., West Palm Beach, Fla., 1996—; also bd. dirs. Mem. Am. Soc. Med. Technologists (cert.), Indpls. Soc. Med. Technologists, Fla. Soc. Med. Technologists, Am. Soc. Clin. Pathologists, Am. Assn. Clin. Chemistry, Royal Soc. Health (London), Internat. Platform Assn., Am. Mus. Natural History, Columbia of Indpls. Club, Harbor Beach Surf Club, Fishing of Am. Club, Marina Bay Club (Ft. Lauderdale), Elks. Republican. E-mail: jack_simpson@msn.com.

**SIMPSON, JAMES S.,** federal agency administrator; BS magna cum laude, St. John's U. Commr. NY State Met. Transp. Authority, 1995—2005; fed. transit adminstr. US Dept. Transp., 2006—. Mem. NY State Job Devel. Authority Bd., NYC Work Force Investment Bd.; observer NY State Fin. Control Bd.; hon. dep. police commr. NYC Police Dept.; chmn. St. Lawrence Seaway Adv. Bd. Dir. NYC Partnership and C. of C.; chmn. Staten Island C. of C.; vice chmn. Snug Harbor Cultural Ctr.; bd. dirs. Staten Island U., St. Vincent's Hosp. Finalist Nat. Entrepreneur of Yr. award, Ernst & Young/NASDAQ; recipient Medal of Achievement, St. John's U., Employer of Yr. award, Am. Moving and Storage Assn. Mem.: NYC Police Dept. Honor Legion (hon.), Nat. Bus. Honor Soc., Nat. Honor Soc. of Economics. Office: Fed Transit Adminstrn 400 7th St SW Washington DC 20590*

**SIMPSON, JESSICA ANN,** vocalist, actress; b. Dallas, July 10, 1980; d. Joe and Tina Simpson; m. Nick Lachey, Oct. 26, 2002 (div. July 2006). Launched edible fragrance, cosmetic and body care line, Dessert Beauty, 2004; co-creator and launched, edible fragrance, cosmetic, and body care line, Taste, 04; nat. spokesperson for Operation Smile. Singer: (albums) Sweet Kisses, 1999, Irresistible, 2001, In This Skin, 2004, Rejoyce: The Christmas Album, 2004, A Public Affair, 2006, (songs) These Boots are Made for Walkin', 2005 (People's Choice award for Favorite Song from a Movie (The Dukes of Hazzard), 2006); actor: (films) The Dukes of Hazzard, 2005; (TV series) Newlyweds: Nick and Jessica, 2003—05, (TV) Nick & Jessica's Variety Hour, 2004, Nick & Jessica's Family Christmas, 2004, Nick & Jessica's Tour of Duty, 2005; co-author: I Do: Achieving Your Dream Wedding, 2003; co-host with husband: Saturday Night Live, 2004; co-host with Dane Cook Teen Choice Awards, 2006, guest appearances (TV series) MadTV, 2000, 2001, That '70s Show, 2002, 2003, Punk'd, 2003, Twilight Zone, 2003, Top of the Pops, 2004, Ashlee Simpson Show, 2004, The Apprentice, 2004. Recipient Movies-Choice Breakout (Female), Teen Choice Awards, 2006. Office: c/o Creative Artists Agy 9830 Wilshire Blvd Beverly Hills CA 90212-1825 also: Epic Records 550 Madison Ave New York NY 10022-3211

**SIMPSON, JOANNE MALKUS,** meteorologist; b. Boston, Mar. 23, 1923; d. Russell and Virginia (Vaughan) Gerould; m. Robert H. Simpson, Jan. 6, 1965; children by previous marriage: David Starr Malkus, Steven Willem Malkus, Karen Elizabeth Malkus. BS, U. Chgo., 1943, MS, 1945, PhD, 1949; DSc (hon.), SUNY, Albany, 1991. Instr. physics and meteorology Ill. Inst. Tech., 1946-49, asst. prof., 1949-51; meteorologist Woods Hole Oceanographic Instn., 1951-61; prof. meteorology UCLA, 1961-65; dir. exptl. meteorology lab. NOAA, Dept. Commerce, Washington, 1965-74; prof. environ. scis. U. Va., Charlottesville, 1974—79, W.W. Corcoran prof. environ. scis., 1974—79; head Severe Storms br. Goddard Lab. Atmospheres, NASA, Greenbelt, Md., 1979—88; chief scientist for meteorology, earth scis. dir. Goddard Space Flight Ctr., NASA, 1988—2004, chief scientist emeritus for meteorology, 2004—; project scientist tropical rainfall measuring mission, 1986—98. Mem. Bd. on Atmospheric Scis. and Climate, NRC/NAS, 1990-93, 97-2000, Bd. on Geophys. and Environ. Data, 1993-96, com. on climate, ecosystems, infectious diseases and human health, 1998-2000; mem. sr. adv. bd. NOAA, 1998-2003. Author: (with Herbert Riehl) Cloud Structure and Distributions Over the Tropical Pacific Ocean; assoc. editor: Revs. Geophysics and Space Physics, 1964-72, 75-77; contbr. articles to profl. jours. Mem. Fla. Gov.'s Environ. Coordinating Coun., 1971-74. Recipient Disting. Authorship award NOAA, 1969, Silver medal Dept. Commerce, 1967, Gold medal, 1972, Vincent J. Schaefer award Weather Modification Assn., 1979, Cmty. Headliner award Women in Comm., 1973, Profl. Achievement award U. Chgo. Alumni Assn., 1975, 92, Lifetime Achievement award Women in Sci. Engring., 1990, Exceptional Sci. Achievement award NASA, 1982, William Nordberg award NASA, 1994, NASA Medal Outstanding Leadership, 1998, I.M.O. prize World Meteorol. Orgn., 2002, U.S. Gov. Presdl. Rank award, 2003, 04; named Woman of Yr., L.A. Times, 1963; Guggenheim fellow, 1954-55, Goddard Sr. fellow, 1984-2004. Fellow Am. Geophys. Union, Am. Meterol. Soc. (mem. coun. 1975-77, 79-81, mem. exec. com. 1977, 79-81, commr. sci. and tech. activities 1982-88, pres.-elect 1988, pres. 1989, publs. commr 1992 08, mem. mem, 1995, Misinga award 1962, Rossby Rsch. medal 1983, Charles Franklin Brooks award 1992, Charles E. Anderson award 2001), World Meterol. Orgn. (IMO prize 2002), Explorers Club, Nat. Acad. Engring., Am. Acad. Arts & Sciences; mem. Royal Meteorol. Soc. (hon.), Cosmos Club, Phi Beta Kappa, Sigma Xi. Home: 540 N St SW Washington DC 20024-4557 Office: NASA Goddard Space Flight Ctr Earth Scis Greenbelt MD 20771-0001 Personal E-mail: nasajoanne@earthlink.net. Business E-mail: simpson@agnes.gsfc.nasa.gov, joanne.simpson_1@nasa.gov.

**SIMPSON, JOE L,** medical educator; b. Birmingham, Ala., Apr. 9, 1943; s. Robert S. and Winnie Leigh Simpson; m. Sandra Carson; children: Scott Alan, Reid Steven. Student, Duke U., Durham, NC, 1961—64, MD, 1968. Bd. cert. ob-gyn. 1975, cert. bd. cert. med. genetics 1982. Assoc. prof. ob-gyn. Northwestern U., 1975—79, prof. ob-gyn., 1979—86; chair ob-gyn. U. Tenn., Memphis, 1986—94; prof. molecular and human genetics, chair ob-gyn. Baylor Coll. Medicine, Houston, 1994—2006, prof. ob-gyn., molecular and human genetics, 2006—. Mem. adv. coun. Nat. Inst. Child Health and Devel. Bethesda, Md., 1994—97, mem. bd. sci. counselors, 2005—; mem. sci. adv. com. March of Dimes, White Plains, NY, 1995—, Klinefelter Syndrome and Assocs. Contbr. chapters to books, articles to profl. jours. Maj. U.S. Army, 1973—75. Recipient Multiple Rsch. awards, NIH, 1977—, Disting. Achievement award, NY Hosp.-Cornell Med. Coll., 2004; fellow ad eunden, Royal Coll. Ob-gyn., 2002. Fellow: Am. Coll. Med. Genetics (pres.-elect 2005—); mem.: Inst. Medicine, Soc. Gynecologic Investigation (pres. 1998—99), Am. Soc. Reproductive Medicine (pres. 1993—94). Republican. Presbyterian. Achievements include research in reproductive genetics and prenatal genetic diagnosis including elucidating disorders of sex differentiation and ovarian failure, safety with prenatal genetic diagnosis; recovery fetal cells from maternal blood. Avocations: opera, tennis, travel. Office: Baylor Coll Medicine 1709 Dryden Rd Houston TX 77030

**SIMPSON, JOE LEIGH,** obstetrics and gynecology educator; b. Birmingham, Ala., Apr. 4, 1943; s. Robert S. and Winnie (Leigh) S.; m. Sandra A. Carson, May 6, 1978; children: Scott, Reid MD, Duke U., Durham, N.C., 1968. Diplomate Am. Bd. Ob-Gyn, Am. Bd. Med. Genetics. Fellow in ob-gyn Cornell Med. Coll., N.Y.C., 1968-73; clin. assoc. N.Y. Blood Ctr., N.Y.C., 1969-73; asst. clin. prof. ob-gyn U. Tex., San Antonio, 1973-75; assoc. prof.,

head ob-gyn Northwestern U. Med. Sch., Chgo., 1975-79, prof. ob-gyn, 1979-86; Faculty prof. chmn. dept. ob-gyn U. Tenn., Memphis, 1986-94; prof. Baylor Coll. Medicine, Houston, 1994—2006, prof. dept. ob-gyn. and prof. molecular and human genetics, 2006—. Mem. genetics grant rev. and adv. bd. HHS, 1979-82; mem. clin. rsch. panel March of Dimes, 1986-94, chmn. adv. panel reproductive hazards, 1988-92, mem. sci. adv. bd., 1994—; mem. accreditation coun. grad. med. edn. Residency Rev. Com. Med. Genetics, 1993-98; mem. adv. com. Nat. Inst. Child Health and Devel., 1994-97; mem. bd. sci. counselors Intramural Rsch. Nat. Inst. Child Health and Devel. 2005—. Author: Disorders of Sexual Development, 1976; author: (with others) Genetics in Obstetrics and Gynecology, 1982, 3d edit., 2003, Obstetrics: Normal and Problem Pregnancies, 1986, 4th edit., 2001; co-editor: Genetic Diseases in Pregnancy, 1981, Material Serum Screening for Fetal Genetic Disorders, 1992, Essentials of Prenatal Diagnosis, 1993; contbr. articles to profl. jours. and chpts. to books. Maj. U.S. Army, 1973-75. Recipient numerous awards Nat. Insts. Child Health and Devel., March of Dimes, Wyeth-Ayerest pub. recognition award Assn. Profs. Ob-Gyn, 1992. Fellow ACOG (chmn. genetics subcom. 1981-84), Am. Coll. Med. Genetics (treas. 1996-02, pres.-elect, 2005-), Royal Coll. Obstetricians and Gynecologists (hon.); mem. NAS, Inst. Medicine, Am. Gynecol. and Obstet. Soc. (mem. coun. 1997-99), Am. Soc. Reproductive Medicine (bd. dirs. 1984-87, pres. 1993-94), Soc. Gynecologic Investigation (pres. 1998-99, Pres.'s Achievement award 1986, Pres. Disting. Scientist award 2002), Soc. Advancement Contraception (pres. 1995-98), Am. Soc. Human Genetics (mem. program com. 1988-91), Internat. Soc. Prenatal Diagnosis (pres. 1994-98), Internat. Fedn. Fertility Socs. (asst. treas. 2004-), Preimplantation Genetic Diagnosis Internat. Soc. (bd. dirs. 2003-05, pres. 2006-). Office: Baylor Coll Medicine Dept Ob/Gyn 1709 Dryden Rd Houston TX 77030-2717 Office Phone: 713-798-8360.

**SIMPSON, JOHN BARCLAY,** academic administrator; b. Oakland, Calif., June 8, 1947; s. Barclay and Joan (Devine) S.; children: Matthew, Melissa. BA, U. Calif., Santa Barbar, 1969; MA, Northwestern U., 1972, PhD, 1973. Research assoc. U. Pa., Phila., 1973-75; from asst. prof. to prof. psychology U. Wash., Seattle, 1975—98, dir. physiology-psychology program, 1984-88, head of the physiological psychology area, 1986—90, assoc. dean for computing, rsch. and facilities, 1991—94, dean of College of Arts and Sciences, 1994—98; exec. vice chancellor, provost U. Calif., Santa Cruz, 1998—2003; president U. at Buffalo, SUNY, 2004—. Vis. researcher U. Calif., San Francisco, 1976-80; vis. prof. Howard Florey Inst. U. Melbourne, Australia, 1983. Contbr. articles to profl. jours. Grantee NIH. Mem. AAAS, Soc. for Neurosci., Soc. Study Ingestive Behavior. Avocations: skiing, sailing, bicycling. Office: U at Buffalo 501 Capen Hall Buffalo NY 14260-1600 Office Phone: 716-645-2901. Office Fax: 716-645-3728. Business E-Mail: simpson@buffalo.edu. E-mail: UBOfficeOfThePresident@vpsa.buffalo.edu.*

**SIMPSON, JOHN M.,** lawyer; b. Ponca City, Okla., Sept. 26, 1950; AB, Harvard U., 1972; JD, Columbia U., 1978. Bar: D.C. 1979, N.C. 1988. Mem. Fulbright & Jaworski L.L.P., Washington. With USMC, 1972—75. Office: Fulbright & Jaworski LLP Market Square 801 Pennsylvania Ave NW Washington DC 20004-2615 Office Phone: 202-662-0200. E-mail: jsimpson@fulbright.com.

**SIMPSON, JOHN NOEL (VIRGINIA SIMPSON),** health facility administrator; b. Durham, N.C., Feb. 27, 1936; m. Virginia Marshall, June 27, 1959; children: John Noel, William M. Asst. adminstr. Riverside Health Sys., Newport News, Va., 1962-65, assoc. adminstr., 1965-70, Richmond (Va.) Meml. Hosp., 1970-74, sr. v.p., adminstr., 1974-77, exec. v.p., 1977-80, pres., 1980-85, Health Corp. Va., 1985-96; chmn. bd. Bon Secours-Richmond Health System, 1996-97, regional v.p., CEO, 1997-2000, divisional cons., 2000—. Preceptor Sch. Health Adminstrn. Duke U. and Med. Coll. Va., Washington U., St. Louis; bd. dirs. Sun Health, Inc./Sun Alliance, 1979-92, vice-chmn., 1984, chmn., 1985-87; vice-chmn. Med./Bus. Coalition, 1981-83; participant Leadership Met. Richmond; bd. dirs. Ctrl. Va. Health Sys. Agy., 1980-84, Richmond cmpt. ARC, 1980-83; mem. Va. Bd. Med. Assistance, 1980-84; mem. joint subcom. studying Va. med. malpractice laws divsn. legal svcs. Gen Assembly of Comm. of Va., 1984; chmn. Va. Health Network, 1989-91; chmn. Hanover Bus. Coun., 1994-95; mem. Gov. Regional Econ. Devel. Adv. Coun., 1994-95. Served with Med. Svc. Corps U.S. Army, 1959-62. Fellow Am. Coll. Healthcare Execs. (Coun. of Regents 1976-82, Edgar C. Hayhow award 1976, bd. govs. 1990-94, regents award sr. exec. level 1995). Fellow Am. Coll. Healthcare Execs. (coun. of regents 1976-82, Edgar C. Hayhow award 1976, bd. govs. 1990-94, regents award sr. exec. level 1995); mem. Am. Hosp. Assn. (chmn. RPBIII 1994-97, del. 1989-93, mem. bd. trustees 1994-97 Va. Hosp. Assn. (dir. 1974-97), del. 1989-93, mem. bd. trustees 1994-97, Va. Hosp. Assn. (dir. 1974-97, chmn.-elect, chmn. 1984-85, Disting. Svc. award 1998), Va. Ins. Reciprocal (chmn. 1977-79), Met. Richmond C. of C. (bd. dirs) (Richmond Acad. Medicine (Disting. Svc. award 2000). Republican. Presbyterian. Office Phone: 804-379-2930. Personal E-mail: JSIMP22736@aol.com.

**SIMPSON, JOHN WISTAR,** utilities executive, consultant; b. Glenn Springs, S.C., Sept. 25, 1914; s. Richard Caspar and Mary (Berkeley) S.; m. Esther Slattery, Jan. 17, 1948; children: John Wistar, Carter B., Patricia A., Barbara J. Student, Wofford Coll., 1932-33, DSc, 1972; BS, U.S. Naval Acad., 1937; MS, U. Pitts., 1941; DSc (hon.), Seton Hill Coll., 1970. With Westinghouse Electric Corp., 1937-77; mgr. Navy and Marine switchboard engring., switchgear div., on leave as mgr. nuclear engring. Daniels pile group, Oak Ridge Nat. Lab., successively as Westinghouse Electric Corp. (Bettis Atomic Power div.), 1949-58; v.p. Westinghouse Electric Corp.; gen. mgr. Westinghouse Electric Corp. (Bettis atomic power lab.), 1958-59, v.p., gen. mgr. atomic power divs., 1959-62. v p engring and research 1962 62, v.p. electic utility group, 1963-69, pres. power systems, corp. exec. v.p., dir., 1971-77; chmn. bd. Internat. Energy Assocs. Ltd., 1976-80; pres. Simpson Bus. Services, Inc., 1980-86; v.p. Sea Pines Assocs., Hilton Head Island, SC, 1989-91, also bd. dirs., 1987-91; bd. dirs. Sea Pines Real Estate Cos., Hilton Head Island, SC, 1987-91. Pvt. energy cons.; mem. adv. bd. Lawrence Livermore Nat. Lab. Fusion, 1975-88; mem. Naval Tech. Mission to Japan, 1945; del. 1st Internat. Conf. on Peaceful Uses Atomic Energy, Geneva, Switzerland, 1955, Conf. on Peaceful Uses Atomic Energy (2d Internat. Conf.), 1958; chmn. Atomic Indsl. Forum, 1974-75; mem. energy research adv. bd. Dept. Energy, 1981-83; chmn. com. on outlook for fusion hybrid and tritium breeding fusion reactors NRC; mem. sci. adv. bd. Notre Dame, 1974-86. Author: Nuclear Power from Underseas to Outer Space, 1994. Mem. governing bd. Nat. Coun. Chs., 1979-81; trustee Seton Hall Coll., 1969-76, Point Park Coll., 1973—, Wofford Coll., 1973-87. Recipient Navy cert. of merit for civilian svc. in World War II, 1947, Gold medal for advancement of rsch. Am. Soc. Metals, 1973, Disting. Alumnus award U. Pitts., 1975. Fellow IEEE (Edison medal 1971), ASME (hon. mem., George Westinghouse Gold medal 1975), Am. Nuclear Soc. (pres. 1973, Henry Dewolf Smyth Nuclear Statesman award 1997); mem. Nat. Acad. Engring., Franklin Inst. (Newcomen Gold medal), Rolling Rock Club (Ligonier, Pa.), Daufuskie Island Club, Bear Creek Golf Club, Sea Pines Club (Hilton Head, S.C.). Home and Office: 36 E Beach Lagoon Rd Hilton Head Island SC 29928-5714 E-mail: jws@hargray.com. *The guiding principles of my career have been to work in an area I considered to be of major importance, to have the most competent people working for me, to know enough technically that I could properly evaluate performance and, as far as possible, always make my position clear to all.*

**SIMPSON, LISA ANN,** physician, educator; b. Lagos, Nigeria, Feb. 9, 1958; (parents Am. citizens); d. Howard Russell and Mary Alice (Turner) Simpson; m. Richard L. Wittenberg; children: Ethan Simpson Wittenberg, Sydney Simpson Wittenberg. MB, B of Surgery, Trinity Coll., Dublin, Ireland, 1981; MPH, U. Hawaii, 1986. Diplomate Am. Bd. Pediat. Resident in pediat. U. Hawaii, Honolulu, 1982-85; resident in preventive medicine U. NC, Chapel Hill, 1987-88; dir. Maternal and Child Health Bur. State Dept. Health, Honolulu, 1988-90, acting dir. family health svcs. divsn., 1990; policy advisor Office of Asst. Sec. for Health HHS, Washington, 1993-94, sr. advisor Agy. for Health Care Policy and Rsch. Rockville, Md., 1994-95, acting dep.

adminstr. Agy. for Health Care Policy and Rsch., 1995-96, dep. adminstr. Agy. for Health Care Policy and Rsch., 1996-99, dep. dir. Agy. Healthcare Rsch. and Quality, 1999—2002; prof., All Children's Hosp. Guild endowed chair child health policy dept. pediat. U. South Fla., St. Petersburg 2003—. Mid-career fellow Inst. Health Policy Studies, San Francisco, 1991-93; adj. faculty dept. health policy and mgmt. Johns Hopkins U., Balt., 1995—; vis. prof. U. Wash., 2000, U. Mich., 2000; nat. dir. child health policy. Nat. Initiative Children's Healthcare Quality, 2004-. Mem. editl. bd. Future Children, Maternal and Child Health Jour., 1996-2005; contbr. articles to profl. jours. Recipient Preventive Medicine traineeship Pub. Health Svc., 1986, Sec. Disting. Svc. award Dept. HHS, 2000, Dir. Disting. Svc. award AHRQ, 2001, Meritorious Rank SES Presdl. award, 2002. Fellow: Am. Acad. Pediat. (Excellence in Svc. award 2002); mem.: APHA (governing coun. 1994—96), Nat. Acad. for Social Ins., Ambulatory Pediat. Assn. (chair pub. policy and advocacy com. 2005—), Acad. Health. Avocations: hiking, cuisine, gardening. Address: 601 4th St South CRI 1008 Saint Petersburg FL 33701 Office Phone: 727-553-3672. Business E-Mail: lsimpso1@hsc.usf.edu.

**SIMPSON, LOUIS A.,** insurance company executive; b. Chgo., Dec. 23, 1936; s. Irving and Lillian (Rubin) S.; m. Margaret Rowley, Dec. 16, 1959; children: Irving, Kenneth, Edward Student, Northwestern U., 1954-55; BA, Ohio Wesleyan U., 1958; AM, Princeton U., 1960. Instr. econs. Princeton U., 1961-62; assoc., ptnr. Stein Roe & Farnham, Chgo., 1962-69; v.p. Shareholders Mgmt., Los Angeles, 1969-70; sr. v.p., exec. v.p., pres. Western Asset Mgmt., Los Angeles, 1970-79; vice chmn. bd. Geico Corp., Washington, 1979-93, pres., chief exec. officer capital ops., 1993—. Bd. dirs. AT & T, Pacific Am. Income Shares, Western Asset Funds, Inc., HNC Software, ResMed, Inc. Trustee Cate Sch., U. Calif. San Diego Found., Urban Inst.; vice chair Woodrow Wilson Sch. Found. Woodrow Wilson fellow, 1958 Mem. San Diego Soc. Fin. Analysts, Scripps Inst. Oceanography Coun., Calif. Club, Arts Club Chgo., Chevy Chase Club, Met. Club. Episcopalian. Office: Geico Corp 1 Geico Plz Washington DC 20076-0005

**SIMPSON, LOUIS ASTON MARANTZ,** language educator, writer; b. Jamaica, W.I., Mar. 27, 1923; s. Aston and Rosalind (Marantz) S.; m. Jeanne Claire Rogers (div. Mar. 1954); 1 child, Louis Matthew; m. Dorothy Mildred Roochvarg, 1955 (div. 1979); children: Anne Borovoi, Anthony Rolf; m. Miriam Butensky Bachner, 1985 (div. 1998). Higher schs. certificate, Munro Coll., Jamaica, 1939; BS, Columbia U., 1948, A.M., 1950, PhD, 1959; D.H.L., Eastern Mich. U., 1977; DLitt, Hampden Sydney Coll., 1990. Editor Bobbs-Merrill Pub. Co., N.Y.C., 1950-55; instr. Columbia U., 1955-59; prof. English U. Calif., Berkeley, 1959-67, SUNY, Stony Brook, 1967-91, Disting. prof., 1991—. Author: (poems) The Arrivistes, 1949, Good News of Death, 1955, A Dream of Governors, 1959, At the End of the Open Road, 1963 (Pulitzer prize for poetry 1964), Selected Poems, 1965, Adventures of the Letter I, 1971, Searching for the Ox, 1976, Caviare at the Funeral, 1980, The Best Hour of the Night, 1983, People Live Here: Selected Poems 1949-83, 1983, Collected Poems, 1988, In the Room We Share, 1990, Jamaica Poems, 1993, There You Are, 1995, The Owner of the House, New Collected Poems, 1940-2000, (transl.) Nombres et poussière, 1996, Modern Poets of France, 1997, Kaviar på begravningen, 1998, François Villon: The Legacy and The Testament, (prose) Riverside Drive, 1962, James Hogg: A Critical Study, 1962, North of Jamaica, 1972, Three on the Tower: The Lives and Works of Ezra Pound, T.S. Eliot and William Carlos Williams, 1975, A Revolution in Taste: Studies of Dylan Thomas, Allen Ginsberg, Sylvia Plath and Robert Lowell, 1978, A Company of Poets, 1981, The Character of the Poet, 1986, Selected Prose, 1989, Ships Going into the Blue, 1994, The King My Father's Wreck, 1995; editor: The New Poets of England and America, 1957, An Introduction to Poetry, 1967. Served with AUS, 1943-45. Decorated Purple Heart, Bronze Star with oak leaf cluster; Hudson Rev. fellow, 1957, Guggenheim fellow, 1962, 70; Am. Coun. Learned Socs. grantee, 1963; recipient Prix de Rome, 1957, Millay award, 1960, Distinguished Alumnus award Columbia U., 1960, medal for excellence Columbia U., 1965; American Acad. of Arts and Letters award in literature, 1976; Centenary medal Inst. of Jamaica, 1980, Jewish Book Coun. award for poetry, 1981, Elmer Holmes Bobst award, 1987, Harold Morton Landon award for translation, 1997. Fellow Am. Acad. in Rome. Home: 7 Stony Rd Stony Brook NY 11790 Office Phone: 631-689-0498. Personal E-mail: louissimpson1@yahoo.com.

**SIMPSON, LYLE LEE,** lawyer; b. Des Moines, Oct. 15, 1937; s. R. Clair and Martha B. (Accola) S. BA, Drake U., 1960, JD, 1963. Bar: Iowa 1963, U.S. Dist. Ct. (so. and no. dists.) Iowa 1963, U.S. Ct. Appeals (8th cir.) 1963, U.S. Tax Ct. 1963, U.S. Supreme Ct. 1970, U.S. Ct. Mil. Appeals 1972. Pvt. practice, Des Moines, 1963—; mem. Beving and Swanson, Des Moines, 1964-68; sr. ptnr. Peddicord, Simpson & Sutphin, Des Moines, 1968-83; pres. Dreher, Simpson & Jensen, PC, 1984—. Gen. counsel campaign com. Gov. Iowa, 1978-98. Contbr. articles to profl. jours. Chmn. bd. trustees Broadlawns Med. Ctr., 1974-80; mem. Iowa Inaugural Com., 1983, 87, 89, 91, 95; bd. dirs. YMCA Boys Camp, 1967-86, Home, Inc., 1981-85, Project H.E.L.P.E.R., 1983-87, Batten Found.; pres., bd. dirs. Polk County Health Svcs., 1972-88; chmn. Iowa Health Facilities Coun. 1988-93; pres. First Unitarian Ch., 1958-70, Iowa Humanities Bd., 1988-94, Humanist Found., 1980—, East High Alumni Found., 1992-2000; treas. Iowa Humanities Found., 1994-99; chmn. Iowa Health Found., 1993—; mem. investment com., fin. com. Iowa Health Sys., 2000—; bd. Iowa Health System, Des Moines, 2005—. Recipient Oren E. Scott award, Class of 1915 award in liberal arts Drake U., 1960. Mem. ABA, Iowa Bar Assn., Polk County Bar Assn., Am. Arbitration Assn., Am. Humanist Assn. (pres. 1979-84), Prairie Club (pres. 1992), Morning Club (pres. 1965), Le Chevaliers de vin Club (pres. 1976-85), YMCA Heritage Club (pres.), Masons, Scottish Rite, Shriner 33 degree, Rotary. Republican. Congregationalist. Address: 222 Equitable Bldg 604 Locust St Des Moines IA 50309-3723 Office Phone: 515-288-5000. Business E-Mail: lsimpson@dreherlaw.com.

**SIMPSON, MARY MICHAEL,** priest, psychotherapist; b. Evansville, Ind., 1925; d. Link Wilson and Mary Garrett (Price) S. BA, BS, Tex. Women's U., 1946; grad., N.Y. Tng. Sch. Deaconesses, 1949, Westchester Inst. Tng. in Psychoanalysis and Psychotherapy, 1976; S.T.M., Gen. Theol. Seminary, 1982. ordained priest Episcopal Ch., 1977. Missionary Holy Cross Mission, Bolahun, Liberia, 1950-52; mem. Order of St. Helena, 1952—; acad. head Margaret Hall Sch., Versailles, Ky., 1958-61; sister in charge Convent of St. Helena, Bolahan, 1962-67, dir. novices, 1968-74; pastoral counselor on staff St. John the Divine, N.Y.C., 1974-87, canon residentiary, canon counselor, 1977-87, hon. canon, 1988—. Pvt. practice psychoanalyst, 1974—; dir. Cathedral Counseling Svc., 1975-87; cons. psychotherapist Union Theol. Seminary, 1980-83; bd. dirs. Westchester Inst. Tng. in Psychoanalysis and Psychotherapy, 1982-84; priest-in-charge St. John's Ch., Wilmot, New Rochelle, N.Y., 1987-88; trustee Coun. Internat. and Pub. Affairs, 1983-87;interim pastor St. Michael's Ch., Manhattan, 1992-94; cons. Diocese of N.Y., 1990—. Author: The Ordination of Women in the American Episcopal Church: The Present Situation, 1981; contbg. author: Yes to Women Priests, 1978. Mem. Nat. Assn. Advancement of Psychoanalysis, N.Y. State Assn. Practicing Psychotherapists, N.Y. Soc. Clin. Psychologists. Home and Office: 151 E 31st St Apt 8H New York NY 10016-9502 Office Phone: 212-951-4316. Personal E-mail: mmsimpson@rcn.com.

**SIMPSON, MICHAEL,** retired metals service center executive; b. Albany, NY, Dec. 10, 1938; s. John McLaren Simpson and Constance (Hasler) Ames; m. Barbara Ann Bodtke, Jan. 5, 1963; children: Leslie Ann, Elizabeth S. Wessel. BA, U. Mich., 1965, MBA, 1966. Product mgr. Armour & Co., Chgo., 1966-68; with A.M. Castle & Co., Franklin Park, Ill., 1968—, pres. Hy-Alloy Steels Co. divsn., 1974-79, v.p. Midwestern region, 1977-79, chmn. bd., 1979—2004, also bd. dirs.; chmn. emeritus, 2004—. Trustee Rush U. Med. Ctr., Chgo., 1991—; mem. exec. com., 1980—, vice chmn., 1991—; trustee Oldfields Sch., Glencoe, Md., 1982-87, 95-2003, chmn. bd., 1998-2000; bd. dirs. Lake Forest (Ill.) Hosp. Found. and Lake Forest Hosp., 1998—; chmn. bd. overseers Rush U., Chgo., 1996—. Office: AM Castle & Co 3400 N Wolf Rd Franklin Park IL 60131-1319 Office Phone: 847-349-2500. Business E-Mail: msimpson@amcastle.com.

**SIMPSON, MICHAEL K.,** congressman; b. Burley, Idaho, Sept. 8, 1950; m. Kathy Johnson, 1971. Student, Utah State U.; DDS, Washington U., St. Louis, 1978. Dentist, Blackfoot, Idaho, 1978—; councilmember Blackfoot City Coun., 1980—84; mem. Idaho Ho. Reps., 1985—99, asst. majority leader, 1989, speaker, 1991—99; mem. US Congress from 2nd Idaho dist., Washington, 1999—. Mem. Ho. Appropriations com., Agr., Resources, Transp. & Infrastructure com., Vet. Affairs com. Served as spkr. majority caucus chmn. and asst. majority leader in Idaho Ho. Reps. Mem. Idaho's Rep. Party Hall of Fame. Recipient Friend of Edn. award, 1994, Citizen of the Yr. award Idaho Family Forum, 1996, Boyd A. Martin award Assn. Idaho Cities. Mem. Idaho State Dental Assn. (Pres.'s award 1998), Am. Legis. Exch. Coun. (state chmn., nat. bd. dirs., Jefferson award 1994). Republican. Avocations: golf, chess, painting. Office: US Ho Reps 1339 Longworth Ho Office Bldg Washington DC 20515-1202 Office Phone: 202-225-5531. Office Fax: 202-225-8216.*

**SIMPSON, MICHAEL MARCIAL,** science specialist, consultant; b. Honolulu, Sept. 24, 1954; s. Marcial Tolentino and Beatrice (Martin) S. AB in Biol. Scis., U. Calif., Berkeley, 1976; MS in Biol. Scis., U. San Francisco, 1977; MS in Energy and Resources, U. Calif., Berkeley, 1979; PhD in Environ. Scis. and Engring., UCLA, 1986. Assoc. researcher NASA, Moffett Field, Calif., 1973; radio program host, producer Sta. KUSF-FM, San Francisco, 1976-78; rsch. asst. Lawrence Berkeley Lab., Berkeley, Calif., 1977-79; rsch. assoc. UCLA/U.S. Dept. Energy, 1979-81; congl. fellow, environ. health U.S. Congress, Washington, 1981-82; specialist in environ. techs., life scis., and terrorism U.S. Congl. Rsch. Svc., Washington, 1982—2006, sci. policy advisor on Homeland Security issues, 2006—. Adv. bd. Banbury Ctr., Cold Spring Harbor, N.Y., 1985—; adj. faculty The Washington Ctr., 1992—. Contbr. articles to profl. jours. Fellow AAAS (Named Congl. Sci. fellow 1981-82); mem. Washington Acad. Sci., Library of Congress Profl. Assn., UCLA in Washington (exec. steering com. 1986-92). Avocations: photography, bicycle touring, short story writing, travel. Business E-Mail: msimpson@crs.loc.gov. E-mail: DrMichaelMSimpson22015@yahoo.com.

**SIMPSON, MIKE,** talent agent; b. Tampa, Fla. BS in Communications, U. Tex., Austin; MA, U. Tex., 1978. Agent trainee program William Morris Agy., 1979, head motion picture packaging dept., 1986, co-head West Coast motion picture dept., 1989—, exec. v.p., mem. bd. dirs. Beverly Hills, Calif. Named one of The 100 Most Powerful People in Hollywood, Premiere Mag., 1998; recipient Warren Skaaren Lifetime Achievement award, Tex. Film Commn., 2001. Office: William Morris Agy 151 S El Camino Dr Beverly Hills CA 90212-2775

**SIMPSON, MURRAY,** electrical engineer, consultant; b. N.Y.C., July 27, 1921; s. George and Sonia (Vernov) Simpson; m. Ethel Gladstein, June 29, 1947; children: Anne Simpson, David, Mindy, Jonathan. BEE, CCNY, 1942; MEE, Polytech. Inst. of NY, 1952. Engr. ITT, NYC, 1942-44; sr. engr. Raytheon Co., Waltham, Mass., 1946-48; sect. mgr. Fairchild Guided Missles div., Farmingdale, NY, 1948-50; v.p. Maxson Elec. Co., NYC, 1950-62; pres. SEDCO Sys. Inc. subs. Raytheon Co., Melville, NY, 1963-86; cons. M. Simpson Assocs., Ft. Lauderdale, Fla., 1986—. Former chmn. bd. dirs. Radyne Corp. Contbr. articles to profl. jours. Former bd. dirs. United Way, L.I. Served to lt. (j.g.) USNR, 1944—46, PTO. Fellow IEEE (chmn. L.I. sect. 1963—64). Avocations: boating, skiing, golf, tennis. *Don't be afraid to take risk in the hope of great reward and satisfaction. The worst that could happen is that you may fail. A much greater loss is that you never tried and perhaps missed the great opportunity of your life.*

**SIMPSON, MURRAY L.,** lawyer; b. Chgo., 1937; BA, U. Ill., 1959; JD, DePaul U., 1961. Staff atty. Securities and Exchange Commn.; atty. priv. practice, 1964—91; CEO, mng. dir. Franklin Templeton Investments-Asia, Hong Kong, 1994—2000; exec. v.p., gen. counsel Franklin Resources, Inc., San Mateo, Calif., 2000—06, exec. v.p., 2006—. Chmn. Hong Kong Investment Funds Assn., 2000; mem. unit trust com. Securities and Futures Commn.; mem. financial services advisory com. Hong Kong Trade Devel. Council; former bd mem. Franklin Resources, Inc. Office: Franklin Resources Inc One Franklin Pkwy San Mateo CA 94403 Business E-Mail: mlsimpson@frk.com.

**SIMPSON, NICOLE B.,** economics professor; b. Winona, Minn., May 9, 1974; d. Ralmond J. and Janice M. Bundy; m. Brendt A. Simpson, Sept. 18, 1999; 1 child, Thomas D. PhD, U. Iowa, Iowa City, 2001. Asst. prof. econs. Colgate U., Hamilton, NY, 2001—. Contbr. articles to profl. jours. Coord. Vol. Income Tax Assistance, Hamilton, 2002—06. Mem.: Com. on the Status of Women in the Econs. Profession (assoc.), Am. Econ. Assn. (assoc.). Avocations: tennis, travel, gardening. Home: 2860 West Hill Rd Hamilton NY 13346 Office: Colgate U Dept Econs 13 Oak Dr Hamilton NY 13346 Office Phone: 315-228-7991. E-mail: nsimpson@mail.colgate.edu.

**SIMPSON, ROBERT G.,** corporate financial executive; Dir. fed. taxes Phillip Morris, Kraft Gen. Foods div.; v.p. tax, gen. mgr. Tenneco Bus Svcs.; v.p. taxation Waste Mgmt. Inc., Houston, sr. v.p., CFO, 2004—. Office: Waste Management Inc Ste 400 1001 Fannin St Houston TX 77002*

**SIMPSON, ROBERT GLENN,** lawyer; b. Seattle, June 27, 1932; s. Harold Vernon and Anna Rondeau (McCabe) S.; m. Josephine Anne Heald, June 7, 1959; children: Jenifer Jane, Thomas Glenn, Mary Elizabeth. BS, U. Oreg., 1954; LLB, Willamette U., 1959. Bar: Oreg. 1959. Assoc. William B. Adams Law Office, Portland, Oreg., 1959-67; ptnr. Adams McLaughlin & Simpson, Portland, 1967-70, Schwabe Williamson & Wyatt, P.C., Portland, 1970—. Trustee, sec. Legacy Good Samaritan Hosp. and Med. Ctr., Portland, 1983-89, mem. cmty. bd., 1989-98; trustee, chancellor Episcopal Diocese of Oreg., Portland, 1988—. Mem. Oreg. State Bar (exec. com. health law sect. 1987-90), Am. Health Lawyers Assn. (program com. 1987-88), Oreg. Health Lawyers Assn.(pres. 1977-78, legis. com. 1989), Multnomah Athletic Club, Univ. Club. Home: 13345 SW Iron Mountain Blvd Portland OR 97219-9306 Office: Schwabe Williamson & Wyatt, PC 1211 SW 5th Ave Ste 1800 Portland OR 97204-3795

**SIMPSON, ROBERT HOMER,** meteorologist, consultant; b. Corpus Christi, Tex., Nov. 19, 1912; s. Clyde Robert and Annie Laurie (Rainey) S.; m. Mazie Houston, Dec. 22, 1935 (div. Dec. 1949); m. Joanne Gerould Malkus, Jan. 6, 1965; children: Peggy A., Lynn S.; stepchildren: David Malkus, Steven Malkus, Karen Malkus. BS, Southwestern U., Tex., 1932, DSc (hon.), 1963; MS, Emory U., 1935; PhD, U. Chgo., 1962. Cert. cons. meteorologist. Observer U.s. Weather Bur., Brownsville, Tex., 1940-42, forecaster New Orleans and Miami, Fla., 1942-45, exec. asst. to dep. chief Washington, 1946-48; established Pacific Region of U.S. Weather Bur., Honolulu, 1948-52; rsch. scientist U.S. Weather Bur., Washington, 1952-56, founding dir. Nat. Hurricane Rsch. Project West Palm Beach, Fla., 1956-61, dep. dir. rsch. severe storms Washington, 1961-64; assoc. dir. ops. Nat. Weather Svc., NOAA, Washington, 1964-67, dir. Nat. Hurricane Ctr. Miami, 1967-74; founding dir. Simpson Weather Assoc., Inc., Charlottesville, Va., 1974—; prof. environ. sci. U. Va. Charlottesville, 1974-80. Established Mauna Loa Summit Obs., Hawaii, 1951. Author: (with Herbert Riehl) The Hurricane and Its Impact, 1981; chief editor: Hurricane: Coping with Disaster, 2002; contbr. articles to profl. jours. Recipient Gold medal Dept. Commerce, 1962, Profl. Achievement award U. Chgo. D.C. Alumni Group, 1998. Fellow Am. Meteorol. Soc. (hon. mem., Cleveland Abbe award 1991), Explorers Club NY; mem. steering com. Wash. Group. Achievements include (with Herbert Saffir) development and implementation of the Saffir-Simpson scale for hurricane damage potential; pioneering research flight in hurricane, Caribbean Sea, W. Pacific Ocean, first over-the-top flight in hurricane, Atlantic Ocean, 1947; many research penetrations of hurricane eyes. Personal E-mail: r.h.simpson @verizon.net.

**SIMPSON, ROBERT LEE,** academic administrator, department chairman, biologist, educator; b. San Francisco, Apr. 3, 1942; s. Robert Lee and Valerie Brinley (Serrick) S.; m. Penelope Sue Flint, June 12, 1970; children: Robert Lee III, Elizabeth Jean. BA in Zoology, Fresno State Coll., 1965, MA in Biology, 1967; PhD in Limnology, Cornell U., 1971. Instr. Cornell U., Ithaca, N.Y., 1970; from asst. prof. to prof. biology Rider Coll., Lawrenceville, N.J., 1970-85, chairperson biology dept., 1972-80; acting dean sch. health professions and nursing William Paterson Coll., Wayne, N.J., 1986-87, prof. biology, 1985-91, dean sch. sci. and maths., 1985-91; provost, vice chancellor acad. affairs U. Mich., Dearborn, 1991—2006, prof. biology, 1991—. Adj. grad. prof. Rutgers U., Camden, N.J., 1976-91; vis. scientist Smithsonian Environ. Rsch. Ctr., Edgewater, N.J., 1977; mem. grad. degree adv. com. N.J. Dept. Higher Edn., Trenton, 1989-91; interim provost, v.p. academic affairs Kettering U., Flint, Mich, 2006-. Editor: (with D. Whigham, R. Good) Freshwater Wetlands: Ecological Processes & Management Potential, 1978, (with M. Leck, V.T. Parker) Ecology of Soil Seed Banks, 1989; contbr. articles to profl. jours. Mem. N.J. Wetlands Mitigation Coun., Trenton, 1988-91; trustee Chilton Meml. Hosp., Pompton Plains, N.J., 1989-91; bd. dirs. Granville Acad., Detroit, 1991-93; chair acad. affairs affairs subcom. Pres. Coun. of State Univs. of Mich., 1997—. Rsch. grantee Office Water Rsch. & Tech., 1975, 79, U.S. EPA, 1976, 78, NSF, 1975, 80, U.S. Geol. Survey, 1983, Challenge to Excellence grantee N.J. Dept. Higher Edn., 1987. Mem. N.J. Acad. Sci. (pres. 1983-85, Outstanding Svc. award 1989), Ecol. Soc. Am., Brit. Ecol. Soc., Soc. Wetland Scientists, Am. Soc. Limnology and Oceanography, Sigma Xi. Home: 2470 Harness Dr West Bloomfield MI 48324-3733 Office Phone: 810-762-7949. Business E-Mail: rlsumd@umich.edu.

**SIMPSON, ROBERT LOUIS,** music educator; b. Orange, N.J., Apr. 17, 1948; s. Robert Gage and Frances Dean Simpson; m. Marianna Parnas, May 29, 1994; children: Laura Helen, Robert Kirkpatrick. AB, Brown U., 1970; M Sacred Music, Union Theol. Sem., Sch. Sacred Music, 1972. Cert. Assoc. Am. Guild of Organists, NY, 1989, Choirmaster Am. Guild of Organists, NY, 1989. Organist-choirmaster Cathedral Ch. St. Luke, Orlando, Fla., 1974—79, Cathedral St. Philip, Atlanta, 1979—93, Christ Ch. Cathedral, Houston, 1993—; founder and artistic dir. Houston Chamber Choir, 1995—; lectr. ch. music Shepherd Sch. Music, Rice U., Houston, 2003—. Musician (conductor): (choral performances) The Blue Estuaries. Recipient S. Lewis Elmer Award, Am. Guild of Organists, 1988. Mem.: Chorus Am. (bd. mem. 2000—06), Assn. Anglican Musicians, Am. Choral Dirs. Assn. Office: Houston Chamber Choir PO Box 53388 Houston TX 77052-3388 Office Fax: 713-222-2412. E-mail: robertsimpson@houstonchamberchoir.org.

**SIMPSON, RUSSELL AVINGTON,** retired lawyer; b. Greybull, Wyo., June 19, 1935; s. William Avington and Margaret E. (Draper) S.; m. Margarita A. del Valle, Dec. 19, 1960; children: Margaret E., Robert A., Alexandra P., Christina M. BS with honors, U. Wyo., 1957; LLB, Harvard U., 1965. Bar: Tex. 1965, Mass. 1966. Assoc. Bonilla, de Pena, Read & Bonilla, Corpus Christi, Tex., 1965-66; asst. dean, dir. admissions Harvard Law Sch., Cambridge, Mass., 1966-75, asst. dean, dir. fin. aid, 1972-78, asst. dean for fin. and gen. adminstrn., 1978-84; dir. adminstrn. Hill & Barlow, Boston, 1984-90; v.p., treas. The Archs. Collaborative, Cambridge, 1991-92, ret., 1992. Chmn. devel. com. Law Sch. Data Assembly Svc., 1969; pres. bd. dirs. Law Sch. Admissions Svcs., Newtown, Pa., 1979-80, bd. dirs., 1989-91; trustee Law Sch. Admission Coun., 1968-70, 72-78, 81-82, chmn. svcs. com. 1972-74, chmn. test devel. and rsch. 1976-78; founder Grad. and Profl. Sch. Fin. Aid Coun. Mem. Belmont (Mass.) Town Meeting, 1975-96, Belmont Sch. Com., 1977-83. Capt. USAF, 1957-62. Mem. Tex. Bar Assn., Rotary (bd. dirs. Belmont 1978-80), Phi Kappa Phi. Democrat. Home: 20 Park St Arlington MA 02474-3314 Home (Winter): 2110 Bernuda Dr Unit 2 Laredo TX 78045-8659 Office Phone: 617-308-8011. Personal E-mail: russellandmaca.simpson@post.harvard.edu.

**SIMPSON, SANDRA KAY,** operations research specialist; b. Rutland, Vt., Feb. 26, 1949; d. Freeman Edward and Ruth Gail (Smith) Campbell. BA, U. Vt., Burlington, 1971; M of Pub. Adminstrn., Troy State U., Europe, 1988, MSc in Internat. Rels., 1991. Instr., trainer U.S. Govt., Ft. McClellan, Ala., 1975-79, asst. logistics officer Kitzingen, Germany, 1979-82, property acctg. officer Ft. Hood, Tex., 1982-86, Wiesbaden, Germany, 1986-93; exec. mgmt. asst. Sport and Sound, Mainz Kastel, Germany, 1993-94; maintenance mgmt. coord. U.S. Govt., Wiesbaden, 1994—, dep. dir. internal logistics, 1999—2002, theater level logistics mgr., 2002—03, 2005—06, def. logistics agy., 2003—05, theater level logistics mgr., 2005—. Cons. U.S. Govt., Heidelberg, Germany, 1994—. With U.S. Army, 1973—93. Mem. Women in Mil. Svc. to Am. Found. (charter mem.), USAREUR Retiree Coun., Wiesbaden/Mainz Retiree Coun. (sec. 1994—), Oxford Club. Avocations: photography, marathons. Home: Cmr 467 Box 1505 APO AE 09096-1505 Office Phone: 49-631-4138063. Business E-Mail: sandy.simpson@us.army.mil.

**SIMPSON, STEVEN DREXELL,** lawyer; b. Sturgis, Mich., Sept. 20, 1953; s. Rex and Lorraine Simpson; m. Peggy Deibert, Apr. 28, 1979; children: Andrew Drexell, Christine Elizabeth, Marianne Tyner. BA, Hillsdale Coll., Mich., 1975; JD, Wake Forest U., 1978; LLM in Taxation, Georgetown U., 1981. Bar: Fla. 1978, D.C. 1980, N.C. 1984. Assoc. Bradford, Williams et al, Miami, Fla., 1978-80, Webster & Chamberlain, Washington, 1980-82, Fisher, Wayland et al, Washington, 1982-84, Maupin, Taylor & Ellis, P.A., Raleigh, NC, 1984-98; ptnr. Law Offices of Steven D. Simpson P.A., 1998—. Author: Tax-Exempt Organizations: Organizational and Operational Requirements, 2000, Tax-Exempt Organizations: Reporting, Disclosure and Other Procedural Aspects, 2000, Taxable Expenditures, 2000, Tax Compliance for Tax-Exempt Organizations, 2005, Multistate Guides to Regulation and Taxation of Nonprofits, 2006; contbr. articles to profl. jours. Mem. ABA (exempt orgns. com.). Republican. Methodist. Avocations: golf, running. Home: 409 Hillandale Dr Raleigh NC 27609-7036 Office: Landmark Center II 4601 Six Forks Rd Ste 530 Raleigh NC 27609-5286 Office Phone: 919-788-9677. Personal E-mail: s.simpsonlaw@verizon.net.

**SIMPSON, THEODORE BRIAN,** set designer, educator; b. Boston, Mar. 14, 1966; s. Robert Reynolds and Helene Marie Simpson. BA, Hampshire Coll., Amherst, Mass., 1985; MFA, Brandeis U., Waltham, Mass., 1989. Set designer/lectr. Tufts U., Medford, Mass., 2002—. Various shows. Achievements include design of over 100 shows for various theater throughout the US. Home: 4 Allen St Newburyport MA 01950 Office: Tufts Univ Dept of Drama and Dance 40 Talbot Ave Medford MA 02155 Office Phone: 617-627-4123. Personal E-mail: tsdesigns@comcast.net. Business E-Mail: ted.simpson@tufts.edu.

**SIMPSON, VINSON RALEIGH,** manufacturing executive, director; b. Chgo., Aug. 9, 1928; s. Vinson Raleigh and Elsie (Passeger) S.; m. Elizabeth Caroline Matte, Sept. 9, 1950; children: Kathleen Simpson Zier, Nancy Simpson Ignacio, James Morgan. SB in Chem. Engring, MIT, 1950; MBA, Ind. U., 1955. With Trane Co., LaCrosse, Wis., 1950-75, mgr. mktg. services, 1957-64, mgr. dealer devel., 1964-66; mng. dir. Trane Ltd., Edinburgh, Scotland, 1966-67; v.p. internat. Trane Co., LaCrosse, Wis., 1967-68, exec. v.p., 1968-70; exec. v.p., gen. mgr. comml. air conditioning div., 1970-73; pres., dir., 1973-75, Simpson and Co., La Crosse, 1975-76; pres., chief operating officer, dir. Marathon Electric Mfg. Corp., Wausau, Wis., 1976-80; chmn., pres., chief exec. officer Marion Body Works, Inc., 1980-93, chmn., 1993—. Bd. dirs. Clintonville Area Found. Past trustee, treas. Fox Valley Tech. Coll.; bd. dirs., past pres. Fox Valley Tech. Coll. Found.; past pres., bd. dir. Wausau Area Jr. Achievement; mem. Marion Minutemen; past 20 yr. trustee, chair endowment com., trustee emeritus Northland Coll.; past dir. Wis. Mfrs. and Commerce; mem. investments com. Comty. Found. for Fox Valley Region, Inc. Decorated Korean War Commendation ribbon. Mem. Am. Legion, Kappa Kappa Sigma, Alpha Tau Omega, Beta Gamma Sigma (dirs. table). Lodges: Masons, Shriners, Lions; past. pres. Marion club, Paul Harris fellow). Congregationalist. Avocations: running, snorkeling, cross country skiing, playing the trombone. Home: 171 Fairway Dr Clintonville WI 54929-1071

**SIMPSON, WILLIAM,** information technology manager, consultant; b. Escondido, Calif., 1953; m. Deborah Simpson. BA in Social Sci., San Diego State U., 1976; MA in Ednl. Tech., U.S. Internat. U., San Diego, 1993. Profl. adminstr. credential Calif. Commn. Tchr. Credentialing, 2003, preliminary adminstrv. svcs. credential Calif. Commn. Tchr. Credentialing, 1993, secondary tchr. credential Calif. Commn. Tchr. Credentialing, 1977. Tchr. Escondido Union Sch. Dist., Calif., 1979—92, coord. tech. and media svcs., 1992—99; dir. staff devel. svcs. San Diego County Office Edn., 1999—. Edn. adv. bd. mem. Apple Computer, Inc., San Diego, 1997—99; co-founder and dir. Innovative Video in Edn., 2001—; dir. Innovative Video in Edn. Adv. Bd.; project dir. techsets San Diego County Office Edn., 2004—; mem. product adv. bd. Learning Frameworks, Inc. Developer: Innovative Video in Education Program (iVIE). Bd. dir. Classroom of the Future Found., San Diego, 1999—2001; mem. program com. San Diego Natural History Mus., 2002—04; edn. com. co-chair Pacific Southwest chpt. NATAS, 2004—. Named Apple Disting. Educator, Apple Computer, Inc., 2003; grantee, Calif. Tech. Assistance Project Region 9 Calif. Dept. Edn., 2003—05, 2005—. Mem.: ISTE, ASCD, Calif. Computer Using Educators (membership chair 1996—97, Tech. Learning Leadership award 2004), Internat. Soc. Tech. in Edn. (Outstanding Leadership 2004). Office: San Diego County Office Edn 6401 Linda Vista Rd San Diego CA 92111 Office Phone: 858-292-3608.

**SIMPSON, WILLIAM ARTHUR,** insurance company executive; b. Oakland, Calif., Feb. 2, 1939; s. Arthur Earl and Pauline (Mikalasic) S.; m. Nancy Dougery Simpson, Mar. 31, 1962; children — Sharon Elizabeth, Shelley Pauline BS, U. Calif.-Berkeley, 1961; postgrad. Exec. Mgmt. Program, Columbia U. CLU. V.p. mktg. Countrywide Life, L.A., 1973-76; v.p. agy. Occidental Life of Calif., L.A., 1976-79; pres., CEO Vol. State Life, Chattanooga, 1979-83; exec. v.p. Transam. Occidental Life Ins. Co., L.A., 1983-86, pres., 1986-88, pres., CEO, COO, 1988-90, also bd. dirs.; dir. USLIFE Corp., N.Y.C., 1990—; pres., CEO All Am. Life Ins. Co., Pasadena, Calif., 1990-94, USLIFE Life Ins. div. USLIFE Corp., 1994, USLIFE Corp., 1995-97. Chmn. Franklin Life Ins. Co. Pres. Chattanooga coun. Boy Scouts Am., 1982, bd. dirs., L.A., 1983, v.p., 1983-85, vice-chmn L.A. area, 1989, chmn., 1989; pres. bd. councillors L.A. County Am. Cancer Soc.; trustee Verdugo Hills Hosp. Found., Ill. Symphony Orch.; bd. dirs. Abraham Lincoln coun. Boy Scouts Am., Meml. Medical Ctr., Springfield, Ill. 1st lt. U.S. Army, 1961—64. Mem. Am. Soc. CLUs, Life Ins. Mktg. and Rsch. Assn. (bd. dirs. 1986-89), Ctl. Ill. Ins. Co. (bd. dirs.). Lodges: Rotary. Republican. Presbyterian. Avocations: golf, skiing. Office: Franklin Life Ins Co 1 Franklin Sq Springfield IL 62713-0002 E-mail: neswas@aol.com.

**SIMPSON, WILLIAM KELLY,** curator, Egyptologist, educator; b. NYC, Jan. 3, 1928; s. Kenneth Farrand and Helen L.K. (Porter) S.; m. Marilyn E. Milton, June 19, 1953; children: Laura Knickerbacker Simpson Thorn, Abby Rockefeller Simpson Mydland. BA, Yale U., 1947, MA, 1948, PhD, 1954; DHL (hon.), Am. U. in Cairo, 2001. Asst. in Egyptian art Met. Mus. Art, 1948-54; rsch. fellow Center Middle East Studies, Harvard U., 1957-58; faculty Yale U., New Haven, 1958—65, prof. Egyptology, 1965—2004, chmn. dept. Near Eastern langs., 1966-69; curator Egyptian and ancient Near Eastern art Mus. Fine Arts, Boston, 1970-86; ltd. partner Kin and Co., 1967-69; ltd. ptnr. Venrock, 1970—. Dir. editor of papers Penn-Yale Archaeol. Expdn. to Egypt, 1960—; mem. adv. council fgn. currency program Smithsonian Instn., 1966-69 Author: Papyrus Reisner I-Records of a Building Project, 1963, Hekanefer and the Dynastic Material from Toshka, 1963, Papyrus Reisner II-Accounts of the Dockyard Workshop, 1965, Papyrus Reisner III: Records of a Building Project in the Early Twelfth Dynasty, 1969, The Terrace of the Great God at Abydos, 1974, The Mastabas of Qar and Idu, 1976, The Offering Chapel of Sekhem-ankh-ptah, 1976, The Offering Chapel of Kayemnofnet in the Museum of Fine Arts Boston, 1992, Papyrus Reisner IV: Personnel Reports, 1986, The Inscribed Material from the Pennsylvania-Yale Excavations at Abydos, 1995, (with others) The Ancient Near East, A History, 2d edit., 1998, The Literature of Ancient Egypt, 1972, The Mastaba of Queen Mersyankh III, 1994. Trustee Am. Sch. Classical Studies, Athens, Am. U. in Cairo, Katonah Mus. Art; mem. internat. council Mus. Modern Art, N.Y.C.; pres. Wrexham Found., 1965-67. Fulbright fellow Egypt, 1955-57; Guggenheim fellow, 1965 Mem. Am. Oriental Soc., Am. Philos. Soc., Archaeol. Inst. Am., Internat. Assn. Egyptologists, Egypt Exploration Soc., Soc. française d'egyptologie, German Archaeol. Inst., Foundation egyptologique Reine Elisabeth. Clubs: Century (N.Y.C.), Met. Opera (N.Y.C.), University (N.Y.C.), Union (N.Y.C.), River (N.Y.C.); Bedford (N.Y.); Golf and Tennis. Home: 129 Katonah Woods Rd Katonah NY 10536-3846 Business E-Mail: william.simpson@yale.edu.

**SIMPSON, WILLIAM M., JR.,** family medicine educator; b. Louisville, Aug. 20, 1947; s. William Maynard and Mary Glynn (Chambers) S.; m. Margaret Elaine Bath, Dec. 20, 1969; children: Jonathan Marc, Kimberly Anne. BS, Clemson U., 1968; MD, Med. U. S.C., 1972. Diplomate Am. Bd. Family Medicne; cert. of added qualification in geriatrics, 1988. Resident in family medicine Med. U. S.C., Charleston, 1972—74, chief resident and instr., 1974—75, asst. prof. family medicine, 1977—84, assoc. prof., 1984—91, prof. family medicine, 1991—, acting chmn. family medicine, 1989—90. With U.S. Army, 1975-77. Grantee HHS, 1986—. Fellow Am. Acad. Family Physicians; mem. Am. Geriatric Soc., Soc. of Tchrs. of Family Medicine. Avocations: tennis, exercise, stamps, coins, guitar. Home: 49 Montagu St Charleston SC 29401-1738 Office: Medical U SC PO Box 250805 Charleston SC 29425-0805 Office Phone: 843-792-3607. Business E-Mail: simpsowm@musc.edu.

**SIMS, BENNETT JONES,** minister, educator; b. Greenfield, Mass., Aug. 9, 1920; s. Lewis Raymond and Sarah Cosette (Jones) S.; children: Laura (Mrs John H. Boucher), Grayson, David. AB, Baker U., 1943, LHD (hon.), 1985; postgrad., Princeton Theol. Sem., 1946-47; BD, Va. Theol. Sem., 1949, DD, 1966, U. South, 1972; Merrill fellow, Harvard U., 1964-65; postgrad., Cath. U., 1969-71. Ordained to ministry Episc. Ch. as deacon, 1949, priest, 1950. Rector Ch. of Redeemer, Balt., 1951-64; dir. continuing edn. Va. Theol. Sem., 1966-72; bishop of Atlanta, 1972-83; vis. prof. theology Emory U., Atlanta, 1980-88, founder Inst. for Servant Leadership, 1988—; priest-in-charge St. Alban's Ch., Tokyo, 1962, 69. Author: Invitation to Hope, 1976, Purple Ink, 1982, Servanthood: Leadership for the Third Millennium, 1997, Why Bush Must Go, A Faith Based Challenge, 2004, The Time of My Life, an Autobiography of Hope, 2006. Trustee U. of South. With USNR, 1943-46. Named Young Man of Yr. Balt. C. of C., 1953; Disting. Alumnus of Yr., Baker U., 1972 Episcopalian. Business E-Mail: admin@servleader.org.

**SIMS, DAVID LLOYD,** lawyer; b. Pine Bluff, Ark., Dec. 31, 1960; s. Lloyd H. Sims Jr. and Betty S. (Shelby) Sims; m. Joan M. Bennett, Aug. 17, 1985; 1 child, Wilson D. BA cum laude, Ouachita Bapt. U., 1983; JD with honors, U. Ark. Sch. Law, 1986. Bar: Ark. 1986, US Dist. Ct., Ea. Dist. Ark. 1987, US Claims Ct. 1989, US Ct. Appeals 8th Circuit 1989, U.S. Supreme Ct. 2005. Assoc. Bridges, Young, Matthews, Holmes & Drake, Pine Bluff, Ark., 1986—91; mem. Bridges, Young, Matthews & Drake PLC, 1991—. Chmn. Am. Cancer Soc. Relay for Life, Pine Bluff, Ark., 1999—2000; adv. bd. Student Cmty. Svc. Project, 1991—94; dir. United Way of SE Ark., 1992—98, Youth Ptnrs. of Pine Bluff/Jefferson County, 2002—; asst. scoutmaster Boy Scouts of Am., 2002—. Mem. ABA, Ark. Bar Assn. (ho. of delegates 1997—2004), Jefferson County Bar Assn., Greater Pine Bluff C. of C., Rotary Club of West Pine Bluff (pres. 1995—96, Paul Harris Fellow 1998). Methodist. Avocations: tennis, hiking, reading, music. Office: Bridges Young Matthews & Drake PLC 315 East 8th Ave Pine Bluff AR 71601 Office Phone: 870-534-5532. Business E-Mail: davidsims@bridgesplc.com.

**SIMS, DOUGLAS D.,** bank executive; b. 1946; Grad., U. Ill., Urbana, 1968. With St. Louis Bank for Cooperatives, St. Louis, 1969-74; v.p. Ctrl. Bank for Coops., 1974-78; pres. St. Louis Bank for Coops., 1978-84; exec. v.p. Farm Credit Banks of St. Louis, 1984-86, pres., 1986-88. Nat. Bank for Cooperatives, Englewood, Colo., 1988-93; CEO CoBank, Englewood, 1994—. Office: CoBank 5500 S Quebec St Greenwood Village CO 80111-1914

**SIMS, EDWARD HOWELL,** editor, writer; b. Orangeburg, SC, May 29, 1923; s. Hugo Sheridan and Jesse Lucile (Howell) S.; m. Frances Dell Hartt, Jan. 5, 1946; m. Martha Lurene Bass, July 18, 1960; children: Edward H., Robert; m. Bente Thorlund Christensen, Oct. 4, 1969; children— Edward Christian, Frederik. AB, Wofford Coll., 1943; postgrad., Emory U., 1946-47. Mng. editor Orangeburg Times and Democrat, 1946, editor, 1952—; Washington corr., founder Washington bur. for number S.C. dailies, 1947. Dir. Sims Pub. Co., Orangeburg. Columnist: Looking South From Washington, 1948—; Washington Bur. chief: Editor's Copy syndicate, 1950-52; editor-pub., 1952—; radio news analyst: The News of The Week In Washington, 1951—; Author: American Aces, 1958, Greatest Fighter Missions, 1962, The Fighter Pilots, 1967, Fighter Tactics 1914-70, 1972, Aces Over the Oceans, 1987; contbr. articles to publs. White House corr. covering Pres.''s confs., 1948—; mem. Senate and House press galleries, 1947—; Am. consul Munich, Germany, 1963-65; cons. Exec. Office of White House, 1966-67; consul gen. Zurich, 1992; apptd. mem. Commn. to Preserve Am. Heritage Abroad, 1987. Served to 1st lt. USAF, World War II. Recipient Young Man of the Year award S.C. Jr. C. of C., 1959 Mem. White House Corrs. Assn., Am. Legion, V.F.W. Clubs: Rotary, Nat. Press; Metropolitan (Washington); R.A.F. (London). Methodist. Home: 3803 Pin Oaks St Sarasota FL 34232-1241 also: PO Box 400 Fairview NC 28730-0400 Office: PO Box 532 Orangeburg SC 29116-0532

**SIMS, ELIZABETH LANEAL,** healthcare association executive; b. Manila, Ark., May 22, 1948; d. Aaron Neal and Mary Elizabeth (Butler) Shedd; m. Jared Preston Sims, Aug. 31, 1968; children: Jared Neal, David Paul, Christopher Wayne. BA in English, James Madison U., Harrisonburg, Va., 1974. Tchr. English Buffalo Gap HS, Augusta County, Va., 1977—79, Wilson Meml. HS, 1981—88, tchr., sponsor, high sch. yr. book The Hornet's Nest, 1981—88; vol. coord., case mgr. Family Children's Svc., Richmond, 1989—93, program adminstr. sr. svcs., 1993—98; exec. dir. Hanover Mental Health Assn., Inc., Ashland, 1998—2005; exec. dir. Va. affiliate Nat. Alliance on Mental Illness, 2005—. Pres. bd. dirs. Hanover Mental Health Assn., 1996-98; bd. dirs. Va. Coalition for Aging Mem. adminstrv. bd. Ctr. United Meth. Ch., 1981—83; mem. staff/parish com. Duncan Meml. United Meth. Ch., 2002—, sec. to adminstrv. bd., 2003—; bd. dirs. United Way, Richmond, 1995—97, campaign cabinet, 1998—2000; v.p. bd. dirs. Urban League Greater Richmond, 1999—2004; bd. dirs. Urban League Found., 2002—04. Recipient Cert. of Appreciation for Profl. Excellence in Edn., Aug. Co., 1987, Cert. of Appreciation, Urban League, 1998, United Way Svcs., 1997, 1998, 1999, 2000. Mem. Internat. Assn. Psychosocial Rehab. Svcs., Mental Health Assn. Va. (bd. dirs. 1998—), Beta Sigma Phi (Laureate Rho chpt. pres. 2003—) United Methodist. Avocation: Boy Scout counseling.

**SIMS, EZRA,** composer; b. Birmingham, Ala., Jan. 16, 1928; s. Ezra G. and Kathryn W. (Wallace) S. BA, Birmingham So. Coll., 1947; postgrad., Birmingham Conservatory Music, 1945-48; MusB in Composition, Yale U. Sch. Music, 1952; MA in Composition, Mills Coll., 1956. Librarian Harvard Music Library, Cambridge, Mass., 1958-62, 65-74; music dir. New Eng. Dinosaur Dance Theatre, Boston, 1968-78; instr. theory New Eng. Conservatory Music, Boston, 1976-78; instr. microtonal theory Mozarteum, Salzburg, 1992-93; freelance composer Cambridge, 1974—. Dir. Dinosaur Annex Music Ensemble, Cambridge, pres. 1977-2003; guest composer 23d Ann. Contemporary Music Festival, Ill. Wesleyan U., 1977; lectr. various colls. including Warwick U., Cleve. Inst. Music, Internat. Christian U., Westport Friends of Music, Schlumberger-Doll Rsch., Webster U., Mozarteum, Northwestern U., Hochschule für Musik, Hamburg. Composer over 100 works, predominantly microtonal music for various mediums including Chamber Cantata on Chinese Poems, 1954, Mass, 1955, Two Folk Songs, 1958, String Quartet, 1959, Sieben-Spencer Lieder, 1960, Sonate Concertanti, 1961, Third Quartet, 1962, Buchlein for Lyon, 1962, Cantata III, 1963, Octet for Strings, 1964, In Memoriam Alice Hawthorne, 1967, Antimatter: Three Dances for Toby, 1968, A Frank Overture: Four Dented Interludes and Coda, 1969, Pastorale, 1970, Clement Wenceslaus Lothaire Nepomucene, Prince Mettermich (1773-1859), In Memoriam, 1970, Real Toads, 1970, Interlope, 1971, Tango Variations, 1971, Museum Piece, 1972, Where the Wild Things Are, 1973, String Quartet #2 (1962), 1974, After Lyle or Untitled, 1975, When the Angels Blow Their Trumpets, 1976, Celebration of Dead Ladies, 1976, Elegie-nach Rilke, 1976, Collage XIII, 1977, Aeneas on the Saxophone, 1977, Come Away, 1978, Midorigaoka, 1978, 5 Songs, 1979, -And, As I Was Saying..., 1979, Two for One, 1980, Sextet, 1981, All Done From Memory, 1980, Phenomena, 1981, Solo After Sextet, 1981, Quartet, 1982, Pictures for an Institution, 1983, Tune and Variations, 1983, Brief Elegies, 1983, String Quartet #4, 1984, The Conversions, 1985, Wedding Winds, 1986, Quintet, 1987, Chase, 1987, Solo in four movements, 1987, AEDM in memoriam, 1988, Flight, 1989, Night Piece: In Girum Imus nocte et Consumimur Igni, 1989, Concert Piece, 1990, Duo, 1992, Invocation, 1992, Stanzas, 1995, If I Told Him, 1996, Duo, 1996, 97, Encores: Three Parlor Songs, 2000, String Quartet #5, 2000, Musing and Recollection, 2003, -furthermore..., 2004, Concert Piece, 2005; contbr. articles to profl. jours. Served as pvt. U.S. Army, 1952-54. Recipient Composers Forum award, 1959, Koussevitzky Found. commn., 1983, Am. Acad. Arts and Letters award, 1985; grantee Cambridge Arts Coun., 1975, 76, Martha Baird Rockefeller Found., 1977; fellow Guggenheim Found., 1962, McDowell Colony, 1966, Nat. Endowment for Arts, 1976, 78, Mass. Artists Found., 1979, Djerassi Found., 1990, Fulbright Sr. Scholar, 1992, Wurlitzer Found., 1998, Camargo Found., 2000. Mem. Broadcast Music, Inc. Home and Office: 229 Hurley St Cambridge MA 02141-2133 Address: Rosalie Calabrese Mgmt Box 20580 Park West St New York NY 10025-1521 Office Phone: 617-864-8781. Personal E-Mail: ezrsims@aol.com.

**SIMS, HENRY P., JR.,** management educator; Prof. mgmt. U. Md., College Park. Author: The Thinking Organization: Dynamics of Organizational Social Cognition, 1986, SuperLeadership: Leading Others to Lead Themselves, 1989, The New Leadership Paradigm: Social Learning and Cognition in Organizations, 1992, Business Without Bosses: How Self-Managing Teams Are Building High-Performance Companies, 1993, Company of Heroes: Unleashing the Power of Self Leadership, 1996, Team Work and Group Dynamics, 1999, The New Superleadership: Leading Others to Lead Themselves, 2001. Office: U Md Van Munching Hall College Park MD 20742-0001 Business E-Mail: hsims@rhsmith.umd.edu.

**SIMS, HOWARD F.,** architectural firm executive; BA in Architecture, MA in Architecture, U. Mich.; Doctorate of Public Service (hon.), Eastern Mich. U. Chmn., CEO Sims Design Group, 1964—. Architectural projects include Museum of African Am. History, various projects at Detroit Metropolitan Airport, Stroh River Place, Cleveland Hopkins Internat. Airport, George Bush Intercontinental Airport Houston, Willow Run Airport. Trustee Community Found. for Southeastern Mich., W. K. Kellogg Found. Office: Sims Design Group 645 Griswold Penobscot Bldg Detroit MI 48226*

**SIMS, HUNTER W., JR.,** lawyer; b. Richmond, Va., Oct. 21, 1944; BS, U. Va., 1967; JD, U. Richmond, 1971. Bar: Va. 1971. Law clk. to Hon. Walter E. Hoffman U.S. Dist. Ct. (ea. dist.), Va., 1971-72; asst. U.S. atty. State of Va. (ea. dist), 1972-75; ptnr. Kaufman & Canoles P.C., Norfolk, Va. Fellow Am. Coll. of Trial Lawyers; mem. ABA, Va. State Bar Com. on Lawyer Discipline (adv. com. on rules of ct. jud. coun. Va. 1998—), Va. Bar Assn. (bd. govs. construction law sect. 1982-85, bd. govs. antitrust sect. 1989-92, bd. dirs. 1990-92), Va. State Bar, Fed. Bar Assn., Va. Beach Bar Assn., Am. Inns of Ct., Norfolk/Portsmouth Bar Assn. (sec. 1981-86), Omicron Delta Kappa, Phi Delta Phi, McNeill Law Soc. Office: Kaufman & Canoles PC PO Box 3037 One Commercial Place Norfolk VA 23514-3037

**SIMS, JOE,** lawyer; b. Phoenix, Sept. 29, 1944; s. Joe and Pauline Jane (Saunders) S.; m. Robin Ann Reed, Jan. 30, 1965; 1 child, Shannon Dane. BS in Fin., Ariz. State U., 1967, JD, 1970. Bar: Ariz. 1970, U.S. Supreme Ct. 1975, D.C 1978. Trial atty. antitrust div. Dept. Justice, Washington, 1970-73; spl. asst. to asst. atty. gen., 1973-75; dep. asst. atty. gen. for policy planning and legislation, 1975-77, dep. asst. atty. gen. for regulatory matters and fgn. commerce, 1977-78; mem. firm Jones, Day, Reavis & Pogue, Washington,

1978-79, ptnr., 1979—; now ptnr., chair antitrust and competition law section and technology issues section Jones Day, Washington. Resident fellow Am. Enterprise Inst. for Pub. Policy Rsch., Washington, 1978-79, vis. fellow, 1979-81; prin. Coun. for Excellence in Govt. Contbr. various articles to prof. jours. Named one of 15 Dealmakers of the Yr., Am. Lawyer mag., 2000, World's Top 10 Antitrust Lawyers, Global Counsel mag., 2001. Mem. ABA (chmn. antitrust law sect. one com. 1987-90, bus. law sect. antitrust law com. 1988-91, antitrust law civil practice and procedure com. 1990-91), Am. Law Inst., D.C. Bar Assn., City Club Washington, Tournament Players Club (Potomac, Md.), Firestone Country Club (Akron, Ohio), Colleton River Plantation (Hilton Head Island, S.C.). Republican. Office: Jones Day 51 Louisiana Ave NW Washington DC 20001-2113 Office Fax: 202-626-1747.

**SIMS, JOHN ERNEST,** biologist, researcher; b. Madison, Wis., Mar. 11, 1947; s. John LeRoy and Anne Schurch Sims; m. Trish Espedal, Oct. 19, 1990; 1 child, Joseph Roy Furlong. PhD, Harvard U., Cambridge, Mass., 1979. Disting. fellow Amgen, 2002—04, exec. sci. dir., 2004—. Contbr. articles to profl. jours. Office: Amgen 1201 Amgen Ct W Seattle WA 98105 Office Phone: 206-265-7005.

**SIMS, JOHN R.,** lawyer; b. 1950; B, U. Mo., 1972, JD, 1975. Various legal positions to v.p., dep. gen. counsel Federated Dept. Stores, Inc., Cin., 1980—2002; exec. v.p., gen. counsel Albertson's Inc., Boise, Idaho, 2002—. Mem.: Law Review, Phi Beta Kappa. Office: Albertsons Inc 250 Parkcenter Blvd Boise ID 83706

**SIMS, KENT OTWAY,** economist; b. Chickasha, Okla., Nov. 2, 1940; s. Jesse Otway and Mable Vela (Bear) S.; m. Jeanette McCollum, June 9, 1961; children: Marketa, Adam. BA, U. Colo., 1963, PhD, 1966. registered investment advisor. Economist Urban Renewal Authority, Denver, 1965-66, U.S. Dept. State mission to Pakistan, 1966-69, Fed. Res. Bank of San Francisco, 1969-71, asst. v.p., 1971-72, v.p., dir. research, 1972-74, sr. v.p., 1974-82, exec. v.p., chief fin. officer, 1982-85; fin. advisor, investment mgr., mgmt. cons. Theodore R. Seton, 1985-89; ptnr. C&K Partnership, 1987-89. Pres. Her Equal Share, Inc., 1986-89, San Francisco Econ. Devel. Corp., 1988-91; dir. econ. planning and devel. Mayor's Office, San Francisco, 1992-93, San Francisco Redevel. Agy., 1993-96; dir. spl. projects City Mgr.'s Office, Oakland, Calif., 1997; dep. dir. Com. Econ. Devel., Oakland, 1997-98; cons. Bay Area Life Scis. Alliance, 1999, San Francisco Planning and Urban Rsch. Assn., 2000, Golden Gate Restaurant Assn., 2001-05, San Francisco Small Property Owners, 2003, San Francisco Small Bus. Alliance, 2003, Burnham & Brown, Attys., 2003-05. Bd. govs. Econ. Lit. Coun. Calif., Long Beach, 1983-88; trustee Strybing Arboretum Soc. Golden Gate Park, San Francisco, 1983-96; bd. dirs. Jewish Community Mus., San Francisco, 1986-93, Design Coun. San Francisco Bay Area, 1989-90, Career Resources Devel. Ctr., 1991-92; adv. bd. St. Lukes Hosp., San Francisco, 1988-96. Mem. Am. Econs. Assn., Nat. Audubon Soc. Am. Clubs: Sierra. Personal E-mail: kentsims@pacbell.net.

**SIMS, LENNIE COLEMAN,** part-time public relations consultant; b. Wellington, Tex., July 31, 1930; d. John Scott Jr. and Ethel Breeding Coleman; m. Billy Mac (William McDowell) Sims, Sept. 1, 1956; children: Richard McDowell Sims, Randall Coleman Sims (twins).* BBA, Abilene Christian U., 1950. Author, choreographer, music arranger (U.S. BiCentennial hist. play) Man & Land & Love, 1972, (all musical) 1976, Collingsworth County Centennial Links of Our Legacy, 1991. Appointed as 1st woman to bd. regents West Tex. State U., 1974 (reappointed 1982, 1st vice chmn., v.p. merger com., W. Tex. A&M U., 1998, Crime Stoppers Adv. Coun. (chair edn. steering com., 1999); Collingsworth County chair Dem. party; 1st v.p. Tex. Dem. Party County Chairs Assn.; appt. State Bar Tex. Mem. Fedn. Women's Clubs (state pres. 1980-82, region Tex., Colo., N. Mex., La., Ariz., Ark.), Internat. Gen. Fedn. Women's Clubs (pres.), 1st chmn. Women's History/Resource Ctr. Internat. Gen. Fedn. Women's Clubs), Tex. Fedn. Music Clubs (state 1st v.p. 1968-70, editor state mag. Lines & Spaces, 1964-75). Home: PO Box 248 Wellington TX 79095-0248

**SIMS, LOWERY STOKES,** museum curator, museum administrator, writer, educator; b. Washington, Feb. 13, 1949; d. John Jacob and Bernice Marion (Banks) S. BA in Art History, Queens Coll., 1970, MPhil, 1989; PhD in Art History, CUNY, 1995; MA in Art History, Johns Hopkins U., 1972; LHD (hon.), Md. Coll. Art, Balt., 1988; ArtsD (hon.), Moore Coll. Art, Phila., 1990; ArtsD, Brown U., Providence, 2003. Mus. edn. assoc. Met. Mus. Art, NYC, 1972-75, asst. curator, 1975-79, assoc. curator, 1979-95, curator, 1995—99; exec. dir. Studio Mus. in Harlem, NYC, 1999—2005, pres., 2005—06, adj. curator, 2006—. Mem. author: (catalogue) Stuart Davis, American Painting, 1991; co-author: (book) Wifredo Lam and the International Avant Guide, 1923, 1982, (catalogue) Wifredo Lam and His Contemporaries, 1994, (catalogue) Challenge of the Modern: African American Arts, 1925-1945, 2002-03, Persistence of Geometry, Cleve. Mus. Art, 2006. Bd. dirs. Caribbean Cultural Ctr. N.Y.C., 1975-80, 90—, Tiffany Found., N.Y.C., 2005—, Met. Mus. Art, 2005—. Recipient award of distinction Am. Women's Econ. Devel., 1993. Mem. Internat. Assn. Art Critics, Coll. Art Assn. (bd. dirs. 1993-97, Mather award for art criticism 1991). Democrat. Avocations: needlepoint, collecting black memorabilia. Office: Studio Museum in Harlem 144 West 125th St New York NY 10027 Personal E-Mail: lsimssmh@aol.com. Business E-Mail: lsims@studiomuseum.org.

**SIMS, MARCIE LYNNE,** language educator, writer; b. Monrovia, Calif., Feb. 22, 1963; d. Charles Eugene and Delores May (Wonert) S.; m. Douglas Todd Cole; children: Marcus Anthony Cole, Thomas Halvor Cole. BA in English, Calif. State Poly., 1986; MA in English, San Diego State U., 1990. Page 113 Jenne, Washington, 19/91 instr. Calif. Conservation Corps, San Diego, 1990; instr. in English Shoreline C.C., Seattle, 1990-94, Seattle Central C.C., 1990-94, Green River C.C., Auburn, Wash., 1994—. Founder Wild Mind Women Writers Workshop, Seattle, 1992—. Author: Soul-Making: John Keats and the Stages of Death, 1990, The Write Stuff, 2005; contbg. author Moms on Line, 1996—; editor Espial Lit. Jour Vol. cons. Camp Fire, Wash., 1994-96. Mem. Am. Fedn. Tchrs., The Keats-Shelley Orgn., Wash. Fed. Tchrs. (exec. bd. mem. 1993-94), Phi Kappa Phi, Sigma Tau Delta. Democrat. Avocations: cooking, tennis. Office: Green River CC 12401 SE 320th St Auburn WA 98092-3622

**SIMS, PAMELA JAN (CERUSSI),** writer, minister; b. Little Rock, Sept. 10, 1933; 2 children. Attended, Mt. St. Mary's Acad., St. Scholastica's Coll., Sydney, Delgado Coll., Nola, Tulane U., 1951; DD (hon.). Lic. rev. in Christian ministry, in specialized svcs. Fla., 2006. Past pres. Ikebana Internat., Le Gals, Inc., 1979—89; pres. Titanic Bead Co.; journalist, notary pub. Fla., 1986—. Tchr. legal secretarial classes, Nola; support writer Pres. George W. Bush, 1999—2007. Prin. works include Ikebana design articles; contbr. articles to mags. and newspapers. Team leader Bush/Cheney Inc., 2002—; mem. Rep. Nat. Com. Rep. Woman's Club, Pensacola Christian Women's Club, United Intercessors Inc. Recipient Cert. of Recognition, Rep. Nat. Party, 2002, Congl. Award of Merit, 2004, Blue and Tri-Color Ribbon awar, Fla. Fedn. Garden Clubs, 2004, Cert. of Appreciation, Rep. Nat. Com., 2005. Mem.: Pensacola Camellia Club. Achievements include patents pending in field. Fax: 850-457-1022. Office Phone: 850-292-1643.

**SIMS, PATTERSON,** curator; b. Phila., Nov. 17, 1947; m. Katy Homans, 1987; 2 children. Student, Trinity Coll., Hartford, Conn.; BA, New Sch. Social Rsch., 1972. Asst. dir. O.K. Harris Works Art, NYC, 1969-76; assoc. curator permanent collection Whitney Mus. Am. Art, NYC, 1976-87; part-time instr. Sch. Continuing Edn. NYU, 1975-77, 84-86; assoc. dir. art and exhbns., curator modern art Seattle Art Mus., 1987—96; dep. dir. edn. and rsch. support Mus. Modern Art, NYC, 1996—2001; dir. Montclair Art Mus., NJ, 2001—. Mem. adv. bds., panels the Fabric Workshop, Phila.; Studio in a Sch. Assn., N.Y.C., Robert Lehman Coll. Art Gallery, N.Y.C., Santa Fe Chamber Mus. Festival, N.Mex., Seattle, Laumier Sculpture Pk., St. Louis, NEA Mus. Implementation Panel, Washington; lectr. in field. Exhbns. include 30 Years Am. Art, 1977, Am. Art 1920-45, Am. Art 1950—, 1977-78,

Tradition and Modernism in Am. Art, 1900-25, Gibbes Art Gallery, Charleston, S.C., 1978, Jan Matulka Retrospective Exhbn., 1979-80, Concentration, 1980-81, Biennial Exhbn., Decade of Transition: 1940-50, 1981, (with Ann D'Harnoncourt) John Cage: Scores and Prints, 1882, (with Emily Rauh Pulitzer) Ellsworth Kelly: Sculpture, 1982-83, (with 3 other curators) Biennial Exhbn.: Minimalism to Expressionism: Painting and Sculpture since 1965, 1983, Viola Frey, 1984, Clare Zeisler, 1984-85, Biennial Exhbn., 1985, Figure as Subject: The Last Decade, 1986, John Storrs Retrospective Exhbn., 1986-87. Figure as Subject: The Revival of Figuration since 1975, 1988, Twentieth Century Am. Art Highlights of the Permanet Collection of the Whitney Mus. Am. Art, 1988, Documents Northwest Series: C.T. Chew, Seattle Art Mus., 1988, Made in N.Y.: The N.Y. Sch.: 1945-65: Jasper Johns: A Selected View: New Work N.Y., Seattle Art Mus., 1989, Documents Northwest Series: Crossed Cultures, Figures of Translucence, Seattle Art. Mus., 1989, Mark Tansey: Art and Source, Seattle Art Mus., 1990; author brochures, catalogs. Home: 11 W 53rd St New York NY 10019-5401 Office: Montclair Art Mus 3 South Mountain Ave Montclair NJ 07042

**SIMS, RICHARD LEE,** retired hospital administrator; b. Columbus, Ohio, Jan. 6, 1929; s. Dorwin Delos and Christine Anna (Hanstein) Sims; m. Marilyn Lou Atkinson, June 2, 1951 (dec. July 2005); children: John Christopher, Steven Paul. BS, Ohio State U., 1951. Pres. Doctors Hosp. Found., Columbus, 1977-95; preceptor faculty Ohio State U. Coll. Health Care Adminstrn.; past chmn. Hosp. Coun. Franklin County; ret., 1995. Past chmn. Hosp. Shared Svc. Inc. Past chmn. 1st Cmty. Village Bd.; past chmn. governing bd. 1st Cmty. Ch.; pres. Scioto Valley Health Systems Agy., 1999-2002; pres. Employment for Srs., 1999-2000, Probus, 2003; past chair Columbus area chpt. ARC, emeritus bd. dirs. Recipient Disting. Svc. award Columbus Jr. C. of C., 1960-63. Fellow Am. Coll. Healthcare Execs. (life); Am. Coll. Osteo. Healthcare Execs. (life); mem. Am. Osteo. Healthcare Assn. (chmn. 1988), Ohio Soc. of Assn. Execs. (past pres.), Ohio Hosp. Assn. (past chmn. bd.), Ohio Osteo. Hosp. Assn. (past pres.), Am. Legion (past post comdr.), Rotary (pres. 1978-79), Columbus Club, Sigma Chi (named Significant Sig 2003). Home: 1180 Kenbrook Hills Dr Columbus OH 43220-4941

**SIMS, ROBERT JOHN,** financial planner; b. Phila., Mar. 18, 1926; s. Stanley Joseph and Marie (Kendrick) S.; m. Gloria MacCarter, Nov. 27, 1965; children: Lisa Byrne, Dana Hospodar, Ernest, William, Peter, Moira. Student, Temple U., 1947-51; MSFS, CLU, ChFC, Am. Coll., Bryn Mawr, Pa., 1957; CFP, Coll. Fin. Planning, Denver. With Provident Mut. Life Ins., Phila., 1947-56, Aetna Life Ins., Phila., 1956-58, Mut. of N.Y., Phila., 1958-68; chmn. Fin-Plan Investments, Inc., Wayne, Pa., 1960—; pres. Fin-Plan Cons., Inc., Wayne, 1960—; Fin-Plan, Inc., Wayne, 1960—; chmn. Sims Fin. Svcs. LLC. Mem. fin. com. Archdiocese of Phila., investment com., trustee Lay Employees Pension Plan. Past trustee Notre Dame Acad. Bd., Radnor, Pa., United Fund; past pres. Phila. Jaycees, past nat. dir. U.S. Jaycees; bd. dirs. Gwynedd Mercy Coll., Phila.; active Big Bros.; mem. adv. bd. St. Charles Borremmeo Sem.; past pres., active Cath. Philopatrian Lit. Inst. With U.S. mil., 1944-46. Mem. Internat. Assn. Fin. Planners (founding pres. Delaware Valley chpt.), Inst. CFPs, Am. Soc. CLU, Phila. Estate Planning Coun., Phila. Assn. Life Underwriters, Golden Key Soc., Union League Phila., Phila. Country Club, Ocean Reef Club. Republican. Roman Catholic. Avocation: golf. Home: 219 Orchard Way Saint Davids PA 19087-4805 Office: Sims Fin Svcs LLC 531 E Lancaster Ave Wayne PA 19087-5112

**SIMS, ROGER W.,** lawyer; b. Cleve., Aug. 3, 1950; BA with high honors, U. Fla., 1972, JD, 1974. Bar: Fla. 1975. Mem. Holland & Knight, Orlando, Fla. Mem. Moot Ct. U. Fla.; contbr. to profl mag. and jour. Mem. ABA (mem. standing com. on environ. law 2000-2003), Fla. Bar Assn. (chmn. environ., land use law sect. 1988-89), Phi Beta Kappa, Phi Kappa Phi, Omicron Delta Kappa, Phi Alpha Delta, Fla. Blue Key. Office: Holland & Knight PO Box 1526 200 S Orange Ave Ste 2600 Orlando FL 32801-3453 Office Phone: 407-425-8500. Business E-Mail: roger.sims@hklaw.com.

**SIMS, WILLIAM D., JR.,** lawyer; b. Kosciusko, Miss., Nov. 19, 1947; BA, U. Miss., 1969; JD, Harvard U., 1972. Bar: Tex. 1972, US Supreme Ct., US Ct. Appeals (5th cir.), US Dist. Ct. (no., ea. we. so. districts) Tex., Tex. Supreme Ct. Ptnr. Vinson & Elkins LLP, Dallas, co-chair Dallas Litig. sect. Named one of The Best Lawyers in Dallas, D mag., 2002—03. Fellow: The Ctr. for Am. & Internat. Law, Internat. Acad. Trial Lawyers. Office: Vinson & Elkins LLP Trammell Crow Ctr 2001 Ross Ave Ste 3700 Dallas TX 75201 E-mail: bsims@velaw.com.

**SIMS, WILLIAM JACK,** secondary school educator; s. William Jackson Sims, Jr. and Helen McNeely Sims; m. Robin Ann Dubrowsky, Sept. 22, 1980; children: Heather McNeely, Benjamin Jackson. BFA in Theater and Speech, N.C. Sch. Arts, Winston-Salem, 1965—68; MS in Edn., Bank St. Coll., N.Y.C., 1992—94. Prodr. dir. Westside Theatre Co., N.Y.C., 1971—79; dir., cons. Periwinkle Nat. Theatre Co., Monticello, 1973—2002; asst. stage dir. N.Y.C. Opera Co., N.Y.C., 1974—79; prodn. stage mgr. Harold Prince Assoc., N.Y.C., 1979—82; spokesman, narrator Video Knowledge, Melville, NY, 1982—; dir., telemarketing svcs. NJ. Symphony Orch., Newark, 1985—92; instr., coord. N.Y.C. Dept. Edn., 1986—2006; dean of students N.Y.C. Dept. Edn., 1986—; dir. Mott Hall After Sch. Learning Acad., N.Y.C., 1995—2000; divsn. leader Manhattan Youth's Downtown Day Camp, N.Y.C., 1999—. actor: (opera) Porgie and Bess; composer: (song collection) Big Apple Tunes, Seven out of Ten Ain't Bad; actor: (film) The Kill Off; dir.: (play) Set It Down in Gold on Lasting Pillars. County com. Dem. Party, Essex County, NJ, 2000—06. Grantee African Lit. and Cinema Studies, NEH, 1991; scholar Summer Inst., Folk Lore Inst., 1993. Mem: Am. Fedn. Tchrs., Actor's Equity Assn. Avocations: dominoes, haiku writer and collector. Office: NYC Dept Edn 71 Convent Ave New York NY 10027 Office Phone: 212-92709466. Personal E-Mail: rsims23@aol.com. Business E-Mail: jsims4@nycboe.net.

**SIMS, WILSON,** lawyer; b. Nashville, Dec. 24, 1924; s. Cecil and Grace (Wilson) S.; m. Linda Bell, Aug. 12, 1948; children: Linda Rickman, Suzanne, Wilson. BA, U. N.C., 1946; JD, Vanderbilt U., 1948. Bar: Tenn. 1948. Since practiced in, Nashville; ptnr. Bass, Berry & Sims; gen. counsel, dir. Baird Ward Printing Co., Southeastern Capital Corp., Martha White Foods, Synercon Corp., Forrest Life Ins. Co., Charter Co., The Bailey Co., Kenworth of Tenn., Inc. Chmn. Tenn. Commn. for Human Devel., Tenn. Commn. on Continuing Legal Edn.; mem. Tenn. Gen. Assembly, 1959-62. bd. dirs. Nashville YMCA, United Cerebal Palsy, Kidney Found., Matthew 25, McKendree Village; trustee Meharry Med. Coll., Webb Sch., Bell Buckle, Tenn.; adv. bd. Jr. League; mem. bd. visitors U.N.C. 1st St. USMCR, 1942-45. 50-52. Fellow Am. Bar Found. (life), Nashville Bar Found.; mem. ABA, Tenn. Bar Assn. (past spkr. ho. of dels., past pres.), Nashville Bar Assn. (past pres., dir., Pub. Svc. award), Tenn. Bar Found. (past chmn.), Am. Judicature Soc., Am. Acad. Polit. Sci., Vanderbilt U. Law Alumni Assn. (past pres., Disting. Svc. award), Belle Meade Country Club (bd. dirs.), High Hampton Colony Club (bd. dirs., pres.). Methodist. Home: 22 Foxhall Close Nashville TN 37215-1862 Office: Bass Berry & Sims AmSouth Ctr Ste 2700 315 Deaderick St Nashville TN 37238-3001 Business E-Mail: wsims@bassberry.com.

**SIMS-CURRY, KRISTY,** women's college basketball coach; b. Olla, La., 1967; m. Kelly Curry, 2 dau. BS in Health and Phys. Edn., N.E. La. U., 1988; MS in Kinesiology, Stephen F. Austin U., Nacogdoches, Tex., 1992. Coach Weston H.S., Mansfield H.S., La.; women's asst. basketball coach Tulane U., 1991-93, Stephen F. Austin U., 1993-94, Tex. A&M U., 1994-96; asst. coach La. Tech. U., 1996-99; head coach Purdue U., West Lafayette, 1999—. Office: care Women's Basketball 1790 Mackey Arena Rm 44 West Lafayette IN 47907-1790

**SIMS IANNELLI, KIMBERLY,** writer; b. Hereford, Tex., Mar. 9, 1964; d. Bob S. and Sue Hess Sims; m. Peter Carmine Iannelli, Sept. 6, 1997; 1 child, Sydney Iannelli. BS, Tex. A&M U., 1986, MPA, 1988, MA, 1999. Legis. aide, com. clk. Tex. Senate, Austin, 1993-95; dir. agr. and conservation policy Office of Gov. George W. Bush, Austin, 1995-97; exec. dir., sec. Tex. Water

Found., Austin, 1998-2000; interim exec. dir. Environ. Edn. Found. Tex., Austin, 2000—01. Adj. faculty South Tex. C.C., McAllen, Tex., 2001—04. Dir. Tex. Women's Alliance, Austin, 2995-2001; mem. adv. coun. Hidalgo County Hist. Mus., Edinburg, Tex., 2000-2001; dir. Friends of Wildlife Corridor, McAllen, 2001. Mem. Tex. Agrl. Lifetime Leadership Evang. Avocations: travel, reading, tennis, cooking.

**SIMSON, BEVLYN,** artist; b. Columbus, Ohio, Sept. 9, 1917; d. Amon and Fannie Florence (Gilbert) Thall; m. Theodore Richard Simson, Mar. 25, 1938; children: Sherran Blair, Douglas A. BFA, Ohio State U., 1969, MFA, 1972. Author, artist Prints and Poetry, 1969. One woman shows include J.B. Speed Art Mus., Louisville, 1970, Huntington Gallery, Columbus, Ohio, 1970, 73, United Christian Ctr., Columbus, 1970, Bodley Gallery, N.Y., 1971, 74, Gilman Galleries, Chgo., 1971, Gallery 200, Columbus, 1972, Hopkins Hall Gallery, Ohio State U., Columbus, 1972, Meth. Theol Sch., Deleware, Ohio, 1973, Columbus Public Lib., 1973, Garfinkels, Washington, 1973, City Hall, Mayor's Office, Columbus, 1974, 82, Capital U., Bexley, Ohio, 1977, Hillel Found., Ohio State U., 1978, Columbus Tech. Inst., 1979, Springfield (Ohio) Art Mus., 1980, Peace Luth. Ch., Gahanna, Ohio, 1981, Franklin U. Gallery, Columbus, 1981, Columbus Mus. Art Collectors Gallery, 1983; exhibited in juried and invitational shows at Columbus Mus. Art-Ohio Art League, 1968, 70, 71, 73, 74, 75, 77, 78, 79, 80, 86, Ohio Statehouse and State Office Tower, Columbus, 1968-78, Battelle Meml. Inst., Columbus, 1969-73, 75, 78, 81-82, Schumacher Gallery, Capital U., Columbus, 1969-85, 87, 88, Salles d'Exposition, Paris, 1969, Am. Cultural Ctr., Kyoto, Japan, J.B. Speed Art Mus. Collector's Gallery, Louisville, 1970-85, Studio San Guiseppe, Mt. St. Joseph Coll., Cin., 1971, Silver Anniversary Coll. Arts, 2nd Biennial Alumni Exhbn., Hopkins Hall Gallery, 1972, 2nd Internat. Art Exhbn., Paramaribo, Serinam, 1974, Mansfield (Ohio) Art Ctr., 1971, Collector's Showroom, Chgo., 1971-82, Gov.'s MansionState of Ohio, 1972, 74, Western Ill. U., 1972, Albatross Gallery, Rome, 1972, Palazzo Dell Exprizioni, Rome, 1972, Place-Allrich Gallery, San Francisco, 1973-75, Chautauqua Assn., N.Y., 1973, Butler Inst. Am. Art, Youngstown, Ohio, 1973, 76, Huntington Gallery, Columbus, 1973, 74, Gallery 200, Columbus, 1972-76, Columbus C. of C., 1974, 75, Zanesville (Ohio) Art Ctr., 1976, Columbus Inst. Contemporary Art, 1978, Nationwide Plaza Gallery, Columbus, 1980, Franklin U., Columbus, 1980, Ohio State U., 1993, Ohio Art League, 1987, Jeffrey Mansion, Bexley, Ohio, 1996, 10th Ann. Women Artists Expo Seal of Ohio Girl Scout Coun. Inc. Columbus, 1996, Financial Group Gallery, Worthington, Ohio, 1997, Ohio Art League, 1997, 4th Hall Gallery, Ohio State U., 1997, Concourse Gallery, Upper Arlington, Ohio, 1998, 13th Ann. Women Artists Expo Art in The Nation Wide Atrium, Columbus, Ohio, 1999, Bexley City Hall Gallery, Jeffrey Mansion, 2000, State Office Towers Exhbn. Gallery, 2003;(Ohio) Art League Mem. Curated Exhbn., Structure/Consequences, 1997, Fourth Biennial Alumni Exhbn.:ReSiDivist, Hopkins Hall Gallery, Ohio State U., 1997, Concourse Gallery, Arlington Ohio, 1998, Bexley Art League, Precision Concepts, Dublin, Ohio, 1999, Art in the Atrium, Columbus, Ohio, 1999, Art on Main Street, Schumacher Gallery, 2002, others; represented in permanent collections Columbus Mus. Arts, J.B. Speed Art Mus., Louisville, Capital U., Bexley, Fordham U., N.Y.C., Kyoto City U. Fine Arts, Springfield (Ohio) Art Mus., Tyler (Tex.) Mus. Art, Wichita (Kans.) Mus. Art, Zanesville (Ohio) Art Ctr., Ohio State U., Columbus, Meth. Theol. Sch., Delaware, Ohio, Yerke Mortgage Co., Columbus, Marcorp, N.Y., Kresge Co., Detroit, IBM, Columbus, Chase Manhattan Bank, N.Y.C., Chase Bank Ohio, Am. Bancorp., Columbus, Ohio Nat. Bank Plaza, Columbus, Pan Western Life Ins. Co., Columbus, First Investment Co., Columbus, Children's Hosp., Phila., Franklin County Crippled Children's Ctr., Columbus, Zenith East, N.Y.C., First Cmty. Bank, Columbus, First City Bank, Columbus, Ohio, Ronald McDonald House, Columbus, Columbia Gas of Ohio, Columbus, Midland Title Security Co., Columbus, Huntington Nat. Bank Ctr., Columbus, Lehman Bros., N.Y.C., Columbus Sch. for Girls, Grand Prix Assocs., Inc., Columbus, Grant Hosp. Med Ctr., Columbus, Libr. and Archs. Ctr. Nat. Mus. Women in Arts, Washington, D.C., Ohio State U. Libr. Rare Books Room Collection, Laredo (Tex.) Pub. Libr.; represented in private collections. Mem. Nat. League Am. Pen Women, Nat. Artists Equity Assn., Bexley Art League, Columbus Mus. Art, Ohio Art League (bd. dirs. 1965-96, treas., sec., pres. 1977), Ohio State U. Alumni Assn., Pres.'s Club (Ohio State U.), Winding Hollow Country Club, Phi Sigma Sigma. Studio: Bevlyn Simson Studio 4300 E Broad St 1st Cmty Bank Bldg Columbus OH 43213-1243 Office Phone: 614-239-4610. Personal E-mail: sherblair@aol.com.

**SIMSON, GARY JOSEPH,** dean, law educator; b. Newark, Mar. 18, 1950; s. Marvin and Mildred (Silberg) S.; m. Rosalind Slivka, Aug. 15, 1971; children: Nathaniel, Jennie Anne. BA, Yale Coll., 1971; JD, Yale U., 1974. Bar: Conn. 1974, N.Y. 1980. Law clk. to judge U.S. Ct. Appeals 2d Cir., 1974-75; from asst. prof. law to prof. law U. Tex., 1975-80; prof. law Cornell U., Ithaca, NY, 1980—2006, assoc. dean, 1997—2004; dean, Hostetler Baker & Hostetler prof. law Case Western Reserve U. Sch. Law, 2006—. Vis. prof. law Cornell U., Ithaca, 1979-80, U. Calif., Berkeley, 1986; chmn. adv. bd. law casebook series Carolina Acad. Press. Author: Issues and Perspectives in Conflict of Laws, 1985, 4th edit., 2005; contbr. articles to profl. jours. Mem. ABA, ACLU, Phi Beta Kappa. Office: Case Western Reserve U Sch Law 11075 E Blvd Cleveland OH 44106 Office Phone: 607-255-3890, 216-368-3283. E-mail: gary.simson@case.edu.

**SIMSON, JO ANNE,** retired anatomy and cell biology educator; b. Chgo., Nov. 19, 1936; d. Kenneth Brown and Helen Marjorie (Pascoe) Valentine; m. Arnold Simson, June 1961 (div.); 1 child, Maria; m. Michael Smith, Nov. 10, 1971 (div.); children: Elisabeth Smith, Briana Smith. BA, Kalamazoo Coll. 1959; MS, U. Mich., 1961; PhD, SUNY, Syracuse, 1969. Fellow Temple U. Health Sci. Ctr., Phila., 1968-70; asst. prof. Med. U. S.C., Charleston, 1970-76, assoc. prof., 1976-83, prof. anatomy and cell biology, 1983-96, prof. emerita, 1996—. With overseas program UMUC, 1999—2004; featured in Smithsonian exhibit Sci. in Am. Life, 1994—. Contbr. articles to profl. jours.; author short stories and poems. Active adult edn. Unitarian Ch., Charleston, 1973-75, social action, 1990-92. Grantee NSF, 1959-60, NIH, 1966-67, 72-87, 91-95. Mem. Am. Assn. Anatomists, Am. Soc. Cell Biology, Histochem. Soc. (sec. 1979-82, exec. com. 1985-89), Fogarty Internat. Fellowship Bioctr. (Basel, Switzerland, 1987-88), Amnesty Internat. (newsletter editor Group 168 1982-86), Phi Beta Kappa. Home: 1760 Pittsford Cir Charleston SC 29412-4110 Business E-Mail: joannesimson@bellsouth.net. *In the end, it is only what a person has created and given to the rest of the world that endures.*

**SIN, YONG WOOK,** researcher, educator; children: Jaimin Elizabeth, Julia Seung-Min. PhD, Ariz. State U., Tempe, 1991—96. Postdoctoral fellowship Ariz. State U., 1997—99; rsch. prof. U. Mo., Rolla, 1999—. Mem.: Electrochemical Soc., Am. Ceramic Soc., Phi Kappa Phi. Office: U Mo 303 Material Research Ctr Rolla MO 65401 Business E-Mail: sinyw@umr.edu.

**SINACORI, JOHN TODD,** surgeon, educator; b. Rochester, N.Y., Apr. 10, 1970; s. Russell R. and Alfia M. Sinacori; m. Faith Lisa Evans, Nov. 26, 1994; children: Zachary J., Leah M., Brooke L. BA, U. of Rochester, 1992; MD, SUNY Health Sci. Ctr., Syracuse, N.Y., 1996. Am. Bd. of Otolaryngology. Clin. asst. instr. dept. otolaryngology SUNY Health Sci. Ctr., Syracuse, NY, 1996—2001; instr., fellow of laryngology dept. otolaryngology Vanderbilt U. Med. Ctr., Nashville, 2001—02; dir. Voice and Swallowing Ctr. Ea. Va. Med. Sch., Norfolk, 2002—, asst. prof., 2002—, dir. residency tng., 2004—06. Contbr. articles to profl. jours. Recipient Resident Rsch. grant, Am. Acad. of Otolaryngology-Head and Neck Surgery, 1999—2000. Methodist. Office: Ea Va Med Sch Ste 510 825 Fairfax Ave Norfolk VA 23507 Office Phone: 757-446-5934. Home Fax: 757-624-2264; Office Fax: 757-624-2264. Business E-Mail: sinacojt@evms.edu.

**SINAGRA, JACK G.,** air transportation executive; b. Queens, NY, Mar. 18, 1950; m. Eileen Cook, 1978; children: Jacklyn, Alexandra, Patrick. Grad. Emporia Coll., 1972. Mem. N.J. Senate, Dist. 18, Trenton, 1992—2002; chmn. Port Author. Board of NY and NJ, 2001—. V.p. Turtle & Hughes, Linden, N.J. Mem. Assn. for a Better Middlesex County. Office: 225 Park Ave S New York NY 10003 Home: PO Box 99 Trenton NJ 08625-0099

**SINAI, ALLEN LEO,** economist, educator; b. Detroit, Apr. 4, 1939; s. Joseph and Betty Paula (Feinberg) Sinai; m. Lee Davis Etston, June 23, 1963; children: Lauren Beth, Todd Michael. AB, U. Mich., 1961; MA, Northwestern U., 1966, PhD, 1969. From asst. prof. to prof. econs. U. Ill., Chgo., 1966-75; v.p., chmn. fin. info. group, chief fin. economist Data Resources, Lexington, Mass., 1971-83; chief economist, mng. dir. Lehman Bros. and Shearson Lehman Bros. Inc., N.Y.C., 1983—88; chief economist, exec. v.p. The Boston Co. Inc., 1988-93; pres., CEO Boston Co. Econ. Advisors Inc., Boston, N.Y.C., 1988-93; mng. dir., chief global economist, dir. global econs. Lehman Bros., N.Y.C., 1993-96; pres., chief global economist, strategist Decision Econs., Inc., Boston, N.Y.C., London, 1996—; chief global economist, vice-chmn. WEFA Group, 1997-2000; global chief economist, exec. v.p. Global Insight, Inc., Lexington, Mass., 2001—03. Cons. Laural Cons., Evanston, Ill., 1966—; vis. assoc. prof. econs. and fin. MIT, Cambridge, 1975—77, vis. faculty Sloan Sch., 1989—91; adj. prof. econs. Boston U., 1977—78, 1981—83, NYU, N.Y.C., 1984—88; adj. prof. econs. and fin. Lemberg Sch., Brandeis U., 1988—95; bd. economists Time Mag., 1991—2003; bd. dirs. Boston Pvt. Fin. Holdings, Inc., 1996—. Contbr. articles to profl. jours.; chapters to books. Mem. reducing fed. budget deficit task force Roosevelt Ctr., Washington, 1984; econ. policy adviser Rep. and Dem. Adminstrns., Washington, 1995—; bd. govs. Com. Developing Am. Capitalism, 1984—96, chmn., 1990—95. Named Top Forecaster, Bus. Week Survey, 1997, USA Today Survey, 2003, 2005, 2006; named one of Ten Smartest Men in Boston, Boston Mag., 1993; recipient Alumnus Merit award, Northwestern U., 1985. Mem.: Am. Econ. Assn., Econometric Soc., Western Econ. Assn. (bd. dirs. 1995—97), Ea. Econs. Assn. (v.p. 1988—89, pres. 1990—91, Otto Eckstein prize 1988), N.Am. Econ. Fin. Assn. (pres. 2004—05, v.p. 2003—04). Jewish. Avocations: tennis, skiing, golf. Office Phone: 617-994-0503, 212-884-9441, 212-884-9441. Office Fax: 212-884-9451. Business E-Mail: asinai@pdeeco.com.

**SINAI, YAKOV G.,** theoretical mathematician, educator; b. Moscow, Sept. 21, 1935; BS, Moscow State U., 1957, PhD in Math., 1960, Doctor Degree, 1963; D Honoris Causa, Warsaw U., 1993, Budapest U. Sci. and Tech., 2002, Hebrew U., Jerusalem, 2005. Sci. rschr. lab. probabilistic and statis. methods Moscow State U., 1960-71; sr. rschr. Landau Inst. Theoretical Physics Acad. Scis., Moscow, USSR, 1971—; prof. math. Moscow State U., 1971-93; prof. math. dept. Princeton (N.J.) U., 1993—. Loeb lectr. Harvard U., 1978; plenary speaker Internat. Congresses Math. Physics, Berlin, 1981, Marseille, 1986, Internat. Congress Math., Kyoto, 1990; disting. lectr., Israel, 1989; S. Lefshetz lectr., Mex., 1990. Recipient Boltzman Gold medal, 1986, Heineman prize, 1989, Markov prize, 1990, Paul Adrian Maurice Dirac medal Internat. Centre for Theoretical Physics, 1992, Wolf prize in math. Wolf Found., Israel, 1997, Moser Prize, 2001, Nemmers Prize in Mathematics, 2002. Mem. Am. Acad. Arts and Sci. (fgn. hon.), Russian Acad. Scis., Hungarian Acad. Scis. (fgn.), London Math. Soc. (hon.), Nat. Acad. Scis. of USA (fgn. assoc.), Brazilian Acad. Scis. (fgn.). Office: Princeton University Dept of Mathematics 708 Fine Hall Washington Rd Princeton NJ 08544-0001 Office Phone: 609-258-4199.

**SINAK, DAVID LOUIS,** lawyer; b. Detroit, Oct. 3, 1953; s. Joseph and Edwina Mae (Collarini) S.; m. Elisabeth Crook; children: Jeffrey David, Margaret Louise, Slade Henry, Calder Crook. BA, U. Notre Dame, 1975; student, London Sch. Econs., 1975-76; JD, Boston Coll., 1979. Bar: Tex. 1979, U.S. Ct. Claims 1981, U.S. Tax Ct. 1981, U.S. Dist. Ct. (no. dist.) Tex. 1984, U.S. Ct. Appeals (fed. cir.) 1982, U.S. Ct. Appeals (5th cir.) 1984. Assoc. Hughes and Luce, Dallas, 1979-84, ptnr., 1984—2002, Gibson, Dunn & Crutcher LLP, Dallas, 2002—. Speaker on taxes to tax insts., law insts. and assns. and legal founds., 1981—. Mem. ABA, Tex. Bar Assn., Dallas Bar Assn. Office: Gibson Dunn & Crutcher LLP 2100 McKinney Ave Ste 1100 Dallas TX 75201 Office Phone: 214-698-3107. Office Fax: 214-571-2914. Business E-Mail: dsinak@gibsondunn.com.

**SINAY, JOSEPH,** retail executive; b. Chgo., Dec. 5, 1920; s. Hyman and Ella S.; m. Ruth Milman, Mar. 7, 1961; 1 dau., Elise Sinay Spilker. Student, Herzl Jr. Coll., 1939. Gen. mgr. Fanchon & Marco Theatres, L.A., 1943-54; v.p., founder Interstate United, Chgo., 1953-56; ptnr. Josam Investment Co., L.A., 1956-97, Sinay Co. L.L.C., L.A., 1997—; pres., CEO R B Industries Inc., L.A., 1956-89, also chmn. bd. dirs., cons.; chmn. bd. dirs. Gorian Sinay Land Co., Inc., L.A., 1997—. Bd. dirs. Am. Acad. Dramatic Arts; pres. Variety Clubs Internat., 1985-87; gen. chmn. United Jewish Welfare L.A., 1976; pres. We. region Am. Friends Hebrew U., 1980; Calif. fin. chmn. Muskie for Pres., 1972; trustee Idyllwild Arts Found., 1968-73; bd. dirs. Constl. Rights Found., 1973-78. Mem. Nat. Home Furnishing Assn. Jewish. Office: Sinay Co LLC 1801 Century Park E Los Angeles CA 90067-2302 Business E-Mail: joe@sinaycompany.com.

**SINBAD, (DAVID ADKINS),** actor, comedian; b. Benton Harbor, Mich. m. Meredith, 1985 (div. 1992); children: Paige, Royce. Student, U. Denver. Stand-up comedian various comedy clubs and concerts nationwide; regular on TV series A Different World, NBC, 1987-91, The Sinbad Show, 1993, (host) Vibe, 1997-98, Hollywood Squares, 1998, other TV appearances include Starch Search (winner stand-up comedian competition 1984), The Cosby Show, Keep on Cruisin, The Redd Foxx Show, Cosby, 1998, 99, Moesha, 2000; occasional co-host Showtime at the Apollo; toured with The Pointer Sisters, Anita Baker, Luther Vandross, Smokey Robinson; appeared in films including That's Adequate, 1989, Necessary Roughness, 1991, Meteor Man, 1993, Coneheads, 1993, Houseguest, 1994, Jingle All The Way, 1996, (voice) Homeward Bound II: Lost in San Francisco, 1996, First Kid, 1996, Good Burger, 1997, Crazy as Hell, 2002, (voice) Hansel & Gretel, 2002, Treading Water, 2002; TV movies: Ready to Run, 2000; author: Sinbad's Guide to Life. Active USAF, to 1983. Address: 12031 Ventura Blvd #3 Studio City CA 91604-2636

**SINCLAIR, ALASTAIR JAMES,** geology educator; b. Hamilton, Ont., Can., Aug. 1, 1935; s. Burton Leslie and Grace (Isherwood) S.; m. Elizabeth Mary Sylvia Hill, June 13, 1964; children: Alison Trevena, Fiona Tamsin. BS, U. Toronto, Can., 1957, MS, 1958; PhD, U. B.C., Can., 1964. Asst. prof. U. Wash., Seattle, 1962-64, U. B.C., Vancouver, 1964-68, assoc. prof., 1968-74, prof., 1974-98, prof. emeritus, 1999—, head dept. geol. scis., 1985-90, dir. Geol. Engring., 1979-80, 81-82, 92-98. Pres. Sinclair Cons. Ltd., Vancouver, 1980—, Internat. Croesus Venture Corp., 2004—. Author: Applied Mineral Inventory Estimation, 2002, Applied Ore Microscopy and Minerolography, 2003, Quality Control of Assay Data, 2004; contbr. numerous articles to profl. jours. Killam Sr. fellow, 1990—91. Fellow Geol. Assn. Can. (treas. mineral deposits divsn. 1978-89, Disting. Svc. award 2001), Soc. Econ. Geologists; mem. Assn. Profl. Engrs. B.C., Assn. Exploration Geochemists (councillor 1992-96), Can. Inst. Mining, Metallurgy and Petroleum (life, disting. lectr. 1999-2000, Robert Elver award 1991), Geol. Soc. Brazil (hon. mem. sci.-tech. commn. geochemistry 1982), Brazilian Geochem. Soc. (hon.). Avocations: classical music, skiing, travel. Home: 2972 W 44th Ave Vancouver BC Canada V6N 3K4 Office: U BC Dept Earth and Ocean Scis Vancouver BC Canada V6T 1Z4 Office Phone: 604-822-3086. Personal E-mail: ajsincon@shaw.ca. Business E-Mail: asinclair@eos.ubc.ca.

**SINCLAIR, CAMERON,** architect; b. London, 1973; BArch, U. Westminster, London; student, Bartlett Sch. Architecture, London. Arch. Lauster and Radu Archs.; project arch. Gensler; co-founder, exec. dir. Architecture for Humanity, 1999—. Adj. prof. Mont. State U. Sch. Architecture; Cass Gilbert vis. prof. U. Minn. Coll. Architecture and Landscape Architecture, 2006; mem. adv. bd. Detroit Collaborative Design Ctr., Kids With Cameras, NYC. Internat. lectr.; co-editor: Design Like You Give a Damn, 2006. Co-recipient WIRED Rave award-Architecture, 2006; recipient Nice Modernist award, Dwell Mag., 2003, Design for Humanity award, Am. Soc. Interior Designers, 2004, TED prize, 2006. Achievements include providing design services to communities in need; selection as one of the Aspen Seven, Fortune Mag., 2004; selection as one of the Fast 50, Fast Co. Mag., 2004.*

**SINCLAIR, CAROL ANN,** accountant, consultant; d. Edward Norman and Doris Mae Nowicki; m. Harold Richard Sinclair, Apr. 7, 1972; children: Matthew John, Catherine Carol, Elizabeth Ann. BA in Acctg. with honors, St. Leo U., Fla., 2004; BA in Art Direction/Design with honors, Coll. Creative Studies, Detroit, 1990. Art dir., designer and illustrator Young & Rubicam Ltd., Detroit, 1992—94, Stone & Simon Advt. Agy., Southfield, 1994—96; acct. accounts receivable nat. accounts Manpower Metro Detroit, Inc., Southfield, 1996—99; acct. Lincare, Inc., Clearwater, Fla., 2000—. Cons. Grosse Pointe Artists Assn., Grosse Pointe, Mich., 1980—95, Assistance League to NE Guidance Ctr., Detroit, 1982—96. Supporting mem. Gulf Coast Mus. Arts, Largo, Fla., 2000—. Recipient Tiffany award, Manpower Metro Detroit, Inc., 1999, Eagle award, 1999, Peer award. Mem.: Nat. Mus. Women in the Arts, Founders Soc. Detroit Inst. Arts, Grosse Pointe Arts Coun. (bd. mem.), Detroit Soc. Women Painters and Sculptors (bd. mem.), Mich. Watercolor Soc. (bd. mem.), Grosse Pointe Artists Assn. (bd. mem.). Avocations: genealogy, reading, travel. Office Phone: 727-431-8316.

**SINCLAIR, CAROLE,** publishing executive, editor; b. Haddonfield, N.J., May 13, 1942; d. Earl Walter and Ruth (Sinclair) Dunham; 1 child, Wendy. Student, U. Florence, Italy, 1963; BA in Polit. Sci., Bucknell U., 1964. Advt. copywriter BBD&O Advertising, N.Y.C., 1966-67; sales promotion mgr. Macmillan Pub. Co., N.Y.C., 1967-71; mktg. mgr. Doubleday & Co., Inc., N.Y.C., 1972-74, promotion dir., 1974-76, advt. mgr., sales and promotion, chmn. mktg. com., 1976-80; v.p. mktg., editorial dir. Davis Pubs., N.Y.C., 1980-83; founder, pub., editorial dir., sr. v.p. Sylvia Porter's Personal Fin. Mag., N.Y.C., 1983-90; pres. The Sylvia Porter Orgn., Inc., N.Y.C., 1980—; founder, pres. Sinclair Media Inc., N.Y.C., 1990—. Mktg. dir. Denver Pub. Inst., summers 1975-78; lectr. Columbia U. Bus. Sch. and Sch. of Journalism, 1976; host nationally syndicated TV show, Sylvia Porter's Money Tips, syndicated daily radio show, Sylvia Porter's Personal Fin. Report, audio cassette series on fin. topics. Author: Keys for Women Starting and Owning a Business, 1991, Keys to Women's Basic Professional Needs, 1991, When Women Retire, 1992; contbg. editor Pushcart Prize, 1977; contbr. The Business of Publishing, 1980. Renaissance Art Program fellow, Florence, Italy, 1963; White House intern, 1962. Mem. Women's Forum, Intercorp. Communications Group, Mag. Pubs.' Assn., Advt. Women in N.Y., Spence Sch. Parent's League. Clubs: Pubs. Lunch. Presbyterian. Avocation: boating.

**SINCLAIR, DAISY,** communications executive; b. Perth Amboy, N.J., Mar. 22, 1941; d. James Patrick and Margaret Mary (McAniff) Nieland; m. James Pratt Sinclair, May 25, 1978; children: Duncan, Gibbons. BA, Caldwell Coll., 1962. Jr. copywriter Young & Rubican, N.Y.C., 1962-64; various positions in casting dept. Ogilvy & Mather, N.Y.C., 1964-90; v.p. dir. casting, 1990—. Mem.: Drama League N.Y. (3d v.p. 1982—), Am. Assn. Advt. (talent agt. com. 1972—), N.Y. Yacht Club, Union Club, Tuxedo Club, Chapaquoit Yacht Club, Edgartown Yacht Club, Knickerbocker Greys (pres.). Republican. Episcopalian. Avocations: opera, theater, sailing, skiing. Home: 4 E 95th St New York NY 10128-0705

**SINCLAIR, GLENN BRUCE,** mechanical engineering educator, researcher; b. Auckland, New Zealand, Mar. 7, 1946; came to U.S., 1969; s. Alan John and Piri (Vincent) S.; m. Della Jane Sutton, Dec. 23, 1972; children— Heidi Lee, Heather Ann, Hillary Colleen, Christopher Alan B.Sc., U. Auckland, 1967, B.E., 1969; PhD, Calif. Inst. Tech., 1972. J. Willard Gibbs instr. mech. engring. Yale U., New Haven, 1972-74; lectr. U. Auckland, 1974-77; asst. prof. Carnegie-Mellon U., Pitts., 1977-80, assoc. prof., 1980-82, prof., 1982-2000, head, 1986-92; vis. prof. Cambridge U., England, 1981; Junneau prof. La. State U., Baton Rouge, 2000—, chmn. dept. mech. engring., 2000—. Research scientist Dept. Sci. and Indsl. Research, Wellington, New Zealand, 1968-69; summer prof. Pratt & Whitney, Hartford, Conn., 1978, Aircraft Corp., West Palm Beach, Fla., 1979; cons. in field. Contbr. articles to profl. jours. Fulbright scholar, 1969-72. Mem. Am. Acad. Mechanics Office: La State U Dept Mech Engring Baton Rouge LA 70803 Office Phone: 225-578-5899. Business E-Mail: sinclair@me.lsu.edu.

**SINCLAIR, JAMES BURTON,** retired plant pathology educator, consultant; b. Chgo., Dec. 21, 1927; s. James Lawrence Sinclair and Helen Marie (Thompson) Owens. BSc, Lawrence U., 1957; PhD, U. Wis., 1955. Grad. rsch. asst. U. Wis., Madison, 1951-55, grad. rsch. assoc., 1955-56; from asst. prof. to assoc. prof. La. State U., Baton Rouge, 1956-65, prof., 1965-68, adminstrv. asst. to chancellor, 1966-68; prof. U. Ill., Urbana, 1968-96, dir. nat. soybean rsch. lab., 1992-96; ret. Co-author: Basic Plant Pathology Methods, 1985, 1995, Principles of Seed Pathology, 1987, 1997, Anatomy and Physiology of Diseased Plants, 1991; contbr. articles to profl. jours. Pres. bd. dirs. W.R. and C.V. Spurlock Mus., Urbana, 1998-00; sec., editor Greater Cmty. AIDS Project, 1996-00; mem. Econ. Devel. Com., Savoy, 2003-; mem. fin. planning com. Carle Hospice, 2001-02; mem. (docent), dir bd. Spurlock Mus. World Culture, 1998-; mem. Coun. Krannert Art Mus. and Kincaid Pavilion, 1998-, docent; mem. Village Savoy Econ. Devel. Com., 2004-. Sgt. US Army, 1946-47. Recipient Soybean Rsch. Recognition award, Am. Soybean Assn., 1983, Prodn. Rsch. award, 1989, Paul A. Funk award, 1984, Disting. Svc. award, USDA, 1988, Phytopathol. Soc. (north ctrl. divsn.), 1991, Rsch. award, Land of Lincoln Soybean Assn., 1992, Lucia R. Briggs Disting. Achievement award, Lawrence U., 2001. Fellow Am. Phytopathol. Soc., Nat. Acad. Scis. (India); mem. Ill. Crop Improvement Assn. (hon.), Am. Soc. Agronomy (hon.) Rotary (chmn. internat. com. Savoy chpt. 1990-91, v.p. 1991-93, pres. 1993-94, chmn. club svc. conf. 2003-04). Home: 408 Arbours Dr Savoy IL 61874-9752 Business E-Mail: jsinclai@uiuc.edu.

**SINCLAIR, KENT,** law educator; b. San Diego, July 8, 1946; s. Kent and Ruth Melva (Wilson) S.; m. Kathryn Spining; children: S. Scott, Keith A. AB, U. Calif., Santa Barbara, 1968; JD, U. Calif. Berkeley, 1971. Bar: Calif. 1972, US Dist. Ct. So. Dist. NY 1972, US Ct. Appeals 2nd Cir. 1972, NY 1973, Va. 1986, US Supreme Ct. 1990. Law clk. to judge James Browning US Ct. Appeals 9th Cir., San Francisco, 1971-72, chief staff atty., 1972; atty. Shearman & Sterling, NYC, 1972—76; US Magistrate Judge US Dist. Ct. So. Dist. NY, NYC, 1976—83; assoc. prof. U. Va. Sch. Law, Charlottesville, 1983—88, prof., 1988—, dir. advocacy and lawyer training, 1983—, assoc. dean, 1990—93. Adj. prof. Fordham U., 1973-83; spl. master US Dist. Ct. So. Dist. NY, 1983-88; dep. spl. master US Supreme Ct., 1989-94; reporter decisions Va. Supreme Ct., Richmond, 1984-; founding dir. Va. Judicial Inst., Charlottesville, 1984-92. Edn. dir. Va. State Bar, 1983-89, mem. Mem. Am. Law Inst., Va. Bar Assn. Avocation: computers. Office: U Va Sch Law 580 Massie Rd Charlottesville VA 22903-1789 Office Phone: 434-924-4663. E-mail: ks3r@virginia.edu.

**SINCLAIR, LINDA DRUMWRIGHT,** educational consultant; b. Norfolk, Va., Aug. 4, 1942; d. Raymond Edward and Evelyn Elizabeth (Edwards) Drumwright; m. Charles Armstrong Sinclair, Oct. 5, 1962; children: William, Dianne, Sandy. BS, U. S.C., 1974, MA, 1976, postgrad. Cert. tchr. in biology, chemistry, physics. Sci. tchr. Keenan H.S., Columbia, S.C., 1976-77; chemistry/physics tchr. Lexington (S.C.) H.S., 1977-93; talented/gifted tchr. U. S.C., Columbia, 1988; tchr. rsch. program Oak Ridge (Tenn.) Nat. Lab., 1989; rschr. Savannah River Ecology Lab., Aiken, S.C., 1991-92; state sci. edn. cons. S.C. Dept. Edn., Columbia, 1993—. Cons. Prentice Hall Pub., Princeton, N.J., 1992-93. Author: Operation Radon, 1993. Adv. bd. S.C. Forestry Common., Columbia, 1993—, S.C. Environ. Coalition, Columbia, 1993—, S.C. Sci. Coun., Columbia, 1989—; mem., com. chair Lexington Woman's Club, 1986—; v.p. Lexington Garden Club, 1983—. Named S.C. Sci. Tchr. of the Yr., S.C. Acad. Sci., 1986, Sigma Xi, 1986, S.C. Chemistry Tchr. of the Yr., S.C. Chem. Soc., 1992; recipient Presdl. Award for Excellence in Sci. Teaching, NSF, 1993. Mem. S.C. Sci. Coun. (v.p., pres.), S.C. Chemistry Tchrs. Assn. (bd. dirs. 1987—), S.C. Acad. Sci. (bd. dirs. 1982—), Sci. Jr. Acad. Sci. (bd. dirs. 1990—), S.C. Environ. Edn. Assn. (bd. dirs. 1990—), Nat. Sci. Tchrs. Assn. (bd. dirs. 1992-94). Lutheran. Avocations: horseback riding, gardening, swimming, water sports. Home: 107 Hermitage Rd Lexington SC 29072-2221 Office: SC Dept Edn 801-B Rutledge Bldg 1429 Senate St Columbia SC 29201-3730 Office Phone: 803-734-0887. Business E-Mail: lsinclai@sde.state.sc.us.

**SINCLAIR, LOUIS,** artist, writer; s. Louis and Rosa Sinclair; 1 child, Owen. MFA, Goddard Coll., 1994. Exhibitions include Farnsworth Mus. (Royal Trust Can. award for Painting, 1976), Bowdoin Coll., U. So. Maine Gallery, Farmington Gallery, U. Maine, Art in Embassies, Nat. Endowment for the Arts, Can. Embassy, Royal Hibernian Acad., Ireland, Nat. Gallery Ireland, Oliver Dowling Gallery, Ireland, United Arts Club, Lincoln Gallery, Robinson Gallery, Ulster Arts Club, Walker Gallery, Moore Gallery; contbr. of poetry and writing in field to various mags. and newspapers. Bd. dirs. Maine Coalition for the Homeless, Augusta, 1988—92; mem. ordinance rev. com. Town of Windham, Maine, 2006—; mem. Task Force for Windham's Future, 2006—; nat. officer Vets. For Peace Inc., 1986—93; pres. Maine Adult Edn. Assn., 1969—70, co-founder, 1969—70; artist assoc. mem. Farnsworth Mus., 2004—. Sgt. U.S. Army, 1963—66, Korea. Mem.: Contemporary Irish Art Soc., Artists Group, United Arts Club. Independent. Avocations: Tae Soo Do, antiques, music, art, reading. Mailing: PO Box 1326 Raymond ME 04071

**SINCLAIR, ROBERT EWALD,** retired physician; b. Columbus, Jan. 19, 1924; s. George Albert and Bertha Florence (Ewald) S.; m. Mary Almira Underwood, Mar. 31, 1945; children: Marcia Ann, Bonnie Sue. BA, Ohio State U., Columbus, 1948; MD, Ohio State U., 1952. Lic. physician, Ohio, Colo., Ala., Kans. Intern Mt. Carmel Hosp., Columbus, 1952—53; resident neurology and psychiatry Columbus State Hosp., 1964—66, chief psychiat. resident adolescent unit, 1965—66; pvt. practice medicine Columbus, 1953—57, Granville, Ohio, 1957—64; dir. student health svc., prof. health edn., team physician Denison U., 1957—64; dir. student health svc., team physician U. Cin., 1966—70; dir. Lafene Student Health Ctr. and U. Hosp.; team physician Kans. State U., Manhattan, 1970—80; dir. Russell Student Health Ctr. and Hosp.; prof. medicine U. Ala., University, 1980—88, ret., 1988. Physician Westinghouse Electric Corp., Columbus, 1953-57; asst. zone chief Civilian Def., Columbus, 1954-57; mem. Licking County Bd. Health, Ohio, 1958-59. Bd. dirs. social health com. Cin. and Hamilton County, Ohio, 1967-70, drug abuse and edn. com., 1968-70. With USNR, 1943-46. Mem. AMA, Ohio Med. Soc., Kans. Med. Soc., Ala. Med. Soc., Columbus Acad. Medicine, Licking County Med. Soc., Riley County Med. Soc. (Kans.), Tuscaloosa County Med. Soc., Nat. Athletic Trainers Assn., Ohio Coll. Health Assn. (editor Newsletter 1968-70, pres. 1970-71), Central Coll. Health Assn. (pres. 1972-73), So. Coll. Health Assn. (pres. 1986), St. Andrews Soc., So. Medicine Assn., Delta Tau Delta (faculty advisor), Nu Sigma Nu, Nu Sigma Nu Alumni Assn. (pres. 1953-54), Kiwanis, Rotary. Home: 1 Rollingwood Tuscaloosa AL 35406-2261 Personal E-mail: unsink2@aol.com.

**SINCLAIR, ROLF MALCOLM,** retired physicist; b. N.Y.C., Aug. 15, 1929; s. Nathan and Elizabeth S.; m. Margaret Lee Andrews, June 13, 1959 (div. 1978); children: Elizabeth Ann, Andrew Caisley; m. Allyn J. Miner, July 29, 1991 (div. 1998); m. Sarah Richards, Mar. 18, 2004. BS, Calif. Inst. Tech., 1949; MA (Reade scholar), Rice U., 1951, PhD (Inst. fellow), 1954. Physicist Westinghouse Rsch. Labs., 1953—56; vis. scientist U. Hamburg, Germany, 1956—57, U. Paris, 1957—58, U.K. Atomic Energy Authority, Culham Lab., England, 1965—66; rsch. physicist Princeton U., 1958—69; program dir. NSF, Washington, 1969—98; ret., 1998. Mem. Solstice Project, 1978-91; NSF rep. U.S. Solar Eclipse Expdn. to Can., 1979, to India, 1980, Amundsen-Scott South Pole Sta., 1995, 96; Disting. vis. prof. N.Mex. State U., 1985; vis. prof. No. Ariz. U., 1986; vis. scientist Los Alamos Nat. Lab., 1988-89, guest scientist, 1989—; cons. to industry, 1960-69, 98—; sr. advisor Centro de Estudios Cientificos, Valdivia, Chile, 1999—. Fellow Am. Phys. Soc. (panel pub. affairs 1976-77, nominating com. 1988-90), AAAS (sec. physics sect. 1972-2000, chair 2005—2006, ret. chair 2006-2007, coun. 1972-73, nominating com. 1982-83); mem. Soc. Am. Archaeology, Sigma Xi. Achievements include research and publs. on physics, archaeoastronomy, tech. and instrumentation. Home: 7508 Tarrytown Rd Chevy Chase MD 20815-6027 E-mail: rolf@santafe.edu.

**SINCLAIR, WILLIAM DONALD,** state legislator, retired church official; b. LA, Dec. 27, 1924; s. Arthur Livingston and Lillian May (Holt) S.; m. Barbara Jean Hughes, Aug. 9, 1952; children: Paul Scott, Victoria Sharon. BA cum laude, St. Martin's Coll., Olympia, Wash., 1975; postgrad., Emory U., 1978-79. Commd. 2d lt. USAAF, 1944; advanced through grades to col. USAF, 1970; served as pilot and navigator Italy, Korea, Vietnam, Japan; ret., 1975; bus. adminstr. 1st United Meth. Ch., Colorado Springs, Colo., 1978-85, Village Seven Presbyn. Ch., 1985-87, Sunrise United Meth. Ch., 1987-89; vice chmn. coun. fin. and adminstrn. Rocky Mountain Conf., United Meth. Ch. U.S.A., 1979-83; mem. Colo. Ho. of Reps., Denver, 1996—, majority whip, 2001—. Pres. Pioneers Mus. Found., 1985—; Rep. candidate for Colo. State Chmn., 1992—93; chmn. bd. dir. Pikes Peak Performing Arts Ctr., 1985—92; bd. dir. Chins Up, Colorado Springs, Colo., 1983—86, Prostate Cancer Edn. Coun., 2000—. Decorated Legion of Merit with oak leaf cluster, DFC, Air medal with six oak leaf clusters, Dept. Def. Meritorious Svc. medal, Vietnam Cross of Gallantry with palms; named Legislator of Yr., Colo. Assn. Commerce and Industry, 1998—99, Colo. Sheriff's Assn., 2001; recipient Frying Pan award, Colo. Restaurant Assn., 1999, 2003, Guardian Small Bus. award, Nat. Fedn. Ind. Bus., 1999—2001, 2003, 2004, Disting. Legislator award, United Vets. Com. of Colo., 2002, Common Sense in the Courtroom award, Colo. Civil Justice League, 2003, 2004, Legis. Yr. award, Colorado Springs C. of C., 2004. Fellow Ch. Bus. Adminstrn. Nat. Assn. (nat. dir., regional v.p., v.p. 1983-85, pres. 1985-87, Ch. Bus. Adminstr. of Yr. award 1983, inducted into Hall of Fame 1995), Colo. Assn. Ch. Bus. Adminstrs. (past pres.), United Meth. Assn. Ch. Bus. Adminstrs. (nat. sec. 1978-81), Christian Ministries Mgmt. Assn. (dir. 1983-85), USAF Acad. Athletic Assn., Colorado Springs Country Club, Garden of Gods Club, Winter Night Club, Rotary (pres. Colorado Springs 1985-86), Order of Daedalians, Tower Club (Dallas). Home: 3007 Chelton Dr Colorado Springs CO 80909-1008

**SINCLITICO, DENNIS J.,** lawyer; b. St. Louis, Jan. 2, 1947. BA, U. San Diego, 1968; JD cum laude, U. Wis., 1971. Bar: Wis. 1971, Calif. 1972, US Dist. Ct. (cen. and so. dists.) Calif. 1972. Prof. Calif. Coll. Law, 1972; ptnr. Sinclitico & Burns PLC, Long Beach, Calif. Arbitrator spl. arbitration plan Los Angeles County Superior Ct., 1975—. Mem. Am. Bd. Trial Advocates (nat. exec. com. 1998—, pres. L.A. chpt., editor newsletter), Long Beach Bar Assn., State Bar Wis., State Bar Calif., Assn. So. Calif. Def. Counsel (program chmn. 1980-81, bd. dirs. 1980—), Cal-Abota (chair 1994), Ball-Hunt Ins of Ct. (barrister), Phi Alpha Delta. Office: Sinclitico & Burns PLC 330 Golden Shore # 410 Long Beach CA 90802 Office Phone: 562-628-1919. Business E-Mail: dsinclitico@sin-burns.com.

**SINCOFF, MICHAEL Z.,** human resources and marketing executive; b. Washington, June 28, 1943; s. Murray P. and Anna F. (Jaffe) S. m. Kathleen M. Dunham, Oct. 9, 1983. BA, U. Md., 1964, MA, 1966; PhD, Purdue U., 1969. Instr. U. Tenn., Knoxville, 1968; asst. prof. Ohio U., Athens, 1969-74, dir. Ctr. for Comm. Studies, 1969-76, assoc. prof., 1974-76; vis. prof. U. Minn., St. Paul, 1974; dir. personnel devel. Celanese Corp., NYC, 1976-79; dir. employee comm. The Mead Corp., Dayton, Ohio, 1979-81, dir. edn. and tng., 1981-83; assoc. dean Sch. of Bus. Adminstrn., Georgetown U., Washington, 1983-84; v.p. human resources ADVO-Sys., Hartford, Conn., 1984—87; v.p. human resources, corp. officer DIMAC Direct Inc., St. Louis, 1987-88; sr. v.p. human resources and adminstrn., sr. corp. officer DIMAC Mktg. Corp. (parent of DIMAC Direct Inc.), St. Louis, 1988-97, also sec., asst. treas., exec. com., 1988-97; sr. v.p. human resources, exec. corp. officer Brooks Fiber Properties, Inc., St. Louis, 1997-98; pres., CEO Michaelson Group Ptnrs., Dayton, Ohio, 1969—. Vis. prof. Wright State U., Dayton, Ohio, 1999-2001, assoc. prof., 2001—; assoc. grad. faculty mem. Ctrl. Mich. U., Mt. Pleasant, 1999—. Author, editor human resources sect. Am. Mgmt. Assn. Mgmt. Handbook, 3d edit.; author approximately 50 books and articles; mem. edtl. adv. bd. Jour. Applied Comm. Rsch., 1991-97. Life mem. Internat. Comm. Assn. (bus. mgr.-exec. sec. 1969-73, fin. com. 1982-85); mem. Am. Mgmt. Assn. (human resources coun. 1990-2000), Printing Industries of Am. (employer resources group 1989-97).

**SINCOSKIE, W. DAVID,** computer engineer; Degree, U. Del. Rsch. scientist Bellcore; v.p. applied rsch. Internet Arch. Rsch. Lab. Telcordia Techs., Inc., Morristown, N.J. Cons. in field; adviser to Taiwan govt. on devel.

of NII; mem. panel high performance computer and comm. initiative NRC; adj. prof. computer and info. sci. U. Del.; mem. adv. com. dean engring. U Pa. Fellow IEEE; mem. NAE, Internet Soc., Def. Advanced Rsch. Projects Agy., Info. Scis. and Tech. Com. Achievements include leading team that produced the experimental Sunshine ATM switch; building of ethernet-based packet telephones; inventor set of extensions to self-learning bridges known as VLANs. Office: Telcordia Techs 1 Telcordia Dr Piscataway NJ 08854-4151

**SINDEN, HARRY,** professional sports team executive; b. Collins Bay, Ont., Can., Sept. 14, 1932; m. Eleanor Sinden; children: Nancy, Carol, Donna, Julie. Defenseman Oshawa Generals, 1951—53, Whitby Dunlops, 1956—59, Hull-Ottawa Canadiens, 1959—60, Kingston Frontenacs, 1960—63, Minneapolis Bruins, 1963—65, Oklahoma City Blazers, 1965—66; head coach Minneapolis Bruins, 1966—70, Boston Bruins, 1966—70, 1979, 1984, gen. mgr., 1972—2000, pres., alt. gov., 1989—2006, sr. advisor to owner, 2006—; chmn. TD Banknorth Garden, Boston, 2002—. Coach Team Can., Summit Series, 1972; mem. bd. dirs. Hockey Hall of Fame. Named to Hockey Hall of Fame, 1983, Internat. Ice Hockey Fedn. Hall of Fame, 1997; recipient Lester Patrick Award, 1999. Achievements include being the coach of Stanley Cup Champion Boston Bruins, 1970. Office: Boston Profl Hockey Assn, Inc TD Banknorth Garden 100 Legends Way Boston MA 02114*

**SINDLER, ALLAN JAY,** chemical engineer, sculptor, educator; b. Bishopville, SC, Oct. 23, 1925; s. Frank and Pauline Ruth Sindler; m. Sophie Payeff Sindler, June 17, 1951; children: Robert, Marc, Michael. BS in Chemistry, U. S.C., 1944, BS in Chem. Engring., 1948, EdM in Pub. Sch. Adminstrn., 1951, postgrad., 1977—81, Stanford U., 1950, U. Del., 1962—64. Registered profl. engr., Del., S.C., 1967. Chem. engr., supr. Du Plan Corp., Winston-Salem, NC, 1948—49; tchr. Dreher H.S., Columbia, SC, 1949—52; chem. engr. E.I. duPont, Inc., Camden, SC, 1952—84, Newark, 1960—65; tchr. Camden H.S., 1984—87; cons., prof. sculptor S.C. Arts Commn., Columbia, 1987—99; founder S.C. Sculptor Orgn. Bd. dirs. Fine Arts Ctr. Kershaw County, Camden. Contbr. articles to several mags. Pres. ARC-Kershaw County Chpt., 1967—68; mem. adv. bd. Kershaw County Detention Ctr., Camden, 2002—; founder, chmn. Save Camden R.R. Sta.; adv. bd. food shelter, Price House, Camden, SC; founder Bi-Racial Forum, Camden; campaign mgr., del. S.C. Dems., 1952—. 2d lt. U.S. Army, 1945—46, ETO, 1st lt. USAR, 1st lt. S.C. N.G. Named Outstanding Young Man in S.C., S.C. Jaycees, 1956; recipient Disting. Svc. award, Camden Jaycees, 1956, medal, Freedom Found., 1956, award, Valley Forge Freedom Found., 1956. Mem.: S.C. Soc. Engrs. (v.p.), Smithsonian Inst. Com. (del. 1990, chmn. save outdoor sculpture Kershaw County 1990), Tri State Sculptors Guild (chair ann. show 1982—). Jewish And Unitarian. Avocations: swimming, diving, writing, architecture, theater. Home: 2006 N Brailsford Rd Camden SC 29020 Office: Sculptured Products Co 2006 N Brailsford Rd Camden SC 29020 Office Phone: 803-432-4865.

**SINDU, PRADEEP,** information technology executive; b. India, 1953; married; 2 children. BA in Electrical Engring., Indian Inst. Tech., Kampur, India; MA in Electrical Engring., U. Hawaii; PhD in Computer Sci., Carnegie Mellon U. Rsch. staff computer sci. lab Xerox Corp., Palo Alto, 1984—91, prin. scientist computer sci. lab, 1987—96, disting. engr. computer sci. lab, 1994—96; vice chmn., CTO, founder Juniper, 1996—. Bd. dirs. Infinera Corp. Achievements include work on design tools that lead to Sun Microsystems first high-performance memory multiprocessors. Mailing: 1194 N Mathilda Ave Sunnyvale CA 94089

**SINEATH, TIMOTHY WAYNE,** librarian, educator, dean; b. Jacksonville, Fla., May 21, 1940; s. Holcombe Asbury and Christine Marcel (Cook) S.; m. Patricia Ann Greenwood, June 8, 1962; children: Philip Greenwood, Paul Byron. BA, Fla. State U., 1962, MS, 1963; PhD (Higher Edn. Act fellow), U. Ill., 1970. Reference librarian U. Ga., 1963-64, catalog librarian, 1964-66; acad. coordinator continuing edn. in library sci. U. Ill., 1966-68; asst. prof. library sci. Simmons Coll., 1970-74, coordinator doctoral program, 1974-77; prof., dean Coll. Libr. Sci. and Info. Sci., U. Ky., Lexington, 1977-87, prof., 1987-97, dir. sch. Libr. and Info. Sci., 1997—. Cons. to libraries, schs., chs., industry; mem. Lexington (Ky.) Public Library Bd., 1978— Author profl. reports; contbr. articles on library and info. sci., gen. info. mgmt., organizational and small group behavior to profl. jours. Mem. ALA, Am. Soc. Info. Sci. and Tech., Assn. for Libr. and Info. Sci. Edn. (pres. 1993). Episcopalian. Home: 3418 Bay Leaf Dr Lexington KY 40502-3804 Office: U Ky M King Bldg Lexington KY 40506-0039 E-mail: tsineath@uky.edu.

**SINEGAL, JAMES D.,** wholesale distribution executive; b. 1936; BA, San Diego State U., 1959. With Fed-Mart Corp., 1954-77, exec. v.p.; v.p. Builders Enporium, 1977-78; exec. v.p. Price Co., 1978-79; with Sinegal/Chamberlin & Assocs., 1979-83; COO Costco Wholesale Corp., Issaquah, Wash., 1983—93, pres., 1993—, CEO, 1988—, bd. dirs. Named one of 100 Most Influential People, Time mag., 2006. Address: Costco Wholesale PO Box 34331 999 Lake Dr Ste 200 Issaquah WA 98027-8982*

**SINEL, NORMAN MARK,** lawyer; b. New Haven, Dec. 8, 1941; s. Nathan and Mona S.; m. Ellen Winnick, June 16, 1963; children— Joshua, Natasha. BA, Yale U., 1963; LL.B., Stanford U., 1966. Bar: Calif. 1967, D.C. 1968. Law clk. to Judge Weigel, Dist. Ct. No. Dist., Calif., 1966-67; assoc. firm Wilmer, Cutler & Pickering, Washington, 1967-71; gen. counsel Public Broadcasting Service, Washington, 1971-73, v.p., gen. counsel, 1973-76, sr. v.p. for corp. mgmt., gen. counsel, 1976-79; ptnr., Transneon Broadcasting Corp., Washington, 1979—. Mem. Calif. Bar Assn., D.C. Bar Assn. Office: Arnold & Porter 555 12th St NW Washington DC 20004-1206 Office Phone: 202-942-5222. Office Fax: 202-942-5999. Business E-Mail: norman.sinel@aporter.com

**SINENKO, SERGEY A.,** biologist, geneticist, researcher; arrived in U.S., 2000; s. Galina Petrovna and Anatolii Grigorievich Sinenko. MS in Biology, Genetics and Molecular Biology, Al-Farabi Kazakh State U., 1994; PhD, Inst. Molecular Biology Biochemistry, Almaty, Kazakhstan, 1999. Postdoctoral rsch. assoc. Dana-Farber Cancer Inst., Boston, 2000—04, UCLA, 2004—. Recipient The best study of young scientist in immunology award, Collegium of Ministry of Sci./Acad. of Sci. Republic of Kazakhstan, 1997; scholar, Biol. Rsch. Ctr. of Hungarian Acad. of Sciences, 1999—2000. Mem.: Genetic Soc. of Am. Democrat. Achievements include discovery of Yantar, a conserved arginine-rich protein that is involved in Drosophila hemocyte development; research in increased expression of Drosophila tetraspanin, Tsp68C, suppresses the abnormal proliferation of ytr-deficient and Ras/Raf-activated hemocytes. Office: University of California Los Angeles 621 Charles E Young Drive LSB 2204 Los Angeles CA 90095 Personal E-mail: s_sinenko@yahoo.com. E-mail: sinenko@mcdb.ucla.edu.

**SINES, RANDY DWAIN,** retail executive; b. Spokane, Jan. 16, 1948; s. Myron Jones and Paula Inez (Walls) S.; m. Irene Cheng, Mar. 18, 1981. Student, Wash. State U., 1966—67, U. Wash., 1968—69. Lic. water well contractor, Wash., Mont. With Boeing Co., 1967, Winchell's Donut House, Inc., Seattle, 1968—71; owner, mgr. bakeries Wash. and Mont., 1972—78; owner, mgr. Sonsine Inc., Great Falls, Mont., 1976—79; pres. Gardian Port Corp., Oxnard, Calif., 1980—82; pres., chmn. SNS Motor Imports, Inc., Oxnard, 1982—86; chmn. Karakal Corp. of Ams., Ventura, Calif., 1986—89; CEO, chmn. Steel Stix, U.S.A., 1990—; chmn. MITT U.S.A. Corp., 1991—; mng. ptnr. Sharps Internat., 1999—. CEO Casinovations Inc., 1995-96; founder, CEO Inven Corp., Spokane, 1996-97; chmn. Digideal Corp., Las Vegas, 1998-2005; chmn. eCardless Bancorp., Spokane, 2000-; CEO Veri-Card, Inc., Spokane, 2000-. Holder more than 50 utility patents. Recipient alumni grant Wash. State U., 1967. Home: 4056 S Madelia St Spokane WA 99203-4227 E-mail: rsincs@digideal.com

**SINFELT, JOHN HENRY,** chemist; b. Munson, Pa., Feb. 18, 1931; s. Henry Gustave and June Lillian (McDonald) Sinfelt; m. Muriel Jean Vadersen, July 14, 1956; 1 child, Klaus Herbert. BS, Pa. State U., 1951; PhD, U. Ill., 1954, DSc (hon.), 1981. Research engr. Exxon Research Engring. Co., Linden, NJ,

1954—57, sr. research engr., 1957—62, research assoc., 1962—68, sr. research assoc., 1968—72, sci. advisor, 1972—79, sr. sci. advisor, 1979—96, sr. sci. advisor emeritus, 1996—. Vis. prof. chem. engring. U. Minn., 1969; Lacey lectr. Calif. Inst. Tech., 1973; Reilly lectr. U. Notre Dame, 1974; Frontiers in Chemistry lectr. Case Western Res. U., Cleve., 1978; Matthew Van Winkle lectr. U. Tex., 1979, disting. vis. lectr. in chemistry, 81; Francois Gault lectr. catalysis Coun. Europe Rsch. Group Catalysis, 1980; Mobay lectr. in chemistry U. Pitts., 1980; Robert Welch Found. lectr. Confs. on Chem. Rsch., 1981; Camille and Henry Dreyfus lectr. UCLA, 1982; Edward Clark Lee Meml. lectr. U. Chgo., 1983; Dow disting. lectr. in chemistry Mich. State U., 1984; Arthur D. Little lectr. Northeastern U., 1985; Vollmer W. Fries lectr. Rensselaer Poly. Inst., 1986; disting. lectr. Ctr. Chem. Physics U. Fla., 1988; David M. Mason lectr. Stanford U., 1995, cons. prof. dept. chem. engring., 1996—. Contbr. articles to profl. jours. Named to Nat'l Inventors Hall of Fame, 1991; recipient Dickson prize, Carnegie-Mellon U., 1977, Internat. prize for new materials, Am. Phys. Soc., 1978, Nat. medal of sci., 1979, Perkin medal in chemistry, Soc. Chem. Industry, 1984, Disting. Alumnus award, Pa. State U., 1985. Fellow: AIChE (Alpha Chi Sigma award 1971, Profl. Progress award 1975), Am. Inst. Chemists (Chem. Pioneer award 1981, Gold medal 1984), Am. Acad. Arts and Scis.; mem.: NAE, NAS (award for indsl. application of sci. 1996), Am. Philos. Soc., Catalysis Soc. (Emmett award 1973), Am. Chem. Soc. (Carothers lectr. Del. sect. 1982, Petroleum Chemistry award 1976, Murphree award 1986). Methodist. Achievements include development of bimetallic clusters as catalysts; invention of polymetallic cluster catalysts used commercially in petroleum reforming. Home: PO Box 364 Oldwick NJ 08858

**SING, WILLIAM BENDER,** lawyer; b. Houston, Oct. 16, 1947; s. William Bender, Sr. and Alice Irene Sing; m. Doris Anne Spradley, Sept. 1, 1967; children: Erin Elaine, Emily Elizabeth. BS cum laude, U. Houston, 1968, JD magna cum laude, 1971; MLA, U. St. Thomas, 1995. Bar: Tex. 1971. Assoc. Fulbright & Jaworski, LLP, Houston, 1973-80, ptnr., 1980—. Past pres., bd. dirs. St. Andrew's Presbyn. Sch., Houston; past pres. Houston CC Place civic Assn.; elder, trustee St. Andrew's Presbyn. Ch., Houston. 1st lt. U.S. Army, 1971—73. Mem.: ABA, Houston Bar Assn., Tex. Bar Assn., U. Houston Alumni Orgn. (life), Order of Barons Law Honor Soc., Omicron Delta Epsilon, Phi Kappa Phi, Phi Delta Phi (life). Avocations: history, literature. Office: Fulbright and Jaworski LLP 1301 Mckinney St Houston TX 77010-3095 Office Phone: 713-651-3709.

**SING, ALAN DANIEL,** artist; b. NYC, June 19, 1950; s. Arthur B. and Edith (Goulfine) S.; m. Anna K. Sears, Sept. 1, 1979; 1 child, Nathaniel. BFA, Cooper Union, 1972; MFA, Cornell U., 1975; student, Yale U., 1971; postgrad., Pratt Inst., 1976-77. Artist, painter, freelance writer, educator, designer, illustrator and curator, 1974—; prof. dept. fine art Rochester Inst. Tech., 1987—; adult edn. instr. N.Y. Bot. Garden, 1985-88; instr. Asa Wright Nature Ctr., Trinidad, W.I., 1978-80. Designer program Franklin Mint Graphics for TDK/Impressions Illustration and Design Exhibits, Bklyn. Botanic Garden, 1987, designs and mechanicals for L.I. U. Brochures/N.C. Zool. Assn., 1986, others; designer, illustrator stamps U.S. Postal Svc., 1980-81, vist. lectr. and artist, Syracuse U., 2006. One-man shows include Hobart William & Smith Coll., Geneva, N.Y., 2001, The Mill Art Ctr., Honeoye Falls, N.Y., 2001, Century Club, Rochester, 1999, Upstairs Gallery: Gallery Arabesque, Ithaca, N.Y., 1998, Germanow-Coffey Gallery, 1997, Angel Fire Gallery, Rochester, N.Y., 1993, 55 Mercer St. Gallery, N.Y.C., 1985, 1992, Haenah-Kent Gallery, N.Y.C., 1991, Bali Miller Gallery, N.Y.C., 1988, Smithsonian Mus. of Natural History, Washington, 1987, Dyer Art Gallery, R.I.T., Rochester, N.Y., 2004, Art and Cultural Coun., 2005, others; group shows include Everson Mus., Syracuse, N.Y., 1999, 2006, Norman Rockwell Mus., Stockbridge, Mass., 2000, Sonnenberg Gardens, Canandaigua, N.Y., 2000, Kew Gardens, Eng., 1997, Buffalo Mus. Sci., 1997, Monroe C.C., 1997, Meml. Art Gallery, Rochester, 1991, 93, Angel Fire Gallery, 1992, Rochester Inst. Tech., 1988, Nat. Acad. Design, N.Y.C., 1986, Cmty. Gallery, Bklyn. Mus., 1985, Coffey Germanow Gallery, 1995, Mill Art Ctr., Honeyoye Falls, N.Y., 2003, Nat. Postal Svc. Mus., 2003, others; author: Wildlife Art, 1999, Botanica 2000, 2000—, Traveling the Erie Canal by Watercolor, 2001; author essays in mus. catalogs, newspapers and jours. Recipient cert. Merit Soc. Illustrators, 1985, Best of Yr. award Postal Commemorative Soc., 1983, Purchase award Nassau C.C., 1976, Pres.'s award Nat. Arts Club, N.Y.C., 1975; Rochester Inst. Tech. grantee, 1991, Faculty Devel. grantee, 1997. Mem. Rochester Print Club (pres.). Avocations: gardening, guitar, hiking. Office: Rochester Inst Tech One Lomb Memorial Dr Rochester NY 14623 E-mail: alan@singerarts.com.

**SINGER, ALFRED,** immunologist, researcher; MD, Columbia U. Clin. training Columbia-Presbyn. Med. Ctr.; fellow in immunology Rockefeller U.; now chief Exptl. Immunology Br. Ctr. Cancer Rsch., Nat. Cancer Inst., Bethesda, Md., also head Lymphatic Devel. Sect. Office: Exptl Immunology Br Ct Cancer Rsch 10 Center Dr Bldg 10 Rm 4B36 Bethesda MD 20892 Office Phone: 301-496-5461. Office Fax: 301-496-0887. E-mail: singera@nih.gov.

**SINGER, ALLEN MORRIS,** lawyer; b. Mpls., Dec. 30, 1923; s. William and Ida (Simenstein) S. JD, U. Chgo., 1948; LLM, Harvard U., Cambridge, Mass., 1958. Bar: Ill. 1948, Calif. 1949. Pvt. practice, 1950-55, 59—; v.p., sec., gen. counsel ABM Industries, San Francisco, 1969-85. Assoc. prof. law U. Oreg., 1955-59; lectr. law Stanford (Calif.) U., 1960-62; of counsel Cooper, White & Cooper, San Francisco, 1970-97. Contbr. articles to profl. jours. Mem. U. Chgo. Nat. Alumni Cabinet, 1978-80. 2nd lt., USAAF, 1943-45. Mem. ABA, San Francisco Bar Assn., Calif. Bar Assn. Office: 1070 Green St Ste 703 San Francisco CA 94133-5414 Office Phone: 415-673-9149.

**SINGER, ARMAND EDWARDS,** foreign language educator; b. Detroit, Nov. 30, 1914; s. Elvin Satori Singer and Mary Rebecca White, Aug. 8, 1940 (dec. Mar. 11, 2004); 1 child, Fredericka Ann Hill. AB, Amherst Coll., 1935; MA, Duke U., 1939, PhD, 1944; Diplôme, U. Paris, 1939; postgrad., Ind. U., 1964. Teaching fellow in sci. Amherst Coll., 1935-36; instr. French and Spanish, part-time Duke U., 1938-40; from teaching fellow Romance langs. to prof. emeritus W.Va. U., Morgantown, 1940—80, prof. emeritus, 1980—. Dir. annual colloquium modern lit. and film W.Va. U., 1976—80, 1985—86, 1996—97, 1999—2001, 2005. Author: A Bibliography of the Don Juan Theme: Versions and Criticism, 1954, The Don Juan Theme, Versions and Criticism: An Annotated Bibliography, 1965, Paul Bourget, 1975, The Don Juan Theme: A Bibliography of Versions, Analogues, Uses, and Adaptations, 1993, supplement, 2003, The Armand E. Singer Tibet, 1809-1975, 1995, supplement, 1998, The Armand E. Singer Nepal, 1772-1961 and Beyond, 1997, The Officials of Tibet, 1999, The Chinese Presence in Tibet, 2002, The Essays and Proofs of Tibet, 2004, 2d edit., 2006,(with J.F. Stasny) Anthology of Readings: Humanities I, 1966, Anthology of Readings: Humanities II, 1967, (with R.F. Gould) A Graded Catalog of Himalayan Mountaineering Correspondence, 2002, 2d edit. rev and enlarged, 2006; editor: West Virginia George Sand Conference Papers, 1981, (with Jürgen E. Schlunk) Martin Walser: International Perspectives, 1987, Doctor Faustus: Archetypal Subtext at the Millennium, 1999; editor W.Va. U. Philol. Papers, 1948-50, 53-55, editor-in-chief, 1951-52, 1955-2004, co-editor, 2005—; editor: 1001 Horny Limericks by Ward Marden, 1996, 500+ of Marden's Favorite Limericks, 2004; editor, contbr. Essays on the Literature of Mountaineering, 1982; bd. editors, The European Legacy, 2003-; contbr. numerous articles to profl. and philatelic jours. Bd. dirs. Cmty. Concert Assn., Morgantown, 1959—60, Humanities Found. W.Va., 1981—87. Recipient 4th Ann. Humanities award, W.Va. Humanities Coun., 1990, Armand E. and Mary W. Singer Professorship in Humanities named in honor of Armand Singer and wife Mary Singer, 1999. Mem. MLA (internat. bibliography com. 1956-59, nat. del. assembly 1975-78), So. Atlantic MLA (exec. com. 1971-74), Am. Assn. Tchrs. Spanish and Portuguese, Am. Philatelic Soc., Nepal and Tibet Philatelic Study Cir. (pres. 1999—), Nepal Philatelic Soc., Collectors Club of N.Y., Phi Beta Kappa. Republican. Home: 1117 University Ave 206 Morgantown WV 26505 Office Phone: 304-293-5121 ext. 5502. Business E-Mail: armand.singer@mail.wvu.edu. *In an age of deteriorating standards, I want to be counted among those educators who stand against the tide. We ask too little of others, we ask too little of ourselves; others ask too little of us. When we constantly encounter shoddy construction, shoddy merchandise, shoddy performances, shoddy ethics, shoddy education, we may be tempted to forswear our standards. But through our hands pass tomorrow's leaders. As teachers we must help stop this erosion of our national pride. If we fail, make no mistake: it could well destroy us all.*

**SINGER, BARBARA HELEN,** photographer; b. NYC, Jan. 29, 1927; d. Robert and Rose (Kaplowitz) S.; m. Nat Herz, Jan. 15, 1956 (dec. Nov. 1964); m. Melvin C. Zalkan, Sept. 7, 1983 (dec. Nov. 1993). BA in Biology, NYU, 1947; studied with Eli Siegel, 1944-76. Registered in diagnostic radiography, in mammography, cert. Women's Bus. Enterprise, 2001, NYC Dept. Small Bus. Svcs., 2005. Radiographer, 1951—; instr. Meth. Hosp. Sch. Radiologic Tech., Bklyn., 1968-72; asst. to Benedict J. Fernandez N.Y.C., 1985-91; asst. to Lucien Clergue New Sch., Parsons, N.Y.C., 1989; photographer N.Y.C., 1983—. Lectr. NY Film Acad., NYC, 2000; panel mem. Phoenix Gallery, NYC, 1999, St. Francis Coll., N.Y.C., 2001. Represented by John Stevenson Gallery, Bridgeman Art Library Internat. Ltd., Getty Images, workbookstock-.com, Getty Images; exhibited in numerous group shows including most recently John Stevenson Gallery, N.Y.C., 1999, 2003, Pietra di Luna Gallery, Fla., 1999, 2000, Park Ave. Armory, N.Y.C., 1999, AIPAD, N.Y.C., 1999, George A. Spiva Ctr. for the Arts, Mo., 2000, Hist. Yellow Springs, Chester, Pa., 2000, Nat. League Am. Pen Women Art Exhbn., N.Y.C., 2000, AIR Gallery, NYC, 2000, Pietra di Luna Gall., Hollywood FL., 2000, St. Francis Coll., NYC, 2001, Modernage, N.Y.C., 2001, Ashforth-Warburg Downtown, N.Y.C., 2002, The Gallery in Stamford, Conn., 2003, WBENC Conf. and Bus. Fair, N.Y.C., 2003, Photo-Plus Expo, N.Y.C., 2003, 04, APA, N.Y.C., 2003, John Stevenson Gallery, 2003, MFA Exhibn. Space, 2005-06, MFA Exhibn. Space, NJ, 2005; CD-ROM Urbane Photography, 1996; photography published in The Murray Hill News, 1983, Profl. Women Photographers Newsletter, 1995, Light and Shade, 1985, Best of Photography Annual 1990, Women of Vision, 1990, Tear Sheet, 1995, Wildlife Conservation Soc. Annual Report, Photonica 21, 1996, In Shape, 1996, Summer of Betrayal, Farrar Straus Giroux, 1997, Wildlife Conservation Mag., 1997, Worldcare Annual Report, 1997, Svenska Missions, 1997, Photonica 25, 1997, Fotophile, 1997, Photonica 34, 1998, Photonica 38, 44, 1999, 49, 2000, Shots, vol. 63, 1999, Photo Dist. News Online, 2003, How Success Happens, 2003, The Picture Professional, 2003, Women's Winners Circle, 2004, Breaking Through, 2004, Roseanne Backstedt, 2005, Partnering For Profit, 2005, www.modernwomentoday.com, 2004, www.thejewishpost.com, 2004, www-.montlyherald.net, 2004, Fancy Living mag., 2005; lit. published in PWP Newsletter, 2001, Tear Sheet, vol. 3, 1995, Today's Great Poems, 1994, Evangelism in America, 1988, Radiologic Tech., 1969, 71; editor, pub. The Impossible Landscapes of Nat Herz and Kurt Seligmann, 1999; appeared in website video, 2003, Manhattan Neighborhood Network TV, 2004; contbr. articles to profl. jours. Photographers' Forum Finalist, 1990; recipient Photography award Beaux Arts Soc., 1994, fiscal sponsorship N.Y. Found. for the Arts, 2000, 2d pl. winner for poetry E.F.S. 1999 Ann. Writing Competition, 2000. Cert. by Women Pres. Ednl. Orgn., 2002, named to Jewish Post list of American's Brightest, Most Talented and Hottest Women of the Yr., 2004, Outstanding Jewish Woman of the Yr., 2004, others; subject of articles ARRC Ann. REport, N.Y. Monthy Herald. Mem.: Acad. Am. Poets, Poetry Soc. Am., Am. Soc. Media Photographers, Am. Soc. Picture Profls. Avocation: ballroom dancing. Office: 319 East 24 St #3A New York NY 10010 Fax: 212-684-1051. Office Phone: 212-689-0395. Personal E-mail: barbara@barbarasinger.com

**SINGER, BRYAN,** film producer, director, writer, actor; b. NYC, Sept. 17, 1965; s. Norbert and Grace Singer. Grad., USC School of Cinema, LA, 1989. Founder Bad Hat Harry Prodn. Co. Dir. (films) Lion's Den, 1988; exec. prodr., dir., writer: (films) Public Access, 1993 (Grand Jury Prize, Sundance Film Festival, 1993); exec. prodr. (films) Burn, 1998, exec. prodr., dir., writer X2, 2003, prodr., dir., writer Superman Returns, 2006, prodr., dir. The Usual Suspects, 1995 (Best Dir. award, Soc. Tex Film Critics, 1995, Best Dir. award, Seattle Film Festival, 1995), Apt Pupil, 1998, prodr., dir., writer Superman Returns, 2006 (WIRED Rave Award in Film, 2006), dir., writer X-Men, 2000 (Saturn Best Dir. award, 2001); actor: (films) Star Trek: Nemesis, 2002, X2, 2003; appearances (films) Cannes Man, 1996, The Book That Wrote Itself, 1999, Round Up: Deposing 'The Usual Suspects', 2002, Keyser Soze: Lie or Legend, 2002, The Uncanny Suspects, 2003, The Visual Effects of X-Men, 2003, X-Factor: The Look of X-Men, 2003, X-Men Production Scrapbook, 2003, My Life with Count Dracula, 2003, The Second Uncanny Issue of X-Men! Making 'X2', 2003, Requiem for Mutants: The Score of 'X2', 2003, Introducing the Incredible Nightcrawler!, 2003, The Secret Origin of X-Men, 2003, Access Nation, 2004, The Shark is Still Working, 2006, (TV specials) Hitchcock: Shadow of a Genius, 1999, The 100 Greatest Movie Stars, 2003, 2nd Annual Spaceys, 2004, (TV series) HBO First Look, 2003, House, M.D., 2005, Sunday Morning Shootout, 2005, exec. prodr., writer The Triangle, 2005, exec. prodr., dir. House, M.D., 2005, exec. prodr. (TV films) The Science of Superman, 2006. Named one of 50 Most Powerful People in Hollywood, Premiere mag., 2006. Office: Bad Hat Harry Productions Inc 150 S Rodeo Dr 3rd Fl Beverly Hills CA 90212*

**SINGER, BURTON HERBERT,** statistics educator; b. Chgo., June 12, 1938; married; 3 children. BS, Case Inst. Tech., 1959, MS, 1961; PhD in Stats., Stanford U., 1967. From asst. to assoc. prof. stats. Columbia U., NYC, 1967-77, prof. math. stats., 1977-85, chmn. dept. math. stats., 1985-89; chmn. biostats. Yale U., New Haven, 1989—91, chmn. and assoc. dean pub. health dept. epidemiology and pub. health, 1989—91, chmn. epidemiology and pub. health, 1991-93, Ira Vaughan Hiscock prof. epidemiology and pub. health, 1991-94, prof. econs. and stats. dept. epidemiology and pub. health, 1991-94; prof. demography and pub. affairs Princeton U., NJ, 1994—, Charles & Marie Robertson prof. pub. & internat. affairs. Research assoc. statistician Princeton U., 1972—73; scientific adv. bd. Santa Fe Inst.; adv. bd. Fogarty Internat. Ctr., NIH; editorial bd. Frontiers of Primary Medicine, Series in Statistics. Commn. Behavioral & Social Sciences & Ed. Nat. Rsch. Coun.; coord. Malaria Task Force, UN Millennium Project. Mem. AAAS, Nat. Acad. Scis., Am. Statis. Assn., Psychometric Soc., Inst. Medicine. Office: Princeton Univ Office Population Rsch 21 Prospect Ave Princeton NJ 08544-2007 Office Phone: 609-258-5938. Office Fax: 609-258-1039. E-mail: singer@princeton.edu.*

**SINGER, CAROL ANN,** librarian, researcher; b. Tarentum, Pa., Mar. 13, 1953; d. Richard Meade and Eleanor (Weir) S. BA, Bowling Green State U., 1975; MLS, Ind. U., 1979. Instr. info. svc. Wayne (Nebr.) State Coll., 1979-84; govt. documents libr. U. Nebr., Omaha, 1984-85, Kenyon Coll., Gambier, Ohio, 1985-91; sr. ref. libr. U.S. Dept. Energy, Washington, 1991-92; ref. libr. USDA, Washington, 1992-97; asst. libr. U.S. Dept. Justice, Washington, 1997-98; ref. libr. Bowling Green (Ohio) State U., 1998—. Instr. Kent State U., Bowling Green, Ohio, 1999; rschr. in field. Contbr. articles to profl. jours. Mem. ALA, Acad. Libr. Assn. Ohio, Ohio Govt. Documents Roundtable. Office: Bowling Green State U Jerome Libr Rm 152 Bowling Green OH 43403 Office Phone: 419-372-9412. Business E-Mail: singerc@bgsu.edu.

**SINGER, CECILE DORIS,** bank executive, former state legislator; BA, Queens Coll.; DHL (hon.), Pace U., 1997. Past rep. Spl. Svcs. for Children, N.Y.C.; past exec. dir. N.Y. State Assembly Social Svcs. and Judiciary Coms., Joint Legis. Com. on Corps., Authorities and Commns.; past pub. rep. Yonkers (N.Y.) Emergency Control Bd.; past coord. Westchester County Assembly Dels.; past chief of staff for dep. minority leader; mem. N.Y. State Assembly, Albany, 1988—94, leadership sec. Rep. Conf., mem. assembly children & families com., mem. various other coms.; bd. dirs. Hudson Valley Bank; prin. Cecile D. Singer Cons. Past rep. Temp. Commn. to Revise Social Svcs. Law; mem. Presdl. Commn. on Privacy Conf., N.Y. State Senate Transp. Conf.; task force on substance abuse Am. Legis. Exch. Coun., task force on econ. devel., crime victims' rights, hosp. crisis, women's issues, com. on mass transit; sec. Rep. Conf. Nat. Adv. Panel Child Care Action Campaign; chmn. Westchester County Commn. on Pub. Financing of Campaigns; chmn. Lower Hudson Valley Adv. Com. N.Y. State Divsn. for Women.; past dir. commn. on poverty and pregnancy, Yonkers IDA, N.Y.; treas. Riverside Corp.; chair, N.Y. State Hudson Valley Coun.; pres. Women's Enterprise Devel. Ctr.; bd. dirs. Hudson Valley Bank, N.Y.; prin. Cecile D. Singer Cons. Chair adv. com. Westchester C.C. Found., Westchester 2000 Rsch., Womens Adv. Bd. Westchester County; task force on certiorari Westchester County Sch. Bds. Assn.; sch. and cmty. chmn. Yonkers PTA; bd. dirs. Yonkers chpt. United Jewish Appeal; v.p. Westchester Sr. Housing; chair Women's Networking, Women in Bus. and the Professions; v.p. Westchester Srs. Housing; trustee, treas. St. John Hosp. Recipient Jenkins Meml. award, Nat. PTA award, Bus. and Profl. award Yonkers C. of C., Millian Vernon award WAWBD, Star award Mental Health Assn., Trustee award St. Johns Hosp., 2005; inducted into Women's Hall of Fame, 1996, Sr. Citizens Hall of Fame, 1996. Mem. Mental Health Assn. (bd. dirs., v.p., nominating and pub. affairs coms. Westchester County chpt.), Rotary. Office: 21 Scarsdale Rd Yonkers NY 10707-3204 Home: 1 Scarsdale Rd Tuckahoe NY 10707-3215

**SINGER, CLIFFORD,** mathematics educator, artist; b. Great Neck, N.Y., May 19, 1955; BFA, Alfred U., N.Y., 1977; MFA, CCNY, N.Y.C., 1990. Tchr. math. Clark County Sch. Dist., Las Vegas, Nev., 2004—. Exhibit curator Geometric Abstraction Nat. Endowment Arts and N.Y. State Coun. Arts Bklyn. Law Sch., 1980, Art & Math. 200 Cooper Union and Albert Nerken Sch. Engring. SUNY, Albany, 2000; commissioned artist Lincoln Ctr. List Art Posters, N.Y.C., 1991, Mostly Mozart Festival, Tokyo, 1991; contr. art and papers to conf. proceedings; lectr. in field. One-man shows include Art Investors Internat., West Palm Beach, Fla., 1986, Vasarely Ctr., N.Y.C., 1988, Thesis Exhibn, Eisner Gallery, CCNY, 1990, Art Rsch. Ctr., Kansas City, Mo., 1992, Fine Arts Forum, Compuserve, 1994, Eich Space, N.Y.C., 1996, Non-Euclid Wide World Web Gallery, Rice U., Tex., 1997, Emden Rm. St. Edmund Hall, U. Oxford, Eng., 2000, Truly Virtual Wab Art Mus., Lastplace-.com, 2000, exhibitions include Soho Ctr. Visual Artists Aldrich Mus. Contemporary Art, N.Y.C., 1980, Aldrich Mus. Contemporary Art, Ridgefield Conn., 1981, 1986, Pace Editions, N.Y.C., 1981, Branchville Soho Gallery, Ridgefield, Conn., 1982, Original Print Collectors Group, N.Y.C. and Paris, 1982, 80 Wash. Sq. East Galleries, N.Y.C., 1983, Thirteen Collection Exhibn. Sotheby Parke Bernet, Inc., 1983, 1984, Hammer Publishing, 1984, The Gallery Albany Inst. History and Art, 1986, Vasarely Ctr., 1987, Art Rsch. Ctr., Kansas City, Mo., 1988, 1995, Ann Jacob Gallery, Atlanta, 1989, Gemini Gallery, West Palm Beach, Fla., 1989, N.Y. Area MFA Ehibn. Coll. Art Assn. Hunter Coll., N.Y.C., 1990, Lincoln Ctr./ Tokyo Bunkamura, N.Y.C. and Tokyo, 1991, 30th Anniversary Lincoln Ctr. Poster and Print Program, N.Y.C., 1993, Bruce McGraw Graphics, N.Y.C., 1994, Am. Online Keyword: Art, 1994, Fine Arts Forum, Compuserve, 1994, Cercle et Carre, Vallejo, Calif., 1996, 1998, Abstract-Art Repository Portfolio Gallery, abstract-art.com, 1997, Boca Raton Mus. Art. Dir.'s Choice, Fla., 1997, Presidents Gallery Darbeth Fine Arts Ctr., Winfield, Kans., 1998, 2001, Bechtel Ctr. U. Caluf., Berkeley, 1998, Mondiale Echo's Mondriinhuis, Amersfoort, Netherlands, 2000—01, Joint Meeting Am. Math. Soc. and Math. Assn. Am., New Orleans, 2001, Ann. Meeting Assn. Women in Math., 2001, Ann. Meeting Nat. Assn. Mathematicians, 2001, Art & Math. 2001 Koussevitsky Art Gallery, Pittsfield, Mass., 2001, Internat. Soc. Interdisciplinary Study of Symmetry Red Ctr. U. NSW, Paddington and Sydney, Australia, 2001, Ringling Sch. Art and Design, Sarasota, Fla., 2002, Monique Goldstrom Gallery, N.Y.C., 2002, AULA Gallery Pedagogical U. FReiburg, Germany, 2002, Holzmann Art Gallery Towson U., Md., 2002, Fire Patrol No. 5 Art, N.Y.C., 2003, U. Granada Art Gallery, Spain, 2003, Cork Gallery Lincoln Ctr., N.Y.C., 2003, Broome St. Gallery, 2004, Joint Math. Meeting Exhibit of Math. Art, Atlanta, 2005, prin. works include Lemma III, Mobil Oil Corp. Hdqs., N.Y.C., 1983, Didecameter Suite, 1985, prin. works include cover art Stagebill Lincoln Ctr. July-Aug., 1992, MUDFISH 9, 1996, FOCUS, 2000, Represented in permanent collections Aldrich Mus. Contemporary Art, Conn., Armand Hammer Collection, N.Y.C., Art Rsch. Ctr., Kansas City, Mo., AT&T, Atlanta, Bank Julius Baer, N.Y.C. and Zurich, Boca Raton Mus. Art, Chemical Bank, N.Y., Citibank, N.A., The Continental Group, Inc., Conn., Gen. Electric Co., Fairfield, Conn., Giant Foods, Mo., IBM Corp., N.Y., Lincoln Ctr. List Art Posters, N.Y.C., McGraw Hill, Mobil Oil Corp., Washington, Mondriaanhuis Archive 90 Reference Collection, Netherlands, Namura Computer Sys., N.Y.C., Needham Harper Worldwide, Inc., Oppenheimer & Co., Inc., Reader's Digest, Pleasantville, N.Y., Revlon, N.Y.C., Southwestern Coll., Winfield, Kansas, Texaco, Inc., N.Y.C., N.Y. Trust Co., Xerox Pub. Group; contbr. chapters to books, scientific papers, articles to profl. jours. Recipient hon. mention, Summit Art Ctr., 1985; grantee, Change, Inc., 1989, IMPACT II, Tchrs. Network, 2001. Home: 4477 El Campana Way Las Vegas NV 89121 Personal E-mail: CliffordhS@aol.com.

**SINGER, CRAIG,** entrepreneur, inventor, investor, consultant; b. N.Y.C., Aug. 13, 1947; s. Albert and Dorothy (Blackman) Singer; m. Ellen Rappaport, Aug. 31, 1969 (separated 2004); children: Chad Adam, Cara Danielle. BS, Cornell U., 1969; JD, Columbia U., 1972. Bar: N.Y. 1973. Exec. Continental Wingage Co., Inc., N.Y.C., 1972-74, Integrated Resources, Inc., N.Y.C., 1974-87; pres. Westminster Fin. Group, Inc., Bedford Corners, NY, 1989—. Chmn. bd. dirs. Integrated Resources Funding Corp., AIM Capital Mgmt. Corp., 1983—87; bus. exec.; entrepreneur; inventor; cons., broker, investor, Bedford Corners, NY, 1988—; reporter. Former mem. editl. adv. bd. Bur. Nat. Affairs Housing and Devel.; former dir. Assn. Govt. Assisted Housing, Inc., 1976—84; former mem. exec. com. Coalition Low and Moderate Income Housing. Home and Office: 148 Meeting House Rd Bedford Corners NY 10549-4241

**SINGER, DANIEL MORRIS,** lawyer; b. Bklyn., Oct. 10, 1930; s. Samuel W. and Fannie G. (Sabloff) S.; m. Maxine Frank, June 15, 1952; children: Amy E., Ellen R., David B., Stephanie F. BA with honors, Swarthmore Coll., 1951; LLB, Yale U., 1954. Bar: N.Y. 1956, U.S. Dist. Ct. D.C. 1957, U.S. Ct. Appeals (D.C. cir.) 1957, U.S. Supreme Ct. 1959. Motions clk. U.S. Ct. Appeals for D.C. Circuit, Washington, 1956-57, law clk. to Judge George T. Washington, 1957-58; assoc. Fried, Frank, Harris, Shriver & Jacobson, Washington, 1958-64, ptnr., 1965-87, counsel, 1987—. Arbitrator complex comml. case and constrn. nat. panels; mediator US Dist. Ct., Washington; vol. atty. Lawyers Com. for Civil Rights Under Law, 1965, 66; mem. exec. com. Washington Lawyers Com. for Civil Rights Under Law, 1973—; spl. asst. corp. counsel, D.C., 1995-2000. Bd. mgrs. Swarthmore Coll., 1987—91; dir., sec.-treas. Coun. for a Livable World, 1962—64; dir. Am. Soc. for Protection of Nature in Israel, 1986—; mem. governing coun., mem. exec. com. Am. Jewish Congress, 1986—96, v.p., 1988—92; bd. dirs., sec.-treas. Nat. Com. Tithing in Investment, 1964—65; bd. dirs. D.C. Developing Families Ctr., 1999—, D.C. Appleseed Ctr., 1996—, chmn. bd., 2000—04. With Signal Corps U.S. Army, 1954—56. Mem.: ABA, D.C. Bar. Home: 5410 39th St NW Washington DC 20015-2902 Office: Fried Frank Harris Shriver & Jacobson 1001 Pennsylvania Ave NW Washington DC 20004-2596 E-mail: daniel.singer@ffhsj.com.

**SINGER, DAVID MICHAEL,** marketing executive, public relations executive; b. Bklyn., Feb. 11, 1957; s. Seymour Allen and Ellen Sybil (Pavnick) S.; m. Pamela Rae Silton, July 20, 1986; children: Max!, Bobby. BA in History, NYU, 1978; MA in Comms., Syracuse U., 1979; MA in Media, New Sch. Social Rsch., 1983; JD, Yeshiva U., 1981. Cons. public. Burson-Marsteller, N.Y.C., 1979-81, The Haas Group, N.Y.C., 1981-84, Braff & Co., N.Y.C., 1987-89; pub.; editor-in-chief Lodestone Pub., N.Y.C., 1984-87; chief oper. officer Pentagon Ent., N.Y.C., 1989-91; v.p. pub. rels. Braff & Co., N.Y.C., 1991-92; v.p. G.S. Schwartz & Co., N.Y.C., 1993-97; v.p. mktg. comm. Imedia, Morristown, NJ, 1998-99; pres. S&S Mktg. Comms. Inc. Lectr. evening div. NYU, 1982-96; dir. media rels. Braff & Co. Contbr. articles and poems to profl. and consumer jours. and mags. Pres. Jewish Cultural Found., N.Y.C., 1976. Named to Outstanding Young Man of Am., Jaycees, 1977; recipient Cert. Recognition Am. Film Inst., 1982, ANDY Design award Advert. Club N.Y., 1983, Proclamation Bklyn. Borough Pres., 1987. Mem. Alpha Epsilon Pi (Bro. of Yr. 1976). Avocations: baseball, politics, ping pong/table tennis, films, theater.

**SINGER, DINAH S.**, federal agency administrator, immunologist, researcher; Grad., MIT, 1969; MPhil, PhD, Columbia U. Post-doctoral fellow Lab. Biochemistry Nat. Cancer Inst., sr. investigator Immunology Branch; sr. scientific officer Howard Hughes Med. Inst., 1998—99; dir. Divsn. Cancer Biology Nat. Cancer Inst., 1999—, also chief Molecular Regulation Sect. of Exptl. Immunology Branch. Mem.: Am. Assn. Immunologists. Office: Nat Cancer Inst Divsn Cancer Biology Executive Plaza North Ste 5000 Bethesda MD 20892-7390 Office Phone: 301-496-8636. E-mail: ds13j@nih.gov.*

**SINGER, DONNA LEA**, writer, editor, educator; b. Wilmington, Del., Oct. 6, 1944; d. Marshall Richard and Sara Emma (Eppihimer) S. BA in English cum laude, Gettysburg Coll., 1966; postgrad., Montclair State Coll., 1972-73, U. Birmingham, Eng., 1977; M of Letters, Drew U., 1985. Asst. to dir. student activities Fairleigh Dickinson U., Madison, crw., 1966-68; tchr., drama coach Morris Hills High Sch., Rockaway, N.J., 1968-84; free-lance editor Basic Books, Inc., N.Y.C., 1983-86; adj. instr. Fairleigh Dickinson U., Madison, 1986-87; free-lance writer, editor Visual Edn. Corp., Princeton, N.J., 1988—; Fact's on File, Bantam, Random House, Fodor's Travel Books, N.Y.C., 1990—, John Wiley & Sons, N.Y.C., 1990—; tchr. Sylvan Learning and Tech. Ctr., Sarasota, Fla., 1999—. Co-founder, co-dir. Traveling Hist. Troupe, Rockaway, 1976-78; tour leader Am. Leadership Study Groups, 1976, 78, 82; theatre studies participant Royal Shakespeare Co., Stratford, Eng., 1978-79, 81; docent, lectr. acting co. Hist. Spanish Point, Osprey, Fla., 1989-2001; grant facilitator NEA, Sarasota, Fla. Author: numerous poems; contbr. chapters to books, articles to profl. jours. Big sister Big Bros./Big Sisters, Sarasota, Fla., 1990-98; NEA grant facilitator Asolo Theater, Sarasota, Fla. Mem. Internat. Women's Writing Guild, West Coast Writers, Met. Mus. Art, Royal Shakespeare Company Assocs., Emerald Coast Writers, Travel Writers Internat. Network. Avocations: dance, theater, travel, antiques. E-mail: shakesds@aol.com.

**SINGER, EMEL**, staffing industry executive; b. Gaziantep, Turkey, Apr. 7, 1944; came to U.S., 1960; d. Mehmet Resit and Nesrin (Kescioglu) Tuzun; m. James Michael Singer, Apr. 28, 1968 (dec. 1987); children: Justin Michael, Jodi Michelle. BBA, Bradley U., 1968. Adminstrv. asst. U. Ky. Med. Ctr., Lexington, 1968; exec. sec. Hoffman Products/Cortron Industries, Chgo., 1968-70; co-founder, adminstr. Banner Pers. Svc., Inc., Chgo., 1970-87, chmn., CEO, 1988—; co-founder Banner Temp. Svc., 1982—; founder Banner Tng. Ctrs., 1996—, Banner Acctg. and Fin., 1999—. Guest spkr. Chgo. Entrepreneurship Program, U. Ill., Chgo., 1993—; fund-raising co-chair U. Chgo., Divsn. Mid. Ea. Studies, 1993-95. Mem. parents bd. Bradley U., Peoria, Ill., 1989-90, assoc. trustee, 1992-93, alumni master, 1993, mem. Bradley coun., 1993-95, bd. trustees, 1995—. Listed in Crains Chgo. Bus. as a Top Woman-Owned Firm, 1989, 90, 91, Today's Chgo. Woman as one of 100 Women Making a Difference, 1997; named to Entrepreneurship Hall of Fame, 1993. Mem. ASTD, Chgo. Orgn. Data Processing Educators, Nat. Assn. Pers. Svcs., Nat. Assn. Temp. Svcs., Ill. Assn. Pers. Svcs., Ill. Assn. Temporary Svcs. Avocations: skiing, scuba diving, travel, sailing. Home: 3750 N Lake Shore Dr Chicago IL 60613-4238 Office: Banner Personnel Service Inc 125 S Wacker Dr #1250 Chicago IL 60606-4424

**SINGER, ERIC T.**, investment banker; b. N.Y.C., 1952; s. Roger M. and Meredith Singer; m. Aet Paaro, Aug. 10, 1974; children: Brett A., Jamison P. BA, SUNY, Stony Brook, 1974; JD, Cornell U., 1977. Assoc. Barrett, Smith et al, N.Y.C., 1977-80; v.p. Smith Barney, N.Y.C., 1980-84; sr. v.p. PaineWebber, N.Y.C., 1984-88; exec. v.p. Metromedia Hotels, N.Y.C., 1988-90; exec. v.p., dir. corp. fin. Gerard Klauer Mattison, N.Y.C., 1990-99; mng. dir., pres. H.C. Wainwright & Co., Inc., N.Y.C., 1999—2003; mng. dir. Burnham Hill Ptnrs., LLC, N.Y.C., 2003—; founder, owner Singer Funds, 2004—, mng. ptnr. Singer Congl. Fund, 2004—. Mem. Cornell Law Rev. Mem. U.S. Maccabiah Squash Team, 1997, 2001, 2005. Mem. Heights Casino Club, Yale Club, Phi Beta Kappa. Home: 72 Hicks St Brooklyn NY 11201-1709 Office Phone: 212-259-2039.

**SINGER, FREDERICK RAPHAEL**, medical researcher; b. St. Louis, June 27, 1939; s. Meyer and Lee (Minkle) S.; m. Sandra Joy Barnes, Aug. 16, 1964; children: Stefanie, Jeffrey. Student, UCLA, 1956—59; BS, U. Calif., Berkeley, 1960; MD, U. Calif., San Francisco, 1963. Diplomate Am. Bd. Internal Medicine, Am. Bd. Endocrinology and Metabolism. Intern UCLA Affiliated Hosp., 1963-64; resident VA Hosp., L.A., 1964-65, 68-69; instr. in medicine Harvard U., Boston, 1971-72; asst. prof. medicine UCLA, 1972-73, U. So. Calif., L.A., 1973-74, assoc. prof., 1974-78, prof., 1978-89, prof. orthop. surgery, 1980-89; dir. Bone Ctr. Cedars-Sinai Med. Ctr., L.A., 1989-92, clin. prof. medicine, 1993—. Dir. Osteoporosis/Metabolic Bone Disease program St. Johns Hosp. and Health Ctr., Santa Monica, Calif., 1992—; dir. Skeletal Biology Lab, John Wayne Cancer Inst., Santa Monica, 1992—; mem. endocrine and metabolic drug adv. com. FDA, USPHS, Bethesda, Md., 1983-87. Author: Paget's Disease of Bone, 1977; contbr. numerous articles, revs. to profl. jours. Vice chmn. cmty. adv. com. Univ. H.S., L.A., 1984. Capt. USAF, 1965-67. Calif. State scholar, 1956-60. Calif. investigator VA, 1971-73. Mem. Endocrine Soc., Am. Soc. Clin. Investigation, Am. Soc. Bone and Mineral Rsch. (chmn. pub. affairs 1981-86, coun. 1987, pres.-elect 1989, pres. 1990), Paget's Disease Found. (chmn. bd. dirs. 1990—). Office: John Wayne Cancer Inst 2200 Santa Monica Blvd Santa Monica CA 90404-2302 Personal E-mail: singerf@yahoo.com.

**SINGER, GARY JAMES**, lawyer; b. LA, Oct. 8, 1952; s. Stanley Merle and Ernestine Alice (Brandstatter) S.; m. Melanie Carol Rabin, Mar. 19, 1978; children: Brian, Kimberly, Andrew. BA magna cum laude, U. Calif., Irvine, 1974; JD cum laude, Loyola U., 1977. Bar: Calif. 1977, U.S. Dist. Ct. (fed. dist.) 1978. Assoc O'Melveny & Myers LLP, LA, 1977-84, Newport Beach, Calif., ptnr., head Irvine, Calif., 1985—, ptnr., head bus. practice group Newport Beach, Calif. Bd. dirs. Irvine Barclay Theatre, 1990-98, chmn. 1993-96; chair bd. dir. Com. on Product Liability and Tort Reform, 1999—; lectr. Continuing Legal Edn., Merger and Acquisition Practice (1997, 1999), Calif. Continuation Edn. of the Bar, Calif. State Bar Assn., Euromoney Conf. Editor-in-chief Loyola of LA Law Review, 1976—77. Bd. dir. Calif. C. of C., Orange County Bus. Com. Arts, 1999—, U. Calif. Irvine Found., 1998—, Human Options, 1982—86, Big Canyon Country Club, 1990—93; past pres. U. Calif. Irvine Chancellor's Club. Named Disting. Alumni Recipient; recipient Lauds and Laurels, 1998. Mem.: ABA, Orange County Bar Assn. (past chmn., corp. and bus. law sect.), St. Thomas More Law Honor Soc., Phi Beta Kappa, Alpha Sigma Nu. Avocations: golf, skiing, reading. Office: O'Melveny & Myers LLP 610 Newport Center Dr 17th Fl Newport Beach CA 92660

**SINGER, HOWARD JACK**, biology professor, researcher; b. Newark, Sept. 4, 1940; s. Nat I. and Rose (Alboum) S.; m. Helena Liisa Niskanen, May 29, 1986; children: Jamie Alexander Niskanen-Singer. BA, Oberlin Coll., 1962; MS, U. Minn., 1966; PhD, Tufts U., 1970. Prof. biology N.J. City U. (formerly Jersey City State Coll.), Jersey City, 1970—. Cons. Proforma Base Corp., Jersey City, 1985-87, Instructivision, Inc., Livingston, N.J., 1988-89; researcher SUNY Downstate Med. Ctr., Bklyn., 1987-89. Contbr. articles to profl. jours. Pres. Van Vorst Pk. Assn., Jersey City, 1977-78; treas. Environ. Voters Alliance, N.J., 1984-90; dir. Hudson County (N.J.) Toxic Task Force, 1980-86; active Scientists Com. for Pub. Info., N.Y.C., 1976-80. Am. Chem. Soc. scholar, 1958-62; fellow NIH, 1966-70, NSF, 1961. Mem.: Am. Fedn. Tchrs. (membership chmn. 1989—), Theobald Smith Soc. (pres. 1996—97, alt. nat. councilor 1997—99, nat. councilor 2000—01, alt. nat. councilor 2002—03, nat. councilor 2003—05, chmn. program com., co-pres. 2006—07), Am. Soc. for Microbiology. Avocations: skiing, art nouveau, scuba, tennis. Home: 297 York St Jersey City NJ 07302-4016 Office: NJ City U 2039 John F Kennedy Blvd Jersey City NJ 07305-1527 Office Phone: 201-200-3310. Business E-Mail: hsinger@njcu.edu.

**SINGER, ISADORE MANUEL**, mathematician, educator; b. Detroit, May 3, 1924; married; 5 children. BS, U. Mich., 1944; MS, U. Chgo., 1948, PhD in Math., 1950; ScD (hon.), Tulane U., 1981; LLD (hon.), U. Mich., 1989, U. Ill., Chgo. Moore instr. math. MIT, Cambridge, 1950—52, prof. math., 1956—70, Norbert Wiener prof., 1970—79, John D. MacArthur prof. math.

---

(1st holder), 1983—, Inst. prof., 1987—; asst. prof. UCLA, 1952—54; vis. prof. math U. Calif., Berkeley, 1977—79, prof., 1979—83, Miller prof. math., 1982—83, prof. math., 1977—83. Vis. asst. prof. math. Columbia U., N.Y.C., 1954—55; mem. Inst. Advanced Study, 1955—56; past steering com. Ctr. for Non-Linear Scis., Los Alamos Nat. Labs.; adv. bd. Inst. Theoretical Physics, U. Calif., Santa Barbara; bd. dirs. Santa Fe Inst.; mem. various organizing coms.; editor procs. for confs. in field. Former editor profl. jours. Recipient Nat. medal of Sci., 1983, Steele prize Lifetime Achievement, 2000, Abel prize, Norwegian Academy of Sci. and Letters, 2004; fellow Alfred P. Sloan, 1959—62, Guggenheim, 1968—69, 1975—76. Mem.: NAS (past councillor, former mem. com. math. and phys. scis., chmn's com.), Internat. Congress Mathematicians (program com.: 1986, Wigner prize 1989), Am. Phys. Soc., Am. Math. Soc. (v.p. 1970—72, past exec. com., Bocher Meml. prize 1969, Pub. Svc. award 1993), Am. Acad. Arts and Scis., Am. Philos. Soc. Office: MIT Dept of Math Bldg 2 Rm 387 77 Massachusetts Ave Cambridge MA 02139-4307

**SINGER, JEFFREY ALAN**, surgeon; b. Bklyn., Feb. 2, 1952; s. Harold and Hilda (Ginsburg) S.; m. Margaret Sue Gordon, May 23, 1976; children: Deborah Suzanne, Pamela Michele. BA cum laude, Bklyn. Coll., 1973; MD, N.Y. Med. Coll., 1976. Diplomate Am. Bd. Surgery. Intern Maricopa County Gen. Hosp., Phoenix, 1976-77, resident, 1977-81, mem. teaching faculty, 1981-96; trauma cons. John C. Lincoln Hosp., Phoenix, 1981-83; pvt. practice Phoenix, 1981-87; group pvt. practice Valley Surg. Clinics, Ltd., Phoenix, 1987—, S.W. Surg. Clinics, P.C., Phoenix, 1996-97. Sec.-treas. med. staff Humana Desert Valley Hosp., Phoenix, 1987-89, chief surgery, 1985-87, 91-93, exec. com., 1993-95; adj. asst. prof. divsn. clin. edn. Ariz. Coll. Osteo. Med., Midwestern U., 1998—, mem. adj. clin. faculty Kirksville (Mo.) Coll. Osteo. Medicine. Assoc. editor Ariz. Medicine, 1994-2000, contbg. writer, 2001—. Rep. precinct committeeman, Phoenix, 1986-2000; mem. exec. com. bd. dirs. Goldwater Inst. for Pub. Policy Rsch., 2002—. Named Top Doc, Phoenix Mag., 1999. Fellow: ACS, Am. Soc. Abdominal Surgeons, Southwestern Surg. Congress, Internat. Coll. Surgeons; mem.: Maricopa County Med. Soc. (v.p. 1998, bd. dirs. 1998—2002), Ariz. Med. Assn. (bd. dirs. polit. com. 1985—, legis com. 1986—, chmn. bd. dirs. polit. com. 1991—93, Walk the Talk award 2001), Ariz. Sch. Choice Trust (bd. dirs. 1998—2004, adv. bd. 2004—), Alpha Omega Alpha. Avocations: philosophy, politics, history, travel, underwater sports, writing. Office: Valley Surg Clinics Ltd 16601 N 40th St Ste 216 Phoenix AZ 85032-3353 Office Phone: 602-996-4747. Personal E-mail: dr4liberty@aol.com. Business E-Mail: jsinger@valleysurgicalclinics.com.

**SINGER, JON DOUGLAS**, foundation administrator, writer; b. N.Y.C. s. Jerome Leonard and Dorothy Gottlieb Singer. BA, NYU, 1974, MA, 1978. Shelver libr. books Yale U. Med. Sch., New Haven, Conn., 1987-88, Willlow Smith Assocs., New Haven, 1996; receptionist Fellowship Club, 2000—. Author: Lost Lands and Cities, 1987, Lost Lands and Cities Beneath the Sea, 1997, Ireland's Mysterious Lands and Sunken Cities, 2001. Campaign asst. Dem. Party, N.Y.C., 1980; mem. Rep. Nat. Com., 2003; mem. U.S. Naval Inst., 2003. Mem. Avocations: archaeology, astronomy, quantum physics. Home: 305 Audubon Ct New Haven CT 06510

**SINGER, JOSEPH WILLIAM**, law educator; b. Long Branch, NJ, May 23, 1954; BA in Polit. Economy, Williams Coll., 1976; AM in Polit. Sci., Harvard U., 1978, JD, 1981. Bar: Mass. 1981, NJ 1982. Prof. law Boston U. Law Sch., Harvard Law Sch., Cambridge, Mass., 1992—. Author: Entitlement: The Paradoxes of Property, 2000, The Edges of the Field: Lessons on the Obligations of Ownership, 2000, Introduction to Property, 2001, Property Law: Rules, Policies & Practices, 2002. Office: Harvard Law Sch 1563 Massachusetts Ave Cambridge MA 02138 Office Phone: 617-496-5292. Office Fax: 617-496-4863. Business E-Mail: jsinger@law.harvard.edu.

**SINGER, JOY DANIELS**, journalist, consultant; b. N.Y.C., Feb. 22, 1928; d. Maurice Blumberg and Anna S. (Kleegman) Daniels; m. Jack Singer, July 30, 1955; children: Merianne B., Daniel C., Richard K. BA, Cornell U., 1948; postgrad., The Sorbonne, Paris, 1949. Advt. copywriter Franklin Spier, George Knoerr & Assocs., Parents Mag., Diener & Dorskind, March Advt., N.Y.C., 1950-68; CEO J.D. Singer, N.Y.C., 1968—. Scriptwriter Can. TV show, Magistrate's Court, 1968-69; syndicated columnist with Marlies Wolf, Women at Work, Feature Assocs., San Rafael, Calif., 1979—. Author: My Mother, The Doctor, 1970. Dem. County committeewoman, 1960-61. Mem. Direct Mktg. Creative Guild (v.p., corp. sec.), Friends Com., Gen. Soc. Libr. (chmn.), NATAS. Home and office: 1725 York Ave Apt 19F New York NY 10128-7811 Office Phone: 212-348-0881. E-mail: imrejoysing@aol.com.

**SINGER, MARKUS MORTON**, retired trade association administrator; b. N.Y.C., Dec. 20, 1917; s. Isadore and Nettie (Stromer) S.; m. Phyllis Berger, June 26, 1945; children— Fredric L., Robert B. B.C.S., NYU, 1939; postgrad., George Washington U., 1951-55. With Nat. Food Brokers Assn., Washington, 1946—, v.p., 1961-65, exec. v.p., 1965-71, pres., 1972-83, pres. emeritus, 1983—, acting pres., chief exec. officer, 1987-88. Lifetime hon. trustee Nat. Food Brokers Assn. Edn. and Tng. Found. Served with AUS, 1942-45. Recipient Pres.'s award as Man of Yr. Can. Food Brokers Assn., 1976 Mem. European Food Brokers Assn. (hon. life), Frozen Food Industry Disting. Order of Zerocrats. Jewish.

**SINGER, MARTIN H.**, Internet company executive; BA, U. Mich.; MA in Exptl. Psychology, PhD in Exptl. Psychology, Vanderbilt U. With Bell Labs., AT&T, Tellabs; v.p., gen. mgr. Wireless Access Bus. Devel. Group. Motorola Cellular Infrastructure Group Motorola, 1990—98; pres., CEO SAFCO, 1998—2001; CEO Pctel Inc., Chgo., 2001, chmn., 2001—. Achievements include patents in field. Office: Pctel Inc 8725 West Higgins Rd Ste 400 Chicago IL 60631

**SINGER, MAXINE FRANK**, retired biochemist, science association director; b. N.Y.C., Feb. 15, 1931; d. Hyman S. and Henrietta (Perlowitz) Frank; m. Daniel Morris Singer, June 15, 1952; children: Amy Elizabeth, Ellen Ruth, David Byrd, Stephanie Frank. AB, Swarthmore Coll., 1952, DSc (hon.), 1978; PhD, Yale U., 1957, DSc (hon.), 1994, Wesleyan U., 1977, U. Md.-Baltimore County, 1985, Cedar Crest Coll., 1986, CUNY, 1988, Brandeis U., 1988, Radcliffe Coll., 2000, Williams Coll., 1990, Franklin and Marshall Coll., 1991, George Washington U., 1991, NYU, 1992, Lehigh U., 1992, Dartmouth Coll., 1993, Harvard U., 1994, Yale U., 1994, U. Nebr., 2004; PhD honoris causa (hon.), Weizmann Inst. Sci., 1995. USPHS postdoctoral fellow NIH, Bethesda, Md., 1956—58, rsch. chemist biochemistry, 1958—74; head sect. on nucleic acid enzymology Nat. Cancer Inst., 1974—79; chief Lab. of Biochemistry, Nat. Cancer Inst., 1979—87, rsch. chemist 1987—88; pres. Carnegie Inst. Washington, 1988—2002. Regents vis. lectr. U. Calif., Berkeley, 1981; bd. dirs. Perlegen Sci., Inc. Mem. editl. bd.: Jour. Biol. Chemistry, 1968—74, Sci. mag, 1972—82, chmn. editl. bd.: Procs. of NAS, 1985—88; co-author (with Paul Berg): 3 books on molecular biology and a sci. biog.; contbr. articles to scholarly jours. Chmn. Smithsonian Coun., 1992—93; trustee Wesleyan U., Middletown, Conn., 1972—75, Yale Corp., New Haven, 1975—90, Carnegie Inst. Wash., 2002—; bd. govs. Weizmann Inst. Sci., Rehovot, Israel, 1978—; bd. dirs. Whitehead Inst., 1985—94, chmn. bd., 2003—04. Named to Washington D.C. Hall of Fame, 2000; recipient award for achievement in biol. scis., Washington Acad. Scis., 1969, award for rsch. in biol. scis., Yale Sci. and Engring. Assn., 1974, Superior Svc. Honor award, HEW, 1975, Dirs. award, NIH, 1977, Disting. Svc. medal, HHS, 1983, Presdl. Disting. Exec. Rank award, 1987, U.S. Disting. Exec. Rank award, 1987, Mory's Cup, Bd. Govs. Mory's Assn., 1991, Wilbur Lucius Cross Medal for Honor, Yale Grad. Sch. Assn., 1991, Nat. Medal Sci., NSF, 1992, Pub. Svc. award, NIH Alumni Assn., 1995, Vannevar Bush award, Nat. Sci. Bd., 1999. Fellow: Am. Acad. Arts and Scis.; mem.: AAAS (Sci. Freedom and Responsibility award 1982, Philip Hauge Abelson prize 2004), NAS (coun. 1982—85, com. sci., engring. and pub. policy 1989—91, treas. 1999—2005), Am. Soc. Cell Biology, Pontifical Acad. of Scis., Inst. Medicine of NAS, Am. Philos. Soc., Am. Chem. Soc. Microbiologists, Am. Soc. Biol. Chemists. Home: 5410 39th St NW Washington DC 20015-2902 Office: Carnegie Inst Washington 1530 P St NW Washington DC 20005-1933

---

**SINGER, MYER R(ICHARD)**, lawyer; b. Everett, Mass., Oct. 24, 1938; s. Nathan and Celia (Rudin) Singer; m. Elaine Doris Ginesky, June 17, 1962; children: Andrew L., Stephen D., Jocelyn G. BSBA, Boston U., 1960, LLB, 1963. Bar: Mass. 1963, U.S. Ct. Appeals (1st cir.) 1963. Atty. Boston Legal Aid Soc., 1963—64; pvt. practice Dennis Port, Mass., 1965—2001; ptnr. Singer & Singer, LLC, 2001—. Trustee, corporator, mem. bd. investment Cape Cod Five Cents Savs. Bank, Harwich Port, Mass.; trustee Cape Cod Mus. of Natural History, 2001—; faculty Mass. Continuing Legal Edn., Inc., 1985, 1990—98; program chmn. Real Estate Devel. Cape Cod-Mass. Bar Inst., 1999; corporator Heritage Mus. and Gardens, 2003—; spkr. in field. Co-author: (book) Creation and Care of Condominiums, 1985, Everything You Need to Know about the Cape Cod Commission Act, 1990. Pres. Dennis Yarmouth Band Parents, 1986—87; mem. adv. bd. Cape Mus. Fine Arts, Dennis, 1988—96; mem. exec. com. Cape Cod Five Cents Savs. Bank Charitable Found. Trust, 2006—; former trustee Cape Cod Synagogue; mem., clk. Yarmouth (Mass.) Zoning Bd. Appeals, 1980—86; former bd. dirs. Cape Cod and Island chpt. of Mass. Heart Assn.; former pres. Legal Svcs. of Cape Cod and Island, Inc. Mem.: ABA, Barnstable County Bar Assn. (mem. exec. com. 1999—2003), Mass. Bar Assn. (chmn. bar assn. program real estate devel. Cape Cod 1999). Avocations: boating, photography. Home: 238 Greenland Circle East Dennis MA 02641-1302 Office: PO Box 67 26 Upper County Rd Dennis Port MA 02639-0067 Office Phone: 508-398-2221. E-mail: mrsinger@singer-law.com.

**SINGER, NIKI**, media consultant; b. Rochester, NY, Sept. 10, 1937; d. Goodman A. and Evelyn (Simon) Sarachan; m. Michael J. Sheets, 1973; children: Romaine Kitty, Nicholas Simon Feramorz. BA cum laude, U. Mich., 1959. Mgr. advt. sales promotion Fairchild Publ., NYC, 1959-67; acct. exec., acct. supr. Vernon Pope Co., NYC, 1967-69, v.p., 1969-71; pres. Niki Singer, Inc., NYC, 1971-93; sr. v.p. M. Shanken Comm., Cigar Aficionado, Wine Spectator, 1994—2002; founder Niki Singer, LLC, 2003—. Mem.: Les Dames d'Escoffier (bd. dirs.), Am. Inst. Wine and Food (bd. dirs.). Office: 1035 5th Ave New York NY 10028-0135 E-mail: sheets@nyc.rr.com.

**SINGER, PAUL MEYER**, lawyer; b. Pitts., May 20, 1943; s. Sidney Morris and Doris (Lyttle) S.; m. Laurie Stern, 1989. BS in Bus., U. Minn., 1965; JD, U. Pitts., 1968; LLM, Harvard U., 1970. Law clk. to presiding justice Pa. Supreme Ct., Pitts., 1970-71; atty. Am. Express Credit Corp., N.Y.C., 1971-73; ptnr. Reed Smith LLP, Pitts., 1973—. Mem. Am. Coll. Bankruptcy (v.p.), Harvard-Yale-Princeton Club, Duquesne Club. Office: Reed Smith LLP 435 6th Ave Pittsburgh PA 15219-1886 E-mail: psinger@reedsmith.com.

**SINGER, PAUL RICHARD**, ophthalmologist; b. NYC, Feb. 1, 1947; m. Katherine W. Singer, June 13, 1970; children: Amy E., Evan P. BA with honors, U. Rochester, N.Y., 1969, MD, 1973. Diplomate Am. Bd. Ophthalmology. Internal medicine intern U. N.C., Chapel Hill, 1973-74, resident in neurology, 1974-75; resident in ophthalmology Washington U. Sch. Medicine, St. Louis, 1975-78, Fight for Sight postdoctoral rsch. fellow dept ophthalmology, 1978-79; pres. Hartford (Conn.) Eye Physicians, 1980—; sr. staff dept. ophthalmology Hartford Hosp., 1980—. Chmn. bd. dirs. Prevent Blindness Conn., Middletown, 1990-92, Combined Health Appeal, Hartford, 1993-95. Recipient Cmty. Svc. award Hartford County Med. Assn., 1993, Robert Polk award for outstanding vol. svc. Prevent Blindness Conn., 1993. Office: Hartford Eye Physicians 55 Nye Rd Ste 103 Glastonbury CT 06033-4394

**SINGER, RICHARD M.**, lawyer; b. Mt. Vernon, NY, 1946; BA, Univ. Pa., 1968, JD, 1971. Bar: NY 1972, DC 1972. Mng. ptnr, ptnr.-in-charge, mem., comm. law practice group Drinker Biddle & Reath LLP, Washington. Mem.: ABA, Fed. Comm. Bar Assn. Office: Drinker Biddle & Reath LLP Ste 1100 1500 K St NW Washington DC 20005-1209 Office Phone: 202-342-8814. Office Fax: 202-842-8465. Business E-Mail: richard.singer@dbr.com.

**SINGER, RICHARD P.**, neurologist, researcher, director; b. NYC, June 19, 1947; MD, SUNY, Buffalo, 1977. Diplomate Am. Bd. Psychiatry and Neurology, 1983. Pres. Neurology Clin. Rsch. Inc., Sunrise, Fla., 1981—; neurologist Sunrise Med. Group. Office: Neurology Clin Rsch Inc 3540 N Pine Island Rd Sunrise FL 33351 Office Fax: 954-472-0556.

**SINGER, ROBERT**, plastic surgeon; b. Buffalo, Oct. 22, 1942; s. Murray and Fay Singer; m. Judith Harris. Student, SUNY, Buffalo, 1960-63; MD, SUNY, 1967. Lic. physician, Calif.; diplomate Am. Bd. Plastic and Reconstructive Surgery. Resident in gen. surgery Stanford Med. Ctr., Palo Alto, Calif., 1967-69, Santa Barbara Cottage and Gen. Hosp., 1972-74; resident in plastic surgery Vanderbilt U., 1974-76; pvt. practice specializing in emergency and trauma San Diego, 1971-72; pvt. practice plastic, reconstructive and aesthetic surgery La Jolla, Calif., 1976—. Prior asst. clin. prof. plastic surgery U. Calif., San Diego; sr. staff, chief plastic surgery Scripps Meml. Hosp., La Jolla, 1980-86, vice chmn. dept. surgery, 1989-91. Contbr. articles to profl. jours. Active San Diego Opera, San Diego Mus. of Man, La Jolla Playhouse, Voices for Children, San Diego Zoo, Mus. Photog. Arts, KPBS, others. Fellow ACS; mem. AMA, Calif. Med. Assn., San Diego County Med. Soc., San Diego Internat. Soc. Plastic Surgeons (pres. 1988-89), Calif. Soc. Plastic Surgeons (pres. 1995-96), Am. Soc. Aesthetic Plastic Surgeons (pres. 1994-95), Internat. Soc. Clin. Plastic Surgeons, Am. Soc. Plastic and Reconstructive Surgeons (trustee 1996—, chmn. bd. trustees 1998-99), J.B. Lynch Soc., Royal Soc. Medicine, Am. Assn. for Accreditation of Ambulatory Surgery Facilities (pres. 1991-2000), San Diego Plastic Surgery Soc. (pres. 1989-90), Aesthetic Surgery Edn. and Rsch. Found. (pres., 2000—). Avocations: tennis, travel, pre-columbian art. Office: 9834 Genesee Ave Ste 100 La Jolla CA 92037-1214

**SINGER, SARAH BETH**, poet; b. N.Y.C., July 4, 1915; d. Samuel and Rose (Dunetz) White; m. Leon Eugene Singer, Nov. 23, 1938; children: Jack, Rachel. BA, NYU, 1934; postgrad., New Sch. Social Research, 1961-63. Tchr. creative writing Hillside Hosp., Queens, N.Y., 1964-75, Samuel Field YMHA, Queens, 1980-82. Mem. Pacific N.W. Writers Conf.; prin. reader Frye Art Mus., 1998, 2000, 01, 03; reader Poetwest, 2005. Author: Magic Casements, 1957, After the Beginning, 1975, Of Love and Shoes, 1987, The Gathering, 1992, contbr. poetry to anthologies, poetry mags. and quars. Recipient Stephen Vincent Benet award Poet Lore, 1968, 71, Dellbrook award Shenandoah Valley Acad. Lit. and Dellbrook-Shenandoah Coll. Writers' Conf., 1978, 79, C.W. Post Poetry award, 1979-80, Best Poem award Lyric Quar., 1981, Biennial award Seattle Br. Nat. League Penwomen, 1988, award Wash. Poets Assn., 1989, 95, 97, 98, four honorable mentions, 1998, 2000, Editor's Choice Haiku award Brussels Sprout, 1992, award Writer's Digest, 1999, 2000, 02, 04, Hon. Mention award Washington Poets Assn., 2001, 02, Hon. Mention, 2001, 03, 2 Hon. Mentions, 2002, 03; cert. merit Muse Mag., 1990; winner Met. Bus. Poetry Project, Seattle, 1992, 96; poem Upon My Demise translated into Russian, recorded 1st prize Marj McAllister award Voices Internat., 1993; Lifetime Achievement award Poets/West, 2003. Mem. PEN, Poetry Soc. Am., Poets and Writers, Nat. League Am. Penwomen (poetry chmn. L.I. br. 1957-87, publicity chmn. 1990, sec. Seattle br. 1990, pres. 1992-94, v.p. 1994—, publicity chmn. State of Wash. 1992—, Marion Doyle Meml. award 1976, 3d place, 2000, 1st prize nat. poetry contest 1976, Drama award 1977, Poetry award 1977, 1st prize modern rhymed poetry 1978, Lectr. award 1980, Sonnet award Alexandria br. 1980, 81, Catherine Cushman Leach award 1982, 3d place, 2000; poetry award Phoenix br. 1983, Pasadena br. 1984, Alexandria br. 1985, 1st prize award Portland br. 1990, structured verse award Spokane br. 1992, Della Crowder Miller Meml. Petrarchan Sonnet award 1994, 2000, Della Crowder Meml. Free Verse award, 2000, Honorable Mention Anita Marie Boggs Meml. award 1994, 2000, Owl award and Ann. award for achievement in poetry Seattle br. 1994, Poet's Choice award Portland br. 1995, 2d prize Internat. Poetry Contest, Palomar br., 1996, 3d prize in internat. poetry 1997, Palomar Branch internat. poetry contest honorable mention, 1998, 1st prize Internat. Poetry Contest Palomar br., 1999, hon. mention, 1999, honorable mention Anita Marx Sestina award 2000, 3d pl. Catherine Cushman Leach Poetry award 2000, 3d pl. Marion Doyle Meml. award 2000, Della Crowder Meml. award for Petrarchan sonnet 2000, Della

Crowder Meml. award for free verse 2000, 3d pl. Anne Marx Sestina award 2002, award for 40 yrs. of svc., 2005), Poetry Soc. Am. (v.p. 1974-78, exec. dir. L.I., 1979-83, James Joyce award 1972, Consuelo Ford award 1973, Gustav Davidson award 1974, 1st prize award 1975, Celia Wagner award 1976), Wash. Poets Assn., Northwest Writer's Conf., Washington Poets Assn., Poetwest (bd. mem., 1998—). Address: 900 University St Apt 6N Seattle WA 98101-2728 Personal E-mail: sarahsing2@aol.com. *As a poet, I have sought never to compromise my standards as to what constitutes poetry, despite fads that come and go. My goal has been to achieve whatever perfection I can in my work, and to preserve enough humility to realize that the best is never good enough. My life has truly been enriched by vision and aspiration. As a poet, the important thing for me is to create something moving and beautiful. Publication is a welcome by-product, but in itself, is not the goal for which I strive.*

**SINGER, S(IEGFRIED) FRED,** geophysicist, educator; b. Vienna, Sept. 27, 1924; came to U.S., 1940, naturalized, 1944; s. Joseph B. and Anne (Kelman) S.; m. Candace Carolyn Crandall, 1990. BEE, Ohio State U., 1943, DSc (hon.), 1970; AM, Princeton U., 1944, PhD in Physics, 1948. Instr. physics Princeton, 1943-44; physicist, applied physics lab. Johns Hopkins, 1946-50; sci. liaison officer Office Naval Research, Am. embassy, London, 1950-53; asso. prof. physics U. Md., College Park, 1953-59, prof., 1959-62; dir. Nat. Weather Satellite Center, Dept. Commerce, 1962-64; dean Sch. Environ. and Planetary Scis., U. Miami, 1964-67; dep. asst. sec. for water quality and research Dept. Interior, Washington, 1967-70; dep. asst. adminstr. EPA, Washington, 1970-71; prof. environ. scis. U. Va., Charlottesville, 1971-87; chief scientist U.S. Dept. Transp., Washington, 1987-89; pres. Sci. and Environ. Policy Project, 1990— Vis. rsch. prof. Jet Propulsion Lab., Calif. Inst. Tech., 1961-62; Fed. Exec. fellow Brookings Instn., 1971; vis. Sid Richardson prof. J.B. Johnson Sch., U. Tex., 1978; sr. fellow Heritage Found., 1982-83; vis. eminent scholar George Mason U., 1984-86, disting. rsch. prof., 1994—; Wesson fellow Hoover Instn., Stanford, 1992, 98; head sci. evaluation group astronautics and space exploration com. U.S. Ho. of Reps., 1958; cons. U.S. Treasury Dept., GAO, Office Tech. Assessment, U.S. Congress; mem. bd. Nat. Com. on Am. Energy Policy; mem. White House Panel on U.S.-Brazil Sci. and Tech. Exch., 1987; guest scholar Nat Air and Space Mus., Smithsonian Instn., 1991, Woodrow Wilson Internat. Ctr. for Scholars, 1991, Hoover Instn., 1992; disting. rsch. rpof. Inst. for Space Sci. and Tech., Gainesville, Fla., 1989-95; bd. dirs. AMREP Corp., Patent Enforcement Fund, Inc. Author: Geophysical Research with Artificial Earth Satellites, 1956, Manned Laboratories in Space, 1970, Global Effects of Environmental Pollution; 1970, Is There an Optimum Level of Population, 1971, The Changing Global Environment, 1975, Arid Zone Development: Potentialities and Problems, 1977, The Economic Effects of Demographic Changes, 1977, Energy, 1979, Price of World Oil, 1983, Free Market Energy, 1984, Global Climate Change, 1990, Origins of The Universe, 1990, The Ocean in Human Affairs, 1990, The Greenhouse Debate Continued, 1992, Hot Talk, Cold Science: Global Warming's Unfinished Debate, 1997, Climate Policy: From Rio to Kyoto, 2000; sci. adv. com. Dept State 1981; vice chmn. Nat. Adv. Com. Oceans and Atmosphere, 1981-86; contbr. articles on space, energy, environment and population problems to profl. publs. Served with USNR, 1944-46, USAFR, 1950-53. Recipient Presdl. commendation, 1958, gold medal for exceptional service Dept. Commerce, 1965; named Outstanding Young Man U.S. Jr. C. of C., 1959 Fellow AAAS (com. coun. affairs 1970), AIAA, Am. Geophys. Union, Am. Phys. Soc.; mem. Internat. Acad. Astronautics, European Acad. for Environ. Affairs, Pan Am. Med. Assn. (pres. sect. on environ. health scis. 1973-85), Cosmos Club (Washington), Colonnade Club (Charlottesville).

**SINGER, STEVEN D.,** lawyer; b. 1954; BA summa cum laude, Tufts Univ., 1976; JD magna cum laude, Harvard Univ., 1979. Bar: Mass. 1979. Ptnr., vice chmn. Corp. dept., co-chmn. Life Sci. dept. Wilmer Cutler Pickering Hale & Dorr, Boston. Mem. bd. overseers Beth Israel Deaconess Med. Ctr.; bd. dir. Beelzebubs Found.; past pres. Temple Beth Shalom, Needham, Mass. Named a Mass. Super Lawyer, Boston Mag., 2004. Mem.: ABA, Mass. Biotechnology Council, Biotechnology Ind. Org. Jewish. Office: Wilmer Cutler Pickering Hale & Dorr 60 State St Boston MA 02109 Office Phone: 617-526-6410. Office Fax: 617-526-5000. Business E-Mail: steven.singer@wilmerhale.com.

**SINGER, SUZANNE FRIED,** editor; b. NYC, July 9, 1935; d. Maurice Aaron and Augusta G. (Ginsberg) Fried; m. Max Singer, Feb. 12, 1959; children: Saul, Alexander (dec.), Daniel, Benjamin. BA with honors, Swarthmore Coll., 1956; MA, Columbia U., 1958. Program asst. NSF, Washington, 1958-60; assoc. editor Bibl. Archaeology Rev., Washington, 1979-84, mng. editor, 1984-96, exec. editor 1996-99, contbg. editor, 1999—; mng. editor Bibl. Rev., Washington, 1984-96, exec. editor, 1994-99; mng. editor Moment, Washington, 1990-99, editor, 1999—2004, contbg. editor, 2004—; exec. editor Archaeology Odyssey, 1998-99, contbg. editor, 1999—2005. Jewish. Address: Barak 1 Jerusalem Israel 93502 Personal E-mail: suzsinger@bogriver.net.

**SINGER, THOMAS KENYON,** international business consultant, fruit grower; b. Wilson, N.Y., Jan. 30, 1932; s. Harold Thomas and Grace (Kenyon) S.; m. Jacqueline Germain Moulin, June 8, 1957; children: Marc Andre, Vivianne Grace Singer Scott, Claire Anne, Michele Moulin Singer Ross, Gail Kenyon Singer Watson. BS in Econs., U. Pa., 1954. Dir. mktg. Europe Kaiser Aluminum & Chem. Corp., London, 1959-66; v.p. Kaiser LeNickel subs., Oakland, Calif., 1967-73, div. mgr., 1973-75; v.p. govt. relations Kaiser Aluminum & Chem. Corp., Washington, 1975-81, corp. v.p. Oakland, Calif., 1982—86; pres. Kaiser Internat. Corp., Oakland, Calif., 1982-86, also dir.; chmn. Singer Farms LLC, Appleton, NY. Dir., pres. IBA Inc., 1986-2000. Trustee United Way of Niagara County, 1998-2004, The Nature Conservancy of Ctrl. and Western N.Y., Niagara Area Found. Capt. USAF, 1955-57. Mem. Army and Navy Club (Washington), Niagara Frontier Country Club. Republican. Episcopalian. Home: 6627 Hummingbird Ln Appleton NY 14008-9693 Office: 6730 Lake Rd Appleton NY 14008-9673 Personal E-mail: jgstks@mac.com.

**SINGER-CHANG, GAIL LESLIE,** medical educator, consultant, social sciences educator; d. Frank Max (Stepfather) and Rona Jane Singer; m. Anthony Chang. BA in Journalism, San Diego State U., 1988; MS in Counseling, Calif. State U., Fullerton, 1992; MA in Clin. Psychology, Calif. Sch. Profl. Psychology, 1994, D of Psychology in Clin. Psychology, 1996. Pupil pers. svcs. credential Calif. Asst. prof. family medicine Western U. of Health Scis., Coll. Osteopathic Medicine of the Pacific, Pomona, Calif., 1999—2005, asst. prof. social and behavioral scis., asst. dean student affairs, 2003—05, program dir., doctor-patient communication program, 1999—2005; med. edn. consultant, 2005—. Orgnl. cons., Irvine, Calif., 1998—99; post-doctoral psychology intern El Toro Marine Base Family Services Ctr., El Toro, Calif., 1997—99; psychology intern Kaiser Permanente, Tustin, Calif., 1995—96, Orange Coast Coll. Student Health Ctr., Costa Mesa, Calif., 1994—95; counseling intern Teen-Age Pregnancy and Parenting Program, Fullerton, Calif., 1991—91; adj. instr. Concordia U., Irvine, Calif., 1998—99, Calif. State U., Fullerton, 1999; presenter in field. Presenter (profl. presentation) Enabling Disability Education: The Value of Using Disabled Persons as Standardized Patients, 10th Internat. Ottawa Conf. Med. Edn., 2002 (Greatest Profl. Promise, 1992), Creative Use of Assessment and Feedback: Increasing Deep Learning and Professionalism, Western Assn. Schs. and Colls., 2002, Psychosocial Aspects of the Physician-Patient Intervention, Soc. Psychol. Anthropology, 2003. Recipient Dedicated Svc. award, Calif. State U., 1998, Recognition cert., El Toro Marine Base Family Svcs. Ctr., 2001—03. Mem.: Assn. Profl. Cons., Am. Anthropol. Assn., Assn. for the Behavioral Scis. and Med. Edn., Soc. of Tchrs. of Family Medicine. Personal E-mail: doctorgail@msn.com.

**SINGH, AMAR V.,** research scientist; b. Ambala, Haryana, India, Feb. 13, 1972; s. Mamchand and Shakuntala Singh; m. Reetu Singh, Apr. 28, 2006. MS, U. Mysore, India, 1993—95. Asst. mgr. Jayson's Agritech Pvt. Ltd, Mysore, 1995—96; project asst. Ctrl. Food Technol. Rsch. Inst., Mysore, 1996—97; rsch. fellow dept. biotech. U. Mysore, 1997—99; clin. data

reviewer Clin. Data Mgmt. Ctr. India (GSK), Bangalore, Karnataka, India, 1999—2000; rsch. scientist in bioinformatics Avestha Gengraine Technologies Pvt. Ltd., Bangalore, 2000—01, group leader bioinformatics, 2001—02; rsch. asst. Thomas Jefferson U., Phila., 2003—03; rsch. assoc. U. Louisville, 2003—05, rsch. scientist, 2005—. Recipient Student & New Investigator Travel award, Teratology Soc., 2006; grantee Lady Tata Meml. fellowship, Lady Tata Meml. Trust, Mumbai, India, 1997—99. Mem.: The Asia Pacific Bioinformatics Network, Bioinformatics Soc. India (planning com., mgmt. mem. 2002), African Soc. Bioinformatics and Computational Biology (assoc.), Internat. Soc. Computational Biologists (assoc.), Teratology Soc. (assoc.; web site com. mem. 2006—). Achievements include design, development, and implementation of periodontal research defects systems manage; design, development, and implementation of birth defects systems manage (http:/sytemsanalysis.louisville.edu); design, development, and implementation of GenProtec for Dr. Monica Riley Marine Biological Laboratory in Mass; design, development, and implementation of laboratory information management system for Avestha Gengraine Technology Pvt. Ltd., India. Home: 2445 Glen Eagle Dr Louisville KY 40222 Home Fax: 501-643-8860. Personal E-mail: amarvsingh@gmail.com.

**SINGH, CHANDRALEKHA,** physics professor; m. Jeremy Levy; children: Akash Levy, Ishan Levy. PhD, U. Calif., Santa Barbara, 1993. Prof. U. Pitts. 1995—2006. Office: Univ Pitts Dept Physics 3941 Ohara St Pittsburgh PA 15260 Office Phone: 412-624-9045.

**SINGH, DELAR K.,** education educator; d. Karam Singh and Darshan Kour; 1 child, Harry. MEd, U. Pitts., 1985, PhD, 1990. Asst. prof. Niagara U., NY, 1998—2001; assoc. prof. Ea. Conn. State U., Willimantic, 2001—. Contbr. articles to profl. jours. Recipient Vincentian Rsch. award, Niagara U., 1999; grantee, Conn. Distance Learning Consortium, 2003; scholar, U. Pitts., 1985—90, Niagara U., 1985—90, 1999. Master: Conn. Coun. Exceptional Children (pres.-elect, pres. 2005—06). Office: Ea Conn State U 83 Windham St Willimantic CT 06226 Office Phone: 860-465-4555. Office Fax: 860-465-5099. Business E-Mail: singhd@easternct.edu.

**SINGH, HARJIT,** medical educator, artist; b. Shimla, Himachal Pradesh, India, Sept. 26, 1936; s. Achal Singh and Sunder Kaur; m. Cecilia Sepulveda, July 17, 1993; children: Namrita Aurora, Arshdeep Cristobal. MB, BS, Govt. Med. Coll., Patiala, India, 1958; MD, Punjabi U., Patiala, 1964. Lic. Punjab Med. Coun., Ludhiana, India, 1958, cert. Ednl. Coun. for Fgn. Med. Grads., 1962, lic. pediat. specialist Dept. Health, Dubai, UAE, 1990. Sr. lectr. in pediat. Govt. Med. Coll., Patiala, Punjab, India, 1965—66, Med. Coll., Rohtak, Haryana, India, 1966—70, asst. prof. pediat., 1970—75, reader in pediat., 1975—76, assoc. prof. pediat., 1976—77, 1978—82, prof. pediat., 1977—78, 1982—84, Arab Med. U., Benghazi, Libya, 1984—88; cmty. pediatrician Am. Hosp., Dubai, United Arab Emirates, 1997—2000; program dir. Hackettstown Regional Med. Ctr., NJ, 2002—. Mem. U. ct. & U. acad. coun. Dayanand U., Rohtak, 1977—82; undergraduate & postgraduate examiner in pediat. M. D. U., Rohtak, 1977—89, other various universities; resource person WHO Nat. Workshop on Pediatric Edn., Jabalpur, Madhya Pradesh, India, 1981; postgraduate examiner in pediat. medicine All India Inst. Med. Scis., New Delhi, 1981; postgraduate examiner in pediat. Punjabi U., Patiala, India, 1982; insp. Med. Coun. India, New Delhi, 1982—82; examiner in pediat. Arab Med. U., Benghazi, 1985—88; mem. rsch. & organizing com. First Internat. Conf. on Infectious Diseases in Arab Countries, Benghazi, 1985; vis. rsch. prof. Sch. Tropical Medicine, Liverpool, 1986—95; observor Arab Bd. in Pediat., Benghazi, 1986; mem. U. rsch. com. Arab Med. U., Benghazi, 1986—88. Exhibitions include Dubai Internat. Art Ctr., 1991—99, Yolo County Art Coun., 2001, Sussex County Art & Heritage Coun., 2002 (Hon. Mention), Warren County Art Coun., 2002, Triveni Art Gllery, New Delhi, 1970, Represented in permanent collections, India, Can., UK, UAE, US. Grantee Rsch. Grants, Indian Coun. Med. Rsch., New Delhi, 1975—88; scholar Course in Devel. of Undergraduate Curriculum in Pediat., WHO, 1982, Course on Devel. of Undergraduate Curriculum on Maternal & Child Health, 1983; fellowship in pediat. hematology, 1974-75. Mem.: Alliance of CME (corr.), Indian Assn. Advancement Med. Edn. (life), Perinatology Forum (life). Office: Hackettstown Regional Med Ctr 651 Willow Grove St Hackettstown NJ 07840 Office Fax: 908-950-6815. E-mail: hsingh@hch.org.

**SINGH, INDERJIT,** internist, nephrologist, medical educator; b. Patiala, India, Oct. 17, 1962; arrived in U.S., 1987; s. Charanjit Singh and Pritinder Kaur; m. Toniya Cheema Singh, June 5, 1994; children: Kunaal Inder, Kabir Inder. MBBS, U. Delhi, 1986. Diplomate Am. Bd. Internal Medicine, Am. Bd. Nephrology. Cert. ACLS. Intern U. Delhi Affiliated Hosps., 1985-86, resident in internal medicine, 1986-87, Easton Hosp.-Hahnemann U. Hosp., 1990-92; rsch. assoc. in endocrinology U. Health Scis.-Chgo. Med. Sch., 1987-88; intern Nassau County Med. Ctr., N.Y., 1988-89; rsch. assoc. in med. transplantation Presbyn. Hosp.-U. Pitts., 1989-90; clin. fellow divsn. nephrology U. Mich., 1992-93, rsch. fellow, 1993-95; clin. asst. prof. internal medicine So. Ill. U. Sch. Medicine, Carbondale, 1995-97; clin. asst. prof. medicine St. Louis U. Sch. Medicine; staff nephrologist BMA Carbondale Dialysis Unit, 1995-97, Marion Nephroplex Dialysis Unit, 1996-97; assoc. med. dir. Jefferson County Dialysis, Festus, Mo., 1999—; med. dir. Washington County Dialysis, Potosi, Mo., 1999—, Perry County Dialysis Unit, 2003—. Med. dir. Arrowhead Point Med. Clinic, Harrisburg, Ill., 1995-97; staff nephrologist BMA Carbondale Dialysis Unit, 1995—, Marion (Ill.) Nephroplex Dialysis Unit, 1996—, Christian NE Hosp., St. Louis, DePaul Hosp., St. Louis, Jefferson Meml. Hosp., Crystal City, Mo., others; chmn. infection control com. Marion Meml. Hosp., 1995-97; instr. Washington U. Sch. Medicine, 1997—; presenter in field. Contbr. articles to profl. jours., chapters to books. Mem. sci. adv. bd. Nat. Kidney Found., 1999—. Fellow ACP; mem. Am. Soc. Nephrology, Nat. Kidney Found., Am. Soc. Internal Medicine. Sikh. Avocations: travel, sports, tennis, opera, music, broadway. Home: 843 Courtwood Ln Ballwin MO 63011-5110 Office: 11125 Dunn Rd Ste 206 Saint Louis MO 63136-6111 Office Phone: 314-741-1600. Personal E-mail: ijsinghmd@yahoo.com.

**SINGH, JAI,** online news executive; b. Agra, India; Exec. editor news InfoWorld, PC Week; head The Source; founding editor, v.p., editor-in-chief CNET News.com, 1996—. Named Most Influential Online Journalist, Marketing Computers Mag., 2001—04; recipient Nat. Mag. award, 2004. Mem.: South Asian Journalists Assn. Office: CNET News.com 235 Second St San Francisco CA 94105

**SINGH, K. PAUL,** telecommunications industry executive; MSEE, S.U.N.Y.; MBA, Harvard U. Vice-pres. global prod. mktg. M.C.I., 1991—94; found., chmn., CEO Overseas Telecommunications Inc.; found. Cygnus Satellite Corp.; found., chmn., CEO Primus Telecommunications Group, 1994, also pres. Office: Primus Telecommunications Group Ste 900 7901 Jones Branch Rd Mc Lean VA 22102*

**SINGH, KRISHNA BINOD,** obstetrician, gynecologist; m. Ualetta Fay Singh, Jan. 1, 1966. MBBS, Patna Med. Coll., Bihar, India, 1958. Assoc. prof. ob-gyn. La. State U. Health Scis. Ctr., Shreveport. Cons. in field.

**SINGH, LOREN CHAN,** writer, educator; b. Palo Alto, Calif., Sept. 10, 1943; s. Shaw Wing and Anna Mae Chan; m. Frances Anastasia Chow, Apr. 19, 1975 (div. Jan. 1988); children: Karen Monique Chan, Pierre Benedict Chan, Marc Henri Chan; m. Sandra Marie Miner, Mar. 14, 2000. AB, Stanford U., Calif., 1965, AM, 1966; MS, Golden Gate U., San Francisco, 1988; PhD, UCLA, 1971. Tchg. asst. UCLA, 1968—69, tchg. assoc., 1969—70; lectr. in history Calif. State U., Northridge, 1970—71, San Jose State U., Calif., 1971—72, asst. prof. history, 1972—76, assoc. prof. history, 1976—80; lectr. history Calif. State U., East Bay, 1980—81; prodn. test technician Nicolet Paratronics Corp., Fremont, Calif., 1982; computer svc. technician Bell-No. Rsch., Mountain View, Calif., 1982—83, rsch. analyst, 1984—85, tech. writer, 1985—87; sr. tech. writer StrataCom, Inc., Campbell, Calif., 1987—88; tech. writer Sun Microsystems, Palo Alto, 1988—90, sr. tech.

writer, 1990—2000; tech. editor Brocade Comms. Sys., Inc., San Jose, 2000—02; instr. adult edn. Santa Clara Unified Sch. Dist., Calif., 2002—03; bus driver Serendipity Land Yachts, Ltd., Santa Clara, 2002—05; adminstrv. asst. Microcontroller Pros Corp., Morgan Hill, Calif., 2005—. Author: Sagebrush Statesman, 1973, Collected Technical Support Notes, 1988, SPARCstation 1 Installation Guide, 1989, Desktop Storage Pack Installation Guide, 1989—90, SPARCstation 2 Installation Guide, 1990, SPARCstation 10 Installation Guide, 1992, SPARCstation 10 Networking and Communication Guide, 1993, SPARCstation 10SX VSIMMs Installation, 1993, SPARCstation 20 HyperSPARC Module Upgrade, 1995, SPARCstation 20 SuperSPARC-II Module Upgrade, 1995, Sun Ultra 1 Reference Material, 1995—96, Sun Ultra 2 Reference Manual, 1996, Sun Ultra 30 Installation Guide, 1997, SPARCstorage FlexiPack Removable Storage Tray Installation Guide, 1997, Sun StorEdge long Wave Gigabit Interface Converter Service Manual, 1999, Sun StorEdge PCI Dual Fibre Channel Host Adapter Installation, 2000; editor: Chinese-American History Reader, 1976; contbr. articles to profl. jours. Radio sta. trustee ARC, Menlo Park, Calif., 1975—80. Recipient Presdl. Sports award, Pres.'s Coun. Phys. Fitness and Sports, 1973. Mem.: Am. Radio Relay League, South Valley YMCA. Democrat. Sikh. Avocations: swimming, amateur radio, stamp collecting/philately. Home: 195 Blossom Hill Rd # 123 San Jose CA 95123-2348 Office: Microcontroller Pros Corp 17408 Blue Jay Dr Morgan Hill CA 95037-6402 Personal E-mail: ad6yu@ecoisp.com.

**SINGH, MANMOHAN,** orthopedic surgeon, educator; b. Patiala, Punjab, India, Oct. 5, 1940; came to U.S., 1969; s. Ajmer and Kartar Singh; m. Manjit Anand, Jan. 1, 1974; children: Kirpal, Gurmeet. MB, BS, Govt. Med. Coll., Patiala, 1964; CM, Panjab U., Chandigarh, India, 1968. Diplomate Am. Bd. Orthop. Surgery. Mem. vis. faculty Mayo Grad. Sch., Rochester, Minn., 1969; rsch. fellow Inst. Internat. Edn., Chgo., 1969-74; resident in orthop. surgery Michael Reese Hosp. and Med. Ctr., Chgo., 1974-78; pvt. practice Chgo., 1979—; mem. attending staff, dir. orthop. rsch. Michael Reese Hosp. and Med. Ctr., Chgo., 1979-94; fellow in orthop. oncology Mayo Clinic and Mayo Found., Rochester, 1979; assoc. prof. U. Ill., Chgo., 1996—. Founder Quantum Health Cir./Enterprises for Holistic Medicine. Developer x-ray method (Singh Index) and bone density method (Radius Index) for diagnosis of osteoporosis. Fulbright travel grantee, 1968. Fellow Am. Acad. Orthop. Surgeons, Am. Orthop. Foot and Ankle Soc.; mem. Orthop. Rsch. Soc., Am. Soc. for Bone and Mineral Rsch., Internat. Bone and Mineral Soc. Democrat. Sikh. Avocations: stamp collecting/philately, photography, meditation. Office: 110 Ridge Rd Munster IN 46321 E-mail: msingh@illianasurgery.com.

**SINGH, NARENDRA,** cardiologist, researcher, medical educator; b. Saraiya, Uttar Pradesh, India, June 10, 1963; Can. U.S.; s. Rudra Prasad and Manorma Singh; m. Mitra Kumari Kandhal, June 26, 1993; children: Shailin Raj, Ishaan Vivek. BS in Biochemistry, Dalhousie U., Halifax, Can., 1983; MD, 1987. Diplomate Am. Bd. Internal Medicine, Am. Bd. Cardiovascular Disease, Am. Bd. Nuclear Cardiology, NASPE Testamur. Rotating intern St. Michael's Hosp., U. Toronto, 1987—88, resident in internal medicine, 1988—91, rsch. fellow in cardiology, 1993—94; cardiologist Centenary Cardiology Assocs., Toronto, Ont., Canada, 1994—2002; dir. Scarborough Cardiology Rsch., Toronto, 1996—2002; cardiologist Northside Cardiology P.C., Atlanta, 2002—, dir. rsch., 2003—; cardiology sect. chair Northside Hosp., Atlanta, 2004—. Lectr. U. Toronto, 1994—2002; med. dir. Pacemaker/ICD Programme, 1995—2002, Cardiac Cath Lab., 1999—2001; co-founder Greater Toronto Area Cmty. Cardiologists, 1995—2001; clin. asst. prof. Emory U. Sch. Medicine, Atlanta, 2002—; mem. regional lipid adv. bd. Merck Can.; spkr. in field. Contbr. articles to profl. jours. Bd. dirs. Hosp. Found., Toronto, 1998—2002. Recipient award plaque in recognition for contbns., Greater Torotno Area Cmty. Cardiologists; scholar, Dalhousie U., 1981, 1983, 1985; Rsch. fellow, U. Toronto, 1993. Fellow: Am. Coll. Cardiology, Royal Coll. Physicians and Surgeons Can. (cert. in cardiology/internal medicine), Am. Heart Assn. (bd. dirs. Atlanta 2005—); mem.: Internat. Soc. Hypertension Blacks, Am. Soc. Nuc. Cardiology, Hearth Rhythm Soc., Heart Assn. Atlanta, Med. Assn. Ga., Can. Med. Assn., Med. Staff Soc. (bd. govs.), mem. med. adv. com. 1995—97, pres. Centenary site, mem. strategic planning com. 1996), Can. Cardiovasc. Soc. (nat. sec. 2000—02, sec., mem. exec. com., chairperson membership com. 2000—02, coun. mem. 1999—2002). Avocations: travel, golf, theater. Office: Northside Cardiology PC 5670 Peachtree-Dunwoody Rd Ste 880 Atlanta GA 30342 Office Phone: 404-256-2575. Office Fax: 404-256-2535. Personal E-mail: narendra.singh@yahoo.com. Business E-Mail: nsingh@atlantanorthsidecardio.com.

**SINGH, RAJENDRA,** mechanical engineering educator; b. Dhampur, India, Feb. 13, 1950; came to U.S., 1973; s. Raghubir and Ishwar (Kali) S.; m. Veena Ghungesh, June 24, 1979; children: Rohit, Arun. BS with honors, Birla Inst., 1971; MS, Indian Inst. Tech., 1973; PhD, Purdue U., 1975. Grad. instr. Purdue U., West Layfayette, Ind., 1973-75; sr. engr. Carrier Corp., Syracuse, NY, 1975-79; asst. prof. Ohio State U., Columbus, 1979-83, assoc. prof., 1983-87, prof., 1987—, Donald D. Glower chair in engring., 2001—. Adj. lectr. Syracuse (N.Y.) U., 1977-79; bd. dirs. Inst. of Noise Control Engring. 1994-96, 99—, v.p. tech. activities, 2000-02, pres., 2003; gen. chmn. Nat. Noise Conf., Columbus, 1985; leader U.S. delegation to India-U.S.A. Symposium on Vibration and Noise Engring., 1996; vis. prof. U. Calif. Berkeley, 1987-88; pres. Inter-Noise 2002 Congress; chmn. India-USA Symposium on Vibration and Noise, 2001; cons., lectr. in field. Author: Emerging Trends in Vibration and Noise Engineering, 1996; contbr. more than 300 articles to profl. jours.; guest editor jours. Recipient Gold medal U. Roorkee, 1973, R. H. Kohr Rsch. award Purdue U., 1975, Excellence in Tchg. award Inst. Noise Control Engring., 1989, Rsch. award Ohio State U., 1983, 87, 91, 96, 2001, 03, Educator of Yr. award GM Tech. Edn. Program, 1998. Fellow ASME, Acoustical Soc. Am., Soc. Auto Engring.; mem. Inst. Noise Control Engring.(cert.), Am. Soc. Engring. Edn. (George Westinghouse award 1993). Achievements include patent for rolling door; development of new analytical and experimental techniques in machine dynamics, acoustics, vibration and fluid control. Home: 4772 Belfield Ct Dublin OH 43017-2592 Office Phone: 614-292-9044. Business E-Mail: singh.3@osu.edu.

**SINGH, RONALD,** social sciences educator, researcher; s. Heeraman and Rajmatti Singh; 1 child, Raymond Anthony D'Angelo. B in Social Sci., U. Guyana, Georgetown, 1986; MS, Hunter Coll., 1999. Trained tchr.'s cert. Ministry Edn., Guyana, 1981. Tchr. St. Lawrence CC & Vreeden Hoop CH Schs., Parika, Vreeden Hoop, 1974—87; planner State Planning Commn., Georgetown, Demerara, 1987—91; rsch. asst. Nat. Exptl. U. Guayana, Puerto Ordaz, Estado Bolivar, Venezuela, 1991—92; pres., dir. Internat. Devel. Consulting, Caracas, Federal District, Venezuela, 1993—98; rsch. assoc. Rsch. Inst. Study Caribbean Diaspora, Queens, 1999—2004; pres., dir. Liberty Tutoring Ctr., Queens, NY, 2000—; v.p. Millennium Photo Inc., Queens, 2002—04. Advisor Nat. Econ. & Social Coun., Georgetown, 1987—91. Author: (poetry) Fragrance of a Dessert-Rose; contbr. articles and chpts. to books; exec. editor Caribbean Jour., Queens, 1999—. V.p. Guyana Venezuela Friendship Assn., Caracas, Federal District, Venezuela, 1995—98; rschr., editor East Indian Diaspora, Inc., Queens, 1998—2002; pres. U. Guyana Assn. of NY, N.Y.C., 1999—2002. Named to Internat. Soc. Poets Hall of Fame, Wash., 1997; recipient Edn. Psychology prize, Cyril Potter Coll. Edn., 1981, Editor's Choice award, Nat. Libr. Poetry, 1995. Mem.: East Indian Diaspora (assoc.; asst. sec. 1999), Internat. Soc. Poets (life Internat. Poet of Merit award 1997), Liberty Knights Sports Club (pres. 2001). Avocations: cricket, travel, reading. Home: 10902 Liberty Ave # 2 South Richmond Hill NY 11419-1704 Office Phone: 718-323-0101.

**SINGH, SANGITA,** information technology and marketing executive; With HCL Technologies, Wipro Technologies, Mountain View, Calif., 1992—; jr. exec., mktg. mgr. e-bus. portfolio, 1999, chief mktg. officer, 2001—, v.p. strategic mktg. Office: Wipro Technologies 2nd Fl 1300 Crittenden Lane Mountain View CA 94043 Office Phone: 650-316-3555. Office Fax: 650-316-3468.*

**SINGH, SEOPAUL,** security firm executive; b. Georgetown, Guyana, Apr. 26, 1946; s. Mooni and D. Singh; m. Gloria Indrouti Birbal, Nov. 6, 1972 (div.); children: Shelly Valini, Paul Rabindranauth, Sharlene Charisma Padmini. Diploma in Pub. Adminstrn., U. Guyana, Georgetown, 1981. Cert. emergency mgr. Va.; ordained min. Internat. Gospels Assemblies, 1977, Assemblies of God, 1979; cert. profl. security mgr. John Jay Coll. N.Y., 2003. Office mgr. UN Urban Planning, Georgetown, 1977—78; trade intelligence exec. Ministry Trade and Consumer Protection, Georgetown, 1978—83, chief allocation distbn., 1978—83; exec. officer CD Commn., Georgetown, 1983—88; resource person Partners Americas, Georgetown, 1988—92; emergency mgmt. specialist UN Volunteers, Geneva, 1992—97; security supr. Morgan Stanley, N.Y.C., 1991—. Advisor emergency relief Nat. Relief Com., Georgetown, 1983—88; advisor emergency mgmt. Partners Americas, 1988—92, Miss., 1988—92; presbyter, missions dir. Assembly God, Georgetown, 1975—83. Author: (book of poetry) Changing Moods; contbr. articles to profl. jours. Co-founder, sec. Guyanese-Am. Assn., Queens, 1992; co founder, pub. rels. officer Assn. Arts & Writers, Queens, NY, 1998. Fellow, Ctrl. U.S. Earth Quake Consortium, 1992, Masonry Inst. Tenn., 1992, Harvard, 1994, Maj. Indsl. Accident Coun. Can. Mem.: NOAA, Assn. Contingency Planners, Internat. Assn. Emergency Mgrs. D-Conservative. International Gospel Assembly. Achievements include development of First Integrated Disaster Response Mechanism, Office of the Prime Minister, Georgetown, Guyana; received Citation for Professionalism in high rise rescue of individual trapped in an elevator; pioneered five churches in five years in Guyana. Avocations: pool, dominoes, chess, poetry reading, christian ministry camping. Home: 139-20 89th Avenue Jamaica NY 11435 Office: Association Artists & Writers 105-27 Liberty Avenue Ozone Park NY 11417 Personal E-mail: seopauls@aol.com.

**SINGH, SHIWENDRA PRASAD,** civil engineer; b. Mukrera, Bihar, India, July 5, 1937; came to U.S., 1969; s. Ramchandra and Dhanna (Devi) S.; m. Sita Singh, Mar. 7, 1962; children: Sarita, Sabita, Kavita, Saket. BSc in Civil Engring., Bihar Coll. Engring., Patna, India, 1961; MSc in Civil Engring., U. Calgary, Alta., Can., 1968. Registered profl. engr., Pa. Asst. bridge engr. Bihar Pub. Works Dept., Patna, 1962-66; sr. project mgr. Pa. Dept. Transp., Clearfield, 1969—. Recipient Gov.'s Meritorious award Pa. State Gov., 1977, Outstanding Managerial Ability award Pa. Dept. Transp., 1982, Sec. award for excellence Pa. Dept. Transp., 1990. Mem. NSPE, Am. Soc. Hwy. Engrs. Home: 2537 Meadow Rd Clearfield PA 16830-1140 Office: Pa Dept Transp 1924 Daisy St Clearfield PA 16830-3224

**SINGH, SURENDRA P.,** agricultural economics professor, consultant; b. Chunar, India, Aug. 16, 1944; arrived in U.S., 1967; s. Dhani Ram and Devi Rama; m. Gita Singh, May 30, 1974; children: Vikas, Yojna. BSc, Agra U., 1963, MSc, 1965; PhD, Pa. State U., 1972. Rsch. assoc. Pa. State U., University Park, 1972; from rsch. assoc. to assoc. prof. Tenn. State U., Nashville, 1980—86, prof. agrl. econ., 1986—. Cons. UN Devel. Prog., India, 1991—92, ACDI/VOCA, Uganda, 1994; cons./PI USAID/USDA, 1991—. Author: Perspectives on the Small Farm, 1986; assoc. editor: So. Jour. Agrl. Econs., 1990—93; contbr. articles to profl. jours. Pres. Hindu Cultural Ctr. Tenn., Nashville, 1988—98, trustee, 1990—98. Recipient Fulbright Scholar award, 1989. Mem.: SAEA, AAEA, IAMA. Hindu. Home: 112 Montcastle Ct Nashville TN 37221 Office: Tenn State Univ 3500 John A Merritt Blvd Nashville TN 37209

**SINGH, VIJAY,** professional golfer; b. Lautoka, Fiji, Feb. 22, 1963; m. Andrea Seth Singh; 1 child, Qass Seth. Profl. golfer PGA Tour, 1993—. Player The President's Cup, 1994, 96, 98, 2000, 03, 05, World Cup, 2002. Named Hon. Chairperson, National Golf Day, 1999; named to World Golf Hall of Fame, PGA Tour, 2006; recipient Samman award, Pravasi Bharatiya Divas, 2005. Achievements include 29 Career PGA Tour victories; winner PGA Championship, 1998, 2004, Masters Tournament, 2002; 22 international victories; Set single season record for earnings, 2004; Ranked No. 1 in the world, 2004. Avocations: snooker, cricket, rugby, soccer. Office: South Fla Sect PGA 10804 W Sample Rd Coral Springs FL 33065-2632*

**SINGHAL, AVINASH CHANDRA,** engineering administrator, educator; b. Aligarh, India, Nov. 4, 1939; s. Shiam Sunder and Pushpa Lata (Jindal) S.; m. Uma Rani Sharma, Sept. 5, 1967; children: Ritu Chanchal, Anita, Neil Raj. BSc, Agra U., India, 1957; BSc in Engring., St. Andrews U., Dundee, Scotland, 1959, degree (hon.) in engring., 1960; MS, MIT, 1961, CE, 1962, ScD, 1964; certificate in bus. mgmt., UCLA, 1971; postgrad., 2005. Registered profl. engr., N.Y., Que., Ariz. Rsch. engr. Kaman Aircraft, Burlington, Mass., 1964-65; prof. Laval U., Quebec, Can., 1965-69; asst. program mgr. TRW, Redondo Beach, Calif., 1969-71; mgr. GE, Phila., 1971-72; mgr. tech. svcs. Engrs. India Ltd., New Delhi, 1972-74; project engr. Weidlinger Assocs., N.Y.C., 1974-77; prof. Ariz. State U., Tempe, 1977—; dir. Cen. Bldg. Rsch. Inst., 1992-93. Dir. Earthquake Rsch. Lab., Ariz. State U., Tempe, 1978—89, grad. coord. structural engring., 1991—92, senator acad. senate, 1995—98, chmn. governance grievance, 1995—96, faculty ombudsman, 1996—97, coord. Computer Aided Design and Modeling, 1997—98, com. acad. freedom and tenure, 1998—99, com. promotion and tenure; cons. McDonnel Aircraft Corp., St. Louis, 1977—78, Sperry Corp., 1979—80, McDonnell Douglas Helicopter Co., 1990—91, Ariz. Nuc. Power Plant, 1991—92; U.S. del. U.S./China Workshop on Arch Dams, Beijing, 1987; Can. del. Shell Structures, USSR, Ukraine, 1964; session chmn. Internat. Conf. on Soil Dynamics and Earthquake Engring., Karlsruhe, Germany, 1991; rsch. prof. Nat. Ctrl. U. Taiwan, 1990; vis. prof. U. Melbourne, Australia, 1983—84, U. Auckland, New Zealand, 1983—84; nodal dir. wood substitute rsch. program, india, 1992—95; instr. Indian Inst. Tech., Madras, 1997—98, Indian Inst. Sci., Bangalore, 1997—98. Mem. editl. bd. Soil Dynamics and Earthquake Engring., 1991—, Advances in Earthquake Engring., 1995—; reviewer Jour. Psychol. Reports, Perceptual and Motor Skills; contbr. Nuclear Waste Storage, 1986, (proc. publ.) Earthquake Behavior of Buried Pipelines, 1989, Wood Substitute: A National Priority, 1992, System Flexibility and Reflected Pressures, 1993, Simulation of Blast Pressures on Flexible Panels, 1994, Dynamic Analysis of Dams with Nonlinear Slip Joints, 1998, Performance of Retrofit Arch Dams, 1998, Ariz. Emergency Ctr. Retrofit, 1998, others; editor: Seismic Performance of Pipelines & Storage Tanks, 1985, Recent Advances in Lifeline Earthquake Engineering, 1987, Seismic Ground Motions Response, Repair and Instrumentation of Pipes and Bridges, 1992; contbr. articles to Jour. Performance of Constructed Facilities, ASCE, Jour. Computers and Structures, Jour. ASME, Jour. Aerospace Engring. ASCE; reviewer, bd. editors Jour. Earthquake Engring. and Structural Dynamics, Structural Engring. Papers Jour. ASCE. Bd. dirs., pres. Las Estadas Homeowner's Assn., Tempe, 1996-97; chmn. bd. dirs. India Assn. Greater Phoenix, 1985-86; pres. India Assn. Greater Boston, 1964-65; v.p., treas. Dobson Ranch Homeowners Assn., Mesa, Ariz., 1988-91; founding mem. Asian Am. Assn. Ariz., Phoenix, 1987-89; founding mem., pres. Asian Am. Faculty Assn., Ariz. State U., Tempe 1986-88; cons. UN Devel. Program New Delhi, 1991-92. McLintock fellow MIT, 1960, Carnegie fellow MIT, 1960-63, fellow Royal Astron. Soc., London, 1961-64; rsch. fellow Kobe U., Japan, 1990; Denninson scholar Instn. Civil Engrs., London, 1959; Henry Adams Rsch. medal Structural Engrs., London, 1972; grantee Can. Def. Rsch. Bd., 1966-69, NSF, 1978-82, Ford Found., 1978-79, U.S. Army Corps Engrs., 1984-86, U.S. Dept. Interior, 1986-88, Office Naval Rsch., 1994. Ariz. Dept. Emergency Mgmt., 1997-98; recipient 1st prize bridge bldg. Instn. Strucural Engrs., Merit award Inst. Engrs., India. Fellow ASCE, Ctrl. Bldg. Rsch. Inst. (chmn. mgmt. coun., chmn. APEX com.), Sigma Xi, Tau Beta Pi, Chi Epsilon. Achievements include research in computer modeling, blast effects on structures, in lifeline engineering, earthquake strengthening of deteriorated dams, steel and concrete buildings, bridges, materials, and non-linear finite element dynamics. Home: 2258 W Monterey Ave Mesa AZ 85202-7330 Office: Ariz State U Dept Civil Engring 2258 W Monterey Cir Mesa AZ 85202-7330 Office Phone: 480-839-1652. Business E-Mail: singhal@asu.edu. *Service to mankind and love for the family and friends is the key to success and happiness.*

**SINGHAL, MEENA,** education educator; b. New Castle, England, Apr. 1, 1968; d. Raj and Mohini Singhal; m. Walid Sabbagh, May 30, 2000. BA, BEd, U. Calgary, Canada, 1992; MEd, McGill U., Montreal, Canada, 1996; PhD, U. Ariz., 1999. Lectr. U. Calif., Irvine, 2000; instr. Long Beach (Calif.) City Coll., 2000—. Editor The Reading Matrix, Irvine, Calif., 2000—. Curriculum project Web-Based Reading Program for Composition Students (Milton Riepe award for Excellence in Tchg., 1999). Fellow, U. of Ariz., 1999; grantee Partnership for Excellence Grant-New Course Proposal, Long Beach City Coll., 2000, Devel. of Integrated Syllabus for Learning Communities Project, 2001, Faculty Devel. and Improvement of Academic Programs: Strengthening Academic Bridges & Support for Success-Methods to Increase Latino Student Retention, 2002. Mem.: Pi Lamba Theta (hon.). Achievements include research in computer-assisted langauge learning and reading. Office: Long Beach City Coll ESL Dept 1305 East Pacific Coast Hwy Long Beach CA 90806 Business E-Mail: msinghal@lbcc.edu.

**SINGHAL, RAJAN,** engineering executive, consultant; b. Saharanpur, Up, India, Oct. 15, 1954; s. Balmukand and Sonadevi Singhal; m. Uma Gangal, June 18, 1979; children: Ekta, Parul. BS in Engring. & Comm., Nat. Inst. Tech., 1976; LLB, Garhwal U., 1997; MBA, Richard Stockton Coll. N.J., 2004. Jr. scientist Solidstate Physics Lab., Delhi, 1976—77; sub divisional officer UP State Electricity Bd., Meerut, 1977—86, exec. engr. Dehradun, 1986—96, superintending engr., 1996—2000; dir. Hi-Tec Sys., Inc., Egg Harbor, NJ, 2000—01, dir. recruiting & placement, 2000—, sr. aviation engr., 2001—04, tech. mgr., 2004—. Guardian Agarwal Com., Dehradun, 1996—2000. Mem.: IEEE (chair 2002—02, Engr. of Yr. 2002), Internat. Test & Evaluation Assn., Am. Inst. of Aeronautics & Astronautics, Internat. Toastmasters (v.p. 2001—02). Office Phone: 609-858-0804. Personal E-mail: rajusa@comcast.net.

**SINGHVI, SURENDRA SINGH,** financial consultant; b. Jodhpur, Rajasthan, India, Jan. 16, 1942; came to U.S., 1962, naturalized 1986; s. Rang Raj and Ugam Kanwar (Surana) S.; m. Sushila Bhandari, July 7, 1965; children: Seema, Sandeep. B in Commerce, Rajasthan U., 1961; MBA, Atlanta U., 1963; PhD, Columbia U., 1967. CPA; cert. mgmt. acct. Asst. prof. fin. Miami U., Oxford, Ohio, 1967-69, assoc. prof. fin., 1969-70; adj. prof. fin., 1970-95; fin. mgr. ARMCO Inc., Middletown, Ohio, 1970-79, asst. treas., 1979-83, gen. fin. mgr., 1983-86; v.p. and treas. Edison Bros. Stores, Inc., St. Louis, 1986-90; pres. Singhvi & Assocs., Inc., Dayton, Ohio, 1990—. Bd. dirs. Columbia Indsl. Sales Corp., Hauer Music Co., Oasis Property Inc., Om Hospitality, Inc., Chester Hospitality Inc. Author: Planning for Capital Investment, 1980; co-editor: Frontiers of Financial Management, 4th edit., 1984, Global Finance 2000-A Handbook of Strategy and Organization (The Conference Board), 1996; contbr. over 90 articles to profl. jours. Bd. trustees South Ctrl. Ohio Minority Bus. Coun., 2000—. Recipient Chancellor's Gold medal Rajasthan U., Ahimsa (Non-Violence) award Fedn. Jaina Assns. in N.Am., 1999. Mem. Inst. Mgmt. Accts. (Bayer Silver medal 1978), Fin. Execs. Inst., Fin. Mgmt. Assn., Dayton Minority Supplier Devel. Coun. (dir. 1997—, chmn. 2000), Rotary (dir. internat. program Middletown chpt. 1973-86, Dayton chpt. 1995—, treas., dir. 2001—02), India Club (pres. Dayton chpt. 1980). Avocations: swimming, kanasta, travel, writing. Home and Office: Singhvi and Assocs Inc 439 Ridge Line Ct Dayton OH 45458-9546 Office Phone: 937-885-7414. Personal E-mail: s.singhvi@yahoo.com.

**SINGLE, THOMAS E.,** paper company executive; b. Gary, Ind., May 31, 1961; BSCE, N.C. State U., 1984, BS in Pulp & Paper Tech., 1984; MBA, U. N.C., 1988. Area mgr. Measurex, Atlanta, 1984—86; mgr. corp. fin. James River, Richmond, Va., 1988—91, dir. energy planning & devel., 1991—95, dir. energy procurement, 1995—98, dir. strategic sourcing & procurement, 1998—2000; v.p. cost reduction & productivity Fort James, Deerfield, Ill., 2000—01; v.p. strategic sourcing and procurement Ga. Pacific Corp., Atlanta, 2001—. Office: Ga Pacific Corp 133 Peachtree St NE Atlanta GA 30303

**SINGLETARY, ALVIN D.,** lawyer; b. Sept. 27, 1942; s. Alvin E. and Alice (Pastoret) Singletary; m. Judy Louise Singletary, Dec. 3, 1983; children: Kimberly Dawn, Shane David, Kelly Diane. BA, La. State U., 1964; JD, Loyola U., New Orleans, 1969. Bar: La. 1969, U.S. Dist. Ct. (ea. dist.) La. 1972, U.S. Ct. Appeals (5th cir.) 1972, U.S. Ct. Appeals (11 cir.) 1981, U.S. Ct. Internat. Trade 1981, U.S. Ct. Customs and Patent Appeals 1982, U.S. Supreme Ct. 1978. Instr. Delgado Coll., New Orleans, 1976—77; sole practice Slidell, La., 1970—. Spl. asst. dist. atty 22d Judicial Dist. Ct., Parish of St. Tammany, La.; sec., treas. St. Tammany Pub. Trust Fin. Authority, 1978—2002. Chmn. sustaining membership enrollment Cypress Dist. Boy Scouts Am., 1989—; treas. Slidell Centennial commn.; councilman-at-large City of Slidell, 1978—2002, interim mayor, 1985; mem. Dem. State Ctrl. Com., 1978—82; mem. Rep. State Ctrl. Com. Dist. 76, La., 1996—2000; del. La.Constl. Conv., 1972—73; chmn. Together We Build Program First Baptist Ch. of Slidell, La.; bd. dir. St. Tammany Coun. on Aging. Mem.: Lions, Delta Theta Phi. Baptist. Office: PO Box 1158 Slidell LA 70459-1158

**SINGLETARY, MICHAEL,** retired professional football player, motivational speaker; b. Houston, Oct. 9, 1958; m. Kim Singletary; children: Kristin, Matthew. BA in Mgmt., Baylor U., 1981. Middle linebacker Chgo. Bears, 1981-93. Motivational spkr. Wash. Speakers Bur., 2004—. Named Defensive MVP, season 1985; named to Pro Bowl team, 1983-91, Sporting News All-Pro team, 1984-89, 91, Sporting News Coll. All-Am. team, 1980. mem. NFL Super Bowl Championship Team, 1985. Office: Wash Spkrs Bur 1633 Prince St Alexandria VA 22314*

**SINGLETARY, PATRICIA ANN,** minister; b. N.Y.C. Mar 3 1948; d George and Minnie Juanita (Williams) Nickens; m. Edward Franklin Singletary, Feb. 5, 1966 (dec.); children: Erik Franklin, Don Andre. BTh, New World Bible Inst. & Sem., 1984, MRE, 1986; AS, BS, SUNY-Empire State Coll., 1991; AA, Va. Sem. and Coll., 1995; MDiv, New Brunswick Theol. Sem., 1995; DD, Tenn. Bapt. Sch. Religion, 1989. Sr. reorgn. underwriter Depository Trust Co., N.Y.C., 1968-90, acct. coord., 1990-98, security specialist, 1998—2003; ret., 2003. Nat. corr. sec. Nat. Bapt. Conv. U.S.A Inc., 1984-87; vice chair Spiritual Life Commn. of Clergywomen, 1987—; assoc. minister Morning Star Missionsry Bapt. Ch. of Jamaica, N.Y. CEO, founder Adoni Econ. Enterprises, Inc., v.p. Queens County Young Pastors, Mins. Evangelist Ea. Bapt. Assn. Author: African-American Guide to Buying Stock Without a Broker; nat editor: Ekklesia, 1986. Pastor Elmendorf Reformed Ch., East Harlem, NY. Recipient Vol. Svcs. award City of N.Y., 1980. Mem. NAFE, Nat. Assn. Negro Bus. and Profl. Women, Interdenominational Bd. Clergywoman (gen. sec. 1985-91), Nat. Bapt. Women Ministers Conv. (bd. mem. pulps. 1983-91), Ea. Bapt. Assn. (instr. 1981-83, v.p. evangelistic unit 1982-83, gen. dir. women's aux. 1988-91), Nat. Coun. Women U.S., Internat. Platform Assn., Bronx Bapt. Ministers Evening Conf. Greater N.Y. and Vicinity, Queens Bapt. Mins. Conf. Greater N.Y. and Vicinity, Assn. Black Seminarians (pres. 1993-95). Office Phone: 212-534-5856.

**SINGLETERRY, GARY LEE,** investment banker; b. Seattle, May 10, 1948; s. Richard W. and Anita J. (Fowler) S.; m. Mary Beth Burfeind, Nov. 29, 1969; children: Douglas, Laura. AB, Harvard U., 1970; MBA, Stanford U., 1974. Assoc. Morgan Stanley & Co., N.Y.C., 1974-79, Wm Sword & Co., Princeton, NJ, 1979-80; v.p. Thomson, McKinnon & Co., N.Y.C., 1981-82; mng. dir. Dean Witter Reynolds, N.Y.C., 1983-85, Prudential-Bache Securities, N.Y.C., 1985-91; pres. Singleterry & Co., Summit, NJ, 1991—. Mem. FNMA Nat. Adv. Coun., 1991. Republican. Office: Singleterry & Co 57 Union Pl Ste 316 Summit NJ 07901-2568 Fax: 908-918-0232. Office Phone: 908-918-0023. E-mail: garysingle@aol.com.

**SINGLETON, DONALD EDWARD,** journalist; b. Morristown, N.J., Nov. 8, 1936; s. Edward Leslie and Charlotte (Angerbauer) S.; m. Maureen Ann McNiff, Aug. 8, 1959 (div. 1977); children: Nancy Ann, Mark Aram, Jill Susan. Student, Fairleigh Dickinson U., 1955-58. Reporter Dover (N.J.) Advance, 1959-61, Morristown Daily Record, 1961-63, Newark Eve. News, 1963-64; feature reporter-writer N.Y. Daily News, 1964—. Organizer Com. to Save Church Sq. Park, Hoboken, N.J.; vice chmn. Hoboken Environment Com.; mem. due process com. ACLU., Mem. bd. edn., City of Hoboken, 1974-77. Recipient Pub. Service award N.Y. Council Civic Affairs, 1967; President's Distinguished Service award N.Y.C. Council, 1969; Newspaper award merit Women's Press Club N.Y.C., 1970, 79; citation VFW, 1970; Heywood Broun Meml. award Am. Newspaper Guild, 1970; Silver medal for pub. service journalism N.Y. chpt. Pub. Relations Soc. Am., 1970; certificate merit Am. Bar Assn., 1971; Page One award Newspaper Guild N.Y., 1970; Feature award Newspaper Reporters Assn. N.Y., 1972; Consistent Excellence award Uniformed Firefighters Assn., 1991. Mem. Am. Newspaper Guild. Clubs: Press (N.Y.C.). Home: 366 Ogden Ave Jersey City NJ 07307-1115 Office: 220 E 42nd St New York NY 10017-5806 Office E-mail: donaldnj@sprynet.com. *In reporting, I try very hard to avoid gathering facts in such a way as to fulfill a preconception. I also attempt to force myself to review constantly my opinions about my subjects, and to keep my mind as open as possible. In writing, I try to ask myself the following questions regularly: "Is this what I really believe? Or am I simply writing this way because I believe that this is what some other person or group would like me to write?" Unless I can answer the first question in the affirmative, and the second in the negative, I am not satisfied with a particular story.*

**SINGLETON, HARRY MICHAEL,** lawyer; b. Meadville, Pa., Apr. 10, 1949; s. Getdins T. and Rose Ann (Fucci) S.; children: Harry M. Jr., Leah Rose DiFucci. BA, Johns Hopkins U., 1971; JD, Yale U., 1974. Bar: D.C. 1975, Pa. 1976, Calif. 1999, Md. 1999, U.S. Dist. Ct. D.C. 1975, U.S. Dist. Ct. Md. 2001, U.S. Ct. Appeals (D.C. cir.) 1975, U.S. Ct. Mil. Appeals 1975; lic. realtor Va., 2004, D.C., 2004. Assoc. Houston & Gardner, Washington, 1974-75, Covington & Burling, Washington, 1976-77; atty. FTC, Washington, 1975-76; dep. minority counsel Com. on D.C./U.S. Ho. of Reps., Washington, 1977-79, minority chief counsel, staff dir., 1979-81; dep. asst. sec. U.S. Dept. Commerce, Washington, 1981-82; asst. sec. U.S. Dept. Edn., Washington, 1982-86; pres. Harry M. Singleton & Assocs., Washington, 1986-91; pvt. practice law Washington, 1991—; pres. Singleton Entertainment, LLC, Washington, 1999-2000; pres., gen. counsel Single Source Tech. Solutions, LLC, Washington, 2001—03; realtor D.C., Va., 2004—, Va. Assn. Realtors, 2004—, Nat. Assn. Realtors, 2004—. Legis. cons. Am. Enterprise Inst., Washington, 1975. Pres. bd. trustees Barney Neighborhood House, Washington, 1978-80; corp. bd. dirs. Children's Hosp. Nat. Med. Ctr., Washington, 1984-88; mem. crime com. Boys and Girls Clubs of Greater Washington, 1994-97; mem. D.C. Rep. State Com., 1991—2004, Rep. Nat. Com., 1992-2000, R.N.C. exec. coun., 1993-95, resolutions com., 1997-2000; mem. Rep. Nat. Hispanic Assembly Washington, 1991-92. Mem. Rep. Nat. Lawyers Assn. (bd. dirs. D.C. chpt. 1990-91), Coun. of 100 Black Reps. (bd. dirs. 1991-92), D.C. Black Rep. Coun. (chmn. 1992-93), Rep. Nat. African-Am. Coun. (nat. chmn. 1993-2001), D.C. Rep. Nat. African-Am. Coun. (chmn. 1993-2001). Republican. Presbyterian. Office: 1250 Connecticut Ave NW Ste 200 Washington DC 20036

**SINGLETON, JAMES KEITH,** federal judge; b. Oakland, Calif., Jan. 27, 1939; s. James K. and Irene Elisabeth (Lilly) S.; m. Sandra Claire Hoskins, Oct. 15, 1966; children: Matthew David, Michael Keith. Student. U. Santa Clara, 1957-58; AB in Polit. Sci., U. Calif., Berkeley, 1961, LLB, 1964. Bar: Calif. 1965, Alaska, 1965. Assoc. Delaney Wiles Moore and Hayes, Anchorage, 1963, 65-68, Law Offices Roger Cremo, Anchorage, 1968-70; judge Alaska Superior Ct., Anchorage, 1970-80, Alaska Ct. Appeals, Anchorage, 1980-90, U.S. Dist. Ct. for Alaska, Anchorage, 1990—2005, chief judge, 1995—2002, sr. judge, 2005—. Chmn. Alaska Local Boundary Commn., Anchorage, 1966-69. Chmn. 3d Dist. Rep. Com., Anchorage, 1969—70. Mem. ABA, Alaska Bar Assn., Phi Delta Phi, Tau Kappa Epsilon. Office: US Dist Ct 222 W 7th Ave Unit 41 Anchorage AK 99513-7504

**SINGLETON, JOAN VIETOR,** publishing executive, writer, film producer; b. LA, Nov. 8, 1951; d. Carl William and Elizabeth Anne (Caulfield) Vietor; m. W. Alexander Sheafe, Apr. 23, 1977 (div. 1981); m. Ralph Stuart Singleton, Dec. 21, 1984. Premiere degree, Universite de Paris, 1971; BA, Hollins Coll., 1972. Asst. to pres. Calif. Fed. Savs., Los Angeles, 1972-73, dir. promotion, publicity, 1973-74; publicist Dave Mirisch Enterprises, Beverly Hills, Calif., 1974-75; owner, pres. Joan Vietor Enterprises, Los Angeles, 1975-79; bus. affairs staff Warner Bros., Inc., Burbank, Calif., 1979-80; pres. Lone Eagle Pub. Co., Los Angeles, 1981—. Assoc. prodr. Stephen King's Graveyard Shift, 1990; prodr. writer Because of Winn-Dixie, 2005. Bd. dirs. The Curtis Sch., 1993—, Crestwood Hills Sch., 1993-95. Mem. Pubs. Mktg. Assn. (bd. dirs. 1984-87). Democrat. Presbyterian. Avocations: skiing, needlepoint, tennis, scuba diving, reading. Office: Lone Eagle Pub Co 2337 Roscomare Rd Los Angeles CA 90077-1851

**SINGLETON, JOHN,** director, screenwriter; b. LA, Jan. 6, 1968; s. Danny Singleton and Sheila Ward.; m. Akosua Busia, Oct. 12, 1996 (div. June 15, 1997); children: Hadar, Cleopatra. BA, U. So. Calif., 1990. Writer, dir.: (films) Boyz N the Hood, 1991 (Acad. award nominee Best Dir. and Best Screenplay 1992), Shaft, 2000; writer, dir., prodr. Poetic Justice, 1993, Higher Learning, 1995, Shaft, 2000, Baby Boy, 2001; dir.: Rosewood, 1997, 2 Fast 2 Furious, 2003, Four Brothers, 2005 (NAACP Image award for Outstanding Direction in a Feature Film, 2006), Hustle & Flow, 2005; exec. prodr.: Woo, 1998, Time Out, 2004. Named to Hollywood Walk of Fame, 2003; recipient New Generation award, LA Film Critics Assn., 1991, Best New Director, NY Film Critics Cir., 1991, MTV Movie award for Best New Filmmaker, 1992. Achievements include being the first African-American and youngest director to be nominated for an Academy Award for Best Director.

**SINGLETON, JONETTA WILLIAMS,** poet, retired special education educator; b. Bunkie, La., June 9, 1920; d. Josephus and Carrie Smith Williams; m. Jonetta W. Singleton; children: Carrie Elizabeth, Lafayette Jr. AA, Balt. Jr. Coll., 1971; BS in Biology and English, Coppins State Coll., 1973, Master's in Spl. Edn., 1974, Master's in Counseling, 1975. Tchr. Balt. Pub. Sch., Baltimore City, Md., 1974—94; ret., 1994. Poet: Poems from the Heart, 2004. Active ARC. Mem.: AAUW, ACLU. Democrat. Methodist.

**SINGLETON, MARVIN AYERS,** state legislator, otolaryngologist; b. Baytown, Tex., Oct. 7, 1939; s. Henry Marvin and Mary Ruth Singleton. BA, U. of the South, 1962; MD, U. Tenn., 1966. Diplomate Am. Bd. Otolaryngology. Intern City of Memphis Hosps., 1966-67; resident in surgery Highland Alameda City Hosp., Oakland, Calif., 1967-68; resident in otolaryngology U. Tenn. Hosp., Memphis, 1968-71; fellow in otolaryngic pathology Armed Forces Inst. Pathology, Washington, 1971; fellow in otologic surgery U. Colo. at Gallup (N.Mex.) Indian Med. Ctr., 1972; practice medicine specializing in otolaryngology/allergies Joplin, Mo., 1972—. Founder, operator Home and Farm Investments, Joplin, 1975—, staff mem. Freeman Hosp., St. John's Hosp., Joplin; cons. in otolaryngology Mo. Crippled Children's Service, Santa Fe R.R.; pres. Ozark Mfg. Co., Inc., Joplin. Mem. Internat. Arabian Racing Bd., 1983-88; mem. Mo. State Senate, 1990-2003; del. Rep. Nat. Conv., 1988, 92. Served with USNG, 1966-72. Fellow Am. Coll. Surgeons, Am. Acad. Otolaryngology Allergy (past pres.), Am. Assoc. Acad. Asthma, Allergy and Immunology; mem. AMA (Mo. del.), Mo. State Med. Assn., Sthrn. Med. Assn., Jasper County Med. Assn., Coun. Otolaryngology, Mo. State Allergy Assn., Ear Nose & Throat Soc. Mo. (past. pres.), Joplin C. of C., Masons (32d degree), Sigam Alpha Epsilon, Phi Theta Kappa, Chi Phi. Republican. Methodist. Office: 1637 W Swain Rd Stockton CA 95207-4172 Home: 4476 Five Mile Rd Seneca MO 64865-8357 Office Phone: 209-476-5623. Personal E-mail: senatorsingleton@hotmail.com.

**SINGLETON, ROBERT CULTON,** academic administrator, theology studies educator; b. Amarillo, Tex., Oct. 17, 1950; s. William Madison and Doris (Culton) S.; m. Stephanie Diane Lawrence, May 17, 1975; children: Kristin Michelle, Robert Culton Jr. BSEE, U. Tex., 1973; ThM in Bible Exposition, Dallas Theol. Sem., 1977; PhD in Higher Edin., U. Tex., 1993. Ordained to ministry Cmty. Bible Chapel, 1981. Campus staff Campus Crusade for Christ, Dallas, 1974-77; dean Nairobi (Kenya) Internat. Sch. Theology, 1978-83; grad. studies staff Campus Crusade for Christ, Austin, U.S.A., 1984-92; dean faculty East Asia Sch. Theology, Singapore, 1993-96; faculty The Orlando

(Fla.) Inst., 1997—. Bd. dirs. Nairobi Internat. Sch. Theology, 1981-83. Contbr. articles to profl. jours. Mem. Kappa Delta Pi, Phi Kappa Phi. So. Bapt. Avocations: personal computers, tennis. Personal E-mail: drbobsing@netscape.net.

**SINGLETON, SHIRLEY,** software development executive; Faculty mem. Mass. pub. schs.; v.p., gen. mgr. N.E. region Logica North Am.; co-founder, pres., CEO Edgewater Tech., Inc., 1992—. Office: Edgewater Technology Inc 20 Harvard Mill Sq Wakefield MA 01880-3209

**SINGLETON, TANYA,** nursing educator; b. Tuscaloosa, Ala., July 23, 1958; d. Crimpton and Inez Virginia (Powe) Singleton; children: David, Edward, Brittany Summerhill; m. Michael B. Brown, Nov. 2003. BS in Nursing, U. Ala., 1982; MPH in Maternal-Child Health, George Washington U., 1997. Cert. high risk perinatal nurse, childbirth educator; cert. lactation cons. Commd. 2d lt. U.S. Army, 1986, advanced through grades to capt., 1988; staff nurse labor and delivery Druid City Hosp., Tuscaloosa, 1982—83, Huntsville (Ala.) Hosp., 1983—86; perinatal counselor Cen. North Ala. Health Svcs. Inc., Huntsville, 1984—86; staff nurse Tripler Army Med. Ctr., Honolulu, 1986—90; asst. head nurse newborn nursery, staff nurse labor and delivery, childbirth counselor and inpatient lactation cons. DeWitt Army Hosp., Ft. Belvoir, Va., 1990—92; maternal infant health educator Providence Hosp., Washington, 1992—95; instr. Montgomery Coll. Sch. of Nursing, 1994; founder Sacred Conceptions Childbirth and Parenting Svcs., 1996—; exec. dir. Women's Wellness Ctr., Fredericksburg, Va., 1999—2000; tobacco cessation coord. MediCorp Health Sys., Fredericksburg, 2001—03; perinatal bereavement coord. Prince William Health Sys., 2002—04, nurse recruiter, 2004—, 2004—. Mem. low risk neonatal test com. Nat. Certification Corp., 1994—95; rsch. assoc. NIH-DC Initiative to Decrease Infant Mortality in D.C. Pride in Parenting Study, 1995—; pres. Rappahannock Teen Abstinence Program; organizer Rappahannock Healthy Families Initiative Planning Bd., Ptnrs. in Prevention VA Planning Dist. XVI. Chair health com. Stafford County br. NAACP. Maj. USAR, 1995—2000, instr. 91C program 80th Tng. Divsn. USAR, res. comp. comdr. 91W transition program USAR, 2001—04, Ft. Lee. Mem. ANA, Assn. Women's Health, Obstetric and Neonatal Nurses, Internat. Childbirth Edn. Assn., Sigma Theta Tau. Home: 6917 Smith Station Rd Spotsylvania VA 22553-1808 Office Phone: 703-369-8007. Personal E-mail: singmo40@aol.com. Business E-mail: tsinglet@pwhs.org.

**SINGLETON, WILLIAM DEAN,** publishing executive; b. Graham, Tex., Aug. 1, 1951; s. William Hyde and Florence E. (Myrick) S.; m. Adrienne Casale, Dec. 31, 1983; children: William Dean II, Paige, Adam Nicholas. Student, Tyler Jr. Coll., Tex.; El Centro Coll., Dallas; BS, U. Tex., Arlington. Vice chmn. and CEO MediaNews Group Inc., Denver, 1983—. Chmn. and pub. Denver Post; chmn. bd. Denver Newspaper Agency; pub. Salt Lake City Tribune; bd. dir. Associated Press, chmn. bd. dir., 2006—; former chmn. Newspaper Assn. Am. Mem. Salvation Army, Am. Heart Assn. of Ft. Bend County. Mem. Newspaper Assn. Am. (bd. govs.), So. Newspapers Assn., New Eng. Newspaper Assn., NJ Press Assn., Tex. Daily Newspaper Assn., Greater Houston Partnership Assn. Baptist. Office: Denver Post 1560 Broadway Denver CO 80202-1577*

**SINGLETON-WOOD, ALLAN JAMES,** communications executive; b. Newport, Monmouthshire, Eng., Feb. 13, 1933; arrived in Can., 1968; s. Charles James and Violet Anne (Bond) S.-W.; m. Joan Davies, June 23, 1956; children: Ceri, Glendon. Student, London U., 1949-51. TV and radio musical dir., 1953-57; TV producer, 1957-61; freelance producer for BBC, 1962-64; indsl. advt. mgr. Western Mail, Cardiff, Wales, 1964; advt. dir. Voice of Brit. Industry Mags., London, 1966; mktg. svcs. exec. The Sun and The People, I.P.C. Newspapers, London, 1966-68; mktg. svcs. mgr. Fin. Post, Toronto, Ont., Can., 1969-71, rsch. mgr., 1971-76, nat. sales mgr., 1976-77; pub. Fin. Post Mag., 1978-79; dir. advt. sales Fin. Post divsn., 1980-83; pub. Small Bus. Mag., 1983-87; v.p. pub. Bedford House Ltd., Toronto, 1987-88; pub. Small Bus. mag., v.p. CB Media Ltd., Toronto, 1988—; v.p. pub. Can. Bus. and Small Bus. mags., Who's Who in Can. Bus., Who's Who in Can. Fin., 1989—; corp. pub., gen. mgr. Sentry Comm., Willowdale, Ont., 1991-92; group pub. Bus. Publs. divsn. MacLean Hunter Ltd., Toronto, 1992-93; pres. Can. Productivity divsn. CB Media Ltd., Toronto, 1994-96; pres., CEO Singleton-Wood Comm. Inc., Victoria, B.C., Canada, 1996—. Pres., CEO, founder Can. Info. Productivity Awards, 1994—2001; lectr., cons. in field. Composer: contemporary music including title theme of Swing High, BBC nat. network series, 1953-57. Mem. Anglican Ch. Achievements include development of first computer media evaluation program for Canadian advertising industry. E-mail: asingleton-wood@shaw.ca.

**SINGLEY, JOHN EDWARD, JR.,** retired environmental scientist, consultant; b. Wildwood, N.J., July 31, 1924; s. John Edward Singley and Dorothy Mae (Pfrommer) S.; children: Gladys, Ann, Margaret, Patricia; m. June Walden Calohan, Apr. 28, 2001; stepchildren: Daniel, Christopher Calohan. BS, Ga. Inst. Tech., 1950; MS, Ga. Inst. Tech., 1952; PhD, U. Fla., 1966. Chemist Redstone Arsenal, Huntsville, Ala., 1950-51; dir. tech. svs. Tenn. Corp., College Park, Ga., 1951-64; lectr. chemistry Ga. State U., Atlanta, 1954-64, assoc. prof., 1964-67; prof. environ. engring. sci. U. Fla., Gainesville, 1967-90, prof. emeritus, 1990—; dir. TREEO Ctr., Gainesville, 1978-86; v.p. James M. Montgomery, Cons. Engrs., Inc., Gainesville, 1984-93, Montgomery Watson Cons. Engrs. Inc., Gainesville, 1993-96; v.p. Environ. Scis. Engring. Inc., Gainesville, 1977-84; prin. Water and Air Rsch., Gainesville, 1970-77; v.p. Metcalf & Eddy, Gainesville, 1996-99; ret., 1999. Cons. Carollo Engrs., Sarasota, Fla., Jones, Edmunds Assocs., Gainesville. Patentee in field of polymers. Mem. Fulton County Rep. Exec. Com., 1962-64; trustee Water for People, 1990-92. With USN, 1943-45. Recipient Donald R. Boyd award Met. Water Agys., 1992. Fellow Am. Inst. Chemists, Inst. Water and Environ. Mgmt.; mem. Am. Water Works Assn. (hon., life, bd. dirs. 1984-87, exec. com. 1986-87, 89-93, v.p. 1989-90, pres.-elect 1990-91, pres. 1991-92, Fuller award 1974, rsch. award 1983, Abel Wolman Excellence award 1995, Disting. Pub. Svc. award 1995, Water Industry Hall of Fame 2000), Fla. Water and Pollution Control Operators Assn. (Flanigan award 1979), Nat. Lime Assn. (Recognition award), Internat. Water Supply Assn., Nat. Assn. Corrosion Engrs., Internat. Ozone Assn. (bd. dirs. 1985-93). Clubs: Gainesville, Civitan (pres. 1972, lt. gov. Fla. dist. 1973-76). Presbyterian. Home: 1719 NW 23rd Ave # PHE Gainesville FL 32605-3027 Office: 1719 NW 23rd Ave PHE Gainesville FL 32605-3027 Office Phone: 352-372-2590. E-mail: h20doceds@aol.com.

**SINGREEN, SHIRLEY ANN BASILE (MRS. HARRY VOSS SINGREEN),** lawyer, consultant; b. New Orleans, Apr. 10, 1941; d. Dominick Joseph and Rose Aile (O'Reilly) Basile; m. Harry Voss Singreen, May 12, 1979; children: Michael Harry, Elizabeth Alexandra. AB, Loyola U., New Orleans, 1962, JD, 1964. Bar: La. 1964. Law clk. Civil Dist. Ct., 1964—65; assoc. Doyle, Smith & Doyle, New Orleans, 1965-66; staff counsel U.S. Ct. Appeals (5th cir.), New Orleans, 1966—68; assoc. Plotkin, Sapir & Bradley, New Orleans, 1968—72; spl. rsch. cons. Henican, James & Cleveland, New Orleans, 1972—73; sr. law clk. 24th Jud. Dist. Ct., Jefferson Parish, La., 1973—76; pvt. practice atty.; ind. legal cons. Appellate counsel, legal cons., trial analyst, New Orleans. Mem. La. State Bar Assn., Assn. for Women Attys., New Orleans Notaries Assn., Phi Alpha Delta. Republican. Roman Catholic. Office: 260 Audubon Blvd New Orleans LA 70125-4125 E-mail: LaLawBrief@aol.com.

**SINGSTOCK, DAVID JOHN,** military officer; b. Oshkosh, Wis., July 19, 1940; s. Arnold William and Viola Rufine (Gerdener) S.; children: Susan, Brian, Elissa, Timothy. BS distinction, Maine Maritime Acad., 1964; student, U.S. Mcht. Marine Acad., 1959—62; BSBA distinction, George Washington U., 1973, MS, 1975. Lic. profl. marine engr. Commd. ensign USN, 1964, advanced through grades to comdr., 1984, various sea assignments including combat duty in Vietnam, 1964—69, engr. officer USS Harold J. Ellison Norfolk, Va., 1969—71, ADP fin. mgr. Cinclantflt, 1971—73, planning and quality assurance officer supr. shipbuilding Portsmouth, Va., 1973—76, prodn./repair officer supr. shipbuilding Bath, Maine, 1976—79, ship maintenance mgr. chief naval ops. Washington, 1980—83, dir. fleet modernization

program space/naval warfare systems command, 1983—86, program mgr. USS Stark restoration naval sea systems command, 1986—88, tech. dir. dep. asst. sec. Navy for internat. programs, 1988—93; mgr. ships program ROH, Inc., Arlington, Va., 1993—95; mgr. ship self def. Vitro, Corp., Arlington, 1996—97; R&D mgr. theater ballistic missile def. Tracor Sys. Techs., Inc., Arlington, 1998—99; mgr. theater ballistic missile def. Marconi Sys. Techs., Inc., Arlington, 1999—2001; dep. dir. Applied Ordnance Tech. Internat., Arlington, 2001—06; sr. tech. dir. Aegis Ballistic Missile Def. Anteon Corp., Arlington, 2001—06; sr. tech. advisor Gen Dynamic's, 2006—. Sr. tech. advisor Royal Saudi Naval Forces Ops. Desert Shield and Desert Storm, 1990-91; sr. naval tech. mem. to Sec. of Def. chartered delegation of sr. U.S. ofcls., Saudi Arabia, 1991; retired U.S. Navy, 1993 Asst. scoutmaster Boy Scouts Am., Dumfries, Va., 1985-90; coach Youth Soccer, Manassas, Va., 1976-84; active local property owners civic orgns., Va., Maine, 1970—; instr. ARC, Seattle, 1967-68 Decorated Navy Commendation medal, Navy Achievement medal, Vietnamese Cross of Gallantry, Meritorious Svc. Medal, Joint Svc. Commendation medal, Bronze Star, Purple Heart; recipient Cert. Appreciation and Gratitude, Comdr. Saudi Arabian Armed Forces, Missile Def. award NDIA. Mem. Am. Soc. Naval Engrs. (dep. com. chmn., spkr. 1988), Nat. Contract Mgmt. Assn. (cert. contracts mgr.), Ret. Officers Assn., Nat. Eagle Scout Assn., Mason (32 degree), Scottish Rite, Shriner Presbyterian. Avocations: sailing, jogging, camping, golf, music. Home: 1125 Portner Rd Alexandria VA 22314-1314 Office: Gen Dynamics IT Divsn 2231 Crystal Dr Ste 600 Arlington VA 22202-3723 Office Phone: 703-892-7966. E-mail: david.singstock@gdit.com.

**SINHA, AKHOURI A.,** cell and development biologist, researcher; b. Churamanpur, Bihar, India, Dec. 17, 1933; arrived in U.S., 1961; s. Akhouri Chandra B. and Bittan Devi Sinha; m. Dorothy Kay Pamer, Sept. 29, 1979. BSc, Allahabad U., India, 1954; MSc, Patna U., India, 1956; PhD, U. Mo., 1965. Lectr. Ranchi (India) U., 1956—61; asst. prof. U. Wis., Eau Claire, 1965—67; sr. scientist U. Minn., Mpls., 1967—69; rsch. scientist VA Med. Ctr., Mpls., 1969—. Prof. U. Minn., 1981—. Contbr. articles to profl. jours. Hindu. Avocations: riding, cross country skiing, photography, travel, reading. Office: Rsch Svcs One Veterans Dr Minneapolis MN 55417 Office Phone: 612-467-2846. Business E-Mail: sinha001@tc.umn.edu.

**SINHA, NEETI,** biophysicist, researcher; d. Rajesh Chandra and Kavita Sinha; m. Sandeep Kumar, July 23, 1997; 1 child, Manushi Raj. PhD, U. Oxford, England, 1998. Postdoctoral rschr. NIH, Frederick, Md., 1998—2003; assoc. rsch. scientist Johns Hopkins U., Balt., 2003—. Asst. dir. Ctrl. Drug Rsch. Inst., Lucknow, India, 2004. Contbr. articles to profl. jours. Postdoctoral fellowship, NIH. Office: Johns Hopkins University Mudd Hall 3400 N Charles St Baltimore MD 21218 Office Phone: 410-516-5379.

**SINHA, RAJ P.,** education educator, researcher; b. Pahsara, Bihar, India, Nov. 11, 1934; arrived in U.S., 1961; s. Kapilded P. and Kaushilya Sinha; m. Rani P. Sinha; children: Rajiv R., Nilu Sinha-Tiwari, Ena. BSc, Patna U., Bihar, India, 1957; MS, U. Wyo., 1963; PhD, U. Manitoba, Can., 1967. Fellow Carleton U., Ottawa, Ontario, Canada, 1968—72; rsch. scientist Food Rsch. Inst., Ottawa, Ontario, Canada, 1972—92; assoc. prof. Chgo. State U., 1992—. Contbr. articles to profl. jours. Recipient Provential Govt. Ontario award, 1980. Office: Chgo State Univ Dept Biology 9501 S King Dr Chicago IL 60628-1598 E-mail: rp.sinha@csu.edu.

**SINHA, RAKESH KUMAR,** computer scientist, researcher; s. RamKrishna and Sanyukta Sinha. PhD in Computer Sci., U. Wash., Seattle, 1995. Asst. prof. Sch. Computer Sci., Miami, Fla., 1995—98; mem. tech. staff Bell Labs., Murray Hill, NJ, 1998—2000; prin. engr. Ciena Core Switching Divsn., Cupertino, Calif., 2000—01; tech. cons. AT&T Labs Rsch., Middletown, NJ, 2001—. Contbr. articles to profl. jours. Recipient Best Paper award, FOCS and FORTE/PSTV. Mem.: IEEE, Assn. Computing Machinery. Achievements include patents in field. Office: Phone: 732-420-9045. Personal E-mail: rakesh_sinha100@yahoo.com. Business E-Mail: sinha@research.att.com.

**SINHA, SUNIL K.,** engineer, educator; b. Patna, India, Mar. 1, 1962; s. Mahesh C. P. and Indu R. Sinha; m. Anju Singh, Jan. 15, 1970; 1 child, Sushruth. B in Engring., Birla Inst. of Tech., 1986; PhD, U. of Waterloo, Can., 2000; MA in sci., U. Waterloo, 1997. Constrn. engr. PACS-MECON Consultants, Lagos, Nigeria, 1986—87; project engr. Govt. of Bihar, Patna, India, 1987—96; rsch. asst. U. of Waterloo, Canada, 1996—2000, postdoctoral fellow, 2000—01; asst. prof. Pa. State U., State College, Pa., 2001—. Contbr. articles to profl. jours. Mem. of adv. bd. Municipality of State Coll., State College, Pa., 2001—. Fellow Post-Doctoral fellowship, Nat. Sci. & Engring. Rsch. Coun. of Can., 2000; scholar U. Grad. Scholarships, U. of Waterloo, 1997, Doctoral Scholarship, Nat. Sci. & Engring. Rsch. Coun. of Can., 1998. Mem.: ASCE (life). Achievements include research in Development of Sustainable Civil Infrastructure Systems. Home: 145 Jay Ln State College PA 16801 Office: Pa State Univ 223 Sackett Bldg State College PA 16802 Business E-Mail: sunil@engr.psu.edu.

**SINHA, SUNIL K.,** aerospace engineer, consultant; b. Patna, Bihar, India, Aug. 19, 1949; arrived in US, 1973; s. Awadh Bihari and Sumitra Kumari Sinha; m. Suman Sinha, Apr. 23, 1978; children: Neena P., Anjuli M. BS, Patna (India) U., 1968; MS, So. Ill. U., 1974; PhD, U. of Ill., Urbana-Champaign, 1977—77; MTech., Indian Inst. of Tech., Bombay, 1973. Sr. rsch. asst. Indian Inst. of Tech., Bombay, 1969—73; grad. tchg. asst. U. of Ill., Urbana-Chapaign, 1974—77; stress and vibration analyst Foster Wheeler Energy Corp., Livingston, NJ, 1977—79; sr. tech. analyst Westinghouse Electric Corp., Boston, 1979—83; sr. engr. GE Appliances, Louisville, 1983—89; sr. staff engr. GE Aircraft Engines, Evendale, Ohio, 1989—2001; prin. engr. GE Aviation, Evendale, 2002—. Mem. LS-Dyna Aerospace Working Group, Livermore, 2000—. Mem. Elfun Soc., Cin., 1989—2006. Mem.: ASME. Non-Partisan. Achievements include research in Pioneering transient dynamics work in the area of rotordynamics such as blade-out and tip-rub, contained and uncontained failure of rotating components; Missile Impact on a Commercial Jet engine; Dynamic Stability of Airfoils; High-speed impact dynamics. Home: 11025 Woodlands Way Cincinnati OH 45241 Office: Imapct Dynamics 1 Neumann Way Cincinnati OH 45215 Office Phone: 513-552-5293. Business E-Mail: sunil@ae.ge.com.

**SINHA, SUNIL KUMAR,** physicist; b. Calcutta, India, Sept. 13, 1939; came to U.S., 1965; s. Sushil Kumar and Romola Sinha; m. Lonny Linde Olsen, Jan. 27, 1962; children: Arjun, Ranjan. BA in Natural Scis., Cambridge U., Britain, 1960, PhD in Physics, 1964. Vis. scientist Bhabha Atomic Rsch. Ctr., Trombay, India, 1965; asst. prof. physics dept. Iowa State U., Ames, 1966-69, assoc. prof., 1969-71, prof. physics, 1972-75; sr. physicist Argonne (Ill.) Nat. Lab., 1975-82; sr. rsch. assoc. Corp. Rsch., Exxon Rsch., Annandale, NJ, 1982-95; sr. scientist and assoc. dir., exptl. facilities div. Argonne (Ill.) Nat. Lab., 1995-2001; prof. physics U. Calif., San Diego, 2001—. Chmn. Div. Condensed Matter Physics Fellowship Com. of Am. Phys. Soc., 1990-91, Conf. X-Ray Physics, 1999; mem. adv. com. US Dept. Energy, 1997-02; co-chair Basic Energy Scis. Advisry Com. subcom. Dept. Energy facilities, 2003. Editor: Ordering in Two Dimensions, 1980, Spin Waves and Magnetic Excitations, 1990; contbr. articles to profl. jours. Recipient Dept. Energy Rsch. Achievement award, 1981, Ernest Orlando Lawrence Meml. award, 1996, Arthur H. Compton award Advanced Photon Source, 2000; Guggenheim fellow, 1982; MRS medal, 2004. Fellow AAAS, Am. Phys. Soc.; mem. Materials Rsch. Soc., Am. Crystallographic Assn. Achievements include research in antiferromagnetism in High Tc materials by neutron diffraction; theory of diffuse X-ray scattering from surfaces. Office: U Calif San Diego Physics Dept 9500 Gilman Dr La Jolla CA 92093 Office Phone: 858-822-5537. Business E-Mail: ssinha@physics.ucsd.edu.

**SINIAWSKI, MATTHEW,** science educator; b. Harvey, Ill., Jan. 1, 1978; m. Catherine Siniawski; 1 child, Lillian McBain. PhD, Northwestern U., Evanston, Ill., 2004. Asst. prof. Loyola Marrymount U., LA. Grantee, NSF, 2005. Mem.: ASME (faculty advisor 2004—06), STLE. Achievements include

research in universal wear model for abrasion. Office: Loyola Marrymount U 1 LMU Dr MS 8145 Los Angeles CA 90045 Office Phone: 310-338-5849. Business E-Mail: msiniawski@lmu.edu.

**SINICK, MARSHALL S.,** lawyer; b. Hartford, Conn., 1942; BA, Boston U., 1964; JD with honors, Ind. U., 1968. Bar: Conn. 1968, DC 1972. Trial atty., Bur. Oper. Rights Civil Aeronautics Bd., 1968—71; prnr. Squire, Sanders & Dempsey LLP, Washington, chmn., Transp. Practice Group. Editl. bd. Ind. U. Law Jour., 1967—68. Mem.: Conn. Bar, DC Bar, Order of Coif. Office: Squire Sanders & Dempsey LLP 1201 Pennsylvania Ave NW PO Box 407 Washington DC 20044-0407 Office Phone: 202-626-6651. Office Fax: 202-626-6780. Business E-Mail: msinick@ssd.com.

**SINISCALCO, GARY RICHARD,** lawyer; b. NYC, Aug. 14, 1943; BA in Econs., Le Moyne Coll., 1965; JD, Georgetown U., 1969. Bar: Calif. Regional counsel, sr. trial atty. EEOC, San Francisco, 1969-78; ptnr. Orrick, Herrington & Sutcliffe, San Francisco, 1978—, past co-chair employment law dept. Mem. adv. bd. Nat. Employment Law Inst.; lectr. in field. Co-author: Manager's Guide to Lawful Terminations, 1991; author: (with others) Employment Discrimination Law, 1979, 3rd edit., 1996; contbr. articles to profl. jours. Mem. ABA (mem. com. on internat. labor rels. and equal employment opportunity, mgmt. co-chairperson equal employment opportunity com. 1996-98), State Bar Calif., Bar Commonwealth Va., Am. Employment Law Coun. (founder). Office: Orrick Herrington 405 Howard St San Francisco CA 94105

**SINISE, GARY,** actor; b. Blue Island, IL, Mar. 17, 1955; s. Robert L. Sinise; m. Moira Harris, 1981; children: Sophie, McCanna, Ella. Ph.D (hon.), Amherst Coll. 2003. Co-founder, artistic dir. Steppenwolf Theatre, 1974-. Chgo. Appeared in (plays) The Indian Wants The Bronx, 1977, Getting Out, 1980 (Joseph Jefferson award), Of Mice And Men, 1980, Loose Ends, 1982, True West, 1983 (also dir., Obie award best dir. 1982-83), Balm in Gilead, 1984, Streamers, 1985, The Caretaker, 1986, Grapes of Wrath, 1990 (Tony award and Drama Desk), Buried Child, 1996 (Tony award nominee, Joseph Jefferson award, 1996), One Flew Over the Cuckoos Nest, 2001; film appearances include A Midnight Clear, 1991, Jack The Bear, 1991, Forrest Gump, 1994 (Acad. award nomination for Best Supporing Actor, 1994, Disabled Am. Veterans Nat. Commanders award, 1994), The Quick and the Dead, 1995, Apollo 13, 1995, Ransom 1996, Albino Alligator, 1996, Snake Eyes, 1998, That Championship Season, 1999, Being John Malkovich, 1999, Reindeer Games, 1999, Mission to Mars, 1999, Bruno, 1999, All the Rage, 1999, The Green Mile, 1999, A Gentleman's Game, 2001, Made-Up, 2002, Mission: Space, 2003, The Human Stain, 2003, The Big Bounce, 2003, This Old Cub, 2004, The Forgotten, 2004; (TV films) True West, 1984, Family Secrets, 1984, The Final Days, 1989, The Grapes of Wrath, 1991, The Witness, 1992, My Name is Bill W., 1989, The Stand, 1994, Truman, 1995 (Cable Ace award 1996, Golden Globe, 1996, Screen Actors Guild Award, 1996), Wallace, 1997 (Emmy award, 1998, Screen Actors Guild award, 1998, Cable ACE Award), That Championship Season, 1999, Path to War, 2002, Fallen Angel, 2003; (TV series) CSI: NY, 2004-; (TV appearances) Knots Landing, 1980, Crime Story, 1986, 1987, Hunter, 1990, Frasier, 1995, CSI: Miami, 2004, 2005; actor, dir. prodr., (films) Of Mice and Men, 1991; actor, prodr. Impostor, 2002; dir., Miles from Home, 1988; dir. (plays) Frank's Wild Years, Action, The Miss Firecracker Contest, Waiting for the Parade, Tracers, Orphans, Landscape of the Body, 1984 Office: care Creative Artists Agy 9830 Wilshire Blvd Beverly Hills CA 90212-1804 also: Licker & Ozurovich 2029 Century Park E Ste 1060 Los Angeles CA 90067-2919*

**SINK, KAYCEE M.,** geriatrician, medical educator; d. Paul Sink and Pauline Sorensen. MD, U. Calif., San Francisco, Calif., 1998, MA in Advanced Studies, 2005. Diplomate Am. Bd. Internal Medicine, 2001, added qualifications in geriatric medicine Am. Bd. Internal Medicine, 2002. Resident internal medicine U. Calif., San Francisco, 1998—2001, clin. fellow in geriat., 2001—02, postdoctoral fellow in clin. rsch., 2002—04; asst. prof. medicine Sch. Medicine Wake Forest U., Winston-Salem, NC, 2004—. Med. dir. Kulynych Memory Assessment Clinic, Winston-Salem, NC, 2005—. Recipient Kathryn Grupe Excellence in Alzheimer's Rsch. award, Alzheimer's Assn. No. Calif. and Nev., 2004; scholar, Claude Pepper Independence Ctr., Wake Forest U., 2005—. Mem.: AMA, Am. Geriat. Soc. (Presdl. Poster award 2004, Best Paper award 2003), Phi Beta Kappa. Avocations: tennis, scuba diving. Office: Wake Forest University One Medical Center Blvd Winston Salem NC 27157 Office Phone: 336-713-8560. Business E-Mail: kmsink@wfubmc.edu.

**SINK, ROBERT C.,** lawyer; b. Racine, Wis., 1938; AB, Duke U., 1959, LLB, 1965. Bar: N.C. 1965. Ptnr. Robinson, Bradshaw & Hinson, P.A., Charlotte, N.C., 1965—. Assoc. editor Duke Law Jour., 1964-65. Trustee Pub. Libr. Charlotte and Mecklenburg County, 1985-90, chmn., 1989-90; bd. dirs. Mus. New South, 1991-97, chmn., 1996-97. Lt. USN, 1959-62, USNR. Mem. ABA (ho. dels. 2001—), N.C. State Bar (councilor 1988-96, pres. 1998-99), Mecklenburg County Bar (pres. 1986-87), Order of Coif, Phi Beta Kappa. Office: Robinson Bradshaw & Hinson PA 101 N Tryon St Ste 1900 Charlotte NC 28246-0103

**SINKFORD, JEANNE CRAIG,** dental association administrator, retired dentist, retired dean, educator; b. Washington, Jan. 30, 1933; d. Richard E. and Geneva (Jefferson) Craig; m. Stanley M. Sinkford, Dec. 8, 1951; children: Dianne Sylvia, Janet Lynn, Stanley M. III. BS, Howard U., 1953, MS, 1962, DDS, 1958, PhD, 1963; DSc (hon.), Georgetown U., 1978, U. Med. and Dentistry of N.J., 1992. Detroit Mercy U., 1996. Instr. prosthodontics Sch. Dentistry Howard U., Washington, 1958—60, faculty dentistry, 1964—, rsch. coord., co-chmn. dept. restorative dentistry, assoc. dean, 1968—75, dean, 1975—91, prof. Prosthodontics Grad. Sch., 1977—84, dean emeritus, prof., 1991—; spl. asst. Am. Assn. Dental Schs., 1991—93, dir. office women and minority affairs, 1993—97, assoc. exec. dir., 1998—. Instr. rsch. and crown and bridge Northwestern U. Sch. Dentistry, 1963—64; cons. prosthodontics and rsch. VA Hosp., Washington, 1965—; resident Children's Hosp. Nat. Med. Ctr., 1974—75; cons. St. Elizabeth's Hosp.; mem. attending staff Freedman's Hosp., Washington, 1964—; adv. bd. DC Gen. Hosp., 1975—; mem. nat. adv. dental rsch. coun. Nat. Bd. Dental Examiners; mem. ad hoc adv. panel Tuskegee Syphilis Study for HEW; sponsor DC Pub. Health Apprentice Program; mem. adv. coun. to dir. NIH; adv. com. NIH/NIDR/NIA Aging Rsch. Coun.; mem. dental devices classification panel FDA; mem. select panel for promotion child health, 1979—80; mem. spl. med. adv. group VA; bd. overseers U. Pa. Dental Sch., Boston U. Dental Sch.; bd. advisors U. Pitts. Dental Sch.; mem. bd. visitors Temple U. Sch. Dentistry, Howard U Coll. Dentistry, Ind. U. Sch. Dentistry, W.Va. U. Health Ctr.; mem. anat. rev. bd. DC NRC Governing Bd.; cons. FDA; mem. Nat. Adv. Dental Rsch. Coun., 1993—96; active NRC Governing Bd. Mem. editl. bd. Jour. Am. Coll. Dentists, 1988—. Mem. Mayor's Block Grant Adv. Com., 1982; mem. parents' coun. Sidwell Friends, 1983; adv. bd. United Negro Coll. Fund, Robert Wood Johnson Health Policy Fellowships; mem. women's health task force NIH; bd. dirs. Girl Scouts U.S.A., 1993—95; bd. visitors Temple U. Sch. Dentistry, W.Va. U. health Scis. Ctr., Howard U. Coll. Dentistry. Fellow Louise C. Ball fellow grad. tng., 1960—63. Fellow: Internat. Coll. Dentists (Merit award), Am. Coll. Dentists (sec.-treas. Wash. met. sect.); mem.: ADA (chmn. appeal bd. coun. on dental edn. 1975—82), Fedn. Dentistis Internat., Links Inc., Dean's Coun. (chair), Smithsonian Assocs., NY Acad. Scis., Am. Soc. Dentistry for Children, Inst. Medicine of NAS (coun.), Nat. Dental Assn., Fed. Prosthodontic Orgn., Am. Prosthodontic Soc., Am. Pedodontic Soc., Leadership in Acad. Medicine (adv. bd.), Health Professions Partnership Initiative (adv. bd.), Assn. Am. Women Dentists, Wash. Coun. Adminstrv. Women, So. Conf. Dental Deans (chmn.), Inst. Grad. Dentists (trustee), Am. Inst. Oral Biology, Dist. Dental Soc., Internat. Assn. Dental Rsch., Am. Soc. for Geriatric Dentistry (bd. dirs.), North Portal Civic League, Golden Key, Beta Kappa Chi, Psi Chi, Omicron Kappa Upsilon, Phi Beta Kappa, Sigma Xi (pres.). Achievements include first female dental dean at Howard U., and in the U.S.A.

**SINKIN, FAY MARIE,** environmentalist; b. N.Y.C., Mar. 24, 1918; d. Joseph E. and Amelia (Kronish) Bloom; m. William R. Sinkin, May 31, 1942; children: Richard, Lanny. BA, Syracuse U., 1938. Pres. LWV, San Antonio, 1947-51; pres., organizer Vis. Nurse Assn., San Antonio, 1952-54; pres. Brandeis U. Women's Com., San Antonio, 1954-56; recruiter, com. U.S. State Dept. (A.I.D.), Washington, 1963-67; pres. Aquifer Protection Assn., San Antonio, 1974-80, Portrait of Am. Women, San Antonio, 1976-82; chair Bexar County/Edwards Underground Water Dist., San Antonio, 1983-89; chairwoman Edwards Aquifer Preservation Trust, San Antonio, 1990. Editor (pamphlet) Is Applewhite Necessary?, 1978. Dedication of Fay's Tree Opening of Govt. Canyon Wilderness Park, 2005. Named Woman of Yr., Express New Publ., 1964, Sunday Woman, San Antonio Light, 1965, Mother of Yr. Avance, 1988, Cmty. Champion, Tex. Assn Cmty. Devel. Corps., 2006; named to, Women's Hall of Fame, San Antonio, 1985; recipient WICI award, Women in Comm., 1989, Spirit of Giving award, J.C. Penney, 1993, Best and Brightest award, U. Round Table, 1998, Star award, LWV, 2005, Fay Sinkin Water Quality award, Edwards Aquifer Authority, 2006. Mem. San Antonio 100, Tex. Internat. Woman's Forum, Bexar Audobon Soc. (Oustanding Cmty. Svc. award 2003), San Antonio Conservation Soc. (award for preservation of the environment 2002). Democrat. Jewish. Avocations: needlepoint, swimming, reading. Home: 311 Nottingham W San Antonio TX 78209 E-mail: fay2646@aol.com

**SINN, JERRY L.,** army officer; m. Cheryl Parant; children: Jacob, Andrew. Grad., U. Mo., Rolla, Command and Gen. Staff Coll. Math. instr. U.S. Mil. Acad., West Point; enlisted U.S. Army, 1968, commd. 2d lt., 1969, advanced through grades to comdr.; dir. for ops. and support, asst. to Sec. of Army for Fin. Mgmt. and Compt., 1995 97; divsn. engr. U.S. Army C.E., Bklyn., 1997-98, comdg. gen. North Atlantic divsn., 1998-99; dep. asst. sec. U.S. Army Budget Office, Washington, 1999—2003; mil. dep. for budget ASA (FM&C), 2003—. Decorated Legion of Merit with 3 oakleaf clusters, Bronze Star medal with V device, Purple Heart with oakleaf cluster, others. Office: ASA/DAS 109 Army Pentagon Rm 3a662 Washington DC 20310-0109

**SINNARD, ELAINE JANICE,** painter, sculptor; b. Fort Collins, Colo., Feb. 14, 1926; d. Elven Orestes and Catherine (Bennet) S. Student, Art Students League, 1948, NYU, 1953, Sculpture Ctr., NYC, 1954, Academie Grande Chaumiere, Paris, 1956. Painter, sculptor. Works exhibited Riverside Mus., NYC, 1955, City Ctr., NYC, 1954-56, Nat. Arts Club, NYC, 1959-90, Lord & Taylor, NYC, 1963-78, Bergdorf Goodman, NYC, 1980-90, Zantman Art Galleries, Carmel-by-the-Sea, Calif., 1970-73, Chevy Chase Gallery, Washington, 1981-88; one woman shows and group exhbns. include: Bergdorf Goodman Nena's Choice Gallery, Sinnard Art Studios; tchr. open workshop for artists, (murals) Trinity Assembly of GOD, Middletown, NY. Mem. Nat. Arts Club NYC. Home: PO Box 304 New Hampton NY 10958-0304 Office Phone: 845-374-8128. Personal E-mail: sinnard@warwick.net.

**SINNER, STEVE,** sculptor; b. Omaha, Nebr., 1942; BS in Industl. Edn., Iowa St. Univ., 1965. Exhibitions include Arrowmont Sch. Arts & Crafts, Gatlinburg, TN, 2001, Minn. Mus. Am. Art, St. Paul, Minn., 2001, Univ. Calif. Davis, 2001, Defining Craft: Collecting for the new Millennium, Davenport Mus. Art, 2002, Put a Lid on It: Containing Human Experience, Am. Assn. Woodturners, 2003, Turned Wood-Small Treasures, del Mano Galleries, LA, 2003—05, Selected Works, 2006, Functional Art Exposition, NYC, 2003—06, Beneath the Bark: 25 Years of Woodturning, BYU, 2004, Against the Grain: Contemporary Turned Wood Urns, Dubuque Mus. Art, 2006, Our Turn Now: Artists Speak out in Wood, 2006. Office: c/o del Mano Gallery 11981 San Vicente Blvd Los Angeles CA 90049*

**SINNING, MARK ALAN,** thoracic and vascular surgeon; b. Holton, Kans., Apr. 24, 1953; s. Henry Harold and Valere Madelene (Davey) S.; m. Kathy Diann Pugh, Sept. 25, 1982 (div.); m. Srinuan Williamson, Sept. 3, 2003; children: Sarah, Emily, Mark, Rachel, Walter, Madalyn. BA, U. Kans., 1975; MD, U. Kans., Kansas City, 1978. Diplomate Am. Bd. Surgery, Am. Bd. Thoracic Surgery. Gen. surgery resident St. Luke's Hosp., Kansas City, Mo., 1978-83, thoracic surgery resident, 1983-85; pvt. practice Coastal Surg. Specialists, PA, New Bern, NC, 1986—. Attending staff Danbury (Conn.) Hosp., 1985-86, Craven Regional Med. Ctr., New Bern, 1986—; asst. clin. prof. East Carolina U., Greenville, 1992—. Fellow ACS, Am. Coll. Chest Physicians; mem. Soc. Thoracic Surgeons, So. Assn. Thoracic Surgery, N.C. Med. Soc., Phi Beta Kappa, Alpha Omega Alpha. Avocations: golf, skiing, music.

**SINNOTT, JOHN THOMAS,** internist, educator; b. Reading, Pa., May 16, 1948; s. John Thomas and Josephine (Mallon) S.; m. Barbara Ballentine, May 30, 1970. BA, Columbus (Ga.) Coll., 1971; MA, U. South Fla., 1973; MD, U. South Ala., 1978. Diplomate Am. Bd. Internal Medicine, Am. Bd. Infectious Diseases. Resident in internal medicine U. South Fla. Coll. Medicine, Tampa, 1978-81, infectious disease resident, 1981-83, asst. prof., 1983-87, assoc. prof., 1987-92, prof. and dir. infectious diseases, 1991—, James Cullison prof. medicine, 2000—, assoc. dean internat. affairs, 2005—; dir. epidemiology Tampa Gen. Healthcare, 1985—, mem. med. exec. bd., 1992—, vice chief staff, 1992-94, chief staff, 1994-96. Dir. S.W. Fla. Tissue Bank, 1987—, dir. epidemiology Shriners Hosp. for Children, 1987; co-founder CHART India, 1998-; mem. adv. bd. Lifelink Fla., 1988-; trustee Tampa Gen. Hosp. Found., 2000-, Hillsborough C.C. Found., 2003-; mem. bd. dirs. FoodTech, 2002- chmn. 2005- Editor jour. Infections in Medicine, 1994—. Recipient hon. alumnus award U. South Fla. Coll. Medicine, 1998, Outstanding Clin. Prof. award, 1986-92; Humanism in Medicine award NBI Healthcare Found., 1998, award For AIDS Care Today, 1998; John T. Sinnott Outstanding Clin Prof. award named in his honor U. So. Fla. Coll. Medicine, 1992. Fellow ACP, Infectious Disease Soc. Am. (pres. com. 1998—); mem. Soc. Hosp. Epidemiology (fin. com. 1990—). Alpha Omega Alpha. Avocations: fishing, flying. Home: 9666 Oak St NE Saint Petersburg FL 33702-2610 Office: Tampa Gen Hosp Dept Infectious Disease Tampa FL 33601-1289

**SINNOTT, STEPHEN P.,** prosecutor; b. May 7, 1955; JD, Loyola U., 1979. 1st asst. US atty. (we. dist.) Wis. US Dept. Justice, Madison, interim US atty., 2005—06.*

**SINOR, DENIS,** history professor, linguist; b. Kolozsvar, Hungary, Apr. 17, 1916; s. Miklos and Marguerite (Weitzenfeld) S.; m. Eugenia Trinajstic (dec.); children: Christophe (dec.), Sophie. BA, U. Budapest, 1938; MA, Cambridge U., Eng., 1948; doctorate (hon.), U. Szeged, Hungary, 1971. Attache Centre National de la Recherche Scientifique, Paris, 1939-48; univ. lectr. Altaic studies Cambridge U., 1948-62; prof. Uralic and Altaic studies and history Ind. U., Bloomington, 1962-81, disting. prof. emeritus Uralic and Altaic studies and history, 1975-86, disting. prof. emeritus Uralic and Altaic studies and history, 1986—, chmn. dept. Uralic and Altaic studies, 1963-1981, dir. Lang. and Area Ctr., 1963-88, dir. Asian studies program, 1965-67, dir. Asian Studies Rsch. Inst., 1967-79, dir. Rsch. Inst. for Inner Asian Studies, 1979-1981, 85-86. Sec. gen. Permanent Internat. Altaistic Conf., 1961—; rsch. project dir. U.S. Office Edn., 1969-70; sec. Internat. Union Orientalists, 1954-64; vis. prof. Inst. Nat. des Langues et Civilisations Orientales, Paris, spring 1974; scholar-in-residence Rockefeller Found. Study Ctr., Bellagio, 1975; vice chmn. UNESCO Commn. for History Civilization Cen. Asia, 1981-2005, consultative com. UNESCO Silk Rd. Project, 1990-97; summer seminar dir. NEH, 1988, 2005; hon. prof. Inst. Oriental Studies, Russian Acad. Scis. Author: Orientalism and History, 1954, History of Hungary, 1959, Introduction à lètude de l'Eurasie Centrale, 1963, Aspects of Altaic Civilization, 1963, Inner Asia, 1968, Inner Asia and Its Contacts with Medieval Europe, 1977, Tanulmányok, 1982, Essays in Comparative Altaic Linguistics, 1990, Studies in Medieval Inner Asia, 1997; editor, contbr.: Modern Hungary, 1977, Studies in Finno-Ugric Linguistics, 1977, Uralic Languages, 1988, Essays on Uzbek History, Culture and Languages, 1993, Cambridge History of Early Inner Asia, Handbook of Uralic Studies, Jour. Asian History, Ind. U. Uralic and Altaic Series; mem. editl. bd. Britannica-Hungarica. Served with Forces Françaises de l'Intérieur, 1943-44; with French Army, 1944-45. Rsch. grantee Am. Coun. Learned Socs., 1962, Am. Philos. Soc., 1963, NEH grant, 1981, 87-88; Guggenheim fellow, 1968-69, 1981-82; recipient Jubilee prize U.

Budapest, 1938, Barczi Geza Meml. medal, 1981, Gold medal Permanent Internat. Altaistic Conf., 1982, 1996, Arminius Vambery Meml. medal, 1983, Thomas Hart Benton Mural medal Hungarian Order of Star, 1986, UNESCO Avicenna medal, 1998, UNESCO 60th Anniversary medal, 2005, medal for outstanding svcs. U. Szeged, 2002. Fellow Körösi Csoma Soc. (hon.); mem. Royal Asiatic Soc. (hon. sec. 1954-64, Denis Sinor medal for Inner Asian Studies named in his honor 1992), Am. Oriental Soc. (pres. Midwest br. 1968-70, nat. pres. 1975-76, medal of honor 1999), Assn. Asian Studies, Am. Hist. Soc., Soc. Asiatique (hon.), Tibet Soc. (pres. 1969-74), Mongolia Soc. (pres. 1987-94), Correspondant de l'Académie des inscriptions et belles lettres (Paris), Hungarian Acad. Scis. (hon.), Acad. Europaea (fgn.), Deutsche Morgenlandische Gesellschaft, Suomalais-Ugrilaisen Seura (hon.), Soc. Uralo-Altaica (v.p. 1964-94, hon.), Internat. Union Oriental and Asian Studies (v.p. 1993—), Cosmos Club Washington, Explorers Club NYC, United Oxford and Cambridge Club London. Achievements include reached the North Pole on a Russian icebreaker, 2004. Home: 5581 E Lampkins Ridge Rd Bloomington IN 47401-8674 Office: Indiana U Dept Ctrl Eurasian Studies Goodbody Hall Bloomington IN 47405 E-mail: sinord@indiana.edu.

**SINOR, HOWARD EARL, JR.,** lawyer; b. New Orleans, Sept. 6, 1949; s. Howard E. and Beverly M. (Bourgeois) S.; children: Sally, Vera Sue, Sarah, Sadie. BA with honors, U. New Orleans, 1971; JD cum laude, Harvard U., 1975. Bar: La. 1975, U.S. Supreme Ct. 1983, U.S. Ct. Appeals (3rd, 5th and 11th cir.), U.S. Dist. Ct. (ea., middle, we.) Dist. La. Ptnr. Jones, Walker, Waechter, Poitevent, Carrere & Denegre, 1975-98, Gordon Arata, New Orleans, 1999—. Contbg. author: La. Appellate Practice Handbook, 1990, 97; editor: CLE Manual of Recent Developments, 1985, contbr. articles to profl. jours. Recipient Pres.'s award, La. State Bar Assn., 1987. Fellow La. Bar Found.; mem. ABA, FBA, La. State Bar Assn. (chmn. antitrust sect. 1987-89). Avocations: golf, hiking.

**SINSHEIMER, ROBERT LOUIS,** retired academic administrator, educator; b. Washington, Feb. 5, 1920; s. Allen S. and Rose (Davidson) S.; m. Flora Joan Hirsch, Aug. 8, 1943 (div. 1972); children: Lois June (Mrs. Wickstrom), Kathy Jean (Mrs. Vandagriff), Roger Allen; m. Kathleen Mae Reynolds, Sept. 10, 1972 (div. 1980); m. Karen Current, Aug. 1, 1981. S.B., MIT, 1941, MS, 1942, PhD, 1948. Staff mem. radiation lab. MIT, Cambridge, 1942-46; assoc. prof. biophysics, physics dept. Iowa State Coll., Ames, 1949-55, prof., 1955-57; prof. biophysics Calif. Inst. Tech., Pasadena, 1957-77, chmn. div. biology, 1968-77; chancellor U. Calif., Santa Cruz, 1977-87, chancellor emeritus, 1987—, prof. Santa Barbara, 1988-90, prof. emeritus, 1990—. Editor: Jour. Molecular Biology, 1959-67, Ann. Rev. Biochemistry, 1966-72. Named Calif. Scientist of Year, 1968; recipient N.W. Beijerinck-Virologie medal Netherlands Acad. Sci., 1969 Fellow Am. Acad. Arts and Scis.; mem. Am. Soc. Biol. Chemists, Biophys. soc. (pres. 1970), AAAS, Nat. Acad. Scis. (mem. council 1970-73, chmn. bd. editors Proc. 1972-80), Inst. Medicine. Achievements include discovery of single-stranded DNA, circular DNA; research in first in vitro replication of infective DNA. Avocations: photography, travel. Office: U Calif MCD Biology Santa Barbara CA 93106 Office Phone: 805-893-8038. Business E-Mail: sinsheim@lifesci.ucsb.edu.

**SINSHEIMER, WARREN JACK,** lawyer; b. NYC, May 22, 1927; s. Jerome William and Elizabeth (Berch) S.; m. Florence Dubin, Mar. 30, 1950; children: Linda Ruth, Ralph David, Alan Jay, Michael Neal. Student, Ind. U., 1943-47; JD cum laude, NY Law Sch., 1950; LLM, NYU, 1957; MPhil, Columbia U., 1977; HLD (hon.), Drew U., 2002. Bar: NY bar 1950. Ptnr. Sinsheimer, Sinsheimer & Dubin, NYC, 1950-78, Satterlee & Stephens, NYC, 1978-86, Patterson, Belknap, Webb & Tyler, NYC, 1986-91; counsel Patterson Belknap Webb & Tyler, NYC, 1991-96; pres., bd. dirs. Neighborhood Bagel Corp., 1994—. Pres. Plessey, Inc., NYC, 1956-70, chmn, CEO, 1970-89; dir. oversees ops. devel. The Plessey Co., Ltd., Ilford, Essex, Eng., 1969-70, dep. chief exec., dir., 1976-89; dir. Plessey, Inc.; trustee NYU Sch. Law, 1996—; pres., bd. dirs. Legal Svcs. Children, Inc., 1998—. Chmn. Com. of 68, 1964-67; Mem. Westchester County Rep. Com., 1956-73; chmn. Nat. Scranton Pres. Com., 1964; mem. NY State Assembly, 1965-66; Bd. visitors Wassaic State Sch., 1962-64; trustee Sch. Law, NYU, 1996—, bd. dirs. Shalom Hartman Inst., Jerusalem, 1991—, treas., 1996—; trustee Citi Bar Fund, 1998-2004. Served with USNR, 1944-45; with USAF, 1950-52. Mem. ABA, Assn. Bar City NY, Torch and Scroll, Century Club (Purchase, NY, gov., treas. 1997—), Century Assn. NYC, Univ. Club, Zeta Beta Tau. Jewish. Home: 22 Murray Hill Rd Scarsdale NY 10583-2828 Office: 271 Madison Ave New York NY 10016-1001 Office Phone: 212-683-7999. Business E-Mail: Sinsheimer@kidslaw.org.

**SINTZ, EDWARD FRANCIS,** librarian; b. New Trenton, Ind., Feb. 6, 1924; s. John and Edith E. (Rudicil) S.; m. Donna Norris, Apr. 12, 1952; children: Ann Kristin, Lesley Elizabeth, Julie Melinda. BA, U. Kans., 1950; MA in L.S, U. Denver, 1954; MS in Pub. Adminstrn, U. Mo., 1965. With Kansas City (Mo.) Pub. Library, 1954-66, asst. dir., 1964-66; assoc. librarian St. Louis Pub. Library, 1966-68; dir. pub. libraries Miami-Dade Pub. Libr., 1968—89, ret. Instr. Washington U., St. Louis, 1966-67; library surveys for Mo. State Library, 1967-68; library bldg. cons., 1965—. Editor: Mo. Library Assn. Quar., 1956—58. Served with USAAF, 1942-45. Mem. ALA, Fla. Library Assn. (pres. 1975-76), Southeastern Library Assn. Clubs: Kiwanian. Home: 7105 Lakeside Dr Charlotte NC 28215 Personal E-mail: edanddonna9@bellsouth.com.

**SIO, JIMMY ONG,** embryologist; b. Manila, Philippines, Mar. 9, 1954; arrived in U.S., 1973; s. Vicente and SiokBee (Ong) Sio. Biology major, U. Philippines, 1971—73; BS in Biology, Calif. State Coll. Bakersfield, 1976; PhD of Cell Biology, U. Tex. Health Sci. Ctr., Dallas, 1985; MD, Emory U., 1985. Diplomate Nat. Bd. Med. Examiners, Am. Bd. Hosp. Physicians, Am. Coll. Ethical Physicians. Resident in anat. pathology Emory U., Atlanta, 1985—86; resident in internal medicine Kem Med. Ctr., Bakersfield, Calif., 1990—93; physician Kaiser So. Calif. Permanente Med. Group, Bakersfield, 1993—, asst. area med. dir., 2006—; Pvt. Philippine Armed Forces, 1971—73. Recipient Businessman of Yr., NRCC, 2003, Man of Yr., IBC and ABI, 2004. Fellow: Am. Biog. Inst.; mem.: Internat. Biog. Assn., NY Acad. Scis., Order of Internat. Fellowship, InterNet Assocs. Avocation: reading. Home: 8604 Dinard Pl Bakersfield CA 93311 Office: Kaiser So Calif Permanente Med Group 8800 Ming Ave Bakersfield CA 93311 Office Phone: 661-664-3706. Personal E-mail: doctorsio@aol.com.

**SION, MAURICE,** mathematics professor; b. Skopje, Yugoslavia, Oct. 17, 1928; came to Can., 1960; s. Max and Sarah (Alalouf) S.; m. Emilie Grace Chisholm, Sept. 15, 1957; children: Crispin, Sarah, Dirk. BA, NYU, 1947, MA, 1948; PhD, U. Calif., Berkeley, 1951. Mathematician Nat. Bur. Stds., Washington, 1951-52; instr. U. Calif., 1952-53; asst. prof. U. Calif., 1957-60; mem. Inst. for Advanced Study, Princeton, NJ, 1955-57, 62; asst. prof. U. B.C., Vancouver, Canada, 1960, assoc. prof., 1961, prof., 1964-89, prof. emeritus, 1989—, head math. dept., 1984-86, dir. Quadra Inst. Math., 1970-89. Author: Introduction to Methods of Real Analysis, 1969, Theory Semi Group Valued Measures, 1973; contbr. articles to profl. jours. With U.S. Army, 1953-55. Mem. Am. Math. Soc., Can. Math. Soc. (v.p. 1972-74). Office: U BC Dept Math Vancouver BC Canada V6T 1Z2

**SIPE, DENA G.,** elementary school educator; b. Washington, Ind., July 18, 1950; d. Roscoe Leon and Wanda Jeanette Smith; m. Kevin Mark Sipe, Aug. 15, 1982; children: Jordan, Allison. BA, Anderson U., 1972; MA, Ball State U., 1978. Tchr. Elwood (Ind.) Cmty. Sch., 1974—. Mem. Nat. State Tchrs. Assn. Mem. Church Of God. Office: Oakland Elem Sch 2100 S P St Elwood IN 46036 Business E-Mail: dsipe@elwood.k12.in.us.

**SIPES, KAREN KAY,** communications executive; b. Higginsville, Mo., Jan. 8, 1947; d. Walter John and Katherine Marie (McLelland) Heins; m. Joel Rodney Sipes, Sept. 24, 1971; 1 child, Lesley Katherine. BS in Edn., Ctrl. Mo. State U., 1970. Reporter/news editor Newton Kansan, 1971—76; sports writer Capital-Jour., Topeka, 1976—83, spl. sects. editor, 1983—85, editl. page editor, 1985—92, mng. editor/features, 1992—2002, asst. editl. page

editor, 2002—03; dir. commn. Kans. Dept. Aging, Topeka, 2003—. Co-chair Mayor's Commn. on Literacy, Topeka, 1995-96; mem. Act Against Violence Com., Topeka, 1995-96, Mayor's Task Force on Race Rels., 1998; mem. planning com. Leadership Greater Topeka, 1997; Great Am. Cleanup, 1999-2001, ERC/Resource and Referral, 2001—; mem. Martin Luther King Living the Dream Bus. Ptnrs. Com., 2001-2004; mem. Centennial planning com. Family Svc. and Guidance Ctr., 2003-04; mem. Project Topeka Com., 2004—, Arthritis Walk Com., 2004-05, Faith in Action-No Place Like Home Coalition, 2003—; bd. dirs. Western Swing Music Soc. Kans., 2003—. Mem. Ctrl. Mo. State U. Alumni Assn. (bd. dirs. 1996-2002, v.p. 1999, pres. 2000). Avocations: music, gardening, art. Office: Kans Dept Aging New England Bldg 503 S Kans Ave Topeka KS 66603-3404 Office Phone: 785-368-7196. Personal E-mail: critterkaren@aol.com. Business E-Mail: karen.sipes@aging.state.ks.us.

**SIPES, THEODORE WARD,** music educator, singer; b. Bay City, Mich., Nov. 30, 1963; s. Ward Nathaniel and Bonnie Lee Sipes. D of Musical Arts, U. Mich., 2004. Min. music McPherson Free Meth. Ch., McPherson, Kans., 1988—95; dir. worship and music Browncroft Cmty. Ch., Rochester, NY, 1995—2001; vis. lectr. music U. Idaho, 2004—06; asst. prof. music Va. Poly. Inst. and State U., 2006—. Mem.: Nat. Assn. of Teachers of Singing, Coll. Music Soc. R-Liberal. Christian. Office: Va Tech Dept Music 167 Squires MC 0240 Blacksburg VA 24061 Office Phone: 540-231-7047. Personal E-mail: taddsipes@juno.com.

**SIPIERA, PAUL P., JR.,** foundation administrator, retired geology and astronomy professor; b. Chgo., Nov. 30, 1948; s. Paul P. and Frances A.; m. Diane M. Vidmar, May 22, 1993; children: Paula Frances, Caroline Antarctica. BA in History, Northeastern Ill. U., 1971, MS in Earth Sci., 1975; PhD in Natural Sci., U. Innsbruck, Austria, 2004. Prof. geology and astronomy Harper Coll., Palatine, Ill., 1976—2006, prof. emeritus, 2006—. Rsch assoc. Field Mus. Natural History, Chgo., 1976—92; exec. bd. Ill. State Acad. Sci., Springfield, 1978—83; rsch. sci. Antarctic search for meteorites NSF, Washington, 1983—84; pres. and CEO Planetary Studies Found., Algonquin, Ill., 1989—. Author: Gerald Ford, 1989, Amundsen & Scott: Race to the South Pole, 1990, Ernest Shackleton: A Life of Antarctic Exploration, 2002; contbr. chapters to books, to profl. publ. Adv. bd. mem. X-Prize Found., St. Louis, 1996—. Recipient Nininger Meteorite Rsch. award, Ariz. State U., 1975—76, Antarctic Svc medal, U.S.A. 1984, Disting. Faculty award, Harper Coll., 1996. Fellow: Ill. State Acad. Sci.; mem.: New Zealand Antarctic Soc., Geol. Soc. New Zealand, Meteoritical Soc. Achievements include asteroid 31931 named in his honor. Avocations: photography, farming. Home and Office: 10 Winterwood Ln Galena IL 61036 E-mail: psipiera@planets.org.

**SIPIORA, LEONARD PAUL,** retired museum director, art appraiser; b. Lawrence, Mass., Sept. 1, 1934; s. Walter and Agnes S.; m. Sandra Joyce Coon, 1962; children— Alexandra, Erika. AB cum laude, U. Mich., 1955, MA, 1956. Dir. museums, City of El Paso, Tex., 1967-90; ret. Co-founder, pres. El Paso Arts Coun., 1969-71; sec.-treas. El Paso Coun. Internat. Visitors, 1968-71; trustee El Paso Mus. Art; bd. dirs. Tex. Com. Humanities, Assn. Roadshow-U.S.A. Bd. dirs. Cmty. Concert Assn. El Paso, El Paso Symphony Orch., El Paso Hist. Soc. Mem. Assn. Mus. Dirs., Mountain Plains Mus. Assn. (pres. 1978-79), Tex. Assn. Museums (pres. 1977-79), Appraisers Assn. Am., Knights of Malta (decorated Grand Cross), Prior of Tex., Kappa Pi. Republican. Lutheran. Home: 1012 Blanchard Ave El Paso TX 79902-2727

**SIPKINS, PETER W.,** lawyer; b. Mpls., 1944; BA, U. Minn., 1966, JD, 1969. Bar: Minn. 1969, Wis. 1982. Spl. asst. atty. gen. State Minn., 1971-73, solicitor gen., 1974-76; mem. Dorsey & Whitney, Mpls., ptnr., trial practice group; co-chmn., products & tech. liability litig. group. Adj. prof. law, legal writing, appellate advocacy William Mitchell Coll. Law, 1974-77. Mem. Phi Delta Phi. Office: Dorsey & Whitney Ste 1500 50 S 6th St Minneapolis MN 55402-1498 Office Phone: 612-343-7903. Office Fax: 612-340-2807. Business E-Mail: sipkins.peter@dorsey.com.

**SIPLER, BARBARA MARIE,** secondary school educator; b. Weatherly, Pa., Aug. 26, 1943; d. Paul Albert Ratajczak and Theresa Lessick; m. Harold Clinton Sipler, Jan. 16, 1960; children: Harold C. Jr., Paul James, Charlaine Powell. BA in English, Wilkes U., 1973; M in Raeding, Bloomsburg U., 1984. Cert. reading supr., elem. and secondary intr. U. Scranton. H.S. English tchr. Weatherly (Pa.) Area Sch. Dist., 1973—84, reading specialist, 1984—. Mem. Weatherly Cmty. Chest, 1998—2005, Lower Luzerne Labor Coun., Hazleton, Pa., 1999—, Fed. Programs Coords., Harrisburg, Pa., 1990—2005. Recipient Pearl award, YMCA, 1990. Mem.: Internat. Reading Assn., Pa. State Edn. Assn. (pres. ea. region, v.p. ea. region). Democrat. Lutheran. Avocations: reading, hiking, writing, crossword puzzles. Home: 500 Fairview St Weatherly PA 18255 Office: Weatherly Area Sch Dist 602 6th St Weatherly PA 18255

**SIPPEL, WILLIAM LEROY,** lawyer; b. Fond du Lac, Wis., Aug. 14, 1948; m. Barbara Jean Brost, Aug. 23, 1970; children: Katharine Jean, David William. BA, JD, U. Wis. Bar: Wis. 1974, U.S. Dist. Ct. (we. dist.) Wis. 1974, Minn. 1981, U.S. Dist. Ct. Minn. 1981, U.S. Ct. Appeals (10th cir.) 1984, U.S. Ct. Appeals (8th cir.) 1985. Research assoc. dept. agrl. econs. U. Wis., Madison, 1974-75; counsel monopolies and comml. law subcom. Ho. Judiciary Com., Washington, 1975-80; spl. asst. to asst. gen. antitrust div. U.S. Dept. of Justice, Washington, 1980-81; from assoc. to ptnr. Doherty, Rumble & Butler, Mpls. and St. Paul, Minn., 1981 99; ptnr. Oppenheimer, Wolff & Donnelly, LLP, Mpls., 1999—. Bd. dirs. Music in the Park, Inc.; adj. faculty antitrust William Mitchell Coll. Law, 2000-01 Co-author: The Antitrust Health Care Handbook, 1988; contbg. author: ABA Energy Antitrust Handbook, 2002. Mem. program com. Minn. World Trade Assn., Mpls., St. Paul, 1985-86, bd. dirs., 1986, Minn.; former dir. Music in the Park, Mpls.; former dir. Person to Person Inc.; chmn. antitrust mktg. orders com. Nat. Coun. Farmer Coops., 2001—. With USAR, 1971-77. Mem. ABA (vice chmn. ins. industry com. 1990-91, contbr. ABA Joint Ventures in Health Care), Minn. Bar Assn. (co-chmn. antitrust sect. 1986-88, internat. law sect. coun. 1986-89, treas. 1989-90, sec. 1990-91, vice chmn. 1995-96, chmn. 1996-97), Minn. Med. Alley Assn. (co-chmn. internat. bus. com. 1990-95, Hennepin County Office Internat. Trade (bd. dirs. 1988-93), Phi Beta Kappa. Roman Catholic. Avocations: reading, photography, computers. Home: 2151 Commonwealth Ave Saint Paul MN 55108-1730 Office: Oppenheimer Wolff Donnelly LLP Plaza VII 45 S Seventh St Ste 3400 Minneapolis MN 55402-1609 Office Phone: 612-607-7251, Business E-Mail: bsippel@oppenheimer.com.

**SIPPEL-WETMORE, FRANCES MARIE,** microbiologist, retired business owner; b. Phila., Apr. 17, 1930; d. Jacob Harry Jr. and Catharine Seachrist (Hershey) Pickle; m. Roy Joseph Sippel, Feb. 8, 1958 (div. June 1979); m. Orville Chase Wetmore, June 14, 1997. Student, Women's Med. Coll., Pa., 1952—54; BA Biology and Chemistry honors, Hood Coll., 1953; MS Microbiology, U. Pitts., 1956. Rsch. asst. to Dr. Jonas Salk U. Pitts., 1955; rsch. asst. to Dr. T.S. Danowski Children's Hosp., Pitts., 1956; bacteriologist Shadyside Hosp., Pitts., 1956—57; rsch. asst. to Dr. Leonard Hayflick Wistar Inst., Phila., 1958—59. Biol. Abstracts, Phila., 1959—60; lit. chemist E.I. du Pont de Nemours & Co., Wilmington, Del., 1960—66; sec.-treas. Can-Am Sales Corp., West Chester, Pa., 1972—73; sales rep. Quick Courier Svc., Phila., 1977—82; owner Color Profile, West Chester, 1982—97. Bd. dirs. Chester County (Pa.) Emergency Med. Svcs., 1980-97; co-chair Holiday House Tour, 1989-93, chair House Acquisitions, 1995; vol. YWCA. Mem. AAUW (Outstanding Woman from West Chester br. 1991), LWV (chmn. Chester County coun. 1993-95), Am. Soc. Microbiologists, Phila. Hood Coll. Club (past pres.), Chester County Hist. Soc. (antiques show coun.), Wilmington Country Club, Sigma Xi Republican. Unitarian Universalist. Avocations: art, music, downhill skiing, travel. Home: 1007 Oriente Ave Wilmington DE 19807-2260

**SIPPEY, ROGER BOYD,** corporate executive; b. Zanesville, Ohio, Feb. 6, 1942; s. Walter Boyd and Ruth Lillian Sippey; m. Janet Elsa Hoehn, Nov. 24, 1943; children: Michael, Nancy Denenburg, Jason, Margarette. BS, Muskingum Coll., New Concord, Ohio, 1960—64. Exec. v.p. Feralloy Corp., Chgo., 1968—. Bd. dirs. Acero Prime Sa de Cv, San Louis Potosi, Mexico. Mem.: Steel Svc. Ctr. Inst., Racquet Club Chgo. Republican. Episcopalian. Avocations: boating, travel. Office: Feralloy Corp 5745 Higgins Road Chicago IL 60645 Home: 218 W St Paul Ave Chicago IL 60614-5712 Office Phone: 773-380-1503. Home Fax: 773-380-1500; Office Fax: 773-380-1812. Business E-Mail: roger@sippey.com.

**SIPPLE, WILLIAM STANTON,** ecologist, educator; b. Camden, N.J., Nov. 16, 1939; s. Gordon R. and Beulah K. (Stetser) S.; m. Geraldine Ann Ruggiano, Apr. 25, 1942; children: Michael W., Michele L., Sean D. BA in Biology, Glassboro State U., 1969; MS in Regional Planning, U. Pa., 1971; postgrad., U. Md., 1974-78. Natural resources planner Md. Dept. Natural Resources, Annapolis, 1971-79; ecologist U.S. EPA, Washington, 1979—2003; pres. W.S. Sipple Wetland & Environ. Tng. Cons., 2003—. Instr. grad. sch. USDA, Washington, 1972-90, No. Va. C.C., Woodbridge, 1993-97, Inst. for Wetland and Environ. Edn. and Rsch., Sherborn, Mass., 1993—, Johns Hopkins U., Balt., 1995-2003, Humboldt Field Rsch. Inst., Steuben, Maine, 1999—, Environ. Concorn, Inc., St. Michaels, Md., 2001—, Towson U., Md., 2003—; mem. scientific adv. bd. Jug Bay Wetlands Sanctuary, Lothian, Md., 1988—; mem. Nat. Tech. Com. for Hydric Soils, Washington, 1986-2003; mem. sci. adv. com. County of Anne Arundel, Annapolis, 1973-76. Author: Through the Eyes of a Young Naturalist, 1991, Days Afield: Exploring Wetlands in the Chesapeake Bay Region; contbr. articles to profl. jours. Mem. Ecol. Soc. Am., Soc. Wetland Scientists, So. Appalachian Botan. Club, Sigma Xi. Republican. Avocations: natural history, bottle collecting, postcard collecting, book collecting. Home and Office: 512 Red Bluff Ct Millersville MD 21108-1478 Office Phone: 410-987-4083. E-mail: bsip333@verizon.com, bsip333@aol.com

**SIPPRELL, GEORGE SIDNEY,** aerospace engineer, consultant; b. Buffalo, Jan. 10, 1949; s. George Gilbert and Eleanor M. Sipprell; m. Kathleen Ann Meyer, July 22, 1972; children: Jeffery David, Benjamin Daniel. BS in Aero. Engring., Rensselaer Poly. Inst., 1970, MEng in Aero. Engring., 1972. Joined Sikorsky Aircraft Corp., Stratford, Conn., 1972, propulsion sys. analyst, 1972—74, helicopter icing lead rsch. engr., 1974—76, UH-60A Black Hawk project engr., 1972—76, engring. mgr. USCG SRR/S76, 1976—79, sr. sys. analyst, LHX, 1979, program mgr., engring. mgr. UH60A Black Hawk ESSS, 1979—83, engring. mgr. LHX Program, 1983—90, engr. mgr. LHX simulation and SHADOW program, 1988—91, dep. program mgr. RAH-66 Comanche Helicopter Program, 1990—2002, chief engr. U.S. Army/DARPA Unmanned Combat Armed Rotorcraft program, 2002—03, dir. engring., sys. requirements and analysis and advanced concepts, 2003—04; ret., 2004. Ind. aerospace sys. engring. cons., 2004—. Recipient AHS Grover Bell award, 1990, U.S. Army Chief Staff award, 1993, Bd. Dirs. Trophy award, United Techs. Corp., 2001. Mem.: Am. Helicopter Soc. (mem. qua. century group), Sikorsky Ski Club (pres. 1980—82, Outstanding Member award 1982). Avocations: model railroading, skiing, toy collecting, British cars and Corvettes. Home and Office: 4 Featherbed Ln Branford CT 06405-6113 Office Phone: 203-481-4866. Personal E-mail: gsipprell@excite.com.

**SIPPY, DAVID DEAN,** dentist; b. Waukesha, Wis., June 22, 1953; s. Lawrence Vern and Myrtle (Lawton) S.; m. Sharon Eleanor Komar, Jan. 8, 1977; children: Sharon Kay, Derek Bradley. MB, U. Wis., Milw., 1972; M in Dental Surgery, Marquette U., 1987. Dentist, New Glarus, Wis., 1988—. Owner Zenter Haus Bed and Breakfast Inn; part-time faculty Sch. Dental Hygiene Madison Area Tech. Coll. Bd. dirs. C. of C., 1989-91. Mem. ADA, Internat. Assn. for Orthodontics, Nat. Trust for Hist. Preservation, Oreg. Geneal. Soc., Am. Orthodontics Soc. (bd. dirs.). Mem. Seventh-Day Aventists. Avocations: genealogy, history, historical architecture, astrophysics. Home: N8588 Zentner Rd New Glarus WI 53574 Office: New Glarus Dental Clinic 119 6th Ave New Glarus WI 53574 also: Family Dental Care 405 1/2 Iowa St Dodgeville WI 53533 Office Phone: 608-930-2121. Personal E-mail: tremeau@tds.net.

**SIPSKI, MARY LEONIDE,** physiatrist, health facility administrator; b. Somerville, N.J., July 6, 1950; d. Joseph John and Sophia Barbara (Marcewicz) Sipski; m. Thomas Edward Lammertse, June 16, 1979; children: Meredith, Matthew, Evan. AB, Rutgers U., 1972; PhD in Phys. Biochemistry, Ohio U., 1976; MD, Ohio State U., 1979; M in Med. Mgmt., U. So. Calif., 2003. Diplomate Am. Bd. Phys. Medicine and Rehab., Am. Bd. Managed Care Medicine, cert. in med. mgmt. Am. Coll. Physician Execs. and U. So. Calif., 2001. Intern, resident in phys. medicine and rehab. Ohio State U. Hosps., 1979-83; dir. phys. medicine and rehab. Gaylord Hosp., Wallingford, Conn., 1983-90; dir. brain injury program, dir. outpatient svcs. Kessler Inst. Rehab., Chester, NJ, 1990-97; chief med. officer Consumer Health Network Solutions, South Plainfield, NJ, 1997—2005, Selective Ins. Managed Care Solutions, Hamilton, NJ, 2002—05. Med. dir. Gaylord/Yale-New haven Ctr. at Long Wharf, 1989-90; asst. clin. prof. dept. orthopedics and rehab. Yale U., New Haven, 1989-90; cons. Bur. Disability Determination, Columbus, Ohio, 1982-83; pvt. practice cons. in brain injury, disability, and expert medicolegal testimony, Far Hills, 1991—. Fellow Am. Acad. Phys. Medicine and Rehab. (sec. Conn. soc.); mem. AMA, Am. Coll. Physician Execs., Am. Coll. Managed Care Medicine, Consumer Health Network Solutions. Office: CHN Solutions 3525 Quakerbridge Rd Hamilton NJ 08619 Office Phone: 800-225-4246. E-mail: dr.sipski@chn.com.

**SIPZNER, HOWARD M.,** real estate executive; MBA, Harvard U. Analyst mcpl. securities Merrill Lynch, 1983—85; v.p. real estate and lodging investment banking Chase Securities, Inc., 1987—89; CFO Equity One, Inc., North Miami Beach, 1999—. Office: 1696 NE Miami Gardens Dr North Miami Beach FL 33179

**SIQUELAND, EINAR,** psychologist, educator; b. Glasgow, Mont., Nov. 15, 1932; s. Harald and Anna Lydia (Kristensen) S.; m. Marian McGrail, Dec. 1960 (div. May 1970); children: Lynne Ruth, Beth Ann; m. Jillian E.A. Godfree, June 29, 1973. BA, Pacific Luth. U., 1954; MS, U. Wash., 1962, PhD, 1963. Rsch. assoc. pharmacology U. Wash., Seattle, 1958-59; clin. intern psychology VA Mental Hygiene Clinic, Seattle, 1960-61; asst. prof. dept. psychology Brown U., Providence, 1965-69, assoc. prof., 1969-88, prof., 1988-99; rsch. scientist dept. Pediatrics Women's and Infants' Hosp., Providence, 1975-93; prof. emeritus Brown U., 1999—. Contbr. articles to profl. jours., chpts. to books. With U.S. Army, 1956-58, Korea. Predoctoral fellow USPHS, 1961-63; postdoctoral fellow, 1963-65. Fellow Am. Psychol. Soc.; mem. AAUP, APA, Soc. Rsch. in Child Devel., Sigma Xi. Office: Brown U Dept Psychology PO Box 1853 Providence RI 02912-1853 E-mail: siquel-e@cox.net.

**SIRAGUSA, CHARLES J.,** judge; BA, Lemoyne Coll., 1969; JD, Albany Law Sch., 1976. Judge U.S. Dist. Ct. (we. dist.) N.Y., 1997—. Office: 1360 US Courthouse 100 State St Rochester NY 14614-1350 Office Phone: 585-613-4050.

**SIRENA, ANTONIA M. FANARA,** artist; b. White Plains, NY, Jan. 13, 1924; d. Lucrezia (Amodio) Mastrocristino; m. Anthony Jack Fanara, Dec. 30, 1950 (div.) Opera singer Vatican, Rome, 1956-89; painter N.Y.C., 1956—. Lectr., cons. in field. Exhibited in group shows at Washington Mus., Md., Arch Diocese N.Y., Art Sci. Mus., Fla., others. Home: 1035 5th Ave New York NY 10028-0135

**SIRGADO, JO ANNE E.,** lawyer; b. Meadville, Pa., May 16, 1960; BA magna cum laude, Villa Maria Coll., 1982; JD, Pace Univ., 1990. Bar: NY 1991. Ptnr., project devel., fin., leasing Hunton & Williams LLP, NYC, and constrn. recruitment com. Office: Hunton & Williams LLP 43rd Fl 200 Park Ave New York NY 10166-0136 Office Phone: 212-309-1093. Office Fax: 212-309-1100. Business E-Mail: jsirgado@hunton.com.

**SIRICA, ALPHONSE EUGENE,** pathology educator; b. Waterbury, Conn., Jan. 16, 1944; s. Alphonse Eugene and Elena Virginia (Mascolo) S.; m. Annette Marie Murray, June 9, 1984; children: Gabrielle Theresa, Nicholas Steven. MS, Fordham U., 1968; PhD in Biomed. Sci., U. Conn., 1971. Asst. prof. U. Wis., Madison, 1979-84; assoc. prof. Med. Coll. Va., Va. Commonwealth U., Richmond, 1984-90, prof. of pathology, 1990—, divsn. chair exptl. pathology, 1992-99, divsn. chair cellular and molecular pathogenesis, 1999—. Vis. prof. Pa. State U. Coll. Medicine, 2000; regular mem. sci. adv. com. on carcinogenesis and nutrition Am. Cancer Soc., Atlanta, 1989—92; metabolic pathology study sect. NIH, Bethesda, 1991—95, ad hoc mem. study sect., 1997—2006. Editor, author: The Pathobiology of Neoplasia, 1989, The Role of Cell Types in Hepatocarcinogenesis, 1992, Cellular and Molecular Pathogenesis, 1996; co-editor, author: Biliary and Pancreatic Ductal Epithelia: Pathobiology and Pathophysiology, 1997; mem. editl. bd. Pathobiology, 1990-99, Hepatology, 1991-94; rev. bd. In Vitro Cellular and Devel. Biology-Animal, 1987—, Exptl. and Molecular Pathology, 1999—, World Jour. Gastroenterology, 2006-; contbr. articles to profl. jours. including Am. Jour. Pathology, Cancer Rsch., Hepatology. Recipient Rsch. Recognition award, Va. Commonwealth U. Sch. Medicine, 2002. Mem.: AAAS, Soc. Toxicology, Han. Popper Hepatopathology Soc., Soc. Exptl. Biology and Medicine, NY Acad. Scis., Am. Gastroenterological Assn., Am. Assn. Study Liver Diseases, Am. Soc. Investigative Pathology (chair program com. 1994—96), Assn. Clin. Scientists, Soc. for In Vitro Biology, Am. Assn. Cancer Rsch. (chmn. Va. state legis. com. 1992—95), Am. Soc. Cell Biology. Achievements include development of collagen gel-nylon mesh system for culturing hepatocytes; first establishment and characterization of hyperplastic bile ductular epithelial cells in culture; research in hepato and biliary carcinogenesis, pathobiology of hepatocyte and biliary epithelial cells and molecular pathogenesis and experimental therapeutics of biliary cancer. Office: Med Coll Va Va Commonwealth U PO Box 980297 Richmond VA 23298-0297 Office Phone: 804-828-9549. E-mail: asirica@hsc.vcu.edu.

**SIRICO, GENARO,** actor; b. Bklyn., July 29, 1942; Actor: (TV series) The Soprano's, 1999—; (TV films) Perfect Witness, 1989, In the Shadow of a Killer, 1992, Gotti, 1996; (films) Hughes and Harlow: Angels in Hell, 1977, Fingers, 1978, The One Man Jury, 1978, Gangsters, 1979, Defiance, 1980, So Fine, 1981, Love and Money, 1982, Exposed, 1983, The Last Fight, 1983, The Pick-Up Artist, 1987, Hello Again, 1987, Cookie, 1989, White Hot, 1989, Goodfellas, 1990, Catchfire, 1990, 29th Street, 1991, Innocent Blood, 1992, Romeo is Bleeding, 1993, Bullets Over Broadway, 1994, The Search for One-eye Jimmy, 1994, Mighty Aphrodite, 1995, Dead Presidents, 1995, Dearly Beloved, 1995, Everyone Says I Love You, 1996, New York Cop, 1996, Cop Land, 1997, Deconstructing Harry, 1997, The Deli, 1997, Mob Queen, 1998, Celebrity, 1998, Mickey Blue Eyes, 1999, It Had to Be You, 2000, Smokin' Stogies, 2001, Turn of Faith, 2001. Office: c/o Arcieri & Assoc Inc Ste 2315 305 Madison Ave New York NY 10165

**SIRIGNANO, MONICA ANN,** performing company executive, playwright; b. Princeton, N.J., May 18, 1971; d. William Alfonso and Molly Wilhelmina Sirignano. BA in English, Stetson U., 1993; postgrad., CUNY. Mng. editor Encore Mag., Miami, Fla., 1993—95; asst. mng. editor PC Mag., N.Y.C., 1995—2000; performer, playwright N.Y.C., 1995—; artistic dir., pres. Screaming Venus Prodns., N.Y.C., 1999—, also bd. dirs. Adjudicator Fringe NYC, 2000, 01; mem. adv. bd. Blue Allied Theatre Co., N.Y.C., 2002—. Contbr. articles to jours.; author: On Zither & Autobiography, 2004, short story pubs. Mem. membership com., mem. creative black tie invitation com. Am. Cancer Soc., Miami, 1993—94; mem. Habitat for Humanity, Ft Lauderdale, Fla., 1994. Recipient award, Off-Off Broadway Rev., 2001; grantee, Harburg Found., 2000. Mem.: Theatre Comm. Group, Dramatists Guild. Avocations: photography, painting, graphic design. Office: Screaming Venus Prodns 29-22 Hoyt Ave S # 21 Astoria NY 11102 Personal E-mail: nicasiri@gmail.com.

**SIRIGNANO, WILLIAM ALFONSO,** aerospace and mechanical engineer, educator; b. Bronx, NY, Apr. 14, 1938; s. Anthony P. and Lucy (Caruso) S.; m. Lynn Haisfield, Nov. 26, 1977; children: Monica Ann, Jacqueline Hope, Justin Anthony. B.Aero.Engring., Rensselaer Poly. Inst., 1959; PhD, Princeton U., 1964. Mem. research staff Guggenheim Labs., aerospace, mech. scis. dept. Princeton U., 1964-67, asst. prof. aerospace and mech. scis., 1967-69, assoc. prof., 1969-73, prof., 1973-79, dept. dir. grad. studies, 1974-78; George Tallman Ladd prof., head dept. mech. engring. Carnegie-Mellon U., 1979-85; dean Sch. Engring., U. Calif.-Irvine, 1985-94, prof., 1994—. Cons. industry and govt., 1966—; lectr. and cons. NATO adv. group on aero. rsch. and devel., 1967, 75, 80; chmn. nat. and internat. tech. congs.; chmn. acad. adv. coun. Indsl. Rsch. Inst., 1985-88; mem. space sci. applications adv. com. NASA, 1985-90, chmn. combustion sci. microgravity disciplinary working group, 1987-90; chmn. com. on microgravity rsch. space studies bd. NRC, 1991-94, Henry Samueli endowed chair in engring., 2004-. Spl. issues editor: Combustion Sci. and Tech., 1969-70, 2000—; assoc. tech. editor Jour. Heat Transfer, 1986-92; contbr. articles to profl. jours. Recipient Disting. Alumni Rsch. award U. Calif. Irvine, 1992, Recognition award Am. Electronics Assn., 1994, Excellence award Orange County Engring. Coun., 1994; United Aircraft rsch. fellow, 1973-74. Fellow: AAAS, ASME (Freeman scholar 1992), AIAA (Pendray Aerospace Lit. award 1991, Propellants and Combustion award 1992, Energy Systems award 2004, Sustained Svc. award 2006), Am. Phys. Soc.; mem.: NAE, Soc. Indsl. and Applied Math., Combustion Inst. (treas. internat. orgn., chmn. ea. sect., Alfred C. Egerton Gold medal 1996), Inst. Dynamics Explosives and Reactive Sys. (v.p. 1991—95, pres. 1995—99, Oppenheim award 1993). Office: U Calif Irvine Sch Engring S3202 Engring Gtwy Irvine CA 92697-3975

**SIRILLA, GEORGE M.,** lawyer; b. Perryopolis, Pa., May 1, 1929; s. Michael and Helen Sirilla; m. Floranne Zalewski Sirilla, Nov. 23, 1968; children: Michael George, Joseph David. BSME, Rensselaer Poly. Inst., Troy, N.Y., 1952; LLB, Georgetown Law Sch., Washington, JD, 1956. Bar: Va. 1956, DC 1956. Assoc. Cushman, Darby & Cushman, Washington, 1955—59, ptnr., 1960, 1968—96, Pillsbury, Madison & Sutro, 1996—, Pillsbury Winthrop, McLean, Va., 2001—05, Pillsbury Winthrop Shaw Pittman, 2005—. Adj. prof. George Washington Law Sch., Washington, 1982—83; mem. mng. bd. Cushman, Darby & Cushman, 1988—89, Pillsbury, Madison & Sutro, 1999—2000. Contbr. articles to law revs. Sgt. U.S. Army, 1946—47, Korea. Named Master, Giles S. Rich Inn of Ct, 1992—2001. Mem.: Am. Coll. Trial Lawyers. Office: Pillsbury Winthrop Shaw 1650 Tysons Blvd Mc Lean VA 22102 Office Phone: 703-770-7784.

**SIRISAENGTAKSIN, ONGARD,** computer scientist, mathematician, educator; Prof. U. Houston, 1986—. Grantee, NSF, 1993, 1994, 1995, 2006, Army Rsch. Office, 1995. Office: University of Houston Downtown One Main Street Houston TX 77002 Office Phone: 713-221-8554. Office Fax: 713-221-8086. Business E-Mail: ongards@dt.uh.edu.

**SIRJANI, MOJTABA B.,** education educator; children: Parsa B., Arsha B. PhD, Old Dominion U., Norfolk, Va., 1998. Assoc. prof. Norfolk State U., Va., 2001—06, prof., 2006—. Asst. prof. Norfolk State U., Norfolk, Va., 1989—2001. Rsch. grant, Lockheed Martin, 1998—2001. Mem.: ASCE, Task Force on Stability (assoc.). Achievements include research in stability analysis of fiber reinforced plastic beams. Office: Norfolk State U 700 Park Ave Norfolk VA 23504 Office Phone: 757-823-9565. Home Fax: 757-823-8427; Office Fax: 757-823-8427. Business E-Mail: sirjani@nsu.edu.

**SIRKECI MERGAN, BIRSEN,** electrical engineer, researcher; b. Eregli, Turkey, Sept. 5, 1976; d. Hayrettin and Aynur Sirkeci; m. Gokhan Mergan, May 24, 2003. BSEE, Mid. East Tech. U., Ankara, 1998; BS Math., Mid. East Tech. U., 1998; MSEE, Northea. U., Boston, 2001. Rsch. asst. Northea U., 1998—2000; engr. Aware Inc., Bedford, Mass., 2000—02; tchg. asst. Cornell U., Ithaca, NY, 2002—04, rsch. asst., 2004—. Recipient Fred Ellersich award, Milcon Conf. com., 2005. Mem.: IEEE.

**SIRKEN, MONROE GILBERT,** statistician; b. N.Y.C., Jan. 11, 1921; s. Irving and Henrietta (Oram) S.; m. Blanche Skalak Hurwitz (div. 1960); children: Robert, Philip. BA, UCLA, 1946, MA, 1947; PhD, U. Wash., 1950. Lectr. Med. Sch. U. Wash., Seattle, 1949; fellow Stats. Lab. U. Calif., Berkeley, 1950; statistician Census Bur., Suitland, Md., 1951-54, Pub. Health Svc., Washington, 1954-60, Nat. Ctr. Health Stats., Hyattsville, Md., 1961—. Cons. NIH, 1980-85, Nat. Inst. Drug Addiction, 1976-80, NSF, 1986—, Health Care Fin. Adminstrn., 1989-90. Contbr. articles to Jour. Am. Statis. Assns., Biometrics, Demography, Jour. APHA, Pub. Health Reports, also others. Home: 3309 Claridge Ct Silver Spring MD 20902-2201 Office Phone: 301-458-4505. Personal E-mail: mgsirken@aol.com. Business E-Mail: mgs2@cdc.gov.

**SIRKIN, JOEL H.,** lawyer; b. Pitts., Jan. 7, 1946; s. Sidney and Marion (Wolkin) S.; m. Karen Sargent, Aug. 7, 1977; children: Alex S., Jacob O. BA magna cum laude, Johns Hopkins U., 1967; JD cum laude, Harvard U., 1972. Bar: Mass. 1972. Prin. Cambridge (Mass.) Pilot Sch., 1970-71; staff atty. Cambridge-Somerville Legal Services, 1972-74; sr. ptnr., chmn. Real Estate dept. Hale & Dorr, Boston, 1974—2004; ptnr., chmn. Real Estate dept., mem. exec. com. Wilmer Cutler Pickering Hale & Dorr, Boston, 2004—. Author: Public School Law. Dir. Mass. Children's Lobby, Boston, 1980-84; mem. fin. com. Town of Wayland, Mass., 1993-96. Named a Mass. Super Lawyer, Boston Mag., 2004. Mem. Phi Beta Kappa. Avocations: gardening, tennis, golf. Home: 10 Wildwood Rd Wayland MA 01778-2122 Office: Wilmer Cutler Pickering Hale & Dorr 60 State St Boston MA 02109-1816 Office Phone: 617-526-6279. Office Fax: 617-526-5000. Business E-Mail: joel.sirkin@wilmerhale.com.

**SIRKIN, MICHAEL S.,** lawyer; b. Newark, Feb. 21, 1947; BS in industl. engring., Rutgers U., 1969; JD, Columbia U., 1972. Bar: N.Y. 1973. Mem. Proskauer Rose LLP, N.Y.C., 1989—. Office: Proskauer Rose LLP 1585 Broadway Fl 27 New York NY 10036-8299 Office Phone: 212-969-3840. E-mail: msirkin@proskauer.com.

**SIRNA, GAIL CAROLYN,** artist, educator; b. Detroit, Apr. 7, 1943; d. John Arthur and Viola Rose McKeown; m. Robert G. Sirna, May 28, 1966; children: Michele Lee Grace, Cheryl Lynn, Anthony McKeown. AB, St. Louis U., 1965; MA, U. Mich., 1969. Tchr., counselor Hazel Park (Mich.) Pub. Schs., 1972—82; shopowner The Fancyworks, Sterling Heights, Mich., 1982—85. Author: (book) In Praise of the Needlewoman: Embroiderers, Knitters, Lacemakers, & Weavers in Art, (bi-monthly column) Needlepoint Now, 2001—. Mem. Needlepoint Guild (nominating com. 2000—03, Best of Show 1999), Nat. Embroidery Tchrs. Assn. (sec. 2002—05, pres. 1985—88), Embroiderers' Guild Am. (region dir. 1990—92, chmn. cert grad. tchr. program 2001—04, cert. grad. tchr.), Nat. Acad. Needlearts (dir. 1990—2000, treas. 2000—, cert. tchr. needlearts, cert. judge, Lifetime Achievement award 2004), Phi Kappa Phi. Roman Catholic. E-mail: gigigail@speakeasy.net.

**SIROIS, CHARLES,** communications executive; b. Chicoutimi, Que., Can., May 22, 1954; children: François-Charles, Marie-Hélène. Doctorate (hon.), U. Québec, Montréal, U. Ottawa (Can.), Concordia U., Montreal, Laval U., Que.; B Fin., Sherbrooke U., Qué.; M Fin., Laval U., Qué. Founder Telesystem Ltd., Montreal, 1984—, Nat. Pagette Ltd., Montreal, 1986-88; chmn., CEO BCE Mobile Comms. Inc., Montreal, 1988-90, Teleglobe Inc., Montreal, 1992-2000; founder, chmn., CEO Telesystem Ltd., Montreal, 1990—; chmn. Microcell Telecomms. Inc., Montreal, 1993—, Telesys. Internat. Wireless, 1997—; global bd. dirs. Enablis. Bd dirs Can Imperial Bank Commerce; mem Global Info Infrastructure Comn, Can Info Hwy. Co-author: (book) The Medium and the Muse, 1995, Organic Management-Creating a Culture of Innovation, 2000. Mem.: Knight Order nat du Que, Order Can (hon.). Office: Telesystem Ltd 38th Fl 1250 René Lévesque Blvd W Montreal PQ Canada H3B 4W8 E-mail: csirois@telesystem.ca.*

**SIROONI, ANAHID ALICE,** composer; Postgrad. diploma, Juilliard Sch., NYC, 1947. Piano tchr. Composer: concert classics recs. Home: 188 Ryder Rd Manhasset NY 11030

**SIROTA, WILBERT H.,** lawyer; b. Balt., 1937; BA, Johns Hopkins Univ., 1958; JD, Univ. Md., 1961; LLM, Georgetown Univ., 1964. Bar: Md. 1961. Law clk. Md. Ct. Appeals, 1961—62; atty. office of chief counsel IRS, 1963; ptnr. DLA Piper, Balt. Lectr. Georgetown Univ. Sch. Law, Univ. Md. Sch. Law, Loyola Coll. Bd. dir. & treas. World Trade Ctr. Inst., Balt.; counsel Econ. Alliance Greater Balt.; mem. bd. vis. Univ. Md. Balt. County; mem. bd. U. Md. Med. Sys., Emerging Tech. Ctr. Office: DLA Piper 6225 Smith Ave Baltimore MD 21209-3600 Office Phone: 410-580-4264. Office Fax: 410-580-3264. Business E-Mail: wilbert.sirota@dlapiper.com.

**SIROTIN, PETER,** musician, conductor; b. Kharkov, Ukraine, Oct. 30, 1973; s. Ilya and Ludmila Sirotin; m. Ya-Ting Chang, Sept. 8, 2000. BA, Moscow State Tchaikovsky Conservatory, 1995; GPD in Violin Performance and Chamber Music, Peabody Conservatory Music/Johns Hopkins U., 1999. Assoc. concert master Harrisburg Symphony Orch., Pa., 1996—; violinist Razumovsky String Quartet, Md., 1997—, Moscow Soloists, Mendelssohn Piano Trio, Potomac, Md., 1997—; artist-in-residence, faculty mem. Messiah Coll., Grantham, Pa., 2003—; ensemble-in-residence Embassy Series. Office: Mendelssohn Piano Trio 9400 Sunnyfield Ct Potomac MD 20854 Personal E-mail: peter@mendelssohnpianotrio.com.

**SIROTY, WILLIAM CHARLES,** physician; b. NYC, June 9, 1951; s. Daniel Hirsch and Eileen (Gusman) S. BS, SUNY, Stony Brook, 1973; MD, Georgetown U., 1977. Diplomate Am. Bd. Internal Medicine, Am. Bd. Allergy-Immunology. Intern in internal medicine Beth Israel Med. Ctr., NYC, 1977-78, resident in internal medicine, 1977-78; fellow allergy and immunology NY Hosp.-Cornell U. Med. Ctr., 1980-82; pvt. practice NYC, 1982-94; staff physician Nashua (NH) Med. Group, 1994—. Mem. adv. bd. Cmty. Rsch. Initiative, 1990-94, HIV Arts Network, 1994-95. Editor: NH News Links, 2000—. Vol. Neighborhood Health Clinic; co-founder, first co-chair Gay People in Medicine Caucus Am. Med. Student Assn., 1976—77; active NH State Dem. Com., 1998—, Hillsborough County Dem. Com., NH, 1998—, vice-chmn., 2004—; del. Dem. Nat. Conv., 2000, 2004; chair Dems. Amherst, 2002—; bd. dirs. Elizabeth Streb Ringside, Inc., NH Civil Liberties Union. Mem. Am. Acad. Allergy, Asthma and Immunology, NH Med. Soc. Office: Nashua Med Group 173 Daniel Webster Hwy Nashua NH 03060-5224

**SIRRI, ERIK R.,** federal agency administrator, economist; BS in Astronomy, Calif. Inst. of Technology, 1979; MBA, U. of Calif.: Irvine, 1984; PhD in Finance, UCLA, 1990. Rsch. scientist Nichols Rsch. Corp., Newport Beach, Calif., 1979—83; asst. prof. Harvard Bus. Sch., Boston, 1989—95, Babson Coll., Babson Park, Mass., 1995—96, assoc. prof., 1999—2004, prof., Walter H. Capenter chair, 2004—; chief economist US SEC, 1996—99, dir. divsn. market regulation, 2006—. Econ. advisory bd. Nasdaq Stock Market, 2000—02, Nat. Assn. Securities Dealers, 2001—05; gov. Boston Stock Exch., 2003—; bd. mem. Boston Options Exch., 2004—; advisory bd. Proxy Governance Inc., 2004—; visiting scholar Harvard Law Sch., 2005—06. Recipient Morgan Stanley Microstructure award, 2005; Olin Fellow, Cornell Law Sch., 2000. Mem.: Am. Fin. Assn., Quantitative Work Alliance for Applied Fin., Edn., and Wisdom (QWAFAFEW). Econ. Fin. Studies. Office: SEC 100 F St NE Washington DC 20549*

**SIRVÉN, JOSÉ E.,** lawyer; b. Camaguey, Cuba, Aug. 28, 1956; AA with honors, Miami-Dade Cmty. Coll., 1976; BBA in Acctg. (hon.), Fla. Internat. U., 1978; JD cum laude, U. Miami Sch. Law, 1981. Ptnr. Holland & Knight LLP, Miami, Fla., mem. dir. com. Author and contbr. editor U. Miami Law Review, 1980—81. Mem.: Cuban Am. Bar Assn., Fla. Bar, Dade County Bar Assn. Office: Holland & Knight LLP 701 Brickell Ave Ste 3000 Miami FL 33131 Office Phone: 305-789-7784. Business E-Mail: jsirven@hklaw.com.

**SIS, PETER,** illustrator, children's book writer, filmmaker, artist; b. Brno, Czech Republic, May 11, 1949; came to U.S., 1982, naturalized, 1988; s. Vladimir and Alena (Petrvalska) S.; m. Terry Ann Lajtha, Oct. 23, 1990; children: Madeleine, Matej. BA, Acad. of Applied Arts, 1968—74; MA, Royal Coll. of Art, 1977. Author, illustrator: Rainbow Rhino, 1987 (Best Illustrated Book award NY Times, 1988), Waving, 1988, Going Up, 1989, Beach Ball, 1990 (Best Illustrated Book award N.Y. Times, 1990), Follow the Dream, 1991 (Best Illustrated Book award N.Y. Times, 1992), An Ocean World, 1992, A Small, Tall Tale from the Far Far North, 1992, Komodo!, 1993, The Three Golden Keys, 1994, Starry Messenger: Galileo Galilei, 1996 (Caldecott Honor Book, 1997), Tibet Through the Red Box, 1998, Madlenka's Dog, 2002, The Tree of Life, 2003; illustrator: Fairy Tales of the Brothers Grimm, 2 vols., 1976, 77, Hexe Lakritze and Buchstabenkonig, 1977, Zizkov Romances, 1978, Hexe Lakritze and Rhino Rhinoceros, 1979, Poetry, 1980, Baltic Fairy Tales, 1981, Little Singer, 1982, Bean Boy, 1983, Stories to solve, 1984, Whipping Boy, 1985 (Newberry medal 1987), Oaf, 1986, Three Yellow Dogs, 1986, Higgledy Piggledy, 1986, Jed and the Space Bandits, 1987, After Midnight, 1987, City Lights, 1987, Scarebird, 1988, Alphabet Soup, 1988, Halloween, 1989, The Ghost in the Noonday Sun, 1989, The Midnight Horse, 1990, More Stories to Solve, 1991, Rumpelstiltskin, 1993, The Dragons Are Singing Tonight, 1993, Still More Stories to Solve, 1994, The 13th Floor, 1995, Monday's Troll, 1996, Sleep Safe Little Whale, 1997; filmmaker: (TV series) Hexe Lakritze, 1982, (short films) Mimikry, 1975, Island for 6,000 Alarm Clocks, 1977, Heads, 1979 (Golden Bear award Berlin Film Festival 1980), Players, 1981 (Grand Prix Toronto Film Festival 1981), You Gotta Serve Somebody, 1983 (CINE Golden Eagle award 1983), Aesop's Fables, 1984, Twelve Months, 1985; artist one man shows include Gallery Martinska, Gallery Nerudova, Gallery Rubin, Prague, 1977-79, Gallery Klostermauer, St. Gallen, 1975, Gallery Ploem, Delft, 1977, Gallery Vista Nova, Zurich, 1980, Gallery Medici, London, 1981, Sch. Art U. Ohio, Athens, 1990. Recipient MacArthur Fellowship, 2003. Office: Farrar, Straus & Giroux Books for Young Readers 19 Union Square West New York NY 10003

**SISCHY, INGRID BARBARA,** editor, art critic; b. Johannesburg, Republic of South Africa, Mar. 2, 1952; came to U.S., 1967; d. Benjamin and Claire S. BS, Sarah Lawrence Coll., 1973; PhD (hon.), Moore Coll. Art, 1987. Assoc. editor Print Collector's Newsletter, N.Y.C., 1974-77; dir. Printed Matter, N.Y.C., 1977-78; curatorial intern Mus. Modern Art, N.Y.C., 1978-79; editor ArtForum Mag., N.Y.C., 1979-88; editor-in-chief Interview, N.Y.C., 1989—. Office: Interview Magazine 575 Broadway Fl 5 New York NY 10012-3230

**SISK, CHERYL,** neuroscientist, educator; b. Waco, Tex., July 4, 1954; BA in Psych., Baylor U., Waco, Tex., 1974; MS in Psych., Fla. State U., Tallahassee, 1976, PhD in Psychobiology/Neuroscience, 1980. Postdoctoral rschr. dept. neurobiology and physiology Northwestern U., 1980—82; rsch. assoc. dept. zoology U. Tex. Inst. Reproductive Biology, Austin, 1983—85; asst. prof. dept. psych. and neuroscience prog. Mich. State U., 1985—89, assoc. prof., 1989, prof., 1995—, adj. assoc. prof., prof. dept. physiology, 1990—. Dir. Interdepartmental Grad. Neuroscience Prog. Mich. State U., 1998—. Contbr. articles to profl. jours., chapters to books; mem. adv. bd.: Jour. Biol. Rhythms, 1995—97, mem. editl. bd.: Endocrinology, 1999—2002, Jour. Exptl. Biology and Medicine, 2004—. Mem.: Soc. Study Reproduction, Soc. Neuroscience, Soc. Behavioral Neuroendocrinology (treas. 2004—), Endocrine Soc., AAAS, Am. Neuroendocrine Soc. Office: Dept Psych Neuroscience Prog Mich State U East Lansing MI 48824 Office Phone: 517-355-5253. Office Fax: 517-432-2744. E-mail: sisk@msu.edu.*

**SISK, DANIEL ARTHUR,** lawyer; b. Albuquerque, July 12, 1927; s. Arthur Henry and Myrl (Hope) S.; m. Katharine Banning, Nov. 27, 1954; children: John, Sarah, Thomas. BA, Stanford U., 1950, JD, 1954. Bar: N.Mex. 1955, Calif. 1954. Ptnr. firm Modrall, Sperling, Roehl, Harris & Sisk, Albuquerque, 1954-70, 71—; justice N.Mex. Supreme Ct., Santa Fe, 1970. Chmn. bd. Sunwest Fin. Svcs., Inc., Albuquerque, 1975-90. Pres. Legal Aid Soc., Albuquerque, 1960-61; trustee Sandia Sch., 1968-72, Albuquerque Acad., 1971-73, A.T. & S.F. Meml. Hosps., Topeka, 1966-82; bd. dirs. N.Mex. Sch. Banking Found., 1981-85. Served with USNR, 1945-46, PTO; to capt. USMCR, 1951-52, Korea. Mem. N.Mex. Bar Assn., Albuquerque Bar Assn. (dir. 1962-63), ABA, State Bar Calif. Presbyn. (elder). Office: 500 4th St NW Albuquerque NM 87102-5324

**SISK, EILEEN VICTORIA,** writer, journalist; b. Henderson, Nev., Nov. 8, 1952; d. Hugh Albert and Susan Apathy (Kuyrkendall) S.; m. Richard James Adams, Dec. 28, 1974 (div. Mar. 1979); m. Stephan Rudolph Tetreault, Aug. 29, 1981 (div. Oct. 1993); children: Jeffrey Hugh Tetreault, Douglas Gerard Tetreault; m. Samuel Ragan Mellar, Apr. 14, 1995 (div. June 2001). BA in Comm., Calif. State U., Fullerton, 1979. Feature writing intern L.A. Times, 1977-78; pub. info. asst. Orange County Transit Dist., Garden Grove, Calif., 1978; copy editor Las Vegas Rev. Jour., 1978-79, Sunday editor, 1979-81; copy editor U.S. C. of L., Washington, 1981-83, The Washington Post, 1982-86, design editor, 1987-92; copy editor II The Tennessean, Nashville, 2000—. Freelance journalist various media outlets including XM Satellite Radio, Continuum Ency., Popular Music of the World, Am. Cowboy, Nev., others. Author: Honky-Tonks: Guide to Country Dancin' and Romancin', 1995. Vol. NOW, Washington, 1981, Gloucester County Pub. Schs., 1992-99. Recipient 4 Merit awards Calif. Photographers Pro Show, 1978. Mem.: Investigative Reporters and Editors, Soc. Profl. Journalists (profl. devel. com. 1986—92). Avocations: running, reading, racquetball, cooking, dance. Office: The Tennessean 1100 Broadway Nashville TN 37203 E-mail: esisk@tennessean.com, westgal@earthlink.net.

**SISK, FRED DEAN,** retired cartographer; b. Johnson City, Tenn., May 26, 1940; s. Aubrey Mackenzie and Vinh I Mae (McCaul) S.; m. Martha Lynn Robinson, Aug. 25, 1963. BS, East Tenn. State U., 1962; MS, George Mason U., 1984. Cartographer Def. Mapping Agy., Brookmont, Md., 1965—79, sr. cartographer, sr. instr., master instr. Ft. Belvior, Va., 1979—81, course mgr., 1981—88, dep. divsn. chief, 1983—88, new employees tng. coord. Bethesda, Md., 1988—89; tng. coord. Def. Mapping Agy. Reston Ctr., Va., 1989—90, security analyst, 1990—95; ret., 1995. Mem. scholarship com. George Mason U. Alumni Assn., Fairfax, 1990; mem. Rep. Nat. Com., Rep. Presdl. Task Force, Washington, 1990—, adv. com. House of Dels., 54th Dist., 1995-2002; officer of election City of Fredericksburg, 1995—, mem. pub. transit adv. bd., 1996—, chmn. memls. adv. commn., 2000-03; notary public, 1996—, security officer, 1996—; pres. Fox Run Homeowners Assn., 1996—. 1st lt. battery commdr. U.S. Army, 1962-64. Mem.: NRA, Internat. Freelance Photographers Orgn. (master photographer 2004—), Lifetime Achievement award in Photography, Master Photographer Regnant), Civil War Round Table. Baptist. Home: 18 Devonshire Dr Fredericksburg VA 22401-2100

**SISK, GREGORY CHARLES,** lawyer, educator; b. Des Moines, May 29, 1960; s. James Anderson and Roberta Jean (Thornburg) S.; m. Melinda Fay Gilchrist, June 14, 1981; 1 child, Caitlin Anne. Student, Western Mont. Coll., 1978; BA in Polit. Sci., Mont. State U., 1981; JD, U. Wash., 1984. Bar: Wash. 1985, Iowa 1992, US Ct. Appeals (3d cir. and 9th cir.) 1986, US Ct. Appeals (2d, 5th, 11th and DC cir.) 1987, US Ct. Appeals (4th, 8th and fed. cir.) 1988, US Ct. Appeals (1st cir.) 1989, US Supreme Ct. 1988. Legis. asst. US Senate, Washington, 1984-85; jud. clk. US Ct. Appeals (9th cir.), Seattle, 1985-86; appellate staff atty. civil div. US Dept. Justice, Washington, 1986-89; assoc. Karr, Tuttle & Campbell, Seattle, 1989-91; asst. prof. Drake U., Des Moines, 1991-94, assoc. prof., 1994-97, prof., 1997—2003, Richard M. and Anita Calkins disting. prof., 1999—2003; prof. U. St. Thomas, Mpls., 2003—. Mem. ABA, Am. Law Inst., Fed. Bar Assn., Christian Legal Soc., Order of Coif, Nat. Order of Barristers, Law and Soc. Assn., Am. Polit. Sci. Assn. Republican. Roman Catholic. Office: Univ St Thomas Sch Law 1000 La Salle Ave Minneapolis MN 55403-2005 Office Phone: 651-962-4923. Business E-Mail: gcsisk@stthomas.edu.

**SISK, JANE ELIZABETH,** economist, educator; b. West Reading, Pa., Sept. 23, 1942; 2 children. BA with honors, Brown U., 1963; MA, George Washington U., 1965; PhD, McGill U., Montreal, Que., Can., 1976. Cons. Nat. Planning Assn., Washington, 1976; scholar VA, Washington, 1978-81; rsch. dir. Office Tech. Assessment, U.S. Congress, Washington, 1976-78, sr. analyst, 1981-84, sr. assoc., 1984-91. Vis. prof. Columbia U. Sch. Pub. Health, N.Y.C., 1990-91, prof., 1992—99; prof. Mt. Sinai Sch. Medicine, N.Y.C., 1999—, dir. divsn. health care stats. Nat. Ctr. for Health Stats., Ctrs. for Disease Control, Hyattsville, Md., 2004—. Co-author: Toward Rational Technology in Medicine, 1981; mem. editl. bd. Internat. Jour. Tech. Assessment in Health Care, 1987—, vol. editor, 1990, 98; asst. editor Am. Jour. Pub. Health, 1990-91; mem. editl. bd. Health Svcs. Rsch., 1994—; contbr. articles to profl. jours. Pres. Internat Soc. Tech. Assessment in Health Care, 1991-93, bd. dirs., 1987-95; mem. N.Y. State Task Force on Clin. Guidelines & Med. Tech. Assessment, 1994-96; mem. study sect. on health care quality and effectiveness rsch. U.S. Agy. for Health Care Policy and Rsch., 1997-2001. Elisah Benjamin Andrews scholar Brown U., 1961, 63; Bronfman fellow McGill U., 1971. Fellow Assn. for Health Svcs. Rsch.; mem. Inst. of Medicine, NAS (mem. cancer policy bd. 1997-2000, inst. medicine, 2001—), Phi Beta Kappa. Office Phone: 301-458-4157.

**SISK, THOMAS DANIEL,** ecologist, educator; b. Albuquerque; BA, Colo. Coll., Colorado Springs, 1983; PhD, Stanford U., 1992. Tropical program coord. Ctr. for Conservation Biology, Stanford U., 1992—94; spl. asst. to dir. Nat. Biol. Svc., U.S. Dept. of Interior, Washington, 1994—96; prof. ecology No. Ariz. U., Flagstaff, 1996—. Mem.: Ecol. Soc. Am. (sr.). Office: No Ariz Uni Ctr for Environ Scis Flagstaff AZ 86011-5694 Office Phone: 928-523-7183. Office Fax: 928-523-7423.

**SISKA, JOHN EDWARD,** foundation administrator, publishing executive; b. Gary, Ind., Oct. 15, 1940; s. Andrew and Ann Mary Siska. AA in Mktg., Ivy Tech., Gary, Ind., 1978; student, Edison 5th Coll., Trenton, N.J., 1959—67. Printer/proofreader Post TriBune, Gary, Ind., 1958—67, Chgo. Tribune, Chgo., 1967—73, Chgo. Sun Times, Chgo., 1967—73, Hammond Times, Ind., 1967—73; owner/mgr. Compass Newspaper, Hammond, Ind., 1973—76; sales WNWI Radio, Valparaiso, 1976—77; adv. mgr. CEN Flo Publs., Chgo., 1978—89; owner, CEO, rep., broker John Edward Siska Mfg., 1989—95. Dir. Portage Twp. Food Pantry, Ind., 2003, Gabriel's Shelter, Ind., 2004, North Shore Health Ctrs., Ind., 2004; CEO John Edward Siska Found., Valparaiso, 2004—. Mem.: Porter County Triad, United Nations Assn. of Am., Chgo. Coun. on Foreign Rels., Acad. Polit. Sci., Portage C. of C. Democrat. Presbyn. Avocations: skiing, birdwatching. Office Phone: 219-764-2158.

**SISKA, ROBERT JOHN,** software engineer; b. Evergreen Park, Ill., May 28, 1949; s. Emil Thomas and Marie Clara Siska; m. Jane Suzan Dwyer, May 25, 1979; children: Johanna, Charlotte. BA, U. Mass., 1974. Advt. coord. Goldblatt Bros., Chgo., 1976-79; tech. writer Calif Fed., L.A., 1980-82; software engr. Informatics Gen. Corp., Canoga Park, Calif., 1982-84, Team Quest Corp., Clear Lake, Iowa, 2005; software programmer Great We. Bank, Northridge, Calif., 1984-86; sr. software engr. Litton Computer Svcs., Woodland Hills, Calif., 1986-90; sr. software devel. Legent Corp., Woodland Hills, 1990-94; sr. systems programmer Nat. Computer Sys., Iowa City, 1994-97; sr. software devel. Storage Tek, Louisville, 1997—2003; sys. programmer State of Colo., Lakewood, 2003—05; software engr. TeamQuest Internat., Clear Lake, Iowa, 2005—. Cons. advisor Johnson County, Iowa City, 1996—97; creator, coord. Craven Maven Record Co., pres., 1995—. Cons. advisor Johnson County Computer Com., Iowa City, 1996—97. Mem.: Network and Sys. Profls. Assn., Johnson County Blues Soc., Colo. Blues Soc. Avocations: record company, marathon running, literature, music. Office: TeamQuest Corp One Team Quest Way Clear Lake IA 50428 Home: 412 Main Ave Clear Lake IA 50428 Office Phone: 641-357-2700. Personal E-mail: bobsiska@aol.com. Business E-mail: bob.siska@teamquest.com.

**SISKE, REGINA,** artist; b. Varen Muritz, Germany, Oct. 11, 1944; d. Peter Paul and Olga Vanda Markunas; m. Roger Charles Siske, May 31, 1969; children: Kelly, Jennifer, Kimberly. BSN, U. Ill., 1966; postgrad. in MSN program, U. Mich., 1968—69; ind. fine art studies, North Shore Art League, Winnetka, Ill., 1970s, Alain Gavin, Art Inst. Chgo., 1980s, Tom James, Wilmette, Ill., 2000—; Asian brush painting and calligraphy studies Lampo Leong, U. Mo., 1998—; Asian brush painting and Chinese calligraphy studies Madeleine Jossem and Qi-Gu Jiang, Art Inst., Chgo., 1999—2002; Asian brush painting and Chinese calligraphy studies Moon Yan Huen, City Coll., San Francisco, 1999—2002; Asian brush painting and Chinese calligraphy studies, Charles Liu, Westmont, Ill., 1999—, numerous workshops, N.Y.C. and Chgo. RN Ill., 1966. Staff med.-surg. nurse Presbyn.-St. Luke's Hosp., Chgo., 1966—67, Mass. Gen. Hosp., Boston, 1967—68; nursing staff devel. VA Rsch. Hosp., Chgo., 1969—70, Evanston/Northwestern Hosp., Evanston, Ill., 1971, St. Francis Hosp., Evanston, Ill., 1971—73; nursing cons. Evanston Hosp., 1971; rsch. and quality control studies VA Hosp., Chgo., 1969—70; cmty. outreach and edn. Evanston and St. Francis Hosps., 1971—73. Chair Asian art exhibit and workshop Suburban Fine Arts Ctr., 2004. Exhibitions include Mobile (Ala.) Mus. Art, 1998, Bayard Cutting Arboretum, Long Island, N.Y., 1999, Suburban Fine Arts Ctr., Highland Pk., Ill., 1999—2006 (award, 2001), Alliance Gallery, Indpls. Mus. Art, 2000—01, Strathmore Hall of Arts, Bethesda, Md., 2000 (award, 2000), 2003 (award, 2003), Courthouse Gallery, Norfolk, Va., 2001, Nat. Juried Virtual Exhbn., Internet, 2002, 2004, Chinese Fine Arts Soc., Westmont, Ill., 2001, Virtual Exhbn., Internet, 2002, 2004, Chgo. Bot. Gardens, Art League Alliance, 2004, J. Harrison Smith Fine Art Gallery, Clearwater, Fla., 2005, Represented in permanent collections. Vol. Kellogg Cancer Rsch. Ctr., Evanston Hosp., 1988—89; bd. dir. St. Elizabeth Nursery Sch., Glencoe, Ill., 1981—82, Josselyn Ctr. for Mental Health, Northfield, Ill., 1989—93, devel. chmn., 1992—93. Named hon. life tima mbr. Josselyn Ctr Mental Health, 1992— Mem. Nat. Serigraph Soc. Am., Midwest Serigraph Soc. (program dir. 2000—06). Avocations: piano, jewelry design, skiing, swimming, tennis. Home and Studio: 248 Hawthorn Ave Glencoe IL 60022 Fax: 847-835-2836. E-mail: sisker@aol.com.

**SISKIN, EDWARD JOSEPH,** engineering company executive, construction company executive; b. Bklyn., Apr. 30, 1941; s. Haskell and Sylvia (Steckler) S.; m. Patricia Ann Moore, June 26, 1965 (div. Apr. 1990); children: Candice P. Howard, Cristin Jo Balchunas; m. Jean Elizabeth Bowen, Dec. 17, 1994. BSEE, U. Pa., 1963; cert., Bettis Reactor Engring. Sch., West Mifflin, Pa., 1965; postgrad., George Washington U., 1963—67. Registered profl. engr., Pa., Mass., N.Y., N.J., Ill., Mich., Fla., W.Va., Ind., S.C., Tex., La., Nebr., Calif., Ala. Engr. U.S. Atomic Energy Commn., Washington, 1963-67, field office mgr. Pitts., 1967-70, Groton, Conn., 1970-77; project mgr. Stone & Webster Engring. Corp., Boston, 1977-78, asst. engring. mgr., 1978-79, engring. mgr. N.Y.C., 1979-83, v.p., mgr., 1984-86, sr. v.p., mgr. Cherry Hill, NJ, 1987-88, exec. v.p., 1988-90, dir. Boston, 1985-90; gen. mgr. Superconducting Supercollider Lab., Dallas, 1990-94; pres. Enerjoin Svcs., Inc., 1994—, 2005—; dir. office fissile materials disposition US Nat. Nuc. Security Adminstrn., 2000—05. Mem. adv. com. Inst. of Nuc. Power Ops., Atlanta, 1987-90, adv. bd. Ctr. for Chem. Plant Safety, N.Y.C., 1988-90. Bd. dirs. PenJerDel Coun., Phila., 1987-90. US LSN, 1963-69. Office: PO Box 445 Voorhees NJ 08043 Personal E-mail: jeananded@comcast.net.

**SISKIND, ARTHUR MICHAEL,** lawyer; b. NY, Oct. 11, 1938; s. William and Sylvia (Schuman) S.; m. Mary Ann Silverman, Nov. 10, 1962; children: Laura, Julie, Kenneth. BA in Liberal Arts, Cornell U., 1960, LLB with distinction, 1962. Ptnr. Squadron, Ellenoff, Plesent & Lehrer, NYC, 1970-91; group gen. counsel News Corp., NYC, 1991—2004, exec. v.p., 1991—96, sr. exec. v.p., 1996—2004, sr. advisor to chmn., 2005—, bd. dirs.; sr. exec. v.p., gen. counsel Fox Entertainment Group. Inc., 1998—2004; also bd. dirs. Adj. prof. Georgetown Law Ctr., 2005—06. Dir. Brit. Sky Broadcasting Group, PLC, NDS plc. Active Cornell Law Sch. Adv. Coun., 1996—; nat. chmn. Cornell Law Sch. Alumni Fund, 1998-2001, Citizens Budget Commn. N.Y.C. Capt. U.S. Army, 1963-65. Mem. ABA, City Bar Assn., Cornell Club, Stockbridge Golf Club. Office: News Corp 1211 Avenue Of The Americas New York NY 10036-8795 Office Phone: 212-852-7007. Business E-Mail: asiskind@newscorp.com.

**SISKIND, DONALD HENRY,** lawyer; b. Providence, Dec. 25, 1937; s. Samuel and Sadie (Wasserman) S.; m. Beth Mohel, July 15, 1962; children: Steven M., Edward M. BS, U. Pa., 1959; LLB, Columbia U., 1962. Bar: Mass. 1962, N.Y. 1963. Assoc. Marshall Bratter Greene Allison & Tucker, N.Y.C., 1962-69, ptnr., 1969-82, Katten Muchin Rosenman, 1982—99, of counsel, 1999—. Mem. adv. bd. Chgo. Title Ins. Co.; chmn. various seminars Practicing Law Inst., 1974—; vis. lectr. Columbia U. Sch. Law, 1993-95; mem. adv. bd. Wharton Real Estate Ctr. Contbr. articles to profl. jours. Pres. Greenville Community Coun., 1974-76; pres. bd. edn. Union Free Sch. Dist., Scarsdale, N.Y., 1978-81 Mem.: ABA, Am. Coll. Real Estate Lawyers (past pres.), Anglo Am. Real Property Inst. (past chmn.), N.Y. State Bar Assn., Assn. of Bar of City of N.Y., Phi Alpha Psi. Home: 876 Park Ave New York NY 10021-1832 Office: Katten Muchin Rosenman 575 Madison Ave Fl 26 New York NY 10022-2585 Office Phone: 212-940-8610. E-mail: donald.siskind@kattenlaw.com.

**SISLEY, BECKY LYNN,** physical education educator; b. Seattle, May 10, 1939; d. Leslie James and Blanche (Howe) S.; m. Jerry Newcomb, 1994. BA, U. Wash., 1961; MSPE, U. N.C., Greensboro, 1964, EdD, 1973. Tchr. Lake Washington H.S., Kirkland, Wash., 1961-62; instr. U. Wis., Madison, 1963-65, U. Oreg., Eugene, 1965-68, prof. phys. edn., 1968—2004, women's athletic dir., 1973-79, head undergrad. studies in phys. edn., 1987-92. Co-author: Softball for Girls, 1971; contbr. over 70 articles to profl. jours. Mem. athletic adv. bd. Women's Sports Found., 1993-96. Named to Hall of Fame, U. Oreg. Athletics, 1998, Hall Fame, N.W. Women's Sports Found., Seattle, 1981, Nat. Masters Track and Field Hall of Fame, 2001; recipient Honor award, N.W. Dist. AAHPERD, 1988, Nat. Assn. for Girls and Women in Sports, 1995, Disting. Alumni award, Sch. Health and Human Performance, U. N.C., Greensboro, 1996. Mem. AAHPERD, Oreg. Alliance Health, Phys. Edn., Recreation and Dance (hon. life mem.), Western Soc. for Phys. Edn. of Coll. Women (hon. mem., exec. bd. 1982-85), Oreg. High Sch. Coaches Assn., N.W. Coll. Women's Sports Assn. (pres. 1977-78), Oreg. Women's Sports Leadership Network (dir. 1987-97), Phi Epsilon Kappa, others. Office: U Oreg Phys Activity & Recreation Svcs Eugene OR 97403

**SISLEY, EMILY LUCRETIA,** psychologist, writer; b. North Charleroi, Pa., May 7, 1930; d. Frederick William and Harriet Watkins (Litman) S. PhD in Clin. Psychology, L.I. U., 1972. Diplomate Am. Bd. Med. Psychotherapists. Mng. editor Med. Jours., Harper & Row, N.Y.C., 1960-67; freelance med. writer-editor N.Y.C., 1967-95; supervising psychologist, dept. psychiatry Roosevelt Hosp., N.Y.C., 1972-77; clin. instr. Columbia Univ. Coll. Physicians and Surgeons, N.Y.C., 1975-77; chief psychologist Gramercy Park Inst., N.Y.C., 1978-84; staff therapist MedcoBehavioral Care Sys., N.Y.C., 1984-95; ret., 1995. Cons. Internat. Jour. Group Tensions, N.Y.C., 1968-72. Illustrator: You and Your Brain, 1963, Thomas Alva Edison award, 1963; co-author: The Vitamin C Connection, 1983; contbr. articles to profl. and lit. jours. Fellow Am. Bd. Med. Psychotherapists; mem. APA, N.Y. Acad. Scis. Democrat. Episcopalian. Avocations: music, golf, skiing, sailing.

**SISLEY, NINA MAE,** physician, public health service officer; b. Jacksonville, Fla., Aug. 19, 1924; d. Leonard Percy and Verna (Martin) S.; m. George W. Fischer, May 16, 1962 (dec. 1990). BA, Tex. State Coll. for Women, 1944; MD, U. Tex., Galveston, 1950; MPH, U. Mich., 1963. Intern City of Detroit Receiving Hosp., 1950-51; resident in gen. practice St. Mary's Infirmary, Galveston, Tex., 1951-52; sch. physician Galveston Ind. Sch. Dist., 1953-56; dir. med. svcs. San Antonio Health Dept., 1960-63, acting dir., 1963-64; resident in pub. health Tex. Dept. Pub. Health, San Antonio, 1963-65; dir. cmty. health svcs. Corpus Christi-Nueces County Dept. Health, Tex., 1964-67; dir. Tb control region 5 Tex. Dept. Health, Corpus Christi, 1967-73; chief chronic illness control City of Houston Health Dept., 1973-78; dir. pub. health region 11 Tex. Dept. Health, Rosenberg, 1978-87; dir. Corpus Christi-Nueces County Dept. Pub. Health, 1987—2002. Lectr. Incarnate Word Coll., San Antonio, 1963-64; adj. prof. U. Tex. Sch. Pub. Health, Houston, 1980—2002; adj. prof. Tex. A&M U., Corpus Christi, 1997—2002; pvt. practice Galveston, Stockdale, Hereford and Borger, Tex., 1952-59; mem. adv. bd. Cmty. Adv. Coun.; clin. instr. U. Tex. Health Sci. Ctr., San Antonio, 1997-2002 Bd. dirs. Coastal Bend chpt. ARC, Corpus Christi, 1990-94, 2003—, pres., 1990-91; bd. dirs. United Way-Coastal Bend, Coastal Bend Coalition on AIDS, 1988-94; mem. Nueces County Child Fatality Rev. Com.; mem. adv. com. Nueces County Hosp. Dist.; mem. adv. bd. Alzheimers Assn.; mem. health adv. bd. Corpus Christi Ind. Sch. Dist.; bd. dirs. Charlie's Place Alcohol and Drug Rehab. Ctr. Fellow Am. Coll. Preventive Medicine, Tex. Med. Assn., Nueces County Med. Soc. (pres. 1997-98), Tex. Assn. Pub. Health Physicians, Tex. Pub. Health Assn. (pres. 1991-92), Local Emergency Planning Assn., Long Term Health Assn., Asthma Coalition. Episcopalian. Avocations: fishing, crossword puzzles, raising african violets. Home: 62 Rock Creek Dr Corpus Christi TX 78412-4214 E-mail: nnsisley@sbcglobal.org.

**SISNEY, NED,** education educator; b. Kansas City, Mo., Feb. 9, 1947; s. Dwight E. and Jeann A. Sisney; m. Mary A. Petersen, Sept. 9, 1988; 1 child, Kaitlyn J. Master's, Concordia U., Mequon, Wis., 2003. Cert. tchr. Wis. 2006. Prof. Concordia U., 1988—. Actor(and dir.): ednl. and profl. theatre. Mem.: Pi Kappa Delta (life), Actor's Equity Assn. (life), Phi Delta Kappa (life), Alpha Psi Omega (life; chpt. pres. 1968—69). Home: 7808 W Rolling Field Dr Mequon WI 53097

**SISSEL, GEORGE ALLEN,** manufacturing executive, lawyer, engineer; b. Chgo., July 30, 1936; s. William Worth and Hannah Ruth (Harlan) S.; m. Mary Ruth Runsvold, Oct. 5, 1968; children: Jenifer Ruth, Gregory Allen. BSEE, U. Colo., 1958; JD cum laude, U. Minn., 1966. Bar: Colo. 1966, Ind. 1973, U.S. Supreme Ct. 1981. Assoc. Sherman & Howard, Denver, 1966-70; with Ball Corp., Broomfield, Colo., 1970—2002, CEO, 1993 2001, chmn. bd., 1996—2002, also bd. dirs. Bd. dirs. Ciber, Inc. Assoc. editor: U. Minn. Law Rev., 1965-66. Served with USN, 1954-65. Mem. Colo. Assn. Commerce & Industry, Order of Coif, MIT Soc. Sr. Execs. (bd. govs. 1987-95), Sigma Chi, Sigma Tau, Eta Kappa Nu. Lodges: Rotary. Methodist.

**SISSMAN, LIRON,** artist, painter; d. Arie and Atara Sissman. BSc magna cum laude, The Hebrew U., Jerusalem, 1987; attended, Avni Fine Art Inst., Tel Aviv, 1988, NY Acad. Art, 1999; MBA, NYU, 1991. One-man shows include Taro Pharms., Hawthorne, NY, 2002 (Purchase award, 2002), Sound Fed. Savs., Cos., Cob, Conn., 2004, Patriot Bank, Old Greenwich, Ct., 2004, Waltuch Gallery, Tenafly, NJ, 2004, Block Gallery, Montclair, NJ, 2005, Shimon and Sara Birnbaum Gallery, Bridgewater, NJ, 2005, The Synaptic Art Gallery, Paramus, NJ, 2005, ADP Hdqrs., 2005, Watchung Arts Ctr., NJ, 2005, Johnson & Johnson World Hdqrs. Gallery, New Brunswick, NJ, 2006, The Pk. Ave Club, Florham Pk., NJ, 2006, commd. oil painting, Bar Scene, Sea Scape, Donna, Donna II, Hanna, Steve Finley, 2004, Coupling, 2005, exhibitions include Cmty. Arts Assn., Ridgewood Art Inst., 2002, Westminster Gallery, 2003, Gallery 214, Montclair, NJ, 2005, Am. Artists Profl. League, Salmagundi Club, NYC, 2005, Newington-Cropsey Mus., Hastings-on-Hudson, NY, 2005, Hudson Valley Art Assn., 2005, Synagogue for the Arts, NYC, 2006, Studio Montclair, St. John on the Mountain, Best Little Art Gallery, Mahwah, NJ, 2005, exhibited in group shows at Madison Gallery, NYC, 2000, Limner Gallery, 2000, The Artist Gallery, Ridgewood, 2001, Ridgewood Art Inst., 2002, Salmagundi Club, 2002, 2003, Midday Gallery, Englewood, NJ, 2004, Montclair State U. Art Galleries, 2004, Port of Call Gallery, Warwick, 2004, Audobon Artists, 2004, Geneva Gallery, Morristown, NJ, 2004, Perkins Gallery, Stoughton, Mass., 2005, Galleria Nuova, Warwick, NY, 2005, C. Magor Gallery, Ridgewood, NJ, 2005, Euro Art Gallery, Montclair, NJ, 2006, Represented in permanent collections PeproTech, Inc., NJ, Taro Pharms., NY, Sq. Bus. Products Inc., NJ, Potomac Homes, Lounge Zen, pvt. collections, Can., U.S., U.K., and Israel; contbr. articles to various publs. featuring artist work. Named Best in Show, Mid Rockland Arts Festival, Nanuet Hebrew Ctr., 2004; recipient Cert. of Achievement, 2004, 1st Pl. Oil award, Bergenfield Arts Festival Collection, 2005. Mem.: Studio Montclair (assoc.), Audobon Artists (assoc.), Allied Artists Am. (assoc.), Am. Artists Profl. League (assoc.). Office Phone: 201-952-1666. E-mail: liron@liron.com.

**SISSOM, LEIGHTON ESTEN,** engineering educator, dean, consultant; b. Manchester, Tenn., Aug. 26, 1934; s. Willie Esten and Bertha Sarah (Davis) S.; m. Evelyn Janelle Lee, June 13, 1953; children: Terry Lee, Denny Leighton. BS, Middle Tenn. State Coll., 1956; BS in Mech. Engring., Tenn. Technol. U., 1962; MS in Mech. Engring., Ga. Inst. Tech., 1964, PhD, 1965. Diplomate Nat. Acad. Forensic Engrs.; registered profl. engr., Tenn. Draftsman Westinghouse Electric Corp., Tullahoma, 1953-57; mech. designer ARO, Inc., Tullahoma, 1957-58; instr. mech. engring. Tenn. Technol. U., Cookeville, 1958-62, chmn. dept. mech. engring., 1965-79, dean engring. 1979-88, dean of engring. emeritus, 1988—; prin. cons. Sissom & Assocs., Cookeville, Tenn., 1962—. Bd. dirs. Accreditation Bd. Engring. and Tech., N.Y.C., 1978-86, treas., 1982-86. Author: (with Donald R. Pitts) Elements of Transport Phenomena, 1972, Heat Transfer, 1977, 1,000 Solved Problems in Heat Transfer, 1991; contbr. An Attorney's Guide to Engineering, 1986; contbr. articles to various publs. Fellow ASME (sr. v.p. 1982-86, gov. 1986-88, Golden medallion), Am. Soc. Engring. Edn. (bd. dirs. 1984-87, pres. 1991-92), Accreditation Bd. Engring. and Tech.; mem. NSPE, Soc. Automotive Engrs., Nat. Engring. Deans Coun. (chmn. 1984-87), Order of the Engr. (chmn. bd. govs. 1994-96), Tau Beta Pi (v.p. 1986-89, councillor 1986-89). Home and Office: 1151 Shipley Church Rd Cookeville TN 38501-7730 Office Phone: 931-526-9123. Business E-mail: sissom@frontier.net.

**SISSON, LAURENCE P.,** artist; b. Boston, Apr. 27, 1928; s. Arthur Foster and Gertrude Davis Sisson; m. Judy Haslee Zimmermann, May 17, 1990; m. Beatrice Bachelder Sisson (div.); children: Mark D., Kerry, David B., Derek Phoenix. Student, Yale U., 1948—49; grad., Worcester Mus. Sch., Mass., 1949; DFA, Maine Coll. Art (formerly Portland Sch. Art), 1992. Artist-in-residence Publick House, Sturbridge, Mass., 1950; guest lectr. Portland Sch. Art, Maine, 1954—58; corporator Worcester Art Mus., Mass., 1972. Artist (cover) Fortune Mag., 1951, artist, actor (film) Maine Harvestors of the Sea, 1969; author: (book) Along Time River, 1975; Represented in permanent collections inclusing Boston U., Berkshire Mus. Bowdin Coll., Clark U., Columbia Mus. Fine Art, Baldwin Mus. Fine Arts, DeCordova Mus., Darthmouth Coll., and others. With U.S. Army, 1946—47. Recipient 4th Am. prize, Hallmark Internat. Show, 1949, 1st prize, Boston Arts Festival, 1956, 1964, Boston Watercolor Soc., 1957. Avocations: golf, croquet. Home: 1408 Camino Amparo NW Albuquerque NM 87107 E-mail: LPSisson@comcast.net.

**SISSON, RAY L.,** retired dean, author; b. Pueblo, Colo., Apr. 24, 1934; s. William Franklin and Lillie Mae (Hall) S.; m. Dixie Lee McConnell, Oct. 1, 1952; children: Mark Lynn, Bryan Keith, Tammy Sue Ann. BSEE, U. Colo., 1960; MSEE, Colo. State U., 1966; AA, Pueblo Coll., 1958; EdD, U. No. Colo., 1973. Electronic technician TV Svcs. Co., Pueblo, 1958, Sid's Appliance Ctr., Tucson; from instr. engring. to asst. prof. So. Colo. State Coll., Pueblo, 1960-63, assoc. prof., 1963-76, engring., electronics dept. head, 1968-70; dean Sch. Applied Sci. and Engring. Tech. U. So. Colo., Pueblo, 1973-84, prof., 1976—, interim dean Coll. Engring. and Sci., 1984-85, dean Coll. Applied Sci. and Engring. Tech., 1985-96, dean prof. emeritus, 1996—; curator Pueblo Weisbrod Aircraft Mus. Cons. Escuela Superior Politecnica del Litoral, Ecuador, 1979-82, SUNY, Alfred, Farmingdale, 1982, Moorhead U, 1985, N.Mex. Highlands U., 1985, 90, Kans. State U., Salina, 1994, Ministry Edn., Republic of Yemen, 1996, Min. Edn., State of Kuwait, 1998. Author: Pueblo Army Air Base 1942-46 A Chronological History, 2001. Bd. dirs. Colo. Transp. Inst., 1993-96; exec. dir. So. Colo. Bus. and Tech. Ctr., 1994-96. With USN, 1952-56. Recipient James H. McGraw award Am. Soc. Engring. Edn., 1990; NSF grantee, 1964, 65, 67, 68, 80-83. Mem. IEEE, ABET (tech. accreditation commn. 1990-96, chmn. definition com, 1991, vice chmn. tech. accreditation commn., 1993-96), Am. Soc. Engring. Edn. (active, spectrum com. 1989-90, chmn. definition com. 1991, fellow 1993), Engring. Tech. Leadership Inst. (founding mem., bd. dirs. 1983-88, chmn. 1984-85), Profl. Engrs. Colo. (So. chpt., assoc. mem., chair young engrs. 1969, scholarship, edn. com. 1990, chair state scholarship com. 1968), Pueblo Pachyderm Club (pres. 1986, 89, 98), Pueblo Hist. Aircraft Soc. (historian 1999—), Retirees Assn. (pres. 1998, 99), Phi Delta Kappa, Eta Kappa Nu, Tau Alpha Pi. Home: 403 Starlite Dr Pueblo CO 81005-2685 Office Phone: 719-948-9219. Personal E-mail: sisson@email.com. Business E-mail: Ray.Sisson@colostate-pueblo.edu.

**SISTO, ELENA,** artist, educator; b. Boston, Jan. 11, 1952; d. Fernando Jr. and Grace Sisto; m. John David Kirkpatrick. BA in Art & Art History, Brown U., 1975; grad., N.Y. Studio Sch., 1977; postgrad., Yale U., Norfolk, Conn., 1975, Skowhegan (Maine) Sch., 1976. Gallery artist Vanderwoude Tananbaum, NYC, 1983-89; gallery artist Damon Brandt Gallery, NYC, 1989-91, Germans Van Eck, NYC, 1991-94. Tchr. RI Sch. Design, Providence, 1987—, NY Studio Sch., NYC, 1987—, SUNY-Purchase, 1988, Bard Coll., summer 1990, Columbia U., NYC, Yale U., Chautauqua Inst., Sch. Visual Arts. Exhibited in one-man shows at Vanderwoude Tananbaum Gallery, 1984, 1986, Damon Brandt Gallery, 1990, Germans Van Eck Gallery, 1991, 1992, Gallery 210, U. Mo., 1991, Stephen Wirtz Gallery, 1993, David Beitzel Gallery, 1995, Greenvile County Mus., SC, 1997, Wurtz Gallerie, San Francisco, Littlejohn Contemporary, 1998, 2001, 2002, 2005, Maier Mus., Va, 1999, Bucheon Gallery, San Francisco, 2003; represented in various pub. and pvt. collections. Fellow Skowhegan Sch., 1970, Yale Norfolk, 1975, NEA, 1983, 89-90, Millary Colony, 1987, Fine Arts Work Ctr., Handhollow Found., Provincetown, Mass., 1995. Address: Littlejohn Gallery 41 East 57th St New York NY 10022 E-mail: elena_sisto@yahoo.com.*

**SISTO, FERNANDO,** mechanical engineering educator; b. La Coruña, Spain, Aug. 2, 1924; s. Fernando Cartelle and Clara (Reiss) S.; m. Grace Jeanette Wexler, June 27, 1946; children: Jane Caroll, Ellen Gail, Todd Frederic. Student, NYU, 1940-43; BS, U.S. Naval Acad., 1946; ScD, MIT, 1952; M Engring. (hon.), Stevens Inst. Tech., 1962. Registered profl. engr., N.J. Commd. ensign USN, 1946, service in the Pacific, ret., 1949; propulsion div. chief Curtiss-Wright Research, Clifton, N.J., 1952-58; prof. mech. engring. Stevens Inst. Tech., Hoboken, N.J., 1959-96, chmn. dept., 1966-79, George Meade Bond prof., 1978-96, prof. emeritus, 1996—, dean of the grad. sch., 1993-94. Bd. dirs., trustee Am. Capital Mut. Funds, Houston, 1960—, chmn. bd., 1992-95; co-chmn. merged bd. Van Kampen Am. Capital, 1995-97, dir. emeritus, 2001—; bd. dir. Dynalysis of Princeton; cons. UN Devel. Program at Nat. Aero. Lab., Bangalore, India, 1978. Co-author: (textbook) A Modern Course in Aeroelasticity, 1978, 5th edit., 2004. Lt. USNR, 1943—49. R.C. DuPont fellow MIT, 1951-52. Fellow ASME; mem. Adirondack Mountain Club. Avocations: skiing, tennis, woodworking, sculling. Office: Stevens Inst Dept Mech Engring Hoboken NJ 07030-5991 Personal E-mail: gsandfs@aol.com. E-mail: sisto_fred@yahoo.com.

**SISULU, SHEILA VIOLET MAKATE,** diplomat, international organization official; m. Lungi Sisulu. BA, U. Lesotho; BE, Witwatersrand U. Various sr. positions South African Com. for Higher Edn., 1988. com. coord. African Bursary Fund South African Coun. Chs., 1988-91; dir. Joint Enrichment Project, 1991-94; spl. advisor Min. Edn., 1994-97; consul-gen. South African Consulate-Gen., NY, 1997-99; amb. extraordinary and plenipotentiary to the U.S South African Govt., 1999—2002; deputy exec. dir. U.N. World Food Programme, 2003—. Organizer, coord. several confs., workshops and seminars on youth and edn.; presenter in field. Mem. ANC Nat. Edn. Com., U.S.A./South Africa Leadership Tng. Program, Cmty. Bank Found.; coun. mem. U. Witwatersrand; trustee Equal Opportunity Found., Women's Devel. Found., Women's Devel. Bank, South African Broadcasting Cooperation. Office: via CG Viola 68 Parco Dei Medici 00148 Rome Italy Fax: 202-265-1607. E-mail: wfpinfo@wfp.org.*

**SITA, MICHAEL JOHN,** pharmacy educator; b. Apr. 28, 1953; s. Julianne Gail; m. Nora Ann Dillon, June 1, 1974 (div. 1996); children: Michael John III, Paul Thomas, Julianne Joyce; m. Christine Elizabeth Nordmann, Aug. 22, 1997; children: Mary Elizabeth, April Christine. BS, St. Louis Coll. Pharmacy, 1976; MBA, So. Ill. U., 1983. Registered pharmacist Mo., Ill. Staff pharmacist Luth. Med. Ctr., St. Louis, 1976-78, asst. chief pharmacist, 1978-81, adminstrv. coord. pharmacy svcs., 1981-85; dir. pharmacy svcs. Jefferson Meml. Hosp., 1985-98; pharmacist Mo. Bapt. Hosp., 1998-2000,

Walgreen's, 2000—. Instr. St. Louis Coll. Health Careers, 1983-86; adj. instr. pharmacy practice St. Louis Coll. Pharmacy, 1980-98; relief pharmacist Dolgins Apothecary, St. Louis, 1976-86, Best Pharmacy, 1986-88, Carraige Drugs, 1989-93, Medicine Shoppe, Festus, Mo., 1990-97, Otto (Mo.) Drug, 1997-2000. Author, editor: Pharmacy Capsule quar., 1977-85. Mem. St. Louis Soc. Hosp. Pharmacists (treas. 1985-87, pres. 1988-89, sec. 1990-92, Pharmacist of Yr. 1994-95), Mo. Soc. Hosp. Pharmacists, Hosp. Assn. Met. St. Louis (chmn. pharmacy tech. adv. com. 1985-86). Avocations: carpentry, rehabbing. Home: 111 Ward Ter Crystal City MO 63019-1707 Office: Walgreens 7339 Gravois Saint Louis MO 63116 Office Phone: 314-752-0722.

**SITARSKI, STEPHEN,** historic site administrator; b. Phila. m. Janice Gangursky; children: Jennifer, Lauren. AA, C.C. Phila.; student, Temple U., 1977-80, U. of the Arts, 1980-82. Pk. ranger Independence Nat. Hist. Pk. Nat. Park Svc., Phila., 1978-80; various mgmt. positions Phila., 1980-90; chief ops., 1991-96; mgr. unit sites Independence Nat. Hist. Park, 1996—2004; chief ranger Interpretation and Visitor Svcs. INDE/EDAL/THKO/GLDE, 2004—. Avocations: travel, drawing and painting, listening to jazz. Office: Independence National Historical Pa 143 S 3rd St Philadelphia PA 19106-2818 E-mail: steve_sitarski@nps.gov.

**SITARZ, ANNELIESE LOTTE,** pediatrician, educator, physician; b. Medellin, Colombia, Aug. 31, 1928; came to U.S., 1935; d. Hans and Elisabeth (Noll) S. BA cum laude, Bryn Mawr (Pa.) Coll., 1950; MD, Columbia U., 1954. Diplomate Nat. Bd. Med. Examiners, Am. Bd. Pediatrics., Am. Bd. Pediatric Hematology and Oncology. Intern Children's Med. Ctr., Boston, 1954—55; resident in pediat. Babies Hosp.-Columbia-Presbyn. Med. Ctr., N.Y.C., 1955—57; mem. faculty Columbia U., N.Y.C., 1957—74, assoc. prof. clin. pediat., 1974—83, prof. clin. pediat., 1983—2000, prof. emerita clin. pediat., spl. lectr. in pediat., 2000—; attending in pediat. Babies and Children's Hosp., N.Y.C., 1983—. Cons. pediatrics, hematology and oncology Harlem Hosp., N.Y.C., 1967—72, Overlook Hosp., Summit, NJ, 1975—2001. Contbr. articles to profl. jours. Pres. Mt. Prospect Assn., Summit, 1987—. Fellow Am. Acad. Pediatrics; mem. Am. Assn. Cancer Rsch., Am. Soc. Clin. Oncology, Am. Soc. Hematology, Internat. Soc. Hematology, Harvey Soc. Republican. Episcopalian. Avocations: gardening, sewing, hiking, stamp collecting/philately, photography. Office: Childrens Hosp of NY Presbyn Irving Pavilion 161 Ft Washington Ave New York NY 10032-3710 Office Phone: 212-305-5808. Business E-mail: als4@columbia.edu.

**SITES, KEVIN,** news correspondent, journalist, web blogger; Masters Degree, Medill Sch. Journalism, Northwestern U. Corr. covering wars and disasters for nat. networks (Iraq, Afghanistan, Columbia and Kosovo, Indonesia 2004 Tsunami, Katrina Hurricane, New Orleans), 2000—; freelance solo journalist NBC News in Asia, 2004, NBC and MSNBC News (Northern and Eastern Alliance forces prior to fall and after fall of Taliban); corr. CNN; war news corr., online news svc., Kevin Sites in the Hot Zone Yahoo! News, 2005—. Covered US Anti-Drug effort in Columbia, 2000—01; broadcast lectr. in journalism Dept. Calif. Polytechnic State, San Luis Obispo, 2000—01. Prodr.: NBC News (Edward R. Murrow award for coverage of the war in Kosovo, nominated for nat. Emmy award for contributions to a series on landmines); worked in local, cable, and network news, including (ABC) This Week with David Brinkley & (NBC) Nightly News with Tom Brokaw, published numerous articles in newspapers and magazines, author of monthly media column NY Times alternative weekly. Named Disting. Lectr. 2000-2001 Academic Yr., Calif. Faculty Assn.; recipient Payne award for Ethics, RAVE award (Blogs), WIRED mag., 2005, Daniel Pearl award for Courage and Integrity in Journalism, LA Press Club, 2006. Travels to major hotspots of the world and reports on various armed conflicts occurring to date; while covering initial invasion of Iraq in 2003 for CNN, was captured and briefly held by Saddam Hussein's militia.*

**SITES, RICHARD LOREN,** lawyer, educator; b. Feb. 16, 1948; s. Loren Richard and Frances Mary (Tellaro) Sites; m. Karen Ann Heazlit, Oct. 6, 1979; children: Brian, David. BA, Coll. Wooster, 1970; JD, U. Denver, 1973, MS, 1975. Bar: Colo. 1973, Ohio 1975, U.S. Dist. Ct. 1973, U.S. Supreme Ct. 1977; cert. health care fin. mgmt. Ohio State U., 1984. Sole practice, Columbus, Ohio, 1973—; atty. HHS, Columbus, 1975—85, Ohio Hosp. Assn., Columbus, 1985—. Assoc. grad. faculty, academic adv. Ctrl. Mich. U., 1992—; faculty Franklin U., Ohio, 1999—2001, Wittenberg U., Ohio, 2002—; exec. dir. OHA Purchasing Solutions, 2004—; trustee Ohio for EDI, Inc., 2002—. Contbr. articles to profl. jours. Co-founder FAMOHIO, Inc., 1992, pres. 1996—98; v.p. LEGAL, 2002—; leader Boy Scouts Am., 1992—2002; alumni admissions rep. Coll. Wooster, Ohio, 1979—85, fund raiser, 1984; v.p. Sycamore Hills Residents Assn., Columbus, 1983, pres., 1984; chair hemophilia adv. coun. Ohio Dept. of Health, 1995—2000. Recipient Spl. Contbn. award, Ohio Soc. for Hosp. Engring., 1988, 1993, Ira Gaffin Meml. award, Famohio, Inc., 1999, Rosie Hass Adv. award, N.W. Ohio Hemophilia Found., 2002. Mem.: Ohio Dept. Health, Newborn Genetic Screening Adv. Coun. Office: Ohio Hosp Assn 155 E Broad St Fl 15 Columbus OH 43215-3609 Office Phone: 614-221-7614.

**SITILIDES, JOHN,** government relations executive; b. Jersey City, Feb. 8, 1962; s. Louis and Frances Sitilides; m. Angela Beth Johnson, Oct. 11, 1997. BA, Queens Coll., 1983; M of Internat. Affairs, Columbia U., 1986. Comm. and legis. affairs U.S. Senator Alfonse M. D'Amato, N.Y.C., 1986—93; pres. The Sitilides Group, Sacramento, 1993—97; exec. dir. Western Policy Ctr., Washington, 1998—2004; pres. JS Assoc., Alexandria, Va., 1998—2004, Trilogy Advisors, Washington, 2005—. Mem. joint sci. and tech. coop. coun. U.S. Commerce Dept/; bd. dirs. BioVest Internat., Inc.; bd. trustees Leadership 100. Policy advisor Dole/Kemp '96, Sacramento, 1996. Mem. World Affairs Coun. Washington, Ahepa (chmn. Cyprus and Hellenic affairs com. 1994—), Wilson Coun., Federalist Soc. Law and Pub. Policy, Nat. Spkrs. Assn., Columbia U. Club Republican. Greek Orthodox. Avocations: reading history current events, baseball. Home: 8121 Dunsinane Ct Mc Lean VA 22102-2719 Office Phone: 202-558-5122.

**SITKEI, GYÖRGY,** engineer, educator; b. Oroskáza, Hungary, Feb. 13, 1931; s. Lajos Sitkei and Erzsébet Szabó; m. Emilia Bereczky, Aug. 18, 1959 (dec. 1993); 1 child, Zsuzsanna. MS, Tech. U., Budapest, Hungary, 1954, PhD, 1960; D Engring. Sci., Hungarian Acad. Scis., Budapest, 1964; D (hon.), U. Gödöllo, 1999, U. Sopron, 2000. Doctorant U. Agr., Moscow, 1954-57; rschr. Tech. U., Budapest, 1957-75; head dept. Agrl. Machinery Trust, Budaörs, Hungary, 1975-80; prof. head U. Sopron, Hungary, 1980-97, prof. emeritus, 1997—. Mem. State Sci. Accreditation Com., Budapest, 1993—. Author: Mixture Formation and Combustion in Diesel Engines, 1964, Heat Transfer and Thermal Loading in IC Engines, 1974, Soil Mechanics Problems of Agricultural Machines, 1976, Mechanics of Agricultural Materials, 1986 (Acad. award 1988). Recipient Szent-Györgyi Albert award Ministry of Edn., 1993, Pattantyus A. Géza award Sci. Soc. Mech. Engring. Budapest, 1994. Mem. N.Y. Acad. Scis., Hungarian Acad. Scis. (mem. com. for agrl. mechanization 1975—, com. for thermal engines 1978—), Internat. Soc. for Terrain Vehicle Sys. Avocation: ornamental trees and shrubs. Home: Székher ut 19 H-1021 Budapest Hungary Office: U Sopron Ady E u 5 H-9401 Sopron Hungary E-mail: dwoodma@fmk.nyme.hu.

**SITNYAKOVSKY, ROMAN EMMANUIL,** scientist, writer, inventor, translator; b. Kiev, Ukraine, Jan. 5, 1934; arrived in U.S., 1988; s. Emmanuil I. and Yevgeniya N. (Glazova) S.; m. Bella Baram, Oct. 4, 1968 (div. Mar. 1992); 1 child, Art. MS in Mech. and Heat Engring., Polytech. Inst., Kiev, Ukraine, 1956; PhD in Heat Theory/Engring., USSR Acad. Scis., Minsk, Belarus, 1967. Project engr. Ural Turbomotor, Sverdlovsk, USSR, 1956-58; mech. engr. Engring Factory, Kiev, Ukraine, 1958-61; project engr. Design Inst., Kiev, Ukraine, 1961-63; sr. engr. Heat and Mass Transfer Inst., Minsk, Belarus, 1963-68; prin. engr. Thermophysics Inst., Kiev, Ukraine, 1968-87; project engr. Hirt Combustion Engring., Montebello, Calif., 1989-90. Cons. Socio-Econ. Sys., LA, 1988-93; translator, Kiev, 1979-87, LA, 1988—; journalist Panorama, LA, 1989-98. Author: I Disagree with Guberman, 1995, Chernobyl is our Fate, 2000, 06, Mollify, not harass hearts, 2003, 06, What is

Love?, 2006, Democrats, Communists, Nationalists, Fascists, 2003, 2006, Fundamentals, 2006, To the Point, 2006; contbr. articles to profl. jours., newspapers and mags. Achievements include over 100 inventions; patentee in field; discoveries of discreteness property of internal heat-mass transfer processes in three-phase media; wave nature of moisture transfer into wet bodies; resonances at heat-mass transfer in three-phase media. Office Phone: 323-654-7111.

**SITOMER, SHEILA MARIE,** television producer, television director; b. Hartford, Conn., Aug. 25, 1951; d. George W. and Mary E. (Chaponis) Bowe; m. Daniel J. Sitomer, Aug. 25, 1985. BA, Smith Coll., 1973. Field producer, dir. Good Morning Am., ABC-TV, N.Y.C., 1981-86; field producer Evening Magazine, WWOR-TV, KDKA-TV, Pitts. and Secaucus, NJ, 1978-79, 88; supervising producer The Reporters, Fox Broadcasting, N.Y.C., 1988; producer Inside Edition, King World Prodns., N.Y.C., 1988-95; co-exec. prodr. Inside Edition and Am. Jour., 1995-98; exec. prodr. Extra, 1998-2000; exec. prodr. program devel. ABC News, N.Y.C., 2000—. Recipient Peabody award, Columbia Dupont award, AWRT Gracie award, 3 Emmys, New England chpt. TV Acad. Arts & Scis., 1975-78, 2 Emmys, N.Y. chpt. TV Acad. Arts & Scis., 1979, 89, recipient first prize Internat. Film & TV Festival N.Y., 1988, No. N.J. Press Club award, 1988, George Polk award, Sigma Delta Chi award, IRE award Nat. Headliners, Columbus Film Festival. Mem. Dirs. Guild Am., Actors Equity Assn. Office: ABC News 47 W 66th St New York NY 10023 E-mail: sheila.sitomer@abc.com.

**SITTON, CLAUDE FOX,** newspaper editor; b. Atlanta, Dec. 4, 1925; s. Claude B. and Pauline (Fox) S.; m. Eva McLaurin Whetstone, June 5, 1953; children: Lea Sitton Stanley, Clinton, Suzanna Sitton Greene, McLaurin. AB, Emory U., 1949. L.H.D., 1984. Reporter Internat. News Service, 1949-50; with U.P., 1950-55, writer-editor N.Y.C., 1952-55; information officer USIA, 1955-57; mem. staff N.Y. Times, 1957-68, nat. news dir., 1964-68; editorial dir. The News and Observer Pub. Co., Raleigh, NC, 1968-90, dir., 1969-90, v.p., 1970-90; editor News and Observer, 1970-90; sr. lectr. Emory U., Atlanta, 1991-94. Active Pulitzer Prize Bd., 1985-94, chmn., 1992-93; bd. counselors Oxford Coll. Emory U., 1993-2001. Lay mem. Commn. on Evaluation of Disciplinary Enforcement, Ga. Supreme Ct., 1995-96; mem. Ga. First Amendment Found. Bd., 1994-97. With USNR, 1943-46, PTO. Recipient Pulitzer prize for commentary, 1983. Home: PO Box 1326 Oxford GA 30054-1326

**SIVAKUMARAN, KUMARASWAMY,** civil engineer, consultant, lawyer; b. Inuvil, Sri Lanka, May 29, 1952; arrived in U.S., 1986; s. Thambipillai and Theivanayaki (Selliah) K.; m. Muthumanimoli Pakkirisamy, June 24, 1982; children: Karthikgeyan, Sabriyan. BS in Civil Engring., U. Sri Lanka, Moratuwa, 1976; MS in Civil Engring., U. Newcastle-upon-Tyne, Eng., 1985; PhD in Civil Engring., Colo. State U., 1989; JD, W.Va. U., 2001. Bar: W.Va. 2002. Irrigation engr. Irrigation Dept., Colombo, Sri Lanka, 1977-80; design engr. Group Engring. Consulting, Colombo, 1981; sr. project engr. Samek Constrn. Co. Ltd., Abia, Nigeria, 1981-84; rsch. asst. Colo. State U., Ft. Collins, 1986-89; guest scientist GKSS Rsch. Ctr., Geesthacht, Germany, 1990-91; assoc., sr. water resources engr. TAMS Consultants, Inc., N.Y.C., 1991—2002; pres. Sterling Legal Svcs. PLLC, 2002—. Adj. asst. prof. W.Va. U., Morgantown, 1998—; pres. Sterling Legal Svcs., PLLC. Travel grantee, Am. Pub. Works Assn., 1986. Mem.: ATLA, ABA, ASCE, U.S. Com. on Large Dams. Home: 154 Edgewood Dr Weston WV 26452-8540 Office: Goff Bldg 321 W Main St Ste 509 Clarksburg WV 26301 Office Phone: 304-622-5770. Personal E-mail: ksivakumaran@earthlink.net. Business E-Mail: ksivakumaran@sterling-legal.com.

**SIVANANTHAN, SIVALINGAM,** science educator; PhD. Dir., microphysics lab. U. Ill., 1994—. Pres. EPIR Technologies Inc., Boolingbrook, Ill., 2003. Author over 160 publications. Mem.: Adv. Bd. for Ill. Coll. of Tech., Nat. Adv. Bd. for Micro fabrication Applications Lab., Editl. Bd. of Jour. of Infrared and Millimeter Waves, Proceeding US workshop on the physics and chemistry of II-VI materials, SPIE (assoc.). Achievements include first to use mercury cadmium telluride (MCT) semiconductor materials in some devices. Office: Dept Physics- UIC 845 W Taylor Str (M/C 273) Room 2236 Chicago IL 60607

**SIVCO, DEBORAH LEE,** materials scientist, researcher; b. Somerville, NJ, Dec. 21, 1957; d. Lawrence M. Skurkay and Elizabeth J. McCulla; m. Gregory Charles Sivco, July 11, 1981; children: Scott Gregory, Michelle Elizabeth, Carolyn Suzanne, David Charles. BA in chem. edn., Rutgers U., 1980; MS in material sci., Stevens Inst., 1988. III-V processing tech. Laser Diode Labs, New Brunswick, NJ, 1980-81; materials scientist Bell Labs. Lucent Technologies, Murray Hill, NJ, 1981—. Contbr. articles to profl. jours. Recipient Newcomb Cleveland prize AAAS, 1993-94, Electronics Letters premium Instn. Elec. Engrs. U.K., 1995, Group Achievement award NASA, 2000. Achievements include 30 patents in field. Office: Bell Labs Lucent Technologies 600 Mountain Ave New Providence NJ 07974-2008 Office Phone: 908-582-2041. Business E-Mail: dls@lucent.com.

**SIVE, REBECCA ANNE,** public relations executive; b. Jan. 29, 1950; d. David and Mary (Robinson) S.; m. Clark Steven Tomashefsky. BA, Carleton Coll., 1972; MA in Am. History, U. Ill., Chgo., 1975. Asst. to chmn. of pres. task force on vocations Carleton Coll., Northfield, Minn., 1972; rsch. assist. Jane Addams Hull House, Chgo., 1974; instr. Loop Coll., Chgo., 1975, Columbia Coll., Chgo., 1975-76; dir. Ill. Women's History Project, 1975-76; founder, exec. dir. Midwest Women's Ctr., Chgo., 1977-81; exec. dir. Playboy Found., 1981-84; v.p. pub. affairs/pub. rels. Playboy Video Corp., 1985—85; v.p. pub. affairs Playboy Enterprises, Inc., Chgo., 1985-86; pres. The Sive Group, Inc., Chgo., 1986—. Instr. Roosevelt U., Chgo., 1977-78; dir. spl. projects Inst. on Pluralism and Group Identity, Am. Jewish Com.; trainer Midwest Acad. Contbr. articles to profl. jours. Commr. Chgo. Park Dist., 1986-88; del.-at-large Nat. Women's conf., 1977; mem. Ill. Human Rights Commn., 1980-87, Ill. coordinating com., Internat Womens Yr.; coord. Ill. Bicentennial Photog. Exhbn., 1977; mem. Ill. Employment and Tng. Coun.; bd dirs. Nat. Abortion Rights Action League and NARAL Found., Ill. div. ACLU, Midwest Women's Ctr. Recipient award for outstanding cmty. leadership YWCA Met. Chgo., 1979, award for outstanding cmty. leadership Chgo. Jaycees, 1988. Office: The Sive Group Inc 1235 N Astor St Chicago IL 60610-5213

**SIVELL, JOHN NORMAN,** language educator; b. Toronto, Ont., Can., June 14, 1946; s. Arthur Leslie and Josephine Ruth (Burgess) S.; m. Chirawibha Pongrueng; children: Vincent, Florent, Wasintara, Chonsawat. BA in English with honors, U. Toronto, 1969; diploma in English, Cambridge (Eng.) U., 1970; PhD in English, U. East Anglia, Norwich, Eng., 1974; MEd, U. Wales, Cardiff, 1983. Asst. prof., head English dept. Jundi Shapur U., Ahwaz, Iran, 1974-78; asst. prof. U. Riyadh, Abha, Saudi Arabia, 1978-79; mai de confs. Faculty of Letters, Rabat, Morocco, 1980-82; vis. lectr. Inst. Am. Univs., Aix-en-Provence, France, 1982-83; instr. English as a 2d lang. Brock U., St. Catharines, Ont., Canada, 1983-86, asst. prof. applied lang. studies, 1986-88, chair dept. applied linguistics, 1988—92, 2001—04, assoc. prof. applied lang. studies, 1988-91, prof. applied linguistics, 1991—, interim dean faculty of humanities, 1994-95, dean faculty of humanities, 1995—2000, founding dir. ctr. internat. studies, 1996—2000, 2001—. Co-editor: Cooperative Learning and Social Change, 1990, Of Special Interest, 1990, Reading Into the Future, 1991; editor: Freinet Pedagogy, 1994; translator: The Wisdom of Matthew, 1990, Education Through Work, 1993; co-author French Elementary Education and the Ecole Moderne, 2000; contbr. articles to profl. publs.; series editor Full Blast Prodns., 1991—; mem. editorial bd. Lang. Teaching Strategies, 1991-94; author numerous pedagogical texts for ESL. Mem. adv. bd. alphabase project Alpha Ont., Toronto, 1992-96. Can. Coun. fellow, 1970-73. Mem. Internat. Assn. Tchrs. of English for Speakers of Other Langs., Ont. Tchrs. ESL (bd. dirs. 1991—, conf. chmn. 1989, 90), Internat. Reading Assn., Comparative and Internat. Edn. Soc., Am. Ednl. Rsch. Assn., Can. Assn. Second Lang. Tchrs. Avocations: gardening, angling, writing. Office: Brock U Saint Catharines ON Canada L2S 3A1 Business E-Mail: jsivell@brocku.ca.

**SIVERTSEN, LINDA JOYCE,** writer, editor, publishing consultant; b. Stanford, Calif., Aug. 31, 1964; d. Alfred Eugene and Joanne Rose Tisch; m. Mark Duanne Sivertsen, Sept. 10, 1988; 1 child, Tosh. Student, U. So. Calif., 1984—87. Life coach, L.A., 1987—89; owner pet sitting bus. Beverly Hills, 1989—94; cons. writing, nat. and internat. 1995—; author Health Comms., Deerfield Beach, Fla., 1998—; West Coast editor Balance Mag., Ft. Lauderdale, Fla., 2002—. Book proposal writer Illiani Co., L.A., 1999—; ghostwriter, co-author Jodere Pub. Group, San Diego, 2001, San Diego, 03, individuals, 2001—; spkr. in field; tchr. Learning Annex, L.A., 2001—03. Author: Lives Charmed: Intimate Conversations with Extraordinary People, 1998 (Earth Island Jour. award, 2000); co-author: Will to Survive: A Mental and Emotional Survival Guide for Law Enforcement Professionals, 2003; contbr. columns in newspapers. Mem.: Nat. Assn. Women Bus. Owners, Delta Gamma (life). Avocations: tennis, gardening, hiking, painting, reading. Office: ILLIANI Co PO Box 41 1893 Los Angeles CA 90041

**SIVILL, JASON RYAN,** music educator; b. Kankakee, Ill., Sept. 22, 1975; s. Joel Franklin and Julie Ray Sivill. BA, We. Ill. U., 1999; MusM, Bowling Green State U., Ohio, 2004. Grad. tchg. asst. Coll. of Musical Arts Bowling Green (Ohio) State U., 2002—04; dir. bands Talawanda H.S., Oxford, Ohio, 2004—. Designer marching band drill Bowling Green (Ohio) State U. Falcon Marching Band, 2003—. Mem.: Music Educators Nat. Conf. Republican. Methodist. Personal E-mail: sivijys@aol.com.

**SIVINSKI, TINA M.,** human resources specialist; Grad. magna cum laude, Springfield Coll. Various positions including v.p. Data Gen. Corp., 1980—99; corp. v.p. mktg. and innovation Sci. Applications Internat. Corp., 2000; v.p. strategic mktg., sales and bus. devel. GrandBasin, 2000—01; pres. energy glow industry solutions group Elec. Data Systems, Plano, Tex., 2001—02, sr. v.p., 2002—03, exec. v.p. human resources, 2003—. Bd. dirs. Tranxition. Office: Elec Data Systems 5400 Legacy Dr Plano TX 75024-3199 Office Phone: 972-604-6000. Office Fax: 972-605-2643.

**SIZEMORE, JOE R.,** music educator, musician; b. Howard, Jr Sizemore and Lois Price; m. Julie P. Sizemore, Apr. 6, 1996; children: Susan G., Catherine P. BS, Old Dominion U., 1976. Cert. music educator NC, 2001. Dir. bands West Craven H.S., Vanceboro, NC, 1976—84; dir. edn. Med. Rev. NC, Raleigh, 1984—85; dir. bands Washington H.S., 1985—2000, East Carteret H.S., Beaufort, 2002—03, Northside H.S., Pinetown, 2003—. Composer: Three Musicians; dir.: NC All Start Jazz Ensemble. Comdr. USCG Aux., Washington, 1993—94. With U.S. Army, 1970—72. Mem.: NC Music Educators (licentiate; dist. pres. 1998—2001, Cert. 1998—2001), Music Educator's Nat. Conf. (licentiate). Achievements include Featured Artist at the Jamaica Jazz Festival 2001, 03, 05, 06; Peformed with Percy Sledge at the 2004 CAMY Awards and Legends Concert. Avocation: sailing. Office Phone: 252-943-6341. Personal E-mail: overboardproductions@myway.com, sizemore_joe@yahoo.com. Business E-mail: nhsbandmaster@yahoo.com.

**SIZEMORE, MICHAEL MAYNARD,** architectural firm executive; b. Detroit, July 20, 1943; s. Arthur Logan and Evelyn (Willer) S.; m. Christine Wick, June 1, 1968; children: Christine Corsaut, James Gawne. BArch, Ga. Inst. Tech., 1966; MArch in Urban Design, Carnegie-Mellon U., 1968. Registered arch. Owner Sizemore & Assocs., Atlanta, 1974-76; v.p. CRS, Sizemore/CRS, Houston and Atlanta, 1976-78; sr. prin. Sizemore Floyd (now Sizemore Group), Atlanta, 1973—. Mem. bd. advisors dist. coun. Urban Land Inst.; trustee The Ga. Conservancy. Author: Energy Planning in Buildings, 1979; prin. works include redesign of hqrs. AIA, Washington, Emory U. Clinic, Hale Ctr. Theatre, Salt Lake City, Atlanta C. of C., master plan of Centennial Olympics, Atlanta, 1996, master plan, feasibility Centennial Olympic Park, hqrs. Atlanta Com. Olympic Games, Smyrna Town Ctr. Design and Devel. (Nat. award Urban Land Inst. 1997). Fellow AIA; mem. Atlanta C of C. (bd. advisors). Office: 1700 Commerce Dr NW Atlanta GA 30318-3123 Office Phone: 404-605-0690.

**SIZEMORE, NICKY LEE,** computer scientist; b. NYC, Feb. 13, 1946; s. Ralph Lee and Edith Ann (Wangler) S.; m. Frauke Julika Hoffmann, Oct. 31, 1974; 1 child, Jennifer Lee Sizemore; 1 stepchild, Mark Anthony Miracle. BS in Computer Sci., SUNY, 1989. Sgt. first class U.S. Army, 1964-68, 70-86; computer operator UNIVAC, Washington, 1968-69, programmer, 1969-70; programmer/analyst Ultra Systems, Inc., Sierra Vista, Ariz., 1986-87; computer scientist Comarco, Inc., Sierra Vista, 1987-92, ARC, Profl. Svcs. Group, Sierra Vista, 1992-93, Computer Scis. Corp., Ft. Huachuca, Ariz., 1994; sr. cons. Inference Corp., 1995; subject matter expert Northrop Corp., Sierra Vista, Ariz., 1995—; sr. info. sys. engr. Harris Corp., Sierra Vista, Ariz., 1996—2001; systems analyst EWA Svcs., Inc., Ft. Huachuca, 2002—. Speaker numerous confs., seminars, symposia; tech. columnist Sierra vista Herald. Mem.: IEEE, Internat. Coun. Sys. Engring., IEEE Computer Soc., Assn. Computing Machinery, Am. Assn. Artificial Intelligence (validation and test of knowledge-based sys. 1988, co-dir. workshop on verification). Avocations: chess, jogging, tai chi. Home: 880 E Charles Dr Sierra Vista AZ 85635-1611 Office Phone: 520-538-2527. Personal E-mail: sizemore@fhu.disa.mil.

**SIZEMORE, RICHARD TOM, III,** government agency administrator; s. Richard Tom, Jr. and Laura Jane Sizemore; children: Eric Christopher, Amy Kathleen, Monica Justine. BS, U.S. Naval Acad., Annapolis, Md., 1972; MD, W.Va. U., Morgantown, 1977. Dep. comdr. Nat. Naval Med. Ctr., Bethesda, Md., 2000—02; dir. ops. & preparedness Dept. Veterans Affairs, Washington, 2003—05; dep. dir. ops. & security programs U.S. HHS, Washington, 2005—. Capt. USN, 1968—2002. Decorated Legon of Merit (4), Def. Meritorious Svc. medal. Fellow: Am. Bd. Ophthalmology (diplomate); mem.: Am Acad Ophthalmology, Am Coll Physician Exces Associations, photography, travel. Home: 14200 Clayton Rd Rockville MD 20853 Office: HHS 200 Independence Ave SW Washington DC 20201 Office Phone: 202-205-1002. Personal E-mail: r.tom.sizemore@1972.usna.com. Business E-mail: tom.sizemore@hhs.gov.

**SIZEMORE, WILLIAM HOWARD, JR.,** journalist; b. South Boston, Va., Dec. 18, 1948; s. W. Howard and Genevieve T. (Walton) S.; m. Mary K. Lamont, Jan. 29, 1972; children: Justin, Jennifer, Julie. BA in Philosophy, Coll. William and Mary, 1971. Editor The Clarksville (Va.) Times, 1972-75; reporter The Roanoke (Va.) Times, 1975-76, The Times-Herald, Newport News, Va., 1976-81; editor, pub. The York Town Crier, Yorktown, Va., 1981-88; copy editor The Ledger-Star, Norfolk, Va., 1982-89, news editor, 1989-95; writer, editor The Virginian-Pilot, Norfolk, Va., 1995—. Recipient various Journalism awards Va. Press Assn., 1972-2006. Avocations: tennis, music, bicycling, camping. Home: 4704 Yarrow St Williamsburg VA 23188-2427 Office: Virginian-Pilot 150 W Brambleton Ave Norfolk VA 23510-2075 Office Phone: 757-446-2276. E-mail: bill.sizemore@pilotonline.com.

**SIZER, PHILLIP SPELMAN,** gas industry executive, retired oil industry executive; b. Whittier, Calif., Apr. 11, 1926; s. Frank Milton and Helen Louise (Saylor) S.; m. Evelyn Sue Jones, Aug. 16, 1952; children: Phillip Spelman Jr., Ves Warner. BSME, So. Meth. U., 1948. Registered profl. engr., Tex. With Otis Engring. Corp., Dallas, 1948-91, project engr., 1958-62, chief devel. engr., 1962-70, v.p. R & D, 1970-73, v.p. engring. and rsch., 1973-76, sr. v.p., tech. dir., 1977-91, bd. dirs., 1978-91; pres. Sizer Engring. Inc., 1992—; prin. Crawford-Sizer Devel. Co., 1996—. Cons. in field; mem. exec. com. Offshore Tech. Conf., 1976-79. Patentee in field Mem. vis. com. dept. mech. engring. U. Tex., 1977-83. Named to Hall of Achievement Coll. Engring., U. Tex., Arlington, 1983 Fellow ASME (chmn. exec. com. petroleum divsn. 1974-75, SPPE-1 chmn. main com. 1981-88, Engr. of Yr. award North Tex. sect. 1971, centennial medal 1980, OILDROP award petroleum divsn. 1982, Dedicated Svc. award 1985, Silver Patent award 1990, region x Clifford H. Shumaker award 1993); mem. Soc. Petroleum Engrs., S.W. Rsch. Inst. (trustee 1982—), Assn. Wellhead Eq. Mfrs. (pres. 1976), Petroleum Engrs. Club of Dallas, Rotary Internat., Kappa Sigma, Tau Beta Pi, Kappa Mu Epsilon. Home: 14127 Tanglewood Dr Dallas TX 75234-3851 Office Phone: 972-247-6087. Personal E-mail: sizer26@comcast.net.

**SIZER, THEODORE R.,** education educator; b. New Haven, June 23, 1932; m. Nancy Faust; 4 children. BA in English Lit., Yale U., 1953; MAT in Social Studies, Harvard U., 1957, Phd in Edn. and Am. History, 1961; PedD (hon.), Lawrence U., 1969; LittD (hon.), Union Coll., 1972; LLD (hon.), Conn. Coll., 1984; LHD (hon.), Williams Coll., 1984; MA ad eundem, Brown U., 1985; LHD (hon.), U Mass., Lowell, 1985, Dartmouth Coll., 1985, Lafayette Coll., 1991, Webster U., 1992, Ind. U., 1993, Mt. Holyoke Coll., 1993, U. Maine, 1993, Iona Coll., 1995, L.I. U., 1996, Bridgewater State Coll., 1996. English and math. tchr. Roxbury Latin Sch., Boston, 1955-56; history and geography tchr. Melbourne (Australia) Grammar Sch., 1958; asst. prof. edn., dir. MA in tchrs. program Harvard U., Cambridge, Mass., 1961-64, dean grad. sch. edn., 1964-72; headmaster, instr. in history Phillips Acad., Andover, Mass., 1972-81; chmn. A Study of High Schs., 1981-84; prof. edn. Brown U., Providence, 1984-96, chmn. edn. dept., 1984-89, Walter H. Annenberg prof. edn., 1993-94, dir. Annenberg Inst. Sch. Reform, 1994-96, univ. prof. emeritus, 1997—. Chmn. Coalition of Essential Schs., 1984—97, chmn. emeritus, 1997—; vis. prof. U. Bristol, England, 1971, Brown U., Providence, 1983; vis. prof. edn. Brandeis U., 2001—. Author: Secondary Schools at the Turn of the Century, 1964, The Age of the Academies, 1964, Religion and Public Education, 1967; author: (with Nancy F. Sizer) Moral Education: Five Lectures, 1970; author: Places for Learning, Places for Joy: Speculations on American School Reform, 1972, Horace's Compromise: The Dilemma of the American High School, 1984, rev. edit., 2004, Horace's School: Redesigning the American High School, 1992, Horace's Hope: What Works for the American High School, 1996; author: (with Nancy Faust Sizer) The Students Are Watching: Schools and the Moral Contract, 1999; author: (with Deborah Meier & Nancy F. Sizer) Keeping School: Letters to Families from Principals of Two Small Schools, 2004; author: The Red Pencil: Convictions from Experience in Education, 2004. Capt. U.S. Army, 1953-55. Named Guggenheim fellow, 1971; recipient citations Am. Fedn. Tchrs., Nat. Assn. Secondary Sch. Prins., Phillips Exeter Acad., Boston C. of C., Andover C. of C., Lehigh U. Edn. Alumni, 1991, Nat. Assn. Coll. Admissions Counsellors, 1991, Anthony Wayne award Wayne State U., 1981, Gold medal for excellence in undergrad. teaching CASE, 1988, Tchrs. Coll. medal Tchrs. Coll., Columbia U., 1991, Harold W. McGraw prize in edn., 1991, James Bryant Conant award Edn. Commn. States, 1992, Disting. Svc. award Coun. Chief State Sch. Officers, 1992, Coun. Am. Private Edn., 1993, Nat. award of Distinction U. Pa., 1993, Alumni award Harvard Grad. Sch. Edn., 1994. Fellow Am. Acad. Arts and Scis., Am. Philos. Soc.; mem. Nat. Acad. Edn. Office: FW Parker Charter Essential Sch Tchrs Ctr 49 Antietam St Devens MA 01432

**SJOBLOM, THOMAS V.,** lawyer; BA summa cum laude, U. Minn., 1974; JD, William Mitchell Coll. Law, 1978; LLM, Georgetown U., 1982. Bar: Minn. 1978, DC 1978, Pa. 2000, N.Y. 2003. Branch chief Div. Market Regulation, Securities and Exchange Commn. (SEC), 1980—82, spl. counsel, 1982—87, asst. chief litig. counsel, 1987—94; spl. asst. U.S. atty. Ctrl. Dist., Calif., 1990—92, We. Dist., NY, 1991—92, Ea. Dist., Pa., 1996—98; litig. ptnr., chair securities practice group Dilworth Paxson LLP, Phila., 1999—2002; ptnr. Chadbourne & Parker LLP, N.Y., NY, 2002—. Mem.: ABA (mem. litig. sect. & bus. law sect.), Am. Conf. Inst. (co-chair "The Corporate Counsel's Guide to Internal Investigations" 2003), Phi Beta Kappa. Office: Chadbourne & Parke LLP 1200 New Hampshire Ave NW Washington DC 20036 also: 30 Rockefeller Plaza New York NY 10112 Office Phone: 202-974-5636. E-mail: tsjoblom@chadbourne.com.

**SJOERDSMA, ALBERT,** research and development company executive; b. Lansing, Ill., Aug. 31, 1924; s. Sam and Agnes S.; m. Fern E. MacAllister, Dec. 2, 1950; children: Leslie, Ann, Albert, Britt. Ph.B., U. Chgo., 1944, BS, 1945, PhD, 1948, MD, 1949. Research asst. U. Chgo., 1947-49, NIH postdoctoral research fellow, 1950; intern U. Mich. Hosp., Ann Arbor, 1949-50; resident physician Michael Reese Hosp., Chgo., 1951; resident in internal medicine USPHS Hosp., Balt., 1951-53; sr. investigator, chief exptl. therapeutics br. Nat. Heart and Lung Inst., Bethesda, Md., 1953-71; v.p. Merrell Internat. Co., Strasbourg, France, 1971-78; v.p. pharm. research and devel. Richardson-Merrell Inc., 1978-81; v.p. pharm. research Merrell Dow Pharms., Cin., 1981-83; pres. Merrell Dow Research Inst., Cin., 1983-89, pres. emeritus, 1989-94; med. scis. cons., 1994—. Vis. spl. fellow Gen. Hosp., Malmo, Sweden, 1959-60; spl. lectr. George Washington U., 1959-71; Anton Julius Carlson lectr. U. Chgo., 1984; hon. chmn. 2d World Conf. on Clin. Pharmacology and Therapeutics, Washington, 1983; clin. prof. medicine U. Cin. Med. Ctr., 1986-91. Mem. AAAS (Theobold Smith award med. scis. 1958), Am. Soc. Pharm. and Exptl. Therapeutics (Harry Gold award in clin. pharmacology 1977, Exptl. Therapeutics award 1990), Am. Soc. Clin. Pharmacology and Therapeutics (Oscar B. Hunter Meml. award in therapeutics 1981), Internat. Soc. Hypertension, Coun. High Blood Pressure Rsch., Am. Heart Assn., Am. Fedn. Clin. Rsch., Am. Soc. Clin. Investigation, Am. Soc. Exptl. Biology and Medicine, Assn. Am. Physicians, Am. Coll. Neuropsychopharmacology. Home and Office: 263 N Dogwood Trail Kitty Hawk NC 27949-3138 Office Phone: 252-261-6761.

**SJOSTRAND, FRITIOF STIG,** biologist, educator; b. Stockholm, Nov. 5, 1912; s. Nils Johan and Dagmar (Hansen) S.; m. Marta Bruhn-Fahraeus, Mar. 24, 1941 (dec. June 1954); 1 child, Rutger; m. Ebba Gyllenkrok, Mar. 28, 1955; 1 child, Johan; m. Birgitta Petterson, Jan. 23, 1969; 1 child, Peter. MD, Karolinska Institutet, Stockholm, 1941, PhD, 1945; PhD (hon.), U. Siena, 1974, North-East Hill U., Shillon, India, 1989. Asst. prof. anatomy Karolinska Institutet, 1945-48, assoc. prof., 1949-59, prof. histology, 1960-61; research assoc. MIT, 1947-48; vis. prof. UCLA, 1959, prof. zoology, 1960-82, prof. emeritus molecular biology, 1982—. Author: Über die Eigenfluoreszenz Tierischer Gewebe Mit Besonderer Berücksichtigung der Säugetierniere, 1944, Electron Microscopy of Cells and Tissues, Vol. I, 1967, Deducing Function from Structure, Vols. I and II, 1990; also numerous articles. Decorated North Star Orden Sweden; recipient Jubilee award Swedish Med Soc., 1959, Anders Retzius gold medal, 1967; Paul Ehrlich-Ludwig Darmstaedter prize, 1971 Fellow Royal Micros. Soc. (hon., London), Am. Acad. Arts and Scis.; mem. Electron Microscopy Soc. Am. (hon., Disting. Scientist award 1992), Japan Electron Microscopy Soc. (hon.), Scandinavian Electron Microscopy Soc. (hon.). Achievements include development technique for high resolution electron microscopy of cells, fluorescence microspectrography; inventor ultramicrotome. E-mail: fsjostra@ucla.edu.

**SJOSTROM, JOAN SEVIER,** retired travel company executive; b. Denver, Nov. 10, 1931; d. George Field and Martha Watson (Turnbull) Sevier; m. Rex William Sjostrom, Mar. 16, 1952; children: Sandra, Anne, John, Sharon. Student, Colo. State U., 1949—51. Bookkeeper U.S. Nat. Bank, Denver, 1951—52, First Nat. Bank, Ft. Collins, Colo., 1952, Larimer County Credit Assn., Ft. Collins, 1953—55, Fox Drug, Castle Rock, Colo., 1974—86; owner, mgr. Travel Haus Inc., Castle Rock, 1987—98; ret., 1998. Vol. Swedish Emergency Ctr., 1976-82, Douglas County Schs. Spl. Edn. Program, 1980-84; mem. Interfaith Task Force Bd., 1987-88, 2001—; mem. Douglas County Bd. dirs., 1978-88; mem. Douglas County Placement Alternative Commn., Castle Rock, 1984-96; mem. D.C. Schs. Sr. Program, Castle Rock, 1992-1995; vol. naturalist Castlewood Canyon State Park, 1997-2000; vol. local history dept., Douglas County Pub. Libr., 2001—. Mem. Castle Rock Rotary (v.p. 1992—, pres. 1993-94, dist. scholarship 1991—). Republican. Lutheran. Avocations: reading, gardening, golf, travel, bowling. Home: 2072 W Wolfensberger Rd Castle Rock CO 80109-9635

**SKABA, MARK PAUL,** music educator; b. Providence, Oct. 12, 1979; s. Paul S. and Mary T. Skaba. MusB magna cum laude, Ithaca Coll., N.Y., 2001. Cert. tchr. N.Y. Music tchr. Nanuet Pub. Schs., Nanuet, NY, 2002—. Pvt. music instr., Rockland County, NY, 2002—. Mem.: Music Educators Nat. Conf., Pi Kappa Lambda, Phi Kappa Phi. Personal E-mail: mskaba1@yahoo.com.

**SKAFF, ANITA L.,** secondary school educator; d. Ferris and Pauline Skaff. BS in Edn., Bowling Green State U., Ohio, 1977, MA in Theatre Arts, 1992. Lic. theatre, speech and English edn. Ohio. Tchr. Rosemont Jr. H.S., Norfolk, Va., 1977—80; Maury H.S. Norfolk, 1980—85, Scott H.S., Toledo, 1985—91, Rogers H.S., Toledo, 1991—. Dir. Toledo Summer Stock Theatre.

Sponsor Red Cross Blood Mobile, Toledo, 1991—. Named Tchr. of Yr., Rogers H.S., 2001. Mem.: Ednl. Theatre Assn. (internat. thespian troupe 1991—), Alpha Delta Pi Alumni. Home: 3509 Cedardale Ct Toledo OH 43623

**SKAFF, JOSEPH JOHN,** state agency administrator, retired military officer; b. Charleston, W.Va., June 13, 1930; s. Michael Joseph and Zahia S.; m. Maree A. Fleming, Aug. 4, 1957; children: Joseph M., Lynn M. Johnson, Gregory M., Nancy E. Kochman. BS, U.S. Mil. Acad., 1955; MS, George Wash. U., 1968. Commd. 2d. lt. U.S. Army, 1955, commd. 1/27 FA bn. Vietnam, 1968-69; mem. staff and faculty U.S. Mil. Acad., 1972-76; advance through grades to maj. gen.; dep. dir. internat. negotiations U.S. Army Joint Chiefs of Staff, Washington, 1979-81; also dep. commr. U.S. Del. Standing Consultative Commn., Geneva, 1979-81; dep. dir. ops. readiness and moblzn. hdqrs. U.S. Army, Washington, 1981-83, dep. comdr./chief staff Japan, 1982-84; dep. comdg. gen. 1st U.S. Army, Fort Devens, Mass., 1985-89; comdg. gen. U.S. Army, Fort Devens, Mass., 1989-95; cabinet sec. mil. affairs and pub. safety W.va., 1989-97. Bd. dirs. Christian Internet Svc. Decorated DSM U.S. Army, Def. Superior Svc. medal, Legion of Merit, Bronze Star, Air medal, others; recipient Disting. W. Va. award. Mem. Assn. Grads. US Mil. Acad., Assn. US Army, Adj. Gens. Assn. US, N.G. Assn. U.S., Fellowship Christian Athletes (regional bd.), Union Mission Ministries (mem. bd.). Eastern Orthodox. E-mail: jjskaff55@aol.com.

**SKAGGS, BEBE REBECCA PATTEN,** college dean, clergywoman; b. Berkeley, Calif., Jan. 30, 1950; d. Carl Thomas and Bebe (Harrison) P. BS in Bible, Patten Coll., 1969; BA in Philosophy, Holy Names Coll., 1970; MA in Bibl. Studies New Testament, Wheaton Coll., 1972, PhD in Bibl. Studies New Testament, Drew U., 1976; MA in Philosophy, Dominican Sch. Philosophy & Theology, 1990; postgrad., U. Calif., Berkeley, 1991-92. Ordained to ministry Christian Evang. Ch., 1963. Co-pastor Christian Cathedral, Christian Evang. Chs. Am., Inc., 1964—; assoc. prof. Patten Coll., Oakland, Calif., 1975-82, dean, 1977—, prof. N.T., 1982—. Presenter in field. Author: Before the Times, 1980, The World of the Early Church, 1990; contbg. author: Internat. Standard Bibl. Ency., rev. edit., 1983, Women's Study Bible, Pneuma Faculty Dialogue. Active Wheaton Coll. Symphony 1971-72, Drew U. Ensemble, 1971-75, Young Artists Symphony, N.J., 1972-75, Somerset Hill Symphony, N.J., 1973-74, Peninsula Symphony, 1977, 80-81, Madison Chamber Trio, N.J., 1973-75. Named one of Outstanding Young Women of Am., 1976, 77, 80-81, 82; St. Olaf's Coll. fellow, 1990. Mem. AAUP, Am. Acad. Religion, Soc. Bibl. Lit., Internat. Biographical Assn., Christian Evang. Chs. of Am., Inc. (bd. dirs. 1964—), Inst. for Bibl. Rsch., Soc. for Pentecostal Studies (pres. 1998-99), Phi Delta Kappa.

**SKAGGS, DAVID L.,** orthopedist, educator; BA in Neurosci. and Psychology, Amherst Coll., Mass., 1985; MD, Columbia U. Coll. of Physicians and Surgeons, N.Y.C., 1989; Masters of Med. Mgmt., Marshal Sch. Bus., U. So. Calif., 2005—06. Diplomate Am. Bd. of Orthop. Surgery, 1998. Intern Columbia-Presbyterian Med. Ctr., NY, 1989—90, resident, 1990—94; Frank E. Stinchfield orthop. rsch. fellowship Columbia U., NY, 1991—92; pediatric orthop. fellowship U. So. Calif., Children's Hosp., LA, 1994—95; asst. prof., divsn. orthop. surgery U. Ala. Sch. Medicine, 1995—96; asst. prof. orthop. surgery U. of So. Calif.-Keck Sch. of Medicine, 1996—2002, assoc. prof. of orthop. surgery, 2002—; assoc. dir. Children's Orthop. Ctr., Children's Hosp. LA, endowed chair, pediatric spinal disorders. Cons. Stryker Spine, Allendale, NJ; instr. Am. Acad. of Orthop. Surgeons, Rosemont, Ill.; cons. Medtronics Sofamor Danek, Memphis; instr., rschr. Stryker Spine, Westchester, Pa. Author: (textbook) Staying Out of Trouble in Pediatric Orthopaedics; contbr. articles to profl. jours.; featured on Miracle Workers (ABC), 2006. Recipient Young Investigator Award, Pediatric Orthopaedic Soc. of N.Am., 2000, Sandoz award, Columbia U. of Coll. of Physicians and Surgeons, 1989; fellow Am., Brit., Can. Traveling Fellow, Am. Orthop. Assn., 2003, Traveling fellow, Pediatric Orthop. Soc. of N.Am., 2002. Mem.: Am. Acad. of Pediat., Sect. of Orthopedics (exec. com.), Am. Acad. of Orthop. Surgeons, Pediatric Orthop.Soc. of N.Am. (bd. of directors, Young Investigators Award, Traveling Fellos 2000, 2002), Scoliosis Rsch. Soc. (program com.), LA Tennis Club, Salt Air Club. Achievements include design of Pediatric spinal instrumentation. Avocations: meditation, tennis, weightlifting, boogie boarding, yoga. Office: Childrens Hospital Los Angeles 4650 Sunset Blvd #69 Los Angeles CA 90027 Office Phone: 323-669-4658. Office Fax: 323-666-4409.

**SKAGGS, MERRILL MAGUIRE,** humanities educator; b. Florala, Ala., Oct. 1, 1937; d. John Henry and Clyde Louise (Merrill) M.; m. Calvin Lee Skaggs, Aug. 19, 1960 (div. Feb. 1994); children: Sylvia Merrill, John Adam. BA, Stetson U., DeLand, Fla., 1958, LLD, 1988; MA, Duke U., 1960, PhD, 1965. Tutor Duke U., 1961-62; lectr. Bklyn. Coll., 1965; assoc. editor The MacMillan Co., NYC, 1966-67; adj. asst. prof. English Drew U., Madison, NJ, 1975-76, adj. assoc. prof., 1976-79, assoc. prof., 1979-85, prof., 1985-86, dean-elect, 1985-86, dean Grad. Sch., 1986-92, Baldwin prof. of humanities, 1992—. Author: The Folk of Southern Fiction, 1972 (Edd Winfield Parks award), After the World Broke in Two: The Later Novels of Willa Cather, 1990; co-author: The Mother Person, 1975; editor: Willa Cather's New York: New Essays on Cather in the City, 2000. Bd. dirs. Willa Cather Pioneer Meml., Red Cloud, Nebr., 1991—, NJ Com. for the Humanities, New Brunswick, 1990-95; clk. Summit Monthly Meeting, 2003-05. Recipient Book of Yr. award, Am. Jour. Nursing, Presdl. award, Drew U., 2006, Lifetime Scholarly Achievement award, 2006. Mem. Soc. for Values in Higher Edn. (bd. dirs. 1988-94), Soc. for Study of So. Lit. (bd. dirs. 1982, 83-85, 87-89). Democrat. Mem. Soc. of Friends. Avocation: tennis. Home: 9 Woodcliff Dr Madison NJ 07940-2006 Office Phone: 973-408-3491. Business E-mail: mskaggs@drew.edu.

**SKAGGS, ROBERT G., JR.,** utilities executive, lawyer; BA, Davidson Coll.; JD, W. Va. Univ.; MBA, Tulane Univ. With Columbia Energy Group, 1981—2000, law dept., 1981—96, pres., Columbia Gas Ohio & Ky., 1996—2000; pres. Bay State Gas, No. Utilities, other Columbia cos. NiSource Inc., 2000—03, exec. v.p., 2003—04, pres., 2004—, CEO, 2005—. Bd. dir. Southeastern Gas Assn.; mem. Midwest Energy Assn.; mem. leadership council Am. Gas Assn. Mem.: ABA, Energy Bar Assn., W. Va. Bar Assn. Office: NiSource Inc 801 E 86th Ave Merrillville IN 46410*

**SKAGGS, RONALD LEE,** controller, history professor, religious studies educator; b. Le Mars, Iowa, Dec. 25, 1952; s. Le Roy and Opal Ruth Skaggs; m. Penny Lee Bycroft, Aug. 15, 1973; 1 child, Tyler Lee. B in Sacred Lit., Ozark Christian Coll., Joplin, Mo., 1979; MA with honors, Pittsburg State U., Kans., 1983. Cert. secondary edn. social studies Mo., 1983. Owner/mgr. Baskin-Robbins 31 Flavors, Joplin, 1973—98; secondary social studies tchr. Coll. Heights Christian Sch., Joplin, 1983—88; adj. instr. history and bibl. studies Ozark Christian Coll., Joplin, 1984—; contr. and head IT dept. Crossroads Transp., Carthage, Mo., 1993—. Pres. O.R.S. Inc., Joplin, 1994—98. Small group discipleship leader Coll. Heights Christian Ch., Joplin, 1987—2006. Named Salutatorian, Ozark Christian Coll., 1979. Conservative. Avocations: tennis, racquetball, chess. Office: Crossroads Transportation 18667 Cedar Rd Carthage MO 64836 Office Phone: 417-782-7146. Business E-mail: mpfincorp@hughes.net.

**SKAGGS, SANFORD MERLE,** lawyer; b. Berkeley, Calif., Oct. 24, 1939; s. Sherman G. and Barbara Jewell (Stinson) Skaggs; m. Sharon Ann Barnes, Sept. 3, 1976; children: Stephen, Paula Ferry, Barbara Gallagher, Darren Peterson. BA, U. Calif., Berkeley, 1961; JD, U. Calif., 1964. Bar: Calif. 1965. Atty. Pacific Gas and Electric Co., San Francisco, 1964-73; gen. counsel Pacific Gas Transmission Co., San Francisco, 1973-75; ptnr. Van Voorhis & Skaggs, Walnut Creek, Calif., 1975-85, McCutchen, Doyle, Brown & Enersen, San Francisco and Walnut Creek, 1985—2002, Bingham McCutchen LLP, 2002—, mng. ptnr.-Walnut Creek office. Dir. John Muir Mt. Diablo Health Sys., 1997—2005. Mem. Calif. Law Revision Commn., 1990—2001, chmn., 1993. Councilman City of Walnut Creek, 1972-78, mayor 1974-75, 76-77; bd. dirs. East Bay Mcpl. Utility Dist., 1978-90, pres., 1982-90; dir. Episcopal Homes Found., 2005-. Mem.: Contra Costa County Bar Assn., Calif. State Bar Assn., Phi Delta Phi, Alpha Delta Phi, Lambda

Alpha. Republican. Office: Bingham McCutchen LLP 1333 N California Blvd Ste 210 Walnut Creek CA 94596-4585 Office Phone: 925-975-5310. Office Fax: 925-975-5390. Business E-Mail: s.skaggs@bingham.com.

**SKAGGS, WAYNE GERARD,** retired diversified financial services company executive; b. Bonneterre, Mo., Dec. 12, 1929; s. Jasper Pinkney and Lattie May (Duren) S.; m. Hana Kaneko, June 1, 1952; children: Robert Kenneth, Melody Jane, Joy Elizabeth. Student, Mo. Inst. Acctg. and Law, 1947-48, U. Mo., Columbia, 1954-55. With Advantage Capital Corp. (formerly Am. Capital Corp.), Houston, 1955-96, ret., 1996; pres., COO Mktg. Group of Cos., Houston, 1976-80, corp. v.p., cons., 1972-90. Served with USAF, 1950-54, Korea. Mem. Nat. Assn. Securities Dealers (nat. vice-chmn. 1977, dist. chmn. 1972), Nat. Bus. Conduct (gov., chmn. 1976), Investment Co. Inst., Am. Legion (life), VFW (life), Optimists (life, pres. 1966). Home: PO Box 726 Wimberley TX 78676-0726 Personal E-mail: hanawayn@anvilcom.com.

**SKAHILL, NATHAN B.,** historian, educator; m. Cory Clark, June 18, 1999; 1 child, Thomas. BA, St. Ambrose U., Davenport, Iowa, 1998; MA, We. Ill. U., Macomb, 2006. Tchr. history Alleman H.S., Rock Island, Ill., 1999—. Office: Alleman High School 1103 40th St Rock Island IL 61201-3199

**SKAINE, JAMES C.,** retired communications educator; b. Monongahela, Pa., Jan. 3, 1936; s. James Skaine, Jr. and Ruth Stamper Skaine; m. Rosemarie Keller, June 4, 1957; children: James Keller, Forrest Todd. BA, Sioux Falls Coll., SD, 1957; MA, U. SD, Vermillion, 1958; Doctoral study, Cornell U., Ithaca, NY, 1958—66, U. Iowa, Iowa City, 1968—78. Lic. to preach Ctrl. Pk. Bapt. Ch., Buffalo, NY, 1954. Grad. asst. U. SD, 1957—58, Cornell U., 1958—60; tchr. George Jr. Republic, Freeville, NY, 1960; prof., comm. Ithaca Coll., Ithaca, NY, 1960—63; asst. prof., comm. Mid. Tenn. State Coll., Murfreesboro, 1963—65, U. No. Iowa, Cedar Falls, 1965—99. Faculty advisor, UNI chpt., Iowa pub. interest rsch. group U. No. Iowa, Cedar Falls, 1976—78, presenter, ofcl. guest, exch. program with China at universities: Beijing Normal, Hebei tchrs., Shaanxi, & Guangxi tchrs., 1991, founders days presdl. com., 1988—90, coll. of humanities & fine arts senator, 1982—83, sec., United Faculty, 1978—79, academic freedom & profl. rights chair, United Faculty, 1980—86, treas., United Faculty, 1986—89, pres., United Faculty, 1989—94; exec. sec. NY State Debate Assn., Ithaca, 1962—63; mem. Speech Comm. Assn., Des Moines, 1965—72, Iowa Comm. Assn., Des Moines, 1972—85; cons., pub. speaking and voice improvement, Cedar Falls - Waterloo, Iowa. Co-author: (book) A Man of the Twentieth Century: Recollections of Warren V. Keller, A Nebraskan; contbr. chapters to books, articles to profl. pubs. Pres. Friends of the Accused, Waterloo, Iowa, 1974—76; parliamentarian Iowa LWV, Des Moines, 1979—81; host in our home Zhu Qizhen, the amb. extraordinary & plenipotentiary of the People's Republic of China to the USA and his wife, Wang Yuqe Iowa US Senator Charles Grassley's Iowa Internat. Trade Symposium III, Cedar Falls, Iowa, 1990; candidate US Congress, Iowa, Dem. Primary Election, Third District, Iowa, 1972—74; min. Presbyn. Ch., Rockvale, Tenn., 1964—65, Bapt. Ch., Enfield, NY, 1960—62, Bapt. Churches, Turkey Valley and Viborg, SD, 1957—58. Mem.: NEA, Iowa State Edn. Assn., Pi Kappa Delta (life). Democrat. Baptist. Avocations: travel, gardening. Home: 2215 Clay St Cedar Falls IA 50613 Office: Author's Castle Publisher 2215 Clay St Cedar Falls IA 50613 Office Phone: 319-266-8163. Home Fax: 319-266-1406; Office Fax: 319-266-1406. Business E-Mail: jskaine@cfu.net.

**SKAINE, ROSEMARIE KELLER,** writer, consultant, publisher; d. Warren V Keller and Marie W Kuehner Keller; m. James Cole Skaine, June 4, 1957; children: James Keller, Forrest Todd. *In his memoirs, "A Man of the Twentieth Century: Recollections of Warren V. Keller," Mrs. Skaine's father recounts life building bridges in Nebraska, South Dakota, and Wyoming. In 1923, his crew constructed their largest, the Green River Bridge on the Lincoln Highway in Wyoming. He describes his trip from Wyoming to Nebraska after leaving the crew: "Highway 30 was not much more than a wagon trail. At times, on the way between Rawlins and Laramie, the road would disappear into sagebrush and, at times, you had to follow the railroad tracks by driving in the ditch to reach your destination." Some of the bridges he built are still standing, though the roads they served have taken different routes.* BA, U. S.D., Vermillion, 1958; MA, U. No. Iowa, Cedar Falls, 1977. Cert. secondary edn. tchr. NY, 1959, SD, 1958. English tchr. Ovid Ctrl. Sch., NY, 1958—60; adminstrv. and legislative asst. Pres. Kennedy's Consumer Adv. Coun. Chairperson, Ithaca, NY, 1963; adj. instr., sociology Wartburg Coll., Waverly, Iowa, 1979—80; adj. instr., composition Hawkeye C.C., Waterloo, Iowa, 1998—98. Cons., institutes on sexual harassment Adult Edn. Bd. YWCA, Waterloo, Iowa, 1992; cons., sexual harassment KCET Pub. TV, Los Angeles, Calif., 1991—94; ct. testimony, sexual harassment Dist. Ct., Waterloo, Iowa, 1989—99; US del. XII Internat. Congress on Family Law, Havana, Cuba, 2002; speaking tour, women of Afghanistan under the Taliban SD Ctr. for the Book's three day program, Maintaining Democracy in an Unstable World, Aberdeen, Brookings, Mitchell and Sioux Falls, SD, 2002; presenter, Am. family, Guilin, Shijiazhuang, Xian, China U. No. Iowa, Cedar Falls, 1993. Co-author (with Warren V. Keller and James C. Skaine): (book) A Man of the Twentieth Century: Recollections of Warren V. Keller, A Nebraskan, 1999; author: Women at War: Gender Issues of Americans in Combat, 1999, Power and Gender: Issues in Sexual Dominance and Harassment, 1996 (Gustavus Myers Ctr. award for the study of human rights in N.Am. for the outstanding work on intolerance in N.Am., 1997), Sexual Harassment: Questions and Answers, 2d revised edit., 1990, (nonfiction book) Female Genital Mutilation: Legal, Cultural and Medical Issues, 2005, (short stories) Lessons in Love and Life, (book) The Cuban Family: Custom and Change in an Era of Hardship, 2004, Questions and Answers about Sexual Harassment, 1980, Paternity and American Law, 2003, The Women of Afghanistan Under the Taliban, 2002, Women College Basketball Coaches, 2001, Female Suicide Bombers, 2006; contbr. articles to profl. jours. Panel mem., women in Afghanistan Cable TV Here and There, Cedar Falls, Iowa, 2001; voters svc. chair, pres. LWV of Waterloo-Cedar Falls, Cedar Falls, Iowa, 1964—69; nat. steering com., hon. mem. Gore 2000 Presdl. Campaign, 2000, Clinton-Gore Presdl. Campaign, 1996; campaign mgr. James Skaine for U.S. Congress, Cedar Falls, Iowa, 1972—74. Recipient award, Women's Studies Undergraduate and Grad. Programs, U. of No. Iowa, Cedar Falls, 1998, So. Poverty Law Ctr., Montgomery, Ala., 2003—. Mem.: Alpha Kappa Delta, Pi Kappa Delta (life). Office: Author's Castle Publishing PO Box 1044 Cedar Falls IA 50613 Office Phone: 319-266-8163. Home Fax: 319-266-1406; Office Fax: 319-266-1406. Personal E-mail: rskaine@cfu.net.

**SKAINS, THOMAS E.,** gas industry executive; BBA, Sam Houston State Univ.; JD, Univ. Houston. Sr. atty. Trans-Continental Gas Pipeline Corp., 1981—86, v.p., 1986—89, sr. v.p. transp. & customer svc., 1989—95; sr. v.p. mktg. & supply svc. Piedmont Natural Gas, Charlotte, NC, 1995—2002, pres., COO, 2002—03, chmn., pres., CEO, 2003—. Bd. dir., mem. exec. com. Am. Gas Assn.; chmn. So. Gas Assn.; regional bd. adv. Wachovia Bank. Bd. dir., mem. exec. com. Charlotte C. of C.; bd. mem. United Way Ctrl. Carolinas; chmn. bd. trustees Providence Day Sch. Mem.: State Bar Tex. Office: Piedmont Natural Gas 4720 Piedmont Row Dr Charlotte NC 28210 Mailing: Piedmont Natural Gas PO Box 33068 Charlotte NC 28233*

**SKAISTIS, RACHEL G.,** lawyer; b. Phila., June 7, 1970; BA, Yale Coll., 1992; JD cum laude, Cornell U., 1997. Bar: NY 1998, US Dist. Ct., So and Ea. Dists. NY 2000. Reporter Fort Worth Star-Telegram, Tex.; assoc. Cravath, Swaine & Moore LLP, NYC, 1997—99, 2000—05, ptnr., litig., 2005—; law clk., Hon. Shira Ann Scheindlin US Dist. Ct., So. Dist. NY, 1999. Mng. editor Cornell Law Rev. Mem.: NY State Bar Assn. Office: Cravath Swaine & Moore LLP Worldwide Plz 825 Eighth Ave New York NY 10019-7475 Office Phone: 212-474-1934. Office Fax: 212-474-3700. Business E-Mail: rskaistis@cravath.com.

**SKALA, GARY DENNIS,** management consultant; b. Bay Shore, N.Y, Oct. 15, 1946; s. Harry A. and Emily Skala. BS in Mgmt. Engring., Rensselaer Polytech. Inst., 1969; MA in Psychology, Hofstra U., 1972; postgrad., Chgo. Theol. Sem., 1996—. Engr. L.I. Lighting Co., Hicksville, NY, 1969-71, labor

rels. coord., 1971-73; mgmt. cons. Gilbert/Commonwealth, N.Y.C., 1973-74; sr. mgmt. cons. Booz, Allen & Hamilton, San Francisco, 1974-78; mgr. utility cons. A.T. Kearney, Chgo., 1978-81; mng. cons. Cresap, div. Towers Perrin, Chgo., 1981-85; pres. Gary D. Skala & Assocs. Mgmt. Cons., Chgo., 1985—. Lectr. utility bus. issues Edison Electric Inst., Utility Exec. Mgmt. Com., Internat. Maintenance Conf., Assn. Rural Electric Coops., Inst. Indsl. Engrs.; subcontracting cons. Arthur D. Little, Inc., Liberty Cons. Group, Ernst & Young, Cresap, A. T. Kearney, Towers Perrin, Michael Paris Assocs. Ltd., Planmetrics. Contbr. articles to profl. jours. Trustee Samaritan Inst. for Religious Studies, 1995—97, chair instnl. advancement com., 1995; bd. dirs. Bailiwick Repertory Theater, 1999—2005, pres., 2001—02, chair mktg./pub. rels. com.; bd. dirs. Good Shepherd Parish Met. Cmty. Ch. of Chgo., 1995—99, vice moderator, 1996—97; mem. bd. Ordained Ministry of Gt. Lakes Dist. of Universal Fellowship Met. Cmty. Chs., 1996—99; vol. The Night Ministry of Chgo. Mem.: Am. Inst. Indsl. Engrs. (chmn. Midwest chpt. utility divsn. 1980—81), Inst. Indsl. Engrs. (sr.; mem. utility divsn. 1978— charter). Office Phone: 773-935-1362.

**SKALAGARD, HANS MARTIN,** artist; b. Skuko, Faroe Islands, Feb. 7, 1924; came to U.S., 1942, naturalized, 1955. s. Ole Johannes and Hanna Elisa (Fredriksen) S.; m. Mignon Diana Haack Haegland, Mar. 31, 1955; 1 child, Karen Solveig Sikes. Pupil, Anton Otto Fisher, 1947. Joined U.S. Mcht. Marine, 1942, advanced through grades to chief mate, 1945; ret., 1965; owner, operator Skalagard Sq. Rigger Art Gallery, Carmel, Calif., 1966—; libr. Mayo Hays O'Donnel Libr., Monterey, Calif., 1971-73; painter U.S. Naval Heritage series, 1973—. Lectr., bd. dirs. Allen Knight Maritime Mus., 1973—, mem. adv. and acquisitions coms., 1973-77; spkr. in field. One-man shows include Palace Legion of Honor, San Francisco, 1960, J.F. Howland, 1963-65, Fairmont Hotel, San Francisco, 1963, Galerie de Tours, 1969, 72-73, Pebble Beach (Calif.) Gallery, 1963, Laguna Beach (Calif.) Gallery, 1969, Arden Gallery, Atlanta, 1970, Gilbert Gallery, San Francisco, Maritime Mus. of Monterey, 1993, 97, Rigger Art Gallery, Carmel, Stanton Ctr., Monterey, 1993, Monterey Maritime Mus., 1993, 1997, St. Francis Yacht Club, San Francisco, 1995, Ventura County Maritime Mus., Oxnard, Calif., 1998; exhibited in group shows at Am. Artists, Eugene, Oreg., Robert Louis Stevenson Exhibit, Carmel Valley Gallery, Biarritz and Paris, David Findley Galleries, N.Y.C. and Faroe Island, Maritime Mus., Calif., 1993, 94, 95, Pacific Coast Lumber Schooners, 1994,. San Francisco Art Expo, 2000, Herrschoff Marine Mus., Bristol, R.I., 2002, Cavalier Galleries, Inc., Nantucket, Mass., 2003, Cavalier Galleries, Inc., Greenwich, Conn., 2003, numerous others; represented in permanent collections Naval Post Grad. Sch. and Libr., Allen Knight Maritime Mus., Salvation Army Bldg., Monterey, Robert Louis Stevenson Sch., Pebble Beach, Anenberg Art Galleries, Chestlibrook Ltd., Skalagard Art Gallery, Carmel; work represented in numerous books including Modern Masters of Marine Art, 1993; featured artist KTEH-TV On-Air Art Auction, 1998; profiled in profl. jours.; subject of cover and article Palette Talk, 1980, Compass mag., 1980; artist (series of paintings) American Revolutionary War at Sea, 2003. Chairperson Mayor's Choice Exhibit, Carmel, 1993-95; co-founder Carmel Gallery Alliance, 2000-. Recipient Silver medal Tommaso Campanella Internat. Acad. Arts, Letters and Scis., Rome, 1970, Gold medal, 1972, Gold medal and hon. life membership Acad. Italia dell Arti e del Honoro, 1980, Gold medal for artistic merit Acad. d'Italia, Statue of Victory award Acad. d'Italia, 2003. Mem. Navy League (bd. dirs. Monterey), Internat. Platform Assn., Sons of Norway (cultural dir. 1974-75, 76-77), Am. Mcht. Marine Vets. Assn. (Golden Gate chpt.), Combat Mcht. Marine WWII Assn. (coun.), Mariners (San Francisco Bay area chpt.). Home: 602 Stony Point Rd Petaluma CA 94952-1048 Office Phone: 707-769-9340. Home Fax: 707-776-4889. E-mail: skalagard@aol.com.

**SKALKA, ANNA MARIE,** molecular biologist; b. NYC, July 2, 1938; AB, Adelphi U., 1959; PhD in Microbiology, NYU, 1964. Am. Cancer Soc. fellow molecular biology genetics rsch. unit Carnegie Inst., 1964-66, fellow, 1966-69; asst. mem. dept. cell biology lab. molecular and biochemical genetics Roche Inst. Molecular Biology, 1969-71, assoc. mem., 1971-76, mem., 1976-80, head, 1980-87; now dir. Inst. Cancer Rsch., Phila., 1987—; sr. v.p. basic sci. Fox Chase Cancer Ctr., Phila., 1987—. Adj. prof. microbiology, Sch. Medicine, U. Pa., 1973—, Rockefeller U., 1975. Mem. AAAS, Am. Soc. Microbiology, Am. Soc. Biol. Chem., Assn. Women Sci., Sigma Xi. Achievements include research in the structure and function of DNA, host and viral functions in the synthesis of viral DNA and RNA, phage DNA as a vehicle for the amplification and study of eukaryotic genes, molecular biology of avian retroviruses. Office: Inst for Cancer Rsch Fox Chase Cancer Ctr 7701 Burholme Ave Philadelphia PA 19111-2412

**SKALL, GREGG P.,** lawyer; b. El Paso, Tex., Mar. 28, 1944; s. Ben Milton and Lottie (Berger) S.; m. Monte Kaye Leake; 1 child, Brandon Cornell. BS, Ohio State U., 1966; JD, U. Cin., 1969. Bar: Ohio 1969, D.C. 1971, D.C. Dist. Ct. 1971, U.S. Dist. Ct. (no. dist) Ohio 1972, D.C. Ct. Appeals 1971, U.S. Supreme Ct. 1978. Atty. gen. State of Ohio, Cleve., summer 1967; intern U.S. Dept. Justice, div. Civil Rights, Washington, summer 1968; tax law specialist IRS, Washington, 1969; gen. atty. FCC, Washington, 1970-72; ptnr. Garber, Simon, Haiman, Gutfeld, Wertheimer & Friedman, Cleve., 1972-75; acting gen. counsel Office Telecommunications Policy Exec. Office of the Pres. of the U.S., Washington, 1975-78; chief counsel Nat. Telecommunications and Info. Adminstrn., Washington, 1978-80; ptnr. Blum, Nash & Railsback, Washington, 1980-84, Baker & Hostetler, Washington, 1984-91, Pepper & Corazzini LLP, Washington, 1991—; with Womble Carlyle Sandridge & Rice PLLC, Washington, 2005—. Professorial lectr. telecomms. law George Washington U. Grad. Sch., Washington, 1978-83; adv. bd. Pike & Fischer Radio Regulation, 1991—; comms. counsel to Minn., Calif. and Nev. Broadcasters Assns., 1990—. Co-author: The Broadcaster's Survival Guide: A Handbook of FCC Rules and Regulations for Radio and TV Stations, 1988; contbr. articles to profl. jours. Named to, Broadcasting Hall Fame, 2003; recipient Corp. Leadership award, Mo. Broadcasters Assn., 2003, Friend Mo. Broadcasters award, 2004. Mem. Fed. Bar Assn. (chmn. regulated industries com. 1979-81), ABA, Fed. Communications Bar Assn., Minn. Broadcasters Assn., Calif. Broadcasters Assn. Lodges: Masons. Office: Womble Carlyle Sandridge & Rice PLLC 1401 I St NW Ste 700 Washington DC 20005-2225 Office Phone: 202-857-4441. Business E-Mail: gskall@wcsr.com.

**SKAMBIS, CHRISTOPHER CHARLES, JR.,** lawyer; b. Painesville, Ohio, Jan. 21, 1953; s. Christopher Charles and Anne (Haritos) S.; m. Susan Elaine Adrianson, Dec. 18, 1976 (div. Mar. 1997); m. Kathleen Louise Maloney, Feb. 1999; children: Adrianne Elaine, Christopher Roy. Student, U. Pa., 1970-72; BA, U. Conn., 1972-74; JD, Ohio State U. Coll. Law, Columbus, 1975-78. Bar: Fla. 1978, U.S. Dist. Ct. (mid. dist.), 1979, U.S. Dist. Ct. (no. and so. dists.) 1997, U.S. Ct. Appeals (5th and 11th cir.) 1981, U.S. Supreme Ct. 1989. Assoc. VandenBerg, Gay & Burke, Orlando, Fla., 1978-81, ptnr., 1982, VandenBerg, Gay, Burke, Wilson & Arkin, Orlando, Fla., 1982-85, Foley & Lardner, Orlando, Fla., 1985—95, Moran & Shams PA, Orlando, Fla., 1996-99; The Skambis Law Firm, Orlando, 2000—. Mem. Orange County Bar Assn., Orlando, Fla., 1978, Fla. Bar 9D Grievance Commn., Orlando, Fla., 1989; arbitrator Fla. Bar 9th Cir. Fee Arbitration Commn., Orlando, Fla., 1987; co-chair Federal and State Trial Practice Com., Orlando, Fla., 1992-93. Mem. Am. Judicature Soc., ABA. Avocation: amateur ham radio operator. Office: The Skambis Law Firm 715 Vassar St Orlando FL 32804-4920 Fax: 407-649-0191. Office Phone: 407-649-0090. E-mail: cskambis@cfl.rr.com.

**SKANCKE, NANCY J.,** lawyer; b. Mar. 24, 1950; d. Frank and LaVerne Hubbard; m. Steven Lynn Skancke, Nov. 29, 1975; children: Matthew David, Carolyn Elizabeth. BS in Math. (hon.), Purdue U., West Lafayette, Ind., 1972; JD (hon.), George Washington U., Washington, D.C., 1975. Bar: Va. 1975, D.C. 1975, U.S.Ct. Appeals (5th, D.C. 11th cirs.), U.S. Supreme Ct., U.S. Ct. Fed. Claims. Ptnr. Ross, Marsh & Foster, Washington, 1980—92, Baller Hammett, Washington, 1992-93, Grammer, Kissel, Robbins & Skancke, Washington, 1993-96, Grammer, Kissel, Robbins, Skancke & Edwards, Washington, 1996—2000, GKRSE, 2000—. Bd. dirs. Found. of Energy Law Jour., 1986—89, 1998—2001. Contbr. articles to profl. jours. Master,

Prettyman-Leventhal Am. Inns of Ct., 1988—2001, pres., 1992—93. Named Disting. Sci. Alumnus, Purdue U., 2006. Fellow: Am. Bar Found.; mem.: ABA (sect. natural resources energy law, sect. adminstrv./regulatory law), Internat. Mcpl. Lawyers' Assn. (program planning com., tech sect. chmn. mcpl. contracts, franchises, Pres. award 2003), Nat. Hydropower Assn. (bd. dirs. 2002—05, treas. 2003—05), Energy Bar Assn. (bd. dirs. 1988—90). Home: 833 Nethercliffe Hall Rd Great Falls VA 22066-2717 Office: Law Offices of GKRSE Ste 330 1500 K St NW Washington DC 20005 Office Phone: 202-408-5400. Business E-Mail: njskancke@gkrse-law.com.

**SKANDERA TROMBLEY, LAURA ELISE,** academic administrator, literature educator; b. LA, Nov. 1, 1960; d. John and Mary Ruth (Chaney) S.; m. Nelson Edmund Trombley, July 13, 1991. BA, Pepperdine U., 1981, MA summa cum laude, 1983; PhD in English Lit., U. So. Calif., 1989. Asst. prof. Dept. English SUNY, Potsdam, 1990—92, assoc. prof., 1993—97, spl. asst. to pres., 1994—97, dir. Tchg., Tenure and Promotion Assistance Program, 1994—97, asst. provost, 1995—97; v.p. academic affairs, dean faculty Coe Coll., Cedar Rapids, Iowa, 1997—2002; pres. Pitzer Coll., Claremont, Calif., 2002—. Asst. lectr. writing program U. So. Calif., 1983—85, 1987; vis. prof. Am. studies U. Eichstaett, Bavaria, Germany, 1985—86, Bavaria, 1987—88; vis. asst. prof. Dept. English Pepperdine U., 1988—90. Author: Epistemology: Turning Points in the History of Poetic Knowledge, 1986, Mark Twain's Literary Marriage, 1992, Mark Twain in the Company of Women, 1994; editor: Critical Essays on Maxine Hong Kingston, 1998; co-editor: Constructing Mark Twain: New Directions in Scholarship, 2001; contbr. articles to profl. jours. Named Quarry Farm fellow Ctr. for Mark Twain Studies, 1988, Finklestein fellow U. Soc. Calif., 1988. Mem.: Internat. Assn. Univ. Prof. English, Internat. Assn. Univ. Pres., Am. Assn. Univ. Women, Mark Twain Circle of Am. Office: Office of Pres Pitzer Coll 1050 N Mills Ave Claremont CA 91711 Office Phone: 909-621-8198. E-mail: president@pitzer.edu.*

**SKARE, ROBERT MARTIN,** lawyer, director; b. Jan. 13, 1930; s. Martin Samuel and Verna Adelle (Forseth) S.; m. Marilyn Hutchinson, Aug. 28, 1954; children: Randolph, Robertson, Rodger, Richard. Student, St. Olaf Coll., 1947-48; BS, U. Minn., 1951, JD, 1954. Bar: Minn. 1956. Clk. Minn. Supreme Ct., 1953-54; assoc. Best and Flanagan, Mpls., 1956-60, ptnr., 1960-90, sr. ptnr., 1970-90, of counsel, 1990—. Corp. mcpl. counsel City of Golden Valley, Minn., 1963—88; founder, dir., gen. counsel, v.p. Luth. Brotherhood-Thrivent Mut. Funds, Mpls., 1969—93; bd. dirs. Vesper Soc. Group, San Francisco, Son of Heaven, Seattle, Aspen Inst. Cmty. Forum, Nat. Coun. Search Inst. Youth Initiative, Venture Catalysts of Calif.; nat. pres. Luth: Human Rels. Assn. Am., 1977—79; founder, dir. Episc. Found. of Aspen, Vinland Nat. Ctr. Disabled; founder Westwood Luth. Found.; adv. bd. P.F. Drucker Grad. Sch. Venture Fin. Inst. Claremont (Calif.) U., 2003—; co-founder Venture Catalysts Mexico, 2006—, SME Mexico Growth Fund and Social Enterprise Venture Fund, 2006—. Trustee Nat. Bd. Am. Luth. Ch.; mem. bd. mgmt. U. Minn. YMCA. Officer Counter-Intelligence Corps U.S. Army, 1954—56. Recipient Pres. award Luth. Human Rels. Assn. Am., 1979, 25 Yr. Pub. Svc. award City of Golden Valley, 1988, Minn., Presdl. award Search Inst., 1997, Disting. Svc. award Luth. Brotherhood, 1992; named Disting. Mil. Student Res. Officers Tng. Corps., U. Minn., 1954. Mem. ABA, Minn. State Bar Assn., Hennepin County Bar Assn., U. Minn. Alumni Club (charter), Mpls. Club, Torske Klubben, Sigma Alpha Epsilon (Alumni Svc. award 1978), Vesper Soc. San Francisco (officer and exec. com. mem. 2004-05). Office: 4000 US Bank Pl 225 South 6th St Ste 4000 Minneapolis MN 55402-4690 also: 780 Mt Laurel Aspen CO 81611 Home (Winter): Box 1390 Fallbrook CA 92088 Home (Summer): 1931 Westhaven Lodge Resort Tower MN 55790 Office Phone: 612-339-7121.

**SKARIE, DAVID P.,** food products executive; BBS, Minn. State Univ. Mgmt. positions through v.p. field sales Ralcorp Holdings Inc., St. Louis, 1986—93, v.p., dir. sales human foods, 1993—94, corp v.p., dir. customer devel. group, 1994—2000, corp. v.p., 2000—03, pres. Ralston Foods, 2000—, pres. Carriage House Co., 2002—, co-CEO, pres., 2003—. Chmn. Private Label Mfr. Assn. Office: Ralcorp Holdings Inc 800 Market St Saint Louis MO 63101*

**SKASANNA, REY,** industrial engineer, department chairman; b. Boston, May 12; s. Don and Mariana Skasanna; m. Julianna Skasanna, Feb. 6, 1990; 1 child, Maria. B in Indsl. Engring., Calif. Nat. U., 1980; D in Indsl. Engring., New Eng. Inst. Tech., 1984. Indsl. engr. The Human Reactor Site, RI, 1985—2000; indsl. engr., chmn. Meriks Wonder Products, Providence, 2000—. Vis. prof. Purdue U., 2003—04; spkr. in field. Author: Making Our Existence More Efficient and Healthier, 2003, Artificial Organs: New Diagnostic and Therapeutic Needs, 2004, The Atom, Just As Large As Our Lives, 2005, Fulfilling Needs in Corporate USA, 2006. Vol. Housing Assocs., 1999—2002; mem. Christ Ch. Group, 2002—05. Mem.: The Environ. and Health Benefits Soc., Indsl. Engrs. Assn., Rotary Club. Roman Catholic. Office: Meriks Wonder Products 69 Governor St 159 Providence RI 02906-3075

**SKEAN, MARK EDGAR,** finance educator, consultant; b. Knoxville, Tenn., Nov. 02; s. James Dan Skean and Nellie Ann Sherrill; m. Diane Gail Ouse, June 15, 1991. AB, Western Ky. U., Bowling Green, 1982; MBA, Ind. U., Bloomington, 1984; PhD, U. N.D., Grand Forks, 1993. CPA Ohio, CMA, Inst. Mgmt. Acctg., CFM, Inst. Mgmt. Acctg., CSA, Inst. Internal Auditors. Sr. fin. analyst Union Underwear, Bowling Green, Ky., 1984—86; sr. field auditor Ky. Revenue Cabinet, Ft. Mitchell, 1986—88; asst. prof. Lees Coll., Jackson, 1988—89, Mayville State U., ND, 1990—93, assoc. prof., 1994—98, prof., 1999—. Rep. N.D. Coun. Coll. Faculties, 1994—96; pres. Assn. N.D. Acctg. Instrs., 2003; presenter in field. Recipient Tchr. of Yr., Mayville State U. Student Senate, 2006; grantee, Bush Found., Mpls., 1998—. Office: Mayville State Univ 330 3rd St NE Mayville ND 58257

**SKEEL, DAVID ARTHUR,** law educator; BA, U. NC, 1983; JD, U. Va., 1987. Asst. prof. Temple U. Sch. Law, 1990—93; vis. assoc. prof. U. Wis. Law Sch., 1993—94; assoc. prof. Temple U. Sch. Law, 1993—98; Olin prof., vis. assoc. prof. law U. Va. Sch. Law, 1996; vis. assoc. prof. U. Pa. Law Sch., Phila., 1997, prof., 1999—2003, S. Samuel Arsht prof. corp. law, 2004—; vis. prof. Georgetown U. Law Ctr., 2004. Law clk. for Hon. Walter K. Stapleton US Ct. Appeals (3rd cir.), 1987—88; assoc. Reorganization and Fin. Dept. Duane, Morris & Heckscher, 1988—90. Author: Debt's Dominion: A History of Bankruptcy Law in America, 2001, Icarus in the Boardroom: The Fundamental Flaws in Corporate America and Where They Came From, 2005; contbr. articles to law jours. Office: U Pa Law Sch 3400 Chestnut St Philadelphia PA 19104 Office Phone: 215-573-9859. Office Fax: 215-573-2025. E-mail: dskeel@law.upenn.edu.

**SKEEN, DAVID RAY,** systems engineer, consultant, engineering executive, educator; b. Bucklin, Kans., July 12, 1942; s. Claude E. and Velma A. (Birney) S.; m. Carol J. Stimpert, Aug. 23, 1964; children: Jeffrey Kent, Timothy Sean, Kimberly Dawn. BA in Math., Emporia State U., 1964; MS, Am. U., 1972; grad., Fed. Exec. Inst., 1983, Naval War Coll., 1984; DSc in Engring. Mgmt., George Washington U. Corr. office automation profl. Computer sys. analyst to comdr.-in-chief U.S. Naval Forces-Europe, London, 1967-70; computer sys. analyst Naval Command Sys. Support Activity, Washington, 1970-73; dir. data processing Office Naval Rsch., U.S. Navy Dept., Arlington, Va., 1973-78; dir. mgmt. info. sys. Naval Civilian Pers. Command, Washington, 1978-80; dep. dir. manpower, pers. tng. automated sys. Dept. Naval Mil. Pers. Command, Washington, 1980-85; dir. manpower, pers. tng. info. resource mgmt. Chief Naval Ops., Washington, 1985-91; assoc. dir. Office of IRM, USDA, Washington, 1992-96; dir. modernization of adminstrn. processes program, 1996-98; dep. dir. office of ops. USDA, Washington, 1998; sr. engring. mgr., cons. Lockheed Martin, Washington, 1998—2000; sys. engrs. cons, GCI, 2004—. Lectr. Inst. Sci. and Pub. Affairs, 1973-76; cons. Electronic Data Processing Career Devel. Programs, 1975—; detailed to Pres.'s Reorg. Project for Automated Data Processing, 1978, spl. Navy IRM studies, SECNAV, 1991, USDA/Office of Mgmt. and Budget IRM, 1993, spl. USDA Field Structure Studies, 1997; adj. prof. Sch. Engring. and Applied Sci. George Washington U., 1985—, Dept. Pub. Adminstrn. George

Mason U., 2005—; mem. Pres.'s Fed. Automated Data Processing Users Group, Washington, 1978-80 Contbr. articles to profl. jours. Capt. USNR, 1960-91. Recipient Outstanding Performance award Interagy. Com. Data Processing, 1976, Adminstrv. Staff Performance award, 1998, Sec.'s cert. Appreciation, 1998. Mem. IEEE, Internat. Coun. on Sys. Engring., Sr. Exec. Assns., Assn. Fed. IRM, Naval Res. Assns., Pres. Fed. Automated Data Processing Users Group. Home: 544 Hidden Cove Ln Lynch Station VA 24571 Personal E-mail: docskeen@earthlink.net.

**SKEES, WILLIAM LEONARD, JR.,** lawyer; b. Indpls., Jan. 26, 1947; s. William Leonard and Marian Catherine (Fagan) S.; m. Cindy Lee Keeton; children: Kristina Suzanne Carlsen, Elizabeth Ann Garrison, Catherine Fagan, William Leonard III (dec.), Samuel Jackson. BA, Ball State U., 1969; JD magna cum laude, Ind. U., 1971. Bar: Ind. 1971, Ky. 1981. Law clk. U.S. Dist. Ct. (no. dist.), Fort Wayne, Ind., 1971-72; mem. Frost Brown Todd, LLC, Louisville, 1981—. Contbr. articles to jours. in field. Mem. bd. visitors Ind. U. Sch. Law, 1975-91; bd. dirs., past pres. Louisville Housing Partnership, 1978—; bd. dirs. Stage One, Louisville Children's Theatre, pres., 1990-91; bd. dirs. Ky. chpt. Nat. SIDS Found.; grad. Leadership Ky., 1996. Mem. ABA, Ky. Bar Assn., Ind. Bar Assn., Louisville Bar Assn., Nat. Assn. Bond Lawyers. Office: Frost Brown Todd LLC 400 W Market St Fl 32D Louisville KY 40202-3346 Office Phone: 502-568-0301. Business E-mail: bskees@FBTLaw.com.

**SKEETE, HELEN WATKINS,** minister, counselor; b. Wallace, N.C., Mar. 2, 1938; d. James Edward Newkirk, Edith Newkirk; m. Paul Louis, Sr. Watkins, Aug. 31, 1958; children: Paul Jr. Watkins, Stella Roys Finch, Trina Joy Gatlin. BTh, Calvary Grace Inst., Columbus, Ohio, 1977. Cert. crisis counselor. Internat. evangelist Soul Saving Sta. Every Nation, N.Y.C., 1959—84; asst. administr., assoc. min. Grace Ch. All Nations, Boston, 1983—88; founder, CEO Love Unlimited Drug Rehab. Outreach Programs, Inc., Boston, 1988—; founder, dir. Love U God's Gang, Brookline, Mass., 1991—; founder, CEO, pastor Love Unlimited Outreach Ministries, Inc., Boston, 1991—; overseer Men & Women of Crossroads Ministries, Dorchester, Mass., 1996—, Gospel Truth Ministries. Mem. adv. bd. New Eng. Med. Ctr. Hosp., Boston, 1981—83, Boston Against Drugs, 1991—96, Living After Murder Program, Inc., Roxbury, Mass., 1993—95. Author: (plays) Life on the Streets in a World of Drugs, 1990 (Proclamation from Mayor Flynn of Boston, 1990), Matriac of Ministry, 2002, Official Resolution - Boston City Council, 2002; co-author: Boston Area Violence Prevention Resource Directory, 1993 (Hon. Cmty. Svc. award, 1993). Facilitator Healthy Boston, 1997—99; mem. AIDS Action Com., Boston, 1995—2001; counselor Boston Safe Neighborhood, 1990—97; mem. evaluation team Boston Against Drugs, 1993—97; dir. March Against Violence, 1991. Recipient Recognition of Achievement, Gov. Paul Cellucci of Mass., 1997, Ofcl. Resolution, Boston City Coun., Recognition of Achievement, Commonwealth of Mass. Ho. Reps., 1997, Letter of Recognition, U.S. Pres. George Bush, 1990, Letter of Appreciation, U.S. Pres. Bill Clinton, 1997, cert. of Appreciation, Boston Police Dept., 1997, Proclamation, City of Boston Mayor Menino, 1997, Letter of Recognition, U.S. Pres. Ronald Regan, 1983; grantee, Boston Safe Neighborhood, 1991. Mem.: Grandparents Raising Their Grandchildren (facilitator 1996—99, cert. of Appreciation 1997). Democrat. Avocations: travel, reading, sewing, singing, writing. Home: 99 Kent St Ste 7-317 Brookline MA 02445-7955 Office: Love Unlimited Drug Rehabilitation Out Brookline MA 02445-7955 Personal E-mail: revhelenwatkinssskeete@yahoo.com.

**SKELLAND, ANTHONY HAROLD PETER,** chemical engineering professor; b. Birmingham, Eng., Feb. 21, 1928; came to U.S., 1959; s. Harold and Hilda Skelland. BSChemE, U. Birmingham, 1948, PhD in Chem. Engring., 1952. Mgr. Procter and Gamble, Eng., 1954-56, R&D engr., 1956-59; asst. prof. Ill. Inst. Tech., Chgo., 1959-62; assoc. prof. U. Notre Dame, South Bend, Ind., 1962-66, prof., 1966-69; Ashland prof. U. Ky., Lexington, 1969-79; prof. Ga. Inst. Tech., Atlanta, 1979—. Cons. Monsanto, Babcock and Wilcox, Union Carbide, E.I. duPont de Nemours, FMC Corp., Westinghouse and others. Author: Non-Newtonian Flow and Heat Transfer, 1967, Diffusional Mass Transfer, 1974; contbr. over 80 articles to profl. jours. Fellow AIChE, Inst. Petroleum; mem. Royal Soc. Chemistry (Eng.), Inst. Chem. Engrs. (Eng.). Avocations: tennis, theater, dining out. Office Phone: 770-399-6694.

**SKELTON, DOUGLAS H.,** architect; b. Cottage Grove, Oreg., Apr. 17, 1939; s. Harry Edward and Mary Jane S.; m. Bonita L. Baker, June 17, 1961; children: Paul D., Cynthia J., Justin D. Student, Oreg. State U., 1957—59; degree in Architecture, U. Oreg., 1963. Registered arch., Oreg. Draftsman Payne & Struble Architecture, Medford, Oreg., 1965-66; intern Wayne Struble Arch., Medford, 1966-70, assoc. arch., 1973-78; project arch. William Seibert Arch., Medford, 1970-73; ptnr. Struble & Skelton Archs., Medford, 1978-83; owner Douglas Skelton Arch., Medford, 1983-89; ptnr. Skelton, Straus & Seibert Archs., Medford, 1989—. Design bldg. renovation (911 Mag. 1991, Excellence in Sch. Architecture AS&U mag. 1987); arch. Jacksonville, Oreg. Libr. (Best Contemp. Design, 2003). Mem. So. Oreg. Regional Econ. Devel. Inc.; bd. dirs. Rogue Valley Christian Ch., 1990—. Recipient Design Competition award Lake Creek Learning Ctr., 1998, Best Contemporary Bldg. Jacksonville Libr. award Hist. Arch. Rev. Commn., 2003. Mem. AIA (pres. So. Oreg. chpt.), AIA Oreg. (treas. 1989), Nation Trust for Hist. Preservation, Rotary (pres. Jacksonville/Applegate chpt. 1998-99), Medford/Jackson County C. of C. Avocations: camping, fishing, boating. Office: Skelton Straus & Seibert Architects and Planners LLP 26 Hawthorne Ave Medford OR 97504-7114

**SKELTON, H. JAY,** retail executive, investment company executive; Various positions KPMG Peat Marwick, Jacksonville, Fla., 1962—78, mng. ptnr., 1978—88; pres., dir. DDI Inc., Jacksonville, Fla., 1989—; chmn. Winn-Dixie Stores, Jacksonville, Fla., 2004—. Bd. dirs. Patriot Transportation Holding, Inc., 2002—, Consolidated-Tomoka Land Co. Pres. Pablo Creek Club, Jacksonville. Office: Winn-Dixie Stores 5050 Edgewood Court Jacksonville FL 32254-3699*

**SKELTON, IKE (ISAAC NEWTON SKELTON IV),** congressman; b. Lexington, Mo., Dec. 20, 1931; s. Isaac Newton and Carolyn (Boone) S.; m. Susan B. Anding, July 22, 1961; children: Ike, Jim, Page. AA, Wentworth Mil. Acad., 1951; student. U. Edinburgh, Scotland, 1953; AB in Hist., U. Mo., Columbia, 1953, LLB, 1956. Bar: Mo. 1956. Asst. Mo. pvt. practice, Lexington, Mo.; pros. atty. Lafayette County, Mo., 1957-60; spl. asst. atty. gen. Mo., 1961-63; mem. Mo. State Senate from 28th dist., 1971—76, US Congress from 4th Mo. dist., 1977—, ranking minority mem. armed svcs. com. Vice chmn. bd. trustees Harry S. Truman Scholarship Found. Named Minuteman of Yr., Res. Officers Assn. of US, 1995; recipient W. Stuart Symington award, Air Force Assn., 1994, Henry M. Jackson Disting. Svc. award, Jewish Inst. Nat. Security Affairs, 1999, Hon. commandant award, Indsl. Coll. Armed Forces, 2005, Mil. Order of Iron Mike award, Marine Corps League. Mem. Phi Beta Kappa, Sigma Chi, Masons, Shriners, Elks, Boy Scouts Am. Bar Assn. Democrat. Mem. Christian Ch. Office: US Ho Reps 2206 Rayburn House Office Bldg Washington DC 20515-2504*

**SKELTON, WILLIAM DOUGLAS,** physician; MD, Emory U., 1963. Sr. v.p. rsch. and health affairs Mercer U., Macon, Ga., 1985—2004; dist health dir. Coastal Health Dist., Savannah, Ga., 2004—. Office: Coastal Health Dist 24 Oglethorpe Professional Blvd Savannah GA 31416 Office Phone: 912-356-2233, 912-644-5210. Business E-mail: wdskelton@dhr.state.ga.com.

**SKERRITT, TOM,** actor; b. Detroit, Aug. 25, 1933; 4 children. Student, Wayne State U., UCLA. Films: War Hunt, 1962, One Man's Way, 1964, Those Calloways, 1964, M*A*S*H, 1970, Wild Rovers, 1972, Fuzz, 1972, Big Bad Mama, 1974, Thieves Like Us, 1974, The Devil's Rain, 1975, The Turning Point, 1977 (Nat. Bd. Rev. Best Supporting Actor), Up In Smoke, 1978, Alien, 1979, Ice Castles, 1979, Silence of the North, 1981, A Dangerous Summer, 1981, Savage Harvest, 1981, Fighting Back, 1982, The Dead Zone,

1983, Top Gun, 1986, Space Camp, 1987, The Big Town, 1987, Wisdom, 1987, Opposing Force, 1987, Maid to Order, 1987, Poltergeist III, 1988, Steel Magnolias, 1989, Big Man On Campus, 1990, The Rookie, 1991, Blue Movie Blue, 1991, Poison Ivy, 1991, A River Runs Through It, 1992, Contact, 1997, The Other Sister, Texas Rangers, 2000, Tears of the Sun, 2003, Swing, 2003,; TV shows: Ryan's Four, 1983, Contact, 1997, On The Edge, 1987, Cheers, 1987-88, Picket Fences, 1992-96 (Emmy award Outstanding Lead Actor in a Drama Series, 1993), Brothers & Sisters, 2006; guest star Will and Grace, 2003, West Wing, 2003, Law & Order: Special Victims Unit, 2004, Huff, 2006; TV films: The Bird Man, The Last Day, Maneaters Are Loose!, Calendar Girl Murders, Miles to Go, True Believer, Parent Trap II, A Touch of Scandal, Poker Alice, Nightmare At Bitter Creek, Moving Target, The Heist, Red King White Knight, The China Lake Murders, Child of the Night, In Sickness and In Health, Getting Up and Going Home, Divided By Hate, 1997, What the Deaf Man Heard, The Heart of the Unicorn Killer, 1998, Aftershock, 1999, American Daughter, 2000, High Noon, 2000, Jacqueline Bouvier Kennedy Onassis: Alife, 2000, Path to War, 2002, Jaqueline Bouvier Kennedy Onassis: A Life, Vinegar Hill, 2004, Desperation, 2006. Office: Guttman Assocs 118 S Beverly Dr Beverly Hills CA 90212-3003*

**SKIBNIEWSKI, MIROSLAW JAN,** engineering educator; MEng, Warsaw Tech. U., 1981; MS, Carnegie-Mellon U., 1983, PhD, 1986; cert. in advanced studies, Harvard U. Grad. Sch. Edn., 2000. Staff engr. engring. dept. Pitts. Testing Lab., 1981-82; rsch. and tchg. asst. dept. civil engring. Carnegie-Mellon U., Pitts., 1982-86; asst. prof. Sch. Civil Engring. Purdue U., West Lafayette, Ind., 1986-90, assoc. prof. Sch. Civil Engring., 1990-95, prof. Sch. Civil Engring., 1995—, asst. exec. vp acad affairs, 1997-2001, assoc provost, 2001—02, dean internat. programs, dir. internat. rsch., 2002—04; A. James Clark endowed chair prof. U. Md., College Park, 2005—. Vis. sr. rsch. scientist divsn. bldg., constrn. and engring. Commonwealth Scientific and Indsl. Rsch. Orgn., Melbourne, Australia, 1992; vis. rsch. prof. Inst. Mechanized Constrn. and Rock Mining, Warsaw, 1993; hon. prof. civil engring. Warsaw Tech. U., 2004—; rsch. engr. Robotics Ctr. Constrn. Engring. Rsch. Lab. U.S. Army C.E., Champaign, Ill., 1993; presenter workshops. Editor-in-chief constrn. techs. and engring. Automation in Constrn.; guest editor Microcomputers in Civil Engring.; mem. editl. bd. Internat. Jour. Cont. Engirng. Edn. and Lifelong Learning, Real Estate Valuation and Investment, Constrn. Mgmt. and Econs., Constrn. Rsch. jours.; contbr. articlest to over 100 profl. jours., chpts. to books. Recipient Best Paper award Am. Soc. Engring. Edn., 1991; named Presdl. Young Investigator NSF, 1987-92. Mem. ASCE Inst. gel. dist. 9 coun. 1986-91) mem. control group aerospace divsn. tsk force on constrn. robotics 1987-89, constrn. rsch. coun. 1987—, expert sys. and artificial intelligence com. 1987—, data base and info. ech. com. 1988—, com. on field sensing and robotics in civil engring. 1990— (Walter L. Huber Civil Engring. Rsch. prize 1998), Internat. Assn. Automation and Robotics in Constrn. (founding mem., co-dir. 1991—, chmn. newsletter com. 1993-95 chmn. Commns. Com. 1997, v.p. 1990-2000, pres. 2000—), Internat. Coun. Bldg. Rsch. Studies and Documentation (Mem. W-75 working commn. on constrn. equipment and mechanization 1989-96, task group on computer-aided learning in constrn. and property, W-89 commn. on bldg. rsch. and edn. 1993— TG27 Task Group on Human Machine Technologies in Constrn.), Internat. Coun. on Tall Bldgs. and Urban Habitat (co-chmn. com. 65 robots and tall bldgs. 1991—, mem. com. on applications of emerging techs 1994-95) Internat. Stds Orgn. (U.S. rep. on behalf of Am. Nat. Stds. Inst. to tech. com. on constrn., machinery and equipment 1994—) Constrn. Industry Inst., Sigma Xi. Achievements include development of a decision support system for managing a fleet of construcotn robotics, a computerized constructabilty review system for advanced construction technologies applications. Office: U Md 1188 Glenn L Martin Hall College Park MD 20742-3021 Fax: (765) 494-0644. Office Phone: 301-405-9364. Office Fax: 301-405-2585. E-mail: mirek@umd.edu.

**SKIDD, THOMAS PATRICK, JR.,** lawyer; s. Thomas Patrick and Anna Skidd; m. Judith Chase Roberts, Sept. 10, 1960; children: Suanne C., Sherry E., Thomas Patrick III, Jody E. BA in Econs. cum laude, Georgetown U., 1958; LLB, Yale U., 1961. Bar: Conn. 1961, U.S. Supreme Ct. 1963. Ptnr., prin. Cummings & Lockwood LLC, Stamford, Conn., 1961—. Mem. Conn. Bar Assn. (real estate sect. and land use sect.), Stamford-Norwalk Regional Bar Assn., Roton Point Club (Rowayton, Conn.). Roman Catholic. Avocation: phonograph record collector. Office: Cummings & Lockwood LLC 6 Landmark Sq 9th Fl Stamford CT 06904-0120 Office Phone: 203-327-1700. Business E-Mail: tskidd@cl-law.com.

**SKIDMORE, HOWARD FRANKLYN,** public relations counsel; b. Bklyn., Sept. 24, 1917; s. William F. and Mae (White) S.; m. Zaza Irina O'Hara, Dec. 4, 1943; children: Joel Michael, Susan Irina. Student, Coll. City N.Y., 1938-39. Editorial staff N.Y. Herald Tribune, 1937-42, 45-47; asst. to dir. pub. relations C. & O. Ry., N.Y.C., 1948, exec. asst. to v.p. passenger traffic, pub. relations, advt. Cleve., 1949-53, dir. pub. relations, 1954-59, spl. asst. to chmn. bd., 1954-77, dir. pub. relations and passenger traffic, 1959-63; v.p. C. & O. Ry., also B. & O. Ry., 1963-77, Western Md. Ry., 1973-77, Chessie System, Inc., 1974-77; pres. Howard Skidmore Co., Inc., Cleve., 1977-83. Trustee Cleve. Music Sch. Settlement, 1958— Served with USNR, 1942-45. Mem. Soc. Silurians, R.R. Pub. Relations Assn. (pres. 1958), Pub. Relations Soc. Am., Soc. Profl. Journalists Clubs: Nat. Press (Washington); Carmel Valley Racquet; Canterbury Golf (Cleve.). Home: 26360 Monte Verde St Carmel CA 93923-9233 E-mail: howzaco@aol.com.

**SKIDMORE, JAMES ALBERT, JR.,** management, computer technology and engineering services company executive; b. Newark, June 30, 1932; s. James A. and Frances W. (Barker) S.; m. Peggy Ann Young, July 10, 1954; children: Jacqueline Sue, James Albert III BA, Muhlenberg Coll., 1954; postgrad., Duke U., 1984. Customer sales rep. N.J. Bell Tel. Co., Newark, 1957-65, then dist. sales mgr., divsn. mktg. mgr.; asst. to pres. for pub. affairs Pepsi Co., Inc., N.Y.C., 1967—69; asst. to Pres. of U.S., 1968-69; v.p. Handy Assoc., N.Y.C., 1969—71, pres., 1972; pres., CEO Sci. Mgmt. Corp., Basking Ridge, NJ, 1972—; chmn. bd. dirs. Newark Brush Co., 1974-79. Bd. dirs. United Jersey Banks, United Jersey Bank, Franklin State Bank; mem. exec. com. UJB Fin.-Summit Bank, 1985-93, Blue Cross & Blue Shield N.J., Inc., Enterprise Holding Co., Inc.; exec. com., trustee Blue Cross of N.J., 1983—; dir. Coca Cola, N.Y., 1980-85, Mariner Comm., 1983-85, Horizon Blue Cross Blue Shield N.J., Pa., N.Y., Del., 1998—; mem., chmn. mktg. com. Seton Hall Commn., 1987; trustee Rutgers U. Grad. Sch. Mgmt., 1989—; trustee Pub. Affairs Rsch. Inst. N.J., 1988-99; lectr. U. Amsterdam, 1967, U. Toronto, U. Helsinki, 1967, Tokyo U. Guest columnist Rotary Internat. mag., 1966-68, Kiwanis mag., 1966-68, Japan Times on Cmty. Responsibility and Leadership, 1965-67. Mem. Nat. Commn. on Youth Employment, 1966-67; state chmn. N.J. Nat. Found. March of Dimes, 1966-73; mem. exec. bd. Watchung Area coun. Boy Scouts Am., 1972-77, dir. N.E. region, 1983-90; mem. Citizen's Adv. Bd. on Youth Opportunity, 1969-75; state chmn. United Citizens for Nixon-Agnew, N.J., 1968; nat. bd. govs. Alpha Tau Omega Found., 1967-73; treas. Jr. Chamber Internat., 1967-68; bd. dirs. Muhlenberg Coll., Allentown, Pa., 1980-92, 2001—, chair governance com., N.E. region Boy Scouts Am., 1983—; trustee Brick Twp. Hosp., Inc., Brick Town, N.J., 1976-80; bd. dirs. Am. Christmas Trains and Trucks, chmn., 1966-67; pres. Project Concern, San Diego, 1966-78; trustee The Scholarship Fund for Inner-City Children, 1997—, Ctr. for Analysis of Pub. Issues, 1999—. Served to capt. USMCR, 1954-57. Decorated Order of St. John (Eng.); recipient Internat. Understanding award, Brussels, 1966, Disting. Svc. award, St. Paul, 1966, Freedom Found. George Washington Medal of Honor award, 1965, Outstanding Achievement in Life award Muhlenberg Coll. Alumni, 1966, Amb. award U.S. Jaycees, 1967, Trinidad and Tobago award Prime Minister of Ireland, 1970, Human Rels. award Soc. Advancement of Mgmt., 1982, Statesman award N.J. Jaycees, 1983, Disting. Citizens award Boy Scouts Am., 1983, Pvt. Sector Initiative award Pres. Reagan, 1985; named among Am.'s Ten Outstanding Young Men, Look Mag. and U.S. Jaycees, 1968; inducted into U.S. Jaycees Hall of Leadership, 1983. Mem. NJ State C. of C. (bd. dirs. 1984-2003), Jr. C. of C., Muhlenberg Coll. Alumni Assn., Alpha Tau Omega, Sky Club (NYC), Baltusrol Golf Club, Longboat Key Club, The Players Club

(chair fin. com., trustee), Union League Club NY. also: 1465 Gulf Of Mexico Dr Longboat Key FL 34228-3447 Office: Sci Mgmt Co LLC 745 US Hwy 202/206 Bridgewater NJ 08807-1760 Office Phone: 908-722-0300.

**SKIDMORE, NANCY LYNNE,** music educator, pre-school educator; b. Lakewood, NJ, May 1, 1947; d. Richard Thayer Skidmore and Mabel Annetta Kummer; m. Wayne L. Reynolds, 1969 (div. 1997); children: Benjamin P. Reynolds, Amy L. Reynolds. BA in Music, William Smith Coll., 1969; postgrad., Georgian Ct. Coll. Cert. tchr. music and elem. edn. NJ. Pvt. piano tchr., Whiting, NJ, 1970—2000, Highlands, NJ, 2000—; substitute tchr. Manchester Twp., NJ, 1990—2000; music tchr. Tutortime Presch., Holmdel, NJ, 1999—2005; lead tchr. Ivy Hill Presch., Rumson, NJ, 2005. Wardrobe mistress Shore Ballet Co. 1987; class fundraiser William Smith Coll., Geneva, NY, 1982—94; Sunday sch. tchr. Episcopal Ch., Whiting, NJ, 1978—97. Mem.: Shore Music Educators Assn., Nat. Guild Piano Tchrs. (Honor Roll Tchr. 2001—05). Avocation: reading. Home: 127 Navesink Ave Rte 36 Highlands NJ 07732

**SKIGEN, PATRICIA SUE,** lawyer; d. David P. and Gertrude H. (Hirschhaut) Skigen; m. Irwin J. Sugarman, May 1973 (div. Nov. 1994); 1 child, Alexander David Sugarman; m. Gary W. Guttman, May 2001. BA with distinction, Cornell U., 1964; LLB, Yale U., 1968. Bar: NY 1968, US Dist. Ct. (so. dist.) NY 1969. Law clk. Anderson, Mori & Rabinowitz, Tokyo, 1966-67; assoc. Rosenman Colin Kaye Petschek Freund & Emil, NYC, 1968-70, Willkie Farr & Gallagher, NYC, 1970-75, ptnr., 1977-95, J.P. Morgan Chase & Co., NYC, 1995—2002, mng. dir., assoc. gen. counsel, 2002—04; gen. coun. fin. svcs. Am. Internat. Group, Inc., 2005—. Asst. supt., gen. counsel NY State Banking Dept., NYC, 1975-77, first dep. supt. banks, 1977; adj. prof. Benjamin Cardozo Law Sch. Yeshiva U., 1979. Contbr. articles to profl. jours. Cornell U. Dean's scholar, 1960-64, Regent's scholar, 1960-64, Yale Law Sch. scholar, 1964-68. Mem.: ABA (corp. banking and bus. law sect.), Assn. of Bar of City of N.Y. (chmn. com. banking 1991—94, long range planning com. 1994—96, audit com. 1994—2001), Phi Kappa Phi, Phi Beta Kappa. Office: 212-770-8805. Business E-Mail: patricia.skigen@aig.com.

**SKILES, JAMES JEAN,** electrical engineer, computer engineer, educator; b. St. Louis, Oct. 16, 1928; s. Coy Emerson and Vernetta Beatrice Skiles; m. Deloris Audrey McKenney, Sept. 4, 1948; children: Steven, Randall, Jeffrey. BSEE, Washington U., St. Louis, 1948; MS, Mo. Sch. Mines and Metallurgy (now U. Mo.-Rolla), 1951; PhD, U. Wis., 1954. Engr. Union Electric Co., St. Louis, 1948-49; instr. U. Mo., Rolla, 1949-51; instr. elec. engring. U. Wis., Madison, 1951—54, prof. elec. engring., 1954-89, prof. emeritus, 1989—, chmn. Dept. Elec. Engring., 1967-72, dir. Univ. Industry Rsch. program, 1972-75, dir. Energy Rsch. Ctr., 1975-95. Cons. in field. Contbr. articles to profl. jours. Mem. Monona Grove Dist. Schs. Bd., Wis., 1961—69; mem. adv. com. Wis. Energy Office, Madison, 1979—80, Wis. Pub. Svc. Commn., 1980—81. Recipient Kiekhofer Tchg. award, 1955, Wis. Electric Utilities Professorship in Energy Engring., U. Wis., 1975—89, Benjamin Smith Reynolds Tchg. award, 1980, Acad. Elec. Engring. award, U. Mo. - Rolla, 1982. Mem.: IEEE (sr.), Am. Soc. Engring. Edn. Home: 8099 Coray Ln Verona WI 53593-9073 Office: Univ of Wisconsin Dept Elec & Computer Engring 1415 Engineering Dr Madison WI 53706-1607 E-mail: skiles@engr.wisc.edu.

**SKILES, SCOTT ALLEN,** professional basketball coach; b. LaPorte, Ind., Mar. 5, 1964; Profl. basketball player Milwaukee Bucks, 1986—87, Ind. Pacers, 1987—89, Orlando Magic, 1989—94, Wash. Bullets, 1994—95, Phila. 76ers, 1995—96; asst. coach Phoenix Suns, 1997-99, head coach, 1999—2002, Chgo. Bulls, 2003—. Office: c/o Chgo Bulls 1901 W Madison St Chicago IL 60612*

**SKILLING, RAYMOND INWOOD,** lawyer; b. Enniskillen, Eng., July 14, 1939; s. Dane and Elizabeth (Burleigh) Skilling; m. Alice Mae Welsh, Aug. 14, 1982; 1 child from previous marriage, Keith A. LLB, Queen's U., Belfast, U.K., 1961; JD, U. Chgo., 1962. Solicitor: English Supreme Ct. 1966, bar: Ill. 1974. Assoc. Clifford-Turner (name now Clifford Chance), London, 1963-69, ptnr., 1969-76; exec. v.p., chief counsel Aon Corp. (and predecessor cos.), Chgo., 1976—2003, sr. advisor, 2004—, also bd. dirs. Recipient McKane medal, Queen's U., Belfast, 1961; Commonwealth fellow, U. Chgo., 1961—62, Bigelow Tchg. fellow, U. Chgo. Law Sch., 1962—63, Fulbright scholar, U.S. Ednl. Commn., London, 1961—63. Mem.: Bucks Club London, Racquet Club Chgo. Office: Aon Corp 200 E Randolph Chicago IL 60601

**SKILLINGSTAD, CONSTANCE YVONNE,** social services administrator, educator; b. Portland, Oreg., Nov. 18, 1944; d. Irving Elmer and Beulah Ruby (Aleckson) Erickson; m. David W. Skillingstad, Jan. 12, 1968 (div. Mar. 1981); children: Michael, Brian. BA in Sociology, U. Minn., 1966; MBA, U. St. Thomas, St. Paul, 1982. Lic. social worker; cert. vol. adminstr., lic. real estate agt. Social worker Rock County Welfare Dept., Luverne, Minn., 1966-68, Hennepin County Social Svc., Mpls., 1968-70, vol. coord., 1970-78, St. Joseph's Home for Children, Mpls., 1978-89, mgr. cmty. resources, 1989-94; exec. dir. Mpls. Crisis Nursery, 1994-97; mem. cmty. faculty Met. State U., St. Paul and Mpls., 1980-97; faculty U. St. Thomas Ctr. Non Profit Mgmt., 1990—2001; asst. adminstr. St. Joseph's Home Children, Mpls., 1997-98; asst. dir. Cath. Charities Archdiocese of St. Paul and Mpls., 1998-2000; dir. mem. svc. Minn. Coun. Fedns., 2001—02; pres. Golden Gulf Homes, Inc., 2001—; exec. dir. Prevent Child Abuse Minn., St. Paul, 2002—. Trainer, mem. adv. commn. Mpls. Vol. Ctr., 1978—90, cons., 1980—, chmn. Contbr. articles to profl. jours. Mem. adv. bd. MADD, Minn., 1986—88, Congregations Concerned for Children, 2002—, Stop It Now!, Minn., 2003—, Grandkids and Me Jail plus Services Network Minn. 2002—. Authentic Voices Internat., Ctr. Grief, Loss and Transition, U. Minn. Children Youth and Family Consortium; vice chmn., chmn. adminstrv. coun., lay leader Hobart United Meth. Ch.; lay rep. Minn. Ann. Conf. Meth. Chs., 1989—92; chmn. social concerns commn. Park Ave. United Meth. Ch., 1992—. Named Woman of Distinction, Mpls. St. Paul Mag./Sta. KARE-TV, 1995; named one of Outstanding Young Women in Am., 1974; recipient Vol. of Yr. 2001, Boca Ballet. Mem.: Minn. Social Svcs. Assn. (pres. 1981, 1998—99, bd. dirs. 1996—2001, mem. legis. com., Disting. Svc. award 1987), Assn. Vol. Adminstrn. (v.p. regional affairs 1985—87, mem. assessment panel 1986—94, coord. nat. tng. team, cert. process vol. adminstr. 1986—92, profl. devel. chair 1990—92), Minn. Assn. Vol. Dirs. (pres. 1975, sec., ethics chmn. 1987—). Dfl. Avocations: bridge, volleyball, travel, reading, accordion. Office: Prevent Child Abuse Minn Ste 202 S 1821 University Ave Saint Paul MN 55104 Home: 28544 Lakewood Dr NW Isanti MN 55040 Business E-Mail: cskillingstad@pcamn.org.

**SKILLMAN, BECKY SUE,** lieutenant governor, former state legislator; b. Bedford, Ind., Sept. 26, 1950; d. Jack Delmar and Catherine Louise (Flinn) Foddrill; m. Stephen E. Skillman, 1969; 1 child, Aaron. Dep. recorder Lawrence County, 1971-76, county recorder, 1977-84; clerk Lawrence County crct. ct., 1985—92; mem. Ind. Senate from 44th dist., 1992—2005; lt. gov. State of Ind., Indpls., 2005—. Co-dir. Lawrence County Young Reps., 1973-78; co-chmn. State Young Reps. Conv., 1975, 77; vice chmn. Lawrence County Rep. Ctrl. Com. Named The Outstanding Elected Official of 2000, Ind. Assn. Area Agencies, "Legislator of the Year", Ind. Library Found., 2002; recipient "Champion of Small Bus." award, Small Bus. Coun, 1995, Disting. Pub. Policy award, Ind. Rural Health Policy Assn., 2003. Republican. Office: Office Lt Governor State Capitol Rm 333 Indianapolis IN 46204 Office Phone: 317-232-4545. Office Fax: 317-232-4788.*

**SKILLMAN, ERNEST EDWARD, JR.,** real estate sales and management executive; b. New Orleans, Oct. 3, 1937; s. Ernest Edward and Helen Cecilia (Klein) S BA, La. State U., 1960, postgrad. in law, 1960-61; postgrad., Southeastern La. U., 1973. intelligence officer USN, 1960—. Commd. USN, 1961—99, advanced through grades to admiral, ret., 1999; Engaged in real estate mgmt. Baton Rouge, 1964—; sales, 1969—. Sustaining mem. Republican Nat. Com., 1976—, life mem., 1980—, mem. congressional com.,

1978—; mem. pres.'s club Democratic Nat. Com., 1979—; mem. Rep. Presdl. Task Force; mem. Jackson (La.) Assembly. Mem.: Grad. Realtors Inst., Rep. Senatorial Inner Circle (Washington), Feliciana C. of C., Mil. Order World Wars (life), U.S. Naval Inst. (life), La. Mem. Aviation Mus. Assn. (charter life), Submarine Force Library and Mus. Assn. (life), Res. Officers Assn. (life), Ret. Officers Assn. (life), Navy League U.S. (life), Am. Contract Bridge League (sr. master), Army and Navy Club (pres. comdr. USS Kidd DD661 Navy Club 1997—98, comdr. 1997—98), Amvets (comdr. 1985—87), Foss-Landry Post #2 1985—87), Kiwanis, Am. Legion, Sigma Chi (life). Roman Catholic. Home: 753 Kenilworth Pky Baton Rouge LA 70808-5716 Office: 4150 Perkins Rd Baton Rouge LA 70808-3027 Office Phone: 225-343-1313. E-mail: ernies1937@aol.com.

**SKILLMAN, WILLIAM ALFRED,** consulting engineering executive; b. Lakehurst, N.J., Jan. 22, 1928; s. Wilbur Newton and Greta Alfreda (Ekman) S.; m. Anne Marie Cavender, Sept. 19, 1948; children: Thomas R., Gregory A., Karen L. BS in Engring. Physics, Lehigh U., 1952; MS in Physics, U. Rochester, 1954. Assoc. engr. Westinghouse Electric Corp., Balt., 1954-56, engr., 1956-58, sr. engr., 1958-61, supervisory engr., 1961-64, adv. engr., 1964-73, sr. adv. engr., 1973-85, cons. engr., 1986-93, cons. electronic systems group, 1993—. Author: Radar Calculations Using the TI-59 Programmable Calculator, 1983; author: (with others) Radar Handbook, 2d edit., 1990; patentee in field Served with USN, 1946-48. Fellow IEEE (life, Dennis J. Picard medal for radar technologies and applications 2003); mem. Aerospace and Electronic Sys. Soc. (Pioneer award 1995), Phi Beta Kappa. Republican. Methodist. Avocations: photography, travel, genealogy, programming. Home and Office: 605 Forest View Rd Linthicum Heights MD 21090-2819 E-mail: wskillman@aol.com.

**SKILLRUD, HAROLD CLAYTON,** minister, retired bishop; b. St. Cloud, Minn., June 29, 1928; s. Harold and Amanda Skillrud; m. Lois Dickhart, June 8, 1951; children: David, Janet, John. BA magna cum laude, Gustavus Adolphus Coll., 1954; STM, Luth. Sch. Theology, Chgo., 1969; DD (hon.), Augustana Coll., 1978, Newberry Coll., 1988. Ordained to ministry Evang. Luth. Ch. in Am., 1954. Supply pastor Saron Luth. Ch., Big Lake, Minn., 1950-51; mem. staff 1st Luth. Ch., Rock Island, Ill., 1951-52; intern, organizer new mission Faith Luth. Ch., Syosset, NY, 1952-53; sr. pastor St. John's Luth. Ch., Bloomington, Ill., 1954-79, Luth. Ch. of the Redeemer, Atlanta, 1979-87; bishop Southeastern Synod Evang. Luth. Ch. in Am., Atlanta, 1987-95, regional rep. bd. pensions, 1995—. Del. to various convs. Luth. Ch. in Am., Luth. World Fedn. in Helsinki, 1963, mem. bd. publ., 1976-84, pastor-evangelist Evang. Outreach Emphasis program, 1977-79, mem. exec. bd. Ill. synod, 1977-79, pres. bd. publ., 1980-84, leader stewardship cluster Southeastern synod, 1983, mem. exec. bd. Southeastern synod, 1984-87; mem. exec. coun., Luth. Ch. in Am., 1984-87; mem. task force on new ch. design Commn. on New Luth. Ch., task force on ch. pub. house, 1985; del. constituting conv. Evang. Luth. Ch. in Am., 1987, del. assemblies Evang. Luth. Ch. in Am., 1989, 91, 93, 95; mem. commn. on clergy confidentiality Luth. Coun. in USA, 1987; co-chair USA Luth.- Roman Cath. Dialogue, 1990-97; mem. Task Force on Theol. Edn. Author: LSTC: Decade of Decision, 1969; co-editor Scripture and Tradition, Lutherans and Catholics in Dialogue, 1995; mem. edtl. bd. Partners mag., 1978-80; contbr. articles and sermons to religious jours. Former bd. dirs. Augustana Theol. Sem.; bd. dirs. Augustana Coll., 1969-77, chmn. bd., 1976-77; bd. dirs. Kessler Reformation Collection, Newberry Coll., Luth. World Relief, Augsburg Fortress; chmn. bd. dirs. Luth. Sch. Theology, Chgo., 1962-69; mem. Leadership Atlanta, 1980-81, United Way, Atlanta, 1980-81; mem. Bishop's Commn. on Econ. Justice, 1985-86; pres. bd. dirs. Atlanta Samaritan House, 1986-87. Recipient Alumni award Luth. Sch. Theology, Chgo., 1976, award Leadership Atlanta, 1981, The Rev. John Bachman award, Luth. Theol. Sem., Columbia, S.C., 1996. Mem. Luth. Sch. Theology Alumni Assn. (pres. 1975-77), Conf. of Bishops, Kiwanis (pres. Midtown chpt. 1984-85). Lutheran. Avocations: travel, photography. Home: 104 Hawthorne Lake Dr Bloomington IL 61704 Personal E-mail: hcskillrud@aol.com.

**SKILTON, JOHN SINGLETON,** lawyer; b. Washington, Apr. 13, 1944; s. Robert Henry and Margaret (Neisser) S.; m. Carmen Fisher, Jan. 28, 1967; children: Laura Anne, Susan Elizabeth, Robert John. BA, U. Wis., 1966, JD, 1969. Bar: Wis. Supreme Ct. 1969, U.S. Dist. Ct. (ea. and we. dists.) Wis. 1969, U.S. Ct. Appeals (7th cir.) 1969, U.S. Supreme Ct. 1989, U.S. Ct. Appeals (Fed. cir.) 1991. Law clk. 7th Cir. Ct. Appeals, Milw., 1969-70; assoc. Foley & Lardner, Milw., 1970-77, ptnr. Madison, Wis., 1977-2000; shareholder Heller, Ehrman, White & McAuliffer, Washington, 2000—. Bd. visitors U. Wis. Law Sch., Madison, 1982-90, chmn., 1988-89; chair Wis. Fed. Nominating Commn., 1994; mem. Gov.'s Task Force on Bus. Ct., 1994-95, Govs. Internat. Trade Coun., 2004-; pres. Wis. Law Found., 2000-02 Recipient Lifetime Achievement award, Equal Justice Fund, 2003. Fellow Am. Bar Found., Am. Coll. Trial Lawyers, Internat. Acad. Trial Lawyers; mem. ABA (mem. standing com. on delivery of legal svcs. 1996-2000, chmn. consortium legal svcs. and pub. 2000-02), Am. Law Inst., Am. Acad. Appellate Lawyers, 7th Cir. Bar Assn. (pres. 1985-86, chmn. 7th cir. adv. com. on rules 1994-2000), State Bar Wis. (pres. 1995-96, Pres.'s award of excellence 1989, Sinykin award for publ svc. 1996), Western Dist. Wis. Bar Assn. (pres. 1992-93), Western Dist. Adv. Group (chmn. 1991), Wis. Law Found. (pres. 2000-02), James E. Doyle Am. Inn of Ct. (chmn. 1992-94), Am. Inns of Ct. Found. (trustee 1995-98), U. Wis. Law Alumni Assn. (bd. dirs. 1991-97, pres. 1993-95), Lawyers Com. Civil Rights (co-chair, 2003-2005). Home: 917 Woodward Dr Madison WI 53704 Office: 1 E Main St Madison WI 53703-5118 Office Phone: 608-663-7474.

**SKINNER, BRIAN JOHN,** geologist, educator; b. Wallaroo, South Australia, Dec. 15, 1928; came to U.S., 1958, naturalized, 1963; s. Joshua Henry and Joyce Barbara Lloyd (Prince) S.; m. Helen Catherine Wild, Oct. 9, 1954; children: Adrienne Wild, Stephanie Wild, Thalassa Wild. B.Sc., U. Adelaide, Australia, 1950; A.M., Harvard U., 1952, PhD, 1955; D Engring. (hon.), Colo. Sch. Mines, 1998; DSc (hon.), U. Toronto, 1998. Lectr. U. Adelaide, 1955-58; research geologist U.S. Geol. Survey, 1958-62, chief br. exptl. geochemistry and mineralogy, 1962-66; prof. geology and geophysics, chmn. dept. Yale U., New Haven, 1966-73, Eugene Higgins prof., 1972—. Hugh Exton McKinstry Meml. lectr. Harvard U., 1978; Alex L. du Toit lectr. Combined Socs. South Africa, 1979; Cecil H. and Ida Green lectr. U. B.C., 1983; Thayer Lindsley Meml. lectr. Soc. Econ. Geologists, 1983; Soc. Econ. Geologists Overseas lectr., 1985; Hoffman lectr. Harvard U., 1986, Joubin-James lectr. U. Toronto, 1987; mem. exec. com. divsn. earth scis. NRC, 1966-69; chmn. com. mineral resources and the environ. Nat. Acad. Scis.-NRC, 1973-75; mem. Lunar Sample Analysis Planning Team, 1968-70, Lunar Sci. Rev. Bd., 1971-72, U.S. Nat. Com. for Geochemistry, 1966-67, U.S. Nat. Com. for Geology, 1973-77, 85-93, chmn., 1987-93, chmn. bd. earth scis. NRC, 1987-88, earth scis. and resources, 1989-90; mem. bd. internat. Geol. Correlation Program, UNESCO-IUGS, 1985-89, 90-96, chmn., 1986-89; cons. Office Sci. and Tech. Policy, 1977-80, NSF, 1977-82; dir. Econ. Geology Pub. Co.; chmn. governing bd. Am. Jour. Sci., 1972-2004; pres. Econ. Geology Pub. Co., 1996-2000. Author: Earth Resources, 1969, 77, 86, Man and the Ocean, 1973, Physical Geology, 1974, 77, 87, Rocks and Rock Minerals, 1979, The New Iron Age Ahead, 1987, Resources and World Development, 1987, The Dynamic Earth, 1989, 92, 95, 2000, 03, The Blue Planet, 1995, 99, 2000, Environmental Geology, 1996, Geology Today, 1999, Oxford Companion to the Earth, 2000; editor: Econ. Geology, 1969-96, Oxford Univ. Press Monographs in Geological Sciences, 1979—, Internat. Geology Rev., 1995—2003; editl. bd. Am. Scientist, 1974-90, chmn., 1987-90. Trustee Hopkins Grammar Sch., 1978-83. Recipient Disting. Contbns. award, Assn. Earth Sci. Editors, 1979, medal, Geol. Assn. Can., 1998, Futer's medal, Inst. of Mining and Metallurgy, London, 2002; fellow, Guggenheim fellow 1970. Fellow Geol. Soc. Am. (councillor 1976-78, chmn. spl. publs. com. 1980-81, chmn. com. on cross. 1983, pres. 1985); mem. Geochem. Soc. (pres. 1972-73), Conn. Acad. Sci. and Engring. (dir. chmn. 1978-80, coun. 1982-87), Soc. Econ. Geologists (pres. 1995, Silver medal 1981, Marsden medal 2003, Penrose medal 2005). Home: PO Box 894 Woodbury CT 06798-0894 Office Phone: 203-432-3175. Personal E-mail: brian.skinner@yale.edu.

**SKINNER, CHRISTOPHER G.,** protective services official, farmer; b. Binghamton, NY, Aug. 15, 1971; s. Gail Ray and Sharyn Skinner; m. Dee Ann Facer; children: Kyle Christopher, Erin Emily. B in Agrl. Engring., SUNY, Cobleskill, 1993. Product support mgr. Case Corp., Racine, Wis., 1995—2000; salesman New Holland Cortland, NY, 2000; trooper NY State Police, Kirkwood, 2000—. Home: 134 Old State Rd Binghamton NY 13901 Office: New York State Police 84 Crescent Dr Kirkwood NY 13795 Office Phone: 607-775-1241. Office Fax: 607-775-2275. Business E-mail: cskinner@troopers.state.ny.us.

**SKINNER, DANIEL THOMAS,** language educator; b. Boston, May 1, 1916; s. Thomas Henson and Esther Hannetta (Jennings) Skinner; m. Vyna May Wingood, Oct. 15, 1944 (dec. Jan. 1995); children: David Edward, John Arnold. AB magna cum laude, Harvard U., 1938, PhD in Romance Lang., 1953; MA in Romance Lang., Boston Coll., 1939. Substitute instr. in French Va. State Coll., Ettrick, 1939—40; instr. in French and Spanish Dillard U., New Orleans, 1940—42; from asst. prof. to prof. French and Latin Morgan State Coll., Balt., 1946—81. Vis. prof. Tex. So. U., Houston, 1953—54, Houston, 1956, Towson State Coll., Balt., 1964; part-time prof. Sojourner-Douglass Coll., Balt., 1981—85, Coppin State Coll., Balt., 1985—90; mem. adv. bd. Directory of Am. Scholars, N.Y.C., 1970—80. Author: U.S. Teacher-Training Program: for France, 1959, Victor Hugo and L. Frechette, 1972, Ustaz Aswad (Black Professor), 1996, Ustaz Aswad No. II (Black Professor), 2005. Pres. PTA, Balt., 1957. Named Rosenwald fellow, Rosenwald Found., Chgo., 1947—48, Fulbright prof. in France, Fulbright Found., Washington, 1956—57; recipient Nat. award, Urban League, Boston, 1949, congratulatory dinner in his honor, French Embassy, Washington, 2003. Mem.: Frisby Hist. Soc. (fin. sec. 2001—02), Henson Family Soc., Phi Beta Kappa. Democrat. Roman Catholic. Avocations: movies, pinochle, sports, foreign travel.

**SKINNER, EULALIA ARDITH,** retired secondary school educator; b. Sterling, Colo., Nov. 28, 1930; d. Ronald R. and Gertrude O. (Hoaglund) Skinner. BA in Phys. Edn., We. State Coll., Gunnison, Colo., 1953. Cert. tchr. Colo. Tchr. Lake Mills (Iowa) Pub. Schs., 1953—54, Pub. Sch. Dist. RE-1, Cortez, Colo., 1954—90; ret., 1990. Named to Hall of Fame, Colo. Volleyball Ofls. Assn., 2001, Class of 2002 Hall of Fame, Colo. HS Activities Assn., 2002; recipient Trailblazer award, Sports Women Colo., 2001. Methodist. Avocations: auto restoration, travel, genealogy, golf, gardening. Home: 725 E 4th St Cortez CO 81321

**SKINNER, G(EORGE) WILLIAM,** anthropologist, educator; b. Oakland, Calif., Feb. 14, 1925; s. John James and Eunice (Engle) S.; m. Carol Bagger, Mar. 25, 1951 (div. Jan. 1970); children: Geoffrey Crane, James Lauriston, Mark Williamson, Jeremy Burr; m. Susan Mann, Apr. 26, 1980; 1 dau., Alison Jane. Student, Deep Springs Coll., Calif., 1942-43; BA with distinction in Far Eastern Studies, Cornell U., Ithaca, N.Y., 1947, PhD in Cultural Anthropology, 1954; LLD (hon.), U. Hong Kong, 2001. Field dir. Cornell U. S.E. Asia program, also Cornell Research Center, Bangkok, 1951-55; rsch. assoc. in Indonesia, 1956-58; assoc. prof., then prof. anthropology Cornell U., Ithaca, NY, 1960-65; asst. prof. sociology Columbia, 1958-60; sr. specialist in residence East-West Ctr. Honolulu, 1965-66; prof. anthropology Stanford, 1966-89; Barbara Kimball Browning prof. humanities and scis., 1987-89; prof. anthropology U. Calif., Davis, 1990—. Vis. prof. U. Pa., 1977, Duke U., 1978, Keio U., Tokyo, 1985, 1988, U. Calif., San Diego, 1986, Hong Kong U., 2002; field rsch. China, 1949-50, 77, S.E. Asia, 1950-51, Thailand, 1951-53, 54-55, Java and Borneo, 1956-58, Japan, 1985, 88, 95; joint com. on contemporary China Social Sci. Research Coun.-Am. Acad. Learned Socs., 1961-65, 80-81, internat. com. on Chinese studies, 1963-64, mem. joint com. on Chinese studies, 1981-83; mem. subcom. rsch. Chinese Soc. Social Sci. Rsch. Coun., 1961-70, chmn., 1963-70; dir. program on East Asian Local Systems, 1969-71; dir. Chinese Soc. Bibliography Project, 1964-73; assoc. dir. Cornell China Program, 1961-63; dir. London-Cornell Project Social Rsch., 1962-65; mem. com. on scholarly communication with People's Republic of China, Nat. Acad. Scis., 1966-70, social scis. and humanities panel, 1982-83; adv. com. Ctr. for Chinese Rsch. Materials, Assn. Rsch. Libraries, 1967-70; bd. dirs. Nat. Ctr. for Geog. Info. and Analysis, 1989-92; policy and planning com. China in Time and Space, 1993-96; mem. mgmt. com. China Hist. GIS, 2000—. Author: Chinese Society in Thailand, 1957, Leadership and Power in the Chinese Community of Thailand, 1958; also articles; Editor: The Social Sciences and Thailand, 1956, Local, Ethnic and National Loyalties in Village Indonesia, 1959, Modern Chinese Society: An Analytical Bibliography, 3 vols, 1973, (with Mark Elvin) The Chinese City Between Two Worlds, 1974, (with A. Thomas Kirsch) Change and Persistence in Thai Society, 1975, The City in Late Imperial China, 1977, The Study of Chinese Society, 1979. Served to ensign USNR, 1943-46. Fellow Center for Advanced Study in Behavioral Scis., 1969-70, Guggenheim fellow, 1969, NIMH spl. fellow, 1970 Mem. NAS, AAAS, Am. Anthrop. Assn., Am. Sociol. Assn., Assn. Asian Studies (bd. dirs. 1962-65, chmn. nominating com. 1967-68, pres. 1983-84), Soc. for Cultural Anthropology, Internat. Union for Sci. Study of Population, Social Sci. History Assn., Am. Ethnol. Soc., Population Assn. Am., Siam Soc., Soc. Qing Studies, Soc. Econ. Anthropology, Phi Beta Kappa, Sigma Xi. Office: U Calif Dept Anthropology 1 Shields Ave Davis CA 95616-5270 Business E-mail: gwskinner@ucdavis.edu.

**SKINNER, HALCYON E.,** lawyer; b. Yonkers, NY, 1946; BA, Wesleyan U., 1968; JD, Duke U., 1973. Bar: Fla. 1973. Ptnr. Mahoney, Adams & Criser (merged with McGuireWoods in 1998), Jacksonville, Fla., McGuire Woods LLP, Jacksonville, Fla., 1998—, mng. ptnr. Jacksonville office, 2000—. Served U.S. Army. Mem.: ABA (bus. law sect.), Jacksonville Bar Assn., Fla. Bar (bus. law sect.). Office: McGuireWoods LLP Bank of Am Tower Ste 3300 50 N Laura St Jacksonville FL 32202-3661 Office Phone: 904-798-2626. Office Fax: 904-360-6324. Business E-mail: hskinner@mcguirewoods.com.

**SKINNER, JAMES A. (JAMES A. SKINNER),** food products executive; b. Davenport, IA; m. Kathleen Skinner; 1 child. Grad. Roosevelt U. Restaurant mgr. trainee to numerous positions within the US Co. McDonald's Corp., 1971—, US zone v.p., 1987—92; sr. v.p., relationship ptnr., 1992—95; exec. v.p., internat. relationship ptnr. McDonald's Ctrl. Europe, Middle East, Africa, India, 1995—97; pres. McDonald's Europe, 1997—2001; pres., COO McDonald's Europe/Asia/Pacific and Middle East, 2001—02, McDonald's Restaurant Group, 2002—03; vice chmn. McDonald's Corp., 2003—04, CEO, 2004—. Adv. dir. bd. dirs. (twice) McDonald's Corp.; bd. dirs. Walgreen Co., 2005—. Bd. mem. Ronald McDonald House Charities. Office: McDonald's Corp McDonald's Plz 2111 McDonalds Dr Oak Brook IL 60523*

**SKINNER, JAMES E.,** corporate financial executive; Grad., Tex. Tech U. CPA. Ptnr. Ernst & Young, 1987—91; chief acctg. officer CompUSA, Dallas, 1991—94, CFO, exec. v.p., treas., 1994—2000; sr. v.p., CFO CapRock Comms. Corp., Dallas, 2000—01; CFO, sr. v.p. Neiman Marcus Group, 2001—. Office: Neiman Marcus Group 1618 Main St Dallas TX 75201

**SKINNER, JAMES LAURISTON,** chemist, educator; b. Ithaca, NY, Aug. 17, 1953; s. G. William and Carol (Bagger) S.; m. Wendy Moore, May 31, 1986; children: Colin Andrew, Duncan Geoffrey. AB, U. Calif., Santa Cruz, 1975; PhD, Harvard U., 1979. Rsch. assoc. Stanford U., Calif., 1980-81; from asst. prof. to prof. chemistry Columbia U., NYC, 1981-90; Joseph O. Hirschfelder prof. chemistry, dir. Theol. Chemistry Inst. U. Wis., Madison, 1990—. Vis. scientist Inst. Theol. Physics U. Calif., Santa Barbara, 1987; vis. prof. physics U. Jos. Fourier, Grenoble, France, 1987, U. Bordeaux, France, 1995. Contbr. articles to profl. jours. Recipient Fresenius award Phi Lambda Upsilon, 1989, Camille and Henry Dreyfus Tchr.-Scholar award, 1984, NSF Presdl. Young Investigator award, 1984, Humboldt Sr. Scientist award, 1993; NSF grad fellow, 1975, NSF postdoctoral fellow, 1980, Alfred P. Sloan Found. fellow, 1984, Guggenheim fellow, 1993. Fellow: AAAS, Am. Acad. Arts & Sciences, Am. Phys. Soc. Achievements include fundamental research in condensed phase theoretical chemistry. Office: U Wis Dept Chemistry Theoretical Chem Inst 1101 University Ave Madison WI 53706-1322

**SKINNER, JAUNETH,** art educator, graphic artist; b. Waco, Tex., Mar. 19, 1958; d. Owen George and Patricia Ann Skinner; 1 child, Miriam Renee Kessler. AS in Comml. Art Tech., Ind. U., Ft. Wayne, 1990, BFA, 1991; MFA, Bowling Green State U., 1993. Cert. Italian lang. and culture tchr. Università per Stranieri, Perugia, Italy, 2004. Asst. prof. visual arts, dept. of visual arts Bemidji State U., Minn., 1994—99, curator Lillian M. Kleven print collection dept. visual arts, 1994—, assoc. prof. visual arts, dept. of visual arts, 1999—2004, prof. visual arts, dept. of visual arts, 2004—, chair dept. of visual arts, 2005—06. Creative dir. Endion Studio, Bemidji, Minn., 1986—; assoc. editor, sr. designer Mid Am. Print Coun. Jour., Chgo., 1994—97; chair exhbn. com. Bemidji Cmty. Arts Ctr., Minn., 1994—97; creative dir., master printer The Quiet Crow Press, Bemidji, Minn., 2000—. Print portfolio, Catch Phrase, print with Gendron Jensen, Umingmaq, broadside print portfolio, Italia, Lake Songs, print portfolio, Women's Self Image, Woman, Sheep, Water, one-woman shows include Impressions: The Graphic Art of Jauneth Skinner, Away: Sabbatical Exhibition, Landscape and Memory, Imprimere: Imprinted on Memory, The Extraordinary in the Prosaic (Works on Paper), All Labels Female, Naked Singularity, internat. juried exhbn., Lessedra World Art Print Annual, Sofia, Bulgaria, 4th Annual Mini Print International Exhibition 2000, 1st Biennial International Miniature Print Exhibition, The World's Women On-Line!, Acm Siggraph, Acm Siggraph, Horizon Club Print, Out of the Woods, exhibited in group shows at The Solarplate Revolution, Women's Work, Traditional and Contemporary: 100 Years of Etchings and Woodblock Prints, APA Memorial Print Project, print published with John Hitchcock, Isolation, exhibited in group shows at Women's Self Image, Minnesota Journal Project 2000, The Foot in the Door Show, Border to Border, Ada: Women and Information Technology, Contemporary Prints - National Invitational, print portfolio, Women's Work, exhibited in group shows at Hare of the Dog Press: Printed Works, Ohio Women's Caucus for Art Exhibition, Chicago Printmakers Collaborative: Paradise Lost, Holograms and Computer Prints, From Greenware to Software, nat. juried exhbn., The Little Prints Exhibit, The 21st National Print Exhibition, 23rd National Small Works Exhibition, Vital Signs:Drawing as Inquiry, Counterpoint 2000: 32nd Annual National Printmaking, Drawing, and Photography Exhibition, Outside Impressions: A Showcase of Contemporary Printmaking, Annual National Small Works Competition, Innovations in Printmaking, Paperworks '99, Community Visual Art Association, Jackson Hole, Wyoming, 12th Annual Parkside National Small Print Exhibition, Hand-Pulled Prints IV, National Works on Paper, Printwork '95, Americanism: Breaking the Mold, Positive/Negative IV, Regional '93, 16th Annual Proscenium 1992, Concepts and Dimensions, Issues of Color and Gender, Reverent/Irreverent, Women's Caucus for Art Third Annual Juried Exhibit, Digital Images 1990, 54th Annual Tri Kappa Regional Artists Exhibition, Indiana: Works on Paper, print portfolio, Memorial, nat. juried exhbm/, Hunterdon Art Center 32nd National Print Exhibition, North Arlington Library Print Exhibition, The Payne Gallery Print Exhibition, internat. juried exhbn., The World's Women On-Line!, international juried exhibition, print with Gendron Jensen, Mandan. Recipient Best of Drawing, Beck Ctr., 1992, First and Second Pl., Preble County Art Assn., 1991, Merit Award, Drawing, Wassenburg Art Ctr., 1991, Third Pl. and Merit Award, Studio Mag. Computer Art Competition, 1989, Merit Award, Third Ann. Liquitex Art Awards Program, 1989, Artist in Residence, Scuola Internazionale di Grafica, Venice, Italy, 2005, Vis. Artist, Kelliher Pub. Sch. and Perpich Ctr., Mpls., MN, 2003, Sch. of Art, U. of SD, Vermilion, SD, 2002, 2001, ND State Coll., Wahpeton, ND, 2002, Artist in Residence, Santa Reparata Stamperia d'Arte Grafica, Florence, Italy, 2001, 2000, Am. U., Corciano, Italy, 2001, Voyageurs Nat. Pk., Internat. Falls, MN, 1999, Vis. Artist, Valley City State U., Valley City, ND, 1997, Ctrl. Lakes Coll., Brainerd, MN, 1997, Disting. Artist Award, McKnight Found. and Region 2 Arts Coun., 1996, Manhattan Arts Internat. Merit Award, 1995, Someone Spl. Vol., United Way, 1995, Charles F. Wassenburg Award, Drawing, Wassenburg Art Ctr., 1993, Best of Show Purchase Award, East Tenn. State U., 1993; grantee McKnight Found. Grant with Dust & Fire: Women's Stories, Region 2 Arts Coun., 1999, Individual Artist Grant with poet CarolAnn Russell, McKnight Found. and Region 2 Arts Coun., 1999, McKnight Found. Grant with Loonfeather Press, 1997, Q-7 Ventures Grant, Minn. State Colleges and Universities, 1996, 1995; scholar Paralyzed Veterans of Am., Paralyzed Veterans of Am., 1989, Fine Arts Scholarship, Dept. of Fine Art, Ind. U., 1986, 1987, 1988, 1989, 1990, 1991, Grad. Tchg. Assoc., Sch. of Art, Bowling Green State U., 1992, Fellowship in Graphic Arts, 1992, 1993, Ely Lilly Scholarship, Ely Lilly Found., 1991. Mem.: Coll. Art Assn., No. Printmakers Alliance, Am. Print Alliance, MidAmerica Print Coun., So. Graphics Print Coun. Achievements include Art work in Cradle Oak Press Collection, Bradley University, Peoria, Illinois; Art work in Scuola Internazionale di Grafica collection, Venice, Italy; Art work in Rossi Library Archives collection, American Academy in Rome, Rome, Italy; Art work in St. Cloud State University collection, St. Cloud, Minnesota; Art work in University Print Library collection, Università di Palermo, Palermo, Italy; Art work in University of Montana collection, Bozman, Montana; Art work in the Lillie M. Kleven Print Collection, Bemidji State University, Bemidji, Minnesota; Art work in University Print Society Collection, Iowa State University, Ames, Iowa; Art work in University of Nebraska, Omaha, Nebraska; Art work in Fogg Art Museum collection, Harvard, Cambridge, Massachusetts; Art work in Harwood Museum of Art collection, University of New Mexico, Santa Fe, New Mexico; Art work in Jerome Library Archives collection, Bowling Green State University, Bowling Green, Ohio; Art work in Kennaháskóli Íslands University Print Collection, Stakkahlíð, Reykjavík, Iceland; Art work in Arizona State University Print Collection, Tempe, Arizona; Art work in King Jigme Singhe Wangchuk of Bhutan Palace Art Collection, Bhutan; Art work in Anoka Ramsey Foundation collection, Anoka Ramsey Community College, Anoka, Minnesota; Art work in School of Art Print Collection, Bowling Green State University, Bowling Green, Ohio. Avocations: travel, reading, gardening. Office: Bemidji State Univ Dept Visual Arts Box 36 1500 Birchmont Dr NE Bemidji MN 56601-2699 Office Phone: 218-755-3741. Office Fax: 218-755-4406. Business E-mail: jskinner@bemidjistate.edu.

**SKINNER, JONATHAN SNOWDEN,** economics educator; b. Boston, Aug. 29, 1955; s. Walter Jay and Sylvia (H.) S.; m. Martha Amy McLafferty, Oct. 17, 1987; children: Owen, Lucy. BA, U. Rochester, 1977; MA, UCLA, 1978, PhD, 1983. Asst. to assoc. prof. U. Va., Charlottesville, 1981-93, prof., 1993—. Cons. The World Bank, Washington, 1984-91; vis. asst. prof. U. Wash., Seattle, 1987; vis. assoc. prof. Stanford (Calif.) U., 1989, Harvard U., Cambridge, Mass., 1992-93. Mem. Sam's Club. Office: Univ Va Dept Econs 114 Rouss Hall Charlottesville VA 22901

**SKINNER, KNUTE RUMSEY,** poet; b. St. Louis, Apr. 25, 1929; s. George Rumsey and Lidi (Skjoldrg) S.; m. Jeanne Pratt; 1953; divorced 1954; 1 child, Frank; m. Linda Kuhn, 1961 (div. 1977); children: Dunstan, Morgan; m. Edna Keil, 1978. Student, Culver-Stockton Coll., 1947-49; BA, U. No. Colo., 1951; MA, Middlebury Coll., 1954; PhD, U. Iowa, 1958. Instr. English U. Iowa, Iowa City, 1955-56, 57-58, 60-61; asst. prof. English Okla. Coll. for Women, 1961-62; lectr. creative writing Western Wash. U., Bellingham, 1962-71, asso. prof. English, 1971-73, prof. English, 1973-97; pres. Signpost Press Inc., nonprofit corp., 1983-95. Author: Stranger with a Watch, 1965, A Close Sky Over Killaspuglonane, 1968, 75, In Dinosaur Country, 1969, The Sorcerers: A Laotian Tale, 1972, Hearing of the Hard Times, 1981, The Flame Room, 1983, Selected Poems, 1985, Learning to Spell "Zucchini," 1988, The Bears and Other Poems, 1991, What Trudy Knows and Other Poems, 1994, The Cold Irish Earth: New and Selected Poems of Ireland, 1965-1995, 1996, An Afternoon Quiet and Other Poems, 1998, Greatest Hits, 1964-2000, 2001, Stretches, 2002, The Other Shoe, 2005; editor: Bellingham Rev., 1977-83, 93-95; contbr. poetry, short stories to anthologies, textbooks, periodicals. Nat. Endowment for the Arts fellow, 1975 Mem. Am. Conf. Irish Studies, Wash. Poets Assn. E-mail: knuteskinner@eircom.net.

**SKINNER, MARY JACOBS,** lawyer; b. 1957; m. Sam Skinner, Aug. 17, 1989; stepchildren: Thomas, Steven, Jane. BA cum laude, Harvard U., 1978; JD, Northwestern U., 1981. Bar: Ill. 1981, D.C. 1990, U.S. Supreme Ct. 1990. With Sidley Austin Brown & Wood, Chgo., 1981—, ptnr., 1989—; counsel to spkr. Ill. Ho. of Reps., Springfield, Ill., 1983—85. Intern White House, 1979. Former trustee RAdcliffe Coll.; participant leadership coun. Greater Chgo.

Fellowship Program, 1984. Named One of Forty under 40 Most Outstanding Leaders in Chco., Crain's Chgo. Bus. Mem. Harvard Alumni Assn. (bd. dirs.), Radcliffe Coll. Alumni Assn. (past pres.). Office: Sidley Austin Brown and Wood Bank One Plz 10 S Dearborn St Chicago IL 60603

**SKINNER, MICHAEL DAVID,** lawyer, lobbyist, consultant; b. Shreveport, LA, Jan. 5, 1950; s. Roger Gilman and Jerry Ann (Sneed) S.; m. Janet Louise Horaist, Jan. 7, 1978. JD, La. State U., 1976. Bar: La. 1977, U.S. Dist. Ct. (we. dist.) La. 1978, U.S. Ct. Appeals (5th and 11th cirs.) 1978, U.S. Dist. Ct. (mid. dist.) La. 1982, U.S. Supreme Ct. 1982, U.S. Dist. Ct. (so. dist.) Tex. 1983. Pvt. practice, Lafayette, La., 1976-84; asst. dist. atty. Lafayette Parish, 1983—84; ptnr. Guilliot, Skinner & Everett, 1984-86; asst. parish atty. Lafayette Parish, 1988—93; ptnr. Goode, Skinner & Hawkland, 1986-93; U.S. atty. West Dist. La., 1993-2000; atty. Onebane Law Firm, Lafayette, La., 2001—. Chmn. La. Democratic Party, 2003—05. Mem. La. State Bar Assn. (mem. ho. of dels.). Democrat. Office: 1200 Camellia Blvd Ste 300 Lafayette LA 70508 Office Phone: 337-237-2660.

**SKINNER, PATRICIA MORAG,** state legislator; b. Glasgow, Scotland, Dec. 3, 1932; d. John Stuart and Frances Charlotte (Swann) Robertson; m. Robert A. Skinner, Dec. 28, 1957; children: Robin Ann, Pamela. BA, NYU, 1953. Mdse. trainee Lord & Taylor, N.Y.C.; adminstrv. asst. Atlantic Products, N.Y.C.; newspaper corr. Salem Observer, NH, 1964-84; mem. N.H. Ho. of Reps., 1972-94, chmn. labor, human resources, and rehab. com., 1975-86, mem. House edn. com., 1987, chmn., 1989-94, exec. com. Nat. Conf. State Legislatures, 1987-90; chmn. N.H. Adv. Coun. Unemployment Compensation, 1984 94. Mem. State Libr. Adv. Coun., 2001. Bd. dirs. Castle Jr. Coll., 1975, chmn. bd., 1988-96; v.p. bd. Swift Water coun. Girl Scouts U.S., v.p., 1987-92; N.H. Voc-Tech. Coll., Nashua, 1978-83; trustee Nesmith Libr., Windham, N.H., 1982—, chmn. bd. trustees, 1994-99; pres. N.H. Fedn. Rep. Women's Clubs, parliamentarian, legis. chmn., 1984-86, 94-96. Mem. Windham Woman's Club (pres. 1981-83), Order Ea. Star. Christian Scientist.

**SKINNER, PEGGY JUNE,** psychology professor, consultant; b. Portales, N.Mex., Nov. 29, 1950; d. Arthur F. and Betty C. (Rogers) Rowland; m. Don Stroud, May 27, 1984 (dec. Oct. 2, 1991); children: Shannon, Derek; m. William Fietz, Apr. 17, 1993. BS, Ea. N.Mex. U., 1973, MA, 1974; PhD, Tex. Tech U., 1983. La. profl. counselor; registered sex offender therapist. Prof., counselor Ea. N.Mex. U., Portales, 1973-78; prof. psychology, dept. chair South Plains Coll., Levelland, Tex., 1978—, dept. chair for behavioral sci. Cons. Levelland Devel. Ctr., 1983—; cons. developmentalist Dept. Protective and Regulatory Svcs., Levelland, 1987—; therapist West Tex. Children's Assessment Ctr., Terry County Juvenile Probation, Hockley County Adult Probation; textbook supplement author McGraw-Hill, Harper Collins. Bd. dirs. Women's Protective Svcs., Lubbock, Tex., 1984—; vol. Family Outreach, Levelland, 1988—. Named Outstanding Tchr., Phi Theta Kappa, 1986, 87, 89. Mem. APA, Tex. Counseling Assn., Soc. for Rsch. in Child and Human Devel., Tex. Conf. on Family Rels., South Plains Perinatal Assn. (bd. dirs., pres. 1978—). Democrat. Avocation: reading. Home: 2042 Longhorn Dr Levelland TX 79336-6702 Office: Behavioral Sci Dept South Plains Coll Levelland TX 79336 Office Phone: 806-894-9611. Business E-mail: pskinner@southplainscollege.edu.

**SKINNER, PETER GRAEME,** retired lawyer; b. London, Ont., Can., July 27, 1944; naturalized, U.S., 1952; s. George Woodley and Marjorie Grace S. AB, Princeton U., 1966; JD, MBA, Columbia U., 1970. Bar: NY 1971. Assoc. Patterson, Belknap, Webb & Tyler, N.Y.C., 1970-77, ptnr., 1977-85; gen. counsel, sec. Dow Jones & Co., N.Y.C., 1985—2004, v.p., 1985—89, v.p., 1989—98, exec. v.p. 1998—2004; ret. 2004. Mem.: ABA, Assn. Bar City N.Y., N.Y. State Bar Assn. Office: Dow Jones & Co Inc 200 Liberty St Fl 12 New York NY 10281-1003 Office Phone: 212-416-3030. E-mail: peter.skinner@dowjones.com.

**SKINNER, RICHARD L.,** federal agency administrator; BS, Fairmount State U.; MPA, George Washington U. Asst. inspector gen. audits Fed. Emergency Mgmt. Agency Dept. Homeland Security, Washington, 1991—96, dep. inspector gen., 1996, acting inspector gen., 2002—03; dep. inspector gen. US Dept. Homeland Security, Washington, 2003—05, acting inspector gen., 2004—05, inspector gen., 2005—. Office: Dept Homeland Security Naval Security Station Nebraska and Massachusetts Avenues NW Washington DC 20528 Office Phone: 202-254-4100. Office Fax: 202-254-4285. E-mail: rick.skinner@dhs.gov.

**SKINNER, ROBERT C., JR.,** retail executive; BA in Political Sci., Middlebury Coll., 1976; grad., Harvard Bus. Sch. Advanced Mgmt. Program, 1992. Pres. Oxford Shirt Group, 1987—99; v.p. Oxford Industries, 1999—2000; pres. Kellwood Menswear, 2000—02; from v.p. to pres., COO Kellwood Co., St. Louis, 2002—03, pres., 2003—, COO, 2003—05, CEO, 2005—, chmn., 2006—. Bd. govs. Young Mens Assn. Office: Kellwood Co 600 Kellwood Pkwy Saint Louis MO 63178 Business E-mail: Bob_Skinner@kellwood.com.*

**SKINNER, ROBERT EARLE,** librarian, writer; b. Alexandria, Va., June 25, 1948; s. Earl Woodrow and Pearle Labar (Capper) S.; m. Linda Sue Long, June 12, 1970 (div. 1976); children: Christopher William, Kelly Sue; m. Patricia Ann Friedmann, Mar. 17, 1979 (div. 1996); children: Esme F., Werner H.; m. Bettye Jean Harrison, June 20, 2001. BA in History, Old Dominion U., 1970; MLS, Ind. U., 1977; postgrad. student, U. New Orleans, 1991-93. Search analyst Strughold Aeromed. Libr., Brooks AFB, Tex., 1977-79; from reference libr. to head med. edn. libr. La. State U. Med. Ctr., New Orleans, 1979-85; spl. cons. Robert L. Siegel & Assocs., New Orleans, 1985-87; univ. libn. Xavier U., New Orleans, 1987 ; mng. editor Xavier Rev. Press, 1988 . Vis. lectr. in Am. studies U.S. Air Force Acad., 2002; spkr. Symposium on African-Am. Detective Fiction, Bucknell U., 2005. Author: The Hard-Boiled Explicator, 1985, The New Hard-Boiled Dicks, 1987, rev. edit., 1995, Two Guns From Harlem, 1989, (with Michel J. Fabre) Chester Himes: An Annotated Primary and Secondary Bibliography, 1992, Fiction in Ellipsis, 1992, (with Thomas Bonner, Jr.) Above Ground, 1993, Immortelles, 1995, (with Michel J. Fabre) Plan B, 1993, Conversations with Chester Himes, 1995, Fiction in Hard Boiled, 1994, Fiction in Crime Yellow, 1994, Skin Deep, Blood Red, 1997, Cat-Eyed Trouble, 1998, Daddy's Gone-A-Hunting, 1999, Blood to Drink, 2000, Pale Shadow, 2001, The Righteous Cut, 2002, guest editor La. Lit., 1998, contbg. guest editor Plots With Guns, 2002-03, contr., 2005; contbr. articles to profl. jours. With USCG, 1970-74. Grantee Mellon Found., 1987-95, La. Divsn. of the Arts, 1993, 95, NEH, 1991—. Mem. ALA. Avocations: hiking, reading, book collecting, antique radios. Home: PO Box 55686 Metairie LA 70055 Office: Xavier U 1 Drexel Dr New Orleans LA 71245-1098 Business E-mail: rskinner@xula.edu.

**SKINNER, ROBERT EARLE, JR.,** civil engineer, engineering executive; b. Washington, Aug. 10, 1946; s. Robert Earle and Dorothy Inez (Ballance) S.; m. Dianne Lynette Sands; children: Martha, Jeffrey. BSCE, U. Va., 1969; MS in Civil Engring., MIT, 1971. Registered profl. engr., Va. Sr. assoc. PRC Voorhees, McLean, Va., 1971-79, v.p., 1979-83; sr. staff officer Transp. Rsch. Bd., Washington, 1983-86, dir. studies and info. svc., 1986-94, exec. dir., 1994—. Exec. com. Hwy. Innovative Tech. Evaluation Ctr., Washington, 1994—; adv. com. Ctr. for Transp. and the Environment, Raleigh, N.C., 1995—; bd. dirs. Innovation Pavement Rsch. Found., Washington, 1999-2002; mem. adv. bd. Ctr. for Urban Transp. Rsch., U. South Fla., 2003—; mem. vis. com. engirng. sys. divsn. MIT, 2004—. Contbr. articles to profl. jours.; mem. editorial bd. Jour. Trans. and Stats., 1997. Mem. adv. coun. U. Va., 1995—; mem. vis. com. on Engring. Sys. Ctr., MIT, 2003—. With U.S. Army N.G., 1970-76. Mem.: ASCE. Methodist. Avocations: woodworking, tennis. Office: Transportation Research Bd of the Nat Acads 500 5th St NW Washington DC 20001-

**SKINNER, THOMAS,** broadcast executive; b. Poughkeepsie, N.Y., Aug. 17, 1934; s. Clarence F. and Frances D. S.; m. Elizabeth Burroughs, June 22, 1957; children: Kristin Jon, Karin Anne, Erik Lloyd. BS, SUNY, Fredonia, 1956; MA, U. Mich., 1957, PhD, 1962. Instr. speech U. Mich., 1960; assoc. prof., exec. producer dept. broadcasting San Diego State U., 1961-66; asst. mgr. Sta. WITF-TV, Hershey, Pa., 1966-70; v.p. Sta. WQED-TV, Pitts., 1970-72; exec. v.p., COO QED Communications Inc. (WQED-TV, WQED-FM, Pittsburgh mag., WQEX-TV), 1972-93; founder, pres., exec. prodr. Windrush Assocs., 1993—; v.p. Programming Resolution Prodns., Burlington, Vt., 1996—; mng. dir. Inland Seas Edn. Assn., 2000—; exec. prodr. Free to Choose Media, 2004—. Exec. prodr.: spls. and series including (for PBS) Nat. Geog. spls. Planet Earth, The Infinite Voyage, Conserving America, (for TBS) Pirate Tales, (for A&E) Floating Palaces, California and the Dream Seekers, The Story of Money, (for Discovery) Battleship, The Secret World of Air Freight, The Life and Ideas of Milton Friedman (for PBS). Recipient award as exec. prodr. DuPont Columbia, 1979, Oscar award as dir. Acad. Motion Picture Arts and Scis., 1967, Emmy award as exec. prodr. Nat. Acad. TV Arts and Scis., 1979, 83-84, 86-87, Peabody award as exec. prodr., 1980, 86. Episcopalian. E-mail: ski361@aol.com.

**SKINNER, THOMAS V.,** federal agency administrator; BA, Lawrence U.; JD, Northwestern U., 1987. Ptnr. Winston & Strawn, Chgo., 1991—99; dir. Ill. EPA, 1999—2001; regional adminstr. Region 5 U.S. EPA, Chgo., 2001—04, acting asst. adminstr. enforcement & compliance assurance Washington, 2004—. Office: EPA Ariel Rios Fed Bldg 1200 Pennsylvania Ave NW Rm 3204 Washington DC 20460

**SKINSTAD, ANNE HELENE,** psychologist, researcher; b. Bergen, Hordaland, Norway, July 8, 1949; d. Alfhild (Hektoen) and Leif Sigurd Skinstad; 1 child, Siri Ødegaard. D in Psychology, U.of Bergen, Norway, 1977; PhD, U.of Bergen, 2001. Diplomate in Clin. Psychology Coll. Problems of Drug Dependence, 1985. Staff psychologist Hjellestad Clinic and Dr. Martens Clinic, Bergen, Norway, Hordaland, Norway, 1977—79; leading psychologist Blå-Kors Social Ctr., Bergen, Norway, 1979—83; facultly mem. U. Iowa, Iowa City, 1990—2001, asst. prof. Coll. Pub. Health, 2001—. Rsch. fellow The U. of Bergen, Norway, 1983—87; leading psychologist treatment ctr. substance abusing women Hjellestad Clinic, Bergen, Norway, 1987—90; program dir. Prairielands Addiction Tech. Transfer Ctr., Iowa City, 1995—2005. Contbr. articles to profl. jours. Recipient numerous grants, Norway, U.S. Mem.: APA, Am. Public Health Assn., Rsch. Soc. Alcoholism, European Roschach Assn. (founding mem. 1989), Nat. ATTC (chmn. liaison com., mem. curriculum com.), Norwegian Psychol. Assn. Avocations: owning Australian sheppards, piano. Office: U Iowa Coll Pub Health E239GH Iowa City IA 52242 Business E-Mail: anne-skinstad@uiowa.edu.

**SKIRDE, EDWARD GEORGE,** academic administrator, consultant; s. Herbert William and Anna Irene Skirde; m. Priscilla Ann Christman, Dec. 20, 1969; children: Deborah Ann Gleeson, Kevin Edward. BA, St. John's U., 1963—67; MA, Pa. State U., 1967—69, PhD, 1969—72. Instr. of speech Pa. State U., U. Pk., 1969—72; asst. dean and chmn., divsn. of interdisplinary studies St. John's U., Jamaica, NY, 1972—78, dir. of alumni rels., 1978—82, adminstrative v.p., 1982—85, v.p. for instl. advancement, 1985—97; v.p. emeritus and exec. dir. of devel. St. John's U. Sch. of Law, 2000—. Cons. Skirde Enterprises, S.I., NY, 1997—. Trustee St. Elizabeth Ann Seton Rehab. Ctr. and Nursing Home, S.I., NY, 1998—2003; bd. of dir. Italian Cultural Ctr. of St. John's U., Jamaica, NY, 1995—2003; trustee St. Vincent's Med. Ctr., S.I., NY, 1988—97; Notre Dame Acad., S.I., NY, 1989—97. Recipient President's medal, St. John's U., 1997, Outstanding Alumni Achievement award, 1992, Outstanding Adminstrv. Achievement award, 1986, Pietas medal, 1981, Nat. Hon. Speech Soc., Delta Sigma Rho - Tau Kappa Alpha, 1970. Mem.: Assn. of Am. Law Schools, Coun. for Advancement and Support of Edn. Avocations: travel, golf. Office: St John's U Sch of Law 8000 Utopia Pkwy Jamaica NY 11439

**SKIRNICK, ROBERT ANDREW,** lawyer; b. Chgo., Apr. 23, 1938; s. Andrew and Stella (Sanders) S.; children: Rebecca, David; m. Maria Ann Castellano, Oct. 4, 1974; 1 child, Gabriella. BA, Roosevelt U., 1961; JD, U. Chgo., 1966. Bar: U.S. Dist. Ct. (no. dist.) Ill. 1966, U.S. Ct. Appeals (7th cir.) 1968, U.S. Supreme Ct. 1970, U.S. Ct. Appeals (5th and 9th cirs.) 1982, N.Y. 1989, U.S. Ct. Appeals (11th cir.) 1992, U.S. Dist. Ct. (so. dist.) Tex. 1992, U.S. Dist. Ct. Ariz. 1993, U.S. Ct. Appeals (4th, 6th and 8th cirs.) 2002. Atty. office gen. counsel honors program HEW, Washington, 1966-68; ptnr. Fortes, Eiger, Epstein & Skirnick, Chgo., 1975-77, Much, Shelist, Freed, Chgo., 1977-79, Wolf, Popper, Ross, Wolf & Jones, N.Y.C., 1979-87, Kaplan, Kilsheimer & Foley, N.Y.C., 1988-89, Wechsler, Skirnick, Harwood, Halebian & Feffer, N.Y.C., 1989-95, Lovell & Skirnick, LLP, N.Y.C., 1995-97, Meredith Cohen Greenfogel & Skirnick, P.C., N.Y.C., 1997—. Cons. Nat. Legal Aid and Def. Assn., Chgo., 1968—69; instr. NYU, 1979—80; spl. asst. atty. gen. Ill. Atty. Gen. Office, Chgo., 1972—73; spl. antitrust counsel State of Conn., 1976—77; mem. adv. bd. Small Bus. Legal Def. Commn., San Francisco, 1982—; lectr. Practicing Law Inst., N.Y.C., 1986—87; spl. master So. Dist. N.Y., 1988—91; ct. apptd. co-lead counsel NASDAQ market makers antitrust litigation, 1994—; ct. apptd. local counsel for instnl. plaintiff AOL TW Securities Litigation, 2002—; adv. bd. Am. Antitrust Inst., Washington, 2004—; sponsor Skirnick Fellowships for Pub. Interest Law Harvard Law Sch. Author: (with others) Federal Subject Matter Jurisdiction of U.S. District Courts, Federal Civil Practice, 1974, Antitrust Class Actions-Twenty Years Under Rule 23, 1986, The State Court Class Action-A Potpourri of Difference in the ABA Forum, Summer 1985; contbg. author: Multiparty Bargaining in Class Actions, Attorneys' Practice Guide to Negotiations, 2d edit., 1996, Survey of Securities Class Actions and Derivative Suits, 2001, ABA Section of Litigation, 2003; bd. editors Ill. Bar Antitrust Newsletter, 1969-73; topic and articles editor Jour. Forum Com. on Franchising, 1981-86. Atty. Office Gen. Counsel Honors Program, U.S. Dept. HEW, 1966-68; chmn. Ill. Legis. Com. Antitrust Section Ill. Bar., 1970-71; Triph and Articles Editor Union Forum Com on Franchising 1001 06 ct apptd. local counsel for instl. plaintiff in AOLTW securities litigation, 2002-. Mem.: ATLA, ABA (co-chair securities law subcom. litigation sect. 1987, mem. com. on regulation of futures and derivative instruments, mem. forum com. on franchising, mem. com. on class actions and derivative suits, mem. internat. antitrust and fgn. competition laws com.), Am. Antitrust Inst. (mem. adv. bd. 2004—), Assn. of the Bar of the City of N.Y. (antitrust and trade regulation com. 2004—), Assn. Bar N.Y. (mem. antitrust and trade regulation com. 2004—), Nat. Assn. Pub. Interest Law (bd. dirs. 1997—, nomination and election com. 1998—99, mem. fin. and investment com. 1998—, chair nominations and elections com. 1999—2000, chair fin. and investment com. 2000—03), Nat. Assn. for Pub. Interest Law Fellowships (bd. dirs. 1991—97, v.p. 1994—97, bd. dirs. 1997—2003, nomination and election coms. 1998—99, mem. budget com. 1998—2003, treas. 2000—03, mem. exec. com., mem. selection com., mem. investment and fin. com.), Ill. Bar Assn. (chmn. antitust sect. Ill. legis. com. 1970—71), N.Y. State Trial Lawyers Assn., N.Y. State Bar Assn. (mem. class action com.), Bar Coun. (mem. com. on second cir. cts. 1983—86, dir. Maria and Robert A. Skirnicle Fund for New Works at Carnegie Hall 2004—), Navy League of U.S. (mem. jour. com. 1995—97, N.Y. coun.), Plandome Country Club, Carlton Club. Office: Meredith Cohen Greenfogel & Skirnick One Liberty Plaza 35th Fl New York NY 10006-1404 Office Phone: 212-240-0020.

**SKIRPAN, RICHARD MICHAEL,** conductor, music educator; b. Phila., Sept. 17, 1980; s. Richard John and Deborah Ann (Gliick) Skirpan. MB, Duquesne U., 2002, MusM, 2004. Dir. choral music Calvert Hall Coll. H.S., Balt., 2004—. Grad. asst. for choral activities Duquesne U., Pitts., 2002—04; asst. condr. Bach Choir of Pitts., 2003—04. Composer: (one-act opera) Masque of the Red Death. Recipient Excellence in Choral Conducting, Beaver Valley (Pa.) Choral Soc., 2002. Mem.: Nat. Assn. for Music Edn., MENC, Am. Choral Dirs. Assn., Golden Key, Pi Kappa Lambda. Roman Catholic. Office: Calvert Hall Coll HS 8102 LaSalle Rd Baltimore MD 21286-8022

**SKIRVIN, DONALD MURRAY,** composer, writer; b. Indpls., Dec. 22, 1946; s. Ralph Carl and Norma Rae Skirvin. BA in French Lang. and Lit., Ind. U., 1971, BA in French, 1971, MS in Applied Linguistics, 1981. Secondary tchg. lic. Ind., cert. ESL instr. Ind. U. Staff writer Alan C. McConnell and Son Pub. Co., Indpls., 1971—77; book order clk., indexer Inst. for Sex Rsch. Bloomington, Ind., 1979—81; sr. editor, mng. editor I.P.F.R. Pub. Inc., NYC, 1982—89; sr. editor Real Estate Investment Network, Pa., 1989—91; freelance desktop pub. cons., editor Wash., 1991—95; software support specialist Adobe Sys. Inc. and Luminous Tech. Corp., Wash. 1996—97; quality assurance lead, tech. writer, editor IPS Inc. and Luminous Tech. Corp., Seattle, 1997—99; quality assurance mgr. print and prepress Adobe Software Sys., Seattle, 1999—2004. Composer-in-residence Esoterics. Composer: (CD) Alchemy, Echoes from the heart, Songs of the Equinox and Solstice, Do Not Weep, (choral composition) We Sing the Dream. Recipient Anthem award, GALA V Festival, 1996, Nat. Endowment for the Arts commissioning award, 2005. Mem.: ASCAP, Wash. Composers Forum. Home: 12539 Evanston Ave N Seattle WA 98133

**SKIVER, STEPHEN ALLEN,** lawyer, physician; b. Toledo, Ohio, Feb. 14, 1949; s. Arnold Leroy and Elizabeth Jane (Boyer) S.; m. Catherine Ann Reynolds, June 26, 1971; children: Tonia, Justin, Ryan, Laura, Elyssa. BS, Ohio U., 1971; MD, Med. Coll. Ohio, 1974; JD, U. Toledo, 1988. Bar: Ohio 1989, U.S. Dist. Ct. (no. dist.) Ohio 1991; Cert. Am. Bd. Internal Medicine. Physician, Maumee, Ohio, 1977-89; clin. asst. prof. medicine Med. Coll. Ohio, Toledo, 1983-89; physician Toledo 1989—; assoc. Jacobson, Maynard, Tuschman, Toledo, 1990-97; ptnr. Buckley, King & Bluso, Toledo, 1997—adr. Home: 30025 E River Rd Perrysburg OH 43551-3430 Office: Buckley King & Bluso 420 Madison Ave Ste 1100 Toledo OH 43604-1209

**SKJERVOLD, GERALDINE REID See REID, GERALDINE**

**SKLANSKY, JACK,** electrical and computer engineering educator, researcher; b. NYC, Nov. 15, 1928; s. Abraham and Clara S.; m. Jerry Joy Weiss, Dec. 24, 1957; children: David Alan, Mark Steven, Jeffrey Paul. BEE, CCNY, 1950; MSEE, Purdue U., 1952; D in Engring. Sci., Columbia U., 1955. Research engr. RCA Labs., Princeton, NJ, 1955-65; mgr. Nat. Cash Register Co., Dayton, Ohio, 1965-66; prof. elec. and computer engring. U. Calif., Irvine, 1966—94; pres. Scanicon Corp., Irvine, 1980-89; prof. radiology Charles R. Drew U. of Medicine and Sci., LA, 1995—. Author: (with others) Pattern Classifiers and Trainable Machines, 1981; editor: Pattern Recognition, 1973, (with others) Biomedical Images and Computers, 1982; editor-in-chief: Machine Vision and Applications, 1987. Recipient best paper award Jour. Pattern Recognition, 1977, 2000; rsch. grantee NIH, 1971-84, Army Rsch. Office, 1984-91, NSF, 1992-96, Office of Naval Rsch., 1995-97, Naval Air Warfare Ctr., 1997-98, Calif. Breast Cancer Rsch. Program, 1997-99, US Army Med. Rsch. and Materiel Command, 1999-2004, Calif. Telehealth and Telemedicine Ctr., 2000-02. Fellow IEEE, Internat. Assn. for Pattern Recognition; mem. ACM. Office: U Calif Dept Elec Engring & Computer Sci MSTB 211 Irvine CA 92697 E-mail: sklansky@uci.edu.

**SKLAR, ALAN CURTIS,** lawyer; b. N.Y.C., Aug. 19, 1959; s. Jerry and Martha (Kolin) S.; m. Linda Susan Catalan, Dec. 26, 1982; twins: Daniel Jay and Jennifer Rachel. BA summa cum laude, U. Pa., 1980, JD, 1982. Bar: Calif., Nev. Assoc. Wolf Block Schorr & Solis-Cohen, Phila., 1980, 81, Rifkind & Sterling, Beverly Hills, Calif., 1982-84, Mitchell Silberberg & Knupp, L.A., 1984-86; mng. dir. Coastal Investment Group, Beverly Hills, 1986-89; ptnr. Warren Clark & Sklar (and predecessor), L.A., 1989—, Gordon & Silver, Las Vegas, Nev., 1991-95, Sklar Warren Conway & Williams LLP, Las Vegas, Nev., 1995—. Dir. Consolidated Mgmt., Inc., N.Y.C., L.A., Las Vegas. Author: Tactics and Techniques in Mergers and Acquisitions, 1985, Recent Developments in Mergers and Acquisitions, 1985, California Corporate Securities Laws, 1985, Corporate Law Overview, 1985, Secured Real Estate Transactions, 1993. Bd. trustees Las Vegas Bowl Organizing Com., 1995, 96, So. Nev. Housing Corp., 1995—; mem. U. Pa. Alumni Secondary Sch. Com., 1998—; counsel Chabad of So. Nev., Las Vegas, 1991-2000. Named Top Corp. Atty., Nev. Bus. Jour. Mem. ABA, State Bar Nev., State Bar Calif., TPC Summerlin Country Club, World Zionist Orgn., Phi Beta Kappa, Phi Alpha Theta. Democrat. Jewish. Office: 8363 W Sunset RD #300 Las Vegas NV 89113-2092 E-mail: asklar@sklar-law.com.

**SKLAR, DANIEL WILLIAM,** lawyer; b. Nashua, NH, Jan. 28, 1953; s. David and Klara S.; m. Debbie-Ann Roth, Nov. 11, 1979; children: Adam R., Stephanie M. BA, U. Pa., 1975; JD, Boston Coll., 1978; LLM in Fed. Tax, Boston U., 1982. Bar: NH 1978, US Dist. Ct. NH 1978, U.S. Ct. Appeals (1st cir.) 1979, US Supreme Ct. 1986. Ptnr. Sheehan, Phinney, Bass & Green, Manchester, NH, 1978-89; pvt. practice Manchester, NH, 1989; ptnr. Nixon Peabody LLP, Manchester, NH. Bd. dirs. regional Bank NH, Manchester; adj. prof. law Franklin Pierce Law Ctr. Dir. Temple Israel, Manchester, 1989, Camp Young Judea, Amherst, NH, 1989. Fellow Am. Coll. Bankruptcy; mem. ABA, NH Bar Assn., Manchester Bar Assn. (pres. 1985-86), Am. Bankruptcy Inst., Am. Immigration Lawyers Assn. Republican. Jewish. Avocations: skiing, tennis. Office: 900 Elm St Manchester NH 03101-2019 Office Phone: 603-628-4008. Office Fax: 603-628-4040. E-mail: dsklar@nixonpeabody.com.

**SKLAR, FREDERICK H.,** neurosurgeon; b. Phila., 1945; m. Alice Sklar; 3 children. BS with highest honors, Pa. State U.; MD, Johns Hopkins U., 1970. Diplomate Am. Bd. Neurol. Surgery, Am. Bd. Pediat. Neurol. Surgery, lic. physician Tex. Halsted intern in surgery Johns Hopkins U., Balt., 1970—71; resident in neurosurgery Johns Hopkins Hosp., 1971—76; clin. assoc. prof. neurol. surgery U. Tex. Southwestern Med. Sch., Dallas; dir. pediat. neurosurgery Children's Med. Ctr. Dallas; founder Neurosurgeons for Children, 1985—. Cons. Tex. Scottish Rite Hosp. for Children, Parkland Meml. Hosp., Dallas. Contbr. to profl. jours. Mem.: Alpha Omega Alpha, Phi Beta Kappa. Office: Children's Med Ctr-Neurosurgery 1935 Motor St Dallas TX 75235

**SKLAR, HOLLY L.,** writer, columnist; b. N.Y.C., May 6, 1955; BA, Oberlin Coll., 1977; MA in Polit. Sci., Columbia U., 1980. Rschr. UN Ctr. Transnat. Corps., N.Y., 1978; writer, rschr. N. Am. Congress Latin Am., N.Y., 1981-82; exec. dir. Inst. New Communications, N.Y., 1982-84; writer, lectr. N.Y., Boston. Review panelist NEH, Washington, 1989; del. Soviet-Am. Women's Summit, N.Y., Washington, 1990. Author: co-author (books) Trilateralism, 1980, Poverty in the American Dream: Women and Children First, 1983, Washington's War on Nicaragua, 1988, Streets of Hope: The Fall and Rise of an Urban Neighborhood, 1994, Chaos or Community? Seeking Solutions, Not Scapegoats for Bad Economics, 1995, Shifting Fortunes: The Perils of the Growing American Wealth Gap, 1999, Raise the Floor: Wages and Policies that Work for All of Us, 2001, A Just Minimum Wage: Good for Workers, Business and Our Future, 2005. Mem. adv. bd. The Progressive Media Project, Polit. Rsch. Assocs.; bd. dirs. United for a Fair Economy, 1996-2000; mem. steering com. Caribbean Basin Info. Project, 1982-85; mem. working group on global econs. Am. Friends Svc. Com., 2002-04. Recipient Outstanding Book award Gustavus Myers Ctr. for Study Human Rights in U.S., 1988, Assocs. award Polit. Rsch. Assocs., Cambridge, 1991-97; fellow Columbia U. Grad. Sch. Arts and Scis., 1978-80. Mem. Nat. Writers Union, Acad. Polit. Sci. Office Phone: 617-522-2923. E-mail: Mediavi@aol.com.

**SKLAR, KATHRYN KISH,** historian, educator; b. Columbus, Ohio, Dec. 26, 1939; d. William Edward and Elizabeth Sue (Rhodes) Kish; m. Robert A. Sklar, 1958 (div. 1978); children: Leonard Scott, Susan Rebecca Sklar Friedman; m. Thomas L. Dublin, Apr. 30, 1988. BA magna cum laude, Radcliffe Coll., 1965; PhD, U. Mich., 1969. Asst. prof., U. Mich., Ann Arbor, 1969-74; assoc. prof. history UCLA, 1974-81, chmn. com. to administer program in women's studies Coll. Letters and Sci., 1974-81, prof., 1981-88; Disting. prof. history SUNY, Binghamton, 1988—, co-dir. Ctr. Hist. Study of Women and Gender, 1998—; Harmsworth prof. U.S. history U. Oxford, 2005—. Pulitzer juror in history, 1976; fellow Newberry Libr. Family and Community History Seminar, 1973; active Calif. Coun. for Humanities, 1981-85, N.Y. Coun. for Humanities, 1992—; Harmsworth prof. Amer. history Oxford U., 2005—. Author: Catharine Beecher: A Study in American Domesticity, 1973 (Berkshire pri e 1974); editor: Catharine Beecher: A Treatise on Domestic Economy, 1977, Harriet Beecher Stowe: Uncle Tom's

Cabin, or Life Among the Lowly: The Minister's Wooing, Oldtown Folks, 1981, Notes of Sixty Years: The Autobiography of Florence Kelley, 1849-1926, 1984, (with Thomas Dublin) Women and Power in American History: A Reader (2 vols.), 1991, (with Linda Kerber and Alice Kessler-Harris) U.S. History as Women's History: New Feminist Essays, 1995, Women's Rights Emerges within the Antislavery Movement: A Short History with Documents, 1830-1870, 2000; co-editor: The Social Survey Movement in Historical Perspective, 1992, Florence Kelley and the Nation's Work: The Rise of Women's Political Culture, 1830-1900, 1995 (Berkshire prize 1996). Social Justice Feminists in the United States and Germany: A Dialogue in Documents, 1885-1933, 1998; mem. editl. bd. Jour. Women's History, 1987—; Women's History Rev., 1990—, Jour. Am. History, 1978-81; contbr. chpts. to books; co-dir. Women and Social Movements in the U.S. 1600-2000: An Online Jour. and Datebase, 1997—. Fellow Woodrow Wilson Found., 1965-67, Danforth Found., 1967-69, Radcliffe Inst., 1973-74, Nat. Humanities Inst., 1975-76, Rockefeller Found. Humanities, 1981-82, Woodrow Wilson Internat. Ctr. for Scholars, 1982, 1992-93, Guggenheim Found., 1984, Ctr. Advanced Study Behavioral and Social Scis., Stanford U., 1987-88, AAUW, 1990-91; Daniels fellow Am. Antiquarian Soc., 1976, NEH fellow Newberry Library, 1982-83; Ford Found. faculty rsch. grantee, 1973-74; grantee NEH, 1976-78, UCLA Coun. for Internat. and Comparative Studies, 1983. Mem. Am. Hist. Assn. (chmn. com. on women historians 1980-83, v.p. Pacific Coast br. 1986-87, pres. 1987-88), Orgn. Am. Historians (exec. bd. 1983-86, Merle Curti award com. 1978-79, lectr. 1982—), Am. Studies Assn. (coun. mem.-at-large 1978-80), Berkshire Conf. Women Historians, Am. Antiquarian Soc., Phi Beta Kappa. Avocation: photography. Office: SUNY Dept History Binghamton NY 13902 Office Phone: 607-777-6202.

**SKLAR, MARTY (MARTIN A. SKLAR),** entertainment company executive; b. New Brunswick, NJ; m. Leah Sklar. Grad., UCLA. Asst. news editor Media Agy. Clients Publs.; with Walt Disney Co., Burbank, Calif., 1956—; v.p. concepts/planning Walt Disney Imagineering, Walt Disney Co., Burbank, Calif., 1974—79, v.p. creative devel., 1979—87, pres., 1987—96, vice chmn., prin. creative exec., 1996—2006, internat. amb., 2006—. One of founders Ryman Program for Young Artists. Contbr. articles to Showman of the World films. Mem. bd. edn. Anaheim City Sch. Dist., 1969, 1973; pres. Orange County, Calif. Sch. Bds. Assn.; commr. Anaheim City; founding chmn. Michael L. Roston Creative Writing Awards. Recipient Cmty. Svc. award for Anaheim, Cypress Coll., 1977, Lifetime Achievement award, Themed Entertainment Assn., 1995; inducted into, Hall of Fame, Internat. Assn. Amusement Pks. and Attractions, 2002. Office: Walt Disney Co 500 S Buena Vista St Burbank CA 91521-9722*

**SKLAR, RICHARD LAWRENCE,** political science professor; b. NYC, Mar. 22, 1930; s. Kalman and Sophie (Laub) S.; m. Eva Molineux, July 14, 1962; children: Judith Anne, Katherine Elizabeth. AB, U. Utah, 1952; MA, Princeton U., 1957, PhD, 1961. Mem. faculty Brandeis U., U. Ibadan, Nigeria, U. Zambia, SUNY-Stony Brook, UCLA; now prof. emeritus polit. sci. UCLA. Mem. fgn. area fellowship program Africa Nat. Com., 1970-73; Simon vis. prof. U. Manchester, Eng., 1975, Fulbright vis. prof. U. Zimbabwe, 1984; Lester Martin fellow Harry S. Truman Rsch. Inst., Hebrew U. Jerusalem, 1979; fellow Africa Inst. of South Africa, 1994—. Author: Nigerian Political Parties: Power in an Emergent African Nation, 1963, Corporate Power in an African State, 1975, African Politics in Postimperial Times, 2002; co-author: Postimperialism: International Capitalism and Development, 1987, African Politics and Problems in Development, 1991; co-editor: Postimperialism and World Politics, 1999; contbr. articles to profl. jours. Served with U.S. Army, 1952-54. Rockefeller Found. grantee, 1967 Mem. Am. Polit. Sci. Assn., African Studies Assn. (dir. 1976-78, 80-83, v.p. 1980-81, pres. 1981-82), AAUP (pres. Calif. Conf. 1980-81) Home: 1951 Holmby Ave Los Angeles CA 90025-5905 E-mail: sklar@polisci.ucla.edu.

**SKLAREW, ROBERT JAY,** biomedical research educator, consultant; b. NYC, Nov. 25, 1941; s. Arthur and Jeanette (Laven) S.; m. Toby Willner, July 15, 1970; children: David Michael, Gary Richard. BA in Zoology, Cornell U., 1963; MS, NYU, 1965, PhD in Biology, 1970. Assoc. rsch. scientist NYU Sch. Medicine, N.Y.C., 1965-70, rsch. scientist, 1971-73, sr. rsch. scientist, 1973-79; rsch. asst. prof. pathology Goldwater Meml. Hosp. Sch. Medicine, N.Y.C., 1979-87, rsch. assoc. prof. pathology, 1987-88; dir. cytokinetics and imaging lab. NYU rsch. svc. Goldwater Meml. Hosp., N.Y.C., 1980-88; prof. cell biology, anatomy and medicine N.Y. Med. Coll., Valhalla, 1988-98. Rsch. assoc. dept. pathology Lenox Hill Hosp., N.Y.C., 1981-88; pres., CEO R.J. Sklarew Imaging Assoc., Inc., Larchmont, N.Y., 1990—2003; chmn. consensus panel for diagnostic cancer imaging Nat. Cancer Inst., 1994. Author: Microscopic Imaging of Steroid Receptors, 1990; sr. author: Cytometry, Jour. Histochem. Cytochem., Cancer, Exptl. Cell Rsch. Group leader Boy Scouts Am., Larchmont, 1978—80; mem., bd. dirs. Pinelake Park Coop, 1998—2001. Grantee Am. Cancer Soc., Nat. Cancer Inst./NIH Conc. for Tobacco Rsch., R.J. Reynolds Industries Found., NYU; recipient Shannon award Nat. Cancer Inst., 1991. Mem. AAAS, Cell Kinetics Soc. (sec. 1983-85, 85-87, v.p. 1987-88, pres. 1988-89, chmn. nominations 1991, 93), N.Y. Acad. Sci., Soc. for Analytic Cytology, Soc. for Cell Biology, Tissue Culture Assn., Union Concerned Scientists, Kappa Delta Rho. Democrat. Achievements include development of methodology, algorithms and Receptogram analytic software for application of microscopic imaging in medical research and in pathodiagnosis of cancer, imaging methods for simultaneous densitometry and autoradiographic analysis; research in diagnostic imaging of steroid receptors, oncogenes and DNA ploidy in cancer, proliferative patterns and cell cycle kinetics of human solid tumors. Home: 8 Vine Rd Larchmont NY 10538-1247 Office: RJ Sklarew Imaging Assoc Inc 8 Vine Rd Larchmont NY 10538-1247 Personal E-mail: rjsklarew@aol.com.

**SKLARSKY, CHARLES B.,** lawyer; b. Chgo., June 13, 1946; s. Morris and Sadie (Brenner) S.; m. Elizabeth Ann Hardzinski, Dec. 28, 1973; children: Jacob Daniel, Katherine Gabrielle, Jessica Leah. AB, Harvard U., 1968; JD, U. Wis., 1973. Bar: Wis. 1973, Ill. 1973, U.S. Dist. Ct. (no. dist.) Ill. 1973, U.S. Ct. Appeals (7th cir.) 1978, U.S. Ct. Appeals (2nd cir.) 1986. Asst. states atty. Cook County, Chgo., 1973-78; asst. U.S. atty. (no. dist.) Ill. US Dept. Justice, Chgo., 1978-86; ptnr. Jenner & Block LLP, Chgo., 1986—. Mem. ABA, Am. Coll. Trial Lawyers, Chgo. Bar Assn. Office: Jenner & Block One IBM Plz Chicago IL 60611-3586 Office Phone: 312-923-2904. E-mail: csklarsky@jenner.com.

**SKLARSKY, FRANK S.,** corporate financial executive; B in Acctg., Rochester Inst. Tech.; MBA, Harvard Bus. Sch., 1983. CPA. Sr. acct. Ernst and Young; v.p. corp. fin. activities DaimlerChrysler Corp., v.p. fin., product quality, cost mgmt. and procurement, v.p. product fin.; exec. v.p., CFO ConAgra Foods, 2004—. Office: ConAgra Foods One ConAgra Dr Omaha NE 68102-5001 Office Fax: 402-595-4000.*

**SKLENAR, HERBERT ANTHONY,** industrial products manufacturing company executive; b. Omaha, June 7, 1931; s. Michael Joseph and Alice Madeline (Spicka) S.; m. Eleanor Lydia Vincenz, Sept. 15, 1956; children: Susan A., Patricia I BSBA summa cum laude, U. Omaha, 1952; MBA, Harvard U., 1954; LLD (hon.), Birmingham-So. Coll., 1996. CPA W.Va. V.p., comptr. Parkersburg-Aetna Corp., W.Va., 1956-63; v.p., dir. Marmac Corp, Parkersburg, 1963-66; mgr. fin. control Boise-Cascade Corp., Idaho, 1966-67; exec. v.p. fin. and adminstrn., sec. Cudahy Co., Phoenix, 1967-72; chmn. emeritus Vulcan Materials Co., Birmingham, Ala., 1972-97, chmn. bd. dirs. emeritus, 1997—. Author (with others): The Automatic Factory: A Critical Examination, 1955. Trustee Leadership Birmingham, Birmingham-So. Coll Recipient Alumni Achievement award U. Nebr.-Omaha, 1977, cert. merit W.Va. Soc. CPAs, Elizah Watts Sells award AICPA, 1965, Brotherhood award NCCJ, 1993; inductee Ala. Acad. Honor, 1997 Mem.: Rotary Club Birmingham (pres.-elect), Birmingham Country Club, Shoal Creek Club, Phi Eta Sigma, Phi Kappa Phi, Omicron Delta Kappa, Delta Sigma Pi. Republican. Presbyterian. Home: 2809 Shook Hill Cir Birmingham AL 35223-2618 Office: Vulcan Materials Co 1200 Urban Center Dr Birmingham AL 35242-2545

**SKLOVSKY, ROBERT JOEL,** naturopathic physician, pharmacist, educator; b. NY; BS summa cum laude, Bklyn. Coll., 1975; MA in Sci. Edn., Columbia U., 1976; PharmD, U. Pacific, 1977; D in Naturopathic Medicine. Nat. Coll. Naturopathic Medicine, 1983. Intern Tripler Army Med. Ctr., Honolulu, 1977; pvt. practice Milwaukie, Oreg., 1983—. Recipient Bristol Labs. award Bklyn. Coll. Pharmacy, 1975, Coll. Gold medal, 1975, NYC Sci. Tchg. award Chemist's Club NY, 1976. Mem.: NY Acad. Sci. Avocations: classical and jazz music, art, gardening, painting. Office: 6910 SE Lake Rd Milwaukie OR 97267-2101

**SKOCHELAK, SUSAN E.,** dean; BS, Mich. Tech. U., 1975, MS in Biol. Sci., 1977; MD, U. Mich., 1981; MPH, U. N.C., 1986. Diplomae Am. Bd. Family Medicine. Intern, resident family medicine U. N.C.-N.C. Meml. Hosp., Chapel Hill, 1977-81; assoc. dean Academic Affairs U. Wis., Madison, 1993—. Cons. in field; assoc. prof. U. Wis. Author: (with others) Preceptor Education Project, Handbook for Clerkship Directors. Mem. Wis. Rural Health Dev. Council, Consortium Primary Care in Wis.; co-dir. Wis. Area Health Edn. Sys. Recipient National award Patient Care mag., 1997. Mem. AMA, Soc. Tchrs. Family Medicine, Assn. Am. Med. Colls., Am. Med. Women's ssn., ACPHE. Office: Univ Wisconsin Med School 1300 University Ave Madison WI 53706-1510

**SKODON, EMIL MARK,** ambassador; b. Chgo., Nov. 25, 1953; s. Emil John and Anne F. (Soltes) S.; m. Dorothea Shaffer, Mar. 6, 1982; children: Catherine Marie, Christine Louise. BA, U. Chgo., 1975, MBA, 1976. Consular officer Am. Embassy, Bridgetown, Barbados, 1977-79, econ. officer East Berlin, Germany, 1979-81; econ. officer Office So. African Affairs, US Dept. State, Washington, 1982-84; econ. officer Am. Embassy, Vienna, 1984-88, Kuwait City, Kuwait, 1989-91; consul gen. Am. Consulate Gen., Perth, Australia, 1991-94; dep. chief mission Am. Embassy, Singapore, 1995-98, dir. office Australia, New Zealand, Pacific Island Affairs Washington, 1998-2000, polit. advisor to USAF chief of staff, 2000—02, deputy chief of Mission Rome, 2002—05, amb. to Brunei Bandar Seri Begawan, 2005—. Decorated Outstanding Civilian Svc. medal U.S. Army, Exceptional Civilian Svc. medal USAF Mem. Nat. Trust for Hist. Preservation. Avocations: visiting historic sites, good food, spending time with family. Office: Am Embassy Bandar Seri Begawan 4020 Bandar Seri Begawan Pl Dulles VA 20189

**SKOGEN, HAVEN SHERMAN,** investment company executive; b. Rochester, Minn., May 8, 1927; s. Joseph Harold and Elpha (Hemphill) S.; m. Beverly R. Baker, Feb. 19, 1949; 1 child, Scott H. BS, Iowa State U., 1950; MS, Rutgers U., 1954, PhD, 1955; MBA, U. Chgo., 1970. Registered profl. engr., Wis. Devel. engr. E.I. duPont, Wilmington, Del., 1955—57; prof. Elmhurst (Ill.) Coll., 1957—58; chief engr. Stackpole, St. Marys, Pa., 1958—62; plant mgr. Magnatronics, Elizabethtown, Ky., 1962—65; mgr. Allen-Bradley, Milw., 1965—70; v.p. Dill-Clithrow, Chgo., 1970—74; oil co. exec. Occidental Oil Co., Grand Junction, Colo., 1974—92; ptnr. H&B Investment Co., 1992—. Author: Synthetic Fuel Combustion, 1984; inventor radioactive retort doping, locus retorting zone. Naval Rsch. fellow, 1951-55. Fellow Am. Inst. Chemists; mem. Internat. Platform Assn., Masons, Elks, Sigma Xi, Phi Beta Kappa, Phi Lambda Upsilon. Republican. Avocations: fly fishing, travel, reading, teaching. Home: 3152 Primrose Ct Grand Junction CO 81506-4147

**SKOGLUND, MARILYN,** state supreme court justice; b. Chgo., Aug. 28, 1946; BA, So. Ill. U., 1971; clerkship, 1977-81. Bar: Vt. 1981, U.S. Dist. Ct. Vt. 1981, U.S. Ct. Appeals (2d cir.) 1983. Asst. atty. gen. Civil Law Divsn., 1981—89, chief, 1988—93, Pub. Protection Divsn., 1993-94; judge Vt. Dist. Ct., 1994-97; assoc. justice Vt Supreme Ct., 1997—. Office: Vt Supreme Ct 109 State St Montpelier VT 05609-0001*

**SKOGSBERGH, JAMES H.,** health facility administrator; BS, Iowa State U.; M in health admin., U. Iowa. Exec. v.p. Iowa Health Sys., Des Moines; pres, CEO Iowa Meth. Med. Ctr., Iowa Luth. Hosp., Blank Children's Hosp.; admin. resident to exec. v.p., chief oper. officer Mem. Health Sys., South Bend, Ind., 1982—91; exec. v.p. Iowa Meth. Med. Ctr., 1991; chief operating officer Advocate Health Care, Oak Brook, Ill., 2001—02, pres., CEO, 2002—. Fellow: Am. Coll. Healthcare Exec.; mem.: Ill. Hosp. Assoc. Advocacy Coun., Metro. Chgo. Healthcare Coun., Young Pres. Organ., Chgo. Econ. Club. Office: Advocate health Care 2025 Windsor Dr Oak Brook IL 60523-1586

**SKOL, MICHAEL,** counter-money laundering consultant; b. Chgo., Oct. 15, 1942; s. Ted and Rebecca (Williams) S.; m. Claudia Serwer, Sept. 29, 1973. BA, Yale U., 1964. U.S. fgn. svc. officer Dept. State, 1965-96; polit. officer U.S. Embassy, Buenos Aires, 1966-67, Saigon, Viet Nam, 1968-70; desk officer Dept. State, Washington, 1970-72; comml. attache U.S. Embassy, Santo Domingo, Dominican Republic, 1972-75; econ. comml. officer U.S. Consulate Gen., Naples, Italy, 1975-76; comml. attache U.S. Embassy, Rome, 1976-78, polit. counselor San Jose, Costa Rica, 1978-82; dep. dir. policy planning Inter-Am. Affairs Bur. Dept. State, Washington, 1982-85; dep. chief of mission U.S. Embassy, Bogota, Colombia, 1985-87; dir. Andean affairs Dept. State, Washington, 1987-88; dep. asst. sec. state for S.Am. U.S. Dept. of State, Washington, 1988-90; amb. U.S. Embassy, Caracas, Venezuela, 1990-93; prin. dep. asst. sec. for Latin Am./Caribbean Dept. State, Washington, 1993-96; sr. v.p. Diplomatic Resolutions, Inc., Washington, 1996-97; pres. Skol & Assoc. Inc., N.Y., Washington, Bogota, 1998—; chmn. US Colombian Bus. Partnership, 1996-99; mng. dir. L.Am. Decision Strategies, N.Y.C., 1998—2005. Pres. Skol, Ospina & Serna, N.Y.C., Washington and Bogota, 2001—03; prin. Skol & Serna, Washington, Bogota, 2003—. Mem.: Coun. on Fgn. Rels., Yale Club of N.Y. Office: 1710 Rhode Island Ave NW Ste 300 Washington DC 20036 Office Phone: 202-331-9464. Personal E-mail: mikeskol@aol.com

**SKOLDBERG, PHYLLIS LINNEA,** music educator, musician; d. August Theodore Skoldberg and Esther Amanda Carlson. MusB with honors, New Eng. Conservatory, 1955, MusM, 1957; M in Music Edn. with high distinction, Ind. U., 1964, Mus D in Performance, 1967. Violinist Houston Symphony Orch., 1957—59, Cin. Symphony Orch., 1959—62; assoc. instr. Ind. U., Bloomington, 1962—64; prof. music SUNY, Oswego, 1964—77; asst. dean fine arts Ariz. State U., Tempe, 1977—84, prof. music, 1977—2001, prof. emeritus, 2001—. Vis. artist Paris Conservatoire, 1973; vis. prof., cons. Australian String Tchrs. Assn.; Brisbane and Sydney, 1984, Shanghai Conservatory Music, 1984; artist-in-residence U. Hong Kong, 1984; adj. prof., coord. string dept. Mesa (Ariz.) CC, 2001—. Author: The Strings: A Comparative View, Vol. I, 1981. Vol. 2, 1982; performer: (solos) Reston (Va.) Music Festival, 1972, 1973, Charles Ives Music Festival, 1975, 1976, Western Music Festival, 1980, (1st violin) Concert Quartet, 2003; soloist Philharmonic. Named winner performance competition, Seattle Philharm. Orch., 1952; recipient Boston Civic Music award, 1954. Mem.: The Phoenix Inst. of Music (founding dir. 2005), Red Rock Music Festival (bd. dirs. 2002—), Music Tchrs. Nat. Assn., Am. String Tchrs. Assn. (adv. bds. 1970—84, Ariz. pres. 1984—86). Home: 12002 S Tuzigoot Ct Phoenix AZ 85044-3467 Office: Mesa CC 1833 W Southern Ave Mesa AZ 85202 Office Phone: 480-461-7575. Office Fax: 480-461-7422. Business E-Mail: phyllis.skoldberg@asu.edu.

**SKOLER, LOUIS,** architect, educator; b. Apr. 5, 1920; s. Harry and Etta (Mitkoff) S.; m. Celia Rebecca Stern, 1952; children: Elisa Anne, Harry Jay. BArch, Cornell U., 1951. Maj. designer Sargent, Webster, Crenshaw & Folley, Syracuse, NY, 1951-59; design critic Cornell U., Ithaca, NY, 1956-57; pvt. practice arch. Syracuse, 1956-69; faculty Sch. Arch. Syracuse U., 1959-92, prof. emeritus, 1990—: Head of arch. masters program, 1980-82, head undergrad. program, 1989-90; programs abroad, London, 1977, Scandinavia, 1985, Japan, 1988; ptnr. Arch. Partnership, Syracuse, 1969-71; pres. Skoler & Lee Archs., P.C., Syracuse, 1971-89; lectr. Nanjing Inst. Tech., China, summer 1986. Named Best in Residential Design, Design-in-Steel,

1968-69. Mem.: AIA. Home: 213 Scottholm Ter Syracuse NY 13224-1737 *A guiding principle over many years of teaching and practice, is the interrelationship of theory and work-of-idea and circumstance, of imagination and the forces generated by day to day life.*

**SKOLFIELD, MELISSA T.,** public relations executive, government official; b. New Orleans, June 25, 1958; m. Frank W. Curtis. BA in Econ. and Behavioral Sci., Rice U., 1980; MA in Pub. Affairs, George Washington U., 1986. Account exec. McDaniel & Tate Pub. Rels., Houston, 1981-84; press sec. Rep. Michael Andrews of Tex., 1985-87; press. sec. Senator Dale Bumpers of Ark., 1987-93; dep. asst. sec. for pub. affairs for policy and strategy Dept. Health and Human Svcs., Washington, 1993-95, asst. sec. pub. affairs, 1995—2001; sr. v.p., dir. healthcare practice group Golin/Harris Internat., Washington, 2001—03; comm. counsel Dem. Leader Nancy Pelosi U.S. House of Reps., Washington, 2003—. Press asst. Dem. Nat. Com., Dem. Nat. Conv., 1988, Clinton Pres. Campaign, Dem. Nat. Com., 1992. Mem. Senate Press Secs. Assn. (pres.), Assn. Dem. Press Assts., Pub. Rels. Soc. Am. Office: US Ho of Reps Office Dem Leader Washington DC 20515

**SKOLL, JEFFREY S.,** philanthropist, former internet company executive; b. Montreal, Jan. 16, 1965; BSEE, U. Toronto, 1987; MBA, Stanford U., 1995; LLD (hon.), U. Toronto, 2003. Founder Skoll Engring., 1987, Micros on the Move Ltd., 1990; mgr. distrbn. channels online news info. Knight-Ridder Info.; co-founder, pres., v.p. strategic analysis and planning eBay Inc., San Jose, Calif., 1995—99; founder, CEO Participant Productions, LA, 2004—. Bd. dirs. e-Bay Found., 1998—; founder, chmn. Skoll Found., 1999—; bd. dirs. Cmty. Found. Silicon Valley; mem. advisory bd. Stanford Grad. Sch. Bus. Named a WIRED Renegade, WIRED Rave Awards, 2006; named one of the most innovative philanthropists of the past decade, BusinessWeek, 2002, 2003, 50 Most Generous Philanthropists, Fortune Mag., 2005, World's Richest People, Forbes, 1999—2004, 100 Most Influential People, Time Mag., 2006; recipient Leafy award, 1999, Visionary award, Software Development Forum, 2001, Outstanding Philanthropist award, Silicon Valley chapter Assn. Fundraising Professionals, 2002, Internat. Assn. Fundraising Professionals, 2003. Office: Skoll Foundation 250 University Ave Ste 200 Palo Alto CA 94301 Office Phone: 650-331-1031. Office Fax: 650-331-1033.*

**SKOLNICK, HOLLY R.,** lawyer; b. NYC, May 7, 1954; BA, Univ. Wis., 1976; JD, Harvard Univ., 1980. Bar: DC 1980, Fla. 1984. Law clk. Hon. Eugene P. Spellman US Dist. Judge (so. dist.) Fla.; staff atty. public defender svc., Washington; shareholder, litig., chair pro bono com. Greenberg Traurig LLP, Miami, Fla. Editor: Harvard Civil Rights-Civil Liberties Law Rev. Bd. dir. Florida Immigrant Advocacy Ctr., Equal Justice Works. Named one of one of the top 250 lawyers in So. Fla., So. Fla. Legal Guide. Office: Greenberg Traurig LLP 1221 Brickell Ave Miami FL 33131 Office Phone: 305-579-0500. Office Fax: 305-579-0717. Business E-Mail: skolnickh@gtlaw.com.

**SKOLNICK, LAWRENCE,** neonatal physician, medical association administrator; b. NYC, July 29, 1947; s. Harry and Sylvia Skolnick; m. Tamar Tumarkin, Apr. 7, 1970; children: Daniel, Michael, Rachel. BS, CUNY, 1968; MD, NYU, 1972; MPH, U. N.C., 1980. Dir. newborn medicine Hosp. of Albert Einstein Coll. Medicine, Bronx, NY, 1977-80; dir. neonatology Morristown (N.J.) Meml. Hosp. 1980—, Overlook Hosp., Summit, NJ, 1999—, Atlantic Health Sys., 1999—; assoc. prof. med. pediat. UNDNJ-N.J.Sch. Medicine, 2001—. E-mail: larry.skolnick@ahsys.org.

**SKOLNICK, MARILYN,** civic worker; b. N.Y.C., Jan. 17, 1925; d. Max and Annie Ruth (Stern) Kassel; n. Herbert Skolnick, Aug. 2, 1948; 1 child, Tamara. BA, Bklyn. Coll., 1946; MA, U. Okla., 1948; postgrad., State U. Iowa, 1948-52. Host, prodr. cable TV program Focus on Issues, 1983—; chair citizen participation com. Transp. Rsch. Bd., Nat. Acad. Sci., 1987-94; sec. local transp. fin. com., 1987—. Bd. dirs. Port Authority of Allegheny County, 1982-95; pres. Allegheny County Transp. Coun., 1997-99, v.p., 1999-2000; mem. Pa. Small Bus. Compliance Adv. Com., 1992—; mem. Penndot Mobility Plan for Pa., 2004—. Chair Monroeville Planning Commn., 1983-85; bd. dirs. Pa. Planning Assn., 1983-85; bd. dirs. Group Against Smog and Pllution; mem. Pa. Transp. Adv. Com., 1983-86; mem. air pollution ctrl. adv. com. Allegheny County Health Dept., 1985—, pollution prevention com. chair, 2004—; mem. Allegheny County Local Emergency Planning Com., 1987—, Allegheny County Comprehensive Plancomm. Pub. Participation Team. Mem. LWV (former bd. dirs.), N.Y. Acad. Scis., Pa. Acad. Scis., Sierra Club (bd. dirs. Pa. chpt. 1986—, chair Allegheny Group 1988-91), Sigma Xi. Home: 109 South Ridge Dr Monroeville PA 15146-4739

**SKOLNICK, S. HAROLD,** lawyer; b. Woonsocket, R.I., June 17, 1915; s. David and Elsie (Silberman) S.; m. Shirley Marshall. AB cum laude, Amherst Coll., 1936; JD, Boston U., 1940. Bar: R.I. 1940, U.S. Supreme Ct. 1946, D.C. 1947, Fla. 1952, U.S. Dist. Ct. (so. dist.) Fla. 1953, U.S. Ct. Appeals (5th cir.) 1960, U.S. Ct. Appeals (11th cir.) 1981. Atty. Dept. of War, Washington, 1940-42; asst. gen. counsel, asst. chief legal dept. Office Chief Ordnance, Dept. of Army, Washington, 1947-50; assoc. Francis I. McCanna, Providence, R.I., 1951-52; ptnr. French & Skolnick, Miami, Fla., 1953-60; sole practice Miami, Fla., 1961—. Served to lt. col. U.S. Army, 1942—47. Mem. ABA, Am. Judicature Soc., Nat. Def. Indsl. Assn. (life), R.I. Bar Assn., D.C. Bar Assn., Dade County Bar Assn., Estate Planning Coun. Greater Miami, Masons, Shriners. Home and Office: 6521 SW 122d St Miami FL 33156-5550

**SKOLNIK, BARNET DAVID,** retired lawyer; b. N.Y.C., Feb. 8, 1941; s. Jack and Edythe (Savitz) S.; m. Patricia L. Krohn; children: Sarah, Deborah, Daniel, Joseph, Benjamin, Rebecca, Zachary. AB in Am. Govt. cum laude, Harvard U., 1962, LLB, 1965. Bar: D.C. 1966, Md. 1984, Maine 1991. Atty. criminal div. U.S. Dept. Justice, Washington, 1966-68; asst. U.S. atty. for Dist. Md., Balt., 1968-78; chief public corruption unit U.S. Atty.'s Office, Balt., 1973-78; pvt. practice law Balt. and Washington, 1978—91, Portland, Maine, 1991—94; ret. Tchr., lectr. on trial practice, white collar criminality, pub. corruption. Recipient Spl. Achievement award Dept. Justice, 1972, 74, Spl. Commendation for Outstanding Svc., Dept. Justice, 1978, Younger Fed. Lawyer award Fed. Bar Assn., 1974, Atty. Gen.'s Disting. Service award, 1974, Legal award Assn. Fed. Investigators, 1977 E-mail: bskolnik@gwi.net.

**SKOLNIK, MERRILL I.,** electrical engineer; b. Balt., Nov. 6, 1927; s. Samuel and Mary (Baker) S.; m. Judith Magid, June 4, 1950; children: Nachama, Martin Allen, Julia Anne, Ellen Charlotte. BEng, Johns Hopkins U., 1947, MSEng, 1949, DEng, 1951. Research scientist Johns Hopkins U., Balt., 1947-54, vis. prof., 1973-74; engring. specialist Sylvania Electric, Boston, 1954; staff mem. MIT Lincoln Lab., Lexington, Mass., 1954-59; research mgr. Electronic Communications, Timonium, Md., 1959-64, Inst. Def. Analyses, Arlington, Va., 1964-65; supr. radar divsn. Naval Research Lab., Washington, 1965-96. radar sys. cons., 1996—. Mem. adv. com. Duke U. Engring. Sch., Durham, N.C., 1976-93; disting. vis. sci. Jet Propulsion Lab., 1990-92; mem. Md. Gov.'s Exec. Adv. Com., 1993-95. Author: Introduction to Radar Systems, 1962, 3d edit., 2001, Radar Handbook, 1970, 2d edit., 1990; editor: Radar Applications, 1988. Recipient Heinrich Hertz premium Instn. Electronic and Radio Engrs., London, 1964, Disting. Alumnus award Johns Hopkins U., 1979, Disting. Civilian Svc. award USN, 1982, Meritorious Exec. award Sr. Exec. Svc., 1986, Johns Hopkins Engring. and Applied Sci. Excellence in Tchg. award, 1998; named to Soc. of Scholars, Johns Hopkins U., 1975. Fellow IEEE (editor Proceedings 1986-89, Harry Diamond award 1983, Centennial medal 1984, Dennis J. Picard medal for radar technologies and applications 2000); mem. Nat. Acad. Engring. Home: 8123 McDonogh Rd Baltimore MD 21208-1005 Office: Naval Rsch Lab Washington DC 20375-5320 E-mail: skolnik@radar.nrl.navy.mil.

**SKOLNIK, RICHARD ALAN,** plastic surgeon; b. NYC, Jan. 7, 1951; BA in biology summa cum laude, C.W. Post Coll., 1972; MD, Cornell U., 1976. Cert. Am. Bd. Plastic and Reconstructive Surgery. Resident gen. surgery Mt. Sinai Med. Ctr., N.Y.C., 1976-79, resident plastic surgery, 1979-82; clin. instr. Mt. Sinai Sch. Medicine, N.Y.C., 1982-84, asst. clin. prof., 1985—2005, assoc. clin. prof., 2005—; assoc. attending Mt. Sinai Med. Ctr., N.Y.C., 1982—, Beth Israel Med. Ctr., N.Y.C., 1984—; courtesy staff Beth Israel North (Doctor's Hosp.), N.Y.C., 1987—. Fellow cleft lip and palate Children's Hosp., Lima, Peru, 1982; vis. prof. Reconstructive Surgery Found., Maceo, Brazil, 1990, Pune, India, 1994, Beijing, China, 1998. Fellow ACS; mem. Am. Soc. of Plastic and Reconstructive Surgeons, N.Y. Regional Soc. Plastic and Reconstructive Surgeons, AMA, Barsky Soc., N.Y. State Med. Soc. Avocations: ceramics, cooking, golf, tennis. Office: 21 E 87th St New York NY 10128-0506 Office Phone: 212-722-1977. E-mail: shanepunum@aol.com.

**SKOLNIKOFF, EUGENE B.,** political science professor; b. Phila., Aug. 29, 1928; s. Benjamin H. and Betty (Turoff) S.; m. Winifred S. Weinstein, Sept. 15, 1957; children: Matthew, Jessica. BS, MS, MIT, 1950, PhD, 1965; BA, Oxford U., Eng., 1952, MA, 1955. Registered profl. engr. Rsch. asst. in elec. engring. Uppsala U., Sweden, 1950; prof. polit. sci. emeritus M.I.T., 1965—, chmn. polit. sci. dept., 1970-74; dir. Center for Internat. Studies, 1972-87. Vis. rsch. prof. Carnegie Endowment Internat. Peace, Geneva, 1969-70; vis. fellow Balliol Coll., U. Oxford, 1989; vis. scholar Yale U., 1997; sys. analyst Inst. Def. Analyses, Washington, 1957-58; mem. White House staff Office Spl. Asst. to Pres. Sci. and Tech., Washington, 1958-63; adj. prof. Fletcher Sch. Law and Diplomacy, Tufts U., Medford, Mass., 1965-72; sr. cons. White House Office Sci. and Tech. Policy, 1977-81, vice chmn. adv. com. on sci., tech. and devel.; mem. policy rev. com. on nat. low-level nuclear waste mgmt., 1980-86; cons. Dept. State, Office of Tech. Assessment, AID, OECD, MacArthur Found., Resources Future, Am. Soc. Internat. Law, Ford Found., Inst. Def. Analyses; chmn., pres. Sci. and Public Policy Studies Group, 1967-73; mem. Internat. Council Sci. Policy Studies; Montague Burton vis. prof. U. Edinburgh, 1977, mem. NRC coms.; chmn. bd. UN U. Inst. New Tech. (INTECH), Maastricht, Holland, 1998-2005; Michael Dukakis vis. prof. pub. policy Am. Coll. Thessaloniki, Greece, 2000. Author: Science, Technology and American Foreign Policy, 1967, International Imperatives of Technology, 1972, The Elusive Transformation: Science, Technology, and the Evolution of International Politics, 1993; co-editor: World Eco-Crisis, 1972, Visions of Apocalypse, End or Rebirth?, 1985, The Implementation and Effectiveness of International Environmental Commitments, 1998; contbr. articles to publs.; chmn. editorial bd. Pub. Sci., 1971-75; mem. editorial bd. Tech. Rev., 1976-78, Social Studies of Sci., 1970-75, Internat. Orgn., 1974-80, Internat. Rels. of Asia Pacific, 2000-; mem. MIT Press Editl. Bd., 2005—; patentee hybrid circuits. Trustee German Marshall Fund, 1979-87, chmn., 1980-86; trustee UN Rsch. Inst. for Social Devel., 1979-85; bd. dirs. Saco Def., 1984-86; mem. Overseas Devel. Coun.; mem. U.S. del. UN Commn. for Social Devel., 1979; mem. State Dept. Adv. Com. on Sci. and Tech., 1987-90. Served with U.S. Army Security Agy., 1955-57. Decorated Comdr.'s Cross Fed. Republic Germany, Order of Rising Sun, Golden Rays, Neck Ribbon, Japan; Rhodes scholar, 1950—52, Rockefeller Found. fellow, 1963—65. Fellow Am. Acad. Arts and Scis. (councillor 1973-77), AAAS (sec. sect. K 1967-69, mem. com. on sci. and pub. policy 1973-74, com. on sci., engring. and pub. policy 1984-89); mem. UN Assn., Fedn. Am. Scientists, (coun. 1981-85), Coun. Fgn. Rels., Am. Assn. Rhodes Scholars, Soc. for Social Studies of Sci., Sigma Xi, Tau Beta Pi, Eta Kappa Nu. Home: 3 Chandler St Lexington MA 02420-3601 Office: MIT E53-373 77 Massachusetts Ave Cambridge MA 02139-4307 Office Phone: 617-253-3140. Business E-Mail: ebskol@mit.edu.

**SKOMAL, EDWARD NELSON,** aerospace company executive, electromagnetic environments consultant; b. Kansas City, Mo., Apr. 15, 1926; s. Edward Albert and Ruth (Bangs) S.; m. Elizabeth Birkbeck, Mar. 4, 1951 (dec. June 1987); children: Susan Beth, Catherine Anne, Margaret Elaine; m. Joan Kerner, Apr. 9, 1988. BA, Rice U., Houston, 1947, MA, 1949. Engr., Socony Rsch. Labs., Dallas, 1949-51; asst. sect. head Nat. Bur. Standards, Washington, 1951-56; project engr. Sylvania Microwave Rsch. Lab., Palo Alto, Calif., 1956-59; mgr. solid state sys. and components applications engring., chief applications engr. Motorola Solid State Systems Div., Phoenix, 1959-63; dir. comms. engring. dept. Aerospace Corp., El Segundo, Calif., 1963-86, ret., 1986; mem. Presdl. Joint Tech. Adv. Com. on Electromagnetic Compatibility, Washington, 1965-70, 71-75. Author: Man Made Radio Noise, 1978, Automatic Vehicle Locating Systems, 1980; Measuring the Radio Frequency Environment, 1985; contbr. articles to profl. jours. Patentee in field of radio systems, solid state devices, radar cross sect. reduction of ballistic reentry vehicles and sold state microwave components. Elder Riverside Presbytery. With USN, 1944-6. Fellow IEEE (asst. editor Trans. Electromatic Compatibility 1978-86, chmn. tech. adv. com. 1982-86, chmn. tech. com. electromagnetic environments 1976-82, standards com. 1980-86, fellow nominating com. 1980-83, nat. com. standards coordinating com. on definitions 1986—, Richard A. Stoddart award 1980, cert. of Achievement 1971, Paper of Yr. award 1970); mem. IEEE Electromagnetic Soc. (life), Am. Phys. Soc., Internat. Union Radio Scientists, Friends A.H. Smiley Pub. Libr., Am. Leghion, Sigma Xi. Republican. Presbyterian. Achievements include research on the theory of man-made radio noise, microwave components the application of stochastic processes. Home: 1802 Morning Dove Ln Redlands CA 92373

**SKONEY, SOPHIE ESSA,** educational administrator; b. Detroit, Jan. 29, 1929; d. George Essa and Helena (Dihmes) Cokalay; m. Daniel J. Skoney, Dec. 28, 1957; children: Joseph Anthony, James Francis, Carol Anne. Ph.B. U. Detroit, 1951; MEd, Wayne State U., 1960, EdD, 1975; postgrad., Ednl. Inst. Harvard Grad. Sch., 1986—. Tchr. elem. sch. Detroit Bd. Edn., 1952-69, remedial reading specialist, 1969-70, curriculum coord., 1970-71, region 6 article 3 title I coord., 1971-83, area achievement specialist, 1984-88; adminstrv. asst. Office Grant Procurement and Compliance, 1988-2000. Mem. dean's adv. com. Coll. Edn. Wayne State U., 1995—; cons. in field. Editor newsletter Alliance to the Mich. Dental Assns., 1993-2000. Recipient Disting. Alumni award Wayne State U., 1993. Mem. ASCD, Wayne State U. Edn. Alumni Assn. (pres. bd. govs. 1979-80, newsletter editor 1975-77, 80—), Macomb Dental Aux. (pres. 1969-70), Mich. Dental Aux. (pres. 1980-81), Alliance Mich. Dental Assn. (pres. 1982-87), Am. Assn. Sch. Adminstrs., Wayne State U. Alumni Assn. (dir., v.p. 1985-86), Internat. Reading Assn., Mich. Reading Assn., Mich. Assn. State and Fed. Program Specialists, Profl. Women's Network (newsletter editor 1981-83, pres. 1985-87, Anthony Wayne award for leadership 1981), Retirees Orgn. Sch. Adminstrs. and Suprs. (pres. 2003—), Anthony Wayne Soc., Delta Kappa Gamma, Beta Sigma Phi, Phi Delta Kappa (v.p. 1988-90, pres. 1990-91, Educator of Yr. 1985, 91, 96, 2000). Roman Catholic. Home: 20813 Lakeland St Saint Clair Shores MI 48081-2104 Personal E-mail: skoneys@aol.com.

**SKONSKY, CAROLINE TRESCHOW,** marriage and family therapist; b. Pitts., Pa., Mar. 13, 1942; d. Godfrey Augustine Treschow and Lillian Marguerite Burns; m. William Lawrence Skonsky, Oct. 14, 1964; children: Sharon Louise, William Lawrence, Bradley James. BA in psychology, Carlow U., 1998; MSW, U. Pitts., 2001. LCSW Pa., 2001. Asst. to dir. New Choices-New Options, Pitts.; vol. mgr. Hospice Care of Pitts., 1998; social worker St. Margaret Senceca Pl., Verona, Pa., 1999; sr. adv. Step by Step, Pitts., 2000; family therapist Holy Family Soc. Svcs., Pitts., 2001—03; dual diagnosis therapist Mercy Behavioral Health, Pitts., 2004—. Vol. Women's Ctr. and Shelter, 1999—2000. Mem.: Pa. Psychological Assn., Nat. Assn. Social Workers. Avocations: genealogy, writing. Home: 116 4th Ave West Mifflin PA 15122 Business E-Mail: ctskonsky01@libcom.com.

**SKOOG, ANDREW,** music educator; b. Jonesboro, Ark., May 27, 1964; s. Alfred and Patty Skoog. MA in Vocal Performance, Stephen F. Austin State U., 1993. Instr. voice and choral music Tyler (Tex.) Jr. Coll., 1995—2003; prof. U. Tenn., Knoxville, Tenn., 2003—. Instr. voice and choral music U. Tex., Tyler, 1993—95. Singer: (Operas) Carnegie Hall, 1997, 2005, Lyric Opera San Antonio, Dallas (Tex.) Symphony, Minn. Orchestra, Toledo (Ohio) Symphony, Baton Rouge (La.) Symphony. Mem.: Am. Choral Dir. Assn., Nat. Assn. Tchrs. Singing (life), Phi Kappa Phi (hon.), Pi Kappa Lambda (life), Phi Mu Alpha Sinfonia Frat. (life; pres. 1987—88). Personal E-mail: skoogsong@aol.com.

**SKOOG, DONALD PAUL,** retired pathologist, educator; b. Sioux City, Iowa, Sept. 29, 1931; m. Mary Ann Bunn, 1955; children: Robert Eugene, David Alan (dec.), Kristin Marie. BA magna cum laude, Midland Lutheran Coll., Fremont, Nebr., 1953; MD cum laude, U. Nebr., 1958; DSci (hon.), Midland Luth. Coll., 1993. Diplomate Am. Bd. Pathology. Intern, then resident in pathology Bishop Clarkson Meml. Hosp., Omaha, 1958-62; resident in pathology Parkland Meml. Hosp., Dallas, 1962-63; fellow in pathology U. Tex. Southwestern Med. Sch., Dallas, 1962-63; practice medicine specializing in pathology Omaha, 1963-92. Pathologist Bishop Carlson Meml. Hosp., 1963-88, chmn. dept. pathology, 1978-80, chmn. med. edn. com., 1978-83, sec.-treas. med. staff, 1982-87, dir. dept., 1986-87; prof. pathology and microbiology U. Nebr. Coll. Med., 1977-93, mem. dean's faculty adv. coun., 1977-79, mem. grad. and continuing edn. com., 1980-85, mem. coun. affiliated instns., 1981-83, mem. admissions com., 1986-91, sr. cons. pathology and microbiology, 1993—; assoc. med. dir. ARC Blood Svcs., Midwest Region, Omaha, 1988, med. dir./dir. 1989-91, dir./prin. officer, 1991-92, mem. computer sys. selection com., 1991; bd. dirs. ARC Blood Svcs., Washington, 1981-, mem. med. affairs com., 1991-92; mem. exec. com. Nebr. Med. Edn. Fund, 1981-, bd. dirs., 1981-, chmn. loan com., 1983-91, sec.-treas., 1984-91; mem. comm. on Pvt. Practice Assocs., Omaha, 1998-2003, mem. credentials and quality improvement com, 1998-2003; chmn. com. Clarkson Legends, Nebr. Med. Ctr., 2005. Mem. editl. bd. Lab. Medicine, 1979—2003; editor, lead author Swedes, Danes, and Norwegions:Oral Histories from Nebraska, 2000; contbr. articles to med. jours. Councilman Luther Meml. Luth. Ch., Omaha, 1966-72, 87-91, vice chmn., 1969-72; trustee Midland Luth. Coll., 1968-87, chmn., 1973-75; mem. Swedish Cultural Com., Omaha, 1975—. Recipient Alumni Achievement award Midland Luth. Coll., 1972, Disting. Svc. award Sch. of Allied Health Program, U. Nebr. Med. Ctr., 1990, Disting. Alumnus award U. Nebr. Coll. Medicine Alumni Assn., 1998. Fellow Am. Soc. Clin. Pathologists (hematology profl. self-assessment com. 1972, 75,78, adv. coun. 1972-78, chmn. coun. hematology 1978-81, editor Hematology Check Sample 1983-88, Disting. Svc. award Commn. on Continuing Edn. 1985, mem. bd. censors 1987-89, mem. nat. meeting activities com. 1989-92, chmn. 1990-92, Israel Davidsohn disting. svc. award 1993), Coll. Am. Pathologists (hematology resource com. 1981-86, vice chmn. 1982-85); mem. AMA, Nebr. Assn. Pathologists, Nebr. Med. Assn., Met. Omaha Med. Soc. (coun. on grievances and profl. ethics 1983-91), Midland Luth. Coll. Alumni Assn. (pres. 1969-70), Alpha Omega Alpha (pres. U. Nebr. chpt. 1976-77, counsellor 1984-90). Republican. Lutheran. Home: 706 S 96th St Omaha NE 68114 Personal E-mail: dpsmd@cox.net.

**SKOOG, DOUGLAS ARVID,** retired chemistry educator, writer; b. Willmar, Minn., May 4, 1918; s. Arvid C. and Hilma E. (Erickson) S.; m. Judith Bone, Oct. 10, 1942; children: James Arvid, Jon Douglas. BS, Oreg. State U., 1940; PhD, U. Ill., 1943. Research chemist Standard Oil Co. of Calif., Richmond, Calif., 1943-47; asst. prof. chemistry Stanford (Calif.) U., 1947-53, assoc. prof., 1953-62, prof., assoc. exec. head dept. chemistry, 1963-76, prof. emeritus, 1976—; visitor Stanford, 1976—. Author: Fundamentals of Analytical Chemistry, 8th rev. edit., 2003, Principles of Instrumental Analysis, 1998, 5th rev. edit., 1992, Analytical Chemistry, 7th rev. edit., 2000; contbr. articles to profl. jours. Fellow AAAS; mem. Am. Chem. Soc. (pres. Santa Clara Valley sect. 1962, Fisher award in analytical chemistry 1999), Sigma Xi, Phi Kappa Phi, Alpha Chi Sigma. Clubs: Bohemian (San Francisco). Avocations: flying, skiing. Home: 401 Webster St Apt 302 Palo Alto CA 94301-1249 Personal E-mail: skoog@stanford.edu.

**SKOOG, GERALD DUANE,** science educator; b. Sioux City, Iowa, Feb. 27, 1936; s. Paul and Mary Ann Skoog; m. Elizabeth Ann Lee, Dec. 28, 1962; children: Jeffrey, John, Sarah. BS, U. Nebr., 1958. Tchr. various schs., Nebr., Ill., 1958-69; instr. U. Nebr., Lincoln, summer 1969; asst. prof. curriculum and instrm. Tex. Tech U., Lubbock, 1969-72, assoc. prof., coordinator program, 1972-74, assoc. dean, secondary edn., 1976-80, prof., chmn. secondary edn., 1980-90, prof., chmn. curriculum and instrm., 1990-97, Helen DeVitt Jones prof., 1997-2001, pres. faculty senate, 1986-87, dean Coll. Edn., 2002—03, Paul Whitfield Horn prof., 2000—04, prof. emeritus, 2005; dir. Ctr. Integration Sci. and Edn. Rsch., 2004—. Vis. prof. We. Ill. U., summer 1972; lectr. in field; participant, facilitator numerous workshops; cons. Contbr. numerous articles to profl. jours., also reviewer articles and papers; co-author secondary sch. science textbooks. Bd. dirs. Gloria Dei Luth. Ch., Lubbock, 1971-74, 92-93; bd. dirs. Luth. Coun. Cmty. Action, 1970-71, Good Neighbor Ministry, 1982-84; leader Boy Scouts Am., 1978-79; foster parent Luth. Social Svcs. Tex.; bd. dirs. Triangle Coalition for Sci. and Tech., 1986-95. Recipient Pres.'s Faculty Achievement award Tex. Tech U., 1986, Disting. Leadership award, 1996, Award of Excellence, U. Nebr., Lincoln Tchrs. Coll. Alumni Assn., 2003; named Notable Alumnus, U. Nebr., Lincoln, Tchrs. Coll., 1998; named to Tex. Sci. Hall of Fame, 2000. Fellow AAAS; mem. ASCD, NSTA (life, bd. dirs. 1977-79, pres. 1985-86, various coms., Disting. Svc. to Sci. Edn. award 1994, Robert H. Carleton award 2004), Nat. Assn. Rsch. Sci. Tchg. Assn. Edn. Tchrs. Sci., Sci. Tchrs. Assn. Tex. (hon., past pres., Skoog Cup award, Robert H. Carleton award 2004), Nat. Assn. Biology Tchrs., Soc. Study Edn., Phi Delta Kappa. Lutheran. Home: 3214 67th St Lubbock TX 79413-6206 Office: Tex Tech U Coll Edn Lubbock TX 79409 Office Phone: 806-742-1997 x 259. E-mail: gerald.skoog@ttu.edu.

**SKOPIL, OTTO RICHARD, JR.,** federal judge; b. Portland, Oreg., June 3, 1919; s. Otto Richard and Freda Martha (Boetticher) Skopil; m. Janet Rae Lundy, July 27, 1956; children: Otto Richard III, Casey Robert, Shannon Ida, Molly Jo. BA in Econs., Willamette U., 1941, LLB, 1946, LLD (hon.), 1983. Bar: Oreg. 1946, U.S. Dist. Ct. Oreg., U.S. Ct. Appeals (9th cir.), U.S. Supreme Ct. 1946. Assoc. Skopil & Skopil, 1946—51; ptnr. Williams, Skopil, Miller & Beck (and predecessors), Salem, Oreg., 1951—72; judge U.S. Dist. Ct., Portland, 1971—79, chief judge, 1976—79; judge U.S. Ct. Appeals (9th cir.), Portland, 1979—85, sr. judge, 1986—. Chmn. com. adminstrn. of fed. magistrate sys. U.S. Jud. Conf., 1980—86; co-founder Oreg. chpt. Am. Leadership Forum; chmn. 9th cir. Jud. Coun. Magistrates Adv. Com., 1988—91; chmn. U.S. Jud. Conf. Long Range Planning Com., 1990—95. Hi-Y adviser Salem YMCA, 1951—52; appeal agt. SSS Marion County (Oreg.) Draft Bd., 1953—66; master of ceremonies 1st Gov.'s Prayer Breakfast for State Oreg., 1959; citizens adv. com. City of Salem, 1970—71; Gov.'s Com. on Staffing Mental Instns., 1969—70; pres., bd. dirs. Marion County Tb and Health Assn., 1958—61; bd. dirs. Willamette U., 1969—71; elder Mt. Park Ch., 1979—81; bd. dirs. Willamette Valley Camp Fire Girls, 1946—56, Internat. Christian Leadership, 1959, Fed. Jud. Ctr., 1979. Lt. USNR, 1942—46. Recipient Oreg. Legal Citizen of Yr. award, 1986, Disting. Alumni award, Willamette U. Sch. Law, 1988. Mem.: ABA, Internat. Soc. Barristers, Assn. Ins. Attys. U.S. and Can. (Oreg. rep. 1970), Def. Rsch. Inst., Oreg. Assn. Def. Counsel (bd. dirs.), Am. Judicature Soc., Marion County Bar Assn., Oreg. Bar Assn. (bd. dirs.), Prayer Breakfast Movement (fellowship coun.), Illahe Hills Country Club (pres., bd. dirs. 1964—67), Exchange Club (pres. 1947), Salem Club. Office: Sr Circuit Judge 827 US Courthouse 1000 SW 3rd Ave Portland OR 97204-2930*

**SKORA, SUSAN SUNDMAN,** lawyer; b. Chgo., Jan. 5, 1947; d. Gordon Manley and Julia Walker (Firebaugh) Sundman; m. Alan Patrick Skora, May 1, 1977. AB, U. Ill., Chgo., 1970; JD, Ill. Inst. Tech., 1980. Bar: Ill. 1980, Mich. 1983, U.S. Dist. Ct. (we. dist.) Mich. 1983. Dir. Chgo. programs U. Ill. Found., 1973—79; asst. dir. bus. affairs U. Ill., Chgo., 1980—81, exec. asst. to exec. v.p., 1981—83; 2d v.p. Nat. Bank Detroit, Grand Rapids, 1983—88; v.p., dept. head bus. devel. NBD Grand Rapids Bank, 1985—88; v.p., trust divsn. head, mem. exec. com. First Bank, Davenport, Iowa, 1988—91; v.p., trust Firstar Bank, Davenport, 1992—97; asst. prof. dept. bus. adminstrn. Black Hawk Coll., 1992; v.p. pvt. client svcs. Wells Fargo Bank, Davenport, 1998—2004; pres., CEO Cmty. Found. of Gt. River Bend, Davenport, 2004—. Author: Cuneen Linguist, 1979 Mem. Harold Cnty. County Osteo. Physicians and Surgeons Aux., 1988-99, treas., 1989, 91-99, v.p., 1990; v.p. West Mich. U. Ill. Alumni Club, 1983-86; mem. Quad City Osteo. Found., 1988- bequest and fin. com. mem., 1988-95, 97-2004, bd. dirs., 1992-95; lead gift com. mem. Davenport Mus. Art, 1988; endowment com. mem. St. Ambrose U., 1988, Quad City Arts, 1992-94; devel. and fin. com. CASI, 1998-2004, bd.

govs., 1992-98, chair trustees com., 1994-98; bd. dirs. Cmty. Found. of Great River Bend, 1998-2003, chair major gifts com., 1998, 2d v.p. 1998-2000, 1st vice chair, 2001, chair, 2002-03; bd. dirs. Quad City Planned Giving Coun., pres., 2000; mem. capital campaign com. Luth. Social Svcs., 1994; mem. Quad City Estate Planning Coun., 1988—; planned giving com. Am. Cancer Soc., 2000-03. Mem. U. Ill. Alumni Assn. (various offices to sec. 1989-91, exec. com. bd. dirs. 1985-91, nominating com. 1991), Quad City Employee Benefits Group (treas. 1993-95, 96-99), Davenport C. of C. (com. 1996-97), Davenport Country Club (fin. com. 1996-2000), Pi Alpha Tau. Avocations: gardening, reading, golf, auctions. Home: 1139 Brookview Dr De Witt IA 52742-9290 Office: Cmty Found of the Gt River Bend 111 E 3d St Davenport IA 52801-1977 Office Phone: 563-326-2840. Personal E-mail: SusanSkora@mail.com. Business E-Mail: susanskora@cfgrb.org.

**SKORA, WAYNE PHILIP,** retired air force officer; b. Chgo., Jan. 16, 1944; s. Felix Anthony Skora and Lillie (Goshko) St. Thomas; m. Dorothy Mae Barrett, June 13, 1966; children: Tanya Christine, Christopher Michael. BS in Engring. Sci., USAF Acad., 1966; MS in Human Resource Mgmt., U. Utah, 1976. Commd. 2d lt. USAF, 1966, advanced through grades to col., 1988, F-4 pilot various locations, 1967-69, 71-79; flight safety officer Hdqrs. Tactical Air Command, Langley AFB, Va., 1979-82; chief safety, A-10 pilot 23d Tactical Fighter Wing, England AFB, La., 1982-84; chief Office Mil. Cooperation, Am. Embassy, Manama, Bahrain, 1984-87; asst. chief logistics 507th Tactical Air Control Wing, Shaw AFB, SC, 1987-88; dep. comdr. for ops. So. Air Div., Howard AFB, Panama, 1988-90; dep. for safety Air Force Devel. Test Ctr., Eglin AFB, Fla., 1990-92; pres. Skora Enterprises, Inc., Colorado Springs, Colo. 1994—. Decorated Legion of Merit, DFC with oak leaf cluster, Air medal with 21 oak leaf clusters, Def. Meritorious Svc. medal, AF Meritorious Svc. medal with oak leaf cluster, AF Commendation medal with oak leaf cluster. Mem. Order of Daedalians (sec. 1988-90), Sertoma. Roman Catholic. Home: 24 Luxury Ln Colorado Springs CO 80921-3300 Office Phone: 719-488-8314. E-mail: wayne@skorateam.com.

**SKORNIA, STACY LYNN,** research scientist; d. Gregory Allen and Deborah Kay Skornia. BS in Biomed. Engring., St. Louis U., 2001, JD, 2006. Rsch. asst. St. Louis U., 2001—. Mem. safety coun. St. Louis U., 2006—. Mem.: Internat. Trademark Assn., Am. Intellectual Property Law Assn., Capoeira Brasil. Office: Saint Louis U 3507 Lindell Blvd Saint Louis MO 63103 Office Phone: 314-977-8286. Office Fax: 314-977-8288.

**SKORTON, DAVID JAN,** academic administrator; b. Milw., Nov. 22, 1949; s. Samuel and Pauline (Millstein) Skorton; 1 child, Joshua Samuel. BA, Northwestern U., 1970; MD, Northwestern U., Chgo., 1974. Diplomate Nat. Bd. Med. Examiners, Am. Bd. Internal Medicine, Am. Bd. Cardiovascular Disease. Resident UCLA, 1974—77, fellow in cardiology, 1977—80, chief resident in medicine, 1978—79; adj. asst. prof., 1978—80; instr. medicine U. Iowa, Iowa City, 1980—81, asst. prof., 1981—82, asst. prof. elec. and computer engring., 1982—84, assoc. prof. medicine and elec. and computer engring., 1984—88, prof. medicine, elec. and computer engring. and biomed. engring., 1988—; acting dir., then dir. div. gen. internal medicine U. Iowa Coll. Medicine, Iowa City, 1985—89, assoc. chmn. for clinical programs, 1989—92, v.p. for rsch. and external rels., 1992—2002; pres. U. Iowa, 2003—06, Cornell U., Ithaca, NY, 2006—. Dir. echocardiology lab. VA Med. Ctr., Iowa City, 1980—89; mem. internat. and coop. projects study sect. NIH, 1988—92, chmn., 1990—92; lectr. in field numerous sci. sessions, nat. and internat. meetings; manuscript reviewer maj. jours. in field. Editor: (book) Cardiac Imaging and Image Processing, 1986, Cardiac Imaging, 1990, Cardiac Imaging, 2d edit., 1996; contbr. articles and abstracts to profl. jours., chapters to books. Named Intern-of-Yr., UCLA, 1975; recipient Rsch. Assoc. Career Devel. award, VA, 1981—84, Rsch. Career Devel. award, Nat. Heart Lung & Blood Inst., 1984—89; scholar Regents', UCLA, 1967—68. Fellow: ACP, Am. Physiol. Soc., Am. Heart Assn., Am. Coll. Cardiology; mem.: AAAS, Internat. Soc. Adult Congenital Cardiac Disease, Assn. Univ. Cardiologists. Jewish. Office: Cornell U Office of Pres 300 Day Hall Ithaca NY 14853 Office Phone: 607-255-5201. Office Fax: 607-255-9924. E-mail: president@cornell.edu.

**SKOTHEIM, ROBERT ALLEN,** botanist, educator; b. Seattle, Jan. 31, 1933; s. Sivert O. and Marjorie F. (Allen) S.; m. Nadine Vail, June 14, 1953; children—Marjorie, Kris, Julia. BA, U. Wash., 1955, MA, 1958, PhD, 1962; LLD (hon.), Hobart and William Smith Colls., Geneva, N.Y., 1975; LittD (hon.), Whitman Coll., 1988; LHD (hon.), Coll. Idaho, 1988, Occidental Coll., 1989, Ill. Wesleyan U., 1990; DFA (hon.), Willamette U., 1989; DFA (hon.), Whittier Coll., 2000; Gustavus Adolphus Coll., 2000. Prof. history U. Wash., 1962-63; prof. history Wayne State U., Detroit, 1963-66; prof. UCLA, 1966-67, U. Colo., Boulder, 1967-72; provost, dean faculty Hobart and William Smith Colls., 1972-75; pres. Whitman Coll., Walla Walla, Wash., 1975-88, Huntington Libr., Art Collections & Bot. Gardens, San Marino, Calif., 1988-2001; ret., 2001. Author: American Intellectual Histories and Historians, 1966, Totalitarianism and American Social Thought, 1971; Editor: The Historian and the Climate of Opinion, 1969; co-editor: American Social Thought: Sources and Interpretations, 2 vols, 1972. Guggenheim fellow, 1967-68 Mem. Phi Beta Kappa (hon.) Home: 10866 Bill Point Dr Bainbridge Island WA 98110

**SKOV, ARLIE MASON,** petroleum engineer, consultant; b. Perry, Okla., Sept. 21, 1928; s. Arnold and Mary (Mason) S.; m. Luella Luticia Sloan, July 31, 1951; children: Gregory Morgan, Jeffrey Markham, Tamara Kay. BS in Petroleum Engring., U. Okla., 1956; postgrad., U. Va., 1966. Engr., Sohio Petroleum Co., Pauls Valley, Oklahoma City, Okla., 1958-66, mgr. spl. projects Oklahoma City, 1966—76; mgr. prodn. planning BP Alaska Inc., San Francisco, 1977-80; project advisor Sohio Gas Pipeline Co., San Francisco, 1980-81; mgr. new tech. devel. Sohio Petroleum Co., San Francisco, 1981-83; dir. prodn. tech. Sohio Petroleum Co. and Standard Oil Prodn., Dallas, 1983-88; sr. cons. BP Exploration, Inc., Houston, 1989-92; owner Arlie M. Skov, Inc. Petroleum Consulting, Houston, 1993—2001. Chair Santa Barbara City Water Commn., 2003—04. Recipient Disting. Svc. award Okla. Petroleum Coun. 1973. Mem. AIME (bd. dirs. 1977-79, trustee 1990-92, 95-97) Soc. Petroleum Engrs. (hon. bd. dirs. 1977-74, exec. com. 1990-92, pres. 1991, pres. Found. 2003-04, Disting. Mem.), Santa Barbara Club, Cosmopolitan Club of Santa Barbara. Avocations: reading, travel. Office Phone: 805-965-5101. E-mail: askov@earthlink.net.

**SKOWRONEK, STEPHEN LEE,** political scientist, educator; b. Somerville, N.J., Mar. 8, 1951; s. Sidney Daniel and Esther (Gordon) S.; m. Susan Jacobs, Dec. 5, 1982; children: Michael. AB, Oberlin Coll., 1973; MA, Cornell U., 1976, PhD, 1979. From asst. to assoc. prof. UCLA, 1978-85; Pelatiah Perit prof. of Pol. & Social Sci. Yale U., New Haven, 1986—. Author: Building A New American State: The Expansion of National Administrative Capacities 1888-1920, 1982, The Politics Presidents Make: Leadership From John Adams to George Bush, 1993, rev. ed. The Politics Presidents Make: Leadership from John Adams to Bill Clinton, 1997; mng. editor Studies in Am. Polit. Devel., 1986—. Woodrow Wilson Internat. Ctr. for Scholars fellow, Washington, 1985-86. Fellow Am. Acad. Arts & Sci.; mem. Am. Political Sci. Assn., Am. Hist. Assn., Social Sci. History Assn., Phi Beta Kappa, Phi Kappa Phi. Office: Yale Univ Dept Polit Sci PO Box 208301 New Haven CT 06520-8301 Business E-Mail: stephen.skowronek@yale.edu.

**SKOWRONSKI, NANCY,** library director; m. Dennis Skowronski. Acting dir. Detroit Pub. Libr., 2001—02, interim dir., 2002, now dir., CEO. Bd. dirs. ProLiteracy Detroit, 2006—. Mem.: ALA, Univ. Cultural Ctr. Assn. (bd. mem.), Mich. Libr. Assn. Office: Cetroit Pub Libr 5201 Woodward Ave Detroit MI 48202 Office Phone: 313-833-3997. Office Fax: 313-833-2327. E-mail: nskowro@detroit.lib.mi.us.*

**SKOWRONSKI, VINCENT PAUL,** musician, recording industry executive; b. Kenosha, Wis., Jan. 22, 1944; MusB, Northwestern U., 1966, MusM, 1968. V.p. Eberley-Skowronski, Inc., Evanston, Ill., 1973-92; internat. dir. mktg. and pub. rels. Vincent Skowronski: Producer of Classical Recordings,

Evanston, 1993—. Internat. broker rare instruments Strings & Things, Evanston, 1973-92; owner Vincent Skowronski: Fine Violins, Evanston, 1993—; internat. dir. mktg. and pub. rels. EB-SKO Prodns., Evanston, 1978-92; dir. media comm. E-S Mgmt., Evanston, 1985-92; internat. violin Northwestern U., 1969-71; asst. prof. violin U. Wyo., 1971-72; pvt. violin tchr., chamber music coach, lectr., master classes. Solo violinist debut Chgo. Youth Orch., 1959; soloist Chgo. Civic Orch., 1968, guest solo artist Am. Artist Gala, Nat. Puerto Rican TV, 1960, guest solo artist Peninsula Music Festival, Fish Creek, Wis., 1965, 66; guest solo artist Young Am. Musicians Sta. WKAR-TV Mich. State U., 1966, N.Am. premiere R. Nanes' Rhapsody Pathetique for violin and orch., Chgo. Cultural Ctr., 1994, Beijing, 1994, DePaul U. Ctr., Chgo., 1994, Skowronski in Recital: 20 Years Remembered, Northwestern U., Evanston, Ill., 1994, IV Internat. Tchaikovsky Competition Commemorative Recital-Moscow Remembered: 1970-95, Evanston, Ill., 1995, J.L. Kellogg Sch. Mgmt. Recital Northwestern Univ., Ill., 1996; featured soloist Artist Showcase, Sta. WGN-TV Chgo., 1966-71, Honors Concert-Northwestern U., 1966, guest solo artist A.M. Am., Sta. ABC-TV, 1977—, Continental Bank Concerts Sta. WFMT-FM Chgo., 1983, 85-86, 88, 90, United Airlines Presents, Live! Sta. WFMT-FM Chgo., Schumann, 1986, Szymanowski, 1987, Bloch, 1988, Saint-Saens, 1989, Grieg, 1991, Excursions in Music: The Artistry of Vincent P. Skowronski, Sta. KQED-FM San Francisco, 1979, Skowronski: Musical Giant, Interlake Profiles, Sta. WFMT-FM Chgo., 1980, Skowronski at 50: A Birthday Celebration Sta. WNIB-FM, Chgo., 1994, Chgo. Musicians Sta. WNIB-FM, 1996-97, Skowronski at 55: A Birthday Celebration Sta. WNIB-FM, Chgo., 1999; guest solo artist, prodr., annotator for LPs Separate But Equal, 1976, All Brahms, 1977; solo artist, exec. prodr., annotator for LPs Gentleman Gypsy, 1978, Strauss and Szymanowski, 1979, Franck and Szymanowski, 1982; exec. prodr., prodr. CDs Skowronski Alone, 1996, Skowronski Plays, Strauss and Szymanowski, 1998, Skowronski Plays, Live in Concert, 2000, Skowronski Plays! Franck, Szymanowski, Bacewicz and Saint-Saens, 2002, Skowronski Plays! Gentleman Gypsy, 2003, Skowronski Plays Beethoven, Live in Concert, 2003 (Top Ten Best Classical CD award, Chgo. Daily Herald, 2003), Skowronski Plays, Avec et Sans, Live in Concert, 2004 (Top Ten Best Classical CD award Chgo. Daily Herald 2004), Honegger, Milhaud, Skowronski Plays! Avec et Sans, Vol. II, Honegger, Milhaud, Engel, Bloch & Szymanowski, Live in Concert, 2006; prodr., annotator for LPs Opera Lady I, 1978, Eberley Sings Strauss, 1980, American Girl, 1983, Opera Lady II, 1984; guest performances numerous TV stas. Bd. dirs. Chgo. Youth Orch., 1973-77, v.p., 1974-77; artistic cons. Classical and Protege Symphony Orchs., Chgo., 1994—; spl. cons. Beck Inst. for Arts, Schaumburg, Ill., 1998-2000; adjudicator ice skating shows and competitions Wilmette (Ill.) Park Dist., 1985-89; guest panelist classical performance-career forum Sch. of Music, Northwestern U., Evanston, 1992, 94; guest cons. career symposium Edwin G. Foreman High Sch., Chgo., 1989; mem. mayor's founding com. Evanston Arts Coun., 1974-75; pres. Vincent Skowronski Music Found., Evanston, 1997—. Recipient Excellence in Performance award Northwestern U., 1958, 59, 60, Nat. H.S. Inst., 1958-60, Roy Harris award Inter-Am. U., San German, P.R., 1960, award Am. Fedn. Musicians, 1961, award Soc. Am. Musicians, 1961, McCormick Found. award Chgo. Tribune, 1965, Wade Fetzer award for excellence in performance Northwestern U., 1966, award Crescendo Musical Club, 1967; selected as one of 7 violinists to represent U.S. in IV Internat. Tchaikovsky Competition, Moscow, 1970; Grammy award entry list Best Chamber Music Performance, 2001, 04—; guest dignitary Papal Audience, The Vatican, 1995. Mem. Internat. Platform Assn. (voting mem.), Nat. Acad. Arts and Scis., Sigma Nu Office Phone: 847-491-9155. Personal E-mail: skowronskirecordings@ameritech.net.

**SKRAINKA, ALAN FREDERICK,** securities analyst; b. St. Louis, May 8, 1961; s. Frederick Ralph and Yvonne M. (Oelawder) S.; m. Julie Lynn Wussler, Jan. 24, 1987. BBA in Acctg. and Fin., U. Mo., 1983; MBA, Washington U., 1990. Chartered fin. analyst. Utility analyst Edward D. Jones & Co., St. Louis, 1983—, ltd. ptnr. Maryland Heights, Mo., 1986-88, gen. ptnr., 1988—, chief market strategist, Investment Policy Adv. Com., 1996—. Mem. Fin. Analysts Fedn. Office: Edward D Jones & Co PO Box 190489 Saint Louis MO 63119-6489*

**SKRAMSTAD, HAROLD KENNETH, JR.,** museum consultant; b. Washington, June 3, 1941; s. Harold K. and Sarah (Shroat) S.; m. Susan Chappelear, Dec. 28, 1963; children: Robert, Elizabeth. AB, George Washington U., 1963, PhD, 1971. Asst. dir. Am. studies program Smithsonian Instn., Washington, 1969-71; spl. asst. to dir. Nat. Mus. Am. History, 1971, chief spl. projects Nat. Mus. Am. History, chief exhibit programs Nat. Mus. Am. History, 1971-74; dir. Chgo. Hist. Soc., 1974-80; pres. Henry Ford Mus. and Greenfield Village, Dearborn, Mich., 1981-96; mus. cons., 1996—. Mem. Nat. Coun. on Humanities, 1994-2000; mem. mus. mgmt. adv. com. J. Paul Getty Trust, L.A., 1984-90; mem. presdl. commn., action plan, Nat. Mus. African Am. Hsitory and Culture, 2003. Chrmn. bd. Met. Detroit Conv. and Visitors Bur., 1993, chmn., mem. exec. com., 1985—; trustee Coll. Art and Design, Detroit, 1981—; mem. Mich. Travel Commn., 1989—. Recipient Charles Frankel prize Nat. Endowment for the Humanities, 1992. Mem. Am. Assn. Mus. (v.p. 1984-88, accreditation commn. 1982, ethics commn. 1992-93), Smithsonian Instn. Nat. Air and Space Mus. (pub. programming adv. com. 1990—), Smithsonian Coun. Office Phone: 505-521-8510.

**SKRETNY, WILLIAM MARION,** federal judge; b. Buffalo, Mar. 8, 1945; s. William S. and Rita E. Skretny; m. Carol Ann Skretny; 3 children. AB, Canisius Coll., 1966; JD, Howard U., 1969; LLM, Northwestern U., 1972. Bar: Ill. 1969, U.S. Dist. Ct. (no. dist) Ill. 1969, N.Y. 1972, U.S. Ct. Appeals (7th cir.) 1972, U.S. Dist. Ct. (we. dist.) N.Y. 1973, U.S. Ct. Appeals (2d cir.) 1976, U.S. Supreme Ct. 1980. Asst. U.S. atty. Office of U.S. Atty. No. Dist. Ill., Chgo., 1971-73, Office of U.S. Atty. We. Dist N.Y., Buffalo, 1973-81, 1st asst., 1975-81; gen. ptnr. Duke, Holzman, Yaeger & Raphn, Buffalo, 1981-83; 1st dep. dist. atty. Office Dist. Atty Erie County, Buffalo, 1983-88; with Gross, Shuman, Brizdle and Gillfillan, PC, Buffalo, 1988, Cox, Barrell, Buffalo, 1989-90; judge U.S. Dist. Ct. (we. dist.) N.Y., Buffalo, 1990—. Mem. jud. conf. com. on security and facilities, 1994; chair subcom. on planning and space mgmt.; com. liaison for long range planning; spl. counsel U.S. Atty. Gen.'s Advocacy Inst., 1979; staff atty., Office of Spl. Prosecutor U.S. Dept. Justice, 1980. Mem. ABA, Fed. Judges Assn., Bar Assn. of Erie County, Di Gamma, Phi Alpha Delta, Alpha Sigma Nu. Republican. Roman Catholic. Office: US District Court 68 Court St Rm 507 Buffalo NY 14202-3405 Office Phone: 716-332-7820.

**SKROMME, LAWRENCE H.,** consulting agricultural engineer; b. Roland, Iowa, Aug. 26, 1913; s. Austin G. and Ingeborg B. (Holmedal) S.; m. Margaret Elizabeth Gleason, June 24, 1939; children: Cherlyn Sue Granrose, Inga Jean Hill, Karen Ann Sequino. BS with honors, Iowa State U., Ames, 1937. Registered profl. engr. Pa. Design and test engr. Goodyear Tire and Rubber Co., Akron, Ohio, 1937-41; project engr. asst. chief engr. Harry Ferguson Inc., Detroit, 1941-51; chief engr Sperry New Holland div. Sperry Corp., New Holland, Pa., 1951-61, v.p. engring., 1961-78; cons. agrl. engr. Lancaster, Pa., 1978—. Mem. adv. bd. U.S. Congresss Com. on Sci. and Tech., 1989—93; cons. AID, World Bank, others, 1978—85, Saudi Arabia, 1985—86. Patentee; contbr. articles to profl. jours. Dir., pres. Farm and Home Found., Lancaster County, 1968—90, Lancaster County Agrl. Land Preservation Bd., 1978—2002, sec.-treas., 1989—99, dir. emeritus, 2002—; rsch. adv. com. U.S. Dept. Agr., Washington, 1964—68; gov.'s com. agr. and land preservation Gov. of Pa., 1969; bd. dirs. awards com. Engrs. Joint Coun., N.Y.C., 1967—75. Fellow: Am. Soc. Agrl. Engrs. (v.p. 1952—55, pres. 1959—60, Gold medal 1974); mem.: NAE (peer and membership com. 1978—82), Am. Soc. Engring. Edn., Internat. Assn. Agrl. Engrs. (v.p. 1974—79, pres. farm machine divsn.), Nat. Soc. Profl. Engrs., Tau Beta Pi, Alpha Zeta, Phi Kappa Phi. Republican. Methodist. Avocations: collecting old tools and antiques, farm machinery history. E-mail: lhsae@aol.com.

**SKROPANIC, JESSICA T.,** sociologist, educator; b. Louisville, Aug. 3, 1966; d. Jan Charles and Marilyn Lee (Hendrickson) Green; m. Zeljko Tomislav Skropanic, Jan. 6, 1990. BA in Anthropology with honors, Humboldt State U., 1989, MA in Anthropology/Sociology with honors, 1992.

Archaeologist Miami U., 1985; rsch. asst. Humboldt State U., Arcata, Calif., 1986—89, rsch. asst. libr./archives, 1989—92, social sci. tutor, 1990—91, grad. tchg. asst., 1991; coord. vol. and docent programs Redding Mus. Art and History, Turtle Bay Pk. and Mus. Corp., 1994; tchr. sociology, social psychology, archaeology Simpson U., Redding, Calif., 1992—. Mng. editor Worldwide Spa Rev. mag., 2004—. Lay Eucharist minister All Sts. Episc. Ch., Redding, 1992-96; vol. Humboldt Jour. Social Rels., 1986-89; vol., mem. various mus. Mem. Am. Sociol. Assn., Shasta County Arts Coun., Phi Kappa Phi, Pi Gamma Mu, Alpha Sigma Lambda (charter faculty). Avocations: creative writing, writing, dance, painting. Office: Simpson U Social Sci Dept 2211 College View Dr Redding CA 96003-8601 Office Phone: 530-226-4711. E-mail: jskropanic@simpsonuniversity.edu.

**SKROWACZEWSKI, STANISLAW,** conductor, composer; b. Lwow, Poland, Oct. 3, 1923; came to U.S., 1960; s. Pawel and Zofia (Karszniewicz) S.; m. Krystyna Jarosz, Sept. 6, 1956; children: Anna, Paul, Nicholas. Diploma faculty philosophy, U. Lwow, 1945; diploma faculties composition and conducting, Acad. Music Lwow, 1945, Conservatory at Krakow, Poland, 1946; L.H.D., Hamline U., 1963, Macalester Coll., 1972; L.H.D. hon. doctorate. U. Minn.; Doctorate (hon.), U. Wroclaw, Poland, 2003. Guest condr. in Europe, S.A., U.S., 1947—; Composer, 1931—; pianist, 1928—; violinist, 1934—; condr., 1939—; permanent condr., music dir. Wroclaw (Poland) Philharmonic, 1946-47, Katowice (Poland) Nat. Philharmonic, 1949-54, Krakow Philharmonic, 1955-56, Warsaw Nat. Philharmonic Orch., 1957-59, Minnesota Orch., 1960-79; prin. condr., mus. adviser Halle Orch., Manchester, Eng., 1984-91; musical advisor St. Paul Chamber Orchestra, 1986-87. First symphony and overture for orch. written at age 8, played by Lwow Philharm. Orch., 1931. Composer: 4 symphonies Prelude and Fugue for Orchestra (conducted first performance Paris), 1948, Overture, 1947 (2d prize Szymanowski Concours, Warsaw 1947); Cantiques des Cantiques, 1951, String Quartet, 1953 (2d Prize Internat. Concours Composers, Belgium 1953), Suite Symphonique, 1954 (first prize, gold medal Composers Competition Moscow 1957), Music at Night, 1954, Ricercari Notturni, 1978 (3d prize Kennedy Center Friedheim Competition, Washington), Concerti for Clarinet and Orch., 1980, Violin Concerto, 1985, Concerto for Orch., 1985, Fanfare for Orch., 1987, Sextett for Oboe, Violin, Viola, Orchestra, 1980, String Trio for Violin, Viola, 1990, Triple Concerto for Violin, Clarinet, Piano, Orchestra, 1992, Fantasie pre Tre (Flute, Oboe, Cello), 1993, Chamber Concerto, 1993, Passacaglia Immaginaria for Orch., 1995, Musica a Quattro for Clarinet, Violin, Viola, Cello, 1998, Concerto for Orch., 1998, Symphony, 2003; also music for theatre, motion pictures, songs and piano sonatas, English horn concerto; rec. by Mercury, Columbia, RCA, Albany, Victor, Vox, EMI, Angel. Decorated comdrs. cross Polonia Restituta; recipient nat. prize for artistic activity Poland, 1953, 1st prize Santa Cecilia Internat. Concours for Condrs., Rome, 1956, Cannes Festival award for best rec. of 19th century symphonic music, 2002, Disting. Artist award McKnight Found., 2004. Mem. Union Polish Composers, Internat. Soc. Modern Music, Nat. Assn. Am. Composers-Condrs., Am. Music Center. Office: PO Box 700 Wayzata MN 55391

**SKRUPKY, ELAINE CHARLOTTE,** art educator; b. Amery, Wis., Nov. 11, 1927; d. Herbert Roy Peterson and Nina Louise Olson; m. Hartford Gay Elaine Charlotte Peterson, June 24, 1950 (dec. Aug. 2, 1982); children: Lynn, Jenene, Van(dec.), Renée, Shawndel(dec.). BSc in Art and English, River Falls U., 1949. Art supr. Rice Lake (Wis.) Schs., 1949—50; art tchr. U. Wis. Ctr., Rice Lake, 1968—69, VIII Pk., Jensen Beach, Fla., 1993—. Author: Poetry Guild Anthology, 1996 (Editors Choice award, 1996), The Best Poems of the 90's, 1997 (named Internat. Poet of Merit, Internat. Soc. Poetry, 1997); Of Moonlight and Wishes, 1997, A Celebration of Poets, 1998, sound of Poetry, 1998. Chmn. and organizer Aquafest Art Show, Rice Lake, 1976—77; chmn. state fine arts Wis. Fedn. Women's Clubs, 1972—74, state drama chmn., 1974—76, dist. art chmn., 1976; pres. Daubers Guild, Rice Lake, 1976—77; chmn. Am. Cancer Dr., Rice Lake, 1979—80, Heart Drive, Rice Lake, 1980; organizer The Red Barn Theatre, Rice Lake. Named Outstanding Woman in Arts, Wis. Federated Woman's Club, 2000; named to Internat. Hall of Fame, Internat. Soc. Poetry, 2000; recipient State Art award, Rural Artists Wis., 1979, 4th runner-up, Ms. Nat. Sr Queen Contest, 1998, State Achievement award, Wis. Federated Woman's Club, 2000, 2001. Mem.: Art League, Alpha Psi Omega, Art Gallery Coop, Poetry Club. Avocations: painting, writing, piano, singing, acting. Home (Summer): 1310 D Orchard Beach Ln Rice Lake WI 54868 Home (Winter): 10701 S Ocean Dr Jensen Beach FL 34957 Personal E-mail: peterson@mailstation.com.

**SKULE, JOHN L.,** pharmaceutical company executive; BS in Economics, Univ. Minn. V.p. Squibb Corp., Bristol-Myers Squibb, v.p. Public Affairs, Corporate Staff, 1993—97, sr. v.p. corp. and environ. affairs, 1998—. Office: Bristol-Myers Squibb Co 345 Park Ave New York NY 10154-0004

**SKULINA, THOMAS RAYMOND,** lawyer; b. Cleve., Sept. 14, 1933; s. John J. and Mary B. (Vesely) S. AB, John Carroll U., 1955; JD, Case Western Res. U., 1959, LLM, 1962. Bar: Ohio 1959, U.S. Supreme Ct. 1964, ICC 1965. Ptnr. Skulina & Stringer, Cleve., 1967-72, Riemer Oberdank & Skulina, Cleve., 1978-81, Skulina, Fillo, Walters & Negrelli, 1981-86, Skulina & McKeon, Cleve., 1986-90, Skulina & Hill, Cleve., 1990-97; atty. Penn Ctrl. Transp. Co., Cleve., 1960-65, asst. gen. atty., 1965-78, trial counsel, 1965-76; with Consol. Rail Corp., 1976-78; pvt. practice Cleve., 1997—. Tchr. comml. law Practicing Law Inst., N.Y.C., 1970; practicing labor arbitrator Fed. Mediation and Conciliation Svc., 1990—; arbitrator Mcpl. Securities Rule-making Bd., 1994-98, N.Y. Stock Exch., 1995—, NASD, 1996—; mediator NASD, 1997—, AAA Comml., 1997—; mediator vol. panel EEOC, 1997-99, contract panel, 1999-2000; arbitrator Better Bus. Bur., 2000—. Contbr. articles to legal jours. Income tax and fed. fund coord. City of Warrensville Heights, Ohio, 1970—77; spl. counsel City of North Olmstead, Ohio, 1971—75; spl. counsel to Ohio Atty. Gen., 1983—93, Cleve. Charter Rev. Commn., 1988, referee, 1986—; fact-finder State Employees Rels. Bd., Ohio, 1986—; hearing officer Human Resource Commn., Summit County, Ohio, 2000—03. With U.S. Army, 1959. Mem. ABA (R.R. and motor carrier com. 1988-96, jr. chmn. 1989-96, alt. dispute resolution com. 1998—), FBA, Assn. Conflict Resolution, Cleve. Bar Assn. (grievance com. 1987-93, chmn. 1997-98, trustee 1993-96, ADR com. 1997—), Ohio Bar Assn. (bd. govs. litigation sect. 1986-98, negligence law com. 1989-96, ethics and profl. responsibility com. 1990-91, alt. dispute resolution com. 1996—), Am. Arbitration Assn. (practicing labor arbitrator 1987—), Nat. Assn. R.R. Trial Counsel (emeritus), Internat. Assn. Law and Sci., Pub. Sector Labor Rels. Assn., Internat. Indsl. Rels. Rsch. Assn., Soc. Fed. Labor and Employee Rels. Profls. Democrat. Roman Catholic. Home: 3162 W 165th St Cleveland OH 44111-1016 Office: 24803 Detroit Rd Westlake OH 44145 Office Phone: 440-899-1911. E-mail: tskulina@sbcglobal.net.

**SKULSKI, TIA,** human resources specialist; b. Buffalo, Jan. 19, 1967; d. Norman Skulski and Christine Yetzer. BS in Mktg., Canisius Coll., Buffalo, 1985—89. Cert. human resources mgmt. UCLA Ext., 2005. Mktg. coord. Pacific Theaters, LA, 1991—93; project coord. Canterbury Designs, LA, 1993—96; human resources mgr. Scour.com, Beverly Hills, Calif., 1999—2000, Vertex Sys., LA, 2000—01; human resources adminstr. Reed Bus. Info., LA, 2001—. Vice-chair LA chpt. Siggraph, 1999—2003. Chair, commr. Commn. on Status of Women, Santa Monica, Calif., 2002—05. Mem.: Profl. Human Resources Assn., Soc. Human Resources Mgmt. Office Fax: 323-549-4174. Personal E-mail: tia_skulski@yahoo.com.

**SKUTNIK, BOLESH J.,** optics scientist, lay worker, lawyer; b. Passaic, N.J., Aug. 19, 1941; s. Boleslaw Stanley and Helen Marie (Dzierzynska) S.; m. Phyllis 'Victoria Wojciechowski, Sept. 2, 1967 (div. July 1991); m. Anita Marie Bacon, Aug. 2, 1997; children: Pam, Janeen, Todd, Darren. BS, Seton Hall U., 1962; MS, Yale U., 1964, PhD, 1967; JD, U. Conn., 1995. Bar: N.Y. 1996, Conn. 1996, U.S. Patent and Trademark Office 1992. Chief scientist Ensign Bickford Coating Co., Simsbury, Conn., 1979-91; prin. B.J. Assocs., New Britain, Conn., 1991-97, West Hartford, Conn., 1997—; patent atty., rsch. scientist Fiberoptic Fabrications, Inc., East Longmeadow, Mass., 1995-97; dir. rsch., dir. patents and licensing Sci. Fiberoptic Fabrications, Inc., East

Longmeadow, Mass., 1997—2002; corp. counsel, dir. rsch. CeramOptec Industries, Inc., East Longmeadow, Mass., 2003—. Lector, mem. parish coun. St. Catherine of Siena, West Simsbury, Conn., 1980-85, St. Maurice, New Britain, Conn., 1985-2000, St. Thomas Apostle, West Hartford, Conn., 1980—; chmn., del. synod Archdiocese of Hartford, Conn., 1990-96; chmn. parish Holy Family Retreat League, New Britain, 1989-2000; pres. Enbic Employees Credit Union, Simsbury, 1988-91; asst. prof. chemistry Fairfield U., Conn., 1973-79. Contbr. articles to profl. jours. Interviewer Yale Alumni Schs. Com., L.I. and Hartford, Conn., 1969—; rep. New Britain Club, 1997-2000; mem. New Britain Mus. Am. Art, Hillstead Mus., Wadsworth Mus., Smithsonian, Ctr. Polish Culture, D.C. Mem. ABA (subcom. chair 1993, 94, 96), Conn. Bar Assn., N.Y. State Bar Assn., Conn. Intellectual Property Lawyers Assn., Am. Intellectual Property Lawyers Assn., Soc. Photo-optical Engrs. (conf. co-chair, 1987-90, 2006), Optical Soc. Am., Am. Ceramic Soc., (coord. symposium 1991), Materials Rsch. Soc. (chair symposium 1987-89), Am. Chem. Soc. (alt. coun. 1988-90. sect. chair 1994, vice chair 1993, bd. dirs. 1985-2002), Porsche Club Am. (various positions Conn. Valley region), Yale Club New Britain (dir. 1994-2000), Yale Club Hartford, Yale Alumni Assn. Roman Catholic. Achievements include patents in field. Home: 51 Banbury Ln West Hartford CT 06107-1102 Office: CeramOptec Industries Inc 515 Shaker Rd East Longmeadow MA 01028-3126 Office Phone: 413-525-8222. Personal E-mail: boleshsj@aol.com. Business E-Mail: bolesh.skutnik@ceramoptec.com. *The human spirit is stronger than anything that can happen to it.*

**SKVORECKY, JOSEF VACLAV,** literature educator, writer; b. Nachod, Czechoslovakia, Sept. 27, 1924; arrived Can., 1969; s. Josef Karel and Anna (Kurazova) S.; m. Zdenka Josefa Salivarova, Mar. 30, 1958 PhD, Charles U., Czechoslovakia, 1951; PhD (hon.), SUNY, 1986, Masaryk U., 1991, U. Calgary, 1992, U. Toronto, 1992. Vis. lectr. U. Toronto, Ont., Canada, 1969-70, writer-in-residence, 1970-71, assoc. prof., 1971-75, prof. English, 1975-90; prof. emeritus, 1990—. Lectr. on lit. topics Voice of Am., 1973—; adv. to Pres. Vaclav Havel, 1990. Editor: Sixty Eight Publ. Corp., 1972—; author: The Cowards, 1958, The End of the Nylon Age, 1967, Republic of Whores, 1969, The Miracle Game, 1972, The End of Lieutenant Boruvka, 1980, The Engineer of Human Souls, 1984, Miss Silver's Past, 1985, Dvorak in Love, 1986, The Bride of Texas, 1992, Headed for the Blues, 1996, The Two Murders in My Double Life, 1996; co-author (with Zdena Salivarova): Brief Encounter, With Murder, 1999, Brief Encounter After Many Years with Murder, 2000, Brief Encounter at the End of an Era, With Murder, 2001, Brief Encounter in the White Lady, With Murder, 2003; co-author: Pulchra, 2003, Ordinary Lives, 2004, An Inexplicable Story, 2002, Brief Encounter in Prague with Murder, 2004; author: (short stories) The Menorah, 1964, The Life of High Society, 1965, The Mournful Demeanor of Lieutenant Boruvka, 1966, A Babylonian Story, 1967, The Bitter World, 1969, Sins for Father Knox, 1973, Oh, My Papa!, 1972, The Edenvale Stories, 1996, When Eve Was Naked, 2001, (plays) The New Men and Women CBC Radio, 1977, God in Your House, 1980 (1st prize Multicultural Theatre Festival Hamilton, 1980), (films) The Tank Battalion, 1991, The Swell Season, 1994, Eine Kleine Jazzmusik, 1996, Poe and the Death of a Beautiful Girl, 1997, The Legend of Emoke, 1998, The Detective Agency, 2000, The Ostrozrak Detective Agency, 2002, (essays) Reading Detective Stories, 1965; author They-Which is We, 1968, All the Bright Young Men and Women, 1972, Working Overtime, 1979, Talkin' Moscow Blues, 1989. Decorated Order of White Lion; apptd. mem. Order of Can., 1992; recipient Neustadt Internat. prize for lit., U. Okla., 1980, Gov. Gen. Can.'s award, 1985, lit. prize Echoing Green Found., 1990, Czech Republic's State Prize for Lit., 1999, Pangea prize 2001, Jaroslev Seifert prize, 2004. Fellow Royal Soc. Can.; mem. Can. Writers' Union, Authors' League Am., Crime Writers Can., Mystery Writers Am., The Internat. PEN Club, Can. br. Czechoslovak Nat. Assn. Can., Order of Can. Conservative. Roman Catholic. Avocation: swing music. Home: 487 Sackville St Toronto ON Canada M4X 1T6 Office Phone: 416-964-8372. Personal E-mail: j.skvorecky@utoronto.ca.

**SKWARCZYńSKI, HENRYK ADAM (HENRYK SKWAR),** writer; b. Lódź, Poland, Aug. 13, 1952; arrived in US, 1980; s. Zdzislaw and Stanislawa Ewa (Laszczyk) S.; m. Eglé Juodvalkis, Sept. 2, 1989 MA, U. Warsaw, 1977; postgrad., Polish Acad. Sci., 1978-80, Sorbonne U. Free-lance writer, N.Y.C., 1980-81, Voice of Am., Washington, 1981-82; instr. Defense Lang. Inst., Monterey, Calif., 1982-84; staff writer Libertas, Paris, 1984-86; free-lance writer Radio Free Europe, Munich, 1987-95; writer Chgo., 1995—. Author: Man in a Cleft, 1979, The Anguish of Becoming American, 1989, Sweeney Among the Nightingales, 2000, The Straw Sea, 2002, A Rose and the Moon in a Coat-of-Arms, 2004; editor-in-chief: Ephemeron, 1974—75; contbr. short stories to mags. Activist Solidarity Movement, 1980—89. Rotary Club grantee, 1982, Hoover Inst. grantee, 1985. Avocation: travel in Africa.

**SKWERES, THOMAS W.,** entrepreneur, writer, poet, investor, consultant, advertising executive; b. Chgo., May 11, 1929; s. Marion John and Sophie Regina (Rataiczyk) Skweres; m. Charmaine Liska, 1950 (div. 2000); m. Carol Lynn, 2004; children: Thomas Allan, Pamela Charmaine, Patricia Ann. AA, Wright C.C., Chgo., 1949; student, Northwestern U., Chgo., 1949—51, student, 1953—56. Prodn. mgr. Reincke, Meyer & Finn, Chgo., 1953—55; v.p., account exec. Hanson and Stevens, Chgo., 1955—61; v.p. sales, gen. mgr. Ross & White, Wheeling, Ill., 1961—84; sales mgr. Graphics Plus, Lisle, Ill., 1984—89, Essig Printing, Lisle, Ill., 1989—91; CEO Tomco Enterprises, Lisle, Ill., 1991—. Staff sgt. U.S. Army, 1951—53, Europe. Achievements include patents in field; research in aviation; chemicals; metals; R.R. products; automotive fields; printing; art direction; real estate; manufacturing industry; finance industry. Avocations: travel, gardening, guidance, conservative gambling, teaching. Home: 5613 Snowdrop Lisle IL 60532 Office: Tomco Printing & Enterprise PO Box 475 Lisle IL 60532

**SKYLER, JAY S.,** medical educator, consultant; b. Phila., Feb. 14, 1947; m. Mercedes Armas Bach, Aug. 9, 2003; children: Jennifer Anne, Alexandra Regina Bach, Marcus Richard Bach. BS, Pa. State U., 1967; MD, Jefferson Med. Coll., 1969. Diplomate in internal medicine, also endocrinology, diabetes and metabolism Am. Bd. Internal Medicine. Intern, resident in internal medicine, fellow in endocrinology and metabolism Duke U., Durham, NC, 1969—73, assoc. then asst. prof., 1972—76; assoc. prof. then prof., medicine, pediatrics and psychology, divsn. endocrinology, diabetes, and metabolism, dept. medicine U. Miami, Fla., 1976—. Pres. Am. Diabetes Assn., Alexandria, Va., 1991—92; v.p. Internat. Diabetes Fedn., Brussels, 1994—2000; bd. dirs. Amylin Pharms., San Diego, DexCom, Inc, San Diego. Founding editor-in-chief (med. jour.) Diabetes Care, 1978—82, scientific editor Internat. Diabetes Monitor, 1989—, assoc. editor Diabetes Technology & Therapeutics, 2006—. With USPHS, 1973—75. Master: ACP (mem. bd. regents 1996—99, chmn., coun. of subspecialty societies); mem.: Internat. Diabetes Fedn. (past v.p.), Soc. for Clin. Investigation, Internat. Diabetes Immunotherapy Group, Am. Diabetes Assn. (past pres.). Independent. Achievements include research in multiple developments for treatment of diabetes. Office: Univ of Miami Diabetes Research Institut Ste 3054 1450 NW 10th Ave Miami FL 33136 Office Phone: 305-243-6146. Office Fax: 305-243-4484. E-mail: jskyler@miami.edu.

**SKYLSTAD, WILLIAM S.,** bishop; b. Omak, Wash., Mar. 2, 1934; s. Stephen Martin and Reneldes Elizzbeth (Danzl) S. Student, Pontifical Coll.Josephinium, Worthington, Ohio, 1946—58; student Wash. State U., 1960—61; MA in Edn., Gonzaga U., 1966. Ordained priest Roman Catholic Ch., 1960; asst. pastor Pullman, Wash., 1960-62; tchr. Mater Cleri Sem., 1961-68, rector, 1968-74; pastor Assumption Parish, Spokane, 1974-76; chancellor Diocese of Spokane, 1976-77; ordained bishop, 1977; bishop Diocese of Yakima, Wash., 1977-90, Diocese of Spokane, Wash., 1990—. V.p. US Conf. of Catholic Bishops, 2001—04, pres., 2004—. Office: Diocese of Spokane PO Box 1453 1023 W Riverside Ave Spokane WA 99210-1103 E-mail: bishop@dioceseofspokane.org.

**SLABACH, STEPHEN HALL,** lawyer; b. Nov. 15, 1934; s. Carl Edward and Alvine A. Slabach; m. Elizabeth Havard Cartwright, Feb. 15, 1958; children: Elizabeth Slabach Schmit, Stephen Edward, William Cartwright.

BSME, Northwestern U., 1957; postgrad., George Washington U. Sch. Law, 1957—59; LLB, Stanford U, 1961. Bar: Calif., U.S. Dist. Ct., Calif. 1962, U.S. Ct. Appeals (9th cir.) 73, U.S. Supreme Ct. 76. Law clk. to judge Calif. First Dist. Ct. Appeal, San Francisco, 1961—62; assoc. Cooley, Corwley, Gather, Godward, Castro & Huddleson, San Francisco, 1962—65, Cushing, Cullinan, Hancock & Rothert, San Francisco, 1965—73, ptnr., 1973—75; sole practice Burlingame, Calif., 1975—88, San Mateo, Calif., 1988—. Legal aid vol. San Mateo County; trustee San Mateo County Law Libr. Com., 1993—2002, v.p., 1998—2002; pres. Pacific Locomotive Assn., 1988—90, gen. counsel, 1980—. Mem.: ABA, State Bar Calif. Republican. Episcopalian. Office: 520 S El Camino Real Ste 700 San Mateo CA 94402-1720 Office Phone: 650-347-7776.

**SLABAUGH, GREGORY GIBRAN,** application developer; b. Garden City, Mich., May 31, 1971; s. Ronald Clinton and Phillis Grace Slabaugh; life ptnr. Stephen John Blanchard. PhD, Ga. Inst. of Tech., Atlanta, 2002. Sr. developer Friendly Software Corp., Maumee, Ohio, 1994—96; mem. tech. staff Siemens Corp. Rsch., Princeton, NJ, 2002—. Mem.: IEEE. Achievements include patents for Computer vision and medical imaging. Home: 13 Angelica Ct Princeton NJ 08540 Office: Siemens Corp Rsch 755 College Rd E Princeton NJ 08540 Office Phone: 609-734-3350.

**SLABE, JAMES F.,** publishing executive; b. Johnstown, Pa., Nov. 29, 1940; s. Frank and Antoinette Marie (Draksler) S.; m. Elaine Werner, July 14, 1973. BA, Washington and Jefferson Coll., 1962; postgrad., U. Md., 1962—64. Divsn. contr. Pfizer, Inc., N.Y.C., 1967—72; treas., contr. Pharmacaps, Inc., Elizabeth, NJ, 1972—73; dir. product planning McGraw-Hill, Inc., N.Y.C., 1973—78; v.p. fin. Parade Publs., Inc., N.Y.C., 1978—79; pres. Exec. Enterprises, Inc., N.Y.C., 1979—95, Sabor & Co., Inc., Mountainside, NJ, 1995—. Bd. dirs. Nat. Assn. Visually Handicapped, Washington and Jefferson Coll., pres. Youth and Family Counseling Svc., 2005—. mem. investment com. Westfield YMCA. Capt. U.S. Army, 1964-66. Mem. Fin. Execs. Inst., Assn. Am. Planners, Assn. Am. Contrs., Phi Beta Kappa. Roman Catholic. Office: Sabor & Co 17 Mountainview Dr Mountainside NJ 07092-2510 Office Phone: 908-232-2704. Business E-mail: jfslabe@quantumforce.net. E-mail: jfslabe@comcast.net.

**SLACHTA, GREGORY ANDREW,** urologist; b. Paterson, N.J., Mar. 17, 1946; s. Andrew Gregory and Mary Catherine (Shimko) S.; children: Gregory Andrew, Lara Ann, Andrea; m. Patricia A. Albano, Nov. 7, 1981. BS, Pa. State U., 1966; MD, Jefferson Med. Coll., 1968. Diplomate Am. Bd. Urology. Intern Lankenan Hosp., Phila., 1968—69; resident urology Temple U. Hosp., Phila., 1969—70, 1973—75; pvt. practice, Springfield, Mass., 1975—97, Hilton Head Med. Group, SC, 1997—99. Author: Inflammatory Diseases of the Male Genital Tract, 1982. Mem. City Coun. Com. for Health Ins., Springfield, 1984, Springfield Planning Bd., 1991; vice-chmn. UROPAC, 2003—. Maj. U.S. Army, 1971-73. Fellow ACS; mem. AMA, Am. Urol. Assn. (chmn. socioecon. com. 1986-91, del. to AMA 1991—), Mass. Med. Soc. (alt. del. to AMA 1986-91, vice chmn. legis. and nat. legis. affairs com. 1987-89), Hampden Dist. Med. Soc. (pres. 1986-88), Mass. Assn. Practicing Urologists (pres. 1985-87), Beaufort County Med. Soc. (pres. 1998-2001). Republican. Roman Catholic. Avocation: golf. E-mail: slachta@aol.com.

**SLACK, CLEMONTENE,** education educator; m. Milton Slack. D in Edn., Nova Southeastern U., 1995. Tchr., counselor Rome City Schs., Ga., 1969—99; dir. Reach-A-Youth Mentor Svc., Rome, 1990—95. ESL instr. Consortium Global Edn., 2004—; spkr. in field. Ministries bd. North Home Church of God; mem. Rome/Floyd Parks and Recreation Assn., 1996—2004. Named Cmty. Resource Person of Yr., Rome Minority Bus. Assn., 1992. Mem.: AAUW (assoc.). Achievements include research in counseling techniques. Office: Shorter Coll 315 Shorter Ave Rome GA 30165 Office Phone: 706-233-7268. Office Fax: 706-233-7437.

**SLACK, DONALD CARL,** agricultural engineer, educator; b. Cody, Wyo., June 25, 1942; s. Clarence Ralbon and Clara May (Beightol) S.; m. Marion Arline Kimball, Dec. 19, 1964; children: Jonel Marie, Jennifer Michelle. BS in Agrl. Engring., U. Wyo., 1965; MS in Agrl. Engring., U. Ky., 1968, PhD in Agrl. Engring., 1975. Registered profl. engr., Ky., Ariz. Asst. civil engr. City of LA, 1965; research specialist U. Ky., Lexington, 1966—70, agrl. engring. advisor Tha Phra, Thailand, 1970—73, rsch. asst. Lexington, 1973—75; from asst. prof. to assoc. prof. agrl. engring. U. Minn., St. Paul, 1975—84; prof. U. Ariz., Tucson, 1984—, head dept. agrl. and biosystems engring., 1991—, prof. watershed mgmt., Cecil H. Miller endowed chair, 2006—. Mem. Mid. East and Mediterranean Desert Devel. Program, 1997—; vis. prof. dept. atmospheric sci. Fed. U. Paraiba, Campina Grande, Brazil, 1997; vis. prof. dept. irrigation Chapingo Autonomous U., Mexico, 2000; tech. adv. Ariz. Dept. Water Resources, Phoenix, 1985—, Tucson active mgmt. area, 1996—; cons. Winrock Internat., Morrilton, Ark., 1984, Water Mgmt. Synthesis II, Logan, Utah, 1985, Desert Agrl. Tech. Sys., Tucson, 1985—, Portek Hermosillo, Mexico, 1989—, World Bank, Washington, 1992—, Malawi Environ. Monitoring Project, 1996, Mex. Inst. for Water Tech., 1997, Nat. Agrl. Rsch. Inst., La Serema, Chile, 1997; cons. F.J. Hansen Inst. for World Peace San Diego State U., 1997—; cons. Internat. Ctr. for Agrl. Rsch. in Dry Areas, 2005; dep. program support mgr. Rsch. Irrigation Support Project for Asia and the Near East, Arlington, Va., 1987—94; mem. adv. team Cearan Found. for Meteorology and Hydrology, Fortaleza, Brazil, 1995—; mem. internat. adv. panel Matrou Resources Mgmt. Project, World Bank, Egypt, 1996—2000; bd. dirs. Sonoita Vineyards, Ltd., Watershed Mgmt. Group, Inc. Contbr. articles to profl. jours. Named Adminstr. of Yr., Coll. Agrl. & Life Scis., 2004—05. Fellow ASCE (Outstanding Jour. Paper award 1988), Am. Soc. Agrl. Engrs. (Ariz. sect. Engr. of Yr. 1993); mem. US Com. on Irrigation and Drainage (life), Am. Soc. Engring. Edn. (program evaluator accreditation bd. for enring. and tech., 2001    ), SAP, Brotherhood of Knights of the Vine (master knight), Rocky Mountain Elk Found. (life), Wyo. Wildlife Fedn. (life); Sigma Xi, Tau Beta Pi, Alpha Epsilon, Gamma Sigma Delta. Democrat. Lutheran. Achievements include patents pending in field; development of infrared based irrigation scheduling device. Avocations: hunting, camping, hiking, model railroading. Home: 9230 E Visco Pl Tucson AZ 85710-3167 Office: U Ariz Agrl Biosystems Engring Tucson AZ 85721-0038 Office Phone: 520-621-7230. Business E-Mail: slackd@email.arizona.edu. *Personal philosophy: Don't take yourself too seriously and don't take anyone else too seriously either.*

**SLACK, EDWARD DORSEY, III,** financial systems professional, consultant; b. Fairmont, W.Va., June 2, 1942; s. Edward Dorsey Jr. and Margaret Elaine (Higgs) S.; m. Donna Jean Carter, Oct. 19, 1944; children: Ted, Robyn. BS in Indsl. Engring., W.Va. U., 1965; postgrad., 1965—66. Registered profl. engr., W.Va. Assoc. sys. and procedures analyst Westinghouse Atomic Power divsn., Pitts., 1966—69; sys. and procedures analyst Westinghouse Nuclear Energy Sys., Pitts., 1969—72, sr. sys. analyst, 1972—75, mgr. payroll and fin. sys., 1975—77; mgr. std. ledger conversion Westinghouse Energy Sys., Pitts., 1977, mgr. fin. sys. and control, 1978—90, mgr. fin. sys. and std. ledger, 1990—91, mgr. payroll, cost and fin. sys. control, 1991—94; data processing analyst & decision support coord. Braddock Med. Ctr., Pa., 1995—96; sys. analyst, decision support coord. U. Pitts. Med. Ctr., Braddock, 1996—. Developer computer programs; designer and installer computer modules, report writer. Mem. NSPE, W.Va. Soc. Profl. Engrs. Avocations: walking, spectator sports, sports and other memorabilia. Home: 179 Autumn Dr Trafford PA 15085-1448 Office: U Pitts Med Ctr Braddock 400 Holland Ave Braddock PA 15104-1599

**SLACK, WARNER VINCENT,** medical educator, researcher; b. East Orange, N.J., June 10, 1933; s. Charles Morse Slack and Evelyn Francis Slack; m. Carolyn Paxton Slack, June 23, 1956; children: Alison Townsend, Charles Warner, Jennifer Cora Slack-Gane. AB, Princeton U., N.J., 1955; MD, Columbia U., N.Y.C., 1959; MS (hon.), Harvard U., Cambridge, Mass. Lic. physician Mass., 1970. Intern then resident in neurology U. Wis., Madison, 1959—61; co-chief divsn. computing dept. medicine Beth Israel Deaconess Med. Ctr., Boston, 1970—; prof. of medicine Harvard Med. Sch., 1999—. Co-pres. Ctr. Clin. Computing Beth Israel Med. Ctr., Boston; editor-in-chief MDComputing, 1989—99. Author: Cybermedicine; contbr. articles to profl. jours. Mem. Med. Com. for Human Rights, Chgo., 1964—70; bd. dirs. Com. of Responsibility, Boston, 1968—73, Princeton Project 55, Princeton, NJ, 1993—99; physician doing primary care medicine in Honduras Cape Cares, Cape Cod, Mass. Capt. Med. Corp USAF, 1962—64. Recipient Outstanding Contributions to Soc. award, Princeton U. Class of 1955, 1995, Morris F. Collen award for Excellence, Am. Coll. of Med. Informatics, 2001. Fellow: Am. Coll. of Medial Informatics (life; one of 50 founding fellows 1986). Achievements include ealy contributor to study of uses of computers in medicine; one of first to offer the idea of patient power that patients who want to should be helped and encouraged to particpate as co-equals with their doctors in medical decisions; research in patient-computer dialogue-the use of a computer to interview patients about their medical histories and to help patients help themselves with medical problems; use and misuse of the SAT and other tests of mental ability. Home: 75 Homer St Newton Centre MA 02459 Office: Beth Israel Deaconess Med Ctr 330 Brookline Ave Boston MA 02215 Office Phone: 617-667-1511. Office Fax: 617-667-1518. E-mail: wslack@bidmc.harvard.edu.

**SLADE, BERNARD,** playwright; b. St. Catharines, Ont., Can., May 2, 1930; s. Frederick and Bessie (Walbourne) Newbound; m. Jill Florence Hancock, July 25, 1953; children: Laurel, Christopher. Actor: Garden Ctr. Theatre, Vineland, Ont., Crest Theatre, Toronto, CBC-TV, Citadel Theatre, Edmonton, Alta.; screenwriter of over 20 hour TV plays for CBC, CBS, ABC, NBC, 1957—; writer/creator (TV series) Love on a Rooftop, The Partridge Family, The Flying Nun, The Girl with Something Extra, Bridget Loves Bernie; story editor, writer 15 episodes of TV series Bewitched; writer/creator (plays) A Very Close Family, 1962, Same Time Next Year (Drama Desk award 1975, Tony award nomination 1975), Tribute, 1978, Romantic Comedy, 1979, Special Occasions, 1981, Fatal Attraction, 1984, Return Engagements, 1986, Sweet William, 1987, An Act of the Imagination, 1987, I Remember You, 1991, You Say Tomatoes, 1993, Everytime I See You, 1994, Same Time, Another Year, Fling!, 2000; feature films: Same Time, Next Year, 1977, Tribute, 1978, Romantic Comedy, 1979, Shared Laughter-a memoir, 2000, Moving Day, 2005, (film biography) Comedic Genius of Bernard Slade, 2003. Recipient Acad. award nomination Motion Picture Arts and Scis., 1978. Mem. Dramatists Guild Am., Writers Guild Am. (award nomination), Acad. Motion Picture Arts and Scis. (Acad. award nomination 1978), Soc. Authors and Artists (France). Avocation: tennis. Address: Apt 1201 1100 Alta Loma RD West Hollywood CA 90069-2439 Personal E-mail: bernslade@aol.com. *I am a prisoner of a childhood dream: to write for the theatre. The fulfillment of that dream has lived up to all my expectations. I believe the theatre should be a celebration of the human condition and that the artist's job is to remind us of all that is good about ourselves. I feel privileged to be given a platform for my particular vision of life, and, whether my plays succeed or fail, I am always grateful for the use of the hall.*

**SLADE, BERNARD NEWTON,** electronics executive; b. Sioux City, Iowa, Dec. 21, 1923; s. William Charles and Katherine Gertrude Slotsky; m. Margot Friedlein, Aug. 18, 1946; children: Steven P., Eric J. BSEE, U. Wis., 1948; MS, Stevens Inst. Tech., 1954. Devel. engr. tube divsn. RCA, Harrison, NJ, 1948-55; devel. engr. RCA Labs., Princeton, NJ, 1955-56; mgr. tech. program IBM, Poughkeepsie, NY, 1956-60; mgr. product ops. Hopewell Junction, NY, 1960-64; mgr. mfg. tech. IBM World Trade Corp., Armonk, NY, 1964-65; corp. dir. of mfg. tech. IBM Corp., Armonk, 1965-84; sr. cons. Arthur D. Little, Inc., Cambridge, Mass., 1984-86, Gemini Cons., Morristown, NJ, 1986-93; founder, v.p., bd. dirs. Yieldup Internat. Corp., 1993-97; bd. dirs. V3 Semiconductors, 1996—2003, Anon, Inc. Co-author: Winning the Productivity Race, 1985; author: Compressing the Product Develop. Cycle, 1992; contbr. articles to profl. jours.; patentee in field; contbg. author: Transistors, 1956, Handbook of Semiconductor Electronics, 1962. 2nd lt. AUS, 1943-46. Mem.: IEEE (sr.), Sigma Xi. Home: 12 Merry Hill Rd Poughkeepsie NY 12603-3214

**SLADE, GEORGE GILBERT,** art historian; b. St. Paul, Jan. 2, 1961; s. George Richard and Ella Carpenter Slade; m. Janet Paine Bisbee, Mar. 31, 1990 (div.); children: Juliet Kotel, Laura Winsor. BA in Am. Studies, Yale U., 1985. Editl. asst. Aperture, N.Y.C., 1985—86; rschr. Magnum Photos, N.Y.C., 1986—87; asst. dir. Archive Pictures, N.Y.C., 1987; freelance writer, rschr. N.Y.C., 1988—89; program dir. U. Minn. McKnight Found. Photography Fellows, Mpls., 1998—; artistic dir. Minn. Ctr. for Photography, Mpls., 2003—. Writer, curator, cons. Re: Photographica, St. Paul, 1989—. Author, editor, consultant (book, commissioning project) Minnesota in Our Time: A Photographic Portrait. Trustee Jerome Found., St. Paul. Dfl. Office: Minn Ctr for Photography 165 13th Ave NE Minneapolis MN 55413 Office Phone: 612-824-5500. Personal E-mail: george@mncp.org.

**SLADE, JOHN DANTON,** lobbyist; b. Balt., Apr. 5, 1939; s. Eldon and Marie (Smith) S.; m. Dale Iris Walden, Mar. 14, 1964 (dec. Dec. 1965); 1 child, Kenyatta Conrad; m. Deborah Faye Douglas, Dec. 11, 1987. BA in Sociology, Morgan State U., 1964; MA in Sociology, CUNY, 1966. Mgmt. trainee IBM, N.Y.C., 1966-69; producer, dir. WBAL-TV, Balt., 1969-71, WGBH-TV, Boston, 1971-73, KPIX-TV, San Francisco, 1973-75; announcer KEST Radio, San Francisco, 1975-76; gen. mgr. Channel 8 Access TV, San Francisco, 1975-79; owner Swansbriar Plantation, Cumberland, Va., 1979-85; asst. prof. military sci., dept. chmn. Howard U., Bowie State U., Georgetown U., Washington, 1985-88; acting chief Nat. Guard Bur., Washington, 1988-92; exec. dir. Assn. Reserve Minority Svc. Members, Inc., Washington, 1992—; founder Iota Phi Theta, Inc. Talk show host WOL Radio, Washington; bd. dirs. Meridian Distributors, St. Thomas, V.I.; guest lectr. Stanford (Calif.) U., Northeastern U., Boston, Morgan State Coll., Balt., Merritt Coll., Oakland, Calif., U. Mass., Amherst; mem. spl. com. San Francisco Chronicle; mem. Balt. Community Rels. Commn.; mem. N.G. Drug Reduction Bd., 1990-91 Author: Last Testament of an American, 1993, Flight of an Angel, 1993, The Founding and Ascendancy of Iota Phi Theta, 1994; Man-Made (Guide to Single Mothers Raising Black Boys Alone), 1994, Iota Phi Theta (Ascending to the Next Millenium), 1999; film producer Breaking the Chains of Bondage, 1972. Mem. exec. council, AARP, DC, 2002; Lt. col. U.S. Army, 1985-92. Recipient Roy Wilkens Renown Svc. award, 1991, Award of Honor, NAACP, Balt., Community Svc. award Les Hommes Civic and Social Club, Hampton, Va., 1991. Mem. Iota Phi Theta (founding mem., bus. mgr. 1963-64, chmn. 2003-). Republican. Office: ARMS 1401 Madison St NW Washington DC 20011-6805 Personal E-mail: iotabooks@comcast.com.

**SLADE, LYNN,** lawyer; b. Santa Fe, Jan. 29, 1948; m. Susan Zimmerman, 1 child, Benjamin, 1 child from a previous marriage, Jessica. BA in Econs., U. N.Mex., 1973, JD, 1976. Bar: N.Mex. 1976, U.S. Dist. Ct. N.Mex. 1976, U.S. Ct. Appeals (10th cir.) 1978, U.S. Ct. Appeals (D.C. cir.) 1984, U.S. Supreme Ct. 1984. Ptnr. Modrall, Sperling, Roehl, Harris & Sisk, PA, Albuquerque, 1976—. Adj. prof. U. N.Mex. Sch. Law, Albuquerque, 1990. Editor N.Mex. Law Rev., 1975-76; contbr. articles to profl. jours. Bd. dirs. N.Mex. First, 1999—, chair, 2005—06; trustee-at-large Rocky Mountain Min. L. Found., 1995—97, 2005—. Mem. ABA (sect. environ. energy and resources, membership officer 1998-00, chair com. on Native Am. natural resources 1991-94, coun. mem. 1995-98, mem. sects. litig., dispute resolution, pub. utilities and comm., and transp. law), N.Mex. State Bar (chair, bd. dirs. sect. natural resources 1983-87, bd. dirs. Indian law sect. 2002-04). Home: 143 Olguin Rd Corrales NM 87048-6930 Office: Modrall Sperling Roehl Harris & Sisk PA 500 4th St NW Ste 1000 Albuquerque NM 87102-2186 Office Phone: 505-848-1828. E-mail: lynn.slade@modrall.com.

**SLADE, MARGOT S.,** editor; d. Melvin S.; m. Nicholas Baxter, Apr. 26, 1981. BA, Wellesley Coll.; MA, Columbia Univ. Various positions NY Times, 1981—2001; editor, sr. dir. Consumer Reports, 2001—. Mem.: Phi Beta Kappa. Office: Consumer Reports 101 Truman Ave Yonkers NY 10703-1044 Office Phone: 914-378-2665. Office Fax: 914-378-2900.*

**SLADE, ROY,** artist, college president, museum director; b. Cardiff, U.K., July 14, 1933; came to U.S., 1967, naturalized, 1975; s. David Trevor and Millicent (Stone) S. N.D.D., Cardiff Coll. Art, 1954; A.T.D., U. Wales, 1954;

D of Arts, Art Inst. So. Calif., 1994. Tchr. art and crafts Heolgam High Sch., Wales, 1956-60; lectr. art Clarendon Coll., Nottingham, Eng., 1960-64; sr. lectr. fine art Leeds Coll. Art, Eng., 1964-67; prof. painting Corcoran Sch. Art, Washington, 1967-68, assoc. dean, 1969-70, dean, 1970-77; dir. Corcoran Gallery of Art, Washington, 1972-77; pres., dir. Cranbrook Acad. Art, Bloomfield Hills, Mich., 1977-94, now dir. emeritus. Sr. lectr. Leeds Coll. Art, England, 1968—69; vis. Boston Mus. Fine Arts, 1970; dir. emeritus Cranbrook Art Mus., 2000—. Exhibited one-man shows Howard Roberts Gallery, Cardiff, Wales, 1958, New Art Ctr., London, 1960, U. Birmingham, 1964, 69, Herbert Art Gallery and Mus., Coventry, 1964, Va. State Art League, 1967, Mus. of Arts and Crafts, Columbus, Ga., 1968, Jefferson Place Gallery, Washington, 1968, 70, 72, 73, Park Sq. Gallery, Leeds, 1969, St. Mary's Coll., Md., 1971, Guelph U., Ont., Can., 1971, Hood Coll., 1974, Pyramid Gallery, Washington, 1976, Robert Kidd Gallery, 1981, 92, Herman Miller, Inc., Mich., 1985; group shows in U.K., Washington, Can.; represented in permanent collections Arts Council Gt. Brit., Contemporary Art Soc., Nuffield Found., Ministry of Works, Eng., Brit. Embassy, Washington, Brit. Overseas Airways Corp., U. Birmingham, Wakefield City Art Gallery, Clarendon Coll., Cadbury Bros., Ltd., Eng., Lord Ogmore, Local Edn. Authorities. Mem. D.C. Commn. on Arts.; bd. dirs. Artists for Environment Found., Nat. Assn. Schs. Art; chmn. Nat. Council Art Adminstrs., 1981. Served with Brit. Army, 1954-56. Decorated knight 1st class Order of White Rose (Finland), Royal Order of Polar Star (Sweden); recipient award Welsh Soc., Phila., 1974, Gov.'s Arts Orgn. award, 1988; Fulbright scholar, 1967-68. Mem. Nat. Soc. Lit. and Arts, AIA (hon. Detroit chpt.), Assn. Art Mus. Dirs. (hon.). Home: 31 Island Way Apt 801 Clearwater FL 33767-2206 Personal E-mail: royslade@verizon.net.

**SLADE, SCOTT,** radio personality; Traffic reporter WSB-AM 750, Atlanta, morning show host, 1992—. Host (radio shows) Atlanta's Morning News, 1992—. Recipient Marconi Radio Award for Large Market Personality of Yr., Nat. Assn. Broadcasters, 2004. Office: Atlanta's Morning News WSB-AM/FM 1601 W Peachtree St NE Atlanta GA 30309-2663 Office Phone: 404-897-6287. Office Fax: 404-876-5126. E-mail: scott.slade@wsbradio.com.*

**SLADE, TOM,** manufacturing executive, political organization worker; b. Albany, Ga., Mar. 13, 1936; s. T.H. and Flora Bell (Jackson) S.; divorced; children: Thomas, Jack, Jeff, Shad. Owner Slade Gas Co., Jacksonville, Fla., 1958-71; pres. Gen. Environ., Jacksonville, 1971-75, Slade & Co., Jacksonville, 1975-80; pres., owner Dozier & Jay Paint Co., Green Cove Springs, 1980—; pres. Tidewater Cons., 1998—. Mem. Fla. Ho. of Reps., Tallahassee, 1962-64, Fla. Senate, 1966-70; vice chmn. Fla. Tax and Budget Reform Commn., 1990—; mem. Fla. High Speed Rail Commn., 1991; active in numerous polit. and civic orgns. Recipient numerous pub. svc. awards. Republican. Avocations: tennis, boating. Office: Dozier & Gay Paint Co 3529 Enterprise Way Green Cove Springs FL 32043-9334 Home: 825 Shipwatch Dr E Jacksonville FL 32225-5416

**SLADEK, JOHN R., JR.,** academic administrator, neurobiology and anatomy educator; b. Chgo., Feb. 6, 1943; s. John R. and Marie (De Benedictis) S.; m. Celia Davis; children: Jonathan Andrew, Stefan Zachary, Jessica Anne. BA, Carthage Coll., 1965; MS, Northwestern U., 1968; PhD, U. Health Scis./Chgo. Med. Sch., 1971. Teaching asst. Chgo. Med. Sch., 1968-70, asst. prof. anatomy, 1971-73, U. Rochester Sch. Medicine, NY, 1973-77, assoc. prof. NY, 1977-82, assoc. prof. brain rsch. NY, 1979-82, prof. NY, 1982-83, prof. neurobiology and anatomy NY, 1982-91, Kilian and Caroline Schmitt prof. NY, 1987-91, chmn. dept. NY, 1982-91, dir. neurosci. grad. program NY, 1987-91; prof., chmn. dept. Neuroscience., dir. Neuroscience. Inst. U. Health Scis./Chgo. Med. Sch., 1991—2001, dir. med. neurosci. course, 1993—2001; vice chancellor rsch. U. Colo. at Denver and Health Scis. Ctr., 2001—06; pres., CEO Calif. Luth. U., Thousand Oaks, 2006—. Vernon Roosa lectr. Trinity Coll., Hartford, Conn., 1989; 1st Irving S. Cooper vis. prof. Mayo Clinic, Rochester, Minn., 1989. Editor: Monoamine Transmitter Histochemistry, 1982, Neural Transplants: Development and Function, 1984, Transplantation into the Mammalian CNS, 1988; editor-in-chief Exptl. Neurology, 1988—; editor Brain Rsch. Bull., 1980-88, Cell and Tissue Rsch., 1992—; mem. editorial adv. bd. Neurobiology of Aging, 1980—; contbr. over 150 articles to profl. jours. Pres. Residents of Bergen (N.Y.) Believe in the Environment and Democracy, 1989-91; mem. spl. com. bd. trustees Carthage Coll., mem. natural scis. adv. com., 1992—, mem. adv. com. career placement and continuing edn. programs, 1993—. Recipient Disting. Alumnus award Carthage Coll., 1983, U. Health Scis./Chgo. Med. Sch., 1990. Mem. Soc. for Neurosci. (nominating com. 1990, fin. com. 1990—), Am. Assn. Anatomists (exec. com. 1972—), Am. Assn. Anatomy Chmn., N.Y. Acad. Scis., Histochem. Soc., Alzheimers Assn. (med. sci. adv. bd.), Coun. Biology Editors. Office: Calif Luth U 60 West Olsen Rd Thousand Oaks CA 91360*

**SLADEK, LYLE VIRGIL,** mathematician, educator; b. Pukwana, S.D., Oct. 13, 1923; s. Charles Frank and Emma Margaret (Swanson) S.; m. Patricia Knotts, Sept. 12, 1948; children: Susan, Ann, Laura, Karen. BS, S.D. State U., 1948; MA, U. S.D., 1949, Stanford U., 1963; PhD, UCLA, 1970. Tchr. high sch., Mitchell, S.D., 1950-56; asst. prof. math. Black Hills State Coll., S.D., 1957-62; prof. math. Calif. Luth. Univ., Thousand Oaks, 1963-94, prof. emeritus, 1994—. Lectr. history WWII. Author, contbr. Lucky Stars and Gold Bars, 2005 (Benjamin Franklin award 2005); contbr. short stories, poems to mags. and newspapers. Pres. congregation Our Savior's Lutheran Ch., Spearfish, S.D., 1961. Served as officer U.S. Army, 1943-46, PTO, ETO. Shell Merit fellow, 1956; NSF fellow, 1956-57, 62-63; recipient Meritorious Achievement award edn. S.D. Mines and Tech., 1957; Fulbright-Hays lectr. Bahamas, 1980-81 Mem. Math. Assn. Am., Blue Key, Pi Kappa Delta, Phi Delta Kappa. Home: 3243 Pioneer St Thousand Oaks CA 91360-2730 Personal E-mail: patlyle@hotmail.com. *I learned from my parents during the dust bowl years that adversity often can be overcome through patience and determination, and that problems provide challenges that add spice to life. I have sought to return full measure to society for all the opportunities and joys of life that have come my way.*

**SLADEK, RONALD JOHN,** physics professor; b. Chgo., Sept. 19, 1926; s. James Joseph and Rose (Vachulka) S.; m. Jeanne T. McFadden, Sept. 19, 1953; children: Linda, James, Frances, Stephen, Rosemarie, Edward. PhB, U. Chgo., 1947, SB, 1949, SM, 1950, PhD, 1954. Rsch. physicist Westinghouse Rsch. Labs., Pitts., 1953-60, fellow scientist, 1960-61; assoc. prof. physics Purdue U., West Lafayette, Ind., 1961-66, prof., 1966-91, prof. physics emeritus, 1992—, acting head dept. physics, 1969-71, assoc. dean sci., 1974-87. Vis. scientist Sci. Center, N.Am. Rockwell Corp., Thousand Oaks, Calif., summer 1967; sabbatical scientist Xerox Rsch. Ctr., Palo Alto, Calif., 1976-77 Contbr. articles to profl. jours. With USNR, 1945-46. AEC fellow U. Chgo., 1952-53. Fellow Am. Phys. Soc. Home: 963 Ridgeview Dr Reno NV 89511-8506

**SLADKUS, HARVEY IRA,** lawyer; b. Mar. 5, 1929; s. Samuel Harold and Charlotte Dorothy Sladkus; m. Harriet Marcia Barske, Nov. 26, 1967 (div.); children: Steven David, Jeffrey Brandon; m. Roberta Frances Pope, Oct. 24, 1986. AB, Syracuse U., 1950; JD, NYU, 1961. Bar: NY 1962, U.S. Supreme Ct. 1967, Conn. 1981. Assoc. Morris Ploscowe, NYC, 1961-66; pvt. practice NYC, 1968—95, 1997—; ptnr. Dweck & Sladkus and Feiden, Dweck & Sladkus, NYC, 1968-95, Dweck & Sladkus, LLP, NYC, 1996; pres. Harvey I. Sladkus, P.C., 1997—. Small claims arbitrator Civil Ct. City of NY, 1977—; adj. prof. law Benjamin N. Cardozo Sch. Law, 1994—95; lectr. family and matrimonial law. Co-author: (book) Practice Under New York's Matrimonial Law, 1971—79; editor-in-chief: Family Law Practice, 1982, contbg. columnist: It's the Law, Suffolk Times, 1999—2002, Bottom Line, 2000—; contbr. articles to profl. jours. 1st lt. U.S. Army, 1962—65, Korea. Decorated Bronze Star, War Svc. medal Korean Govt.; named Arbitrator of Yr., NY Civil Small Claims Ct., 2002, Civil Ct. NY County, 2002; recipient George Washington Honor medal, Freedoms Found., Valley Forge, 1953. Mem.: Suffolk County Bar Assn., Am. Arbitration Assn. (nat. panel arbitrators), Internat. Acad. Matrimonial Lawyers, Am. Acad. Matrimonial Lawyers, Assn. Bar City of

NY, NY State Bar Assn. Jewish. Office: 425 Park Ave New York NY 10022-3506 Office Phone: 212-754-9400. E-mail: hisatty@nyc.rr.com. *Notable cases include: Burns vs. Burns, first to constitute a tenant in occupancy to subscribe to shares of an apt. corp. going coop.; Brown vs. Brown, case of first impression recluse in agreement of ex-wife living with another man.*

**SLAFF, ALLAN PAUL,** military officer, academic administrator, educator, entrepreneur; b. Mt. Vernon, N.Y., Feb. 2, 1923; s. Frank Alfred and Augusta Raye (Scher) S.; m. Mary Lee Schaeffer; children: Randolph Elliott, Valerie Anne. BS, U.S. Naval Acad., 1944; postgrad., U.S. Naval Post Grad Sch., 1949-50, U.S. Naval War Coll., Newport, R.I., 1959-60, Harvard U., 1967. Commd. ensign USN, 1944, advanced through grades to capt., 1965, WWII Battleship Mass. Fast Carrier TF, 1944-46, personal aide to CNO Adm. Arleigh Burke, 1950-51, spl. security officer commd. in Korean War Navy, comdr. USS Lester, Davis, Luce, Albany, 1957-70, sr. naval advisor to Vietnam Navy, 1967-68, ret., 1970; dean, mem. faculty Bus. Sch. Harvard U., Boston, 1970-80; chmn. Luzerne Co. News Co., Wilkes Barre, Pa., 1980-86, LABSPHERE, Inc., N. Sutton, N.H., 1983-94. Cons. Harvard Bus. Sch., 1980-84. Author (autobiography): (book) A Sailor's Story, 2004; contbr. numerous articles to profl. jours. and mags. Bd. dirs. numerous schs., clubs, corps., civic and polit. orgns. Decorated Legion of Merit, Bronze Star, Nat. Order of Vietnam, numerous other decorations U.S. Navy, 1941-70; recipient Disting. Grad. award Wyoming Sem., Kingston, Pa., 1990. Mem. Port Royal Club (sec. bd. dirs.), The Naples Yacht Club (treas., bd. dirs.), Royal Poinciana Golf Club, Port Royal Property Owners Assn. (bd. dirs.), Lake Sunapee Yacht Club, Baker Hill Golf Club. Republican. Episcopalian. Avocations: golf, travel, photography, gardening. Home: 4151 Gulf Shore Blvd N # 601 Naples FL 34103-2292 also: PO Box 1836 27 Highland Rdg New London NH 03257-4321 E-mail: allanslaff@aol.com.

**SLAFKA, KRISTI LYNNE,** journalist; b. McKeesport, Pa., Aug. 18, 1978; d. Kenneth Edward and Debra Lynne Slafka. BA, Washington and Lee U., 2000; web prodr. cert., Georgetown U., 2002. Assoc. editor Hotline, Washington, 2000—04; assoc. prodr./booker Fox News Channel, Washington, 2004—05; stringer People mag., Washington, 2002; prodr. Washington Jour. C-SPAN, Washington, 2005—. Mem.: Radio and TV News Dirs. Assn., Soc. Profl. Journalists, Washington and Lee U. Alumni Assn., Kappa Delta. Office: C-SPAN 400 N Capitol St NW Ste 650 Washington DC 20001

**SLAGER, DONALD W.,** waste management executive; Various mgmt. positions Gen. Waste Svcs., 1985—90, gen. mgr., 1990—92; dist. mgr. Chgo. metro dist. Allied Waste Industries, Scottsdale, Ariz., 1992—96, regional v.p. west region, 1996—97, asst. v.p. ops., 1997—98, v.p. ops., 1998—2001, sr. v.p. ops., 2001—03, exec. v.p., COO, 2003—04, pres., COO, 2005—. Office: Allied Waste Industries Ste 100 15880 N Greenway-Hayden Loop Scottsdale AZ 85260*

**SLAGLE, TOM,** medical products executive; BBA, U. Toledo. With ortho diagnostics divsn. Johnson & Johnson; with Baxter Healthcare; mem. staff to exec. v.p. East Coast Distbn. Cardinal Health, Inc., Dublin, Ohio, 1996—99, exec. v.p. franchise devel. Medicine Shoppe Internat., pres., CEO Medicine Shoppe Internat., grp. pres. Med. Supply Chain bus. Office: Cardinal Health Inc 7000 Cardinal Pl Dublin OH 43017*

**SLAIGHT, GARY,** broadcast executive; b. Edmonton, Alta., Can., 1951; married; 2 children. BA in English, U. Western Ont. Media estimator McLaren Advt., 1973; promotion mgr. Quality Records, 1974-75, WEA Records, 1975; account exec. Q107, 1977, program dir., 1978, v.p., gen. mgr., 1982, MIX 99.9, 1987-2000; pres., CEO Std. Radio Inc., Toronto, 1987—Std. Broadcasting Corp., Ltd., 2000. Bd. dirs. Can. Acad. Recording Arts and Scis. Bd. dirs. Walk of Fame, Moontaxi, Hosp. for Sick Children. Recipient ann. music industry awards Gen. Mgr. of Yr., 1986, Program Dir. of Yr., 1987, Broadcast Exec. of Yr., 1992, 93, 96, 98, Outstanding Cmty. Svc. by an Individual Broadcaster award, CAB, 2004; inductee Can. Music Industry Hall of Fame, 2005. Office: Standard Radio Inc 2 St Clair Ave W Toronto ON Canada M4V 1L6

**SLAMON, DENNIS J.,** research scientist; married; 2 children. MD, PhD, U. Chgo. Chief divsn. hematology-oncology, prof. and exec. vice chair Jonsson Comprehensive Cancer Ctr. UCLA Sch. Medicine; dir. Revlon/UCLA Women's Health Rsch. Program, Revlon/UCLA Women's Cancer Rsch. Program. Mem. sci. adv. bd. Coastview Capital Inc., New Biotics Inc.; named to Pres. Clinton's Cancer Panel, 2000. Named one of five Men for the Cure, GQ mag. and Concept:Cure, 1999; recipient Salk Inst. award, U. Calif., San Diego, 1999, Landon AACR prize, Am. Assn. Cancer Rsch., 2003. Achievements include development of the drug Herceptin for treating breast cancer. Office: UCLA Sch Medicine Divsn Hematology Oncology 3360 Ueberroth Bldg mail code 707707 Los Angeles CA 90095

**SLANINA, LYNNSEY D.,** costume designer, educator; d. Gary S. and Donielle A. Slanina. BS in Apparel Merchandising, Utah State U., 1998; MFA in Costume Design & Tech., NC Sch. Arts, 2003. Costume shop mgr. Billings Studio Theatre, Mont., 1998—99; costume shop mgr., instr. Utah State U., Logan, 1999—2000; grad. asst. NC Sch. Arts, Winston-Salem, NC, 2000—03; costume designer Little Theatre Winston-Salem, 2002; costume design prof. Fla. Sch. Arts, Palatka, Fla., 2003—. Mem. US Inst. Theatre Tech., Inc., 1999—. Recipient Zelma H. Weisfeld award, US Inst. Theatre Tech., Inc., 2003. Avocations: knitting, spinning, drawing, sheep herding. Office: Fla Sch Arts 5001 St Johns Ave Palatka FL 32177

**SLANSKY, JERRY WILLIAM,** investment company executive; b. Chgo., Mar. 8, 1947; s. Elmer Edward and Florence Anna (Kosobud) S.; m. Marlene Jean Cannella, Jan. 29, 1950; children: Brett Matthew, Blake Adam. BA, Elmhurst Coll., 1969; MA, No. Ill. U., 1971. Mktg. rep. Bantam Book Co., Chgo., 1972-73, Charles Levy Circulating Co., Chgo., 1973-76; account exec. Merrill Lynch, Chgo., 1976-77, Oppenheimer & Co., Inc., Chgo., 1977—, asst. v.p., 1978, v.p., 1979, sr. v.p., 1981, mng. dir., 1986, ptnr., 1986—. Bd. dirs. Lake Geneva (Wis.) Beach Assn., 1987-02, Glen Ellyn Youth Ctr., Glenbard West H.S., pres., 1998-99; bd. dirs. Buttonwood Cove, Longboat Key, Fla., 2006-; mem. bus. affairs com. Presbytery of Chgo., 1999-04. Mem. Nat. Assn. Securities Dealers (arbitrator 1988—), N.Y. Stock Exch., Chgo. Bd. Options, Am. Arbitration. Assn, Omaha C- of C. Presbyterian. Avocations: swimming, water-skiing, golf, skiing, kayaking. Office: Oppenheimer & Co Ste 4000 500 W Madison St Chicago IL 60661 Office Phone: 312-360-5553. Personal E-mail: jerry.slansky@opco.com.

**SLARK, MARTIN P.,** electronics executive; BSE, Reading Univ., England, 1977; MBA, Ea. London Univ. Mgmt. positions Molex Inc., Lisle, Ill., 1976—99, exec. v.p., 1999—2001, pres., COO, 2001—05, vice-chmn., CEO, 2005—. Bd. dir. Hub Group Inc. Office: Molex Inc 2222 Wellington Ct Lisle IL 60532*

**SLASH, (SAUL HUDSON),** guitarist; b. Stoke-on-Trent, Eng., July 23, 1965; s. Anthony and Ola Hudson; m. Renée Suran, Oct. 10, 1992 (div. 1997); m. Perla Ferrar Oct. 15, 2001-; children: London Emilo, Cash Anthony. Guitarist Guns n' Roses, 1985—96; founder, guitarist Slash's Snakepit, 1994—2001; guitarist Velvet Revolver, 2002—. Albums: (with Guns N' Roses) Live Like a Suicide, 1986, Appetite for Destruction, 1987 (Am. Music awards Favorite Rock Album, 1990, VH1: 100 Greatest Albums, 2001, #1. Spin mag.'s Greatest Metal Albums, 2002, one of 500 Greatest Albums of All Time, Rolling Stone, 2003), GN'R Lies, 1988, Use Your Illusion I, 1991, Use Your Illusion II, 1991, The Spaghetti Incident?, 1993, (with Slash's Snakepit) It's Five O'Clock Somewhere, 1995, Ain't Life Grand, 2000, (with Velvet Revolver) Contraband, 2004; songs: (with Guns N' Roses) Welcome to the Jungle, 1987 (one of 500 Songs That Shaped Rock & Roll, Rock & Roll Hall of Fame, 1997, one of 100 Greatest Videos Ever Made, MTV, 1999), Sweet Child O' Mine, 1987 (Am. Music awards Favorite Rock Single, 1989, MTV Video Music awards Best Heavy Metal video, 1989, one of 100 Greatest Videos Ever Made, MTV, 1999, one of 100 Greatest Pop Songs,

Rolling Stone & MTV, 2000, #3, VH1's 100 Best Songs of Past 25 Yrs., 2003), November Rain, 1991 (MTV Video Music awards Best Cinematography, 1992, one of 100 Greatest Videos Ever Made, MTV, 1999, one of 100 Greatest Videos, VH1, 2001); contbr.: (films) The Dead Pool, 1988, Cocktail, 1988, Lean on Me, 1989, Black or White, 1991, Interview with the Vampire, 1994, Jackie Brown, 1997, Rated X, 2000, Hulk, 2003, Ray, 2004 (video games) Grand Theft Auto: San Andreas, 2004); worked as guitarist with Iggy Pop, Bob Dylan, Michael Jackson, Lenny Kravitz. Named Best New Artist, MTV Video Music awards, 1988, Favorite Hard Rock Artist, Am. Music awards, 1990, 1992, World's Best Selling Hard Rock Artist of Yr., World Music awards, 1993; named one of 100 Greatest Artists of Hard Rock, VH1, 2001, Sexiest Artists, 2002, Top Pop Artists of Past 25 Yrs., 2004; recipient Video Vanguard award, MTV Video Music awards, 1992. Office: RCA Records 1540 Broadway New York NY 10036*

**SLATE, FLOYD OWEN,** retired engineering educator; b. Carroll County, Ind., July 26, 1920; s. Ora George and Gladys Marie (Miller) Slate; m. Margaret Mary Magley, Oct. 14, 1939; children: Sally Lee Slate McEnteer, Sandra Kay Slate Miller, Rex Owen. BS, Purdue U., 1941, MS, 1942, PhD, 1944. Chemist Manhattan Project, Columbia U., N.Y.C. and Decatur, Ill., 1944-46; asst. prof. civil engring. Purdue U., Lafayette, Ind., 1946-49; v.p., dir. Geotechnics & Resources Inc., White Plains, NY, 1959-63; prof. engring. materials Cornell U., Ithaca, NY, 1949-87; prof. emeritus, 1987. Internat. lectr.; cons. concrete, low-cost housing. Author; contbr. articles to profl. jours. Recipient Excellence in Engring. Tchg. award, Cornell U., 1976; sr. fellow, East-West Ctr., 1976, rsch. grantee, NSF, 1960—86. Fellow: Am. Inst. Chemists, Am. Concrete Inst. (hon. Wason Rsch. medal 1957, 1965, 1974, 1986, Anderson award 1983); mem.: ASTM, ASCE, Am. Chem. Soc. Achievements include research in internal structure of concrete vs. properties; chemistry applied to engineering problems and low-cost housing for developing countries. Home: 255 The Esplanade N Apt 306 Venice FL 34285-1518 *Think positively and be optimistic. Be considerate of others, try to help others, and enjoy life.*

**SLATE, JOE HUTSON,** psychologist, educator; b. Hartselle, Ala., Sept. 21, 1930; s. Murphy Edmund and Marie (Hutson) S.; m. Rachel Holladay, July 1, 1950; children: Marc Allan, John David, James Daryl. BS, Athens Coll., 1960; MA, U. Ala., 1965, PhD, 1970. Mem. faculty Athens (Ala.) State Coll., 1965-92, prof. psychology, 1974-92, chmn. behavioral scis., 1974-92; pvt. practice psychology Athens, 1970-92, Hartselle, 1992—; v.p. Slate Security Systems, Hartselle, Ala., 1984—. Author: Psychic Phenomena, 1988, Self-Empowerment, 1991, Psychic Empowerment, 1995, Psychic Empowerment for Health and Fitness, 1996, Astral Projection, 1998, Aura Energy for Health Healing, and Balance, 1999, Rejuvenation: Strategies for Living Younger, Longer and Better, 2001, Psychic Vampires, 2002, Beyond Reincarnation, 2005. Named hon. prof. U. Montevallo, 1973, prof. emeritus Athens State U., 1992. Mem. APA, Am. Soc. Clin. Hypnosis, Inst. Parapsychol. Rsch. (founder), Coun. for Nat. Register Health Svc. Providers in Psychology, NEA, Ala. Edn. Assn., Delta Tau Delta, Phi Delta Kappa, Kappa Delta Pi. Home: 1807 Highway 31 NW Hartselle AL 35640-4442 Office: 310 E Main St Hartselle AL 35640 Personal E-mail: joehslate@aol.com.

**SLATE, JOHN BUTLER,** biomedical engineer; b. Schenectady, NY, Sept. 27, 1953; s. Herbert Butler and Violet (Perugi) S. BSEE, U. Wis., 1975, MEE, 1977, PhDEE, 1980. Spl. fellow of cardiovascular surgery U. Ala., Birmingham, 1980-81, dept. biomed. research engr., 1981-82; microbiology fellow, 1981-82; sr. research engr. IMED Corp., San Diego, 1982-83, sr. research scientist, 1983-86; sci. dir. Pacesetter Infusion Ltd. (dba MiniMed Technologies) Sylmar, Calif., 1986-87; v.p. tech. MiniMed Technologies, Sylmar, Calif., 1987-91; v.p. R & D Siemens Infusion Systems, Sylmar, Calif., 1991-93; v.p. tech. devel. Via Med., San Diego, 1993-94; pres. Slate Engring., San Diego, 1997—2003, Avant Drug Delivery Sys., Inc., San Diego, 1997—2002; v.p. ops. Avant Med. Corp., San Diego, 2002—, pres., 2002—. Mem. IEEE (IEE Ayrton award), Sigma Xi. Office: Avant Med Corp 10225 Barnes Canyon Rd Ste A113 San Diego CA 92121 Office Phone: 858-202-1560 Ext. 1. E-mail: jslate@avantmedical.com

**SLATER, ALLEN J.,** music educator; s. Kermit and Ruth Slater; m. Rebecca Slater, Sept. 3, 1977; children: Benjamin, Megan. MusB in Edn., U. Mont., Missoula, Mont., 1978; MusM in Edn., VanderCook Coll., Chgo., Ill., 1989. Dir. choir First Immanuel Luth. Ch., Missoula, Mont., 1978—79; tchr. music Harlem (Mont.) Schs., 1979—80, Shelby (Mont.) Pub. Schs., 1980—88; dir. bands Flathead H.S., Kalispell, Mont., 1988—, chmn. Dept. Music, 1991—. Dir. choir United Meth. Ch., Shelby, 1980—83; pres. dist. music festival, Shelby, Mont., 1980—88, Kalispell, Mont., 1989—2006. Bd. dirs. Glacier Symphony Orch., Kalispell, Mont., 1996—2001. Named Arts Educator of Yr., Kalispell Arts Assn., 1999; recipient Gold Star Excellence award, Sta. KCFW-TV, Staples, 2001; fellow, Flubright Meml. Fund, Japanese Govt., 2001. Mem.: NEA, Mont. Music Educators Assn. (state mgr. 2006—, chmn. membership 2006—), Nat. Bandmasters Assn. (state pres. 1988—2006), Mont. Bandmaster Assn. (pres. 1988—93), Am. Sch. Band Dirs. Assn., Mortor Bd. (v.p. 1977—78), Phi Beta Mu (treas. 1990—98), Meth. Avocations: music, woodworking. Home: 468 2nd Ave WN Kalispell MT 59901 Office: Flathead High School 644 4th Ave W Kalispell MT 59901 Office Phone: 406-751-3554. Office Fax: 406-751-3505. Business E-Mail: slatera@sd5.k12.mt.us.

**SLATER, BRIAN (RAVEN SLATE),** writer; b. Arlington Heights, Ill., June 19, 1973; s. Robert Vincent and Kathe Lynn Slater; m. Debra Renee Staudt (div. Feb. 27, 2002). Prin. Slate Raven Novels, Ill., 1993—. Author: (novels) Civilized War 2023, 2000, Fresh Start, 2001, Magician's Box, 2005. Mem.: Knights in Shining Leather (life; swordfighting trainer 1991—2002). Avocations: swimming, martial arts, sword collecting. Office Phone: 847-359-2894. Personal E-mail: author@slateraven.com.

**SLATER, C. STEWART,** chemical engineering educator; b. Feb. 24, 1957; s. Clarence S. and Elizabeth Slater. BS, Rutgers U., Piscataway, N.J., 1979, MS, 1981, MPh, 1982, PhD, 1983. Process devel. engr. Procter & Gamble Co., Cin., 1979-81; teaching asst., project mgr. Rutgers U., 1981-83; prof. chem. engring. Manhattan Coll., Riverdale, NY, 1983-95; prof. and chair chem. engring. dept. Rowan U., Glassboro, NJ, 1995—. Cons. to major U.S. corps. Contbr. over 100 articles to profl. publs., several chpts. to books. Recipient Ralph R. Teetor award Soc. Automotive Engrs., 1986. Fellow Am. Soc. for Engring. Edn. (divsn. chmn. 2003, program chmn. 1990, New Engring. Educator Excellence award 1987, Dow Outstanding Faculty award 1989, John Fluke award 1992, George Westinghouse award 1996, Chester Carlson award 1999, Joseph J. Martin award 1998, 99), Mem. Am. Chem. Soc., Am. Inst. Chem. Engrs., Am. membrance Soc., Sigma Xi, Tau Beta Pi, Omega Chi Epsilon. Achievements include research in membrane technology. Office: Rowan Univ Dept Chem Engring 201 Mullica Hill Rd Glassboro NJ 08028-1702 Business E-Mail: slater@rowan.edu.

**SLATER, CARMEN ROCHELLE,** elementary school educator; b. Fort Worth, Tex., Mar. 3, 1973; d. Carl Leslie, Sr. and Billie Faye Slater. BA in Communication & Elem. Edn., U. Tex., Arlington, 1991—96, BA in English & Elem. Edn., 1991—96. Cert. Elem. Sch. tchr. Tex. State Bd. Edn., 1996, Elem. Speech Comm. tchr. Tex. State Bd. Edn., 1996, Early Childhood Edn. tchr. Tex. State Bd. Edn., 2000. Kindergarten tchr. Paul L. Dunbar Elem. Sch., Dallas, 1996—. Reading/lang. arts rep. (K-3), Campus Instrnl. Leadership Team Paul L. Dunbar Learning Ctr., Dallas, 1999—, grade level chair, 1999—, campus early childhood rep., 1999—, new tchr. mentor, 2000—03, campus headstart liaison, 2001—, kindergarten sponsor, Benjamin Banneker Math Club, 2001—. Mem.: Internat. Reading Assn., Am. Fedn. Tchrs., Delta Sigma Theta, Phi Delta Kappa (xinos sponsor 1999—2003). Conservative. Baptist. Avocations: reading, singing, travel. Home: 5509 Kilpatrick Ave Fort Worth TX 76107 Personal E-mail: crslater73@hotmail.com.

**SLATER, CHRISTIAN,** actor; b. NYC, Aug. 18, 1969; s. Michael Hawkins and Mary Jo Slater; m. Ryan Haddon, Feb. 12, 2000; children: Jaden Zach Haddon-Slater, Eliana Sophia Haddon-Slater. Actor: (films) Legend of Billie Jean, 1985, Name of the Rose, 1986, Twisted, 1986, Tucker, 1988, Gleaming the Cube, 1989, Heathers, 1989, Beyond the Stars, 1989, The Wizard, 1989, Tales from the Darkside: The Movie, 1990, Young Guns II, 1990, Pump Up the Volume, 1990, Robin Hood: Prince of Thieves, 1991, Mobsters, 1991, Star Trek VI: The Undiscovered Country, 1991, Kuffs, 1992; (films, voice) FernGully: The Last Rainforest, 1992; (films) Where the Day Takes You, 1992, Untamed Heart, 1993, True Romance, 1993, Jimmy Hollywood, 1994, Interview with the Vampire: Vampire Chronicles, 1994, Murder in the First, 1995, Bed of Roses, 1995, Broken Arrow, 1996, Austin Powers: Internat. Man of Mystery, 1997, The Tears of Julian Po, 1997, (& co-prodr.) Hard Rain, 1998, Basil, 1998, (& exec. prodr.) Very Bad Things, 1998, Love Stinks, 1999, White Lies, 1999, The Contender, 2000, 3000 Miles to Graceland, 2001, Who Is Cletis Tout, 2001, Windtalkers, 2002, Run for the Money (aka Hard Cash), 2002, Masked & Anonymous, 2003, Mindhunters, 2004, The Good Shepherd, 2004, Pursued, 2004, Churchill: Hollywood Years, 2004, (& exec. prodr.) The Deal, 2004, Alone in the Dark, 2005, A License to Steal, 2005; dir.: Mus. of Love, 1996; actor: (TV films) Sherlock Holmes: The Strange Case of Alice Faulkner, 1981, The Hunted Mansion Mystery, 1983, Living Proof: The Hank Williams Jr. Story, 1983, Secrets, 1986, Desperate for Love, 1989, Merry Christmas, George Bailey, 1997; (TV series) One Life to Live, 1977, Ryan's Hope, 1985, LA Law, 1988, Saturday Night Live, 1991, 1993, 1994; (TV series, voice) Prehistoric Planet, 2002; (TV series) The West Wing, 2002, (voice) Adventures of Jimmy Neutron: Boy Genius, 2003, Alias, 2003; (plays) Music Man, 1980, Between Daylight & Boonville, 1980, Copperfield, 1981, Macbeth, 1982, Merlin, 1983, Landscape of the Body, 1984, Dry Land, 1986, One Flew Over the Cuckoo's Nest, 2004—05, The Glass Menagerie, 2005. Named one of 100 Sexiest Stars in Film History, Empire Mag., 1995. Office: Creative Artists Agy 9830 Wilshire Blvd Beverly Hills CA 90212

**SLATER, CODY,** retail executive; Founder BW Tech. Ltd., 1987; pres., CEO BW Tech. Ltd. (acquired as subsidiary by First Tech. Innovative Solutions, 2004), Calgary, Alberta, Canada, 1987—. Office: BW Tech 2840 2nd Ave SE Calgary AB Canada T2A 7X9 Office Phone: 403-248-9226. Fax: 403-273-3708.

**SLATER, EVE E.,** former federal agency administrator; b. May 16, 1945; 2 children. Grad., Vassar Coll. Cert. internal medicine and cardiology. Intern and resident Mass. Gen. Hosp., chief resident medicine, 1976; chief hypertension unit, asst. prof. medicine Harvard Med. Sch., 1977—82; sr. dir. biochem. endocrinology Merck Rsch. Labs., 1983—88, sr. v.p. clinical & regulatory devel., 1994—2001, sr. v.p. external policy, v.p. corp. pub. affairs, 2001—02; acting asst. sec. for health US Dept. Health & Human Services, Washington, 2001—02, asst. sec. for health, 2002—03; Lloyd H. Smith vis. prof. med. U. Calif., San Francisco, 2003. Adj. assoc. clinical prof. med. Columbia U., 1983—2002; chmn. Internat. Conf. on Harmonization Com. on the Structure and Content of Clin. Studies Reports; chmn. regulations adv. bd. Ctr. for Medicine Rsch.; mem. Keystone Nat. Policy Dialogue on HIV; founder Forum for HIV Rsch.; bd. dirs. Vertex Pharmaceuticals Inc. Cambridge, Mass., 2004—, AnorMED, 2005—, Theravance, Inc., 2005—, Phase Forward Inc., 2005—. Recipient Virginia Kneeland Frantz '22 Disting. Women in Med. award, Columbia U. Coll. Physicians & Surgeons, 2003, Caring Heart award, NJ Assn. for Biomedical Rsch., 2004. Mem.: Phi Beta Kappa. Avocation: flute.*

**SLATER, JAMES MUNRO,** radiation oncologist; b. Salt Lake City, Jan. 7, 1929; s. Donald Munro and Leone Forestine (Fehr) S.; m. JoAnn Strout, Dec. 28, 1948; children: James, Julie, Jan, Jerry, Jon. BS in Physics, U. Utah, Utah State U., 1954; MD, Loma Linda U., 1963; PhD (hon.), Andrews U., Berrien Springs, Mich., 1996. Diplomate Am. Bd. Radiology. Intern Latter Day Saints Hosp., Salt Lake City, 1963-64, resident in radiology, 1964-65; resident in radiotherapy Loma Linda U. Med. Ctr., White Meml. Med. Center, L.A., fellow in radiotherapy, 1967-68, U. Tex.-M.D. Anderson Hosp. and Tumor Inst., Houston, 1968-69; dir. radiation oncology sect. Loma Linda U. Med. Ctr., Calif., 1970—79, dir. radiation sect. Calif., 1975—79, chmn. dept. radiation scis. Calif., 1978—90, chmn. dept. radiation medicine Calif., 1990—2001, dir. Cancer Inst., 1993—97, treas. Calif., 1995-96, exec. v.p. Calif., 1994—95; founder, dir. Loma Linda U./NASA Radiation Biology Lab., Calif., 1997—; vice chair radiation medicine Loma Linda U. Med. Ctr., 2003—. Co-dir. cmty. radiology oncology program L.A. County-U. So. Calif. Comprehensive Cancer Ctr., 1978-83; mem. cancer adv. coun. State of Calif., 1980-85; clin. prof. U. So. Calif., 1982—; founding mem. Proton Therapy Coop. Group, 1985—, chmn. 1987-91; cons. charged particle therapy program Lawrence Berkeley Lab., 1986-94; cons. R&D monoclonal antibodies Hybritech Inc., 1985-94, bd. dirs., 1985-94; cons. Berkeley lab., 1986-94; mem. panel cons. Internat. Atomic Energy Agy. UN, 1994-98; cons. Sci. Applications Internat. Corp., 1979, 89-91. Bd. dirs. Am. Cancer Soc., San Bernardino/Riverside, 1976-84, exec. com., 1976—; pres. Inland Empire chpt., 1981-83. NIH fellow, 1968-69; recipient exhbn. awards Radiol. Soc. N.Am., 1973, exhbn. awards European Assn. Radiology, 1975, exhbn. awards Am. Soc. Therapeutic Radiologists, 1978, Alumnus of Yr. award, 1993-94. Fellow Am. Coll. Radiology; mem. AAAS, AMA, ACS (liaison mem. to commn. on cancer 1976-84), Am. Radium Soc., Am. Soc. Clin. Oncology, Am. Soc. Therapeutics Radiologists, Assn. Univ. Radiologists, Soc. for Clinical Trials, N.Y. Acad. Scis., Calif. Med. Assn., Calif. Radiol. Soc., Gilbert H. Fletcher Soc. (pres. 1981-82), Loma Linda U. Med. Sch. Alumni Assn., Radiol. Soc. N.Am., Bernardino County Med Soc., Soc. Chairmen Of Acad. Radiation Oncology Programs, Alpha Omega Alpha. Achievements include development of world's first proton accelerator system for treating patients with cancer and some benign diseases in a hospital environment; development of world's first computer assisted radiation treatment planning system utilizing patient's digitized anatomic images with overlying radiation distribution images; development and direction of radiation molecular biology laboratories at Loma Linda U.; expansion of core laboratories for physics, engineering, chemistry and micro imaging under design at Loma Linda U. Office: Loma Linda Univ Med Ctr 25590 Prospect Ave Apt 27c Loma Linda CA 92354-3150 Business E-Mail: jmslater@dominion.llumc.edu.

**SLATER, JIM,** sportswriter, journalist; b. Williamsburg, Va., May 31, 1961; s. James and Iva Slater. BA in Journalism and Sociology, Ind. U., Bloomington, 1982. Sports journalist UPI, Indpls., 1983—91, Watertown Daily Times, NY, 1991—93; sports editor Agence France-Presse, Washington, 1993—. Recipient Second pl. nat. sports news writing/circulation 50, 000 and under, AP, 1992, 1993, Hon. Mention sports features and in-depth investigative sports reporting/circulation 50, 000 or less, 1992, 1993. Office: Agence France Presse 1500 K St NW Ste 600 Washington DC 20005-1200

**SLATER, LORI ANNETTE,** project manager; b. Houston, Aug. 8, 1964; d. Ted Gerald Patterson, JoAnn Patterson. AAS in Bus., Blinn Coll., 1984; BA in Applied Behavioral Sci., Nat. Louis U., 2000. Cert. profl. project mgr. Sec. Century Coating, Houston, 1984—85; asst. Ted's Post Co., Houston, 1985—88; sec. Freestone County Attorney's Office, Fairfield, Tex., 1989—90; dispatcher Tex. Instruments, Inc., Houston, 1990—93, Hewlett Packard Co., Atlanta, 1993—95; global accounts tech. adminstr. Hewlett Packard Co., Atlanta, 1995—98; bus. process analyst Hewlett Packard Co., Atlanta, 1998—2000, project/program mgr., 2000—. Mem. Friends of the Ctr. So. Poverty Law Ctr., Montgomery, 2001—, founding mem. Nat. Campaign for Tolerance, 2001—. Mem.: Project Mgmt. Inst. Avocations: reading, tennis, watching old movies. Business E-Mail: lori.slater@hp.com.

**SLATER, RALPH EVAN,** lawyer; b. Bklyn., July 14, 1948; s. Ralph Groff and Silvia Helen (Montanelli) S.; m. Cynthia Elaine Mann, Aug. 29, 1970; children: Robert Evan, Andrew Montgomery, Steven Edward. AB, Princeton U., 1970; JD, U. Pa., 1973. Bar: Conn. 1973, U.S. Dist. Ct. Conn. 1984, U.S. Tax Ct. 1984, U.S. Supreme Ct. 1987. Assoc. Gregory & Adams, Wilton, Conn., 1973-79, ptnr., 1980-93; prin. Gregory & Adams P.C., 1994—, pres., 1996—. Chmn. bd. The Wilton Bank, 1986—; atty. Planning and Zoning

Commn., Zoning Bd. Appeals, Ridgefield, Conn., 1979—81. Chmn. bd. edn. 1st Congl. Ch., Ridgefield, Conn., 1982—84, chmn. bd. trustees, 1985—87. Mem. Conn. Bar Assn. (exec. com. estates and probate sect. 1984-86, 93-99), Western Conn. Estate and Tax Planning Coun. Inc. (dir. 1992-96), Wilton C. of C. (dir., 2004—). Republican. Mem. Ch. of Christ. Home: 30 Strawberry Ridge Rd Ridgefield CT 06877-6019 Office: Gregory & Adams 190 Old Ridgefield Rd Wilton CT 06897-4023 Office Phone: 203-762-9000. E-mail: rslater@gregoryandadams.com.

**SLATER, RODNEY E.**, lawyer, emergency management executive, former secretary of transportation; b. Tutwyler, Miss., Feb. 23, 1955; m. Cassandra Wilkins; 1 child. BS, Ea. Mich. U., 1977; JD, U. Ark., 1980. Asst. atty. gen. State of Ark., 1983-85, exec. asst. for community and minority affairs Gov. of Ark., 1983-85, exec. asst. for econ. and community programs, 1985-87; dir. intergovernmental rels. Ark. State U., 1987-93; adminstr. fed. hwy. adminstrn. U.S. Dept. Transp., Washington, 1993-97, sec., 1997-2001; ptnr. Patton Boggs LLP, Washington, 2001—; and vice chair & sr. advisor James Lee Witt Associates, LLC, Washington, 2004—. Mem. Ark. State Hwy. and Transp. Commn., 1987-93, chair, 1992-93; dep. campaign mgr., sr. traveling advisor Clinton for Pres. Campaign, 1992; dep. to chair Clinton/Gore Transition Team, 1992-93; bd. dirs. Africare, 2001—, Joint Ctr Polit. and Econ. Studies, 2001— Ark. liaison Martin Luther King, Jr. Fed. Holiday Commn., 1983-87; mem. Ark. Sesquicentennial Commn., 1986. Mem. Ark. Bar Assn. (sec.-treas. 1989-93), W. Harold Flowers Law Soc. (pres. 1985-92). Democrat. Office: Patton Boggs 2550 M St NW Washington DC 20037

**SLATER, THOMAS GLASCOCK, JR.**, lawyer; b. Washington, Mar. 15, 1944; s. Thomas G. and Hylton R. Slater; m. Scott Newell Brent, Aug. 31, 1996; children: Thomas Glascock, Tacie Holden Norris, Andrew Fletcher. BA, Va. Mil. Inst., 1966; LLB, U. Va., 1969. Bar: Va. 1969, U.S. Dist. Ct. (ea. dist.) Va. 1970, U.S. Ct. Appeals (4th cir.) 1975, DC 1980, U.S. Ct. Appeals (5th cir.), U.S. Ct. Appeals DC 1980, U.S. Supreme Ct. 1981. Assoc. Hunton & Williams LLP, Richmond, Va., 1969-76, ptnr., 1976—, co-head litig. practice. Bd. dirs. Tredegar Industries. Pres. VMI Found., 1995—97, VMI Bd. Visitors, 2003—; bd. trustees Va. Hist. Soc.; mem. vestry St. Mary's Episcopal Ch.; bd. dirs. Central Va. Legal Aid Soc. Fellow: Va. Law Found., Am. Coll. Trial Lawyers, Am. Bar Found.; mem.: Richmond Bar Assn. (pres. 1989—90), DC Bar Assn., Va. State Bar Coun. (exec. com.), 4th Cir. Jud. Conf., Va. Mil. Inst. Alumni Assn. (past pres.). Office: Hunton & Williams LLP Riverfront Plz East Tower 951 E Byrd St Richmond VA 23219-4074 Office Phone: 804-788-8475. Business E-Mail: tslater@hunton.com.

**SLATER, VALERIE A.**, lawyer; b. Passaic, NJ, Oct. 13, 1952; BA magna cum laude, Allegheny Coll., 1974; JD, Cath. U. Am., 1977. Bar: DC 1977, US Ct. Appeals (DC cir.) 1978, US Dist. Ct. (DC dist.) 1982, US Ct. Internat. Trade 1984, US Ct. Appeals (fed. cir.) 1984. Ptnr. Akin Gump Strauss Hauer & Feld LLP, Washington, ptnr., chair internat. trade practice group, 1990—. Mem.: Phi Beta Kappa. Office: Akin Gump Strauss Hauer & Feld LLP 1333 New Hampshire Ave NW Washington DC 20036-1564 Office Phone: 202-887-4112. Office Fax: 202-887-4288. Business E-Mail: vslater@akingump.com.

**SLATER, WANDA MARIE WORTH**, property manager; b. Thurston, Ohio, Feb. 18, 1927; adopted d. Daniel Harrison and Grace Marie (Neel) Worth; m. Charles Edwin Slater (dec. Sept. 2005); children: Margaret Grace(dec.), Daniel Worthington(dec.), Donald Rowe. Student, Denison U., 1941-45, Bethany Coll., 1945-46. Recipient certs. Ohio Ho. Reps. and Senate, 116th Ohio Assembly, Creative Living, Columbus. Sub. tchr. Licking County Schs., Union Twp., Ohio, 1946; clerical typist Farm Bur. Ins. Co., Columbus, Ohio, 1947-49; salesperson Avon Co., Clyde, Ohio, 1954-63; dep. registrar Sandusky County, Ohio, 1960-64; notary pub. State of Ohio, Clyde, 1965-78, Hebron-Buckeye Lake, Ohio, 1978-98. Owner, mgr. rental property. Editor OFWC Buckeye mag., 1970-74, 88-98. Pres. Welcome Wagon, Clyde, 1957, Clyde Jr. League of Women, 1966, Leads-Licking County Cmty. Action Com., 1988, 94, 2000-01. Recipient Disting. Leadership award 1992, certificate of appreciation CARE. Mem.: Twentieth Century Club (pres. 1976—77), Order Eastern Star (worthy matron Clyde chpt. 1965, 1978, Hebron Eagon chpt. 1989, 1994, 2001), Mut. and Civic Improvement Club (pres. 1994—), Ohio Fedn. Women's Clubs (pres. 1986—88), Gen. Fedn. Women's Clubs Marionettes (pres. 1988—). Republican. Avocations: monologues, flower arranging, travel, crafts. Home and Office: 36 Worth Dr Hebron OH 43025-9760

**SLATKIN, LEONARD EDWARD**, conductor, musician, music director; b. LA, Sept. 1, 1944; s. Felix and Eleanor (Aller) Slatkin; m. Linda Hohenfeld, Mar. 29, 1986; 1 child, Daniel. Began violin study, 1947; piano study with, Victor Aller and Selma Cramer, 1955; composition study with, Castelnuovo-Tedesco, 1958; viola study with, Sol Schoenbach, 1959; conducting study with, Felix Slatkin, Amerigo Marino and Ingolf Dahl; student, Ind. U., 1962, L.A. City Coll., 1963, Juilliard Sch.; student (Irving Berlin fellow in musical direction), beginning 1964; student of, Jean Morel and Walter Susskind; doctorate (hon.), Juliard Sch. Music dir. Nat. Symphony Orch., Washington, 1996—; chief conductor. BBC Symphony Orch., 2000—04. Condr. St. Louis Symphony Orch., 1968—96, music dir., 1979—96, condr. laureate 1996—; founder, music dir.; condr. St. Louis Symphony Youth Orch., 1969—, mus. advisor, 1979—80; prin. guest condr. LA Philharmonic, Hollywood Bowl, 2005—; Royal Philharmonic Orch., 2005—; with ICM Artist, Ltd., Harold Holt, Ltd., Konzertdircktion/Schmidt; founder, dir. Nat. Conducting Inst. Conducting inst. asst. condr. Youth Symphony of N.Y., Carnegie Hall 1966, asst. condr. Juilliard Opera Theater and Dance Dept., 1967, St. Louis Symphony Orch., 1968—71, assoc. condr., 1971—74, guest condr. Concertgebouw, Royal Danish Orch., Tivoli, English Chamber Orch., BBC Manchester, London Philharm., London Symphony Orch., Royal Philharm. Orch., 1974, Nat. Orch. Paris, Scottish Nat. Orch., NHK Tokyo, 1986, Vienna State Opera, Lyric Opera Chgo., Stuttgart Opera, Stockholm, Oslo, Israel, Goteborg, Berlin, debut Chgo. Symphony Orch., 1974, NY Philharm., 1974, Phila. Orch., 1974, USSR Orchs., 1976—77, Met. Opera, 1991, prin. guest condr. Minn. Orch., 1974—, summer artistic dir., 1979—89, music dir. New Orleans Philharm. Symphony Orch., 1977—78, artistic dir. Great Woods, 1990, artistic adminstr. Blossom, 1991; composer: The Raven, Dialogue for Two Cellos and Orchestra, Ext. 1, 2, 3, 4; rec. artist RCA, Angel EMI, Vox, Telarc, Philips, Warner Bros. Recipient 2 Grammy awards, Prokofiev Symphony No. 5 with St. Louis Symphony, 1985, Declaration of Honor in Silver, Austrian Govt., 1986. Mem.: NARAS (bd. govs. Chgo. chpt.). Office: John F Kennedy Ctr 2700 F St NW Washington DC 20566 also: Askonas Holt Ltd Lonsdale Chambers 27 Chancery Ln London WC2A 1PF England Office Phone: 20 7400-1700. Office Fax: 20 7400-1799.*

**SLATNER, THOMAS ALLEN**, bookseller; b. Marple, Cheshire, Eng., May 1, 1940; arrived in U.S., 1947; s. Hugo and Edith (Elsner) S.; m. Eve Naomi Silberberg, Aug. 11, 1961; children: Nicole, Claude, Genevieve. BA, CCNY, 1961. Mgr. Richard Abel & Co., London, 1968-73; dir. Thomas Slatner & Co., London and N.J., 1978—. Home: 2 Wellfield Ave London N10 2EA England Office: 1127 Kennedy Blvd North Bergen NJ 07047-1839

**SLATON, CHARLES R.**, hospital administrator; b. Quanah, Tex., Nov. 28, 1956; s. Charles L. and Margaret S. (Graham) S.; m. Lori Renee Downs, Oct. 11, 1979; children: Charles M., Preston H., McKinsay L. BBA in Mgmt., Tex. Tech. U., 1979, MBA in Health Orgn. Mgmt., 1988. Exec. dir. physe ventures St. Mary Hosp., Lubbock, 1986-89; v.p. strategic devel. Santa Rosa (Calif.) Meml. Hosp., 1989-94; v.p. physician rels. to pres., CEO St. Francis Hosp Tenet Healthcare, Memphis, 1994—97, v.p. operations, Central States Region Little Rock, 1997—99, v.p. operations, 1999—2000; v.p. operations, 2000—03; exec. v.p. MedCath Inc., 2003—04, COO Charlotte, NC, 2003—05, pres., 2004—, CEO, 2005—. Office: MedCath Inc 10720 Sikes Pl Ste 300 Charlotte NC 28277

**SLATON, GWENDOLYN CHILDS**, academic administrator; b. Phila., June 19, 1945; d. George Alexander and LaFronia (Dunbar) Childs; m. Harrison Allen Slaton, Sept. 17, 1966; children: Kimberly Dawn, Leigh Alison. BA in History, Pa. State U., 1970; MA in Edn., Seton Hall U., 1976; MLS, Rutgers U., 1981. Lic. profl. librarian, N.J. Tchr. Project A.C.T.I.O.N., New Brunswick, N.J., 1969-70; prodn. coord. Essex County Coll., Newark, 1972-75, non-print media spl., 1975-81, dir. libr., 1981—97, assoc. dean learning resources, 1997—. Sec. Maplewood Cultural Commn., 1983-89; mem. adv. bd. Family Svc. Child Guidance Ctr. of the Oranges, Maplewood and Millburn, 1976-82; bd. dirs., North Jersey Minerva Found., 2004—. Mem. ALA, N.J. Libr. Assn., Essex Hudson Regional Libr. Coop. (sec. exec. bd. 1988-89), Assn. Two Yr. Coll. Libr. Dirs. (pres. 1984), North Jersey Minerva Found., Delta Sigma Theta (North Jersey Alumnae chpt., v.p. 1992-94, pres. 1994-96, parlimentarian 2003—). Office: Essex County Coll 303 University Ave Newark NJ 07102-1719 Office Phone: 973-877-3233. Business E-Mail: slaton@essex.edu.

**SLATTERY, JAMES JOSEPH (JOE SLATTERY)**, actor; b. Memphis, Feb. 7, 1922; s. James Joseph and Katie May (Carlin) S.; m. Mary Margaret Costello, May 23, 1944 (dec. Aug. 1987); children: James Joseph, John P., Ann, Mary, Nancy; m. Marilyn Daus, Sept. 16, 1989. AB, Hendrix Coll., Conway, Ark., 1942. Pres. Am. Fedn. TV and Radio Artists, 1976-79. Actor. Served with USAAF, 1942-46; to lt. col. USAF (ret.) Recipient Disting. Grad. award Hendrix Coll., 1986. Mem. Screen Actors Guild. Roman Catholic. Address: 5 The Court Of Bayview Northbrook IL 60062-3201 Personal E-mail: marilynd.slattery@comcast.net.

**SLAUGH, LYNN H.**, retired chemist; With Shell Devel. Co., Houston. Holder 160 patents; inventor two indsl. processes; contbr. articles to profl. jours. Recipient Indsl. Chemistry award Am. Chem. Soc., 1995. Achievements include 160 patents. Office: Shell Chem Comp PO Box 1380 Houston TX 77251-1380

**SLAUGHTER, ALEXANDER HOKE**, lawyer; b. Charlottesville, Va., Nov. 24, 1937; s. Edward Ratliff and Mary (Hoke) S.; m. Virginia Borah, 1964 (div.); 1 child, David A.; m. Mary Peeples, 1971. BA, Yale U., 1960; LLB, U. Va., 1963. Ptnr. McGuire, Woods, Richmond, Va., 1969—. Episcopalian. Home: 3016 Rugby Rd Richmond VA 23221-3936 Office: McGuire Woods One James Ctr 901 E Cary St Richmond VA 23219-4030 Office Phone: 804-775-4346. E-mail: aslaughter@mcguirewoods.com.

**SLAUGHTER, ANNE-MARIE**, dean; m. Andrew Moravcsik; children: Edward, Alexander. Grad. magna cum laude, Princeton U., 1980; JD cum laude, Harvard U., 1985; MPhil, Oxford U., 1982, DPhil, 1992. Tchr. law U. Chgo.; rschr. Harvard U., J. Sinclair Armstrong prof. internat., fgn., and comparative law, dir. internat. legal studies program; Bert G. Kerstetter univ. prof. politics and internat. affairs Princeton U., dean Woodrow Wilson sch. pub. and internat. affairs, 2002—. Bd. dirs. McDonalds Corp., Coun. Fgn. Rels., New Am. Found., Can. Inst. Internat. Governace Innovation; spkr. in field. Author: (book) A New World Order; contbr. articles to profl. jours. Covener, acad. co-chair Princeton Project on Nat. Security. Recipient Francis Deak Prize, Am. Jour. Internat. Law, 1990, 1994. Fellow: Am. Acad. Arts and Scis.; mem.: Am. Soc. Internat. Law (pres. 2002—04). Office: Princeton Univ 424 Robertson Hall Princeton NJ 08544-1013 E-mail: slaughtr@princeton.edu.

**SLAUGHTER, DJUANIQUE NATÉ**, healthcare analyst, project manager, consultant; BS in Criminal Justice, Grambling State U., 1993; MPA, Calif. State U., Dominguez Hills, 1998. Med. clinic asst. Green Clinic, Ruston, La., 1993—97; pub. health intern Dept. Health and Human Svcs., Long Beach, Calif., 1997—98; project mgmt. specialist Scan Health Plan, Long Beach, 1998; adminstrv. asst. Salick Healthcare, LA, 1998—99, healthcare analyst, cons., project mgr., 1999; managed care report analyst Health Care Ptnrs., Torrance, Calif., 1999—2000; project mgr. Ops. Health Care Ptnrs., Torrance, 2000—03; mgr. claims adminstrn. Kaiser Permanent, Pasadena, Calif., 2003—04, cons. quality and risk mgmt., 2004—. HIV/AIDS peer counselor Campus Awareness Prevention, Grambling, La., 1993. Mem. Reach 2010, Reach 2010 Project, 2001—. Am. scholar Grambling State U. Personal E-mail: dedeaka@aol.com.

**SLAUGHTER, EDWARD RATLIFF, JR.**, lawyer; b. Raleigh, N.C., Sept. 15, 1931; s. Edward Ratliff and Mary McBee (Hoke) S.; m. Anne Limbosch, July 25, 1957; children: Anne-Marie, Hoke, Bryan. AB, Princeton U., 1953; postgrad. (Rotary Found. fellow), U. Brussels, 1955-56; LLB, U. Va., 1959. Bar: Va. 1959, D.C. 1981. Assoc. firm McGuire, Woods & Battle (now McGuire Woods) and predecessors, Charlottesville, Va., 1959-64; ptnr. McGuire, Woods & Battle and predecessors, 1964-79, head dept. litig., 1964-79, spl. asst. for litig. to atty. gen. U.S., 1979-81; ptnr. firm Whitman & Ransom, Washington, 1981-84; prin. Slaughter & Redinger, P.C., Charlottesville, 1984-95, Slaughter, Izakowitz, Clarke & Nunley, P.C., 1995-96, Woods, Rogers & Hazlegrove, P.L.C., 1996—2002, of counsel, 2002—03, Michie, Hamlett, Lowry, Rasmussen, & Tweel, PLLC, 2003—. Vis. lectr. trial advocacy U. Va., 1970-77, Va. procedure, 1986-91; disting. lectr. U. Tunis, 1996; mem. standing com. on commrs. of accounts Jud. Coun. of Va., 1993—, chmn., 1995-2001. Chmn. Albemarle County (Va.) Dem. Com., 1969-73; pres. Charlottesville-Albemarle United Way, 1972; commr. accounts Albemarle County, 1986—; trustee Lime Kiln Arts, Inc., 1992-98. Served with USNR, 1953-55. Recipient William J. Brennan award U. Va. Trial Advocacy Inst., 1996 Fellow Am Bar Found, Am Coll Trial Lawyers; mem D C Bar, Charlottesville-Albemarle Bar Assn. (pres. 1976-77), Va. Bar Assn. (pres. 1978), Va. State Bar (bd. govs. internat. practice sect. 1992-2000, bd. govs. sr. lawyers conf. 2004—), Thomas Jefferson Inn Ct. (pres. 1995-96), Farmington Country Club. Home: 200 Tuckahoe Farm Ln Charlottesville VA 22901-5531 Office: Michie Hamlett Lowry Rasmussen & Tweel PLLC 500 Court Sq Ste 300 PO Box 298 Charlottesville VA 22902-0298 Office Phone: 434-295-8310. Business E-Mail: eslaughter@mhlrt.com.

**SLAUGHTER, FREEMAN CLUFF**, retired dentist; b. Estes, Miss., Dec. 30, 1926; s. William Cluff and Vay (Fox) S.; m. Genevieve Anne Parks, July 30, 1948; children: Mary Anne, Thomas Freeman, James Hugh. Student, Wake Forest U., 1944, Emory U., 1946-47; DDS, Emory U. Sch. of Dentistry, 1951. Lic. real estate broker. Practice gen. dentistry, Kannapolis, N.C., 1951-89; ret. Mem. N.C. State Bd. Dental Examiners, 1966-75, pres., 1968-69, sec.-treas., 1971-74; chief dental staff Cabarrus Meml. Hosp. (now N.E. Med. Ctr.) Concord, N.C., 1965-66, 75; mem. N.C. Adv. Com. for Edn. Dental Aux. Pers.-N.C. State Bd. Edn., 1967-70; advisor dental asst. program Rowan Cabarrus C.C., 1974-76; Duke Med. Ctr. Davison Century Club. Trustee N.C. Symphony Soc., 1962-68, pres. Kannapolis chpt., 1961; mem. Cabarrus County Bd. Health, 1977-83, chmn., 1981-83, acting health dir. 1981; vice chmn. Kannapolis Charter Commn., 1983-84; mem. City Coun. Kannapolis, 1984-85; Mayor protem, Kannapolis, 1984-85; past active Boy Scouts Am., Eagle scout with silver palm. QM2C asst. navigator on USS Xenia AKA 51, co-navigator on USS Gen. George O. Squier AP 130 with USN, 1944-46, WW II, ETO, MTO. Recipient Kannapolis Citizen of Yr. award, 1982. Fellow Am. Coll. Dentists (life); mem. ADA (life), Am. Legion, Kannapolis Jr. C. of C. (v.p. 1952), Toastmasters Internat. (pres. Kannapolis chpt. 1963-64), Am. Assn. Dental Examiners (Dentist Citizen of Yr. 1975, v.p. 1977-79, Recognition plaque, 1980), So. Conf. Dental Deans and Examiners (v.p. 1969), N.C. Dental Soc. (resolution of commendation 1975), N.C. Dental Soc. Anesthesiology (pres. 1964), Southeastern Acad. Prosthodontics, So. Acad. Oral Surgery, Am. Soc. Dentistry for Children (pres. N.C. unit 1957), Internat. Assn. Dental Rsch. Cabarrus County Dental Soc. (pres. 1953-54, 63-64, 69), N.C. Assn. Professions (Dr. Friend 1976-80), Kannapolis Music Club (pres. 1962-63), Emory U. Corpus Cordis Aureum (Emory U. disting. alumnus award 2006), Masons, Shriners, Rotary (dir. 1977-80), Omicron Kappa Upsilon, Alpha Epsilon Upsilon.

**SLAUGHTER, JAMES H.**, lawyer; b. Concord, N.C., July 29, 1964; s. Freeman C. and Genevieve A. (Parks) S.; m. Tamara A. Vincent, Oct. 1, 1988; children: Freeman J., McKinley J., Wyatt T. BA with highest honors, U.N.C., 1986, JD, 1989. Bar: N.C. 1989, U.S. Dist. Ct. (mid. and we. dists.) N.C. 1989, U.S. Ct. Appeals (fed. cir.) 1992, Supreme Ct. US; cert. profl. parliamentarian; profl. reg. parliamentarian. Assoc. Henson, Henson, Bayliss & Sue, Greensboro, NC, 1989—91; Floyd & Jacobs, LLP, Greensboro, NC, 1991—96; ptnr. Floyd & Jacobs, Greensboro, NC, 1996—2001, Forman Rossabi Black, Pa., 2001—, pres. Pa., 2003—. Mem. of faculty Williamsburg Practicum of the Am. Inst. of Parliamentarians, 1994—. Tech. editor: The Complete Idiot's Guide to Robert's Rules, 2004; contbg. author: Labor Union Law and Regulation, 2005; legal guest columnist News & Record, Greensboro, 1991-95. Pres. Young Dems. of N.C., 1992-93, Greensboro Hist. Mus., 2006-; chmn. State Dem. Coun. of Rev., N.C., 1994-96, 2001-, Nat. Conf. Com. Justice (Triad Chpt.), 2004-06; mem. Gov.'s Crime Commn., N.C., 1982-85; mem. N.C. Progress Bd., 1996-98; dir. Greensboro chpt. ARC, 1996-99, sec., 1997-98; bd. dirs. Greensboro chpt. NCCJ, 1996-99; bd. trustee Greensboro Hist. Mus., 1996-99; elder First Presbyn. Ch., 2000-03, clerk of session, 2001-02. U.S. Truman Scholar, 1984. Master Am. Funds of Court; mem. Rotary (Greensboro Crescent club 1993—, Paul Harris fellow), Greensboro Bar Assn. (pres. 1991-92), Nat. Assn. Parliamentarians Ethics (chmn., 2005-), Am. Inst. Parliamentarians (chmn., 2005-), Ethics Phi Beta Kappa. Presbyterian. Home: 2206 Granville Rd Greensboro NC 27408-5012 Office: Forman Rossabi Black PA PO Box 41027 Greensboro NC 27404

**SLAUGHTER, KENNETH S.**, lawyer; b. Washington, July 5, 1951; AB, Brown Univ., 1973; JD, Georgetown Univ., 1976. Bar: DC 1976. Atty. advisor U.S. Dept. Treasury, Washington, 1976 79; asst. gen counsel Nat. Cooperative Bank, 1979—83, corp. v.p., gen. counsel, 1983—87; ptnr., State & Local Govt. practice Venable LLP, Washington & Baltimore. Bd. mem. SEED Public Charter Sch., Heads Up, Boys & Girls Clubs of Greater Washington, Venture Philanthropy Ptnrs. Mem.: Nat. Bar Assn., Internat. Assn. Gaming Attorneys, DC Bar Assn. Office: Venable LLP 575 7th St NW Washington DC 20004 also: Venable LLP 1800 Mercantile Bank & Trust Bldg 2 Hopkins Plz Baltimore MD 21201 Office Phone: 202-344-8385, 410-244-7715. Office Fax: 202-344-8300. Business E-Mail: ksslaughter@venable.com.

**SLAUGHTER, LOUISE MCINTOSH**, congresswoman; b. Lynch, Ky., Aug. 14, 1929; d. Oscar Lewis and Grace (Byers) McIntosh; m. Robert Slaughter, 1956; children: Megan Rae, Amy Louise, Emily Robin. BS in Microbiol., U. Ky., Lexington, 1951, MPH, 1953; D (hon.), U. Ky., 2006. Bacteriologist Ky. Dept. Health, Louisville, 1951-52, U. Ky., 1952-53; market rschr. Procter & Gamble, Cin., 1953-56; mem. Monroe County Legislature, NY, 1976—79; regional coord. Staff of Sec. State Mario Cuomo, NY, 1976—78, Staff of Lt. Gov. Mario Cuomo, NY, 1979—82; mem. NY State Assembly, 1982—86, US Congress from 28th NY dist., 1987—, ranking minority mem. rules com., Dem. chair Congl. Arts Caucus, Dem. chair Congl. Pro-Choice Caucus, mem. Dem. steering and policy com., mem. Comm. Security and Cooperation in Europe. Del. Dem. Nat. Conv., 1972, 76, 80, 88, 92, 96; mem. Nat. Ctr. for Policy Alternatives Adv. Bd., League of Women Voters, Nat. Women's Polit. Caucus. Named Lay Educator of Yr., Phi Delta Kappa Internat., Rochester chpt., 1999; recipient Disting. Pub. Health Legislator award, Pub. Health Assn., 1997, Award for Outstanding Arts Leadership in the US Ho. Reps., US Conf. Mayors and Ams. for the Arts, 1998, Humane Legislator of Yr., Am. Humane Assn., 2003, Woman of Vision award, Women in Film and Vision, 2004, Sidney R. Yates Nat. Arts Advocacy award, Nat. Assembly State Arts Agencies. Democrat. Episcopalian. Office: US Ho Reps 2469 Rayburn Ho Office Bldg Washington DC 20515-3228 Office Phone: 202-225-3615.*

**SLAUGHTER, MATTHEW J.**, federal official, economics professor; BA in Econ., Notre Dame, 1990; Ph.D in Econ., MIT, 1994. Asst. prof. econ. Dartmouth Coll., Hanover, NH, 1994—2001, assoc. prof. econ., 2001—02, assoc. prof. bus. adminstrn. Tuck Sch. Bus., 2002—; mem. Coun. Econ. Advisers Exec. Office of the Pres., Washington, 2005—. Faculty rsch. fellow Nat. Bur. Econ. Rsch., 1995—2002; vis. fellow Inst. for Internat. Economics, 1997—; mem. Coun. Fgn. Rels., 2000—05; vis. scholar Fed. Reserve Bank, 1998, 2002, IMF, 1996, 97; panel mem. NAS, 2004—; bd. acad. advisors Internat. Tax Policy Forum, 2005—; bd. economists Time mag., 2004; cons. The World Bank, 1995—97, 2000, 02, Emergency Com. for Am. Trade, 1996—2003, Nat. Fgn. Trade Coun., 2003, Com. for Fair Internat. Taxation, 2004, Org. for Internat. Investment, 2004. Recipient Bronze award, AMEX Bank Review Essay Competition, 1994, John M. Manley Huntington Teacher award, Dartmouth Coll., 2001; fellow, NSF, 1990—93; grantee MIT Industrial Performance Ctr. Doctoral Fellowship, Sloan Found., 1993—94, Nat. Fellowship, Nat. Bur. Econ., 2000—01; Elizabeth R. & Roland A. Jeffe Fellowship, Dartmouth Coll., 2001—02. Office: Coun Econ Advisers 1800 G St NW Washington DC 20502

**SLAUGHTER, NATHANIEL G., III**, lawyer; b. Athens, Ga., July 22, 1944; s. N.G. Jr. and Nancy (Ivey) S.; m. Jerilene Southwell, Aug. 12, 1967; 1 child, Nat. BBA cum laude, U. Ga., 1966, JD cum laude, 1969. Bar: Ga. 1969. Law clerk Judge Richard T. Rives, U.S. Ct. Appeals 5th Cir., Montgomery, Ala., 1969-70; assoc. King & Spalding, Atlanta, 1970-76; gen. counsel E.T. Barwick Industries, Inc., Atlanta, 1976-78; ptnr. Killorin & Schroder, Atlanta, 1979-84, Slaughter & Virgin, Atlanta, 1984—. Editor-in-chief: Georgia Law Review, 1968-69. Mem. Atlanta Estate Planning Coun. mem. ABA, State Bar Ga. (chmn. corp. and banking law sect. corp. code revision com. 1979-83, chmn. corp. and banking law sect. 1984-85), Atlanta Bar Assn. Episcopalian. Avocations: golf, reading, wine, travel. Office: Slaughter & Virgin 1201 Peachtree St NE Ste 1110 Atlanta GA 30361-6313 Office Phone: 404-897-1110. Personal E-mail: slaughvirg@aol.com.

**SLAUGHTER, RICHARD ARTHUR**, political scientist, economist, educator; b. Twin Falls, Idaho, Nov. 20, 1943; s. Walter Arthur and Mary Viola Slaughter; m. Susan Kay Clark, Aug. 11, 1966; children: Scott, Ryan. BA in Polit. Sci., U. Idaho, 1966; MA in Internat. Rels., U. Denver, 1968, PhD in Internat. Politics, 1974. Asst. prof. polit. sci. West Ga. Coll., Carrollton, 1972-76; economist divsn. fin. mgmt. State of Idaho, Boise, 1976-80, chief economist, 1980-84; pres. Richard Slaughter Assocs., Boise, 1984—; dir. Martin Inst. for Peace Studies U. Idaho, 1996—2000; internat. economist Cen. Asia, 1998—2001; cons. economist Climate Impacts Group, U. Wash., 2000—. Vol. exec. dir. Boise Com. on Fgn. Rels., 1989-; mem. adv. bd. Martin Inst., U. Idaho, 1990-96, 2005—; co-founder Am. Coms. on Fgn. Rels., treas. 1995-2001, v.p., 2005—. Editor Idaho Econ. Forecast jour., 1977-84; author articles on Third World econ. devel. and nation-bldg., global climate change policy. Bd. dirs. Capitol Youth Soccer Assn., Boise, 1980-89, soccer commr., 1983-86. Mem. Coun. Fgn. Rels. Home and Office: 907 Harrison Blvd Boise ID 83702-4079 Office Phone: 208-850-1223. Business E-Mail: richard@rsaboise.com.

**SLAUGHTER, VERNON LEROY**, recording industry consultant; b. Omaha, Nov. 10, 1950; m. Lauren M. Callwood; children: Christopher, Michael. BA, U. Nebr., 1972; JD, Whittier Coll., 1990. Coll. rep. CBS Records, Lincoln, Nebr., 1970-73, local promotion mgr. Washington, 1973-76, dir. promotion N.Y.C., 1976-77, v.p. mktg., 1977-81; v.p. promotion Columbia Records, N.Y.C., 1981-86; v.p. rhythm and blues promotion A&M Records, L.A., 1987; pres. Vernon Slaughter, Inc., L.A., 1986—. Mem. Nat. Assn. Recording Arts & Scis.

**SLAVEN, TIMOTHY WILLIAM**, theater educator, set designer; b. Ft. Dodge, Iowa, June 15, 1959; s. George Emmett and Vivian Margaret Slaven; m. Colette Marie Ceilley, June 21, 1986; children: Katherine Amelia Salven, Sean Edward Salven, William Timothy Salven, Quinn Harrison Salven. AA, Iowa Ctrl. CC, Ft. Dodge, 1979; BA, U. No. Iowa, Cedar Falls, 1982, MA, 1990. Cert. tchr. Iowa. Designer/tech. dir. Clinton Area Showboat Theatre, Iowa, 1991, Old Creamery Theatre Co., Amana, Iowa, 1991—92; theatre instr. Ea. Ariz. Coll., Thatcher, Ariz., North Iowa Area CC, Mason City, Iowa, 1992—. Performer, bd. dirs. Mason City Cmty. Theatre, Iowa, 1997—2000; lighting designer/choreographer Stebens Children's Theatre, Mason City,

2004—05. Designer, choreographer, singer, dancer: numerous plays and musicals. Reader for blind IRIS, Mason City, 2004—06. Mem.: Mensa. Avocations: music, sports, dance. Home: 3389 Saratoga Ct Mason City IA 50401 Office: N Iowa Area CC 500 College Dr Mason City IA 50401 Office Phone: 641-422-4274. Business E-Mail: slavetim@niacc.edu.

**SLAVENS, THOMAS PAUL,** library science professor; b. Cincinnati, Iowa, Nov. 12, 1928; s. William Blaine and Rhoda (Bowen) S.; m. Cora Hart, July 9, 1950; 1 son, Mark Thomas. BA, Phillips U., 1951; MDiv, Union Theol. Sem., 1954; MA, U. Minn., 1962; PhD, U. Mich., 1965. Ordained to ministry Christian Ch., 1953. Pastor First Christian Ch., Sac City, Iowa, 1953-56, Sioux Falls, SD, 1956-60; librarian Divinity Sch., Drake U., Des Moines, 1960-64; teaching fellow Sch. Info., U. Mich., Ann Arbor, 1964-65; instr. U. Mich., Ann Arbor, 1965-66, asst. prof., 1966-69, assoc. prof., 1969-77, prof., 1977—2003, prof. emeritus, 2003—. Vis. prof. U. Minn., 1967, U. Coll. of Wales, 1978, 80, 93; vis. scholar U. Oxford, Eng., 1980; cons. Nutrition Planning Abstracts-UN, N.Y.C., 1977-79. Author-editor: Library Problems in the Humanities, 1981, (with John F. Wilson) Research Guide to Religious Studies, 1982, (with W. Eugene Kleinbaur) Research Guide to the History of Western Art, 1982, (with Terrence Tice) Research Guide to Philosophy, 1983, Theological Libraries at Oxford, 1984, (with James Pruett) Research Guide to Musicology, 1985, The Literary Adviser, 1985, A Great Library through Gifts, 1986, The Retrieval of Information, 1989, Number One in the U.S.A.: Records and Wins in Sports, Entertainment, Business, and Science, 1988, Doors to God, 1990, Sources of Information for Historical Research, 1994, Introduction to Systematic Theology, 1992, Reference Interviews Questions and Materials, 3d edit., 1994, Using the Financial and Business Literature, 2004. Served with U.S. Army, 1946-48. Recipient Warner Rice Faculty award U. Mich., 1975; H.W. Wilson fellow, 1960; Lilly Endowment fellow Am. Theol. Libr. Assn., 1963. Mem. Assn. Libr. and Info. Sci. Edn. (pres. 1972), Beta Phi Mu.

**SLAVICK, ANN LILLIAN,** retired art educator; b. Chgo., Sept. 29, 1933; d. Irving and Goldie (Bernstein) Friedman; m. Lester Irwin Slavick, Nov. 21, 1954 (div. Mar. 1987); children: Jack, Rachel. BFA, Sch. of Art of Chgo., 1973, MA in Art History, Theory, Criticism, 1991. Dir. art gallery South Shore Commn., Chgo., 1963-67; tchr. painting, drawing, crafts Halfway House, Chgo., 1972-73; tchr. studio art Conant H.S., Hoffman Estates, Ill., 1973-74; tchr. art history and studio arts New Trier H.S., Winnetka and Northfield, Ill., 1974-80; tchr. 20th century art history New Trier Adult Edn. Program, Winnetka, 1980-81; tchr. art adult edn. program H.S. Dist. 113, Highland Park, Ill., 1980-81; rschr., writer Art History Notes McDougall-Littel Pub., Evanston, Ill., 1984-85; tchr. art and art history Highland Park and Deerfield (Ill.) H.S., 1980-2000; tchr. art history Coll. of Lake County, Grayslake, Ill., 1986-88; ret., 2000. Faculty chair for visual arts Focus on the Arts, Highland Park H.S., 1981-85, faculty coord. Focus on the Arts, 1987-2005; panelist Ill. Arts Coun. Arts Tour, 1999, Evanston Arts Coun., 2000-02. Ill. Arts Coun. Multidisciplinary Grant Awards, 2001-03; reader advanced placement art history exams, 2003, 04, 06. One woman show Bernal Gallery, 1979, U. Ill., Chgo., 1983, Ann Brierly Gallery, Winnetka, 1984; exhibited paintings, drawings, prints and constrns. throughout Chgo. area; work represented by Art Rental and Sales Gallery, Art Inst. Chgo., 1960-87, Bernal Gallery, 1978-82; group shows at Bernal Gallery; work in pvt. collections in Ill., N.Y., Calif., Ariz., Ohio. Recipient Outstanding Svc. in Art Edn. award Ea. Ill. U., 1992, Mayors award for contbn. to the arts, Highland Park, 1995. Mem.: Ill. Art Edn. Assn., Nat. Art Edn. Assn. Avocations: cooking, reading, theater. Home: 5057 N Sheridan Rd Chicago IL 60640-3127 Office: Highland Park High Sch 433 Vine Ave Highland Park IL 60035-2099 E-mail: annlslavick@aol.com.

**SLAVICKAS, RIMAS ANTHONY,** industrial engineer, educator; s. Silvestras Kasimeras and Sofija (Koncavicius) Slavickas; m. Wilma Johanna Van Sinderen, Sept. 13, 1969; 1 child, Paul Anthony. Diploma Elec.Engring., Gordon Inst. Tech., Geelong, Victoria, Australia, 1962; BSc Math. & Physics magna cum laude, Laurentian U., Sudbury, Ont., Can., 1969; BSc Elec. Engring. honours, Queens U., Kingston, Ont., Can., 1971; MSc Applied Sci., U. Toronto, Can., 1974; PhD, McMaster U., Can., 1998. Profl. Engr., Ont., 1972. Pres., CEO Welland Hydro-Electric Sys. Corp., Ont., Canada, 1974—2003; prof. industry U. Fla., Gainesville, 2004—. Adv. bd. mem. Savo Tech Inc., Toronto, 2003—; cons. W&E Internat. Corp., Markham, Ont., Canada. Assoc. editor: Internat. Jour. Power and Energy Sys., 1998—; contbr. articles to profl. jours. Recipient Best Paper award, Internat. Conf., 2000. Mem.: IEEE (A number of awards for tech. excellence at confs.), Assn. Profl. Engrs. Australia, Profl. Engrs. Ont. (licentiate; chmn. Niagara chpt. 1985—86). Home: 76 Bridlewood Drive Ontario Welland Canada L3C 6K8 Office: University Florida 320 Benton Hall Gainesville FL 32611-6200 Office Phone: 352-392-3291. Personal E-mail: lpa@collaborative-research.com. E-mail: ras@ece.ufl.edu.

**SLAVIN, ARLENE,** artist; b. N.Y.C., Oct. 26, 1942; d. Louis and Sally (Bryck) Eisenberg; m. Neal Slavin, May 24, 1964 (div. 1979); m. Eric Bregman, Sept. 21, 1980; 1 child, Ethan. BFA, Cooper Union for the Advancement of Sci. and Art, 1964; MFA, Pratt Inst., 1967. One-woman shows include Fischbach Gallery, N.Y., 1973, 1974, 2003, Brooke Alexander Gallery, 1976, Alexander Milliken Gallery, N.Y., 1979, 1980, 1981, 1983, U. Colo., 1981, Pratt Inst., N.Y.C., 1981, Am. Embassy, Belgrad, Yugoslavia, 1984, Heckscher Mus., Huntington, N.Y., 1987, Katherine Rich Perlow Gallery, 1988, Chauncey Gallery, Princeton, N.J., 1990, The Gallery Benjamin N. Cardoza Sch. Law, 1991, Norton Ctr. for Arts, Danville, Ky., 1992, Kavesh Gallery, Ketchum, Idaho, 1993, exhibited in group shows at Bass Mus. Art, Fla., Whitney Museum of Art, 1973, The Contemporary Arts Center, Cin., 1974, Indpls. Mus. Art, 1974, Madison (Wis.) Art Ctr., Santa Barbara (Calif.) Mus., Winnipeg (Can.) Art Gallery, Gensler Assocs., San Francisco, 1986, Eliane Benson Gallery, Bridgehampton, N.Y., 1987, 1989, 1991, 1993, 2004, City of N.Y. Parks and Recreation Central Park, N.Y.C., 1989, Benton Gallery, Southampton, N.Y., 1991, Parish Mus., Southampton, 1991, Michele Miller Fine Art, 1993, Dillon Gallery, N.Y.C., 1998, Hebrew Union Coll., 2000—01, Fischbach Gallery, 2003, Am. Inst. Archs., 2003, Represented in permanent collections Met. Mus. of Art, N.Y.C., Fogg Art Mus., Cambridge, Mass., Hudson River Mus., Yonkers, N.Y., Heckscher Mus., Huntington, N.Y., Cin. Art Mus., Readers' Digest, Pleasantville, N.Y., pub. commns., N.C. Zoo, 1999, N.Y.C. Parks and Recreation, 1999, NJ Transit, Hoboken Terminal and Middletown Station, NJ, 1999—2002, Forest City Ratner, Ct. St Devel., 2000, Assunpink (NJ) Wildlife Ctr., 2004; subject: bibliography Arlene Slavin: Mediating Public Space, 2001; pub. commns., Town of Chapel Hill, N.C., 2002, PS 89, NYC, 2003, Island Beach State Pk., N.J., 2006, one-woman shows include Fischbach Gallery, N.Y., 2003; artist mem. design team Hillsborough Area Regional Transit, Tampa, Fla., 2003—05. Grantee, Nat. Endowment for Arts, 1977—78, Threshold Found., 1991. Home: 119 E 18th St New York NY 10003-2107 Office Phone: 212-777-3042. E-mail: slavin@arleneslavin.com.

**SLAVIN, PETER L.,** hospital administrator; AB, Harvard U., 1979, MD, 1984, MBA, 1990. Sr. v.p., chief med. officer Mass. Gen. Hosp., Boston, 1994—97; pres. Barnes-Jewish Hosp., St. Louis, 1997-99; med. dir. Mass. Gen. Physicians Orgn., Boston, chair., CEO, 1999—2003; pres. Mass. Gen. Hosp., Boston, 2003—. Office: Mass Gen Hosp 55 Fruit St Boston MA 02114-2622 Office Phone: 617-724-9300.

**SLAVIN, RAYMOND GRANAM,** allergist, immunologist; b. Cleve., June 29, 1930; s. Philip and Dinah (Baskind) S.; m. Alberta Cohrt, June 10, 1953; children: Philip, Stuart, David, Linda. AB, U. Mich., 1952; MD, St. Louis U., 1956; MS, Northwestern U., 1963. Diplomate Am. Bd. Internal Medicine, Am. Bd. Allergy and Immunology (treas.). Intern U. Mich. Hosp., Ann Arbor, 1956-57; resident St. Louis U. Hosp., 1959-61; fellow in allergy and immunology Northwestern U. Med. Sch., 1961-64; asst. prof. internal medicine and microbiology St. Louis U., 1965-70, assoc. prof., 1970-73, prof., 1973—; dir. divsn. allergy and immunology, 1965—. Mem. NIH study sect., 1985-89; cons. U.S. Army M.C. Contbr. numerous articles to med. publs.; editl. bd.: Jour. Allergy and Clin. Immunology, 1975-81. Chmn. Bd.

Asthma and Allergy Found. Am., 1985-88. With M.C., U.S. Army, 1957-59. Grantee NIH, 1967-70, 84—, Nat. Inst. Occupl. Safety and Health, 1974-80. Master: ACP; fellow: Am. Acad. Allergy and Immunology (exec. bd., historian, pres. 1983—84, Disting. Svc. award 1995, Disting. Clinician award 2005); mem.: AAAS, Ctrl. Soc. Clin. Rsch., Am. Assn. Immunologists. Democrat. Jewish. Home: 631 E Polo Dr Saint Louis MO 63105-2629 Office: 1402 S Grand Blvd Saint Louis MO 63104-1004 Office Phone: 314-977-8829. Business E-Mail: slavinrg@slu.edu.

**SLAVIT, DAVID HAL,** otolaryngologist; b. N.Y.C., Sept. 5, 1960; s. Leonard S. and Barbara H. (Levine) S.; m. Robin E. Feldman, July 31, 1983; children: Danielle, Evan, Roni. BS, Cornell U., 1982; MD, Mt. Sinai U., 1986. Cert. in otolaryngology. Intern Mayo Clinic, Rochester, Minn., 1986-87, resident in otolaryngology, 1987-91; with Lenox Hill Hosp., N.Y.C. Asst. prof. Health Sci. Ctr.-SUNY Downstate; cons. Juilliard Sch. Music, N.Y.C., 1994-99; dir. Ames Vocal Dynamics Lab., N.Y.C., 1998-2001. Author, editor: (book) Essentials of Otolaryngology, 1993; author: (books) Voice Disorders, 1995, Rhinologic Diagnosis and Treatment, 1996, Systemic Disease of the Nasal Airway, 1993; contbr. articles to profl. jours. Fellow ACS; mem. AMA, Am. Acad. Otolaryngology-Head and Neck Surgery, Am. Acad. Facial Plastic and Reconstructive Surgery, Am. Rhinologic Soc. Office Phone: 212-517-9177.

**SLAVITT, DAVID WALTON,** retired lawyer; b. Chgo., Mar. 15, 1931; s. Isaac and Fay (Goldstein) S.; m. Roberta Chelnek, July 26, 1953; children: Steven, Denise, Howard. BS, UCLA, 1952, JD, 1955. Bar: Calif. 1956; C.P.A., Calif. Since practiced in Los Angeles; pres. Slavitt & Borofsky (P.C.), 1969-87. Moderator continuing edn. programs. Author articles in field. Served with USNR, 1955. Mem. Am. Assn. Atty.-C.P.A.s (pres. 1964), ABA, State Bar Calif., Calif. Assn. Atty.-C.P.A.s (pres. 1963), Beverly Hills Bar Assn. (vice chmn. continuing edn. of bar 1970, asst. chmn. law practice mgmt. com. 1973).

**SLAVKIN, HAROLD CHARLES,** dean, biologist; b. Chgo., Mar. 20, 1938; m. Lois S. Slavkin; children: Mark D., Todd P. BA in English lit., U. So. Calif., 1961, DDS, 1965; Doctorate (hon.), Georgetown U., 1990, U. Paris, 1996, U. Md., 1997. Mem. faculty U. So. Calif. Sch. Dentistry, L.A., 1968—, mem. faculty gerontology inst., 1969, chmn. dept. biochemistry and nutrition, 1969—75, prof., 1974—, chmn. grad. program in craniofacial molecular biology, 1975-85, founding dir. Ctr. for Craniofacial Molecular Biology, 1989-95, George & Mary Lou Boone prof. craniofacial molecular biology, 1989-95, dean, 2000—, G. Donald and Marian James Montgomery Dean's Chair in Dentistry, 2000—; dir. Nat. Inst. Dental and Craniofacial Rsch., NIH, Bethesda, Md., 1995—2000. Vis. prof. Israel Inst. Tech., Haifa, 1987-88; cons. U.S. News and World Report, 1985-95, L.A. Edn. Partnership, 1983-95, Torstar Books, Inc., 1985-95. Contbr. articles to profl. jours. Mem. sci. adv. bd. Calif. Mus. Sci. and Tech., 1985-95. Rsch. scholar U. Coll. London, 1980. Mem. AAAS, Am. Assn. Anatomists, Am. Inst. Biol. Scis., Am. Soc. for Cell Biology, Am. Assn. for Dental Rsch. (pres. 1993-94), N.Y. Acad. Scis., Inst. Medicine of NAS, Internat. Coll. Dentistry, Am. Coll. Dentistry, Los Angeles County Art Mus. Assocs. Office: 925 W 34th St Los Angeles CA 90089 Office Phone: 213-740-2811. Office Fax: 213-740-1509. E-mail: slavkin@usc.edu.*

**SLAWSKY, DONNA SUSAN,** librarian, singer; b. N.Y., Jan. 18, 1956; d. Samuel Slawsky and Lillian (Freizer) Alexander. BA, City Coll. N.Y., 1977; M of Infor. Libr. Sci., Pratt Inst., 1998. Coord. NYNEX Market Info. Ctr., White Plains, NY, 1985—87; dir. Info. Ctr./Archives, exhbns. curator HarperCollins Pubs., N.Y.C., 1988—99; singer N.Y.C., 1987—; dir. content devel. BuyerWeb, Inc., N.Y.C., 1999—2000; founder Info Diva, N.Y.C., 2001—02, Mixed Beadia Jewelry, 2004—; mgr. indexing for digital archive Scholastic, Inc., N.Y.C., 2002—. Contbr. articles to profl. jours. Pres. Assn. HarperCollins Employees, N.Y.C., 1990-94; dir. Tenants Assn., N.Y.C., 1994. Recipient Schubertiade Lieder Competition award 3d St. Y, N.Y.C., 1990. Mem.: Am. Soc. Info. Sci. and Tech., Assn. Ind. Info. Profls., Profl. Women Singers Assn. (treas. 1992—96, mem.-at-large 1997—, webmaster 2001—), Spl. Librs. Assn., Beta Phi Mu. Avocations: bicycling, theater, jewelry designing. Office: Scholastic Inc 568 Broadway Rm 1045 New York NY 10012 Office Phone: 212-343-7716. E-mail: dslawsky@scholastic.com.

**SLAWTER, JOHN DAVID, JR.,** oil industry executive; b. Winston-Salem, May 11, 1917; s. John David and Carrie Wess (Linville) S.; children: Suzanne Marie, Sheila Margaret; m. Joan Margaret Pirek, July 7, 1946. Student, U. N.C., 1935—37, U.N.C., 1938—40. V.p. B&B Gas and Petroleum, Corpus Christi, Tex., 1950-59; exec. v.p. Cal-O-Tex Oil, Columbus, Ohio, 1959-65; pres. Atlantic Internat. Oil, Charleston, W.Va., 1966-73; CEO Interstate Hotels, Inc., 1975, Pacific Internat. Prodn. Holding Co. for Activated Carbon Corp. Am., Dallas, 1989, Mid-Continent Oil, 1974—, OFG Corp., 1995—, EMTEC, 1997—, HTS, 1999—. Chmn. advisory bd. Cal-O-Tex, 1966—, Atlantic Internat. Oil, 1974—, Pacific Internat., 1974—, Black Diamond Coal Co., 1978—, Southwest Interstate Support Sys., 1985—, Activated Carbon Corp., 1989—; vice chair AIOC Trust, Slawter Trust (lifetime). Author: (patents and copyrights) purification and desalination sys., 1991, pumping unit tech., 1995, oil field gen., 1996, oil field mobile remote control unit, 1998, heat transfer sys., 1999. Mem. Rep. Nat. Nom. Com., Washington, 1994-2000. Maj. Engrs. 1941-45, WWII, PTO. Decorated Purple Heart, Silver Star, Bronze Star with oak leaf cluster, Presdl. Citation, 4 Battle Stars. Mem. internat. petroleum clubs, Geneva Exec. Club (v.p. 1970-78), Chi Phi. Avocations: aviation, golf. Office: Pacific Internat Prodn/Subs Ste 8108 4350 Trinity Mills Rd Dallas TX 75287-7037 also: PO Box 795273 Dallas TX 75379-5273 Office Phone: 972-380-5560. Personal E-mail: joslawter2@earthlink.net.

**SLAYDEN, JAMES BRAGDON,** retired retail executive; b. Seattle, Sept. 28, 1924; s. Philip Lee and Ruth Alwin (Bragdon) S.; m. Barbara Marie McBride, May 7, 1955; children: Tracy Anne, James Bragdon. BA, U. Wash., 1948; MBA, U. So. Calif., 1949. Buyer Frederick & Nelson, Seattle, 1949-59, div. mdse. mgr., 1959-65; gen. mgr. Bullocks Westwood, Los Angeles, 1965-69; exec. v.p., gen. mdse. mgr. May D&F Co. dept. store, Denver, 1969—72; exec. v.p. Robinson dept. store, L.A., 1972—73; pres. J.W. Robinson dept. store, 1974—78; exec. v.p. ops. Marshall Field & Co., Chgo., 1978—80; gen. mgr. Bullocks Del Amo, 1980—85; lectr. mktg. U. So. Calif., 1985—93. Active United Crusade United Way, L.A., 1973-78, Chgo. Heart Assn., 1978-79; chmn. Pvt. Industry Coun., 1982-95; cons. Internat. Exec. Svc. Corps., 1987—; mem. traffic com. Rancho Palos Verdes, 1994-97, planning commn., 1997-2000, view restoration com., 2000—04. With U.S. Army, 1943-45. Mem. Phi Kappa Psi. Republican. Christian Scientist. Home: 37 Mela Ln Palos Verdes Peninsula CA 90275-5086

**SLAYMAN, CAROLYN WALCH,** geneticist, educator; b. Portland, Maine, Mar. 11, 1937; d. John Weston and Ruth Dyer (Sanborn) Walch; m. Clifford L. Slayman; children: Andrew, Rachel BA with highest honors, Swarthmore Coll., 1958; PhD, Rockefeller U., 1963; DSc (hon.), Bowdoin Coll., 1985. Instr., then asst. prof. Case Western Res. U., Cleve., 1967; from asst. prof. to prof. genetics Yale U. Sch. Medicine, New Haven, 1967—, Sterling prof. genetics, 1991—, chmn. dept. genetics, 1984-95, dep. dean acad. and sci. affairs, 1995—. Chmn. genetic basis of disease rev. comm. NIH, 1981—85, nat. adv. gen. med. scis. coun., 1989—93; bd. dirs. J. Weston Walch Pub., Portland, Maine, Applera Corp.; mem. sci. rev. bd. Howard Hughes Med. Inst., 1992—97. Mem. editl. bd. Jour. Biol. Chemistry, 1989-94; contbr. articles to sci. jours. Trustee Foote Sch., New Haven, 1983—89, Hopkins Sch., New Haven, 1988—93; bd. overseers Dartmouth Med. Sch., 1997—, Woods Hole Oceanographic Instn., 1997—, Bowdoin Coll., Brunswick, Maine, 1976—88, trustee, 1988—2001. Recipient Deborah Morton award Westbrook Coll., 1986. Mem. Am. Soc. Biol. Chemists, Genetics Soc. Am., Soc. Gen. Physiologists, Am. Soc. Microbiology, Inst. Medicine, Phi Beta Kappa

**SLAYTON, GUS,** foundation administrator; b. Pocahontas, Ark., Jan. 20, 1937; s. Alvin M. and Eula Inis (Milam) S.; m. Ruth Virginia Furr, May 27, 1961 (dec. Nov. 1989). BA, U. Md., College Park, 1973. Enlisted U.S. Army,

1957, commd. 2nd lt., 1963, advanced through grades to lt. col., 1978; various operational and research and devel. assignments, including The Pentagon, 1974-78; ret., 1980; exec. dir. Assn. of Old Crows, Alexandria, Va., 1980-92, AOC Ednl. Found., 1992—. Decorated Legion of Merit (2), Bronze Star (2) Republican. Avocation: real estate investment. Home: 152 Mill Cove Ln Ponte Vedra Beach FL 32082-4135 E-mail: slaytonag@earthlink.net.

**SLAZBERG, BARRY,** corporate financial executive; Degree in acctg., Bklyn. Coll.; JD, Bklyn. Law Sch.; LLM in taxation, NYU Sch. Law. Mng. ptnr. Deloitte & Touche USA LLP, 2003—; bd. dirs. Deloitte & Touche, mem. and chair exec. com. Recipient CEO Diversity Leadership award, Bus. Women's Network, 2004. Mem.: NYSSCPA, AICPA, NY County Lawyers Assn. Office: Deloitte & Touche 1633 Broadway New York NY 10019-6754 Office Phone: 212-489-1600. Office Fax: 212-489-1687.

**SLECHTA, JIRI,** theoretical physicist; b. Havlickuv Brod, Bohemia, Czechoslovakia, Apr. 26, 1939; came to Eng., 1969; s. Josef and Marie (Posikova) S.; m. Miriam Vydrarova, July 17, 1971; children: Vera, Martin. DrRerNat, Charles U., Prague, Czechoslovakia, 1962. Sr. lectr. dept. theoretical physics Charles U., Prague, 1964-69; rsch. fellow dept. physics U. Warwick, Coventry, Eng., 1969-71; sr. rsch. assoc. Sch. Math. and Physics U. East Anglia, Norwich, Eng., 1971-74; rsch. fellow dept. physics U. Leeds, England, 1976-77. Chair 3 Symposiums 13th Internat. Congress on Cybernetics, Namur, Belgium, 1992; co-chmn. symposium 17th World Congress SVU, Prague, 1994, chair symposium 14th Internat. Congress on Cybernetics, Namur, 1995, Knowledge Transfer 96, London; rschr. and presenter in field. Author 67 papers and 42 contbns. at nonpub. confs.; editor Informatica; patentee in field 2d lt. Czechoslovakia mil., 1962-64. Benevolent Fund Inst. of Physics ann. grantee, London, 1979—; recipient Gold Coins Am. Biog. Inst., 1994, 95, 96. Assoc. fellow Inst. Math. and Applications; mem. Am. Phys. Soc., Internat. Acad. Scis. San Marino, Inst. Physics, European Phys. Soc., Brit. Cybernetic Soc., Internat. Assn. Cybernetics, Internat. Cybernetics Acad., N.Y. Acad. Scis., Czechoslovak Math. Union, Czech Soc. Arts and Sci. Mem. Conservative party. Achievements include theory of disordered materials and self-organizing systems (brain, economy, society) and cybernetics; mathematical theory of Darwinism. Home and Office: 5 Beckhill Chase Leeds LS7 2RQ England Office Phone: 44 113 216 5654. E-mail: jirislechta@hotmail.com, jiri_slechta@amserve.net, jiri_slechta@yahoo.co.uk.

**SLEDD, ROBERT C.,** food products executive; Dir. Taylor & Sledd Industries, 1974—87, pres. & CEO, 1984—87; dir. Performance Food Group, 1987—, pres., 1987-95, CEO, 1987—2001, 2004—06, chmn., 1995—. Bd. dir. SCP Pool Corp., Internat. Foodservice Distributor Assn. Vice chmn. Homeward, 2000—; bd. dir. Better Housing Coalition, 2000—, Va. Found. for Performing Arts; trustee Va. Found. of Independent Colleges; chmn. bus. adv. bd. Hilliard House. Office: Performance Food Group 12500 West Creek Pkwy Richmond VA 23238*

**SLEDGE, LELA BELL,** minister; b. Madisonville, Tenn., July 8, 1938; d. Henry and Hattie Louella (Freeman) Bowers; m. Fred Thomas Sledge, Aug. 8, 1953 (dec.); children: Benny Ray, Wanda Faye Pico, Timothy Fred, Pamela Darlene McKee. DDiv, United Christian Bible Inst., Cleveland, Tenn., 1997; D.Bible Knowledge, United Christian Bible Inst., 1985. Ordained to ministry United Christian Ch., 1969. Minister, evangelist, missionary Full Gospel Bible Ch., Cleveland, Tenn., 2000—. Author: The Girl Who Found Life in the Graveyard, 1978. Mem.: Full Gospel Bible Ministries (pres.). Avocations: reading, travel, sewing, puzzles, exercise. Office Phone: 423-472-6237.

**SLEED, JOEL,** columnist; b. NYC, Jan. 29, 1929; m. MaryLou Kalwara, Nov. 15, 1983; children: Jodie, Jill, Jeffrey, Kristin Kalwara, Karen Hepler. Former travel editor The Star-Ledger, Newark, Newhouse News Svc., Washington; columnist travel sect. Sunday Rep., Springfield, Mass.; travel editor Palm Beach Post. mag. Office: Newhouse Newspapers 711 Third Ave New York NY 10017 E-mail: joelsleed@msn.com.

**SLEEMAN, ANITA MARIE,** education educator, academic administrator, director; b. East Chgo., Ind., Aug. 1, 1960; d. Daniel T. and Mary Margaret Ranker; m. Brian J. Sleeman, July 16, 1983; children: Brian J., Matthew. MusB, St. Mary's Notre Dame, Notre Dame, Ind., 1982. Fine arts dept. chair St. Joseph's Cath. Sch., Greenville, SC. Comm. chair S.C. Thespians, Columbia. Recipient SCTA Tchr. of the Yr., 2005. Office: St Joseph s Cath Sch 100 St Joseph s Dr Greenville SC 29607 Office Phone: 864-234-9009.

**SLEEMAN, DONALD GEORGE,** construction executive, contractor; BS in Acctg., Miami U. Treas. Turner Corp., Dallas, 1992—, v.p., 1994—, controller, 1996—, exec. v.p., CFO, 2003—.

**SLEIGH, SYLVIA,** artist, educator; b. Llandudno, North Wales; came to U.S., 1961; d. John Harold and Katherine Amy (Miller) S.; m. Lawrence Alloway, June 28, 1954. Student, Sch. Art, Brighton, Sussex, Eng., 1932-36; diploma, U. London Extra-Mural Dept., 1947. Vis. asst. prof. SUNY-Stony Brook, 1978; instr. New Sch. Social Research, N.Y.C., 1974-77, 78-80; Edith Kreeger Wolf disting. prof. Northwestern U., Evanston, Ill., 1977; vis. artist Baldwin Seminar Oberlin Coll., Ohio, 1982, New Sch. Social Rsch., N.Y.C. One person show include Bennington (Vt.) Coll., 1963, Soho 20 Art Gallery, N.Y.C., 1974, 76, 80, 82, A.I.R. Gallery, N.Y.C., 1974, 76, 78, Ohio State U., Columbus, 1976, Matrix, Wadsworth Atheneum, Hartford, Conn., 1976, Marianne Deson Gallery, Chgo., 1990, G.W. Einstein, Inc., N.Y.C., 1980, 83, 85, U. Mo., Saint Louis, 1981, Zaks Gallery, Chgo., 1985, 95, Milw. Art Mus., Butler Inst., Youngstown, Ohio, 1990, Stiebel Modern, N.Y.C., 1992, 94, Gallery 609, Denver, Canton (Ohio) Art Inst., Soho 20 Gallery, 1999, Deven Golden Fine Arts, N.Y., 1999, The Art of Sylvia Sleigh and Lawrence Alloway Phila. Art Alliance, Phila., 2001; exhibited in group shows Newhouse Gallery, S.I., N.Y., Stamford (Conn.) Mus., 1985, Albany (N.Y.) Inst. Art, Cin. Art Mus., New Orleans Mus. Art, Denver Art Mus., Pa. Acad. Fine Arts, 1989, Carlsten Art Gallery, Stevens Point, Wis., 1993, Stiebel Modern, N.Y.C., 1994, Soho 20, N.Y.C., 1993, 96, Katzen Brown Gallery, N.Y.C., 1989, Zaks Gallery, Chgo., 1986, Steinbaum Krauss Gallery, 1997, Deven Golden Fine Arts, Ltd., N.Y.C., 1997, Rutgers U., New Brunswick, N.J., 1984, 86, RioArriba Gallery, Abiquiu, N.Mex., 1996, Milw. Art Mus., 1996, Steinbaum Krauss Gallery, 1997, N.Y. Mus. exhbn. traveling until 2001, David and Alfred Smart Mus., Chgo., Broome St. Gallery, N.Y.C., Deven Golden Fine Arts, N.Y.C., A.I.R. Gallery, N.Y.C., Apex Art Co., N.Y.C., 1998, McKee Gallery, N.Y.C., 1998, Royal Coll. Art, London, 1998, Heckscher Mus. Art, Huntington, N.Y., 1999, Printworks Gallery, 2000, SoHo 20, N.Y.C., 2004, Snug Harbor Cultural Ctr., N.Y.C., 2005, Mason Gross at Rutgers U., N.J., 2005, Mus. Contemp. Art, L.A., 2006. Panelist Creative Artists Pub. Service Program, N.Y.C., 1976. Nat. Endowment for Arts grantee, 1982, Pollock-Krasner Found. grantee, 1985. Home: 330 W 20th St New York NY 10011-3302 Personal E-mail: ssallway@verizon.net.

**SLEIK, THOMAS SCOTT,** lawyer; b. La Crosse, Wis., Feb. 24, 1947; s. John Thomas and Marion Gladys (Johnson) S.; m. Judith Mattson, Aug. 24, 1968; children: Jennifer, Julia, Joanna. BS, Marquette U., 1969, JD, 1971. Bar: Wis. 1971, U.S. Dist. Ct. (we. dist.) Wis. 1971. Assoc. Hale Skemp Hanson Skemp & Sleik, La Crosse, 1971-74, ptnr., 1975—. Bd. mem. Wis. Lawyer Mut. Ins. Co., 1999—. State pres. Boy Scouts Am., 1981—83, bd. dirs. Gateway Area Coun., 1973—99, pres., 1980—81; trustee La Crosse Pub. Libr., 1981—, chair. bd. trustees, 2006—; bd. dirs. Children's Mus. of La Crosse, 1997—2002, Greater La Crosse Area United Way, 1985—92, campaign chmn., 1986, pres., 1987; bd. dirs. La Crosse Bd. Edn., 1973—77, v.p., 1977; festmaster Oktoberfest (LaCross Festivals Inc.), 2001, trustee, 2001—; bd. mem. Franciscan Skemp Healthcare, 2003—. Fellow Am. Acad. Matrimonial Lawyers (pres. Wis. chpt. 1999-2000); mem. ABA, State Bar Wis. (bd. govs. 1997-99, chmn. 1992-93). Roman Catholic. Home: 4082 Glenhaven Dr La Crosse WI 54601-7503 Office: Hale Skemp Hanson Skemp & Sleik 505 King St Ste 300 La Crosse WI 54602-1927 Business E-Mail: tss@haleskemp.com.

**SLEMMONS, ROBERT SHELDON,** architect; b. Mitchell. Nebr., Mar. 12, 1922; s. Matthew Garvin and K. Fern (Borland) S.; m. Dorothy Virginia Herrick, Dec. 16, 1945; children: David (dec.), Claire, Jennifer, Robert, Timothy. AB, U. Nebr., 1947, BArch, 1948. Draftsman Davis & Wilson, Archs., Lincoln, Nebr., 1947-48; chief designer, project arch. Office of Kans. State Arch., Topeka, 1948-54; assoc. John A. Brown, Arch., Topeka, 1954-56; ptnr. Brown & Slemmons, Arch., Topeka, 1956-69; v.p. Brown-Slemmons-Krueger, Archs., Topeka, 1969-73; owner Robert S. Slemmons, A.I.A. & Assocs., Archs., Topeka, 1973—. Cons. Kans. State Office Bldg. Commn. 1956-57; lectr. in design U. Kans., 1961; bd. dirs. Kaw Valley State Bank & Trust Co., Topeka, 1978-92. Prin. archtl. works include Kans. State Office Bldg., 1954, Topeka Presbyn. Manor, 1960-74, Meadowlark Hills Ret. Cmty., 1979, Shawnee County Adult Detention Facility, 1985. Bd. dirs. Topeka Civic Symphony Soc., 1950-60, Midstates Ret. Cmtys., Inc., 1986-92, Topeka Festival Singers; cons. Solutions for Aging, Inc., Topeka, 1984-97; mem. Topeka Bd. Bldg. and Fire Appeals, Kans., 1977-97, Com. for Employer Support of the Guard and Res. With USNR, 1942-48. Mem. AIA (Topeka pres. 1955-56, Kans. dir. 1957-58, com. on housing, com. for hist. resources), Internat. Conf. Bldg. Ofcls., Topeka Art Guild (pres. 1950), Am. Corrections Assn., Kans. Coun. Chs. (dir. 1961-62), Shawnee County Hist. Soc., Greater Topeka C. of C. (sr. coun., pres.), Downtown Topeka Inc. (v.p. 1992-99), Topeka, Shawnee County Libr. (vice friends of the libr.), St. Andrews Soc. (pres.), SAR (pres. state soc., pres. chpt.), Soc. of Antiquaries of Scotland (fellow), U. Nebr. Alumni Assn. (life), Band Alumni Assn., Kiwanis (pres. 1966-67), Topeka Knife and Fork Club. Presbyterian (elder, deacon, chmn. trustees). Office: Slemmons Assocs Archs 534 S Kansas Ave Ste 140 Topeka KS 66603 3473 Personal E mail: rdslem@hotmail.com.

**SLEMMONS, ROD,** museum director, art educator, curator; BA, U. Iowa, MA in English; MFA, Rochester Inst. Tech., 1976—78. Curator prints and photog. Seattle Art Mus., 1982—96; dir. Mus. of Contemporary Photog., Columbia Coll., Chgo., 2002—. Tchr. hist. photog. and grad. mus. studies U. Wash., Seattle. Curator Eye of the Mind/Mind of the Eye, 1988, Water: The Renewable Metaphor, 1997, Beyond Novelty: New Digital Art, 2000. Office: Mus Contemporary Photog Columbia Coll Chgo 600 S Michigan Ave Chicago IL 60605

**SLEMON, GORDON RICHARD,** electrical engineering educator; b. Bowmanville, Ont., Can., Aug. 15, 1924; s. Milton Everitt and Selena (Johns) S.; m. Margaret Jean Matheson, July 9, 1949; children: Sally, Stephen, Mark, Jane. BASc., U. Toronto, 1946, MASc., 1948; D.I.C., Imperial Coll. Sci., London U., Eng., 1951, PhD, 1952; D of Engring. (hon.), Meml. U. Nfld., 1994. Asst. prof. elec. engring. N.S. Tech. Coll., Can., 1953-55; assoc. prof. U. Toronto, Ont., Can., 1955-63, prof. Ont., 1964-90, chmn. dept. elec. engring. Ont., 1966-76, dean of faculty of applied sci. and engring. Ont., 1979-86, prof. emeritus Ont., 1990—. Colombo plan adviser, India, 1963-64; pres. Elec. Engring. Consociates, 1976-79; bd. dirs. Inverpower Controls Ltd., Innovations Found. Author: (with J.M. Ham) Scientific Basis of Electrical Engineering, Magnetoelectric Devices, (with A. Straughen) Electric Machinery; (with S.B. Dewan, A. Straughen) Power Semiconductor Drives, Electric Machines and Drives; contbr. articles to profl. jours. Chmn. Innovations Found., 1980-93, vice chmn., 1993—97; chmn. Microelectronics Devel. Ctr., 1983-88. Decorated officer Order of Can.; recipient excellence in tchg. award Western Electric, 1965, Can. Centennial medal, 1967, Ross medal, 1978, 83, Gold medal Jugoslav Union of Nikola Tesla Socs., Engring. Alumni medal, Educator of Yr. award Can. Engrs., 1992, Hall of Distinction award U. Toronto, 1992, Achievement award IEEE Magnetics Soc., 1997, Arbor award U. Toronto, 1997. Fellow Can. Acad. Engring. (pres. 1998-99), Engring. Inst. Can., Instn. Elec. Engrs. (hon. fellow 1995), IEEE (Centennial medal 1984, Nikola Tesla award, Millennium medal 2000, Prof. Engrs. Engring. Excellence award 2005); mem. Am. Soc. Engring. Edn., others. Achievements include patents in field. Home: 40 Chatfield Dr Don Mills ON Canada M3B 1K5 Office: U Toronto Fac Applied Sci and Engring Toronto ON M5S 3G4 Canada E-mail: g.slemon@utoronto.ca.

**SLETTEHAUGH, THOMAS CHESTER,** retired art educator; b. Mpls., May 8, 1925; s. Melvin Joseph and Gertrude Mary (Henry) Slettehaugh; m. Mary Madonna Rude, June 18, 1946; children: Mary Lee, John Thomas, MaryPaul Karen, Joan Diane, Peter Ford. Diploma naval air fighter pilot and aero. engring., Williams Coll., U. SC and U. Ga., 1943—45; BS, U. Minn., 1949, MEd, 1950; student, Syracuse U., 1954; EdD, Pa. State U., 1956; student, Kossuth U., 1990. Grad. tchg. asst. U. Minn., 1949—50; art educator Mpls. Pub. Schs., 1950, Albert Lea H.S., Minn., 1950—52; prof., head art dept. State Tchrs. Coll., Springfield, SD, 1952—54; art instr., ednl. TV artist Pa. State U., University Park, 1954—56; prof. art State Coll. at Slippery Rock, Pa., 1956—62; vis. prof. art edn. Ctr. for Syracuse U., Chautauqua, NY, 1957—58; prof. art, head art and art edn. Frostburg State Coll., Md., 1962—68; prof. art, head fine arts, dir. gallery and mus. Miss. U. for Women, 1968—70; assoc. prof. art edn., mem. grad. sch. Coll. Edn. and Human Devel. U. Minn., Mpls., 1970—87, prof. emeritus, 1987—. Vis. prof. art Cambridge U., 1976—77, Leicester Poly., 1976—77, Heidelburg U., Germany, 1976—77, Fine Arts Ctr., Almeria, Spain, 1976—77, Cultural Ctr., Zagreb, Croatia, 1976—77, Pedagogy Inst., Budapest, Hungary, 1976—77, Fine Art Sch., Vienna, 1976—77, Friendship Ctr., Moscow, 1976—77; vis. scholar Ednl. Bur., Xian, China, 1981, Cath. U., Montevideo, Uruguay, 1984, Centro Artistico Artesanal, Buenos Aires, 1984, Kenyatta U., Nairobi, 1986—88, Casa Strobele, Borgo/Valsugana, Italy, 1991, Museu de Arte Contemporanea da Univ., São Paulo, 1991, Internat. Creativita Arte Sella, 1992, Humboldt U., Germany, 1993, U. Lisbon, 2004. Numerous articles to profl. jours., exhibitions include Minn. State Fine Arts Exhbn., Mpls. Inst. Fine Arts, Washington County Mus. Fine Art, Md., Mpls. Pub. Libr., numerous others, Walker Art Ctr. Mpls, The Woman IKKONN photo montage Lisbon 2004, prin works include outdoor sculptures Shrine St. Anthony, Forrestville, Pa., 1958, Symbol of Excellence at MSCW campus, Columbus, Miss., 1969, prin. works include Apollo 14 Moon Art, 1971; author: Mexico Visto Por Sus Ninos, 1981, Art in Education: An International Perspective, 1984. Aviation cadet USN, 1943—45. Recipient 50 Yr. Artistic Participation award, 2003, Minn. Fine Arts Pinnacle of Achievement award, Cambridge, Eng., 2006, 100 Disting Alumni Centennial award, U. Minn. Coll. Edn. and Human Devel., 2006, Archimedes Medal of Honour, 2006;, Pa. State U. scholar, 1954—56. Mem.: Scottish Soc. Art and Psychopathology, Internat. Union Archs., Internat. Coun. on Edn. for Tchg., Internat. Assn. Empirical Aesthetics, Internat. Soc. Aesthetics, Internat. Congress Art Historians, Internat. Soc. Edn. through Art (U.S. rep. on world coun.), U.S. Soc. for Edn. through Art, Nat. Art Edn. Assn., Ptnrs. of Ams., Minn./Uruguay, U. Minn. Woman's Club (quasi-mem. art sect. 2004). Home: 49 Williams Ave SE Minneapolis MN 55414-3449 Office: Slettehaugh-Studio Gallery 49 WIlliams Ave SE Minneapolis MN 55414-3449 E-mail: slett001@tc.umn.edu.

**SLEZAK, ERIN KATHLEEN,** elementary school educator; b. Allentown, Pa., Feb. 02; d. Maureen and Robert Slezak. BA, Ohio State U., 2003. Texas Educator Certificate State Bd. of Educator Cert. Tchr., dept. chair YES Coll. Prep., Houston, Tex., 2005—; alumna Teach for Am., McAllen, Tex., 2003—05. Mem.: Nat. Coun. for the Social Studies. D-Liberal. Office Phone: 713-208-7588. E-mail: eslezak@yesprep.org.

**SLEZKINE, YURI,** history professor; b. Moscow, Feb. 7, 1956; came to U.S., 1983; s. Lev Y. and Karma M. (Goldstein) S.; m. Lisa C. Little, Nov. 21, 1984; 1 child, Peter A. BA, MA, Moscow State U., 1978; PhD, U. Tex., 1989. Transl., Port Beira, Mozambique, 1978-79; editor Progress Pub., Moscow, 1980-82; instr. Linguacoop Lang. Inst., Lisbon, Portugal, 1982-83; instr. Slavic Studies U. Tex., 1983-86; asst. prof. history Wake Forest U., Winston-Salem, NC; prof. of history, dir. Ctr. for Slavic, East European & Eurasian studies Univ. Calif., Berkeley. Author: The Jewish Century, 2004, Arctic Mirrors: Russia and the Small Peoples of the North, 1994; co-author: Speak Russian, 1990; asst. editor Slavic Rev., 1985-87; co-editor: In the Shadow of Revolution: Life Stories of Russian Women from 1917 to the Second World War, 2000, Between Heaven and Hell: The Myth of Siberia in Russian Culture, 1993. Pew grantee Wake Forest U., 1990; Postdoctoral fellow Social Sci. Rsch. Coun., 1990—; Fgn. Lang. and Area Studies fellow U. Tex., 1988-89, Univ. fellow U. Tex., 1987-88. Mem. Am. Hist. Assn., Am. Assn. Advancement Slavic Studies. Office: UC Berkeley History Dept 2220 Dwindle Hall Berkeley CA 94720

**SLICHTER, CHARLES PENCE,** physicist, researcher; b. Ithaca, NY, Jan. 21, 1924; s. Sumner Huber and Ada (Pence) S.; m. Gertrude Thayer Almy, Aug. 23, 1952 (div. Sept. 1977); children: Sumner Pence, William Almy, Jacob Huber, Ann Thayer; m. Anne FitzGerald, June 7, 1980; children: Daniel Huber, David Pence AB, Harvard U., 1946, MA, 1947, PhD, 1949; DSc (hon.), U. Waterloo, 1993; LLD (hon.), Harvard U., 1996. Rsch. asst. Underwater Explosives Rsch. Lab., Woods Hole, Mass., 1943-46; faculty U. Ill., Urbana, 1949—, prof. physics, 1955-97, prof. Ctr. for Advanced Study, 1968-97, prof. chemistry, 1986-97, rsch. prof. physics, 1997—, prof. emeritus, 1997—. Morris Loeb lectr. Harvard U., 1961; mem. Pres.'s Sci. Adv. Com., 1964-69, Com. on Nat. Medal Sci., 1969-74, Nat. Sci. Bd., 1975-84, Pres.'s Com. Sci. and Tech., 1976 Author: Principles of Magnetic Resonance, 1963, 3d edit., 1989; Contbr. articles to profl. jours. Former trustee, mem. corp Woods Hole Oceanog. Instn.; mem. Harvard Corp., 1970-95. Recipient Langmuir award Am. Phys. Soc., 1969, Buckley prize, 1996; Alfred P. Sloan fellow, 1955-61. Fellow AAAS, Am. Phys. Soc., Internat. Electron Paramagnetic Resonance Soc.; mem. NAS (Comstock prize 1993), Am. Acad. Arts and Scis., Am. Philos. Soc., Internat. Soc. Magnetic Resonance (pres. 1987-90, Trienniel prize 1986). Home: 61 Chestnut Ct Champaign IL 61822-7121

**SLICKER, FREDERICK KENT,** lawyer; b. Tulsa, Aug. 21, 1943; s. James Floyd and Lucille Geneva (Nordling) S.; children: Laura, Kipp. BA, U. Kans., 1965, JD with highest distinction, 1968; LLM, Harvard U., Cambridge, Mass., 1973. Bar: Kans. 1968, U.S. Ct. Mil. Appeals 1968, U.S. Supreme Ct. 1972, Tex. 1973, Okla. 1980. Prin. founder Slicker Law Firm, P.C., 2000—. Author: A Practical Guide to Church Bond Financing, 1985, Angels All Around, 1999, Seeking God's Heart, 2004. Capt. U.S. Army, 1965—72. Mem. ABA, Okla. Bar Assn., Order of Coif. Democrat. Methodist. Avocation: Christian men's ministries. Office: 4444 E 66th Str #201 Tulsa OK 74136-4206 Office Phone: 918-496-9020. Business E-Mail: fslicker@swbell.net.

**SLIFKIN, DANIEL,** lawyer; b. London, Eng., June 14, 1965; BA first class honors, Oxford Univ., Eng., 1987, BCL first class honors, 1988; JD magna cum laude, Harvard Univ., 1991. Bar: NY 1991. Assoc. Cravath Swaine & Moore LLP, NYC, 1991—98, ptnr., litig., 1998—. Articles editor Harvard Law Rev. Mem.: ABA, NY State Bar Assn. Office: Cravath Swaine & Moore LLP Worldwide Plz 825 Eighth Ave New York NY 10019-7475 Office Phone: 212-474-1438. Office Fax: 212-474-3700. Business E-Mail: dslifkin@cravath.com.

**SLIGER, BERNARD FRANCIS,** academic administrator, economist, educator; b. Chassell, Mich., Sept. 30, 1924; s. Paul and Hazel (MacLauchlin) S.; m. Greta Taube, Sept. 1, 1945; children: Nan, Paul, Greta Lee, Sten. BA in Econs. with high hons., Mich. State U., 1949, MA, 1950, PhD, 1955; postgrad., U. Minn., 1961-62. Mem. faculty La. State U., 1953-61, prof. econs., 1961, head dept., 1961-65, vice chancellor, dean academic affairs, 1965-68; sec. adminstrn. State of La., 1968—69; sec.-treas. La. Office Bldg. Corp., 1969-72; organizer, exec. dir. La. Coordinating Council Higher Edn., 1969-72; prof. econs. Fla. State U., Tallahassee, 1973—2003, prof. econ. emeritus, 2003—, exec. v.p. Tallahassee, 1972-76, chief acad. officer, 1973-76, pres., 1977-91, interim pres., 1993, dir. univ.'s London Study Ctr., 1975, pres. emeritus, 1992—2003; ret., 2003. Mem. staff sci. and tech. com. Fla. Ho. of Reps., 1979; mem. V.P. Mondale's Select Com. on Sci. and Tech., 1980; mem. bd. dirs. Fed. Res Bank of Atlanta, 1983-88; cons. econ. theory and pub. fin. to pvt. and pub. commns., orgns.; mem., chief cons. Gov. La.'s tax study com., 1968; formerly La. commr. adminstrn. and chief budget officer; mem. NCAA pres.'s comm., 1987-91. Author: (text) Public Finance, 1964, rev. edit., 1970, (with others) Municipal Finance Administration, 1976, rev.; contbr. to profl. publs. Vol. economist Tallahassee C. of C., 1977, Fla. C. of C., 1978; mem. Acad. Task Force for Review of the Ins. and Tort Systems, 1986-88; trustee The Nature Conservancy, 1986—; trustee Am. Coll. Testing Corp., 1981-87, chmn. 1985-87; ex-officio mem. Fla. Coun. 100. With C.E., U.S. Army, 1943-46. Named Dir. Practical Politics La. Ho. of Reps., 1969; Bernard F. Sliger Eminent scholar Chair in Econ. Edn. created in his name by Fla. State U., 1987, Bernard F. Sliger Bldg. dedicated at univ.-related rsch. park, Bernard F. Sliger Tower in Univ. Ctr. Bldg. dedicated, 1999. Mem. Kiwanis, Phi Beta Kappa, Omicron Delta Kappa, Phi Kappa Phi, Omicron Delta Epsilon, Alpha Kappa Psi, Beta Gamma Sigma, Phi Eta Sigma. Presbyterian. Home: 3341 E Lakeshore Dr Tallahassee FL 32312-1440 Office: Gus A Stavros Ctr Adv Free Enterprise & Economic Edu 250 S Woodward Ave Tallahassee FL 32306-4220 Office Fax: 850-644-9866. E-mail: sliger@mailer.fsu.edu/sliger@garnet.acns.fsu.edu.

**SLIM, MICHEL S.,** surgeon, educator, health facility administrator; b. Nov. 18, 1929; s. Saliba and Julia Slim; m. Norma Gebara, Sept. 4, 1958; children: Julie, Lina, Nayla. MD, Am. U., Beirut, Lebanon, 1954. Diplomate Am. Bd. Surgery, Am. Bd. Pediatric Surgery, Am. Bd. Thoracic Surgery. Prof. surgery Am. U., Beirut, 1963-86, N.Y. Med. Coll., 1986—; attending Westchester Med. Ctr., Valhalla, 1986—, chief pediatric trauma, 1991—, chief pediatric surgery, 1994—2002. Editl. cons. Pediatric Surg. Internat., 1985-2004; reviewer Ann. Thoracic Surgery, Jordan Med. Jour. Jour. Jordan Royal Med. Svcs.; contbr. articles to profl. jours Evarts Graham Traveling fellow Am. Assn. Thoracic Surgery, 1970-71. Fellow ACS, Am. Acad. Pediat., Am. Coll. Chest Physicians five Critical Care Medicine; mem. Am. Pediatric Surgery Assn., Brit. Assn. Pediatric Surgery, Internat. Soc. Pediatric Surgery, Eastern Assn. for Surgery of Trauma. Office: NY Med Coll Munger Pavilion Valhalla NY 10595 Office Phone: 914-493-7620. E-mail: mslimpedsurg@hotmail.com.

**SLINGER, MICHAEL JEFFERY,** law librarian, director; b. Pitts., Apr. 12, 1956; s. Maurice and Mary Helen (Kengerski) S.; m. Cheryl Blaney, Apr. 19, 1980; children: Rebecca, Sarah. BA, U. Pitts., 1978; M Librianship, U. S.C., 1979; JD, Duquesne U., 1984. Reference libr. Duquesne U. Sch. Law, Pitts., 1983-84; rsch. libr. U. Notre Dame (Ind.) Sch. Law, 1984-85, head rsch. svcs., 1985-86, assoc. dir. pub. svcs., 1986-90; law libr. dir., assoc. prof. law Suffolk U. Sch. Law, Boston, 1990-93, law libr. dir., prof. law, 1994-95; law libr. dir., prof. law, assoc. dean Cleve. State U., 1995—. Contbr. articles to profl. jours., chpt. to book. Mem.: ALA, ABA, Ohio Regional Assn. Law Librs. (v.p. 1987—88, pres. 1988—89, Pres. award 1989), New Eng. Law Libr. Consortium (treas. 1992—95), Am. Assn. Law Schs. (exec. bd. sect. on law librs. 1993—94), Am. Assn. Law Libs. (chair acad. law libr. spl. interest sect. 2005—). Avocations: reading, sports. Office: Cleveland-Marshall Coll Law Law Libr 1801 Euclid Ave Cleveland OH 44115-2223 Office Phone: 216-687-3547. Business E-Mail: michael.slinger@law.csuohio.edu.

**SLINGERLAND, MARY JO,** writing educator; b. Lansing, Mich., Oct. 19, 1958; d. Thomas James and Maxine Margaret Slingerland; 1 child, Nicole Charisse Ballesteros. BA in English/Journalism, Mich. State U., 1983; MA in Tchg., Wayne State U., 2005. Owner, writer, editor Vision Decisions, SCS, Mich., 1982—; proposal writer Mich. State U., 1989—90; writer, editor Daimler-Chrysler Corp., Auburn Hills, Mich., 1995—98; writer, editor for CDI Ford Motor Co., Livonia, Mich., 1999—2001; instr. English lit./composition, tech. writing/speaking Wayne County Coll., Detroit, 2002—06; coord. Tutorial Lab. Baker Coll., Detroit, 2006—. Instr. Baker Coll., 2005—. Editor: Arthroscopic Surgery, 1986; contbr. articles to profl. jours. Scholar, Wayne State U., 2004—05, Grad. Profl. scholar, 2005; Wheaton Tutor scholar, Mich. State U., 1980. Mem.: Internat. Reading Assn., Mich. Reading Assn., Nat. Coun. Tchrs. English, Mich. Coun. Tchrs. English, Mich. Assn. Computer Users Learners, Internat. Tech. Assn., Nat. Mgrs. Women Bus. Owners. Avocations: golf, tennis, sailing, fishing. Home: 17771 Feather Ln Brownstown MI 48192 Office Phone: 586-764-8630. Personal E-mail: mslinger2@netzero.net.

**SLIPMAN, RONALD (SAMUEL SLIPMAN),** hospital administrator; b. New Orleans, Aug. 24, 1939; s. Jake and Esther (Steinman) S.; m. Carole Marie Green, July 1, 1961 (div. Feb. 1982); children: Susan Rachel, Lawrence Jay; m. Marilyn Morais, Feb. 5, 1983 (dec. June 1985); m. Lelia Ruth Foster, Jan. 12, 1986; children: Ronald Andrew, Brian Edward. BS, Tulane U., 1961; cert. in supervision techniques, La. State U., 1984; postgrad., NE La. U., 1978-79, 80-81. Design progress estimator Boeing Co., New Orleans, 1964-66; interviewer Tex. Employment Commn., Tyler and Lufkin, 1977-78; pers. technician State of La., Baton Rouge, 1961-62, 63-64, 73-75, 81; rsch. statistician La. Ins. Commn., Baton Rouge, 1968-69; labor market analyst La. Dept. Labor, Baton Rouge, 1969-70, 77; pers. dir. Royal Orleans Hotel, New Orleans, 1966-67; mgmt. analyst for quality assurance Earl K. Long Hosp., Baton Rouge, 1981-84, dir. ancillary svcs., 1984-86; mgmt. analyst, spl. asst. to dir. for total quality mgmt. Dept. Vets. Affairs Med. Ctr., Alexandria, La., 1987-88, 89-90; mgmt. cons., 1990-91. Cubmaster pack 10 Boy Scouts Am., 1993-94, 96-98, asst. cubmaster, 1994-96, chmn. pack com., 1998-99, mem. pack com., 1999—2004; trustee Kent Plantation House, Inc., 2000-03; mem. Ann. Tom Peyton Meml. Arts Festival Com., 2003—; mem. adminstrv. bd. 1st United Meth. Ch., 2003-, chmn. presch. bd. Mem. La. Soc. Hosp. Pharmacists, Ctrl. La. Soc. for Human Resource Mgmt., S.W. La. Bridge Assn. (pres., bd. dirs.). Republican. Methodist. Avocations: duplicate bridge, tennis. Home and Office: 105 Foxfire Ln Alexandria LA 71302-8638 Personal E-mail: Rancher2000@aol.com.

**SLIPSAGER, HENRIK C.,** building services company executive; CFO ISS Internat. Svc. Sys., Inc., 1984-85, exec. v.p., COO, 1985-88, pres., CEO, 1988-94; exec. v.p. janitorial svcs. Am. Bldg. Maintenance Industries Inc., San Francisco, 1994 99, sr. v.p., 1997 99, pres. Am. Bldg. Maintenance Co., 1999-2000, CEO, pres., 2000—. Office: ABM Industries 160 Pacific Ave San Francisco CA 94111

**SLITKIN, BARBARA ANN,** artist; b. Newark, Oct. 15, 1948; d. Lewis Leonard and Charlotte Deborah Rothgessor Small; m. Kenneth Bernard Slitkin, Sept. 23, 1967 (div. July 12, 1991); 1 child, Tiffany Simone. Faculty Art Sch. Ednl. Alliance, NYC, 1999—; presenter in field. Actor: (plays) Dolly Pardon Me, 1999; one-woman shows include Ortho Diagnostics, Raritan, N.J., 1986, Tompkins Sq. Gallery, NYC, 1992—93, 1998, 2001, 2004, exhibited in group shows at Paterson (N.J.) Mus., 1987, Krasdale Gallery Bronx (NY) Mus., 1989, Blue Mountain Gallery, NYC, 1997—98, 2000—02, 2004—05, exhibitions include Avanian Awards Gallery, NY, 1988—90, N.Y.C., 2004, Bass Mus. Broward C.C., 1996, 1997, Represented in permanent collections Franklin Furnace Archive Mus. Modern Art, NYC, Mid Hudson Arts Ctr., Poughkeepsie, N.Y., New Eng. Ctr. Contemporary Art, Conn., Das Deutsche Gartenzwerg Mus., Germany, Sharajah Mus., United Arab Emigrates, Willem Coll., Tilberg, Internat. Mus. Collage and Assemblage Construction, Mex. Scholar, Internat. Fine Arts, 1966—67. Mem.: The Nat. Mural Soc. Office: 175 East 96 St 12-0 New York NY 10128 Personal E-mail: barbaraslitkin@yahoo.com. E-mail: slitkin@msn.com.

**SLIVE, SEYMOUR,** museum director, art educator; b. Chgo., Sept. 15, 1920; s. Daniel and Sonia (Rapoport) S.; m. Zoya Gregorevna Sandomirsky, June 29, 1946; children: Katherine, Alexander, Sarah. AB, U. Chgo., 1943, PhD, 1952; MA (hon.), Harvard U., 1958, Oxford U., Eng., 1972. Instr. fine arts Oberlin (Ohio) Coll., 1950-51; chmn. art dept. Pomona (Calif.) Coll., 1952-54; mem. faculty Harvard U., Cambridge, Mass., 1954—, prof. fine arts, 1961—, Gleason prof. fine arts, 1973-91, Gleason prof. fine arts emeritus, 1991—, chmn. dept. fine arts, 1968-71, dir. Fogg Art Mus., 1975-82; Elizabeth and John Moors Cabot dir. emeritus Harvard art museums, 1982. Exchange prof. Leningrad (USSR) U., 1961; Ryerson lectr. Yale U., 1962; Slade prof. Oxford (Eng.) U., 1972-73 Author: Rembrandt and His Critics, 1630-1730, 1953, The Rembrandt Bible, 1959, Catalogue of the Paintings of Frans Hals, 1962, Drawings of Rembrandt, 1965, (with Jakob Rosenberg and E.H. ter Kuile) Dutch Art and Architecture 1600-1800, 2nd edit., 1978, Rembrandt's Drawings, 1965, Frans Hals, 3 vols., 1970-74, Jacob van Ruisdael, 1981, Frans Hals, 1989, Dutch Painting: 1600-1800, 1995, 2d edit., 1998, Jacob van Ruisdael: A Complete Catalogue of His Paintings, Drawings and Etchings, 2001, Jacob Van Ruisdael: Master of Landscape, 2005. Trustee Solomon R. Guggenheim Found., 1978—, Norton Simon Mus., 1989-91; bd. dirs. Burlington mag. Found., 1987—. Lt. (j.g.) USNR, 1943-46, PTO. Decorated officer Order Orange Nassau Netherlands, 1962; Fulbright fellow Netherlands, 1951-52; Guggenheim fellow, 1956-57, 78-79; Fulbright research scholar Utrecht (Netherlands) U., 1959-60 Fellow Am. Acad. Arts and Scis.; mem. Karel van Mander Soc. (hon.), Coll. Art Assn. (dir. 1958-62, 65-69), Renaissance Soc., Dutch Soc. Scis. (fgn. mem.), Brit. Acad. (corr. fellow). Office: Harvard U Sackler Art Museum Cambridge MA 02138 Office Phone: 617-495-9151.

**SLIWA, CURTIS,** radio personality, volunteer; b. Bklyn., Mar. 26, 1954; s. Chester and Francesca Sliwa; m. Lisa Evers, Dec. 24, 1981 (div. 1993); m. Mary Sliwa; 1 child, Anthony Chester. Founder, head Guardian Angels, 1979—; talk show host WNYW, 1993—96, Monday Night Flights, 1996, WABC, 1990—92, talk show host, Curtis and Kuby in the Morning, 2002—, MSNBC, 2002—03. Spkr. in field. Actor: (films) The Siege, 1998; contbr. articles to numerous profl. jours. Named Top Talk Show Host Yr., Radio and Records Mag., 2004. Mem.: Guardian Angels. Achievements include host of number one rated morning talk-show in NYC. Office: The Guardian Angels Ste 401 717 Fifth Ave New York NY 10022 Office Fax: 212-545-7666.*

**SLJIVIC-SIMSIC, BILJANA B.,** Slavic and Baltic languages educator; b. Belgrade, Yugoslavia, Jan. 20, 1933; arrived in US, 1962; d. Branko M. and Radojka (Pesic) S.; m. Branislav S. Simsic, Jan. 21, 1953 (div. 1963); 1 child, Violet Ljubica. Diploma, U. Belgrade, 1955; MA, Harvard U., 1963, PhD, 1966. Asst. U. Belgrade, 1957 62; lectr. U. Clermont Ferrand, France, 1959-61; vis. lectr. UCLA, 1964-65, vis. asst. prof., 1965-66; asst. prof. U. Ky., Lexington, 1966-67, U. Pa., Phila., 1967-73; vis. lectr. Princeton (N.J.) U., 1967-69; assoc. prof. U. Ill., Chgo., 1973-86, head of dept., 1981—96, prof. dept. Slavic and Baltic langs. and lit., 1986—. Exch. prof. U. London and Cambridge (Eng.) U., 1989—90, U. Amsterdam, 2002; cons., panelist U.S. Dept. Edn., Fulbright Fellowship, Washington; sr. writer Ohio State U., summers, 1983, 84, 85, 86, 88. Co-author: Serbo-Croatian-English Dictionary, 1972 (grant), Judeo-Spanish Ballads from Bosnia, 1972 (grant); author: Serbo-Croatian, Just For You, 1985 (grant 1983-84); major author 8 vols. of Serbo-Croatian Textbooks for Individualized Studies, 1983-88. Grantee, U. Pa., Phila., 1972; scholar, Radcliffe Coll., 1962—63, Harvard U., 1963—64. Mem.: Am. Assn. for Advancement of Slavic Studies, N.Am. Soc. Serbian Studies (sec.-treas. 1976—82, pres. 1982—84, mem. exec. bd. 1984—86), Assn. Serbian Writers Belgrade, Chgo. Hort. Soc., Harvard and Radcliffe Clubs Chgo. Serbian Orthodox. Avocations: photography, travel, gardening. Office: U Ill Chgo Dept Slavic & Baltic Langs & Lit 601 S Morgan St Chicago IL 60607-1716 Office Phone: 312-996-4412. E-mail: bibi@uic.edu.

**SLOAN, ALLAN HERBERT,** journalist; b. Bklyn., Nov. 27, 1944; s. Samuel and Doris (Shanblott) Sloan; m. Nancy Nolan, June 29, 1969; children: Sharon R., Susan M., Dena A. Bklyn. Coll., 1966, MS, Columbia U., 1967. Reporter, sports writer Charlotte Observer, NC, 1968-72; reporter Detroit Free Press, 1972-79; assoc. editor, staff writer Forbes Mag., NYC, 1979-81, sr. editor, 1984-88; staff writer Money Mag., NYC, 1982-84; columnist NY Newsday, NYC, 1989-95; Wall St. editor Newsweek Mag., NYC, 1995—. Contbr., Marketplace Pub. Radio Internat.; frequent commentator, Nightly Bus. Report PBS TV. Author: Three Plus One Equals Billions: The Bendix-Martin Marietta War, 1982. Named Alumnus of Yr., Columbia Grad. Sch. Journalism, 1999; recipient Hancock award for fin. journalism, Hancock Found., 1992, Loeb award for fin. journalism, Loeb Found., UCLA Anderson Sch. Mgmt., 1974, 1984, 1991, 1993, 1998, Lifetime Achievement award, 2001, Disting. Achievement award, Am. Bus. Editors and Writers, 2001. Office: Newsweek 251 W 57th St New York NY 10019-1802

**SLOAN, ANNE ELIZABETH,** food scientist, writer; d. Thomas and Anne Sloan; m. James Murtland, June 14, 2003. BS, Rutgers U., 1973; PhD, U. Minn., 1976. Mgr. nutrition comm. Gen. Mills, Mpls., 1976—78; dir. Good

Housekeeping Inst., N.Y.C., 1978—85; editor-in-chief McCall's Mag., N.Y.C., 1985—92; pres. Sloan Trends and Solution, Stuart, Fla., 1993—2003, Sloan Trends, Escondido, Calif., 2004—. Author: Food For Thoughts, 1977, Contemporary Nutrition Controversies, 1979; contbr. articles to numerous profl. jours. and mag. Recipient Pub. Rels. award, John W. Hill Found.; George Cook scholar, Rutgers U., 1973. Office: Sloan Trends PO Box 461149 Escondido CA 92046

**SLOAN, DANIEL KAY,** electrical engineer; b. Walla Walla, Wash., Oct. 20, 1944; s. James Lester and Bertha Louise (Ulstrup) S.; m. Janice Kay Christensen, Jan. 31, 1965 (dec.); m. Patrica Ann Purdy, Feb. 8, 2003. BSEE, Wash. State U., 1967. Product line controls engr. Beloit (Wis.) Corp., 1967-72, product line mgr.-controls, 1972-79; elec. engr. U & I Inc., Kennewick, Wash., 1979-81; elec. project engr. Boise-Cascade, Wallula, Wash., 1981-86; sr. elec. project engr. Simpson Tacoma (Wash.) Kraft Co., 1986—. Staff sgt. U.S. Air Guard, 1967-73. Mem. IEEE, Instrumentation, Systems and Automation Soc., Elks. Office: Simpson Tacoma Kraft Co 801 Portland Ave Tacoma WA 98421-3098 Office Phone: 253-596-0291. E-mail: dsloan@simpson.com.

**SLOAN, DAVID B.,** lawyer; b. Martin, Ky., Sept. 20, 1950; BA, Berea Coll., 1972; JD, No. Ky. Univ., 1976. Ptnr. O'Harra, Ruberg, Taylor, Sloan & Sergent. Mem.: Am. Bar Assn., Ky. Bar Assn. (pres.-elect 2004), No. Ky. Bar Assn. (bd. dir.). Office: O'Hara Ruberg Taylor Sloan & Sergent 25 Crewstview Hills Mall Rd Ste 2001 PO Box 17411 Bromley KY 41017-0411 Business E-Mail: dsloan@ortlaw.com.

**SLOAN, DAVID EDWARD,** retired finance company executive; b. Winnipeg, Man., Can., Mar. 29, 1922; s. David and Annie Maud (Gorvin) S.; m. Kathleen Lowry Craig, Dec. 26, 1947; children: Pamela Jane, John David, Kathleen Anne. B.Commerce, U. Man., 1942. With Monarch Life Assurance Co., Winnipeg, 1946-47, Can. Pacific Ltd., 1947-88, treas., 1969-88; pres. and chief exec. officer Can. Pacific Securities Ltd., 1985-88. Mem. adv. com. Can. Pension Plan, Can. Govt., 1967-76, chmn., 1974-76. Lt. Royal Can. Army Service Corps, 1942-45. Mem. Fin. Exec. Inst. Can. (past pres. Montreal chpt.), Toronto Soc. Fin. Analysts, Soc. Internat. Treas. (internat. chmn. 1985-86, mem. coun. advisors 1978-87), Assn. Investment Mgmt. and Rsch., U. Man. Alumni Assn., The Toronto Hunt Club. Mem. United Ch. Can. Home: 316 Rosemary Rd Toronto ON Canada M5P 3E3

**SLOAN, DAVID SCOTT,** lawyer; b. Rochester, NY, Dec. 13, 1959; BS, Binghamton U. (SUNY), 1982; JD, Albany Law Sch. of Union U., 1985; LLM in Taxation, Boston U. Sch. Law, 1987. Bar: Mass. 1985, NY 1986, US Tax Ct. Ptnr. Holland & Knight LLP, Boston, mem. dir. com., bd. dir., dep. sect. leader, private wealth svcs., past chmn., Boston private wealth svcs. group, trustee, trusts, chmn., investment com., chmn, strategic planning com.; bd. mgr. Holland & Knight Consulting, LLC. Mem. faculty, grad. tax program Boston U. Sch. Law, 1989—91. Articles editor Boston U. Jour. Tax Law, 1986—87, editor-at-large, 1987—89, co-editor-in-chief, 1989—91; contbr. articles to profl. jours., newspapers, and mags. Recipient Boston U. Sch. Law Graduate Tax Alumni Academic Achievement award, 1987. Fellow: Am. Coll. of Trust and Estate Counsel; mem.: Boston Probate Forum, NY State Bar Assn., Mass. Bar Assn. (chmn., estate planning com. 1988—90, chmn., taxation sect. 1991—94, chmn. tax legislation com., mem. budget and fin. com.), Boston Bar Assn. (co-chmn., estate planning com. 2000—02), Boston Estate Planning Coun. Office: Holland & Knight LLP 10 St James Ave 11th Fl Boston MA 02116 Office Phone: 617-573-5803. Business E-Mail: dsloan@hklaw.com.

**SLOAN, DONNIE ROBERT, JR.,** lawyer; b. Nashville, July 24, 1946; s. Donnie R. Sr. and Mary Catharine (Willis) S. BS in Indsl. Engring., Ga. Inst. Tech, 1968; JD cum laude, U. Ga., 1971; LLM, Harvard U., 1975. Bar: Ga. 1971, U.S. Dist. Ct. (no. dist.) Ga. 1971, U.S. Ct. Appeals (11th cir.). Atty. Southwire Co., Carrollton, Ga., 1971-74; assoc., ptnr. Hyatt & Rhoads, P.C., Atlanta, 1975-89; pvt. practice, 1989-96; ptnr. Davidson, Fuller & Sloan, LLP, 1996—. Instr. legal rsch. U. Ga., Athens, 1970-71; instr. music law Ga. State U., Atlanta, 1976. Mem. editl. bd. Ga. Law Rev., 1969-71. Treas. Ga. Wheelchair Athletic Assn., Atlanta, 1981-84; pres., treas. Dixie Wheelchair Athletic Assn., Atlanta, 1984-87. Recipient Appreciation award Ga. Wheelchair Sports and Recreation Assn., 1979; named one of Outstanding Young Men of Am., 1981; named to Dixie Wheelchair Athletic Assn. Hall of Fame, 1990. Mem. Am. Judicature Soc., Phi Kappa Phi, Alpha Phi Mu, Ga. Tech. Club, Harvard Club. Presbyterian. Avocations: skiing, jogging, swimming. Home: 820 Saddlehill Rd Roswell GA 30075 Office: 11330 Lakefield Dr Bldg 1 Ste 250 Duluth GA 30097-1578 Office Phone: 770-662-4700. Business E-Mail: drsloan@dfslaw.com.

**SLOAN, EARLE DENDY, JR.,** chemical engineering educator; b. Seneca, S.C., Apr. 23, 1944; s. Earle Dendy and Sarah (Bellotte) S.; m. Marjorie Nilson, Sept. 7, 1968; children: Earle Dendy III, John Mark. BSChemE, Clemson U., 1965, MSChemE, 1972, PhD in Chem. Engring., 1974. Engr. Du Pont, Chattanooga, 1965-66, Seaford, Del., 1966-67; cons. Parkersburg, W.Va., 1967-68, sr. engr. Camden, S.C., 1968-70; postdoctoral fellow Rice U., 1975; prof. chem. engring. Colo. Sch. Mines, Golden, 1976—; dir. Ctr. for Rsch. on Hydrates and Other Solids, 1990—, Gaylord and Phyllis Weaver dist. prof. chem. engring., 1992—. Inaugural pres. faculty senate Colo. Sch. Mines, 1989-90, disting. lectr., 1997-98, appointed senator, 1998; Tokyo Electric Power Co. chair Keio U., Japan, 1996; Erskine fellow U. Canterbury, Christchurch, N.Z., 2002; chmn. Codata Hydrate Database Task Force Group, 2005-06. Author: Clathrate Hydrates of Natural Gases, 1990, 2d edit., 1998, Hydrate Engineering, 2000; chmn. pub. bd. Chem. Engring. Edn., 1990—. Scoutmaster local Cub Scouts, 1978-81; elder Presbyn. Ch., Golden, Colo., 1977-79, 92-94; elder Ctrl. Presbyn. Ch., Denver, 1999—. Recipient Donald L. Katz award for rsch., Gas Processors Assn. Fellow AIChE (chmn. area Ia thermodynamics and transport 1990-93); mem. Am. Soc. for Engring. Edn. (chmn. ednl. rsch. methods divsn. 1983-85, chmn. chem. engring. divsn. 1984), Am. Chem. Soc., Soc. Petroleum Engrs. (Disting. Lectr. 1996-97). Avocations: bicycling, cello, philosophy. Office: Colo Sch of Mines Ctr for Hydrate Rsch Golden CO 80401 Personal E-Mail: edendysloan@comcast.net. Business E-Mail: esloan@mines.edu.

**SLOAN, FRANK ALLEN,** economist, educator; b. Greensboro, N.C., Aug. 15, 1942; s. Harry Benjamin and Edith (Vortrefflich) Sloan; m. Paula Jane Rackoff, June 22, 1969; children: Elyse Valerie, Richard Matthew. AB, Oberlin Coll., 1964; PhD, Harvard U., 1969. Rsch. economist Rand Corp., Santa Monica, Calif., 1968—71; asst. prof. econs. U. Fla., Gainesville, 1971—73, assoc. prof., 1973—76; prof. econs. Vanderbilt U., Nashville, 1976—84, Centennial prof. econs., 1984—93, chmn. dept., 1986—89; J. Alexander McMahon health policy and mgmt., prof. econs. Duke U., Durham, NC, 1993—, prof. health policy and mgmt., 1994—, dir. Ctr. for Health Policy, Law and Mgmt., 1998—. Dir. Health Policy Ctr. Vanderbilt U. Inst. Pub. Policy Studies, 1976—93; mem. Inst. Medicine, Washington, 1982—, mem. prospective payment rev. commns., 1996—; mem. Nat. Coun. Health Care Tech., Washington, 1979—81, Nat. Allergy and Infectious Disease Coun., Washington, 1971—74; cons. adv. coun. Social Security, Washington, 1983. Co-author: Private Physicians and Public Programs, 1978, Hospital Labor Markets, 1980, Insurance, Regulation and Hospital Costs, 1980, Uncompensated Hospital Care: Rights and Responsibilities, 1986, Insuring Medical Malpractice, 1991. Mem.: Western Econ. Assn., Soc. Econ. Assn., Am. Econ. Assn. Office: Duke University Ctr for Health Policy PO Box 90253 Durham NC 27708-0253

**SLOAN, F(RANK) BLAINE,** law educator; b. Geneva, Nebr., Jan. 3, 1920; s. Charles Porter and Lillian Josephine (Stiefer) S.; m. Patricia Sand, Sept. 2, 1944; children: DeAnne Sloan Riddle, Michael Blaine, Charles Porter. Grandfather Charles H. Sloan was a Republican Congressman for ten years, serving on the Ways and Means and the Agriculture Committees of the House of Representatives. He is recognized for his work in the eradication of Bovine Tuberculosis and Hog Cholera. He voted against entry to World War I, but

once America was involved, he supported the war effort and gave his three sons to the service. His oldest son, Frank Blaine Sloan, died overseas. His second son, Charles Porter, enlisted in the Army Air Service in the pioneering days of military aviation. AB with high distinction, U. Nebr., 1942, LLB cum laude, 1946; LLM in Internat. Law, Columbia U., 1947. Bar: Nebr. 1946, N.Y. 1947. Asst. to spl. counsel Intergovtl. Com. for Refugees, 1947; mem. Office Legal Affairs UN Secretariat, N.Y.C., 1948—78; gen. counsel Relief and Works Agy. Palestine Refugees, Beirut, 1958—60; dir. gen. legal divsn., dep. to legal counsel UN Legal Office, N.Y.C., 1966—78, rep. of Sec. Gen. to UN Commn. Internat. Trade Law, 1969—78, rep. to Legal Sub-com. on Outer Space, 1966—78; rep. UN Del. Vietnam Conf., Paris, 1973, UN Conf. on Carriage of Goods by Sea, Hamburg, 1978; prof. internat. law orgn. and water law Pace U., 1979—87, prof. emeritus, 1987—. Law lectr. Blaine Sloan Internat., 1988—. Blaine Sloan served in the UN Legal Office in New York and abroad for over thirty years, the last twelve as Director, General Legal Division. His wife Patricia, an artist and writer, and their children accompanied him on missions in Jerusalem and Beirut. His 1948 British Year Book of International Law article, for many years the leading study on UN General Assembly Resolutions, was quoted by the Supreme Court of Israel in the Eichmann case and by a dissenting judge in the unfortunate 1966 South West Africa cases. He is currently working on a treatise on the UN Charter as a Constitution. Author: United Nations General Assembly Resolutions in Our Changing World, 1991, United Nations Memories, 2005, (with Kathryn Sloan Ashby) A Hsitory of the Sloan, Porter, Fournell and Stiefer Families, 2005; contbr. articles to legal jours. Cons. UN Office of Legal Affairs, 1983-84, UN Water Resources Br., 1983; supervisory com., Pace Peace Ctr.; legal advisor Korean Missions, 1951, 53, UNTSO, Jerusalem, 1952, UNEF I, Gaza, 1957-58; prin. sec.UN Commn. to investigate Sec.-Gen. Hammarskjold's crash, 1961-62. Navigator AC, U.S. Army, 1943-46 Decorated Air medal. Mem. Am. Soc. Internat. Law, Am. Acad. Polit. and Social Sci., Am. Arbitration Assn., Order of Coif, Phi Beta Kappa, Phi Alpha Delta (hon.). Republican. Roman Catholic. Home: HCR-68 Box 72 Foxwind-Forbes Park Fort Garland CO 81133 Office: 78 N Broadway White Plains NY 10603-3710 also: 375 Soubry Pl Forbes Park Fort Garland CO 81133

**SLOAN, HARRY EVANS,** film company executive; BA, UCLA, 1971; JD, Loyola Law Sch., 1976. Founder, entertainment lawyer Sloan, Kuppin and Ament, LA, 1976—83; co-chmn. New World Entertainment Ltd., Los Angeles, 1983—89; chmn. SBS Broadcasting S.A., Luxembourg, 1990—2002, CEO, 1993—2001, exec. chmn., 2002—05; chmn., CEO Metro-Goldwyn-Mayer Inc., 2005—. Dir. ZeniMax Media Inc. Office: Metro Goldwyn Mayer Inc 10250 Constellation Blvd Los Angeles CA 90067

**SLOAN, HERBERT ELIAS,** physician, surgeon; b. Clarksburg, W.Va., Oct. 10, 1914; s. Herbert Elias and Luella (Dye) S.; m. Doris Edwards, May 3, 1943; children: Herbert, Ann, Elizabeth, John, Robert. AB, Washington and Lee U., 1936; MD, Johns Hopkins U., 1940. Diplomate Am. Bd. Surgery, Am. Bd. Thoracic Surgery (bd. dirs. 1966-86, v.p. 1971-73, sec. 1973-86). Resident in surgery Johns Hopkins Hosp., 1941-44; instr. dept. surgery Johns Hopkins U., 1943-44; resident in thoracic surgery U. Mich. Hosp., Ann Arbor, 1947-49, instr. thoracic surgery, 1949-50; asst. prof. U. Mich., Ann Arbor, 1950-53, assoc. prof., 1953-62, prof. surgery, 1962-87, head sect. thoracic surgery, 1970-85; chief clin. affairs U. Mich. Hosps., Ann Arbor, 1982-86, med. dir. operating room, 1986-87, prof. emeritus surgery, 1987—; med. dir. managed health care U. Mich., Ann Arbor, 1989-96, Herbert Sloan Collegiate Professorship in cardiac surgery, 2003. Mem. staff VA Hosp., Ann Arbor, 1953—, cons., 1968—. Author: The American Board of Thoracic Surgery: A Fifty Year Perspective, 1998, (with Marvin M. Kirsh) Blunt Chest Trauma, General Principles of Management, 1987; editor Annals of Thoracic Surgery, 1969-85; contbr. (with Marvin M. Kirsh) chpts. to books, articles to profl. jours. Served to maj. M.C. U.S. Army, 1944-47. Recipient Bruce Douglas award in thoracic diseases, 1974, Med. Alumni Svc. award Johns Hopkins Sch. Medicine, 1973, Disting. Svc. award Johns Hopkins U. Sch. Medicine, 1983, Disting. Svc. award Mich. Med. Ctr. Alumni Soc., 1988, Herbert Sloan Collegiate Prof. Cardiac Surgery award, 2003; named to Hall of Honor, U. Mich. Med. Sch., 2006. Mem. ACS, Am. Surg. Assn., Am. Heart Assn., Am. Assn. Thoracic Surgery (pres. 1979-80), Soc. Thoracic Surgeons (pres. 1974-75, Disting. Svc. award 1981), Central Surg. Assn., Soc. Univ. Surgeons, So. Thoracic Surgery Assn. (hon.), Thoracic Soc. Gt. Britain (hon.), John Alexander Soc., Western Thoracic Surg. Assn. (hon.), Cardiovascular Surgeons Club, Detroit Heart Club. Am. Trudeau Soc., Mich. Heart Assn., Mich. Trudeau Soc., Am. Acad. Pediatrics, Soc. Vascular Surgery, Frederick A. Coller Surg. Soc., U. Mich. Med. Alumni Soc. (Disting. Svc. award 1988), U. Mich. James Angell Soc., Rsch. Club, Phi Beta Kappa, Alpha Omega Alpha, Omicron Delta Kappa, Sigma Xi. Clubs: Ann Arbor Golf (pres. 1965-66). Home: 471 Barton North Dr Ann Arbor MI 48105-1017 Office: 1500 E Medical Center Dr Ann Arbor MI 48109 Business E-Mail: hsloan@umich.edu.

**SLOAN, HUGH WALTER, JR.,** automotive executive; b. Princeton, NJ, Nov. 1, 1940; s. Hugh Walter and Elizabeth (Johnson) Sloan; m. Deborah Louise Murray, Feb. 20, 1971; children: Melissa, Peter, Jennifer, William. AB in History with honors, Princeton U., 1963. Staff asst. to Pres. U.S. White House, Washington, 1969-71; treas. Pres. Nixon's Re-election Campaign, Washington, 1971; spl. asst. to pres. Budd Co., Troy, Mich., 1973-74, exec. asst. internat., 1974-77, mgr. corp. mktg., 1977-79; pres., gen. mgr. Budd Can. Inc., Kitchener, Ont., Canada, 1979-85; pres. automotive Woodbridge Group, Troy, 1985-98, dep. chmn., 1998—. Bd. dirs. Woodbridge Foam Corp., Mfrs. Life Ins. Co., Wescast Industries. Trustee Cranbrook Ednl. Cmty., Beaumont Hosp. Lt. USNR, 1963—65. Recipient Outstanding Bus. Leader award, Wilfrid Laurier U., 1987. Mem.: Bloomfield Hills (Mich.) Country Club. Republican. Office: Woodbridge Group 1515 Equity Dr Troy MI 48084-7146 Office Phone: 248-280-6571. Business E-Mail: hugh_sloan@woodbridgegroup.com

**SLOAN, JEANETTE PASIN,** artist; b. Chgo., Mar. 18, 1946; d. Antonio and Anna (Baggio) Pasin; children: Eugene Blakely, Anna Jeanette. BFA, Marymount Coll., Tarrytown, N.Y., 1967; MFA, U. Chgo., 1969. One-woman shows include G.W. Einstein Gallery, N.Y.C., 1977—85, Landfall Press Gallery, Chgo., N.Y.C., 1978, 1987, Roger Ramsay Gallery, Chgo., 1987, 1989, 1992, Tatischeff Gallery, Santa Monica, Calif., 1989, Steven Scott Gallery, Balt., 1989, Butters Gallery, Portland, Oreg., 1989, 1991, 1994, 1996, 1999, Tatistcheff & Co. Inc., 1995, 1997, 1999, Quartet Editions, N.Y.C., 1995, Elliot Smith Gallery, St. Louis, 1994, Peltz Gallery, Milw., 1994—95, 1999, 2006, Gerhard Wurzer Gallery, Houston, 1997, 2001, Cline Fine Arts Gallery, Santa Fe, 1998, 2001, J. Cacciola Gallery, N.Y.C., 2004—05, Amarillo Mus. Art, Tex., 2006, Represented in permanent collections Art Mus. Chgo., Cleve. Mus. Art, Ill. State Mus., Indpls. Mus. Art, Canton (Ohio) Art Inst., Ball State Bus., Mpls. Inst. Art, Fogg Mus. Harvard U., Yale U. Art Gallery, Snite Mus. U. Notre Dame, Met. Mus. Art, N.Y.C., Herbert F. Johnson Mus. Cornell U., Ithaca, N.Y., Valpariaso (Ind.) Mus. Art, Nat. Gallery Art, Washington, exhibited in group shows; subject of book by Gerritt Henry Jeanette Pasin Sloan, 2000, subject of book by by James Yood The Prints of Jeanette Pasin Sloan, 2003. Studio: 301 Loma Arisco Santa Fe NM 87501 Office Phone: 505-699-9234. Personal E-Mail: jeanettepasin@aol.com.

**SLOAN, JERRY (GERALD EUGENE SLOAN),** professional basketball coach; b. McLeansboro, Ill., Mar. 28, 1942; m. Bobbye (dec. 2004); 3 children: Kathy, Brian, Holly. Student, Evansville (Ind.) Coll., 1965. Professional basketball player, Baltimore, 1965-66, Chicago Bulls, NBA, 1966-76; head coach Chicago Bulls, 1979-82; scout Utah Jazz, NBA, Salt Lake City, 1983-84, asst. coach, 1984-88, head coach, 1988—. Player 2 NBA All-Star games; named to NBA All-Defensive First Team, 1969, 72, 74, 75. Office: c/o Utah Jazz Delta Ctr 301 W South Temple Salt Lake City UT 84101-1216*

**SLOAN, JULIE L.,** stained glass artist, consultant; d. Sheldon Ross and Catherine Cain Sloan; m. Albert L. Lewis, Nov. 15, 1986. MSc, Columbia U., 1982. Pvt. practice stained glass cons., North Adams, Mass., 1983—. Adj. prof. Columbia U., NYC, 1985—97, Salve Regina U., Newport, RI, 2004. Author: Conservation of Stained Glass in America, (exhibition catalog) Light

Screens: The Leaded Glass of Frank Lloyd Wright; Stained Glass Dome, Boldt Castle, Thousand Islands, NY, stained-glass window design, Christmas and Easter, First Congregational Ch., Adams, MA; curator (exhibitions) Light Screens: The Leaded Glass of Frank Lloyd Wright. Grantee, Graham Found. Advanced Studies in the Fine Arts, 1987, Nat. Endowment Arts, 1989, 1994; Mid-Career Grant for Preservation Professionals, James Marston Fitch Found., 1994-95, Rsch. grant, Arts and Crafts Fund, 2005. Mem.: Internat. Inst. Conservation, Victorian Soc. Am., Assn. Preservation Tech., Soc. Archtl. Historians, Am. Inst. Conservation (assoc.). Home: 54 Cherry St North Adams MA 01247 Personal E-Mail: jlsloan@jlsloan.com.

**SLOAN, KATHERINE (KAY SLOAN),** college president; DArts in English, Carnegie Mellon U. Pres. Greenfield C.C., 1988—94, North Hennepin C.C., Mpls., 1994—96, Mass. Coll. Art, Boston, 0199—. Office: Office of President Mass College of Art 621 Huntington Ave Boston MA 02115 Office Phone: 617-879-7100.

**SLOAN, MACEO KENNEDY,** lawyer, investment company executive; b. Phila., Oct. 18, 1949; s. Maceo Archibald and Charlotte (Kennedy) S.; m. Melva Iona Wilder, July 3, 1971; children: Maceo S., Malia K. BA, Morehouse Coll., 1971; MBA with honors, Ga. State U., 1973; JD with honors, N.C. Cen. U., 1979. CFA. Investment analyst N.C. Mut. Life Ins. Co., Durham, 1973-77, asst. to treas., 1977-78, asst. v.p., 1978-83, treas., 1983-85, v.p., treas., 1985-86; pres. NCM Devel. Group subs. N.C. Mut. Life Ins. Co., Durham, 1985-86; of counsel Moore & Van Allen, Durham, 1985-86; pres., CEO NCM Capital Mgmt. Group, Inc., Durham, 1986-91, chmn., pres., CEO, 1991—, Sloan Fin. Group, Inc., Durham, N.C., 1991—. Adj. vis. prof. N.C. Ctrl. U., Durham, 1978-86, workshop rev. leader Study Seminar for Fin. Analysts, Windsor, Ont., Can., 1980—; bd. dirs. Mechanics & Farmers Bank, Durham, 1979—, chmn. trust com., 1979-93; networking leader Black Enterprise mag., 1987—; bd. trustees Coll. Retirement Equities Fund, 1991—, ERISA Adv. Coun. U.S. Dept. Labor, 1991-93; bd. dirs. News and Observer Pub. Co. Bd. dirs. United Way, Durham, 1980-87, Urban Ministries, Durham, 1983-88, Internat. Found. Edn. and Self Help, 1993—, N.C. Air Cargo Airport Authority, 1993—; bd. visitors N.C. Ctrl. U. Sch. Law, Durham, 1979-86, U. N.C., Chapel Hill, 1990—. Recipient Outstanding Svc. award Better Bus. Bur., 1980, Freedom Guard award Durham Jaycees, 1982, Outstanding Leadership award United Way Durham, 1984, Resolution in Appreciation Durham City Coun., 1983. Fellow Life Mgmt. Inst.; mem. ABA, Fin. Analysts Fedn., N.C. Soc. Fin. Analysts (v.p. 1977-78), N.C. State Bar Assn., Durham C of C., Nat. Investment Mgrs. Assn. (founder, chmn.), Nat. Assn. Securities Profls., Treyburn Country Club (Durham), Univ. Club (Durham), The George Town (Washington). Democrat. Baptist. Avocations: reading, jogging, weight training, golf, tennis. Home: 24000 S Lowell Rd Bahama NC 27503-9693 Office: Sloan Fin Group Inc 103 W Main St Fl 4 Durham NC 27701-3638 also: NCM Mgmt/Sloan Financial 2634 Durham-Chapel Hill Blvd Ste 206 Durham NC 27707-1958

**SLOAN, MARY JEAN,** retired media specialist; b. Lakeland, Fla., Nov. 29, 1927; d. Marion Wilder and Elba (Jinks) Sloan. BS, Peabody Coll., Nashville, 1949; MLS, Atlanta U., 1978, SLS, 1980. Cert. libr. media specialist. Music dir. Pinecrest Sch., Tampa, Fla., 1949-50, Polk County Schs., Bartow, Fla., 1950-54; pvt. music tchr. Lakeland, 1954-58; tchr. Clayton County Schs., Jonesboro, Ga., 1958-59; media specialist Eastualley Sch., Marietta, Ga., 1959-89; ret., 1989. Coord. conf. Ga. Libr. Media Dept., Jekyll Island, 1982-83, sec., Atlanta, 1982-83, com. chmn. ethnic conf., Atlanta, 1978, pres., 1984-85, state pres., 1985-86; program chmn. Ga. Media Orgns. Conf, Jekyll Island, 1988. Contbr. to bibliographies. Recipient Walter Bell award Ga. Assn. Instrnl. Tech., 1988, Disting. Svc. award, 1991. Mem. ALA (del. 1984, 85, 90), NEA, Southeastern Libr. Assn., Am. Assn. Sch. Librs., Soc. for Sch. Librs., Internat., Ga. Assn. Educators (polit. action com. 1983), Beta Phi Mu, Phi Delta Kappa. Republican. Methodist. Home: 797 Yorkshire Rd NE Atlanta GA 30306-3264

**SLOAN, MICHAEL ALLAN,** neurologist; b. Detroit, July 26, 1954; s. Eugene and Mildred Jody Sloan (Stepmother); children: Jessica Barry, Brittany Erin. MD, Wayne State U., 1980; MS, Rush U., 2003. Diplomate neurology Am. Bd. Psychiatry and Neurology, 1988, internal medicine Am. Bd. Internal Medicine, 1984, vascular neurology Am. Bd. Psychiatry and Neurology, 2005. Assoc. prof. neurology U. Md. Med. Ctr., Balt., 1988—97; neurologist Harbin Clinic, Rome, Ga., 1998—2000; assoc. prof. neurology U. Rush, Chgo., 2000—05; dir. stroke program Carolinas Med. Ctr., Charlotte, NC, 2005—; adj. prof. neurology U. NC, Chapel Hill, 2005—. AMA del. Am. Soc. Neuroimaging, 2001. Fellow: Am. Coll. Cardiology, Am. Acad. Neurology. Avocations: politics, music, performing arts, travel, sports. Office Phone: 704-355-5694. Office Fax: 704-355-9296. Business E-Mail: michael.sloan@carolinashealthcare.org.

**SLOAN, MICHAEL DANA,** information systems specialist, management consultant; b. Santa Monica, Calif., Sept. 30, 1960; s. Avery and Beverly Rae (Krantz) S.; m. Barbara Rogers; 1 child, Ashley Harrison. BS in Bus. Adminstrn., Calif. State U., Northridge, 1983; MBA, Pepperdine U., 1987. Programmer/analyst TICOR, Inc., L.A., 1979-80; data processing analyst Deluxe Check Printers, Inc., Chatsworth, Calif., 1980-83; fin. systems analyst Wismer & Assocs., Inc., Canoga Park, Calif., 1983-84; sr. systems analyst Coast Savs. & Loan, Granada Hills, Calif., 1984-86; microcomputer systems specialist Litton Industries, Woodland Hills, Calif., 1986-87; systems mgr. info. resources mgr. TRW, Inc.- Space and Def., Redondo Beach, Calif., 1987-93; project mgr. Health Net, Woodland Hills, 1993-95; mgr. fin. and sales systems Merisel Ams. Inc., El Segundo, Calif., 1995-97; sr. mgr. web tech. & devel. Ingram Micro Inc., Santa Ana, Calif., 2000—01; with Ptnrs. Cons. Svcs., Inc., Laguna Beach, Calif., 2001—02, Consulting Solutions, Inc., Calabasas, Calif., 2002—05; mgmt. cons. Strategic Cons. Solutions, Ltd., Redondo Beach, Calif., 2005—. Cons. Data Most, Inc., Chatsworth, 1982—83, Home Savs. & Loan, North Hollywood, Calif., 1987, Micro Tech., L.A., 1987, TRW, Inc.-Space and Def., Redondo Beach, Calif., 1993—2000, Pacificare Health Systems, Inc., 1997, Nissan North America (formerly Nissan Motor Corp., USA), 1998—99, Prosum Info. Techs., Inc., 2000—01, Am. Honda Motors, Inc., 1999—2000, Toyota Fin. Svcs., 2001—02, Warner Bros. Studios, 2002—05, Oakwood Worldwide, 2005—. Mem. IEEE Computer Soc., Salle Gascon Fencing Club, U.S. Fencing Assn., Delta Sigma Pi. Republican. Avocations: fencing, comedy improvisation, tennis, volleyball, travel. Office: Strategic Consulting Solutions Ltd Ste 1 2607 Vanderbilt Ln Redondo Beach CA 90278

**SLOAN, O. TEMPLE, JR.,** automotive equipment executive; b. Sanford, N.C., Feb. 21, 1939; s. Orris Temple and Thelma (Hamilton) S.; m. Carol Carson; children: C. Carson Henline, O. Temple Sloan III, Mark H. Sloan. BA in Bus. Adminstrn., Duke U., 1961. Founder, chmn., CEO Gen. Parts Inc., Raleigh, NC, 1961—. Chmn. bd. dir. Highwoods Properties Inc., Raleigh; bd. dir. CARQUEST Corp., Raleigh, Bank Am., Charlotte, Lowe's Cos., Inc., Golden Corral, Global Transpark Found. Trustee Boys and Girls Homes N.C., Lake Waccamaw, 1973; campaign chmn. Wake County United Way, 2001; mem. Centennial Authority, 1995—2005, trustee. Presbyn. Ch. com. fin. com.; elder Presbyn. Ch.; exec. bd. Occoneechee coun. Boy Scouts Am., capital campaign chmn. Occoneechee coun., 2004—05, past v.p.Occoneechee coun., past treas. Occoneechee coun.; bd. visitors Peace Coll., Raleigh, 1985—87, trustee, 1987—97, vice chmn. bd. trustees. Recipient Silver Beaver award Boy Scouts Am., Disting. Eagle Scout award Boy Scouts Am., Disting. Svc. citation Automotive Hall of Fame, 1997; named Northwood U. Outstanding Bus. Leader, 1999. Mem. Automotive Warehouse Distbrs. Assn. Inc. (dir. 1969—, chmn. 1976-77, Scholarship award 1977, Automotive Man of Yr. award 1989), The Fifty Group (past pres.), Carolina Country Club (Raleigh). Avocations: fishing, hunting, ranching. Home: 3026 Randolph Dr Raleigh NC 27609-6942 Office: Gen Parts Inc PO Box 26006 Raleigh NC 27611 Business E-Mail: licanipe@gpi.com.

**SLOAN, ROBERT BRYAN, JR.,** academic administrator; b. Coleman, Tex., 1949; m. Sue Collier; children: Charissa, Bryan, Eraina, Michael, Alathea, Sophia, Paul. BA cum laude, Baylor U., 1970; MDiv magna cum laude,

Princeton Theol. Sem., 1973; doktor der theologie insigni cum laude, U. Basel, 1978. Faculty Hardin-Simmons U., Abilene, Southwestern Bapt. Theol. Sem., Fort Worth, 1980—83; faculty, religion Baylor U., Waco, Tex., 1983, George W. Truett chair in Evangelism, 1990—95, dean Truett Sem., 1993—95, pres., CEO, 1995—2005, chancellor, 2005—. Mem. Cooper Found. Bd., Compass Bank Adv. Bd.; pastor, interim pastor over 20 chs., Tex., Okla., N.J., Germany; mem., treas. Big 12 Exec. Com.; bd. dirs. Salado Inst. for the Humanities. Inducted Little League Hall of Excellence. Mem. Studiorum Novi Testamenti Societas, Soc. of Bib. Lit., Inst. for Bib. Rsch. Office: Baylor U Office of Chancellor PO Box 97132 Waco TX 76798-7132 Office Phone: 254-710-2012. Office Fax: 254-710-3126.*

**SLOAN, ROBERT D.,** energy executive, lawyer; b. Ill., Oct. 27, 1947; m. Dauphine de Montlaur Sloan; children: Alexandra, Caroline, Edward. BA, U. Mich.; JD, Harvard U. Gen. counsel to Minority U.S. Senate Permanent Subcommittee on Investigations; asst. legal adviser, worked on nuclear non-proliferation and politico-military matters U.S. State Dept.'s Office of Legal Adviser; gen. counsel Multinational Force and Observers, Rome, 1981—84; v.p., dir. Sovereign Credit Mgmt. Divsn. 1st Nat. Bank Chgo., 1985—92; ptnr. Pepper, Hamilton and Sheetz Law Firm, Washington, Sloan, Lehner & Ruiz; mng. ptnr. Brussels office McKenna and Cuneo LLP, 1993—98; v.p., gen. counsel GE Indsl. Sys., Plainville, Conn., 1998—2003; sr. v.p., gen. counsel, sec. Entergy Corp., New Orleans, 2003—. Adj. prof. law Georgetown Law Ctr., Washington. Bd. dir. Ctr. for Internat. Bus. Edn., U. Mich., New Orleans Ballet Theatre.

**SLOANE, BEVERLY LEBOV,** writer, consultant, writing instructor; b. NYC, May 26, 1936; d. Benjamin S. and Anne (Weinberg) LeBov; m. Robert Malcolm Sloane, Sept. 27, 1959 (dec. May 16, 2002); 1 child, Alison Lori Sloane Gaylin. AB, Vassar Coll., 1958; MA, Claremont Grad. U., 1975, postgrad., 1975—76; cert. in exec. mgmt., UCLA Grad. Sch. Mgmt., 1982, grad. exec. mgmt. program, 1982, cert. in advanced exec. mgmt., 1995, grad. advanced exec. mgmt. program, 1995; grad. profl. pub. course, Stanford U., 1982, grad. exec. refresher course in profl. pub., 1994; grad. intensive bioethics course Kennedy Inst. Ethics, Georgetown U., 1987, advanced bioethics course, 1988; grad. Summer Bioethics Inst., Loyola Marymount U., 1990; grad. Annual Summer Inst. on Teaching of Writing, Columbia U. Tchrs. Coll., 1990; grad. Annual Summer Inst. on Advanced Teaching of Writing, Columbia Tchrs. Coll., 1993; grad. Annual Inst. Pub. Health and Human Rights, Harvard U. Sch. Pub. Health, 1994; grad. women's campaign sch., Yale U., 1998; grad. writing and thinking course, Inst. Writing and Thinking, Bard Coll., 2005; Ethics Fellow, Loma Linda U. Med. Ctr., 1989. Circulation libr. Harvard Med. Libr., Boston, 1958-59; social worker Conn. State Welfare, New Haven, 1960-61; tchr. English Hebrew Day Sch., New Haven, 1961-64; instr. creative writing and English lit. Monmouth Coll., West Long Branch, NJ, 1967-69; writer, cons., 1970—. V.p. coun. grad. students, Claremont Grad. U., 1971-72; adj. dir. Writing Ctr. Speaker Series, 1993-2000, spkr., 1996-98, Claremont Grad. U.; mem. Strategic Planning Task Force Com. Campaign Pre-eminence. 1986-87, Alumni Coun.; bd. dirs. Alumni Assn., 1993-96; mem. Vol. Devel. Com., 1994-96, Alumni Awards Com., 1993-96; bd. visitors Claremont Grad. U. Ctrs. for Arts and Humanities, 2001—; adv. coun. tech. and profl. writing Dept. English, Calif. State U., Long Beach, 1980-82; adv. bd. Calif. Health Rev., 1982-83; mem. Foothill Health Dist. Adv. Coun. LA County Dept. Health Svcs., 1987-93, pres., 1989-91; vis. scholar Hastings Ctr., 1996; spkr. NY State Task Force on Life and the Law, 1996; panel spkr. Annual Conf. Am. Assn. Suicidology, 1998; adj. instr. English composition Marist Coll., Poughkeepsie, NY, 2005—. Author: From Vassar to Kitchen, 1967, A Guide to Health Facilities: Personnel and Management, 1971, 2nd edit., 1977, 3d edit., 1992, Introduction to Healthcare Delivery Organization: Functions and Management, 4th edit., 1999. Co-chmn. Vassar Christmas Showcase Vassar Club, New Haven, 1965—66; pub. rels. bd. Monmouth County Mental Health Assn., 1968—69; co-chmn. Vassar Club So. Calif. Annual Book Fair Vassar Coll., 1970—71; chmn. creative writing group Calif. Inst. Tech. Woman's Club, 1975—79; mem. task force edn. and cultural activities City of Duarte, 1987—88; class rep. Vassar Coll. Alumnae Assn., 1989; chmn. creative writing group Yale U. Newcomers, 1965—66; dir. creative writing group Yale U. Women's Group, 1966—67; mem. Exec. Program Network UCLA Grad. Sch. Mgmt., 1987—2000; trustee Ctr. Improvement Child Caring, 1981—83; mem. League Crippled Children, 1982—, treas. for gen. meetings, 1990—91, chmn. hostesses com., 1988—89, pub. rels. com., 1990—91; del. Task Force on Minorities in Newspaper Bus., 1987—89; rep. cmty. County Health Network Tobacco Control Program, 1991; mem. NY Citizens Com. Health Care Decisions, bd. dirs., 2005—; mem. Vassar Coll. Class Gift Com., 1998; chmn. 1st ann. Rabbi Camillus Angel Interfaith Svc. Temple Beth David, 1978, v.p., 1983—86; cmty. rels. com. Jewish Fedn. Coun. Greater LA, 1985—87; bd. dirs. League Crippled Children, 1988—91; ethics com., human subjects protection com. Jewish Home for Aging, Reseda, Calif., 1994—97; various positions and coms. Claremont Grad. U., 1986—; bd. visitors Claremont Grad. U. Ctr. Arts and Humanities, 2001—; bd. dirs. LA Commn. Assaults Against Women, 1983—84; class corr. Vassar Coll. Quar. Alumnae Mag., 1993—98; class of 1958 coms. Vassar Coll., class v.p., 1998—2000, class co-pres., 2000—01, class pres., 2001—03, program chmn. 40th reunion, 1998. Recipient cert. of appreciation City of Duarte, 1988, County of LA, 1988, Ann. Key Mem. award LA Dept. Health Svcs., 1996; Coro Found. fellow, 1979, Ethics fellow Loma Linda U. Med. Ctr., 1989; named Calif. Communicator of Achievement, Woman of Yr. Calif. Press Women, 1992. Fellow: Am. Med. Writers Asn. (Pacific S.W. del. to nat. bd. 1980—87, dir. 1980—93, chmn. nat. book awards trade category 1982—83, chmn. Nat. Networking Luncheon 1983—84, nat. chmn. freelance sect. 1984—85, workshop leader, Nat. Ann. Conf. 1984—89, gen. chmn. Asilomar Western Regional Conf. 1985, workshop leader, Asilomar Western Regional Conf. 1985, nat. exec. bd. dirs. 1985—86, nat. admnr. sects. 1985—86, pres.-elect Pacific Southwest chpt. 1985—87, chmn. gen. session nat. conf. 1986—87, chmn. Walter C. Alvarez Mem. Found award 1986—87, program co-chmn. 1987, program chmn. nat. conf. 1987, moderator gen. session. nat. conf. 1987, pres. Pacific S.W. chap. 1987—89, workshop leader, Asilomar Western Nat. Conf. 1988, spkr. Pacific S.W. chpt. 1988—89, program co-chmn. 1989, workshop leader, Asilomar Western Nat. Conf. 1989, Pacific Southwest deleg. to nat. bd. 1989—91, immediate past pres. 1989—91, workshop leader, Nat. Ann. Conf. 1990—92, bd. dirs. 1991—93, workshop leader, Nat. Ann. Conf. 1995, chmn. conv. coms., Appreciation award for outstanding leadership 1989, named to Workshop Leaders Honor Roll 1991); mem.: AAUP, APHA, AAUW (creative writing chmn. Arcadia Br. 1973—74, 1st v.p. program dir. 1975—76, legis. chmn. Arcadia Br. 1976—77, networking chmn. 1981—82, spkr. 1987, chmn. task force promoting individual liberties 1987—88, pres.-elect 1998—99, educ. equity chmn. 1998—99, chmn. deleg. to national conv. 1999, chmn. Technical Trek Sci. Camp Scholarship for Girls 1999, Career Day 1999, pres. Arcadia br. 1999—2000, writer in res Calif. State Am. Assn. Univ. Women 1999—2000, diversity chmn. Arcadia br. 2000—01, LA Interbr. Coun. Arcadia br. repr. 2000—02, Calif. State diversity com. 2000—02, program vice-chmn. LA County Interbr. Coun. 2000—02, Woman of Achievement Arcadia br. 1986, cert. of appreciation 1987), Calif. State AAUW (program co-v.p. 2002), Town Hall Calif. (vice chmn. cmty. affairs sect. 1982—87, faculty-instr. Exec. Breakfast Inst. 1985—86, Exec. Breakfast Inst. spkr. 1986), Pasadena Athletic, Claremont Cols. Faculty House, Women's City (Pasadena), Nat. Writer's Union, Authors Guild, Assn. Writing Programs, NY Acad. Medicine (met. NY Ethics Network), Soc. Health and Human Values, Kennedy Inst. Ethics, Nat. Fedn. Press Women (chmn. state women of achievement comt. 1986—87, nat. co-chmn. task force recruitment minorities 1987—89, bd. 1987—89, bd. dirs. 1987—93, nat. dir. spkrs. bur. 1989—93, Plenary past pres. state 1989—, workshop leader, spkr. annual nat. conf. 1990, editor spkrs. bur. directory 1991—92, editor spkrs. bur. addendum dir. 1992, cert. of appreciation 1991, 1st runner up, Nat. Communicator of Achievement 1992, cert. of appreciation 1993), Hastings Cent. (vis. scholar 1996), Ind. Writers So. Calif. (bd. dirs. corp. 1988—89, bd. dirs. 1989—90, dir. at large 1989—92, dir. specialized groups 1989—90, dir. speech writing group 1991—92), NY Acad. Scis., Calif. Press Women (v.p. programs L.A. chpt. 1982—85, pres. 1985—87, state pres. 1987—89, immediate past state pres. 1989—91, chmn. state speakers bur.

1989—95, deleg. nat. bd. 1989—95, dir. family literacy day Calif. 1990, moderator, ann. spring conv. 1990, chmn. nominating comt. 1990—91, Calif. literacy dir. 1990—92, dir. state literacy com. 1990—92, moderator, ann. spring conv. 1992, Cert. of Appreciation 1991, Calif. Communicator of Achievement 1992), Am. Soc. Law, Medicine, Ethics, AAUW Calif. State Comns. Comt. (writer in residence 1999—2000), Coro Nat. Alumni Assn. (bd. dirs. 1999—, continuing edn. com. 2003—), Am. Assn. Higher Edn., Women in Comm. Inc. (N.E. area rep. 1980—81, bd. dirs. 1980—82, v.p. cmty. affairs 1981—82, chmn. awards banquet 1982, chmn. LA chpt. Agnes Underwood Freedom Info. Awards banquet 1982, nominating com. 1982—83, seminar leader, spkr., ann. nat. profl. conf. 1985, program adv. com. LA chpt. 1987, com. Women of the Press awards luncheon 1988, bd. dirs. 1989—90, v.p. activities 1989—90, Recognition award 1983), Duarte Rotary Club. Home and Office: 22 East Knoll Rhinebeck NY 12572 Office Phone: 845-876-0738. Business E-Mail: beverly.sloane@marist.edu.

**SLOANE, CARL STUART,** corporate executive, educator, management consultant; b. NYC, Feb. 9, 1937; s. George and Dorothy (Cohen) S.; m. Toby Tattlebaum, Dec. 27, 1958; children: Lisa Beth, Amy Rachel, Todd Cowan. BA, Harvard U., 1958, MBA, 1960. Asst. to pres. Revlon, Inc., N.Y.C., 1960-62; mgmt. cons. Harbridge House, Inc., Boston, 1962-69; pres., CEO, chmn. Temple, Barker & Sloane, Inc., Lexington, Mass., 1970—91; prof. bus. adminstrn. Harvard Grad. Sch. Bus. Adminstrn., Lexington, 1991—2001; co-chair Alex Ptnrs. and Questor Funds, 2005—. Policyholders' examining com. N.W. Mut. Life Ins. Co.; bus. adv. com. Transp. Ctr., Northwestern U., 1984-91; adv. com. Ctr. for Sci. and Internat. Affairs, Kennedy Sch. Govt., Harvard U., 1984-94; bd. dirs. Rayonier, Inc., Brinks Co. Bd. dirs. Harvard-Radcliffe Hillel, Cambridge, Mass., 1987-98, chmn., 1994-98; bd. dirs., trustee Beth Israel Deaconess Med. Ctr., Boston, 1993—, vice-chmn., 1996-2002, chmn. 2002-05; nat. fund chmn. Harvard Bus. Sch., 1987-89, vis. com. Mem. Assn. Mgmt. Cons. Firms (chmn. 1984-86), Harvard U. Bus. Sch. Alumni Assn. (v.p. 1989, pres. 1989-91), Boston Yacht Club (Marblehead), Kernwood County Club (Salem), Harvard Club N.Y.C. Office: Harvard Bus Sch Soldiers Fld Boston MA 02163-1317 Home: 402 Paradise Rd Apt 2G Swampscott MA 01907 Office Phone: 781-639-2922. Business E-Mail: csloane@hbs.edu.

**SLOANE, HOWARD G.,** lawyer; b. San Francisco, Dec. 7, 1950; BA, Wesleyan U., Ohio, 1972; JD, Suffolk U., 1976. Bar: NY 1977, DC 1981. Law clk. US Dist. Ct. (Ea. Dist.) NY, 1976—77; co-adminstr. ptnr. Cahill Gordon & Reindel LLP, ptnr., Litig. Practice Group. Chmn. bd. Heckscher Found. for Children, 1995—; trustee Horace Mann Sch., 1998—, Sisulu Victory Acad. Charter Sch., 2000—03, Leadership for a Diverse Am., 2004—; bd. dir. Mcpl. Art Soc., 1990—. Office: Cahill Gordon & Reindel LLP 80 Pine St New York NY 10005-1702 Office Phone: 212-701-3321. Office Fax: 212-378-2369. Business E-Mail: psloane@cahill.com.

**SLOANE, J.P.,** television producer, theologian, entertainer, writer; b. Hollywood, Calif., Sept. 6, 1942; s. Jimmy Jackson and Anita (Thibodeaux) Barrios. Cert. in TV prodn., Purdue U., 1981; grad., Oral Roberts U., 1985; diploma, Inst. Jewish-Christian Studies, Dallas, 1992; grad., Moody Bible Inst., Chgo., 1998; student, IBEX Campus, Abu Ghosh, Israel, 2001; BA summa cum laude, Master's Coll., N.Y.C., 2003, MA, 2004; DA, Trinity Theol. Sem., 2006. Biblical scholar and lectr.; appeared on major Christian networks. Guest Art Linkletter's House Party (age 5), CBS Radio Network; played Billy Kettle in Ma and Pa Kettle movie series; appeared on Memory Lane TV show, Hollywood; recorded High on a Mountain, 1960, Linda Darling, 1960; lead singer The Brothers Grimm, 1965-68; featured act with Charlie Rich; mem. J.P. Sloane & Co. group, 1973-78; albums include Solid Gold; co-author (with Shannon Sloane) You Can Be a Virgin Again, The Christian Counselor's Guide to Restoring Virginity, 2006; tv and radio prodr. Recipient Excellence in Media Angel awards for Outstanding TV Prodr., Outstanding Male Vocalist and Outstanding Music Video, Medal of Merit, Pres. Ronald Reagan; named Hon. Sheriff, L.A. County, Hon. Ky. Col., Hon. Lt. Gov. State of Ind., Hon. Citizen, Tulsa, Met. Nashville, 22d Internat. Angel award best multiple character voices, 1999, others; nominee Cleo award, 1980; key to cities Nashville and New Orleans, others. Mem.: Nat. Scholars Honor Soc. (life). Office: Angeles Crest Productions Ste 407 2219 E Thousand Oaks Blvd Thousand Oaks CA 91362-2930 Business E-Mail: jp@jpsloane.com.

**SLOANE, NEIL JAMES ALEXANDER,** mathematician, researcher; b. Beaumaris, Wales, Oct. 10, 1939; came to U.S., 1961; s. Charles Ronald and Jessie (Robinson) S.; m. Susanna Stevens Cuyler, Mar. 8, 1980. BA with honors, U. Melbourne, Australia, 1959, BEE, 1960; MS, Cornell U., 1964, PhD, 1967. Asst. prof. Cornell U., Ithaca, NY, 1967-69; mem. tech. staff AT&T Bell Labs., Murray Hill, NJ, 1969-96; prin. mem. tech. staff AT&T Rsch. Labs., 1996—, fellow, 1998. Author: Handbook of Integer Sequences, 1973; co-author: (with F.J. MacWilliams) Theory of Error-Correcting Codes, 1977, (with J.H. Conway) Sphere-Packings, Lattices and Groups, 1988, 32d edit., 1998, (with A.D. Wyner) Claude Elwood Shannon:Collected Papers, 1993, (with S. Plouffe) Encyclopedia of Integer Sequences, 1995, (with A.S. Hedayat and J. Stufken) Orthogonal Arrays, 1999, (with P. Nick) Rock Climbing New Jersey, 2000, (with G. Nebe and E.M. Rains) Self-Dual Codes and Invariant Theory, 2006. Fellow IEEE (editor in chief Trans. Info. Theory jour. 1978-80, Hamming medal 2005); mem. NAE, Math. Assn. Am. (Chauvenet prize 1979, Earle Raymond Hedrick lectr. 1984), Am. Math. Soc., Am. Stat. Assn. Avocation: rock climbing. Office Phone: 973-360-8415. E-mail: njas@research.att.com.

**SLOANE, PHYLLIS LESTER,** artist; b. Worcester, Mass., Sept. 27, 1921; d. Nathan and Goldie (Pollock) Lester; m. David J. Sloane, Nov. 25, 1943 (div. July 1986); children: Diana, Nathaniel, Lisa. BFA, Carnegie Mellon U., 1943. Freelance product designer, N.Y.C., 1944-45; co-owner PDA Design Co., Cleve., 1946-48, Sloane O'Sickey Gallery, Cleve., 1970-72; gallery dir. New Orgn. for Visual Arts, Cleve., 1972-74; freelance artist Cleve., 1974—. One-woman shows include Gallery 200, Columbus, Ohio, 1974, 1978, Cleve. Play House Gallery, 1972, 1974, 1976, 1981, 1983, 1985, Mansfield (Ohio) Art Ctr., 1977, 1996, Wooster (Ohio) Coll. Art Mus., 1978, Massillon (Ohio) Mus., 1979, Janus Gallery, Santa Fe, 1981, Women's City Club, 1982, 1988, Florence O'Donnell Wasmer Gallery, Ursiline Coll., 1987, Frank Croft Fine Art, Santa Fe, 1987, 1988, 1996, William Engle Gallery, Indpls., 1987, 1988, Bonfoey Gallery, Cleve., 1990, 1992, 1994, 1996, Harris-Stanton Gallery, Akron, 2002, Las Vegas (Nev.) Art Mus., 2004, N.Mex. Printmakers Gallery, 2006, exhibited in group shows at Mansfield Art Ctr., 1984, 1993, Pratt Graphics Ctr., N.Y., 1986, Calif. Coll. Arts & Crafts, 1987, Oreg. Sch. Arts & Crafts, Portland, 1987, Hudson River Mus., Yonkers, N.Y., 1987, Cleve. Ctr. Contemporary Art, 1987, Sigma Gallery, N.Y., 1990, Harris-Stanton Gallery, Akron, 2000, Eldridge, McCarthy Gallery, Santa Fe, 2003, 2004, Represented in permanent collections Cleve. Mus. Art, Hunterdon Art Ctr., Clinton, N.J., Phila. Art Mus., Massillon (Ohio) Mus., Rutgers U. Archives, N.J., Cleve. Pub. Libr., N.Mex. Mus. Fine Arts, Santa Fe, U. N.Mex. Art Mus., Las Vegas (Nev.) Art Mus. Recipient Purchase award, Hunterdon Nat. Print Exhbn., 1977, Print Club Phila., 1977, Anderson Winter Show, 1985, N.C. Print and Drawing Assn., 1985, Graphics award, Cleve. Mus. Art, 1978, Visual Arts award, City of Cleve., 1982, 1st prize, Miami Internat. Print Biennial, 1984, Nationwide Ins. award, Ohio Watercolor Soc., 1984. Mem.: Santa Fe Printmakers Gallery, Artists Archives Western Res., Cleve. Soc. Contemporary Art, Boston Printmakers (Purchase award 1984), Santa Fe Etchers Club, Print Club Cleve. (trustee 1991—2000). Home: 501 Calle De Leon Santa Fe NM 87505

**SLOANE, THOMAS O.,** speech educator; b. West Frankfort, Ill., July 12, 1929; s. Thomas Orville and Blanche (Morris) S.; m. Barbara Lee Lewis, Nov. 1, 1952; children:— Elizabeth Alison, David Lewis, Emily. BA, So. Ill. U., 1951, MA, 1952; PhD, Northwestern U., 1960. Instr. English, Washington and Lee U., 1958-60; asst. prof. speech U. Ill., 1960-65, assoc. prof., 1965-70, assoc. head dept., 1967-68, asst. dean liberal arts and scis., 1966-67; prof. rhetoric, chmn. rhetoric dept. U. Calif., Berkeley, 1970-92, pres.'s chair, 1987-90, prof. emeritus, 1993—. Dir. Nat. Endowment Humanities Summer Seminar for Coll. Tchrs., 1979 Editor: The Oral Study of Literature, 1966, The

Passions of the Minde in Generall (Thomas Wright), 1971, (with Raymond B. Waddington) The Rhetoric of Renaissance Poetry, 1974, (with Joanna H. Maclay) Interpretation, 1972; Donne, Milton and the End of Humanist Rhetoric, 1985, On the Contrary, 1997, (with Peter Oesterreich) Rhetorica Movet, 1999; editor in chief: Encyclopedia of Rhetoric, 2001; contbr. articles to profl. jours. Served to lt. USNR, 1952-55. Faculty research fellow, 1964; U. Ill. instructional devel. awardee, 1965; Henry H. Huntington Library research awardee, 1967; U. Calif. humanities research fellow, 1974; Guggenheim fellow, 1981-82 Office: U Calif Berkeley CA 94720-0001 E-mail: tos@berkeley.edu.

**SLOAT, BARBARA FURIN,** cell biologist, educator; b. Youngstown, Ohio, Jan. 20, 1942; d. Walter and Mary Helen (Maceyko) Furin; m. John Barry Sloat, Nov. 2, 1968; children: John Andrew, Eric Furin. BS, Denison U., Granville, Ohio, 1963; MS, U. Mich., 1966, PhD, 1968. Lic. and cert. emergency med. technician, paramedic. Lab. asst. U. Ghent, Belgium, 1964; tchg. fellow, lectr. U. Mich., Ann Arbor, 1964-66, 68-70, asst. rsch. biologist Mental Health Rsch. Inst., 1972-74, vis. asst. prof., lectr. Ann Arbor and Dearborn, 1974-76, dir. women in sci. Ann Arbor, 1980-84, assoc. dir. honors, 1986-87, rsch. scientist, 1976-, lectr. Residential Coll., 1984—, assoc. Inst. Humanities, 1991—. Author: Laboratory Guide for Zoology, 1979, Summer Internships in the Sciences for High School Women (CASE Silver medal, 1985, Excellence in Edn. award, U. Mich., 1993). Bd. dirs. Jewel Heart Tibetan Cultural Ctr., Ann Arbor, Mich., 2005—, Jewel Heart Health Ctr. and Cmty. Hospice, Ann Arbor, 2003—. Recipient Acad. Women's Caucus award, U. Mich., 1984, Grace Lyon Alumnae Award, Denison U., 1988; grantee NSF, U.S. Dept. Edn., Warner Lambert Found., others. Mem. AAAS, Am. Soc. Cell Biology, N.Y. Acad. Scis., Nat. Assn. Women Deans, Adminstrs. and Counselors, Assn. for Women in Sci. (councilor 1988-90, pres. elect 1990, mentor of yr. award Detroit area chpt. 1994), Phi Beta Kappa, Sigma Xi. Avocations: hiking, yoga, tibetology. Home: 240 Indian River Pl Ann Arbor MI 48104-1825 Office: U Mich Residential Coll 216 Tyler East Quad Ann Arbor MI 48109-1245 Business E-Mail: bsloat@umich.edu.

**SLOAT, RICHARD JOEL,** artist; b. Easton, Pa., Sept. 18, 1945; s. Samuel Michael and Florence Elizabeth (Cohen) S.; m. Su-Li Hung, Aug. 18, 1972; 1 child, Benjamin Hung-Hur. BA, U. Pa., 1969; postgrad., Art Students League, N.Y.C., 1971-72. One-man shows include Moon St., Westport, Conn., 1974, Spring Gallery, Taipei, 1979, Martin Summers, N.Y.C., 1987, Wood and Stone Gallery, Taipei, 1990, F.D.R. Gallery, N.Y.C., 1993, The Old Print Shop, N.Y.C., 1995, The Ottendorfer Libr., N.Y.C., 1996, Sonnenshein, Nath & Rosenthal, N.Y.C., 1998, Paul McCarron, N.Y.C., 2001, Howard Salon, Taiwan, 2001, Old Print Shop, 2004, Safe-T-Gallery, N.Y.C., 2005; two-person show Falkenstern Fine Art, N.Y.C., 1990, Port Washington Pub. Libr., 1998, Michael Ingbar Gallery, N.Y.C., 2005; exhibited in group shows at NAD, 1974, 86, 88, 94, 1999, 2000, 03, 04, 05, Taipei Mus., 1976, Terry/Chassman, N.Y.C., 1990, Blum Helman Warehouse, N.Y.C., 1989, Fine Arts Assn., Hanoi, 1991, Curtiba Print Mus., Brazil, 1992, Michael Ingbar Gallery, N.Y.C., 1993, 94, 96, 97, 98, 2000, 01, 05, 06, Duxbury (Mass.) Mus., 1994, 97, 2004, Paul McCarron Gallery, N.Y.C., 1994, 2004, Child's Gallery, Boston, 1994, Br. Consulate, N.Y.C., 1995, Mus. Fine Art, Springfield, Mass., 1995, Kanagawa Prefectural Gallery, Japan, 1995, 97, Roopankar Mus. Fine Arts, India, 1995, Kala Inst., Calif., 1996, Frederick Baker, Chgo., 1996, Fed. Hall, N.Y.C., 1996, NY Transit Mus., N.Y.C., 1997, 2003, Mass. Coll. Art, Boston, 1997, Newark Pub. Libr., 1997, 2000, Daniel Peretz Gallery, N.Y.C., 1997, The Old Print Shop, 1998, 2001, 03, 04, 05, Krasdale Gallery, N.Y.C., 1998, Housatonic Mus. Art, Conn., 1998, Macau Mus. Art, 2000, Albrecht-Kemper Mus. Art, Mo., 2000, Springfield Art Mus., 2001, 05, Mus. Modern Art, N.Y.C., 2002, Mus. City N.Y., 1982, 2002, N.Y. Hist. Soc., N.Y.C., 2002, 2004, Susan Teller Gallery, 2004, UBS Paine Weber Art Gallery, 2002, NobleMaritime Collection, 2006, Hollar Soc., Prague, 2006; group shows inlcude AFP Gallery, N.Y.C., 2006, Noble Maritime Collection, S.I., N.Y., 2006; represented in permanent collections Mus. City of N.Y., N.Y. Pub. Libr., Taipei Mus., Printmaking Workshop, N.Y.C., Fogg Mus., Cambridge, Mass., Nat. Mus. Fine Art, Hanoi, Boston Pub. Libr., Davison Art Ctr., Middletown, Conn., Israel Mus., Jerusalem, British Mus., London, Libr. of Congress, Washington, Portland (Oreg.) Art Mus.; author: Journey of Faces, 1985, Mythic City & Friends. Recipient Watercolor Tr. award Washington Square Art Show, N.Y.C., 1976, Leo Meissner prize NAD, 1986, 94, Annual prize Audubon Artists, 1974, 96, 97, 98, 99, 2001, 02, Cash award Springfield Mus., 2005. Mem. Alliance Figurative Artists (program dir. 1982-85), Print Consortium, Printmaking Workshop, Boston Printmakers, Soc. Am. Graphic Artists (coun. 1995—, v.p. 1999-2002, pres. 2003—),Fedn. Modern Painters & Sculptors, Nat. Acad. Art. Jewish. Avocations: bird watching, travel. Home: 170 2nd Ave 7B New York NY 10003-5754 Studio: 27 Essex St Apt 5A New York NY 10002-4662

**SLOBODNIK, RICCI,** mathematician, educator; b. Belleville, Ill., Oct. 7, 1969; d. Robert L. Underwood and Diana L. Heilman; m. Jason W. Slobodnik, May 24, 1998. BS in Math., U. Utah, Salt Lake City, 1994; MEd in Tech. Leadership, U. Nev., Las Vegas, 2002. Math. educator Cimarron-Meml. H.S., Las Vegas, 2000—05, learning strategist, 2005—. V.p. So. Nev. Math. Coun., Las Vegas, Nev., 2003—04, pres., 2004—06. Grantee, Best Buy, 2004. Mem.: Nat. Coun. Tchrs. Math. (rep. Nev. Math. Coun. 2006). Personal E-mail: rxs453@interact.ccsd.net.

**SLOCOMBE, WALTER BECKER,** lawyer, former federal agency administrator; b. Albuquerque, Sept. 23, 1941; m. Ellen Seidman; children: Sarah Cody, Merrin Hayes, Benjamin William BA, Princeton U., 1963; Rhodes scholar, Balliol Coll., Oxford U., 1963-65; LL.B., Harvard U., 1968. Bar: D.C. 1970. Law clk. to Justice Abe Fortas, US Supreme Ct., Washington, 1968-69; mem. staff Nat. Security Coun., 1969-70; tech. assoc. Internat. Inst. Strategic Studies, London, 1970-71; assoc. Caplin & Drysdale, Washington, 1971—74, mem., 1974-76, 81-93, 2001—03, 2003—; prin. dep. asst. sec. for internat. security affairs US Dept Def., Washington, 1977—79, dep. undersec. for policy planning, 1979-81, prin. dep. under-sec. for policy planning, 1993-94, under-sec. for policy, 1994—2001; sr. advisor for nat. def. Coalition Provisional Authority, Baghdad, Iraq, 2003. Dir. US Dept. Def. Task Force on Strategic Arms Limitation Talks II (SALT II), 1977—81; mem. Commn. on the Intelligence Capabilities of the US Regarding Weapons of Mass Destruction, 2004. Rhodes scholar, 1963-65; recipient Disting. Pub. Svc. medal, 1981, 85, 97, 2001, 04, Joseph Kruzel award for Disting. Svc. in the Pursuit of Peace, 2004. Mem. ACLU, Coun. Fgn. Rels., Internat. Inst. Strategic Studies. Democrat. Home: Caplin & Drysdale 1 Thomas Cir Washington DC 20005 Office Phone: 202-862-5060. E-mail: wbs@capdab.com.

**SLOCUM, DONALD HILLMAN,** consumer products company executive; b. Flushing, N.Y., Jan. 6, 1930; s. John G. and Frances H. S.; m. June Manning, Sept. 22, 1952 (dec. 1976); children: Richard, Mark, Carol; m. Barbara M. Ruane, Nov. 1, 1985. BS, Davis and Elkins Coll., 1951; MS, U. Vt., 1956; PhD, Ohio State U., 1958; LLD, Fla. Tech. Inst., 1968; MBA, Rider Coll., 1971; Dr. Profl. Studies, Pace U., 1974; ScD, Davis and Elkins Coll., 2000. Rsch. chem. Charles Pfizer, Inc., Bklyn., 1954; rsch. scientist Procter & Gamble, Cin., 1958—60; mgr. product devel. E.I. DuPont de Nemours & Co., Wilmington, Del., 1960-68; dir. new ventures N.L. Industries, N.Y.C., 1968-71; dir. fin. planning Hoffmann LaRoche, Nutley, NJ, 1971-74; v.p. Curtiss-Wright Corp., Woodridge, NJ, 1974-78; sr. v.p. Masonite-USG/Internat. Paper, Chgo., 1978-85; pres. Doner-Viking Corp., Madison, NJ, 1985-87, Woodtec, Inc. subs. Masco, Taylor, Mich., 1987-89; Versitec Industries, 1996—. Author: New Venture Methodology, 1974; contbr. articles to tech. and bus. publs.; patentee in field. Lt. U.S. Army, 1951-54, Korea, Col. Res., ret. Achievements include patent of DuPont Corian. Home: 61 Chimney Ridge Dr Morristown NJ 07960-4722 Office: SRA 3400 Bee Ridge Rd Sarasota FL 34239-7223 Personal E-mail: drdslocum@optonline.net.

**SLOCUM, DONALD WARREN,** chemist, researcher; m. Laurel Hopper, 1990 (dec. May 1997); children from previous marriage: Warren, Matthew. BS in Chemistry, BA in English, U. Rochester; PhD in Chemistry, NYU, 1963. Postdoctoral rsch. assoc. Duke U., Durham, NC, 1963—64; asst. prof.

chemistry Carnegie Inst. Tech., Pitts., 1964—65; from asst. to assoc. prof. chemistry So. Ill. U., Carbondale, 1965—72, prof., 1972—81, adj. prof., 1981—84; program dir. chem. dynamics sect., chemistry divsn. NSF, Washington, 1984—85; program leader divsn. ednl. programs, sr. scientist chem. tech. divsn. Argonne Nat. Lab., Ill., 1985—90; head dept. chemistry We. Ky. U., Bowling Green, 1990—95, prof. chemistry, 1995—2005, emeritus prof. chemistry, 2005—. Sr. scientist Gulf R&D Co., Pitts., 1980-82; vis. prof. U. Ill., 1970, U. Bristol, Eng., 1973, U. Cin., 1976; vis. fellow U. Bristol, 1972; vis. lectr. Carnegie-Mellon U., 1983-84, U. Pitts., 1983-84; organizer symposia on organometallic chemistry and catalysis; bd. dirs. Ctrl. States Univs., Inc., 1986-88, Arts at Argonne, 1988-90; com. in field; mem. nat. organizing com. XV Internat. Conf. on Organometallic Chemistry Wayne State U., Detroit, 1990; mem. internat. adv. bd. XV Internat. Conf. on Organometallic Chemistry, Warsaw, 1992; mem. NSF/EPSCoR subcom., Ky., 1993-94; mem. coun. on organometal. rsch. Instnl. Liaison Rep. to We. Ky. U., 1995—Co-editor: Advances in Chemistry Series of Am. Chem. Soc., Vol. 230, 1992, Methane and Alkane Activation (Plenum), 1995; mem. editl. bd. Synthesis and Reactivity in Inorganic, Metal-Organic and Nano-Metal Chemistry, 1971—, Natural Product Rsch., 2006—; regional editor Letters in Organic Chemistry, 2004-05, mem. editl. bd., 2005—; contbr. over 80 articles to profl. jours., chpts. to books Recipient Rsch./Creativity award Ogden Coll. of Sci., Tech. and Health, We. Ky. U., 1996, Sci. award honoring Brian Andreen, Cottrell Coll. Sci., 1999. Mem. Am. Chem. Soc. (sec. gen. elect catalysis and surface sci. secretariat 1992, sec. gen. chair, organic divsn. rep. to catalysis and surface sci. secretariat, 1993-98, co-chmn. symposium, San Diego, 1994), Chem. Soc. Gt. Britain, Catalysis Soc., Bowling Green Chamber Singers, Sigma Xi. Avocations: music, literature, sports. Office: Western Ky U Dept Chemistry Bowling Green KY 42101 Office Phone: 270-745-5239. Business E-Mail: donald.slocum@wku.edu.

**SLOCUM, JUDITH ANN,** retired elementary school educator; b. Kimberly, Wis., Apr. 11, 1942; d. Julius Lawrence and Adele Van Handel; m. Richard Eugene Slocum, June 20, 1964; children: Catherine Jean Wolfla, Susan Marie. BS, U. Wis., LaCrosse, 1964; MS, Ind. U., Bloomington, 1983. Cert. English and speech tchr. Ind. Bd. Edn., 1966, reading specialist/middle sch. specialist Ind. Bd. Edn., 1983. English tchr. Northmont Schs., Englewood, Ohio, 1964—66, Ellettsville (Ind.) Schs., 1966—68, Martinsville (Ind.) Schs., 1974—80; reading specialist Washington Twp. Schs., Indpls., 1980—94, English tchr., bapt. chair, 1994—2004. Grant writer Martinsville Schs., 1978—80; in-service presenter on reading across the curriculum Washington Twp. Schs., Indpls., 1980—2004, co-authored curriculum document, 2000—04. Author: McGrammar, 2003. Mem.: Nat. Coun. Tchrs. of English (assoc.). Achievements include development of system of teaching grammar and writing in McGrammar. Avocations: sailing, swimming, reading. Home: 8876 Crystal River Dr Indianapolis IN 46240

**SLOCUM, ROBERT BIGNEY,** retired librarian; b. Brockton, Mass., Apr. 6, 1922; s. George Weeden and Florence Alice (Heustis) S.; m. Christine Stanfield, Aug. 23, 1953; children: Robert Stanfield, Kathryn Slocum Goodwin. BA, Boston U., 1946; MA, Columbia U., 1947; BSLS, Simmons Coll., 1949. Libr. intern Libr. of Congress, Washington, 1949-50; asst. to dir. librs. Simmons Coll., Boston, 1950-51; libr. cataloger, instr. U. Ill. Libr., Urbana, 1951-54; assoc. catalog libr. Cornell U. Libr., Ithaca, N.Y., 1954-88. Author: Sample Catalog Cards, 1962, Biographical Dictionaries and Related Works, 1967-78, 2d edit., 1986, Sample Cataloging Forms, 1968, rev. edit., 1980; editor Manual of Cataloging Procedures, 1959, rev. edit., 1969, New England in Fiction, 1994; contbr. articles to profl. jours. Active Am. for Dem. Action, Pub. Citizen, Am. Farmland Trust, steering bd. Cornell U. Retirees Vols. in Svc.; co-chmn. Dryden Bicentennial Com. With U.S. Army, 1942-45, ETO. Mem.: AARP, ALA, AAUP, Cornell U. Libr. Assoc., Newark Valley Hist. Soc., N.Y. State Hist. Assn., Libr. Congress Assoc., Dryden Hist. Soc., Am. Hist. Assn. (founder Nat. History Ctr.), Peace Action, Common Cause, Wilson Ctr. Assoc., Drake Group, Cornell Assn. Profs. Emeriti, Smithsonian Assoc. Presbyterian. Avocations: hiking, movies, literature. Home: 92 W Main St Dryden NY 13053-9706 E-mail: rbs8@cornell.edu.

**SLOCUM, ROSEMARIE,** physician services consultant, recruiter; b. Port Arthur, Tex., Dec. 19, 1948; d. Edly and Ella (McNeely) Raccard; m. James Rubenstein; 1 child from previous marriage, Blair Ashton Slocum. BS in Secondary Edn., La. State U., Baton Rouge, 1971; MA in Bus. Comm., Jones Internat. U., Englewood, Colo., 1999. Cert. tchr. La. Edn. specialist La. Dept. Occupl. Stds., Baton Rouge, 1971—74; account exec. UARCO, Inc., 1974—77; owner, broker Rosemarie Slocum Real Estate, 1977—85; physician recruiter MSI, New Orleans, 1985—86; assoc. dir. physician recruitment Physician Svcs. Cons., Fairfax, Va., 1986-88; spl. cons. Caswell/Winters Physician Search Cons., Milw., 1988—89; v.p. U.S. Med. Search, Inc. subs. of Caswell/Winters, 1988—89; dir. physician recruitment/mktg. East Range Clinics, Ltd., Virginia, Minn., 1989—91; pres. RSI Physician Svcs. Cons., Virginia, 1991—96, Mpls., 1996—. Office: RSI Physician Svcs Cons 3622 W 44th St Minneapolis MN 55410-1366 Office Phone: 612-703-0410. E-mail: rsrsi@earthlink.net.

**SLOMAN, MARVIN SHERK,** lawyer; b. Fort Worth, Apr. 17, 1925; s. Richard Jack and Lucy Janette (Sherk) S.; m. Margaret Jane Dinwiddie, Apr. 11, 1953; children: Lucy Carter, Richard Dinwiddie. BA, U. Tex., 1948; LLB with honors, 1950. Bar: Tex. 1950, N.Y. 1951. Assoc. Sullivan & Cromwell, N.Y.C., 1950-56, Carrington, Coleman, Sloman & Blumenthal LLP and predecessor, Dallas, 1956-60, ptnr., 1960-97; sr. counsel, 1998—. Office: Carrington Coleman Sloman & Blumenthal LLP 901 Main St Ste 5500 Dallas TX 75202-3767

**SLOMANSON, LLOYD HOWARD,** architect, musician, photographer; b. NYC, July 31, 1928; s. Albert Jerome and Dorothea (Jacobson) S.; m. Joan Barbara Kanel; children: Peter, Eric. BArch, Syracuse U., 1949. Registered architect, 18 states including N.Y. and N.J.; NCARB; registered profl. planner, N.J. Archtl. draftsman Rich & Conn Architects, Bklyn., 1949-50; project architect Fordyce & Hamby/Raymond Loewy, N.Y.C., 1951-53; project architect, assoc. ptnr. Serge P. Petroff, Architect, N.Y.C., 1953-58; project dir. Robert W. Hegardt, Architect, N.Y.C., 1959-60; project architect, ptnr. Fordyce & Hamby Assocs., N.Y.C., 1960-67; ptnr. Fordyce, Hamby & Kennerly, N.Y.C., 1967-69, Hamby, Kennerly & Slomanson, N.Y.C., 1969-72, Kennerly, Slomanson & Smith, N.Y.C., 1972-81; mng. ptnr. Slomanson, Smith & Barresi, N.Y.C., 1981-99; pvt. practice, 1999—. Arbitrator Am. Arbitration Assn. and NASD Dispute Resolution, N.Y.C. Author articles. Served with U.S. Army, 1950-51. Recipient 1st prize for design S.I. C. of C., 1967, 84. Mem. AIA, N.Y. Soc. Architects (Store of Yr. award 1985, Design award 1993), N.Y. State Assn. Architects, Bldg. Ofcls. Conf. Am., Univ. Club, The Players. Avocations: music, photography. Office: 137 W 78th St New York NY 10024-6702 Office Phone: 917-441-0067. Personal E-mail: woodpics@aol.com.

**SLONAKER, NORMAN DALE,** lawyer; b. Havre, Mont., Sept. 16, 1940; s. Frederick and Agnes (Monson) S.; m. Helen Bogumil, Aug. 29, 1964. BS, U. Wash., Seattle, 1962; LLM, Harvard U., 1965. Bar: NY 1966. Assoc. Sidley Austin LLP, NYC, 1965—72, ptnr., 1973—. Office Phone: 212-839-5356. Business E-Mail: nslonaker@sidley.com.

**SLONCZEWSKI, CRAIG (CRAIG SLON),** composer; b. Poughkeepsie, N.Y., Mar. 27, 1958; s. John and Esther Slonczewski. BA Liberal Arts, Sarah Lawrence Coll., 1982. Composer: (unpub. symphonic music) Sorrow's Road, Yukiku and Robert Lunday, 2005—; sound designer with film dir. Abbe Chopra, N.Y.C., 2004; composer (with film dir.): Steve Koh, 2006, Craig McNeil, 2005; composer: (with video artist) Molly Stevens, 2004. Music therapist Royal Blind Sch., Edinburgh, Scotland, 1986, Stafford Ctr., Edinburgh, Scotland, 1987—88. Recipient Craft award for Original Score, First Run Film Festival, 2003; grant, Artlink, 1986. Mem.: Am. Music Ctr. Achievements include design of audio computer; an electro-acoustic prepared guitar; development of titanium sheet percussion instrument; prepared piano. Home: 172 Prospect Pk W Brooklyn NY 11215 Office: Aracu Studio 172 Prospect Pk W 2R Brooklyn NY 11215 Personal E-mail: aracu@juno.com.

**SLONE, SANDI,** artist; b. Boston, Oct. 1, 1939; d. Louis and Ida (Spind) Sudikoff; children: Erric Solomon, Jon Solomon. Student, Boston Mus. Fine Arts Sch., 1970-73; BA magna cum laude, Wellesley Coll., 1974. Sr., grad. painting faculty Boston Mus. Fine Arts Sch./Tufts U., 1975—; instr. grad. program Sch. Visual Art, N.Y.C., 1989-90; lectr. painting Harvard U., Cambridge, Mass., 1982; artist-in-residence City Hall, Barcelona, 1987, 1989; NY Artists resident Santa Fe Art Inst., 2002. Vis. artist Triangle Artists Workshop, NY, 1982, 87, 90; co-founder, dir. Art/Omi Internat. Artists Found., NYC, 1992—; bd. dirs. The Fields Sculpture Pk. and ART OMI, 1991-. One-woman shows include ICA, Boston, 1977, Harcus Krakow Gallery, Boston, 1978, 79, 80, 82, 84, 86, Acquavella Contemporary Art, N.Y., 1977, 79, 80, 82, 84, Stephen Rosenberg Gallery, N.Y., 1988, Levinson Kane Gallery, Boston, 1989, Smith Jariwala Gallery, London, 1990, Jersey City Mus., 1996, The Artists Mus., Lodz, Poland, 1997, Cristinerose Gallery, N.Y.C., 1999, Savage Gallery, Portland, Oreg., 2001, Art Resources Transfer, NYC, 2002, The Santa Fe Art Inst., N.Mex., 2002, The Tower Gallery, Hong Kong, 2004; exhibited in group shows at Mus. Fine Arts, Boston, 1977, Corcoran Gallery of Art 35th Biennial, Washington, 1977, Edmonton Art Mus., 1977, 85, Hayden Gallery MIT, Cambridge, Mass., 1978, New Generation Andre Emmerich Gallery, N.Y., 1980-81, Am. Ctr., Paris, 1980-81, Amerika Haus, Berlin, 1980-81, Carpenter Ctr., Harvard U., Ctr. de la Cultura Contemporania, Barcelona, 1987, Federated Union of Black Artists, Johannesburg, South Africa, 1989, Jan Weiss Gallery, N.Y., 1990, Olympia Internat. Art Fairs, London, 1991, Gallery Korea, N.Y., 1992, Klarfeld Perry Gallery, N.Y., 1994, Out of the Blue Gallery, Edinburgh, Scotland, 1994, Gallery One, Toronto, 1996, Fine Arts Ctr., U. R.I., Kingston, 1996, Crieger Dane Gallery, Boston, 1996, Visual Arts Gallery, N.Y., 1997, TransHudson Gallery, N.Y., 1997, Butler Inst. of Am. Art, Youngstown, Ohio, 1998, 45th Biennial Corcoran Mus. Art, Washington, 1998, Lombard-Freid Fine Arts, N.Y., 1999, 00, Cyclorama, Boston, 2000, Cristinerose Gallery, N.Y., 2001, Queens U., Toronto, 2001, Art Resources Transfer, 2002, U. Cambridge, Eng., 2003, Art in Gen., NYC, 2004, Savage Gallery, Portland, Oreg., 2004, The Transformer Rm. Queens U. Belfast, Ireland, 2006, others; represented in permanent collections Mus. Modern Art, N.Y.C., Mus. Contemporary Art, Barcelona, Mus. Fine Arts, Boston, Hirshhorn Mus., Washington, Corcoran Gallery & Mus. Art, Washington. Mus. Fine Arts Boston fellow, 1977, 81; Ford Found. grantee, 1979. Studio: 13 Worth St New York NY 10013-2922 E-mail: sslone@rcn.com.

**SLONE, WESLEY SHAUN,** network engineer; b. Huntsville, Ala., Sept. 2, 1977; s. Connie Earp and Donald Slone, David Michael Earp (Stepfather). B in MIS, Auburn U., Ala., 1999. Cert. CCNA Cisco Systems, 2006. STAT group (top tier support group) ITC—Deltacom, Huntsville, 2000—03; network engr. Sanmina-SCI, Huntsville, 2004—. Contbr. articles to coll. newspaper. Mem.: Mensa. Home: 2104 Rodgers Dr Huntsville AL 35811 Personal E-mail: wesslone@yahoo.com.

**SLONEM, HUNT,** artist; b. Kittery, Maine, July 18, 1951; s. Charles and Louise W. Slonem. Student, Skowhegan Sch. Painting and Sculpture, 1972; BA, Tulane U., 1973. Represented by Marlborough Gallery. Numerous one-man shows, 1977—, including Tilden-Foley Gallery, New Orleans, 1991, Charlotte Milburn Fine Art Mus., Oslo, 1991, Pulitzer Gallery, Amsterdam, 1991, Witteveen Gallery, Amsterdam, 1991, Marlborough Chelsea, 2005; numerous others; exhibited in numerous group shows, 1977—, including Laguna Gloria Mus., Austin, Tex., 1990, Bergen Mus. Art & Sci., Paramus, NJ, 1990, Meredith Long Gallery, Houston, 1990, Marlborough Gallery, NYC, Solomon R. Guggenheim Mus., NYC, Centro Cultural Recoleta, Buenos Aires, 2000, Heriard Cimino Gallery, New Orleans, 2000, Vanier Gallery, Scottsdale, Ariz., 2000, Harmon Meek Gallery, Naples, Fla., numerous others; represented in numerous permanent collections Metropolitan Mus. Art, NYC, Contemporary Mus., Honolulu, Guggenheim Mus., NYC, Miro Found., Spain, Chrysler Mus., Norfolk, Va., Columbus (Ohio) Mus. Art, Oklahoma Art Ctr., Oklahoma City, Portland (Maine) Mus. Art, Wichita (Kans.) Art Mus., many others; exclusively represented by Marlborough Gallery, NYC. Resides in his legendary NYC loft with his seventy exotic birds. McDowell fellow, 1983, 84, 86, Ragsdale Found. fellow, 1983; Elizabeth T. Greenshields Found. grantee, 1976, NEA grantee, 1991; recipient award Millay Colony, 1982. Avocation: aviculture. Mailing: c/o Marlborough Gallery 40 West 57th St New York NY 10019

**SLOSBERG, MIKE,** advertising executive; b. Phila., Aug. 29, 1934; s. Sam M. and Florence (Frank) S.; m. Joan Shidler, Aug. 29, 1957 (div. 1984); children: Sydney Ellen (dec.), Robert Morton; m. Janet Cohn, June 10, 1987. BSBA, U. Denver, 1960. With Young & Rubicam, Inc., N.Y.C., 1960-78; pres. Wunderman, Rocotta & Kline, N.Y.C., 1978-83; exec. v.p., exec. creative dir. Marsteller, Inc., N.Y.C., 1983-84, Bozell Jacobs, Kenyon & Eckhardt, N.Y.C., 1984-86, pres. direct mktg. div., 1986-87; exec. creative dir. Bronner Slosberg Humphrey, Boston, 1987-96; vice chmn., chief creative officer Digitas (formerly Bronner Slosberg Humphrey), Boston, 1996-2000; co-founder Digitas, Inc.; ret., 2003. Author: The August Strangers, 1978, The Hitler Error, 2006. Avocation: writing novels. Personal E-mail: mslosberg@digitas.com.

**SLOSBURG-ACKERMAN, JILL ROSE,** artist, educator; b. Omaha, Aug. 28, 1948; d. Harold Walter and Marion (Gill) Slosburg; m. James Sloss Ackerman, Aug. 8, 1987; 1 child, Jesse August Ackerman. Diploma, Boston Mus. Sch., 1971; BFA, Tufts U., 1971, MFA, 1983. Prof. art Mass. Coll. Art, Boston, 1973—; vis. artist Cranbrook Acad. Art, Bloomfield, Mich., 1993. One-woman shows include Harcus-Krakow-Rosen-Sonnabend Gallery, Boston, 1978, 1980, Helen Shlien Gallery, 1980, 1982, Cohen Arts Ctr., Tufts U., Medford, Mass., 1982, Van Buren/Brazellon/Cutting Gallery, Cambridge, Mass., 1985, Genovese Gallery, Boston, 1995, Manwaring Gallery Cumings Art Ctr., Conn. Coll., New London, 1995, Rose Art Mus., Brandeis U., Waltham, Mass., 1996, Atrium Gallery, U. Mass., Dartmouth, 1999, Judy Ann Goldman Fine Art, Boston, 1999, 2004, exhibited in group shows at Naga Gallery, 1980, DeCordova Mus., Lincoln, Mass., 1980, Jewett Art Ctr., Wellesley, Mass., 1982, Helen Shlien Gallery, Boston, 1982, Cherry Stone Gallery, Wellfleet, Mass., 1984, Quadrum Gallery, Chestnut Hill, Mass., 1985, Fed. Res. Gallery, Boston, 1986, Danforth Mus., 1986, Conseil de la Sculpture, Montreal, 1986, North Hall Gallery, Boston, 1987, Artists Found. Gallery, 1990, Mus. Decorative Arts, Prague, 1991, Nancy Margolis Gallery, N.Y.C., 1991, Bellevue (Wash.) Art Mus., 1992, Artwear, N.Y., 1992, Genovese Gallery, Albany, N.Y., 1992, Judy Ann Goldman Fine Art, Boston, 1997, 2002, Mills Gallery, 1997—98, 2004, Boston Mus. Fine Arts, 1999, DeCordova Mus., Lincoln, 2000, Nat. Mus. China, Beijing, 2001, Forest Hills Cemetery, Boston, 2002, 2004, Coll. Holy Cross, Worcester, Mass., 2003, Fuller Craft Mus., 2005, Represented in permanent collections J. L. Brandeis & Sons, Omaha, Mass. Coll. Art, Boston, Boston Pub. Libr., City of Cambridge, Forest Hills Cemetery, Jamaica Plain, Mass.; contbr. articles to profl. jours. Founder mem. Boston Women's Action Coalition; bd. dirs. Cambridge (Mass.) Multi-Cultural Ctr., Gallery at Green St., 1993. Recipient Patricia Jellinek Hallowell prize for Jewelry, 1984, Disting. Svc. award, Mass. Coll. Art, 1980, 4th prize sterling silver design competition, Nat. Guild Sterling Silversmiths, 1970; fellow, Haystack Mountain Sch. Crafts, 1972, 1976, Nat. Endowment Arts, 1974, 1986, The Artists Found., 1984, Mary Ingraham Bunting Inst., 1985—86; grantee, Artist's Resource Trust, 2001, New Eng. Art Critics Assn., 2004, 2006; Profl. Devel. grantee, Mass. Coll. Art, 1987, Polaroid Corp. Photography grantee, 1988, New Eng. Found. Arts fellow, 1998, Mass. Cultural Coun. Artist's grantee, 1999, 2006. Jewish. Home: 12 Coolidge Hill Rd Cambridge MA 02138-5510 Studio: One Fitchburg St Apt C415 Somerville MA 02143-2128 Office Phone: 617-625-4056. Personal E-mail: jsackerman44@comcast.net.

**SLOSS, JOHN,** lawyer; b. Detroit, Apr. 29, 1956; s. Richard and Marjory (Feerer) S. BA, U. Mich., 1978; JD, U. Mich. Sch. Law, 1981. Bar: N.Y. Assoc. Cahill, Gordon & Reindel, N.Y.C., 1981-84, Parker, Auspitz, Neeseman & Delehanty, N.Y.C., 1984-87; from assoc. to ptnr. Morrison & Foerster, N.Y.C., 1987-93; pvt. practice law N.Y.C., 1993—; mng. ptnr. Sloss Law Office LLP/Cinetic Media Inc., N.Y.C.; founding ptnr. Ind. Digital Entertainment (InDigEnt), 1999—. Exec. producer movies The Ballad of Little Jo, The

Secret of Roan Inish, Before Sunrise, American Buffalo, She's the One, Lone Star, Ulee's Gold, The Newton Boys, The Last Days of Disco, The Fog of War, Pieces of April, Far From Heaven, Before Sunset; sales agent (through Cinetic Media) for Super Size Me, Napoleon Dynamite. Bd. dirs. Dance Theatre Workshop, N.Y.C., 1986—. Ind. Feature Project, N.Y.C., 1996—. Office: Sloss Law Office LLP 555 West 25th St Fourth Floor New York NY 10001

**SLOSSON, CONSTANCE SWEET,** retired music educator; b. New Brighton, Pa., Jan. 31, 1942; d. W. Coburn, Jr. and Nancy McIlwain Sweet; m. George F. Slosson, Aug. 15, 1964; children: Deborah Tilmont, Sharon Bucks, Barbara Boulerice, Ronald. BS in Christian edn., Baldwin-Wallace Coll., Berea, Ohio, 1964; MS in music edn., SUNY, Potsdam, 1963—66. Cert. Music Edn. K-12 NY State Edn. Dept., 1966. Music tchr. Cumberland Head Elem. Sch., Plattsburgh, NY, 1963—67; elem. music tchr. St. Mary's Acad., Champlain, NY, 1989—85; music tchr. Northside Elem. Sch., Peru, NY, 1986—89, Plattsburgh City Sch. Dist., 1989—97; pvt. music instrn. Slosson Music Studios, Plattsburgh, 1997—. Ch. organist Glenville Presbyn. Ch., Cleve., 1957—60, Plattsburgh AFB Chapel, 1963—66, First Meth. Ch., 1968—71; asst. choir dir. Ch. Nazarene, 2001—. Mem., com. chmn. Plattsburgh Mothers Club, 1968—74; music chmn., gen. co-chm. BiCentennial Celebration 1976, Chazy, 1974—76; co-chairman West Chazy BiCentennial Field Days, 1974—76; girl scout troop leader Chazy Jr. Girl Scout Troop, NY, 1974—82; tchr. Congl. Ch., Berea, Ohio, 1961—63; ch. sch. tchr., supt. Chazy Presbyn. Ch., 1974—81; ch. sch. tchr. Ch. Nazarene, 1986—89; mem., officer West Chazy Grange #979, 1964—90. Mem.: AAUW (rec. sec. 1968—71), Am. Orff Schulwerk Assns., Clinton County Music Educators Assn. (corresponding sec. 1965—68), Music Educators Nat. Conf., NY State Sch. Music Assn., NY State Ret. Tchrs. Assn. (life). Avocations: singing, swimming, travel, mentoring. Home: 76 Slosson Rd West Chazy NY 12992

**SLOTKIN, MARVIN BERNARD,** surgeon; b. Bklyn., Sept. 29, 1931; s. Mark and Lena (Tuckman) S.; m. Evelyn Ruth Kroll, Sept. 6, 1959; children: David, Michael, Terri. BA, NYU, 1952; MD, U. Tenn., 1956. Diplomate Am. Bd. Surgery. Intern Michael Reese Hosp., Chgo., 1957; fellow exptl. surgery U. Miami Jackson Meml. Hosp., 1958; resident surgery U. Miami, 1958—61, chief resident surgery, 1961—62; pvt. practice surgery, 1962-95; ret. Fellow ACS, Southeastern Surg. Congress; mem. Beta Beta Beta, Alpha Omega Alpha. Jewish. Personal E-mail: evmar123@yahoo.com.

**SLOTKIN, RICHARD SIDNEY,** literature educator; b. Bklyn., Nov. 8, 1942; s. Herman and Roselyn B. (Seplowitz) S.; m. Iris F. Shupack, June 23, 1963; 1 child, Joel Elliot. BA, Bklyn. Coll., 1963; PhD, Brown U., 1967; MA (hon.), Wesleyan U., Middletown, Conn., 1976. Mem. faculty Wesleyan U., 1966—, prof. English, 1976—, Olin prof., 1982—, chmn. dept. Am. studies, 1976—. Author: Regeneration Through Violence: The Mythology of the American Frontier, 1600-1860, 1973 (Albert Beveridge award Am. Hist. Assn.), (with J.K. Folsom) So Dreadfull a Judgement: Puritan Responses to King Philip's War, 1675-1677, 1978, The Crater: A Novel of the Civil War, 1980, The Fatal Environment: The Myth of the Frontier in the Age of Industrialization, 1800-1890, 1985, The Return of Henry Starr, 1988, Gunfighter Nation: The Myth of the Frontier in Twentieth Century America, 1992 (National Book award nominee, 1993), Abe: A Novel of the Young Lincoln, 2000 (Michael Shaara Civil War Fiction award, 2000), Lost Battalions: The Great War and the Crisis of American Nationality, 2005; and articles. Fellow Center Humanities; fellow Wesleyan U., 1969-70, 74-75, 80—; fellow NEH, 1973-74, Rockefeller Found., 1976-77; recipient Don D. Walker prize AQ; lit. award Little Big Horn Assocs., 1986 Fellow Soc. Am. Historians; mem. AAUP, PEN, Am. Film Inst., Am. Studies Assn. (Mary Turpie prize for tchg. and program-bldg. 1995), Am. Hist. Assn., Orgn. Am. Historians, Authors Guild. Jewish. Office: Wesleyan U Ctr For The Americas Middletown CT 06459-0001

**SLOTKIN, TODD,** diversified financial services company executive; b. Detroit, Mar. 19, 1953; s. Hugo and Babette Slotkin; m. Judy Scavone, Jan. 30, 1988; children: Matthew, William, Thomas, Peter. BS, Cornell U., 1974, MBA, 1975. With Citicorp, 1975-92, sr. credit officer, 1984-92, head divsn. corp. fin., 1988-90, sr. mng. dir., 1990-92; with MacAndrews & Forbes Holdings, Inc., N.Y.C., 1992—, sr. v.p., 1992-98, exec. v.p., 1998—, CFO, 1999—; dir. CBIZ, Inc., 2003—. Dir. Food Allergy Initiative, 1999—. Home: 888 Park Ave Apt 12 B New York NY 10021 Office: MacAndrews & Forbes Holding 35 E 62nd St New York NY 10021-8032

**SLOTNICK, MORTIMER H.,** artist; b. N.Y.C., Nov. 7, 1920; s. Max S. and Sarah B. S.; m. Phyllis June Gluckin, July 26, 1953; children: Debra Jan, Mark Stuart. BSS, CCNY, 1942; MA, Tchrs. Coll., Columbia U., 1942. Tchr. visual arts, public schs., New Rochelle, NY, 1946-64; supr. arts and humanities City Sch. Dist., 1964-72; prin. Davis Elem. Sch., 1972-84. Adj. prof. art CCNY, 1964-72; prof. art. New Rochelle, N.Y., 1972-78; adj. prof. edn. Pace U., 1988-93. One-man shows include Ada Ahrtz Galleries, N.Y.C., 1959, Westport (Conn.) Art Gallery, 1986, New Rochelle Coun. on the Arts, 1989; exhibited in group shows Nat. Acad. N.Y., World Trade Ctr., N.Y.C., Lever House, N.Y.C., Am. Artists Profl. League, Nat. Arts Club, Salmagundi Club, Kent (Conn.) Art Gallery; represented in permanent collections Nat. Mus. Am. Art, Smithsonian Instn., New Britain Mus. Am. Art, Johnson Mus. Art Cornell U., Nat. Archives, Washington, Truman Home, Independence, Mo., F.D.R. Mus., Hyde Park, N.Y.; also pvt. and corp. collections; works published in Artists of Am. Calendar. Mem. City Art Commn. New Rochelle, 1977-80. Served with AUS, 1942-46, ETO, PTO. Mem. N.Y. Artists Equity Assn., Allied Artists Am., Am. Artists Profl. League, Coll. Art Assn., Nat. Assn. Humanities Edn., Art Pub., Am. Artists Group, Bernard Picture Co., McLeery-Cumming Co., Donald Art. Co., Scafa-Tornabene Art Publ., A. B. Franklin Gallery, Internet, Masons. Home and Office: 43 Amherst Dr New Rochelle NY 10804-1814 E-mail: Phyllmor@gateway.net, phyllmor@aol.com. *An artist must respect the totality of his art. His work must express his integrity, his honesty and his wish to communicate with the viewer. It must strive toward the sublime. Anything less is unworthy of being called art.*

**SLOTNICK, ROBERT D,** food products executive; B in bus. adminstrn., Fairleigh Dickinson U. Systems analyst to mgr. of distbn. systems Warner-Lambert Co., 1980—85; MIS dir. AFI, 1985, v.p. ops., 1987, gen. mgr., 1992, co-pres., 1997; sr. v.p. Performance Food Group, 2003—, CIO, 1999—. Office: Performance Food Group P O Box 29269 Richmond VA 23242

**SLOTSVE, GEORGE AARON,** economist, educator, consultant; b. Estevan, Saskatchewan, Can., Sept. 5, 1959; s. Stanley and Mary Elizabeth Slotsve. BA honors, Queen's U., Kingston, 1981; MA in Econ., U. We. Ont., 1982; MS in Econ., U. Wis., 1985, PhD in Econ., 1989. Prof. Vanderbilt U., Nashville, 1988—96, No. Ill. U., DeKlab, 1996—. Vis. prof. Queen's U., Kingston, Ont., Canada, 1992, U. Philippines, Quezon City, 1999. Author: (book) Are We Becoming Two Societies?: Income Polarization and the Myth of the Declining Middle Class in Canada. Office: Northern Ill Univ Dept Econ Zulauf Hall Dekalb IL 60115 Business E-Mail: gslotsve@niu.edu.

**SLOUJITEL, JACOB BEN,** mathematics professor, researcher; b. Moscow, Nov. 1, 1945; arrived in U.S., 1994; s. Ben Leo Sloujitel and Bertha Gilel Sloujitel-Shamis; m. Mira Noah Rudaya, Aug. 31, 1968; children: Kate, Lev. BS, Inst. Elecs. and Mining Mechanics, 1966; MS, Moscow Mining U., 1968; PhD, State Rsch. Inst., 1976. Cons. Acad. Natural Sci., Moscow, 1993—95; prof., coord. math. Globe Inst. Tech., NYC, 1997—. Adj. prof. physics CUNY, 1995—98; vis. prof. math. Ramapo Coll., Mahwah, NJ, 1997—, Fairleigh Dickinson U., Madison, 2002—; pres. J and M Smartel Cons. Ctr., Fair Lawn, 1999—. Author: Underground Melting of Sulphur, 1981. Mgr. Soccer Club, Fair Lawn, 1994—. Fellow, State Rsch. Inst. Moscow, 1968—94. Mem.: Math. Assn. Avocations: soccer, ping pong/table tennis, chess. Home: 38 Beverly Ct Fair Lawn NJ 07410 Office: Globe Inst Tech 291 Broadway New York NY 10007 Office Phone: 212-349-4330 x 151. Business E-Mail: jsloujit@globe.edu.

**SLOVIK, SANDRA LEE,** retired art educator; b. Elizabeth, N.J., Mar. 22, 1943; d. Edward Stanley and Frances (Garbus) S. BA, Newark State Coll., 1965, MA, 1970. Cert. art tchr. Art tchr. Holmdel (N.J.) Twp. Bd. Edn., 1965-99, ret., 1999. Computer art in-sv. tng. Holmdel Bd. Edn., 1990; computer art workshop Madison (N.J.) Bd. Edn., 1991; presenter Nat. Edn. Computer Conv., 1999. Charter supporter, mem. Statue of Liberty/Ellis Island Found., 1976—; charter supporter Sheriffs' Assn. N.J., 1993—; mem. PTA, Holmdel, 1965—. Recipient Curriculum award NJ ASCD, 1992; grantee Holmdel Bd. Edn., 1989, 90, N.J. Bus., Industry, Sci., Edn. Consortium, 1990. Mem. NEA, Nat. Art Edn., Assn., N.J. Art Educators Assn., N.J. Edn. Assn., Monmouth County Edn. Assn., Holmdel Twp. Edn. Assn. (sr. bldg. rep. 1977-79). Avocations: travel, sports. Office: Village Sch 67 Mccampbell Rd Holmdel NJ 07733-2299 E-mail: sslovik@hotmail.com.

**SLOVITER, DOLORES KORMAN,** federal judge; b. Phila., Sept. 5, 1932; d. David and Tillie Korman; m. Henry A. Sloviter, Apr. 3, 1969 (dec. May 2003); 1 child, Vikki Amanda. AB in Econs. with distinction, Temple U., 1953, LHD (hon.), 1986; LLB magna cum laude, U. Pa., 1956; LLD (hon.), Dickinson Sch. Law, 1984, U. Richmond, 1992, Widener U., 1994. Bar: Pa. 1957. From assoc. to ptnr. Dilworth, Paxson, Kalish, Kohn & Levy, Phila., 1956—69; mem. Harold E. Kohn PA, Phila., 1969—72; assoc. prof. Temple U. Law Sch., Phila., 1972—74, prof., 1974—79; judge U.S. Ct. Appeals (3rd cir.), Phila., 1979—, chief judge, 1991—98. Bd. overseers U. Pa. Law Sch., 1993—99; bd. trustees Nat. Constitution Ctr., 1998—; mem. Jud. Conf. of U.S., 1991—98. Chair Pa. Rhodes Scholarship Selection Com., 2003—04; mem. S.E. region Pa. Gov.'s Conf. on Aging, 1976—79, Com. of 70, 1976—79; U.S. com. Bicentennial Constn., 1987 90; com. on Rules of Practice and Procedure, 1990—93; com. to Rev. Cir. Coun. Conduct and Disability Orders, 2004—; mem. Dist. IV Selection Com., Rhodes Scholarship Competitions, 2005—; trustee The Pa. Women's Forum, 1996—, Jewish Publ. Soc. Am., 1983—89. Recipient Juliette Low medal, Girl Scouts Greater Phila., Inc., 1990, Honor award, Girls High Alumnae Assn., 1991, Jud. award, Pa. Bar Assn., 1994, James Wilson award, U. Pa., 1996, Cert. of Honor award, Temple U., 1996; Disting. Fulbright scholar, Chile, 1990. Mem.: ABA, Phila. Bar Assn. (gov. 1976—78, Sandra Day O'Connor award 1997), Am. Judicature Soc. (bd. dirs. 1990—95), Nat. Assn. Women Judges, Am. Law Inst., Fed. Judges Assn., Fed. Bar Assn., The Pa. Women's Forum, Order of Coif (pres. U. Pa. chpt. 1975—77), Phi Beta Kappa. Office: US Ct Appeals 18614 US Courthouse 601 Market St Philadelphia PA 19106-1713*

**SLOWIK, RICHARD ANDREW,** air force officer; b. Detroit, Sept. 9, 1939; s. Louis Stanley ad Mary Jean (Zaucha) S.; 1 stepchild, Amber Dawn Evans. BS, U.S. Air Force Acad., 1963; BS in Bus. Adminstrn., No. Mich. U., 1967; LLB, LaSalle Extension U., 1969; MBA, Fla. Tech. U., 1972; MS in Adminstrn., Ga. Coll., 1979; MA, Georgetown U., 1983; postgrad. cert., Va. Poly. Inst. and State U., 1986. Commd. 1st lt. U.S. Air Force, 1963, advanced through grades to lt. col; pilot Craig AFB, Ala., 1963-64, Sawyer AFB, Mich., 1964-68; forward air contr. Pacific Air Forces, South Vietnam, 1968-69; pilot SAC, McCoy AFB, Fla., 1969-71; asst. prof. aerospace studies Va. Poly. Inst. and State U., Blacksburg, 1972-76; br. chief current ops. br. Robins AFB, Ga., 1976-80; asst. dep. chief ops. group Hdqrs Air Force, Pentagon, Washington, 1980-82; Western Hemisphere and Pacific Area desk officer Nat. Mi. Command Ctr., Pentagon, Washignton, 1982-83; mil. rep Ops. Ctr., Dept. State, Washington, 1983-85; ops. officer 97th Bombardment Wing, Blytheville AFB, Ark., 1985-87; chief base ops. and tng. divsn. 97th Combat Support Group, Blytheville AFB, Ark., 1987-88; chief airfield mgmt. divsn. Eaker AFB, Ark., 1988-91; freelance writer, 1991—. Contbr. articles to profl. jours. Group ops. officer CAP, Marquette, Mich., 1967-67, Orlando, Fla., 1970-72, sr. programs officer, Blacksburg, 1972-76, Warner Robins, Ga., 1976-80, wing plans and programs officer, Washington, 1980—. Decorated Def. Meritorious Svc. medal, 10 Air medals, 3 Air Force Meritorious Svc. medals, 2 Commendation medals, Corss of Gallantry with palm, Presdl. Legion of Merit, Presdl. Medal of Merit (3), Presdl. Achievement award (3), others; recipient Bill Baker Short Story award Miss. County Writers Guild, 1995. Mem. Acad. of Mgmt., Air Force Assn., Cato Inst., Heritage Found., Mil. Order World Wars, Am. Def. Preparedness Assn., Am. Security Coun., Order of Daedalians. Roman Catholic. Home and Office: 1708 N Broadway St Blytheville AR 72315-1320 E-mail: slowik@blyonline.com, ras6@georgetown.edu.

**SLOYAN, GERARD STEPHEN,** theology studies educator, priest; b. N.Y.C., Dec. 13, 1919; s. Jerome James and Marie (Kelley) S. AB, Seton Hall U., 1940; S.T.L., Cath. U. Am., 1944, PhD, 1948; DLitt, Seton Hall U., 1984; HHD, St. Ambrose U., 1995. Ordained priest Roman Cath. Ch., 1944. Asst. pastor in, Trenton, Maple Shade, N.J., 1947-50; mem. faculty Cath. U. Am., Washington, 1950-67, chmn. dept. religion, 1957-67; prof. N.T. studies Temple U., Phila., 1967-90, chmn. dept. religion, 1970-74, 84-86. Disting. lectr. Georgetown U., 1997—; vis. prof. Cath. U. Am., Washington, 1992—, Iowa State U., 1995. English editor: N.T., The New American Bible, 1970; author: Jesus on Trial: A Study of the Gospels, 2d edit., 2006, Historical Atlas of the Religions of the World, 1974, Is Christ the End of the Law?, 1978, Jesus in Focus, 1983, 2d edit., 1993, The Jesus Tradition, 1986, John: "Interpretation" Commentary, 1988, Jesus, Redeemer and Divine Word, 1989, What Are They Saying About John?, 1991, rev. edit., 2006, Walking in the Truth: 1, 2, and 3 John, 1995, The Crucifixion of Jesus, History, Myth, Faith, 1995, Open Catholicism, The Tradition at Its Best, 1997, Holy Week and Easter, 1999, What Men Owe to Women, Men's Voices from World Religions, 2001, Preaching from the Lectionary: An Exegetical Commentary, 2005, Why Jesus Died, 2004. Recipient Pro Ecclesia et Pontifice medal, 1970, Johannes Quasten medal Cath U. Am., 1985, Michael Mathis award Notre Dame Ctr. Pastoral Liturgy, 1994. Mem. AAUP, Cath. Bibl. Assn., Soc. Bibl. Lit., Cath. Theol. Soc. Am. (John Courtney Murray award 1981, pres. 1993-94), Coll. Theology Soc. (pres. 1964-66), Liturg. Conf. (pres. 1962-64, v.p. 1970-71, 75-88, chmn. bd. dirs. 1980-88), N.Am. Acad. Liturgy (Berakah award 1986). Democrat. Personal E-mail: gerard.sloyan@att.net.

**SLOYAN, PATRICK JOSEPH,** journalist; b. Stamford, Conn., Jan. 11, 1937; s. James Joseph and Annamae (O'Brien) Sloyan; m. Phyllis Hampton, Nov. 19, 1960; children: Nora, Amy, Patrick, John. BS, U. Md., 1963. Reporter Albany (N.Y.) Times-Union, 1957—58, Balt. News Post, 1958—60, UPI, Washington, 1960—69, Hearst News Svc., Washington, 1969—74, Newsday, Washington, 1974—81, bur. chief London, 1981—86, Washington, 1986—88, sr. corr., 1988—2001; assoc. editor Digital Journalist.org, 2002—. Dir. Fund for Investigative Journalism, Washington, 1987—. With U.S. Army, 1955—57. Recipient Best Writing award, Am. Soc. Newspaper Editors, 1982, War Reporting award, George Polk Awards, 1992, Pulitzer Prize for internat. reporting, 1992, Raymond Clapper award, 1996; Alicia Patterson Found. fellow, 2000. Mem.: Gridiron Club. Roman Catholic. Avocations: gardening, swimming, tennis. Home: 17115 Simpson Cir Paeonian Springs VA 20129-1735 Personal E-mail: pjs338@yahoo.com.

**SLUBERSKI, THOMAS RICHARD,** international educator, journalist, theologian; b. Jersey City, Dec. 7, 1939; s. Walter and Anna Louise (Gall) S. BA with honors, Concordia U., 1962; MDiv with high honors, Concordia Sem., 1966; postgrad., U. Vienna, Austria, 1966, U. Erlangen-Nuremberg, Fed. Republic Germany, 1966-68; MA in English Lit., Washington U., 1970; ThD with honors, U. Heidelberg, Fed. Republic Germany, 1973, NYU, 1978. Ordained to ministry Luth. Ch.-Mo. Synod, 1969. Vicar Zion Luth. Ch., Wausau, Wis., 1964-65; asst. to dean chapel., lectr. dept. theology Valparaiso (Ind.) U., 1969-70; prof. English, religion, humanities Concordia Univ. Sys., Bronxville, N.Y., 1972—, Duda chair in religion, 2000—; pastor St. Matthew's Luth. Ch., Hastings-on-Hudson, N.Y., 1977-87; exec. dir. Am. Luth. Publicity Bur., 1987-89; guest prof. Luth. U. of Brazil, Canoas, Brazil, 2004—. Rsch. assoc., editor Luth. World Fedn., Geneva, 1968—69; judge Nat. Physique com., 1983—87. Russian Fedn. Body Builders, 1992—94; coord. 9th and 10th Inter-Luth. forums, 1988—90; bd. dirs. Luth. Soc. Worship, Music and Arts, 1971—73; lectr. U. St. Petersburg, U. Omsk, Merchant Marine Acad., Vladivostok, Russia, U. Khabarovsk, U. Vladivostok, Alexander von Herzen U., Russia; staff Russian-Am. Press Ctr.; warden U.S. Consulate at St. Petersburg; coord. vols. St. Petersburg Goodwill Games,

1994; tchr. sports mktg. Sports Couns. of Singapore, Hong Kong and Kuala Lumpur, Malaysia, 1995; prof. Russian Luth. Sem., 1992—94, Deacon's Tng. Sch., 1992—94; instr., bd. mem. Ben Weider Coll. Bodybldg., St. Petersburg, 1993—94; advisor Internat. Shaping Fedn., 1992—94; mem. exec. bd. 15th Ann. Workshop on Jewish Christian Rels., Stamford, Conn.; bd. dirs. Peterschule, St. Petersburg, 1993—94. Asst. editor Seminarian jour., 1965-66; lit. survey editor, rsch. asst. Luth. World Fedn., Geneva, Switzerland, 1968-69; judge (TV) Emmy's, 1995—; contbr. articles to profl. jours. Juror Am. Film Festival, N.Y.C., 1976-87; mem. nat. faculty of U.S. Sports Acad., Daphne, Ala., 1995—. Austrian State scholar, 1966, Bavarian State scholar, 1966-67; World Coun. Chs. fellow, 1967, Nat. Merit scholar, 1958, Luth. World Fedn. scholar, 1967, Deutscher Akademischer Austauschdienst fellow, 1970-72, Ctr. for Creative Persons fellow, 1975, 76; Aid Assn. for Luths. Faculty Study grantee, 1972. Fellow Christian Writers Inst.; mem. Nat. Acad. TV Arts and Scis., Disting Fulbright Inst., Am. Film Inst., Soc. Arts, Religion and Culture. Office: ULBRA U Canoas Brazil Home: 529 Bastogne Dr Akron OH 44303-1606

**SLUDIKOFF, STANLEY ROBERT,** publisher; writer; b. Bronx, NY, July 17, 1935; s. Harry and Lillie (Elberger) S.; m. Ann Paula Blumberg, June 30, 1972; children: Lisa Beth, Jaime Dawn, Bonnie Joy. B.Arch., Pratt Inst., 1957; grad. student, U. So. Calif., 1960-62. Cert. planner Am. Inst. Cert. Planners. Project planner Robert E. Alexander, F.A.I.A. & Assos., Los Angeles, 1965-66, Daniel, Mann, Johnson & Mendenhall (City and Regional Planning Cons.), Los Angeles, 1967-70; pres., editor, pub. Gambling Times Inc., also Two Worlds Mgmt., Inc., Los Angeles, 1971—2003; v.p. Prima Quality Farms, Inc., PR: chmn. Creative Games, Inc., 1992—. Pres. Las Vegas TV Weekly, also Postal West, Las Vegas, 1975-79; founder Stanley Roberts Sch. Winning Blackjack, 1976; instr. city and regional planning program U. So. Calif., 1960-63; founding mem. Mfrs. Direct, 1996. Author: (under pen name Stanley Roberts) Winning Blackjack, 1971, How to Win at Weekend Blackjack, 1973, Gambling Times Guide to Blackjack, 1983; author: The Beginner's Guide to Winning Blackjack, 1983, Begin to Win at Blackjack, 1997, Begin to Win at Video Poker, 1997, Begin to Win at Craps, 1997; also monthly column, 1977—; creator & tournament dir. The World Casino Games; editor/pub. Poker Player Newspaper, 1982-88, 2003—; pres. Heavenlit Championship of Poker Tournament, 2005-; inventor Daily Digit lottery game, Straight Out casino game; founder www.gamblingtimes.com, www.pokerplayernewspaper.com; patentee in field. Mem. Destination 99 Forum, Citizens Planning Group, San Fernando Valley, Calif., 1966-67, Rebuild L.A. land use com., 1992-94. Served to lt. col. U.S. Army, now Aus. ret. Recipient commendation from mayor Los Angeles for work on model cities funding, 1968 Mem. AIA, Am. Planning Assn., Am. Inst. Cert. Planners, Internat. Casino Assn. (sec. 1980-85), Res. Officers Assn. (life), Mensa (life) Achievements include invention of Straight Out gambling game. Office: 3883 W Century Blvd Inglewood CA 90303-1003 Office Phone: 310-674-3365. Business E-mail: srs@gamblingtimes.com. *The challenge of being alive lies in the development of one's maximum potential. To do less is to fly in the face of the gifts of creation, to shorten the aspect of one's life and to deny the fullness of existence. "The weakness of the flesh" prevents anyone's full development from reaching fruition but the personal and societal loss lies in giving up too soon, before we have fully tested our limits.*

**SLUSHER, KIMBERLY GOODE,** researcher; b. Benham, Ky., Oct. 4, 1960; d. Herschel James and Nevelyn Faye (Hayes) Goode; m. Joe Allan Slusher, May 1, 1985; children: Tarah Rena, Preston Cole. BS in Agr., Ea. Ky. U., 1982; MS in Agr., U. Tenn., 1989. Rsch. asst. U. Tenn., Knoxville, 1983-89; info. analyst Oak Ridge (Tenn.) Nat. Lab., 1989—, tchr. cons. sci. honors program, 1993. Author: (army study) Drinking Water Contamination Study, 1995; contbr. chpt.: Teratogens: Chemicals Which Cause Birth Defects, 1993. Methodist. Avocations: gardening, piano. Office: Human Gene Info Analysis Sect 1060 Commerce Park Dr # Ms6480 Oak Ridge TN 37830-8043 Business E-Mail: kfg@ornl.gov.

**SLUSS, DOROTHY LOUISE,** education educator, researcher; b. Hurley, Va., Aug. 02; d. Monroe Irvin and Mildred A. Dotson Justus; m. James Roger Sluss, Sr.; 1 child, James Roger II. BS, U. of Va., 1978; MS (magna cum laude), Va. Tech., 1983, PhD, 1995. Commonwealth of Va. Postgrad. Proff. Cert. Va. State Dept. of Edn., 1983. Elem. tchr. Coeburn Primary and Mid. Schs., Va., 1978—92; adj. prof. Va. Tech., Blacksburg, 1993—94; vis. professor Emory & Henry Coll., Va., 1994—95; from asst. prof. to assoc. prof. East Tenn. State U., Johnson City, 1995—2001, program coord., 2000—01; assoc. prof., program coord. Clemson (SC) U., 2001—. V.p. Va. Assn. for the Edn. of Young Children, 1994—95; dir. project TIES East Tenn. State U., Johnson City, SC, 1996—2001; panel chair, grants reviewer U.S. Dept. of Edn., Washington, 2000; pres. The Assn. for the Study of Play, 2000—01; adv. bd. Playing for Keeps, Wilmette, Ill., 2003—. Editor (guest editor): National Newsletter; editor: The Association for the Study of Play; contbr. chapters to books; author: Supporting Play: Birth to Age Eight, Effects of Peer Interaction on Play. Clk. of the session, elder Castlewood Presbyn. Ch., Va., 1985—99. Recipient Darden Soc. award, U. of Va. at Wise, 1978, W.D. Richmond award in Edn., 1978; grantee Towards Inclusion in Edn. Project (TIES), U.S. Office of Edn., 1996—2002. Mem.: Nat. Assn. for the Edn. of Young Children, Soc. for Rsch. in Child Devel. (assoc.), Kappa Omicron Nu (treas. 1993—94), Phi Delta Kappa (assoc.; sec. 2002—03), Phi Kappa Phi (assoc.). Office: Clemson U 406 Tillman Hall Clemson SC 29634 Office Phone: 864-656-5099. Personal E-mail: dsluss@charter.net. Business E-Mail: djsluss@clemson.edu.

**SLUSSER, EUGENE ALVIN,** electronics executive, consultant; b. Denver, Mar. 13, 1922; s. Jesse Alvin and Grace (Carter) S.; m. Anne L. Longley, Oct. 2, 1943; children: Robert, Jon, Carolyn BS Physics, U. Denver, 1947. Registered profl. engr., N.H. Mem. staff Radiation Lab. MIT, Cambridge, 1942—45, project engr. Helland Rsch. Co., Denver, 1945—47, cons. Ocn. Tel. Sys., N.Y.C., 1947—51; project engr. Airborne Inst. Lab., Mineola, NY, 1951—53; v.p. N.E. Electronics Corp., Concord, NH, 1953—58; pres. Aerotronic Assocs., Inc., Contoocook, NH, 1958—84, N.H. Automatic Equipment Corp., Concord, 1962—90, N.H. Realty Corp., Concord, 1990—96; pres., cons. E.A. Slusser & Assocs., Concord, 1996—. Patentee electronics field Chmn. Hopkinton (N.H.) Water Bd., 1962-69, Hopkinton Planning Bd., 1971-77, Hopkinton Precinct Bd. Adjustment, 1977 Mem. Aircraft Owners and Pilots Assn. (cert. pilot), Captiva Island (Fla.) Yacht Club (past commodore), Wharf Rat Club, Anglers Club, Pacific Club (Nantucket, Mass.), Masons (32d degree) Personal E-mail: easlusser@caol.net.

**SLUSSER, ROBERT WYMAN,** aerospace transportation executive; b. Mineola, NY, May 10, 1938; s. John Leonard and Margaret McKenzie (Wyman) S.; m. Linda Killeas, Aug. 3, 1968. BS, MIT, 1960; MBA, U. Pa., 1962; ERC, Ft. Belvior Def. Sys. Mgmt. Sch., 1977; AMP, Claremont, 1982. Assoc. adminstr.'s staff NASA Hdqrs., Washington, 1962-65; with Northrop Corp., Hawthorne, Calif., 1965-96; adminstr. Space Labs., 1965-68; mgr. bus. and fin. Warnecke Electron Tubes Co. divsn., Chgo., 1968-71; mgr. bus. adminstrn. YF-17 Program Aircraft Divsn., 1971-75, mgr. adminstrn. F-18/Cobra programs, also mgr. F-18 design to cost program, 1975-79, mgr. engring. adminstrn., 1980-82, acting v.p. engring., 1982, v.p. info. resources, 1983-91, mgr. long range planning, 1991-93, program mgr.-bus. F/A-18E/F program, 1994-96, cons., 1996—. Bd. dirs., CFO So. Calif. Hist. Aviation Found., 1987-90, chmn. bd., pres., 1990-97; treas. Flight Path Learning Ctr. So. Calif., 1996-2001; contracting officer, PDES, 1991-97; dirs. adv. bd. SC Rsch. Authority, 1991-95. Grumman Aircraft Engring. scholar, 1956—60. Fellow AIAA (assoc., membership chmn. L.A. sect. 1996-98); mem. So. Calif. Soc. Hist. Mgmt. (mem. exec. com. 1987-91), Northrop Mgmt. Club (bd. dirs. 1992-93, Man of Yr. 1991-92). Avocation: private pilot. Home: 7270 Berry Hill Dr Palos Verdes Peninsula CA 90275-4402

**SLUSSER, WILLIAM PETER,** investment banker; b. June 20, 1929; s. Eugene and Thelma (Donovan) S.; m. Joanne Eleanor Briggs, June 20, 1953; children: Kathleen E., Martin E., Wendelin M., Caroline E., Sarah A. BA cum laude, Stanford U., 1951; MBA, Harvard U., 1953. Mgr. spl. situations dept. Dean Witter & Co., NYC, 1955-60; ptnr., sr. v.p. corp. fin. dept. Shields &

Co., NYC, 1960-75; sr. v.p. Paine Webber, Inc., NYC, 1975-80; mng. dir., head merger and acquisitions dept., mem. mgmt. com. Blyth Eastman Paine Webber, Inc., NYC, 1980—88; pres. Slusser Assocs., Inc., NYC, 1988—. Bd. dirs. Ampex Corp., Sparton Corp., Magellan Group Ltd., Unigene Labs., Inc. Contbr. articles to profl. jours. Founding stockholder Assoc. Mortgage Cos., Cap Gemini Sogetti; bd. fin. advisors Columbia U. Bus. Sch., Calif. Senate Commn. on Local Govt. Investments; mem. Calif. Senate Commn. on Corp. Governance. 1st lt. USAF, 1953—55. Mem. Soc. Calif. Pioneers, Knickerbocker Club, Stanford Assocs., Harvard (N.Y.C.) Club, Lawrence Beach Club, Stanford of N.Y. Club, Alpha Delta Phi (exec. coun. 1956-62, treas. 1961). Home: 901 Lexington Ave New York NY 10021-5924 also: Slusser Ranch Windsor CA 95492 Office: Slusser Assocs Inc 1 Citicorp Ctr Ste 5100 153 E 53d St New York NY 10022-4611

**SLUTSKY, LEONARD ALAN,** finance executive, consultant; b. N.Y.C., July 25, 1945; s. Hyman and Ruth (Neuman) S.; m. Sharlene Alexis Farber, Oct. 20, 1968; children: Jacquelyn Anne, Jason Ian, Adam Jeffrey. Student, U. Ariz., 1963-66. Chmn., pres., chief exec. officer Republic Pension Svc. Inc., Melville, N.Y., 1981-83; pres., chief exec. officer Am. Money Svc. Corp., Huntington, N.Y., 1977-97; chmn. bd. Peoples Nat. Bank of Rockland, N.Y., 1983-85, Millbrook Equity Corp., N.Y.C., 1985-86; chmn., chief exec. officer Republic Advisors, Inc., Lake Success, N.Y., 1981-95; chmn. Am. Money Co., Inc., Huntington, 1982-90; pres. Windsor Funding Corp., West Hills, N.Y., 1987-90. Bd. dirs. Triad Temporary Agy., Inc., Triad Employee Leasing LLC. Sgt. N.Y. N.G., 1966-71. Recipient Disting. Service award Rockland County, 1984, Com. Service award Dist. Atty. Rockland, 1984, Distinguished Service award 6th Congl. Dist., Washington, 1984, Yeshiva U., N.Y.C., 1984. Mem. Am. Soc. C.L.U., KP Republican. Jewish. Avocations: swimming, fishing, camping, golf. Home: 20 Equestrian Ct Huntington NY 11743-6636 Office: 790 Management Co 790 New York Ave Huntington NY 11743-4499 Office Phone: 631-424-2400.

**SLUTSKY, LORIE A(NN),** foundation executive; b. NYC, Jan. 5, 1953; d. Edward and Adele (Moskowitz) S. BA, Colgate U., 1975; MA in Urban Policy Analysis, New Sch. Social Rsch., NYC, 1977. Program officer NY Cmty. Trust, NYC, 1977-83, v.p., 1983-87, exec. v.p., 1987-89, pres., CEO, 1990—. Former mem. and chmn. bd. Coun. on Founds., Inc., Washington, 1986-95. Trustee emerita, former chmn. budget com. Colgate U., Hamilton, N.Y., 1989-98; former mem. bd. dirs. Found. Ctr., Inc., N.Y.C., L.A. Wallace Fund for Met. Mus. Art, N.Y.C., D. Wallace Fund for Meml. Sloan Kettering, United Way of N.Y.C.; bd. dirs. BoardSource, Alliance Capital; trustee New Sch. U. Office: NY Community Trust 22d Fl 909 3d Ave New York NY 10022

**SLUTZ, PAMELA JO HOWELL,** ambassador; b. Chgo., 1949; d. Robert and Rose Slutz; m. Ronald Deutch; 2 children. B in Politics, Hollins U., 1970; M in Asian Studies and Polit. Sci., U. Hawaii, 1972. Office of Korean Affairs Bur. East Asian and Pacific Affairs US Dept. of State (FSO), 1981—82, Office of China and Mongolia Affairs Bur. East Asian and Pacific Affairs, 1995—97, Office of East Asian and Pacific Regional Security and Policy Planning Bur. East Asian and Pacific Affairs, 1997—99, amb., fgn. svc. officer Shanghai, 1991—94, Am. Inst. Taiwan, 2001—03. Mem. U.S. del. to Nuc. and Space Talks with Russia, Geneva, 1987—89. Fellow, East West Ctr., 1970—72. Home and Office: 4410 Ulaanbaatar Pl Washington DC 20521-4410 Fax: 976-11-320776.

**SLUYTER, ANDREW,** geographer, educator; b. Kitimat, British Columbia, Can., Nov. 24, 1958; s. Nicolaas Sluyter and Lena Arnoudina Gotzen; m. Carina Giusti, Apr. 9, 2004; 1 child, Sophia. BA, U. BC, Vancouver, Can., 1987; MA, U. BC, Vancouver, BC, Can., 1990; PhD, U. Tex., Austin, 1995. Prof. Pa. State U., University Park, Pa., 1995—2002, La. State U., Baton Rouge, 2003—. Author: (nonfiction book) Colonialism and Landscape (Blaut CAPE award, Assn. of Am. Geographers, 2004); contbr. articles to profl. jours. U.S. rep. Geography and Regional Planning Commn. Orgn. of Am. States, 2006—. Fellow Global Change Rsch. Program, NASA, 1992—95; grantee Rsch. grant, Nat. Geog. Soc., 2000, 2001, Rsch. grants, EPA, 2001; Rsch. grant, Nat. Geog. Soc., 1999, NSF, 1998, 1999, 2000, 2001, Rsch. grants, EPA, 2002. Mem.: Assn. of Am. Geographers (splty. group chair 2000—02). Office: La State Univ 227 Howe Russell Baton Rouge LA 70803 Office Phone: 225-578-4261. Office Fax: 225-578-4420. Business E-Mail: asluyter@lsu.edu.

**SLY, RIDGE MICHAEL,** pediatrician, educator, allergist, immunologist; b. Seattle, Nov. 3, 1933; s. Ridge Joseph and Eva Jean (Ruddell) S.; m. Ann Turner Jennings, June 12, 1957; children: Teresa Ann Perper, Cynthia Marie Schattenfield. AB, Kenyon Coll., Gambier, Ohio, 1956; MD, Washington U., St. Louis, 1960. Diplomate Am. Bd. Pediat., Am. Sub-Bd. Pediat. Allergy, Am. Bd. Allergy and Immunology. Intern, resident in pediat. St. Louis Children's Hosp., 1960—62; chief resident in pediat. U. Ky. Med. Ctr., Lexington, 1962—63; fellow in allergy and immunology UCLA Med. Ctr., 1965—67; from asst. prof. to prof. pediat. La. State U. Med. Ctr., New Orleans, 1967—78; head sect. allergy and immunology Children's Nat. Med. Ctr., Washington, 1978—; prof. pediat. George Washington U., Washington, 1978—. Author: Textbook of Pediatric Allergy, 1985; mem. editl. bd. Annals of Allergy, Asthma, & Immunology, 1982-98, 99-2002, Jour. Asthma, 1982-93, Clin. Revs. in Allergy, 1982-2001, Pediat. Asthma, Allergy, & Immunology, 1987—; assoc. editor Annals of Allergy, Asthma, & Immunology, 1989-90, editor, 1990-98; contbr. articles to profl. jours. Served to capt. USAF, 1963-65 Recipient La. plaque Am. Lung Assn. of La., 1978 Fellow Am. Acad. Allergy, Asthma & Immunology (chmn. com. on drugs 1981-87), Am. Acad. Pediats. (sect. on allergy com. 1972-75), Am. Coll. Allergy, Asthma, and Immunology (Disting. Fellow award 1993, Bela Schick award 1997, chmn. ethics com. 1997-99); mem. Am. Thoracic Soc., Assn. for Care of Asthma (pres. 1980-81, dir. postgrad. courses 1980—, Realian Maml award 1983), Ctr. for Bioethics and Human Dignity, Phi Beta Kappa. Republican. Baptist. Avocations: music, piano, organ. Office: Children's Nat Med Ctr 111 Michigan Ave NW Washington DC 20010-2970

**SLY, WILLIAM S.,** biochemist, educator; b. East St. Louis, Ill., Oct. 19, 1932; MD, St. Louis U., 1957. Intern, asst. resident ward medicine Barnes Hosp., St. Louis, 1957-59; clin. assoc. nat. heart inst. NIH, Bethesda, Md., 1959-63, rsch. biochemist, 1959-63; dir. divsn. med. genetics, dept. medicine and pediatrics, sch. medicine Washington U. St. Louis, 1964-84, from asst. prof. to prof. medicine, 1964-78, from asst. prof. to prof. pediatrics, 1967-78, prof. pediatrics, medicine and genetics, 1978-84; prof. biochemistry and pediat. St. Louis U., 1984—, chmn. Edward A. Doisy dept. biochemistry-molecular biology, 1984—. Vis. physician Nat. Heart Inst., 1961-63, pediatric genetics clinic U. Wis., Madison, 1963-64; Am. Cancer Soc. fellow lab. enzymol Nat. Ctr. Sci. Rsch., Gif-sur-Yvette, France, 1963, dept. biochemistry and genetics U. Wis., 1963-64; attending physician St. Louis County Hosp., Mo., 1964-84; asst. physician Barnes Hosp., St. Louis, 1964-84, St. Louis Children's Hosp., 1967-84; genetics cons. Homer G. Philips Hosp., St. Louis, 1969-81; mem. genetics study sect. divsn. rsch. grants NIH, 1971-75; mem. active staff Cardinal Glennon Children's Hosp., St. Louis, 1984—; mem. med. adv. bd. Howard Hughes Med. Inst., 1989-92. Recipient Merit award NIH, 1988; elected to Nat. Acad. Sci., 1989; named Passano Found. laureate, 1991. Mem. NAS, AMA, AAAS, Am. Soc. Human Genetics (mem. steering com. human cell biology program 1971-73, com. genetic counseling 1972-76), Am. Soc. Clin. Investigation, Am. Chem. Soc., Genetics Soc. Am., Am. Soc. Microbiology, Soc. Pediatric Rsch., Sigma Xi. Achievements include research on lysosomal enzyme replacement in storage diseases, inherited carbonic anhydrase deficiencies, and hereditary hemochromatosis. Office: St Louis U Med Sch Dept Biochemistry 1402 S Grand Blvd Saint Louis MO 63104-1004

**SLYDE, JIMMY (JAMES T. GODBOLT, KING OF SLIDES),** tap dancer; b. Atlanta, 1927; Attended, New England Conservatory of Music; D of Performing Arts (hon.), Okla. City U. Mem. (with Jimmy "Sir Slyde" Mitchell) The Slyde Brothers; instr. to Savion Glover. Instr. Chgo. Human Rhythm Project, 2005. Performer: (films) The Jazz Adventure, The Cotton Club, 1984, 'Round Midnight, 1986, TAP, 1989, (Broadway plays) Black and

Blue, 1989—91 (Tony award nomination, 1989), (TV Spl.) Motown Returns to the Apollo, 1985, Tap Dance in America, 1989, Performance at the White House, 1998. Named Living Treasure in Am. Dance, Okla. City U.; recipient Dance mag. award, 2005; Nat. Heritage fellowship award, NEA, 1999, Guggenheim fellowship for choreography, 2003. Achievements include innovative tap style mixed with jazz, stressing sliding cascades of taps close to floor. Mailing: c/o Chgo Human Rhythm Project 2936 N Southport Chicago IL 60657*

**SMAGALSKI, CAROLYN M.,** publishing executive, webmaster, director; b. Phila., Aug. 28, 1952; d. Raymond L and Mary K Hanisco; children: Michael M, Tyler A. BA Cum Laude, Temple U., Philadelphia, 1971—75. Lic. private pilot SEL with IFR rating and Complex Aircraft Rating US Dept. of Transp./Fed. Aviation Adminstrn., 1996. Account mgr. Brown Printing Co., East Greenville, Pa., 1996—; exec. dir., author, webmaster, internetwork marketer CQ Web Wide LLC, Harleysville, Pa., 2002—. Beer and brewing advisor Gluten Free Beer Festival U.K., 2006—. Author (editor): (website mag.) Beer and Brewing, 2004—; creator Beer Fox, 2004, guest appearance Beer Fox/Beer Chef, Beer Radio. Beer and brewing advisor Gluten Free Beer Festival, England, 2006—. Mem.: Better Internet Bur., Internat. Assn. Home Bus. Entrepreneurs, Internat. Orgn. Women Pilots, Aircraft Owners & Pilot's Assn. Avocations: information technology, aviation, psychology of brain & socio-emotional challenges, gourmet cooking, public relations & travel. Home: 805 Continental Drive Harleysville PA 19438 Office: CQ Web Wide LLC 805 Continental Drive Harleysville PA 19438 Office Phone: 215-541-2723. Personal E-mail: carolsmagalski@comcast.net. E-mail: cs1@cqwebwide.com.

**SMAGNER, JOHN PATRICK,** applied behavior analyst, educator; b. Jamestown, N.Y., July 27, 1974; s. Linda Smagner. B. Edinboro U., Pa., 1996; M, D, U. Kans., Lawrence, 2003. Applied behavior analyst, Chgo., 2003—. Adj. prof. U. Chgo., 2004—, Chgo. Sch. for Profl. Psychology, 2004—. Author: Research on Social Work Practice, Behavioral Interventions. Mem.: Assn. for Behavior Analysis. Home: 4677 N Virginia Ave Chicago IL 60625 Office: U Chgo 969 E 60th St Chicago IL 60637 Personal E-mail: johnsmag@uchicago.edu.

**SMAGORINSKY, PETER,** education educator; b. Princeton, N.J., Oct. 24, 1952; s. Joseph and Margaret (Knoepfel) Smagorinsky; m. Anne O'Gorman, July 10, 1982 (dec. Aug. 1982); m. Jane E. Farrell, Oct. 12, 1985; children: Alysha, David. BA, Kenyon Coll., 1974; MA in Tchg., U. Chgo., 1977, PhD, 1989. English tchr. Westmont (Ill.) H.S., 1977-78, Barrington (Ill.) H.S., 1978-85, Oak Park (Ill.) and River Forest H.S., 1985-90; asst. prof. U. Okla., Norman, 1990-95, assoc. prof., 1995-98, U. Ga., Athens, 1998-2001, prof., 2001—. Author: Standards in Practice, 1996; co-author: How English Teachers Get Taught, 1995, The Language of Interpretation, 1995; co-editor: Rsch. Tchg. English, 1996—2003, Reading Rsch. Quar. Rev. Ednl. Rsch., Am. Jour. Edn., Written Comm., Reading and Writing Quar. Recipient Steve Cahir award for Rsch. in Writing, Am. Ednl. Rsch. Assn., 1991, Raymond B. Cattell award for Disting. Programmatic Rsch., 1999. Mem.: Nat. Coun. Tchrs. English (chair standing com. rsch. 1995—96, co-chair assembly rsch. 1996, trustee rsch. found. 1997—2003, chair 2000—03, pres. nat. conf. rsch. lang. and literacy 2001, English Jour. Writing award 1989, Edwin M. Hopkins award 2000, Janet Emig award 2003). Home: 175 Emerald Dr Athens GA 30605-4106 Office: U Ga 125 Aderhold Hall Athens GA 30602 E-mail: smago@uga.edu.

**SMAIL, DANIEL LORD,** history professor; b. Ithaca, N.Y., Oct. 5, 1961; s. John R.W. and Laura L. Smail; m. Kathleen M. M. Mulkern, June 8, 1985; children: Irene E., Gregory L., Benedict A. PhD, U. of Mich., 1994. Prof. of history Fordham U., Bronx, 1995—2005, Harvard U. Cambridge, Mass., 2006—. Author: (scholarly monograph) Imaginary Cartographies: Possession and Identity in Late Medieval Marseille (Herbert Baxter Adams prize, 2000), The Consumption of Justice: Emotions, Publicity, and Legal Culture in Marseille, 1264-1423 (James Willard Hurst prize (co-winner), 2004). Recipient fellowship for univ. tchrs., NEH, 1999; fellow, Am. Coun. of Learned Socs., 1998. Office: Harvard U Dept History Cambridge MA 02138 Office Phone: 1-617-496-0149.

**SMAIL, LESLIE ANNE,** librarian; b. Pitts., July 25, 1958; d. Laurence Mitchell and Nancy (Fried) S.; m. Eric D. Hunley, July 10, 1998. BA, Christopher Newport Coll., 1980; MSLS, Cath. U., 1982. Libr. intern Tng. and Doctrine Command, Ft. Monroe, Va., 1982-84; libr. Ft. Story (Va.) Libr., 1985-2000; libr. dir. Bryant & Stratton Coll. Libr., Virginia Beach, Va., 2000; libr. Gwinnett County Pub. Libr., Lawrenceville, Ga., 2000—01; contractor retrospective conversion project Tortolita Vet. Svcs., PC, Tucson, 2002—03; reference libr. Davis-Monthan AFB Libr., 2003—04; libr. dir. Bateman Libr., Langley AFB, Va., 2004—. Recipient Exceptional Performance award U.S. Army, Ft. Eustis, Va., 1985-99, Comdr.'s award for civilian svc., 1995, 2000; named SVS Contractor of Yr., 2005, Outstanding Program Mgr. TRADOC, Ft. Monroe, 1988-89, ISVS Contractor of Yr. award, 2005. Mem.: Sigma Tau Delta. Avocations: arts and crafts, antiques, gardening, genealogy. Office: Bateman Libr 42 Ash Ave Langley Afb VA 23665 Office Phone: 757-764-2906. Business E-Mail: leslie.smail@langley.af.mail.

**SMALDONE, EDWARD JAMES,** composer; b. Wantagh, NY, Nov. 19, 1956; m. Karen Ajamian, Aug. 5, 1979; children: Laura, Gregory, Julia. BA in Music, Queens Coll., 1978, MA in Music, 1980; PhD in Music, CUNY, 1986. Lectr. SUNY, Purchase, 1986-90; adj. asst. prof. Hofstra U., Hempstead, NY, 1988-90; vis. asst. prof. New Sch. for Social Rsch., N.Y.C., 1988; adminstrv. dir. Speculum Musicae, N.Y.C., 1988-89; artistic dir. Sounds for the Left Bank, Rego Park, NY, 1985-92; asst. prof. Copland Sch. of Music, CUNY, Flushing, 1990-99, assoc. prof., 1994—2005, prof., 2005—; dir. Copland Sch. Music CUNY, Flushing, 2002—. Composer in residence N.Y.C. Pub. Schs., 1994, 95; Carlisle Project Choreographer and Composer Collaboration Commn., 1994; assoc. composer Atlantic Ctr. Arts, 1999, vis. fac. Univ. Coll. Chichester, Eng., 1999, 01. Composer: Two String Quartets, 1980, 86, Dialogue for orch., 1987, Double Duo (flute, clarinet, violin, cello), 1987, Transformational Etudes (solo piano), 1990, Rhapsody for piano and orch., 1992, Suite for violin and piano, 1993, Three Scenes from "The Heartland" for solo piano, 1994, Saxophone Quartet, 1995, Rituals: Sacred and Profane for flute, cello and piano, 1996, American Spiritual Fantasy for string orch., 1997, Psalm of the Phoenix for Shakuhachi and cello, 1998, Suite for violin and 12 instruments, 2000, Letters from Home, mezzo soprano, flute, clarinet, and piano, 2000, String Quartet No. 3, 2001, Life Imagined, Life Engaged for piccolo and chamber orch., 2001, Trio Concertante for violin, horn and piano with string orch., 2004; dance compositions: The Chair, The Table and Tatyana's Letter (choreography by Yin Mei), 1999; albums include Scenes from the Heartland, Transformational Etudes, String Quartet No. 2. Recipient Standard award ASCAP, 1986—, Creative Incentive award CUNY Rsch. Found., 1992, 95, 97; residency fellow Yaddo Corp., 1986, 87, Composer's fellow Charles Ives Ctr. for Am. Music, 1990, residency fellow MacDowell Colony, 1994, Goddard Lieberson fellow Am. Acad. Arts and Letters, 1993; prize winner Percussive Arts Soc., 1994. Home: 228 Manhasset Ave Manhasset NY 11030 Business E-Mail: edward.smaldone@qc.cuny.edu.

**SMALHEISER, NEIL RAYMOND,** neurobiologist; b. NYC, Dec. 10, 1954; BA with honors, U. Iowa, 1974; MD, Phd, Yeshiva U., 1982. Asst. prof. U. Ill., 1996—, U. Chgo., 1981-96. Achievements include research on cell morphogenesis and neurite extension, laminin-binding proteins in axonal guidance, synaptic specificity, neuroinformatics. Office: UIC Psychiat Inst MC 912 1601 W Taylor St Chicago IL 60612-4310

**SMALL, BERTRICE W.,** writer; b. N.Y.C., Dec. 9, 1937; d. David Roger Williams, Doris Melissa (Maud) Steen; m. George Sumner Small, Oct. 5, 1963; 1 child, Thomas David. Student, Western Coll. for Women, Oxford, Ohio, Katherine Gibbs Sectl. Sch., N.Y.C., 1959. With Young & Rubicon, N.Y.C., 1959—60, Weed Radio & TV, N.Y.C., 1960—61, Edward Petry &

Co., N.Y.C., 1961—63. Author: The Kadin, 1978, Sky O'Malley, 1980, All The Sweet Tomorrows, 1984, Amount In Time, 1991, Betrayal, 1998, The Innocent, 1999, Rosamund, 2002, 25 others. Vestrywoman Redeemer Episc. Ch., Mattituck, NY, 1998—2001. Recipient Career Achievement Reviewers Choice award, Romantic Times Mag., 1983, 1988, 1995, 2001. Mem.: L.I. Romance Writers (bd. dirs. 1999—2001), Romance Writers of Am., Authors Guild. Episcopalian. Avocation: gardening. Mailing: PO Box 765 Southold NY 11971

**SMALL, CLARENCE MERILTON, JR.,** lawyer; b. Birmingham, Ala., July 24, 1934; s. Clarence Merilton and Clara (Roberts) S.; m. Jean Russell, Nov. 18, 1935; children: William Stephen, Elizabeth Ann, Laura Caro. BS, Auburn U., 1956; LLB, U. Ala., 1961. Founding ptnr. Christian & Small, Birmingham, 1961—. Served to 1st lt., arty. AUS, to capt. JAGC. Fellow Am. Bar Found., Internat. Acad. Trial Lawyers, Am. Coll. Trial Lawyers, Ala. Law Found.; mem. ABA (ho. of dels. 1984-86), Ala. Bar Assn. (pres. 1992-93), Birmingham Bar Assn. (pres. 1979), Ala. Def. Lawyers Assn., Internat. Assn. Def. Counsel. Office: 1800 Financial Ctr Birmingham AL 35203-4611 Office Phone: 205-795-6588. Business E-Mail: cmsmall@csattorneys.com.

**SMALL, DONALD MACFARLAND,** biophysics professor, department chairman, gastroenterologist, researcher; b. Newton, Mass., Sept. 15, 1931; s. Grace (MacFarland) S.; m. Elisabeth Chan, July 8, 1957 (div. 1979); children: Geoffrey, Philip; m. Kathryn Ross, July 26, 1986 (div. 1999); 1 child, Samuel. BA, Occidental Coll., 1954; MA (hon.), Oxford (Eng.) U., 1964; MD, UCLA, 1960. Intern, asst. resident in medicine Mass. Meml. Hosps., Boston, 1960-62; sr. resident Boston City Hosp., 1962-63, vis. physician med. svcs., 1965—90; asst. prof. medicine Boston U. Sch. Medicine, 1968-69, assoc. prof. medicine and biochemistry, 1969-73, prof., 1973—, prof. biophysics, chmn. dept., 1989-2000, dir. Biophysics Inst., 1972—, prof. chmn. dept. physiology and biophysics, 2000—. Spl. tng. in phys. chemistry of lipids Inst. Pasteur, Paris, 1963-65; mem. adv. bd. Gladstone Found Labs., San Francisco, 1980—; George Lyman Duff Meml. lectr. Coun. Arteriosclerosis, Am. Heart Assn., 1986; cons. Nat. Inst. Arthritis and Metabolic Diseases, NIH, 1968-72, mem. task force Nat. Heart, Lung and Blood Inst., 1990; also others. Author, editor: Physical Chemistry of Lipids, 1986; mem. editl. bd. Gastroenterology, 1967-74, Arteriosclerosis, Thrombosis and Vascular Biology, 1980-2002, Jour. Biol. Chemistry, Current Opinions in Structural Biology, 1990—, Structure, 1992-98; sub-editor: Jour. Lipid Rsch., 1974-78, editor, 1979-83; editor: (with R. Havel) Advances in Lipid Rsch., 1989-99; mem. internat. bd. editors Jour. Nutritional Biochemistry, 1989—; contbr. articles and revs. to profl. jours.; author: (with A. Adams) The Healthy Meateaters Cookbook, 1991. Recipient Eppinger prize IV Internat. Congress on Liver Disease, 1976, Disting. Achievment award Modern Medicine, 1978, Disting. Alumni award UCLA Sch. Medicine Alumni Assn., 1988; Marshall scholar Magdalen Coll., Oxford, 1956-58, Aesculapian scholar UCLA, 1958-60, Markle scholar, 1966-70; others. Mem. AAAS, Am. Heart Assn. (fellow coun. arteriosclerosis, chmn. program coun. 1988-90, chmn. coun. 1992-94), Am. Assn. Physicians, Am. Soc. Biol. Chemists, Biophys. Soc., Am. Soc. Clin. Investigation, Am. Gastroent. Assn. (Ann. Disting. Achievement award 1972, Beaumont prize 2000), Am. Oil Chemists Soc. (Alton E. Bailey award 1998), Am. Fedn. Clin. Rsch., Am. Soc. Clin. Nutrition, Mass. Med. Soc., Suffolk Dist. Med. Soc., Phi Beta Kappa, Alpha Omega Alpha, Sigma Xi. Achievements include patents for on method for making meat products having a reduced saturated fat and cholesterol content. Office: Boston U Sch Medicine Dept Physiology and Biophysics 715 Albany St W302 Boston MA 02118-2526 Office Phone: 617-638-4001. E-mail: dmsmall@bu.edu.

**SMALL, ELISABETH CHAN,** psychiatrist, educator; b. Beijing, July 11, 1934; came to U.S., 1937; d. Stanley Hong and Lily Luella (Lum) Chan; m. Donald M. Small, July 8, 1957 (div. 1980); children Geoffrey Brooks, Philip Willard Stanley; m. H. Sidney Robinson, Jan. 12, 1991 (div. 2001). Student, Immaculate Heart Coll., L.A., 1951-52; BA in Polit. Sci., UCLA, 1955, MD, 1960. Intern Newton-Wellesley Hosp., Mass., 1960-61; asst. dir. for venereal diseases Mass. Dept. Pub. Health, 1961-63; resident in psychiatry Boston State Hosp., Mattapan, Mass., 1965-66, Tufts New Eng. Med. Ctr. Hosps., 1966-69, psychiat. cons. dept. gynecology, 1973-75; asst. clin. prof. psychiatry Sch. Medicine Tufts U., 1973-75, assoc. clin. prof., 1975-82, asst. clin. prof. ob-gyn, 1977-80, assoc. clin. prof. ob-gyn, 1980-82; from assoc. prof. to prof. psychiatry U. Nev. Sch. Med., Reno, 1982-95; practice psychiatry specializing in psychological effects of bodily changes on women, 1969—; emeritus prof. psychiatry and behavioral scis. U. Nev. Sch. Medicine, Reno, 1995—, from assoc. prof. to clin. assoc. prof. ob-gyn, 1982-88; mem. staff Tufts New Eng. Med. Ctr. Hosps., 1977-82, St. Margaret's Hosps., Boston, 1977-82, Washoe Med. Ctr., Reno, 1983—2006, St. Mary's Regional Med. Ctr., Reno, Truckee Meadows Hosp., Reno, St. Mary's Hosp., Reno; chief psychiatry svc. Reno VA Med. Ctr., 1989-94. Lectr., cons. in field; mem. psychiatry adv. panel Hosp. Satellite Network; mem. office external peer rev. NIMH, HEW; psychiat. cons. to Boston Redevelopment Authority on Relocation of Chinese Families of South Cove Area, 1968-70; mem. New Eng. Med. Ctr. Hosps. Cancer Ctr. Com., 1979-80, Pain Control Com., 1981-82; reproductive sys. curriculum com. Tufts Univ. Sch. Medicine, 1975-82. Mem. editorial bd. Psychiat. Update Am. (Psychiat. Assn. ann. rev.), 1983-85; reviewer Psychosomatics and Hosp. Community Psychiatry, New Eng. Jour. of Medicine, Am. Jour. of Psychiatry Psychosomatic Medicine; contbr. articles to profl. jours. Immaculate Heart Coll. scholar, 1951-52, Mira Hershey scholar UCLA, 1955; fellow Radcliffe Inst., 1967-70. Fellow Am. Coll. Psychiatrists (sci. program com. 1989-98); mem. AMA, Am. Psychiat. Assn. (life, rep. to sect. com. AAAS, chmn. ad hoc com. Asian-Am. Psychiatrists 1975, task force 1975-77, task force cost effectiveness in consultation 1984—, caucus chmn. 1981-82, sci. program com. 1982-88, courses subcom. chmn. sci. program com. 1986-88), Nev. Psychiat. Assn., Assn. for Acad. Psychiatry (fellowship com. 1982), Washoe County Med. Assn., Nev. Med. Soc. Avocations: skiing, cooking. Home and Office: 825 Caughlin Crossing Reno NV 89509-0647

**SMALL, GEORGE LEROY,** geographer, educator; b. Malden, Mass., Mar. 27, 1924; s. George Arthur and Alice Mildred (Weston) S.; m. Geraldine H. Koepke, July 4, 1970; 1 dau., Elizabeth Mary. BA, Brown U., 1950; M.I.A., Columbia U., 1952, PhD, 1968. French tchr. pvt. schs., Ariz., 1955-62; instr. geography Hunter Coll., 1964-68; assoc. prof. geography Coll. S.I., CUNY, 1968—. Cons. problems of whaling to environ. groups. Author: The Blue Whale, 1971. Served with U.S. Army, 1942-46. Recipient Nat. Book award, 1972; Rotary Found. fellow, 1952-53 Mem. Assn. Am. Geographers. Office: CUNY Coll Staten Is New York NY 10314

**SMALL, HAMISH,** chemist; b. Newtown Crommelin, No. Ireland, Oct. 5, 1929; s. Johnston and Jean (Wilson) S.; m. Beryl Maureen Burley, Mar. 27, 1954; children: Deborah Jane, Claire Leslie. BS, Queens U., Belfast, Northern Ireland, 1949, MS, 1953. Chemist U.S. Atomic Energy Authority, Harwell, England, 1949-55; rsch. scientist Dow Chem. Co., Midland, Mich., 1955-83; chemist Rsch. and Invention, 1983—. Author: Ion Chromatography, 1990; contbr. articles to profl. jours. Recipient Albert F. Sperry award Instrument Soc. Am., 1978, A.O. Beckman award, 1983, Herbert H. Dow Gold Medal Dow Chem. Co., 1983, Stephen Dal Nogare award, 1984, Am. Chem. Soc. award in Chromatography, 1991. Mem. Am. Chem. Soc. Achievements include 46 patents in field. Avocations: painting, sketching. Home: 4176 Oxford Dr Leland MI 49654-9716

**SMALL, JONATHAN ANDREW,** lawyer, consultant; b. NYC, Dec. 26, 1942; s. Milton and Teresa Markell (Joseph) S.; m. Cornelia Mendenhall, June 8, 1969; children: Anne, Katherine. BA, Brown U., 1964; student, U. Paris, 1962-63; LLB, Harvard U., 1967; MA, Fletcher Sch. of Law and Diplomacy, 1968; LLM, NYU, 1974. Bar: NY 1967. VISTA vol., Washington and Cambridge, Mass., 1968; law clk. to judge US Ct. Appeals (2d cir.), 1968-69; assoc. Debevoise & Plimpton, NYC, 1969-75, ptnr., 1976-99; pres. Nonprofit Coord. Com. N.Y., 2000—05; spl. cons. Govt. Rels., 2005—. Cons. Spl. Task Force of NY State Taxation, 1976; bd. overseers Fletcher Sch. Law and Diplomacy Tufts U., 2003—. Trustee Brearley Sch., 1985-95; bd. dirs. Nonprofit Coordinating Com. of NY, 1985-2005, Muscular Dystrophy Assn.,

1986-88, Human Svcs. Coun. NYC, Inc., 2000-05, Investor Responsibility Rsch. Ctr., Inc., 2000-06, Lawyers Alliance for NY, 2000—, Americans for the UN Population Fund, 2000—. Mem. ABA, Am. Law Inst., NY State Bar Assn. (chmn. tax sect. com. exempt orgns. 1980-82, cons. 1995), Assn. Bar City NY, Nonprofit Forum, Phi Beta Kappa. Home: 60 E End Ave New York NY 10028-7907 Office: Debevoise & Plimpton 919 Third Ave New York NY 10022

**SMALL, LAWRENCE M.,** museum executive; b. NY, Sept. 14, 1941; m. Sandra Small; 2 children. BA, Brown U., 1963; JD (hon.), Morehouse Coll. Vice chmn. bd., chmn. exec. com., dir. Citicorp, N.Y.C., 1964-91; pres., COO Fannie Mae, Washington, 1991-2000; CEO., sec. Smithsonian Instn., Washington, 2000—. Bd. dirs. Chubb Corp., Marriott Internat. Trustee emeritus Brown U., Morehouse Coll., Atlanta, 1973-99, Mt. Sinai-NYU Med. Ctr., Nat. Bldg. Mus.; bd. dirs. Spanish Repertory Theatre, Fannie Mae Found.; ex officio trustee Nat. Gallery Art. Office: Smithsonian Instn 1000 Jefferson Dr SW Washington DC 20560-0009

**SMALL, MARIO L.,** sociologist, educator; Degree in Sociology, Harvard U. Sociologist Princeton U., 2001—. Office: Dept Sociology Princeton Univ Princeton NJ 08544

**SMALL, MELVIN,** historian, educator; b. N.Y.C., Mar. 14, 1939; s. Herman Z. and Ann (Ashkinazy) S.; m. Sarajane Miller, Oct. 23, 1958; children: Michael, Mark. BA, Dartmouth Coll., 1960; MA, U. Mich., 1961, PhD, 1965. Asst. prof. history Wayne State U., Detroit, 1965-68, assoc. prof., 1968-76, prof., 1976—, chmn. dept. history, 1979-86, disting. prof., 2004—. Vis. prof. U. Mich., Ann Arbor, 1968, Marygrove Coll., Detroit, 1971, Aarhus (Denmark) U., 1972—74, 1983, Windsor (Ont. Can.) U., 1977—78. Author: Was War Necessary, 1980, Johnson, Nixon and the Doves, 1988, Covering Dissent, 1994, Democracy and Diplomacy, 1996, The Presidency of Richard Nixon, 1999, Antiwarriors, 2002, At The Water's Edge, 2005; co-author: Wages of War, 1972, Resort to Arms, 1982; editor: Public Opinion and Historians, 1970; co-editor: International War, 1986, Appeasing Fascism, 1991, Give Peace a Chance, 1992, The Good Fight Continues, 2006; mem. editl. bd. Internat. Interactions, 1987-91, Peace and Change, 1989—; restaurant critic Detroit Metro Times, 1982-95; reviewer Detroit Free Press, 1988-95 Mem. hon. bd. Swords into Plowshares Mus., 1992—; bd. dirs. Abraham Lincoln Brigade Archives, 1998—, Ctr. on Peace and Liberty, 2003—, David S. Wyman Inst. for Holocaust Studies, 2003—. Recipient Disting. Faculty award Mich. Assn. Governing Bds., 1993; Am. Coun. Learned Socs. fellow, 1969; Stanford Ctr. for Advanced Study fellow, 1969-70, Rsch. fellow NATO, 1996; grantee Am. Coun. Learned Socs., 1983, Johnson Libr., 1982, 88, Can. Govt., 1987; named to Hewlett-Woodmere Alumni Hall of Fame, 2005. Mem. Coun. on Peace Rsch. in History (nat. coun. 1986-90, pres. 1990-92), Am. Hist. Assn., Atlantic Coun. (acad. assoc.), Orgn. Am. Historians, Soc. for Historians of Am. Fgn. Rels. (Warren Kuehl prize 1989). Home: 1815 Northwood Blvd Royal Oak MI 48073-3919 Office: Wayne State U Dept History 3119 Fab Detroit MI 48202 Office Phone: 313-577-6138. E-mail: M.Small@Wayne.edu.

**SMALL, MELVIN D.,** physician, educator; b. Somerville, Mass., May 22, 1925; s. Sidney J. and Ida (Gelbsman) Small; m. Judith Nogee, Dec. 23, 1962; children: Michael Dorian, Michele. AB, U. Wis., 1953; MD, Duke U., 1959; studied under Dr. Gregory Pincus, Worcester Found. Exptl. Biol. and Medicine, 1950-53; studied under Prof. Brian Abel-Smith, London Sch. Econs., 1986-90, MPhil, 1988. Lic. physician Fla., Md., DC, Va. Intern Georgetown U. Hosp., Washington, 1959-60, resident, 1960-61, chief gastrointestinal rsch., 1961-64, instr. medicine, 1961-66, asst. prof., 1966-67, asst. clin. prof., 1967-83, 93—; chief gastroenterology sect. Georgetown divsn. DC Gen. Hosp., 1964-68. Chief animal experimentation cancer rsch. under Dr. Sidney Farber Children's Med. Ctr., Boston, 1948—50; rsch. asst. Boston U. Sch. Medicine, 1956—57; lectr. hygiene and preventive medicine Peace Corps groups, Ethiopia, Turkey, Brazil, and Columbia Georgetown U., 1961—62; active staff Fairfax (Va.) Hosp., 1961—73, Arlington (Va.) Hosp., 1961—85, Cir. Terr. Hosp., Alexandria, 1965—85, Commonwealth Drs. Hosp., Fairfax, 1969—74, Mt. Vernon Hosp., Alexandria, 1976—85; attending physician DC Gen. Hosp., 1961—68, Georgetown U. Hosp. 1961—81, 1993—, Mt. Sinai Hosp. Miami Beach, Fla., 1992—; cons. Children's Hosp., Washington, 1962—66; chmn. dept. medicine Alexandria Hosp., 1974—75, hon. staff mem., 1985—89, 1992—; founder, chmn. No. Va. Consortium Continuing Med. Edn., 1974—86; chmn. emeritus No. Va. Consotium Continuing Med. Edn., 1986; witness subcom. small bus. U.S. Senate, 1967; lectr in field; founder, chmn. Nat. Coun. State Coms. Continuing Med. Edn., 1977—79. Author: publs. in field. Nominated candidate Palm Beach (Fla.) Town Coun., 1995—96; trustee Jefferson Meml. Hosp., 1965—74, mem. founding group, 1965, chmn. pharmacy com., 1965—76, co-chmn. tissue com., 1965—74; Fellow, Mallory Inst. Pathology, 1953—59, Gastroenterology Rsch., Evans Meml. Hosp., 1951—53. Mem.: ACP, AMA, Palm Beach County Med. Soc., Alexandria Med. Soc. (v.p. 1979—80), Med. Soc. Va. (chmn. commn. continuing med. edn. 1978—81), DC Med. Soc., Am. Soc. Gastrointestinal Endoscopy, Am. Physiol. Soc., Am. Inst. Nutrition, Am. Gastroent. Assn., Am. Coll. Gastroenterology. Home: 47 Saint George Pl Palm Beach Gardens FL 33418 Office Phone: 561-596-4025. Personal E-mail: drmelv@davisp.com.

**SMALL, NATALIE SETTIMELLI,** retired pediatric mental health counselor; b. Quincy, Mass., June 2, 1933; d. Joseph Peter and Edmea Natalie (Bagnaschi) Settimelli; m. Parker Adams Small, Jr., Aug. 26, 1956; children: Parker Adams III, Peter McMichael, Carla Edmea. BA, Tufts U., 1955; MA, EdS, U. Fla., 1976, PhD, 1987. Cert. child life specialist. Pediatric counselor U. Fla. Coll. Medicine, Gainesville, 1976-80, Shands Hosp.-U. Fla., Gainesville, 1980-87, supr. child life dept. patient and family resources, 1987—2003; pres. Small Group Cons.com, 2003—. Adminstrv. liaison for self-dir. work teams, mem. faculty Ctr. for Coop. Learning for Health and Sci. Edn., Gainesville, 1988-2003, assoc. dir., 1996, supr. pastoral svcs., 1998-2003; cons. and lectr. in field. Author: Parents Know Best, 1991; co-author team packs series for teaching at risk adolescent health edn. Building Strong Families, 1998. Bd. dirs. Ronald McDonald House, Gainesville, 1980—, mem. exec. com., 1991-05; bd. dirs. Gainesville Assn. Creative Arts, 1994—; mem. health profl. adv. com. March of Dimes, Gainesville, 1986-96, HIV prevention planning partnership, 1995-96; mem. Teen Pregnancy Prevention Action Com., 1994-00, exec. com. Children's Hosp., 1998-03. Recipient Thayer Acad. Humanitarian award, 2006, Caring and Sharing award Ronald McDonald House, 1995, Appreciation award March of Dimes, 1996; Boston Stewart Club scholar, Florence, Italy, 1955; grantee Jessie Ball Du Pont Fund, 1978, Children's Miracle Network, 1990, 92-95, 97, 2000, 01-03. Mem. ACA. Roman Catholic. Avocations: travel, reading, swimming. Home: 3454 NW 12th Ave Gainesville FL 32605-4811 E-mail: smallgroup2@aol.com.

**SMALL, PARKER ADAMS, JR.,** pediatrician, educator; b. Cin., July 5, 1932; s. Parker Adams and Grace (McMichael) S.; m. Natalie Settimelli, Aug. 26, 1956; children: Parker Adams, Peter McMichael, Carla Edmea. Student, Tufts U., 1950-53; MD, U. Cin., 1957; BS extraordinent, 1986. Med. intern Pa. Hosp., Phila., 1957-58; rsch. assoc. Nat. Heart Inst. NIH, Washington, 1958-60; rsch. fellow St. Mary's Hosp., London, 1960-61; sr. surgeon NIMH, Washington, 1961-66; prof. immunology and med. microbiology U. Fla., 1966-95, chmn. dept., 1966-75, prof. pediat., 1979—2003, prof. emeritus, 2003—, prof. pathology, 1995—2003, prof. emeritus, 2003—, adj. prof. large animal sci., 1999—2003; pres. PigVax Inc., 2000—01. Dir. Ctr. for Coop. Learning for Health Sci. Edn., U. Fla., 1998-2003; vis. prof. U. Lausanne, Switzerland, 1972, U. Lagos, Nigeria, 1982, Al Hada Hosp., Saudi Arabia, 1983; rsch. assoc. Nat. Acad. Sci., Washington, 1973; assoc. life scis. panel Nat. Acad. Scis., 1981-88, co-chmn., 1982-83; bd. dirs. Biol. Sci. Curriculum Study, 1984-90, exec. bd., 1987-90; mem. adv. com. Nat. Fund Med. Edn., 1984-87; mem. study com. Nat. Bd. Med. Examiners, 1983-85, mem. nat. vaccine adv. com., 1987-91, chmn. subcom. on new vaccines, 1987-91; v.p. smallgroupconsultants.com, 2003—; mem. Truro Shellfish Advisory Com.; cons. in field. Creator patient oriented problem solving system/POPS, for tchg. immunology and coop. learning to med.

students and Team Packs for tchg. K-12 & coll. students health edn. and coop. learning; co-dir. Fla. Ptnrs. in Prevention of Substance Abuse, 1997-2003; editor: The Secretory Immunologic System, 1971; mem. editl. bd. Infection and Immunity, 1974-76, Jour. Med. Edn., 1978-80; cons. editor Microbios, Cytobios; patentee in field; contbr. more than 150 articles to profl. jours. Sec., treas. Oakmont, Md., 1964-65, mayor, 1965-66; chmn. Citizens for Pub. Schs. Gainesville, Fla., 1969-70; mem. Teen Pregnancy Prevention Action Com., 1998-2000, Truro Shellfish Adv. Com., 2004-. With USPHS, 1958-60, 61-66. Named Tchr. of Yr. U. Fla. Coll. Medicine, 1978-79, Disting. Lectr. AMA, 1986; recipient Presdl. medallion U. Fla., 1987, Nat. Basic Sci. Disting. Tchg. award Alpha Omega Alpha, 1993, Jacob Ehrenzeller award, 1995, Pres.'s Faculty Humanitarian award U. Fla., 1996, Pep award U. Fla., 1998, Lifetime Achievement award U. Fla. Coll. Medicine, 2003; NIH spl. fellow, 1960-61, rsch. grantee, 1966-91, U. Fla. Tchr./Scholar and commencement spkr., 1987; invited lectr. Assn. Am. Med. Colls., 1992. Mem. AAAS, Am. Assn. Immunologists (edn. com. 1983-86), Physicians for Social Responsibility, Fla. Med. Assn., Phi Beta Kappa, Sigma Xi, Alpha Omega Alpha, Theta Delta Chi. Home: 3454 NW 12th Ave Gainesville FL 32605-4811 Office: U Fla Coll Med PO Box 100275 Gainesville FL 32610-0275 Personal E-mail: smallgroup2@aol.com. Business E-Mail: small@pathology.ufl.edu.

**SMALL, PARKER ADAMS, III,** investment banker; b. Phila., Feb. 1, 1958; s. Parker Adams Jr. and Natalie (Settimelli) S.; m. Katherine Currier, Aug. 24, 1985; children: Margaret Edmea, Elizabeth Parker. BA, Dartmouth Coll., 1980; MBA, Harvard U., 1985. Account exec. Leo Burnett Advt., Chgo., 1980-83; assoc. Merrill Lynch-Becker Paribas, N.Y.C., 1984; product mgmt. The Gillette Co., Boston, 1985-86; mgmt. cons. Arthur D. Little Inc., Cambridge, Mass., 1986-89; v.p. Butler Capital Corp., N.Y.C., 1989-92. Pres. S.R.S. Sera Co., Gainesville, Fla., 1976-91; bd. dirs. Julius Koch USA Inc., Strine Printing Co., Lancaster Press Inc. Author: Understanding Immunology, 1976; producer Dartmouth Coll. video. 1980. Reunion chmn. Dartmouth Coll., 1990, mem. alumni coun., 1999; bd. dirs. Wellesley Edn. Found. Avocations: skiing, tennis, scuba diving. Home: 11 Westwood Rd Wellesley MA 02482-7015

**SMALL, RAY,** university administrator; b. Winters, Tex., Aug. 2, 1915; s. George Norman Small and Etta Thompson; m. Dollee Georgia Meyer, Aug. 6, 1938 (div. Jan. 1981); children: Marilynn, Andra; m. Maria Victoria De Leon, Aug. 14, 1998. BA, West Tex. A&M, 1937; MA, U. Tex., 1941, PhD, 1958. Prin. Quail (Tex.) Pub. Sch., 1937-38; tchr. Wayside (Tex.) Sch., 1938-40, prin., 1940-41; tchr. Horace Mann Sch., Amarillo, Tex., 1941—43; prof. Amarillo Coll., Tex., 1946—61; prof., asst. to pres. Tex. Western Coll., El Paso, 1961-63; prof., dean U. Tex., El Paso, 1963-79, acting dir. student publication, 1985-90, editl. advisor-student publs., 1990-95, acad. advisor-comms., 1995—2005. Emeritus dean liberal arts U. Tex., 1979, emeritus prof. English, 1981, emeritus prof. comm., 1995. Served to comdr. USNR, 1943—75. Presbyterian. Home: 603 E Baltimore Dr El Paso TX 79902

**SMALL, RICHARD DONALD,** travel company executive; b. West Orange, NJ, May 24, 1929; s. Joseph George and Elizabeth (McGarry) S.; m. Arlene P. Small; children: Colleen P., Richard Donald, Joseph W., Mark G., Brian P. AB cum laude, U. Notre Dame, 1951. With Union-Camp Corp., NYC, 1952-62, Chgo., 1962—; chmn. Alumni Holidays, Inc., 1962—, AHI Internat. Corp., 1962—; pres. All Horizons, Inc., 1982—2000; cons. in field, 2001—. Chmn. AHI, Inc., 1982-89; bd. dirs. French Cruise Lines, Des Plaines, Ill., Russian Cruise Lines, Alumni Campus Abroad, 1994—. Recipient Munich Ptnr. award, 1989. Mem.: Carlton Club (Chgo.), Univ. Club Chgo. Home: Water Tower Pl 180 E Pearson St # 3306 Chicago IL 60611-6730 also: Wailea Golf Estates 3954 Waakaula Pl Wailea HI 96753 Personal E-mail: royals@hawaii.rr.com.

**SMALL, SARAH MAE,** volunteer; b. Salisbury, N.C., Nov. 16, 1923; d. Clint and Lillie Mae (Wilbourn) Evans; m. Jesse Small Sr., May 4, 1941; children: Jesse Jr., Jean Carol Small Bell. Cert., Cortez Bus. Sch., 1948. File clk. gen. acctg. office Fed. Govt., Washington, 1941-47; sec., stenographer CIA, Washington, 1948-52, adminstrv. asst. McLean, Va., 1952-65, ret., 1965. Elected pres. Energetic Crusaders, Inc., 1993—. Pres. Energetic Crusaders, Inc., 1993; bd. dirs. ARC, Washington, 1986-87, Children's Edn. Found., Inc., 1989—. Recipient Outstanding and Dedicated Vol. Svc. award Kiwanis Club of Capital Centre, 1985, Plaque in Recognition of Dedicated and Outstanding Vol. Svc. to the Corps and Washington D.C., Cmty. Jr. Citizen's Corps., 1989, Appreciation award for Outstanding and Dedicated Vol. Svc. to Corps, Jr. Citizens Corps., Inc., 1990, Appreciation award Jr. Citizens Corp., Inc., 1990, Cmty. Svc. award for leadership and youth advocacy Bus. and Profl. Women's League, Inc., 1991, Vol. award achievement excellence svc. youths of Jr. Citizens Corps., Inc., 1992, others. Mem. Jr. Citizens Corps (life, pres. 1985—, Dedicated Cmty. Svc. award 1983, Bus. and Cmty. Svc. award 1986), Bus. and Profl. Women's League (treas. 1982-86), Women in Arts (chartered, pres. 1984—), Nat. Coun. Negro Women, World Affairs Coun. Washington, Agrl. Coun. Am. Democrat. Baptist. Avocations: travel, photography, walking, swimming. Home: 2010 Upshur St NE Washington DC 20018-3244

**SMALL, WILFRED THOMAS,** surgeon, educator; b. Boston, June 13, 1920; s. Fred Wentworth and Isabelle (Scott) S.; m. Muriel Yoe Gratton, Sept. 15, 1948; children: Wilfred Thomas, Richard Gratton, James Stewart, John Wentworth. BS, Bowdoin Coll., 1943; MD, Tufts U., 1946. Diplomate Am. Bd. Surgery. Intern surg. svc. The Boston Children's Hosp., 1946-47, rsch. fellow, 1947-48; assoc. in surgery Peter Bent Brigham Hosp./Harvard U., 1949-50; resident, chief resident in surgery New Eng. Med. Ctr., Tufts U., 1950-53; practice medicine specializing in surgery Worcester, Mass., 1953-88; mem. staff Meml. Hosp., 1953-88, chief divsn. surgery, 1973-81; from assoc. prof. to prof. surgery Tufts U., Mass., Worcester, 1973—, Instr. Harvard U., 1949-50, Tufts U., 1952-60. Contbr. articles to profl. jours. Active Worcester Art Mus., Worcester County Music Assn.; sec. bd. dirs. Indian River UN Assn. Served to lt. (j.g.) USN, 1947-49. Fellow ACS (pres. Mass. chpt. 1979); mem. AMA, New Eng. Surg. Soc., New Eng. Cancer Soc., Soc. Surgery Alimentary Tract, Mass. Med. Soc., Pan Am. Med. Soc., Am. Trauma Soc., Indian River Hosp. Assn. (bd. dirs.), Vis. Nurses Assn. (bd. dirs.), Worcester Econs. Club (past pres.), Worcester Coun. on Fgn. Rels., Tatnuck Country Club, Sakonnet Golf Club, Riomar Golf Club (Vero Beach, Fla.). Episcopalian. Home: 16 Warrens Point Rd Little Compton RI 02837-1433 E-mail: Thecuff80@aol.com.

**SMALL, WILLIAM EDWIN, JR.,** association and recreation executive; b. Jackson, Mich., Jan. 18, 1937; s. William Edwin and Lena Louisa (Hunt) S.; m. Ruth Ann Toombs, Mar. 28, 1959; children: Suzanne Marie, William Edwin III, Bryan Anthony. As. Jackson C.C., 1959; BS in Geology, Mich. State U., 1961, MA in Journalism, 1964. Reporter Sci. Svc., Washington, 1961-62; writer sci. U. Chgo., 1963-64; staff, sci. info. officer Pa. State U., State College, 1964-66; corr. McGraw-Hill, Washington, 1966-69; staff com. pub. works U.S. Senate, 1969—71; founding editor Biomed. News, 1969-71; dir. pub. info. Nat. Bur. Standards, Washington, 1972-76; editor Am. Pharmacy Jour., 1979-82; dir. media and info. svcs. AMA, Washington, 1982-86; exec. dir. Nat. Found. Infectious Diseases, Washington, 1986-91, Assn. Biotech. Cos., 1991-93; CEO, Bioconfs. Internat., Bethesda, Md., 1993-95, WESmall & Assocs., Assn. Execs., Louisa, Va., 1976—. Owner recreation resort Small Country Campground, Louisa, 1976—; exec. dir. Va. Biotech. Assn., 1996-2000, Va. Campground Assn., 2001-03; developer Weswood Estates properties, Louisa, 2004-. Author: Third Pollution, 1971. With Security Agy., AUS, 1955-59. Recipient Superior Accomplishment award U.S. Dept. Commerce, 1974. Fellow AAAS; life mem. Nat. Assn. Sci. Writers. Office: PO Box 343 Louisa VA 23093-0343

**SMALLEY, CHRISTOPHER JOSEPH,** pharmaceutical company professional; b. Phila., June 26, 1953; s. Charles Wilfred and Verna May (Coulter) S.; m. Maria Visnieske, Aug. 9, 1974; children: Christa Maria, Mark Charles, Lora Loray. BS, Phila. Coll. Pharmacy and Sci., 1976; MBA, Temple U., 1982; PhD, LaSalle U., 1991. Ordained elder, Presbyn. ch., 1992. Mfg. pharmacist supr. McNeil Labs., Fort Washington, Pa., 1976-77; mfg. pharmacist group supr. McNeil Consumer Products Co., 1978-79, mfg. pharmacist

mgr., 1980-85; tech. svcs. mgr. Janssen Pharmaceutica, 1985-88, plant mgr., 1988-94; quality assurance dir. Sanofi rsch. divsn. Sanofi Pharms., Inc., Malvern, Pa., 1994-98; dir. validation compliance Wyeth-Ayerst Pharms., St. Davids, Pa., 1998—. Mem. Reg. Nat. Com., 1979—. With USNR Med. Corps., 1986-95, with USAF, 1995—. Mem. Am. Pharm. Assn., Assn. Mil. Surgeons of U.S., Am. Assn. Pharm. Scientists, Internat. Soc. Pharm. Engrs., Aerospace Med. Assn., Am. Acad. Med. Adminstrs., Assn. Med. Svc. Corps Officers, Pa. Pharm. Assn., Inst. Environ. Scis., Eastern Assn. GMP Trainers, Parenteral Drug Assn. (chmn. tng. com.), Pharm. Mfrs. Assn. (prodn. sect.), Phila. Pharm. Forum, USN Inst., NRA, Kappa Psi. Presbyterian. Home: 816 Kenmara Dr West Chester PA 19380-2022 Office: 240 N Radnor Chester Rd Saint Davids PA 19087-5106

**SMALLEY, ROBERT MANNING,** diplomat; b. Los Angeles, Nov. 14, 1925; s. William Denny and Helen (McConnell) S.; m. Lois Louisa Williamson, Nov. 28, 1948 (div.) m. Rosemary Sumner, Jan. 4, 1957; children— Leslie Estelle, David Christian. Student, UCLA, 1946-48. Radio news editor Mut. Radio Broadcasting System, Los Angeles, 1950-55; mgr. Agrl. Info. Inc., Sacramento, 1957-59; with Whitaker & Baxter, San Francisco, 1956-57, 59-61; sec. Mayor, San Francisco, 1961-63; asst. dir. pub. relations Republican Nat. Com., 1964; press sec. Republican vice presdl. candidate William E. Miller, 1964; dir. pub. relations Republican Nat. Com., 1965; v.p. Whitaker & Baxter, San Francisco, 1966-68; asst. press sec. Republican vice presdl. candidate Spiro Agnew, 1968; spl. asst. Sec. Commerce, Washington, 1969-72; adminstrv. asst. U.S. Senator Robert P. Griffin, Washington, 1972-73; dir. corp. affairs Potomac Electric Power Co., Washington, 1973-75; U.S. rep. devel. assistance com. O.E.C.D., Paris, 1975-77; spl. asst. U.S. Senator Robert P. Griffin, Washington, 1977-78; asst. to campaign mgr. Reagan for Pres. Com., Washington, 1979; sr. advisor mgmt. communications IBM, 1979-82; dep. asst. sec. of state pub. affairs Dept. of State, Washington, 1982-87, U.S. amb. to Kingdom of Lesotho, 1987-89; lectr. in U.S. politics and pub. policy. Author: (book) The Admiralities at War 1944-45, 2002. Campaign mgr. Senator Robert P. Griffin, MIch., 1966, 72. Served with USN, 1944-46, PTO. Republican. Episcopalian. Home: 3131 Connecticut Ave NW Apt 2302 Washington DC 20008

**SMALLWOOD, CAROL,** writer; b. Cheboygan, Mich., May 3, 1939; d. Lloyd Gouine and Lucille Drozdowska; m. T.M. Smallwood, 1963 (div. 1976); children: Michael, Ann. BS, Ea. Mich. U., 1961, M in History, 1963; MLS, We. Mich. U., 1976. Tchr. Mich. Pub. Schs., 1961—64; grad. asst. Western Mich. U., Kalamazoo, 1975-76; Title I libr. cons. Northland (Mich.), Grand Traverse (Mich.) Library Systems, 1976-77; head media dir. Pellston (Mich.) Pub. Schs., 1977—97; writer, libr. cons. classes Mt. Pleasant, 1998—. Asst. dir. Northland Libr. System, Alpena, Mich., 1977; developer, operator ednl. materials clearinghouse, 1981-83; adult edn. tchr. Cheboygan Area Schs., 1985-86. Author: Free Michigan Materials for Educators, 1980, 2nd edit., 1986, Free Materials Resource Disk, 1983, Exceptional Free Library Resource Materials, 1984, Free Resource Builder, 1985, 2d edit., 1992, A Guide to Selected Federal Agency Programs and Publications for Librarians and Teachers, 1986, Health Resource Builder, 1988, An Educational Guide to the National Park System, 1989, Current Issues Builder, 1989, Library Puzzles and Word Games, for Grades 7-12, 1990, Reference Puzzles and Word Games for Grades 7-12, 1991, Michigan Authors, 1993, Helpful Hints for the School Library, 1993, Recycling Tips for Teachers and Librarians, 1995, An Insider's Guide to Libraries, 1997, Free or Low-Cost Health Information, 1998; (with S. McElmeel) WWW Almanac, 1999; (with B. Hudson, A. Riedling, J. Rotole) Internet Sources on Each U.S. State, 2005, Educators as Writers: Publishing for Personal and Professional Development, 2006; author 100 poems in English Jour., Poesia, others; contbr; columnist Detroit News; others. Charter bd. mem., publicity chmn. Cheboygan Area Arts Coun.; founder, pres. Cheboygan County Humane Soc.; co-founder Humane Animal Treatment Soc. Recipient 1st prize for fiction, Byline Mag., 2004. Mem.: Doris Day Animal Found. Mailing: PO Box 1485 Mount Pleasant MI 48804 E-mail: smallwood@tm.net.

**SMALLWOOD, GLENN WALTER, JR.,** utility marketing management executive; b. Jeffersonville, Ind., Oct. 12, 1956; s. Glenn Walter and Darlene Ruth (Zeller) S. BSBA, S.E. Mo. State U., 1978; MA in Bus., Webster U., 1992, MBA, 1993. Cert. econ. developer Inst. Econ. Devel. Cert., counselor, energy mgr. Customer svc. advisor Union Electric Co., Mexico, Mo., 1979—95, Cape Girardeau, Mo., 1995—97; cmty. devel. exec. Ameren Svcs., Cape Girardeau, 1997—98, bus. devel. exec., 1998—. Instr. Mexico Vo-Tech Sch., 1981; panelist on home design Mo. Extension Svc., 1984; co. advisor Mo. Bus. Week. Coord. local United Way, 1984; mem., chair Gt. Rivers coun. Boy Scouts Am., chair Shawnee dist. Eagle Scout advancement com., 1999-2001, chair Shawnee Dist. com., 2002--; panelist Mo. Freedmon Forum, 1990; charter mem. class Mo. Leadership; chmn. Leadership Mexico Program; coordinating advisor Jr. Achievement, Mexico H.S.; committeeman, chmn. Republican Party of Audrain County; bd. dirs. Mo. Rep. Grassroots Caucus, S.E. Mo. Univ. Found., 1998—chmn. Cape Girardeau Planning and Zoning Commn., 2004—; adv. coun. Cape Girardeau County Jr. Achievement, 2005-06. Named among Ten Outstanding Young Missourians, Mo. Jaycees, 1993; recipient Disting. Svc. award, Mexico, Mo. Jaycees, 1993. Mem. Am. Mktg. Assn. (profl.), Nat. Eagle Scout Assn. (bd. dirs. St. Louis coun.), Cooper Dome Soc., Boy Scouts Am. Alumni Family, Mexico Area C. of C. (bd. dirs. 1993-95), Cape Girardeau C. of C. (chair govtl. affairs com.), S.E. Mo. U. Alumni Assn., Inst. Cert. Profl. Mgrs. (cert. mgr.), Assn. Energy Engrs. (cert. energy mgr.), Adminstrv. Mgmt. Soc., Optimists (Youth Appreciation award 1974), Kiwanis (cert. appreciation 1984), Mexico Noon (bd. dirs. 1990, treas. 1990-91, v.p. 1991-92, pres. 1993-94), Audrain County Pachyderm Club (bd. dirs., 2d v.p. 1990-92, pres. 1993), S.E. Mo. Univ. Found. (bd. dirs.), S.E. Mo. Pachyderm Club (founder, pres. 1997-98), Mo. Fedn. Pachyderm Clubs (bd. dirs.), Honorable Order Ky. Cols. (comml. Ky. col. 1995), Sons of Confederate Vets., Disting. Hoosier Soc. (State of Ind. 1999), Rotary (treas. 2004-05, pres. elect 2005-06), 1889er Soc. Republican. Avocations: music, sports, baseball, basketball, tennis. Office: Ameren Svcs 2222 Kent Dr Cape Girardeau MO 63701 Business E-Mail: gsmallwood@ameren.com.

**SMALLWOOD, ROBERT ALBIAN, JR.,** retired secondary education educator; b. Phila., Oct. 3, 1946; s. Robert Albian and Mildred May (Miller) S.; m. Geraldine Ann Boozan, May 27, 1972; children: Amy Lynn, Daniel James. BSc, Rider Coll., 1969, MA, 1976; EdS, Rutgers U., 1986. Cert. social studies tchr., secondary sch. prin., super. curriculum and instrn., Pa.; cert. social studies and gen. bus. tchr., prin., supr., sch. bus. adminstr., asst. supt. bus., sch. adminstr. (supt.) N.J. Tchr. social studies Trenton Bd. Edn., 1973-76, tchr. bus. edn., 1975-76, sch. disciplinarian, 1976-84, 94-97; acting asst. prin. Jr. High Sch. 2, 1980-83, tchr. U.S. history, 1983-87, chmn. social studies dept., 1984-85; acting asst. prin. Carroll Robbins Elem. Sch., Jr. High Schs. #1 and #5, 1987-88; tchr. gifted and talented social studies Dunn Jr. High Sch., 1989-93, social studies tchr., 1997-99, whole sch. reform site facilitator, 1999—2005; ret., 2005. Mem. Dist.'s Affirmative Action Adv. Council; mem. Nat. Tchr. Corps Project, Trenton Area; fin. advisor M.S. Prin., 1998-2005. Asst. ops. officer Trenton CD Unit, 1974-76, asst. disaster analysis officer, 1976, disaster analysis officer, 1976-79; trustee N.J. Coun. for Alcohol/Drug Edn., 1983-99, mem. exec. coun., 1985-95, 96-99, chmn. nominating com., 1985, 86, treas., 1987-95, acting exec. dir., 1994-95, v.p., 1996-98, pres. 1998-99. With U.S. Army, 1969-72. Decorated Bronze Star, Army Commendation medal with oak leaf cluster, Joint Svc. Commendation medal. Mem. NEA, Vietnam Vets. Am., Va. Geneal. Soc., Md. Geneal. Soc., Md. Hist. Soc., Geneal. Soc. Pa., Nat. Geneal. Soc., Assn. Profl. Genealogists, Phi Delta Kappa. Home: 2 Leese Ave Trenton NJ 08609-1828 E-mail: RASteach@aol.com.

**SMALLY, DONALD JAY,** consulting engineering executive; b. Cleve., 1922; s. Daniel James and Alice (Rohrheimer) S.; m. Ruth Janet Glasser, July 8, 1944; children: Alan Jon, Leonard Arthur. BME, U. Cin., 1949. Prodn. engr. N. Ransohoff, Inc., Cin., 1949-50; chief engr. Mosby Engring. Assocs., Sarasota, Fla., 1952-55; prin. Smally, Wellford & Nalven, Inc., Sarasota, 1956-91. Mem. tech. adv. com. Manatee Community Coll., Sarasota, 1965-

90; mem. adv. com. Vocat.-Tech. High Sch., Sarasota, 1968-80 V.p. Sarasota YMCA, 1968-71, Sarasota Opera Assn., 1975-88, pres., 1988-89; chmn. Sarasota Vol. Talent Pool, 1973-76; sec.-treas. Civitan Found., 1965-79; bd. dirs. Suncoast Heart Assn., 1976; mem. Fla. Coordinating Coun. for Vocat. and Adult Edn., 1984-95, chmn., 1987-88; chmn. Sarasota Hist. Preservation Bd., 1988-91; pres. Sarasota County Rd. Improvement Task Force, 1990-93; mem. Sarasota County Pub. Sch. Found., 1990-95, chmn., 1990-91; v.p. Hist. Soc. Sarasota, 1990-91, Children's Haven and Adult Cmty. Svcs., 1983-99, pres., 1991-94; pres. John Ringling Ctr. Found., 1991-98; mem. Plymouth Harbor Bd., 1994-99; bd. dirs. Sarasota Alliance for Hist. Preservation, 2004—. Recipient Good Citizenship award SAR, 1975, Disting. Alumni award U. Cin. Engring. Coll., 1985, Outstanding Svc. award Myakna Chpt. Fla. Engring. Soc., 1993; named Citizen of Yr. Sarasota Civitan Club, 1975, Engr. of Yr. Sarasota-Manatee Engrs. Soc., 1976. Fellow Am. Coun. Engring. Cos. (treas. 1980-82), Fla. Engring. Soc. (pres. Sarasota-Manatee chpt. 1956-58); mem. Sarasota County C. of C. (past dir., v.p. 1983), Cons. Engrs. Council Fla. (pres. 1968), Fla. Soc. Profl. Land Surveyors (chpt. pres. 1973), Am. Water Works Resources Assn. (pres. Fla. Soc. 1981), Sarasota-Manatee Engring. Soc.

**SMARDZ, ZOFIA JADWIGA,** editor, writer; b. Reinbek, Germany, Oct. 20, 1950; arrived in U.S., 1950; d. Stanislaw Kostka and Krystyna Maria Smardz; m. Daniel Felix Arnaud, Oct. 11, 1975 (div. 1984); m. Charles Anson Franklin, Feb. 27, 1987; children: Andrew, Roman. BA, Vassar Coll., 1972; M Journalism, U. Calif., Berkeley, 1975. Reporter Washington Star, 1976—81; fgn. corr. Newsweek, Bonn, Germany, 1981—84, corr. Washington, 1984—86; editorial Washington Post, 2000. Freelance editor, cons., Washington, 1986—2000. Co-author: Special Trust, 1994; writer, editor: Awakening Intuition, 1997. Bd. edn. Our Lady of Victory Sch., Washington, 1997—99. Fellow, Alicia Patterson Found., Washington, 1986; scholar, Woodrow Wilson Ctr., Washington, 1986; Fulbright fellow, 1972. Republican. Roman Catholic. Avocations: music, voice, piano, flute, gardening. E-mail: smardzz@washpost.com.

**SMARR, TRACY JEAN,** psychologist; b. Warrensburg, Mo., Nov. 16, 1976; d. Kenneth B. and Susan J. Smarr. Degree in edn. specialist, U. Mo., 2002. Lic. sch. psychologist Kans., 2001. Sch. psychologist WYCO SPED Coop., Kansas City, 2001—. Mem.: Nat. Assn. Sch. Psychologist. Office: Wyandotte Spl Edn Coop 4601 State Ave Ste 38/SPED Kansas City KS 66112 Office Phone: 913-627-5685.

**SMART, ALLEN RICH, II,** retired lawyer; b. Chgo., July 3, 1934; s. Jackson W. Smart and Dorothy (Byrnes) Bowles. Student, Deerfield Acad., 1949-52; AB magna cum laude, Princeton U., 1956; LLB, Harvard U., 1961. Bar: Ill. 1961. Assoc. Bell Boyd & Lloyd, Chgo., 1961-69, ptnr., 1970-91, of counsel, 1992—2001. Bd. dirs. Rec. for Blind, Inc., Chgo., 1984-95, vice-chmn., 1987-90; co-chmn. zoning com. Old Town Triangle Assn., Chgo., 1987-94; bd. dirs. Lawrence Hall Sch. for Boys, 1965-70, Old Masters Soc., Art Inst., 1987—; governing mem. Orchestral Assn. Lt. USNR, 1956-58. Mem.: ABA, Chgo. Opera Theater (dir. 2002—), Renaissance Soc. Chgo. (bd. dirs. 1988—), Inst. for Psychoanalysis (dir. 2001—), Friends of the Pks. Chgo. (bd. dirs. 1986—), Infant Welfare Soc. Chgo. (bd. dirs. 1971—95, pres. 1982—86), Racquet Club Chgo., Arts, Lawyers Econ. Clubs of Chgo., Univ. Club (bd. dirs. 1986—89). Home: 1732 N North Park Ave Chicago IL 60614-5710 Office: Bell Boyd & Lloyd 3200 Three First Nat Pl Chicago IL 60602

**SMART, CATHERINE ANNE,** retired administrative assistant; b. Milw., Mar. 24, 1920; d. John Roberts and Cecelia Poteracki; m. Chester Irwin Smart (dec.); adopted children: Richard Paul(dec.), Dianne Lezotte. Student, U. Wis., Milw. Notary pub. With Allis Chalmers Mfg., 1942—44; bookkeeper, sec. Murphy Diesel Co., Milw., 1944—48; sec.-treas. A-1 Machining Inc., Hales Corners, Wis., 1954—70; adminstrv. asst. to assoc. dean Marquette U. Med. Sch., Milw., 1956—58; adminstrv. asst. Charles W. Yoder, Architect, Milw., 1957—58, Nat. Small Bus. Assn., Milw., 1958—60. Pres. YWCA Bus. & Profl. Women's Club, 1941; Sunday sch. tchr. St. John's Ch., Hot Springs, Ark., 1995—99. Mem.: AARP (bd. dirs.), KC (historian, pres. ladies aux.), Good Sam Camping Club (sec.). Roman Catholic. Home: 215 Ostego St Hot Springs AR 71901-7839

**SMART, GEORGE M.,** energy executive, former packaging company executive; BS, Defiance Coll.; MBA, Wharton Sch., U. Penn. With Central States Can Co. (div. of Van Dorn Co.), 1970—78, pres., CEO, 1978—93; chmn., pres. Phoenix Packaging Corp., 1993—2001; pres. Sonoco- Phoenix, Inc., 2001—03; bd. dirs. FirstEnergy Corp., Akron, Ohio, 1997—, chmn., 2004—. Bd. dirs. Ohio Edison Co., 1988—, Ball Corp., 2005—. Office: FirstEnergy Corp 76 S Main St Akron OH 44308*

**SMART, JAMES ANTHONY,** music educator; b. Marietta, Ga., July 21, 1959; s. James Bryant Smart and Patricia Morgan Williams; m. Robin Arlene McDaniel, May 26, 1990; children: Laurel Morgan, Andrew Forrest. MusB, Jacksonville State U., 1982; MusM, Ga. State U., 1985; student in Music Edn., Boston U., 2006—. Adj. prof. U. West Ga., Carrollton, 1995—2001; dir. of bands Cobb County Schs., Mableton, Ga., 2000—; tchg. asst. Auburn U., 1994—96. Orch. dir. First Bapt. Ch., Lithia Springs, Ga., 1995—2005. Office Phone: 770-819-2496. Personal E-mail: james.smart@cobbk12.org.

**SMART, JILL BELLAVIA,** financial consultant; b. Chgo., Oct. 16, 1959; d. Salvatore and patricia (Foran) B.; m. Stephen D. Smart; two children. BS, U. Ill., 1981; MBA, U. Chgo., 1991. Assoc. ptnr. Accenture Ltd., Chgo., 1981—89, mng. ptnr. human resource delivery/Chgo. office, lead ptnr., 1989—. Bd. trustee Accenture Found. Vol. Treehouse Animal Found., Chgo., 1986-90, Chgo. Area Runners Assn., 1986—; bd. dirs. Goodman Theater, Chgo.; dir. United Way Met. Chgo.; mem. pres. adv. coun. U. Ill. Named one of Chgos. 100 Most Influential Women, Crain's Chgo. Bus., 2004. Republican. Roman Catholic. Avocations: jogging, aerobics, travel, reading, skiing. Office Phone: 312-693-0161.

**SMART, JUDITH ANN,** mathematics professor; d. Paul Frederick and Keneta Mae Decker; m. Philip Amos Smart, Aug. 22, 1970; children: Renée Annette, Eric Philip. BS in Edn. and Math., Otterbein Coll., Westerville, Ohio, 1970; MA in Edn., Heidelberg Coll., Tiffin, Ohio, 1999. Math. tchr. Lakota H.S., Rising Sun, Ohio, 1970, Upper Arlington Schs., Ohio, 1970—71, Newport News Schs., Va., 1971—73; subsitute math tchr. Clyde-Green Springs Schs., Ohio, 1973—80; math. instr. Terra C.C., Fremont, Ohio, 1983—. Mem. adv. bd. for apprentices Terra C.C., Fremont, 2005—. Choir mem. Trinity United Meth. Ch., Fremont, 1965—, Sunday sch. tchr., 1973—, fin. sec., 1976—. Recipient Adj. Faculty Excellence award, Terra C.C., 1991, Nat. Inst. Staff and Devel. ORgnl. Devel. Excellence award, 2001, U. Tex., Austin, 2001, Cir. Excellence award, Terra C.C., 2006. Mem.: Beta Sigma Phi (v.p., Order of the Rose). Republican. Avocations: crocheting, flower arranging, gardening, playing piano for quartet. Home: 1455 CR 31 Fremont OH 43420 Office: Terra CC 2830 Napolean Rd Fremont OH 43420

**SMART, MARY-LEIGH CALL (MRS. J. SCOTT SMART),** civic worker; b. Springfield, Ill., Feb. 27, 1917; d. S(amuel) Leigh and Mary (Bradish) Call; m. J. Scott Smart, Sept. 11, 1951 (dec. 1960). Diploma, Monticello Coll.; 1934; student, Oxford U., 1935; BA, Wellesley Coll., 1937; MA, Columbia U., 1939, postgrad., 1940—41; NYU, 1940—41; painting student, with Bernard Karfiol, 1937—38. Dir. mgmt. Cen. Ill. Grain Farms, Logan County, 1939—; owner Lowtrek Kennel, Ogunquit, Maine, 1957-73, Cove Studio Art Gallery, Ogunquit, 1961-68; art collector, donor, Pa. publicist, 1954—. Cons. in field. Editor: Hamilton Easter Field Art Found. Collection Catalog, 1966; originator, dir. show, compiler of catalog Art: Ogunquit, 1967; Peggy Bacon-A Celebration, Barn Gallery, Ogunquit, 1979. Program dir., sec. bd. Barn Gallery Assoc., Inc., 1958-69, pres., 1969-70, 82-87, asst. treas. 1987-92, hon. dir., 1970-78, adv. trustee, 1992-94, v.p. 1994-2003; curator Hamilton Easter Field Art Found. Collection, 1978-79, curator exhbn., 1979-86, chair exhbn. com., 1987-94; acquisition com. DeCordova Mus.,

Lincoln, Mass., 1966-78; chancellor's coun. U. Tex., 1972—; pres. coun. U. NH, 1978—; bd. dir. Ogunquit C. of C., 1966, treas., 1966-67, hon. life mem. 1968—; bd. overseers Strawbery Banke, Inc., Portsmouth, NH, 1972-75, 3d vice chmn., 1973, 2d vice-chmn., 1974; bd. advisors U. Art Galleries, U. NH, 1973-89; pres., 1981-89; bd. dir. Old York Hist. and Improvement Soc., York, Maine, 1979-81, v.p., 1981-82; adv. com. Bowdoin Coll. Mus. Art Invitational exhibit, 1975, '76 Maine Artists Invitational Exhbn., Maine State Mus., Maine Coast Artists, Rockport, 1975-78, All Maine Biennial '79, Bowdoin Coll. Mus. Art juried exhbn.; mem. jury for scholarship awards Maine com. Skowhegan Sch. Painting & Sculpture, 1982-84; nat. com. Wellesley Coll. Friends of Art, 1983—; adv. trustee Portland Mus. Art, 1983-85, fellow, 1985—; mus. panel Maine State Commn. on Arts and Humanities, 1983-86; adv. com. Maine Biennial, Colby Coll. Mus. Art, 1983; coun. advisors Farnsworth Art Mus., Rockland, Maine, 1986-98; collections com. Payson Gallery, Westbrook Coll., Portland, 1987-91; dir. Greater Piscataqua Cmty. Found., NH Charitable Fund, 1991-97; com. to establish artist's advancement grant, 2001; mem. corp. Ogunquit Mus. Am. Art, 1988-90, 95-2000; active Maine Women's Forum, 1993—; mem. art com. York Pub. Libr., 2002—; pres. Class of 1937, Wellesley Coll., 2001—. Lt. (j.g.) WAVES, 1942-45. Recipient Deborah Morton award Westbrook Coll., 1988, Friend of the Arts award Maine Art Dealers Assn., 1993. Mem. Springfield Art Assn., Jr. League Springfield Ill., Western Maine Wellesley Club. Episcopalian. Address: 30 Surf Point Rd York ME 03909-5053

**SMART, THOMAS A.,** lawyer; AB summa cum laude, Dartmouth Coll., 1971; JD, U. Pa., 1974. Bar: NY 1976, So. and Ea. Dist. NY, US Ct. Appeals, 2nd, 3rd, 9th and 10th Cir., US Supreme Ct. Ptnr. litig., co-chair Intellectual Property and Patent Litig. Group Kaye Scholer LLP, NYC. Mem.: Phi Beta Kappa. Office: Kaye Scholer LLP 425 Park Ave New York NY 10022 Office Phone: 212-836-8761. E-mail: tsmart@kayescholer.com.

**SMARTSCHAN, GLENN FRED,** educational consultant; b. Allentown, Pa., Dec. 11, 1946; s. Fred Gotfred and Joyce Isabel (Hensinger) S.; m. Linda Susan Bastinelli, Mar. 18, 1972; children: Erin Joy, Lauren Nicole. BS in Edn., Kutztown State Coll., 1968; MS in Edn., Temple U., 1972; EdD in Ednl. Adminstrn., Lehigh U., 1979. Cert. tchr. history and comprehensive social studies, secondary prin., supt., Pa. Tchr. 8th grade social studies South Mountain Jr. H.S., 1968-76; adminstrv. asst. to prin. to prin. Raub Jr. H.S., 1976-80, dist. dir. curriculum, 1980-84, asst. to supt. for curriculum and cmty. svcs., 1984-86; supt. schs. Brandywine Hts. Area Sch. Dist., Topton, Pa., 1986-90, Mt. Lebanon Sch. Dist., Pitts., 1990—2003. Adj. prof. Cedar Crest Coll., 1986-88, Duquesne U., 1997, 2005, 06, U. Pitts., 2001; CEO Ednl. Dynamics Cons.; spkr. and cons. Multiple Client Feedback (MCF), Stakeholder Surveys Pay for Performance Plans, Match of Written, Taught and Tested Curriculum, Criterion Referenced Testing, Strategic Planning; ednl. planner Burt Hill, 2003—; cons. Tri-State area study coun. U. Pitts for planning and accountability, 2003— Bd. dirs. Alternative House, Inc., Bethlehem, Pa., 1976-81, chmn. program com., 1977-78, v.p., 1979, pres., 1980; adv. com. Lehigh County (Pa.) Hist. Mus., 1980-86; bd. dirs. Girls Club Allentown, 1983-86, v.p., 1985. Mem. ASCD, Pa. Assn. Supervision and Curriculum Devel. (exec. com., registrar ea. regional meeting, v.p. Ea. region, pres. 1988), Am. Assn. Sch. Adminstrs. (Pa. State Supt. of Yr. 1999), Pa. Assn. Sch. Adminstrs. (pres. 1996), Pa. Sch. Bds. Assn., Juvenile Diabetes Assn. (bd. dirs.), Alumni Coun. Lehigh U. (pres. 1986), Phi Delta Kappa, Fleetwood Club, Rotary (charter mem. Allentown club, exec. com. 1985). Roman Catholic. Home: One Spalding Cir Pittsburgh PA 15228 Office Phone: 412-344-8663. Business E-Mail: edcsmartschan@adelphia.net.

**SMARTT, BILL,** air courier company executive; CFO DHL Airways Inc., Redwood City, Calif.; exec. v.p., CFO, chief administrv. officer DHL Worldwide Express, Redwood City, Calif. Office: Dhl 1200 S Pine Island Rd Ste 170 Plantation FL 33324-4469

**SMATHERS, JAMES BURTON,** medical physicist, educator; b. Prairie du Chien, Wis., Aug. 26, 1935; s. James Levi and Irma Marie (Stindt) S.; m. Sylvia Lee Rath, Apr. 20, 1957; children: Kristine Kay, Kathryn Ann, James Scott, Ernest Kent. B.Nuclear Enging., N.C. State Coll., 1957, MS, 1959; PhD, U. Md., 1967. Diplomate Am. Bd. Radiology, Am. Bd. Health Physics. Am. Bd. Medical Physics; cert. in radiation oncology physics; registered profl. engr., D.C., Tex., Calif. Research engr. Atomics Internat., Canoga Park, Calif., 1959, Walter Reed Army Inst. Research, Washington, 1961-67; prof. nuclear engring. Tex. A. and M. U., College Station, 1967-80, prof., head bioengring., 1976-80; prof., head med. physics, dept. radiation oncology UCLA, 1980-2001, prof. emeritus, 2001— Cons. U.S. Army, Dept. Energy, also pvt.; industry. Served with U.S. Army, 1959-61. Recipient Excellence in Teaching award Gen. Dynamics, 1971; Excellence in Research award Tex. A. and M. U. Former Students Assn., 1976 Mem. Health Physics Soc., Am. Assn. Physcists in Medicine, Sigma Xi, Sigma Pi Sigma, Phi Kappa Phi. Home: 18229 Minnehaha St Northridge CA 91326-3427 E-mail: smathers@ucla.edu.

**SMAW, SHERCODA GENEE,** research scientist; b. Norwalk, Conn., Aug. 18, 1973; BS, Northeastern U., 1996; MS, Howard U., 2002, PhD, 2006. Med.tech. Northeastern U., Boston, 1991—92, Brigham & Women's Hosp., 1992—96, Polestar Labs., Inc., Silver Springs, Md., 1996—98; intern AISES/NIH, Bethesda, 1998; grad. tchg. asst. Howard U., Washington, 1998—99, NSF/Howard U., 1999—2002; biology lab. tech. Prince George's C.C., Largo, Md., 2002—03; grad. tchg. asst. Howard U., 2002—03; substitute tchr. D.C. Pub. Schs., 2002—03; grad. tchg. asst. Howard U., 2003—; staff scientist, night supr. Midwest Rsch. Inst., Rockville, Md., 2004—. Adj. faculty Prince George's C.C., 2003—04. Fellow, Howard U., 1999—2002, Arthur Ashe Jr. Sports scholar, 2001; scholar, AIBS, 2002. Mem.: AAAS, Assn. Southeastern Biologists, Am. Inst. Bio. Scis., Am. Bryological and Lichenological Soc., Am. Indian Sci. & Engring. Soc., Am. Soc. Clin. Pathologists (assoc.), Beta Kappa Chi, Sigma Xi, Alpha Kappa Alpha. Democrat. Baptist. E-mail: ssmaw@hotmail.com.

**SMAY, CONNIE R.,** educational media specialist, educator; b. Benton Harbor, Mich., May 27, 1953; d. Victor Wier and Lois Reynolds; m. James Robert Smay, Aug. 11, 1979; children: Robert James, Thomas Victor, Rebekah Josephine. Student, Western Mich. U., Kalamazoo, 1975, 76; BS in Edn., Ctrl. Mich. U., Mt. Pleasant, 1975; MS in Edn. with honors, No. Ill. U., DeKalb, 1979. Tchr.'s aide Coloma (Mich.) Migrant Program, 1971, 73-76, tchr., 1977; factory prodn. line worker Voice of Music, Benton Harbor, 1972; student tchr. Wyoming (Mich.) Sch. Dist., 1975; libr., media specialist Cmty. Sch. Dist. 300, Dundee, Ill., 1975-79, Cmty. Sch. Dist. 115, Ouqawka, Ill., 1980; children's libr. Warren County Pub. Libr., Monmouth, Ill., 1980-81; ednl. media specialist Parsippany Troy Hills (N.J.) Bd. Edn., 1990—. Computer liaison Parsippany Troy Hills Bd. Edn., 1993-98, insvc. trainer for dist., 1995—, integrator of technology and NJ Core Content Stds. into content curriculum areas, 1990—; Internet trainer, 1997—, dist. tech. com., 2002-, coord. NetDay, 1997-98. Grantee EBSCO Pub., Ipswich, Mass., 1996-97; recipient dist. mini-grant Sci. Is for Everyone, 1996, Hit the Nail on the Head, 1997, Integrating Core Curriculum Stds. in Sci. and Math. Mem. DAR, ALA, Am. Assn. Sch. Libr., NJ Reading Assn., NJ Statewide Systemic Initiative, NJ Edn. Assn., Parsippany Tech. Com. (sci. standing com., learning resources and media svcs. com.), Ednl. Media Specialists Assn., Ednl. Media Assn. NJ, Morris County Media Specialist Assn., Disting. Flying Cross Soc. (assoc.). Methodist. Home: 152 Orben Dr Landing NJ 07850-1828 Office: Parsippany Troy Hills Sch Dist Brooklawn Mid Sch Parsippany NJ 07054 Office Phone: 973-428-7551 3003. Business E-Mail: csmay@pthsd.k12.nj.us.

**SMEALL, CHRISTOPHER,** lawyer; b. Aug. 17, 1951; BA, U. Mich., 1973; MA, U. Calif., Berkeley, 1975, CPhil, 1976; JD, Yale U., 1979. Law clerk US Ct. Appeals, Second Cir., 1979—80; assoc. Debevoise & Plimpton LLP, NYC, 1980—88, corp. ptnr., 1988—. Mem.: ABA, Coun. Foreign Rels., Assn. of Bar of City of NY, Internat. Bar Assn. Office: Debevoise & Plimpton LLP 919 Third Ave New York NY 10022 Office Phone: 212-909-6457. E-mail: csmeall@debevoise.com.

**SMEALLIE, KEVIN WAYNE,** engineering company executive, consultant; b. Willoughby, Ohio, Sept. 24, 1965; s. Wayne Henry and Nancy Jane Smeallie; 1 child, Devin Wayne. AS, ETI, 1984; BS in mech. engring. magna cum laude, U. Wexford, 1994. Designer Barce Equipment, Painesville, Ohio, 1984—90; project mgr., sr. designer SMS Engring., Painesville, 1990—93, project engr., mgr., sr. designer; project mgr., sr. designer Leveltek Internat., Grand River/Painesville, 1998—2000, gen. mgr., 2000—04; ret., 2004. Mem.: AISE. Achievements include invention of cart for a golf bag and method for usage. Avocation: golf. Personal E-mail: kwaynes@netzero.net.

**SMEDINGHOFF, THOMAS J.,** lawyer; b. Chgo., July 15, 1951; s. John A. and Dorothy M. Smedinghoff; m. Mary Beth Smedinghoff. BA in Math. Knox Coll., 1973; JD, U. Mich., 1978. Bar: Ill. 1978, U.S. Dist. Ct. (no. dist.) Ill. 1978. Assoc. McBride, Baker & Coles and predecessor McBride & Baker, Chgo., 1978—84, ptnr., 1985—99, Baker & McKenzie, Chgo., 1999—2006, Wildman, Harrold, Allen & Dixon LLP, Chgo., 2006—. Adj. prof. computer law John Marshall Law Sch., Chgo.; adj. prof. bus. law Grad. Sch. Bus. Dominican U., Chgo., 2004—; chair Ill. Commn. on Electronic Commerce and Crime, 1996—; mem. U.S. Del. to UN Commn. on Internat. Trade Law. Author: Online Law, 1996. Mem.: ABA (chair electronic commerce divsn. 1995—2003, chmn. sect. Sci. and Tech. Law 1999—2000). Office: Wildman Harrold Allen & Dixon LLP 225 W Wacker Dr Ste 3000 Chicago IL 60606 Office Phone: 312-201-2021. Business E-Mail: smedinghoff@wildmanharrold.com.

**SMEDLEY, CHARLES VINCENT,** social studies educator; b. Washington, Sept. 1, 1955; s. Frederick Joseph Smedley and Ruth (Bouknight) McGee; m. Sue Marie Prosser, Aug. 28, 1976; 1 child, Sarah Jane. BS cum laude, U. S.C., 1978; MA, U. Ill., 1980, PhD, 1986. Asst. prof. U. Charleston, W.Va., 1986-88, Charleston (S.C.) So. U., 1988—. Mem. editorial adv. bd. Roxbury Pub. Co., 1989—, Collegiate Press, 1991—; editor Behavioral Sci. update Charleston So. U., 1989—. Mem. 1st Scots Presbyn. Ch., Charleston, 1990—. Fellowship U. Ill., 1978-79, 85 Fellow Soc. Applied Anthropology; mem. AAAS, Am. Sociol. Assn., Am. Anthropol. Assn., N.Y. Acad. Scis., Am. Acad. Polit. and Social Sci., Soc. for Advancement of Socio-econs., Soc. Psychol. Study Social Issues, Soc. Southeastern Social Psychologists, Archaeol. Inst. Am., S.C. Sociol. Assn., Soc. Applied Anthropology, Mo. Archaeol. Soc., Nat. Trust for Historic Preservation, U. S.C. Alumni Assn., U. Ill. Alumni Assn., U. S.C. Gamecock Club, Berkeley County Soc. for Prevention of Cruelty to Animals, Phi Beta Kappa, Phi Kappa Phi, Pi Gamma Mu, Alpha Kappa Delta. Republican. Home: 111 Dominion Cir Goose Creek SC 29445-5512 Office: Charleston So U PO Box 118087 Charleston SC 29423-8087

**SMEDLEY, LAWRENCE THOMAS,** retired organization executive; b. Lorain, Ohio, Sept. 2, 1929; s. Robert E. and Gerda Sofia (Johnson) S.; m. Carmen Nancy Suarez, June 29, 1962; children: Lorraine, Robert, Lawrence, Richard. BA, Bowling Green State U., 1952; MA, U. Mich., 1957; PhD, Am. U., 1972. Analyst Social Security dept. AFL-CIO, Washington, 1962-65, asst. dir. dept., 1965-73, assoc. dir. dept. occupation safety-health-social security, 1973-88; exec. dir. Nat. Coun. Sr. Citizens, Inc., Washington, 1988-96. Former mem. numerous presdl. task forces and coms. on older Ams. and disabled; mem. planning and adv. coms. White House Conf. on Aging, 1971, 81; former mem. adv. coun. on employee welfare and pension plans Dept. Labor, also former mem. spl. task force examining policies relating to asset reversions from over-funded pension plans; bd. dirs. Nat. Coun. Sr. Citizens. Co-chmn. Leadership Coun. Aging Orgns., Washington, 1988-95; mem. exec. bd. Com. for Nat. Health Ins., WAshington, 1989—; mem. policy conv. White House Conf. on Aging, 1995; chair Montgomery County Com. Aging. With M.I., U.S. Army, 1952-55, Korea. Recipient Svc. award Commn. on Accreditation of Facilities of Rehab., 1975, Dedicated Svc. award White House Conf. on Handicapped, 1977, award of honor Industry-Labor Coun., 1981, Outstanding Svc. award Pres.'s Com. on Employment of Handicapped, 1987. Democrat. Lutheran. Home: 3154 Gravefield Rd Apt 217 Silver Spring MD 20904 Personal E-mail: ltsmed@aol.com.

**SMEDS, EDWARD WILLIAM,** retired food company executive; b. Chgo., Feb. 15, 1936; s. Sigvard A. and Ida S.; m. Alice J. Lawler, Jan. 26, 1957; children: Ellen R., Brad W. BS, Carthage Coll., 1957; MS, U. Ill., 1959; grad. advanced mgmt. program, Harvard U., 1977. With Borg Warner Corp., 1958-61, Kraft Foods div. Kraft Inc., 1961-75, v.p., dir. personnel, ops. group, 1976-78, v.p. human resources, 1978-79, sr. v.p. human resources, 1979-80, sr. v.p. fin. and adminstrn., 1980-84; pres. Kraft Asia Pacific, 1984-88; chmn. Kraft Foods Ltd., Australia, 1984-88; pres. Kraft Ltd. Can., 1988-89; sr. v.p. ops. and logistics Kraft Gen. Foods, Glenview, Ill., 1990-94; pres. customer svc. and ops. Kraft, Northfield, Ill., 1993-94, ret., 1994. Chmn. bd. Thrivent Mut. Funds. Chmn. bd. trustees Carthage Coll. Mem. Econ. Club of Chgo., Sunset Ridge Country Club, Club at Pelican Bay, Olde Fla. Home: 10 Regentwood Rd Northfield IL 60093-2728 also: 7575 Pelican Bay Blvd Naples FL 34108-8218 E-mail: esmeds@comcast.net.

**SMEETON, THOMAS ROONEY,** government affairs consultant; b. Evanston, Ill., Sept. 26, 1934; s. Cecil Brooks, Jr. and Florence Mary (Rooney).; m. Susan Diane Tollefson, Feb. 23, 1963; children: Sean, Timothy, Shannon, Brendan, Colin. BS in History, Marquette U., 1958; postgrad., U. Notre Dame, 1958-59; grad., Armed Forces Staff Coll., 1972. Intelligence officer U.S. CIA, Langley, Va., 1962-73; v.p., gen. mgr. Nowicki Fla. Devel. Corp., Ft. Lauderdale, 1973-75; cons. spl. projects com. on fgn. affairs U.S. House Reps., Washington, 1975-86, minority counsel permanent select com. on intelligence, 1986-92, minority staff dir. Iran/Contra com., 1987-88, exec. dir. Rep. policy com., 1993-94; adminstr., chief investigator House Judiciary Com., Washington, 1995-96; govtl. affairs cons., 1996—. Contbg. author: (with Hyde) For Every Idle Silence, 1985. Bd. dirs. Sylvan Beach Found. With U.S. Army, 1959-62. Recipient Agy. Seal medallion CIA, 1993. Mem. Assn. Former Intelligence Officers, Ctrl. Intelligence Retirees Assn., Am. Legion, Amelia Island Club, Capitol Hill Club, The Notre Dame Club of North Fla. Republican. Roman Catholic. Avocation: golf. Home and Office: PO Box 8029 Fernandina Beach FL 32035-8029

**SMEGAL, THOMAS FRANK, JR.,** lawyer; b. Eveleth, Minn., June 15, 1935; s. Thomas Frank and Genevieve (Andreachi) S.; m. Susan Jane Stanton, May 28, 1966; children: Thomas Frank, Elizabeth Jane. BS in Chem. Engring., Mich. Technol. U., 1957; JD, George Washington U., 1961. Bar: Va. 1961, D.C. 1961, Calif. 1964, U.S. Supreme Ct. 1976. Patent examiner U.S. Patent Office, Washington, 1957-61; staff patent atty. Shell Devel. Co., San Francisco, 1962-65; patent atty. Townsend and Townsend, San Francisco, 1965-91, mng. ptnr., 1974-89; sr. ptnr. Graham and James, San Francisco, 1992-97; ptnr. Knobbe, Martens, Olson & Bear, San Francisco, 1997—2005. Mem. U.S. del. to Paris Conv. for Protection of Indsl. Property; mem. adv. com. Ct. of Appeals for Fed. Cir., 1992-96. Contbr. articles to profl. jours. Pres. bd. dirs. Legal Aid Soc. San Francisco, 1982-84, Youth Law Ctr. 1973-84; bd. dirs. Nat. Ctr. for Youth Law, 1978-84, San Francisco Lawyers Com. for Urban Affairs, 1972—, Legal Svcs. for Children, 1980-88; bd. dirs., presdl. nominee Legal Svcs. Corp., 1984-90, 1993-2003. Capt. Chem. Corps, U.S. Army, 1961-63. Recipient St. Thomas More award, 1982. Mem. ABA (chmn. PTC sect. 1990-91, ho. of dels. 1988-2000,2006, mem. standing com. Legal Aid and Indigent Defendants 1991-94, 2004—, chair sect. officer conf. 1992-94, bd. govs. 1994-97, standing com. on Pro Bono and Pub. Svc. 1997-2001, standing com. on Gavel awards 2001-04), Intellectual Property Law Assn. (chmn. nat. coun. 1989), Nat. Inventors Hall of Fame (pres. 1988), Calif. Bar Assn. (v.p. bd. dirs. 1986-87), Am. Patent Law Assn. (pres. 1986), Internat. Assn. Intellectual Property Lawyers (pres. 1995-2001), Bar Assn. San Francisco (pres. 1979), Patent Law Assn. San Francisco (pres. 1974), World Trade Club, Olympic Club, Golden Gate Breakfast Club, Claremont Club (Berkeley). Republican. Roman Catholic. Office: One Sansome Ste 3500 San Francisco CA 94104 Home: 107 King Ave Piedmont CA 94610 Office Phone: 415-217-8383. Business E-Mail: tomsmegal@smegallaw.com.

**SMELSER, DOUGLAS MARTIN,** music educator; b. St. Charles, Mo., Mar. 4, 1970; s. Earl Franklin and Brenda Sue Smelser; m. Robyn Ann Mueller, Aug. 4, 1990; children: Brad, Drake. AA, Jefferson Coll., 1990; B Music Edn., SE Mo. State U., 1992, M Music Edn., 2001. Tchr., band dir. Twin Rivers HS and Mid. Schs., Broseley, Mo., 1992—95, Herculaneum (Mo.) HS and Mid. Schs., 1995—. Mem.: NEA, Mo. Band Masters, Mo. Music Edn. Assn., Music Educators Nat. Conf. Home: 9723 Roundtable Ct Hillsboro MO 63050 Office: Herculaneum HS 4 Blackcat Dr Herculaneum MO 63048

**SMELSER, NEIL JOSEPH,** sociologist; b. Kahoka, Mo., July 22, 1930; s. Joseph Nelson and Susie Marie (Hess) S.; m. Helen Thelma Margolis, June 10, 1954 (div. 1965); children: Eric Jonathan, Tina Rachel; m. Sharin Fateley, Dec. 20, 1967; children: Joseph Neil, Sarah Joanne. BA, Harvard U., 1952, PhD, 1958; BA, Oxford U., Eng., 1954, MA, 1959; grad., San Francisco Psychoanalytic Inst., 1971. Mem. faculty U. Calif., Berkeley, 1958-94, prof. sociology, 1962—, asst. chancellor ednl. devel., 1966-68; assoc. dir. Inst. of Internat. Studies, Berkeley, 1969-73, 80-89; prof. sociology U. Calif., Berkeley, 1972-94; prof. emeritus, 1994—; dir. edn. abroad program for U. Calif., Berkeley, 1977-79, spl. advisor Office of Pres., 1993-94, dir. Ctr. for Advanced Study in Behavioral Scis., 1994-2001. Bd. dirs. Social Sci. Rsch. Coun., chmn., 1971-73, com. econ. growth, 1961-65; trustee Ctr. for Advanced Study in Behavioral Scis., 1980-93, 94-, chmn., 1984-86; trustee Russell Sage Found., 1990-2000; subcom. humanism Am. Bd. Internal Medicine, 1981-85, 89-90, adv. com., 1992-99, chmn. adv. com., 1995-99; chmn. sociology panel Behavioral and Social Scis. survey NAS and Social Sci. Rsch. Coun., 1967-69; com. on basic rsch. in behavioral and social scis. NRC, 1980-89, chmn., 1984-86, co-chmn., 1986-89; chmn. com. of selection Guggenheim Found., 1996-; chmn. Commn. for Behavioral and Social Scis. and Edn. (NAS/NRC), 1996-2003, German-Am. Acad. Coun., 1999-2000. Author: (with T. Parsons) Economy and Society, 1956, Social Change in the Industrial Revolution, 1959, Theory of Collective Behavior, 1962, The Sociology of Economic Life, 1963, 2d edit., 1975, Essays in Sociological Explanation, 1968, Sociological Theory: A Contemporary View, 1971, Comparative Methods in the Social Sciences, 1976, (with Robin Content) The Changing Academic Market, 1980, Sociology, 1981, 2d edit., 1984, 3d edit., 1987, 4th edit., 1991, 5th edit., 1995, Social Paralysis and Social Change, 1991, Effective Committee Service, 1993, Sociology, 1994, Problematics of Sociology, 1997, The Social Edges of Psychoanalysis, 1999; editor: (with W.T. Smelser) Personality and Social Systems, 1963, 2d edit., 1971, (with S.M. Lipset) Social Structure and Mobility in Economic Development, 1966, Sociology, 1967, 2d edit., 1973, (with James Davis) Sociology: A Survey Report, 1969, Karl Marx on Society and Social Change, 1973, (with Gabriel Almond) Public Higher Education in California, 1974, (with Erik Erikson) Themes of Work and Love in Adulthood, 1980, (with Jeffrey Alexander et al) The Micro-Macro Link, 1987, Handbook of Sociology, 1988, (with Hans Haferkamp) Social Change and Modernity, 1992; (with Richard Munch) Theory of Culture, 1992; (with Richard Swedberg) The Handbook of Economic Sociology, 1994; (with Jeffrey Alexander) Diversity and Its Discontents, 1999; (with William Julius Wilson and Faith Mitchell) American Becoming: Racial Trends and their Consequences, 2001, (with Paul B. Baltes) International Encyclopedia of the Social and Behavioral Sciences, 2001; editor Am. Sociol. Rev., 1962-65; adv. editor Am. Jour. Sociology, 1960-62. Rhodes scholar, 1952-54; Jr. fellow Soc. Fellows, Harvard U., 1955-58, fellow Russell Sage Found., 1989-90. Mem. Am. Sociol. Assn. (coun. 1962-65, 67-70, exec. com. 1963-65, pres. elect 1995-96, pres. 1996-97), Pacific Sociol. Assn., Internat. Sociol. Assn. (exec. com. 1986-94, v.p. 1990-94), Am. Acad. Arts and Scis. (hon.), Fedn. State Med. Bds. (bd. dirs. 2006-), (Am. Philos. Soc. (hon.), Nat. Acad. of Scis. (hon.) Business E-Mail: nsmelser@berkeley.edu.

**SMELSER, THELMA ANN,** writer, tax specialist; b. Piedmont, Ala., June 7, 1941; d. Rufus Milton and Florence Inez Steward; m. William Guy Smelser, Jr., June 11; children: Joseph Milton, William Preston. BA in English, Huntingdon Coll., 1964; postgrad., U. Ga., 1973—79. Tic. SEC. Tchr. Montgomery (Ala.) Bd. Edn., 1964—66, DeKalb County Bd. Edn., Decatur, Ga., 1966—85; owner Everlasting Images Wholesale, Snellville, Ga., 1985—98; tax profl. H&R Block, Loganville, Ga., 1998—; owner TAS Publs., 2004—. SEC fin. advisor H&R Block, Loganville, Ga., 2003—. Author: Strawberries & Honeysuckle, 1985; columnist: Loganville Post, 2004—. Tax advisor The Loganville Post, 2004; team mom Little League Baseball Team, Gwinnett County, Ga., 1986; mem. charity com. First Bapt. Ch., Loganville, 1997. Recipient Yearbook award, Walker H.S., 1977, Scrapbook award, Snellville Middle Sch., 1988. Republican. Baptist. Avocations: wildlife, boating, rug hooking, painting, reading. Home: 4201 Cannon Rd Loganville GA 30052 Office: H&R Block 4325 Atlanta Hwy Loganville GA 30052 Office Phone: 404-444-7279. E-mail: asmelser@bellsouth.net.

**SMELTZER, DEBRA JEAN,** botanist; b. Camden, Ark., Oct. 13, 1953; d. William Dewey and Frankie Jean (Braswell) S.; m. James Richard Ziesler, Sept. 1, 1984. Cert. in interior design, Bauder Fashion Coll., Arlington, Tex., 1973; BA in Botany, U. Tex., 1985. Biol. rsch. asst. U.S. Dept. Interior, Everglades Nat. Park, Fla., 1980; biologist, surveyor Great Lakes Dredge and Dock, Miami Beach, Fla., 1981-82, 1984, biologist, surveyor, drafter Port Everglades, Fla., 1984; biologist, lab. tech. J.B. Reark and Assocs., Miami, 1982-84; fisheries biologist Kathryn Chandler and Assocs., Alexandria, Va., 1981-84; pres. Greensleeves, Inc., Miami and San Juan, P.R., 1985—; San Juan, P.R., 1991-95. Bd. govs. Nat. Coun. for Interior Hort. Cert., Columbus, Ohio, 1989-92; licensee Interior Landscape Internat. Corp., Dade, Monroe, Caribbean, 1990-92. Eucharistic min. St. Timothy Cath. Ch. Recipient Best Project award Interiorscape Mag., 1989, 1996, State Award of Excellence Fla. Nurserymen and Growers Assn., 1989, award of recognition, 1999. Mem. Associated Landscape Contractors Am. (award of Distinction 1989, 91, 92, Grand award 1990, 2001), South Fla. Interior Landscape Assn. (ednl. com. 1987-89, bd. dirs. 1986-87, author newsletter articles 1986-89, founder 1986), Coral Gables C. of C. (trustee coun.), Calif. Interior Plantscape Assn. (judges award, 2001, Distinction award 2001, 02). Republican. Avocations: waterskiing, skiing, scuba diving, photography.

**SMERDON, ERNEST THOMAS,** engineering educator; b. Ritchey, Mo., Jan. 19, 1930; s. John Erle and Ada (Davidson) Smerdon; m. Joanne Duck, June 9, 1951; children: Thomas, Katherine, Gary. BS in Engring., U. Mo., 1951, MS in Engring., 1956, PhD in Engring., 1959, DSc (hon.), 2003. Registered profl. engr., Ariz. Chmn. dept. agrl. engring. U. Fla., Gainesville, 1968-74, asst. dean for rsch., 1974-76; vice chancellor for acad. affairs U. Tex. System, Austin, 1976-82; dir. Ctr. for Rsch. in Water Resources U. Tex., 1982-88; dean Coll. Engring. and Mines U. Ariz., Tucson, 1988-92, vice provost, dean Engring. 1992-97; sr. adm. assoc. NSF, Arlington, Va., 1997-00; prof. civil engring. and hydrology U. Ariz., Tucson, 2000—01, dean emeritus, 2001—. Mem. bd. sci. and tech. internat. devel. NRC, 1990—94, mem. com. planning and remediation irrigation-induced water quality problems, 1990—96, chair com. Yucca Mountain peer rev., 1995, mem. com. study rsch.-doctorate programs U.S., 1991—95, mem. com. Missouri River Ecosystem Sci., 1999—2001; chair com. Water Resources Mgmt. Instream Flow and Salmon Survival in Columbia River, 2002—04, Sci. Bases Colorado River Water Mgmt., 2005—, others. Editor: Managing Water Related Conflicts: The Engineer's Role, 1989. Mem. Ariz. Gov.'s Sci. and Tech. Coun., Tucson, 1989—96; bd. dirs. Greater Tucson Econ. Coun., 1990—95. Recipient Disting. Svc. in Engring. award, U. Mo., 1982, Lifetime Achievement award, Environ. and Water Resources Inst., 2002. Fellow: NAE (acad. adv. bd. 1989—95, tech. policy options com. 1990—91, chair com. career-long edn. engrs. 1997—2000, acad. adv. bd. 1998—99, peer com. 2002—05, chmn. sect. 12 2003—04, com. capacity U.S. Engr. Rsch. Enterprise 2004, peer com. 1986—90, 2002—, steering com. engr. 2020, policy com. Engr. 2020), ASCE (hon. Outstanding Svc. award irrigation and drainage divsn. 1988, Royce Tipton award 1989, Robert C. Park Outstanding Civil Engr. award 2005); mem.: Ariz. Soc. Profl. Engrs. (Engr. of Yr. award 1990), Univ. Coun. Water Resources, Am. Geophys. Union, Am. Soc. Engring. Edn. (chmn., bd. dirs. engring. dean's coun. 1995—97, pres. 1998—99), Am.

Water Resources Assn. (Icko Iben award 1989); Am. Soc. Agrl. Engrs., Pi Mu Epsilon, Tau Beta Pi, Phi Kappa Phi, Sigma Xi. Avocations: hiking, golf, scuba diving, painting. Office: U Ariz AME Bldg Rm N521 Tucson AZ 85721-0001

**SMERGE, RAYMOND G.,** finance company executive; b. Portales, N.Mex. m. Patricia Smerge; children: Paul, Jessica, Mark. BS. No. Ill. U., 1967; JD, De Paul U. Law, 1971. Closing officer Centex Corp., 1968—72, v.p.; gen. counsel, 1972—85, v.p., 1985—93, chief legal officer, 1985—, sec., chief legal officer, 1993—2005, exec. v.p., 1997—2005; ret., 2005. Mem.: Dallas Bar Assn., ABA. Office: Centex Corp 2728 N Harwood St Ste 200 Dallas TX 75201-1591 Office Phone: 214-981-6530. E-mail: rsmerge@centex.com.

**SMETANA, MARK,** food products executive; CFO Eby-Brown Co., Naperville, Ill. Office: 280 Shuman Blvd Ste 280 Naperville IL 60563-2578

**SMETANKA, MARY JANE,** reporter; Grad., U. Minn.-Twin Cities. Reporter, Minn., ND, Conn.; higher edn. reporter Mpls. Star Tribune, Mpls. Mem.: Edn. Writers Assn. (pres.). Achievements include being a Minn. Master Gardener. Office: Mpls Star Tribune 425 Portland Ave Minneapolis MN 55488-1511

**SMETANKA, SALLY S.,** small business owner; b. Athens, N.Y., Aug. 26, 1944; AS, Valencia C.C., Orlando, Fla., 1981; BA, Rollins Coll., Winter Park, Fla., 1991. With labor rels. Walt Disney World, Orlando, Fla., 1978—81, asst. to pres., 1983—2005; owner Carriage Ho. Antiques, Orlando, Fla., 2005—. Home and Office: 1253 Nottingham St Orlando FL 32803 Office Phone: 407-898-5393.

**SMETHERAM, HERBERT EDWIN,** management consultant; b. Seattle, Sept. 9, 1934; s. Francis Edwin and Grace Elizabeth (Warner) S.; m. Beverly Joan Heckert, Sept. 7, 1963; children: Alice, Helen, Charles. BA, U. Wash., 1956; diploma, Naval Intelligence Sch., 1962; MA, U. Md., 1971; diploma in Swedish, U.S. Fgn. Svc. Inst., 1978; MBA, Rollins Coll., 1991. Ensign USN, 1956, advanced through grades to capt., 1976; comdr. USS Lind (DD-703), 1971-73; attache to Sweden USN, Stockholm, 1978-81; comdr. Naval Adminstrn. Command, Orlando, Fla., 1981-84; ret. USN, 1984; strategic planner electronics, info. and missiles group Martin Marietta Corp., Orlando, 1985-93; exec. dir. re-use com. Naval Trng. Ctr., Orlando, 1993-97, mil. base closure cons., 1991-98. Mgmt. cons., ZHA, Inc., 1998—. Mem. ARC Ctrl. Fla.; mem. Ctrl. Fla. coun. USO, Orlando, 1981—93, pres., 1991—93; mem. steering com. U.S. Congressman McCollum for Re-election, 1992—96; mem. U.S. Senator Hawkins Naval Acad. Nominating Com., Orlando, 1982—86, Fla. Gov.'s Def. Reinvestment Task Force, 1992—93; treas. St. Mathews Episcopal Parish, Orlando, 2000—03; bd. dirs. Episcopal Diocese Ctrl. Fla., 2002—05, exec. com. Decorated Royal Order of North Star (Sweden). Mem. SAR, Electronics Industry Assn. (requirements com. 1985-93), Nat. Assn. Installation Developers (southeast regional dir. 1996-97, treas. 1996-2000, bd. dirs. 1996-2000), Fla. Def. Alliance, Ret. Officers Assn., Fla. Econ. Devel. Coun., Navy League, Univ. Club of Winter Park, Fla. (bd. dirs. 2003-06), U.S. Tennis Assn., Fla. Tennis Assn., Army Navy Country Club, Orlando Tennis Ctr., Royal Lawn Tennis Club Stockholm, Winter Park (Fla.) Tennis Ctr., Delta Kappa Epsilon. Republican. Episcopalian. Avocation: tennis. Home: 3985 Lake Mira Dr Orlando FL 32817-1643 E-mail: hesmetheram@msn.com.

**SMETHURST, E(DWARD) WILLIAM, JR.,** investment banker; b. Newark, Apr. 15, 1930; s. Edward William and Helen Lea (Wiener) S.; m. Ludlow Bixby, June 30, 953; children: James, Andrew, Katherine. AB, Amherst Coll., 1952; MBA, Harvard U., 1958. Credit analyst Chase Manhattan Bank, N.Y.C., 1958-60; mgr. securities Irwin Mgmt. Co., Columbus, Ind., 1961-64; ptnr. Wertheim & Co., N.Y.C., 1965-79; sr. v.p. Cyrus J. Lawrence Inc., N.Y.C., 1980-87; mng. dir. Wertheim Schroder & Co. Inc., N.Y.C., 1988-95; pres., chief investment officer Schroder Wertheim Investment Svcs., N.Y.C., 1990-96; chmn., trustee Wertheim Series Trust, N.Y.C.; retired, 1996; mng. dir. Byram Capital Mgmt., Greenwich, Conn., 2002—. Trustee Mount Holyoke Coll., South Hadley, Mass., 1982—98. Lt. USN, 1952—55. Episcopalian. Home: 861 Bingham Rd Ridgewood NJ 07450-2111 Office: Byram Captial Mgmt 41 West Putnam Ave Greenwich NY 06830 Office Phone: 203-869-5570. Business E-Mail: ewill@bryamcapital.com.

**SMICK, SUSAN SCHNEE,** manufacturing executive, tile designer, marketing professional; b. Bklyn., July 12, 1947; d. Henry and Rhoda (Noskin) Schnee; m. Edward Lewis Smick, Feb. 5, 1972 (separated 1994); 1 child, Joshua Henry. BA with honors, C.W. Post Coll., 1970; postgrad., NYU, 1970-71. Cert. tchr., N.Y. Customer svc. and campus rep. Trans World Airlines, N.Y.C., 1966-71, strategic airline mktg. planner, 1971-72, fleet planning analyst, 1972-73; propr. Sailor's Valentine, Chatham, Mass., 1974-76; ednl. and corp. tour developer Crimson Travel, Cambridge, Mass., 1977-80; propr., tile designer, mfr. Cape Cod Tile Co., 1986-97; founding ptnr. TileGraphics, Weston, Mass., 1994-97; founding ptnr. tile designer, mfr. Great Am. Tile Works, Weston, Mass., 1997—. Cons. U.S. Dept. Transp., 1975. Author (ednl. tours) The Flying Classroom, 1977-80; ceramic artist; author mktg. software. Friends of McLean, McLean Hosp., Belmont, Mass., 1997; mem. Mass. Horticulture Soc., 1995—; bd. dirs. Women's Cmty. League of Weston, 1999, chmn. ways and means com., 2000; chmn. of events Pub. Action for the Arts, 1999, adv. bd. mem., 2000. Recipient Howard Gold Polit. Sci. scholarship Howard Gold Meml. Fund, 1965, acad. scholarship C.W. Post Coll., 1967-70, Nat. Profl. Devel. Act fellowship NYU Grad. Sch. Edn. and History, 1970. Mem. Soc. Glass and Ceramic Decorators, Pi Gamma Mu, Phi Beta Kappa. Avocations: interior and fashion design, horticulture, fundraising, American folk art. Home: 199 Coolidge Ave Apt 513 Watertown MA 02472-1572 E-mail: ssmick@mediaone.net.

**SMIDDY, JOSEPH CHARLES,** retired academic administrator; b. Jellico, Tenn., June 20, 1920; s. Joseph F. and Sara Nan (Tye) Smiddy; m. Reba Graham, Sept. 6, 1985; children: Joseph F., Elizabeth Lee. BA, Lincoln Meml. U., 1948, LHD (hon.), 1970; MA, Peabody Coll., 1952; LLD, U. Richmond, 1975; LHD (hon.), Coll. William and Mary, 1986; DAm (hon.), Cumberland Coll., 1993. Tchr. Jonesville H.S., 1948—51, prin., 1951—52; sec.-treas. Powell Valley Oil Co., Big Stone Gap, Va., 1952—53; prof. biology Clinch Valley Coll., U. Va., Wise, 1956—57, dean, 1957—68, dir., 1968—85, chancellor, 1968—85, chancellor emeritus, 1985—. Mem. Charter Day Award Emory and Henry Coll., 1980; mem. Commonwealth Day Award James Madison U., 1985. Musician, singer. Trustee Lincoln Meml. U. With U.S. Army, 1942—45, PTO. Recipient Laurel Leaves award, Appalachian Consortium, 1995, Kanto Ednl. award, Wise County, 1995. Mem.: Bapt. Gen. Assn. Va. (pres. 1974—), Kiwanis, Shriners, Masons. Home: Ridgefield Acres Wise VA 24293 Office: PO Box 3160 Wise VA 24293-3160

**SMIDT, SEYMOUR,** economics professor; b. Chgo., Nov. 2, 1928; s. Joseph and Harriet (Morrison) S.; m. Rita Barbara Liss, Jan. 28, 1951; children—Tamar Rachelle, Stanley Adam. AB, U. Chgo., 1948; MA, 1952, PhD, 1954. Asst. prof. econs. and fin. Cornell U. Johnson Grad. Sch. Mgmt., Ithaca, NY, 1956-59, assoc. prof., 1959-65, prof., 1965-78, Nicholas H. Noyes prof., 1978—2005, prof. emeritus, 2005—. Assoc. dir. Instl. Investor Study, SEC, 1969-70; dean faculty of adminstrv. scis. Koç U., Istanbul, Turkey, 1993-95. Author (with Harold Bierman, Jr.) The Capital Budgeting Decision, 1960, 66, 71, 75, 80, 84, 88, 92 (with others) Management Decision-Making Under Uncertainty, 1969; contbr. articles to profl. jours. Mayor Village of Lansing, N.Y., 1977-81. Served with U.S. Army, 1954-56. Mem. Am. Econ. Assn., Am. Fin. Assn., Fin. Mgmt. Assn. Office: Cornell U Johnson Grad Sch Mgmt Ithaca NY 14853-4201

**SMIDTS, CAROL,** mechanical engineer, educator; d. Freddy and Julienne Smidts. PhD, U. Libre, Brussels, 1991. Faculty rsch. assoc. Ecole Poly. U. Libre, Brussels, 1991—92; faculty rsch. assoc. dept. materials and nuc. engring. U. Md., College Park, 1992—94, asst. prof. dept. materials and nuc. engring., 1994—2000, assoc. prof. dept. materials and nuc. engring.,

2000—03, assoc. prof. dept. mech. engring., 2003—; assoc. dir. rsch. Nat. Ctr. Sci. Rsch., Toulouse, France, 2000. Assoc. chair reliability engring. program U. Md., College Park, 2000—01; CEO TestSolvers, Bethesda, Md., 2005—; vis. scientist Inst. for Systems Engring. & Informatics, Italy, 1992, JRC, Italy, 1992, European Communities Commn., Italy, 1992. Organizing com. Jeunesses Scientifiques Belgique, Brussels, 1987—91. Recipient award, Belgian Nuc. Soc., 1986, Flight Safety award, NASA, 1998, Rotary Nat. award, 1998, Achievement award, 1998, Software Assurance Symposium award, 2003; fellow, Inst. pour l=Encouragement de la Rsch. Sci. dans l'Industrie Agr., Belgium, 1986—88, Fonds Nat. de la Rsch. Sci., Belgium, 1989; grantee, TEDCO, 2005. Mem.: AIAA, ANS (Best Paper award 1991), IEEE (sr.). Achievements include patents for QRAS 1.0 software; method and apparatus for a common-cause failure module for probabilistic risk assessment tools; patents pending for domain specific test design automation, domain specific test design automation. Office: 3125 Glenn Martin Hall College Park MD 20742 Office Phone: 301-405-7314. Business E-Mail: csmidts@umd.edu.

**SMIGEL, IRWIN,** dentist; b. NYC, Oct. 9, 1924; m. Lucia Shvetz, Sept. 30, 1956; children: Bellanca Smigel Rutter, Robert. WSC, DDS, NYU, 1950. Diplomate Am. Bd. Aesthetic Dentistry. Dentist pvt. practice, N.Y.C., 1950—. Vis. prof. Pitts. Dental Sch., 1980-83, Case Western U., 1990—; lectr. SUNY Buffalo, U. Mo., Kansas City, U. Minn.; cons., lectr. in field. Author: Dental Health, Dental Beauty, 1978; contbr. editor Dentistry Today, 1980-, dental adv. bd.; contbr. articles to dental jours. With INF., 1943-45. Irwin Smigel Chair in Aesthetic Dentistry established NYU Sch. Dentistry, 1996, Smigel Prize; recipient Outstanding Contbrn. to Aesthetic Dentistry award, Am. Acad. Cosmetic Dentistry, 1994 Fellow Am. Soc. Dental Aesthetics (founder, pres. 1976-2006); mem. Am. Dental Assn., Acad. Gen. Dentistry, Fedn. Dentaire, First Dist. Dental Soc. Achievements include invention of the Supersmile Whitening brand mouthrinse, toothpaste, floss and brush, tooth bonding technique. Avocations: reading, tennis, racewalking, art, music. Office: 635 Madison Ave New York NY 10022-1009

**SMILEY, FREDERICK MELVIN,** education educator, consultant; b. Yuba City, Calif., Apr. 13, 1943; s. Lester Boomer and Claire Leone (DeChesne) S. AA, Yuba Coll., 1963; BA, Chico State U., 1966; MA in Edn., Chapman Coll., 1973, MA in English, 1978, MA in Spl. Edn., 1982; PhD, U. Santa Barbara, 1982; EdD, Okla. State U., 1992. Tchr., coach, v.p. McDermitt (Nev.) High Sch., 1978-80; resource specialist Eagle Mt. (Calif.) High Sch., 1980-81; instr. spl. edn. Mary Stone Sch., San Mateo, Calif., 1981-86; dept. leader Quaezar Corp., Bridgeport, Conn., 1986-87; cons., researcher Multifunctional Resource Ctr., Stillwater and Norman, Okla., 1988-91; prof. edn. Cameron U., Lawton, Okla., 1991—. Contbr. articles to profl. jours.; contbg. editor Thiel', The Writing Teacher, Okla. Assn. Tchr. Eductors Jour., ATE Jour. Mem. AAUP, Am. Assn. for Teaching and Curriculum, Am. Soc. Curriculum Devel., Am. Coun. Rural Spl. Edn., Am. Assn. Colls. for Tchr. Edn., Coun. for Exceptional Children, Okla. Assn. Tchr. Educators (pres. 2001—), Soc. Educators and Scholars, Kappa Delta Pi, Phi Delta Kappa, Phi Kappa Phi. Democrat. Lutheran. Avocations: reading, writing, racing, tennis, golf. Office: Cameron U 2800 W Gore Blvd Lawton OK 73505-6377 Home: 2001 Alford Park Dr Kenosha WI 53140-1929 E-mail: freds@cameron.edu.

**SMILEY, JACQUELYN,** voice educator; b. Baxley, Ga., June 28, 1977; MusB in Edn., Ga. State U., 2000. Cert. Music Edn. K-12 Profl. Standards Commn., State Ga. Voice, choral faculty North Springs H.S., Atlanta, 2000—01; choral dir. Pine Mountain Mid. Sch., Kennesaw, Ga., 2001—03; vocalist First Presbyn. Ch. Atlanta, 2005—; choral dir. Garrett Mid. Sch., Austell, Ga., 2003—. Cons. Music Alive Mag., N.Y.C., 2005—06. Singer: Superbowl Halftime Show, Atlanta Hawks Pregame Show, Atlanta Braves Pregame Show. Mem.: Ga. Music Educators Assn., Am. Choral Dirs. Assn., Music Educators Nat. Conv., Phi Beta Kappa. Home: 701 Highland Ave 2236 Atlanta GA 30312 Office: Garrett Mid Sch 5235 Austell-Powder Springs Rd Austell GA 30106 Office Phone: 770-819-2466. Home Fax: 770-819-2468; Office Fax: 770-819-2468. Personal E-mail: jackiesmiley2001@hotmail.com. Business E-Mail: jacquelyn.smiley@cobbk12.org.

**SMILEY, JOHN CLINTON,** lawyer; b. Chgo., Jan. 27, 1960; s. John Wallace and Kay Alice Smiley; m. Pamela Kay St. John, Aug. 12, 1983; children: Nicholas H., Alison R. BS, Colo. State U., 1983; JD, U. Wyo., 1986. Bar: Colo. 1986, Wyo. 1986, U.S. Dist. Ct. Colo., U.S. Dist. Ct. Wyo., U.S. Ct. Appeals (10th cir.). Assoc. Sherman Howard, Denver, 1986—90, Lindquist & Vennum PLLP, Denver, 1991—93, ptnr., 1994—, ptnr.-in-charge, 2001—. Co-coord faculty led. adws. Bankruptcy Pro Bono Program, Denver, 2002—05; mem. 10th Cir. BAP Rules Com., 2005—. Avocations: fly fishing, skiing, reading. Office: Lindquist & Vennum PLLP 600 17th St Ste 1800-S Denver CO 80202 Office Phone: 303-454-0508. Business E-Mail: jsmiley@lindquist.com.

**SMILEY, LAURA CICELY,** theater educator, performing company executive; b. New Brunswick, N.J., June 1, 1965; d. Ralph and Alicia Alejandro Smiley. BFA in Acting. Cath. U. Am., Washington, D.C., 1983—87; MFA in Acting, U. Pitts., Pa., 1992—96. Artistic dir. The Unseam of Shakespeare Co., Pitts., 1993—; adj. faculty U. Pitts., 1996—99, asst. prof., theatre, 1999—2000; adj. faculty Point Pk. U., Pitts., 1998—2001; asst. prof., theatre Ind. U. Pa., 1997, 2001, Slippery Rock U., 2003—. Grantee, Pa. Coun. on Arts, 1999—2006, Howard Heinz Small Arts Initiative, Pitts., Pa., 1997—2006. Mem.: AFTRA, SAG, Shakespeare Theatre Assn. Am., Actors Equity Assn. Roman Catholic. Office: Slippery Rock Univ 301B Miller Auditorium Slippery Rock PA 16057

**SMILEY, MARILYNN JEAN,** musicologist; b. Columbia City, Ind., June 5, 1937; d. Orla Raymond and Mary Jane (Bailey) S. BS (State scholar), Ball State U., 1954; MusM, Northwestern U., 1958; cert., Ecoles d Art Americaines, Fontainebleau, France, 1959; PhD (Grad. scholar, Delta Kampa Gamma scholar), U. Ill., 1970. Public sch. music tchr., Logansport, Ind., 1954-61; faculty music dept. SUNY-Oswego, 1961—, Disting. Teaching prof., 1974—, chmn. dept., 1976-81. Presenter papers at confs. Contbr. articles to profl. jours. Bd. dirs. Oswego Opera Theatre, 1978—, Oswego Orch. Soc., 1978—, Penfield Libr. Assocs., 1985—. Recipient Chancellor's award for Excellence in Tchg., 1973; SUNY Rsch. Found. fellow, summers, 1971, 1972, 1974, NEH grantee, 1990—91. Mem.: AAUW (grantee 1984, pres. Oswego br. 1984—86, br. coun. rep. dist. III, N.Y. State divsn. 1986—88, br. coun. coord. N.Y. State divsn. 1988—90, N.Y. divsn. area intererst rep. cultural interests 1990—92, N.Y. divsn. diversity dir. 1993—96, Oswego br. diversity chair 1995—, N.Y. state unofcl. historian 2000—04, N.Y. state historian 2004—), NOW, Oswego County Hist. Soc., Early Music Am., Am. Recorder Soc., Soc. Am. Music (membership chair 1998—2003), Renaissance Soc. Am., Coll. Music Soc., Music Libr. Assn., Medieval Acad. Am., Am. Musicol. Soc. (chmn. N.Y. chpt. 1975—77, chpt. rep. to AMS coun. 1993—96, bd. dirs. N.Y. State-St. Lawrence 1993—96, mem. status of women com. 1997—2000), Oswego Recorder Consort, Ontario Singers, Heritage Found. of Oswego, Phi Kappa Phi, Kappa Delta Pi, Sigma Tau Delta, Sigma Alpha Iota, Pi Kappa Lambda, Delta Phi Alpha, Phi Delta Kappa, Delta Kappa Gamma (music chair State of Ind. 1961, music chair State of N.Y. 1968). Methodist. Office: SUNY Dept Music Oswego NY 13126 Office Phone: 315-312-3054. Business E-Mail: smiley@oswego.edu.

**SMILEY, RICHARD WAYNE,** researcher; b. Paso Robles, Calif., Aug. 17, 1943; s. Cecil Wallace and Elenore Louise (Hamm) S.; m. Marilyn Lois Wenning, June 24, 1967; 1 child. Shawn Elizabeth. BSc in Soil Sci., Calif. State Poly. U., San Luis Obispo, 1965; MSc in Soils, Wash. State U., 1969, PhD in Plant Pathology, 1972. Asst. soil scientist Agrl. Rsch. Svc., USDA, Pullman, Wash., 1966-69; rsch. asst. dept. plant pathology Wash. State U., Pullman, 1969-72; soil microbiologist Commonwealth Sci. and Indsl. Rsch. Orgn., Adelaide, Australia, 1972-73; rsch. assoc. dept. plant pathology Cornell U., Ithaca, NY, 1973-74, asst. prof., 1975-80, assoc. prof., 1980-85; supt. Columbia Basin Agr. Rsch. Ctr., 1985-2000; prof. Oreg. State U., 1985—. Vis. scientist Plant Rsch. Inst., Victoria Dept. Agr., Melbourne, Australia, 1982-83. Author: Compendium of Turfgrass Diseases, 1983, 3d edit., 2005; contbr. more than 200 articles to profl. jours. Postdoctoral fellow

NATO, 1972. Fellow Am. Phytopath. Soc. (sr. editor APS Press 1984-87, editor-in-chief 1987-91); mem. Coun. Agrl. Sci. and Tech., Rotary (pres. Pendleton chpt. 1991-92, Paul Harris fellow 1993). Achievements include discovery of the etiology of a serious disease of turfgrasses, which led to a redefinition of studies and disease processes in turfgrasses. Office: Oreg State U Columbia Basin Agr Rsch Ctr PO Box 370 Pendleton OR 97801-0370 Business E-Mail: richard.smiley@oregonstate.edu.

**SMILEY, ROBERT WILLIAM, JR.,** investment banker; b. Lansing, Mich., Nov. 17, 1943; s. Robert William Sr. and Rebecca Lee (Flint) S. AB in Econs., Stanford U., 1970; postgrad., San Fernando Valley Coll. Law, 1973—75; MBA in Corp. Fin., City U. L.A., 1979; LLB, LaSalle U., 1982. Bar: Calif. 1984. Sr. v.p. mktg. Actuarial Systems Inc., San Jose, Calif., 1972-73; founder, chmn. Benefit Systems Inc., L.A. and S.E. Nev., 1973-84, Brentwood Sq. Savs. and Loan, L.A., 1982-84; chmn., CEO The Benefit Capital Cos. Inc., L.A. and S.E. Nev., 1984—. Lectr. U. Calif. Ext., L.A. and Berkeley, 1977—; instr. Am. Coll. Life Underwriters. Editor, contbg. author: Employee Stock Ownership Plans: ESOP Planning, Implementation, Law and Taxation, 1989, 3d edit. 2006; contbg. author: The Handbook of Employee Benefits, 1984, 7th edit., 2005; contbr. articles to profl. jours. Mem. nat. adv. coun., trustee Reason Found., L.A., 1983-91; bd. dirs. Nat. Ctr. for Employee Ownership, Oakland, Calif.; former trustee The Employee Ownership Found., Washington, 2000-04. With USN, 1961-64, Vietnam. Recipient Spl. Achievement award Pres.' Commn. on Pension Policy, 1984. Fellow Life Mgmt. Inst.; mem. Employee Stock Ownership Plan Assn. (founder, pres., bd. dirs., lifetime dir.), Assn. for Corp. Growth, Western and SW Pension Confs., Nat. Assn. Bus. Economists, ABA, Calif. Bar Assn. Office: The Benefit Capital Cos Inc PO Box 542 Logandale NV 89021-0542 Office Phone: 702-398-3222.

**SMILEY, TAVIS,** radio talk show host; b. Biloxi, Miss., Sept. 13, 1964; s. Emory G. and Joyce M. Smiley. Grad., Ind. U., 1986, D (hon.). Asst. to Mayor Tomilea Allison, L.A., 1984—85; coun. aide, 1987; spl. asst. to exec. dir., 1978—88; adminstrv. aide to Mayor Tom Bradley, 1988—90; commentator The Smiley Report, 1990—2001; contbr. CNN, 2001—, HuffingtonPost.com; spl. correspondent ABC-TV, 2001—; commentator Tom Joyner Morning Show; pres., CEO Smiley Group, Inc. Host (TV series) BET Tonight with Tavis Smiley, 1999—2001, supervisory prodr. Tavis Smiley, 2004— (Outstanding TV News, Talk or Information (Series or Spl.), NAACP Image award, 2006), TV appearances include For Your Love, 1999, The Parkers, 2000, Any Day Now, 2001, American Dreams, 2004; author: (books) Hard Left: Straight Talk about the Wrongs of the Right, 1996, Doing What's Right: How to Fight for What You Believe and Make a Difference, 2000, How to Make Black America Better: Leading African Americans Speak Out, 2002, Keeping the Faith: Stories of Love, Courage, Healing and Hope from Black America, 2002, (foreword) Ruminations: KRS-One, 2003, (introduction) Reclaim Your Power: A 30-Day Guide to Hope, Healing, and Inspiration for Men of Color, 2003; editor: The Covenant with Black America, 2006; author: (novels) What I Know for Sure, 2006. Founder Tavis Smiley Found.; bd. dirs. Challengers Boys and Girls Club, Black Coll. Tour, L.A.; mem. adv. bd. Martin Luther King Jr. Ctr. Non-Violent Social Change, 1992—93, Inner City Found. Excellence in Edn., 1989—91, After Class Scouting, Scouting USA, 1991; chmn. ops. com. Young Black Profls., L.A., 1988—90; mem. steering com. United Way Greater L.A., 1989—90. Named one of 50 Most Promising Young Leaders, Time Mag., 100 Most Influential Black Americans, Ebony mag., 2006; named to Hall of Fame, Vanity Fair, 1996; recipient Outstanding Bus. Profl. award, Dollars & Sense Mag., 1992, Image award, NAACP, 2000, Mickey Leland Humanitarian award, Nat. Assn. Minorities in Communications. Office: 3870 Crenshaw Blvd Ste 391 Los Angeles CA 90008

**SMILEY, VIRGINIA A.,** elementary school educator; d. Yancy and Ella W Felder; m. Clarence H. Smiley, Oct. 16, 1982; children: Jacobi T., JaVarius T., JaQuzes T. Bachelor, Ala. State U., 1982, M in Elem. Edn., 1996, M in Ednl. Adminstrn., 2001. Educator/tech. coord. Montgomery Pub. Schs., Ala., 1989—98, lead tchr./tech. coord., 1998—. Advisior Motivation for Acad. Performance, Montgomery, Ala., 1989—98; facilitator Nat. Coalition for Equality in Learning, Montgomery, Ala., 1993—95, Mid. Sch. Action Team, Montgomery, Ala., 1994—95. Vol. Envision Montgomery 2020, Ala., 2000—05. Sci. Lab. grant, Ctrl. Ala. Cmty. Found., 1996, Reading grant, 1999, Comprehensive Sch. Reform grant, Modern Red School House, 2004. Baptist. Avocations: reading, ceramics. Office: Hayneville Road Elem Sch 3315 Hayneville Rd Montgomery AL 36108

**SMIRNOV, ALEXEI VLADIMIROVICH,** research scientist, consultant; s. Vladimir Fedorovich Smirnov and Iraida Izmailovna Smirnova; m. Svetlana Georgievna Kadysheva; children: Ivan, Anna Smirnova, Ilya, Sergey, Anastasia Smirnova. Masters cum laude (hon.), Moscow Engring. Physics Inst., 1982, postgrad., 1985; PhD, Supreme Certifying Com., 1986. Tchr., lectr. math. Moscow Inst. Radio-Electronics and Automatics, 1990—91; reviewer dissertations and projects Russian Rsch. Ctr. Kurchatov Inst., Moscow, 1992—98; IBM network product mgr. UNIT Group Internat., Moscow, 1995—96; cons. head analytical dept. GI Cons., Moscow, 1996—99; patent expert Patent Inst., Moscow, 1998—99; tech. reviewer manuscripts DULY Rsch. Inc., Rancho Palos Verdes, Calif., 2001—02, scientist, 1999—. Contbr. articles to profl. jours., including Am. Inst. Phys. Procs.; author: The Role of Consulting in Enterprise Restructuring, 1998. Trade union mgr. dept. Russian Rsch. Ctr. Kurchatov Inst., Moscow, 1986—90. Named Winner contest Young Scientists and Engrs.-Rschrs., I.V. Kurchatov Inst. Atomic Energy, 1990; recipient prize Best Engring. Devel., Sci. Coun. Russian Rsch. Ctr., Kurchatov Inst., 1995; grantee, Internat. Sci. Found., Soros Found., 1993, 1994, Internat. Sci. Found., 1995. Mem.: American Physical Society APS. Achievements include invention of section of PBG Klystron; transverse coupler, computation methods for magnets and wakefields; linear electron accelerator with RF-energy compression, planar electromagnetic and twisted undulators, linear accelerator of electrons with RF energy compression and an RF device. Home: 1934 Trudie Dr Rancho Palos Verdes CA 90275 Office Phone: 310-548-0290. Personal E-mail: alexei_sav@hotmail.com.

**SMISEK, JEFFERY A.,** airline company executive; b. Washington, Aug. 17, 1954; married; 2 children. AB, Princeton U., 1976; JD, Harvard U., 1982. Bar: Mass., 1982, Tex. 1983. Ptnr., exec. v.p. Vinson & Elkins, LLP, Houston, 1983-95; sr. v.p., gen. counsel Continental Airlines, Inc., Houston, 1995—96, exec. v.p., gen. counsel and sec., 1996—2001, exec. v.p., corp., 2001—03, exec. v.p., 2003—04, pres., 2004—. Bd. dirs. Varco Internat., Inc., Orbitz, Inc. Office: Continental Airlines Inc 1600 Smith St Dept Hdqs Houston TX 77002-7362*

**SMISKO, NICHOLAS RICHARD,** bishop, educator; b. Perth Amboy, N.J., Feb. 23, 1936; s. Andrew and Anna (Totin) S. BTh, Christ the Saviour Sem., 1959; BA, U. Youngstown, 1961; Lic. in Theology, Halki (Greece) Sch. Theology, 1965. Ordained priest Carpatho-Russian Orthodox Greek Cath. Ch., 1959; elevated to rank of met. bishop, 1997. Pastorate Sts. Peter and Paul Ch., Windber, Pa., 1959-62; prefect of discipline Christ the Saviour Sem., Johnstown, Pa., 1963-65; pastor Sts. Peter and Paul Ch., Homer City, Pa., 1965-71, St. Michael's Ch., Clymer, Pa., 1971-72; pastorate St. Nicholas Ch., N.Y.C., 1972-77; abbot Monastery of the Annunciation, Tuxedo Park, NY, 1978-83; bishop of Amissos Carpatho-Russian Orthodox Diocese, 1983—. Mem. del. Ecumenical Patriarchate World Coun. Chs. 6th Gen. Assembly, Vancouver, B.C., Can.; mem. standing conf. Canonical Orthodox Bishops in Am.; active Orthodox-Cath. Consultation of Hierarchs. Mem. Halki Alumni Assn. Am., Christ the Saviour Sem. Alumni Assn., Am. Soc. Constantinople. Carpatho-Russian Orthodox. Home and Office: 312 Garfield St Johnstown PA 15906-2122

**SMISKO, RICHARD G. See NICHOLAS**

**SMIT, HANS,** law educator; b. Amsterdam, Netherlands, Aug. 13, 1927; came to U.S. 1952; s. Eylard Albertus and Trijntje (de Jong) S.; m. Beverly M. Gershgol, Aug. 1, 1954; children: Robert Hugh, Marion Tina. LLB with highest honors, U. Amsterdam, 1946, JD with highest honors, 1949; AM, Columbia U., 1953, LLB with highest honors, 1958; D. (hon.), U. Paris I, 1991. Bar: Supreme Ct. Netherlands 1946, NY 1974. Ptnr. Bodenhausen, Blackstone, Rueb, Bloemsma & Smit, The Hague, 1952-58; assoc. Sullivan & Cromwell, NYC, 1958-60; mem. faculty law Columbia U., NYC, 1960—, assoc. prof., 1960-62, prof., 1962—, Stanley H. Fuld prof. law, 1978—. Dir. Parker Sch. Fgn. and Comparative Law, Columbia U., 1980-98, Ctr. for Internat. Arbitration and Litig. Law, 1997-, Ctr. for East European Law, 1998, Project on Internat. Procs; vis. prof. U. Paris, Sorbonne-Pantheon, 1975-76, 89-90, 92-94; reporter U.S. Com. on Internat. Rules Jud. Procedure, 1960-67; bd. dirs. Project on European Legal Inst., 1968, Leyden-Amsterdam-Columbia Summer Program in Am. Law; cons. internat. comml. transactions, internat. litig.; arbitrator ICC and AAA. Author: International Co-operation in Litigation, 1963, (with others) Elements of Civil Procedure, 5th edit., 1985, International Law, 3d edit., 1993, (with Pechota) World Arbitration Reporter, 1986, (with Herzog) The Law of the European Economic Community, 1978; editor-in-chief Am. Rev. of Internat. Arbitration. Mem. All-Dutch Waterpolo team 1946-48, All-Am. Waterpolo team, AAU, 1954. Knight Order of Netherlands Lion, 1987. Mem. ABA, Internat. Bar Assn., Am. Fgn. Law Assn., Assn. of Bar of City of NY, Am. Soc. Internat. Law, German-Am. Lawyers' Assn., Internat. Assn. Jurists of U.S.A.-Italy, Internat. Acad. Comparative Law, Royal Dutch Soc. Arts and Scis. (assoc.), Am. Arbitration Assn., Internat. C. of C. Home: 351 Riverside Dr New York NY 10025-2739 Office: Columbia U Sch Law 435 W 116th St New York NY 10027-7297 Office Phone: 212-854-2631. Business E-Mail: hsmit@law.columbia.edu.

**SMIT, NEIL,** telecommunications industry executive; BS, Duke U.; M in internat. bus., Tufts U. Mgmt. positions Pillsbury Co.; regional v.p. Nabisco; with Am. Online, Inc., 2000—05, COO Mapquest.com, COO AOL Local, sr. v.p. product and programming team, exec. v.p. mem. services, 2002—03, exec. v.p. mem. devel., 2003—04, press. access bus., 2004—05; press., CEO Charter Comm., Inc., St. Louis, 2005—, also dir., 2005—. Served to lt. comdr. Navy SEALS USN. Office: Charter Comm Inc Ste 1000 12405 Powerscourt Dr Saint Louis MO 63131-3660*

**SMITH, A. ROBERT,** editor, author; b. York, Pa., Feb. 13, 1925; s. Arthur R. and Inez (Dunnick) S.; m. Yvonne Franklin, 1945 (div. 1965); 1 child, Dana C.; m. Elizabeth McDowell Morgan, 1967 (div. 1988); children: Philip S. Morgan IV, Edward A. M. Morgan, Elizabeth A. Morgan; m. Jane Dreifus, 1993 (dec. 1999). BS, Juniata Coll., 1950; postgrad., George Washington U., 1950. Reporter Huntingdon (Pa.) Daily News, 1947, Evening Star, Washington, 1950; Washington corr. Eugene (Oreg.) Register-Guard, 1951-78, Portland Oregonian, 1952-72, King Broadcasting, 1976-78; assoc. editor Virginian-Pilot, Norfolk, 1978-83; editor Venture Inward, Assn. Rsch. and Enlightenment mag., Virginia Beach, Va., 1984—2003. Author: The Tiger in the Senate, 1962, Hugh Lynn Cayce: About My Father's Business, 1988, The Lost Memoirs of Edgar Cayce, 1997, Misdiagnosed: Was My Wife a Casualty of America's Medical Cold War?, 2001, No Soul Left Behind, 2005; co-author: (with Eric Sevareid and Fred J. Maroon) Washington: Magnificent Capital, 1965; (with James V. Giles) An American Rape, 1975 With USNR, 1943-46, PTO. E-mail: abob@cox.net.

**SMITH, ABBIE OLIVER,** college administrator, educator; b. Augusta, Ga., Jan. 31, 1931; d. Rowland Sheppard and Abigail Seabrook (Hanahan) Oliver; m. William Parkhurst Smith, Jr., July 2, 1953; children: William Parkhurst Smith, III, Oliver Hamilton. BS, George Washington U., 1953, MEd, 1958, EdDin Higher Edn., 1986. Tchr. St. Mary's Acad., Monroe, Mich., 1954-55; tchr., coach Washington-Lee H.S., Arlington, Va., 1955-58; homemaker, cmty. vol. Bethesda, Md., 1959-64; asst. professorial lectr. George Washington U., Washington, 1965-69, adminstr. continuing edn., 1969-80, asst. dean, dir., 1981-89, acting dean divsn. continuing edn., 1989-93, asst. v.p., asst. to dean institutional advancement, 1993—. Panelist TV series WETA, Washington; mem. exec. bd., newsletter editor Tng. Officers Conf., 1989—, chair charter expansion 1992—. Co-author: (workbook) Developing New Horizons for Women, 1975, Manual for Counselors for Developing New Horizons for Women, 1975. Mem. adv. bd. Washington Bd. Trade, 1975-77, women's branch adv. bd. State Nat. Bank, Bethesda, Md., 1978-81; collegiate adv. bd. Episcopal Diocese of Washington, 1977-79. Recipient Leadership in Adult Edn. award, 1976, GW award for outstanding contbn. to univ. life Episcopal Diocese of Washington, 1977-79; Recipient Leadership in Adult Edn. award, 1976, GW award for outstanding contbn. to univ. life Office of GW Pres., 1991, Washington Women of Achievement, Washington Edn. TV Assn., 1980. Mem. Nat. U. Continuing Edn. Assn. (awards chair divsn. women's edn. 1977-78, nat. chair 1977-78, chair-elect divsn. part-time students program 1984-86, nat. chair 1984-86, chair coun. human resources 1985-86, nat. spl. com. on couns. and divsn. 1984-86, nat. exec. bd. 1984-86, nat. bd. dirs. 1984-98, nat. charters and bylaws coms. 1987-89, sec.-elect divsn. cert. and nontraditional degree programs 1987-89, chair-elect 1989-90, nat. chair 1990-91, nat. ann. planning coms. 1987, 92, sec. region II 1989-90, chair-elect, ann. conf. chair, single host instn. ann. conf. region II 1990-91, chair region II 1991-92, awards com. chair 1992, Walton S. Bittner Svc. Citation 1994, hon. mention for program catalog nat. divsn. mktg. 1988, Floyd B. Fisher Leadership award 1996), Phi Delta Kappa Internat. (G.W. chpt., v.p. for programs 1995-96, press. 1996-97, newsletter editor 1977—, Newsletter Award Merit 1998-99, Outstanding Newsletter award 1999-2000, 2000-01). Democrat. Episcopalian. Avocations: writing, painting, swimming, dance, travel. Home: 3751 Jocelyn St NW Washington DC 20015-1836 Office: George Washington U 2134 G St NW Washington DC 20037-2797 E-mail: asmith@gwu.edu.

**SMITH, ADA LAVERNE,** state legislator; b. Amherst County, Va. d. Thomas and Lillian Smith. Grad., CUNY. Dep. clk. N.Y.C.; state senator N.Y. Legislature, Albany, 1988—, mem. various coms., ranking corp. commn. and authorities, 1994, minority whip, 1994—2003, chair Senate Dem. Conf., 2003—05, asst. Dem. leader, policy and adminstrn., 2005—. Mem. Senate Minority Puerto Rican and Hispanic Task Force. Trustee, life dir. Coll. Fund Baruch Coll. Recipient Outstanding Alumni award Baruch Coll. Mem. NY Assn. State Black and Puerto Rican Legislators, Baruch Coll. Alumni Assn. (press., Disting. Svc. award, Outstanding Achievement award), Nat. Black Caucus of State Legislators (bd. dirs., vice chair telecomms. com.), Women in Govt. (state bd. dirs.). Office: NY State Senate Rm 808 Legis Office Bldg Albany NY 12247 also: Queens Dist Office 11643 Sutphin Blvd Jamaica NY 11434-1526 Office Phone: 518-455-3531. E-mail: smith@senate.state.ny.us.

**SMITH, ADAM See GOODMAN, GEORGE**

**SMITH, ADAM,** congressman; b. Washington, June 15, 1965; s. Ben Smith; m. Sara Bickle-Eldridge, Aug. 1993; 2 children. BA, Fordham U., 1987; JD, U. Wash., 1990. Driver United Parcel Svc., 1985-87; mem. Wash. State Senate, 1990-96; atty. Cromwell, Mendoza and Belur, 1991—92; asst. pros. atty. Seattle, 1993—95; pro tem judge, 1996; mem. US Congress from 9th Wash. dist., 1997—, mem. armed svcs. com., mem. internat. rels. com. Mem. Kent Drinking Driver Task Force, Highline Citizens for Schs., Kent Meridian HS Site-Based Coun.; bd. mem. Judson Pk. Retirement Home. Mem.: Kiwanis Internat. Democrat. Office: US Ho Reps 227 Cannon Ho Office Bldg Washington DC 20515 Office Phone: 202-225-8901.*

**SMITH, ADRIAN DEVAUN,** architect; b. Chgo., Aug. 19, 1944; s. Alfred D. and Hazel (Davis) S.; m. Nancy L. Smith, Aug. 17, 1968; children: Katherine, Jason. Student, Tex. A&M U., 1962-66; BArch, U. Ill., Chgo., 1969. Registered architect, Ill., Mass., Fla. Design ptnr. Skidmore, Owings, & Merrill, Chgo., 1967—2003, CEO, 1993—95, cons. ptnr., 2004—. Vis. faculty Sch. Architecture, U. Ill., Chgo., 1984; chmn. U. Ill. Sch. Archtl. Alumni Assn., AIA Jury on Inst. Honors; adv. jury AIA gold metal and architecture firm award, 2000; chmn. nat. AIA awards jury for architecture and 25 yr. award, 2004; chmn. Skidmore Owings Merrill Found., 1989-95; press. Chgo. Ctrl. Area, 1997-99; bd. dirs. Greater State Street Coun. trustee; bd. govs. Sch. Art Inst. Chgo., 1999—; repr. RIBA British Archtl. Libr. Trust, British Schs. and Univ. Found.; dir. U. Ill. Alumni Found., 88-89; cons. and lectr. in field. Designer numerous projects including Three First Nat. Plaza, Chgo., 1982, 919 North Michigan Ave, Chgo., 1982, Capitol Square, Des Moines, Iowa, 1983, Woodmont Place, Rockville, Maryland, 1983, Chgo.

Ctrl. Area Plan, 1984, 1992 Chgo. World's Fair, 1980-85, Arborlake Ctr., Deerfield, Ill., 1985, Lake Cook Office Ctr., Deerfield, 1985, Harbortown, Detroit, Mich., 1986, Loop Transporatation Ctr./203 North LaSalle, Chgo., 1986, Olympia Ctr., Chgo., 1986, Trump Tower Chgo., GM Hdqrs., Renn Ctr., Detroit, 222 N. LaSalle, Chgo., 1986 (Disting. Bldg. award CCAIA 1988), Art Inst. Chgo. 2nd Fl. Galleries, 1987 (CCAIA Disting. Bldg. award 1987), 225 West Washington, Chgo., 1986, Arthur Anderson Tng. Ctr., St. Charles, Ill., 1987 (Masonry award 1988), Rowes Wharf, Boston, 1988 (Build Am. award 1988, Build Mass. award 1989, ULI award 1989, PCI Profl. Design award 1989, CCAIA Hon. award 1998, Nat. AIA Honor award 1994), Chgo. Tranist Authority Red Line, AT&T Corp. Ctr., Chgo., 1989 (recipient Gold Metal Ill. Ind. Masonry award), NBC Tower at Cityfront Ctr., Chgo. 1989 (Chgo. Sun Times Bldg. of Yr. award 1991, CCAIA Disting. Bldg. award 1990, PCI Design award 1989), 75 State St., Boston, 1989 (Archtl. Woodwork Inst. award 1989, Nat. Comml. Builder's Coun. Merit award 1990, Bldg. Stone Inst. Tucker Archtl. award 1990), Continental Bank First Fl. Renovation, Chgo., 1990, Dearborn Tower, Chgo., 1991, USG Hdqs., Chgo., 1991, Washington Univ. Psychology Bldg., Lab., & Animal Facility, St. Louis, 1996, Chgo. Transit Authority, Green Line Rehabilitation, Chgo., 1995, Commonwealth Edison, East Lake Transmission & Distribution Ctr., Chgo., 1995, St. Charles, Ill., Heller Internat. Tower, Chgo., State St. Renovation (spl. achievement award 1997, AIA honor award urban design 1998), 1996, Riverport Casino Ctr., Maryland Heights, Mo.,1997, Metro. Ctr. II, Mpls., Minn., 1997, 301 South Wacker Drive, Chgo., 1999, Washington Univ. Arts & Scis. Bldg., St. Louis, Mo., 2000, Campus Crusade for Christ Internat., Orlando, Fla., 2000, Sun Plaza, Las Vegas, Nevada, 2000, Metro. Fin. Corp., Mayfield Heights, Ohio, 2000, Millennium Park, Chgo., 2002, United Airlines World Hdqrs., Chgo., 2002, 7 South Dearborn Tower, Chgo., 2002, Manulife Fin., Boston, 2003, GM Global Hdqrs. at Resaissance Ctr., Detroit, 2003, Lakeshore East, Chgo., Trump Internat. Hotel & Tower, Chgo.; designer numerous fgn. projects including: Monterey Cultural Ctr., Mex., 1978, Hyatt Regency Surabaya, Indonesia, 1979, Banco de Occidente, Guatemala City, 1980 (CCAIA Interior Architecture award 1981, NAIA Honor award 1982), Bally of Switzerland, 1982, Broadgate, London, 1987-92, Hdqs. Canary Wharf Fin. Ctr., London, Eng., 1988, United Gulf Bank, Manama, Bahrain, 1986 (Progressive Architecture award 1984, CCAIA Disting. Bldg. award 1988, NAIA Honor award 1988, CCAIA Detail Honor award 1989), 10 Ludgate (CCAIA 1994 Honor award, Brit. Civil Trust award), 10 Fleet Place, Ludgate Office Bldg., London, 1992, 100 Ludgate Hill, Ludgate Office Bldg., London, 1992, Aramco Hdqrs., Dhahran, Saudi Arabia, 1993, Aramco Hdqrs. Office Bldg., 1993, Xiamen Posts & Telecommunications Bldg., China, 1994, Frankfurter Allee, 1991, Phase I implementation, Berlin, Germany, 1995, Tower Palace III, Seoul, Korea, 1996, Kowloon MTR Tower, Hong Kong, Pidemco GSCP MSCP Towers, Singapore, 1997, Aramco Hdqs. Dharan Saudi Arabia, McGraw Hill European Headquarters, Canary Wharf (FC-2), London, 1990, Canary Wharf, London, 1991, Canary Wharf (DS4), CSFB European Headquarters, Canary Wharf (DSI), Morgan Stanley Headquarters for Europe (HQI), Canary Wharf, Burj Dubai Tower (World's Tallest Bldg.), United Arab Emirates, Jin Mao Tower (World's Tallest Mixed-Use Project), Shanghai, China (Nat. AIA award for interior architecture 2000), 1998, BankBoston Hdqrs., Sao Paulo, Brazil, 2000, Broadgate Phase, London, Eng., 2002, Nanjing Guozi Greenland Fin. Ctr., Nanjing, China, Sinopec China Energy, Bejing, China, Russia Tower, Moscow,Tower Palace for Samsung Group,Seoul, Korea, 2003, Chemsunny Plaza, Beijing,China,; author: Monograph of Adrian P. Smith, 2002; contbr. articles to profl. jours.; subject numerous pubs. in architecture. Mem. com. Task Force for New City Plan, Chgo., Light Up Chgo., Ctrl. Area Com. Task Force Chgo.; chmn. Senator Richard A. Newhouse Bldg. Competition Jury, 1982, Progressive Architecture Design Jury, 1985; bd. dirs. State St. Coun.; lifetime gov., Urban Land Inst. Found.; trustee, Chgo. Architecture Found., 93-99, Bldg. Experiences Trust, 91-95. Recipient U. Ill. Alumni Achievement award. Fellow AIA (mem. Young Architects Award Design July, 1987, Mich. Jury 1988, chmn. nat. jury arch. and 25 yr. award 2004, Disting. Bldg. award 1990), Royal Inst. Brit. Architects, Archtl. Registration Coun., U.K., Nat. Coun. Archtl. Registration Bds., Architecture Soc. of Art Inst. Chgo., Chgo. Arch. Found., Chgo. Archtl. Club, Urban Found. (bd. trustees) University Club, Arts Club; Am. Acad. Rome (Midwest dir., 85-86); mem. Economic Club Chgo. Office: Skidmore Owings & Merrill LLP 224 S Michigan Ave Ste 1000 Chicago IL 60604 Office Phone: 312-554-9090. Office Fax: 312-360-4545.

**SMITH, ADRIAN J.R.,** management company executive; b. Liverpool, Eng. married; 4 children. Grad., Liverpool Law Sch., 1966. With Procter & Gamble Ltd., 1966-79; v.p. European consumer ops. Ecolab Inc., Minn., 1979-90; pres. Ecolab Can. Ltd.; with Arthur Andersen and Co., 1990-96; CEO Grant Thornton LLP, Chgo., 1996. Mem. Am. Bus. Conf. Bd. dirs. March of Dimes, Chgo., Montessori Sch., Lake Forest, Chgo. Sinfonietta.

**SMITH, AGNES EYVONDA,** writer; b. Nashville, Tenn., Apr. 24, 1959; d. Robert Jackson and Agnes Marieo Odom; m. Harold Haywood Smith, Aug. 3, 1999; m. James G. Parker, Dec. 12, 1982 (div. Apr. 25, 1993); children: Tangla S. Odom, Gary J. Parker, Steven J. Parker. At sch. of nursing, Tenn. State U., 1979. Cert. Nashville Area Vocat. Sch., 1980. LPN Carriage Ho., Nashville, 1980—92; coach operator Metro. Transit Authority, Nashville, 1992—2000; writer T.H.A.T. Pub., Nashville, 1999—. Author: (books) Wonderful Soul Food, 2001, Entering into the Unknown, 2002. Bd. mem. Amalgamated Transit Union, Nashville, 1991—2003. Mem.: Ea. Star, Sarai Chpt. 419 (worthy matron 2002—03). Home: 1111 S Douglas Ave Nashville TN 37204 Office: THAT Publisher PO Box 40781 Nashville TN 37204 E-mail: 0957@bellsouth.net.

**SMITH, AGNES MONROE,** history professor; b. Hiram, Ohio, Aug. 8, 1920; d. Bernie Alfred and Joyce (Messenger) Monroe; m. Stanley Blair Smith; children: David, Doris, Darl, Diane. BA, Hiram Coll., 1940; MA, W.Va. U., 1945; PhD, Western Res. U., 1966. Social sci. tchr. Freedom (Ohio) High Sch., 1940-44; instr. of history W.Va. U., Morgantown, 1945; instr. of social sci. Hiram Coll., 1946; instr. history and social sci. Youngstown (Ohio) State U., 1964-66, asst. prof. to prof. of history, 1966-84, prof. history emeritus, 1984—; vis. prof. history Hiram Coll., 1988-90. Co-editor: Bourgeois, Sans Culottes and other Frenchmen, 1981; contbr. articles to profl. jours. Mem. Ohio Acad. History, Delta Kappa Gamma, Phi Alpha Theta, Pi Gamma Mu. Mem. Christian Ch. (Disciples Of Christ). Home: 16759 Main Market Rd West Farmington OH 44491-9608

**SMITH, ALAN MICHAEL,** music educator, musician; b. Austin, Tex., Oct. 2, 1945; s. Jackson Buford Smith and Katherine Elizabeth Webb; m. Diana Lou Barker, Dec. 28, 1968; 1 child, Hillary Kay. MusB, U. Tex., 1967, MusM, 1969, D of Musical Arts, 1977. Instr. cello Shenandoah U., Winchester, Va., 1970—72; asst. prof. cello U. NC, Chapel Hill, 1974—80; prof. cello Bowling Green (Ohio) State U., 1980—. Vis. assoc. prof. cello Oberlin (Ohio) Conservatory of Music, 1990; vis. prof. cello U. Ariz., Tucson, 1992—93; music dir., coord. Bowling Green Symphony Orch., 1994—2004; assoc. dean Coll. Musical Arts Bowling Green State U., 2001—; mem. adv. bd. STRINGS Mag., San Rafael, Calif., 2003—. Performer (CD) The Guarneri Duo, 2004. Tech. sgt. USAF, 1969—72. Recipient Young Artist award Midland-Odessa (Tex.) Symphony, 1965, Eric Sorantin award, San Angelo (Tex.) Symphony, 1968, Young Artist award, Denver Symphony Orch., 1970. Mem.: Am. Fedn. Musicians, Chamber Music Am., Coll. Music Soc.

**SMITH, ALAN WADE,** music educator; b. Elizabeth City, N.C., Oct. 8, 1964; s. Gilbert Richard and Marilyn Kay Smith. AA in music edn., St. Petersburg (Fla.) Jr. Coll., 1986; BS, U. South Fla., 1990. Cert. Secondary Social Studies Edn. S.C., 2005, Fla., 2004. Social studies tchr. Seminole (Fla.) Mid. Sch., 1993—2004; global studies tchr. Dorman HS Freshman Campus, Roebuck, SC, 2004—06; assoc. marching band dir. Dorman HS, Roebuck, SC, 2004—06. Visual designer (marching band competitive field shows) Marching Band Competitive Field Show (Bands of Am. Regional Champions/Nat. Finalists). Recipient Tchr. of the Yr., Seminole Mid. Sch., 1997. Mem.: Music Educator's Nat. Conf., Nat. Coun. for Social Studies

(assoc.). Home: PO Box 665 Roebuck SC 29376 Office: Dorman HS Freshman Campus 1225 Cavalier Way Roebuck SC 29376 Personal E-Mail: alan88888@aol.com. Business E-Mail: smithaw@spart6.org.

**SMITH, ALBERT ALOYSIUS, JR.,** electrical engineer, consultant; b. Yonkers, N.Y., Dec. 2, 1935; s. Albert Aloysius and Jean Mary (Misiewicz) S.; m. Rosemarie Torricelli, Apr. 4, 1964 (dec. 1982); children: Denise, Matthew. BSEE, Milw. Sch. Engring., 1961; MSEE, NYU, 1964. Staff engr. Adler/Westrex, New Rochelle, NY, 1961-64; adv. engr. IBM, Kingston, NY, 1964-78, sr. engr. Poughkeepsie, NY, 1978-85, Kingston, 1985-91; cons., 1991—. Author: Coupling of External Electromagnetic Fields to Transmission Lines, 1977, Measuring the Radio Frequency Environment, 1985, Radio Frequency Principles and Applications, 1998. Com. chmn. Woodstock Boy Scout Troop 34, 1978-79; com. chmn. Woodstock Cub Pack 34, 1976-78. Served with USN, 1953-56. Recipient Outstanding Alumnus award Milw. Sch. Engring., 1981; Invention Achievement award IBM, 1979, 90, Div. award, 1981. Fellow IEEE (tech. com. on electromagnetic environments, assoc. editor Trans. on EMC); mem. Am. Nat. Standards Com. Roman Catholic. Home: 4507 Burnett St Valatie NY 12184-2516

**SMITH, ALBERT CROMWELL, JR.,** investment company executive, writer; b. Norfolk, Va., Dec. 6, 1925; s. Albert Cromwell and Georgie (Foreman) Smith; m. Laura Thaxton, Oct. 25, 1952; children: Albert, Elizabeth, Laura. BSCE, Va. Mil. Inst., 1949; MS in Govtl. Adminstrn., George Washington U., 1965; MBA, Pepperdine U., 1975; PhD in Bus. Adminstrn., LaSalle U., 1994. Enlisted USMC, 1944, advanced through grades to col., 1970, comdr. inf. platoons, coss., landing force; assigned to staffs, U.K. Joint Force, U.S. Sec. Navy, Brit. Staff Coll., Marine Staff Coll., U.K. Staff Coll. and Latimer Staff Coll.; advisor, analyst amphibious sys. USMC; ret., 1974; press. A. Cromwell-Smith, Ltd., Charlottesville, Va., 1973; head broker, cons. A. Cromwell Smith, Investments, La Jolla and Coronado, Calif., 1975—. Author: The Individual Investor in Tomorrow's Stock Market, 1977, The Little Guy's Stock Market Survival Guide, 1979, rev. edit., 2000, Wake Up Detroit: The EVs are Coming, 1982, The Little Guy's Tax Survival Guide, 1984, Little Guy's Real Estate Success Guide, 1990, Little Guy's Stock Market Success Guide, 1992, Little Guy's Stock Market Future Effectiveness, 1994, The Little Guy's Sailboat Success, 1996, The Little Guy's Business Success, 1997, Business Success, 1997, Stock Market Success, 1998, Semper Fidelis in Peace and War, 1999, revised edit., 2003, Sailboat Success, 1999, Tax Survival Guide, 1999, The EVs are Coming, 1999, Real Estate Success, 2000, The EVs and Hyboards Are Here, 2005; contbr. articles to profl. jours. Bd. dirs. La Jolla Reps., 1975—76; vestryman St. Martin's Episcopal Ch., 1971—73. Decorated Legion of Merit with oak leaf cluster with V device, Bronze Star with V device with oak leaf cluster, Air medal with two oak leav clusters, Purple Heart, Vietnamese Galantry Cross with gold star. Mem.: VFW, SAR, ASCE, So. Calif. Options Soc., Stockbrokers Soc., Coronado Bd. Realtors, San Diego Bd. Realtors, Calif. Assn. Realtors, Nat. Assn. Realtors, Mil. Order Purple Heart. Address: 1810 Ave del Mundo # 106 Coronado CA 92118

**SMITH, ALBERT E.,** areonautics company professional; BSEE, Northeastern U., Boston. With CIA, Washington, 1972—85, Lockheed Martin Missiles & Space, 1985-96; press. electronics systems sector Harris Corp., 1996-98; press. Sanders Divsn. Lockheed Martin Aerospace Electronics Systems, 1998-99; exec. v.p. Lockheed Martin Space Systems, 1999—2003; exec. v.p., integrated Systems and Solutions (IS&S) Lockheed Martin Corp., 2003—. Mem. Security Affairs Support Assn., Assn. of U.S. Army, Assn. of Old Crows, Armed Forces Comms. and Electronics Assn. Office: Lockheed Martin Corp 6801 Rockledge Dr Bethesda MD 20817-1836

**SMITH, ALDO RALSTON, JR.,** brokerage house executive; b. Yonkers, N.Y., Mar. 19, 1947; s. Aldo Ralston Sr. and Maggie (Allen) S.; m. Linda McKenney Davila, Oct. 15, 1983; children: Damian Allen, Caitlin Victoria McKenney. BA in Psychology summa cum laude, Talladega Coll., 1973; postgrad., CUNY, 1973-76. Account exec. trainee Advest Inc., N.Y.C., 1978-79; account exec. Merrill, Lynch, Pierce, Fenner & Smith, N.Y.C., 1979-80, Lehman Brothers Kuhn Loeb, N.Y.C., 1980-82; fin. cons. Shearson Am. Express, N.Y.C., 1982-84; v.p. instl. mcpl. bond sales A.L. Haven Securities, N.Y.C., 1984; v.p. Prescott Ball & Turben, Inc., N.Y.C., 1984-85; v.p. instl. sales Baird Patrick & Co Inc., N.Y.C., 1985-91, Lincoln Pvt. Bank, 1991—; account exec. North Fork Bank Corp., 1995. Bd. dirs. Hale House for Human Potential, N.Y.C., 1978-80, Yonkers Family Svc. Assn., 2002—, Lower Hudson Valley Legal Svcs.; v.p.r Yonkers Family Svc. Assn.; mem. Mayor's Citizens Adv. Budget Com., 1993; chmn. Yonkers Police Citizens Profl. Standards Adv. Com., 1992. With U.S. Army, 1967-70. Named Outstanding Young Men of Am. Nat. Jr. C. of C., 1981; decorated Sovereign Mil. Order of Knights of Jerusalem, The Most Venerable Order of the Hosp. of St. John of Jerusalem. Mem. Yonkers Lions Club (bd. dirs. 1985—, press. 1991-92, zone chmn. 1992-93), Masons (dist. dep. grand master 4th Manhattan dist.), Sovereign Mil. Order Knights of Jerusalem, Most Venerable Order Hosp. St. John of Jerusalem, Alpha Chi. Republican. Episcopalian. Avocations: scuba diving, photography, horticulture, cooking. Home: 96 Edgecliff Ter Yonkers NY 10705-1609

**SMITH, ALEX,** professional football player; b. Seattle, Wash., May 7, 1984; s. Doug, Pam. Bachelor's degree in Econ., Utah Univ., 2003. Quarterback San Francisco 49ers. Named Nat. Player Yr., The Sporting News, 2004. Achievements include first over-all selection in NFL draft, 2005. Office: San Francisco 49ers Marie P DeBartolo Sports Ctr 4949 Centennial Blvd Santa Clara CA 95054*

**SMITH, ALEXANDER WYLY, JR.,** lawyer; b. Atlanta, June 9, 1923; s. Alexander Wyly and Laura (Payne) S.; m. Betty Rawson Haverty, Aug. 31, 1946; children— Elizabeth Smith Crew, Clarence Haverty, Laura Smith Brown, James Haverty, Edward Kendrick, Anthony Marion, William Rawson. Grad., Marist Sch., 1941; student, Holy Cross Coll., 1941-42; BBA, U. Ga., 1947, LL.B. cum laude, 1949. Bar: Ga. 1948. Practiced in, Atlanta, 1948-98; ret. ptnr. Smith, Gambrell & Russell and predecessor, 1994—. Bd. dirs. Our Lady of Perpetual Help Free Cancer Home; bd. dirs., planning and devel. coun. Cath. Archdiocese Atlanta, Marist Sch., Atlanta, John and Mary Franklin Found. Served with USAAF, 1943-46. Mem. Ga. Bar Assn., Atlanta Bar Assn., Phi Delta Phi, Chi Phi, Peachtree Driving Club Atlanta, Peachtree Golf Club Atlanta (pres. 1989-91). Home: 2771 Peachtree Rd #5 Atlanta GA 30305-3523 Office: 3100 Promenade II Atlanta GA 30309-3574 Office Phone: 404-815-3507.

**SMITH, ALICE DAVIS,** retired biology educator, retired art educator; b. Hill City, SD, Feb. 25, 1917; d. John Oliver Davis and Medora Alice Morehouse; m. Dwaine Casey Smith, June 21, 1941 (dec. 1991); children: Richard, Ronald, Brian, Dee, Doreen. BSc, ND State Coll., 1940; degree in art, Black Hills Tchg. Sch., 1960. Botany lab instr. S.D. State U., 1946—48; jr. high. gen. svc. Pierre Sch. Dist., 1953—56, biology tchr., 1955—65, art and biology tchr., 1965—70, art tchr., 1970—75; ret., 1975. Mem. Hill City Arts Coun., SD, We. Women in the Arts, Black Hills Writers; presenter in field. Author: (poetry) Potpourri, Medley of Life, (plays) A Port and Points in Time; contbr. articles to profl. jours. Mem. H-Camp; mem., trustee Friends of Libr. Nominee Spirit of Dakota award, Gov.'s Art award, 2000; recipient Award of Honor, Nat. Coun. State Garden Clubs, 1999. Mem.: AAUW, Pierre Edn. Assn., Hill City C of C (life), SD State Poetry Soc. (bd. dirs.), Canvas Backs Art Club, Hill City Garden Club. Avocations: fishing, swimming, photography, gardening, writing.

**SMITH, ALISON LEIGH,** lawyer; b. Brownsville, Tex., Sept. 24, 1952; d. Arthur Lee and June (Allen) Smith; m. Dean A. Burkhardt, Apr. 24, 1981. B in Journalism summa cum laude, U. Tex., 1974, JD cum laude, 1977. Bar: Tex. 1977, U.S. Dist. Ct. (so. dist.) Tex. (1978), U.S. Ct. Appeals (5th cir.) 1981, U.S. Dist. Ct. (no. dist.) Tex. 1987, U.S. Ct. Appeals (D.C. cir.) 1989. Assoc. Vinson & Elkins LLP, Houston, 1977-84, ptnr., 1984—89, 1991—2004; dep. asst. atty. gen. antitrust divsn. U.S. Dept. Justice, Washington, 1989-91; ptnr. Dewey Ballantine LLP, Houston, 2004—05, Haynes and Boone, LLP, Houston, 2005—. Adj. prof. law U. Tex., Austin, 1992-93. Alternate del. Rep. Nat. Conv., New Orleans, 1988; mem. ethics com. City of Houston, 1988-89; chair Mayor's Animal Protection Task Force, 2005. Mem. ABA (antitrust law sect., chair transp. industry com., 1992-95, co-chmn. pvt. antitrust litig. com. 2001-04, vice chmn. Sherman Act sect. one com. 2004-05, econ. evidence task force 2005—); Am. Law Inst., Tex. Bar Found., Houston Bar Assn. Home: 2125 Bolsover St Houston TX 77005-1617 Office: Haynes and Boone LLP 1221 McKinney Ste 2100 Houston TX 77010 Office Phone: 713-547-2673. Business E-Mail: alison.smith@haynesboone.com.

**SMITH, ALLAN LASLETT,** research scientist, educator; b. Newark, N.J., June 21, 1938; s. Arthur Laslett and Dorothy Preisler Smith; m. Charity Fletcher, Aug. 28, 1960; children: Fletcher, Nadja. BA, Harvard U., Cambridge, Mass., 1960; PhD, MIT, Cambridge, Mass., 1965. Asst. prof. Yale U., New Haven, 1966—75; assoc. prof. Drexel U., Phila., 1975—84, prof., 1984—; pres., founder Masscal Corp., Chatham, Mass., 2001—. Contbr. over 75 articles to profl. jours. Bd. dirs., chmn. Daycroft Sch., Greenwich, Conn., 1978—82; bd. dirs. Singing City, Phila., 1994—99. Grantee, NSF, 1976—82, U.S. Dept. Energy, 1976—2004.

**SMITH, ALLIE MAITLAND,** engineering educator; b. Lumberton, NC, June 9, 1934; s. Allie McCoy and Emma Hattie (Wright) S.; m. Sarah Louise Whitlock, June 16, 1957; children: Sara Leianne, Hollis Duval, Meredith Lorren. BME with honors, N.C. State U., Raleigh, 1956, MS, 1961, PhD, 1966. Assoc. engr. Martin Co., Balt., 1956-57; devel. engr. Western Electric Co., 1957-60; mem. tech. staff Bell Tel. Labs., Burlington, NC, 1960-62; instr., then asst. prof. extension N.C. State U., 1958-62; rsch. project engr. Rsch. Triangle Inst., Durham, NC, 1962-66; rsch. supr. Sverdrup/ARO, Inc., Arnold Air Force Sta., Tenn., 1966-79; adj. prof. U. Tenn., Tullahoma, 1967-79; prof. mech. engring. U. Miss., University, 1979—, dean Sch. Engring., 1979—2000. Bd. dirs., scholarship bd. Miss. Mineral Resources Inst.; exec. chmn. 14th conf. Southeastern Conf. on Theoretical and Applied Mechanics, exec. com. 13th-16th confs., ops. com. and policy com., 1990-99, session chair, 1994; organizing com., internat. sci. adv. bd., plenary session presiding officer Internat. Conf. on Hydrosci. and Engring., 1993, 95; organizing com., plenary session chair Conf. on Mgmt. of Landscapes Disturbed by Channel Incision, 1997; keynote lecture and plenary sessions chair, 3rd Internat. Conf. on Hydrosci. and Engring., Berlin, 1998 Author: Fundamentals of Silicon Integrated Device Technology, Vol. I: Oxidation, Diffusion and Epitaxy, 1967, also articles, revs.; editor: Radiative Transfer and Thermal Control, 1976, Thermophysics of Spacecraft and Outer Planet Entry Probes, 1977, Fundamentals and Applications of Radiation Heat Transfer, 1987, Developments in Theoretical and Applied Mechanics, Vol. XIV, 1988, Radiation Heat Transfer: Fundamentals and Applications, 1990, Fundamentals of Radiation Heat Transfer, 1991, Radiative Heat Transfer: Theory and Applications, 1993, Solution Methods for Radiative Heat Transfer in Participating Media, 1996, Radiative Heat Transfer, 1997. Fellow AIAA (chmn. thermophysics tech. com. 1975-77, ASME (aerospace heat transfer com. 1975—, chmn. radiative heat transfer I and II sessions, Pitts. 2000, chmn. radiation heat transfer II session, St. Louis, 2002), chmn. terrestrial energy sys. tech. com. 1979-81, chmn. confs. 1975, 79, assoc. editor jour. 1975-77, 1986—, nat. publ. com. 1979-83, Nat. Thermophysics award 1978, Hermann Oberth award 1984-85, Space Shuttle Flag Challenger plaque 1984, supernumerary dir. Ala.-Miss. sect. 1994—2000); mem. AAUP, NSPE (pres. N.E. Miss. chpt. 1990-91), Am. Soc. Engring. Edn. (host Nat. Engring. Deans' Inst. 1991), NY Acad. Scis., Sigma Xi, Phi Kappa Phi, Tau Beta Pi, Pi Tau Sigma, Upsilon Pi Epsilon, Sigma Pi (scholar 1955), Order of the Engr., Rotary Achievements include discovery of anomalous refraction maxima phenomenon. Home: PO Box 1857 University MS 38677-1857 Office: U Miss 205 Carrier Hall University MS 38677 Office Phone: 662-915-5842. Business E-Mail: enas@olemiss.edu.

**SMITH, ALVIN WINFRED,** veterinarian, educator; b. Kooskia, Idaho, Sept. 25, 1933; m. Gladdie Colleen Jones. D of Vet. Medicine, Wash. State U., 1957. Diplomate Am Vet. Med Assn., 1968. Prof. Oreg. State U., Corvallis, 1980—. Contbr. scientific papers. With USAF, 1958—80. Decorated Air Force Meritorious Svc. USAF. Mem.: Oreg. Vet. Med. Assn. (life; pres. 1989—90). R-Consevative. Christian. Achievements include patents in field. Avocation: fishing. Home: 26833 Sulphur Springs Rd Corvallis OR 97330 Personal E-mail: calicit@qwest.net.

**SMITH, AMOS BRITTAIN, III,** chemist, educator; b. Lewisburg, Pa., Aug. 26, 1944; s. Amos Brittain and Mildred (Cornelius) S.; m. Janet L. Duyckinck; children: Amos Matthew MacMillan, Kathryn Schuyler. BS, MS, Bucknell U., 1966; PhD, Rockefeller U., 1972; MA (hon.), U. Pa., 1978. Rsch. assoc. Rockefeller U., N.Y.C., 1972-73; asst. prof. U. Pa., Phila., 1973-78, assoc. prof., 1978-81, prof., 1981—, chmn. dept. chemistry, 1988—96, Rhodes-Thompson prof. chemistry, 1990—, mem. Lab. Rsch. Structure Matter, 1976—2000. Vis. dir. Kitasato Inst., Tokyo, 1990—; ad hoc mem. medicinal chemistry A and bioorganic and natural products chemistry rev. panel, NIH, 1980-83, mem. medicinal chemistry study sect., 1983-87, chmn. study sect. workshop on medicinal chemistry, 1986, mem. study sect. for AIDS and related rsch., 1989; vis. prof. Columbia U., N.Y.C., 1980, Cambridge (Eng.) U., 1982; Arthur D. Little lectr. Northeastern U., 1986, H. Martin Friedman lectr. Rutgers U., 1988, Merck-Frosst lectr., Ottawa, Can., 1988, U. Sherbrooke, Québec, Can., 1993; Phillips lectr. Haverford Coll, 1992; Soc. Francaise de Chimie lectr., Paris, 1988, lectr. at French-speaking univs., Switzerland, 1989; bd. dirs. Organic Reactions, Inc. Mem. editl. bd. Jour. Organic Chemistry, 1982-86, 94-97, Jour. Am. Chem. Soc., 1988-93, Organic Reactions, 1987—, Organic Syntheses, 1990—, Jour. Chem. Soc., Perkin I., 1992—; Synlett, 1995-97, Fullerene Sci. and Tech., 1993—; guest editor Tetrahedron Symposium in Print, Fullerene Chemistry, 1993, regional editor Fullerene Sci. and Tech., 1997—; bd. cons. editors Tetrahedron Publs., Jour. of Antibiotics, 1999—; editor-in-chief Organic Letters, 1999—; editl. adv. bd. Synlett, 1995-98; contbr. numerous articles to profl. jours., chpts. in books, revs., others. Recipient Camille and Henry Dreyfus Tchr.-Scholar award, 1978-83, Career Devel. award NIH, 1980-85, Arthur C. Cope Scholar award, 1991, Alexander von Humboldt Rsch. award for sr. U.S. scientists, 1992, Ernest Guenther award in the chemistry of essential oils, 1993, Alumni award for outstanding profl. achievement Bucknell U., 1993, Centenary medal Royal Soc. Chem., London, 2002, Yamada prize Tokyo, Japan, 2003, Order of Rising Sun Gold Rays with Neck Ribbon, Govt. Japan, 2004; J.S. Guggenheim Found. fellow, 1985-86, Japan Soc. for Promotion Sci. fellow, 1986-87. Mem. Am. Chem. Soc. (chmn. nominating com. organic chemistry divsn. 1985, exec. officer Nat. Organic Symposium 1993, chair-elect, chair, past chair Divsn. Organic Chemistry, 1995, 96, 97, canvassing com. 1989—, Phila. sect award 1986), Internat. Soc. Chem. Ecology (counselor), Gordon Rsch. Conf. (vice chmn. organic reaction and processes 1979, chmn. 1980), Franklin Inst. (com. on scis. and arts 1985—), Phila. Organic Chemists Club (chmn. 1978, award 1991), Pharm. Soc. of Japan (hon. mem. 1999); fellow AAAS, 2002, Am. Acad. Arts and Sciences, 2006. Avocations: hunting, fishing. Office: Univ Penn Dept Chemistry 231 S 34th St 440 N Philadelphia PA 19104-3803 Office Phone: 215-898-4860. E-mail: smithab@sas.upenn.edu.*

**SMITH, AMY B.,** mechanical engineer, engineering educator; BSc, MIT, 1984, MSE, 1995. Vol. Peace Corps, Botswana, 1986—90; inventor, instr. MIT Edgerton Ctr., Cambridge, Mass., 2000—. Co-founder MIT IDEAS competition (Innovation, Devel., Enterprise, Action, Svc.); and co-founder Internat. Devel. Initiative. Named a MacArthur Fellow, 2004; recipient Lemelson-MIT Student prize, 2000. Office: MIT Edgerton Ctr Rm 4-405 77 Mass Ave Cambridge MA 02139*

**SMITH, ANDREW ALFRED, JR.,** urban planner; b. Lynchburg, Va., Oct. 3, 1947; s. Andrew Alfred and Josephine (Vaughan) S. BArch (cum laude), Howard U., 1972; M in City Planning, MIT, 1980. Archtl. designer The Architects Collaborative Inc., Cambridge, Mass., 1972-76; archtl. coordinator Fay, Spofford & Thorndike Inc., Boston, 1977-79; assoc. city planner N.Y.C. Planning Commn., 1980—. Active Briarwood (N.Y.) Community Assn.,

1985—, Jamaica YMCA, Queens, N.Y.; Newark Area Planning Assn., 1968, Peoples Involvement Corp., Washington, 1971-72, Mission Hill Planning Commn., Boston, 1978-80. HUD grantee, 1978-80; recipient Hallmark medal, 1989. Mem. Am. Planning Assn., Inst. Urban Design, Nat. Assn. Housing and Redevel. Ofcls. (exec. v.p. N.Y. Met. chpt. 1996—), Urban Land Inst. (assoc.), Howard U. Alumni Assn. (regional rep. 1978-79, 82-86, pres. L.I. chpt. 1983-85), Sierra Club, Nat. Travel Club, Mpcl. Art Soc. Democrat. Avocations: scuba diving, horseback riding, travel photographing, fundraising, arts and crafts collecting. Home: 84-55 Daniels St Apt 6L Briarwood NY 11435-2014 Office: NYC Planning Commn 22 Reade St New York NY 10007-1216 E-mail: asmith1@planning.nyc.gov;

**SMITH, ANDREW DONALD,** plastic surgeon; s. Donald Raymond and Susan Blair Smith; m. Erin Patricia Wayne, Aug. 10, 1997; children: Hunter James, Claire Emma, Jillian Erin. BS, U. Mich., 1991; MD, George Washington U., 1995. Diplomate Am. Bd. Plastic Surgery, Am. Bd. Surgery. Resident gen. surgery George Washington U., Washington, 1995—98; post-doctoral rsch. fellow plastic and reconstructive surgery U. Calif., L.A., 1998—99, resident, 2001—03; resident gen. surgery Med. Ctr. The U. Calif., Irvine, Calif., 1999—2001; pvt. practice Irvine, Calif., 2003—; staff Salleback Meml. Med. Ctr., 2003—, Orange Coast Meml. Med. Ctr., 2003—, Irvine (Calif.) Regional Med. Ctr., 2003—, Mission Hosp., 2003—05, Laguna Hills (Calif.) Surgery Ctr., 2003—, Saddleback Valley Outpatient Surgery Ctr., 2003—. Fellow pathology George Washington U., Washington, 1991; surgeon Hosp. Regional Univ., Lille, France, 1992; asst. rschr. surg. oncology NIH, Bethesda, Md., 1995. Contbr. chapters to books, articles to profl. jours. Mem.: AMA, ACS, Am. Soc. Plastic Surgeons, Alpha Omega Alpha. Office: 16300 Sand Canyon Ave 911 Irvine CA 92618

**SMITH, ANDREW JAMES THOMAS,** music educator; b. Isleworth, England, Sept. 9, 1968; arrived in U.S., 1996; s. James Smith and Ann Madelaine Veronica (Collette) Gane; m. Andrea Elizabeth Mills, May 25, 2003; m. Margaret Mary Kane. Diploma, Royal Acad. Music, 1991, cert. in Advanced Solo Studies, 1992; D in Musical Arts, Hartt Sch., 2003. Concertmaster European Chamber Opera, London, 1992—95; asst. prof. Valparaiso (Ind.) U., 2000—05; dir. Suzuki Music Sch., Westport, Conn., 2005—. Concertmaster Orquestra da Fafe, Portugal, 1992; assoc. concertmaster D'Oyly Carte Opera Orchestra, Birmingham, England, 1992—94; dir. Stamford (Eng.) Internat. Music Festival, 2004—; guest artist Andrews U., Mich., 2002, Shanghai (China) Conservatory, 2003, Am. String Tchrs. Assn., Valparaiso, 2002, 05, Dame Myra Hess Concerts, Chgo., Fetzer Soc. Concerts, 2004; artist in residence La Porte Symphony; asst. Emerson String Quartet; guest concertmaster Ill. Philharmonic, Kalamazoo Symphony; asst. concertmaster London Pops Orch. Musician: (albums) Glazunow Violin Concerto, 2001, My True Gift's To Come, 2004, Castillon Piano Trio. Dir. The Copland Century Festival, Hartford, Conn., 2000; artistic dir. Bach At The Brauer Mus., Valparaiso, 2002—05; artistic dir. Da Capo Concert Series Southport, Conn., 2005—. Recipient Farjeon prize, Royal Acad. Music, 1992, Celt award, Valparaiso (Ind.) U., 2002, Alumni award, 2002. Mem.: Suzuki Assn. The Americas, Cobbett Assn. Chamber Music, Am. String Tchrs. Assn. Office: Suzuki Music School Westport 212 Post Road West Westport CT 06880 Office Phone: 203-227-9474. E-mail: violin@att.net.

**SMITH, ANNA DEAVERE,** actress, educator, playwright; b. Balt., Sept. 18, 1950; d. Deavere Young and Anna (Young) S. BA, Beaver Coll., Pa., 1971, doctorate (hon.); 1973; MFA, Am. Conservatory Theatre, 1977; doctorate (hon.), U. NC, 1995; degree (hon.), Wheelock Coll., 1995, Colgate U., 1997, Sch. Visual Arts, 1997, Wesleyan U., 1997, Northwestern U., 1997, Coll. Holy Cross, 1997. Ann O'Day Maples prof. arts and drama Stanford U. Artist-in-residence Ford Found., 1997. Playwright, performer one-woman shows On the Road: A Search for American Character, 1983, Aye, Aye, Aye, I'm Integrated, 1984, Piano, 1991 (Drama-Logue award), Fires in the Mirror, 1989 (Obie award 1992, Drama Desk award 1992, N.Y. Drama Critics spl. citation 1993-94), Twilight: Los Angeles 1992 (Obie award, 2 Tony award nominations, Drama Critics Cir. spl. citation, Outer Critics Cir. award, Drama Desk award, Audelco award, Beverly Hills, Hollywood NAACP theatre awards), House Arrest, 1997; writer libretto for Judith Jamison, performer Hymn, 1993; appeared in (films) Dave, 1993, Philadelphia, 1993, The American President, 1995, Twilight: Los Angeles, 2000. Founding dir. The Inst. on Arts and Civic Dialogue Harvard U., 1998; trustee, Mus. Modern Art, N.Y.C. Named One of Women of Yr., Glamour mag., 1993; fellow Bunting Inst., Radcliffe Coll.; genius fellow The MacArthur Found., 1996. Office: 1460 4th St Ste 212 Santa Monica CA 90401-3414 also: Stanford U Dept Drama Memorial Hall Stanford CA 94305

**SMITH, ANNA NICOLE (VICKIE LYNN HOGAN),** television personality, model; b. Mexia, Tex., Nov. 28, 1967; d. Donald Eugene and Virgie (Hart) Hogan; m. Billie Smith, Apr. 4; 1985 (div. 1987); 1 child, Daniel (dec.); m. J. Howard Marshall II, June 27, 1994 (dec. Aug. 4, 1995); 1 child. Former model for Guess? jeans; weekly gossip columnist Nat. Enquirer, 2005—. Spokesperson Trim Spa X32 (Ephedra Free), 2003—. Actress (films) Naked Gun 33 1/3: The Final Insult, 1994, The Hudsucker Proxy, 1994, To the Limit, 1995, Skyscraper, 1997 (also assoc. prodr.), Be Cool, 2005; (TV series) N.Y.U.K., 2000, The Anna Nicole Smith Show, 2002-04 (also creative cons.); prodr., screenwriter, dir. (video) Anna Nicole Smith: Exposed, 1988; guest TV appearance include MadTV, 1998, Veronica's Closet, 1999, Ally McBeal, 1999, and several talk show appearances. Named Playmate of the Month, 1992, Playmate of the Yr., 1993.

**SMITH, ANNICK,** writer; b. Paris, May 11, 1936; came to U.S., 1937; d. Stephen and Helene Deutch; m. David James Smith (dec. 1974); children: Eric, Stephen, Alex, Andrew. Student, Cornell Univ., 1954-55. U. Chgo., 1955-57, BA, U. Wash., 1961. Editor U. Wash. Press, Seattle, 1961-61. Montana Bus. Quarterly, U. Montana, Missoula, 1971-72; founding bd. mem. Sundance Film Inst., Sundance, Utah, 1981-85; founding mem. Ind. Film Project, N.Y.C., 1981-84; acting dir. Montana Com. for the Humanities, Missoula, 1983-84; devel. dir. Hellgate Writers, Inc., Missoula, 1986-96; creative dir. Yellow Bay Writers Workshop, U. Montana Continuing Edn. Dept, Missoula, 1987-98. Freelance filmmaker, producer, arts administrator, writer, Mont., 1974—; past H.S. tchr., cmty. organizer, environ. worker. Exec. prodr. Heartland, 1981; co-produ. A River Runs Through It, 1992; co-editor (with William Kittredge) The Last Best Place; author: Homestead, 1994, Big BlueStem A Journey into the Tall Grass, 1996, In This We Are Native, 2001; contbr. to anthologies including Best Am. Short Stories, 1992. Recipient Western Heritage award Cowboy Hall of Fame, 1981; Mont. Humanites award Mont. Com. for Humanities, 1988, Okla. Book award, 1997, Bancroft Prize Denver Pub. Libr., 1998. Mem. Trout Unlimited, Blackfoot Challenge. Democrat. Office: 898 Bear Creek Rd Bonner MT 59823

**SMITH, ANTHONY L.,** utilities executive; Grad. with honors, Whittier Coll.; MBA, U. So. Calif., M in Bus. Taxation; grad. pub. utility exec. program, U. Mich.; grad. exec. fin. program, U. Pa. Joined Edison Internat., 1970, mgmt. trainee, various mgmt. and supervisory positions, tax assts. asst. contr., 1988, v.p., dir. tax So. Calif. Edison subs., v.p., dir. tax Rosemead, Calif., 1999—. Former chair Calif. Taxpayer's Assn.; mem., former chair taxation com. and tax analysis and rsch. subcom. Edison Electric Inst. Mem.: Internat. Tax Inst., Tax Execs. Inst., Calif. Assessor's Assn. Office: Edison Internat 2244 Walnut Grove Ave Rosemead CA 91770 Office Phone: 626-302-2004. E-mail: anthony.smith@sck.com.

**SMITH, ARLAN ROBERT,** plastic and reconstructive surgeon; b. Surabaja, Indonesia, Aug. 3, 1948; arrived in Holland, 1954; m. Paulina Jacoba de Jong, May 25, 1990; children: Arlana Dominque, Darryl Nathaniël, Beau Aurora Fabiana, Chloé Aphrodite Zoë. Student, St. Ignatius Coll., Amsterdam, The Netherlands, 1961-66; PhD, U. Amsterdam, The Netherlands, 1972, MD, 1974. Cert. plastic and reconstructive surgeon. Gen. surgery tng. dept gen. surgery U. Maastricht, The Netherlands, 1975-79; clin. and rsch. fellow Mass. Gen. Hosp., Harvard Med. Sch., Boston, 1977-79; specialist in plastic and reconstructive surgery dept. plastic surgery U. Hosp. Dijkzigt Rotterdam, The Netherlands, 1979-82, chef de clinique in microsurgery and hand surgery

dept. plastic and reconstructive surgery, 1979-86; head dept. plastic and reconstructive surgery Holy Hosp. Vlaardingen, The Netherlands, 1985-96; vis. prof. plastic and reconstructive surgery U. Kristen Idonesia Jakarta, Indonesia, 1989-91; dir. and owner Clinic Holystaete Vlaardingen, Netherlands, 1991—. Contbr. articles to profl. jours. Mem. Dutch Soc. for Hand Surgery, Dutch Soc. Esthetic Surgery, Dutch Soc. Plastic and Reconstructive Surgery, Internat. Microsurg. Soc., Found. Moshe Yemin clinic Holystaete (chmn. bd.), the Netherlands. Avocations: gardening, pre-Columbian art, modern art, Egyptian and African art. Office: Clinic Holystaete Churchillsingel 480 3137XB Vlaardingen Netherlands Business E-Mail: info@kliniekholystaete.nl. E-mail: abr.smith@planet.nl.

**SMITH, ART,** chef; b. Jasper, Fla. Attended, Fla. State U., Walt Disney Magic Kingdom Coll. Prog. Internship Greenbrier Resort; exec. chef Fla. Gov. Mansion; chef Am. European Express Train; personal chef to Oprah Winfrey, 1997—. Spkr. Celebration of Reading, Barbara Bush Found. for Family Literacy; bd. of dir. Kid's Cafe, Mpls.; chef's coun. Chefs for Humanity, 2005—. Author: Back to the Table: The Reunion of Food and Family, 2001 (James Beard Found. award, 2002, Gourmand World Cookbook award, 2001), Kitchen Life (Gourmand World Cookbook award, 2004); contbg. editor: O Mag. Co-founder Common Threads, 2002—. Office: Common Threads c/o Linda Novick 345 N Canal Ste 1601 Chicago IL 60606 Office Phone: 312-876-1289. Office Fax: 312-876-1038.*

**SMITH, ARTHUR B., JR.,** lawyer; b. Abilene, Tex., Sept. 11, 1944; s. Arthur B. and Florence B. (Baker) S.; m. Marya Argetsinger, 1968 (div. 1996); children: Arthur C., Sarah R.; m. Tracey L. Truesdale, 1999; children: Thomas A. BS, Cornell U., 1966; JD, U. Chgo., 1969. Bar: Ill. 1969, N.Y. 1976. Assoc. Vedder, Price, Kaufman & Kammholz, Chgo., 1969-74; asst. prof. labor law N.Y. State Sch. Indls. and Labor Rels., Cornell U., 1975-77; ptnr. Vedder, Price, Kaufman & Kammholz, Chgo., 1977-86; founding mem. Murphy, Smith & Polk, Chgo., 1986-98; shareholder Ogletree, Deakins, Chgo., 1999—. Guest. lectr. Northwestern U. Grad. Sch. Mgmt., 1979, Sch. Law, spring 1980; mem. hearing bd. Ill. Atty. Registration and Disciplinary Commn. Author: Employment Discrimination Law Cases and Materials, 5th edit., 2000, supplement, 2004, Construction Labor Relations, 1984, supplement, 1993; co-editor-in-chief: 1976 Annual Supplement to Morris, The Developing Labor Law, 1977; chpt. editor: The Developing Labor Law, 4th edit., 2000, supplement, 2005; contbr. articles to profl. jours. Recipient award for highest degree of dedication and excellence in tchg. N.Y. State Sch. Indsl. and Labor Rels., Cornell U., 1977; listed in The Best Lawyers in Am., 2003—. Fellow Coll. Labor and Employment Lawyers; mem. ABA (co-chmn. com. on devel. law under Nat. Labor Rels. Act, Sect. Labor Rels. Law 1976-77), N.Y. State Bar Assn., Phi Eta Sigma, Phi Kappa Phi, Chgo. Athletic Assn., Mid-Day Club. Presbyterian. Office: Ogletree Deakins et al 2 First National Plz F5 Chicago IL 60603 Office Phone: 312-558-1230. Business E-Mail: Arthur.Smith@ndnss.com.

**SMITH, ARTHUR JOHN STEWART,** physicist, researcher; b. Victoria, B.C., Can., June 28, 1938; s. James Stewart and Lillian May (Geernaert) S.; m. Norma Ruth Askeland, May 20, 1966; children: Peter James, Ian Alexander. BA, U. B.C., 1959, MSc., 1961; PhD, Princeton U., 1966. Postdoctoral fellow Deutsches Electronen-Synchrotron, Hamburg, Germany, 1966—67; mem. faculty dept. physics Princeton U., 1967—, prof., 1978—, Class of 1909 prof., 1992—, assoc. chmn. dept., 1979—83, chmn. dept. physics, 1990—98, chair Physics Bd., 2005—. Vis. scientist Brookhaven Nat. Lab., 1967—, chair sci. and tech. steering com. Brookhaven Sci. Assocs., 1997—2005, bd. dirs., 2005—; vis. scientist Fermilab, 1974—, Stanford Linear Accelerator Ctr., 1996—, vis. prof., 2000—02, spokesperson BaBar experiment, 2000—02. Assoc. editor Phys. Rev. Letters, 1986-89; contbr. articles to profl. jours. Fellow Am. Phys. Soc. (chmn. divsn. of particles and fields 1991). Achievements include research on experimental high-energy particle physics; kaon decays, physics of the B particles and quark structure of hadrons. Home: 4 Ober Rd Princeton NJ 08540-4918 Office: PO Box 708 Princeton NJ 08544-0001

**SMITH, ARTHUR KITTREDGE, JR.,** academic administrator, political scientist, educator; b. Derry, N.H., Aug. 15, 1937; s. Arthur Kittredge and Rena Belle (Roberts) S.; m. June Mary Dahar, Nov. 28, 1959; children: Arthur, Valerie, Meredith. BS, U.S. Naval Acad., 1959; MA, U. N.H., 1966; PhD, Cornell U., 1970. Vis. prof. El Colegio de Mexico, Mexico City, 1968-69; asst. prof. polit. sci. SUNY-Binghamton, 1970-74, assoc. prof., 1974-84, prof., 1984-88, provost for grad. studies and research, 1976-83, v.p. for administrn., 1982-88; prof. govt. and internat. studies U. S.C., Columbia, 1988-91, exec. v.p. for acad. affairs, provost, 1988-90, 91, interim pres., 1990-91; pres., prof. polit. sci. U. Utah, Salt Lake City, 1991-97; chancellor U. Houston Sys., 1997—2003; pres. U. Houston, 1997—2003, prof., 2003—. Author: (with Claude E. Welch, Jr.) Military Role and Rule: Perspectives on Civil-Military Relations, 1975; contbr. articles to profl. jours. With USN, 1959-65. Lehman fellow, 1966-69, NDEA fellow, 1969-70 Mem. Am. Polit. Sci. Assn., L.Am. Studies Assn., Inter-Univ. Sem. on Armed Forces and Soc., Am. Coun. on Edn., World Affairs Coun. (pres. Binghamton chpt. 1976-76), Bus.-Higher Edn. Forum, Phi Beta Kappa, Pi Sigma Alpha, Omicron Delta Kappa, Phi Delta Kappa, Beta Gamma Sigma, Phi Kappa Phi. Office: Univ Houston 4500 University Dr Rm 2000K Houston TX 77204-6056 Office Phone: 832-443-3008. E-mail: aksmith@uh.edu.

**SMITH, ARTHUR LEE,** lawyer; b. Davenport, Iowa, Dec. 19, 1941; s. Harry Arthur Smith and Ethel (Hoffman) Duerre; m. Georgia Mills, June 12, 1965 (dec. Jan. 1984); m. Jean Bowler, Aug. 4, 1984; children: Juliana, Christopher, Andrew, Wendy. BA, Augustana Coll., Rock Island, Ill., 1964; MA, Am. U., 1968; JD, Washington U., St. Louis, 1971. Bar: Mo 1971, DC 1983. Telegraph editor Davenport Morning Democrat, 1963-64, ptnr. Peper Martin Jensen Maichel & Hetlage, 1971-95, Husch & Eppenberger, St. Louis, 1995—. Arbitrator Nat Asn Security Dealers, 1980—, Am Arbitration Assn. 1980—2004. Columnist: St Louis Lawyer, syndicated columnist: Technolawyer.com and other publications. Dir. P. Buckley Moss Found. for Children's Edn., 2001—03. Lt USN, 1964—68. Fellow: St. Louis Bar Found. (dir. 2004—, v.p. 2005—); mem.: ABA (co-chair electronic discovery subcom.), Bar Assn. Met. St. Louis (chmn law mgt comt 1993—96, chair technology comt 1996—99, Pres.'s award Exceptional Service 1995, 2003), P. Buckley Moss Soc. (dir 1994—, v.p. 1998—2000, exec vpres 2001—02, pres. 2002—), Mo. Bar Assn. (vice-chair ins programs comt 1981—83, vice-chair antitrust comt 1981—83, chair admin law comt 1995—97), D.C. Bar Assn. (chmn law practice mgt 1990—91), Order of Coif. Office: Husch & Eppenberger Ste 600 190 Carondelet Plz Saint Louis MO 63105-3441 Office Phone: 314-480-1500. E-mail: arthur.smith@husch.com.

**SMITH, B. SCOTT,** automotive executive; Grad., Rollins Coll., 1991. Gen. mgr. Town & Country Ford, Charlotte, NC, 1992—97; pres., COO Sonic Automotive Inc., Charlotte, NC, 1997—2002, vice chmn., chief strategic officer, 2002—. Office: Sonic Automotive Inc 5401 Independence Blvd Charlotte NC 28212*

**SMITH, BAKER ARMSTRONG,** management executive, lawyer; b. Oct. 3, 1947; s. William Armstrong and Priscilla (Baker) S.; m. Deborah Elizabeth Ellis, Nov. 13, 1982; children: Ellis Armstrong, Elizabeth Anne, Everett Baker, Emery Manning. BS, U.S. Naval Acad., 1969; MBA, Northeastern U., 1975; JD cum laude, Suffolk U., 1977; LLM in Labor, Georgetown U., 1981. Bar: Ga. 1977, D.C. 1978, U.S. Supreme Ct. 1980; cert. turnaround profl., 1994; fellow Family Firm Inst. Commd. ensign USN, 1969, advanced through grades to lt., 1974; exec. dir., founder Ctr. on Nat. Labor Policy, Inc., North Springfield, Va., 1977-81; asst. to sec., dir. labor rels. U.S. Dept. HUD, Washington, 1981-83; exec. v.p. U.S. Bus. and Indsl. Coun., Nashville, 1983-84; pres. Am. Quality Builders, Inc., Nashville, 1984-86; v.p. Hopeman Bros., Inc., Waynesboro, Va., 1986-88, Morris, Anderson, Atlanta, 1988—. Sec., founder U.S. Constnl. Rights Legal Def. Fund, Inc., Atlanta, 1983—; trustee Leadership Inst., Springfield, Va., 1978—; v.p., 1998—; v.p. Turnaround Mgmt. Assn., Chgo. 1998-99; pres. Assn. Cert. Turnaround Profls., Boston, 1997-98; mem. Coun. for Nat. Policy, Washington, 1981—, Civil

Rights Reviewing Authority U.S. Dept. Edn., Washington, 1984-88; transition team leader Office of the Pres.-Elect of the U.S., NLRB, Occupl. Safety and Health Rev. Commn., Fed. Mediation and Conciliation Svc., Nat. Mediation Bd., Fed. Labor Rels. Authority, Washington, 1980-81; instr. law, faculty sec. No. Va. Law Sch., Alexandria, Va., 1980-83; instr. law D.C. Law Sch., Washington, 1978-80. Contbg. author: Mandate for Leadership, 1981; contbr. articles to profl. jours. Recipient Outstanding Contbr. to the Turnaround Profession award, 1999. Fellow Family Firm Inst.; mem. ABA (Nat. Law Day chmn. 1976-77, Silver Key award 1977), St. George's House, Windsor Castle (assoc.), Phila. Soc., U.S. Supreme Ct. Hist. Soc., Federalist Soc., Beta Gamma Sigma, Phi Delta Phi (pres. 1989-91), Capitol Hill Club (Washington), Piedmont Club (Winston-Salem). Republican. Presbyterian. Home: 3360 E Terrell Branch Ct Marietta GA 30067-5164 Business E-Mail: bsmith@morris-anderson.com

**SMITH, BARBARA,** food service executive, model; b. Everson, Pa., Aug. 24, 1949; m. Dan Gasby; 1 stepdaughter. Owner B. Smith Restaurant Group; former model. Mem. adv. bd. Culinary Inst. Am., 1995—. Author: B. Smith's Cooking and Entertaining for Friends, 1995; host (syndicated weekly TV show) B. Smith With Style; founder B. Smith Style mag. Mem.: Screen Actors Guild, Feminist Press (founding bd. mem.), NY Women's Found. (founding bd. mem.), Times Sq. Bus. Improvement Dist. (founding bd. mem.). Achievements include appeared in over 100 radio, print, and TV ads; First African Am. woman elected to bd. trustees Culinary Inst. Am. Avocation: family activities. Mailing: 320 W 46th St New York NY 10036

**SMITH, BARBARA ANNE,** health facility administrator, consultant; b. N.Y.C., Oct. 10, 1946; d. John Allen and Lelia Maria (De Silva) Santoro; m. Joseph Newton Smith, Feb. 5, 1966 (div. Sept. 1984); children: J. Michael, Robert Lawrence. Student, Oceanside/Carlsbad Coll. Real estate agt. Routh Robbins, Inc., Washington, 1973-75; gen. mgr. Mall Shops, Inc., Kansas City, Kans., 1975-80; regional mgr. FAO Schwarz, N.Y.C., 1980-84; clin. adminstr. North Denver Med. Ctr., Thornton, Colo., 1984-88; adminstrv. dir. Country Side Ambulatory Surgery Ctr., Leesburg, Va., 1989-91; pres. SCS Healthcare Mgmt., Inc., Washington, 1991—. Bd. dirs. Franz Carl Weber Internat., Geneva, 1982-84; mng. dir. Nat. Healthcare Consortium, 1997—; mng. assoc. Monarch Assocs. in Healthcare. Pres. Am. Women Club, 1968; v.p. Oak Park Assn., Kansas City, 1977-78, pres., 1978-79; vol. Visitor Info. and Assn. Reception Ctr. program Smithsonian Instn., Washington. Mem. NAFE, Network Colo., Profl. Bus. Women Assn., Med. Group Mgmt. Assn., Federated Ambulatory Surgery Assn.

**SMITH, BARBARA JEAN,** lawyer; b. Washington, Jan. 9, 1947; d. Harry Wallace and Jean (Fraser) S.; m. Philip R. Chall, July 13, 1991; children: Brian C.S. Brown, Craig F.S. Brown, Amy E. Spiers, Carrie A. Chall. BA, Old Dominion Coll., 1968; MBA, Pepperdine U., 1974; JD, Case Western Res. U., 1977. Bar: Ohio 1977. Assoc. Squire, Sanders & Dempsey, Cleve., 1977—88, ptnr., 1988—93; shareholder McDonald, Hopkins, Burke & Haber Co., L.P.A., Cleve., 1993—2003; ptnr. Shottenstein, Zox & Dunn Co., LPA, Cleve., 2003—05; founding mem. Smith & Hultin LLC, Chagrin Falls, Ohio, 2005—. Bd. editors Health Law Jour. of Ohio, 1989-95; contbr. articles to health jours. and periodicals. Trustee Urban Community Sch., Cleve., 1984-86, Alzheimer's Assn. Greater Cleve., 2000-2005. Mem. Ohio Women's Bar Assn. (pres. 1994-95), Cleve. Bar Assn. (pres. 1998-99, trustee 1992-95, chair health law sect. 1991-92), Am. Health Lawyers Assn., Ohio State Bar Assn. (health law com. 1991—), Soc. Ohio Hosp. Attys., Sci. Edn. Coun. Ohio. Democrat. Mem. United Ch. of Christ. Avocations: reading, hiking. Home: 416 Fairway Vw Chagrin Falls OH 44023-6718 Office: Smith & Hultin LLC 100 N Main St Ste 350 Chagrin Falls OH 44022 Office Phone: 440-247-2620. Business E-Mail: smith@smithhultin.com

**SMITH, BARBARA JEANNE,** retired librarian; b. Jersey Shore, Pa., Apr. 14, 1939; d. Moyer Emmerson and Mary Kathryn (Ebner) S. BS in Edn. (Biology), Pa. State U., 1961, DEd in Higher Edn., 1981; MS in Edn. (English), SUNY, Oswego, N.Y., 1967; MLS, U. Pitts., 1970. Reference libr. Pa. State U. Librs., University Park, 1970-75, commonwealth campus coord., 1975-82, asst. dean librs., head commonwealth campus librs. divsn., 1982-89; dir. Smithsonian Instn. Librs., Washington, 1989-98. Gen. sci. tchr., Binghampton (N.Y.) City Schs., 1961-62; English tchr., North Syracuse (N.Y.) Ctrl. Schs., 1970-75; mem. Smithsonian Instn. Rsch. Info. Svc. (chair 1993-95), Planning Adv. Group, 1989-93; chair Internet Implementation Com., Smithsonian Instn. Librs. User Adv. Com., 1989-97; founding dir. Chesapeake Info. and Rsch. Libr. Alliance, 1996-98. Contbr. articles to profl. jours.; speaker in field. UCLA Grad. Sch. of Libr. and Info. Sci. Sr. fellow, 1982. Mem. AAUW, ALA (mem. coun. 1987-91), Centre County (Pa.) Hist. Soc. (life), U. Pitts. Alumni Assn. (bd. dirs. 1991-94), Beta Phi Mu. E-mail: bsmith5598@pennswoods.net.

**SMITH, BARBARA KATHRYN,** retired elementary school educator; b. Monroe, Mich., Mar. 13, 1951; d. Gus J. and Betty K. (Stadelman) Hochradel; m. Lancel R. Smith, Mar. 21, 1970; children: Cheryl Lynn, Michael John. BS, Ea. Mich. U., 1981, MA, 1985. Cert. tchr. all subjects, English lit. and lang, spl. edn., reading. Tchr., diagnostician U. Mich., Ann Arbor, 1981—85; tchr. Walled Lake Consolidated Schs., Mich., 1985—2006; ret., 2006. Mem. Mich. Assn. Learning Disability Eduators. Home: 1851 Ayrshire Dr Commerce Township MI 48390-2947 Personal E-mail: teachei@aol.com.

**SMITH, BARNARD ELLIOT,** management educator; b. Mpls., May 6, 1926; s. Sheldon Strong and Jessie (Gould) S.; m. Betty Lou Strohschein, Aug. 28, 1949; children: Carolyn Louise, Eileen Elizabeth. BS in Mech. Engring. with distinction, U. Minn., 1949, MS, 1950; PhD, Stanford U., 1961; MA (hon.), Dartmouth Coll., 1971. Asst. prof. mech. engring. U. Minn., 1950-51; mfg. specialist A.O. Smith Co., Milw., 1951-54; asst. prof. indsl. engring. Oreg. State Coll., 1954-58, Stanford U., 1958-61; asso. prof. mgmt. Sloan Sch. Mgmt., MIT, 1961-68; prof. mgmt. Indian Inst. Mgmt., Calcutta, 1965-68; prof. engring. Thayer Sch. Engring. Dartmouth Coll., 1968-71; dean Stuart Sch. Mgmt. and Finance, Ill. Inst. Tech., 1971-75, prof. mgmt., 1975-80; David M. French disting. prof. mgmt. U. Mich., Flint, 1980-89, emeritus, 1989; pres. Vineyards of the Acad., 1989, The Acad. of Wine of Oreg. Inc., 1993—. Cons. in field. Served with USNR, 1944-46. Mem. Phi Tau Sigma, Beta Gamma Sigma. Home: 18200 Highway 238 Grants Pass OR 97527-8631 Office Phone: 541-846-6817.

**SMITH, BARRY HAMILTON,** foundation administrator, physician; b. Orange, N.J., Oct. 6, 1943; s. Kenneth Wright and Harriet (Barr) S.; m. Carley Eldredge, Dec. 13, 1969; children: Christopher, Sara. BA, Harvard U., 1965; PhD, MIT, 1968; MD, Cornell U., 1972. Intern, resident N.Y. Hosp., N.Y.C., 1971—75; resident Mass. Gen. Hosp., Boston, 1975—78; program dir. Neuroscis. Rsch. Program MIT, Boston, 1977-78; dep. dir. Surg. Neurology Br. NIH, Bethesda, Md., 1978—83; dir. sci. & med. Dreyfus Med. Found., N.Y.C., 1983—88; dir. Dreyfus Health Found., N.Y.C., 1988—. Sr. v.p. Rogosin Inst., 1990—; prof. surgery Cornell U., Peking U. Med. Coll. Editor Ency. Neurosci., 1995-2005; contbr. articles to profl. jours. Bd. dirs. Desmond Tutu Peace Found., Kornfeld Found., N.Y.C. Rescue Mission., Global Health Action Comdr. USPHS, 1978—83. Recipient Commendation Medal award, USPHS, 1982, EEO award, 1983. Mem. AMA, AAAS, Soc. Neurosci., Am. Pain Soc. (audit com. 1983-85), Nat. Coun. Internat. Health (governing bd. 1990-95, chair 1993-95), Global Health Coun. Soc. Critical Care Medicine, Phi Beta Kappa, Sigma Xi, Alpha Omega Alpha Avocations: sailing, writing. Home: 1192 Park Ave Apt 10B New York NY 10128-1314 Office: Dreyfus Health Found 205 E 64th St Rm 404 New York NY 10021-6635 Office Phone: 212-750-5075. Business E-Mail: bsmith@dhfglobal.org.

**SMITH, BARRY SAMUEL,** physiatrist; b. Windber, Pa., Jan. 15, 1947; MD, Jefferson Med. Coll., 1969. Diplomate Am. Bd. Phys. Medicine and Rehab. Intern Reading (Pa.) Hosp., 1969-70; resident in phys. medicine and rehab. Inst. Phys. Med. Rehab., Louisville, 1970-73; now with Baylor U. Med. Ctr., Dallas, chief in phys. medicine and rehab. Mem. AMA, Am. Acad.

Phys. Medicine and Rehab., Am. Congress Rehab. Medicine, Assn. Acad. Physiatrists, Am. Assn. Electrodiagnostic Medicine, Nat. Bd. Med. Examiners (diplomate). Office: Baylor U Med Ctr Dept Phys Medicine and Rehab 3500 Gaston Ave Dallas TX 75246-2096

**SMITH, BERNADINE M.,** radio personality, filmmaker, writer, film producer, film director; d. Bernice and Dudley Smith; 1 child, Evan Dudley. Student, Am. Internat. Coll., Springfield, Mass., 1971—73. Founder/owner Every Woman Filmworks, Bklyn., 1980—, Queen Bee Multi-Media Advt. & Consulting Agy., Bklyn., 1988—; mgr. Nat. Amusements, Bklyn., 1998—2000; founder/owner GGTG WORLDWIDE Media, 2002—. Editor: (religious programming) Holiness is Right, (religious and gospel programming) GGTG Radio, (religious programming) JC-1; writer/dir. (play) Sweet Pea's Place of Prayer, LUPUS, (feature film) Bad Kids, writer/dir. They Mines; dir.: (book) How He Made A Woman Out of Me/LIFE 101.da real skool; author: Bushwhackers from Texas...A Political Essay; playwright: 3 Women and a Man, Comin' Out, BROKEN; author: (songs) (radio drama) From the Table to the Heart, (sit-com) Max Warlock P.I. Chairperson, incorporator Big Sisters of Hampden County, Springfield, Mass., 1981—82; mem. Mt. Sinai Cathedral Ch. of God in Christ, 2000—. Recipient awards prodn. value and prodn. content, N.Am. Women in Cable, 1995, First Time Film Maker's Camera Package, Panavision Corp., 2001; prodn. grantee, The Endowment Channel, 1996. Democrat. Pentacostal. Avocations: writing, producing, teaching, mentoring. Office: Every Woman Filmworks Queen Bee Media 63 Lafayette Ave Brooklyn NY 11217 Office Phone: 917-202-6972. E-mail: blkonblk99@aol.com.

**SMITH, BERNALD STEPHEN,** retired pilot; b. Long Beach, Calif., Dec. 24, 1926; s. Donald Albert and Bernice Merrill (Stephens) Smith; m. Marilyn Mae Spence, July 22, 1949; children: Lorraine Ann Smith Foute, Evelyn Donice Smith DeRoos, Mark Stephen, Diane April(dec.). Student, U. Calif., Berkeley, 1944-45, 50-51. Cert. airline transport pilot, flight engr. FAA. Capt. Transocean Airline, Oakland, Calif., Transocean Air Lines, Tokyo, 1951-53, Hartford, Conn., 1954-55; 1st officer United Air Lines, Seattle, 1955, San Francisco, 1956-68, tng. capt. Denver, San Francisco, 1961—68, capt., 1968-86, 2d officer, 1986-93; ret., 1993. Founder, v.p. Avia Am., Palo Alto, Calif., 1970—72, Avia Internat., Palo Alto, 1972—74; founder, trustee AirSailing, Inc., 1970—, Soaring Safety Found., 1985—; cons. Caproni Vizzola, Milan, 1972—84; instr. aviation Ohlone Coll., Fremont, 1976; prin., cons. Internat. Aviation Cons. and Investments, Fremont, Calif., 1985—; founder Pacific Soaring Coun. Author, editor: American Soaring Handbook, 1975, 1980; contbr. articles to profl. jours. Trustee Nat. Soaring Mus., 1975—2001, pres., 1975—78; active RTCA; SSA del., 1992—; FAI del., 1996—. Comdr. USNR. Named Barnaby Lectr., Nat. Soaring Mus., 2003; recipient Gold medal, 2002. Fellow: Internat. GPS Svc. Geodynamics; mem.: AIAA (pub. bd. 1977—94), Civil GPS Svc. Interface Com., Inst. Navigation, Commn. de Vol A Volle (U.S. del. 1970—71, 1978, 1985—97, v.p. 1988—96), Fedn. Aeronatique Internat. (environ. commn. v.p., U.S. del. 1995—, mem. airspace mgmt. group 1998—, del. environ. com. 2002—, Paul Tissandier diploma 1992, Lilienthal medal 1993, Bronze medal 2003), Seaplane Pilots Assn., Orgn. Scientifique et Technique Internat. du Vol a Voile (hon.; bd. dirs., U.S. del. 1981—97), Airline Pilots Assn., Exptl. Aircraft Assn., Nat. Aero. Assn., Soaring Soc. Am. (bd. dirs. 1963—97, pres. 1969—70, chmn. pub. bd. 1971—84, chmn. ins. com. 1975—93, hon. vice-chmn. bd. dirs. 2000—, Exceptional Svc. award 1970, 1975, Warren Eaton Meml. trophy 1977, Exceptional Svc. award 1982, named to Hall of Fame 1984, Exceptional Svc. award 1988, 1991, Exceptional Achievement award 1996, Warren Eaton Meml. trophy 1997, Schweizer Lifetime Svc. award 2003), Aircraft Owners and Pilots Assn., U. Calif. Alumni Assn. (life). Democrat. Methodist. Office: Internat Aviation Cons Investments PO Box 3075 Fremont CA 94539-0307

**SMITH, BETTY,** writer, not-for-profit developer; b. Bonham, Tex., Sept. 16; d. Sim and Gertrude (Dearing) S. Student, Stephens Coll.; BJ, U. Tex. Women's editor Daily Texan; pres. Hope Assocs. Corp., N.Y.C.; pres., owner Betty Smith Assocs., N.Y.C. Author: A Matter of Heart, 1969. Bd. dirs. Melchior Heldentenor Found., N.Y.C., 1968—, pres., 1987-97; pres., CEO Gerda Lissner Found., 1994—; bd. dirs. Herman Lissner Found., 1990—, CEO, 2004—. Mem. Author's Guild. Office: care Lissner Found 135 E 55th St 8th Fl New York NY 10022-4049 Office Phone: 212-826-6100. E-mail: bsmithassocs@aol.com.

**SMITH, BETTY DENNY,** county official, administrator, fashion executive; b. Centralia, Ill., Nov. 12, 1932; d. Otto and Ferne Elizabeth (Beier) Hasenfuss; m. Peter S. Smith, Dec. 5, 1964; children: Carla Kip, Bruce Kimball. Student, U. Ill., 1950-52; student, L.A. City Coll., 1953-57, UCLA, 1965, U. San Francisco, 1982-84. Freelance fashion coordinator, L.A., N.Y.C., 1953-58; tchr. fashion Rita LeRoy Internat. Studios, 1959-60; mgr. Mo Nadler Fashion, L.A., 1961-64; showroom dir. Jean of Calif. Fashions, L.A., 1965—. Freelance polit. book reviewer for community newspapers, 1961-62; staff writer Valley Citizen News, 1963. Bd. dirs. Pet Assistance Found., 1969-76; founder, pres., dir. Vol. Services to Animals L.A., 1972-76; mem. County Com. To Discuss Animals in Rsch., 1973-74; mem. blue ribbon com. on animal control L.A. County, 1973-74; dir. L.A. County Animal Care and Control, 1976-82; mem. Calif. Animal Health Technician Exam. Com., 1975-82, chmn., 1979; bd. dirs. L.A. Soc. for Prevention Cruelty to Animals, 1984-94, Calif. Coun. Companion Animal Advocates, 1993-97; dir. West Coast Regional Office, Am. Humane Assn., 1988-97; mem. adv. com. Moorepark Coll., 1988-97; CFO Coalition for Pet Population Control, 1987-92; trustee Gladys W. Sargent Found., 1997—, Coalition to End Pet Overpopulation, 1998—; cons. Jungle Book II, Disney Studios, 1997; mem. adv. com. Wishbone Prodn., 1995-97; mem. govt. rels. and pub. affairs com. Motion Picture & TV Industry Assn., 1992-97; mem. Coalition to Protect Calif. Wildlife, 1996-97, Spl. Commn. Spay/Neuter City L.A., 1998-99; adv. com. La. Dept. of Animal Reg. 2000; mem. adv. com. Calif. Dept. Fish & Game Animal Care, 2003; pres., bd. dirs. Fauna Found., 2004-; mem. Calif. Rep. Cen. Com., 1964-72, mem. exec. com., 1971-73; mem. L.A. County Rep. Cen. Com., 1964-72, mem. exec. com., 1966-70; chmn. 29th Congl. Cen. Com., 1969-70; sec. 28th Senatorial Cen. Com., 1967-68; mem. speakers bur. George Murphy for U.S. Senate, 1970; campaign mgr. Los Angeles County for Spencer Williams for Atty. Gen., 1966; mem. L.A. County Art Mus., L.A. Libr. Assn. Mem. Internat. Platform Assn., Mannequins Assn. (bd. dirs. 1967-68), Lawyer's Wives San Gabriel Valley (bd. dirs. 1971-74, pres. 1972-73), L.A. Athletic Club, Town Hall. Home: 1766 Bluffhill Dr Monterey Park CA 91754-4533 Office Phone: 323-262-1815.

**SMITH, BETTY ROBINSON,** elementary school educator; b. Athens, Ga., Jan. 31, 1941; d. Willie Martin and Leila Mary Robinson; m. Freddie Smith; children: Natalie Yvonne, Rewa Patrice. BSEd, Tuskegee (Ala.) Inst., 1964; MS in Early Childhood Edn., Nova U., Ft. Lauderdale, Fla., 1979; cert. early childhood, U. S. Fla. Head tchr. in headstart program Perkins Elem. Sch., St. Petersburg, Fla., 1965; tchr. Orange Grove Elem. Sch., Tampa, Fla., 1967-68, Largo (Fla.) Ctrl. Elem. Sch., 1970-71, North Shore Elem. Sch., St. Petersburg, Fla., 1971-99; head tchr. Gulfport Elem. Montessori Acad., 2000—; resource cons., bd. dirs. Mt. Zion Christain Acad., 1999—. Head tchr. Early Success Program; active Appreciate Cultures Program for sch. improvement plan Pinellas County; chair Multicultural Club; organizer ann. Elem. workshop; network trainer, Gulfport Elem., 2000—; head multicultural com., acad network trainer Gulfport Elem. Montessori Acad., 2002-2004; head multicultural tural liason, 2000-05. Dir. youth choir, active community and religious roles; mem. mass choir Mt. Zion Progressive Baptist Ch.; organizer 55+ Club; head multicultural com. North Shore Elem. Sch. Mem. PCTA, Am. Montessori Soc., Zeta Gamma Zta, PREP (rep. for Pinellas County, Fla.). Home: 4301 Cortez Way S Saint Petersburg FL 33712-4024 Office Phone: 727-893-2643.

**SMITH, BETTY W.,** librarian; b. Lincoln, Nebr., June 29, 1919; d. Clem and Edith Margaret (Stanley) Wilder; m. Dulaney Dale Smith, Mar. 20, 1946; children: Douglas D., Diane E., Richard W. BA, Wayne U., 1940; BS, U. Minn., 1941; MA, Mich. State U., 1955. Cert. libr. Br. libr. Pub. Libr., Park Ridge, Ill., 1941-42; reference libr. Dearborn, Mich., 1942-44; U.S.C.G.

SPAR, libr. asst. U.S.C.G. Acad., New London, Conn., 1945-46; reference libr. Libr. Hawaii, Honolulu, 1946-47; libr. Hawaiian Econ. Found., Honolulu, 1947-49; reference libr. Lansing Pub. Libr., Mich., 1967-86, substitute libr., 1986-98. Mem. Citizens for Actions in Mental Health, 1980—86; steering com. Long-Range Planning Mich. Dept. Mental Health, 1986—90; bd. dirs. Tri-Co. Cmty. Mental Health, Lansing, 1992—98; founding and exec. com. mem. Alliance for Mentally Ill, Mich., 1985—2003, now v.p.; adv. coun. Mich. Forensic Ctr., 1988—, Lafayette Clinic, Detroit, 1986—92. Mem. LWV, Mental Health Assn., Mich. Assn. Emotionally Disturbed Children (bd. dirs. 1963-68), Mich. Mental Health (adv. coun. 1986-90), Phi Alpha Theta. Home: 1782 Eifert Rd Holt MI 48842-1976

**SMITH, BILL,** religious organization administrator; b. NYC, June 24, 1940; s. Harry John and Catharine Marie (Wheeler) S.; m. Judith Ann Carroll, Mar. 18, 1961; children: Shawn, Kevin, Susan, Kurt, Eric. BA, Iona Coll., 1962; MS, USN Postgrad. Sch., 1971; MPA, Golden Gate U., 1982. Credentialed city mgr. ICMA, credentialed spl. dist. mgr. Calif. Spl. Dist. Assn. Adminstrv. analyst City of Monterey (Calif.), 1982-84; city adminstr. City of Sonora (Calif.), 1984-86; asst. city mgr. City of Monterey, 1986-90; city mgr. City of Manhattan Beach (Calif.), 1990-94, City of Westminster, Calif., 1994-97; gen. mgr. Ventura (Calif.) Regional Sanitation Dist., 1997—2005; regional asst. to Cath. Bishop of Santa Barbara Pastoral Region Calif., 2005—. Instr. USN Postgrad. Sch., Monterey, 1979-82; adj. prof. Golden Gate U., San Francisco, 1984-90. Contbr. articles to profl. jours. Bd. dirs. Monterey County AIDS Project, 1987-90. Lt. col. USMC, 1962-82. Decorated Silver Star, Bronze Star, PurpleHeart, Joint Svc. Commendation medal. Mem. Am. Soc. Pub. Adminstrn. (chpt. pres. 1983-84), Internat. City Mgrs. Assn., Retired Officers Assn., Disabled Am. Vets., VFW, Am. Legion. Home: 261 Cherry Hills Ct Thousand Oaks CA 91320-4171 Office: Santa Barbara Pastoral Regon 3240 Calle Pinon Santa Barbara CA 93105-2760 Office Phone: 805-682-0442. Business E-Mail: billsmith@sbpr.org. E-mail: judy_billy@msn.com.

**SMITH, BOB,** lawyer, educator, state senator; b. Scranton, Pa., Mar. 25, 1947; s. Philip and Ruth (Delmar) S.; m. Ellen Theresa Foster; children: Karen Elizabeth, Lisa. BA in History, U. Scranton, 1969, MS in Chemistry, 1970; MS in Environ. Sci., Rutgers U., 1973; JD, Seton Hall U., 1981. Bar: N.J. 1981. Sci. tchr. Lourdesmont H.S., Clark Summit, Pa., 1968-70; environ. health sci. curriculum coord. Middlesex County Coll., Edison, NJ, 1972-73, adminstrv. asst. to dean sci., 1974-77, instr., 1970-74, asst. prof., 1974-76, assoc. prof., 1976-79, prof. chemistry and environ. sci., 1979-86; law clk. N.J. Dept. Environ. Protection, Trenton, 1980; prin. pvt. practice law Bob Smith and Assocs., Piscataway, NJ, 1981—. Prosecutor East Brunswick, 1997—, South Brunswick, 1998—; Mayor of Piscataway Twp., 1981-86; N.J. assemblyman N.J. 17th Legis. Dist., 1986-2001, mem. appropriations com. and environ. quality com., assembly select com. on ocean pollution, 1988, assembly energy and hazardous waste com. policy and rules, 1994; mem. N.J. State Senate, 2002—, chmn. environ. com., 2004-, mem. jud. com. and environment com.; parliamentarian Assembly Dem. Caucus, 1988-90, chmn. task force on environment, 1987; chmn. Piscataway Dem. Orgn., 1981-90; counsel N.J. State Dem. Platform Com., 1987, 89; chmn. Middlesex County Dem. Orgn., 1991-92; Assembly Dem. Dept. Minority Leader, 1993-95; councilman-at-large Piscataway Twp., 1977-80, pres. coun., 1979, v.p. 1978; mem. Middlesex County Transp. Coordinating Com., 1980-86; chmn. Piscataway Planning Bd., 1981-86, sec., 1975, chmn., 1976; bd. dirs. N.J. Conf. Mayors, 1984-86; mem. tech. adv. com. air pollution Middlesex County Planning Bd., 1973-74; mem. Greenbrook Basin com. Area 208 Mgmt. Planning Program, 1975-76; mem. commr's adv. com. N.J. Dept. Environ. Protection, 1972-86. Recipient Disting. Citizen award Piscataway Jewish Congregation B'nai Shalom, 1982; named Legis. of Yr. Eden Inst., N.J. State VFW, 1998, Environ. Legislator of Yr., N.J. Environ. Fedn., 1990, Environ. Legislator of Yr., N.J. Environ. Lobby, 2005; Presdl. scholar U. Scranton, 1965-69. Mem. Middlesex County Bar Assn., NJ State Bar Assn Roman Catholic. Office: 216 Stelton Rd B-1 Piscataway NJ 08854-3284 also: 216 Stelton Rd E-5 Piscataway NJ 08854-2600

**SMITH, BRAD,** journalist; Picture editor Sports Illustrated, Sports Illustrated Women; sports photo editor New York Times. Spkr. in field. Co-editor: (books) Sports of the Times, 2003. Office: NY Times Sports Desk 229 W 43rd St New York NY 10036 Office Phone: 212-556-7371. Office Fax: 212-556-5848.*

**SMITH, BRADFORD LEE,** information technology executive, lawyer; b. Milw., Jan. 17, 1959; m. Kathy Surace-Smith; 2 children. AB summa cum laude, Princeton U., 1981; JD, Columbia U., 1985; student, Univ. Geneva Grad. Inst. Internat. Studies, Geneva, Switzerland, 1984. Former ptnr. Covington & Burling, Washington; mgr., European Law & Corp. Affairs group, Microsoft, Paris, 1993—96, dep. gen. counsel for worldwide sales Redmond, Wash., 1996—2001, sr. v.p., gen. counsel for law and corp. affairs, 2001—. Lectr. Hague Acad. Internat. Law. Contbr. articles. Office: Microsoft One Microsoft Way Redmond WA 98052-6399

**SMITH, BRADLEY E.,** anesthesiologist; b. Cedar Vale, Kans., Jan. 4, 1933; MD, U. Okla., 1957. Diplomate Am. Bd. Anesthesiologists. Resident U.S. Naval Hosp., NYC, 1957-60; fellow Columbia Presbyn. Hosp., NYC, 1960—61; faculty Yale U., 1962-63, U. Miami, 1963-69; chmn., prof. dept. anesthesiology Vanderbilt U., Nashville, 1969-93, prof., 1993—, prof. emeritus, 2004—, prof. clin. anesthesiology, 2005—. Mem.: AMA, ACOG (assoc.), Am. Soc. Anesthesiologists. Office: Vandy Med Ctr Rm 209 Oxford House Nashville TN 37232-4125 Office Phone: 615-936-0718.

**SMITH, BRADLEY YOULE,** lawyer; b. N.Y.C., Feb. 11, 1948; s. Bradley and Christine (Brown) S.; m. Anne Barre, Dec. 31, 1986; children: Evelyn McLaren, Andrew Robert, Lauren Barre, Timothy James, Lynden Eleanor, Christina McLaren. BA in History cum laude, Yale U., 1970; JD, NYU, 1974. Bar: N.Y. 1975, U.S. Dist. Ct. (so. dist.) N.Y. 1975, U.S. Ct. Appeals (2d cir.) 1975. With Davis Polk & Wardwell, N.Y.C., 1974—; ptnr., 1980—. Trustee Royal Coll. Surgeons Found., Inc. Mem. ABA (chmn. subcom. secured transactions 1983-87, moderator and panelist com. banking law and uniform comml. code), Am. Law Inst., N.Y. State Bar Assn. (mem. banking law com.). Office: Davis Polk & Wardwell 450 Lexington Ave New York NY 10017-3982 Office Phone: 212-450-4000. Business E-Mail: bradley.smith@dpw.com.

**SMITH, BRANSON M.,** computer technology company executive; BSc in Bus. Adminstrn., U. Ariz. Prin. Southwest Automation; from v.p. distbn. and sr. v.p. fulfillment svcs. Insight Direct USA, Inc. to pres. Insight Enterprises, Inc., Tempe, Ariz., 1992—2001, pres., 2001—. Office: Insight Enterprises Inc 1305 W Auto Drive Tempe AZ 85284

**SMITH, BRIAN D.,** lawyer; AB, Brown Univ., 1972; JD, Univ. of Va. Law School; PhD, Cambridge Univ., 1986. Bar: Calif.; N.Y., Am. Bar Assoc. Atty., real estate, shareholder Heller, Ehrman, White, & McAuliffe LLP, San Francisco, 1991—. Mem.: Lambda Alpha Internat. Office: Heller Ehrman 333 Bush St San Francisco CA 94104 Office Phone: 415-772-6534. Fax: 415-772-6268. E-mail: bsmith@hewm.com.

**SMITH, BRIAN RICHARD,** hematologist, oncologist, pathologist; b. Glen Cove, N.Y., May 7, 1952; s. Frank C. and Gloria R. S.; m. Keiren Donovan, Apr. 17, 1993. AB in Chemistry summa cum laude, Princeton U., 1972; MD, Harvard U., 1976; MA (hon.), Yale U., 1997. Diplomate Am. Bd. Internal Medicine, HEmatology and Med. Oncology, Am. Bd. Pathology Hematopathology. Resident/fellow Harvard U., Brigham and Women's Hosp., 1976-80; instr. medicine Harvard Med. Sch., 1981—84; assoc. physician Brigham & Women's Hosp., Children's Hosp., Dana-Farber Cancer Ins, Boston, 1981-88; asst. prof. Harvard Med. Sch., 1985-88; assoc. prof. medicine, lab. medicine & pediatrics sch. med. Yale U., New Haven, 1988-96; prof. medicine, lab medicine & pediatrics, 1996—; dir. immunohematology; vice chmn. dept. lab. medicine Yale Med. Sch.-Yale New Haven Hosp., 1997—; DeCamp lectr. biomed. ethics Princeton U., NJ, 1992. Contbr. over 140 articles to med. publs. Trustee Richard D. Frisbee III Found.; chair study sect. Am. Heart Assn. Recipient George A. Howe prize Princeton U., 1976; Am. Cancer Soc. fellow, 1981-84, Leukemia Soc. fellow, 1982-88; Leukemia Soc. Am. scholar, 1989, Stohlman scholar, 1993, Nat. Blood Found. scholar, 1996. Fellow ACP, Coll. Am. Pathologists; mem. NIH (recombinant DNA adv. com. 1992-97), Acad. Clin. Lab. Physicians and Scientists (exec. coun. 2000—), Phi Beta Kappa, Sigma Xi, Alpha Omega Alpha. Roman Catholic. Office: Yale U Sch Med PO Box 208035 333 Cedar St New Haven CT 06520-8035

**SMITH, BRIAN WILLIAM,** lawyer, former government official; b. NYC, Feb. 3, 1947; s. William Francis and Dorothy Edwina (Vogel) S.; m. Donna Jean Holverson, Apr. 24, 1976; children: Mark Holverson, Lauren Elizabeth. BA, St. John's U., N.Y.C., 1968, JD, 1971; MS, Columbia U., 1981. Bar: N.Y. 1972, D.C. 1975, U.S. Dist. Ct. (ea. and so. dists.) N.Y. 1975, U.S. Supreme Ct. 1976, U.S. Dist. Ct. D.C. 1986. Atty. Am. Express Co., N.Y.C., 1970-73, CIT Fin. Corp., N.Y.C., 1973-74; assoc. counsel, mng. atty. Interbank Card Assn. (named changed to Master Card Internat., Inc.), N.Y.C., 1974-75, sr. v.p., corp. sec., gen. counsel, 1975-82; chief counsel Compt. of Currency, Washington, 1982-84; ptnr. Stroock & Stroock & Lavan, Washington, 1984-92, mng. ptnr., 1986-92; ptnr. Mayer, Brown, Rowe & Maw, LLP, Washington and N.Y.C., 1992—2004, Latham & Watkins LLP, Washington, 2004—. Lectr. fin. industry. Editor: E-Commerce, 2003, Financial Products and Services, 2004. Capt. USAR, 1970—78. Mem. ABA, N.Y. State Bar Assn., D.C. Bar Assn., Assn. Bar City N.Y., Fed. Bar Assn., N.Y. Athletic Club, Met. Club (N.Y.), Met. Club (Washington). Home: 35 W Lenox St Chevy Chase MD 20815-4208 Office: Latham & Watkins LLP 555 11th St NW Washington DC 20004 1304 Office Phone: 202 637 2288.

**SMITH, BRUCE ALFRED,** oil industry executive; b. Coffeyville, Kans., Oct. 12, 1943; s. George Alfred and Isabel (Andrews) S.; m. Cynthia Denton Doughat, Aug. 7, 1969 (div. Jan. 1987); children: Denton Todd, Bruce Chandler, John Paul, Joseph Williams, Charles Pinson Smith; m. Gail Hutchison, Nov. 10, 1990. BA, Westminster Coll., 1965; MBA, U. Kans., 1967; postgrad., U. Chgo., 1971. With Ford Motor Co., Dearborn, Mich., 1967-69; banking officer met. divsn. Continental Ill. Nat. Bank and Trust Co. Chgo., Chgo., 1971-73, 2nd v.p. multinat. divsn., 1973-75, v.p. mining divsn., 1975-77, v.p., sect. mgr. Chgo. and London, 1977-80, v.p. mgr. internat. energy divsn. Chgo., 1980-82, v.p., mgr. S.W. group, comml. banking Houston, 1983-86; corp. v.p., treas. Valero Energy Corp. and Valero Natural Gas Ptnrs., San Antonio, 1986-92; v.p. Tesoro Petroleum Corp., San Antonio, 1992-93, CFO, 1992-95, exec. v.p., 1993-95, exec. v.p. Tesoro Exploration and Prodn. Co., 1993-95, exec. v.p., COO, dir., 1995, pres., CEO, 1995-96, chmn., CEO, pres., 1996—. Bd. dirs. Noble Energy, Inc., Nat. Petrochemical & Refiners Assn. Bd. dirs. San Antonio Sports Found. With U.S. Army, 1969-71. Rem. Fin. Execs. Inst. (past pres. San Antonio chpt.). Office: Tesoro Petroleum Corp 300 Concord Plaza Dr San Antonio TX 78216-6903*

**SMITH, BRUCE I.,** state legislator; b. Harrisburg, Pa., Feb. 19, 1934; s. Bruce I. and Margaret M. (Zerbe) S.; m. Patricia A. Ninkovich; children: Rhonda J., Renee N. BA, Elizabethtown Coll., 1956; MEd, Pa. State U., 1961. Chmn. Newberry Twp. (Pa.) Recreation Bd., 1971-77, Newberry Twp. Bd. Supr., 1978-83; mem. Pa. Ho. of Reps., Harrisburg, 1980—. Chmn. game and fisheries com., 1995—, agrl. and rural affairs com., 1993-94; chmn. Ctrl. Pa. Rep. Caucus, 1995—. Rep. committeeman, 1976-80; active Newberry Twp. Planning Commn., 1978-80; tchr. Cedar Cliff H.S., West Shore. Sgt. USAR, 1958-64. Named Conservation Legislator of Yr., York County, Pa., 1987, 1994—98, Conservationist of Yr., York County, 1999, Pa., 2001, Legislator of Yr., Pa. Trappers Assn., 2001, Sportmens Legislator of Yr., Pa. Fedn. Sportsmen's Clubs, 2002. Mem. Shrine Club, Pinchot Der Passe Walton League (charter). Address: Fairview Indsl Pk 540B Industrial Dr Lewisberry PA 17339-9534

**SMITH, BRUCE R.,** language educator; b. Jackson, Miss., Mar. 21, 1946; Student, U. Birmingham, England, 1966-67; BA magna cum laude in English with honors, Tulane U., 1968; MA, U. Rochester, 1971, PhD with distinction, 1973. From asst. prof. to assoc. prof. English Georgetown U., Washington, 1972-87, prof. English, 1987—2003, U. So. Calif., 2003—04, Disting. Coll. prof. English, prof. theater, 2004—; faculty Bread Loaf Sch. English, Middlebury Coll., 1994—. Seminar dir. Folger Inst., 1994, 98-99. Author: Ancient Scripts and Modern Experience on the English Stage 1500-1700, 1988, Homosexual Desire in Shakespeare's England: A Cultural Poetics, 1991, Roasting the Swan of Avon: Shakespeare's Redoubtable Enemies and Dubious Friends, 1994, The Acoustic World of Early Modern England, 1999, Shakespeare and Masculinity, 2000; editor: Shakespeare, Twelfth Night: Text and Contexts, 2001; editl. bd. Shakespeare Quar., 1995—, PMLA, 2000-02, Studies in English Lit., 2003—; contbr. chpts. to books, articles to profl. jours. Summer grantee Georgetown U. Acad. Rsch., 1976, 84, 87, 89, 91, 92, 99, grantee Intercultural Curriculum Devel., 1982, Agecroft Assn., 1991; Mellon fellow Huntington Libr., 1996, jr. fellow Folger Inst., 1985, fellow, 1990, 96, ACLS fellow, 1979-80, NEH fellow, 1987-88, 99, Va. Found. Humanites fellow, 1989, Internat. Globe fellow Shakespeare's Globe, London, 1997, Guggenheim fellow, 2001-02, Brit. Acad.-Huntington Libr. fellow, 2004; recipient Roland Bainton pize for lit. 16th Century Studies Assn., 2000, Disting. Scholar award U. Rochester, 2002. Mem. MLA, Soc. Study Early Modern Women, Renaissance Soc. Am., Shakespeare Assn. Am. (pres. 1994-95), Com. for Lesbian and Gay History. Office: U So Calif Dept English Taper Hall 404 Los Angeles CA 90089-0354

**SMITH, BRUCE VAUGHN,** electrical engineer; b. Kingsville, Tex., July 28, 1953; s. Robert Vaughn and June Estelle (Link) S.; m. Astrid Marie Ryerson, July 17, 1976; 1 child, Leslie Michelle. BSEE, Iowa State U., 1975, MEEE, 1980, PhD, 1991; Prof. engrn. Iowa. Sr. prin. avn. engr. Rockwell Collins Avionics, Cedar Rapids, Iowa, 1975—. Owner Cottonwood Sys. Design, Co., 2001—; adj. prof. Iowa State U., Ames, 1991—, grad. faculty, 1999—; program evaluator, engr. commr., exec. com. Accreditation Bd. Engring. & Tech., Balt., 1995—, mem. exec. com.; state problem capt. Odyssey of the Mind, 1996-2000. Bd. dirs. North Linn Sch. Dist., Troy Mills, Iowa, 1993-95. Mem. IEEE (com. on engring. accreditation activities), Internat. Coun. Sys. Engring. (sec.-treas. Heartland chpt. 2000-), Sigma Xi. Office: Rockwell 400 Collins Rd NE Cedar Rapids IA 52498-0001 E-mail: smithb@mchsi.com.

**SMITH, C. D.,** civil engineering educator; BSc in Civil Engring., U. Alta, Can., 1948; MSc in Hydraulic Engring., U. Sask., 1963. Cons. hydraulic engr., prof. civil engring. U. Sask., Saskatoon, Can., to 1991, prof. emeritus civil engring., cons. hydraulic engr., 1991—. Author: two books; contbr. to over 70 profl. jours. Recipient C. Dagenais award Can. Soc. Civil Engring., 1986, T.C. Keefer medal, 1962, 91, Engring. Achievement Silver medal Profl. Engrs. of Sask., 1991, Engr. of Yr., Saskatoon Engring. Soc., 1993, Julian Smith medal Engring. Inst. Can., 2000. Fellow ASCE; mem. Can. Soc. Civil Engring. (past pres.). Home: 120 7th St E Saskatoon SK Canada S7H 0W8 Office Phone: 306-242-8421. E-mail: cds.hyd.eng@shaw.ca.

**SMITH, C. GRANT,** scriptwriter, film producer; b. St. Louis, Mar. 1, 1967; s. Lynwood M. and Peggy M. Smith; m. Hannah King, June 17, 1971; 1 child, Samuel Owen; 1 child, Caroline K. Cert., Am. Film Inst., LA, 1998; MA, Webster U., 2006. Cert. Acctg., Sanford Brown Bus. Coll., 1988. Mcht. developer Maritz, Inc., Fenton, Mo., 1995—97; flight attendant coord. TWA, St. Louis, 1999—2001; co-owner BlackSmith Pictures, Inc.; prodn. engr. Quick Study Radiology. Co-writer, prodr.: screenplays Hunting Ground; co-author Jersey Shore (finalist L.A. Screenwriting Expo., 2003), Hawkins, The Willows, 2006, Chain Letter, 2006. Democrat. Achievements include development of screenwriting application through MS Office 2000/Access. Home: 1075 Wilson Ave Saint Louis MO 63130 Office Phone: 314-713-6872. E-mail: cgsgrant@yahoo.com.

**SMITH, C. LAMONT,** sports association executive, lawyer; B magna cum laude, Clark Atlanta Univ.; JD, Howard Univ., 1984. Pres., founder All Pro Sports & Entertainment Inc., Denver, ELETE Sports Couture, Denver. Named

9th Most Powerful African-Am. in Sports, Savoy Mag.; recipient Agent of Yr. award, Black Sports Agents Assn., 2001. Mem.: Sports Lawyers Assn., Black Entertainment & Sports Law Assn. (past chmn., mem., BESLA Hall of Fame). Office: All Pro Sports & Entertainment Inc Ste 100 The Smith Ctr 36 Steele St Denver CO 80206 Office Phone: 303-320-4004. Office Fax: 303-320-4019.

**SMITH, C. LEMOYNE,** retired publishing executive; b. Atkins, Ark., Sept. 15, 1934; s. Cecil Garland and Salena Bell (Wilson) S.; m. Selma Jean Tucker, May 23, 1964; 1 child, Jennifer Lee BS, Ark. Tech. U., 1956; M.Ed., U. Ark., 1958. Tchr. pub. schs., Little Rock, 1956-58; instr. bus. adminstrn. Ark. Tech. U., Russellville, 1958-60; sales rep. South-Western Pub. Co., Cin., 1960-67, editorial staff, 1967-82, pres., chief exec. officer, 1982-90, chmn., 1990-91, ret., 1991. Bd. dirs. Cin. Council on World Affairs, 1983-95. Mem.: Nat. Bus. Edn. Assn., Delta Pi Epsilon. Republican. Presbyterian. Avocations: bridge, travel, golf. Office: South-Western Pub Co 5191 Natorp Blvd Mason OH 45040-7980

**SMITH, CARA,** editorial executive; Mng. editor Am. Jour. Internat. Law Am. Soc. Internat. Law, Washington. Office: Am Jour Internat Law 2223 Massachusetts Ave NW Washington DC 20008

**SMITH, CARL BERNARD,** education educator; b. Feb. 29, 1932; s. Carl R. and Elizabeth Ann (Lefeld) S.; m. Virginia Lee Cope, Aug. 30, 1958; children: Madonna, Anthony, Regina, Marla. BA, U. Dayton, 1954; MA, Miami U., Oxford, Ohio, 1961; PhD, Case Western Res. U., 1967. Tchr. Cathedral Latin H.S., Cleve., 1954-57; customer corr. E.F. MacDonald Co., Dayton, 1958-59; tchr. Kettering (Ohio) H.S., 1959-61; editor Reardon Baer Pub. Co., Cleve., 1961-62; tchr., rschr. Case Western Res. U., Cleve., 1962-65, Cleve. Pub. Schs., 1966-67; asst. prof. edn. Ind. U., Bloomington, 1967-69, assoc. prof., 1970-72, prof., 1973—99, prof. emeritus, 1999—. Dir. ERIC Ctr., 1988-2004, Family Literacy Ctr., 1990—; pres. Grayson Bernard Pub. Co., 1988—, Am. Family Learning Corp., 1996—. Author: Reading Instruction through Diagnostic Teaching (Pi Lambda Theta Best Book in Edn. award 1972), Getting People to Read, 1978; sr. author: Series r, 1983, New View, 1993, Teaching Reading and Writing Together, 1984, Connect! Getting Your Kids to Talk to You, 1994, Word History A Resource Book, 1995, Self-Directed Learner Curriculum, 1998, (videotape) Make a Difference, 1996, Improving Your Child's Writing Skills, 1999, Gotcha Grandpa, 2000, Talk to Your Children About Books, 2001, Teaching Children to Learn, 2002, Reading to Learn, 2003, Parents Guide to Character Development, 2003, The Spriritual Family, 2005. Pres. Bd. Edn., St. Charles Sch., Bloomington, 1976-80. Recipient Sch. Bell award NEA, 1967, Literacy award Ind. State Reading Assn., 1997. Mem. ASCD, Internat. Reading Assn., Nat. Coun. Tchrs. of English, Am. Ednl. Rsch. Assn., Phi Delta Kappa. Republican. Roman Catholic. Home: 4915 E Cedarcrest Dr Bloomington IN 47401 Office: Reading and English Clearinghouse Smith Rsch Ctr Bloomington IN 47405 Office Phone: 812-855-5847. Business E-Mail: smith2@indiana.edu.

**SMITH, CARNICE,** music educator, director; b. Jackson, Mississippi, Miss., June 8, 1954; d. James Edward and Mary Lee Smith. B in Music Edn., Jackson State U., 1976, M in Music Edn., 1979; Orff cert., Miss. State U., 1993. Nat. bd. cert. tchr. Music tchr. Morrison Elem. Sch. Jackson Pub. Sch., Miss., 1987—95; choral dir. Blackburn Mid. Sch. Jackson Pub. Schools, Miss., 1995—. Dir., sponsor Miss. Songfest Jackson Pub. Schools, 1998—2005. Music scholar, Jackson State U., 1972—76. Mem.: Delta Sigma Theta (life) Internat. Reading Assn. Home: 3627 Fontaine Ave Jackson MS 39213 Office: Blackburn Mid Sch 1311 W Pearl St Jackson MS 39203 Personal E-mail: csharp54@yahoo.com.

**SMITH, CAROL ANN,** academic administrator; b. Waterbury, Conn., Dec. 22, 1941; d. Prosper Mark and Emma Edna (Dumschott) Zailskas; m. Gordon B. Jobe; children from previous marriage: Amy, Christian, Meghan. BSN, Boston Coll., 1965; MSN, Boston U., 1971, PhD in Adminstrn., 1977. Chmn. grad. nursing dept. Boston Coll. Sch. Nursing, 1973—78; coord. Harvard Med. Sch. program Boston Coll., 1975—78; dir. baccalaureate nursing program Coll. of Our Lady of Elms, 1978—80; dean sch. nursing Duquesne U., 1980—83, acting acad. v.p., 1983—85; vis. v.p. for acad. affairs Carnegie-Mellon U., 1985—86; acad. v.p. Marshall U., Huntington, W.Va., 1985—89; pres. Mater Dei Coll., Ogdensburg, NY, 1989—. Field reader US Dept. Edn., 1990—91. Exec. com. Sisters of St. Joseph Consortium, 1990—; bd. dirs. Commn. Ind. Colls. and Univs., 1990—, Boys and Girls Club, A. Barton Hepburn Hosp. Found. Mem.: LWV, St. Lawrence C. of C. (bd. dirs.), Boston Coll. Club, Rotary, Delta Gamma Kappa, Phi Delta Kappa, Sigma Theta Tau, Delta Kappa Gamma. Roman Catholic. Office: Mater Dei College PO Box 794 Ogdensburg NY 13669-0794

**SMITH, CAROLE DIANNE,** retired lawyer, editor, writer, product developer; b. Seattle, June 12, 1945; d. Glaude Francis and Elaine Claire (Finkenstein) S.; m. Stephen Bruce Presser, June 18, 1968 (div. June 1987); children: David Carter, Elisabeth Catherine. AB cum laude, Harvard U., Radcliffe Coll., 1968; JD, Georgetown U., 1974. Bar: Pa. 1974. Law clk. Hon. Judith Jamison, Phila., 1974—75; assoc. Gratz, Tate, Spiegel, Ervin & Ruthrouff, Phila., 1975—76; freelance editor, writer Evanston, Ill., 1983—87; editor Ill. Inst. Tech., Chgo., 1987—88; mng. editor LawLetters, Inc., Chgo., 1988—89; editor ABA, Chgo., 1989—95; product devel. mgr. Midwest Market Ctr. West Group, Deerfield, Ill., 1996—97; mkt acquisitions, bus. and fin. group CCH, Inc., Riverwoods, Ill., 1997—2002; ret. Author Jour. of Legal Medicine, 1975, Selling and the Law: Advertising and Promotion, 1987; (other pseudonym Sarah Tracy) 78 children's books and stories, 1984-2002, editor The Brief, 1990-95, Criminal Justice, 1989-90, 92-95 (Gen. Excellence award Soc. Nat. Assn. Pubs. 1990, Feature Article award-bronze Soc. Nat. Assn. Pubs. 1994), Franchise Law Jour., 1995; mem. editl. bd. The Brief, 1995-2000, editor-in-chief, 1998-2000. Dir. Radcliffe Club of Chgo., 1990-93; mem. parents coun. Latin Sch. Chgo., 1995-96; trustee Winnetka-Northfield Libr. Dist., 2003—, pres. trustees, 2005—; mem. Winnetka Plan Commn. 2003-05, Winnetka Forestry Commn., 2004-05 Mem. ABA (editor-in-chief The Brief 1998-2000, mem. publs. editl. bd. tort trial and ins. practice sect. 2003-05, chair 2005—).

**SMITH, CATHERINE ARNOTT,** medical informatics educator, researcher; d. Peter Douglas Arnott and Eva Charlotte Schenkel; m. Mark Brampton Smith, Jan. 12, 1991; 1 child, Simon Peter Brampton. AM of Libr. Sci., U. Mich., 1992, MA, 1992, MS in Info. Sci., 2000; PhD, U. Pitts., 2002. Asst. editor Harcourt Brace Jovanovich, N.Y.C., 1981—83; reference libr. Northwestern U., Evanston, Ill., 1992—93; med. info. sys. mgmt. specialist Lincoln Nat. Reinsurance, Ft. Wayne, Ind., 1993—97; asst. prof. Sch. of Info. Studies, Syracuse, NY, 2002—06, U. Wis. Sch. Libr. and Info. Studies, Madison, 2006—. Author: (annotated bibliography) Tennessee Williams On File. Mem. adv. bd. Episcopal Chaplaincy, Syracuse U., 2005. Recipient Nat. Libr. Medicine fellow, 1997—2002, Ctr. for Healthcare Mgmt. Rsch. stipend, 2003; electronic docs. fellow, Nat. Hist. and Pub. Records Commn., 2005. Mem.: Am. Soc. for Info. Sci. and Tech. (chair med. informatics spl. interest group 2005—06), Med. Libr. Assn. (chair med. informatics sect. 2005—06, Donald A. B. Lindberg Rsch. fellowship 2002). Episcopalian. Avocation: choral music. Office: U Wis 4217 Helen C White Hall Madison WI 53706

C.S. Mott Found., 2001. Mem.: Coll. Art Assn. (assoc.). Democrat. Home: 824 S Leroy St Fenton MI 48430 Office: Mott CC 1401 E Court St Flint MI 48503 Office Phone: 810-762-0443. E-mail: womeninpants1@sbcglobal.net.

**SMITH, CATHERINE MARIE,** science educator; b. Bridgeport, Conn., Dec. 28, 1958; d. Arthur Vincent Giles, Sr. and Lila Catherine (Auger) Giles; m. Roger K. Smith, July 16, 1982. BS, U. Bridgeport, 1980; MBA, Sacred Heart U., 1994. Cert. Med. Technologist Am. Soc. Clin. Pathologists, 1981. Medical technician Bridgeport Hosp., Conn., 1980—88; med. technologist St. Joseph Med. Ctr., Stamford, Conn., 1988—94; lab. mgr. Stamford Medical Group, Stamford, 1994—99; chemistry and biology tchr. Wilbur Cross HS, New Haven, 1999—2003, New Canaan HS, Conn., 2003—. Donor Am. Red Cross, Conn., 1984—; tchr. participant Jr. Sci. & Humanities Symposium, U. Conn., 2000—03; youth min. Our Lady of Assumption, Fairfield, Conn., 1989—2004; emmaus team mem. Holy Family, Fairfield, Conn., 2000—, St. Aloysius, New Canaan, Conn., 2004—. Mem.: NSTA, So. Poverty Law, Am. Soc. Clin. Pathologists, Conn. Nat. Sci. Tchrs. Assn., Pi Lambda Theta, Delta Mu Delta. Roman Catholic. Avocations: car racing, dog training. Personal E-mail: cmbgs@aol.com.

**SMITH, CATHERINE PARSONS,** music educator; b. Rochester, N.Y., Nov. 4, 1933; d. Judson A. and Frances H. Parsons; children: Walter, Anne, Courtney. AB magna cum laude, Smith Coll., Northampton, Mass., 1954; MMus, Northwestern U., 1957; D Mus. Arts, Stanford U., 1969. Lectr. music dept. U. Nev., Reno, 1969-76, asst. prof., 1976-79, assoc. prof., 1979-86, prof. music, 1986—2000, emerita, 2000—. Prin. flute Reno Philharmonic, 1979-99. Author: (with others) Mary Carr Coore American Composer, 1987, (English transl.) On Playing Oboe, Recorder, and Flageolet, 1992, William Grant Still: A Study in Contradictions, 2000; contbr. articles to mus. jours. NEH fellow, 1983, 89, Danforth fellow, 1967-69. Office: U Nev Music Dept 226 Reno NV 89557-0001 E-mail: smithcp@unr.edu.

**SMITH, CATHY GAYE,** elementary school educator; b. Tulsa, Nov. 25, 1957; d. Morris Dean and Mayce Aileen Herring; m. Donald Eugene Smith, May 27, 1989; 1 child, Christie Gayeleen 1 stepchild, Amber Renee. BA, Northeastern State U., 1984; M in edn., U. Ctrl. Okla., 1994. Tchr. Pleasant Grove Elem., Shawnee, Okla., 1985—86, White Rock Elem., McLoud, Okla., 1986—2004, Luther Elem., Okla., 2004—. Chairperson Textboat Com., White Rock Sch.; mem. Sch. Improvement Com., White Rock Sch.; tutor Reading. Named Tchr. of Yr, White Rock Sch., 1991—92, Meeker Masonic Tchr. of Yr., 1991—92. Mem.: Okla. Educators Assn., Okla. Early Childhood Assn., Okla. Reading Assn., Great Expectations. Democrat. Baptist. Avocations: reading, puzzles, movies.

**SMITH, CECE,** venture capitalist; b. Washington, Nov. 16, 1944; d. Linn Charles and Grace Inez (Walker) S.; m. John Ford Lacy, Apr. 22, 1978. BBA, U. Mich., 1966; M in Liberal Arts, So. Meth. U., 1974. CPA, Tex. Staff acct. Arthur Young & Co. (CPAs), Boston, 1966-68; staff acct., then asst. to contr. Wyly Corp., Dallas, 1969-72; contr., treas. subs. Univ. Computing Co., Dallas, 1972-74; contr. Steak and Ale Restaurants Am., Inc., Dallas, 1974-76, v.p. fin., 1976-80, exec. v.p., 1980-81, Pearle Health Services, Inc., 1981-84, pres. Primacare divsn., 1984-86; gen. ptnr. Phillips-Smith-Machens Venture Ptnrs., 1986—; pres. Le Sportsac Dallas, Inc., 1981-87. Bd. dirs. Brinker Internat. Inc., Michaels Stores, Inc.; chmn. Fed. Res. Bank Dallas, 1994—96; past v.p., dir. IWF-Dallas; mem. pres. adv. group U. Mich.; treas, mem. exec. bd. Dallas Symphony Assn. Past co-chmn. pres.'s rsch. coun. U. Tex. S.W. Med. Ctr. Dallas; past vis. com. U. Mich. Bus. Sch.; exec. bd. So. Meth. U. Cox Sch. Bus.; past v.p., bd. dirs. Jr. Achievement Dallas; past pres. Charter 100; past treas. Dallas Assembly; exec. bd., treas. Dallas Symphony Assn. Mem.: Com. of 200. Home: 3710 Shenandoah St Dallas TX 75205-2121 Office: 5080 Spectrum Dr Ste 805 W Addison TX 75001-4648 Office Phone: 972-387-0725.

**SMITH, CHAD A.,** band director; b. Ft. Dodge, Iowa, July 27, 1976; s. Robert A. and Chris L. Smith. MusB, U. Iowa, 1999. Cert. Teacher Iowa, 1999. Color guard staff Cavaliers Drum and Bugles Corps, Rosemont, Ill., 1999—2005; dir. of bands Chaminade Coll. Prep, West Hills, Calif., 2001—. Office: Chaminade Coll Prep 7500 Chaminade Ave West Hills CA 91304 Office Phone: 818-347-8300. Office Fax: 818-348-8374. E-mail: csmith@chaminade.org.

**SMITH, CHAD CORNTASSEL,** Native American tribal leader; s. Nelson and Pauline Smith; m. Bobbie Gail Smith; children: Chris, Kiah, Anaweg. BSEd, U. Ga., 1973; MPA, U. Wis., 1975; JD, U. Tulsa, 1980. Pvt. law practice; pub. defender Tulsa County; prosecutor Creek County; adminstr. Cherokee Nation Tax Commn.; prosecutor Cherokee Nation, prin. chief, 1999—. Has taught Indian law at Dartmouth Coll., Northeastern State U., Rogers State U. Office: Cherokee Nation Attn: Principal Chief PO Box 948 Tahlequah OK 74465 Office Phone: 918-456-0671 ext. 2882. E-mail: csmith@cherokee.org.*

**SMITH, CHAD GAYLORD,** musician, recording artist; b. St. Paul, Oct. 25, 1962; m. Maria St. John, 1996 (div. 1997); 1 child; m. Nancy Mack Smith, May 2004; 1 child. Drummer The Red Hot Chili Peppers, 1988—. Musician: (albums) The Red Hot Chili Peppers, 1984, Freaky Styley, 1985, The Uplift Mofo Party Plan, 1987, Mother's Milk, 1989, Blood Sugar Sex Magik, 1991, One Hot Minute, 1995, Californication, 1999, By the Way, 2002, Live in Hyde Park, 2004, Stadium Arcadium, 2006, (songs) Dani California, 2006 (MTV Video Music award for best Art Direction, 2006). Office: care Q Prime 131 S 11th St Nashville TN 37206 Office Phone: 615-258-1050. Office Fax: 615-258-1040. E-mail: info@qprime.com.*

**SMITH, CHARLES ANTHONY,** foundation administrator, director; b. Santa Fe, Sept. 16, 1939; s. Frances (Mier) Vigil; m. Paula Ann Thomas, June 26, 1965; 1 child, Charlene Danielle. Student various adminstrv. & law courses. Circulation mgr. Daily Alaska Empire, 1960-63; agt. Mut. of N.Y. Life Ins. Co., Juneau, Alaska, 1964-65; mng. ptnr. Future Investors in Alaska and Cinema Alaska, Juneau, 1961-62; SE Alaska rep. K & L Distbrs., 1966-68; mgr. SE Alaska Alaska Airlines Newspapers, 1969; dep. Alaska Retirement Sys., Juneau, 1970-71; apptd. dir. hwy. safety, gov.'s hwy. safety rep. Juneau, 1971-83; pres. Valley Svc. Ctr., I Nc., 1984-94; chmn. 3-S Alaska Employee Support of the Guard and Reserve, 1992—; pres. 3-S Corp., 1995—. Apptd. chmn. S.E. Alaska for ESGR, 1995; apptd. Alaska state dir. Selective Svc., 1996—. Author various hwy. safety manuals and plans. Alaska pres. Muscular Dystrophy Assn. Assn.; mem. SE Alaska Emergency Med. Svcs. Coun., 1965-72; state dir. Selective Svc., 1996. Served to maj. Army N.G., 1964-88. Named Alaska Safety Man of Yr., 1977. Mem. Am. Assn. Motor Vehicle Adminstrs., Alaska Peace Officers Assn., Nat. Assn. Gov.'s Hwy. Safety Reps., N.G. Assn., Internat. Platform Assn., Elks (Juneau). Roman Catholic. Home: PO Box 32856 Juneau AK 99803-2856

**SMITH, CHARLES COURTLAND, JR.,** lawyer, state legislator; b. Edgewood, Md., Feb. 27, 1946; s. Charles Courtland and Nell Jeanette (Martin) S.; m. Patricia Arlene Cassens, Aug. 31, 1974; children: Brian Courtland, Joel McQuarrie. BA, U. Ga., 1968, JD, 1973. Ptnr. Nichols, Lavigao, Smith & Rice, Conyers, Ga., 1973-74, Smith & Floyd, St. Marys, Ga., 1976—; trial asst. dist. atty. Fulton County Dist. Atty., Atlanta, 1974-76; rep. Ga. Gen. Assembly, Atlanta, 1993—2003, adminstrn. fl. leader, 1999—2003. City atty. City of St. Marys, 1979-81. Chmn. bd. dirs. St. Marys United Meth. Ch., 1983. Fellow Kiwanis Internat.; mem. USN League (life), Am. Numis. Assn., Am. Radio Relay League (life), Camden-Kings Bay Navy League (charter), Camden-Kings Bay C. of C. (charter), St. Marys Kiwanis Club (pres. 1979). Democrat. Avocations: flying, scuba diving, skiing, amateur radio, woodturning. Office: Smith & Floyd PO Drawer 766 1815 Osborne Rd Saint Marys GA 31558-9140

**SMITH, CHARLES HADDON,** geologist, consultant, retired federal agency administrator; b. Dartmouth, N.S., Can., Sept. 3, 1926; s. Albion Benson and Dora Pauline (McGill) S.; m. Mary Gertrude Saint, Sept. 5, 1949;

children: Charles Douglas, Richard David, Alan Michael, Timothy McGill. B.Sc. and Diploma in Enring, Dalhousie U., Can., 1946, M.Sc. in Geology, 1948; MS, Yale U., 1951, PhD in Econ. Geology, 1952. Instr. Dalhousie U., Halifax, N.S., 1946-48; geologist Cerro de Pasco Copper Corp., Morococha, Peru, 1949, Geol. Survey of Can., Ottawa, Ont., 1952-64, chief petrological scis. div., 1964-67, chief crustal geology div., 1967-68; sci. adviser Sci. Council Can., Ottawa, 1968-70; dir. planning Dept. Energy Mines and Resources, Ottawa, 1970-71, asst. dep. minister sci. and tech., 1971-75, sr. asst. dep. minister, 1975-81; pres. Charles H. Smith Cons., 1982-94. Mem. adv. coun. dept. geology and geophysics Princeton U., 1967-76; sci. advisor Can. commn. for UNESCO, 1989-93; exec. dir. Can. Nat. Com./World Energy Conf., 1983-90; bd. govs. Can. Inst. Radiation Safety, 1983-86; hon. mem. Energy Coun. Can., 1991—; coord. 150th anniversary Geol. Survey Can., 1990-93. Mem. editl. bd. Am. Jour. Sci., 1967-72, Mineralium Deposita, 1968-83, Jour. Petrology, 1966-70, Econ. Geology, 1960-70; contbr. articles to profl. jours. Fellow Royal Soc. Can. (fgn. sec. 1986-90), Mineral. Soc. Am., Soc. Econ. Geologists (v.p. N.Am. 1968-70), Canadian Acad. Engring.; mem. Can. Inst. Mining and Metallurgy (life mem., v.p. 1982-84), Assn. Profl. Engrs. Ont., Geol. Assn. Can., Can. Geosci. Coun. (pres. 1984), Rotary.

**SMITH, CHARLES HYDE,** librarian, historian; b. Winsted, Conn., Sept. 30, 1950; s. George Nelson and Hazel Munson Smith; m. Alesia Maltz, 1978 (div. 1984). BA in Geology, Wesleyan U., Middletown, Conn., 1972; MA in Geography, Ind. U., Bloomington, 1980; PhD in Geography, U. Ill., Champaign-Urbana, 1984; MLS, U. Pitts., 1995. Sci. libr., asst. prof. libr. pub. svcs. Western Ky. U., Bowling Green, 1995—2000, sci. libr., assoc. prof. libr. pub. svcs., 2000—04, sci. libr., prof. libr. pub. svcs., 2004—. Editor: (anthology and bibliography) Alfred Russel Wallace: An Anthology of His Shorter Writings, (anthology) Alfred Russel Wallace: Writings on Evolution 1843-1912; compiler/maintainer (informational website) Nineteenth Century Exploration of Australia, Early Classics in Biogeography, Distribution, and Diversity Studies: 1951-1975, Some Biogeographers, Evolutionists and Ecologists: Chrono-Biographical Sketches, Malvina Reynolds: Song Lyrics and Poems, The 111 Greatest (Anglo-American) Folk Music Artists, The Alfred Russel Wallace Page (Sci. Am. Best Five History of Sci. Websites, 2003), HERPFAUN, The Classical Music Navigator, MAMMFAUN, Early Classics in Biogeography, Distribution, and Diversity Studies: To 1950, author/maintainer (website) The Once and Future Wallace, compiler (bibliography) Biodiversity Studies: A Bibliographical Review (The Oberly award, 2001); author: (monographic analysis) Alfred Russel Wallace: The Evolution of an Evolutionist. Mem.: History of Sci. Soc., Soc. for the History of Natural History, Ky. Libr. Assn. Office: Western Kentucky University 1906 College Heights Blvd Bowling Green KY 42101 Office Phone: 270-745-6079. Business E-Mail: charles.smith@wku.edu.

**SMITH, CHARLES ISAAC,** geology educator; b. Hearne, Tex., Feb. 9, 1931; s. Walter Lee and Nellie Lucille (Clearwater) S.; m. Anita Lou Howell, Aug. 22, 1961; children: Lanita Maylene, James Emmett, Timothy Stephen, Sheila Nell. BS, Baylor U., 1952, MA, La. State U., 1955; PhD, U. Mich., 1966. Geologist Shell Devel. Co., Houston, 1955-60, 62-65; prof. geology U. Mich., Ann Arbor, 1965-77, chmn. dept., 1970-77; prof. geology U. Tex., Arlington, 1977-93, prof. emeritus, 1994—, chmn. dept., 1977-89, cons. geologist, 1993—. Contbr. articles to profl. jours. Home: 3814 Tridens Trl San Angelo TX 76904-7223 Office: Univ Tex Dept Geology Arlington TX 76019-0001

**SMITH, CHARLES JEFFREY,** radiologist, educator, research scientist; b. Independence, Mo., Apr. 24, 1969; s. Charles Wayne and Judith Ann Smith; m. Monica Kaye Meyer, Oct. 29, 2000; children: Caitlyn JoAnn, Morgyn Kay. PhD, U. Mo. Columbia, 1997. Rsch. asst. prof. internal medicine U. Mo. Columbia, 2003—; adj. prof. Nuc. Sci. and Engring. Inst., Columbia, 2003—; rsch. asst. prof. Mo. U. Rsch. Reactor, Columbia, 2004—; asst. prof. radiology U. Mo. Sch. Medicine, Columbia, 2004—; rsch. scientist Harry S. Truman Meml. Vet. Hosp., Columbia, 2005—. U.S. amb. IAEA, Vienna, 2002—; mem. editl. bd. Synthesis and Reactivity in Inorganic, Metal-Organic, and Nano-metal Chemistry, Phila., 2004—. Contbr. articles to profl. jours. Chairperson bd. trustees Trinity Luth. Ch., Columbia, 2005—; pres. Barclay Ridge Homeowners' Assn., Columbia, 2005—06. With U.S. Army, 1990—92. Recipient Biology Clin. and Basic Sci. award, World Fedn. Nuc. Medicine, 2002; grantee Preparation of Low-valent Tc/Re(I) Imaging/Therapeutic Agents, U.S. Dept. VA, 2005—08, Devel. of 3-Dimensional Fluorescence Molecular Tomography for In Vivo Fusion Molecular Imaging, NIH, 2005—07, Preparation of Low-valent Tc(I) Imaging Agents, 2004—05. Mem.: Internat. Soc. Radiopharma. Chemistry and Biology, Am. Chem. Soc. (assoc.), Soc. Nuc. Medicine (assoc.). R-Consevative. Achievements include patents in field. Home: 2011 Keystone Dr Columbia MO 65203 Office: Univ Mo Columbia Dept Radiology 1 Hospital Dr Columbia MO 65211 Home Fax: 573-882-1663; Office Fax: 573-882-1663. Business E-Mail: smithcj@health.missouri.edu.

**SMITH, CHARLES OLIVER,** retired engineer; b. Clinton, Mass., May 28, 1920; s. Oliver E. and Flora (Small) S.; m. Mary J. Boyle, Feb. 9, 1946; children: Mary J., Charles M., John P., Susan M., Peter G., Robert A., Katherine M. BS in Mech. Engring., Worcester Poly. Inst., 1941; SM, MIT, 1947, ScD in Metallurgy, 1951. Instr. mech. engring. Worcester Poly. Inst., 1941-43; instr., then asst. prof. Mass. Inst. Tech., 1946-51; research engr. Alcoa Research Lab., 1951-55, Oak Ridge Nat. Lab. 1955-65; prof. engring. U. Detroit, 1965-76, U. Nebr., 1976-81, Rose-Hulman Inst. Tech., 1981-86. Author: Product Liability: Are You Vulnerable?, Nuclear Reactor Materials, Science of Engineering Materials, Introduction to Reliability in Design; also numerous papers on materials, design, product liability, engring. edn. Served with USNR, 1943-46. Recipient St. George award Boy Scouts Am. Fellow ASME (Triodyne Safety award 1992, Machine Design award, 1993), Am. Soc. Engring. Edn. (Fred Merryfield award 1981); mem. AIME, Am. Soc. Metals, Sigma Xi, Tau Beta Pi, Pi Tau Sigma, Phi Kappa Theta. Home: 1717 Homewood Blvd Apt 156 Delray Beach FL 33445-6899

**SMITH, CHARLES WILLIAM,** social sciences educator; b. Providence; s. Joseph and Clara (Loitman) S.; m. Rita Cope, Sept. 3, 1963; children: Abigail Cope, Jonathan Cope. AB, Wesleyan U., 1960; MA, Brandeis U., 1966, PhD in Sociology, 1966. Instr. sociology Simmons Coll., Boston, 1964-65; from lectr. to assoc. prof. Queens Coll., Flushing, NY, 1965-71, from assoc. to prof. sociology, 1979—; grad. faculty Grad. Ctr. CUNY, 1986—. Vis. scholar Nuffield Coll., Oxford, Eng., 1979-80, Wesleyan U., Middletown, Conn., 1987-88; chair dept. sociology Queens Coll., Flushing, 1988-91, 97-00, acting dean of faculty social sci., 1991-92, dean faculty social sci., 1992-97; cons. auctions, 1986—. Author: Critique of Sociological Reasoning: An Essay in Philosophic Sociology, 1979, Auctions: The Social Construction of Values, 1989, Success and Survival on Wall Street: Understanding the Mind of the Market, 1999, Market Values Im American Higher Education, 2000; editor Jour. for Theory of Social Behavior, 1983—. Bd. dirs., pres. Cmty. Action Program of White Plains, N.Y., 1974-79; bd. trustees, v.p. Temple Israel Ctr. of White Plains, 1975-94; class agt., alumni activities Wesleyan U., Middletown, Conn., 1960—. Recipient FIPSE award, Dept. Edn., 1993—96, Ford Found. Diversity grant, 1990—93, 1996—98. Office: Queens Coll CUNY 65-30 Kissena Blvd Flushing NY 11367-1575 Office Phone: 718-997-2840. Business E-Mail: charles.smith@qc.cuny.edu.

**SMITH, CHARLES Z.,** retired state supreme court justice; b. Lakeland, Fla., Feb. 23, 1927; s. John R. and Eva (Love) S.; m. Eleanor Jane Martinez, Aug. 20, 1955; children: Carlos M., Michael O., Stephen P., Felica L. BS, Temple U., 1952; JD, U. Wash., 1955. Bar: Wash. 1955. Law clk. Wash. Supreme Ct., Olympia, 1955-56; dep. pros. atty., asst. chief criminal div. King County, Seattle, 1956-60; ptnr. Bianchi, Smith & Tobin, Seattle, 1960-61; spl. asst. to atty. gen. criminal div. U.S. Dept. Justice, Washington, 1961-64; judge criminal dept. Seattle Mcpl. Ct., 1965-66; judge Superior Ct. King County, 1966-73; former assoc. dean, prof. law U. Wash., 1973—83; justice Wash. Supreme Ct., Olympia, until 2002. Mem. adv. bd. NAACP, Seattle Urban League, Wash. State Literacy Coun., Boys Club, Wash. Citizens for Migrant Affairs, Medina Children's Svc., Children's Home Soc. Wash., Seattle Better

Bus. Bur., Seattle Foundation, Seattle Symphony Orch., Seattle Opera Assn., Community Svc. Ctr. for Deaf and Hard of Hearing, Seattle U., Seattle Sexual Assault Ctr., Seattle Psychoanalytic Inst., The Little Sch., Linfield Coll., Japanese Am. Citizens League, Kawabe Meml. Hous, Puget Counseling Ctr, Am. Cancer Soc., Hutchinson Cancer Rsch. Ctr., Robert Chinn Found.; pres. Am. Bapt. Chs. U.S.A., 1976-77, U.S. Commn. on Internat. Religious Freedom, 1999-2000. lt. col. ret. USMCR Mem. ABA, Am. Judicature Soc., Washington Bar Assn., Seattle-King County Bar Assn., Order of Coif, Phi Alpha Delta, Alpha Phi Alpha. Mailing: PO Box 146 Olympia WA 98507-0146 Office Phone: 360-273-0964. E-mail: czsmith@usa.net.

**SMITH, CHARLOTTE REED,** retired music educator; b. Eubank, Ky., Sept. 15, 1921; d. Joseph Lumpkin and Cornelia Elizabeth (Spenser) Reed; m. Walter Lindsay Smith, Aug. 24, 1949; children— Walter Lindsay IV, Elizabeth Reed. B.A. in Music, Tift Coll., 1941; M.A. in Mus. Theory, Eastman Sch. of Music, 1946; postgrad. Juilliard Sch., 1949. Asst. prof. theory Okla. Bapt. U., 1944-45, Washburn U., 1946-48; prof. music Furman U., Greenville, S.C., 1948-92; chmn. dept. music, 1987-92. Editor: Seven Penitential Psalms with Two Laudate Psalms, 1983; author: Manual of Sixteenth-Century Contrapuntal Style, 1989. Mem. Internat. Musicological Soc., Am. Musicological Soc., Soc. for Music Theory, AAUP (sec.-treas. Furman chpt. 1984-85), Nat. Fedn. Music Clubs, Pi Kappa Lambda. Republican. Baptist.

**SMITH, CHESTER,** broadcast executive; b. Mar. 29, 1930; s. Louis L. and Effie (Brown) Smith; m. Naomi L. Crenshaw, July 19, 1959 (div. 2002); children: Lauri, Lorna, Roxanne; m. Ann Lesley Huntington, Dec. 2003. Country western performer Capitol Records, TV, Radio, 1947-61, Sta. KLOC, Ceres-Modesto, Calif., 1963-81, KCBA-TV, Calif., 1963—81; owner, gen. ptnr. KCSO-TV, Modesto-Stockton-Sacramento, 1966—97, KCVU-TV, Paradise-Chico-Redding, Calif., 1986—, KBVU-TV, Eureka, 1990—, KXVU-LP, Chico, KNSO-TV, Merced-Fresno, 1996—2003, KCSO-LP, Sacramento, 1996—, KRVU-LP, Redding, 1997—, Univision, Chico, KUCO-LP, K46HI, Redding, K08NH, Oroville, K38FQ, Anderson and Central Valley, K17EH, Eureka, K31EW, K33FN, K52FK, K67GU, KFBI-LP, Medford, Oreg., K14LG, K41ID, Klamak Falls, Oreg., 2006—. Original rec. Wait A Little Longer Please Jesus in Country Music Hall of Fame, Nashville, 1955, albums California Blend (with Merle Haggard), 2001, Captured by Love (with Ann-Lesley), 2005. Inductee Western Swing Hall of Fame, Sacramento, 1988, Nat. Traditional Country Music Assn. Hall of Fame, 2003; recipient cert. of recognition for 50 years of cmty. svc. Calif. Assembly, 1997, Lifetime Achievement award Modesto Area Musicians Assn., 2002, Broadcaster of Yr. Calif. Broadcasters Assn. 2003. Mem.: Calif. Broadcasters Assn. Republican. Mem. Christian Ch. Address: Sainte Partners II L P PO Box 4159 Modesto CA 95352-4159 E-mail: csmith@sainte.tv.

**SMITH, CHRISTOPHER (KIT SMITH),** lawyer; b. Evanston, Ill., Nov. 12, 1947; AB, Wabash Coll., 1969; JD, U. Kans., 1972. Bar: Kans. 1972, DC 1973, US Supreme Ct. 1976. Ptnr. Arent Fox Kintner Plotkin & Kahn, Washington, mng. ptnr., 1997—2002; ptnr. Sonnenschein Nath & Rosenthal LLP, Washington, 2003—. Office: Sonnenschein Nath & Rosenthal LLP Ste 600, E Tower 1301 K St NW Washington DC 20015 Office Phone: 202-408-9231. Office Fax: 202-408-6399. Business E-Mail: kitsmith@sonnenschein.com.

**SMITH, CHRISTOPHER ALLEN,** information technology executive, financial executive; b. Rockford, Ill., Nov. 16, 1961; s. Robert Lee and Martha Ann (Moody) S.; m. Mary G. Meany, Apr. 13, 1991. BA, postgrad., Ind. U., 1983, Golden Gate U., San Francisco, 1986—87; MA, U. Phoenix, Ariz., 2003. Rates analyst North American Van Lines, Ft. Wayne, Ind., 1984-85; mgr., investor rels. BRAE Corp., San Francisco, 1985-87; fin. analyst CIS Corp., San Francisco, 1987-89; dir., corp. devel. Affiliated Computer Systems, Inc., San Francisco, 1989-96; v.p. Sci. Applications Internat. Corp., San Francisco, 1996—. Alumni Dept. of Def. Joint Civilian Orientation Conf. Contbr. articles to profl. jours. Vol. Rep. Party, Foster City, Calif., 1988; apptd. dir. Pvt. Industry Coun. Contra Costa County. With USMCR, 1982-83. Mem. Equipment Leasing Assn. Am. (Jour. award 1991), Ind. U. Alumni Assn. Republican. Roman Catholic. Avocations: writing, photography, gardening. Office: Sci Applications Internat Corp 2200 Powell St Ste 920 Emeryville CA 94608-1895 Office Phone: 510-652-7302 ext. 12. Business E-Mail: christopher.a.smith-2@saic.com.

**SMITH, CHRISTOPHER HENRY,** congressman; b. Rahway, NJ, Mar. 4, 1953; s. Bernard Henry and Katherine Joan (Hall) Smith; m. Marie Hahn, July 2, 1977; children: Melissa, Christopher, Michael, Elyse. Student, Worcester Coll. Eng., 1973-74; BA in Bus. Adminstrn., Trenton State Coll., NJ, 1975. Exec. dir. NJ Right to Life Com., Inc., 1976-78; dir. instl. sales Leisure Unlimited Inc., Woodbridge, NJ, 1978-80; legis. agt. NJ Gen. Assembly, 1979; mem. US Congress from 4th NJ dist., 1981—, vice chair internat. rels. com., co-chair security and cooperation in Europe commn., co-chair Pro-Life Caucus. US rep. to UN internat. conf. on immunizing world's children. Active in human rights movements Romania, China, former Soviet Union, Vietnam Named Legislator of Yr. VFW, Internat. Assn. Chiropractors, JWV of Am., 1996, Leader of the Yr., NJ State Postal Workers Union, 2002, William Wilberforce award, 2002; recipient Leader for Peace award Peace Corps, George (Buck) Gillispie Congl. award, Meritorious Svc. Blinded Am. Vets. Found., 2003. Mem.: Nat. Fedn. Ind. Bus. Republican. Roman Cath. Office: US Ho Reps 2373 Rayburn Ho Office Bldg Washington DC 20515-3004 Office Phone: 202-225-3765.*

**SMITH, CHRISTOPHER T.,** environmental health officer; BS Environ. Health Sci., Ea. Ky. U., Richmond, 2001; MPH, Fla. Internat. U., Miami, 2004. Registered Environ. Health Specialist Ky, 2006. Regulatory ops. officer US FDA, Rockville, Md., 2004—. Lt. US Pub. Health Svc., 2001. Scholar Environ. Health, Ky Assn. Milk, Food, and Environ. Sanitarians, 2000. Mem.: Nat. Environ. Health Assn.

**SMITH, CLAIRE,** chef; Grad., Calif. Culinary Acad., San Francisco; grad. in art and art history, Rice U. Chef Green and Oliveto, San Francisco Bay area, The Daily Review Cafe, Houston, 1994—. Office: 3412 W Lamar Houston TX 77019

**SMITH, CLARE,** art appraiser; Grad, Oxford Univ., Courtauld Inst. Art, London. Specialist, Victorian picture dept. Christie's, NYC, 1999, now specialist, sporting art, also US rep. for British & Irish art. Project coord., sale, Forbes collection, Victorian art Christie's, 2003. Office: Christie's 20 Rockefeller Plz New York NY 10020 Office Phone: 212-636-2084. Office Fax: 212-636-4925. Business E-Mail: claresmith@christies.com.

**SMITH, CLYDE CURRY,** historian, educator; b. Hamilton, Ohio, Dec. 16, 1929; s. Charles Clyde and Mabel Ethel Ola (Curry) S.; m. Ellen Marie Gormsen, June 13, 1953; children: Harald Clyde, Karen Margaret Boettge. BA in Physics cum laude and MS, Miami U., Oxford, Ohio, 1951; BDiv. U. Chgo., 1954, MA, 1961, PhD, 1968; DLitt honoris causa, Fairfax U., 1999. Ordained to ministry Christian Ch. (Disciples of Christ), 1954. Exec. asst. to dean Disciples Div. House, Chgo., 1956-57; lectr. in O.T., Univ. Coll. U. Chgo., 1957; asst. prof. St. John's Coll. U. Manitoba, Winnipeg, Can., 1958-63; instr. Brandeis U., Waltham, Mass., 1963-65; prof. ancient history and religions U. Wis., River Falls, 1965-90, prof. emeritus, 1990—. Vis. prof. religious studies Culver-Stockton Coll., Canton, Mo., 1990, U. Newcastle-upon-Tyne, Eng., 1992-94; vis. lectr. div., Edge Hill Coll. of Edn., Ormskirk, Eng., 1970-71; postdoctoral fellow Johns Hopkins U., Balt., 1977; NEH fellow-in-residence U. Calif., Santa Barbara, 1978-79; vis. rsch. fellow, lectr. religious studies U. Aberdeen, Scotland, 1980, 85-86; sr. acad. visitor Wolfson Coll., Cambridge U., 2001—; scholar-in-residence Overseas Ministries Study Ctr., New Haven, 2004—. Contbr. articles to profl. jours. Mem. Pierce County Hist. Assn., River Falls, 1965—, Wis. Dems. 1965—, Dem. Nat. Com. 1983—; charter mem. Sci. Mus. of Minn., St. Paul, 1973—; charter assoc. Libr. of Congress, 1994—; founding mem. River Falls Cmty. Arts Base,

1996—, Kinnikinnic River Land Trust, 1996—; bd. dirs. River Falls Libr. Found., 1997—. Recipient Gov.'s Spl. award State of Wis., 1990, several grants. Mem. Assn. Ancient Historians, Can. Soc. Ch. History (founder, treas. 1960-63), N.Am. Patristics Soc., Can. Soc. for Mesopotamian Studies, Soc. Old Testament Study (Gt. Britain), Soc. for Promotion Roman Studies of London, Hellenic Soc. London, Brit. Sch. Archaeology in Iraq, Brit. Inst. Archaeology in Ankara, Internat. Soc. Anglo-Saxonists, Oriental Inst. U. Chgo., Phi Beta Kappa. Democrat. Avocations: outerspace, battleships, dinosaurs. Home: 2642 Golf View Dr River Falls WI 54022-7502 Office Phone: 715-425-6383. *We can begin thought with the assumption that there is a world which knows neither origin nor end but which includes us; we can conclude with the affirmations that there was a "when" whatever is was not, and that whatever is will with time cease to be. Our concern then can be to enhance value and empower others, especially those who follow.*

**SMITH, CLYDE RAY,** dean; b. Bassett, Va, Apr. 21, 1935; s. William Henry and Ava I. (Roberson) S.; m. Phyllis Jane Watkins, Mar. 25, 1959; children: Anthony William, Cheryl Ann, Theresa Jane. BA, Bridgewater Coll., 1956; MBA, U. Va., 1958; D in Bus. Adminstrn. (hon.), Bridgewater Coll., 2004. Instr. U. Va. - Darden, Charlottesville, Va., 1961-64, asst. prof., 1964-67, assoc. prof., 1967-72, prof., 1972—, assoc. dean MBA program, 1972-94, assoc. dean exec. edn., 1994-97, interim dean, 1997-98; exec. dir. Darden Sch. Found., 1998—2003; prof. emeritus U. Va. - Darden, Charlottesville, Va., 2003—. Adminstrv. dir. Inst. Chartered Fin. Analysts, Charlottesville, 1962-69; bd. trustees Bridgewater Coll. Co-author: (books) Executive's Guide to Mgmt. Accounting and Control Sys., 1998, Fin. Accounting for Mgmt., 1981. Capt. (res.) US Army, 1958-68. Named Disting. Alumnus Bridgewater Coll., Va., 1991. Mem. AICPA, Am. Real Estate Soc., Colonade Club, Farmington Country Club, Raven Soc., Beta Gamma Sigma, Omicron Delta Kappa. Home: 39 Canterbury Rd Charlottesville VA 22903-4700 Office: Univ Va - Darden Sch PO Box 6550 Charlottesville VA 22906-6550 Office Phone: 434-924-4799. E-Mail: crs6n@virginia.edu.

**SMITH, CONSTANCE,** retired elementary school educator; b. Bklyn., Jan. 29, 1966; d. Edward and Constance Byrnes; m. Patrick Smith, Aug. 29, 1987. BA, U. SC, Spartanburg, 1991; M, U. SC, Columbia, 1999. Cert. elem. edn., mid. sch. sci., mid. sch. social studies SC. Tchr. New Prospect Elem., Inman, SC, 1993—2004. Home: PO Box 214 Landrum SC 29356 Personal E-mail: constancesmith@alltel.net.

**SMITH, CRAIG R.,** health products executive; m. Cynthia Smith; 2 children. BA, Univ. So. Calif. With Owens & Minor, Glen Allen, Va., 1989—, divsn. v.p., group v.p., sr. v.p. distbn. and info. sys., 1989—95, exec. v.p., COO, 1995—99, pres., COO 1999—2005, pres., CEO, 2005—. Bd. mem. Inst. for Diversity in Health Mgmt., Health Ind. Dist. Assn.; mem. bd. vis. St. Gertrude High Sch., Richmond; mem. bus. council Va. Mus. Fine Arts; bd. dir. Greater Richmond YMCA. Office: Owens & Minor 4800 Cox Rd Glen Allen VA 23060-6294*

**SMITH, CRAIG R.,** lawyer; BS in Civil Engring., Manhattan Coll., 1992; MS in Environmental Engring., U. Ill., 1994; JD, NYU, 1997. Bar: Mass. 1997. Principal Fish & Richardson, Boston. Mem. bd. dirs. Greater Boston Legal Svcs. Named a Super Lawyer-Rising Star, Boston Mag., 2005; recipient Norman S. Ostrow Moot Ct. award, 1996. Mem.: ABA. Office: Fish & Richardson 225 Franklin St Boston MA 02110-2804 Office Phone: 617-542-5070. Office Fax: 617-542-8906.

**SMITH, CRAIG RICHEY,** thoracic surgeon; b. Cleve., Nov. 17, 1948; AB, Williams Coll., 1970; MD, Case Western Res. U., 1977. Diplomate Am. Bd. Thoracic Surgery, Am. Bd. Surgery. Intern U. Rochester (N.Y.) Hosp., 1977-78, resident, 1978-82; fellow in cardiothoracic surgery Columbia-Presbyn. Med. Ctr., N.Y.C, 1982-84, chief, divsn. cardiothoracic surgery N.Y.C., 1996—; prof. surgery Columbia U. Coll. Physicians & Surgeons, 1997—2001, Calvin F. Barber prof. surgery, 2001—. Assoc. prof. surgery Columbia U. Hosp., N.Y.C. Mem. AMA, ACS, Am. Assn. Thoracic Surgery, Am. Heart Assn., Am. Surgical Assn., Internat. Soc. for Heart Transplantation, Am. Coll. Cardiology, NY Soc. for Thoracic Surgery, Assn. for Academic Surgery. Office: 177 Fort Washington Ave New York NY 10032-3713

**SMITH, CULLEN,** lawyer; b. Waco, Tex., May 31, 1925; s. Curtis Cullen and Elizabeth (Brient) S.; m. Laura Risher Dossett, Mar. 6, 1948; children: Sallie Smith Wright, Alethea Risher Smith Gilbert, Elizabeth Brient Smith. Student, Emory U., 1943-44, Duke U., 1944; BBA, Baylor U., 1948, JD, 1950. Bar: Tex. 1950. Ptnr. firm Smith, McIlheran & Smith, Weslaco, Tex., 1950-53, Naman, Howell, Smith & Lee LLP, Waco, 1953—. Lectr. law Baylor U. Sch. Law, 1964-72 Contbr. articles to legal publs. Mem. standing com. Episcopal Diocese of Tex., 1960-63, 74-75; trustee Episcopal Theol. Sem. of S.W., 1962-67; mem. Waco City Coun., 1983-86; chmn. bd. Vanguard Sch., 1975; bd. dirs. G.H. Pape Found., 1993-94; bd. dirs., vice chmn. Tex. Ctr. for Legal Ethics and Professionalism, 1994-99; mem. adv. coun. Baylor U. Coll. Arts and Scis., 1998-2003. 1st lt. USMCR, 1943-46. Named One of 5 Outstanding Young Texans Tex. Jr. C. of C., 1957, Baylor Lawyer of Yr., 1980; recipient Disting. Alumnus award Waco Ind. Sch. Dist. Edn. Found., 2002. Fellow Am. Bar Found., Tex. Bar Found. (chmn. bd. 1973-74, 50 Yr. Lawyer award 2000), fellow Coll. of Law Practice Mgmt.; mem. ABA, standing com. econs. law practice 1965-69, chmn. spl. com. on law book pub. practices 1970-72, chmn. gen. practice sect. 1973-74, mem. house of dels. 1974-81), Am. Law Firm Assn. (mem. 1989-90), Waco-McLennan County Bar Assn. (pres. 1956-57), Mont. Bar Assn. (hon.), State Bar Tex. (pres. jr. bar 1957-58, chmn. profl. econs. com. 1959-61, chmn. spl. com. on revision Tex. Canons Ethics 1969-71, dir. 1971-74, pres. 1978-79), Philos. Soc. Tex., Baylor U. Law Alumni Assn. (pres. 1962-63), Order of Coif, Delta Sigma Phi, Phi Delta Phi, Am. Inns Ct. (master), Ridgewood Country Club (pres. 1965), Hedonia Club (pres. 1957), Rotary. Avocation: photography. Home: Oak Grove Farm 447 Meandering Way China Spring TX 76633-2905 Office: Naman Howell Smith & Lee LLP Tex Ctr PO Box 1470 Waco TX 76703-1470 Office Phone: 254-755-4100.

**SMITH, CYNTHIA JANESE,** science educator; b. Chgo., Aug. 23, 1950; d. James Edward and Margie Maxine Duke; m. Jerome Lyaton Smith, Aug. 30, 1991; children: Twana, Shariff. BS in Edn., Chgo. State U., 1973. Std. elem. tchg. cert. Ill., std. secondary tchg. cert. Ill. Home econs. tchr. Archdiocese Parochial Schs., Chgo., 1976—82; sci. tchr. Kohn Sch. Chgo. Pub. Schs., 1975—76, tchr. 6th grade Kohn Sch., 1982—87, tchr. 7th and 8th grade sci. Lawndale Sch., 1987—93, tchr. 7th and 8th grade sci. Park Manor Sch., 1993—2002, tchr. environ. sci. Hyde Park H.S., 2002—. Named Exemplary Sci. Tchr., Chgo. Pub. Schs., 2000; recipient Blum-Kovler Tchr. award, U. Chgo., 2004—05. Mem.: Nat. Sci. Tchrs. Assn. Lutheran. Avocations: computers, sewing. Office: Hyde Park H S 6220 S Stony Island Ave Chicago IL 60637

**SMITH, CYNTHIA S.,** writer; b. NYC, Dec. 29, 1934; d. Harry and Sarah (Cohen) Sharfin; m. David Smith, May 21, 1953 (dec. May 1985); 1 child, Hillary Smith Pannier. BA, Hunter Coll, N.Y.C. 1954. Advt. dir. Joshua Meier Co., Inc., N.Y.C., 1955; pres. C/D Smith Advt., Inc., Rye, 1966-01; assoc. adj. prof. Mgmt. Inst. NYU 1992—. Author: How to Get Big Results from a Small Advertising Budget, 1978, Doctors' Wives, 1981, Step by Step Advertising, 1985, Seven Levels of Marriage, 1988, Why Women Shouldn't Marry, 1990, What Has She Got?, 1995, Woman's Guide to Starting Business, 1996, Noblesse Oblige, 1996, Misleading Ladies, 1997, Impolite Society, 1997, Silver and Guilt, 1998, Royals and Rogues, 1998. Mem. Authors' Guild, Mystery Writers of Am., Sisters in Crime, Internat. Assn. Crime Writers. Avocations: tennis, chorale singing. Personal E-mail: cynthiassmith@verizon.net.

**SMITH, D. BROOKS,** federal judge; b. 1951; BA, Franklin and Marshall Coll., 1973; JD, Dickinson Sch. Law, 1976. Pvt. practice Jubelirer, Carothers, Krier, Halpern & Smith, Altoona, Pa., 1976-84, mng. ptnr., 1981—83; judge Ct. Common Pleas of Blair County, Pa., 1984-88, U.S. Dist. Ct. (we. dist.)

Pa., 1988—2002, chief judge, 2001—02; judge U.S. Ct. Appeals 3d Cir., 2002—. Asst. dist. atty. Blair County, part-time, 1977-79, spl. prosecutor, 1981-83, dist. atty. part-time, 1983-84; instr. Pa. State U., Altoona campus, 1977—, St. Francis Coll., 1986—; adv. com. on criminal rules U.S. Jud. Conf., 1993-99. Trustee St. Francis Coll., 1992—2004, Phila. U., 2005—. Mem. Am. Law Inst., Pa. Bar Assn., Am. Judicature Soc., Pa. Soc., Amen Corner, Blair County Game, Fish and Forestry Assn., Fed. Judges Assn. (bd. dirs. 1993-97, 2002—), Inns of Ct., Allegheny County Bar Assn., Pi Gamma Mu. Office: Allegheny Profl Ctr 1798 Old Rte 220 N Ste 203 Duncansville PA 16635*

**SMITH, D(AISY) MULLETT,** publisher; b. Washington, Aug. 17, 1948; d. Gordon Hunt and Suzanne Myrick (Mullett) Smith. BA, Am. U., 1970; cert. computer programming, U. So. Calif., Arlington, Va., 1986; cert. in records mgmt., Assn. Records Mgrs. Am., Prairie Village, Kans., 1987. Christian Sci. practitioner The First Ch. of Christ, Scientist, Boston, 1970-86; clk. Fifth Ch. of Christ, Scientist, Washington, 1971-74; Christian Sci. campus counsellor The Am. U., Washington, 1976-81; editor, computer specialist, desktop pub. Mullett-Smith Press, Washington, 1984-89, owner, pub., 1989—, music copyist, pub. on computer, 1990—, web weaver, 1996—, pub., typesetting, 2004—; ptnr. H. James Enterprises and JoJames. Cons., spkr. in field; started webhosting svc. partnership with H. James Enterprises and Bluebirdartworks.com. Author: AB Mullett, His Relevance in American Architecture, 1990 (Printers award 1990); editor: AB Mullett, Architect Engineer 1862-90, 1985; contbr. articles to profl. jours. Participant White House Conf. on Children, 1970; active Save Pioneer Post Office, Portland, Oreg., 1996—; fundraising com. U.S. Treasury Bill Restoration Fund, 1998-2000; libr. Christian Sci. Reading Rm., 1999-2002; renovator TH-7, 2003, Hist. Townhouse Wheat Row, 2003-06; commrs. Jefferson County, W.Va., 2003; interviewer PBS radio, saving Jefferson County Jail. Recipient Key to the City, Mayor Lincoln, Nebr., 1989. Mem. Nat. Soc. Arts and Letters (editor/pub. directory 1971-2006, treas. 1988-90, web weaver 1996—, web host 2006—), Nat. Trust for Hist. Preservation, Assn. Records Mgrs. and Adminstrs., Assn. for Info. and Image Mgmt. Internat., U.S. Treasury Hist. Assn., U.S. Capitol Hist. Soc. Avocations: art, design, guitar, windsurfing, computers. Office Phone: 202-479-4333. Business E-Mail: mspress@mullett-smithpress.com.

**SMITH, DAN,** chef; b. NYC; life ptnr. Steve McDonagh; 1 adopted child, Nate. Actor; model; chef Francine Maroukian; co-founder The Hearty Boys catering co., Bethel, Maine, Chgo., The Cafe at Hearty Boys, Lakeview, Ill., 2003—, HB restaurant, The Cafe at Hearty Boys, Lakeview, Ill., 2005—. Co-host Party Line with the Hearty Boys; co-author: Solving the Run of the Mill; featured in Chgo. Mag., guest appearances on ABC, NBC, CBS, FOX, CLTV. Achievements include co-winning The Next Food Network Star with ptnr. Steve McDonagh, 2005. Office: The Hearty Boys Caterers 3404 N Halsted Chicago IL 60657 Office Phone: 773-244-9866. Office Fax: 773-244-8088.*

**SMITH, DAN F.,** oil industry executive; With Atlantic Richfield Co, Los Angeles, Calif., 1967—88; exec. v.p., CFO Lyondell Chem. Co., Houston, dir., 1988—, COO, 1993—96, pres., 1994—, CEO, 1996—. Bd. dir. Cooper Industries. Office: Lyondell Chemical Co 1221 McKinney St Ste 700 Houston TX 77010*

**SMITH, DANIEL,** oncologist, gynecologist; b. Cushing, Okla., Feb. 12, 1946; MD, Harvard Med. Sch., 1972. Diplomate Am. Bd. Surgery, Am. Bd. Obstetrics and Gynecology with subspecialty in gynecologic oncology. Intern Mass. Gen. Hosp., Boston, 1972—73, resident, 1973—75, 1978, L.A. County/U. So. Calif. Med. Ctr., L.A., 1975—78; fellow Meml. Sloan-Kettering Cancer Ctr., 1979—81; oncologist, ob-gyn. Columbia Presbyn. Med. Ctr., N.Y.C., 1981—2003; assoc. prof. ob-gyn. Columbia Coll. Physicians and Surgeons. Office: 20 Prospect Ave Ste 703 Hackensack NJ 07601 Office Phone: 201-996-5373. Business E-Mail: dsmith@humed.com.

**SMITH, DANIEL C.,** dean, finance educator; B in bus. adminstrn., U. Toledo, 1980, M in bus. adminstrn., 1982; PhD in bus. adminstrn., U. Pitts., 1988. Asst. prof. U. Wis. Sch. Bus., Madison; asst. to assoc. prof. U. Pitts. Joesph M. Katz Grad. Sch. Bus.; joined faculty Kelley Sch. Bus., Ind. U., 1996, MBA program chair, 1998—2001, chair mktg. dept., 2002—03, Clare W. Barker chair mktg., 2002—, assoc. dean academics, 2003—04, interim dean, 2004—05, dean, 2005—. Mem. editl. rev. bd. Jour. Mktg., Jour. Acad. Mktg. Sci., Jour. Competitive Intelligence, Jour. Personal Selling and Sales Mgmt., Jour. Market Focused Mgmt. Avocation: fly fishing. Office: Ind Univ Kelley Sch Bus 1309 E Tenth St Bloomington IN 47405 Office Phone: 812-855-8489. Business E-Mail: dansmith@indiana.edu.

**SMITH, DANIEL CLIFFORD,** lawyer; b. Cin., Aug. 9, 1936; s. Clifford John and Vivian Aileen (Stone) S.; m. Carroll Cunningham; children: Edward, Andrew, Scott. BS, Ariz. State U., 1960; postgrad., George Washington U., 1961—62; JD, Am. U., 1965. Bar: D.C. 1965, U.S. Ct. Appeals (D.C. cir.) 1966, U.S. Ct. Appeals (Fed. cir.) 1983, U.S. Dist. Ct. D.C. 1966, Va. 1967, U.S. Supreme Ct. 1969, U.S. Ct. Appeals (4th, 5th, 6th, 7th, 9th and 11th cirs.), U.S. Ct. Claims, U.S. Ct. Customs and Patent Appeals, U.S. Tax Ct. Assoc. Alpern & Feissner, Washington, 1963-66; atty. FTC, Washington, 1966-70; ptnr. Arent, Fox, Kintner, Plotkin & Kahn, Washington, 1970-93, Canfield & Smith, Washington, 1993—. Pres., dir. Country Pl. Citizens Assn., Inc., 1974-77; bd. dirs. Sea Watch Condominium, Ocean City, Md., 1978—, treas., 1982-86, pres. 1986—; active Supreme Ct. Hist. Soc., The Federalist Soc., Smithsonian Inst. Assocs., Ariz. State Soc. Served with USMC. Mem. D.C. Bar Assn. (bd. dirs. 1974-76, common protection com. 1972-74, chmn. D.C. affairs sect. 1975-76), Va. State Bar Assn., Fed. Bar Assn., Assn. Trial Lawyers Am., Nat. Field Selling Assn. (gen. counsel), Am. State C. Alumni Assn., Rotary Club (pres. 1987-88, 96-97), Optimist (pres. 1972-73), Internat. Town and Country Club (dir. 1969-73), Masons, Delta Theta Phi. Office: Canfield & Smith Ste 800 910 17th St NW Washington DC 20006-2606

**SMITH, DANIEL ELON,** physical education educator; b. Van Nuys, Calif., Nov. 14, 1952; s. Elon Vernielle and Eileen Palmer S.; m. Wendy Willison, Aug. 4, 1973; children: Spencer Daniel, Calrk Elon, Torrey Camielle. BS, Brigham Young U., 1974, MS, 1975; PhD, U. Ill., 1987. Cert. sport psychology cons. Instr., basketball coach Placerita Jr. High Sch., Newhall, Calif., 1975-76; phys. edn. faculty supr., asst. basketball coach Coll. of the Canyons, Valencia, Calif., 1975-76; phys. edn. instr./volleyball coach Rio Hondo Coll., Whittier, Calif., 1976-77; men's volleyball coach Calif. State Polytechnic U., Pomona, Calif., 1977; phys. edn. instr., basketball coach Brigham Young U./Hawaii Campus, Laie, 1977-80; tchg. asst., asst. basketball coach U. Ill., Champaign, 1980-83, athletic dept. sport psychologist, 1983-86; assoc. prof. phys. edn. SUNY, Brockport, 1987—. Cons. Buffalo Sabres Profl. Hockey Team, N.Y., 1989—, Ind. Pacers Profl. Basketball Team, Indpls., 1992-93, Chgo. White Sox Profl. Baseball Team, 1985-86, Chgo. Bulls Profl. Basketball Team, 1985; del. People to People Internat., Moscow, Leningrad; toured East Germany and Soviet Union as sport psychologist. Contbg. author: Mental Imagery, 1991, Competitive Anxiety in Sport, 1990; contbr. articles to profl. jours. Varsity Boy Scout Leader, Boy Scouts Am., Brockport, 1989—. Named to Outstanding Young Men of Am., 1984; selected mem. Citizen Ambassador Program, Leipzig, Germany, 1989. Mem. AAHPERD, Assn. Advancement of Applied Sport Psychology. Mem. Lds Ch. Avocations: running, volleyball, golf. Office: Dept Phys Edn SUNY Brockport NY 14420

**SMITH, DAVID,** music educator; b. Newton, Kans., June 17, 1962; s. Bobby Smith, Twyla and Roy Rumfelt (Stepfather); m. Audry Johnson, June 2, 2001. AA with honors, Cowley County CC, 1984; BS, S.W. Bapt. U., 1986; MSc, Pittsburg State U., 1990; M in Ch. Music, Midwestern Bapt. Theol. Sem., 1997. Cert. in Microsoft Word 2003, 2006, in Microsoft Power Point 2003, 2006; Voice Music Tchr. Music Tchrs. Nat. Assn., 2004. Admissions counselor, adj. instr. music Cowley County CC, Arkansas City, Kans., 1990—91;

instr. vocal music Highland CC, Kans., 1992—94, Ctrl. CC, Columbus, Nebr., 2000—01; min. music edn. First Bapt. Ch., Kearney, Mo., 1994—95; coll. coord. Blue River CC, Blue Springs, Mo., 1995—2000; grad. tchg. asst. U. Kans., Lawrence, 1997—2000; instr. music Neosho County CC, Chanute, Kans., 2001—. Mem. First Bapt. Ch., Independence, Kans., 2005—. Named an Outstanding Music Grad., S.W. Bapt. U., 1986; recipient Excellence award, Nat. Inst. Staff and Orgnl. Devel., 2006. Mem.: Coll. Music Soc., Music Tchrs. Nat. Assn., Am. Choral Dirs. Assn., Music Educators Nat. Conf. R-Conservative. Avocations: reading, golf, travel. Office: Neosho County Community Coll 800 W 14th Chanute KS 66720 Business E-Mail: dksmith@neosho.edu.

**SMITH, DAVID A.,** medical services executive; BS, Univ. No. Fla. CPA. Public acctg., 1983—87; regional mgr., gen. mgr., sales mgr. and opers. mgr. PSS/World Medical Inc., Jacksonville, Fla., 1987—93, v.p., 1992—96, chmn. bd. dirs., 1993—, exec. v.p., 1996—2000, pres., 2000—, CFO, 1992—2002, CEO, 2002—. Mem. exec. bd. Health Industry Distributors Assn. Office: PSS World Med Inc 4345 Southpoint Blvd Jacksonville FL 32216*

**SMITH, DAVID BURNELL,** lawyer, state legislator; b. Charleston, W.Va., Apr. 8, 1941; s. Ernest Dayton and Nellie Dale (Tyler) S.; m. Rita J. Hughes, Sept. 25, 1967. BA, U. Charleston, 1967; JD, U. Balt., 1972; MJS, U. Nev., 1995. Bar: Colo. 1972, Md. 1972, U.S. Supreme Ct. 1980, Ariz. 1983, U.S. Dist. Ct. Md. 1972, U.S. Dist. Ct. Colo. 1972, U.S. Ct. Appeals (4th Cir.) 1972, U.S. Ct. Appeals (9th cir. 1972, U.S. Ct. Appeals (10th cir.) 1983. Sales rep. Gulf Oil, Washington, 1967-72; pvt. practice Littleton, Colo., 1972-83, Glendale, Ariz., 1983-86, Phoenix, 1986-88, Scottsdale, Ariz., 1988—; mem. Ariz. Ho. of Reps., 2005—, vice-chmn. judiciary com., 2005—. Pro-tempore judge Wickenburg Mcpl. Ct., 1986—; presiding judge Peoria (Ariz.) Mcpl. Ct., 1987-94, Cave Creek Mcpl. Ct., 1995-98. Appeared as actor in movie Dead Girls Don't Tango, 1990. V.p. South Jefferson County Reps., Lakewood, Colo., 1979, pres., 1990; candidate Dist. 6 for Congress; 2nd vice-chmn. Dist. 7 Rep. Party, pres. Ariz. Rep. Assembly Dist. 28, bd. dirs. Scottsdale (Ariz.) Constitution Commemorative Com., 1995-2003, pres., 2002-; elected Ariz. Ho. of Reps., Dist. 7, 2005—. With USCG, 1959-66. Mem. ATLA, ABA (vice-chmn. family law 1983), Nat. Assn. Criminal Lawyers, Am. Judicature Soc., Nat. Assn. Criminal Def. Attys., Ariz. Magistrates Assn., Colo. Bar Assn., Ariz. Bar Assn., Scottsdale (Ariz.) Bar Assn. (sec. 2001-2002, v.p. 2002-2003, pres., 2003-2004), Md. Bar Assn., Colo. Trial Lawyers Assn., Maricopa County Bar Assn., Scottsdale Bar Assn. (pres. 1994—, pres., 1999—, pres.), Masons, Shriners, Elks. Home: PO Box 5145 36418 N Wildflower Rd Carefree AZ 85377-5145 Office: 4310 N 75th St Scottsdale AZ 85251-3578 Office Phone: 480-990-7500. Personal E-mail: dbsdbsatty@yahoo.com.

**SMITH, DAVID CLARK,** research scientist; b. Owensboro, Ky., Feb. 8, 1937; s. Robert Emmitt and Mary Margaret (Flaherty) S.; m. Kathleen Sue Kohne, June 27, 1964; children: Christine, Jennifer, Paula. BSME, U. Dayton, 1959; MS, Northwestern U., 1961, PhD, postgrad., Northwestern U., 1964. Rsch. scientist United Techs. Rsch. Ctr., East Hartford, Conn., 1965-67, sr. rsch. scientist, 1967-68, prin. scientist, 1968-80, mgr. exptl. optics, 1980-82, mgr. optical physics, 1982-91; cons. DCS Assoc., Inc., 1992-99, Conn. Tech. Assocs., 1992—, DCS Lasers/Optics LLC, 1997—. Author: (with G. Bekefi) Principles of Laser Plasmas, 1976; contbr. articles to profl. jours. Chmn. Youth and Family Resource Ctr. Commn., 1979-84; bd. dirs. Glastonbury A Better Chance, Conn., 1970-78; mem. Glastonbury Energy Com., 1979-83; tutor YMCA Read to Succeed Literacy; vol. Habitat for Humanity. Recipient Outstanding Svc. award, 1985, Glastonbury, Conn., United Techs. Outstanding Svc. award, 1987; named Man of Yr., Friends of Glastonbury Youth, 1984. Fellow: Am. Soc. Laser Medicine and Surgery; mem.: SPIE, IEEE, AIAA, AAAS, Am. Phys. Soc., Sigma Xi. Democrat. Roman Catholic. Achievements include patentee in field. Home: 514 Main St Old Saybrook CT 06475 Office: DCS Lasers & Optics LLC PO Box 167 East Glastonbury CT 06025-0167 Office Phone: 860-267-7547. E-mail: kohne@aol.com.

**SMITH, DAVID COVENTRY,** lawyer; BA cum laude, Wake Forest Univ., 1981, JD cum laude, 1984. Bar: NC 1984, Maine 1986, US Dist. Ct. (ea., we., middle dist. NC), US Ct. Appeals (4th cir.). Ptnr., bus. litigation Kilpatrick Stockton LLP, Winston-Salem, NC. Co-author (& co-editor): North Carolina Trial and Appeal, 1998; contbr. articles to profl. jours. Bd. dirs. Legal Aid Soc., Children's Law Ctr. Named NC Lawyer of the Year, Legal Aid Soc. N.W. NC, 2001—04, Best Lawyers in Am. Bus. Litig., 2004—06; named to NC Legal Elite, 2006. Mem.: NC Bar Assn. (Commendation pub. svc. 2005), NC Acad. Trial Lawyers, Forsyth County Bar Assn., Am. Inns of Ct. Barrister. Office: Kilpatrick Stockton LLP 1001 W 4th St Winston Salem NC 27101-2400 Office Phone: 336-607-7392. Office Fax: 336-734-2611. Business E-Mail: dcsmith@kilpatrickstockton.com.

**SMITH, DAVID EDWARD,** small business owner, aerospace engineer, aerospace scientist; b. Battle Creek, Mich., Sept. 16, 1939; s. Hebdin Leslie and Dureatha Rosella (Stephens) S.; m. Margaret Eugenia Clark, June 13, 1964; 1 child, Wendy Leigh. Student, Kellogg C.C., 1957—58; BSME, Mich State U., 1962; MS in Real Estate Investing (hon.), Meta U., Salt Lake City, 1992. Engr., scientist Douglas Aircraft Co., Santa Monica, Calif., 1962-63, McDonnell Douglas Astronautics Co., Cape Kennedy, Fla., 1963-78; broker salesman Cape Kennedy Realty, Inc., Cape Canaveral, Fla., 1978-87; pres., founder Cash Flow Seminars, Merritt Island, Fla., 1979—, Cash Flow Systems, Inc., Merritt Island, Fla., 1983—; prof. fin. Meta U., Salt Lake City, 1992-94. Lectr. fin. convs. and orgns. including Fed. GSA, Pub. Bldg. Svc., Am. League of Savs., Fin. Instns. Mktg. Assn., Acad. Real Estate, Am. Congress Real Estate; prof. fin. Meta U., Salt Lake City, 1992-94; distbr. Hewlett Packard Corp., 1985-88; dir. comml. investment divsn. CKBOR, Merritt Island, 1978-79; adv. bd., lectr. Fin. Freedom Report, Nat. Inst. Fin. Planning, both Salt Lake City, 1985-92; instr. Fla. Real Estate Commn., La. Real Estate Commn., Fla. Bd. Accountancy, Am. Inst. Real Estate Appraisers. Author: Turbo-Diesel, The Time Value of Money, Creative Financing Techniques; contbr. articles to profl. jours. and mags. Mem.: Internat. Platform Assn., Fla. Real Estate Exchangors, Iron Butt Assn., Gold Wing Rd. Riders Assn. Republican. Avocations: flying, transcontinental bicycling, motorcycle touring. Office: Cash Flow Seminars PO Box 540634 Merritt Island FL 32954-0634

**SMITH, DAVID ELVIN,** physician; b. Bakersfield, Calif., Feb. 7, 1939; s. Elvin W. and Dorothy (McGinnis) S.; m. Millicent Buxton; children: Julia, Suzanne, Christopher Buxton-Smith, Sabree Hill-Smith. Intern San Francisco Gen. Hosp., 1965; fellow pharmacology and toxicology U. Calif., San Francisco, 1965-67; clin. prof. U. Calif., San Francisco Med. Ctr., 1967—dir. psychopharmacology study group, dir. Inst. of Health, 1966-70, assoc. clin. prof., rsch. physician Med. Sch.; clin. prof. U. Calif., San Francisco, practice specializing in toxicology/addiction medicine San Francisco, 1965—. Physician Presbyn. Alcoholic Clinic, 1965—67, Contra Cost Alcoholic Clinic, 1965—67; dir. alcohol and drug abuse screening unit San Francisco Gen. Hosp., 1967—68; co-dir. Calif. drug abuse info. project U. Calif. Med. Ctr., 1967—72; founder, pres., med. dir. Haight-Ashbury Free Med. Clinic, San Francisco, 1967—2006; rsch. dir. Merritt Peralta Chem. Dependency Hosp., Oakland, Calif., 1984—2003; med. dir. Drug Abuse Scis., 1999—2003, Calif. Alcohol and Drug Programs, U. Calif. San Francisco Substance Abuse Policy Ctr., 1999; exec. med. dir. Prometa Ctr., Santa Monica, Calif.; asst. med. dir., med. rev. officer Betty Ford Ctr. Profl. Recovery Program; chmn. Nat. Drug Abuse Conf., 1977, Calif. Gov.'s Commn. on Narcotics and Drug Abuse, 1977—; nat. health adviser to former U.S. Pres. Jimmy Carter; mem. Pres. Clinton's Health Care Task Force on Addiction and Nat. Health Reform, 1993; with Office Drug Abuse Policy, White House Task Force Physicians for Drug Abuse Prevention; dir. Benzodiazepine Rsch. and Tng. Project, Substance Abuse and Sexual Concerns Project, PCP Rsch. and Tng. Project; med. editor AlcoholMD.com, OpiateMD.org, Alcohol MD (CD-ROM); vis. assoc. prof. U. Nev. Med. Sch., 1975—; clin. prof. U. Calif. San Francisco Med. Ctr.; v.p. corp. med affairs Hythiam; cons. in field; chief Addiction Medicine Svcs. Bayside Marin, San Rafael, 2006—; med. dir. Centerpoint, 1996—. Author: Love Needs Care, 1970, The New Social Drug: Cultural, Medical and Legal Perspectives on

Marijuana, 1971, The Free Clnic: Community Approaches to Health Care and Drug Abuse, 1971, Treating the Cocaine Abuser, 1985, The Benzodiazepines: Current Standard Medical Practice, 1986, Physicians' Guide to Drug Abuse, 1987; co-author: It's So Good, Don't Even Try it Once: Heroin in Perspective, 1972, Uppers and Downers, 1973, Drugs in the Classroom, 1973, Barbiturate Use and Abuse, 1977, A Multicultural View of Drug Abuse, 1978, Amphetamine Use, Misuse and Abuse, 1979, PCP: Problems and Prevention, 1981, Sexological Aspects of Substance Use and Abuse, Treatment of the Cocaine Abuser, 1985, The Haight Ashbury Free Medical Clinic: Still Free After All These Years, Drug Free: Alternatives to Drug Abuse, 1987, Treatment of Opiate Dependence, Designer Drugs, 1988, Treatment of Cocaine Dependence, 1988, Treatment of Opiate Dependence, 1988, The New Drugs, 1989, Crack and Ice in the Era of Smokeable Drugs, 1992, Clinical Guide to Substance Abuse, 2001, others; also drug edn. films; founder, editor Jour. Psychedelic Drugs (now Jour. Psychoactive Drugs), 1967—; co-author: Clinical Guide to Substance Abuse; contbr. over 300 articles to profl. jours. Mem. Physicians for Prevention White House Office Drug Abuse Policy, 1995; pres. Youth Projects, Inc.; founder, chmn. bd., pres. Nat. Free Clin. Coun., 1968-72; med. dir. Calif. Alcohol and Drug Programs, 1998, U. Calif. Drug Policy Ctr., San Francisco, 1998—, Drug Abuse Scis., 1998—. Named one of Best Doctors in U.S., 1995, 1996, 1997, 2002; recipient Rsch. award, Borden Found., 1964, AMA Rsch. award, 1977, Cmty. Svc. award U. Calif., San Francisco, 1974, Calif. State Drug Abuse Treatment award, 1984, Vernelle Fox Drug Abuse Treatment award, 1985, UCLA Sidney Cohen Addiction Medicine award, 1989, U. Calif. San Francisco medal of honor, 1995, Lifetime Achievement award for sr. workers, Gov. of Calif., 2003. Mem. AMA (alt. del.), Calif. Med. Assn. (alt. del.), Am. Soc. on Addiction Medicine (bd. dirs., pres. 1995), San Francisco Med. Soc., APHA, Calif. Soc. on Addiction Medicine (pres., bd. dirs.), Am. Soc. Addiction Medicine, Cosmos Club, 2006, Sigma Xi, Phi Beta Kappa. Methodist. Home: 289 Frederick St San Francisco CA 94117-4051 Office: David E Smit MD and Assocs 856 Stanyan San Francisco CA 94117 Office Phone: 415-487-3688, 415-518-8380. E-mail: dsmith4619@aol.com.

**SMITH, DAVID ENGLISH,** pathologist, educator; b. San Francisco, June 9, 1920; s. David English and Myrtle (Goodin) S.; m. Margaret Elizabeth Bronson, June 9, 1948; children: Ann English Smith Elbert, David Bronson, Mary Margaret. AB, Central Coll. Mo., 1941; MD cum laude, Washington U., St. Louis, 1944. Intern, resident pathology Barnes Hosp., St. Louis, 1944-46; instr. pathology Washington U. Med. Sch., 1948-51, asst. prof., 1951-54, asst. head dept., 1953-54, assoc. prof., 1954-55; prof. pathology U. Va. Sch. Medicine, 1955-73, chmn. dept., 1958-73; dir. div. U. Va. Sch. Medicine (Cancer Studies), 1972-73; prof. pathology Northwestern U. Sch. Medicine, 1974-75, U. Pa. Sch. Medicine, 1976-80, Tulane U. Sch. Medicine, 1980-85, assoc. dean, 1980-85; prof. pathology U. Tex. Med. Br., 1986—. Assoc. dir. Am. Bd. Med. Spltys., 1974-75; v.p., sec., dir. undergrad. evaluation Nat. Bd. Med. Examiners, 1975-80; trustee Am. Bd. Pathology, 1966-73, v.p., 1973; mem. Nat. Bd. Med. Examiners, chmn. pathology test com., 1966-72; chmn. test com. Ednl. Commn. for Fgn. Med. Grads., 1979-91; eligibility & due process com. Nat. Commn. Cert. Physician Assts., 1990-2001. Editor: Survey of Pathology in Medicine and Surgery, 1966-70; contbr. articles to profl. publs. Pres. Va. div. Am. Cancer Soc., 1967-69. Served from 1st lt. to capt. M.C. AUS, 1946-48. Named Disting. Alumnus, Wash. U. Med. Sch., 2004; recipient Preclin. Tchr. award, U. Tex. Med. Br., 1999; Paul Brindley Disting. scholar, 1997. Mem. Va. Soc. Pathology (pres. 1960), Am. Assn. Pathologists, Internat. Acad. Pathology (council 1956-59, pres. 1964-65), Am. Soc. Clin. Pathologists (co-dir. self assessment program 1970-75, Path Educator award 2000), AMA, Am. Assn. Neuropathologists, AAAS, Sigma Xi, Alpha Omega Alpha, Phi Beta Pi, Alpha Epsilon Delta. Home: 59 Colony Park Cir Galveston TX 77551-1737 E-mail: descolpkga@aol.com.

**SMITH, DAVID EUGENE,** business administration educator; b. Boise, Idaho, Dec. 14, 1941; s. Roy Arthur and Anna Margaret (Fries) S.; m. Patricia Stroy, Aug. 4, 1973; 1 child, Zachary Adam. BS in Applied Stats., San Francisco State Coll., 1964, MS in Mgmt. Sci., 1966; MBA, PhD in Bus. Adminstrn., U. Santa Clara, 1969. Asst. to dir. mgmt ctr. Grad. Sch. Bus., U. Santa Clara, Calif., 1966-69, lectr. mktg., 1968; asst. prof. bus. adminstrn. dept. mktg./decision Scis. San Jose State U., Calif., 1969—71, assoc. prof. bus. adminstrn. dept. mktg./decision Scis., 1971—76, prof. bus. adminstrn. dept. mktg./decision Scis., 1976—, chmn. dept. mktg./decision Scis., 1986—89. Author: Quantitative Business Analysis, 1977, Internat. Edit., 1979, 1982; contbr. articles to profl. jours. Mem.: DSI, INFORMS, Beta Gamma Sigma, Phi Kappa Phi. Republican. Avocations: tennis, fishing, skiing. Home: 22448 Tim Tam Ct Los Gatos CA 95033-8521 Office: San Jose State U Mktg/Decision Scis One Washington Sq San Jose CA 95192

**SMITH, DAVID HARRY WATROUS,** retired secondary school educator; b. Ashtabula, Ohio, Oct. 10, 1938; s. David Lincoln Smith and Catherine (Watrous) Lookenott; m. Jane Francis Ottley, Sept. 11, 1965; children: Olivia Jane, Adam Lawrence. BFA with honors, Goodman Theatre, Art Inst. Chgo., 1965; MA, Hunter Coll., 1968; PhD, Cornell U., 1979. Stage mgr. N.Y. Shakespeare Festival, N.Y.C., 1962-70; Theatre of Living Arts, Phila., 1964-65; dir. Rochester (N.Y.) Cmty. Players, 1978-79; prof. Monroe CC, Rochester, NY, 1972—2004, prof. emeritus, 2004—. Dir. Rochester Shakespeare Players, 1996. Author: (plays) Beauty and the Beast, 1984, Kari and the Ice Cream Cone, 1988, The Golden Fish, 1993; co-author, dir. A Christmas Carol, 2005; translator: How the Errant Husband Was Delivered, 1992. Office: Monroe Community Coll 1000 E Henrietta Rd Rochester NY 14623-5701 Home: 5353 W Lake Rd Geneseo NY 14454-9575 E-mail: dhwsmith@rochester.rr.com.

**SMITH, DAVID HORTON,** retired social sciences educator; b. L.A., May 2, 1939; s. Paul Roosevelt Smith and Helen Ethel (Frechem) Mitchell; divorced; children: Gregory David, Laura Ghislaine. AB magna cum laude, U. So. Calif., 1960; MA, Harvard U., 1962, PhD, 1965. Asst. prof. U. So. Calif., L.A., 1966-68; assoc. prof. Boston Coll., Chestnut Hill, Mass., 1968-76, prof., 1976—2004. Rsch. fellow, lectr. Harvard U., 1965-66; cons. to govt. agys. and nonprofit orgns., including Nat. Ctr. for Voluntary Action, Brit. Nat. Vol. Ctr., Ctr. for Voluntary Soc., Filer Commn. on Pvt. Philanthropy and Pub. Needs, Union of Internat. Assns. Author: Latin American Student Activism, 1973, Grassroots Associations, 2000; co-author: Becoming Modern, 1974 (award 1975), Voluntary Sector Policy Research Needs, 1974, Participation in Social and Political Activities, 1980, Why People Recreate, 1987, A Dictionary of Nonprofit Terms and Concepts, 2006; editor: Voluntary Action Research, 1972, 73, 74, Voluntarism, Voluntary Assns. and Devel., 1981, Internat. Perspectives on Voluntary Action Rsch., 1983; contbr. numerous articles to profl. jours.; contbr. chapts. to books; founding editor-in-chief Jour. Voluntary Action Rsch. (now Nonprofit and Voluntary Sector Quar.), 1971-76. Founding bd. dirs. Nat. Com. for Responsive Philanthropy, 1976-78, Alliance for Volunteerism; dir. rsch. Ctr. for Voluntary Soc., Washington, 1970-74. NSF grad. fellow, 1960-63; Woodrow Wilson Hon. fellow, 1960. Mem. Assn. Rsch. on Non-Profit Orgns. and Voluntary Action (founder, pres. 1971-73, Lifetime Achievement award 1993), Authors Guild, Sarasota Fiction Writers, Harvard Club of Sarasota, Phi Beta Kappa, Phi Kappa Phi. Mem. Unity Ch. Avocations: reading, photography, fiction writing, jazz, foreign travel. E-mail: dhortonsmith@hotmail.com.

**SMITH, DAVID JAMES,** corporate lawyer; b. 1955; BS, Western Ill. U.; JD, John Marshall Law Sch. Asst. sec. Archer Daniels Midland, Decatur, Ill. 1988-97, asst. gen. counsel, 1995-97, v.p., gen. counsel, 1997—2001, sr. v.p., sec., gen. counsel, 2002—03, exec. v.p., sec. and gen. counsel, 2003—. Office: Archer Daniels Midland Co 4666 E Faries Pkwy Decatur IL 62526-5666

**SMITH, DAVID JEDDIE,** American literature educator; b. Portsmouth, Va., Dec. 19, 1942; s. Ralph Gearld and Catherine Mary (Cornwell) S.; m. Deloras Mae Weaver, Mar. 31, 1966; children: David Jeddie, Lael Cornwell, Mary Catherine. BA, U. Va., 1965; MA, So. Ill. U., 1969; PhD, Ohio U., 1976. Staff creative writing Bennington (Vt.) Coll. summer prog., 1980-87; instr. English We. Mich. U., Kalamazoo, 1973-74; asst. prof. English Cottey Coll., Nevada,

Mo., 1974-75; assoc. prof. English U. Utah, Salt Lake City, 1976-80; vis. prof. English SUNY, Binghamton, 1980-81; assoc. prof. English U. Fla., Gainesville, 1981-82; prof. Am. lit. Va. Commonwealth U., Richmond, 1982-89; prof. La. State U., 1990—2002; prof. poetry Johns Hopkins U., 2002—. Lectr. in field; cons. in field. Author: Local Assays, 1985, The Roundhouse Voices: Selected and new Poems, 1985, The Morrow Anthology of Younger American Poets, 1985, Gray Soldiers, 1984, Southern Delights, 1984, In the House of the Judge, 1983, The Pure Clear Word: Essays on the Poetry of James Wright, 1982, Onliness, 1981, Homage to Edgar Allan Poe, 1981, Cuba Night, 1990, Night Pleasures: New and Selected Poems (England), 1992, Fate's Kite: Poems 1991-1995, 1996, Floating on Solitude: Three Books of Poems, 1996, The Wick of Memory: New and Selected Poems 1970-2000, 2000, Little Boats, Unsalvaged, 2005, others; editor New Va. Rev., 1987, The Back Doors: A Poetry Mag., Southern Rev., 1990; contbr. articles to profl. jours. Recipient Va. Prize in Poetry, 1988, Prairie Schooner poetry prize, 1980, Portland Rev. poetry prize, 1979, Sou'wester poetry prize, 1973, others; Guggenheim fellow, 1981, Lyndhurst fellow, 1987, 88, 89, others. Mem. MLA, So. MLA, Poetry Soc. Am., Poetry Soc. Va., PEN, Nat. Book Critics Cir., Assn. Writing Progs., Acad. Am. Poets, Fellowship of So. Writers. Office: 14 E Bishops Rd Baltimore MD 21218-2312 also: Johns Hopkins U The Writing Seminars 3400 N Charles St Baltimore MD 21218 Office Phone: 410-516-3409. E-mail: djstrucker2@cs.com.

**SMITH, DAVID JOHN**, physicist, researcher; b. Melbourne, Australia, Oct. 10, 1948; arrived in U.S., 1984; s. Arthur and Agnes Frances Smith; m. Gwenneth Paula Bland, Sept. 18, 1971 (div. 1992); children: Heather F., Marion J. BSc with honors, U. Melbourne, Australia, 1970, PhD, 1978, DSc, 1988. Post-doctoral rsch. asst. Cavendish Lab. U. Cambridge, England, 1976-78, sr. rsch. assoc., 1979-84; assoc. prof. Ariz. State U., Tempe, 1984-87, prof., 1987—, regents prof., 2000—, dir. Ctr. Solid State Sci., 2001—04. Dir. high resolution electron microscope Cambridge U., 1979—84; dir. Ctr. High Resolution Electron Microscopy NSF, Tempe, 1991—96. Editor: 18 conf. procs.; contbr. chapters to books, over 400 articles to profl. jours. Recipient Faculty Achievement award, Burlington Resources Found., 1990. Fellow: Am. Phys. Soc., Inst. Physics (U.K.) (Charles Vernon Boys prize 1985); mem.: Microscopy Soc. Am., Material Rsch. Soc. Office: Ariz State U Dept Physics Tempe AZ 85287-1504 Office Phone: 480-965-4540. Business E-Mail: david.smith@asu.edu.

**SMITH, DAVID JOHN, JR.**, plastic surgeon; b. Indpls., Feb. 20, 1947; s. David John and Carolyn (Culp) S.; m. Nancy Loonsten, June 7, 1975; children: Matthew, Peter, Hadley. BA, Wesleyan U., 1969; MD, Ind. U., 1973. Diplomate Am. Bd. Plastic Surgery. Resident Emory U.-Grady Hosp., Atlanta, 1973-78; resident Ind. U. Med. Ctr., Indpls., 1978-80; Christine Kleinert fellow in hand surgery, 1979; asst. prof. surgery Ind. U. Sch. Medicine, 1980-84; assoc. prof. of surgery Wayne State U. Sch. Medicine, 1984-87; assoc. plastic surgery, surgery sect. head U. Mich. Med. Ctr., Ann Arbor, 1987-92, prof. surgery sect. head, 1992—2001; prof. surgery Coll. Medicine U. South Fla., 2004—, Juan Bolivar chair in surg. oncology, dir. divsn. plastic and reconstructive surgery, 2004—. Mem. Residency Rev. Com. for Plastic Surgery, 1992-2000, vice chmn., 1994, chmn. 1996-99; vis. prof. Ctr. Cutaneous Rsch. Queen Mary U., London, Eng., 2004—, Anglia Polytech. U., Cambrige, Eng., 2004—. Mem. editl. bd. Jour. of Surg. Rsch., 1989-95, Annals of Plastic Surgery, 1992-2002, assoc. editor, 1994-2002, Yearbook of Hand Surgery, 1989—; guest reviewer Surgery, 1988—, Plastic and Reconstructive Surgery, 1988—; contbr. articles to profl. jours. Recipient numerous grants. Fellow ACS (many coms.), Am. Assn. Plastic Surgeons, Am. Surg. Assn., Am. Bd. Plastic Surgeons (vice chmn. 1997-98, chair-elect 1998-99, chmn. oral exam 1995-97, chmn. 1999-2000), Ctrl. Surg. Assn., Am. Soc. for Surgery of the Hand, Am. Soc. Plastic Surgeons, Plastic Surgery Ednl. Found. (bd. dirs. 1988-99, treas. 1994, v.p., pres.-elec., pres., chair nominating com. 1997-98), Plastic Surgery Rsch. Coun., Am. Burn Assn. (chmn. com. on organization and delivery of burn care 1995-98), Am. Burn Life Support Nat. Faculty, Am. Assn. for Hand Surgeons (pres. 1994), Assn. Acad. Chmn. Plastic Surgery (pres.-elect 1997, pres. 1998-99, chmn. nominating com. 1999-2000). Home: 3107 Prospect Rd Tampa FL 33629 Office: Divsn Plastic Surgery 4 Columbia Dr Ste 650 Tampa FL 33606 E-mail: dsmith3@hsc.usf.edu.

**SMITH, DAVID JULIAN**, educational consultant; b. Boston, Apr. 24, 1944; s. Julian John and Anita Regina (Goldman) S.; m. Suzanne Marilla Shaw, June 18, 1966. AB, Harvard U., 1966; MAT, Reed Coll., 1967. Cert. elem. tchr., Mass., Hawaii, Oreg. 10th grade tchr. Punahou Sch., Honolulu, 1967-69; 7th, 9th grades tchr. U. Hawaii Lab. Sch., Honolulu, 1969-70; 7th grade head tchr. Shady Hill Sch., Cambridge, Mass., 1970-92; pvt. practice ednl. cons. Cambridge, Mass., 1992—. Author: Mapping the World By Heart, 1992, CEESA Web-Site Manual, 1998, If the World Were a Village, 2002, Emergency Procedures Manual for Overseas Schools, 2004; contbr. articles to profl. jours. Bd. dirs. Cambridge Mental Health Assn., 1991-96, Cambridge Ctr. for Adult Edn., 1998; active Cambridge Civic Assn. Recipient Breaking the Mold award US Dept. Edn., 1992. Mem. Nat. Coun. Social Studies, Nat. Coun. Geog. Edn., Assn. Am. Geographers (chair cartographic splty. group 1997). Office: Mapping the World by Heart 4 Blanchard Rd Cambridge MA 02138-1009 Personal E-mail: djsmapping@gmail.com.

**SMITH, DAVID KINGMAN**, retired oil company executive, consultant; b. Malone, N.Y., June 5, 1929; s. Ernest DeAlton and Louisa Kingman (Bolster) S.; m. Lois Louise Wing, June 13, 1959; children: Mara Louise, David Andrew. BS in Engring., Princeton U., 1952. Registered profl. engr., Tex. Civil engr., supt. Raymont Internat. Inc., N.Y.C., 1952-55, asst. v.p., 1970-71, v.p., 1971-74, group v.p. Houston, 1974-80; mgr. Raymond-Brown and Root, Maracaibo, Venezuela, 1955-70; sr. engring. assoc. Exxon Prodn. Rsch. Co., Houston, 1980-81, supr., 1982-95; cons. project mgmt., 1995—. Pres. Yorkshire Civic Assn., Houston, 1979-80, trustee, 1985-97. With U.S. Army, 1946-48, PTO. Mem. ASCE, NSPE, Soc. Petroleum Engrs. (continuing edn. com. Gulf Coast chmn. 1989-93, treas. 1987-88, nat. continuing edn. com. 1991-93, dir. Gulf Coast sect. 1994-95), Tex. Soc. Profl. Engrs., Men's Garden Club Houston, Am. Legion, Princeton Alumni Assn. (dir. Houston sect.), Cen Ners In Square Dance Club (pres. 1996-97), Exxon Mobil Meml. Area Retirees Club (pres. 2005-06). Republican. Methodist. Avocations: photography, gardening, tennis, golf, square dancing. Home: 611 W Forest Dr Houston TX 77079-6915 Personal E-mail: smithdktx@aol.com.

**SMITH, DAVID LEE**, retired editor; b. Shelby, Ohio, Apr. 4, 1939; s. Ferris Francis and Rita Ann (Metzger) S.; m. Betty Stewart Walker, Sept. 10, 1960; children: Stacie Lynn, Stefanie Linn, David Lee, II (dec.). Student, Pontifical Coll. Josephinum, Worthington, Ohio, 1953-56, Ohio State U., Mansfield, 1961. Sports writer Mansfield News-Jour., 1960-61; sports editor Ashland (Ohio) Times-Gazette, 1961-63, Miami (Fla.) News, 1963-67, Ft. Lauderdale (Fla.) News, 1967-70, Boston Globe, 1970-78, Washington Star, 1978-81; dep. mng. editor, exec. sports editor Dallas Morning News, 1981—2005, sports dir. AH Belo pub. and new media divsns., 1998—2003, v.p., 2003—05, ret., 2005. Condr. seminars. Mem. adv. bd. Dallas Stars Found., Dallas Alliance for the Mentally Ill, SMU Athletics, Jesuit Sch. Found.; bd. dirs. Field Scovell Scholarship Found., Doak Walker Nat. Running Back Award, GTE-SMU Athletic Forum. With USMC, 1957—60. Mem. AP Sports Editors Assn. (1st pres. 1974-75), Baseball Writers Assn. (Red Smith award for major contbns. to sports journalism 1990), Football Writers Assn., Golf Writers Assn., SMU Athletic Forum (bd. dirs.), Bent Tree Country Club, Salesmanship Club of Dallas. Roman Catholic. Home: 16 Mad Turkey Crossing Savannah GA 31411 Personal E-mail: studie.dave@comcast.net.

**SMITH, DAVID MARTYN**, retired forestry educator; b. Bryan, Tex., Mar. 10, 1921; s. John Blackmer and Doris (Clark) S.; m. Catherine Van Aken, June 16, 1951; children: Ellen, Nancy. BS, U. R.I., 1941; postgrad., NYU, 1942; MF, Yale U., 1946, PhD, 1950; DSc (hon.), Bates Coll., 1986, U. R.I. 1993. From instr. to prof. Sch. Forestry and Environ. Studies, Yale U., 1946-90, asst. dean, 1953-58; Morris K. Jesup prof. silviculture Yale U., 1967-90, ret., 1990, Morris K. Jesup prof. emeritus, 1990—. Vis. prof. U. Munich, 1981. Author: Practice of Silviculture, 1954, 4th edit., 1997. Capt.

Weather Svc., USAAF, 1942-45. Fellow Soc. Am. Foresters (Disting. Svc. New Eng. sect. award 1969, 93); mem. Am. Forests (Disting. Svc. award 1990), Nat. Acad. Forest Scis. Mex. (corr.), Ecol. Soc. Am., Conn. Forest and Park Assn. (dir.), Sigma Xi, Phi Kappa Phi. Mem. United Ch. of Christ. Home: 200 Leeder Hlll Dr Apt 425 Hamden CT 06517-2728 Personal E-mail: david.m.smith@yale.edu.

**SMITH, DAVID PAUL**, psychologist, researcher; b. Pittsfield, Mass., Apr. 4, 1961; s. Cathleen Francis Smith; m. Laura Marie Finnegan, May 18, 1997; 1 child, Matthew Leo Finnegan. PhD, U. Chgo. Cert. clin. psychologist Ill., 2000. Rschr. U. Chgo., 1998—2005; pvt. practice Inst. Clin. Hypnosis and Rsch., Chgo., 2000—06. Contbr. articles to profl. jours., chapters to books. Mem.: Soc. Psychotherpay Rsch. D-Liberal. Home: 1454 East 56th St Chicago IL 60637 Office: Inst Clinical Hypnosis & Rsch 1525 East 53rd St Ste 934 Chicago IL 60615 Office Phone: 773-363-0600. Office Fax: 773-363-0600. Personal E-mail: drdaveps@comcast.net.

**SMITH, DAVID STUART**, anesthesiology educator, physician; b. Detroit, May 29, 1946; s. Philip and Eleanor (Bishop) S.; m. Suzanne Wanda Zeleznik, Aug. 17, 1969; children: Katherine Michele, Lisa Anne. BA, Oakland U.; MD, PhD, Med. Coll. Wis., 1975. Intern dept. medicine Med. Coll. Wis., Milw., 1975-76; resident dept. anesthesia U. Pa., Phila., 1976-78, fellow dept. anesthesia, 1978-80; dir. divsn. neuroanesthesia Hosp. U. Pa., Phila., 1982-2001, attending anesthesiologist, 1980—; asst. prof. U. Pa., Phila., 1980-89, assoc. prof., 1989—. Co-editor: Anesthesia and Neurosurgery, 3d edit., 1994, 4th edit., 2001; mem. editl. bd. Jour. Neurosurg. Anesthesia, N.Y.C., 1987-97; author and co-author of numerous sci. papers, revs., and book chpts. Sr. fellow, Nat. Rsch. Svc. award, Phila., 1985-87. Fellow Coll. Physicians Phila.; mem. Am. Soc. Anesthesiologists, Soc. Neurosurg. Anesthesia and Critical Care (sec., treas. 1987-89, v.p. 1989-90, pres. elect 1990-91, pres. 1991-92), Assn. U. Anesthesiologists, Internat. Soc. Cerebral Blood Flow and Metabolism. Jewish. Office: Hosp U Pa Dept Anesthesia 3400 Spruce St Philadelphia PA 19104-4206

**SMITH, DAVID THORNTON**, lawyer, educator; b. Pawtucket, R.I., Dec. 11, 1935; s. Herbert Jeffers and Harriet Amelia (Thornton) S.; m. Sandra June Gustavson, Dec. 20, 1958; children: David T., Douglas A., Daniel H. BA, Yale U., 1957; JD cum laude, Boston U., 1960. Bar: Mass. 1961, U.S. Supreme Ct. 1964. Instr. law Ind. U., Bloomington, 1960-62; asst. prof. law Duquesne U., Pitts., 1962-63, Case Western Res. U., Cleve., 1963-65, assoc. prof., 1965-68; assoc. prof. law U. Fla., Gainesville, 1968-69, prof., 1969—2003, prof. emeritus, 2003—. Lectr. Fla. Bankers Assn., Fla. Trust Sch., 1973—; vis. prof. law U. Ga., 2004, Wake Forest U., 2006. Author: (with M. Sussman and J. Cates) The Family and Inheritance, 1970, Florida Probate Code Manual, 1975. Mem. Am. Bar Assn., Mass. Bar Assn., Am. Law Inst., Am. Judicature Soc., AAUP (past pres. U. Fla. chpt.), Fla. Blue Key, Selden Soc., Omicron Delta Kappa, Phi Alpha Delta. Lutheran. Office: Univ Fla Coll Law Gainesville FL 32611

**SMITH, DAVID WAYNE**, psychologist, educator; b. Ind., Apr. 16, 1927; s. Lowell Wayne and Ruth Elizabeth (Westphal) S.; m. Marcene B. Leever, Oct. 20, 1948; children: David Wayne, Laurreen Lea. BS, Purdue U., 1949; MS, Ind. U., 1953, PhD, 1955. Diplomate Am. Bd. Psychol. Specialities. Prof. rehab., dir. Rehab. Center; asso. dean, later asst. v.p. acad. affairs Ariz. Health Scis. Center, U. Ariz., Tucson, 1955-80; research prof. rehab., adj. prof. medicine, cons. in research S.W. Arthritis Center, Coll. Medicine, 1980-87; prof. rehab. and rheumatology, dept. medicine U. Ariz., 1987—, also dir. disability assessment program. Pres. allied health professions sect. Nat. Arthritis Found.; bd. dirs. Nat. Arthritis Found. (S.W. chpt.); nat. vice chmn. bd. dirs.; mem. NIH Nat. Arthritis adv. Bd., 1977-84; also chmn. subcom. community programs and rehab.; mem. staff Ariz. Legislature Health Welfare, 1972-73; Mem. Gov.'s Council Dept. Econ. Security, 1978-85; pres., bd. dirs. Tucson Assn. for Blind, 1974-86; chmn. Gov.'s Council on Blind and Visually Impaired, 1987—; active Gov.'s Coun. on Arthritis and Musculoskeletal Disease, 1987—, Gov.'s State wide Coun. on Rehab., 1998—, Am. Bd. Forensic Examiners, 1997—. Author: Worksamples; contbr. chpts. to books and articles to profl. jours. Mem. Gov.'s State Rehab. Coun., 1998—, commr. Commn. on Civil Rights, Az., 2002. Recipient Gov.'s awards for leadership in rehab., 1966, 69, 72; awards for sci. and vol. services Nat. Arthritis Found., 1973, 75; 1st nat. Addie Thomas award Nat. Arthritis Found., 1983, Benson award, 1989, Govt. Affairs award, 1989; Arthritis Found. fellow, 1983. Mem. Am. Psychol. Assn. (div. 17 counseling psychology), Am. Coll. Forensics, Assn. Schs. Allied Health Professions, Nat. Rehab. Assn., Ariz. Psychol. Assn. Home: 5765 N Camino Real Tucson AZ 85718-4213 Office: U Ariz Arizona Health Scis Ctr Tucson AZ 85724-0001 Personal E-mail: davesfolly@earthlink.net.

**SMITH, DEAN**, communications advisor, arbitrator; b. N.Y.C., Aug. 10, 1925; s. Franklin Grant and Anna Lucille (Kranebell) S.; m. Andree Marie Praileur, Aug. 9, 1947; children: David F., Christopher P. Student, NYU, 1945-46, Columbia U., 1946-47, N.Y. Sch. Printing, 1946-47. Editor Show-Bill Mag., N.Y.C., 1945-47; news editor Boulder City (Nev.) Daily News, 1947-49; owner, pub., editor Tucson Sun-News, 1951-53; dir. radio and TV news Sta. WBEN/WBEN-TV, Buffalo, 1951-53; dir. pub. svc. and promotion Indpls. Times, Buffalo, 1953-56; v.p., gen. mgr Kendall Assocs., Inc., N.Y.C., 1956-60; dir. Office Publs. and Info., Commerce Dept., Washington, 1961-70, dir. publs. div., 1970; asst. dir. Nat. Tech. Info. Svc., Springfield, Va., 1971-81, dir. office of market devel., 1982-83; assoc. dir. NTIS, Springfield, Va., 1984-85, self-employed communications advisor, 1986—. Chmn. for fed. mail list policy Vice Pres.'s Com. on Right of Privacy; chmn. presdl. domestic policy rev. work group on fed. acquisition of fgn. tech., 1979; bd. dirs. Commerce Fed. Credit Union. Served with AUS, 1943-45 Decorated Silver Star with oak leaf cluster, Bronze Star, Purple Heart with oak leaf cluster; recipient award Ariz. Newspaper Assn., 1950, Ind. Photo Journalism award, 1954 Mem. Am. Arbitration Assn. (panelist), Washington Book Pubs., Soc. Mayflower Descs., Sons of Revolution (treas.), Flagon and Trencher, Soc. for the Descs.of the Colonial Clergy, Soc. Descs of Founders of Hartford, Oldest Inhabitants of DC., St. Nicholas Soc. of N.Y.C. Democrat. Home and Office: 2325 49th St NW Washington DC 20007-1002 Personal E-mail: dc49@comcast.net.

**SMITH, DEAN EDWARDS**, retired men's college basketball coach; b. Emporia, Kans., Feb. 28, 1931; s. Alfred Dillon and Vesta Marie (Edwards) S.; m. Linnea Weblemoe, May 21, 1976; children: Sharon, Sandy, Scott, Kristen, Kelly. BS in Math. and Phys. Edn., U. Kans., 1953. Asst. basketball coach USAF Acad., 1955-58; asst. basketball coach U. N.C., 1958-61, head basketball coach, 1961-97, now cons. basketball and athletic dept. Mem. U.S. and Canadian Basketball Rules Com., 1967-73; U.S. basketball coach Olympics, Montreal, Que., Can., 1976; lectr. basketball clinics, Germany, Italy. With USAF, 1954-58. Named Coach of Year, Atlantic Coast Conf., 1967, 1968, 1971, 1976, 1977, 79, Nat. Basketball Coach of Year, 1977, Nat. Coach of Yr., U.S. Basketball Writers, 1979, one of Top 5 Coaches of the 20th Century, ABC-TV and ESPN; named to Naismith Basketball Hall of Fame, 1982 Mem. Nat. Assn. Basketball Coaches (Nat. Basketball Coach of Yr. 1976, dir. 1972—, pres. 1981-82), Fellowship Christian Athletes (dir. 1965-70) Baptist. Office: U NC Basketball Office PO Box 2126 Chapel Hill NC 27515-2126

**SMITH, DEBORAH L.**, music educator, secondary school educator; b. Santurce, P.R., Aug. 28, 1964; d. Richard M. Smith and Carmen M. Cruz. Student, U. Surrey, Guildford, Eng., 1985—86; MusB cum laude, U. Mass., 1987; MusM in Choral Conducting, U. Conn., 1992. Cert. tchr. grades 5-12 Mass. Choral music dir. Granby (Mass.) Jr.-Sr. H.S., 1987—88, Claremont (N.H.) Pub. Schs. 1988—90; grad. tchg. asst. in theory U. Conn., Storrs, 1990—92; dir. choral music Lincoln-Sudbury (Mass.) Regional H.S., 1992—2004, Concord-Carlisle H.S., 2005—. Founder, condr. Chamber Singers U. Surrey, Guildford, England, 1985—86; conductor Reading (Mass.) Cmty. Singers, 1995—2002, Braintree Choral Soc., 2002. Mem.: Mass. Tchrs. Assn., Mass. Music Educators Assn. (adjudicator dist. festivals 1987, 1996, 1999, asst. mgr. Mass. All-State Chorus 2000—01, mgr. Mass. All-State

Chorus 2001—02, adjudicator dist. festivals 2005), Music Educators Nat. Conf., Am. Choral Dirs. Assn. (clinician workshop at state conf. 2000), Pi Kappa Lambda. Avocations: theater, dance, travel. Office Phone: 978-341-2490 7155. E-mail: dsmith@colonial.net.

**SMITH, DEBRA A.**, osteopath; d. Larry Lee Smith DO and Lola V. BA in Internat. Econs., Youngstown State U., 1989; DO, Nova Southeastern U., 1993; M in Internat. Health Mgmt., Thunderbird Sch., Glendale, Ariz., 1996, MBA in Internat. Mgmt., Treasury Mgmt., 1996. Cert. Am. Osteo. Bd. of Preventive Medicine, 2000, Am. Bd. of Ind. Med. Examiners, 2001, diplomate Am. Bd. of Quality Assurance and Utilization Rev. Physicians, 2001, Am. Bd. Preventive Medicine, 2004. Corp. med. dir. Highmark Life & Casualty Group, Pitts., 2001—03; clin. asst. prof. U. North Tex. Health Scis. Ctr.-Coll. Osteopathic Medicine, Ft. Worth, 2005—; regional med. dir., disability and workers compensation Delphi Corp., Dayton, Ohio, 2005—. Mem. Coun. on Internat. State. Med. Edn. of the Am. Osteo. Assn., Chgo., 2000—; clin. assoc. prof. Tex. Coll. Osteo. Medicine U. North Tex., Ft. Worth, 2005—. Grantee Stipend for Fgn. Students Studying in Austria, Austrian Ministry of Sci. and Rsch., 1992; YSU Found. scholar, Youngstown State U., 1986-1989. Fellow: Am. Coll. Preventive Medicine, Am. Osteo. Coll. Occupl. and Preventive Medicine (trustee 2003—); mem.: Omicron Delta Epsilon. Personal E-mail: drdebraasmith@zoominternet.net.

**SMITH, DEBRA L.**, lawyer; BS, Boston U., 1975; JD, New Eng. Sch. Law, Boston, 1982. Bar: Mass. 1983, Colo. 1992, U.S. Dist. Ct. Mass. 1984, U.S. Ct. Appeals (1st cir.) 1984, U.S. Supreme Ct. 1989. Coord. family law program Cambridge (Mass.) Somerville Legal Svcs. Inc., 1987-88; pvt. practice Watertown, Mass., 1984—. Tchr. Nat. Acad. Paralegal Studies Inc., Chestnut Hill and Framingham, Mass., 1989-94, Mt. Ida Coll., Newton, Mass., 1988-89. Assoc. editor Middlesex County Bar Assn. News and Comments, 1995, 96. Mem., leader Appalachian Mountain Club, Boston, 1990—; bd. dirs. Children Behavioral Health Care Inc., Waltham, Mass., 1990-96; tutor Watertown Lit. Project, 1993-94; bd. dirs. Mass. Coun. Family Mediation, Inc., 2002—. Mem. Mass. Coun. on Family Mediation, Inc., Boston Bar Assn. Avocations: biking, skiing, swimming, dancing. Office: 134 Main St Watertown MA 02472-4416 Office Phone: 617-924-6728. Office Fax: 617-924-6797. Business E-Mail: lawdeb@aol.com.

**SMITH, DENISE LORRAINE**, accountant; b. De Kalb, Ill., Apr. 27, 1963; d. Frank Vincent S. and Shirley Ann (Miller) Engstrom. BS, Northern Ill. U., 1985; MS, U. Denver, 1993, MAcc, 2003. CPA Colo. Student tchr. Craigslea High Schs.lo.) Schs., Brisbane, Australia, 1985; substitute tchr. Colorado Springs (Colo.) Schs., 1986-88; ATM tech. Wells Fargo Automatic Teller Machine Svc., Denver, 1986-90; tchr., computer Denver Pub. Schs., 1988-89, tchr., math., 1989—2000; computer programmer Am. Mgmt. Sys., 2000—01; acct. Bansek & Co., 2003—04; agent IRS, 2004—. Coach, Mathcounts, Denver, 1988-92. Mem. AICPA, Nat. Coun. Tchrs. Math., NEA, Colo. Coun. Tchrs. Math., Colo. Edn. Assn., Colo. Soc. CPA's, Denver Coun. Tchrs. Math. Avocations: camping, dance. Personal E-mail: denise4cpa@yahoo.com.

**SMITH, DENNIS (EDWARD SMITH)**, publishing executive, writer; b. N.Y.C., Sept. 9, 1940; s. John and Mary (Hogan) S.; m. Patricia Ann Kearney, Aug. 24, 1963 (div. May 1988); children: Brendan, Dennis, Sean, Deirdre and Aislinn (twins); m. Katina Arts Meyer, Dec. 25, 1997. BA, NYU, 1970, MA, 1972. Adj. asst. prof. Coll. New Rochelle, 1973-74; fireman City of N.Y., 1963-80; founder, pub., editor in chief Firehouse Mag., N.Y.C., 1976-89; chmn. First Responders Fin., LLC, 2005—. Author: Report from Engine Co. 82, 1972, Final Fire, 1975, Firehouse, 1977, Dennis Smith's History of American Firefighting, 1978, Glitter and Ash, 1980, The Aran Islands—A Personal Journey, 1980, Steely Blue, 1985, Firefighters, Their Lives in Their Own Words, 1988, The Little Fire Engine That Saved the City, 1990, A Song for Mary, 1999, Report From Ground Zero, 2002, Brassy the Fire Engine, 2005, San Francisco Is Burning, 2005. Chmn. First Responders Fin., LLC; mem. bd. advisors Boys and Girls Clubs Am., N.Y.C., The New York Fire Safety Found.; bd. dirs. Kips Bay Boys and Girls Club, N.Y.C., N.Y. Police & Fire Widows' & Children's Benefit Fund; bd. dirs., chmn. emeritus N.Y. Acad. Art; bd. dirs., pres. First Responders Found. With USAF, 1957-60. Recipient Christopher award for non-fiction, 1973. Mem. Century Assn. Club. Roman Catholic. Home and Office: 545 Fifth Ave New York NY 10017 Personal E-mail: dennissmith@mindspring.com, dennis@dennissmith.com.

**SMITH, DENNIS B.**, neurologist, educator; b. Albany, N.Y., Sept. 6, 1939; s. Bernard Y. and Virginia Shultes Smith; m. Bonnie Wimburn Smith, July 6, 1984; children: Kimberly, Kendall, Jennifer. BA, Wesleyan U., 1961; MD, Albany U., 1965. Cert. neurology, Am. Bd. Clinical Neurophysiology (CNP). Resident, instr. Yale U., 1965—70; asst. prof. U. Vt., Burlington, 1970—74; assoc. prof. to prof. Med. Coll. Ga., Augusta, 1974—84; chief staff Va Hosp., Hampton, Va., 1984—86; assoc. dean Ea. Va. Med. Sch., Norfolk, 1984—86; dir. Oreg. Epilepsy Program Legacy Health Sys., Portland, 1986—91; assoc. undersec. for health Dept. VA, Washington, 1991—94; prof. neurology Oreg. Health Scis. U., Portland, 1994—. Dir. Office of Stds. in Human Studies Rsch. Dept. VA, Washington, 1994—2000; cons., adv. bd. Oreg. Mus. Sci. and Industry, Portland, 2000—; cons. Nat. Ctr. Auditory Rsch. Dept. VA, Portland, 1997—. Editor: (books) Undergraduate Neurol Education, 1974, Epilepsy, Dx and Rx, 1990, Neurobehavioral Problems in Epilepsy, 1991. Mem. profl. adv. bd. exec. com. Epilepsy Found. Am., Washington, 1987—90; cons., advisor Exec. Office of the Pres., Washington, 1994; bd. dirs. Epilepsy Assn. Oreg., Portland, 1990, 1991. Fellow: Am. Acad. Neurology (edn. chair 1985—90); mem.: So. EEG Soc. (pres. 1984—85), Am. Neurol. Assn., Am. Epilepsy Soc. (exec. bd. 1991—94), Am. Coll. Healthcare Execs. Democrat. Avocations: sailing, painting. Home: 827 NW 25th Ave Portland OR 97210 Office: Oreg Health Scis U Sam Jackson Rd Portland OR 97201 Personal E-mail: smithden1@comcast.net. Business E-Mail: smithden@ohsu.edu.

**SMITH, DENNIS G.**, federal agency administrator; married; 4 children. B in Polit. Sci., Ill. State U.; MPA, George Mason U. Mem. Senate Fin. Com., 1996; dir. dept. med. assistance svcs. Commonwealth of Va., 1998—2001; chief liaison to Bush-Cheney transition team U.S. Dept. Health and Human Svcs., dir. Ctr. for Medicaid and State Ops., Ctrs. for Medicare and Medicaid Svcs., 2001—03, acting administr. Ctrs. for Medicare and Medicaid Svcs. Washington, 2003—. Office: US Dept HHS Ctrs for Medicare and Medicaid Svcs 200 Independence Ave SW Washington DC 20201

**SMITH, DEREK ARMAND**, information technology executive; b. Hamilton, Ont., Can., Sept. 2, 1953; came to U.S., 1981; s. Alastair A.G. and Jessie Mead (Maben) S.; m. Rebecca Oldfield, Oct. 10, 1981; 1 child, Alastair Maben Oldfield. BCom., U. Toronto, 1976. Chartered acct.; CPA, Mass. Staff acct. Office of Auditor Gen., Ottawa, 1976-78; chartered acct. Peat Marwick Thorne, Ottawa, 1978-79; v.p. fin. administrn. Can. Dry Bottling Ltd., Kingston, Ont., 1979-81; supervising sr. Peat Marwick, Boston, 1981-82; mgr. corp. reporting Warren, Gorham & Lamont, Inc., Boston, 1981-82, asst. contr. N.Y.C., 1982-84, sr. v.p., CFO, 1988-90, Penguin Books USA Inc., N.Y.C., 1990-96; exec. v.p. 1995-96; exec. v.p., CFO Addison Wesley Longman Inc., Reading, Mass. 1996-98; v.p., chief adminstrv. officer Orgnl. Dynamics, Inc., Burlington, Mass., 1998-2000; CFO First Knowledge Ptnrs. Inc., Boston, 2000—02; CFO, v.p. adminstrn. Castel, Inc., Beverly, 2002—. Pres. Trinity Coll. Sch. Fund, Beverly, Mass., 1992; bd. govs. Trinity Coll. Sch., Port Hope, Ont., 1992-2003, trustee 2003—. Trustee John Hart Hunter Ednl. Found., N.Y.C., 1992. Mem. AICPA (bd. examiners 1998-2003), Assn. Chartered Accts. U.S. Ltd. (treas. 1990-93, dir. 1989-94, hon. dir. 1994—), Kappa Alpha Soc. (exec. com., v.p. 1991-93, pres. 1993-95). Episcopalian. Avocations: skiing, sailing, tennis, paddle tennis, golf. Office: Castel Inc 100 Cummings Ctr Ste 157H Beverly MA 01915 Office Phone: 978-232-7612. Personal E-mail: derekasmith@comcast.net.

**SMITH, DEREK V.,** risk management consultant; Various positions Equifax, 1981, v.p., corp. v.p., treas., 1990-91, sr. v.p., CFO, 1991-93, v.p., group exec. ins. svcs. group, 1993; chmn., pres., CEO ChoicePoint, 1997—. Office: ChoicePoint 1000 Alderman Dr Alpharetta GA 30005-4199

**SMITH, DIANA BARKER,** music educator; b. Houston, Tex., Sept. 1, 1941; d. Irving Willis Barker and Mary Martine Kelly; m. Alan Michael Smith, Dec. 28, 1968; 1 child, Hillary Kay. Student, Aspen Sch. Music, Colo., 1961; MusB, U. Houston, 1963; MusM, U. Tex., 1966. Instr. piano SW Tex. State U., San Marcos, 1968—69, Colo. Coll., Colorado Springs, 1969—71; adj. prof. piano Duke U., Durham, NC, 1974—79, Bowling Green (Ohio) State U., 2000—. Mem. Guarneri Duo; musician: (performances include) Kennedy Ctr., Phillips Collection, Nat. Gallery of Art, Sala Chopin, Sala Carlos Chavez, (soloist) Houston Symphony. Recipient 1st pl. award Young Artist Competition, Houston Symphony, 1955, Phi Beta award Nat. Young Artist Competition, 1960, Young Artist Competition award, KRBE FM, Tex., 1962.

**SMITH, DIANA MARIE,** business educator; b. Des Moines, Oct. 25, 1940; d. Nathan Henry and Helen (Hall) Kitchen; m. Robert Nelson Smith, Jan. 26, 1971 (dec. 12-7-2004); 1 child, Stephen Ba, Drake U., 1968, MA, 1971. Cert. tchr., Iowa. Stenographer Polk County Welfare Dept., Des Moines, 1960—67; typist Polk County Auditor, Des Moines, 1968, Ctrl. Life Assurance Co., Des Moines, 1976—79; computer oper. IRS, Des Moines, 1988; lead specialist II Norwest Bank, Des Moines, 1978—2002; sec. Shive-Hattery Engrs., Des Moines, 1976—90; instr. adult edn. Des Moines Ind. Dist., 1969—2001; tchr. bus., computers Des Moines Pub. Schs., 1968—2000; instr. computers St. Paul Ch. and Saks Inc., Des Moines, 2000—04. Ind. computer cons.; instr.-authorized tng. assoc. program for Word Perfect, 1994; Mary Kay beauty cons., 1993— Chair meml. com. Burns United Meth. Ch., Des Moines, 1988—, Sunday sch. tchr., 1961-83, 92-98, 2005—, sec. adminstrv. bd., 1983-2004 Democrat. Avocations: reading, computers. Office: Saks Inc 701 Walnut Des Moines IA 50309 Office Phone: 515-246-3189. Personal E-mail: dsmith1034@aol.com.

**SMITH, DIANE JANS,** librarian, educator; b. Chgo., May 10, 1951; d. Steven Fred and Lillian Ann Jans; m. John H. Smith, July 22, 1989; stepchildren: Laurie, Tammy. BA in English, Calif. State U., Fullerton, 1973; MLS, U. So. Calif., L.A., 1974. Children's libr. Riverside Co. Libr. Sys., Indio, Calif., 1979—81, Orange Co. Pub. Libr., Mission Viejo, Calif., 1981—85, br. mgr., 1987—89, Laguna Beach, 1985—87, bibliog. svcs. supr. Santa Ana, 1990—94, program adminstr., 1994—2002; ref. libr., br. mgr. Riverside Co. Libr. Sys., San Jacinto, Calif., 2002—. Libr., faculty mem. U. N.D., Williston, 1974—77. Mem. City of Mission Viejo Libr. Design Task Force, Calif., 1994—96; tchr. Ch. on Northside, La Habra, Calif., 1987—90, El Toro Baptist Ch., Lake Forest, Calif., 1992—2002, Hemet Valley Baptist Ch., Calif., 2002—. Recipient Cmty. Svc. Award, City of Mission Viejo, Calif., 1989. Baptist. Avocations: hiking, canoeing, kayaking, dance, reading. Office: Riverside Co Libr Sys San Jacinto Libr 500 Idyllwild Dr San Jacinto CA 92583

**SMITH, DINAH MAXWELL,** painter, photographer; b. N.Y.C. d. Francis Eugene and Jane Frances (Maxwell) S. Student, L'Acad. Julian, Paris; BFA, R.I. Sch. Design, 1963; student, Santa Fe Inst. W. Thiebaud, 1988. Watercolor instr. Parrish Art Mus., Southampton, N.Y., 1979, painting instr. oils on paper, 1997-98. One-woman shows include Nat. Arts Club, N.Y.C., 1975, City Center, Kulicke Gallery, N.Y.C., 1976, Sarah Y. Rentschler Gallery, N.Y.C., Bridgehampton, N.Y., 1982, The Townhouse Gallery, N.Y.C., 1984, Union League Club, N.Y.C., 1988, 92, Mark Humphrey Gallery, Southampton, N.Y., 1993, AHI/Lizan-Tops, N.Y.C., 1995, East Hampton 1996, New Light Arts, Water Mill, N.Y., Coach Gallery, East Hampton, N.Y., Mecox Gardens, Southampton, N.Y., 1998, Wessel Gallery, Hamburg, Germany, 1998, 2001, Cook-Pony Farm, Sag Harbor, NY, Franco-Allemand Ch. of Commerce, Paris, 2001, Holstein Gallery, Emmendingen, Germany, 2001, Bancotec, Stuttgart, Germany, 2001, Paradise Cafe, Sag Harbor, 2002, Hampton Road Gallery, 2003, Southampton; works also listed in Palette Talk mag., 1988 and Am. Artist mag., 1998, 2002; contbr. articles to mags. and jours. Episcopalian. Avocations: tennis, gardening. Home and Office: 1421 Berninghaus Rd Taos NM 87571 Office Phone: 505-758-4876.

**SMITH, DONALD ARCHIE,** religious business executive, consultant; b. Dayton, Ohio, Feb. 23, 1934; s. Archie Ford and Catherine Rosella (Rabold) S.; m. Joan Sandra Speedie, May 18, 1955; children: Douglas Alan, Keith Cameron, Deirdre Lynn, Neal Ramsey. BA in Sci. and Math., Harvard U., 1956; cert., Indsl. Coll. of Armed Forces, 1971. Mgmt. Acct., 1977, Enrolled Agt., 1996. Nuclear rsch. and project engr. N.Am. Aviation Co., 1956-62; fin. software specialist Nat. Cash Register, 1962-63; mgr. sys. engring. N.Am. Aviation, 1963-67; mgr. bus. planning, mktg. svcs. and pub. rels. N.Am. Rockwell, Columbus, Ohio, 1967-72, mgr. internat. sales and mktg., 1968-73; mgr. strategic planning Rockwell Internat. Corp., Columbus, 1973-76, program mgr. Condor weapons sys., 1976-77, dir. guided bomb programs, 1977-78, dir. bus. devel. and legis. liaison, 1978-80; v.p. fin. applied tech. group Arvin Industries, Columbus, Ind., 1980-84; v.p. fin. Calspan Corp., Columbus, Ind., 1980-82, v.p. fin. and adminstrn., 1982-84, CFO, treas., dir., 1983-84; bus. dir. Franklin United Meth. Home, 1984-86; dir. fin. and adminstrn. North Ind. Conf. of the United Meth. Ch., 1986-92; sr. assoc. gen. sec. health benefits/gen. bd. of pensions United Meth. Ch., 1992-96; staff devel. cons. legal ednl. software, 1996-2000; pres. Kid Solve, Inc., 1999—. Ops. rsch. cons., 1962-64; instr. math. Sinclair Coll., Dayton, Ohio, 1961-63; mem. U.S.-U.K. Bipartite Com. on Nuclear Weapons, 1958-61; industry chmn. Mil. Specifications and Stds. Rev. Com., 1972-79; mgmt. cons., 1984—. Author: Financial Recordkeeping Handbook for Local Churches, Past pres., treas., trustee Players Theatre of Columbus, 1975—80; v.p. Ohio Assn. U.S. Army, 1979—80; dist. commr. Boy Scouts Am., 1970—73, cubmaster, 1965—70; squadron comdr. CAP, 1976; treas., dir. Franklin United Meth. Home, 1982—84; auditor First United Meth. Ch., 1981—84; ch. adminstr. Greenwood United Meth. Ch., 1997—2002; dir., treas. South Ind. United Meth. Found., 2002—; treas., trustee Columbus Arts Guild, 1980—83; mem. audit and rev. com. Gen. Coun. on Fin. and Adminstrn., 1988—92; chmn. Commn. on Racism in Columbus Pub. Schs., 1972; trustee Indpls. East Dist. United Meth. Ch., 2002—. Recipient Nat. award Jr. Achievement, Inc., 1954; Letters of Commendation govt. agys., Am. Def. Preparedness Assn., Boy Scouts Am., 1958-78; Leadership award Nat. Mgmt. Assn., 1979. Mem.: NAEA, NAA, NRA, SAR, AIA (nat. chmn. soc. and aerospace tech. com. 1980—83, nat. pub. policy com.), AARP (state chmn. Ill. 1993—95, mem. nat. tech. com. 1996—98, state adminstr. Ind. 1996—2003), Royal Inst. Nav., Nat. Mgmt. Assn. (v.p., trustee), Nat. Tng. Com. (chmn. 1998—2003, Gt. Lakes regional coord. 2003—), Army and Navy Club, Harvard Club (Ind.), Palatines to Am., Shriners, Masons. Home and Office: 7 E Hill Valley Dr Indianapolis IN 46227-2624 Office Phone: 319-889-0771.

**SMITH, DONALD CAMERON,** retired preventive medicine physician; b. Peterborough, Ont., Can., Feb. 2, 1922; arrived in U.S., 1952, naturalized, 1960; m. Jean Morningstar, Sept. 11, 1946. MD, Queen's U., 1945; MSc in Medicine, U. Toronto, Ont., 1948, DPH, 1949. Diplomate Am. Bd. Preventive Medicine, Am. Bd. Pediatrics. Intern Victoria Hosp., London, Ont., Canada, 1945-46; fellow in physiology U. Toronto, 1947—49; med. officer health Kent County (Ont.) Health Unit, 1950—52; Commonwealth Fund fellow in pediat. U. Mich. Hosp., 1952-55; prof. maternal and child health Sch. Pub. Health U. Mich., prof. pediat. Med. Sch., chmn. dept. health and human devel., 1961-79; prof. psychiatry and behavioral scis. Northwestern U. Med. Sch., Chgo., 1979-85; ret., 1985. Chmn. Medicaid Adv. Coun., 1969—72; vis. prof. maternal and child health Harvard U., 1969—72; prin. advisor health and med. affairs to gov., Mich., 1972—78; dir. Mich. Dept. Mental Health, 1974—78; chmn. State Pub. Health Adv. Coun., 1982—90; chmn. health care policy bd. Mich. Dept. Corrections, 1986—91; med. dir. Sisters Mercy Health Corp., 1981—91. Surgeon lt. Royal Can. Navy, 1946—47. Address: # 408 807 Asa Gray Dr Ann Arbor MI 48105 Business E-mail: leelo@umich.edu.

**SMITH, DONALD E.,** broadcast engineer; b. Salt Lake City, Sept. 10, 1930; s. Thurman A. and Louise (Cardall) S.; m. Helen B. Lacy, 1978. BA, Columbia U., 1955; BS, U. Utah, 1970; postgrad., U. So. Calif., U. Utah, Harvard U.; PhD (hon.), Columbia U., 1985. Engr. Iowa State U. (WOI-TV), 1955-56; asst. chief engr. KLRJ-TV, Las Vegas, 1956-60; studio field engr. ABC, Hollywood, Calif., 1960; chief engr. Teletape, Inc., Salt Lake City, 1961; engring. supr. KUER, U. Utah, Salt Lake City, 1962-74, gen. mgr., 1975-85. Freelance cinematographer, 1950—; cons. mgmt. engr., 1965—. Mem. Soc. Motion Pictures and TV Engrs., Lambda Chi Alpha. Home: 2233 S 500 E Unit #115 Salt Lake City UT 84106-1485 E-mail: donald.smith2@comcast.net.

**SMITH, DONALD RAY,** magazine dealer; b. Louisville, Dec. 12, 1934; s. Henry Bland and Margaret Frances (Corbett) S. Student pvt. schs., Louisville. Clerk Huber & Huber Motor Express, Louisville, 1951-52, Retail Credit Co., Louisville, 1952-53, Louisville & Nashville R.R., Louisville, 1953-65; owner, appraiser, cons. Don Smith's Nat. Geog. Mags., Louisville, 1969—. Author: Nat. Geog. Mag. for Collectors, 1975, 2d edit., 1978, 3d rev. edit., 1985, 4th rev. edit., 1988, 5th rev. edit., 1992, 6th rev. edit., 1996, Gone With the Wagons, 1980; composer song My Dreams Desire Another Way, 1968, poem Calico Waltz, 1986, Beyond Repast, 1986, The Essence of Darkness, 1986, The Dominant Submissive, 1987, Agony's Prelude, 1987, The Unmoving Distance, 1988, Exercise, 1997, Doris Jean, 1998, Cranfling's Release, 1998, Mr. Gally, 1999, Every Time I Hear My Favorite Song, 1999; price guide booklet for collectors of Nat. Geog. Mag., 2000, Nat. Geog. Collector's Newsletter, 2000, Torell's First Love, 2001, Put Your Dreams in a Cup, 2001, I Heard Your Melody of Words, 2002, The Sealed Doorway, 2003, The Picture of Helga Harwell, 2004, Hopeless Surrender, 2004, The Valley of the Morons, 2005, The Lady on the Wall, 2005, Symbols are Written on the Walls, 2005, The Third Profile, 2005, A Gift from the Heavens, 2006; contr. pamphlets and articles on collecting mags. Democrat. Roman Catholic. Avocations: finger syle guitar, drawing, painting. Home and Office: 3930 Rankin St Louisville KY 40214-1748

**SMITH, DONALD RAYMOND,** librarian; b. Highland, Ill., Sept. 25, 1946; s. Raymond Stanley and Gladys Loraine (Martin) S.; m. Elaine Marie Neudecker, Apr. 12, 1969; 1 child, Benjamin Christopher. BA, So. Ill. U., 1968, MA, 1972, MS, 1978; MLS, U. Mo., 1976. Acad. adv. So. Ill. U., Edwardsville, 1970-73, libr. instr., 1973-78, edn. libr., 1978-82; assoc. dir. pub. svc. and collection devel. U. Tulsa, 1982-88, assoc. dir. pub. svcs., 1988-93; dir. libr. N.E. La. U., Monroe, La., 1993-96; dean info. svcs. U. La., Monroe, 1996—2003, dean libr., 2003—. Cons. Hayner Pub. Libr., Alton, Ill., 1977-82, Tulsa City County Libr., 1984; cons. facilitator Tulsa Area Libr. Coop., 1987-88, 90; collection evaulator Okla. Jr. Coll., Tulsa, 1984. Author: Newspaper Indexing Handbook, 1981; editor and compiler newspaper index, 1976-77. Cataloger Our Lady Queen of Peace Sch., Belleville, Ill., 1979-82; campaign worker Dem. Party, Belleville, 1972; chair bd. dirs. Tulsa Area Libr. Coop., 1991-93; mem. La. Libr. Network Commn., 2004—. With U.S. Army, 1969-70. Recipient Millicent C. Palmer award Friends of Lovejoy Library, So. Ill. U., 1974, H.W. Wilson scholar, 1974, Higher Edn. Coordinating Act grantee Ill. State Library, 1980-81, Workshop award U. Okla. Sch. Library Sci., 1984. Mem.: ALA, La. Libr. Network (commn. 2004—), Tech. Consortium Tchr. Edn., Trailblazer Libr. Dirs. Bd. and Commn., La. Acad. Libr. Info. Network Consortium (at-large exec. bd. dirs. 1994—96, chmn. rsch. and devel. com. 2001—03), La. Assn. Coll. and Rsch. Librs. (automation and tech. com. 2000—, v.p., pres.-elect 2003—05), La. Libr. Assn. (sec. scholarship trust 1994—2004, co-chair ann. conf. 2003—04, network commn. 2004—), Okla. Libr. Assn. (chmn. contig. edn. com. 1985—86, chmn. adminstrn. roundtable 1989—90, chair automation roundtable 1991—92), Assn. Coll. and Rsch. Librs., Phi Delta Kappa, Phi Kappa Phi. Roman Catholic. Avocations: travel, history, reading. Office: U La Univ Libr 700 University Ave Monroe LA 71209-0720 Office Phone: 318-342-1050. Business E-mail: dosmith@ulm.edu.

**SMITH, DOROTHY OTTINGER,** apparel designer, volunteer; b. Indpls., 1922; d. Albert Ellsworth and Leona Aurelia (Waller) Ottinger; m. James Emory Smith, June 25, 1943 (div. 1984); children: Michael Ottinger, Sarah Anne, Theodore Arnold, Lisa Marie. Student, Herron Art Sch. of Purdue U. and Ind. U., 1941-42. Comml. artist William H. Block Co., Indpls., 1942-43, H.P. Wasson Co., 1943-44; dir. Riverside (Calif.) Art Ctr., 1963-64; jewelry designer Riverside, 1970—; numerous design commns. Adviser Riverside chpt. Freedom's Found. of Valley Forge; co-chmn. fund raising com. Riverside Art Ctr. and Mus., 1966-67, bd. dirs. Art Alliance, 1980-81; mem. Riverside City Hall sculpture selection panel Nat. Endowment for the Arts, 1974-75; chmn. fundraising benefit Riverside Art Ctr. and Mus., 1973-74, trustee, 1980-84, chmn. permanent collection, 1981-84, co-chmn. fund drive, 1982-84, trustee, 1998—; chmn. Riverside Mcpl. Arts Commn., 1974-76, Silver Anniversary Gala, 1992; juror Riverside Civic Ctr. Purchase Prize Art Show, 1975; mem. pub. bldgs. and grounds subcom., gen. plan citizens com. City of Riverside, 1965-66; mem. Mayor's Commn. on Civic Beauty, Mayor's Commn. on Sister City Sendai, 1965-66; bd. dirs., chmn. spl. events Children's League of Riverside Community Hosp., 1952-53; bd. dirs. Crippled Children's Soc. of Riverside, spl. events. chmn., 1952-53; bd. dirs. Nat. Charity League, pres. Riverside chpt., 1965-66; mem. exec. com. bd. trustees Riverside Arts Found., 1977-91, fund drive chmn., 1978-79, project rev. chmn., 1978-79, advisor Eveing for the Arts, 1998, juror Gemco Charitable and Scholarship Found., 1977-85; mem. bd. women deacons Calvary Presbyn. Ch., 1978-80, elder, 1989-92; mem. incorporating bd. Inland Empire United Fund for the Arts, 1980-81; bd. dirs. Hospice Orgn. Riverside County, 1982-84; trustee Riverside Art Mus., 1998—; mem. Calif. Coun. Humanities, 1982-86. Recipient cert. Riverside City Coun., 1977, plaque Mayor of Riverside, 1977, Spl. Recognition Riverside Cultural Arts Coun., 1981, Disting. Svc. plaque Riverside Art Ctr. and Mus., Jr. League Silver Rainross Community Svc. award, 1989. Cert Appreciation Outstanding Svc. to the Arts Community Riverside Arts Found., 1990, Top Dog award Riverside Art Mus., 1999. Mem. Riverside Art Assn. (pres. 1961-63, 1st. v.p. 1964-65, 67-68, trustee 1959-70, 80-84, 87-92), Art Alliance of Riverside Art Ctr. and Museum (founder 1964, pres. 1969-70). Address: 3979 Chapman Pl Riverside CA 92506-1150

**SMITH, DORRANCE (J. DORRANCE SMITH),** federal agency administrator; BA, Claremont Men's Coll. Asst. to the Pres. for media affairs The White House; exec. prodr. Nightline ABC News, exec. prodr. This Week with David Brinkley; sr. media advisor & cons. Fed. Emergency Mgmt. Agy. (FEMA); sr. media advisor Coalition Provisional Authority, Iraq; media cons. Joint Com. on Inaugural Ceremonies US Ho. Reps.; asst. sec. for pub. affairs US Dept. Def., Washington, 2006—. Office: US Dept Defense 1400 Defense Pentagon Rm 2E556 Washington DC 20310-1400 Office Phone: 703-697-9312. Office Fax: 703-695-4299.*

**SMITH, DWIGHT CHICHESTER, III,** lawyer; b. Ft. Meade, Md., June 24, 1955; s. Dwight Chichester Jr. and Rachel (Stryker) S.; m. Mindy L. Kotler, Aug. 18, 1985; children: Dwight C. IV, Cornelia R. BA, Yale U., 1977, JD, 1981. Bar: DC 1982, NY 1982. Para-legal House Ethics Com., Washington, 1977-78; law clk. to Hon. Hugh Bownes U.S. Ct. Appeals (1st cir.), Concord, NH, 1981-82; assoc. Kaye, Scholer, Fierman, Hays & Handler, Washington, 1982-84, Covington & Burling, Washington, 1984-90; dep. chief counsel for legal policy Office of Thrift Supervision, Dept. of Treasury, Washington, 1990-94, dep. chief counsel for bus. transactions, 1995-99; counsel Alston & Bird, LLP, Washington, 1999—2001, ptnr., fin. svcs., products group, 2002—. Article and book rev. editor Yale Law jour., 1980-81; contbr. articles to profl. jours. Mem. Potomac Boat Club, City Tavern Club. Presbyterian. Avocation: rowing. Home: 1606 32nd St NW Washington DC 20007-2930 Office: Alston & Bird LLP North Bldg 11th Fl 601 Pennsylvania Ave NW Washington DC 20004-2601 Office Phone: 202-756-3325. E-mail: dcsmith@alston.com.

**SMITH, DWIGHT MORRELL,** chemistry professor, academic administrator; b. Hudson, NY, Oct. 10, 1931; s. Elliott Monroe and Edith Helen (Hall) S.; m. Alice Beverly Bond, Aug. 27, 1955 (dec. 1990); children— Karen

Elizabeth, Susan Allison, Jonathan Aaron; m. Elfi Nelson, Dec. 28, 1991. BA, Ctrl. Coll., Pella, Iowa, 1953; PhD, Pa. State U., 1957; ScD (hon.), Ctrl. Coll. 1986; LittD (hon.), U. Denver, 1990. Postdoctoral fellow, instr. Calif. Inst. Tech., 1957—59; sr. chemist Texaco Rsch. Ctr., Beacon, NY, 1959—61; asst. prof. chemistry Wesleyan U., Middletown, Conn., 1961—66; assoc. prof. Hope Coll., Holland, Mich., 1966—69, prof., 1969—72; prof. chemistry U. Denver, 1972—, chmn. dept., 1972—83, 1999—2001, vice chancellor for acad. affairs, 1983—84, chancellor, 1984—89; pres., bd. trustees Hawaii Loa Coll., Kaneohe, 1990—92. Mem. Registry for Interim Coll. and Univ. Pres.; mem. adv. bd. Solar Energy Rsch. Inst., 1989—91; mem. vis. com. Zettlemoyer Ctr. for Surface Studies Lehigh U., 1990—99; dept. chemistry and geochemistry Colo. Sch. Mines; mem. sci. adv. bd. Denver Rsch. Inst.; sr. advisor Rocky Mountain Ctr. Homeland Def. Editor Revs. on Petroleum Chemistry, 1975-78; editl. adv. bd. Recent Rsch. Devels. in Applied Spectroscopy, 1998—; contbr. articles to profl. jours. Chmn. Chs. United for Social Action, Holland, 1968-69; mem. adv. com. Holland Sch. Bd., 1969-70; bd. commrs. Colo. Rsch. Inst., 1984-88, Univ. Senate, United Meth. Ch., Nashville, 1987-88, 91-93; mem. adv. bd. United Way, Inst. Internat. Edn., Japan Am. Soc. Colo., Denver Winter Games Olympics Com.; mem. ch. bds. or consistories Ref. Ch. Am., N.Y., Conn., Mich., United Meth. Ch., Colo. DuPont fellow, 1956-57, NSF fellow Scripps Inst., 1971-72; recipient grants Rsch. Corp., Petroleum Rsch. Fund, NSF, Solar Energy Rsch. Inst., Camille & Henry Dreyfus Found., Inc. Mem. AAAS, Am. Assn. Aerosol Rsch., Am. Chem. Soc. (chmn. Colo. 1976, sec. we. Mich. 1970-71, joint coun. and bd. com. on sci. 1997-98, award Colo. sect. 1986), Soc. Applied Spectroscopy, Mile High Club, Sigma Xi. Achievements include patents for selective hydrogenation. Home: 1931 W Sanibel Ct Littleton CO 80120-8133 Office: U Denver Dept Chem & Biochem Denver CO 80208-0001 Office Phone: 303-871-2938. Personal E-mail: elfidwight@comcast.net. Business E-Mail: dwismith@du.edu.

**SMITH, E. BERRY,** television and radio consultant; b. Daytona Beach, Fla., Feb. 21, 1926; s. Samuel Rogers and Rosemary (Berry) S.; m. Mary Terese Hoffman, Apr. 3, 1948 (dec.); children: Kevin B., Martin J. BS, Butler U., 1949. Account exec. Sta. WIRE Radio, Indpls., 1949-54; dir. advt. and pub. relations Franklin Fin. Co., Hartford City, Ind., 1954-56; account exec. CBS Radio Network, Detroit, 1956-57; v.p. Sta. WFIE-TV, Evansville, 1957-61, Sta. WFRV-TV, Green Bay, Wis., 1961-62; exec. v.p. Sta. WLKY-TV, Louisville, 1962-64; pres. Sta. WTVW-TV, Evansville, 1964-80, Sta. WSBT, South Bend, Ind., 1981-89; sr. v.p. Schurz Commn. Inc., South Bend, 1989-2001, cons., 2001—. Dir. adv. bd. CBS-TV Affiliates Assn., 1984-87, sec., treas., 1988-90, chmn., 1990-91. Dir. Goodwill Industries, South Bend, 1984-85, Jr. Achievement Michiana, South Bend, 1984-91. Served to 1st lt. U.S. Army, 1944-46, PTO. Recipient Silver medal Am. Advt. Fedn., Evansville, Ind., 1973; named to Ind. Broadcasters Assn. Hall of Fame, 1989; appointed Sagamore of the Wabash, 1993. Mem. South Bend C. of C. (bd. dirs. 1988-92), Ind. Soc. Chgo., Nat. Press Club, Mensa, Notre Dame U. Club, Elks. Roman Catholic. Office: 5182 Finch Dr South Bend IN 46614-5491 Office Phone: 574-291-9664.

**SMITH, E. FOLLIN,** corporate financial executive; b. Miss. m. John Gerdy; children: E. Wallace Gerdy, James F. Gerdy. BA, Davidson Coll.; MBA, U. Va. With treas.'s office GM, NYC, 1985; treas. GM Canada Ltd., 1994-97; v.p. fin. GMAC; asst. treas. GM, 1994-97; CFO Delphi Cahssis, Dayton, Ohio, 1997-98; v.p., treas. Armstrong World Industries, Inc., Lancaster, Pa., 1998-2000, sr. v.p., CFO, 2000—01, Constellation Energy, Balt., 2001—03, exec. v.p., CFO, CAO, 2003—. Bd. dir. Ryder Sys. Inc. Trustee, chair audit com. Darden Sch., Univ. Va.; mem. bd. vis. Davidson Coll.; bd. dir. Balt. Mus. Art. Office: Constellation Energy 750 E Pratt St Baltimore MD 21202*

**SMITH, EARL CHARLES,** nephrologist, educator; b. Pitts., Mar. 1, 1936; s. Mose and Irene Smith. BS, Tufts U., 1957; MD, U. Pitts., 1961. Diplomate in internal medicine and nephrology Am. Bd. Internal Medicine. Intern Montefiore Hosp., Pitts., 1961-62; resident, fellow Cleve. Clinic, 1964-68; physician Cook County Hosp., Chgo., 1968-71; chief nephrology divsn. Mt. Sinai Hosp., Chgo., 1971—, pres. med. staff, 1985-87, vice chair medicine, 1987—, interim chair medicine, 1994—95, 2005—; chief nephrology divsn. Chgo. Med. Sch., 1994—, prof. medicine, 1995—. Cons. Internat. Jour. Artificial Organs, Milan, 1986—; med. adv. bd. Kidney Found. Ill., Chgo., 1980—. Co-author: Medical Exam Book-Nephrology, 1976, Self Assessment in Internal Medicine, 1980; assoc. editor Kidney jour., 1991—; contbr. articles to profl. jours. Chair hypertension com. Chgo. Heart Assn., 1973-75. Capt. USAF, 1962-64. Recipient Meritorious Svc. award, Chgo. Heart Assn., 1975. Fellow Am. Coll. Physicians, Am. Soc. Nephrology; mem. Am. Soc. Artificial Internal Organs, Am. Soc. Hypertension Specialist in Clin. Hypertension, Internat. Soc. Nephrology, Phi Beta Kappa, Alpha Omega Alpha, Sigma Xi. Office: Mount Sinai Hosp 15th and California Ave Chicago IL 60608 Office Phone: 773-257-6554. Business E-Mail: smie@sinai.org.

**SMITH, EDGAR EUGENE,** biochemist, educator, academic administrator; b. Hollandale, Miss., Aug. 6, 1934; s. Sam and Augusta Lillie (McCoy) S.; m. Inez Oree Wiley, May 27, 1955; children— E. Donald, Anthony R., Stephen S., Gregory S. BS, Tougaloo Coll., 1955; MS, Purdue U., 1957, PhD, 1960; degree (hon.), Morehouse Sch. Medicine, 1989, U. Mass., 2000, Tongalo Coll., 2002. Rsch. fellow in surgery (biochemistry) Harvard Med. Sch., Boston, 1959-61, rsch. assoc., 1961-68; assoc. in surg. rsch. Beth Israel Hosp., Boston, 1959-68; asst. prof. surgery (chemistry) Boston U. Sch. Medicine, 1968-70, assoc. prof. biochemistry, 1970-74, U. Mass. Med. Sch., Worcester, 1974-80, prof. emeritus biochemistry and molecular biology, 1991—, assoc. dean acad. affairs, 1974-77, provost, 1975-83; asst. dean minority affairs, prin. investigator Bur. Health Manpower Spl. Project grant Boston U. Sch. Medicine, 1977-74; v.p. acad. affairs U. Minn. System, 1983-91; v.p. Nellie Mae, 1990-93; acting pres. Tougaloo Coll., 1995, edn. cons., 1996-98; sr. advisor to pres. Tougaloo Coll., 2002—; dir. AHEC program U. Miss. Med. Ctr., 1998-2000. Mem. governing bd. Robert Wood Johnson Health Policy Fellowship Program, Inst. Medicine, NAS, 1978-85. Contbr. writings to sci. publs. Chmn. bd. overseers Sch. Medicine Morehouse Coll.; trustee Tougaloo Coll., Metco Scholarship Fund, Lexington, Mass.; bd. dirs. Dimock Community Health Center, Boston, New Urban League of Greater Boston, So. Edn. Found., 1979; chmn. Boston Com. for Nat. Med. Fellowships, Inc. Recipient research career devel. award Nat. Cancer Inst., 1969-74, award for outstanding achievement in biochemistry Nat. Consortium for Black Profl. Devel., 1976, human relations award Mass. Teachers Assn., 1977, health award NAACP, 1977; Robert Wood Johnson Health Policy fellow Inst. Medicine, Nat. Acad. Scis., 1977-78; named Alumnus of Yr. Tougaloo Coll., 1969, Disting. Alumnus Nat. Assn. for Equal Opportunities in Higher Edn., 1979, 92, Old Master Purdue U., 1978 Fellow Am. Inst. Chemists; mem. Am. Soc. Biol. Chemists, Am. Chem. Soc. (div. biol. chemists), AAAS, N.Y. Acad. Scis., Am. Assn. for Cancer Research, Boston Cancer Research Assn., Am. Polit. Sci. Assn., Am. Soc. Biol. Chemists (com. on minorities 1980-83), Josiah Macy, Jr. Found. Scholarship Com. Marine Biol. Lab., Woods Hole, Mass., Sigma Xi, Phi Lambda Upsilon, Alpha Phi Alpha. Home: 5934 Paddock Pl Jackson MS 39206-2135 E-mail: Esmithahec@aol.com.

**SMITH, EDWARD KENDRICK,** lawyer; b. Atlanta, Dec. 9, 1956; s. Alexander Wyly and Elizabeth (Haverty) Smith; m. Caryl Greenberg Smith, Oct. 16, 1983; children: Gina Leigh, Jacob Ryan. BA, U. NC, Chapel Hill, 1974—78; JD, U. Ga., Athens, 1978—81. Bar: Ga. 1981, US Ct. Appeals (11th cir.), US Dist. Ct. (no. mid. & so. dist). Ptnr. Smith Gambrell & Russell, LLP, Atlanta, 1981—2005, Jones Day, Atlanta, 2005—. Instr. Lorman Bus. Inst, 1989—. Inst. Continuing Legal Edn., Nat. Bus. Inst., Inc. Chmn. Rsch. Atlanta, 1993—97; program chair Leadership Ga., Atlanta, 1997—98; chmn. Servants of Relief for Incurable Cancer, Atlanta, 2000—05, The Bridge, Inc.; mem. exec. com. Atlanta Downtown Partnership, 1990—92; pres. The Bridge, Atlanta, 1991—99; trustee SW Hosp. & Med. Ctr., Atlanta, 1991—2002; bd. dirs. Atlanta Progress, Atlanta, 1994—2005; bd. mem. Bd. Visitors U. Ga. Law Sch., Athens, 2004—05; bd. mem. Zoo Atlanta, Atlanta, 2004—05; bd. dirs., trustee SW Hosp. & Medical Ctr., Atlanta. Recipient Ga. Legal Elite, Ga. Trend Mag., 2003, 2004, 2005, Ga.

Super Lawyer, Atlanta Mag., 2003, 2004, 2005, Ga. Legal Leader, James Mag., 2005. Mem.: ABA, Nat. Dicesan Attys. Assn., Ga. Hosp. Assn., Am. Acad. Hosp. Lawyers, Inst. Profls. Taxation, Piedmont Driving Club. Avocations: squash, jogging, piano. Office: Jones Day 1420 Peachtree St Ste 800 Atlanta GA 30309 Office Fax: 404-581-8330. Business E-Mail: eksmith@jonesday.com.

**SMITH, EDWARD PAUL, JR.,** lawyer; b. Westbury, N.Y., Jan. 13, 1939; s. Edward Paul Sr. and Margaret (Eisenhauer) S.; m. Mary Elizabeth Neagle, Mar. 29, 1980; children: Nora, Edward, Brian, Thomas, Brendan. BA, Coll. of the Holy Cross, 1960; LLB, Columbia U., 1963. Bar: NY 1964, Fla. 1966. Assoc. Chadbourne & Parke LLP, NYC, 1964-75, prin., 1975—, ptnr. corp. dept., employment dept. Corp. sec. Am. Bur. Metal Statis., NYC, 1978—. Contbr. articles to profl. jour. Capt. USAF, 1964-67. Mem. NY State Bar Assn., Fla. Bar Assn. Roman Catholic. Office: Chadbourne & Parke LLP 30 Rockefeller Plz Fl 31 New York NY 10112-0129 Office Phone: 212-408-5100. Office Fax: 212-541-5369. Business E-Mail: esmith@chadbourne.com.

**SMITH, EDWIN E.,** aerospace transportation executive; b. West Point, Miss., Dec. 16, 1968; s. William Earl and Beth Clay Smith. Interior installation team leader Dassault Falcon Jet, Little Rock, Ark., 1999—. Author: (poetry collection) One Stranger to Another. Instigator Ghost Pub., Little Rock, 2003—06. Buddhist. Personal E-mail: edwinesmith@edwinesmith.com.

**SMITH, EDWIN ERIC,** lawyer; b. Louisville, Sept. 29, 1946; s. Lester Henry and Nancy Joy (Heyman) S.; m. Katharine Case Thomson, Aug. 16, 1969; children: Benjamin Clark, George Louis, Andrew Laurence. BA, Yale U., 1968; JD, Harvard Law Sch., 1974. Bar: Mass. 1974, NY, 2005, US Dist. Ct. Mass. 1974. Assoc. Bingham McCutchen LLP, Boston, 1974—81, ptnr., 1981—, co-chmn. fin. instn. practice group. Lectr. in field; Mass. commr. on uniform state laws; articles 5 and 9 drafting com. Uniform Comml. Code, chmn. payments article divsn. drafting com., editl. bd., 2005—; U.S. del. to receivables assignment working group UN Commn. on Internat. Trade Law Trustee Uniform Law Found. Lt. USNR, 1969-71. Recipient Achievement Medal USN, 1971. Mem. ABA (chmn. uniform comml. code com., law sect. 1995-99, permanent editl. bd. uniform comml. code 1999-), Am. Law Inst. (Uniform Comml. Code article 9 study com.), Am. Coll. Comml. Fin. Lawyers (pres. 2002-03), Assn. Comml. Fin. Attys., Nat. Bankruptcy Conf., Am. Coll. Bankruptcy. Office: Bingham McCutchen LLP 150 Federal St Boston MA 02110-1713 Office Phone: 617-951-8615. Office Fax: 617-951-8736. Business E-Mail: edwin.smith@bingham.com.

**SMITH, ELAINE DIANA,** foreign service officer; b. Glencoe, Ill., Sept. 15, 1924; d. John Raymond and Elsie (Gelbard) S. BA, Grinnell Coll., 1946; MA, Johns Hopkins U., 1947; PhD, Am. U., 1959. Commd. fgn. svc. officer U.S. Dept. State, 1947; assigned to Brussels, 1947-50, Tehran, Iran, 1951-53, Wellington, New Zealand, 1954-56, Dept. State, Washington, 1956-60, Ankara, Turkey, 1960-69, Istanbul, Turkey, 1969-72, Dept. Commerce Exch., 1972-73; dep. examiner Fgn. Svc. Bd. Examiners, 1974-75; Turkish desk officer Dept. State, Washington, 1975-78. Consul gen. Izmir, Turkey, 1978—. Author: Origins of the Kemalist Movement, 1919-1923, 1959. Recipient Alumni award Grinnell Coll., 1957. Mem. U.S. Fgn. Svc. Assn., Phi Beta Kappa. Home: The Plaza 800 25th St NW Apt 306 Washington DC 20037-2207

**SMITH, ELDEN LEROY,** recreational vehicle company executive; b. Berwyn, Ill., June 1, 1940; s. Frederick M. and Margaret I. (Larson) S.; B.A. in Bus. Adminstrn., Whittier Coll., 1962; m. Barbara G. Whaley, Apr. 4, 1963; children— Jill Marie, David Elden. Market analyst Autonetics div. N.Am. Aviation, Anaheim, Calif., 1963-66; sales mgr. Pendleton Tool Industries, Los Angeles, 1966-68; plant gen. mgr. Fleetwood Enterprises, Inc., Hancock, Md., 1969-71, v.p. recreational vehicle group, Riverside, Calif., 1972-88, sr. v.p., 1988-97, pres., dir. & CEO 2005-. Trustee Whittier (Calif.) Coll., 1991-99. Served with USNR, 1962-63. Mem. Recreation Vehicle Industry Assn. (chmn. 1980-82, dir. 1975-97). Office: Fleetwood Enterprises 3125 Myers St Riverside CA 92503

**SMITH, ELDON,** cardiologist, physiologist, educator; MD, Dalhousie U., Halifax, N.S., Can., 1967. From asst. prof. to assoc. prof. medicine and physiology Dalhousie U., 1973—80; prof. medicine and physiology and biophysics U. Calgary, Canada, 1980—2004, prof. emeritus, 2004—, chief divsn. cardiology, 1980—86, chair dept. medicine, 1985—90, assoc. dean clin. affairs, 1990—92, dean faculty of medicine, 1992—97; trustee Alta. Heritage Found. for Med. Rsch., Canada, 2000—; dir., pres. Peter Lougheed Med. Rsch. Found., 1999—, mem. Premier's adv. coun. of health, 2000—02, mem. health professions adv. bd., 2002—. Corp. dir. Can. Natural Resources, Ltd., 1997—, Vasogen, Inc., 1998—, Pheromone Scis. Corp., 2000—, Overlord Fin., Inc., 2005—. Editor-in-chief: Can. Jour. Cardiology, 1991—. Recipient officer Order of Can. Fellow: Can. Acad. Health Scis., Am. Heart Assn., Internat. Acad. Cardiovasc. Scis., Am. Coll. Cardiology, Royal Coll. Physicians and Surgeons Can. Office: U Calgary Faculty Medicine 3330 Hosp Dr Calgary AB Canada T2N 4N1 Office Phone: 403-220-5500. Business E-Mail: esmith@ucalgary.ca.

**SMITH, ELDRED GEE,** church leader; b. Lehi, Utah, Jan. 9, 1907; s. Hyrum Gibbs and Martha E. (Gee) S.; m. Jeanne A. Ness, Aug. 17, 1932 (dec. June 1977); children: Miriam Smith Skeen, Eldred Gary, Audrey Gay Smith Vance, Gordon Raynor, Sylvia Dawn Smith Isom; m. Hortense H. Child, May 18, 1978; stepchildren: Carol Jane Child Burdette (dec.), Thomas Robert Child. Employed with sales div. Bennett Glass & Paint Co., Salt Lake City, 6 years; mech. design engr. Remington Arms Co., 2 years; design engr., prodn. equipment design Tenn. Eastman Corp., Oak Ridge, Tenn., 3 years; now presiding patriarch Ch. Jesus Christ of Latter-day Saints. Mem. Lds Ch. Home: 2942 Devonshire Cir Salt Lake City UT 84108-2526 Office: 47 E South Temple Salt Lake City UT 84150-9701

**SMITH, ELEANOR JANE,** retired university chancellor, consultant; b. Circleville, Ohio, Jan. 10, 1933; d. John Allen and Eleanor Jane (Dade) Lewis; m. James L. Banner, Aug. 10, 1957 (div. 1972); 1 child, Teresa M. Banner Watters; m. Paul M. Smith Jr. (dec. Apr. 30, 2004). BS, Capital U., 1955; PhD, The Union Inst., Cin., 1972. Tchr. Columbus (Ohio) Pub. Schs., 1956-64, Worthington (Ohio) Pub. Schs., 1964-72; from faculty to administrator U. Cin., 1972-88; dean Smith Coll., Northampton, Mass., 1988-90; v.p. acad. affairs, provost William Paterson Coll., Wayne, NJ, 1990-94; chancellor U. Wis.-Parkside, Kenosha, 1994-97, ret., 1997; ind. cons. in higher edn. Dir. Afrikan Am. Inst., Cin., 1977-84; adv. bd. Edwina Bookwalter Gantz Undergrad. Studies Ctr., Cin.; mem. Gov.'s Tobacco Tax adv. coun.; lectr. in field. Performances include (concert) Black Heritage: History, Music and Dance, 1972—. Spl. Arts Night Com., Northampton, 1988-89; bd. dirs. Planned Parenthood No. and Ctrl. Ariz., Am. Lung Assn. Ariz./N.Mex. Named career woman of achievement YWCA, Cin., 1983. Mem. AAUW, Nat. Assn. Women in Higher Edn., Am. Assn. for Higher Edn., Leadership Am. (bd. dirs., treas. 1993-95), Nat. Assn. Black Women Historians (co-founder, co-dir. 1979-82), Am. Coun. on Edn. (mem. com. on internat. edn. 1994-97, bd. dirs. 1995-97), Am. Assn. State Colls. and Univs. (mem. com. on policies and purposes 1994-97). Avocations: music, pen and ink drawing, travel, reading. Home: 1208 Verona Way Keller TX 76248

**SMITH, ELISE FIBER,** international non-profit development agency administrator; b. Detroit, June 14, 1932; d. Guy and Mildred Geneva (Johnson) Fiber; m. James Frederick Smith, Aug. 11, 1956 (div. 1983); children Gregory Douglas, Guy Charles; life ptnr. Jac Smit, 1990. BA, U. Mich., 1954; postgrad., U. Strasbourg, France, 1954-55; MA, Case Western Res. U., 1956. Tchr. U.S. Binat. Ctr., Caracas, Venezuela, 1964-66; instr. English Am. U., 1966-68; prof. lang. faculty Catholic U., Lima, Peru, 1968-70; coord. English lang. and culture program, lang. faculty El Rosario U., Bogota, Colombia, 1971-73; lang. specialist. mem. faculty Am. U., English Lang. Inst., 1975-78; exec. dir. OEF Internat. (name formerly Overseas Edn. Fund), Washington,

1978-89, bd. dirs.; dir. Global Women's Leadership Program Winrock Internat., 1989-98, sr. policy advisor on gender, 1998—. Co-founder, founding chair Women's EDGE, 1997—; v.p. Pvt. Agys. Collaborating Together, NYC, 1985-90; trustee Internat. Devel. Conf., Washington, 1983-2001, exec. com., 1985-90; hon. com. for Global Crossroads Nat. Assembly, Global Perspectives in Edn., Inc., NYC, 1984, Washington, 1984-92, gen. assembly, 1992; nat. com. Focus on Hunger '84, LA; ofcl. observer UN Conf. on Status Women, 1980, UN 3rd World Conf. on Women, 1985, del. NGO Forum, UN 4th World Conf. on Women, del. NGO Forum, 1995; mental health adv. com. Dept. State, 1974-76; U.S. del. planning seminar integration women in devel. OAS, 1978; participant Women, Law and Devel. Forum; exec. com., chair commn. advancement women interaction Am. Coun. for Vol. Internat. Action, co-founder, co-chair, 1982-84, exec. com., 1985-88; adv. bd. Global Links Devel. Edn., Washington, 1985-86; adv. coun. Global Fund for Women, 1988-93; US del. Vital Voices Conf. Women and Democracy, Iceland, 1999, Women in Democracy Conf., Lithuania, 2000, Baltic Women in Democracy Conf., Estonia, 2003. Co-editor: Toward Internationalism: Readings in Cross-cultural Communication, 1979, 2d edit. 1986; author: (book chpt.) Developing Power: How Women Transformed International Development, 2004. Bd. dirs. Internat. Ctr. Rsch. on Women, 1992-2001, Sudan-Am. Found.; adv. com. on vol. fgn. aid US AID, 1994—; women and conservation adv. com. World Wildlife Fund, 1998-2002; state dept. adv. com. US Internat. Econ. Policy, 2000—. Rotary Internat. ambassadorial scholar Strasbourg, France, 1954-55; grantee Dept. State, 1975. Mem. Assn. Women in Devel., UNIFEM, Coalition Women in Internat. Devel. (co-founder 1979, chair 1993-96),pvt. Agys. in Internat. Devel. (co-chmn. 1980-82, pres. 1982-85), Nat. Assn. Fgn. Student Affairs (grantee 1975), U. Mich. Alumni Assn., Women's Fgn. Policy Group, Rotary Internat. (mem. global com. Women in Future Soc. 1996). Unitarian Universalist. Home: 4701 Connecticut Ave NW Apt 304 Washington DC 20008-5617 Office Phone: 202-362-6234. Business E-Mail: esmith@winrock.org.

**SMITH, ELIZABETH ANGELE TAFT,** curator; Degree art history, Columbia U. Curator Mus. Contemporary Art, LA, 1983—99, James W. Alsdorf Chief Curator Chgo., 1999—. Adj. prof. pub. art studies program U. So. Calif., 1992—98; bd. advisors Independent Curators Internat., NYC; bd. overseers, Sch. Architecture, Ill. Inst. Tech., Chgo. Curator (exhibitions) Blueprints for Modern Living: History and Legacy of the Case Study Houses, Mus. Contemporary Art, LA, 1989, Urban Revisions: Current Projects for the Public Realm, 1994, Cindy Sherman: Retrospective, 1997, At the End of the Century: One Hundred Years of Architecture, 1998, The Architecture of R.M. Schindler, 2001 (Named Best Architecture or Design Exhibition of Yr., Internat. Assn. Art Critics/USA, 2001), Matta in America: Painting and Drawings of the 1940s, Mus. Contemporary Art, Chgo., 2001, Donald Moffett: What Barbara Jordan Wore, 2002, Lee Bontecou: A Retrospective, 2003 (Named Best Monographic Mus. Show Nationally, Internat. Assn. Art Critics/USA, 2004); author: (books) Techno Architecture, 2000, Case Study Houses: The Complete CSH Program 1945-66, 2002; co-editor: Lee Bontecou: A Retrospective of Sculpture and Drawing, 1958-2000, 2003. Named Woman of Yr., Chgo. Soc. Artists, 2004. Office: Mus Contemporary Art 220 E Chgo Ave Chicago IL 60611

**SMITH, ELIZABETH MACKEY,** retired financial consultant; b. Phila., Mar. 23, 1941; d. William Norman and Celeste (Parvin) Mackey; m. George Van Riper Smith, Aug. 15, 1964; children: Douglas George, Todd Mackey. BA, Gettysburg Coll., 1963; MAT in French, Ga. State U., 1978. ChFC. Tchr. fgn. lang. Haverford (Pa.) H.S., 1963-65; registered rep. Am. Express Fin. Advisors, Inc., Macon and Savannah, Ga., 1979-2000, br. mgr. Tybee Island, Ga., 2000—05, ret., 2005. Reader Atlanta Serv for the Blind, 1968; hostess Atlanta Coun Int Visitors, 1972—74; foreign exchange student coord Loisirs Culturels a l'Etranger, 1990; staff protocol vol sailing venue Olympic Games, Savannah, 1996. Mem.: Delta Gamma, Delta Phi Alpha, Phi Sigma Iota. Avocations: tennis, swimming. Home: 104 Landings Way North Savannah GA 31411-1512 Personal E-mail: islandwoman64@earthlink.net.

**SMITH, ELLIS CARLTON,** history educator, consultant; b. Quantico, Va., Nov. 15, 1937; s. Ellis Carlton Smith and Eunice Wells; children from previous marriage: Catherine, Caron. BGS, Chaminade U., Honolulu, 1972; MA, Pepperdine U., Malibu, Calif., 1973. Chief master sgt. U.S. Air Force, 1955—81; tchr. social studies Bastrop Mid. Sch., Tex., 1981—83, Dripping Springs H.S., Tex., 1983—. Advanced placement cons. Coll. Bd. Southwest Region, Austin, Tex. Named Top Tex. Tchr., Republic of Tex. Press, 2002; recipient Spl. Recognition award, Coll. Bd. Southwest Region, 1997, Excellence in Tchg. award, Dripping Springs Ind. Sch. Dist. Edn. Found. Bd., 2003. Mem.: Tex. Fedn. Tchrs., U.S. Tennis Assn., Phi Delta Kappa. Methodist. Avocation: tennis. Office: Dripping Springs HS Hwy 290 and Tiger Ln Dripping Springs TX 78620-0479 Home: Apt B 357 Fantail Loop Lakeway TX 78734-4191

**SMITH, ELMER,** telecommunications industry executive; Grad., Tulane U. Numerous positions The Berry Co.; pres., CEO The Berry Co. (now Bellsouth Corp.); pres. advt. and pub. Bellsouth Corp., Atlanta, 2001—. Mem.: Assn. Directory Mktg. (bd. dirs.), Yellow Pages Integrated Media Assn. (chmn. 2003—04). Office: Bellsouth Corporation 472 Ivy Park Ln Ne Atlanta GA 30342-4554

**SMITH, ELWIN EARL,** mining and oil company executive; b. Ellicottville, NY, Sept. 30, 1922; s. Henry B. and Beatrice M. (Spellman) S.; m. Mary Ellen Kirchmaier, Nov. 4, 1944; children: Peter E., Michael E., Timothy E. Student, U. Ala., 1941-43, NYU, 1954, Harvard Bus. Sch., 1962. Sales engr. Cities Service Oil Co., N.Y.C., 1949-55; gen. sales mgr. Climax Molybdenum Co., N.Y.C., 1955-64; exec. v.p., dir. Lithium Corp. Am., Gastonia, N.C., 1964-69, pres., CEO, 1969-77; v.p. Gulf Resources & Chem. Co., Houston, 1970-77; pres., dir. Asia Lithium Corp., Osaka, Japan, 1970-77; pres. Amax Iron Ore, Greenwich, Conn., 1977-80, corp. v.p., group exec. for indsl. minerals and resources group, 1978-80; exec. v.p. Amax Inc., Greenwich, 1981-82, sr. exec. v.p., 1982-85; prin. Elwin Smith Internat. Sales Engrs., Darien, Conn., 1986—. Bd. dirs. Am. Metal & Coal Co., Greenwich, Ct., Ethanol Corp., Sydney, Australia, First Dynasty Mines, Denver, IMR Industries, Ltd., London; chmn. Seven Seas Cinema, Stamford, Conn., 1985-95. 1st lt. U.S. Army Paratroopers, 1943-48. Decorated Combat Inf. badge, Bronze Star, sr. parachute badge. Mem. AIME, Am. Petroleum Inst., Am. Chem. Soc., Am. Australian Assn., Japan Soc., Asia Soc., Mining and Petroleum Club of Sydney, Copper Club N.Y., Weeburn Country Club, Masons. Republican. Home and Office: 7 Tokeneke Trl Darien CT 06820-6126 Office Phone: 203-655-9129. E-mail: thesquare@aol.com.

**SMITH, EMIL L.,** biochemist, educator; b. NYC, July 5, 1911; s. Abraham and Esther (Lubart) S.; m. Esther Press, Mar. 29, 1934; children— Joseph Donald, Jeffrey Bernard BS, Columbia U., 1931, PhD, 1936. Instr. biophysics Columbia U., N.Y.C., 1936-38; John Simon Guggenheim fellow Cambridge U., Eng., 1938-39, Yale U., New Haven, 1939-40; fellow Rockefeller Inst., N.Y.C., 1940-42; biophysicist, biochemist E. R. Squibb & Sons, New Brunswick, N.J., 1942-46; assoc. prof. to prof. biochemistry U. Utah, Salt Lake City, 1946-63; prof. biol. chemistry Sch. Medicine UCLA, 1963-79, prof. emeritus, 1979—Cons. NIH, Am. Cancer Soc., Office Naval Research Author: (with others) Principles of Biochemistry, 7th edit., 1983; also numerous articles Recipient Stein-Moore award Protein Soc., 1987. Mem. NAS, Am. Acad. Arts and Scis., Am. Philos. Soc., Am. Soc. Biochemistry and Molecular Biology, Am. Chem. Soc., Protein Soc., Acad. Scis. Russia (fgn.). Office: UCLA Sch Medicine Los Angeles CA 90095-1737

**SMITH, EMMITT J., III,** retired professional football player; b. Pensacola, Fla., May 15, 1969; s. Emmitt Jr. and Mary Smith. Student, U. Fla. Running back Dallas Cowboys, 1990—2003, Ariz. Cardinals, 2003—04. Player Pro-Bowl, 1990—95, 1998—99, Super Bowl XXVII, 1992, Super Bowl XXVIII, 1992; owner Emmitt Inc. Named Running Back, Sporting News Coll. All-Am. team, 1989, Offensive Rookie of Yr., 1990, Running Back, Sporting News NFL All-Pro team, 1992, 1993, NFL Player of Yr., Sporting News, 1993; named to NFC Pro-Bowl Team, 1990—95, 1998—99, Coll.

Football Hall of Fame, 2006; recipient MVP award for season, 1993, MVP award for Super Bowl, 1993. Achievements include recognized as NFL's all-time leading rusher, 2002; leading NFL in rushing, 1991-93, 95; leading NFL running backs in scoring, 1992, 95; leading NFL in rushing Touchdowns, 1992, 1994-1995; being a member of Super Bowl Champion Dallas Cowboys, 1992, 1993, 1995. Office: Ariz Cardinals PO Box 888 Phoenix AZ 85001-0888*

**SMITH, EPHRAIM PHILIP,** academic administrator; b. Fall River, Mass., Sept. 19, 1942; s. Jacob Max and Bertha (Horvitz) S.; m. Linda Sue Katz, Sept. 3, 1967; children: Benjamin, Rachel, Leah. BS, Providence Coll., 1964; MS, U. Mass., 1965; PhD, U. Ill., 1968. Chmn. dept. acctg. U. R.I., Kingston, 1972-73; dean Sch. Bus. Shippensburg State Coll., Pa., 1973-75; dean Coll. Bus. Adminstrn. Cleve. State U., 1975-90; dean Sch. Bus. Adminstrn. and Econ. Calif. State U., Fullerton, 1990-98, v.p. acad. affairs, 1998—. Co-author: Principles of Supervision: First and Second Level Management, 1984, Federal Taxation-Advanced Topics, 1995, Federal Taxation-Basic Principles, 2006, Federal Taxation Comprehensive Topics, 2006; contbr. articles to profl. jours. Mem. Am. Acctg. Assn., Am. Taxation Assn., Am. Inst. for Decision Scis., Fin. Execs. Inst., Beta Gamma Sigma, Beta Alpha Psi. Office: Calif State Univ - Fullerton VPAA Office MH-133 800 N State College Blvd Fullerton CA 92831-3599 Business E-Mail: esmith@fullerton.edu.

**SMITH, ERIC LEDELL,** historian; b. Detroit, Oct. 9, 1949; s. Warren Cornelius and Henrietta Volena Smith. BA in Humanities, Mich. State U., 1971, MA in Philosophy, 1973, student, 1973—78; MLS, U. Mich., 1980; MA in Performance Studies, NYU, 1985. Sales clk. Dawn Treader Bookshop, Ann Arbor, Mich., 1980—90; asst. Libr. U. Mich., Ann Arbor, 1980—90; curator jr. edn. Detroit (Mich.) Hist. Mus., 1990—92; curator African Am. Mus., Phila., 1992—93; historian Pa. State Archives, Harrisburg, Pa., 1993—2001, State Mus. Pa., Harrisburg, 2001—. Archivist R.E. Olds Mus., Lansing, Mich., 1985; curator jr. edn. Dossin Great Lakes Mus., Detroit, 1989; curator exhbns. Author: Bert Williams: A Biography of the Pioneer Black Comedian, 1992 (nominee Pulitzer prize in biography, 1992), Blacks in Opera: A Biographical Dictionary of People and Companies, 1873-1993, 1995, African Americans in Pennsylvania: Shifting Historical Perspectives, 1997, Commemorating African American History in Pennsylvania: The First Twenty-five Years of the Conference on Black History in Pennsylvania, 2002, African American Theater Buildings, 2003 (Ray and Pat Browne Book award, 2003), The State Museum of Pennsylvania: A Centennial History, 2005; co-author: The African Americans in Pennsylvania, 1997, African Americans of Harrisburg, 2005; mem. editl. bd.: Pa. History, 1999—2001, Pa. Mag. History and Biography, 2004—; author: (plays) African Americans at the Capital Making Jazz History, 1999, When Lincoln Came to Harrisburg, 2000, The Liberation of Jim Phillips, 2001; contbr. articles to profl. jours. and mags. Bd. dirs. U.S. Colored Troops Inst., Harrisburg, Pa., 2002—03, African Am. Mus., Harrisburg, 1994—97; dir. exec. bd. Fedn. State Cultural Ednl. Profls., 2005—. Finalist Excellence Hist. Recorded Sound Rsch. award, Assn. Recorded Sound Collections, 1993; recipient Contbn. award, Pa. Dept. Edn., 1999, Individual Achievement award, Pa. Fedn. Mus. and Hist. Socs., 2003. Mem.: Hist. Harrisburg Assn., Dauphin County Hist. Soc. (bd. dirs. 1994—97), African Am. Mus. Phila., Assn. Study African Am. History, Pa. Hist. Assn. (Philip S. Klein award 1999), Org. Am. Historians. Democrat. Roman Cath. Home: 101 S 2nd St 1202 Harrisburg PA 17101 Office: The State Mus of Pa 300 North St Harrisburg PA 17120

**SMITH, ERIC PARKMAN,** retired railroad executive; b. Cambridge, Mass., Mar. 23, 1910; s. B. Farnham and Helen T. (Blanchard) S. AB, Harvard U., 1932, MBA, 1934. Staff fed. coord. transp., Washington, 1934; with traffic and oper. dept.s N.Y. New Haven & Hartford R.R., Boston and New Haven, 1934-53; with Maine Ctrl. R.R., Portland, 1953-82, sec. adv. bd. retirement trust plan, 1958-82, asst. treas., dir. cost analysis, 1970-82, bd. dirs., 1981-82. Author: Verses on an Icelandic Vacation, 1965, The Church in Concord and its Ministers, 1971, In All That Dwell Below the Skies, 1972; contbr. The Meeting House on the Green, 1985. Trustee parish donations 1st Parish in Concord, Unitarian-Universalist Ch., 1960-96, trustee emeritus, 1996—. Mem. New Eng. R.R. Club (hon.; pres. 1973-74), Louisa May Alcott Meml. Assn. (dir. 1984-99, treas. 1987-99), The Thoreau Soc. (dir. 1987-95, treas. 1987-95). Home and Office: 35 Academy Ln Concord MA 01742-2431

**SMITH, ERNEST KETCHAM,** electrical engineer; b. Peking, China, May 31, 1922; (parents Am. citizens); s. Ernest Ketcham and Grace (Goodrich) S.; m. Mary Louise Standish, June 23, 1950; children: Priscilla Varland, Nancy Smith Johnson, Cynthia Jackson. BA in Physics, Swarthmore Coll., 1944; MSEE, Cornell U., 1951, PhD, 1956. With Mut. Broadcasting Sys., 1946-49, chief plans and allocations engr., 1949; with radio propagation lab. Nat. Bur. Stds., Boulder, Colo., 1951-65, chief ionosphere rsch. sect., 1957-60, divsn. chief, 1960-65; dir. Telecom. Scis., 1968, dir. univ. rels., 1968-70; assoc. dir. Inst. Telecom. Scis. Office of Telecom., Boulder, 1970-72, cons., 1972-76; tech. staff Jet Propulsion Lab. Calif. Inst. Tech., Pasadena, 1976-87; adj. prof. dept. elec. and computer engring. U. Colo., Boulder, 1987—. Vis. fellow Coop. Inst. Rsch. on Environ. Scis., 1968; assoc. Harvard Coll. Obs., 1965-75; adj. prof. U. Colo., 1969-76; internat. vice-chmn. study group 6, Internat. Radio Consultative Com., 1958-70, chmn. U.S. study group, 1970-76; mem.-at-large U.S. nat. com. Internat. Sci. Radio Union, 1985-88; convenor Boulder Gatekeepers to the Future, 1990—. Author: Worldwide Occurrence of Sporadic E, 1957; (with S. Matsushita) Ionospheric Sporadic E, 1962. Contbr. numerous articles to profl. jours. Editor: Electromagnetic Probing of the Upper Atmosphere, 1969; assoc. editor for propagation IEEE Antennas and Propagation Mag., 1989—. Mem. 1st Congl. Ch., moderator, 1995-97. Recipient Diplôme d'Honneur, Internat. Radio Consultative Com., Internat. Telecom. Union, 1978; named to Gallery of Disting. Scientists, Engrs. and Adminstrs., Nat. Bur. Stds., Nat. Stds. and Tech., Gaithersburg, Md., 2003. Fellow IEEE (fellow com. 1993, 94, 95), AAAS; mem. Am. Geophys. Union, Electromagnetics Acad., Svc. Club, Kiwanis, Athenaeum (Pasadena), UN Assn. of U.S. (treas. 1994-2005), Sigma Xi (pres. U. Colo. chpt. 1994-95, v.p. 95-98). Home: 350 Ponca Pl Apt 179 Boulder CO 80303-3802 Office: U Colo Dept Elec & Computer Engring Campus Box 425 Boulder CO 80309-0425 Personal E-Mail: n6hqkek@aol.com. Business E-Mail: ernest.smith@colorado.edu. *A weakness of many large organizations is that it is difficult for senior administrators to step down after peaking in their 40s. I'm grateful for a crisis at age 50 which resulted in my taking early retirement at age 54 and then accepting a more modest job until age 65.*

**SMITH, ESTHER THOMAS,** communications executive; b. Jesup, Ga., Mar. 13, 1939; d. Joseph H. and Leslie Thomas; m. James D. Smith, June 2, 1962; children: Leslie, Amy, James Thomas. BA, Agnes Scott Coll., 1962. Staff writer Sunday women's editor Atlanta Jour.-Constn., 1961-62; mng. editor Bull. of U. Miami Sch. Medicine, 1965-66; corr. Atlanta Jour.-Constn. and Fla. Times-Union, 1964, 67-68; founding editor Bus. Rev. of Washington, 1978-81; founding editor, gen. mgr. Washington Bus. Jour., 1982; pres., bd. dirs. TechNews, Inc., 1986-96, CEO, 1995-96; founder, editor-at-large Washington Tech., 1986-97, Tech. Transfer Bus. Mag., 1992-95; co-chair editl. bd. TechCapital Mag., 1997-99; prin. Poretz Group Investor Rels., McLean, Va., 1998—2000; ptnr. Qorvis Comm. LLC (successor to Poretz Group), McLean, 2000—. Bd. dirs. Provant Inc., Women Connect.com, telezoo inc., World Affairs Coun. Washington, The Atlantic Coun., Netpreneur Program Morino Inst., 1996—2002; mem. internat. adv. bd. Kilby Awards Found.; mem. MIT Enterprise Forum of Washington/Balt., 1981—82, Internat. Women's Forum, 1991—, No. Va. Bus. Round Table. Lectr. Tech. 1993—98; mem. adv. bd. Va. Math Coalition, 1991—94; commr. NACD Blue Ribbon Commn., 2001; trustee Ctr. for Excellence in Edn., 1993—96; bd. dirs. trustee Capital Region Technology Investors Conf.; bd. advisors George Washington U., Va., 1996—99; trustee George Mason U. Found., 2004— Named to, Washington Bus. Hall of Fame, 2002; recipient Lifetime Achievement award, Women in Tech., 2000. Mem.: Md. High Tech. Coun., No. Va. Tech. Coun. (sr. adv. bd. 1998—2000, exec. com., bd. dirs., Earle C. Williams

Leadership award 1999), Assn. Tech. Bus. Couns. (chmn. bd. advisors 1989—94). Office: Qorvis Comm LLC 8484 Westpark Dr 8th Fl Mc Lean VA 22102 Office Phone: 703-744-7812. Business E-Mail: esmith@qorvis.com.

**SMITH, EUGENE WILSON,** retired academic administrator, education educator; b. Forrest City, Ark., June 10, 1930; s. Milton Saumel and Frank Leslie (Wilson) S.; m. Lucinda Anne Slaughter, May 27, 1956; children: Lucinda Anne, Bradley Eugene. BA, Ark. State U., 1952; M.Ed., U. Miss., 1955, Ed.D, 1958. Mem. faculty Ark. State U., State University, 1958-92, prof. edn., 1971-92, v.p. adminstrn., 1968-71, dean Grad. Sch., 1971-84, interim pres., 1981-82, pres., v.p., 1980-84, pres., 1984-92, 94-95; pres. emeritus Ark. State U., State University, 1992—; interim pres., 1994-95. Pres. Jonesboro Indsl. Devel. Corp., 1983-94; mem. exec. com. Conf. So. Grad. Schs., 1973-74, Ark. State Coun. on Econ. Edn., 1987-90; pres. Am. South Athletic Conf., 1987-89; dir. Mercantile Bank of Jonesboro, Union Planters Bank of Northeast Ark., Regions Bank of N.E. Ark. Alderman, City of Jonesboro, 1982-84, dir., pres. The Kays Found. Served to 1st lt. AUS, 1952-54, Korea. W.K. Kellogg Found. rsch. fellow, 1954-58 Mem. Ark. Adv. Council Elem. and Secondary Edn., Jonesboro C. of C. (dir. 1967-69, 80-85, v.p. 1981-82, pres. 1982-83), Phi Kappa Phi, Phi Delta Kappa, Kappa Delta Pi. Clubs: Rotary (pres. 1974-75). Home: 407 Lynne Ct Jonesboro AR 72401-8807

**SMITH, EUGENIA SEWELL,** funeral home executive; b. Albany, Ky., Oct. 24, 1922; d. Leo Matheny and Marjorie (Warinner) Sewell; m. James Frederick Smith, June 25, 1948; 1 child, Bryson Sewell (dec.). Student Berea Coll., 1937-41, Bowling Green Coll. Commerce, 1944-45. Owner, operator Sewell Funeral Home, Albany, 1977—; bd. dir. Citizens Bank of Albany, Ky., 1989—. Sec. Albany Woman's Club, 1950-54; den mother Cub Scouts, Boy Scouts Am., 1958-62; pres. Clinton County Homemakers, Albany, 1968-70, Modern Homemakers, 1992-98; mission action chmn. Missionary Baptist Ch., 1965-91; v.p. Modern Homemakers Club of Albany, 1990-92, pres., 1994-98. Democrat. Lodge: Demolay Mother's (pres. Albany club 1966-67), Order Eastern Star (former assoc. conductress, former Martha and Esther). Home: RR 5 Box 104 Burkesville Rd Albany KY 42602-9310 Office: Sewell Funeral Home 115 Cross St Albany KY 42602

**SMITH, FERN M.,** judge; b. San Francisco; children: Susan, Julie. AA, Foothill Coll., 1970; BA, Stanford U., 1972, JD, 1975. Bar: Calif. 1975. Assoc. Bronson, Bronson & McKlinnon, San Francisco, 1975-81, ptnr., 1981—86; judge San Francisco County Superior Ct., 1986-88, U.S. Dist. Ct. (no. dist.) Calif., 1988—. Dir. Fed. Jud. Ctr., Wash., 1999-2003; mem. adv. com. on Jud. Conf. U.S., Rules of Evidence, 1993-96, chair, 1996—. mem. exec. com. Ninth Cir. Jud. Conf., 1994-96, Ninth Cir. State-Fed. Jud. Coun., 1990-93, Calif. Jud. Coun. 1987-88, mem. adv. Task Force on Gender Bias, 1988-90, hiring, mgmt. and pers. coms., active recruiting various law schs.; faculty Inst. Study and Devel. Legal Sys., 1992, Egypt & Bolivia, 1994, Mexico and Tunisia, 1995, Israel, Jordan, Greece and Egypt, 1996, India, 1998, Jordan and Italy, 1998, Italy, Israel and France, 2000, India, Israel and Russia, 2001, Morocco, Thailand and China, 2002, Turkey, Bahrain, the Netherlands and Russia, 2003, Jordan and Brazil, 2004, ISDLS Rule of Law Conf., Berkeley, Calif.; bd. vis. Law Sch. Stanford U., 1990-92, 99—; chair U.S. Jud. Conf. Com. on Internat. Jud. Rels., 2003—. Contbr. articles to legal publ. Mem. ABA, Queen's Br. Nat. Assn. Women Judges, Calif. Women Lawyers Assn., Bar Assn. San Francisco. Fed. Judges Assn., 9th Cir. Dist. Judges Assn., Am. Judicature Soc., Calif. State Fed. Jud. Coun., Phi Beta Kappa.

**SMITH, FLOYD LESLIE,** insurance company executive; b. Silver Creek, N.Y., Nov. 12, 1931; s. Harry Lee and Fanny Diem (Arnold) S.; m. Jane Kathryn Elters, Feb. 18, 1956; children: Keith Arnold, Bruce Erik. AB, Oberlin Coll., (Ohio), 1953; MBA, NYU, 1962. Investment analyst Mut. of N.Y., N.Y.C., 1953-64, dir. investments, 1964-66; asst. v.p. securities investment Mut. of N.Y., N.Y.C., 1966-69; 2d v.p. securities investment Mut. of N.Y., N.Y.C., 1969-74, v.p. securities investment, 1974-78, sr. v.p., 1978-81, chief investment officer, 1981-83, exec. v.p., chief investment officer, 1983-89, vice chmn., chief investment officer, 1989-91; trustee The Mut. Life Ins. Co. of N.Y., 1988-91; dir. MONY Series Fund, 1983—2005, Empire Fidelity Investments Life Ins. Co., 1994—. Trustee MONY Real Estate Investors, N.Y.C., 1981-90; bd. dirs., chmn. exec. com. Ins. Systems Am., Atlanta, 1974-82. Trustee Friends Sem., N.Y.C., 1975-84, Village of Saltaire, 1984-87; dir. St. Maarten Condo. Assn., Naples, Fla., 1993—; mem. Saltaire (N.Y.) Zoning Bd. Appeals, 1982-84; mem. fin com. N.Y. Quarterly Meeting Soc. of Friends, 2004—. With Signal Corps, U.S. Army, 1954-56. Mem. Ft. Worth Boat Club, Edgewater Club.

**SMITH, FRANK EARL,** retired trade association administrator; b. Fremont Center, N.Y., Feb. 4, 1931; s. Earl A. and Hazel (Knack) S.; m. Caroline R. Gillin, Aug. 14, 1954; children: Stephen F., David S., Daniel E. BS, Syracuse U., 1952. With Mellor Advt. Agy., Elmira, NY, 1954-55; asst. mgr. Elmira Assn. of Commerce, 1955-56; retail dept. mgr. C. of C., Binghamton, NY; mgr. Better Bus. Bur., Broome County, NY, 1956-60; exec. v.p. C. of C., Chemung County, Elmira, 1960-65, Schenectady County (N.Y.) C. of C., 1965-69, Greater Cin. C. of C., 1969-78; pres. Greater Detroit C. of C., 1978-95. Dir. Presbyn. Devel. Corp. Detroit, Inc. 1995; bd. dirs., sec. Presbyn. Devel. Corp. of Detroit, Inc. Served to 1st lt. USAF, 1952-54. Named Young Man of Yr. Jr. C. of C. Elmira, 1964. Mem. C. of C. Execs. Mich., Am. C. of C. Execs. (past chmn.), N.Y. State C. of C. Execs. (past pres.), Ohio C. of C. Execs. (past pres.), C. of C. of U.S. (past bd. dirs. Ctr. Internatl Pvt. Enterprise, past chmn. nat. bd. regents, Inst. for Orgn. Mgmt.). Presbyterian. Home: 173 Windwood Pointe Dr Saint Clair Shores MI 48080

**SMITH, FRANK G., III,** lawyer; b. Greenville, Miss., June 6, 1952; BA cum laude, Davidson Coll., 1974; JD, Stanford Univ., 1977. Bar: Ga. 1977. Ptnr., head, intellectual property litig. group Alston & Bird LLP, Atlanta. Contbr. articles to profl. journals. Mem.: Order of Coif, Phi Beta Kappa. Office: Alston & Bird LLP One Atlantic Ctr 1201 W Peachtree Street NE Atlanta GA 30309-3424 Office Phone: 404-881-7240. Office Fax: 404-253-8184. Business E-Mail: fsmith@alston.com.

**SMITH, FREDERICK COE,** retired manufacturing executive; b. Ridgewood, NJ, June 3, 1916; s. Frederick Coe and Mary (Steffee) S.; m. Ruth Pfeiffer, Oct. 5, 1940; children: Frederick Coe, Geoffrey, Roger, William, Bart. BS, Cornell U., 1938; MBA, Harvard U., 1940. With Armstrong Cork Co., Lancaster, Pa., 1940-41; with Huffy Corp., Dayton, Ohio, 1946-86, pres., chief exec. officer, 1961-72, chmn., chief exec. officer, 1972-76, chmn., 1976-78, chmn. exec. com., 1979-86. Past chmn. Sinclair C.C. Found.; past chmn. nat. bd. dirs. Planned Parenthood Fedn.; past dir. Internat. Parenthood Fedn.; past chmn. Dayton Found.; trustee emeritus Alan Gutmacher Inst., Ohio United Way; past chmn. employment and tng. com. Gov.'s Human Investment Coun. Lt. col. USAAF, 1941-46. Decorated Legion of Merit. Office Fax: 937-223-1441. Personal E-Mail: dotti8@aol.com.

**SMITH, FREDERICK H.,** archaeologist, educator; b. Columbus, Ohio, Mar. 7, 1966; s. William Lee and Mona Frank Smith; m. Rachel W. Bulf, Aug. 6, 1994; 1 child, Rachel W. BA, George Mason U., Fairfax, Va., 1989; MA, Coll. William and Mary, Williamsburg, Va., 1994; PhD, U. Fla., Gainesville, 2001. Asst. prof. Western Mich. U., Kalamazoo, 2002—05, Coll. William and Mary, 2005—. Vis. prof. U. Fla., 1999—2001. Author: (book) Caribbean Rum: A Social and Economic History, 2005. Mem.: Soc. Hist. Archaeology (assoc.), Barbados Mus. and Hist. Soc. (life). Achievements include research in archaeology of Barbados.

**SMITH, FREDERICK ORVILLE, II,** agricultural products executive, retired military officer; b. Cambridge, Mass., July 17, 1934; s. Harry Francis and Dorothy Spaulding (Zeller) S.; m. Mabel Roxy Moore, June 6, 1965; children: Sarah Zeller, Jennifer Joy, Erika Hildred. BA, Bowdoin Coll., 1956; MA in Polit. Sci., U. Vt., 2000. Deck officer, 1st lt. USN, 1957-59; officer US Naval Sta., Adak, Alaska, 1959-60; clk. & exec. Fred O. Smith Mfg. Co., New

Vineyard, Maine, 1960-71, pres., treas., 1971—; res. officer Naval Res. Tng. Ctr., Augusta, Maine, 1960-69, Bangor, Maine, 1970-79 (ret.). Co-owner Sugarwood Gallery, Inc., 2000—. Editor: New Vineyard, Maine 1802-2002, Its Settlement, Its People, Its History, A New Vineyard Historical Society Document, 2002. Notary pub., 1978—; chair, mem. nat. com. Young Reps., Maine, 1960—68, pres. New Eng. coun., 1962—64; chmn. Franklin County (Maine) Rep. Com., 1976—80, v.p. state conv., 1994; mem. Maine Rep. State Com., 1980—86, 1992—94, 1998—2002, 2006—; mem. state com. ASCO, 1998—2002; town chmn. Rep. Com., New Vineyard, 1972—86, Farmington, Maine, 1992—, Paul Harris fellow Farmington Rotary Club, 1996. Mem.: Porter Lake Assn. (bd. dirs. 2005—), Franklin County Arts and Crafts (v.p. 2002—05), Up Country Artists (bd. dirs. 1996—2003, v.p. 1997, pres. 1998—2000, bd. dirs. 2000—03, v.p., bd. dirs. 2005—), Shriners, Masons, Kora Temple Shrine. Congregationalist. Avocations: photography, cabinet making & design, skiing, hiking, writing. Home: 127 Anson St Farmington ME 04938-5734 Office: The Fred O Smith Mfg Co PO Box 248 New Vineyard ME 04956-0248 Fax: 207-779-0716. Office Phone: 207-778-4177. E-mail: fosmith@somtel.com.

**SMITH, FREDERICK WALLACE,** delivery service executive; b. Marks, Miss., Aug. 11, 1944; s. Frederick Smith; m. Diane Avis., div. BS in Econs., Yale U., 1966. Cert. comml. pilot. Owner Ark Aviation, 1969-71; founder FedEx Express Corp., Memphis, 1971—, pres., 1971—75, CEO, 1977—98, chmn. bd., 1975—; CEO FedEx Corp., 1998—. Served with USMC, 1966-70, co-chmn. WWII Meml. Campaign. Named one of 400 Richest Ams., Forbes mag., 2006; recipient Eagle of Aviation award, Embry-Riddle Aero. award, 2001, Champion of Workplace Learning and Performance award, Amer. Soc. Tng. and Devel., 2002. Office: FedEx Corp 942 S Shady Grove Rd Memphis TN 38120-4117*

**SMITH, FREDRICA EMRICH,** rheumatologist, internist; b. Princeton, NJ, Apr. 28, 1945; d. Raymond Jay and Carolyn Sarah (Schleicher) Emrich; m. Paul David Smith, June 10, 1967. AB, Bryn Mawr Coll., 1967; MD, Duke U., 1971. Intern, resident U. N.Mex. Affiliated Hosps., 1971-73; fellow U. Va. Hosp., Charlottesville, 1974-75; pvt. practice, Los Alamos, N.Mex., 1975—. Chmn. credentials com. Los Alamos Med. Ctr., 1983—; chief staff, 1990, 2003; bd. dirs. N.Mex. Physicians Mut. Liability Ins. Co., Albuquerque, 1988-97; regional adv. bd. Am. Physicians Assurance, 1997-. Contbr. articles to med. jours. Mem. bass sect. Los Alamos Symphony, 1975—; mem. Los Alamos County Parks and Recreation Bd., 1984-88, 92-96, Los Alamos County Med. Indigent Health Care Task Force, 1989—2003; mem. ops. subcom. Aquatic Ctr., Los Alamos County, 1988—. Fellow ACP, Am. Coll. Rheumatology; mem. N.Mex. Soc. Internal Medicine (pres. 1993-96), Friends of Bandelier. Democrat. Avocations: swimming, music, reading, hiking. Office: Los Alamos Med Ctr 3917 West Rd Los Alamos NM 87544-2275 Office Phone: 505-662-9400.

**SMITH, GARDNER WATKINS,** physician; b. Boston, July 2, 1931; s. George Van Siclen and Olive (Watkins) S.; m. Susan Elizabeth Whiteford, Sept. 6, 1958; children: Elizabeth Whiteford, Rebecca Tremain, George Van Siclen II. Grad., Phillips Acad., 1949; MD, Harvard U., 1956; AB, Princeton U., 1969. Diplomate: Am. Bd. Surgery, Am. Bd. Thoracic Surgery. Intern Johns Hopkins Hosp., Balt., 1956-57, asst. resident, 1958-59, fellow, 1957-58, asst. in surgery, 1957-59, prof. surgery, 1970-96, emeritus prof. surgery, 1996—, dep. dir. dept. surgery, 1978-85. Asst. resident U. Va., Charlottesville, 1959-61, resident, 1961-62, asst. in surgery, 1959-63, cardiovascular resident, 1962-63, instr., 1963-65, asst. prof., 1965-67, assoc. prof., 1967-70, surgeon, 1963-70; chief surgery Balt. City Hosp., 1970-79, vis. surgeon, 1979-85; chmn. sect. surg. scis. Johns Hopkins Bayview Med. Ctr., 1985-96; bd. dirs. Blue Hill Meml. Hosp. Found., 1998-06, chair, 1999-00; bd. dirs. Blue Hill Meml. Hosp., 1998-05, chair, 2000-04; cons. Greater Balt. Med. Ctr., 1970-91, Loch Raven VA Hosp., Balt., 1971-92, Walter Reed Army Med. Ctr., 1976-90, Nat. Naval Med. Ctr., 1984-90; trustee Kneisal Hall, 2005—. Contbr. articles to med. jours. Mem. ACS, Soc. U. Surgeons, Am. Surg. Assn., So. Surg. Assn., Am. Gastroenterol. Assn., Assn. for Acad. Surgery, Balt. City Med. Soc., Halsted Soc., Med. and Chirurgical Faculty of Md., Soc. Surgery Alimentary Tract, Soc. Vascular Surgery, Internat. Cardiovascular Soc., So. Soc. Clin. Surgeons, Southeastern Surg Congress, So. Assn. Vasular Surgery, Va. Surg. Assn., Cum Laude Soc., Alpha Omega Alpha, Nu Sigma Nu. Home and Office: 95 Plumb Point Rd PO Box 565 Deer Isle ME 04627-0565 Personal E-Mail: gwsmith@hughes.net.

**SMITH, GARY RICHARD,** technology educator; b. Little Rock, Ark., Jan. 21, 1929; s. C. Ray and Maureen (Martin) S.; m. Mary Clare Beacom, June 16, 1956; children: Raymond, Timothy, Daniel, Laura, Carolyn. BA, Cornell Coll., 1952; MEd, Nat. Coll. Edn., Evanston, Ill., 1954; PhD, Northwestern U., 1960. Asst. editor Chem. Processing Mag., Chgo., 1952-53; tchr. various elem. schs. Evanston, Ill., 1954-58; instr. Northwestern U., Evanston, 1958-60; asst. prof. Wayne State U. Detroit, 1960-63, assoc. prof., 1964-69, prof., 1970—. Edn. rsch. cons. Mich. Senate Edn. Com., Lansing, 1973-74, Mich. Com. to Redistrict Detroit Pub. Schs., 1981. Contbr. articles to profl. jours With U.S. Army, 1948-49. Mem. Internat. Soc. for Technology in Edn. Home: 3514 Arrowvale St Orchard Lake MI 48324-1506 Office: Wayne State U Rm 227 Edn Bldg Detroit MI 48202

**SMITH, GARY W.H.,** retired sales executive; s. Howard Frederick and Violet Irma Smith; m. Donna Jean Schallert, July 28, 1962; children: Darren H.F., Brian R.A., Garrick D.S. Student, Phoenix Coll., 1959—62, Fresno City Coll., 1963—64; BS in Psychology, Edgewood Coll., 2001. Regional mktg. dir. Berven Carpets Corp., Fresno, Calif., 1962—69; terr. mgr. Phila. Carpet Co., Dalton, Ga., 1969—75; pres., owner G. Wentworth Smith, Inc., Columbus, Wis., 1975—2003; v.p. ops., CEO Royal Impex Corp., Watertown, Wis., 1978—79; v.p. sales and mktg. Jacolde Wholesale Inc., Madison, Wis., 1983—86; pres., CEO Simuwear Corp., Columbus, 1995—2003; ret., 2003. Con. Human Movement Disorders Lab. U. Pitts. Sch. Medicine, 1990—2003. Editor-in-chief: Comml. Carpet Digest, 1979—92, columnist: Gralla Pubs. Trade Press, 1990. Chmn. Dane County Rep. Party Campaign Sch., Madison, 1980; campaign mgr. Rep. Party, Wis., 1982, del. various state conventions Wis.; cons. gubernatorial, congl. and legis. candidates. Recipient J.B. Campbell award, Dane County Rep. Party, 1980. Mem.: Masons (jr. warden 1979). Republican. Mem. Congregational Ch. Achievements include patents for foot force simulator. Avocations: writing, singing, composing. Home: 913 Vernon Ave Madison WI 53714

**SMITH, GEORGE,** marketing professional; Assoc. Sci. in Liberal Arts, Monroe Community Coll., Rochester, NY. Field sales rep. Elec. Components, Avnet, Inc. 1978—80, gen. mgr. Rochester, NY, 1980—84, Boston, 1984—88; N.E. regional v.p. Avnet, Inc., 1989—91; ea. area mgr. Avnet Computer Mktg., 1991; sr. v.p. sales North Am. Avnet Computer Mktg. Group, 1992—94; exec. v.p. Avnet Computer, 1994; exec. v.p. Hall-Mark Computer Products Avnet, Inc., 1995, pres. Hall-Mark Computer Products, 1996; regional pres. Avnet Computer Mktg. Europe, 1997; pres. Avnet Electronics Mktg. EMEA, Phoenix, 1998—2003; pres. computer mktg. Europe Avnet Computer Mktg.-Avnet Applied Computing, 2001—03; pres. Avnet Computer Mktg.-Avnet Applied Computing, Asia, 2003—; v.p. Avnet, Inc., 1996—. Office: Avnet Inc 2211 S 47th St Phoenix AZ 85034

**SMITH, GEORGE BUNDY,** state appeals court judge; b. New Orleans, Apr. 7, 1937; m. Alene L. Smith; children: George, Jr., Beth Beatrice. Cert. Polit. Studies, Institut d'Etudes Politiques, Paris, 1958; BA, Yale U., 1959, JD, 1962; MA in Polit. Sci., NYU, 1967, PhD, 1974; M of Jud. Process, U. Va., 2001. Staff atty. NAACP, 1962-64; law sec. to Hon. Jawn Sandifer, 1964-67; law sec. to Hon. Edward Dudley, 1967-71; law sect. to Hon. Harold Stevens, 1972-74; adminstr. model cities City of NY, 1974-75; interim judge Civil Ct. NYC, 1975-76, judge, 1976-79; NY State Supreme Ct., 1980-86, assoc. justice appellate divsn., 1st dept., 1987-92; assoc. judge NY State Ct. Appeals, NYC, 1992—. mem. NY State Ethics Commn. Unified Ct. System, 1989-90; adj. prof. law Fordham U., 1981—. Author: (with Alene L. Smith) You Decide: Applying the Bill of Rights to Real Cases; contbr. articles to profl. jours. Trustee Grace Congl. Ch., Harlem, NY, Horace Mann-Barnard

Sch., Bronx, NY, 1977-99; bd. dirs. Harlem-Dowling Westside Ctr. for Children and Family Svcs., NYC; former alumni trustee Phillips Acad., Andover, Mass. Mem. Met. Black Bar Assn. (founding, former pres. Harlem Lawyers Assn., bd. dirs., chmn. 1984-88), Assn. of Bar of City of NY (v.p. 1988-89), Judicial Friends. Office: NY Court Appeals 29th Fl 61 Broadway Rm 2900 New York NY 10006-2802 also: Ct of Appeals Hall 20 Eagle St Albany NY 12207-1009*

**SMITH, GEORGE CURTIS,** judge; b. Columbus, Ohio, Aug. 8, 1935; s. George B. and Dorothy R. Smith; m. Barbara Jean Wood, July 10, 1963; children: Curtis, Geoffrey, Elizabeth Ann. BA, Ohio State U., 1957, JD, 1959. Bar: Ohio 1959, U.S. Dist. Ct. (so. dist.) Ohio 1987. Asst. city atty. City of Columbus, 1959-62; exec. asst. to Mayor of Columbus, 1962-63; asst. atty. gen. State of Ohio, 1964; chief counsel to pros. atty. Franklin County, Ohio, 1965-70; pros. atty., 1971-80; judge Franklin County Mcpl. Ct., Columbus, 1980-85, Franklin County Common Pleas Ct., 1985-87; sr. judge U.S. Dist. Ct., 2002—. Mem. 2003 Ohio Bicentennial Com.; mem. Historical Marker com., 2003; mem. Ohio Supreme Ct. Coun. on Victims Rights; judge in residence Law Sch. U. Cin.; chair Fed. Ct. Case Settlement Seminar; faculty Ohio Jud. Coll., Litig. Practice Inst.; chmn., Fed. Bench-Bar Conf.; lectr. ABA Anti-Trust Sec.; alumni spkr. law graduation Moritz Coll. Law, Ohio State U.; pres. Young Rep. Club; chmn. Perry Group, 2005; exec. com. Franklin County Rep. Party, 1971-80 Elder Presbyn. Ch. Recipient Superior Jud. Svc. award Supreme Ct. Ohio, Outstanding Pub. Svc. award Fr. Co. Rep. Orgn., 2001, Judge W.K. Thomas award Ohio State U. Law Alumni, 2005, Disting. Jurist, 2006, Ohio Pros. of Yr. award Ohio Pros. Attys. Assn., Hon. Leadership award. Mem. Columbus Bar Assn., Columbus Bar Found., Columbus Athletic Club (pres., dir.), Lawyers Club of Columbus (pres.), Masons (pres. 33 deg.), Shriners, Gyro Club (pres.). Office: 85 Marconi Blvd Columbus OH 43215-2823 Office Phone: 614-719-3220.

**SMITH, GEORGE DRURY,** publishing executive; b. Dayton, Ohio, Mar. 10, 1927; s. Martin Jefferson and Viola (Haas) S.; m. Anne Liard Jennings, Apr. 1967 (div. 1977); life ptnr. Leston Chandler Buell, 1996. AB cum laude, Marietta Coll., 1953; Diplome de Phonetique, U. Grenoble, 1950; student, U. Madrid, 1950-51, Heidelberg U., 1951-52, U. Minn., 1953-55, U. Calif.-Berkeley, 1965, UCLA, 1968. CFO Argonaut newspaper, 1972—. Editor: Beyond Baroque, 1968-80, NewLetters, 1969-75, (book series) NewBooks, 1976-78. Founder Beyond Baroque Found., Venice, Calif., 1968, chmn., 1968-80, chmn. emeritus, 1980—; mem. Mcpl. Arts Adv. Bd., L.A., 1980-82; chmn. Save Westminster Auditorium Com., Venice, 1977-80. With U.S. Army, 1945-47. Grantee Nat. Endowment for Arts, 1973-80, Calif. Arts Coun., 1977-80, Mcpl. Arts Commn., 1977-80, Coordinating Coun. Lit. Mags., 1974-80. Home Fax: 323-443-3808. Personal E-mail: georgedrurysmith@yahoo.com. *I believe that if we can live without fear; that the universe is benevolent if we can love unconditionally; that we can live righteously and prosper if we are honest and seek divine guidance; and that our mission is to enjoy life and strive for beauty.*

**SMITH, GEORGE PATRICK, II,** lawyer, educator; b. Wabash, Ind., Sept. 1, 1939; s. George Patrick and Marie Louise (Barrett) S. BS, Ind. U., 1961, JD, 1964; certificate, Hague Acad. Internat. Law, 1965; LLM, Columbia U., 1975; LLD, Ind. U., 1998. Bar: Ind. 1964, U.S. Supreme Ct. 1968. Kannert teaching fellow Ind. U. Sch. Law, 1964-65; instr. law U. Mich. Sch. Law, 1965-66; practiced in Ind. and Washington, 1965—; legal adviser Fgn. Claims Settlement Commn., Dept. State, Washington, 1966; asst. prof., asst. dean State U. N.Y. at Buffalo Law Sch., 1967-69; vis. asst. prof. law George Washington U., Nat. Law Center, summer 1968; assoc. prof. law U. Ark., 1969-71; spl. counsel EPA, Washington, 1971-74; adj. prof. law Cath. U. Law Sch., Washington, 1973-74, prof., 1977—. Spl. counselor environl. affairs Gov. Ark., 1969—71; mem. Ark. Waterway Commn., 1970—71; mem. com. hwy. rsch. NRC, NAS, 1971—81; adj. prof. law Georgetown U., 1971—75; assoc. prof. law U. Pitts., 1975—78; numerous vis. prof. positions including most recently; vis. fellow Law Sch. Fordham U., 1999; fellow Emmanuel Coll. Cambridge (England) U., 1999; vis. prof. U. New South Wales, Australia, 2001, U. Sydney, Australia, 2003; disting. vis. prof. Macquarie U., Sydney, 2005; numerous vis. fellowships including most recently; vis. fellow Program Law and Pub. Health Johns Hopkins U., Washington, 2001—02; vis. fellow Australlnoan Inst. Ethics and Professions U. Queensland, Brisbane, Australia, 2003; vis. fellow Inst. Health Law Loyola U., Chgo., 2004; vis. fellow Ctr. Interdisciplinary Study Religion Emory U., Atlanta, 2005; numerous vis. scholar positions including most recently; vis. scholar Ctr. Clin. Bioethics Georgetown U., Washington, 1998—99; vis. scholar Ctr. Theology and Natural Scis. U. Calif., Berkeley, 1999; vis. scholar Ctr. Study Sci. and Religion Columbia U., 2002; vis. scholar Reily Ctr. Sci., Tech. and Values Notre Dame U., 2002, vis. scholar Ctr. Ethics in Culture, 03; vis. scholar Law Sch. Cardiff (Wales) U., 2002; cons. in field; lectr. in field; vis. fellow Rothermeer Inst., Oxford U., 2006; vis. scholar Inst. Spirituality and Health George Washington U., 2006; vis. scholar Ctr. for the Study of Religion and Politics U. St. Andrews, Scotland, 2006; vis. fellow Rothermere Am. Inst. Oxford U., England, 2006. Author: Restricting the Concept of Free Seas, 1980, Legal, Ethical and Social Issues of the Brave New World, 1980, Genetics, Ethics and the Law, 1981, Medical-Legal Aspects of Cryonics, 1983, The New Biology, 1989, Final Choices: Autonomy in Health Care Decisions, 1989, Bioethics and the Law, 1993, Legal and Healthcare Ethics for the Elderly, 1996, Family Values and the New Society: Dilemmas of the 21st Century, 1998; Human Rights and BioMedicine, 2000, The Christian Religion and Biotechnology, 2005; contbr. articles to profl. jours. U. Ark. del. Pacem In Maribus Conf., Malta, 1970. Recipient Disting. Alumni award Ind. U. Bd. Trustees, 1985, citation for Path-Breaking Work; establishment of George P. Smith II Disting. Professorship of Law, Ind. U., Bloomington, 1986. Mem. ABA (rep. UN Conf. on Human Environ. Stockholm 1972, rep. Law of Sea Conf., UN, N.Y.C. 1976, Switzerland 1979, cons. UNESCO Declaration on the Production of the Protection of the Human Genome, Paris 1995-97), Am. Law Inst., Soc. Ind. Pioneers, Am. Friends of Cambridge U., Order of St. John Hospitaller, Alpha Kappa Psi, Phi Alpha Delta, Sigma Alpha Epsilon, Order of Omega. Clubs: Cosmos (Washington). Republican. *Think big, work hard and, above all, have a dream: these are the simple guideposts for a fulfilling life.*

**SMITH, GEORGE THORNEWELL,** retired state supreme court justice; b. Camilla, Ga., Oct. 15, 1916; s. George C. and Rosa (Gray) S.; m. Eloise Taylor, Sept. 1, 1943 (dec.). Grad., Abraham Baldwin Agrl. Coll., 1940; LLB, U. Ga., 1948. Bar: Ga. 1947. Assoc. Cain & Smith, Cairo, Ga., 1947-71; city atty. Cairo, 1949-58; atty. Grady County, 1950-59; solicitor Cairo City Ct., 1951-59; mem. Ga. Ho. of Reps., 1959-67, speaker of the house, 1963-67; lt. gov. State of Ga., 1967-71; city atty. East Point, Ga., 1973-76; judge Ga. Ct. Appeals, 1976-81; justice Ga. Supreme Ct., Atlanta, 1981-91, presiding justice, 1990-91; of counsel Browning & Smith LLC, Marietta, Ga., 1992—. Past mem. exec. com. Nat. Coll. Appellate Judges; vice chmn. Nat. Conf. Lt. Govs. Trustee Nat. Arthritis Found. Lt. comdr. USN, 1940-45. Only person in the state's history to serve in an elective capacity in all 3 brs. of govt. Mem. State Bar Ga., Cobb County Bar Assn., Lawyers Club Atlanta, Am. Legion, VFW, Moose, Kiwanis. Avocations: hunting, golf. Office: Browning & Smith 31 Atlanta St Ste 201 Marietta GA 30060 Office Phone: 770-424-1500.

**SMITH, GEORGE VINAL,** librarian; b. Chgo., May 14, 1943; s. Earl Wesley and Frances (Kenney) S.; m. Chrystal Jean Stillings, Jan. 29, 1966; children: Rebecca Tyson, Morgen Elizabeth. BA, Whitman Coll., 1965; MA, Wash. State U., 1967; PhD, No. Ill. U., 1974; MS, U. Ill., 1975. Reference libr. Illinet/U. Ill., Urbana, 1975-76; info. svcs. cons. Lincoln Trail Libr. System, Champaign, Ill., 1977-79; circulation and network svcs. supr. Oreg. State Libr., Salem, 1979-81, adminstr. of libr. devel., 1983-85; dir. Canby (Oreg.) Pub. Libr., 1981-82, Woodburn (Oreg.) Pub. Libr., 1982-83; dep. dir. Alaska State Div. of Libr., Archives and Mus., Juneau, Alaska, 1985—91, acting dir., 2002—05; assoc. dep. dir. state programs Inst. of Mus. and Libr. Svcs., Washington, 2005—. Vol. Peace Corps, Thailand, 1967-69; vis. asst. prof. Grad. Sch. Libr. Sci., U. Ill., 1977-78; instr. Chemekata C.C., Salem, 1980-83, Marylhurst Coll., Lake Oswego, Oreg., 1982; course mentor Grad. Sch. Libr. Sci., U. Ariz., Juneau, Alaska, 1992-94; mem. State of Alaska

Personnel Reinvention Com., 1996; Library Fellow to Bulgaria, US State Dept., 2000. Author: The Dutch in 17th-Century Thailand, 1977; co-editor and author: Contributions to Asian Studies, 15, 1980. Pres., bd. dirs., coach Juneau Soccer Club, 1992-94; dir., adminstrv. staff Arctic Winter Games/Team Alaska, Fairbanks, 1992—2005; coach, referee, referee trainer, Juneau Parks and Recreation Dept., 1986—2005; vol., patron Alaska Folk Festival, 1986—. NDEA fellow No. Ill. U., 1972-73; recipient Gov.'s Mgmt. Recognition award, Gov. Oreg., 1985. Mem. ALA (Libr. fellow to Nat. Libr. Cambodia 1994-95), Pacific N.W. Libr. Assn. (pres., v.p. 1987-89), Alaska Libr. Assn., Oreg. Libr. Assn. (pres., v.p. 1984-85). Avocations: fishing, hiking, backpacking, soccer coaching and refereeing. Office: Inst of Mus and Libr Svcs 1100 Pennsylvania Ave NW Washington DC 20506 Office Phone: 202-653-4650. E-mail: vinal1@verizon.net.

**SMITH, GEORGE WOLFRAM,** physicist, researcher; b. Des Plaines, Ill., Sept. 19, 1932; s. Murray Sawyer and Alice Lucile (Wolfram) S.; m. Mary Lee Sackett, Sept. 7, 1956; children— Dean, Grant. BA, Knox Coll., 1954; MA, Rice U., 1956, PhD, 1958. Welch Found. fellow Rice U., 1958-59; sr. rsch. physicist GM, Warren, Mich., 1959-76, dept. rsch. scientist, 1976-81, sr. staff rsch. scientist, 1981-87, prin. rsch. scientist, 1987-99; retired, 1999. Lectr. physics and astronomy Cranbrook Inst. Sci., Bloomfield Hills, Mich., 1963-87, mem. sci. adv. com., 1989—; instr. Lawrence Inst. Tech., 1963-65; vice chmn. Gordon Rsch. Conf. on Orientational Disorder in Crystals, 1976, chmn., 1978; co-chmn. Internat. Symposium on Particulate Carbon, 1980; mem. rev. com. Liquid Crystal Inst., Kent (Ohio) State U., 1984-85; mem. adv. com. Conf. on Electrorheological Fluids, 1991, 93; mem. adv. bd. NSF Sci. and Tech. Ctr. for Advanced Liquid Crystalline Optical Materials, 1996-00; physics co-chair Internat. Sci. and Engring. Fair, 2000; invited spkr. Ill. Assn. Physics Tchrs., 2003. Co-editor: Particulate Carbon: Formation During Combustion, 1981; editl. cons. Ency. Applied Physics, 1988-00; contbr. Handbook of Chemistry and Physics; contbr. 100 articles to sci. and tech. jours.; patentee on temperature measuring device, liquid crystal device tech., dielectric heating, graphite fiber growth, polymer-dispersed liquid crystals. Mem. Mich. Regtl. Civil War Roundtable, 1965—, pres., 1971-72. Recipient Knox Coll. Achievement award 1977, John M. Campbell Research award, 1980, Charles L. McCuen Achievement award, Gen. Motors, 1985. Fellow Am. Phys. Soc. (com. on applications of physics 1988-91, chmn. 1991, chmn. com. on tutorials 1991, mem. Pake Prize Com. 1993-94); mem. Soc. Info. Display (program com. 1990-93), Detroit Zool. Inst. (docent 2001-03, sr. docent 2003—), Am. Contract Bridge League, Phi Beta Kappa, Sigma Xi (chpt. pres. 1980-81), Phi Delta Theta, Alpha Delta. Home: 1882 Melbourne St Birmingham MI 48009-1163

**SMITH, GERARD PETER,** neuroscientist; b. Phila., Mar. 24, 1935; s. Stanley Alward and Agnes Marie (McLarney) S.; m. Barbara McInnis, May 12, 1962; children: Christopher, Mark, Hilary, Maura. BS, St. Joseph's U., Phila., 1956; MD, U. Pa., 1960; ScD (hon.), U. Camerino, Italy, 2002. Intern, resident N.Y. Hosp., 1960-62; with dept. neuroendocrinology Walter Reed Army Inst. Rsch., 1962—64; asst. prof. physiology U. Pa. Sch. Medicine, Phila., 1964-68; from asst. to assoc. prof. Cornell U., N.Y.C., 1968—; prof. psychiatry (behavioral neurosci.), 1973—. Vis. prof. MIT, 1973—74, Rockefeller U., 1979—80, adj. prof., 1982—86; cons. NIH; Curt Richter lectr. Johns Hopkins U., 1976; Leon lectr. U. Pa., 1990, Stellar lectr., 93; Rushton lectr. Fla. State U., 1992; Merck, Sharpe, and Dohm prof. neurosci. U. Flinder, Australia, 1992; Loucks lectr. U. Wash., 1995; dir. Eating Disorders Inst. N.Y. Hosp.-Cornell Med. Ctr., 1984—88. Recipient Rsch. Scientist, USPHS, 1982; grantee, NIH. Mem. AAAS, Am. Physiol. Soc., Soc. for Study Ingestive Behavior (pres., Disting. Career award 2004), Internat. Behavioral Neurosci. Soc. (pres., Myers Lifetime Achievement award 2001), Alpha Omega Alpha, Alpha Sigma Nu. Office: NY Presbyn Hosp Westchester Divsn 21 Bloomingdale Rd White Plains NY 10605-1504 Office Phone: 914-682-9100 x 2666. Business E-Mail: gpsmith@med.cornell.edu.

**SMITH, GLADYS ANN,** counselor, military medic; b. Leland, Miss., July 19, 1960; d. Gladys Rose. B in Healthcare Mgmt., So. Ill. U., 1993; M in Health Sci., Washington U., St. Louis, MO, 1997; MEd, U. Mo., 2001. Lic. substance abuse counselor, advanced substance abuse counselor, provisional lic. counselor. Mental health counselor Webster U., St. Louis, 2001—, petty officer, 1984—. Counselor, educator St. Louis County Corrections. Recipient Navy Achievement awards, 1992, 1997, 2001. Mem.: Nat. Counselors Assn., Nat. Assn. Drug Abuse Counselors (none), Coalition of 100 Black Women. Democrat. Mem. A.M.E. Ch. Avocations: dance, running, reading. Home: 7006 Stanford Saint Louis MO 63130 Office: Webster U 470 E Lockwood Saint Louis MO 63119 Personal E-mail: GSmith2222@aol.com. Business E-Mail: gasmith@webster.edu.

**SMITH, G(ODFREY) T(AYLOR),** college president; b. Newton, Miss., Nov. 12, 1935; s. Taylor and Edna (Blanton) S.; m. Joni Eaton, Sept. 1, 1956; children: Paul Brian, Sherry Lynn. BA, Coll. of Wooster, 1956; MPA with distinction, Cornell U., 1960; LLD (hon.), Bethany Coll., 1979. Assoc. dir. devel. Cornell U., Ithaca, NY, 1960-62; dir. devel. Coll. Wooster, Ohio, 1962-66, v.p., 1966-77; pres. Chapman U., Orange, Calif., 1977-88, pres. emeritus, 1988—; exec. dir. Talaris Rsch. Inst., Seattle, 2001—03; pres. Bethany Coll., Bethany, W.Va., 2004—. Lectr. in field. Contbr. numerous articles to profl. publs. Bd. dirs. Wayne County (Ohio) Indsl. Devel. Corp., 1966-72, World Affairs Coun. Orange Coun., Calif., 1978-89, Orange County chpt. NCCJ, 1979-86, Orange County coun. Boy Scouts Am., 1980-85, Coun. Ind. Colls., 1985-87; bd. dirs. div. higher edn. Christian Ch. (Disciples of Christ), 1980-86, chmn., 1984-86; bd. dirs., mem. exec. com. Ind. Colls. So. Calif., 1979-88, pres., 1981-82; mem. exec. com. Assn. Ind. Calif. Colls. and Univs., 1980-88, treas., 1982-87. Recipient William A. Galpin prize The Coll. Wooster, 1956, Steuben Apple award for tchg. excellence Coun. for Advancement and Support Edn., 1984, Disting. Alumnus award Coll. of Wooster, 1991, Faith and Reason award Christian Ch. (Disciples of Christ), 1993, Laureate award for Lifetime Achievement Inst. for Charitable Giving, 1997; Smith Hall dedicated at Chapman U., 1988; Alfred P. Sloan fellow Cornell U. 1960. Presbyn. Home: PO Drawer S Bethany WV 26032 Office: Bethany Coll 110 Old Main Bethany WV 26032 Office Phone: 304-829-7111. Business E-Mail: buck@bethanywv.edu. *If we treat people as they are, they will stay as they are. But if we treat them for what they might be and might become, they will become those better selves.*

**SMITH, GOFF,** industrial equipment manufacturing executive; b. Jackson, Tenn., Oct. 7, 1916; s. Fred Thomas and Mabel (Goff) S.; m. Nancy Dall, Nov. 28, 1942 (dec. 1972); children: Goff Thomas, Susan Knight; m. Harriet Schneider Oliver, June 23, 1973 (dec. 1998). BSE, U. Mich., 1938, MBA, 1939; MS, MIT, 1953. Trainee Bucyrus Erie, South Milwaukee, Wis., 1939-40; mem. sales staff Amsted Industries, Chgo. and N.Y.C., 1946-55, subsidiary pres. Chgo., 1955-60, v.p., 1960-69, pres., dir., 1969-74, CEO, dir., 1974-80, chmn., 1980-82. Pres. Village of Winnetka, Ill., 1967—69; pres., bd. dirs. United Way Chgo., 1976—85; bd. dirs. Rehab. Inst., Chgo., 1979—99, Chgo. Theol. Sem., 1979—99, Presbyn. Home, Evanston, Ill., 1979—2005. Maj. U.S. Army. Sloan Fellow MIT, 1952-53. Republican. Avocations: hunting, fishing, golf. Office Phone: 847-446-5756.

**SMITH, GORDON H.,** civil engineer, consultant, forensic engineer consultant; b. NYC, Mar. 17, 1916; s. Henry and Theodora (Augenstern) S.; m. Norma Kaplan, Feb. 28, 1960; children: Randy Smith Bamp, Robin Smith. B in Engring., Yale U., 1957. Registered profl. engr., Mich., NY, Fla. V.p., chief engr. Albro Metal Products Corp., N.Y.C., 1957-69, pres., 1969-75, Gordon H. Smith Corp., N.Y.C., 1975—, Gordon H. Smith PE, N.Y.C., 1998—. Guest lectr. Yale U. Sch. Arch., MIT, Am. Inst. Archs., Constrn. Specification Inst., Nat. Glass Assn., Glass Assn. N.Am.; protective glazing coun. N.Y. Inst. Tech. Contbr. articles to Archtl. Record, Progressive Arch., ASTM, Chgo. High Rise Com. Mem. NSPE, ASTM, ASCE, AIA (Inst. Honors 1994, 2003), Nat. Assn. Archtl. Metal Mfrs. (v.p., pres., bd. dirs.), Archtl. Aluminum Mfrs. Assn. (v.p., dir.), Nat. Assn. Miscellaneous, Ornamental and Archtl. Metal Mfrs. (bd. dirs.), Constrn. Specifications Inst. Office: Gordon H Smith Corp 200 Madison Ave New York NY 10016-3903 Business E-Mail: ghsmith@gordonhsmithcorp.com.

**SMITH, GORDON HAROLD,** senator; b. Pendleton, Oreg., May 25, 1952; s. Milan Dale and Jessica (Udall) S.; m. Sharon Lankford; children: Brittany, Garrett (dec.), Morgan. BA in History, Brigham Young U., 1976; LLB, Southwestern U., 1979. Law clk. to Justice H. Vernon Payne N.Mex. Supreme Ct.; pvt. practice Ariz.; pres., CEO Smith Frozen Foods, 1981—97; mem. Oreg. State Senate, 1992-95, pres., 1995-96; US Senator from Oreg., 1997—. Mem. com. Indian affairs US Senate, com. fin., com. energy and natural resources, com. commerce, sci. and transp., commn. security and cooperation in Europe; mem. Presdl. Adv. Commn. Holocaust Assets in US. Author: Remembering Garrett: One Family's Battle with a Child's Depression, 2006. Recipient Torch of Liberty award, Nat. Conf. Soviet Jewry, 2001, Cmty. Health Defender award, Nat. Assn. Cmty. Health Centers, 2003, Homeownership Hero award, Homeownership Alliance, 2004. Republican. Ch. Latter Day Saints. Office: US Senate 404 Russell Senate Off Bldg Washington DC 20510-0001 also: Jager Bldg Ste 3 116 South Main St Pendleton OR 97801 Office Phone: 202-224-3753, 541-278-1129. Office Fax: 202-228-3997, 541-278-4109.*

**SMITH, GORDON PAUL,** management consultant; b. Salem, Mass., Dec. 25, 1916; s. Gordon and May (Vaughan) S.; m. Daphne Miller, Nov. 23, 1943 (div. 1968); m. Ramona Chamberlain, Sept. 27, 1969; children: Randall B., Roderick F. BS in Mgmt., U. Mass., 1947; MS in Govt. Mgmt, U. Denver, 1948; postgrad. in polit. sci, NYU, 1948-50; DHL (hon.), Monterey Inst. Internat. Studies, 1994. With Econ. Rsch. Tax Found., Inc., N.Y.C., 1948—51, Booz, Allen & Hamilton, 1951-70, partner San Francisco, 1959-62, v.p., 1962-67, mng. pntr. Western U.S., 1968-70; ptnr. Harrod, Williams and Smith, San Francisco, 1962—69; dir. fin. State of Calif., 1967—68; pres. Gordon Paul Smith & Co., Mgmt. Cons., 1968—; pres., CEO Golconda Corp., 1972—74, chmn. bd., 1974-85. Pres. Cermetek Corp., 1978-80; adviser task force def. procurement and contracting Hoover Commn., 1954-55; spl. asst. to pres. Republic Aviation Corp., 1954-55; cons., Hawaii, 1960-61, Alaska, 1963; cons. Wash. Hwy. Adminstrn., 1964, Am. Baseball League and Calif. Angels, 1960-62, others; bd. dirs. Monterey Coll. Law; chmn. Ft. Ord Econ. Devel. Adv. Group, 1991; chmn. Coalition on Rsch. and Edn., 1993—97; spkr. in field. Contbr. articles to profl. jours. Mem. Calif. Select Com. on Master Plan for Edn., 1971—73; mem. alumni coun. U. Mass., 1950—54, bd. dirs. alumni ass., 1964—70; chmn. West Coast Cancer Found., 1976—87, Coalition Rsch. and Edn., 1993—, Jim Tunney Youth Found., 1994—; trustee, chmn. Monterey Inst. Internat. Studies, 1978—92, trustee emeritus, 1995—; trustee Northfield Mt. Hermon Sch., 1983—93, Robert Louis Stevenson Sch., 1993—; mem. devel. coun. Cmty. Hosp. of Monterey Peninsula, 1983—84; sr. advisor Pres. Calif. State U., Monterey, Calif., 1998—; mem. 15 bds. and commns. State of Calif., 1967—72; bd. dirs. Alumni Assn. Mt. Hermon Prep. Sch., 1963; bd. dirs. Stanford Med. Ctr., 1960—62, pres., chmn., 1962—66; bd. dirs. Friends of the Performing Arts, 1985—, Monterey County Symphony Orch., 1991—96, Monterey Bay Futures Project, 1992—, Ctr. for Nonproliferation of Weapons of Mass Destruction, 1998—, Calif. Inst. for Local Self Govt., 2000—. Recipient spl. commendation Hoover Commn., 1955, Alumni of Yr. award U. Mass., 1963, Trustee of Yr. award Monterey-Peninsula, 1991, Monterey-Peninsula Outstanding Citizen of Yr. award, 1992, Laura Bride Powers Heritage award, 1991, U.S. Congl. award, 1992, Calif. Senate and Assembly Outstanding Citizen award, 1992, Wisdom award of honor Wisdom Soc., 1992; permanent Gordon Paul Smith Disting. Chair for Internat. Studies established at Monterey Inst. Internat. Studies; Gordon Paul Smith Scholarship Fund named in his honor Northfield Mt. Hermon Sch.and Robert Louis Stevenson Sch.; named to Honorable Order of Ky. Cols. Mem. Monterey History and Art Assn. (bd. dirs. 1987-92, pres. 1985-87, chmn. 1987-92, hon. lifetime dir. 1992—), The Stanton Heritage Ctr. (chmn. 1987-92, chmn. emeritus 1992—), Salvation Army (bd. dirs., chmn. hon. cabinet), Monterey Peninsula Mus. Art, Carmel Valley (Calif.) Country Club, Monterey Peninsula Country Club, Old Capitol Club, Edgartown Yacht Club. Home: 253 Del Mesa Carmel CA 93923 Personal E-mail: gp1225@aol.com. *If the quest for personal success is only for an accumulation of prestige, power or wealth, then personal failure will be assured. Genuine personal success can surely be found, however, through a significant and lasting contribution toward helping the progress of others and raising the human worth. This is the true mark of leadership.*

**SMITH, GORDON RAY,** utilities executive; b. San Francisco, Feb. 26, 1948; s. Margaret C. Orlando; m. Elizabeth Anne Rulfo, Sept. 26, 1981; children: Adam R., Alexandra R. BS in Fin., U. Calif., Berkeley, 1970; MBA in Fin., U. San Francisco, 1974. Fin. analyst Pacific Gas & Electric Co., San Francisco, 1970-76, sr. fin. analyst, 1976-78, dir., project financing, 1978-80, asst. treas., 1980-82, treas., 1982-83, v.p. fin., treas., 1983-87, v.p. fin. and rates, 1987—91, CFO, 1991—97, pres., CEO, 1997—. Mem. Mayor's Fiscal Adv. Com., San Francisco, 1986, Investment Rev. Com., San Francisco Found., 1986; dir. Calif.Chamber of Commerce, Bay Area Council, trustee, Monterey Bay Aquarium. Mem. Fin. Officers No, Calif., Pacific Coast Electric Assn., Pacific Coast Gas Assn., Bankers Club San Francisco, Moraga Country Club.

**SMITH, GREGG,** brewing industry executive, writer; b. Somerville, NJ, Sept. 28, 1952; s. Joseph E. Smith and Mary Louise (Menapace); m. Lisa Marie Bobbins; children: Darcy Michelle Romaniello, Jessica Faber. BS, So. Ill. U., SUNY; MS, No. Ill. U.; PhD, Windsor U. Chief petty officer USN, 1972—81; dir. tng. NY Power Authority, White Plains, 1981—91; gen. mgr. Idaho Brewing Co.; plant engr. G Modelo. Faculty Excelsior Coll., Albany, NY, 1983—; bd. mem. Edn. and Tng. Divsn. Am. Nuc. Soc.; mem. N.Am. Brewers Assn., 1995—. Author: (beer history book) Beer Enthusiast's Guide, Beer: A History (Silver Tankard, N.Am. Guild Beer Writers, 1996), Beer Drinker's Bible (Silver Tankard, N.Am. Guild Beer Writers, 1997), Beer in America (Gold Tankard, N.Am. Guild Beer Writers, 1998). Dir. Beer Judge Certification Program, 1996—98. Chief petty officer USN. Named Beer Writer of Yr., N.Am. Guild Beer Writers, 1997, 2001. Mem.: Elks. Avocations: sailing, camping, golfing, bicycling. Home: 2845 Holly Pl Idaho Falls ID 83402 Office: G Modelo 5005 S 15th West Idaho Falls ID 83402 Office Phone: 208-552-5539 1150. Home Fax: 208-524-6490; Office Fax: 208-552-5538. Personal E-mail: gsmithbeer@aol.com.

**SMITH, GREGORY ALLGIRE,** academic administrator; b. Washington, Mar. 31, 1951; s. Donald Eugene and Mary Elizabeth (Reichert) Smith; m. Susan Elizabeth Watts, Oct. 31, 1980; 1 child, David Joseph Smith-Watts. BA, Johns Hopkins U., 1972; MA, Williams Coll., 1974. Adminstrv. asst. Washington Project for Arts, 1975; intern Walker Art Ctr., Mpls., 1975—76; asst. devel. officer Sci. Mus. Minn., St. Paul, 1977; asst. dir. Akron Art Inst., Ohio, 1977—80; asst. to dir. Toledo Mus. Art, 1980—82, asst. dir. adminstrn., 1982—86; exec. v.p. Internat. Exhbns. Found., Washington, 1986—87; dir. Telfair Mus. Art, Savannah, Ga., 1987—94, Art Acad. Cin., 1994—98, pres., 1998—. Trustee Greater Cin. Consortium of Colls. and Univs., vice chmn., 2001—03, chmn., 2003—05; trustee Assn. Ind. Colls. of Art and Design; grad. Leadership Savanah, 1990—92, Leadership Cin., 2003—04. Mem.: Coll. Art Assn., Ohio Found. on the Arts (v.p. 1981—83, trustee 1981—84), Assn. Art Mus. Adminstrs. (founder 1984—85), Am. Assn. Mus., Rotary (dir. Cin. club 2000—01, sec.-treas. 2001—02, pres. 2002—03), Univ. Club. Avocation: collecting arts and crafts movement objects, landscape design, gardening. Home: 8380 Springvalley Dr Cincinnati OH 45236-1356 Office: Art Academy Of Cincinnati 1212 Jackson St Cincinnati OH 45202-7106 Office Phone: 513-562-8743. E-mail: gasmith@artacademy.edu.

**SMITH, GREGORY C.,** lawyer; b. Salt Lake City, 1963; BA with distinction, Stanford U., 1985; JD Harlan Fiske Stone Scholar, Columbia Law School, 1988. Bar: Calif. 1988. Ptnr. Skadden, Arps, Slate, Meagher & Flom LLP. Corp. author, gen. editor Start-up and Emerging Companies, 2004. Dir. Friends of Music, Stanford U. Named one of The World's Leading Lawyers Bus., Chambers Global, 2002—04, 2004—05, Am.'s Leading Bus. Lawyers, Chambers USA, 2004—05. Mem.: Phi Beta Kappa. Office: Skadden 525 University Avenue Suite 1100 Palo Alto CA 94301 Office Phone: 650-470-4590.

**SMITH, GREGORY WHITE,** writer; b. Ithaca, N.Y., Oct. 4, 1951; s. William R. and Kathryn (White) S. BA, Colby Coll., 1973; JD, Harvard U., 1977, MEd, 1980. Bar: Mass., 1980. Fellow Thomas J. Watson, 1973-74; co-founder & editor Woodward/White, Inc. (publishers of Best Lawyers in Am., Best Doctors in Am., Best Dentists in Am.), 1981—. Author: (with Steven Naifeh) Moving Up in Style, 1980, Gene Davis, 1981, How to Make Love to a Woman, 1982, What Every Client Needs to Know About Using a Lawyer, 1982, The Bargain Hunter's Guide to Art Collecting, 1982, Why Can't Men Open Up?: Overcoming Men's Fear of Intimacy, 1984, The Mormon Murders: A True Story of Greed, Forgery, Deceit, and Death, 1988, Jackson Pollock: An American Saga, 1989 (Nat. Book award nomination for nonfiction 1990, Pulitzer Prize for biography 1991), Final Justice: The True Story of the Richest Man Ever Tried for Murder, 1993, A Stranger in the Family: A True Story of Murder, Madness, and Unconditional Love, 1995, On a Street Called Easy, In a Cottage Called Joye: A Restoration Comedy, 1996, Making Miracles Happen, 1997; editor: (with Naifeh) The Best Lawyers in America series, The Best Doctors in America series, The Best Dentists in America series. Chmn. Aiken Historic Preservation Commn. Office: Woodward/White 129 First Ave SW Aiken SC 29801 E-mail: gsmith@bestlawyers.com.

**SMITH, GRIFFIN,** editor; b. Fayetteville, Ark., June 29, 1941; s. Griffin and Mildred Smith; m. Mary Elizabeth Routh, Sept. 1, 1979. BA in History, Rice U., 1963; MA in Polit. Sci., Columbia U., 1965; postgrad. in philosophy, Oxford U., 1966; JD, U. Tex., 1969. Bar: Tex. 1969, U.S. Dist. Ct. (ea., we., no. and so. dists.) Tex. 1969, Ark. 1981, U.S. Dist. Ct. (ea. and we. dists.) Ark. 1981. Spl. asst. to Senator Fulbright U.S. Senate, Washington, 1968-69; atty. estate and gift tax div. IRS, Houston, 1970; rsch. dir. Tex. gubernatorial campaign Paul Eggers, 1970; chief counsel constl. amendments com. Tex. Senate, 1971, chief counsel drug law reform com., 1971-73; editor natural areas survey Lyndon B. Johnson Sch. Pub. Affairs U. Tex., Austin, 1973-77; speech writer Pres. of U.S., 1977-78; ptnr. Smith & Nixon (formerly Smith, Smith, Nixon & Duke), Little Rock, 1984-92. Author: (book) A Consumer Viewpoint on Taxation, 1971, Marijuana in Texas, 1972, The Best of Texas Monthly, 1978, Texas Monthly's Political Reader, 1978, 1980, Journey into China, 1982, Forgotten Texas: A Wilderness Portfolio, 1983, The Great State of Texas, 1985; sr. editor: Tex. Monthly Mag., 1973—77, exec. editor: Ark. Dem. Gazette Newspaper, 1992—. Fellow Woodrow Wilson, 1964. Mem.: Tex. Inst. Letters (award for best work of journalism in Tex. 1974, 1976), State Bar Tex., Ark. Episcopalian-Reformed. Office: Ark Dem Gazette 121 E Capitol Ave Little Rock AR 72201-3819 Office Phone: 501-399-3610.

**SMITH, GROVER C(LEVELAND),** language educator; b. Atlanta, Sept. 6, 1923; s. Grover C. and Lillian Julia (McDaniel) S.; m. Phyllis Jean Snyder, June 19, 1948 (div. 1965); children: Alice Elizabeth, Charles Grover; m. Dulcie Barbara Soper, Dec. 29, 1965; children: Stephen Kenneth, Julia Margaret. BA with honors, Columbia U., 1944, MA, 1945, PhD, 1950. Instr. English Rutgers U., 1946-48, Yale U., 1948-52, Duke U., 1952-55, asst. prof., 1955-61, assoc. prof., 1961-66, prof., 1966-93, prof. emeritus, 1993—. Mem. summer faculty CUNY, 1946, 47, 48, Columbia U., 1963, 64, NYU, 1963, Wake Forest U., 1966, vis. lectr., 1963, 64; instr. coll. entrance exam bd. Summer Inst. Commn. on English, 1962. Author: The Poems of T.S. Eliot 1909-1928: A Study in Symbols and Sources, 1950, T.S. Eliot's Poetry and Plays: A Study in Sources and Meaning, 1956 (Poetry Chapbook award) rev. edit., 1974, Archibald MacLeish, 1971, Ford Madox Ford, 1972, The Waste Land, 1983, T.S. Eliot and the Use of Memory, 1996; editor: Josiah Royce's Seminar, 1913-1914: As Recorded in the Notebooks of Harry T. Costello, 1963, Letters of Aldous Huxley, 1969. Mem. Christian Gauss Award com., 1973-75; mem. com. of sponsors Sir Julian Huxley Tribute, NY Soc. for Ethical Culture, 1975. With U.S. Army, 1943. Alexander M. Proudfit fellow Columbia U., 1945-46; Guggenheim fellow, 1958; Am. Philos. Soc. grantee, 1965; Am. Learned Socs. grantee, 1965; NEH grantee, 1979, fellow, 1980. Mem. T.S. Eliot Soc. (hon., Eliot Meml. Lectr. 1986, bd. dirs. 1986-94, 96-99, v.p. 1986-88, editor News and Notes, 1987-88, 90-91, pres. 1989-91, supr. elections 1992-94, sec. 1996-99), Am. Lit. Assn. (rep. to coun.of Am. Author Socs. 1990-91), Nat. Assn. Scholars. Home: 2 Silver Maple Ct Durham NC 27705-5642

**SMITH, H. KERNER,** manufacturing executive, heavy; b. 1944; BS Marine Engring., U.S. Merchant Marine Acad., King Point, N.Y., 1966; MBA, Boston U., 1973. Chmn. bd., CEO Riley Consolidated, Inc., Worcester, Mass., 1988—; v.p. Babcock & Wilcox; pres. & CEO Deutsche Babcock Technologies, Worcester, Mass, 1993-96, Stone & Webster, Inc., Boston, Mass, 1996—, chmn., 1997—. Office: Riley Consolidated Inc 5 Neponset St Worcester MA 01606-2714

**SMITH, H. MORGAN,** environmental scientist, educator; b. Orlando, Fla., Dec. 31, 1926; s. Claude Earle Smith and Pearl Adelaide Morgan; m. Marjori Blank (div. 1962); m. Charles V. Smith. BS in Anthropology, Fla. State U., 1953; postgrad., U. Ala., Troy State U.; PhD (hon.), U. Peru, Iquitos, 2002. Prof. environ. sci. State of Ala., U. USAF; rsch. scientist, tchr., adminstr. fed. svc.; ret., 1981. Lectr. univs., schs., profl. and civic groups; conductor security, survival tng. people, India, Australia, Europe, and U.S., 2001—; tchr. rainforest ecology workshops ethnobotany, Peruvian Amazon, Panama; vol. prof. environ. sci. Selwyn Sch., Denton, Tex. Author (editor) numerous pubs.; scriptwriter (5 major edml. videos cross-cultural comm. and emergency survival). Decorated WWII Asia Pacific Combat medal. Office Phone: 940-891-1133. Business E-Mail: vieje7@charter.net.

**SMITH, HAMILTON OTHANEL,** molecular biologist, educator; b. NYC, N.Y., Aug. 23, 1931; s. Bunnie Othanel and Tommie Harkey S.; m. Elizabeth Anne Bolton, May 25, 1957; children: Joel, Barry, Dirk, Bryan, Kirsten. Student, U. Ill., 1948-50; AB in Math, U. Calif., Berkeley, 1952; MD, Johns Hopkins U., 1956. Intern Barnes Hosp., St. Louis, 1956-57; resident in medicine Henry Ford Hosp., Detroit, 1959-62; USPHS fellow dept. human genetics U. Mich., Ann Arbor, 1962-64, rsch. assoc., 1964-67; asst. prof. molecular biology and genetics Sch. Medicine Johns Hopkins U., Balt., 1967-69, assoc. prof., 1969-73, prof., 1973—, emeritus prof. molecular biology and genetics; scientist Celera Genomics. Asso. Inst. für Molekularbiologie der U. Zurich, Switzerland, 1975-76; assoc. Rsch. Inst. Molecular Pathology, Vienna, 1990-91; trustee The Inst. for Genomic Rsch. Contbr. articles to profl. jours. Served to lt. M.C. USNR, 1957-59. Recipient Nobel prize in physiology or medicine, 1978; Guggenheim fellow, 1975-76. Mem. Am. Soc. Microbiology, AAAS, Am. Soc. Biol. Chemists, Nat. Acad. Sci.*

**SMITH, HARMON LEE, JR.,** clergyman, theology studies educator; b. Ellisville, Miss., Aug. 23, 1930; s. Harmon Lee Sr. and Mary (O'Donnell) S.; children: Pamela Lee, Amy Joanna, Harmon Lee III. AB, Millsaps Coll., 1952; BD, Duke U., 1955, PhD, 1962. Ordain to priest Episcopal Ch., 1972. Asst. dean Duke U. Divinity Sch., Durham, NC, 1959-65, asst. prof. Christian ethics, 1962-68, assoc. prof. moral theology, 1968-73, prof. moral theology, 1973-99, prof. community and family medicine, 1974-99, ret., 1999, prof. emeritus moral theology and cmty. family medicine. Cons. med. ethics; vis. prof. U.N.C., 1964, 70, 72, U. Edinburgh, Scotland, 1969, U. Windsor, Ont., 1974 Author books on Christian theology, ethics and med. ethics; sr. editor Social Science and Medicine, 1973-89; contbr. articles on Christian ethics to various publs. Lilly Found. fellow, 1960; Gurney Harris Kearns Found. fellow, 1961; Nat. Humanities Ctr. fellow, 1982-83 Mem. Am. Assn. Theol. Schs., Am. Soc. Christian Ethics, Am. Acad. Religion, Soc. for Religion in Higher Edn., Soc. Health and Human Values. Home: 3510 Randolph Rd Durham NC 27705-5347 E-mail: orare@aol.com.

**SMITH, HAROLD B.,** manufacturing executive; b. Chgo., Apr. 7, 1933; s. Harold Byron and Pauline (Hart) S. Grad., Choate Sch., 1951; BS, Princeton U., 1955; MBA, Northwestern U., 1957. With Ill. Tool Works, Inc., Chgo., 1954—, exec. v.p. 1968-72, pres., 1972-81, vice chmn., 1981, chmn. exec. com., 1982—, also bd. dirs. Bd. dirs. W.W. Grainger, Inc., No. Trust Corp Mem. Rep. Nat. Com., 1976-99; chmn. Ill. Rep. Com., 1993-99; del. Rep. Nat. Conv., 1964, 76, 88, 92, 96, 2000, 04; bd. dirs. Adler Planetarium, Boys and Girls Clubs Am., Northwestern U., Rush U. Med. Ctr., Newberry Libr. Mem.: Chicago, Commercial, Commonwealth, Economic, Northwestern, Princeton (Chgo.). Office: Ill Tool Works Inc 3600 W Lake Ave Glenview IL 60026-1215

**SMITH, HAROLD CHARLES,** pension fund administrator; b. NYC, Jan. 11, 1934; s. Harold Elmore and Hedwig Agnes (Gronke) S. BA cum laude with honors, Ursinus Coll., 1955; MBA, NYU, 1958; M in Div., Union Theol. Sem., N.Y.C., 1958; DD (hon.), 1993; DD (hon.), Ursinus Coll., 1997; DHum (hon.), Springfield Coll., 1998. CFA; ordained minister United Ch. Christ, 1959. V.p. YMCA Retirement Fund, Inc., N.Y.C., 1958-69, portfolio mgr., 1960—, assoc. sec., 1969-77, v.p., 1977-80, exec. v.p., 1980-82, pres. elect, 1982-83, pres., 1983-2000; assoc. prof. bus. and fin. L.I. U., 1969-71. Trustee Bank Mart, Bridgeport, Conn., 1983-91; bd. dirs. Y Mut. Ins. Co., treas. 1988—. Author: Getting It All Together in Retirement, 1977. Trustee YWCA Greater Bridgeport, 1975—79, Pension Funds United Ch. of Christ, 1968—, Springfield Coll., Mass., 1983—, United Ch. Found., 1968—, vice chmn., 1995—98, chmn., 1998—99; chmn. bd. trustees NY State YMCA; pastor 1st E&R Ch., Bridgeport, Conn., 1958—88, Unity Hill United Ch. of Christ, 1988—2000, 1st Congl. Ch., Union, NJ, 2001—02, River Edge, NJ, 2002—03; treas. United H. Homes of N.J. Inc., 2001—; exec. coun. UCC, 2000—; bd. dirs. United Ch. Residencies, 1962—65, YMCA Greater N.Y., 2002—04, 1983—97, Bridgeport Area Found., 1989—2000, Ursinus Coll., Pa., 1994—, Coun. of Chs. Greater Bridgeport, 1995—96, Silver Bay Christian Conf. Ctr., 1997—2003. Mem. Am. Econs. Assn., N.Y. Soc. Security Analysts, Fin. Analysts Fedn., Masons, Order Ea. Star. Personal E-mail: hcsmith1@email.msn.com.

**SMITH, HAROLD HASKEN,** university administrator; b. Cin., Mar. 16, 1942; s. Harold C. and Ruth V. (Hasken) S.; m. Karen A. Willis, Dec. 20, 1969; children: Amy Elizabeth, Andrew David, Anne Cameron. AB, Centre Coll., 1964; MBA, Am. U., 1968; LLD (hon.), Cumberland Coll., 2003. Admissions counselor Centre Coll., Danville, Ky., 1964-66, assoc. dir. admissions, 1968-70, dir. admissions, 1970-73, dean admissions, 1973-80, y.p., den students, 1980-83, lectr. econs. mgmt., 1973-80; v.p. devel. Muskingum Coll., New Concord, Ohio, 1983-97; pres. Pikeville (Ky.) Coll. and Coll. Osteo. Med., Ky., 1997—. Cons. in edn. Dir. Boyle-Mercer County (Ky.) YMCA, 1979-83; mem. bd. trustees S.E. Ohio Regional Med. Ctr., 1987-97; bd. dirs. Southeast Ohio Symphony Orch., 1983-97, Renew Environment of New Concord, 1983-97, Leadership Ky., 2002—. Recipient Disting. Chmn. award Rotary Found., 1981-82. Mem. Ctr. Coll. Athletic Hall of Fame, 1994, Assn. Ind. Ky. Colls. and Univs. (exec. com. 2004—), Nat. Assn. Student Personnel Adminstrs., Am. Coll. Personnel Assn., Nat. Assn. Intercollegiate Athletics (coun. pres. 2004—), Cambridge C. of C. (bd. dirs. 1984-97), Nat. Assn. Coll. Admissions Counselors, So. Assn. Colls. and Schs. (commr. coll. commn. 2005—), Rotary (pres. 1979-80, dist. gov.'s rep. 1981-82), Zanesville Country Club, Green Meadow Country Club. Office: Pres's Office Pikeville Coll Pikeville KY 41501 Office Phone: 606-218-5261. Business E-mail: halsmith@pc.edu.

**SMITH, H(AROLD) LAWRENCE,** lawyer; b. Evergreen Park, Ill., June 27, 1932; s. Harold Lawrence and Lorna Catherine (White) Smith; m. Madonna Jeanne Koehl, June 9, 1956 (div. 1968); children: Lawrence Kirby, Sandra Michelle, Madonna Clare Galloway; m. Nancy Leigh Baum, May 2, 1970 (dec. 1983); m. Louise Fredericka Jeffrey, Nov. 2, 1984 (div. 1994); m. Marianne Lorraine Laug, Apr. 19, 1997. BS, US Naval Acad., 1956; JD, John Marshall Law Sch., 1965. Bar: Ill. 1965, Mich. 1986, U.S. Dist. Ct. (no. dist.) Ill. 1965, U.S. Ct. Appeals (7th cir.) 1965, U.S. Ct. of Customs and Patent Appeals, 1976, U.S. Ct. Appeals (fed. cir.) 1982, U.S. Patent and Trademark Office 1968. Asst. prof. naval sci. U. Notre Dame, 1960-61; tech. asst. Langner, Parry, Card & Langner, Chgo., 1961-65, assoc., 1965-69; patent atty. Borg-Warner Corp., Chgo., 1970-74; sr. patent atty. Continental Can Co., Inc., Chgo. and Oak Brook, Ill., 1974-82. asst. gen. counsel Stamford and Norwalk, Conn., 1982-86; ptnr. Varnum, Riddering, Schmidt & Howlett, Grand Rapids, Mich., 1986-96, counsel, 1996-97; ptnr. Rader, Fishman, Grauer & McGarry, Grand Rapids, 1997—2001; of counsel McGarry Bair LLP, Grand Rapids, 2001—03; cons., 2003—. Adj. prof. patent law Cooley Law Sch., 1991—. Served to lt. USN, 1956-61. Fellow Mich. State Bar Found.; mem. Intellectual Property Law Assn. Chgo., Chartered Inst. Patent Agts. (London 1971-2003), World Affairs Coun. Western Mich. (bd. dirs. 1996-2002, treas. 1998-2000. Office: 39533 Woodward Ave Ste 140 Bloomfield Hills MI 48304 E-mail: hls@mcgarrybair.com.

**SMITH, HARRISON HARVEY,** journalism consultant; b. Wilkes-Barre, Pa., Oct. 24, 1915; s. Ernest Gray and Marjorie (Harvey) S.; m. Joanne Christopher, June 7, 1940 (div.); children: Barbara DeWitt, Marjorie Harvey, Susan C. (dec. 1999); m. Margaret Simons, July 18, 1947 (dec. May 1978); children: Rosanne Jameson, Elizabeth Simons; m. Dorothy Wright Welborn, June 22, 1989. Diploma in lit., Wyoming (Pa.) Sem., 1936; postgrad., Northwestern U., 1937-38. Asst. to pub. Wilkes-Barre Times-Leader, 1938-39, v.p., asst. sec., 1939-46, pres., 1946-79; editor Wilkes-Barre Record, 1962-72; newspaper cons. Key Biscayne, Fla., 1979—. Dir. emeritus 1st Ea. Bank Wilkes-Barre; pres. Pa. AP, 1953. Chmn. Wyoming Valley ARC, 1954-55; v.p. bd. dirs. Wilkes-Barre Gen. Hosp., 1954-76. With U.S. Army, 1945-46, Korea. Mem. Am. Soc. Newspaper Editors, Nat. Conf. Editl. Writers, Soc. Profl. Journalists, Pa. Newspaper Pubs. Assn. (mem. exec. com. 1954-62), Wyoming Valley Hist. Soc. (pres. 1971-74), Newcomen Soc. Am. Legion, VFW, Poor Richard Club (Phila.), Mirador Club (Geneva), Westmoreland Club, Sankaty Head Golf and Beach Club (Nantucket Island, Mass.), Country Club Coral Gables, Key Biscayne Yacht Club, Masons (33 degree). Republican, Presbyterian. Home (summer): 10 Lyons La PO Box 180 Siasconset MA 02564-0180 Office Phone: 508-257-6177.

**SMITH, HARRY DELANO,** education administrator; b. Florence, Ala., June 10, 1954; s. Cornelius Everett and Nadine (Olive) S.; m. Wanda Joy Skipworth, Nov. 23, 1978; children: Benjamin Delano, Rebekah Joy. BS, U. North Ala., 1975, MA, 1977, EdS, 1983; EdD, U. Ala., Tuscaloosa, 1989. Cert. class AA supr.-prin., Ala. Exec. dir. Christian Student Ctr., Florence, 1980-83; head instr. math Mars Hill Bible Sch., Florence, 1983-87; tchr. math. and physics Muscle Shoals (Ala.) High Sch., 1975-80, asst. prin., 1987-88, prin., 1989—. Farmer, Killen, Ala., 1974-80; tchr. summer sch. Sheffield (Ala.) High Sch., 1977-78; dir. scholars program Muscle Shoals Schs., 1987-88; asst. prin. Avalon Mid. Sch., Muscle Shoals, 1987-88, prin., 1988-89; math. cons. Cartersville (Ga.) City Schs., 1991-92; curriculum cons. Eufaula (Ala.) High Sch., 1991-92; co-chmn. Ala. Learner Outcomes Com., Montgomery, 1991-92; dist. judge All-State Acad. Team, Athens, Ala., 1991-92; coach Ala. Mathcounts team NSPE, Birmingham, 1985. Dir. music and edn. Shoals Ch. of Christ, 1992. Named Outstanding Young Educator, No. Dist. Ala. Jaycees, 1987; Beeson fellow Samford U., 1987. Mem. ASCD, Nat. Assn. Secondary Sch. Prins., Am. Assn. Sch. Adminstrs., Ala. Coun. Sch. Adminstrs. and Suprs., Ala. Assn. Secondary Sch. Prins., Kappa Delta Pi, Phi Kappa Phi. Avocations: travel, stamp collecting/philately, reading, bowling. Office: Muscle Shoals High Sch 100 Trojan Dr Muscle Shoals AL 35661-3173 Home: 2077 County Road 71 Killen AL 35645-5119

**SMITH, HARVEY ALVIN,** mathematics professor, consultant; b. Easton, Pa., Jan. 30, 1932; s. William Augustus and Ruth Carolyn (Krauth) S.; m. Ruth Wismer Kolb, Aug. 27, 1955; children: Deirdre Lynn, Kirsten Nadine, Brinton Averil. BS, Lehigh U., 1952; MS, U. Pa., 1955, AM, 1958, PhD, 1964. Asst. prof. math Drexel U., 1960-65; mem. tech. staff Inst. Def. Analyses, Arlington, Va., 1965-66; assoc. prof. math Oakland U., 1966-68; ops. research scientist Exec. Office of Pres., Washington, 1968-70; prof. math. Oakland U., 1970-77; prof. Ariz. State U., Tempe, 1977—2003, prof. emeritus, 2003—; cons. Inst. Def. Analyses, 1967-69, Exec. Office Pres., 1967-73, U.S. Arms Control and Disarmament Agy, 1973-79, Los Alamos Nat. Lab., 1980-93. Author: Mathematical Foundations of Systems Analysis, 1969. NSF fellow, 1964-65; recipient Meritorious Service award Exec. Office

of Pres., 1970 Mem. Soc. Indsl. and Applied Math., Am. Math. Soc., AAAS, Sigma Xi Home: 18 E Concorda Dr Tempe AZ 85282-3517 Office: Ariz State U Dept Math Tempe AZ 85287-1804 Office Phone: 480-968-6813. Business E-Mail: hsmith@math.asu.edu.

**SMITH, HEATHER LYNN,** psychotherapist, recreational therapist; b. Modesto, Calif., May 31, 1956; d. Gary Fremont and Marilyn Rae (Brown) S. BS, Calif. State U., Fresno, 1979; MA, U. San Francisco, 1989. Lic. marriage, family and child counselor, Calif. Recreational therapist Casa Colina Rehab. Hops., Pomona, Calif., 1979-82; evaluator developmentally delayed, coord. family edn. Cath. Charities, Modesto, 1982-87; bereavement counselor Hospice, Modesto, 1983-87; high risk youth counselor Ctr. Human Svcs., Modesto, 1987—; pvt. practice, family therapist Modesto, 1988—. Program dir. chemically dependent treatment program Stanislaus County Juvenile Hall, 1990—; program adminstr. First Step, 1999—. Named Outstanding Young Woman of Stanislaus County, 1986, Citizen of Yr., Civitan, 1986, Outstanding Individual award Stanislaus County, 1992. Mem. Calif. Assn. Marriage and Family Therapists, Kappa Kappa Gamma. Republican. Roman Catholic. Avocations: skiing, running, backpacking, tennis. Office: PO Box 577456 Modesto CA 95357-7456 Office Phone: 209-521-7254. Business E-Mail: serenitymft@comcast.net.

**SMITH, HEDRICK LAURENCE,** journalist, television producer; b. Kilmacolm, Scotland, July 9, 1933; s. Sterling L. and Phebe (Hedrick) S.; m. Ann Bickford, June 29, 1957 (div. Dec. 1985); children: Laurel Ann, Jennifer Laurence, Sterling Scott, Lesley Roberts; m. Susan Zox, Mar. 7, 1987. BA, Williams Coll., 1955, LittD (hon.), 1973; postgrad. (Fulbright scholar), Balliol Coll., Oxford, Eng., 1955-56; LittD (hon.), Wittenberg U., 1985, N.H. Coll., 1991; LHD (hon.), Columbia Coll., 1992; LittD (hon.), Amherst Coll., 1992; LHD (hon.), U. S.C., 1992; LittD (hon.), Furman U., 1996. With U.P.I., Memphis, Nashville, Atlanta, 1959-62; with N.Y. Times, 1962-88, Washington and S.E., 1962-63, Vietnam, 1963-64; Middle East corr. N.Y. Times, Cairo, U.A.R., 1964-66, diplomatic news corr. Washington, 1962-64, 66-71, Moscow Bur. chief, 1971-74, dep. nat. editor, 1975-76, Washington Bur. chief, 1976-79, chief Washington corr., 1980-85; Washington correspondent N.Y. Times mag., 1987-88. Vis. journalist Am. Enterprise Inst., 1985-87; fellow Fgn. Policy Inst., Johns Hopkins U. Sch Advanced Internat. Studies, 1989-97; panelist Washington Week in Rev., PBS, 1969-95. Author: The Russians, 1975 (Overseas Press Club award, 1976), The Power Game: How Washington Works, 1988, The New Russians, 1990 (Overseas Press Club citation, 1991), Rethinking America, 1995; co-author: The Pentagon Papers, 1972, Reagan the Man, the President, 1981, Beyond Reagan: The Politics of Upheaval, 1986, Seven Days That Shook the World, 1991, (TV documentaries) Star Wars, 1985, Moscow Jews, 1986, Space Bridge, Chernobyl: Three Mile Island, 1987, 4-part Power Game series, PBS, 1989, Countdown to White House: The Bush Transition, 1989, 4-part series Inside Gorbachev's USSR, 1990 (George Polk award, Gold Baton award Columbia-DuPont), Guns, Tanks and Gorbachev (Frontline), 1991, Soviets, 1991 (George Peabody award), After Gorbachev's USSR (Frontline), 1992, 4-part series PBS, Challenge to America, 1994 (Cine Golden Eagle award, Rias award), Across the River, PBS, 1995 (Hillman award), The People and the Power Game, 1996 (Silver award Houston Film Festival), Surviving the Bottom Line, 1998 (Cine Golden Eagle award), Seeking Solutions, 1999 (nat. award for pub. svc. Sigma Delta Chi, spl. gold medal Houston Film Festival), Duke Ellington's Washington, 2000 (N.Y. Film Festival Bronze prize), Critical Condition, 2000 (Emmy nomination), Dr. Solomon's Dilemma (Frontline), 2000 (Chris award), Juggling Work and Family, 2001, Rediscovering Dave Brubeck, 2001, Inside the Terror Network (Frontline), 2002 (co-winner Columbia-Dupont Gold Baton), Bigger Than Enron (Frontline), 2002 (Cine Gold Eagle), The Wall Street Fix (Frontline), 2003 (Emmy award, Cine Gold Eagle, Chris award), Tax Me If You Can (Frontline), 2004 (Emmy nomination), Is Walmart Good for America?, 2004 (Writer's Guild award nomination), Making Schools Work With Hedrick Smith, 2005, Can You Afford to Retire, 2006. Trustee Williams Coll., 1982-97, Nat. Ctr. for Humanities, 2005—; mem. Aspen Inst. Domestic Strategy Group, 1997-2002; bd. dirs. New American Schs., 1996-2004; mem. steering com. Concerned Journalists, 2001—. With USAF, 1956-59. Recipient Pulitzer prize for pub. svc. Pentagon Papers Series, 1972, for internat. reporting from Soviet Union and Ea. Europe, 1974, William Allen White award U. Kans., 1996; Nieman fellow Harvard U., 1969-70. Mem. Gridiron Club, Phi Beta Kappa. Office: Hedrick Smith Prodns Inc 6935 S Wisconsin Ave Chevy Chase MD 20815 Office Phone: 301-654-9848. E-mail: hsmithprod@aol.com.

**SMITH, HENRY CHARLES, III,** symphony orchestra conductor; b. Phila., Jan. 31, 1931; s. Henry Charles Jr. and Gertrude Ruth (Downs) S.; m. Mary Jane Dressner, Sept. 3, 1955; children— Katherine Anne, Pamela Jane, Henry Charles IV. BA, U. Pa., 1952; artist diploma, Curtis Inst. Music, Phila., 1955. Solo trombonist Phila. Orch., 1955-67; condr. Rochester (Minn.) Symphony Orch., 1967-68; assoc. prof. music Ind. U., Bloomington, 1968-71; resident condr., ednl. dir. Minn. Orch., Mpls., 1971-88; prof. music U. Tex., Austin, 1988-89, Frank C. Erwin Centennial Prof. of Opera, 1988-89; music dir. S.D. Symphony, Sioux Falls, 1989-2001; prof. Ariz. State U., Tempe, 1989-93, prof. emeritus, 1993—. Vis. prof. U. Tex., Austin, 1987-88; founding mem. Phila. Brass Ensemble, 1956—; music dir. World Youth Symphony Orch., Interlochen, Mich., 1981-96; artistic advisor, prin. guest conductor Cedar Rapids Symphony, Iowa, 2004-. Composer 5 books of solos for trombone including Solos for the Trombone Player, 1963, Hear Us As We Pray, 1963, First Solos for the Trombone Player, 1972, Easy Duets for Winds, 1972; editor 14 books 20th century symphonies lit. Served to 1st lt. AUS, 1952-54. Recipient 3 Grammy nominations, 1967, 76, 1 Grammy award for best chamber music rec. with Phila. Brass Ensemble, 1969. Mem. Internat. Trombone Assn. (dir.), Am. Symphony Orch. League, Music Educators Nat. Conf., Am. Guild Organists, Am. Fedn. Musicians, Tubist Universal Brotherhood Assn., Acacia Fraternity. Republican. Congregationalist. Home: 8032 Pennsylvania Rd S Bloomington MN 55438-1135

**SMITH, HENRY E.,** law educator; AB, Harvard U., 1986; AM in German, Stanford U., 1987, PhD in Linguistics, 1992; JD, Yale U., 1996. Bar: Ill. 1997. Law clk. to Hon. Ralph K. Winter US Ct. of Appeals (2nd Cir.), 1996—97; asst. prof. Northwestern U., 1997—2000, assoc. prof., 2000—01, prof., 2001—02; vis. prof. U. Chgo., 2000, Yale U., New Haven, 2001—02, prof. law, 2002—. Author: Restrictiveness in Case Theory, 1996; contbr. articles to law jours. Office: Yale Law Sch PO Box 208215 New Haven CT 06520 E-mail: henry.smith@yale.edu.

**SMITH, HENRY HELLER,** music educator, director; s. Martin Post and Doris Winefred (Bauch) Smith. BA, Buchnell U., Lewisburg, Pa., 1986; MusM, Rider U., Princeton, N.J., 1996. Dir. Oread Singers U. Kans., Lawrence, 2003—. Assoc. music dir. Trinity Episc. Ch., Lawrence, 2004—. Composer: (songs) Dedication to My Choir Master, 1976, Prolude II Garden City Prelude, 1978. Chmn. Lake George Antique Boat Mus., Bolton Landing, NY, 1995—, Saratoga Antiques Mus., Saratoga Springs, NY, 1998—2002. Avocation: boat collector. Home: 1301 West Campus Rd Lawrence KS 66044

**SMITH, HERBERT G., II,** lawyer; b. Newport News, Va., Mar. 15, 1958; BA cum laude, Washington & Lee Univ., 1980, JD, 1983. Bar: Va. 1984, DC 1996. Ptnr., Comml. Litigation, Product Liability & Toxic Torts practices Venable LLP, Washington. Contbr. articles to profl. jours. Mem.: Va. State Bar Assn., DC Bar Assn. Office: Venable LLP 575 7th St NW Washington DC 20004 Office Phone: 202-344-4858. Office Fax: 202-344-8300. Business E-Mail: hgsmith@venable.com.

**SMITH, HILARY CRANWELL BOWEN,** investment banker; b. Balt., Nov. 1, 1937; s. Henry Bowen and Clayton (Cranwell) S.; m. Janet Simmons, June 9, 1962. BA, Colgate U., 1960; MBA, U. Va., 1967. V.p. Goldman, Sachs & Co., N.Y.C., 1969-74, E. F. Hutton & Co., N.Y.C., 1974-77; sr. v.p. Blyth Eastman Dillon, N.Y.C., 1977—90; mng. dir. Salomon Bros., N.Y.C., 1990—2004, UBS, N.Y.C., 1990—2004; sr. advisor Greenhill & Co., N.Y.C., 2004—. Bd. dirs. Forest 2 Market. Trustee Wheaton Coll., 1997-2003,

Chesapeake Maritime Mus., 1998-2004, Greenwich Acad., 1988-94, Mystic Seaport, 2005, Nat. Maritime Hist. Soc., 2006—. Lt. USN, 1960-63. Office: Greenhill and Company 300 Park Ave New York NY 10022 Office Phone: 212-389-1557.

**SMITH, HOWARD I.,** former insurance company executive; BBA in Acctg., CCNY. CPA, N.Y. In charge N.Y. office ins. practice, N.Y.C.; with Coopers & Lybrand LLP, 19 yrs; comptr. Am. Internat. Group, Inc., N.Y.C., v.p., 1984-87, sr. v.p., 1987-95, exec. v.p., 1995—2005, CFO, 1996—2005, vice chmn., 2002—05, chief admin. officer, 2002—05, also mem. bd. dirs. Mem. AICPA, N.Y. Soc. CPA's, Fin. Execs. Inst.

**SMITH, HOWARD RUSSELL,** manufacturing executive, director; b. Clark County, Ohio, Aug. 15, 1914; s. Lewis Hoskins and Eula (Elder) S.; m. Jeanne Rogers, June 27, 1942; children: Stewart Russell, Douglas Howard, Jeanne Ellen Smith James. AB, Pomona Coll., 1936. Security analyst Kidder, Peabody & Co., N.Y.C., 1936-37; economist ILO, Geneva, 1937-40; asst. to pres. Blue Diamond Corp., Los Angeles, 1940—; v.p., gen. mgr., dir. Avery Dennison Corp., Pasadena, Calif., 1946-56, pres., 1956-75, chmn. bd., 1975-84, chmn. exec. com., 1984-95; dir. emeritus, 1995—; chmn. bd. Kinsmith Fin. Corp., San Marino, Calif., 1979—. Bd. dirs., past pres., chmn. Los Angeles Philharm. Assn.; chmn. emeritus, bd. trustees Pomona Coll., Claremont, Calif.; past chmn. bd. Children's Hosp. Los Angeles, Community TV of So. Calif. (Sta. KCET), Los Angeles. Lt. USNR, 1943-46. Home: 1458 Hillcrest Ave Pasadena CA 91106-4503 Office: Avery Dennison Corp 150 N Orange Grove Blvd Pasadena CA 91103 3534 Office Phone: 626-304-2153.

**SMITH, HOWARD THOMPSON,** manufacturing executive; b. Camden, Ark., Apr. 30, 1937; s. Howard Thompson and Pauline Virginia (Rogers) S.; m. Ann Monroe; children: Paul R., Elizabeth M. BS, Tulane U., 1960; postgrad. studies, La. State U., 1961-63; EPBA, Columbia U., 1978. Dir. planning Ethyl Corp., Baton Rouge, La., 1970-76; exec. v.p., gen. mgr. William Bonnell Co. subs. Ethyl Corp., Newman, Ga., 1976-81; pres. Steelcraft, Cin., 1981-84; v.p., group exec. Am. Standard, Cin., 1984-89, sr. v.p. N.Y.C., 1989-94, also bd. dirs., 1989—; pres., CEO The Trane Co., N.Y.C., 1989-94; mng. ptnr. Septa Assocs., 1994—; gen. ptnr. Rutledge Capital, 2000—. Pres. Thompson Smith Found., 1993—; chmn. bd. dirs. Trinity Mother Francis Health Sys., 1996—, Adobe, 2000—, Framed Picture Enterprises, 1999-; bd. dirs. CROM Corp. Bd. dirs. Salvation Army, 1988—, Tex. Rsch. League, Austin, 1989, U. Tex., Tyler, 1990—, Mother Francis Hosp. Found., 1991—; chmn. bd. dirs. East Tex. Communities Found., 1993—; elder, trustee 1st Presbyn. Ch.; trustee U. Tex., Tyler, East Tex. Pres. Found., Union Theol. Sem., 1994— Mem. Tex. Assn. Taxpayers (dir.), Smith County C. of C. (bd. dirs. 1988-91), Tyler Petroleum Club, Hollytree Country Club, Willowbrook Country Club, Sawgrass Country Club. Republican. Presbyterian. Avocations: golf, tennis. Office: The Trane Co PO Box 9010 Tyler TX 75711-9010 also: 819 Spinnakers Reach Dr Ponte Vedra Beach FL 32082-3408

**SMITH, HOWARD WELLINGTON,** education educator, retired dean; b. Granby, Mo., Jan. 19, 1929; s. Howard W. and Margaret L. (Sanderson) S.; m. Margaret E. Bell, Mar. 1, 1953; 1 child, Christopher Alan. BS, S.W. Mo. State U., 1954; MEd, U. Mo., 1955, EdD, 1959. Tchr. Newton County (Mo.) Pub. Schs., 1948-51; instr. U. Mo., Columbia, 1955-59; asst. prof. So. Meth. U., Dallas, 1959-61; from asst. to full prof. U. North Tex., Denton, 1961-97, dean emeritus. Assoc. dean Coll. Edn. U. North Tex., 1972-76, assoc. v.p. acad. affairs, 1976-79, v.p. acad. affairs, 1979-82, interim dean, 1994-97; interim chancellor U. North Tex. Coll. Osteo. Medicine, Denton and Ft. Worth, 1981; sr. cons. Am. Assn. State Colls. and Univs., Washington, 1982; cons. Srinakharinwirot U., Thailand, 1986, Tex. Internat. Edn. Consortium, Austin, 1992, sr. author Operation Manual Al Akhawayn U., 1993; vis. prof. Shanxi Ednl. Coll. Taiyuan, China, 1993. Contbr. articles to ednl. jours. Prin. investigator Micro Tchg. Lab., 1967—69; chair Ret. Instrs., Pers. and Spouses U. North Tex., 2001; accreditation cons. Art Inst. Dallas, 2001—; chair Denton County Hist. Soc., 1999—2004; exec. coun. U. North Tex. Friends of Libr., 2005—; trustee Art Inst. Dallas, 2005—; adv. bd. Coll. Edn. U. North Tex., 1997—2005, adv. bd. Bill J. Priest Ctr. for C.C. Edn., 1999—2002, Coll. of Edn. devel. bd., 1999—2002; adv. bd. Coll. Edn., 2006—; pres. bd. dirs. Tex. Lakes Trail, 2002—04. With USAF, 1951—53. Democrat. Presbyterian. Avocations: travel, reading. Office: U North Tex Coll Edn PO Box 311319 Denton TX 76203-1337

**SMITH, HUGH CADHAM,** cardiovascular diseases physician; b. Winnipeg, Manitoba, Canada, July 14, 1939; BS, U. Manitoba, Winnipeg, MD, 1965. Intern U. Maitoba, 1965, resident in internal med., 1966—68; fellow in pulmonary disease U. Wash. Hosps., Seattle, 1968—70; resident in cardiology Mayo Clinic, Rochester, Minn., 1970—73, staff mem., 1970—. Chair bd. govs. Mayo Clinic, 1999—; prof. med.; v.p., mem. bd. trustees Mayo Found. Office: Mayo Clinic 200 First St SW Rochester MN 55905

**SMITH, IAN CORMACK PALMER,** biophysicist; b. Winnipeg, Man., Can., Sept. 23, 1939; s. Cormack and Grace Mary Smith; m. Eva Gunilla Landvik, Mar. 27, 1965; children: Brittmarie, Cormack, Duncan, Roderick. BS, U. Man., 1961, MS, 1962; PhD, Cambridge U., Eng., 1965; PhD (hon.), U. Stockholm, 1986; DSc (hon.), U. Winnipeg, 1990, Brandon U., 2001, Cracow Polish Acad. Sci., Poland, 2006; diploma in tech. (hon.), Red River Coll., 1996. Fellow Stanford U., 1965-66; mem. rsch. staff Bell Tel. Labs., Murray Hill, NJ, 1966-67; rsch. officer divsn. biol. scis. NRC, Ottawa, Canada, 1967-87, dir. gen., 1987-91, Inst. Biodiagnostics, Winnipeg, Canada, 1992—. Adj. prof. chemistry and biochemistry Carleton U., 1973—90, U. Ottawa, 1976—; adj. prof. biophysics U. Ill., Chgo. 1974—80, adj. prof. chemistry, radiology, physics and anatomy U. Man., 1992—; allied scientist Ottawa Civic Hosp., 1985—98, Ottawa Gen. Hosp., 1989—98, Ont. Cancer Found., 1989—91, St. Boniface Hosp., 1992—, Health Scis. Ctr., 1993—, Econ. Tech. Innovation Coun., Man., 1994—98, mem. exec. com., Man., 1996—98, Man. Health Rsch. Coun., 1996—98, chmn., 1998—2002; mem. adv. bd. Loeb Inst., Ottawa, 1999—2001, Keystone Ventures, 1999—2002, Western Life Scis. Fund, 2002—, Novadaq, 2004—, St. Boniface Hosp. Rsch. Enterprise, 2006—, Cancer Care Man.; bd. dirs. ENSIS Growth Fund, DIASPEC Holdings, IMRIS Inc., Magnetic Resonance Vets., Photonics Rsch. Ont., Spectex Pty., Biomed. Commercialization Can., Rover Imaging Inc., Ontario Centres of Excellence, Genome Prairie, Cancer Care Man., St. Boniface Hosp. Rsch. Ctr. Contbr. chapters to books, articles to profl. jours. Mem. adv. bd. Smart Winnipeg, 2000—03; mem. Premier's Econ. Adv. Bd., Man., 2001—, exec. com. Man., 2004—; bd. govs. U. Man., 2000—06. Decorated Order of the Star of Romania; recipient Barringer award, Can. Spectroscopy Soc., 1979, Herzberg award, 1986, Organon Teknika award, Can. Soc. Clin. Chemists, 1987, Sr. Scientist award, Sigma Xi, 1995, Queen's Jubilee medal, 2003, Star of Romania, 2004. Fellow: Soc. Magnetic Resonance Medicine (mem. exec. com. 1989—94), Royal Soc. Can. (Flavelle medal 1996), Chem. Inst. Can. (Merck award 1978, Labatt award 1984); mem.: Internat. Union Pure and Applied Biophysics (mem. coun. 1993—, v.p. 1996—99, 2000—05, pres. 2005—), Biophys. Soc. Can. (pres. 1992—94), Can. Biochem. Soc., Biophysical Soc., Internat. Coun. Sci. Unions (mem. gen. com. 1989—94), U. Man. Alumni Assn. (bd. dirs. 1994—2000 bd. 1997—98, pres. 1998—99). Office: Inst Biodiagnostics Winnipeg MB Canada R3B 1Y6 Office Phone: 204-983-7526. Business E-Mail: ian.smith@nrc-cnrc.gc.ca.

**SMITH, IRVING,** gerontologist; b. Washington, June 4, 1948; s. Alfonso Marcellus and Nannie (Hunter) S.; children: Bryan, Rashard, Irving, Nevada, Ryan. M in Human Svcs., Lincoln U., 1995, grad. cert. advanced gerontology, 1995; PhD in Health and Human Behavior, Walden U., 2002. Lic. profl. counselor D.C. Dir. Sr. Ctr. Md.-Nat. Capital Park and Planning Commn., Prince George's County, Md., 1969—71, 1989—; prof. psychology Grad. Sch. Internat., nat. forum spkr. on leisure and aging issues; founder Prince George's County Centenarian Celebration; prin. investigator Prince George's County, Md. Centenarian Rsch. Study; bd. dirs., regional dir. Leisure and Aging. Mem. Nat. Recreation and Park Assn. (state rep. leisure and aging, bd.

dirs. leisure and aging sect., dir. Mid-Atlantic region), Pi Gamma Mu. Democrat. Baptist. Home: 4311 23d Pky #505 Temple Hills MD 20748 Personal E-mail: ismith@starpower.net.

**SMITH, ISABEL FRANCIS,** financial planner; b. Detroit, May 21, 1935; d. Edward Hugh and Isabel (Winegar) Francis; m. Lawrence Smith, June 7, 1958; children: Mark, Hugh, Claire. Student, Newton Coll. 1953—54; BA, U. Mich., 1957, MA, 1958, postgrad., 1975—76. Registered investment adviser. Tchr. Edison Sch., Hazel Park, Mich., 1958—61, Warren Valley Sch., Dearborn Heights, Mich., 1958—61; counselor Riverside HS, Dearborn Heights, 1961—62; pres. Isabel Francis Smith Ltd., Farmington Hills, Mich., 1980—, Integrated Fin. Strategies Ltd., Farmington Hills, 1980—. Registered rep., dist. mgr. Investors Diversified Svcs., Oak Park, Mich., 1978—80; instr. Oakland CC, 1979—; cons. to women's orgns.; dir. pres. Oakland County Fin. and Estate Planning Coun., 1988—94; writer, profl. radio and TV personality. Lectr., trustee Bloomfield Twp. Libr., 1978—99, Interlochen Ctr. Arts, 1989—; founder Interlochen Friends, Vol. Network for Women. Recipient Heart of Gold award, United Found., 1976, Outstanding New Rep. award, Investors Diversified Svcs., 1979. Mem.: AAUW, Inst. Cert. Fin. Planners (nat. dir. 1980—86, dean retreat 1987, 1989, past regional dir., leadership devel. com., cert. fin. planner), Internat. Assn. Fin. Planners (past pres. S.E. Mich. chpt.), Nat. Assn. Women Bus. Owners, U. Mich. Alumni Assn., Interlochen Alumni Founder Assn. (past pres., award), Village Club, Mut. Svcs. Corp. (pres. club 1992—2002, Outstanding Rep. award 1981—90), Women's Econ. Club, Phi Beta Kappa (nat. chmn., past pres., exec. com. Pres. award Detroit assn.). Home: 7110 Paterese Dr Bloomfield Hills MI 48301-3764 Office: 3184 Northwestern Hwy Farmington Hills MI 48334-1628 Office Phone: 248-932-9329. Business E-Mail: isabel@ifs-ltd.com.

**SMITH, J. GORDON,** automotive executive; BA in Acctg., U. Mass.; grad., GE Fin. Mgmt. Program. Chief fin. officer comml. fin. units GE, 1990—2003; sr. v.p., chief fin. officer Asbury Automotive Group, Stamford, Conn., 2003—. Office: Asbury Automotive Group 3 Landmark Sw Stamford CT 06901

**SMITH, J. KELLUM, JR.,** foundation administrator, lawyer; b. N.Y.C., June 18, 1927; s. James Kellum and Elizabeth Dexter (Walker) S.; m. Sarah Tod Lohmann, July 22, 1950 (div. 1993); children: Alison Andrews, Timothy Kellum, Jennifer Harlow, Christopher Lohmann; m. Angela Marina Brown, Feb. 3, 1995. Grad., Phillips Exeter Acad., 1945; AB magna cum laude, Amherst Coll., 1950; LL.B., Harvard, 1953. Bar: N.Y. 1955. Assoc. Lord, Day & Lord, N.Y.C., 1953-59; asst. sec. John Simon Guggenheim Meml. Found., 1960-62; mem. staff Rockefeller Found., 1962-74, asst. sec., 1963-64, sec., 1964—74; v.p., sec. Andrew W. Mellon Found., N.Y.C., 1974—89, sr. fellow, 1989-92; sr. advisor, 1992-98; pvt. practice cons. and writer. Trustee Nat. Sculpture Soc., 1955-71, Nat. Ins. Archtl. Edn., 1961-69, St. Bernard's Sch., N.Y.C., 1968-78, Found. for Child Devel., 1968-74; trustee Brearley Sch., N.Y.C., 1964-80, pres., 1973-78; trustee Am. Acad. in Rome, 1964-96, treas., 1965-66, 2d v.p., 1968-72, 84-88, sec., 1973-84, 89-95. With USAAF, 1945-46. Mem. Phi Beta Kappa. Clubs: Century Association (N.Y.C.). Home: 550 Number 37 Rd Saranac NY 12981-2956

**SMITH, JACK CARL,** import/export company executive; b. Cleve., Sept. 11, 1928; s. John Carl and Florence Agnes (O'Rourke) S.; m. Nannette June Boyd, Dec. 1, 1962; 1 dau., Colleen Wentworth. Student, Baldwin Wallace Coll., 1948-51, postgrad., 1958; BA, Ohio U., 1954. Rep. Flying Tiger Line, Inc., Los Angeles, 1958-61; prin. Pub. Rep. bus., Cleve., 1961-64; pub. Penton Pub., Cleve., 1964-90; spl. advisor Am. Fgn. Policy Coun., Washington, 1990—. Dir. Central Cleve. Corp., Nat. Distbn. Terminals; graduated Air Tng. Command Intelligence Officer Sch., served from 1958-62 AFR. Trustee Presdl. task force, Rep. Senatorial Inner Circle, Coun. of Logistics Mgmt., U.S. Bus. and Indsl. Coun. With USAF, 1954-58. Mem. Am. Mgmt. Assn., Material Handling Inst., Am. Trucking Assn., Nat. Council Phys. Distbn. Mgmt., Family Motor Coach Assn., Recreation Vehicle Industry Assn., Am. Bus. Press, Mag. Pubs. Assn., Sci. Research Soc., Internat. Platform Assn., Sigma Xi, Sigma Chi Clubs: Wings (N.Y.C.). Home: 457 Devonshire Ct Bay Village OH 44140-3009 Office: Am Fgn Policy Coun 1521 16th St NW Washington DC 20036-1463 *Do your best and God will forgive you the rest.*

**SMITH, JACK DAVID,** lawyer; b. Honolulu, Jan. 4, 1946; s. Jack David and Gloria June (Slater) S.; m. Mary Elizabeth Zasadny, Sept. 17, 1977; children: Amy Elizabeth, Amanda Marie. BA in Polit. Sci., George Washington U., 1968, JD, 1971. Bar: Va. 1971, U.S. Ct. Mil. Appeals 1971, U.S. Ct. Appeals (1st and D.C. cirs.) 1975, U.S. Ct. Appeals (2d and 7th cirs.) 1976, U.S. Supreme Ct. 1976, D.C. 1986. Atty. litig. div. FCC, Washington, 1974-81, dept. chief common carrier bur., 1981-83, chief common carrier bur., 1983-84, gen. counsel, 1984-86; dep. gen. counsel Fed. Home Loan Bank Bd., Washington, 1986-89, Fed. Deposit Ins. Corp., Washington, 1989—. Served to capt. USMC, 1971-74. Mem. Va. Bar Assn., D.C. Bar Assn. Avocations: tennis, running, skiing. Office: Fed Deposit Ins Corp 550 17th St NW Washington DC 20429-0002 Home: 400 Madison St No 1705 Alexandria VA 22314 Business E-Mail: jsmith@fdic.gov.

**SMITH, JACK LEE,** bank executive; b. Yale, Okla., Feb. 2, 1948; s. George W. and Alta E. (Tilley) S.; m. Rose Mary Cantrell, Feb. 3, 1968 (div. Feb. 1980); children: Anissa Kay, Melany Elaine; m. Janice A. Houston, Aug. 2, 1981(div. Feb. 2000). BS, Okla. State U., 1972. State v.p. Production Credit Assn., 1972-76; v.p., office mgr. Mountain Plains Prodn. Credit Assn., Ft. Collins, 1976-81; dist. mgr. Ralston Purina, St. Louis, 1981-83; 2d v.p. Omaha Nat. Bank, 1983-85; v.p., office mgr. FirsTier Bank, N.A., Omaha, Ft. Collins, 1985-93, mgr. western area agrl. lending Omaha, 1993-96; sr. v.p. agribus. fin. group Farm Credit Svcs., Greeley, Colo., 1996—. Bd. dirs. Colo. Cattle Feeders Assn.; chmn. Allied Industry Coun. for Agr. Mem. Am. Bankers Assn., Colo. Bankers Assn., Nat. Cattlemen's Assn., Kans. Livestock Assn., Colo. Cattlemen's Assn., Elks. Republican. Avocations: photography, hiking, fishing, camping. Home: 2613 Jewelstone Ct Fort Collins CO 80525-6118 Office: AgriBusiness Finance Group Farm Credit Svcs 4505 29th St Greeley CO 80634-8763

**SMITH, JACLYN,** actress; b. Houston, Oct. 26, 1947; d. Jack and Margaret Ellen S.; m. Dennis Cole (div. 1981); m. Tony Richmond, Aug. 4, 1981; 1 dau., Spencer Margaret. Student, Trinity U., San Antonio. Worked as model. Motion picture appearances include The Adventurers, 1970, Bootleggers, Deja Vu; TV film appearances include Bogen County, 1977, The Users, 1978, Rage of Angels, 1980, Nightkill, 1980, Jacqueline Bouvier Kennedy, 1981, Sentimental Journey, 1984, George Washington (miniseries), 1984, Florence Nightingale, 1985, The Night They Saved Christmas, 1986, Wind Mills of the Gods (miniseries), 1988, The Bourne Identity, 1988, Settle the Score, 1989, Danielle Steele's Kaleidoscope, 1990, Lies Before Kisses, 1991, The Rape of Dr. Willis, 1991, In The Arms Of A Killer, 1992, Love Can Be Murder, 1992, Family Album, 1994, Cries Unheard: The Donna Yaklich Story, 1994, My Very Best Friend, 1996, Married to a Stranger, 1997, Before He Wakes, 1998, Three Secrets, 1999, Freefall, 1999; one of prin. roles TV series Charlie's Angels, 1976-80, (ABC Saturday Night Movie) Christine Cromwell, 1989-90; other TV appearances include Get Christy Love, McCloud, The Rookies, Love Boat, Switch, Navigating the Heart, 2000, The District, 2000; appeared in numerous TV commls. Mem. AFTRA. Office: ICM 8942 Wilshire Blvd Beverly Hills CA 90211-1934

**SMITH, JAMES A.,** lawyer; b. Akron, Ohio, June 11, 1930; s. Barton H. and Myrna S. (Young) S.; m. Melda I. Perry, Jan. 17, 1959; children: Hugh, Sarah Louise. AB, Western Res. U., 1952; postgrad., Columbia U., 1954-56, LLB, 1961; postgrad., Yale U., 1956-58. Bar: Ohio 1961, U.S. Dist. Ct. (no. dist.) Ohio 1963, U.S. Ct. Appeals (6th cir.) 1973, U.S. Supreme Ct. 1974, U.S. Ct. Appeals (11th cir.) 1983, U.S. Ct. Appeals (D.C. cir.) 1984. Assoc. Squire, Sanders and Dempsey, Cleve., 1961-70, ptnr., 1970-91, counsel, 1991-96; adj. prof. Case Western Res. U. Sch. Law, 1997-98, ret., 1994. Mem. spl. adv. com. Nat. Conf. Commrs. on Uniform State Laws, 1972-74. Trustee Chagrin Falls Park Cmty. Ctr., 1968-78, Greater Cleve. Neighborhood Ctrs. Assn.,

1973-78, Legal Aid Soc. Cleve., 1977-80, Cleve. Inst. Music, 1994—; mem. Charter Rev. Commn., Chagrin Falls, 1966. Lt. (j.g.) USNR, 1952-54. Fellow Am. Coll. Trial Lawyers; mem. ABA, Ohio Bar Assn., Cleve. Bar Assn. (trustee 1988-92), U.S. Ct. Appeals for 6th Cir. Jud. Conf. (life), Ohio Ct. Appeals for 8th Jud. Dist. Conf. (life), Ct. of Nisi Prius (clk. 1975-76, judge 1994-95), Appalachee Vill. Assn. (pres. 2004-05), Phi Beta Kappa, Omicron Delta Kappa, Delta Sigma Rho. Democrat. Personal E-mail: jasasmith1@aol.com.

**SMITH, JAMES ALBERT,** lawyer; b. Jackson, Mich., May 12, 1942; s. J William and Mary Barbara (Browning) S.; m. Lucia S. Santini, Aug. 14, 1965; children: Matthew Browning, Aaron Michael, Rachel Elizabeth. BA, U. Mich., 1964, JD, 1967. Bar: Mich. 1968, U.S. Dist. Ct. (ea. dist.) Mich., U.S. Ct. Appeals (6th and D.C. cirs.), U.S. Supreme Ct. Assoc. Bodman, Longley & Dahling, Detroit, 1967-75, ptnr., 1975—. Mem. panel Atty. Discipline Bd., Wayne County, Mich., 1980—; arbitrator Am. Arbitration Assn., 1975—; mem. Banking Commrs. com. on Contested Case Adminstrn., 1978. Mem. pro bono referral group Call For Action, Detroit, 1982—. Mem. ABA, State Bar Mich., Detroit Bar Assn. Roman Catholic. Avocations: sailing, travel. Office: Bodman Longley & Dahling 100 Renaissance Ctr Ste 34 Detroit MI 48243-1001

**SMITH, JAMES COPENHAVER,** bank executive; s. Harold Webster Smith; m. Cathy Smith, 1987; 2 children. BA, Dartmouth Coll., 1971. Adminstrv. banking officer First Federal (renamed Webster Bank in 1995), 1975; pres. Webster Bank, 1982—87, CEO, 1987—, Webster Financial Corp., 1987—, chmn., 1995—. Mem. Fed. Advisory Coun.; bd. dirs. MacDermid Inc. Bd. dirs., exec. com. St. Mary's Hosp., Waterbury, Conn.; chmn. bd. dirs. Palace Theater, Waterbury, Conn. Mem.: Conn. Bankers Assn. (exec. com.). Avocations: running, bicycling, golf, hiking. Office: Webster Fin Corp Webster Plaza WFD730 Waterbury CT 06702*

**SMITH, JAMES FINLEY,** economist, educator; b. Dallas, Nov. 4, 1938; s. Emerson Russell and Achsah Elizabeth (Foster) S.; children: Carter Emerson, Jamie, Curtis Noel, Marshall Edward; m. Linda M. Topp, Aug. 5, 2001. BA, So. Meth. U., 1961, MA, 1964, PhD, 1971. Mah. analyst Sears, Roebuck & Co., Oak Brook, Ill., 1965-68, adminstrv. asst. to v.p. and treas. Chgo., 1968-69, dir. econometric rsch., 1969-75; sr. economist Bd. Govs. FRS, Washington, 1975-77; dir. credit rsch. Sears, Roebuck & Co., Chgo., 1977-80; chief economist Union Carbide Corp., Danbury, Conn., 1980-85; dir. regional svcs. and U.S. cons. Wharton Econometric Forecasting Assocs., Phila., 1986; dir., chief economist Bur. Bus. Rsch. U. Tex., Austin, 1987-88; prof. fin. U. NC, Chapel Hill, 1988—; sr. fellow Kenan Inst. Pvt. Enterprise, 2002—; chief economist Nat. Assn. Realtors, Washington, 1999—2000; dir. Ctr. for Bus. Forecasting, U. N.C., 2002—; chief economist Soc. Indsl. and Office Realtors, Washington, 2002—06, Parcec Fin. Mgmt., Asheville, NC, 2006—. Econ. adv. bd. U.S. Dept. Commerce, 1977-80, 83-93; cons. Pres.'s Coun. of Econ. Advisers, Washington, 1978-83; pres. Nat. Bus. Econ. Issues Coun., N.Y.C., 1981-83; dir. Nat. Bur. Econ. Rsch., Cambridge, Mass., 1992-95; bd. advisors Thurston Arthritis Rsch. Ctr., Chapel Hill, N.C., 1994-99; dir. Am. Fin. Svcs. Assn. Edn. Found., 1997—. Author: (quarterly) UNC Business Forecast, 1988-2005, Jim Smith's Econ. Outlook, 2005—; (with others) Economic Growth and Investment in Higher Education, 1987, The New Texas Economy, 1988; (with Elsie Echeverri-Carroll) The Economic Impact of Travel on Texas Counties: 1986, 1988; contbr. articles to profl. jours. Served to lt. U.S. Army, 1961-62. Fellow NDEA, 1962—65. Fellow Nat. Assn. Bus. Econ. (v.p. 1988-89, pres. 1989-90, dir. 1980-92); Nat. Economists Club (bd. govs. 1984-87), Am. Econ. Assn., Economists Group Switzerland, Fin. Mgmt. Assn., Bus. Economists U.K. Methodist. Office: U NC Kenan Flagler Bus Sch Dept Fin McColl Bldg Campus Box 3490 Chapel Hill NC 27599-3490 Business E-Mail: j_smith@unc.edu.

**SMITH, JAMES LAWRENCE,** research physicist; b. Detroit, Sept. 3, 1943; s. William Leo and Marjorie Marie (Underwood) S.; m. Carol Ann Adam, Mar. 27, 1965; children: David Adam, William Leo. BS, Wayne State U., 1965; PhD, Brown U., 1974. Mem. staff Los Alamos Nat. Lab., N.Mex., 1973—82, fellow, 1982—86, dir. ctr. materials sci., 1986—87, fellow, 1987—; chief scientist Superconductivity Tech. Ctr., 1988—99; N.Am. editor Philos. Mag., 1990—95; editor Philos. Mag. B., 1995—2002, Philos. Mag., 2003—. Scientific editor: Los Alamos Rsch. Quar., 2002-03; contbr. articles to profl. jours. Recipient E.O. Lawrence award, 1986, Disting. Alumni award Wayne State U., 1993. Fellow Am. Phys. Soc. (internat. prize for new materials 1990); mem. AAAS, Materials Rsch. soc., Minerals Metals Materials Soc., Am. Crystallographic Assn., Brown Alumni Assn. (bd. govs. 1998-2000), Phi Beta Kappa. Achievements include patents for design of magnetic field and high-strength conductors. Office: Los Alamos Nat Lab Mail Stop G770 Los Alamos NM 87545-0001

**SMITH, JAMES M.,** dean; b. Houston, Sept. 14, 1965; s. C.F. and Hallie Ann Smith; m. Sheryl M. Smith, Aug. 6, 1994; children: Madison, Zachary. BS, Sam. Houston State U., Huntsville, Tex., 1993; MEd, U. Houston Clear Lake, 2005. Tchr. Lamar Consol. Ind. Sch. Dist., Rosenburg, Tex., 1993—2005; dean instrn. Employment Tng. Ctr., Houston, 2005—. Republican. Baptist. Avocations: camping, hiking, baseball. Home: 9503 Cardinal Rd Beasley TX 77417 Office: ATLA 8329 Lawndale Houston TX 77012

**SMITH, JAMES PATRICK,** economist; b. Aug. 3, 1943; s. James P. and Winefred (Harrison) S.; m. Sandra Berry, Oct. 25, 1983; children: Gillian Clare, Lauren Theresa. BS, Fordham U., 1965; PhD, U. Chgo., 1972. Rsch. assoc. Nat. Bur. Econ. Rsch., N.Y.C., 1972-74; sr. economist Rand Corp., Santa Monica, Calif., 1974—; dir. of rsch. labor and population, 1977-93. Bd. mem. Occupl. Safety and Health Standards State Calif. Editor: Female Labor Supply, 1980, The New Americans, 1997, The Immigration Debate, 1998, Wealth, Work, and Health, 1999; bd. editors: Am. Econ. Rev., 1980-83; author articles in field. Recipient Merit award NIH, 1995—. Mem. NIA (monitoring com., health and retirement survey, chair NAS panel on immigration, prin. investigator New Immigrant Survey), Am. Econ. Assn., Phi Beta Kappa. Office: RAND PO Box 2138 Santa Monica CA 90407-2138 Office Phone: 310-451-6925. Business E-Mail: smith@rand.org.

**SMITH, JAMES TODD** *See* **LL COOL J**

**SMITH, JAMES W., JR.,** state supreme court justice; b. Louisville, Miss., Oct. 28, 1943; BS, U. So. Miss., 1965; JD, Jackson St. Law, 1972; MEd with honors, Miss. Coll., 1973. Bar: Miss. 1972, U.S. Dist. Ct. (no. and so. dists.) Miss. 1973, U.S. Ct. Appeals (5th cir.) 1974. Pvt. practice, Pearl, Miss., 1972-78, Brandon, Miss., 1979-80; pres. atty. City of Pearl, 1973-80; prosecutor Rankin County, Miss., 1976; dist. atty. 20th Jud. Dist., Miss., 1977-82; judge Rankin County, 1982-92; justice Miss. Supreme Ct., 1993—, chief justice, 2004—. Instr. courtroom procedure and testifying Miss. Law Enforcement Tng. Acad., 1980-91. With U.S. Army, 1966-69. Named Wildlife Conservationist of Yr. Rankin County, 1988, Lawyer of Yr. Mo. Coll. Sch. Law, 2006; recipient Outstanding Positive Role Model for Today's Youth award, 1991, Child Forever award Miss. Voices of Children and Youth, 1992, You've Made a Difference award 1995, Alumnus of Yr. award Hinds C.C., 1996, Disting. Pub. Servant award U. So. Mo., 2006; Juris Sodalitas fellow 2006; named to Hall Fame, U. So. Mo. Fellow Miss. Bar Found. (bd. dirs. 1998); mem. Miss. State Bar Assn., Rankin County Bar Assn. Office: Carroll Gartin Justice Bldg PO Box 117 Jackson MS 39205-0117 Office Phone: 601-359-2093.

**SMITH, JAMES WALKER,** lawyer; b. S.I., N.Y., May 11, 1957; s. James Patrick and Ann Catherine (Sullivan) S.; m. Erin Patricia Murphy, Aug. 15, 1982; children: Patrick James, Daniel Timothy, Meghan Kathleen, James John. BA magna cum laude, Fordham U., 1979, JD, 1982; LLM, NYU, 1988. BAr: N.Y. 1983, N.J. 1984, Pa. 1993, U.S. Supreme Ct. 1994. Assoc. Mendes & Mount, N.Y.C., 1982, Costello Shea & Gaffney, N.Y.C., 1982-86; ptnr. Anderson Kill Olick & Oshinsky P.C., N.Y.C., 1986-96, Smith Abbot, LLP, N.Y.C., 1996—. Arbitrator N.Y.C. (N.Y.) Civil Ct., 1987-89; faculty chair-

person hosp. law Fordham Law Sch., N.Y.C., 1989-93; mediator U.S. Dist. Ct. (so. dist.) N.Y., N.Y.C., 1992-96. Author: Hospital Liability, 1985—; editor-in-chief: New York Practice Guide, 1993-97; contbg. editor: Medical Malpractice Law and Strategy, 1993—; bd. editors Fordham Urban Law Jour., 1981-82. Mem. N.Y. County Lawyer's Assn. (com. on tort law 1993-95), Assn. of the Bar of the City of N.Y. (com. on tort law 1990-92, com. on state cts. 1994—). Roman Catholic. Avocations: golf, coaching youth basketball. Home: 15 Flagg Ct Staten Island NY 10304-1157 Office: Smith Abbot LLP 100 Maiden Ln New York NY 10038-4818

**SMITH, JAMES WARREN,** pathologist, educator, microbiologist, parasitologist; b. Logan, Utah, July 5, 1934; s. Kenneth Warren and Nina Lou (Sykes) S.; m. Nancy Chesterman, July 19, 1958; children: Warren, Scott. BS, U. Iowa, 1956, MD, 1959. Diplomate Am. Bd. Pathology. Intern Colo. Gen. Hosp., Denver, 1959—60; resident U. Iowa Hosps., Iowa City, 1960—65; asst. prof. pathology U. Vt., Burlington, 1967—70; prof. pathology Ind. U., Indpls., 1970—98, chmn. dept. pathology and lab. medicine, 1992—98, Nordshow prof. of lab. medicine, 1997—98, prof. emeritus, 1998—. Contbr. articles to profl. jours. Served to lt. comdr. USN, 1965-67. Recipient Outstanding Contbn. to Clin. Microbiology award South Ctrl. Assn. Clin. Microbiology, 1977. Fellow Coll. Am. Pathologists (chmn. microbiology resource com. 1981-85); mem. AMA, Infectious Disease Soc. Am., Am. Soc. Investigative Pathology, Royal Soc. Tropical Medicine and Hygiene, Am. Soc. Clin. Pathology, Am. Soc. Microbiology, Am. Soc. Tropical Medicine and Hygiene, U.S.-Can. Acad. Pathology, Assn. Pathology Chairs, Binford Dammin Soc. Infectious Disease Pathologists, Soc. Protozoologists. Home: 4375 Cold Spring Rd Indianapolis IN 46228-3327 Office: Ind U Med Ctr 635 Barnhill Dr Rm A128 Indianapolis IN 46202-5126

**SMITH, JANE SCHNEBERGER,** retired city administrator; b. Chgo., Aug. 9, 1928; d. Frank R. and Marion (Durante) Schneberger; m. Z. Erol Smith Jr., Oct. 28, 1950 (div. 1974); children: Suzan MacKenzie Smith, Tracy Smith Cawley, Cameron Farley, Z. Erol III, Kimberly Van Den Elzen, Scott. BA in Chemistry, U. Colo., 1950; MA in Comm., Mich. State U., East Lansing, 1978, PhD in Ednl. Adminstrn., 1987. Chemist Kellogg Switchboard, Chgo., 1950-51; v.p. South Cook County Girl Scouts, Harvey, Ill., 1967-69, staff advisor, 1970-72; tchr. Crab Orchard Sch., Palos Heights, Ill., 1969-70; program and tng. dir. Mich. Capitol. Coun. Girl Scouts, Lansing, Mich., 1972-75; dir. svc. learning ctr. Mich. State U., East Lansing, 1975-81; city clk. City of Ashland, Wis., 1981-89, interim city adminstr., 1989-90; ret., 1990; acting city clk. City of Ashland, 2003, 2006. Cons. vol. adminstrn., Mich., Wis., 1975—. Co-editor: Looking Backward Moving Forward, 1987, Roots and Wings, 2002; contbr. articles to profl. jours. V.p. Mich. Capitol Girl Scout Coun., Lansing, 1976-78; bd. dirs. Lansing RSVP, 1976-81, Ashland Mus., 1985-87, Ptnrs. in Recovery, 1985-87; v.p. Friends of the Libr., 1992-97, pres., 1997-99; sec. New Horizons, 1985-90, New Day Shelter, 1990-99, v.p., 1993-95, pres., 1995-97, sec., 1997-99; pres. LWV of Ashland Bayfield County, 1992-93, 96-98; sec. No. Wis. History Ctr., 1992-94; commr. Ashland Water and Wastewater Utility, 1993-96; mem. Ashland Beautification Com., 1993—, Big Top Chautauqua, 1996-2003, vice chair Alliance for Sustainability, 1994-99; v.p. GFWC/Ashland Monday Club, 1994-98, pres., 1998-2000, 1st v.p. 10th Dist. GFWC-W1, 2000-02; mem. Ashland County Human Svcs. Bd., 1998—, vice chair, 2003-04, Restore the Depot Com., 2001—; co-chair comprehensive plan update com., 2002—05. co-chair comprehensive plan implementation com., 2006—; mem. tree bd. City of Ashland, 2002—, planning commn., 2004—. Recipient cert. appreciation Mich. Capitol Girl Scout Coun., 1975, Thanks Badge, 1972, Tribute to Excellence award LWV of Wis., 1999. Mem. Internat. Mcpl. Clks., Wis. Mcpl. Clks. Assn. (dist. dir. 1984-86), Am. Bus. Women's Assn. (scholarship chmn. 1985), Zonta (pres. 1979-81), Ashland Hist. Soc. (bd. dirs.). Roman Catholic. Avocations: stained glass, gardening, stamp collecting/philately, genealogy. Home: 700 MacArthur Ave Ashland WI 54806-2903 Personal E-mail: snowmont@cheqnet.net.

**SMITH, JANET BREWER,** secondary school educator; b. Pinehurst, NC, July 5, 1969; d. Vernon L. Brewer and Frances Brewer Rush; m. John Wesley Smith, July 11, 1993; children: Richard Austin, Nicholas Weston, Sarah Elizabeth. BA, NC State U., Raleigh, 1991. Cert. tchr. NC. Social studies tchr., dept. head North Moore HS, Robbins, NC, 1992—. Sunday sch. tchr. Pine Grove Bapt. Ch., Eagle Springs, NC, 1993. Named Tchr. of Yr., North Moore HS, 2005—06. Mem.: Profl. Educators NC. Southern Baptist. Home: 149 Cheyenne Rd Robbins NC 27325 Office: North Moore High Sch PO Box 9 Robbins NC 27325 Office Phone: 910-464-3105. Business E-Mail: jsmith@mcs.k12.nc.us.

**SMITH, JANET HUGIE,** lawyer; b. Logan, Utah, Aug. 1, 1945; BA magna cum laude, Utah State U., 1967; MA cum laude, Stanford U., 1969; JD, U. Utah, 1976. Bar: Utah 1976, U.S. Supreme Ct. 1992, U.S. Ct. Appeals (10th cir.) 1977, (9th cir.) 2003, US Dist. Ct. Colo. 2004. Shareholder, exec. com. Ray, Quinney & Nebeker, Salt Lake City, 1983—. Mem. ABA (labor and employment law sect.), Utah State Bar (labor and employment law sect.), CUE (labor lawyers adv. coun.), Am. Law Coun., Am. Coll. Trial Lawyers, Aldon J. Anderson Am. Inns of Ct. Office: Ray Quinney & Nebeker 36 S State St Ste 1400 Salt Lake City UT 84111-1431 Business E-Mail: jhsmith@rqn.com.

**SMITH, JANET MARIE,** sports executive; b. Jackson, Miss., Dec. 13, 1957; d. Thomas Henry and Nellie Brown (Smith) S. BArch, Miss. State U., 1981; MA in Urban Planning, CCNY, 1984. Draftsman Thomas H. Smith and Assocs. Architects, Jackson, 1979; mktg. coord. The Eggers Group, P.C. Architects and Planners, N.Y.C., 1980; program assoc. Ptnrs. for Livable Places, Washington, 1980-82; coord. asst. Lance Jay Brown, Architect and Urban Planner, N.Y.C., 1983-84; coord. architecture and design Battery Park City Authority, N.Y.C., 1982-84; pres., chief exec. officer Pershing Sq. Mgmt. Assn., L.A., 1985-89; v.p. stadium planning and devel. Balt. Orioles Oriole Park at Camden Yard, 1989-94; v.p. sports facilities Turner Properties, Atlanta, 1994-97; v.p. planning and devel. Atlanta Braves, Braves, 1994—; pres. TBS Sports Devel., Inc., 1997-2000; with Struever Brothers, Eccles & Rouse, Inc., Balt., 2000—; sr. v.p. planning Boston Red Sox, 2002—. Bd. dirs. Assn. Collegiate Schs. Architecture, Washington, 1979-82, Assn. Student Chpts. AIA, Washington, 1979-82. Guest editor: Urban Design Internat., 1985; assoc. editor: Crit, 1979-82; contbr. articles to profl. jours. Named Disting. Grad., Nat. Assn. State Univs. and Land Grant Colls., 1988, One of Outstanding Young Women of Am., 1982; recipient Spirit of Miss. award, Sta. WLBT, Jackson, 1987, Disting. Grad. award Nat. Assn. State Univs., 1988, Outstanding Alumni award Miss. State U., 1994, Andrew White medal Loyola Coll., 1997, Ptnrs. Livable Cmtys. award, 1998, City Coll. N.Y. award, 1998. Mem. AIA (assoc.), Urban Land Inst. Democrat. Episcopalian. Office Phone: 443-573-4342. E-mail: jm.smith@sber.com.

**SMITH, JANET SUE,** systems specialist; b. Chgo., Jan. 15, 1945; d. Curtis Edwin and Margaret Louise (Yost) Smith. BA, Ind. U., 1967. Sales mgr. Marshall Field & Co., Chgo., 1968-70, programmer, 1970-72; sr. programmer, analyst Trailer Train Co., Chgo., 1972-75; mgr. data base and systems devel. Railinc-Assn. Am. R.R., Washington, 1975-85, asst. v.p., corp. sec., 1985-93, asst. v.p. bus. svc., 1993-98, sec. dir. Interline Svc., 1998-99, asst. v.p. bus. svc., 1999—2001; owner JSSmith Consulting LLC, Chapel Hill, NC, 2002—05, Bloomington, Ind., 2005—. Nat. student v.p. YWCA, 1966-67; bd. dir. v.p. planning and fin. Guide Internat.; advisor Jr. Achievement; mem. alumni bd. dir. Coll. Arts and Scis. Ind. U., co-chair colloquium for women, mem. internat. studies adv. coun. Mem.: Woodburn Guild, Am. Coun. R.R. Women, Ind. U. Alumni Assn. (life). Home and Office: JSSmith Cons LLC 3141 E Wyndam Ct Bloomington IN 47401-4495

**SMITH, JARED RUSSELL WILLIAM,** research executive, research scientist, consultant; b. Cleve., Mar. 24, 1950; s. Russell Floyd William Smith and Mary Wiltrude Lee; m. Deborah Jane Parriott; children: Russell Jared Webster, Heather Frances. BA cum laude, NYU, 1973, MA, 1976. V.p. The Energy Bur., Inc., N.Y.C., 1976—86; assoc. dir. Inst. Gas Tech., Des Plaines, Ill., 1986—99; spl. appointee Argonee Nat. Lab., Ill., 1999—2000;

cons., 2001—. Adj. faculty NYU, N.Y.C., 1974-76; mem. adv. bd. La. State U., Baton Rouge, 1999—; adviser to Pres.'s Commn. on Critical Infrastructure Protection, Washington, 1997—; bd. dirs., adviser N.Y. Quar. Literary Found., N.Y.C., 1986. Author: (poetry books) Song of the Blood, 1983, Dark Wing, 1986, Keeping the Outlaw Alive, 1988, Walking the Perimeters of the Plate Glass Window Factory, 2000, Lake Michigan adapted to stage by David Lightner, 2003, Lake Michigan and Other Poems, 2005, (CD) Seven Minutes Before the Bombs Drop, 2006; editor: (books) Integrating Microelectronics into Gas Distribution, 1987, Gas, Oil and Coal Biotechnology, 1990 Election dist. leader Dem. Party, White Plains, N.Y., 1972; chmn. nominating com. Sch. Dist. 181, Hinsdale, Ill., 1993; adv. bd. mem. N.Y. Quar., 2005 Mem. Chgo. Poets Club, Poets and Patrons (pres.), Ill. State Poetry Soc. Democrat. Avocations: literature, fishing, hiking, painting, music. Home: 2630 Longview Dr Lisle IL 60532 E-mail: smithjrw@comcast.net.

**SMITH, JASON A. B.,** lawyer; b. Washington, Aug. 21, 1971; BA, Columbia Univ., 1993; JD, NYU, 1996. Bar: NY 1998. Ptnr., structured fin. and derivatives practice Weil Gotshal & Manges, N.Y.C. Mem.: ABA, NY State Bar Assn. Office: Weil Gotshal & Manges 767 Fifth Ave New York NY 10153 Office Phone: 212-310-8914. Office Fax: 212-310-8007. Business E-Mail: jason.smith@weil.com.

**SMITH, JAY See SMITH, ROBERT JR.**

**SMITH, JAY LAWRENCE,** financial planning company executive; b. Detroit, June 10, 1954; s. Paul Edward Smith and Gloria D. Lawrence; m. Janice Irene Acheson, May 21, 1978; children: Kevin Hamilton, Travis Jay. Student, Oakland U., 1972-75. CFP. Asst. tng. dir Equitable Co., Troy, Mich., 1978-81, pres. JLS Fin. Planning Corp., Oxford, Mich., 1978—. Adj. faculty Oakland U., Rochester, Mich., 1986-87; commentator TV show Your Money and You, 1987. Cons. Practicing Fin. Planning, 1990; contbr. articles to profl. jours. Mem. Internat. Assn. Fin. Planning (v.p. 1985-87, bd. dirs. 1987-89), Inst. Cert. Fin. Planners (bd. dirs. 1988-90), Inst. Cert. Fin. Planners-Mich. (pres. 1992-93), Fin. Profl. Adv. Panel, Internat. Bd. Cert. Fin. Planners, Rotary (bd. dirs. 1984-86, treas. 1985-87, pres. Oxford 1992-93). Republican. Methodist. Avocations: skiing, music, raquetball. Office: Investment Mgmt & Rsch Inc PO Box 4 28 S Washington St Oxford MI 48371-4985

**SMITH, J.E. GUIDO,** marketing professional; Student, U. Ariz.; BS, MBA, Hamilton U. Regional salels mgr. TR-3 Cheml Corp., Orange, Calif., 1980—81, nat. sales mgr., 1981—82, v.p.l, 1982—83; exec. v.p., CMO Simple Green (Sunshine Makers, Inc.), Huntington Beach, Calif., 1983—90; v.p. mktg. Blue Coral Inc., Cleve., 1990—92; ptnr. Premier Mktg. Solutions, LLC, Geneva, Ill., 1992—2000; sr. bus. strategist/e-bus. strategies and branding marchFIRST, Inc., Chgo., 2000; mng. ptnr. The Six Sigma Group, Southaven, Miss., 2000—02; v.p. sales and mktg. Moltan Co., L.P., Memphis, 2002—. Author: Successful Trade Show Marketing Strategies; co-author: Management Team, Marketing Masters; contbr. articles to profl. jours.; mem. editl. bd. Greener Mgmt. Internat. Recipient Disting. Sales Mgmt. award, Sales and Mktg. Execs. Internat., Presdl. Award of Merit. Mem.: Project Mgmt. Inst., Am. Mktg. Assn. Home: 8143 Waterford Cir #106 Memphis TN 38125

**SMITH, JEAN KENNEDY,** former ambassador; b. Brookline, Mass., Feb. 20, 1928; d. Joseph P. and Rose Kennedy; m. Stephen E. Smith (dec. 1990); 4 children. BA, Manhattanville Coll.; Degree (hon.), NYU, Fordham U., Nat. U. Ireland, Dublin City U. Founder, dir. chair Very Spl. Arts, 1974—; amb. to Ireland Dublin, 1993-98. Author: (with George Plimpton) Chronicles of Courage, 1993; contbr. articles on the disabled to profl. jours. Trustee John F. Kennedy Ctr. Performing Arts, 1964— Recipient Sec.'s award Dept. Vets. Affairs, Vol. of Yr. award People-to-People Com. Handicapped, Margaret Mead Humanitarian award Coun. Cerebral Palsy Auxs., Jefferson award Am. Inst. Pub. Svc., Spirit of Achievement award Yeshiva U., Humanitarian award Capital Children's Mus., Irish Am. of Yr. award Irish Am. Mag., 1995, Rotary One Internat. award Rotary Club Chgo., 1997, Terence Cardinal Cooke Humanitarian award, 1997.

**SMITH, JEAN WEBB (MRS. WILLIAM FRENCH SMITH),** civic worker; b. LA; d. James Ellwood and Violet (Hughes) Webb; m. George William Vaughan, Mar. 14, 1942 (dec. Sept. 1963); children: George William Vaughan, Merry Vaughan; m. William French Smith, Nov. 6, 1964. BA summa cum laude, Stanford U., Calif., 1940. Mem. Nat. Voc. Adv. Coun., 1973—76, vice chmn., 1974—76; dir. Beneficial Std. Corp., 1976—85; bd. dirs. Cmty. TV So. Calif., 1979—93. Bd. dirs. United Way, Inc., 1973—80, Nat. Symphony Orch., 1980—85; nat. bd. dirs. Boys' Club Am., 1977—80; mem. Pres.'s Commn. White House Fellowships, 1980—90, Nat. Coun. Humanities, 1987—90, Calif. Arts Commn., 1971—74, vice chmn., 1973—74; bd. dirs. The Founders, Music Ctr., LA, 1971—74; bd. dirs. costume coun. Los Angeles County Mus. Art, 1971—73; bd. dirs. LA chpt. NCCJ, 1977—80, LA World Affairs Coun., 1990, LA chpt. ARC, 1994—95; mem. adv. bd. Salvation Army, 1979—; bd. overseers Hoover Instn. War, Revolution and Peace, 1989—94; bd. govs. Calif. Cmty. Found., 1990—; bd. dirs. Hosp. Good Samaritan, 1973—80, mem. exec. com., 1975—80; bd. fellows Claremont U. Ctr. and Grad. Sch., 1987—; bd. regents Children's Hops. LA, 1993—. Named Woman of the Yr. for Cmty. Svc., LA Times, 1958; recipient Citizens of the Yr. award, Boys Clubs Greater LA, 1982, Life Achievement award, LA Coun. Boy Scouts Am., 1985. Mem.: Kappa Kappa Gamma, Assn. Jr. Leagues Am. (dir. region XII 1956—58, pres. 1958—60), Jr. League LA (pres. 1954—55, Spirit of Volunteerism award 1994), Phi Beta Kappa. Home: 11718 Wetherby Ln Los Angeles CA 90077-1348

**SMITH, JEFFREY A.,** lawyer; b. Trenton, Tenn., Sept. 27, 1963; s. Nathan L. and Mary Jane (Ledinger) b. DD in Acctg., U. Tenn. at Martin, 1985; JD, MBA, Memphis State U., 1991. Cost acct. Goodyear Tire & Rubber, Union City, Tenn., 1986-88; atty. Bill Barron, Atty., Trenton, Tenn., 1991-93, Kizer, Bonds, Crocker & Hughes, Milan, Tenn., 1993-95, Jeffrey A. Smith, Trenton, Tenn., 1995—. City atty. City of Dyer, Tenn., 1993-95, City of Kenton, Tenn., 1996—; bd. dirs. United Way of West Tenn., Jackson, 1997—. Elected mem.-alderman Bd. of Mayor & Aldermen, Rutherford, Tenn., 1993—; elected mem.-commr. Gibson County Bd. County Commrs., 1994—. Office: Jeffrey A Smith Atty PO Box 462 Trenton TN 38382-0462 Home: 16 Mcwherter Ln Rutherford TN 38369-9605

**SMITH, JEFFREY ANDREWS,** musician, educator, sound recording engineer; b. Tulsa, Aug. 25, 1955; s. Charles Lee Smith and Dorothy Germon Babcock; m. Robin Karen Hock, 1986. MusB with distinction, U. Kans., Lawrence, 1977; MusB in Edn. with honors, U. Tulsa, 1978, MA in Music Edn., 1979; MusM, Cleve. Inst. Music, 1983. Cert. tchr. State of Okla., 1983. Prin. violist Signature Symphony Orch., Tulsa, 1978—, Bartlesville Symphony Orch., Bartlesville, Okla., 1985—, Internat. String Orch., Graz, Austria, 1996; instrumental music dir. Allison Jr. H.S. Wichita, Kans., 1979—83, Bell Mid. Sch., Tulsa, 1983—88, Edison Prep. Sch., Tulsa, 1988—; pres., CEO SongSmith Records, Tulsa, 1986—; violist Signature String Quartet, Tulsa, 2000—; adj. faculty Okla. Wesleyan U., Bartlesville, Okla., 2002—. Prodr: (CD) All Strings Attached, 2002, Christmas at the Capital, 2001, Tulsa Bagpipe Band, 2003. Recipient Excellence award, Tulsa Pub. Schs., 1998; scholar U. So. Calif. String Congress, Am. Fedn. Musicians, 1973. Mem.: NEA, Tulsa Classroom Tchrs. Assn., Okla. Music Educators Assn. (all state chmn. 1992), Am. Fedn. Musicians, Local 94, Am. String Tchrs. Assn., Okla. Chpt. (pres. 1996—98, Tchr. of Yr. 2003). Avocations: model aircraft, racecars, motorcycling. Home: 6025 N Lions Ave Broken Arrow OK 74012 Personal E-mail: songsmithrecords@cox.net.

**SMITH, JEFFREY AUSTEN,** lawyer; b. Queens, NY, Sept. 6, 1952; AB cum laude, Harvard U., 1974; JD, U. Pa., 1981. Bar: Pa. 1981, NY 1994. US Ct. of Appeals (3d cir.) 1982. Assoc. Cravath Swaine & Moore LLP, NYC, 1992—98, ptnr., 1998—, mng. ptnr. adminstn., 2000—05. Contbr. articles to profl. jours. Mem. adv. bd. Urban Assembly. Mem.: ABA (chmn. com.

environ. disclosure), Urban Assembly (adv. bd.). Office: Cravath Swaine & Moore LLP Worldwide Plz 825 Eighth Ave New York NY 10019-7475 Office Phone: 212-474-1514. Office Fax: 212-474-3700. Business E-Mail: jsmith@cravath.com.

**SMITH, JEFFREY CHIPPS,** art educator; MA, Columbia U., 1975, MPhil, 1977, PhD, 1979. Kay Fortson chair in European art U. Tex., Austin, 1979—. Author: Nuremberg, A Renaissance City, 1500-1618, 1983, German Sculpture of the Later Renaissance, c. 1520-1580: Art in an Age of Uncertainty, 1994, Sensuous Worship: Jesuits and the Art of Early Catholic Reformation in Germany, 2002, The Northern Renaissance, 2004, The Art of the Goldsmith in Late Fifteenth Century Germany: The Virgin and Her Bishop, 2006; editor: New Perspectives on the Art of Renaissance Nuremberg: Five Essays, 1985; editor: (introduction to) E. Panofsky, The Life and Art of Albrecht Durer, 1943—2005; reviewer in field, —; contbr. articles to profl. jours. Alexander von Humboldt-Stiftung fellow, Bonn, Germany, ACLS grantee, NEH grantee, Getty Found. grantee, Guggenheim Found. grantee, Kimbell Art Found. grantee, Zentralinstitut Kunstgeschicht fellow. Mem.: Sixteenth Century Soc. and Conf. (bd. dir. 2004—), Renaissance Soc. Am. (bd. dirs. 2000—, editor Renaissance Quarterly 2003—06), Coll. Art Assn. (bd. dir. 1996—2000). Office: U Tex Dept Art and Art History Austin TX 78712 Office Phone: 512-232-2609. Business E-Mail: chipps@mail.utexas.edu.

**SMITH, JEFFREY G.,** lawyer; b. Mineola, N.Y., Feb. 21, 1948; s. Robert R. and Helen E. (Graham) S.; m. Lynn J. Fielden, June 16, 1974; children: Allyson M., Graham H., Brendan C. AA, Dutchess CC, 1972; AB, Vassar Coll., 1974; M in Pub. Adminstn., Princeton U., N.J., 1977; JD, Yale U., New Haven, Conn., 1978. Bar: N.Y. 1979, Calif. 1988, U.S. Dist. Ct. (so. and ea. dists.) N.Y. 1979, U.S. Dist. Ct. (so. dist.) Calif. 1989, U.S. Dist. Ct. (ctrl. dist.) Calif. 1990, U.S. Dist. Ct. Colo. 1998, U.S. Dist. Ct. Nev. 2000, U.S. Ct. Appeals (6th, 8th and 9th cirs.) 1985, U.S. Ct. Appeals (2d cir.) 1987, U.S. Ct. Appeals (3d cir.) 1992, U.S. Ct. Appeals (4th cir.) 1998, U.S. Ct. Appeals (5th cir.) 2000, U.S. Tax Ct. 1979, U.S. Supreme Ct. 1983. Assoc. Fried, Frank, Harris, Shriver & Jacobson, N.Y.C., 1978-81, Wolf Haldenstein Adler Freeman & Herz, LLP, N.Y.C., 1981-86, ptnr., 1987—. Bd. dirs. Osborne Assn., N.Y.C., Dutchess C.C. Found., Poughkeepsie, N.Y Mem. ABA, ATLA, N.Y. State Bar Assn., Calif. State Bar Assn., Assn. of Bar of City of N.Y. Avocations: scuba diving, sailing. Office: Wolf Haldenstein et al 270 Madison Ave New York NY 10016-0601 Office Phone: 212-545-4600. E-mail: smith@whafh.com.

**SMITH, JEFFREY GREENWOOD,** gas industry executive, retired military officer; b. Ft. Sam Houston, Tex., Oct. 14, 1921; s. Henry Joseph Moody and Gladys Adrienne (Haile) S.; m. Dorothy Jane Holland, June 2, 1948; children: Meredith B. Exnicios, Jennifer H. Smith, Jeffrey Greenwood, Tracy E. McDonald, Melissa A. Deutsch, Ashley A. Pollock. BS in Civil Engring, Va. Mil. Inst., 1943; MS in Mech. Engring, Johns Hopkins U., 1949; MA in Internat. Affairs, George Washington U., 1964. Commd. 2d lt. U.S. Army, 1944, advanced through grades to lt. gen., 1975; service in CBI, Korea, Germany and Vietnam; comdr. 2d Inf. Div., Korea, 1971-73; dep. chief staff ops. Hdqrs. Army Forces Command, Ft. McPherson, Ga., 1973-74, chief staff, 1974-75; comdr. 1st U.S. Army, Ft. Meade, Md., 1975-79; ret., 1979; dir. govt. rels. Ethyl Corp., Washington, 1980—, v.p. govt. rels., 1992—, ret., 1994. Decorated D.S.M., Silver Star, Legion of Merit with 3 oak leaf clusters, D.F.C., Bronze Star with V device and 2 oak leaf clusters, Air medal with 12 oak leaf clusters, Army Commendation medal with oak leaf cluster, Purple Heart with oak leaf cluster, Combat Inf. badge (2); breast Order Yun Hui Republic China; Order Security Merit Korea; Gallantry Cross with silver and gold stars (Vietnam) Army Distinguished Service Order Mem. Assn. U.S. Army, Mil. Order Carabao, U.S. Cavalry Assn., Kappa Alpha, Tau Beta Pi. Clubs: Army and Navy. Home: 3000 Sevor Ln Alexandria VA 22309-2221 E-mail: genjeffrey@aol.com.

**SMITH, JEFFREY HARTMAN,** lawyer; b. Salina, Kans., Oct. 24, 1944; s. Robert B. and Alice Mae (Williams) S.; m. Claudia Jean Chyle, June 18, 1966; children: Amy Elisabeth, Katherine Ann. BS, U.S. Mil Acad., 1966; JD, U. Mich., 1971. Bar: Mich. 1971, DC 1989. Asst. legal advisor Office of Legal Advisor Dept. of State, Washington, 1975-84; minority counsel Senate Armed Svcs. Com., Washington, 1984—86, gen. counsel, 1986-88; ptnr. Arnold & Porter, Washington, 1988—95; gen. counsel CIA, 1995—96; ptnr., Govt. Contracts Practice Group & Public Policy/Legislative Practice Group Arnold & Porter, Washington, 1996—. Mem. bd. dirs. The Henry L. Stimson Ctr., Washington, 1990-; mem. Commn. to Review Roles & Missions of Armed Svcs. & chmn., Joint Security Commn., US Dept. Def.; chief, Clinton Transition team, US Dept. Def., 1992-1993. Mem. Bd. Vis., US Mil. Acad., 1993-; bd. vis., Univ. Mich. Law Sch.; gen. counsel The Goldwater Found., Washington, 1988—; trustee Aerospace Corp., El Segundo, Calif., 1990—. Atty. JAG Corps U.S. Army, 1971—75. Mem. Am. Soc. Internat. Law, Coun. Fgn. Rels. Office: Arnold & Porter 555 12th St NW Washington DC 20004-1206 Office Phone: 202-942-5115. Office Fax: 202-942-5999. Business E-Mail: jeffrey.smith@aporter.com.

**SMITH, JEFFREY MICHAEL,** lawyer; b. Mpls., July 9, 1947; s. Philip and Gertrude E. (Miller) S.; 1 son, Brandon Michael. Student, U. Malaya, 1967—68; BA summa cum laude, U. Minn., 1970, JD magna cum laude, 1973. Bar: Ga. 1973. Assoc. Powell, Goldstein, Frazier & Murphy, 1973-76; ptnr. Rogers & Hardin, 1976-79, Bondurant, Stephenson & Smith, 1979-85, Arnall, Golden & Gregory, 1985-92, Katz, Smith & Cohen, 1992-98; prin. shareholder Greenberg Traurig LLP, 1998—. Vis. lectr. Duke U., 1977-79, 79-80, 89-93; adj. prof. Emory U., 1976-79, 81-82; lectr. Vanderbilt U., 1977-82. Editor, reviewer Accountant s Legal Liability, 1981; co-author: Preventing Legal Malpractice, 1999, Legal Malpractice, 2006, Legal Opinions in Business Transactions, 2005. Bd. visitors Law Sch. U. Minn., 1976-82. Mem. ABA (vice-chmn. com. profl. liability 1980-82, mem. standing com. lawyer's profl. liability 1981-85, chmn. 1985-87, standing com. lawyer competency 1993-95), State Bar Ga. (chmn. profl. liability and ins. com. 1978-89, trustee Inst. Cont. Legal Edn. in Ga. 1979-80), Order of the Coif, Phi Beta Kappa. Home: 145 15th St NE Unit 811 Atlanta GA 30309-3559 Office Phone: 678-553-2333. Business E-Mail: smithj@gtlaw.com.

**SMITH, JENNIE,** artist; b. San Francisco, 1981; Student, Burren Coll Art, Ireland, 2002; BFA in Drawing, Mpls. Coll. Art & Design, 2004. Prin. works include Migration, 2004, Animal Its Habitat, 2004, Animals Slumber, 2004, Kite Wars, 2004, We'll Never Tell You Where We Have Gone, 2004, exhibited in group shows at Made at MCAD, Mpls., 2005, Sr. Exhbn., Mpls. Coll. Art & Design, 2005, Drawing Show, Soo Vac Gallery, Mpls., 2005, Grp. Drawing Show, The Gen. Store, Milw., 2005, Four Color Drawing Show, Van Harrison Gallery, Chgo., 2005, Whitney Biennial: Day for Night, Whitney Mus. Am. Art, 2006, exhibitions include Bull. Bd. Project 008, Calif. Coll. Arts Wattis Inst. Contemporary Arts, San Francisco, 2006, Rena Bransten Gallery, San Francisco, 2006. Mailing: c/o Rena Bransten Gallery 77 Geary St San Francisco CA 94108*

**SMITH, JEROME,** not-for-profit developer, film producer, writer; b. Birmingham, Ala., Sept. 10, 1956; s. Herny Horace and Susie Govan Smith. BS in Edn., Daniel Payne Coll., Birmingham, Ala., 1979. Cert. tchr. Ala., Ohio. Tchr. Birmingham Bd. of Edn., Ala., 1979—84, Cleve. Bd. of Edn., 1984—95; CEO Poise Entertainment Edn., Cleve., 1999—. Ednl. prodr. Urban League, Cleve., 2001—03, United Black Fund, Cleve., 2000—03, Rock and Roll Hall of Fame, Cleve., 1999—, dir. cmty. svc., 2003—; songwriter Hilltop Records, Hollywood, Calif., 2004—; TV host You Can Do It Program. Author: Poise Entertainment Edn. Co.'s You Can Do It Program, 2004; host, prodr. Poise Entertainment Edn. Co.'s You Can Do It Program Hall of Fame and Mus. Named to Nat. Dean's List; recipient Best Song honors, Hilltop Records, Best Songwriter honors, Americord, Cmty. Svc. award, Help Educate for Svc.; grantee, Urban League, 2002, United

Black Fund, 2003, Ward 7 City of Cleve., 2004. Baptist. Avocations: songwriting, horseback riding. Office: Poise Entertainment Edn Co 15115 Elm Ave Cleveland OH 44112 Office Phone: 216-561-0277. Business E-Mail: poise-ed@sbcglobal.net.

**SMITH, JERRY EDWIN,** federal judge; b. Del Rio, Tex., Nov. 7, 1946; s. Lemuel Edwin and Ruth Irene (Henderson) Smith; m. Mary Jane Blackburn, June 4, 1977; children: Clark, Ruth Ann, J.J. BA, Yale U., 1969, JD, 1972. Bar: Tex. 1972. Law clk. to judge U.S. Dist. Ct. (no. dist.) Tex., Lubbock, 1972—73; assoc. then ptnr. Fulbright & Jaworski, Houston, 1973—84; dir. Harris County housing auth., Tex., 1978—80; special asst. office of atty. gen., Tex., 1981—82; Chmn. Houston Civ. Svc. Comm., 1982—84; city atty. City of Houston, 1984—87; cir. judge U.S. Ct. Appeals (5th cir.), Houston, 1988—. Chmn. Harris County Rep. Party, Houston, 1977—78; committee-man State Rep. Exec. Com., Tex., 1976—80. Mem.: Houston Bar Assn., State Bar Tex. Methodist. Office: US Ct Appeals Bob Casey US Courthouse 515 Rusk St Rm 12621 Houston TX 77002-2698*

**SMITH, JESSE GRAHAM, JR.,** dermatologist, educator; b. Winston-Salem, NC, Nov. 22, 1928; s. Jesse Graham and Pauline Field (Griffith) S.; m. Dorothy Jean Butler, Dec. 28, 1950; children: Jesse Graham, Cynthia Lynn, Grant Butler. BSM, Duke U., 1962, MD, 1951. Diplomate: Am. Bd. Dermatology (dir. 1974-83, pres. 1980-81). Intern VA Hosp., Chamblee, Ga., 1951—52; resident in dermatology Duke U., 1954—56, assoc. prof. dermatology, 1960—62, prof., 1962—67; resident U. Miami, 1956—57, asst. prof., 1956—60; prof. dermatology Med. Coll. Ga., 1967—91, chmn. dept. dermatology, 1967—91, acting chmn. dept. pathology, 1973—75, acting v.p. devel., 1984—85; chief staff Talmadge Meml. Hosp., Augusta, Ga., 1970—72; chief divsn. of dermatology U. South Ala., Mobile, 1991—98, prof. dermatology, 1991—99, prof. emeritus, 1999—. Mem. adv. coun. Nat. Inst. Arthritis, 1975-79 Mem. editl. bd. Archives of Dermatology, 1963-72, Jour. Investigative Dermatology, 1966-67, Jour. AMA, 1974-80; mem. editl. bd. So. Med. Jour., 1976-2000, assoc. editor, 1991-92, editor, 1992-2000; editor Jour. Am. Acad. Dermatology, 1978-88; contbr. chpts. to books, articles to profl. jours. Served with USPHS, 1952-54. Recipient Disting. Alumnus award Duke U. 1981 Fellow ACP, Royal Soc. Medicine; mem. Am. Acad. Dermatology (hon., dir. 1971-74, 78-88, pres.-elect 1988-89, pres. 1989-90, master 2003), Can. Dermatol. Assn. (hon.), Am. Dermatol. Assn. (hon. sec. 1976-81, pres. 1981-82), Soc. Investigative Dermatology (dir. 1964-69, pres. 1979-80), S.E. Dermatol. Assn. (sec. 1970-71, pres. 1975-76), Ga. Soc. Dermatology (pres. 1979-80), So. Med. Assn. (chmn. sect. dermatology 1973-74, Disting. Svc. award 2005), Assn. Profs. Dermatology (dir. 1976-77, 80-82, pres. 1984-86), Med. Rsch. Found. Ga. (bd. dir. 1967-91, pres. 1974-75), Alpha Omega Alpha Home: 4272 Bit and Spur # 4 Mobile AL 36608 Office: Diagnostic and Med Clinic 1700 Spring Hill Ave Mobile AL 36604-1407 Office Phone: 251-435-1200. E-mail: skeesmith@mindspring.com.

**SMITH, JESSIE P. DOWLING,** retired social services administrator; b. Sturgills, NC, June 15, 1918; d. Robe V. and Stella Pennington (Eller) Smith; m. F. P. Smith, July 22, 1983. AB, Berea Coll., 1939; MSW, Columbia U., 1945. Social work assignments WPA, Ky., 1939—43; social worker ARC, New Orleans, 1943—45, Bklyn., 1943—45, Huntington, W.Va., 1946—56, Washington, 1946—56; instr. Sch. Social Work W.Va. U., Morgantown, 1953—54; cons. W.Va. Dept. Mental Health, Charleston, 1954—55; program supr. USPHS Clin. Ctr., Bethesda, Md., 1956—62; cons., social work NIMH, Chgo., 1962—66, NYC, 1962—66; assoc. regional health dir. Mental Health Programs, NYC, 1966—81; ret., 1981; v.p. adv. bd. Mental Retardation Substance Abuse Programs Davidson County Mental Health, NC, 1987—89, pres., 1988—89. Mem.: NASW (exec. bd. 1968—70, pres. Washington Met. Area chpt., pioneer steering com. 1999—), Columbia U. Alumni Fedn. Bd., Columbia U. Sch. Social Work Alumni Assn. (pres. 1979—81), Columbia U. Sch. Social Work (adv. coun.), Social Casework (editl. adv. bd. 1968—70), NC Coun. of Cmty. Mental Health Programs (adv. bd. 1987—92). Home: Apt 703 1330 Massachusetts Ave NW Washington DC 20005-4154

**SMITH, JIMMY WAYNE, SR.,** forensic specialist; s. William Moody Smith and Virginia M. Howard, Robert D. Howard (Stepfather); m. Kathleen B. Chandler; children: Tonya N., Jimmy Jr. W. BS in Acctg., U. Sci. and Arts of Okla., 1984, BS in Sociology, 1984. Cert. Am. Bd. Forensic Document Examiners. Lt. Chickasha (Okla.) Police Dept., 1969—85; investigator, forensic document examiner Okla. Insp. Gen., Oklahoma City, 1985—95; forensic document examiner Las Vegas (Nev.) Met. Police Dept., 1995—. Author: (research) Using an Alternative light Source to Restore Writing (Publ. JFS). Fellow: Am. Acad. Forensic Scis. (sec. 2005—); mem.: Assn. Cert. Fraud Examiners, Southwestern Assn. Forensic Document Examiners (new letter editor 1994—98, bd. dirs. 1995—99). Achievements include research in using an alternative light source to restore writing. Office: Las Vegas Metropolitan Police Department 5605 W Badura Ave Ste 120B Las Vegas NV 89118 Office Phone: 702-229-3964. Personal E-mail: cherokee48@cox.net. Business E-Mail: j4927s@lvmpd.com.

**SMITH, JO ANNE,** writer, retired communications educator; b. Mpls., Mar. 18, 1930; d. Robert Bradburn and Virginia Mae S. BA, U. Minn., 1951, MA, 1957. Wire and sports editor Rhinelander (Wis.) Daily News, 1951-52; staff corr., night mgr. UPI, Mpls., 1952-56; interim instr. U. N.C., Chapel Hill, 1957-58; instr. U. Fla., Gainesville, 1959-65, asst. prof. journalism, communications, 1965-68, assoc. prof., 1976-88, profl. emeritus, 1977, prof. emeritus. Author: JM409 Casebook and Study Guide 1976 Mass Communications Law Casebook, 1979, 3d edit., 1985. Active, Friends of Libr., Alachua County Humane Soc. Recipient outstanding Prof. award Fla. Blue Key, 1976; Danforth assoc., 1976-85. Mem. Women in Communications, Assn. Edn. in Journalism, Phi Beta Kappa, Kappa Tau Alpha. Democrat. Unitarian Universalist. Home: 208 NW 21st Ter Gainesville FL 32603-1732

**SMITH, JOANN CARROLL,** library and information scientist; m. Michael Smith; children: Jenifer Jeané Wilkinson, Jonna Jarie Hawkins. BS, U. Ala., Tuscaloosa, 1972; MA, U. of Ala., Tuscaloosa, 1974; EdS, U. Ala., 1979; M in Libr. Svc., U. of Ala., Tuscaloosa, 1984, EdS level in Libr. Svc., 1993. Cert. Tchr. Tenn., 1997, Ala., 1972. Libr. media specialist Sullivan East HS, Bluff City, Tenn., 1997—2001, Sullivan South HS, Kingsport, Tenn., 2001—. Treas. PACE Polit. Action No Johnson City Bapt., Johnson City, Tenn., 2004—06; dist. 1 chr. Tenn. Edn. Assn., Nashville, 2002—05. Recipient Oustanding Svc. to Ala. Librs., Libr. and Media Profls., 1996—97. Mem.: NEA, Tenn. Edn. Assn. (chair nea concerns com. 2002—04, bd. dirs. 2002—05, chair human rels. com. 2004—05), Sullivan County Edn. Assn. (pres. 1999—2001, treas. 2001—06, pres. 2006—), Tenn. Assn. Sch. Librarians (chair constn. and bylaws 2006—). Baptist. Avocations: reading, singing, travel. Home: 141 Bentley Parc Johnson City TN 37615 Office: Sullivan South HS Libr 1236 Moreland Dr Kingsport TN 37664 Office Phone: 423-354-1312. Home Fax: 423-283-9037. Personal E-mail: joannsmi@yahoo.com.

**SMITH, JOE DORSEY, JR.,** retired newspaper executive; b. Selma, La., Apr. 6, 1922; s. Joe Dorsey and Louise (Lindsay) S.; 1 child, Lawrence Dorsey. BA, La. Coll. Pineville, 1939-43. Gen. mgr. Alexandria Daily Town Talk, La., 1958—, pub., 1965—; pres. McCormick & Co., Inc., 1968—, chmn., 1990-96. Served with USAF, 1942-45. Mem. Alexandria Golf and Country Club, Boston Club, New Orleans Club. Democrat. Episcopalian. Home: 2804 Georges Ln Alexandria LA 71301-4723 Office: Ste 1003 Hibernia Bldg 934 3rd St Alexandria LA 71301-8383 Office Phone: 318-448-3598. Personal E-mail: smith7462@aol.com.

**SMITH, JOHN B.,** publishing executive; b. LaGrange, Ga. s. John Watson and Pressarene Whitfield Smith; m. Frances M. Evans; children: Pamela, Lori, John Jr. BS, Morehouse Coll.; MA, Atlanta U. Pub., CEO Atlanta Inquirer. Bd. dirs. Atlanta Fair & Exposition, Grade Homes Boys' Club, Boy

Scouts of Am. Named one of Most Influential Black Americans, Ebony mag., 2006. Mem.: Nat. Newspaper Publishers Assn. (mem. bd. dirs., pres., Publisher of Yr. Award). Office: Nat Newspaper Pub Assn 3200 13th St, NW Washington DC 20010*

**SMITH, JOHN BREWSTER,** library administrator; b. Bryan, Tex., June 26, 1937; s. Elmer Gillam and Sara Roland (Lull) S.; m. Ida Hawa, Dec. 28, 1963; children: Susan Helen, Rona Esther. BA, Tex. A & M U., 1960; MS, Columbia U., 1963, cert. advanced librarianship, 1984, DLS, 1991. Asst. law librarian Columbia U., N.Y.C., 1963-66; asst. library dir. for pub. services Tex. A & M U., College Station, 1966-69, dir. libraries, 1969-74; dir. libraries, dean library scis. SUNY, Stony Brook, 1974-96, dir. library and info. sci. tchg. program, 1996-97; chief libr. Bronx Cmty. Coll., CUNY, 1997-2000, cons. on libr. mgmt., 2000—. Named Librarian of Year Tex. Library Assn. 1972 Mem. ALA. Home and Office: 108 Inverness Dr Montgomery TX 77356-5877 Office Phone: 936-588-0203. Personal E-mail: counterpoint@flex.net.

**SMITH, JOHN EDWIN,** philosophy educator; b. Bklyn., May 27, 1921; s. Joseph Robert and Florence Grace (Dunn) S.; m. Marilyn Blanche Schulhof, Aug. 25, 1951; children: Robin Dunn, Diana Edwards. AB, Columbia U., 1942, PhD, 1948; BD, Union Theol. Sem., N.Y.C., 1945; MA, Yale U., 1959; LL.D., U. Notre Dame, 1964. Instr. religion and philosophy Vassar Coll. 1945-46; instr., then asst. prof. Barnard Coll., 1946-52; mem. faculty Yale U., 1952—, prof. philosophy, 1959—, chmn. dept., 1961—, Clark prof. philosophy, 1972-91, Clark prof. philosophy emeritus, 1991—. Vis. prof. Union Theol. Sem., 1959, U. Mich., 1958; guest prof. U. Heidelberg, Germany, 1955-56; Fagothey chair of philosophy U. Santa Clara, 1984, vis. prof. Boston Coll., 1992; Dudleian lectr. Harvard, 1960; lectr. Am. Week, U. Munich, Germany, 1961; Suarez lectr. Fordham U., 1963; pub. lectr. King's College, Univ. London, 1965; Aquinas lectr. Marquette U., 1967; Warfield lectr. Princeton Theol. Sem., 1970; Fulbright lectr. Kyoto U., Japan, 1971; Sprunt lectr. Union Theol. Sem. Va., 1973; Mead-Swing lectr. Oberlin Coll. 1975; H. Richard Niebuhr lectr. Elmhurst Coll., Ill., 1977; Merrick lectr. Ohio Wesleyan U., 1977; Roy Wood Sellars lectr. Bucknell U., 1978; O'Hara lectr. U. Notre Dame, 1984; Winston Churchill lectr. Bristol (Eng.) U., 1985; Hooker disting. vis. prof. Mc Master U., 1985; mem. adv. com. Nat. Humanities Inst., New Haven, 1974, dir., 1977-80; Winston Churchill lectr. Bristol U., Eng., 1985. Author: Royce's Social Infinite, 1950, Value Convictions and Higher Education, 1958, Reason and God, 1961, The Spirit of American Philosophy, 1963, 2d edit., 1983, The Philosophy of Religion, 1965, Religion and Empiricism, 1967, Experience and God, 1968, revised edit., 1995, Themes in American Philosophy, 1970, Contemporary American Philosophy, 1970, The Analogy of Experience, 1973, Purpose and Thought: The Meaning of Pragmatism, 1978, America's Philosophical Vision, 1992, Jonathan Edwards, Puritan, Preacher, Philosopher, 1992, Quasi-Religions: Humanism, Marxism, Nationalism, 1994, Reason, Experience, and God, 1997; translator: (R. Kroner): Kant's Weltanschauung, 1956; editor: (Jonathan Edwards): Religious Affections, Vol. 2, 1959, An Edwards Reader, 1995; gen. editor, Yale edit.: Works of Jonathan Edwards, 1965-91, gen. editor emeritus, 1992—; Editorial bd.: Monist, 1962—, Jour. Religious Studies, Philosophy East and West, Jour. Chinese Philosophy, The Personalist Forum, Jour. Faith and Philosophy, Jour. Speculative Philosophy. Named Hon. Alumnus, Harvard Div. Sch., 1960; recipient Herbert W. Schneider award Soc. for Advancement of Am. Philosophy, 1990, Founder's medal Metaphys. Soc. Am., 1996, Am. Coun. Learned Socs. fellow, 1964-65. Mem. Culvary Inst. Am. (dir. New Haven affiliate). Am. Philos. Assn. (v.p. 1980, pres. 1981), Am. Theol. Soc. (pres. 1967-68), Metaphys. Soc. Am. (pres. 1970-71, founder's medal, 1996), Hegel Soc. Am. (pres. 1971), Charles S. Peirce Soc. (pres. 1992). Home: 300 Ridgewood Ave Hamden CT 06517-1428 Office: PO Box 201562 New Haven CT 06520-1562 E-mail: john.smith@yale.edu.

**SMITH, JOHN FRANCIS,** materials science educator; b. Kansas City, Kans., May 9, 1923; s. Peter Francis and Johanna Teresa (Spandle) S.; m. Evelyn Ann Ross, Sept. 1, 1947 (dec. July 1994); children—Mark Francis, Letitia Ann Smith Harder; m. Eileen R. Ross, Apr. 12, 1997. BA with distinction, U. Mo.-Kansas City, 1948; PhD, Iowa State U., 1953. Grad. asst. Iowa State U., Ames, 1948-53, faculty and research scientist, dept. chmn., div. chief Ames Lab., 1966-70, prof. emeritus, 1988. Cons. Tex. Instruments, Inc., Dallas and Attleboro, Mass., 1958-63, Argonne Nat. Lab., Ill., 1964-70, Iowa Hwy. Commn., Ames, Los Alamos Nat. Lab., N.Mex., 1984-88, bur. standards Nat. Inst. Standards and Tech., Gaithersburg, Md., 1988-91, Sandia Nat. Lab., Albuquerque, N.M., 1991-92, ASM Internat., Cleve., 1992—. Patentee ultrasonic determination of texture in metal sheet and plate, lead-free solder; author: Phase Diagrams of Binary Vanadium Alloys; Hellcats Over the Philippine Deep; co-author: Thorium: Preparation and Properties, 1975; editor: Calculation of Phase Diagrams and Thermochemistry of Alloy Phases, 1978; editor Jour. Phase Equilibria and Diffusion, 1988—; contbr. articles to profl. publs. Mem. former comdr. Ames-Boone Squadron CAP, 1970-75. With USN, 1942-46, PTO, comdr. USNR, 1946-64. Decorated Air medal with cluster; recipient Disting. Svc. award CAP, Maxwell AFB, Ala., 1979, faculty citation Iowa State U. Alumni Assn., Ames, 1977. Fellow Am. Inst. Chemists, ASM (chmn. Des Moines chpt. 1966); mem. AIME, Materials Rsch. Soc., Am. Legion, Silent Knights, Inc. (trustee 1980-96), Exptl. Aircraft Assn., Alpha Sigma Mu (trustee 1984-86). Roman Catholic. Avocation: flying. Home: 2919 S Riverside Ames IA 50010-8605 Office: Iowa State U Ames Lab 136F Wilhelm Hall Ames IA 50010

**SMITH, JOHN FRANCIS, JR., (JACK SMITH),** retired automotive executive; b. Worcester, Mass., Apr. 6, 1938; s. John Francis and Florence E.C. (Sullivan) S.; children: Brian, Kevin; m. Lydia G. Sigrist, Aug. 27, 1988; 1 stepchild, Nicola. BBA, U. Mass., 1960; MBA, Boston U., 1965. Fisher Body div. mgr. GM, Framingham, Mass., 1961-73, asst. treas N.Y.C., 1973-80, comptroller Detroit, 1980-81, dir. worldwide product planning, 1981-84, pres., gen. mgr. Oshawa, Ont., Canada, 1984-85; exec. v.p. Gen. Motors Europe, Glattbrugg, Switzerland, 1986-87, pres., 1987-88; exec. v.p. internat. ops. GM, Detroit, 1988-90, vice chmn. internat. ops., 1990, bd. dirs., mem. fin. com., 1990-98, pres., COO, 1992-98, CEO, pres., 1992-98, chmn. bd., CEO, pres., 1996-98, chmn. bd., CEO, 1998-2000, chmn. bd. 1996—2003. Mem. U.S. Japan Bus. Coun.; bus. coun. Meml. Sloan-Kettering Cancer Ctr.; bd. dirs. Procter & Gamble Co., Swiss Re, Delta Air Lines Inc., 2000-, non-exec. chmn., 2004-; chmn. adv. bd. Alix Ptnrs. LLC/Questor Ptnrs. Funds. Mem. chancellor's exec. com. U. Mass., dir.; trustee United Way S.E. Mich., New Am. Revolution, Boston U.; bd. dirs. The Nature Conservancy. Mem. Am. Soc. Corp. Execs., Am. Auto Mfrs. Assn. (bd. dirs.), Econ. Club Detroit (bd. dirs.), The Bus. Coun., Beta Gamma Sigma, Dirs. Table. Roman Catholic. Office: Delta Air Lines Inc Hartsfield Atlanta Internat Airport 1030 Delta Blvd Atlanta GA 30320-6001

**SMITH, JOHN FRANCIS, III,** lawyer; b. White Plains, N.Y., Sept. 24, 1941; s. John Francis and Mary Dake (Mairs) S.; m. Susan Brown; children: John, Stephen, Peter. AB, Princeton U., 1963; LLB, Yale U., 1970. Bar: Pa. 1970, U.S. Supreme Ct. 1985. Assoc. Dilworth, Paxson, Kalish & Kauffman, Phila., 1970-75, ptnr., 1975-86, sr. ptnr., 1986-91; sr. litigation ptnr. Reed Smith LLP, Phila., 1991—, mem. exec. com., 1993-04; chancellor Reed Smith U., 2004—. Mem. exec. com. Employment Discrimination Referral Project, 1971-74; pres. Society Hill Civic Assn., 1975-76, Phila. Chamber Ensemble, 1977-80; bd. govs. Pa. Economy League (ea. divsn.), 1983—, sec. 1995-97; vice chair Health Care Task Force, 1993-96; bd. dirs. World Affairs Council Phila., 1983-87, chmn. program com., 1986-87; Burn Found., 1987-95, Internat. House Phila., chmn. bd. trustees, 2005-; moderator Main Line Unitarian Ch., 1986-89, 00—; founder and pres. Found. for Individual Responsibility and Social Trust (FIRST), 1995—. Served to lt. (j.g.) USNR, 1963-67; Vietnam. Fellow Am. Bar Found.; mem. ABA, Phila. Bar Assn., Unitarian Universalist Assn. (pres.'s coun.), Yale Law Sch. Alumni Assn. (exec. com. 1982-88, sec. 1987-88), Princeton Club (Phila.). Office: Reed Smith LLP 2500 One Liberty Pl Philadelphia PA 19103 Office Phone: 215-241-7920. E-mail: jsmith@reedsmith.com.

**SMITH, JOHN KERWIN,** lawyer; b. Oct. 18, 1926; 1 child, Cynthia. BA, Stanford U.; LLB, Hastings Coll. Law. Ptnr. Haley, Purchio, Sakai & Smith, Hayward, Calif.; pres. Calhoun Heights LLC, Garin Vista LLC. Pres. bd. dirs. Rowell Ranch Rodeo, Hastings Coll. Lawpres. Gen. ptnr. Oak Hills Apts., City Ctr. Commercial, Creekwood I and II Apts.; Road Parks commn. 1957; city coun. 1959-66, mayor 1966-70; chmn. Alameda County Mayors conf. 1968, revenue taxation com. League Calif. Cities, 1968; former vice chmn. Oakland-Alameda County Coliseum; vol. Hastings 1066 Found. (pres., vol. svc. award 1990), Martin Kauffman 100 Club; bd. dirs. Hastings Coll. of Law, 1999—, pres. bd. dirs., 2004—. Named Alumnus of Yr., Hastings Coll. Law, 1989. Mem. ABA, Calif. Bar Assn., Alameda County Bar Assn. Am. Judicature Soc., Rotary, 100 Club (chmn. bd. dirs.) Office: Haley Purchio Sakai & Smith 22320 Foothill Blvd Ste 620 Hayward CA 94541-2700 Office Phone: 510-538-6400. Personal E-mail: hpssckb@aol.com.

**SMITH, JOHN W(ESLEY), JR.,** data processing executive, consultant; b. Bklyn., Jan. 6, 1946; s. John Wesley and Eunice (Davis) S.; m. Carolyn Ferrebbee, Aug. 19, 1971 (div. 1980); children: John Wesley III, Janine Carol. Student, NYU, 1989—. Supr. computer ops. Shearson Lehman Stone, Inc., N.Y.C., 1967—70; sr. analyst Fin. Data Svcs., Inc., N.Y.C., 1977—77; coord. tng. program Chem. Bank, N.Y.C., 1977—78; sr. hardware analyst ADP, Clifton, NJ, 1978—79; administr. data base Depository Trust Co., N.Y.C., 1979—81; mgr. data ctr. ops. Leviton Mfg. Co., Littleneck, NY, 1981—83; dir. corp. info. svcs. Reed Robert's Assocs., Inc., Uniondale, 1983—86; dir. prodn. planning and control Human Resource Adminstrn., N.Y.C., 1986—87; mgmt. cons. Asbach/Sci., Inc., N.Y.C., 1987—. Mem. Data Processing Mgmt. Assn., Am. Soc. Notaries, Am. Mgmt. Assn., Am. Arbitration Assn. (comml. panel 1983—), Inst. Certification Computer Profls. (cert systems profl.). Avocation: real estate. Office: Smith Wesley Assocs Inc 1072 Barbey St Brooklyn NY 11207-9202

**SMITH, JONATHAN DAVID,** medical educator; b. Cleve., Jan. 10, 1955; BS, U. Calif., Santa Cruz, 1978; PhD, Harvard U., 1984. Postdoctoral fab. Biochem. Genetics and Metabolism The Rockefeller U., N.Y.C., 1984-89, asst. prof., 1989-96, assoc. prof., 1996—. Contbr. articles to profl. jours. Recipient Nat. Rsch. Svc. award NIH, 1985-87, Program Project award, 1995—. Mem. AAAS, Am. Heart Assn. (Investigatorship award N.Y.C. affiliate 1989-92, Grant-in-Aid 1989-92, 92-95, Established Investigator 1994—). Achievements include identification of genes that regulate atherosclerosis; development of animal models useful for testing therapies to proevent atherosclerosis; characterization of novel functions of apolopoprotein E which are relevant to Alzheimer's disease, cardiovascular disease and longevity. Home: 22687 Westchester Rd Shaker Heights OH 44122-2976

**SMITH, JUANITA BÉRARD,** lawyer, artist; b. St. Martinsville, La., Oct. 23, 1947; d. Zachary Joseph and Lucille Bourque Bérard; m. Mark Christian Smith III, Mar. 16 (dec. 2003); children: Mark IV, Brett, Robyn, Tara. BA in History, Loyola U., 1979, JD, 1982. Bar: La. 1982. Pvt. practice, New Orleans, 1982—; pres. 730 Bienville Inc., New Orleans, 2003—, TSL Properties Inc., New Orleans, 2003—, Century Hotels Inc., New Orleans, 2003—; owner, pres. St. Louis Hotel, New Orleans, 2003—, St. Ann Hotel, New Orleans, 2003—, Louis XVI Restaurant, New Orleans, 2003—, La Louisiane Restaurant, New Orleans, 2003—, Woodstone Subdivsn., Mandeville, 2003—, McCrory's, New Orleans, 2003—, Hotel Marie Antoinette, New Orleans, Mark Smith Enterprises, New Orleans, 2004. Exhibited in group shows at Alexander and Victor Gallery Fine Art, New Orleans, Alexander and Victor Gallery, Coral Gables, Fla., Palma Gallery, New Orleans, one-woman shows include La. Gallery, 2004. Named one of Women of Yr. 2004, New Orleans City Bus. Mem.: La. State Bar Assn., New Orleans Bar Assn. Avocations: skiing, theology. Home: 730 Rue Bienville St New Orleans LA 70130 Office: 730 Bienville Partners Ltd 1000 Iberville St New Orleans LA 70130 Studio: 106 Mariners Island Mandeville LA 70448 Mailing: PO Box 57929 New Orleans LA 70157 Personal E-mail: jbsmith1947@charter.net.

**SMITH, JULIA LADD,** oncologist, physician; b. Rochester, N.Y., July 26, 1951; d. John Herbert and Isabel (Walcott) Ladd; m. Stephen Slade Smith; 1 child. BA, Smith Coll., 1973; MD, N.Y. Med. Coll., 1976. Diplomate Am. Bd. Internal Medicine, Am. Bd. Med. Oncology, Am. Bd. Hospice and Palliative Medicine. Intern in medicine N.Y. Med. Coll., N.Y.C., 1976-77; resident in medicine Rochester Gen. Hosp., 1977-79; internist Genesee Valley Group Health, Rochester, 1979-80; oncology fellow U. Rochester, 1980-82, asst. prof. oncology in medicine sch. medicine and dentistry, 1986—2003; oncologist Med. Ctr. Clinic, Ltd., Pitts., 1982-83; oncologist, internist Rutgers Community Health Plan, New Brunswick, NJ, 1983-86; med. dir. Genesse Region Home Care Assn./Hospice, Rochester, 1988—; med. oncologist Genesee Hosp., Rochester, 1996—2001; chief hematology/oncology, 1996—2001; med. oncologist Rochester Gen. Hosp., 2001—. Bd. dirs. Am. Cancer Soc., Monroe County, 1988-92. Nat. Cancer Inst. rsch. grantee, 1993—95. Fellow Acad. Hospice Physicians; mem. ACP, Am. Soc. Clin. Oncology. Unitarian-Universalist. Avocations: sailing, reading, movies, bridge. Office: Lipson Blood and Cancer Ctr 1425 Portland Ave Rochester NY 14621 Office Phone: 585-922-4020.

**SMITH, JULIAN CLEVELAND, JR.,** chemical engineering professor; b. Westmount, Que., Can., Mar. 10, 1919; s. Julian Cleveland and Bertha (Alexander) S.; m. Joan Elsen, June 1, 1946; children: Robert Elsen, Diane Louise Smith Brook, Brian Richard. B.Chemistry, Cornell U., 1941, Chem. Engr., 1942. Chem. engr. E. I. duPont de Nemours and Co., Inc., 1942-46; mem. faculty Cornell U., 1946—, prof. chem. engring., 1953-86, prof. emeritus, 1986—, dir. continuing engring. edn., 1965-71; assoc. dir. Cornell U. (Sch. Chem. Engring.), 1973-75, dir., 1975-83. Vis. lectr. U. Edinburgh, 1971-72; cons. to govt. and industry, 1947-2001; UNESCO cons. Universidad de Oriente, Venezuela, 1975 Author: (with W. L. McCabe and P. Harriott) Unit Operations of Chemical Engineering, 1956, 7th edit., 2005, also articles; sect. editor: Perry's Chemical Engineers' Handbook, 1963. Fellow Am. Inst. Chem. Engrs.; mem. Am. Chem. Soc., Paleontologic Rsch. Instn., Ithaca Country Club, Savage Club, Sigma Xi, Tau Beta Pi, Phi Kappa Phi, Alpha Delta Phi. Home: 427 Savage Farm Dr Ithaca NY 14850-6507 Business E-Mail: jcs29@cornell.edu.

**SMITH, JULIOUS PERRY, JR.,** lawyer; b. Richmond, Va., Jan. 10, 1943; s. Julious Perry and Mary Inez (Whitlow) S.; m. Sherrill Marie Poehler, July 28, 1967; children: Julious P. III, S. Hayes, Sarah Graham. BS, Hampden-Sydney (Va.) Coll., 1965; LLB, U. Va., 1968. Bar: Va. 1968, U.S. Dist. Ct. (ea. dist.) Va. 1969. Assoc. Williams Mullen, Richmond, 1968-73, shareholder, 1973—, pres., 1983—99, chmn., CEO, 1999—. Bd. dirs. Quarles Petroleum, Inc., Mut. Assurance Soc. of Va., LandAm. Fin. Group, Inc., Hilb Rogal and Hobbs Co.; spkr. Joel A. Rose Conf. on Law Firm Mgmt., 1995, 98, 2000, 04. Chmn. profl. divsn. United Way, 1990—92, campaign chmn., 1994—95, de Tocqueville Chair, 2000; Va. state chair U.S. Olympic Com., 1996—2000; trustee Hampden-Sydney Coll., 1996—, vice chmn., 2004—06; bd. dirs. Theater Va., 2001—02; chair Multiple Sclerosis Dinner, 2002, CCA-Fin.-Am. Cancer Soc. Golf Championship, 2004; mem. sch. bd. St. Bridget's Cath. Ch., Richmond, 1981—88, chmn. capital fund raising campaign, 1991. Recipient Micheli award Richmond Touchdown Club, 1981, Patrick Henry award Hampden-Sydney Coll., 2003; named to Salvation Army Boys and Girls Club Hall of Fame, 1997 Fellow: Va. Law Found., Am. Coll. Trust and Estate Counsel; mem.: ABA, Best Lawyers in Am., Va. Legal Elite, Richmond Mgmt. Round Table, Soc. Internat. Bus. Fellows (Va. chair 1996—97), Richmond Bar Assn. (chmn. young lawyers sect. 1973—74, bd. dirs. 1985—87, 1989—92, pres. 1995—96, Hill-Tucker Pub. Svc. award 2005), Va. Bar Assn., Kinloch Golf Club, Farmington Country Club, Forum Club, Country Club Va., Commonwealth Club (bd. govs. 1997—2000, v.p. 2005—). Roman Catholic. Avocations: reading, sports, travel. Office: Williams Mullen 2 James Center PO Box 1320 Richmond VA 23218-1320 Office Phone: 804-783-6408. Business E-Mail: jsmith@williamsmullen.com.

**SMITH, JUSTIN P.,** technology analyst, lab consultant; b. Fort Polk, La., Dec. 26, 1984; s. Mark and Mary Smith. Student, U. of Minn., Mpls., 2003—. Cert. networking adminstr. Cisco Sys. Tech. analyst U. of Minn. Found.,

Mpls., 2005—; lab cons. Carlson Sch. of Mgmt., Mpls., 2005—. Mem. constrn. crew Habitat for Humanity, Mpls., 2005—06. Mem.: Phi Kappa Psi (risk mgmt., fin. chair, historian, ho. mgr., summer boss 2004—06). Lutheran. Home: 1609 University Ave SE Minneapolis MN 55414 Office: U Minn Found Ste 500 200 Oak St SE Minneapolis MN 55455 Office Phone: 612-624-3333. Personal E-mail: nirvanakng@hotmail.com.

**SMITH, K. CLAY,** machinery transport company executive; b. New Orleans, Aug. 29, 1937; s. Kenneth Eugene and Yvonne Smith; children: Elizabeth, K. Clay, Andrew. BBA, U. Notre Dame, 1960; JD, Georgetown U., 1964; DBA (hon.), Marian Coll., Indpls., 1988. Bar: Ind. 1964. Spl. agt. FBI, Los Angeles, 1964-68; assoc. Kightlinger, Gray, Indpls., 1968-71; pres., chief exec. officer Underwood Machinery Transport, Indpls., 1971—. Bd. dirs. Marsh Supermarkets, Inc., Specialized Carriers; former vice chmn. Ind. Horse Racing Commn. Chmn. lic. rev. bd., City of Indpls., 1974; mem. reciprocity com., State of Ind., 1988. Mem. Ind. Bar Assn., Indpls. Bar Assn., Indpls. Athletic Club (bd. dirs. 1986-92, pres. 1992), Highland Country Club. Republican. Roman Catholic. Avocations: reading, music, golf, tennis. Home: PO Box 977 Indianapolis IN 46206-0977 Office: Underwood Cos 940 W Troy Ave Indianapolis IN 46225-2244

**SMITH, KAREN A.,** lawyer; b. Newark, May 26, 1962; BA, Lafayette Coll. 1984; JD, Cornell U., 1987. Bar: NJ 1987, NY 1988, DC 1989. Ptnr., co-head Bus. & Internat. Sect. Vinson & Elkins LLP, NYC. Mem.: ABA. Office: Vinson & Elkins LLP 666 Fifth Ave, 26 Fl New York NY 10103-0040

**SMITH, KAREN B.,** educational consultant; b. Monahans, Tex., Oct. 15, 1946; d. Ralph J. and Christine W. Barnes; m. Jack W. Smith, July 19, 1997. BS, No. Tex. State U., Denton, 1965—68; postgrad., Angelo State U., San Angelo, Tex., 1970—73. Provisional Tchg. Cert. 1968. Tchr. Fort Worth ind. sch. dist., Tex., 1968—70; tchr. and vocat. adjustment coord. San Angelo ind. sch. dist., Tex., 1973—91; site base com. mem. Ctrl. H.S., San Angelo, Tex., 1990—91; vocat. adjustment coord. San Angelo ind. sch. dist., Tex., 1997—. Instr. displaced workers Concho Valley Coun. Govts., San Angelo, Tex., 1994—97; v.p. of bd. dirs. Candlelight Apts., Inc., Concho Resource Ctr.; bd. dirs. Promised Wisdom Learning Ctr., com. chair. Active Tom Green County Rep. Women, San Angelo, Tex., 1982—90; past pres. C. of C. Concho Cadre, San Angelo, Tex., 1992—; exhibits com. mem. San Angelo Stock Show and Rodeo, Tex., 1990—; com. mem. Concho Valley Alliance for Transition, San Angelo, Tex., 1999—, Concho Valley Social and Health Resources Coalition, San Angelo, Tex., 2000—; transition task force mem. Mental Svcs. for Concho Valley, San Angelo, Tex., 2001—; vice chair Make a Wish Found., San Angelo, Tex., 1983—84; chair membership Mayor's Com. for Persons with Disabilites, San Angelo, Tex., 1984—86; GROW com. Glen Meadows Baptist Ch., San Angelo, Tex., 2001—; active San Angelo Mus. Fine Arts, 2000—01; vol. Fort Concho Nat. Hist. Landmark and Miss Hattie's Mus., San Angelo, Tex., 1991—. Named Pub. Employee of Yr., Mayor's Com. for Disabled Persons, 1988, Cadre Person of Yr., San Angelo C. of C., 1996; recipient Cmty. Accessibility Recognition award, Shannon Rehab. Ctr., 2002, 2003. Mem.: Guardianship Alliance (nomination com. mem. and bd. dirs. 2001—03), Ctrl. H.S. PTA, Tex. Assn. Vocat. Adjustment Coords., Tex. Classroom Tchrs. Assn. Baptist. Home: 219 Dellwood San Angelo TX 76903 Office: San Angelo Ctrl HS 100 Cottonwood San Angelo TX 76901

**SMITH, KAREN E.,** mathematician, educator; b. Red Bank, New Jersey, May 9, 1965; married; children: Sanelma, Tapio, Helena. BA in Math., Princeton U., 1987; PhD, U. Mich., 1993. Tchr. math. N.J. Pub. Schs., 1987—88; NSF postdoctoral fellow Purdue U., West Lafayette, Ind., 1993—94; Moore instr., asst. prof. MIT, Cambridge, 1994—97; prof. math. U. Mich., Ann Arbor, 1997—. Vis. prof. U. Jyvaskyla, Finland, 2001. Author: An Invitation to Algebraic Geometry, 2000; assoc. editor Jour. Am. Math. Soc., mem. editl. bd. Am. Math. Monthly. Recipient Ruth Lyttle Satter prize, 2001; fellow, Fulbright Found.; grantee, NSF, Alfred P. Sloan Found. Mem.: Nat. Rsch. Coun. (bd. dirs. Math. Scis.). Office: Dept Math Rm 2832 East Hall Univ Michigan 530 Church St Ann Arbor MI 48109 Office Phone: 734-763-5048. Fax: 734-763-0937. E-mail: kesmith@umich.edu.*

**SMITH, KATHLEEN TENER,** bank executive; b. Pitts., Oct. 19, 1943; d. Edward Harrison Tener Jr. and Barbara Elizabeth (McCormick) Tener; m. Roger Davis Smith, May 30, 1970 (div.); children: Silas Wheelock, Jocelyn Tener, Luke Ewing Taft. BA summa cum laude, Vassar Coll., 1965; MA in Econs., Harvard U., 1968. Rsch. assoc. Harvard U. Grad. Sch. Bus., Cambridge, Mass., 1967—69; from assoc. economist to 2d v.p. Chase Manhattan Bank, NYC, 1969—72, v.p., 1973—98, sec. asset-liability mgmt. com., 1980—90, treas. Global Bank, 1990—91; network ptnr. Smith Barney, Citigroup Global Markets, 1999—. Editor: Commodity Derivatives and Finance, 1996. Trustee Eleanor Roosevelt Ctr. Val-Kill Found., 2000—03, chmn. fin. com., 2002—03; mem. subcom. on edn. Chase Manhattan Found., N.Y.C., 1985—90; trustee Huguenot Hist. Soc. New Paltz, 1999—2002, chair fin. com., 1999—2002, trustee, JEBGA, 2000—04; mem. working com. Huguenot Heritage, 1999—; chair Pyramid Soc. Vassar Coll., Poughkeepsie, 2001—05, trustee, 1979—91, mem. exec. com., 1987—91, class pres., 2000—05. Fellow, NSF, 1965—67. Mem.: Yale Club, Phi Beta Kappa. Republican. Episcopalian. Address: PO Box 129 New Paltz NY 12561-0129

**SMITH, KATHY L.,** elementary school educator, cosmetics executive, consultant; b. Gillespie, Ill., Mar. 8, 1959; d. William G. and Phyllis L. Russell; m. Thomas A. Smith, Aug. 30, 1980; children: Ashley M., Blake T. BA, So. Ill. U., Edwardsville, 1981, MA, 1988. Cert. Nat. Bd. Cert. Tchr. Fla., 2002. Tchr. 1st, 4, th and 6th Bunker Hill Sch. Dist., Bunker Hill, Ill., 1984—89; tchr. kindergarten, 1st, and 2nd Marion County Sch. Dist., Weirsdale, Fla., 1989—96; tchr. 1st grade Lake County Sch. Dist., Eustis, Fla., 1996—99, intensive reading tchr. Leesburg, Fla., 1999—; beauty cons. Mary Kay, Fruitland Park, Fla., 2003—. Facilitator U. Ctrl. Fla., Orlando, Fla., 2004—. Author: (novels) Powerful Classroom Stories from Accomplished Teachers. Family fun Women of the Moose, Leesburg, Fla., 2005—; vol. Morrison United Meth. Ch., Leesburg, Fla., 1999—2001. Mem.: Cert. Accomplished Tchrs. (assoc.), So. Ill. U. Alumni Assn. (life), Women of the Moose (assoc.). Avocations: reading, travel, swimming. Home: 4209 Idlewild Dr Fruitland Park FL 34731 Office: Carver Mid Sch 1200 N Beecher St Leesburg FL 34748 Office Phone: 352-787-7868. Personal E-mail: kathysmarykay4u@aol.com.

**SMITH, KATIE (KATHERINE MAY SMITH),** professional basketball player; b. Logan, Ohio, June 4, 1974; d. Don Smith. Degree in zoology, Ohio State U., 1996. Profl. basketball player Columbus Quest, ABL, 1997—98, Minn. Lynx, WNBA, 1999—, Lotos VBW Clima, EuroLeague, Gdynia, Poland, 2001—02. Named Ohio State Female Athlete of the Century, Columbus Touchdown Club, 2002; named to ABL All-Star Team, 1997, 1998, All-ABL First Team, 1998, WNBA All-Star Team, 2000, 2001, 2002, 2003, All-WNBA First Team, 2001, 2003. Achievements include mem., Columbus Quest ABL Championship Team, 1997, 98; mem., US Women's Basketball Gold Medal Team, FIBA World Championships, 1998, 2002; mem., US Women's Basketball Gold Medal Team, Sydney Olympics, 2000; mem., US Women's Basketball Team, Athens Olympics, 2004; first female in history of Ohio State U. to have number retired, Jan. 21, 2001. Office: Minn Lynx 600 First Ave North Minneapolis MN 55403

**SMITH, KAYE TRAIN,** artist; b. Camden, N.J., July 15, 1927; d. William Matthew Biddle and Jennie May Leibensperger; m. Robert L. Smith, Aug. 18, 1995; m. John Martin Train, June 3, 1945 (dec. Jan. 2, 1993); children: Jeanne Carole Train, Suzanne Kathryn Coffee, Kurt Robert Train. Airbrush artist Norcross Greetings Corp., N.Y.C., 1945—46; profl. in-house model Jo Collins Sportswear Corp., St. Louis, 1947—48; freelance artist Fremont, Roseville, Calif., 1967—2005. Exhibit coord. Placerville Art Assn., 1971—72. Recipient Nat. Design award, Am. Greetings Corp., 1966. Mem.: Roseville Arts Ctr., Sun City Roseville Art Club (pres. 1996—97, various coms., signature painting, 8th ann. show 2003). Home: 7260 Timberrose Way Roseville CA 95747

**SMITH, KEITH ALLEN,** secondary school educator; b. Purdin, Mo., June 25, 1950; s. Erwin Eugene and Delores Rea Smith; m. Diana Kay Stanger, June 21, 1975; 1 child, Kylee Marie. BS in Secondary Edn., NW Mo. State U., Maryville, 1972, MA in History, 1987. Tchr. Lafayette County C-1 Schs., Higginsville, Mo., 1974—77; tchr., chmn. dept., coach Maysville (Mo.) HS, 1977—81, Maryville HS, 1981—. Inspector, supr. Pioneer Hi-Bred Internat., Johnston, Iowa, 1979—. Recipient Tchr. of Yr. award, Maryville HS, 1986. Mem.: Nat. Coun. History Edn., Nat. Coun. Social Studies, Nat. Coun. Geog. Edn. (mem. exec. bd. 1981—84, Merit Tchr. award 1981). Avocation: barbershop singing. Office: Maryville R-II HS 1503 S Munn Ave Maryville MO 64468

**SMITH, KENNETH ALAN,** chemical engineer, educator; b. Winthrop, Mass., Nov. 28, 1936; s. James Edward and Alice Gertrude (Walters) S.; m. Ambia Marie Olsson, Oct. 14, 1961; children: Kirsten Heather, Edward Eric, Andrew Ian Beaumont, Thurston Garrett. BS, MIT, 1958, MS, 1959, DSc, 1962; postgrad., Cambridge U., Eng., 1964-65. Asst. prof. chem. engring. MIT, 1961-67, assoc. prof., 1967-71, prof., 1971—, acting head dept., 1976-77, assoc. provost, 1980-81, assoc. provost, v.p. rsch., 1981-91, dir. Whitaker Coll. Health Sci. and Tech., 1989-91. Cons. chem. and oil cos. NSF fellow, 1964-65, Overseas fellow, Churchill Coll., (Eng.), 1993, 01. Mem. Am. Inst. Chem. Engrs., Nat. Acad. Engring., Am. Chem. Soc., AAAS, Sigma Xi, Phi Lambda Upsilon, Tau Beta Pi. Episcopalian. Home: 32 School St Manchester MA 01944-1336 Office: MIT Bldg 66-540 Cambridge MA 02139 Office Phone: 617-253-1973. E-mail: kas@mit.edu.

**SMITH, KENNETH DALE,** civil engineer, consultant; s. Zella and Butler Barker Smith; m. Hayrunisa Palanci, June 1988; children: Ethan, Logan. BS in civil engring., Purdue U., West Lafayette, Ind., 1990—95, BS in land surveying, 1990—95. Cert. profl. engr., Ind., 2000. Dir. ops., civil engring. Fanning/Howey Assocs., Inc., Lafayette, Ind., 1996—. Cons. Fanning/Howey Assocs., Inc., Lafayette, Ind., 1996—. Author: A Study of the Popular Linear Compactor. Water com. Lafayette C. of C., Ind., 2003. Staff sgt. U.S. Army, 1983—90, Fort Campbell, Kentucky, Germany. Decorated Army Commendation Medal, Meritorious Svc. U.S. Army. Mem.: Ind. Soc. Profl. Land Surveyors (assoc). Conservative. Home: 3421 Covington St Lafayette IN 47906 Office: Fanning Honey Assocs 9025 River Rd Ste 200 Indianapolis IN 46240-6436 E-mail: ksmith@fhai.com.

**SMITH, KENNETH JUDSON, JR.,** chemistry professor; b. Raleigh, N.C., Sept. 4, 1930; s. Kenneth Judson and Irene (Strickland) S.; m. Dorothy Margaret Ratcliffe, Mar. 6, 1953; children: Patricia Lynne Smith Pittman, Pamela Jean. AB, East Carolina U., 1957; MA, Duke U., 1959, PhD, 1961. Research chemist Chemstrand Research Center, Durham, N.C., 1961-65, sr. research chemist, 1965-68; asst. prof. polymer research SUNY Coll. Environ. Sci. and Forestry, Syracuse, 1968-70, assoc. prof., 1970-73, prof., 1973-95, emeritus prof., 1995—, asst. dir. Polymer Research Center, 1971-79, acting dir., 1979-83, dir. Organic Materials Sci. Program, 1971-75, chmn. dept. chemistry, 1972-84. Vis. researcher Instituto di Chimica Industriale, U. Genoa, Italy, 1979; cons. U.S. Army Materials and Mechanics Ctr., Watertown, Mass., 1973-75, cert. of appreciation 1973, NRC, Washington, 1980-87; mem. adv. coun. Syracuse Met. Transp. Coun., 1975-84; mem. adv. bd. confs. in polymer sci. and tech. SUNY, New Paltz, 1975-85; mem. rsch. found. joint com. on procedures SUNY, Albany, 1974-81; cons. Hong Kong Rsch. Coun., 1995—. Contbr. articles to profl. jours. Served with USMC, 1951-54. Recipient cert. Appreciation U.S. Army Materials and Mechanics Rsch. Ctr., 1973. Mem. AAAS, Am. Chem. Soc. (dir. Syracuse sect. 1977-79, chmn. 1978, councilor 1979-82), Am. Phys. Soc. (com. on internat. freedom of scientists, small coms.), Am. Inst. Chemists, Soc. Plastics Engrs., Math. Assn. Am., N.Y. Acad. Scis., Sigma Xi, Phi Lambda Upsilon, Kappa Delta Pi. Achievements include research on statistical mechanics, mechanical properties and theoretical studies of polymers; rubber elasticity and thermoelasticity; crystallization of networks; structure-property relationships; ultimate properties of fibers; thermodynamic theory of polymer fiber properties; thermodynamic theory of fiber strength. Office: Coll Environ Sci and Forestry Suny Syracuse NY 13210

**SMITH, KENNETH RODGER,** finance educator; b. Vancouver, B.C., Can., May 12, 1942; arrived in US, 1962; s. John Douglas and Marion (Cannon) S.; m. Esther J. Davenport, July 26, 1977; children from previous marriage: Morgen Jennifer, Jason Andrew BA, U. Wash., 1964; PhD, Northwestern U., 1968. Vis. rsch. fellow Universite Catholique de Louvain, Belgium, 1968-69; asst. prof. economics Health Economics Rsch. Ctr., U. Wis., Madison, 1969-71, assoc. prof., 1971-75; prof., program dir. Grad. Sch. Mgmt., Northwestern U., Evanston, Ill., 1975-79; Eller Disting. Svc. prof. Eller Coll. Mgmt., U. Ariz., Tucson, 1980—, dean, 1980—95, interim dean, 2004—05; vice provost U. Ariz., Tucson, 1992—95. Vis. assoc. prof. U. Calif.-San Diego, 1971-72; bd. dirs. The FINOVA Group, Apache Nitrogen Products, Ventana Corp. Co-author: Hospital Cost Containment Programs: A Policy Analysis, 1978 Bd. dirs. U. Achievement of Tucson, 1980-88, St. Joseph Hosp., Tucson, 1980-83; vice chmn. Ariz. Commn. on Long Term Care, 1983-84; mem. nat. adv. com. Robert Wood Johnson Found. Program for Prepaid Health Care, 1983-88. Mem. Assn. to Advance Collegiate Schools of Bus. (bd. dirs., 1990-96, pres., 1994-95). Office: U Ariz Eller Coll Mgmt Dept Economics PO Box 210108 Tucson AZ 85721-0108 Office Phone: 602-621-2633. Office Fax: 520-621-8450. Business E-Mail: ksmith@eller.arizona.edu.*

**SMITH, KENT ASHTON,** information scientist, consultant; b. Boston, Sept. 3, 1938; s. Kent Wooliscroft and Dorothy Patten Smith; m. Mary Margaret Gaffney; children: Holly L. Smith, Kent W. BA, Hobart Coll., 1960; MBA, Cornell U., 1962; postgrad., Am. U., 1978-79. Mgmt. analyst Office of Sec., HEW, Washington, 1962-65; adminstrv. officer divsn. rsch. facilities and resources NIH, Bethesda, Md., 1965-67, asst. exec. officer divsn. rsch. facilities and resources, 1967-68, exec. officer divsn. rsch. resources, 1968-71, asst. dir. adminstrn. Nat. Libr. Medicine, 1971-78, dep. dir., 1978—2004, PHS spl. expert-info. scientist, 2000—02; cons. Nat. Ctr. for Biotechnology Info., 2004—, Office Sci. and tech. Info. Dept. Energy, 2005—. Mem. exec. bd. and bur. Internat. Coun. Sci. and Tech. Info., Paris, 1983—2001; v.p. U.S. Nat. Com. of UNESCO-PGI, Washington, 1983—85; mem. exec. adv. bd. Fed. Libr. and Info. Ctr. Com., Washington, 1984—89; exec. com. CENDI-Info. Consortia, Washington, 1985—; treas. Internat. Coun. Sci. and Tech. Info., Paris, 1986—89; pres. Nat. Fed. Abstracting and Info. Svcs., Phila., 1988—89, v.p., 1987—88; chmn. Info. Policy Com., 1988—89, CENDI-Info. Consortia, Washington, 2001—04; mem. US Nat. Commn. for CODATA, 1990—2001, Science.gov Alliance, 2002—04, NISO Blue Ribbon Panel, 2004; pres. Internat. Coun. Sci. and Tech. Info., Paris, 1990—94; mem. panel on Dept. Energy Info. Infrastructure NAS, 2000; reviewer study digital strategy for Libr. Congress NRC, 2000; mem. panel on Nat. Tech. Info. Svc. Nat. Commn. Libr. and Info. Sci., 2000; long-range planning panel mem. Nat. Libr. Medicine, 2005—06. Contbr. articles to profl. jours., chpt. to book: Management of Federally Sponsored Libraries, 1995. Mem. Citizens Com. for Pub. Libr. Montgomery County, Bethesda, 1981-82; fin. dir. Christ Ch., Rockville, Md., 1990-91. Recipient Asst. Sec. for Health Exceptional Achievement award USPHS, 1978, Sr. Exec. Svc. award, 1996, 97, 98, 99, HEW Superior Svc. medal 1974, Nat. Fedn. Abstracting Info. Sci., 1998, Miles Conrad hon. lectureship, Hammer award V.P. US, 1999. Fellow Nat. Fedn. Abstracting and Info. Svcs.; mem. ASPA (vice chmn. 1971-72), AAAS, Int. Assn. Sci. Tech. and Med. Pubs., Am. Mgmt. Assn., Am. Soc. Info. Svc., Med. Libr. Assn. (hon.; Pres. award 1997, ICSTI Disting. Svc. award 2001), Assn. Rsch. Librs. (Alfred Zipf fellow com. chair 2001-04), Cosmos Club. Episcopalian. Avocations: golf, baseball, genealogy, theater, birdwatching, antiques. Home and Office: 17517 Hidden Garden Ln Ashton MD 20861 Office Phone: 301-496-5359.

**SMITH, K(ERMIT) WAYNE,** computer company executive; b. Newton, NC, Sept. 15, 1938; s. Harold Robert and Hazel K. (Smith) S.; m. Audrey M. Kennedy, Dec. 19, 1958; 1 son, Stuart W. BA, Wake Forest U., 1960; MA, Princeton U., 1962, PhD, 1964; postgrad., U. So. Calif., 1965; LLD (hon.),

Ohio U., 1992; LHD (hon.), Ohio State U., 1998. Instr. Princeton U., 1963; asst. prof. econs. and polit. sci. U.S. Mil. Acad., 1963-66; spl. asst. to asst. sec. def. for sys. analysis Washington, 1966-69; program mgr. def. studies RAND Corp., Santa Monica, Calif., 1969-70; dir. program analysis NSC, Washington, 1970-72; group v.p. planning Dart Industries, L.A., 1972-73, group pres. resort devel. group, 1973-76; exec. v.p. Washington Group, Inc., 1976-77; mng. ptnr. Coopers & Lybrand, Washington, 1977-80, group mng. ptnr., 1980-83; chmn., CEO World Book, Inc., 1983-86; prof. Wake Forest U., 1986—88, 2001—; CEO OCLC Online Computer Libr. Ctr., Inc., Dublin, Ohio, 1989-98, pres. emeritus, 1998—. Sr. cons. Dept. Def., Dept. State, NSC, NASA, Dept. Energy, OMB, GAO; bd. dirs. Nat. City Bank, K. Wayne Smith and Assocs.; con. prof. (hon.) Tsinghua U., Beijing, 1996; chmn. Rainbow Care For Kids Found., 1999-2000. Author: How Much is Enough? Shaping the Defense Program, 1961-69, 1971, reprinted as RAND classic, 2005; editor: OCLC 1967-97: Thirty Years of Furthering Access to the World's Information, 1998; contbr. articles to profl. jours. Mem. vis. com. Brookings Instn., Washington, 1971-79; mem. bd. visitors Wake Forest U., 1974-78, 82-90, chmn. bd. visitors, 1976-78, trustee, 1991-95, 96-00, 01-05, 06-, vice chmn., 2006-; mem. bd. visitors Def. Sys. Mgmt. Coll., 1982-85, Lenoir Rhyne Coll., 1988-94, Mershon Ctr. Ohio State U., 1990-92, Columbus Assn. for Performing Arts, 1991-95, U. Pitts. Sch. Libr. and Info. Sci., 1992-95; mem. bd. visitors Bowman Gray Bapt. Hosp. Med. Ctr., 1992-95, chmn. bd. visitors, 1993-95. Danforth fellow, Woodrow Wilson fellow Princeton U., 1962-64. Mem. ALA (hon., life), Coun. Fgn. Rels., Internat. Inst. Strategic Studies, Inst. Internat. Edn., Coun. Higher Edn., Am. Assn. Higher Edn., Chgo. Club, Lakes Golf and Country Club, Capital Club, Phi Beta Kappa, Omicron Delta Kappa, Kappa Sigma. Methodist. Home: 2606 Sigmon Dairy Rd Newton NC 28658-7609 Office: Online Computer Libr Ctr Inc 6565 Frantz Rd Dublin OH 43017-5308

**SMITH, KERRY CLARK,** lawyer; b. Phoenix, July 12, 1935; s. Clark and Fay (Jackson) S.; m. Michael Waterman, 1958; children: Kevin, Ian. AB, Stanford U., 1957, JD, 1962. Bar: Calif. 1963, U.S. Supreme Ct. 1980. Assoc. Chickering & Gregory, San Francisco, 1962-70, ptnr., 1970-81, Pettit & Martin, San Francisco, 1981-95, Hovis, Smith, San Francisco, 1995-99; pvt. practice San Francisco 1999—. Mem. editl. bd. Stanford Law Rev., 1961-62. Lt. USN, 1957-60. Mem. ABA (bus. law sect.), Calif. Bar Assn., San Francisco Bar Assn., Orinda County Club, Palms Golf Club, La Quinta Citrus Golf Club, San Francisco World Trade Club. Office: Smith Law Offices 601 California St Ste 1600 San Francisco CA 94108-2821 E-mail: kerrysmith50965@msn.com.

**SMITH, KEVIN,** film director, writer, actor; b. Red Bank, NJ, Aug. 2, 1970; m. Jennifer Schwalbach, Apr. 25, 1999; 1 child, Harley Quinn. LHD (hon.), Illinois Wesleyan University. Owner Jay and Silent Bob's Secret Stash Comic Book Store, Red Bank, NJ, View Askew Productions, 1996—. Dir., writer, actor (films): Clerks, 1994, Mall Rats, 1996, Chasing Amy, 1997, Dogma, 1999; dir., writer, actor: Jay and Silent Bob Strike Back, 2001; exec. prodr.: Good Will Hunting, 1997, Vulgar, 2000, Reel Paradise, 2005, Small Town Gay Bar, 2006; dir., producer, writer (films): Jersey Girl, 2004, Clerks II, 2006; screenwriter: (TV film) Roadside Attractions, 2002; dir., screenwriter: (TV film) The Flying Car, 2002; writer, actor, exec. prod. (TV series) Clerks, 2000; appeared in films: Scream 3, 1999, Daredevil, 2003, Bottom's Up, 2006, Southland Tales, 2006, (voice) Doogal, 2006; Author: Silent Bob Speaks: The Collected Writings of Kevin Smith, 2005*

**SMITH, KIKI,** artist; b. Nuremberg, Germany, Jan. 18, 1954; d. Tony Smith. One-woman shows include The Kitchen, N.Y.C., 1982, Fawbush Gallery, 1988, 1992, 1993, Galerie René Blouin, Montreal, 1989, 1991—92, 1994, Dallas Mus. Art, 1989, Ezra and Cecile Zilkha Gallery Ctr. for the Arts Wesleyan U., Middletown, Conn., 1989, Tyler Gallery Tyler Sch. Art Temple U., Phila., 1990, Ctr. d'Arte Contemporaine, Geneva, 1990, Inst. Art and Urban Resources The Clocktower, Long Island, N.Y., 1990, Inst. Contemporary Art, Amsterdam, 1990, Mus. Modern Art, N.Y.C., 1990—91, Shoshana Wayne Gallery, Santa Monica, Calif., 1991, 1992, 1992—93, MAK Galerie, Vienna, 1991, U. Art Mus., Berkeley, Calif., 1991, Art Awareness, Inc., Lexington, N.Y., 1991, Corcoran Gallery Art, Washington, 1991, Greg Kucera Gallery, Seattle, 1991, Rose Art Mus. Brandeis U., Waltham, Mass., 1992, Österreichisches Mus. angewandte Kunst, Vienna, 1992, Moderna Mus., Stockholm, 1992, Bonner Kunstverein, Bonn, 1992, Galerie M & R Fricke, Düsseldorf, Germany, 1992—93, Williams Coll. Mus. Art, Williamstown, Mass., 1992—93, Ohio State U., Columbus, 1992—93, Anthony d'Offay Gallery, London, 1993, 1995, Phoenix Art Mus., 1993, U. Art Mus., Santa Barbara, Calif., 1994, La. Mus. Modern Art, Humlebaek, Denmark, 1994, The Israel Mus., Jerusalem, 1994, Barbara Gross Galerie, Munich, 1994, Laura Carpenter Fine Art, Santa Fe, 1994, Pace Wildenstein, N.Y., 1994, Royal LePage Gallery, Toronto, 1994—95, Barbara Krakow Gallery, Boston, 1994—96, Whitechapel Art Gallery, London, 1995, San Francisco Mus. Modern Art, 2005, Contemporary Art Mus., Houston, 2006, numerous others, exhibited in group shows at Brooke Alexander Gallery, N.Y., 1980, 1991, White Columns, N.Y., 1981, 1983, 1990, Artists Space, 1981, 1990, Barbara Gladstone Gallery, 1982, Hallwalls, Buffalo, N.Y., 1983, Susan Caldwell Gallery, N.Y., 1984, 1987, Galerie Engstrom, Stockholm, 1984, Art City, N.Y., 1985, Moderna Mus., Stockholm, 1985, Cin. Art Mus., 1985, Bklyn. Mus., 1986, 1989, Curt Marcus Gallery, N.Y., 1986, Fawbush Gallery, 1987, 1989, 1990, Mus. Modern Art, N.Y.C., 1988, 1992, IBM Gallery, N.Y., 1988, Arch Gallery, Amsterdam, 1988, Tom Cugliani Gallery, 1989, Simon Watson Gallery, N.Y., 0190, Mus. Fine Arts, Boston, 1990, Hunter Coll. Art Gallery, 1991, Milw. Art Mus., 1992, Paula Cooper Gallery, 1993, Serpentine Gallery, London, 1994, PaceWildenstein, N.Y., 1995, 1997, 1998, Ace Gallery, Mex., 1997, Yale U. Art Gallery, New Haven, Conn., 1998, John Berggruen Gallery, San Francisco, 2005, numerous others. Named one of 100 Most Influential People, Time Mag., 2006. Mem.: AAAL. Office: c/o Pace Wildenstein 32 E 57th St New York NY 10022-2513*

**SMITH, KIMMIE CHRISTINE,** small business owner; b. Redding, Calif., Apr. 28, 1971; d. Steven Burton Tyler and Kim Kassina Hern; m. Kenneth Thomas Smith, Nov. 12, 1988; 1 foster child, Savannah children: Stephanie, Shannon, Steven, Shelby, Danika. AAS, U. Alaska, Sitka, 2003, AA, 2004, BLA, 2005. Owner, adminstr. Krissy's Playland Childcare Ctr., Wrangell, Alaska, 1995—. Sec., treas., com. mem. Cub Scouts Am., Wrangell, Alaska, 2000—04; v.p. Emblem Club #87, 2006—. Named Family Childcare Provider of Year, AEYC-SEA, 2005. Avocations: hunting, scrapbooks, fishing. Home: PO Box 615 Wrangell AK 99929 Office: Krissy's Playland PO Box 615 Wrangell AK 99929 Office Phone: 907-874-4307. Business E-Mail: krissysplayland@aptalaska.net.

**SMITH, L. DENNIS,** former academic administrator; b. Muncie, Ind., Jan. 18, 1938; s. Thurman Lewis and Dorothy Ann (Dennis) S.; m. Suzanne F. Metcalfe; children: Lauren Kay, Raymond Bradley. AB, Ind. U., 1959, PhD, 1964; DSc (hon.), Purdue U., 2000. Asst. embryologist Argonne (Ill.) Nat. Lab., 1964-67, assoc. biologist, 1967-69; assoc. prof. Purdue U., West Lafayette, Ind., 1969-73, prof. biology, 1973-87, assoc. head dept. biol. scis., 1979-80, head dept., 1983-87; prof. dept. devel. and cell. U. Calif. Irvine, 1987-94, dean Sch. Biol. Scis., 1987-90, exec. vice chancellor, 1990-94; pres. U. of Nebr., 1994—2004, pres. emeritus, prof. biol. scis., 2004—. Instr. embryology Woods Hole (Mass.) Marine Biology Lab., 1972-74, mem. Space Studies Bd., Washington, 1986-91; chmn. Space Biology and Medicine, space sci. bd., 1986-91; cell biology study sect. NIH, Bethesda, Md., 1971-75; chmn., 1977-79, bd. sci. counselors Nat. Inst. Child Health and Human Devel., 1990-95, chmn., 1992-95; space biology peer rev. bd. AIBS, 1980-85. Mem. Bus. Higher Edn. Forum, 1995—, chair, 2000—02; bd. dirs. Nebr. Arts Coun., Nebr., Nebr. Indsl. Competitiveness Alliance. Fellow Guggenheim, 1987; Sci. Freedom and Responsibility award, AAAS, 2002. Mem. AAAS, Am. Soc. Biochemistry and Molecular Biology, Internat. Soc. for Devel. Biology, Soc. for Devel. Biology, Am. Soc. Cell Biology, Am. Soc. for Microbiology. Office: Alex West Ste 135 312 No 14th St Lincoln NE 68588-0430 Office Phone: 402-472-7154.

**SMITH, LAMAR SEELIGSON,** congressman; b. San Antonio, Nov. 19, 1947; s. Campbell and Eloise Keith (Seeligson) Smith; m. Elizabeth Schaefer, Mar. 20, 1992; children: Nell Seligson, Tobin Wells. BA, Yale U., New Haven, 1969; JD, So. Meth. U. Sch. Law, Dallas, 1975. Mgmt. intern SBA, Washington, 1969-70; bus. writer Christian Sci. Monitor, Boston, 1970-72; assoc. Maebius & Duncan, Inc., San Antonio, 1975-76; chmn. Rep. Party of Bexar County, San Antonio, 1978—82; mem. Tex. State Ho. Reps. from Dist. 57-F, San Antonio, 1981-82; commr. Bexar County Precinct 3, Tex., 1982—85; mem. US Congress from 21st Tex. dist., 1987—. mem. judiciary com., chmn. courts, the internet and intellectual property subcommittee, mem. sci. com., mem. homeland security com., mem. standards of ofcl. conduct com. Ptnr. Lamar Seeligson Ranch, Premont, Tex., 1975—. Named Legislator of Yr., Info. Tech. Industry Coun., 2005; named one of 50 Most Influential People in the World of Intellectual Property, Mng. IP Mag., 2006, 100 Most Influential People in Washington, DC, Nat. Jour.; recipient Congl. Leadership award, Semiconductor Industry Assn. Republican. Christian Scientist. Office: US Ho Reps 2184 Rayburn Ho Office Bldg Washington DC 20515-4321 Office Phone: 202-225-4236.*

**SMITH, LANCE L.,** career military officer; BA in Bus. Mgmt., Va. Poly. Inst., 1969; MA in Bus. Mgmt, Ctrl. Mich. U., 1978; grad., Air command Staff Coll., 1982, Army War Coll., 1990, J. L. Kellog Grad. Sch. Mgmt., 1994. Commd. 2d. lt. USAF, 1970, advanced through grades to gen., 2005; pilot tng. Columbus AFB, Miss., 1970-71; A-1 combat crew tng. Hurlburt Field, Fla., 1971-71; A-1 pilot 1st Spl. Ops. Squadron, Nakhom Phanom Royal Thai AFB, Thailand, 1971-72; instr. pilot tng. Randolph AFB, Tex., 1972-73; instr. pilot, chief 96th Flying Tng. Squadron, Williams AFB, Ariz., 1973-77; staff ofice Air Staff Tng. Program, Washington, 1977-79; A-7 Corsair Conversion Tng., A-7D aircraft comdr., flight comdr. and asst. ops. officer 76th Tactical Fighter Squadron Eng. Airforce Base, La., 1979-81; air staff officer The Pentagon, Washington, 1982-86; chief safety, asst. dep. comdr. for ops. 354th Tactical Fighter Wing, Myrtle Beach AFB, S.C., 1986-89; comdt. NATO Sch. Obermammergau, Germany, 1992-93; vice comdr, then comdr. 27th Fighter Wing, Cannon AFB, N.Mex., 1992-93; asst. dir. ops. Hdqs. Air Combat Command, Langley AFB, Va., 1993-95; comdr. 4th Wing, Seymour Johnson AFB, N.C., 1995-97; vice comdr. 7th Air Force, U.S. Air Forces Korea, chief staff, Osan Air Base, South Korea, 1997-98; comdt. Air War Coll., 1998-99; vice comdr. Air Univ., Maxwell AFB, Ala., 1998-99; comdr. Airforce Doctrine Ctr., Maxwell AFB, Ala., 1999—2001; dep. comdr. UN Command, Osan AFB, Republic of Korea, 2001—03; dep. comdr. US Forces Korea, comdr. Air Component Command Republic of Korea/US Combines Forces Command, 2001—03; comdr. 7th Air Force, Pacific Air Forces, Osan AFB, 2001—03; dep. comdr. US Ctrl. Command, MacDill AFB, Fla., 2003—05; comdr. US Joint Forces Command, Norfolk, Va., 2005—; supreme allied comdr. for transformation NATO, 2005—. Decorated Silver Star with two oak leaf clusters, Def. Superior Svc. medal, Dinsting. Svc. medal, Legion of Merit with oak leaf cluster, D.F.C. with two oak leaf clusters, Purple Heart, Meritorious Svc. medal with three oak leaf clusters, Air medal with one silver and four bronze oak leaf clusters, Aerial Achievement medal with oak leaf cluster, Air Force Commendation medal, Army Commendation medal, Humanitarian Svc. medal, Armed Forces Expeditionary medal, Rep. Vietnam Gallantry Cross with Palm, Honor Cross of the Bundeswehr medal (Republic of Germany), Order Nat. Sec. Merit Cheonsu medal, Order Nat. Security Merit Gukseon medal (Rep. Korea) Office: US Joint Forces Command 1562 Mitscher Ave Ste 200 Norfolk VA 23551*

**SMITH, LANTY L(LOYD),** lawyer, corporate financial executive; b. Sherrodsville, Ohio, Dec. 13, 1942; s. Lloyd H. and Ellen Ruth (Newell) S.; m. Margaret Hays Chandler, June 11, 1966; children: Abigail Lamoreaux Presson, Margaret Ellen Smith-Rhee, Amanda Prescott Lacoff. BS in Math. with honors, Wittenberg U., Springfield, Ohio, 1964; LLB with honors, Duke U., 1967. Bar: Ohio 1967. Assoc. Jones, Day, Cockley & Reavis, Cleve., 1967-73; ptnr. Jones, Day, Reavis & Pogue, Cleve., 1974-77; exec. v.p., sr. gen. counsel Burlington Industries, Inc., Greensboro, NC, 1977-86, pres., 1986-88; chmn. Precision Fabrics Group Inc., Greensboro, 1988—, The Greenwood Group, Inc., Raleigh, NC, 1992—, Soles Brower Smith & Co., 1998—. Bd. dirs., chmn. exec. com., lead ind. dir. Wachovia Corp.; bd. dirs., lead ind. dir. Wikoff Color; pres., CEO MediWave Star Tech. Inc., 1999—. Mem. bd. visitors Duke U. Sch. Law; trustee The Duke Endowment; vice chmn. exec. com. Duke U. Mgmt. Co.; mem. exec. com. The Herring Ridge YMCA Retreat. Mem.: NC Inst. Medicine. Episcopalian. Home: 1401 Westridge Rd Greensboro NC 27410-2912 Office: Soles Brower Smith & Co Wachovia Tower Ste 925 Greensboro NC 27401-2167 Business E-Mail: lsmith@solesbrower.com.

**SMITH, LARRY STEVEN,** financial analyst, accountant, farmer; b. Jasper, Tenn., Sept. 30, 1950; s. Samuel Lester and Stella Mae (Barnes) Smith. BA in Econs., U. Ala., Tuscaloosa, 1972, MBA, 1975. Laborer Lester Smith Farms, Scottsboro, Ala., 1975-76; acct. Ala. Hwy. Dept., Montgomery, 1976-77, Ala. State Agy. Social Security, Montgomery, 1977-78; acct., analyst Ala. Pub. Svc. Commn., Montgomery, 1978-79, utilities analyst II, 1980-81, supr., 1981-89, chmn. computer oversight com., 1988-91, supr. telecom. divsn., 1989—; sales assoc. Jack Hendrix Real Estate, Montgomery, 1979-80. Interim dir. telecom. divsn. Ala. Pub. Svc. Commn., Montgomery, 1993, mem. telecom. task force, 1996—99. Mem. Montgomery Jaycees, 1978—81, bd. dirs., 1979, 1980, Ala. Jr. Miss., Montgomery, 1979—81; mem. Ala. Reps., 1983—. Nat. Grad. Coun. Fellowship grantee, 1973. Mem.: Am. Assn. Ind. Investors, Sierra Club, Nat. Wildlife Fedn., Amnesty Internat., Environ. Def. Fund, Wilderness Soc., Nat. Audubon Soc., N.Am. Limousin Found. Baptist. Avocations: photography, skiing, hunting, hiking, fly-fishing, backpacking. Home: 1600 Cobblestone Ct Montgomery AL 36117-1702 Office: Alabama Public Service Commission PO Box 304100 Montgomery AL 36130-4200

**SMITH, LAUREN ASHLEY,** lawyer, clergyman, physicist, journalist; b. Clinton, Iowa, Nov. 30, 1924; s. William Thomas Roy and Ethel (Cook) S.; m. Barbara Ann Mills, Aug. 22, 1947; children: Christopher A., Laura Nan Smith Pringle, William Thomas Roy II. BS, U. Minn., 1946, JD, 1949; postgrad., U. Chgo., 1943-49; MDiv, McCormick Theol. Sem., 1950; postgrad., U. Iowa, 1992. Bar: Colo. 1957, Iowa 1959, Ill. 1963, Minn. 1983, U.S. Supreme Ct. 1967; ordained to ministry Presbyn. Ch., 1950. Pastor Presbyn. Ch., Fredonia, Kans., 1950-52, Lamar, Colo., 1952-57, Congl. Ch., Clinton, 1975-80; editor The Comml., Pine Bluff, Ark., 1957-58; ptnr. Schoenauer Smith & Fullerton ASP, Clinton, 1995—. CEO LASCO Pub. Group, Clinton, 1995—; CEO, founder Interlink for the Internet Generation; internat. conferee Stanley Found., Warrenton, Va., 1963—72; legal observer, USSR, 1978; co-sponsor All India Renewable Energy Conf., Bangalore, 1981; law sch. conferee U. Minn., China, 1983; lectr. law, religion, physics, nat. policy U. Wis., 2001, Spl. lectr. contemporary physics and religion, 01. Author: (jurisprudence treatise) Forma Dat Esse Rei, 1975, (monograph) First Strike Option, 1983; co-author: India On to New Horizons, 1989; columnist Crow Call, 1986—; co-editor Press and News of India, 1978-82; pub. Crow Call; pseudonym Christopher Crow, 1981—; writer BBC World Svc., London; editor Asian Econ. Cmty. Jour.; contbr. articles to religious pubs. Assoc. Westar Inst. (The Jesus Seminar); Santa Rosa, Calif.; active Quad City Estate Planning Coun.; minister-at-large Presbyn. Ch. U.S.A., Iowa, 1987—; bd. dirs. Iowa divsn. UN Assn. U.S.A., Iowa City, 1970—85; fellow Molecular Nanotechnology Foresight Inst., Palo Alto, Calif., Franciscans UN Non Govt. Orgn.; founder, CEO Interlink relating quantum mechanics and religion, Clinton, Iowa 1998—; founding dir. Project 67/74, Clinton, 2002—. Recipient World Wide Essay Contest award, Radio China Internat., 2003—04. Mem. ABA, Iowa Bar Assn., Ill. Bar Assn., St. Andrews Soc., Clinton County Bar Assn. (pres. 1968, Best in Iowa citation), Clinton Ministerial Assn., Samaritan Health Systems Chaplain Corps. (pres.), European Soc. for Study of Sci. and Religion, Quad City Estate Planning Coun., Quaker Internat. Yokefellow, Nat. Network for New Spiritual Formation Presbyn. Ch. USA, Franciscans Internat., Parish Without Walls (founding dir.), City Club of Quad Cities (bd. dirs.), Cath. Order St. Francis (assoc., founder project 67/74), New Rd. Map for Am. (founder). Office: 230 4th Ave S Clinton IA 52732-4311

**SMITH, LAURENCE ROGER,** journal editor; b. N.Y.C., Sept. 30, 1939; s. John and Edith (Haabestad) S.; m. Betty Ann Larsen, Oct. 9, 1965; children: Erik Lars, Alesa Ann. AAS, Staten Island Community Coll., 1962; BS, SUNY, Oswego, 1965; MBA, St. John's U., 1975. Cert. in bus. and exec. coaching NLP & Coaching Inst. Calif., Inst. HeartMath, Heart Math. Inner Quality Mgmt., bus. tchr. NY, indsl. arts tchr. NY. Dir. cmty. devel. S.I. (N.Y.) C. of C., 1965-77; exec. v.p. CEO, Yonkers (N.Y.) C. of C., 1977-78; chief exec. officer Greater Lawrence (Mass.) C. of C., 1978-91; pres. The LeaderShip, North Andover, Mass., 1991-94; editor in chief Jour. Innovative Mgmt. (Goal/QPC), Salem, NH, 1994—. Dir., clk. Lawrence Downtown Parking Assocs., 1979-91; dir., asst. treas. Greater Lawrence Revolving Loan Fund, 1979-91; mem. U.S. C. of C. Com. on Edn. and Tng., 1990-91; dir. Mgmt. Innovations Group, GOAL/QPC, 1997—. Author: Godfidence, 1991. Chmn. Lower Merrimack Valley Pvt. Industry Coun., Lawrence, 1981; treas. Lawrence YMCA, 1985; vice-chmn. literacy com. Mass. Regional Employment Bd., 1989-90; bd. dirs. Greater Lawrence Red Cross; apptd. to Mass. Dept. Edn. Sch.-Bus. Partnership Com., 1990-91. With USCG, 1958-60. Recipient Pvt. Sector award Presdl. Commn., 1985, Flood Relief award ARC, 1987; named to U. Notre Dame Acad. Orgn. Mgmt., 1989, CUNY Hall of Fame. 1990. Mem. Am. C. of C. Execs., New Eng. Assn. C. of C. Execs. (pres., 1986), Mass. Assn. C. of C. Execs. (pres. 1984). Democrat. Episcopalian. Avocations: singing, acting. Home: The LeaderShip 233 Osgood St North Andover MA 01845-4025 Office: Jour Innovative Mgmt Goal/QPC 12B Manor Pkwy Salem NH 03079 Office Phone: 603-890-8800. E-mail: lsmith@goalqpc.com.

**SMITH, LAVENSKI R. (VENCE SMITH),** federal judge; m. Trendle Smith; 2 children. BA, U. Ark., 1981, JD, 1987. Law clerk Hall, Wright & Morris, 1985—87; staff lawyer Ozark Legal Svcs., 1987-91; pvt. practice Springdale, 1991-94; asst. prof. John Brown U., 1994-96; regulatory liaison Ark. Gov. Off., 1996—97; interim assoc. justice Ark. State Supreme Ct., 1999—2000; commr. Ark. Pub. Serv. Commn., 2001; judge U.S. 8th Circuit Court, 2002—. Bd. dirs. N.W. Ark. Christian Justice Ctr.; trainer Ptnrs. for Family Tng., 1993-96; chmn. Ark. Pub. Svc. Commn., 1996-98. Republican. Office: Fed Bldg Rm 316 35 E Mountain St Fayetteville AR 72702*

**SMITH, LAWRENCE S.,** communications executive; Grad., Ithaca Coll., 1969. CFO Advanta Corp.; tax ptnr. Arthur Anderson & Co., Phila., head Phila. internat. bus. practice and merger & acquisition practice; exec. v.p. Comcast, Phila., 1988—, co-CFO. Bd. dir. E! Entertainment Television, Inc., QVC, Inc., The Golf Channel. Bd. dir. Meadowood Corp., Perkiomen Sch.; YMCA of Greater Phila. Co-recipient CFO of Yr. award, Broadcast Cable Fin. Mgmt. Assn., 2004; named one of America's Best CFOs, Instl. Investor mag., 2004. Office: Comcast Corp 1500 Market St Philadelphia PA 19102-2100 Office Fax: 215-981-7790.*

**SMITH, LEE ELTON,** surgery educator, retired military officer; b. Ventura, Calif., July 19, 1937; s. Raymond Elroy and Edith Irene (Jordan) S.; m. Carole Sue Smith; children: Justine Diane, Alexander Loren. BS, U. Calif., Berkeley, 1959; MD, U. Calif., San Francisco, 1962. Diplomate Am. Bd. Surgery, Am. Bd. Colon and Rectal Surgery (pres. 1992-93). Commd. ens. USN, 1960, advanced through grades to capt., 1977; intern U. Utah, Salt Lake City, 1962-63; resident USN, San Diego, 1966-70, staff surgeon Bremerton, Wash., 1970-72; resident colorectal surgery U. Minn., Mpls., 1972-73; dir. colorectal surgery Nat. Naval Med. Ctr. USN, Bethesda, Md., 1973-82, ret., 1983, Seattle, 1982; clin. prof. surgery Uniformed Svcs. U., Bethesda, 1976—; prof. surgery George Washington U., Washington, 1983-96, Georgetown U., Washington, 2001—; dir. sect. of colon and rectal surgery Washington Hosp. Ctr., 1996—. Pres. Am. Bd. Colon and Rectal Surgery, 1993-94. Editor: Practical Guide to Anorectal Physiology, 1990, 2d edit., 1995; assoc. editor Diseases of the Colon and Rectum, 1984-96, Perspectives in Colon and Rectal Surgery, 1989-2000. Mem. ACS (pres. Met. Washington chpt. 1993-94), Soc. Am. Gastrointestinal Endoscopic Surgeons (pres. 1989-90), Am. Cancer Soc. (v.p. D.C. chpt. 1985-93), Am. Soc. Colon & Rectal Surgeons (pres. 1998-99). Home: 7512 16th St NW Washington DC 20012 Office: Washington Hosp Ctr 106 Irving St NW Washington DC 20010-2975 Office Phone: 202-877-8484. E-mail: lee.e.smith@medstar.net.

**SMITH, LEILA HENTZEN,** artist; b. Milw., May 20, 1932; d. Erwin Albert and Marian Leila (Austin) Hentzen; m. Richard Howard Smith, Sept. 12, 1959; 1 child, Jennie. BFA, Miami U., 1955; cert., Famous Artists Schs., 1959. Quilting tchr. Milw. Pub. Schs., 1975-79. One-woman shows include Boerner Bot. Gardens, Whitnall Park, Wis., 1995, 2 person show, Firefly Gallery, Wauwatosa, Wis., 2003, exhibited in group shows at Milw. Art Ctr., 1961, West Bend Gallery Fine Arts, 1963, 1993, 1996, 1999, 2002, 2005, Wustum Mus. Art, Racine, Wis., 1966, Mount Mary Coll., Milw., 1969—2001, Mapledale Sch. Gallery, Bayside, Wis., 1977, 1981, Artist's World Gallery, Cedarburg, Wis., 1975, Ozaukee Art Ctr. 1982—86, John Michael Kohler Arts Ctr., Sheboygan, Wis., 1984, 1987, 1989—2002, 2005, Cedarburg Cultural Ctr., 1988—2001, Ozaukee Art Ctr, Cedarburg, Wis., 1993, Rahr-West Art Mus., Manitowoc, Wis., 1994, Gallery 110 North, Plymouth, Wis., 1996, Rahr-West Art Mus., Manitowoc, Wis., 1997, Cardinal Stritch U., 1998—2003, Represented in permanent collections Milw. County Art Commn. Women's aux. vol. Salvation Army, Milw.; mem. dean's adv. coun. U. Wis. Milw. Sch. Arts. Recipient Honorable Mention for painting Bayshore Merchants Assn, 1969, Delta Gamma Art Fair, 1981, Best of Show for painting John Michael Kohler Arts Ctr., 1988. Mem. AAUW, Cedarburg Artists Guild, Wis. Watercolor Soc., Seven Arts Soc. Milw. (pres. 1967-68, painters group chmn. 1962-63), DAR (Milw. chpt. Holiday Folk Fair chmn. 1965-76, libr. historian 1974-77, corr. sec. 1977-80, dir. 1983-86, rec. sec. 1992-95, regent 1995-98, Outstanding Jr. Mem. 1966), Wis. Soc. Daus. of Founders and Patriots of Am. (pres. 1964-66, 2d v.p. 1966-68, 70-73, corr. sec. 1976-79), Wis. Ct. Assts., Nat. Soc. Women Descendants Ancient and Hon. Arty. Co. Boston, Wis. Soc. Mayflower Descendants (sec. 1999-02), Delta Zeta. Congregationalist. Avocations: needlecrafts, swimming, quilting.

**SMITH, LEONORE RAE,** artist; b. Chgo. d. Leon and Rose (Hershfield) Goodman; m. Paul Carl Smith, Apr. 17, 1943; children: Jill Henderson, Laurie Christman. Student, Chgo. Art Inst., 1935-40, U. Chgo., 1939—. Performer in many Broadway shows, with Met. Opera Quartet, Carnegie Hall, nat. concerts; portrait, landscape painter; signature artist Oil Painters of Am., Chgo., 1992-2006, Am. Acad. of Women Artists, 1997-98; ofcl. artist U.S. Coast Guard, Washington, 1989-2000; cert. artist Am. Portrait Soc., Huntington Harbor, Calif., 1985; nat. adv. bd. The Portrait Club, N.Y.C., 1983. Pres. Pacific Palisades Rep. Women, Calif. Named one of Master Artists of the World, Internat. Artist Mag., 1996; recipient Best of Show awards, Salamagundi U.S. Coast Guard, 1989, Pacific Palisades Art Assn., 1987, 1st prize in oils, Greater L.A. Art Competition, Santa Monica, Calif., 1995, prize, The Artist's Mag., 1995, Internat. Soc. Artists, 1977, 1st pl. award, Dream Studio competition, 1996, 1st pl. in portrait, O.P.A. Nat. Show, 2001, award, Northlight Art Mag., 2002, Internat. Artist Mag., 2002, several awards, Calif. Art Club, shown at Nat. Mus. Naval Aviation, Carnegie Mus., Frederick Weisman Mus., Malibu, Calif. Mem. Am. Acad. Women Artists (signature), Salmagundi Club, Pacific Palisades Art Assn. (past pres.), Calif. Art Club, Oil Painters Am. (signature, 1st Pl. 2001), Am. Portrait Soc. (nat.) Achievements include moer than 50 oil paintings of fallen military in Iraq and Afghanistan. Avocations: singing, acting, poetry. Office Phone: 310-454-4223. E-mail: leonorpaul@aol.com.

**SMITH, LESLIE EDGAR,** vocational school administrator; b. Pitts., Dec. 28, 1950; s. Joel David and Margaret Elizmath Smith; m. Pamela S. Ghost, June 17, 1994; children: Bethani E. Thomas, Kylene D. Clickner, Andrew J. Clickner. BA, Calif. U. Pa., 1972. Vocat. instr. Steel Ctr. AVTS, Jefferson Hills, Pa., 1989—99, vocat. adminstr., 1999—. Baptist. Home: 400 Bunola River Rd Bunola PA 15020 Office: Steel Center AVTS 565 Lewis Run Rd Jefferson Hills PA 15025 Office Phone: 412-469-3200 129. Personal E-mail: lps50@msn.com. E-mail: leslie.smith@aiu3.net.

**SMITH, LESLIE ROPER,** hospital administrator, health facility administrator; b. Stockton, Calif., June 20, 1928; s. Austin J. and Helen (Roper) S.; m. Edith Sue Fincher, June 22, 1952; children: Melinda Sue, Leslie Erin, Timothy Brian. AB, U. Pacific, 1951; MS in Pub. Adminstrn, U. So. Calif., 1956. Adminstrv. asst. Ranchos Los Amigos Hosp., Downey, Calif., 1953-57; asst. adminstr. Harbor Gen. Hosp., Torrance, Calif., 1957-65; adminstr. Harbor UCLA Med. Ctr., 1966-71; acting regional dir. Los Angeles County Coastal Health Services Region, 1973; pres. San Pedro Peninsula Hosp., San Pedro, Calif., 1974-86; exec. dir. Los Angeles County/U. So. Calif. Med. Center, 1971-73; adminstr. Long Beach (Calif.) Hosp., 1965-66; asso. clin. prof. community medicine and pub. health, also emergency medicine U. So. Calif., 1968-78; instr. U. So. Calif. (Sch. Pub. Adminstrn.), 1968; preceptor hosp. adminstrn. UCLA Sch. Pub. Health, 1964—; chief exec. officer French Hosp. Med. Ctr. and Health Plan, 1986-87; dir. health care services McCormack & Farrow, 1987—. Lectr. in field, 1963—; cons. emergency health services HEW, 1970-73; chmn. com. disaster preparedness Hosp. Council So. Calif., 1966-72, sec., 1971—, pres., 1973; mem. Calif. Assembly Com. on Emergency Med. Services, 1970, Calif. Emergency Med. Adv. Com., 1972-75, Los Angeles County Commn. on Emergency Med. Services, 1975-83, Los Angeles Health Planning and Devel. Agy. Commn., 1980-83; bd. dirs. Blue Cross of So. Calif.; mem. hosp. relations com. Blue Cross of Calif.; mem. adv. com. on emergency health services Calif. Dept. Health, 1974-75; bd. dirs., mem. exec. com. Truck Ins. Exchange of Farmers Ins. Group, 1977-82; bd. dirs. Hosp. Council of So. Calif., 1966-76, 81-86, Health Resources Inst., 1985-86; chmn. Preferred Health Network, 1983-86 Mem. goals com., Torrance, 1968—; pres. Silver Spur Little League, Palos Verdes, 1969-70. With U.S. Army, 1946—48. Recipient Silver Knight and Gold Knight award Nat. Mgmt. Assn., 1970, 85, Walker Fellowship award, Calif. Hosp. Assn, 1976 Fellow Am. Coll. Health Care Execs. (life); mem. Am., Nat. mgmt. assns., Am. Hosp. Assn. (chmn. com. on community emergency health services 1973), Calif. Hosp. Assn. (chmn. com. emergency services 1965-70, trustee 1973-76, bd. dirs. Calif. Ins. Service Group 1980-82), County Suprs. Assn. Calif. (chmn. joint subcom. on emergency care 1970) Presbyn. (elder, trustee). Methodist. Personal E-mail: leslie.smith@cox.net.

**SMITH, LEWIS J.,** medical educator, researcher; b. N.Y.C., Oct. 17, 1948; m. Ellen J. Jarrow; children: Laura M.Lang, Deborah S. Wood. BA, CCNY, 1969; MD, U. Rochester, 1973. Diplomate in internal medicine and pulmonary medicine Am. Bd. Internal Medicine. Intern, resident Strong Meml. Hosp., Rochester, NY, 1973—76; pulmonary fellow Boston U., 1976—79; prof. medicine Northwestern U. Feinberg Sch. Medicine, Chgo., 1991—. Office: Northwestern Univ 750 N Lake Shore Dr Chicago IL 60611 Office Phone: 312-503-0501. Business E-Mail: ljsmith@northwestern.edu.

**SMITH, LEWIS MOTTER, JR.,** retired advertising and direct marketing executive; b. Kansas City, Mo., Nov. 4, 1932; s. Lewis Motter and Virginia (Smith) S.; m. Alice Allen, June 28, 1975; children: Katherine Allen, Patience Allen. Student, Kenyon Coll., 1951-53, Columbia U., 1956-58. Copywriter mail order divsn. Grolier Soc., Inc., N.Y.C., 1957-59; free lance copywriter Santa Fe, 1960-61; v.p. creative svcs. Grolier Enterprises Inc., N.Y.C., 1962-67; v.p. creative planning dir. Wunderman, Ricotta & Kline, Inc., N.Y.C., 1968-72; exec. v.p., creative dir., 1972-79; exec. v.p. Young & Rubicam Direct Mktg. Group, 1980; sr. v.p., dir. mktg. Book-of-the-Month Club, Inc., 1980-84, dir., 1981-84; exec. v.p., creative dir. SSC&B: Vos Direct Inc., N.Y.C., 1985-87; pres., dir. creative services Lintas: Direct Inc. (formerly SSC&B: Vos Direct Inc.), N.Y.C., 1987-89; pres. Lew Smith & Assocs., Inc., Hyde Park, NY, 1989—2001. Bd. dirs. Young Concert Artists, Inc., N.Y.C., 1966-67, Harlem Sch. Arts, 1967-68. Served with U.S. Army, 1953-56. Mem. Delta Phi. Episcopalian. Home: 215 East Dr Hurley NY 12443 E-mail: lmsjr@earthlink.net.

**SMITH, LINDA A.,** retired congresswoman; m. Vern Smith; children: Sheri, Robi. Office mgr.; former mem. Wash. State Ho. of Reps.; mem. Wash. State Senate; congresswoman Wash. 3rd Dist. U.S. House Reps., Washington, 1995-98; mem. resources com., small bus. com.; founder, dir. Shared Hope Internat., Vancouver, Wash., 1998—. Republican. Home: 10009 NW Ridgecrest Ave Vancouver WA 98685-5159 Office: Shared Hope Internat PO Box 65337 Vancouver WA 98665

**SMITH, LINDA SANTOS,** psychologist, medical educator; d. Amadeu and Linda Santos; m. James Todd Smith, May 19, 2001; children: Aidan James, Corbin Matthew. BA in Psychology, Adelphi U., Garden City, NY, 1995; MS in Clinical Psychology, Columbia U., NYC, 1999, PhD, 2003. Lic. psychologist Mass. Asst. dir. Comprehensive Family Evaluation Ctr Tufts New Eng. Med. Ctr., Boston, 2001—. Mem.: Mass. Assn. Guardians (bd. dirs. 2002—), Mass. Psychol. Assn., Am. Psychol. Assn. Office: Tufts New Eng Med Ctr Comprehensive Family Evaluation Ctr 750 Washington St Box 531 Boston MA 02111

**SMITH, LIZ (MARY ELIZABETH SMITH),** columnist, newscaster; b. Ft. Worth, Tex., Feb. 2, 1923; d. Sloan and Sarah Elizabeth (McCall) S. B.J., U. Tex., 1948. Editor Dell Publns., N.Y.C., 1950-53; assoc. producer CBS Radio, 1953-55, NBC-TV, 1955-59; assoc. Cholly Knickerbocker newspaper column, N.Y.C., 1959-64; film critic Cosmpolitan mag., 1966; columnist Chgo. Tribune-N.Y. Daily News Syndicate (now Tribune Media Services), 1976-91; TV commentator WNBC-TV, N.Y.C., 1978-91; commentator Fox-TV, N.Y.C., 1991—; columnist Newsday, L.A. Times Syndicate, 1991—, Family Circle mag., 1993—; freelance mag. writer; commentator Gossip Show E! Entertainment, 1993—; columnist N.Y. Post, N.Y.C., 1995—, 1995—. Author: The Mother Book, 1978, Natural Blonde, 2000, Munich at Your Door, 2003, Dishing, 2005. Home and Office: 160 E 38th St New York NY 10016-2651 *A Career in Journalism? Any career at all? I say learn to type. Read a lot. Keep on keeping on. Work is its own reward and success is loving your work. And remember, never give up. After the Middle Ages comes the Renaissance.*

**SMITH, L.J.,** professional football player; b. Highland Park, NJ, May 13, 1980; s. John, Kathy. BA in Labor Studies, Rutgers U., 2003. Tight end Phila. Eagles, 2003—. Named to All-Big-East Team, 2002—03. Achievements include ranking second among Tight Ends in Rutgers University history with 122 receptions for 1,458 yds. and 10 TDs. Office: Phila Eagles 1621 Franklin Mills Cir Philadelphia PA 19154 Office Phone: 215-632-4495.*

**SMITH, LLOYD,** musician; b. Cleve., Dec. 1, 1941; s. Thomas George Russell and Anita May (Speer) S.; m. Rheta R. Naylor, Mar. 30, 1967 (div. Nov. 1994); 1 child, Peter Eldon; m. Nancy R. Bean, June 6, 1995. MusB, Curtis Inst. Music, 1965. Tchr. Settlement Music Sch., 1970-72, 92—. Cellist Pitts. Symphony, 1965-67, Phila. Orch., 1967—, asst. prin. cello, 1988-2002, acting assoc. prin. cello, 2002-2003, ret., 2003; soloist Indpls. Symphony, 1958, 68, Garden State Philharm., 1964, Lansdowne Symphony, 1965, West Jersey Chamber Orch., 1991, Haverford-Bryn Mawr Symphony, 1992, The Phila. Orch., 1994, Ocean City Symphony, 2001, The Brn Athym Orch., 2003, The Everett Symphony, 2004; mem. Huntingdon Trio, 1974-93, Wister quartet, 1988—; composer Sonata for cello and piano, Op. 1, 1997, Quintet, Op. 2 for Saratoga Chamber Music Festival, 1998, duet for cello Four Hands, 1999, "You're Invited" for string quartet and violin, 1999, Suite for accordion and strings, Op. 4, 2000, String Quartet Op. 3, 2000, Full Circle for cello Op. 5, 2003, Ceremonial, Op. 6 for 8 cellos, 2004, Trio for cellos, Op. 7, 2004. Alumni rep. Curtis Inst. Music Bd. Trustees, chmn. Parents' Com., 1989-90; bd. dirs. Phila. Youth Orch., 1987-91, Cmty. Out Reach Partnership, 1988-90, Musical Fund Soc. Phila., 2005—. Recipient C. Hartman Kuhn award for outstanding achievement, Phila. Orch., 2002. Mem. Am. Soc. Ancient Instruments (asst. artistic dir. 1975-77, music dir. 1977-80), Curtis Inst. Music Nat. Alumni Assn. (treas., bd. dirs. 1989-90), 1807 & Friends (bd. dirs. 1994—). Home and Office: 5639 E Wister St Philadelphia PA 19144-1522 E-mail: frnd1807@verizon.net.

**SMITH, LLOYD HOLLINGSWORTH,** physician; b. Easley, SC, Mar. 27, 1924; s. Lloyd H. and Phyllis (Page) S.; m. Margaret Constance Avery, Feb. 27, 1954; children— Virginia Constance, Christopher Avery, Rebecca Anne, Charlotte Page, Elizabeth Hollingsworth, Jeffrey Hollingsworth. AB, Washington and Lee U., 1944, D.Sc., 1969; MD, Harvard, 1948. Intern, then resident Mass. Gen. Hosp., Boston, 1948-50, chief resident physician 1955-56; mem. Harvard Soc. Fellows, 1952-54; asst. prof. Harvard Soc. Fellows (Med. Sch.), 1956-63; vis. investigator Karolinska Inst., Stockholm, 1954-55, Oxford (Eng.) U., 1963-64; prof. medicine, chmn. dept. U. Calif. Med. Sch., San Francisco, 1964-85, assoc dean, 1985-2000. Mem. Pres.'s Sci. Adv. Com., 1970-73 Bd. overseers Harvard, 1974-80. Served to capt, M.C. AUS, 1950-52. Mem. Am. Acad. Arts and Scis., Am. Soc. Clin. Investigation (pres. 1969-70), Western Soc. Clin. Rsch. (pres. 1969-70), Assn. Am. Physicians (pres. 1974-75), Am. Fedn. Clin. Rsch. Achievements include special research genetic and metabolic diseases. Home: 309 Evergreen Dr Kentfield CA 94904-2709 Office: U Calif San Francisco Med Ctr San Francisco CA 94143-0001 E-mail: lloydhsmith@aol.com.

**SMITH, LOIS ARLENE,** actress, writer; b. Topeka, Kans., Nov. 3, 1930; d. William Oren and Carrie D. (Gottshalk) Humbert; m. Wesley Dale Smith, Nov. 5, 1948 (div. 1973); 1 child, Moon Elizabeth. Student, U. Wash., 1948-50; studied with Lee Strasberg, Actor's Studio, NYC, 1955—. Guest dir. Juilliard Sch., 1987; Clarence Ross fellow Am. Theater Wing at Eugene O'Neill Theater Ctr., 1983; mem. adv. panel program fund Pub. Broadcasting Service, 1981-82; hon. founder Harold Clurman Theatre Artists Fund, Ctr. for Arts, SUNY-Purchase, 1981 Author: play All There Is, 1982; debut in Time Out for Ginger, 1952; actress Broadway and off-Broadway prodns., 1952—; stage appearances include Theater of the Living Arts, Mark Taper Forum, Long Wharf Theater, Balt. Centerstage and Steppenwolf Theater Co.; appears on network and pub. TV programs; stage appearances include, The Young and the Beautiful, 1955, The Glass Menagerie, 1956, Blues for Mr. Charlie, 1964, Orpheus Descending, 1957, Miss Julie, 1966, Uncle Vanya, 1965, 69, The Iceman Cometh, 1973, Harry Outside, 1975, Hillbilly Women, 1979, 81, the Vienna Notes, 1985, The Stick Wife, April Snow, 1987, The Grapes of Wrath, 1988-89, 90, Measure for Measure, Beside Herself, 1989, Escape from Happiness, 1993, Buried Child, 1995-96, Defying Gravity, 1997, Impossible Marriage, 1998, Mrs. Warren's Profession, 1999, Give Me Your Answer, Do, 1999, Mother Courage, 2001, The Trip to Bountiful, 2005 (Lucille Lortel award, outstanding actress 2006, Outer Critics' Cir. award outstanding actress in a play 2006, OBIE award Village Voice 2006, Drama Desk award outstanding actress in a play, 2006, Kingsley-Evans award, 2006); films include East of Eden, 1955, Five Easy Pieces, 1970, Next Stop Greenwich Village, 1975, Resurrection, 1980, Green Card, 1990, Fried Green Tomatoes, 1991, Falling Down, 1993, How to Make an American Quilt, 1995, Dead Man Walking, 1995, Larger than Life, 1996, Twister, 1996, Tumbleweeds, 1998, Minority Report, 2002, The Laramie Project, 2002, Iron-Jawed Angels, 2004, Best Thief in the World, 2004, P.S., 2004, Sweet Land, 2005, Little Fugitive, 2006, Hollywoodland, 2006, Kill Shot, 2006. Named Best Supporting Actress for Five Easy Pieces, Nat. Soc. Film Critics, 1971; named to named to Filmdom's Famous Fives for East of Eden, Failm Daily mag., 1955; recipient Tony nominations, for Grapes of Wrath, 1990, Buried Child, 1996, Steppenwolf Ensemble Nat. Medal of Arts, 1998. Mem. SAG, AFTRA, Actors Equity Assn., Dramatists Guild, Actors Studio, Ensemble Studio Theater, Steppenwolf Theatre Co. Ensemble, Acad. Motion Picture Arts and Scis.

**SMITH, LOREN ALLAN,** federal judge; b. Chgo., Dec. 22, 1944; m. Catherine Yore; children: Loren Jr., Adam (dec.). BA in Polit. Sci., Northwestern U., 1966, JD, 1969; LLD (hon.), John Marshall Law Sch., 1995, Capital U. Law Sch., 1996, Campbell U., 1997. Bar: Ill. 1970, U.S. Ct. Mil. Appeals 1973, U.S. Ct. Appeals (D.C. cir.) 1974, U.S. Supreme Ct. 1974, U.S. Ct. Claims, 1985, U.S. Ct. Appeals (fed. cir.) 1986, U.S. Ct. Fed. Claims. Host nightly radio talk show What's Best for America?, 1972; cons. Sidney & Austin, Chgo., 1972-73; gen. atty. FCC, 1973; asst. to spl. counsel to the pres. The White House, Washington, 1973-74; spl. asst. US atty US Dept. Justice, Washington, 1974-75; chief counsel Reagan for Pres. campaigns, 1976, 80; prof. Del. Law Sch., 1976-84; dep. dir. Office Exec. Br. Mgmt. Presdl. Transition, 1980-81; chmn. Adminstrv. Conf. U.S., 1981-85; judge US Ct. Fed. Claims, Washington, 1985—2000, chief judge, 1986-2000, sr. judge, 2000—. Disting. lectr. Columbus Sch. Law U. Am., 1996—; Disting. adj. prof. law George Mason U. Sch. Law, 1998—; past mem. Pres.'s Cabinet Coun. on Legal Policy, Pres.' Cabinet Coun. on Mgmt. and Adminstrn.; chmn. Coun. Ind. Regulatory Agys.; served as disting. jurist in residence U. Denver; Allen chair U. Richmond Sch. Law, 1995, internat. elections observer Chile and Serbia; internat. speaker in field; internat. appearances on TV and radio. Co-author: Black America and Organized Labor: A Fair Deal?, 1979; contbr. articles to profl. jours. Adv. bd. mem. WETA Pub. Radio Cmty. Adv. Bd. Recipient Presdl. medal Cath. U. Am. Law Sch., 1993, Romanian medal of justice Romanian Min. of Justice, 1995, Ronald Reagan Pub. Svc. award Nat. Property Rights Conf., 1997. Mem. Bar Assn. D.C. (hon. mem., judicial honoree award 1997), Univ. Club (Washington, named club mem. of the yr. 1991, chmn. entertainment com., centennial com.). Republican. Jewish. Office: US Ct of Fed Claims 717 Madison Pl NW Suite 328 Washington DC 20005

**SMITH, LOUIS ROYCRAFT, JR.,** guidance and counseling educator, administrator; b. Demopolis, Ala., Apr. 12, 1945; s. Louis Roycraft and Trice (Dryer) S.; m. Carole Stewart Williams, Aug. 31, 1968; children: Louis Roycraft III, Cullen H., Jack D. BA, Birmingham-So. Coll., 1967; MA, U. N.C., 1969; student, U. Colo., 1971; PhD, U. Ala., Tuscaloosa, 1988. Tchr. Anniston (Ala.) High Sch., 1968-69; instr. Patrick Henry Jr. Coll., Monroeville, Ala., 1969-73; headmaster Sumter Acad., York, Ala., 1973-79; store owner The Market Place, Livingston, Ala., 1979-86; vis. prof. U. Montevallo, Ala., 1986-88; dir. Student Devel. Ctr., asst. prof. guidance-counseling Livingston U., 1989—. Cons. Macy Bio Prep. program U. Ala., Tuscaloosa, 1987—; workshop cons. Sumter County Bd. Edn., Livingston, 1990, Linden (Ala.) City Schs., 1991. Contbr. book revs. to profl. jours. Chmn. Livingston Sesquicentennial Celebration, 1984; mem. coun. Boy Scouts Am., Livingston, 1987—, Sumter County Heart Fund, Livingston, 1989—. Recipient Colonial Dames award, Birmingham, 1967; NSF grantee, 1971; Friends of the Archives scholar, 1987. Mem. AACD, Assn. for Counselor Edn. and Supervision, Ala. Assn. Counseling and Devel., So. Hist. Assn., Ala. Hist. Assn., Phi Delta Kappa (pres. 1990—), Ala. State Beta Club (coun. 1978-80). Presbyterian. Avocations: hunting, swimming, reading. Office: Livingston U Sta # 33 Livingston AL 35470 Home: 1064 N Montgomery St Apt B Starkville MS 39759-2287

**SMITH, LOVIE,** professional football coach; b. Gladewater, Tex., May 8, 1958; m. MaryAnne Smith; children: Mikal, Matthew, Miles. BA, Tulsa Univ., 1979. Head coach Big Sandy High School Football Team 1980, Cascia Hall Prep, Tulsa, 1981, Tulsa U., 1983—86, U. Wis., 1987, Ariz. State U., 1988—91, U. Ky, 1992, U. Tenn., 1993—94, Ohio State U., 1995; linebacker coach Tampa Bay Buccaneers, 1996—2001; defensive coord. St. Louis Rams, 2001—03; head coach Chgo. Bears, 2004—. Named Coach of the Yr., AP, 2005; recipient two-time All-American, three-time All-Missouri Conference. Office: Chicago Bears 1000 Football Dr Lake Forest IL 60045*

**SMITH, LUELLA MARGARET,** special education educator; b. Greensburg, Pa., Nov. 8, 1947; d. William Elmer Peace and LaRue (Matson); m. Edwin Stewart Smith, Oct. 17, 1970; children: Laura LaRue Zendarski, William Daniel. BS, Indiana U. of Pa., 1990; MEd, Gannon U., Erie, Pa., 2000. Cert. prin. Spl. edn. tchr. Blairsville-Saltsburg Sch. Dist., Blairsville, Pa., 1990—. Mem.: ASCD (assoc.), Coun. for Exceptional Children (assoc.). Democrat-Npl. Lutheran. Avocations: golf, scrapbooks. Home: 4416 Rte 819 Avonmore PA 15618 Personal E-mail: edwlue@kiski.net.

**SMITH, MABEL HARGIS,** retired secondary school educator, musician; b. Ruby, La., Mar. 29, 1917; d. Ildephonso Albinos Hargis and Stella Gertrude Baker; m. Thomas Leonard Smith, Dec. 29, 1950; 1 child, Susan Claire Smith McLaughlin. BA, La. Coll., 1938; MusM, Northwestern U., 1952. Tchr. Tioga H.S., La., 1938—75; pianist-organist children's choir Tioga First

Bapt. Ch., Tioga, 1941—2002. Named Sr. Adult of Yr., First Bapt. Ch., 1989, Disting. Alumna, La. Coll., 1977; named one of Women of Century, Daily Town Talk, Alexandria, La., 1999; recipient Cmty. Svc. award, Matinee Music Club, 1953—54, Recognition for musical contbns., Curtis T. Hines Masonic Lodge, 1997. Mem.: La. Music Educators (Hall of Fame 1999), Music Educator's Nat. Conf., Delta Omicron Internat., Delta Kappa Gamma. Baptist. Avocations: sewing, cooking, reading, gardening. Home: 27 Purser Pineville LA 71360

**SMITH, DAME MAGGIE (MARGARET NATALIE SMITH CROSS),** actress; b. Ilford, Eng., Dec. 28, 1934; d. Nathaniel and Margaret Hutton (Little) S.; m. Robert Stephens, 1967 (div. 1974), 2 children; m. Beverley Cross, 1974 (dec. 1998). Grad., Oxford High Sch. Girls; D.Litt. (hon.), St. Andrews, 1971; DLitt (hon.), Oxford U., 1994. Asst. stage mgr., actor Oxford Playhouse, 1951—53. Stage and film actress, 1952—, stage appearances include Twelfth Night, 1952, New Faces, debut N.Y.C. 1956, Share My Lettuce, 1957, The Stepmother, 1958, Rhinoceros, 1960, Strip the Willow, 1960, The Rehearsal, 1961, The Private Ear and the Public Eye, 1962 (Evening Standard award for best actress, 1962), Mary, Mary, 1963 (Variety Club award named actress of yr., 1963), Othello, 1964, Hay Fever, 1964, 1977, Master Builder, 1964, Much Ado About Nothing, 1965, 1980, Miss Julie, 1965, Black Comedy, 1965, Hedda Gabbler, 1970 (Evening Standard award, 1970), Three Sisters, 1970, 1976, Private Lives, 1972, 1974 (Variety Club award, 1972), 1978, Cleopatra, 1976, Way of the World, 1976, 1984—85 (Evening Standard award for best actress, 1984), A Midsummer Night's Dream, 1977, Richard III, 1977, As You Like It, 1977, Macbeth, 1978, Night and Day, 1979—80, Virginia, 1980 (Evening Standard award for best actress, 1982), Interpreters, 1985—86, Lettice and Lovage, 1987—88 (Tony Award for best actress, 1990), 1990, The Importance of Being Earnest, 1993, Three Tall Women, 1994—95 (Evening Standard award for best actress, 1994, Variety Club award for best actress, 1994), Talking Heads, 2004, Bed Among the Lentils, 1996, A Delicate Balance, 1997—98, Lady in the Van, 1999—2000, Breath of Life, 2002—03, and several others, appearances at Old Vic, 1959—60, charter mem. Royal Nat. Theatre, London, 1963—; actor: (films) Child in the House, 1956, Nowhere to Go, 1958, Go to Blazes, 1962, The VIPs, 1963, The Pumpkin Eater, 1964, Young Cassidy, 1965, Othello, 1965, The Honey Pot, 1967, Oh What a Lovely War, 1968, Hot Millions, 1968, The Prime of Miss Jean Brodie, 1969 (Brit. Acad. of Film & TV Arts for best actress, 1969, Film Critic's Guild for best actress, 1969, Acad. award for best actress, 1970, Variety Club for film actress of yr., 1988), Travels with My Aunt, 1973, Love and Pain and the Whole Damn Thing, 1973, Murder by Death, 1976, Death on the Nile, 1978, California Suite, 1978 (Golden Globe for best supporting actress, 1979, Acad. award for best supporting actress, 1979), Quartet, 1981 (Evening Standard award for best actress, 1981), Clash of the Titans, 1981, Evil under the Sun, 1981, Better Late Than Never, 1982, The Missionary, 1983, A Private Function, 1984 (Brit. Acad. of Film & TV Arts for best actress, 1984), A Room with a View, 1986 (Brit. Acad. of Film & TV Arts for best supporting actress, 1986, Golden Globe for best supporting actress, 1986), The Lonely Passion of Judith Hearn, 1988 (Brit. Acad. of Film & TV Arts for best actress, 1989), Paris by Night, 1988, Hook, 1991, Sister Act, 1992, The Secret Garden, 1993, Sister Act 2: Back in the Habit, 1993, Richard III, 1995, The First Wives Club, 1996, Washington Square, 1997, Tea with Mussolini, 1999 (Brit. Acad. of Film & TV Arts for best supporting actress, 2000), The Last September, 2000, Harry Potter and the Sorcerer's Stone, 2001 (Golden Satelite (Internat. Press Assn.) for best supporting actress, 2002), Gosford Park, 2001 (NY Critics Online for best supporting actress, 2002, SAG award for best ensemble in a motion picture, 2002), Divine Secrets of Ya-Ya Sisterhood, 2002, Harry Potter and the Chamber of Secrets, 2002, Harry Potter and the Prisoner of Azkaban, 2004, Ladies in Lavender, 2004, Harry Potter and the Goblet of Fire, 2005, Keeping Mum, 2005; (TV films) Night of the Plague, 1957, Boy Meets Girl, 1957, The Widower, 1958, The Curious Savage, 1958, Sunday Out of Season, 1958, A Phoenix Too Frequent, 1959, For Services Rendered, 1959, Guardian Angel, 1960, The Savages, 1961, Hay Fever, 1965, Penelope, 1965, Much Ado About Nothing, 1967, Home and Beauty, 1967, On Approval, 1968, Man and Superman, 1968, The Merchant of Venice, 1972, The Millionairess, 1972, Mrs. Silly, 1983, Lily in Love, 1983, Bed Among the Lentils, 1988 (Brit. Acad. of Film & TV Arts for best actress, 1987, Baniff (Can.) for best actress, 1987), Memento Mori, 1992, Suddenly Last Summer, 1993, Curtain Call, 1998, David Copperfield, 1999, All the King's Men, 1999, My House in Umbria, 2003 (Emmy award for best actress miniseries or movie, 2003);, performer albums and tapes. Recipient Best Film Actress award Soc. Film and TV Arts U.K., 1968, Best Actress LA Critics, 1970, Taomina Gold award, 1985, Hanbury Shakespeare prize, FVS Found. 1991, Lifetime Achievement award, Brit. Acad. of Film & TV Arts, 1992, William Shakespeare award for Classical Theatre, Wahington, DC's Shakespeare Theatre, 1999; decorated Commdr. British Empire, 1970, Dame of the British Empire, 1990; named to Theater Hall of Fame, 1994. Fellow: British Film Inst., British Acad. Film & Television Arts. Office: 41 Warbeck Rd London W12 8NS England

**SMITH, M(AHLON) BREWSTER,** retired psychologist, educator; b. Syracuse, NY, June 26, 1919; s. Mahlon Ellwood and Blanche Alice (Hinman) S.; m. Jean Dresden Schwartz, June 1942 (div. 1945); m. Deborah Anderson, June, 1947; children: Joshua H., T. Daniel, Rebecca M., J. Torquil. Student, Reed Coll., Portland, Oreg., 1935- 38; AB, Stanford U., 1939, AM, 1940; PhD, Harvard U., 1947. Jr. analyst Office Coordinator of Info., U.S. Govt., 1941; Rantoul scholar Harvard U., 1940-41, Social Sci. Research Council fellow, 1946-47, asst. prof. social psychology, dept. social rels., 1947-49; prof. psychology, chmn. dept. Vassar Coll., 1949-52; staff Social Sci. Rsch. Coun., 1952-56; prof. psychology NYU, 1956-59, U. Calif. at Berkeley, 1959-68, dir. Inst. Human Devel., 1965-68; prof., chmn. dept. psychology U. Chgo., 1968-70; prof. psychology U. Calif. at Santa Cruz, 1970-88, prof. emeritus, 1988—, vice chancellor social scis., 1970-75, ret., 1988. Fellow Ctr. Advanced Studies Behavioral Scis., 1964-65, v.p. Joint Commn. Mental Illness and Health, 1955-61. Author: Social Psychology and Human Values, 1969, Humanizing Social Psychology, 1974, Values, Self and Society, 1991, For a Significant Social Psychology, 2003; co-author: The American Soldier, vol. 2, 1949, Opinions and Personality, 1956; editor: Jour. Social Issues, 1951-55, Jour. Abnormal Soc. Psychology, 1956-61; contbr. articles to profl. jours. Rsch. officer Info. and Edn. divsn. War Dept., 1943-46; rsch. assoc. spl. com. on soldier attitudes Social Sci. Rsch. Coun. 1946. Maj. AUS, 1942-46 Decorated Bronze Star medal; NIMH fellow, 1954-55, NEH fellow, 1975-76; Belding scholar Found. for Child Devel., 1982-83; Gold medal award Am. Psychol. Found., 1992 Fellow AAAS, APA (pres. 1978, Disting. Contbn. to Pub. Interest award 1988, Henry A. Murray award 1993); mem. Soc. Psychol. Study Social Issues (pres. 1959, Kurt Lewin Meml. award 1986, Presdl. citation 2004), Western Psychol. Assn. (pres. 1986, Lifetime Contbn. award 1996), Psychologists for Social Responsibility (pres. 1987-90), Internat. Soc. Polit. Psychology (Harold Lasswell award 1993), Internat. Assn. Applied Psychology (pres. divsn. polit. psychology 1994-98), Soc. Peace, Conflict and Violence (Lifetime Contbn. to Peace Psychology award 1999), Cosmos Club (Washington), Phi Beta Kappa, Sigma Xi. Democrat. Home: 316 Escalona Dr Santa Cruz CA 95060 Business E-Mail: brsmith@ucsc.edu.

**SMITH, MALCOLM BARRY ESTES,** philosopher, educator, lawyer; b. Houston, Oct. 24, 1939; s. Fairleigh Estes and Norna Barry (McNab) S.; m. Patricia Sweetser; children: Malcolm, Eric. BA, Va. Mil. Inst., 1961; PhD, Cornell U., 1969; JD, U. Calif., Berkeley, 1994. BarL Mass. 1985, U.S. Supreme Ct. 1992. Instr. philosophy Smith Coll., Northampton, Mass., 1967-69, asst. prof. philosophy, 1969-74, assoc. prof., 1974-79, prof., 1979—2002, prof. emeritus, 2002—. Served to capt. USAR, 1964-66. Mem. Mass. Bar Assn., Am. Philos. Assn. Home: 9 Park St Northampton MA 01062-1236 Office: Smith Coll Dept Philosophy PO Box 839 Northampton MA 01061-0839 Office Phone: 413-586-0679. Business E-Mail: mbsmith@smith.edu.

**SMITH, MALCOLM BERNARD,** investment company executive; b. Lynn, Mass., May 27, 1923; s. Philip and Ida (Zenis) S.; m. Betty Booth, June 20, 1948; children: Eric, Daniel. BA summa cum laude, Dartmouth Coll., 1944;

MA in Econs., Harvard U., 1948; degree (hon.), New Sch. Social Rsch., 1995. Sec. Gen. Am. Investors Co., N.Y.C., 1956-57, treas., 1957-59, v.p., 1958-61, pres., 1961-89, vice chmn., 1989-97; sr. cons., 1997—. Chmn. fin. com. N.Y. Found., 1973—82, treas., 1979—82, trustee, 1973—89; chmn. N.Y. Found., 1982—85; chmn. New Sch. for Social Rsch., N.Y.C., 1985—95, trustee, 1982—, treas., 1982—84, chmn. ednl. policy com., 1984—85, chmn. exec. com., 1985—95; mem. investment com. Phi Beta Kappa Found., 1987—96; bd. dirs. Learning Smith, Inc., 1992—93, Cybersmith, Inc., 1994—97; mem. investment com. Fedn. Jewish Philanthropies, NY, 1975—96; bd. dirs. Human Rights Watch, 1993—2001, emeritus, 2001—; trustee John Simon Guggenheim Meml. Found., 1982—95, chmn. fin. com., 1975—95; mng. trustee Permanent Fund of MLA, 1987—. With U.S. Army, 1943—46. Mem. AAAS (chmn. investment and fin. com. 1975—), Investment Co. Inst. (bd. govs. 1987-95), Assn. Publicly Traded Investment Funds (bd. dirs. 1970-87, chmn. 1971-79, Coun. on Fgn. Rels.), N.Y. Soc. Security Analysts, Harvard Club (bd. mgrs. 1984-86), N.Y.c. (treas., bd. mgrs. 1999-2003), Phi Beta Kappa Fellows (adv. com. 1984-93, bd. dirs. 1993—), Phi Beta Kappa. Home: PO Box 358 Pound Ridge NY 10576-0358 Office: 1150 Park Ave New York NY 10128-1244

**SMITH, MALCOLM SOMMERVILLE,** bass; b. Rockville Centre, N.Y., June 22, 1933; s. Carlton Newell and Margaret (Sommerville) S.; m. Margaret Yauger, Oct. 4, 1975. B.Music Edn., Oberlin Coll., 1957, B.Mus., 1960; MA in Ednl. Adminstrn, Columbia Tchrs. Coll., 1958; student, Ind. U. Sch. Music, 1960-62. Dir. choral music Ramapo Regional H.S., Wyckoff, NJ, 1958—60. Mem. artist faculty U. So. Maine, 2004—06. Bass: Lyric Opera, bass soloist: Russian tour, Robert Shaw Choral, 1962, leading bass N.Y.C. Opera, 1965—70, Deutsche Oper Am Rhein, Dusseldorf, Germany, 1971—, Vienna State Opea, 1973—74, 86 Met. Opera, Japan tour, 1975, Met. Opera, N.Y.C., 1975—77, Paris Opera, 1978, Barcelona Opera, 1978, Sao Paulo, Brazil, 1978, Mexico City, 1979, 80, Berlin Opera, 1979, 80, Montreal Symphony, 1979, 80, 81, 82, Hamburg Opera, 1981, Koln Opera, 1980, Stuttgart Opera, 1980, Frankfurt Opera, 1980, Rome Opera, 1980, Trieste (Italy) Opera, 1981, Berlin Staatsoper, 1982, 85, Lyric Opera Phila., 1982, L.A. Philharm. at Hollywood Bowl, 1984, Mannheim Opera, Germany, 1986, Turin Opera, Italy, 1986, 88, Bordeaux, France, 1987, Dresden Opera, Germany, 1987, Staats Opera Berlin Japan tour, 1987, Polish TV, 1989, Oslo Opera, 1987, Paris Radio, 1988-89, Orange Festival, France, 1988, Penderecki Festival, Krakow, Poland, 1988, maj. soloist Schleswig Holstein Festival, Germany, 1989, Krakow Philharmonic, Poland, 1988, Maggio Musicale, Florence, Italy, 1988, Boston Symphony, Minn., Cin., Houston, Utah, Seattle, Chgo., Phila., Balt. Symphony, 1993, Mex. Nat. Symphony, 1993, nat. symphonies, also Cin. Summer Opera, Central City (Colo.), Summer Opera, Festival of Two Worlds, Spoleto, Italy, Saratoga Festival, 1985, debut La Scala, Milan, Italy, 1982, Salzburg Festival, 1986, Athens Festival, 1987, Bordeaux (France) Opera, 1987, Ft. Worth Opera, 1988, Orange Festival, France, 1988, Staatsoper Munich, 1990, Bastille Opera, Paris, 1991, Heidelberg Summer Festival, 1991, 92, Brussels Opera, 1992, 93, 94, 97, Opera Nice, France, 1992, Opera Montpelier, France, 1992, Cin. Opera, 1994, 2000, Dusseldorf Opera, 1994, Japan tour, 1994, Bregenz (Austria) Festival, 1996, Honolulu Opera, 1996, 98, Balt. Opera, 1996, Prague Autumn Festival, 1997, Cin. Opera, 1998, 2000, Grand Rapids Opera, 2000, Dusseldorf Opera, 2001, 2002, Portland Opera, 2001, Portland Symphony, 2002, recorded War and Peace, 1986, Penderecki Requiem, 1990, Aspen Music Festival, 1997; musician: Portland Symphony Orch., 2002—05, Schwerin Opera Festival, 2003, Opera Orch. NY, 2005, Springfield Festival, 2006, Spoleto Festival, 2006, Port Opera, 2006. Served with AUS, 1954-56. Recipient Kämmersanger title Dusseldorf (Germany) Opera, 1996. Congregationalist. Office: care Thea Dispeker Artists Rep 59 E 54th St New York NY 10022-4211 *Hard work and a sense of humor.*

**SMITH, MARCIA K.,** government agency administrator; b. Yakima, Wash., Dec. 7, 1953; d. Richard C. Stewart and Joyce M. Gardner; m. Jerry D. Smith, Mar. 18, 2001; children: Brittany M. Palmer, Benjamin T., Alysia D. AAS, Spokane C.C., Wash., 1974. Author: (novel) The Goddess Speaks, (poetry) My Son (Golden Poets award Writers Guild, 1992, 1993, 1994). Area rep. Coun. Magical Arts, Austin, Tex., 1992—2003; denom. svc. leader US Army, Fort Hood, Tex., 1996—98. Sgt. US Army, 1974—80. Mem.: ACLU. Libertarian. Achievements include first to 1st Druid High Priestess of US Mil.'s 1st officially sanctioned and federally protected Pagan Open Circle. Avocations: writing, art. Personal E-mail: silth_elentari@yahoo.com.

**SMITH, MARGARET ANN,** retired art educator; b. Floyd, Va., May 27, 1930; d. Floyd Patterson and Annie Mallie (William) Smith. BA in Art Edn., Radford Coll., 1951; M in Elem. Edn., U. Va., 1973. Cert. tchg. State of Va. Counselor Camp Carysbrook, Riner, Va., 1950—51; tchr. Marion (Va.) HS, 1951—52, Floyd (Va.) Elem. Sch., 1952—53; clerk Floyd Municipal Bldg., 1953—54; tchr. Check (Va.) HS, 1954—56, Patrick Henry Elem. Sch., Martinsville, Va., 1956—59, Draid Hills Sch., Martinsville, 1958—80, Albert Harris Mid. Sch., Martinsville, 1980—90; ret., 1990. Com. mem. State of Va., Lang. Art Dept., Richmond, Va., 1978—79. Exhibitions include Chains of Modern Man, 1973 (1st prize junk sculpture, 1973), Alaskan Triangle, 1982 (2d prize, 1982), In The Manner of Matisse, 1988. Named Vol. of Month, Piedmont Arts Assn.; recipient War Bond Poster Contest award, County of Floyd, Va., 1942, Purchase award, Foot of Hills Show, 1993, Pres. award, Lynwood Artists Show, 1994, Purchase award, Expressions Show, 2002. Mem.: DAR (treas. 2000—, former regent, vice regent), Martinsville Edn. Assn. (v.p., chmn. polit. action com.), Va. Edn. Assn. (chmn. dist. 7 polit. action com., bd. of dir.), Nat. Edn. Assn., Floyd Hist. Soc. (v.p. 2004—), Jacksonville Art and Design Ctr. (bowtouth Ctr. for Visual Design, Danville Fine Arts Mus., Piedmont Arts Assn. (bd. of dirs. sec. 1973—76, 1st prize 1973, 2d prize 1982, Hon. Mention 1988, award 2002, Purchase award 2003, Hon. Mention 1996, Pres.' award 1996, Purchase award 2001), Docent Guild of Piedmonts Arts Assn. (program com. 2005), Lynwood Artists of Piedmont Arts Assn., Va. Mus. of Fine Arts, Colonial Dames of 17th Century, Weavers Exchange (v.p.), United Daughters of the Confederacy (sec. 1998—2005), Delta Kappa Gamma (v.p. 1973). Democrat. Presbyterian. Avocations: weaving, watercolor painting, silver jewelry fabrication.

**SMITH, MARGARET TAYLOR,** volunteer; b. Roanoke Rapids, N.C., May 31, 1925; d. George Napoleon and Sarah Luella (Waller) T.; m. Sidney William Smith Jr., Aug. 15, 1947; children: Sarah Smith, Sidney William Smith III, Susan Smith, Amy Smith. BA in Sociology, Duke U., 1947. Chair emeritus bd. trustees Kresge Found., Troy, Mich., 1985—; chmn. Trinity Bd. Visitors NC 1988-98; chair emeritus. Chmn. bd. visitors Wayne State U. Med. Sch., 1993; bd. dirs., mem. exec. com. Detroit Med. Ctr.; mem. bd. govs. Detroit Med. Ctr. Recipient the Merrill-Palmer award Wayne State U., Detroit, 1987, Zimmerman award Gtr. Detroit Health Coun., Athena award C. of C., 1998, Women of Achievement award Mich. Women's Fedn., 1999, disting. svc. award Wayne State U., 1999; named disting. alumna award Duke U. Mem. The Village Club, Internat. Women's Forum, Pi Beta Phi, Phi Beta Kappa. Methodist. E-mail: sidmyth@aol.com.

**SMITH, MARIE EDMONDS,** real estate agent, property manager; b. Quapaw, Okla., Oct. 5, 1927; d. Thomas Joseph and Maud Ethel Edmonds; m. Robert Lee Smith, Aug. 14, 1966 (dec. 1983). Grad. vocat. nurse, Hoag Hosp., Costa Mesa, Calif., 1953; BA, Vanguard U., 1955; MS, U. Alaska, 1963. Lic. vocat. nurse, Calif.; cert. sci. tchr., Alaska. Nurse Calif. Dept. Nurses, Costa Mesa, 1952-60; tchr. Alaska Dept. Edn., Aniak and Anchorage, 1955-60; tchr. sci. Garden Grove (Calif.) Sch. Dist., 1960-87; property mgr. Huntington Beach, Calif., 1970—; agent Sterling Realtors, Huntington Beach, 1988—. Author: Ocean Biology, 1969. Bd. dirs., tchr. Newport Mesa Christian Ctr., Costa Mesa, 1983-2001; com. chmn. Garden Grove Unified Sch. Dist. PTA, 1977. NSF grantee, 1960-62. Mem. AAUW, Vanguard U. Alumnae Assn. Republican. Avocations: skin diving, travel. Home: 83ll Reilly Dr Huntington Beach CA 92646 Office: L8l53 Brookhurst St Fountain Valley CA 92708

**SMITH, MARIE F.,** lobbyist, small business owner, writer, retirement association executive; b. East St. Louis, Ill., Mar. 12, 1939; d. David and Christina Ford; m. Richard Stanley Smith, Dec. 13, 1986; stepchildren: Jeffrey, Reginald, Laurie Debrotz. BA, Fisk U., 1961. Dir. manpower mgmt. and orgn. planning Social Security Adminstrn.; realtor assoc., 1987—; small bus. owner, 1987—; freelance writer, 1987—; commr. Status of Women; chair Nat. Legis. Coun. AARP, Washington, spokesperson Women's Initiative Program, mem. audit and fin. com., 2000—02, mem. exec. dir. search com., 2000—02, treas. found. bd. dirs., 2000—02, pres. elect, 2002—04, pres., 2004—. Active Interfaith Vol. Caregivers; sec. bd. dirs. Maui Adult Day Care Ctr.; pres. bd. dirs. Maui Vol. Ctr. Named one of Am.'s 100 most influential African Am. leaders, Ebony mag., Most Influential Black Americans, 2006; recipient Woman of Excellence award, Commn. on the Status of Women, Circle of Women award, County Commn. on the Status of Women. Mem.: Zonta Internat., Nat. Assn. Ret. Fed. Employees (pres.), African Am. Heritage Found. Maui (pres.). Avocations: writing, travel, golf. Office: AARP 601 E St NW Rm A10-331 Washington DC 20049 E-mail: mfsmith@aarp.org.*

**SMITH, MARION PAFFORD,** retired avionics company executive; b. Waycross, Ga., Dec. 12, 1925; s. Rossa Elbert and Lillian Solee (Pafford) S.; m. Esther Pat Davis, Nov. 23, 1952; children: Bryan P., Danton D., Patricia Anne. Student, Okla. State U., 1944, Yale U., 1945; BS in EE, La. State U., 1949; postgrad., U. So. Fla., 1966-70. Engr. Bell Telephone Co., Baton Rouge, 1949-51; mgr. engring. Vitro Labs., Silver Spring, Md., 1952-57; design engring. mgr. dept. design and constrn. flight hand contrs. Space Shuttle and Space Sta. Honeywell Avionics Div., Clearwater, Fla., 1957-98. Vice chmn., bd. dirs. First Union, Largo, Fla., 1985-93; cons. U.S. Army Mgmt. Engring. Tng. Agy., 1975-79; U.S. Del. Internat. Elec. Tech. Commn., 1965-85, chmn. chief U.S. tech. adviser com. on reliability and maintainability, 1975-85, v.p., exec. com. U.S. nat. com., 1975-84; U.S. del. NATO Quality Conf., 1973; mem. White House Summit Conf. on Inflation, 1975; del. White House Conf. on Handicapped, 1977; mem. nat. adv. coun. on devel. disabilities HEW, 1974-78, Fla. Devel. Disabilities Coun., 1974-78; pres. Fla. Advocacy Ctr. for Persons with Disabilities, Inc., 1997-2000; commr. State of Fla. Occupl. Access Commn., 2000-2002; mem. devel. coun. Morton Plant Hosp., Clearwater, 1971-74. 1st lt. Signal Corps, AUS, 1944-45, 51-52. Served to 1st lt. Signal Corps AUS, 1944-45, 51-52. Recipient McDonald award Fla. Rehab. Assn., 1968; Bilgore award Citizen of Year Clearwater, Fla., 1969; Outstanding Service award Am. Soc. Quality Control, 1968-69; United Comml. Travelers award Most Outstanding Service Retarded Fla., 1970; named Engr. of Year Fla. W. Coast, 1970; Service to Mankind award Sertoma Clubs, 1977 Fellow IEEE (dir., Nat. Reliability award 1979); mem. Assn. Retarded Citizens USA (pres. 1973-75, nat. govt. affairs chmn. 1975-83), Am. Assn. Mental Deficiency, Nat. Symposium Reliability Quality Control (gen. chmn.), Sigma Chi. Presbyterian elder. Club: Kiwanis (Marion P. Smith award established in his honor). Home: 1884 Oakdale Ln N Clearwater FL 33764-6441 Personal E-mail: m.paffordmps2@verizon.net. *True turning points in life are sometimes difficult to recognize, but for those who have become parents of a handicapped child, particularly a mentally retarded child, then that turning point is easy to recognize. After the difficult period of adjustment, one becomes aware of a realization that all persons have human dignity and worth and can make a contribution to humanity and to society.*

**SMITH, MARK ANTHONY,** biochemist, educator; b. Leicester, Eng., Aug. 15, 1965; came to U.S., 1992; s. John and Rita Joyce (Haywood) S. BSc with honors, Durham (U.K.) U.. 1986; PhD, Nottingham (U.K.) U., 1990. Postdoctoral biochemist Sandoz Forschungsinstitut, Vienna, 1990-91, Karl Landsteiner rsch. fellow, 1991-92; rsch. assoc. Case Western Res. U., Cleve., 1992-94, instr. in biochemistry, 1994-95, asst. prof., 1995—99, assoc. prof., 1999—2002, prof., 2002—. Cons. StressGen Biotechs. Corp., Victoria, B.C., 1999, Panacea Pharms., Potomac, 2000—, Prion Devel. Labs., Vernon Hills, 2001—, Voyager Pharmacies, Raleigh, NC, 2001—; chief exec. cons. World Events Forum, Chgo., 2001—. Editor Biomed. Jour., 1994-95; guest editor Molecular Chemistry Neuropathology; mem. editl. bd. Internat. Jour. Exptl. Pathology; contbr. articles to profl. jours.; rsch. findings presented on WQHS-TV 61 sta. Dalland fellow Am. Philos. Soc., 1995; recipient Ruth Salta Investigator award, 1995, Young Scientist Lectr. award Internat. Soc. Neurochem., Nathan Shock New Investigator award Gerontol. Soc. Am. Mem. AAAS, Am. Assn. Neuropathology, Microscopic Soc. Northeast Ohio (pres. elect 1997—), N.Y. Acad. Scis., Internat. Soc. Neurochemistry. Avocations: golf, soccer, music, current affairs. Office: Case Western Res U Inst Pathology 2085 Adelbert Rd Cleveland OH 44106-2622 Home: 7416 Chagrin Rd Chagrin Falls OH 44023-4435

**SMITH, MARK ARTHUR,** information scientist, educator; s. Marvin (Mark) Ira and Cora S. Smith. AAS in Music, Nassau CC, 1977; MusB in Music Edn., SUNY, Fredonia, 1980; MS in Edn., Elmira Coll., Fredonia, 1987; MLS, U. Buffalo, 1992. Cert. music edn. tchr. N.Y., 1980, sch. libr. media specialist N.Y. Dept. Edn., 1992. Vocal music tchr. Canisteo Ctrl. Sch., NY, 1981—91; info. sys. libr. NY State Coll. Ceramics, Alfred U., 1994—; mem. adv. com. info. techs. South Ctrl. Rsch. Coun., 2002—. Provost adv. com., liaiason SUNY Librs., Albany, 1998—; pres. State Univ. of N.Y. Librs. Assn., 1999—2000. Musician (choral condr.): Hornell Cmty. Choir; contbr. articles to profl. jours. Actor, dir. Hornell Rotary Club, NY, 1992; dir. Orpheus Chorale Hornell; bd. dirs. Hornell Area Arts Coun., NY, 2004—06. Recipient Chancellors Award for Excellence in Librarianship, SUNY, 2004. Mem.: ALA, South Ctrl. Rsch. Libr. Coun. (chair adv. com. on info. techs. 2005), Libr. and Info. Tech. Assn., Assn. of Coll. and Rsch. Libr. Am. Choral Dir. Assn., SUNY Librs. Assn., Phi Beta Mu, Phi Kappa Phi. Avocations: music performance, theatrical performance, choral directing. Office: NYS Coll of Ceramics Alfred Univ 2 Pine St Alfred NY 14802 Office Phone: 607-871-2942. Personal E-mail: mark@opus57.com. Business E-Mail: msmith@alfred.edu.

**SMITH, MARK CHRISTOPHER,** lawyer; b. Denver, Colo., Sept. 21, 1962; s. Frederick Trussel and Joon Eleanor Smith. BA, Colo. State U., 1984; JD, U. Denver, 1994. Atty Smith & Assoc., Greenwood Village, Colo. Office: Smith & Assoc 7400 East Orchard Rd Ste 160 Englewood CO 80111

**SMITH, MARK LEE,** architect; b. L.A., Nov. 16, 1957; s. Selma (Moidel) Smith. BA in History of Architecture, UCLA, 1978, MA in Architecture, 1980. Registered architect Calif., Nev., Oreg., Wash., Tenn., Colo., N.Y., Ohio. Designer, drafter John B. Ferguson and Assocs., L.A., 1976-83, architect, 1983; pvt. practice architecture L.A., 1984—. Mem. L.A. County Archtl. Evaluation Bd.. 1990-2004; spkr. Western Pool and Spa Show, 1997—2001. Author: A Bridge Across the Continents, 2003; essay columnist AIA/SFV monthly, 1997—; founding editor ARCHimpressions.org mag., 2003-2005, When Stones Could Speak, 2005; contbr. articles to profl. jours Bd. govs. UCLA John Wooden Ctr., 1978-80; judge Bank Am. Achievement Awards, 1998—2000, chair, 1999-2000. Regents scholar, U. Calif., Berkeley, UCLA, 1975-78; UCLA Grad. Sch. Architecture Rsch. fellow, 1979-80. Mem. AIA (treas. San Fernando Valley chpt. 1986, bd. dirs. 1995—, v.p. 1987, pres. 1988, Design award 1988, 89, 90, 91, 99, chmn. Design awards 1994, bd. dirs. Calif. coun. 1989-94, v.p. 1991-94, chmn. continuing edn. 1991-93, chmn. 1992 Office.), Phi Beta Kappa. Office: 18340 Ventura Blvd Ste 225 Tarzana CA 91356-4278

**SMITH, MARK P.,** foundation administrator; b. Charleston, W. Va., July 27, 1949; s. Bernard Henry and Josephine S. (Polan) Smith; m. Jane Stephens, May 6, 1978; children: Stephen Noble, Allison Baxter. BA, Princeton U., 1971; JD, Yale U., 1978. Bar: admitted to practice. Assoc. to exec. dir. ABA, Chgo., 1996-79 v.p. Ctr. Am. and Internat. Law, Richardson, Tex., 1989—; dir. Inst. for Transnational Arbitration, 1993—98, Mcpl. Legal Studies Ctr., 1998—; sec. W. Va. Legal Svc. Plan, Inc., Charleston, 1987—88. Pres. bd. dirs. Kanawha County Coalition for Homeless, 1986—87; pres. Vol. Ctr. Collin County, 2001—03; mem. bd. Vol. Ctr. North Tex., 2001—; chair Dallas Com. for Internat.

Visitors, 2003—. Mem.: Nat. Assn. Bar Execs. (chmn. continuing ed. com. 1981—82, mem. exec. com. 1984—86), Saigling Elem. Sch. PTA (pres. 1991—92). Office: Ctr Am and Internat Law PO Box 799030 Richardson TX 75379-9030

SMITH, MARK W., management consultant; BA in Acctg., Hillsdale Coll., Mich. CPA AICPA. Mgr. Arthur Andersen; various fin. positions Ryder Sys., Inc., Miami; from v.p. fin. to CFO Spherion Corp., Ft. Lauderdale, Fla., 1997—2003, CFO, 2003—. Mem.: Mich. Assn. CPAs and Fin. Execs. Internat. Office: Spherion corp 2050 Spectrum Blvd Fort Lauderdale FL 33309

SMITH, MARSCHALL IMBODEN, lawyer; b. San Antonio, Oct. 3, 1944; s. Lowell B. and Jacqueline I. Smith; m. Elizabeth Braswell (div. 1973); m. Ann McNamara, June 3, 1976; children: Catherine, Elizabeth, Margaret, Austin, Lillian. AB in history cum laude, Princeton U., 1966; LLB, U. Va., 1973; MBA, U. Chgo., 1987. Bar: NY 1974, Ill. 1981. Assoc. Debevoise & Plimpton, NYC, 1973-75, Paul Weiss Rifkind Wharton & Garrison, NYC, 1975-81; atty. Baxter Travenol Labs., Deerfield, Ill., 1980-82, Baxter Internat. Inc., Deerfield, Ill., 1982-83, 1983-85, asst. gen. counsel, 1985-87, assoc. gen. counsel, 1987—92; v.p., gen. counsel Am. Med. Holdings Inc., 1992—93; sr. v.p., gen. counsel, sec. IMC Global Inc. (formerly IMC Fertilizer Group Inc.), Northbrook, Ill., 1993—99; exec. v.p., gen. counsel Digitas Inc., Boston, 1999—2001; v.p., gen. counsel, corp. sec. Brunswick Corp., Lake Forest, Ill., 2001—. Adj. faculty Lake Forest Grad. Sch. Mgmt., 1985—88. Maj. USMC, 1966—73, Vietnam. Mem.: U.S. Supreme Court Counsel, Christian Legal Soc., Chgo. Bar Assn. Office: Brunswick Corp 1 N Field Ct Lake Forest IL 60045-4811 Office Phone: 847-735-4430.

SMITH, MARSHA H., state agency administrator, lawyer; b. Boise, Idaho, Mar. 24, 1950; d. Eugene F. and Joyce (Ross) Hatch; 2 children. BS in Biology/Edn., Idaho State U., 1973; MLS, Brigham Young U., 1975; JD, U. Wash., 1980. Bar: Idaho, U.S. Dist. Ct. Idaho, U.S. Ct. Appeals (9th cir.), U.S. Ct. Appeals (D.C. cir.). Dep. atty. gen. Bus./Consumer Protection Divsn., Boise, 1980-81, Idaho Pub. Utilities Commn., Boise, 1981-89, dir. policy and external rels., 1989-91, commr., 1991—, pres., 1991-95. Mem. Harvard Electricity Policy Group, Nat. Coun. on Electricity Policy; com. for regional electric power coop. Western Interstate Energy Bd., 1999-2005; dir. Western Electricity Coordinating Coun., 2002—; mem. adv. coun. Electric Power Rsch. Inst. Legis. dist. chair Ada County Democrats, Idaho, 1986-89. Mem. Nat. Assn. Regulatory Utility Commrs. (bd. dirs. 1999—), chair electricity com. 2000-03, 2nd v.p. 2005). Office: Idaho Pub Utilities Commn PO Box 83720 Boise ID 83720-0074 Office Phone: 208-334-3912.

SMITH, MARSHALL SAVIDGE, foundation executive; b. East Orange, NJ, Sept. 16, 1937; s. Marshall Parsons and Ann Eileen (Zulauf) S.; m. Carol Goodspeed, June 25, 1960 (div. Aug. 1962); m. Louise Nixon Claiborn, Aug. 1964; children: Adam, Jennifer, Matthew, George. AB, Harvard U., 1960, EdM, 1963, EdD, 1970. Systems analyst and computer programmer Raytheon Corp., Andover, Mass., 1959-62; instr., assoc. prof. Harvard U., Cambridge, Mass., 1966-76; asst., assoc. dir. Nat. Inst. Edn., Washington, 1973-76; asst. commr. HEW, Washington, 1976-79, chief of staff to U.S. Dept. Edn. sec., 1980; prof. U. Wis., Madison, 1980-86, Stanford (Calif.) U., 1986—2003, dean Sch. Edn., 1986—94; under-sec. edn. U.S. Dept. Edn., 1993-2000, acting dep. sec. edn., 1996-2000; program dir. Hewlett Found., 2001—. Task force, chmn. Clinton Presdl. Transition Team, 1992-93; chmn. PEW Forum on Ednl. Reform; chmn. bd. internat. com. studies in edn. NAS, 1992-93. Author: The General Inquirer, 1967, Inequality, 1972; contbr. articles to profl. jours, chpts. to books. Pres. Madison West Hockey Assn., 1982-84. Mem. Nat. Acad. Rsch. Assn. (chmn. orgn. instl. affiliates 1985-86), Nat. Acad. Edn. Democrat. Avocations: environmental issues, philanthropy. Home: 1256 Forest Ave Palo Alto CA 94301 Office: Wm & Flora Hewlett Found Menlo Park CA Business E-Mail: msmith@hewlett.org.

SMITH, MARTHA A., academic administrator; b. Bradford, Pa., Aug. 31, 1948; BA, Slippery Rock State U., Pa., 1970; MEd, U. Hawaii, 1972; PhD, U. No. Colo., 1974. Dir. Hawaii Open program U. Hawaii, 1975—77; v.p. student affairs Coll. of St. Teresa, 1977—81; dean of students Dundalk CC, 1982—87, acting pres., 1987, pres., 1988—94, Anne Arundel CC, Arnold, Md., 1994—. Bd. dir. Inst. CC Devel. at Cornell U.; mem. Gov.'s Workforce Investment Bd., Md. Ednl. Coun., Nat. Edn. Commn. of the States; charter mem. Nat. Cmty. Coll. Adv. Bd. Campaign chair Anne Arundel County United Way, 1999; mem. adv bd. Chesapeake Innovation Ctr.; mem ACE Commn. on Adult Learning and Ednl. Credentials; bd. dirs. League for Innovation in the C.C., Leadership Anne Arundel, Greater Balt. Com. Named Bus. Leader of Yr., Anne Arundel Trade Coun., 1996—97, Power Elite, Daily Record, 2003; named one of Md.'s Top 100 Women, 1998, 2000, 2002; recipient First Women award, YWCA of Annapolis and Anne Arundel County, 1995, Tribute to Women in Industry award, YWCA, 1995, Cmty Trustee award, Leadership Anne Arundel, 2001, Inside the Field Nat. Leadership award, Nat. Coun. Continuing Edn., 2001, Fannie Lou Hamer award, Dr. Martin Luther King awards com., 2002, Kathleen Kennedy Townsend award of excellence, Women in Govt. Studies, 2001, Employer of the Yr., BWI Bus. Partnership, 2004. Mem.: Md.Assn. of CC (exec. com.). Office: Anne Arundel CC 101 College Pkwy Arnold MD 21012-2222 Office Phone: 410-777-1177. E-mail: masmith@aacc.edu.

SMITH, MARTHA LEE, lawyer; b. Austin, Tex., 1968; BA in English, cum laude, Washington & Lee U., 1990; JD, U. Tex., 1993. Bar: Tex. 1993. Ptnr., Banking/Fin. Andrews Kurth LLP, Houston, co-chmn. recruiting com. Mem.: Houston Bar Assn., ABA, State Bar Tex. Office: Andrews Kurth LLP 600 Travis St Ste 4200 Houston TX 77002-3090 Office Phone: 713-220-4372. Office Fax: 713-238-7202. Business E-Mail: martysmith@andrewskurth.com.

SMITH, MARTIN BERNHARD, journalist; b. San Francisco, Apr. 20, 1930; s. John Edgar and Anna Sophie (Thorsen) S.; m. Joan Lovat Muller, Apr. 25, 1953; children: Catherine Joan, Karen Anne. AB, U. Calif., Berkeley, 1952, M Journalism, 1968. Reporter, city editor Modesto (Calif.) Bee, 1957-64; reporter, mng. editor Sacramento Bee, 1964-75; polit. editor, columnist McClatchy Newspapers, Sacramento, 1975-92; ret., 1992. Episcopalian. Personal E-Mail: Joan_and_Marty@msn.com.

SMITH, MARTIN CRUZ, author; b. Reading, Pa., Nov. 3, 1942; s. John and Louisa (Lopez) S.; m. Emily Stanton Arnold, June 15, 1968; children: Ellen, Luisa, Samuel. BA, U. Pa., 1964. Author: Gorky Park, 1981, Stallion Gate, 1986, Polar Star, 1989, Red Square, 1992, Rose, 1996, Havana Bay, 1999, December 6, 2002, Wolves Eat Dogs, 2004.

SMITH, MARTIN HENRY, retired pediatrician; b. Gainesville, Ga., Nov. 3, 1921; s. Charles E. and Mamie Mae (Emmett) S.; m. Mary Gillis, Feb. 25, 1950; children: Susan, Margaret, Mary MD, Emory U., 1945. Diplomate Am. Bd. Pediatrics. Intern City Hosp. System, Winston-Salem, NC, 1945-46; fellow in infectious diseases Grady Meml. Hosp., Atlanta, 1948-49; resident Henrietta Egleston Hosp., Atlanta, 1949-50, Children's Hosp., Washington, 1950-51; practice medicine, specializing in pediatrics Gainesville, Ga.; ret., 1988; clin. asst. prof. Emory U. Hosp., Atlanta; chief of staff Hall County Hosp., Gainesville, 1965-66. Mem. Nat. Vaccine Adv. Commn., 1990—, chmn., 1991. Contbr. articles to profl. jours. Chmn. Nat. Vaccine Adv. Com., 1991—. Capt. M.C., U.S. Army, 1946-48 Fellow Am. Acad. Pediatrics (chpt. chmn. 1966-69, dist. chmn. 1977-83, pres.-elect 1984-85, pres. 1985-86); mem. Hall County Med. Soc. (pres. 1960), Ga. Pediatric Soc. (pres. 1965-66). Med. Assn. Ga., AMA, Alpha Omega Alpha Clubs: Chattahoochee Country (Gainesville); Piedmont Driving (Atlanta). Episcopalian. Personal E-mail: drmsmith@earthlink.net.

SMITH, MARTIN JAY, advertising executive, marketing executive; b. NYC, Feb. 1, 1942; s. Nathan and Helen (Schwartz) S.; m. Ellen Susan Chadakoff, Dec. 20, 1964; children: Hilary, Nancy. BA, U. Pitts., 1963. With sta. clearance dept. ABC Radio Network, N.Y.C., 1965-66; asst. account exec.

Norman Craig & Kummel, N.Y.C., 1966-67, account exec., 1967-68, Gotham, Inc., N.Y.C., 1968-72, account supr., 1972-74, v.p., 1974-78, sr. v.p., 1978-80, exec. v.p., 1980-84, vice chmn., 1995—2005; chief strategy officer Agency Sacks, N.Y.C., 2005—. Sgt. USAR, 1963-69. Mem. Am. Advt. Assn. Am. (mem. mgmt. com. 1987). Avocations: flying, tennis, golf. Home: 920 Park Ave New York NY 10028-0208 Office: Agency Sacks 345 7th Ave New York NY 10001 Office Phone: 212-225-9327. Business E-Mail: msmith@agencysacks.com.

SMITH, MARTIN JAY, physician, biomedical research scientist; b. Bklyn., May 21, 1934; s. I. Richard and Marilyn (Bernard) S.; m. Joyce Ellen Gleason, June 26, 1960 (div. Nov. 1968); children: Danielle, Robert, Alexander; m. Ruby Helen Rhodes, Apr. 7, 1972. BA, Hofstra Coll., 1955; MD, Columbia U., 1959. Diplomate Am. Bd. Internal Medicine, Am. Bd. Internal Medicine in Hematology, Am. Bd. Pathology in Clin. Pathology, Am. Bd. Pathology in Immunopathology. Intern Meth. Hosp., N.Y.C., 1959-60, resident in medicine, 1960-61, Montefiore Hosp., N.Y.C., 1963-64; rsch. fellow in medicine Harvard Coll., Cambridge, Mass., 1964-66; clin. and rsch. fellow in medicine Mass. Gen. Hosp., Boston, 1964-66; physician Gundersen Clinic and Luth. Hosp., La Crosse, Wis., 1966-99, chmn. dept. internal medicine, 1971-73; dir. spl. hematology lab. Gundersen Clinic, La Crosse, 1967-99, chmn. dept. lab. medicine, 1973-96; dir. lab. medicine Luth. Hosp., La Crosse, 1973-96. Dir. rsch. Gundersen Med. Found., 1975-88; med. dir. Med. Lab. Tech. Program Western Wis. Tech. Inst., 1978-99. Contbr. articles to New Eng. Jour Medicine, Jour. Lab. Clin. Medicine, Blood, Ann. Internal Medicine, Biochim, Biophys. Acta, Jour. Infectious Diseases, Thrombosis and Haemostasis, Clin. Chemistry. Capt. USNR, ret. Fellow ACP, Coll. Am. Pathologists (inspector labs. 1983-99); mem. Am. Assn. for Cancer Rsch., Am. Soc. Hematology, Internat. Soc. Hematology, Assn. Med. Lab. Immunologists, Phi Beta Kappa. Home: 1428 Main St La Crosse WI 54601-4225

SMITH, MARY LEE, civil engineer, technician; b. Tell City, Ind., June 8, 1953; d. Russell Eugene Cassidy and Mary Helen Cronin Cassidy; m. James Houston Smith, Mar. 3, 1973; children: LeAnn Michelle Jackson, Randi Lynelle. Seamstress Gozzards, Huntingburg, Ind., 1971—72; dist. sec. (part-time) Perry County Soil & Water Conservation Dist., Cannelton, Ind., 1972—79; clerk-typist (part-time) USDA, Soil Conservation Svc., 1972—79, soil conservation technician, 1979—95, USDA, Natural Resources Conservation Svc., Rockport, Ind., 1995—2006, civil engring. technician, 2005—. Mem., com. sec. USDA, NRCS, Ind. Civil Rights Com., Indpls., 2006—; mem. USDA, NRCS, Ind. Field Employees Coun., 2005—, NRCS Ind. Operational Improvements Team, Ind., 2006—. Quilt making instr. Perry Ctrl. Continuing Edn., Leopold, Ind., 2000—; com. mem. Perry Ctrl. After Prom Com., 1991—97; sec. Leopold Twp. Trustee, Leopold, Ind., 2000—03; coun. sec. St. Mark Parish Coun., Ind., 2005—; religious instr. St. Mark Cath. Ch., 1987—95. Recipient Effort to Encourage Drug & Alcohol Free Schools award, Perry Ctrl. Schs., 1993, Cert. Merit award, USDA, Soil Conservation Svc., 1979, 1985. Mem.: Orgn. Profl. Employees of USDA (assoc.), Soil and Water Conservation Soc. (assoc.). Roman Catholic. Avocations: quilting, hiking, gardening, photography; volunteering. Office: USDA Natural Resources Conservation Svc 2827 West State Rd 66 Ste C Rockport IN 47635-9260 Office Phone: 812-649-9136. Office Fax: 812-649-4796. E-mail: marylee.smith@in.usda.gov.

SMITH, MARY W., secondary school educator, artist; b. Ft. Lewis, Wash. 1 child, Lara Smith Blair. Grad. in music edn., James Madison U., Va., 1966. Drama tchr. Franklin H.S., Seattle, 1985. Founder, dir. FAME Co. Seattle Pub. Schs., 1985—. Actor: Am. Hous Theatre, Frankfurt Playhouse, Seattle Repertory Theatre, Va. Stage Co. Named Outstanding Theatre Educator, Seattle Repertory Theatre, 1998, Outstanding Regional Theatre Educator, Cmty. Philanthropists, 2004. Mem.: AFTRA, SAG. Office: Franklin High Sch 3013 S Mt Baker Blvd Seattle WA 98144-6199

SMITH, MAURA ABELN, lawyer, paper company executive; b. Reading, Pa., Oct. 3, 1955; d. Henry Joseph and Lynn (Blashe) Abeln; children: Gwendolyn Casebeer, Karl Casebeer; m. Steven A. Smith, Dec. 18, 1999. AB, Vassar Coll., 1977; M Philosophy, Oxford U., 1979; JD, U. Miami, 1982. Bar: Fla. 1982, Ohio 1999. Assoc. Steel, Hector & Davis, Miami, 1982—87; ptnr. Baker & McKenzie, Miami, 1987-91; v.p., gen. counsel GE Co./Plastics, Pittsfield, Mass., 1991-98; sr. v.p., gen. counsel, sec. Owens Corning, Toledo, 1998-2000, chief restructuring officer, sr. v.p., gen. counsel, sec., 2000—03, bd. dirs.; sr. v.p., gen. counsel, sec., pub. affairs Internat. Paper, Memphis, 2003—. Rhodes scholar, Oxford Eng., 1977-79; John M. Olin fellow in law and econs., Olin Found., 1979-82. Mem.: Phi Beta Kappa. Avocations: skiing, horseback riding, tennis, golf. Office: 6400 Poplar Ave Memphis TN 38197 Office Phone: 901-419-3829. E-mail: maura.abelnsmith@ipaper.com.

SMITH, MERRITT ROE, history professor; b. Waverly, N.Y., Nov. 14, 1940; s. Wilson Niles and Mary Eleanor (Fitzgerald) S.; m. Bronwyn M. Mellquist, Aug. 24, 1974. AB, Georgetown U., 1963; MA, Pa. State U., 1965, PhD, 1971; LHD (hon.), Rensselaer Poly. Inst., 1997. Assst. prof. history Ohio State U., Columbus, 1970-74, assoc. prof., 1974-78; vis. prof. history and sociology of sci. U. Pa., Phila., 1976; prof. history tech. program in sci., tech. and society M.I.T., Cambridge, 1978—, Metcalfe prof. engring. and liberal arts, 1989-92, dir. program in sci., tech. and society, 1992—96, 2000—02, Leverett and William King Cutten prof., 1993—. Author: Harpers Ferry Armory and the New Technology, 1977, Military Enterprise and Technological Change, 1985, Science, Technology and the Military, 2 vols., 1988, Does Technology Drive History?, 1994, Major Problems in the History of American Technology, 1998, Inventing America, 2002, 2d edit., 2006; mem. editl. bd. Tech. and Culture, 1973-91, Bus. History Rev., 1978-85, MIT Press, 1986-91, Archimedes, 1995—2001. Mem. Mass. Hist. Soc.; bd. advisors MIT Mus. Recipient Cert. of Commendation Am. Assn. State and Local History, 1978, Disting. Tchg. award Ohio State U., 1978, Founders Day award Charles River Mus. Industry, 2003; grantee Ohio State U., 1972, Am. Philos. Soc., 1974, Harvard Bus. Sch., 1974-75, Eleutherian Mills-Hagley Found., 1978-79, Alfred P. Sloan Found., 1994-2002; Guggenheim fellow, 1983-84, Regents fellow Smithsonian Instn., 1984-85. Mem. AAAS, Am. Acad. Arts and Scis., Soc. History Tech. (mem. exec. coun., Dexter Prize com., Da Vinci medal 1994, mus. com., v.p., pres. 1989-91), Orgn. Am. Historians (Frederick Jackson Turner award 1977, Disting. lectr. 2004—), Bus. History Conf., Am. Antiquarian Soc., Newcomen Soc. N.Am., Soc. Indsl. Archeology, History Sci. Soc. (Pfizer award 1978), Phi Kappa Phi, Phi Alpha Theta. Home: 17 Longfellow Rd Newton MA 02462-1505 Office: STS Program MIT 77 Massachusetts Ave Rm E51-185 Cambridge MA 02139 Office Phone: 617-253-4008. E-mail: roesmith@mit.edu.

SMITH, MICHAEL, academic administrator; b. St. Joseph, Mo., Jan. 30, 1941; s. Walton Joseph and Margaret Dorothy (Chubb) S.; m. Connie Stanton, Oct. 27, 1965; children: Jeffrey, Timothy. AD, Mo. Western Community Coll., 1960; BS, N.E. Mo. State U., 1967; PhD, U. Nebr., 1975. Ins. investigator Retail Credit Co., St. Joseph, Mo., 1963-65; instr. Havana HS, Ill., 1967-68, West Bend High Sch., Iowa, 1968-70, U. Nebr., 1972-75; asst. prof. English Albany Jr. Coll., Ga., 1975-78; chmn. arts and scis., dir. internat. programs U. Minn., Crookston, 1978-80; chief exec. officer, coll. dean N.D. State U., Bottineau, 1980-87; provost, dean of faculty Richard Bland Coll., Coll. William and Mary, 1987-89; chancellor La. State U., Eunice, 1989-95; pres. Our Lady of the Lake Coll., Baton Rouge, 1995—2006. Commr. North Cen. Assn. Colls. and Schs., 1984-, accreditation cons./evaluator, 1982-87, vis. prof. English, U. New Orleans, 1995-98. With U.S. Army, 1960-63. Office: Our Lady of the Lake Coll 7434 Perkins Rd Baton Rouge LA 70808-4374 Office Phone: 225-768-1710. Business E-Mail: msmith@ololcollege.edu.

SMITH, MICHAEL (CARL MICHAEL SMITH), lawyer, former federal agency administrator; b. Oklahoma City, Oct. 11, 1944; s. Carl W. Jr. and Nina (Furr) S.; m. Sharon Kay Lewis, June 5, 1971. BA, U. Okla., 1966, JD, 1969. Bar: Okla. 1969, U.S. Dist. Ct. (we., no. and ea. dists.) Okla. 1976, U.S. Ct. Appeals (10th cir.) 1976, U.S. Supreme Ct. 1976. Mem. firm Lawrence, Smith & Harmon, Oklahoma City, 1977-80; pres. Red Rock Exploration, Inc., Oklahoma City, 1980-83; mem. firm Lawrence & Ellis, P.A., Oklahoma City,

1983—95; sec. Okla. Dept. Energy, Oklahoma City, 1995—2002; asst. sec. for fossil energy US Dept. Energy, Washington, 2002—04; of counsel Dunlap, Codding & Rogers, Washington, 2004—. Mem. Blue Ribbon Commn. on Natural Gas, Oklahoma City, 1982; chmn. Okla. Polit. Action Com., Oklahoma City, 1986-90; mem. Okla. Legis. Interim Task Force on Environ. Regulation, Oklahoma City, 1991-92; sec. Okla. Energy Resources Bd., 1992-94; Capt. U.S. Army, 1969-71, Vietnam. Mem. Okla. Ind. Petroleum Assn. (pres. 1994-95). Office: Dunlap Codding & Rogers PC 1000 Farragut Sq 1025 Connecticut Ave NW Washington DC 20036 Office Phone: 202-327-5495. E-mail: cmike_smith@okatents.com.*

SMITH, MICHAEL EARL, jockey; b. Roswell, N.Mex., Aug. 10, 1965; Winner Preakness Stakees, 1993, Fla. Derby, 1994, Blue Grass, 1994, Travers, 1994, Haskell, 1994, Met Mile, 1994, Woodward, 1994, Breeder's Club Turf, 1994, Breeder's Cup Sprint, 1994, Caeser's Internat., 1994, Ala., 1994. Office: care Jockeys Guild 250 W Main St Lexington KY 40507-1714 also: Jockeys Guild Inc PO Box 150 Monrovia CA 91017-0150

SMITH, MICHAEL JAMES, industrial engineering educator; b. Madison, Wis., May 12, 1945; s. James William and Ruth Gladys (Murphy) S.; m. Patricia Ann Bentley, June 22, 1968; children: Megan Colleen, Melissa Maureen. BA, U. Wis., 1968, MA, 1970, PhD, 1973. Rsch. analyst Wis. Dept. Industry Labor, Madison, 1971-74; rsch. psychologist Nat. Inst. for Occupational Safety and Health, USPHS, Cin., 1974-84; prof. U. Wis., Madison, 1984—. Owner, prin. M.J. Smith Assocs. Inc., Madison, 1991—. Contbr. articles to profl. jours. Mem. APA, Inst. Indsl. Engrs. (sr.), Human Factors Soc., Assn. Computer Machinery, Am. Soc. Testing and Measurement. Avocation: tennis. Home: 6719 Shamrock Glen Cir Middleton WI 53562-1144 Office: U Wis Dept Indsl Engring Human Factors Rsch Lab 1513 University Ave Madison WI 53706-1539 Office Phone: 608-263-6329. Business E-Mail: mjsmith@engr.wisc.edu.

SMITH, MICHAEL L., transportation company executive; b. 1948; BA, DePauw U., 1970. V.p. Coll. Mktg. & Rsch. Corp., 1968-70; with Arthur Andersen & Co., 1970-75; div. contr. Mayflower Group, Carmel, Ind., 1975-77, group v.p., warehouse div., 1977, then exec. v.p., now pres., chief oper. officer, 1989—95, also bd. dirs.; with Mayflower Transit Co. subs. Mayflower Group, Carmel, 1975—95, then sr. v.p., chmn., CEO, 1989—95, also bd. dirs.; CFO WellPoint, Inc., 1999—2005.

SMITH, MICHAEL PETER, social sciences educator, researcher; b. Dunkirk, N.Y., Aug. 2, 1942; s. Peter Joseph and Rosalie Barbara (Lipka) S.; m. Patricia Anne Lendway, Aug. 21, 1965. BA magna cum laude, St. Michael's Coll., 1964; MA in Polit. Sci., U. Mass., 1966, PhD in Polit. Sci., 1971. Instr., asst. prof. dept. govt. Dartmouth Coll., Hanover, NH, 1968—71; asst. prof. dept. polit. sci. Boston U., 1971—74; assoc. prof., prof. dept. polit. sci. Tulane U., New Orleans, 1974—86; prof. cmty. studies U. Calif., Davis, 1986—, chmn. dept. applied behavioral scis., 1986—91, chmn. cmty. studies and devel. program, 2001—. Vis. prof. pub. policy U. Calif., Berkeley, 1981, city planning U. N.C., Chapel Hill, 1982, city planning U. Calif., Berkeley, 1985; vis. scholar in govt. U. Essex, Eng., 1979; vis. scholar polit. and social sci. U. Cambridge, Eng., 1982; vis. scholar Inst. Urban and Regional Devel., U. Calif., Berkeley, 1990, 94 Internat. Ctr. for Advanced Studies, NYU, 1998, Ctr. Migration, Policy and Soc., Oxford U., 2005 Author: The City & Social Theory, 1979, City, State and Market, 1988, Transnational Urbanism, 2001; co-author: Restructuring the City, 1983, California's Changing Faces, 1993; editor: Cities in Transformation, 1984, Breaking Chains, 1991, After Modernism, 1992, Marginal Spaces, 1995, Comparative Urban & Community Research, 1986—; co-editor: The Capitalist City, 1987—, The Bubbling Cauldron, 1995, Transnationalism from Below, 1998, City and Nation: Rethinking Place and Identity, 2001, The Human Face of Global Mobility, 2006; mem. editl. bd. Global Networks, 1999—. Office: Dept Human & Cmty Devel Univ Calif Davis CA 95616 Office Phone: 530-752-2243. Business E-Mail: mpsmith@ucdavis.edu.

SMITH, MICHAEL ROBERT, electro-optical engineer, physicist; b. Tela, Honduras, Aug. 24, 1937; s. Ike Morgan and Edith Helen (Hudson) S.; m., div., remarried Lorraine L. Smith, Apr. 26, 2002; children: Stephen, Monica, Meryl. BME, Ga. Inst. Tech., 1959, MS in Nuclear Engring., 1961; PhD, Case Inst. Tech., 1965. Mem. tech. staff Hughes Rsch. Labs., Malibu, Calif., 1965-68; v.p., dir. rsch. Britt Corp., L.A., 1968-73; sr. staff engr. Singer/Librascope divsn., Glendale, Calif., 1973-78; pres. Exocor Tech., Newbury Park, Calif., 1978-95; asst. prof., head physics program Calif. Luth. U., Thousand Oaks, 1990-96; design leader LIGO project Calif. Inst. Tech., Pasadena, 1996—. Contbr. articles to profl. jours.; inventor emergency vehicle warning and traffic control sys., emergency vehicle warning sign, flat electro-optic display panel, high power mirror, laser recording film with opaque coating, pulsed gas laser with radiation cooling, infrared laser photocautery device; 8 U.S. patents; 9 fgn. patents. Greek folk dance tchr. Arts Coun., Thousand Oaks, Calif., 1991-97. Mem. IEEE, Laser Electro-Optic Soc. (chair 1995-97), Sigma Xi, Pi Tau Sigma. Republican. Home: 1611 N Roosevelt Ave Pasadena CA 91104-1927 Business E-Mail: smith@ligo.caltech.edu.

SMITH, MICHELLE, education educator; b. Lawton, Okla., Aug. 2, 1968; d. Howard and Sharon Smith; 1 child, Brittany Wolfe. EdD, Okla. State U., Stillwater, Okla., 1999. Cert. tchr. elem. edn. Okla., 1992, tchr. psychometrist Okla., 1993. Asst. prof. McMurry U., Abilene, Tex., 1999—2000; assoc. prof. Cameron U., Lawton, Okla., 2000—. Mem.: Delta Kappa Gamma (pres. 2004—, v.p. 2004—). Democrat. Home: 6713 NW Oak Dale Drive Lawton OK 73505 Office: Cameron University 2800 W Gore Blvd Lawton OK 73505 Office Phone: 580-581-2203. Personal E-Mail: michells0802@sbcglobal.net. Business E-Mail: michells@cameron.edu.

SMITH, MICHELLE RENE, elementary school educator; b. Burnet, Tex., Mar. 20, 1967; d. Wayne William and Mildred Martha Green; m. William Lloyd (Skip) Smith, June 10, 1989; children: Madison Paige, Minley Jade. BS, U. Tex., Austin, 1990. Tchr. grade 4-6 gen. edn. and sci. Thrall Ind. Sch. Dist., Tex., 1991—94; tchr. math. 6th grade Chisholm Trail Mid. Sch., Round Rock, 1994—96; tchr. math. 7th grade and algebra 8th grade Thorndale Ind. Sch. Dist., 1996—97; tchr. math. 7th grade Chisholm Trail Mid. Sch., Round Rock, 1997—2000; tchr. math. 7th grade, dept. head Leander Mid. Sch., 2000—. Tchr. religious edn. St. Elizabeth's Cath. Ch., Pflugerville, Tex., 2003—, tchr. vacation bible sch., 2004—, St. William's Cath. Ch., Round Rock, 2000—05. Mem.: Assn. Tex. Profl. Educators. Roman Catholic. Avocations: scrapbooks, photography.

SMITH, MICHELLE SUN, psychologist; b. Balt., June 9, 1971; d. Nelson Cang and Laura Gamber Sun; m. Michael Timothy Smith, Nov. 22, 1997; children: Nolan Sean, Hailey Elizabeth. PhD, Calif. Sch. of Profl. Psychology, Berkeley, 1998. Lic. psychologist Md., 2001, N.Y., 1999. Staff psychologist, sr. instr. psychiatry U. Rochester, NY, 1999—2001; staff psychologist, coord. eating disorder svcs. Johns Hopkins U. Counseling Ctr., Balt., 2001—03; clin. psychologist MedPsych Assocs., Lutherville, Md., 2003—; asst. prof. U. Md. Dental Sch., Md., 2004—. V.p. program devel. bMed Techs., Rochester, NY, 2001—; cons. Ruxton Orthop. Assocs., Towson, Md., 2004—. Contbr. articles to profl. jours. Recipient Ruth C. Wylie prize in psychology, Goucher Coll., 1993; fellow, Okura Mental Health Leadership Found., 1997. Mem.: APA, Md. Psychol. Assn., Interdisciplinary Coun. of Learning Disorders, Psi Chi. Avocation: autism awareness & early intervention. Office: 2324 West Joppa Rd Ste 220 Lutherville MD 21093 Office Phone: 410-583-2623. Business E-Mail: msunsmith@comcast.net.

SMITH, MIEKO KOTAKE, education educator; b. Osaka, Japan, Sept. 19, 1941; arrived in U.S. 1968; d. Kohei and Toshiko Kotake; m. James Allen Smith; 6 children. BA, Tsuda Coll., Tokyo, Japan, 1964; MA, Kent State U., 1972, Ednl. Specialist Degree, 1972; PhD, Case Western Res. U., 1980. LCSW ind. social worker Ohio. Student activities coord., internat. student advisor Cleve. State U., 1972—78; rsch. assoc. Case Western Res. U.,

1978—81; dir. aftercare Murtis H. Taylor Multi-Svcs. Ctr., 1981—82; dir. rsch. and tng. Hill House Mental Health Rehab. and Rsch., Inc., 1982—87; ind. cons. Beachwood, Ohio, 1987—90; asst. prof. Cleve. State U., 1990—93, assoc. prof., 1993—2000, prof., 2000—. Cons. Summit County Children Svcs. Bd., Akron, Ohio, 1988—90. Contbr. chapters to books, articles to profl. jours. Bd. dirs., v.p., pers. com. chair Cleve. YWCA, 1975—87; bd. dirs., edn. chair Women's City Club of the Greater Cleve., 1991—96; trustee Help Found., Cleve., 1994—96; chairperson Women Celebrating the Bicentennial, Cleve., 1994—97; trustee, com. chair Women's Cmty. Found., Cleve., 1991—97; bd. governance, chair Multi-Cultural Tng. Inst., Cleve., 1993—98; trustee Phoenix Soc., Cleve., 1996—98; bd. govs., first vice chair, program planning and policy com. chair Cuyahoga County Cmty. Mental Health Bd., Cleve., 1998; bd. dirs. Univ. Christian Movement, Cleve., 1992—94. Recipient Rsch. Recognition award, Ohio Program Evaluators' Group, 1992; grantee, Ohio Dept. Mental Health, 1985, 1990, 1999, U.S. Dept. Edn., 1999, City of Cleve., 1999, 2000, 2001, U.S. Dept. Health and Human Svcs., 2000. Mem.: AAUP, NASW, Am. Evaluation Assn. Democrat. Presbyterian. Avocation: reading.

**SMITH, MILAN DALE, JR.,** federal judge; b. Pendleton, Oreg., May 19, 1942; BA cum laude, Brigham Young U., 1966; JD, U. Chgo., 1969. Bar: Calif. 1970, D.C. 1972, U.S. Supreme Ct. 1977, U.S. Tax Ct. 1978. Assoc. O'Melveny & Myers, Los Angeles, 1969-72; ptnr. Smith Crane Robinson & Parker LLP (formerly Smith & Hilbig LLP), Torrance, Calif., 1972—2006; cir. judge US Ct. Appeals (9th cir.), 2006—. Pres. Los Angeles State Office Bldg. Authority, 1983-92, Informed Voters League, Torrance, 1975-77; vice chmn. bd. Ettie Lee Homes for Youth, 1973-82, Calif. Fair Employment and Housing Commn., 1987-91; mem. Cabinet of the Interfaith Coalition to Heal L.A., head econ. devel. subcom.; bd. trustees Deseret Trust Co. Calif.; sec.-treas. Criminal Justice Legal Found.; chair, bd. visitors Sch. Religion, Claremont U., 2005-06. Recipient Super Lawyer award, 2006; Nat. Honor scholar, 1966-69, U. Chgo. Mem. Brigham Young U. Alumni Assn. (bd. dirs. 1982-86). Office: US Ct Appeals 125 S Grand Ave Pasadena CA 91105-1510

**SMITH, MOLLY D.,** theater director; b. Yakima, Wash. d. Kay. BA, Cath. U.; MA in Theatre, Am. U., PhD (hon.), 2001. Founder Perserverance Theatre, Juneau, Alaska, 1979—98; artistic dir. Arena Stage, Washington, 1998—. Creative advisor Sundance Inst. New Plays; lit. advisor Banff Playwright's Colony, Canada; bd. dir. Theatre Comms. Group; panelist Ctr. Internat. Theatre Devel.; spkr. in field; prof. Arts, Music and Theatre Dept. Georgetown U.; judge Susan B. Blackburn Prize. Dir.: (plays). Named Artist of Yr., Alaska State Coun. Arts; named one of 100 Most Powerful Women, Washingtonian Mag., 2001; recipient Cmty. Leader award, U. Alaska Southeast. Office: Arena Stage 1101 6th St SW Washington DC 20024

**SMITH, MORTON EDWARD,** ophthalmology educator, dean; b. Balt., Oct. 17, 1934; BS, U. Md., 1956, MD, 1960. Bd. cert. Ophthalmology Bd.; lic. physician Mo., Md., Wis. Rotating intern Denver Gen. Hosp., 1960-61; resident, nat. inst. of neorol. diseases and blindness fellow in opthalmology Washington U. Sch. Medicine-Barnes Hosp., 1961-63; NIH spl. fellow in ophthalmic pathology Armed Forces Inst. of Pathology, Washington, 1964; chief resident, instr. ophthalmology Washington U. Sch. Medicine, St. Louis, 1965-66, instr. ophthalmology, 1966-67, assoc. prof. ophthalmology and pathology, 1967-69, assoc. prof. ophthalmology and pathology, 1969-75, prof. ophthalmology and pathology, 1975—, asst. dean, 1978-91, assoc. dean, 1991-96, prof. emeritus, assoc. dean emeritus, 1996—; prof. ophthalmology U. Wis., Madison, 1995-2001. Vis. scholar Eye Inst., Columbia Presbyn. Med. Ctr., N.Y.C., 1966; prof./lectr. Montefiore Hosp., Pitts., 1969, U. Ark., 1970, 77, 80, 82, 84, 86, 88, U. Fla., 1972, 81, U. Tex. and Lackland AFB, San Antonio, 1973, U. Colo., 1974, 82, U. Mo., 1974, 79, 80, 88, So. Ill. U., Springfield, 1974, U. Md., 1975, Montreal (Can.) Gen. Hosp., 1975, U. Wis., 1976, 87, 93, U. Pitts., 1977, 83, 87, U. Iowa, 1977, 87, Cleve. Clinic, 1978, Colo. Ophthalmol. Soc., 1978, Brooke Army Hosp., San Antonio, 1979, Wills Eye Hosp., Phila., 1980, USPHS Hosp., San Francisco, 1981, U. Calif., Davis, 1981, Sinai Hosp., Balt., 1985, 89, 94, U. Calif., San Diego, 1985, Tufts U., Boston, 1985, Cornell U., N.Y.C., 1988, U. Wash., Seattle, 1990, Brown U., Providence, 1990, Vanderbilt U., Nashville, 1991, Duke U., Durham, N.C., 1992; Chandler lectr. Harvard U., 1988; The Lois A. Young-Thomas Meml. lectr. U. Md., 1991; Braley lectr. U. Iowa, 1993; Havener Meml. lectr. Ohio State, 1994. Editor pathology sect.: Perspectives in Ophthalmology, 1977; mem. editl. bd. Ophthalmic Plastic & Reconstructive Surgery, 1986-90; contbr. articles to profl. jours. With USAR M.C., 1958-66. Scholar U. Md., 1958, 59. Fellow Am. Acad. Ophthalmology (ophthalmic pathology com. 1977-83, chmn. ophthalmic com. 1979-83, Honor award for svc. 1981, Sr. Honor award 1992); mem. AMA, Am. Bd. Ophthalmology (diplomate, bd. dirs. 1992—), Assn. for Rsch. in Vision and Ophthalmology (chmn. sect. pathology ann. meeting 1971), Am. Assn. Ophthalmic Pathologists (pres. 1977-80), Assn. Am. Med. Colls. (group med. edn. 1985—), Mo. Med. Assn., Mo. Ophthalmol. Soc., Verhoeff Soc., Theobald Soc., St. Louis Med. Soc., St. Louis Ophthalmol. Soc., Soc. Med. Coll. Dirs. for Continuing Med. Edn., Alpha Omega Alpha (sec.-treas. chpt. 1993-95, councillor 2003—). Home: 1275 Castle Gate Dr Saint Louis MO 63132 Office: Campus Box 8096 660 S Euclid Ave Saint Louis MO 63110-1093 Office Phone: 314-747-5559. Business E-Mail: smithm@vision.wustl.edu.

**SMITH, MORTON HOWISON,** religious organization administrator, educator; b. Roanoke, Va., Dec. 11, 1923; s. James Brookes and Margaret Morton (Howison) S.; m. Lois Virginia Knopf, July 7, 1925; children: Samuel Warfield, Susanne Rochet Margaret. BA, U. Mich., 1947; BD, Columbia Theol. Sem., 1953; ThM, ThD, Free U., Amsterdam, The Netherlands, 1962. Ordained to ministry Presbyn. Ch., 1954. Pastor Springfield-Roller Presbyn. Chs., Carroll County, Md., 1954; prof. bible Belhaven Coll., Jackson, Miss., 1954-63; guest lectr. Westminster Theol. Sem., Phila., 1963-64; prof. Re formed Theol. Sem. in Jackson, 1961-79, stated clk. gen. assembly Presbyn. Ch. in Am., Decatur, Ga., 1973-88; prof. systematic theology Greenville Presbyn. Theol. Sem., 1987—, dean faculty, 1987-98. Moderator gen. assembly Presbyn. Ch. Am., 1986-98, bd. dirs.; mem. bd. dirs. Presbyn. Jour., Asheville, N.C., 1965-87; lectr. on theology Republic of So. Africa, June-July, 1988, Riga, Latvia, 1992, Budapest, Hungary, 1994, Prague, Czech Republic, 1994, 95, Trinidad and Tobago, 1995, Zlin, Czech Republic, 1998, 99, on missions, Republic of Korea, June-July, 1989, Munkton, Can., 1998, 99, Recife, Brazil, 1998, 2002, Reformed Sem., St. Petersburg, Russia, New Zealand, 2003. Author: Studies in Southern Presbyterian Theology, 1962, 2d edit. 1987, How Is the Gold Become Dim, 1973, republished 1998, (pamphlet) Reformed Evangelism, 1970, Testimony, 1986, Commentary on the Book of Church Order of the Presbyterian Church in America, 1990, Harmony of the Westminster Confession and Catechisms, 1990, Systematic Theology, 1994; contbr. articles to profl. jours. Trustee Covenant Coll., Lookout Mountain, Tenn., 1982-90. 1st lt. USAAF, 1942-45. Fulbright fellow U.S. Govt., 1958. Mem. N.Am. Presbyn. and Reformed Coun. of Chs. (sec. 1977-92). Presbyterian. Avocations: flying, travel, genealogy. Office: Greenville Presbyn Theol Sem PO Box 690 Taylors SC 29687-0014 Office Phone: 864-322-2717. Personal E-mail: wcflcsc@citcom.net.

**SMITH, MYRON JOHN, JR.,** librarian, author; b. Toledo, May 3, 1944; s. Myron John and Marion Oliva (Herbert) S.; 1 son, Myron John III. Student, Coll. Steubenville, 1962; AB, Ashland Coll., 1966; MLS, Western Mich. U., 1967; MA, Shippensburg U., 1969; postgrad., U. Wis., Purdue U.; LittD, Cardinal Newman Coll., 1982. Rsch. librarian G.W. Blunt White Libr., Mystic Seaport, Conn., 1967-68; asst. librarian Western Md. Coll., Westminster, 1969-72; libr. dir. Huntington (Ind.) Pub. Libr., 1972-76; prof. history and libr. sci., dir. librs. Benedum Libr. Salem-Teikyo U.; then assoc. dir. aviation program Salem (W.Va.) Coll., 1976-90; prof. history and libr. sci., libr. dir. Tusculum Coll., Greeneville, Tenn., 1990—. Mem. Am. Com. on History 2d World War, Assn. for Bibliography of History Author: American Naval Bibliography Series, vol. 1, Huntington Centennial Handbook, 1973, The Sophisticated Lady: The Battleship Indiana in World War II, 1973, World War II at Sea: A Bibliography of Sources in English, 1976, (with Robert Webber)

Sea Fiction Guide, 1976, The Cloak and Dagger Bibliography, 1976, World War I in the Air, 1977, Air War Chronology 1939-45, 1977, Air War Bibliography Series, 1977—, The Mountain State Battleship: USS West Virginia, 1979, Air War Southeast Asia, 1979, The Soviet Navy, 1941-1978, 1979, The Secret Wars Series, 1980-81, The Soviet Air and Strategic Rocket Forces, 1941-1980, 1981, The Soviet Army, 1941-1980, 1981, Equestrian Studies: The Salem College Guide, 1981, The Cloak and Dagger Fiction Guide: An Annotated Guide to Spy Thrillers, 1981, (with Terry White) 3d edit., 1994, The Mountaineer Battlewagon: USS West Virginia, 1982, The Keystone Battlewagon: USS Pennsylvania, 1983, The Golden State Battlewagon: USS California, 1983, Watergate: A Bibliography, 1983 World War II: Mediterranean and European Theaters, 1984, The United States Navy and Coast Guard, 1946-1983: A Bibliography of English Language Works and 16mm Films, 1984, U.S. Television Network News: A Guide to Sources in English, 1984, Battleships and Battlecruisers, 1884-1984: A Bibliography and Chronology, 1985, Baseball: A Comprehensive Bibliography, 1986, 99th Infantry Division Bibliography, 1986, The Airline Bibliography: The Salem College Guide to Sources on Commercial Aviation, Vol. I, The United States, 1986, Vol. II, Airliners and Foreign Carriers, 1987, Passenger Airliners of the United States, 1926-86: A Pictorial Guide, 1987, rev. edit. through 1991, 1991, 3d rev. edit. through 1995, 4th revised edit., 2002, Brooklyn/Los Angeles Dodgers: A Bibliography, 1987, American Warplane Bibliography, 1989, Volunteer Battlewagon: The U.S.S. Tennessee (BB-43), 1989; editor: Sports Teams and Players Bibliography Series, 1987, Battle and Leaders Bibliography Series, 1988, 100 Years of Opportunity: A Pictorial History of Salem College, 1888-1988, 1988, Pro Football Bio-Bibliography, 1920-1988, 1989, Pearl Harbor, December 7, 1941: An Annotated Bibliography, 1991, Battles of the Coral Sea and Midway, 1942: A Bibliography, 1991, World War II at Sea, 1974-1989: A Bibliography, 1990, Professional Football: The Official Pro Football Hall of Fame Bibliography, 1993, Baseball: A Comprehensive Bibliography-1st Supplement: 1985-1991, 93, The College Football Bibliography, 1994, Glimpses of Tusculum College: A Pictorial History, 1794-1994, 1994, Baseball: A Comprehensive Bibliography-2d Supplement: 1992-1997, 1998, The Airline Encyclopedia, 1909-2000, 2002, The Baseball Bibliography, 2d edit., 2006; contbr. articles to various jours. Recipient Nelson Ross award Profl. Football Rsch. Assn., 1993; 1st am. recipient Richard Franck Gold medal Bibliothek für Zeitgeschichte, Stuttgart, Fed. Rep. Germany, 1981. Mem. ALA, U.S. Naval Inst., U.S. Mil. Inst., U.S. Air Force Found. Assn. Bibliog. of History (pres. 1981-82), Alliance of Librs. in Northeast Tenn. (pres. 1997—), Beta Phi Mu, Phi Alpha Theta. Clubs: Optimist. Office: Tusculum Coll PO Box 5005 Greeneville TN 37743-0001 Office Phone: 423-636-7320.

**SMITH, NANCY ANGELYNN,** federal agency administrator; b. Nashville, Mar. 28, 1950; d. Russell Monroe and Louise (Stephenson) Smith; m. Richard Christian Egan, Jan. 1, 1999. Student, Blair Acad. Music, 1966, Am. Internat. Acad. Europe, 1970; BA in Psychology with distinction, Rhodes Coll., Memphis, Tenn., 1972; MS with honors, U. Tenn., 1974; cert. in acctg., U. New Orleans, 1985, U. SC, Columbia, 1987. Contract administr. State of Tex. Dept. Health and Human Svcs., Houston, 1976-78; dept. Head Coop. Edn. Program No. Va. C.C., Annandale, 1978-81; revenue agt. IRS Dept. of Treasury, Nashville, 1988-99, mgr., adminstr. IRS, 1999—. Faculty rep. Faculty Senate No. Va. C.C., Annandale, 1979—81; comm. rep. IRS, 2002—. Author: numerous poems; contbr. articles to profl. jours. Vol. Voter Registration program, Denver, 1981—84, Adopt-a-Sch., Nashville, 1993—97, Tenn. State Guard; disaster relief coord. Ky. and Tenn., 1998—99, Red Cross Inst., 1976—78, VITA, 1990—95; vol. Congresswoman Pat Shroeder, Denver, 1981—84, Al Gore for Senate, Nashville, 1987—88, Federica Pena for Mayor, Denver, 1981—; bd. dirs. No. Va. C.C., Annandale, 1978—81. Mem.: DAR, Advancement Individual Minorities, Profl. Mgrs. Assn., Cert. Fraud Examiners Assn., Gamma Beta Phi, Alpha Omicron Pi (chmn. bd. dirs. Colo. chpt.), Omicron Nu (hon.), Phi Kappa Pi (hon.). Avocations: painting, skeet shooting, camping, historical battlefields, collecting edged weapons.

**SMITH, NANCY HOHENDORF,** sales executive, marketing professional; b. Detroit, Jan. 30, 1943; d. Donald Gerald and Lucille Marie (Kopp) Hohendorf; m. Richard Harold Smith, Aug. 21, 1978 (div. Jan. 1984). BA, U. Detroit, 1965; MA, Wayne State U., 1969. Customer rep. Xerox Corp., Detroit, 1965-67, mktg. rep. Univ. Microfilms subs. Ann Arbor, Mich., 1967-73, mktg. coord., 1973-74, mgr. dir. mktg., 1975-76, mgr. mktg. Can., 1976-77, major account mktg. exec. Hartford, Conn., 1978-79, New Haven, 1979-80, account exec. State of N.Y. N.Y.C., 1981, N.Y. region mgr. customer support Greenwich, Conn., 1982, N.Y. region sales ops. mgr., 1982, State of Ohio account exec. Columbus, 1983, new bus. sales mgr. Dayton, Ohio, 1983, major accounts sales mgr., 1984, info. systems sales and support mgr., quality specialist Detroit, 1985-87, new product launch mgr., ops. quality mgr., 1988, dist. mktg. mgr., 1989-92, major accounts sales mgr., 1992—; graphics arts industry sales mgr., 1998—; sales mgr. corp. accounts Sprint- Nextel Comms., Farmington Hills, Mich., 2005—. Reg. graphic arts industry cons. mgr., 1999. Mem. exec. leadership team Am. Heart Assn. Named to Outstanding Young Women of Am., 1968, Outstanding Bus. Woman, Dayton C. of C., 1984, Women's Inner Circle of Achievement, 1990. Mem. NAFE, Am. Mgmt. Assn., Am. Heart Assn. (mem. exec. leadership team 2005-06), Women's Econ. Club Detroit, Detroit Inst. Arts Founders' Soc., Detroit Hist. Soc., Detroit Hist. Soc., Greater Detroit C. of C. Republican. Roman Catholic. Avocations: interior decorating, reading, music, art. Home: 6462 West Oaks Dr West Bloomfield MI 48324-3269 Office Phone: 248-866-0601. Personal E-mail: nancyhsmith@sbcglobal.net.

**SMITH, NANCY L.,** information technology executive; BS in Mgmt. and Orgnl. Behavior, U. San Francisco. Western regional sales mgr., nat. sales mgr. Electronic Arts, Redwood City, Calif., 1984, v.p. sales, 1988—93, sr. v.p. N.Am. sales and distbn., 1993—96, exec. v.p. N Am sales, 1996, 98 exec. v.p., gen. mgr. N AM. pub., 1999—. Office: Electronic Arts Inc 209 Redwood Shores Pkwy Redwood City CA 94065-1175

**SMITH, NANCY LEE,** communications official; b. Junction City, Kans., May 10, 1953; d. James Emerson and Donna Lee (Cousins) Smith. BA with hons., Stephens Coll., Columbia, Mo., 1975; MPA with hons., Am. U., 1990. Appt. sec. to chief of staff The White House, Washington, 1975; appt. sec. to sec. of def. Dept. Def., Washington, 1975-77; sec., office mgr. to various congressmen U.S. Ho. of Reps., Washington, 1977-83; Congl. specialist U.S. Geol. Survey, Washington, 1983-84; staff asst. to sec. of land and mineral mgmt. U.S. Dept. Interior, Washington, 1984-85; Congl. liaison officer Office of Surface Mining, Reclamation and Enforcement, Washington, 1985-95, comms. officer, 1995-2000; group mgr. legis. affairs Bur. of Land Mgmt., Washington, 2000—. Mem.: Pi Alpha Alpha, Alpha Lambda Delta. Avocations: white-water rafting, photography, reading, origami, exercise. Office: Bur of Land Mgmt 1849 C St NW 401L5 Washington DC 20240-0001

**SMITH, NANCY WOOLVERTON,** journalist, real estate agent, antique appraiser; b. San Antonio, July 31, 1947; d. Tillman Louis and Enid Maxine (Woolverton) Brown; 1 dau., Christina Elizabeth Woolverton Jones; m. William F. Pry II, Mar. 7, 1998 (div. July 31, 2003). Student, Ecole Nouvelle de la Suisse, Romande, Lausanne, Switzerland, 1962, Vanderbilt U., 1964; BA, So. Meth. U., 1968, postgrad., 1969-70. Cert. S.E. Paralegal Inst., Ancien Regime Christie's (London), antiques and residential contents. Tchr. spl. edn. Hot Springs Sch. Dist. (Ark.), 1970-72; reporter, soc. editor Dallas Morning News, 1974-82; soc./celebrity columnist Dallas Times Herald, 1982-91; owner, pub. High Society, Society Fax; bus. editor DFW Cmty. Newspapers divsn. Lionheart Newspapers Inc., Plano, Tex., 1999—2003; co-founder Decorative Arts Soc. Dallas, For Worth; pub. Decorative Arts Mag.; owner Personal Property Appraisal Svc., 2005—; realtor Keller Williams. Realtor, Ebby Halliday Realtors; stringer Washington Post, 1978; owner Nancy Smith Pub. Rels. Contbg. editor Ultra mag., Houston, 1981-82, Tex. Woman mag., Dallas, 1979-80, Profl. Woman mag., Dallas, 1979-80; mem. bd. advisors Ultra Mag., 1985—; columnist North Dallas People; appeared on TV series Jocelyn's Weekend, Sta. KDFI-TV, 1985. Bd. dirs. TACA arts support orgn., Dallas, 1980—, asst. chmn. custom auction, 1978-83; judge Miss Tex. USA Contest, 1984; bd. dirs. Am. Parkinson Disease Assn. (Dallas chpt.), mem.

adv. bd. Cattle Baron's Ball Com., Dallas Symphony Debutante presentations; mem. bd. dirs. Dallas Opera Women's Bd., Northwood Inst. Women's Bd., Dallas Symphony Leauge; mem. Friends of Winston Churchill Meml. and libr., Dallas Theatre Ctr. Women's Guild, Childrens' Med. Ctr. Aux.; mem. women's com. Dallas Theatre Ctr.; hon. mem. Crystal Charity Ball Com.; mem. Cmty. Coun. Greater Dallas Cmty. Awareness Goals Com. Impact '88, 1985—; com. mem. Dallas Arboretum, Preservation Dallas; co-chmn. Multiple Sclerosis San Simeon Gala, 1988; celebrity co-chmn. Greer Garson Gala of Hope 1990-91; gala chmn. Greer Garson Gala of Hope for Am. Parkinson's Disease Assn., 1991-93; chmn. gala benefit Northwood U., 1994; co-chmn. star-studded stomp Mar. Dimes, 1994; mem. Femmes du Monde spl. activities com., 1999 luncheon com., com. Dallas Coun. World Affairs; bd. dirs. Dallas Ballet's Lone Star Adagio; pub. rels. vol. Habitat for Humanity, 2005. Mem.: DAR, Internat. Soc. Appraisers (accredited; antiques and residential contents cert.), Nat. Press Club, Soc. Profl. Journalists (v.p. coms. 1978—79), Nat. Soc. Newport County, Decorative Arts Soc. Dallas/Ft. Worth (CEO, appraiser, co-founder), French Heritage Soc., Lancaster Hist. Soc., Daus. of Republic of Tex. (registrar 1972), Dallas So. Meml. Assn., Dallas County Heritage Soc. (bd. dirs.), Dallas Mus. Art League, Dallas Opera Guild, City of Plano Sister Cities Com., Flagler Mus., Dallas Glass Club, Rotary Club (gala chmn. North Tex. dist. 5810 2007, dist. 5810 gala chmn. 2007), Park Cities Rotary Club, Bent Tree Country Club, Dallas Knife and Fork Club, S'Amuser, Kermis Club, Coterie Club, Thalia Club, Rondo/Carrousel Club, The 500 Club (Dallas), Argyle Club (sec. 1983—84, 1st v.p. 2005—), Pub. Affairs Luncheon Club, Trippers Club, Tower Club. Home: 5727 Covehaven Dr Dallas TX 75252-4934 Office Phone: 214-625-1162. Personal E-mail: nancywoolvertonsmith@comcast.net, nancysmithpry@aol.com.

**SMITH, NEIL,** former professional sports team executive; b. Toronto, Ont., Can., Jan. 9, 1954; m. Katia Smith. Student, We. Mich. U. Selected NHL amateur draft NY Islanders, with scouting dept., 1980-81; from dir. profl. scouting to dir. farm sys. Detroit Red Wings, 1982; dir. scouting, player procurement, gen. mgr., gov. Adirondack Red Wings (Am. Hockey League); gen. mgr. NY Rangers, 1989-2000, pres., 1992-2000; cons. Anaheim Mighty Ducks, Pitts. Penguins, 2002; gen. mgr. NY Islanders, 2006. Hockey analyst ESPN, OLN, 2005—06. Bd. dirs. Nat. Child Abuse Prevention Ctr. Named All-Am. Defenseman We. Mich. U., to Hall of Fame, 1991, NHL Exec. Yr. Sporting News. Avocations: raquetball, movies.*

**SMITH, NICK H.,** former congressman, archivist, farmer; b. Addison, Mich., Nov. 5, 1934; s. LeGrand John and Blanche (Nichols) S.; m. Bonnalyn Belle Atwood, Jan. 1, 1960; children: Julianna, Bradley, Elizabeth, Stacia. BA, Mich. State U., 1957; MS, U. Del., 1959. Radio & TV farm editor Sta. WDEL, Wilmington, Del., 1957-59; radio editor Sta. KSWD, Wichita Falls, Tex., 1959-60; capt. intelligence USAF, Tex., 1959-61; mem. twp. bd. Somerset Twp., Addison, 1962-68; asst. dep. administr. USDA, Washington, 1972-74; state rep. Mich. Ho. of Reps., Lansing, 1978-82; state senator Mich. State Senate, Lansing, 1982-92; mem. U.S. Congress from 7th Mich. dist, 1993—2005, mem. agr., sci., and internat. rels. coms. Mem. fin. com. Mich. State Senate, 1990—92, mem. budget com., 2006—, chmn. sci. rsch. com., 2006—. Del. Am. Assembly on World Population & Hunger, Washington, 1973; nat. del. on U.S.-Soviet Cooperation and Trade, 1991; former trustee Somerset Congl. Ch. Capt. USAF, 1959-61. Fellow Kellogg Found., 1965; named Hon. FFA State Star Farmer, 1987, SCF Conservator of Yr. Hillsdale County, 1988. Mem. Mich. Farm Bur. (bd. dirs.), Jackson C. of C., Mich. State U. Alumni Club, Masons. Republican.

**SMITH, NORA NUNNERY,** information scientist, educator; b. Roanoke, Va., Aug. 19, 1947; d. James Clifford and Oma Lucille (Cox) Nunnery. AS in Bus. Adminstrn., Va. We. C.C., 1977; BSBA, Radford U., 1981; MS in Vocat. & Tech. Edn., Va. Poly. Inst., 1996. Trainer, instr. Va. We. C.C., Roanoke, 1998—2002; instr. electronics, comm. programming and info sys. Tech. Coll., Roanoke, 2003—. Adj. instr. Nat. Bus. Coll., Roanoke, 1996-97, New River C.C., Dublin, Va., 1997. Treas. Unitarian Universalist Ch., Roanoke, 1999—. Mem.: ASTD, Southeast Region Bus. Edn. Assn., Toastmasters, Omicron Tau Theta, Delta Pi Epsilon, Phi Delta Kappa. Avocations: horseback riding, bridge, golf, photography. Home: 1135 Lynchburg Tpke Salem VA 24153-5316 Office: PO Box 14007 Roanoke VA 24038-4007 Office Phone: 540-563-8000. E-mail: norasmit@yahoo.com.

**SMITH, NORMAN OBED,** retired physical chemist, educator; b. Winnipeg, Man., Can., Jan. 23, 1914; came to U.S., 1950, naturalized, 1958; s. Ernest and Ruth (Kilpatrick) S.; m. Anna Marie O'Connor, July 1, 1944; children: Richard Obed, Graham Michael, Stephen Housley. B.Sc., U. Man., 1935, M.Sc., 1936; PhD, NYU, 1939. Teaching fellow NYU, 1936-39; mem. faculty dept. chemistry U. Man., Winnipeg, 1939-50, asst. prof., 1946-49, assoc. prof., 1949-50, Fordham U., N.Y.C., 1950-65, prof. chemistry, 1965-84, prof. emeritus, 1984—, chmn. dept., 1974-78; ret., 1984. Sr. phys. chemist Arthur D. Little, Inc., Cambridge, Mass., 1957; indsl. cons. Author: (with others) The Phase Rule and Its Applications, 1951, Chemical Thermodynamics, A Problems Approach, 1967, Elementary Statistical Thermodynamics, A Problems Approach, 1982; contbr. to: Ency. Brit, 1974. Fellow Chem. Inst. Can.; mem. Am. Chem. Soc., Asso. Can. Coll. Organists, Am. Guild Organists (dir. chpt. 1964-66, 79-82, 91-92), Sigma Xi, Phi Lambda Upsilon. Home: 811 E Central Rd Apt 112 Arlington Heights IL 60005-3293

**SMITH, NORMAN RAYMOND,** academic administrator; b. Toronto, Ont., Can., Oct. 24, 1946; s. William Raymond and Jeanne (Malin) S.; m. Susan Robinson, Dec. 26, 1981; 1 child, Caroline Robinson. BS, Drexel U., 1969, MBA, 1971; EdD, Harvard U., 1984; HLD (hon.) (hon.), Phila. U., 2001, Wagner Coll., 2002. Assoc. dean students Drexel U., Phila., 1971-73; v.p., dean of students, professor Phila. Univ., 1973-78; asst. dean Harvard Grad. Sch. Edn., Cambridge, Mass., 1978-80, John F. Kennedy Sch. Govt., Harvard U., Cambridge, 1980-84; exec. v.p. Moore Coll. Art, Phila. 1984-87; pres., prof. Wagner Coll., S.I., NY, 1988—2002, pres. emeritus, 2002—; pres., prof. Richmond, The Am. Internat. U. London, 2002—. Dir. Dime Bancorp; assoc. Harvard U. Philosophy of Edn. Rsch. Ctr., Cambridge, 1982—. Author: Selecting the Right College, 6th edit., 2000. Chair mayor's cabinet transition search City of Boston, 1983-84; trustee N.Y. Coun. of Ind. Colls. and Univs., 1994-97. Lt. U.S. Army, 1969-73. Recipient U. medal Drexel U., 1993, Pres.'s medal NYU, 1994. Mem. Ind. Coll. Fund N.Y. (sec.-treas.), Harvard Club of N.Y.C., Richmond County Country Club. Office: Richmond U Queens Rd Richmond-upon-Thames TW10 6JP England Home: 9 Albert Hall Mansions London SW7 5NA England Office Phone: 020-8332-8246. Business E-Mail: smithn@richmond.ac.uk.

**SMITH, NUMA LAMAR, JR.,** lawyer; b. Rock Hill, S.C., Nov. 22, 1915; s. Numa Lamar and Grace (Hanes) S.; m. Mary Catherine Gray, Mar. 24, 1941; children: Patricia Gray (dec.), Elizabeth Hanes, Lamar Douglas. AB, Furman U., 1938; LL.B. with distinction, Duke U., 1941. Bar: N.Y. 1942, D.C. 1946. Assoc. firm White & Case, N.Y.C., 1941-42, Miller & Chevalier, Washington, 1946-49, partner, 1949-83, counsel, 1983—; bd. visitors, 1973-83. Sr. fellow Duke U. Law Sch., 1979-80 Assoc. editor: Duke Law Jour, 1940-41. Served with U.S. Army, 1942-46; with Judge Adv. Gen. Corps 1944-46. Recipient Gen. Excellence award Furman U., 1938 Fellow Am. Bar Found.; mem. ABA, D.C. Bar Assn., Am. Law Inst., Duke Law Alumni Assn. (pres. 1967-69); Order of Coif, Met. Club (Washington), Burning Tree Club (Bethesda, Md.), Washington Golf Club (Arlington, Va.), The Club at Pelican Bay, Sigma Alpha Epsilon. Baptist. Home: 7515 Pelican Bay Blvd Naples FL 34108-6520

**SMITH, O. BRUTON,** automotive company executive; Founder Charlotte Motor Speedway, 1959, CEO & dir. 1975—; chmn., CEO Sonic Automotive, Inc., Charlotte, NC, Speedway Motor Sports, Inc., Charlotte, 1994—; owner operator Town and Country Ford and various other pvt. bus., Charlotte, NC. Founder Speedway Children's Charities, 1984. Named to, Greater Charlotte Sports Hall of Fame, 2005; recipient Award of Excellence, NASCAR, 1997. Office: Sonic Automotive Inc 6415 Idlewild Rd Ste 109 Charlotte NC 28212*

**SMITH, OCTOBER,** elementary school educator; b. Milw., Apr. 12, 1977; d. Jerry Clark and Debby DuBois; m. Wade Smith, June 22, 1996; children: Stacey children: Sydney. BS in Biology and Elem. Edn., Houston Bapt. U., 2000. Tchr. Lamar Consolidated Ind. Sch. Dist., Richmond, Tex., 2000—. Home: 9323 Hillhaven Ct Rosenberg TX 77469

**SMITH, OLLEN BRUTON,** sports association executive; divorced; 4 children. Founder, exec. officer, dir. Lowe's Motor Speedway, Concord, NC, 1959—61, CEO, dir., 1975—; CEO, pres., dir. Atlanta Motor Speedway, 1990—; CEO, chmn. Speedway Motorsports, 1994—; chmn., pres. Bristol Motor Speedway, 1996—, Sears Point Raceway, 1996—, Tex. Motor Speedway, 1996—; owner, operator Town & County Ford, Inc. Named one of Forbes' Richest Americans, 2006. Office: Speedway Motorsports 5555 Concorde Pkwy S Concord NC 28027*

**SMITH, ORIN C.,** retired food products executive; MBA, Harvard U., 1967; BA in Fin., Econ., Acctg. and Statis., U. Wash., 1965. With Touche Ross & Co., 1969—77, 1980—85, State of Wash. Office Mgmt. and Budget, 1977—80, 1985—87, No. Air Freight and Danzas Corp., 1987—90; from v.p., CFO to pres., COO Starbucks, Seattle, 1990—2000, pres., CEO, 2000—05. Bd. dirs. Nike, Inc., Wash. Mutual, Walt Disney Co., 2006—. Bd. dirs. Conservation Internat.; advisory bd. U. of Wash. Sch. Bus.; bd. dirs. U. of Wash. Medicine. Avocations: golf, skiing, reading. Office: Starbucks PO Box 34067 Seattle WA 98124-1067*

**SMITH, ORIN ROBERT,** chemical company executive; b. Newark, Aug. 13, 1935; s. Sydney R. and Gladys Emmett (DeGroff) S.; m. Stephanie M. Bennett-Smith; children: Lindsay, Robin; 1 stepchild, Brendan. BA in Econometrics, Brown U., 1957; MBA in Mgmt., Seton Hall U., 1964; PhD in Econs. (hon.), Centenary Coll., 1991; LLD (hon.), Monmouth Coll., 1994. Various sales and mktg. mgmt. positions Allied Chem. Corp., Morristown, NJ, 1959-69; dir. sales and mktg. Richardson-Merrell Co., Phillipsburg, NJ, 1969-72; with M&T Chems., Greenwich, Conn., 1972-77, pres., 1975-77; with Engelhard Minerals & Chems. Corp., Menlo Park, Edison, NJ, 1977-81, corp. sr. v.p., 1978-81, pres. div. minerals and chems., 1978-81, also bd. dirs. 1979-81, pres., dir. various U.S. subs., 1979-81; exec. v.p., pres. div. minerals and chems. Engelhard Corp., Menlo Park, Edison, 1981-84, bd. dirs., 1981—, pres., CEO, Iselin, NJ, 1984-95, chmn., CEO, 1995—; also bd. dirs. Bd. dirs. Summit Bank Co., The Summit Bancorp, Vulcan Materials Co., PE Corp., Ingersoll-Rand Co., Engelhard Corp., Mfrs. Alliance. Trustee N.J. State C. of C., Inst. for Tech. Advancement; mem. bd. overseers N.J. Inst. Tech.; trustee Plimoth Plantation; 1st vice chmn. bd. trustees Centenary Coll.; past dir. Minorco, La. Land and Exploration Co.; past trustee Henry R. Kessler Found., Inc.; past chmn. Ind. Coll. Fund N.J.; past dir.-at-large U. Maine Pulp and Paper Found. Lt. (j.g.) USN, 1957-59. Mem. Chem. Mfrs. Assn. (past bd. dirs.), Econ. Club (N.Y.C.), Union League Club (N.Y.C.), Duxbury Yacht Club, New Bedford Yacht Club, N.Y. Yacht Club. Office: Engelhard Corp 101 Wood Ave S Iselin NJ 08830-2703

**SMITH, ORVILLE AUVERNE,** physiology educator; b. Nogales, Ariz., June 16, 1927; s. Orville Auverne and Bess (Gill) S.; m. Clara Jean Smith; children— Nanette, Marcella. BA in Psychology, U. Ariz., 1949; MA, Mich. State U., 1950, PhD, 1953. Instr. psychology Mich. State U., East Lansing, 1953-54; fellow U. Pa., Phila., 1954-56; trainee dept. physiology and biophysics U. Wash., Seattle, 1956-58, instr. physiology and biophysics, 1958-59, asst. prof., 1959-61, 62-63; asst. dir. Regional Primate Research Ctr., 1962-69, assoc. prof., 1963-67, prof., 1967-97; assoc. dir. Regional Primate Research Center, 1969-71, dir., 1971-88, prof. emeritus, 1997—. Contbr. articles to profl. jours. Mem. Am. Physiol. Soc., Am. Soc. Primatologists (pres. 1977-79), Internat. Congress Physiol. Scis., Am. Assn. Anatomists, AAAS, Pavlovian Soc. N.Am. (pres. 1977-78), Internat. Primatological Soc., AAUP, Neurosci. Soc. Home: 30311 201st Ct SE Kent WA 98042-5920 Office: U Wash Nat Primate Rsch Ctr PO Box 357330 Seattle WA 98195-7330

**SMITH, OZZIE (OSBORNE EARL SMITH),** retired professional baseball player; b. Mobile, Ala., Dec. 26, 1954; m. Denise Jackson, Nov. 1, 1980; children: Osborne Earl Jr., Dustin Cameron. Grad., Calif. State Poly. U., San Luis Obispo. Shortstop San Diego Padres Baseball Club, Nat. League, 1977—82, St. Louis Cardinals Baseball Club, Nat. League, 1982—96; baseball analyst St. Louis Cardinals Sta. KPLR, St. Louis, 1997—. Named Member of World Series Championship Team, 1982; named to All-Star Team, Nat. League, 1981—92, 1994, Sporting News, 1982, 1984—87, Baseball Hall of Fame, 2002; recipient Most Valuable Player award, Nat. League Championship Series, 1985, Golden Glove award, 1980—92, Silver Slugger award, 1987. Avocations: jazz, word puzzles, backgammon. Office: 2250 Ball Dr Saint Louis MO 63146-8602

**SMITH, PAMELA HYDE,** ambassador; b. Tacoma, July 1945; m. Sidney G. Smith (dec.); 2 children. BA in Art History, Wellesley Coll., 1967. Joined US Info. Agy., 1975; asst. & cultural attaché US Embassy, Bucharest, 1976—77; special asst. to USIA Dir., 1977—81; cultural asst. US Embassy, Belgrade, 1982—86; dep. chief Acad. Exch. Program USIA, 1986—91; press attaché US Embassy, Jakarta, 1991—95; dir. Office Geog. Liaison U.S. Info. Agy., 1995—97; pub. affairs officer US Embassy, London, 1997—2001; U.S. amb. to Moldova Dept. State, 2001—.

**SMITH, PAMELA LATRICE,** school psychologist; b. Monroe, La., Jan. 11, 1975; d. Tommy Lee Smith and Lovely Marie Bams. BA, N.E. La. U., Monroe, 1997, MS, 1999. Cert. specialist in sch. psychology 2000, supr. sch. psychol. svcs. 2004. Sch. psychologist Westside Alternative Sch., Tallulah, La., 1999—2000; sch. psychologist Office Spl. Ednl. Svcs. Monroe City Schs., 2000—. Instr. psychology U. La., Monroe, 2002—; instr. Crisis Prevention Inst., Monroe, 2001. Founding mem. Wall of Tolerance, Montgomery, Ala., 2002—; mem. Southern Poverty Law Ctr., 2005—. Recipient Outstanding Academic Achievement, 1992—93; scholar La. Honor's Scholarship award, 1993. Mem.: AAUW, La. Sch. Psychol. Assn., So. Property Law Ctr., Cooking Club of Am. (life), Mortar Bd. Honor Soc., Phi Kappa Phi, Psi Chi Nat. Honor Soc., Delta Sigma Theta Sorority Inc. Democrat. Avocations: travel, reading, music, shopping. Home: 507 Auburn Ave Monroe LA 71201 Office: Divsn Student Support Svcs PO Box 4180 Monroe LA 71211 Personal E-mail: psmith@bayou.com.

**SMITH, PATRICIA (PAT) ANN,** elementary school educator; b. Wichita, Kans., Dec. 30, 1947; d. Orville Stark Kildow and Jean Robison, Ann Stipe (Stepmother); m. Wilton Ray Smith, Aug. 26, 1967; children: Kevin Ray, Lee Clayton. BA in Edn., Wichita State U., Kans., 1969. Elem. tchr. Derby Pub. Sch., Kans., 1969—70, Broken Arrow Pub. Sch., Okla., 1978—2003. Edn. cons. Houghton Mifflin Pub. Co., Dallas, 2004—. Adv. com. mem. Journey Through the Universe Challenger Ctr., Alexandria, Va., 1998—2005; vol. Tulsa Air and Space Mus., 1997—2006. Named Tchr. of Yr., WalMart, Ea. Okla., 2001; named to teach Bookers, by John Yow, 2001, Udvar-Hazy Wall of Honor, Washington, DC, 2005; recipient Unsung Heroes award, Reliastar/No. Life, 2001, Golden Apple award, Broken Arrow Sch. Bd., 2004; grantee, Nat. Geog., 2003; Christa McAuliffe fellow, Okla., 1995, 1998. Mem.: Okla. Ret. Tchrs. Assn., Alpha Delta Kappa (pres. 2006—08). Achievements include Teacher in Space; Ambassador on the Governor's Education Team, OASIS. Personal E-mail: smithpathmco@valornet.com.

**SMITH, PATRICIA GRACE,** federal official; b. Nov. 10, 1947; d. Douglas and Wilhelmina (Griffin) Jones; m. J. Clay Smith, Jr., June 25, 1983; children: Eugene Douglas, Stager Clay, Michelle L., Michael L. BA in English, Tuskegee Inst., 1968; postgrad., Auburn U., 1969-71, Harvard U., 1974, George Washington U., 1983, Fed. Exec. Inst. 1997. Cert. exec. mgmt ng. devel. assignments Dept. Def., 1986, U.S. Senate Commerce Com., 1987. Instr. Tuskegee Inst., Ala., 1969-71; program mgr. Curber Assocs., Washington, 1971-73; air placement Nat. Assn. Broadcasters, Washington, 1973-74, dir. pub. affairs, 1974-77; assoc. prodr. Group W Broadcasting, Balt., 1977, prodr., 1977-78; dir. affiliate rels. and programming Sheridan Broadcasting

Network, Crystal City, Va., 1978-80; dep. dir. policy, assoc. mng. dir. pub. info./reference svc. FCC, Washington, 1992-94, acting assoc. mng. dir., pub. info. and reference svcs., 1994—. Chief of staff office assoc. adminstr. for comml. space transp. FAA, U.S. Dept. Transp., 1994-96, dep. assoc. adminstr. for comml. space transp., 1996-97, acting assoc. adminstr., 1997, assoc. adminstr., 1998—. Vice-chmn. Nat. Conf. Black Lawyers Task Force on Comms., Washington, 1975-87; trustee, mem. exec. com., nominating com., youth adv. com. Nat. Urban League, 1976-81; mem. comms. com. Cancer Coordinating Coun., 1977-84; mem. Braintrust Subcom. on Children's Programming, Congl. Black Caucus, 1976—; mem. adv. bd. Black Arts Celebration, 1978-83; mem. NAACP; mem. journalism and comms. adv. coun. Auburn U., 1976-78; mem. Washington Urban League, 1985—; bd. dirs. Black Film Rev., 1989-91; mem. D.C. Commn. on Human Rights, 1986-88, chmn., 1988-91; mem. adv. coun. NIH, 1992-96; mem. bd. advisors The Salvation Army, 1993-2000. Named Outstanding Young Woman of Yr., Washington, 1975, 78; recipient Sustained Superior Performance award FCC, Washington, 1982-95, Disting. Alumnus award Tuskegee U., 1996, C. Alfred Anderson award, 2002. Mem. Women in Comms., Inc. (mem. nat. adv. com.), Broadcasters Club (bd. dirs. 1976-77), Lambda Iota Tau. Democrat. Baptist. Avocations: writing, swimming. Home: 4010 16th St NW Washington DC 20011-7002 Office: DOT/AST 800 Independence Ave SW Rm 331 Washington DC 20591-0001 Office Phone: 202-267-7793.

**SMITH, PATRICIA LYNNE,** artist; b. Camden, N.J., Nov. 3, 1955; d. Thomas Patrick Connelly and Elizabeth Jean (Swope) Shober; m. William Clarence Smith, Nov. 30, 1973 (div. June 1980); children: Travis, Taryn. BA, Rutgers U., Camden, N.J., 1980; MFA, Rutgers U., New Brunswick, N.J., 1984. Adj. instr. Rutgers U., New Brunswick, NJ, 1983-84, Trenton State Coll., 1989-90. One-woman shows include Piezo Electric Gallery, N.Y.C., 1986, S.O.M.A. Gallery, Berlin, 1994, A.I.R. Gallery, N.Y.C., 1994, St. Peter's Ch., 1994, Croxhapox Gallery, Belgium, 1995, Black and Herron Gallery, N.Y.C., 1996, Studio Five Beekman, 1997, Front Room Gallery, Bklyn., 2006, others, exhibited in group shows at Art Exch. Fair, N.Y.C., 1996, 1997, Bklyn. Mus. Art, 1997, Cornerhouse, Manchester, Eng., 1997, Gas Works, London, 1997, Gramercy Art Fair, 1997, Rotunda Gallery, 1997, Kunstlerhause, Vienna, 1998, Vassar Coll., Poughkeepsie, N.Y., 1998, Bard Coll., Rheinbeck, N.Y., 1998, Eyewash Gallery, Bklyn., 1994, 1999—2000, Project Space, Toronto, Can., 2001, Sideshow Gallery, Bklyn., 2001, Exit Art, N.Y.C., 2002, Voorkamer, Lier, Belgium, 2002, 2006, Art Ctr. Coll. Design, Pasadena, Calif., 2002, U. Md., College Park, 2003, Solway Jones Gallery, LA, 2003, Carlsbad Mus., N.Mex, 2003, Krasdale Gallery, N.Y., 2004, Stadt Mus., Lier, Belgium, 2004, Stedelijk Mus., Aalst, Belgium, 2004, 2006, Ill. State U., 2004, Gallery 32, London, 2004, Shore Inst. Contemporary Art, Long Branch, N.J., 2005, Pierogi, N.Y., 2005, Galerie In Situ, Aalst, Belgium, 2006, Weatherspoon Art Mus., N.C., 2006, Voorkamer, Lier, Belgium, 2006. Recipient Stedman Purchase prize, Rutgers U., 1980; Garden State fellow, 1982—84, Exhbn. grantee, Artist's Space, 1988, 1990. E-mail: smithpl@frontiernet.net.

**SMITH, PATRICIA M. (PATTI SMITH),** state supreme court justice; married; 2 children. BA, Troy State U., 1973; JD, Jones Sch. of Law, 1976. Atty. Bell, Johnson and Medaris; asst. dist. atty. Shelby County, Ala., 1976—80, dist. judge Ala., 1980—2004; assoc. justice Ala. Supreme Ct., 2005—. Organized Shelby County's Children's Policy Council; mem. Governor's Commn. on Crime, Commn. on Future of Juvenile Justice System, Ala. Jud. System Study Commn. on Sentencing; chmn. Task Force on Dependency, Interagency Conference on Youth. Named Judge of the Yr., Nat. Ct. Appointed Special Advocates, 2001. Mem.: Ala. State Bar Assn., Shelby County Bar Assn., Ala. Assn. of Juvenile and Family Ct. Judges, Ala. Assn. of Dist. Ct. Judges. Office: Ala Supreme Ct 300 Dexter Ave Montgomery AL 36104 Office Phone: 205-670-6400.*

**SMITH, PATRICK W. (RICK SMITH),** manufacturing executive; BA in Biology cum laude, Harvard U., 1991; MBA, U. Chgo., 1993; Masters Degree in Internat. Finance, U. of Leuven, Leuven, Belgium, 1993. Co-founder, CEO, dir. Taser Internat., 1993—. Named the fasted growing small public company in America, Fortune mag., 2005. Office: Taser International 17800 N 85th St Scottsdale AZ 85255 Office Phone: 480-905-2000. Office Fax: 480-991-0791. Business E-mail: rick@taser.com.

**SMITH, PATSY JUANITA,** financial executive; b. Dallas, Aug. 3, 1939; d. Roland Murl and Ruby Esther (Whiteside) Stephens; m. Jerry Arlin Kerby, June 7, 1957 (div. Nov. 1971); children: Timmy Wayne, Pamela Anita; m. Charles Albert Smith, June 17, 1977. Student, Ins. Inst., Dale Carnegie Sch. Claims adjuster Crum & Forster, Dallas, 1967—77, Atlantic Mut. Co., Dallas, 1978—79, Am. States Ins. Co., Dallas, 1979—81, Trinity Adjusting Co., Dallas, 1981—83; beauty cons. Mary Kay Cosmetics, Dallas, 1980—83, sales dir., 1983—84; loan officer Westco Fin. Svcs., Dallas, 1984—. Precinct chmn. Dem. Party, Dallas, 1981, election judge, 1981, 1982. Named Queen of Recruiting, 1982; recipient Claims Profl. of Yr. award, Ins. Women Dallas, 1998, Ins. Woman of Yr. award, 1999. Mem.: Am. Bus. Womans Assn., Dallas (Tex.) Claims Assn. (pres. 2002—03), Women's Coun. Realtors (state pub. rels. com.), Greater Dallas Bd. Realtors, Mortgage Bankers Assn., Am. Bus. Women Assn. (sec. 1980), Ins. Women of Dallas (pres. 1981—82, 2000—02, Claimswoman of Yr. 1979, 1980, Ins. Woman of Year 1998), Order Blue Goose. Home: 9922 Burnham Dr Dallas TX 75243-2412 E-mail: patjsmith1@sbcglobal.net.

**SMITH, PAUL LETTON, JR.,** geophysicist; b. Columbia, Mo., Dec. 16, 1932; s. Paul Letton and Helen Marie (Doersam) S.; m. Mary Barbara Noel; children: Patrick, Melody, Timothy, Christopher, Anne. BS in Physics, Carnegie Inst. Tech., 1955, MSEE, 1955, PhD in Elec. Engring., 1960. From instr. to asst. prof. Carnegie Inst. Tech., Pitts., 1955-63; sr. engr. Midwest Rsch. Inst., Kansas City, Mo., 1963-66; from rsch. engr. to sr. scientist and group head Inst. Atmospheric Scis., S.D. Sch. Mines and Tech., Rapid City, 1966-81; vis. prof. McGill U., Montreal, Que., Canada, 1969-70; chief scientist Air Weather Svc. USAF, Scott AFB, Ill., 1974-75; dir. Inst. Atmospheric Scis., S.D. Sch. Mines and Tech., Rapid City, 1981-96, prof. emeritus, 1996—. Lectr. Tech. Svc. Corp., Silver Spring, Md., 1972-91; vis. scientist Alberta Rsch. Coun., Edmonton, Can., 1984-85; dir. S.D. Space Grant Consortium, Rapid City, 1991-96; Fulbright lectr. U. Helsinki, 1986; nat. assoc. Nat. Acads., 2004—. Contbr. over 60 articles to profl. jours. Fellow Am. Meteorol. Soc. (Editor's award 1992, Remote Sensing lectr. 2006); mem. IEEE (life, sr.), NRC (assoc.), Weather Modification Assn. (Thunderbird award 1995), Sigma Xi. Home: 2107 9th St Rapid City SD 57701-5315 Office Phone: 605-394-2291. Business E-mail: paul.smith@sdsmt.edu.

**SMITH, PAUL VERGON, JR.,** retired gas industry executive; b. Lima, Ohio, Apr. 25, 1921; s. Paul Vergon and Aleta Rose (Bowers) S.; m. Alta Fern Chipps, Mar. 2, 1945; children: Douglas, Marsha, Jeffrey, Alison AB, Miami U., Oxford, Ohio, 1942; MS, U. Ill., 1943, PhD, 1945. With Exxon Rsch. & Engring. Co., 1946—66; with Exxon Rsch, & Engring Co., 1972—86, mgr. pub. affairs, 1972—86, mgr. ednl. and profl. soc. rels. Florham Park, NJ, 1981—86; asst. dir. chem. rsch. Esso Petroleum Co., Abingdon, England, 1966—67; dir. chem. rsch. Esso Rsch. S.A., Brussels, 1967—71; mem. adv. bd. Cache, Inc., Austin, Tex., 1979—86; pres. APS Assocs., Westfield, NJ, 1986—90. Bd. dirs., treas. Jets, Inc., Alexandria, Va.; dir. CENTCOM, Ltd.; mem. exec. bd. N.J. Bus./Industry/Sci. Edn. Consortium Patentee in field; contbr. numerous articles to profl. jours., chpts. to books Bd. dirs. United Way Union County, N.J., 1980-86; chmn. rsch. adv. coun. Miami U., 1980-84 Recipient Pres.'s award Am. Assoc. Petroleum Geologists, 1955; Spl. award N.J. Sci. Tchrs. Assn., 1985 Mem. AAAS, Am. Chem. Soc. (dir. 1978-86, chmn. bd. 1984-86; Belden award 1984), Am. Soc. Eng. Edn. (dir. 1980-86, v.p. 1980-86), Country Club Naples, Phi Beta Kappa, Sigma Xi, Omicron Delta Kappa, Phi Eta Sigma, Alpha Chi Sigma, Pi Mu Epsilon, Sigma Pi Sigma, Phi Lambda Upsilon Republican. Methodist.

**SMITH, PAULA YVETTE,** education educator; b. Kansas City, Mo., Mar. 17, 1961; d. Curley B. Adams and Jannie Mae Smith; children: Shane, Caleb Jackson. BS, U. Ark., 1998; Masters, Capella U., Mpls., 2004. Grad. cert.

social and cmty. svc. 2004. Pres. PTA, Little Rock, 2001—04; tchr. U. Ark. Med. Sci/Head Start, Little Rock, 2004—. Exec. dir. Single Parents In Edn., Little Rock, 2000—04. Com. mem. Little Rock Sch. Dist. Nutrition and Physical Activity Advisory Com., Little Rock, 2003—04. Mem.: Nat. Orgn. for Human Svc. Methodist. Home: 6405 Shady Brook Dr Little Rock AR 72204-5533 Home Fax: 501-244-0715. Personal E-mail: pysmith@arkansas.net.

**SMITH, PETER WALKER,** finance company executive; b. Syracuse, NY, May 19, 1923; s. Stanley Sherwood and Elizabeth Wilkins (Young) S.; m. Lucile Elizabeth Edson, June 22, 1946; children: Andrew E., Laurie Smith-Frailey, Pamela C. (Mrs. Denison W. Schweppe), Stanley E. B.Chem. Engring., Rensselaer Poly. Inst., 1947; MBA, Harvard U., 1948; LL.B., Cleve. Marshall Law Sch., 1955. Bar: Ohio 1955; Registered profl. engr., Ohio. Div. controller Raytheon Co., Lexington, Mass., 1958-66; v.p. finance, indsl. systems and equipment group Litton Industries Inc., Stamford, Conn., 1966-70; v.p. finance, treas. Copeland Corp., Sidney, Ohio, 1970-74; v.p. fin., treas., dir. Instrumentation Lab. Inc., Lexington, Mass., 1974-78; chief fin. officer, treas. Ionics, Inc., Watertown, Mass., 1978-80; v.p. fin., treas. Data Printer Corp., Malden, Mass., 1980-84, Orion Research Inc., Boston, 1984-87; pvt. practice cons. Concord, Mass., 1987—. Mem. fin. adv. bd.; Northeastern U., Boston. Sgt. C.E., AUS, 1943-46, ETO, 1st lt., 1950-52, Korea and Japan. Decorated Commendation medal. Mem. Fin. Execs. Inst., Am. Prodn. and Inventory Control Soc. (founding), Rensselaer Soc. Engrs., Sigma Xi, Tau Beta Pi.

**SMITH, PETER WILLIAM EBBLEWHITE,** electrical engineer, educator, research scientist, physicist; b. London, Nov. 3, 1937; m. Jacqueline Marie Mankiewicz, June 18, 1966; children: Christal, Dawn N. BSc, McGill U., Montreal, Que., Can., 1958, MSc, 1961, PhD, 1964. Profl. physicist. Mem. of staff Can. Marconi Co., Mont., 1958-59; mem. tech. staff Bell Labs. Holmdel, NJ, 1963-83; dist. mgr. Bellcore, Red Bank, NJ, 1984-88, div. mgr., 1988-92; prof. elec. and computer engring. U. Toronto, 1992—2003, prof. emeritus, 2003—; exec. dir. Ont. Laser and Lightwave Rsch. Ctr., 1992-95; dir. Nortel Inst. Telecom., 1999—2003. Editor-in-chief IEEE Press Progress in Lasers and Electro-Optics Series, 1987—92, Optics Letters, 1989—95; contbr. over 300 articles to profl. jours., chapters to books. Bd. dirs. Monmouth Arts Found., Red Bank, 1965-82; pres. The Circle for Children Found., 2003—. Recipient Sr. Scientist award NATO, 1979. Fellow IEEE (life, Quantum Electronics award 1986, Third Millennium medal 2000), Optical Soc. Am. (bd. dirs., chmn. bd. editors), Inst. Physics U.K.; mem. IEEE Lasers and Electro-Optics Soc. (pres. 1984). Achievements include first demonstration of waveguide gas laser, non-linear optical interface; development of hybrid bistable optical devices; 34 patents in field. Office: U Toronto Dept Elec & Computer Engring Toronto ON Canada M5S 3G4 E-mail: peter.smith@utoronto.ca.

**SMITH, PETER WOLFGANG,** physicist, artist; b. Rostock, Germany, May 16, 1929; s. Hans Schmidt-Isserstedt and Gertrude Calo; m. Marie Smith, Sept. 8, 1954; children: Nicholas, Lydia, Caroline. Scholar, King's Coll. Choir Sch., Cambridge, Eng., 1940—43, Felsted Sch., Essex, Eng., 1943—48; student, Cambridge Art Coll., Eng., 1950; BS with 1st honors in natural philosophy, St. Andrews U., 1952; postgrad., Edinburgh U., 1952—54. Sci. officer Admiralty Signal and Radar Establishment, Portsmouth, England, 1954—60; scientist Plessey Co., Hampshire, England, 1960—67; supr. Norden Sys., Norwalk, Conn., 1967—89; cons. Peter Smith, Westport, Conn., 1989—; artist Pierre Cochon, Westport, 1993—. Patentee in field; contbr. articles to profl. jours.; artist exhibiting in Wessex shows, U.K., 1956-60, various Conn. shows, 1996—. Mem. Inst. of Physics of London. Avocations: music, art history, golf. Home and Office: 7 Darbrook Rd Westport CT 06880-3611 Office Phone: 203-226-5162.

**SMITH, PHILIP DANIEL,** academic administrator, education educator; b. Dayton, Ohio, Dec. 25, 1933; s. Hubert Edgar and Edith (Parker) S.; m. Marilyn Brown, Nov. 25, 1953; children: Carolyn Smith Valentine, Norman Daniel, Stanley Nathan. BS cum laude, Bob Jones U., 1955; MEd, Miami U., Oxford, Ohio, 1956; EdD, Pa. State U., 1964. Dean coll. arts and sci. Bob Jones U., Greenville, SC, 1961-65, registrar, 1965-81, prof. edn., 1956—2005, provost, 1981—2005, provost emeritus, 2005—. Mem. edn. adv. bd. One Touch Systems, Inc., 1995-96. Cons. for BJ Help Network, BJ Linc, and BJU Press books Beginnings for Christian Schools, English Skills for Christian Schools, Handwriting for Christian Schools. Pres. Bob Jones U. Alumni Assn., Greenville, 1970-71; mem. coll. parallel adv. com. Tri-County Tech. Coll., Pendleton, S.C., 1973-86. Mem. Assn. Ednl. Communications and Tech. (life mem.; membership coord. profl. assns. 1969-72, vice chair nat. membership com. 1972-73, chair nat. membership com. 1973-75, council del. S.C. chpt. 1972-73, audiovisual instrn. editorial adv. com. 1974-75, del. to Lake Okoboji ednl. media leadership conf. 1972, 74), Assn. Ednl. Communications and Tech. of S.C. (bd. dirs. 1970-75, pres. 1972-73, award for outstanding contbns. and service 1971), Am. Assn. Collegiate Registrars and Admissions Officers, Phi Delta Kappa. Republican. Baptist. Office: Bob Jones U Office Provost Greenville SC 29614-0001 Office Phone: 864-242-5100. Business E-Mail: psmith@bju.edu.

**SMITH, PHILIP G.,** lawyer; b. Louisiana, Mo., Oct. 4, 1946; m. Andrea K. Smith; children: Andrew Gentry, James Lyndon. BS, N.E. Mo. State U., 1968; JD, U. Mo., 1972. Atty. Mem. Rotary Club, Elks, Masons, Mo. Alumni Assn., Mo. State U. Alumnus assn. Home: PO Box 486 Louisiana MO 63353-0486

**SMITH, PHILIP JONES,** lawyer; b. York, Pa., May 14, 1941; s. Clark S. and Margaret Ann (Jones) S.; m. Ann F. Johnson, Apr. 21, 1973; 1 child, James M. BA cum laude, Williams Coll., 1963; LLB, U. Va., 1966. Bar: Mass. 1967. Assoc. Ropes & Gray, Boston, 1967-76, ptnr., 1976—. Lectr. Boston U. Sch. of Law, 1984—98. Contbr. chapters to books, articles to profl. jours. Bd. dirs., pres. Greater Boston Youth Symphony Orch., Boston, 1978-2000; bd. dirs., v.p. pres. Keewaydin Found., Salisbury, Vt., 1980—, pres., 2002-2005; bd. dirs., past treas. Project STEP, Boston, 1987-95; overseer, chair facilities com. New Eng. Conservatory, Boston, 1989-95 Fulbright scholar, U. Madrid, 1966—67. Mem.: ABA, Essex County Club, N.Y. Yacht Club, Eastern Yacht Club (sec. 1977—83, bd. dirs. 2001—), Order of Coif. Home: 35 Harbor Ave Marblehead MA 01945-3636 Office: Ropes & Gray One Internat Pl Boston MA 02110-2624 Office Phone: 617-951-7744. Business E-Mail: p.smith@ropesgray.com.

**SMITH, PHILIP MEEK,** science administrator, consultant; b. Springfield, Ohio, May 18, 1932; s. Clarence Mitchell and Lois Ellen (Meek) Dudley. BS, Ohio State U., 1954, MA, 1955; DSc (hon.), NC State U., 1986. Mem. staff U.S. Nat. Com. for Internat. Geophys. Yr., Nas, 1957-58; program dir. NSF, 1958-63, dir. ops. U.S. Antarctic Rsch. program, 1964-69, dep. head divsn. polar programs, 1970-73, exec. asst. to dir. and spl. advisor to pres., 1974-76; chief gen. sci. br. Office Mgmt. and Budget Exec. Office of Pres., 1973-74; assoc. dir. Office Sci. and Tech. Policy, Exec. Office of Pres., 1976-81; exec. officer NRC-NAS, Washington, 1981-94; ptnr. McGeary and Smith, Washington, 2004—; chmn. external adv. com. Nat. Computational Sci. Alliance, 1997—2001, mem., 2002—03; prin. Smith Sci. Policy and Mgmt., Santa Fe, 2004—. Bd. dirs. Aurora Flight Scis. Corp.; adv. cons. bd. U. Ala. Geophys. Inst., 1994-98, adv. bd. Sci.'s Next Wave, 1998—2002; advisor Com. for Econ. Devel., 1997; com. on sci., tech. and health aspects fgn. policy agenda US NRC, 1998—2000, com. on sci. and tech. counterism, 2001—02, mem. com. sci. bases Colo. River Basin water mgmr., 2005—06, mem. com. sci. basis decision making internat. sustainable devel. orgns., 2002—05; chair com. orgn. & strategy Sci. Com. Antarctic Rsch., 1999—2000; co-chair adv. bd. Calif. Inst. Telecom. & Info. Tech., 2000—; mem. US Nat. Com. Internat. Polar Yr., 2003—05; history of geophysics com. Am. Geophys. Union, 2004—; bd. dirs. found. Los Alamos Nat. Lab., 2006—. Author: (with others) The Frozen Future, a Prophetic Report from Antarctica, 1973; contbr. articles to profl. jours. Bd. dirs. Washington Project for Arts, 1983-84, Washington Sculptors Group, 1983-84.

1st lt. U.S. Army, 1955-57. Mem. AAAS, Antarctican Soc., Cosmos Club (Washington), Am. Alpine Club (Golden, Colo.), Sigma Xi. Office: Smith Sci Policy & Mgmt 767 Acequia Madre 2 Santa Fe NM 87505-2868 Business E-Mail: pmsmith@erols.com.

**SMITH, PHILLIPS GUY,** banker; b. Orange, N.J., Sept. 15, 1946; s. Phillips Upham and Helen Otilie (Voderberg) S.; m. Ann Dixon Schickhaus, Dec. 29, 1973; children: Guy Dixon, William Schickhaus, Louisa Upham. B in engring., Stevens Inst. Tech., Hoboken, N.J.; MBA, U. Pa., 1975. Comml. banking rep. The Bank of N.Y., N.Y.C., 1976-78, asst. treas., 1978-79, asst. v.p., 1979-80, v.p., 1980-85, sr. v.p., 1985-93; mng. dir. Internat. Strategy Svcs., Inc., N.Y.C., 1993-2000; prin. Sippican Group LLC, Greenwich, Conn., 2000—. Vestryman Ch. of The Heavenly Rest, N.Y.C., 1983-88, treas., 1985-87; trustee Tabor Acad., Marion, Mass., 1987—, treas., 1991—. Lt. USN, 1970-74, Vietnam. Mem. Racquet and Tennis Club, Down Town Assn., Rockaway Hunting Club, Nantucket Yacht Club. Episcopalian. Home: 9 E 94th St New York NY 10128-0611 Office: Sippican Group LLC 15 E Putnam Ave Ste 3280 Greenwich CT 06830-5424 Business E-Mail: psmith@sippicangroup.com.

**SMITH, PHYLLIS MAE,** healthcare consultant, educator; b. Coeur d'Alene, Idaho, May 2, 1935; d. Elmer Lee Smith and Kathryn Alice (Newell) Wilson. Diploma, Luth. Bible Inst., Seattle, 1956, Emanuel Hosp. Sch. Nursing, Portland, Oreg., 1959, Coll. San Mateo, Calif., 1971. Staff nurse in surgery Emanuel Hosp., Portland, 1962-63; head nurse ctrl. svc. Sacred Heart Hosp., Eugene, Oreg., 1964-69; dir. ctrl. svcs. Peninsula Hosp., Burlingame, Calif., 1969-74; pres. Phyllis Smith Assocs. Inc., Lewiston, Idaho, 1975-88; sr. tech. advisor. dir. ednl. programs Parkside Material Mgmt. Svcs., Park Ridge, Ill., 1988-90; AIDS coord. Asotin County Health Dist., 1989-2000. Lectr., cons. in field in over 14 countries. Contbr. to manuals and profl. jours. Mem. NAFE, Internat. Assn. Hosp. Ctrl. Svc. Mgmt. (dir. edn. 1973-88, chmn. technician edn. and affairs com. 1978-88, John Perkins award 1977, Cheshire award 1977, Lifetime Achievement award 2003), Assn. for Advancement Med. Instrumentation. Lutheran. Avocations: fishing, walking, photography, chess, reading. Home and Office: 1415 Chestnut St Clarkston WA 99403-2429 Office Phone: 509-751-1180.

**SMITH, R. GORDON,** lawyer; b. Roanoke, Va., May 28, 1938; BA with highest honors, U. Va., 1960; LLB magna cum laude, Harvard U., 1964. Bar: Va. 1964. Law clk. to judge U.S. Ct. Appeals (5th cir.), 1964-65; ptnr. McGuire, Woods, Battle & Boothe, Richmond, Va., 1969—. Exec., legislation editor Harvard Law Rev., 1963-64; bd. dirs. Scott & Stringfellow Fin., Inc., Trigon Healthcare, Inc., Va. C. of C. Fellow Am. Bar Found.; mem. Va. Bar Assn. (pres. 1987-88), Am. Law Inst., Phi Beta Kappa, Omicron Delta Kappa. Office: McGuire Woods 901 E Cary St Richmond VA 23219-4057 Office Phone: 804-775-4347.

**SMITH, R. JEFFREY,** reporter; b. Milw. s. Robert J. and Eileen Smith; m. Marjorie E. Sun, May 14, 1983. With Sarasota Herald-Tribune, NY, Des Moines Register, Iowa, Milw. Jour., Science mag., Washington, 1979—86; nat. security corr. Washington Post, 1986—98, bur. chief Rome, 1998—2001, nat. news staff reporter Washington, 2001—. Recipient Sci.-in-Soc. Journalism award, Nat. Assn. Sci. Writers, 1982, Pulitzer Prize for investigative reporting, 2006. Office: Washington Post 1150 15th St NW Washington DC 20071*

**SMITH, RALPH ALEXANDER,** cultural and educational policy educator; b. Ellwood City, Pa., June 12, 1929; s. J. V. and B. V. Smith; m. Christiana M. Kolbe, Nov. 16, 1955. AB, Columbia Coll., 1954; MA, Columbia U., 1959, EdD, 1962. Faculty art history and arts edn. Kent (Ohio) State U., 1959-61, Wis. State U., Oshkosh, 1961-63, SUNY, New Paltz, 1963-64; faculty edn. and art edn. U. Ill., Urbana-Champaign, 1964—, prof. cultural and ednl. policy & aesthetic edn., prof. emeritus, 1996—. First Italo DeFrancesca Meml. lectr. Kutztown State U., 1974; Leon Jackman Meml. lectr., Perth, Australia, 85; Dean's lectr. Coll. Fine Arts and Comm., Brigham Young U., 1985; disting. vis. prof. Ohio State U., 1987; sr. scholar Coll. Edn., U. Ill., 1991; Dunbar lectr. Millsaps Coll., 1993; John Landrum Bryant lectr. Harvard U., 1999. Founder, editor: Jour. Aesthetic Edn., 1966—2000; editor: (book) Aesthetics and Criticism in Art Education, 1966, Aesthetic Concepts and Education, 1970, Aesthetics and Problems in Education, 1971, Regaining Educational Leadership, 1975, Cultural Literacy and Arts Education, 1991, Discipline-Based Art Education, 1989; editor: (with Alan Simpson) Aesthetics and Arts Education, 1991; editor: (with Bennett Reimer) The Arts, Education and Aesthetic Knowing, 1992; editor: (with Ronald Berman) Public Policy and the Aesthetic Interest, 1992; editor: General Knowledge and Arts Education, 1994, Excellence II: The Continuing Quest Art Education, 1995, Online Bibliography: Discipline Based Art Education, 1997, Readings in Discipline-Based Art Education: A Literature of Educational Reform, 2000; co-author: Research in the Arts and Aesthetic Education: A Directory of Investigators and Their Fields of Inquiry, 1978, Excellence in Art Education: Ideas and Initiatives, 1987, The Sense of Art: A Study in Aesthetic Education, 1989, Culture and the Arts in Education, 2006; author (with Albert William Levi): (book) Art Education A Critical Necessity, 1991; contbg. editor: Arts Edn. Policy Rev., 2001—. With Med. Svc. U.S. Army, 1954—57. Recipient spl. merit recognition, Coll. Edn., U. Ill., 1975, Disting. Lectr. Studies in Art Edn. award, 1991. Fellow: Nat. Art Edn. Assn. (Disting., Manuel Barkan Meml. award 1973, Nat. Educator award 2000); mem.: Ill. Art Edn. Assn. (Disting.), Coun. Policy Studies Art Edn. (1st exec. sec. 1978—82). Home: 2909 Heathwood Ct Champaign IL 61822-7659 Office: 360 Education 1310 S 6th St Champaign IL 61820-6925 Business E-Mail: ras@uiuc.edu.

**SMITH, RALPH HARRISON,** lawyer; b. Albuquerque, Nov. 2, 1951; s. Robert Tatum and Harriet Smith; m. Helen Elizabeth Oakley, July 13, 1974; children: Harrison, William, Robert BA, Washington and Lee U., 1973; MA, Oxford U., 1976; JD, Yale U., 1979. Bar: D.C. 1979, Ala. 1982. Assoc. Covington & Burling, Washington, 1979—82, Cabaniss, Johnston, Gardner, Dumas & O'Neal, Birmingham, Ala., 1982—84; ptnr. Johnston, Barton, Proctor & Powell LLP, Birmingham, 1984—2004; gen. counsel U. Ala. Sys., 2004—; adjunct prof. U. Ala. Honors Coll., 2005—. Disting. lectr. law U. Ala. Law Sch., 2005—; pres.'s adv. coun. Birmingham So. Coll., 1987-88; leadership coun. U. Ala., Birmingham, 1988-91, Med. Clinics Bd., Birmingham, 1997; dir. Comm. on Fgn. Rels., Birmingham, 1996-2002; selection com. Rhodes Scholarship, 1982-87, 98—; Ala. sec. Rhodes Scholarship Trust, 2003-04, dist. sec., 2005—; adj. prof. U. Ala. Honors Coll., 2005—. Trustee Highland's Day Sch., Birmingham, 1985-89; pres. bd. St. Martin's in the Pines Nursing Home, Birmingham, 1990; dir. Ala. Sch. Fine Arts Found., Birmingham, 1993-98, Farrah Law Soc., U. Ala. Law Sch.; mem. Leadership Birmingham, 1988, membership coun., 1998-2001; chancellor Episcopal Diocese of Ala., 2000-2003 Rhodes scholar, 1973. Mem. Birmingham Bar Assn., Tuscaloosa Bar Assn., D.C. Bar Assn., Birmingham C. of C. (trustee 1993-2004), Rotary Club Birmingham (dir., v.p. 1989-91, 90-91, 2001-02, Paul Harris fellow 2001) Episcopalian. Home: 3519 Country Club Rd Birmingham AL 35213-2826 Office: 1818 U Blvd Tuscaloosa AL 35401 Office Phone: 205-348-8345. Business E-Mail: rsmith@uasystem.ua.edu.

**SMITH, RALPH LEE,** writer, musician; b. Phila., Nov. 6, 1927; s. Hugh Harold and Barbara (Schatkin) S.; m. Betty H. Smith, Sept. 1954 (div. Jan. 1963); children: David Bruce, Robert Hugh; m. Mary Louise Hollowell, 1971 (div. 1977); m. Shizuko Maruyama, 1977; 1 child, Lisa Koyuki. BA, Swarthmore Coll., Pa., 1951; MEd, U. Va., Charlottesville, 1987. Folk musician on Appalachian dulcimer; recs. include Dulcimer: Old Time and Traditional Music, 1973, Tunes of the Blue Ridge and Great Smoky Mountains, 1983, Across the Blue Ridge, 2005; author: The Story of the Dulcimer, 1986, Appalachian Dulcimer Traditions, 1997, Songs and Tunes of the Wilderness Road, 1999, Folk Songs of Old Kentucky, 2003. Recipient writing awards Columbia U. Grad. Sch. Journalism, U. Mo. Grad. Sch. Journalism, AMA. Home: 1662 Chimney House Rd Reston VA 20190-4302 E-mail: rls2@erols.com.

**SMITH, RALPH WESLEY, JR.,** retired federal judge; b. Ghent, N.Y., July 16, 1936; s. Ralph Wesley and Kathleen S. (Callahan) S.; m. Nancy Ann Fetzer, Dec. 30, 1961 (div. 1981); children: Mark Owen, Tara Denise, Todd Kendall; m. Barbara Anne Milian, Nov. 8, 1982; stepchildren: Kim Highter, Jeffrey Highter, Eric Highter. Student, Sorbonne, U. Paris, Paris, 1954-55; BA, Yale U., 1956; LLB, Albany Law Sch., 1966. Bar: N.Y. 1966, U.S. Dist. Ct. (no. dist.) N.Y. 1966. Assoc. Hinman, Straub Law Firm, Albany, N.Y., 1966-69; chief asst. dist. atty. Albany County, N.Y., 1969-73, dist. atty. N.Y., 1974; regional dir. state nursing home investigation Asst. Atty. Gen., Albany, 1975-77; dir. State Organized Crime Task Force, 1978-82; U.S. magistrate judge U.S. Dist. Ct. (no. dist.) N.Y., Albany, 1982-2001. Judge moot ct. Albany Law Sch., 1983-2001; lectr. N.Y. State Bar Assn., 1985—, Am. Inns of Ct., 1994-99. Capt. USNR, 1957-82, ret. Mem. Fed. Magistrate Judges Assn. (dir. 2d cir. 1992-99), Columbia County Magistrates Assn. Independent. Roman Catholic. Avocations: fishing, bicycling, skiing, sailing, camping. Home: 40 Wequasset Rd Harwich Port MA 02646

**SMITH, RAYMOND LLOYD,** former university president, consultant; b. Vanceboro, Maine, Jan. 25, 1917; s. Ivan and Genevieve (Gatcomb) S.; m. Beatrice Bennett, Dec. 4, 1943 (dec. Apr. 16, 1998); children: Bennett Charles, Martin Lloyd; m. Rachel Malcolm, March 10, 2002. BS in Mining Engring. cum laude, U. Alaska, 1943; MS in Metall. Engring, U. Pa., 1951, PhD in Metall. Engring, 1953; D.Sc. (hon.), Western Mich. U.; LL.D., No. Mich. U.; D.Eng. (hon.), Mich. Technol. U., S.D. Sch. Mines and Tech. Instr. math. U. Alaska, 1946-47, asst. prof. metallurgy, 1948-49; rsch. assoc. dept. metallurgy U. Pa., 1949-53; sr. rsch. metallurgist Franklin Inst. Labs., Phila., 1953, sect. chief metallurgy, 1954-56, head solid state physics, 1957, tech. dir., 1958-59; prof., head metall. dept. Mich. Technol. U., Houghton, 1959-64, coord. rsch., 1960-64, pres., 1965-79, Am. Soc. Metals, 1979-80, Houghton (Mich.) Daily Mining Gazette, 1979-81, R. L. Smith, Inc. Am. Soc. Metals/The Metallurgical Soc. joint disting. lectr. in materials; lectr. in field. Contbr. numerous articles to metall. sci. jours.; patentee in field. With AUS, 1943—46. Recipient Distinguished Alumnus award U. Alaska, Clair M. Donovan award Mich. Tech. U., D. Robert Yarnall award U. Pa. Engring. Sch.; Outstanding Service award Air Force ROTC; Rotary Paul Harris fellow. Fellow Metall. Soc., AIME (Henry Krumb meml. lectr. 1981), Am. Soc. for Metals (hon.); mem. Scabbard and Blade, Blue Key, Tau Beta Pi, Alpha Sigma Mu (hon. lectr. 1982), Alpha Phi Omega, Phi Kappa Phi, Theta Tau. Home: PO Box 726 Green Valley AZ 85622-0726 Personal E-mail: raysmith726@aol.com. *A sense of humor is one of the important building blocks for that firm sense of balance so necessary to meet the challenges of life. It's like the seasoning of a chef's masterpiece.*

**SMITH, RAYMOND THOMAS,** anthropology educator; b. Oldham, Lancashire, Eng., Jan. 12, 1925; s. Harry and Margaret (Mulchrone) S.; m. Flora Alexandria Tong, June 30, 1954; children: Fenela, Colin, Anthony. BA, Cambridge U., Eng., 1950, MA, 1951, PhD, 1954. Sociol. research officer govt., Brit. Guiana, 1951-54; research fellow U. W.I., 1954-59; prof. sociology U. Ghana, 1959-62; sr. lectr. sociology, prof. anthropology U. West Indies, 1962-66; prof. anthropology U. Chgo., 1966-95, prof. emeritus, 1995—, chmn. dept. anthropology, 1975-81, 84-85, 94-95. Vis. prof. U. Calif.-Berkeley, 1957-58, McGill U., Montreal, 1964-65; mem. com. on child devel. rsch. and pub. policy NRC, 1977-80; dir. Caribbean Consortium Grad. Sch., 1985-86. Author: The Negro Family in British Guiana, 1956, British Guiana, 1962, 2d edit., 1980, Kinship and Class In The West Indies, 1988, The Matrifocal Family, 1996; co-author: Class Differences in American Kinship, 1978; editor: Kinship Ideology and Practice in Latin America, 1984; contbr. articles to profl. jours. Co-investigator urban family life project U. Chgo., 1986-90. Served with RAF, 1943-48. Guggenheim fellow, 1983-84 Fellow Am. Anthrop. Assn.; mem. Assn. Social Anthropologists. Office: Univ Chicago Dept Anthropology 1126 E 59th St Chicago IL 60637-1580 E-mail: r-smith@uchicago.edu.

**SMITH, RAYMOND W.,** investment banking executive; b. Pitts., 1937; BS, Carnegie-Mellon U., 1959; MBA, U. Pitts., 1969. Budget dir. AT&T, 1976-77; v.p.-regulatory Bell of Pa. and Diamond State Tel., Phila., 1981-83; pres., CEO Bell of Pa. & Diamond State Tel., Phila., 1983-85; vice chmn., CFO, dir. parent co. Bell Atlantic Corp., Phila., 1985-88, pres., COO, 1988, chmn., CEO Phila., 1989-98, Rothschild North America, Inc., NYC, 1999—; founding ptnr. Arlington Capital Partners, 1998—. Bd. dirs., U.S. Airways, CBS Corp., Banneker Technologies; mem. Bus. Roundtable, 1990—; mem. nat. adv. bd. Pvt. Sector Coun., 1990—; mem. James Madison nat. coun. Libr. of Congress, 1990—. Pub. playwright. Mem. Lincoln Ctr., Pres. Commn.-Arts and Humanities, WETA, Carnegie Corp., Carnegie Mellon, Rockham Ventures; trustee, Rockefeller Found., 2006-; With Signal Corps, U.S. Army, 1959-60. Office: Rothschild North Am Inc 1251 Avenue Of The Americas New York NY 10020-1104 also: Arlington Capital Ptnrs Ste 660 600 New Hampshire Ave NW Washington DC 20037*

**SMITH, REBECCA LYNN,** language educator; b. Camp Springs, Md., Oct. 16, 1967; d. D. E. and Edith M. Smith. A in bus., San Antonio Coll., 1989; BA in English, U. Tex. San Antonio, 2000, M in English, 2003. Supr. Roy Maas' Youth Alternatives, Boerne, Tex., 1993—97. Mem.: Beth Sichma, Alpha Phi, Sigma Tau Delta. Avocations: watercolor painting, travel. Home: 12205 Wilderness Trail San Antonio TX 78233 Office: NW Vista Coll 3535 N Ellison Dr San Antonio TX 78251

**SMITH, REGINALD BRIAN FURNESS,** retired anesthesiologist, educator; b. Warrington, Eng., Feb. 7, 1931; s. Reginald and Betty (Bell) S.; m. Margarete Groppe, July 18, 1963; children: Corinne, Malcolm. MB, BS, U. London, 1955; DTM and H, Liverpool Sch. Tropical Medicine, 1959. Intern Poole Gen. Hosp., Dorset, England, 1955-56, Wilson Meml. Hosp., Johnson City, NY, 1962-63; resident in anesthesiology Med. Coll. Va., Richmond, 1963-64, U. Pitts., 1964-65, from clin. instr. to prof., 1965-78, acting chmn. dept. anesthesiology, 1977-78; anesthesiologist in chief Presbyn. Univ. Hosp., Pitts., 1976-78; dir. anesthesiology Eye and Ear Hosp., Pitts., 1971-76; prof., chmn. dept. U. Tex. Health Sci. Ctr., San Antonio, 1978-98, anesthesiologist in chief hosps., 1978-98, clin. prof. anesthesiology, 1999—, clin. prof. rehab. medicine, 2003—, med. dir. hyperbaric medicine and woundcare unit Univ. Hosp., 1993-2000, mem. med. staff Univ. Hosp., 2003—; ret., 2000. Contbg. editor: Internat. Ophthalmology Clinics, 1973, Internat. Anesthesiology Clinics, 1983; contbr. articles to profl. jours. Served to capt. Brit. Army, 1957-59. Fellow ACP, Am. Coll. Anesthesiologists, Am. Coll. Chest Physicians; mem. AMA, Internat. Anesthesia Rsch. Soc., Am. Soc. Anesthesiologists (pres. Western Pa. 1974-75), Tex. Soc. Anesthesiologists, San Antonio Soc. Anesthesiologists (pres. 1990), Tex. Med. Assn., Bexar County Med. Soc. Home: 76 Bristol Green San Antonio TX 78209-1104

**SMITH, REX WILLIAM,** journalist; b. Danville, Ill., Oct. 19, 1952; s. Ralph William and Lillian Grace (Hart) S.; m. Marion Roach, July 15, 1989. BA cum laude, Trinity U., San Antonio, 1974; MS with highest honors, Columbia U., N.Y.C., 1980. Mag. editor Rensselaer (Ind.) Rep. newspaper, 1974-75; legis. asst. U.S. Rep. Floyd J. Fithian, Washington, 1975-79; reporter, spl. writer Newsday, L.I., NY, 1980-87, chief Albany (N.Y.) bur., 1987-91; editor The Record, Troy, NY, 1991-95; mng. editor Times Union, Albany, NY, 1995—2002, editor, v.p., 2002—. Vice chair NY Fair Trial Free Press Conf., 2002—. Contbr. numerous articles to newspapers and mags. Recipient Cmty. Svc. award Rensselaer C. of C., 1975, Media award World Hunger Fund, 1983, Disting. Svc. medal Soc. Profl. Journalists, 1987, Editl. award Common Cause, 1992, Disting. Cmty. Svc. award N.Y. State Pubs. Assn., 1994; Rotary fellow, 1979, Pulitzer Travel fellow Columbia U., 1982; named Citizen of Yr. N.Y. State LWV, 1999. Mem. N.Y. State Assoc. Press Assn. (pres. 1998). Home: 3 Middle Hill Rd Troy NY 12180-6827 Office: Times Union PO Box 15000 Albany NY 12212-5000 Office Phone: 518-454-5040. Business E-Mail: rsmith@timesunion.com.

**SMITH, RICHARD A.,** manufacturing executive; b, U. Chgo.; MBA, Northwestern U.; JD, St. Louis U. Former asst. treas., asst. to CFO Ralston Purina; former v.p. and treas., v.p. and contr. of Payless Show Source divsns. May Dept. Stores; former v.p. fin., CFO Arvin Industries, Inc. (now Arvin Meritor, Inc.); CFO, chief adminstrn. officer Zonetrader.com, 2000—01; CFO Lennox Internat., Richardson, Tex., 2001—. Mem.: Mo. Bar, Mfrs. Alliance, Fin. Execs. Inst. Office: Lennox Internat 2140 Lake Park Blvd Richardson TX 75080

**SMITH, RICHARD ALAN,** publishing and specialty retailing executive; b. Boston, 1924; married. BS, Harvard U., 1946; LLD (hon.), Boston Coll., 1988. With Smith Mgmt. Co.: 1947-61; chmn. bd., CEO Gen. Cinema Corp. (name changed to Harcourt Gen., Inc. 1993), Chestnut Hill, Mass., 1961-91; chmn., CEO Harcourt Gen. Inc., Chestnut Hill, Mass., 1993—; chmn. bd., CEO Neiman Marcus, Chestnut Hill, Mass., 1987—; chmn., CEO, pres. GC Cos., Inc., Chestnut Hill, Mass., 1993-95, chmn., CEO, 1995—. Address: GC Companies Inc 1280 Boylston St Chestnut Hill MA 02467

**SMITH, RICHARD BERNARD,** music educator; MusB, N.W. La. State U., 1968, MusM, 1969; MusD, La. State U., 1976. Asst. prof. Sam Houston State U., Huntsville, Tex., 1976—83; prof. piano Ctrl. Mo. State U., Warrensburg, Mo., 1993—. Office: Central Missouri State University Department of Music Warrensburg MO 64093 E-mail: rbsmith@cmsu1.cmsu.edu.

**SMITH, RICHARD BOWEN,** retired national park superintendent; b. Grandville, Mich., Mar. 8, 1938; s. William Jr. and Mary Elizabeth (Bowen) S.; m. Katherine Theresa Short, Sept. 21, 1980. BA in History, Albion Coll., 1960; MA in English, Mich. State U., 1967. Tchr. Grand Rapids (Mich.) Jr. H.S., 1960-66; vol. Peace Corps, Asuncion, Paraguay, 1968-70; ranger Nat. Pk. Svc., Yosemite, Calif. 1971-76, ranger. instr. Grand Canyon, Ariz., 1976-78, ranger, legis. specialist Washington, 1978-80, asst. supt. Everglades, Fla., 1980-83, assoc. regional dir. ops. Phila., 1984-86, supt. Carlsbad Caverns, N.Mex., 1986-88, assoc. regional dir. ops. Santa Fe, 1988-89; assoc. regional dir. resources mgmt. Nat. Park Service, Santa Fe, 1990-94; cons. on protected area mgmt. in L.Am., 1994—; temp. supt. Yellowstone Nat. Pk., 1994—; owner R & K Internat., 1994—2000; assoc. Orgnl. Quality Assocs., 2000—. Pres. Assn. Nat. Park Rangers, 1977-78; coord. Congress of Internat. Ranger Fedn., San Jose, Costa Rica, 1997, v.p., 1998-2000, pres., 2000-03. Bd. dirs. Yellowstone Assn., 1995-97, Ptnrs. in Parks, 1998-2000. Recipient Meritorious Svc. award Dept. Interior, 1992, Disting. Alumnus award Albion Coll., 2006. Mem. Assn. Nat. Park Rangers (chmn. internat. com. 1997-2000), George Wright Soc. (bd. dirs. 1998—2004), Coalition of Nat. Park Svc. Retirees (exec. coun. 2004—). Home: 2 Roadrunner Trl Placitas NM 87043-9424 E-mail: rsmith0921@earthlink.net.

**SMITH, RICHARD C. (DICK),** lawyer; b. Jackson, Miss., 1946; BA, Univ. Fla., 1968; JD, Harvard Univ., 1971. Bar: Fla. 1971, US Dist. Ct. (so. dist. Fla.), US Ct. Appeals (5th, 11th cir.). Ptnr., bus. litigation, antitrust & trade regulation practices Shook Hardy & Bacon LLP, Miami, Fla. Editor (legis.): Harvard Jour. on Legislation; editor: partnership & corp. litigation chpt., Southeast Litigation Guide. Mem. Fla. Humanities Council. Served to Lt. JAGC USNR, 1972—75. Mem.: ABA, Assn. Trial Lawyers Am., Acad. Fla. Trial Lawyers, Fla. Bar, Dade County Bar Assn. Office: Shook Hardy & Bacon LLP Suite 2400 Miami Ctr 201 S Biscayne Blvd Miami FL 33131-4332 Office Phone: 305-960-6924. Office Fax: 305-358-7470.

**SMITH, RICHARD CHARLES,** not-for-profit administrator, educator, consultant, advocate; b. St. Paul, July 30, 1947; s. Arthur George Smith, Edna Alma Smith; m. Joan Rita Oxendine. BA, Calif. State U., San Bernardino, 1976; MBA, U. Calif., Riverside, 1981. Dir. mktg. SCW and Assoc., Riverside, Calif., 1981—84; dir. mktg. and ops. Thomas and Assoc., Riverside, 1984—85; v.p. br. adminstrn. First Fed. Savings and Loan, Ridgecrest, Calif., 1985—90; gen. mgr. KLOA Radio, Ridgecrest, 1990—92; dir. mktg. Ridgecrest Auto Ctr., Ridgecrest, 1992—94; exec. dir. Partnership to Preserve Indep. Living for Srs. and Persons with Disabilities, Riverside, 1994—. Mem. Riverside County C.A.R.E. Team, 2001—; sr. advisor The Beverly Found., 2004—; mem. Am. Soc. on Aging, 2005—; cons., spkr. in field. Prodr.: (ednl. videos) Health Education Program Series, 2002; contbr. articles to profl. jours. E5 Army, 1966—69, Vietnam. Office: Partnership for Independent Living 6296 Rivercrest Dr Ste K Riverside CA Office Phone: 951-867-3800. Personal E-Mail: rsmith@vitalco.net.

**SMITH, RICHARD EMERSON (DICK SMITH),** make-up artist; b. Larchmont, NY, June 26, 1922; s. Richard Roy and Coral (Brown) S.; m. Jocelyn De Rosa, Jan. 10, 1949; children: Douglas Todd, David Emerson. BA, Yale U., 1944. Pioneer dir. first TV make-up dept. NBC-TV, N.Y.C., 1945-59; make-up dir. David Susskind Prodns., N.Y.C., 1959-61; freelance make-up artist, cons., 1961—. Lectr. Yoyogi Animation Sch., Tokyo, 1992—, Polytek Devel. seminar, 1996; key spkr. Internat. Make-up and Effects Trade Show, 1997-99; featured make-up expert in Movie Magic tv documentaries, Monster Effects, 1994, Aging Effects, 1995; lectr. on spl. make-up effects Douglas Edn. Ctr., Monessen, Pa., 2004— Credits include Requiem for a Heavyweight, 1962, The World of Henry Orient, 1963, Mark Twain, Tonight!, 1967 (Emmy award 1967), Midnight Cowboy, 1968, Little Big Man, 1969, The Godfather, 1971, The Exorcist, 1973, The Godfather, Part II, 1974, The Sunshine Boys, 1975, Taxi Driver, 1975, Altered States, 1979, Scanners, 1980, Ghost Story, 1981, The Hunger, 1982, Amadeus, 1983 (U.S. Acad. award 1984, Brit. Acad. award 1985), Starman, 1984, Poltergeist III, 1987, Everybody's All-American, 1988, Sweet Home (Japanese film), 1988, Dad, 1989, Death Becomes Her, 1991, Forever Young, 1992; author: The Advanced Professional Make-Up Course, 1985, The Basic 3-D Make-up Course, 2002; permanent exhbn. of make-up work from Little Big Man, The Exorcist, Amadeus, others, at N.Y. Mus. of the Moving Image, 1992—; columnist Makeup Artist Mag., 1997—. Honored on his 50th ann. in make-up by Am. Film Inst., Visionary Cinema, Cinefex mag. 1995, 60 Yrs Achievement in Makeup, Internat. Make-Up Artists Trade Show, 2005. Home and Office: 27 Wilford Ave Branford CT 06405-3822 Office Phone: 203-488-8111. Personal E-mail: pros355@aol.com.

**SMITH, RICHARD F.,** financial services company executive; BS, Purdue Univ., 1983. Sales rep. Owens Corning, Kans. City, Kans., 1981—83; various mgmt. positions GE, 1983—2005; sales rep. GE Plastics Bus. Group, Itasca, Ill., mktg. mgr.; gen. mgr.; pres., CEO GE Capital Modular Space, Malvern, Pa., GE Capital Fleet Services, Eden Prairie, Minn., GE Global Property & Casualty Reinsurance, Overland Park, Kans.; COO GE Ins. Solutions, Overland Park, Kans.; pres., CEO Equifax Inc., Atlanta, 2005, chmn., pres., CEO, 2006—. Office: Equifax Inc 1550 Peachtree St NW Atlanta GA 30309 Mailing: Equifax Inc PO Box 4081 Atlanta GA 30302*

**SMITH, RICHARD HOWARD,** banker; b. Tulare, Calif., Aug. 27, 1927; s. Howard Charles and Sue Elizabeth (Cheyne) S.; B.A., Principia Coll., 1958; LL.B., LaSalle U., 1975; postgrad. Sch. Banking U. Wash., 1970-72; m. Patricia Ann Howery, Mar. 12, 1950 (dec. Sept. 2001); children: Jeffrey Howard, Holly Lee, Gregory Scott, Deborah Elaine; m. Charlene Burruel, Mar. 27, 2004. Prin., Aurora Elementary Sch., Tulare, 1951-53; prin. Desert Sun Sch., Idyllwild, Calif., 1953-55; trust adminstr. trainee Bank of Am., San Diego, 1955-58, asst. trust officer, Ventura, Redlands, Riverside and L.A., 1958-65; asst. trust officer Security Pacific Bank, Fresno, Calif., 1965-68; trust officer, 1968-72, v.p., mgr., 1972-88, Pasadena, 1988-94; v.p. Bank of Am., L.A., 1994-95; ret., 1995; pres. Fiduciary Svcs., Fresno, 1995—; instr. San Bernardino Valley Coll., 1962-, Fresno City Coll., 1977-. With USN, 1945-46. Home: 3222 W Dovewood Ln Fresno CA 93711-2125 Office: Smith Fiduciary Svc 163 7081 N Marks Ave #104 Fresno CA 93711-0232 Office Phone: 559-432-6573.

**SMITH, RICHARD JACKSON,** elementary school educator; b. Mt. Airy, N.C., Feb. 17, 1947; s. Robert Wayne and Ruth (Jackson) S.; m. Sue Monday, Sept. 10, 1971 (dec. Nov. 21, 1981); 1 child, Richard Jackson Jr. BA, A.N.C., 1972; MA, Appalachian State U., 1975; EdD, U. N.C. 1994. Elem. tchr. Surry County Schs., Dobson, NC, 1967-96, Title I parent coord., 1992-96, K-5 instnl. specialist, 1996—2003; project coord. Reading Is Fundamental, 1996-2000. Part-time instr. grad. equivalency diploma/adult basic edn. and effective tchr. tng. classes Surry C.C., Dobson, 1988-92, tchr. literacy class,

1999-2000; adj. faculty Lees-McRae Coll., 2003—; cons. Eckerd Family Youth Alternatives, Inc., 1994-96. Local and dist. chmn., state treas. N.C. Polit. Action Com. Edn., Raleigh, 1976-81; state exec. com. N.C. Dem. Party, Raleigh, 1981-83; trustee, deacon First Bapt. Ch. of Pilot Mountain, 1988—, Sunday sch. dir. 1991—, mem. nominating com., 1991—; sec. bd. deacons 1990-91, vice chmn. 1996-97, chmn. 1997-99; trustee Charles M. Stone Meml. Libr., 1997-2000, vice chmn., 1998-99, chmn., 1999-2000; chaplain Gideon Internat., pilot camp, 2000-2004, sec.; scripture chair, 2004—; bd. dirs. Surry County chpt. ARC, chmn. bd. dirs., 2000-05, vice chmn., 2003-2004, chair, 2004-2005; v.p. Pilot Mountain Civic Club, 2006. Mem. ASCD, NEA (congressional lobbying 1976-80), Internat. Reading Assn. (local unit chair 1986-90), N.C. Assn. Educators (local, dist. pres. 1979-81, local, dist., state chmn. legis. commn. 1980-81), Pilot Mountain Jaycees (life, charter, pres. 1979-80, Officer of Yr. 1978, 79), Geneal. Soc. Rockingham & Stokes Counties, Stokes County Hist. Soc., SCV (Stokes County camp 1994—), Masons (32 degree, Scottish Rite, amb. 1990—, lodge master 1990, edn. chmn. 1986—, scholarship chmn. 1986—, Cert. of Meritorious Svc. 1988, adv. bd. Masonic Home for Children at Oxford 2001—, dist. dep. grand master Grand Lodge of N.C. 2001-2004, chmn. grand lodge com. masonic edn. chair 2004—), Pilot Mtn. Civc Club (v.p. 2006). Home: PO Box 127 517 E Main St Pilot Mountain NC 27041-8519 E-mail: drrichardsmith@yahoo.com.

**SMITH, RICHARD JAMES,** retired music educator; b. Baton Rouge, Nov. 28, 1950; s. Jimmie P. and Agnes Mae Smith; m. Dewanna Ann Davis, July 3, 1992 (div. Apr. 30, 2003); m. Lenora Faye McMillon, Mar. 3, 1981 (div. Feb. 28, 1988); m. Elissa Sisk Parks, Oct. 14, 2003; 1 child, James. MusB Edn., La. State U., 1972, MusM Edn., 1977, PhD, 1986. Cert. tchr. La. State Dept. Edn., 1972. Band dir. Northside H.S., Atlanta, 1972—73, Redemptorist H.S., Baton Rouge, 1973—74, East Beauregard H.S., DeRidder, La., 1974—77, Hammond H.S., Hammond, La., 1977—78, Silliman Inst., La., 1978—81, Mansfield H.S., Mansfield, La., 1981—83; dir. band and choir Breaux Bridge H.S., Breaux Bridge, La., 1984—85; band dir. Raynaud Mid. Sch., Lake Charles, La., 1985—86, Tallulah H.S., Tallulah, La., 1988—91, Pointe Coupee Ctrl. H.S., LaBarre, La., 1991—94, Glen Oaks H.S., Baton Rouge, 1994—95, Claiborne Acad., Haynesville, La., 1995—97, Jonesboro-Hodge H.S., Jonesboro, La., 1997—98; piano instr. Recreation and Parks Commn., Baton Rouge, 1998—99; band dir. East Iberville H.S., St. Gabriel, La., 1999—2000; piano instr. Recreation and Pks. Commn., Baton Rouge, 2000—. Composer: Symphonic Essay for Band, 1973, March Triumphe, 1974, Go, Ye Trojans, 1975, Adagio for unaccompanied flute, 1975, Serenade for Unaccompanied Flute, 1975, Noble Knights, 1976, In Memoriom, 1976, Requiem Mass in D minor, 1977, Fight On!, 1978, Sillman Inst. Alma Mater, 1978, Elegy, 1980, The Silver Star, 1980, Freedom Express, 1982, Marche Royale, 1984, Hail to Liberty, 1986, Hall of Justice, 1986, Freedom and Unity, 1988, First Pl. in Mansfield Christmas Parade - Mansfield H.S. Band, Mansfield, LA, Chamber of Commerce, 1981. Mem.: NEA (life), U.S. Achievement Acad. (nat. adv. bd. 1983—2002), La. Bandmasters Assn., La. Music Educators Assn., Music Educators Nat. Conf., La. Educators Assn. (life), Pi Kappa Lambda, Kappa Kappa Psi (life Outstanding pledge 1969). Avocations: travel, reading, music, building 3-d puzzles, miniature golf. Home: 10515 Tallowwood Ave Baker LA 70714 Office: Recreation and Parks Commission 3140 N Sherwood Forest Dr Baton Rouge LA 70814 Office Phone: 225-262-1956. Personal E-mail: rjsmith4@cox.net.

**SMITH, RICHARD MILLS,** editor-in-chief; b. Detroit, Jan. 12, 1946; s. William Steele Smith and Janet (Mills) Morrison; m. Lee Ann Vanderstoep (div.); children: Scott William, Anna Mills; m. Soon-Young Yoon, Oct. 20, 1978; 1 child, Song-Mee. BA summa cum laude, Albion Coll., 1968; postgrad., Columbia U., 1968—69, MS, 1970; LLD (hon.), Albion Coll., 1993. Reporter Associated Press, NY, 1969; assoc. editor foreign dept. Newsweek, NY, 1970—73, gen. editor nat. affairs dept. NY, 1973—74, editor Asian region, bur. chief Hong Kong Hong Kong, 1974—77; mng. editor Newsweek Internat., NY, 1977—81; asst. mng. editor Newsweek, NY, 1982, exec. editor, 1983, editor in chief, 1984—, pres., 1991—98, chmn., 1998—. Chmn. Mag. Pub. Am., 1996—97. Trustee Albion Coll; bd. dirs. Cooper-Hewitt Nat. Design Mus., Smithsonian Instn., Harvard AIDS Inst. Recipient Disting. Alumni award, Albion Coll., 1974, Henry Johnson Fisher award, Mag. Pub. of Am., 2001. Mem.: Century Assn., Coun. on Fgn. Rels., Mag. Pubs. Assn. (chmn.), Am. Soc. Mag. Editors (mem. exec. com. 1985—88), Phi Beta Kappa. Office: Newsweek Inc 251 W 57th St New York NY 10019-1802*

**SMITH, RICHEY,** manufacturing executive; b. Akron, Ohio, Nov. 11, 1933; s. Thomas William and Martha (Richey) S.; m. Sandra Cosgrave Roe, Nov. 25, 1961; children: Mason Roe, Parker Richey. Grad., Hotchkiss Sch.; BS, U. Va., Charlottesville, 1956. Asst. to pres. Sun Products Corp., Barberton, Ohio, 1960-64, v.p., 1964-67, gen. mgr., dir., 1967-69, chmn., CEO, 1969-76; prin. A.T. Kearney Co., Cleve., 1977-87; chmn., CEO Richey Industries, Inc., Medina, Ohio, 1987—. Bd. dirs. Jaite Packaging, Inc. Exec. com. Gt. Trail coun. Boy Scouts Am.; chmn. capital funds dr. Summit County Planned Parenthood; trustee, found. pres. Old Trail Sch., Barberton Citizens Hosp., Medina County Arts Coun., Akron Regional Devel. Bd.; treas. Friends of Metro Park; found. trustee, vestryman St. Paul's Episcopal Ch.; corp. bd. Cleve. Mus. of Art; bd. govs. The Hotchkiss Sch. Lt. USN, 1957—60, lt. comdr. USNR, 1961—69. Mem. Ohio Commodores, Bluecoats (trustee), Navy League (pres. Akron coun. 1972-73), Young Pres. Orgn., Portage Country Club (bd. dirs.), Mayflower Club, Sawgrass Country Club (Fla.) Farmington Country Club (Charlottesville, Va.), Rotary (trustee Akron 1974-75), Yale Club (N.Y.C.), Rockwell Springs Trout Club, Chi Psi (pres.). Home: 721 Delaware Ave Akron OH 44303-1303 Office: 910 Lake Rd Medina OH 44256-2453 Office Phone: 330-725-4997 x 304. E-mail: rsmith@richeyind.com.

**SMITH, RICK,** professional sports team executive; b. Sept. 3, 1969; BA, Purdue Univ., Ind., 1992. Asst. strength and conditioning coord. Purdue Univ., 1993—94, defensive backs coach, 1994—95; defensive unit coach Denver Broncos, 1996—99, also pro personnel ops., 1999—2005, asst. gen. mgr., 2006; gen. mgr. Houston Texans, 2006—. Achievements include being NFL's youngest gen. mgr., 2006. Office: Houston Texans Two Reliant Park Houston TX 77054 Office Phone: 832-667-2000.*

**SMITH, RISE LOUISE,** librarian; b. Ft. Wayne, Ind., Sept. 16, 1952; d. Dallas Fisher and Leah Loretta (Nyffeler) S.; m. Eugene Allan Fosnight, Oct. 30, 1973; 1 child, Teal Helena Fosnight. BA, Kalamazoo Coll., 1974; MA, U. Mich., 1976; MLS, San Jose State U., 1981. Reference and serials librarian Santa Teresa Lab. IBM, San Jose, Calif., 1981; archives asst. Sioux Falls (S.D.) Coll., 1982-84, circulation supr., 1983-84, learning resources dir., 1984; acting dir. Mundt Library Dakota State Coll., Madison, S.D., Apr. to Aug., 1986, pub. svcs. libr., 1984-90; tech. svcs. libr., 1990—92; pub. svcs. libr., 1994—. Named Libr. of Yr., S.D. Libr. Assn. Mem. AAUW (pres. Madison chpt. 1988-90), ALA, Assn. Coll. and Rsch. Librs., S.D. Libr. Assn. (treas. 1990-91, chmn. acad. sect. 1985-86, pres. 1996-97). Home: 6285 Dakota Ave Madison SD 57042-9444 Office: Dakota State U Mundt Libr Madison SD 57042 Office Phone: 605-256-7126. E-mail: rise.smith@dsu.edu.

**SMITH, ROBERT BOULWARE, III,** vascular surgeon, educator; b. Atlanta, June 15, 1933; s. Robert Boulware Jr. Smith and Mary Eva (Black) Fanning; m. Florence Chance Limehouse, Aug. 22, 1953; children: Victoria Joanne Smith Harkins, Robert Boulware IV, Brian Scott. MD, Emory U., 1957. Diplomate Am. Bd. Surgery, Am. Bd. Vascular Surgery. Intern in surgery Columbia Presbyn. Hosp., N.Y.C., 1957-58, resident in surgery, 1960-65; asst. prof. surgery Emory U. Sch. Medicine, Atlanta, 1966-69, assoc. prof., 1969-77, prof., 1977—, head gen. vascular surgery, 1984-98. Chief surg. svc. VA Med. Ctr., Atlanta, 1969-88; assoc. med. dir. Emory U. Hosp., 1993-95, med. dir., 1995—. Contbr. numerous articles, book chpts. to profl. publs.; co-editor: Trauma to the Thorax and Abdomen, 1969, Medical Management of the Surgical Patient, 1982, 3d edit., 1995. Capt. M.C., U.S. Army, 1958-60. Mem. ACS, Am. Surg. Assn., So. Assn. Vascular Surgery (sec. 1986-91, pres. 1992-93), Soc. Vascular Surgery, Assn. VA Surgeons (pres. 1983-84, Disting. Svc. award 1988), Ga. Surg. Soc. (pres. 1992-93), Atlanta Vascular Soc. (pres. 1986-88), Internat. Soc. for Cardiovasc. Surg. (pres. 1996-97). Phi Beta Kappa, Alpha Omega Alpha. Republican. United Methodist. Avocations: music, travel. Home: 2701 Coldwater Canyon Dr Tucker GA 30084-2358 Office: Emory Univ Hosp B207 1364 Clifton Rd NE Atlanta GA 30322-1013 Office Phone: 404-727-8145. Business E-Mail: robert.smith@emory.edu.

**SMITH, ROBERT CARLISLE,** department administrator, welding educator; b. St. Albans, W.Va., Sept. 2, 1939; s. Clarence Mack (stepfather) and Artimitia (Blake) Smith Fowler; m. Janet Lee Koehn, Dec. 28, 1958; children: Teresa Lynn, Stephen Carlisle. BA, Glenville State U., 1984; MSc, Marshall U., 1994. Cert. welding inspector, non-destructive tester. Br. mgr. Va. Welding, Charleston, W.Va., 1963—76; prin. Weld Inspection and Cons., St. Albans, 1976—94; mgr. quality assurance Kanawha Mfg., Charleston, 1988—2003; dept. head, instr. welding W.Va. U., Parkersburg, 1981—2003. Contbr. articles. Lt. ROTC 1957-71; committeeman Rep. Party, Kanawha County, 1968-69; former Sun. sch. tchr. Highlawn Baptist Ch.; presenter Nat. Educators Workshop NASA, Langley Space Flight Ctr., 1993. Recipient Disting. West Virginian award Gov. W.Va., 1968, Tchr. of Excellence award Nat. Inst. for Staff and Orgnl. Devel.; named Outstanding Prof. of Yr. W.Va. U. Parkersburg campus, 2005. Mem. Am. Welding Soc. (chmn. 1971-72, program chairperson 1989-90, educator of yr. 1990, 92, 2003-04), Am. Soc. Non-Destructive Testing (membership recruiter 1988), W.Va. Edn. Assn., W.Va. C.C. Assn. Protestant. Avocations: autos, trucks, writing, fishing, banjo. Home: 2302 S Walnut Dr Saint Albans WV 25177-3947 E-mail: carlsmith@mail.wvu.edu.

**SMITH, ROBERT CLINTON,** former senator; b. Trenton, N.J., Mar. 30, 1941; s. Donald and Margaret (Eldridge) S.; m. Mary Jo Hutchinson, July 2, 1966; children: Jennifer L., Robert Clinton, Jason H. AA, Trenton Jr. Coll., 1963; BA, Lafayette Coll., 1965; postgrad., Long Beach State U., 1968-69. Tchr., realtor, Wolfeboro, N.H., 1970-85; chmn. Gov. Wentworth Dist. Sch. Bd., 1978-84; mem. 99th-101st Congresses from 1st N.H. dist., Washington, 1985-90, U.S. Senate from N.H., Washington, 1990—2003. Mem. armed svcs., environ. and pub. works, chmn. ethic com., chmn. and sen. judiciary com. With USN, 1962-69, Vietnam. Mem. Am. Legion, Theta Xi. Republican. Roman Catholic. Office: The Everglades Foundation PO Box 1436 Osprey FL 34229-1436

**SMITH, ROBERT EARL,** space scientist; b. Indpls., Sept. 13, 1923; s. Harold Bennett and Bernice (McCaslin) S.; m. Elizabeth Lee Usak, Jan. 3, 1947 (dec. 1984); children: Stephanie Lee, Robert Michael, Cynthia Ann, Kelly Andrew; m. Lyla Lee Lewellen, July 1, 1988. BS, Fla. State U., 1959, MS, 1960, U. Mich., 1969, PhD, 1974. Enlisted US Army Air Force, 1943-44; advanced through grades to maj. U.S. Air Force, 1955; airway traffic controller Berlin, 1945; staff weather reconnaissance officer 9th Air Force, 1956; ret., 1963; project scientist Atmospheric Cloud Physics Lab.; dep. chief atmospheric scis. div. NASA/Marshall Space Flight Ctr., Ala., 1963-86; sr. scientific cons. Univs. Space Rsch. Assn., Huntsville, Ala., 1986-87; sr. computer cons. Computer Scis. Corp., Huntsville, 1987-89; chief space sci. and applications div. FWG Assocs., Inc., Huntsville, 1989-92; NASA program mgr. Physitron, Inc., Huntsville, 1992-96; sr. computer scientist Computer Scis. Corp., Huntsville, 1996—2002. Mem. AIAA, Pi Mu Epsilon, Sigma Phi Epsilon. Avocation: golf. Home: 125 Westbury Dr SW Huntsville AL 35802-1619

**SMITH, ROBERT EVERETT,** lawyer; b. NYC, Mar. 15, 1936; s. Arthur L. and Augusta (Cohen) S.; m. Emily Lucille Lehman, July 17, 1960; children: Amy, Karen, Victoria. BA, Dartmouth Coll., 1957; LLB, Harvard U., 1960. Bar: N.Y. 1960, U.S. Dist. Ct. (so. dist.) N.Y. 1962, U.S. Ct. Appeals (2d cir.) 1963, U.S. Supreme Ct. 1967, U.S. Dist. Ct. (ea. dist.) N.Y. 1969, U.S. Ct. Appeals (3d cir.) 1982, U.S. Ct. Appeals (9th cir.) 1988. Assoc. Paul, Weiss, Rifkind, Wharton & Garrison, N.Y.C., 1960-65; from assoc. to ptnr. Baar, Bennett & Fullen, N.Y.C., 1965-74; ptnr. Guggenheimer & Untermyer, N.Y.C., 1974-85; Rosenman & Colin LLP, N.Y.C., 1985-98, chmn., 1994-97, counsel, 1998—2002, Katten Muchin Rosenman LLP, N.Y.C., 2002—. With U.S. Army, 1961-64. Mem. ABA, N.Y. State Bar Assn., Assn. of Bar of City of N.Y., Fed. Bar Coun., N.Y. County Lawyers Assn., Internat. Bar Assn., Am. Arbitration Assn. (nat. panel arbitrators), Am. Law Inst. Office: Katten Muchin Rosenman LLP 575 Madison Ave Fl 26 New York NY 10022-2585 Office Phone: 212-940-8850. E-mail: robert.smith@kattenlaw.com.

**SMITH, ROBERT FREEMAN,** history professor; b. Little Rock, May 13, 1930; s. Robert Freeman and Emma Martha Gottlieb (Buerkle) S.; m. Alberta Vester, Feb. 1, 1951 (dec. 1985); children: Robin Ann, Robert Freeman III; m. Charlotte Ann Coleman, Sept. 9, 1985. BA, U. Ark., 1951, MA, 1952; PhD, U. Wis., Madison, 1958. Instr. U. Ark., Fayetteville, 1953; asst. prof. Tex. Luth. Coll., Seguin, 1958-62; assoc. prof. U. R.I., Kingston, 1962-66, U. Conn., Storrs, 1966-69; prof. history U. Toledo, 1969-86, disting. univ. prof., 1986—. Vis. prof. U. Wis., Madison, 1966-67. Author: The United States and Cuba: Business and Diplomacy 1917-1960, 1961 (Tex. Writers' Roundup award 1961), What Happened in Cuba: A Documentary History of U.S.-Cuban Relations, 1963, The United States and Revolutionary Nationalism in Mexico, 1916-1932, 1973 (Ohio Acad. History award 1973), The Era of Caribbean Intervention, 1890-1930, 1981, The Era of Good Neighbors, Cold Warriors, and Hairshirts, 1930-82, 1983, The Caribbean World and the United States: Mixing Rum & Coca-Cola, 1994; contbr. to numerous publs. Retired Col. 7th Inf. Detachment, Ohio Mil. Res. 1st lt. U.S. Army, 1953-55. Knapp fellow in history U. Wis., 1957; Tom L. Evans rsch. fellow Harry S. Truman Libr., Independence, Mo., 1976-77, Mexican Ministry Fgn. Rels. fellow, 1991-92. Mem. Soc. Historians of Am. Fgn. Rels., Soc. Mil. History, U.S. Naval Inst., Ohio Acad. History, So. Hist. Assn., Orgn. Am. Historians, Assn. U.S. Army, State Guard Assn. of U.S., Am. Legion, Masons, Scottish Rite, Shriners, Army Hist. Found., Inst. Land Warfare, Sons of Confederate Vets., Phi Beta Kappa, Phi Alpha Theta. Episcopalian. Avocation: photography. Home: 4110 Dunkirk Rd Toledo OH 43606-2217 Office: U Toledo Dept History Toledo OH 43606

**SMITH, ROBERT G.,** lawyer; b. Washington, Oct. 4, 1943; BA, Johns Hopkins U., 1965; LLB, Harvard U., 1968. Bar: Md. 1969. Ptnr., Environ., Appellate Litigation practices Venable LLP, Balt. & Washington, 1970—. Contbr. articles to profl. jours. Mem. ABA, Assn. Trial Lawyers Am., Def. Rsch. Inst., Air & Waste Mgmt. Assn., Md. C. of C. (Air Quality com.), Md. Bar Assn., Bar Assn. Balt. City. Office: Venable LLP 1800 Mercantile Bank & Trust Bldg 2 Hopkins Plz Baltimore MD 21201 also: Venable LLP 575 7th St NW Washington DC 20004 Office Phone: 410-244-7590, 202-344-4056. Office Fax: 410-244-7742. Business E-Mail: rgsmith@venable.com.

**SMITH, ROBERT HUGH,** retired engineering construction company executive; b. Wichita, Kans., Dec. 29, 1936; s. Richard Lyon and E. Eileen (O'Neal) S.; m. Melinda Louise Fitch, Sept. 26, 1959 (div. Dec. 1969); children: Robert Blake, Thomas Hugh; m. Margaret Anne Moseley, Dec. 11, 1971; 1 child, Steven Richard. BS, Kans. State U., 1959; MS, U. Kans., 1964, PhD, 1970. Sr. process engr. FMC Corp., Lawrence, Kans., 1959-64; rsch. engr. Phillips Petroleum Co., Bartlesville, Okla., 1964-66; group leader

Standard Oil of Ohio, Warrenville Heights, Ohio, 1966-67; sr. rsch. assoc., group leader Atlantic Richfield, Plano, Tex., 1970-80; regional mgr., sr. mgr., sales mgr. Fluor Daniel, Houston and Marlton, NJ, 1980-90; v.p., gen. mgr. Badger Design & Construction, Tampa, Fla., 1990-93; exec. v.p., COO Process divsn. Black & Veatch, Overland Park, 1993-2000; ret., 2000. Patentee in the field; contbr. to profl. jours. Adv. bd. dept. chem. engring. coll. of engring. U. Kans., Lawrence, 1993—; mem. adv. bd. coll. engring. Kans. State U., 1998-2005. Recipient Disting. Svc. award Kans. State U., 1998; named to Engring. Hall of Fame Kans. State U., Chem. and Petroleum Engring. Hall of Fame, U. Kans., 2000. Fellow AIChE (chmn., vice chmn., sec. Dallas chpt. 1962—, Engr. of Yr. award Dallas chpt. 1980, exec. bd. Engr. and Cons. Contracting divsn., 1995-97, bd. dirs. 2002-04, career and edn. ops. coun. 2002-03), Phi Lambda Upsilon. Avocations: tennis, sailing, skiing, reading. Personal E-mail: bobsmith29@everstkc.net.

**SMITH, ROBERT J., JR.,** real estate executive; b. Rochester, N.Y., June 1, 1951; s. Robert and Irene (Frisbie) S.; m. Sherry L. Silberman, July 5, 1981; 1 child, Jordan. Student, Ohio U., 1969-73. CPA, Ohio. Gen. mgr. Televac, Inc., Athens, 1975—; CFO, gen. mgr. Practice Mgmt., Inc. (PMI), Cleve., 1988—. Mem. AICPA. E-mail: televac@aol.com.

**SMITH, ROBERT JOHN,** anthropology educator; b. Essex, Mo., June 27, 1927; s. Will Dan and Fern (Jones) S.; m. Kazuko Sasaki, Aug. 22, 1955. BA summa cum laude, U. Minn., 1949; MA, Cornell U., 1951, PhD, 1953. Engaged in cultural anthrop. field research, N.S., Canada, 1950, Japan, 1951-52, 55, 57-58, Brazil, 1966-67; mem. faculty Cornell U., 1953—, prof. anthropology, 1963-74, Goldwin Smith prof. anthropology, 1974-97, prof. emeritus, 1997—, chmn. dept. Asian studies, 1961-66, chmn. dept. antropology, 1967-71, 76-82, prof. emeritus, 1997—. Vis. prof. anthropology U. Ariz., 1971, U. Hawaii, 1978, Nat. Mus. Ethnology, Osaka, Japan, 1982 Author: (with Cornell) Two Japanese Villages, 1956, (with Cornell, Saito and Maeyama) Japanese and Their Descendants in Brazil, 1967; editor: (with Beardsley) Japanese Culture: Its Development and Characteristics, 1962, Social Organization and the Applications of Anthropology, 1974, Ancestor Worship in Contemporary Japan, 1974, Kurusu: The Price of Progress in a Japanese Village, 1951-75, 1978, (with Wiswell) Women of Suye Mura, 1982, Japanese Society: Tradition, Self and the Social Order, 1983, (with K. Smith) Diary of a Japanese Innkeeper's Daughter, 1984 Served with AUS, 1944-46. Tng. grantee Social Sci. Rsch. Coun., Japan, 1951-52; recipient Individual Exch. award to Japan Inst. Internat. Edn., 1957-58; Fulbright lectr. Tokyo Met. U., 1962-63; NSF rsch. grantee, 1965-67; Japan Found. grantee, 1979; awarded Order of the Rising Sun, Govt. of Japan, 1993. Fellow Assn. Asian Studies (v.p. 1987-88, pres. 1988-89), Soc. Applied Anthropology (editor jour. Human Orgn. 1961-66). Home: 322 Savage Farm Dr Ithaca NY 14850 E-mail: rjs6@cornell.edu.

**SMITH, ROBERT K.,** music educator, director; m. Holly Smith. MA in Music Edn., Auburn U., Ala., 2000. Cert. tchr. Ala. Dept. Edn., 2005. Grad. tchg. asst. Auburn U., 1999—2000; dir. bands Leeds HS, Ala., 2003—. Mem.: Ala. Music Educators Assn., Music Educators Nat. Conf., Ala. Bandmasters Assn., Phi Mu Alpha Sinfonia. Office: Leeds HS Band 8404 Greenwave Dr Leeds AL 35094 Office Phone: 205-699-7106. Office Fax: 205-699-4515. Business E-Mail: smith@leedsband.com.

**SMITH, ROBERT LOUIS,** construction company executive; b. Parkersburg, W.Va., Apr. 19, 1922; s. Everett Clerc and Janet (Morrison) S.; m. June Irene Odbert, Oct. 25, 1948; children: Peter Clerc, Morrison James, Edna Louise. BS in Civil Engring., Lehigh U., 1944. Design engr. Chrysler Corp., 1944-46; engr. Harrison Constrn. Co., Charleston, W.Va., 1946-47; sr. engr. Creole Petroleum Co., Las Piedras, Venezuela, 1947-55; v.p. Rea Constrn. Co., Charlotte, N.C., 1955-64; exec. v.p. Warren Bros. Co., Cambridge, Mass., 1964-68, pres., 1968-79; also dir.; sr. v.p. Ashland Oil, Inc., Ky., 1974-79; pres. Robert L. Smith & Assocs., Lexington, 1979—; pres., dir. Tree Farm Devel. Corp., Cambridge, 1979—. Dir. Panastalto (S.A.), Wilder Constrn. Co., Inc., J.H. Shears Sons, Inc. Fellow ASCE; mem. Nat. Asphalt Pavement Assn. (dir.), Phi Beta Kappa, Tau Beta Pi, Sigma Chi. Republican. Unitarian Universalist. Home office: 1010 Waltham St Apt A412 Lexington MA 02421-8065 Office Phone: 781-861-0489. Personal E-mail: rlouissmith@comcast.net.

**SMITH, ROBERT MICHAEL,** lawyer, mediator, arbitrator; b. Boston, Nov. 4, 1940; s. Sydney and Minnie (Appel) S.; m. Catherine Kersey, Apr. 14, 1981 (dec. 1983); m. Clarissa Redmond, Feb. 11, 1999 (dec. 2001). AB cum laude, Harvard Coll., 1962; diploma, Centro de Estudos de Espanol, Barcelona, 1963; MA in Internat. Affairs, Columbia U., 1964, MS in Journalism with high honors, 1965; JD, Yale U., 1975. Bar: Calif., N.Y., D.C., U.S. Supreme Ct.; barrister Inner Temple, London; solicitor Supreme Ct. of Eng. and Wales; accredited mediator Hong Kong Internat. Arbitration Ctr.; chartered arbitrator, Eng.; registered mediator Ctr. de Mediation et d'Arbitrage Paris. Intern in econ. devel. UN, Geneva, 1964; corr. Time Mag., N.Y.C., 1965-66, The N.Y. Times, Washington, 1968-72, 75-76; atty. Heller, Ehrman, White & McAuliffe, San Francisco, 1976-78; spl. asst. Office of Atty. Gen. of U.S., Washington, 1979-80; dir. Office Pub. Affairs U.S. Dept. Justice, Washington, 1979-80; mem. U.S. delegation U.S. v. Iran Internat. Ct. of Justice, The Hague, 1980; asst. U.S. atty. No. Dist. Calif., San Francisco, 1981-82; counsel, sr. counsel to sr. litigation counsel Bank of Am. NT & SA, San Francisco, 1982-86; vis. fellow Ctr. for Effective Dispute Resolution, London, 2005—, dir. mediation, 2005—. Lectr. FBI Acad., Quantico, Va., 1980, Internat. Bankers Assn. Calif., 1994, Calif. Bankers Assn., 1994, Cmty. Bankers No. Calif., 1994, 95; judge Golden Medallion Broadcast Media awards State Bar of Calif., 1985; judge pro tem Mcpl. Ct. City and County of San Francisco, 1989—; conciliator Peninsula Conflict Resolution Ctr.; panelist World Intellectual Property Orgn., Geneva; arbitrator internat. Commercial arbitration ctrs., Vancouver, Cairo, Singapore, Kuala Lumpur, India; CPR Panel of Disting. Neutrals; mem. panel Nat. Assn. for Dispute Resolution; disting. vis. fellow CEDR, London, 2005. Author: Alternative Dispute Resolution for Financial Institutions, 1995, revised, 1996, 97, 98; bd. editors Yale Law Jour., 1974-75; editor Litigation, jour. ABA litigation sect., 1978-81; mem. editl. adv. bd. Bancroft-Whitney, 1991-94; contbr. articles to profl. jours. Bd. dirs. Neighborhood Legal Assistance Found., San Francisco 1985-87, Nob Hill Assn., San Francisco, 1985-93; bd. dirs., fin. com. St. Francis Found., San Francisco, 1993-94. 1st lt. inf., USAR, 1965-71. Recipient UPI Award for Newswriting, 1958; Harvard Coll. scholar, 1958-62, Fulbright scholar, 1962-63; Columbia U. Internat. fellow, 1964-65. Fellow Internat. Acad. Mediators, Am. Coll. Civil Trial Mediators, Hong Kong Inst. Arbitrators, Chartered Inst. Arbitrators (London); mem. ABA (corp. counsel com. 1986-96, alternative dispute resolution sect. 1994-98), Assn. Atty. Mediators (v.p. No. Calif. chpt. 1995), State Bar of Calif. (pub. affairs com. 1982-85, litigation sect. 1990-96), Bar Assn. of San Francisco (bench-bar media com. 1985-96, alternative dispute resolution com. 1994-98), Assn. Bus. Trial Lawyers No. Calif., Assn. of Former U.S. Attys. No. Dist. Calif., Am. Arbitration Assn. (mem. comml. arbitration panel, No. Calif. adv. coun., mediator Am. Arbitration Ctr. for Mediation), Nat. Assn. Dispute Resolution, The Mediation Soc. (chmn. bd., pres.). Profl. Atty. Mediators, Cmty. Bds. of San Francisco (conciliator), French-Am. C. of C., German-Am. C. of C. West U.S., Harvard Club of San Francisco (bd. dirs. 1986-94, pres. 1992-94), Yale Club of San Francisco (bd. dirs. 1989-94), Soc. Profls. in Dispute Resolution, Columbia U. Alumni Club of No. Calif. (exec. com. 1978-92). Office: Ctr Effective Dispute Resolution 70 Fleet Street London EC4Y 1EU England E-mail: rms@robertmsmith.com.

**SMITH, ROBERT POWELL,** former ambassador, retired foundation administrator; b. Joplin, Mo., Mar. 5, 1929; s. Powell Augusta and Estella (Farris) S.; m. Alice Irene Rountree, Aug. 22, 1953; children: Michael Bryan, Steven Powell, Karen Louise, David Robert. BA, Tex. Christian U., 1954, MA, 1955. Fgn. svc. officer Dept. State, 1955-81; press officer Washington, 1955; vice-consul Lahore, Pakistan, 1956—58; 2d sec. Beirut, 1959-61; consul and prin. officer Enugu, Nigeria, 1962-65; officer-in-charge Ghanaian Affairs, 1966; officer-in-charge Nigerian Affairs, dep. dir. Office West African Affairs, 1967-69; dep. chief of mission, counselor of embassy Pretoria, South

Africa, 1970-74; amb. to Malta, 1974-76; amb. to Ghana, 1976-79; amb. to Liberia, 1979-81. Pres. Africa Wildlife Leadership Found., 1981-85. Served with USMCR, 1946-49, 50-52. Decorated Air medal; recipient Meritorious Honor award State Dept., 1967 Mem. Am. Fgn. Service Assn. Baptist.

**SMITH, ROBERT RUTHERFORD,** dean, communications educator; b. Buffalo, Nov. 18, 1933; s. Thomas Newlands and Mary Jane (Rutherford) S.; m. Suzanne Louise Stines, June 7, 1958; children: Eric Anthony, Gwendolyn Anne. BA cum laude, U. Buffalo, 1955; MA, Ohio State U., 1956, PhD, 1963. Prof. communication, chmn. divsn. broadcasting and film Sch. Pub. Communication, Boston U., 1961-78; prof., dean. Sch. Communication and Theater Temple U., Phila., 1978-95. Author: poems Participations, 1972; criticism Beyond the Wasteland, 1980, (with G. Ingram and R. Marler) Fishing the Delaware Valley, 1997; editor TV Quar., 1971, Feedback, 1973-76; contbr. articles to profl. jours. Mem. communication con. Mass. Coun. Chs., 1971-76. Served with USAR, 1959-64 Mem. Broadcast Edn. Assn. (pres. 1984-85), Broadcast Pioneers (pres. Phila. 1985-86), Soc. Profl. Journalists (pres. 1983-85, Quarter Century Wireless Assn. (Yankee chpt. pres. 2006—) Home: 6 Trout Farm Ln Plympton MA 02367-1617 Office Phone: 781-585-0117. Personal E-mail: suzrobs@cs.com. Business E-Mail: kk3p@arrl.net.

**SMITH, ROBERT SHERLOCK,** state appeals court judge; b. NYC, Aug. 31, 1944; s. Robert and Janet W. (Welt) S.; m. Dian Goldston Smith, Aug. 31, 1969; children: Benjamin Eli, Emlen Matthew, Rosemary Friedman. BA with great distinction, Stanford U., 1965; LLB magna cum laude, Columbia U., 1968. Bar: N.Y. 1968, U.S. Dist. Ct. (so. dist.) N.Y. 1969, U.S. Dist. Ct. (ea. dist.) N.Y. 1977, U.S. Ct. Appeals (2d cir.) 1970, U.S. Ct. Appeals (4th cir.) 1986, U.S. Ct. Appeals (1st cir.) 1988, U.S. Ct. Appeals (7th cir.) 1989, U.S. Ct. Appeals (6th cir.) 1995, U.S. Ct. Appeals (D.C. and 8th cirs.) 1997, U.S. Ct. Appeals (5th cir.) 1999, U.S. Tax Ct. 1974, U.S. Supreme Ct. 1979. Assoc. Paul, Weiss, Rifkind, Wharton & Garrison, NYC, 1968-76, ptnr., 1976—2003; individual practitioner, spl. counsel Kornstein, Veisz, Wexler & Pollard, NYC, 2003—04; assoc. judge NY State Ct. Appeals, NYC, 2004—. Vis. prof. Columbia Law Sch., N.Y.C., 1980-81, lectr. law, 1981-90. Editor-in-chief Columbia Law Review. Mem. ABA, N.Y. State Bar Assn. (vice chair com. ct. adminstrn. 2001-), Assn. Bar City N.Y. (com. fed. legis. 1981-84, com. on judiciary 1984-87, com. on bicentennial of U.S. Constitution 1988-91), Federalist Soc. N.Y. (pres. lawyers chpt. 1994-2003). Republican. Mem. Reformed Ch. Office: 71 Thomas St New York NY 10013 also: State NY Ct Appeals 20 Eagle St Albany NY 12207-1095 Office Phone: 646-386-3824. Business E-Mail: rssmith@courts.state.ny.us.

**SMITH, ROBERT VICTOR,** academic administrator, educator; b. Glendale, N.Y., Feb. 16, 1942; s. Robert Arthur and Marie Marlene (Florence) S. BS in Pharm. Sci., St. John's U., Jamaica, N.Y., 1963; MS in Pharm. Chemistry, U. Mich., 1964, PhD in Pharm. Chemistry, 1968. Asst. prof., then assoc. prof. U. Iowa, Iowa City, 1968-74; assoc. prof., asst. dir. U. Tex., Austin, 1974-77, area coordinator basic pharmaceutics, 1975-76, assoc. dir. Drug Dynamics Inst., 1977-78, dir. Drug Dynamics Inst., Coll. Pharmacy, 1979-85, James E. Bauerle Centennial prof. Coll. Pharmacy, 1983-85; prof., dean Coll. Pharmacy, Wash. State U., Pullman, 1985-86, vice provost for rsch., dean Grad. Sch., 1987-97; vice provost for rsch. and grad. edn., dean Grad. Sch., U. Conn., Storrs, 1997-2000; provost, vice chancellor acad. affairs U. Ark., Fayetteville, 2000—. Cons. E.R. Squibb, New Brunswick, N.J., 1979-82, Upjohn Co., Kalamazoo, 1982-85; external examiner U. Malaysia, Penang, 1981-82; mem. sci. adv. bd. Biodecision Labs., Pitts., 1985-86; Wash. Exposition Sci. Tech. Found., 1989-90; mem. noms. com. Coun. Grad. Schs., Washington, 1990-91, 96-97; accreditation evaluator Northwest Assn. Schs. and Colls., Seattle, 1991-97; mem. exec. com. grad. deans African-Am. Inst., N.Y., 1992-2000; bd. dirs. Coun. Grad. Schs., 1998, Grad. Record Exam, 1999-2003; exec. sec. U. Ark. 2010 Commn., 2000—; chair Southeastern Conf. Provosts Group, 2003-04. Author: Textbook of Biopharmaceutic Analysis, 1981, Graduate Research: A Guide for Students in the Sciences, 1998, Development and Management of University Research Groups, 1986, The Elements of Great Speechmaking: Adding Drama and Intrigue, 2004, Pedestals, Parapets and Pits: The Joys, Challenges and Failures of Professional Life, 2005, Where You Stand is Where You Sit: An Academic Administrator's Handbook, 2006. Bd. dirs. Wash. Tech. Ctr., 1990-92; exec. sec. 2010 Commn. Grantee NIH, 1974-83; fellow Acad. Pharm. Scis., 1981, Am. Assn. Pharm. Scientists, 1987; recipient Disting. Alumnus award Coll. Pharmacy U. Mich., 1990, Outstanding Svc. award Wash. State U., Grad. and Profl. Student Assn., 1993, 95. Mem. Am. Assn. Colls. Pharmacy (chmn. research and grad. affairs com. 1983-84), U.S. Pharmacopeia (revision com. 1985-90), Acad. Pharm. Scis. (chmn., vice chmn. 1983-85, 90, Presdl. citation 1985), Wash. Rsch. Found. (bd. dirs. 1989-97). Unitarian Universalist. Home: 665 Samara Cir Fayetteville AR 72701-3035 Office: U Ark Adminstrn Bldg Fayetteville AR 72701 Office Phone: 479-575-5459. Business E-Mail: bobsmith@uark.edu.

**SMITH, ROBERT W., JR., (JAY SMITH),** lawyer; b. Balt., Aug. 1, 1951; BS magna cum laude, Univ. Pa., 1973; JD with honors, Univ. Md., 1977. Bar: Md. 1977. Ptnr., chair corp. and securities practice group, mem. exec. com. DLA Piper Rudnick Gray Cary, Balt. Bd. trustees McDaniel Coll., Center Stage. Mem.: ABA, Md. State Bar Assn., Order of Coif. Office: DLA Piper Rudnick Gray Cary 6225 Smith Ave Baltimore MD 21209-3600 Office Phone: 410-580-4266. Office Fax: 410-580-3266. Business E-Mail: jay.smith@dlapiper.com.

**SMITH, ROBERTA,** art critic; b. NYC; d. Thomas R. and Eleanor Smith. BA, Grinnell Coll., IA, 1969; ind. study program, Whitney Mus. Am. Art, NYC, 1969. Sr. ed. Art in America, NYC, 1976—80; art critic Village Voice, NYC, 1981-85, NY Times, 1986—. Tchr. in field, govt. curator & catalogue essayist Kansas U. Spencer Mus. Art, Lawrence, Kans., 1981; contbr. Arts, Artsforum, Art in America; contbr. to various exhibition catalogues. Author: Rhapsody, 1985; co-author: NY Times Traveler's Guide to International Art Museum Exhibitions, 2005; Illustrator The Stories Huey Tells, 1997. Recipient Frank Jewett Mather award, Coll. Art Assn., 2003; grantee, Natl. Endowment for the Arts, 1975, 1980. Office: NY Times Culture Desk 229 W 43rd St New York NY 10036 Office Phone: 212-556-1345. Office Fax: 212-556-1516.

**SMITH, ROBIN E.,** music educator; b. Buffalo, Dec. 1, 1978; d. Thomas William and Maureen Diane Oates; m. Gary Joseph Smith, July 24, 2004. MusB in Performance and Edn., SUNY, Fredonia, 2001, MusM in Edn., 2005—. Cert. music tchr. N.Y. Music educator Alden (N.Y.) Mid. Sch., 2001—02, Gowanda (N.Y.) Mid. and HS, 2002—. Artistic dir. Gowanda Thespian Musical Prodns., 2002—, music dir., 2002—; co-dir.: Student Opera Theatre Assn., 2006; dir.: (prodn.) Joseph and the Amazing Technicolor Dreamcoat, 2005—06; singer: (soloist) Rutter Requiem, 2006. Mem.: N.Y. State Sch. of Music Assn., Erie County Music Educator's Assn. (Svc. award 2004—05, 2003—04). Avocations: theater, singing, softball. Home: 4079 Fairview Pkwy Blasdell NY 14219 E-mail: rsmith@gowcsd.org.

**SMITH, ROBIN ERROL,** pediatrician, neurologist, educator; b. Johannesburg, Gaugteng province, South Africa, Dec. 11, 1961; s. Siegmund and Shulamith Smith; m. Jessica Smith, Feb. 2, 1962; 1 child, Mikhail. MBBch, U. Witwatersrand, South Africa, 1985. Asst. prof. pediat. and neurology Albert Einstein Coll. Medicine, NYC, 2002—; attending physician Schneider Children's Hosp., New Hyde Park. Office: North Shore Long Island Health System 269-01 76th Ave New Hyde Park NY 11040 Office Phone: 718-470-3450. Office Fax: 718-343-5826.

**SMITH, ROD,** professional football player; b. May 15, 1970; Postgrad in econ. & fin., Mo. So. State Coll., postgrad in gen. bus., postgrad in mktg. & mgmt. Wide receiver Denver Broncos, 1994—. Named to NFL Pro-Bowl, 2000—01, 2005. Achievements include being a member of Super Bowl Champion Denver Broncos, 1997, 1998; being the only undrafted NFL reciever to catch over 10,000 yards. Office: Denver Broncos Football Club 13655 Broncos Pky Englewood CO 80112*

**SMITH, RODERICK JOEL,** behavioral consultant, researcher, educator; b. Ft. Worth, Nov. 15, 1946; s. Bill Joel and Vicky Marrarow Smith; m. Patricia Lee Payne, Sept. 30, 1978; children: Rachael Jena, Adam Joel. BA in Anthropology, San Francisco State U., 1972, MA in Spl. Edn., 1973. Tchr. John Swett Sch. Dist., Selby, Calif.; v.p.; dir. Vallejo (Calif.)-Benicia Assn.; resource cons. Washoe County Schs., Reno, Smith/Peltier & Assocs., Reno. Adj. prof. Sierra Nevada Coll., Incline, Nev. Mem. Nev. State Bully Free Task Force, Carson City, 2000—; appointed Calif. Devel. Disabilities Bd. Area III, Sacramento, 1982—86. Mem.: NEA, Am. Coun. on Rural Spl. Edn., Phi Delta Kappa. Avocations: teaching, learning, improving the lives of children. Home and Office: Smith/Peltier & Assocs 861 Barber Way Gardnerville NV 89460

**SMITH, RODGER FIELD,** financial executive; b. Milw., Jan. 23, 1941; s. Millard Beale and Alice Catherine (Field) S.; m. Sarah Godfrey, June 19, 1964 (dec. Dec. 1999); children: Rodger F. Jr., Scott G., Reid W. BSChemE, U. Wis., 1964, MBA in Fin. with distinction, 1965. V.p. Allis Chalmers, Milw., 1966-76; mng. dir. Greenwich (Conn.) Assocs., 1976—. Trustee Harbor Funds, Toledo, 1987—; bd. dir. Arlington Capital, London, 1992—; dean's adv. bd. U. Wis. Bus. Sch.; mem. Tokeneke Tax Dist. Author articles and spkr. on investing pension funds. Fund raiser United Way, Milw., 1966—76. Mem.: Bascom Hill Soc., U. Wis. Alumni Assn. (nat. bd. dir. 1994—2000), Tokeneke Tax Dist. 1, Wee Burn Country Club (fin. com.), Beta Gamma Sigma, Tau Beta Pi (chmn. trust adv. com. 1986—). Avocations: travel, golf, tennis, coin collecting/numismatics. Office: Greenwich Assocs Office Park Fight Greenwich CT 06831 5195 Office Phone: 203 629 1200. E-mail: rodger@greenwich.com.

**SMITH, ROGER WINSTON,** retired political theory educator; b. Birmingham, Ala., July 9, 1936; s. Buford Houston and Sarah Louise (Travis) S.; m. Martha Christin Daniels, Jan. 16, 1960; children— Louisa, David AB magna cum laude, Harvard U., 1958, postgrad. in law, 1958-59; MA in Polit. Sci., U. Calif.-Berkeley, 1963, PhD in Polit. Sci., 1971. Teaching assoc. U. Calif.-Berkeley, 1965-66; asst. prof. govt. Coll. William and Mary, Williamsburg, Va., 1967-72, assoc. prof., 1972-80, prof. 1980-2001, prof. emeritus, 2001—. Sr. lectr. politics Glasgow U., 1977-78; lectr. NEH, 1988; cons. Nelson-Hall Pubs., Chgo.; mem. coun. Inst. Internat. Conf. on the Holocaust and Genocide, Jerusalem; chair acad. adv. bd., dir. genocide and human rights univ. program Zoryan Inst., Toronto; v.p. Inst. Study of Genocide, NY. Co-author, editor: Guilt: Man and Society, 1971; co-author: Genocide and the Modern Age, 1987, Genocide, vol. 2, 1991, Bearing Witness to the Holocaust, 1939-89, 1987, The Coming Age of Scarcity, 1998, Pioneers of Genocide Studies, 2002, When Will Genocide Ever End?, 2002, On the Edge of Scarcity, 2002, Race and Ethnic Relations, 15th ann. edit., 2005, A Encyclopedia of Genocide and Crimes Against Humanity, 2004; editor: Genocide, 1999; contbg. editor Internet on the Holocaust and Genocide; contbr. articles to profl. jours. Served to 1st lt. U.S. Army, 1960-62, Japan Fellow NSF, 1966, College of William and Mary, 1977 Mem. Am. Polit. Sci. Assn., Internat. Assn. Genocide Scholars (co-founder, v.p., past pres.), Human Rights Watch, PETA. Democrat. Protestant. Avocations: gardening, walking, opera. Home: 102 Lake Dr Williamsburg VA 23185-3113 Office: Coll William and Mary Dept Govt Williamsburg VA 23187

**SMITH, ROGERS MOOD,** political scientist, educator; b. Sept. 20, 1953; s. Henry Dale and Betty (Mood) Smith. BA in Polit. Sci., Mich. State U., 1974; MA, Harvard U., 1978, PhD, 1980. Asst. prof. polit. sci. Yale U., New Haven, 1980—85, assoc. prof., 1985—89, Alfred Cowles prof. govt, 1989—2001; Browne Disting. prof. polit. sci. U. Pa., Phila., 2001—. Author: Liberalism and American Constitutional Law, 1985, Citizenship Without Consent, 1985, Stories of Peoplehood, 2003, The Unsteady March, 1999, Civic Ideals, 1997; contbr. articles to profl. jours. Fellow: Am. Acad. Arts & Sci.; mem.: New Eng. Polit. Sci. Assn. (Pres.'s award 1982), Social Sci. History Assn. (Sharlin award), Orgn. Am. Historians (Curie prize), Am. Polit. Sci. Assn. (Greenstone prize, Bunche prize, Easton prize). Avocation: baseball. Office: Univ Pa Dept Political Science 208 S 37th St Philadelphia PA 19104-6215 Office Phone: 215-898-7662. E-mail: rogerss@sas.upenn.edu.

**SMITH, RONALD EDWARD,** ophthalmologist; b. Walkersville, Md., Oct. 7, 1942; s. Harry Otto and Marjorie Lee Smith; m. Sara Gutelius Watt, Sept. 4, 1965 (div. Oct. 1977); children: Kelly, Matt; m. Suzette Edith Le Blanc, Sept. 6, 1980. BA, Johns Hopkins U., 1964, MD, 1967. Diplomate Am. Bd. Ophthalmology. Intern Johns Hopkins Hosp., Baltimore, Md., 1967—68; resident opthalmology Johns Hopkin's Hosp., Baltimore, Md., 1968—72; asst. prof. U. So. Calif., L.A., 1975—78, assoc. prof., 1978—81, prof., 1981—95, prof., chmn. dept. ophthalmology, 1995—. Co-author: Intraocular Inflammation, 1980, Vitrectomy Techniques, 1983, Uveitis: A Clinical Approach, 1986. Lt. comdr. USPHS, 1973—78. Recipient gold medal, Internat. Uveitis Study Group, 1998, Light award, Braille Inst., 1998. Mem.: Am. Acad. Ophthalmology (pres. 1994—95, 1998—, chmn. found. 1998—99). Avocations: golf, skiing, tennis. Office: USC Dept Ophthalmology 2617 E Chapman No 301 Orange CA 92829

**SMITH, RONALD THOMAS,** environmental scientist; b. Palmerton, Pa., Feb. 17, 1952; s. Albert Hubert and Jeanne Alice (Kemmerle) S.; m. Jeri Lee Hammond, June 21, 1997; children: Clara Lucy, Curran Troy. BA in English, U. Notre Dame, 1974; MS in Environ. Sci., Ind. U., 1983. Chemist City of Bloomington (Ind.), 1984-91; rsch. sci. Ind. Geol. Survey, Bloomington, 1994—. Sci. advisor and activist McRae & McRae Attys., Bloomington, 1987, People Against the Incinerator, 1988-92, Thousands of People, 1983-87 Environ activist Citizens Clearinghouse on Hazardous Waste, Arlington, Va., 1987; founder Ind. Voters Party, 1991; pro se litigant Schalk & Smith vs. Lee Thomas, U.S. Ct. Appeals (7th cir.), 1990. Notre Dame scholar, 1970-74; recipient Giraffe Award for Pub. Svc., Giraffe Soc. Am., Everett, Wash., 1992. Mem.: AAAS, Pi Alpha Alpha. Avocations: writing, music, politics, outdoors activities. Office: Ind U Ind Geol Survey 611 N Walnut Grv # S427 Bloomington IN 47405-2208

**SMITH, ROWLAND JAMES,** educational administrator; b. Johannesburg, Aug. 19, 1938; s. John James and Gladys Spencer (Coldrey) S.; m. Catherine Anne Lane, Sept. 22, 1962; children: Russell Claude, Belinda Claire. BA, U. Natal, 1959, PhD, 1967; MA, Oxford U., Eng., 1967. Lectr. English U. Witwatersrand, Johannesburg, 1963-67; asst. prof. Dalhousie U., Halifax, N.S., Canada, 1967-70, assoc. prof. English, 1970-77, prof., 1977-88, McCulloch prof., 1988-94, chmn. English dept., 1977-83, 85-86, dir. Centre for African Studies, 1976-77, asst. dean arts and scis., 1972-74, dean arts and social scis., 1988-93, provost Coll. Arts and Scis., 1988-89, 90-91, 92-93; vis. prof., rsch. assoc. Multidisciplinary Ctr. Can. Studies, U. Rouen, 1994; prof. Wilfrid Laurier U., Waterloo, 1994—2004, v.p. acad., 1994—2004; prof. English U. Calgary, 2004—, dean humanities, 2004—. Author: Lyric and Polemic: The Literary Personality of Roy Campbell, 1972; editor: Exile and Tradition: Studies in African and Caribbean Literature, 1976, Critical Essays on Nadine Gordimer, 1990, Postcolonizing the Commonwealth: Essays in Literature and Culture, 2000. Bd. govs. Halifax Grammar Sch., 1972-74, Neptune Theatre Found., 1977-78; selection com. IODE Meml. Scholarships for N.S., 1969-71, Rhodes Scholarships N.S., 1972-74; com. Victoria Gen. Hosp., 1986-90; dir. publicity and promotion N.S. Rugby Football Union, 1987-89; chair liaison com. edn. dept. N.S. U., 1990-93; book prize jury Can. Fedn. for Humanities, 1990, regional judge (Can. and the Caribbean) Commonwealth Writers Prize, 1991; chair com. on employment and ednl. equity Coun. Ont. Univs., 1996-99, chair working group on post-diploma degrees, 1999-2001; bd. dirs. Opera Ontario, 2001-04; active Coll. Univ. Consortium Coun., 2000-02; chmn. Ontario Coun. Acad. V.P., 2002-04. Recipient Transvaal Rhodes scholar, 1960; vis. fellow Dalhousie U., 1965-66, vis. scholar Ctr. Canadian Studies U. Western Sydney, Macarthur, New South Wales, 1996; Can. Council leave fellow, 1974-75, research grantee, 1977; grantee Social Scis. and Humanities Research Council of Can., 1978, internat. grantee, 1985, grantee Cultural Personalities Exchange program Assn. Canadian Studies in Australia and New Zealand, 1996, grantee Cultural Personalities Exch. Program, Assn. in Can. Studies in German Speaking Countries, 1997. Mem. Assn. Can. Univ. Tchrs. English (sec.-treas. 1968-70, Profl. concern com. 1979-81), Can. Assn. for Commonwealth Lit. and Lang. Studies (exec. mem. 1989-92, pres. 1995-96), Can. Assn. Chmn. English (v.p. 1981-82, pres. 1982-83, exec. mem.-at-large 1985-86), Can. Fedn. Humanities (aid to scholarly publs. com. 1979-85, bd. dirs. 1992-94), MLA (div. chmn. 1984, mem.), Social Scis. and Humanities Rsch. Coun., Can. (chair rsch. grants adjudication com. 1994-96), Can. Rsch. Chairs Program (Coll. Reviewers 2000—), Internat. Coun. for Can. Studies (Can. scholarship and fellowship selection com. 2003—), Can. Fedn. for the Humanities and Social Scis. (aid to scholarly publs. com. 2004—). Office: Office Dean Humanities Univ Calgary Calgary AB Canada T2N 1N4 Office Phone: 403-220-2272. Business E-Mail: rowsmith@ucalgary.ca.

**SMITH, ROY,** lawyer; b. 1958; m. Donna Lee Shira, Sept. 9, 1989. AB cum laude, Princeton U., 1980; JD, Columbia U., 1983. Bar: NY 1984. Assoc. Cahill, Gordon & Reindell, 1983—92; atty. Am. Cyanamid Co., 1992—94; sr. atty. Cytec Industries, Inc., West Paterson, NJ, 1994—98, asst. gen. counsel, 1998—2001, v.p., gen. counsel sec., 2002—. Editor: Columbia Law Review. Office: Cytec Industries Inc Five Garret Mountain Plz West Paterson NJ 07424 Office Phone: 973-357-3100. Office Fax: 973-357-3058.

**SMITH, ROY PHILIP,** judge; b. S.I., NY, Dec. 29, 1933; s. Philip Aloysius and Virginia (Collins) S.; m. Elizabeth Helen Wink, Jan. 23, 1965; children: Matthew P., Jean E. BA, St. Joseph's Coll., Yonkers, N.Y., 1956; JD, Fordham U., 1965. Bar: NY. Asst. reg. counsel FAA, N.Y.C., 1966-79; adminstrv. law judge U.S. Dept. Labor, Washington, 1979-83; adminstrv. appeals judge Benefits Rev. Bd., Washington, 1983—, chmn., chief adminstrv. appeals judge, 1988-90. Adj. prof. aviation law Dowling Coll., Oakdale, N.Y., 1972-79; adj. prof. transp. law Adelphi U., Garden City, N.Y., 1975-79; vis. prof. Georgetown U. Law Sch., 1989—. With U.S. Army, 1957—59. Mem.: Fed. Adminstrv. Law Judges Conf. (treas. 1983—84, exec. com. 1982—83), Assn. Bar of City of N.Y. (sec.-treas. aeronautics com. 1978—79), Georgetown U. Libr. Assocs., Friendly Sons of St. Patrick, Edgemoor Club. Avocation: tennis. Home: 6700 Pawtucket Rd Bethesda MD 20817-4836 Office: Benefits Rev Bd 200 Constitution Ave NW Washington DC 20210-0001 Business E-Mail: smith-roy@dol.gov.

**SMITH, RUBY LUCILLE,** retired librarian; b. Nobob, Ky., Sept. 19, 1917; d. James Ira and Myrtie Olive (Crabtree) Jones; m. Kenneth Cornelius Smith, Dec. 25, 1946; children: Kenneth Cornelius, Corma Ann. AB, Western Ky. State Tchrs. Coll., 1943, MA, 1966. Tchr. rural schs., Barren County, Ky., 1941-42; tchr. secondary sch. English, libr. Temple Hill Consol. Sch., Glasgow, Ky., 1943-47, 49-51, 53-56, sch. libr. 1956-83. Sec. Barren County Cancer Soc., 1968—70, Barren County Fair Bd., 1969—70; leader 4-H Club, 1957—72; coord. tax-aide program AARP, 1985—88, dist. dir. 1988—2000, local chpt. v.p., 1996—98, pres., 1999—2000, instr. 55 Alive Mature Driving, 1993—; sec. Oak Grove Bapt. Ch., 1979—; coun. mem. Barren County; bd. dirs. Barren County Hist. Found., Inc., 1997—; trustee Mary Wood Weldon Meml. Libr., 1964—, Barren County Pub. Libr. Bd., 1969—2001; sec. Barren County Pub. Libr., 2001; trustee Barren County Hist. Found., 1996—. Mem. NEA (life), Ky. Edn. Assn., Ky. Sch. Media Assn. (sec. 1970-71), 3d Dist. Libr. Assn. (pres. 1944, 66), Barren County Edn. Assn. (pres. 1960-62, treas. 1979-80), 3d Dist. Ret. Tchrs. Assn. (pres. 1991-92), Ky. Ret. Tchrs. Assn. (v.p. 1992-93, pres.-elect 1993-94, pres. 1994-95), Glasgow-Barren County Ret. Tchrs. Assn. (pres. 1984-86, 96-98, sec. 1989, treas. 1990), Ky. Libr. Trustee Assn. (bd. dirs. 1985-98, pres. 1986-88, 93-95, dir. Barren River region 1987-89), Barren County Rep. Women's Club, Monroe Assn. Woman's Missionary Union (dir. 1968-72, 79-83, sec. 1985-98), Monroe Assn. Bapts. (libr. dir. 1972-88), Ky. Edn. Assn., South Ctrl. Hist. Soc. (v.p. 1997-98, pres. 1998-2000), DAR (chaplain Edmund Rogers chpt. 1998—), Delta Kappa Gamma (pres. Delta chpt. 1996-98).

**SMITH, RUSSELL FRANCIS,** transportation executive; b. Washington, Mar. 26, 1944; s. Raymond Francis and Elma Gloria (Daugherty) S. Student, East Carolina U., 1964, N.C. State U., 1964—65; BS with honors, U. Md., College Park, 1969, MBA, 1975. Exec. asst. mgr. Hotel Corp. Am. Internat. Inn and Mayflower Hotel, Washington, 1966—68; sr. venture capital cons. Initiative Investing Corp., Washington, 1968—69; pres., gen. mgr. Associated Trades Corp., Washington, 1970—74; cons. in fin. Greenbelt, Md., 1974—76; mng. cons. Bradford Nat. Corp., Washington, 1976—79; v.p. OAO Corp., Washington, 1979—81; ptnr. for fin. evaluation and ops. analysis Blake, Brunell, Lehmann & Co., Washington, 1981—86; v.p. mgmt. svcs. adminstrn. United Airlines Svcs. Corp., Lakewood, Colo., 1986—91; cons. Venture Fund of Washington, 1991—. Chmn. com. on wildlife Soc. for Prevention of Cruelty to Animals, Hyattsville, 1971—75, Prince George Humane Soc., Hyattsville, Md., 1968—71. With U.S. Army, 1963—66. Decorated Silver Star medal, Bronze Star medal with V device, Purple Heart. Mem.: Assn. MBA Execs. (registered investment adviser), Internat. Assn. Math. Modeling, N.Am. Soc. Corp. Planners, Am. Acctg. Assn., Ops. Rsch. Soc. Am., Am. Fin. Assn., Beta Alpha Psi, Beta Gamma Sigma. Libertarian.

**SMITH, RUSSELL JACK,** diplomat, consultant; b. Jackson, Mich., July 4, 1913; s. Lee C. and Georgia L. (Weed) S.; m. Rosemary Thomson, Sept. 5, 1938; children: Stephen M., Scott T., Christopher G. AB, Miami U., Oxford, Ohio, 1937; PhD, Cornell U., 1941. Asst. instr. English Cornell U., 1937-41; instr. English Williams Coll., 1941-45; with OSS, 1945; asst. prof. English Wells Coll., 1946-47; with CIA, 1947-74, mem. bd. nat. estimates, 1957-62, dir. current intelligence, 1962-66, dep. dir. for intelligence, 1966-71; spl. asst. U.S. Embassy, New Delhi, 1971-74; cons., 1975—82. Assigned Nat. War Coll., 1951-52, U.S. rep. Brit. Joint Intelligence Com., Far East, Singapore, 1951 56. Author: John Diplo d, & Study in Controversy, 1941, The Unknown CIA: My Three Decades with the Agency, 1989, The Little Red House that Jack Built, 2002, Rosemary: A Memoir, 2004, (novels) The Secret War, 1986, The Singapore Chance, 1991, Lodestone, 1993, Whirligig, 1994, Always Afternoon, 1997, Time's Prism, 2000, Downriver, 2001, The Listener, 2002, Lodestar, 2004, Winterset, 2005. Recipient Nat. Civil Svc. League award, 1971, Disting. Intelligence medal CIA, 1974. Mem. Phi Beta Kappa, Phi Delta Theta, Omicron Delta Kappa. Home: 1138 Bellview Rd Mc Lean VA 22102-1104

**SMITH, RUSSELL LOUIS,** lawyer; b. Atlanta, Sept. 9, 1946; s. Nathan Harry and Edith (Carfield) S.; m. Judith Beth Lavine, June 20, 1971; 1 child, Harris Charles Smith. BA, Vanderbilt U., 1968; JD, U. Ga., 1972. Bar: D.C., 1973, U.S. Supreme Ct., 1977, U.S. Ct. Appeals, (D.C. cir.), 1978. Atty.-advisor U.S. Dept. Treasury, Washington, 1972-76; Washington counsel Consol. Rail Corp., Phila., 1976-82; dir. Office of Automotive Industry Affairs U.S. Dept. Commerce, Washington, 1982-84; minority counsel Com. on Energy and Commerce U.S. Ho. Reps., Washington, 1984-88; assoc. McNair Law Firm, Washington, 1988-89; spl. counsel Govt. Rels. Dept. Willkie Farr & Gallagher LLP, Washington, 1989—. Republican. Jewish. Office: Willkie Farr & Gallagher LLP 1875 K Street, NW Washington DC 20006 Office Phone: 202-303-1116. E-mail: rsmith@willkie.com.

**SMITH, RYAN ARTHUR HAROLD,** mental health services professional, writer; b. Port Jervis, N.Y., Aug. 27, 1977; s. Craig Steven and Isabel Hodges Smith; m. Michelle Leigh Boff, Dec. 21, 2002; 1 stepchild, Darby Autumn Shae McCaslin 1 child, Connor Riley. BA in Psychology, Sage State U., 2001; MA in Psychology, Suffield U., 2003. Processing and cognitive enhancement tng., cert. applied behavioral analysis (level 3), discrete trial instrn. (level 3); protective immobilization/passive restraint. Data analyst Ctr. Applied Behavioral Scis. Pa. State U., University Park, 2000; processing and cognitive enhancement trainer/counselor Harmonic Progressions, State College, Pa., 2001; therapeutic support staff New Hope of Pa., Inc., Wyoming, 2002, adminstrv. case mgr., 2002—03; intensive case mgr. Allegheny Children's Initiative, Pitts., 2003—04; family-based mental health sr. clinician, 2004—. Therapeutic support staff Western Psychiat. Inst. and Clinic, Pitts., 2003—; cons. in field. Petition co-organizer Allegheny County Green Party, Pitts., 2003—; mem. Soka Gakkai Internat., Pa., 2002—03. Mem.: APA (assoc.), Psi Chi (life; philanthropy com. 2000—01). Buddhist. Avocations: neurotheology, evolutionary psychology, religious study, writing/poetry, yoga/meditation. Office: Allegheny Children's Initiative 2304 Jane St Pittsburgh PA 15203 Office Phone: 412-390-3825. Personal E-mail: ras229@adelphia.net. E-mail: rsmith@citizencare.org.

**SMITH, S. KINNIE, JR.,** lawyer; BA econ., Yale U., 1953; JD, U. Wisc. Law Sch., 1956. Ptnr. Sidley & Austin, Chgo., 1964—75; gen. counsel through vice chmn., ANR subsidiary, & sr. v.p. Coastal Corp., 1975—87; pres. CMS Energy, Jackson, Mich., 1988—96; counsel Skadden, Arps, Slate, Meagher & Flom, 1996—2002; vice chmn., gen. counsel CMS Energy, Jackson, Mich., 2002—. Mem. bd. vis. Univ. Wis. Law Sch. Mem.: ABA, Mich. Bar Assn. Chgo. Bar Assn. Office: CMS Energy One Energy Plaza Jackson MI 49201 Office Phone: 517-788-1671. Office Fax: 517-788-1859.

**SMITH, SALLYE WRYE,** librarian; b. Birmingham, Ala., Nov. 11, 1923; d. William Florin and Margaret (Howard) Wrye; m. Stuart Werner Smith, Sept. 20, 1947 (dec. June 1981); children: Carol Ann, Susan Patricia, Michael Christopher, Julie Lynn, Lori Kathleen. BA, U. Ala., 1945; MA, U. Denver, 1969. Psychometrician U.S. Army, Deshon Gen. Hosp., Butler, Pa., 1945-46, U.S. Vet. Adminstrn, Vocat. Guidance, U. Ala., Tuscaloosa, 1946; clin. psychologist U.S. Army, Walter Reed Gen. Hosp., Washington, 1946-47, U.S. Army, Fitzsimons Gen. Hosp., Denver, 1948, U.S. Vets. Adminstrn., Ft. Logan, Colo., 1948-50; head sci.-engring. libr. U. Denver, Colo., 1969-72; instr., reference libr. Penrose Libr., U. Denver, 1972-80, asst. prof., reference libr., 1980-90, interim dir., 1990-92, asst. prof. emerita, 1992—. Vis. prof. U. Denver Grad. Sch. Libr. Info. Mgmt., 1975-77, 83; info. broker Colo. Rschrs., Denver, 1979—; cons., presenter The Indsl. Info. Workshop Inst. de Investigaciones Tecnologicas, Bogota, Colombia, 1979, LIPI-DRI-PDIN workshop on R&D mgmt., Jakarta, Indonesia, 1982; mem. BRS User Adv. Bd., Latham, N.Y., 1983-86. Indexer: Statistical Abstract of Colorado 1976-77, 1977. Recipient Cert. of Recognition, Sigma Xi, U. Denver chpt., 1983. Mem. ALA, Spl. Libr. Assn., Colo. Assn. Librs., Phi Beta Kappa, Beta Phi Mu. Office: Colo Researchers PO Box 22779 Denver CO 80222-0779

**SMITH, SAM,** columnist; writer; b. Bklyn., Jan. 24, 1948; s. Leon and Betty (Pritzker) S.; m. Kathleen Ellen Rood, Jan. 24, 1976; children: Connor, Hannah-Li. BBA in Acctg., Pace U., N.Y.C., 1970; MA in Journalism, Ball State U., Muncie, Ind., 1974. Acct. Arthur Young & Co., N.Y.C., 1970-72; reporter Ft. Wayne (Ind.) News Sentinal, Ft. Wayne, 1973-76, States News Svc., Washington, 1976-79; press sec. U.S. Senator Lowell Weicker Jr., 1979; writer/reporter Chgo. Tribune, 1979-90, columnist, 1991—. Commentator ESPN Radio. Author: The Jordan Rules, 1991, Second Coming, 1995; co-author: Total Basketball Encyclopedia, 2004, The Perfect Team, 2006; contbr. columns to mags., articles to radio. With USAR, 1970-76. Named Ball State U. Journalism Alumnus of Yr.; named to Ball State U. Journalism Hall of Fame, 2002; recipient Journalism awards, AP, UPI, Sigma Delta Chi, Sports Local Emmy award, WGN-TV. Mem.: Basketball Writers Assn. (pres. 1998—2005). Office: Chicago Tribune 435 N Michigan Ave Chicago IL 60611-4066

**SMITH, SAMANTHA DENICE AKERS,** primary school educator; b. Oklahoma City, Okla., June 2, 1980; d. Mark Eugene and Norma Denice Akers; m. Benjamin Michael Smith, Feb. 19, 1980. BS Edn., Okla. Bapt. U., 2002; MEd Reading, U. Ctrl. Okla., 2004. Tchr. first grade Moore Pub. Schs., Okla., 2002—05; tchr. kindergarten Little Lake City Sch. Dist., Norwalk, Calif., 2005—; dir. Akers Reading Clinic, Lomita, Calif., 2006—. Mentor/facilitator Okla. Close-Up, Oklahoma City, 1999—2001. Mem.: Internat. Reading Assn. R-Consevative. Baptist. Avocations: reading, scrapbooking, travel. Home: 1629 W Pacific Coast Hwy #57 Wilmington CA 90744

**SMITH, SAMANTHA JUNE,** literature and language educator; b. FairChild AirForce Base, Wash., Sept. 7, 1974; d. Marcus Clifford and Nelda Marie Gold; m. Channing Lamar Smith, June 14, 2003. AA in Pre-Edn. Secondary, Cleve. C.C., 1994; BS in English, Appalachian State U., 1996. Lic. English secondary tchr. N.C. Dept. Edn., 1997. Deli clk., cashier Harris Teeter Grocery Store, Shelby, NC, 1993—98; tchr. English Shelby City Schs., 1997—98; tchr. asst. Charlotte Mecklenburg Schs., 2002—03; tutor lang. arts Paws Tutoring Svc., 2004—. Owner Paws Tutoring Svc., 2003—. Author: (poetry) Coming Out Of My Shell, (children's book) A Tail of Two Cats; painter (private exhibition) collection. Mem.: Resident Adv. Coun. (assoc.) sec. Gladedale bd. 2004—05). Independent. Presbyterian. Avocations: sewing, painting, writing, knitting, weaving. Home: 5829 Apt A Old Providence Rd Charlotte NC 28226 Office Phone: 704-877-7698. Personal E-mail: saphiregold_2003@yahoo.com

**SMITH, SAMUEL CLAYTON,** history professor; b. Clarkesville, Ga., May 27, 1959; s. George Clayton and Annie Ruth Smith; m. Rebecca Kay Brown, Oct. 5, 1991; children: Kendra Ann, Logan Clayton, Kayla Ruth, Haddon Robert. BA in Bible Studies, Bob Jones U., Greenville, SC, 1977—81, MA in Ch. History, 1982—84; PhD in History with distinction, U. SC, Columbia, 1994—99. Advanced profl. in adminstrn. and history Ga. Assn. Christian Schs., 2001. Tchr. Ctrl. Heights Christian Sch., Mt. Airy, Ga., 1984—90, prin., 1990—94; headmaster Westminster Christian Sch., Gainesville, Ga., 2000—04; asst. prof. history Liberty U., Lynchburg, Va., 2004—. Advanced placement reader Ednl. Testing Svc., Princeton, NJ, 2001—06. Contbr. articles to mags., chapters to books. Lay min., Sunday sch. tchr. Broad River Bapt. Ch., Baldwin, Ga., 1984—2000, Westminster Presbyn. Ch., Gainesville, 2000—04. Recipient award, Soc. Mayflower Descendants in State SC, 1997, Outstanding Young Men am., 1988, Distinguished Rsch. Fellowship award, U. SC, 1999, Charles Coolidge Post-doctoral Tchg. Fellowship award, 1999—2000. Mem.: Conf. Faith & History. Evangelical. Achievements include first to founding and organization of two private high schools. Home: 1183 Macon Loop Lynchburg VA 24503 Office: Dept History Liberty Univ 1971 University Blvd Lynchburg VA 24502

**SMITH, SCOTT A.,** lawyer; b. Grand Forks, N.D., July 17, 1957; married. BA, Stanford U., 1978; JD, U. Calif., Berkeley, 1981. Bar: Wash. 1981, U.S. Ct. Appeals (9th cir) 1982, U.S. Dist. Ct. (Ea. and We. dists.) Wash. Law clk. to Hon. Jerome Farris 9th Cir. U.S. Ct. of Appeals, 1981—82; assoc. Preston, Gates & Ellis, Seattle, 1982—88; ptnr. Short, Cressman & Burgess, Seattle, 1988—2004, Riddell Williams, Seattle, 2004—. Chair Wash. State Access to Justice Bd., Seattle, 2002—04. Recipient Pro Bono award, Wash. State Bar Assn., Allies for Justice award, LEGALS of Wash. Fellow: Am. Bar Found.; mem.: King County Bar Assn. (pres. 1996—97, trustee 1991—97, Helen Geisness award Exemplary Svc.). Office: Riddell Williams Ste 4500 1001 Fourth Ave Plaza Seattle WA 98154 Office Phone: 206-624-3600. Business E-Mail: SSmith@riddellwilliams.com.

**SMITH, SCOTT C.,** lawyer, legal association administrator; b. Atlanta, Apr. 26, 1960; BA cum laude, Wake Forest U., 1982; JD magna cum laude, Mercer U., 1985. Bar: Ga. 1985. V.p., corp. counsel Genuine Parts Co., Atlanta. Mng. editor Mercer U. Law Rev., 1984-85, mem., 1983-85; contbr. articles to law jours. Capt. U.S. Army, 1985-89. Mem. State Bar Ga., Brainerd Currie Honor Soc., Phi Kappa Phi Office: 2999 Circle 75 Pkwy SE Atlanta GA 30339-3050

**SMITH, SCOTT CLYBOURN,** media company executive; b. Evanston, Ill., Sept. 13, 1950; s. E. Sawyer and Jerolanne (Jones) S.; m. Martha Reilly, June 22, 1974; children: Carolyn Baldwin, Thomas Clybourn. BA, Yale U., 1973; M.Mgmt., Northwestern U., 1976. With Northern Trust Co., Chgo., 1973-77, Tribune Co., Chgo., 1977—93, sr. v.p., chief fin. officer, 1989-91, sr. v.p. for devel., 1991-93; pres., CEO, pub. Sun Sentinel Co., Ft. Lauderdale, Fla., 1993-97; pres., pub., CEO Chgo. Tribune Co., 1997—. Episcopalian. Office: Chgo Tribune Co 435 N Michigan Ave Chicago IL 60611-4066

**SMITH, SELMA MOIDEL,** lawyer, composer; b. Warren, Ohio, Apr. 3, 1919; d. Louis and Mary (Oyer) Moidel; 1 child, Mark Lee. Student, UCLA, 1936-39, U. So. Calif. Law School, 1939-41; JD, Pacific Coast U., 1942. Bar: Calif. 1943, U.S. Dist. Ct. 1943, U.S. Supreme Ct. 1958. Gen. practice law;

mem. firm Moidel, Moidel, Moidel & Smith, 1943—. Field dir. civilian adv. com. WAC, 1943—45; charter mem. nat. bd. Med. Coll. Pa. (formerly Woman's Med. Coll. Pa.), 1953—, mem. exec. bd., 1976—80, pres., 1980—82, chmn, past pres. com., 1990—92, spkr., honoree 50th anniversary gala, 2003. Author: A Century of Achievement: The National Association of Women Lawyers, 1998, The First Women Members of the ABA, 1999; composer: Espressivo-Four Piano Pieces (orchestral premiere, 1987, performance Nat. Mus. Women in the Arts, 1989), numerous works. Decorated La Orden del Merito Juan Pablo Duarte (Dominican Republic), 1956. Fellow Am. Bar Found. (life); mem. ASCAP, ABA (jr. bar. conf., 1946-52, activities com., 1948-49), Sr. Lawyers divsn. ABA (vice-chair editl. bd. Experience mag. 1997-99, chair arts com. 1998-99, chair editl. bd. Experience Mag. 1999-2001, exec. coun. 1999-2003, Experience mag. adv. bd. 2001—, nominating com. 2003-04, co-chair newsletter 2003-04, chair 2004-05, asst. sec., 2005—, Dist. Svc. award 2003-05), Calif. Supreme Ct. Hist. Soc. (bd. dirs. 2001—, programs and pubs. com., 2004—, State Bar program coord., 2006), Assn. Learning in Retirement Orgns. in West (pres. 1993-94, exec. com. 1994-95, Disting. Svc. award 1995), Plato Soc. UCLA (discussion leader Constitution Bicentennial Project 1985-87, moderator extension lecture series 1990, Toga editor 1990-93, sec. 1991-92, chmn. colloquium com. 1992-93, Exceptional Leadership award 1994), Euterpe Opera Club (chair auditions 1972, chair awards 1973-75, v.p. 1974-75), Docents L.A. Philharm. (press and pub. rels. 1972-75, cons. coord. 1973-75, v.p 1973-83, chair Latin Am. Cmty. Rels., Recognition and Honor award, 1978), Calif. Fedn. Music Clubs (chair Am. music 1971-75, conv. chair 1972), Nat. Fedn. Music Clubs (vice-chair Western region 1973-78), Nat. Assn. Composers USA (dir. 1974-79, luncheon chair 1975), Calif. Pres. Coun. (1st v.p.), L.A. Bus. Women's Coun. (pres. 1952), Calif. Bus. Women's Coun. (dir. 1951), Coun. Bar Assns. L.A. County (charter sec. 1950), Inter-Am. Bar Assn., League of Ams. (dir.), Nat. Assn. Women Lawyers (regional dir. western states, Hawaii 1949-51, jud. adminstrn. com. 1960, nat. chair world peace through law com. 1966-67, liaison to ABA Sr. Lawyers Divsn. 1996—, chair bd. elections 1997-98, centennial com. 1997-99, chair com. unauthorized practice of law, social commn. UN, Lifetime Svc. award 1999, honoree annual Selma Moidel Smith law student writing competition 2005—), L.A. Lawyers Club (pub. defenders com. 1951), L.A. Bar Assn. (servicemen's legal aid com. 1944-45, psychopathic ct. com. 1948-53, Outstanding Svc. award 1993), State Bar Calif. (conf. com. on unauthorized practice of medicine 1964, Disting. Svc. award 1993), Women Lawyers Assn. LA (formerly So. Calif. Women Lawyers Assn.)(hon life; pres., 1947, 48, chair law day com. 1966, subject of oral hist. project 1986, 2001), Iota Tau Tau Legal Scholastic Soc. (dean L.A. 1947, supreme treas. 1959-62, 1st prize 1942). Home: 5272 Lindley Ave Encino CA 91316-3518

**SMITH, SERAFINA GANGEMI,** artist; b. Phila., Sept. 1, 1919; d. Guiseppe I. and Maria Josephine (Meo) Gangemi; widowed, 1988; children: FRancisco Sidney, Guiseppe Scott, Maria Leslie. AA, U. Hawaii Windward Coll., Kaneohe, 1982; BA, U. Hawaii West Oahu, Pearl City, 1985; BA profl. studies, U. Hawaii, 1997. Cert. guardian ad litem for judiciary State of Hawaii. Ind. art instr., Forrest Heights, Md., 1963-67; stable mgr. Camp Smith Marine Base, Aiea, Hawaii, 1973-74; counselor Rehab. Hosp. of Pacific, Honolulu, 1979; counselor, cons. Hina Mauka Alcohol Rehab. Ctr., Kaneohe, 1980-82. State del. Al-Anon, Honolulu, 1982-84; bd. dirs. Pacific Inst. Chem. Dependency, Honolulu, 1983—; speaker on alcholism and family systems, 1981—; mgr. art gallery Hawaii Maritime Ctr., 1992—; studied with Guido del Corso, Verona, Italy, 1956-60, Lester Cook, Nat. Gallery, Washington, 1963-67, Dr. Chan, Oriental Inst. of Art, Washington, 1964-65, J. Woodward, Washington, 1965-66, Renzetti, Phila. Acad. of Arts, 1966-67, Douglas Walton, La. Tech., 1988—. Exhibited in group shows at Hawaii Watercolor Soc. Exhbn., 1992 (Bank of Hawaii award), 91 (Cresent Bd. award), Water Color Encounter, La. Tech. U., 1990 (Best in Show-Proffecial Judging award); one-women show Hawaii Maritime Mus., 1992; author: My Sicilian Family's Favorate Recipes, 2003. Vol. Hospice Hawaii, Honolulu, 1981-83, Suicide Crisis and Prevention Hotline, Honolulu, 1986-90, Hawaii Maritime Ctr., Honolulu, 1988—. Mem. AAUW (bd. dir. Hawaii unit 1986-87), Assn. for Christian Character Develop., team sponsor, Nat. Italian-Am. Found. (coun. mem.), Hawaii Joint Police Assn., U. Hawaii West Oahu Alumni Assn., Assn. Hawaii Artists (publicity chair 1990—), Hawaii Watercolor Soc., Nat. Mus. Women in Arts. Democrat. Roman Catholic. Avocations: cooking, designing clothes, travel.

**SMITH, SHARMAN BRIDGES,** state librarian; b. Lambert, Miss. BS, Miss. U. for Women, Columbus, 1972; MLS, George Peabody Coll., Nashville, 1975. Head libr. Clinton (Miss.) Pub. Libr., 1972-74; asst. dir. Lincoln-Lawrence-Franklin Regional Libr., Brookhaven, Miss., 1975-77, dir., 1977-78; info. svcs. mgr. Miss. Libr. Commn., Jackson, 1978-87, asst. dir. libr. ops., 1987-89, dir. libr. svcs. div., 1989-92; state libr. State Libr. Iowa, Des Moines, 1992—2001; exec. dir. Miss. Libr. Commn., Jackson, Miss., 2001—. Recipient Iowa Computer Using Educators Friend of Edn. award, 1995, Iowa Libr. Assn. Mem. of Yr. award, 1996. Office: Miss Libr Commn 3881 Eastwood Dr Jackson MS 39211 Office Phone: 601-432-4039. Business E-Mail: sharman@mlc.lib.ms.us.

**SMITH, SHERWOOD HUBBARD, JR.,** retired electric utilities executive; b. Jacksonville, Fla., Sept. 1, 1934; s. Sherwood Hubbard and Catherine Gertrude (Milliken) S.; m. Eva Hackney Hargrave, July 20, 1957; children: Marlin Hamilton Dohlman, Cameron Hargrave Callaway, Eva Hackney Davis. AB, U. N.C., 1956, JD, 1960; D civil laws, St. Augustine's Coll., 1988; LDD, Campbell U., 1990; HHD, Francis Marion Coll., 1990. Bar: N.C. 1960. Assoc. Lassiter, Moore & Van Allen, Charlotte, 1960-62; ptnr. Joyner & Howison, Raleigh, 1962-65; assoc. gen. counsel Carolina Power & Light Co., Raleigh, 1965-70, sr. v.p., gen. counsel, 1971-74, exec. v.p., 1974-76, pres., 1976-92, CEO, 1979-96, chmn. bd., 1980-99, chmn. emeritus, 1999—; with Progress Energy Co., 2005—. Former dir. NorTel Network, Northwestern Mut. Life Ins. Co., Wachovia Corp., Durham Corp., Springs, Ind. Trustee Z Smith Reynolds Found., 1978-96, Nat. Humanities Ctr., 1990-93; bd. dirs. NC Citizens Bus. and Industry, chmn., 1985-86; bd. dirs. Rsch. Triangle Found. NC, NC Inst. Medicine; mem. bd. govs. Ctr. Creative Leadership; mem. chmn. Triangle Univs. Ctr. Advanced Studies, 1986—; dir. Franklin St. Ptnrs.; former chmn. bd. trustees, chmn. Rex Hosp.; gov. Boys and Girls Clubs Am. Recipient Nat. Humanitarian award Am. Lung Assn., 1993, Outstanding Leadership award in Mgmt. scis. Am. Soc. Mech. Engrs., 1983, A.E. Finley Disting. Svc. award Greater Raleigh C. of C., 1985, Disting. Citizenship award N.C. Citizens Bus. and Industry, 1997; named to N.C. Bus. Hall of Fame, 1999. Mem.: Greater Raleigh C. of C. (pres. 1979), Phi Beta Kappa. Home: 408 Drummond Dr Raleigh NC 27609-7006 Office: Progress Energy Co PO Box 1551 Raleigh NC 27602-1551

**SMITH, SHIRLEY,** artist; b. Wichita, Kans., Apr. 17, 1929; d. Harold Marvin and Blanche Carrie (Alexander) S. BFA, Kans. State U., 1951; postgrad., Provincetown (Mass.) Workshop, 1962-66. One-woman shows include 55 Mercer St. Gallery, N.Y.C., 1973, Wichita Art Mus., Kanas, 1978, Stamford Mus. and Nature Ctr., Conn., 1987, Aaron Gallery, Washington, 1987, 1988, Joan Hodgell Gallery, Sarasota, Fla., 1987, Marianna Kistler Beach Mus. 38 Yr. Retrospective, Kans. State U., 1999—2000, John Jay Gallery, NYC, 2000, Represented in permanent collections Whitney Mus. Am. Art, Phoenix Art Mus., The Aldrich Mus. Contemporary Art, Ridgefield, Conn., Ulrich Mus., Wichita State U., Kans., Everson Mus., Syracuse, N.Y., U. Calif. Berkeley Art Mus., Marianna Kistler Beach Mus., Kans. State U., Manhattan, Telfair Mus. of Art, Savannah, Ga. Recipient Grumbacher Cash award for mixed media New Eng. Exhibition, Silvermine, Conn., 1967, Acad. Inst. award Am. Acad. Arts and Letters, N.Y.C., 1991, Richard Florsheim Art Funds grantee, 1998, Retrospective Opening grantee, 1999. Mem. Artist Equity. Democrat. Presbyterian. Home: 141 Wooster St New York NY 10012-3163

**SMITH, SHIRLEY A.,** state legislator, state representative; b. 1950; 2 children. AA, Cuyahoga CC; BA, Cleve. State U. Rep. Ohio State Ho. Reps., Columbus, 1998—. Mem. banking, pensions and securities com. Ohio State Ho. Reps., mem. juvenile and family law com., mem. fin. instns., real estate

and securities com., ranking minority mem. health com., mem. joint legis. com. on health care oversight. Vice chair Ohio Women's Dem. Caucus; chair region IX exec. com. Nat. Black Caucus of State Legislators; sec. Ohio Legis. Black Caucus; active Cuyahoga County Dem. Del. Mem.: NOW, Ohio Legis. Women's Caucus, Nat. Black Caucus of State Legis., Women in Govt., Emily's List. Democrat. Office: Ohio State House Reps 77 South High Street 10th Floor Columbus OH 43215-6111

**SMITH, SIBLEY JUDSON, JR.,** historic site administrator, educator; b. Alexandria, La., June 26, 1955; s. Sibley Judson and Eunice Lee (Raulins) S.; children: Jacob Lee, Casey Raulins. Student, N.E. La. U., 1973-76; BA in History magna cum laude, Christopher Newport Coll., 1985; MA in Am. Studies, Coll. of William and Mary, 1992. Mus. interpreter Colonial Williamsburg (Va.) Found., 1979-87; coord. of interpretation Hist. Hudson Valley, Inc., Tarrytown, NY, 1987-88; historic site mgr. Philipse Manor Hall State Hist. Site, Yonkers, NY, 1988-91; exec. dir. Hist. Allaire (N.J.) Village, Inc., 1991-97; dir. edn. Vietnam Era Ednl. Ctr., N.J. Vietnam Vets. Meml. N.J. Dept. Mil. and Vet. Affairs, Holmdel, 1997—. Mem. Alpha Chi, Alpha Psi Omega. Avocations: gardening, theater, movies, mus. Office: Vietnam Era Ednl Ctr 1 Memorial Ln PO Box 648 Holmdel NJ 07733-0648 Office Phone: 800-648-8387. Business E-Mail: sjsmith2@njvvmf.org.

**SMITH, SIDNEY OSLIN, JR.,** lawyer; b. Gainesville, Ga., Dec. 30, 1923; s. Sidney Oslin and Isabelle Caroline (Charters) S.; m. Patricia Irwin Horkan, Aug. 4, 1944 (dec. Oct. 19, 2001); children— Charters Smith Wilson, Ellen Smith Andersen, Sidney Oslin III; m. Carolyn S. Reed, Nov. 29, 2004. AB cum laude, Harvard Coll., 1947; LL.B. summa cum laude, U. Ga., 1949. Bar: Ga. 1948. Ptnr. Telford, Wayne & Smith, Gainesville, Ga., 1949-62; asst. solicitor Superior Cts., Northeastern Jud. Cir. Ga., 1951-61, judge, 1962-65, U.S. Dist. Ct. (no. dist) Ga., 1965-68, chief judge, 1968-74; ptnr. Alston, Miller & Gaines, Atlanta, 1974-82, Alston & Bird, Atlanta, 1982-94, of counsel, 1994—. Chmn. Gainesville Bd. Edn., 1959-62; trustee Brenau Coll., Gainesville, 1974—, chmn., 1976-84; mem. state bd. regents Univ. System of Ga., 1980-87, chmn., 1984-85. Served to capt. U.S. Army, 1943-46, ETO. Fellow ABA, Am. Coll. Trial Lawyers; mem. Am. Law Inst., Am. Judicature Soc., Commerce Club, Chattahoochee Club, Phi Beta Kappa, Phi Kappa Phi, Phi Delta Phi, Phi Delta Theta. Republican. Episcopalian. Home: 3206 Club Pointe Way Gainesville GA 30506-1638 Office: Alston & Bird 1 Atlantic Ctr Atlanta GA 30309-3400 E-mail: smit977@bellsouth.net.

**SMITH, SIDNEY RUFUS, JR.,** linguist, educator; b. Greensboro, N.C., Sept. 18, 1931; s. Sidney Rufus and Page (Johnston) S.; m. Vera Pautzsch, Apr. 19, 1969 (div. 1975); children: Stephanie Alice, Eric Brian. BA, Duke U., 1953; PhD, U. N.C., 1965. Asst. prof. U. Conn., Storrs, 1965-66, U. N.C., Chapel Hill, 1966-71, assoc. prof., 1971-79, prof., 1979—, chmn. Germanic langs., 1979-89, 94-97, chmn. linguistics, 1981-84, prof. emeritus, 1997—. Author numerous articles for profl. publs. Local troop leader Girl Scouts U.S.A. Served to sgt. AUS, 1953-56. Recipient Stephen Freeman award N.E. Conf. Teaching Langs., 1969, cert. of merit Goethe Inst., 1997. Mem.: Am. Assn. Tchrs. German, Soc. Advancement Scandinavian Study. Democrat. Office: U NC Dept Germanic Langs Chapel Hill NC 27599-0001 Business E-Mail: srsmith@email.unc.edu. E-mail: srsmith@mindspring.com.

**SMITH, SPENCER BAILEY,** engineering and business educator; b. Ottawa, Ont., Can., Jan. 31, 1927; s. Sidney B. and Etta (Bailey) S.; m. Mildred E. Spidell, Dec. 31, 1954 B in Engring., McGill U., 1949; MS, Columbia U., 1950, DSc in Engring., 1958. Adminstrv. engr. Mergenthaler Linotype Co., N.Y.C., 1953-58; ops. research mgr. Raytheon Co., Newton, Mass., 1958-61; ops research mgr. Montgomery Ward & Co., Chgo., 1961-66; assoc. prof., then prof. Ill. Inst. Tech., 1966-96, prof. emeritus, 1996—, chmn. dept. indsl. and systems engring., 1971-77, dir. Stuart Sch. Office of Research, 1977-82. Tchr. TV courses Nat. Tech. U. Author: Computer-Based Production and Inventory Control, 1989; contbr. articles to profl. jours.; patentee on order quantity calculator, 1964. Vol. cons. on sch. redistricting Elem. Sch. Dist., Evanston, Ill., 1972-74 Research grantee Harris Trust and Savs. Bank, 1968-70, Ill. Law Enforcement Commn., 1972-74, U.S. Army C.E., 1981, Am. Prodn. and Inventory Control Soc., 1980 Mem. INFORMS, ASME, Inst. Indsl. Engrs., Univ. Club (Chgo.). Presbyterian. Home: 2530 Lawndale Ave Evanston IL 60201-1158 E-Mail: montrosemillennium@comcast.net.

**SMITH, STAN VLADIMIR,** economist, finance company executive; b. Rhinelander, Wis., Nov. 16, 1946; s. Valy Zdenek and Sylvia Smith; children: Cara, David. BS in Ops. Research, Cornell U., 1968; MBA, U. Chgo., 1972, PhD in Econs., 1997. Diplomate Am. Bd. Disability Analysts. Lectr. U. Chgo., 1973; economist bd. govs. Fed. Res. System, Washington, 1973-74; staff economist First Nat. Bank of Chgo., 1974; assoc. December Group, Chgo., 1974-77; founding pres. Seaquest Internat., Chgo., 1977-85; mgr., ptnr. Ibbotson Assocs., Chgo., 1981-85; pres. Smith Econ. Group Ltd. divsn. Corp. Fin. Group, Chgo., 1985—. Expert econ. witness in field; adj. prof. DePaul U. Coll. Law, Chgo., 1990. Author: Economic/Hedonic Damages, 1990; founding editor Stocks, Bonds, Bills and Inflation yearbook, 1983-01; editor Jour. Forensic Econs., 1990-01; contbr. articles in field. Founder, exec. dir. Inst. for Value of Life, 1996. Fellow Allied Chem., 1967, John McMullen Trust, 1969; grantee Ford Found., 1972, U.S. Fed. Res., 1973. Fellow: Am. Coll. Forensic Examiners (bd. cert. 1996—); mem.: Soc. Litig. Economists (bd. govs. 1999—), Acad. Econ. and Fin. Experts, Am. Bd. Forensic Examiners, Nat. Future Assn. (arbitrator), Am. Arbitration Assn. (arbitrator 1994—96), Nat. Acad. Econ. Arbitrators (founder 1989—), Nat. Assn. Forensic Econs. (v.p. 2000—03), Am. Fin. Assn., Am. Econ. Assn., Alpha Delta Phi. Office: Smith Econ Group Ltd Ste 600 1165 N Clark St Chicago IL 60610-7861 Office Phone: 312-943-1551. Business E-Mail: stan@smitheconomics.com.

**SMITH, STANLEY ROGER,** retired professional tennis player; b. Pasadena, Calif., Dec. 14, 1946; s. Charles Kenneth and Rhoda (Widmer) S.; m. Marjory Logan Gengler, Nov. 23, 1974; children: Ramsey Gengler, Trevor Austin, Logan Widmer, Austin Church. BA, U. So. Calif., 1969; L.H.D., Greenville Coll., 1974, Winthrop Coll., N.C. Profl. tennis player, 1968—; mem. U.S. Davis Cup Team, 1968-79, 81; adviser Pres.'s Council on Phys. Fitness, 1971-75; chmn. Stan Smith Design, Inc.; dir. coaching USTA. Cons. Sea Pines Plantations, 1971—, Adidas, Landersheim, France, 1971—, Fischer G.m.b.H., Austria, 1980-86, Prince Adv. Staff, 1986—; bd. dirs. Hilton Head br. Citizens & So. Nat. Bank S.C. Writer: nationally syndicated newspaper column Stan Smith's Tennis Tips, 1971—; Author: Inside Tennis, 1974, Stan Smith's Six Tennis Basics, 1974, The Executive Tennis Diary 1975, 1974, Stan Smith's Guide to Better Tennis, 1975, (with Bob Lutz) Modern Doubles, 1975, It's More Than Just a Game, 1977; also video with Arthur Ashe, Vic Braden: Tennis Our Way. Bd. dirs. Greater Los Angeles Big Bros. Am., 1966-71; hon. tennis chmn. Duke's Children's Classic, 1982—; hon. chmn. Am. Festival Fitness and Sport, 1987. Served with AUS, 1970-72. Decorated D.S.M.; named Martini and Rossi Player of Year, 1971, 72; holder 26 U.S. singles and doubles titles, including U.S. Open singles, 1971, U.S. Open doubles, 1968, 74, 78, 80; ranked number one in U.S. doubles, 1968, 69, 1970, 71, 72, 74; number one in U.S. singles, 1969, 71, 72, 73; winner Wimbledon singles title, 1972, 6 World championship tennis titles in 1973, including; World Championship of Tennis Finals in singles; also: Rothman's World Doubles title; ranked world's number one tennis player, 1972, 73; Lebair Sportsmanship Trophy, 1969; Johnston Sportsmanship Trophy, 1968; champion 35 & Over Cir. Singles and Doubles Championships, 1982, 84, 86; named to U.S. Collegiate Hall of Fame, 1984, to Carolina Tennis Hall of Fame, 1986, to Internat. Hall of Fame, 1987. Mem. Assn. Tennis Profls. (dir. 1972-79, 81-83), Men's Internat. Profl. Tennis Council, Athletes in Action, Beta Theta Pi. Clubs: Sea Pines Plantation, Los Angeles Tennis, All England, West Side Tennis, No. Century XXI, Balboa Bay. Republican. Presbyterian. Office: 1101 Wilson Blvd Ste 1800 Arlington VA 22209-2248 *God has given me certain talents. I feel a great opportunity and responsibility to develop and use these talents to their fullest on and off the tennis courts. I see great potential in our country and especially in our youth today, and I hope to* *provide some leadership and direction that this youth will need to develop their potential constructively. God has given me a great life so far and I plan to rely on His guidance to take me the rest of the way.* 

**SMITH, STANTON KINNIE, JR.,** lawyer; b. Rockford, Ill., Feb. 14, 1931; s. Stanton Kinnie Smith and Elizabeth (Brown) Stanton; m. Mary Beth Sanders, July 11, 1953; children: Stanton E., Kathryn A., Dana. BA, Yale U., 1953; JD, U. Wis., 1956. Bar: Ill. 1956, Mich. 1976. Ptnr. Sidley & Austin Law, Chgo., 1964—87; sr. v.p. The Coastal Corp., Houston, 1985—87; vice chmn., gen. counsel CMS Energy Corp., Jackson, Mich., 1987—88, pres., 1988—92, vice chmn., 1992—96, vice chmn., bd. 2002—05; sr. spl. counsel Skadden, Arps, Slate, Meagher & Flom, N.Y.C., 1996—2002; vice chmn. Trans-Elect, Inc., 2002. Bd. dirs. Clarcor Corp., Mich. Natural Corp., Mich. Nat. Bank. Trustee Founders Soc., Detroit Inst. Arts, Rockford Coll.; devel. bd. mem. Yale U.; trustee Mich. Opera Theatre; bd. advisors U. Wis. Law Sch., Mich. State U.; Pub. Utility Inst. Mem.; ABA, Chgo. Bar Assn., Mich. Bar Assn. Office: CMS Energy Corp One Energy Plaza Jackson MI 49201 Business E-mail: sksmith@cmsenergy.com

**SMITH, STEPHEN ALLEN,** mathematician, educator; s. William Francis and Gertrude Elizabeth Smith; m. Karen Ann Jensen, Apr. 27, 2002; children: Gregory, Daniel. BS in Math., U. Cin., 1965; MS in Math., Stevens Inst. Tech., 1967; PhD in Engring.-Econ. Sys., Stanford U., 1972. Rsch. scientist Xerox Rsch. Ctr., Palo Alto, Calif., 1972—82; J.C. Penney prof. Leavey Sch. Bus. Santa Clara U., Calif., 1982—. Prin. Pricing Strategy Assocs., Berkeley, Calif., 1984—95; mem. adv. bd. Spotlight Solutions, Inc., Cin., 1998—2003, StoreSight Sys., Palo Alto, 2000—, Profit Logic, Inc., Cambridge, Mass. Author: New Service Opportunities for Electric Utilities, 1993; mem. editl. bd.: Ops. Rsch. Jour., 1984—2000, Inst. Indsl. Engring., 1997—; contbr. articles to profl. jours. Recipient award for best pub. paper, Jour. Retailing, 1991. Mem.: Inst. Ops. Rsch. and Mgmt. Sci. (chmn. bus. applications 1986—90, sr. editor Mfg. and Svc. Ops. Mgmt. Jour. 2002—). Office: Santa Clara Univ Dept OMIS 500 El Camino Real Santa Clara CA 95053 E-mail: ssmith@scu.edu.

**SMITH, STEPHEN F.,** food service executive; b. El Dorado, Ark. m. Jan Smith; 6 children. Student, South Ark. U. Mgr. Sysco Corp., Jackson, Minn., 1980—81, v.p. wholesale co. El Paso, Tex., 1981—83, pres., CEO Atlanta, 1983—87, Little Rock, 1987—95, Orlando, 1995—2002, sr. v.p. food svc. ops. Ocoee, Fla., 2002—. Office: Sysco Corp 200 W Story Rd Ocoee FL 34761-0130

**SMITH, STEPHEN GRANT,** journalist; b. N.Y.C., Mar. 6, 1949; s. John J. and Nora O.S.; m. Sarah Rowbotham Bedell, May 22, 1982; children: R. Kirk Bedell, Elisabeth DeCou Bedell, David Branson Smith. Student, Deerfield Acad.; BA, U. Pa., 1971. City Hall reporter Daily Hampshire Gazette, Northampton, Mass., 1971-73; spl. assignment reporter Albany Times-Union, 1973-74; dep. regional editor Phila. Inquirer, 1974-76; asst. met. editor Boston Globe, 1976-78; sr. editor Horizon Mag., 1978; staff writer Time Mag., 1978-80, sr. editor, 1980-82, Nation editor, 1982-85, acting asst. mng. editor, 1985-86; exec. editor Newsweek Mag., 1986-91; Washington news editor Knight Ridder newspapers, 1991-94; founding editor Civilization Mag., Washington, 1994-96; editor Nat. Jour., 1996-98, U.S. News and World Report, 1998-2001; exec. v.p. Winner & Assocs., 2001—02; v.p., dir. comm. Brookings Instn., 2003—04; Wash. bur. chief Houston Chronicle, 2004—. Mem. bd. Nat. Press Found., 2005—. Mem. bd. overseers U. Pa., 2001—; mem. bd. U. Pa. Press, 2005—. Mem.: Overseas Press Club, Nat. Press Club, U. Pa. Alumni Soc. (exec. com. 1994—2000), World Affairs Coun. Washington, Coun. on Fgn. Rels., Royal St. George's Golf Club, Fourth Estate Golf Soc., Sakonnet Golf Club, Penn Club, White's Club, Beefsteak Club, Chevy Chase Club, Met. Club, Century Club, Brook Club. Office: Houston Chronicle Ste 1000 1850 K St NW Washington DC 20006 Personal E-mail: sgrasmith@gmail.com.

**SMITH, STEPHEN K.,** minister; s. Leon C. and Oneta B. Smith; m. Cynthia K. Smith, Dec. 14, 1955; 1 child, Danchal K. BA, Okla. Bapt. U., 1978; MusM, Southwestern Bapt. Theol. Sem., 1986. Min. music Emmaus Bapt. Ch., Oklahoma City, 1987—91; min. music and edn. Pleasant Ter. Bapt. Ch., Dallas, 1991—95, Regency Pk. Bapt. Ch., Moore, Okla., 1995—2001; min. worship Choctaw Rd. Bapt. Ch., 2001—. Soloist Singing Churchmen Okla., Oklahoma City, 1995—. Home: 12428 Goldsborough Rd Midwest City OK 73130

**SMITH, STEPHEN MARK,** music educator; b. Columbia, Mo., Feb. 23, 1954; s. Elmer Lee and Josephine Ann Smith; m. Pamela Layne Snella, July 30, 1978; 1 child, Christopher Stephen. A of Music, Morton Coll., 1974; BS in Music Edn., U. Ill., 1977; M of Spl. Edn., U. North Fla., 1995, postgrad., 2001—02. Cert. tchr. Fla. Dept. Edn., 1988. Commd. ensign USN, 1978, advanced through grades to lt., ret., 1988; music resource tchr. special edn. Duval County Sch. Dist. Music Dept., Jacksonville, Fla., 1988—. Presenter in field. Cubmaster Boy Scouts of Am., Jacksonville, 1988—90, scoutmaster 1992—93, merit badge counselor, 1994—2002. Decorated Sea Svc. Ribbon, Sea Svc. Ribbon First Star, Navy Expeditionary Medal, Pistol Marksman Ribbon, Rifle Marksman Ribbon, Navy Achievement Medal; named Arts Educator of Yr., Cultural Coun., Jacksonville, 1997, Feature Article Educator Teaches in the Key of Success, The Times Union Newspaper, Jacksonville, 1998; recipient cert. of Appreciation, Future Educators Am., 1998; grantee, U.S. Dept. Edn., 1995, 1996, Duval Pub. Edn. Found., Jacksonville, 1996, 1996, Duval Pub. Edn. Found., 1996, U.S. Dept. Edn., 1997, The Cultural Coun. Greater Jacksonville, 1997, U.S. Dept. Edn., 1998, Duval County Pub. Found, 1998, U.S. Dept. Edn. 1999, Duval Pub. Edn. Found., 1999, The Cultural Coun. of Greater Jacksonville, 1999, Jacksonville Elec. Authority and The Alliance for World Class Edn., 2000, The Alliance for World Class Edn., 2000, Individuals with Disabilities Edn. Act, 2005, Severely Emotionally Distrubed Network, 2004—05, Sednet, 2004—06. Mem.: Fla. Elem. Music Educators Assn. (state dist. rep. 1990—91), Fla. Music Educators Assn., Appalachian Tr. Assn., The Am. Legion, Pi Lambda Theta, Delta Sigma Pi. Democrat-Npl. Roman Catholic. Avocations: digital gaming, computing, computer gaming, flying. Office: Duval County Sch Bd Music Dept 1701 Prudential Dr Jacksonville FL 32207 Personal E-mail: baden@fdn.com.

**SMITH, STEPHEN RANDOLPH,** aerospace executive; b. Des Moines, Apr. 17, 1928; s. Norvin Ellis and Helen (Heberling) S.; m. Margaret Anne Graves, Dec. 20, 1950; children: Stephen Randolph Jr., Susan Canning, Sara Kutler, Anne Barrette, Julia Carroll. BSME, Stanford U., 1951, MSME, 1952; MBA Advanced Mgmt. Program, Harvard U., 1974. Registered profl. engr., Calif. Sr. analyst, preliminary design engr. Northrop & Garrett Corps., L.A. and Hawthorne, Calif., 1952-55; propulsion lead design engr. Northrop Corp., Hawthorne, 1955-59, engring. rep. ea. dist. Washington, 1959-60, T-38/F-5/F-5X program mgr. Hawthorne, 1960-75, v.p. Iran ops. Tehran, 1975-78, v.p. advanced stealth projects Hawthorne, 1978-83, v.p. engring. and advanced devel., 1983-86, v.p., program mgr. F-20/YF-23A, 1986-88, corp. v.p., gen. mgr. aircraft divsn., 1988-92; cons. tech. mgmt. Palos Verdes, Calif., 1992—. Bd. mem. Quarterdeck Ptnrs., Inc., L.A. and Washington, 1992—; NASA Advanced Aeronautics Com., 1984-86; invited lectr. aircraft design USAF Acad., 1983. Author, designer, patentee in field. Bd. dirs. Boy Scouts Am., L.A. coun., 1986—, explorer exec. com., 1943—; pres. Penn Srs., Palos Verdes, Calif., 1996; trustee Western Mus. Flight; jr. warden St. Francis Ch. Sgt. U.S. Army, 1946-48. Recipient Disting. Civilian Svc. medal for Tacit Blue, U.S. Dept. Def., Washington, 1983. Fellow AIAA (chmn. L.A. sect. 1985-86, adv. bd. 1988—, Spl. Citation 1994), Inst. Advancement Engring.; mem. Soc. Automotive Engrs. (chmn. aerotech. 1986-87, honors 1987), Sierra Club, Trailfinders Conservation Coun. (life, coun. chief 1940), Redondo Beach Yacht Club (charter), King Harbor Yacht Club (charter). Republican. Episcopalian. Avocations: competitive sailing, tennis, backpacking, skiing, running. Home and Office: 2249 Via Guadalana Palos Verdes Estates CA 90274

**SMITH, STEPHEN ROSS,** endocrinologist; b. Iowa City, Mar. 5, 1938; s. Wendell Ross and Ruth Anne (Frudenfeld) S.; m. Elaine Cashman Frazier, July 4, 1964 (div. Dec. 1990); children: Julia Helene, Stuart Ross; m. Regina Alilada Clarito, Dec. 26, 1990; 1 child, Alexander Ross. AB, Princeton U., 1959; MD, Harvard U., 1963. Instr. medicine Johns Hopkins U. Sch. Medicine, Balt., 1970-72, asst. prof. medicine, 1972-73, 82—; chief endocrinology Kern County Hosp., Bakersfield, Calif., 1973-76; assoc. prof. medicine Tex. Tech. U. Sch. Medicine, El Paso, 1977-80; chief medicine Thomason Gen. Hosp., El Paso, 1977-80, Bon Secours Hosp., Balt., 1980-83, Security Forces Hosp., Riyadh, Saudi Arabia, 1984-88; pvt. practice Balt., 1988—; med. dir. Nat. Clin. Rsch. Ctrs., Bethesda, Md., 1988-93. Pres. med. staff Univ. Specialty Hosp., Balt., 1996—; rsch. assoc. Johns Hopkins Ctr. Med. Rsch. and Tng., Calcutta, India, 1970—72; bd. dirs. El Paso Diabetes Assn., 1978—80; cons. Liberty Med. Ctr. Diabetes Mgmt. Ctr., Balt., 1991—98, pharm. industry, 1993—. Contbr. articles to profl. jours. Capt. USAF, 1965-67. Fellow ACP; mem. Am. Diabetes Assn., Princeton Club Md., Hampton Swim Club, Bodie Island Beach Club (pres. 2002-, bd. dirs. 2000-). Republican. Avocations: swimming, travel, history. Office: 8709 Harford Rd Baltimore MD 21234-4607 Office Phone: 410-882-4741.

**SMITH, STEVE,** professional football player; b. LA, May 12, 1979; Attended, U. Utah. Wide receiver Carolina Panthers, 2001—. Named NFL Comeback Player of the Yr., 2005; named to NFC ProBowl Team, 2005, NFL All-Pro Team, 2005. Office: Carolina Panthers 800 So Mint St Charlotte NC 28202*

**SMITH, STEVEN RAY,** law educator; b. Spirit Lake, Iowa, July 8, 1946; s. Bynard L. and Dorothy V. (Fischbeck) S.; m. Lera Baker, June 15, 1975. BA, Buena Vista Coll., 1968; JD, U. Iowa, 1971, MA, 1971. Bar: Iowa 1971, Ky. 1987, Ohio 1992. From asst. to assoc. dean Sch. Law U. Louisville, 1974-81, acting dean, 1974-75, 76, prof. law, 1971-88, assoc. in medicine Med. Sch., 1983-88; dep. dir/ Assn. Am. Law Schs., 1987-88; dean, prof. law Cleve. State U., 1988-96; pres., dean and prof. Calif. Western Sch. of Law, 1996—. Author: Law, Behavior and Mental Health: Policy and Practice, 1987; contbr. chpts. to books, articles to profl. jours. Trustee U. Louisville, 1980-82, SCRIBES, 1993—; pres. Ky. Congress of Senate Faculty Leaders, 1982-84; bd. trustees Am. Bd. Profl. Psychology, 1994-2001; bd. dirs. Nat. Register of Health Svc. Providers in Psychology, 2002—, San Diego Vol. Lawyers Program, 1998—, Nat. Conflict Resolution Ctr., 2003—; sec., bd. dirs. Assn. for Accreditation of Human Rsch. Protection Programs, 2001—. Recipient Grawemeyer award Innovative Teaching. Metroversity Consortium, 1983. Fellow Ohio State Bar Found., ABA (stds. rev. com. 1991-95, govt. rels. com. 1993-95, joint commn. ABA/Assn. Am. Law Schs. financing of legal edn. 1993-94, 97-98, coun. sect. legal edn. and admission to the bar 1997—, chmn.-elect sect. on legal edn. and admission to the bar 2004—); mem. APA (pub. mem. ethics com.), Am. Econs. Assn., Assn. Am. Law Schs. (chmn. librs. com., dep. dir. 1987-88, mem. accreditation com. 1993-96, chair accreditation com. 1994-96), Ohio State Bar Assn. (coun. of dels. 1992-96), Order of Coif, City Club of Cleve. (pres. 1994-95). Office: Calif Western Sch Law Office of Dean 225 Cedar St San Diego CA 92101-3046

**SMITH, STEVEN SIDNEY,** molecular biologist; b. Idaho Falls, Idaho, Feb. 11, 1946; s. Sidney Ervin and Hermie Phyllis (Robertson) Smith; m. Nancy Louise Turner, Dec. 20, 1974. BS, U. Idaho, 1968; PhD, UCLA, 1974. Asst. rsch. scientist Beckman Rsch. Inst. City of Hope Nat. Med. Ctr., Duarte, Calif., 1982-84, staff Cancer Ctr., 1983—; asst. rsch. scientist depts. Thoracic Surgery and Molecular Biology, 1985-87, assoc. rsch. scientist, 1987-95; rsch. scientist City of Hope Nat. Med. Ctr., Duarte, 1995-00, prof. molecular sci., 2000—; dir. dept. cell and tumor biology City of Hope, Duarte, Calif., 1990—2002, assoc. dir. rsch. Prostate Cancer Program, 2003—. Vis. prof. in basic med. scis. Okla. State U., 1995—96; cons. Molecular Biosystems Inc., San Diego, 1981—84, Am. Inst. Biol. Scis., Washington, 1994, Okla. Ctr. for Advancement of Sci. and Tech., 2001—. Editl. bd. mem. Analytical Biochemistry, 1997—2000, exec. editor, 2000—, editl. bd. mem. Inscight Acad. Press., 1998—; contbr. articles to profl. jours. Named Honors Laureate, Computer World, 2001; fellow Swiss Nat. Sci. Found. fellow, U. Bern, 1974—77, fellow, Scripps Clinic and Rsch. Found., 1978—82, Scripps Clinic fellow, NIH, 1979—81. Mem.: Am. Chem. Soc., Am. Assn. Cancer Rsch., Am. Soc. Cell Biology, Phi Beta Kappa. Achievements include 5 U.S. patents. Avocation: backpacking. Office: Kaplan Clin Rsch Lab City of Hope 1500 E Duarte Rd Duarte CA 91010-3011 Office Phone: 626-357-9711 ext. 68316. Business E-Mail: ssmith@coh.org.

**SMITH, STUART A.,** lawyer; b. NYC, Mar. 16, 1941; s. Sydney S. and Gertrude (Blinder) S.; m. Helaine Levi, Mar. 14, 1982. AB, Columbia Coll., N.Y.C., 1961; LLB, Harvard U., 1964. Bar: N.Y. 1964, U.S. Tax Ct. 1965, U.S. Supreme Ct. 1967, D.C. 1970. Law clk. to chief judge U.S. Tax Ct., Washington, 1964-66; atty. U.S. Dept. Justice Tax Div., Washington, 1966-70; pvt. practice Washington, 1970-73; tax asst. to solicitor gen. U.S. Dept. Justice, Washington, 1973-83; pvt. practice N.Y.C., 1983—. Author: How You Can Get the Most from the New Tax Law, 1982; contbr. articles to law revs. Mem. ABA (chmn. tax sect. subcom.), Assn. of Bar of City of N.Y (fed. taxation com.), Am. Law Inst. (tax adv. group), Univ. Club (N.Y.C., Washington), RAC Club (London). Office: 750 Lexington Ave New York NY 10022 Office Phone: 212-759-8285.

**SMITH, STUART LYON,** psychiatrist, corporate financial executive; b. Montreal, Que., Can., May 7, 1938; s. Moe Samuel and Nettie (Krainer) S.; m. Patricia Ann Springate, Jan. 2, 1964; children: Tanya, Craig. BSc, McGill U., 1958, MD, CM, 1962, diploma in psychiatry, 1967; LLD (hon.), Mt. Allison U., 1992, Royal Rds U., 2000; B.Ap.Sc. (hon.), Humber Coll., 2005. Intern. Montreal Gen. Hosp., 1962-63, resident in psychiatry, 1963-67; from asst. prof. to assoc. prof. medicine McMaster U., Hamilton, Ont., Canada, 1967-75; leader Ont. Liberal Party Ont. Legislature, 1976-82, leader of the opposition, 1977-82; chmn. Sci. Coun. Can., Ottawa, 1982-87; pres. Rock-Cliffe Rsch. and Tech. Inc., 1987—, Philip Utilities Mgmt. Corp., Toronto, Ont., 1994-97. Chmn. com. inquiry Can. U. Edn., 1989—91; chmn. Ensyn Tech. Inc., 1990—; sr. adv. ICF Cons., 2002; chmn. Nat. Round Table on Environment and Economy, Ottawa, 1995—2002; chmn. bd. dirs. Humber Coll., 2002—04, Esna Tech., Inc., 2004—. Decorated knight Nat. Order of Merit (France); McLaughlin travel fellow, 1964-65. Fellow Royal Coll. Physicians and Surgeons of Can. Personal E-mail: smithstuart@rogers.com.

**SMITH, STUART SEABORNE,** writer, government official, union official; b. N.Y.C., Jan. 27, 1930; s. Purcell Leonard and Elizabeth (Wright) S.; m. Birte Moeller Jacobsen, Apr. 27, 1956 (div. 1972); children: Stuart Seaborne, Bjarne Moeller; m. Editha Maria Fuchs, Jan. 3, 1973; children: Cornelia Gerda, Melanie Carla. Student, Princeton U., 1948—51, U. Heidelberg, Germany, 1953—54, U. Madrid, 1954—55, U. Copenhagen, 1955—56. Reporter Balt. Sun, 1957-65, fgn. corr. chief Bonn (Germany) bur., 1965-69, corr. Washington Bur., 1969-70; with ABA, 1970-71, Dept. Justice, Washington, 1971—; exec. dir. Capitol Employees Organizing Group, 1979—; pub. Balt. Banner, 1965. Served with AUS, 1951-53. Recipient Spl. award for meritorious svc. Washington-Balt. Newspaper Guild, 1965, Meritorious Svc. award Dept. Justice, 1985, 87, Sustained Superior Performance award Dept. Justice, 1992, 93. Mem. Am. Fedn. State, County and Mcpl. Employees (pres. coun. 26 1977-80, 87-95, chief steward Local 2830 1975-80, 81-82, pres. 1982—, Meritorious Svc. award Local 2830, 1980). Home: 10522 Tyler Ter Potomac MD 20854-4059 Office: Office Of Justice Programs Washington DC 20531-0001 Office Phone: 202-307-0784. Personal E-mail: stuart.smith20@verizon.net. Business E-Mail: stuart.smith@usdoj.gov. E-mail: stu219@hotmail.com. *I believe in honor and democracy and social justice. I further believe that for the most part we are the ignorant slaves of political and philosophical superstitions, but in the end the truth shall set us free.*

**SMITH, SUE FRANCES,** newspaper editor; b. Lockhart, Tex., July 4, 1940; d. Monroe John Baylor and Myrtle (Krause) Mueck; m. Michael Vogtel Smith, Apr. 20, 1963 (div. July 1977); 1 child, Jordan Meredith; m. Kirkland Gideon Smith, Apr. 17, 1999. B of Journalism, U. Tex., 1962. Feature writer,

photographer Corpus Christi Caller Times, 1962-64; feature writer, editor Chgo. Tribune, 1964-76; features editor Dallas Times Herald, 1976-82; sales assoc. Bumpas Assocs., Dallas, 1982-83; asst. mng. editor for features Denver Post, 1983-84, assoc. editor, 1984-91; asst. mng. editor in charge of Sunday paper Dallas Morning News, 1991-94, asst. mng. editor Lifestyles, 1994-96, dep. mng. editor Lifestyles, 1996—2001, dep. mng. editor recruiting/devel., 2001—. Active Coun. Press, 1993; juror Pulitzer Prize, 2002, 03. Mem. Am. Assn. Sunday and Feature Editors (pres. 1993), Newspaper Features Coun. (pres. 2002), Tex. AP Mng. Editors (pres. 1999-00, Jack Douglas award disting. svc. 2005, Am. com. conf. 2005, 06), Delta Gamma. Home: 6241 Park Meadow Ln Plano TX 75093-8863 Office: 508 Young St Dallas TX 75202-4893 E-mail: ssmith@dallasnews.com.

**SMITH, SURVILLA MARIE,** social services administrator, artist, poet; b. Chattanooga, Oct. 17, 1933; d. Charlie and LeGusta (Robinson) Prater; children: Charles, Calvin, Robin. Student, Mass. Bay C.C., Boston, 1965—66, Northeastern U., 1967-79, Mus. Sch. Fine Arts, 1989—91, U. Mass., 1989—96, Simmons Grad. Sch. Mgmt., 1995—97. Exec. sec. The Ecumenical Ctr., Roxbury, Mass., 1965-67, Roxbury Fedn. of Neighborhoods, 1965-68; bus. mgr. Coun. of Elders, Inc., Boston, 1969-72; exec. sec., asst. bookkeeper Edn. Renewal, Inc., Boston, 1972-73; asst. dir. METCO Inter-Dist. Transfer Inc., Roxbury, 1973-75; pupil pers. coord. Met. Coun. for Ednl. Opportunity, Roxbury, 1975-78; with Vis. Nurse Assn. of Boston, 1978-79; sec. Bay State Banner Newspaper, Roxbury, 1980; sr. outreach coord. Mattahunt Community Sch Sr. Outreach, Mattapan, Mass., 1989-95. Founder, chmn., CEO S.P.A.C.E. An Artistic Comty. Inc.; founder, chmn., CEO LED, 1995—. Exhibitions include Steppin Out, Boston, 1993, Treasured Legacy Gallery, 1995, Urban League Ea. Mass., Roxbury, 1997—98, Codman Sq. Br. Libr., Dorchester, Mass., 1997—2002, New Art N.Eng. Libr. Arts Ctr., Newport, N.H., 1997, Dorchester Hist. Soc., 1996, 1997, 1998, Dorchester Art Assn., Boston, 1996, 1997, 1998, Open Studios, South End, Mass., 1998, Roxbury Cmty. Coll. Media Arts Ctr., 1998, Reggie Lewis Ctr., Roxbury, 1998, Rothschild Gallery, Radcliffe Coll., Cambridge, Mass., 1998, Boston City Hall Scollary Sq. Gallery, Boston, 1998, 1999, 2000, Pan African Historical Mus., Springfield, Mass., 1999, Grove Hall Br. Libr., Roxbury, 2000, Egleston Br. Libr., Mass., 2000, Parker Hill Br. Libr., Roxbury, 2000, South End (Mass.) Open Studios, 2000, CVS Windows-The Mall at Grove Hall, Roxbury, 2002, Codman Sq. Br. Libr., Dorchester, 2004—05, CVS Window Porter Sq., Cambridge, 2002—05, Macy's Windows, 2000, 1999, Codman Sq. Libr., Mass., 2004—, North River Cmty. Ch., 2006—, Boston Bus. Assistance Ctr., Roxbury, Mass., 2005—. Represented in permanent collections N.Eng. Zoo, pvt. collections, artwork published, Art New Eng., ArtsMedia, Art & Antiques; author: (poetry book) Days, Years to Remember: A Collection of Poems, 2003. Active Women's Caucus Art, Boston chpt., Coalition Black Women, Nat. Coun. Negro Women; chmn. health campaign Grove Hall/Franklin Park AARP, Boston, 1990—; vol. Experiment in Internat. Living, Mass., Mattapan/Franklin Park Jubilee Task Force, WGBH, Am. Cancer Soc.; artwork auction donor various orgns. Grantee, New Eng. Found. for the Arts; scholar, U. Mass., Amherst, 1999; Americans for the Arts scholar, 1999. Mem.: PEN N.E., NAACP, Boston Afro-Am. Artists, Nat. Poetry Soc., South End Artists, Mass. Advocates for the Arts, Scis. & Humanities, Dorchester Art Assn., Am. for the Arts, Nat. Writer's Assn., Poetry Soc. Am. Avocations: writing, painting, reading. Home: 4 Wentworth St Dorchester MA 02124-3517 Office Phone: 617-436-1063. E-mail: 1space@gte.net, 1space@verizon.net.

**SMITH, SUSAN CARLTON,** artist, illustrator; b. Athens, Ga., June 30, 1923; d. Edward Inglis and Hart Wylie Smith; m. George Stanley Terence Cavanagh, Oct. 25, 1977. *In 1962, Ms. Smith's husband, Terry Cavanagh, became Director of Duke University's Medical Center Library and Curator of the Trent Collection, retiring in 1989 as Emeritus Professor of Medical Literature. He was responsible for publishing "The Four Seasons of Human Life," a book derived from four fugitive sheets; the only book known to exist. He authored and published "The Panorama of Vesalius, a 'Lost' Design from Titan's Studio," which was an important contribution to medicine and art. An Antiquarian Bookseller noted worldwide, he offered medical books under Old Galen Books and Emeritus Books and he created The Sacrum Press and The Gazebo Press.* BS in Zoology, U. Ga., 1947, MFA in Drama, 1961. Sci. illustrator US Pub. Health Communicable Disease Ctr., Atlanta, 1952; artist archeology dept. U. Ga., 1953—, costume designer, speech tchr., drama dept, 1956—61, sci. illustrator biology dept., 1964—65; conservator, asst. curator Med. Ctr. Libr., Duke U., Durham, NC, 1967—90; biological and botanical illustrator Duke U., 1967—90; botanical illustrator U. NC, 1967—90. Lectr. in field. Illustrator Jack & Jill Magazine, 1960—62, (book) Plant Variations and Classification, 1967, Wildflowers of NC, 1968, A Child's Book of Flowers, 1976, A Book of Flowers, 1987, illustrator, text contr. (book) Lady Bug, Lady Bug, 1969 (Top 50 Best Children's Books of Yr., 1969), (Book) Hey Bug!, and Other Poems About Little Things, 1972 (Printers Industries of Am. award), 3 Famous Artists-Naturalists of the Colonial Period, John Abbot, William Bartram, Mark Catesby- A Coloring Book for all Ages, 2002; contbr. various sci. jours.; exhibitions include eleventh Internat. Botanical Congress, Seattle, 1969, Internat. Exhbn. Botanical Art, Johannesburg, South Africa, Second Internat. Exhbn. Twentieth Cent. Botanical Art and Illustration, Carnegie-Mellon U., 1968—69, Duke U. Mus. Art, U. Ga. Mus. Art, State Botanical Garden, Ga. Vol. U. NC Botanical Gardens, 1967—89, State Botanical Gardens, Ga., 1989—2006. Mem.: Trent Soc. History of Med., Duke U., Am. Assn. History of Med., Nat. Soc. Colonial Dames, Jr. Ladies Garden Club, Garden Club Am. (Eloise Payne Lequer medal 1969), Puppeteers of Am., Chi Omega, Phi Kappa Phi. Episcopalian. Avocation: sculpting. Home: 755 EPPS Bridge Pky #404 Athens GA 30606 Address: 755 Eppa Bridge Pkwy Cottage 404 Athens GA 30606 Personal E-mail: gotcavan@regis.net

**SMITH, SUSAN ELIZABETH,** guidance director; b. Phila., Mar. 24, 1950; d. E. Burke Hogue and Janet Coffin Hogue Ebert; m. J. Russell Smith, June 17, 1972 (div. June 1989); 1 child, Drew Russell. BS in Elem. Edn., E. Stroudsburg Coll., 1972; MEd in Counseling, U. Okla., 1974, postgrad., 1976-77, Trenton State Coll., 1989-90; EdM in Devel. Disabilities, Rutgers U., 1992, postgrad., 1994—. Cert. elem. tchr., N.C.; cert. elem. tchr., early childhood edn. tchr., guidance and counseling, Okla.; cert. elem. tchr., guidance and counseling, tchr. of handicapped, psychology tchr., supr. instrn., dir. student pers. svcs., N.J. Elem. tchr. Morton Elem. Sch. Onslow County Schs., Jacksonville, N.J. 1971-72; instr. U. Isfahan, Iran, 1974-76; guidance counselor Moore (Okla.) Pub. Schs., 1976-77; counselor Johnstone Tng. Ctr. N.J. Divsn. Devel. Disabilities, Bordentown, 1988-90; spl. edn. tchr. Willingboro (N.J.) Schs., 1990-91; guidance counselor Haledon (N.J.) Pub. Schs., 1991-92; spl. edn. adj. tchr. Gateway Sch., Carteret, N.J, 1991-93; guidance counselor Bloomfield (N.J.) Pub. Schs., 1992-94; dir. guidance Somerville (N.J.) Pub. Schs., 1994-95. Adj. prof. in spl. edn. Essex County (N.J.) Coll., 1994; guidance Ft. Lee (N.J.) Schs., 1995-2001; guidance dir. Bogota Schs., N.J., 2001-02, Closter Schs., Closter, N.J., 2002—; cons., seminar and workshop presenter on behavior mgmt., parenting skills, and behavior modification techniques; cons. N.J. Fragile X Assn. Author: Motivational Awards for ESL Students, 1993, Parent Contracts to Improve School Behaviors, 1996; contbr. articles to profl. jours. Leader Boy Scouts Am., Oklahoma City, 1983-84; devel. com. chmn., Redmond, Wash., 1987-88. Recipient Rsch. award ERIC/CAPS, 1992. Svc. award N.J. Fragile X Assn., 1993. Mem. ACA, Am. Sch. Counselor Assn. (grantee 1992), N.J. Counseling Assn., N.J. Sch. Counseling Assn., Assn. for Multicultural Counseling and Devel., AAUW, Assn. for Counselor Edn. and Supervision, N.J. Assn. for Counselor Edn. and Supervision, N.J. Prins. and Supra. Assn., Nat. Assn. Coll. Admissions Counselors (grantee 1995), Alpha Omicron Pi. Episcopalian. Home: 916 Lincoln Pl Teaneck NJ 07666-2572

**SMITH, SUSANNA S.,** school system administrator; 2 children. Degree, Calif. State U., LA, 1977; MEd, Calif. State U., 1981, adminstrv. credential, 1992. Elem. sch. tchr. Mountain View Sch. Dist., El Monte, Calif., 1978—95; asst. prin. Bassett Unified Sch. Dist., La Puente, Calif., 1995—98, prins. mid. sch., 1998—2000; dir. curriculum and instrn. El Rancho Sch. Dist., Pico Rivera, Calif., 2000—02, asst. supt. edn., 2003—. Ednl. judge LA County

Fair, Pomona, Calif., 2002—. Bd. dirs. I'm Going to Coll. Found., Pico Rivera, 2003—. Fellow: Calif. Assn. Bilingual Adminstrs., Assn. Calif. Adminstrs. (Adminstr. of Yr. for Mid. Sch. 1999); mem.: Soroptimist Internat. (sec., v.p.). Avocations: tennis, hiking, movies, reading. Fax: 562-942-1598.

**SMITH, SYDNEY,** elementary school educator; b. Birmingham, Ala., Aug. 17, 1957; d. E. Erle and Virginia J. Smith. BS, U. Montevallo, 1979, EdM, 1986. Nat. bd. cert. tchr. Aquatics dir. Girls Club, Bessemer, Ala.; phys. edn. tchr. Shelby County Bd. Edn., Vincent, Ala., 1979; aquatic dir. YWCA, Birmingham, 1980; kindergarten tchr. Talledega County Bd. Edn., Sycamore, Ala., 1984, Jefferson County Bd. Edn., Warrior, Ala., Birmingham Bd. Edn., 1987, reading recovery tchr., 0199—. Facilitator/mentor nat. bd. cert. Birmingham Bd. Edn., Ala., 2005—06. Mem. pet assisted therapy team Delta Soc./Critter Companions, Birmingham, 1998—. Mem.: Reading Recovery Coun. N.Am., Internat. Reading Assn., Pi Lambda Theta.

**SMITH, TAD RANDOLPH,** lawyer; b. El Paso, Tex., July 20, 1928; s. Eugene Rufus and Dorothy (Derrick) S.; m. JoAnn Wilson, Aug. 24, 1949; children: Laura Borsch, Derrick, Cameron Ann Compton. LLB, U. Tex., 1951, BBA, 1952. Bar: Tex. 1951. Assoc. firm Kemp, Smith Duncan & Hammond P.C., El Paso, Tex., 1951-52, ptnr., 1952-81, CEO, 1975—98, shareholder, 1981—99; of counsel Kemp Smith, LLP, El Paso, 1999—. Active United Way of El Paso; chmn. El Paso County Reps., 1958-61, Tex. Rep. State Exec. Com., 1961-62; alt. del. Rep. Nat. Conv., 1952, 62, del. 1964, dir. El Paso Elec. Co., 1961-90, State Nat. Bank of El Paso, 1969-90, The Leavell Co., 1970-94; trustee Robert E. and Evelyn McKee Found., 1970-90, Property Trust of Am., 1971-91; mem. devel. bd. U. Tex., El Paso, 1973-81, v.p., 1975, chmn. 1976; dinner treas. Nat. Jewish Hosp. and Rsch. Ctr., 1977, chmn. 1978, presenter of honoree, 1985; bd. dirs. NCCJ 1965-76, chmn. 1965-78; bd. dirs. Southwestern Children's Home, El Paso, 1959-78; trustee Hervey Found., 1990-99, Lydia Patterson Inst., 1994-99 Named Outstanding Young Man, El Paso Jaycees; named to Bd. of Fellows, U. Tex., El Paso, 1997—2001; recipient Humanitarian award, El Paso chpt. NCCJ, 1983. Fellow Am. Bar Found.; mem. ABA, Tex. Bar Found.; mem. ABA (pres. 1971-72), El Paso C. of C. (dir. 1979-82), Sigma Chi. Republican. Methodist. Address: 20 Stratford Hall Cir El Paso TX 79912 Personal E-mail: tadjoann@msn.com.

**SMITH, TEFFT WELDON,** lawyer; b. Evanston, Ill., Nov. 18, 1946; s. Edward W. and Margery T. (Weldon) S.; m. Nancy Jo Smith, Feb. 25, 1967; children: Lara Andrea, Tefft Weldon II. BA, Brown U., 1968; JD, U. Chgo., 1971. Bar: Ill. 1971, D.C. 2000, U.S. Supreme Ct. 1977. Sr. litigation ptnr. Kirkland & Ellis LLP, Chgo., 1971—, chair, competition and antitrust practice group. Mem. adv. bd. Bur. Nat. Affairs Antitrust and Trade Regulation Reporter; instr. trial advocacy. Contbr. numerous articles on trial practice and antitrust issues to law jours. Mem. ABA (litigation sect., antitrust law sect.), Econ. Club., Univ. Club, Mid-Am. Club, Sea Pines Country Club (Hilton Head, S.C.). Avocations: squash, ferraris, sculpture. Office: 655 15th St NW Washington DC 20005-5701 also: Kirkland & Ellis 200 E Randolph St Fl 54 Chicago IL 60601-6636 Home: 700 New Hampshire Ave NW Washington DC 20037 Office Phone: 202-879-5212. Business E-Mail: tsmith@kirkland.com.

**SMITH, TERRY JAY,** endocrinology educator; b. Kansas City, Mo., Nov. 23, 1949; s. Samuel Ira and Violet (Kline) S.; m. Kathleen Amorose, Aug. 5, 1982 (div. Dec. 10, 1987); m. Linda Polonsky, Dec. 18, 1987. Student, Tulane U., 1968-71; MD, U. Mo., 1975. Diplomate Nat. Bd. Med. Examiners. Intern U. Ill., Chgo., 1975-76; resident Sinai Hosp., Balt., 1976-77; fellow U. Calif., San Francisco, 1977-78, Columbia U., N.Y.C., 1978-81; endocrine resident U. Chgo., 1979-81; asst. prof. Rockefeller U., N.Y.C., 1981-83; assoc. prof. Med. Coll. Ga., Augusta, 1982-86, SUNY, Buffalo, 1986-90; prof. Albany (N.Y.) Med. Coll., 1990—. Editorial reviewer Endocrinology, 1984—, Am. Jour. Physiology, 1989—, Jour. Clin. Endocrinology and Metabolism, 1984—; author: (with others) Clinical Methods, 1990; contbr. articles to profl. jours. Charles D. Tandy Clin. scholar Rockefeller U., 1981-83; recipient Career Devel. award VA, 1983-86. Mem. Am. Thyroid Assn., Am. Fedn. for Clin. Rsch., Am. Soc. Biochemists and Molecular Biologists, Phi Eta Sigma, Beta Beta Beta, Alpha Epsilon Delta. Achievements include elucidation of the molecular mechanisms involved in the pathogenesis of hypothyroid myxedema; demonstration of the role of thyroid hormone in the regulation of heme metabolism and melanin pigment formation; contributions to the pathophysiology of Graves' ophthalmopathy. Office: Albany Med Coll Dept Medicine 47 New Scotland Ave Albany NY 12208-3412

**SMITH, THEODORE GLENN,** webmaster; b. Willowbrook, Calif., Oct. 19, 1957; s. Thomas Eugene and Marilyn Glenna Smith; m. Kathleen Ione, May 27, 1978; children: Melissa Lauren, Melanie Kelly. AAS in Electronic Engring., Clark County CC, North Las Vegas, Nev., 1984; BBA magna cum laude, Nat. U., San Diego, 1987; MEd, U. Nev., Las Vegas, 2001; postgrad., Capella, Mpls. Lic. educator Nev.; Tex. Electronic technician E.G.&G. Inc. Nev. Test Site, Mercury, 1978—90; tech. instr. Garside Jr. HS, Las Vegas, 1992—99; bus./acctg. instr. Clark HS, Las Vegas, 1999—2001; computer instr. Bob Miller Mid. Sch., Las Vegas, 2001—02; cons., tutor Nev. Edn. Cons., Las Vegas, 2002—03; online facilitator Clark County Team Acad., Las Vegas, 2003—. Mem. Internat. Surfing Mus., Huntington Beach, Calif., 1972—, Friends of Sea Otter, Monterrey, Calif., 1995—. Mem.: Internat. Soc. Tech. Edn. (cons. 2001—), Tex. State Hist. Assn., Alpha Kappa Phi. Republican.

**SMITH, THEODORE S.,** lawyer; b. Summit, NJ, 1955; BArch, Univ. Syracuse, 1978, BS in Mgmt., 1978; JD, Univ. Pa., 1983. Bar: NJ 1983. Law clerk, Hon. Frederick B. Lacey US Dist. Ct., NJ; joined Drinker Biddle & Reath LLP, 1984, ptnr., litig. dept. Florham Park, NJ, co-chair, construction law practice group. Arbitrator Am. Arbitration Assn. Mem.: Am. Inst. Architects (chair). Office: Drinker Biddle & Reath LLP 500 Campus Dr Florham Park NJ 07932-1047 Office Phone: 973-549-7210. Office Fax: 973-360-9831. Business E-Mail: theodore.smith@dbr.com.

**SMITH, THOMAS A.,** lawyer, investment company executive; b. Springfield, Ill., Dec. 14, 1956; BA, Wabash Coll., 1978; JD, St. Louis U., 1983, MBA, 1984. Bar: Ill. 1984, Mo. 1985, N.Y. 1990; lic. series 7 Nat. Assn. Securities Dealers, series 24 Nat. Assn. Securities Dealers. Enforcement atty. Ill. Securities Dept., 1984—85; staff atty. divsn. investment mgmt. U.S. SEC, 1986—89; sr. assoc. Wilkie Farr & Gallaghar, 1989—91; asst. gen. counsel Dreyfus Corp., 1991—93, N.Y. Life Ins. Co., NYC, 1994—96, assoc. gen. counsel, 1996—97, v.p., assoc. gen. counsel, 1997—99; exec. v.p., gen. counsel Van Kampen Investments, Inc., 1999—2001; mng. dir., gen. counsel U.S. investment mgmt. Morgan Stanley, NYC, 2001—. Co-author: (book) Regulation of Investment Companies. Office: Morgan Stanley Law Dept 1221 Ave of the Americas 5th Fl New York NY 10020

**SMITH, THOMAS CLAIR,** retired manufacturing company executive; b. Indiana, Pa., Mar. 14, 1925; s. William Bryan and Edna Louise (Thomas) S.; m. Marilyn Louise Globisch, May 29, 1948; children: Claudia Lynn Smith Holtry, Craig Randall. BSME, Pa. State U., 1946; A. Alexander Hamilton Bus. Inst., 1949. Registered profl. engr., Pa., N.J., Del. Structural test engr. Chance Vought Aircraft Co., Bridgeport, Conn., 1946-48; test engr. Fed. Mogul Bearings Co., Lancaster, Pa., 1949-51; fuse engr. to mgr. materials Hamilton Watch Co. (name now Hamilton Tech.), Lancaster, Pa., 1952-70; plant mgr. Woodstream Corp., Lititz, Pa., 1970-79, v.p mktg., 1980—87, ret., 1987. Faculty, coach Lacrosse Franklin and Marshall Coll., Lancaster, 1950-53. Pub. Smith, Bryan, Allison & Morris Geneal. Chart, 1989; author and pub. of 1600 person geneal. chart in Libr. of Congress, 1989; patentee electric watch, 1957, swivel snap, 1975; author Penna Law 110 of 1992 and Pa. Law 22 of 1994/saving ancestral cemetaries. Pres. bd. dirs. Lancaster County Mental Health Assn., 1952-60, Lancaster County Cmty. Svc. Ctr., 1968-78; pres., bd. dirs. Am. Cancer Soc., 1970-72, bd. dirs., 1965-97, life bd. dirs., 1998—; bd. dirs. Hearing Conservation Assn., Lancaster, 1955-60, ARC, Lancaster, 1967-86, United Way, Lancaster, 1968-72, Ephrata (Pa.)

Area Rehab. Ctr., 1986—, Grave Concern, Inc., 1994—; pres. Ephrata (Pa.) Area Rehab. Found., 1997—; mem. All-Am. Lacrosse Team, 1945, Heritage Ctr. Lancaster, 1980—, Ind. County Hist. Soc., 1984—, Greene County Hist. Soc., Waynesburg, Pa., 1985—, Selective Svc. Bd., 1992—; trustee Lancaster County Hist. Soc., 1992-98, mem., 1983—; judge elections, Lancaster County, 1994-2001. Named Boss of Yr., Am. Bus. Women's Assn., 1978, Vol. of Yr., Am. Cancer Soc., 1998, Tennis Family of Yr. Pa. N.J., Del., 1970; named to Lancaster County Tennis Hall of Fame, 2001; recipient Outstanding Svc. award, Mental Health Assn. Lancaster, 1961, Edward D. Eshelman award as Humanitarian of Yr., Am. Cancer Soc., 1991. Mem. Order of Crown of Charlemagne in U.S.A. (life), Pa. State U. Alumni Club (life), Pa. Sons of Revolution (bd. dirs., sec. 1990—), Phi Delta Theta (pres. Pa. State U. chpt. 1945), Wheatland Tennis Club (v.p. 1990-94, pres. 1995-96). Clubs: Lancaster Country (chmn. tennis com. 1960-75). Republican. Presbyterian. Avocations: genealogy, tennis, skiing. Home: 3877 Sterling Way Columbia PA 17512-9026 *You only go through this life on earth once. Don't waste that time. Put it to use in helping to make the earth a better place.*

**SMITH, THOMAS E.,** social studies educator; s. Karen and Thomas Smith; m. Donna K. Baker. BA in History, Towson State U., Md., 1993; MA in New Profl. Studies, Tchg., George Mason U., Alexandria, Va., 2004. Tchr. social studies Denmark-Olar HS, Denmark, SC, 1994—98, Louisa County HS, Mineral, Va., 1998—, curriculum facilitator, 2003—. Named Educator of Yr., Louisa County High Sch., 2003. Mem.: NEA, Am. Ednl. Rsch. Assn., Nat. Coun. Social Studies.

**SMITH, THOMAS EUGENE,** investment company executive, financial consultant; b. Brown's Summit, NC, Aug. 23, 1930; s. Howard Cleveland and Annie May (Warren) S.; m. Joan Cretcher Hopkins, Sept. 22, 1948; 1 dau., Vicki Joan. Student, George Washington U., 1948-50, Am. U., 1950-55 (intermittently). Pres., dir. T. Eugene Smith, Inc. investment co. and real estate and fin. cons. co., Falls Church, Va., 1950—; pres. The Potomac Corp., Falls Church, Va., 1960-74; pres., dir. Nat. Bank of Fairfax, Va., 1975-81, dir. Va.; exec. v.p. First & Mchts. Nat. Bank, Richmond, Va., 1981-83; chmn., dir. Decisions and Designs, Inc., McLean, Va., 1983-86; ptnr. Braddock-Ravensworth Ltd. Partnership, 1964—; sec., dir. Port Royal, Inc., 1965—; ptnr. Lee Graham Shopping Ctr., 1969—; chmn., pres., dir. Am. Mobile Home Towns, Inc., holding co., 1969-85; dir., pres. Topsail, Inc., 1983-89; ptnr. Potomac Greens Assn., 1986—. Bd. dirs. Growth Fund of Washington, Am. Funds Tax Exempt Series I, Washington Mut. Investors, M.G. Thalheimer Realty Advisors, Inc.; chmn., bd. dirs. River Capital Corp., Alexandria, Va., 1986-89, J. Webb, Inc., 1986—; acting dir., mgmt. com. Alexandria 20/20, 1988-91, acting dir., 1988-89; pres., dir. Pender Marina Holdings, Inc., 1988—, Pender Land Holdings, Inc., 1990—; adv. bd. CSX Realty, 1992-2003. Bd. dirs. Wolftrap Found., Washington, 1974-84; trustee Sta. WETA-TV, 1978-86; mem. Nat. Capital Planning Commn., Washington, 1980-83, vice chmn., 1981-83; mem. Va. Hwys. and Transp. Commn., Richmond, 1982-86; trustee Ch. Schs., Diocese of Va., 1983-88; mem. Va. Gov.'s Coun. Econ. Advisors, 1985-94, Met. Washington Airports Authority, 1986-94; chmn. Fairfax County Transp. Commn. for the Future, 1988-89; dir. Air and Space Heritage Coun., 1987-90. Mem.: Nat. Assn. Small Bus. Investment Cos. (treas. and bd. dirs. 1962—66), Met. Club (Washington). Democrat. Episcopalian. Office Phone: 703-243-2041. E-mail: tes.mclean@cox.net.

**SMITH, THOMAS GORDON,** architect; b. Oakland, Calif., Apr. 23, 1948; s. Sheldon Wagers and Margaret (Prendergast) S.; m. Marika Wilson, Dec. 19, 1970; children— Alan, Stuart, Demetra, Andrew, Philip, Duncan. A.B., U. Calif.-Berkeley, 1970, M.Arch., 1975. Lic. architect, Calif. Prin. Thomas Gordon Smith, Architect, Chgo., 1980—; instr. archtl. history Coll. of Marin, Kentfield, Calif., 1976-77; guest instr. archtl. design So. Calif. Inst. Architecture, Santa Monica, 1983; guest lectr., seminar leader Kunstegeschichtliches Institut der Philipps Universität, Marburg, W.Ger., 1983; guest lectr. U. Ill., Chgo., UCLA, 1984; assoc. prof. U. Ill., Chgo.; chmn. Sch. Architecture U. Notre Dame, Ind., 1989-98. Exhibited art in shows at Santa Barbara Mus. Art, 1977, Cooper-Hewitt Mus., Chgo. Art Inst., 1980, Louisiana Mus. Modern Art, Copenhagen, 1981, Venice Biennale, 1980, Smith Coll. Mus. Art, 1981, La Jolla Mus. Modern Art, Calif., 1982, Deutsches Architektur-museum, Frankfurt, W.Ger., 1984; revision of Modern IBM Gallery, N.Y., 1987; author: Classical Architecture: Rule and Invention, 1987, Vitruvius on Architecture, 2003. Bd. dirs. Soc. Cath. Liturgy. U. Calif. grad. fellow, 1974, John K. Branner fellow, 1975, Rome Prize fellow, Am. Acad., 1979; grantee Graham Found. Advanced Study in Fine Arts, 1984, 87, Am. Philos. Soc., 1987. Mem. AIA (Grad. fellow 1973), Soc. Archtl. Historians. Home: 1903 Dorwood Dr South Bend IN 46617-1818 Office: 2025 Edison Rd South Bend IN 46637 E-mail: archtgs@aol.com.

**SMITH, THOMAS HUGH (T. KILGORE SPLAKE),** poet, writer, photographer; b. Three Rivers, Mich., Dec. 8, 1936; s. Emery Crum and Margaret Louise Smith; m. Olga Irma Korzen Muir, July 7, 1977 (div. July 1990); children: Henry Korzen, Heidi Korzen. BA, Western Mich. U., 1959, MA, 1963; postgrad., Mich. State U., 1963—64, U. Maine, 1976. Hs tchr. Comstock (Mich.) Sch., 1959—63; jr. high tchr. Lansing (Mich.) Sch. Sys., 1963—64; prof. Kellogg CC, Battle Creek, Mich., 1964—89, Western Mich. U., Kalamazoo, 1973—74. Photographer (cover) Poesy Mag.; author: numerous poems; contbr. articles and photographs to popular mags.; author: Backwater Graybeard Twilight, 2002. Home: PO Box 508 Calumet MI 49913

**SMITH, THOMAS J.,** surgeon, educator; BA cum laude, Amherst Coll. 1967; MD, Tufts U. Sch. Medicine, 1971. Diplomate Am. Bd. Surgery, Nat. Bd. Med. Examiners. Intern, resident in surgery Tufts New Eng. Med. Ctr., Boston, 1971-73, chief resident in surgery, 1975-78; clin. assoc. surgery br. Nat. Cancer Inst., Bethesda, Md., 1978-80; from asst. prof. to assoc. prof. surgery Tufts U. Sch. Medicine, 1980-94; assoc. prof. U. South Fla., 1994; asst. prof. clin. surgery Columbia U., N.Y.C., 1995—97. Clin. prof. surgery U. Medicine and Dentistry N.J. Med. Sch., 1997—2002. Editl. bd. Internat. Jour. Cancer Rsch. & Treatment, Oncology; contbr. articles, abstracts to profl. jours. Mem. Am. Coll. Physician Execs., Am. Soc. Clin. Oncology, Soc. Surg. Oncology (edn. com. 1988—), Am. Cancer Soc. (Sword of Hope award com.). Office: Everett Clinic 3901 Hoyt Ave Everett WA 98201 Office Phone: 425-339-5442. Business E-Mail: tsmith@everettclinic.com.

**SMITH, THOMAS KENT,** retired radiologist; b. Bowling Green, Ohio, Aug. 21, 1934; s. Robert O. and Roslyn Smith; m. Jaleh Saidi, Feb. 1, 1974; children: Jeffrey, Todd, Mark, Blake, Tyler. BS with high honors, U. Cin., 1957; MD, Case Western Res. U., 1961. Intern Nat. Naval Med. Ctr., Bethesda, Md., 1961-62; resident in radiology VA Med. Ctr., Long Beach, Calif., 1965-69; fellow in radiologic pathology Armed Forces Inst. Pathology, Washington, 1968; dir. radiology Harriman Jones Med. Group, Long Beach, 1969-88; fellow in MRI/CT U. Calif., San Francisco, 1988-89; dir. MRI Orange County MRI, Fountain Valley, Calif., 1989-90; chmn. dept. diagnostic imaging Kaiser Permanente Med. Ctr., Honolulu, 1990-2000, dir. MRI, 1994-2000; ret. Mem. adv. bd. Hawaii Permanente Med. Group, Honolulu, 1990—2000; assoc. clin. prof. radiology U. Hawaii, Honolulu, 1990—2000; asst. clin. prof. U. Calif., Irvine, Calif., 1970—88, clin. instr., San Francisco, 1988—89, asst. clin. prof., 1989—99; cons. in radiologic devel. Kaiser Permanente Internat., 1996—98; owner Rubaiyat Vineyard, Sonoma County, Calif. Lt. Med. Corps, Nuc. Submarine Svc. USN, 1961—65. Fellow Am. Coll. Radiology; mem. Hawaii Radiol. Soc. (pres. 1992-93), Radiol. Soc. N.Am., Internat. Soc. Magnetic Resonance in Medicine, Margulis Soc., Alpha Omega Alpha, Sonoma County Grape Growers Assn., Sonoma Valley Vintners and Growers Alliance, Rhone Rangers,. Avocations: fishing, travel, viticulture. Home: Rubaiyat Vineyard 5409 Sonoma Mountain Rd Santa Rosa CA 95404-8884 Fax: 707-544-4117. Personal E-mail: rubaiyatvineyard@aol.com.

**SMITH, THOMAS P.,** manufacturing executive; m. Deanna Smith; 2 children. BS in Ecology and Evolutionary Biology, U. Ariz.; MBA, N. Ariz. U. Cons. operations, distribution and logistics Anderson Consulting, 1991—92; programmer analyst Jostens Learning, 1992—93; co-founder, pres., dir. Taser Internat., 1993—. Named the fastest growing small public

company in America, Fortune mag., 2005; recipient Entrepreneur of the Year award, Arizona Ernst & Young, 2002. Avocations: scuba diving, skiing, water-skiing, piano, photography, flying. Office: Taser International 17800 N 85th St Scottsdale AZ 85255 Office Phone: 480-905-2000. Office Fax: 480-991-0791. Business E-Mail: tom@taser.com.

**SMITH, THOMAS PATRICK,** music director; b. Kansas City, Mo., Jan. 31, 1947; s. Harold and Mary O'Keefe Smith. BA, Rockhurst Coll., Kansas City, 1969; MusM, U. of Mo.-Kansas City, 1975. Organist/choir dir. St. Augustine's Cath. Ch., Kansas City, Mo., 1966—69; dir. of music Cathedral of St. Joseph, St. Joseph, Mo., 1969—72, 1978—; music tchr. Macon County R-IV Schools, New Cambria, Mo., 1976—77, St. Joseph Pub. Schools, St. Joseph, Mo., 1977—78. Boy scout leader Boy Scouts of Am., St. Joseph, Mo., 1979—2006. With US Army, 1970—73, Kaiserslautern, Germany, with USAR, 1973—2000. Mem.: Am. Guild of Organists (assoc.). Roman Catholic. Avocation: hiking. Home: 112 W Highland Ave Saint Joseph MO 64505 Office: Cathedral of St Joseph 519 N 10th St Saint Joseph MO 64501 Office Phone: 816-232-7763. Personal E-mail: tpsmith@stjoelive.com.

**SMITH, THOMAS RAMSAUR, JR.,** lawyer; b. Feb. 12, 1938; AB, Princeton U., 1960; LLB, U. Va., 1963. Assoc. Brown & Wood, NYC, 1963-71, ptnr., 1971-96, mng. ptnr., 1996—2001; ptnr. Sidley Austin Brown & Wood LLP (following merger), NYC, 2001—, vice chmn. mgmt. com., 2001—03, mem. exec. com., 2001—04. Chmn. 2000 Law Firm Appeal Lawyers Alliance for NY. Bd. dir. Legal Aid Soc. Office: Sidley Austin Brown & Wood LLP 787 7th Ave New York NY 10019 Office Phone: 212-839-5535. Business E-Mail: tsmith@sidley.com.

**SMITH, THOMAS RAYMOND, III,** software engineer; b. Phila., Dec. 6, 1946; s. Thomas Raymond and Naomi (Hart) S.; m. Marguerite Anne LeMoyne de Martigny, Sept. 6, 1969; children: Michelle Renée, Heather Anne, Thomas Raymond IV. Student, MIT, 1964-68. Sr. analyst Dabcovich and Co., Lexington, Mass., 1969—71; sr. analyst, prin. Multi-Logic Corp., Burlington, Mass., 1970—73; cons. engr. Digital Equipment Corp. (now Hewlett-Packard Co.), Palo Alto, Calif., 1974—. Co-editor: IEEE Dictionary, 1993; author, co-editor numerous stds. books for Internat. Electrotech. Commn. and IEEE, 1984-93. Mem.: IEEE (chmn. various stds. coms. 1980—). Home: 36 Toppans Ln Newburyport MA 01950-3843 Office: Hewlett-Packard Co ZK01-3/H42 110 Spit Brook Rd Nashua NH 03062-2711 Business E-Mail: smith@alum.mit.edu.

**SMITH, THURSTON SINCLAIR,** mental health services professional, consultant, community activist; b. N.Y., Aug. 7, 1962; s. Thurston Sinclair and Alethia Helena Smith; children: Jermaine Sinclair, Na'eema Iman. BA, Graceland U., 1998; postgrad., Ctrl. Wesleyan Coll., 1993—94. Cert. addictions counselor, nationally cert. compulsive gambling counselor, cert. alcohol and drug counselor Ga., clin. counselor S.C.; instr. trainer U.S. Army Res. Dir. client and prevention svcs. ACCESS Network, Beaufort, SC, 1996—98; mental health care coord. Ralph H. Johnson VA Med. Ctr., Charleston, SC, 1998—. Addictions therapist Clark Ctr.-Meml. Med. Ctr., Savannah, Ga., 1996; cons. S.C. Dept. Alcohol and Other Drug Abuse Svcs., Columbia, SC, 1997—2004; adminstrv. program surveyor CARF: The Accreditation Commn., Tucson, 1999—; counter drug team S.C. Army Nat. Guard, Columbia, 1999—2000; chmn. NAADAC Southeast Regional Leadership Conf., Jekyll Island, 2000; presenter in field. Co-author: Masculinity: Identity Issues in Addictions Treatment, 1999, Compulsive Gambling, The Hidden Addiction, 1997—, Substance Abuse Use Disorders and The Veterans Population, 2004; contbg. author: Advocates: A Publication of the South Carolina Governor's Office Division of Foster Care Review, 2001; reviewer A Provider's Guide to Substance Abuse Treatment, U.S. Dept. Health & Human Svc., Ctr. for Substance Abuse Treatment, 2001; contbr. articles to profl. publs. Foster care rev. bd. mem. S.C. Gov.'s Office, Columbia, 2001—, chmn. First Foster Care Legislative Luncheon, 2001; bd. dirs. Father to Father Project, Charleston, SC, 2002—04; planning com. Ga. Conf. on HIV and AIDS, Augusta, 2000; EEO adv. com. Dept. Vet. Affairs, Charleston, 1999—2001; del. to Columbia, S. Am. S.C. Ptnrs. Am./U.S. Dept. State-Office Ednl. and Cultural Affairs, Washington, 2000; co-chmn. Beaufort (S.C.) and Jasper County HIV Prevention Collaboration, Beaufort, 1997—98; chmn. Evaluation com. Beaufort County EEO Commission, 1997; region IV rep. S.C. Assn. Alcoholism and Drug Abuse Counselors, Columbia, 1996—98; chmn. Charleston County Foster Care Rev. Bd., 2004—; bd. mem. Charleston Dorchester Mental Health Com., 2004—06; del. S.C. Dem. Party, Columbia, 2000—01; candidate Charleston City Coun., SC, 2005; bd. dirs. Crisis Ministries Charleston, SC, 2001—03. Sgt. USARNG, 1981. Named Counselor of Yr., S.C. Assn. Alcoholism and Drug Abuse Counselors, 1997; recipient Leadership Beaufort Cert. of Achievement, Beaufort County C. of C., 1998, Cert. of Honor, U. Del Valle Sede Buga, Colombia, 2000, SATTC Svc. award, Morehouse Sch. Medicine, 2003, Key to City, Mayor of Clemson, S.C., 2004, Vets. Integrated Svc. Network 7 Recognition, Lora Roe Meml. Alcoholism and Drug Abuse Counselor of Yr., 2004, Carey award, Bd. Examiners Vets. Health Adminstrn., 2006, Veteran's Health Adminstrator's Carry award, Bd. Examiners, 2006. Mem.: Vets. Integrated Svc. Network, Assn. Addiction Profls. (Exec. Com. Svc. award 2004, Fla. Svc. award 2005, Ralph H. Johnson VA Med. Ctr. Pub. Safety Recognition 2005), Nat. Assn. Alcoholism and Drug Abuse Counselors (officer, membership chmn. 1998—2000, conf. chmn. 1999, S.E. regional v.p. 2000—04, legis. luncheon chmn. 2001, One to One Membership Campaign award 1996, Ralph H. Johnson VA Med. Ctr. Merit award 2002, named Lora Roe Meml. Alcoholism and Drug Abuse Counselor of Yr. 2003, Ralph H. Johnson VA Med. Ctr. Merit award 2004), S.C. Ptnrs. Am. (com. chmn. 2000, S.C. liaison to S.E. Addiction Tech. Transfer Ctr. 2002—03). Methodist. Avocations: music, travel. Office: Ralph H Johnson VA Med Ctr 109 Bee St Charleston SC 29401-5799 Personal E-Mail: teesmith1@comcast.net. Business E-Mail: thurston.smith@med.va.gov.

**SMITH, TIMOTHY K.,** editor; b. NYC; m. Priscilla Painton; children: Anthony, Isabel. BA in History, Brown U., 1979; grad., La Sorbonne, Paris. Page one editor The Wall Street Journal Europe; copy editor The Wall Street Journal, 1982, writer & editor Washington, Atlanta, NYC; editor Fortune mag., 1994—, asst. mng. editor. Recipient Lawrence Minard Editor award, UCLA Anderson Sch. Mgmt., 2005. Office: Fortune Time & Life Building Rockefeller Ctr New York NY 10020-1393 Office Phone: 212-522-7367.*

**SMITH, TODD A.,** lawyer; b. Chgo., Aug. 27, 1949; married; 2 children. BSB, U. Kans., 1971; MBA, Northwestern U., 1973; JD, Loyola U., 1976. Bar: Ill. 1976, U.S. Dist. Ct. (no. dist.) Ill. 1980, U.S. Ct. Appeals (7th cir.) 1991, U.S. Supreme Ct. 1980. Asst. Cook County Public Defender, Chgo.; atty. Corboy & Demetrio P.C., Chgo., ptnr., Powers, Rogers, & Smith P.C., Chgo. Adj. prof. law De Paul Coll., 1985—88; mock trial judge, 1978—83; bd. dir. Trial Lawyers Club of Chicago, 1987—; lectr. John Marshall Law Sch., 1985, Loyola U. Sch. Law, 1981—85, 1988; bd. gov Assoc. Trial Lawyers of Am. (ATLA), 1985—, mem. exec. comm., 1999—, treas., 2000—01, sec., 2001—02, v.p., 2002—03, pres. elect, 2003—04, pres., 2004—05; bd. dir. ATLA Endowment, 1999—, ISBA Mutual Insurance Co., 1995—, Ill. Bar Found. 2000—. Assoc. editor: Ill. Trial Lawyers Jour.; contbr. articles to profl. jours. Named Person of the Yr., Chicago Lawyer Mag., 1998; named one of The Best Lawyers in Am., 1997—2004; fellow Internat. Soc. of Barristers, 1996, Am. College of Trial Lawyers, 1996, Am. Bar Found., 1996, Internat. Acad. of Trial Lawyers, 1998, Am. Bd. of Trial Advocates, 1999. Fellow: Am. Coll. Trial Lawyers, Internat. Soc. Barristers, Internat. Acad. Trial Lawyers; mem.: Ill. State Bar Assn. (past pres.). Office: Powers, Rogers, Smith 70 W Madison St 55th Fl Chicago IL 60602

**SMITH, TODD D.,** museum director; BA, Duke U.; MA, Ind. U. With Dayton Art Inst., Ohio, Mint Mus., Charlotte, NC; pres., CEO Plains Art Mus., Fargo, ND; exec. dir. Knoxville Museum of Art, Tenn., 2002—. Office: Knoxville Mus Art 1050 World's Fair Park Knoxville TN 37916-1653 Office Phone: 865-525-6101 x256. E-mail: tsmith@kmaonline.org.

**SMITH, TODD LEE,** protective services official; b. Lubbock, Tex., May 6, 1964; s. Charles and Sharon Smith; m. Lena Smith, Mar. 29, 1971; children: Lindsy, Payton. Tex. peace officer TCLOESE-Tex., Tex. peace officer instr. TCLEOSE, Tex., fingerprint comparison Sirchie Labs, N.C. Investigator Hockley County DA Office, Levelland, Tex., 1997—2001; chief investigator Lubbock County CDA, 2001—. Mem. faculty Tex. Dist. and County Attys. Assn., Austin, Tex., 2000, Nat. Coll. of Dist. Attys., Columbus, SC, 2005—06. Office Phone: 806-775-1195. Personal E-mail: smith693@cox.net. Business E-Mail: tsmith@co.lubbock.tx.us.

**SMITH, TRENTON GARRY,** education educator; b. Walnut Creek, Calif., Jan. 15, 1968; s. Garry H. and Dottie Z. Smith; m. Valeri Lee Schillberg, Aug. 16, 1996; 1 child, Semolina Limuw Schillberg. BAS, Stanford U., Calif., 1990, MS, 1993; MA, U. Calif., Santa Barbara, 1997, PhD, 2002. Cert. profl. engr., Wash., 1996. Postdoctoral rsch. fellow dept. econs. U. Bonn, Germany, 2002—03; global fellow UCLA Internat. Inst., L.A., 2003—04; asst. prof. Wash. State U. Sch. Econ. Scis., Pullman, 2004—. Author: (jour. article) The McDonald's Equilibrium: Advertising, Empty Calories, and the Endogenous Determination of Dietary Preferences, A Theory of Natural Addiction. Avocations: mountaineering, zymology. Office: Wash State Univ Sch Econ Scis Box 646210 Pullman WA 99164-6210 Office Phone: 509-335-2865. Office Fax: 509-335-1173. Business E-Mail: trentsmith@wsu.edu.

**SMITH, TRINA,** academic administrator; b. Rogersville, Ala., Sept. 18, 1971; d. Will Buford and Margaret Cannon Smith. BS, Athens State U., 1993; MS, U. Ala., Huntsville, 2000; M of Accountancy, U. Ala., 2001. Cert. Notary Pub. Br. ops. supr. Union Planters Bank, Athens, Ala., 1994—2000; acct. Calhoun Coll., Decatur, Ala., 2000—. Dir. Habitat for Humanity, Athens, 1994—2000; mem. adv. bd. Dogwood Festival Com., Athens, 1999. Vol. Jr. Achievement, Decatur, Ala., 1997—2000, Care Assurance Sys. for Aging and Homebound, Athens, 1995—99, Found. of Aging, Athens, 1999—2002. Recipient Outstanding Support award, Habitat for Humanity, 1996. Mem.: NAFE, NAACP, Am. Inst. of Cert. Pub. Accts., Nat. Assn. Black Accts., Am. Acctg. Assn., Am. Soc. Women Accts., Nat. Notary Assn., Inst. Mgmt. Accts. Baptist. Avocations: gardening, photography, collecting antiques, investments, outdoor activities. Home: 13708 Dart Cir Athens AL 35611 Office: Calhoun Cmty Coll Hwy 31 S Decatur AL 35609 Personal E-mail: TSmith3671@aol.com.

**SMITH, TROY ALVIN,** aerospace research engineer; b. Sylvatus, Va., July 4, 1922; s. Wade Hampton and Augusta Mabel (Lindsey) S.; m. Grace Marie (Peacock) Bres, Nov. 24, 1990. BCE, U. Va., 1948; MS in Engring., U. Mich., 1952, PhD, 1970. Registered profl. engr., Va., Ala. Structural engr. U.S. Army C.E., Norfolk, Va., Wilmington, NC, Washington, 1948-59; chief structural engr. Brown Engring. Co., Inc., Huntsville, Ala., 1959-60; structural rsch. engr. U.S. Army Missile Command, Redstone Arsenal, Ala., 1960-63, aerospace engr., 1963-80, aerospace rsch. engr., 1980-96; engr. emeritus U.S. Army Aviation and Missile Command, Redstone Arsenal, Ala., 1996—2003, U.S. Army Rsch., Devel., and Engring. Command, Aviation and Missile Rsch., Devel., and Engring. Ctr., Redstone Arsenal, Ala., 2003—. Contbr. articles AIAA Jour., Jour. Sound and Vibration, 17 major U.S. Army tech. reports on analysis of shells and other structures. With USNR, 1942-46, PTO. Fellow, Dept. Army, 1969. Mem. N.Y. Acad. Scis., Assn. U.S. Army, Elks, Sigma Xi. Achievements include research on procedures for analysis of structures. Home: 2202 Yorkshire SE Decatur AL 35601-3470

**SMITH, TURNER TALIAFERRO, JR.,** lawyer; b. Washington, Dec. 16, 1940; s. Turner Taliaferro and Lois (Fisk) S.; m. Christine H. Perdue; children: Turner T., III, John Webb Tyler. BA magna cum laude, Princeton U., 1962; LLB cum laude, Harvard U., 1968. Bar: Va. 1968, D.C. 1977. Ptnr. Hunton & Williams, Richmond, Va., 1975—2006, sr. counsel; tchr. environ. law Washington and Lee U., 1978, Coll. William and Mary, 1979, 80, U. Va. Law Sch.; tchr. internat. environ. law George Mason Law Sch., 2004, tchr. war crimes seminar, 2005, 06. Mem. ABA (chmn. standing com. environ. law 1983, 84, 85, chmn. environ., banking and bus. law sect. com. on environ. controls 1973-80), Va. Bar Assn. Office: Hunton & Williams 1900 K St NW 12 Fl Washington DC 20001 Office Phone: 202-955-1692. Business E-Mail: tsmith@hunton.com.

**SMITH, V. KERRY,** economics professor; b. Jersey City, Mar. 11, 1945; s. Vincent C. and Dorothy E. (Linehan) S.; m. Pauline Anne Taylor, May 10, 1969; children: Timothy, Shelley. AB, Rutgers U., 1966, PhD, 1970. Asst. prof., then assoc. prof. Bowling Green State U., Ohio, 1969-72; rsch. assoc. Resources for Future, Washington, 1971-73; assoc. prof. SUNY, Binghamton, 1973-75, prof., 1975-78; sr. fellow Resources for Future, Washington, 1976-79; prof. U. N.C., Chapel Hill, 1979-83; Centennial prof. Vanderbilt U., Nashville, 1983-87; univ. disting. prof. N.C. State U., 1987-94, univ. disting. prof., dir. Ctr. Environ. and Resource Econ. Policy, 1999—; Arts and Scis. prof. environ. econs. Duke U., 1994-99. Adviser energy div. Oak Ridge Nat. Lab., 1978-80, U. N.C. Inst. Environ. Studies, 1980-83; mem. panel NSF, 1981-83, sci. adv. bd. EPA. Author: Monte Carlo Methods, 1973, Technical Change, Relative Prices and Environmental Resource Evaluation, 1974, The Costs of Congestion: An Econometric Analysis of Wilderness Recreation, 1976, Structure and Properties of a Wilderness Travel Simulator: An Application to the Spanish Peaks Area, 1976, The Economic Consequences of Air Pollution, 1976, Scarcity and Growth Reconsidered, 1979, (with others) Explorations in Natural Resource Economics, 1982, (with others) Environmental Policy Under Reagan's Executive Order, 1984, (with W.H. Desvousges) Measuring Water Quality Benefits, 1986, (with others) Environmental Resources and Applied Welfare Economics, 1988, (with R J Kopp) Valuing Natural Assets: The Economics of Natural Resource Damage Assessment, Resources for the Future, 1993, Estimating Economic Values for Nature, 1996, (with others) The Smoking Puzzle: Information, Perception and Choices, 2003; editor Advances in Applied Micro Econs. series; contbr. numerous articles to profl. jours. Guggenheim fellow, 1976; grantee Resources for Future, 1970, 73, 74, 86, Fed. Energy Adminstrn. 1975, N.Y. Sea Grant Inst., 1975, Ford Found., 1976, NSF, 1977, 79, 83, Electric Power Rsch. Inst., 1978, Nat. Oceanic and Atmospheric Adminstrn., 1980, Sloan Found., 1981, 86, EPA, 1983-88, N.C. Sea Grant Program, 1987-93. Russell Sage Found., 1989-91; recipient Frederick V. Waugh medal Am. Agrl. Econ. Assn., 1992. Fellow Am. Agrl. and Econ. Assn., Assn. Environ. and Resource Economists (bd. dirs. 1975-79, v.p. 1979-80, chmn. com. 1982-83, pres. 1985-86, Disting. Svc. award 1989); mem. NAS, Am. Econ. Assn., Am. Statis. Assn., Econometric Soc., So. Econ. Assn. (exec. com. 1981-83, 1st v.p. 1987, pres.-elect 1988, pres. 1989). Business E-Mail: kerry.smith@ncsu.edu.

**SMITH, VALENE LUCY,** anthropologist, educator; b. Spokane, Wash., Feb. 14, 1926; d. Ernest Frank and Lucy (Blachly) S.; m. Edwin Chesteen Golay, June 7, 1970 (dec. June 1980); m. Stanley George McIntyre, Nov. 26, 1983 (dec. Oct. 2000); m. George Addison Posey, Oct. 5, 2005. BA in Geography, U. Calif., 1946, MA in Geography, 1950; PhD in Anthropology, U. Utah, 1966. Cert. travel counselor. Prof. earth sci. L.A. City Coll., 1947-67; prof. anthropology Calif. State U., Chico, 1967—. Owner World Tourism Orgn., Madrid, 1987. Editor: Hosts and Guests: The Anthrop. 1989, Tourism Alternatives: Potentials and Problems in the Development of Tourism, 1992, Hosts and Guests Revisited, 2001. Mem. Soroptimist Internat., Chico, 1968—; founding pres. Chico Mus. Assn., 1978. Named Fulbright prof., Peshawar, Pakistan, 1953—54; recipient Athena award, U.S. C. of C., 1988. Mem. Internat. Acad. for Study Tourism, Cert. Travel Counselors, Am. Anthrop. Assn., AAUW, Canyon Oaks Country Club, Soroptimists. Republican. Avocations: travel, aviation, photography. Office: U Calif State Dept Anthropology Chico CA 95929-0004 Office Phone: 530-891-1155. Business E-Mail: vsmith@csuchico.edu.

**SMITH, VALERIE,** curator; Curator Artists Space, NYC; curator, dir. exhibitions Queens Mus. Art, NYC. Curator (exhibitions) Sonsbeek Sculpture Exhbn., Arnhem, The Netherlands, 1993 (Named one of the top 10 shows of the 1990s, Artforum mag.), Joan Jonas: Five Works, Queens Art Mus., 2003—04 (Award for Best Exhbn. of Time Based Art, Internat. Assn. Art Critics/USA, 2005). Office: Queens Mus Art NYC Bldg Flushing Meadows Corona Pk Corona NY 11368

**SMITH, VAN P.,** diversified financial services company executive; b. Oneida, N.Y., Sept. 8, 1928; m. Margaret Ann Kennedy, Nov. 19, 1960; children: Lynn Ann Smith Walters, Mark Charles, Paul Gregory, Susan Colleen Smith Newell, Victor Patrick. AB in Pub. Adminstrn. and Econs., Colgate U., 1950; JD, Georgetown U., 1955; LLD (hon.), Ball State U., 1980; D of Bus. (hon.), Vincennes U., 1985; LLD (hon.), Ind. State U., 1986; LLD (hon.), Colgate U. Bar: D.C., Ind. Assoc. Warner, Clark & Warner, Muncie, Ind., 1955-56; co-founder, dir. Ontario Corp. of Muncie, 1956-63, sec. then v.p. sales, 1956-63, pres., CEO, 1963-97, also chmn. bd., 1978—. Chmn. bd. Ontario Corp. Found., all in Muncie, and other subs. Ontario Corp.; chmn. bd. Hoosier Motor Club, Indpls.; ptnr. Smittie's Men's Store, Village Developers, all in Muncie. Rep. mem. Ind. Ho. of Reps., 1960-62; del. Ind. and Nat. Rep. Conv.; pres. Muncie Police & Fire Commn., 1963-66; mem. parochial sch. bd. St. Mary's Sch., Muncie, 1968-70; mem. Ind. Employment Security Bd., 1969-71, Ind. Commn. Higher Edn., 1971-93, Nat. Adv. Council SBA, 1982-87, Gov.'s Fiscal Policy Adv. Council, 1982-87, Ind. Labor & Mgmt. Council, 1983-90, Ind. Econ. Devel. Council, 1985-90, Presdl. Observation Team Phillipine Nat. election, 1986, Presdl. Trade Mission to several Far Eastern countries, 1984; bd. dirs. Bus.-Industry Polit. Action Com., 1984-98; trustee Colgate U., 1985-96, chmn. emeritus; trustee La Lumiere Sch., 1983-87, Acad. for Community Leadership, 1975—; bd. dirs. Muncie Symphony Assn., 1980-88, pres. 1986-87; pres. Del. County United Way, 1969-70; bd. dirs. Newman Found. Ind., 1969-90, Religious Heritage Am. 1986-88; active St. Mary's Cath. Parish, Muncie; mem. Diocese of Lafayette Bishop's Com. 100, 1969-80, pres. 1969-70; bd. regents Cath. U. Am., Washington, 1986-90, trustee 1993-2003, vice chmn. bd., 2001-03; trustee Interlochen (Mich.) Ctr. for Arts, 1991—, vice chmn., 2001. Served 1st Lt. USAF, 1951-53. Named one of Outstanding Young Men of Am., Jaycees, 1960; recipient Bus. and Layman award, Religious Heritage Am., 1984, Ind. Cath. Layman award, Faith, Family & Football of Ind., Inc. 1985, Civic Service award, Ind. Assn. Cities and Towns, 1985; invested Knight Comdr. of Equestrian Order of Holy Sepulchre of Jerusalem, 1986. Mem. ABA, Ind. Bar Assn., Ind. Mfrs. Assn. (chmn. 1978-80, bd. dirs. 1978—), Forging Industry Assn. (pres. 1976-77), Alliance of Metalworking Industries (chmn. 1978-80), U.S. C. of C. (chmn. numerous coms., active panels and councils 1977—), Ind. State C. of C. (exec. com. 1982—), Rotary (past pres.), Elks, K.C., Meridian Hills Country Club, Theta Chi (pres. Iota chpt. 1950), Delta Theta Phi, Beta Gamma Sigma (hon.), Delta Sigma Pi (hon.). Clubs: Columbia, Skyline (Indpls.); Ind. Soc. of Chgo. Home: PO Box 2757 Muncie IN 47307-0757

**SMITH, VERNE V.,** astronomer; b. Boone, Iowa, July 16, 1954; s. Marguerite O'Daniels and Verne V. Smith; m. Katia Cunha; children: Mariana Martins, Nicholas. BA, U. Iowa, 1976, MS, 1978; PhD, U. Wash., Seattle, 1983. Rsch. fellow U. Tex., Austin, 1983—88; rsch. scientist U. of Tex. at Austin, McDonald Obs., Austin, Tex., 1988—2006; prof. physics and astronomy U. Tex., El Paso, 1996—2004; dir., gemini sci. ctr. Nat. Optical Astronomy Obs., Tucson, 2004—. Office: Nat Optical Astronomy Observatory 950 N Cherry Ave Tucson AZ 85719 Office Phone: 520-829-1072. E-mail: vsmith@noao.edu.

**SMITH, VERNON G.,** education educator, state legislator; b. Gary, Ind. BS, Ind. U., 1966, MS, 1969, EdD, 1978; postgrad., Ind.U.-Purdue U., 1986-90. Tchr. Gary Pub. Schs. Systems, 1966-71, resource tchr., 1971-72; asst. prin. Ivanhoe Sch., Gary, 1972-78; prin. Nobel Sch., Gary, 1978-85, Williams Sch., Gary, 1985-92; part-time counselor edn. div. Ind. U. N.W., Gary, 1967-69, adj. lectr., 1987-92, assoc. prof., 1992—; mem. Ind. Ho. of Reps., Indpls., 1990—. Columnist Gary Crusader, 1969-71; speaker Devel. Tng. Inst., 1986—. Author: (with D. McClam) Building Bridges Instead of Walls—History of I.U. Dons, Inc., 1979; also articles. Mem. Gary City Coun., 1972-90; precinct committeeman Gary Dem. Com., 1972-92; founder, chmn. Gary City-wide Festival Com.; bd. dirs. N.W. Ind. Urban League; founder, pres. I.U. Dons, Inc.; past pres. Gary Cmty. Mental Health Bd.; v.p. Gary Common Coun., 1982, 85-87, pres., 1976, 83-84, 88; past mem. bd. dirs. Little League World series; founder, past sponsor Youth Ensuring Solidarity, Young Citizens' League; chmn. Ind. Commn. on Status of Black Males, 1992—; mem. Gov.'s Commn. for Drug-Free Ind., 1990—. Recipient citation in edn. Gary NAACP, 1970, Good Govt. award Gary Jaycees, 1977, Outstanding Svc. award Gary Young Dems., 1979, Businessman of Yr. award Gary Downtown Mchts., 1979, Bd. Dirs. Svcs. award Gary Cmty. Health Ctr., 1982, G.O.I.C. Dr. Leon H. Sullivan award, 1982, Gary Jaycees Youth award, 1983, Info Newspaper Outstanding Citizen of N.W. Ind. and Info. Newspaper's Outstanding Educator award, 1984, Post Tribune Blaine Marz Tap award, 1984, Gary Cmty. Sch. Corp. Speech Dept. Recognition award, 1984, Gary Cmty. Mental Health Ctr.'s 10th Yr. Svc. award, 1985, Roosevelt H.S. Exemplary Svc. award, 1985, Gary Crusader 25th Anniversary award, 1986, Purdue U. Ednl. Opportunity Programs Black History Svc. award, 1986, Educator Par Excellence award Williams Sch., 1987, Black Woman Hall of Fame Found. Success award, 1987, Black Women Hall of Fame Bethune-Tubman-Truth award, 1987, Our Lady of Perpetual Help Ch. Hom. Mem. award, 1987, Gary Educator of Christ Adminstr. Leadership award, 1988, NBC-LEO Appreciation award, 1988, Gary Cmty. Schs. Presenters award, 1991, Mr. G.'s Svc. award, 1991, Appreciation award Ind. Assn. Chiefs Police, 1992, Meth. Hosp., 1992, Bros. Keeper, 1992, Svc. award Ind Assn Elem. and Mid. Sch. Prins., 1992, N.W. Ind. Black Expo's Sen. Carolyn Mosby Above and Beyond award, 1995, In the Bethune Tradition award Nat. Coun. Negro Women, 1996, Citizen Yr. award NASW (Ind. chpt.), 1997, 98, Appreciation award Ind. chpt., 1997, Presenters award, Gary Cmty. Sch. Corp. Parent Involvement Program, 1996, Appreciation award, Pitman Square Sch., 1997, 98, 99, Alumni Appreciation award, Froebel High Sch., 1997, 98, 2002, Svc. award, Ind. League Municipal Clerks and Treas., 1998, Facet Excellence in Tchg. award, 1998, Brothers Keeper Appreciation award, 1999, Appreciation award, Lake County Assn. for the Retarded, 1999, New Hope award, 1999, New Hope Men's Day award, 2000; featured cover story Big Brothers Big Sisters Am. Newsletter for Diversity, 2000, Appreciation award, Hoosier Boys Town, 2000, Appreciation award, Gary Reading Coun., 2000, Outstanding Commitment award, Nat. Assn. Social Workers Region I, 2000, Svc. award, Ivanhoe Sch., 2002, Drum Major award, Gary Frontiers, 2002, Majestic Star award, 2002, Appreciation award, City of Lake Station, 2002, New Hope African Am.- Frederic Douglas award, 2003. Mem.: NAACP (life Ovington award 1999), No. Ind. Assn. Black Sch. Educators (founder), Ind. Assn. Sch. Prins., Ind. U. N.W. Alumni Assn. (life Disting. Educator award 1992), Phi Delta Kappa (25 Yr. award (N.W. Ind. chpt.) 1996), Omega Psi Phi (life Omega Man Yr. award 1974, Citizen Yr. award 10th dist. 1989, appreciation award Omicron Rho chpt. 1991, Citizen Yr. award (Alpha Kappa Kappa chpt.) 2003, Man Yr. award (Alpha Kappa Kappa chpt.) 2003). Baptist. Home: PO Box M622 Gary IN 46401-0622 Office: Ind U NW 3400 Broadway # 339 Gary IN 46408-1101 Office Phone: 219-980-7120. Business E-Mail: vesmith@iun.edu.

**SMITH, VERNON LOMAX,** economist, researcher; b. Wichita, Kans., Jan. 1, 1927; s. Vernon Chessman and Lula Belle (Lomax) S.; m. Candace C. Smith, Mar. 13, 2002. BSEE, Calif. Inst. Tech.; 1949; MA in Econs., U. Kans., 1952; PhD in Econs., Harvard U., 1955; D of Mgmt. (hon.), Purdue U., 1990. Asst. prof. econs. Purdue U., West Lafayette, Ind., 1955-58, assoc. prof., 1958-61, prof., 1961-65, Krannert prof., 1965-67; prof. Brown U., Providence, 1967-68, U. Mass., Amherst, 1968-74, U. Ariz., Tucson, 1975—2001, Regents' prof., 1988—2001; prof. econs. & law George Mason U., 2001—. Contbr. articles to profl. jours. Fellow Ctr. for Advanced Study in Behavioral Scis., Stanford, Calif., 1972-73; Sherman Fairchild Disting. Scholar Calif. Inst. Tech., Pasadena, 1973-74; adj. scholar CATO Inst., Washington, 1983—; recipient Nobel prize in econs., 2002. Fellow AAAS, Am. Acad. Arts and Scis., Econometric Soc., Am. Econ. Assn. (Disting. fellow); mem. NAS, Pvt. Enterprise Edn. Assn. (Adam Smith award). Office: George Mason U Interdisc Ctr for Econ Sci 4400 University Blvd MSN 1B2 Fairfax VA 22030-4444*

**SMITH, VERONICA LATTA,** real estate company officer; b. Wyandotte, Mich., Jan. 13, 1925; d. Jan August and Helena (Hulak) Latta; m. Stewart Gene Smith, Apr. 12, 1952; children: Stewart Gregory, Patrick Allen, Paul Donald, Alison Veronica Hurley, Alisa Margaret Lyons, Glenn Laurence. BA in Sociology, U. Mich., 1948. Tchr. Coral Gables (Fla.) Pub. Sch. Sys., 1949—50; COO Latta Ins. Agy, Wyandotte, 1950—62; treas. L & S Devel. Co., Grosse Ile, Mich., 1963—84; v.p. Regency Devel., Riverview, Mich., 1984—. Active U. Mich. Bd. Regents, 1985-92, regent emeritus, 1992—; mem. Martha Cook Bd. Govs., U. Mich., pres., 1976-78; del. Rep. County Conv., Grand Rapids, Mich., 1985, 87, 89, 91, 92, 94, 96, Lansing, Mich., 1996, Detroit, 1986, 88, 90, 92, 97; mem. pres. adv. com. Campaign for Mich., 1992-97, mem. campaign steering com., 1992-97. Mem. Mich. Lawyers Aux. (treas. 1975, chmn. 1976, 77, 78, 79), Nat. Assn. Ins. Women (cert.), Faculty Women's Club U. Mich. (hon.), Radrick Farms Golf Club (Ann Arbor), Pres.'s Club U. Mich., Investment Club (pres. 1976, sec. 1974-75, treas. 1975-76), Alpha Kappa Delta. Home: 22225 Balmoral Dr Grosse Ile MI 48138-1403

**SMITH, VICKIE M.,** chemicals executive; Asst. contr. Helena Chem. Co., sr. dir. info. tech., 2000—. Named one of Premier 100 IT Leaders, Computerworld, 2005. Office: Helena Chem Co 225 Schilling Blvd Collierville TN 38017*

**SMITH, VIN,** editor, small business owner, writer; b. Whittier, Calif., May 19, 1944; s. M. Clifford and Anna Eugenia (Hill) S.; m. Marthea Karen Callaham, May 15, 1966 (div. 1979); children: Jayare Smith, Eric Smith; m. Ginger Hammon, Oct. 20, 1984; children: Amy Michelle, Stacey Erin, Kellie Rae. Student, Columbia Sch. Broadcasting, San Francisco, 1967; AA, Cuesta Coll., 1974; grad., Am. Sch. of Piano Tuning, 1978; DD, Ancient Order of the WA, 2004. Sales mgr. Sta. KTAT, Frederick, Okla., 1967-69; announcer KOCY, Oklahoma City, 1969; owner Melmart Markets, San Luis Obispo, Calif., 1971-73; Am. Direct Sales, Grover City, Calif., 1973-79; instr. piano Valley View Acad., Arroyo Grande, Calif., 1977-78, Long Piano Co., San Luis Obispo, 1977-79, piano technician, 1978-79; owner Chocolate Piano, Yreka, Calif., 1979—; instr. piano Makah Indian Tribe, Neah Bay, Wash., 1981-82; sports editor Yreka News Digest, Bakersfield, Calif., 1988—. Cons., stress evaluator seminar Yreka Stress Therapy Clinic, 1986-87; reporter Vinco Distbrs. (formerly Vinco Enhancement Sys.), 1998; chair piano dept. Bogus Sch., 1999-2004, internat. relationship counselor Ask Me com., 2000-03, askdrpiano.com., 2000. Author: (novel) Neon Streets, 2002, Lincoln Park, 2003, Ride the High Waves, 2004, Lucky Pierre's, 2004, The Outrageous Views of Professor Fogelman, 2004, a.k.a. Mandi Wire, 2004, A Bullet for Slade, 2005, Get Mandi Wire, 2005, Jimamon and the Air Kids, 2005; sports columnist New Words Digest, 1987-91; guest columnist Siskiyou Daily News, 1991-94; nat publicist chamber music concerts So. Oreg. State Coll., 1993—; host (TV Show) Vin and Friends, 2003; host, prodr. (nat. broadcast CRN Digital Talk) Vin Smith's Midnight Bookworm, 2005—; contbr. articles to profl. jours. Chmn. heart fund Tillman County Okla., 1968; pub. co-chmn. Siskiyou County No-Prop 174, 1994; campaign worker Ken Jourdan for sheriff, Yreka, 1986; publicity dir. Gene Breceda for supr., 1993-94. Recipient Cert. of Appreciation, Siskiyou County, 1988, Achievement award, 1988, Golden Poet award World of Poetry, 1989, Living Treasure award Siskiyou County, 2003. Mem. Nat. Writers Club (chmn. student com. Yreka chpt. 1988), Author's Guild Inc., Author's League of Am., Mystery Writers Am., Soc. Children's Book Writers, Jr. C. of C. (sgt.-at-arms Frederick chpt. 1967-69), Kiwanis, Moose. Avocations: horse shoe pitching, photography, reading. Home: 710 Knapp St Yreka CA 96097-2343 Office: Chocolate Piano Svcs PO Box 447 Yreka CA 96097-0447 Office Phone: 530-842-7672. E-mail: drpiano@earthlink.net.

**SMITH, VINCENT MILTON,** Feng Shui consultant, educator, writer; b. Barbourville, Ky., Nov. 21, 1940; s. Virgil Milton and Louis (McGalliard) Smith; children: Jessica Todd, Duncan. BA, Harvard U., 1962; LLB, Yale U., 1965. Bar: N.Y. 1966. Assoc. Breed, Abbott & Morgan, N.Y.C., 1965-70, Debevoise & Plimpton, N.Y.C., 1970-75, ptnr., 1975-95; CEO Lang, Winslow & Smith Co., Chatham, NJ, 1995-98; owner VMS Feng Shui Design Co., 1998—, Panergetics, LLC, 2002—. Mem. adv. bd. Chgo. Title Ins. Co., N.Y.C., 1979—2002; vis. Feng Shui prof. Berea (Ky.) Coll., 1999, Williams Coll., Williamstown, Mass., 2001—02; Feng Shui lectr. N.Y. Open Ctr., 1999—; co-founder, chmn. bd. Keen Co., 2000—. Author: Feng Shui: A Practical Guide for Architects and Designers. Trustee Chatham (N.J.) Players, 1967—77, 1987—91, Summit Friends Meeting, Chatham, 1973—99, N.J. Shakespeare Festival, Madison, 1975—80, Playwrights Theatre N.J., 1989—91. Mem.: N.Y. Athletic Club, Harvard Club. Mem. Soc. Of Friends. E-mail: vmsdesign@aol.com.

**SMITH, W. KEITH,** bank executive; b. Regina, Sask., Can. B in Commerce, U. Sask., Can.; Master's, U. Western Ont., Can. Chartered acct. Exec. Booz, Allen & Hamilton, Inc., Ctrl. Nat. Chgo. Corp., Ctrl. Nat. Bank, Chgo.; sr. v.p. acctg. and control Bank of Montreal, Can.; exec. v.p., CFO Crocker Nat. Bank; mgr. fin. and leasing subsidiaries and corp. staff dept. PACCAR, Inc.; vice chmn., CFO Mellon Bank Corp. and Mellon Bank, N.A., Pitts., 1987-90, head svc. products businesses, 1990-93, vice chmn., dir., 1993—. Mem. Fin. Execs. Inst., Bankers Roundtable. Bd. dirs. Dentsply Internat., St. Margaret Meml. Hosp., River City Brass Band. Office: The Dreyfus Corp 200 Park Ave Fl 7W New York NY 10166-0039

**SMITH, W. PRESTON,** publishing executive, educator, real estate broker; b. Little Rock, Oct. 30, 1938; s. Arthur W. and Syble M. Smith; children: Cynthia Ann Smith Jones, Carey R. BS, U. Ark., Little Rock, 1959; postgrad., Henderson State U., Arkadelphia, Ark., 1968-69, Ark. State U., 1969, Texarkana Coll., 1981-82, U. Ark., Pine Bluff, 1983, Tulane U., Miss. County C.C., 1985; MEd, U. Ark., 1984. Cert. sch. adminstr., social studies tchr., Laubach reading instr. Tchr. math. and social studies 4th Sch. Jr. H.S., North Little Rock, 1959-61; owner Walker Enterprises, Hot Springs Village, Ark., 1964—; tchr. Malvern (Ark.) Pub. Schs., 1967-68, Prattsville (Ark.) H.S., 1968-69, Poyen (Ark.) H.S., 1969-70, Horatio (Ark.) H.S., 1981-82, Bingham Rd. Acad., Little Rock, 1982-83, Luxora (Ark.) H.S., 1985, Stanton Rd. Sch., Little Rock, 1986; tchr., prin. Dept. Correction Sch. Dist., Ark., 1989-95; ret., 1995. Sci. textbook selection com., Prattsville H.S., 1968-69; math. stds. com. Ark. Coun. Tchrs. Math., Little Rock, 1983; lectr. Zero Down seminars on creative real estate financing; owner Silver Dollar Press, Inc. Author, pub.: Jokebook of the Century, 1989; author: Jokebook of the Century, vol. II, 1990, vol. III, 1991, How To Start Your Own Business, 1992, Forms For Business, vol. I and II, 1995, Consumers Should Know, vols. I-IV, 1996, vols. V-IX, 1997, vols. X-XVIII, 2002, How to Adjust and Repair Your Sewing Machine, 2005, Jokebook of the Century, Vol 4, Color A Laugh! Create a Colorful Comic, 2003, vol. I-II, The Spirit Tales of Silver Wolf and His People, 2003, The Adventures of Jake Hardy and His Friends, Vol. 1, 2004, Free E-Book About Free E-Books, Vol. 1, 2004, Three Children's Stories, 2005 Past pres., song leader Sunday Sch. class; former mem. Ch. choir. Mem. AARP (past pres. England, Ark. chpt., chpt. specialist), Ark. Assn. Ednl. Adminstrn. (assoc.), Ark. Ret. Tchr. Assn. (state membership chmn. 1998-2001), Lonoke County Ret. Tchr. Assn. (pres. 1997-2000). Lodges: Order of DeMolay (master councillor). Avocations: candlemaking, refinishing furniture, tape recording classical music. Home and Office: Po Box 8394 Hot Springs Village AR 71910-8394

**SMITH, WALTER JOHN,** lawyer; b. Omaha, Apr. 19, 1948; s. Walter H. and Margaret A. (Ortman) S.; m. Mary Lou Dreves, June 20, 1970; children: Benjamin, Michael, Jeffrey. JD, Creighton U., 1972; LLM, Harvard U., 1975. Bar: Nebr. 1972, Tex. 1975. Law clk. to Judge E.A. Tamm U.S. Ct. Appeals (D.C. cir.), 1972-73; assoc. Monen, Seidler, McGill, Festerson & Koley, Omaha, 1973-74; mng. ptnr. & mem. exec. com. Baker & Botts, Houston, 1975—. Editor (in chief): Creighton Law Rev. Dir. Univ. Houston Law

Found., Casa de Amma, Inc., San Juan Capistrano, Calif., Ctrl Houston Inc., Greater Houston Partnership, Hobby Ctr. for Performing Arts; trustee Riverview Sch., Ea. Sandwich, Mass. Sustaining life fellow, Houston Bar Found.; mem. Houston Bar Assn., Coronado Club. Office: Baker & Botts LLP One Shell Plz 910 Louisiana St Houston TX 77002-4995 Office Phone: 713-229-1614. Office Fax: 713-229-7714. Business E-mail: wsmith@bakerbotts.com.

**SMITH, WALTON NAPIER,** lawyer; b. Macon, Ga., Feb. 26, 1942; s. Robert Monroe and Marion Rose (Napier) S.; m. Susan Rush (Baum), Oct. 10, 1970; children: Rush Hendley, Berkeley Bosman. BA, Dartmouth Coll., 1964; JD, Harvard U., 1967. Bar: Ga., 1966; D.C., 1972; Ill., 1978; U.S. Supreme Ct., 1971. Counsel Nat. R.R. Passenger Corp., Washington, 1971-75; assoc. Lord, Bissell, and Brook, Washington and Chgo., 1975-79, ptnr. Chgo. and Atlanta, 1980—2004. With Am.'s Watershed Land Keeper. Capt. JAGC U.S. Army, 1964—71. Decorated Bronze Star, Army Commendation Medal. Mem. State Bar Ga. Democrat. Episcopalian. Personal E-mail: wnsmith@soquesmiths.com.

**SMITH, WARREN ALLEN,** writer, director, columnist; b. Minburn, Iowa, Oct. 27, 1921; s. Harry Clark and Ruth Marion (Miles) S. BA, U. No. Iowa, 1948; MA, Columbia U., 1949. Chmn. dept. Eng. Bentley Sch., N.Y.C., 1949-54, New Canaan (Conn.) H.S., 1954-86; founder, pres., chmn. bd. Variety Sound Corp., N.Y.C., 1961-90; pres. Afro-Carib Records, 1971-90, Talent Mgmt., 1982-90, AAA Rec. Studio, 1985-90; founder, pres. Variety Rec. Studio, 1961-96; founder Philosopedia.org, 2005—. Instr. Columbia U., 1961-62. Author: Who's Who in Hell, 2000, Celebrities in Hell, 2002, Cruising the Deuce, 2005, Gossip From Across the Pond, 2005; book rev. editor: The Humanist, 1953—58; editor: (jour.) Taking Stock, 1967—93, Pique, 1990—93, Van Rijn's Pad, 1991, Janestreeter, 1997—98; contbr. book revs. Libr. Jour.; editl. assoc.: Free Inquiry, 1992—2000, columnist: Gay and Lesbian Humanist, 1996—, GHQ Humanist, 2005—, syndicated columnist: Manhattan Scene in W.I. newspaper; syndicated columnist Humanist Pot-pourri in Free Inquiry, 1994—98; drama critic: Brontë Newsletter, 1995—2000, book reviewer: New Humanist, 1997—2000, CD prodr.: Man-uel Salazar: Costa Rica's Forgotten Tenor, writer: The Villager, 2002—. Pres. Taursa Fund, 1971-73; bd. dirs. Jane Street Corp. Treas. Secular Humanist Soc. N.Y., 1988-93; sec. Jane St. Corp., 1995-97, 98-99; with Jane Street Authors, 2000—; with ACT UP, Hume Soc.; founding mem. Voltaire Soc. Am. With AUS, 1942-46; signer Humanist Manifesto II, 1973, Humanist Manifesto, 2000, Humanist Manifesto III, 2003. Recipient Leavey award Freedoms Found. at Valley Forge, 1985. Mem.: ASCAP, Chelpress (pres. 2004—), N.Y. Soc. Ethical Culture, Bertrand Russell Soc. (bd. dirs. 1973—, v.p. 1977—80), Brit. Humanist Assn., Conn. Edn. Assn., Rationalist Press Assn., Am. Unitarian Assn., Internat. Press Inst., N.Y. Skeptics Soc. (bd. dirs. 1990—94), Asociación Iberoamericana Ético Humanista (hon.), Stonewall Vets. Orgn. (treas. 1998—99), Mensa, Omaha Beach Vets. Assn., Mensa Investment Club (chmn. 1967—2001), Humanist Book Club (pres. 1957—62). Avocation: teratology. Home and Office: 31 Jane St Apt 10 D New York NY 10014-1980 Personal E-mail: wasm@mac.com.

**SMITH, WARREN JAMES,** optical scientist, consultant, lecturer, author; b. Rochester, NY, Aug. 17, 1922; s. Warren Abrams and Jessie Madelyn (Forshay) S.; m. Mary Helen Geddes, May 18, 1944 (dec. 1999); children: David Whitney, Barbara Jamie; m. Dung My Luong, Dec. 24, 2000. BS, U. Rochester, 1944; postgrad., U. Calif., Santa Barbara, 1960. Physicist Clinton Engr. Works, Tenn. Eastman Co., Oak Ridge, 1944-46; chief optical engr. Simpson Optical Mfg. Co., Chgo., 1946-59; mgr. optical sect. Raytheon Corp., Santa Barbara, 1959-62; v.p. R & D, Infrared Industries, Santa Barbara, 1962-87; chief scientist Kaiser Electro-Optics, Inc., Carlsbad, Calif., 1987—2005; cons. Rockwell Collins Optronics, Carlsbad, 2005—. Lectr. U. Wis., Madison, 1972—; Genesee Computer Ctr., Rochester, 1982—93, U. Rochester, 1988—92, Sinclair Optics, 1994—2000; cons. in field; expert witness. Author: Modern Optical Engineering, 1966, 3d edit., 2000, Modern Lens Design, 1992, 2nd edit., 2004, Practical Optical System Layout, 1997; editor McGraw-Hill series Optical and Electro-Optical Engineering; also articles. Recipient honored, Tribute Conf., San Diego, 2005. Fellow: Optical Soc. Am. (nat. pres. 1980, organizer, chmn. tech. confs., Fraunhofer medal 2001), Internat. Soc. Optical Engring. (life; nat. pres. 1983, organizer, chmn. tech. confs., Gold medal 1985, Dirs. award 1992), Sigma Chi. Avocations: tennis, sailing. Home: 1165 Countrywood Ln Vista CA 92081-5334 Office: Rockwell Collins Optronics 2752 Loker Ave W Carlsbad CA 92010-6603 Office Phone: 760-438-9255 ext. 234. Business E-mail: wjsmith1@rockwellcollins.com.

**SMITH, WAYNE CALVIN,** chemical engineer, consultant; b. Beaver, Okla., Mar. 19, 1935; s. Dean C. and Loraine S.; m. Suellyn Joyce Canon, Aug. 18, 1984. BS, Okla. U., 1958, MSChemE, 1964; PhDChemE, Colo. U., 1974. Registered profl. engr., Tex., Okla., Colo.; cert. emergency response special-ist. Process engr. Shell Oil Co., Deer Park, Tex., 1958-59; sr. devel. engr. Monsanto, Pensacola, Fla., 1965-66; project leader Phillips Petroleum Co., Bartlesville, Okla., 1967-69; acting chief process control EPA Nat. Enforce-ment Investigations Ctr., Denver, 1971-78; firm wide mgr. pollution control Dames & Moore, Golden, Colo., 1978-81; regional mgr. Hittman Assocs., Englewood, Colo., 1981-82; pres. Environ Environs Control Svcs., Golden, Colo., 1982-83; chief hazardous waste mgmt. Woodword-Clyde Cons., Englewood, 1983-84; exec. cons. Kellogg Corp., Littleton, Colo., 1984-86; program mgr. Radian Corp., Austin, Tex., 1986-93; prin. engr., program mgr. Tetra Tech, Inc., Oklahoma City, 1993—2003; project mgr. FPM Group Ltd., Midwest City, Okla., 2003—04, ret., 2004—. Contbr. over 30 articles to profl. jours. Capt. USMC, 1959-62. Scholar Magnolia Petroleum Co., 1958-58; fellow Phillips Petroleum Co., 1962-64, Marathon Oil Co., 1966-67, Gulf Oil Co., 1969-71. Mem. AIChE, Am. Arbitration Assn., The Greens Country Club, Sigma Xi. Baptist. Avocations: golf, woodworking. Personal E-mail: wcssjs@sbcglobal.net.

**SMITH, WAYNE RICHARD,** lawyer; b. Petoskey, Mich., Apr. 30, 1934; s. Wayne Anson and Frances Lynetta (Cooper) S.; m. Carrie J. Swanson, June 13, 1959; children: Stephen, Douglas (dec.), Rebecca. AB, U. Mich., 1956, JD, 1959. Bar: Mich. 1959. Asst. atty. gen. State of Mich., 1960-62; pros. atty. Emmet County (Mich.), 1963-68; dist. judge 90th Jud. Dist., Mich., 1969-72; city atty. City of Petoskey, 1976-98. Trustee North Central Mich. Coll. 1981-98, chmn., 1992-97; trustee/chmn. N. Ctrl. Mich. Coll. Found., 1999—; mem. No, Mich. Community Mental Health Bd., 1972-92, chmn., 1979-81. Mem. Emmet-Charlevoix Bar Assn. (pres. 1967), State Bar Mich., Mich. State Bar Found. Presbyterian. Home and Office: 365 E Main St PO Box 4677 Harbor Springs MI 49740-4677 Office Phone: 231-526-1684.

**SMITH, WAYNE THOMAS,** healthcare company executive; b. Jan. 29, 1946; BS, Auburn Univ, 1968, MS, 1969; M in hosp. adminstrn., Trinity U.; postgrad., King's Fund Coll. Hosp. Adminstrn. With Trinity Univ, 1971-73; Humana Inc, Louisville, 1973-75, v.p. ctrl. hosp. region, 1978-80, sr. v.p., 1980-85, exec. v.p., 1985-86, pres., COO group health divsn., 1986-96, also bd. dirs.; exec. v.p. Humana Health Care Ops., Louisville, 1991-96; ret. Humana Inc., 1996; pres., CEO, Cmty. Health Sys., Brentwood, Tenn., 1996—, chmn. bd., 2001—. Exec. v.p health plan ops., bd. dirs. Humana Health Plan, Inc., Louisville; pres. Humana Ins Nev., Inc., Humana Health Plan Fla., Inc.; exec. v.p. Humana Health Plan Ohio, Inc., Humana Health Chgo. Ins. Co., Humana Kansas City, Inc.; pres., COO Humana Health Plan Tex., Prime Health Mgmt. Svcs.; pres., bd. dirs. HMPK, Inc.; bd. dirs. Praxair, Inc.; chmn. bd. Fedn. Am.'s Hosps. Bd. dirs. Gov.'s Scholars Program, Ky., Actors Theatre of Louisville, Ky. Ctr. for the Arts, The Louisville Orchestra; bd. overseers U. Louisville; mem. exec. com. Greater Louisville Fund for the Arts; past chair bd. dirs. Louisville Collegiate Sch. With U.S. Army, 1969-73, capt., 1973. Mem. Group Health Assn. Am. (bd. dirs.), Health Ins. Assn. Am. (bd. dirs.). Office: Community Health Systems 155 Franklin Rd Ste 400 Brentwood TN 37027-4646*

**SMITH, WENDY HAIMES,** federal agency administrator; b. Tex. m. Jay L. Smith. BA in Econs., U. Mich.; postgrad., Ohio State U., Am. U., Washington Studio Sch., Aspen Inst., Wye, M., 1997. Cert. real estate agt. Office mgr. Haimes Travel Agy., Ohio, 1972-73; mgmt. intern US Dept. Commerce, Washington, 1973-75, country specialist for Korea, 1973, spl. asst. to dep. asst. sec. for internat. commerce, 1973-74, project officer, maj. projects divsn., 1974-75, project mgr. indsl. sys., maj. projects divsn., 1975-77, country specialist for Brazil, 1978, project mgr., hydrocarbons and chem. process plants, maj. export projects divsn., 1977-79, exec. asst. to dep. asst. sec. of commerce for export devel. and staff dir. Pres. Export Coun., 1979-81, dir. Pres. Export Coun., 1981-92, acting dir. Office Planning and Coordina-tion, 1988-89, dir. adv. coms. and pvt. sector programs Internat. Trade Adminstrn., 1992-97; dir. Trade Info. Ctr., Washington, 1997—, acting dir. office of export promotion, 1999, 2000-01; acting dir. Office Export Assis-tance and Bus. Outreach, 2003—04; deputy dir. U.S.A. Trade Promotion, 2005—; sr. advisor Nat. Acad. Pub. Adminstrn., 2005—. Author, editor US Trade in Transition: Maintaining the Gains, 1988, co-author, editor The Export Imperative, 1980, Coping with the Dynamics of World Trade in the 1980s, 1984; Exhibited in group shows at Courtyard Gallery, Brian Logan Artspace, Artists Mus., Washington, Designer's Art Gallery, Bethesda, Md., one-woman shows include Courtyard Gallery, Washington, 2001. Active Art League, Smithsonian Instn., Washington Opera Guild; bd. dir. Washington Studio Sch; one man show Courtyard Gallery, 2001.

**SMITH, WENDY L.,** foundation executive; b. Chgo., Sept. 12, 1950; d. John Arthur and Dolores Mae (Webb) Rothenberger; m. Alan Richard Smith; children: Angela Fuhs, Erica Smith. Student, Oakton CC, Des Plaines, Ill. 1986, Mundelein Coll., 1990. Purchasing clk. AIT Industries, Skokie, Ill., 1975-76; purchasing agt. MCC Powers, Skokie, 1976-78; office mgr. Spartan Engring., Skokie, 1978-80, Brunswick Corp., Skokie, 1980—; successively sr. sec., coord. indsl. rels., dir. Brunswick Found., Lake Forest, Ill., 1982-89, pres., 1989—. Asst. sec. Brunswick Pub. Charitable Found., Lake Forest, 1989—; mem. adv. com. Found. for Ind. Higher Edn., Stamford, Conn., 1989—, Coun. Better Bus. Burs., Arlington, Va., 1988-90; bd. dirs. Associ-ated Colls. of Ill., 1991—; bd. dirs., mem. trustees com., mem. compensation and benefits com. Donors Forum of Chgo., 1988-93. Bd. dirs. INROADS/Chgo., Inc., 1994—; mem. steering com. Dist. 57 Edn. Found., Mt. Prospect, Ill., 1996—. Recipient Pvt. Sector Initiative Commendation, U.S. Pres., 1987-89. Mem. Donors Forum Chgo. (treas. 1988-91, bd. dirs., mem. exec. com., chairperson audit and fin. com., mem. trustees com. 1992—), Coun. on Founds., Ind. Sector Suburban Contbns. Network (chair-person 1987-89), Women in Philanthropy Corp. Founds. (mem. cmty. rels. com. 1985-87), Chgo. Women in Philanthropy. Avocations: antique restora-tion, pleasure reading, bowling, golf.

**SMITH, WILBUR LAZAR,** radiologist, educator; b. Warwick, NY, Oct. 11, 1943; s. Wilbur and Betty (Norris) S.; m. Rebecca Rowlands, June 19, 1965; children: Jason, Daniel, Joanna, Noah, Ethan, Jacob. BA, SUNY, Buffalo, 1965, MD, 1969. Diplomate Am. Bd. Radiology, Am. Bd. Pediat., Am. Bd. Pediatric Radiology. Intern, then resident Buffalo Children's Hosp., 1969-71; resident in pediatric radiology Cin. Gen. and Children's Hosp., 1971-74; asst. prof. pediatrics and radiology Ind. U., Indpls., 1975-78, assoc. prof., 1978-80, acting dir. pediatric radiology 1979-80; assoc. prof. U. Iowa, Iowa City, 1980-82, prof., 1982—, dir. med. edn. in radiology, 1980-86, vice chmn. dept. radiology, 1986-94, interim head, 1994-96, dir. pediatric radiology 1980-92; chmn. dept. radiology Henry Ford Health Sys., Detroit, 1998-99; prof. radiology Wayne State U., Detroit, 2000—, chmn. dept. radiology, 2002—; staff radiologist Mich. Children's Hosp., Detroit, 2000—. Vice chmn. radiology for academics Wayne State U., 2001, radiology residency dir., 01, prof., chmn. dept. radiology, 2002—. Assoc. editor Gastrointestinal Imaging in Pediatrics, Acad. Radiology, 1992—, Quar. Rev. Child Abuse, 1998, Radiology 101, co-author, 2d edit. 2004; exec. assoc. editor Acad. Radiology, 1997-2000, assoc. editor, 2000—02; contbr. articles to profl. jours. Vol. soccer coach, 1980-99; physician cons. in child abuse, 1980-; mem. equity adv. com. Iowa City Sch. Bd., 1983-87. With USAR, 1969—77, hon. discharge USAR. Fellow Am. Acad. Pediatrics, Am. Coll. Radiology; mem. AMA, Radiol. Soc. N.Am.(second v.p. 2004-05), Iowa Radiol. Soc. (pres. 1987-88), Assn. Univ. Radiologists (pres. 1995-96, sr. adv. 2001—, Gold medal 2006), Soc. Pediat. Radiology (treas. 1995-98, rep. coun. Acad. Socs. of AAMC 1996-02), Mich. Radiol. Soc. (bd. dirs. 2004—). Mem. Soc. Of Friends. Avocation: photog-raphy. Home: 10124 Lasalle Blvd Huntington Woods MI 48070-1162 Office: Detroit Receiving Hosp Dept Radiology (3L8) 4201 St Antoine Detroit MI 48201 Office Phone: 313-745-4443. Business E-Mail: wlsmith@med.wayne.edu.

**SMITH, WILL,** actor, rap artist; b. Phila., Sept. 25, 1968; s. Caroline and Willard Smith; m. Sheree Smith, May 9, 1992 (div. 1995); 1 child, Willard III; m. Jada Pinkett Smith, Dec. 31, 1997; children: Jaden Christopher Syre, Willow Camille Reign. Ptnr. Overbrook Entertainment. Albums (as The Fresh Prince with DJ Jazzy Jeff): And in this Corner..., 1989, Homebase, 1991, Rock the House, 1987, He's the DJ, I'm the Rapper, 1988, Code Red, 1993, Big Willie Style, 1997, Willennium, 1999, Maximum Will Smith, 2000, Born to Reign, 2002, Greatest Hits, 2002, Lost and Found, 2005; (singles) Just One of Those Days, 1987, Girls Ain't Nothing But Trouble, 1988, Brank New Funk, 1988, A Nightmare on My Street, 1988, Jazzy's Groove, 1989, I Think I Can Beat Mike Tyson, 1989, Parents Just Don't Understand, (Grammy award for Best Rap Performance, 1988), The Things That U Do, 1991, Summertime, 1991 (Grammy award), Ring My Bell, 1991, I'm Looking for the One (To Be With Me), 1993, Boom! Shake the Room, 1993; Actor: (TV series)The Fresh Prince of Bel-Air, 1990-96, (also exec. prodr. 1994-96), Happily Ever After: Fairy Tales for Every Child (voice), 1995, All of Us, 2003 (also writer, exec. prodr.); (TV appearances) Blossom, 1991, All of Us, 2003; (films) Where the Day Takes You, 1992, Made in America, 1993, Six Degrees of Separation, 1993, Bad Boys, 1995, Independence Day, 1996 (Blockbuster Entertainment award Favorite Actor Sci-Fi), Men In Black, 1997 (MTV Movie awards Best Fight, Best Movie Song, ASCAP award Most Performed Songs for Motion Picture, Blockbuster Entertainment award Favorite Actor Sci-Fi), Welcome to Hollywood, 1998, Enemy of the State, 1998, Wild Wild West, 1999, The Legend of Bagger Vance, 2000, Ali, 2001, Men in Black II, 2002, Bad Boys II, 2003, I, Robot, 2004 (also exec. prodr.), Shark Tale (voice), 2004, Hitch, 2005 (also prodr.); exec. prodr., Showtime, 2002, The Seat Filler, 2004; prodr. Saving Face, 2004, ATL, 2006. Recipient ShoWest Conv. awards Actor of Yr., 1999, Spl. Internat. Box Office Achievement award 1997, BET award for Best Actor, 2002, Am. Music Award, Favorite Male Artist, 2005; named one of 50 Most Powerful People in Hollywood, 2004-06, 100 Most Influential People, Time Mag., 2006*

**SMITH, WILLARD GRANT,** psychologist; b. Sidney, NY, June 29, 1934; s. Frank Charles and Myrtle Belle (Empet) S.; m. Ruth Ann Dissly, Sept. 14, 1957; children: Deborah Sue Henri, Cynthia Lynn Koster, Andrea Kay Richards, John Charles. BS, U. Md., 1976; MS, U. Utah, 1978, PhD, 1981. Diplomate Am. Bd. Forensic Examiners, Am. Bd. Psychol. Specialities, Am. Bd. Disability Analysts, cert. forensic cons.; lic. psychologist Utah, cert. sch. psychologist nat. Tchg. asst. dept. ednl. psychology U. Utah; rsch. asst. U. Utah Med. Ctr., 1976-78; rsch. cons. Utah Dept. Edn., 1977; program evaluator Salt Lake City Sch. Dist.; program evaluator, auditor Utah State Bd. Edn., 1978; sch. psychologist Jordan Sch. Dist., Sandy, Utah, 1978-82, tchr., 1979-80; exec. dir. Utah Ind. Living Ctr., Salt Lake City, 1982-83; spl. edn. cons. Southeastern Edn. Svc. Ctr., Price, Utah, 1983-85; sch. psychologist Jordan Sch. Dist., Sandy, Utah, 1985-96; assoc. psychologist Don W. McBride & Assocs., Bountiful, Utah, 1989-91; pvt. practice Sandy, Utah, 1991—. Master sgt. USAF, 1953-76. Decorated Air Force Commendation medal with 2 clusters. Fellow Am. Coll. Forensic Examiners (life) mem. APA, Nat. Assn. Sch. Psychologists, Air Force Assn., Air Force Sgts. Assn., Ret. Enlisted Assn., Am. Legion, VFW, Phi Kappa Phi, Alpha Sigma Lambda. Home: 8955 Quail Hollow Dr Sandy UT 84093-1903 Office Phone: 801-942-5356. E-mail: dr_bill5@msn.com.

**SMITH, WILLIAM ASHLEY,** lawyer, investment banker, energy execu-tive; b. Birmingham, Ala., Sept. 14, 1944; S. Robert Wesley and Nancy Victoria (Davis) S.; m. Blakeley Dean Dent, Sept. 2, 1967; children: William Ashley, Andrew Lindsey BA, U. Va., 1966; JD, U. Ala., 1969. Bar: Ala 1972. Atty. Sonat, Inc., Birmingham, Ala., 1970-73, asst. sec., 1973-79, asst. v.p., asst. sec., 1979-80, asst. v.p., asst. sec., assoc. gen. counsel, 1980-81, v.p., gen. counsel, sec., 1981-84, v.p., gen. counsel, 1984-87, sr. v.p., gen. counsel, 1987-89, sr. v.p., 1989-91, exec. v.p., 1991-94, exec. v.p., gen. counsel, 1995—99; vice chmn. Sonat Exploration, Birmingham, Ala., 1994-97; exec. v.p. El Paso Corp., 1999—2002; chmn. El Paso Global Gas Group, 2001—02; ptnr. Galway Group, Houston, 2002—. Pres. So. Natural Gas Co., 1989—, chmn., 1991-94. Mem. ABA, Ala. Bar Assn. Episcopalian. Office: Galway Group LP 3050 Post Oak Blvd Ste 1300 Houston TX 77056

**SMITH, WILLIAM CHARLES,** retired lawyer; b. Batavia, NY, June 9, 1930; s. William F. and Verna B. (Busmire) S.; m. Lucia P. Pierce, July 10, 1954; children: William Charles, Leonard P., Victoria J. BA, U. Buffalo, 1952; LLB, Harvard U., 1955. Bar: Maine 1955, D.C. 1962, Fla. 1995, U.S. Dist. Ct. Maine, 1956, U.S. Tax Ct. 1960, U.S. Ct. Appeals (1st cir.) 1977, U.S. Ct. Claims 1985, U.S. Supreme Ct. 1960. Assoc., Portland, Maine, 1955-57; ptnr. Hutchinson, Pierce, Atwood & Allen, Portland, 1957-59; counsel Office Tax Legis. Counsel, U.S. Treasury Dept., Washington, 1959-61; ptnr. Pierce Atwood, Portland, 1961-96, of counsel, 1996—2005. Exec. com. Fed. Tax Inst., New Eng. Vice chmn. budget com. United Community Services, 1966-68, chmn., 1968-70, nat. budget and consultation com., 1969-71; bd. dirs. Portland Goodwill, Inc., 1967-69, United Way, Inc., 1968-74, 75-80, Portland Widow's Wood Soc., 1962—2005; trustee Portland Regional Op-portunity Program, 1967-68, Freyburg Acad., 1976-96, Found. Blood Re-search, 1979-85. Mem. ABA, Maine Bar Assn., Cumberland County Bar Assn., Am. Law Inst., Am. Coll. Trust and Estate Counsel, Am. Coll. Tax Counsel, Portland County Club, Mid-Ocean Club (Bermuda), Meadows Country Club (Fla.), Cumerland Club (Maine). Republican. Unitarian Uni-versalist. Personal E-mail: wsmith2@maine.rr.com.

**SMITH, WILLIAM DOUGLAS,** lawyer; b. Spartanburg, S.C., Apr. 3, 1958; s. Milton Alfred and Suzanne (Earnhardt) S.; m. Alison Evans Smith; children: Cameron McIver, Anna Douglas. BA, Wofford Coll., 1980; JD, U. S.C., 1983. Bar: S.C. 1983, U.S. Dist. Ct. S.C., U.S. Ct. Appeals S.C. Assoc. Johnson, Smith Firm, Spartanburg, S.C., 1983-86, ptnr., 1986—. Mem. S.C. Ho. of Reps., 1990—, spkr. pro tempore, 2000—. Mem. S.C. Bar Assn., Spartanburg County Bar Assn., S.C. Golf Assn. (bd. dirs. 1995). Republican. Presbyterian. Avocation: golf. Home: 21 Springdale Ln Spartanburg SC 29302-3410 Office: Johnson Smith 220 N Church St Spartanburg SC 29306-5104

**SMITH, WILLIAM FRENCH, II,** safety engineer; b. Bay City, Tex., Nov. 30, 1941; s. William and Willie Mae (Perry) S.; m. Sylvia Knight, Feb. 4, 1977; children: William III, Maurice. BS, Tuskegee U., 1964; postgrad., Washington U., 1968—70. Equipment engr. Boeing Co., Huntsville, Ala., 1964-67; plant design engr. McDonnell Douglas Corp., St. Louis, 1967-69; project engr. St. Louis County Govt., 1969-72; divsn. engr. E.I. duPont de Nemours & Co., Inc., Wilmington, Del., 1972-74, Victoria, Tex., 1972-74; engring. mgr. Westinghouse Corp., Millburn, NJ, 1974-76; bldg. safety engr. Denver Pub. Schs., 1976—; project adminstr., 1977—, energy conservation-ist, 1978—; pres. Smith Environ. Consulting, Denver, Las Vegas, Nev. Dir. hazardous materials Tuskegee U., Denver, 1985—88, environ. safety dir., 1988—; reservist Fed. Emergency Mgmt. Agy.; pres. Smith Environ. Con-sulting. Bd. dirs. Denver Opportunities Industrialization Ctr., 1979-80, Nat. Commn. on Future of Regis Coll.; mem. Mayor's Citizens Adv. Com. on Energy, 1980—, City of Lakewood Sr. Citizens Adv. Coun., Lakewood Bd. Appeals, Lakewood Code Enforcement Com.; past bd. dirs. Colo. Alliance Environ. Edn., Colo. Emergency Planning Commn.; past v.p. The Rocky Mountain Poison and Drug Ctr. Served with USNR, 1979—. Recipient Pres.'s Nat. award for energy conservation, 1980. Mem. Am. Soc. Safety Engrs., Colo. Assn. Sch. Energy Coords., Am. Assn. Blacks in Energy, Denver Pub. Schs. Black Adminstrs. and Suprs. Assn. (treas.), Colo. Environ. Health Assn., Nat. Asbestos Coun., Colo. Hazardous Waste Mgmt. Soc., Colo. Hazardous Materials Assn. (past treas.), Denver Emergency Planning Commn., Civil Air Patrol, Colo. Renewable Energy Soc., Colo. Energy Network, Nat. Assn. Minority Contractors, Environ. Consulting (pres.), Internat. Hazardous Ma-terials Assn., Tuskegee U. Alumni Assn. Republican. Home: 102 S Balsam St Lakewood CO 80226-1344 Office: Denver Public Schs 2800 West 7th Ave Denver CO 80204-4117 E-mail: wmfrenchsmith1@aol.com.

**SMITH, WILLIAM HENRY PRESTON,** freelance/self-employed writer, editor, former telecommunications industry executive; b. Pleasanton, Tex., Sept. 8, 1924; s. Sidney Newton and Willie Gertrude (Cloyd) S.; m. Frances Dixon, July 1, 1950; children: Juliet, Dixon, David. B.J., U. Tex., 1949. Reporter Dallas Morning News, 1949-52; advt. asst. Dallas Power & Light Co., 1952-55; dir. pub. relations Greater Boston C. of C., 1955-58; with New Eng. Telephone and Telegraph Co., Boston, 1958-86, asst. v.p., 1966-75, corp. sec., 1975-83, dir. pub. relations, 1983-86; free-lance writer Dover, Mass., 1986—. Editor: Bus. Ethics Resource Newsletter. Bd. dirs., v.p. Mass. Soc. for Prevention Cruelty to Children; bd. dirs. Bus. Ethics Found., Urban Dynamics Adv. Coun.; mem. support policies com. United Way Mass; bd. advisors to pres. Andover Newton Theol. Sch. With paratroopers U.S. Army, 1943-46. Decorated Purple Heart, U.S. Army, Bronze Star, U.S. Army. Mem. Am. Soc. Corp. Secs., Friars, Dedham Country and Polo Club, Down Town Club, Wellesley Coll. Club, Sigma Delta Chi, Delta Kappa Epsilon. Repub-lican. Home and Office: 3236 Wingfield Lake Rd Williamsburg VA 23185-7519

**SMITH, WILLIAM JAY,** author; b. Winnfield, La., Apr. 22, 1918; s. Jay and Georgia (Campster) S.; m. Barbara Howes, Oct. 1, 1947 (div. June 1965); children: David Emerson, Gregory Jay; m. Sonja Haussmann, Sept. 3, 1966. Student, Institut de Touraine, Tours, France, 1938; BA, Washington U., St. Louis, 1939, MA, 1941; postgrad., Columbia U., 1946-47; postgrad. Rhodes scholar, Oxford U., 1947-48; postgrad., U. Florence, Italy, 1948-50; Litt.D., New Eng. Coll., 1973. Asst. in French Washington U., 1939-41; instr. English and French Columbia U., 1946-47; lectr. English Williams Coll., 1951, poet in residence, lectr. English, 1959-64, 66-67; Ford Found. fellow Arena Stage, Washington, 1964-65; writer in residence Hollins Coll., 1965-66, prof. English, 1967, 70-80, prof. emeritus, 1980. Poet laureate Libr. Congress, Washington, 1968-70, hon. cons. in Am. letters, 1970-76; vis. prof., acting chmn., writing divsn. Sch. Arts, Columbia U., 1973, 74-75; mem. staff Salzburg (Austria) Seminar, 1975; mem. jury Nat. Book award, 1962, 70, 75, Neustadt Internat. prize for lit., 1978, Com. of Pegasus Prize for Lit., 1979-98; poet in residence Cathedral St. John the Divine, N.Y., 1985-88. Author: Poems, 1947, Celebration at Dark, 1950, Laughing Time, 1955, Poems, 1947-57, Boy Blue's Book of Beasts, 1957, Puptents and Pebbles: A Nonsense ABC, 1959, Typewriter Town, 1960, The Spectra Hoax, 1961, What Did I See, 1962, Ho for a Hat, 1964, (with Louise Bogan) The Golden Journey; Poems for Young People, 1965, The Tin Can and Other Poems, 1966, If I Had a Boat, 1966, Poems from France, 1967, Mr. Smith and Other Nonsense, 1968, New and Selected Poems, 1970, The Streaks of the Tulip, selected criticism, 1972, Poems from Italy, 1973, Venice in the Fog, 1975, The Telephone, 1977, Laughing Time, 1980, The Traveler's Tree, New and Selected Poems, 1980, Army Brat, a Memoir, 1980, A Green Place: Modern Poems, 1982, Plain Talk: Epigrams, Epitaphs, Satires, Nonsense, Occasional Concrete and Quotidian Poems, 1988, Ho for a Hat (rev.), 1989, Collected Poems 1939-1989, 1990, Laughing Time: Collected Nonsense, 1990, Birds and Beasts, 1990, Big and Little, 1992 (with Carol Ra) Behind the King's Kitchen: A Roster of Rhyming Riddles, 1992, The Cyclist, 1995 (with Carol Ra) The Sun is Up: A Child's Year of Poems, 1996, The World Below the Window: Poems 1937-1997, 1998, Here is My Heart: Love Poems, 1999, The Cherokee Lottery: A Sequence of Poems, 2000, Around My Room, 2000, The Spectra Hoax (paperback reissue), 2000, The Girl in the Glass: Love Poems, 2002; translator: (with Emanuel Brasil) Brazilian Poetry 1950-80, 1984, (with Ingvar Schousboe) The Pact: My Friendship with Isak Dinesen by Thorkild Bjørnvig, 1983, (with J.S. Holmes) Dutch Interior: Post-War Poetry of the

Netherlands and Flanders, 1984, Scirocco by Romualdo Romano, 1951; Poems of a Multimillionaire by Valery Larbaud, 1955, Selected Writings of Jules Laforgue, 1956, Children of the Forest by Elsa Beskow, 1969, Two Plays by Charles Bertin: Christopher Columbus and Don Juan, 1970, The Pirate Book by Lennart Hellsing, 1972, (with Leif Sjöberg) Agadir by Artur Lundkvist, 1979, Moral Tales of Jules Laforgue, 1985, Collected Translations: Italian, French, Spanish, Portuguese, 1985, (with Dana Gioia) Poems from Italy, 1985, (with Leif Sjöberg) Wild Bouquet: Nature Poems by Harry Martinson, 1985, (with Sonja Haussmann Smith) The Madman and the Medusa by Tchicaya U Tam'Si, 1989, Songs of Childhood by Federico Garcia Lorca, 1994; Berlin: The City and the Court, 1996, (with Leif Sjöberg) The Forest of Childhood: Poems from Sweden, 1999, Gyula Illyés: Selected Poems, 1999; editor: Herrick, 1962, Light Verse and Satires by Witter Bynner, 1978, (with F.D. Reeve) An Arrow in the Wall: Selected Poetry and Prose by Andrei Voznesensky, 1986 (one of 16 Best Books of 1986, N.Y. Times), Life Sentence: Selected Poems of Nina Cassian, 1990. Mem. Vt. Ho. of Reps., 1960-62. Served to lt. USNR, 1941-45. Recipient Alumni citation Washington U., 1963; prize Poetry mag., 1945, 64; Henry Bellamann Major award, 1970; Russell Loines award Nat. Inst. Arts and Letters, 1972; Gold medal Labor Hungary 1978; Golden Rose award New Eng. Poetry Club, 1979, médaille de vermeil French Acad., 1991, Pro Cultura Hungarica medal, Hungary, 1993; Nat. Endowment for Arts fellow, 1972, 95; NEH fellow, 1975, 89; Ingram Merrill fellow, 1982; Camargo Found. fellow, 1986, René Vásquez Díaz prize Swedish Acad., 1997. Mem. Am. Acad. Arts and Letters (v.p. for literature 1986-89), Am. Assn. Rhodes Scholars, Acad. Am. Poets, Authors Guild, P.E.N. Clubs: Century. Home: 63 Luther Shaw Rd Cummington MA 01026-9787 Address: 52-56 rue d'Alleray 75015 Paris France

**SMITH, WILLIAM L.,** telecommunications industry executive; BS with honors, No. Carolina St. Univ., 1979. Rsch. asst. Bell Communications, 1979—87; mktg., tech., ops. BellSouth, 1987, head DSL, Internet Wholesale, Bus. units, now Chief Tech. Officer. Chmn. bd. dir. Alliance for Telecom. Indus. Solutions. Bd advisors No. Carolina St. Univ. Grad. Sch.; exec. bd. Atlanta Area Council Boy Scouts Am., Make-A-Wish Found., Ga. Office: BellSouth 1155 Peachtree St, NE Atlanta GA 30309-3610

**SMITH, WILLIAM RANDOLPH (RANDY SMITH),** health facility administrator; b. Spartanburg, SC, July 23, 1948; s. Jesse Edward and Helen (Knox) S.; m. Donna Marie HAwthorne, July 18, 1970; children: Kirstin Leigh, Andrea Marie. BA, Furman U., 1970; MHA, Duke U., 1972. Exec. dir. Riverside Hosp., Wilmington, Del., 1974-79; assoc. exec. dir. Brookwood Med. Ctr., Brimingham, Ala., 1979-81, exec. dir., 1983-85; v.p. ops. Am. Med. Internat., Atlanta, 1981-89, interim CFO Beverly Hills, Calif., 1989—90, chief administrv. officer Dallas, 1990, exec. v.p. ops., 1990-95; exec. v.p. Tenet Health Corp, Dallas, 1995—2003, pres. Western divsn., 2003. Bd. dirs. EPIC Healthcare Group, Dallas, 1989-92. Bd. dirs. Ala. Symphony Assn., Birmingham, 1985, State of Ala. Ballet, Birmingham, 1983-85, Esoterix, Inc., 1997—. Lt. U.S. Army, 1972-74. Mem. Fedn. Am. Health Systems (bd. dirs. 1989-99, pres. 1993, chmn. 1994). Episcopalian. Avocations: skiing, tennis, automobiles. Office: Tenet Healthcare Inc 14001 Dallas Pkwy Ste 200 Dallas TX 75240-4346

**SMITH, WILLIAM RAYMOND,** farmer, horse breeder; b. Bowling Green, Ky., June 5, 1932; s. William Raymond and Rose Velta (Biggerstaff) Smith; m. Robin Sommers, July 12, 1954 (div. July 1977); children: Dana Leslie Henning, Lauren Reneé Imgrund; m. Lee Ann McClatthey, Dec. 31, 1994 (div. May 2003). BA in Liberal Arts, U. Chgo., 1953, MA in English, 1959, PhD in History of Culture, 1961. Lic. thoroughbred trainer. Asst. prof. English Pa. State U., Univ. Park, 1961-63, Haverford (Pa.) Coll., 1963-66, Scripps Coll., Claremont, Calif., 1966-67, exec. officer literature divsn., 1966-67; chmn. integrative studies Shimer Coll., Mt. Carroll, Ill., 1967-70; asst. prof. humanities Reed Coll., Portland, 1970; prof. history and philosophy U. Pitts., Johnstown, Pa., 1971-98, acad. dean, 1971-72; ret., 1998. Fulbright prof. Am. studies U. Utrecht, Netherlands, 1969—70. Author: History as Argument, 1966, The Rhetoric of American Politics, 1969; co-author: The Colonial Legacy, 1971, Nineteenth Century Literary Criticism, 1986. With U.S. Army, 1955—57. Fellow, Union Rsch. Higher Edn., 1968. Avocation: fox hunting rider. Home: Loghouse Farm 445 Mt Zion Rd Dillsburg PA 17019 Office Phone: 717-432-1554. Personal E-mail: loghousefarm@aol.com.

**SMITH, WILLIAM REECE, JR.,** lawyer; b. Athens, Tenn., Sept. 19, 1925; s. William Reece and Gladys (Moody) S. BS, U. SC, 1946, LLD, 1981; JD, U. Fla., 1949; Rhodes scholar, Oxford U., 1949-52; LLD, U. So. Fla., 1973, Rollins Coll., 1980, U. Fla., 1980, Stetson U., 1985, Nova Southeastern U., 2005; DCL, Central Meth. Coll., 1980, New Eng. Coll., 1980; DHL, Calif. West Sch. Law, 1981; DBA, Tampa Coll., Fla., 1991; LHD, U. So. Fla., 1990. Bar: Fla. 1949. Mem. firm Carlton, Fields, Ward, Emmanuel, Smith and Cutler, Tampa, 1953—, now chmn. emeritus; interim pres. U. So. Fla., 1976-77; city atty. Tampa, 1963-72. Asst. prof. law U. Fla., 1952-53; adj. prof. law Stetson U., 1954-59, 91—; past pres. Fla. Legal Svcs., Inc., Tampa Philharmonic Assn., Fla. Gulf Coast Symphony, Inc. Sec. Fla. Rhodes Scholar Selection Com., 1969-94. Midshipman and ensign USNR, 1943—46. Named Outstanding Young Man of Tampa, 1961; recipient Good Govt. award Fla. Jr. C. of C., 1965, Disting. Am. award Tampa Chpt. Nat. Football Found., 1977, Humanitarian award B'nai B'rith Found., 1977, Pres.'s award Fla. Assn. Retarded Citizens, 1978, Von Briesen award Nat. Legal Aid and Defender Assn., 1980, Brotherhood award NCCJ, 1980, Herbert Harley award Am. Judicature Soc., 1983, Citizen of Yr. award Civitan Club, 1986, Algernon Sydney Sullivan award, U. SC, 1987, Pub. Svc. award Stetson U. Coll. Law, 1990, C.H.I.E.F. award Fla. Ind. Colls. and Univs., 1990, Professionalism award Am. Inns of Ct., 2002; inaugural mem. Hall of Fame Stetson U. Coll. [illegible], Fla. Trial Lawyers, Internat. Acad. Trial Lawyers, Fla. Bar Found. (past pres.); mem. ABA (chmn. jr. bar conf. 1960-61, life, ho. dels., sec. 1967-71, pres. 1980-81, Gold medal 1989, Pro Bono Publico award 1994), Am. Bar Found., Am. Bar Endowment, Internat. Soc. Barristers, Am. Law Inst. (mem. coun.), Internat. Bar Assn. (past pres.), Inter-Am. Bar Assn. (mem. exec. coun. 1972-77), Fla. Bar Assn. (pres. 1972-73), Hillsborough County Bar Assn. (pres. 1963), Nat. Conf. Bar Pres. (pres. 1978-79), Greater Tampa C. of C. (pres. 1986-87). Methodist. Home: PO Box 3239 Tampa FL 33601-3239 Office: Carlton Fields Ward Emmanuel Smith & Cutler Corp Ctr 3 10th Flr 4221 W Boy Scout Blvd Tampa FL 33607 Office Phone: 813-223-7000. Business E-Mail: rsmith@carltonfields.com.

**SMITH, WILLIAM S., JR.,** education association administrator; BS in Chemistry, Tex. A&M U., 1970, PhD in Chemistry, 1974. Postdoctoral rschr. U. Calif., Irvine, 1974—77; program mgr. FAA; graduate rsch. Tex. A&M U. 1971—74; phys. scientist FAA, U.S. Dept. Transp., 1977—85; sci. advisor subcom. on space, com. on sci., space and tech. U.S. Ho. of Reps., 1985—88, staff dir. subcom., 1988—90, dep. Dem. chief of staff, 1994—98; v.p. for programs Assn. Univs. for Rsch. in Astronomy, Inc., Washington, 1998—2000, interim pres., 1999—2000, pres., 2000—. Recipient Exceptional Svc. award, NASA, Sci. and Tech. Fellowship award, Dept. Commerce, 1984. Office: AURA Inc Ste 350 1200 New York Ave NW Washington DC 20005 E-mail: wsmith@aura-astronomy.org.

**SMITH, YEARDLEY,** actress; b. Paris, July 3, 1964; Voice of Lisa Simpson, Maggie Simpson and others The Simpsons, 1989—. Actor: (films) Heaven Help Us, 1985, The Legend of Billie Jean, 1985, Maximum Overdrive, 1986, Three O'Clock High, 1987, Listen to Me, 1989, Zwei Frauen, 1989, City Slickers, 1989, Toys, 1992, Jingle All the Way, 1996, Just Write, 1997, As Good As It Gets, 1997, (voice only) We're Back! A Dinosaur's Story, 1993,; (TV films) Mom's On Strike, 1984, Tickets, Please, 1988; (TV series) Brothers, 1984, The Tracey Ullman Show, 1987-89, Herman's Head, 1991, Dharma & Greg, 1997—99, 2001—02, (TV guest appearance) Tales from the Darkside, 1986, Mama's Family, 1986, Mathnet, 1987, Sydney, 1990, Likely Suspects, 1992, Hey Hey, It's Sunday, 1994, Empty Nest, 1994, Smart Guy, 1997, Teen Angel, 1997, Sports Night, 1998, Nash Bridges, 1999, Becker, 2003, (theatre) More, 2004.

**SMITH, YOLANDA IPPOLITO,** law educator, researcher, writer; b. Raleigh, NC, Oct. 12, 1943; d. Luciano and Blanche Ruth Mason Ippolito; m. Ralph Clemens Smith III, May 21, 1999; m. John Jacob Christensen, Nov. 27, 1965 (div.); children: Elizabeth Kristen Christensen, Peter John Christensen. BS, U. Md., College Park, 1965; MA, Vt. Coll., Northfield, 1981; JD, U. oMd., Balt., 1993. Bar: Md. 1993, DC 1995, U.S. Ct. Appeals (4th cir.) 1995, U.S. Dist. Ct. Md. 1995. Bus. franchisee Wicks 'N' Sticks, Gautier, Miss., 1980—81; prof. No. Va. C.C., Alexandria, 1995—. Cons., spkr. in field; adj. faculty No. Va. C.C., 1986—95. Author: Needlepoint Simplified, The Needlepoint Book, rev. edition, Worry-Free Retirement Living: Choosing a Full Service Retirement Community, Bargello Stitchery, Trapunto, Cross Stitchery, Applique and Reverse Applique, The Needlepoint Book, Teach Yourself Needlepoint, Needlepoint: The Third Dimension, The Needlepoint Scraps Book.

**SMITH, YOUNG MERRITT, JR.,** lawyer; b. Hickory, N.C., July 25, 1944; s. Young Merritt and Christine Ellen (White) S.; m. Louise Garner Price, Sept. 6, 1966 (div. Aug. 1974); 1 child, Patrick Adam; m. Charlie Mae Early, Nov. 19, 1977 (div. May 1985); m. Mary Gayle Jones, June 8, 1985; children: Mary Gaither, Jennifer Gayle. AB, U. N.C., 1966; JD, Duke U., 1969. Bar: N.C. 1969. Pres. The Litchfield Plantation Co., Pawleys Island, S.C., 1969-74, The Figure Eight Island Co., Wilmington, N.C., 1971-74; ptnr. Smith and Smith, Hickory, N.C., 1974-87; lawyer in pvt. practice Hickory, 1987—. Trustee Fund for Peace, N.Y.C., 1970-79, United Health Services N.C., Durham, 1971-73, N.C. Design Found., Raleigh, 1973-76. Mem. N.C. Bar Assn., Delta Kappa Epsilon. Democrat. Episcopalian. Office: Young M Smith Jr Atty PO Drawer 1948 Hickory NC 28603 Office Phone: 828-327-4101. E-mail: ysmith@youngsmithlaw.com

**SMITH, ZADIE (SADIE SMITH),** writer; b. London, Eng., Oct. 27, 1975; m. Nick Laird, 2004. Grad. in English, Cambridge U., 1997; postgrad., Harvard U. Writer-in-residency Inst. Contemporary Arts; Radcliffe Inst. fellow Harvard U., 2002—03. Author: (novels) White Teeth, 2000 (First Book award, Guardian newspaper, Whitbread First Novel award, Commonwealth Writers prize, Ethnic and Multicultural Media Award, best book/novel, Ethnic and Multicultural Media Award, best female newcomer, James Tait Black Meml. prize for fiction, 2000, WH Smith award, best new talent, 2001, (UK miniseries, 2002; aired on PBS in US), The Autograph Man, 2002 (Wingate Literary prize for fiction, Jewish Quarterly, 2003), On Beauty, 2005 (Orange prize for fiction, 2006, Somerset Maugham award, 2006), (nonfiction) Fail Better, 2006; editor: (anthology) Pieces of Flesh, 2001; author (of introduction): The Burned Children of America, 2003. Named one of 100 Most Influential People, Time Mag., 2006. Mailing: c/o Georgia Garrett AP Watt Ltd 20 John St London WC1N 2DR England also: Hamish Hamilton Ltd c/o Penguin Ltd 80 Strand London WC2R ORL England Office Phone: 20 7405 6774. Office Fax: 20 7831 2154. E-mail: zsmith@literati.net.*

**SMITH, ZAK,** artist; b. Syracuse, NY, July 16, 1976; BFA, Cooper Union, NY, 1994—98; attended, Skowhegan Sch. Painting & Sculpture, Maine, 1999; MFA, Yale U., 1999—2001. One-man shows include 20 Eyes in My Head, Fredericks Freiser Gallery, NY, 2002, Paintings That Look Good and Were Hard to Make, 2003, Hope You Like It, Franklin Art Works, Mpls., 2004, Fredericks Freiser Gallery, NY, 2005, exhibited in group shows at I See You 2, 2001, Comic Release: Negotiating Identity for a New Generation, Carnegie Mellon University, Pitts., 2002, Hello, My Name Is..., 2002, Upstream Gallery, Amsterdam, 2004, Whitney Biennial, Whitney Mus. Am. Art, NY, 2004, Contemporary Mus., Balt., 2004, Feeling Strangely Fine, Estrany De La Mota, Barcelona, Spain, 2005, Represented in permanent collections, Progressive Corporation, Mayfield, OH. Mailing: c/o Fredericks Freiser Gallery 504 West 22nd St New York NY 10011

**SMITH, ZANNIE O.,** retired career officer; b. Columbia, S.C., Mar. 27, 1943; BA in History, U. Tampa; M in Bus. Mgmt., Webster U., St. Louis. Enlisted 82d airborne divsn. U.S. Army, 1962, commd. 2d lt., advanced through grades to maj. gen.; chief of staff U.S. Army Res. Command, Atlanta, 1995; asst. divsn. comdr. ops. 10th Mountain Divsn. and Ft. Drum, 1997; dep. comdg. gen., chief of staff I Corps and Ft. Lewis, 1998—2003; ret., 2003. Decorated Def. Superior Meritorious Svc. award, Legion of Merit with 5 oak leaf clusters, Def. Meritorious Svc. medal, Meritorious Svc. medal with 4 oak leaf clusters, Army Commendation medal with 2 oak leaf clusters, Armed Forces Expeditionary medal, four Vietnam Svc. medals, Good Conduct medal, Bronze Star medal with V and 2 oak leaf clusters, Air medal with oak leaf cluster; recipient Combat Infantryman's badge, Ranger Tab, Air Assault badge.

**SMITHART-OGLESBY, DEBRA LYNN,** food service executive; b. Apr. 24, 1959; BA in Acctg., U. Tex.; MBA, So. Methodist U. Asst. contr. Brinker Internat., Inc., Dallas, 1985—86, contr., 1986—88, v.p., contr., 1988—91, v.p. fin., 1991, exec. v.p., CFO, 1991—97; pres. corp. services, CFO First Am. Autootive Inc., 1997—99; pres. Dekor, Inc., 1999—2000, O/S Partners, 2000—06; chmn. Denny's Corp., Spartanburg, SC, 2006—. Bd. dirs. Brinker Internat., Inc., 1997—97, Denny's Corp., 2003—, Noodles & Co. Office: Dennys Corp 203 E Main St Spartanburg SC 29319*

**SMITH-DOERR, LAUREL,** sociologist; b. Hampton, Va., Feb. 27, 1969; d. Norman D. and Kathleen M. Smith; m. Bill Doerr, May 23, 1991; 1 child, Gene Doerr. BA, Pomona Coll., 1991; PhD, U. Ariz., Tucson, 1999. Asst. prof. Boston U., 1999—; Jean Monnet fellow European U. Inst., Ctr. for Advanced Studies, Florence, Italy, 2004—05. Author: (book) Women's Work: Gender Equality vs. Hierarchy in the Life Sciences, (journal article) Administrative Science Quarterly, (book chpt.) Handbook of Economic Sociology; [illegible] articles in [illegible] jours. (Award for scholarly Contbn., 2002). Sr. min. search com. Old South Ch., Boston, 2002—04. Mem.: Ea. Sociol. Soc., Tech. Transfer Soc., Soc. for Social Study of Sci., Am. Sociol. Assn. (coun. mem. sci./knowledge and tech. sect. 1997—99, 2006—), Phi Beta Kappa. United Church Of Christ, Congregational. Office: Boston U Dept of Sociology Boston MA 02215 Office Phone: 617-353-2591. E-mail: ldoerr@bu.edu.

**SMITH-EPSTEIN, MARY KATHLEEN,** dancer; b. Austin, Tex., Sept. 12, 1940; d. Walter Bentley Jr. and Kathleen Beatrice (Lancaster) Smith; m. Witaly Osins, June 6, 1967 (div. 1975); m. Howard Irwin Epstein, June 20, 1987. Grad. high sch., Dallas. Demi soloist Am. Festival Ballet, European Tour, 1961; prin. dancer HET Nat. Ballet, Amsterdam, Holland, 1962-67; guest artist Berliner Ballet, Berlin, 1964, Ballet De L'Atlantique, Nantes, France, 1967-68, Cologne, Fed. Republic Germany, 1968-70, Ballet Spectacular, Miami, Fla., 1973-74; prin. dancer Opernhaus, Hannover, Fed. Republic Germany, 1968-70, Musiktheater, Gelsenkirchen, Fed. Republic Germany, 1968-71, Ballet Van Vlaanderen, Antwerp, Belgium, 1971-73, Ballet De Wallonie, Charleroi, Belgium, 1973-74, Irish Nat. Ballet, Cork, Ireland, 1975-85, Chgo. Ballet, 1977-78, Ballet Met., Columbus, Ohio, 1978-79; founder, co-dir. Conservatory Classical Dance, Eugene, Oreg., 1989—. Founder N.W. Chamber Ballet, 1988—; artistic dir. 8 Dance Ensemble; guest tchr. Imperial Kirvek Ballet, 2000-01, Internat. Ballet Sch., 2000. Choreographer: (ballet) Opus 1, 1978, For Him From Her, 1982, The Catalyst, 1983 (Bursary Irish Arts Council award 1985), Pas De Deux, 1985 (Bursary Irish Arts Council 1985), Logic of the Heart, 1988, Masquerade Suite, 1988, Tango, 1999, Nocturne, 1998, Pro-Fun-Ditties, 1997, No One Knew, 1997; choreographer Ballet N.W., Performing Ensemble Conservatory Classical Dance, 1989—. Treas. Neighborhood Watch, Vida, Oreg., 1988-89, bd. dirs., sec. to ops. Lane Arts Coun., 1993-96; dir. bldg. fund pres. McKenzie R. Mus., 1998-99; house dist. chair Lane County Dem. Party, 2005—. Alexandra Danilova scholar, Dallas, 1958. Buddhist. Personal E-mail: khepsteinor@comcast.net.

**SMITHER, HOWARD ELBERT,** musicologist, educator; b. Pittsburg, Kans., Nov. 15, 1925; s. Elbert S. and Ethel (Schwab) S.; m. Doris J. Arvin (div. 1976); children: Thomas A., Jesse N. Woodsmith; m. Ann M. Woodward. AB magna cum laude, spl. honors in music, Hamline U., 1950; MA in musicology, Cornell U., 1952; postgrad., U. Munich, 1953-54; PhD in musicology, Cornell U., 1960. Instr. Oberlin Coll. and Conservatory of Music, Oberlin, Ohio, 1955-57, asst. prof., 1957-60, U. Kans., Lawrence, 1960-63; assoc. prof. Tulane U., New Orleans, 1963-68; U. N.C., Chapel Hill, 1968-71, prof., 1971-79, dir. grad. studies in music, 1977-79, 83-84, 86-88, James Gordon Hanes prof. humanities in music, 1979-92, James Gordon Hanes prof. emeritus humanities in music, 1992—; John Bird prof. of music U. Wales, Cardiff, 1993-95. Lectr., chmn. panels regional, nat. and internat. meetings, confs., symposiums, 1964-90. Author: A History of the Oratorio, Vol. 1, The Oratorio in the Baroque Era: Italy, Vienna, Paris, 1977 (transl. Italian), Vol. 2, The Oratorio in the Baroque Era: Protestant Germany and England, 1977 (Deems Taylor award ASCAP 1978), Vol. 3 The Oratorio in the Classical Era, 1987, Vol. 4, Oratorio in the 19th and 20th Centuries, 2000; editor Oratorios of the Italian Baroque 1983—, The Italian Oratorio 1650-1800, Vols. 1-3, 6, 8, 11-13, 16, 18-20, 24-25, 27, 1986-87; Oratorios of the Italian Baroque, 1983—; editor, translator poems in Alfred Einstein's The Italian Madrigal, 1971; music rev. editor Notes, 1967-69; mem. editorial bd. Detroit Monographs in Musicology, 1971-87; chmn. editorial bd. Early Musical Masterworks: Editions and Commentaries, 1978-83; mem. editorial bd. Videodisc Music Series, NEH, 1982-86; contbr. articles to profl. jours. Fellow Cornell U., 1953-54, NEH, Italy, 1972-73, England, 1979-80, Guggenheim, 1984-85; Fulbright sr. rsch. grant in Italy, 1965-66, sr. Fulbright lectr. Moscow State Conservatory, 1990. Mem. Am. Mus. Soc. (hon; chmn. S.E. chpt. 1969-71, mem. coun. 1969-71, 75-77, bd. dirs. 1977-79, pres. 1980-82, del. to Am. Coun. Learned Socs. 1984-88, to Internat. Congress Strasbourg 1982), Music Libr. Assn. (bd. dirs. 1968-70), Soc. for Am. Music, Internat. Assn. Jazz Educators, Internat. Trumpet Guild. Avocations: hiking, jazz trumpet performance.

**SMITHER, NICK,** automotive executive; b. 1959; Engr. prod. devel., European Divsn. Ford Motor Co., 1980, systems analyst, 1983, mgr. prod. devel., info. tech. integration, So. Am., 1995—2000, sr. v.p., finance sys. teams, exec. dir., global IT, bus. ops., v.p., CIO, 2006—. Office: Ford Motor Co 1 American Way Dearborn MI 48126-2798*

**SMITHERAM, MARGARET ETHERIDGE,** health facility administrator, director; b. Atlanta, Jan. 5, 1938; d. Philip Fitzgerald and Mary Catharine (Dwyer) E.; m. Roy Charles McCracken, May 5, 1975; m. William Bertram Smitheram, Aug. 17, 1985. BA, Emory U., 1960; M in Health Adminstrn., Washington U., St. Louis, 1973. Registered record administr., 1960-71; spl. asst. to dir. VA Med. Ctr., Roseburg, Oreg., 1973-74; hosp. administrn. specialist VA Central Office, Washington, 1974-75; asst. dir. trainee VA Med. Ctr., Phila., 1976, assoc. dir. Hampton, Va., 1976—80, Buffalo, 1980-81; presdl. exchange exec. Kimberly Clark Corp., Neenah, Wis., 1981-82, Roswell, Ga., 1981-82; dir. VA Med. Ctr., Grand Island, Nebr., 1982-94; interim dir. Grand Island-Hall County Health Dept., 1996-97; instr. Cerritos Coll., 1969-70. Bd. dirs. Project 2M Coordinating Coun., Inc., Grand Island, 1985-87, Hall County Leadership Unlimited, Inc., 1990. Bd. dirs. Grand Island Area United Way, 1987-90 (pres. 1989), Grand Island Concert Assn, 1987-92, Ctrl. Nebr. Goodwill Industries, Inc., 1987-93 (pres. 1991-92). Fellow Am. Coll. Healthcare Execs. (life); mem. rev. bd. State of Nebr. Foster Care, Am. Hosp. Assn., Fed. Exec. Assn. (pres. Grand Island chpt. 1987), Nebr. Hosp. Assn., Grand Island C. of C. (bd. dirs. 1988-92, legis. affairs com 1984-85, priorities com. 1984-85, govtl. affairs com. 1984-88, nominating com. 1991-92, 94-95, audit com. 1992-93, pres. club 1993-94), Rotary Internat. Club #1485 (v.p. 1998-2000, pres. 2000-2001, District 5630 Group Study Exchange Team Leader to South Korea District 3710, 1999, Paul Harris fellow). Home: 221 Trail of the Flowers Georgetown TX 78628

**SMITHEY, DONALD LEON,** airport authority director; b. St. Louis, Aug. 31, 1940; children: Kelly, Jill. Student, St. Ambrose Coll., 1962; BS in Bus. Mgmt., So. Ill. U., 1966; postgrad., U. Mo., St. Louis, 1973-74. Asst. ops. dispatcher Ozark Airlines, 1971-72; transp. analyst Olin Corp., 1972-78, cost acct., 1978-80; commr. St. Louis Regional Airport Authority, 1971-80, chmn., 1974-80, airport dir., 1980-83; asst. dir. Cedar Rapids Mcpl. Airport, 1983-85; dir. adminstrn. Omaha Airport Authority, 1985-87, dep. exec. dir., 1987-89, exec. dir., 1989—. With USN Air Res. 1963-66, USN, 1966-68. Mem. Am. Assn. Airport Execs. (Great Lakes chpt.), Airports Coun. Internat., Iowa Airport Exec. Assn. (past pres.), Ill. Pub. Airports Assn. (past v.p.), Kepft. Aircraft Assn., Omaha Rotary Club, Masonic Lodge (Bethalto, Ill.), Tangier Shrine (Omaha), Quiet Birdmen Assn., Silver Wings Fraternity. Office: Omaha Airport Authority 4501 Abbott Dr Omaha NE 68110-2698

**SMITH FAWZI, MARY C.,** epidemiologist; b. New Brunswick, N.J., Sept. 29, 1965; d. Maureen A. and Robert R. Smith; m. Wafaie W. Fawzi, June 18, 1994; 1 child, Roseanne Viola Fawzi. DSc, Harvard Sch. Pub. Health, Boston, 1988—94. Epidemiologist Partners In Health, Boston, 1997—; instr. Harvard Med. Sch., 1998—. Cons. FAO, Baghdad, Iraq, 1995. Recipient Albert Schweitzer award, Harvard Sch. Pub. Health, 1994. Democrat. Roman Catholic. Achievements include research in on diseases that disproportionately impact those living in poverty, particularly HIV, other sexually transmitted diseases, TB, and psychiatric disorders. Office Phone: 617-432-2574.

**SMITH-GONZALEZ, APRIL RENEE,** music educator; b. Kettering, Ohio, Oct. 11, 1973; d. Michael Charles and Linda Lucille Smith; m. Isaac Gonzalez, Dec. 16, 2000. AA, Palm Beach C.C., Lake Worth, FL, 1996; BA, MA, Fla. Atlantic U., 2001. Lic. massage therapist Fla. Piano tchr. Apr. Smith Piano Studio, West Palm Beach, Fla., 1988—. Vol. min. Christian Congregation of Jehovah's Witnesses, West Palm Beach, 1986—2005. Mem.: Holographic Repatterning Assn. (chmn. jour. com. 2005—06), Am. Coll. Osteo. Family Physicians (v.p. local student chpt. 2006—). Home: 6904 Manatee Ave W Apt 3D Bradenton FL 34209

**SMITHIES, OLIVER,** geneticist, educator; b. Halifax, Eng., June 23, 1925; naturalized; PhD in Biochemistry, Oxford U., Eng., 1951; DSc (hon.), U. Chgo., Duke U. Postdoctoral fellow phys. chemistry U. Wis., Madison, 1951—53, from asst. prof. to prof. genetics and med. genetics, 1960—63, Leon J. Cole prof., 1971—80, Hilldale prof., 1980—88; rsch. asst., assoc. Connaught Med. Rsch. Lab., Toronto, Canada, 1953—60; Excellence prof. dept. pathology and lab. medicine U. N.C., Chapel Hill, 1988—. Mem. nat. adv. med. sci. coun. NIH, 1985. Contbr. articles to profl. jours. Recipient William Allen Meml. award, Am. Soc. Human Genetics, 1964, Karl Landsteiner Meml. award, Am. Assn. Blood Banks, 1984, Internat. award, Gairdner Found., 1990, 1993, State of N.C. award, 1994, Alfred P. Sloan Jr. prize, 1994, Hypertension Rsch. award, CIBA, 1996, Cardiovasc./Metabolic Disease Rsch. award, Bristol-Meyers Squibb, 1997, Rsch. Achievement award, AHA, 1998, Albert Lasker award for Med. Rsch., 2001, Max Delbruck award, 2002, Wolf prize in medicine, 2003, Prize in Devel. Biology, March of Dimes, 2005; scholar Markle, 1961. Fellow: AAAS; mem.: NAS, Inst. Medicine, Genetics Soc. Am. (v.p. 1974, pres. 1975), Am. Acad. Arts & Sci. Achievements include research in targeted modification of specific genes in living animals. Office: Univ N C Dept Pathology & Lab Med Chapel Hill NC 27599-0001 Office Phone: 919-966-6913. E-mail: oliver.smithies@pathology.unc.edu.*

**SMITH-KIELLAND, INGVALD ALAIN,** product designer; b. Oslo, Apr. 29, 1974; arrived in US, 1996; s. Ingvald Smith-Kielland and Chantal Cocmeteux. BS, Art Ctr. Coll. Design, Calif., 1999. Product designer Playhut, City of Industry, Calif., 2000, Universal Electronics, Cypress, Calif., 2000—03; sr. product designer, project mgr. RKS Design, Thousand Oaks, Calif., 2003—. With Army, 1992—93, Norway. Recipient Bronze Idea award, Indust. Design Excellence Awards, 2003. Achievements include patents for interface info; cord mgmt. sys. Avocations: snowboarding, golf, jogging, travel. Home: 7111 Latisera Blvd Apt B101 Los Angeles CA 90045 Office: RKS Design 350 Conejo Ridge Ave Thousand Oaks CA 91361-4928 E-mail: ingvaldsk@hotmail.com.

**SMITH-MEYER, LINDA HELENE (LINDA SMITH),** artist; b. Manhattan, Nov. 18, 1947; d. Murray and Beatrice Victory (Waters) Smith; m. Charles Emil Meyer, Oct. 28, 1995. BFA, SUNY, 1969; MFA, NYU, 1973.

One-woman shows include Sushi Gallery, West Hollywood, Calif., 1983, The Ivey Gallery, L.A., 1987, Schwartz Cierlak Gallery, Santa Monica, Calif., 1990; group shows include Cicchinelli Gallery, N.Y.C., 1981, Proteus Gallery, Beverly Hills, Calif., 1981, Elizalde Gallery Internat., Laguna Beach, Calif., 1981, 82, Gallery Helene, West Hollywood, 1982, Factory Place Gallery, L.A., 1983, 84, The Ivey Gallery, 1986, Ratliff-Williams Gallery, Sedona, Ariz., 1990-91, Spago Restaurant, Hollywood, Calif., 1985-2001, Orlando Gallery, Tarzana, Calif., Craft and Folk Art Mus. Shop, L.A., 2005, Beatrice Wood Ctr. Arts, Ojai, Calif., 2006, others; represented in permanent collections at Peter Selz, Berkeley, Calif., Cedars-Sinai Med. Ctr. L.A., Martin Blinder/Barry Levine-Martin Lawrence Galleries, L.A., Ms. Found. for Women, N.Y.C., also pvt. collections; contbr. articles to profl. jours. Home: 1261 S Highland Ave Los Angeles CA 90019-1731 Personal E-mail: linda@lindasmithceramicsplus.net.

**SMITH-MILLER, HENRY HOUCK,** architect; b. NYC, Feb. 9, 1942; s. Theodore Roosevelt and Mary Elizabeth (Houck) Smith-Miller. BA, Princeton U., NJ, 1964; BArch, Yale U., New Haven, 1964-65; MArch, U. Pa., 1966. Registered architect, NY, Pa., Md., NC, Calif. Archtl. designer Michael Graves & Peter Eisenman Architects, Princeton, NJ, 1964; architect Richard Meier & Ptnrs., Arch., NYC, 1970-77; ptnr. Rubin & Smith-Miller, Archs., NYC, 1977-81, Smith-Miller & Hawkinson, Archs., NYC, 1981—. Vis. critic architecture U. Va. Sch. Architecture, Charlottesville, 1978-79, Columbia U. Sch. Architecture, NYC, 1981, 84, Harvard U. Grad. Sch. Architecture, Cambridge, Mass., 1987; Thomas Jefferson prof. architecture U. Va. Sch. Architecture, 1989—. Trustee Creative Time, NYC, 1986—. Recipient Architecture Record awards; Fulbright scholar, 1967-69. Mem. AIA (Design awards NY chpt. 1986, 87, 89, 91, 92, 94), Contemporary Coun. Mus. Modern Art. Democrat. Home and Office: Smith-Miller & Hawkinson Architects 305 Canal St New York NY 10013-2569

**SMITH-MOONEY, MARILYN PATRICIA,** city government official, management consultant; b. Jamaica, NY, July 5, 1942; d. Raymond Lionel and Katherine Marie (Doepp) Cowan; m. Jack (John) J. Mooney, Sept. 1, 2002; 1 child, Paul William Hibner. Student various aviation schs., St. Joseph's Coll., N.Y. cert. in Leadership and Human Resources Devel., Goldratt Inst., Conn., JONAH cert. Inst. Elected Ofcls., Advanced Inst. for Elected Ofcls., Leadership Charlotte Class of 97-98, Local Govt. Leadership Fla., Class IV-99. Exec. sec. to chief design Wiedersum Assoc., Arch. and Engr., Valley Stream, NY, 1960-61; office mgr., arch. apprentice, interior designer Keith I. Hibner, Arch., Hicksville, Garden City, NY, 1961-73; owner, pres. Hibner Atelier, Ltd., Garden City, 1968-75; interior design and gen. constrn. Garden City, 1968-76; office mgr., tech. planning, manual writer for county dept. structure & operation Ward Assoc./Planning Assoc., Arch. and Engr., Bohemia, NY, 1975-76; chief pilot, flight/ground aviation instr. Islip Aviation Ltd., NY, 1974-77; exec. asst. to pres. Arkay Packaging Corp., Hauppauge, NY, 1977-86; in-house constrn. mgr., 1980-82; adminstrn. and human resources mgr. Arkay Packaging Corp., Hauppauge, NY, 1986-89, dir. corp. devel., 1989, dir. materials mgmt., 1989-90. Cert. assoc. Goldratt Inst. for LI/Metro NY area, 1990-92; owner Concepts for Constructive Change, Educators and Facilitators for Continuous Improvement, Lake Grove, NY, 1990-92; ind. aviation flight/ground instr. airplane and instrument, 1977—; safety counselor FAA, 1974-92, FAA Ea. region counselors coord., 1985-86; mem. city charter rev. com. City Punta Gorda, Fla., 1996; mem. city coun. City of Punta Gorda, Fla., 1996—, vice mayor, 1998-99, 2000-01, first woman mayor, 2001-02, 2002-03; selected "top 100" west influential in Charlotte County by "Charlotte SUN", 2002, 2003; past bd. dir., officer Aviation Coun. LI; founder Seminar on Air Travel for Everyone (S.A.F.E.), 1979, Fly-T-Cure/W Air Condition People, 1979; city coun. appointee to S.W. Fla. Regional Planning Coun., 1999—, Charlotte County tourist devel. coun., 1998—, Charlotte County Assembly, 1998, 2001, Punta Gorda Historic Mural Soc., past mem. bd. dir.; county appointee Enterprise Charlotte Econ. Devel. team. Author articles, seminar syllabus. Past mem. nat. panel Consumer Arbitrators, Nat. Consumer Arbitration Program, Better Bus. Bur.; lic. comml. pilot, flight and ground instr.; mem. bd. Charlotte Skatepark, Inc.; past Bd. mem., past officer Punta Gorda Elks Lodge 2606. Past chmn. ninety-nines L.I. chpt., founding internat. chmn. safety edn., Amelia Earhart Bronze medal 1975, Old Punta Gorda, Inc.; mem. various cmty. non-profit org., (past mem. bd. dir.). Home: 654 Andros Ct Punta Gorda FL 33950-5809

**SMITH-SANDERS, CAROL ANN,** physical therapist, music therapist, psychologist; b. Montgomery County, Tenn., Apr. 19, 1951; d. Carl and Ruth (Gettinger) S. BME in Music Therapy, U. Kans., 1974; MA in Clin. Psychology, Mid. Tenn. State U., 1977; EdS in Human Svc. Mgmt., Vanderbilt U., 1979; EdD in Ednl. Adminstrn., Auburn U., 1997. Gen. therapeutic recreation specialist VA Med. Ctr., Murfreesboro, Tenn., 1973-79, music therapist Marion, Ind., 1979, chief recreation therapy service Tucson, 1979-84, chief recreation therapy Northport, N.Y., 1984-87, health systems specialist Dir.'s Office Cleve., 1987-88, adminstrv. asst. to assoc. dir., 1988-91, adminstrv. asst. to chief of staff Tuskegee, Ala., 1991-97; sr. health sys. specialist, med. dir. clin. programs Ctrl. Ala. Vets. Health Care sys., 1997—. Adj. instr. Mid. Tenn. State U., part-time 1978—; guest speaker, 1975—; facilitator AchieveGlobal. Contbr. articles to profl. jours. Mem. Am. Psychol. Assn. (assoc.), Nat. Assn. Music Therapy (cert.), NAFE, Phi Kappa Phi. Home: 1003 Wallace Ave Opelika AL 36801-6958 E-mail: carol.sanders@med.va.gov.

**SMITH-SINGARES, EDUARDO,** trauma surgeon, researcher; s. Edward Smith and Mitzi Y. Singares; m. Izaskun Melania Iglesias, Feb. 27, 1998; children: Iratxe Smith, Clive Xesu Smith. BS, Colegio Javier, Compañia de Jesus, 1987; MD, Universidad de Panama, 1994. Diplomate Ednl. Commn. for Fgn. Med. Graduates, 1997, cert. surgeon Am. Bd. Surgery, 2005. Surgery fellow The Johns Hopkins U. Sch. Medicine, Balt., 1999—2001; gen. surgeon Robert Wood Johnson U. Hosp., New Brunswick, NJ, 2001—04; assoc. U. Medicine and Dentistry of NJ., Piscataway, NJ, 2001—04; trauma surg. critical care specialist SUNY, Stony Brook, NY, 2004—05, clin. instr. surgery, 2004—05; chief surgeon McKenzie Hosp., 2005—; attending surgeon Bapt. Meml. Hosp., Huntingdon, Tenn., 2005—; clin. asst. prof. surgery Bethel Coll. Sch. Physician Assistants, McKenzie, 2006. Mem.: ACS (assoc.), Assn. Academic Surgery. Office Phone: 731-352-6627. E-mail: eduarsmith@gmail.com.

**SMITH-SMITH, PEOLA,** principal, not-for-profit executive; Prin. Neptune Middle Sch., NJ. Named one of Most Influential Black Americans, Ebony mag., 2005, 2006. Mem.: Nat. Assn. of Negro Bus. & Profl. Women's Clubs (nat. pres.). NANBPWC, Inc 1806 New Hampshire Ave, NW Washington DC 20009 Office Phone: 202-483-4206. E-mail: PSmith@nanbpwc.org.*

**SMITHSON, CHARLES WAYNE,** economist, consultant; b. Dallas, Sept. 29, 1946; s. Charles Winston and LaVerne (Putman) S.; m. Cynthia Ann Thomas, May 18, 1973; children: Nathan Thomas, Charles Matthew. BA in Econs., U. Tex., Arlington, 1969, MA, 1973; PhD, Tulane U., 1976. Instr. econs. U. New Orleans, 1975—76; asst. prof. Tex. A&M U., College Station, 1976—82; assoc. prof., 1983—85; sr. economist FTC, CPSC, 1982—83; v.p. Chase Manhattan Bank, N.Y.C., 1985—87, mng. dir. risk mgmt. rsch., 1990—94, sr. v.p., 1994—95; AT&T resident mgmt. fellow Simon Grad. Sch. Bus. U. Rochester, NY, 1987; profl. fin., dir. PhD program U. North Tex., Denton, 1987—88; v.p. product devel., risk mgmt. products Continental Bank, Chgo., 1988—89, mng. dir. rsch., product devel. global trading, distbn., 1989—90; mng. dir. rsch. fin. products CIBC World Markets, N.Y.C., 1995—99; mng. ptnr. Rutter Assocs., N.Y.C., 1999—. Mem. working group Group of 30 Derivatives Project. Author: (with others) The Economics of Mineral Extraction, 1980; (with S.C. Maurice) Managerial Economics, 1981, The Doomsday Myth: 10,000 Years of Economic Crisis, 1984; (with others) Managing Financial Risk, 1990, 3rd edit., 1998; editor: (with C.W.Smith) Handbook of Financial Engineering, 1990, Credit Portfolio Management, 2003; assoc. editor Financial Management; adv. bd. Jour. Applied Corp. Fin.;

contbr. articles to profl. jours. 1st lt. USAF, 1969—73. Mem.: Internat. Assn. Fin. Engrs., Fin. Mgmt. Assn. Avocations: fishing, boating, snorkeling. Home: 4010 NE Joes Point Rd Stuart FL 34996 Office Phone: 212-949-1180. E-mail: csmithson@rutterassociates.com.

**SMITH-THOMPSON, PATRICIA ANN,** public relations consultant, educator; b. Chgo., June 7, 1933; d. Clarence Richard and Ruth Margaret (Jacobson) Nowack; m. Tyler Thompson, Aug. 2, 1992; children from previous marriage: Deborah, Kurt, Nancy, Janna, Gail, Lori. Student, Cornell U., 1951—52; BA, Centenary Coll., Hackettstown, N.J., 1983. Prodn. asst. Your Hit Parade Batten, Barton, Durstine & Osborne, 1953-54; pvt. practice polit. cons., 1954-66; legal sec., asst Atty. John C. Cushman, 1966-68; field dep. L.A. County Assessor Office, 1968-69; pub. info. officer L.A. County Probation Dept., 1969-73; dir. consumer rels. Fireman's Fund, San Francisco, 1973-76; spl. projects officer L.A. County Transp. Commn., 1977-78; tchr. Calif. State U., Dominguez Hills, 1979-86. Editor, writer Jet Propulsion Lab., 1979—80; pub. info. dir. L.A. Bd. Pub. Works, 1980—82; pub. info. cons. City of Pasadena, Calif., 1982—84, pub. rels. cons., 1983—90; cmty. affairs cons. Worldport L.A., 1990—92; tchr. Kern County Schs., 2002—. Contbr. articles to profl. jours. Active First United Meth. Ch. Commn. Missions and Social Concerns, 1983—89; bd. dirs. Depot, 1983—87; mem. devel. com. Pasadena Guidance Clinics, 1984—85; pres. Cultural Arts Assn., Bear Valley Springs, 1999—2000, Calif. Press Women, Bay Area, 1975-89. Recipient Pro award, L.A. Publicity Club, 1978, Outstanding Achievement award, Soc. Consumer Affairs Profls. Bus., 1976, Disting. Alumni award, Centenary Coll., 1992. Mem.: Nat. Assn. Mental Health Info. Officers (3 regional awards 1986), Calif. Press Women (pres. Bay area 1975—76, award 1974, 1978, 1983, 1984, 1985, Cmty. Rels. 1st pl. winner 1986, 1987, 1988, 1989), Nat. Press Women (Calif. chpt. pres. 1975—76, Pub. Rels. award 1986), Pub. Rels. Soc. Am. (accredited mem., consumer program award 1977, 2 awards 1984, Joseph Roos Cmty. Svc. award 1985). Republican. Home and Office: 24145 Jacaranda Dr Tehachapi CA 93561-8309 Office Phone: 661-821-3804.

**SMITS, EDWARD JOHN,** historian, consultant; b. Freeport, NY, Dec. 11, 1933; s. Karl M. and Jennie (Spring) S.; m. Ruth K. Hall; children: E. John, Robert K., Theodore R. BA, Hofstra U., 1955; MA, NYU, NY, 1959. Curator Nassau County Hist. Mus., East Meadow, NY, 1956-70; dir. Div.sn Mus. Svc. Nassau County, Syosset, NY, 1971-92. Nassau County historian, 1985—; planning coord. Mus. at Mitchel Ctr., 1994-2001; chmn. Nassau County Centennial Com.; CEO, Museums at Mitchel Cradle of Aviation, 2002-04. Author: Long Island Landmarks, 1970, Creation of Nassau County, 1959, Nassau, Suburbia USA, 1974. Trustee Friends for L.I.'s Heritage, Nassau County Hist. Soc.; trustee, past pres. Levittown Libr. Bd. 1st lt. U.S. Army, 1955-56. Fulbright grantee, 1965; recipient Nassau County disting. svc. award, 1970, alumni disting. svc. award Hofstra U., 1970, Achievement award N.Y. State Historians, 2004 Mem. Am. Assn. Mus. Avocations: book collecting, antique toys, golf. Home: 14 Wavy Ln Wantagh NY 11793-1202

**SMITS, HELEN LIDA,** medical education administrator, educator; b. Long Beach, Calif., Dec. 3, 1936; d. Theodore Richard Smits and Anna Mary Wells; m. Roger LeCompte, Aug. 28, 1976; 1 child, Theodore. BA with honors, Swarthmore Coll., 1958; MA, Yale U., 1961, MD cum laude, 1967. Intern, asst. resident Hosp. U. Pa., 1967—69; fellow Beth Israel Hosp., Boston, 1969-70; chief resident Hosp. U. Pa., 1970-71; chief med. clinic U. Pa., 1971-75; assoc. adminstr. for patient care svcs. U. Pa. Hosp., 1975-77; v.p. med. affairs Community Health Plan Georgetown U., Washington, 1977; dir. health standards and quality bur. Health Care Financing Adminstrn., HHS, Washington, 1977-80; sr. rsch. assoc. The Urban Inst., Washington, 1980-81; assoc. prof. Yale U. Med. Sch., New Haven, 1981-85; assoc. v.p. for health affairs U. Conn. Health Ctr., Farmington, 1985-87; prof. community medicine U. Conn. Sch. Medicine, Farmington, 1985-93; hosp. dir. John Dempsey Hosp., Farmington, 1987-93; dep. administr. Health Care Financing Adminstrn., Washington, 1993-96; pres., chmn. Health Right, Inc., Meriden, Conn., 1996-99; vis. prof. Robert F. Wagner Grad. Sch. Pub. Svc., NYU, 1999—2001. Commr. Joint Com. on Accreditation Hosps., Chgo., 1989-93, chair, 1991-92; mem., co-chair strategic framework bd. Nat. Forum on Health Care Quality Measurement and Reporting, 2000—01; Fulbright lectr. faculty medicine Eduardo Mondlane U., Maputo, Mozambique, 2001-04. Contbr. numerous articles to profl. jours. Bd. dirs. The Ivoryton Playhouse Fedn., Inc., 1990-92, The Connecticut River Mus., 1990-93, Hartford Stage, 1990-93; mem. Dem. Town Com., Essex, Conn., 1982-89; vol. The William J. Clinton Found., Mozambique, 2000-04. Recipient Superior Svc. award HHS, Washington, 1982; Royal Soc. Medicine Found. fellow, London, 1973; Fulbright scholar, 1959-60. Mem. ACP (master, regent 1984-90), Inst. Medicine (vice chmn. com. for evaluation of PEPPAR implementation 2005—), Nat. Acad. Scis., Phi Beta Kappa, Alpha Omega Alpha. Episcopalian. Avocations: sailing, cooking, gardening.

**SMITS, JIMMY,** actor; b. Bklyn., July 9, 1955; m. Barbara Smits 1981 (div. 1987); 2 children. BA in Theatre, Bklyn. Coll., 1980; MFA, Cornell Univ., 1982. Appearances include Off-Broadway prodns., tours with regional theatres, Anna in the Tropics, 2005; (TV series) Miami Vice, 1984, L.A. Law, 1986-91 (Emmy award Outstanding Actor in Dramatic Series 1990), NYPD Blue, 1994-98, The West Wing, 2004-06 (Outstanding Actor in a TV Series, Nat. Coun. La Raza ALMA award (Am. Latin Media Arts), 2006); (TV movies) Rockabye, 1986, The Highwayman, 1987, Glitz, 1988, The Broken Cord, 1991, Stephen King's The Tommyknockers, 1993, The Cisco Kid, 1994, Solomon & Sheba, 1995, Marshal Law, 1996, (voice) Mother Goose: A Rappin' and Rhymin' Special, 1997, Lackawanna Blues, 2005; (films) Running Scared, 1986, The Believers, 1987, Old Gringo, 1988, Vital Signs, 1989, Fires Within, 1989, Switch, 1990, Gross Misconduct, 1992, The Cisco Kid, 1993, Solomon & Sheba, 1994, My Family, 1994, Marshal Law, 1995, Murder in Mind, 1996, Lesser Prophets, 1997, Bless the Child, 2000, The Million Dollar Hotel, 2000, Price of Glory, 2000, Star Wars: Episode II - Attack of the Clones, 2002, Angel, 2003, Star Wars III - Revenge of the Sith, 2005. Co-founder, mem. bd. dirs. Nat. Hispanic Found. Arts. Avocations: football, basketball, softball, reading. Office: care Sherman Mgmt 1516 S Beverly Dr Apt 304 Los Angeles CA 90035-3059 also: Nat Hispanic Found Arts Waterfront Center 1010 Wisconsin Ave NW Ste 650 Washington DC 20007*

**SMITS, RONALD FRANCIS,** language educator, poet; b. Bayonne, NJ, Dec. 22, 1943; s. Edwin Joseph and Florence Ann Smits; m. Bonnie Lee Brown, June 10, 1970 (div. Mar. 1976); 1 child, Ronald Thomas. AB, Rutgers U., 1966; MS, Ind. State U., 1969; PhD, Ball State U., 1978. Instr. English Kaskaskia Coll., Centralia, Ill., 1969-74; instr. Ball State U., Muncie, Ind., 1976-78; asst. prof. English, Indiana U. Pa., 1979-92, assoc. prof., 1992-96, prof., 1996—. Contbr. poems to jours. 1st lt. U.S. Army, 1966-68, Vietnam. Doctoral fellow Ball State U., 1974-78; Disting. Faculty Award, Creativ Arts, Indiana U. Pa, 1993; recipient Outstanding Faculty award English Assn. of Pa. State U., 2002. Avocations: walking, nature hikes, nature study, reading. Home: PO Box 466 Ford City PA 16226-0466 Office: Indiana U of Pa Northpointe Campus 167 Northpointe Blvd Freeport PA 16229-2699 Office Phone: 724-294-3300. Business E-Mail: rfsmits@iup.edu.

**SMITTLE, NELSON DEAN,** military analyst, artist; b. Peebles, Ohio, Sept. 19, 1934; s. Nelson John and Alma Katherine (Green) S.; m. Claire Wiggins, May 5, 1973. BS, BFA, U. Cin., 1962, MA, 1971. Commd. 2d lt. US Army, 1962; staff officer US Army Photo Agy. Pentagon, Washington, 1966; detachment comdr. tactical comms. Vietnam, 1967-68; commn. transferred to USAF, 1970; instr. art U. Cin., 1972; combr. 907th comunications squadron Rickenbacker AFB, Ohio, 1972; dir. ops. fixed communications Air Combat Command Langley AFB, Va., 1982; dir. info. systems AWACS Saudi Arabia, 1984-85; dep. chief of staff standard systems Air Material Command Wright-Patterson AFB, Ohio, 1985; comdr. engring. installation divsn. Tinker AFB, Okla., 1988; commd. col. ret. USAF, Cin., 1988, 91, ret., 1991; pres. Falcon Techs., Cin. 1991-98; tchr. Princeton City Sch. Dist., Cin., 1992-94; pres. Thumbs Up Aerospace Art, Cin., 1998—; instr. art history Cin. State Tech. & Cmty. Coll., 2000—; mil. analyst 700 WLW AM Radio, Cin., 2001—, WCPO TV, 2003— WXIX TV, 2001—, WWNC AM Radio,

2006—, WNKU FM Radio, 2006—; lectr. Thumbs Up Am., Ams. at War, 2001—. Lectr. USAF Mus., Ams. at War, 2002—; cons. Air War Coll., Air U., Maxwell AFB, Ala., 1987—; Def. Systems Mgmt. Coll., Ft. Belvoir, Va., 1988—; faculty Cin. Acad. Leadership U. Cin. Coll. Law, 2003—. Author: Army Visual Presentation, 1966 (medal 1966), Famous Moments in Aerospace History, 1997; exhibited in group shows Mus. of Flight, Seattle, 1997, Midland Arts Ctr., Mich., 1997, Wichita Ctr Arts, 1998, Ralice Studio, Cin., 1998, Master Works Exhibit, Cin., 1999, Cin. Mus. Ctr., 1998, Mus. Aviation, Warner Robbins, Ga., 1999, Pub. Libr. Cin., Hamilton County, Ohio, 1999, Cin. Art Club, 2001, Kathy McCoy Design Studio, Batavia, Ohio, 2004, The Miterbox Studio, Cin., 2005; mil. cons. costume dept. Across the Universe, film prodn., 2006; author cover art Jour. of League of World War I Aviation Historians, Jour. WWI Aviation Historians, 1999. Mem. Batavia City Coun., Ohio, 1972; pres. Ohio Buckeye Wing Assn., Columbus, 1973; mem. Air Force Policy Coun., Washington, 1978; congl. campaign mgr., 1993; bd. dirs. Cin. Art Club, 1995-96. Decorated Commendation medal; recipient Meritorious Svc. medal Dept. Def., 1986, 91. Mem.: VFW, DAV, Mil. Officers Assn. Am. (v.p., dir. pub. affairs Cin. chpt.), Am. Soc. Aviation Artists, Res. Officers Assn., Air Force Assn., Spl. Ops. Warrior Found., 82d Airborne Assn., Aircraft Owners and Pilots Assn. Avocations: writing, walking, science fiction. Home and Office: Thumbs Up America 198 Palisades Pointe Cincinnati OH 45238-5653 Office Phone: 513-922-6018. Personal E-mail: deanstargate@aol.com.

**SMOAK, EVAN L.,** lawyer; b. Columbia, SC, Jan. 30, 1967; s. Lewis E. and Phyllis Anderson. BA cum laude, U. S.C., 1989; JD, U. Va., 1992. Bar: Conn. 1992, NY 1993, US Dist. Ct. (so. and ea. dists.) NY 1993, US Ct. Appeals (2d cir.) 2000, US Ct. Appeals (7th cir.) 2004. Actor S.C. Ednl. Television, Columbia, 1977-86; atty. Werner & Kennedy, N.Y.C., 1992-97; assoc., ptnr. Barger & Wolen, N.Y.C., 1997—. Art auction co-chair Empire State Pride Agenda, NYC, 1996-98, devel. com., 1999-2005, bd. dirs., 2000-2005, N100 fundraiser co-chair, 2001-02, exec. com. 2002-05, bd. counsel, 2002-04; vice-chair fall dinner fundraiser, 2002, co-chair, 2003; bd. dirs. Empire State Pride Agenda Found., 2005—; arbitrator cert. com., AIDA Reinsurance and Insurance Arbitration Soc., 2005—. Recipient Thomas Moore Craig award U. S.C., 1988; Carolina scholar, 1985-89, Nat. Merit scholar, 1985-89. Mem. ABA, Assn. Bar of City of N.Y., Phi Beta Kappa, Omicron Delta Kappa. Democrat. Home: 450 W 24th St New York NY 10011 Office: Barger & Wolen LLP 10 E 40th St 40th Fl New York NY 10016 Office Phone: 212-557-2800.

**SMOAK, LEWIS TYSON,** lawyer; b. Orangeburg, S.C., Feb. 11, 1944; s. William B. and Louise (Dempsey) S.; m. Elizabeth Adams Babb, July 16, 1969; children— Katherine, Blair, Tyson. B.A., Furman U., 1966; J.D., U. S.C., 1969. Bar: S.C. 1969, D.C. 1982. Founder, Ogletree, Deakins, Nash, Smoak and Stewart, Greenville, S.C., 1969—. Fellow Coll. Labor and Employment Lawyers; mem. ABA, Greenville County Bar Assn., S.C. Bar Assn., D.C. Bar Assn., Poinsett Club, Greenville Country Club, Wade Hampton Golf Club (Cashiers, N.C.), Doonbeg (Ireland) Golf Club. Office: 300 N Main St Greenville SC 29601 Office Phone: 864-271-1300.

**SMOAK, RANDOLPH DUNCAN, JR.,** surgeon; b. Bamberg, SC, May 5, 1933; MD, Med. Coll. S.C., 1959. Diplomate Am. Bd. Surgery. Intern Grady Meml. Hosp., Atlanta, 1959-60; resident surgery Med. U. S.C.-Teaching Hosps., 1962-65, resident, tchg. fellow, 1965-66; fellow surgery MD Anderson Cancer Ctr., Houston, 1966-67; surg. staff Orangeburg (S.C.) Calhoun Regional Hosp., 1967-87, emeritus staff, 1987; clin. prof. surgery Med. U. S.C., Charleston, 1987—, U.S.C. Sch. Medicine, Columbia, 86—. Fellow ACS; mem. AMA (pres. 2000-01), So. Med. Assn., Soc. Head and Neck Surgeons, So. Soc. Clin. Surgeons, Soc. Clin. Oncology. Office: 275 Mason Rd Orangeburg SC 29118-8201 Personal E-mail: randysmoak@earthlink.net. Business E-Mail: smoak@ama-assn.org.

**SMOCK, DONALD JOE,** information technology manager, political scientist; b. Ponca City, Okla., Sept. 24, 1964; s. Joe Clellan and Ruth Esther Smock. BA in Polit. Sci., U. Ctrl. Okla., 1991, MA in Urban Affairs, 1993. Rschr. The Nigh Inst. State Govt., Edmond, 1993—94; govt. liaison Elizey Electric Motor Co., 1994—96; govt. affairs dir. Oklahoma City Met. Assn. Realtors, 1997—2002; sr. zoning analyst Zoning-Info. Inc., 2003—06; zoning project mgr. Bock & Clark Corp., 2006. U. Ctrl. Okla. del. to Ctr. Study of Pres. Symposium, Washington, 1993 Charter founder Ronald Reagan Rep. Ctr., 1989; del. State of Okla. Rep. Presdl. Task Force, 1996; mem. Rep. Presdl. Trust, 1996. Recipient Okla. Rep. Blue Key award, 1984, Presdl. Commn., 1992, Merit cert. Rep. Nat. Com., 1990; named to Ronald Reagan Rep. Ctr. Presdl. Commemorative Honor Roll, 1991; by order of President George Bush flag dedicated in name Rotunda of U.S. Capitol, 1990. Mem. Tau Kappa Epsilon (Delta Nu colony inductee, chpt. advisor 1990-92, Fraternity for Life inductee, David Crain Leadership award 1986, Ed Howell Leadership award 1988-89, Red Carnation Ball dedicated in name 1989-90, 94, Top Alumnus 1990-91), Pi Sigma Alpha. Republican. Mem. Ch. of Christ. Home: PO Box 6323 Edmond OK 73083-6323 Office Phone: 405-525-2998 x105. Personal E-mail: donaldjsmock@yahoo.com.

**SMOCK, RAYMOND WILLIAM,** historian; b. Jeffersonville, Ind., Feb. 8, 1941; s. Richard and Lottie (Paciorek) S.; m. Phyllis Lee Chadwick, Feb. 12, 1961 BA, Roosevelt U., Chgo., 1966; PhD, U. Md., College Park, 1974. Rsch. asst. Md. Constl. Conv., Annapolis, 1967-68; lectr. in history U. Md., College Park, 1968-72; co-editor The Booker T. Washington Papers, 14 vols., 1972-83; pres. Instructional Resources Corp., Lanham, Md., 1976-83, Rsch. Materials Corp., College Park, 1982-83, dir., 1982-85; historian, dir. Office for Bicentennial, U.S. Ho. of Reps., Washington, 1983-89, Office of Historian, U.S. Ho. of Reps., Washington, 1989-95. Mem. editl. advisors Md. Historian, College Park, 1971—95; exec. dir. Robert C. Byrd Ctr. for Legis. Studies, Shepherd U., Shepherdstown, W.Va., 2002—. Author: A Talent for Detail: The Photographs of Miss Frances Benjamin Johnston 1889-1910, 1974; co-editor: A Guide to Manuscripts in the Presidential Libraries, 1985, Masters of the House, 1998; editor: Booker T. Washington in Perspective: The Essays of Louis R. Harlan, 1988; author, editor: Landmark Documents on the U.S. Congress, 1998. Bd. dirs. W.Va. Humanities Coun., 2006—, Ford Found. fellow, 1970; recipient Philip M. Hamer award Soc. Am. Archivists, 1979 Mem. Nat. Coun. Pub. History, Assn. for Documentary Editing (pres. 1983-84), Orgn. Am. Historians, So. Hist. Assn., Soc. History in Fed. Govt. (v.p./pres.-elect 2000—), Assn. Crs. for Study of Congress (pres. 2005—), W.Va. Humanities Coun. (bd. mem. 2006—). Avocations: photography, astronomy. Office Phone: 304-876-5670. E-mail: RaySmock@aol.com, rsmock@shepherd.edu.

**SMOCK, TIMOTHY ROBERT,** lawyer; b. Richmond, Ind., June 24, 1951; s. Robert Martin and Thelma Elizabeth (Cozad) S.; m. Martha Carolene Middleton, Apr. 4, 1992; children: Andrew Zoller, Alison Pierce. BA, Wittenberg U., 1973; JD cum laude, Ind. U., 1977. Bar: Ind. 1977, Ariz. 1979, U.S. Dist. Ct. (so. dist.) Ind. 1977, U.S. Dist. Ct. Ariz. 1979, U.S. Ct. Appeals (7th cir.) 1977, U.S. Ct. Appeals (9th cir.) 1979. Jud. clk. Ct. of Appeals of Ind., Indpls., 1977-79; assoc. Lewis and Roca, Phoenix, 1979-82; assoc./shareholder Gallagher & Kennedy, Phoenix, 1982-89; ptnr. Scult, French, Zwillinger & Smock, Phoenix, 1989-94, Smock and Weinberger, Phoenix, 1994-99, Richards and Smock, Phoenix, 1999—2005, Zwillinger & Georgelos, 2005—. Judge, pro tempore Maricopa County Superior Ct., Phoenix, 1989—; faculty, State Bar Course on Professionalism, Ariz. Supreme Ct/State Bar, Phoenix, 1992—; speaker, Continuing Legal Edn., Maricopa County and Ariz. State Bar, 1988—. Mem. ABA, Ariz. Bar Assn., Maricopa Bar Assn. Office: Zwillinger & Georgelos Ste 600 2425 E Camelback Rd Phoenix AZ 85016 Office Phone: 602-224-7888. E-mail: Timothy.Smock@azbar.org.

**SMOKER, ROY ELLIS,** retired military officer; b. Richmond, Ind. Dec. 7, 1943; s. Vernon Willard and Emma May (Creager) S.; m. Linda Carol Kensinger, Sept. 7, 1969; children: Cheryl Lynn, Deborah June; m. JoAnn Bratcher, May, 2001. BA in Econs. and Math., Blackburn Coll., 1965; MA in Econs., U. N.D., 1967; PhD, U. Mo., 1984. Commd. 2d lt. USAF, 1971, advanced through grades to col., 1992, chief rsch. integration Office Productivity and Rsch., 1980-82, sr. mil. estate program analyst Office Sec. Def., 1982-84, sr. logistics analyst, 1984-85, dep. dir., dir. program control Milstar Joint Program Office, 1985-89, chief econ. analysis asst. sec. USAF for fin. mgmt., 1989-90, chief space and strategic def., 1990-91; dir. bus. ops. Titan Sys. Program Office, 1991-93; comptroller Arnold Engring. Devel. Ctr., 1993-95, Air Force Devel. TestCtr., 1995-97, Air Force Space and Missile System Ctr., 1997-2000; dir. program mgmt. MCR Fed., LLC, 2001—. Bd. dirs. Aerospace Fed. Credit Union, 1998-2000; fin. advisor Alzheimer's Assn., Tullahoma, Tenn., 1993-95; chmn. bd. trustees 1st United Meth. Ch., Huntington Beach, Calif., 1987-89. Decorated Joint Svc. Achievement medals, Air Orgnl. Excellence award, and numerous others. Mem. Mo. U. Alumni Assn., Air Force Assn., Soc. Cost Estimating and Analysis, Am. Soc. Mil. Comptrollers (pres. L.A. chpt. 1998), Franklin County C. of C. (bd. dirs. 1993-95). Office Phone: 310-640-0005.

**SMOLANSKY, BETTIE MORETZ,** sociology educator; b. Columbia, S.C., June 1940; d. Walter Jennings Sr. and Opal (Ledford) Moretz; m. Oles M. Smolansky, Dec. 29, 1966; children: Alexandra Smolansky Zentmeyer, Nicholas Jennings. AB in Sociology, Lenoir-Rhyne Coll., 1962; MA in Sociology, Duke U., 1964; PhD in Sociology, Pa. State U., 1984. From instr. sociology to prof. Moravian Coll., Bethlehem, Pa., 1964—88, prof., 1988—, chmn. Dept. Sociology, 1991—97, 2005—, interim dean faculty, 1998—99, dean acad. affairs, 2000—01. Trustee Moravian Coll., 1977-81, 91-95, NEH visitor core curriculum workshop, 1985, sec. presdl. search com., 1996-97; mem. curriculum evaluation conf. Bklyn. Coll., 1988. Co-author: The USSR and Iraq, 1991 (AAAS Marshall Schulman prize 1992), The Lost Equilibrium, 2001. Bd. dirs. Northampton County Area on Aging, Bethlehem, 1984-90, 2003—; vice chair United Way Allocations Panel, Bethlehem, 1984-90; chair YWCA Commn. on Status of Women, Bethlehem, 1992-94; bd. dirs. YWCA of Bethlehem, 1993-97, 98-2002, 1st v.p., 1998-2000, pres., 2001-02. Recipient NDEA fellow, 1962-64, Disting. Alumnus award Lenoir-Rhyne Coll., 1995. Mem. Am. Sociol. Assn., Ea. Sociol. Assn., Lehigh Valley Assn. Acad. Women (pres. 1988-89, Woman of Yr. 1995-96), ODK (advisor 1987-90), AKD (advisor 1991—). Home: 3665 Walt Whitman Ln Bethlehem PA 18017-1553 Office: Moravian Coll Dept Sociology 1200 Main St Bethlehem PA 18018-6650 Office Phone: 610-861-1317. Office Fax: 610-625-7811. E-mail: mebms01@moravian.edu.

**SMOLANSKY, OLES M.,** retired humanities educator; b. Ukraine, USSR, May 2, 1930; came to U.S. 1950; s. Mykola S. and Irene (Plinto) S.; m. Bettie Moretz, Dec. 29, 1966; children: Alexandra, Nicholas. BA, NYU, 1953; MA, Columbia U., 1955, PhD, 1959. Instr. UCLA, 1960-62; asst. prof. Lehigh U., Bethlehem, Pa., 1963-66, assoc. prof., 1966-70, prof., 1970-85, univ. prof., 1985—2005, emeritus univ. prof., 2005—. Author: The Soviet Union and the Arab East Under Khrushchev, 1974, The USSR and Iraq: The Soviet Quest for Influence, 1991; co-editor: Russia and America: From Rivalry to Reconciliation, 1993, Regional Power Rivalries in the New Eurasia: Russia, Turkey, and Iran, 1995, The Lost Equilibrium: International Relations in the Post-Soviet Era, 2001; contbr. articles to profl. jours. Recipient joint fellowship, Rockefeller Found. and Ford Found., N.Y.C., 1962-63, sr. rsch. joint fellowship, Rsch. Inst. on Communist Affairs and Mid. East Inst., Columbia U., N.Y.C., 1972-73, rsch. fellowship, Ford Found., N.Y.C., 1980-81. Mem. Internat. Studies Assn., Am. Assn. for Advancement of Slavic Studies (Marshall Shulman award 1992), Mid. East Studies Assn., Mid. East Inst. Democrat. Greek-Orthodox. Avocations: music, sports. Home: 3665 Walt Whitman Ln Bethlehem PA 18017-1553 Office: Lehigh U Dept Internat Rels Bethlehem PA 18015 Office Phone: 610-758-3388. Business E-mail: oms0@lehigh.edu.

**SMOLEN, LEE M.,** lawyer; b. 1960; BS with highest honors, Univ. Ill., 1982; JD, Univ. Chgo., 1985. CPA; bar: NY 1985. Assoc. Sidley Austin Brown & Wood, Chgo., 1985—93, ptnr. real estate practice, 1993—, and mem. practice devel. com. Mem.: ABA. Office: Sidley Austin Brown & Wood LLP Bank One Plz 10 S Dearborn St Chicago IL 60603 Office Phone: 312-853-7823. Office Fax: 312-853-7036. Business E-Mail: lsmolen@sidley.com.

**SMOLENSKI, LISABETH ANN,** physician; b. Pitts., Oct. 1, 1950; d. Anthony Edward and Betty Jean (Gross) S.; m. William Ward Daniels, May 24, 1980; 1 child, Kathryn Elizabeth. BA, Carlow Coll., 1972; MD, Hahnemann U., 1982. Diplomate Am. Bd. Family Practice. Resident in family practice West Jersey Health Sys., Voorhees, N.J., 1982-85; pvt. practice, Somerville, Tenn., 1985-90, Memphis, 1990—2003; with Spectrum Pain Clinics, Franklin-Nashville, Tenn., 2003—04; Cumberland Back Pain PC, Cookeville, Tenn., 2005—, Clarksville, Tenn., 2005—. Sec. exec. com. med. staff Meth. Hosp. Somerville, 1988-90. Fellow: Am. Acad. Family Physicians. Republican. Avocation: reading. Office: Cumberland Back Pain Clinic PC 440 Med St Cookeville TN 38501 also: Cumberland Back Pain Clinic PC 271 Med Park Dr Clarksville TN 37043-6310 Office Phone: 931-520-8104, 931-647-5747.

**SMOLENSKY, EUGENE,** economics professor; b. Bklyn., Mar. 4, 1932; s. Abraham and Jennie (Miller) S.; m. Natalie Joan Rabinowitz, Aug. 16, 1952; children: Paul, Beth. BA, Bklyn. Coll., 1952; MA, Am. U., 1956; PhD, U. Pa., 1961. Prof. econs. U. Wis., Madison, 1968-88, chmn. dept., 1978-80, 86-88; dir. Inst. for Research on Poverty, U. Wis., 1980-83; dean Grad. Sch. Pub. Policy, U. Calif., Berkeley, 1988-97, prof. pub. policy, 1997—. Author: Public Expenditures, Taxation and the Distribution of Income: The U.S., 1950, 61, 70, 77. Mem. Nat. Acad. Pub. Adminstrn., 1994; mem. com. on child devel. rsch. and pub. policy NAS, Washington, 1982-87, mem. com. on status of women in labor market 1985-87. With USN, 1952-56. Mem. Am. Econs. Assn. Democrat. Jewish. Avocation: master etching and lithograph collecting. Home: 669 Woodmont Ave Berkeley CA 94708-1233 Office: U Calif Dept Pub Policy 2607 Hearst Ave Berkeley CA 94720-7305 Office Phone: 510-643-3979. Business E-mail: geno@berkeley.edu.

**SMOLIN, LEE,** physicist, researcher, writer; b. NYC, June 6, 1955; s. Michael and Pauline (Selman) Smolin. BA, Hampshire Coll., Amherst, Mass., 1975; AM, Harvard U., 1978, PhD in Theoretical Physics, 1979. Mem. Inst. Advanced Study, Princeton, NJ, 1979, 1981—83; postdoctoral physicist Inst. Theoretical Physics, Santa Barbara, Calif., 1980-81; postdoctoral rschr. U. Chgo. Enrico Fermi Inst., 1983—84; asst. prof. Yale U., New Haven, 1984—88; assoc. prof. Syracuse U., NY, 1988-91, prof., 1991—93, Pa. State U., 1993—2001; mem. faculty Perimeter Inst. Theoretical Physics, Waterloo, Ont., Canada, 2001—. Adj. prof. physics dept. U. Waterloo, Canada, 2001—. Contbr. articles to profl. jours.; author: Life of the Cosmos, 1997, Three Roads to Quantum Gravity, 2000, The Trouble with Physics, 2006. Active Clamshell Alliance, 1978; organizer Star Wars Pledge Campaign, 1984-86. Co-recipient First award essay Gravity Rsch. Found., 1985, 2nd award, 1981, 83. Mem. Internat. Soc. Gen. Relativity and Gravitation. Avocations: jazz guitar, sailing, philosophy. Office: Perimeter Inst Theoretical Physics 31 Caroline St N Waterloo ON Canada N2L 2Y5 E-mail: lee@Qgravity.org.*

**SMOLKE, CHRISTINA,** chemical engineer; BSChemE summa cum laude, U. So. Calif., 1997; PhD in Chem. Engring., U. Calif., Berkeley, 2001. Postdoctoral rschr. U. Calif., Berkeley, 2001—03; asst. prof. chem. engring. Calif. Inst. Tech. Contbr. articles to profl. jours. Named one of Top 100 Young Innovators, MIT Tech. Review, 2004; Postdoctoral fellow, NIH, 2001. Office: Calif Inst Tech Bioengring Faculty MC 210-41 236 A Spalding Pasadena CA 91125

**SMOLLA, RODNEY ALAN,** dean, law educator; b. Pueblo, Colo., Mar. 13, 1953; s. Richard Paul and Harriet (Waskowiak) S. BA, Yale U., 1975; JD, Duke U., 1978. Bar: Ill. 1979, U.S. Supreme Ct. 1987. Law clk. to presiding judge U.S. Ct. Appeals, Jackson, Miss., 1978-79; assoc. Mayer, Brown & Pratt, Chgo., 1979-80; asst. prof. De Paul U. Sch. Law, Chgo., 1980-81, U. Ill. Coll. Law, 1981-83; prof. U. Ark. Sch. Law, 1983-87; vis. prof. U. Denver Coll. Law, 1987-88; Arthur B. Hanson prof. constl. law Coll. of William and

Mary, Williamsburg, Va., 1988-98, dir. Inst. Bill of Rights Law, 1988-96; dean, George E. Allen prof. U. Richmond Sch. Law, 1998—. Author: Suing the Press: Libel, The Media & Power, 1986 (cert. of merit ABA 1987), Law of Defamation, 1986, Jerry Falwell v. Larry Flynt: The First Amendment on Trial, 1988; (with Banks and Braveman) Constitutional Law: Structure and Rights in Our Federal System, 1991, 3rd edit., 1996, Free Speech in an Open Society, 1992 (William O. Douglas Prize 1993), Smolla and Nimmer on Freedom of Speech, 1994, 3rd edit., 1996, Federal Civil Rights Acts, 1994; editor: A Year in the Life of the Supreme Court, 1995 (ABA Silver Gavel award), Deliberate Intent: A Lawyer Tells the True Story of Murder by the Book, 1999. Fellow, cons. Annenberg Washington Program in Communications, 1987-96; project dir. Annenberg Libel Reform Task Force, 1988-89; reporter Bill of Rights Adv. Com. to the Commn. on the Bicentennial of U.S. Constitution, 1989—. Recipient Recipient Disting. Prof. of Yr. award, U. Ark., 1986, Outstanding Faculty award, Va. State Coun. Higher Edn., 2002. Mem. ABA, Ill. Bar Assn., AAUP (mem. litigation com. 1988—). Office: U Richmond TC Williams Sch of Law Richmond VA 23173 Home: 1848 W Grace St Richmond VA 23220 Office Phone: 804-289-8197. Office Fax: 804-289-8994. E-mail: rsmolla@richmond.edu.

**SMOLLER, BRUCE MELVYN,** psychiatrist; b. Chgo., Sept. 19, 1944; s. Norman and Beatrice Betty (Janows) Smoller; m. Cosette Nieporent, Aug. 20, 1967; children: Jamie, Lauren. AB, Cornell U., 1965; MD, Tulane U., 1969. Diplomate Am. Bd. Psychiatry and Neurology. Intern Maimonides Med. Ctr., N.Y.C., 1969-70; resident in orthopedic surgery Einstein Med. Ctr., N.Y.C., 1970-73; resident in psychiatry Cornell Med. Ctr., N.Y.C., 1973-76; pvt. practice in psychiatry with emphasis on clin. and rsch. aspects of pain Bethesda, Md., 1976—; chmn. dept. psychiatry Holy Cross Hosp., Silver Spring, Md., 1980-83; assoc. clin. prof. psychiatry George Washington U., 1977-91, clin. prof. psychiatry, 1991—. Cons. NIH, 1979—2001. Co-author: Pain Control: The Bethesda Program; editor: Md. Medicine, The State Med. Soc.'s Jour. With Med. Corps USAR, 1970—78. Mem.: Med. and Chirurgical Faculty of Md. (trustee), Montgomery County Med. Soc. (pres. 2004—05). Office: 5530 Wisconsin Ave Bethesda MD 20815-4404 Office Phone: 301-951-4466. E-mail: bsmoller@radix.net.

**SMOLTZ, JOHN ANDREW,** professional baseball player; b. Warren, Mich., May 15, 1967; With Detroit Tigers, 1985—87; pitcher Atlanta Braves, 1987—. Named Nat. League Pitcher of the Yr., Sporting News, 1996, NLCS MVP, 1996; named to All-Star Game, Nat. League, 1989, 1992, 1993, 1996, 2002, 2003; recipient Roberto Clemente award, 2005, Cy Young award, Baseball Writers' Assn. Am., 1996, Rolaids Relief Man, 2002. Achievements include leading Nat. League in strikeouts, 1992. Office: Atlanta Braves Turner Field PO Box 4064 Atlanta GA 30302-4064*

**SMOLYANSKY, JULIE,** consumer products company executive; d. Michael and Ludmila Smolyansky. BA, U. Ill., 1996. Dir. sales and mktg. Lifeway Foods Inc., Morton Grove, Ill., 1997—2002, pres., 2002—, CEO, 2002—, CFO, 2002—, treas., 2002—, dir. Avocation: running. Office: Lifeway Foods Inc 6431 West Oakton Ave Morton Grove IL 60053

**SMOOT, BURGESS HOWARD,** federal official; b. Washington, Mar. 28, 1947; s. James Elias and Frances Galdinia (Hawkins) S.; m. Ann Louise Gordon, Aug. 9, 1982; children: Frederick Hawkins, Chanel Gordon, Ervine Gholston, Shemerrian. Cook Freedmans Hosp., Washington, 1968-70; mail & file clk. asst. Chief of Staff Intelligence, Washington, 1970-74; adminstrv. asst. logistics Office Joint Chiefs of Staff, Pentagon, Washington, 1974-77, adminstrv. asst. policy & plans, 1977-80. Author: (poetry) Lost in the Beginning. Capt. Neighborhood Watch Group, Fort Washington, Md., 1995-97; presdl. election official, 2000—, primary election judge for Md., 2002, primary and gen. presdl. election judge, 2004; judge for Md. gov., 2002; pres. Sunday Schs. 12rs. through adult Capital Ward, 2002—04, libr., 2004—; judge primary and gen. elections Md., 2006. With U.S. Army, 1965-68, Civil Air Patrol, 1964-65. Decorated Army Commendation medal, Combat Infantry badge, Good Conduct medal, Nat. Def. medal, Vietnam Svc. medal, Vietnam Campaign ribbon, Sharp Shooter's Medal. Mem. Disabled Am. Vets. (comdr., svc. officer, sgt. at arms, hon. guard). Democrat. Mem. Lds Ch. Avocations: baseball, football, wrestling, bowling, pool. Home: 10103 Kathleen Dr Fort Washington MD 20744-2530

**SMOOT, DAVID PAUL,** finance company executive; b. Guthrie, Okla., Jan. 9, 1947; s. Jerry Edward and Katherine Ann (Doyle) S.; m. Marie Kathleen Stokes, Aug. 6, 1971; children: Aimee, Melissa. Student, Cumberland Coll., 1965—67, Glassboro State Coll., 1967, U. Cin., 1968—69. Regional mgr. Dennison Mfg., Chgo., 1969-77, Wordstream, Chgo., 1978-79; dist. mgr. AM Jacquard, San Francisco, 1979-82; co-founder, v.p. sales Phaser Systems Pub. Co., San Francisco, 1980-82; dir. ctrl. ops. Digital Rsch., Schaumburg, Ill., 1982-85; founder, chmn. bd., CEO Software Funding Internat., Deerfield, Ill., 1985-89, Software Funding Internat. (acquired by The Meridian Group), Deerfield, Ill., 1989; pres. Meridian Software Funding, 1989-92, Am. Indian Svcs. Inc., 1992-95; pres., founder Airborne Remote Mapping, 1995-98, Am. Indian Fin. Svcs. LLC, 1998—; founder, CEO Native Am. Water, LLC, 2002—. Mem. Native Vision program Johns Hopkins U. Hosp., NFL Players Assn. and Nick Lowery Found. Mem. bd. of consult Little City Home for Retarded, Palatine, Ill., 1986; founder, CEO Pro Players Classic Golf Invitational to Benefit Indigenous Youth, 1999—; founding mem. Robert B. Huff Scholarship Found., Chgo.; bd. dirs. Sports Legends Prostate Cancer Found., Phoenix, Ariz.; ptnr. Social Venture Ptnrs. Ariz. Served with U.S. Army, 1960-75. Mem. Assn. Data Processing Svc. Orgns., Software Publ. Assn., Syntopicaon XII, IBM PC User's Group (spkr.). Avocations: basketball, sailing, camping, fishing, tennis. Office: Natawa Corp 11 Sundial Cir Ste 19 PO Box 3800 Carefree AZ 85377 Office Phone: 480-595-5506.

**SMOOT, FRED,** professional football player; b. Jackson, Minn., Apr. 17, 1979; Attended, Miss. State, 2001. Corner back Wash. Redskins, 2001—04, Minn. Vikings, 2005—. Vol. Redskins Relief Fund, Wash., 2001—04. Recipient BJ Blanchard award, 2004, Ed Block Courage award, Redskins, 2003. Office: Minn Vikings Winter Park Admin Offices 9520 Viking Dr Eden Prairie MN 55344*

**SMOOT, LEON DOUGLAS,** chemical engineer, educator, retired dean; b. Provo, Utah, July 26, 1934; s. Douglas Parley and Jennie (Hallam) S.; m. Marian Bird, Sept. 7, 1953; children: Analee, Claudia, Michelle, Melinda Lee. BS, Brigham Young U., Provo, Utah, 1956; B in Engring. Sci., Brigham Young U., 1957; MS, U. Wash., Seattle, 1958; PhD, U. Wash., 1960. Registered profl. engr., Utah. Engr. Boeing Corp., Seattle, 1956; teaching and research asst. Brigham Young U., 1954-57; engr. Phillips Petroleum Corp., Arco, Idaho, 1957; engr., cons. Hercules Powder Co., Bacchus, Utah, 1961-63, asst. prof. Brigham Young U., 1960-63; engr. Lockheed Propulsion, Redlands, Calif., 1963-67; vis. asst. prof. Calif. Inst. Tech., 1966-67; assoc. prof. to prof. Brigham Young U., 1967—2003, prof. emeritus, 2003—, chmn. dept. chem. engring., 1970-77, dean Coll. Engring. and Tech., 1977-94, dean emeritus, 1994—; prin. Combustion Resources, Inc., 1994—. Expert witness on combustion and explosions; founding dir. Advanced Combustion Engring. Research Ctr. (NSF), 1986-97; cons. Hercules, Thiokol, Lockheed, Teledyne, Atlantic Research Corp., Raytheon, Redd and Redd, Billings Energy, Ford, Bacon & Davis, Jaycor, Intel Com Radiation Tech., Phys. Dynamics, Nat. Soc. Propellants and Explosives, France, DFVLR, West Germany, Martin Marietta, Honeywell, Phillips Petroleum Co., Exxon, Nat. Bur. Standards, Eyring Research Inst., Systems, Sci. and Software., Los Alamos Nat. Lab., others. Author 5 books on coal combustion; contbr. over 200 articles and rsch. jours. Recipient Nichols award, Am. Soc. Mech. Engring., 2002, Homer H. Lowry Gold Medal, U.S. Dept. Energy, 2002. Mem. AIChE, Nat. Fire Protection Assn., Combustion Inst., Nat. Soc. Am., Sigma Xi, Tau Beta Pi. Republican. Mem. Lds Ch. Office: Brigham Young U Chem Engring Dept 435 T CTB Provo UT 84602

**SMOOT, OLIVER REED, JR.,** lawyer, trade association administrator; b. San Antonio, Aug. 24, 1940; s. Oliver Reed and Angie Frances (Watters) Smoot; m. Sandra Lee Curry, July 25, 1964; children: Stephen Reed, Sheryl Anne. BS, MIT, 1962; JD, Georgetown U., 1966. Bar: DC 1966, Va. 1967. Computer sys. mgr. Inst. Def. Analyses, Arlington, Va., 1962-69; from program mgr., v.p., to exec. v.p. and treas. Info. Tech. Industry Coun. (formerly Computer & Bus Equipment Mfrs. Assn.), Washington, 1969-2000; v.p. external vol. stds. rels. Info Tech Industry Coun., Washington, 2000—04. Author (with others): (book) Computers and the Law, 3d edit., 1991; chpt. editor: book Toward a Law of Global Communications Networks, 2001. Pres. Internat. Orgn. Standardization, 2003—04; chmn. Am. Nat. Stds. Inst., 2001—02. Mem.: ABA (chmn. sci. and tech. sect. 1989—90), Assn. Computing Machinery, Computer Law Assn. (pres. 1990—91). Methodist. Avocations: alpine skiing, gardening.

**SMOOT, SKIPI LUNDQUIST,** psychologist; b. Aberdeen, Wash., Apr. 10, 1934; d. Warren Duncan and Miriam Stephen (Bishop) Dobbins; m. Harold Richard Lundquist, June 2, 1951 (div. Mar. 1973); children: Kurt Richard, Mark David, Ted Douglas, Blake Donald; m. Edward Lee Smoot, June 14, 1975. BA in Psychology, Coll. of William and Mary, 1978; MA, Pepperdine U., 1980; PhD, Calif. Sch. of Profl., Psychology, San Diego, 1985. Lic. clin. psychologist, Calif.; lic. marriage and family therapist, Calif. Owner, operator McDonald's Restaurants, San Pedro and Torrance, Calif., 1965-76, Williamsburg, Va., 1965-76; psychotherapist Coll. Hosp., Cerritos, Calif., 1979-81, Orange County Child Guidance, Laguna Hills, Calif., 1981-82, Calif. State Police, Costa Mesa, 1982-83, Anaheim, 1983-84; psychologist Orange County Mental Health, Santa Ana, Calif., 1984-85, Psychol. Ctr., Orange and El Toro, Calif., 1985-91; clin. dir. Career Ambitions, Lake Forest, Calif., 1991-98, Psychol. Decisions, Irvine-Laguna Hills, Calif., 1991-94. Psychol. cons. seminars and workshops for bus., Irvine and Laguna Hills, 1991-98. Mem. APA, Calif. Psychol. Assn. Democrat. Avocations: music, travel, rsch. Office: Psychol Decisions Career Ambitions Unltd 23832 Rockfield Blvd # 165 Lake Forest CA 92630-6822 Office Phone: 949-770-2675. Personal E-mail: skipilsmootphd@cox.net.

**SMORAL, VINCENT J.,** electrical engineer; b. Syracuse, N.Y., May 13, 1946; s. Anthony Vincent and Stephanie (Koutin) S.; m. Theresa W. Gut, Aug. 5, 1967; children: Jennifer, Laura, Anne. BSEE, Syracuse U., 1967. Jr. engr. Fed. Sys. Div. IBM, Owego, NY, 1967-68, adv. engr. logic design, 1968-80, sr. engr./sys., 1980-90, sr. engr./program mgr., 1990-93; sr. engr. Lockheed Martin Fed. Sys. Co., Owego, 1994—2000; program mgr. Eastman Kodak C&GS, Rochester, 2000—. Designer 688 Class Sonar, An/UYS-1 Signal Processor, AWACS Computer, 3838 Array Processor, 1968-80; mgr. AN/UYK-43 Computer, AWACS Computer, Rugged Processor, F117 Processor, 1980-93; patentee in field. Fellow AIAA (assoc.; mem. nat. computer systems tech. com. 1990-95); mem. IEEE, KC. Democrat. Roman Catholic. Avocations: swimming, sailing, fishing, skiing. Home: 12 Founders Grn Pittsford NY 14534-2165 Office: Eastman Kodak Co Commerical & Govt Sys 1447 Paul St Rochester NY 14653-7214 Office Phone: 585-726-5401. E-mail: vsmoral@rochester.rr.com.

**SMOTHERMON, REBA MAXINE,** elementary school educator; b. Liberal, Kans., July 8, 1933; d. Albert Isaac and Georga Maxine (Long) Shank; m. Wendell Scott Smothermon, Sept. 6, 1953; children: Jennifer Lynn Smothermon Kirby, Wendell Brent Smothermon. BA in Edn., Wichita State U., 1955; MA in Ednl. Psychology and Guidance, U. No. Colo., 1959. Cert. tchr. Kans., Calif., Colo., arthritis instr. Tchr. second grade Unified Sch. Dist. 480/Washington Sch., Liberal, Kans., 1955-57, Adams County Sch. Dist. Skyline Vista Sch., Westminster, Colo., 1957-61; elem. tchr. Ventura Unified Santa Ana Sch., Ojai, Calif., 1964-80, Unified Sch. Dist. #480, Southlawn McKinley Schs., Liberal, 1980-95; ret., 1995. Literary coun. mem. Southwest Reading Coun., Liberal, 1985-95. Participant devel. sch. curriculum, 1977-79. Sec. to pres. Evergreen Garden Club, Liberal, 1980-05; youth sponsor, pres. women's group 1st United Meth. Ch., Liberal, 1945—; mem. Liberal Panhellenic, 1980-96; bd. dir. pres. Community Concerts of Liberal, 1987-91; pres. Liberal Woman's Club, 1995—; mem. Kans. Coun. on Travel and Tourism, 2002-05; pres. Book Club I, sec.-treas., tchr. swimming, arthritis support groups. Recipient Lifetime Achievement award, Southwest Daily Times, 2006. Mem. AAUW (pres. local chpt. 1980—, Woman of Yr. 1985, state chmn. internat. rels. com. 1985-90),DAR (regent chaplain 1972-), PEO (various to pres. 1985—), Aurora Club, Ladies' Oriental Shrine N.Am., Delta Kappa Gamma (various to pres. 1981—). Republican. Avocations: music, reading. Home: 830 S Clay F3 PO Box 470 Liberal KS 67905-0470 Personal E-mail: smutsmut@swko.net.

**SMOTHERS, RONALD,** journalist; Reporter New York Times. Panelist NYU Multinational Inst. Am. Studies, 1998. Author: (articles) In Plea Deal a Banker Outlines Money Laundering in Caymans, 1999, Gas Stations Violated Pricing Laws, New Jersey Says, 2005. Office: New York Times Newark Bur 111 Mulberry St Newark NJ 07102 Office Phone: 973-623-3904. Office Fax: 973-802-1877.*

**SMOTHERS, TOM,** actor, singer; b. Feb. 2, 1937; s. Thomas B. and Ruth Smothers; children: Tom, Bo, Riley Rose; m. Marcy Carriker, Sept. 9, 1990. Student, San Jose State Coll. Owner winery, Kenwood, Calif. Nightclub appearances in Reno, Lake Tahoe, Las Vegas, Nev., and various venues in the U.S.; co-star TV situation comedy Smothers Brothers Show, 1965-66, Smothers Brothers Comedy Hour, CBS-TV, 1967-69, 70, weekly variety show The Smothers Brothers Show, NBC-TV, 1975; starred in films The Silver Bears, Get To Know Your Rabbit, A Pleasure Doing Business, Serial, There Goes the Bride, Pandemonium, Speed Zone; starred on Broadway in I Love My Wife, 1978-79; appeared in TV movie Tom of the Hill, 1987; starred in Smothers Brothers Spl. and Series, 1988-89. Office: Knave Prodns Ste 107B 6442 Coldwater Canyon Ave North Hollywood CA 91606-1137 Office Phone: 818-754-0351. E-mail: SMOBRO1@AOL.COM.

**SMOTRICH, DAVID ISADORE,** architect; b. Norwich, Conn., Oct. 6, 1933; s. Max Z. and Ida (Babinsky) S.; m. Bernice D. Strachman, Mar. 25, 1956; children: Ross Lawrence, Maura Faye, Hannah. AB, Harvard Coll., 1955, MArch, 1960. Master planning team, Town of Arad, State of Israel, 1961-62; assoc. Platt Assocs., N.Y.C., 1963-65; gen. ptnr. Smotrich & Platt, N.Y.C., 1965-74, Smotrich Platt & Buttrick, N.Y.C., 1975-76, Smotrich & Platt, N.Y.C., 1976-85, David Smotrich & Ptnrs., N.Y.C., 1985—. Cons. to Jerusalem Master Plan Office, Israel Ministry of Housing, 1967. Planning bd. Town of New Canaan, N.Y.C., 1974-81; exec. bd. Road Rev. League, Bedford, N.Y., 1966-70. With AUS, 1955-57. Recipient Bard award, 1969, 85, Archtl. Record award, 1971, 73-75, 78, Design award HUD, 1980. Mem. AIA (Nat. Honor award 1969, N.Y. State Honor awards 1984, 94, Cmty. Design awards 1991, 93, AIA Coll. of Fellows 1993), Assn. Engrs. and Archs. in Israel, Phi Beta Kappa, Harvard Club (N.Y.C.). Home: 7 Mayberry Close Chappaqua NY 10514-1113 Office: David Smotrich & Ptnrs 443 Park Ave S New York NY 10016-7322 Office Phone: 212-889-4045. Personal E-mail: ds@dsmotricharch.com.

**SMOUSE, H(ERVEY) RUSSELL,** lawyer; b. Oakland, Md., Aug. 13, 1932; s. Hervey Reed and Vernie (Rush) Smouse; m. Creta M. Staley, June 15, 1955; children: Kristin Anne, Randall Forsyth, Gregory Russell. AB, Princeton U., 1955; LLB, U. Md., 1958. Bar: Md. 58, U.S. Tax. Ct. 79, U.S. Ct. Appeals (4th cir.) 60, U.S. Supreme Ct. 74. Atty. Atty. Gen.'s Honors Program, Dept. Justice, Washington, 1958—60; asst. U.S. atty. Dist. Md., 1960—62; assoc. Pierson and Pierson, Balt., 1962—64; atty. B.&O. R.R., Balt., 1964—66; mem. Pierson and Pierson, 1966—69; Clapp, Somerville, Black & Honemann, Balt., 1969—74; pvt. practice Law Offices H. Russell Smouse, 1974—81; mem. Melnicove, Kaufman, Weiner & Smouse, P.A., Balt., 1981—89, chmn. litigation, 1985—89; mem. Whiteford, Taylor & Preston, Balt., 1989—93, chmn. litigation dept., 1989—93; head gen. litigation Law Offices Peter G. Angelos, 1993—; gen. counsel Balt. Orioles, 1993—. Permanent mem. jud. conf. U.S. Ct. Appeals (4th cir.); vice chmn. Legal Aid Bur. Balt. City, 1972—73. Named Best Lawyers in America, 2005—06. Fellow: Am. Coll. Trial Lawyers; mem.: ATLA, ABA, Nat. Assn.

R.R. Trial Counsel (exec. com., v.p. ea. region 1986—92), Bar Assn. Balt. City (chmn. grievance com. 1969—70, chmn. judiciary com. and nominating com. 1980, mem. exec. com. 1969—70, 1980, chmn. exec. com. lawyers' com. for ind. judiciary 1989—96), Md. State Bar Assn. (gov. 1981—83), Am. Law Inst. Republican. Presbyterian. Office Phone: 410-649-2000. Business E-Mail: djmiller@lawpga.com.

**SMOUSE, PETER E.,** ecologist, educator; BS in Forestry, U. Calif., Berkeley, 1965; PhD in Genetics, NC State U., Raleigh, 1970. Postdoctoral rschr. zoology U. Tex., Austin, 1970—72; asst. prof. to prof. human genetics U. Mich., 1972—89, prof. biology, 1985—89; prof. II marine and coastal scis. Rutgers U., 1989—96, prof. II ecology, evolution and natural resources, 1996—. Vis. prof. demographic and population genetics U. Tex., 1984—85; assoc. dir. Ctr. Theoretical and Applied Genetics Rutgers U., 1989—96, assoc. dean scis., 1993—95, acting assoc. provost scis., 1993—95, chair ecology, evolution and natural resources, 1997—2001; mem. DNA subcommittee NY State Forensic Commn., 1995—98; vis. scholar Australian Nat. U., 1996—97; mem. adv. com. Columbia Earth Inst., 1998; mem. adv. bd. ecology and evolutionary biology Columbia U., 2001—; mem. adv. bd. Land Inst., 2001—. Contbr. articles to sci. jours.; assoc. editor Theoretical Population Biology, 1979—82, Evolution, 1987—89, Jour. Heredity, 1990—92, mem. editl. bd.: Internat. Jour. Quantitative Anthropology, 1988—91. Office: Dept Ecology Evolution and Natural Resources Rutgers U Cook Coll 14 Coll Farm Rd New Brunswick NJ 08901-8551 E-mail: smouse@aesop.rutgers.edu.*

**SMUCKER, RICHARD K.,** food products executive; m. Emily Delp; 1 child. Grad., Miami U., Ohio; MBA, Wharton Sch. Bus., U. Penn. Pres. The J.M. Smucker Co., 1987—, co-CEO, 2001—. Bd. dirs. The J.M. Smucker Co., Wm. Wrigley Jr., Co., Internat. Multifoods, The Sherwin-Williams Co., Internat. Foodservice Mfr. Assoc.; bd. trustees Cleveland Orchestra, Culinary Inst. Am. Office: 1 Strawberry Ln Orrville OH 44667-1241

**SMUCKER, TIMOTHY P.,** food products executive; m. Jennifer Coddington; 3 children. BS Economics, Coll. of Wooster, 1967; MBA Mktg., Wharton Sch. Bus., U Penn, 1969. Chmn. The J.M. Smucker Co., 1984—, co-CEO, 2001—. Bd. dirs. The J.M. Smucker Co., Huntington BancShares, Inc., Dreyer's Grand Ice Cream, Inc., Grocery Mfr. Am., Inc.; bd. trustees Coll. of Wooster; mem. steering com. Heartland Edn. Community. Office: 1 Strawberry Ln Orrville OH 44667-1241

**SMUKAL, MICHAEL WILLIAM,** music educator, composer, musician; s. Paul Herbert and Carol Hannen Smukal; children: Michael Adam, Stephen Andrew. BA, MusM, U. Nev., Las Vegas, 1985. Dir. of bands Silvestri Jr. H.S., Clark County Sch. Dist., Las Vegas, 1985—. Composer, arranger Warner Bros. Music Publs., Las Vegas. Music arranger: educational jazz publs. Now Rock, Ye Rested Gentlemen (Editor's Choice, 2004), Song Of The Volga Boatmen, trombonist: with Elvis Presley, 1975—77, Elvis in Concert, CBS TV spl., Spring Tours '77, Elvis Presley, Moody Blue, Elvis Presley, Elvis: A Canadian Tribute, Elvis Presley, Platinum: A Life in Music, Elvis Presley, Elvis in Concert, Elvis Presley, This is Elvis, Elvis Presley, Elvis Aaron Presley. State pres. Nat. Assn. Of Jazz Educators, Las Vegas, Nev., 1984—86. Tech. sgt. USAF, 1971—75, Washington, DC. Named SW Region Disting. Educator of the Yr., Clark County Sch. Dist., 2003—04. Mem.: Internat. Assn. Jazz Educators, Nev. Music Educators Assn., Music Educator's Nat. Conf. Personal E-mail: smukal@cox.net.

**SMUTNY, JOAN FRANKLIN,** academic director, educator; b. Chgo. d. Eugene and Mabel (Lind) Franklin; m. Herbert Paul Smutny; 1 child, Cheryl Anne. BS, MA, Northwestern U. Tchr. New Trier H.S., Winnetka, Ill.; mem. faculty, founder, dir. Nat. H.S. Inst. Northwestern U. Sch. Edn., Chgo.; faculty, founder, dir. h.s. workshop critical thinking/edn. Nat. Coll. Edn., Evanston, Ill., exec. dir. h.s. workshops, 1970-75; founder, dir. Woman Power Through Edn. Seminar, 1969-74; dir. Right to Read Seminar in critical reading, 1973-74; dir. seminar gifted h.s. students, 1973; dir. gifted programs for 6th, 7th, 8th graders Evanston pub. schs., 1978-79; dir. gifted programs 1st-8th grade Glenview (Ill.) pub. schs., 1979—. Dir. gifted programs Nat.-Louis U., Evanston, 1980-82, dir. Ctr. for Gifted, 1982—; dir. Bright and Talented Project, 1986—, North Shore Country Day Sch., Winnetka, 1982—; dir. Job Creation Project, 1980-82; dir. New Dimensions for Women, 1973; dir. Thinking for Action in Career Edn. Program 1976-79; dir. TACE, dir. Humanities Program for Verbally Precocious Youth, 1978-79; co-dir., instr. seminars in critical thinking Ill. Family Svc., 1972-75; writer ednl. filmstrips in lang. arts and lit. Soc. Visual Edn., 1970-74; spkrs. bur. Coun. Fgn. Rels., 1968-69; adv. com. edn. professions devel. act U.S. Office Edn., 1969—; state team for gifted, Ill. Office Edn., Office of Gifted, Springfield, Ill., 1977; writer, cons. Radiant Ednl. Corp., 1969-71; cons. ALA, 1969-71, workshop leader and spkr. gifted edn., 1971—; coord. career edn. Nat. Coll.Edn., 1976-78, dir. Project 1987—, dir. Summer Wonders, 1986—, Creative Children's Acad., bd. dirs., Worlds of Wisdom and Wonder, 1978—; dir. Future Tchrs. Am. Seminar in Coll. and Career, 1970-72; cons. rsch. & devel. Ill. Dept. Vocat. Edn., 1973—; evaluation cons. DAVTE, IOE, Springfield, Ill., 1977, mem. Leadership Tng. Inst. Gifted, U.S. Office Edn., 1973-74; dir. workshops for h.s. students; cons., spkr. in field; dir. Gifted Young Writers and Young Writers confs., 1978, 79; dir. Project '92 The White House Conf. on Children and Youth; mem. adv. bd. Educating Able Learners, 1991—; chmn. bd. dirs. Barbereux Sch., Evanston, 1992—; asst. editor, editl. bd. Understanding our Gifted, 1994—. Author: (with others) Job Creation: Creative Materials, Activities and Strategies for the Classroom, 1982, A Thoughful Overview of Gifted Education, 1990, Your Gifted Child—How to Recognize and Develop the Special Talents in Your Child from Birth to Age Seven, 1987, paperback, 1991, Education of the Gifted: Programs and Perspectives, 1990, Teaching Gifted Young Children in the Regular Classroom, 1997, Gifted Girls, 1998, Stand Up For Your Gifted Child, 2001, Gifted Education: Promising Practices, 2003, Differentiated Instruction, 2003, Differentiating For the Young Child, 2004; editor: The Young Gifted Child: Potential and Promise: An Anthology, 1998, Underserved Gifted Populations, 2003; contbg. editor Roper Rev., 1994—; asst. editor Understanding Our Gifted, 1995—; editor, contbr. Maturity in Teching; writer ednl. filmstrips The Brothers Grimm, How the West Was Won, Mutiny on the Bounty, Dr. Zhivago, Space Odyssey 2001, Christmas Around the World; editor IAGC Jour. for Gifted, 1994—; adv. bd. Gifted Edn. Press Quar., 1995—; contbr. editor numerous books in field; contbr. articles to profl. jours. including Chgo. Parent Mag.; reviewer programs for Gifted and Talented, U.S. Office Edn., 1976-78; editor Creativity Series Ablex, 1998—. Mem. AAUP, Nat. Assn. Gifted Child (nat. membership chmn. 1991—, co-chmn. schs. and programs, co-editor newsletter early childhood divsn.), Nat. Soc. Arts & Letters (nat. bd., 1st and 3d v.p. Evanston chpt. 1990-92), Mortar Bd., Outstanding Educators of Am. 1974, Pi Lambda Theta, Phi Delta Kappa (v.p. Evanston chpt. rsch. chmn. 1990-92). Home: 633 Forest Ave Wilmette IL 60091-1713 *Commitment to education is defined as contribution. We who are privileged to work in education know that the focus is the educant-the learner. Gifted education is particularly vital in that it discerns the needs of bright, talented children who have an immense amount to contribute to our country and our world. Gifted children are our country's most neglected resource--and most needed. It is my privilege to work in this area, to work with children, parents and teachers. The community of mankind is needed to support the talent and growth of the gifted. Then we are really contributing to the educant.*

**SMYNTEK, JOHN EUGENE, JR.,** editor; b. Buffalo, Aug. 24, 1950; BA, U. Detroit, 1972. Asst. instr. Mich. State U., East Lansing, 1981; features editor Free Press, Detroit, 1985-92; dir. online svcs. and dir. libr. Free Press Plus, Detroit, 1992-95, spl. features and syndicate editor, 1995—; asst. instr. U. Detroit Mercy, 2000—01. Vis. fellow in journalism Duke U., 1988; profl. student publs. advisor U. Detroit Mercy, 1992—94; bd. visitors Wayne State U. Coll. Fine, Performing and Comm. Arts, 2001—05. Recipient Fine Arts Reporting award, Detroit Press Club, 1985. Roman Catholic. Office: Detroit Free Press 600 W Fort St Detroit MI 48226-2706 Office Phone: 313-222-5169. Business E-Mail: jsmyntek@freepress.com.

**SMYTH, CRAIG HUGH,** fine arts educator; b. N.Y.C., July 28, 1915; s. George Hugh and Lucy Salome (Humeston) S.; m. Barbara Linforth, June 24, 1941; children: Alexandra, Edward Linforth (Ned). BA, Princeton U., 1938, MFA, 1941, PhD, 1956; MA (hon.), Harvard U., 1975. Sr. mus. aid, rsch. asst. Nat. Gallery Art, Washington, 1941-42; officer-in-charge, dir. Cen. Art Collecting Point, Munich, 1945-46; lectr. Frick Collection, N.Y.C., 1946-50; asst. prof. Inst. Fine Arts NYU, 1950-53, assoc. prof. Inst. Fine Arts, 1953-57, prof. Inst. Fine Arts, 1957-73, acting dir. Inst. Fine Arts, acting head dept. fine arts Grad. Sch. Arts and Scis., 1951-53, dir. inst., head dept. fine arts Grad. Sch., 1953-73; prof. fine arts Harvard U., 1973-85, prof. emeritus, 1985—; Samuel Kress prof. Ctr. for Advanced Study in Visual Arts Nat. Gallery Art, Washington, 1987-88; dir. Villa I Tatti Harvard U. Ctr. Italian Renaissance Studies, Florence, 1973-85. Art historian in residence Am. Acad. in Rome, 1959-60; mem. U.S. Nat. Com. History Art, 1955-85; alt. U.S. mem. Comité Internat. d'Histoire de l'Art, 1970-83, U.S. mem., 1983-85; chmn. adv. com. J. Paul Getty Rsch. Inst. History of Art and Humanities, 1982-99; mem. architect selection com. J. Paul Getty Trust, 1983-84; mem. organizing com., keynote speaker 400th Anniversary of Uffizi Gallery, 1981-82; vis. scholar Inst. Advanced Study, Princeton, N.J., 1971, mem., 1978, visitor, 1983, 85-86; vis. scholar Bibliotheca Hertziana, Max Planck Soc., Rome, 1972, 73; mem. vis. com. dept. art and archaeology Princeton U., 1956-73, 85-89; mem. adv. com. Villa I Tatti, 1985-92; trustee Hyde Collection, Glens Falls, N.Y., 1985-87, The Burlington mag., 1987—; mem. commn. Ednl. & Cultural Exch. between Italy and U.S., 1979-83. Author: Mannerism and Maniera, 1963, rev. edit. with introduction by E. Cropper, 1992, Bronzino as Draughtsman, 1971, Michelangelo Architetto (with H.M. Millon), 1988, English edit., 1988, Repatriation of Art from the Collecting Point in Munich After World War II, 1988; editor: Michelangelo Drawings (Nat. Gallery of Art), 1992; editor (with Peter M. Lukehart), contbr.: The Early Years of Art History in the United States, 1993; founding chmn. (periodical) I Tatti Studies: Essays in the Renaissance, 1984-85; contbr. to profl. jours. Hon. trustee Met. Mus. Art, N.Y.C., 1968—; trustee Inst. Fine Arts, NYU, 1973—; mem. mayor's com. Piazza Della Signoria, Florence, 1975-78. Lt. USNR, 1942-46. Decorated Chevalier Legion of Honor France, U.S. Army Commendation medal, Netherlands Medal for Svc. to the State; sr. Fulbright Rsch. fellow, 1949-50, honored by establishment of CHS professorship, Inst. of Fine Arts NYU, 1999. Mem. Am. Acad. Arts and Scis., Am. Philos. Soc., Coll. Art Assn. Am. (bd. dirs. 1953-57, sec. 1956), Accademia Fiorentina delle Arti del Disegno (academician, assoc.), Accademia di San Luca (hon. 1995), Harvard Club (N.Y.C.), Century Assn. (N.Y.C.), Phi Beta Kappa. Address: PO Box 539 Cresskill NJ 07626-0039

**SMYTH, DAVID,** writer, editor; b. Buenos Aires, Feb. 7, 1929; came to U.S. 1962, naturalized 1970; s. Currell Hutchinson and Jessie Rodger (Dodds) S.; m. Elli Helene Dusterhoft, Nov. 9, 1968; 1 child, Clifford Dieter. BA, Cambridge (Eng.) U., 1951, MA, 1967. Tech. writer, copywriter, 1953-55; movie promotion writer, 1956; owner Ace Translation Agy., Buenos Aires, 1957-58; sec. Found. Econ. Edn., 1959; cables editor Buenos Aires Herald, 1960; lexicographer Simon & Schuster English-Spanish Dictionary, 1961; Latin Am. desk editor UPI, N.Y.C., 1962-63, AP, N.Y.C., 1963-73, world svcs. fin. editor, 1973-96; freelance writer, translator, editor, 1997—. Author: You Can Survive Any Financial Disaster, 1977, Worldly Wise Investor, 1988; co-author: The Speculator's Handbook, 1974, Unusual Investments That Could Make You Rich, 1978, No Cost/Low Cost Investing, 1987. Served with Argentine Army, 1952. Mem. N.Y. Fin. Writers Assn. Home: 8 Beechwood Ave Metuchen NJ 08840-2107 E-mail: Currell@aol.com.

**SMYTH, DONALD MORGAN,** chemistry professor, researcher; b. Bangor, Maine, Mar. 20, 1930; s. John Robert and Selma (Eubanks) S.; m. Elisabeth Luce, Aug. 1, 1951; children: Carolyn, Joanne. BS in Chemistry, U. Maine, 1951; PhD in Inorganic Chemistry, MIT, 1954. Sr. chemist Sprague Electric Co., North Adams, Mass., 1954-58, sect. head, 1958-61, dept. head, 1961-71; assoc. prof. Lehigh U., Bethlehem, Pa., 1971-73, prof., 1973-95, dir. Materials Rsch. Ctr., 1971-92, Paul B. Reinhold prof. materials sci., engring. and chemistry, 1988-95; emeritus, 1995—. Mem. various coms. Lehigh U., 1973-95; mem. materials rsch. adv. com. NSF, 1984-88, mem., 1985-86, co-chair ad-hoc com. to brief dir., 1986; mem. coun. materials sci. Dept. Energy, 1986-90; presenter in field. Contbr. articles to profl. jours. Recipient Libsch Rsch. award Lehigh U., 1990, Buessem award Dielectrics Rsch. Ctr., Pa. State U., 1991; grantee in field. Fellow Am. Inst. Chemists, Am. Ceramic Soc. (com. edn. electronics divsn. 1974-78, chmn. Lehigh Valley sect. 1978-79, counselor 1982-00, assoc. editor jour. 1988-92, best paper award 1987, 95, Kraner award Lehigh Valley sect. 1990, Sosman lectr. 1996); mem. Am. Chem. Soc., Nat. Acad. Engring., Materials Rsch. Soc., Electrochem. Soc. (various coms., sec. dielectrics and insulation divsn. 1967-69, vice chmn. 1969-70, chmn. 1970-71, rsch. award battery divsn. 1960). Achievements include patents (with others) for Solid-State Battery Cell with Complex Organic Electrolyte Material, Capacitor with Dielectric Film Having Phosphorous-Containing Component Therein, Solid Barrier Electrolyte Incorporating Additive, others; research in defect chemistry and electrical properties of complex oxides. Home: 3429 Mountainview Cir Bethlehem PA 18017-1807 Office: Lehigh Univ Ctr Advanced Material and Nanotech 5 E Packer Ave Bethlehem PA 18015-3102 Office Phone: 610-758-3852. Business E-Mail: dms4@lehigh.edu.

**SMYTH, JOEL DOUGLAS,** newspaper executive; b. Renovo, Pa., Nov. 8, 1941; s. Bernard John and Eva Mae (Stone) S.; m. Madonna Robertson, Nov. 29, 1959; children: Deborah Sue, Susan Kelly, Michael Robertson, Patricia Ann, Rebecca Lee, Jennifer Neilia. Student, Lycoming Coll., 1959. Reporter Del. State News, Dover, 1960-62, news editor, 1962-65, mng. editor, 1965-70, editor, pres., 1970-78; editor Del. Sunday News, 1964-65; pres. Ind. Newspapers, Inc., Dover, 1970-89, chmn., CEO, 1989—. Founding pres. Valley Citizen's League, 1987-90. Recipient writing awards. Mem. AP Mng. Editors Assn. (dir.), Am. Soc. Newspaper Editors, Young Pres.'s Orgn., Sigma Delta Chi. Home: 39833 N 100th St Scottsdale AZ 85262-2975 Office: Independent Newspaper Inc PO Box 70001 Dover DE 19903

**SMYTH, JOSEPH PATRICK,** retired military officer, physician; b. Norwalk, Conn., Mar. 2, 1933; s. Patrick and Helen (Heffernan) Smyth; m. Ursula Marie Kirwin, Feb. 22, 1961; children: Donna, Jennifer, Joseph. BA, Fairfield U., 1960; MD, Creighton U., 1964. Diplomate Am. Bd. Med. Examiners. Commd. ensign USN, 1963, advanced through grades to rear adm., 1988; intern Phila. Naval Hosp., 1964-65, internal medicine resident, 1965-68, staff physician, 1968-69; internist, chief of medicine U.S. Naval Hosp., DaNang, Vietnam, 1969-70, Orlando, Fla., 1970-76, chief of medicine, exec. officer Yokosuka, Japan, 1976-80, exec. officer Oakland, Calif., 1980-82, comdg. officer, 1984-86, Okinawa, Japan, 1982—84, Naval Med. Command European Region, London, 1986-90; dep. dir. for med. readiness The Joint Staff, Pentagon, Washington, 1990-92; retired US Navy, 1992; med. dir. Volusia County (Fla.) Dept. of Corrections, 1994—2005. Instr. medicine Jefferson Med. Coll., 1966—69; preceptor USN Physician Asst. Program, Orlando, 1971—76; instr. mgmt. course Navy Med. Dept., Washington, 1986; med. coord. entire Gulf War buildup to Joint Chief Staff chmn. Gen. Colin Powell Operation Desert Shield/Storm, Saudi Arabia, 1990—91; med. dir. Volusia County Dept. Corrections, Fla., 1994—2005. Physician Orange County Fla. Alcohol Ctr., Orlando, 1974—76. Decorated Def. Superior Svc. medal, Legion of Merit, Meritorious Svc. medals with 2 oak leaf clusters, Navy Commendation medal with combat V. Mem.: AMA, Orange County Med. Soc., Am. Acad. Physician Execs., Fla. Med. Assn., Am. Acad. Med. Adminstrs. (Levandowski award 1991), Assn. Mil. Surgeons U.S. Republican. Roman Catholic. Home: 400 Sweetwater Blvd Longwood FL 32779-3422

**SMYTH, JOSEPH VINCENT,** manufacturing executive; b. Belfast, Ireland, July 18, 1919; s. Joseph Leo and Margaret M. (Murray) S.; m. Marie E. Cripe, Mar. 22, 1941; children: Kevin W., Brian J., Ellen M., Vincent P. BS cum laude, U. Notre Dame, 1941. With Arnolt Corp., Warsaw, Ind., 1946-63, exec. v.p., gen. mgr., until 1963; pres., gen. mgr. Hills-McCanna Co., Carpenters-

ville, Ill., 1963-72; pres. Lunkenheimer Co., Cin., 1972-79; v.p. Condec Flow Control Group, Chgo., 1979-82; cons., 1982—. Mem.: K.C. Address: 7656 Spring Bay Cove Orlando FL 32819-7208 Business E-Mail: j.smyth1@cfl.rr.com.

**SMYTH, NICHOLAS PATRICK DILLON,** surgeon; b. Dublin, Apr. 1, 1924; arrived in U.S., 1951; s. Patrick Joseph and Nano Elizabeth (Dillon) S.; m. Elizabeth Stavely Long; children: Sheila, Brian, Nicholas, Augustine, Patrick. BSc, Univ. Coll. Dublin, 1946, MSc, 1948, MB, BChir, 1949; MS, U. Mich., 1954. Diplomate Am. Bd. Surgery, Am. Bd. Thoracic Surgery. Intern Mater Misericordiae Hosp., Dublin, 1949-50, Norfolk and Norwich Hosp., England, 1950-51; resident in gen. surgery Henry Ford Hosp., Detroit, 1951-55; resident in thoracic surgery George Washington U. Hosp., Washington, 1957-59; pvt. practice Washington, 1959-86; clin. prof. surgery emeritus George Washington U. Sch. Medicine, Washington. Mem. staff Washington Hosp. Ctr., George Washington U. Med. Ctr. Contbr. articles to profl. jours.; patentee in field. Capt. M.C., U.S. Army, 1955-57. Fellow: ACS, Am. Coll. Cardiology; mem.: N.Am. Soc. Pacing and Electrophysiology, So. Thoracic Surg. Assn., Soc. Thoracic Surgery, Am. Assn. Thoracic Surgery. Republican. Roman Catholic. Avocation: writing.

**SMYTH, PAUL BURTON,** lawyer; b. Phila., Aug. 15, 1949; s. Benjamin Burton and Florence Elizabeth (Tomlinson) S.; m. Denise Elaine Freeland, May 31, 1975. BA, Trinity Coll., 1971; JD, Boston Coll., 1974. Bar: Conn. 1974, D.C. 1975, U.S. Dist. Ct. D.C., 1980, U.S. Supreme Ct., 1985. With Dept. Interior, 1974—. Atty. Office of Hearings and Appeals, Arlington, Va., 1974—76, acting atty., 1993—94, dep. assoc. solicitor for land and water resources, 1995—; atty. Office of Solicitor, Washington, 1976—82, asst. solicitor for land use and realty, 1982—87, dep. assoc. solicitor for energy and resources, 1987—95; lectr. environ. law George Washington U. Law Sch., Washington, 1997—2001. Editor: Federal Reclamation and Related Laws Annotated, Reclamation Reform Act Compilation, 1982—88; contbr. articles to legal pubs. Bd. dirs. EcoVoce, 1998—; trustee Rocky Mtn. Mineral Law Found., 1999—2001. Mem. ABA (coun. 1991-94, budget officer 1994-98, sec. natural resources, energy and environ. law, exec. editor Nat. Resources and the Environ. 1989-91). Office: Office of Solicitor Dept Interior 18th And C Sts NW Washington DC 20240-0001 Office Phone: 202-208-4506. E-mail: paulb.smyth@verizon.net.

**SMYTH, RICH,** publishing executive; b. Bronx; married; 2 children. BA in Comm., Boston Coll. With Carnation Co. (now Nestle Foods), Dallas, 1985—88; joined So. Living, 1988, nat. sales mgr. NYC, 1996—98, advt. dir., 1998—2000, v.p., 2000—, pub., 2003—. Office: Southern Living PO Box 523 2100 Lakeshore Drive Birmingham AL 35209 Mailing: Southern Living 20th Floor 1271 Ave of Americas New York NY 10020-1391 Office Phone: 888-254-9654, 212-522-1212. Office Fax: 212-522-4199. E-mail: rich_smyth@timeinc.com.*

**SMYTH, RYAN,** professional hockey player; b. Banff, Alta., Can., Feb. 21, 1976; m. Stacey Smyth. Left wing Edmonton Oilers, 1994—. Mem. Team Can., Olympic Games, Salt Lake City, 2002, Team Can., World Cup of Hockey, 2004. Achievements include being a member of gold medal Canadian Hockey team, World Junior Championships, 1995, Salt Lake City Olympic Games, 2002; being a member of World Cup Champion Team Canada, 2004. Office: Edmonton Oilers 11230-110 St Edmonton AB T5G 3H7 Canada*

**SMYTHE, CHEVES MCCORD,** internist, geriatrician, educator, dean; b. May 25, 1924; Student, Yale Coll., 1942—43; MD cum laude, Harvard, 1947. Diplomate Am. Bd. Internal Medicine, Am. Bd. Geriatrics. Intern, asst. resident Harvard Med. Svc., Boston City Hosp., 1947—49, chief resident, 1954—55; resident chest svc. Bellevue, 1949—50; rsch. fellow Presbyn. Hosp., N.Y.C., 1950—52; assoc. medicine Med. Coll. S.C. Sch. Medicine, 1956—58, asst. prof. medicine, 1958—60, assoc. prof. medicine, 1960—66, dean, 1963—65; attending physician Wesley Meml., Cook County North Side VA Hosps., Chgo., 1967—70; with Aga Khan U. Hosp., Karachi, Pakistan, 1990—91; dean faculty health scis., prof. medicine Aga Khan U., Karachi, Pakistan, 1982—85, prof., chmn. dept. medicine, 1990—91; chief Med. Svcs. at LBJ Hosp., Houston, 1991—95; chief divsn. gen. medicine dept. internal medicine U. Tex. Med. Sch., Houston, 1970—, dean, 1970—75, dean pro tem, 1995—96. Assoc. med. dir. Hermann Hosp., 1996—. Bd. dirs. Assn. Am. Assoc. Med. Colls., Office: U Tex Med Sch 6431 Fannin St 1-108 Houston TX 77030-1501

**SMYTHE, WILLIAM RODMAN,** physicist, researcher; b. LA, Jan. 6, 1930; s. William Ralph and Helen (Keith) S.; m. Carol Richardson, Nov. 27, 1954 (dec. Dec. 1987); children: Stephanie, Deborah, William Richardson, Reed Terry; m. Judith Brean Travers, Jan. 1, 1989. BS, Calif. Inst. Tech., 1951, MS, 1952, PhD, 1957. Engr. Gen. Electric Microwave Lab., Palo Alto, Calif., 1956-57; asst. prof. U. Colo., 1958-63, assoc. prof., 1963-67, prof., 1967-95, chmn. nuclear physics lab., 1967-69, 81-83, 90-92, prof. emeritus, 1995—. Mem. Am. Phys. Soc. Clubs: Colorado Mountain (Boulder). Achievements include inventing negative ion cyclotron. Home: 2106 Knollwood Dr Boulder CO 80302-4706 E-Mail: Rod.Smythe@colorado.edu.

**SNADER, JACK ROSS,** publishing company executive; b. Athens, Ohio, Feb. 25, 1938; s. Daniel Webster and Mae Estella (Miller) S.; m. Sharon Perschnick, Apr. 4, 1959; children: Susan Mae, Brian Ross. BS, U. Ill., 1959. Cert. mgmt. cons. With mktg. Richardson-Merrell, Cin., 1959-65, Xerox Corp., N.Y.C., 1965-67, Sieber & McIntyre, Chgo., 1967-69; pres. Systema Corp., Northbrook, Ill., 1969—. Mem. exec. adv. bd. bus. program Trinity Internat. U. Author Systematic Selling, 1987, The Sales Relationship, 1988. Mem. ASTD, Inst. Mgmt. Cons. Office: Systema Corp 900 Northshore Dr Ste 166 Lake Bluff IL 60044

**SNAPP, ELIZABETH,** librarian, educator; b. Lubbock, Tex., Mar. 31, 1937; d. William James and Louise (Lanham) Mitchell; m. Henry Franklin Snapp, June 1, 1956 (div. Dec. 2001). BA magna cum laude, North Tex. State U., Denton, 1968, MLS, 1969, MA, 1977. Asst. to archivist Archive of New Orleans Jazz Tulane U., 1960-63; catalog libr. Tex. Woman's U., Denton, 1969-71, head acquisitions dept., 1971-74, coord. readers svcs., 1974-77, asst. to dean Grad. Sch., 1977-79, instr. libr. sci., 1977-88, acting Univ. libr., 1979-82, dir. librs., 1982—2002, dir. librs. emeritus, 2002—, univ. historian, 1995—2002; adj. prof. dept. history and govt. Tex. Woman's U., Denton, 2002—; rsch. assoc. Tex. Woman's U. Libr., Denton, 2002—. Chair-elect Tex. Coun. State U. Librs., 1988—90, chmn., 1990—92; adv. com. on libr. formula Coord. Bd. Tex. Coll. and Univ. Sys, 1981—92; Libr. Sys. Act adv. bd. Tex. State Libr. and Archives Commn., 1999—2002; del. OCLC Nat. Users Coun., 1985—87, by-laws com., 1985—86, com. on less-than-full-svcs. networks, 1986—87; trustee AMIGOS Libr. Svcs., 1994—2000, sec. bd. trustees, 1996—97, vice-chmn. bd. trustees, 1997—99, chair bd. trustees, 1999—2000; project dir. NEH consultancy grant on devel. core curriculum for women's studies, 1981—82; chmn. Blue Ribbon com. 1986 Gov.'s Commn. for Women to select 150 outstanding women in Tex. History; project dir. math./sci. anthology project Tex. Found. Women's Resources; co-sponsor Irish Lecture Series, Denton, 1968, 70, 73, 78. Asst. editor Tex. Academe, 1973—76; co-editor: Read All About Her! Texas Women's History: A Working Bibliography, 1995; contbg. author Women in Special Collections, 1984, Special Collections, 1986, book reviewer Libr. Resources and Tech. Svcs., 1973—2002; contbr. articles to profl. jours. Trustee, treas. Adult Day Care of North Tex., 2002—04; v.p., 2004; sec. Denton County Dem. Caucus, 1970. Recipient Ann. Pioneer award, Tex. Woman's U., 1986, Women's Studies Vision award, 1998. Mem.: AAUW (legis. br. chmn. 1973—74, br. v.p. 1975—76, pres. 1979—80, state historian 1986—88, treas. 1998—99), ALA (stds. com. 1983—85), AAUP, Tex. Assn. Coll. Tchrs. (pres. Tex. Woman's U. chpt. 1976—77), So. Conf. Brit. Studies, Women's Collecting Group (chmn. ad hoc com. 1984—86), Tex. Hist. Commn. (judge for Farenbach History prize 1990—93), Tex. Libr. Assn. (program com. 1978, Dist. VII chmn. 1985—86, archives and oral history com. 1990—92, co-chair conf. program com. 1994, Tall Texan selection com. 1995—96, treas. exec. bd. 1996—99, Centennial com. 2000—02), AAUW Ednl. Found. (tech. and awards panel 1990—94), Alliance Higher Edn. (chair coun. libr. dirs. 1993—95), Rotary Internat. (sec. local chpt. 1999—2002), Soroptomist Internat. (pres. Denton chpt. 1986—88), Women's Shakespeare Club (pres. 1967—69), Pi Delta Phi, Alpha Lambda Sigma (pres. 1970—71), Alpha Chi, Beta Phi Mu (sec. chpt. 1976 1978, sec. nat. adv. assembly 1978—79, pres. 1979—80, nat. dir. 1981—83). Methodist. Office: TWU Sta PO Box 424093 Denton TX 76204-4093 E-mail: snappe@charter.net. *The idealistic dreams of youth can be translated into making a difference in the work place and in your personal life if you develop a big picture that includes the ideas of individuals of diversity and if you give life your full attention, enthusiasm and courage and give a few your steadfast friendship.*

**SNAPP, HARRY FRANKLIN,** historian, educator; b. Bryan, Tex., Oct. 15, 1930; s. H.F. and Ethel (Manning) Snapp; m. Elizabeth Mitchell, June 1, 1956 (div. Dec. 20, 2001). BA, Baylor U., 1952, MA, 1953; PhD, Tulane U., 1963. Instr. U. Coll. Tulane U., 1960—62; asst. prof. history Wofford Coll., 1963—64, U. North Tex. (formerly North Tex. State U.), Denton, 1964—69, assoc. prof., 1969—94; dir. Tex. Rsch. Ctr. Biog. Study of Women, Denton, 1995—; pres., dir. Read All About Her Tex. Women's Biographic Ctr., Inc., 1995—. Editor: Brit. Studies Mercury, 1970—84, Tex. Acad., 1973—76; co-editor: Read All About Her! Texas Women's History: A Working Bibliography, 1995, enlarged edit., 1997; author (with others): West Texas Historical Assn. Year Book, 1994, 1996; contbr. articles to profl. jours. Mem. Bridwell Assocs. of So. Meth. U., Friends of Southwestern Art, Am. Com. Irish Studies; mem. adv. com. on acad. freedom and tenure policy, coord. bd. Tex. Coll. and Univ. System. Recipient North Tex. State U. Faculty Rsch. award, 1966, 1967. Mem.: AAUP (pres. North Tex. chpt. 1968—69, pres. Southwestern regional conf. 1971—72, pres. Tex. conf. 1974—76, nat. coun. 1976—86), Butler Soc. (Ireland), Northamptonshire Record Soc., Libr. History Round Table, Libr. Rsch. Round Table, Hist. Assn. (London), Tex. State Hist. Assn., Panhandle-Plains Hist. Soc., West Tex. Hist. Assn. (bd. dirs 1997—), Am. Hist. Assn., So. Conf. Brit. Studies (sec.-treas. 1969—84), Tulane U. Alumni Assn., Lambda Chi Alpha, Alpha Chi. Democrat. Methodist. Home: 1904 N Lake Trl Denton TX 76201-0602 Office: Read All About Her Tex Women's Biographic Ctr Inc PO Box 424053 Denton TX 76204-4053

**SNAPPER, ERNST,** mathematics professor; b. The Netherlands, Dec. 2, 1913; came to U.S., 1938, naturalized, 1942; s. Isidore and Henrietta (Van Buuren) S.; m. Ethel Lillian Klein, June 1941; children: John William, James Robert. MA, Princeton U., 1939, PhD, 1941; MA (hon.), Dartmouth Coll. 1964. Instr. Princeton, 1941-45, vis. asso. prof., 1949-50, vis. prof., 1954-55; asst. prof. U. So. Calif., 1945-48, asso. prof., 1948-53, prof., 1953-55; NSF post-doctoral fellow Harvard, 1953-54; Andrew Jackson Buckingham prof. math. Miami U., Oxford, Ohio, 1955-58; prof. math. Ind. U., 1958-63, Dartmouth, 1963—, Benjamin Pierce Cheney prof. math., 1971—79. Mem. Am. Math. Soc., Math. Assn. Am. (pres. Ind. sect. 1962-63, Carl B. Allendoerfer award 1980), Assn. Princeton Grad. Alumni (governing bd.). Soc. for Preservation Bridges of Konigsburg, Phi Beta Kappa (hon.), Pi Mu Epsilon (hon.). Home: PO Box 67 Norwich VT 05055-0067

**SNARE, CARL LAWRENCE, JR.,** retired accountant, financial planner; b. Oct. 25, 1936; s. Carl Lawrence and Lillian Marie (Luoma) Snare. BBA, Northwestern U., 1968; postgrad., San Francisco State U., 1976—77, Roosevelt U.; BS, SUNY, 1995. CPA Calif.; CFP Calif. Asst. sec., contr. Bache Halsey Stuart & Shields Inc. (now Prudential Securities), Chgo., 1968—73; contr. Innisfree Corp. divsn. Hyatt Corp., Burlingame, Calif., 1973—76; cash mgr. Portland GE, 1976—79; CFO, contr. Vistar Fin. Inc., Marina del Rey, Calif., 1979—82; pres. Snare Properties Co., Long Beach, Calif., 1984—96, Snare Fin. Svcs. Corp., Rialto, Calif., 1985—89, Carl Snare & Assocs., Long Beach; v.p., treas. Carson Estate Co., Rancho Dominguez, Calif., 1988—96; pres., CEO Glenshire Homes, Inc., Phoenix, 1996—98, Glenshire Tech., Boulder, Colo., 1997—99; acct., fin. planner Calif.; ret. Mem.: AICPA, Founder Cash Mgmt. Assn. E-mail: carl.snare@lycos.com.

**SNARE, LEROY EARL,** physicist, physics educator; b. Garden City, Mo., Nov. 6, 1931; s. Joseph Claude and Mildred Ella (Harvey) S.; m. Mary Lou Seabright, Feb. 6, 1960; children: Jonathan Lee, Sarah Elizabeth, Judith Irene. BA in Physics and Maths., U. Mo., 1953, MS in Physics, 1959; MS in Aeronautics and Astronautics, MIT, 1962. Cert. sec. sch. tchr., Mo. Head dynamic analysis and simulation br. Naval Avionics Ctr., Indpls., 1963-72, applied rsch. sr. staff, 1972-76, dir. systs. analysis divsn., 1976-80, dep. dir. applied rsch., 1980-84, dep. dir. engring., 1984-86, rsch. and tech. coord., 1986-91; asst. prof. phys. sci. Ivy Tech. State Coll., Indpls., 1991—2000. Nat. bd. advs. Rose-Hulman Inst. Tech., Terre Haute, Ind., 1984-91. Author: Ivy Tech. State Coll. Ctrl. Campus Physics, Physical Sci. Laboratory Manuals; contbr. Ind. state plan comm. Ind. State Corp. Sci. and Tech., Indpls., 1985-88. Scholar Donnelly Garment Co., Kansas City, 1949-53. Mem. IEEE (sr.), Am. Assn. Physics Tchrs., Masons, Sigma Xi. Presbyterian. Achievements include definition (with others) of equipment and procedures to initialize all navy aircraft inertial guidance systems; upgraded curriculum, added labs. to Ivy Tech. State Coll. Physics Courses which enabled credit transfers to four year colls. Home: 6626 N Olney St Indianapolis IN 46220-3757

**SNAREY, JOHN ROBERT,** psychologist, educator; b. 1948; s. John Herbert and Esther Snarey; m. Carol Dunn Snarey, 1970; children: Johnny, Elizabeth. BS, Geneva Coll., Beaver Falls, Pa., 1969; MA, Wheaton Coll., Ill., 1973; EdD, Harvard U. Cambridge, Mass., 1982. Postdoctoral rsch fellow dept. psychiatry Harvard U., Cambridge, Mass., 1982-84; assoc. rsch. psychologist Wellesley Coll., 1984-85; assoc. prof. human devel. and edn. Northwestern U., Evanston, Ill., 1985-87; prof. human devel. and ethics Sch. Theology and dept. psychology Emory U., Atlanta, 1987—. Mem. senate Emory U., Atlanta, 2001—05, pres. 2003—04. Author: How Fathers Care for the Next Generation, 1993; contbr. articles to profl. jours.; editor: Conflict and Continuity: A History of Ideas on Social Equality and Human Development, 1981, Remembrance of Lawrence Kohlberg, 1988, Race-ing Moral Formation: African Am. Perspectives on Care and Justice, 2004; mem. editl. bd. Harvard Ednl. Rev., 1979—81, Jour. Psychology and Theology, 1986—90, Jour. Moral Edn., 1998—, Am. Ednl. Rsch. Jour., 2001—04, mem. editl. adv. bd. Lawrence Erlbaum Assocs., 1988—90. Recipient Exemplary Dissertation award, Nat. Coun. Social Studies, 1982, Kuhmereker Dissertation award, Assn. Moral Edn., 1983, Outstanding Human Devel. Rsch. award, Am. Ednl. Rsch., 1988, James D. Moran Book award, Assn. Family and Consumer Sci., 1994, Marie C. Keel, Excellence in Mentoring award, 2003. Mem.: APA, Assn. Moral Edn. (exec. bd. 1986—, treas. 2001—04, pres. 2004—, program chair 1997, Dissertation award 1983), Am. Ednl. Rsch. Assn. (divsn. E exec. bd. 1990—2000, moral devel. and edn. spl. interest group co-chair 1994—96, sec. divsn. E 1997—99, Moral Devel. and Edn. Book award 2006). Office: Emory U Bishops Hall 66 Atlanta GA 30322-0001 Office Phone: 404-727-4185. Business E-mail: jsnarey@emory.edu.

**SNAVELY, LOANNE,** library director; b. Waterloo, Iowa, Oct. 2, 1950; d. John Ernest and Lois Mow Snavely; m. Gary Gyekis, Apr. 1, 1979; children: Joseph Gyekis, Elody Gyekis. BS, Juniata Coll., Huntingdon, Pa., 1972; M in Librarianship, Emory U., 1975; MS in Tchg., Rochester Inst. Tech., 1978. Reference libr. Bucknell U., Lewisburg, Pa., 1975—87; assoc. prof. Bloomsburg (Pa.) U., 1988—92; head arts libr. Pa. State U. Librs., University Park, 1992—97, acting head arts and humanities libr., 1997—99), head instrnl. programs, 1999—. Author: Designs for Active Learning: A Sourcebook of Classroom Strategies for Information Education; contbr. articles to profl. jours. Head environ. edn. programming Pa. Valley Conservation Assn., Aaronsburg, 2001—06. Recipient U. Librs. award, Pa. State U. Librs., 2004. Mem.: ALA/Assn. Coll. and Rsch. Librs. (chair instrn. sect. 1996—97, inst. info. literacy, chair 2003—05, Profl. Liaison award 1992, Miriam Dudley Instrn. Libr. award 2003), Pa. Libr. Assn. (exec. bd. 1984—85), Art Librs.

Soc. N.Am. (column editor 1995—96). Home: 614 Lingle Valley Rd Spring Mills PA 16875 Office: Pa State U 306 Pattee Libr University Park PA 16802 Office Phone: 814-865-3064. Office Fax: 814-865-9256. E-mail: lsnavely@psu.edu.

**SNEAD, DAVID N.,** music educator; b. Danville, Va., May 26, 1959; s. Rodney Easley and Lynwwod Alver (Motley) Snead; m. Kimberly Susan Ingram, July 30, 1988; children: Kelly Amanda, Noah Alexander. B in music edn., Va. Commonwealth U., 1986; MusM, James Madison U., 1989. Music performer numerous bands, Va. Ga. NC, 1980—; tchr. Va. Beach City Public Sch, Va. Beach, Va., 1990—. Dept. head fine arts Bayside Mid. Sch., Va. Beach, Va., 1991—, prin. adv. com., 2001—. Composer: various marching bands, 1977—. Mem.: Citizens for the Preservation of Rural Chesapeake. Avocations: softball, fishing, church, muscle cars, coaching youth baseball. Office: Bayside Mid Sch 965 Newtown Rd Virginia Beach VA 23462 Office Phone: 757-473-5080 60435. E-mail: davidsnead@juno.com.

**SNEAD, GEORGE MURRELL, JR.,** military officer, research scientist, consultant; b. San Diego, Nov. 6, 1922; s. George Murrell and Helen (Olsen) S.; m. Kathleen Hill Dawson, Apr. 26, 1947; children: George Murrell III, James M., William M., John P., Edward W. BS, Va. Mil. Inst., 1943; MS, U. Ill., 1948; PhD, U. Va., 1953. Commd. 2d lt. U.S. Army, 1943, advanced through grades to brig. gen., 1969; with Central Germany campaign 805th Signal Co., Europe, 1945-46; Aleutian sector comdr. Alaska Communication System, 1948-50; sta. at Electronic Warfare Center Ft. Monmouth, N.J. and Ft. Huachuca, Ariz., 1953-56; student U.S. Army Command and Gen. Staff Coll., 1956-57; signal adviser MAAG Vietnam, 1957-58; signal officer Dept. Army, 1958-60; acting dir. research ballistic missile def. Advanced Research Projects Agy., 1960; with U.S. Army Satellite Communications Agy. Ft. Monmouth, 1960-63; student Nat. War Coll., 1963-64; div. signal officer 24th Inf. Div., 1964-65; comdg. officer 7th Signal Group, 1965; dir. Communication /ADP Lab. Ft. Monmouth, 1966-68; exec. asst. chief of staff Communications Electronics, Dept. Army, 1968; dir. army research Dept. Army Washington, 1968-71; dep. comdr. Army Strategic Communications Command, 1971-73; prin. scientist Gen. Research Corp. McLean, Va., 1973-82; pres. Nat. Sci. Ctr. Found., Burke, Va., 1982-84. Chmn. bd. Am. Fed. Savs. & Loan Assn., Lynchburg, Va., 1985-86; sci./bus. cons., 1986—. Active Boy Scouts Am., 1958-68; bd. dirs. Ctrl. Youth Summer Activities, Ft. Monmouth, 1960-63, Arthritis Found., Washington, 1981-84, Lynchburg Symphony, 1990-95; pres. Acad. Music Theatre, Lynchburg, 1985-95; trustee, vice chmn. bd. dirs. Westminster-Canterbury, Lynchburg, 1991-99; trustee Sci. Mus. Va., 1995—; elder Presbyn. Ch., 1986—. Decorated D.S.M., Legion of Merit with two oak leaf clusters, Bronze Star, Air medal, Army Commendation medal with 4 oak leaf clusters. Mem. Assn. U.S. Army, Armed Forces Communications and Electronics Assn. (sec. Washington chpt. 1968-69), Sigma Xi, Kappa Alpha. Office: PO Box 3306 Lynchburg VA 24503-0306 Personal E-mail: g_snead@msn.com.

**SNEAD, JAMES ARRINGTON,** architect; b. Richmond, Va., June 24, 1950; s. John Elwood and Anna Ruth (Reiche) S. BA, U. N.C., 1972; MArch, Va. Tech. U., 1978. Assoc. CS&D Architects, Balt., 1980-84; v.p., pres. Ziger Hoopes & Snead, Balt., 1984-93; pres. Ziger/Snead Architects, Balt., 1994—. Trustee Gilman Sch., Balt., 1990—, treas. 1998—; mem. adv. bd. Md. Inst. Sch. Continuing Studies, Balt., 1991—, chmn., 1998—. Mem. AIA. Democrat. Presbyterian. Avocations: golf, travel, sailing, skiing. Office: Ziger/Snead Architects 1006 Morton St Baltimore MD 21201-5411

**SNEDDON, THOMAS WILLIAM, JR.,** prosecutor; b. LA, 1941; m. Pam Sneddon. BA, U. Notre Dame, 1963; JD, UCLA, 1966; grad., Nat. Dist. Atty. Sch., U. Houston, 1972, Nat. Homicide Acad., 1977. Dep. dist atty. Santa Barbara County, 1969—71, supr. criminal ops., 1977—82, dist. atty., 1983—. Mem. faculty Santa Barbara Coll. Law, 1989—; chair Com. for Child Support Enforcement, 1991—; advisor Am. Prosecutor's Rsch. Ctr.; pres. Calif. Dist. Atty. Assn., 1989—90; co-chair Nat. Dist. Atty. Child Support Com., Nat. Dist. Atty. Assn. Nat. Coun., 1997, v.p., 2000—. Served in U.S. Army, 1967—69. Recipient Leadership award, Calif. Dept. Social Services, 1993, Director's award, Calif. Family Support Coun., 1995, Disting. Faculty award, Nat. Dist. Atty. Coll., 2000. Office: Thomas W Sneddon Jr 1112 Santa Barbara St Santa Barbara CA 93101-2008

**SNEDEKER, JOHN HAGGNER,** university president; b. Plainfield, N.J., May 30, 1925; s. Alfred H. and Anna Marie (Ward) S.; m. Noreen I. Davey, Dec. 30, 1950; children—John D., Philip A., Patrick W. BS cum laude, N.Y. U., 1951, MA, 1951; Ed.D., Ind. U., 1959. Dir. lab. human devel. U. Mont., 1952-56; cons. psychologist research Purdue U., 1955; assoc. prof., dir. bur. research Ball State U., 1956-61; prof. higher edn., research asso. Ind. U., 1958; prof., dean Western Wash. State U., Bellingham, 1961-62; pres. Western N.Mex. U., Silver City, 1962—. Mem. exec. bd. Internat. Coun. Spl. Edn., 1952-56; Rocky Mountain regional rep. APA, 1953-56; mem. Gov. Wash. Com. Licensing Tchr. Edn., 1961, Wash. State Legislature Rsch. Tech. Com., 1961. Author or co-author rating scales, attitude and opinion measurement devices; contbr. jours. Bd. dirs. Nat. Sci. Fair; trustee N.Mex. Health Found. Served with U.S. Army, 1943-48. Fellow AAAS; mem. Midwest Psychol. Assn., Inter-Am. Soc. Psychology, Am. Ednl. Research Assn., Holland Soc. N.Y. Address: 2200 Pinon St Silver City NM 88061-7735

**SNEDIKER, DAVID E.,** lawyer; b. Chgo., Oct. 2, 1947; BS, U. Notre Dame, 1969; JD, St. John's U., 1975. Bar: N.Y. 1976, Conn. 1983. Ptnr. Paul, Hastings, Janofsky & Walker LLP, Stamford, Conn., mng. ptnr.-Stamford Office. Mem. ABA (com. creditors' rights in real estate financing 1984—, com. land surveys 1985-93, sect. real property, probate, trust law), Pension Real Estate Assn. (govt. affairs com. 1997—), Internat. Assn. Attys. in Corp. Real Estate (bd. dirs. 1991—, vice chmn. 1995—). Office: Paul Hastings Janofsky & Walker 9th Fl 1055 Washington Blvd Fl 9 Stamford CT 06901-2216 Office Phone: 203-961-7401. Office Fax: 203-359-3031. Business E-Mail: davidsnediker@paulhastings.com.

**SNEED, GUY WAYNE,** surgeon; b. Paris, Tex., Feb. 1, 1968; s. Stanley Ulysses Sneed and Margie Lee Brock; m. Catherine Ann Thornbrugh, Feb. 28, 2004; 1 child, Brock. BS, Okla. State U., 1990; DO, Okla. State U., Tulsa, 1994; MBA, Okla. City U., 1998. Diplomate Am. Bd. Ob-gyn Surgery. Chief med. officer Creek Nation Health Svs., Okmugee, Okla., 1995—98; chief resident Tulsa Regional Med. Ctr., 1998—2002, resident ob-gyn. surgery, 2002; pvt. practice ob-gyn. surgeon Tulsa, 2002—. Founder Adoption Svcs. Okla., 2004—. Author: (poetry) This House That I Have Built, 1994; contbr. articles to profl. jours. Hon. chmn. bus. adv. coun. Nat. Rep. Congl. Com., 2004—06. Mem. With U.S. Army, 2004—05. Named Rookie Physician of Yr., Okla. Osteo. Assn., 2004. Fellow: Am. Coll. Osteo. Ob-gyns.; mem.: Am. Osteo. Assn., Am. Coll. Physician Execs. Republican. Avocations: horseback riding, art, exercise. Home: 20190 E 72d St N East Concord NY 14055 Office: Northeast Oklahoma Womens Ctr 1222 N Florence Ave Ste C Claremore OK 74017 Business E-Mail: guy.sneed@triadhospitals.com.

**SNEED, JOSEPH TYREE, III,** federal judge; b. Calvert, Tex., July 21, 1920; s. Harold Marvin and Cara (Weber) Sneed; m. Madelon Juergens, Mar. 15, 1944 (dec. Dec. 1998); children: Clara Hall, Cara Carleton, Joseph Tyree IV. BBA, Southwestern U., 1941; LLB, U. Tex., Austin, 1947; SJD, Harvard, 1958. Bar: Tex. 1948. From instr. bus. law to prof. U. Tex., Austin, 1947—57, asst. dean, 1949—50; counsel Graves, Dougherty & Greenhill, Austin, 1954—56; prof. law Cornell U., 1957—62; prof. Stanford Law Sch., 1962—71; dean, prof. of law Duke Law Sch., 1971—73; dep. atty. gen. U.S. Justice Dept., 1973; judge U.S. Ct. Appeals (9th cir.), San Francisco, 1973—87, sr. judge, 1987—. Author: The Configurations of Gross Income, 1967, Footprints on the Rocks of the Mountain, 1997; contbr. articles to profl. jours. With USAF, 1942—46. Mem.: ABA, NY Bar Assn., Fed. Bar Assn., Assn. of Am. Law Schs., Am. Jud. Soc., Am. Law Inst. (cons. estate and gift tax project 1960—69), State Bar Tex., Order of Coif. Office: US Ct Appeals PO Box 193939 San Francisco CA 94119-3939 also: US Ct Appeals 9th Cir 95 Seventh St San Francisco CA 94103-1526*

**SNEED, PAULA ANN,** food products executive; b. Everett, Mass., Nov. 10, 1947; d. Thomas Edwin and F. Mary (Turner) S.; m. Lawrence Paul Bass, Sept. 2, 1978; children: Courtney Jameson. BA, Simmons Coll., 1969; MBA, Harvard U., 1977; D Bus. Adminstrn. (hon.), Johnson & Wales U., 1991. Ednl. supr., femal coord. Outreach Program for Problem Drinkers, 1969-71; dir. plans, program devel. and evaluations Ecumenical Ctr. in Roxbury, Mass., 1971-72; program coord. Boston Sickle Cell Ctr., 1972-75; asst. product mgr. Gen. Food Corp., White Plains, N.Y., 1977-79, assoc. product mgr., 1979-80; product mgr. Gen. Foods Corp., White Plains, N.Y., 1980-82, sr. product mgr., 1982-83, product group mgr., 1983-86, category mgr., 1986-87, v.p. consumer affairs, 1986-90, pres. food svc. div., sr. v.p., 1990-95; sr. v.p. mktg. svcs. Kraft Foods N.Am., 1995, group v.p., pres. e-commerce and mktg. services, 2000—04; sr. v.p. global mktg. resources Kraft Foods Inc., 2004—05, exec. v.p. global mktg. resources & initiatives, 2005—. Mem. bd. dirs. Hercules Inc., 1994-2002, Airgas Inc., 99-, Charles Schwab Corp., 2002-. Bd. dirs. Crispus Attucks Scholarship Fund, Ridgewood, N.J., 1982, Westchester/Fairfield Inroads; trustee Simmons Coll., Teach for Am., Chgo. Children's Museum. Recipient Benevolent Heart award Graham-Windham, 1987, Black Achiever award Harlem YWCA, 1982, MBA of Yr. Harvard Bus. Sch., 1987, Benevolent Heart award Graham Windham Soc., 1987; named MBA of Yr. Harvard Bus. Sch. Black Alumni Orgn., 1987; named one of 100 Top Black Women in Corp. Am. Ebony Mag., 1990, 91, 21 Most Influential African Ams. in Corp. Am., 1991, 97 (One of 40 Most Influential, 1993), Breakthrough 50 Exec. Female Mag., 50 Most Powerful Women Mgrs., 1994, 25 Most Influential Mothers Working Mother Mag., 1998; inducted Acad. Women Achievers N.Y. YWCA, 1990. Mem. AAUW, Exec. Leadership Coun., Chgo. Network, adv. coun. to dean Howard U. Bus. Sch., Nat. Assn. Negro Bus. and Profl. Women, Coalition of 100 Black Women, Soc. Consumer Affairs Profls., Women's Forum. Office: Kraft Foods Inc Three Lakes Dr Northfield IL 60093-2753

**SNEED, RONALD ERNEST,** retired project engineer, engineering educator; b. Oxford, NC, Nov. 23, 1936; s. Henry Ernest and Jewel Leigh (Hughes) S.; m. Shelba Jean Walters, June 8, 1958; children: Kathy Geneva Grosvenor, Jennie Leigh Berrier. BS in Agrl. Engring., N.C. State U., 1959, PhD in Biol. and Agrl. Engring., 1971. Registered profl. engr., NC; cert. irrigation designer, contractor, landscape irrigation auditor, and irrigation specialist. Sales trainee John Deere Co., 1959-60; ext. specialist NC State U., 1960-62, ext. instr., 1962-69, 70, ext. asst. prof., 1971-75, ext. assoc. prof., 1971-80, prof., 1980-92, prof. emeritus, 1993—; project engr. Agri-Waste Tech., Inc., 1993-2000, Irrigation Consulting, Inc., 1995—; project engr. divsn. soil and water NC Dept. Environment and Natural Resources, 1997-99, project engr. divsn. water quality, 2003—05, Carolina Turkeys, 2004, NC Dept. Adminstrn., 2004—05. Maj. gen. U.S. Army, 1960-95, ret. Recipient Outstanding Paper award So. region Am. Soc. Hort. Sci., 1986, 91; Ronald E. Sneed Irrigation Soc., Inc. scholarship established in his honor, 1991. Fellow Am. Soc. Agrl. Engrs. (ednl. aids competition Blue Ribbon 1963-64, 68, 78-79, 85, 89, 91-92, Gunlogson Countryside Engring. award 1992, Outstanding Paper award 1984), The Irrigation Assn. (life tech. mem., Man of Yr. 1981), NC Irrigation Soc., Inc. (Oustanding Contbn. to Irrigation award 1973, former tech. advisor), Soil and Water Conservation Soc., Carolinas Irrigation Assn. (hon.), Res. Officers Assn. (life), Civitan (Civitan of Yr. 1998). Democrat. Baptist. Office: 3405 Malibu Dr Raleigh NC 27607-6505 Office Phone: 919-782-7867. Personal E-mail: rsneed@intrex.net.

**SNEERINGER, STEPHEN GEDDES,** lawyer; b. Lancaster, Ohio, Mar. 27, 1949; s. Stanley Carlylle and Mary Eleanor (Fry) S.; m. Kristine Karen Serfling, Oct. 6, 1974; children: Mary Rhonda, Robyn Kathleen. BA magna cum laude, Denison U., Granville, Ohio, 1971; JD, Washington U., St. Louis, 1974. Bar: Mo. 1974. Sr. v.p. A.G. Edwards & Sons Inc., St. Louis, 1974—. Arbitrator N.Y. Stock Exch., NASD Dispute Resolution, Nat. Futures Assn., Am. Arbitration Assn. Editor: Urban Law Am., 1973-74; bd. editors Securities Arbitration Commentator. Am. Jurisprudence scholar, 1974. Mem. ABA (dispute resolution sect., arbitration com.), Mo. Bar Assn., Securities Industries Assn. (arbitration com.), Futures Industries Assn., Nat. Assn. Securities Dealers (mem. nat. arbitration and mediation com. 1992-94, 2001-03). Office: AG Edwards & Sons Inc 1 N Jefferson Ave Saint Louis MO 63103-2205

**SNEIDER, JOYCE PAPPACHRISTOU,** dietician, educator; b. Springfield, Mass., May 15, 1932; d. Hector and Henrietta (Hemerling) Flores; m. Stanley Sneider; children: Dianne, Donna, Paul Jr., Gary. AA, Nassau Community Coll., 1970; BA in Math., Sci. and Home Econs. with honors, Queens Coll., 1973; MA, MS in dietetics/nutrition, NYU, 1976; postgrad., Nova U., 1989—. Cert. tchr., N.Y.C., N.Y., tchr. home econs., health edn., sci., Fla.; lic. dietitian, nutritionist Fla. Tchr. Roslyn High Sch., Elmont Meml. High Sch.; dietitian L.I. (N.Y.) Jewish Hosp.; dietician St. Mary's Hosp.; instr. nutrition Cath. Med. Ctr. Nursing, 1974-76; chief dietician Jamaica (N.Y.) Hosp., 1976-80; tchr. Broward Coutny (Fla.) Bd. Educators, 1981—2000; pvt. practice, 2000—. Adj. prof. Nassau Community Coll., Fla. Internat. U., 1980-81. Contbr. articles to profl. jours. Mem. Am. Dietetics Assn., Am. Home Econs. Assn. (cert.), Fla. Dietetics Assn., Fla. Assn. Computer Educators, Fla. Correctional Edn. Assn., Fla. Assn. Alternative Educators, Phi Beta Kappa, Kappa Delta Pi. E-mail: Joysta@earthlink.net.

**SNEIDER, ROBERT M.,** petroleum exploration engineer; PhD in Geology and Mining Engring., U. Wis. With Shell Oil, Shell Devel.; ptnr. Sneider and Meckel Assocs., Inc., 1974-81; pres. Robert M. Sneider Exploration, Inc., Houston, 1981—. Disting. lectr. in field. Mem.: MAE, Soc. Petroleum Engrs., Petroleum Exploration Soc. Australia, Am. Assn. Petroleum Geologists. Office: Exploration Inc 419 Wycliffe Dr Houston TX 77079

**SNELL, BRUCE M., JR.,** retired judge; b. Ida Grove, Iowa, Aug. 18, 1929; s. Bruce M. and Donna (Potter) Snell; m. Anne Snell, Feb. 4, 1956; children: Rebecca, Brad. AB, Grinnell Coll., 1951; JD, U. Iowa, 1956. Bar: Iowa 1956, N.Y. 1958. Law clk. to presiding judge U.S. Dist. Ct. (no. dist.) Iowa, 1956-57; asst. atty. gen., 1961-65; judge Iowa Ct. Appeals, 1976-87; justice Iowa Supreme Ct., Des Moines, 1987—2001; ret., 2001. Comments editor: Iowa Law Rev. Mem.: ABA, Am. Judicature Soc., Iowa State Bar Assn., Order Coif. Methodist. Home: PO Box 192 Ida Grove IA 51445-0192

**SNELL, LINDA S.,** internist, educator; b. Salford, Eng., Apr. 24, 1952; BA, U. Alta., 1971, MD, 1975; MHPE, U. Ill., Chgo., 1997. Sr. physician Royal Victoria Hosp., Montreal, 1990—; assoc. dean continuing med. edn. McGill U., Montreal, 1994-2000, dir. divsn. gen. internal medicine, 1994—2004; assoc. physician-in-chief McGill U. Health Ctr., Montreal, 2004—. Fellow ACP, Royal Coll. Physicians Can.; mem. Can. Soc. Internal Medicine (pres. 1994-96), Can. Assn. Med. Edn. (treas. 2004—). Office: McGill U Health Ctr Dept Medicine 687 Pine Ave W Rm M3-07 Montreal PQ Canada H3A 1A1 E-mail: linda.snell@mcgill.ca.

**SNELL, MICHAEL STEVEN,** music educator; b. Pocatello, Idaho, Oct. 23, 1961; s. Harold Alfred and Marilyn Elizabeth Snell; m. Molly Ann McAllister, Apr. 11, 1997; children: Megan Marie, Christopher James. MA in Instrnl. Tech., U. Colo., Denver, 1998. Instrumental music tchr. Parker Jr. H.S., Parker, Colo., 1986—96; condr. Colo. Honor Band, Denver, 1990—98; instrumental music dir. ThunderRidge H.S., Highlands Ranch, Colo., 1996—. Exec. sec. Colo. Bandmasters Assn., Denver, 2000—03. Music Tech. grant, Douglas County Edn. Found., 1998. Mem.: Music Educators Nat. Conf., Am. Sch. Band Directors Assn., Colo. Bandmasters Assn. (life; exec. sec. 2000—03, Svc. award 2003). Avocations: woodworking, travel, music. Office: ThunderRidge HS 1991 Wildcat Reserve Pkwy Highlands Ranch CO 80129 Office Phone: 303-387-2123.

**SNELL, PATRICIA POLDERVAART,** librarian, consultant; b. Santa Fe, Apr. 11, 1943; d. Arie and Edna Beryl (Kerchmar) Poldervaart; m. Charles Eliot Snell, June 7, 1966. BA in Hist., U. N.M., 1965; MSLS, U. So. Calif., 1966. Asst. edn. libr. U. So. Calif., L.A., 1966—68; med. libr. Bedford (Mass.) VA Hosp., 1968—69; asst. law libr. U. Miami, Coral Gables, Fla.,

1970—71; acquistions libr. U. N.Mex. Law Sch. Libr., Albuquerque, 1971—72; order libr. Los Angeles County Law Libr., 1972—76, cataloguer, 1976—90; libr. Parks Coll., Albuquerque, 1990—92; records technician Technadyne Engring. Cons. to Sandia Nat. Labs., 1992—93; libr. Tireman Learning Materials Ctr. U. N.Mex., Albuquerque, 1993—96, instr. libr. sci. program Coll. Edn., 1991—; rsch. technician City of Albuquerque, 1996—2006; legal rsch. tch. Bernadillo County, 2006—. Ch. libr. Beverly Hills Presbyn. Ch., 1974-90, ch. choir libr., 1976-90. Southwestern Library Assn. scholar, 1965. Mem.: ALA, N.Mex. Libr. Assn., Pi Lambda Theta. Avocations: travel, reading. Office: Law Libr BCMDC 5800 Shelly Rd SW Albuquerque NM 87151 Business E-Mail: psnell@berno.gov.

**SNELL, RICHARD SAXON,** anatomist; b. Richmond, Surrey, Eng., May 3, 1925; came to U.S., 1963; s. Claude Saxon and Daisy Lilian S.; m. Maureen Cashin, June 4, 1949; children: Georgina Sara, Nicola Ann, Melanie Jane, Richard Robin, Charles Edward. MB, BS, Kings Coll., U. London, 1949, PhD, 1955, MD, 1961. House surgeon Sir Cecil P.G. Wakeley, Kings Coll. Hosp. and Belgrave Hosp. for Children, London, 1948-49; lectr. anatomy Kings Coll., U. London, 1949-59, U. Durham, Eng., 1959-63; asst. prof. anatomy and medicine Yale U., 1963-65, assoc. prof., 1965-67, vis. prof. anatomy, 1969; prof., chmn. dept. anatomy N.J. Coll. Medicine and Dentistry, Jersey City, 1967-69; vis. prof. anatomy Harvard U., 1970, 71, 80, 86; prof. anatomy Coll. Medicine, U. Ariz., Tucson, 1970; prof., chmn. dept. anatomy George Washington U. Med. Ctr., Washington, 1972-88, prof. emeritus, 1988—. Author: Clinical Embryology for Medical Students, 1972, 3d edit., 1983, Clinical Anatomy for Medical Students, 1973, 6th edit., 2000, Clinical Anatomy, 7th edit., 2003, Atlas of Normal Radiographic Anatomy, 1976, Atlas of Clinical Anatomy, 1978, Gross Anatomy Dissector, 1978, Clinical Neuroanatomy, 1980, 6th edit., 2006, Student's Aid to Gross Anatomy, 1986, Clinical Anatomy for Anesthesiologists, 1988, Clinical Anatomy of the Eye, 1989, 2d edit., 1997, Gross Anatomy: A Review with Questions and Explanations, 1990, Neuroanatomy: A Review with questions and Explanations, 1992, Clinical Anatomy for Emergency Medicine, 1993, Clinical Neuroanatomy: An Illustrated Review with Questions and Explanations, 3d edit., 2001, Clinical Anatomy: An Illustrated Review with Questions and Explanations, 4th edit., 2003 Clinical Anatomy by Systems, 2006; contbr. articles to med. jours. Med. Rsch. Coun. grantee, 1959; NIH grantee, 1963-65 Mem. Anat. Soc. Gt. Britain, Am. Soc. Anatomists, Alpha Omega Alpha. Home: 518 Boston Post Rd Madison CT 06443-2930

**SNELLING, BARBARA W.,** retired state legislator; b. Fall River, Mass., Mar. 22, 1928; d. Frank Taylor and Hazel (Mitchell) Weil; m. Richard Arkwright Snelling, June 14, 1947 (dec. Aug. 1991); children: Jacqueline, Mark, Diane, Andrew. AB magna cum laude, Radcliffe Coll., 1950; D of Pub. Svc. (hon.), Norwich U., 1981; LLD (hon.), Middlebury Coll., 1997; LLD (hon.), St. Michaels Coll., 2002. Pres. Snelling and Kolb, Inc., 1982-95; lt. gov. State of Vt., 1993-97; mem. U.S. Senate, Montpelier, Vt., 1997—99, 2001—02, ret., 2002. Bd. dirs. U.S. Inst. Peace; mem. adv. bd. Westaff Inc. Vt., 1997—. Mem. bd. sch. dirs. Champlain Valley Union HS, 1962—69, chmn., 1962—68, others; mem. Vt. Bd. Edn. Adv. Coun., 1968—71, New Eng. Tchr. Edn. Adv. Com., 1968—70, Shelburne Sch. Bd., 1958—73, Vt. Alcohol and Drug Rehab., 1970—73, Vt. State Bd. Edn., 1971—77, Vt. Ednl. Partnerships, 1992—2000, New. Eng. Bd. Dollars for Scholars, 1997—2002, Champlain Valley Area Health Edn. Coun., 1997—2002; bd. dirs. Vt. Cmty. Found., 1986—94, Shelburne Mus., 1988—98, Vt. Program Quality, 1997—2002; trustee Champlain Coll., 1971—74, Radcliffe Coll., 1990—95; v.p. devel. and external affairs U. Vt., 1974—82. Named Vt. Citizen of the Yr., Vt. State C. of C., 2002; recipient Laymen's award, Vt. Edn. Assn., 1965, Fanny G. Shaw award for Disting. Cmty. Svc., Burlington Cmty. Coun., 1972, Hope award, MS Cmty. Champion, 1996, Philanthropy Day award, Nat. Soc. Fundraising Execs., 1997, Susan B. Anthony award, YWCA Vt., 2001, Robert Skiff Cmty. Svc. award, Lake Champlain C. of C., 2002, Vt. Children's Trust Found. award, 2002, Patricia S. Walton award, Vt. Soc. Pub. Adminstrn., 2002, AHEC Bi State Primary Care Assn. award, 2002, Vt. Alzheimer's Assn. award, 2002, Gold heart, Am. Heart Assn., 2002. Office Phone: 802-985-2121. Personal E-mail: ulfkiel@aol.com.

**SNELLING, JAMES ANTHONY,** biology professor, technologist; b. Omaha, Nebr., Mar. 30, 1949; s. Lawrence Jack and Tina Maria Snelling; m. Mary Antionette Monico, Feb. 15, 1969; children: Kymberly Dawn Snelling-Donlan, Michelle Marie Dougherty, JoAnn Marie Higgins, Anthony James. BA in Biol. Scis., U. Nebr., Omaha, 1975, MA in Biol. Scis., 1978. Cert. med. technologist Am. Soc. Clin. Pathology, 1989. Med. technologist VA Med. Ctr., Omaha, 1970—2003, Alegent Health MV Hosp., Mo. Valley, Iowa, 2003—. Hospitalman, edn. staff USNR, Omaha, 1968—92; instr. Omaha Coll. Health Careers, 1981—2001; adj. instr. Met. C.C., Omaha, 2003—, Iowa We. C.C., Coun. Bluffs, Iowa, 2003—, Coll. St. Mary, Omaha, 2003—. With med. corps. USNR, 1970—71, Vietnam. Mem.: VFW, Am. Legion. Home: 815 Edgewood Blvd Papillion NE 68046 Personal E-mail: jamesandmary2@cox.net.

**SNELLING, ROBERT ORREN, SR.,** employment executive; b. Aug. 16, 1932; s. Louis Raymond and Gwendolyn Anne (Preble) S.; m. Joan E., 1951 (dec. 1979); children: Robert, Krista; m. Anne Morris, June 30, 1979; children: Rick Spragins, Leigh Crews, Linda Paulk. Student, Pa. State U., 1951-52; Dr. Lit. (hon.), Albright Coll., 1968. Profl. employment counselor Snelling & Snelling, Phila., 1952-53, gen. mgr., 1954—62, pres., 1962—96, chmn. bd. dirs., 1969—2000, CEO, 1997—2000; bus. and franchising cons., 2000—. Spkr., lectr. in field. Author: The Opportunity Explosion, 1969, Jobs—What They Are-Where They Are-What They Pay, 1985, rev. edit., 1992, The Right Job, 1987, rev. edit., 1992; contbr. articles to profl. jours. Mem. long-range planning Sarasota 2000, 1976; mem. pvt. sector employment svcs. com. Dept. Labor, 1982; mem. Com. on Skilled Employment Brokering Svcs., 1984; mem. White Ho. Com. on Small Bus., 1986; mem. adv. com. to U.S. Sec. William Brock, 1986; mem. Gov.'s Select Com. on Workforce 2000, 1988—89, chmn. govtl. regulations and benefits subcom., 1989; apptd. to Nat. Com. for Employment Policy, 1994—97; trustee Regent U., 1988—, Found. for Thought and Ethics, 1990—, Acts 29, 1999—. With U.S. Army, 1953—54. Recipient Golden Plate award, 1964, W.O. Blanchet award, Pa. Assn. Pers. Svc., 1976, Outstanding Citizen award, Assn. Pers. N.Y., 1977, award for excellence, Am. Acad. Achievement, 1964, Harold B. Nelson award, 1985. Mem. Internat. Franchise Assn., Nat. Assn. Pers. Cons., Nat. Assn. Temp. Svcs., U.S. C. of C. Republican. Office Phone: 214-618-2523. Personal E-mail: bsnelling@grandecom.net.

**SNELLING, TROY WAYNE,** history educator; b. Excelsior Springs, Mo., 1965; s. Kenneth Wayne and Shirley Louise Snelling. BA in History, Park Coll., 1991, MA in Edn., 1999. History educator Park Hill Sch. Dist., Kans. City, Mo., 1992—, chmn. Dept. Social Studies H.S., 1998—. Bd. dir. Tchg. History Through Reality, Kans. City. Mem.: Orders and Medals Soc. Am., Masons, Phi Alpha Theta. Republican. Episc. Avocations: coin collecting/numismatics, rare books, antiques, trapshooting, vintage cars. Home: 30422 NE 158th Excelsior Springs MO 64024 Office: Park Hill High School 7701 NW Barry Rd Kansas City MO 64153 Personal E-mail: snellingt@hotmail.com.

**SNIDER, BARRY B.,** organic chemist; b. Chgo., Jan. 13, 1950; s. Gordon L. and Ruth C. (Tobias) S.; m. Katalin Boros, July 12, 1975; 1 child, Emily L. BS in Chemistry, U. Mich., 1970; PhD, Harvard U., 1973. Postdoctoral fellow Columbia U., NYC, 1973-75; asst. prof. Princeton U., NJ, 1975-81; assoc. prof. Brandeis U., Waltham, Mass., 1981-85, prof., 1985—, chmn. dept. chemistry, 1992-95. Breskin prof. organic chemistry, 1998—. Recipient scholar award Dreyfus Found., 1982; Sloan Found. fellow, 1979; Japan Soc. for Promotion of Sci. fellow, 1999. Mem. Am. Chem. Soc. (Arthur C. Cope scholar 1995), Royal Soc. Chemistry. Office: Brandeis U Dept Chemistry Waltham MA 02454 Office Phone: 781-736-2550. E-mail: snider@brandeis.edu.

**SNIDER, DARRYL,** lawyer; BA Phi Beta Kappa, Univ. of Mich., 1971; JD magna cum laude, Univ. of Mich. Law School, 1974; PhD Economics, Highest Distinction, Univ. of Mich., 1975. Bar: Calif., U.S. Supreme Ct., Am. Bar Assoc. Adjunct prof. Law Golden Gate Univ., 1977—78, Univ. San Francisco, 1979; atty., shareholder Heller, Ehrman, White, & McAuliffe LLP, Los Angeles, Calif., 1998—. Panel mem. Inst. on Securities Litigation, 1996—97. Office: Heller Ehrman 601 South Figueroa Street 40th Fl Los Angeles CA 90017 Office Phone: 213-689-7577. Office Fax: 213-614-1868. E-mail: dsnider@hewm.com.

**SNIDER, DEE (DAVID DANIEL SNIDER),** rock singer, composer, radio personality; b. Massapequa, NY, Mar. 15, 1955; s. Bob and Marge S.; m. Suzette Guilot; children: Jesse, Shane, Cody, Cheyenne. Lead singer Twisted Sister, 1976—87, 1997—; Desperado, Widowmaker, the SMFs; host Dee Snider Radio WMRQ FM-104.1, Hartford, Conn., 1999—2002, WMMR 93.3-FM, Phila., 2004—05; host House of Hair syndicated radio show, 2005—; co-host Fangoria Radio, 2006—. Singer (with Twisted Sister): (albums) Ruff Cutts, 1982, Under the Blade, 1982, You Can't Stop Rock 'N' Roll, 1983, Stay Hungry, 1984, Come Out and Play, 1985, Love is for Suckers, 1987, Still Hungry, 2004, Twisted Christmas, 2006, (songs) Bad Boys of Rock 'n' Roll, 1982, I'll Never Grow Up Now!, 1982, We're Not Gonna Take It, 1984, The Price, 1984, Be Chrool to Your Scuel, 1985; singer: (with Desperado) (albums) Bloodied but Unbowed; singer: (with Widowmaker) Blood & Bullets, 1992, Stand by for Pain, 1994; singer: (solo albums) Never Let the Bastards Wear You Down, 2000; writer, actor (films) Strangeland, 1998, actor Deepwater, 2005, (TV films) Warning: Parental Advisory, 2002, writer, narrator (radio program) Van Helsing's Curse, 2004—05. Office: Mgmt & Bookings PO Box 77 Lindenhurst NY 11757-0077*

**SNIDER, DIANE MEIER,** organist, choir director, music educator; b. Montreal, Quebec, Canada, Sept. 24, 1962; d. Louis Alois and Judith Ann Meier; m. Curtis Wayne Snider, June 8, 1985; children: Christopher James, Michael Andreas. MusB, Westminster Choir Coll., NJ, 1984, MusM, 1986. Asst. interim organist Bryn Mawr Presbyn. Ch., Bryn Mawr, Pa., 1981; asst. organist, choir dir. St. Michael's Episc Luth. Ch., Paris, 1984—85; organist Hist. St. Peter's Episc. Ch., Perth Amboy, NJ, 1984—86; min. of music Collingwood Presbyn. Ch., Toledo, 1987—92; organist, asst. dir. of music First United Meth. Ch., Pine Bluff, Ark., 1993—2000; adj. instr. of music history and appreciation SE Ark. Coll., 1998—2000; parish musician Trinity Luth. Ch. and Sch., Newport News, Va., 2000—05. Organ recitalist Tidewater Chpt. AGO, Va., 2004—; dir. music, organist 1st United Ch. of Christ, Hampton, Va., 2005—; accompanist Va. Choral Soc., Newport News, Va., 2005—, asst. musical dir., 2006—. Recipient Music Hon., Pi Kappa Lambda, 1984, Accompanist, Oratorio Choir, Westminster Choir Coll., 1981—82; scholar Alexander McCurdy award in Organ Performance, 1980—81. Mem.: United Ch. Christ Musicians Nat. Network, Inc., Am. Guild of English Handbell Ringers. Avocations: gardening, bicycling. Home: 103 Saddle Dr Newport News VA 23602 Personal E-mail: toccatagirl@aol.com.

**SNIDER, EDWARD MALCOLM,** professional hockey club executive; b. Washington, Jan. 6, 1933; s. Sol C. and Lillian (Bonas) Snider; children: Craig Alan, Jay Thomas, Lindy Lou, Tina Suzanne, Sarena Lynn, Samuel Everett. BS, U. Md., 1955. CPA Md. Maj. stockholder, exec. v.p. Edge Ltd., Washington, 1957—63; v.p. Phila. Eagles Football Club, 1964—67; owner Phila. Flyers Hockey Club, 1967—; chmn. bd. Spectrum Arena, Phila. 1967—; bd. govs. NHL, 1967—. Established Spectacor (now Comcast-Spectacor), chmn. bd., 1996; adv. bd. Sol C. Snider Entrepreneurial Ctr. U Pa.; bd. overseers Wharton Sch. U. Pa.; bd. dirs. Inst. for Cancer and Blood Diseases Hahnemann U., Simon Weisenthal Ctr.; bd. trustees Inst. for Objectivist Studies. Co-recipient Lester Patrick Trophy for outstanding service to hockey in US, 1980; named Phila.'s greatest sports mover and shaker, Phila. Daily News, 1999; named to Hockey Hall of Fame, 1988, Phila. Flyers Hall of Fame, 1989. Office: Phila Flyers Phila 76ers First Union Center, 3601 S Broad St Philadelphia PA 19148-5250

**SNIDER, GEORGE RUNYON, JR.,** franchising company executive; b. Huntington, W.Va., Jan. 25, 1941; s. George R. and Marjorie Steuart S.; m. Nora C. Jacobs, Aug. 26, 1988; children: George R. III, Jeremy W. BA, Yale U., 1962. Assoc. dir. pub. affairs Procter & Gamble Co., Cin., 1972-76; dir. pub. rels. BF Goodrich Co., Akron, Ohio, 1977-82; dir. mktg. BF Goodrich Chem. Group, Cleve., 1982-88; dir. mktg. and comms. Walter & Haverfield, Cleve., 1988-92; pres., CEO SRA Internat., Inc., Akron, 1992—. Trustee Old Trail Sch., Bath, Ohio, 1982-88, trustee emeritus, 1989—. Named one of 100 Most Influential People in Recruiting Industry, Recruiter Mag., 2002. Mem.: Soc. Cin., Nat. Assn. Pers. Svcs. (dir., chmn. govt. affairs com. 1997—2000, chmn. pub. rels. 2000—01), Mory's Assn. (New Haven), The Club at Key Ctr. (Cleve.). Office: SRA Internat Inc 3737 Embassy Pkwy Ste 200 Akron OH 44333-8369

**SNIDER, GORDON LLOYD,** physician; b. Toronto, Apr. 11, 1922; came to U.S., 1946, naturalized, 1956; s. Isadore Leonard and Rebecca (Freeman) S.; m. Ruth Charlotte Tobias, May 18, 1945; children: Barry Bernard, Martin David, Rebecca Eve. MD, U. Toronto, 1944. Intern Toronto Gen. Hosp., 1944-45; resident in medicine Bronx Hosp., N.Y.C., 1946-47; resident in pathology Mass. Meml. Hosps., Boston, 1947-48; fellow in medicine Lahey Clinic, Boston, 1948-49; fellow in pulmonary medicine Trudeau San., Trudeau, NY, 1949-50; asst. dir. chest dept. Michael Reese Hosp., Chgo., 1950-61; attending physician Winfield (Ill.) Hosp., 1950-61; cons. physician, dir. pulmonary function lab. Mcpl. Tb San., Chgo., 1954-68; chief div. thoracic medicine Mt. Sinai Hosp., Chgo., 1961-66; acting chmn. depts. medicine Chgo. Med. Sch. and Mt. Sinai Hosp., 1965-66; chief pulmonary disease sect. Wood VA Hosp.; attending physician Milwaukee County Gen. Hosp., Wood, Wis., 1966-68. Asst. prof. Chgo. Med. Sch., 1958-61, assoc. prof., 1961-64, prof., 1964-66; prof. Marquette U. Sch. Medicine, 1966-68; prof. medicine, head pulmonary medicine sect. Boston U. Sch. Medicine, 1968-87; chief pulmonary medicine sect., Boston VA Med. Ctr., 1968-88, chief med. svc., 1986-2000, physician med. svc. VA Boston Healthcare Sys., 2000-2001; pulmonary sect. mem. Evans Dept. Clin. Rsch., U. Hosp., Boston, 1968-2000; Maurice B. Strauss prof. medicine Boston U. and Tufts U. Schs. Medicine, 1986-93, Boston U. Sch. Medicine, 1993—; Presdl. lectr. Soc. European Pulmonologists, Stressa-Milan, Italy, 1986, Blankenhorn lectr. Cin. Soc. Ind. Medicine, 1989; Parker B. Francis lectr. Thomas L. Petty Aspen Lung Conf., 1991, Theodore Badger Meml. lectr. Mass. Thoracic Soc., 1995; vis. prof. U. Cin. Sch. Medicine, 1989; Frank T. Fulton vis. physician-in-chief pro tempore R.I. Hosp. and Brown U., Providence, 1988; med. adv. bd. Puritan-Bennett Corp.; chmn. sci. adv. com. Norman B. Salvesen Emphysema Trust, U. Edinburgh, 1981-93; Theodore Badger Meml. lecture Mass. Thoracic Soc., 1995, Irving Kass lectr. U. Nebr., 1992 Chair sci. adv. com. Am. Lung Assn., 2002. Served to capt. M.C. Royal Can. Army, 1945-46. Co-recipient Alton Ochsner award, 1990; NIH grantee, 1962-91; Francis S. North travel fellow, 1978; 6th Robert K. Match Disting. scholar L.I. Jewish Hosp., 1991; recipient David M. Worthen for academic excellence award Dept. Vets. Affairs, 1998; Gordon and Ruth Snider Professorship in Pulmonary Medicine established at Boston U. Sch. Medicine, 2000; Gordon L. Snider Critical Workshop Series of Alpha-1 Found. established 2002. Fellow Am. Coll. Chest Physicians (Simon Rodbard lectr. 1985, Selman A. Waksman lectr. NJ chpt. 2003), ACP; mem. Am. Fedn. Clin. Research, Am. Thoracic Soc. (pres. 1986, Amberson lectr. 1992), Central Soc. Clin. Research, Sigma Xi, Alpha Omega Alpha. Jewish. Personal E-mail: glsnider@comcast.net.

**SNIDER, JAMES RHODES,** radiologist; b. Pawnee, Okla., May 16, 1931; s. John Henry and Gladys Opal (Rhodes) S.; m. Lynadell Vivion, Dec. 27, 1954; children: Jon, Jan. BS, U. Okla., 1953, MD, 1956. Intern Edward Meyer Meml. Hosp., Buffalo, 1956—57; resident radiology U. Okla. Med. Ctr., 1959—62; radiologist Holt-Krock Clinic and Sparks Regional Med. Ctr., Ft. Smith, Ark., 1962—66; dir. Fairfield Comty. Land Co. Little Rock 1968—87, Fairfield Comtys., Inc., 1968—87. Assoc. editor: Computerized Tomography, 1976—88. Mem. Ark. Bd. Pub. Welfare, 1967—70; bd. visitors U. Okla.; bd. dirs. U. Okla. Assn., 1967—70, U. Okla. Alumni Devel. Fund, 1970—74. Lt. comdr. USNR, 1957—62. Mem.: AMA, Am. Roentgen Ray

Soc., Radiol. Soc. N.Am., Am. Coll. Radiology, Phi Beta Kappa, Alpha Epsilon Delta, Beta Theta Pi. Home: 5814 Cliff Dr Fort Smith AR 72903-3845 Office: 1500 Dodson Ave Fort Smith AR 72901-5128

**SNIDER, JEROME GUY,** lawyer; b. Mar. 14, 1950; s. Theodore Charles and Minnie Snider; m. Naomi S. Herman, Sept. 20, 1981; children: Benjamin Herman, Todd Nathaniel. AB with highest honors, Rutgers U., 1972; attended, Hebrew U., Jerusalem, 1970—71; JD, U. Pa., 1975. Bar: N.Y. 1976, U.S. Dist. Ct. (so. and ea. dists.) N.Y. 1976, U.S. Dist. Ct. (no. dist.) Calif. 1979, U.S. Dist. Ct. D.C. 1983, U.S. Ct. Appeals (6th cir.) 1984, U.S. Ct. Appeals (D.C. cir.) 1986, U.S. Supreme Ct. 1980. Law clk. to chief judge U.S. Dist. Ct. (so. dist.) N.Y., N.Y.C., 1975—77; assoc. Davis Polk & Wardwell, N.Y.C., 1977—82, ptnr. Washington, 1983—94, N.Y.C., 1994—, co-head litig. practice group, 2000—05. Mem.: ABA, Bar Assn. of the City of N.Y. Jewish. Office: Davis Polk & Wardwell 450 Lexington Ave New York NY 10017-3911 Office Phone: 212-450-4060. Office Fax: 212-450-3060. Business E-Mail: jerome.snider@dpw.com, snider@dpw.com.

**SNIDER, L. BRITT,** federal official; b. Rocky Mount, NC, Jan. 12, 1945; s. Arnold Holmes and Kate Mills (Suiter) S.; m. Virginia Lansford, Aug. 24, 1974; 1 child, Britt Arnold. BA, Davidson Coll., NC, 1966; JD, U. Va., 1969. Counsel judiciary subcom. on constl. rights U.S. Senate, Washington, 1971-75, counsel select com. on intelligence, 1975-76; ptnr. Ketner & Snider, Salisbury, NC, 1976-77; counsel govt. ops. subcom. on govt. info. U.S. Ho. Reps., Washington, 1977; asst. dep. undersec. counterintelligence and security Dept. Def., Washington, 1977-87; minority counsel U.S. Senate Intelligence Com., Washington, 1987-89, gen. counsel, 1989-95, staff dir. commn. on roles and capabilities of U.S. Intelligence Cmty., 1995-96; sr. fellow Ctr. for Study of Intelligence, 1996-97; spl. counsel to dir. CIA, 1997-98, inspector gen., 1998-2001. Staff dir. Commn. to Rev. Security Practices and Procedures Dept. Def., Washington, 1985; adj. prof. Sch. Foreign Svc. Georgetown U., 2005 Served to capt. U.S. Army, 1969-71, Vietnam. Mem.: DC Bar Assn., Va. Bar Assn. Democrat. Episcopalian. Avocations: golf, jogging, reading.

**SNIDER, MARIE ANNA,** syndicated columnist; b. Croghan, N.Y., Aug. 9, 1927; d. Nicholas and Dorothy (Moser) Gingerich; m. Howard Mervin, Nov. 27, 1954; children: Vada Marie, Conrad Howard. BS, Goshen Coll., 1949; M in Religious Edn., Mennonite Bibl. Sem., 1957; MS, Kans. State U., 1980. High sch. tchr. Rockway Collegiate, Kitchener, Ont., Can., 1949-53; freelance writer, 1953-54; pub. rels. Goshen Coll., Ind., 1955-57; free-lance writer, homemaker, 1957-67; info. editor Prairie View, Inc., Newton, Kans., 1967-76, dir., pub. info. & edn., 1976-85, dir. communications, 1985-91; freelance writer, columnist North Newton, 1991—; syndicated columnist "This Side of 60", 1992—. Bd. dirs. Health Systems Agy. of S.E. Kans. 1981-86, v.p., 1986-87; workshop presenter Nat. Coun. of Community Mental Health Ctrs., Atlanta, 1980, N.Y., 1982, 89, Miami, 1987. Editor: Media and Terrorism--The Psychological Impact, 1976; columnist: This Side of 60. Pres. City Council, N Newton, 1977-79, pres. 1980. Recipient 1st Pl. MacEachern award Assn. of Hosp. Pub. Rels., 1981, 1st Pl. Media award Nat. Coun. Community Mental Health Ctrs., 1977, 84, runner-up Pub. Rels. award Nat. Assn. Pvt. Psychiat. Hosps., 1980. Mem. Nat. Soc. Newspaper Columnists. Democrat. Avocations: research on role of women in american comics (speaker and media interviews on this topic), empowerment in aging. Home and Office: PO Box 332 North Newton KS 67117-0332 E-mail: thisside60@aol.com.

**SNIDER, RICHARD DOUGLAS,** music educator, director; b. Oklahoma City, Nov. 6, 1945; s. Norman and Natalie Campbell Snider; m. Sandra G. Snider, Aug. 12, 1972; children: Britten C., Miles D. MusB in Edn., Tex. Tech U., 1968; MusM in Edn., Tex. Tech. U., 1968. Cert. tchr. N.Mex Dept. Edn., 2006. Tchr. music Santa Fe (N.Mex.) Pub. Schs., 1972—2000; dir. bands St. Michael's H.S., Santa Fe, 2001— Arranger (orch.) Pavane by Gabriel Faure. Served with Army bands U.S. Army, 1968—71. Named one of Tchrs. Who Inspire, Santa Fe (N.Mex.) Partners in Edn., 1994. Mem.: Tex. Bandmasters Assn., Santa Fe (N.Mex.) Music Educator's Assn. (instr. 2002—), N.Mex Music Educator's Assn. (named to Hall of Fame 2002). Home: 625 Webber St Santa Fe NM 87505 Office Phone: 505-983-7353.

**SNIDER, ROBERT LARRY,** management consultant; b. Muskogee, Okla., Aug. 10, 1932; s. George Robert and Kathryn (Smiser) S.; m. Gerlene Rose Tipton, Nov. 26, 1953; children: Melody Kathryn Porter, Rebecca Lee. BS in Indsl. Engring., U. Houston, 1955, postgrad., 1956, Pomona Coll., 1960. Cert. mgmt. cons. Instr. U. Houston Coll. Engring., 1955-56; sr. indsl. engr. Sheffield Steel Corp., Houston, 1955-59, Kaiser Steel Co., Fontana, Calif., 1959-60; cons. Arthur Young & Co. L.A., 1960-61; mgmt. analyst Iranian Oil Exploration & Producing Co., Masjidi-Suliman, Iran, 1961—65; v.p., Dallas office mgr. operating methods divsn. Booz, Allen & Hamilton, Inc., 1966—68, v.p. internat. prodn. and inventory control divsn., 1968—69; prin., gen. cons. practice Peat Marwick Mitchell, CPAs, Houston, 1969-71; exec. v.p. mfg. Sterling Electronics Corp., Houston, 1971-72, COO, pres., 1972-77; CEO, pres. Rapoca Energy Corp., Cin., 1977-79; mng. ptnr., cons. Coopers & Lybrand, Southwest, Houston, 1979-81; mng. dir. S.W. region Korn Ferry Internat., Houston, 1981-86; ptnr.-in-charge Houston Mgmt. Cons. Practice, 1986-91; ptnr. cons. Southwest Enterprise Coopers & Lybrand, Houston, 1991-92, S.W. Mfg. Cons. Process Improvement Group, 1992-93, internat. cons. ptnr., 1993-95; mng. ptnr. RLS Profl. Svcs. LLC, 1995—; chmn., dir. L&G Snacks, 1997-2000. Chmn. L&G Snacks. Trustee Gene Cragg Caring Forever Found., 1997—99; sr. trustee R. Larry and Gerri R. Snider Native Am. scholarship trust Cullen Coll. Engring., U. Houston, 2004—; sr. trustee Kipten Native Am. female scholar trust U. Houston, Cullen Coll. Engring.; past chmn. bd. mem. found. bd. and adminstrv. bd. Chapel Wood Meth.Ch.; former mem. adminstrv. bd. Memorial Dr. Meth. Ch., Houston, 1997—99; sr. trustee United Meth. Found. Remainder Trust, 2002—; chmn. adminstrv. bd. 1st United Meth. Ch., Willis, Tex., 2001—02; deacon, steward, video coord. 1st Christian Ch., Conroe, Tex., 2003—05; past bd. dirs. Houston Jr. Achievement, exec. com.; ret. exec. com. Houston Grand Opera, bd. dirs.; sr. trustee Tipton-Snider Minister Edn. Fund., 1999—; mem. Cullen Coll. Leadership bd. U. Houston. With C.E. AUS, 1956. Recipient Outstandng Mil. Engr. award Soc. Mil Engrs., 1955; named Disting. Alumni, Cullen Coll. Engring., U. Houston, 1991, named Disting. Indsl. Engring. Alumni, 2005. Mem.: Bridge Builder Soc., U. Houston Alumni Assn. (life; exec. com. 1985—94, pres. and chmn. bd. 1990—93, past bd. dirs., named to Cir. of Excellence), Phi Kappa Phi, Phi Theta Kappa. Home and Office: 9387 Escondido Dr Willis TX 77318-6621 Personal E-mail: rlarry32@earthlink.net.

**SNIDER, STACEY,** film company executive; b. Phila., Apr. 29, 1961; m. Gary Jones; children: Katie, Natalie. BA, U. Penn., 1982; JD, U. Calif. LA, 1985. Dir. of devel. Guber-Peters Entertainment Co., 1986—90, exec. v.p., 1990—92; pres. prodn. TriStar Pictures, 1992-96; co-pres. prodn. Universal Pictures, Universal City, Calif., 1996—98, pres. prodn., 1998—99, chmn., CEO, 1999—2006; co-chmn., CEO DreamWorks SKG, Glendale, Calif., 2006—. Bd. dirs. Am. Film Inst. Bd. dirs. Spl. Olympics of So. Calif.; bd. trustees Art Ctr. Coll. of Design, Pasadena, Calif. Named one of 100 Most Powerful Women in Entertainment, Hollywood Reporter, 2005, Most Powerful Women, Forbes mag., 2005, 50 Most Powerful People in Hollywood, Premiere mag., 2004—05, 100 Most Powerful Women in Bus., Fortune mag., 2005—06; recipient Dorothy and Sherrill C. Corwin Human Rels. Award, Am. Jewish Com. 2003. Office: DreamWorks SKG 1000 Flower St Glendale CA 91201*

**SNIDER, TIMOTHY R.,** mining executive; BS in Chemistry and Geology, No. Ariz. U., 1979; grad. advanced mgmt. program, U. Pa., 1996. Joined Phelps Dodge Corp., 1970; pres. Phelps Dodge Morenci Inc., Morenci, Ariz.; pres., COO Phelps Dodge Mining Co., 1998—; sr. v.p. Phelps Dodge Corp., 1998, pres., COO Phoenix, 2003—. Office: Phelps Dodge Corp One North Central Ave Phoenix AZ 85004*

**SNIFFEN, FRANCES P.,** artist; d. Esther Wade; m. Richard Sniffen; children: William, Kevin, Jeffrey, John, Caroline. BFA, Corcoran Coll. Art and Design, 1996. Resident artist Arlington Arts Ctr., Arlington, Va., 2001—; tchr. art summer workshop; studio Millennium Art Ctr., Washington, 2003. Mem. women's com. Nat. Mus. Women in Arts, Washington, 2001—. Author (with Caroline Sniffen): Coloring Shadows, 1994 (Dorothy Tabak Meml. award NAWA, 2002); exhibitions include Artscape 97, Balt., Md., 1997, WPA Space, Washington, 1998, Bristol (RI) Art Mus., 2001, The DCCA, Wilmington, Del., 2002, Russian Embassy Cultural Ctr., Washington, 2002, Attleboro (Mass.) Mus., 2002, IASG, 2002, Tsinghua U., Bejing, China, Gallery K, Washington, 2002, Biennale Internazionale Dell'Arte Contemporanea Citta di Firenze, 2003, one-woman shows include Gallery K, Wash., 2003, mentioned in critical review by John Blee, Art Critics Rev., Georgetowner Newspaper, 2003. Mem. gala com. Imperial Collections, State Hermitage Mus. for Nat. Mus. Women in the Arts, Washington, 2003; vol. White House, Washington, 1992—93; mem. art com., event chmn. Hospitality Info. Svc. Meridian House Internat., Washington, 1986—; mem. women's com., event chair Nat. Symphony Orch. Kennedy Ctr., Washington, 1986—; women's bd. exec. vol. Georgetown U. Hosp., Washington, 1988—2002. Mem.: Nat. Assn. Women Artists, Inc. (juried membership, N.Y.C.). Avocations: creative writing, music, sports, politics, nutrition.

**SNIPES, WESLEY,** actor, film producer; b. Orlando, Fla., July 31, 1962; m. April Snipes, 1984 (div. 1990); 1 child, Jelani Asar; 1 child, Isnet. Grad. SUNY, Purchase, 1980, D (hon.) in Humanities and Fine Arts. Appeared in Broadway plays Boys of Winter, Execution of Justice, Death and King's Horsemen; (films) Streets of Gold, 1986, Vietnam War Story (ACE award for best actor 1989), Mo'Better Blues, 1989, Major League, 1989, King of New York, 1990, New Jack City, 1991 (NAACP Image award for outstanding actor), Jungle Fever, 1991, The Waterdance, 1992, White Men Can't Jump, 1992, Passenger 57, 1992, Rising Sun, 1993, Demolition Man, 1993, Boiling Point, 1993, Sugar Hill, 1994, Drop Zone, 1994, To Wong Foo, Thanks for Everything, Julie Newmar, 1995, The Money Train, 1995, The Fan, 1996, Murder at 1600, 1997, U.S. Marshals, 1998, One Night Stand, 1998 (Venice Film Festival Volpi Cup award for best actor), Play it to the Bone, 1999, Liberty Stands, 2002, Zigzag, 2002; actor, prodr., martial arts choreographer Blade, 1998; actor, prodr. Blade II, 2002, Blade: Trinity, 2004; actor, exec. prodr. Art of War, 2000, Undisputed, 2002; prodr. The Big Hit, 1998, Down in the Delta, 1998, Dr. Ben, 2001; (TV) H.E.L.P., 1990, The Real Malcolm X, 1992, America's Dream, 1996 (NAACP Image award for best actor in a TV movie/series); actor, prodr. (TV) Future Sport, 1998; actor, exec. prodr. Disappearing Acts, 2000; TV guest appearances include The Bernie Mac Show, 2001. Recipient Star on Hollywood Walk of Fame, 1998.

**SNITKOFF, GAIL GOODMAN,** immunologist, educator; d. Alvin and Muriel Goodman; m. Louis Steven Snitkoff, June 12, 1976; children: Joshua, Benjamin. PhD, N.Y. State Downstate Med. Ctr., Bklyn., 1974—79. Instr. Union Coll., Schenectady, NY, 1984—86; rsch. asst. prof. Albany Med. Ctr., NY, 1986—91; asst. prof. Albany Coll. Pharmacy, NY, 1991—96, assoc. prof., 1996—. Contbr. articles to profl. jours. Mem. Planned Parenthood, 1980—2005; pres. Schenectady Hadassah, NY, 2003—05; mem. NARAL, 1990—2004; mem., bd. trustees Congregation Gates of Heaven, Schenectady, NY, 1986—92; pres. Schenectady Area Midrasha, NY, 1995—2005. Fellow, NSF, 1979—80, NIH, 1980—82; grantee, 1987—90. Mem.: AAAS (assoc.), N.Y. Acad. Sci. (assoc.), Sigma Xi (assoc.), Am. Assn. Microbiology (assoc.), N.Y.C. Ballet Guild (assoc.), Glass Art Soc. (assoc.), Saratoga Performing Arts Ctr. (life). Jewish. Achievements include patents for immunogenic composites capable of selectively inducing antibody production; research in pharmaceutical compositions employing the same method of selectively inducing antibody production. Avocations: performing arts, contemporary crafts, knitting, reading, travel. Home: 2154 Lynnwood Dr Niskayuna NY 12309 Office: Albany Coll Pharmacy 106 New Scotland Ave Albany NY 12208 Office Phone: 518-694-7227. Business E-Mail: snitkofg@acp.edu.

**SNITZER, ELIAS,** physicist; b. Lynn, Mass., Feb. 27, 1925; s. Isaac and Jenny (Sussman) Snitzer; m. Shirley Ann Wood, Nov. 22, 1950; children: Sandra, Barbara, Peter, Helen, Louis. BSEE, Tufts U., 1946; MS in Physics, U. Chgo., 1950, PhD, 1953. Rsch. physicist Honeywell Corp., Phila., 1954-56; assoc. prof. Lowell Technol. Inst., Mass., 1956-58; dir. rsch. Am. Optical Co., Southbridge, Mass., 1959-76; mgr. applied physics United Technologies Rsch., East Hartford, Conn., 1977-84; mgr. fiber optics Polaroid, Cambridge, Mass., 1984-88; prof. Rutgers U., 1989-97, prof. emeritus, 1997—. Contbr. articles to profl. jours. With USN, 1943—46. Fellow: Am. Phys. Soc., Ceramic Soc. (Corning Stookey Discovery award 2006), Optical Soc. Am. (John Tyndall award 1994); mem.: IEEE (George Morey award 1971, Quantum Electronics award 1979, Charles Townes award 1991, Otto Schott award 1999, Opto-Electronic Rank prize 2000, LEOS Millenium award 2001), NAE. Democrat. Jewish. Achievements include invention of glass laser; fiber laser amplifier. Home and Office: 78 Ivy Rd Wellesley MA 02482 Office Phone: 781-431-2605. Personal E-Mail: snitzer27@yahoo.com.

**SNODDY, CHRIS RAYMOND,** athletic trainer; b. Nashville, Nov. 19, 1959; s. Raymond Thomas and Farris (Duke) S. BS, Lipscomb U., 1981; MA, Appalachian State U., 1987. Lic. athletic trainer. Real estate salesperson McKinney & Co., Nashville, 1980-89; head athletic trainer Lipscomb U., Nashville, 1981-91; sr. athletic trainer Ctr. Sports Medicine, Bapt. Hosp., Nashville, 1993—; coord. sports medicine Bapt. Hosp., Nashville, 1997—99, mgr., 1999—2003, dir., 2003—; head athletic trainer Skyline Med. Ctr., 2003—. Dir. sports medicine Pinnacle Rehab., Nashville, 1991-92; cons. sports medicine David Lipscomb H.S., Nashville, 1982-91; adj. faculty Free Will Bapt. Bible Coll., Nashville; cons. Lipscomb U. Sports Medicine. Editor: Where to Go Camping Guide, 1980; contbr. articles to Flying Eagle mag. Recipient Mayor's medallion City of Nashville, 1986, Silver Beaver award Boy Scouts Am., 1995; named Eagle Scout, 1976, Ohio Athletic Trainer of Yr., 1992, 2003, Athletic Trainer of Yr., Southeastern Athletic Trainers Assn., 2005; named to Lipscomb U. Hall of Fame, 2004. Mem. Nat. Athletic Trainers Assn., Tenn. Athletic Trainers Soc. (named to Hall of Fame, 2005). Mem. Ch. of Christ. Lodges: Civitan (bd. dirs. Nashville 1986-87, pres. 1990), Wa-Hi-Nasa (lodge advisor 1995—), Order of Arrow (assoc. advisor Tenn. and Ky. sects. 1984-87, 2004-05, Founder's award 1976). Avocation: skiing. Home: 315 Bowwood Dr Nashville TN 37217-2301 Office Phone: 615-769-7576.

**SNODDY, JAMES ERNEST,** education educator; b. Perrysville, Ind., Oct. 6, 1932; s. James Elmer and Edna May (Hayworth) S.; m. Alice Joanne Crowder, Aug. 15, 1954; children: Ryan Anthony, Elise Suzanne. BS, Ind. State U., 1954; MEd, U. Ill., 1961, EdD, 1967. Tchr. Danville (Ill.) Pub. Schs., 1954-57, prin., 1961-64; instr. U. Ill., Champaign, 1965-67; prof. edn. Mich. State U., East Lansing, 1967-72, 78-96, chmn. dept. elem. and spl. edn., 1972-78, ret., 1996, prof. emeritus, 1997—; dir. Program CORK, 1978-82. With U.S. Army, 1955-57. Mem. Am. Assn. for Adult and Continuing Edn., Commn. of Profs. of Adult and Continuing Edn. Methodist. Home: 1926 Creek Lndg Haslett MI 48840-8704 Office: Mich State U 419 Erickson Hall East Lansing MI 48824-1034 Office Phone: 517-339-6548. Business E-Mail: jsnoddy@msu.edu.

**SNODGRASS, W. D.,** writer, educator; b. Wilkinsburg, Pa., Jan. 5, 1926; s. Bruce DeWitt and Jesse Helen (Murchie) S.; m. Lila Jean Hank, June 6, 1946 (div. 1953); 1 child, Cynthia Jean; m. Janice Marie Ferguson Wilson, Mar. 19, 1954 (div. Aug. 1966); children— Kathy Ann Wilson (stepdau.), Russell Bruce; m. Camille Rykowski, Sept. 13, 1967 (div. 1977); m. Kathleen Brown, June 20, 1985. Student, Geneva Coll., 1943-44, 46-47; BA, State U. Iowa, 1949, MA, 1951, MFA, 1953; doctorate (hon.), Allegheny Coll., 1991. Faculty English dept. Cornell U., Ithaca, N.Y., 1955-57; faculty English dept. U. Rochester, N.Y., 1957-58; prof. English Wayne State U., Detroit, until 1968; prof. English and speech Syracuse U., N.Y., 1968-76; Disting. prof. of creative writing and contemp. poetry U. Del., Newark, 1979-94, retired, 1994. Faculty Morehead Writers' Conf., Ky., summer 1955, Antioch Writers' Conf., Yellow Springs, Ohio, summer 1958, 59; disting. vis. prof. Old Dominion U., Norfolk, Va.; instr. Narrative Poetry Workshop SUNY, Binghamton, 1977, Cranbrook Writers' Conf., Birmingham, Mich., 1981. Author: (poems) Heart's Needle (Pulitzer prize 1960), 1959, After Experience, 1968, Remains (under pseudonym S.S. Gardons) 1970, The Fuhrer Bunker, 1977, If Birds Build With Your Hair, 1979, The Boy Made of Meat, 1982, Magda Goebbels (poems from The Fuhrer Bunker, 1983), Heinrich Himmler (poems from The Fuehrer Bunker) 1983, D.D. Byrde Calling Jennie Wrenne, 1984, A Colored Poem, 1986, The House the Poet Built, 1986, 1987, Selected Poems, 1957-87, W.D.'s Midnight Carnival: Poems by W.D. Snodgrass and Paintings by DeLoss McGraw, 1988, The Death of Cock Robin: Poems by W.D. Snodgrass and Paintings by DeLoss McGraw, 1989, Autumn Variations, 1990; translator: (with Lore Segal) Gallows' Songs of Christian Morgenstern, Six Troubadour Songs, 1977, Traditional Hungarian Songs, 1978, Six Minnesinger Songs, 1983, The Four Seasons (translations of Vivaldi's Sonnets) 1984, (essays) In Radical Pursuit, 1975, Star and Other Poems, 1990, Five Romanian Ballads, 1991, Snow Songs, 1992, Each in His Season, 1993, The Fuehrer Bunker: The Complete Cycle, 1995; contbr. essays, poems, translations to lit. mags. Recipient Ingram-Merrill award, 1958, Longview lit. award, 1959, spl. citation Poetry Soc. Am., 1960, Pulitzer prize for poetry, 1960, Guinness Poetry award, 1961, Miles Modern Poetry award, 1966; Hudson Rev. fellow in poetry, 1958-59; fellow Guggenheim Found., 1972-73, Acad. Am. Poets, 1973, Bi-Centennial Medal William and Mary Coll., 1976, Centennial Medal Govt. Romania, 1977; Ingram-Merrill fellow 1979; sabbatical grantee Nat. Council on Arts, 1966-67, Ctr. for Advanced Study U. Del. grantee, 1983-84. Mem. PEN, Nat. Inst. Arts and Letters (grantee 1960), Poetry Soc. Am.*

**SNOEYINK, VERNON L.,** civil engineer, educator; BS in Civil Engring., U. Mich., 1964, MS in Sanitary Engring., 1966, PhD in Water Resource Engring., 1968. Assoc. prof. sanitary engring. U. Ill., Urbana, 1969-73, from assoc. prof. to prof. environ. engring., 1973—, Ivan Racheff prof. environ. engring., 1989—2004, prof. emeritus, 2004—. Mem.: NAE. Office: U Ill Dept Civil Engring Newmark Civil Engring Lab 205 N Mathews Ave Urbana IL 61801 Business E-Mail: snoeyink@uiuc.edu.

**SNOOK, PAUL,** real estate company executive; b. Swindon, Wilt, Eng., Dec. 31, 1949; arrived in U.S., 1979; s. Eric Arthur and Era Glynis Snook; m. June Chambers, Apr. 17, 1971 (div. Sept. 1977); m. Elizabeth Keefe, June 25, 1979 (div. Jan. 2003); children: Sarah, Erica. Student, Northampton (Eng.) Coll. Exec. property mgr. Zaremba Mgmt. Svcs. Inc., Cleve., 1979-85, dir. mktg. ops., 1985-88; sr. v.p. Riverview Mgmt. Co., Akron, Ohio, 1988-96; pres. Strategic Property Mgmt., Cleve., 1999—; Paul Snook & Assocs., Cleve. Contbr.: Professional Apartment Rental Techniques, 1999. Recipient Cmty. Improvement award City of Mayfield Heights, 1986. Mem. No. Ohio Apt. Assn. (life trustee, Mgr. of Yr. 1994, Pres. award 1987-90), Inst. of Real Estate Mgmt. (Pres. award 1987-90, cert. property mgr.), Cleve. Area Bd. of Realtors. Avocation: sailing.

**SNOOP DOGG, (CALVIN BROADUS),** vocalist, actor; b. Long Beach, Calif., Oct. 20, 1972; s. Beverly Tate; m. Shante Taylor, June 1997; 1 child, Corde Calvin Broadus;children from previous marriage: Cordell Broadus, Cori Broadus. Founder, owner Doggy Style Records, Inc. (formerly Dogg-House Records), 1999—. Musician: (albums) Doggystyle, 1993, Tha Dogg-father, 1996, Da Game Is To Be Sold Not To Be Told, 1998, No Limit Top Dogg, 1999, Tha Last Meal, 2000, Doggy Style Allstars: Welcome to Tha House, 2002, Paid Tha Cost to Be da Bo$$, 2002, Soundtrack Raw N Uncut, Vol. 1, 2002, Welcome to Church: Mix Tape, Vol. 1, 2003, R&G - Rhythm and Gangster: The Masterpiece, 2004, Dogg Pound Mix, 2005, Me & My Homies, 2005, Tha Blue Carpet Treatment, 2006, The Chronicalz, Vol. 1: The Mixed Up Album, 2006, (CD singles) Vapors, 1997; actor: (films) Half Baked, 1998, I Got the Hook Up, 1998, Ride, 1998, Caught Up, 1998, Urban Menace, 1999, The Wrecking Crew, 1999, Hot Boyz, 1999, Tha Eastsidaz, 2000, Baby Boy, 2001, Training Day, 2001, Bones, 2001, The Wash, 2001, Crime Partners, 2001, Malibu's Most Wanted (voice), Starsky & Hutch, 2004, Soul Plane, 2004, (voice) Racing Stripes, 2005,; (guest appearance in film) Old School, 2003, (guest appearance in TV show) Just Shoot Me, 2001; author: Tha Doggfather: The Times, Trials, and Hardcore Truths of Snoop Dogg, 1999. Founder Snoop Youth Football League, Calif., 2005. Office: Doggy Style Records 1142 S Diamond Bar Blvd #504 Diamond Bar CA 91765*

**SNORTLAND, HOWARD JEROME,** financial consultant; b. Sharon, N.D., June 22, 1912; s. Thomas and Aline (Vig) S.; m. Anna Adeline Anderson, Sept. 1, 1940; children— Jan Signe, Kristi Jo, Howard Jay. BA, U. Ill., 1937, MS, 1958. Cashier R.D. Workmen's Compensation Bur., 1937-42, N.D. State Treas.'s Office, 1945-48; with N.D. Dept. Pub. Instrn., Bismarck, 1948-81, supt. pub. instrn., 1977-81; edn. fin. cons., 1981—. Pres. State Econ. Coun., 1978; nat. pres. Com. Ednl. Data Systems, 1965-67 Chmn. Burleigh ARC, 1963-67, bd. dirs., 1946—, vice chmn., 1964—; bd. dirs. Burleigh County Tb Assn., 1950—; stated clk. United Presbyterian Ch., 1942—; pres. N.D. United Christian Campus Fellowship, 1964-67, N.D. Westminster Found., 1963-70; mem. N.D. Synod Coun., 1970—; chmn. United Way Fund, 1983. Served with USAAF, 1942-45. Recipient Summit Conf. award for outstanding pub. svc., 1976. Mem. NEA, N.D. Edn. Assn., N.D. Sch. Bus. Ofcls., N.D. Assn. Administrs., Nat. Assn. Administrs., N.D. Assn. Ret. Employees (pres. 1987—), Am. Assn. Ret. Persons (vice chmn. N.D. legis. com. 1992-94, chmn. 1994—), Kiwanis, Phi Beta Kappa, Phi Delta Kappa (br. emeritus).

**SNOUFFER, NANCY KENDALL,** literature and language educator; b. Long Branch, N.J., Aug. 22, 1941; d. Percival Wallace and Ruby Mae (Braswell) Kendall; m. Eugene Joseph Snouffer, Aug. 27, 1966; 1 child, Kendall Ann. BA in English, Gettysburg (Pa.) Coll., 1962; MA in English and Journalism, U. N.C., 1964; MS in Edn. and Reading, Western Ill. U., 1974; postgrad., U. Mo. 1976/78 Univ. English U. N.C., Wilmington, 1965-66; Shaw U., Raleigh, N.C., 1965-66; from instr. to asst. prof. English Wright Coll. and Chgo. City Colls., 1967-74; from instr. to asst. prof. reading Western Ill. U., Macomb, 1974-81; prof. comm., lang. and reading Del Mar Coll., Corpus Christi, Tex., 1982—, reading coord., 2001—. Mem. adv. bd. Tex. A&M U., Corpus Christi, 1993—; cons. in field. Author: College Reading Power, 5th edit., 1976-83; assoc. editor jour. Epistle, 1980-83, mem. editorial bd., 1983-85; contbr. articles to profl. jours. Master Tchr. Del Mar, 1986. Grantee Western Ill. U., 1974-81, Del Mar Coll., 1982—, NISSOD Tchg. Excellence award, 1993, Coll. Acad. Support Program Tex. State level Lifetime Achievement award. Mem. Tex. Assn. Developmental Educators, Tex. Coll. Reading Learning Assn. (chair So. membership 1994—, state sec. 1995-97, pres.-elect 1997-98, pres. 1998-99, past pres. 1999-2000, Lifetime Achievement award 2002), Nat. Assn. Devel. Educators (co-chair nat. com. profl. liaison), Internat. Reading Assn., Corpus Christi Literacy Coun. (bd. dirs. 1986-2003, sec. 1988-93, vice-chmn. 1991-92, v.p.-elect 2000-01, chmn. 2001-02), Harbor Playhouse (bd. dirs. 1988, 91-93), Alliance Francaise. Republican. Episcopalian. Avocations: tennis, travel, reading. Home: 4206 Acushnet Dr Corpus Christi TX 78413-2004 Office: Del Mar Coll 101 Baldwin Blvd Corpus Christi TX 78404-3805 E-mail: snouffer@delmar.edu.

**SNOW, CLAUDE HENRY, JR.,** information services executive, consultant; b. Lumberton, N.C., Feb. 25, 1954; s. Claude Henry and Vada Isabelle (Simpson) S.; m. Sarah Catherine Turnbull, Sept. 26, 1981. BA, U. N.C., 1976, MA, 1978. Communications systems rep. So. Bell Tel. & Tel., Charlotte, N.C., 1978-82; systems mgr. Sykes Datatronics, Atlanta, 1982-83; strategic planning mgr. Lockheed-Ga. Co., Marietta, 1983-86; regional mgr. communications Wang Labs., Atlanta, 1986-88, regional mgr. mktg., mfg., 1989; mgr. Deloitte & Touche, Atlanta, 1989-94; mng. dir. IBM Healthcare Consulting divsn., 1994-2000; exec. dir. IBM Pub. Sector Divsn. Global Svcs., 2000—02; global v.p. health ins. industry Electronic Data Systems, Plano, Tex., 2002—. Mem. U N.C. Libr. Bd., 1995—; bd. dirs. Ctrs. Disease Control Found., 1999—; bd. visitors U. N.C., Chapel Hill, 2001--. Mem. SAR, U. N.C. Alumni Assn. (pres. Atlanta chpt. 1985, mem. adv. bd. 1986-89), United Sons of Confederacy, Old Guard Atlanta, Chancellors Club of N.C. Democrat. Episcopalian. Avocations: golf, Scottish games, historic preservation. Office Phone: 919-824-7669. Business E-Mail: claude.snow@eds.com.

**SNOW, DASH,** photographer; b. NYC, 1981; Exhibited in group shows at Interstate, Nicole Klagsbrun Gallery, 2005, Whitney Biennial: Day before Night, Whitney Mus. Am. Art, 2006, exhibitions include Silence Is The Only True Friend That Shall Never Betray You, Rivington Arms Gallery, NYC, 2006. Mailing: c/o Rivington Arms Gallery 4 E 2nd St 1st Fl New York NY 10003*

**SNOW, DAVID B.,** pharmaceutical executive; BS Sci. and Econ., Bates Coll.; MS Healthcare Admin., Duke Univ. Sr. vice-pres. Am. Internat. Healthcare, Rockville, Md., 1988—89; pres. and CEO Managed Healthcare Systems, Reston, Va., 1989—93; exec. vice-pres. Oxford Health Plans, Norwalk, Conn.; pres. and CEO WellChoice, New York, NY, 1999—2003. Office: Medco Health 100 Parsons Pond Franklin Lakes NJ 07417

**SNOW, EDWIN FAWCETT,** management consultant; s. Edwin James and Suzanne Fawcett Snow; m. Mary Anna Siemion, June 28, 1986; m. Cynthia Suzanne Ramsey, June 24, 1961 (div. Dec. 5, 1983); children: John Edwin, Cynthia Currie Nickell. BSME, U. Ill., 1959; MBA and MS in Indsl. Engring., Carnegie Mellon U., 1964. EIT Ill., registered profl. engr., Ky. Detail and sr. draftsman Internat. Harvester, East Moline, Ill., 1955—56; lab. technician Am. Air Filter, Moline, Ill., 1957; layout draftsman Internat. Harvester, East Moline, 1958; staff asst., sales engr. Westinghouse Electric Corp., Pitts., 1959—64; sr. assoc. rsch. dir. Batton Barton Durstine & Osborne, N.Y.C., 1964—68; asst. to the pres., mgr. Andre Debrie divsn. Applied Devices Corp., N.Y.C., 1968—71; mgr. mktg. and govt. projects USC Inc., Pitts., 1971—72; mgr. mktg. comm. rsch. GE, Louisville, 1972—78; dir. mktg. rsch. Glenmore Distilleries Co., Louisville, 19/8—83; mgmt. cons., exec. supr. George S. May Internat. Co., Park Ridge, Ill., 1984; dir., survey rsch. and analysis Urban Studies Ctr., U. of Louisville, 1984—85; mktg. and sales dir. Nemeth Engring., Crestwood, Ky., 1988—2002; owner, mktg. and mgmt. cons. EF Snow and Assocs., Crestwood, 1985—. Mktg. dir. EVA, Goshen, Ky., 2000—; adj. prof. mktg. decision making Ind. U. S.E., New Albany, 1983—84; adj. prof. mktg. mgmt. Carnegie Mellon U. Grad. Sch. Indsl. Adminstrn., Pitts., 1967. Co-author: (cost benefit model) Brookings Institute Press, (chpt.) Applications of Management Science in Marketing, Models of Buyer Behavior. Scoutmaster Boy Scouts of Am., Louisville, 1977—79. 1st lt. U. S. Army Corps of Engrs., 1959—62. Recipient Harvard Book award, Moline H.S., 1955, Herman Nelson Meml. scholarship, U. of Ill., Coll. of Engring., 1957. Master: Masons; mem.: ASME, Inst. for Ops. Rsch. and Mgmt. Sci., Am. Legion, U. Ill. Alumni Assn., Plantation Swim Club (pres., chmn. bd. 1976—78), Tau Beta Phi, Pi Tau Sigma, Phi Eta Sigma, Delta Phi (pres. Tau chpt. 1956—58). Republican. Episcopalian. Achievements include development of measuring effectiveness of advertising applications of the DEMON model; new product early warning sys; mixed goal programming for non-linear budgetary decisions; patents for leak detection sys. for a nuc. reactor; sampling slide valve (nuclear reactor); remote controlled highwall mining sys. (coal); remote controlled mining sys. (coal). Avocations: sailing, tennis, gardening, computers, photography. Home: 2213 W Highway 22 Crestwood KY 40014 Office Phone: 502-241-4944. Personal E-Mail: nedsnow@bellsouth.net.

**SNOW, GARTH,** professional sports team executive, former professional hockey player; b. Wrentham, Mass., July 28, 1969; m. Erica Snow; 1 child, Glenn. Grad., U. Maine, 1992. Goalie U. Maine, 1988—93, Quebec Nordiques, 1993—95, Phila. Flyers, 1995—98, Vancouver Canucks, 1998—2000, Pitts. Penguins, 2000—01, NY Islanders, 2001—06, gen. mgr., 2006—. Named to Second All-Star Team, Hockey East, 1992, 1993, Championship All-Tournament Team, NCAA, 1993. Office: NY Islanders Nassau Veterans Meml Coliseum 1255 Hempstead Turnpike Uniondale NY 11553*

**SNOW, GEORGE BARTLETT,** accountant, city manager; b. Feb. 23, 1943; s. Frank Batchelder and Corinne Althea (Fuller) Snow; m. Tuula Anita Kahila, Feb. 6, 1965; children: Frank Edwin II, James Hooper. BS in Acctg., Babson Coll., Mass. Acct. Morgan & Morgan, Boston, 1965—70; town acct. Town of Marblehead, Mass., 1970—, data processing coord., 1986—, fin. dir., 1994—. Treas., bd. dirs. Employees Fed. Credit Union, Marblehead, 1979—; mem. com. to rewrite Uniform Mcpl. Acctg. Sys. Manual, 1983—94; acctg. tchr. Mass. Mcpl. Auditors and Accts. Assn., Amherst, 1981—. Clk. Town of Marblehead Bd. Selectmen, 1970—75; mem. Marblehead Retirement Bd., 1970—; trustee Abbot Fund, Town of Marblehead, 1970—90; mem., clk. schs. bldg. com. Town of Marblehead, 1971—72; mem. Marblehead Harbor Study Com., 1997—98. Mem.: Sugarloaf Condo. Pres.' Assn. (pres. 1995—2001), Sugarloaf Phase VII Condo. Assn. (pres. 1988—), Govtl. Fin. Officers Assn., Mass. Govtl. Fin. Officers Assn. (v.p. 1986—87, pres. 1987—88), Mass. Mcpl. Auditors and Accts. Assn. (pres. 1981—82, chmn. legis. com. 1983—88), North Shore Auditors and Accts. Assn. (pres. 1981—82), Onamor Hills Neighborhood Assn. (treas. 1988—94), Pleon Yacht Club (dir. 1979—82), Boston Yacht Club (treas. 1974—78). Home: 242 W Shore Dr Marblehead MA 01945-1324 Office: Town of Marblehead Mary A Alley Bldg 7 Widger Rd Marblehead MA 01945 E-mail: snowb@town.marblehead.ma.us.

**SNOW, GORDON RAYMOND,** composer, conductor, bass; s. Herbert Raymond and Marcheta Eloise Snow. BA in Music and Religion, Ill. Wesleyan U., 1986; postgrad., Western Ill. U., 1987—88; student of, Winifred Faix Brown, 1993—97. With Carl Fischer, Chgo., 1991—99; dir. music ministry Hickory Hills Presbyn. Ch., 1999—; with Gamble Music Co., Chgo., 2000—; sr. artistic dir. Northwest Ind. Youth Chorus, Highland, 2001—; operatic basso Da Corneto Opera, Chgo., 2002—. Composer: The Magi, 1992; editor: (historical jour.) In Quest For Peace, 2002—, author of poems Mem. Am. Guild Organists, Am. Guild Handbell Ringers, Phi Mu Alpha. Democrat. Presbyterian. Avocations: rock collecting, cooking, interior decorating, writing.

**SNOW, JACK (JOHN WILLIAM SNOW),** former secretary of the treasury; b. Toledo, Aug. 2, 1939; s. William Dean and Catherine (Howard) S.; m. Fredrica Wheeler, June 11, 1964 (div. 1973); children: Bradley, Ian; m. Carolyn Kalk, Aug. 31, 1973; 1 child, Christopher. BA, Kenyon Coll./U. Toledo, 1962; PhD in Economics, U. Va., 1965; LLB, George Washington U., 1967. Asst. prof. econs. U. Md., College Park, 1965-67; assoc. Wheeler & Wheeler, Washington, 1967-72; asst. gen. counsel US Dept. Transp., Washington, 1972-73, dep. asst. sec. for policy, plans and internat. affairs, 1973-74, asst. sec. for govtl. affairs, 1974-75, dep. under sec., 1975-76; adminstr. Nat. Hwy. Traffic Safety Adminstrn., Washington, 1976-77; v.p. govt. affairs Chessie System Inc., Washington, 1977-80; sr. v.p. corp. services CSX Corp., Richmond, Va., 1980-84, exec. v.p., 1984-85; pres., CEO Chessie System R.R.s, Balt., 1985-86, CSX Rail Transport, Jacksonville, Fla., 1986-87, CSX Transp., Jacksonville, Va., 1987-88; pres., COO CSX Corp., Richmond, Va., 1988-89, pres., CEO, 1989-91, chmn., pres., CEO, 1991—2003; sec. US Dept. Treasury, Washington, 2003—06. Adj. prof. law George Washington U., 1972-75; vis. prof. econs. U. Va., Charlottesville, spring 1977; vis. fellow Am. Enterprises Inst., Washington, spring 1977. Ex officio trustee Nat. Gallery Art. Mem. Va. State Bar. Clubs: Chevy Chase, Metropolitan (Washington); Country of Va. (Richmond). Episcopalian.

**SNOW, JAMES BYRON, JR.,** otolaryngologist, research administrator, educator; b. Oklahoma City, Mar. 12, 1932; s. James B. and Charlotte Louise (Andersen) S.; m. Sallie Lee Ricker, July 16, 1954; children: James B., John Andrew, Sallie Lee Louise. BS, U. Okla., Norman, 1953; MD cum laude, Harvard U., Cambridge, Mass., 1956; MA (hon.), U. Pa., 1973. Diplomate Am. Bd. Otolaryngology (dir. 1972-90). Intern Johns Hopkins Hosp., Balt., 1956-57; resident Mass. Eye and Ear Infirmary, Boston, 1957-60; prof., head dept. otorhinolaryngology Sch. Medicine U. Okla., Oklahoma City, 1962-72; prof., chmn. dept. otorhinolaryngology and human communication U. Pa., 1972-90; dir. Nat. Inst. on Deafness and Other Comm. Disorders, NIH, Bethesda, Md., 1990-97; convener, corr. Tinnitus Rsch. Consortium, 1998—. Mem. nat. adv. coun. neurol. and communicative disorders and stroke NIH, 1972-76, 82-86; chmn. Nat. Com. Rsch. Neurol. and Communicative Disorders, 1979-80. Editor: Am. Jour. Otolaryngology, 1979-83; Contbr. articles to sci. and profl. jours. Officer, M.C., U.S. Army, 1960-62. Recipient Regents award for superior tchg. U. Okla., 1970, Golden award Internat. Fedn. Otorhinolaryngological Socs., 1989, Disting. Achievement award Deafness Rsch. Found., 1993, Presdl. Meritorious Exec. Rank award; named to Soc. Scholars Johns Hopkins U., 1991. Fellow Japan Broncho-Esophagological Soc. (hon.), Am. Laryngological Assn. (hon.); mem. ACS (regent 1982-90), AMA (coun. on sci. affairs 1975-86), Soc. Univ. Otolaryngologists (pres. 1975), Am. Acad. Otolaryngology-Head and Neck Surgery, Assn. Acad. Depts. Otolaryngology (pres. 1981-82), Am. Laryngol., Rhinol. and Otol. Soc., Am. Otol. Soc. (merit award 2003), Am. Laryngol. Assn. (editor 1983-89, pres. 1990-91), Am. Broncho-Esophagol. Assn. (editor trans. 1973-77, pres. 1979), Collegium Otorhinolaryngologicum (pres. 2000-02), Phi Beta Kappa, Alpha Omega Alpha. Home: 327 Greenbriar Ln West Grove PA 19390-9490 Personal E-mail: jandssnow@comcast.net.

**SNOW, JOEL ALAN,** research director; b. Brockton, Mass., Apr. 1, 1937; s. George H. Jr. and Mary W. (Sproul) S.; m. Laetitia Harrer, June 29, 1957 (div. 1983); children: Jonathan E., Nicholas H.; m. Barbara Kashian, Feb. 7, 1992; stepchildren: James, Alexander. BS in Physics, U. N.C., 1958; MA in Physics, Washington U., St. Louis, 1963, PhD in Physics, 1967. Fellow Ctr. Advanced Study U. Ill., Champaign, 1967-68; program dir. for theoretical physics NSF, Washington, 1968-70, head office of interdisciplinary rsch., 1969-71, dep. asst. dir. for sci. and tech., rsch. applications, 1971-74, dir. office of planning and resources mgmt., 1974-76, dir. div. of policy rsch. and analysis, 1976; sr. policy analyst, office of sci. and tech. policy Exec. Office of the Pres., Washington, 1976-77; assoc. dir. for rsch. policy U.S. Dept. Energy, Washington, 1977-81, dir. sci. and tech. affairs, 1981-88; assoc. v.p. for rsch. Argonne Nat. Lab., U. Chgo., 1988-92; dir. Inst. for Phys. Rsch. and Tech. Iowa State U., Ames, 1993-98, prof. elec. and computer engring., 1993—, prof. polit. sci., 1998-2000, exec. assoc. dir. Internat. Inst. Theoret./Applied Physics, 1998—. Rsch. assoc. dept. physics U. Ill., Urbana, 1967-68; instr. physics and electronics U.S. Navy Nulcear Power Shc., New London, Conn., 1958-61; sci. tech. organizer Pres.'s Conf. on Superconductivity, 1987, NSF program rsch. applied to nat. needs, 1971, designer, mgr., founder NSF program interdisciplinary rsch. relevant to problems of society, 1969. Contbr. over 130 articles to mags. and profl. jours. Lt. (j.g.) USN, 1958-61. Recipient Meritorious Svc. award NSF, 1972, Meritorious award William A. Jump Found., 1973, Arthur S. Fleming award Downtown Jaycees, 1974; NSF postdoctoral fellow Ctr. for Advanced Study U. Ill., 1967-68; NSF fellow, 1963-65. Fellow AAAS, Am. Phys. Soc.; mem. IEEE, Am. Chem. Soc., Am. Nuc. Soc., World Future Soc., Sigma Xi, Phi Beta Kappa, Phi Kappa Phi. Achievements include pioneering devel. of federal programs in environment, solar and geothermal energy and energy conservation, sustainable development; fed. programs in technology transfer to industry; developed collaborations between univ., govt. and industry; fostering internat. collaboration in sci., engring. and edn. E-mail: jasnow@iastate.edu.

**SNOW, KARL NELSON, JR.,** public management educator, academic administrator, retired state senator; b. St. George, Utah, July 1, 1930; s. Karl Nelson and Wanda (McGregor) S.; m. Donna Jean Dain, Jan. 29, 1960; children: Karl Nelson, III, Melissa, Daniel D., Jeanmarie, Elisabeth, Howard H. BS, Brigham Young U., Provo, Utah, 1956; MA, U. Minn., 1958; MPA, U. So. Calif., 1965, DPA, 1972. Budget examiner Minn. Dept. Adminstrn., 1956-59; staff asst., instr. Sch. Pub. Adminstrn. U. So. Calif., 1959-62; mem. faculty Brigham Young U., Provo, Utah, 1962-96, dir. Inst. Govt., 1969-79, prof. pub. mgmt., 1979—, asst. exec. v.p., 1987-91; state legis. fiscal analyst, 1966-70; mem. Utah Senate from 16th Dist., 1972-85, majority leader, 1981-85. Chmn. Utah State House Fellowship Commn., 1973-79, Utah Constl. Revision Commn., 1977-89; bd. dirs. Legis. Leaders Found., 1981-85; chmn. bd. trustees Utah Tech. Fin. Corp., 1983-94; pres., trustee Utah Tech. Equity Found., 1994-96; chmn. Conf. of State Sponsored Seed and Venture Funds, 1993-96; internat. affairs rep. LDS Ch., N.Y.C., 1997-2000. Bd. editors Public Adminstrn. Rev, 1969-70, State and Local Govt. Rev, 1977-83; contbr. articles to profl. jours. Missionary Mormon Ch., 1950-52, mem. stake high coun., 1975-85, 93-97, bishop, 1985-90, dir. ch. internat. affairs, N.Y.C., 1997-2000; mem. Warren Burger Prison Task Force, 1983-87; bd. dirs. Utah Innovation Found., 1984-88. Adminstrv. fellow State of Minn., U. Minn., 1956-57; Univ. fellow U. So. Calif., 1959-61. Mem. Am. Soc. Pub. Adminstrn. (chpt. pres. 1968-69), dir. nat. council (1969-72), Sons Utah Pioneers.

**SNOW, MARINA,** writer; b. Boston, Apr. 9, 1937; d. Charles Ernest Snow and Katherine Alice Townsend; m. Richard DeVere Horton, 1958 (div. 1968); children: Heather Kertchem, James Horton; m. Charles A. Washburn, 1978 (div. 1979). BA, U. Iowa, 1958; MA in Speech Pathology, N.Mex. State U., 1967; MA in Librarianship, San Jose State U., 1976; MA in Theatre Arts, Calif. State U., Sacramento, 1979. Cert. clin. competence Am. Speech and Hearing Assn. Tchr. ESL Inst. Colombo-Americano, Cali, Colombia, 1958-59; tchr. Las Cruces (N.Mex.) Pub. Schs., 1964-66; speech therapist Sutter County Schs., Yuba City, Calif., 1967-72; reference libr. Calif. State U., Sacramento, 1976-95. Author: (novels) The Walking Wounded, 2001 (Best First Novel of 2001-2002 award Bay Area Ind. Pub. Assn., 2001), Look No Further, 2004, (plays) Apricot Coffee, Alkali Flat, (short stories) (in Artisan) The Black Iris, 1999; contbr. articles to profl. jours. Pres. Alkali Flat Neighborhood Assn., Sacramento, 1987—94. Mem.: Calif. Writer's Club, Sacramento Old City Assn. Avocations: theater, historic preservation, gardening.

**SNOW, MARLON O.,** trucking executive, state agency administrator; m. Ann; children. Gen. mgr. spl. commodities Milne Truck Lines, Phoenix, LA, 1970-81; gen. mgr. spl. commodities, sales Motor Cargo, Salt Lake City, 1981-82; owner MST Trucking, Inc., Salt Lake City, 1982—. V.p. Utah Motor Carriers for State of Utah, 1997-98; mem. adv. bd. Zions Bank. Mem. State Bd. Edn., 1994-97, chair, 1995-97; trustee Utah Valley State Coll., 1998; mem. Ho. of Reps., Utah, 1999-2001; bd. regents Bd. Higher Edn. State of Utah, 2001—; bd. dirs. Children's Justice Ctr., State of Utah, 2002-, Riverside Country Club; mem. bd. I.H.C. Hosp. Utah County. Mem. Utah Valley State Coll. Found. (bd. dirs. 1991—), Alpine Sch. Dist. Found. (bd. dirs. 1990-94). Office: 1247 E 430 N Orem UT 84097-5400

**SNOW, MICHAEL D.,** health facility administrator; BS in Acctg., U. Alabama; MBA, Troy State U. CEO Doctor's Hosp., Metairie, La.; v.p., oper. Gulf Coast Divsn., 1995—96; pres. Gulf Coast Divsn., HCA, 1996—2004; COO HealthSouth Corp., Birmingham, Ala., 2004—. Chmn. bd. trustees Tex. Hosp. Assn., 2002—03. Tex. Governor's Spl. Com. on Medicaid Reform; Am. Hosp. Assn. Reg. Policy Bd. Mem.: Am. Heart Assn. (chmn. Houston Chpt.). Office: HealthSouth One HealthSouth Pkwy Birmingham AL 35243

**SNOW, THEODORE PECK,** astrophysics educator; b. Seattle, Jan. 30, 1947; s. Theodore P. and Louise (Wertz) S.; s. Constance M. Snow, Aug. 23, 1969; children: McGregor A., Tyler M., Reilly A. BA, Yale U., 1969; MS, U. Wash., 1970, PhD, 1973. Rsch. staff Princeton (N.J.) U., 1973-77; prof. U. Colo., Boulder, 1977—, dir. Ctr. for Astrophysics and Space Astronomy, 1986-96, dir. Fiske Planetarium, 2000—. Mem. instrument devel. teams for far Ultraviolet Spectroscopic Explorer, 1999—, Cosmic Origins Spectrograph to be installed in Hubble Space Telescope. Author: (textbook) The Dynamic Universe, 1983, 4th edit., 1991, Essentials of the Dynamic Universe 4th edit., 1993 (textbook excellence award Text and Academic Authors Assn. 1994), Physics, 1986, Universe: Origins and Evolution, 1997; contbr. over 200 articles to profl. jours. Fellow Royal Astron. Soc.; mem. Am. Astron. Soc., Astron. Soc. Pacific, Sigma Xi. Achievements include discovery, through observations in ultraviolet visible, and infrared wavelengths, and through laboratory measurement of chemical reactions, of several important processes involving interstellar gas and dust, and their roles in star formation and late stages of stellar evolution. Office: U Colo Ctr Astrophysics Space Astronomy 389 UCB Boulder CO 80309-0389 Business E-Mail: tsnow@casa.colorado.edu.

**SNOW, TIFFANY,** writer, healer, composer; b. Vista, Calif., 1962; d. Fred Archer and Trisha Ann Wallace; children: Jenni, Sierra, Jesse, Timothy. MS in Theology, Suffield Coll. and Univ., West Hartford, Conn., PhD in

Psychology; M in Usui Reiki Sys., Sacred Cir. Spiritual Healing; DD (hon.), World Christianship Ministries, Fresno, Calif. Lic. CE provider, Bd. Registered Nursing, Calif. Healer Divine Wellness Inst., Escondido, Calif., 1999—; pres. Spirit Journey Books, San Diego, 2003—. Inspirational and motivational spkr., tchr. Author: (nonfiction book) Psychic Gifts in the Christian Life - Tools to Connect, The Power of Divine: A Healer's Guide - Tapping into the Miracle (USA Book News Awards 2004 finalist, 2004, Finalist 2004 Reader's Preference Editor's Choice award, 2004, Finalist San Diego Books award, 2004), Forward From the Mind - Distant Healing, Prayer & Remote Viewing, The Holy Frail - The Power of Brokenness: Mending Your Spirit During Trauma, (poetry book) Homesick: A Healer Remembers God - NDE Prayers & Poems of the Mystic Soul, 2006, (nonfiction book) Medical Intuition & Prague in a Quantum World, 2006; songwriter: country music CD Tiffany Snow - Two Wild Horses; composer: (instrumental CD) Indian Desert, Private Island; contbr. articles to jours. and mags., forewards and chpts. to books. Mem.: BMI (songwriter, composer, musician), PMA (pub.), Internat. Assn. Reiki Practitioners (registered tchr. and practitioner 2004), Internat. Assn. Raiki Practitioners, Order of St. Luke the Physician, Publs. Mktg. Assn., Internat. Assn. for Near-Death Studies (corr.), Acad. Religion and Paranormal Studies (life). Office: Divine Wellness Inst PO Box 61 San Marcos CA 92079 Office Phone: 800-535-5474. E-mail: adm@tiffanysnow.com.

**SNOW, TONY,** White House press secretary, political commentator, analyst; b. Berea, Ky., June 1, 1955; m. Jill Snow, 1987; 3 children. BA in Philosophy, Davidson Coll., NC, 1977. Editl. writer Greensboro Record, 1979, Virginian Pilot, Norfolk, Va.; editl. page writer Daily Press in Newport News, Washington Times; dep. editl. page editor Detroit News, nationally syndicated columnist Mich., 1993—2001; columnist USA Today, 1994—2000; with FOX News Channel, 1996—, host FOX News Sunday, 1996—2003; host Tony Snow Show and Weekend Live with Tony Snow, polit. analyst; host Tony Snow Show Fox News Radio; asst. to Pres., press sec. The White House, Washington, 2006—. Dep. asst. for comm., dir. of speech writing to President George H. W. Bush, 1991—92; dep. asst. for media affairs to President George H. W. Bush, 1991. Tchr. physics and East African geography in Kenya; advocate for the mentally ill and developmentally disabled NC. Avocation: musician with Beats Workin'. Office: FOX News Channel 1212 Avenue of the Americas New York NY 10036 also: The White House 1600 Pennsylvania Ave NW 1st Fl Washington DC 20500 Office Phone: 202-456-2673. Office Fax: 202-456-0126. Business E-Mail: tonysnow@foxnews.com.*

**SNOW, TOWER CHARLES, JR.,** lawyer; b. Boston, Oct. 28, 1947; s. Tower Charles and Margaret (Harper) S. BA in English, Dartmouth Coll., 1969; JD, U. Calif., Berkeley, 1973. Bar: Calif. 1973, U.S. Dist. Ct. (no. dist.) Calif. 1973, U.S. Ct. Appeals (9th cir.) 1973, U.S. Supreme Ct. 1976, U.S. Dist. Ct. (ea. dist.) Calif. 1979, U.S. Ct. Appeals (fed. cir.) 1980, U.S. Ct. Claims 1980, U.S. Ct. Appeals (2d cir.) 1987, N.Y. 1988, U.S. Dist. Ct. (ea. and so. dists.) N.Y. 1988, U.S. Dist. Ct. (ctrl. dist.) Calif. 1989, U.S. Dist. Ct. (no. dist.) Tex. 1995, U.S. Dist. Ct. (so. dist.) Calif. 1996, U.S. Dist. Ct. Ariz. 1996. Ptnr., chmn. litigation dept. Orrick, Herrington & Sutcliffe, San Francisco, 1973-89; ptnr. Shearman & Sterling, San Francisco, 1989-94; ptnr., chmn. securities litigation group, mem. policy com. Brobeck, Phleger & Harrison, LLP, San Francisco, 1995-97; chmn., CEO Brobeck, Phleger & Harrison, San Francisco, 1998—2001; ptnr., mem. Americas Mgmt. Group, Clifford Chance, LLP, 2002—04, cons., 2005—06. Arbitrator Nat. Assn. Securities Dealers, Am. Stock Exch., N.Y. Stock Exch., Pacific Coast Stock Exch., Superior Ct. City and County San Francisco, Am. Arbitration Assn.; lectr. in field. Author numerous law handbooks and articles to prof. jours. Mem. San Francisco Mus. Soc., San Francisco Symphony, San Francisco Ballet, San Francisco Opera, Am. Conservatory Theatre. Named Best Lawyer in the U.S. in his Field, Corp. Bd. Member Mag., 2001; named one of 100 Most Influential Lawyers in Am., Nat. Law Jour., 2000, 100 Most Influential Lawyers in Calif., Calif. Law and Bus., 2000, 2002, 100 Most Influential Lawyers in World, Lawyer Mag. (U.K.), 2002, America's Leading Lawyers for Bus., Chambers USA, 2003, 2004, 2005; Rufus Choate scholar, Dartmouth Coll., 1969. Mem. ABA (chmn. subcom. pub. offering litig. 1984-88, co-chair task force on securities arbitration 1988-93, vice chair securities litig. com. 1986-88), Continuing Edn. Bar (bus. law inst. planning com. 1986), Securities Industry Assn., Nat. Inst. Trial Advocacy, San Francisco Bar Assn. (pres. securities litig. sect. 1995). Democrat. Avocations: travel, skiing, running, scuba diving, films. Home: 177 Ridge Dr Napa CA 94558-9777 Office Phone: 707-252-6802. Business E-Mail: tower.snow@gmail.com.

**SNOWBARGER, VINCE,** former congressman; b. Kankakee, Ill., Sept. 16, 1949; s. Willis Edward and Wahnona Ruth (Horger) S.; m. Carolyn Ruth McMahon, Mar. 25, 1972; children: Jeffrey Edward, Matthew David. BA in History, So. Nazarene U., 1971; MA in Polit. Sci., U. Ill., 1974; JD, U. Kans., 1977. Bar: Kans. 1977, U.S. Dist. Ct. Kans. 1977, Mo. 1987. Instr. Mid-Am. Nazarene Coll., Olathe, Kans., 1973—76; ptnr. Haskin, Hinkle, Slater & Snowbarger, 1977—84, Dietrich, Davis, Dicus et al, 1984—88, Armstrong, Teasdale, Schafly & Davis, Overland Park, 1989—92, Holbrook, Heaven & Fay, P.C., Merriam, 1992—94, Snowbarger & Veatch LLP, Olathe, 1994—96; mem. 105th Congress from 3rd Kans. dist., 1997—99; exec. dir. Kans. Assn. Am. Educators, 2000—01; dep. exec. dir. Pension Benefit Guaranty Corp., Washington, 2002—. Mem. Kans. Legislature, Topeka, 1985-96; majority leader Ho. of Reps., 1993-96; mem. Olathe Planning Commn., 1982-84, Leadership Olathe; divsn. chmn. United Way, Olathe, 1985-88, chmn. citizen rev. com., 1991-95. Mem. Olathe Area C. of C. (bd. dirs. 1984). Republican. Nazarene. Avocation: politics. Office: 1200 K St NW Washington DC 20005-4026 Home: 12676 Lace Falls Loop Bristow VA 20136-1295 Office Phone: 202-326-4010. Business E-Mail: snowbarger.vince@pbgc.gov.

**SNOWDEN, DAVID L.,** protective services official; BA, Calif. State U., Fullerton. Chief of police, Beverly Hills, Calif. Recipient Am.'s Star award U.S. Marshal's Office, Sherman Block Law Enforcement Profl. of Yr. award Calif. Peace Officers Assn., 2003. Mem. Calif. Police Chiefs Assn. (past pres.), Orange County Chiefs and Sheriffs Assn. (past pres.), L.A. County Chiefs Assn. (past pres.). Office: 464 N Rexford Dr Beverly Hills CA 90210 E-mail: dsnowden@beverlyhills.org.

**SNOWDEN, LAWRENCE FONTAINE,** retired air transportation executive, retired military officer; b. Charlottesville, Va., Apr. 14, 1921; s. Lawrence Fontaine Snoddy and Beatrice M. (Huffman) S.; m. Martha Roselyn Ham, Nov. 17, 1942; children: John Stephen, Brian Fontaine. Student, Stetson U., 1938-39; BS, U. Va., 1942; MA, Northwestern U., 1950; postgrad., Harvard U., 1968; grad., Indsl. Coll. Armed Forces, 1967. Commd. 2d lt. USMC, 1942, advanced through grades to lt. gen., 1975; comdr. 7th Marine Regt., Vietnam, 1966; ops. officer III Marine Amphibious Force, Vietnam, 1967; asst. dir. personnel Hdqrs. Marine Corps, Washington, 1968-69, dir. systems support group, 1969-70; dir. Marine Corps Devel. Ctr., Quantico, Va., 1970-72; chief of staff U.S. Forces, Japan, 1972-75; U.S. chmn. UN Bd., Japan, 1975-77; chief of staff Hdqrs. U.S. Marine Corps, 1977-79; ret., 1979; v.p. Far East Internat. Service Co. Hughes Aircraft Co., 1979-86, group v.p. Internat. Ground Systems Group Fullerton, Calif., 1986-88; pres. Snowden Internat. Assocs., Tallahassee, Fla., 1988—. Recipient Silver Beaver award Boy Scouts Am., Disting. Eagle Scout award; decorated Disting. Svc. medals (2), Legion of Merit (5), Army Commendation medal, Navy Commendation medal, Purple Heart (2), Cross of Gallantry (3) Vietnam, Second Order of Sacred Treasure Japan) Mem. Marine Corps League, U.S. Navy League, Am. C. of C. in Japan, Am.-Japan Soc., Marine Corps Assn., Econ. Club Fla., Sigma Nu. Clubs: Tokyo.

**SNOWDEN, RUTH O'DELL GILLESPIE,** artist; b. Gary, W.Va., Apr. 16, 1926; d. Haynes Thornton and Blanche Beaula (Boling) Gillespie; m. Eugene Louis Snowden, Dec. 21, 1946; children: Wanda Snowden Ballard, Eugene III, Ronald, Marian Snowden Warren, Jeffry. RN, Natharith Coll., 1946; student Sch. Art, Transylvania U., 1983-84, U. Ky., 1985-89. RN. Painter, publicity chmn. Artists's Artic Inc., Lexington, Ky., 1988-89. Exhibited in group shows at U. Ky. Art Mus., Lexington, 1988, 5th Internat. Juried Exhibition Pastels, Nyack, N.Y., 1988, Small Paintings Nat., Ky. Highlands

Mus., Ashland, 1988, The Appalachian Cen., U. Ky., 1988, Ft. Wayne (Ind.) Mus. Art, 1986, John Howard Sanden Nat. Artists Seminar, Washington, Nat. Artists' Seminar, Chgo., Huntington (W.Va.) Galleries, Nat. Nursing Art Exhibit, Meth. Med. Cen., Peoria, Ill., Chautauqua Art Assn. Galleries, N.Y., 1990, Central Bank gallery, Chatauqua, 1990, Pastel & Chisel Acad. Fine Arts, 1990, Opera House Gallery, 1990, Sacramento Fine Arts Ctr., 1990, Ariel Gallery, Soho, N.Y., 1990, 91, Sumi-e Soc. Am., Inc., 1993, Watercolor Soc. Ala., 1994; represented in the Director of American Portrait Artists, Am. Portrait Soc., Huntington Harbour, Calif., Audubon Artists Exhibit, N.Y.C., 2003, 2004; numerous local and nat. shows; in pvt. collections. Recipient Assn. Alliance award Am. Frame Co., 1993, Elizabeth Morris Genious award, 2002, Winsor Newton Merchandising award Summie Soc. Am., 2002. Mem. Oil Pastel Assn., Winchester Art Guild, Lexington Art League, Ky. Watercolor Assn. (Bluegrass regional dir. 1988, 89, 90, 91, 92), Ky. Guild Artists and Craftsmen, Inc., Northwest Pastel Soc., Degas Pastel Soc., Pen & Brush Soc. (Perfect Proportion award). Avocations: golf, bowling. Home and Studio: 2800 Old Boonesboro Rd Winchester KY 40391-8805 Office Phone: 859-744-6693.

**SNOWE, OLYMPIA J.,** senator; b. Augusta, Maine, Feb. 21, 1947; d. George John and Georgia G. Bouchles; m. John McKernan. BA, U. Maine, 1969; LLD (hon.), U. Maine, Orono, 1981, Nasson Coll., 1981, U. Maine, Machias, 1982, Bowdoin Coll., 1982, Colby Coll., 1985; LHD (hon.), Thomas Coll., 1987; LLD (hon.), Suffolk U., 1994; DSc (hon.), Maine Maritime Acad., 1995; LLD (hon.), Colby Coll., 1996, U. New England, 1996; degree (hon.), Harvard U., 1997; LLD (hon.), Bates Coll., 1998. Businesswoman; mem. Maine Ho. of Reps., 1973-76, Maine Senate, 1976-78, 96th-103d Congresses from 2d Maine Dist., 1979-94, mem. budget com., foreign affairs com., com. on aging, 1979-94; co-chair Congl. Caucus for Women's Issues, 1983-94; U.S. senator from Maine, 1995—. Mem. Senate com. armed svcs., 1997-2001, chair, seapower subcom., Senate com. on commerce, sci. and transp., 1995—, chair, oceans and fisheries subcom., Senate Budget com., 1995—, Senate com. small business, 1995—, Senate com. Fgn. Rels., 1995-97; counsel to asst. majority leader, 1997—, House Budget com., 1991-95, House Fgn. Affairs com., 1979-95, House Aging com. 1979-95, Congl. Caucus on Women's Issues 1979-84, co-chair 1983-95; dep. Repub. Whip, 1984-95; dep. Whip, 1996-97; corporator Mechanics Savs. Bank. Recipient Homeric award for adv. of human rights Chian Fedn., 1999, award for "Excelling in Standing up for Choice" Women's Campaign Fund, 1999, Spirit of Enterprise award U.S. Chamber of Commerce, 1997, 99, Woman of Yr. award Glamour Mag., 1998, David and Sherry Huber award for leadership on family planning, women's health issues, Family Planning Assn. of ME, 1998, Golden Bulldog award Watchdogs of the Treasury, Inc., Wash., 1994, 96, 98, Guardian of Small Business award Nat. Fedn. Indep. Bus., Wash., 1994, 96, 98, Responsible Choices award Planned Parenthood of Am., 1998, Spl. honor Nat. Assn. Devel. Orgns., 1998, Disting. Pub. Svc. award Am. Legion, Wash., 1998, Neil W. Allen award Greater Portland Chamber of Commerce, 1997, Legis. award for outstanding svc. to schs. and pub. librs., White Ho. Conf. on Libr. and Info. Svcs. Task Force, Wash., 1997, Pub. Leadership award, Nat. Breast Cancer Coalition, 1997, Magnificent Seven award Bus. & Profl. Women/USA, Wash., 1997, Deborah Morton award Westbrook Coll., Portland, ME, 1997, Golden Gavel award U.S. Senate Leadership, Wash., 1996, Nat. Osteoporosis Assn. award for leadership, Wash., 1996, award for leadership U.S. Distance Learning Assn., Crystal City, Va., 1996, award for leadership United Hellenic Am. Cong., 1995, William H. Natcher Disting. Svc. award Com. for Edn. Funding, 1995, Pub. Svc. award Am. Coll. Obstetricians and Gynecologists, 1995, Nat. Security Leadership award Am. Security Coun., Wash., 1994, Thomas Jefferson award Nat. Am. Wholesale Grocers Assn./Internat. Foodsvc. Distbrs. Assn., 1994, Grace Caucus award Citizens Against Govt. Waste, 1994, Sound Dollar award Free Cong. Found., 1994, Appreciation award Agrl. Stblzn. and Conservation Com. Somerset County chpt., Lifetime Achievement award Am. Hellenic Inst., 1994, Golden Heart award Assn. for Children for Enforcement of Support, ME chpt., 1993, Am. Social Health Assn. award on behalf of women's health issues, 1993, Medal of St. Andrew presented by His All Holiness Dimitrios Ecumenical Patriarch of Constantinople, Wash., 1990, Congrl. Waste Watchers award Coalition to Reform the Davis-Bacon Act, 1990; named to "CQ 50" Congrl. Quarterly Mag., Wash., 1999, Maine Women's Hall of Fame, 1999, Washingtonian Mag. 100 Most Powerful Women, 1997, All Maine Women Honor Soc. U. Maine, 1996, Deficit Reduction Honor Roll Concord Coalition, 1994, Honor Roll for dairy farmer support Associated Milk Prodrs., 1993; named Taxpayer's Hero for preventing govt. waste Citizens Against Govt. Waste, 1997, No Nonsense Am. Women, No Nonsense Coun. on Women's Issues, 1995, Congresswoman of Yr. Nat. Assn. for Transp. Alternatives, 1986; honored by Nat. Coalition for Osteoporosis and Related Bone Diseases, 1999, Edn. and Libr. Networks Coalition, 1997, Am. Assn. Univ. Pres., 1996, Pub. Policy Com. for Hellenic-Am. Women, 1995, Nat. Vietnam Vet. Coalition, 1994; named one of most powerful women, Forbes mag., 2005. Mem.: Philoptochos Soc. Republican. Greek Orthodox. Office: US Senate 154 Russell Senate Bldg Washington DC 20510-1903 E-mail: olympia@snowe.senate.gov.*

**SNOWHOOK, ANN LAFERTY,** social services administrator; b. N.Y.C., May 25, 1929; d. Paul Gause and Anna Gladys (Braun) Laferty; m. John David Snowhook, Sept. 13, 1952; children: Eileen M., Elizabeth J., David P., J. Jordan, Nancy P. BA in Math., UCLA, 1953, postgrad., 1965, 70. Mathematician missiles divsn. The Rand Corp., L.A., 1951-52; substitute tchr. math. Spastic Children's Found., L.A., 1958-60; sec. women's aux. Exceptional Children's Found., L.A., 1960-63; chmn. and treas. parents group, chmn. fundraising, subsitute tchr. Exceptional Children's Class Pacific Palisades, L.A., 1963-73; chmn. area guild, mgr. sch. lunch program Corpus Christi Ch., L.A., 1972-74; statistician, rsch. asst. in mental retardation, family therapy and anorexia nervosa Neuropsychiatric Inst. UCLA, 1974-90; mem. program/policy bd. Kennedy Regional Ctr. for Developmentally Disabled, L.A., 1974-78; del. program devel. fund grants review Los Angeles County Area Bd. X, 1978-82; del. We. Regional Ctr. Assn. Regional Ctr. Contracting Agys., L.A., 1981-82; bd. dirs., pres., corp. sec. We. Regional Ctr. for Developmentally Disabled, L.A., 1978-82; founding dir., corp. sec., treas. Home Ownership Made Easy, L.A., 1988-91; bd. dirs., corp. sec., treas. Found. for Developmentally Disabled, L.A., 1982—; bd. dirs., corp. treas. Marian Homes for Physically Handicapped and Devel. Disabled, L.A., 1992—95. Rsch. assoc. Family Therapy: An Overview, 1980, Anorexia Nervosa: A Body Image Disturbance, 1978, Autism: A Study for Chromosomal Abnormalities, 1979, Family Therapy Today, Estrogen Therapy in Menopausal Women, 1991; rsch. coms. Estrogen Therapy in Menopausal Women, Family Therapy Today; bd. mem. Programs for the Developmentally Handicapped, 1995—; v.p. 1997-98, 2003-; bd. mem. Jay Nolan Cmty. Svcs., 1995-, v.p. 1997-98, chmn. human resources, 2001—; v.p. Jay Nolan v.p. 2005—, sec. 2003-05; program chair and bd. dirs. Easter Seals So. Calif., 1996—, treas., 2002—. Mem. Autism Soc. L.A. (v.p., program chair 1993-95, pres. 1995-99, 2001-02). Roman Catholic. Avocations: reading, swimming, antiques. Home: 901 Iliff St Pacific Palisades CA 90272-3826

**SNOW-SMITH, JOANNE INLOES,** art history educator; b. Balt. d. Henry Williams and Elsie Orrick (Bagley) Snow; m. Robert Porter Smith (dec.); children: Joanne Tyndale Darby, Henry Webster Smith, III (dec.), Constance Elizabeth Bagley, Cynthia Porter Bloom, Robert Porter Smith, Jr.; m. Robert Edward Willstadter (dec.) BA, Goucher Coll.; MA, U. Ariz., 1968; PhD, UCLA, 1976. Prof. Italian Renaissance art history U. Wash., Seattle, 1981—; Program dir. of art history U. Wash. Rome Ctr. in Palazzo Pio, Rome, 1998, 2000, 2002. Author: (book) The Salvator Mundi of Leonardo da Vinci, 1982 (Internat. award 1983), The Primavera of Sandro Botticelli: A Neoplatonic Interpretation, 1993; contbr. numerous articles to profl. jours. Recipient Rsch. Professorship to study in Oxford and London, U. Wash. Grad. Sch., 1986. Mem. Nat. Soc. Colonial Dames of Am., Renaissance Soc. of Am., Leonardo Soc./U. London, Calif. Art Assn., Seattle Art Mus., Met. Mus. Art, Ashmolean Mus. (Oxford, Eng.). Home: 1414 Shenandoah Dr E Seattle WA 98112-3730 Office: Univ Wash PO Box 353440 Seattle WA 98195-3440 E-mail: jsnowsmi@u.washington.edu.

**SNYDER, ALAN CARHART,** finance company executive; b. NYC, May 25, 1946; s. John I. and Elfrida (Bendix) S.; m. Mary Burgoyne, Feb. 9, 1974. BS, BA, Georgetown U., 1968; MBA, Harvard U., 1973. Cons. Reynolds Securities, N.Y.C., 1972-73; exec. v.p. Dean Witter Reynolds, N.Y.C., 1975-85; sole proprietor Shinnecock Ptnrs., N.Y.C., 1985-89, mng. ptnr., 1989—; pres., chief oper. officer, bd. dirs. First Exec. Corp., L.A., 1990-91; COO, Exec. Life Ins. Co., L.A., 1991-93; CEO, Aurora Nat. Life Assurance Co., LA, 1993-94, cons. L.A., 1994-95; mng. ptnr. Shinnecock Group L.L.C., L.A., 1994—; chmn., CEO, pres. Answer Fin. Inc., L.A., 1997—. Baker scholar Harvard Bus. Sch., 1973.

**SNYDER, ALLEN ROGER,** lawyer; b. Washington, Jan. 26, 1946; s. Henry and Sylvia (Oxenburg) S.; m. Susan Port, Aug. 10, 1969; children: Joanna, Carolyn. BA with distinction, George Washington U., 1967; JD magna cum laude, Harvard U., 1971. Bar: D.C. 1973, U.S. Dist. Ct. D.C., Md., U.S. Ct. Appeals (D.C., 4th, 5th, 6th, 8th, 11th cirs.), U.S. Supreme Ct. Temp. assoc. Williams, Connolly & Califano, Washington, 1971; law clk. to assoc. justice J. Harlan U.S. Supreme Ct., 1971, law clk. to assoc. justice W. Rehnquist, 1972; assoc. Hogan & Hartson, Washington, 1972-78, ptnr., 1979—2001; of counsel, 2001—. Mem., then chmn. D.C. Cir. Commn. on Admissions and Grievances, 1984-90, D.C. Cir. Appeals Bd. Profl. Responsibility, 1978-84; mem. D.C. Cir. Adv. Com. on Procedures, 1986-92; mem. com. on pro se litigation U.S. Dist. Ct., 1991-2001. Bd. dirs. Jewish Found. Group Homes, Rockville, Md., 1982-86. Served with USAR, 1968-74. Fellow Am. Acad. of Appellate Lawyers; mem. D.C. Bar Unified (chmn. steering com. div. cts., lawyers and adminstrn. justice 1974-77, long range planning com. 1976, bd. govs. 1977-78), Washington Coun. Lawyers (bd. dirs. 1976-91), Am. Psychiat. Assn. (exec. sec. com. jud. action 1974-77). Office: Hogan & Hartson 555 13th St NW Ste 800E Washington DC 20004-1161 E-mail: ARSnyder@HHLaw.com.

**SNYDER, ARNOLD LEE, JR.,** retired military officer, research director; b. Washington, Oct. 12, 1937; s. Arnold Lee and Frances May (Humbert) S.; m. Patricia Dorine Ward, July 6, 1963; children: Heinrick Jason, Sonya Doreen, Ross Nansen. BCE, George Washington U., 1960; MS, U. Colo., 1966; PhD, U. Alaska, 1972. Command. 2d lt. USAF, 1960; advanced through grades to col., 1981; chief space environ. support sys. devel. sect. Air Force Global Weather Central, Offutt AFB, Nebr., 1972-76; chief ionospheric dynamics br. Geophysics Lab., Hanscom AFB, Mass., 1976-80; test dir. CONUS OTH-B radar system, Columbia Falls AFB, Maine, 1980-81, program dir. Hanscom AFB, 1981-85; dir. Office of Tech. Support, 1985-87; tech. dir. U. Lowell Ctr. Atmospheric Rsch., 1987-89; with The Mitre Corp., 1989-96; pvt. practice, 1996—. Adj. prof. U. Lowell, 1987-89. Contbr. articles to sci. jours. Recipient Legion of Merit, Meritorious Svc. medal with one oak leaf cluster, Commendation medal USAF, R&D award, 1981; Def. Value Engring. award, 1984; Henry Harding scholar, 1955-56. Mem. Am. Geophys. Union, Am. Meteorol. Soc., Air Force Assn., Sigma Xi. Home and Office: PO Box 530 Stockton Springs ME 04981 Personal E-mail: palsnyder@aol.com.

**SNYDER, ARTHUR,** publishing executive; b. Valley Stream, NY, Feb. 6, 1925; s. Arthur and Kathryn (Staubitzer) Snyder; m. Betty Lain Harper, July 8, 1950; children: Susan, Arthur, Betsy, Jack, Heidi, Bonnie. B in Metall. Engring., Cornell U., 1950, MBA, 1952. Mfg. engr. Norton Co., Worcester, Mass., 1952-56, chief acct., 1956-58, asst. contr., 1958-59, mgr. data processing, 1959-61, contr., 1961-65; exec. v.p. A.M. Best Co., Oldwick, NJ, 1965-67, pres., 1968—, chmn., 1971—. Author: (book) Principles of Inventory Control and Managing Capital Expenditures. 1st lt. AUS, 1942—45. Decorated Battlefield Commn., Bronze Star with oak leaf cluster, Purple Heart. Mem.: U. Srs. Golf Assn., Cornell Soc. Engrs., Fin. Execs. Inst., Lyford Cay Club (Nassau, Bahamas), Baltusrol Golf Club (Springfield, NJ). Presbyterian. Home: 111 Lloyd Rd Bernardsville NJ 07924-1710 Office: A M Best Company Inc Ambest Rd Oldwick NJ 08858 Business E-Mail: snydera2@ambest.com.

**SNYDER, BARBARA K.,** pediatrician, educator; MD, George Washington U., 1979. Diplomate in pediatrics and adolescent medicine Am. Bd. Pediatrics. Intern Children's Nat. Med. Ctr., Washington, 1979—80, resident in pediatrics, 1980—82; fellow in adolescent medicine U. Rochester (N.Y.) Sch. Medicine, 1986—88; chief divsn. adolescent medicine, dept. pediatrics Robert Wood Johnson Med. Sch., New Brunswick, NJ, 1990—, assoc. prof., 1994—, dir. eating disorders program, adolescent medicine program, 1990—. Office: U Medicine and Dentistry NJ-Robert Wood Johnson Med Sch Dept Pediats New Brunswick NJ 08903-0019 Office Phone: 732-235-7896.

**SNYDER, BARBARA LOU,** retired educational association administrator; b. Denison, Iowa, July 13, 1935; d. Alfred Howard and Elsie May Bowen; children: Steven, Terry, Richard, Jonathan. BA, Simpson Coll., 1957; MEd, Mid. Tenn. State U., 1975. Cert. insurance agent TN. Tchr. Huntsville City Schs., Huntsville, Ala., 1966—68, Huntsville Achiev. Sch., 1968—70; resource tchr. Tullahoma City Schs., Tullahoma, Tenn., 1971—95; ins. agent Nat. Health Administr., 1996—2004; lobbyist Tenn. Retired Tchrs. Assn., Nashville, 2001—, assoc. exec. dir. to exec. dir., 2003—04. Legislative chair Tenn Retired Tchrs. Assn., Nashville, 1995—2001. Treas. Tenn. Federation Democratic Women, Nashville, 1997—99, cooresponding sec., 1995—97; convention co-chair 41st Annual Tenn. Federation Democratic Women, Manchester, Tenn., 1998; recording sec. Tenn. Federation Democratic Women, Nashville, 1999—2001; mem. Coffee County Dem. Exec. Com., 1992—, sec., 1998—. Named First Hometown Hero, Tullahoma News, 2001, Mrs. Democrat, Highland Rim Democratic Club, 2000. Mem.: Coffee County Retired Tchrs., Tenn. Retired Tchrs. Assn., Nat. Retired Tchrs. Assn. Democrat. Unitarian. Avocations: reading, gardening, walking, politics. Home: 320 E Fort St Tullahoma TN 37388 Office: Tenn Retired Tchrs Assn 801 Second Ave N Nashville TN 37201 Office Phone: 615-242-8392 x 350. Personal E-mail: bsnyder@cafes.net.

**SNYDER, BARBARA ROOK,** academic administrator; BA, Ohio State U., 1976; JD, U. Chgo., 1980. Bar: Ill. 1980. Law clk. for Judge Luther M. Swygert U.S. Ct. Appeals for the Seventh Cir.; with Sidley & Austin, Chgo.; joined law faculty Case Western Res. U., 1983, Ohio State U., Columbus, 1988, assoc. dean for acad. affairs, 2000—01, vice provost for acad. policy and human resources, 2001—03, interim provost, 2003—04, exec. v.p., provost, 2004—, Joanne W. Murphy/Class of 1965 professorship Moritz Coll. Law. Office: Ohio State U Office Acad Affairs 203 Bricker Hall 190 N Oval Mall Columbus OH 43210 Office Phone: 614-292-5881. Business E-Mail: snyder.7@osu.edu.

**SNYDER, BARRY E., SR.,** Native American tribal leader; Owner Seneca Hawk; pres. Seneca Nation of Indians, 2004—. Office: Seneca Nation of Indians William Seneca Bldg 12837 Rt 438 Irving NY 14081 Office Phone: 716-539-4900 ext. 5004.*

**SNYDER, BROCK ROBERT,** lawyer; b. Topeka, Sept. 18, 1935; s. Ralph and Helen (Fritze) S.; m. Carol Lee Cunningham, June 5, 1957 (div. Nov. 1976); children: Lori, Holli, Staci; m. Sheryl Anita Clarke, Apr. 1, 1985 (div. Apr. 1997); children: Brock Robert II, Samantha. BS, U. Kans., 1957; JD, Washburn U., 1964. Bar: Kans. 1964. Ptnr. Eidson, Lewis, Porter & Haynes, Topeka, 1964—82; pvt. practice Topeka, 1982—. Lectr. on sch. discipline and due process, 1975-80; pres. Kans. Legal Services, Topeka, 1977-80. Served to capt. USMC, 1957-61. Fellow Kans. Bar Assn. (chmn. legal assts. com. 1983-84); mem. ABA, Kans. Trial Lawyers Assn. (bd. govs.), Topeka Bar Assn., Topeka Legal Aid Soc. (bd. govs., pres. 1976-78). Republican. Lutheran. Avocation: scuba. Office: 1401 SW Topeka Blvd Topeka KS 66612-1818 Office Phone: 785-232-1700. E-mail: brsnyder@inlandnet.net.

**SNYDER, BURTON HAROLD,** lawyer; b. York, Pa., Nov. 7, 1947; m. Carol A. Oyler. BA in math., Lehigh U., 1969; JD, Harvard U., 1975. Bar: Pa. 1975. Staff counsel Hershey Foods Corp., Hershey, Pa., 1979—82, sr. counsel, 1982—85, ops. dir., gen mgr. for Far East and Middle East Hershey Internat. Ltd., 1985—89, asst. gen. counsel, 1993—2000, v.p., asst. gen. counsel, 2000—02, sr. v.p. pub affairs, gen. counsel, sec., 2002, sr. v.p. internat., gen. counsel, sec., 2002—03, sr. v.p., gen. counsel, sec., 2003—; ptnr. McNees, Wallace & Nurick, Harrisburg, Pa., 1989—93. Mem.: Assn. of Corp. Counsel, ABA. Office: The Hershey Co 100 Crystal A Dr Hershey PA 17033-0810

**SNYDER, C. BYRON,** electric power industry executive; Owner, CEO S.W. Graphics Internat., Inc., Relco Refrigeration Co., 1992—98; founder, sr. mng. dir. Main St. Equity Ventures II, chmn. bd. dir. Integrated Electrical Services. Office: Integrated Electrical Svcs Ste 500 1800 West Loop South Houston TX 77027 Office Phone: 713-860-1500.

**SNYDER, CAROLYN ANN,** education educator, librarian, director; b. Elgin, Nebr., Nov. 5, 1942; d. Ralph and Florence Wagner. Student, Nebr. Wesleyan U., 1960—61; BS cum laude, Kearney State Coll., 1964; MS in Librarianship, U. Denver, 1965. Asst. libr. sci. and tech. U. Nebr., Lincoln, 1965—67, asst. pub. svc. libr., 1967—68, 1970—73; from pers. libr. to interim dean Ind. U. Librs., Bloomington, 1973—89, interim devel. officer, 1989—91; adminstrv. army libr. Spl. Svcs. Agy., Europe, 1968—70; dean libr. affairs So. Ill. U., Carbondale, 1991—2000, prof. libr. affairs, 2000—, dir. found. rels., 2000—. Team leader Midwest Univs. Consortium for Internat. Activities-World Bank IX project to develop libr. sys. and implement automation U. Indonesia, Jakarta, 1984-86; libr. devel. cons. Inst. Tech. MARA/Midwest Univs. Consortium for Internat. Activities Program in Malaysia, 1985; ofcl. rep. EDUCAUSE, 1996-2000; mem. working group on scholarly comm. Nat. Commn. on Librs. and Info. Sci., 1998-2000. Editor: Library and Other Academic Support Services for Distance Learning, 1997; contbr. chpt. to book and articles to profl. jours. Active Carbondale Pub. Libr. Friends, 1991-, Morris Libr. Friends, 1991—; br. pres. AAUW, Carbondale, 2004-05; bd. dirs. Carbondale Cmty. Arts Bd., 2006-, Carbondale Info. and Telecomm. Commn., 2006-. Cooperative Rsch. grant Coun. on Libr. Resources, Washington, 1984. Mem. ALA (councilor 1985-89, Bogle Internat. Travel award 1988, H.W. Wilson Libr. Staff devel. grant 1981), Libr. Adminstrn./Mgmt. Assn. (pres. 1981-82, numerous others), Com. on Instnl. Coop./Resource Sharing (chair 1987-91), Coalition for Networked Info. (So. Ill. U. at Carbondale rep. 1991-00), Coun. Dirs. State Univ. Librs. in Ill. (chair 1992-93, 99-00), Coun. on Libr. and Info. Resources Digital Leadership Inst. Steering Com. (Assn. Rsch. Librs. rep. 1998-00), Ill. Assn. Coll. and Rsch. Librs. (chair Ill. Bd. Higher Edn. liaison com. 1993-94), Ill. Network (bd. dirs.), Ind. Libr. Assn. (chair coll./univ. divsn. 1982-83), U.S. Grant Assn. (bd. dirs. 1992—), Ill. Libr. Computer Sys. Orgn. (policy coun. 1992-95, 96-00), Nat. Assn. State Univs. and Land-Grant Colls. (commn. on info. tech. and its distance learning and libr. bds. 1994-96), NetIllinois (bd. dirs. 1994-96), OCLC Users Coun. (elected rep. 1995-98), Big 12 Plus Libr. Consortium (chair 1997-98), Nat. Commn. on Librs. and Info. Sci. Working Group on Scholarly Comm., Assn. Rsch. Libr. (vis. program officer 2000-01). Avocations: antiques, theater, movies, reading. Office: So Ill U Ctrl Devel Carbondale IL 62901-6632 Office Phone: 618-453-1447. Business E-Mail: csnyder@lib.siu.edu.

**SNYDER, CHARLES AUBREY,** lawyer; b. Bastrop, La., June 19, 1941; s. David and Shirley Blossom (Haas) S.; m. Sharon Rae Veta, Aug. 29, 1963; children: David Veta, Shelby Haas, Claire Frances. BBA, Tulane U., 1963; JD, La. State U., 1966. Bar: La. 1966. Assoc. firm. Milling Benson Woodward, LLP and predecessors, New Orleans, 1966-69, ptnr., 1969—. Bd. dirs. Delta Petroleum Co., Terre aux Boeufs Land Corp., Kemper and Leila Williams Found., v.p., 2004-. Bd. dirs. New Orleans Speech and Hearing Ctr., pres., 1978-80; bd. dirs. City Pk. Commn., 1991-98, pres., 1995, dir. emeritus 1999—; bd. dirs. New Orleans Mus. Art, 1996-2002, 2004-, v.p., 1998-99, sec., 1999-2000. Fellow Am. Bar Found., La. Bar Found.; mem. ABA, La. Bar Assn. (chmn. sect. on corp. and bus. law 1982-83), New Orleans Bar Assn., Am. Law Inst., La. Law Inst. (coun. 2000-, coms. on mineral code and revision of partnership law, property law), Plimsoll Club, Bienville Club, Beta Gamma Sigma. Home: 74724 River Rd Covington LA 70435-2222 Office Phone: 504-569-7230. E-mail: csnyder@millinglaw.com.

**SNYDER, CHARLES ROYCE,** sociologist, educator; b. Haverford, Pa., Dec. 28, 1924; BA, Yale U., 1945; MA, 1949, PhD, 1954. Mem. staff Ctr. Alcohol Studies Yale U., 1950-60, asst. prof. sociology, 1956-60; prof. sociology So. Ill. U., Carbondale, 1960-85, chmn. dept., 1964-75, 81-85, prof. emeritus, 1985—. Vis. prof. human genetics Sackler Sch. Medicine, Tel Aviv U., 1980; cons. behavioral scis. tng. com. Nat. Inst. Gen. Med. Scis., NIH, 1962-64; mem. planning com., chmn. program 28th Internat. Congress Alcohol and Alcoholism, 1964. Author: Alcohol and the Jews, 1958; editor: (with D.J. Pittman) Society, Culture and Drinking Patterns, 1962; editorial bd. Quar. Jour. Studies on Alcohol, 1957-83; assoc. editor Sociol. Quar., 1960-63. Mem. theol. commn. United Ch. of Christ, 1964-71; bd. dirs. Ill. Stewardship Alliance, 1990-95. With USNR, WWII. Fellow Am. Sociol. Assn.; mem. Soc. Study Social Problems (v.p. 1963-64, rep. to council Am. Sociol. Assn. 1964-66), Midwest Sociol. Soc. (bd. dirs. 1970-71), AAUP. Home: Apt 1606 8680 E Alameda Ave Denver CO 80247

**SNYDER, CLARICE JANE,** music educator, musician; b. New Albany, Ind., Dec. 31, 1947; d. Clarence Valentine and Earleen Francis Engleman; children: Sarah Elizabeth, Scott Andrew. MusB, Wittenberg U., Springfield, Ohio, 1970; MusM, Northwestern U., Evanston, Ill., 1971; student in Organ and Harpsicord, Toulouse Conservatory, France, 1978—79. Cert. Music Edn. State of Ind., 2002. Pvt. and class piano and organ tchr., 1962—2002; organist/choir dir. Holy Trinity Luth. Ch., Englewood, 1961 for organist Hopewell United Presbyn. Ch., Franklin, Ind., 1969—70, Canterbury at Northwestern U., Evanston, Ill., 1970—73; dir. of music St. John's United Ch. of Christ, Evanston, Ill., 1973—74; liturgical music coord. St. Peter's Roman Cath. Ch., LaPorte, 1974—77; music dir. St. Mary's Roman Cath. Ch., Mich. City, Ind., 1977; organist/choir master St. Thomas Episcopal Ch., Plymouth, Ind., 1980—83; dir. music St Paul's United Ch. of Christ, LaPorte, Ind., 1983—85; organist St. Thomas Episcopal Ch., Plymouth, Ind., 1986—90; interim organist Northern Ind., Southern Mich., 1990—91; dir. music Holy Trinity Luth. Ch., South Bend, Ind., 1991—2002; band and choir tchr. Marian H.S., Mishawaka, Ind., 1993—95; band tchr. St Jude Cath. Sch., South Bend, Ind., 1994—95, St Bavo Cath. Sch., Mishawaka, Ind., 1994—95; accompanist and asst. dir. Michiana Young Men and Boy Choir, South Bend/Mishawaka, Ind., 1994—2000; adj. faculty (music) Southwestern Mich. Coll., Dowagiac, Mich., 1996—98; accompanist Elkhart Boy Choir, Elkhart, Ind., 1996—99; choir dir. Sacred Heart of Jesus, Lakeville, Ind., 2000—02; music keyboard tchr. Paul Pub. Charter Sch., Washington, 2002—06; minster of music Ch. of the Ascension (Sligo Parish), Silver Spring, Md., 2002—. Founder and dir. Laporte Symphonic Chorus, LaPorte, Ind., 1988—95. Musician recitals, concerts. Mem., treas., presenter, South Bend Area Music Tchrs. Assn., South Bend, Ind., 1988—2002. Scholar, Johnson County Choral Assn., 1966. Mem.: South Bend Area Music Tchrs. Assn. (Local Chpt. MTNA) (cooresponding sec., treas., presenter), South Bend Chpt. of The Am. Guild of Organists (sub-dean, dean, historian, bd. mem., presenter), Music Educator's Nat. Conf., Am. Guild of Organists - No. Va. Chpt., Alexandria Choral Soc., Sigma Alpha Iota (life). Personal E-mail: musicjs2001@yahoo.com.

**SNYDER, COLLEEN M.,** music educator; b. Sanger, Calif., Apr. 24, 1946; d. Tarance Smith and Loramae Hockett Magee; m. C. Ray Slape, Apr. 19, 1980; children: K. C. Simba-Torres, Isaac Slape; m. Arthur M. Snyder, Aug. 27, 1966 (div. 1970). BA, Stanford U., 1968, MA, D of Mus. Arts, 1975. Instr. Lower Columbia Coll., Longview, Wash., 1978—81, Kelso (Wash.) Unified Sch. Dist., 1981—89; dir. instrumental music Reedley Coll., Calif., 1989—2003, chmn. music dept., 2003—. Conductor Kings Symphony Orch., Hanford, Calif., 1991—; asst. conductor Tulare County Symphony Orch., Visalia, Calif., 1992—; guest condr. Fresno-Madera County Honor Orch., San Luis Obispo County Honor Band, Tulare County Honor Band. Mem.: Calif. Orch. Dirs. Assn. (bd. dirs. 2000—, pres. 2004—06).

**SNYDER, DANIEL,** professional sports team executive, communications executive; b. Nov. 23, 1964; m. Tanya Snyder. Founder, chmn., CEO Snyder Communications, Inc. (sold to Havas), 1985—2000; chmn. bd., owner Washington Redskins, 1999—; non-exec. chmn. Six Flags Inc., 2005—. Bd. dirs. McLeod USA, Ventiv Health; mem., broadcast com. and ventures com. NFL. Bd. dirs. Ctr. for Missing and Exploited Children, Parents in Charge; exec. leadership cabinet Martin Luther King, Jr. Nat. Meml. Found. Project; bd. dirs. Wash. Children's Nat. Med. Ctr.; founder Wash. Redskins Leadership Coun. Mem.: Wash. Bd. Trade, Bus. Executives for Nat. Security. Office: c/o Washington Redskins 21300 Redskin Park Rd Ashburn VA 20147

**SNYDER, DARIN W.,** lawyer; b. Kansas City, Mo., 1963; BA cum laude, Georgetown U., 1985; JD cum laude, U. Chgo., 1988. Bar: Calif. 1988, US Dist. Ct., (Ctrl, No., Ea., and So. Dists. of Calif.), US Ct. of Appeals (Ninth and Fed. Circuits), US Ct. Veterans Appeals. Head O'Melveny & Myers LLP, San Francisco, co-chair patent and tech. litig. practice group, head intellectual property and tech. dept. No. Calif. Divsn. LA. Bradley Law & Government Fellow, 1987—88. Mem.: Am. Intellectual Property Law Assn., Santa Clara County Bar Assn., San Francisco County Bar Assn., ABA (former co-chair intellectual property com., co-chair trade secrets subcommittee litig. sect. 1997—98). Office: O'Melveny & Myers LLP Embarcadero Ctr West 275 Battery St San Francisco CA 94111-3305 Office Phone: 415-984-8846. Office Fax: 415-984-8701. Business E-Mail: dsnyder@omm.com.

**SNYDER, DARLENE NOOTENS,** science educator, mathematics educator; b. Chgo., Feb. 15, 1949; d. Joseph Nootens and Adeline Marie Snell; m. Thomas Moroe Snyder, July 7, 1986; children: Lara, Daniel, Michael, Gregory. BS in Biology, U. Houston, 1979; AAS, Lincoln Land CC, Springfield, 1993; MS in Biology, U. Ill., Springfield, 2004. RN Ill. Dept. Profl. Regulation, 1993. Math. instr. Lincoln Land CC, Springfield, Ill., 1991—; instr. environ. sci. U. Ill., 2004—; instr. dept. chemistry and microscopy SCI-Ban, 2006—. Author and editor: textbook Math 081-082, 2005—06, author and editor: sci. curricula and course outlines. Mem.: AAAS, Nat. Assn. Biology Tchrs., Ill. Math. Assn. of CC. Home: 2308 Heather Mill Ct Springfield IL 62704 Office Phone: 217-786-4039.

**SNYDER, DAVID RICHARD,** lawyer; b. Kalamazoo, Mich., Oct. 9, 1949; s. Richard E. and Margaret L. (Vanderplough) S.; m. Phyllis Alford, Aug. 14, 1971; children: Jason Richard, Carrie Lynn. BA with high honors, Mich. State U., East Lansing, 1971; JD with distinction, Cornell U., Ithaca, N.Y., 1974. Bar: Calif. 1974. Assoc. Jenkins & Perry, San Diego, 1974-77, ptnr., 1978-83, Aylward, Kintz & Stiska, San Diego, 1983-86, Luce, Forward, Hamilton & Scripps, San Diego, 1986-93, Pillsbury Madison & Sutro LLP, San Diego, 1993—2005; mng. bd. Pillsbury Winthrop LLP, San Diego, 1999—2005, vice chmn., 2000—05; chair bus. dept., ptnr., corp & securities practice, mem. mng. bd. Pillsbury Winthrop Shaw Pittman LLP, San Diego, 2005—. V.p., dir. San Diego Venture Group, 1989-91; adj. prof. Calif. Western Sch. Law, San Diego, 1982-84; lectr. Calif. Continuing Edn. of Bar, 1983—. Co-author: Drafting Legal Instruments, 1982; editor Cornell Law Rev., 1973-74. Bd. dirs. Boys Club Chula Vista, Calif., 1979-83, San Diego Symphony Orch. Assn., 2006-; pres. Corpus Christi Parish Coun., Bonita, Calif., 1988-90; trustee Children's Hosp. Found., San Diego, 1988-2004, chmn., 1990-92. Mem.: ABA (fed. securities law com. 1987—, chmn. subcom. on ann. rev. fed. securities regulation dir. corp. dirs. forum), Corp. Dirs. Forum (bd. dirs. 2001—), San Diego County Bar Assn., State Bar Calif., Am. Electronics Assn. (bd. dirs., mem. exec. com. San Diego chpt. 1991—93), Order of Coif, Phi Beta Kappa. Republican. Roman Catholic. Office: Pillsbury Winthrop Shaw Pittman LLP 501 W Broadway Ste 1100 San Diego CA 92101-8298 Office Phone: 619-544-3369. Office Fax: 619-236-1995. Business E-Mail: dave.snyder@pillsburylaw.com.

**SNYDER, DONALD EDWARD,** finance company executive; b. Rochester N.Y., Nov. 10, 1928; s. Benjamin Orman and Arlien Henrietta (Wing) S.; m. Dorothy Edna Stanke, Oct. 16, 1954; children: Donald Edward, Anne Arlien Snyder Marone, Barbara Lynn Snyder Mitchell, Richard John Snyder. AB, Cornell U., 1950, JD, 1952; postgrad., Ind. U., 1962. Bar: N.Y. 1953. Pvt. practice law, 1953-56; with Eastman Savs. and Loan Assn., 1956-68, pres., 1970-75, chmn. bd., 1979-88; asst. to treas. Eastman Kodak Co., Rochester, 1968-70, gen. credit mgr., 1975-77, with Comptroller's div., 1977-78, asst. treas., 1978-79, treas., 1979-88; chmn. Eastman Kodak Credit Corp., 1955-88; chief exec. officer, chmn. bd., pres. Corp. Officers and Dirs. Assurance Ltd., Hamilton, Bermuda, 1990-93. Bd. dirs. Greater Rochester chpt. Epilepsy Found. Am., 1979-85, Allendale Mut. Ins. Co., 1983-92; bd. dirs. Luth. Ch.-Mo. Synod, 1983-95; vice chmn. bd., chmn. fin. com., chmn. audit com., 1989-95; bd. dirs., mem. exec. com. ACE Ltd., 1985-90, EXEL Ltd., 1985-90, CODA Ltd., 1986-93; mem. investment rev. com. United Way of Greater Rochester, 1979-2000; trustee Seneca Zool. Soc., 1983-90. With USNR, 1946-48. Mem. N.Y. State Bar Assn., Monroe County Bar Assn., Rochester C. of C. (trustee 1980-86), Cornell Club (Rochester), Phi Kappa Tau (nat. fin. advisor, mem. nat. coun 1988-95, treas., mem. exec. com. Phi Kappa Tau Found. 1991-2002). Home and Office: 14 Hidden Springs Dr Pittsford NY 14534-2897 also: 2700 N AIA Ste 705 Fort Pierce FL 34949

**SNYDER, EDWARD ADAMS,** dean, economics professor; b. Danville, Pa., July 3, 1953; s. Harry Coolidge and Fay (Adams) S.; m. Kimberly Marie Snyder; children: Alison Marie, Jeffrey Adams, Kevin James. BA in Econs. and Govt., Colby Coll., 1975; M of Pub. Policy, U. Chgo., 1978, PhD in Econs., 1984. Staff economist Antitrust div. U.S. Dept. Justice, Washington, 1978—82; asst. prof. bus. econs. and pub. policy Sch. Bus. Adminstrn. U. Mich., Ann Arbor, 1982—90, assoc. prof. Sch. Bus. Adminstrn., 1990-94, prof. Sch. Bus. Adminstrn., 1994-98, chair bus. econ. and pub. policy, U.S. Bus. Adminstrn., 1997—03, dean Darden Bus. Sch. U. Va., Charlottesville, 1998—2001; dean U. Chgo. Grad. Sch. Bus., 2001—, prof., 2001—02, George Pratt Shultz prof., 2002—. Rsch. fellow Office for Study of Pub. and Pvt. Instns., U. Mich.; cons. Antitrust div. U.S. Dept. Justice, Chgo., 1982-85, Fed. Home Loan Bank Bd., Washington, 1989; antitrust expert, 1985—; John M. Olin vis. assoc. prof. U. Chgo., 1991-92; dir. William Davidson Inst. Mich. Bus. Sch., 1992-95. Author: Crisis Resolution in the Thrift Industry, 1989; contbr. articles to econ. jours. and law revs., 1985-99. Avocations: foreign policy, sports, sailing. Office: U Chgo Grad Sch of Bus 5807 S Woodlawn Ave Chicago IL 60637 Office Phone: 773-702-1680. E-mail: tsnyder@chicagogsb.edu.

**SNYDER, EVAN,** cloning and stem cell company administrator, educator, neuroscientist; MD and PhD in Neuroscience, U. Pa., 1981. Resident in pediatrics and neurology Children's Hosp.-Boston; postdoctoral rsch. Harvard Med. Sch., instr. neurology 1992—96, asst. prof. neurology, 1996—2001; prof., dir. stem cell and regeneration prog. Burnham Inst., La Jolla, Calif., 2001—. Contbr. articles in profl. jours. Office: Burnham Inst 10901 N Torrey Pines Rd La Jolla CA 92037 Fax: 858-646-3199. Business E-Mail: esnyder@burnham.org.

**SNYDER, GEORGE EDWARD,** lawyer; b. Battle Creek, Mich., Feb. 7, 1934; s. Leon R. and Edith (Dullaban) S.; m. Mary Jane Belt, July 27, 1957 (div. Sept. 23, 1982); children: Sara Lynn, Elizabeth Jane; m. Claudia Gage Brooks, Feb. 25, 1984 BS, Mich. State U., 1957; JD, U. Mich., 1960. Bar: Mich. 1961, U.S. Dist. Ct. (we. and ea. dists.) Mich. 1961. With Gen. Electric Co., 1957-58; asso. firm Miller, Johnson, Snell & Commisky, Grand Rapids, 1960-62, Goodenough & Buesser, Detroit, 1962-66; partner firm Buesser, Buesser, Snyder & Blank, Detroit and Bloomfield Hills, 1966-85, Meyer, Kirk, Snyder & Lynch PLLC, Bloomfield Hills, 1985—. Chmn. bd. dirs. Bill Knapps Mich., Inc., 1998-2000. Chmn. E. Mich. Environ. Action Council, 1974-78; mem. inland lakes and streams rev. com. Mich. Dept. Natural Resources, 1975-76. Served as 2d lt. AUS, 1957. Fellow Am. Acad. Matrimonial Lawyers (pres. Mich. chpt. 1991-92), Am. Coll. Family Trial Lawyers, Am. Bar Found., Internat. Acad. Matrimonial Lawyers, Mich. Bar Found; mem. ABA, Am. Judicature Soc., Am. Arbitration Assn. (panel arbitrators), State Bar Mich. (chmn. family law com. 1964-72, mem. rep. assembly 1972-78, chmn. rules and calendar com. 1977-78, mem. family law sect. coun. 1973-76, environ. law sect. coun. 1980-85, prepaid legal svcs.

com. 1973-82, com. on judicial selection 1974, com. on specialization 1976-82), Detroit Bar Assn. (chmn. family law com. 1966-68), Oakland County Bar Assn., Delta Upsilon (chmn. trustees, alumni chpt. dep. 1965-70), Tau Beta Pi, Pi Tau Sigma, Phi Eta Sigma. Detroit Athletic Club, Birmingham (Mich.) Athletic Club, Bloomfield Hills Country Club. Episcopalian. Home: 32965 Outland Trl Bingham Farms MI 48025-2555 Office: Meyer Kirk Snyder & Lynch PLLC Ste 100 100 W Long Lake Rd Bloomfield Hills MI 48304-2773 Office Phone: 248-647-5111. Business E-Mail: gsnyder@meyerkirk.com.

SNYDER, GRAYDON F., religion educator; b. Peru, Ind., Apr. 30, 1930; s. Clayton Fisher and Irene Elizabeth (Fisher) S.; m. Lois Hannah Horning, June 13, 1953; children: Jonathan Edvard, Anna Christine, Stephen Daniel. BA, Manchester Coll., 1951; MDiv, Bethany Theol. Sem., 1954; ThD, Princeton Theol. Sem., 1961. Asst. prof. Bibl. studies Bethany Theol. Sem., Chgo., 1959—65, prof. Oak Brook, Ill., 1965—79, dean, 1975—86, Wieand prof. New Testament studies, 1979—88; acad. dean, prof. New Testament Chgo. Theol. Sem., 1986—90, prof. New Testament, 1990—96, adj. prof. New Testament, 1996—99. Mem. accrediting commn. Assn. Theol. Schs., 1976-82. Author: Ante Pacem, 1985, First Corinthians, 1992, Health and Medicine in the Anabaptist Tradition, 1995, Inculturation of the Jesus Tradition, 1999, Irish Jesus, Roman Jesus, 2002, Ante Pacem, rev. edit., 2003, The People are Holy, 2005; mem. editl. bd. Bibl. Rsch., 1965-95, Brethren Life and Thought, 1962-94. Mem. Bd. Edn. # 88, Elmhurst, Ill., 1970-73; chmn. bd. trustees Bethany Hosp., Chgo., 1979-92; del. governing bd. Nat. Coun. Chs., 1986-91. Fellow Westar Inst.; mem. Soc. Bibl. Lit., Chgo. Soc. Bibl. Rsch. (pres. 1969), Studiorum Novi Testamenti Societas. Mem. Ch. of The Brethren. Avocation: early christian art. Home: 5475 S Ridgewood Ct Chicago IL 60615-5314 E-mail: graydonsny@aol.com.

SNYDER, HENRY LEONARD, historian, educator, writer; b. Hayward, Calif., Nov. 3, 1929; s. Henry Runyon and Mary (Rosenberg) S.; m. Janette Marie Hannus, July 21, 1961; children: Michael Jesse, Christopher Henry, David Lyle. BA, U. Calif., Berkeley, 1951, MA, 1960, PhD, 1963. Sr. buyer Dohrmann Comml. Co., San Francisco, 1951—59; instr. to prof. U. Kans., Lawrence, 1963—78, assoc. dean to dean arch. adminstrn., 1967—78; prof. history U. Calif., Riverside, 1986—; dir. Ctr. for Bibliog. Studies, 1989—; dean humanities and social scis. U. Calif., Riverside, 1986; vis. lectr. Bedford Coll., U. London, 1965—66; Fulbright lectr., rsch. scholar U. Hamburg, Germany, 1974; dir. English Short Title Catalogue for N.Am., 1978—. Editor: The Marlborough Godolphin Correspondence, 1975; co-editor: The Scottish Heritage, 1981. Pres. Baton Rouge Opera, 1981-83, Riverside Opera, 1987-90; pres. United Way, Lawrence, 1977; bd. dirs. Arts and Humanities Com., Baton Rouge, 1981-85; Sigmund, Martin, Heller Traveling fellow U. Calif.-Berkeley, 1962-63. Am. Council Learned Soc. sr. fellow, 1969-70 Fellow Royal Hist. Soc. Gt. Brit. Bibliog. Soc. London; mem. Am. Soc. 18th Century Studies (pres. 1980-81), Conf. Brit. Studies (exec. com. 1978-83), Am. Hist. Assn., Internat. Fed. Librs. (chair rarebooks and ms. sect. 1995—). Republican. Congregationalist. Home: 220 Trinity Ave Kensington CA 94708-1139 Office: U Calif Ctr For Bibliog Studies Riverside CA 92521-0154 Office Phone: 951-827-5841. Personal E-mail: hlsnyder@earthlink.net.

SNYDER, JEAN MACLEAN, lawyer; b. Chgo., Jan. 26, 1942; d. Norman Fitzroy and Jessie (Burns) Maclean; m. Joel Martin Snyder, Sept. 4, 1964; children: Jacob Samuel, Noah Scot. BA, U. Chgo., 1963, JD, 1979. Bar: Ill. 1979, U.S. Dist. Ct. (no. dist.) Ill. 1979, U.S. Ct. Appeals (7th cir.) 1981. Ptnr. D'Ancona & Pflaum, Chgo., 1979-92; prin. Law Office of Jean Maclean Snyder, Chgo., 1993-97, 2004—; trial counsel The MacArthur Justice Ctr. U. Chgo. Law Sch., 1997—2004, of counsel, 2004—05. Contbr. articles to profl. jours. Bd. dirs. Citizens Alert, 2005—. Mem.: Lawyers for the Creative Arts (bd. dirs. 1995—97), ACLU of Ill. (bd. dirs. 1996—99), ABA (mem. coun. on litigation sect. 1989—92, editor-in-chief Litigation mag. 1987—88, co-chair First Amendment and media litigation com. 1995—96, co-chair sect. litigation task force on gender, racial and ethnic bias 1998—2001, standing com. on strategic comms. 1996—2001). Office Phone: 773-285-5100. Business E-Mail: jeansnyder@sbcglobal.net.

SNYDER, JED C., foreign affairs specialist; b. Phila., Mar. 24, 1955; s. David and Lynn S. BA, Colby Coll., 1976; MA, U. Chgo., 1978, postgrad., 1978—79. Rsch. assoc. U. Chgo., 1979; asst. rschr. Pan Heuristics divsn. R & D Assocs., Marina del Rey, Calif., 1979-80, assoc. rschr., asst divsn. mgr., 1980-81, cons., 1982-83, Sci. Applications, Inc., 1979-81, Rand Corp., Santa Monica, Calif., 1979-81, Los Alamos (N.mex.) Nat. Lab., 1984; sr. spl. assist. to dir. Bur. of Politico-Mil. Affairs, Dept. State, Washington, 1981-82; rsch. assoc. Internat. Security Studies Program, Woodrow Wilson Internat. Ctr. for Scholars, Smithsonian Instn., Washington, 1982-84; dep. dir. nat. security studies Hudson Inst., 1984-87; sr. rsch. fellow Nat. Strategy Info. Ctr., 1988-90; mgr. internat. strategic planing MPRI, Inc., 1997-2000; sr. nat. security advisor Dyncorp, 2001—02; sr. analyst CNA Corp., 2002—; cons. Strategic Planning and Internat. Affairs, Washington, 2002—. Cons. Rand Corp., 1983—88; founder, chmn. Washington Strategy Seminar, 1984—90, pres., corp. dir., 1984—93; appointee U.S. Bush's Adv. Task Force on Mid-East, 1987—88; cons. Office of Sec. of Def., 1988—92; apptd. supervisory rsch. prof., sr. fellow and team leader Inst. for Nat. Strategic Studies Nat. Def. U., 1992—97. Contbr. articles to profl. jours. Trustee Kents Hill (Maine) Sch., 1987-92. Recipient U.S. Navy award for Superior Civilian Svc., 2005; guest scholar Sch. Advanced Internat. Studies, Johns Hopkins U., 1982-83; fellow U. Chgo., 1979, Inter-Univ. Seminar on Armed Forces and Soc., 1980, MacArthur Sr., 1985-86, Herman Kahn, 1985-86, Smith Richardson, 1987-88, John M. Olin, 1985-86; selected as a Young Am. Leader, Am. Coun. on Fed. Republic of Germany, 1984. Mem. Internat. Inst. for Strategic Studies, Royal United Svcs. Inst., U.S. Naval Inst., Fgn. Policy Rsch. Inst., Coun. on Fgn. Rels. Office: CNA Corporation 1718 M St NW #197 Washington DC 20036-4504 Office Phone: 703-824-2225. Personal E-mail: snyder7@attglobal.net.

SNYDER, JOAN, artist; b. Highland Park, N.J., Apr. 16, 1940; d. Leon D. and Edythe A. (Cohen) S.; 1 child, Molly Fink. AB in Sociology, Douglass Coll., 1962; M.F.A., Rutgers U., 1966. Mem. faculty SUNY, Stony Brook, 1967-69, Yale U., 1974, U. Calif., Irvine, 1975, San Francisco Art Inst., 1976, Princeton U., 1975-77, Parsons, 1992, 93. One-woman exhbns. include, Paley and Lowe, New Brunswick, N.J., 1971, 73, Michael Walls Gallery, San Francisco, 1971, Parker 470, Boston, 1972, Los Angeles Inst. Contempory Art, 1976, Portland (Oreg.) Center Visual Arts, 1976, Carl Solway Gallery, NYC, 1976, Neuberger Mus., Purchase, N.Y., 1978, Hamilton Gallery Contemporary Art, 1978, 79, 82, 83, Nielson Gallery, Boston, 1983, 86, 91, Hirshl & Adler Modern Art Mus., NYC, 1985-87, 88, 90, 92, Compass Rose Gallery, Chgo., 1988, 89, Victoria Munroe, N.Y., 1990, Gibbs Mus. Art, Charleston, N.C., 1992, Artists Space, N.Y., 1992, Michael Walls Gallery, N.Y., 1992, Victoria Monroe Gallery, N.Y., 1993, Richard Anderson Gallery, N.Y., 1993, Nielson Gallery, 1993, 2002, Fine Arts Work Ctr., Mass., 1993, Allentown Art Mus., Pa., 1993, Nina Bransten Gallery, Calif., 1993, Jay Gorney Modern Art, NYC, 1993, Hirschl/Adler Modern, NYC, 1994, Nielsen Gallery, Mass., 1994, Rose Art Mus. Brandeis U., Waltham, Mass., 1994, Brooklyn Mus. Art, 1998, Robert Miller Gallery, NY, 2001, Elena Zang Gallery, NY, 2003, Betty Cuningham Gallery, 2004, Alexandre Gallery, NY, 2004, Sawhill Gallery, James Madison Univ., Harrisburg, Va., 2005; travelling one-woman show, San Francisco Art Inst., Grand Rapids Art Mus., Renaissance Soc., U. Chgo., Anderson Gallery, Va. Commonwealth U., Richmond, 1979-80, The Jewish Mus., NYC, Danforth Mus., Framington, Mass., 2005—; group exhbns. include Whitney Am., 1972, Whitney Bienniel, 1974, 80, Corcoran Bienniel, 1975, 87, Mus. Modern Art, NYC, Am Jaffe Gallery, Bay Harbor Island, Fla., 1991, Cynthia Mcallister Gallery, NYC, Bixler Gallery, NYC, Parrish Art Mus., Southampton, N.Y., Acad. Arts and Letters, NYC, Tribeca 148 Gallery, NYC. Grantee Nat. Endowment Art, 1974; Guggenheim fellow, 1981-82

SNYDER, JOAN PAULA, lawyer; b. Woodbury, N.J., July 8, 1956; d. Paul W., Jr. and Anna May (Mollet) Snyder; m. Philip S. VanderWeele, May 19, 1984; children: Kathryn VanDerWeele, Jennifer VanDerWeele. BS in Chemistry, U. Del., 1978; JD cum laude, U. Mich., 1984. Bar: Mich. 1984, Oreg. 1986, U.S. Dist. Ct. Oreg., U.S. Dist. Ct. (we. dist.) Mich., U.S. Ct. Appeals (6th cir.). Law clk. to Hon. Benjamin F. Gibson U.S. Dist. Ct. (we. dist.) Mich., Grand Rapids, 1984-86; assoc. atty. Stoel Rives, L.L.P., Portland, Oreg., 1986-93, ptnr., 1993—. Editor: U. Mich. Your. Law Reform, 1985—86; co-editor: Oreg. State Bar Environ. and Natural Resources Law, 2002. Mem. N.W. Environ. Bus. Coun., 2004—. Mem.: Oreg. State Bar (chair environ. and natural resources law sect. 1996—97, mem. CLE com.), Multnomah County Bar Assn. (mem. alt. dispute resolution com. 1998—2000, Disting. Svc. award 1989). Democrat. Lutheran. Office: Stoel Rives LLP 900 SW 5th Ave Ste 2600 Portland OR 97204-1229 E-mail: jpsnyder@stoel.com.

SNYDER, JOHN GORVERS, lawyer; b. Boston, June 20, 1960; s. Philip Francis and Sylvia (Gorvers) S.; m. Hinda Mala Simon, July 8, 1984; children: Monica Paige, Kimberly Blaine. BA, Johns Hopkins U., 1982; JD, Cornell U., 1987. Bar: Mass. 1988, U.S. Dist. Ct. Mass. 1989. Assoc. banking law, bus. law and corp. law dept. Craig and Macauley P.C., Boston, 1987—94, ptnr. banking law, bus. law and corp. law dept., 1995—2000; sr. v.p. and gen. coun. Simon Cos., LP, Braintree, Mass., 2000—. Lectr. New England Coll. Fin., 1994-2000. Active Combined Jewish Philanthropies, Boston, 1991—, Anti-Defamation League, Boston, 1993-94, Amherst Coll. Parents Fund, 2004—, Buckingham, Browne and Nichols Sch. Ann. Fund, 1999-, Amherst Coll. Parents Fund 2004—. Mem. Mass. Bar Assn., Boston Bar Assn., Phillips Exeter Acad. Alumni Assn., Phi Alpha Delta Internat., Omicron Delta Kappa (Johns Hopkins U. chpt., pres. 1981-82), Delta Upsilon (Johns Hopkins U. chpt.). Avocations: golf, tennis. Home: 7 Laurus Ln Newton Center MA 02459-3138 Address: The Simon Cos LP Attn: John G Snyder SVP 639 Granite St Braintree MA 02184-5366 E-mail: jsnyder@simoncompanies.com

SNYDER, JOHN HENRY, computer science educator, consultant; b. Wichita, Kans., Mar. 16, 1947; s. Melvin Henry and Cathleen Ann (Collins) S.; m. Patricia Reilly, Mar. 11, 1984; children: Matthew Melvin George, Mark John Joseph. BA, U. Kans., 1970; MS, Nova U., Ft. Lauderdale, Fla., 1984. Cert. tchr. Nev., N.D. Computer sci. tchr. Hyde Park Jr. High Sch., Las Vegas, Nev., 1981-86, Chaparral High sch., Las Vegas, 1986-91, Cimarron Meml. High Sch., Las Vegas, 1991-94; chair dept. sci. & tech. Advanced Tech. Acad., Las Vegas, 1994—. Copywriter pub. info. office CCSD, Las Vegas, 1982—84; chmn. gifted children spl. interest group Am. Mensa, 1984; mem. tech. com. Nev. State Network Internet Com., 1994—95; vice chair NW Accreditation Team, 2002—04; cons. Office Supt. Clark County Sch. dist., Las Vegas, 1984, Las Vegas, 85, IBM Corp., Atlanta, 1991—96; systems analyst Homes & Narver (summer), 1988; adminstrv. aide EG&G Energy Measurements, Las Vegas, 1989; adj. instr. computer sci. Nova U., 1984—93, U. Nev., Las Vegas, 1990—, The Meadows Sch., 1991—96; nat. coord. Milken Educator States Network, 2000—, Milken Educator Listserve, 2001—; chmn. Nev. State Tchrs. of the Yr., 2000—, 2d v.p., 2001—02, nat. conv. chmn., 2002. Newsletter editor Nat. State Tchrs. of Yr., 1991-93, nat. newsletter editor, webmaster, 1999—; contbr. articles to profl. jours. Cochmn. Ednl. Exposition, Las Vegas, 1984; tech. cons. Harry Reid for U.S. Senate, 1986, 92; mem. Nevada 2000 Tech. Subcom., 1993, Nev. State Network Internet Com., 1993—. Named Tchr. of Yr., State of Nev., 1989-90, Burger King, 1989-90, U. Nev., Las Vegas, Southland Tchr. of Yr., 1990, Tandy Tech. Scholar, 1991, Nev. Educator of Yr., Milken Family Found., 1992, Nev. Tchr. of the Yr. Microsoft Corp./Technology & Learning Mag., 1995; recipient Innovative Teaching award Bus. Week Mag., 1990, Dolly Parton Chasing Rainbows award, 2003; Impact Innovator grantee, 1996; McAuliffe fellowship, 1994, 97. Mem.: KC (sec., v.p., pres., local lodge newsletter editor), Am. Legion, Phi Delta Kappa (newsletter editor Overall Excellence award 1990). Democrat. Roman Catholic. Avocations: programming, didjeridu, classical music, website construction, virtual reality. Office: Advanced Tech Acad 2501 Vegas Dr Las Vegas NV 89106-1643 Business E-Mail: jsnyder@web.wiz-lv.com.

SNYDER, JOHN JACOB, researcher; b. Harrisburg, Pa., Sept. 21, 1946; s. John Jacob and Evelyn R. (Gutshall) Snyder. BA. Dickinson Coll., 1968; MA., U. of Deleware, 1976. Hist. rsch. Loise Steinman Von Hess Found., Columbia. Pa., 1975—78; cons. arch. hist. Hist. Preservation Trust of Lancaster County, 1978—83, rsch. cons., 1983—. Bd. mem. James Buchanan Found., Lancaster, Pa., 1976—92, Heritage Ctr. Museum, Lancaster, Pa., 1988—97; cons. Montgomery House Restoration, Lancaster, 2004—. Co-author: Clocks of Lancaster County, 1977, Clocks of Berks County, 1995; contbr. articles to jour. Pres. Rock Ford Found., Lancaster, Pa., 1992—94, chmn. Acquisitions com., 1994—. Mem.: Hist. Soc. York County, Hist. Soc. Perry County, Hist. Soc. Lancaster County, Hist. Soc. Chester County, Hist. Soc. Berks County. Republican. Lutheran. Home and Office: PO Box 40 1938 Water St Washington Boro PA 17582 Office Phone: 717-684-6232.

SNYDER, JOHN MICHAEL, lobbyist, public relations executive; b. Kingston, N.Y., Dec. 18, 1939; s. John Ignace and Agatha (Flick) S.; m. Ling-Ling Woo, Jan. 1, 1996. BA, Georgetown U., Washington, D.C., 1961, MA, 1968. Legis. sec. U.S. Ho. of Reps., Washington, 1964-65; assoc. editor The Am. Rifleman, Washington, 1966-74; chief lobbyist, dir. publs. and pub. affairs Citizens Com. for Right to Keep and Bear Arms, Washington, 1975—; mgr. Telum Assoc. LLC, 2000—. Author: (book) Gun Saint, 2003—; editor: (newsletter) Point Blank, 1974—; editor: (Capitol Hill editor) Gun Week 1986—. Active Arlington County Rep. Com., 1994-2002. Recipient Grand Knighthood award Order of Michael the Archangel, 1988, Cicero award Nat. Assn. Federally Licensed Firearms Dealers, 1996. Mem. Am. Fedn. Police (nat. v.p. pub. rels. 1989—), Nat. Assn. Chiefs of Police (v.p. pub. affairs 1995—, v.p. Washington Liaison 2000—), Second Amendment Found. (treas. 1986—), St. Gabriel Possenti Soc. Inc. (pres. 1989—), Coun. for Am. (dir.), The Asia Soc., Internat. Platform Assn., Kiwanis Internat., Coun. for Am. (bd. dirs.), Nat. Press Club, Pub. Rels. Soc. Am., Capitol Hill Club, Am. League Lobbyists (hon.). Republican. Roman Catholic. Avocations: swimming, bicycling, reading, movies, theater. Home: PO Box 2844 Arlington VA 22202 Office: Citizens Com Right to Keep and Bear Arms 1250 Connecticut Ave NW Ste 200 Washington DC 20006 Office Phone: 202-326-5259. E-mail: gundean@aol.com, john0849@aol.com.

SNYDER, JON DAVID, dean; b. Portland, Mar. 14, 1953; s. Max M. and Nancy F. Snyder; 1 child, J. B. BA, Wash. State U., 1977, MA, 1980; EdD, Columbia U., 1992. Assoc. dir. honors program Wash. State U., Pullman, 1979—80; tchr. elem. sch. Vancouver Pub. Schs., Wash., 1977—84; mgr. product Hosts Corp., Vancouver, 1984—87; assoc. dir. rsch. Nat. Ctr. Restructuring Edn., N.Y.C., 1990—92; sr. rschr. Nat. Commn. Tchg., N.Y.C., 1997—2002; dir. tchr. edn. U. Calif., Santa Barbara, 1992—2001; dean Bank St. Coll., N.Y.C., 2001—. Cons. Albertson's Found., Boise, 1997—2000. Author: Makers of Meaning in a Learning Centered School, Dare to Dream, 1996, A Teaching Quality System for Excellence in Equity, 1999. Commr. Calif. Coalition Tchr. Crediting, Sacramento, 1996—2000; cons. Ark. Tchr. Lic. Task Force, Little Rock, 1996, Nat. Assn. State Bds. Edn., Washington, 1992—93. Recipient EPIC award, Internat. Assn. Bus. Comm., 1996; scholar, Wash. State U., Pullman, 1977. Mem.: Nat. Soc. Study Edn., Am. Edn. Rsch. Assn., Phi Delta Kappa. Office: Bank St Coll 610 W 112th St New York NY 10025 Office Phone: 212-875-4466. Business E-Mail: jsnyder@bankstreet.edu.

SNYDER, LARRY, priest, social services administrator; BA, Ill. Benedictine Coll.; MDiv, St. Paul Sem.; MPA, Hamline U. High Sch. St. Bede Acad., Peru, Ill., Marquette HS, Ottawa, Ill.; ordained priest Archdiocese of St. Paul & Mpls., 1988; assoc. pastor Epiphany Cath. Ch., Coon Rapids, Minn., 1988—90, Nativity of Mary Ch., Bloomington, Minn., 1990—91; assist to the dir. Cath. Charities of St. Paul & Mpls., 1991—92, assoc. dir., 1992—99, exec. dir., 1999—2005; chaplain Cath. St. Catherine, St. Paul & Mpls.; pres. & CEO Cath. Charities USA, Alexandria, Va., 2005—. Roman Catholic. Office: Cath Charities USA 1731 King St Alexandria VA 22314

SNYDER, LEWIS EMIL, astrophysicist, educator; b. Ft. Wayne, Ind., Nov. 26, 1939; s. Herman Lewis and Bernice (McKee) S.; m. Doris Jean Selma Lautner, June 16, 1962; children: Herman Emil, Catherine Jean. BS, Ind. State U., 1961; MA, So. Ill. U., 1964; PhD, Mich. State U., 1967. Research assoc. Nat. Radio Astronomy Obs., Charlottesville., Va., 1967-69; prof. astronomy dept. U. Va., Charlottesville, 1969-73, 74-75; vis. fellow Joint Inst. for Lab. Astrophysics, U. Colo., Boulder, 1973-74; prof. astronomy dept. U. Ill., Urbana, 1975—2005, prof. emeritus, 2005—, chair astronomy dept., 2002—05. Co-editor: Molecules in the Galactic Environment, 1973; contbr. articles to sci. jours. NASA-Am. Soc. Engring. Edn. summer fellow, 1972, 73; Alexander von Humboldt Found. sr. U.S. scientist award, 1983-84. Mem. AAAS, Am. Phys. Soc., Am. Astron. Soc., Internat. Astron. Union, Union Radio Scientifique Internationale, Alexander von Humboldt Assn. Am. Lutheran. Office: U Ill 1002 W Green St Urbana IL 61801-3074

SNYDER (MACKLEY), LOUISE MARIE, speech pathology/audiology services professional, consultant; d. Gordon Joseph and Audrey Augusta (Garvelman) Mackley. BS, Western Mich. U., 1972; MA, 1972; PhD, Mich. State U., 1993. Cert. tchg. elem. edn., speech pathology Dept. Edn., Mich., 1972, clin. competence Am. Speech-Lang.-Hearing Assn., 1975, myofunctional therapy Inst. Myofunctional Therapy, 1986, pre-primary impaired tchg. endorsement Office of Spl. Edn./Dept. Edn., Mich., 1993, lic. speech-lang. pathology Ind., 1995. Speech-lang. pathologist Port Huron Area Sch. Dist., Mich., 1974—75, Br. Intermediate Sch. Dist., Coldwater, Mich., 1975—, Speech and Lang. Svcs., Coldwater, 1992—; cons. Pines Behavioral Health Svcs., Coldwater, 1993—2003; speech-lang. pathologist Laurels Health Care, Coldwater, 1999—, Sundance Rehab., Angola, Ind., 2000—; instr. Kellogg CC, Battle Creek, 2001—03. Cons. speech pathology Office Spl. Edn.-Dept. Edn., Lansing, 1993—96, Venture Behavioral Health, Battle Creek, 1997—2003. Author: (doctoral dissertation) Contextual Factors in Receptive Vocabulary Development of Three-Year-Old Children in Homogeneous and Heterogeneous Day Care. Pres. Early Bird Exch. Club, Coldwater, Mich., 1997—98, 2000—01, 2004—. Recipient Exchangite of Yr., Early Bird Exch. Club, 1995, 2004, ACE, Am. Speech-Lang.-Hearing Assn., 1996. Mem.: Am. Speech-Lang.-Hearing Assn. (licentiate), Nat. Exch. Club. Avocations: miniature pinschers, Norman Rockwell memorabilia, gardening.

SNYDER, MARION GENE, lawyer, retired congressman; b. Louisville, Jan. 26, 1928; s. M. G. and Lois (Berg) S.; 1 son, Mark; m. Patricia C. Robertson, Apr. 10, 1973; 2 step-children. LLB cum laude, Jefferson Sch. Law, Louisville, 1950; JD, U. Louisville, 1969. Bar: Ky. bar 1950, D.C. bar 1970. Practiced law, Louisville, 1950-76; ret.; farmer, 1957-80; city atty. Jeffersontown, 1953-57; magistrate 1st dist. Jefferson County, 1957-61; real estate broker, 1949—89; mem. 88th Congress from 3d Ky. Dist., 1963-65, 90th-99th congresses from 4th Ky. Dist., 1967-87, ret., 1987; sole practice, 1987-91. V.p. Ky. Magistrates and Commrs., 1958. Vice pres. Jeffersontown Civic Center, 1953-54; pres. Lincoln Republican Club Ky., 1960-61, 1st Magisterial Dist. Rep. Club, 1955-57. Mem. Ky. Bar Assn., Ky. Farm Bur., Optimists (pres. Jeffersontown club 1957-58), Jesters, Shriners, Masons. Home (Winter): 383 Juli Fe Dr Naples FL 34110-1123 Personal E-mail: genesnyder@aol.com.

SNYDER, MARK JEFFREY, financial planner, actuary; b. Bklyn., May 16, 1947; s. Milton A. and June (Freed) S.; m. Gloria Carol Beskin, May 31, 1969; children: Chad Alan, Heather Lynn. B of Engring. Sci., SUNY, Stony Brook, 1969. CLU, chartered fin. cons., registered fin. planner. Ins. agt. Mass. Mut. Life Ins., Holbrook, N.Y., 1971-79; dist. mgr. Guardian Life Ins. Co., Port Jefferson, N.Y., 1979-81; v.p. pensions Exec. Planners, Ronkonkoma, N.Y., 1981-84; pres. CAS Adv. Services, Inc., Patchogue, N.Y., 1984-93; mng. exec. Integrated Resources Equity Corp., Patchogue, 1986-89, Royal Alliance Assocs., Inc., Patchogue, 1990—; pres. Snyder Fin. Svcs., Patchogue, 1986-91, Snyder Kresh Pension Svcs. Inc., Patchogue, 1989-97, Snyder Kresh Fin. Svcs., Inc., Medford, N.Y., 1990-98, Mark J. Snyder Fin. Svcs., Medford, 1998—. Spkr. in field. Moderator, host Moneywise, Brookhaven Cable TV, Port Jefferson Sta., N.Y., 1987-88; host WLIM Radio program; contbr. articles to profl. jours. Mem. South Setauket (N.Y.) Civic Assn., 1972—, Three Village Dem. Club, Setauket, 1984—; bd. dirs., pres. Suffolk Estate Planning Coun., 1991-92; chmn. planned giving com. Suffolk County coun. Boy Scouts Am., 1985-87, 93—, mem. exec. bd. 1985—, v.p. 94—, mem. trust coun. 1989-98, chmn. Boy Scouts Am. endowment devel. trust com., 1985-87, 93—; v.p. Suffolk County Coun.; pres. SUNY at Stony Brook Alumni Assn., 2000—. Named one of top 300 fin. planners in the country, Worth mag., 1998, top 250, 1999, 2001; named to Rsch. Mag. Advisor Hall of Fame; recipient top 250, Worth mag., 2002. Mem. Soc. Fin. Svcs. Profls.Registered Fin. Planners L.I. (bd. dirs., pres. 1986-87), Pension Forum L.I. (bd. dirs., chmn. pub. rels. 1986-88), Rotary Internat., KP. Democrat. Jewish. Avocations: racquetball, swimming. Office: Royal Alliance Assocs Inc 1731 N Ocean Ave Medford NY 11763-2649 Office Phone: 631-284-4226. Business E-Mail: marl@markjsnyder.com.

SNYDER, MARVIN, neuropsychologist; married; 1 child. BA (N.Y. State Regents scholar 1958-62, Meml. award psychology 1962), Bklyn. Coll., 1962; PhD (NDEA fellow 1962-65, USPHS fellow 1965-66, trainee 1966-67), Duke U., 1967. Rsch. psychologist NIMH, 1967—71, Nat. Eye Inst., 1971—72; program dir. neuroscis. Nat. Inst. Drug Abuse, 1974—79, dir. divsn. rsch., 1979—90, dir. Office of Sci. Policy, Edn. and Legislation, 1990—94, acting dep. dir., 1992—93; dir. life scis. rsch. office Fedn. Am. Socs. for Exptl. Biology, 1995—97; pres. Snyder Assocs., 1997—. Mem. NIH sr. exec. svc. USPHS exec. com. AIDS, 1983-85; mem. Dept. Health and Human Svcs. Orphan Products Bd., 1982-88; mem. The White House Task Force on Drug Abuse Health Issues; co-chmn. Interagy. Com. on Smoking and Health, Interagy. Com. on New Therapies for Pain and Discomfort; exec. sec. Interagy. Com. on Pain and Analgesia, chmn. subcom. on edn. and tng., 1985—; cons. to WHO on drug abuse policy issues, 1985-87, Ctr. Substance Abuse Treatment, 1999-2000, biosensor devel., 2000-02; testifier on drug abuse sci. and policy issues to U.S. Congress; mem. Fed. Coordinating Com. for Sci., Engring. and Technology, Com. on Brain and Behavior, 1990-91, Devel. Guidelines for Protecting Human Subjects in Drug Abuse Studies, 1991; sci. adv. Dynamac Corp., 1999—; adv. bd. Bus.-Higher Edn. Forum, Rsch. Collaboration Initiative, 1999—2001. Author papers and reports on comparative neurology, drug abuse, nutrition, and health and sci. policy. Recipient Devel. of Naltrexone award ADAMHA, 1985, Pub. Svc. award, 1986, Michael Morrison award for excellence in sci. adminstrn. Com. on Problems of Drug Dependence, 1988, Presdl. Meritorious Rank award 1990. Personal E-mail: tupaia@yahoo.com. Mem. E-mail: sibbaldus@hotmail.com.

SNYDER, MICHAEL F., telecommunications industry executive; Various positions ADT Security Svcs. Inc. Tyco Internat. Ltd., 1977—97, pres., 1997—2006; CEO Vonage Holdings Corp., 2006—, bd. dirs., 2006—. Office: Vonage Holdings Corp 23 Main St Holmdel NJ 07733 Office Phone: 732-528-2600. Office Fax: 732-287-9119. E-mail: michael.snyder@vonage.com.*

SNYDER, NADINE ELDORA, music educator; d. Clair Ernest and Eldora Irene Snyder. BA in Music, Moravian Coll., 1982; MS in Edn., Temple U., 1987. Cert. music tchr. N.J. Dept. Edn., 1982, music tchr. instrml. I Pa. Dept. Edn., 1982, music tchr. instrn. II Pa. Dept. Edn., 1989. Music tchr. Voorhees H.S., Glen Gardner, NJ, 1982—83, Palisades Jr./Sr. H.S., Ottville, Pa., 1983—84, Lehighton (Pa.) Area Schs., 1984—85; supr. Wee Care Nursery Sch., Palmerton, Pa., 1985—88; music tchr. Pleasant Valley Schs., Brodheadsville, Pa., 1988—, music dept. chair, 1992—. Mem. curriculum coun. Pleasant Valley Sch. Dist., Brodheadsville, 1992—, mem. prin. adv. coun., 2000—; pvt. music instr., Pa., 1980—; organist, choir dir. various chs., Allentown, Pa., 1983—93. Recipient Lioness award, Lehigh Twp. Lioness Club, 1994; Thursby scholar, Moravian Coll., 1979, 1980, 1981. Mem.: ASCD, Kimmel Ctr. for the Performing Arts, Am. Choral Dirs. Assn., State Theater Easton, Moravian Coll. Music Alliance, Monroe County Arts Coun., Monroe County Arts Coun., Pa. State Edn. Assn., Pa. Music Educators Assn., Music Educators Nat. Conf., Moravian Coll. Alumni Assn., Order Ea. Star

(Gnaden Huetten chpt.), Phi Delta Kappa (Recognition award 2001). Democrat. Avocations: walking, reading, swimming, travel, drama/musicals. Office: Pleasant Valley Sch Dist School Ln Brodheadsville PA 18322 Office Phone: 570-402-1000 x3152.

**SNYDER, NATHAN,** entrepreneur; b. Hartford, Conn., Oct. 7, 1934; s. Saul and Betsy (Wand) S.; m. Geraldine Wolff, Dec. 27, 1964; children: Hannah Abigail, Alexander Lowell Wolff. AB, Harvard U., 1956; JD, Columbia U., 1963; postgrad. in bus., NYU, 1967-68. Bar: N.Y. 1963. Assoc. Paul, Weiss, Rifkind, Wharton & Garrison, N.Y.C., 1963-66; v.p., sec. Randolph Computer Corp., Greenwich, Conn., 1966-69, exec. v.p., assoc. counsel, bd. dirs., 1969-73; exec. v.p., chief operating officer BanCal Tri-State Corp. (holding co. Bank of Calif.), San Francisco, 1974-76; v.p. acquisitions CBS Inc., N.Y.C., 1976-87; pres. VS & A Communications Ptnrs., N.Y.C., 1987-89, The Snyder Co., New Canaan, Conn., 1989—. Lectr. mgmt. Golden Gate U., San Francisco, 1974-76, Annenberg Sch. Commns., Phila., 1982-87. Editor: Columbia Law Rev., 1962-63. Vol. legal services Office Econ. Opportunity, 1963; bd. dir. S.W. Regional Planning Agy. Served to lt. USNR, 1956-60. Harlan Fiske Stone scholar, 1964-65 Mem. Harvard Club (N.Y.C.), Harvard Club (bd. dirs. Fairfield County). Personal E-mail: naterun7@hotmail.com.

**SNYDER, NATHAN PAUL,** music educator, musician; b. Carlisle, Pa., Oct. 8, 1979; s. Robert Lee and Paula Gail Snyder; m. Jessica Lynn Calaman, June 15, 2002. MusB in Music Edn., Susquehanna U., 2002. Cert. music tchr. Pa. Band dir. William Penn Sch. Dist., Yeadon, Pa., 2002—04; music tchr. South East Delco Sch. Dist., Folcroft, Pa., 2004, North Penn Sch. Dist., Lansdale, Pa., 2005; music tchr., musical theater dir. Gurnee (Ill.) Sch. Dist., 2005—. Prin. bass clarinetist North Penn Symphony Orch., 2004—05; bass clarinetist Northshore Concert Band, 2005—06; v.p. United Meth. Men., Lansdale, 2003—05; condr. Gloria De handbell choir Christ United Meth. Ch., Lansdale, 2003—05. Mem.: Music Educators Nat. Conf. Republican. Avocation: reading.

**SNYDER, PETER M.,** medical educator, medical researcher; BA in Biology summa cum laude, Luther Coll., 1984; MD, U. Iowa, 1989. Diplomate Am. Bd. Internal Medicine, Am. Bd. Cardiovasc. Disease. Resident in internal medicine U. Tex., Dallas, 1989—92; fellow in cardiovasc. diseases Dept. Internal Medicine U. Iowa Hosp. & Clinics, Iowa City, 1992—96, asst. prof. Dept. Internal Medicine, 1996—2000, assoc. prof. internal medicine and physiology and biophysics, 2000—. Contbr. articles to profl. jours. Recipient Clinician Scientist award, 1996, Katz Basic Sci. award, 1998; fellow Student Rsch., U. Iowa, 1985, Student, Am. Heart Assn., 1987—88. Mem.: ACP, Alpha Omega Alpha. Achievements include research in sodium channel structure and function. Office: U Iowa Coll of Medicine Dept Internal Medicine 200 Hawkins Dr Iowa City IA 52242-1009

**SNYDER, RICHARD GERALD,** research scientist, administrator, educator, consultant; b. Northampton, Mass., Feb. 14, 1928; s. Grant B. and Ruth (Putnam) S.; m. Phoebe Jones, March 2, 1949; children: Dorinda, Sherrill, Paul, Jeff, Jon, David. Student, Amherst Coll., 1946-48; BA, U. Ariz., 1956, MA, 1957, PhD, 1959. Diplomate Am. Bd. Forensic Anthropology. Tchg. asst. dept. anthropology U. Ariz., Tucson, 1957-58, assoc. rsch. engr. Applied Rsch. Lab., Coll. Engring., 1958-60, mem. staff Ariz. Transp. and Traffic Inst. 1959-60, assoc. prof. sys. engring., 1960; chief phys. anthropology Civil Aeromed. Rsch. Inst. FAA, Oklahoma City, 1960-66, rsch. pilot, 1962-66, acting chief Protection and Survival Labs., 1963-66; mgr. biomechanics dept. Office Automotive Safety Rsch. Ford Motor Co., Dearborn, Mich., 1966-68, prin. rsch. scientist, 1968; assoc. prof. anthropology U. Mich., Ann Arbor, 1968-73, prof., 1973-85; rsch. scientist Hwy. Safety Rsch. Inst. U. Mich. Trans. Rsch. Inst., Ann Arbor, 1968—85; head biomed. dept. U. Mich., Ann Arbor, 1969-84, dir. NASA Ctr. of Excellence in Man-Vehicle Syss., 1984-85, prof. emeritus, 1985—, rsch. scientist emeritus, 1989—, named chair, R.G. Snyder disting. univ. prof. indsl. and ops. engring, 2004—; pres. Biodynamics Internat., Tucson, 1986—. Pres., bd. dirs. George Snively Rsch. Found., 1992-98; assoc. prof. sys. engring. U. Ariz., 1960; adj. assoc. prof. U. Okla., 1963; rsch. assoc. Zoller Lab., U. Chgo., 1964-65, rsch. assoc. dept. anthropology, 1965-67; assoc. prof. Mich. State U., East Lansing, 1967-68; cons. USAF Aerospace Med. Rsch. Labs., Nat. Acad. Scis., U.S. Dept. Transp., adv. com. Office Naval Rsch. Dept. Navy, numerous others. Assoc. editor Jour. of Comm., 1961—63, cons. editor Jour. Biomechanics, 1967—81, mem. editl. bd. Product Safety News, 1973, adv. bd. Aviation Space and Environ. Medicine, 1980—91, 1994, mem. editl. rev. bd. Stapp Car Crash Jour., 2001—03; contbr. chapters to books, numerous articles to profl. jours. Judge Internat. Sci. Fair, Detroit, 1968; mem. coun. Explorer Scouts, Ann Arbor, 1968-70; dir. Am. Bd. Forensic Anthropology, 1978-84, 85-91; dir. Snell Meml. Found., 1990—; bd. dirs. N.Mex. Rsch. Inst., 1996-2000. 1st lt. USAF, 1949-54, Korea. Decorated Disting. Flying Cross, 3 Air Medals; recipient Met. Life award Nat. Safety Coun., 1970, Admiral Luis de Flores Flight Safety award Flight Safety Found., 1987; named to Safety and Health Hall of Fame Internat., 1993, Ariz. Aviation Hall of Fame, 1998. Fellow AAAS, Aerospace Med. Assn. (Harry G. Moseley award 1975, Profl. Excellence award 1978, John Paul Stapp award in aerospace biomechanics 1994), Royal Anthrop. Inst., Am. Anthrop. Assn., Am. Acad. Forensic Scis. (T. Dale Stewart award 1992), Soc. Automotive Engrs. (Arch T. Colwell Merit award 1973, Aerospace Congress award 1982, Tech. Contbns. to Air Transport Safety), Explorers Club; mem. AIAA (assoc. fellow), Ariz.-Nev. Acad. Sci., Internat. Soc. Aircraft Safety Investigators, Aerospace Physiologists Soc., Sigma Xi, Beta Beta Beta. Republican. Congregationalist. Avocations: aviation, aerospace medicine, forensic anthropology. Home: 3720 N Silver Dr Tucson AZ 85749-9709 Office: BioDynamics Internat Tucson AZ 85749

**SNYDER, RICK (RICHARD D. SNYDER),** computer company executive; BGS with high distinction, Univ. Mich., 1977. MBA with high distinction, 1979, JD, 1982. CPA; bar: Mich. Acct. Coopers & Lybrand, 1982—88, ptnr., 1988—91; exec. v.p. Gateway, Inc., Irvine, Calif., 1991—97, pres. & COO, 1996—97, dir., 1991—97, chmn., 2005—, interim CEO, 2006; pres. Avalon Investments, 1997—2000; founder, CEO, chmn. Ardesta LLC, Ann Arbor, Mich., 2000—. Adj. prof. acctg. U. Mich., 1982—84; dir. Launch Media Inc. Trustee The Henry Ford; bd. mem. U. Mich. Coll. Engring. Nat. Adv. Com.; mem. tech. transfer nat. adv. com. U. Mich.; mem. Gov. e-Mich. Adv. Council; mem. adv. bd. Samuel Zell & Robert H. Lurie Inst. for Entrepreneurial Studies, NanoBus. Alliance; mem. vis. com. Purdue Univ. Sch. Engring.; chmn. Ann Arbor SPARK; mem. The Nature Conservancy, Mich. Chpt. Mem.: Mich. Bar Assn. Office: Gateway Inc 7565 Irvine Center Dr Irvine CA 92618*

**SNYDER, ROBERT ELLIS,** retired music educator, minister; b. Columbus, Ohio, June 22, 1930; s. Ellis Emmanuel and Pauline Walker Snyder; m. Paula Schumacher, Aug. 27, 1966; children: Carol Elizabeth, Paul Robert. BA in Music, Capital U., 1952; BDiv, Trinity Luth. Sem., 1956; MusM, U. Colo., 1956; PhD in Choral Conducting and Lit., U. Iowa, 1970. Ordained min. 956. Min. Faith Luth. Ch., Detroit, 1956—66; prof. music Ea. Ill. U., Charleston, 1968—95; ret., 1995. Mem.: Am. Choral Dirs. Assn. (nat. treas.). Avocations: golf, tennis, bridge, travel. Home: 114 Longwood Green Ct Aiken SC 29803

**SNYDER, ROBERT LYMAN,** materials scientist, educator; b. Plattsburgh, NY, June 5, 1941; s. George Michael and Dorothy (Lyman) M.; m. Sheila Nolan, Sept. 1, 1963; children: Robert N., Kristina M. BA, Marist Coll., 1963; PhD, Fordham U., 1968. Postdoctoral fellow NIH U. Pitts., 1968; NRC fellow NASA Elec. Rsch. Ctr., Cambridge, Mass., 1969; asst. prof. ceramic sci. Alfred (N.Y.) U., 1970-77, assoc. prof., 1977-83, prof., 1983-96, dir. Inst. Ceramic Superconductivity, 1987-96; prof., chmn. dept. materials sci. and engring. Ohio State U., Columbus, 1996—2002; prof., chmn. Sch. Materials Scis. and Engring. Ga. Inst. Tech., Atlanta, 2003—. Vis. prof. Lawrence Livermore (Calif.) Lab., 1977, 78, U.S. Nat. Bur. Stds., Gaithersburg, Md., 1980, 81, Siemens AG Ctrl. Rsch. Labs., Munich, 1983, 91; invited prof. U. Rennes, France, 1996. Author: Introduction to X-Ray Powder Diffractometry, 1996; author, editor 8 books; contbr. chpts. to books and over 270 articles to profl. jours. Deputy mayor Village of Alfred, 1973-77; pres. Alfred Vol. Fire

---

Co., 1979-88. Recipient Chancellor's award SUNY, 1980, numerous research grants; named Faculty Exch. scholar SUNY, 1978-96. Fellow Am. Ceramic Soc. (Outstanding Educator award 1999), Am. Soc. Metals (disting.), Internat. Ctr. Diffraction Data (Hanawalt award, 2004); mem. TMS (Leadership award 2002), NAS (U.S. nat. com. on crystallography 1991-95, Codata 2001—), Nat. Inst. Ceramic Engrs., Am. Crystallography Assn. (chmn. applied crystallography div. 1988-92), Materials Rsch. Soc., Ceramic Ednl. Coun., Internat. Ctr. Diffraction Data (bd. dirs. 1986-92, elected chmn. bd. dirs. 1996-2000), Internat. X-ray Analysis Soc. (pres. 2000-2001), Edward Orton Jr. Ceramic Found. (bd. dirs. 1996—), Alfred and Allegany County Fire Assn., Sigma Xi, Phi Kappa Phi. Democrat. Achievements include numerous patents for practical superconductors. Office: Ga Inst Tech Sch Materials Sci and Engring 771 Feist Dr Atlanta GA 30332-0245 Home: 195 14th St NE Ste 1 Atlanta GA 30309-2682 Office Phone: 404-894-2888. Business E-Mail: robert.snyder@mse.gatech.edu.

**SNYDER, ROGER ALAN,** physician, neurologist; b. Phila., Apr. 8, 1939; s. Harry Z. and Ida Snyder; m. Margaret Zemel, June 23, 1962 (div. Apr. 1996); children: Richard Owen, Karen Dana. AB, Harvard Coll., 1961; MD, U. Pa., 1965. Diplomate Am. Bd. Psychiatry and Neurology. Intern, med. resident U. Rochester, 1965-67; rsch. assoc. NIH, 1967-70; neurology resident U. Pa., 1970-73; fellow Mass Eye and Ear Infirmary, 1972; clin. instr. Georgetown U. Med. Ctr., Washington, 1974-76, clin. asst. prof., 1976—. Bd. dirs. N.Va. chpt. Am. Heart Assn., 1979-83. Fellow Am. Acad. Neurology; mem. Harvard Alumni Assn. (dir. 1990-93), Harvard Club (Washington, pres. 1986-88). Avocations: sailing, tennis. Office: 8303 Arlington Blvd 202 Fairfax VA 22031 Office Phone: 703-573-5150.

**SNYDER, SOLOMON HALBERT,** psychiatrist, pharmacologist; b. Washington, Dec. 26, 1938; s. Samuel Simon and Patricia (Yakerson) S.; m. Elaine Borko, June 10, 1962; children: Judith Rhea, Deborah Lynn. MD cum laude, Georgetown U., 1962; PhD (hon.), Ben Gurion U., 1990; DSc (hon.), Georgetown U., 1986, Northwestern U., 1981, Technion Inst., 2002, Mt. Sinai Med. Sch., 2004, U. Maryland, 2006. Intern Kaiser Found. Hosp., San Francisco, 1962-63; rsch. assoc. NIMH, Bethesda, Md., 1963-65; resident psychiatry Johns Hopkins Hosp., Balt., 1965-68; assoc. prof. psychiatry and pharmacology Johns Hopkins Med. Sch., 1968-70, prof., 1970-77, disting. svc. prof. psychiatry and pharmacology, 1977-80, disting. svc. prof. neurosci., psychiatry, and pharmacology, 1980—, dir. dept. neurosci., 1980—. Wellcome disting. prof. U. Wash., 1999; lectr. in field; lectr. Gross Found., 2005. Author: Uses of Marijuana, 1971, Madness and the Brain, 1973, Opiate Receptor Mechanisms, 1975, The Troubled Mind, 1976, Biologic Aspects of Mental Disorder, 1980, Drugs and the Brain, 1986, Brainstorming, 1989; editor Perspectives in Neuropharmacology, 1971, Frontiers in Catecholamine Research, 1973, Handbook of Psychopharmacology, 1974; contbr. articles to profl. jours. Served with USPHS, 1963-65. Recipient Outstanding Scientist award, Md. Acad. Scis., 1969, John Jacob Abel award, Am. Pharmacology Soc., 1970, A.E. Bennett award, Soc. Biol. Psychiatry, 1970, Gaddum award, Brit. Pharm. Soc., 1974, F.O. Schmitt award in neurosci., MIT, 1974, Rennebohm award, U. Wis., 1976, Stanley Dean award, Am. Coll. Psychiatrists, 1978, Lasker award, 1978, Wolf prize, 1983, Dickson prize, 1983, Sci. Achievement award, AMA, 1985, Claa-Giegy-Drew award, 1985, Strecker prize, 1986, Edward Sachar Meml. award, Columbia U., 1986, Sense of Smell award, Fragrance Rsch. Found., 1987, J. Allyn Taylor prize, 1990, Pasarow Found. award, 1991, Bower award, Achievement Sci. Franklin Inst., 1991, Joseph Priestley prize, Dickinson Coll., 1992, Baxter award, Am. Assn. Med. Colls., 1995, Bristol-Myers-Squibb Neurosci. prize, 1996, City of Medicine award, 2000, Gerard prize, Soc. Neurosci., 2000, Salmon medal, 2001, Lieber prize, NARSAD, 2001, Disting. lectr., U. Tex., Houston, 2002, Presdl. lectr., Sloan-Kettering Cancer Inst., N.Y., 2002, Goldman-Rakic prize, NARSAD, 2003, Nat. medal sci., US Pres., 2005. Fellow: Am. Philos. Soc., Am. Acad. Arts and Scis., Am. Psychiat. Assn. (Hofheimer award 1972, Disting. Svc. award 1989, Judd Marnor award 2000), Am. Coll. Neuropsychopharmacology (Daniel Efron award 1974); mem.: Inst. Medicine, Am. Pharmacology Soc., Am. Soc. Biol. Chemists, Soc. for Neurosci. (pres. 1979—80, Presdl. lectr. 2000, History of Neurosci. lectr. 2001), Nat. Acad. Scis. (Sarnat prize in mental health 2001). Home: 3801 Canterbury Rd Unit 1102 Baltimore MD 21218-2379 Office: Johns Hopkins U Med Sch Dept Neurosciences 725 N Wolfe St Baltimore MD 21205-2105 Office Phone: 410-955-3024. Business E-Mail: ssnyder@jhmi.edu.

**SNYDER, STEPHEN EDWARD,** lawyer, mediator; b. Albuquerque, Sept. 14, 1942; s. John Royden and Elaine Stella (Draper) S.; m. Judith Anne Swall, Oct. 27, 1967; children: Sara, Katherine. BBA, U. N.Mex., 1965, MBA, 1967; JD, U. Tex., 1972. Bar: Colo. 1973, N.Mex. 1984. Ptnr. Holme Roberts & Owen, Denver, 1973-96. Author: Commercial Bankruptcy Litigation, 1989. Chmn. bd. trustees Mile High Transplant Bank, Denver, 1995; trustee The Transplant Found., 1992-96, Allosource, 1994-96; bd. trustees N.Mex. Ctr. for Dispute Resolution, 1999—. Lt. (j.g.) USN, 1967-70.

**SNYDER, TIMOTHY DAVID,** history professor, writer; b. Kettering, OH, Aug. 18, 1969; s. Estel Eugene and Christine Hadley Snyder; m. Marci Shore, June 10, 2005. BA, Brown U., 1991; PhD, U. Oxford, 1995. Assoc. prof., dept. history Yale U., New Haven, 2001—. Author: (history book) Sketches from a Secret War, Reconstruction of Nations, Nationalism, Marxism, and Modern Central Europe. Marshall scholarship, UK Govt., 1991-1994, Acad. scholarship, Harvard U., 1998-2000. Office: Yale Univ Dept History Box 208324 New Haven CT 06520-8324 Business E-Mail: timothy.snyder@yale.edu.

**SNYDER, TODD,** retail executive; BA in Apparel Design, Iowa State U., 1992. Men's wear designer Ralph Lauren, NYC, 1997, Old Navy: v.p. men's design J Crew, 2003: cofounder (with Steve King) Tailgate Clothing Co. Corp. Office: J Crew 770 Broadway New York NY 10003 also: Tailgate Clothing Co Corp 2805 SW Snyder Dr Ste 530 Ankeny IA 50021*

**SNYDER, VIC,** congressman, physician; b. Medford, Oreg., Sept. 27, 1947; m. Betsy Singleton; 1 child, Charles Pennington. BA in Chemistry, Willamette U., 1975; MD, U. Oreg. Health Scis. Ctr., 1979; JD, U. Ark., Little Rock, 1988. Resident family practice U. Ark. Med. Scis., 1979-82; physician family practice Ark., 1982—; mem. Ark. State Senate, 1991-96, US Congress from 2d Ark. dist., 1997—; mem. armed srvc. com., veterans affairs com. Med. missions to Cambodian regufee camps, Thailand, El Salvadoran regufee camps, Honduras, mission hosp., Sierra Leone, Africa, Ethiopian refugee camp, Sudan. With USMC, 1967-69. Democrat. Methodist. Office: US Ho Reps 1330 Longworth Ho Office Bldg Washington DC 20515-0402 also: Dist Office Ste 150 1501 N Univ Little Rock AR 72207 E-mail: snyder.congress@mail.house.gov.*

**SNYDER, WILLARD BREIDENTHAL,** lawyer; b. Kansas City, Kans., Dec. 18, 1940; s. N.E. and Ruth (Breidenthal) S.; m. Lieselotte Dieringer, Nov. 10, 1970 (dec. Nov. 1975); 1 child, Rolf; m. T.J. Sewall, May 17, 1996. BA, U. Kans., 1962, JD, 1965; postgrad., Hague Acad. Internat. Law, The Netherlands, 1965-66, U. Dijon, France, 1966; grad., Command and Gen. Staff Coll., Ft. Leavenworth, Kans., 1977. Bar: Kans. 1965, Mo. 1986, U.S. Tax Ct. 1977, U.S. Ct. Mil. Appeals 1981, U.S. Dist. Ct. Kans. 1965, U.S. Supreme Ct. 1977. Atty., Kansas City, 1970-80, 85—; trust officer, corp. trust officer Security Nat. Bank., Kansas City, 1980-83, corp. sec., 1983—; pres. Real Estate Title Co., Leawood, Kans., 1984—; adv. dir. United Mo. Bank, 1985-90. Bd. dirs. Blue Ridge Bank, mem. trust com. Bank Holding Co., 1991—; German Consul (H) for Kans., Western Mo., 1972—. Mem. Platte Woods City Coun., Mo., 1983—84; bd. govs., past pres. Liberty Meml. Assn.; pres. MacJannett Found., Talloires, France; chmn. Breidenthal-Snyder Found.; nominating and exec. com. Hoover Pres. Libr.; bd. dirs., v.p. Unicorn Theatre, 1998—2004; vice dean Kansas City Consular Corp.; bd. dirs. FBI Citizens Acad., KC Actors Theatre, Kansas City Metro Crime Commn., Truman Found., Kansas City; pres. Wyandotte County Kans. Cmty. Found.; trustee St. Mary Coll., 1984—2001; bd. regents Rockhurst U., trustee, gen. counsel; bd. dirs., vol. Kansas City Cmty. Kitchen; bd. dirs., pres. Navy UDT & SEAL Mus.; dir. and gen. counsel Army Command and GS Found.; bd.

---

dirs., pres. Kansas City Kans. Cmty. Found. Col. inf. U.S. Army, ret. USAR, ret. Kans. Army N.G. Decorated Bundesverdienst Kreuz IKL Bundeswehr Kreuz (silver), Bundeswehr Kreuz (gold) Germany, Legion of Merit, KARNG medal of excellence, Mil. Order of WW award; named to Hon. Order Ky. Cols., OCS Hall of Fame; recipient Golden Honour medal, German Vet. Orgn., Bavaria, 1988. Mem. Mo. Bar Assn., Kansas City Bar Assn., Kansas City Hosp. Attys., Mil. Order of World Wars (chpt. comdr. 1983-84, regional comdr. 1987-91, Patrick Henry award), Nat. Eagle Scout Assn. Avocations: scuba diving, hunting, notgeld collections, cartridge collection. Office: 8014 State Line Rd Ste 203 Shawnee Mission KS 66208-3712 Business E-Mail: wbs11@kc.rr.com.

**SNYDER, WILLIAM BURTON,** insurance company executive; b. Clarksburg, W.Va., July 9, 1929; s. William Burton and Mary Catherine (Cornwell) Snyder; m. Georgie Gaye, Oct. 27, 1951 (dec.); children: William Burton, Melissa Ann; m. Sally Marie Snyder, May 17, 2003. BBA in Acctg. cum laude, Tex. Tech U., 1955. With Travelers Ins. Co., 1955-77, v.p., 1970-77; with Govt. Employees Ins. Co., Washington, 1977-93; chmn., pres., CEO GEICO Corp., 1985-93; chmn. bd. dirs. Auto Body Am., Inc., 2004—. Dir. Nat. Capital Area coun. Boy Scouts Am. Capt. USAF, 1950—53. Decorated Air medal. Mem.: Kenwood Country Club (Bethesda, Md.). Republican. Baptist. Office Phone: 727-599-6170. Personal E-mail: wbs111@aol.com.

**SNYDER, WILLIAM W.,** corporate financial executive; m. Valerie Snyder; 2 children. BSBA, U. Mo., M in Accountancy. CPA. With pub. acctg. Deloitte & Touche; v.p., controller, v.p. leasing and adminstrn. promoted to sr. v.p., chief info. officer Fleet Svs.; corp. contr. Enterprise Rent-A-Car, 1984—89, asst. v.p., 1989, v.p., v.p. fleet adminstrn., 1994, v.p. info. sys., 1995, sr. v.p., chief info. officer, 1998, sr. v.p., 2002—03, CFO, 2002—, exec. v.p., 2003—. Office: Enterprise Rent-A-Car 600 Corporate Park Dr Saint Louis MO 63105

**SNYDERMAN, NANCY,** surgeon, medical journalist; m. Doug Snyderman; 3 children. PhD in medicine, U. Nebr. Med. Sch. Cert. otolaryngology U. Pitts.; UMDA. Resident in pediatrics and ear, nose, and throat surgery U. Pitts.; dir. head and neck surgery U. Ark. Med. Scis., 1983—87; surgical practice Calif. Pacific Med. Ctr., San Francisco, 1988—; med. corr. Good Morning Am., 1987—2003, 20/20, 1987—2003, ABC News, 1987—2003; v.p. med. affairs corp. staff Johnson & Johnson, 2003—06; chief med. editor NBC News, 2006—. Contbr. to med. jour.; author: Dr. Nancy Snyderman's Guide to Good Health for Women Over Forty, Necessary Journeys, Girl in the Mirror: Raising Adolescent Daughters. Mem.: Am. Acad. of Otolaryngology Head and Neck Surgery (bd. dirs.). Achievements include reporting on med. topics affecting both men and women; traveled and reported extensively from Eastern and Western Europe, Saudi Arabia during Persian Gulf War, Russia, Somalia, Kosovo, Pakistan, and Afghanistan. Office: NBC 30 Rockefeller Plz New York NY 10112

**SNYDERMAN, RALPH,** medical educator, physician; b. Bklyn., Mar. 13, 1940; 1 child, Theodore Benjamin. BS, Washington Coll., Chestertown, Md., 1961; MD magna cum laude, SUNY, Bklyn., 1965, DSc (hon.) Health Sci. Ctr., 1996. Diplomate Am. Bd. Internal Medicine, Am. Bd. Allergy and Immunology. Intern Duke U. Hosp., Durham, 1965-66, med. resident, 1966-67; public health officer NIH, 1967-72; Howard Hughes med. investigator, asst. prof. medicine and immunology Duke U. Hosp., Durham, N.C., 1972-74, assoc. prof., 1974-77, chief divsn. rheumatology and immunology, 1975-87, prof. medicine and immunology, 1980-87, Frederic M. Hanes prof. medicine and immunology, 1984-87, adj. prof. medicine, 1987-89; surgeon USPHS, NIH, Bethesda, Md., 1967-69; sr. staff fellow Nat. Inst. Dental Rsch., NIH, Bethesda, Md., 1969-70, sr. investigator immunology sect. lab. microbiology and immunology, 1970-72; chief divsn. rheumatology Durham VA Hosp., Bethesda, Md., 1972-75; v.p. med. rsch. and devel. Genentech, Inc., South San Francisco, Calif., 1987-88, sr. v.p. med. rsch. and devel., 1988-89; chancellor for health affairs, dean Sch. Medicine Duke U., Durham, NC, 1989—2004, James B. Duke prof. medicine, 1989—2004, CEO Duke U. Health Sys., Durham, 1998—2004. Howard Hughes med. investigator, Durham, 1972-77; dir. Lab Immune Effector Function, Howard Hughes Med. Inst., Durham, 1977-87; adj. prof. medicine U. Calif., San Francisco, 1987-89. Editor: Contemporary Topics in Immunobiology, 1979, Inflammation: Basic Concepts and Clinical Correlates, 1988, 2nd edit., 1992, Medical Clinics of North America, 1997, Journ. Integrated Med., 1997, Proceedings of Amer. Physician, 1997; contbr. articles to profl. jours. Recipient McLaughlin award, 1978, Alexander von Humboldt award Fed. Republic Germany, 1985, award for lifetime achievements in inflammation rsch. Ciba-Geigy Morris Ziff, 1992, Bonazinga award Soc. for Leukocyte Biology, 1993, Disting. Alumni Achievement award SUNY Bklyn., 1995, Disting. Alumni achievement award Washington Coll., 1995, Disting. Alumni citation, 1996, Lifetime Achievement award Arthritis Found., Eastern Reg., 1997, Lifetime Achievement award Argentine Nat. Acad. Medicine, 1998, others. Mem.: NAS, Am. Acad. Arts and Scis., Soc. for Med. Adminstrs., Assn. Am. Med. Colls. (chair task force on clin. rsch. 1998, chmn. coun. deans 1999—2000, chmn. 2001—02), Am. Coll. Rheumatology, Assn. Acad. Health Ctrs., Am. Soc. for Biochemistry and Molecular Biology, Assn. Am. Physicians, Am. Fedn. Clin. Rsch., Soc. for Leukocyte Biology, Am. Assn. Cancer Rsch., Am. Acad. Allergy, Am. Soc. Clin. Investigation, Am. Assn. Immunologists, Assn. Am. Physicians (pres. 2003—04), Inst. Medicine, Sigma Xi.

**SNYDERS, DIRK JOHAN,** electrophysiologist and biophysicist educator; b. Wilrijk, Antwerpen, Belgium, July 18, 1955; arrived in U.S., 1984; s. Godlief Stefaan and Mariette L. Snyders. BS in Med. Sci., U. Antwerp, Belgium, 1976, MD with great honor, 1980. Lic. physician, cert. cardiologist Belgium. Resident then fellow in internal medicine and cardiology Univ. Hosp. Antwerp, 1980—84; postdoctoral fellow U. Calif., San Francisco, 1984—85; instr. medicine Vanderbilt U., Nashville, 1986—87, asst. prof., 1987—95, assoc. prof. medicine and pharmacology, 1995—. With V.I.B. dept. biophysics and pharmacology Antwerp U., 1998—2003; prof. biochemistry U. Antwerp, 1998—, vice-chair dept. biochemistry, 1999—2001, chair dept. biomed. scis., 2001—, prof. biomed. scis., 2001—, vice chair rsch. coun., 2004—. Co-author: The Heart and the Cardiovascular System, 1991; mem. editorial bd. Circulation Rsch.; reviewer Jour. Gen. Physiology, Cardiovascular Rsch., Jour. Molecular and Cellular Cardiology, Molecular Pharmacology, European Jour. Pharmacology, Biophys. Jour., Jour. Biol. Chemistry; contbr. articles to profl. jours. Lt. Med. Svc. Belgian Army, 1987—88. Recipient Specia award Specia NV., Belgium, 1980; hon. fellow Belgian Am. Ednl. Found.; NATO rsch. fellow, 1984, med. rsch. fellow Alta. Heritage Found., 1984; rsch. grantee NIH, Am. Heart Assn. Fellow Am. Heart Assn. (basic sci. coun.); mem. AAAS, Biophys. Soc., Soc. Gen. Physiologists, European Working Group (cardiac cellular electrophysiology bd. mem.) Achievements include research on mechanism of action of "specific brady-cardiac agents", use-dependent unblocking and voltage clamp validation of modulated receptor theory (cardiac sodium channels and antiarrhythmic agents), electrophysiology and pharmacology of cloned channels molecular localisation of antiarrhythmic drug binding sites, cardiac potassium channels (including human), molecular ion channel structure-function relationships, molecular basis of congenital excitability disorders. Office: Antwerp U Dept Biomed Scis Universiteitsplein 1 T4 2160 Antwerp Belgium Address: Fazantenlaan 6 Antwerp B2610 Belgium Office Phone: 011-32-3-820-2335. E-mail: dirk.snyders@ua.ac.be.

**SNYDMAN, DAVID RICHARD,** infectious diseases specialist, educator; b. Phila., Sept. 23, 1946; m. Diane Canter, June 26, 1971; children: Laura Kate, Alexander Julian. BA, Williams Coll., 1968; MD, U. Pa., 1972. Diplomate Am Bd. Infectious Disease, Am. Bd. Internal Medicine. Intern New Eng. Med. Ctr., Boston, 1972-73, resident in medicine, 1973-74; asst. prof. Sch. Medicine Tufts U., Boston, 1979-84, assoc. prof., 1984-90, prof. medicine and pathology, 1990—; hosp. epidemiologist New Eng. Med. Ctr., Boston, 1979-89, 1999—, dir. clin. microbiology, 1987-98, chief divsn. infectious diseases, 1998—. Epidemic intelligence svc. officer CDC, Atlanta, 1974—76. Assoc. editor: Yearbook of Infectious Diseases, 1986-98, Yearbook of Medicine, 2003—; contbr. to 14 books; contbr. over 200 articles to profl. jours. Lt. comdr. USPHS, 1974-76. Grantee NIH, 1982-93, 2004—; recipient

U. Pa. A.O.J. Kelly prize, 1972, citation Mass. Dept. Pub. Health, 1994. Fellow Infectious Disease Soc. (Bristol fellow 1978-79, Ken Kaplan Clinician award Mass. chpt., 2003, Emanuel Wolinsky award 2004); mem. ACP (Tchng. and Rsch. scholar 1979-82), Soc. Hosp. Epidemiologists, Am. Soc. Transplant Physicians, Mass. Infectious Diseases Soc. (Ken Kaplan clinician 2003). Achievements include first description of Lyme arthritis; rsch. in hosp. infections, intravenous catheter-associated infections, transplant-related infectious diseases, antibiotic resistance, sepsis, cytomegalovirus prevention; developer of cytomegalovirus immune globulin. Office: New Eng Med Ctr 750 Washington St Boston MA 02111-1526 Office Phone: 617-636-5788. Business E-Mail: DSnydman@tufts-nemc.org.

**SNYGG, JOHN,** mathematician, educator; b. Oswego, N.Y., Dec. 2, 1937; s. Donald and Elaine (Morrow) S.; m. Virginia Snygg, Mar. 22, 1965; children: Suzanne, Zachary, Spencer. BA, Harvard Coll., 1959; PhD, NYU, 1967. Lectr. Hunter Coll., N.Y.C., 1963-66; from asst. prof. to prof. Upsala Coll., East Orange, N.J., 1967-95; prof. Wagner Coll., Staten Island, N.Y., 1996, St. Peter's Coll., Jersey City, N.J., 1997—. Author: Clifford Algebra, 1997. Recipient Lindback award for Disting. Tchg., The Christian R. and Mary F. Lindback Found., 1977. Mem. Math. Assn. Am. Achievements include patent for silhouette of the vane in rotary vane device. E-mail: jsnygg@earthlink.net.

**SO, JUNGMIN,** computer scientist, researcher; b. Seoul, Korea (South), Feb. 20, 1979; s. Hyunsoo So and Sueok Shin. In Computer Engring., Seoul Nat. U., Korea, 2001. Rsch. asst. U. Ill., Urbana, 2003—. Small group leader Inveraarity Christian Fellowship, Seoul, Korea (South), 1999—2000. Recipient scholarship, Korea Found. for Advanced Studies, 2001-2006; Illiac fellow, U. Ill., Computer Sci. Dept., 2001. Mem.: IEEE, Assn. Computing Machinery. Office Phone: 217-244-5791.

**SO, KEVIN,** singer; b. Boston; BA in Jazz Studies, U. So. Calif. Former keyboardist Premier Cruise Lines; former singer, keyboardist, guitarist XPO; solo artist, 1995—. Played Kerrville Music Festival, Tex., Fillmore West, San Francisco, Buddy Guy's Legends, Chicago, Kennedy Ctr., Washington, Beacon Theater, NYC, Bottom Line, NYC. Musician: (albums) Pendulum, 1996, Individual, 1997, Along the Way, 1999, Different, 2000, That Oriental Guy, 2001, Shirts N' Skinz, 2002, Leaving the Lights On, 2003, The So Must Go On, 2005. Office: c/o Musicians Concept 3411 W Bryn Mawr Ave Ste 2 Chicago IL 60659

**SO, YUEN T.,** neurologist, educator; s. Wing Yee So and Yuk Wa Chan; m. Susan E. So, June 16, 1979; children: Andrew, Cynthia. BS, Northwestern U., 1974; PhD, Rockefeller U., 1979; MD, Yale U., 1983. Diplomate Am. Bd. Psychiatry and Neurology. Asst. prof. neurology U. Calif., San Francisco, 1989—94; assoc. prof. neurology Oreg. Health Scis. U., Portland, 1994—99; prof. neurology Stanford (Calif.) U., 1999—, dir. neurology clinic Med. Ctr., 1999—, prof. neurology, dir. neurology residency program. Author more than 90 chpts. and other pubs.; contbr. chapters to books. Named Outstanding Tchr., U. Calif., San Francisco, 1993, Oreg. Health Scis. U., 1998, Stanford U., 1999. Fellow: Am. Assn. Electrodiagnostic Medicine; mem.: Am. Acad. Neurology, Am. Neurol. Assn. (hon.). Office: Stanford U Dept Neurology Stanford U Med Ctr #5235 Stanford CA 94305-5235

**SOARIES, DEFOREST B., JR.,** former state official; m. Donna Soaries; 2 children. Ph.D (hon.), Drew U.; BA, Fordham U.; MDiv, Princeton Theol. Sem.; DMin, United Theol. Sem., Dayton, Monmouth U. Ordained minister Bapt. Ch., 1990. Sr. pastor First Bapt. Ch. of Lincoln Gardens, Somerset, NJ, 1990—; sec. of state State of N.J., Trenton, 1999—2002. Internat. lectr. in field.; founder First Bapt. Cmty. Devel. Corp., Renaissance Cmty. Devel. Credit Union, CDC Properties, Renaissance Employment & Tng. Acad.; faculty Princeton Theol. Sem., Drew U. Theol. Sch., Kean U., Mercer County Coll. Contbr. articles to profl. jours. Vol. Urban League, Newark, Operation PUSH, Chgo.; advocate for at-risk youth; addressee Pres.'s Summit for Am.'s Future in Phila. Office: First Baptist Church of Lincoln Gardens Ste 101-102 630 Franklin Boulevard Somerset NJ 08873

**SOAVE, ANTHONY,** manufacturing executive; Pres., CEO, founder City Mgmt. Corp., Detroit, 1974—98, Soave Enterprises LLC, Detroit. Dir. Titan Internat., Inc., 1994—. Office: Soave Enterprises 3400 E Lafayette St Detroit MI 48207-4962

**SOAVE, ROSEMARY,** internist; b. NYC, Jan. 23, 1949; BS, Fordham U., 1970; MD, Cornell Med. Coll., 1976. Diplomate Am. Bd. Internal Medicine, Subspecialty Bd. in Infectious Diseases. Intern, resident N.Y. Hosp., N.Y.C., 1976-79; chief med. resident Meml.-Sloan Kettering Cancer Ctr., N.Y.C., 1979-80; fellow infectious diseases N.Y. Hosp., N.Y.C., 1980-82, asst. prof. medicine, 1982-89, assoc. prof. medicine and pub. health, 1989—. Spkr. in field; mem. Nat. Insts. Allergy and Infectious Diseases-AIDS and Related Diseases Study Sect. Contbr. numerous articles to profl. jours., chpts. to books, reviews and abstracts to profl. jours. Recipient Mary Putnam Jacobi fellowship for rsch., 1981-82, Leopold Schepp Rsch. fellowship, 1983-84, Nat. Found. for Infectious Diseases Young Investigator Matching Grant award, 1984-85; NIH grantee, 1986-89, 83-86, 87-90, 99-00. Fellow ACP, Infectious Diseases Soc. Am.; mem. AAAS, Am. Fedn. Med. Rsch., N.Y. Acad. Scis., Am. Soc. for Microbiology, Harvey Soc., Sigma Xi. Office: NY Presbyn Hosp Weill Cornell Med Ctr Box 125 1300 York Ave New York NY 10021-4805 Office Phone: 212-746-6319.

**SOBEHART, HELEN C.,** academic administrator, educator; b. Pitts., Mar. 5, 1948; d. Leonard Arthur Zaremski and Helen Olga Baric; m. Joseph A Sobehart, Jan. 25, 1969; children: Michael J Anthony J. BA, Slippery Rock U., 1971; MS, Duquesne U., 1976; DA, Carnegie Mellon U., 1986. Dir. spl. edn. North Hills Sch. Dist. and Pa. State Sys., 1969—88; dir. Spl. Edn. Consortium, Greenville, Pa., 1988—90; supr. Fox Chapel Area Sch. Dist., Pitts., 1989—97; assoc. dir. Lab. for Student Success, Phila., 1997—98; dir. lead instr. and Interdisciplinary Program Ednl. Leaders Duquesne U., Pitts., 1998—2005, assoc. academic v.p., 2006—. Bd. dir. Ednl. Policy and Issues Ctr., Pitts., Pa. Assn. Sch. Adminstrn. Women's Caucus, Harrisburg, Pa. Leadership and Devel. Ctr., Harrisburg, Pa.; presenter in field. Guest editor Internat. Monograph on Leadership, 2000—04; editor: Am. Assn. Sch. Adminstrn. Women's Conf., 2002—, Pa. Assn. Sch. Adminstrn. Women's Caucus, 2001—. Ch. lector, eucharistic min. Epiphany Ch., Pitts.; chmn. bd. Bradley Ctr. for Children and Youth, Pitts.; homeless bd. Homeless Children and Families Fund, Pitts.; bd. dir. Negro Ednl. Emergency Dr. Recipient Goldstar award, Pitts. Coun. on Pub. Edn., 2002. Mem.: AAUW, Pa. Assn. Sch. Adminstrs., Am. Assn. Sch. Adminstrs., Phi Delta Kappa. Avocations: walking, gardening, travel, classical music. Office: Duquesne Univ Assoc Academic VP 314 Old Main Pittsburgh PA 15282 Office Fax: 412-396-1393. Business E-Mail: sobehart@duq.edu.

**SOBEL, ALAN,** electrical engineer, physicist; b. NYC, Feb. 23, 1928; s. Edward P. and Rose (Naftalison) S.; m. Marjorie Loebel, June 15, 1952; children: Leslie Ann, Edward Robert. BSEE, Columbia U., 1947, MSEE, 1949; PhD in Physics, Poly. Inst. Bklyn., 1964. Lic. Profl. Engr., N.Y. and Ill. Asst. chief engr. The Electronic Workshop, N.Y.C., 1950-51; head, functional engr. Fairchild Controls Corp., 1951-56; project engr. Skiatron Electronics and TV Corp., 1956-57; sr. rsch. engr. Zenith Radio Corp., Glenview, Ill., 1964-78; v.p. Lucitron inc., Northbrook, Ill., 1978-87, pres., 1987; pvt. practice cons. Evanston, Ill., 1988—; v.p. Machine Vision and Control Internat. Inc., 1994—2003, LightWave Technologies Corp., 2000—. Asst., instr. Poly. Inst. Bklyn.,1957-64; mem. program coms. SID Internat. Symposium, Internat. Display Rsch. Conf., 1970—. Inventor: 14 patents on various display and electron devices; editor Jour. Soc. Info. Display, 1991-99; adv. editor Info. Display Mag.,1991-2003; assoc. editor IEEE Trans. on Electron Devices, 1970-77; contbr. articles to profl. jours. Mem. Dem. Party of Evanston. NSF fellow, 1959, 60. Fellow Soc. Info. Display (Lewis and

Beatrice Winner award 2002); mem. IEEE (sr., life), SPIE, Am. Phys. Soc., Sigma Xi. Democrat. Home and Office: 633 Michigan Ave Evanston IL 60202-2552 Office Phone: 847-869-5607. Business E-Mail: as1285@columbia.edu.

**SOBEL, BURTON ELIAS,** internist, educator; b. N.Y.C., Oct. 21, 1937; s. Lawrence J. and Ruth (Schoen) Sobel; m. Susan Konheim, June 19, 1958; children: Jonathan, Elizabeth. AB, Cornell U., 1958; MD magna cum laude, Harvard U., 1962. Intern Peter Bent Brigham Hosp., Boston, 1962-63, resident, 1963-64, 66-67; clin. asso., cardiology br. NIH, Bethesda, Md., 1964-66, 67-68; asst. prof. medicine U. Calif. at San Diego, La Jolla, 1968-71, asso. prof. medicine, dir. myocardial infarction research unit, dir. coronary care, 1971-73; asso. prof. medicine Barnes Hosp.-Washington U., St. Louis, 1973-75; adj. prof. chemistry Washington U., St. Louis, 1979-94; prof. medicine Barnes Hosp.-Washington U., 1975—, dir. cardiovascular div., 1973—, program dir. specialized ctr. rsch. ischemic heart disease, 1975-89, program dir. specialized ctr. rsch. in coronary and vascular diseases, 1990-94, program dir. principles in cardiovascular rsch., 1975-94; chmn. and E.L. Amidon prof. medicine, prof. biochemistry U. Vt., Burlington, 1994—; physician-in-chief Med. Cr. Hosp. Vt., Burlington, 1994—2005, Fletcher Allen Health Care, Burlington, 1995—2005; dir. Cardiovasc. Rsch. Inst. U. Vt., Burlington, 2005—. Program dir. Collaborative Clin. Trial Therapy to Protect Ischemic Myocardium Washington U., 1977, prin. investigator Specialized Ctr. of Rsch. in Ischemic Heart Disease, 1975—95, program dir. Principles in Cardiovasc. Rsch., 1975—95, program dir. Nat. Rsch. and Demonstration Ctr. in Ischemic Heart Disease, 1985—95; prin. investigator BARI, II, NIH Fibrinalysis and Coagulation Core U. Vt., 2000; chmn. cardio renal drugs U.S Pharmacopeial Conv., 1990—; bd. dirs. Scios Corp., Corvas Corp., Ariad Corp., Bristol Myers Squibb Corp., Fletcher Allen Health Care, New River Pharm., Inc, Nuvelo Corp.; scientific adv. bd. CV Therapeutics, Inc.; sci. adv. bd. Epix Med., Inc., New River Pharm., Inc.; chmn. HaptoGuiard, Inc. Assoc. med. editor: Heart Bull, 1971—72; editor: Clin. Cardiology, 1971—74; mem. circulation bd. Clin. Guides to Med. Mgmt., 1971—; editor: Clin. Guides to Med. Mgmt., 1996—, Circulation, 1983—88; cons. editor Circulation; mem. editl. bd.: Circulation Rsch., 1974—, Annals Internal Medicine, 1976—, Am. Jour. Cardiology, 1976—, Cardiology Digest, 1976—77, Jour. Clin. Investigation, 1977—, Jour. Continuing Edn. Cardiology, 1978—, Am. Jour. Physiology: Heart and Circulatory Physiology, 1978—, Cardiology in jElderly, 1991—, Current Med. Lit., —, Churchill Livingstone edtl. adv. bd.: Internat. Seminars Cardiovascular Medicine, 1978—, Cardiology in Rev., 1992—; mem. editl. bd.: Internat. Jour. Cardiology, Fibrinolysis, 1986; assoc. editor: Internat. Jour. Cardiology, Fibrinolysis, 1990—, mem. editl. bd.: Current Opinion in Cardiology, —; editor, 1989—; mem. editl. bd. Can. Jour. Cardiology, 1995—, Arteriosclerosis, Thrombosis, and Vascular Biology, 1996—, Clin. Therapeutics, 1996, Clin. Insights in Diabetes, 1999, Heart Disease, 2000, Diabetes Treatment Today, 2000, Am. Jour. Geriatric Cardiology, 2000, Diabetes Care, 2002—, Current Diabetes Revs., 2004—; editor: Coronary Artery Disease, 1989—. Served to lt. comdr. USPHS, 1964—68. Recipient Career Rsch. Devel. award, USPHS, 1972, Internat. Recognition award, Heart Rsch. Found., 1981, Disting. Achievement award, Am. Heart Assn. Sci. Couns., 1984, award, Robert J. and Claire Posatow Found., 1988, Va. Heart Ctr., 1991, Drake award, Maine Heart Assn., 1992. Master: ACP, ASIM; fellow: AAAS (councilor 1997—), Am. Coll Angiology, Am. Coll. Cardiology (Disting. Scientist award 1987), Am. Heart Assn. (coun. on basic cardiovasc. scis., clin. coun., circulation and arteriosclerosis, thrombosis and vascular biology, James B. Herrick award 1992, Spl. Recognition award coun. on arteriosclerosis, thrombosis and vascular biology 1999), Molecular Medicine Soc., Royal Soc. Medicine; mem.: Inst. Biomed. Scis. and Tech., Internat. Acad. Cardiovascular Scis., Internat. Soc. Applied Cardiovasc. Biology, Soc. Exptl. Biology and Medicine (councilor 1998—, pres. bd. govs. 2002—, pres.-elect 2005—), Assn. Profs. Cardiology (pres.-elect 1992), Internat. Soc. Fibrinolysis and Thrombolysic (councilor), Western Soc. Clin. Rsch., Cardiac Muscle Soc., Am. Physiol. Soc., Assn. Am. Physicians, Am. Soc. Clin. Investigation (councilor, instnl. rep. 1997—), Assn. Univ. Cardiologists, Am. Fedn. Clin. Rsch. (councilor), Alpha Omega Alpha. Home: 17 Lost Cove Rd Colchester VT 05446-7473 Office: Fletcher Allen-MCHV Campus Fletcher 311 Burlington VT 05401 Business E-Mail: burt.sobel@vtmednet.org.

**SOBEL, CLIFFORD M.,** ambassador; b. 1949; m. Barbara Sobel; 2 children. Student, U. Vt.; BS in Govt., NYU; LLD (hon.), Kean U., 1999. Chmn., pres. SJJ Investment Corp. and CMS Realty Co.; founder, bd. mem. Norcrown Bank of Roseland, NJ, 1985—91; founder, chmn. several cos. that designed, manufactured and imported fixtures in retail environments; chmn. Net2Phone, Inc.; US amb. to the Netherlands US Dept. State, The Hague, Netherlands, 2001—05, US amb. to Brazil Rio de Janeiro, 2006—. Mem. Holocaust Meml. Coun., Washington, 1994—95. Bd. dirs. N.J. Performing Arts Ctr.; apptd. by Sec. Def. to bd. visitors Naval Post Grad. Sch., Monterey, Calif., 1993—97; adv. bds. Empower Em. and Rep. Leadership Coun.; del. Rep. Nat. Conv., 1996, 2000; N.J. fin. chmn. primary and presdl. campaigns of George W. Bush, 2000; bd. dirs., mem. policy com. Bus. Execs. for Nat. Security; apptd. U.S. Govt. Industry Sector Internat. Trade bd., 1987—89; exec. com. Prosperity N.J., United Jewish Fedn. Metrowest N.J.; bd. dirs. Lexington Inst., Arlington, Va.; chmn. bd. overseer Alexis de Tocqueville Instn. Office: US Embassy 3090 Rio de Janeiro Pl Washington DC 20052-3090

**SOBEL, DEAN,** museum director, curator, artist; Curator contemporary art Milwaukee Art Mus.; dir., chief curator Aspen Art Mus., Colo., 2000—05; project dir. (proposed) Clyfford Still Mus., Denver, 2005—. Author: One Hour Ahead: The Avant-Garde in Aspen, 1945-2004.

**SOBEL, GERALD,** lawyer; BEE, CCNY, 1960; JD, NYU, 1963; MA in Econs., New Sch. Social Rsch., N.Y.C., 1967. Bar: N.Y., U.S. Ct. Appeals (2d and fed. cirs.), U.S. Dist. Ct. (so., ea. and no. dists.) N.Y., U.S. Supreme Ct. Law clerk to Hon. Richard H. Levet U.S. Dist. Ct. (so. dist.) N.Y., N.Y.C., 1964-65; atty., ptnr., sr. litig. ptnr. Kaye, Scholer, Fierman, Hays & Handler, N.Y.C., 1965—. Adj. assoc. prof. Sch. Law NYU; lectr. Columbia Sch. Law, Stanford Sch. Law. Contbr. articles on litigation, patents and antitrust to profl. jours. Fellow: ABA, Am. Intellectual Property Law Assn., Assn. NY Intellectual Property Law; mem.: Fed. Cir. Bar Assn. Office: Kaye Scholer LLP 425 Park Ave New York NY 10022-3506 Office Phone: 212-836-8515. Business E-Mail: gsobel@keyeschoar.com.

**SOBEL, HOWARD D.,** dermatologist; b. 1950; MD, Albert Einstein Coll. of Medicine, Bronx, NY, 1973. Cert. in Dermatologic and Cosmetic Surgery. Residency in dermatology and dermatologic surgery Emory U. Sch. Medicine, Atlanta; clin. attending physician in dermatology and dermatologic surgery Lenox Hill Hosp., Beth Israel Hosp., and Cabrini Med. Ctr.; dir. Skin and Spa Cosmetic Surgery Ctr., NY. Editor-in-chief Internat. Jour. of Cosmetic Surgery and Aesthetic Dermatology, appeared on numerous television and radio programs (including: Sally Jesse Raphael Show, Home Show, Good Day NY, CNBC, MSNBC, New York 1, and Channels 2, 4, 5, and 7 News programs). Fellow: Am. Acad. Cosmetic Surgery; mem.: Am. Soc. Laser Surgery, Am. Soc. Hair Restoration Surgery, Am. Soc. Liposuction Surgery, Am. Acad. Dermatological Surgery, Am. Acad. Dermatology. Achievements include helping to pioneer the union of dermalogy with cosmetic surgery; the first surgeon in 1986 to perform liposuction using the tumescent solution purely under local anesthesia; founder and chmn. of HDS Labs, the manufacturer of DDF (Doctor's Dermatologic Formula). Avocations: skiing, tennis. Office: Skin and Spa Cosmetic Surgery Ctr 960A Park Ave New York NY 10028 Office Phone: 212-288-0060. E-mail: hdsobel-md@nyc.rr.com.*

**SOBEL, ROBERT A.,** retired orthopedic surgeon; b. Detroit, Feb. 18, 1916; s. David L. Sobol and Sarah Losh; m. Flora Hannah Rosenbaum, Nov. 9, 1941; children: Susan, Daniel, Joel. AB, U. Mich., 1936, MD, 1939. Capt. U.S. Army, 1942—46. Mem.: ACS, Am. Acad. Orthoped. Surgeons. Home: 25800 W Eleven Mile Rd Apt 258 Southfield MI 48034

**SOBELLE, RICHARD E.,** lawyer; b. Cleve., Mar. 18, 1935; BA, Stanford U., 1956, JD, 1960; LLM, U. So. Calif., 1967. Bar: Calif. 1961, U.S. Supreme Ct. 1969. Exec. Tracinda Corp. Mem. ABA (corp., banking and bus. law sect. 1969-95), State Bar Calif. (del. to conf. state bar dels. 1965-77, exec. com. bus. law sect. 1977-78), L.A. County Bar Assn. (exec. coun., jr. barristers 1965-68, exec. com. bus. and corps. sect. 1973-75). Office: Tracinda Corp 150 S Rodeo Dr Ste 250 Beverly Hills CA 90212-2417 Office Phone: 310-271-0638.

**SOBERAL, ISABEL M.,** minister, music educator, social worker; b. Arecibo, PR, Aug. 22, 1940; d. Jesús Soberal and Justina Román; children: Isabel M., Maria T., Ana M., Miguel A. Rodriguez. BA, Catholic U., 1962; MDiv, Evangelical Sem., 1997, MA in Religion, 2001; postgrad., Instituto Teologico Internacional de Puerto Rico, 2002—. Ordained min. Meth. Ch., 2005; LCSW 1963. Social worker Health Dept., PR, 1963—88; handbell choir dir. Samuel Aun Weor handbell choir, PR, 1986—2004; music tchr. Dept. Edn., PR, 1994—2004; pastor United Meth. Ch., Hopkinsville, Ky., 2004—05, Meth. Ch., PR, 2002—04. Hand bell choir dir. Sala Festivales-Centro Bellas Artes, 2002—04; interpreter Cabinet for Health and Family Svcs. Disability Determination Svcs. Named one of, Musicians Arts Corp., 2003. Mem.: Assn. de Maestros de PR, Am. Guild English Handbell Ringers. Home: 2820 S Virginia St Hopkinsville KY 42240 Office: St John Corona de Vida 2808 S Virginia St Hopkinsville KY 42240 Office Phone: 270-886-1049. Office Fax: 270-886-0391. E-mail: isabelm@hesenergy.net, isbsb@aol.com.

**SOBERON, PRESENTACION ZABLAN,** state bar administrator; b. Cabambangan, Bacolor, Pampanga, Philippines, Feb. 23, 1935; came to U.S., 1977; naturalized, 1984; d. Pioquinto Yalung and Lourdes (David) Zablan; m. Damaso Reyes Soberon, Apr. 2, 1961; children: Shirley, Sherman, Sidney, Sedwin. Office mgmt., stenography, typing cert., East Cen. Colls., Philippines, 1953; profl. sec. diploma, Internat. Corr. Schs., 1971; A in Mgmt. Supervision, Skyline and Diablo Coll., 1979, LaSalle Ext. U., 1980-82; AA, cert. in Mgmt. and Supervision, Diablo Valley Coll. With U.S. Fed. Svc. Naval Base, Subic Bay, Philippines, 22 yrs, clerical, stenography and secretarial positions, 1955-73, adminstrv. asst., 1973-77; secretarial positions Mt. Zion Hosp. and Med. Ctr., San Francisco, 1977, City Hall, Oakland, Calif., 1978; with State Bar Calif., San Francisco, 1978-79; secretarial positions gen. counsel divsn. and state bar ct. divsn., adminstrv. asst. fin. and ops. divsn., 1979-81; office mgr. sects. and coms. dept., profl. and pub. svcs., 1981-83; appointment adminstr. office of bar rels., 1983-86; adminstr. state bar sects. bus. law sect., estate planning, trust and probate law sect., labor and employment law sect., office of bar rels., 1986-89; adminstr. antitrust and trade regulation law sect., labor and employment law sect., workers' compensation sect., edn. and meeting svcs., 1989-96; adminstr. criminal law sect., 1996—; labor and law employment law sect., 1996—; internat. law sect., 1996—; workers' compensation sect., 1996—; edn. and meeting svcs., 1996-98; ret., 1998. Lectr. in min. Our Lady of the Queen of the World Ch.; disc jockey, announcer Radio Sta. DZYZ, DZOR and DWHL, Philippines, 1966-77 Organizer Neighborhood Alert Program, South Catamaran Circle, Pittsburg, Calif., 1979-80. Recipient 13 commendation certs. and outstanding pers. monetary awards U.S. Fed. Svc., 1964-77, 20 Yr. U.S. Fed. Svc. cert., 1975, Nat. 1st prize award Nat. Inner Wheel Clubs Philippines, 1975, Kaiser Vol. Svc. Mem.: NAFE, Am. Soc. Assn. Execs., Our Lady Queen Ch. Filipino Assn., SRF Tigers No. Calif., Castillejos Assn. No. Calif., Olongapo-Subic Bay Assn. Am. (Pitts. rep. 1982—87, bus. mgr. 1988—89, pub. rels. officer 1993—94, bus. mgr. 1997—, bus. mgr. Ulo Ng Apo chpt. 2003—). Roman Catholic. Home: 207 South Catamaran Circle Pittsburg CA 94565-3613 Office: State Bar of Calif 180 Howard St San Francisco CA 94105-1639 Personal E-mail: pzsoberon@comcast.net.

**SOBEY, DAVID FRANK,** food company executive; b. Stellarton, N.S., Can., 1931; s. Frank Hoyse and Irene S.; m. Faye B. Naugle, June 2, 1953; children: Paul David, Janis Irene Hames. D of Commerce (hon.), St. Mary's U., 1991. With Sobeys Inc., Stellarton, 1949—, store mgr., dir. merchandising and advt., v.p., exec. v.p., pres., dep. chmn., chief exec. officer, dir., 1981-85, chmn., 1985—2001, chmn. emeritus, 2001—. Mem. Order of Can., 1996; bd. dirs. Empire Co. Ltd., Sobeys Inc.; chmn. The Sobey Found., Frank H. Sobey Fund for Excellence in Bus. Studies. Bd. dirs. The Sobey Art Found., Boy Scouts Can., Atlantic Salmon Fedn. Mem.: Abercrombie Golf Club, City Club (New Glasgow), Halifax Club. Office: Sobeys Inc 115 King St Stellarton NS Canada B0K 1S0

**SOBEY, DONALD CREIGHTON RAE,** real estate developer; b. New Glasgow, N.S., Can., Oct. 23, 1934; s. Frank Hoyse and Irene (MacDonald) S.; m. Elizabeth H. Purvis; children: Robert George Creighton, Irene Elizabeth, Kent Richard. B of Commerce, Queen's U.; LLD (hon.), Dalhousie U., 1989. Dir. Alliance Atlantis Comm., 1989—; pres. Empire Co. Ltd., 1969, chmn., 1985—, chmn. emeritus, 2004—; also bd. dirs. Bd. dirs. Sobeys Inc., World Wildlife Found., Stora Enso Port Hawksbury; bd. suprs. Trader Classified Media NV. Gov. Olympic Trust Can.; chair Nat. Gallery Can.; mem. Can. group The Trilateral Commn. Avocations: skiing, tennis, music, art, travel. Office: Empire Co Ltd 115 King ST Stellarton NS Canada B0K 1S0

**SOBEY, EDWIN J. C.,** museum director, consultant, oceanographer; b. Apr. 7, 1948; s. Edwin J. and Helen (Chapin) S.; m. Barbara Lee, May 9, 1970; children: Ted Wooddall, Andrew Chapin. BS, U. Richmond, 1969; MS, Oreg. State U., 1974, PhD, 1977. Rsch. scientist Sci. Applications, Inc., Boulder, Colo., 1977-79, divsn. mgr., 1979-81; exec. dir. Sci. Mus., West Palm Beach, Fla., 1981-88, Mus. Sci. and History, Jacksonville, Fla., 1988, Nat. Invention Ctr., Akron, Ohio, 1989-92, Fresno Met. Mus., Calif., 1993-95; ednl. cons., 1995—. Exec. dir. A.C. Gilbert's Discovery Village, Salem, Oreg., 1997-99; pres. Northwest Invention Ctr., 1999—; founder Nat. Toy Hall of Fame, 1998; instr. mus. mgmt. U. Wash., 1998-2001. Author: Complete Circuit Training Guide, 1980, Strength Training Book, 1981; author: (with others) Aerobic Weight Training Book, 1982; author: The Whole Backpacker's Catalog, 1988, Increasing Your Audience, 1989, Inventing Stuff, 1995, Wrapper Rockets and Trombone Straws-Science at Every Meal, 1996, Car Smarts, 1997, Just Plane Smart, 1998, Young Inventors at Work, 1999, How to Enter and Win an Invention Contest, 1999, Fantastic Flying Fun with Science, 2000, Wacky Water Fun with Science, 2000, Inventing Toys: Kids Having Fun Learning Science, 2001, How to Build Your Own Prize-Winning Robot, 2002, Loco-Motion, 2005, Rocket-Powered Science, 2005, A Field Guide to Roadside Technology, 2006; mem. editl. adv. bd. Invent Mag., 1989—92; exec. prodr.: (TV show) Idea Factory, Sta. KFSN-30, 1995—97; co-host (ednl. TV show) Blow the Roof Off, 1992. Alumni v.p. Leadership Palm Beach County; expdn. leader Expdn. '92, 1991; instr., N.E., S.E. Alaska, 1980; mem. U.S. Antarctic Rsch. Program, 1974; founder, bd. dirs. Visually Impaired Sports Program, Boulder, 1978-81; fitness instr. YMCA Boulder, 1977-81; convener 1st Nat. Conf. Sports for the Blind, 1979; bd. dirs. Leadership Palm Beach; vice chmn. County Com. on Artificial Reefs; treas. Leadership Akron Alumni Assn., 1990-91, class pres. Leadership Akron; v.p. Leadership Akron, 1991-92, pres., 1992-93; bd. dirs. Fla. Mus. Assn., 1988-89; mem. adv. bd. Marine Sci. Inst., 1990—. Lt. USN, 1970-73. Fellow Explorers Club (chair Pacific Midwest chpt. 2002—); mem. Marine Tech. Soc. (sect. chmn. 1982-84), Coral Reef Soc. (chpt. pres. 1982-87), Nat. Inventive Thinking Assn. (bd. dirs. 1989—). Home: 2420 178th Ave NE Redmond WA 98052-5820 Office Phone: 425-861-8685. Personal E-Mail: sobey@gte.net.

**SOBH, LOU,** automotive executive; b. Mex. arrived in US, 1960; m. Georgia Zurbriggen; children: Michael, Laurie. Joined McAnary Ford, Gary, Ind., 1967, named ptnr., 1972; owner furniture store, Torreon, Mexico; with automobile dealership, Mishawaka, Ind.; founder, pres. Lou Sobh Automotive Inc., Conyers, Ga., 1990—; now owns dealerships in Ariz., Calif., Fla, Ga., and Ill. Office: Lou Sobh Automotive Inc 1800 Iris Dr SW Conyers GA 30094*

**SOBIESKI, JAROSLAW,** aerospace engineer; b. Wilno, Poland, Mar. 11, 1934; came to U.S., 1966; naturalized, 1971. s. Stanislaw and Sabina Sobieszczanski; m. Wanda Dlugosz, Dec. 31, 1958; children: Margaret Ann,

Ian Patrick. BS aeros., Tech. U. Warsaw, 1955, MS aeros., 1957, DEng. 1964. Cons. Polish Aircraft Industries, Warsaw, 1957-64; asst. and adj. prof. Tech. U. Warsaw, Warsaw, 1955-64; rsch. assoc. Tech. U. Norway, Trondheim, 1964-66; assoc. prof. St. Louis U., 1966-71; aerospace engr. NASA Langley Rsch. Ctr., Hampton, Va., 1971-89, head rsch. office, 1979-93, chief scientist, 1993—96, multidisciplinary rsch. coord., 1994—2001, mgr. Computational AeroScis. team, 1996—2001, sr. rsch. scientist, 2001—06, disting. rsch. assoc., 2006—. Mem. faculty George Washington U., 1971-2003, U. Va., 1992-99, Va. Poly. Inst., 2004—; pres. and cons. engr. Tech. Analysis Optimization, Inc. Hampton, Va., 1982-02. Co-editor: Structural Optimization jour., 1989-2005; contbr. articles to profl. jours. Recipient Wright Bros. medal, SAE, 2000. Fellow AIAA (mem. tech. com., Nat. Multidisciplinary Design Optimization award 1996); mem. International Soc. for Structural and Multidisciplinary Optimization (founding mem. exec. bd. 1992—2003). Achievements include research in and problem solving for aeronautics, space flight, and high performance computing; multidisciplinary design optimization. Home: 518 Elizabeth Lake Dr Hampton VA 23669-1724 Office: NASA Langley Rsch Ctr MS 188E Hampton VA 23681-0001 Office Phone: 757-864-2799. E-mail: jaroslaw.sobieski-1@nasa.gov.

**SOBKOWICZ, HANNA MARIA,** neurologist, researcher; b. Warsaw, Jan. 1, 1931; arrived in U.S., 1963; d. Stanislaw and Jadwiga (Ignaczak) S.; m. Jerzy E. Rose, Mar. 12, 1972. BA, Girls State Lyceum, Gilwice, Poland, 1949; M.D. Med. Acad., Warsaw, 1954, PhD, 1962. Intern. 1st Internal Med. Clinic Med. Acad., Warsaw, 1954-55; resident 1st Internal Med. Clinic, Med. Acad., Warsaw, 1955-59, Neurol. Clinic, Med. Acad., 1959, jr. asst., 1959-61, sr. asst., 1961-63; research fellow neurology Mt. Sinai Hosp., N.Y.C., 1963-65; Nat. Multiple Sclerosis Soc. fellow Columbia U., N.Y.C., 1965-66; asst. prof. neurology U. Wis., Madison, 1966-72, assoc. prof., 1972-79, prof., 1979—2006, prof. emerita, 2006—. Contbr. articles to profl. jours. NIH rsch. grantee, 1968—2002. Mem. Internat. Brain Rsch. Orgn., Soc. Neurosci., Internat. Soc. Devel. Neurosci. (editl. bd. 1984—). Office: U Wis Dept Neurology 1300 University Ave Madison WI 53706-1510 Office Phone: 608-262-1246. Business E-Mail: hmsobkow@wisc.edu.

**SOBLE, MARK RICHARD,** lawyer; b. San Francisco, Dec. 25, 1964; life ptnr. Leslye Soble, Nov. 2000. BA with deptl. honors, Stanford U., 1985; JD, U. Mich., 1988. Bar: Calif. 1988, U.S. Dist. Ct. (cen. dist.) Calif. 1988, U.S. Dist. Ct. (ea. dist.) Calif. 1990, U.S. Dist. Ct. (no. and so. dists.) Calif. 2003. Law clk. to chief judge U.S. Dist. Ct. for S.D., Pierre, 1988-89; assoc. Lewis, D'Amato, Brisbois & Bisgaard, L.A., 1989-90; counsel enforcement div. Fair Polit. Practices Commn., Sacramento, 1990-96, sr. counsel, 1996—2001; dep. atty. gen. civil div. Office of Calif. Atty. Gen., 2001—. Note editor U. Mich. Jour. Law Reform, 1987-88. Raymond K. Dykema scholar U. Mich. 1987. Mem. State Bar Calif., Sacramento County Bar Assn. (mng. editor Docket 1997, mem.-at-large bar coun. 1998-00). Business E-Mail: mark@4lawyer.net.

**SOBOL, ELISE SCHWARCZ,** music educator; b. Chgo., June 12, 1951; d. Morton and Harriet Jacobsohn Schwarcz; m. Lawrence Paul Sobol, Aug. 21, 1977 (div. Sept. 1989); children: Marlon I., Aaron L. AA, Simon's Rock Bard Coll., 1971; student, Mannes Coll. Music; 1971—73, Juillard Sch. Music, 1973—74; BA, New Sch. Social Rsch., 1985; MA, Columbia U., 1987. Staff auditorium events, concerts, lectures Met. Mus. Art, 1972-73; sec. to pres. Harry Beall Mgmt. Inc., N.Y.C., 1973-76; sales rep. M.L. Falcone Pub. Rels., N.Y.C., 1976-77; asst. to pres. Jacques Leiser Artist Mgmt., N.Y.C., 1977-78; artist rep. Elise Sobol Mgmt. Inc., South Huntington, NY, 1978-82; dir. early musical devel. program children Calling All Kids, South Huntington, 1981—86; tchr. music Roslyn Mid. Sch., 1987—88, Nassau Boces Divsn. Spl. Edn., 1988—; dir. LI Music Workshop, 1992—. Tchr. young and adult piano students, 1968—; instr. SUNY, Farmingdale, 1993—98; piano adjudicator, NY, 1993—; guest lectr. NYU, NY, 1999; adj. prof. NYU, Steinhardt Sch. Edn., N.Y.C., 2000—; advisor arts and humanities Internat. Biog. Ctr., Cambridge, England; guest lectr. Hofstra, 2000; adj. faculty C.W. Post Coll. LI U., 2000. Musician: (piano concerts) Chamber Music series at U.S. Mil. Acad., N.Y./N.J. met. area concerts, Disting. Artists series, 2002—03, Met. Area Concerts, 2003, Am. Assn. Univ. Women Commentary and Concerts, 2003; musician: (commentary and concert) A Gentlewoman's Pursuit, AAUW, 2003, concerts in New Zealand, Australia, Eng., Ireland, Can. and U.S.; contbg. author: Spotlight in Making Music with Special Learners, 2004; author: (signature series) A Gentleman's Pursuit, 2003—04; author: An Attitude and Approach for Teaching Music to Special Learners, 2001. Active Nassau Boces Elem. Program PTA, cultural arts coord., 1988—; Nominee N.Y. Senate Women of Distinction Program, 2003; named Internat. Musician of the Yr., 2004; recipient award of Honor, LI Very Spl. Arts Festival, 1993, Spl. citation, N.Y. State Assembly Ames Elem. Program, 1998, Spl. recognition, Nassau Music Educators Assn., 1999, 1st prize, Dr. Martin Luther King Jr. Performing Arts Competition Exceptional Students Nassau County, 1999—2001, Internat. Peace prize, United Cultural Conv., 2002, citation, Town of Oyster Bay, 2002, award, Ernest Kay Internat. Found., 2004. Mem.: AAUW, ASCD, NAFE, Music Educators Nat. Conf., N.Y. State Sch. Music Assn. (chair music spl. learners 1993—). Home: 21 Saxon St Melville NY 11747 E-mail: ESSOBOL@aol.com.

**SOBOL, ROBERT E.,** medical company executive; BA in Philosophy, Boston U.; MD, Chgo. Med. Sch. Diplomate Am. Bd. Internal Medicine with subspecialty in med. oncology. Resident U. So. Calif. Med. Ctr., U. Calif., San Diego; founder GeneSys Therapeutics; founder, v.p. IDEC Pharms. Corp.; dir. clin. sci. Sidney Kimmel Cancer Ctr., San Diego; exec. v.p., COO GenStar Therapeutics, San Diego, 1996—, pres., 1996—2000, CEO, dir., 1998—. Achievements include development of clinical applications of immuno therapy and gene therapy for the treatment of cancer; research in gene therapy protocols for treatment of colon carcinoma; treatment of brain tumor patient with cytokine gene therapy.

**SOBOL, THOMAS,** education educator; b. Jan. 11, 1932; m. Harriet Sobol; three children. BA in English, Harvard U., 1953, grad., 1954; PhD, Columbia U., 1969. Head dept. English pub. sch. system, Bedford, N.Y., 1961-65; dir. instrn., 1965-69; asst. supt. instrn. pub. sch. system Great Neck, N.Y., 1969-71; supt. sch. systems Scarsdale, N.Y., 1971-87; commr. N.Y. State dept. Edn. Albany, 1987-95; Christian A. Johnson Prof. Columbia Univ. Teacher's College, N.Y.C., 1995—, dir. ednl. administrs. Office: Columbia Univ Teachers College 525 W 120th St New York NY 10027-6625

**SOBOL, ZBIGNIEW W.,** orthopedist, surgeon; b. Chelmno, Poland, Feb. 25, 1926; arrived in U.S., 1949; s. Wladyslaw and Wanda Caroline Sobol; m. Eve Frances Harvey, Sept. 13, 1956; children: Stefan, Christine, Peter, Andrew. B in Medicine and Surgery, Edinburgh U., Scotland, 1948. Diplomate Am. Bd. Orthopedic Surgery. Intern in surgery Bolton Royal Infirmary, England, 1949; resident in internal medicine Overlook Hosp., Summit, NJ, 1950, resident surgery, 1951; resident orthop. surgery Columbia Presbyn. Med. Ctr. N.Y. Orthop. Hosp., 1952—56; orthopedic surgeon Meml. Hosp., South Bend, Ind., 1962—, St. Joseph Med. Ctr., Mishawaka, Ind., 1962—, chmn. dept. orthopedic surgery, 1991—95. Med. missionary Christian Med. Soc., Jamaica, 1984, Kenya, 1996; hon. cons. Polish hosps., 1986—. Fellow: ACS, Academy Orthopedic Surgeons; mem.: Polish Orthop. and Traumatol. Soc. (hon.). Home: 19072 Summers Dr South Bend IN 46637 Office: 320 W 4th St Mishawaka IN 46544 Office Phone: 574-255-5219.

**SOBOLEWSKI, JOHN STEPHEN,** computer scientist, director, consultant; b. Krakow, Poland, July 14, 1939; came to U.S., 1966; s. Jan Zygmund and Stefania (Zwolinska) S.; m. Helen Skipper, Dec. 17, 1965 (div. July 1969); m. Carole Straith, Apr. 6, 1974; children: Anne-Marie, Elisa, Martin. BE, U. Adelaide, Adelaide, South Australia, 1962, ME, 1966; PhD in Computer Sci., Wash. State U., 1971. Sci. officer Weapons Research Establishment, Salisbury, South Australia, 1964-66; asst. prof. computer U. Wash. State U., Pullman, 1966-73; dir. research, assoc. v.p. Wash., Seattle, 1973-80, dir. computer svcs., 1980-88; assoc. v.p. computing U. N.Mex., Albuquerque, 1988—. Cons. govt. and industry, Seattle, 1973—; mem. bd. trustees Fisher Found., Seattle, 1984—. Author: Computers for the Dental

Office, 1986; contbr. articles to profl. jours. Served as engr. with Royal Australian Army, 1957-60. Australian govt. scholar, 1954-60, Elec. Res. Bd. scholar CSIRO, Melbourne, Australia, 1961-64. Mem. IEEE, Computer Soc. Roman Catholic. Avocation: mineral collecting. Home: 18422 57th Ave NE Kenmore WA 98028 Personal E-mail: nwminerals@hotmail.com.

**SOBRATO, JOHN A.,** construction executive; married; 3 children. Real estate agt., Palo Alto, 1957; founder, prin. Sobrato Devel. Cos., Cupertino, Calif. Trustee U. Santa Clara; vice chmn. Nat. Hispanic U. Named Philanthropist of Yr., NSFRE, 1998; named one of Forbes' Richest Americans, 2006. Office: Sobrato Devel Cos Ste 200 10600 N De Anza Blvd Cupertino CA 95014-2075*

**SOBRERO, KATE (KATHRYN MICHELE SOBRERO),** professional soccer player; b. Pontiac, Mich., Aug. 23, 1976; BA in Bus., U. Notre Dame, 1997. Mem. U.S. Nat. Women's Soccer Team, 1995—2001; profl. soccer player Boston Breakers (WUSA), 2001—03. Mem. U.S. Under-20 Nat. Team, 1993—. Named Defensive Most Valuable Player, NCAA Final Four, 1995. Achievements include on cover of Soccer Am. mag., 1995; member Notre Dame NCAA National Championship Team, 1995; member U.S. World Cup Championship Team, 1999; member U.S. Olympic Silver Medal Team, 2000. Office: US Soccer Fedn 1801-1811 S Prairie Ave Chicago IL 60616

**SOBUS, KERSTIN MARYLOUISE,** physician, physical therapist; b. Washington, June 16, 1960; d. Earl Francis and Dolores Jane (Gill) G.; m. Paul John Jr., March 10, 1990; children: Darlene Marie, Julieann Marie, Gwendolyn Rose Marie. BS in Phys. Therapy summa cum laude, U. N.D., 1981, MD, 1987. Clinic instr. pediatric physical therapy U.N.D. Sch. Medicine, Grand Forks, 1981-83; pediat. phys. theraist child evaluation-treatment program Med. Rehab. Ctr., Grand Forks, 1981-83, med. dir. program, 1997—; asst. prof. dept. pediatrics, asst. prof. dept. physical medicine and rehab. U. Ark. for Med. Scis., Little Rock, 1992-96; resident in internal medicine Sinai Hosp. Balt., 1987-88; resident in phys. medicine and rehab. Johns Hopkins program Sinai Hosp., Balt., 1988-91; pediatric rehab. clin. and rsch. fellow Alfred I. DuPont Inst., Wilmington, Del., 1991-92; pediatric physiatrist Altru Health System, Grand Forks, 1997—. Contbr. articles to med. jours. Mem. Am. Acad. Cerebral Palsy and Devel. Medicine, Alpha Omega Alpha Honor Soc. Office: Altru Health Sys PO Box 6002 1300 S Columbia Rd Grand Forks ND 58201-4012 Home: 7451 S 25th St Grand Forks ND 58201 Office Phone: 701-780-2482.

**SOCHEN, JUNE,** history professor; b. Chgo., Nov. 26, 1937; d. Sam and Ruth (Finkelstein) S. BA, U. Chgo., 1958; MA, Northwestern U., 1960, PhD, 1967. Project editor Chgo. Superior and Talented Student Project, 1959-60; high sch. tchr. English and history North Shore Country Day Sch., Winnetka, Ill., 1961-64; instr. history Northeastern Ill. U., 1964-67, asst. prof., 1967-69, assoc. prof., 1969-72, prof., 1972—. Author: The New Woman, 1971, Movers and Shakers, 1973, Herstory: A Woman's View of American History, 1975, 2d edit., 1981, Consecrate Every Day: The Public Lives of Jewish American Women, 1981, Enduring Values: Women in Popular Culture, 1987, Cafeteria America: New Identities in Contemporary Life, 1988, Mae West: She Who Laughs Lasts, 1992, From Mae to Madonna: Women Entertainers in 20th Century America, 1999; editor: The New Feminism in 20th Century America, 1972, Women's Comic Visions, 1991; contbr. articles to profl. jours. Nat. Endowment for Humanities grantee, 1971-72 Office: Northeastern Ill U 5500 N Saint Louis Ave Chicago IL 60625-4679 Office Phone: 773-442-5607. Business E-Mail: j-sochen@neiu.edu.

**SOCHET, MARY ALLEN,** psychotherapist, educator, writer; b. Plattsburgh, N.Y., Feb. 10, 1938; d. Edwin Elisha and Mary Elizabeth (Thomson) Allen; m. Marvin J. Sochet, 1963; children: Melorra, David. BS in Childhood Edn., SUNY, Plattsburgh, 1958; MA in Human Rels., NYU, 1961, PhD in Human Devel., 1963. Tchr. kindergarten L.I. Pub. Schs., 1958-62; tchr. N.Y.C. Pub. Schs., 1962-64; prof. early childhood edn., child devel. and psychology Bklyn. Coll., 1964-71; program dir., acting exec. dir. Newark Pre-Sch. Coun., 1965-66; psychotherapist N.Y.C. Community Guidance Svc., 1966-78; staff cons. Human Resources Inst., 1966—; pvt. practice psychotherapy N.Y.C., 1966—. Writer, lectr., ednl. cons. and editorial cons. in field. Author: (with Robert Allen) Toward a Caring Community, 1980; contbr. articles on edn., community orgns., peace and mental health to various jours. Founding mem. Community Loft, 1971-74, Neighbor's Network, 1979—; organizing mem. Children's Free Sch., 1969-81; co-chair Perhaps Kids Meeting Kids Can Make a Difference, 1982—. NCCJ fellow, 1961-61; recipient Founder's Day award NYU, 1963. Mem. Am. Psychol. Assn., Soc. Psychol. Study Social Issues, Psychologists for Social Responsibility. Home and Office: 380 Riverside Dr New York NY 10025-1858 Business E-Mail: kidsmtgkids@igc.org.

**SOCHYNSKY, YAROSLAV,** lawyer, arbitrator, mediator; b. Feb. 5, 1946; BA in English, Colgate U., 1967; JD, Georgetown U., 1970. Bar: Calif., N.Y. Assoc. White & Case, N.Y.C., 1970-71; law clerk to Hon. William T. Sweigert U.S. Dist. Ct. (no. dist.) Calif., 1971-73; assoc. Landels, Ripley & Diamond LLP, San Francisco, 1973-76; sr. ptnr. Landels, Ripley & Diamond, San Francisco, 1976-2000; mediator Am. Arbitration Assn., San Francisco, 2000—. Lectr. Calif. Continuing Edn. Bar, 1985, Equity Asset Mgr.'s Assn., 1987, Calif. Dept. Real Estate, 1986-89). Originator, co-author California ADR Practice Guide, 1992; co-author Real Property Practice and Litigation, 1990; case and notes editor, mem. editorial bd. Georgetown Law Jour.; contbr. articles and monographs to profl. jours. Fellow, Coll. Comml. Arbitrators. Fellow Chartered Inst. Arbitrators (London); mem. ABA (mem. exec. coun. sect. on real property, probate and trust, lectr. 1988, 89, 91), Am. Arbitration Assn. (cert. mediator, mem. pres.' panel of mediators, large and complex case panel, internat. panel, real property valuation panel, No. Calif. adv. coun., lectr. 1990, speaker various panels, No. Calif. Outstanding Mediator award 1991), San Francisco Bar Assn.

**SOCOL, MICHAEL LEE,** obstetrician, gynecologist, educator; b. Chgo., Oct. 3, 1949; s. Joseph and Bernice (Bofman) S.; m. Donna Kaner, Dec. 17, 1972. BS, U. Ill., 1970; MD, U. Ill., Chgo., 1974. Diplomate Am. Bd. Ob-Gyn., Am. Bd. Maternal-Fetal Medicine. Resident obstetrics and gynecology U. Ill. Hosp., Chgo., 1974-77; clin. rsch. fellow dept. obstetrics and gynecology L.A. County-U. So. Calif. Med. Ctr., 1977-79; assoc. attending physician Northwestern Meml. Hosp., Chgo., 1980-86, attending physician dept. ob-gyn., 1986—; co-dir. Northwestern Perinatal Ctr., Chgo., 1987—; chief obstetrics Northwestern Meml. Hosp., Chgo., 1987—, dir. maternal-fetal medicine fellowship program, 1987-99, asst. prof. obstetrics and gynecology, 1979-84, assoc. prof., 1984-92, prof., 1992—. Vice chmn. dept. ob-gyn Northwestern Meml. Hosp., Chgo., 1992—. Author: (with others) Clinical Obstetrics and Gynecology, 1982, 1984, Diagnostic Ultrasound Applied to Obstetrics and Gynecology, 1987, Principles and Practice of Medical Therapy in Pregnancy, 1992; peer reviewer Am. Jour. Obstetrics and Gynecology, 1980—, Obstetrics and Gynecology, 1984—; contbr. numerous articles to profl. jours. Fellow Am. Coll. Ob-Gyn., Soc. Maternal-Fetal Medicine, Soc. for Gynecol. Investigation, Am. Gynecol. and Obstet. Soc.; mem. Assn. Profs. Gynecology and Obstetrics. Avocation: marathon running. Office: 333 E Superior St Ste 410 Chicago IL 60611-3015 Office Phone: 312-926-7518.

**SOCOL, SHELDON ELEAZER,** university official; b. N.Y.C., July 10, 1936; s. Irving and Helen (Tuchman) S.; m. Genia Ruth Prager, Dec. 26, 1959; children: Jeffrey, Steven, Sharon, Robyn, Leslie, Steven Warren. BA, Yeshiva U., 1958; JD, NYU, 1963. From asst. bursar to dir. student fins. Yeshiva U., N.Y.C., 1958-70, sec. 1970—, chief fiscal officer, 1971-72, v.p. bus. affairs, 1972—2003, v.p. and counselor to the pres., 2003—05; exec. asst. to chmn. Bd. of Overseers, 1986—. Mem. N.Y. State Adv. Coun. on Fin. Assistance to Coll. Students, 1969-76; asst. dir. Tng. Inst. for Fin. Aid Officers, Hunter, Coll., CUNY, 1970-71; mem. presdl. adv. com. Temple U., 1986; mem. regents adv. task force N.Y.C. Regional Plan for Higher Edn., 1971-73; bd. dirs. N.Y. Structural Biology Ctr., 2000; spkr. in field. Pres.

Minyon Park Estates, Inc. Mem. NEA, Nat. Assn. Coll. and Univ. Attys., Met. N.Y.C. Fin. Aid Adminstrs. Assn., Ea. Assn. Student Fin. Aid Officers, Am. Mgmt. Assn., Am. Assn. for Higher Edn., Nat. Assn. Coll. and Univ. Bus. Officers, Soc. Coll. and Univ. Planning, Mid. States Assn. Colls. (evaluation team Commn. on Higher Edn., U. Medicine and Dentistry N.J., 1985, Upstate Health Sci. Ctr. 1986, Carnegie-Mellon U. 1988, Albany Med. Ctr. 1989). Office: Yeshiva U Resnick Campus Albert Einstein Coll Medicine 1300 Morris Park Ave Bronx NY 10461 Office Phone: 718-430-4140. Business E-Mail: dses@yu.edu. E-mail: dses@ymail.yu.edu.

**SOCOLOW, ARTHUR ABRAHAM,** geologist; b. Bronx, N.Y., Mar. 23, 1921; s. Samuel and Yetta (Solomon) S.; m. Edith S. Blumenthal, Apr. 10, 1949; children: Carl, Roy. Jeff. BS, Rutgers U., 1942; MA, Columbia U., 1947, PhD, 1955. Reg. profl. geologist, Commonwealth Pa. Photogrammetrist, U.S. Army Air Corps, 1942-46; with Eagle Picher de Mexico, 1947; instr. geology So. Methodist U., 1948-50; dir. geology field camp Colo., 1948-50; asst. prof. Boston U., 1950-55; geologist Def. Minerals Exploration Authority, Alaska, 1952; assoc. prof. U. Mass., 1955-57; econ. geologist Pa. Geol. Survey, 1957-61, dir., state geologist, 1961-86; cons. geologist Gloucester, Mass., 1986—; prof. environ. geology Salem (Mass.) State Coll., 1993-98; dir. New Eng. Govs. Conf. Project on Aggregate Resources New Eng., 1990-97. Mem. Outer Continental Shelf Policy Com., 1974-88, Pa. rep., 1978-88; lectr. mineral conservation Pa. State U., 1959-75; mem. conf. earth sci. source materials NSF, 1959; chmn. ann. field conf. Pa. Geologists, 1961-86; past mem. U.S. Nat. Com. on Tunnelling Tech.; mem. com. on N.Y. State low level waste program Nat. Acad. Sci.; past mem. gov.'s adv. com. Nat. Coun. on Environ. Quality; past chmn. Pa. Water Resources Coordinating Com.; geol. advisor Boston Mus. Sci., 1955-57. Former editor Pa. Geol. Bull.; mem. editorial bd. Northeastern Geol. Jour.; contbr. over 100 publs. and papers on environ. and econ. geology to profl. jours. Served with USAAF, 1942-46. Fellow AAAS (past pres. geography-geology sect.), Geol. Soc. Am. (sec.-treas. N.E. sect., past nat. councilor), Mineral Soc. Am., Soc. Econ. Geologists; mem. AAUP, Am. Geol. Inst., Nat. Assn. Geology Tchrs. (past regional pres., Ralph Digman award for contbns. to geologic edn. 1980), Am. Meteoritical Soc., Assn. Am. State Geologists (past pres., editor, compiler State Geol. Surveys-A History 1988, Disting. Svc. award 2004), Am. Geophys. Union, Am. Commn. Stratigraphic Nomenclature (past chmn.), Gloucester Conservation Commn. (chmn.), Fgn. Policy Assn. (past chpt. pres.), Sigma Xi. Clubs: Internat. Torch (past pres. chpt.). Home and Office: 26 Salt Island Rd Gloucester MA 01930-1945 Office Phone: 978-283-7490. Personal E-mail: artsoc@verizon.net. *I have great respect for the individualism of man in the midst of a society and a world where there is an unavoidable interrelationship and interdependence of man upon man, and of man upon his environment. While we strive to maintain our individualism, we must share our common resources and our common aspirations. This is the challenge that makes our lives worth living.*

**SOCOLOW, DAVID JACOB,** state agency administrator; b. New Haven, Conn., Jan. 31, 1969; s. Robert H. and Elizabeth A. (Sussman) Socolow; m. Erin Marie Spinello, Nov. 20, 1999; 2 children. AB magna cum laude, Harvard U., 1991; MPA, Rutgers U. Phila. 1991. fin. coord. U.S. Senator Harris Wofford's campaign, Phila., 1991; N.Y. state fin. dir. Bob Abrams for U.S. Senate, N.Y.C., 1991-92; v.p. Fundraising Mgmt. Group, Washington, 1993-94; dir. Am. Resources Info. Network, Washington, 1995-96; chief staff to Congressman Robert E. Andrews U.S. Ho. of Reps., Washington, 1996—2001; assoc. dir. congressional affairs US Labor Dept., 2001; dir. unemployment ins. NJ Dept. Labor and Workforce Devel., Trenton, NJ, 2002—06, acting commr., 2006, commr., 2006—. Bd. dirs. Ctr. for Environ. Citizenship, Washington, 1995—; rsch. asst. Clinton-Gore Transition Team, Washington, 1992-93. Democrat. Jewish. Office: NJ Dept Labor and Workforce Devel PO Box 110 Trenton NJ 08625-0110*

**SOCOLOW, ELIZABETH ANNE,** poet, educator, artist, writer; b. NYC, June 15, 1940; d. Ralph Maurice and Frances Irene (Goldberg) Sussman; m. Robert H. Socolow, June 10, 1962 (div. Apr. 1982); children: David Jacob, Seth Louis. BA, Vassar Coll., 1962; MA, Harvard U., 1963, PhD, 1967. Lectr. in English and composition U. Mich., Dearborn, 1993—99; lectr. in English Wayne State U., 1993—99, Lawrence Technol. U., Southfield, Mich., 1994—98; lectr. Bucks County C.C., 1999—2001, Rutgers/Camden at Freehold, 2001—. Poetry editor newsletter Soc. for Lit. and Sci., Athens, Ga., 1989—. Author: Laughing at Gravity: Conversations With Isaac Newton, 1988 (Barnard Women Poets Series prize 1987). Avocations: computer, graphics, cards.

**SOCOLOW, ROBERT HARRY,** engineering educator; b. NYC, Dec. 27, 1937; s. A. Walter and Edith (Gutman) S.; m. Elizabeth Anne Sussman, June 10, 1962 (div. Apr. 27, 1982); children: David, Seth; m. Jane Ries Pitt, May 25, 1986; stepchildren: Jennifer, Eric. BA summa cum laude in Physics, Harvard Coll., 1959; MA in Physics, Harvard U., 1961, PhD in Physics, 1964. NSF predoctoral fellow, 1960—64; NSF postdoctoral fellow physics U. Calif. Berkeley and European Ctr. Nuc. Rsch. (CERN), 1964—66; asst. prof. dept. physics Yale U., New Haven, 1966-71; assoc. prof. dept. aerospace and mech. scis., mem. Ctr. Environ. Studies Princeton U., NJ, 1971-77, prof., 1977—79, prof. dept. mech. and aerospace engring., 1979—. Rsch. assoc. dept. geology and geophysics Yale U., 1971; mem. Inst. Advanced Study Princeton U., 1971; dir. Princeton U. Ctr. Environ. Studies, 1977—78, acting dir., 1978—79; dir. Princeton U. Ctr. Energy and Environ. Studies, 1979—98; chmn. bd. Am. Coun. Energy Efficient Econ., 1989—93; bd. dirs. Nat. Audubon Soc., 1992—99; mem. environ. sci. adv. com. Environ. Def. Fund, 1999—2001; co-dir. Carbon Mitigation Initiative. Contbr. articles to profl. jours., chapters to books; co-editor: Patient Earth, 1971. Efficient Use of Energy 1975, Boundaries of Analysis: An Inquiry into the Tocks Island Dam Controversy, 1976, Indsl. Ecology and Global Change, 1994, Environmentally Significant Consumption, 1997; editor: Saving Energy in the Home: Princeton's Expts. at Twin Rivers, 1978; assoc. editor: Ann. Rev. Energy and Environment, 1988—92; editor, 1992—2002; contbg. editor: Environment, 1999—, mem. mng. bd.: Jour. Indsl. Ecology, mem. editl. bd.: Perspectives in Energy, Energy and Bldgs. Grantee John Simon Guggenheim fellowship, 1976—77, German Marshall Fund fellowship, 1976—77. Fellow: Am. Phys. Soc. (Leo Szilard Lectureship award 2003), AAAS. Jewish. Office: Princeton Environ Inst Princeton U 139 Guyot Hall Washington Rd Princeton NJ 08544 E-mail: socolow@princeton.edu.*

**SODANO, SALVATORE F.,** former stock exchange executive; b. Jan. 17, 1956; m. Anne Sodano; 2 children. BA, Hofstra U., 1977, MBA in Banking and Fin., 1983. Staff acct. Price Waterhouse & Co.; asst. to treas. Morgan Guaranty Internat. Fin. Corp., 1979—83; with Bankers Trust Co., 1983—90, v.p., group head; v.p., dep. controller NY Branch Westpac Banking Corp., 1990—91, v.p., controller, 1991—93, v.p. controller Am. Div., 1993—94, sr. v.p., CFO, 1994—95, sr. v.p., chief mgr., prin. oper. officer, 1995—96; exec. v.p., CFO Nat. Assn. Securities Dealers (NASD), 1997—98, dep. COO, CFO, 1998—2000, vice chmn., 2001—02; acting pres. Am. Stock Exch. LLC, NYC, 1999, chmn., CEO, 1999—2005; dean Frank G. Zarb Sch. Bus. Hofstra U., Hempstead, NY, 2006—. Bd. dirs. Securities Ind. Automation Corp., 1999—2002; bd. trustees Hofstra U., 2001—05, chmn., 2002—05, co-chair endowment com., mem. fin. and devel. coms., mem. dean's exec. coun. Frank G. Zarb Sch. Bus., mem. bus. adv. bd. Merrill Lynch Ctr. for Study of Internat. Fin. Svcs. and Markets, exec.-in-residence. Mem. oversight com. Cath. Health Svcs. of LI; advisor to fin. com. Good Samaritan Hosp.; mem. Chinese Econ. Zone Adv. Bd. Zhongguancun Sci. Park, 2001. Named a Knight, Sovereign Military of Malta, 2003; named Man of Yr., Am. Stock Exch. S&20 Club, 2001; named to Disting. Post of Knight, Sacred Military Constantinian Order of Saint George, 2001; recipient Alumi Achievement award, Hofstra U., 2000, 100 Black Men Investors Club Performance award, 2002, Spl. Achievement award in Bus., Nat. Italian Am. Found, 2003, Monsignor Thomas J. Hartman Award, Telecare, 2004. Mem. Club NY (Ellis Island Medal of Honor award 2000). Office: Hofstra U Frank G Zarb Sch Bus Weller Hall Hempstead NY 11549-1000 Office Phone: 516-463-5678. Office Fax: 516-463-5268. E-mail: Salvatore.F.Sodano@hofstra.edu.*

**SODEN, RICHARD ALLAN,** lawyer; b. Feb. 16, 1945; s. Hamilton David and Clara Elaine (Seale) S.; m. Marcia LaMonte Mitchell, June 7, 1969; children: Matthew Mitchell, Mark Mitchell. AB, Hamilton Coll., 1967; JD, Boston U., 1970. Bar: Mass. 1970. Law clk., Hon. George C. Edwards Jr. U.S. Ct. Appeals (6th cir.), 1970-71; assoc. firm Goodwin, Procter & Hoar LLP, Boston, 1971-79; ptnr., bus. law dept. Goodwin Procter LLP (formerly Goodwin, Procter & Hoar LLP), Boston, 1979—; mem., diversity com. Goodwin Procter LLP, Boston. Instr. Law Sch. Boston Coll., Chestnut Hill, Mass., 1973-74. Mem. South End Project Area Com.; hon. dir. United South End Settlements, pres., 1977-79; chmn. Boston Mcpl. Rsch. Bur., 1996-97, pres., 1997-99; pres. Boston Minuteman coun. Boy Scouts Am.; trustee Judge Baker Children's Ctr., chmn., 1994-96, pres., 1992-94; trustee New Eng. Aquarium, Boston U., 1995-2001; bd. visitors Boston U. Goldman Sch. Grad. Dentistry; mem. bd. overseers WGBH; mem. Mass. Minority Bus. Devel. Commn.; mem. Adv. Task Force on Securities Regulation; mem. Adv. Com. on Legal Edn.; steering com. Lawyers Com. for Civil Rights under Law, chmn., 1992-94. Mem. ABA (chmn. standing com. on bar svcs. and activities, Commn. on Lawyer Assistance Programs Adv. Coun. on Diversity 1998-2000), Nat. Bar Assn., Mass. Bar Assn. (past vice chmn. bus. law coun. 1990-91), fellow Am. Bar Found., Boston Bar Found. Office: Goodwin Procter LLP Exchange Pl 53 State St Boston MA 02109-2803 Office Phone: 617-570-1533. Office Fax: 617-523-1231. Business E-Mail: rsoden@goodwinprocter.com.

**SODERBERG, DALE LEROY,** language educator, drama director, producer; b. Warren, Pa., Apr. 24, 1929; s. Leroy Wilbur and Olive Hazel (Conboy) S.; m. Marjorie Ann Hamm, Aug. 19, 1951; children: David J., Valli K., W. Mark, Lisa T., Kathi L. BA, Gettysburg Coll., 1951; BD, Luth. Theol. Sem., Gettysburg, Pa., 1954. Cert. secondary English tchr., N.Y., 1968; ordained mins. Luth. Ch., 1954. Pastor Grace Luth. Ch., Clarion, Pa., 1954-57; mission developer, 1st pastor Our Saviour's Luth. Ch., Horseheads, N.Y., 1957-60; dir. Ecclesia Tours (Luth. Fgn. Tours), Horseheads and North Syracuse, N.Y., 1958-67; mgr. Soderberg Travel Svc., Corning, N.Y., 1960-62; pastor St. John's Luth. Ch., Syracuse, N.Y., 1962-66; guest chapel preacher Wittenberg U., Ohio, 1966; tchr. English Ft. Myers (Fla.) High Sch., 1967-68; tchr. English, dir. drama Hamilton (N.Y.) Cen. Sch., 1968-92; retired, 1992; sermon and story writer Ecclesia Svcs., Hamilton, 1984-96. Lay preacher Upstate N.Y. Synod Evang. Luth. Ch. Am., Syracuse, 1968—; advisor student tchrs.at Hamilton Cen. Sch. for Colgate U., Hamilton, 1975-92; clk. Hamilton Stores, Yellowstone Nat. Park, summer 1948, 93. Author: (novels) Pawns, 1980, The Amsterdam Connection, 1999, A Time for Choosing, 2001, Mr. Protestant, 2002, The Winds of Change, 2003, The Manipulators, 2004, Sirocco, 2005, The View from the Pew, 2006. Dir. tours to Europe, Holy Land and Luth. mission fields in Brit. Guiana, East and West Africa, and India; bd. dirs. Luth. Homes Found., 1993-96; vol. missionary religious edn. tchr. U. of Papua New Guinea, Goroka, spring 1996; mem. Global Missions Team, Upstate N.Y. Synod Evang. Luth. Ch. Am., Syracuse, 1999—; organizer and dir. Bishop's tour to Zimbabwe, 2001. Mem.: N.Y. State Ret. Tchrs. Assn., Hamilton Tchrs. Assn., N.Y. State United Tchrs., World Wildlife Fund, Defenders of Wildlife Nat. Pk. Conservation Assn. Wilderness Soc., Sierra Club. Democrat. Avocations: travel, photography, home video, creative writing, Hemingway specialization. Home: 1907 Preston Hill Rd Hamilton NY 13346-2321 E-mail: dsoderbe@twcny.rr.com.

**SODERBERG, LEIF G.,** electronics company executive; BA, Harvard Coll.; MS in Mgmt., MIT. Various positions with ptnr. McKinsey & Co., Cleveland and Scandinavia, 1978-93; head bus. strategy Land Mobile Products Sector, Network Svcs. Bus. Motorola Inc., 1993-94, v.p., gen. mgr. Network Svcs. and Bus. Strategies Group Ill., 1994—98, sr. v.p. Systems Solutions Group Ill., 1998—2000, sr. v.p., gen. mgr., strategy, business development and industry relations, 2000—02, sr. v.p., dir., Motorola's global strategy and corporate development organization, 2002—. Mem. Clearnet's Nominating Com. Office: Motorola 1301 E Algonquin Rd Schaumburg IL 60196-1078

**SODERBERG, NANCY,** former court official, writer; b. San Turce, P.R., Mar. 13, 1958; d. Lars Olof and Nancy (MacGilvrey) S. BA in French and Econs., Vanderbilt U., 1980; MS in Fgn. Svc., Georgetown U., 1984. Del. selection asst. Mondale-Ferraro Com., Washington, 1983, fgn. policy advisor, 1984; dep. issues dir. fgn. policy Dukakis for Pres. Com., Boston, 1988; fgn. policy advisor Senator Edward M. Kennedy, Washington, 1985-88, 89-92; fgn. policy dir. Clinton/ Gore Campaign, Little Rock, 1992; dep. asst. dir. transition nat. security Clinton/ Gore Transition, Little Rock, 1992-93; dep. asst. to Pres. for nat. security affairs Nat. Security Coun., Washington, 1993—97; amb. (alt. rep.) UN, NYC, 1997—2001; v.p., dir. NY office Internat Crisis Group, 2001—05; dist. vis. scholar U. North Fla., Jacksonville, 2006—. TV and radio commentator MSNBC; mem. Coun. Fgn. Rels. Author: The Superpower Myth: The Use and Misuse of American Might, 2005. Home: 121 Lanternwick Pl Ponte Vedra Beach FL 32082 Office Phone: 212-813-0820, 646-591-0912. Office Fax: 212-813-0825. Personal E-mail: nsoderberg@aol.com.

**SODERBERG, PETER H.,** health products executive; B in engring., Yale Univ. Mgmt. positions Johnson & Johnson, 1968—89; pres. Johnson & Johnson Health Mgmt., 1989—93; group v.p., COO Welch Allyn Inc., Skaneateles Falls, NY, pres., CEO, 2000—06, Hillenbrand Industries Inc., Batesville, Ind., 2006—, Hill-Rom, 2006—. Bd. dir. Greatbatch Inc., AdvaMed. Vice-chmn. Syracuse Symphony Orch., Met. Develop. Authority Ctrl. NY; chmn. CNY Medtech. Office: Hillenbrand Industries Inc 700 State Rte 46 E Batesville IN 47006-8835*

**SODERBERG, SUSAN COOKE,** historian, writer; b. Richmond, Va., July 7, 1944; d. Earle Truesdale and Ann Shirley Cooke; m. William Charles Soderberg, June 13, 1970; children: Anna Kristina, Jenka Melinda, Keir Stephen. BA in Art History, Coll. of William and Mary, Williamsburg, Va., 1967; MA in Am. Civilization, George Washington U., Washington, 1992. Radio announcer Coll. of William and Mary, Williamsburg, Va., 1965—67; docent Nat. Gallery of Art, Washington, 1968—70; edn. and outreach planner Montgomery County Dept. of Pk. and Planning, Silver Spring, Md., 1999—; free-lance writer Germantown, Md., 1989—. Cons. on the civil war trails Md. Office of Tourism, Balt., 2003—05; cons. on restoration of 1790s store Hist. Medley Dist., Poolesville, Md., 1991—93; lectr. in art history Montgomery Coll., Germantown, Md., 1989—91; conf. publicity chmn. La Leche League Internat., Washington, 1985. Author: (non-fiction book) A Guide to Civil War Sites in Maryland: Blue and Gray in a Border State, (book) The Met: A History of the Metropolitan Branch of the B & O Railroad, Lest We Forget: A Guide to Civil War Monuments in Maryland, A History of Germantown, Maryland; editor (cons.): (film) Trails to Germantown (Montgomery Cable Television-2nd prize, 1998). Mem. Gov.'s Commn. on Mil. Monuments, Annapolis, Md., 2001—06, Montgomery County Hist. Preservation Commn., Silver Spring, Md., 1995—99, County Execs. Town Ctr. Com., Germantown, Md., 1990—91; pres./v.p. and founder Germantown Hist. Soc., 1990—2006; pres. Germantown Citizens Assn., 1986—89; bd. mem. Germantown Alliance, 1983—2001; leader La Leche League, Germantown, 1978—89; Girl Scouts of U.S., Germantown, 1979—90. Named Citizen of the Yr., Germantown Citizens Assn., 1995. Mem.: Oral History Assn. of the Mid-Atlantic Region (assoc.), Small Mus. Assn. (assoc.), Md. Assn. of History Mus. (assoc.), Assn. of Living History Farm Mus. (assoc.), Md. Hist. Soc. (assoc.), Montgomery County Hist. Soc. (assoc.). Avocations: gardening, quilting, swimming, travel. Office: Montgomery County Department of Park and 8787 Georgia Ave Silver Spring MD 20910 Office Phone: 301-563-3400.

**SODERBERGH, STEVEN ANDREW,** filmmaker; b. Atlanta, Jan. 14, 1963; s. Peter Andrew and Mary Ann (Bernard) S.; m. Elizabeth Jeanne Brantley, Dec. 1, 1989 (div. Oct. 1994). Writer, dir., editor: (films) Sex, Lies, and Videotape, 1989 (Palme d'Or award Cannes Film Festival 1989), King of the Hill, 1993, Schizopolis, 1996, Solaris, 2002; dir., editor: (film) Kafka, 1991, Bubble, 2006; exec. prodr.: (films) Suture, 1994, Good Night and Good Luck, 2005, The Big Empty, 2005 Syriana, 2005, Rumor Has It..., 2005,

PU-239, 2006; prodr.: The Daytrippers, 1997, Pleasantville, 1998; dir.: (films) The Underneath, 1995, Gray's Anatomy, 1996, Out of Sight, 1998, The Limey, 1999, Erin Brokovich, 2000, Traffic, 2000, Ocean's Eleven, 2001, Full Frontal, 2002; dir., prodr.: Ocean's Twelve, 2004, Bubble, 2006; writer: (film) Nightwatch, 1998; dir., prodr. (TV series) K St., 2003 Named a WIRED Renegade, WIRED Rave Awards, 2006. Mem. AMPAS, Dirs. Guild Am. Democrat.*

**SODERLIND, STERLING EUGENE,** newspaper industry consultant; b. Rapelje, Mont., Sept. 6, 1926; s. William John and Florence (Longbotham) S.; m. Helen Boyce, Apr. 9, 1955; children: Steven (dec.), Sarah, Lori. BA, U. Mont., 1950; Rhodes Scholar, Oxford U., Eng., 1950-52. Reporter Mpls. Tribune, 1952-55; reporter Wall St. Jour., Chgo., 1955-56, Southeastern bur. chief Jacksonville, Fla., 1956-57, mem. page one editing staff N.Y.C., 1957-65, asst. mng. editor, 1966-70, mng. editor, 1970; econs. editor Dow Jones & Co., Inc., N.Y.C., 1970-77, asst. to pres., 1975-77, v.p., 1977-91; newspaper industry cons., 1992—. Served with USNR, 1944-46. Congregationalist. Home: 58 Wellington Ave Short Hills NJ 07078-3308

**SODERQUIST, RONALD BRUCE,** minister, consultant, religious organization administrator; b. Pine City, Minn., Mar. 16, 1943; s. Russell Eugene and Abigail Mae (Berger) S.; m. Carol Lynn Peterson, Aug. 20, 1966; children: Peter Gustav, Ingrid Ann-Marie, Anna Kristine. BA, Northwestern Coll., 1965; MA, U. Wis., 1967; DMin, Bethel Theol. Sem., 1993. Ordained min. So. Bapt. Conv., 1988. Acad. dean Kings Inst. Coll., Koronodal, Cotabato, The Philippines, 1967-69; asst. prof. English Trinity Coll., Deerfield, Ill., 1969-70; student ministry staff Campus Crusade for Christ, LA., Mpls., Madison, 1970-77, regional dir. midwest, 1977-80, internat. rep. in Sweden Gothenburg, Sweden, 1980-84; spl. rep. Christian Embassy, Washington, 1984-87, dir. mil. ministry, 1987-98; adj. prof. MS in Orgnl. Leadership Program Geneva Coll., 1998; min., cons. Campus Crusade's U.S. Ministry, 1999—2001; city dir. Priority Assocs., Mpls., 2001—. Recipient Disting. Alumnus award, Northwestern Coll. St. Paul, 1999. Avocations: travel, photography, reading. Home: 5371 S Park Dr Savage MN 55378 Office Phone: 612-730-7037. E-mail: ron@servantleadership.com.

**SODHANI, ARVIND,** computer company executive; Bachelor's, Master's, U. London; MBA, U. Mich., 1978. Asst. treas. Intel Europe Intel Corp., 1981—84, asst. treas., 1984—88, asst. treas., 1988—90, v.p. and treas., 1990—. Office: 2200 Mission College Blvd Santa Clara CA 95052

**SODINI, PETER J.,** food service executive; b. Jan. 26, 1941; With Fazio's div. of Fisher Foods Inc., 1976-78, Boys Markets Inc., L.A., 1978-1990, Buttrey Food & Drug Co., Great Falls, Mo., 1990-91; pres., EEO, Purity Supreme, North Billerica, Mass., 1991-98; pres., CEO Pantry Inc., Sanford, NC, 1998—. Office: Pantry PO Box 1410 Sanford NC 27331-1410

**SODOLSKI, JOHN,** retired professional society administrator; b. Menasha, Wis., Apr. 11, 1931; s. L.V. and L.W. (Pinkowski) S.; m. C.J. Eppard BS, U. Wis., 1953. Vice pres. Electronic Industries Assn., Washington, 1961-83; pres. U.S. Telephone Assn., Washington, 1983-93; ret., 1993. Served to 1st lt. USMC, 1955 Home: PO Box 1014 Middleburg VA 20118-1014

**SODREL, MICHAEL EUGENE,** congressman, small business owner; b. Louisville, Dec. 17, 1945; s. Robert Eugene Sodrel and Nora Baily (Vermillion) Keller. m. Marquita Dean, Nov. 24, 1967; children: Michael Noah, Keesha. Student, Ind. U., Jeffersonville, 1963. Dir. maintenance Sodrel Truck Lines, Inc., Jeffersonville, 1969-72, dir. ops., 1972-74, v.p., 1974-76, exec. v.p., 1976-81, pres., chief exec. officer, 1981—2004; mem. US Congress from 9th Ind. dist., 2005—; mem. sci. com., small bus. com., transp. and infrastructure com. Pres., chief exec. officer, Salem Stage, Inc., Jeffersonville, 1974-2004, The Free Enterprise System, Inc., 1976-2004. Bd. dirs. George Rogers Clark council Boy Scouts Am., New Albany, Ind., 1988—. Served to staff sgt. Nat. Guard U.S. Army, 1966—73. Recipient Spl. Tourism award State of Ind., 1987; named to Hon. Order Ky. Col, 1983. Mem. Nat. Star Route Mail Contractor's Assn. (pres., chmn. bd. 1978-88), Am. Bus. Assn. (bd. dirs. 1987—), So. Ind. C. of C. Clubs: Skal (pres. 1986-87). Lodges: Rotary (pres. 1988—, Paul Harris fellow 1976). Republican. Presbyterian. Office: US Ho Reps 1508 Longworth Ho Office Bldg Washington DC 20515-1409 Office Phone: 202-225-5315. Office Fax: 202-226-6866.

**SODROSKI, JOSEPH G.,** medical educator; b. Coaldale, Pa. BS, Allentown Coll., 1976; MD, Jefferson Med. Coll., 1980. Intern in medicine New Eng. Deaconess Hosp., Boston, 1980—81; rsch. fellow in microbiology Dana-Farber Cancer Inst., Sch. Pub. Health Harvard U., Boston, 1981—84, from instr. to assoc. prof. div. human retrovirology Dana-Farber Cancer Inst., 1984—96, prof. div. human retrovirology Dana-Farber Cancer Inst., 1996—97, from instr. assoc. prof. pathology Med. Sch., 1984—96, prof. dept. pathology Med. Sch., 1996—, assoc. prof. dept. cancer biology Sch. Pub. Health, 1992—96, prof. dept. cancer biology Sch. Pub. Health, 1996—97, prof. dept. cancer immunology and AIDS Dana-Farber Cancer Inst., 1997—, prof. dept. immunology and infectious diseases Sch. Pub. Health, 1997—. Chief div. human retrovirology Dana-Farber Cancer Inst. Harvard U., Boston, 1993-97; dir. Ctr. AIDS rsch. Dana-Farbert Inst. Beth Israel Deaconess Med. Ctr./Children's Hosp., Boston, 1994—; mem. sci. adv. bd. Ariel Project for prevention on HIV transmission from mother to infant, 1992—; mem. various coms. confs. in field; mem. external sci. adv. com. div. infectious diseases Mass. Gen. Hosp., 2000; mem. various coms. NIH; mem. sci. adv. bd. Aaron Diamond AIDS Rsch. Ctr. City N.Y., 1989—; mem. sci. adv. bd. Ctr. Human Retrovirology Thomas Jefferson U., 1995, Editor: Jour. Virology, 1993—98; editor: (assoc. editor) AIDS Scis., 1995—; reviewing editor AIDS, 1987—90, Jour. AIDS, 1988— (Howard Temin award for basic sci., 1993), AIDS Rsch. and Human Retroviruses, 1990—, Virology, 1991—, Jour. Virology, 1998—. Recipient Scholar award, Leukemia Soc. Am., 1986, Stohlman Meml. Scholar award, 1991, David Gottlieb Meml. Lectureship, U. Ill., 1993, Best of What's New award, Popular Sci. mag., 1998, Harvey Lectr., 2005, Retrovirology prize, 2006; fellow, Am. Found. AIDS Rsch., 1986; grantee, NIH, 1986—2005, Dept. Army, 1987—90, Am. Found. AIDS Rsch., 1987—88; postdoctoral fellow, NIH, 1981, Damon Runyon-Walter Winchell fellow, Damon Runyon-Walter Winchell Found., 1982, Spl. fellow, Leukemia Soc. Am., 1985. Mem.: AAAS, Clin. Immunology Soc., Am. Soc. Virology, Am. Soc. Microbiology, Delta Epsilon Sigma, Alpha Omega Alpha, Sigma Xi. Office: Dept Cancer Immunology and AIDS Dana-Farber Cancer Inst 44 Binney St Jimmy Fund Bldg Rm 824 Boston MA 02115 Office Phone: 617-632-3371. Business E-Mail: joseph_sodroski@dfci.harvard.edu.

**SODUMS, DZINTARS,** writer; b. Riga, Latvia, May 13, 1922; arrived in U.S., 1963; s. Andrejs and Ella Brastins Sodums; m. Skaidrite Kronbergs, Feb. 23, 1946 (dec. May 1999); children: Andris, Marcis. Student, Lynn C.C., 1975—80. Transl.: Ulysses, 1960, 93, Narziss und Goldmund, 1951, 2002, Waste Land, 1990, Four Quartets, 1999 Mem. Latvian Writers Assn. in Exil Democrat.

**SOEJIMA, DAISUKE,** diversified financial services company executive, economist; b. Tokyo, Jan. 17, 1959; s. Aritoshi and Hiroko Soejima; m. Kiyomi Soejima, Sept. 26, 1987; children: Sayuri, Taiga, Chiaki. BS in Econs., Tokyo U., 1983; MBA, Georgetown U., 1991. Assoc. cons., mgr. coord. Mitsubishi Corp., Tokyo, 1991-95; mgr. Mitsubishi Internat. Corp., Washington, 1995-97, mgr. project and planning N.Y.C., 1997-98, mgr. chem. groups M&A divestitures, 1998-2001; dir. E-Commerce Devel., 1999—2004, unit mgr. investment and devel., 2001—04; pres., CEO Mitsubishi Internat. Food Ingredients Inc., N.Y.C., 2004—, Mitsubishi Food Ingredients (MC) Can., Ltd., 2005—. Sr. rschr. Japan Inst. for Econ. Rsch., Tokyo, 1981—83; founding assoc. Inst. Strategic Leadership, Japan. Grad. adv. bd. Georgetown U. Mem.: Cornell Club, Tokyo Club, Alpha Mu Alpha, Beta Gamma Sigma. Home: 71 Hoyt St Darien CT 06820-3116 Office: 1 Bridge Plz Ste 270 Fort Lee NJ 07024 Address: 5200 Blazer Pkwy DA3 Dublin OH 43017 Office Phone: 201-944-5280. E-mail: daisuke.soejima@mitsubishicorp.com.

**SOENEN, MICHAEL J.,** consumer products company executive; BA, Kalamazoo Coll., 1992. Mem. staff Salomon Brosthers Inc., 1993-96; assoc. Perry Corp., 1996; dir. sales promotion FTD Inc., 1997-98. v.p. mktg., 1998; pres., CEO, dir. FTD.Com, Inc., Downers Grove, Ill., 1999—. Office: FTD Com Inc 3113 Woodcreek Dr Downers Grove IL 60515-5412

**SOERGEL, KONRAD HERMANN,** physician; b. Coburg, Germany, July 27, 1929; came to U.S., 1954, naturalized, 1962; s. Konrad Daniel and Erna Henrietta (Schilling) S.; m. Rosina Klara Rudin, June 24, 1955; children: Elizabeth Ann, Karen Theresa, Marilyn Virginia, Kenneth Thomas. MD, U. Erlangen, Germany, 1954, Dr. med., 1958. Intern Bergen Pines County Hosp., Paramus, NJ, 1954-55; resident in pathology West Pa. Hosp., Pitts., 1955-56; rsch. asst. U. Erlangen, Germany, 1956-57; resident in medicine Mass. Meml. Hosp., Boston, 1957-58; fellow in gastroenterology Boston U. Med. Sch., 1958-60, instr., 1960-61; mem. faculty Med. Coll. Wis., Milw., 1961—, prof. medicine, 1969—2002, prof. medicine emeritus, 2003—, prof. physiology, 1993—2002, chief sect. gastroenterology, 1961-93. Chmn. gastroenterology and clin. nutrition study sect. NIH, 1979-80 Contbr. articles to profl. jours., chpts. to books. Recipient Research Career Devel. award USPHS, 1963-72; Alexander von Humboldt Found. sr. fellow, 1973-74 Mem. Am. Gastroenterol. Assn., Am. Soc. Clin. Investigation, Am. Assn. Physicians, German Soc. for Digestive and Metabolic Disorders (hon.), Ger. Soc. Internal Medicine (hon.). Home: 14245 Hillside Rd Elm Grove WI 53122-1677 Office: Med Coll Wis 9200 W Wisconsin Ave Milwaukee WI 53226-3522 Personal E-mail: k.soergel@comcast.net.

**SOETEBER, ELLEN,** journalist, editor; b. East St. Louis, Ill., June 14, 1950; d. Lyle Potter and Norma Elizabeth (Osborn) S.; m. Richard M. Martins, Mar. 16, 1974. BJ, Northwestern U., 1972. Edn. writer, copy editor Chgo. Today, 1972-74; reporter Chgo. Tribune, 1974-76, asst. met. editor, 1976-84, assoc. met. editor, 1984-86, TV and media editor, 1986, met. editor, 1987-89, assoc. mng. editor for met. news, 1989-91, dep. editor editorial page, 1991-94; mng. editor South Fla. Sun-Sentinel, Ft. Lauderdale, 1994-2001; editor St. Louis Post-Dispatch, 2001—05. Fellow journalism U. Mich., Ann Arbor, 1986-87; guest instr. Poynter Inst. for Journalism Studies; leader mgmt. seminars, 2006—. Named to Hall of Achievement, Medill Sch. of Journalism, 2003. Office Phone: 954-522-9287. Personal E-mail: ellsoeteber@aol.com.

**SOETEDJO, HARIYADI,** materials scientist, researcher; b. Sragen, Central Java, Indonesia, Jan. 24, 1966; PhD, U. Essex, 1999. Sr. rschr. Measurement and Sensor Lab., Oulu U., Kajaani, Finland, 2002; rschr. Tuebingen U., Germany, 2003, Cordoba U., Andalusia, Spain, 2003—04; prin. rschr. Telekom R & D, Serdang, Selangor, Malaysia, 2005—. Contbr. articles to profl. jours. Vol. Andalusia Found. Indonesia, Yogyakarta, Yogyakarta, 2002. Fellow, Tuebingen U., Germany, 2003; grantee, Oulu U., Finland, 2002, Cordoba U., Spain, 2003—04; scholar, King Faisal Found., 1995—98; Rsch. Grant, U. Malaysia Sabah, 1999—2000. Mem.: European Optical Soc. (corr.), Indonesian Physics Soc. (corr.). Achievements include patents for Patent for measurement method in electronic devices. Home: Jalan Kaliurang Km 10 9 Sleman Yogyakarta Indonesia Office: Telekom R&D Sdn Bhd Ump-Mtdc Selangor Serdang 43400 Malaysia Office Phone: +60-3-89451784. Office Fax: +60-3-8945-1591. E-mail: andalusia40@lycos.com.

**SOFAER, ABRAHAM DAVID,** lawyer, educator, judge, consultant; b. Bombay, May 6, 1938; arrived in U.S., 1948, naturalized, 1959; m. Marian Bea Scheuer, Oct. 23, 1977; children: Daniel E., Michael J., Helen R., Joseph S., Aaron R., Raphael J. BA in History magna cum laude, Yeshiva Coll., 1962; LLB cum laude, NYU, 1965. Bar: N.Y. 1965, D.C. 1988. Law clk. to Hon. J. Skelly Wright U.S. Ct. Appeals (D.C. cir.), Washington, 1965-66; law clk. to Hon. William J. Brennan Jr. U.S. Supreme Ct., Washington, 1966-67; asst. U.S. atty. U.S. Dist Ct. (so. dist.) N.Y., N.Y.C., 1967-69; prof. law Columbia U., N.Y.C., 1969-79; judge U.S. Dist. Ct. (so. dist.) N.Y., 1979-85; legal advisor U.S. Dept. State, Washington, 1985-90; ptnr. Hughes Hubbard & Reed, Washington, 1991-94; George P. Shultz disting. scholar, sr. fellow Hoover Instn., Stanford U., 1994—. Hearing officer N.Y. Dept. Environ. Conservation, 1975-76. Author: War, Foreign Affairs and Constitutional Power: The Origins, 1976; contbr. articles to legal, polit., fgn. jours.; editor-in-chief: NYU Law Rev. 1964-65. Served with USAF, 1956-59. Root-Tilden scholar NYU, 1965. Mem. ABA, Fed. Bar Assn., N.Y.C. Bar Assn., N.Y. Bar Assn., Am. Law Inst. Jewish. Office: Stanford Univ The Hoover Instn Stanford CA 94305-6010 Office Phone: 650-725-3763. Office Fax: 650-723-2103. Business E-Mail: sofaer@hoover.stanford.edu.

**SOFAIR, ANDRE,** epidemiologist, researcher; m. Mary Sofair. MD, Albert Einstein Coll. Medicine, Bronx, N.Y., 1986. Diplomate Am. Bd. Internal Medicine. Attending physician, asst. prof. medicine, epidemiology, and pub. health Yale U. Sch. Medicine, New Haven, 2000—. Bd. dirs. Am. Liver Found., Conn. Mem.: Phi Beta Kappa. Achievements include research in emerging diseases. Office Phone: 203-573-6574.

**SOFFER, OLGA,** archaeologist, educator; d. Alexander and Galina Shabunin; 1 child, Alexandra Lara Beattie. PhD, CUNY, NYC, 1984. Asst. prof. U. Ill., Urbana-Champaign, Ill., 1985—88, assoc. prof., 1988—92, prof., 1992—. Scholar, U. Ill., 1989. Mem.: Am. Anthrop. Assn. Achievements include discovery of Paleolithic textile technology. Office: University of Illinois 109 Davenport Hall 607 S Mathews Urbana IL 61801 Office Phone: 217-333-2100. Office Fax: 217-244-3490. E-mail: n.a.

**SOFFRONOFF, PIERCE,** physician; b. Phila., Jan. 14, 1949; s. Ernest Carl Gustave and Jane Kynett (Coggeshall) S.; m. Strachelle Barry, Jan. 1, 1976; children: Strachelle B., Alexandra J. Cesny P. BA in Biology, Baylor U., 1970; MD, U. Tex., 1974. Diplomate Am. Bd. Ob-Gyn. Resident in ob-gyn. U. Pitts., 1974-77; pvt. practice, attending physician Magee Women's Hosp., Pitts., 1978—; asst. clin. prof. dept. ob-gyn. Sch. Medicine U. Pitts., 1978-90, assoc. clin. prof., 1990—. Fellow ACOG; mem. AMA, Pitts. Ob-Gyn. Soc., Allegheny County Med. Soc., Pa. Med. Soc. Office: Magee Womens Hosp 300 Halket St Pittsburgh PA 15213-3180 Office Phone: 412-828-6870.

**SOFIA, R. D.,** pharmacologist; b. Ellwood City, Pa., Oct. 8, 1942; BS, Geneva Coll., 1964; MS, Fairleigh-Dickenson U., 1969; PhD in Pharmacology, U. Pitts., 1971. Rsch. biologist Lederle Labs., N.Y., 1964-67; rsch. assoc. pharmacology Union Carbide Corp., 1967-69; sr. pharmacologist Pharmakon Labs., Pa., 1969, sr. rsch. pharmacologist, 1971-73, dir. dept. Pharmacology and Toxicology, 1973-76, v.p. biology rsch., 1976-80, v.p. R&D, 1980-82; v.p. pre-clin. and clin. rsch. Wallace Labs., Cranbury, 1982—. Cons. Pharmakon Labs., 1969-71. Mem. Am. Soc. Pharmacology and Experimental Therapeutics, Soc. Toxicology, SOc. Neuroscience, Internat. Soc. Study Pain, Am. Rheumatism Assn. Achievements include research in pharmacology and toxicology of various constituents of marijuana, development of new drugs for cardiovascular pulmonary and central nervous system diseases and pain relief. Office: Carter Wallace Pharmaceutical 265 Davidson Ste 300 Somerset NJ 08873-4120

**SOFTIC, TANJA,** artist; BFA, U. Sarajevo, Bosnia and Herzegovina, 1988; MFA, Old Dominion U./Norfolk State, 1992; student bookbinding, letterpress, Ctr. Book Arts, N.Y.C., 1993; student hand papermaking, Dieu Donne Paper Mill, N.Y.C. 1993. Printer Kathy Caraccio Printmaking Workshop, N.Y.C., 1991; adj. instr. Norfolk (Va.) State U., 1991—92; asst. prof. art Rollins Coll., 1992—2000; assoc. prof. art Richmond (Va.) U., 2000—. Asst. to gallery dir. Old Dominion U. Gallery, Norfolk, 1991—92; juror various exhbns., 1993—94; instr. workshops on printmaking history and techniques for docents Ctr. Flat Art Mus., 1992—95; presenter in field. One-woman shows include various mus.: Dubrovnik, Yugoslavia, 1989, Stanley Gallery, Norfolk, 1990, Collegium Artisticum, Sarajevo, 1991, Peninsula Fine Arts Ctr., Newport News, Va., 1992, Cornell Fine Arts Mus., Rollins Coll., Winter Park, Fla., 1994, Wyndy Moorehead Fine Arts, New Orleans, 1994, Coker Coll. Art Gallery, Hartsville, S.C., 1995, Kendall Gallery of Miami-Dade C.C., Miami, Fla., 1996, Allen R. Hite Art Inst., U. Louisville, 1996,

Catherine J. Smith Gallery, Appalachian State U., Boone, N.C., 1997, exhibited in group shows at City Hall Gallery, Orlando, Fla., 1994 (Purchase award), Jacksonville (Fla.) C.C. Gallery, 1995 (hon. mention), U. Wis. at Parkside Gallery, Kenosha, 1995, Niagara C.C. Art Gallery, Buffalo, 1995, Catherine D. Smith Gallery, Appalachian State U., Boone, 1995, Kanagawa Prefectural Gallery, Japan, 1995, Paul Mesaros Gallery, W.Va. U., Morgantown, 1996, Hokkaido Mus. Modern Art, Sapporo, Japan, 1996, others, Represented in permanent collections, exhibited in group shows at Emerson Gallery, McLean, Va., 2004. Recipient Best Debut prize, XV Biennial of Watercolor of Yugoslavia, 1989, Purchase award, Valencia Small Works, 1994, Orlando Biennial, 1994; fellow Grad. fellow, Old Dominion U. Coll. Arts and Letters, 1989; grantee Visual Artist grantee, Southeastern Coll. Art Conf., 1994; scholar Charles Sibley Grad. scholar, 1990—91, Artist scholar, Acad. Arts and Scis. of Bosnia and Herzegovina, 1990—91. E-mail: tsoftic@richmond.edu.

**SOFTNESS, DONALD GABRIEL,** marketing professional, manufacturing executive; b. Bklyn. s. Burt H. and Ida (Kaiser) S.; m. Sydell Meyerson; children: Michael, Anita May, Beth. AB, NYU, 1949, MBA, 1959; L.H.D., St. John's U., 1979. Chmn. Softness Group, Inc., N.Y.C., 1960-79; pres. Softness Groupe, N.Y.C., 1979—, SecureVue, Inc., N.Y.C., 1984—. V.p., maj. prin. Radio Stas. WVJ-AM-FM, Newark and N.Y.C.; mem. faculty Advt. Week seminars Advt. Age; prodr., promoter Bklyn. Rollathon (skating marathon). Co-author: Cardiologists' Guide to Health and Fitness Through Exercise, 1979; contbr. articles to bus. and trade jours. Patentee in mech. field. Served with USN. Mem. Public Relations Soc. Am., Internat. Radio TV Soc., Am. Coll. Sports Medicine Clubs: N.Y. Yacht. Home and Office: 28 Trues Dr West Islip NY 11795-5139 Office: SecureVue Inc 251 E 51st St New York NY 10022-6534 Office Phone: 212-752-5960. E-mail: don@securevue.net.

**SOFTNESS, JOHN,** public relations executive; b. Bklyn., Nov. 7, 1930; s. Burt H. and Ida (Kaiser) S.; m. Carol Brady Blades; children: Barney, David, Daniel. BA, U. Miami, 1955. Reporter Miami Herald, 1953; reporter Sta. WTVJ, Miami, Fla., 1954; asso. pub. relations dir. aviation dept. Shell Oil Co., N.Y.C., 1958-60; pres., chief exec. officer The Softness Group, Inc., N.Y.C., 1960-91, chmn., 1992-98; spl. asst. to dean Sch. Bus. U. Miami, 1998-2000. Spl. counselor to Bklyn. Borough pres., 1966-76; adj. prof. comm. arts St. John's U., 1981-98; adj. prof. speechwriting U. Miami, 2006; counselor comms. com. N.Y. Heart Assn.; mem. comm. coun. U. Miami; speechwriter, comm. advisor to Miami-Dade Mayor. Author: (autobiography) Boy Outta Brooklyn. Dir. Alliance for Ethical Govt., Miami. Served to capt. USAF, 1955-58. Mem. Pub. Rels. Soc. Am., Pride and Alarm (chmn.), Counselors' Acad. Home and Office: 2 Grove Isle Dr Apt 210 Coconut Grove FL 33133-4102 E-mail: softysr@aol.com.

**SOGG, WILTON SHERMAN,** lawyer; b. Cleve., May 28, 1935; s. Paul P. and Julia (Cahn) S.; m. Saralee Frances Krow, Aug. 12, 1962 (div. July 1975); 1 child, Stephanie; m. Linda Rocker Lehman, Dec. 22, 1979 (div. Dec. 1990); m. Nancy Rosenfield Walsh, June 2, 1991. AB, Dartmouth Coll., 1956; JD, Harvard U., 1959; postgrad., London Grad. Sch. Bus. Studies, 1974-76. Bar: (Ohio) 1960, (Fla) 1970, (U.S. Tax Ct.) 1961, (U.S. Supreme Ct.) 1969. Assoc. Gottfried, Ginsberg, Guren & Merritt, 1960-63, ptnr., 1963-70, Guren, Merritt, Feibel, Sogg & Cohen, Cleve., 1970-84; of counsel Hahn, Loeser, Freedheim, Dean and Wellman, Cleve., 1984-85; ptnr. Hahn Loeser & Parks LLP, Cleve., 1986-2000; of counsel McCarthy, Lebit, Crystal & Liffman Co., Cleve., 2001—. Trustee, pres. Cleve. Jewish News; adj. prof. Cleve. State U. Law Sch., 1960—; lectr. Harvard U. Law Sch., 1978-80. Author: (with Howard M. Rossen) new and rev. vols. of Smith's Review Legal Gems series, 1969—; editor: Harvard Law Rev.; contbr. articles to profl. jours. Trustee Jewish Cmty. Fedn. of Cleve., 1966-72; bd. overseers Cleveland Marshall Coll. Law, Cleve. State U., 1969—, vis. com. Coll. Bus. Adminstrn., 1996-2001, 2003-; mem. U.S. and State of Ohio Holocaust commns.; pres. bd. trustees Ohio Audubon Adv. Bd., 2005—. Fulbright fellow U. London, 1959-60. Mem. Ohio Bar Assn., Fla. Bar Assn., Germany Philatelic Soc., Oakwood Club, Chagrin Valley Hunt, Rowfant Club, Phi Beta Kappa. Home: PO Box 278 Gates Mills OH 44040-0278 Office: McCarthy Lebit Crystal & Liffman 101 W Prospect Ave Ste 1800 Cleveland OH 44115-1088 Office Phone: 216-696-1422. Business E-Mail: wss@mccarthylebit.com.

**SOGIN, MITCHELL L.,** biologist, educator; BS in Chemistry and Microbiol., U. Ill., Urbana, 1967, MS in Indsl. Microbiol., 1969, PhD in Microbiol. and Molecular Biology, 1972. NIH postdoctoral fellowship Nat. Jewish Ctr., Denver, 1972—76, sr. staff scientist dept. molecular and cellular biology, 1976—89; asst. prof. dept. biochemistry and biophysics U. Colo. Health Scis. Ctr., 1980—86, assoc. prof. dept. microbiol. rsch., 1987—89; sr. scientist Marine Biol. Lab., Woods Hole, Mass., 1989—, dir. Josephine Bay Paul Ctr. Comparative Molecular Biology and Evolution, 1997—; prof. dept. molecular biology, cell biology and biochemistry Brown U., Providence, 2004—. Assoc. fellow Can. Inst. Advanced Rsch., 1986—99; vis. Miller rsch. prof. U. Calif., Berkeley, 1997—98; sci. adv. Integrated Genomics, Chgo. Contbr. articles to sci. jours.; mem. editl. bd.: Molecular Biology and Evolution, 1994—2000, Jour. Eukaryotic Microbiol., Molecular Phylogenetics and Evolution, Jour. Molecular Evolution, Protist, Environ. Microbiol., Astrobiology. Recipient Stoll Stunkard award, Am. Soc. Parasitologists, 1993. Fellow: Am. Acad. Arts & Scis., Am. Acad. Microbiol., AAAS; mem.: Am. Soc. Cell Biology, Soc. Molecular Biology and Evolution, Internat. Soc. Evolutionary Protozoologists, Soc. Protozoologists, Am. Soc. Microbiol. Office: Josephine Bay Paul Ctr Marine Biol Lab Woods Hole 7 MBL St Woods Hole MA 02543 E-mail: sogin@mbl.edu.*

**SOH, CHUNGHEE SARAH,** anthropology educator; b. Taegu, Korea, May 1, 1947; came to U.S. 1970; d. Sang Yung and Ok Yun (Choi) S., m. Jerry Dee Bouchet. BA in English summa cum laude, Sogang U., 1971; postgrad., U. Calif., Berkeley, 1971; MA in Anthropology, U. Hawaii, 1983, PhD in Anthropology, 1987. Staff instr. English Korean Air Lines, Edn. & Tng. Ctr., Seoul, 1978-79; instr. anthropology Ewha Womans U., Seoul, 1985; postdoctoral assoc. Inst. of Culture and Comm., East-West Ctr., Honolulu, 1987; asst. prof. U. Hawaii, 1990; asst. prof. anthropology Southwest Tex. State U., San Marcos, 1991-94, San Francisco State U., 1994-96, assoc. prof. anthropology, 1996—2006, prof., 2006—. Guest lectr. Chaminade U. Honolulu, 1988; vis. asst. prof. anthropology U. Ariz., 1990-91; adj. prof. Intercultural Inst. Calif., 1996-98; cons. in field. Author: The Chosen Women in Korean Politics: An Anthropological Study, 1991, Women in Korean Politics, 1993; contbr. articles to profl. jour. Bd. dirs. Women Devel. Inst. Internat., 2000—. Grantee East-West Ctr., 1981-87, NSF, 1985-86; fellow Korea Found., 1993, Japan Found., 1997-98, Inst. Social Sci., U. Tokyo, 1997-98, Leiden U. Internat. Inst. for Asian Studies, The Netherlands, 1998, Inst. for Corean-Am. Studies, 1998—; Hoover Inst. scholar, 1996-97, Stanford U. Inst. for Rsch. on Women and Gender scholar, 2000-01; Rsch. and Writing grantee John D. and Catherine T. MacArthur Found., 2000-01. Fellow Am. Anthrop. Assn. (treas. East Asia sect. 2001-03), Inst. for Corean-Am. Studies; mem. Am. Ethnological Soc., Soc. Psychol. Anthropology, Assn. Asian Studies (exec. bd. Com. Women Asian Studies 1995-97), Korean Assn. Womens Studies, Royal Asiatic Soc. Korean Br. Office: San Francisco State U Dept Anthropology 1600 Holloway Ave San Francisco CA 94132-1722 Business E-Mail: soh@sfsu.edu.

**SOHAILI, HUSHMAND,** lawyer; BA summa cum laude, Univ. So. Ill., 1975; JD, Univ. So. Calif., 1979. Bar: Calif. 1979, US Dist. Ct. (ctrl. dist.) Calif., US Tax Ct. Ptnr. Finley, Kumble, Wagner, Underberg, Manley, Myerson & Casy, LA; ptnr., real estate transactional matters Kaye Scholer Fierman Hays & Handler LLP, LA, 1987—97; ptnr., head, real estate fin. practice group LA Akin Gump Strauss Hauer & Feld LLP, LA, 1997—. Mem.: State Bar of Calif., LA County Bar Assn. (real estate sect.), Order of Coif, Phi Alpha Delta. Office: Akin Gump Strauss Hauer & Feld LLP Ste 2400 2029 Century Pk E Los Angeles CA 90067-3012 Office Fax: 310-229-1060, 310-229-1001. Business E-Mail: hsohaili@akingump.com.

**SOHAILI, MONIRA,** retired special education educator; b. Pune, India, Nov. 4, 1933; d. Ispandiar and Keshvar Yaganegi; m. Shahpur Sohaili, Oct. 15, 1953 (dec. Dec. 2000). BA in Edn., Northeastern Ill. U., 1981, MA, 1982. Cert. behavioral therapy Behavioral Therapy Tng. Ctr., L.A., 1996. Tchr. Parramalta Marist H.S., Australia, 1970—71; guide Bahai House of Worship, Chgo., 1973—83; ESL instr. Cuban/Hatian Refugee Program, Chgo., 1983—84, Chgo. Bd. Edn., 1984—87; ESL and Eng. instr. Santa Monica (Calif.) City Coll., 1987—89; ESL, Eng. and reading tchr. Le Conte Mid. Sch., L.A., 1989—96; head dept. Ctr. Mid. Sch., 1994—96, spl. edn. tchr. L.A., 1996—2005, dept. head, 1996—2000; tchr. spl. edn. J. Burroughs Mid. Sch., L.A., 2000—05; ret., 2005. Storyteller in field, 2002—. Author: Monira's Fables, 2000, From Earth and Beyond, 2003, Spotty the Wonder Dog, Family History. Coord. childproof medicine vials donation, Papua New Guinea, 1995—97. Recipient Cert. of Achievement, L.A. USD Lang. Acquisition, 1993, I Made a Difference award, L.A. Dept. Edn., 1995. Mem.: NEA (reading and writing program 1990—), Calif. Tchrs. Assn. (assisted in program 1990—). Avocations: reading, writing, travel, swimming. Home: PO Box 590 Santa Monica CA 90406-0590

**SOHLMAN, MICHAEL,** foundation administrator; b. Stockholm, 1944; s. Rolf R. and Zinaida (Yarotskaya) S. BA, U. Uppsala, Sweden, 1964, postgrad. in econs. and polit. sci., 1968, U. Stockholm, 1968. Asst. sec. to Commn. Environ. Problems, 1969; with Ministry of Industry, 1972-74; with internat. divsn. Ministry of Fin., 1974-76, with budget dept., 1976, head of planning econ. dept., 1982-84, dir. of budget, 1985-87; fin. counsellor, permanent Swedish del. OECD, 1977-80; with rsch. dept. Social-Dem. Parliamentary Group, 1981-82; under-sec. of state Ministry of Agriculture, 1987-89; under-sec. of state for fgn. affairs Ministry for Fgn. Affairs, 1989-91; exec. dir. Nobel Found., Stockholm, 1992—. Chmn. bd. dirs. Royal Dramatic Theatre, Stockholm, 1993-96; chmn. bd. dirs. Post Pension Fund; bd. dirs. Axel Johnson Internat. Mem. Royal Swedish Acad. Scis., Acad. of Engring. Scis. Office: Nobel Foundation PO Box 5232 102 45 Stockholm Sweden

**SOHMER, BERNARD,** mathematics professor, administrator; b. N.Y.C., July 16, 1929; s. Sol and Florence (Schonfeld) S.; m. Margot Rosette, July 27, 1952; children: Emily Sohmer Tai, Olivia Sohmer Rosenbaum. BA, NYU, 1949, MS, 1951, PhD, 1958. Lectr. CCNY, NYC, 1952—57; asst. prof. NYU, NYC, 1957—58; faculty CCNY, NYC, 1958—2005, prof. math., 1969—2005, prof. emeritus, 2005—. Founding mem. SEEK program CCNY, NYC, 1964, dean students, 1969—72, v.p. student affairs, 1972—75, chmn. faculty senate, 1977—79, NYC, 1985—91, NYC, 2002—03, chmn. liberal arts and sci. faculty coun., 1979—85, ombudsman, 1991—98, NYC, 2002—03; trustee PSC-CUNY Welfare Fund, 1982—97; pres. Hillel, 1988—2001; sec. U. Faculty Senate CUNY, NYC, 1992—94, vice chair, 1994—98, chair, 1998—2002, ex officio bd. trustees, 1998—2002. Mem. AAAS, AAUP (pres. CCNY chpt. 1966-67, sec. 1977-78), Am. Math. Soc., Math. Assn. Am. (pres. elect NY Met. sect. 1989-90, pres. 1992-93, past pres. 1993-94, gov. 1996-98), Profl. Staff Congress (chair CCNY chpt. 1993-96, exec. coun. 1997-2000). Home: 3345 92nd St Jackson Heights NY 11372-1851 also: 176 E 77th St New York NY 10021 E-mail: bsohmer@earthlink.net.

**SOHN, CATHERINE ANGELL,** pharmaceutical executive, pharmacist; b. San Francisco, Mar. 21, 1953; d. Vincent Herbert and Margaret Ann Ware Angell; m. John Edwin Sohn, Aug. 10, 1974; children: Karen Elizabeth, Jennifer Michele. Student, U. Calif., Davis; PharmD, U. Calif., San Francisco, 1977. Registered pharmacist, Calif., Pa. Pharmacist Kaiser Permanent, San Francisco, 1977-78; asst. prof. pharmacy Phila. Coll. Pharmacy and Sci., 1978-82; mgr. med. affairs Smith Kline & French, Phila., 1982-86; assoc. dir. bus. devel. pharm. divsn. Smith Kline Beecham, Phila., 1986-88, product dir., 1988-93, v.p. worldwide strategic product devel., 1994-97; v.p. worldwide bus. devel. Glaxo Smith Kline Consumer Healthcare, Phila., 1998—. Lectr. St. Andrew the Apostle, Gibbsboro, NJ, 1989—; adv. bd. Healthcare Bus. Women's Assn., N.Y.C., NY, 1996—; bd. overseers U. Calif. Sch. Pharmacy, San Francisco, 1997—; health adv. bd. Johns Hopkins U. Sch. Pub. Health, Balt., 1998—. Author: (with others) Applied Clinical Therapeutics, 1980, Handbook of Non-Prescription Drugs, 1980, rev. edit., 1982; contbr. chpts. to profl. pubs. Mem. Am. Pharm. Assn., Calif. Pharmacists Assn., Consumer Healthcare Products Assn. (chmn. internat. affairs com. 1998—, bd. dirs. 1999—), Licensing Exec. Soc., Rho Chi. Roman Catholic. Avocations: swimming, bicycling. Office: GlaxoSmithKline FP1370 200 N 16th St Philadelphia PA 19102-1282

**SOHN, HONG YONG,** chemical engineer, metallurgical engineer, educator; b. Kaesung, Kyunggi-Do, Republic of Korea, Aug. 21, 1941; arrived in U.S. 1966; s. Chong Ku and Soon Deuk (Woo) Sohn; m. Victoria Bee Tuan Ngo, Jan. 8, 1971; children: Berkeley Jihoon, Edward Jihyun. BSChemE, Seoul Nat. U., Republic of Korea, 1962; MSChemE, U. NB, Can., 1966; PhD, U. Calif., Berkeley, 1970. Engr. Cheil Sugar Co., Busan, Republic of Korea, 1962-64; rsch. assoc. SUNY, Buffalo, 1971-73; rsch. engr. DuPont Co., Wilmington, Del., 1973-74; prof. metall. engring., adj. prof. chem. engring. U. Utah, Salt Lake City, 1974—. Cons. Lawrence Livermore Nat. Lab., 1976—, Cabot Corp., 1984—, DuPont Co., 1987—, Utah Power and Light Co., 1987—, H. C. Starck, 1997—. Co-author: (book) Gas-Solid Reactions, 1976; co-editor: Rate Processes of Extractive Metallurgy, 1979, Extractive Metallurgy of Refractory Metals, 1980, Advances in Sulfide Smelting, 2 vols., 1983, Recycle and Secondary Recovery of Metals, 1985, Gas-Solid Reactions in Pyrometallurgy, 1986, Flash Reaction Processes, 1988, Metallurgical Processes for the Year 2000 and Beyond, 1988, Metallurgical Processes for the Early Twenty-First Century, 2 vols., 1994, Proceeding of the Julian Szekely Memorial Symposium on Materials Processing, 1997, Value-Addition Metallurgy, 1998, Sulfide Smelting, 2002, Metallurgical and Materials Processing: Principles and Technologies, 3 vols., 2003; contbr. articles to profl. jours. Recipient Fulbright Disting. lectureship, 1983; Camille and Henry Dreyfus Found. Tchr. scholar, 1977, Japan Soc. Promotion Sci. fellow, 1990. Mem.: AIChE, AIME (James Douglas Gold medal 2001), Korean Inst. Chem. Engrs., Korean Acad. Sci. and Tech. (Fellow award 1998), Minerals, Metals and Materials Soc. (past dir., Extractive Metallurgy Lectr. award 1990, Extraction and Processing Sci. award 1990, champion H. Mathewson Gold medal award 1993, Extraction and Processing Sci. award 1994, 1999). Achievements include patents for process for treating sulfide-bearing ores, continuous solvent extraction with bottom gas injection. Office: U Utah 135 S 1460 E Rm 412 Salt Lake City UT 84112-0114 Office Phone: 801-581-5491. Business E-Mail: hysohn@mines.utah.edu. *Fortunate are those who earn a living by doing what they would rather be doing even if they do not have to do it to earn a living. Material wealth accumulated by doing what one does not enjoy doing is not worth the effort.*

**SOHN, JUNGYUL,** education educator; b. Seoul, Korea (South); s. Dongin Sohn and Youngsoo Kim; m. Soo Kyoung Oh, Jan. 7, 2006. BA with honors, Seoul Nat. U., 1987—91, MA, 1991—93; PhD, U. of Ill., 1996—2002. Rsch. asst. U. Pa., Phila., 1997, U. Ill., Urbana, 1998—2001; rsch. assoc. U. Md., College Park, 2002—04; asst. prof. U. Memphis, 2004—06, Seoul Nat. U., 2006—. Affiliate prof. U. Md., 2004—. Mem. editl. bd. Geog. Jour. of Korea, 2003—; contbr. articles to profl. jours., chapters to books. Cpl. Korean Army, 1993—95, Gyeonggi Province, Korea. Scholar, Woosan Found., 1991—93; Grad. Coll. Conf. Travel grant, U. Ill., 2001. Mem.: Regional Sci. Assn. Internat. Avocations: travel, movies, sports. Office: Seoul Nat Univ Dept Geography San 56-1 Sillim-dong Gwanak-gu Seoul 151-746 Republic of Korea Office Phone: 82-2-880-4055. Office Fax: 82-2-876-9498. Business E-Mail: jsohn@snu.ac.kr.

**SOHN, MICHAEL N,** lawyer; b. May 11, 1940; AB, Columbia Univ. 1960; JD cum laude, Harvard Univ. 1963. Bar: N.Y. 1964, D.C. 1969, US Supreme Ct. 1969. Atty. Gen. Counsel Office, NLRB, Washington, 1964—69; gen. counsel FTC, Washington, 1977—80; chmn. of firm & chmn Policy Com. Arnold & Porter, Washington, 1996—. Mem. exec. com. Regulatory Council of the U.S., 1978—80; mem. council Adminstrv. Conf. of U.S., 1978—83. Office: Arnold & Porter 555 Twelfth St NW Washington DC 20004-1206 Office Phone: 202-942-5005. Office Fax: 202-942-5999. Business E-Mail: michael.sohn@aporter.com.

**SOHN, RAYNA MAYER,** medical researcher, legal association administrator; b. Chgo., Jan. 14, 1938; d. Jacob DeCosta and Dorothy Mayer; widowed; children: Andrew, Douglas; m. Herbert Sohn (div. 1969); children: Marc, Tracy, Dana Teitler. BA with honors, UCLA, 1958. Pres. Vista Del Mar, L.A.; asst. to sr. v.p. Calif. Fed. Savings, L.A.; medical-leaal analyst John D. Hayes & Assocs., Chgo. Translator laws SDL, Dominican Republic. Coord. campaign Sen. Arthur Berman; former lobbyist disabled, Chgo. and Washington. Mem. Phi Beta Kappa, Alpha Epsilon. Democrat. Jewish.

**SOHN, YONGHO,** science educator; m. Hye Shin, July 28, 1994; children: Yewon Danielle, Yejoon Joshua. BS, Worcester Poly. Inst., 1991, MS, 1993; PhD, Purdue U., 1998. Rsch. scholar U. of Conn., Storrs, 1999—2000; prof. U. Cen. Fla., Orlando, 2001—. Recipient Career award, NSF, 2003—08. Mem.: ASM (tech. com.), Am. Soc. of Engring. Edn., Am. Ceramic Soc., Metals, Minerals and Materials Soc. (tech. com.). Achievements include research in Diffusion in Solids; High Tempeature Coatings; Materials Characterization and Electron Microscopy. Office: U Cen Fla AMPAC-MMAE 4000 Central Florida Blvd Orlando FL 32816-2455 Office Phone: 407-882-1181. Office Fax: 407-882-1462. Business E-Mail: ysohn@mail.ucf.edu.

**SOIFER, AVIAM,** dean, law educator; b. Worcester, Mass., Mar. 18, 1948; married; 2 children. BA cum laude, Yale U., 1969, MA in Urban Studies, 1972, JD, 1972. Bar: Conn. 1974, U.S. Dist. Ct. Conn. 1974, U.S. Supreme Ct. 1994. Law clk. to judge Jon O. Newman U.S. Dist. Ct. Conn., 1972-73; asst. prof. U. Conn. Sch. Law, 1976-77, assoc. prof., 1977-78, 1978-80, Boston U. Sch. Law, 1980—93, 1998—2003; dean Boston Coll. Law Sch., 1993-98, U. Hawaii, Sch. Law, Honolulu, 2003—. Vis. prof. Boston U. Sch. Law, 1979-80; vis. colleague William S. Richardson Sch. Law, 1999-2000. Author: Law the the Company We Keep, 1995 (Alpha Sigma Nu Nat. Jesuit Book Prize, 1998); contbr. articles to profl. jours. Vice chair Supreme Jud. Ct. Mass. Task Force on Jud. Edn., 1996-2001; mem. steering com. 1st Cir. Task Force on Gender, Race and Ethnicity, 1995-99; trustee New Eng. Med. Ctr., 1997-2002, Cambridge Health Alliance, 2002-03. Recipient Disting. Sr. Rsch. award Boston Coll., 2001-02; named Disting. Scholar Legal Studies Inst., U. Wis., 2001-; Harvard Program in Law and Humanities fellow, 1976-77; Kellog Nat. fellow, 1981-84. Mem. ABA (commn. on coll. and univ. legal studies 1996-2000. Office: William S Richardson Sch Law U Hawaii 2515 Dole St Honolulu HI 96822 E-mail: soifer@hawaii.edu.

**SOJKA, GARY ALLAN,** biologist, educator, academic administrator; b. Cedar Rapids, Iowa, July 15, 1940; s. Marvin F. and Ruth Ann (Waddington) Sojka Green; m. Sandra Kay Smith, Aug 5, 1962; children: Lisa Kay, Dirk Allan. BS, Coe Coll., 1962; MS, Purdue U., 1965, PhD, 1967, DSc (hon.), 2002; DL (hon.), Lycoming Coll., 1995. Rsch. assoc. Ind. U., Bloomington, 1967-69, asst. prof., 1969-73, assoc. prof., 1973-79, prof., 1979-84, assoc. chmn. biology, 1977-79, chmn. biology, 1979-81, dean arts and scis., 1981-84; pres. Bucknell U., Lewisburg, Pa., 1984-95, prof. biology, 1984—2006, prof., pres. emeritus, 2006. Mem. higher edn. commn. Mid. States Assn. Colls. and Schs., 1992-96, chmn. task force on instnl. effectiveness, 1999-2000; chmn. tax policy subcom. Nat. Assn. Ind. Colls. and Univs., 1991-93; mem. study group on internat. edn. Am. Coun. Edn., 1992-94. Mem. So. Ind. Health Sys. Agy., Bedford; vice-chair Am. Livestock Conservancy, 2003—05, chmn. of bd., 2005—; chmn. bd. dirs. Stone Belt Coun. Ret. Citizens, Bloomington, 1977—95; mem. nominating com. Ind. Assn. Ret. Citizens, Indpls., 1979; bd. dirs. Geisinger Med. Found., Danville, Pa., 1985—97, 2003—06, mem. regional bd., 1997—2003; chmn. Pa. Assn. Ind. Colls. and Univs., 1989—90; mem. pres.'s commn. NCAA, 1993—95; mem. planning adv. com. Snyder County, Pa., 1996—98, mem. planning commn., 2001—; bd. dirs. Bethesda Found., Lewisburg, 1996—98; trustee, bd. dirs. Am. Livestock Conservancy, 2001—, vice chair, 2003—05, chair bd., 2006—; dir. WITF Public Broadcasting, Harrisburg, bd. trustees, 2003—; gov. Inst. European Studies, 0989—1994, Citizen for the Future of Pa., 1999—. Recipient Ind. U. Sr. Class Tchg. award, 1975, Frederick B. Lieber award, 1977, Coe Coll. Alumni award of merit, 1982, Gary A. Sojka award Bucknell U., 1992, Cmty. Leadership award Susquahanna Valley Boy Scouts, 1994, Sheepskin award for Disting. Svc. to Higher Edn. Pa. Assn. Colls. and Univs., 2000, ECAC Appreciation award, Bucknell U., 2003, Adam Smith award Econ. Pa., 2003, Disting. Svc. medal Reading (Pa.) Ind. Day Coms., 2004; named to Coe Coll. Athletic Hall of Fame, 1988, Bucknell U. Athletic Hall of Fame, 2006; Gary A. Sojka Pavillion named in his honor, 2003. Mem.: AAAS, Pa. Assn. Coll. and Univs. (interim pres. 1997—98, exec. com. Sheepskin award 1999, Sheepskin award 2000), Phila. Soc. Promotion of Agriculture, Am. Coun. Edn. (study group on internat. edn. 1992—94), Nat. Assn. Independent Colls. and Univs. (subcom. chmn. 1991—93), Am. Soc. Biol. Chemists, Am. Acad. Microbiology, Am. Soc. Microbiology, Phi Beta Kappa (hon.), Omicron Delta Kappa, Sigma Nu, Sigma Xi. Baptist. Office: Bucknell U Dept Biology Lewisburg PA 17837 Office Phone: 570-577-3812. Business E-Mail: gsojka@bucknell.edu.

**SOKAL, ALLEN MARCEL,** lawyer; b. Phila., Dec. 17, 1946; s. Michael Rudolf and Olga (Pories) Sokal; m. Judith Ann Berkowitz, May 25, 1968; children: Michelle Paula, Shira Hermine; m. Sharon Greenfield, Mar. 23, 2003. BSChemE cum laude, U. Pa., 1968; JD, Georgetown U., 1972. Bar: Va. 1973, DC 1974, lic.: US Tax Ct. (DC Dist.) 1978, US Ct. Appeals (Fed. Cir.) 1982, US Supreme Ct. 1987; registered: US Patent & Trademark Office 1973. Patent examiner US Patent Office, Washington, 1968—73; assoc. Sughrue, Rothwell, Mion, Zinn & Macpeak, Washington, 1973—74; tech. advisor, law clk. to Hon. Jack R. Miller US Ct. Customs & Patent Appeals, Washington, 1974—76; assoc. Finnegan, Henderson, Farabow, Garrett & Dunner LLP, Washington, 1976—82, ptnr., Biotech./Pharm. Practice Group, 1982—, leader, Appellate Sect. Mem. Georgetown Law Jour., 1971—72. Contbr. articles to profl. jours.; spkr. in field. Recipient spl. achievement award, US Patent Office, 1970, 1971, 1972. Mem.: Va. State Bar, Bar Assn. DC, ABA, Assn. Former Ct. Customs & Patent Appeals Law Clks. & Tech. Advisors (sec. 1980), Am. Patent Law Assn. (chmn. current ct. cases subcom., chem. practice com. 1979—81), DC Bar (vice chmn. patent, trademark & copyright divsn. 1983—84, chmn. patent, trademark & copyright divsn. 1984—85), Phi Lambda Upsilon, Tau Beta Pi. Dem. Jewish. Office: Finnegan Henderson Farabow Garrett & Dunner LLP 901 New York Ave NW Washington DC 20001-3315 Office Phone: 202-408-4000. Office Fax: 202-408-4400. Business E-Mail: allen.sokal@finnegan.com.

**SOKAL, ROBERT REUVEN,** biology professor, writer; b. Vienna, Jan. 13, 1926; came to U.S., 1947, naturalized 1956; s. Siegfried and Klara (Rattner) S.; m. Julie Chen-Chu Yang, Aug. 12, 1948; children: David Jonathan, Hannah Judith. BS in Biology, St. John's U., Shanghai, Republic of China, 1947; PhD in Zoology, U. Chgo., 1952; DSc (hon.), U. Crete, Greece, 1990. From instr. to prof. U. Kans., Lawrence, 1951-69; prof., then leading prof., Disting. prof. SUNY, Stony Brook, 1969-95, dept. chmn., 1980-83, vice provost for rsch. and grad. studies, 1981-82, disting. prof. emeritus, 1995. Fulbright vis. prof. Hebrew/Tel Aviv U., Israel, 1963-64, U. Vienna, Austria, 1977, 78, 84; vis. prof. Inst. Adv. Studies, Oeiras, Portugal, 1971-80; vis. disting. prof. U. Mich., 1975-76; vis. prof. Coll. de France, Paris, 1989. Author: Principles of Numerical Taxonomy, 1963, Biometry, 1969, 3d rev. edit., 1995, Statistical Tables, 1969, 3rd rev. edit. 1995, Introduction to Biostatistics, 1973, 2d rev. edit., 1987, Numerical Taxonomy, 1973; editor Am. Naturalist, 1969-74. Recipient Charles Darwin Lifetime Achievement award in phys. anthropology, 2004; Career investigator NIH, 1964-69; sr. fellow NSF, 1959-60, NATO fellow, 1974, Guggenheim fellow, 1975-76, 84; Ctr. Advanced Study in Behavioral Sci. fellow, 1992-93. Fellow AAAS, Am. Acad. Arts and Scis.; mem. Soc. Study Evolution (pres. 1977), Am. Soc. Naturalists (hon. mem., pres. 1984), The Classification Soc. (pres. 1969-71),

Internat. Fedn. Classification Socs. (pres. 1988-89), Nat. Acad. Scis., Linnean Soc. London (fgn.), Soc. Systematic Zoology (hon.), Natural History Mus. (Paris, corr. mem.), B'nai Brith Lodge (mem. 1966). Democrat. Jewish.

**SOKLER, BRUCE DOUGLAS,** lawyer; b. Newark, May 2, 1949; s. Lester and Aline Irma (Lasner) Sokler; m. Barbara Adele Cunningham, June 1, 1974; children: Sean, Brendan. AB cum laude, Princeton U., 1971; JD, Georgetown U., 1974. Bar: DC 1975, Mass. 1984, US Dist. Ct. (Dist. DC), US Dist. Ct. (Dist. Mass.), US Ct. Appeals (DC Cir.), US Ct. Appeals (2nd Cir.), US Ct. Appeals (8th Cir.), US Supreme Ct. Law clk. to Judge Edward Allen Tamm US Ct. Appeals (DC Cir.), Washington, 1974-75; assoc. Covington & Burling, Washington, 1975-82; ptnr. Mintz, Levin, Lohn, Ferris, Glovsky & Popeo PC, Washington, 1982—, mgr. Fed. Sect. Editor-in-chief Georgetown Law Jour., 1973—74. Mem.: DC Bar Assn., ABA (Antitrust Law Sect., Adminstrv. Litig. Sect.), Fed. Comm. Bar Assn. Office: Mintz Levin Lohn Ferris Glovsky & Popeo PC 701 Pennsylvania Ave NW Washington DC 20004-2608 Office Phone: 202-434-7303. Office Fax: 202-434-7400. Business E-Mail: bdsokler@mintz.com.

**SOKOL, DAVID L.,** energy services provider company executive; b. Omaha, Nebr., 1956; married; children: D.J.(dec.), Kelly. BSCE, U. Nebr., Omaha, 1978; doctorate (hon.), Bellevue U., Nebr. With Citicorp, Henningson, Durham and Richardson, Inc.; pres., CEO, bd. dirs. Ogden Projects, Inc.; pres., CEO Peter Kiewit Energy Company, 1991; chmn., CEO MidAm. Energy Holdings Co. (succesor to CalEnergy Co., Inc.), Des Moines, 1991—, pres., from 1991. Co-chmn. for Campaign Nebr., U. Nebr. Found.; dir.; mem. Met. Omaha Conv., Sports and Entertainment Authority; bd. dirs. Creighton U., Coll. World Series Omaha, Inc., Omaha Airport Authority, Strategic Command Consultation Co., Joslyn Art Mus., River City Roundup and Rodeo, Nebr. Easter Seal Soc. Mt. Michael Abbey H.S., Archdiocese of Omaha, Girls, Inc., Mid-Am. coun. Boy Scouts Am., Muscular Sclerosis Soc.-Midlands Chpt., United Way Midlands, Edison Electric Inst., Creighton U.; bd. govs. Knights of Ak-Sar-Ben; leadership adv. bd. bd. dir. NCAA; adv. com. arts JFK Ctr.; chmn. Met. Entertainment and Convention Authority Named CEO of Yr., Fin. Times Energy, 2000; recipient Individual Achievement award, Energy Daily, 2001. Mem. Del. Assn. Profl. Engrs., Neb. Soc. Profl. Engrs.; life mem. Horatio Alger Assn. Avocations: hockey, hunting, fishing, running, horseback riding. Office: MidAm Energy Holdings Co 666 Grand Ave PO Box 657 Des Moines IA 50303-0657

**SOKOL, JAN D.,** lawyer; b. NYC, May 27, 1952; BS magna cum laude, Rutgers U., 1974; JD Northwestern Sch. of Law, Lewis and Clark Coll., 1977. Bar: Oreg. 1978, U.S. Dist. Ct. (dist. Oreg.), U.S. Ct. Appeals (9th cir.) 1981, U.S. Claims Ct. 1982, U.S. Supreme Ct. 1984. Law clerk to Hon. George A. Juba U.S. Dist. Ct. (dist. Oreg.), 1978-79, law clerk to Hon. Gus J. Solomon, 1979-80, law clerk to Hon. James A. Redden, 1980; mng. mem. Stewart, Sokol & Gray, 1994. Case note and comment editor Environmental Law, 1976-77. Mem. ABA (mem. forum com. on the construction industry, fidelity and surety, forest resources com.), Multnomah County.

**SOKOL, JENNIFER MARIE,** musician; b. Seattle, Wash., Mar. 26, 1958; d. Vilem and Agatha Sokol. BA in violin performance, Ind. U. Founder, first violinist, mgr. Cameo String Quartet. Contbr. articles various profl. jours. Recipient Pres. award for Literary Excellence. Nat. Authors Registry, 2004. Roman Cath. Avocations: reading, ballet, outdoor recreation. Home: 6303 NE 185th St Kenmore WA 98028 Office Phone: 425-485-8380. E-mail: jennifermsokol@aol.com.

**SOKOL, ROBERT JAMES,** obstetrician, gynecologist, educator; b. Rochester, NY, Nov. 18, 1941; s. Eli and Mildred (Levine) S.; m. Roberta Sue Kahn, July 26, 1964; children: Melissa Anne, Eric Russell, Andrew Ian. BA in Philosophy with highest distinction, U. Rochester, 1963, MD with honors, 1966. Diplomate Am. Bd. Ob-gyn. (assoc. examiner 1984-86), Sub-Bd. Maternal-Fetal Medicine. Intern Barnes Hosp., Washington U., St. Louis, 1966—67, resident in ob-gyn., 1967—70, asst. in ob-gyn., 1966—70, rsch. asst., 1967—68, instr. clin. ob-gyn., 1970; Buswell fellow in maternal fetal medicine Strong Meml. Hosp.-U. Rochester, 1972—73; fellow in maternal-fetal medicine Cleve. Met. Gen. Hosp.-Case Western Res. U., 1974—75, assoc. obstetrician and gynecologist, 1973—83, asst. prof. ob-gyn., 1973—77; asst. program dir. Perinatal Clin. Rsch. Ctr., 1973—78, co-program dir., 1978—82, program dir., 1982—83, acting dir. obstetrics, 1974—75, co-dir., 1977—83, assoc. prof., 1977—81, prof., 1981—83, assoc. dir. dept. ob-gyn., 1981—83; prof. ob-gyn. Wayne State U., Detroit, 1983—2000, dist. prof. ob-gyn., 2000—, chmn. dept. ob-gyn., 1983—89, mem. grad. faculty dept. physiology, 1984—, interim dean Med. Sch. 1988—89, dean, 1989—99, pres. Fund for Med. Rsch. and Edn., 1988—99, interim dir. Applied Genomics Ctr., 2004—; chief ob-gyn. Hutzel Hosp., Detroit, 1983—89; interim chmn. med. bd. Detroit Med. Ctr., 1988—89, chmn. med. bd., 1989—99, sr. v.p. med. affairs, 1992—99, trustee, 1990—99; past pres. med. staff Cuyahoga County Hosps.; mem. adv. bd. Educated Childbirth Inc., 1976—80; dir. C.S. Mott Ctr. for Human Growth and Devel., 1983—89, 1999—. Mem. surg. team Johns Hopkins U. (Balt. Md.), 1965. Contbr. articles profl. jours., chpts. to books. Mem. editorial bd. Am. Jour. Ob-Gyn., 1981-86, sect. editor, 1986-88; mem. editorial bd. Jour. Maternal-Fetal Medicine, 1991—, editor-in-chief Am. Jour. Obstetrics and Gynecology; reviewer med. jours.; mem. editl. bd. Jour. Perinatal Medicine; editor-in-chief Interactions: Programs in Clinical Decision-Making, 1987-90; rsch. computer applications in perinatal medicine, alcohol-related birth defects, perinatal risk and neurobehavioral devel.; contbr. chpts. to books and articles to profl. jours. Mem. Pres.'s leadership coun. U. Rochester, 1976—80, permanent trustee, 1986—; mem. exec. com. bd. trustees Southeast Mich. Ctr. Med. Edn., 1987—2000; chmn. Friends of the Grand Theatre, 2005—; mem. rsch. adv. com. Wayne State U., 2005—; mem. fetal alcohol spectrum disorders prevention adv. com. CDC and Prevention, 2005—; bd. dirs. Am. U. Caribbean, 2001—; Grand Theatre, London, Ont., Canada, 2002—; mem. bd. trustees Stratford Am., 2004—. Maj. M.C. USAF, 1970—72. Recipient 15 sci. rsch. awards, 1986—, Disting. Svc. award, Wayne State U. Mem.: APHA, ACOG (chmn. steering com. drug and alcohol abuse contract 1986—87, rep. ctr. for disease control & prevention task force 2000—, editor-in-chief ACOG Update 2001—, Outstanding Dist. Svc. Excellence award), NAS (Inst. of Medicine, com. to study fetal alcohol syndrome 1994—96), AMA, Soc. Maternal-Fetal Medicine Found. (found. bd. chmn. 2003—), Soc. Physicians Reproductive Choice and Health, World Assn. Perinatal Medicine, Internat. Soc. Computers in Obstetrics, Neonatology, Gynecology (v.p. 1987—89, pres. 1989—92), Soc. for Neuroscics. (Mich. chpt.), Am. Med. Soc. on Alcoholism and Other Drug Dependencies, Am. Gynecol. and Obstet. Soc., Neurobehavioral Teratology Soc., Soc. Perinatal Obstetricians (pres.-elect 1987—88, pres. 1988—89, v.p., Achievement award 1995), Rsch. Soc. Alcoholism, Ctrl. Assn. Obstetricians-Gynecologists (pres.-elect 1997—99, pres. 1999—2000), Detroit Acad. Medicine (pres.-elect 1999—2001, pres. 2001—02), Wayne County Med. Soc., Mich. Med. Soc., Royal Soc. Medicine, Am. Profs. Ob-gyn., Perinatal Rsch. Soc., Soc. Gynecologic Investigation, Am. Med. Informatics Assn., Chgo. Gynecol. Soc. (hon.), Detroit Physiol. Soc. (hon.), Wayne State U. Acad. Scholars, Alpha Omega Alpha, Sigma Xi, Phi Beta Kappa. Republican. Jewish. Home: 7921 Danbury Dr West Bloomfield MI 48322-3581 Office: Wayne State U CS Mott Ctr for Human Growth and Devel Detroit MI 48201 Office Phone: 313-577-1337. Business E-Mail: rsokol@moose.med.wayne.edu. *The drive for academic accomplishment was instilled early in childhood in a home environment which placed value on a multiplicity of interests in science and the arts. My parents taught me what to do. In retrospect, exposure to strong role models-professors of philosophy, pathology, psychiatry and obstetrics-gynecology-takes on increased importance-these individuals showed me how*

*to do it. My family continues to support me in seeking and meeting new challenges. The opportunity to develop and transmit new knowledge sustains a high level of activity. I enjoy what I do.*

**SOKOL, RONALD JAY,** pediatric gastroenterologist, researcher; b. Chgo., July 18, 1950; s. Max Charles and Edith Sokol; m. Lori Lubman, Aug. 20, 1989; children: Skylar Paul, Jared Todd. BS, U. Ill., 1972; MD, U. Chgo., 1976. Diplomate Am. Bd. Pediat., Am. Bd. Pediatric Gastroenterology. Asst. prof. pediat. U. Colo., Denver, 1983—88; assoc. prof. pediat. U. Colo. Sch. Medicine, Denver, 1989—95, prof. pediat., 1995—, vice chair pediat., 1999—. Program dir. Pediatric Gen. Clin. Rsch. Ctr., Denver, 1998—, head sect. pediat. gastroenterology, hepatology and nutrition, 2006—. Editor: (med. textbook) Liver Disease in Children. Chair children's liver coun. Am. Liver Found., NYC, 1997—2003. Rsch. grantee, NIH, 1985—. Fellow: Am. Acad. Pediat. (nutrition rsch. award 2003); mem.: Am. Pediat. Soc., N. Am. Soc. for Pediat. Gastroenterology, Hepatology and Nutrition (pres. 1996—98), Am. Assn. for Study of Liver Disease, Soc. Pediat. Rsch., Am. Gastroent. Assn. Achievements include patents for antioxidant solution for treatment of cholestatic liver disease and for treatment of non-alcoholic steatohepatitis. Office: Childrens Hosp 1056 E 19th Ave Denver CO 80218 E-mail: sokol.ronald@tchden.org.

**SOKOLOFF, AUDREY L.,** lawyer; b. Providence, R.I., 1966; AB, Dartmouth Coll., 1987; JD, UCLA, 1990. Bar: Calif. 1990, N.Y. 1999. Atty. Skadden, Arps, Slate, Meagher & Flom LLP, New York, 1999—. Office: Skadden Arps Slate Meagher & Flom LLP Four Times Sq New York NY 10036

**SOKOLOFF, LOUIS,** physiologist, neuroscientist; b. Phila., Oct. 14, 1921; married; 2 children. BA, U. Pa., 1943, MD, 1946; Dr. (hon.), Philipps U. Marburg, Germany, 1990; MD (hon.), U. Rome, 1992; ScD (hon.), Georgetown U., 1992, Mich. State U., 1993, U. Pa., 1997. Intern Phila. Gen. Hosp., 1946-47; rsch. fellow in physiology U. Pa. Grad. Sch. Medicine, 1949-51, instr., then assoc., 1951-56; assoc. chief, then chief sect. cerebral metabolism NIMH, Bethesda, Md., 1953-68, chief lab. cerebral metabolism, 1968—. Chief editor Jour. Neurochemistry, 1974-78. Served to capt. M.C. U.S. Army, 1947-49. Recipient F.O. Schmitt medal in neurosci., 1980, Albert Lasker clin. med. research award, 1981, Karl Spencer Lashley award Am. Philos. Soc., 1987, Disting. Grad. award U. Pa., 1987, Nat. Acad. Scis. award in Neurosci., 1988, Georg Charles de Hevesy Nuclear Medicine Pioneer award Soc. Nuclear Medicine, 1988, Mihara Cerebrovascular Disorder Rsch. Promotion award, 1988. Mem. NAS, Inst. Medicine (sr.), Am. Physiol. Soc., Assn. Rsch. Nervous and Mental Diseases, Am. Biophys. Soc., Am. Acad. Neurology, Am. Neurol. Assn., Am. Philos. Soc., Am. Soc. Biol. Chemists, Am. Soc. Neurochemistry. Achievements include development of methods for measurement of cerebral blood flow and metabolism in animals and man. Office: NIMH/NIH Bldg 49 Rm 1C80 9000 Rockville Pike Bethesda MD 20892-4030 Office Phone: 301-496-1371. Business E-Mail: louissokoloff@mail.nih.gov.

**SOKOLOV, RICHARD SAUL,** real estate company executive; b. Phila., Dec. 7, 1949; s. Morris and Estelle Rita (Steinberg) S.; m. Susan Barbara Saltzman, Aug. 13, 1972; children: Lisa, Anne, Kate. BA, Pa. State U., 1971; JD, Georgetown U., 1974. Assoc. Weinberg & Green, Balt., 1974-80, ptnr., 1980-82; v.p., gen. counsel The Edward J. DeBartolo Corp., Youngstown, Ohio, 1982-86, sr. v.p. devel., gen. coun., 1986-94; pres., CEO DeBartolo Realty Corp., Youngstown, Ohio, 1994-96; pres., COO Simon DeBartolo Group, Indpls., 1996-98; pres, COO Simon Property Group, Indpls., 1998—. Mem. investment com. Jewish Fedn., Youngstown, 1992—; trustee U. Wis.-Madison Ctr. for Urban Land Econs. Rsch., Youngstown/Mahoning Valley United Way. Alumni fellow Pa. State U., 2000. Mem. Internat. Coun. Shopping Ctrs. (trustee 1994—, chmn. 1998-99), Urban Land Inst. (assoc.). Office: Simon Property Group 115 W Washington St Ste 1465 Indianapolis IN 46204-3464

**SOKOLOWSKI, LINDA ROBINSON,** artist, educator; b. Utica, NY, May 20, 1943; d. Walter Prentice and Doris Helene Robinson; m. Robert Louis Sokolowski, May 27, 1967; 1 child, Devon Robert. BFA, R.I. Sch. Design, 1965; MA, U. Iowa, 1970, MFA, 1971. Prof. art Harpur Coll., SUNY, Binghamton, 1971—2004. One-woman shows include Kraushaar Galleries, N.Y.C., 1976, 1979, 1982, 1986, 1989, 1991, 1994, 1998, 2001, 2004, exhibited in group shows at Pushkin Mus., Moscow, 1973, Mt. Holyoke Coll., 1974, Miami U., Oxford, Ohio, 1976, U. N.C., 1978, Emporia State U., 1979, Butler Inst. Am. Art, 1979, 1980, 1992, Nat. Mus. Art Smithsonian, 1981, Columbia (S.C.) Mus. Arts and Scis., 1984, NAD, 1986, Fed. Res. Bd., 1987, numerous others, Represented in permanent collections IBM, Inc., Pepsico, Oak Ridge Art Ctr., Libr. Congress, others. Recipient Childe Hassam award Am. Acad. Arts and Letters, 1978; SUNY rsch. grantee, 1976, 90. Mem. United Univ. Professions. Democrat. Office: SUNY Dept Art And History Binghamton NY 13902 Office Phone: 845-292-4375. Personal E-mail: soko1@usadatanet.net.

**SOKOLOWSKY, BRIAN WILLIAM,** archivist, historian; b. Bremerton, Wash., Sept. 17, 1953; s. Victor and Elizabeth Sokolowsky; m. April Ann Sommerset, Mar. 17, 1984; children: Frederick, William, Katherine. BA in Art and Design, Brigham Young U., 1977; BA in History, Western Wash. U., 1984, MA in History, 1987. Cert. archivist Acad. Cert. Archivists. Lt. col., historian USAFR, Hill AFB, Utah, 1986—; archivist LDS Ch., Salt Lake City, 1986—. C-130 navigator USAF, 1978—80. Bishop Copperhill 10th Ward LDS Ch., West Valley City, Utah, 1996—2001. Capt. USAF, 1977—83. Mem.: Soc. Am. Archivists. E-Mail: lowsky@earthlink.net.

**SOKOLSKY, ROBERT LAWRENCE,** journalist; b. Boston, May 18, 1928; s. Henry and Lillian (Gorodetzky) S.; m. Sally-Ann Moss, Aug. 11, 1955; 1 son. Andrew E. AB, Syracuse U., NY, 1950. Reporter Springfield (Mass.) Union, 1950; asst. dir. pub. info. ARC, Syracuse, 1952-54; entertainment editor Syracuse Herald-Jour., 1954-61, Buffalo Courier Express, 1961-72, Phila. Bull., 1972-82; entertainment writer Riverside (Calif.) Press-Enterprise, 1983-2000; syndicated TV columnist Ottaway News Svc., 1988-96, Scripps Howard, 1996-2000; freelance writer, radio commentator pub. radio, 2000—; columnist San Bernardino Sun, 2001—; entertainment editor Inland Empire News Radio, 2001—. Radio show host; freelance writer; guest lectr. Contbr. columns in newspapers, 2001, articles to profl. jours. Bd. dirs. Brush Hollow Civic Assn., Eversham Twp., N.J. Served with U.S. Army, 1950-52. Recipient Sigma Delta Chi award for feature writing, 1950, award for entertainment coverage Twin Counties Press Club, 1984, 87, Lifetime Achievement award Inland Theatre League, 2001. Mem. Am. Newspaper Guild (Page One award for opinion writing), Syracuse Press Club, Greater Buffalo Press Assn., TV Critics Assn., Soc. Profl. Journalists (Excellence in Journalism award 1989, 93), Pen and Pencil Club of Phila., Variety Club. Republican. Jewish. Home and Office: 3080 Saratoga St Riverside CA 92503-5435 Office Phone: 951-785-0798. E-mail: rsokolsky@charter.net.

**SOKULSKI, GARY A.,** law firm executive; BSBA, Robert Morris Coll., 1979. CPA Price Waterhouse, 1981—92; joined Reed Smith LLP, Pitts., 1992, now COO, mem. mgmt. com. & exec. com. Mem.: Pitts. Legal Administrators Assn., Pa. Inst. CPAs, Assn. Legal Administrators, Am. Inst. CPAs. Office: Reed Smith LLP 435 Sixth Ave Pittsburgh PA 15219 Office Phone: 412-288-4232. Office Fax: 412-288-3063. Business E-Mail: gsokulski@reedsmith.com.

**SOLA, AUGUSTO,** pediatrician, educator; m. Marta Rogido; children: Mariana, Carolina, Augusto Jr., Ignacio. BS (Bilingual), Belgrano Day Sch., Buenos Aires, Argentina, 1967; MD, Buenos Aires Nat. U. Sch. of Medicine, Argentina, 1973. Dir. neonatal clin. services U. of Calif., San Francisco, 1991—97, prof. pediat., 1995—97; dir. divsn. of neonatology Cedars-Sinai Med. Ctr., LA, 1997—2001; prof. pediat. U. of Calif., LA, 1997—2001; dir. divsn. of neonatal-perinatal medicine Emory U. Sch. of Medicine, Atlanta, 2001, co-director, devel. progress clinic, 2001—, prof. pediat. and obstetric-

s,gynecology (tenured), Goddard scholar, 2001—. Prof. pediat., dir. neonatology U. Buenos Aires, 1985—91; dir. neonatal fellowship program Cedars-Sinai Med. Ctr., LA, 1998—2001; cons. Am. Assn. of World Health, 1998—. Author: (book) Cuidados Intensivos Neonatales-Fisiopatologia y Terapeutica, Cuidados Especiales del Feto y Recien Nacido, Fisipatologia y Terapeutica, (manuscript) Jour. of Pediats. Nominee Ten Outstanding Young Profl. of the World, Internat. Jr. Chamber, 1989; recipient E.H. Christopherson award on Internat. Child Health, Am. Acad. of Pediat., 1999. Fellow: Am. Acad. of Pediat.; mem.: AAAS, Am. Acad. of Pediat. Sect. on Internat. Child Health, Soc. of Pediatric Rsch. Office: Emory Univ 2040 Ridgewood Dr Atlanta GA 30322 E-mail: asola2@emory.edu.

**SOLA, JURE,** electronics executive; BSEE, San Jose State U., 1972. Various mgmt. positions Lika Corp., Stockton, Calif., 1972-80; co-founder, held various mgmt. positions Sanmina Corp. and predecessor, 1980—, now pres. & chmn., 1991—2001; co-chmn. Sanmina-SCI, 1999—2002, CEO, 2001—, chmn., 2002—. Recipient Ernst & Young Master Entrepreneur of Yr. award, 2004. Office: Sanmina Corp 2700 N 1st St San Jose CA 95134-2015*

**SOLA, SRIKANTH,** cardiologist; s. Venkateswara Rao and Vasantha Lakshmi Sola; m. Ramya Ravindran, June 4, 1998; 1 child, Sridhar. BS, Stanford U., 1993; MD summa cum laude, U. Louisville, 1998. Diplomate Am. Bd. Internal Medicine. Resident in internal medicine Duke U. Med. Ctr., Durham, NC, 1999—2001; chief fellow divsn. of cardiology Emory U. Sch. of Medicine, Atlanta, 2004—05; assoc. staff cardiologist Cleve. Clinic Found., 2005—. Contbr. articles to profl. jours. Recipient George P. Caldwell award in internal medicine, U. Louisville Sch. of Medicine, 1998, Peter K. Knoefel award in pharmacology, 1998, Frank Lecocq award for best sr. resident lecture in internal medicine, Duke U. Med. Ctr., 2001, Young Investigator's award, Am. Coll. Cardiology, 2004. Mem.: AMA, Am. Heart Assn., N.Am. Soc. for Cardiovasc. Imaging, Soc. for Cardiovasc. Magnetic Resonance, Am. Coll. Cardiology, Alpha Omega Alpha. Achievements include patents for Angiotensin receptor blockers and alpha-lipoic acid in the metabolic syndrome. Avocations: community service, hiking, hatha yoga. Office: Cleve Clin Found Dept Cardiovasc Medicine Desk F-15 9500 Euclid Ave Cleveland OH 44195

**SOLÁ, VICTORIA M.,** announcer, writer; b. Englewood, N.J., Nov. 11, 1952; d. Salvador Felix and Hedda Blanc (Westhead) Solá; 1 child, Frank Salvador Solá Grillo. Student, Fairleigh Dickinson U., N.J., 1970—72. Radio host and prodr. jazz WFDU-FM Radio, Teaneck, NJ, 1981—83, jazz dir., 1982—86, radio host and prodr. Latin, 1983—, Latin music dir., 1983—. Contbg. editor Descarga Catalog, N.Y.C., 1996—2002; columnist Latin Beat Mag., Gardena, Calif., 1998, Latin London Mag., 1999; Latin jazz planning com. adv. Smithsonian Inst. Traveling Exhbn. Svc., Washington, 1999—2002, narrator, 2002. Coord. ann. on-air fundraiser for Latin music programming WFDU-FM, Teaneck, NJ, 1983—; participant on-air blood donor drive Bergen Cmty. Regional Blood Ctrs., Paramus, NJ, 1986; vol. fund raiser Operation Rescue North Shore Animal League Am., 2006. Mem.: Internat. Latin Music Hall of Fame (adv. com. 1999—, Spl. Recognition award 2001). Democrat. Avocations: reading, photography, drawing, writing. Office: WFDU-FM 1000 River Rd Teaneck NJ 07666 Office Phone: 201-692-2806 ext. 10. Office Fax: 201-692-2807. E-mail: vickisola1@aol.com.

**SOLAND, NORMAN R.,** corporate lawyer; b. Duluth, Minn., Oct. 17, 1940; m. Carol A. Isaacson, Aug. 29, 1964; children: Kirk, Lisa, Kari, Chad. BA, U. Minn., 1963; JD, Am. Univ., 1972. Bar: Minn. 1973. Analyst CIA, 1963-73; assoc. Thompson, Hessian, Fletcher, McKasy & Soderberg, Thompson, Fletcher, Stone & Morse, 1973-79; gen. counsel Nash-Finch Co., Mpls., 1979-84, asst. sec., counsel, 1984-86, sec., gen counsel, 1986-88, v.p., sec. & gen. counsel, 1988-98, sr. v.p., sec., gen. counsel, 1998—. Mem. ABA, Minn. State Bar Assn., Hennepin County Bar Assn., Am. Corp. Counsel Assn. Office: Nash Finch Co PO Box 355 Minneapolis MN 55440-0355

**SOLANO, CARL ANTHONY,** lawyer; b. Mar. 26, 1951; s. Nick D. and Catherine A. (Occhiato) S.; m. Nancy M. Randazzo, 1989; children: Melanie A., Carla Nicole. BS magna cum laude, U. Scranton, 1973; JD cum laude, Villanova U., 1976. Bar: Pa. 1976, U.S. Dist. Ct. (ea. dist.) Pa. 1978, U.S. Ct. Appeals (3d cir.) 1980, U.S. Ct. Appeals (5th cir.) 1981, U.S. Supreme Ct. 1982, U.S. Ct. Appeals (9th cir.) 1986, U.S. Dist. Ct. (mid. dist.) Pa. 1988, U.S. Ct. Appeals (6th cir.) 1988, U.S. Ct. Appeals (7th cir.) 1989, U.S. Ct. Appeals (6th cir.) 1988, U.S. Ct. Appeals (7th cir.) 1996. Law clk. Hon. Alfred L. Luongo U.S. Dist. Ct. (ea. dist.) Pa., Phila., 1976—78; assoc. Schnader, Harrison, Segal & Lewis, Phila., 1978—84, ptnr., 1985—. Adj. prof. Villanova U. Sch. Law, 1999—2001. Mem.: ABA, Justinian Soc., St. Thomas More Soc., Phila. Bar Assn. (chair bar news media com. 2003), Pa. Bar Assn. (statutory law com. 1980—95), Am. Law Inst., Order of Coif, Pi Gamma Mu. Roman Catholic. Home: 5 Barrister Ct Haverford PA 19041-1137 Office: Schnader Harrison Segal & Lewis LLP 1600 Market St Ste 3600 Philadelphia PA 19103-7287 Office Phone: 215-751-2202. Business E-Mail: CSolano@Schnader.com.

**SOLANO, HENRY L.,** lawyer; m. Janine Solano; children: Mateo, Amalia, Guadalupe. BS in Mech. Engring., U. Denver; JD, U. Colo.; LLD (hon.), U. Denver. Asst. atty. gen. Human Resources divsn. Colo. Dept. Law, 1977-82; asst. U.S. atty. Dist. Colo., 1982-87; U.S. atty. for Colo. U.S. Dept. Justice, Denver, 1994-98; solicitor U.S. Dept. Labor, Washington, 1998-2001; ptnr. LeBoeuf, Lamb, Greene & MacRae L.L.P., Denver, 2001—. Exec. dir. Colo. Dept. Instns., 1987-91, Colo. Dept. Regulatory Agys., 1987; acting exec. dir Colo. Dept. Corrections, 1989-90; chair Cabinet Coun. on Families and Children, 1990-91; mem. adv. com. U.S. Atty. Gen., 1994-95; lectr. Kennedy Sch. Govt. Bd. dirs. Nat. Latino Children's Inst., Mex.Am. Legal Def. Edn. Fund, Denver Housing Authority, Denver Women's Commn., Colo. Dept. Social Svcs., Colo. Transit Constrn. Authority, Regional Transit Dist. Office: 1875 Coon Ave NW Ste 1200 Washington DC 20009-5728 Office Phone: 202-986-8056. E-mail: hsolano@llgm.com.

**SOLANO, JULIO RAFAEL,** priest, educator; b. Barranquilla, Atlantico, Colombia, Sept. 12, 1946; came to U.S., 1971; s. Domingo Rafael Solano and Christine Balderrama. Degree in acctg., Centro Intensificacion Comml., Bogota, Colombia, 1970; BA, St. John Vianney Coll. Sem., Miami, Fla., 1989; MDiv, St. Vincent de Paul Regl. Sem., Boynton Beach, Fla., 1993. Transitional deacon St. Louis Cath. Ch., Miami, 1992—93; asst. pastor St. Elizabeth Cath. Ch., Pompano Beach, Fla., St. Patrick Cath. Ch., Miami Beach, Fla., 1996—98; parochial vicar St. Coleman Cath. Ch., Pompano Beach, 1998—99, St. Elizabeth of Hungary Cath. Ch., Pompano Beach, 1999—2001, St. Vincent Cath. Ch., Margate, Fla., 2001—02; pastor Our Lady Queen of Heaven Cath. Ch., North Lauderdale, Fla., 2002—06, Little Flower Cath. Ch., Hollywood, Fla., 2006—. Tchr. La Salle H.S., Miami, 1996-98; asst. chaplain Serra Club Internat. Pompano Beach, 1994-95. Mem. KC, Assn. Sacerdotes Hispanos. Democrat. Roman Catholic. Avocations: travel, reading, writing, stamps, coins. Office Phone: 954-922-3517. Personal E-mail: frsolano@bellsouth.net.

**SOLARO, ROSS JOHN,** physiologist, biophysicist; b. Wadsworth, Ohio, Jan. 9, 1942; s. Ross and Lena (Chuppa) S.; m. Kathleen Marie Cole, Sept. 18, 1965; children: Christopher, Elizabeth. BS, U. Cin., 1965; PhD, U. Pitts., 1971. Asst. prof. Med. Coll. Va., Richmond, 1973-77; assoc. prof. pharmacology and physiology U. Cin., 1977-81, prof. pharmacology and cell biophysics, 1981-85, prof. physiology, 1981-88; prof. physiology, head U. Ill., Chgo., 1988—, disting. univ. prof., 1998—. Sec. gen. Internat. Soc. Heart Rsch., 1989-93, sec./treas., 1995-98, pres., 1999; assoc. chair dept. physiology U. Cin., 1987-88. Editor: Protein Phosphorylation in Heart Muscle, 1986, Handbook of Physiology: The Heart, 2001; co-editor Handbook of Physiology: The Heart, 2001; contbr. articles to profl. jours. including Nature, Jour. Biol. Chemistry, Circulation Rsch. Chmn. rsch. coun. Am. Heart Assn., Met. Chgo., 1990-92. Grantee NIH, 1977—, Fogarty fellow, 1986; Brit. Am. Heart fellow Am. Heart Assn., 1974-75; Sr. Internat. fellow U. Coll. London, 1987.

Mem. Am. Physiol. Soc. (chmn. subgroup), Am. Soc. Pharm. Exptl. Therapeutics, Biophys. Soc. (chmn. subgroup 1983-84). Office: U Ill at Chgo MC901 Physiology & Biophysics 835 S Wolcott Ave Chicago IL 60612-7340 Business E-Mail: solarorj@uic.edu.

**SOLARZ, ALAN H.,** lawyer; BS magna cum laude, SUNY, Albany, 1978; JD cum laude, SUNY, Buffalo, 1983; LLM, NYU, 1987. Bar: NY 1984, US Tax Ct. 1984, US Dist. Ct., So. and Ea. Dists. NY 1992. Ptnr., group co-leader Tax Advice and Controversy Bryan Cave LLP, NYC. Office: Bryan Cave LLP 1290 Ave of the Americas New York NY 10104 Office Phone: 212-541-2075. E-mail: ahsolarz@bryancave.com.

**SOLBERG, ELIZABETH TRANSOU,** public relations executive; b. Dallas, Aug. 10, 1939; d. Ross W. and Josephine V. (Perkins) Transou; m. Frederick M. Solberg Jr., Mar. 8, 1969; 1 son, Frederick W. BJ, U. Mo., 1961. Reporter Kansas City (Mo.) Star, 1963-70, asst. city editor, 1970-73; reporter spl. events, documentaries Sta. WDAF-TV, Kansas City, Mo., 1973-74; prof. dept. journalism Park Coll., Kansas City, Mo., 1975-76, advisor, 1976-79; mng. ptnr. Fleishman-Hillard Inc., Kansas City, Mo., then exec. v.p., sr. ptnr., gen. mgr. Kansas City br., now regional pres., sr. ptnr.; pres. Fleishman-Hillard/Can., 1994—99. Mem. Kansas City Commn. Planned Indsl. Expansion Authority, 1974-91; bd. dirs. Ferrellgas, Midwest Airlines. Mem. long range planning com. Heart of Am. coun. Boy Scouts Am., 1980-82, bd. dirs., 1986-89; mem. Clay County (Mo.) Devel. Commn., 1979-88; bd. govs. Citizens Assn., 1975—; mem. exec. com. bd. Kansas City Area Devel. Coun., 1989-96, co-chair, 1991-93; trustee Pembroke Hill Sch., 1987-93, U. Kansas City, 1990-2002, exec. com., 1992-2002, Midwest Rsch. Inst., 1995-2002; bd. dirs. Greater Kansas City Cmty. Found. and Affiliated Trusts, 1996-2005, Starlight Theatre, 1996-2002, Union Sta. Bd., 1998-2002, Mo. Devel. Fin. Bd., 2000—, chair, 2003—; regent Rockhurst Coll., 1984-96, active Rus. Coun., Nelson Gallery Found., Nelson-Atkins Mus. Art, 1990—; bd. dirs. Civic Coun. Greater Kansas City, 1992—, chair civic coun., 2003-2005; mem. Jr. League Kansas City. Recipient award for contbn. to mental health Mo. Psychiat. Assn., 1973, Arthur E. Lowell award for excellence in orgn. comm. Kansas City/IABC, 1985, Kansas City Spirit award Gillis Ctr., 1994. Mem. Pub. Rels. Soc. Am. (nat. honors and awards com., co-chmn. SilverAnvil com. 1983, Silver Anvil award 1979-82, chair nat. membership com. 1989-91, assembly bd.-at-large 1995-96), Counselor's Acad. (exec. com. 1991-92), Mo. C. of C. Pub. Rels. Coun., Greater Kans. City C. of C. (chair 1994-95, bd. exec. com.), River Club, Carriage Club. Office: Fleishman Hillard Inc 2405 Grand Blvd Ste 700 Kansas City MO 64108-2522

**SOLBERG, MARY ANN,** federal official; Grad., Western Mich. U. Dep. dir. Office Nat. Drug Control Policy Exec. Office of Pres., Washington, 2001—; exec. dir. Coalition of Health Comtys., Troy (Mich.) Cmty. Coalition for Prevention of Drug and Alcohol Abuse; various positions Troy Adult and Cmty. Edn., 1977—91. Mem. adv. com. to develop a nat. prevention sys. Nat. Ctr. for Substance Abuse Prevention; mem. adv. com. Nat. Ad Coun.'s Cmty. Anti-Drug Campaign; mem. Pres.'s Commn. on Drug-Free Cmtys., 1998, co-chairperson. Office: Exec Office of Pres Office Nat Drug Control Policy 750 17th St NW Washington DC 20503

**SOLBERG, WINTON UDELL,** historian, educator; b. Aberdeen, SD, Jan. 11, 1922; s. Ole Alexander and Bertha Georgia (Tschappat) S.; m. Ruth Constance Walton, Nov. 8, 1952; children— Gail Elizabeth, Andrew Walton, Kristin Ruth. AB magna cum laude, U. S.D., 1943, LHD (hon.), 1987; student, Biarritz Am. U., France, 1946; A.M., Harvard, 1947, PhD, 1954. Instr., then asst. prof. social scis. U.S. Mil. Acad., 1951-54; instr., then asst. prof. history Yale U., 1954-58; fellow Pierson Coll., 1955-58, Morse fellow, 1958; James Wallace prof. history Macalester Coll., 1958-62; vis. prof. U. Ill. 1961-62, assoc. prof. history, 1962, prof., 1967—, chmn. dept. history, 1970-72. Rsch. fellow Ctr. Study History of Liberty in Am., Harvard U., 1962-63; rsch. scholar Henry E. Huntington Library, San Marino, Calif., 1959; dir. Coe Found. Am. Studies Inst., summers 1960-62; lectr., cons. Army War Coll., 1959-62; lectr. U.S. Command and Gen. Staff Sch., 1963-64; Fulbright lectr. Johns Hopkins U. Bologna, 1967-68, Moscow (USSR) State U., 1978, U. Calcutta India, 1993; vis. prof. Konan U., Kobe, Japan, 1981; USIA Lectr., Korea and Malaysia, 1985, Korea, 1992. Author: The Federal Convention and the Formation of the Union of the American States, 1958, The Constitutional Convention and the Formation of the Union, 1990, The University of Illinois, 1867-1894, An Intellectual and Cultural History, 1968, Redeem the Time: The Puritan Sabbath in Early America, 1977, History of American Thought and Culture, 1983, Cotton Mather, The Christian Philosopher, 1994, The University of Illinois, 1894-1904: The Shaping of the University, 2000; also articles. Mem. Ill. Humanities Council, 1973-75; sec. Council on Study of Religion, 1981-85. Maj. inf. AUS, 1943-46, 51-54; lt. col. U.S. Army Res. Recipient Faculty Achievement award Burlington No. Found., 1986, Disting. Teaching award U. Ill. Coll. Liberal Arts and Scis., 1988; NEH sr. fellow, 1974-75; Rsch. grantee NSF, 1981-82 Mem. Am. Hist. Assn., So. Hist. Assn., Orgn. Am. Historians, Am. Studies Assn. (pres. Mid-Am. 1985-86), Am. Soc. Ch. History (pres. 1985-86), AAUP (chpt. pres. 1965-66, mem. council 1969-72, 1st v.p. 1974-76), Phi Beta Kappa. Episcopalian. Home: 8 Lake Park Rd Champaign IL 61822-7101 Office: U Ill History Dept Urbana IL 61801 Office Phone: 217-333-4193. Business E-Mail: wsolberg@uiuc.edu.

**SOLBRIG, HAROLD RALPH,** systems analyst; s. Alfred William and Doris Solbrig; m. Barbara Christine Baldwin, June 21, 1985; children: William, Sarah Elizabeth, Mary Katherine. BS, Westminster Coll., 1993. Sr. systems analyst 3M, Salt Lake City, 1989—99; tech. specialist Mayo Clinic, Rochester, Minn., 1999—. Editor, primary author: OMG Terminology Query Services (TQS) Standard, ANSI/HL7 Common Terminology Services Specification. Named Vol. of Yr., Health Level Seven, 2005; named to Cir. of Tech. Excellence, 3M, 1990. Achievements include design and development of the lexical grid, a federated, distributed ontology and terminology publishing system, Home 781 Shenandoah Ln NW Rochester MN 55901 Office: Mayo Clinic 200 First Street SW Rochester MN 55905 Office Phone: 507-284-0753. Business E-Mail: solbrig@mayo.edu.

**SOLBRIG, INGEBORG HILDEGARD,** literature educator, writer; b. Weissenfels, Germany, July 31, 1923; arrived in U.S., 1961, naturalized, 1966; d. Reinhold J. and Hildegard M. A. (Ferchland) Solbrig. Grad. in chemistry, U. Halle, Germany, 1948; student, Delmar Coll., 1961; BA summa cum laude, San Francisco State U., 1964; postgrad., U. Calif., Berkeley, 1964-65; MA, Stanford U., 1966, PhD in Humanities and German, 1969. Asst. prof. U. R.I., 1969-70, U. Tenn., Chattanooga, 1970-72, U. Ky., Lexington, 1972-75; assoc. prof. German U. Iowa, 1975-81, prof., 1981-93, prof. emerita, 1993—. Domestic and abroad lectr.; former presenter The Light from the East, Coptic Christians/Egypt, 2004. Author: Hammer-Purgstall und Goethe, 1973, Orient-Rezeption, 1996, Orient-Rezeption, Fischer Lexikon Literatur, 1996, 2d edit., 2000, Modulationen von Gold und Licht in Goethes Kunstmärchen, 1997, Momentaufnahmen, 2000, J.G. Herder: Echo of the Cultural Philospher's Ideas in Early African-American Intellectual Writing, 2000, Maria Sibylla Merian..., 2001, The Light from the East: The Coptic Christians of Egypt; main editor: Rilke Heute, Beziehungen und Wirkungen, 1975; editor (and translator): Reinhard Goering: Seeschlacht/Seabattle, 1977; mem. editl. bd.: Kairoer Germanistische Studien, vol. 9 & 10, 1998; contbr. articles to profl. jours., chpts. to books. Mem. Iowa Gov.'s Com. 300th Anniversary German-Am. Rels. 1683-1983, 1983. Named Ky. Col., 1975; recipient Hammer-Purgstall Gold medal, Austria, 1974; fellow, Stanford U., 1965—66, 1968—69, Austrian Ministry Edn., 1968—69; Delta Phi Alpha Deutsche Ehrenverbindung, U. Ky., 1973, Old Gold fellow, Iowa, 1977, Am. Coun. Learned Socs. grantee, German Acad. Exch. Svc. grantee, 1980, Sr. Faculty Rsch. fellow in humanities, 1983, NEH grantee, 1985, May Brodbeck fellow in humanities, 1989, numerous summer faculty rsch. grants. Mem.: MLA (life), Soc. for History Alchemy and Chemistry, Internat. Herder Soc. (founding mem.), Goethe Soc. N.Am. Inc., Can. Soc. 18th Century Studies, Am. Soc. 18th Century Studies, Deutsche Schiller Gesellschaft, Goethe Gesellschaft, Internat. Vereinigung fur Germanische Sprach und Lit. Wiss., Egyptian Soc. Lit. Criticism (hon.), World Peace and Diplomacy Forum (life).

Avocations: horseback riding, photography, writing, travel, theology. Home and Office: 1126 Pine St Iowa City IA 52240-5711 *The circumstances of my life took me to many places and cultures. Despite the discord and problems plaguing many parts of this planet, let us not forget that it's the home of the human family, our home. Always remember: Life is, by definition, change.*

**SOLDAN, ANGELIKA,** political science educator, philosopher; b. Hennigsdorf, Germany, Feb. 10, 1953; d. Hans and Erika Potempa; m. Wolfgang Karl Soldan, May 8, 1987; 1 child, Anja Soldan. MA in Philosophy, Humboldt U., 1975, PhD, 1990, Martin Luther U., Halle-Wittenberg, Germany, 1982. Assoc. prof. philosophy, polit. ethics Humboldt U., Berlin, 1989-91; adj. prof. philosophy, ethics, govt. U. Tex., Brownsville, 1991-98, lectr. social issues and philosophy, 1999—2000, asst. prof., 2000—05, assoc. prof., 2005—. Contbr. articles to profl. jours. Co-founder Gesellschaft für Solidarische Entwicklungszusammenarbeit, 1990. Mem. Am. Philos. Assn., Internat. Fromm Soc., Internat. Nietzsche Soc., Internat. Assn. Women in Philosophy. Office: U Tex Brownsville 80 Fort Brown St Brownsville TX 78520 Office Phone: 956-882-8890. E-mail: angelika.soldan@utb.edu.

**SOLDNER, PAUL EDMUND,** artist, ceramist, educator; b. Summerfield, Ill. s. Grover and Beulah (Geiger) S.; m. Virginia I. Geiger, June 15, 1947; 1 child, Stephanie. BA, Bluffton Coll., 1946; MA, L. Colo., 1954; MFA, L.A. County Art Inst., 1956; DFA (hon.), Westminster Coll., 1992. Tchr. art Medina (Ohio) County Schs., 1946-47; supr. art, asst. county supr. Wayne County Schs., Wooster, Ohio, 1951-54; tchr. adult edn. Wooster Coll., 1952-54; vis. asst. prof. ceramics Scripps Coll., 1957-66, prof., 1970-91, prof. emeritus, 1991. Prof. Claremont (Calif.) Grad. Sch., 1957-66, prof., 1970-92; prof. U. Colo., Boulder, 1966-67, U. Iowa, Iowa City, 1967-68, pres. Soldner Pottery Equipment, Inc., Aspen, Colo., 1956-77; mem. steering com. Internat. Sch. Ceramics, Rome, 1965-77; advisor Vols. for Internat. Assistance, Balt. 1966-75; craftsman, trustee Am. Craft Coun., N.Y.C., 1970-74, trustee emeritus, 1976-77; dir. U.S. sect. World Craft Coun., 1970-74; dir. Anderson Ranch Ctr. for Hand Art Sch., 1974-76; speaker 6th Internat. Ceramics Symposium Syracuse, 1989; participant Internat. Russian Artists Exchange Program, Riga, Latvia, 1989; cons. in field. Author: Kilns and Their Construction, 1965, Raku, 1964, Paul Soldner, A Retrospective View, 1991; contbr. articles to profl. jours.; subject of 5 films; 156 one-man shows including Cantini Mus. Modern Art, Marseille, France, 1981, Thomas Segal Gallery, Boston, 1982, Elements Gallery, N.Y., 1983, Louis Newman Gallery, L.A., 1985, Susan Cummins Gallery, Mill Valley, Calif., 1989, Great Am. Gallery, Atlanta, 1986, Patricia Moore Gallery, Aspen Colo., 1987, Coleg Prifysgol Cymru, Aberystwyth, Wales, 1987, Joan Hodgell Gallery, Sarasota, Fla., 1988, Esther Saks Gallery, Chgo., 1986, 88, El Camino Gallery Art, Toraance, Calif., 1987, San Antonio Art Ctr., San Angelo, Tex., 1988, traveling exhibit, 12 U.S. mus., 1992—, Besson Gallerie, London, 1996, Bernard Palissy Mus., France, 1996; 335 group shows including Nelson-Atkins Mus., Kansas City, Mo., 1983, Los Angeles Mcpl. Art Gallery, 1984, 27th Ceramic Nat. Exhibition, Everson Mus. Art, Syracuse, N.Y., 1986, Victoria & Albert Mus., London, 1986, Chicago Internat. New Art Forms Exposition, 1986, Hanover Gallery, Syracuse, N.Y., 1987, L.A. County Mus. of Art, 1987, Crain/Wolov Gallery, Tulsa, 1987, Contem Crafts Gallery, Portland, Oreg., 1988, Oakland (Calif.) Art Mus., 1988, Munson Gallery, Santa Fe, 1988, Japanese Influence on Am. Ceramics, Everson Mus., Syracuse, N.Y., 1989, traveling retrospective, 1991-93; hon. vis. artist Shigaraki Ceramic Cultural Park, Japan, 1994; works in permanent collections, Nat. Mus. Modern Art, Kyoto, Japan, Victoria and Albert Mus., London, Smithsonian Instn., Washington, Los Angeles County Mus. Art, Oakland Art Mus., Everson Mus. Art, Syracuse Australian Nat. Gallery, Taipei Fine Arts Mus.; curator Mirror Images Exhibit, Craft Alliance Gallery, St. Louis, 1989. Served with U.S. Army, 1941-46. Decorated Purple Heart; grantee NEA, 1991, Louis Comfort Tiffany Found., 1966, 72, Nat. Endowment for Arts, 1976, Colo. Gov.'s award for the Arts & Humanities, 1975; voted one of Top Twelve Potters World-Wide, Ceramics Monthly mag., 1981; Scripps Coll. Faculty Recognition award, 1985; named Hon. Mem. Coun., Nat. Coun. on Edn. for Ceramic Arts, 1989. Fellow Collequum of Craftsmen of the U.S.; mem. Internat. Acad. Ceramics, Nat. Coun. on Edn. for Ceramic Arts. Achievements include being the originator of Am. Raku philosophy and techniques in ceramics. Home: PO Box 90 Aspen CO 81612-0090

**SOLE, MICHAEL JOSEPH,** cardiologist; b. Timmins, Ont., Can., Mar. 5, 1940; s. Fred and Lillian Sole; m. Susan Karen Samuels, May 26, 1964; children: David Frederick, Leslie Meredith. BSc, U. Toronto, Ont., Can., 1962, MD, 1966. Cert. Coll. Physicians and Surgeons Ont.; diplomate Am. Bd. Internal Medicine. Rotating intern, jr. asst. resident, sr. asst. resident in internal medicine Toronto Gen. Hosp., 1966-69; cardiology fellow Cardiovasc. Rsch. Inst., U. Calif., San Francisco, 1969-71; cardiology fellow Peter Bent Brigham Hosp., Boston, 1971-73; jr. asst. medicine, 1973-74; rsch. assoc. MIT, Cambridge, 1973-74; instr. medicine Harvard Med. Sch., 1973-74; from asst. to assoc. prof. medicine U. Toronto, 1974-83, prof. medicine and physiology, 1983—, mem. staff inst. med. sci., 1978—, dir. cardiology rsch., 1987-89, dir. centre cardiovasc. rsch., 1989-99, Searle chair cardiovasc. rsch., 1998—; staff cardiologist Toronto Hosp., 1974-89, dir. non-invasive cardiology 1974-79, dir. cardiology rsch., 1979-89, dir. divsn. cardiology, 1989-98, dir. cardiovasc. program, 1992—97, dir. Peter Munk Cardiac Ctr., 1992-97. Vis. prof. Harvard U., 1975, NIH, Bethesda, Md., 1981, U. B.C., 1982, 91, 92, Capital Med. Sch. and Beijing Hosp., 1985, U. Tokyo, 1992, others; mem. Can. Govt. Task Force Diagnostic Ultrasound, 1976-78; vice-chmn. econs. com. dept. medicine Toronto Gen. Hosp., 1977, chmn., 1978, 79, chmn. emeritus, 1980, mem. various coms., 1981-98, chmn. cardiology rsch. com., 1988-89, mem. cardiovasc. collaborative practice group, 1989-92; rsch. assoc. Ont. Heart Found., 1979-89; assoc. rsch. inst. pediat. Hosp. Sick Children, Toronto, 1979—; mem. med. staff Mt. Sinai Hosp., Toronto, 1979—; mem. adv. bd. Merck Pharms., 1983— Roots Pharms 1992-93; mem. Health Rsch. inst. Devel. Coun., Province of Ont., 1983-86, mem. exec. com., 1984-86; Levesque lectr. Montreal Heart Inst., 1984; mem. cardiovasc. panel Med. Rsch. Coun. Can., 1985-87; mem. heart and blood vessel rsch. adv. com. Toronto Hosp., 1986-89; chmn. cardiovasc. rsch. adv. com. faculty medicine U. Toronto, 1986-87, mem. various coms., 1987—, chmn. rsch. com. dept. medicine, 1987-88, mem. rsch. adv. bd., 1989-97, chair life scis. com., 1990-92, chair decanal promotions com. faculty medicine, 1992-94; mem. Centre Cardiovasc. Rsch., 1998-99, chmn. sci. com., 1989-99, mem. exec. com. cardiovasc. clin. rsch. lab., 1992-99, chmn. rsch. com., 1992-99; Pfizer vis. fellow Clin. Rsch. Inst., Montreal, 1988; mem. sr. adv. com. Toronto Western Hosp., 1989-90; Katz vis. prof. U. Chgo., 1989; mem. provincial working group cardiovasc. svcs. Ministry of Health, 1990-91, mem. ctrl. east region cardiovasc. patient care mgmt. group, 1990-91; mem. trial devel. com. diabetes atherosclerosis intervention study WHO and Fournier Pharms., 1991-93, mem. trial exec. com., 1993-2000; mem. Joint Med. Rsch. Coun. Can./Pharm. Mfrs. Assn. Can. Adv. Com. Sci., 1993; mem. organizing coms. various sci. meetings; presenter in field. Mem. editl. bd. Can. Jour. Cardiology, 1988—, Index and Revs. Congestive Heart Failure, 1988-90, Hypertension Can., 1988-90, European Jour. Pharmacology, 1992-96, Cardiosci., 1993, Jour. Heart Failure, 1994—, Circulation, 1996—, Jour. Molecular Medicine, 1996—, Jour. Molecular Cell Cardiology, 1999-2001; mem. internat. editl. bd. Cardiology Digest, 1992—; contbr. chpts. to books and articles to profl. jours.; patentee in field. Recipient Robert Beamish Leadership award, Inst. CV Sci., U. Man., 2001; fellow Ivan Smith Rsch. fellow, U. Toronto, 1964, Hunter fellow, Ont. Heart Found., 1973; grantee Grantee, Heart & Stroke Found. Ont., 1969—; Med. Rsch. Coun. Can., 1982—92, 1994—97; scholar Walter Watkins scholar, U. Toronto, 1962. Fellow Am. Coll. Cardiology (abstract reviewer 1989, 91), Royal Coll. Physicians and Surgeons, Can. Acad. Health Sci.; mem. Am. Soc. Clin. Investigation, Assn. Am. Physicians, Am. Heart Assn. (fellow couns. clin. cardiology, hypertension, circulation and basic sci., mem. exec., basic sci. coun. 1986-89, mem. Katz prize selection com. 1988-90), Can. Inst. Acad. Medicine, Can. Soc. Clin. Investigation, Can. Cardiovasc. Soc. (mem. young investigators award panel 1982-84, mem. student presentation award com. 1988-90, mem. nat. task force cardiovasc. sci. 1992-93, Ann. Rsch. award 1975, Rsch. Achievement award 1989), Heart and Stroke Found. Can. (mem. sci. rev. bd. 1976-79, vice-chmn. 1980-83, chmn.

hypertension and cardiovasc. pharmacology panel 1982-83, chmn. molecular biology, biochemistry, pathology panel 1989-90), Can. Med. Assn. (mem. coun. 1982-87), Am. Fedn. Clin. Rsch., Ont. Med. Assn. (alt. del. Toronto Gen. Hosp. bd. 1988-90), Heart and Stroke Found. Ont. (mem. med. rsch. com. 1978-81, bd. dirs. 1986-92, 96—, mem. fin. com. 1986-90, 96-97, mem. corp. rels. com. 1990-92, mem. rsch. policy com. 1991-93, 96-97, chmn. 1997-99, mem. exec. com. 1997-99, nomination com. 1997-99, chmn. 50th anniversary com., mem. audit com., Disting. Rsch. Prof. 1998-99, Murray Robertson Meml. lectr. 1989), Internat. Soc. Heart Rsch. (exec. Am. sect. 1979-88, lectr. Latin Am. sect. 1995), Banting Rsch. Found. (hon. sec.-treas. 1979-81), Gairdner Found. (mem. rev. panel 1979-94), Heart Failure Soc. Am. (publs. com. 2000-03, nominating com. 2001-04), Maple Downs Golf and Country Club (Toronto; bd dirs 2001—, exec. bd. 2003—), Alpha Omega Alpha. Office: Toronto Gen Hosp Eaton 585 University Ave Rm 4N488 Toronto ON Canada M5G 2N2 Office Phone: 416-340-3471. Business E-Mail: michael.sole@uhn.on.ca.

**SOLECKI, R. STEFAN,** anthropologist, educator; b. Bklyn., Oct. 15, 1917; s. Kazimierz John and Mary (Tarnawski) S.; m. Rose Muriel Lilien, June 24, 1955; children— John Irwin, William Duncan. B.Sc., City Coll. N.Y., 1941; MA, Columbia, 1950, PhD in Anthropology, 1958. Archaeologist Smithsonian Instn., 1948-54; archaeol. asst. anthropology Columbia U., N.Y.C., 1954-55, mem. faculty, 1959-88, prof. anthropology, 1965-88, prof. emeritus, 1989—, chmn. dept., 1975-78; adj. prof. dept. anthropology Tex. A&M Univ., College Station, 1989—; assoc. curator old world U.S. Nat. Mus., 1957-59. Archael. expdns. to Alaska, 1949, 61, Iraq, 1950-51, 53, 56-57 (field dir.), 60, 78, Sudanese Nubia, 1961, Turkey, 1963, Syria, 1963, 64, 65, 88, 89, Iran, 1968, Lebanon, 1969-73, France, 1975, Ea., Midwestern and Western U.S.; collaborator in archaeology Smithsonian Instn., 1953; cons. UNESCO, 1959. Served with AUS, 1943-45. Fulbright scholar, Iraq, 1952-53; William Bayard Cutting travelling fellow Columbia, 1956-57; Fulbright-Hays faculty research awardee Syria, 1980-81; Fulbright fellow, Iraq, 1988-89. Fellow Am. Anthrop. Assn., Arctic Inst. Am., N.Y. Acad. Scis. (chmn. anthropology sect. 1977-79); mem. N.Y. Archaeol. Assn. (pres. 1960-62), N.Y. Oriental Club (pres. 1965), Profl. Archeologists of N.Y.C. (pres. 1980-81), Soc. Archaeology, Am. Schs. Oriental Research (assoc. trustee 1969-71), Prehistoric Soc., Deutsches Archaeologisches Inst., Soc. Préhistorique Français, Archaeol. Inst. Am. (exec. com. 1968-70), Assn. Field Archaeology (pres. 1972-74). Home: 86 Park Pl South Orange NJ 07079-2303 Office: Columbia U Dept Anthropology New York NY 10027

**SOLENDER, MICHAEL S.,** lawyer; Bachelors summa cum laude, Columbia College; JD, Yale Law Sch. Gen. counsel Consumer Product Safety Commn.; ptnr. Arnold & Porter; sr. mng. dir., legal dept. Bear Stearns Cos. Inc., N.Y.C., 2002—04, gen. counsel, 2004—. Office: The Bear Stearn Cos Inc 383 Madison Ave New York NY 10179

**SOLENDER, ROBERT LAWRENCE,** retired real estate company executive, retired publishing executive; b. Rochester, NY, Sept. 1, 1923; s. Samuel S. and Catherine (Goldsmith) S.; m. Ellen Van Raalte Karelsen, Nov. 25, 1948; children: Elizabeth, Jefferson, Katherine. BA, Oberlin Coll., 1943. Asst. to pres. Craven & Hedrick, Inc., N.Y.C., 1946-49; with Dallas Times Herald, 1949-75, v.p., advt. dir., 1964-69, v.p., gen. mgr., 1969—71, v.p. sales, 1971—75; dir. NorthPark Nat. Bank, 1973—93; prin. Robert L. Solender & Assocs., Dallas, 1975—; mng. ptnr. The Devonshire Co., Dallas, 1978-95. Interim chmn., CEO, AccuBanc Mortgage Corp., 1992. Trustee SW Med. Found.; bd. dirs. Friends Dallas Pub. Libr.; pres. Dallas Child Guidence Clinic, 1956, Dallas Mental Health Assn., 1959, Hope Cottage Children's Bur., 1973; past bd. dirs. Dallas Theatre Ctr., Child Care Dallas, Tex. Mental Health Assn., Dallas Civic Music Assn., Dallas County United Way, exec. com.; adv. bd. Cmtys. Found. Tex.; assoc. Dallas Mus. Art. Mem.: Masons. Home: 9131 Devonshire Dr Dallas TX 75209-2411

**SOLENSTEN, JOHN MARTIN,** retired English and American studies educator, writer; b. Madelia, Minn., Sept. 16, 1929; s. Martin Christian and Agnes Lucille Solensten; children: Peter John, Peggy Ann. BA, Gustauvs Adophus U., 1951; PhD, Bowling Green State U., 1968. Asst. prof. Wittenberg U., Springfield, Ohio, 1964—68; assoc. prof. Mankato State U., Minn., 1968—74; prof., chmn. divsn. Concordia U., St. Paul, 1975—93; ret., 1993. Cultural rsch. Sons of Norway, Mpls., 1993—. Author: Good Thunder, 1985, The Boys of War (Turkey), 1992, In the Belly of the Horse, 2005, Swing, 2005, 2 short story collections, poetry chapbook, 3 plays; contbr. poems to lit. publs. Bd. dirs. Octagon Ctr. for Arts, Ames, Iowa, 1994—97. Sgt. U.S. Army, 1951—53, Korea. Recipient Minn. Voices award, New Rivers Press, 1983, award, Assoc. Writing Program, Fairfax, Va., 1985, Native Am. Play Camp award, 1985; Blandin grantee, 1993. Avocations: river exploration, writing. Home: 519 Oliver Cir Ames IA 50014

**SOLER, ESTA,** foundation administrator; Founder, pres. Family Violence Prevention Fund, 1980—. Cons. and adv. Dept. Justice, U.S. Dept. Health and Human Svcs., CDC, others; bd. dirs. The Ctr. on Fathers, Families and Pub. Policy. Co-author: Ending Domestic Violence: Changing Public Perceptions/Halting the Epidemic, 1997. Bd. dirs. Blue Shield Calif. Found., Bay Area United Way Safe Cmtys. Cabinet. Recipient Koret Israel Prize, 1989, Public Health Heroes award, U. Calif., 1998; fellow, Kellogg Found. Nat. Leadership, 1990. Office: 383 Rhode Island St Ste 304 San Francisco CA 94103-5133

**SOLET, MAXWELL DAVID,** lawyer; b. Washington, May 15, 1948; s. Leo and Pearl (Rose) S.; m. Joanne Marie Tolksdorf, Sept. 27, 1970; children: David Marc, Paul Jacob. AB, Harvard U., 1970, JD, 1974. Bar: Mass. 1974, U.S. Tax Ct. 1976, U.S. Ct. Claims 1976, U.S. Supreme Ct. 1976. Assoc. Gaston Snow & Ely Bartlett, Boston, 1974-79, Mintz, Levin, Cohn, Ferris, Glovsky & Popeo, P.C., Boston, 1979-82, ptnr., 1982—. Mem. IRS advisory com. on tax exempt and gov. entities, 2005—. Mem.: ABA, Cambridge Health Alliance (bd. mem. 2005—), Nat. Assn. Bond Lawyers (mem. steering com. bond atty.'s workshop 1992—95), Boston Bar Assn. (chmn. tax sect. 1987—89, mem. multidisciplinary practice task force 2000—01, mem. audit com. 2003—), Mass. Bar Assn., Cambridge Hist. Soc. (bd. mem. 1999—2000, sec. 2001—05, v.p. 2005—). Home: 15 Berkeley St Cambridge MA 02138-3409 Office: Mintz Levin Cohn Ferris Glovsky & Popeo PC One Financial Ctr Boston MA 02111 Office Phone: 617-348-1739. Business E-Mail: msolet@mintz.com.

**SOLEY, DAVID BENJAMIN,** composer; b. Ancón, Panama, July 11, 1962; arrived in U.S., 1979; s. Alfred T. Soley and Gladys S. Beckford. MusB, Calif. State U., Northridge, 1987; D in Musical Arts, Stanford U., 1993. Asst. prof. music Stanford (Calif.) U., 1995—99, Rice U., Houston, 1999—2001; composer N.Y.C., 2001—. Composer: (songs) Camaïeu, 1997, tondo (...unreceding on.), 2002, "...", 2003, Laberinto IV, 2004. With U.S. Army, 1980—83. Recipient award to student composers, Broadcast Music, Inc., 1986, 1987, Bearns prize, Columbia U., 1987; Guggenheim fellow, John Simon Guggenheim Meml. Found., 1993. Office: Church St Station PO Box 3360 New York NY 10008

**SOLEY, ROBERT LAWRENCE,** plastic surgeon; b. N.Y.C., Feb. 26, 1935; s. Max and Saide (Leader) S.; m. Judy Wasserman, June 16, 1963; children: John, Jill. BS, Yale U., 1956; MD, NYU, 1959. Diplomate Am. Bd. Surgery, Am. Bd. Plastic Surgery. Intern Bellevue Hosp., N.Y.C., 1955—60; resident in gen. surgery Mt. Sinai Hosp., N.Y.C., 1960—65; resident in plastic surgery Hosp. U. Pa., Phila., 1967—69; practice medicine specializing in plastic surgery White Plains, NY, 1969—. Mem. staff, mem. med. bd. White Plains Hosp., 1985—88, chief sect. plastic surgery, 1988—94. Contbr. articles to profl. jours. Capt. M.C., USAF, 1965-67. Grantee USPHS, 1968-69. Fellow ACS; mem. Am. Soc. Plastic Reconstructive Surgery, Am. Soc. Aesthetic Surgery, N.Y. State Med. Soc. (ho. of dels.), Westchester County Med. Soc.

(pres. 1996-97, bd. dirs.), Rotary (bd. dirs. White Plains chpt. 1982-85). Home: 30 Griffin Ave Scarsdale NY 10583-7661 Office: Associated Plastic Surgeons Westchester PC 30 Griffen Ave Scarsdale NY 10583-7661 E-mail: bob@soley.com.

**SOLGANIK, MARVIN,** real estate executive; b. Chgo., Nov. 7, 1930; s. Harry and Dora (Fastoff) S.; m. Judith Rosenberg, Sept. 11, 1960; children: Randall, Janet, Robert. BBA, Case Western Res. U., 1952. Real estate broker, Cleve., 1950-65, Herbert Laronge Inc., Cleve., 1965-68; sr. v.p. real estate Revco D.S., Inc., Twinsburgh, Ohio, 1968—, corp. dir., 1974—. Adj. prof. Ohio No. U.; guest lectr. Cleve. State U., Case Western Res. U. Sch. Law, Cuyahoga C.C., Ohio No. U., Cleve. Real Estate Bd., CASE Sch. Law. Vol. jewish Welfare Fund, Shaker heights, Ohio; chmn. capital and budget coms. Jewish Fedn.; chmn. Agnon Sch. Bdlg. Com.; bd. dirs. Bellfair-J.C.B.-Home for Emotionally Disturbed Children, Visconsi Cos. Cleve. Inst. Music. Recipient Appreciation award Am. Soc. Real Estate Appraisers, Akron-Cleve. chpt., 1971 Mem. Nat. Assn. Corp. Real Estate Officers, Internat. Council Shopping Ctrs. Office: D S Revco 22925 Holmwood Rd Shaker Heights OH 44122-3005

**SOLIDAY, MICHAEL DAVID,** secondary school and special educator; b. Durant, Okla., Feb. 25, 1955; s. David Norman and Patsy Marceille (Mansfield) S.; 7 foster children. BS in Edn., Utah State U., 1979; MEd in Deaf Edn., Western Md. Coll., Westminster, 1982; postgrad., Drake U., Des Moines, 1986. Itinerant tchr. for hearing impaired Heartland, AEA II, Des Moines, 1979-80, tchr. for hearing impaired, 1983-85, 86-87; tchr. Fla. Sch. for the Deaf, St. Augustine, 1982-83; liaison State of Iowa/Deaf Svcs., Des Moines, 1985-86; tchr. resource and 4th grade White Pine County Sch. Dist., Ely, Nev., 1987-94; tchr. h.s. deaf Brevard County Sch. Bd., Titusville, Fla., 1994—; resource tchr. White Pine County Sch. Dist., 1995—. Chairperson sch. improvement Nev. Dept. Edn., Ely, 1990-91. Soccer commr. Steptoe Valley Soccer Club, Ely, 1989-94, 95-96; foster parent Children's Svcs., State of Nev., 1989-93; bd. dirs. White Pine County Family Recreation Ctr., 1996—. Named Nev. Tchr. of the Yr., Dept. of Edn., Nev., 1993; recipient Supt.'s award White Pine County Sch. Dist., 1992, 93. Avocations: backpacking, bicycling, canoeing, fishing.

**SOLIDUM, JAMES,** finance and insurance executive; b. Honolulu, Mar. 12, 1925; s. Narciso and Sergia (Yabo) S.; m Vickie Mayo, Aug. 14, 1954; children: Arlin James, Nathan Francis, Tobi John, Kamomi Teresa. Student, U. Hawaii, 1949-50; BA, U. Oreg., 1953. CLU. Promotional salesman Tongg Pub. Co., 1953—54; editor Hi-Tan. Tribune, 1954—55; master planning technician Fed. Civil Svc., 1955—57; publs. editor Hawaii Sugar Planters Assn., 1957; field agt. Grand Pacific Life Ins. Co., 1957—59, home office asst., 1959—60, supr., 1960—62, asst. v.p., 1962—64; propr. J. Solidum & Assoc., Honolulu, 1964—; pres. Fin. Devel. Inst., 1967—. Contbg. writer Paradise of Pacific Mag., 1957-58, Hawaii Agrl. Mag., 1957-58; gen. ptrn. R.Z. Limited Partnership, 1981—; v.p Grand Pacific Life Ins. Co., 1983-90; bd. dirs. Hawaii Econ. Devel. Corp., 1982-89; mem. adv. com. Honolulu dist. SBA, 1971-77; bd. advisors Philippine Consulate of Hawaii, 1959. Pres. Keolu Elem. PTA, 1960-62; mem. satisfaction com. Hawaii Visitors Bur., 1963-66; chmn. budget and rev. panel IV, Aloha United Way, 1966-72, bd. dir., 1971-77, 82-88, chmn. bd., 1984; mem. mgmt. svcs. com., 1977, mem. cen. com., 1977-82, chmn. budget and allocations com., 1982-84; chmn. Kamehameha Dist. fin. com. Aloha coun. Boy Scouts Am., 1966; vice chmn. Businessmen's Cancer Crusade, 1965; chmn. Operation Bayanihan, Hawaii Immigration Task Force, 1970; participant Oahu Housing Workshop, State of Hawaii, Hawaii chpt. HUD, 1970; mem. task force on housing and transp. Alternative Econ. Futures for Hawaii, 1973; chmn. Bicentennial Filipiniana, 1976; campaign chmn. State Rep. Rudolph Pacarro, 1964-68; mem. exec. com. Campaign for Reelection U.S. Senator Hiram L. Fong, 1970, Gov. William Quinn for U.S. Senate, 1976; Rep. candidate for Hawaii Ho. of Reps., 1972; mem. Rep. Citizens Task Force on Housing, 1973; trustee St. Louis Alumni Found., 1970—, Kuakini Med. Ctr., 1984-86, Palama Settlement, 1975-82, v.p., 1976, treas., 1980-82; bd. mgrs. Windward YMCA, 1964-67; bd. advisers St. Louis H.S., 1963-64; bd. gov. Goodwill Industries, 1964; bd. dir. Children's Ctr., Inc., 1975-77, Hawaii Multi-Cultural Arts Ctr., 1977-81, treas., 1979; fin. chmn. St. Stephen's Parish Coun., 1974—; bd. dir. St. Louis Fine Arts Ctr., 1985-88; mem. steering com. Conf. Filipino Voter Registrars, 1962. With U.S. Army, 1945-47. Recipient Man of Yr. award Filipino C. of C., 1965, cert. of merit Aloha United Way, 1971, Wisdom mag. honor award, 1974, Outstanding Alumnus honor medal St. Louis High Sch., 1976, Island Treasure award Cath. Ch. Hawaii, 2003. Mem. Hawaii State C. of C. (bd. dir. 1964-67, chmn. legis. com. 1966-67, v.p. 1970, chmn. election judges 1971, mem. ad hoc com. bus.-youth rels. 1970—), Filipino C. of C. (past pres. 1965, com. chmn.), Am. Soc. CLU, Soc. Fin. Svcs. Profls., Honolulu Assn. Life Underwriters (bd. dir. 1963-66, del. nat. conv. 1967, chmn. life underwriters trng. coun. 1962-67), Hawaii Estate Planning Coun., Hawaii Plantation Indsl. Editors Assn. (sec.-treas. 1957), St. Louis Alumni Assn. (bd. dir., chmn. fin. 1969-75, pres. 1976, treas. 1977—), Phi Kappa Sigma. Republican. Roman Catholic. Home: 2622 Waolani Ave Honolulu HI 96817-1362 Office: 225 Queen St Apt 12-a Honolulu HI 96813-4603

**SOLINGER, JANET W.,** museum executive; b. Cin., Dec. 20, 1921; d. Fred and Dorothy G. (Gross) Weiland; widowed; children: Dorothy, Regina, Martha. BA, U. Cin., 1943; MA, NYU, 1973; DFA (hon.) Corcoran Coll. of Art, 1998. Asst. to pres. Hebrew Union Coll., Cin., 1957-60; administr. Jewish Mus., N.Y.C., 1961-65; exec. dir. Finch Coll., N.Y.C., 1965-66; dir. pub. info. and spl. events NYU, 1966-72; dir. Smithsonian resident assoc. program Smithsonian Instn., Washington, 1972-93; v.p. Corcoran Gall. of Art, Washington, 1994—. Lectr. in field. Author: Museums and Universities: New Paths for Continuing Education, 1990, Marketing the Arts, 1992; contbr. articles to profl. jours. Named Washingtonian of Yr., Washingtonian mag., 1984, Outstanding Woman Pioneer in Arts, Smithsonian Archives Am. Art, 2005; recipient decorations, Belgium, 1980, The Netherlands, 1981, Germany, 1982, Gold medal, Smithsonian Inst., 1990, Wash. Woman of the Millenium award, Art Table, 2000, Art Spark award, 2005; Fulbright Fellow, New Zealand, 1992. Mem. AIA (hon.), Washington Archtl. Found. (bd. dirs. 1996-2001), Art Table (bd. dirs. 1994-2000), Faberge Found. (bd. dirs. 1991—), Cosmos Club. Democrat. Jewish. Avocations: golf, bridge, reading, travel. Home: 2801 New Mexico Ave NW Washington DC 20007-3921 Office: Corcoran Gall of Art 500 17th St NW Washington DC 20006-4804 Office Phone: 202-639-1771. Business E-Mail: jsolinger@corcoran.org.

**SOLIS, CARLOS,** lawyer; b. Managua, Nicaragua, May 15, 1945; came to U.S., 1952; s. Carlos and Luisa (Serrano) S. BA, U. San Francisco, 1967, JD, 1969. Bar: Calif. 1970, U.S. Dist. Ct. (cen. and no. dists.) Calif. 1970, U.S. Ct. Appeals (9th cir.) 1970, U.S. Dist. Ct. (ea. dist.) Calif. 1972, U.S. Dist. Ct. (so. dist.) Calif. 1973, U.S. Supreme Ct. 1973. Assoc. Kindel & Anderson, LA, 1976, ptnr., 1976—96, Heller Ehrman LLP, 1996—2005; pvt. practice, 2005—. Exec. legal counsel, bd. dirs. internat. student ctr. UCLA, 1976-86, exec. v.p., 1981-86; instr. atty. asst. program UCLA, 1977-79; bd. advisors Los Angeles Internat. Trade Devel. Corp., 1981-87; bd. dirs. Pub. Counsel of L.A. Assoc. editor U. San Francisco Law Rev., 1968-69; contbr. articles to profl. jours. Bd. dirs. ARC, L.A., 1978-93, 95-05, chmn. audit com., 1985-88, bd. advisors, 1993-05; bd. dirs. March of Dimes, L.A., 1982-87, L.A. Pub. Theater Found., 1978-81, Young Musicians Found., 1979-80, Boys and Girls Club East L.A., 1986-89; bd. dirs. Am. Diabetes Assn., L.A., 1986-93, chmn., 1989-91, bd. dirs. Calif., 1988-93, chmn., 1992-93, mem. nat. minority initiative task force, 1986-92, bd. dirs. Nat., 1993-95; vice chmn. bd. L.A. United Way, 1982-83, bd. dirs., 1980-03, corp. bd. dirs., 1982-96, treas., 1989-93; pres. L.A. Open Golf Found., 1979-80. Recipient Alumni award U. San Francisco, 1969, Province award Phi Delta Phi, 1969. Mem. Los Angeles Jr. Chamber (pres., chmn. bd. dirs. 1980-81, Most Improved com. award 1975, Dir. of Yr. award 1977, Outstanding Bus. Leader award 1980), Assocs. Los Angeles C. of C., Los Angeles Area C. of C. (bd. dirs. 1979-80), U. San Francisco Alumni Assn. (pres. San Gabriel Valley chpt. 1976-80), Latin Am. Ctr. Assocs. (pres. 1980-82, bd. advisors 1980-88), Alpha Sigmu Nu, Phi Delta Phi. Home: 201 La Vereda Rd Pasadena CA 91105-1227 Personal E-mail: carlossolis1@earthlink.net.

**SOLIS, HILDA LUCIA,** congresswoman, educational administrator; b. LA, Oct. 20, 1957; d. Raul and Juana (Sequiera) S.; m. Sam H. Sayyad, June 26, 1982. BA in Polit. Sci., Calif. State Poly U., 1979; MA in Pub. Adminstrn., U. So. Calif., 1981. Interpreter Immigration and Naturalization Service, Los Angeles, 1977-79; editor in chief Office Hispanic Affairs, The White House, Washington, 1980-81; mgmt. analyst Office Mgmt. and Budget, Washington, 1981-82; field rep. Office Assemblyman Art Torres, L.A., 1982; dir. Calif. Student Opportunity and Access, Whittier, 1982—; rep. 57th assembly dist. Calif. State Assembly, Sacramento, 1992-94; mem. Calif. Senate from 24th dist., 1994-2000, U.S. Congress from Calif. 32nd dist., Washington, 2001—; mem. resources com., energy & commerce com., former mem. edn. and workforce com. Cons. South Coast Consortium, L.A., 1986—; mem. South Coast Ednl. Opportunity Pers. Consortium. Bd. dirs. Calif. Commn. on Status of Women, 1993—; corr. pres. Friendly El Monte (Calif.) Dem. Club, 1986—; mem. credentials com. Calif. Dem. Com., 1987-88; trustee Rio Hondo C.C., 1985-92. Recipient Meritorious Svc. award Dept. Def., 1981, Young Careerist award El Monte Bus. and Profl. Women, 1987; fellow Nat. Edn. Inst., Kellogg Found., 1984-85. Mem. Western Assn. Ednl. Opportunity Pers. (sec. bd. dirs. 1986—), Comision Feminil de Los Angeles (bd. dirs. 1983-84, edn. chmn.), Women of Moose. Democrat. Roman Catholic. Office: 1725 Longworth House Office Bldg Washington DC 20515-0532 also: Ste 211 4401 Santa Anita Ave El Monte CA 91731

**SOLISH, JONATHAN CRAIG,** lawyer; b. Monticello, NY, May 27, 1949; s. David Julius and Gertrude (Hellman) S.; m. Dhana Krushkhov, Dec. 30, 1981; 1 child, Nickolas Brewster. BA, U. Calif., Santa Cruz, 1971; JD, UCLA, 1975. Bar: Calif. 1975, US Dist. Ct. Ctrl. Dist. Calif. 1977, US Ct. Appeals 9th Cir. 1979, US Ct. Appeals Fed. Cir. 1988, US Dist. Ct. So. Dist. Calif. 1988, US Dist. Ct. Ea. Dist. Calif. 1992, US Dist. Ct. No. Dist. Calif. 1993, US Supreme Ct 2000. Ptnr. Solish, Jordan & Wiener, LA, Solish Arbiter & Gehring (merged with Jenkens & Gilchrist), LA; shareholder Jenkens & Gilchrist, P.C., LA, 1997—, firm co-leader franchise & distribution practice group. Assoc. editor Franchise Law Jour., 1992-97, editor-in-chief, 1997-2000; contbr. articles to profl. jours. Mem. LA Olympics Citizens Adv. Com., 1981-84, LA Olympics Cultural and Fine Arts Adv. Com., 1981-84. Mem. ABA (forum com. on franchising 1984-, appellate advocacy com. 1989-, antitrust sect. & subsect. on franchising 1990-, litig. & dispute resolution steering com. 2001-), LA County Bar Assn. (appellate practice 1989-, atty.-client rels. com. 1985-, Pacific Rim com. 1990—, antitrust section 1990—), State Bar Calif. (internat. law sect. 1990-) Office: Jenkens & Gilchrist PC 12100 Wilshire Blvd 15th Fl Los Angeles CA 90025-7120 Office Phone: 310-442-8804. Office Fax: 310-820-8859. Business E-Mail: jsolish@jenkens.com.

**SOLIVAN, NEIDA M.,** librarian, educator, school system administrator; d. Santos Soliván and Felicita Rolón; m. Luis R. Abraham, July 28, 1972; children: Joel R. Abraham, Luis R. Abraham, Neida L. Abraham. BE, U. PR, Rio Piedras, 1968—72, MLS, 1983—86; MEd & Sch. Administrn., U. Phoenix, Puerto Rico Campus, 1984—86. Cert. sci. tchr. PR Dept. Edn. 1972, sch. libr. PR Dept. Edn., 1987, sch. dir. PR Dept. Edn., 1987, sch. libr. prof. Turabo U., 2000, sch. supr. PR Dept. Edn., 2000. Sci. tchr. Aibonito Mid. Sch., PR, 1972—76, Bonifacio Sanchez HS, Aibonito, 1977—83; sch. libr. Federico Degetau I Sch., Aibonito, 1984—85; profl. libr. Interamericana U., Barranquitas, PR, 1985—86; sch. libr. S.U. Pasto Sch., Aibonito, 1986—89; sch. libra regional supr. Ednl. Caguas Region, PR, 1995—96; sch. libr. edn. prof. Turabo U., Gurabo, PR, 1995—; sch. libr. dir. PR Dept. Edn., Hato Rey, 1996—98, sch. aux. supt. Aibonito, 2000—; sch. libr. Pont Flores Sch., Aibonito. Sch. libr. cons. Turabo U., Gurabo, PR, 2000—. Contbr. articles to profl. jours. Pub. libr. collaborator Aibonito Pub. Libr., PR, 1999—2005; cath. young instr. Aibonito Cath. Ch. Recipient Honor Plate award, Aibonito Dist. Sch. Libr., 1990, Excellence in Tchr. award, Pont Flores Sch., 1993, Honor Plate award, Federico Degetau II Sch. Libr., 2000, Aibonito Dist. Sci. Fair, 2005, Libr. Recognition award, Aibonito Sch. Dist., 2005, Honor Plate award, Caguas Ednl. Region Sci. Fair, 2005. Mem.: PR Tchr. Assn. (assoc.), PR Sch. Libr. Assn. (assoc. Found. Meml. Honor Plate award 1986), Lion Club (Lady of Yr. 1995). Catholic. Avocations: reading, travel, music, poetry, writing. Personal E-mail: adiensun2003@yahoo.com.

**SOLJACIC, MARIN,** physicist, educator; b. Zagreb, Croatia, Feb. 7, 1974; arrived in U.S., 1992; s. Ivo and Marija Soljacic; m. Mihaela Papa, Apr. 2, 1976; 1 child, Fran Daniel. BA in Physics, MIT, 1996, BA in elec. engring., 1996; PhD, Princeton U., 2000. Pappalardo fellow MIT, Cambridge, Mass., 2000—03, prin. rsch. scientist, 2003—05, asst. prof., 2005—. Cons. OmniGuide Comm. Inc., Cambridge, Mass., 2001—; spkr. in field. Contbr. chapters to books, 56 articles to sci. jours. Recipient Adolph Lomb medal, Optical Soc. Am., 2005. Mem.: Phi Beta Kappa. Achievements include 11 patents; 5 patents pending. Office: Room 12-112 MIT 77 Mass Ave Cambridge MA 02139 Office Phone: 617-253-2467.

**SOLKOFF, JEROME IRA,** lawyer, educator; b. Rochester, N.Y., Feb. 15, 1939; s. Samuel and Dorothy (Krovetz) S.; m. Doreen Hurwitz, Aug. 11, 1963; children: Scott Michael, Anne Lynn. BS Sch. Indsl. Rels. and Labor Rels., Cornell U., 1961; JD, U. Buffalo, 1964. Bar: N.Y. 1965, Fla. 1974, U.S. Dist. Ct. (we. dist.) N.Y. 1965; cert. elder law atty., Fla. Bar, Nat. Elder Law Found. of Nat. Acad. of Elder Law Attys., ABA. Assoc. Nusbaum, Tarricone, Weltman, Bilgore & Silver, Rochester, N.Y., 1964-66, Mousaw, Vigdor, Reeves, Heilbronner & Kroll, Rochester, 1966-70; sr. mcpl. atty. Urban Renewal Agy., Rochester, 1970-73; sole practice Rochester, 1970-73; chief legal counsel Arlen Realty Mgmt., Inc., Miami, Fla., 1973-75; assoc. Britton, Cohen, Kaufman, Benson & Schantz, Miami, 1975-76; chief legal counsel First Mortgage Investors, Miami Beach, Fla., 1976-79; ptnr. Cassel & Cassel, P.A., Miami, 1979-82; sole practice Deerfield Beach, Fla., 1982—. Lectr. on fgn. investment practices in U.S., Eng., 1981-88, Montreal, Que., Can., 1981, estate planning, 1982—; medicaid law and elder law, 1988—. Author: Fundamentals of Foreign Investing in American Real Estate and Businesses, 1981, Checklist of N.Y. Mortgage Foreclosure Procedures, 1970, History of Municipal Employee Unions, 1964, Practice Guide for Florida Elder Law, 1996, National Elder Law Forms Manual, 2005, and yearly supplements. Bd. dirs. Broward Homebound Program, 1990-2001, pres. 1998-99; bd. dirs. Jewish Cmty. Ctrs. of South Broward, Fla., 1979-90, NE Alzheimers Daycare Ctr., Inc., 1990-92; mem. exec. bd. dirs. Broward Alzheimers Assn., 1995—; co-chair Fla. Alzheimers Pub. Policy steering com., 1999-2001. Named Advocate of Yr., Broward County Legal Aid Assn., 2003. Mem. ABA (mem. sects. real property, trust and probate law), Fla. Bar Assn. (sects. real property, trust and probate law, vice-chmn. com. on the elderly 1987-91, lectr. estate planning for the aging and disabled 1989—, founder, chmn. elder law sect. 1994-95, elder law sect., chmn. ethics com. 1998-2000), Nat. Acad. Elder Law Attys., Elder Law Attys., Fla. Acad. Elder Law Attys.

**SOLKOFF, SCOTT M.,** lawyer; b. Rochester, NY, July 5, 1966; s. Jerome Ira and Doreen Solkoff; m. Lauren Resa Kalish, Nov. 23, 1996; children: Jacob Solomon, Lola Danielle. BA, U. Fla., 1991; JD cum laude, Nova Southeastern U., 1994. Bar: Fla. 1994, U.S. Dist. Ct. (so. dist.) Fla. 1995, U.S. Ct. Appeals (11th cir.) 1995, bd. cert. elder law atty.: Prin. Solkoff & Assocs. PA, Boynton Beach & North Miami Beach, Fla., 1994—. Chair elder law sect. Fla. Bar, Tallahassee, 2003—; bd. dirs. Fla. State Guardianship Assn. Contbr. articles to profl. jours. Mem. adv. bd. State of Fla. Office Pub. Guardian, Tampa, 2000—01; bd. dirs. Palm Beach County, Fla., 2002. Recipient Charlotte Brayer Pub. Svc. award, Fla. Bar, 1998. Mem.: Nat. Acad. Elder Law Attys. (mem. bd. dirs.), Acad. Fla. Elder Law Attys. (faculty, pres. emeritus, past pres.). Office: Solkoff & Assocs PA 1901 S Congress Ave #350 Boynton Beach FL 33426 Office Phone: 561-733-4242. E-mail: clientservices@solkoff.com.

**SOLLENDER, JOEL DAVID,** management consultant, financial executive, accountant; b. NYC, Nov. 11, 1924; s. Samuel and Flora (Blumenthal) S.; m. Dorothy Leaf, Aug. 6, 1958; children: Jeffrey D., Jonathan L. BS, N.Y. U., 1946. CPA N.Y., 1947. Staff auditor Ernst & Young, N.Y.C., 1946-50; with United Mchts. & Mfrs., Inc., N.Y.C., 1950-86, chief acctg. officer, 1976—, corp. contr., 1977—, sr. v.p., 1980—, mem. exec. mgmt. com. also bd. dirs.

subsidiary cos.; assoc. dir. N.Y. Hist. Soc., N.Y.C., 1986—89; mem. adv. coun. to Office of Charities Registration Dept. State, N.Y. State, 1988-89; v.p. fin. Piedmont Industries, N.Y.C., 1989-90; exec. v.p., CFO Earthworm Inc., 1990—92; fin. mgmt. cons.; sr. cons. Internat. Exec. Svc. Corps Agy. for Aid for Internat. Devel., Kazakstan, 1996—. Adv. coun. San Diego State U., 1997—; audit com. San Diego Mus. Art, 1997-2002; fin. com. Globe Theater, 2003-04, audit com., 2004—. With U.S. Army, WW II. Decorated Combat Infantry Badge, Purple Heart with oak leaf cluster, Prisoner of War medal, Bronze Star. Mem. AICPA, N.Y. State Soc. CPAs (chief fin. officer com.), Am. Inst. Corp. Contrs., Rancho Bernardo (Calif.) Men's Club, Bailiwick Club (Greenwich, Conn.), Greenhaven Yacht Club (Rye).

**SOLLERS, JOSEPH SEDWICK, III,** lawyer; b. Balt. AB, Princeton Univ., 1977; JD with honors, Univ. Md., 1982. Bar: D.C. 1983. Law clk. Judge Norman P. Ramsey, US Dist Ct. Md.; ptnr., Spec. Matters & Govt. Investigations Practice Group King & Spalding LLP, Washington. Fellow: Am. Col. Trial Lawyers (co-chmn D.C. subcom., Criminal Litigation com.); mem.: ABA. Office: King & Spalding LLP 1700 Pennsylvania Ave NW Washington DC 20006 Office Phone: 202-626-5612. Office Fax: 202-626-3737. Business E-Mail: wsollers@kslaw.com.

**SOLLMAN, GEORGE HENRY,** venture capitalist; b. Michigan City, Ind., Nov. 2, 1941; s. Henry Charles and Margaret Elisabeth (Gockel) S.; m. Maureen Tosh, July 12, 1968; children: Jennifer, Erich. Spl. student, MIT, 1965—66; BSEE, Northwestern U., 1964; MSEE, Northeastern U., 1967. Engring. dir. Honeywell Info. Systems, Waltham, Mass., 1964—73; product line mgr. Control Data, Hawthorne, Calif., 1973—76; v.p., gen. mgr. Shugart/Xerox, Sunnyvale, 1976—84; spl. ptnr. Sand Hill Venture Group, Menlo Park, 1984; pres., CEO Centigram Corp., San Jose, 1985—97, AtMotion Inc. (now OpenWave Corp.), Redwood City, Calif., 1997—2000, Arabesque Investments LLC, Atherton, Calif., 2000—; chmn. First Virtual Corp., Redwood Shores, Calif., 2004—, Corticon Techs., San Mateo, Calif., 2000—. Bd. dirs. T-Ventures, Venture Capital arm of Deutsche Telecom, Bonn, Germany, 2001-; chmn. nat. bd. dirs. Am. Elec. Assn.; presdl. nomination Semicondr. Tech. Coun.; co-chmn. Alexis d'Toqueville Soc.; mem. adv. coun. Joint Venture Silicon Valley; chmn. adv. bd. Leavey Sch. Bus., Santa Clara U., 2000-. Patentee in field. Co-chmn. United Way of Santa Clara County; mem. steering com. George Lucas Ednl. Found., Marin County. Home: 242 Polhemus Ave Atherton CA 94027-5439 Office: Arabesque Investments LLC 242 Polhemus Ave Atherton CA 94027-5439 Office Phone: 650-365-8186. Personal E-mail: george_sollman@hotmail.com.

**SOLLORS, WERNER,** literature and language educator; PhD, Freie U., Berlin, 1975. Wissenschaftlicher asst., asst. prof. John F. Kennedy Inst. Freie U., Berlin; from asst. to assoc. prof. English and Comparative Lit. Columbia U.; Henry B. and Anne M. Cabot Prof. English Lit., prof. Afro-Am. studies Harvard U., Cambridge, Mass. Author: Amiri Baraka/LeRoi Joines: The Quest for a Populist Modernism, 1978, Beyond Ethnicity: Consent and Descent in American Culture, Neither Black Nor White Yet Both: Thematic Explorations of Interracial Literature, 1997; contbr. chapters to books Das amerikanische Drama der Gegenwart, 1976, The Harvard Encyclopedia of American Ethnic Groups, 1980, Reconstructing American Literary History, 1986, 1986, Columbia Literary History of the United States, 1988, 1988, Critical Terms for Literary Study, 1990, 1990, Looking Inward, Looking Outward: From the 1920s through the 1940s, 1990, 1990, Nationale und kulturelle Identitat: Studien zur Entwicklung des kollektiven Bewusstseins in der Neuzeit, 1991, Immigrants in Two Democracies: French and American Experience, 1992, Intersecting Boundaries: The Theatre of Adrienne Kennedy, 1992, Il razzismo e le sue storie, 1992, Swedes in America: Intercultural and Interethnic Perspectives on Contemporary Research, 1993, Multiculturalism and the Canon of American Culture, 1993, Configurations de l'ethnicite aux Etats-Unis, 1993, History & Memory in African-American Culture, 1994, Thematics: New Approaches, 1995, Thematics Reconsidered: Essays in Honor of Horst Jr. Daemmrich, 1995, Performances in American Literature and Culture, 1995, New Essays on Henry Roth's Call It Sleep, 1996, Families, 1996, Cultural Difference and the Literary Text, 1996, Beyond Pluralism, 1998, The Sally Hemings-Thomas Jefferson Relationship, 1999, Columbia Companion to 20th Century American Short Fiction, 2001, Dream-Fluted Cane: Essays on Jean Toomes and the Harlem Renaissance, 2001, Not English Only: Redefining "American" in American Studies, 2001, American Studies and Peace, 2001, Mixed-Race Literature, 2001; editor: A Bibliographic Guide to Afro-American Studies, 1972, A Bibliographic Guide to Afro-American Studies Supplement I, 1974; co-editor: Bibliographie amerikanistischer Veröffentlichungen in der DDR bis, 1968, 1976, Varieties of Black Experience at Harvard, 1986, The Invention of Ethnicity, 1989, The Life Stories of Undistinguished Americans as Told by Themselves, 1990, 1999, The Return of Thematic Criticism, 1993, Cane, 1993, Blacks at Harvard: A Documentary History of African-American Experience at Harvard and Radcliffe, 1993, The Black Columbiad: Defining Moments in African-American Literature and Culture, 1994, Theories of Ethnicity: A Classical Reader, 1996, The Promised Land, 1997, Multilingual America: Transnationalism, Ethnicity and the Languages of American Literature, 1998, The Multilingual Anthology of American Literature, 2000, The Norton Critical Edition of Olaudah Equiano, 2000, Interracialism: Black-White Intermarriage in American History, Literature and Law, 2000, The Adrienne Kennedy Reader, 2001, German? American? Literature?: New Directions in German-American Studies, 2002, Interracial Literature: An Anthology of Black-White Contacts in the Old World and the New, 2004, Frank J. Webb: Fiction, Essays and Poetry, 2005; contbr. articles to profl. jours. Recipient Constance Rourke prize Am. Studies Assn., 1990; John Simon Guggenheim Meml. fellow, Andrew W. Mellon faculty fellow Harvard U., Walter Channing Cabot fellow Harvard U., 1997-98; NEH fellow, 1999-00. Fellow: Am. Acad. of Arts and Scis. Office: Harvard U Barker Center 12 Quincy St Cambridge MA 02138-3804

**SOLLS, MARK A.,** lawyer; b. 1956; married; 3 children. BA in Finance, U. Ill., 1977; JD, So. Ill. U., 1980. Bar: Ill. 1980, Tex. 1982, cert.: mediator. Pvt. practice; v.p., gen. counsel, sec. Pronet, Inc., 1993—97, Dal-Tile Internat., Inc., 1998—2002; exec. v.p., general counsel, sec. Wyndham Internat., Inc., Dallas, 2002—.

**SOLLY, RICHARD PETER,** music educator; s. Richard Gibson and Jane Ruth Solly. BA, Coll. N.J., 1975, MA, 1976. Cert. tchr. Pa., N.J. Asst. organist Trinity Episcopal Ch., Trenton, NJ, 1975—77; organist, choirmaster, dir. St. Paul's Luth. Ch., Doylestown, Pa., 1972—; tchr. music North Penn Sch. Dist., Lansdale, 1978—. Adj. faculty Bucks County C.C., Newtown, Pa., 1977—78; program annotator Bucks County Symphony Orch., Doylestown, 1988—. Composer: The Hymnal, 1982, Hymnal for the Hours, 1989. Recipient Srs. Choice award, North Penn Sch. Dist., 1996, 1997, 1998. Mem.: Am. Guild Organists, Kappa Delta Pi. Avocations: travel, baseball, railroading. Home: PO Box 264 Doylestown PA 18901-0264

**SOLMAN, JOSEPH,** artist; b. Vitebsk, Russia, Jan. 25, 1909; came to US, 1912; s. Nathan and Rose (Peskin) S.; m. Ruth Romanofsky (dec. July 1999); children: Paul, Ronni., Nat. Acad. of Design, 1927-30. Easel painter WPA, N.Y.C., 1935-41; pvt. art instr. N.Y.C., 1951-66; art instr. CUNY, N.Y.C., 1967-75; artist N.Y.C., 1935—. One-man shows: Contemporary Arts Gallery, NYC, 1934, ACA Gallery, 1950, 1968, 77, 86; Exhibitions: Retrospective at Phillips Mem. Mus., Washington, 1949, Retrospective at Wichita (Kansas) Mus. of Art, 1984, Robert Brown Contemporary Art, Washington, 1985, Mercury Gallery, Boston and Rockport, Mass., 1995, 96, 98, 99, 2000, 03, 04, 05, Simmons Gallery, San Francisco, 2004, 05; author: books, Joseph Solman, Crown Publishers, 1966. Monotypes of Joseph Solman, Da Capo Press, 1977, Mozartiana, 1990, Joseph Solman, Da Capo Press, 1995; editor-in-chief, Art Front Mag. 1937-38; artist: several paintings. Recipient of several awards for paintings and portraits including the Nat. Inst. of Arts & Letters, 1961, and 8 prizes from the Nat. Acad. of Design Annuals, 1967-89. Mem. Nat. Acad. of Design (treas. 1979-85, academician, 1974-), Fedn. of Modern Painters & Sculptors (exec. bd. 1968-89); fellow (life) Art Student League.

**SOLMER, RICHARD,** surgeon; b. South Bend, Ind., Feb. 11, 1947; MD, U. Mich., 1972. Diplomate Am. Bd. Plastic Surgery. Surgical intern Hosp. of the U. Pa., Phila., 1972-73; gen. surgical resident Calif. Hosp. Med. Ctr., L.A., 1976-80; plastic surgery resident Allentown (Pa.) Affiliated Hosp., 1980-82; pvt. practice Huntington Beach, and Newport Beach, Calif., 1982—. Fellow Am. Coll. Surgeons; mem. Am. Soc. Plastic Surgeons. Office: 307 Placentia Ave Ste 208 Newport Beach CA 92663-3308 Office Phone: 949-548-0227.

**SOLMSSEN, PETER,** retired academic administrator; b. Berlin, Nov. 1, 1931; m. Kathleen Mailliard, Dec. 2001. AB, Harvard U., 1952; JD, U. Pa., 1959. Atty. Ballard, Spahr, Andrews & Ingersoll, Phila., 1959-60; with U.S. Fgn. Service, 1961; vice consul Singapore, 1962-63; asst. to under sec. of state, 1963-65; 2d sec. Rio de Janeiro, 1965-67; Cultural attache U.S. Dept. State, Sao Paulo, Brazil, 1967-70; adviser on arts Washington, 1974-80; dep. ambassador at large for cultural affairs, 1981-83; pres. Phila. Coll. Art, 1983-87, U. of the Arts, Phila., 1987-2000. One-man photography exhbns. include: Mus. Art, Sao Paulo. Author and illustrator. Mem.: Philadelphia; Century Assn.

**SOLNIK, MEIR JONATHON,** gynecologist, director; MD, U. Tex., Houston, 1994—98. Lic. dr. Am. Bd. Obstetrics & Gynecology, 2005. Clin. instr. minimally invasive surgery Magee-Womens Hosp., Pitts., 2002—03; asst. clin. prof. Irvine Med. Ctr. U. Calif., Orange, Calif., 2003—06; dir., Ctr. Minimally Invasive Gynecologic Surgery Cedars-Sinai Med. Ctr., LA, 2006—. Fellow: Am. Coll. Obstetricians & Gynecologists. Office: Cedars-Sinai Med Ctr 8635 W Third St Ste 160W Los Angeles CA 90048 Personal E-mail: jonathonsolnik@yahoo.com.

**SOLNIT, REBECCA,** writer, critic; Author Secret Exhibition: Six California Artists of the Cold War Era, 1994, Savage Dreams: A Journey into the Landscape Wars of the American West, 1995, A Book of Migrations: Some Passages in Ireland, 1998, Wanderlust: A History of Walking, 2001, As Eve Said to the Serpent: On Landscape, Gender and Art, 2001, Hollow City: The Siege of San Francisco and the Crisis of American Urbanism, 2002, Motion Studies: Time, Space and Eadweard Muybridge, 2003, River of Shadows, 2003 (Nat. Book Critics Circle award, 2004). Grantee Guggenheim Fellowship, NEA Fellowship. Office: c/o Bloomsbury USA 175 5th Ave New York NY 10010

**SOLO, JOYCE RUBENSTEIN,** volunteer; b. Buffalo, N.Y., Feb. 14, 1924; d. Jay Harry and Rose (Maisel) Rubenstein; m. Richard D. Solo, Jan. 6, 1946; children: Harry Jay Solo, Eleanor Solo, Sally Solo. BA, Wellesley Coll., 1945. Mem. S.E. Pa. Health Coord. Coun., 1978—84; chair reach to recovery Phila. divsn. Am. Cancer Soc., 1985—87; sec. Sarasota County Health Care Coord. Adv. Coun., Fla., 1993—95; chair sr. adv. com. Sarasota Meml. Hosp., 1996—98; vol. Reach to Recovery Breast Cancer Task Force, Manatee County Am. Cancer Soc.; mem. numerous other health and civic orgn. activities; pres. women's bd. Temple Beth Israel, 1996—98, bd. dirs., 1998—2000; mem. governing bd. Health Systems Agy. S.E. Pa., 1977—86. Mem.: LWV (v.p. Pa. chpt. 1969—73, pres. Phila. 1975—77, pres. Sarasota County 1990—92, healthcare com. chair 1988—90, 1992—), Phi Beta Kappa. Personal E-mail: rjoysolo14@comcast.net.

**SOLO, ROBERT ALEXANDER,** economist, educator; b. Phila., Aug. 2, 1916; s. Louis C. and Rebecca (Muchnick) S.; m. Roselyn Starr; 1 dau., Tova Maria. BS, Harvard U., 1938; MA, Am. U., 1941; PhD, Cornell U., 1953. Economist fed. and war agys., 1939-41; author, script chief Sta. WCAU-TV, Phila., 1949-50; mem. faculty Rutgers U., New Brunswick, N.J., 1953-55, McGill U., Montreal, Que., Can., 1955-56, CCNY, 1956-58; sr. research economist Princeton U., 1965-66; prof. dept. econs. Mich. State U., East Lansing, 1966-87, prof. emeritus, 1987—; dir. Inst. Internat. Bus. and Devel. Studies, 1966-68. Mem. faculty Johns Hopkins U., Balt., summer 1953, U. Mich., Ann Arbor, summer 1958; lectr. L'Ecole Pratique des Hautes Etudes, Sorbonne, Paris, 1964-65; research Institut Recherch Economique et Planification, lectr. U. Grenoble, France, 1972-73; prof. associe U. Paris IV, Dauphine, 1971, 73; cons. NASA, 1965-67, OECD, 1963-65, Commonwealth of P.R., 1959-61, U.S. Dept. Justice, 1994-96; project chmn. Study on Info. Tech., Nat. Conf. Bd., 1969-72; project dir. Nat. Planning Assn., Washington, 1961-63; U.S. del. Yugoslavian Conf. on Transfer of Tech., Belgrade, 1974; mem. Alan T. Waterman award Com., 1976-77; expert witness Dept. Justice, Washington, L.A., 1995-97. Author: Economics and the Public Interest, 1955, Synthetic Rubber: A Case Study in Technological Development under Public Direction, 1959 (reprinted as Across the High Technology Threshold 1980), Economic Organizations and Social Systems, 1967 (reissued 2001), (with Everett Rogers) Inducing Technological Change for Economic Growth and Development, 1973, The Political Authority and the Market System, 1974, Organizing Science for Technology Transfer in Economic Development, 1975, The Positive State, 1981, (with Charles Anderson) Value Judgement and Income Distribution, 1981, Opportunity Knocks: American Economic Policy after Gorbachev, 1991, The Philosophy of Science and Economics, 1991, The Super Power and the Serb, 1998, The Song of Songs: The Harvard Version, 1998, also other books in field; contbr. chpts. to books, articles to profl. jours. Fulbright fellow, 1972-73 Mem. Council European Studies (steering com., exec. com., chmn. research com. 1974-77). Home: 4609 Chippewa Dr Okemos MI 48864-2009 Personal E-mail: solo@mail.msu.edu.

**SOLODKY, HOWARD N.,** lawyer; b. Buffalo, June 28, 1951; BA in Psychology (hon.), Clark U., 1973; JD cum laude, SUNY, Buffalo, 1976; LLM in Taxation (hon.), George Washington U., 1980. Bar: NY 1977, DC 1980. Jud. clk. appellate divsn. 3rd dept. NY State Supreme Ct., 1976—77; atty. advisor office of chief counsel IRS, Washington, 1977—81; assoc. to ptnr. Melrod, Redman & Gartlan, Washington, 1981—93; prin. David, Hagner, Kuney & Davison, Washington, 1993—98; mem. Womble Carlyle Sandridge & Rice PLLC, Washington, 1998—, chair tax practice group. Office: Womble Carlyle Sandridge & Rice PLLC 7th Fl 1401 Eye St NW Washington DC 20005 Office Phone: 202-857-4424. Office Fax: 202-261-0024. Business E-Mail: hsolodky@wcsr.com.

**SOLOFF, LAURA J.,** academic administrator; BA in English, minor in Art History, UCLA. Human resources position Broadway Dept. Stores; dir. career planning & placement Fashion Inst. Design & Merchandising, Calif., campus dir. Calif., regional dir. Calif., dir. student financial svcs. Calif.; dir. human resources & adminstrn. Sony Pictures Entertainment, Culver City, Calif.; mem. Edn. Mgmt. Corp., 1998—; pres. Art Inst. Calif.-Orange County, 2000—03, Art Inst. Calif.-LA, 2003—; regional v.p. Edn. Mgmt. Corp., 2004—. Office: Office Pres Art Institute California LA 2900 31st St Santa Monica CA 90405-3035

**SOLOMON, ANDREW P.,** lawyer; b. Newark, 1953; BA, Brown U., 1975; JD, Harvard U., 1984. Bar: NY 1985. Ptnr. Sullivan & Cromwell, NYC, 1992—, now mng. ptnr. tax group. Mem.: NY State Bar Assn. (tax section exec. com., co-chair, com. on fin. intermediaries). Office: Sullivan & Cromwell 125 Broad St New York NY 10004-2489 Office Phone: 212-558-4000. Office Fax: 212-558-3588. Business E-Mail: solomona@sullcrom.com.

**SOLOMON, ANDREW WALLACE,** author; b. N.Y.C., Oct. 30, 1963; s. Howard and Carolyn Ruth (Bower) S. BA in English magna cum laude, Yale U., 1985; BA, Jesus Coll., Cambridge U., Cambridge, Eng., 1987, MA in English, 1987. Editl. intern Met. Mus. Art, NYC, 1981, editl. asst., 1982, asst. editor, 1983, editor, 1986; intern dept. old master paintings Sotheby's NY, 1984; galleries corr., contbg. editor Harpers and Queen, London, 1987-91; contbg. editor HG, 1991-93; contbg. writer The NY Times Mag., 1993—2000. Author: The Irony Tower: Soviet Artists in a Time of Glasnost, 1991, A Stone Boat, 1994, The Noonday Demon: An Atlas of Depression, 2001 (Nat. Book award, finalist Pulitzer Prize); contbr. articles to profl. jours. Bd. dirs. World Monuments Fund, Alliance for the Arts, The American Coun. for Cultural Policy, The Victoria and Albert Mus., The Alex Fund, Depression Ctr. of U. Mich., The Worcester (Mass.) Found., Cold Spring Harbor Lab Jesus Coll. Travel grantee, Cambridge U., 1986; Yale Conservation Project

fellow for travel, 1985; Brit.-Am. Project fellow; Bogliasco fellow, 1998; recipient Nat. Book award Books for a Better Life, 2001, New Visions award QPB, Ken award Nat. Alliance for Mentally Ill., Charles T. Ruby Loss award, 2002, Silvano Arieti award, 2002, Didi Hirsch Cmty. Svc. award, 2002, Lambda award ALA. Mem. Groucho Club, Oxford & Cambridge Club, Chelsea Arts Club, Century Assn., Nat. Arts Club, Lotos Club, Explorers Club, Coun. on Fgn. Rels., Conservators Coun. of NY Pub. Libr. Democrat.

**SOLOMON, ARTHUR CHARLES,** pharmacist; b. Gary, Ind., May 30, 1947; s. Laurence A. and Dorothy B. (Klippel) S.; m. Janet Evelyn Irak, Aug. 23, 1969; children: Thomas, Michael, Mark, Jill. BS in Pharmacy, Purdue U., 1970, MS in Clin. Pharmacy, 1972; PharmD. Registered pharmacist; cert. nuclear pharmacist. Clin. prof. pharmacy U. Tex., Austin, 1972-75; v.p. Nuclear Pharmacy, Inc., Atlanta, 1975-83; exec. v.p., COO Diagnostek, Inc., Albuquerque, 1983-95; pres. Health Care Svcs., Inc., 1990-95; exec. v.p., COO Value Rx, Albuquerque, 1995-96; pres. Solomon and Assocs., Albuquerque, 1996-97; pres., CEO, dir. SP Pharms. LLC, Albuquerque, 1997—2001; sr. v.p. Cardinal Health, Albuquerque, 2001—04; COO PharmaFab, Grand Prairie, Tex., 2004—. Adj. prof. U. N.Mex., 1992—. Contbr. articles to profl. jours. Named Disting. Alumnus Purdue U., 1998. Fellow Am. Soc. Cons. Pharmacists, Parental Drug Assn.; mem. Am. Pharm. Assn., Am. Assn. Pharm. Scis., Am. Soc. Hosp. Pharmacy, Nat. Assn. Retail Druggists, Nat. Coun. Prescription Drug Programs, Am. Managed Care Pharmacy Assn. (pres., dir.), Rho Chi, Pi Kappa Phi. Republican. Roman Catholic. Avocations: golf, woodworking, gardening. Home: 6709 Alpine Ln Colleyville TX 76034-7290 Office: ThermaFab 2940 N Hwy 360 Grand Prairie TX 75050 E-mail: asolomon@pharmafab.com.

**SOLOMON, BARRY JASON,** human services administrator, consultant; b. Boston, May 16, 1934; s. Samuel and Ethel (Fleishman) Solomon; m. C. Priscilla Fugate, June 29, 1958; children: R. Stephen, Jon, Julie Ellen. BS in Biology and Chemistry, Tufts U., 1955; MBA in Health Care Adminstrn., Xavier U., Cin., 1960; MPH in Health Care Adminstrn., U. N.C., 1989. Chief med. record adminstr. USPHS Hosp., Lexington, Ky., 1956-59; asst. dir. Union Meml. Hosp., Balt., 1960-61; asst. adminstr. James Lawrence Kernan Hosp., Balt., 1961-67; asst. to dean, lectr. health edn. and med. care sects. Yale U. Sch. Medicine, New Haven, 1967-70; dir. health svcs., clin. asst. prof. pharmacy adminstrn. U. R.I., Kingston, 1970-76; assoc. dir. for adminstrn. USPHS Hosp., Norfolk, Va., 1976-81; dir., COO, sr. fellow in social medicine Montefiore Hosp., Bronx, NY, 1981-84; assoc. v.p. for med. affairs, mem. exec. coun. of Med. Sch. U. South Fla., Tampa, 1984-89; assoc. prof., acting chmn. dept. comprehensive medicine U. So. Fla., Tampa, 1984-89, assoc. prof. Coll. Pub. Health, 1984-89; cons. in health adminstrn., Columbia, Md., 1989-93; v.p. for acad. affairs North Broward Hosp. Dist., Ft. Lauderdale, Fla., 1993-96; chmn. bd. dirs. Sr. Benefit Ctrs. Am., Inc., 1998-2000. 1st v.p. bd. trustees, CEO Count and Countess de Hoernle Alzheimer's Pavillion, 2000—06, cons. to bd. dirs., 2006—; pres. Villa D'Este Condominium, Inc., 1999—2001; exec. com., nominating com. Vis. Nurse Assn. Tampa Bay, 1987—90; planning com. bd. trustees Hillsborough County Hosp. Authority, 1986—88; profl. affairs com. bd. trustees H. Lee Moffitt Cancer Ctr. and Rsch. Inst., 1986—88; affiliation com. S.W. Fla. Blood Bank, 1988—89; instr. hosp. adminstrn. Xavier U., 1960; course asst., instr. Am. Med. Record Assn., 1962—72; instr. Howard U. Coll. Continuing Edn., Washington, 1993; cons. St. Elizabeth Hosp., Covington, Ky., 1959, City Hosp. Ctr. Elmhurst, 1965, Hall-Brooke Hosp., Westport, Conn., 1968—69, Conn. Mental Health Ctr., New Haven, 1969—70, South County Hosp., Wakefield, RI, 1970—76, Centurion Hosp., Tampa, 1989, Primary Care Svcs., Tampa, 1991, Holland & Knight, Tampa, 1991, NCC Internat., Colchester, England, 1991, F. W. Assocs., Tampa, 1989—92, Decking Design, Norfolk, 1986—93, SMinc., Columbia, 1993, Internat. Flooring & Protective Coatings, Inc., Norfolk, 1993—; sr. cons. Meisel Assocs., Inc., N.Y.C., 1983—. Contbr. articles to profl. jours. Mem. Nat. Com. Religion and Health, 1982—84; mem., vice chmn. Chariho Sch. Bd., Richmond, RI, 1974—76; mem. Broward Econ. Devel. Coun., Inc.; trustee Montefiore-Morrisania Cmty. Ctr., 1981—84. Lt. USPHS, 1956—59, capt. USPHS, 1976—81. Recipient citation, Suncoast chp. Am. Heart Assn., 1988. Fellow: Am. Coll. Healthcare Execs.; mem.: APHA. Avocation: tennis. Home: 2863 Via Venezia Deerfield Beach FL 33442-8633

**SOLOMON, BILLY K.,** army officer; b. Oakwood/Fairfield, Tex., Nov. 16, 1944; BS in Agr. Edn., Prairie View A&M Coll.; MA in Contracting and Acquisition Mgmt., Fla. Inst. Tech.; student, Armed Forces STaff Coll., Logistics Exec. Devel. Course, Indsl. Coll. Armed Forces, DoD CAPSTONE Worldwide Tng. Program for Gen. Officers. Commd. 2d lt. U.S. Army, 1966, advanced through grades to lt. gen.; chief of staff U.S. Army Materiel Command, to 1997; dir. logistics and security assistance U.S. Army Ctrl. Command, MacDill AFB, Fla., 1997-99; commdg. gen. Combined Support Command, Fort Lee, Va., 1999—2002; ret. Decorated Def. DSM with oak leaf cluster, DSM, Legion of Merit with 2 oak leaf clusters, Bronze Star with oak leaf cluster, Def. Superior Svc. medal, Meritorious Svc. medal with three oak leaf clusters, Army Commendation medal with 1 oak leaf cluster, Army Achievement medal, Armed Forces Res. medal, others

**SOLOMON, BRUCE MICHAEL,** mathematician, educator; b. San Diego, Calif., July 22, 1953; s. Herbert Joel and Elene Gordon Solomon; m. Susan Harriet Swartz, Dec. 27, 1996; children: Naima, Lonica, Leah. PhD, Princeton U., Princeton, N.J., 1982. Assoc. prof. Ind. U., Bloomington, Ind., 1983—. Mem.: Am. Math. Soc. Jewish. Achievements include research in classification of embedded constant mean curvature surfaces in R—3; the absence of skew loops characterizes ellipsoids among compact surfaces in R—3. Office: Indiana University Rawles Hall Bloomington IN 47405 Office Phone: 812-855-4900.

**SOLOMON, DAVID HARRIS,** geriatrician, educator; b. Cambridge, Mass., Mar. 7, 1923; s. Frank and Rose (Roud) Solomon; m. Ronda L. Markson, June 23, 1946; children: Patti Jean Sinaiko, Nancy Ellen. AB, Brown U., 1944; MD, Harvard U., 1946. Intern Peter Bent Brigham Hosp., Boston, 1946—47, resident, 1947—48, 1950—51; fellow endocrinology New Eng. Center Hosp., Boston, 1951—52; faculty UCLA Sch. Medicine, 1952—, prof. medicine, 1966—93, vice chmn. dept. medicine, 1968—71, chmn. dept., 1971—81, assoc. dir. geriatrics, 1982—89; dir. UCLA Ctr. on Aging, 1991—96; prof. emeritus UCLA, 1993—. Chief med. svc. Harbor Gen. Hosp., Torrance, Calif., 1966—71; cons. Wadsworth VA Hosp., L.A., 1952—93, Sepulveda VA Hosp., 1971—93; cons. metabolism tng. com. USPHS, 1960—64, endocrinology study sect., 1970—73; cons. RAND Corp., 1997—. Editor: Jour. Am. Geriatric Soc., 1988—93; contbr. numerous articles to profl. jours. Recipient Ollie Randall award, Nat. Coun. on the Aging, 2004. Master: ACP (John Phillips Meml. award 2002); mem.: AAAS, Gerontol. Soc. Am. (Freeman award 1997), Am. Geriatrics Soc. (bd. dir. 1985—93, Milo Leavitt award 1992, Disting. Svc. award 1993, Edward Henderson award 1999, David H. Solomon Disting. Svc. award named in his honor), Am. Fedn. Aging Rsch. (Irving S. Wright award 1990), Western Assn. Physicians (councillor 1972—75, pres. 1983—84), Inst. Medicine Nat. Acad. Sci., Am. Thyroid Assn. (pres. 1973—74, Disting. Svc. award 1986), Endocrine Soc. (Robert H. Williams award 1989), We. Soc. Clin. Rsch. (councillor 1964—65, Mayo Soley award 1986), Am. Soc. Clin. Investigation, Assn. Am. Physicians, UCLA Med. Alumni Assn. (Extraordinary Merit award 2002), Assn. Profs. of Medicine (pres. 1980—81), Alpha Omega Alpha, Sigma Xi, Phi Beta Kappa. Achievements include The Parlow-Solomon Chair on Aging named in his honor at UCLA School of Medicine. Home: 2103 Ridge Dr Los Angeles CA 90049-1153 Office Phone: 310-471-5256. Personal E-mail: dsolomon1@earthlink.net.

**SOLOMON, EDWARD IRA,** chemistry professor, researcher; b. NYC, Oct. 20, 1946; s. Mordecai L. and Sally S. Solomon; m. Darlene Joy Spira, Sept. 15, 1984; children: Mitchell Landau, Paige Elana. BS, Rensselaer Poly. Inst., 1968; PhD, Princeton U., 1972. Rsch. assoc. Princeton (N.J.) U., 1972-73; postdoctoral fellow H.C. Ørsted Inst., Copenhagen, 1973-74, Calif. Inst. Tech., Pasadena, 1974-75; asst. prof. MIT, Cambridge, Mass., 1975-79, assoc. prof., 1979-81, prof., 1981-82, Stanford (Calif.) U., 1982-91, Monroe E.

Spaght prof. humanities and sci., 1991—, SSRL prof., 2005—. Cons. prof., World Bank lectr. Xiamen U., People's Republic of China, 1984: O.K. Rice lectr. U. N.C., 1984, Reilly lectr. U. Notre Dame, 1985; invited prof. U. Paris, 1987; 1st Glen Seaborg lectr. U. Calif., 1990; Frontiers in Chem. Rsch. lectr. Tex. A&M U., 1990; ACS lectr. Argentina, 1992; invited prof. Tokyo Inst. Tech., 1992; Xerox lectr. U. Alta., 1993; lectr. NSC Republic of China, 1993; Leermakers lectr. Wesleyan U., 1994; Amoco lectr. Ind. U., 1995; Kahn lectr. U. N.Mex., 1996, Golden Jubilee invited prof. Tata Inst., India, 1996; Karcher lectr. U. Okla., 1997; Colloquium 3eme Cucle, Switzerland, 1998; FMC lectr. Princeton U., 1999; A.D. Little lectr. MIT, 1998, Nobel Found. lectr. Stockholm U., 2000; invited prof. Tata Inst. Bombay, India, 2000; Crawford lectr. in spectroscopy U. Minn., 2004; McElvain lectr. U. Wis., numerous other lectureships. Assoc. editor Inorganic Chemistry, 1985—; mem. editl. adv. bd. Chem. Revs., 1990—, Jour. Inorganic Biochemistry, Chemtracts, Chemistry and Biology, Jour. Biol. Inorganic Chemistry, Coord. Chem. Revs.; mem. editl. bd. Indian Jour. Chemistry, Cen. European Jour. Chemistry, Inorganica Chemica Acta; author. 470 articles to profl. publs., including Jour. Am. Chem. Soc., Inorganic Chemistry, Procs. of NAS, Phys. Rev. Sci. Mem. panels NIH, NSF, Washington; mem. vis. coms. Exxon, U. Calif., Santa Cruz. Recipient Ramsen award Md. ACS and Johns Hopkins U., 1994, NIH Merit award, 1995, Dean award for disting. tchg., 1990, G.W. Wheland medal, U. Chgo., 2001, ACS award Inorganic Chem., 2001, Frontiers Biol. Chem. award, Max Planck Inst., NIH Merit award, 2002, Centenary medal and lectureship Royal Soc. U.K., 2003; Sloan fellow. Fellow AAAS, NAS, Japan Soc. for Promotion of Sci., Am. Acad. Arts and Scis.; mem. Am. Chem. Soc. (chmn. bioinorganic divsn., award for disting. svc. in advancement of inorganic chemistry 2006), Am. Phys. Soc., Internat. EPR Soc., Soc. Biol. Inorganic Chemistry, Sigma Xi. Achievements include research in structure/function correlations in copper cluster proteins, in electronic structure of the blue copper active site, in spectroscopic definition of the active site in the Cu/ZnO methanol synthesis catalyst, in new spectroscopic probes of non-heme iron enzymes, in excited state potential energy surfaces of inorganic complexes and their contribution to reactivity, on new methods of inorganic spectroscopy; covalency in transition metal complexes. Office: Stanford U Dept Chemistry Roth Way Stanford CA 94305 Office Phone: 650-723-9104. E-mail: edward.solomon@stanford.edu.

**SOLOMON, ELINOR HARRIS,** economics professor; b. Boston, Feb. 26, 1923; d. Ralph and Linna Harris; m. Richard A. Solomon, Mar. 30, 1957; children: Joan S. Griffin, Robert H., Thomas H. AB, Mt. Holyoke Coll., 1944; MA, Radcliffe U., 1945; PhD, Harvard U., 1948. Jr. economist Fed. Res. Bank Boston, 1945-48; economist Fed. Res. Bd. Govs., Washington, 1949-56; internat. economist U.S. State Dept., Washington, 1957-58; professorial lectr. Am. U., Washington, 1964-66; sr. economist antitrust div. U.S. Dept. Justice, Washington, 1966-82; prof. econs. George Washington U., Washington, 1982—. Econ. cons., Washington, 1982—; expert witness antitrust, fin. networks, electronic funds transfer cases, Washington, 1988—. Author: Virtual Money, 1997; author, editor: Electronic Funds Transfers and Payments, 1987, Electronic Money Flows, 1991; contbr. articles on econs., banking and law to profl. jours. Mem. Am. Econs. Assn., Nat. Economists Club (bd. govs. 1997-98), The Cosmos Club (chmn. Frontiers of Sci. 2001-04, chmn. program com. 2004-06, bd. mgmt. 2006—). Home: 6805 Delaware St Chevy Chase MD 20815-4164 Office: George Washington U Dept Econ Washington DC 20052-0001 Personal E-mail: rsolomonhome@earthlink.net.

**SOLOMON, GAIL ELLEN,** physician; b. Bklyn., May 26, 1938; d. Samuel and Estelle (Suffin) S.; m. Harvey Hecht, Oct. 28, 1962; children: Daniel, Jonathan, Elizabeth. AB, Smith Coll., 1958; MD, Albert Einstein Coll. Medicine, 1962. Diplomate Am. Bd. Pediats., Am. Bd. Psychiatry and Neurology (assoc. examiner), Am. Bd. Electroencephalography, Am. Bd. Electroencephalography and Neurophysiology, Am. Bd. Clin. Neurophysiology. Intern in pediat. Bronx Mcpl. Hosp. Ctr., 1962—63, resident in pediat., 1963—64, N.Y. Hosp.-Cornell U. Med. Coll., N.Y.C., 1964—65; NIH vis. fellow in neurology and child neurology Columbia-Presbyn. Med. Ctr., N.Y.C., 1965—68, NIH vis. fellow in clin. neurophysiology and electroenceph.; instr. neurology Columbia U. Coll. of Physicians and Surgeons, N.Y.C., 1968—69, asst. prof. neurology and pediat., 1970—76, assoc. prof. clin. neurology and pediat., 1976—2004, prof. clin. neurology and pediat., 2004—; asst. prof. Cornell U. Med. Coll., 1969—70, prof. clin. neurology and and pediat., 2004—; asst. attending in neurology and pediat. N.Y. Hosp., N.Y.C., 1969—76, dir. electroencephalography, 1969—, assoc. attending in neurology and pediat., 1976—, assoc. attending neurologist in psychiatry, 1983—. Mem. joint com. for stroke facilities NIH; mem. FDA Peripheral and CNS Adv. Com., 1979-83, chmn., 1983, cons., 1983-84; mem. med. audit com. N.Y. Hosp., mem. utilization rev. com.; mem. profl. adv. bd. N.Y. State Epilepsy Assn.; adj. attending physician in neurology Meml.-Sloan Kettering Cancer Ctr., 1982-93; assoc. attending pediatrician Hosp. Spl. Surgery, 1987—; neurology cons. Blythedale Children's Hosp., Valhalla, N.Y., 1991—, Meml.-Sloan Kettering Cancer Ctr., 1993—. Author: (with F. Plum) Clinical Management of Seizures: A Guide for the Physician, 1976, (with Plum and Kutt) 2d edit., 1983; editor: (with Kaufman and Pfeffer) Child and Adolescent Neurology for Psychiatrists, 1992, Neurologic Disorders: Developmental and Behavioral Sequelae, 1999; contbr. articles to profl. jours., chpts. to med. books. Fellow: Am. Acad. Neurology, Am. Acad. Pediats., Am. Electroencephalographic Soc.; mem.: AMA (Physician's Recognition award in Continuing Med. Edn.)), NY State Med. Soc., NY County Med. Soc., Am. Med. Women's Assn., Am. Epilepsy Soc., Am. Acad. Clin. Neurophysiology, Eastern EEG Soc., Am. Med. EEG Assn., Child Neurology Soc., Internat. Child Neurology Assn., Tristate Child Neurology Soc., Assn. for Rsch. in Nervous and Mental Diseases, NY Acad. Sci. Avocations: art museums, reading literature, french language, travel. Office: NY Presbyn Hosp Cornell U Med Coll 525 E 68th St New York NY 10021-4870

**SOLOMON, HENRY,** university dean; b. Bronx, N.Y., Nov. 28, 1926; s. Max and Tillie (Gilerowitz) S.; m. Jacqueline Mona Cohen, May 31, 1953; 1 son, Michael Robert. BA, Bklyn. Coll., 1949; MA, NYU, 1950, PhD, 1960. Rsch. assoc., then sr. staff investigator and dep. prin. investigator Logistics Rsch. Project George Washington U., 1950—66, prof. econs., chmn. dept., 1962—74, 1991—96, dean Grad. Sch. Arts and Scis., 1974—90, prof. and dean emeritus, 1996—. Dep. asst. adminstr. econs., acting asst. adminstr. planning, research and analysis SBA, 1966-67; cons. in field. Assoc. editor: Naval Research Logistics Quar., 1957-90. Served with U.S. Army, 1945-46. Recipient Founder's Day award N.Y. U., 1960 Mem.: Am. Econ. Assn. Home: # 603 5450 Whitley Park Terr Bethesda MD 20814 E-mail: henry20814@aol.com.

**SOLOMON, HILDA PEARL,** wholesale executive; b. Conway, S.C., Dec. 15, 1948; d. Ezel and Dorothy (Gottlieb) S. BFA, U. S.C., 1968. Buyer Solomon Bros. Dept. Store, Conway, 1969-73; coutourier sales Julius Lewis, Memphis, 1973-75; buyer Helen of Memphis, 1975-78, George M. Muse Clothing Co., Atlanta, 1978-83; sales rep. Whiting & Davis Co. Inc., Plainville, Mass., 1983-84, exec. sales mgr. southeast dist., 1984-92; owner Solomon, Atlanta, 1992—. Sec. bd. dirs. Bur. Wholesale Accessory Reps., Atlanta, 1983-87, Accessories On 6 Atlanta Apparel Mart, 1986-87; dir. trade shows, key accounts, export mgr., 1994-98; nat. key account mgr. Westminster, Inc., 1999-2000; dir. sales Decorative Expressions, Inc., Atlanta, 2000—. Prin. works include Posh Petals, Atlanta, 1986—. Mem. Atlanta Hist. Soc., Young Careers High Mus. Art. Jewish. Avocations: design, travel, writing, art. Home: 2917 Hamilton Sq Decatur GA 30033-1140 Office Phone: 770-300-9735 x103.

**SOLOMON, HOWARD,** pharmaceutical executive; b. Aug. 12, 1927; s. David and Faye (Gussow) S.; m. Carolyn Ruth Bower, Dec. 17, 1961 (dec. 1991); children: Andrew Wallace, David Frederic; m. Sarah Durie Billinghurst, Aug. 27, 2003 BA, CCNY, 1949; LLB, Yale U., 1952. Bar: NY 1952. Atty. Moses & Singer, NYC, 1952-55, Kay Scholer, Fierman Hays & Handler, NYC, 1956-60; pres. Hildred Mgmt. Corp., NYC, 1967-83; dir. Forest Laboratories Inc., NYC, 1964—, CEO, 1977—98, chmn., CEO, 1998—. Dir. Pharmax Ltd., Bexley, Kent., UK, 1979—; bd. trustees NY-

Presbyn. Hosp. Bd. dirs. Met. Opera, Lincoln Ctr. for Performing Arts; exec. com. mem., chmn. emeritus NYC Ballet; mem. Sch. AM. Ballet. Mem. N.Y. State Bar Assn., Yale Club, Harmonie Club of N.Y. Office: Forest Labs Inc 909 3rd Ave New York NY 10022-4731

**SOLOMON, JACK AVRUM, JR.,** lawyer, automotive executive, art dealer; b. Omaha, Oct. 25, 1928; s. John A. and Matilda (Bienstok) S.; m. Josephine J. Kleiman, June 1948 (div. Mar. 1971); children: Debra, Alisa, Michael, Rena; m. Carolyn Summers, Dec. 1973. BS, U. Nebr., 1950, LL.B. cum laude, 1952; LL.M. (Cook fellow), U. Mich., 1953. Bar: Nebr. 1950, Ill. 1951. Practice law, Chgo., 1950—; with firm Stiefel, Greenberg, Burns, Baldridge & Solomon, 1953-66, ptnr., 1958-66, Solomon, Rosenfeld, Elliot & Stiefel, and predecessor, 1966—, sr. ptnr., 1966—. Dir. Amco Industries, Inc., Chgo., 1968—, chmn. bd., 1968-69, sec., gen. counsel, 1969—; sec., dir. Mogen David Wine Corp., Chgo., 1964-71; chmn. bd., dir. Arts and Leisure Corp., 1969-76; pres., chmn. bd., dir. Circle Fine Art Corp., 1968-94; chmn. bd. S2 Art Group, Ltd., 1996—; Re Society, 1997—, Art of the Movies.com, 1999—; pres. The Las Vegas Art Dist., 2002-, mng. dir. C&J Properties LLC, 2005-; chmn., CEO Jack Gallary, Inc., High Stakes Art, Inc. Commr. Las Vegas Arts Commn., 2005—. Mem. Ill., Nebr. bar assns.; mem. Fine Art Pubs. Assn. (pres. 1982—); Mem. Order of Coif. Jewish (pres. temple 1959-61). Club: Nat. Arts (N.Y.C.). Home: 2870 Augusta Las Vegas NV 89109 Office: 1 E Charleston Las Vegas NV 89104 Office Phone: 702-868-7880. Personal E-mail: jsolomon@s2art.com.

**SOLOMON, JACK DAVID,** investment banker; b. Detroit, July 27, 1930; s. Alexander C. and Anita Ruth Solomon; m. Karla Marie Frantzve, Mar. 26, 2002; children: Jacqueline Cheryl Tal, David Neal, Gregg Harvey, Diana Ruth Rothstein, Moriah Chloé Dee. AA, L.A. City Coll., 1954; BA, L.A. State Coll., 1956, Calif. State Univ., 1958. V.p. JSH Electronics Corp., 1954—60; dir. Harwit Internat. Corp., 1954—60; pres. Fed. Electronics, 1960—66; pres., chmn. Advanced Patent Tech. Corp., 1976—83, APT Games Inc., 1978—80; co-found., dir. Am. Bank of Commerce, 1978—83; found., chmn. New Age Corp., 1980—94; pres. Genesis investment Corp., 1986—. Dir. Houston Fearless Corp., 1962—65, Western Transistor Corp., 1962—68; chmn. of the bd. dirs. Western Fed. Fin. Corp., 1964—66; dir. Fed. Land and Devel. Corp., 1964—90, Fed. Rsch. and Devel., 1965—83; chmn. of the bd. Advanced Patent tech., 1967—83. Nat. dir. Equal Opportunities Found., 1963—66; sponsor Nat. Hosp. Denever, Colo.; co-founder Israeli Armored Corps Mus.; patron Orr Chadash Orphanage Israel; vice chmn. Calif. Dem. Coun., 1966—70; candidate Calif. State Sen., 1966; dir. United Jewish Fed., 1965—67; mem. com. L.A. C. of C.; mem. World Affairs Coun.; mem. of pres. cabinet Am. Israel pub. Affairs Com.; mem. Las Vegas C. of C.; dir. Utah Shakespeareon Festival, 1999—2000. Sgt. USAF, 1948—52, serv. on the Berlin Airlift in Germany. Decorated Medal for Humane Action USAF; recipient Man of the Yr., Southern Calif., 1963, Marshall Medal for Outstanding Social Svc., 1964, Carson White award, 1964, Disting. Svc. award, L.A. Affairs Com., 1966, Disting. Citizen award, City of Montreal, 1966, Meritorious award, Dem. Party, 1966, Ken. Col., 1970, Wall of Honor, Hebrew Univ. of Jerusalem, 1976, Israeli State Med., 1990, Pres. Medal, Suleiman Demirel Pres. of Turkey, 1992. Mem.: Am. Air Mus. in Britian (found. mem.), Armed Forces Commn. and Electronics Assn., Nat. Aeronautics Assn., Internat. Assn. of Bus. and Profl. (hon.), B'nai B'rith, Pres. Club Utah Valley State Coll., Pres. Club Brigham Young Univ., Pres. Club World Jewish Congress (life), 32nd Degree Mason, Scottish Rite (life). Achievements include funded and restored the ancient Zion's Gate and Plaza in Jerusalem; constructed the Colo. Belle Hotel and Casino one of the first of its kind in Laughlin, Nev. Avocation: art. Office Phone: 801-359-3755.

**SOLOMON, LIBERTINA,** pharmacist, educator; b. Botosani, Romania, Feb. 5, 1926; d. Harry and Betty Segal; m. Monel Solomon, June 12, 1948; children: Silviu, Aniela. PhD in Biology, U. Bucharest, 1970. Registered pharmacist. Asst. prof. U. Al. I. Cuza, Iasi, Romania, 1949—59, assoc. prof., 1959—72, prof., 1972—89, rschr., 1959—89, chief dept. animal biology, 1975—80; pharmacist asst. Bronx Lebanon Hosp., N.Y.C., 1990—. Mem. Com. of According Drs. Degree, Romania, 1975—80. Contbr. more than 80 articles and rsch. papers to profl. jours., chapters to books. Mem.: N.Y. Acad. Sci. Achievements include discovery of 16 new species of gamasida (Acari) and over 160 new species of Romanian fauna; soil and parasitic gamasides. Avocation: travel. Home: 729 W 186 St Apt 2E New York NY 10033

**SOLOMON, LOUIS PAUL,** theater educator, actor, director; s. Louis M. and Marcelle N. Solomon; m. Michelle Louise Mills, June 24, 2000; children: Brad, Paul. BS, U. Maine, Presque Isle, 1979; MFA, Fla. Atlantic U., Boca Raton, 1992. English tchr., dir. theatre South Portland Sch. Dept., Maine, 1980—94; tchg. artist Learning through Enhanced Arts Programs, N.Y.C., 1998—2002; instr. theatre Brevard C.C., Cocoa, Fla., 2003—. Prodr., dir. Oceanside Theatre Co., Portland, Maine, 1985—87. Actor: Oberon in A Mid Summer Night's Dream, Fla. Atlantic U., 1989, Osmond in King Arthur, Boston Early Music Festival, 1995, Harpagon in The Miser, Nat. Theate Performing Arts, 1996, Instant Shakespeare, NY Renaissance Faire, 1997; dir.: The Happy Journey, Maine Drama Festival (Divsn. II state co-winner, 1993), The Solid Gold Cadillac, Brevard CC, 2006. Esther Griswold Theatre scholar, Fla. Atlantic U., 1988. Mem.: SAG, Actors Equity Assn. Avocations: sports, cooking. Personal E-mail: solomonl@brevardcc.edu.

**SOLOMON, MARILYN KAY,** primary school educator, consultant, small business owner; b. Marshall, Mo., Oct. 16, 1947; d. John W. and Della M. (Dille) S. BS, Ctrl. Mo. State U., 1969; MS, Ind. U., 1974. Cert. in early childhood and nursery sch. edn., Mo., Ind. Tchr. Indpls. Pub. Schs., 1969—74; dir. Singer Learning Ctrs., Indpls., 1974—78; v.p. ECLC Learning Ctrs., Inc., Indpls., 1978—95; pres., CEO, owner Early Learning Ctrs., Inc., Indpls., 1995—; owner, pres., CEO Solomon Antique Restoration, Inc., Indpls., 1996—, The Shoppes at Guilford Junction, 2002—; pres., CEO Woodbridge Group, 1995—. Mem. OJT tng. task force Dept. Labor, Washington; mem. nat. task force for parenting edn. HEW, Washington; cons. to numerous corps. on corp. child care; built 29 child care ctrs. for corps., hosps. and govt. Co-author curricula. Founding bd. dirs. Mid City Pioneer, Indpls., 1977; mem. adv. bd. Enterprise Zone Small Bus. Incubator, Indpls., 1995-2002; founding bd. dirs. Family Support Ctr., Indpls., 1983, pres. bd. dirs., 1985-87; founding mem., co-chair Voices for Children, 1996—2004; mem. White Rivers Gardens State Park, Indpls. Mus. Art, 500 Festival Assn. Recipient Outstanding Leadership award Ind. Conf. on Social Concerns, 1975, 76, 77, Children's Mus. Edn. award, 1974; named to Outstanding Young Women of Am., 1984. Mem. Indpls. Mus. Art, Ind. Lic. Child Care Assn. (v.p. 1992, pres. 1974, 75), State of Ind. Quality and Tng. Coun. (chair 1992), Step Ahead-Marion County (rep. for child care 1992—2005, co-chair educare com. 1999—2005), Ind. Alliance for Better Child Care (bd. dirs. 1992, adv. bd. 1990-95), Pub. Broadcasting (tng. com. 1992-99, child devel. tng. com. 1996-99), Indpls. Zool. Soc. (charter), Order Eastern Star. Office: Early Learning Ctrs Inc 1315 S Sherman Dr Indianapolis IN 46203-2210 E-mail: earlylearn@indy.rr.com.

**SOLOMON, MARK RAYMOND,** lawyer, educator; b. Pitts., Aug. 23, 1945; s. Louis Isadore and Fern Rhea (Josselson) S. BA, Ohio State U., 1967; MEd, Cleve. State U., 1971; JD with hons., George Washington U., 1973; LLM in Taxation, Georgetown U., 1976. Bar: Ohio, Mich., U.S. Dist. Ct. (ea. dist.) Mich., U.S. Ct. Appeals (6th cir.), U.S. Tax Ct., U.S. Ct. Fed. Claims. Tax law specialist corp. tax for Nat. Office of IRS, 1973—75; assoc. Butzel, Long, Gust, Klein & Van Zile, Detroit, 1976—78; dir., v.p. Shatzman & Solomon, P.C., Southfield, Mich., 1978—81; prof., chmn. tax/bus. law dept., dir. MS in Taxation Program Walsh Coll., Troy, Mich., 1981—; of counsel in tax matters Meyer, Kirk, Snyder & Lynch, PLLC, Bloomfield Hills, Mich., 1981—1. Adj. prof. law U. Detroit, 1977-81. Editor: Cases and Materials on Consolidated Tax Returns, 1978, Cases and Materials on the Application of Legal Principles and Authorities to Federal Tax Law, 1990. Mem.: Mich. Bar Assn., Phi Eta Sigma. Avocation: bridge (life master). Home: 2109 Golfview Dr Apt 102 Troy MI 48084-3926 Office: Meyer Kirk Snyder & Lynch PLLC

100 W Long Lake Rd Ste 100 Bloomfield Hills MI 48304-2773 also: Walsh Coll 3838 Livernois Rd Troy MI 48083-5066 Office Phone: 248-823-1277. Business E-mail: msolomon@walshcollege.edu.

**SOLOMON, MARSHA HARRIS,** draftsman, artist; b. Tulsa, Oct. 21, 1940; d. Ruel Sutton and Anna May (Fellows) Harris; m. Robert E. Collier, Aug. 13, 1960 (div. Dec. 1968); 1 child, Craig Robert Collier. m. Louis G. Solomon, Sept. 5, 1984. Student, U. Tex., 1958-61; BFA, U. Houston, 1966. Chief draftsman Internat. Paper, Petroleum and Minerals Divsn., Houston, 1985—2003; artist, ptnr. Archway Gallery, Houston, 1994. Mem. Nat. Mus. Women in Art (charter). Mem. Watercolor Art Soc. Houston (bd. dirs. 1984-91, treas. 1987-89, pres. 1990-91), Tex. Watercolor Soc. (signature mem., Purple Sagebrush), N.Mex. Watercolor Soc. (signature mem.), Okla. Watercolor Soc. (signature mem.), Ariz. Watercolor Soc. (signature mem., Royal Scorpion mem.). Home: 5832 Valley Forge Dr Houston TX 77057-2248

**SOLOMON, MAYNARD ELLIOTT,** musicologist, retired recording industry executive; b. N.Y.C., Jan. 5, 1930; s. Benjamin and Dora (Levine) S.; m. Eva Georgiana Tevan, Jan. 22, 1951; children: Mark Jonathan, Nina Stephanie, Maury David. BA, Bklyn. Coll., 1950; postgrad., Columbia U., 1950-51; MusD (hon.), New Eng. Conservatory Music, 2005. Co-founder, co-owner Vanguard Rec. Soc., Inc., N.Y.C., 1950-86; faculty grad. div. CUNY, 1979-81. Vis. prof. SUNY Stony Brook, 1988, Columbia U., N.Y.C., 1990, Harvard U., Cambridge, Mass., 1992, Yale U., New Haven, 1994-95; scholarly advisor Beethoven Archive, Bonn, 1997—; faculty grad. divsn. Juilliard Sch., 1998—. Author: Marxism and Art, 1973, Beethoven, 1977 (translated into German, French, Spanish, Portuguese, Japanese, Italian, Bulgarian), Myth, Creativity and Psychoanalysis, 1978, Beethoven's Tagebuch, 1982, Beethoven's Tagebuch, German translation, 1990, Italian translation, 1992, Japanese translation, 2001, Beethoven Essays, 1988, Italian translation, 1998; Mozart: A Life, 1995 (translated into Swedish, Italian, Japanese, German, Portuguese, Hungarian), Late Beethoven, 2003; editor: Joan Baez Songbook, 1964; contbg. editor: Beethoven Forum, Am. Imago; mem. editl. bd. Beethovenhaus edit. Beethoven's Letters; editor: Memories of Beethoven, 1992; prodr. over 100 folk music albums; contbr. articles to profl. jours. Recipient Deems Taylor award ASCAP, 1978, 89, 96, Disting. Vis. award U. Toronto, 1996. Mem. PEN, Am. Musicol. Soc. (bd. dirs. 1984-86, Otto Kinkeldey award 1989, hon. mem. 1999), Authors Guild, N.Y. Inst. for Humanities, Phi Beta Kappa. Home: 1 W 72nd St New York NY 10023-3486 Personal E-mail: maynardsol@aol.com.

**SOLOMON, NEAL EDWARD,** management consultant, executive recruiter, social theorist, entrepreneur, author; b. San Diego, Mar. 9, 1960; s. Donald Jay and Roberta Yvonne (Recht) S. BA in Philosophy, Reed Coll., Portland, Oreg., 1981; AM in Philosophy, U. Chgo., 1982. Founder Calif. Legal Search, 1983—, Catalyst Learning Strategies, 2002; chmn., CEO Solomon Rsch., 2004—. Author: A Turning Point in World History?, 1992, High Performance Venture Characteristics, 1992, Dilemmas of Democracy (3 vols.: A Critique of Liberalism, A Critique of Political Ideology, The Limits of Social Theory), 1992, The Problem of Modernity, 1993, Theoretical Foundations of Dynamic Macroeconomics, 1993, The Evolution of Philosophy, 1995, Legal Management Theory, 2d edit., 1997, Transformation of the Corporate Law Firm, 1998, others. Democrat. Achievements include inventions regarding electronic commerce, robotics, proteomics, databases, and intelligent systems. Address: Ste 1600 580 California St San Francisco CA 94104 E-mail: ulysses@well.com.

**SOLOMON, PATTY JO,** elementary school educator; b. Richmond, Mo., Mar. 25, 1965; d. Glen B. and Joyce A. (Briggs) Solomon. AA Bus., Wentworth Jr. Coll., 1985; B Elem. Edn., Ctrl. Mo. State U., 1987; M Elem. Edn., N.W. Mo. State U., 1996. Cert. lifetime tchg. grades 1-8 Mo. Dept. Elem. and Secondary Edn. Tchr. 3d grade Richmond R-XVI Sch. Dist., 1988—98, tchr. 2d grade, 1998—. Coach Mo. Accelerated Schs., Richmond, 1998—. Mem. exec. bd. Federated Women's Dem. Club Ray County, Richmond, 1986—96. Mem.: AAUW (treas. 1988—98), PTA (exec. bd. 1992—), Richmond Cmty. Tchr's Assn. (exec. bd. 1988—, Outstanding Leader of Yr. 1993—94, Outstanding Educator of Yr. 2003—04), Mo. State Tchrs. Assn. (del. to conv. 1987—, Profl. Devel. Com. ctrl. region 1996—2002), Phi Kappa Phi, Delta Kappa Gamma (chpt. Beta Tau 1997—2000), Kappa Delta Pi. Democrat. Baptist. Achievements include helping to formulate a MSTA resolution that led to the passage of legislation in the Missouri Assembly, that returned lifetime certification to Missouri teachers. Avocations: reading, walking, travel, collecting historical artifacts. Office: Sunrise Elem Sch 401 Matt Waller Dr Richmond MO 64085

**SOLOMON, PAUL ROBERT,** neuropsychologist, educator; b. Bklyn., Aug. 27, 1948; s. Maynard and Norma Harris (Ruben) S.; m. Suellen Zablow, Aug. 16, 1970; children: Todd, Jessica. BA in Psychology, SUNY, New Paltz, 1970, MA in Psychology, 1972; PhD in Psychology, U. Mass., 1972. Diplomate Am. Coll. Forensic Examiners; lic. psychologist, Mass. Prof. psychology and neurosci. Williams Coll, Williamstown, Mass., 1976—; neurosci. program chmn., 1990-95; dir. memory disorders clinic S.W. Vt. Med. Ctr., Bennington, 1990—; pres. Clin. Neurosci. Rsch. Assocs., 1997—. Bd. dirs. No. Berkshire Mental Health Assn., North Adams, Mass. Author: Scientific Writings, 1985, Memory, 1989, Psychology 4th edit., 1993; contbr. articles to profl. jours. Bd. dirs. W. Mass. Alzheimers Assn., 1992—. Recipient Distinguished Teaching award U. Mass., Amherst, 1975; Rsch. grantee EPA, NIH, NSF, 1978—; Rsch. fellowships NIH, 1979, NSF, 1980. Fellow APA, AAAS, Am. Psychol. Soc.; mem. Soc. for Neuroscience. Home: 130 Forest Rd Williamstown MA 01267-2029 Office: Williams Coll Dept Psychology Williamstown MA 01262

**SOLOMON, PEARL GOLD,** education educator, consultant; d. Joseph and Rose Gold; m. Milton Solomon, Feb. 12, 1950; children: Ellen Heidi Burke, Nancy Whitney Grunwald. BA, Hunter Coll., 1949, MA, 1952; EdD, Columbia U., 1977. Cert. tchr. math. and sci. N.Y. State, sch. dist. administr. N.Y. Tchr. elem. edn. and h.s. N.Y.C. schs., 1949—68; tchr. h.s., prin., dir. curriculum Pearl River (N.Y.) Schs., 1968—91; prof. emerita St. Thomas Aquinas Coll., Sparkill, NY, 1991—. Profl. cons. Pk. Ridge Schs., NJ, 2000—05, Edvotek, Inc. 1998—, Columbia U., N.Y.C., 2005—, NYU, N.Y.C., 2005—. Author: (tchrs. text.) The Curriculum Bridge (Outstanding Academic Book. award ALA, 1994), (tchrs. text) No Small Feat, (text) The Math WE Need to Know and Do (Finalist, Book of Yr. Award Am. Assn. of Colls. of Tchr. Edn., 2002), The Assesment Bridge. Founder, dir. Pearl River Comm. Coun., 1975—91. Named Woman of the Yr., Orgn. for Rehab. and Tng., 1979; recipient Cert. Merit, Assembly of State of N.Y., 1987, Disting. Svc. award, County of Rockland, 1987, Liberty Bell award, Rockland County Bar Assn., 1981, Dedication and Contbn. to Cmty. Svc. award, Orangetown Police Dept., 1987. Mem.: Am. Ednl. Rsch. Assn. Office: St Thomas Aquinas Coll Rte 340 Sparkill NY 10976 Office Phone: 845-398-4000. Personal E-mail: pgsolomon@msn.com. E-mail: psolomon@stac.edu.

**SOLOMON, RANDALL LEE,** lawyer; b. Dayton, Ohio, June 8, 1948; BA summa cum laude, Wright State U., 1970; JD, Case Western Res. U., 1973. Bar: Ohio 1973, U.S. Dist. Ct. (no. dist.) Ohio 1973, U.S. Ct. Appeals (6th cir.) 1973, U.S. Ct. Appeals (fed. cir.) 1988, U.S. Supreme Ct. 2002. Ptnr. Baker & Hostetler, Cleve. Life mem. Sixth Circuit Jud. Conf., Eighth Dist. Jud. Conf., Ohio; speaker in field. Fellow Am. Coll. Trial Lawyers; mem. ABA (mem. litigation, tort and ins. practice sects.), Ohio State Bar Assn., Cleve. Bar Assn. (chair litig. sect. 1991-92), Nat. Inst. Trial Advocacy (mem. nat. session 1978), Def. Rsch. Inst., Anthony J. Celebrezze Inn. of Ct. (master). Office: Baker & Hostetler LLP 3200 Nat City Ctr 1900 E 9th St Ste 3200 Cleveland OH 44114-3475 Office Phone: 216-861-7327. Business E-Mail: rsolomon@bakerlaw.com.

**SOLOMON, RAYMAN LOUIS,** dean, law educator; b. Helena, Ark., Sept. 5, 1947; s. David and Miriam (Rayman) S.; m. Carol Avins, Aug. 10, 1975. BA, Wesleyan U., 1968; MA in History, U. Chgo., 1972, JD, 1976, PhD in History, 1986. Bar: Ill. 1976, U.S. Ct. Appeals (7th cir.) 1978, U.S. Ct.

Appeals (6th cir.) 1979. Dir. court history project U.S. Ct. Appeals (7th cir.), Chgo., 1976-78; law clk. to presiding judge U.S. Ct. Appeals (6th cir.), Cin., 1978-79; Bigelow fellow instr. U. Chgo. Law Sch., 1979-80; research fellow Am. Bar Found., Chgo., 1980-89, assoc. dir., 1986-89; assoc. dean Northwestern U. Sch. Law, Chgo., 1989—98; dean Rutgers U. Sch. Law, Camden, 1998—. Instr. Kent-Ill. Inst. Tech. Coll. Law, Chgo. 1982, Northwestern U., Evanston, Ill. 1986. Author: History of the Seventh Circuit, 1981; editor Am. Bar Found. Research Jour., 1985-87. Bd. dirs. Family Counseling Svc. of Evanston, 1985—, BPI, 1990—. Served with USN, 1969-70. Mem. ABA, Law and Soc. Assn., Selden Soc., Am. Soc. Legal Hist. (bd. dirs. 1985-88). Democrat. Jewish. Office: Rutgers State U Sch Law 217 North Fifth St Camden NJ 08102 Office Phone: 856-225-6191. Office Fax: 856-225-6487. E-mail: raysol@camlaw.rutgers.edu.*

**SOLOMON, RICHARD HARVEY,** think-tank executive; b. Phila., June 19, 1937; s. Bertram Harvey and Ellen (Harris) S.; m. Anne G. Keatley, Dec. 16, 1991. Student, Harvard U., 1959-63, Yale U., 1961, 63-64; SB, MIT, 1960, PhD, 1966. Tech. photographer, lab. worker Photon, Inc., Cambridge, Mass., 1957; rschr. Polaroid Corp., 1959-61; rsch. assoc. Ctr. for Chinese Studies U. Mich., Ann Arbor, Mich., 1966-71, from asst prof. to prof. polit. sci., 1966-71; staff mem. NSC, Washington, 1971-76; head. polit. sci dept. The Rand Corp., Santa Monica, Calif., 1976-86, program dir. Internat. Security Policy Research, 1977-83; mem. Pres.' Commn. on Fgn. Lang. and Internat. Studies Washington, 1978-80; mem. Chief of Naval Ops. exec. panel, 1983—; dir. policy planning staff Dept. of State, Washington, 1986-89, asst. sec. of state for East Asian and Pacific affairs, 1989-92; U.S. ambassador to Philippines, 1992-93; pres. U.S. Inst. of Peace, Washington, 1993—. Author: Mao's Revolution and the Chinese Political Culture, 1999, Chinese Political Negotiating Behavior, 1999, Exiting Indochina, 2000; contbr. articles to profl. jours. Office: US Inst of Peace 1200 17th St NW Ste 200 Washington DC 20036-3011 Business E-Mail: usip_requests@usip.org.

**SOLOMON, RICHARD HUGH,** art dealer, publishing executive; b. Boston, May 12, 1934; m. Ann Weinbaum; Solomon; children: John, James. BA, Harvard U., 1956, MBA, 1958. Mktg. exec. Stop & Shop Inc., Boston, 1958-67; advt. exec. Clairol, N.Y.C., 1967-70; pres. Pace Edits. Inc. and subs., N.Y.C., 1970—; chmn. Pace/McGill, N.Y.C., 1984-92. Mem. Art Dealers Assn. Am. (bd. dirs. 1990-92, pres.), Internat. Fine Print Dealers Assn. (bd. dirs. 1992—). Office: Pace Prints/Pace Editions 32 E 57th St New York NY 10022-2513 Office Phone: 212-219-8000.

**SOLOMON, RISA GREENBERG,** clinical social worker, child and family therapist, former entertainment industry executive; b. NYC, June 22, 1948; d. Nathan and Frances (Guttman) Greenberg; m. Philip Howard Solomon, June 21, 1970 (dec. 1994); children: Elycia Beth, Cynthia Gayle. BA, NYU, 1969, MA, 1970, MSSW, 1996. Asst. editor Redbook Mag., N.Y.C., 1969-70; assoc. editor Greenwood Press, Westport, Conn., 1970-71; mng. editor Dushkin Pub., Guilford, Conn., 1971-72; freelance editor Yale U. Press, New Haven, 1972-75; v.p. ops. Videoland, Inc., Dallas, 1980-82; v.p. Video Software Dealers Assn., Cherry Hill, N.J. and Dallas, 1981-83; pres. Videodome Enterprises, Dallas, 1983-94; clin. social worker, child and family therapist pvt. practice, Dallas, 1994—. Cons. Home Rec. Rights Coalition, Washington, 1983—84; spkr. in field of child and adolescent therapy. Bd. dirs. Congregation Anshai Emet, Dallas, 1985-86. Mem. Video Software Dealers Assn. (founder, dir. 1981-82). Democrat. Jewish. Avocations: skiing, travel, tennis, scuba diving. Office: 17103 Preston Rd Ste 100 Dallas TX 75248 Personal E-mail: rgs8961@msn.com.

**SOLOMON, ROBERT,** economist; b. NYC, May 2, 1921; s. Sol and Betty (Brownstone) S.; m. Fern Rice, Sept. 11, 1946 (dec. 2001); children: Carol Ann, Barbara Betty, Anne Eleanor. BA, U. Mich., 1942; MA, Harvard U., 1947, PhD, 1952. With Fed. Res. Bd., 1947-76, assoc. adviser research div., 1963-65, adviser research div., 1965, adviser to bd. govs., 1965-76, dir. div. internat. fin., 1966-72; sr. fellow Brookings Instn., Washington, 1976-80, guest scholar, 1980—. Pres. RS Assos., pub. Internat. Econ. Letter, 1981—2005; vice chmn. deps. of com. of 20 IMF, 1972-74; adj. prof. Am. U., 1962-67; sr. staff economist Coun. Econ. Advisers, 1963-64 Author: The International Monetary System, 1945-81, 1982, Partners in Prosperity, 1991, Money on the Move, 1999, The Transformation of the World Economy, 1999; contbr. articles to profl. jours. 1st lt. USAAF, 1942—45. Decorated D.F.C., Air medal; named Officier Legion of Honor France; recipient Rockefeller Pub. Service award, 1971. Mem. Am. Econ. Assn., Coun. on Fgn. Relations. Clubs: Cosmos (Washington). Home and Office: 8502 W Howell Rd Bethesda MD 20817-6827 Office Phone: 301-365-5224. E-mail: Rsolo52178@aol.com.

**SOLOMON, ROBERT A.,** law educator; BA, Rutgers U., 1969; JD, George Washington U., 1972. Bar: Pa. 1972, Conn. 1979. Staff atty, mng. atty. Legal Aid Society, Bucks County, Pa., 1972—77; mng. atty., exec. dir. New Haven Legal Assistance Assn., 1978—85; ptnr. Pittman, Sheehan, Solomon and Swaine, 1986—91; Selma A. Levine lectr. in clin. studies Yale U., New Haven, 1985—86, lectr. in clin. studies, 1986—89, adj. clin. prof., 1989—91, clin. prof., 1991—. Interim exec. dir. Housing Authority of City of New Haven, 1999—2002. Contbr. articles to law jours. Office: Yale Law Sch PO Box 208215 New Haven CT 06520 E-mail: robert.solomon@yale.edu.

**SOLOMON, ROBERT CHARLES,** philosopher, educator; b. Detroit, Sept. 14, 1942; s. Charles M. and Vita (Petrosky) S. BA, U. Mich., 1963; MA, U. Mich., 1965, PhD, 1967. Teaching fellow U. Mich. Ann Arbor, 1965-66; lectr. Princeton (N.J.) U., 1966-67, 67-68; asst. prof. U. Pitts., 1969-71, CUNY, 1971-72; assoc. prof. philosophy U. Tex., Austin, 1972-77, prof., 1977—, Quincy Lee Centennial prof., 1986-97, disting. tchg. prof., 1997—. Vis. prof. U. Pa., UCLA, U. Auckland, N.Z., La Trobe U., Melbourne, Australia, U. B.C.; chmn. Phi Beta Kappa Emerson Award Com.; cons. in field. Author: From Rationalism to Existentialism, 1972, The Passions, 1976, Introducing Philosophy: Problems and Perspectives, 1977, History and Human Nature: A Philosophical Review of European History and Culture, 1750-1850, 1979, Love: Emotion, Myth and Metaphor, 1981, In the Spirit of Hegel, 1983; (with C. Calhoun) What Is an Emotion?, 1984, It's a Good Business, 1985; (with Kristine Hanson) Above the Bottom Line, 1983, From Hegel to Existentialism, 1987, Continental Philosophy After 1750, 1988, About Love, 1988, A Passion for Justice, 1990, Ethics: A Briefer Introduction, 1991, Ethics and Excellence, 1992, Entertaining Ideas, 1992; (with J. Solomon) Up the University, 1993; (with Kathleen Higgins) A Short History of Philosophy, 1996, A Passion for Wisdom, 1997, A Better Way to Think About Business, 1999, The Joy of Philosophy, 1999, What Nietzsche Really Said, 2000; (with Fernando Flores) Building Trust, 2000, Spirituality for the Skeptic, 2002, Not Passions Slave, 2003, Living with Nietzsche, 2003, In defense of Sentimentality, 2004; editor: Phenomenology and Existentialism, 1972, Nietzsche, 1973, Existentialism, 1974; (with Kathleen Higgins) Reading Nietzsche, 1988, From Africa to Zen, 1993, The Age of German Idealism, 1993, (with Mark A. Murphy) What Is Justice?, 1990, Wicked Pleasures: Meditations on the Seven Deadly Sins, 1999, What is an Emotion, 2003, Thinking about Feeling, 2004; contbr. articles to profl. jours. Recipient Outstanding Tchr. award Standard Oil Co., 1973, Pres.' Teaching Excellence award, 1985, 96., Chad Oliver Honors Tchg. award, 1998; named to Acad. Disting. Tchrs., 1997. Mem. Am. Philos. Assn., N.Am. Nietzsche Soc., Internat. Soc. Rsch. on Emotions (pres.), Soc. for Bus. Ethics, Acad. Disting. Tchrs.

**SOLOMON, SAMUEL,** biochemistry educator, administrator; b. Brest Litovsk, Poland, Dec. 5, 1925; s. Nathan and Rachel (Greenberg) S.; m. Sheila R. Horn, Aug. 11, 1953 (div. 1974); children: David Horn, Peter Horn, Jonathan Simon; m. Augusta M. Vineberg, July 12, 1974. BS with honors, McGill U., 1947, MS, 1951, PhD in Biochemistry, 1953. Rsch. asst. Columbia U., 1953-55, assoc. in biochemistry, 1958-59, asst. prof., 1959-60; assoc. prof. biochemistry and expti. medicine McGill U., 1960-66, prof., 1967-95, prof. emeritus, 1995—, prof. ob-gyn., 1976-95; dir. endocrine lab. Royal Victoria Hosp., Montreal, Que. 1965-95, dir. research inst., 1982-85; affilate dept. pharmacology U. Sherbrooke, 1995—. Mem. endocrinology and metabolism grants com. Med. Rsch. Coun. Can., 1967-71, regional dir. for Que., 1993-95; vis. prof. endocrinology U. Vt., 1964; cons. in field; Joseph Price orator, 1982, Am. OB-GYN Soc.; mem. steering com. Pharm. Mfg. Assn. Med. Rsch. Coun. Can. Partnership, 1993—; Med. Rsch. Coun. Can. dir. for McGill U., 1993-95. Co-editor: Chemical and Biological Aspects of Steroid Conjugation, 1970; mem. editl. bd. Endocrinology, 1962; assoc. editor Can. Jour. Biochemistry, 1967-71, Jour. Med. Primatology, 1971; contbr. articles to profl. jours. Mem. bd. govs. McGill U., 1975-78; mem. steering com. European Study Group on Steroid Hormones, 1974-99, chmn. steering com., 1983-99, chmn. program com., 1990-91; mem. Dubin Commn. on Inquiry Drugs in Athletes, 1988-90. Decorated officer Order of Can. 1997; recipient McLaughlin medal Royal Soc. Can., 1989, Michel Sarrazin prize, 1997. Fellow Chem. Inst. Can., Am. Ob-Gyn. Soc. (hon.), Perinatal Rsch. Soc. Am. (pres. 1976), Soc. Gynecol. Investigation (program chmn. 1980), Endocrine Soc. (publ. com. 1986-89). Home: 239 Kensington Ave 804 Montreal PQ Canada H3Z 2H1 Business E-Mail: samuel.solomon@mcgill.ca.

**SOLOMON, SEAN CARL,** geophysicist, lab administrator; b. LA, Oct. 24, 1945; BS geophysics, Calif. Inst. Tech., 1966; PhD geophysics, MIT, 1971. From asst. prof. to prof. geophysics MIT, Cambridge, 1972-92; dir. dept. terrestrial magnetism Carnegie Instn. Washington, 1992—. Vis. scientist Lunar Sci. Inst., 1975, Lawrence Livermore Nat. Lab., 1978, Jet Propulsion Lab., 1990—91; guest investigator Woods Hole Oceanographic Inst., 1979—92; vis. faculty Inst. Geophysics and Planetary Physics, dept. earth and space scis. UCLA, 1982—83; Roland and Jane Blumberg vis. prof. planetary scis. U. Tex., Austin, 1988; vis. assoc. divsn. geol. and planetary scis. Calif. Inst. Tech., 1990—91; mem. various groups, teams, coms. NASA, 1974—; earthquake hazards reduction program peer rev. panel U.S. Geol. Survey, 1975, 85; lunar and planetary sci. coun. Univs. Space Rsch. Assn., 1978—80, 1991—93; tech. rev. panel, geophysics rev. panel Dept. Def., 1981—85; chmn. steering com. space sci. working group Assn. Am. Univs., 1987—89; rev. panelist NSF, 1986, 88, 95, 96, 2001, 03, 2006—; chmn. standing com. global seismic network Inc. Rsch. Instns. Seismology, 1988—90; participant numerous oceanographic expeditions, 1967—88. Editor (assoc. editor): Proceedings of the Lunar and Planetary Sci. Conf., 1976, 1978, Jour. Geophys. Rsch., 1976—78, Physics of the Earth and Planetary Interiors, 1977, Eos Transactions of Am. Geophys. Union, 1979—81, Geophys. Rsch. Letters, 1986—88; editor: Tectonophysics, 1981; mem. editl. bd.: Physics and Chemistry of Earth, 1981—85, Astrobiology, 2001—, Earth and Planetary Sci. Letters, 2001—, mem. editl. com.: Ann. Rev. Earth and Planetary Scis., 1993—97; contbr. articles to profl. jours. Recipient Arthur L. Day prize, NAS, 1999, Public Svc. medal, NASA, 2004, Disting. Alumni award, Calif. Inst. Tech., 2006; fellow Grad., NSF, 1966—68, Postdoctoral, 1971—72, Fannie and John Hertz Found., 1968—71, Alfred P. Sloan Rsch., 1977—81, John Simon Guggenheim Meml., 1982—83. Fellow: AAAS, Geol. Soc. Am. (G.K. Gilbert award 1999), Am. Geophys. Union (pres. elect and pres. 1994—98, pres. planetology sect. 1984—88, chmn. geophys. monograph bd. 1983—84, numerous coms., H.H. Hess medal 2005), Am. Acad. Arts and Scis.; mem.: NAS, Seismol. Soc. Am., Am. Astron. Soc. (divsn. planetary scis.), Tau Beta Pi. Office: Carnegie Instn Dept Terrestrial Magnetism 5241 Broad Branch Rd NW Washington DC 20015-1305 Office Phone: 202-478-8850. E-mail: scs@dtm.ciw.edu.

**SOLOMON, SEYMOUR,** neurologist, consultant; b. Milw., May 27, 1924; s. Morris and Sylvia (Heifetz) S.; m. Ethel Marion Ross, Mar. 28, 1948; children: Robert, Debora. Student, Marquette U., 1942-44, MD, 1947. Diplomate Am. Bd. Psychiatry and Neurology. Intern Mt. Sinai Hosp., Milw., 1947-48, resident in internal medicine, 1948-50; resident in neurology Montefiore Hosp., N.Y.C., 1950-52; chief neurology Phila. Gen. Hosp., 1952-53; instr. neurology Temple U. Sch. Medicine, Phila., 1952-55, Woman's Med. Coll., Phila., 1952-55; attending neurologist Montefiore Med. Ctr., Bronx, N.Y., 1955—, dir. headache unit, 1980—; asst. clin. prof. neurology Columbia U. Coll. Physicians and Surgeons, N.Y.C., 1958-64; assoc. prof. neurology Albert Einstein Coll. Medicine, Bronx, 1980-83, prof. neurology, 1983—. Author: The Headache Book, 1991; author 220 book chpts. and revs.; editor abstracts Jour. Headache, 1987-96; editor Headache Rev., 1988-92; contbr. 150 articles to profl. jours. Capt. USAF, 1953-55. Fellow Am. Acad. Neurology, Am. Headache Soc. (pres.); mem. AMA, Am. Neurol. Assn., Am. Coun. Headache Edn., Internat. Assn for Study of Pain, Internat. Headache Soc., Assn. for Rsch. in Nervous and Mental Diseases. Avocations: photography, travel. Office: Montefiore Med Ctr 1575 Blondell Ave Bronx NY 10461 Office Phone: 718-405-8360. Business E-Mail: ssolomon@montefiore.org.

**SOLOMON, SUSAN,** chemist, scientist; b. Chicago, Ill., Jan. 19, 1956; d. Leonard Marvin and Alice (Rutman) Solomon; m. Barry Lane Sidwell, Sept. 20, 1988. BS in Chemistry, Ill. Inst. Tech., 1977; MS in Chemistry, U. Calif., Berkeley, 1979, PhD in Chemistry, 1981; D (hon.), Tulane U., Williams Coll., SUNY at Stony Brook, Ill. Inst. Tech., U. Colo. Sr. scientist aeronomy lab. NOAA, Boulder, Colo., 1981—88, program leader middle atmosphere group aeronomy lab., 1988—. Adj. faculty U. Colo., 1982—; head project sci. Nat. Ozone Expdn., McMurdo Station, Antarctica, 1986, McMurdo Station, Antarctica, 87; co-chair Intergovernmental Panel on Climate Change. Co-author: Aeronomy of the Middle Atmosphere, 1984; contbr. articles to sci. jours. Named Solomon Glacier and Solomon Saddle in honor of leadership in Antarctic rsch., 1994; named to Hall of Fame, Women in Tech. Inst., 2004; recipient Gold medal, U.S. Dept. Commerce, 1989, Scientist of the Yr. award, 1992, Nat. Medal of Sci., 2000, Arthur S. Flemming awrd, Common Wealth award, Common Wealth Trust, Ozone award, UN Environ. Programme. Fellow: Am. Geophys. Union (J.B. McElwane award 1985), Am. Meteorol. Soc. (Henry G. Houghton award, Carl-Gustaf Rossby award 2000), Royal Meteorol. Soc.; mem.: NAS, European Acad. Scis. (foreign assoc.), French Acad. Scis. (foreign assoc.), US Nat. Acad. Scis., Am. Acad. Arts and Scis. Avocations: creative writing, crafts, scuba diving. Office Phone: 303-497-3483. Business E-Mail: ssolomon@al.noaa.gov.

**SOLOMON, WILLIAM TARVER,** general construction company executive; b. Dallas, Aug. 11, 1942; s. Marion Bryant and Margaret (Moore) S.; m. Gay Ferguson, Feb. 15, 1964; children: William Tarver Jr., Meredith M. BSCE, So. Meth. U., 1965; MBA, Harvard U., 1967. With Austin Industries, Inc., Dallas, 1967—, chmn., pres., CEO, 1970—; chmn. Austin Comml., Inc., Dallas, Brit. Am. Ins. Co., Dallas; chmn., CEO Austin Industries, Inc., Dallas, now chmn. Bd. dirs. A.H. Belo Corp., Nat. Bank Tex. Past chmn. Dallas Citizens Coun. and Greater Dallas C. of C.; bd. dirs. Baylor U. Med. Ctr. Found., Dallas Mus. Art; trustee Southwestern Med. Found., So. Meth. U. Recipient citation of honor Dallas chpt. AIA, 1985, Humanitarian award NCCJ, Dallas, 1982, Champion of Free Enterprise award Associated Builders and Contractors, 1985, Outstanding Alumni award Southern Meth. U., 1988, Charles Cameron Sprague Cmty. Svc. Award Southwestern Med. Found., 2004, So. Meth. U. Sch. Engring. Hall of Leaders Disting. Alumni Award, 2005, Linz Award, 2005; inductee Tex. Bus. Hall of Fame, 1996. Mem. ASCE, Young Pres.'s Orgn. (past chmn. Dallas chpt.), Dallas Assembly, Salesmanship Club Dallas, Dallas C. of C. (bd. dirs.). Republican. United Methodist Home: 3830 Windsor Ln Dallas TX 75205-1743 E-mail: bsol@austin-ind.com.

**SOLOMONS, GUS, JR., (GUSTAVE MARTINEZ),** choreographer, dancer, writer; b. Boston; s. Gustave Martinez and Olivia Mae. Student, Boston Conservatory of Music, 1956-59; BArch, MIT, 1961; postgrad., Martha Graham Sch., N.Y.C., 1961-66. Dance soloist Martha Graham Co., N.Y.C., 1964-65, Donald McKayle Co., 1961-64, Merce Cunningham Co., N.Y.C., 1965-68; artistic dir. The Solomons Dance Co., N.Y.C., 1972—; dean, artistic dir. Calif. Inst. of the Arts, Valencia, 1976-78. Vis. artist-in-residence U. Calif., Santa Cruz, Calif. State U., Long Beach, others; dance panelist Nat. Endowment Arts; various other other state art couns., 1983—; assoc. prof. dance numerous colls., univs., including UCLA, U. Nev.-Las Vegas, Tex. Christian U., York, Simon Fraser, NYU; mem. faculty Tisch Sch. of Arts, 1994—; USIA cons. to Nat. Dance Co., Tanzania, East Africa, 1988, Argentina, 1994. Appearances on TV networks, Sta. WGBH-TV, Boston;

choreographr for various univs. and dance cos.; writer dance criticism for Village Voice, Dance Mag., others. Grantee Nat. Endowment for Arts, 1983—, N.Y. State Coun. on the Arts, 1972—; fellow Nat. Endowment for Arts, 1978-80; recipient Master Tchr. award NYU/Tisch, 1996, Bessie award, 2000, Robert A. Muh award for disting. MIT artist/alumnus, 2001, Balasaraswat/Beineke Disting. Tchg. award, 2004. Studio: 889 Broadway New York NY 10003-1212 E-mail: gus.solomonsjr@nyu.edu. *The content of a good dance is the truth about its maker. Performing it is a confession to the audience. The dancer places himself in the position of ultimate vulnerability each time he performs; it is at once cleansing, fulfilling, and courageous.*

**SOLOMONS, MARK ELLIOTT,** lawyer, art dealer, entrepreneur; b. Buffalo, Mar. 4, 1946; s. Alvin and Trude (Salant) Solomons; m. Jill E Kent, Aug. 20, 1978. BA, U. Rochester, 1967; JD, U. Pa., 1970; LLM, George Washington U., 1973. Staff atty. U.S. Dept. Labor, Washington, 1970-73, counsel coal miners benefits, 1973-77, legis. counsel, 1977-80; prin. Kilcullen Wilson & Kilcullen, Washington, 1980-86; ptnr. Arter and Hadden, Washington, 1986-2001, mem. exec. com., 1989-98; shareholder Greenberg Traurig, Washington, 2001—, nat. co-chair appellate practice group. Guest lectr law and hist SUNY, Stony Brook, 1970—76, Univ Mich, 1977—78, Hobart Col, 1972—76; prin Coun for Excellence in Govt, 1991—; co-owner Frogeye Co; chmn Atlantic Threadworks, 1998—2001; del Atlantic Treaty Asn Gen Assembly, 2000—. Contbr. articles to profl jours. Trustee China Found, 1997—, chair, nominating com., 1997—. Master: Am Inn of Ct (counselor 1996—97); mem.: ABA (chair workers compensation and employers liability comt 1987—88, sr. vice chair 1988—, vice chair appellate advocacy comt), NY Bar Asn, DC Bar Asn, Fed Bar Asn (chair regulatory reform comt 1988—89). Republican. Office: Greenberg Traurig LLP 800 Connecticut Ave NW Washington DC 20006 Office Phone: 202-533-2361. Business E-Mail: solomonsm@gtlaw.com.

**SOLOMONSON, GLEN TERRANCE,** music educator, musician; b. Jamestown, NY, June 19, 1953; s. Glen Earl and Matilda Carlson Solomonson; m. Elizabeth Denton Whitfield, May 15, 1976; children: Laura Meredith, Glen Andrew. B in Music Edn., Murray State U., Ky., 1975; M in Music Edn., U. Louisville, 1978. Adj. instr. tuba Bradley U., Peoria, Ill., 1980—, music dir. WCBU-FM, 1980—95; prin. tuba Peoria Symphony Orch., 1985—, Opera Ill., Peoria, 1985—; asst. prof. tuba Western Ill. U., Macomb, 1988—. Prodr., author, engr. Why Did They Come? (Ill. Humanities Coun., 1984), recording prodr., engr. Music from the Heartland (Ill. Arts Coun., 1985), Classical Wizards!, Camerata Woodwind Quintet, Pipes on the Prairie (NEA Grant, 1983). Mem.: Nat. Conf. Music Educators, Coll. Music Soc. (assoc.), IMEA (assoc.), ITEC (assoc.), NACWPI (assoc.), Phi Mu Alpha Sinfonia (life; chpt. advisor 1998—2005). Office: Western Ill Univ 1 University Circle Macomb IL 61455 Office Phone: 309 298-2199. Personal E-mail: mfgts@wiu.edu.

**SOLON, LEONARD R(AYMOND),** retired physicist, educator, consultant; b. White Plains, N.Y., Sept. 11, 1925; s. Morris and Rebecca (Bobrov) S.; m. Charlotte Rothman, June 30, 1946; children: Miriam Solon Weintraub, Matthew Benjamin, Emily Solon Bader. BA, Hamilton Coll., 1947; MSc, Rutgers U., 1949; PhD, NYU, 1960. Cert. Am. Bd. Health Physics. Physicist Nuc. Devel. Assocs., Inc., White Plains, 1950-52; asst. chief, then chief radiation br. AEC, N.Y.C., 1952-60; dir. applied nuc. tech. Tech. Rsch. Group, Inc., Syosset, N.Y., 1960-62; cons. Burns & Roe, N.Y.C., 1962-64, Servo Corp. Am., Hicksville, N.Y., 1962-64; mgr. R&D Electronics Corp., Mt. Vernon, N.Y., 1964-67; founder, exec. v.p., tech. dir. Hadron, Inc., Yonkers, N.Y., 1967-75; dir. bur. radiation control N.Y.C. Dept. Health, 1975-91; ret., 1991. Lectr., then adj. assoc. prof. N.Y.U. Inst. Environ. Medicine, 1955-93; environ. & radiol. health cons.; prof. health physics U.S. Mcht. Marine Acad., 1963. Contbr.: Dictionary of American Biography, 1995, The Scribner Encyclopedia of American Lives, vol. 1, 2, 3, 4, 5, 1998-2002; contbr. articles to profl. jours. Served with inf. U.S. Army, 1944-46, ETO. Decorated Combat Inf. badge, Bronze Star. Mem. AAAS, Am. Nuc. Soc., Health Physics Soc., Am. Phys. Soc., N.Y. Acad. Scis., Conf. Radiation Control Program Dirs., Radiol. and Med. Physics Soc. N.Y., Phi Beta Kappa, Sigma Xi. Achievements include co-patentee for laser photocauterizer used in treatment of detached retina; powering lasers using nuclear sources. Office Phone: 631-673-1134.

**SOLOSKI, JOHN,** journalism and communications educator; AB cum laude, Boston Coll., 1974; MA in journalism, Univ. Iowa, 1976, PhD, 1978. Copy editor, reporter Iowa City Press Citizen, 1977-78; instr. Univ. Iowa, 1977-78, asst. prof. sch. journalism and mass communication, 1978-84, assoc. prof. sch. journalism and mass communication, 1984-85, assoc. prof., head of grad. studies, 1985-92, prof., head of grad. studies, 1992-94, prof., acting dir., 1994-95, prof. sch. of journalism and mass communication, 1995-96, prof., dir. sch. of journalism and mass communication, 1996—, prof. law, 1996—2001; dean Grady Coll. Journalism and Mass Comm. U. Ga., 2001—. Con. Ottumwa Courier, 1976-77, Iowa City Press-Citizen, 1976-77; speaker in field; vis. prof. Univ. Tech., Sydney, Australia, 1995. Co-author: Reforming Libel Law, 1992, Libel and the Press: Myth and Reality, 1987, Taking Stock: Journalism and the Publicly Traded Newspaper Company, 2001; contbr. numerous articles to profl. jours.; editor: Journalism and Communication Monographs, 1994—. Recipient Soc. of Profl. Journalists Disting. Svc. award, 1988; numerous rsch. grants. Mem.: Assn. Schs. Journalism and Mass Comm. (pres. 2003—04). Office: Henry W Grady College of Journalism and Mass Communication The University of Georgia Athens GA 30602-3018 Office Phone: 706-542-1704. Business E-Mail: jsoloski@uga.edu.

**SOLOW, MICHAEL BARRY,** lawyer; b. Chgo., Jan. 6, 1959; s. Gilbert and Eunice (Eres) S.; m. Dale Susan Weinbaum, Aug. 23, 1983; children: Corey Francis, Andrew Wenbaum. AB summa cum laude, U. Ill., 1981; JD, Harvard U., 1984. Bar: Ill. 1984, NY 2003, U.S. Dist. Ct. (no. dist.) Ill. 1984, U.S. Dist. Ct. (no. dist.) Tex. 1987, U.S. Dist. Ct. Ariz. 1991, U.S. Dist. Ct. (we. dist.) Mich. 2003, U.S. Dist. Ct. (so. dist.) NY 2004, U.S. Ct. Appeals (7th cir.) 1984, U.S. Ct. Appeals (8th cir.) 1992, U.S. Ct. Appeals (4th cir.) 1993, U.S. Ct. Appeals (6th cir.) 1997, U.S. Supreme Ct. 1993. Law clk. to presiding justice Ill. Supreme Ct., 1984-85; assoc. Hopkins and Sutter, Chgo., 1985-90, ptnr., 1990—2001; ptnr., co-chair Bus. Reorganization and Creditors' Rights Dept., mem. Exec. Com. Kaye Scholer LLP, Chgo., NYC, 2001—. Mem. ABA, Chgo. Bar Assn., Phi Beta Kappa. Office: Kaye Scholer LLP 3 First Nat Plaza, Ste 4100 70 West Madison St Chicago IL 60602 also: 425 Park Ave New York NY 10022 Office Phone: 312-583-2310, 212-836-7240. Business E-Mail: msolow@kayescholer.com.

**SOLOW, ROBERT MERTON,** economist, educator; b. Bklyn., Aug. 23, 1924; s. Milton Henry and Hannah Gertrude (Sarney) Solow; m. Barbara Lewis, Aug. 19, 1945; children: John Lewis, Andrew Robert, Katherine. BA, Harvard U., 1947, MA, 1949, PhD, 1951, DLitt (hon.), 1992; LLD (hon.), U. Chgo., 1967, Brown U., 1972, U. Warwick, 1976, Tulane U., 1983, Dartmouth Coll., 1990, Rensselaer Poly. Inst., 2003; DLitt (hon.), Williams Coll., 1974, Lehigh U., 1977, Wesleyan U., 1982, Boston Coll., 1986, Harvard U., 1992, Colgate U., 1990; DSc (hon.), U. Pa., 1975, U. Geneva, 1982, Bryant Coll., 1988; D of Social Sci. (hon.), Yale U., 1976, U. Mass., Boston, 1989; D Social Sci. (hon.), U. Helsinki, 1990, SUNY, Albany, 1991, U. Glasgow, 1992, Rutgers U., 1994; D (hon.), U. Chile, 1992; Conservatoire, Nat. des Arts et Mètiers, Paris, 1994; D in Engring., Colo. Sch. Mines, 1996; postgrad, U. Buenos Aires, 1999; D in Lit. Humanities, NYU, 2000, New School U., 2006. Mem. faculty MIT, 1949—95, prof. econs., 1958—95, inst. prof., 1973—95, prof. emeritus, 1995—; W. Edwards Deming prof. NYU, 1996—97. Sr. economist Coun. Econ. Advisers, 1961—62, cons., 1962—68, RAND Corp., 1952—64; Marshall lectr., fellow commoner Peterhouse Cambridge (Eng.) U., 1963—64; Eastman vis. prof. Oxford U., 1968—69; overseas fellow Churchill Coll., Cambridge; sr. fellow Soc. Fellows, Harvard U., 1975—89; bd. dirs. Boston Fed. Res. Bank, 1975—80, chmn., 1979—80; active President's Commn. on Income Maintenance, 1968—70, President's Com. on Tech., Automation and Econ. Progress, 1964—65, Carnegie Commn. Sci., Tech. and Govts., 1988—93, Nat. Sci. Bd., 1994—2000; found. fellow Russell Sage Found., 2001—. Author (with R. Dorfman, P. Samuel-

son): Linear Programming and Economic Analysis, 1958; author: Capital Theory and the Rate of Return, 1963, The Sources of Unemployment in the United States, 1964, Growth Theory, 1970, Price Expectations and the Behavior of the Price Level, 1970; author: (with M. Dertouzos, R. Lester) Made in America, 1989; author: The Labor Market as a Social Institution, 1990; author: (with F. Hahn) A Critical Essay on Modern Macroeconomic Theory, 1995; author: Learning from "Learning by Doing", 1997; author: (with J. Taylor) Inflation, Unemployment and Monetary Policy, 1998; author: Monopolistic Competition and Macroeconomic Theory, 1998, Work and Welfare, 1998; editor (with Alan Krueger): The Roaring Nineties, 2002. Bd. dirs., mem. exec. com. Nat. Econ. Rsch.; trustee Inst. for Advanced Study, Princeton U., 1972—78, Woods Hole Oceanographic Inst., 1988—, Alfred P. Sloan Found., 1992—; Resources for the Future, 1994—2003, Urban Inst., 1994—, German Marshall Fund of U.S., 1994—2002, Ctr. Advanced Study Behavioral Scis., 1982—95, chmn., 1987—95. With U.S. Army, 1942—45. Decorated Bronze Star U.S. Army; recipient David A. Wells prize, Harvard U., 1951, Seidman award in polit. economy, 1983, Nobel prize in Econs., 1987, Nat. Medal of Sci., 2000; fellow, Ctr. Advanced Study Behavioral Scis., 1957—58, Russell Sage Found., 2000—. Fellow: Am. Acad. Arts and Scis., Brit. Acad. (corr.); mem.: NAS (coun. 1977—80, 1995), AAAS (v.p. 1970), Internat. Econ. Assn. (pres. 1999—2002), Econometric Soc. (pres. 1964, exec. com.), Am. Econ. Soc. (exec. com. 1964—66, v.p. 1968, pres. 1979, John Bates Clark medal 1961), Royal Irish Acad. (hon.), Order Pour le Merite (Germany), Acad. dei Lincei, Am. Philos. Soc. Home: 528 Lewis Wharf Boston MA 02110-3920 Office: MIT Dept Econs Cambridge MA 02139

**SOLOWAY, ALBERT HERMAN,** medicinal chemist; b. Worcester, Mass., May 29, 1925; s. Bernard and Mollie (Raphaelson) S.; m. Barbara Berkowicz, Nov. 29, 1953; children: Madeleine Rae, Paul Daniel, Renee Ellen. Student, U.S. Naval Acad., 1945-46; BS, Worcester Poly. Inst., 1948; PhD, U. Rochester, 1951. Postdoctoral fellow Nat. Cancer Inst. at Sloan-Kettering Inst., N.Y., 1951-53; research chemist Eastman Kodak Co., Rochester, NY, 1953-56; asst. chemist Mass. Gen. Hosp., Boston, 1956-61, asso. chemist, 1961-73; asso. prof. med. chemistry Northeastern U., Boston, 1966-68, prof. medicinal chemistry, chmn. dept., 1968-71, prof. medicinal chemistry and chemistry, chmn. dept. medicinal chemistry and pharmacology, 1971-74; dean Coll. Pharmacy and Allied Health Professions, 1975-77; dean Coll. Pharmacy Ohio State U., Columbus, 1977-88, prof. medicinal chemistry, 1977-98, Kimberly prof. pharmacy, 1997-2000, dean, prof. emeritus, 1998—. Author rsch. in medicinal chemistry, boron neutron capture therapy of cancer. Recipient Disting. Achievements in Boron Sci. award, Boron USA, 1994. Fellow AAAS, Acad. Pharm. Soc.; mem. AHS (50 Yr. mem.), Am. Chem. Soc., Am. Assn. Coll. Pharmacy, Am. Assn. Cancer Rsch., Torch Club Columbus (pres. 2004-05) Office: Ohio State U 500 W 12th Ave Columbus OH 43210-1214 Business E-Mail: soloway.1@osu.edu.

**SOLOWAY, DANIEL MARK,** lawyer; b. Buffalo, Jan. 21, 1959; s. Sol Murray and Shirley (Prashker) S.; m. Natalie Ann-Marie Chin, June 10, 1989; children: Rachael Ann, Rebecca Leigh. BA cum laude, SUNY, Buffalo, 1982; JD with honors, Fla. State U., 1985. Bar: Fla. 1985, U.S. Dist. Ct. (no. dist.) Fla. 1985, (mid. dist.) Fla. 1995, (so. dist.) Ala. 1986, U.S. Ct. Appeals (11th cir.) 1985, U.S. Supreme Ct. 1989; bd. cert. in civil trial law, Fla.; cert. Nat. Bd. Trial Advocacy, 1998, civil et. mediator, 2000. Law clk. Circuit Judge, Tallahassee, 1983-84, Douglass, Davey, Cooper & Coppins, Tallahassee, 1984-85; ptnr. McKenzie & Soloway, Pensacola, Fla., 1985-98; pvt. practice Daniel M. Soloway, P.A., Pensacola, 1998—. Author: Criminal Justice: An Analysis Toward Reform, 1981; contbr. articles to profl. jours.; editor Escambia-Santa Rosa Bar Assn. newsletter, 1989-90, Dry Shoes, Fla. Bar Jour., 1992. Profl. adv. bd. N.W. Fla. Epilepsy Soc., Pensacola, 1989—; speaker on AIDS, State of Fla. Dept. HRS, 1989—; active Escambia County Human Rels. Commn., 1996-98. Recipient Pro Bono Svc. award Escambia-Santa Rosa Bar, 1989-90, Pro Bono Svc. Pres.'s award Fla. Bar, 1990. Mem. Million Dollar Advocates Forum (diplomat), ABA, Assn. Trial Lawyers Am., Escambia-Santa Rosa Bar Assn. (editor newsletter 1989-90), Acad. Fla. Trial Lawyers (speaker 1993—), Nat. Orgn. Social Security Claimants Reps. Democrat. Jewish. Avocation: writing. Office: 901 Scenic Hwy Pensacola FL 32503-6866 Office Phone: 850-435-0555.

**SOLOWAY, RICHARD LEWIS,** electronics executive; b. Long Branch, NJ, Feb. 27, 1946; Studied, N.Y. Inst. Tech., Old Westbury. V.p. Nat. Alarm Products Co., Farmingdale, NY, 1970—72; co-founder Napco Security Sys. Inc., Amityville, NY, 1972, v.p., 1972—83, sec., treas., 1975—, chmn. bd., 1981—. Named Entrepreneur of Yr. in Mfg., Ernst & Young, 2001. Office: NAPCO Security Sys Inc 333 Bayview Ave Amityville NY 11701-2800 Office Phone: 631-842-9400 x120.

**SOL'SAX,** artist, educator; BFA, Cooper Union, 1992; MFA, Yale U., 1996. Lectr. art Medgar Evers Coll., CUNY. One-man shows include Recognize the Real, Silverstein Gallery, 1995, The Wild Herb of Bushwick Presents: My Tea Blessed Heads of Kind County, Rush Arts Gallery, 1997, Hood Flags, NYC Libr., 2001, These Hands Me Down Black and Blue Jeans, PS. 1, 2002, The Other Mainstream: Selections from the Collection of Mikki and Stanley Weithorn, Ariz. State U. Art Mus., 2005. Represented in permanent collections Bronx Mus., Mus. of City of NY. Fellow Guggenheim Meml. Found., 2004. Office: c/o ASU Art Mus PO Box 872911 Tempe AZ 85287-2911

**SOLSO, THEODORE M.,** manufacturing executive; m. Denny; 3 children. BA, DePauw U., 1969; MBA, Harvard U., 1971. Asst. to v.p. personnel Cummins Engine Co., Inc., Columbus, Ind., 1971—72; employment dir. Holset Engring. Co., Ltd. (Cummins' U.K. subs.), Columbus, 1972—74, dir. devel. & tng., 1974—77; exec. dir. personnel Cummins Engine Co. Inc., Columbus, 1977-80, v.p. spl. engine markets, 1984-86, v.p. mktg., 1986-88, v.p., gen. mgr. engine bus., 1988-92, exec. v.p. opers., 1992—94, exec. v.p. & COO, 1994—95, pres. & COO, 1995-00, chmn., CEO, 2000—; dir. administrm. CAEMI Cummins., Brazil; v.p., mng. dir. Holset Engring. Co., Ltd. (Cummins' U.K. subs.), 1980-84. Bd. dirs. Ashland, Inc., Cyprus Amax Minerals, Inc. Bd. trustees DePauw U.; bd. advisors U. Mich. Sch. Bus.; past bd. dirs. Heritage Fund Bartholomew County, Ind.; chmn. campaign Bartholomew County United Way; bd. dirs. Otter Creek Golf Course, Columbus, Ind. Mem. Mfrs. Alliance (bd. trustees). Office: Cummins Inc 500 Jackson St Columbus IN 47201*

**SOLTANIAN-ZADEH, HAMID,** research scientist, educator; arrived in U.S., 1987; s. Mirza-Ahmad Soltanian-Zadeh and Fatemeh Rismanian; m. Nahid Raee-Ezabadi, June 22, 1971; children: Sepeedah, Somayyeh, Sameeraa. PhD, U. of Mich., 1992. Sr. staff scientist Henry Ford Health Sys., Detroit, 1993—. PhD advisor U. of Mich., Ann Arbor, 1997—2001, Wayne State U., Detroit, 1998—. Conf. presenter (hon. Mention award, 1999, 2000, 2002, 2003); contbr. articles to profl. jours. Named Outstanding Rschr., Dept. of Justice, 1993; rsch. grantee, NIH, 1993—99, NSF, 2000—03. Mem.: IEEE, Soc. for Molecular Imaging, Internat. Soc. for Optical Engring., Internat. Soc. of Magnetic Resonance in Medicine. Achievements include research in Medical Image Analysis Algorithms and Software. Office: Henry Ford Health Sys 1 Ford Pl 2F Detroit MI 48202 E-mail: hamids@rad.hfh.edu.

**SOLTERO-HARRINGTON, LUIS RUBÉN,** retired surgeon, educator; b. San Juan, PR, Sept. 4, 1925; s. Augusto Rafael Soltero and Anna Lila Harrington; m. Alice Joyce Carpenter, Apr. 24, 1958; children: Luis Ruben, Kathleen Ann, Susan Joyce, Robert Richard, Sharon Theresa. BS in Agr., U. P.R., Rio Piedras, 1945; BM, MD, Northwestern U., Chgo., 1949. Diplomate Am. Bd. Surgery, Nat. Be. Med. Examiners, P.R. Rd. Med. Examiners. Intern Michael Reese Hosp., Chgo., 1949-50; resident in gen. surgery Aguadilla (P.R.) Dist. Hosp., 1950-51; resident in gen. surgery, instr. Baylor U. Coll. Medicine and Affiliated Hosps., Houston, 1954-59; resident in gen. surgery Jefferson Davis, VA and M.D. Anderson Hosps., Houston, 1954-57; resident in pediatric, thoracic and cardiovasc. surgery St. Luke's-Tex. Children's Hosp., Houston, 1957-59; asst. prof. surgery U.P.R. Sch. Medicine, 1960-64, assoc. clin. prof., 1972-73, assoc. clin prof., 1973—, in charge devel. heart surgery program 1960-64, dir. surgery residency tng. program, 1961-64; pvt.

practice San Juan, 1959—2003; ret., 2003. Prof. surgery U. del Caribe Sch. Medicine, Cayey, P.R., 1981—; cons. in cardiovasc. and thoracic surgery Med. Examing Bd. P.R., San Juan, 1989; chief thoracic and cardiovasc. surgery Tchrs. Hosp., San Juan, from 1959; dir. surgery residency tng. program Univ. Hosp., Rio Piedras, from 1961; cons. in thoracic and cardiovasc. surgery San Juan City Hosp., 1962—; cons. in surgery, 1964—; cons. in surgery Presbyn. Hosp., 1972—, Mimiya's Hosp., 1987—; cons. in thoracic and cardiovasc. surgery Indsl. Hosp., San Juan, 1975—, Hosp. Met., 1982—, Clinic Fernández García, 1983—; chief surgery Ruiz Arnau Hosp., Bayamon, P.R., 1978—; asst. dir. ICU, Hosp. del Maestro, 1987—; bd. dirs. Rsch. Found. Cardiovasc. Surgery Tex., 1984—, Am. Cancer Soc.; 1974; mem. Nat. Adv. Cun. Mended Hearts, Inc., 1969. Author: (textbook) The Management of the Acutely Ill Patient, 2002; contbr. articles to med. jours.; patentee partial occlusion vascular clamp to be used in small blood vessels; inventor respirator for infants based on electronic equipment. Capt., M.C., USAF, 1953-54. Recipient award for outstanding work in cardiovasc. surgery Lions Club, Hato Rey, 1961. Fellow: Am. Acad. Pediat., Am. Coll. Legal Medicine (assoc.); mem. AMA (physician recognition award 1980); mem. Denton A. Cooley Cardiovasc. Surg. Soc., Michael E. De Bakey Internat. Cardiovasc. Soc., Pan Am. Med. Assn. (coun. pediatric surgery), P.R. Soc. Cardiology, Am. Heart Assn., P.R. Hear Assn., Phi Chi. Avocations: travel, horticulture, bridge.

**SOLTYS, FLORENCE GRAY,** social worker; d. Olsie Glenn Gray and Addie Rebecca Hill; m. John Joseph Soltys; children: Jacqueline, Rebecca. BS, U. TN, 1958; RD, Mass. Gen. Hosp., 1959; MSW, U. NC, 1984. Clin. dietitian Mass. Gen. Hosp., Boston, 1960—63; dir. social work & bereavement Triangle Hospice, Chapel Hill, NC, 1985—87; assoc. clin. prof. U. NC Sch. Medicine, Chapel Hill, 1998—; assoc. clin. prof. and chair aging U. NC Sch. Social Work, Chapel Hill, 1998—; adj. assoc. prof. U. NC Sch. Nursing, Chapel Hill, 1998—. Chair Chapel Hill Parks and Recreation, 1981—87, Orange County Aging Bd., Chapel Hill, 1992—, Master Aging plan for Orange County, Chapel Hill, 2000—. Editor (author): American Society on Aging; author: (documentary) An Unlikely Friendship. Bd. Intervention Reminiscing Svc., Wis., 1995; leadership coun. Am. Soc. on Aging, San Francisco, 1993; bd. chair Dept. on Aging, Chapel Hill, 2000; vice chair Carol Woods Retirement, Chapel Hill. Named Trustee of Yr., Am. Assn. Homes and Svcs. to Aging, 2003; recipient Disting. Tchg., U. NC at Chapel Hill, 2001, Trustee Yr., Non-Profit Homes State NC, 2001, Leadership in Aging, Duke U., 2002, Sharon W. Wilder award, Long Term Care Assistance Advocacy, 2003. Fellow: Inst. Aging (assoc.); mem.: NASW (assoc.; bd. mem. 1986—91), N.C. Commn. on Aging, Am. Soc. Aging (assoc.; leadership coun. 1993—2003). Office: Sch Social Work 301 Pittsboro St CB# 3550 Chapel Hill NC 27599-3550 E-mail: fgsoltys@email.unc.edu.

**SOLTYS, JOHN JOSEPH,** lawyer; b. Portsmouth, Va., Feb. 4, 1942; children: John J. III, Amy Elaine. BS, USCG Acad., 1963; JD, Willamette U., 1970. Bar: Wash. 1970, U.S. Dist. Ct. (we. and ea. dists.) Wash. 1970. From assoc. to sr. ptnr. Karr, Tuttle, Seattle, 1970-89; sr. ptnr. Cozen, O'Connor, Seattle, 1999—. Writer, spkr. in field of product liability, med. malpractice and toxic torts; editor Wash. State Bar Assn. Motor Vehicle Accident Litig. Deskbook, 2000-01; elected super lawyer Wash. State Lt. (j.g.) USCG, 1963-67. Mem. Wash. Def. Trial Lawyers (pres. 1986-87), Fedn. Def. and Corp. Counsel. Avocations: fishing, hunting, gardening. Office: Cozen O'Connor 1201 3rd Ave Ste 5200 Seattle WA 98101-3071 Office Phone: 206-340-1000. Business E-mail: jsoltys@cozen.com.

**SOLTZ, JUDITH E.,** insurance company executive, retired lawyer; BA, Barnard Coll., 1968; JD cum laude, Boston Coll., 1971; LLM in Taxation, NYU, 1978. Tax atty. Conn. Gen. Corp., 1973—85; from asst. gen. counsel to exec. v.p., gen. counsel Cigna Corp., Phila., 1985—2001; sr. v.p., assoc. gen. counsel, 1998—2001, exec. v.p., gen. counsel, 2001—06, ret., 2006. Trustee Acad. Natural Scis. Phila. Mem.: ABA (tax and bus. law sects.).

**SOLUM, JOHN HENRY,** flutist, educator, author; b. New Richmond, Wis., May 11, 1935; s. Irwin M. and Helen L. (Anderson) S.; m. Millicent Kemp Hunt, July 30, 1960; children: Eric, Andrew. AB, Princeton U., 1957. Concert flutist, 1957—; tchr. Ind. U., Bloomington, 1973, Vassar Coll., Poughkeepsie, NY, 1969-71, 77—, Oberlin (Ohio) Conservatory, 1976. Dir. Bath (Eng.) Summer Sch. Baroque Music, 1979-89; artistic dir. Conn. Early Music Festival, New London, 1982-89; pres. N.Y. Flute Club, 1983-86; mem. music adv. panel NEA, 1990-93; arts adv. panel N.H. Arts Coun., 1995-98. *In addition to his activities related to music, in 1994 Solum began championing the work of the pioneering American modernist artist, James Daugherty (1887-1974). Solum's initiatives have led to special exhibitions of Daugherty's art, lectures, television documentaries, articles, and the recovery and restoration of ten of his large scale murals, including four in Cleveland's State Theater at Playhouse Square and six New Deal murals in Greenwich, Stamford and Darien, Connecticut.* Composer Cadenzas for Mozart's Flute Concertos, 1964; editor flute music; music critic for Notes, Pro Musica, The Consort; author: The Early Flute, 1992; contbg. editor: New Grove Dictionary of Musical Instruments, New Grove Dictionary of Music and Musicians; contbr. articles to Mus. Am., Flutist Quar., FLute Talk, Hist. Performance Mag., Woodwind World, Traversieres, Revue de la Société Liégeoise de Musicologie, Pan; flutist throughout N.Am., 1957—, Europe, 1962—, Asia, 1969—, S.Am., 1978—, Russia, 1983—; rec. artist Albany, Arabesque, Boston Skyline, Brunswick, Cambridge, Chesky, Columbia, CRI, Decca Gold Label, EMI, Epiphany, Innova, MCA Westminster, MSR, Philips, RCA, Seraphim, Smithsonian, Vanguard, others. Chmn. Hanoverian Found., 2000—. Recipient Phila. Orch. Youth Contest award, 1957. Mem. Nat. Flute Assn. (treas. 1989-94, Disting. Svc. award 1998), Dolmetsch Found. (bd. dirs.), Galpin Soc., Am. Musical Instrument Soc., Century Assn. (N.Y.). Home: 10 Bobwhite Dr Westport CT 06880-1001 E-mail: jhsolum@optonline.net.

**SOLURI, PATRICK J.,** composer; b. Sao Paulo, Brazil, Feb. 17, 1975; s. Michael R Soluri and Maria Judite dos Santos. Undergradute Studies, Bennington Coll., 1993—95; MusB in classical composition, Manhattan Sch. of Music, 1995—99; M on music in composition theory, U. of Louisville, 2000—02. Moritz von Bomhard fellow U. of Louisville, 2000—02; composer in residence Manhattan Virtuosi Chamber Orch., 1998—2000. Composer: (ballet) Madame X, (cello concerto w/orchestra) Lyric Concerto for Cello & Orchestra, (chamber orchestra w/chorus) To the Planets, (songs for soprano & piano) I Sang & Other Songs, (chamber music with singers) Inferno of Dante: A Study, (chamber music w/soprano) Fear, (chamber music) Fantasia Trio, Septet, (brass quintet) Retornando a Compostela, (chamber music) String Quartet, Duest for Cello & Piano; composer: (producer) (ballet) Ngoni (Cert. of Merit from the Nat. Young Composers Competition, 1997); composer: (electronic music) Nuances #1 (for voice & electronics), Nuances #2 (for viola & electronics); composer: (sound designer) (film score) Dead Serious; composer: (opera) Inferno of Dante: Canto V; composer: (producer, librettist) Figaro's Last Hangover; composer: (cameo actor, librettist) A Dialogue on Time Upon the New Millennium; composer: (producer) Inferno; composer: (orchestral work) Inferno: Symphonic Poem, Nuances, Fantasia for String Trio & Orchestra. Recipient ASCAP Plus, Am. Soc. of Composers, Authors & Publishers, 2004; Margaret Fairbank Jory Copy grant, Am. Music Ctr., 1998. Mem.: Opera Am., Am. Composers Forum, Am. Music Ctr., ASCAP. Avocations: travel, swing dancing, cooking, fencing. Personal E-mail: patrick@soluri.com.

**SOLYMOSY, EDMOND SIGMOND ALBERT,** marketing professional, retired military officer; b. Budapest, Pest, Hungary, Sept. 3, 1937; came to U.S., 1949; s. Sigmond Ladislas and Gabrielle (Lindelof) S.; m. Mary Ellen Via, Sept. 9, 1961; children: Edmond S.A. Jr., Stephan G., Philip A. BSME, Tex. A&M U., 1960, BBA, 1961, MBA, 1970; postgrad., Mich. U., 1985, Harvard U., 1991. Commd. 2d lt. U.S. Army, 1961, advanced through grades to gen., 1985; student Nat. Def. U., Washington, 1980-81; commdr. 1st Air Def. Arty. Brigade, Ft. Bliss, Tex., 1981-83; chief of staff U.S. Army Air Def. Ctr., Ft. Bliss, 1983; dir. Human Resources Directorate, Hqdrs. Dept. Army, Washington, 1983-85; dep. commdr. U.S. Army Community and Family

Support Ctr., Alexandria, Va., 1985-86; chief of staff U.S. Army I Corps, Ft. Lewis, Wash., 1986-88; chief exec. U.S. Office of Def. Coop., Athens, Greece, 1988-91; ret., 1991; pres. Global Project Mgmt., Houston, 1991—, Am. Southwest Properties Inc., 1993-95, Prime Daniel Asset Mgmt. Corp., 1997-2001; sr. ptnr. Solymosy Investment Assocs., 2000—; owner Bar-O-S Ranch. Advisor Sec. of Army Panel, Washington, 1983-86, Hellenic-Am. C. of C., Athens, 1988-91; bd. dirs. Am. Ikarus Inc., Maxoil Inc., So. Nat. Bank Tex., SNB Bankshares, Tex. A&M U. Rsch. Found., Fin. Literacy Found.; hon. consul Republic of Hungary; chmn. Houston Com. on Fgn. Rels. Author: Continental Economic Alliances, 1981. Sponsor Spl. Olympics, Ft. Lewis, 1986; advisor Mil. Mus., Ft. Lewis, 1986-88; regional v.p. Mediterranean coun. Boy Scouts Am., Athens, 1988-91; mem. devel. com. Tex. A&M U., College Station, 1991, advisor ctr. for Internat. Bus.; mem. bd. advisors Mosher Inst. for Internat. Policy Studies; mem. Mil. Com., Houston. Decorated D.S.M., Def. D.S.M., Combat Infantryman's Badge, Airborne Parachutist's Badge, Army Ranger, Legion of Merit (3); recipient U.S. and Vietnamese awards for heroism, Greek Disting. Svc. award, 1991. Mem.: VFW, Assn. U.S. Army (Svc. to Soldiers award 1985), Am. Quarter Horse Assn., Armed Forces YMCA (chmn. com. 1982, nat. vol. of yr. award 1983), Am. Palomino Horse Breeders Assn., Internat. Propeller Club (Greece advisor 1989), Kiwanis Club Houston, Hungarian Knights Hospitaller of Order of St. John. Republican. Lutheran. Avocations: sports, jogging, sailing, fishing, hunting. Home: 10150 Dogwood Tr College Station TX 77845-6740 Office: Global Project Mgmt 10150 Dogwood Tr College Station TX 77845 E-mail: essglobal@aol.com.

**SOLZ, HERMANN,** plastic surgeon; b. São Paulo, Brazil, May 5, 1952; s. Hermann and Hilde (Sihler) Solz; m. Jeanette Solz, Feb. 29, 1980; children: Sandra, Alex. MD, U. Sul Fluminense, Rio de Janeiro, 1976. Resident in internal medicine Hosp. Matarazzo, São Paulo, 1976; resident in plastic surgery BG Unfallklinik, Ludwigshafen, Germany, 1977—79, Marienhosp. Stuttgart, Germany, 1979—80, St. Markus Krankenhaus, Frankfurt, Germany, 1980; prof. plastic surgery U. Santa Cecilia, Santos, Brazil, 1983—88; plastic surgeon Hosp. Beneficencia Portuguese, Santos, 1983—88; chief plastic surgeon Mannheimer Clinic Plastic Surgery, Germany, 1989—. Fellow: Brazilian Soc. for Plastic Surgery, German Assn. Aesthetic Surgery, German Soc. Plastic Surgery. Avocations: diving, snowboarding, motorsports, languages. Office: Mannheimer Klinik für Plastische Chirurgie Mollstrasse 45 Mannheim D-68165 Germany Office Phone: +49-621-14740/152800. Office Fax: 0621 14849. Business E-mail: info@beautyclinic.de. E-mail: drsolz@aol.com.

**SOMASUNDARAN, PONISSERIL,** surface and colloid engineering educator; b. Pazhookara, Kerala, India, June 28, 1939; arrived in U.S., 1961; s. Kumara Moolayil and Lakshmikutty (Amma) Pillai; m. Usha N., May 25, 1966; 1 child, Tamara. BS, Kerala U., Trivandrum, India, 1958; BE, Indian Inst. Sci., Bangalore, 1961; MS, U. Calif., Berkeley, 1962, PhD, 1964. Rsch. engr. U. Calif., 1964, Internat. Minerals & Chem. Corp., Skokie, Ill., 1965-67; rsch. chemist R.J. Reynolds Industries, Inc., Winston-Salem, NC, 1967-70; assoc. prof. Columbia U., NY, 1970-78, prof. mineral engring., 1978-83, La Von Duddleson Krumb prof., 1983-97; dir. NSF Industry U. Coop. Rsch. Ctr. in Novel Surfactants, 1998—; hon. prof. Wuhan Inst. Chem. Tech., 2001—. Chmn. Henry Krumb Sch. Chem. Engring., Materials Sci. and Mining Engring., Columbia U., 1988—97; dir. Langmuir Ctr. for Colloids and Interfaces Columbia U., 1987—; mem. panel NRC; chmn. numerous ianternat. symposia and NSF workshops; mem. adv. panel Bur. Mines Generic Ctr., 1983—91; keynote and plenary lectr. internat. meetings; hon. prof. Ctrl. South U. Tech., China; Brahm Prakash prof. metallurgy and material sci. Indian Inst. Sci., Bangalore, 1990; hon. rsch. advisor Beijing Gen. Rsch. Inst., 1991—; Henry Krumb lectr. AIME, 1988; cons. in field. Editor: Fine Particles Processing, 1980; editor-in-chief: Encyclopedia of Surface and Colloid Sci.; hon. editor-in-chief Colloids and Surfaces, 1980—; contbr. articles to profl. jours. Pres. Keralasamajam of Greater NY, NYC, 1974-75; bd. dirs. Fedn. Indian Assocs., NYC, 1974-95, Vols. in Svc. to Edn. in India, Hartford, Conn., 1974—; mem. planning bd. Village of Piermont, NY, 1995-2000, mem. zoning bd. appeals, 2000—, mem. citizens adv. com., 2000—. Recipient Disting. Achievement in Engring. award, AINA, 1980, Antoine M. Gaudin award Soc. Mining Engrs.-AIME, 1983, Achievements in Applied Sci. award 2d World Malayalam Conf., 1985, Robert H. Richards award, AIME, 1986, Arthur F. Taggart award Soc. Mining Engrs.-AIME, 1987, honor award Assn. Indian in Am., 1988, VHP award of Excellence, Ellis Island medal of Honor, 1990, Commendations citation State of N.J. Senate, 1991; named Mill Man of Distinction, Soc. Mining Engrs.-AIME, 1983, Disting. Alumnus award Indian Inst. Sci., Bangalore, 1989, Outstanding Contbns. and Achievement award Cultural Festival India, 1991, Recognition award SIAA, 1992, Asian-Am. Heritage award Asian Am. Higher Edn. Coun., 1994, award for outstanding contbn. to sci. and tech. Hudson Valley Malayalee Assn., 2005, AIME Edn. award, 2006. Fellow Russian Acad. Nat. Scis. (fgn.), Chinese Acad. Engring. (fgn.) Indian Nat. Acad. Engring., Instn. Mining and Metallurgy (UK); mem. AICE, NAE, Soc. Mining Engrs. (bd. dirs. 1982-85, Disting. mem. award, also others), Engring. Found. (chmn. bd. 1993-95, chmn. conf. com. 1985-88, bd. exec. com. 1985-88, bd. dirs. 1991—, Frank Aplan award 1992), Am. Chem. Soc., NY Acad. Scis., Russian Acad. Natural Scis. (fgn.), Internat. Assn. Colloid and Surface Scientists (councillor 1989-92), Indian Material Rsch. Soc. (hon.), Sigma Xi. Achievements include patents in field. Office Phone: 212-854-2926. E-mail: ps24@columbia.edu.

**SOMER-GREIF, PENNY LYNN,** lawyer; b. New Hyde Park, N.Y., Mar. 30, 1970; d. Stanley Jerome and Janice Somer; m. Brian Scott Greif; 1 child, David Joseph Somer Greif. BS, SUNY, Binghamton, 1992; JD, Am. U., 1995. Bar: N.J. 1996, N.Y. 1996, D.C. 2000. Atty.-advisor U.S. SEC, Washington, 1995-2000; assoc. Arnold & Porter, Washington, 2000—06, Ober, Kaler, Grimes & Shriver, Balt., 2006—. Avocations: reading, exercise. Office: 120 E Baltimore St Baltimore MD 21202-1643 Office Phone: 410-347-7341, 202-962-6402. Business E-mail: penny_somer-greif@sports.com.

**SOMERHALDER, IAN JOSEPH,** actor; b. Covington, La., Dec. 8, 1978; Student, William Esper Studio, NYC. Model for Calvin Klein, Dolce & Gabanna, Gucci, Versace, Guess. Actor, prodr. (films) Recess, 2004; actor: (films) Life as a House, 2001, Changing Hearts, 2002, Rules of Attraction, 2002, In Enemy Hands, 2004, The Old Man and the Studio, 2004, Pulse, 2006; (TV films) Anatomy of a Hate Crime, 2001; (TV series) Young Americans, 2000, Smallville, 2004, Lost, 2004—05 (Outstanding Performance by an Ensemble in a Drama Series, Screen Actors Guild award, 2006). Avocations: writing, yoga, horseback riding, snow skiing, water-skiing. Address: care Innovative Artists 1505 Tenth St Santa Monica CA 90401 Mailing: care Innovative Artists 7th Fl 235 Park Ave S New York NY 10003*

**SOMERHALDER, JOHN W., II,** energy executive; m. Rebecca Somerhalder; 4 children. BSCE, Univ. Ariz. Sr. v.p. El Paso Corp., Houston, 1992—96, pres. El Paso Energy Reorganization, 1996—, exec. v.p. pipeline group, pres. pipeline group, 2001—05, exec. v.p., 2001—05; pres., CEO AGL Resources Inc., Atlanta, 2006—. Bd. dir., past chmn. Interstate Natural Gas Assn. Am.; bd. dir. Interstate Nat. Gas Assn. Am.; bd. mem. Am. Gas Assn. Bd. mem. Metro Atlanta C. of C., Ga. C. of C. Office: AGL Resources Inc 10 Peachtree Pl Atlanta GA 30309 Mailing: AGL Resources Inc PO Box 4569 Atlanta GA 30302-4569*

**SOMERMAN, MARTHA J.,** dean, dental educator; m. Norm Schiff. DDS, NYU, 1975; PhD, U. Rochester, 1980. Diplomate Am. Acad. Periodontology. Asst. prof., periodontics and pharmacology Balt. Coll. Dental Surgery, 1984—87, assoc. prof., pharmacology, 1987—91; William K. and Mary Anne Najjar prof., dept. periodontics, prevention and periodontics U. Mich. Sch.

Dentistry, 1991—2002, chair dept. periodontics, prevention and geriatrics, 1991—2001, assoc. dean rsch., 2001—02; assoc. prof., pharmacology U. Mich. Med. Sch., 1991—95, prof., pharmacology, 1995—2002; dean U. Wash. Sch. Dentistry, 2002—. Adv. coun. mem. Nat. Inst. of Dental and Craniofacial Rsch. Contbr. articles to profl. jours. Recipient Rsch in Oral Biology Award, Internat. Assn. Dental Rsch., 2005. Fellow: AAAS; mem.: Am. Assn. Dental Rsch. (past pres.). Office: RM D-322 Box 356365 Seattle WA 98195 Office Phone: 206-543-5982. Office Fax: 206-616-2612. Business E-mail: somerman@u.washington.edu.*

**SOMERS, ANNE RAMSAY,** retired medical educator; b. Memphis, Sept. 9, 1913; d. Henry Ashton and Amanda Vick (Woolfolk) Somers; m. Herman Miles Somers, Aug. 31, 1946; children: Sara Ramsay, Margaret Ramsay. BA, Vassar Coll., 1935; postgrad., U. N.C., 1939—40; DSc (hon.), Med. Coll. Wis., 1975. Ednl. dir. Internat. Ladies Garment Workers Union, 1937—42; labor economist U.S. Dept. Labor, 1943—46; rsch. assoc. Haverford Coll., 1957—63; rsch. assoc. indsl. rels. sect. Princeton U., 1964—84; prof. U. Medicine and Dentistry of N.J.-R. Wood Johnson Med. Sch. (formerly Rutgers Med. Sch.), 1971—84, adj. prof., 1984—2002. Adj. prof. geriat. medicine U. Pa. Sch. Medicine, 1990—2002; mem. Nat. Bd. Med. Examiners, 1983—86; cons. in health econs., health edn., geriats., gerontology, realted areas. Author: Hospital Regulation: The Dilemma of Public Policy, 1969, Health Care in Transition: Directions for the Future, 1971; author: (with H.M. Somers) Workmen's Compensation: The Prevention, Rehabilitation and Financing of Occupational Disability, 1954; author: Medicare and the Hospitals, 1967, Doctors, Patients and Health Insurance, 1961, Health and Health Care: Policies in Perspective, 1971; author: (with N.L. Spears) The Continuing Care Retirement Community: A Significant Option for Long Care?, 1992; editor (with D.R. Fabian): he Geriatric Imperative: An Introduction to Gerontology and Clinical Geriatrics, 1981. Mem. bd. visitors Duke U. Med. Ctr., 1972—77, U. Tex. Health Scis. Ctr., Houston, 1982—86. Named to Health Care Hall of Fame, 1993; recipient Elizur Wright award, Am. Risk and Ins. Assn., 1962. Fellow: Coll. Physicians Phila. (hon.), Am. Coll. Hosp. Adminstrs. (hon.); mem.: Nat. Acad. Social Ins., Inst. Medicine of NAS, Soc. Tchrs. of Family Medicine (hon.). Home: Pennswood Village # C-202 Newtown PA 18940-2401

**SOMERS, CLIFFORD LOUIS,** lawyer; b. Portland, Maine, Dec. 27, 1940; s. Norman Louis and Adeline Wilhemina (Witzke) Somers; m. Jennie Sierra Somers; children from previous marriage: Alan Mark, Penelope Lee. BA, U. Fla., Gainesville, 1965, JD, 1967. Bar: Fla. 1967, U.S. Ct. Mil. Appeals 1968, U.S. Dist. Ct. (mid. dist.) Fla. 1972, cert.: civil trial lawyer, mediator. Ptnr. Burton, Somers & Reynolds, Tampa, Fla., 1975—77, Miller, McKendree & Somers, Tampa, 1977—85, McKendree & Somers, Tampa, 1985—89, Somers and Morgan, Tampa, 1989—91, Somers and Assocs., Tampa, 1991—99, Barr, Murman, and Tonelli, Tampa, 1999—. Instr law U. Fla, Gainesville, 1967; sec. treas. Chester H. Ferguson-Morris S. White Inn Am. Inns Ct., 1987—89, pres.-elect Chester H. Ferguson-Morris S. White Inn, 1989—90, pres. Chester H. Ferguson-Morris S. White Inn, 1990—91. Contbr. articles to profl. jours. With U.S. Army, 1961—64, Vietnam, capt. JAG U.S. Army, 1968—72, mil. judge JAG U.S. Army, 1971—72. Mem.: Am. Bd. Trial Attys. (v.p. Tampa chpt 1990—91), Def. Rsch. Inst. (chmn. 2d dist. area west coast 1985—95), Fla. Bar Assn. (chmn. civil procedure rules com 1991—92), Brandon Vets. Post and Park, Am. Legion (comdr. Post 278 1975). Avocations: writing, weightlifting. Office: Barr Murman and Tonelli Ste 1700 201 E Kennedy Blvd Tampa FL 33602-5829 Home: 5700 Mariner St #404 Tampa FL 33609 Office Phone: 813-223-3951. Business E-Mail: csomers@barrmurman.com.

**SOMERS, JOHN ARTHUR,** insurance company executive; b. Cin., Feb. 24, 1944; s. Arthur Edward and Margaret Mary (Netschke) S.; m. Ann-Christin Ahlander, Dec. 28, 1968; children: Monica Ann, Christina Elizabeth, Mark Edward BS in Econs., Villanova U., 1966; postgrad., Sch. Law, U. Conn., 1966-67; With U. Conn., 1972. Asst. town mgr. Town of Newington, Conn., 1970-72; v.p. Prudential Ins. Co. Am., Newark, 1972-81; sr. v.p. Tchrs. Ins. & Annuity Assn., N.Y.C., 1981—, exec. v.p., 1996—. Bd. dirs. Cmty. Preservation Corp., Guardian Life. Roman Catholic. Office: Tchrs Ins & Annuity Assn Am 730 3rd Ave New York NY 10017-3206 Office Phone: 212-916-4400.

**SOMERS, LOUIS ROBERT,** retired food company executive; b. Pontiac, Mich., Aug. 8, 1926; s. Jay G. and Maggie (Gee) S.; m. Rynda Horinga, July 28, 1950; children: Linda, Laurie. BS, Mich. State U., 1950. With Kellogg Co., Battle Creek, Mich., 1955-88; controller Kellogg Internat., 1967-70, 72-75; fin. dir. Kellogg Gt. Brit. Ltd., 1970-72; v.p. fin., treas. Kellogg Co., 1975-85, sr. v.p. fin., 1985-88. Trustee Alma Coll., 1982—2001; bd. govs. ARC, 1985—92, chmn. audit com.; bd. dirs. Mich. State U. Devel. Fund, 1983—88.

**SOMERS, SHELLEY ALLEN,** elementary school educator; b. Elkin, N.C., May 25, 1959; d. Harold Frederick and Tracy Caudle Allen; m. Danny Van Somers; children: Daniel Brett, Tyler Jesse, Cameron Malachi. BA in Early Childhood Edn., Appalachian State U., Boone, N.C., 1981. Cert. K-6 edn. and mid. sch. math/sci. N.C. Tchr. asst. Wilkes County Schs., Wilkesboro, NC, 1982—84, tchr., 1985—. Advisor envirothon competition team East Wilkes Mid. Sch., Ronda, NC, 2002—. Author: North Carolina Young Authors. Named Tchr. of the Yr., Boomer-Ferguson Elem. Sch., 1990—91, Math. Tchr. of the Yr., Wilkes County Schs., 1996, Educator of the Yr., Wilkes Soil and Water Conservation Dist., 2004, N.C. Secondary Tchr. of the Yr., N.C. Assn. Soil and Water Conservation Dists., 2004, Tchr. of the Yr., East Wilkes Mid. Sch., 2005—06. Mem.: Profl. Educators of N.C. Avocations: gardening, sports, music. Home: 186 Mitchell Cir North Wilkesboro NC 28659 Office: East Wilkes Middle School 2202 Macedonia Church Rd Ronda NC 28670

**SOMERS, SUZANNE MARIE,** actress, writer, singer; b. San Bruno, Calif., Oct. 16, 1946; d. Frank and Marion Mahoney; m. Greg Somers (div.); 1 child; m. Alan Hamel, 1977. Student, Lone Mountain Sch., San Francisco Coll. for Women; studies with Charles Conrad. Owner, founder Suzanne Somers Collection. Actress: (theater) The Blonde in the Thunderbird, 2004; (films) American Graffiti, 1973, Billy Jack Goes to Washington, 1977, Yesterday's Hero, 1979, Nothing Personal, 1980, Rusty: A Dog's Tale, 1997; (TV films) Sky Heist, 1975, It Happened at Lakewood Manor, 1977, Happily Ever After, 1978, Zuma Beach, 1978, Goodbye Charlie, 1985, Totally Minnie, 1988, Rich Men, Single Women, 1990, Seduced by Evil, 1994, Devil's Food, 1996, Love-Struck, 1997, No Laughing Matter, 1998, The Darklings, 1999; (TV series) Anniversary Game, 1969, High Rollers, 1974, Three's Company, 1977-81, She's the Sheriff, 1987-89, Step by Step, 1991—98; (TV miniseries) Hollywood Wives, 1985; actress, co-exec. prodr.: (films) Exclusive, 1992; host: (TV series) The Suzanne Somers Show, 1994, VH1's 8-Track Flashback, 1995, Candid Camera (co-host), 1997-2000; performer Las Vegas (Nev.) Hilton, MGM Grand, Las Vegas, Sands Hotel, Atlantic City, USO, various TV commls.; author: Touch Me Again, 1973, Keeping Secrets (autobiography), 1988, Suzanne Somers' Eat Great, Lose Weight, 1997, After the Fall: How I Picked Myself Up, Dusted Myself Off and Started All Over Again (autobiography), 1998, Suzanne Somers' Get Skinny on Fabulous Food, 1999, Suzanne Somers 365 Ways to Change Your Life, 1999, Eat, Cheat, and Melt the Fat Away, 2001, The Sexy Years: Discover the Hormone Connection, 2004. Named Las Vegas Entertainer of Yr., 1986; named an hon. mem., US Military, 2005; recipient Humanitarian award, Nat. Council on Alcoholism, 1992, President's award, Nat. Assoc. of American Drug Counselors.

**SOMERSET, HAROLD RICHARD,** retired retail executive; b. Woodbury, Conn., Sept. 25, 1935; s. Harold Kitchener and Margaret Mary (Roche) S.; m. Marjory Deborah Ghiselin, June 22, 1957 (dec. Jan. 1984); children: Timothy Craig, Paul Alexander; m. Jean MacAlpine DesMarais, Jan. 2, 1985; stepchildren: Cheryl Lyn DesMarais, James Fenelon DesMarais. BS, U.S. Naval Acad., 1957; B.C.E., Rensselaer Poly. Inst., Troy, N.Y., 1959; LL.B., Harvard U., 1967. Bar: Mass. 1967, Hawaii 1973. Commd. ensign U.S. Navy, 1957, advanced through grades to lt., 1961; service in U.S. and Hawaii;

resigned, 1964; with firm Goodwin, Procter & Hoar, Boston, 1967-72; corp. counsel Alexander & Baldwin, Inc., Honolulu, 1972-74, v.p.: gen. counsel, 1974-78, group v.p.-sugar, 1978-79, exec. v.p.-agr., 1979-84; with Calif. & Hawaiian Sugar Co., San Francisco, 1984-93, exec. v.p., chief operating officer, 1984-88, pres., chief exec. officer, 1988-93, bus. cons., 1994—2002; pres., CEO Longs Drug Stores Corp., 2002—03; ret. Bd. dirs. Longs Drug Stores Corp., Brown and Caldwell; bus. cons., 2003-. Mem. adv. bd. San Francisco Nat. Maritime Mus. Home: 19 Donald Dr Orinda CA 94563-3646

**SOMERVILLE, CHRISTOPHER ROLAND,** botanist, educator; b. Oct. 11, 1947; naturalized, US, 1995; BSc in Math., U. Alta., Can., 1974, MSc in Genetics, 1976, PhD in Genetics, 1978; DSc (hon.), Queen's U., 1993, U. Alta., 1997, Wageningen U., 1998. Rsch. assoc. dept. agronomy U. Ill., 1978—81; asst. prof. dept. genetics U. Alta., 1981; assoc. prof. dept. botany and plant pathology Mich. State U., 1982-86, prof., 1986—93; prof. dept. biol. scis. Stanford U., Calif., 1994—; dir. dept. plant biology Carnegie Instn. Washington, Stanford, Calif., 1994. Panel mem. fed. support for soybean rsch. USDA-ARS, 1981; mem. adv. bd. molecular genetics Mass. Gen. Hosp., 1989—92; mem. plant adv. group Cold Spring Harbor Lab., 1990; mem. adv. bd. The Inst. Genomic Rsch., 1992—, Noble Found., 1993—97, Danforth Ctr., 1999—2001; mem. bd. agr. NRC, 1994—96; mem. vis. com. Swedish Found. for Strategic Rsch., 1995, Cornell U. Plant Biology, 1998; mem. President's Adv. Panel on Plant Biodiversity, 1997—98, Alta. Heritage Found., 2000—; vis. prof. U. Glasgow, 1998—; mem. sci. adv. bd. Wellcome Trust, 1999—2001; mem. adv. com. life scis. Cornell U., 2001—; mem. adv. com. U. Wis. Structural Biology Ctr., 2001—; CEO Mendel Biotechnology, 2002—. Contbr. articles to sci. jours.; mem. editl. com.: Photosynthesis Rsch., 1984—87, Plant Physiology, 1985—91, Development, 1986—93, Archives Biochemistry and Biophysics, 1986—2003, Devel. Genetics, 1989—91; editor: The Plant Jour., 1990—94; co-editor: Biochemistry and Molecular Biology of Membrane and Storage Lipids of Plants, 1993, Arabidopsis, 1994, The Arabidopsis Book, 2002; assoc. editor: Ann. Rev. Plant Physiology and Plant Molecular Biology, 1993—97, The Plant Cell, 1995—2000, mem. editl. bd.: Current Biology, 1996—, Procs. NAS, 1997—2000, mem. bd. reviewing editors: Science, 1996—, mem. sr. editl. com.; 2001—; editor: Current Opinion in Plant Sci., 1997—. Recipient Young Presdl. Investigator award, NSF, 1984, Humboldt Sr. Rsch. award, 1992, Kuhmo award, 2001, Mendel medal, Genetics Soc., 2004. Fellow: AAAS, Royal Soc. London, Royal Soc. Can.; mem.: Internat. Soc. Plant Molecular Biology (bd. mem. 1993—97), Academia Europaea, NAS, Am. Soc. Plant Physiologists (mem. publ. com. 1989—91, Gibbs medal 1993, Schull award 1987). Office: Dept Plant Biology Stanford U Carnegie Instn 260 Panama St Stanford CA 94305-4101 E-mail: crs@stanford.edu.*

**SOMERVILLE, GEORGE ARNOLD,** lawyer; b. Parkersburg, W.Va., Dec. 1, 1951; s. G. Talmage and Mary Frances (Moats) S.; m. Elizabeth Pairet; children: Matthew C., Thomas A., David R., Stephen E. AB in English magna cum laude, W.Va. U., 1973; JD, U. Va., 1980. Bar: Pa. 1980, U.S. Dist. Ct. (we. dist.) Pa. 1980, Va. 1982, U.S. Dist. Ct. Va. 1982, U.S. Ct. Appeals (3d and 4th cirs.) 1982, U.S. Supreme Ct. 1989. Law clk. to Hon. Ruggero J. Aldisert U.S. Ct. Appeals (3d cir.), Pitts., 1980-82; assoc. Mays & Valentine, Richmond, Va., 1982-88, ptnr., 1989—2000, Troutman Sanders LLP, Richmond, 2001—. Mem. ABA (mem. water resources com., natural resources and environ. law sect.), Va. Bar. Assn., Richmond Bar Assn., Va. State Bar (chair legal edn. Va. sect.), Order of the Coif. Avocations: running, music. Office: Troutman Sanders LLP PO Box 1122 Richmond VA 23218-1122 Home: 10307 Meadbrook Pl Richmond VA 23238 Office Phone: 804-697-1291. Business E-Mail: george.somerville@troutmansanders.com.

**SOMERVILLE, RICHARD CHAPIN JAMES,** atmospheric scientist, educator; b. Washington, May 30, 1941; s. James William and Mollie (Dorf) S.; m. Sylvia Francisca Bal, Sept. 17, 1965; children: Anatol Leon, Alexander Chapin. BS in Meteorology, Pa. State U., 1961; PhD in Meteorology, NYU, 1966. Postdoctoral fellow Nat. Ctr. Atmospheric Rsch., Boulder, Colo., 1966-67; rsch. assoc. geophysical fluid dynamics lab. NOAA, Princeton, NJ, 1967-69; rsch. scientist Courant Inst. Math. Scis., N.Y.C., 1969-71; meteorologist Goddard inst. space studies NASA, N.Y.C., 1971-74; adj. prof. Columbia U., NYU, 1971-74; head numerical weather prediction sect. Nat. Ctr. Atmospheric Rsch., Boulder, 1974-79; prof. meteorology Scripps Inst. Oceanography, U. Calif.-San Diego, La Jolla, 1979—. Author: The Forgiving Air: Understanding Environmental Change, 1996. Fellow: AAAS, Am. Meteorol. Soc.; mem.: Am. Geophys. Union. Office: U Calif San Diego Scripps Inst Oceanography 9500 Gilman Dr Dept 0224 La Jolla CA 92093-0224

**SOMES, JOAN MARIE,** critical care nurse; b. St. Paul, Aug. 17, 1952; d. Richard and Jane (Blaiser) Friesen; m. Michael Somes, Nov. 15, 1975. BA in Nursing, Coll. of St. Catherine, St. Paul, 1974; paramedic cert., Inver Hills C.C., Inver Grove Heights, Minn., 1976; MSN, U. Minn., 1989; PhD in Health Administrn., Columbia So. U., Orange Beach, Ala., 2002. RN, Minn.; cert. emergency nurse, geriatrics nurse; nat. registered EMT-paramedic; cert. ACLS instr., PALS instr.; cert. TNCC instr.; cert. CATN instr., ENPC instr.; cert. ACLS-EP instr. Paramedic A.L.F. Ambulance, Apple Valley, Minn., 1987-97; charge nurse emergency dept. Divine Redeemer Hosp., South St. Paul, Minn., 1974-94; staff nurse emergency dept. St. Joseph's Hosp., St. Paul, 1994—, emergency dept. educator/staff nurse, 1999—. Instr. numerous local cmty. colls., hosps. and ambulance svcs.; item writer CEN exam., 1994-96, 96-98; edn. specialist Regions Emergency Med. Svcs., 1994—; spkr. in field; co-chair Cornerstones Emergency Nursing Conf., 2000; mem. regional faculty PALS Am. Heart Assn., 2004—; mem. magnet steering com. Health East, 2005—. Author nursing home study courses; consulting editor Man. of Emergency Dept. and Urgent Care Instrns., 2001—; contbr. articles to profl. jour. Grantee Glaxo Pharm. Co., 1989, Health East Found. 1991, 94, 97, 98, recipient Mary Piper award Minn. Emergency Nurses Assn. State Coun. 1994-2006 Fellow: Acad. Emergency Nurses; mem.: Vision Coun. for Profl. Devel., Nat. Emergency Nurses Assn. (chair geriatric com. 2003—04, mem. exam item writer com. 2003—, mem. geriat. com. 2005—), Emergency Nurses Assn. (chair state trauma com. 1994—95, sec. treas. Minn. state coun. 1994—95, sec. 1996—98, sec. treas. Minn. state coun. 1997—98, 1999—2000, treas. Greater Twin Cities chpt. 2001—02, state coun. rep. 2001—03, sec-treas. Minn. state coun. 2004—, dir./state coun. liaison Greater Twin Cities chpt., Nurse Competency in Aging award 2005, Deanna Earle award Greater Twin Cities chpt.).

**SOMIDE, ADEGBOYEGA ADESINA,** financial analyst, educator, state official; arrived in U.S., 1983; s. Benjamin Emannuel I. Somide and Esther Akinreti; m. Karen O. Gilpin, Sept. 27, 2003; children: Joanne O., Jessica T., Denise F. BA, Berea Coll., Ky., 1986; MA, Ea. Ky. U., Richmond, 1987; PhD, U. at Albany SUNY, 2006. Cert. secondary tchr. NY State Edn. Dept., 1992. Tchr. N.Y.C. Pub. Schools, 1990—96; rschr. and tchr. U. at Albany SUNY, 1996—2006; sr. fin. and legis. analyst N.Y. State Senate, 2001—. Contbr. chapters to books, articles to profl. jours. Sunday sch. tchr. First United Meth. Ch., Delmar, NY, 2004—05. Recipient C. Louis Smith award, Berea Coll. 1986; grantee, U. at Albany SUNY, 1998, 1999, 2000, Democracy and Diversity Inst. New Sch. U., 2000. Mem.: Am. Polit. Sci. Assn., Internat. Polit. Sci. Assn., African Studies Assn., Internat. Honor Soc. Social Sci. Avocations: reading, travel, running, international politics. E-mail: somide@yahoo.com.

**SOMLO, VALESKA BARBARA,** medical/surgical nurse; d. Christian Staudt and Otillia Jenschke; m. Lawrence Alexander Somlo, Sept. 27, 1971. BSN, Incarnate Word Coll., 1956; grad., Santa Rosa Sch. Nursing, San Antonio, 1943. RN Tex., 1943, cert. anesthesiology, Ill., 1951. Joined Army Nurse Corps, 1943, advanced through grades to 1st lt., 1947, discharged, 1947; 1st lt. USAF Nurse Corps, 1948, advanced through grades to lt. col., 1966, ret., 1971. With USAF, 1966—71. Decorated Army Commendation medal, Air medal, Asiatic Pacific Campaign medal, WWII Victory medal, Philippine Liberation ribbon, Philippine Ind. ribbon, Nat. Def. Svc. medal with 5 oak leaf clusters, Air Force Outstanding Unit award with 5 oak leaf clusters, Air Force Longivity Svc. medal with 1 silver oak leaf cluster. Mem.: Mil.

---

Officers, Aviation, Space and Environ. Medicine, USAF Med. Svc. Corps Assn. (life), Soc. Ret. Air Force Nurses, WWII Flight Nurse Assn. Home: 100 W El Prado Dr #207 San Antonio TX 78212-2067

**SOMMA, THOMAS P.,** art historian, museum director; b. Somerville, NJ, Sept. 8, 1949; s. Thomas P. and Anne Somma; m. Marie A. Dacchille, Dec. 2, 1983. MA, Rutgers U., 1983; BS, Marietta Coll., Ohio, 1972; PhD, U. Del., 1990. Mus. dir. U. Mary Washington, Fredericksburg, Va., 1998—; adj. prof. Georgetown U., Washington, 2001—; asst. prof., mus. dir. Ithaca Coll., 1991—98, instr. semester Washington program, 2001—. Co-project dir. NEH landmarks of Am. History Summer Workshops, Washington, 2004—. Author: (book) The Apotheosis of Democracy (U. of Del. Am. Manuscript Competition Winner, 1992); co-author: The Library of Congress: The Art and Architecture of the Thomas Jefferson Building, Perspectives on American Sculpture before 1925, 2003; co-editor, contbr.: book American Pantheon; contbr. jour. Recipient U. S. Capitol Hist. Soc. fellowship, 1987, 1991. Mem.: Am. Assn. of Mus., Coll. Art Assn. Avocations: chess, literature, travel. Home: 11016 Naples Ct Fredericksburg VA 22407 Office: U of Mary Washington Galleries 1301 College Ave Fredericksburg VA 22401-5358 Office Phone: 540-654-1013. Office Fax: 540-654-1171. Business E-Mail: tsomma@umw.edu.

**SOMMARUGA, CORNELIO,** foundation administrator, diplomat; b. Rome, Dec. 29, 1932; s. Carlo and Anna Maria (Valagussa) S.; m. Ornella Marzorati; 6 children. LLD, U. Zurich, Switzerland, 1957; D of Polit. Affairs (hon.), U. Fribourg, Switzerland, 1985; D in Internat. Rels. (hon.), U. Minho, Portugal, 1989; D of Medicine (hon.), U. Bologna, Italy, 1991; D in Law (hon.), U. Nice, Sophia-Antipolis, France, 1992; Seoul Nat. U., Republic of Korea, 1992; PhD in Law (hon.), U. Hamburg, 1993; LHD (hon.), Webster U., 1998. Various diplomatic positions Swiss Confedn.'s Svc., 1960-73; dep. sec. gen. European Free Trade Assn., Geneva, 1973-75; minister plenipotentiary Dept. Pub. Economy, Berne, Switzerland, 1976-77, amb. plenipotentiary, 1977-80, del. Swiss Govt. for Trade Agreements, 1980-83, state sec. external econ. affairs, 1984-86; pres. Internat. Com. Red Cross, Geneva, 1987-99, Assn. Initiatives of Change Internat., Caux, Switzerland, 2002—. Pres. Geneva Internat. Ctr. for Humanitarian Demining, 2000—. Chmn. bd. Karl Popper Found., Zug, 2000—; bd. dirs. Found. for the Future; pres. bd. Found. Internat. Union Against Lance, Geneva. Recipient Presdl. award Tel-Aviv U., 1995, North-South prize Coun. of Europe, 2001, Dr. Jean Mayer Global Citizenship award Tufts U., 2003. Home: 16 chemin Crets-de-Champel CF-1206 Geneva Switzerland Office: GICHD BP 1300 CH-1211 Geneva Switzerland Office Phone: +41 22 906 16 97. E-mail: c.sommaruga@gichd.ch.

**SOMMER, ALFRED,** ophthalmologist, medical educator, researcher; b. N.Y.C., Oct. 2, 1942; s. Joseph and Natalie Sommer; m. Jill Abramson Sommer, Sept. 1, 1963; children: Charles Andrew, Marni Jane. BS summa cum laude, Union Coll., 1963; MD, Harvard U., 1967; MHS in Epidemiology, Johns Hopkins U., 1973. Diplomate Am. Bd. Ophthalmology, Nat. Bd. Med. Examiners. Tchg. fellow in medicine Harvard U. Med. Sch., Boston, 1968—69; dir. Nutritional Blindness Prevention Rsch. Program, Bandung, Indonesia, 1976—79; vis. fellow Inst. Ophthalmology U. London, 1979—80; founding dir., Dana Ctr. for Preventive Ophthalmology Johns Hopkins Med. Insts., Balt., 1980—90; assoc. prof. Johns Hopkins U., Balt., 1981—85, prof. ophthalmology, epidemiology and internat. health, 1985—, dean Johns Hopkins Sch. Hygiene and Pub. Health, 1990—2005, dean emeritus, 2005—. Vis. prof. ophthalmology U. Padjadjaran, Indonesia, 1976—79; cons., advisor Helen Keller Internat., N.Y.C., 1973—; cons., chmn. com. NIH, Bethesda, Md., 1981—; bd. dirs. Internat. Agy. for the Prevention of Blindness, Geneva; cons., com. mem. NAS, Washington, 1989; chmn. program adv. group on blindness prevention WHO, Geneva, 1989—90, com. mem., 1978—90, expert com., 1990—; chmn. steering com. Internat. Vitamin A Cons. Group Micronutrient Forum, Washington, 1975—; pres. Internat. Fedn. of Tissue Banks; chmn. sci. adv. bd. Edna McConnell Clark Found.; mem. Internat. Coun. Ophthalmology; dir. Becton Dickenson Corp., 1998—, T. Rowe Price Group, 2003—, Internat. Trachoma Initiative Found. of NIH, 2004—, Lasker Found., 2004—; chair expect cmty. health global governance initiative World Econ. Forum; lectr. in field. Author: Epidemiology and Statistics for the Ophthalmologist, 1980, Nutritional Blindness: Xerophthalmia and Keratomalacia, 1982, Vitamin A Deficiency: Health, Survival and Vision, 1995, Detection and Control of Vitamin A Deficiency and Xerophthalmia, 1978, 1982, 1995; chmn. bd. overseers Am. Jours. Epidemiology and Epidemiologic Revs., 1990—2005, also bd. dirs., —; contbr. articles to profl. jours. Recipient Charles A. Dana Found. award for Pioneering Achievement in Health, 1988, Disting. Svc. award for Contbn. to Vision Care, APHA, 1988, E.V. McCollum Internat. Lectureship in Nutrition, Am. Inst. Nutrition, 1988, Second Ann. Am. Coll. Advancement in Medicine Achievement award in Preventative Medicine, 1990, Disting. Contbn. to World Ophthalmology award, Internat. Fedn. Ophthal. Socs., 1990, Smadel award, Infectious Diseases Soc. Am., 1990, Doyne Meml. award, Oxford, 1995, Albert Lasker award Clin. Rsch., 1997, Helmut Horten Rsch. award, 1997, Gold medal, Singapore Ophthalmology Soc., 1997, Duke Elder Gold medal, Internat. Coun. Ophthalmology, 1998, Prince Mahidol award for contbns. to pub. health, 1998, Bristol-Meyers Nutrition Rsch. award, 2001, Danone Internat. award in nutrition rsch., 2001, Warren Alpert Found. prize, Harvard Med. Sch., 2003, Howe medal, Am. Opthal. Soc., 2003, Pollin prize, Columbia U., 2004, Helen Keller Rsch. Fund prize, 2006, Gonin medal, Swiss Ophthal. Soc., 2005, Spirit of Helen Keller award, 2006. Mem.: IOM, NAS, Acad. Ophthalmology Internat., Internat. Coun. Ophthalmology (Gonin medal), Chgo. Ophthal. Soc. (Gifford Meml. award 1997), Pa. Coll. Physicians (de Schweinitz award 1996) Assn. Schs. of Pub. Health (pres.), Internat. Assn. to Prevent Blindness (bd. dirs. 1978—), Nat. Soc. to Prevent Blindness (bd. dirs. 1989), Am. Acad. Ophthalmology (chmn. pub. health com. 1982—88, chmn. Quality of Care/Clin. Guidelines 1986—90, Hon. award 1986, Sr. Hon. award 1997, blindness prevention award 1998, Jackson Meml. lectr. award 1999), Inst. Medicine of NAS (Food and Nutrition bd.). Achievements include first to detail and publish epidemiologic approach disaster assessment; nutritional indices predict subsequent mortality in children, surveillance and containment is effective intervention strategy for controlling smallpox; vitamin A deficiency increases childhood mortality and vitamin A supplementation decreases childhood mortality; nerve fiber layer is valuable diagnostic and prognostic sign of early glaucoma; routine preventive services cost-effective in eye disease; clinical guideline development and importance of outcome assessment; research in epidemiologic and public health approaches to ophthalmology, blindness prevention, and improved health and survival. Office: Johns Hopkins U Bloomburg Sch Pub Health 615 N Wolfe St Rm 1041 Baltimore MD 21205-2103 also: Becton Dickinson 1 Becton Dr Franklin Lakes NJ 07417-1880 Fax: 410-955-0121. Office Phone: 410-502-4167. Business E-Mail: asommer@jhsph.edu.

**SOMMER, JAMES KOCH,** lawyer; b. Crawfordsville, Ind., June 5, 1932; s. Edwin John and Sophia Kurth (Koch) Sommer; m. Michael Jean Stewart, Feb. 23, 1963; children: John Stewart, Whitney Suzanne. BA, Yale U., 1954; LLB, Harvard U., 1959. Bar: Ind. 1959, U.S. Supreme Ct. 1970. Assoc. Barnes, Hickam, Pantzer & Boyd, Indpls., 1959—62; founding ptnr. and dir. Sommer Barnard (and certain predecessor firms), Indpls., 1962—2003, of counsel, 2003—. Chmn. Indpls. Regulatory Study Commn., 1992—93. Fellow: Indpls. Bar Found. (Disting. mem.: ABA, Bar Assn. Seventh Fed. Ct., Ind. Bar Assn. Home: 105 Curacao Ln Bonita Springs FL 34134 Office: Sommer Barnard One Indiana Sq Ste 3500 Indianapolis IN 46240 Office Phone: 317-713-3500. Business E-Mail: jsommer@sommerbarnard.com.

**SOMMER, JEFF,** journalist; BA in History with distinction, Cornell U., 1974; MS in Journalism, Columbia U., 1977; MS in Regional Studies-East Asia, Harvard U., 1978. Local reporter The Albany (NY) Knickerbocker News, 1977-79; The Record, Bergen County, NJ, 1979-81; Newsday, 1981-82, Asia bur. chief Beijing, 1983-86, chief corr. Soviet & East European affairs Moscow, 1986-89, fgn. editor, 1989; now sect. editor, Sunday Bus. NY

---

Times. Recipient Hal Boyle award Overseas Press Club, 1985, Knight-Bagehot Fellow Columbia Univ., 2001; edited Pulitzer prize-winning coverage in internat. news, 1992, 93. Office: Sunday Business NY Times 229 W 43rd St New York NY 10036*

**SOMMERER, JOHN,** accountant, former mayor; b. Mt. Holly, N.J., Oct. 30, 1947; s. John Price and Barbara Elizabeth (Davis) S.; m. Diane Catherine Kuszaj, Aug. 5, 1967; children: James Peter, John Joseph, Paul Andrew, Matthew Thomas. BS, U. Hartford, 1969; MBA, U. Toronto, 1972; postgrad., Columbia U., 1972-74. CPA, Fla., N.J., N.Y. Sr. cons. Deloitte and Touche, N.Y.C., 1974-78; dir. mgmt. info. systems Pantry Pride Enterprises, Ft. Lauderdale, Fla., 1978-82; mng. ptnr. John Sommerer and Co., P.A., Coral Springs, Fla., 1982—; mayor City of Coral Springs, 1994—2004. Treas. Coral Springs Cmty. Chest, 1988-94. Mem. Coral Springs Kiwanis (bd. dirs. 1990, 92, treas. 2004-), Coral Springs C. of C. (pres. 1987, treas. 1986, bd. dirs. 1986-88). Roman Catholic. Home: 9501 NW 44th Pl Coral Springs FL 33065-6602 Office: John Sommerer and Co PA 3300 N University Dr Coral Springs FL 33065-6309 E-mail: cpa@accountant.com.

**SOMMERER, JOHN CURTIS,** physicist, educator; b. Milw., Aug. 5, 1957; s. Curtis John and Phyllis Marie (Merten) S.; m. Suzette Jacques Sommerer, May 20, 1979. BS summa cum laude, Washington U., St. Louis, 1979; MS (hon.), Johns Hopkins U., 1987; PhD, U. Md., 1991. Rsch. assoc. Washington U. Sch. Medicine, St. Louis, 1979-80; supr. Tactics and Ops. Johns Hopkins Applied Physics Lab., Laurel, Md., 1980-91; physicist, 1991-93; deputy dir. M.S. Eisenhower Rsch. Ctr., 1994-96; dir. M.S. Eisenhower Rsch. Ctr., 1996—2005, dir. sci. and tech., chief tech. officer, 2005—. Adjunct grad. faculty The Johns Hopkins U., Balt., 1991—; mem. USN Nonacoustic Coord. Com., Washington, 1983-86. Contbr. articles to profl. jours. Supporting mem. Democratic Nat. Com., Washington, 1992; vice chair USN Rsch. Adv. Com., 2005—. Recipient Nat. Def. Sci. and Engring. fellowship Dept. Def., Washington, 1989, R.W. Hart Prize for Rsch. The Johns Hopkins U., Balt., 1992; named Disting. Young Scientist Md. Acad. Scis., Balt., 1994. Mem. Soc. for Indsl. and Applied Math., Am. Phys. Soc. Office: Applied Physics Lab The Johns Hopkins Univ Laurel MD 20723-6099 Office Phone: 240-228-6242. Business E-Mail: john.sommerer@jhuapl.edu.

**SOMMERFELD, DAVID WILLIAM,** lawyer, educator; b. Detroit, Jan. 21, 1942; s. Henry Anthony and Hilda (Diffley) S.; m. Anne Marlaine Toth, June 27, 1964; children: Catherine, David Jr., Michael, Caroline. BS, U. Detroit, 1963; JD, Detroit Coll., 1967. Trust officer Nat. Bank Detroit, 1963-68; tax supr. Ernst & Ernst, 1968-73; ptnr. Monaghan, Campbell, LoPrete & McDonald, Detroit, 1973-77; prof. Detroit Coll., 1977-86; ptnr. Butzel Long, Detroit, 1987—. Lectr. Ind. Soc. CPAs, Indpls., 1980-93, Ohio Soc. CPAs, Columbus, 1987, W.Va. Soc. CPAs, Charleston, 1983-86, 91. Editor Mich. Probate and Trust Law Jour., 1981-83. Fellow Am. Coll. of Trust and Estate Counsel; mem. Mich. Bar Assn., Detroit Bar Assn., Am. Inst. CPA's, Mich. Assn. CPA's, Forest Lake Country Club, Detroit Athletic Club. Roman Catholic. Avocations: bowling, spectator sports, gardening. Office: Butzel Long 41000 Woodward Ave Stoneridge W Bloomfield Hills MI 48304 Business E-Mail: sommerfeld@butzel.com.

**SOMMERFELD, MARIANNA,** retired social worker, writer; b. Frankfurt, Germany, Jan. 25, 1920; d. Martin and Helene (Schott) S. BA, Smith Coll., 1940; MA, Radcliffe Coll., 1946; MSW, Simmons Coll., 1957. Lic. ind. social worker. Tchr. Latin, German, English Burnham Sch. Girls, Northampton, Mass., 1940-43; German translator Yale Inst. Human Rels., New Haven, 1943-44; tchr. Northfield (Mass.) Sch. Girls, 1944-45; psychiat. social worker McLean Hosp., Belmont, Mass., 1957-59, Gaebler Children's Unit/Met. State Hosp., Waltham, Mass., 1959-62, Boston U./Boston City Hosp., 1962-67, New Eng. Med. Ctr., Boston, 1967-71; pvt. practice Cambridge, Mass., 1962-68; supr. clin. social work Erich Lindemann Mental Health Ctr., Boston, 1971-90; writer, 1976—. Author: Marianna Sommerfeld: Diary of a Single Woman, 1991. Vol. Cambridge Sch., 1993. Mem. NOW, AFL-CIO, Planned Parenthood, Nat. Writers Union, Women's Nat. Book Assn., PEN New Eng. (assoc.). Office Phone: 617-354-1801.

**SOMMERFELDT, JOHN ROBERT,** historian, educator; b. Detroit, Feb. 4, 1933; s. Melvin John and Virginia Zita (Gruenheck) S.; m. Patricia Natalie Levinske, Aug. 25, 1956; children: Ann, James, John, Elizabeth. AB, U. Mich., 1954, AM, 1956, PhD, 1960. Instr. history Stanford U., 1958-59; from instr. to prof. Western Mich. U., 1959-78; prof. history U. Dallas, 1978—; chmn. dept. history, 1984-87, univ. pres., 1978-80. Dir. Medieval Inst., Western Mich. U., 1961-76; exec. dir. Inst. Cistercian Studies, 1973-78; dir. Center Contemplative Studies, 1976-78; pres. Cistercian Publs., 1973-79, chmn. bd., 1976-79. Author: The Spiritual Teachings of Bernard of Clairvaux, 1991, Bernard of Clairvaux On the Life of the Mind, 2004, Bernard of Clairvaux On the Spiritualty of Relationship, 2004, Aelred of Rievaulx: Pursuing Perfect Happiness, 2005, Aelred of Rievaulx On Love and Order in the World and in the Chuch, 2006; editor: Studies in Medieval Culture, 12 vols., 1964-78, Studies in Medieval Cistercian History, II, 1977, Cistercian Ideals and Reality, 1978, Simplicity and Ordinariness, 1980, The Chimaera of His Age: Studies in Bernard of Clairvaux, 1980, Abba: Guides to Wholeness and Holiness, East and West, 1981, Erudition at God's Service, 1987, Bernardus Magister, 1992, Studiosorum Speculum, 1993, Studies in the Theology of St. Thomas Aquinas, 1995. Fulbright scholar, 1954-55; Univ. fellow U. Mich., 1956-57. Mem. Medieval Acad. Am., Am. Hist. Assn., Am. Catholic Hist. Assn., Am. Soc. Ch. History, Phi Beta Kappa, Phi Eta Sigma, Phi Kappa Phi. Republican. Roman Catholic. Home: 2809 Warren Cir Irving TX 75062-8938 Office: U Dallas Dept History Irving TX 75062-4736 Office Phone: 972-721-5370. Business E-Mail: jrsommer@udallas.edu.

**SOMMERLAD, ROBERT EDWARD,** environmental research engineer; b. Jersey City, Aug. 27, 1937; s. Herman Francis and Helen Rita (Joyce) S.; m. Margaret Doreen Breen, Sept. 9, 1961; children: Sharon K., Michael E., Ellen J. BSME, N.J. Inst. Tech., 1960, MSME, 1963, postgrad., 1965. Cert. profl. engr., State of NJ, 1964. Devel. engr., rsch. assoc. Foster Wheeler Energy Corp., Livingston, NJ, 1960-71, head air pollution control sect., 1971-74; v.p. contract ops. Foster Wheeler Devel. Corp., Livingston, 1974-84; pres. Enviresponse Inc., Livingston, 1985-86; dir. bus. devel. Energy and Environ. Rsch. Corp., Edison, NJ, 1987-88; cons., 1988-89; dir. environ. bus. devel. Midwest Rsch. Inst., Falls Church, Va., 1989-90; mgr. combustion tech. Rsch.-Cottrell Cos., 1990-92, cons., 1992-93; mktg. dir. PSI Powerserve, Andover, Mass., 1993-94, cons., program mgr., 1994-95; cons. Gas Rsch. Inst., Chgo., 1995-98, GE Energy and Environ. Rsch. Corp., Gurnee, Ill., 1998—2003; pvt. cons., 2003—; cons. Coll. Lake County, Grays Lake, Ill., 2004—; strategic acct. mgr. Loesche Am., Inc., 2005—. Mem. coal combustion and applications working group U.S. Dept. Energy U. San Diego, 1981-84. Patentee in field. V.p. Cranford (N.J.) Cmty. Pools Parents Assn., 1975-77, 86-87, pres., 1977-79, 84-89; chmn. N.J. Swimming and Diving Conf., Cranford, 1986-89; v.p. Stonebrook Crossings Homeowners Assn., Gurnee, 1998-2000, pres., 2000—; cons. for family aquatic ctr. Gurnee Park Dist., 1996-2002; mem. dept. pub. works com. Village of Gurnee, 2002—; mem. St. Paul the Apostle Choir, 2000-, Parish Pastoral Coun., 2003-. Recipient Outstanding Achievement award Westfield YMCA, 1975. Fellow ASME (mem. rsch. com. indsl. and mcpl. waste 1971—, vice chmn. 1972-74, sec. 1987-91, mem. environ. affairs com. 1982-92, mem. dioxin com. 1985-92, mem. bd. performance test codes 1986-97, chmn. boiler-calorimeter com. 1986-89, numerous com. and conf. chairmanships, Cert. Achievement, Bd. on Codes and Standards, 1997); mem. Air and Waste Mgmt. Assn. (mem. AE-1 com. on particulate and associated acid gases, sec. 1991-94, vice chair 1996), Watchung Amateur Ski Club (mem. exec. bd. 1986-87); diplomate Am. Acad. Environ. Engr. (bd. trustees 2003-). Roman Catholic. Home: 1368 Knottingham Dr Gurnee IL 60031-5632 Office Phone: 847-856-1390.

**SOMMERS, ALEXIS NIGEL,** university administrator, engineering educator, manufacturer; b. London, Oct. 9, 1941. B. Mech. Engring., Cornell U., 1964; MS., Rutgers U., 1966; PhD., Purdue U., 1968; s. Alexis and Joan (Lanchester) S.; children: Robin Alexis, Guinevere Rose; m. Pamela Coffey, Oct. 17, 1990. Chief project engr. El-Tronics, Inc., Warren, Pa., 1963-64;

exptl. mathematician Allison div. Gen. Motors, Indpls., 1966-68; transp. systems analyst Vitro Labs., Silver Spring, Md., 1968-70; assoc. dean grad. sch. U. New Haven, 1970-74, provost, 1974-91, prof. indsl. engring., 1991—; interim pres. Newton-New Haven Co., Inc., North Haven, Conn., 1995-96. Contbr. articles to profl. jours. Chmn. South Cen. Conn. chpt. ARC, 1986-88; sec. Bethany Conservation Trust (Conn.), 1980-86; chmn. Bethany Conservation Commn., 1982-88; apptd. bd. zoning appeals Town of Guilford, Conn., 1991—. Recipient Sterling award ARC, 1988. Mem. Inst. Indsl. Engrs. (sr.), Ops. Research Soc. Am., Soc. Logistics Engrs. (Adm. Eccles medal 1994), Conn. Assn. Purchasing Mgrs. (pres. 2003—). Democrat. Congregationalist. Home: 71 Broad St Guilford CT 06437-2636 Office: Newton-New Haven Co 408 Saint Ronan St New Haven CT 06511-2251

**SOMMERS, GEORGE R.,** lawyer; b. N.Y.C., Jan. 27, 1955; BA, U. So. Fla., 1975; JD, NYU, 1987. Bar: N.J. 1987, U.S. Dist. Ct. N.J. 1987, N.Y. 1988, U.S. Dist. Ct. (all dists.) N.Y. 1988, U.S. Ct. Appeals (3d cir.) 1988, U.S. Ct. Appeals (2d cir.) 1989, U.S. Supreme Ct. 1992. Assoc. Sullivan & Cromwell, N.Y.C., 1987-90; pvt. practice lawyer N.Y.C., 1990—. Pres. Bill of Rights Found., N.Y.C., 1994—. Seidler scholar NYU Sch. Law, N.Y.C., 1985. Mem. Hoboken Bar Assn. (pres. 1994). Jewish. Avocations: boxing, chess. Office: 51 Newark St Hoboken NJ 07030-4548 Office Phone: 212-709-8389, 201-656-6575.

**SOMMERS, MARK,** lawyer; b. Chgo., Mar. 29, 1956; BA, Ohio Wesleyan U., 1978; JD, U. Northern Ill., 1982; LLM, U. London, Eng., 1983. Bar: Ill. 1982, NY 1985, Mass. 1985, DC 1989. Ptnr. Finnegan, Henderson, Farabow, Garrett & Dunner LLP, Washington, leader, Trademark & Copyright Sect. Named top 5 trademark attys. in US, Mng. Intellectual Property, top 10 trademark attys. in world. Office: Finnegan Henderson Farabow Garrett & Dunner LLP 901 New York Ave NW Washington DC 20001-3315 Office Phone: 202-408-4000. Office Fax: 202-408-4400. Business E-mail: mark.sommers@finnegan.com.

**SOMMERS, ROBERT THOMAS,** editor, writer; b. Balt., Aug. 6, 1926; s. Thomas Michael and Pearl Florence (Glendenning) S.; m. Helen Louise Ray, Oct. 19, 1952; children — Thomas Michael II, Patricia Ray. BS, U. Md., College Park, 1950. Reporter Evening Sun, Balt., 1950-62; reporter Evening Star, Washington, 1962-66; editor U.S. Golf Assn. Jour., N.Y.C., 1966-72, Far Hills, N.J., 1972-92. Author: The Oxford Book of Golf Anecdotes, 1995, 2d edit., 2004, The U.S. Open: Golf's Ultimate Challenge, 1987, 2nd edit., 1996, Bobby Jones in Chapman's Library of Golf, 1992; co-author: Great Shots, 1989; contbr. articles to profl. jours. Served with U.S. Coast Guard, 1944-46, PTO. Mem. Golf Writers Assn. Am., Assn. Golf Writers Gt. Britain, Authors Guild, Ballybunion Golf Club (Ireland), Royal and Ancient Golf Club of St. Andrews (Scotland), The Legacy Golf and Tennis Club (Fla.). Republican. Episcopalian. Avocations: reading, golf, music. Home and Office: 8083 Spendthrift Ln Port Saint Lucie FL 34986-3122 Personal E-mail: r.sommers@worldnet.att.net.

**SOMMERS, SAMUEL R,** psychologist; PhD, U. Mich., 2002. Asst. prof. Tufts U., Medford, Mass., 2003—. Office: Tufts U Dept Psychology 490 Boston Ave Medford MA 02155 Office Phone: 617-627-5293. Business E-Mail: sam.sommers@tufts.edu.

**SOMMERS, STEPHEN,** film director, scriptwriter, film producer; b. Indianapolis, IN; Motion picture dir., writer, prodr. Writer, dir. Catch Me If You Can, 1989, The Adventures of Huck and Finn, 1993, The Jungle Book, 1994, Deep Rising, 1998, The Mummy, 1999; The Mummy Returns, 2001; writer, prodr. Tom and Huck, 1995, The Scorpion King, 2002; writer, prodr., dir., Van Helsing, 2004; prodr. T.V. movie Oliver Twist, 1997; dir. Terror Eyes, 1989; writer Gunmen, 1994. Office: c/o Jim Wiatt William Morris Agy 151 El Camino Dr Beverly Hills CA 90212

**SOMMERS, STEPHEN ANTHONY,** lawyer; b. Atlanta, Ga., Sept. 27, 1967; s. Richard Clarence and Sara Richwine Sommers. BA, East Carolina U., 2000; JD, Northeastern U., Boston, 2002. Bar: Calif. 2003. Vol. US Peace Corps, Moa, Kanem-Borno, Chad, 1990—91; regional dir. Citizen Action, Pitts., 1991—93; union organizer United Radio Machine Workers of Am., Pitts., 1993—94; internat. rep. Union of Needletrades Indsl. and Textile Employees, Atlanta, 1994—99; atty. Beeson, Tayer & Bodine, Oakland, Calif., 2002—03, Sommers Law Group, San Francisco, 2004—. Activist Dem. Party, San Francisco, 2002—06. Mem.: Calif. Bar Assn., The Men's Cir. (vision body 2005—06). Achievements include brought and settled lawsuit for sexual harassment against The Gorilla Foundation, home of Koko; traveled coast to coast in United States by bicycle. Avocations: art, travel. Office: Sommers Law Group 870 Market St Ste 1142 San Francisco CA 94102 Office Phone: 415-260-5457. Home Fax: 415-956-0878; Office Fax: 415-956-0878. Personal E-mail: stevesommers@gmail.com.

**SOMMERS, WILLIAM PAUL,** management consultant, research and development company executive; b. Detroit, July 22, 1933; s. William August and Mary Elizabeth (Baietto) S.; m. Josephine A. Sommers; children: William F., Clare M., John C. Hughes, Joanna M. Weems, Russell L. Hughes. BSE (scholar), U. Mich., 1955, MSE, 1956, PhD (Riggs fellow, Texaco fellow, Univ. fellow), 1961. Rsch. assoc. U. Mich. Inst. Sci. and Tech., Ann Arbor, 1958-61; chief chem. propulsion space and missile sys. Martin Marietta Corp., Balt., 1956-58, 61-63; v.p. Booz, Allen & Hamilton, Inc., Bethesda, Md., 1963-70, pres. Tech. Mgmt. Group, 1973-79, sr. v.p., 1979-92; exec. v.p. Iameter, Inc., San Mateo, Calif., 1992-94; pres., CEO SRI Internat., Menlo Park, Calif., 1994-98, ret. 1998. Bd. dirs. Gukenheimer Enterprises, H2 Gen. Contbr. articles to profl. jours., also chpt. in book. Pres. Washington chpt. U. Mich. Alumni Club, 1970-71; v.p. Wildwood manor Citizens Assn., 1968-70; chief Adventure Guide program YMCA, 1971-72; bd. visitors Coll. Engring. U. Calif., Davis; mem. nat. adv. bd. Coll. Engring. U. Mich.; mem. conf. bd. Internat. Coun. on Innovation and Tech. Mem.: Hyannis Yacht Club, Ponte Vedra Lodge and Club, Ponte Vedra Inn and Club, Nat. Club (D.C.), Marsh Landing Country Club, Wianno Yacht Club, Pi Tau Sigma, Tau Beta Pi, Sigma Xi. Republican. Roman Catholic. Home (Summer): 49 Warren St Osterville MA 02655 Office Phone: 904-543-1425. Personal E-mail: williamp.sommers@comcast.net.

**SOMMERVILLE, DANIEL VERNE,** mechanical engineer; b. San Jose, Calif., Sept. 26, 1976; s. Ronald William and Ruby Anne Sommerville; m. Jesse Rose West, Dec. 21, 2002. BS in Mech. Engring., Calif. Poly. State U., San Luis Obispo, 1999—99; MSME, Santa Clara U., Calif., 2004. Engr. in tng., Calif., 1998. Structural analyst GE Energy Nuc. Power, San Jose, Calif., 2001—04, tech. lead scale model testing, 2004—. Mem. US Nat. Vaulting Team, 1990—94. Mem.: ASME, Soc. Automotive Engrs. Achievements include patents pending for Boiling Water Reactor jet pump riser brace vibration mitigation device; Boiling Water Reactor steam dryer vibration mitigation device; scale model test methodology and apparatus for predicting acoustic loads on Boiling Water Reactor steam dryer. Office Phone: 408-202-1948. Business E-Mail: daniel.sommerville@ge.com.

**SOMMESE, ANDREW JOHN,** mathematics professor; b. N.Y.C., May 1948; s. Joseph and Frances S.; m. Rebecca Rooze DeBoer, June 7, 1971; children: Rachel, Ruth. BA in Math., Fordham U., 1969; PhD in Math., Princeton U., 1973. Gibbs instr. Yale U., New Haven, 1973-75; asst. prof. Cornell U., Ithaca, NY, 1975-79; assoc. prof. U. Notre Dame, Ind., 1979-83, prof. of math. Ind., 1983—, chair dept. math. Ind., 1988-92, Vincent J. Duncan and Annamarie Micus Duncan chair math. Ind., 1994—, dir. Ctr. Applied Math. Ind., 2005—. Mem. Inst. for Advanced Study, Princeton, N.J., 1975-76; guest prof. U. Bonn, Germany, 1978-79; guest rschr. Max Planck Inst. for Math., Bonn, 1992-93; cons. GM Rsch., Warren, Mich., 1986-97. Editor: Manuscripta Mathematica jour., 1986-93, Advances in Geometry, 2000;mem. editl. bd. Milan Jour. Math., 2002; contbr. articles to profl. publs.

---

Recipient Rsch. award for Sr. U.S. Scientists, Alexander Von Humboldt Found., 1993; A.P. Sloan Found. rsch. fellow, 1979. Mem. Am. Math. Soc., Soc. for Indsl. and Applied Math.. Phi Beta Kappa. Office: U Notre Dame Dept Math Notre Dame IN 46556

**SOMORJAI, GABOR ARPAD,** chemist, educator; b. Budapest, Hungary, May 4, 1935; came to U.S., 1957, naturalized, 1962; s. Charles and Livia (Ormos) S.; m. Judith Kaldor, Sept. 2, 1957; children: Nicole, John. BS, U. Tech. Scis., Budapest, 1956; PhD, U. Calif., Berkeley, 1960; Dr. Honoris Causa (hon.), Tech. U., Budapest, 1989, U. Pierre et Marie Curie, Paris, 1990, U. Libre Brussels, 1992, U. degli de Ferrara, Italy, 1998, Jozsef Attila U., Szeged, Hungary, 1999, Royal Inst. Tech., Stockholm, 2000; D (hon.), U. Manchester, Eng., 2001. Mem. research staff IBM, Yorktown Heights, N.Y., 1960-64; dir. Surface Sci. and Catalysis Program Lawrence Berkeley Lab., Calif., 1964—; mem. faculty dept. chemistry U. Calif.-Berkeley, 1964—, assoc. prof., 1967-72, prof., 1972—, Miller prof., 1978, univ. prof., 2002. Unilever prof. dept. chemistry U. Bristol, Eng., 1972; vis. fellow Emmanuel Coll., Cambridge, Eng., 1989; Baker lectr. Cornell U., Ithaca, N.Y., 1977; edit. bd. mem. Catalysis Reviews J. Am. Chem. Soc., 2004—. Author: Principles of Surface Chemistry, 1972, Chemistry in Two Dimensions, 1981, Introduction to Surface Chemistry and Catalysis, 1994; editor-in-chief Catalysis Letters, 1988—; contbr. articles to profl. jours. Recipient Emmett award Am. Catalysis Soc., 1977, Kokes award Johns Hopkins U., 1976, Albert award Precious Metal Inst., 1986, Sr. Disting. Scientist award Alexander von Humboldt Found., 1989, E.W. Mueller award U. Wis., Chemical Pioneer award Am. Inst. of Chemists, 1995, Von Hippel award Materials Rsch. Soc., 1997; Guggenheim fellow, 1969, Wolf prize in chemistry, Wolf Found., Israel, 1998. Fellow: AAAS, Am. Phys. Soc.; mem.: NAS, Catalysis Soc. N.Am., Am. Chem. Soc. (chmn. colloid and surface chemistry 1981, Surface and Colloid Chemistry award 1981, Peter Debye award 1989, Arthur W. Adamson award 1994, Award for creative rsch. in homogeneous and heterogeneous catalysis 2000, Cotton medal 2002), Hungarian Acad. Scis. (hon. Pauling medal 1990, Nat. Medal of Sci. 2001), Am. Acad. Arts and Scis. Home: 665 San Luis Rd Berkeley CA 94707-1725 Office: U Calif Dept Chemistry D 58 Hildebrand Hl Berkeley CA 94720-0001 E-mail: somorjai@socrates.berkeley.edu.

**SON, GWI-RYUNG,** medical educator; arrived in U.S., 1987; d. Byung Cheon Son and Young Boon Lee; m. Hyun Dae Hong, Nov. 22, 1986; children: Lee Kyung Hong, Daniel Jacob Hong. BS, HanYang U., Seoul, 1983; MS, U. Conn., Storrs, 1994; PhD, Case Western Res. U., Cleve., 1998. RN Ohio, clin. nurse specialist, Ohio. Staff nurse Ewha Woman's Univ. Hosp., Seoul, 1983—85, St. Joseph's Living Ctr., Windham, Conn., 1989—94; lectr. HanYang U., Seoul, 1997—98, Inha U., Incheon, Republic of Korea, 1997—98; postdoctoral fellow U. Mich., Ann Arbor, 1998—2000, asst. rsch. scientist, 2001—06, rsch. asst. prof., 2006—. Reviewer Jour. Nursing Scholarship, 2002—; mem. adv. com. Greater Cin. Alzheimer's Assn., Cin., 2003—06. Contbr. articles to profl. jours. Tchr. Cin.-Korean Am. Sch., 2004—06. Recipient Marie Houg Student award, Case Western Res. U., 1996, Lucile and Clayton Clark Faculty Rsch. award, U. Mich., 2001, New Investigator award, Soc. Urological Nurses Assn., 2004, Judith Braun award for Rsch. Excellence, Nat. Gerontological Nursing Assn, 2006. Mem.: Soc. Urol. Nurses and Assocs. (New Investigator award 2004), Gerontol. Soc. Am., Midwestern Nursing Rsch. Soc. Avocations: reading, movies.

**SON, SEUNG UK,** chemistry professor, researcher; b. Milyang, Kyungsangnam-Do, Republic of Korea, Nov. 26, 1972; s. Jin Taek Son and Sun Hee Kim. PhD, Seoul Nat. U., Seoul, 2001. Post doc, Inst. Basic Sci., Seoul Nat. U., Republic of Korea, 2001—03; post doc Inst. Engring., Seoul Nat. U., 2003—05; asst. prof., rschr. Sungkyunkwan U., Suwon, Kyunggi-Do, Republic of Korea, 2005—; vis. prof. Brown U., Providence, 2005—06. Contbr. articles various profl. jours. Achievements include research in development of new transition metal catalysts and novel functional nanomaterials. Avocations: table tennis, badminton. Office: Sungkyunkwan U Chemistry Dept CheonCheon-Dong Kyunggi-Do Suwon 440-746 Republic of Korea Office Phone: 82-31-290-5932. Home Fax: 82-31-299-4572; Office Fax: 82-31-299-4572. Business E-Mail: sson@skku.edu.

**SON, YOUNG-JUN,** industrial engineering professor, researcher; b. Taegu, Kyungbook, Republic of Korea; m. Hyewon Shin, Jan. 5, 2003; 1 child, Natalie Hee-Ju. PhD, Pa. State U., 2000. Asst. prof. U. Ariz., Tucson, 2000—06, assoc. prof., 2006. Sec. IIE Ariz. Chpt., 2005. Assoc. editor: Journal of Manufacturing Systems, International Journal of Modeling and Simulation. Recipient Outstanding Young Mfg. Engr. award, Soc. Mfg. Engrs., 2004, Outstanding Young Indsl. Engr. award, Inst. Indsl. Engrs., 2005. Office Phone: 520-626-9530.

**SONBERG, STEVEN,** lawyer; b. NYC, May 10, 1947; BS in Acctg., NYU Leonard N. Stern Sch. Bus., 1969; JD, U. Miami Sch. Law, 1972; LLM in Taxation, NYU Sch. Law, 1973. Bar: Fla. 1972, US Tax Ct. 1979. Ptnr. Holland & Knight LLP, Miami, Fla., Fort Lauderdale, Fla., chair, bus. law sect., served as mem. dir. com., co-chair, corp. governance nat. practice group. Spkr. in field. Contbr. articles to profl. jours. Bd. trustee U. Miami; bd. dir. Diabetes Rsch. Inst. Found., Inc., 1980—, pres., 1984—86, chmn. bd. dirs., 1990—96. Mem.: Am. Bar Found., Fla. Bar (mem. bus. law sect., internat. law sect., tax sect.), ABA (mem. bus. law sect., internat. and tax sects.), Dade County Bar Assn., Broward County Bar Assn. Office: Holland & Knight LLP 701 Brickell Ave Ste 3000 Miami FL 33131 Address: Holland & Knight LLP One East Broward Blvd Ste 1300 Fort Lauderdale FL 33301 Office Phone: 305-789-7794, 954-468-7816. Business E-Mail: ssonberg@hklaw.com.

**SONDAG, MARY JO,** elementary school educator, education educator; b. Harlan, Iowa, Nov. 29, 1950; d. Leroy J. and Gladys M. Anastasi; m. Tony Sondag; 1 child, Andy. AA, Iowa Western Coll., Council Bluffs, 1989; BA, Buena Vista U., Storm Lake, Iowa, 1990; MAT, Morningside Coll., Sioux City, Iowa, 1994. Chpt. I reading tchr. Harlan (Iowa) Cmty. Schs., 1990—94, tchr. sci. grade 5, 1994—95, tchr. kindergarten, 1995—2004, tchr. prekindergarten, 2004—. Adj. instr. Buena Vista U., Denison, Iowa, Western Iowa Tech. Coll., Iowa Western Coll., Hanan. Named Outstanding Faculty Mem., Buena Vista U., 2001. Mem.: NEA, ASCD, Harlan Edn. Assn. Home: 1405 College Blvd Harlan IA 51537 Office: Harlan Cmty Schs 2102 Durant Harlan IA 51537

**SONDAK, ARTHUR,** retired management consultant; b. N.Y.C., Oct. 16, 1929; s. Louis and Eva (Dolin) S.; m. Sylvia Mayran, Jan. 17, 1953 (div. 1975); children: Janet, Steven, Donald; m. Susan Altman, Oct. 17, 1999. BBA, Baruch Coll., 1950, MBA, 1958. Employment mgr. Saks Fifth Ave, N.Y.C., 1954-57; wage and salary adminstr. Royal Typewriter Co., N.Y.C., 1957-61; employment mgr. Sperry Rand Corp., N.Y.C., 1961-62; compensation dir., region personnel mgr. Royal Typewriter Co., N.Y.C., 1962-66; mgr. personnel program planning MAI, N.Y.C., 1966-69; personnel dir. ITEl Corp., White Plains, N.Y., 1969-73; dir. personnel and adminstrn. MAI, N.Y.C., 1973-75; instr. Baruch Coll. Grad. Sch., N.Y.C., 1969-70; prin. Personnel Mgmt. Svcs., Delray Beach, Fla., 1975-99. Editorial adv. bd. AMACOM, N.Y.C., 1986-96; contbr. articles to profl. jours. Adv. bd. Cmty./Advancement Resource Ctr., Middlesex Coll., Edison, 1985-90; career guidance counselor USAF, 1950-54. Avocations: photography, nostalgia, sports, golf. Home: 6320 Crystal View Ln Boynton Beach FL 33437-4041

**SONDE, THEODORE IRWIN,** lawyer; b. NYC, Jan. 7, 1940; s. Martin and Anne (Greenbaum) S.; m. Susan Kolisch, Sept. 10, 1964; children: Andrea Martine, David Ian. BA, CCNY, 1961; LLB, NYU, 1964; LLM, Georgetown U., 1967. Bar: N.Y. 1964, D.C. 1978, U.S. Supreme Ct. With SEC, Washington, 1964-80, asst. gen. counsel Office Gen. Counsel, 1970-74, assoc. dir. divsn. enforcement, 1974-80; prin. Office Enforcement, FERC, Washington, 1980-81; mem. firm Cole, Corette & Abrutyn, 1982—90, Dechert, Price & Rhodes, 1990—2002, Crowell & Moring, Washington, 2002—04, Hogan & Hartson, Washington, 2005—. Adj. prof. Georgetown U. Law Sch.

---

1977-95, George Washington U. Nat. Law Ctr., 1976-82. Contbr. articles to law jours. Office: Hogan & Hartson 555 13th St NW Washington DC 20004 Office Phone: 202-637-3569. Business E-Mail: tsonde@hhlaw.com.

**SONDEL, PAUL MARK,** pediatric oncologist, educator; b. Milw., Aug. 14, 1950; s. Robert F. and Audrey J. (Dworkus) S.; m. Sherie Ann Katz, Jan. 1, 1973; children: Jesse Adam, Beth Leah, Elana Rose, Jodi Zipporah. BS with honors, U. Wis., 1971, PhD in Genetics, 1975; MD magna cum laude, Harvard Med. Sch., Boston, 1977. Diplomate Nat. Bd. Med. Examiners, Am. Bd. Pediatrics; lic. physician, Wis. Postdoctoral rsch. fellow Harvard Med. Sch., Boston, 1975-77; intern in pediatrics U. Minn. Hosp., Mpls., 1977-78; resident in pediatris U. Wis. Hosp. and Clinics, Madison, 1978-80; asst. prof. pediatrics, human oncology and genetics U. Wis., Madison, 1980-84, assoc. prof., 1984-86, prof. pediatrics, human oncology and genetics, 1987—, head divsn. pediatric hematology/oncology, program leader, 1990—; assoc. dir. U Wisc. Cancer Ctr., 1996-99, 2006—; vice chair rsch. dept. pediatrics U. Wis., Madison, 2006—. Sub-fellow pediat. oncology; Midwest Children's Cancer Ctr., Milw., 1980; vis. scientist dept. cell biology Weizmann Inst. Sci., Rehovot, Israel, 1987, 2000; chmn. immunology com. Children's Cancer Group 1990-2001; cancer ctr. rev. com. Nat. Cancer Inst., 1997-2000, bd. sci. counselors, 2005—. Sr. editor Clin. Cancer Rsch., 1996-99; mem. editl. bd. Jour. Immunology, 1985-87, Jour. Nat. Cancer Inst., 1987—, Jour. Biol. Response Modifiers, 1990—, BLOOD, 1992—, Natural Immunity, 1992—; contbr. articles to Jour. Exptl. Medicine, Jour. Immunology, Cellular Immunology, Immunol. Revs., Med. Pediatric Oncology, Wis. State Med. Jour., Jour. Biol. Response Modifiers, Jour. Pediatrics, Jour. Clin. Oncology, Jour. Clin. Investigation, others State of Wis. Regents scholar, 1968; J.A. and G.L. Hartford Found. fellow, 1981-84. Mem. Am. Assn. Immunologists, Am. Assn. Clin. Histocompatibility Typing, Am. Fedn. Clin. Rsch., Am. Soc. Pediatric Hematology/Oncology, Am. Assn. Cancer Rsch., Am. Soc. Transplant Physicians, Am. Soc. Clin. Oncology, Am. Acad. Pediatrics, Leukemia Soc. Am. (bd. dirs. Wis. chpt. 1987-90 Achievements include patent for Typing Leukocyte Antigens; research on clinical and immunological effects of human recombinant Interleukin-2 and monoclonal antibodies. Home: 1114 Winston Dr Madison WI 53711-3161 Office: U Wis K4/448 Clin Sci Ctr 600 Highland Ave Madison WI 53792-3284 Office Phone: 608-263-9069. Business E-Mail: pmsondel@facstaff.wisc.edu.

**SONDERBY, SUSAN PIERSON,** federal judge; b. Chgo., May 15, 1947; d. George W. and Shirley L. (Eckstrom) Pierson; m. James A. De Witt, June 14, 1975 (dec. 1978); m. Peter R. Sonderby, Apr. 7, 1990. AA, Joliet Jr. Coll., Joliet, Ill., 1967; BA, U. Ill., 1969; JD, John Marshall Law Sch., 1973. Bar: Ill., 1973; U.S. Dist. Ct. (cen. and so. dists.) Ill., 1973; U.S. Dist. Ct. (no. dist.) Ill., 1984; U.S. Ct. Appeals (7th Cir.), 1984. Assoc. O'Brien, Garrison, Berard, Kusta, and De Witt, Joliet, Ill., 1973-75, ptnr., 1975-77; asst. atty. gen. consumer protection div., litig. sect. Office of the Atty. Gen., Chgo., 1977-78, asst. atty. gen., chief consumer protection divsn. Springfield, Ill., 1978-83; U.S. trustee (no. dist.) Ill. Chgo., 1983-86; judge U.S. Bankruptcy Ct. (no. dist.) Ill., Chgo., 1986—, chief fed. bankruptcy judge, 1998—2002. Mem. law faculty Fed. Jud. Tng. Ctr., Ill., Practicing Law Inst., Ill., U.S. Dept. Justice, Ill., Nat. Bankruptcy Inst., Ill. Ill. Continuing Edn.; spl. asst. atty. gen., Ill., 1972—78; adj. faculty De Paul U. Coll. Law, Chgo., 1986; past mem. U.S. Trustee adv. com., Ill.; consumer adv. coun. Fed. Res. Bd., Ill.; past sec. of State Fraudulent I.D. com. Dept. of Ins. Task Force on Improper Claims Practices, Ill.; former chair pers. rev. bd., mem. task force race and gender bias, U.S. Dist. Ct.; jud. conf. planning com. 7th Cir. Jud. Conf.; former mem. Civil Justice Reform Act Adv. Com., Adminstrv. Office of the U.S. Cts. Bankruptcy Judges Adv. Group, Ct. Security com., Adminstrv. Office of the U.S. Cts. Budget and Fin. Coun. Contbr. articles to profl. jour. Mem. Fourth Presbyn. Ch., Art Inst. Chgo.; past mem. Westminster Presbyn. Ch., Chgo. Coun. of Fgn. Rels.; past bd. dirs. Land of Lincoln Coun. Girl Scouts U.S.; past mem. individual guarantors com. Goodman Theatre, Chgo.; past chair clubs and orgns. Sangamon County United Way Capital campaign; past bd. dirs., chair house rules com. and legal subcom. Lake Point Tower; past mem. Family Svc. Ctr., Aid to Retarded Citizens, Henson Robinson Zoo. Named Young Career Woman, Bus. and Profl. Women, One of Ten Outstanding Bankruptcy Judges, Turnarounds and Workouts, 2002; named one of 500 Leading Judges in Am., Law Dragon mag., 2006; recipient Spl. Achievement Award, Dept. Justice, 1984, Disting. Svc. Alumni Award, Joliet Jr. Coll., 1987, Disting. Alumni Award, John Marshall Law Sch., 1988, Dir. Award, Exec. Office U.S. Trustee, Leadership Award, Internat. Orgn. Women Exec., Outstanding Svc. to Bench, Am. Bankruptcy Inst., 1990. Master: Abraham Lincoln Marovitz Inn of Ct. (former pres., membership com.); fellow: Am. Coll. Bankruptcy (circuit admissions com.); mem.: ATLA, Comml. Law League Am. (former exec. coun. mem., bankruptcy and insolvency sect., coord. with nat. conf. bankruptcy judges com.), Nat. Conf. Bankruptcy Judges (co-chair ednl. program com. conf. 2001, liaison with bankruptcy rev. commn. com.), Bar Assn. (7th cir.) (former treas., judicial conf. planning com.), Am. Bankruptcy Inst. (bd. dirs. Chgo. chpt.), Fed. Bar Assn., Chgo. Archtl. Found., John Marshall Law Sch. Alumni Assn. (bd. dirs.), Nordic Law Club (past legis. com.), Lawyers Club Chgo. (hon.). Avocations: travel, flying, interior decorating. Office: US Bankruptcy Ct 219 S Dearborn St Ste 638 Chicago IL 60604-1702

**SONDHEIM, STEPHEN JOSHUA,** composer, librettist, lyricist; b. NYC, Mar. 22, 1930; s. Herbert and Janet (Fox) Sondheim. BA, Williams Coll., 1950. Composer, lyricist. Vis. prof. contemporary theatre Oxford U., England. Lyricist West Side Story, 1957 (Tony award), Gypsy, 1959, music and lyrics A Funny Thing Happened on the Way to the Forum, 1962, Anyone Can Whistle, 1964, lyricist Do I Hear a Waltz?, 1965, Evening Primrose, 1966, Company, 1970 (Tony award, 1971), Follies, 1971 (Tony award, 1972), A Little Night Music, 1973 (Tony award, 1973), The Frogs, 1974, Pacific Overtures, 1976, Sweeney Todd, 1979 (Tony award, 1979), Merrily We Roll Along, 1981, Sunday in the Park with George, 1984 (Pulitzer prize, 1985), Into the Woods, 1987 (Tony award, 1988), Assassins, 1991, Passion, 1994 (Tony award, 1994), Bounce, 2003, The Frogs, 2004, Chita Rivera: The Dancer's Life, 2005, (incidental music) Girls of Summer, 1956, Invitation to a march, 1961, Twigs, 1971, additional lyrics Candide, 1973, (anthologies) Side by Side by Sondheim, 1976, Marry Me a Little, 1981, You're Gonna Love Tomorrow, 1983, Putting It Together, 1993, (film scores) Stavisky, 1974, Reds, 1981; composer: songs for film Dick Tracy, 1990 (Acad. award); co-author: (films) The Last of Sheila, 1973, Birdcage, 1996, Getting Away with Murder, 1996. Founder Young Playwrights Inc., 1981—. Recipient Creative Arts medal, Brandeis U., 1982, Grammy awards, 1970, 1973, 1975, 1979, 1984, 1988, Kennedy Ctr. Honor for Lifetime Achievement, 1993, Nat. medal of arts, NEA, 1997, Praemium Imperiale, 2000, The Jason Robards award for excellence in theatre, Roundabout Theatre Co., 2005. Mem.: Am. Acad. and Inst. Arts and Letters.*

**SONDIK, EDWARD J.,** health science administrator; BEE, MEE, U. Conn.; PhD in Elec. Engring. U. Stanford U. Faculty dept. engring econ. sys. Stanford U.; acting dir. Nat. Cancer Inst., acting dept. dir., dept. dir. divsn. cancer prevention and control, assoc. dir. surveillance program; dir. Nat. Ctr. Health Stats., Ctrs. Disease Control Prevention, Hyattsville, Md., 1996—. Sr. adv. health stats. Sec. Health Human Svcs.*

**SONE, HIRO,** chef, restaurant owner, writer; b. Ichihasama, Japan; m. Lissa Doumani. Grad., Ecole Technique Hoteliere Tsuji, Osaka, Japan. From dishwasher to sous chef Italian restaurant, Tokyo; from mem. staff to head chef Spago, L.A.; former sous chef Tokyo; co-owner, chef Terra, St. Helena, Calif., 1988—. Author (with Lissa Doumani): Terra, Cooking from the Heart of the Napa Valley, 2001. Nominee Am. Express Best Chef, Calif., James Beard Found., 2001; recipient James Beard Best Chef Calif. award, 2003. Office: Terra 1345 Railroad Ave Saint Helena CA 94574

**SONE, YUTAKA,** artist; b. Shizuoka, Japan, 1965; BFA, Tokyo Geijutsu U., 1988, MA in Architecture, 1992. One-man shows include One hand clapping, Yokohama Galleria, Japan, 1993, Her 19th Foot, Contemporary Art Ctr., Art Tower Mito, Japan, 1993, Space Luxury Art, Hosomi Gallery, Tokyo, Japan, 1994, Departures, Roentgen Kunst Institute, Tokyo, Japan, 1995, Future

Perfect, Bunkamura Gallery, Tokyo, Japan, 1996, Scoop, Mitaka City Arts Found., Tokyo, Japan, 1996, Amusement, Gallery Side 2, Tokyo, Japan, 1997, At the End of All the Journeys, Shiseido Art House, Kakegawa, Japan, 1998, David Zwirner, NY, 1999, Double Six, Artpace, San Antonio, 2000, Travel to Double River Island, Toyota Mcpl. Mus. Art, Toyota City, Japan, 2002, Yutaka Sone: Jungle Island, Mus. Contemporary Art, LA, 2003, Amusment Romana, David Zwirner, NY, 2004, exhibited in group shows, Shinjuku Shonen Art, Tokyo, Japan, 1994, Ripple Across the Water, Watari Mus. Contemporary Art, Watari-um, Tokyo, 1995, Join Me! One Night Artist's Cafe, Spiral Wacoal Art Ctr., Tokyo, 1996, Cities on the Move 1, Wiener Secession,Vienna, Austria, 1997, Unfinished History, Walker Art Ctr., Mpls., 1998, Cities on the Move 3, PS1 Contemporary Art Ctr., Queens, NY, 1998, Cities on the Move 5, Hayward Gallery, London, 1999, From a Distance: Landscape in Contemporary Art, Inst. Contemporary Art, Boston, 2000, Déjà Vu, Ctr. Curatorial Studies, Bard College, Annandale-on-Hudson, NY, 2000, New Works: 00.4, ArtPace, A Foundation for Contemporary Art, San Antonio, 2001, Pub. Offerings, Mus. Contemporary Art, LA, 2001, Is NY, David Zwirner, NY, 2001, The Gift. Generous offering, insidious hospitality, Scotsdale Mus. Contemporary Art, Ariz., 2002, Loop, P.S. 1 Contemporary Art Ctr., Long Island City, NY, 2002, Metascape, Cleve. Mus. Art, 2003, 100 Artists See God, Ind. Curators Internat., NY, 2004, Whitney Biennial, Whitney Mus. Am. Art, NY, 2004, Universal Experience: Art, Life & the Tourists Eye, Mus. Contemporary Art, Chgo., 2005. Mailing: c/o David Zwirner 525 West 19th St New York NY 10011

**SONEGO, IAN G.,** assistant attorney general; b. Louisville, May 27, 1954; s. Angelo and Zella Mae (Causey) S. BA in Polit. Sci. with high honors, U. Louisville, 1976, JD, 1979. Bar: Ky. 1979, U.S. Dist Ct. (ea. dist.) Ky. 1980, U.S. Dist. Ct. (we. dist.) Ky. 1989, U.S. Ct. Appeals (6th cir.) 1989, U.S. Supreme Ct. 1990. Asst. atty. Office Commonwealth's Atty. Pike County, Pikeville, Ky., 1980, sr. asst. atty., 1988-89; assoc. John Paul Runyon Law Firm, Pikeville, 1981-87; asst. atty. gen. Office Atty. Gen., Frankfort, Ky., 1989—. Lectr. criminal law Ky. Bar Assn., Jenny Wiley Park, 1981, Ky. Prosecutors Conf., 1989, 93; mem. Atty. Gen.'s task force child sexual abuse, 1992-94, Nat. Conf. on Domestic Violence, 1996. Contbg. editor Ky. Prosecuter Newsletter, 1991—. Recipient Kesslman award, U. Louisville, 1975, Bd. trustee award, 1979, Outstanding Prosecutor award, Ky. Atty., Award Outstanding Advocacy, Assn. Govt. Attys. in Capital Litigation, 2001. Mem.: Assn. Govt. Attys. in Capital Litig., Ky. Commonwealth's Attys. Assn. (hon.; lectr. 1987, 90, chmn. com. ethics 1984—86, bd. dirs. 1983—85, Spl. award 1987). Office: Office Atty Gen Criminal Appeals Office 1024 Capital Center Dr Frankfort KY 40601-8204 Office Phone: 502-696-5342. E-mail: ian.sonego@ag.ky.gov.

**SONENSHEIN, ABRAHAM LINCOLN,** biology professor, researcher; b. Paterson, N.J., Jan. 13, 1944; s. Israel Louis and Celia (Rabinowitz) S.; m. Gail Entner, Jan. 28, 1967; children: Dina Miriam, Adam Israel. AB, Princeton U., 1965; PhD, MIT, 1970. Postdoctoral fellow U. Paris, Orsay, France, 1970-72; asst. prof. Tufts U., Boston, 1972-78, assoc. prof., 1978-82; prof. molecular biology and microbiology Tufts U. Sch. Medicine, Boston, 1982—, dir. molecular biology program. Vis. prof. U. Paris, 1998. Rsch. grantee NIH, 1972—; fellow Am. Cancer Soc., 1970-72. Mem. AAAS, Am. Soc. for Microbiology, Am. Acad. Microbiology, Fedn. Am. Scientists, Sigma Xi. Office: Tufts U Dept Microbiology 136 Harrison Ave Boston MA 02111 Office Phone: 617-636-6761, 617-636-6762. Office Fax: 617-636-0337. Business E-Mail: linc.sonenshein@tufts.edu.

**SONETT, JOSHUA ROBERT,** medical educator, surgeon; b. 1962; BA cum laude, Duke U., 1984; MD, E. Carolina U., 1988. Cert. Am. Bd. Thoracic Surgeons, Am. Bd. Surgery. Resident gen. surgery U. Mass. Med. Ctr., Worcester, Mass., 1988—93, rsch. fellow cardiothoracic surgery, 1990—91; resident cardiothoracic surgery U. Pitts. Med. Ctr., Pitts., 1993—96; fellow thoracic surgery Sloan-Kettering Meml. Hosp., NYC, 1995—96; asst. prof. surgery U. Md., Balt., 1996—2001, dir. lung transplant program, 1998—2001, co-dir. Photodynamic Therapy Treatment Ctr., 1999—2001, assoc. prof. surgery, 2001, Columbia U., NYC, 2001—; dir. lung transplant program NY Presbyterian Hosp./Columbia U. Med. Ctr., NYC, 2001—, attending surgeon divsn. cardiothoracic surgery, 2001—. Chief thoracic surgery Balt. Veterans Affairs Ctr., Balt., 1996—2001; mem. adv. panel Med. Soc. State of NY Organ Donation. Mem. editl. bd. Jour. Transplantation; contbr. articles to profl. jours. Named one of Best Doctors, NY mag., 2002—04. Mem.: NY Soc. Thoracic Surgery, Am. Coll. Surgeons, Am. Coll. Chest Physicians, Soc. Thoracic Surgeons, So. Thoracic Assn., Gen. Thoracic Surgery Club, Cardiothoracic Surgery Network. Office: Columbia U 622 W 168th St PH 14 East Rm 104 New York NY 10032 Office Phone: 212-305-8086. Office Fax: 212-342-5382. E-mail: js2106@columbia.edu.

**SONFIELD, ROBERT LEON, JR.,** lawyer; b. Houston, Oct. 28, 1931; s. Robert Leon and Dorothy Harriett (Huber) S.; 1 dau., Sheree. BA, U. Houston, 1956, LLB, JD, 1959; PhD (hon.), U. Eastern Fla., 1962; LLD (hon.), London Inst. Applied Rsch., 1973; cert. fed. taxation, NYU, 1973; cert. securities regulation, Harvard U., 1983. Bar: Tex. 1959, U.S. Supreme Ct. 1959, U.S. Dist. Ct. Tex. 1960, U.S. Tax Ct. 1960, U.S. Ct. Appeals 1960, U.S. Ct. Claims 1974. Mng. dir. Sonfield & Sonfield, Houston, 1959—. Mem. nat. adv. coun. Nat. Fedn. Ind. Bus. Author: Corporate Financing by Sale of Securities to the Public, 1969, Mergers and Acquisitions, 1970, Student Rights, 1971, The Limited Partnership as a Vehicle for Real Estate Investment, 1971, Integration of Partnership Offerings, 1974, The Grantor Trust Rules After The Tax Reform Act of 1986, Incentive Equity Program, Corporate Name Protection Along With Name Registration, A Guide to SEC Corporate Filing, Organizational Professionals' Residual Litigation and Investment Strategy, Comparing California, Delaware and Nevada: Corporate Laws in Light of California Corporations Code Section 2115 and Offering of Unregistered Securities Only to Accredited Investors, Disclosure Policies, Practices and Procedures For Public Companies, Regulation of Franchises, How to Become a Publicly Held Company Via the Registered Distribution of a Percentage of Your Company's Stock to Shareholders, numerous others. Recipient St. John Garwood award, 1957, Frio-Finnegan Outstanding Alumnus award, 1970-71, citation for outstanding contbn. to legal profession, 1971. Mem. Am. Tax Lawyers Assn. (pres.), Lawyers Soc. Houson, Am. Judicature Soc., ABA, Tex. Bar Assn. (dist. com. on admission to state bar, chmn. clients security fund com.), Houston Bar Assn. (com. chmn. coun., tax sect.), Tex. Equal Access to Justice Found., Houston Bar Found., Real Estate Securities and Syndication Assn., Huguenot Soc. of London, Order Stars and Bars, SAR, Sons Confederate Vets., Mil. Order World Wars, Mil. and Hospitaller Order St. Lazarus of Jerusalem, Knightly Assn. St. George the Martyr, Smithsonian Assocs., Houston Heritage Soc., Houston Mus. Fine Arts, Newcomen Soc. N.Am., Phi Delta Phi, Delta Sigma Phi, Met. Club (N.Y.C.), Argyle Club (San Antonio), Houstoon Club, Houstonian Club. Office: Sonfield & Sonfield 770 S Post Oak Ln Houston TX 77056-6665 Office Phone: 713-877-8333. E-mail: robert@sonfield.com.

**SONG, DANNY,** radiation oncologist; BA, So. Adventist U., Chattanooga, 1992; MD, Med. Coll. Ga., Augusta, 1996. Intern Sinai Hosp. of Balt., 1996—97; resident in radiation oncology Johns Hopkins U., Balt., 2001; asst. prof. Va. Commonwealth U., Richmond, Va., 2001—04; faculty depts. oncology and urology Johns Hopkins U., Balt., 2004—, asst. prof. radiation oncology, 2004—. Contbr. articles to profl. jours. Named one of Best Pediat. Drs. in Richmond, Richmond mag., 2002; recipient Faculty Tchg. award, Va. Commonwealth U. Dept. Radiation Oncology, 2002, Tchr. of the Yr. award, Assn. Residents in Radiation Oncology, 2002. Mem.: AAPM (stereotactic body-radiotherapy task group), Am. Brachotherapy Soc., Am. Soc. Therapeutic Radiology and Oncology, ACS. Office: Johns Hopkins Sch Medicine Weinberg Ste 1441 401 N Broadway Baltimore MD 21231*

**SONG, DAVID,** plastic surgeon, medical educator; b. 1970; MD, UCLA. Cert. Plastic Surgery. Surg. resident Univ. Chgo. Hospitals, plastic surgeon, chief plastic surgeon, 2004—. Spkr. in field. Contbr. articles to numerous

profl. jours. Med. Aid for Children Latin Am. Named one of 40 Under Forty, Crain's Bus. Chgo., 2005. Mem.: Am. Coll. Plastic Surgeons, Am. Coll. Surgeons. Office: Univ Chgo Hosps MC 6035 5841 S Maryland Ave Chicago IL 60637*

**SONG, JESSICA CHUYUNN,** pharmacist, educator; b. Seattle, Wash., July 8, 1967; d. Choong Nae and Sung Nyun Song. PharmD, U. Calif., San Francisco, 1998. Pharmacy faculty U. Pacific, Stockton, Calif., 2001—; coord. pharmacy residency Santa Clara Valley Med. Ctr., 2004—. Cons. Schering-Plough Pharm., San Jose, 2005—. Con. edn. coord. Quatra Chpt, Calif. Health Systems Pharmacist, San Jose, 2004—06. Recipient Tchr. of the Yr. award, U. Pacific, Sch. Pharmacy, 2003. Conservative. Avocations: travel, cooking. Office: Santa Clara Valley Med Ctr 751 South Bascom Ave San Jose CA 95128 Office Phone: 408-885-2321. E-mail: jessica.song@hhs.co.santa-clara.ca.us.

**SONG, JIE,** chemistry professor; PhD, U. N.D., Grand Forks, 2002. Asst. prof. U. Mich., Flint, 2004—. Office Phone: 810-762-3110.

**SONG, JOSEPH,** pathologist, educator; b. Pyong Yang, Korea, May 11, 1927; s. Ha Ju and Hwa Soon (Koh) S.; m. Kumsan Ryu, Apr. 12, 1958; children: Patricia, Michael, Jeff. MD, Seoul U. Sch. Medicine, 1950; MS in Pathology, U. Tenn., Memphis, 1956; MD, U. Ark. Med. Sch., 1965. Diplomate Am. Bd. Pathology. Pathologist in charge State Cancer Detection Survey, Providence, 1956—59; assoc. pathologist Providence Lying-In Hosp., 1958—61; assoc. prof. pathology U. Ark. Med. Ctr., Little Rock, 1961—64; dir. lab. Mercy Hosp., Des Moines, 1965—92, rschr. cancer, 1993—95; clin. prof. pathology Creighton U. Sch. Medicine, Omaha, 1968—95; med. dir. Corning Clin. Labs., Des Moines, 1995—97; ret., 1997. Cons. EPA, Washington, 1975-85; pres. med. staff Mercy Hosp., Des Moines, 1981 Author: (book) The Human Uterus, 1964, Pathology of Sickle Cell Anemia, 1971 (award 1975), Beyond the Horizon, 1995. Elder Winsdor Presbyn. Ch., Des Moines, 1964; com. mem. Aldersgate Meth. Ch., Des Moines, 1995. Major Med. Corps, 1950-52, Korea. Recipient Martin Luther King Med. Achievement award, So. Christian Leadership Conf., Statesmanship award Am. Assn. Med. Adminstrs., Las Vegas, Nev., 1987. Fellow ACP, Coll. Am. Pathologists, Am. Soc. Clin. Pathology, Am. Assn. Cancer Rsch. Methodist. Avocation: classical music. Home: 2345 Park Ave Des Moines IA 50321-1505

**SONG, SUN-JU,** materials scientist; s. Gilnam and Guinim (Yoon) Song; m. Hyemin Hwang, 1974; 1 child, Rosa. PhD, U. Fla., 2003. Rsch. scientist Argonne Nat. Lab., Ill., 2004—. Catholic. Office Phone: 630-252-7761. Business E-Mail: song@anl.gov.

**SONG, XUBIN,** mechanical engineer, researcher; b. Yi Wu, China; s. Sengui Song and Yueqing Hu; m. Rongrong Zhou; 1 child, Justin Jia-Wen. BS in Engring., Nanjing U. Aeronautics and Astronautics, Nanjing, China, 1986; MS in Engring., China Acad. Launch Vehicle Tech., Beijing, China, 1988; MS in Mech. Engring., N.C. A&T State U., 1996; PhD, Va. Tech. U., 1999. Engr. China Acad. Launch Vehicle Tech., Beijing, 1988—2004, MSX Internat., Auburn Hills, Mich., 1999—2000; tech. profl. Visteon Corp, Dearborn, Mich., 2000—04; prin. engr. Eaton Corp, Southfiled, Mich., 2004—. Gen. mgr. XYZ Tech. Corp., Canton, Mich. 2003. Contbr. over 30 articles to profl. jours. Mem.: ASME (mem. vehicle design com. 2003), IEEE, Detroit Chinese Bus. Assn. (sr. bus. mgr. 2001—), Soc. Automotive Engrs. (mem. comml. vehicle powertrain and drivetrain com. 2004), Phi Kappa Phi. Achievements include five patents in field; development of torsional vibration control for commercial vehicles; adaptive control for magneto-rheological damper based suspension systems; research in automated optimization design and control of large nonlinear flexible structures; four patents pending; ten inventions related to powertrain control under patent application. Office: Eaton Corp 26201 Northwestern Highway Southfield MI 48076 Office Phone: 248-226-1738. Personal E-mail: xusong@vt.edu. Business E-Mail: xubinsong@eaton.com.

**SONG, YONGYI,** librarian; b. Shanghai, Dec. 15, 1949; arrived in U.S., 1989; s. Changrui Song and Meiqing Jia; m. Xiaohua Helen Yao, Jan. 1, 1980; 1 child, Xiao. BA, Inst. Shanghai Edn., 1985; MA, U. Colo., 1992; MLS, Ind. U., 1995. Instr. comparative lit. Pa. State U., State College, 1992—93; Chinese bibliographer U. Pitts., 1995—97; sr. libr. East Asian studies/langs. and area studies Dickinson Coll., Carlisle, Pa., 1997—2004; libr. tch. svcs. and collection devel. Calif. State U., L.A., 2004—. Author: The Cultural Revolution: A Bibliography, 1966-1996, 1998, The Cultural Revolution and Heterodox Thoughts, 2001, Historical Dictionary of the Chinese Cultural Revolution, 2006; chief editor The Chinese Cultural Revolution Database, 2002. Recipient 21st Century Nat. Libr. award, Syracuse U. Sch. Info. Studies, NY, 2004; grantee, Chan's Journalism and Culture Found., NYC, 2000; scholar, Pa. Libr. Assn., 2001. Mem.: ALA (Paul Howard award 2005). Office: Calif State U 5151 State Univ Dr Los Angeles CA 90033 Office Phone: 323-343-4884. Business E-Mail: ysong2@calstatela.edu.

**SONG, ZHEN,** electrical engineer, researcher; b. Beijing, Mar. 10, 1975; s. Kongzhi Song and Xiaoxia Yan; m. Hong Yan; 1 child, Calla Xueyan. MS, Utah State U., Logan, Utah, 2006. Cert. IRB tng., Utah State U., 2004, Responsible conduct of rsch., Utah State U., 2004. Rsch. asst. Utah State U., Logan, Utah, 2000—05; intern Siemens Corp. Rsch., Princeton, NJ, 2006—. Contbr. scientific papers to profl. jour. Recipient 2nd Pl. of Smart Dust Challenge, Crossbow Inc., 2005; Dissertation Fellowship, Utah State U., 2005, Rsch. v.p. Fellowship, 2003. Mem.: ACM, SIAM, IEEE. Achievements include research in Wireless Sensor Network; development of Robots. Home: 1401 Fox Run Dr Plainsboro NJ 08536 Office: Siemens Corp Rsch 755 Coll Rd E Princeton NJ Personal E-mail: zhensong@ieee.org.

**SONGER, SUSAN KAY,** secondary school educator; b. Coudersport, Pa., Dec. 17, 1952; d. Burton Rendell Shirey and Edith Marie Machtley-Shirey; m. Michael Bruce Songer, July 22, 2000; children from previous marriage: Tracy Lee Shaffer, Sean Michael Patten, Ryan Andrew Patten. BS in Secondary Comm., Lock Haven State U., Pa., 1979; Master's Equivalent in Devel./Remedial Reading, Pa. State U., University Park, 1983. Tchr. English Brockway Area Jr./Sr. H.S., Pa., 1974—76; indsl. rels. rep. Piper Aircraft Corp., Lock Haven, Pa., 1976—80; tchr. English/drama Penns Valley Area Jr./Sr. H.S., Spring Mills, Pa., 1980—. Dir.: over 100 high sch. plays and musicals. Mem. Grace United Ch. of Christ, Spring Mills, 2000—. Named Tchr. Who Makes a Difference, Penns Valley Sch. Bd., 2006. Democrat. Church Of Christ. Avocations: camping, boating, reading, theater. Home: PO Box 14 Coburn PA 16832 Office: Penns Valley Area HS 4595 Penns Valley Rd Spring Mills PA 16875 Office Phone: 814-422-8854. E-mail: bude58@verizon.net.

**SONKA, MILAN,** electrical and computer engineering educator; b. Prague, Czechoslovakia, June 5, 1955; came to U.S., 1990; s. Zdenek and Jirina (Haskova) S. MSEE, Czech Tech. U., Prague, 1979, PhD, 1984. Asst. prof. elec. engring. Czech Tech. U., Prague 1984-90; vis. asst. prof. elec. and computer engring. U. Iowa, Iowa City, 1990-93, vis. assoc. prof., 1993-94, assoc. prof., 1994—99, prof., 2000—. Author: Computer Vision (in Czech), 1992, Image Processing, Analysis and Machine Vision, 1993, 2d edit., 1998, Handbook of Medical Imaging--Medical Image Processing and Analysis, 2000; contbr. articles to profl. jours. Grantee-in-aid Am. Heart Assn., NIH, NSF. Fellow IEEE, Am. Inst. for Med. and Biol. Engring.; mem. Internat. Assn. Pattern Recognition. Achievements include devel. of knowledge-based automated methods for analysis of med. image data from angiography, ultrasound, computer tomography, magnetic resonance, positron emission tomography, others, more robust and accurate than conventional. Office: U Iowa 4322 SC Dept Elec Engring Iowa City IA 52242 Home: 832 Forest Hill Dr Coralville IA 52241-3455

**SONLEITNER, FRANK JOSEPH,** zoology educator; b. Chgo., Jan. 23, 1932; s. Frank Joseph Sr. and Lucille (Hamilton) S.; m. Nancy Kate Pierce, Sept. 13, 1974 (div. Feb. 1987); children: Bonnie, Catherine, Carol. AB, U.

Chgo., 1951, BS, 1956, PhD, 1959. Postdoctoral fellow NSF, Sydney, Australia, 1959-61; lectr. in zoology U. Calif., Berkeley, 1961-62; asst. prof. entomology U. Kans., Lawrence, 1962-65; asst. prof. zoology U. Okla., Norman, 1965-69, assoc. prof. zoology, 1969—2002; prof.zoology emeritus, 2002. Bd. dirs. Nat. Ctr. for Sci. Edn. With U.S. Army, 1954-55. Office of Surgeon Gen. U.S. Army rsch. grantee, 1963-65. Mem. AAAS, Am. Inst Biol. Scis., Ecol. Soc. Am., Entomol. Soc. Am., Okla. Acad. Sci., Nat. Ctr. for Sci. Edn., Phi Beta Kappa. Office: U Okla Dept Zoology Norman OK 73019-0001 Business E-Mail: frank.j.sonleitner-1@ou.edu.

**SONNECKEN, EDWIN HERBERT,** management consultant; b. New Haven, July 22, 1916; s. Ewald and Pauline (Halfmann) S.; m. Elizabeth Gregory, June 3, 1939; children: William H., Richard G., Paul D. BS, Northwestern U., 1938; MBA, 1940. With Montgomery Ward & Co., Chgo., 1940-42; price adminstr. OPA, Chgo., 1943; mgr. sales B.F. Goodrich Co., Akron, Ohio, 1943-53; dir. planning Ford Motor Co., Dearborn, Mich., 1953-57; pres. Market Planning Corp., N.Y.C., 1957-61; from dir. corp. planning and research to v.p. corp. bus. planning Goodyear Tire & Rubber Co., 1961-80; chmn. Mktg. Sci. Inst., Cambridge, Mass., 1980-84, also trustee, chmn. research policy com.; mgmt. cons., Akron, 1985—. Pres. Akron (Ohio) chpt. Am. Mktg. Assn., 1950, v.p. Detroit chpt., 1955, nat. v.p., dir., 1957, nat. pres., 1964-65, mem. global mktg. coun., 1986—. Pres. YMCA, Akron, 1978; chmn. trustees First Congl. Ch., Akron, 1985, chmn. endowment trust, 1987—. Served with AUS, 1945-46. Mem. Am. Statis. Assn., Am. Assn. Pub. Opinion Research, Nat. Assn. Bus. Economists, Am. Mktg. Assn., Internat. Mktg. Fedn. (pres.), European Soc. for Opinion and Market Research, Beta Gamma Sigma, Portage Country (Akron). Avocation: golf. Home and Office: Apt 333 100 Brookmont Rd Akron OH 44333-3094

**SONNEDECKER, GLENN ALLEN,** pharmaceutical historian, educator; b. Creston, Ohio, Dec. 11, 1917; s. Ira Elmer and Leta (Linter) S.; m. Cleo Bell, Apr. 3, 1943; 1 child, Stuart Bruce. BS, Ohio State U., 1942; MS, U Wis., 1950, PhD, 1952; Dr. Sci. honoris causa, Ohio State U., 1964, Phila. Coll. Pharmacy and Sci., 1989; PharmD honoris causa, Mass. Coll. Pharmacy, 1974. Lic. pharmacist. Mem. editorial staff Sci. Service, Washington, 1942-43; asst. prof. U. Wis., 1952-56, assoc. prof., 1956-60, prof., 1960-81, Edward Kremers prof., 1981-86; sec. Am. Inst. History of Pharmacy, 1949-57, dir., 1957-73, 81-85, hon. dir. life, chmn. bd., 1988-89; editor-in-chief RPh, 1978-80. Sec., bd. dirs. Friends of Hist. Pharmacy, 1945-49; chmn. Joint Com. on Pharmacy Coll. Librs., 1960-61; U.S. del. Internat. Pharm. Fedn., 1953, 55, 62; U.S. rep. to Mid. East Pharm. Congress, Beirut, 1956; sec. sect. history of pharmacy and biochemistry Pan-Am. Congress Pharmacy and Biochemistry, 1957. Co-author books; contbr. to pharm. and hist. publs. Recipient Edward Kremers award (for writings), 1964, Nat. award Rho Chi, 1967, Schelenz plaquette Internat. Soc. for History of Pharmacy, 1971, Remington honor medal Am. Pharm. Assn., 1972, Urdang medal, 1976, Folch Andreu prize, Spain, 1985, Profile award Am. Found. Pharm. Edn., 1994; Am. Found. fellow, 1948-52, Guggenheim fellow, 1955, Fulbright Rsch. scholar, Germany, 1955-56. Mem. Am. Pharm. Assn. (life; sec. sect. history of pharmacy 1949-50, vice chmn. 1950-51, chmn. 1951-52, rsch. assoc. 1964-65, chmn. joint task force with Acad. Pharm Scis. 1985, hon. chmn. bd. trustees 1985), Internat. Acad. History Pharmacy (1st v.p. 1970-81, pres. 1983-91, hon. pres. 1991—), Am. Assn. History of Medicine (exec. coun. 1966-69), Internat. Gesellschaft fur Geschichte der Pharmazie (exec. bd. 1965-89), hon. mem. socs. for history of pharmacy of Italy, Benelux, pan-Arab, Spain; mem. Sigma Xi, Rho Chi (mem. nat. exec. coun. 1957-59), Phi Delta Chi. Unitarian Universalist. Home: 2030 Chadbourne Ave Madison WI 53726-4047

**SONNEK, KARLA JEAN,** secondary school educator; b. Wells, Minn., Mar. 28, 1961; d. Albert Peter and Mary Jane Sonnek; life ptnr. Randall Fletcher. B, Mankato State U., 1984; MEd (hon.), S.W. Tex. State U., 2003; postgrad., U. Tex. Cert. tchr. Tex. ESL tchr. Manor (Tex.) Mid. Sch., 1999—. Head English dept. Manor Mid. Sch., 1999—2004, team leader, 2000—02. Contbr. articles to popular mags. Mem.: Kappa Delta Pi (life). Democrat. Avocations: motorcycling, sewing, writing, reading. E-mail: sonneckboom@earthlink.net.

**SONNEMAN, EVE,** artist; b. Chgo., 1946; d. Eric O. and Edith S. BFA, U. Ill., 1967; MFA, U. N.Mex., 1969. One-woman shows include Castelli Gallery, N.Y.C., 1976, 78, 80, 82, 84-86, Tex. Gallery, Houston, 1976, 78, 80, 82, 85, Galerie Farideh Cadot, Paris, 1978, 80, 83, François Lambert Gallery, Milan, Italy, 1980, 87, Mpls. Inst. Arts, 1980, La Noveau Musée, Lyon, France, 1980, Musée de Toulon, France, 1983, Centre Georges Pompidou, Paris, 1984, Circus Gallery, L.A., 1989, 97, Jones Troyer Fitzpatrick, Washington, 1989, Zabriskie Gallery, N.Y., 1990, Gloria Luria Gallery, Miami, 1990, Grand Central Terminal, N.Y.C., 1991, Charles Cowles Gallery, 1992, Sidney Janis Gallery, N.Y.C., 1996, La Geode Mus., Paris, 1996, Cirrus Gallery, 1997, Bruce Silverstein Gallery, N.Y., 2002, Jadite Gallery, N.Y., 2002, 03, 04, 05, 06, Galeria Turchi, Siena, Italy, 2002, I Space, Chgo., 2005, Mingle Salon, Tokyo, 2005; author: America's Cottage Gardens, 1990, Where Birds Live, 1992; co-author: How To Touch What, 2000; photographs subject of book Real Time, 1976. Grantee Nat. Endowment Arts, 1971, 78, Polaroid Corp., 1978; Cartier fellowship, France, 1989. Address: 446 W 47th St Apt 5C New York NY 10036-2381 Office Phone: 212-582-9375. Personal E-mail: evesonneman@earthlink.net.

**SONNEMANN, HARRY,** electrical engineer, consultant; b. Munich, Sept. 3, 1924; came to U.S., 1938, naturalized, 1944; s. Leopold and Emmy (Markus) S.; m. Shirley E. Battles, Nov. 25, 1949; children Carol Jo an, Joyce Blanc, Patricia Ann. BS, Poly. Inst. Bklyn., 1954. Research electroence-phalography, 1944-47; asst. to dir. electronics dept. AEC contract, Columbia U., 1947-50; supr. electronics shop Columbia Hudson Labs., 1951-53, head electronics dept., 1954-59; asst. dir. Project Artemis, 1959-64, Project Artemis (Hudson labs.), 1961-64; asst. dir. field engring. Advanced Research Projects Agy., Nuclear Test Detection Office, 1964-67; acting dep. dir. Nuclear Test Detection Office, 1967-68; spl. asst. in electronics to asst. sec. navy for research and devel. Navy Dept., 1968-76, spl. asst. to asst. sec. navy for research and devel., 1976-77; asst. to chief engr. NASA, 1977-78, dep. chief engr., 1978-84, asst. chief engr., 1984-86, cons., 1986—2000; pres. SBC Assocs., McLean, Va., 1988-95. Chmn. Dept. Def. Tactical Satellite Exec. Steering Group, 1968-69, chmn. Dept. Def. nav. satellite exec. steering group, 1969-70, 72-73 Treas. Art League. No. Va., 1967-68; pres. Rotonda Condominium Unit Owners Assn., 1982-84, 97-98, 99-2000. Mem.: Washington Figure Skating (dir. 1968-73, treas. 1969-72), Ice Club of Washington (pres. 1974-76). Home and Office: 7452 Spring Village Dr # 434 Springfield VA 22150-4951 E-mail: hssbc@aol.com.

**SONNENBERG, HARDY,** data processing executive, researcher, electrical engineer; b. Schoensee, Fed. Republic Germany, Apr. 12, 1939; s. Gustav and Wanda (Neumann) S.; m. Doris Linda Adam, June 20, 1964; children: Kevin, Denise. BS, U. Alta., 1962; MS, Stanford U., 1964, PhD, 1967. Registered profl. engr., Ont. Advanced devel. engr. GTE Sylvania, Mountain View, Calif., 1966-68, engring. specialist, 1968-70; sr. engr., 1970-73; dir. rsch. Optical Diodes Inc., Palo Alto, Calif., 1973-74; mem. rsch. staff Xerox Rsch. Centre Can., Mississauga, Ont., 1975-78, area mgr., 1978-80, lab. mgr., 1980-86, mgr. rsch. ops., 1986-87, mgr. tech. and engring. systems, 1987-94, v.p. rsch. and tech., 1994-96; pres. Calixo Cons., Freelton, Ont., 1997—. Chmn. indsl. adv. coun. McMaster U., Hamilton, Ont., 1990-93, active, 1987-94. Contbr. articles to profl. jours.; patentee in field. Chmn. bd. dirs. local ch., Hamilton, Ont., 1983-85, 89-93, 98-2002; pres. Sheridan Park Assn., Mississauga, 1988-89; chmn. Conf. Bd. Can. Rsch. Mgrs. Forum, 1991-93. Recipient cert. of recognition for invention NASA, 1973, 74, Achievement award Xerox Corp., 1981, Charles E. Ives Engring. award, 1983. Mem.: IEEE (sr.), Assn. Profl. Engrs. Ont., Am. Phys. Soc., Sigma Xi. Avocations: outdoor activities, singing, church participation. Home and Office: 900 Hwy 97 Freelton ON Canada L0R 1K0 E-mail: hsonnenb@ieee.org.

**SONNENBLICK, EDMUND HIRAM,** medical educator, cardiologist; b. New Haven, Oct. 7, 1932; s. Ira J. and Rosalind (Helfand) S.; m. Linda Bland, Dec. 21, 1954; children: Emily Sonnenblick Offit, Charlotte Sonnenblick Van Doren, Annie E. (dec.). BA, Wesleyan U., Middletown, Conn., 1954; MD, Harvard U., 1958. Diplomate Am. Bd. Internal Medicine. Resident in medicine Presbyn. Hosp., N.Y.C., 1958-60, 62-63; sr. investigator Nat. Heart Inst., Bethesda, Md., 1960-62, 63-68; asst. prof. medicine Harvard Med. Sch., Boston, 1968-70, assoc. prof., 1970-75; co-dir. cardiology Peter Bent Brigham Hosp., Boston, 1968-75; dir. cardiovasc. rsch., 1970-75; Olson prof. medicine, chief carddiology Albert Einstein Coll. Medicine, Bronx, NY, 1975—96, Edmond J. Safra prof. medicine, 1996—, chief emeritus cardiology, 1996—. Vis prof. medicine NY Med. Coll.; assoc. dir. Cardiovasc. Rsch. Inst., Valhalla, NY; editor Progress in Cardiovasc. Diseasess; contbr. over 600 articles to med. jours. Author 15 books and chpts. in books. Trustee Wesleyan U., 1994-97. Sr. surgeon USPHS, 1960-62. Fellow ACP, Am. Coll. Cardiology (Disting. Scientist award 1989), Internat. Soc. for Heart Rsch.; mem. Am. Heart Failure Soc. Am., Am. Hypertension Soc. (co-founder), Am. Coll. Physicians, Am. Assn. Physicians, Century Assn., Am. Soc. Clin. Investigation, Am. Physiol. Soc., Interurban Club, NY Yacht Club, Noroton Yacht Club, Woods Hole Yacht Club. Avocation: sailing. Home: 138 Goodwives River Rd Darien CT 06820-5807 Office: Albert Einstein Coll Medicine Weiler Hosp 1825 Eastchester Rd Bronx NY 10461-2301 Office Phone: 718-904-2932. E-mail: esonnenbli@aol.com.

**SONNENFELD, BARRY,** director, cinematographer; b. NYC, Apr. 1, 1953; m. Susan Ringo, 1989; 1 child. Grad., NY U., 1978. Cinematographer (films) In Our Water, 1982, Blood Simple, 1984, Compromising Positions, 1985, Three O'Clock High, 1987, Raising Arizona, 1987, Throw Momma from the Train, 1987, Big, 1988, When Harry Met Sally..., 1989, Miller's Crossing, 1990, Misery, 1990, (TV movies) How to Be a Perfect Person In Just Three Days, 1983, Out of Step, 1984 (Emmy award best cinematography 1984), Double Take, 1985, Welcome Home, Bobby, 1986, Classified Love, 1986; dir. (films) The Addams Family (uncredited cameo appearance), 1991, Addams Family Values (also actor), 1993, Get Shorty, 1995 (also exec. prodr., actor), Men In Black, 1997, Maximum Bob (TV series, also exec. prodr.), 1998, Wild Wild West, 1999 (also prodr.), Chippendales, 2000, Men In Black II, 2002 (also actor), R.V., 2006; dir., co-prodr.: For Love or Money, 1993; exec. prodr.: (films) Out of Sight, 1998, Lemony Snicket's A Series of Unfortunate Events, 2004, (TV Series) Fantasy Island, 1998, (TV) Partners, 1999; prodr. (TV Series) Secret Agent Man, 2000 (also creator), The Tick, 2001 (also dir.), Karen Sisco, 2003, (film) The Crew, 2000, Big Trouble, 2002 (also dir.), Ladykillers, 2004. Office: Creative Artists Agy c/o Fred Specktor 9830 Wilshire Blvd Beverly Hills CA 90212 also: United Talent Agency 9560 Wilshire Blvd Fl 5 Beverly Hills CA 90212-2401*

**SONNENFELDT, HELMUT,** former government official, educator, consultant, writer; b. Berlin, Sept. 13, 1926; came to U.S., 1944, naturalized, 1945; s. Walter H. and Gertrud (Liebenthal) S.; m. Marjorie Hecht, Oct. 4, 1953; children—Babette Sonnenfeldt Lubben, Walter H., Stewart H. AB, Johns Hopkins, 1950, MA, 1951. With Dept. State, Washington, 1952-77; formerly dir. Office Rsch. and Analysis for USSR and Eastern Europe, 1965-69; lectr. Sch. Advanced Internat. Studies, Johns Hopkins U., 1958-69, vis. scholar, 1977-78; guest scholar Brookings Instn., Washington, 1978—. Sr. mem. Nat. Security Coun., 1969-74; counselor Dept. State, 1974-77. Former gov. UN Assn. of U.S.; dir. Atlantic Coun. of U.S., World Affairs Coun. Washington; trustee Johns Hopkins U. With AUS, 1945-46. Mem. Coun. on Fgn. Rels. N.Y., Pi Delta Epsilon. Home: 5600 Wisconsin Ave Apt 1505 Chevy Chase MD 20815-4412 Office: Brookings Instn 1775 Massachusetts Ave NW Washington DC 20036-2103 Office Phone: 202-797-6028. Business E-Mail: hsonnenfeldt@brookings.edu.

**SONNENSCHEIN, DAVID,** music educator, composer, conductor; b. Hamburg, Germany, Nov. 2, 1928; s. Abraham and Elsa Sonnenschein; m. Tamar Gronemann, June 23, 1957; children: Iris, Nurit, Orna. Mus D, Boston U., 1976; MusM, New Eng. Conservatory, Boston, 1968. Dir. Tiberias Conservatory, Tiberias, Israel, 1962—66; music tchr. Reali Sch., Haifa, Israel, 1962—66; instr. Emmanuel Coll., Boston; assoc. prof. music Northeastern U., Boston, chair dept. music, 1993—99. Condr. Chamber Orch., Hamburg, Germany, 1959—62, Hamburg, 1959—61; guest condr. Hamburg Symphony Orch., Hamburg, Germany, 1959—61; condr. Haifa Chamber Choir, Haifa, Israel, 1962—63; assoc. condr. Haifa Symphony Orch., Haifa, Israel; condr. Melrose Symphony Orch., Melrose, Mass., Polymnia Choral Soc., Melrose, Mass., 1971—81; guest condr. Boston Pops Orch., Boston, 1974—79; condr. Northeastern U. Symphony Orch., Boston, 1972—88, Concert Arts Orch., Boston, 1973—84. Author: (music courseware) The Anatomy of Music. Recipient Innovative Excellence in Learning, Tchg. and Tech., Ninth Internat. Conf. on Coll. Tchg., Learning and Tech., 1998; fellow, Brandeis U., 1968—70, Lady Davis, Haifa Technion, 1980—81; scholar, New Eng. Conservatory, 1966—68. Achievements include first to Developer of Music Courseware and Learning Modules for Distance Learning. Avocations: sailing, hiking, cross country skiing. Home: 169 Bonad Rd Chestnut Hill MA 02467 Office: Northeastern University Huntington Ave 373 Ryder Hall Boston MA Office Phone: 617-373-2441. Personal E-mail: dsonnens@rcn.com.

**SONNENSCHEIN, HUGO FREUND,** academic administrator, writer, economist, educator; b. NYC, Nov. 14, 1940; s. Leo William and Lillian Silver Sonnenschein; m. Elizabeth Gunn, Aug. 26, 1962; children: Leah, Amy, Rachel. AB, U. Rochester, 1961; MS, Purdue U., 1963, PhD, 1964, PhD (hon.), 1996; PhD (hon.), Tel Aviv U., 1993; D (hon.), U. Autonoma Barcelona, Spain, 1994; PhD (hon.), Lake Forest Coll., 1995, North Ctrl. Coll., 2001. U. Chgo., 2002. Faculty dept. econs. U. Minn., 1964—70, prof., 1968—70; prof. econs. U. Mass., Amherst, 1970—73, Northwestern U. 1973—76, Princeton (N.J.) U., 1976—87, Class of 1926 prof., 1987—88, provost, 1991—93; dean, Thomas S. Gates prof. U. Pa. Sch. Arts & Scis., Phila., 1988—91; pres. U. Chgo., 1993—2000, Hutchinson disting. prof., pres. emeritus, 2000—. Vis. prof. U. Andes, Columbia, 1965, Tel Aviv U., 1972, Hebrew U., 1973, U. Paris, 1978, U. Aix-en-Provence, France, 1978, Stanford U., 1984—85; bd. dirs. Van Kampen Mutual Funds. Editor: Econometrica, 1977—84; mem. editl. bd.: Jour. Econ. Theory, 1972—75, Jour. Math. Econs., 1974—; SIAM Jour., 1976—80; contbr. articles to profl. jours. Trustee U. Rochester, 1992—, U. Chgo., 1993—. Fellow, Social Sci. Rsch. Coun., 1967—68, NSF, 1970—, Ford Found., 1970—71, Guggenheim Found., 1976—77. Fellow: Econometric Soc. (pres. 1988—89), Am. Acad. Arts and Scis.; mem.: NAS, Am. Philos. Soc. Business E-Mail: h-sonnenschein@uchicago.edu.

**SONNENSCHEIN, RALPH ROBERT,** physiologist; b. Chgo., Aug. 14, 1923; s. Robert and Flora (Kieferstein) S.; m. Patricia W. Niddrie, June 21, 1952; children—David, Lisa, Ann. Student, Swarthmore Coll., 1940—42, U. Chgo., 1942—43; BS, Northwestern U., 1943, BM, MS, Northwestern U., 1946, MD, 1947; PhD, U. Ill., 1950. Research asst. in physiology Northwestern U. Med. Sch., 1944-46; intern Michael Reese Hosp., Chgo., 1946-47; successively research fellow clin. sci., research asst. psychiatry, research asso. psychiatry U. Ill. Med. Sch., Chgo., 1947-51; mem. faculty U. Calif. Med. Sch., Los Angeles, 1951-88, prof. physiology, 1962-88, prof. emeritus, 1988—; liaison scientist Office Naval Research, London, 1971-72. Author papers on pain, innervation of skin, peripheral circulation. Served with AUS, 1943-46. Spl. research fellow USPHS, 1957-58; fellow Swedish Med. Research Council, 1964-65; grantee USAF; grantee Office Naval Research; grantee NIH; grantee NSF. Mem. Am. Physiol. Soc., Microcirculatory Soc., Soc. Exptl. Biology and Medicine, AAAS, Hungarian Physiol. Soc. (hon.). Home: 18212 Kingsort Dr Malibu CA 90265-5636 Office: U Calif Sch Medicine Dept Physiology Los Angeles CA 90095-1751

**SONNIER, JOSEPH A.,** lab administrator, physician; MD, La. State U. Sch. Medicine, 1979. Cert. in Anatomic and Clin. Pathology 1983. Mng. dir. Unipath Ltd.; regional mng. dir., southwest region AmeriPath, pres., 2003—. Office: AmeriPath Inc 7111 Fairway Dr Ste 400 Palm Beach Gardens FL 33410 Office Phone: 561-712-6200.

**SONNIER, PATRICIA BENNETT,** business management educator; b. Park River, ND, Mar. 25, 1935; d. Benjamin Beekman Bennett and Alice Catherine (Peerboom) Bennett Brenckinridge; m. William McGregor Castellini (dec.); m. Cecil Sherwood Sonnier (dec.); m. Joseph N. Pagano; children: Bruce Bennett Wells (Nabil Subhani), Barbara Lea Ragland. AA, Allan Handcock Coll., Santa Maria, Calif., 1964; BS magna cum laude, U. Great Falls, 1966; MS, U. N.D., 1967, PhD, 1971. Fiscal acct. USIA, Washington, 1954-56; pub. acct. Bremerton, Wash., 1956; statistician USN, Bremerton, Wash., 1957-59; med. svcs. accounts officer USAF, Vandenberg AFB, Calif., 1962-64; instr. bus. adminstrn. Western New Eng. U., 1967—69; vis. prof. econs. Chapman Coll., 1970; vis. prof. U. So. Calif. Sys., Griffith AFB, NY, 1971-72; assoc. prof., dir. adminstrv. mgmt. program Va. State U., 1973-74; assoc. prof. bus. adminstrn. Oreg. State U., Corvallis, 1974-81, prof. mgmt., 1982-90, emeritus prof. mgmt., 1990—, univ. curriculum coord., 1984-86, dir. adminstrv. mgmt. program, 1974-81, pres. Faculty Senate, 1981. Mem. Interinstl. Faculty Senate, 1986-90, pres., 1989-90; exec. dir. Bus. Enterprise Ctr., 1990-92, Enterprise Ctr. LA, Inc., 1992-95; commr. Lafayette Econ. Devel. Authority, 1994-2000, treas., 1995-96, vice chmn., 1996-97, chmn., 1997-98, past chmn., 1998-99, sec., chmn. bldg. com., 1999-2000; cons. process tech. devel. Digital Equipment Corp., 1981. Pres., chmn. bd. dirs. Adminstrv. Orgnl. Svcs., Inc., Corvallis, 1976—83, Dynamic Achivement, Inc., 1983—92; cons. Oregonians in Action, 1990—91, sec., 1999, 2000; cert. adminstrv. mng. pres. TYEE Mobile Home Park, Inc., 1987—92; mem. Leadership LA, 1986; del various convs.; mem. parish coun. St. Patrick's Cath. Ch., 1998—2000, Risen Savior Ch., 2005—06. Fellow: Assn. Bus. Comm. (internat. bd. 1980—86, v.p. Northwest 1981, 2d v.p. 1982—83, 1st v.p. 1983—84, pres. 1984—85); mem.: AAUP (chpt. sec. 1973, chpt. bd. dirs. 1982, pres. Oreg. conf. 1983—85, chpt. bd. dirs. 1984—89, pres. chpt. 1985—86), Corvallis Area C. of C. (v.p. chamber devel. 1987—88, pres. 1988—89, chair bd. 1989—90, Pres.'s award 1986), La. Bus. Incubation Assn. (sec.-treas. 1993—95), Nat. Assn. Tchr. Edn. for Bus. Office Edn. (pres. 1976—77, chair pub. rels. com. 1978—81), Better Bus. Bur. (sec. 1994, treas. 1995, vice-chair 1996, chair 1997, past chair 1998, sec. 1999, chair nominating com. 1999, chair pub. rels., Lafayette Blue Ribbon 1999—2000), Nat. Bus. Edn. Assn., Associated Oreg. Faculties, Am. Vocat. Assn. (nominating com. 1976), Adminstrv. Mgmt. Soc., Assn. Info. Sys. Profls. (chpt. v.p. 1977, chpt. pres. 1978—81), Am. Bus. Women's Assn. (chpt. v.p. 1979, pres. 1980, Top Businesswoman in Nation 1980, Bus. Assoc. of Yr. 1986), Albuquerque Federated Rep. Women (hospitality chair 2003—04, 1st v.p. 2004—), Acadiana Rep. Women (gen. chmn. La. Fedn. Rep. Women's Clubs State Conv. 1997, 1st v.p. 1997—98, pres. 1998—2000, asst. state CAP chmn. 1999—2000, Ahrens for Gov. Com. 2002), Rotary (co-chmn. fundraiser com. 2002), Boys and Girls Club of Corvallis (pres. 1991—92), Lafayette Rotary (cmty. svc. dir. 1993—94, bd. dirs. 1993—2000, treas. 1995—96, sec. 1996—97, v.p. 1997—98, pres. 1998—99, Dist. 6200 Found. award 2000), Rotary of Albuquerque del Norte (silent auction chair 2001—02, dep. dir. internat. svc. com. 2002, dist. 5520 dep. dir. permanent fund, asst. gov. 2003—04, chair 2003—, chmn. shrimp fiesta 2005, dist. 5520 found. chair 2003—06, dist. 5520 internat. chmn. 2004—06, Svc. Above Self award 2003, Dist. 5520 Found. award 2003, 2004, 2005, Svc. Above Self award 2004—05, 2005—06), Sigma Kappa. Office Phone: 505-298-1248. Personal E-mail: patriciasonnier@aol.com.

**SONNTAG, BERNARD H.,** agronomist, researcher, public information officer; b. Goodsoil, Sask., Can., June 27, 1940; s. Henry R. and Annie (Heesing) S.; m. Mary L. Ortman, Aug. 10, 1963; children: Calvin, Galen, Courtney Anne. BSA, Sask. U., Saskatoon, 1962, MSc, 1965; PhD, Purdue U., 1971. Economist Agriculture Can., Saskatoon, 1962-66; cons. D.W. Carr & Assoc., Ottawa, Ont., Canada, 1966-68; economist Agriculture Can., Lethbridge, Alta., 1968-79, Saskatoon, 1979-80, dir. rsch. sta. Brandon, Man., 1980-86, Swiftcurrent, Sask., 1986-89, Lethbridge, 1989-95; dir. gen. Prairie Farm Rehab. Adminstrn., Regina, Sask., Canada, 1996-01; pres. Sonntag Agrl. Svcs., Saskatoon, Sask., Canada, 2001—. Pres. Man. Inst. Agrologists, Brandon, 1984. Recipient Leadership award Bell Can., 1993; named Disting. Agrologist, Alta. Inst. Agrologists, 1995. Fellow Agrl. Inst. Can.; mem. Rotary. Roman Catholic. Home: Sonntag Agrl Svcs 318 Collinsster Rd Saskatoon SK Canada S7N 4K7

**SONO, MASAYUKI,** architect, artist; b. Kobe, Japan, 1971; MArch, U. Wash., Seattle, 1996, Kobe U., Japan, 1998. Arch. Voorsanger & Assocs., NYC, 1998—2003; prin. arch. Masayuki Sono Archs., NYC, 2003—. Over 60 exhibitions, prin. works include Postcards: The Staten Island Sept. 11th Meml., NY (Merit award, Small Project, NY Constrn. News, 2004), Asia Soc. and Mus. renovation and addition, NYC, U. Va. Art Mus., Charlottesville, LaGuardia Internat. Airport Control Tower, Queens, NY, Aspen Residence, Colo., World Trade Ctr. Site Perimeter Enclosure, NYC, Ashiya Art Gallery, Hyogo, Japan, Shofu-den renovation and addition, Sullivan County, NY. Co-recipient Achievement in the Arts award, Coun. on the Arts & Humanities for Staten Island, 2004. Office: Masayuki Sono Architects 308 Mott St Ste 3F New York NY 10012 E-mail: msono@masasono.com.*

**SONSINI, LARRY W.,** lawyer; b. Rome, NY, Feb. 5, 1941; AB, U. Calif., Berkeley, 1963; LLB, U. Calif., 1966; PhD (hon.), Pacific Grad. Sch.of Psychology. Bar: Calif. 1966. With Wilson, Sonsini, Goodrich & Rosati, Palo Alto, 1966—, ptnr., chmn. CEO; prof. securities regulation Boalt Hall Sch. law U. Calif., Berkeley, 1985—. Bd. dirs. N.Y. Stock Exchange (NYSE), 2001—03, Silicon Valley Bancshares, 2001—, Brocade Communications Systems, Inc., Echelon Corp., LSI Logic Corp., Lattice Semiconductor Corp., Pixar, Inc.; chmn. Regulation, Enforcement and Listing Standards Com., Legal Adv. Com., 2003—. Trustee Santa Clara U. Named one of Top Ten Lawyers in Bay Area, San Francisco Chronicle, 2003; recipient Spl. Achievement Award in Commerce and Law, Nat. Italian Am. Found. (NIAF), 2003, Cmty. Svc. award exemplary leadership, Nat. Conf. Cmty. & Justice, 1993, Visionary award, Software Devel. Forum, 2000. Mem.: ABA (com. on fed. regulation securities, subcom. on registration statements), Am. Acad. Arts and Scis., Am. Law Inst. Office: Wilson Sonsini Goodrich & Rosati 650 Page Mill Rd Palo Alto CA 94304-1050 Office Phone: 650-493-9300. Office Fax: 650-493-6811. E-mail: lsonsini@wsgr.com.*

**SONSTEBY, CHARLES M.,** food service executive; Dir. tax, treasury and risk mgmt. depts. Brinker Internat. Inc., Dallas, 1990—94, v.p., treas., 1994—97, sr. v.p. fin., 1997—2001, exec. v.p., CFO, 2001—. Office: 6820 LBJ Fwy Dallas TX 75240

**SONTAG, ED,** former federal agency administrator; BA in Spl. Edn., SUNY, MA in Elementary Sch. Adminstrn. and Supervision; PhD in Spl. Edn. Adminstrn., Syracuse U. Resident scholar for Wis. Gov. Tommy G. Thompson; deputy asst. sec. US Dept. Interior, 1989—92; prof. U. Wis. - Stevens Point Sch. Edn., 1992—99; senior-level positions Ill. State Bd. Edn., US Dept. Edn., Ind. U., Wis. and NY pub. sch. sys.; dep. chief of staff for mgmt. and ops. US HHS, 2001, asst. sec. adminstrn. and mgmt., 2002. Recipient U. Wis.-Steven Point Vice Chancellor Merit award, Dept. Interior Disting. Safety award. Office: US Dept Health and Human Svcs 200 Independence Ave SW Rm 309 Washington DC 20201

**SONTAG, FREDERICK EARL,** philosophy educator; b. Long Beach, Calif., Oct. 2, 1924; s. M. Burnett and Cornelia (Nicholson) S.; m. Carol Furth, June 10, 1950; children: Grant Furth, Anne Burnett Karch. BA with great distinction, Stanford U., 1949; MA, Yale U., 1951, PhD, 1952; LLD (hon.), Coll. Idaho, 1971. Instr. Yale U., 1951-52; asst. prof. philosophy Pomona Coll., Claremont, Calif., 1952-55, assoc. prof., 1955-60, prof., 1970—, Robert C. Denison prof. philosophy, 1972—, chmn. dept. philosophy, 1960-67, 76-77, 1980-84; chmn. coord. com. in philosophy Claremont Grad. Sch. and Univ. Ctr., 1962-65. Vis. prof. Union Theol. Sem., NYC, 1959-60, Collegio de Sant' Anselmo, Rome, 1966-67, U. Copenhagen, 1972; theologian-in-residence Am. Ch. in Paris, 1973; fulbright regional vis. prof., India, East Asia, Pacific areas, 1977-78; nat. adv. coun. Kent Fellowship Program of Danforth Found., 1963-66. Author numerous books, the most recent being: Love Beyond Pain: Mysticism Within christianity, 1977, Sun Myung Moon and the Unification Church, 1977, also German, Japanese and Korean transl.; (with John K. Roth) God and America's Future, 1977, What Can God Do?, 1979, A Kierkegaard Handbook, 1979, The Elements of Philosophy, 1984, (with John K. Roth) The Questions of Philosophy, 1988, Emotion, 1989, The Return of the Gods, 1989, Willgenstein and the Mystical, 1995, Uncertain Truth, 1995, The Descent of Women, 1997, The Acts of the Trinity, 1997, Truth and Imagination, 1998, 2001: A Spiritual Odyssey, 2001, The Mysterious Presence, 2002. Pres. bd. dirs. Claremont Family Svc., 1960-64; trustee The Coro Found., L.A. and San Francisco, 1967-71; bd. dirs., chmn. ways and means com. Pilgrim Place, Claremont, 1970-77. With AUS, 1943-46. Vis. scholar Ctr. for Study Japanese Religions, Kyoto, Japan, spring 1974; vis. fellow East-West Ctr., Honolulu, summer 1974; Wig Disting. prof. award, 1970, 76. Mem. Am. Philos. Assn., Metaphys. Soc. Am. Soc. on Religion in Higher Edn. (Kent fellow 1950-52), Am. Acad. Religion, Phi Beta Kappa. Congregationalist. Office: Pomona Coll 551 N College Ave Claremont CA 91711-4410

**SONTAG, JAMES MITCHELL,** oncologist, researcher; b. Denver, Dec. 8, 1939; s. Samuel Henry and Rose Hazel (Silverman) S.; m. Elizabeth Crockett Tunis; children: Ariella, Eythan. BS, Lamar State Coll. Tech., Beaumont, Tex.; MS, U. Ill., 1967; PhD, Weizmann Inst. Sci., Rehovot, Israel, 1971; MPH, Harvard U., 1982. Postdoctoral fellow Damon Runyon Meml. Fund Cancer Rsch., 1971-72; guest worker Nat. Cancer Inst., NIH, Bethesda, Md., 1972-73, staff fellow, 1973-74, exptl. oncologist, 1973-76, mgr. carcinogen bioassay program, 1973-76, asst. to divsn. dir. cancer cause and prevention, 1976-80; exec. sec. Clearinghouse on Environ. Carcinogens, 1976-80, asst. dir. for interagy. affairs Office of Dir., 1980-82, spl. asst. epidemiology and biostatistics program, 1982-96; chief office divsn. ops. & analysis divsn. cancer epidemiology and genetics Nat. Cancer Inst., 1996-99; vol. with grassroots articans, med. mission L.Am., 1999—. Author, editor in field. ESL tchr. 2004-; Served with AUS, 1956-59. Beaumont LWV scholar, 1963-65 Mem. Beta Beta Beta. Personal E-mail: jim18y@msn.com.

**SOOD, MANU RAJ,** pediatrician, consultant; b. Shimla, Himachal, India, May 23, 1962; arrived in Eng., 1990; s. Satinder Kumar and Ram Dulari Sood; m. Anjla Sharma, Nov. 7, 1993; children: Nikita, Riya. MB BS, Indra Gandhi Med. Coll., Shimla, 1989; MD, Manchester U., Eng., 2001. Sr. house officer Birmingham (Eng.) Children's Hosp., 1992—93, registrar, 1996—2000; clin. fellow Children's Hosp. Orange County, 2000—01; cons. Royal Manchester Children's Hosp., 2002; assoc. prof. Med. Coll. Wis., Milw., 2004. Contbr. articles to profl. jours. Mem.: European Soc. Pediat. Gastroenterology Hepatology and Nutrition, N.Am. Soc. Pediat., Gastroenterology and Nutrition (brain rsch. group), Am. Motility Soc., Brit. Soc. Pediat. Gastroenterology and Nutrition, Royal Coll. Pediat. and Child Health. Avocations: cricket, chess, tennis. Home: 2355 Macaulay Dr Brookfield WI 53045

**SOOD, NEERAJ,** economist, researcher; s. Sood; m. Ashlesha Datar, Dec. 28, 2000. MA in Econs., Ind. U., Indpls., 1999; PhD, RAND Grad. Sch., Santa Monica, Calif., 2003. Economist RAND, Santa Monica, 2003—; assoc. prof. Pardee RAND Grad. Sch., Santa Monica, Calif., 2003—. Faculty rsch. fellow Nat. Bur. of Econ. Rsch., Cambridge, Mass.; mng. editor forum for health policy and econs. BEPRESS, Berkeley, Calif., 2006—. Contbr. articles to profl. jours. and chpts. to books in field of econs., med. and health policy. Recipient Gen. Distinction award, RAND Grad. Sch.; fellow, Delhi U.; grantee, NIH, 2003—06, Calif. Healthcare Found. Mem.: Am. Econs. Assn. Achievements include patents pending for Internet-based tool that computes optimal contributions to health care reimbursement accounts. Office: RAND Corp 1776 Main St Los Angeles CA 90066 Office Phone: 310-393-0411 6809.

**SOO HOO, TSUNG (BILL) YAO,** security studies educator, consultant; s. Yin and Chui Woo Soo Hoo; m. Rachel Ann Cammorato, Nov. 3, 1984; 1 child, Carolyn Yu-yi. PhD, Seton Hall U., 2005. Cert. firearms instr. N.J., 1986. Spl. agt. FBI, West Paterson, NJ, 1970—2001; prof., profl. security studies program coord. N.J. City U., Jersey City, 2002—, chair profl. security studies dept. Exec. com. Am. Soc. Indsl. Security, Ltd., Internat., NJ, 2002— Author: An Alternative Problem-based Collaborative Learning Model and Student Experiences. Mem.: Am. Soc. Indsl. Security (exec. bd. mem. 2005). Office: NJ City U 2039 Kennedy Blvd Rm P216 Jersey City NJ 07305-1597 Office Phone: 201-200-2000.

**SOON, BOON YI,** engineer; b. Singapore, Oct. 18, 1971; s. Ren Joo Soon and Yoke Lan Lee. MS in Electro-Optics, U. Dayton, 1997, MS in Applied Math., 2000, PhD in Electro-Optics, 2002. 06optical designer Thales Electro-Optics Pte Ltd, Singapore, 2003—; sr. transceiver designer Finisar Singapore Pte Ltd, Singapore, 2006—. Contbr. articles to profl. jours. Charles Buckley scholar, 1993-95, Dayton Area Grad. Studies Inst. scholar, 1998-2002. Mem. Tau Beta Pi, Eta Kappa Nu, Phi Kappa Phi, Pi Mu Epsilon, Golden Key. Avocations: running, surfing the net, movies. Office: Finisar Singapore PTE LTD 10 Ang Mo Kio St 65 05-01/02/03 Techpoint Singapore 569059 Singapore Personal E-mail: boonyi@yahoo.com.

**SOON, WILLIE WEI-HOCK,** environmental scientist; s. Gim-Chuan Soon and Chiew-See Chua; m. Julia Pham; 1 child, Benjamin Yue-Jian. PhD, U. So. Calif., Los Angeles, 1991. Post-doctoral scientist Harvard-Smithsonian Ctr. for Astrophysics, Cambridge, Mass., 1991—97; astronomer Mt. Wilson Obs., Mount Wilson, Calif., 1992—2004; vis. prof. U. of Putra, Serdang, Selangor, Malaysia, 1999—2000; astrophysicist Harvard-Smithsonian Ctr. for Astrophysics, Cambridge, Mass., 1997—; receiving editor New Astronomy, Netherlands, 2002—; chief scientist Ctr. for Sci. and Pub. Policy, Washington, 2003—. Sr. rsch. fellow and contbr. techcentralstation.com, Washington, 2001—; chief scientist Ctr. for Sci. and Pub. Policy, Washington, 2003—. Author: (book) The Maunder Minimum and the Variable Sun-Earth Connection. Sci. testimony U.S. Senate's Environment and Pub. Works Com., Washington, 2003. Recipient Nuc. and Plasma Sciences Soc. Grad. Scholastic award, IEEE, 1989, Rockwell Dennis Hunt Scholastic prize, U. So. Calif., 1991, award, Smithsonian Instn., 2003, Petr Beckmann award, Doctors for Disaster Preparedness, 2004. Office: Harvard-Smithsonian Ctr for Astrophys 60 Gardent St MS 16 Cambridge MA 02138 Office Phone: 617-495-7488. Office Fax: 617-495-7095. E-mail: wsoon@cfa.harvard.edu.

**SOON-SHIONG, PATRICK,** pharmaceutical executive; MSc, U. Brit. Columbia; MD, U. Witwatersrand. CEO, chmn. bd. VivoRx, Inc., 1994—98; pres., CFO, dir. Am. BioScience, Inc., 1994—; CEO, chmn. bd. Am. Pharm. Partners, Inc., Schaumburg, Ill., 1996—, pres., 2001—. Named one of Forbes' Richest Americans, 2006. Fellow: ACS, Royal Coll. Physicians and Surgeons Can. Achievements include patents in field. Office: Am Pharmaceutical Partners Ste 300 E 1501 E Woodfield Rd Schaumburg IL 60173-5837

**SOORIYAARACHCHI, GAMINI SARATHCHANDRA,** oncologist, hematologist, educator; b. Kosgama, Sri Lanka; m. Chandrika Senerath; children: Jasmine, Marcus. MBBS with honors, U. Ceylon, Colombo, Sri Lanka, 1970; diploma in child health, Conjoint Bd. Examiners, London, 1975; diploma in obstetrics, Royal Coll. Ob-Gyn Gt. Britain, 1975; MBA, U. Tenn., Knoxville, 2004. Diplomate Am. Bd. Internal Medicine, Am. Bd. Geriatric Medicine, Am. Bd. Med. Oncology, Am. Bd. Hematology, cert. physician exec. Cert. Comm. Med. Mgmt., 2005. Intern U. Ceylon Tchg. Hosps., 1970-71; sr. house officer Guildford Hosps., England, 1971-73; registrar St. Helens Hosp., England, 1973-75; sr. house officer Royal Marsden Hosp. and Inst. Cancer Rsch., Sutton, England, 1973-74; fellow in med. oncology and hematology U. Wis. Comprehensive Cancer Ctr., Madison, 1975-77; cons. med. oncologist and hematologist Rockford Clinic and Rockford Meml. Hosp., Ill., 1977-83, Oncology Hematology West and Alegent Bergan Mercy Cancer Ctr., Omaha, 1983—; med. dir. Alegent Bergan Mercy Cancer Ctr., Omaha, 1984—; co-dir. bone marrow transplantation program Oncology Hematology West and Alegent Bergan Mercy Med. Ctr., Omaha, 1993—. Asst. clin. prof. medicine U. Ill. Sch. Medicine, Rockford, 1977—83; bd. dirs. Cancer Biotherapy Rsch. Group, Franklin, Tenn.; mem. at-large exec. com. Alegent Bergan Mercy Med. Ctr., 2002—03, pres.-elect, vice chmn., 2003—04; pres., chief med. staff Alegent Bergan Mercy Med. Ctr., 2005—; bd. dirs. Missouri Valley Cancer Consortium, Omaha, pres., 1999—2001, prin. investigator, 2006—; assoc. clin. prof. medicine Creighton U. Sch. Medicine, Omaha, 1984—96, clin. prof., 1996—; chmn. prof. edn. Am. Cancer Soc., 1986, Nebr. divsn., 87, bd. dirs. Douglas and Sarpy Counties, Neb., 86, Nebr. divsn., 87; med. dir., founding mem. No. Ill. Hospice Assn., Rockford, 1980—83; mem. exec. com., novel therapeutics com., audit com., ethnic diversity com North Ctrl. Cancer Treatment Group, Mayo Clin., Rochester, Minn.; mem. governing coun. Am. Med. Assn. Sec. of Internat. Med. Graduates; alt. delegate AMA House Delegates; alt. rep. AMA Commn. to End Healthcare Disparities. Contbg. author: Cancer Genetics in Women, 1987; contbr. over 50 articles and astracts to med. jours., including Jour. Clin. Oncology, Blood, Archives Surgery, Jour. Immunotherapy, Cancer Investigation, Annals Pharmacotherapy, Jour. Am. Acad. Dermatology, Jour. Clin. Pathology. Recipient Leadership award (Internat. Med. Grad. Physician), AMA Found., 2006. Fellow ACP, Royal Coll. Physicians (London), Soc. for Biol. Therapy; mem. AMA (alt. del. to House of Dels. 2006-, alt. rep. Commn. to End Healthcare Disparities 2006-), Royal Coll. Surgeons (Eng.), Am. Soc. Clin. Oncology, Am. Soc. Hematology, Am. Soc. for Blood and Marrow Transplantation, Nebr. Med. Assn. Office: Alegent Health Bergan Mercy Cancer Ctr 7710 Mercy Rd Ste 122 Omaha NE 68124-2346

**SOOUDI, MATTHEW M.,** retired surgeon; b. Iran, Oct. 24, 1934; came to U.S., 1962; s. Yahya and Iran (Nicknejad) S.; m. Joyce J. Sooudi, Oct. 2, 1965; 2 children. MD, U. Iran, 1962. Diplomate. Am. Bd. Surgery, Am. Bd. Colon and Rectal Surgery, Internat. Bd. Proctology. Intern. Bon Secours Hosp., Grosse Pointe, Mich., 1962-63; resident Grace Hosp., Detroit, 1963-67, Ferguson Clinic, Grand Rapids, Mich., 1967-68; pvt. practice St. Elizabeth Hosp., Tex., Beaumont (Tex.) Med. Hosp., Bapt. Hosp., Tex.; ret., 1996. Fellow ACS, Am. Soc. Colon and Rectal Surgeons, Internat. Assn. Proctologists; mem. AMA, Am. Assn. Phys. Surgeons, So. Med. Assn., Tex. Med. Assn., Tex. Soc. Colon and Rectal Surgeons. Address: 980 Thomas Rd Beaumont TX 77706-4621

**SOOY, WILLIAM RAY,** information technology executive; b. Jan. 12, 1951; s. Edward Leinau and Alice Elizabeth (Franklin) S.; m. Jean Marie Sooy, Sept. 17, 1976; children: Jennifer, Karen, Diana, Julia. BSEE, U. Miami, 1973, MS, 1977. Registered profl. engr., Fla. Engr. Fla. Power and Light, Miami, 1973-80, prin. engr. nuc. instrumentation and control, power sys. controls, sys. protection designer, 1981-97; engr. Harris Corp., Melbourne, Fla., 1980—81; tech. rsch. svcs., designer internet svcs., mgr. sys. ops. Energy Mktg. and Trading, Fla. Power and Light, 1998-2000; sr. fin. analyst Energy Mktg. and Trading, 2000—02; sr. engr. Progress Energy, Lake Mary, Fla., 2002—03; sr. dir. info. tech. Garden of Life, West Palm Beach, Fla., 2004—; sr. engr. Sgt. and Lundy, Juno Beach, 2005—. Adj. prof. elec. engring., physics Palm Beach C.C., 2000—. Mem.: IEEE (sr.), MENSA. Home: 12735 Ellison Wilson Rd North Palm Beach FL 33408-2113 Personal E-mail: wrsooy@hotmail.com.

**SOPANEN, JERI RAINER,** photography director; b. Helsinki, Finland, Aug. 14, 1929; arrived in US, 1950; s. Rainer and Helvi Raakel (Salminen) S.; m. Carolyn Maier, 1952 (div. 1956); 1 child, Erik; m. Eileen A. Humeston, 1961 (div. 1980); ptnr. Christine Huneke, 1975 (separated 1991); children: Anya Maarit, Mark; m. Marja Roth, 2000. MusB, Lawrence Coll., 1952; BA, U. So. Calif., 1956. Ind. dir. photography Sopanen Films, Inc., N.Y.C., 1966—. Dir. photography: (films) My Dinner With Andre, 1982, The Gig, 1986, The Luckiest Man in the World, 1989; (documentaries) The Brain, 1986, The Ring of Truth, 1987, The Mind (Emmy award 1989); dir. photography Nova programs, 1991—, Gardens of the World with Audrey Hepburn, 1993. With U.S. Army, 1952-54. Mem. Dirs. Guild Am., Internat. Assn. Theatrical Stage Employees. Democrat. Avocation: cross country skiing. Home and Office: 100 W 89th St Apt 8D New York NY 10024-1936 Office Phone: 212-799-0679. E-mail: jrsopanen@aol.com.

**SOPER, JEANNINE,** real estate agent; b. N.Y.C., Nov. 24, 1929; d. Antonio Bruno and Marie Kapuscinski; widowed; children: Erik, Wayne. Grad., Scudder Secretarial Coll., 1948, Realtors Inst., 1970. Sec. Std. Brands Inc. N.Y.C., 1948—52, Armstrong Rubber Co., Norwalk, Conn., 1952—53; real estate sales assoc. V, Ducale Real Estate, Norwalk, 1960—63; owner Sopers Real Estate, Norwalk, 1963—66; owner, ptnr. Siegel and Soper, Realtors, Norwalk, 1966—86; realtor, sales mgr. Prudential Real Estate, Norwalk, 1986—91; realtor Wm Pitt Real Estate, Norwalk, 1991—. Pres. Women's Coun. Realtors, Conn., 1970, Norwalk Bd. Realtors, 1979. Exhibited in group shows at Rowayton Art Ctr., Darien Art Ctr., others. Chmn. Bd. Assessment Appeals, Norwalk, 1989—; pres., treas. Rowayton (Conn.) Art Ctr., 2000—. Mem.: Wilson Cove Yacht Club (life 1st Woman Commodore 1991). Office: Wm Pitt Sothebys Internat Real Estate 162 East Ave Norwalk CT 06851 Office Phone: 203-838-0018. Personal E-mail: jlsoper@optonline.net.

**SOPER, PHILIP,** law educator; Grad. summa cum laude, Washington U., St. Louis, 1964, MA; PhD in philosophy, Washington U.; JD magna cum laude, Harvard U., 1969. Law clk. to Justice Byron R. White US Supreme Ct.; atty. Gen. Counsel's Office, Coun. on Environ. Quality, Washington, DC; faculty mem. U. Mich. Law Sch., Ann Arbor, 1973—; James V. Campbell Prof. Law. Author: A Theory of Law and The Ethics of Deference; contbr. articles to law jours. Office: U Mich Law Sch 533 Legal Research 625 S State St Ann Arbor MI 48109-1215 Office Phone: 734-763-1067. Office Fax: 734-764-8309. E-mail: psoper@umich.edu.

**SOPHER, VICKI ELAINE,** appraiser; b. Streator, Ill., May 22, 1943; d. Donald Bird and Thelma Elsie (Saxton) Watson; m. Terry Ray Sr., Jan. 20, 1962 (div. July 1982); 1 child, Terry Ray Jr. AA, No. Va. Community Coll., 1973; BA, Am. U., 1976; MS, Bank State Coll. Edn., 1986; Cert., Getty Mus. Mgmt. Inst., 1998. Cert. in appraisal courses George Washington U., 2004. Adminstrv. asst. Decatur & Wilson House, Washington, 1977-81; asst. dir. Decatur House/Nat. Trust for Hist. Preservation, Washington 1981-84, dir. 1984-95; exec. dir. Hammond-Harwood House Assn., Annapolis, Md., 1996-98; curator Nat. Am. Red Cross, Washington, 1999—2004; pres. Vintage Appraisals, Inc., Tampa, Fla., 2005—. Cons.; founder, pres. Historic House Mus. Met. Washington. Mem. Am. Assn. Mus., Mid-Atlantic Assn. Mus., Am. Assn. State and Local History, Victorian Soc. Am. (bd. dirs.), Am. Soc. Appraisers. Home and Office: Vintage Appraisals 3116 W Wallcraft Ave Tampa FL 33611-1943 Office Phone: 815-300-9200. Personal E-mail: vsopher@verizon.net.

**SOPHIR, ERIC L.,** lawyer; b. NYC, Dec. 14, 1976; s. Stephen P. and Jan P. Sophir; m. Vanessa L. Frohwirth, Aug. 11, 2002. BS in Materials Sci. and Engring., Cornell U., 1999; JD, Franklin Pierce Law Ctr., 2002. Bar: U.S. Patent and Trademark Office 2001. Va. 2002, DC 2003. Assoc. Kilpatrick Stockton LLP, Washington, 2002—04, Greenberg Traurig, McLean, Va., 2004, Kilpatrick Stockton LLP, Washington, 2005—. McMullan Dean's scholar, Cornell U. Office: Kilpatrick Stockton LLP 607 14th St NW Ste 900 Washington DC 20005 Office Phone: 202-508-5812. Office Fax: 202-585-0039. Business E-mail: esophir@kilpatrickstockton.com.

**SOPRANOS, ORPHEUS JAVARAS,** manufacturing executive; b. Evanston, Ill., Oct. 4, 1935; s. James Javaras and Margoula (Papalexatou) S.; m. Angeline Buches, Dec. 31, 1959; children—Andrew, Katherine. AB, MBA, U. Chgo., 1957. Mgmt. trainee Ford Motor Co., Chgo., 1958-59; with Amsted Industries, Chgo., 1959—, dir. bus. research, 1966-70, treas., 1970-80, v.p., 1980—; pres. Amsted Internat., 1991-93, corp. v.p., 1993-2000, ret. Served with U.S. Army, 1958, 61-62. Mem. Univ. Club (Chgo.), Skokie Country Club.

**SORA, SEBASTIAN ANTONY,** business machines manufacturing executive, educator; b. N.Y.C., June 29, 1943; s. Joseph Louis and Angelina Maria (Maletta) S.; m. Janet Lee Dietz, Apr. 11, 1970 (dec. July 1972); 1 child, Joseph Walter; m. Mary Frances Elizabeth Boscketti, Oct. 12, 1974; children: Joseph Walter, Sebastian Nicholas, Frances Ann, Jenny Concetta. BS, Bklyn. Coll., 1964; MBA, Iona Coll., 1974, PMC, 1976; DPS, Pace U., 1989. Math. modeller Assoc. Univs. Inc., 1964-66; with U.S. Coast and Geodetic Survey,

Washington, 1967-70; mgr. programming IBM, Yorktown, NY, 1966-67, 70-75, programmer, modeller, 1970-72, mgr. program system and design Fishkill, NY, 1971-77, analyst on market models Harrison, NY, 1977-81, sr. programmer Boeblingen, Fed. Republic Germany, 1981-82, mgr. rsch. staff 1st Josephson system Yorktown, 1982-84, program dir. Systems Rsch. Inst. N.Y.C., 1984-87; mgr. edn. program World Trade Corp. IBM, North Tarrytown, NY, 1989-90; mgr. promotional-artificial intelligence systems IBM, White Plains, NY, 1990—; assoc. prof. MIS Montclair State Coll., Upper Montclair, NJ, 1992-95; pres. Bus. Edn. Systems Tech., 1992-95. Assoc. prof. info. sci. Pace U., White Plains, N.Y., 1977-96; asst. prof. telecomm. Iona Coll., New Rochelle, N.Y., 1986; asst. prof. mgmt. Manhattan Coll., Bronx, N.Y., 1988; cons. AID, Washington, 1989; vis. prof. L.I. U., 1997; assoc. prof. computer sci. Marymount Coll., Tarrytown, 1999, mgmt. and info sys. Adelphi U., 2002—; spkr. in field. Editor Jour. Value Based Mgmt., 1987—, Jour. Cross Cultural Mgmt., Jour. of Am. Mgmt., 1994-99; pub. Paradegon Shifts in Edn: Paradise Lost or Regained, U. Press of Am., Info. Sys. Ethics, Northeast Decision Sci. Inst., 2004; contbr. articles to profl. jours.; patentee fluxless solder. Mem. IEEE (technol. leadership com. 1986—, info. policy com. 1986-95), Data Processing Mgmt. Assn., Assoc. Computing Machinery. Roman Catholic. Home and Office: Internat Bus Edn Sys Techs 1 Christie Ct Somers NY 10589-2430 E-mail: sora@us.ibm.com, sailor@attglobal.net.

**SORBELLO, JOSEPH CHARLES,** retired lawyer; b. Redlands, Calif., Apr. 8, 1925; s. Salvatore and Maria (Gallotto) S.; m. Sharon Broome, June 3, 1945, Margaret Pillsbury, June 10, 1969 (dec. June 1995); m. Marguerite Geftakys, Apr. 23, 1997. BS in Pharmacy, Wash. State U., 1951; JD, Lincoln U., 1975. Bar: Calif. 1975; lic. pharmacist Calif., Wash. Owner Community Pharmacy, Edgemont, Calif., 1955-60; pharmacist Owens Pharmacy, Bishop, Calif., 1961-69; supervising insp. Calif. State Bd. Pharmacy, San Francisco, L.A., 1969-87; pvt. practice Westminster, Calif. 1987-95; ret., 1996. Lectr. in pharmacy law U. So. Calif., L.A., 1984, 85, 86. Bd. dirs. Moreno Valley Sch. Dist., Sunny Mead, Calif. Staff sgt. USMC, 1942-46, PTO. Mem. Masons, Nu Beta Epsilon, Rho Chi. Democrat. Avocation: amateur radio. Home: 3942 S Mission Rd Fallbrook CA 92028-9455

**SORBER, CHARLES ARTHUR,** academic administrator; b. Kingston, Pa., Sept. 12, 1939; s. Merritt Walter and Marjory (Roachford) S.; m. Linda Ellen Babcock, Feb. 20, 1972; children: Kimberly Ann, Kingsley Charles. BS in Sanitary Engring., Pa. State U., 1961, MS in Sanitary Engring., 1966; PhD, U. Tex., 1971. Sanitary engr. U.S. Army, France and Fed. Republic Germany, 1961-65; chief gen. engring. br. U.S. Army Environ Hygiene Agy., Edgewood Arsenal, Md., 1966-69; comdr. U.S. Army Med. Environ. Rsch. Unit, Edgewood Arsenal, Md., 1971-73; dir. environ. quality divsn. U.S. Army Med. Bioengring. R&D Lab., Frederick, Md., 1973-75; asst. dean coll. scis. and math. U. Tex., San Antonio, 1976-77, acting dir. divsn. earth & phys. scis., 1977-80, dir. Ctr. Applied Rsch. & Tech., 1976-80, assoc. dean coll. engring. Austin, 1980-86, L.B. (Preach) Meaders prof., 1985; dean sch. engring. U. Pitts., 1986-93; pres. U. Tex.-Permian Basin, Odessa, 1993-2001; prof. U. Tex., Austin, 2001—; interim vice chancellor for spl. engring. programs U. Tex. Sys., 2002—03; interim pres. U. Tex., Arlington, 2003—04, spl. engring. advisor. Bd. dirs., advy. coun., cons. various cos. and agys. Author, co-author more than 140 papers, book chpts., reports on land application of wastewater and sludges, water and wastewater reuse, water and wastewater disinfection and higher edn. Recipient Disting. Alumnus award Wilkes Coll., 1987, Disting. Grad. award Coll. of Engring., U. Tex., Austin, 1994, Outstanding Engring. Alumnus award Pa. State U., 1994; John A. Focht teach fellow U. Tex.-Austin, 1982. Fellow: ASCE; mem.: NSPE, Coun. Pub. Univ. Presidents and Chancellors (exec. com. Tex. 1994—95, sec.-treas. 1999—2001), Am. Water Works Assn., Am. Soc. Engring. Edn., Water Environ. Fedn. (com. chmn. 1983—85, 1988—89, 1993—96, bd. control 1988—94, v.p. 1990—91, pres.-elect 1991—92, pres. 1992—93, Svc. award 1985, 1989, 1990, 1996), Am. Acad. Environ. Engrs. (trustee 1994—97, 2002—, diplomate, Gordon Maskew Fair award 1993), The U. Tex. Club. Office Phone: 512-322-3776. Business E-mail: csorber@utsystem.edu.

**SORBY, DONALD LLOYD,** dean; b. Fremont, Nebr., Aug. 12, 1933; s. Lloyd A. and Orpha M. (Simmons) S.; m. Jacquelyn J. Burchard, Nov. 7, 1959; children: Thomas, Sharon. BS in Pharmacy, U. Nebr., 1955; MS, U. Wash., 1958, PhD, 1960. Dir. pharm. services U. Calif., San Francisco, 1970-72; chmn. dept. pharmacy practice Sch. Pharmacy, U. Wash., Seattle, 1972-74; dean Sch. of Pharmacy, U. Mo., Kansas City, 1974-84, Sch. of Pharmacy, U. Pacific, Stockton, Calif., 1984-95, dean emeritus, 1995—. Contbr. articles to profl. jours. Named Disting. Alumnus, U. Nebr. Coll. Pharmacy, 2000. Mem. Am. Pharm. Assn. (Linwood F. Tice award 1995), Am. Assn. Colls. of Pharmacy (pres. 1980-81), Calif. Pharm. Assn., Calif. Soc. Health-Sys. Pharmacists, Sigma Xi, Phi Kappa Phi, Rho Chi. Home: 4362 Yacht Harbor Dr Stockton CA 95204-1126 E-mail: dsorby@att.net.

**SORDELLO, STEVE,** communications executive; b. 1970; BA in Fin. and Mgmt., Santa Clara U., MBA. Cert. Mgmt. Acct. Various positions in finance and acctg. Syntex Corp., Palo Alto, Calif.; sr. dir., fin. planning Adobe Systems, Inc.; joined Ask Jeeves, Inc., Oakland, Calif., 1999, dir., fin. planning and analysis, 1999—2000, v.p. fin. planning and analysis, 2000, acting CFO, 2000—01, exec. v.p., CFO, 2001—05; CFO TiVo Inc., 2006—. Office: TiVo Inc PO Box 2160 Alviso CA 95002-2160 Office Phone: 510-985-7400. Office Fax: 510-985-7412.*

**SORDO, MARGARITA,** medical researcher; d. Francisco Sordo and Margarita Sanchez. BSc in Computer Engring. with honors, Instituto Tecnologico Autonoma de Mex., 1994; MSc in Artificial Intelligence, U. Edinburgh, 1995; PhD in Computer Sci. and Artificial Intelligence, U. Sussex, 1999. Rsch. assoc. Advanced Computation Lab. Imperial Cancer Rsch. Fund, London, 1999—2001; rsch. assoc., instr. radiology Decision Systems Group Harvard Med. Sch., Boston, 2002 , Mem. Am. Med. Informatics Assn. (assoc.), HL7 - Decision Support Group (assoc.). Achievements include development of ANSI-approved - GELLO: A standard expression language for developing clinical guidelines. Office: Decision Systems Group Harvard Med 75 Francis St THORN 309 Boston MA 02115 Office Phone: 617-732-6271. E-mail: msordo@dsg.harvard.edu.

**SOREL, EDWARD,** artist; b. N.Y.C., Mar. 26, 1929; s. Morris and Rebecca (Kleinberg) Schwartz; m. Nancy Caldwell, May 29, 1965; children: Jenny, Katherine; children by previous marriage: Madeline, Leo. Diploma, Cooper Union, 1951; DFA (hon.), Art Inst. Boston, 1998. Co-founder Pushpin Studio, 1953; free-lance artist, 1956—; syndicated Sorel's News Service, 1969-70, King Features. Author, illustrator: Making the World Safe for Hypocrisy, 1972; exhibited in Pushpin Studio retrospective at the Louvre, 1970, other European galleries, 1970-71; exhibited one-man show, Graham Galleries, N.Y.C., 1973, 78, Galerie Bartsch & Chariau, Munich, 1986, Retrospective Exhibition Cooper Union, 1987, Susan Conway Galleries, Washington, 1992, Soc. Illustrators Am. Mus. Illustration, N.Y.C., 1993, Davis and Langdale Galleries, N.Y.C., 1994, 97, 2006, Nat. Portrait Gallery, Washington, 1999; illustrator: Pablo Paints a Picture, 1961, Gwendolyn the Miracle Hen, 1963 (N.Y. Herald Tribune Book award for illustration 1962), What's Good for a Five-Year-Old, 1969, The Duck in the Gun, 1969, Word People, 1970, Magical Storybook, 1972, Superpen, 1978, The Zillionaire's Daughter, 1990, First Encounters, 1994, Unauthorized Portraits, 1997, Johnny on the Spot, 1998, The Saturday Kid, 2000, Literary Lives, 2006; contbr. to The Nation, The New Yorker, American Heritage and The Atlantic mags. Recipient awards Soc. Illustrators, Art Dirs. Club N.Y.; Augustus St. Gauden's medal Cooper Union; George Polk award for satiric drawing, 1981; Page One award Newspaper Guild of N.Y. for best editorial cartoon (magazines), 1988, Hamilton King award Soc. Illustrators, 1990, John Singleton Copley medal Smithsonian Instn., 1999, Art Dirs. Hall of Fame, 2001, Karikaturpreis Deutschen Anwaltschaft 2002. Office Phone: 212-665-0698. Office Fax: 212-665-0699. Personal E-mail: edwardsorel@hotmail.com.

**SORELL, KITTY JULIA,** public relations executive; b. Vienna, Apr. 20, 1937; came to U.S. 1938; d. Bruno Alexander and Ilse (Fischl) Singerman. BA, Syracuse U., 1959. Lic. realtor Real Estate Bd. N.Y. Spl. events coord.

Gimbel's, N.Y.C., 1966—69; pub. rels./account exec. Hamra Assocs., N.Y.C., 1969—71; spl. events/pub. rels. dir. Stern Bros., Paramus, NJ, 1972; pub. rels. account exec. Zachary & Front, N.Y.C., 1972—76; dir. pub. rels. RSM&K Advt., N.Y.C., 1976—77; owner Kitty Sorell Pub. Rels., N.Y.C., 1977—; realtor, v.p., assoc. broker Corcoran Group, N.Y.C., 1994—. Reporter Wisdom's Child, 1981-84, The Villager, 1986-88; lectr. in field. Contbg. editor Mktg. Maker mag., 1976. Fundraiser WNET-TV, N.Y.C., 1974-75; vol. pub. rels. Sheridan Sq. Triangle Assn., N.Y.C., 1984-89; pres. bd. dirs. Apt. House Coop., 1991—; bd. dirs. Greenwich Village Alliance, 1994—; mem. Greenwich Village Soc. for Hist. Preservation, 1999—. Mem. Am. Soc. Profl. and Exec. Women, Publicity Club. Democrat. Jewish. Avocations: books, theater. Office: Kitty Sorell Pub Rels 250 W 57th St New York NY 10107 Office Phone: 212-539-4968. E-mail: kjs@corcoran.com.

**SORELLE, RUTH DOYLE,** writer, journalist; b. Port Arthur, Tex., Oct. 9, 1948; d. Richard Thomas and Ruth Elaine (Droddy) D.; m. Paul Charles SoRelle, Apr. 10, 1970; children: Danielle Amanda, Richard Paul. BJ, U. Tex., 1971; MPH, U. Tex., Houston, 1988. Reporter Port Arthur News, summer 1968, 69, Univ. and Info. Svc., Austin, Tex., 1970-71; med. editor U. Tex. MD Anderson Hosp., Houston, 1973-74; editor Resources Devel. Corp., Houston, 1974-76; med. editor Baylor Coll. Medicine, Houston, 1977-78; copy editor Houston Chronicle, Houston, 1978-79, med. writer, 1979-99; sr. dir. for spl. projects Baylor Coll., 1999—, editor 2 online newsletters. Instr. U. Houston, 1986, 87, 89; editor websites. Leader Presbyn. Youth Fellowship, Houston, 1989; co-chair Tex. State Strategic Health Partnership. Recipient John P. McGovern award Am. Med. Writers Assn., Community Svc. award Tex. Assoc. Press, 1993, Katie award Dallas Press Club, 1992, 93, Anson Jones award Tex. Med. Assn., 1981, 83, 85, 86, 88, 90, 92, 95, 96, 98, Francis C. Moore award Harris County Med. Assn., 1984-98, Silver Star Tex. award Tex. Hosp. Assn., 1984, 86, 89, 92, Tex. Pub. Health Assn. award, 1981, 89, 90, 91, 94, Houston Area Health Care Coalition's Health Policy Leadership award, 1990, Paul Ellis award Am. Heart Assn., 1988, 95, Nat. Multiple Sclerosis Soc. award for med. writing, 1998, Inernat. Health Reporting award Pan Am Health Orgn., 1998, others. Mem. Am. Med. Writer's Assn. (bd. dirs. southwest chpt. 1994-95), Press Club of Houston (Deadline Coverage award 1984, Investigative Series award 1990, Mag. Feature award 1994). Democrat. Avocations: bicycling, reading, swimming. E-mail: dsorelle@bcm.tmc.edu.

**SORELL STEHR, DEBORAH K.,** lawyer; b. NYC, 1962; m. Mark Stehr; children: Daniel, Julia. AB, Princeton U., 1984; JD, Northwestern U., 1987. Bar: 1987. With Kronish Lieb Weiner & Hellman, O'Sullivan Graev & Karabell; assoc. gen. counsel Nine West Group Inc., 1996—98; gen. counsel Iconix Brand Group, Inc., 1998—, v.p., 1998—99, sr. v.p., 1999—. Office: Iconix Brand Group Inc 215 W 40th St New York NY 10018 Office Phone: 212-730-0030. Office Fax: 212-391-2057.*

**SOREN, DAVID,** archaeologist, educator, writer, filmmaker; b. Phila., Oct. 7, 1946; s. Harry Friedman and Erma Elizabeth (Salomon) Soren; m. Noelle Louise Schattyn, Dec. 22, 1967. BA, Dartmouth Coll., 1968; MA, Harvard U., 1972, PhD, 1973. Cert. Rome Classics Ctr. Curator of coins Fogg Art Mus., Cambridge, Mass., 1972; asst. prof. U. Mo., Columbia, 1972-76, assoc. prof., dept. head, 1976-81; prof. U. Ariz., Tucson, 1982-97, Regents prof., 1997—, dept. head, 1984-89. Guest curator Am. Mus. Natural History, N.Y.C., 1983—90, lectr, 1993—; creator, dir. Kourion Excavations, Cyprus, 1982—89, Portugal, 1983—84, Am. Excavations, Lugnano, Italy, 1988—93; pot cons., field dir. Tunisa Excavations, Chgo. Oriental Inst./Smithsonian Instn., 1973—78; dir. excavations Chianciano, Terme, Italy, 1995—; dir. Orvieto (Italy) Inst. Classical Studies, 2002—; resident in classical archaeology Am. Acad., Rome, 2002. Author: (book) Unreal Reality, 1978, Rise and Fall of Fantasy Film, 1980, Carthage, 1990, Carthage, French edit., 1994, Vera-Ellen: The Magic and the Mystery, 1999, 2d edit., 2003, Lugnano! Excavation of a Roman Villa, 1999, Kourion: Search for a Lost Roman City, 1988, Corpus des Mosaiques de Tunisie, 1972, Corpus des Mosaiques de Tunisie, 3d rev. edit., 1986, Carthage: A Mosaic of Ancient Tunisia, 1987; editor: Excavations at Kourion I, 1987; contbg. editor Archaeology Mag.; prodr.: (films) Carthage: A Mirage of Antiquity, 1987; creator, guest curator (internt traveling exhbn.) Carhtage: A Mosaic of Ancient Tunisia, 1987—92; editor, founder: Roscius, 1993—95; creative cons. (TV miniseries) Lost Civilizations, 1994; contbr. articles to profl. jours.; prodr.: (documentaries) BBC-TV documentary Malaria and the Fall of Rome, 2002; author: Vera-Ellen: The Magic and the Mystery; 2d edit., 2003; cons.: The History Channel, 2004; cons., on-screen contbr. Where on Earth, History Channel, 2004, The Colosseum, 2005, Where Did It Begin. Named Outstanding Am. Under 40, Esquire Mag., 1985, hon. Italian citizen, Lugnano, Italy, 1989; recipient Cine Golden Eagle, 1980, Angenieux Film award, Indsl. Photography Mag., 1980, Oustanding Am. Under 40 award, C. Johns Hopkins-Britain's Royal Inst. Internat. Affairs, 1985; grantee, NEH, 1979, 1987, Fulbright, Lisbon, 1983. Fellow: Brit. Royal Inst. Internat. Affairs; mem.: Am. Acad. Rome (mem. internat. com. 2003—, bd. dirs. 2003—), Luso-Am. Commn. (citation 1983—84), Archaeol. Inst. Tucson (pres. 1983—86), Am. Sch. Oriental Rsch. (dept. rep. 1981—85), Nat. Geog. Soc. (project dir. 1983—84). Office: U Ariz Dept Classics 371 Mlb Tucson AZ 85721-0001 Office Phone: 520-621-1689. Business E-mail: soren@u.arizona.edu.

**SORENSEN, ALLAN CHRESTEN,** service company executive; b. Edson, Alta., Can., Apr. 27, 1938; arrived in U.S., 1962, naturalized, 1965; s. Henry and Vivien A. Sorensen; children: Scott, Jody, Rosey. BS in Pharmacy, Drake U., 1961. Salesman Hoffman LaRoche Pharm. Co., Kitchener, Ont., Canada, 1961-62; salesman Personnel Pool of Am., Inc., Chgo. 1962-63, regl. mgr. 1963-67, dir. pres. 1967-80, chief exec. officer, 1978-91, chmn. interim svcs., 1989-97; vice chmn., co-founder Interim Healthcare Inc., Ft. Lauderdale, 1997—2004, pres., CEO, 2004—; dir. Republic Svcs., Inc., Ft. Lauderdale, 1998—. Mem. Am. Staffing Assn. (past pres., bd. dir.), Am. Assn. for Homecare (past chmn., bd. dir.), Broward Workshop. Republican. Home: 333 Sunset Dr #708 Fort Lauderdale FL 33301 Office: Interim Healthcare Inc 1601 Sawgrass Corporate Pkwy Sunrise FL 33323-2827

**SORENSEN, ANDREW AARON,** academic administrator; b. Pitts., July 20, 1938; s. Albert Aaron and Margaret (Lindquist) S.; m. Donna Ingemie, Aug. 4, 1968; children: Aaron Ashley, Benjamin Samuel. BA, U. Ill., 1959; BDiv, Yale U., 1962, MPhil, 1970, PhD, 1971; MPH, U. Mich., 1966. Asst. prof. Cornell U., Ithaca, NY, 1971-73, U. Rochester, NY, 1973-76, assoc. prof. NY, 1976-83; prof., dean U. Mass., Amherst, 1983-86, Johns Hopkins U., Balt., 1986-90, exec. dir. AIDS Inst.; provost, v.p. acad. affairs U. Fla., Gainesville, 1990-96; pres. U. Ala., Tuscaloosa, 1996—2002, U. SC, Columbia, 2002—. Chmn. adminstrv. bd. Whitney Marine Biol. Lab., 1990—96; chmn. editl. bd. Univ. Press. Fla., 1990—96; vis. fellow U. Cambridge, 1979—80; past pres. So. U. Conf. Author 7 books; contbr. over 100 articles to profl. jours. Vice-chmn., bd. dirs. Chautauqua Instn., 1996-98; bd. mem. Nat. Sci. Advisory Bd. for Biosecurity, 2005-. U.S. Dept. Edn. fellow Lincoln U., 1966-67, NSF fellow Harvard U., 1975-76; named mem. of NY Greater Columbia C of C. Mem.: So. Univ. Conf. (past pres.), Univ. Rsch. Assn. (trustee), Southeastern Univs. Rsch. Assn. (past chmn. coun. presidents). Presbyterian. Office: Office of Pres U SC Osborne 206 Columbia SC 29208 Office Phone: 803-777-2001. E-mail: sorensen@sc.edu.

**SORENSEN, CARL EDWARD,** manufacturing executive; b. San Diego, Sept. 21, 1964; s. Carl Edward and Bonnie Jean Sorensen; m. Cynthia Ann Sorensen, June 5, 1987; 1 child, Carl Edward. B Bus. Mgmt., St. Leo Coll., Norfolk, Va., 1995; M Bus. Fin. and Acctg., Mont. State U., Bozeman, 1998. Commd. USN, 1983, advanced through grades to comdr., 1998; owner, pres., CEO Sorensen Enterprises Inc., Virginia Beach, Va., 1998—. Adv. bd. chmn. Rural Bus. Enhancement, Virginia Beach; chmn. Pennys From Heaven, Sunbury, S.C. Mem. DAV, WW II Meml. Fund, Elks. Republican. Methodist. Avocations: buying small companies, improving and selling them, antique collecting. Home and Office: Sorenson Enterprises 5049 Hunt Club Chase Suffolk VA 23435-3203

**SØRENSEN, ERIK,** retired diversified financial services company executive; b. Randers, Denmark, July 19, 1944; s. Christen and Erna Sørensen; m. Brigitte Berg; children: Anne Marie, Thomas, Anne Louise, Anne Mette, Anne Sophie. MS in Chemistry, Tech. U. Denmark, 1968; MBA in Internat. Fin., Cph Sch. Econs., 1971. Sr. economist Novo Industri A/S, Bagsvaerd, Denmark, 1970-71, mgr. econs. and planning, 1972-74, v.p. sales and mktg., 1974-80, pres. bioindsl. group, 1980-88; pres. Health Care Grp Novo Nordisk A/S, 1988-1995; pres., CEO Christian Hansen Group, Denmark, 1995—; ret., 2005. Bd. dirs., chmn. ISS A/S. Lt. Danish Army, 1968-70. Office: Chr Hansen Group Bøge Allé 10 2970 Horsholm Denmark

**SØRENSEN, GILLIAN MARTIN,** United Nations official; b. Columbus, Ohio, Mar. 4, 1941; d. John Butlin and Helen (Hickam) Martin; m. Theodore C. Sorensen, June 28, 1969; 1 child, Juliet. BA, Smith Coll., 1963. Commr. N.Y.C. Commn. for UN and Consular Corps, 1978-90; pres. Nat. Conf., 1990-93; undersec gen., spl. advisor for pub. policy UN, N.Y.C., 1993-97, UN asst. sec. gen. for external rels., 1997—2003; sr. advisor UN Found., N.Y.C., 2003—. Del. Dem. Nat. Conv., 1976, 84, 88. Mem.: Acad. Coun. on the UN, Women's Forum, Coun. on Fgn. Rels. Democrat. Office: UN Found 801 Second Ave Ste 404 New York NY 10017 Office Phone: 212-697-3315. Business E-Mail: gsorenson@unfoundation.org.

**SØRENSEN, JOHN B.,** surgeon; s. Bruce F. and Suzanne B. Sorensen. MD, Temple U., 1986. Cert. surgery Am. Bd. Surgery, 1992, critical care Am. Bd. Surgery, 1995, transplantation surgery U. Pitts., 1993. Dir. transplantation LDS Hosp., Salt Lake City, 1993—2005; chief sect. transplantation dept. surgery U. Utah, Salt Lake City, 2005—. Med. dir. Intermountain Donor Services, Salt Lake City, 2004—. Lt. col. U.S. Army, 2002. Decorated Combat Med. Badge, Bronze Star U.S. Army. Fellow: ACS; mem.: Am. Soc. Transplant Surgeons, Sigma Chi. Mem. Lds Ch. Office: Univ Utah Dept Surgery 30 North 1900 East Salt Lake City UT 84132 Office Phone: 801-585-2816.

**SØRENSEN, JOHN NOBLE,** retired mechanical and nuclear engineer; b. Mpls., Jan. 2, 1934; s. Alfred Noble and Helen Viola (Baker) S.; m. Joan Elizabeth Reiche, Sept. 15, 1954; children: Laura Elizabeth, Nancy Helen, Karen Lynn. BSME, U. N.D., 1955; MSME, U. Pitts., 1958. Cert. engr. Sr. engr. Westinghouse Electric, Pitts., 1955-67; v.p., gen. mgr. NUS Corp., Rockville, Md., 1967-86; v.p., dir. Grove Engring., Inc., Rockville, 1986-93; tech. asst. to commr. NRC, Washington, 1993-97, sr. fellow adv. com. on reactor safeguards, 1997—2001, sr. fellow adv. com. on nuclear waste, 1997—2001, spl. asst. spent fuel project office, 2002—03; prin. cons. Project Enhancement Corp., 2004—. Mem. ASME, NSPE, Am. Nuclear Soc., Sigma Xi. Home: 629 Crocus Dr Rockville MD 20850-2046 Office: Project Enhancement Corporation 20300 Century Blvd Ste 175 Germantown MD 20874-1189 Office Phone: 240-686-3059. Personal E-mail: jsoren5605@aol.com.

**SØRENSEN, LINDA,** lawyer; b. Eureka, Calif., Mar. 3, 1945; BS, U. Wis., 1967; JD, U. Calif., 1976. Bar: Calif. 1976, U.S. Dist. Ct. (no. dist.) Calif. 1976, U.S. Ct. Appeals (9th cir.) 1976, U.S. Dist. Ct. (ea. dist.) Calif. 1977. Assoc., ptnr. Rothschild, Phelan & Mortali, San Francisco, 1976-88; dir. Howard, Rice, Nemerovski, Canady, Falk & Rabkin, San Francisco, 1988-95; shareholder Feldman, Waldman & Kline, P.C., San Francisco, 1997-99; pvt. practice Berkeley, Calif., 1999—; of counsel Stromsheim & Assoc., 2001—. Mem. ABA (mem. subcom. on avoiding powers, bus. bankruptcy com. 1983-95), Bar Assn. of San Francisco (chmn. comml. law and bankruptcy sect. 1984, editor fed. cts. com., no. dist. Calif. digest 1979-82). Office: PO Box 325 Bodega Bay CA 94923 Office Fax: 510 845 1785. Personal E-mail: lindasorensen@earthlink.net.

**SØRENSEN, POUL HENRIK BREDAHL,** physician, research scientist, pathologist; b. Copenhagen, Oct. 11, 1956; s. Paul Bredahl and Inger Sørensen, Alex Eisenberg; 1 child, Derek Lee. BS, U. B.C., Can., 1980, MD, 1984, PhD, 1988. Cert. Anatomic Pathology Royal Coll. of Physicians and Surgeons of Can., 1991. Postdoctoral fellowship U. of Minn., Mnpls., 1991—92, U. of So. Calif., LA, 1992—93; clin. asst. prof. U. of Brit. Columbia, Vancouver, Canada, 1993—96, clin. assoc. prof., 1996—98, assoc. prof., 1998—. Dir. molecular pathology lab. Children's and Women's Health Ctr. of Brit. Columbia, Vancouver, Canada, 1993—; chair and dir. clin. program pediat. oncology basic and translational rsch. Depts. of Pathology and Pediat., U. of Brit. Columbia, Vancouver, Canada, 1999—; chair biopathology and translational rsch. com. Children's Oncology Group, Bethesda, Md., 2002—. Recipient Lotte-Strauss award, Soc. for Pediat. Pathology, 1994, Young Investigator award, 1996, Children's Oncology Group, 1999, Translational Rsch. award, 2003; Centennial Fellowship, Med. Rsch. Coun. of Can., 1991—93. Mem.: Soc. for Pediat. Pathology (rsch. com. mem. 1993—), Children's Oncology Group (soft tissue sarcoma com. 1996—2003, chair, biopathology and translational rsch. com. 2002—). Achievements include research in Identification of series of genetic changes thought to underlie malignant transformation in specific subtypes of childhood cancer; Discovery of first known chromosomal translocation leading to a genetic alteration as a primary event in human breast cancer (human secretory breast carcinoma); application of signal transduction analysis for the identification of potential therapeutic targets in childhood cancer; development of series of molecular genetic tools used world-wide for diagnosis of specific subtypes of childhood cancers. Office: BC Cancer Rsch Ctr Rm 1 114 675 W 10th Ave Vancouver BC V5Z 1L3 Canada Office Phone: 604-675-8203. Office Fax: 604-675-8218. Business E-Mail: sberkow@bccrc.ca.

**SØRENSON, ARNE M.,** hotel executive; b. Tokyo; BA, Luther Coll., 1980; JD, U. Minn., 1983. Law clk. to Hon. Ellsworth Van Graafeiland U.S. Ct. Appeals (2d cir.), 1983—84; assoc. attorney Latham & Watkins, Washington, 1984—90; ptnr. Latham & Watkins, Washington, 1990—96; sr. v.p. bus. devel. Marriott Internat. Inc., Washington, 1996-98, exec. v.p., CFO, 1998—, pres., continental European lodging, 2003—. Office: Marriott Internat Inc 1 Marriott Dr Washington DC 20058-0001

**SØRENSON, GEORGIA LYNN JONES,** political science professor; b. Abilene, Tex., Aug. 23, 1947; d. Wyly King and Olive M. (Sorenson) Jones; 1 child, Suzanna Simmonds Strasburg. BA, Am. U., 1974; MA, Hood Coll., 1976; PhD, U. Md., 1992. Social scientist Nat. Inst. Edn., Washington, 1978-79, U.S. Commn. Civil Rights, Washington, 1976-79; sr. policy analyst The White House, Washington, 1979-80; founder, sr. scholar James MacGregor Burns Acad. Leadership U. Md., College Park, 1980—; Inaugural chair and prof. transformation U.S. Army, Army War Coll., 2005—. Adv. mem. W.K. Kellogg Found. Nat Fellows, Battle Creek, Mich., 1996-99; inaugural choir, prof. transformation U.S. Army, U.S. Army War Coll., 2005-06. Co-author: (with James MacGregor Burns) Dead-Center: Clinton-Gore Leadership and the Perils of Moderation, 1999; editor: (with George Goethals and James MacGregor Burns) Encyclopeida of Leadership, 2004; contbr. articles to profl. jours. Chair Md. Women's Polit. Caucus, 1991-94; mem. White House Productivity Coun., Washington, 1979; mem. V.P. Youth Employment Task Force, 1979-80. Mem. Am. Polit. Sci. Assn., Internat. Soc. Polit. Psychologists, A.K. Rice Inst. Office: James MacGregor Burns Acad Leadership Univ Md College Park MD 20742-0001 Office Phone: 301-405-6100. Business E-Mail: gsorenson@academy.umd.edu.

**SØRENSON, GRETCHEN HARTLEY,** elementary school educator; b. Muncie, Ind., Dec. 3, 1935; d. James Ross and Lois (Reed) Hartley; m. Ray L. Valour, June 6, 1959 (div. June 1988); 1 child, Virginia; m. George W. Sorenson, June 17, 1988. BFA, Colo. U., 1957; MA in Edn., Ball State U., 1961; cert. elem. edn. administrn., Ariz. State U., 1980. Cert. elem. art, elem. classroom, elem. administr. art tchr. Jefferson County (Colo.) Schs., Jefferson County, Colo., 1957-59; tchr. Delaware County Schs., Selma, Ind., 1959-60, Beverly (Mass.) Schs., 1960-61, Delaware County Schs., Muncie, Ind., 1961-66, Park Forest (Ill.) Schs., 1966-68, Scottsdale (Ariz.) Pub. Schs. 1968—95, Trinity Luth. Sch., Fountain Hills, Ariz., 1995—. Trainer of tchrs. Ariz. Bar Found., Phoenix, 1988-93; mem. site-based mgmt. team Laguna

Sch., 1990-91. Author: (book) Fifth of Fun, 1986. Mem. ch. bd. Paradise Valley (Ariz.) United Meth. Ch., 1970-74, Desert Hills Presbyn. Ch., Carefree, Ariz., 1975-87, Shepherd Desert Luth. Ch., Scottsdale, 1988—; mem. exec. bd. Luth. Hispanic Ministry; mem. Scottsdale Bicentennial Commn., 1987-90. Recipient Outstanding Young Educator, C. of C., Park Forest, 1968. Mem. Phi Delta Kappa (treas. 1988-91, Outstanding Educator award 1992). Lutheran. Avocations: travel, reading. Home: 15043 E Greene Valley Dr Fountain Hills AZ 85268-1339 E-mail: g2sorenson@att.net.

**SØRENSON, JAMES LEVOY,** research and development company executive; b. Rexburg, Idaho, 1921; m. Beverley Sorenson; 8 children. Pharmaceutical salesman Upjohn Co., 1946; co-founder Deseret Pharm., 1957; founder LeVoy's (lingerie bus.), 1960, Sorenson Rsch. Co. (now Abbott Critical Care Sys.), 1972. Exec. bd. mem. Nat. Conf. Christians and Jews. Missionary Ch. Jesus Christ Latter-day Saints New Eng. Named one of Forbes; Richest Americans, 2006; recipient Giant of Our City award, Salt Lake City, 2006. Achievements include patents for the first computer-based real-time heart monitor, 1975; invention of Sorenson VP-100 videophone, a device which assists the deaf and hard of hearing in communication; disposable surgical mask and the disposable venous catheter. Home: Sorenson Molecular Genealogy Found 2511 SW Temple Salt Lake City UT 84115

**SØRENSON, KATHERINE ANN,** elementary school educator; b. Hastings, Minn., Aug. 30, 1947; d. Fredrick William Nearing and Marguerite Lucille Keene-Nearing; m. Michael Alfred Sorenson; children: Brock, Scott. BS in Edn., Black Hills State Coll., 1972; MA in Early Childhood Edn., U. Colo., Denver, 1995. Profl. tchr. lic. Colo.; cert. reading recover tchr. Tchr. Maternity Mary Cath. Sch., St. Paul, 1967—68, St. Andrew's Cath. Sch., St. Paul, 1968—70, Hill City Pub. Sch., 1972—73, Groton Pub. Sch., 1973—75; substitute tchr. Billings Pub. Sch., 1975—76; tchr. Livingston Pub. Sch., 1977—85; asst. dir. childcare Children's Creative Encounters, Littleton, Colo., 1986—87; tchr. Cherry Creek Sch. Dist., Eastridge Elem., Aurora, Colo., 1987—96, 1996—, creator immersion program for mobile at risk students, edn. cons., 2004—. Co-author: Blue Ribbon Application, 1998 (Blue Ribbon School, 1999), Reading Recovery Longitudinal Analysis, National Association for Year Round Education Application. Pack leader Boy Scouts Am., Parker, 1988—94, bd. dirs., 1988—94; mem. Cherry Creek Schs. North Area Task Force, Aurora, 2001—03; Sunday sch. tchr. St. Mary's Cath. Ch., Livingston, 1978—84, religious edn. coord., 1981—82; Sunday sch. tchr. Ave Maria Cath. Ch., Parker, 1992—94; mem. team fundraising Parker Baseball, 1989—92; sec. Moorhead Foster Parent Assn., 1976—77. Recipient Dewitt Wallace Libr. Power award, Dewitt Wallace Found., 1997, Exemplary Reading Program award, Colo. Coun. Internat. Reading, 1998-1999, Tchr. of the Yr. award, Cherry Creek Sch.-Eastridge Elem., 2003, Reading Recovery Excellence award, Morgridge, 2004. Mem.: Cherry Creek Edn. Assn., Reading Recovery Assn., Colo. Coun. Internat. Reading Assn. Avocations: reading, travel, southwest history, quilting. Home: 11182 Cambridge Ct Parker CO 80138 Office: Eastridge Elem Sch 11777 E Wesley Ave Aurora CO 80014

**SØRENSON, LIANE BETH MCDOWELL,** director, state legislator; b. Chgo., Aug. 13, 1947; d. Harold Davidson McDowell and Frances Elanor (Williams) Daisey Van Kleeck; m. Boyd Wayne Sorenson, June 30, 1973; children: Nathan, Matthew, Dana. BS in Edn., U. Del., 1969, M in Counseling with honors, 1986. Tchr. Avon Grove Sch. Dist., West Grove, Pa., 1969-70, Alexis I. duPont Sch. Dist., Wilmington, Del., 1970-73, Barrington (Ill.) Sch. Dist., 1973-75; counseling intern Medill Intensive Learning Ctr.-Christina Sch. Dist., Newark, Del., 1985; counselor Family Violence Shelter CHILD, Inc., Wilmington, 1985, 86-87; dir. parent edn. programs, 1987-88; dir. Office Women's Affairs, exec. dir. Commn. on Status of Women U. Del., Newark, 1988—; mem. Dist. 6 Del. Senate, Dover, 1992—, minority whip. Chair Del. Ho. Edn. Com., 1992—, edn. Bd. Del. Breast Cancer Coalition, 1998—; commr. Edn. Commn. State Del.; mem. tng. com. Nat. Conf. State Legislatures; mem. Bd. Women's Network Nat. Conf. State Legislatures; mem. joint sunset com. Del. Legislature, Del. House of Reps., 1992-94, Del. Senate, 1994—, Del. Legis. Joint Fin. Com. Del. Legis., 1994—, Coun. State Govts. Toll Fellowship. Presenter papers various meetings & confs. Pres. bd. dirs. Nursing Mothers, Inc., 1980-81; trustee Hockessin Montessori Sch., 1982-84, enrollment chair, 1982-83; trustee Hockessin Pub. Libr., 1982-84, pres. bd., 1982-84; bd. dirs. Del. Coalition for Children, 1986-88; bd. dirs. Children's Bur. Del., 1984-87, sec., 1985-87; pres. Jr. League Wilmington, 1986-87, rsch. coun. v.p., 1985-86; bd. dirs. YWCA New Castle County, 1989-91; pres. Del. Women's Agenda, 1986-88; vice-chair Women's Leadership Ctr., 1992—; mem. Del. Work Family Coalition; bd. dirs. Del. divsn. Am. Cancer Soc., 1993—. Grantee Del. Dept. Svcs. to Children, Youth and Their Families, 1987-88, 1988, State of Del. Gen. Assembly, 1992; recipient Disting. Legis. Svc. award Del. State Bar Assn., 1997, Del Tufo award Delaware Humanities Forum, 1999. Mem.: Hockessin Hist. Soc. (bd. mem. 2000—), Del. Family Law Commn., Del. Alliance for Arts in Edn., Del. Greenway and Trails Coun., Am. Assn. for Higher Edn. (chair women's caucus 1991—92, program chair women's caucus 1990—91, pre-conf. workshop coord. women's caucus 1990 Ann. Conf.), Rotary (charter mem. Hockessin Pike Creek club 1994—). Republican. Methodist. Avocations: camping, hiking. Office: State of Delaware Legislative Hall Rm 210 PO Box 1401 Dover DE 19903-1401

**SØRENSON, SCOTT K.,** manufacturing executive; BSc, U. Utah; MBA, Harvard U. Mgmt. cons. McKinsey & Co.; exec. Phelps Dodge Corp.; CFO Power Generation Div. and Comm. and Sys. Div. Westinghouse Electric Corp./CBS, 1996—98; exec. v.p., CFO Pliant Corp., 1998—2001; v.p., CFO Hillenbrand Industries Inc., Batesville, Ind., 2001—. Office: Hillenbrand Industries Inc 700 State Rte 46 E Batesville IN 47006-8835

**SØRENSON, STEPHEN JAY,** prosecutor; b. Salt Lake City, Aug. 9, 1949; s. Peter Jay and Jeannette (Hanks) S.; m. Corinne Clyde, Jan. 24, 1974; children: Jeannette, Peter, Richard, Michael, Rebecca. Student, Yale U., 1967-69; BA, U. Utah, 1973, JD, 1977. Bar: Utah 1977, U.S. Dist. Ct. Utah 1977, U.S. Ct. Appeals (10th cir.) 1982. Asst. atty. gen. State of Utah, Salt Lake City, 1977-90, chief litigation divsn., 1986-90; asst. U.S. atty. Dist. Utah US Dept. Justice, Salt Lake City, 1990—98, chief civil divsn., 1995-98, first asst. US atty., 1998—, acting US atty., 2006. Mem. Utah Bar Assn. Office: US Atty's Office 185 S State St Ste 400 Salt Lake City UT 84111-1552

**SØRENSTAM, ANNIKA,** professional golfer; b. Stockholm, Oct. 9, 1970; m. David Esch. Student, U. Ariz. With Women's Profl. Golf European Tour, 1992—, LPGA, 1993—. Swedish Nat. Team, 1987-92, Solheim Cup Team, 1994, 96, 98; playing editor Golf Digest, 2006—, Golf for Women, 2006—. Recipient Vare Trophy award, 1998, Espy Awards for Best Female Golfer, ESPN, 1996, 1998, 1999, 2002-2004, Espy Award for Best Female Athlete, 2006; named Rolex Player of Yr., 1995, 97, 98, 2000-2003, Female Athlete of Yr., AP, 2003. Achievements in Tournaments won include: Australian Ladies Open, 1994, U.S. Women's Open, 1995, 96, 2006, Ladies Masters, 1995, 2000, 2002, LPGA Championship, 1997, 2002-2004, Women's British Open, 2003, first woman since 1945 to appear in a PGA Tour event, 2003, inducted into World Golf Hall of Fame, 2003, 61 career LPGA Tour victories, topped $2 million in earnings 2001-2004, only woman in LPGA history to ever go over $2 million in one season. Office: LPGA 100 International Golf Dr Daytona Beach FL 32124-1092

**SOREY, THOMAS LESTER, JR.,** architect, educator; b. Wichita Falls, Tex., Jan. 26, 1927; s. Thomas Lester and Katherine (Peak) S.; m. Carolyn Drake, Dec. 24, 1959 (div. 1973); 1 child, Drake. Student, U. Okla., 1944—47; BArch, Okla. State U., 1952; MArch, Harvard U., 1954. Registered arch., Okla. Designer McKim Mead & White, Archs., NYC, summer 1954; ptnr. Sorey Hill & Sorey Archs., Oklahoma City, 1958-70; pvt. practice Oklahoma City, 1971-95; vis. prof. architecture U. Okla., Norman, 1972-74, prof. architecture, 1975-90, prof. emeritus architecture, sculptor, 1991—. Work included in books: Oklahoma Landmarks, 1967, Houses Architects Design for Themselves, 1974, Architecture in Oklahoma: Landmark and Vernacular, 1978, Affordable Houses Designed by Architects, 1979, Oklahoma Homes Past and Present, 1980; sculptor in one-man and group exhbns.

Oklahoma City, Norman, Tulsa, 1977—. Mem. prof. adv. com. Okla. State U. Sch. Architecture, Stillwater, 1967-69, Neighborhood Alliance, Inc., Oklahoma City, 1971-73; founding dir. Contemporary Arts Found., Oklahoma City, 1965-67; dir. Sunbeam Family Svcs., Oklahoma City, 1967-75; trustee Oklahoma City Art Mus., 1968-77, v.p., 1975; mem. Citizens League of Ctrl. Okla., Interfaith Alliance. With U.S. Army, 1954-56. Recipient Award of Excellence for House Design, Archtl. Record, 1968, Assocs. Disting. Lectr. award U. Okla., 1984-86. Mem. AIA (Okla. chpt. sect. 1965, bd. dirs. Okla. chpt. 1968-69, 75-77), Men's Dinner Club. Democrat. Avocations: photography, travel, reading non-fiction. Home and Office: 3801 Ives Way Norman OK 73072-4009 Office Phone: 405-364-1624.

**SORGE, KAREN LEE,** printing company executive, consultant; b. Warwick, N.Y., May 27, 1958; d. Wesley Thomas and Margaret Anne (Storms) Kervatt; m. David W. Farquhar, July 16, 1982 (div. Feb. 1990); 1 child: Lauren Nicole; m. Thomas E. Sorge, May 16, 1997; children: Natalie MaKalen Sorge, Ryan Thomas. AS, Roger Williams Coll., 1978, BS cum laude, 1980. Office mgr. Price-Rite Printing Co., Dover, NJ, 1975—76; cons. SBA, Bristol, RI, 1978—80; account exec. P.M. Press Inc., Dallas, 1980—90, sales trainer, 1984—85; v.p. KDF Bus. Forms Inc., Dallas, 1984—90; account exec. Jarvis Press, Dallas, 1990—; pres. Print Trends, Dallas, 1990—. Printer Tex. Aux. Charity Auction Orgn., Dallas, 1985, Cystic Fibrosis, Dallas, 1989—93, Life Enhancement Assn. Programs Found., 1992—, Dallas Soc. Visual Comm., 1992, AIDS Resources Com., Dallas chpt. Cerebral Palsy, 1994, Lloyd-Paxton AIDS Benefit, 1994, Feast for the Eyes Gala-Benefit to Prevent Blindness, 2001, Genesis Women's Shelter, 2002, others. Recipient award, Clampitt Paper Co., Dallas, 1982, P.M. Press Inc., 1983—89, Mead Paper Co., 1985—96, Feast for the Eyes Gala, 2001, Gold award, Adrian Advt., 2004, Silver award, 2005, 2006. Mem. Printing Industry in Am. (recipient Judges Favorite award 1992, Best of Show Hon. Mention award 1994, gold award Best of Tex. 1996), Internat. Assn. Bus. Communicators, Nat. Bus. Forms Assn. Republican. Baptist. Avocation: piano. Home: 2600 Raintree Dr Southlake TX 76092-5536 Office Phone: 817-424-5252. E-mail: printtrends@aol.com.

**SORGENFREI, ROBERT L.,** retired trust company executive; b. Wawaka, Ind., Sept. 25; s. Harold and Flo Sorgenfrei; children: Robert, John. LLB, Ind. U., 1953. Trust coun., mgr. trust legal divisn. Security Pacific Nat Bank, LA, 1975—84, assoc. trust coun., 1962—75.

**SORGI, LEONARD,** lawyer; b. Bklyn., Sept. 4, 1959; BS in Mech. Engring., Polytechnic U., NY, 1982; JD cum laude, NY Law Sch., 1987. Bar: NY 1988, NJ 1988, registered: US Dist. Ct. (So. Dist.) NY 1988, US Dist. Ct. (Ea. Dist.) NY 1988, US Dist. Ct. NJ 1988, US Ct. Appeals Fed. Cir., US Ct. Appeals (11th Cir.), US Patent & Trademark Office. Ptnr., intellectual property dept. Schulte Roth & Zabel LLP, NYC. Contbr. articles to profl. jour.; spkr. in field; editor: NY Law Sch. Law Rev., 1985—86. Mem.: Am. Intellectual Property Lawyers Assn., Licensing Exec. Soc., ABA, NY County Bar Assn., Am. Soc. Mech. Engrs. (chmn. NY Chpt. Govn. Relations Com. 2000—03). Office: Schulte Roth & Zabel LLP 919 Third Ave New York NY 10022 Office Phone: 212-756-2545. Office Fax: 212-593-5955. Business E-Mail: leonard.sorgi@srz.com.

**SORGI, MERCEDES PRIETO,** psychologist; b. Havana, Cuba, Sept. 8, 1953; came to the U.S., 1961; d. Roberto Isaac and Dora Natalia (Fernandez) Prieto; m. John David Sorgi, Sept. 2, 1978; children: James, John, Roberto. BA in Psychology, Vanderbilt U., 1974; MA in Spl. Edn., George Peabody Coll., 1976; EdS in Spl. Edn., U. Miami, 1978; PhD in Sch. Psychology, Kent State U., 1994—. Cert. sch. psychologist, Ohio. Lead tchr. Mailman Ctr. for Child Devel., Miami, Fla., 1976, parent tng. coord., 1976-78; owner, buyer, salesperson The Land of Make Believe Shop, Hudson, Ohio, 1979-87; pre-sch. owner Mother's Day Out, Hudson, 1984-87; Open Doors program dir. Hattie Larlham Found., Mantau, Ohio, 1986-91, dir. cmty. alternatives, 1988-92; pvt. cons. N.E. Ohio Agys., 1992-93; sch. psychology intern Orange (Ohio) Sch. Dist., 1996-97; sch. psychologist Seton Elem. Sch., Hudson, 1997-98; tchg. fellow Kent State U., 1997-99; bilingual sch. psychologist Cleve. City Schs., 1998—. Bd. mem., chair various coms. Summit County Assn. for Retarded Citizens, Akron, Ohio, 1980—; mem. adv. bd. Pre-Sch. Parents Assn., Hudson, 1982-85, Chem. Abuse Reduction Through Edn., Hudson, 1983-85; founding mem., chair Hattie Larlham League Hudson, 1985—. Mem. Rep. Women's League, Hudson, 1983-94; coun. mem. St. Mary Parish Coun., Hudson, 1985-88. Mem. APA, Nat. Assn. Sch. Psychologists, Ohio Assn. Sch. Psychologists, Cleve. Assn. for Sch. Psychologists, Support Spl. Edn. in Hudson (founder), Grad. Orgn. Sch. Pscyhology Studies (founder, chair). Roman Catholic. Avocations: gardening, horses, antiques. Home: 333 Aurora St Hudson OH 44236-2917

**SORIANO, ALFONSO GUILLEARD,** professional baseball player; b. San Pedro De Macoris, Dominican Republic, Jan. 1, 1978; Profl. baseball player N.Y. Yankees, 1999—2003, Texas Rangers, 2003—05, Wash. Nationals, 2005—. Named All-Star Game MVP, 2004; named to Am. League All-Star Game, 2002—04; recipient Silver Slugger award, MLB, 2005. Achievements include led Am. League in Hits (209), Runs 128, and Stolen Bases (41), 2002. Office: Wash Nationals RFK Stadium 2400 E Capitol St Washington DC 20003*

**SORIANO, NANCY MERNIT,** editor-in-chief; married; 1 child. Degree in Art History, Bard Coll. Former editor Good Food; former contbg. editor Cosmopolitan, Food & Wine, Brides; joined Country Living, 1982, assoc. decorating editor, home bldg. and arch. editor, exec. editor, 1995—98, editor-in-chief, 1998—. Founder Country Living Restoration Mag., 1996. Design editor (book series) American Country Design, Time Life Books, editor spl. interest publ. Country Living Dream Homes; co-author: (books) Country Living Decorating Style: The New Look of Country, 1999, Country Living Decorating with Baskets: Accents for Every Room, 2000, Country Living Decorating with Candles, 2000, Country Living Handmade Christmas: Decorating Your Tree and Home, 2001, Country Living Handmade Halloween, 2002, Stylish Renovations: Design Ideas for Old and New Houses, 2002. Office: Heart Corp Country Living 224 W 57th St Fl 7 New York NY 10019-3212*

**SORKIN, AARON,** scriptwriter, television producer, playwright; b. NYC, June 9, 1961; m. Julia Bingham, Apr. 13, 1996 (div. 2006); 1 child, Roxy. Student, SUNY, Purchase; BFA in Musical Theatre, Syracuse U. Creator, prodr. (TV series) Sports Nights, 1998—2000 (Humanitas prize 1999); creator, writer, exec. prodr.: TV series The West Wing, 1999—2003 (Emmy award for Best for Outstanding Writing in a Drama Series, 2000, 2001, 2002, 2003, Humanitas prize, 2000, 2002, Writer Guild Am. award, 2001, Television Prodr. of the Yr. Producers Guild Am. Golden Laurel award, 2002); creator, writer, exec. prodr. (TV series) Studio 60 on the Sunset Strip, 2006—; writer: screenplays A Few Good Men, 1992, Malice, 1993; writer: (films) The American President, 1995; writer: Broadway plays A Few Good Men, 1989 (Outer Critics Circle award as Outstanding American Playwright, 1989), Hidden in this Picture, 1990, Making Movies, 1992. Office: Endeavor Talent Agy # 1000 9701 Wilshire Blvd Beverly Hills CA 90212*

**SORKIN, ALAN LOWELL,** economist, educator; b. Decatur, Ill., Nov. 2, 1941; s. Martin and Sally Eileen (Steinberg) S.; m. Sylvia Jean Smardo, Sept. 9, 1967; children: David, Suzanne. BA, Johns Hopkins U., 1963, MA, 1964, PhD, 1966. Rsch. assoc. Brookings Instn., Washington, 1967-69; asst. prof. internat. health and econs. Johns Hopkins U., Balt., 1969-72, assoc. prof. internat. health and econs., 1972-74, adj. prof. dept. internat. health Sch. Hygiene and Pub. Health, 1986—; prof., chmn. dept. econs., 1974—; also adj. prof. preventive and social medicine Med. Sch. U. Md., 1974—. Author: Education, Unemployment and Economic Growth, 1974, Health Economics: An Introduction, 1975, 2d edit., 1983, 3d edit., 1992. The Urban American Indian, 1978, Economic Aspects of Natural Hazards, 1982, Health Care and the Changing Economic Environment, 1986, Monetary and Fiscal Policy and Business Cycles in The Modern Era, 1988, Public Health and Development,

1988, (with others) Female Labor Force and Development, 1990, Nutrition, Food Policy and Development, 1995, (with Irina Farquhar) Economic and Social Aspects of Occupational and environmental Health, 1998, others; contbr. articles to profl. jours. Mem. Am. Econs. Assn., Phi Beta Kappa, Delta Omega. Republican. Lutheran. E-mail: sorkin@umbc2.umbc.edu, asorkin@jhsph.edu Home: 1694 Campbell Rd Forest Hill MD 21050-2342 Office: U Md Dept Econ 5401 Wilkens Ave Baltimore MD 21250-1000 Office Phone: 410-455-2173. Business E-Mail: sorkin@umbc.edu. *Personal relationships are more important than material possessions. Persons with many friends have a sense of well-being that can never be embodied in materialism.*

**SORKIN, ANDREW ROSS,** reporter, columnist; b. Feb. 19, 1977; BS, Cornell U., 1999. European mergers and acquisitions reporter NY Times, London, 1999—2000, chief mergers and acquisitions reporter, 2000—, columnist SundayBusiness; founding editor DealBook (online financial report published by the Times). Frequent guest appearances on (NBC) Today Show, (PBS) The NewsHour with Jim Leher, (PBS) The Charlie Rose Show, (CNBC) Kudlow & Cramer.(CNBC) Closing Bell, (MSNBC) Abrams Report, (NPR) Talk of Nation, (BBC) World Service and several others. Named one of 30 Most Influential Fin. Journalists in the Nation Under the Age of 30, TJFR/NewsBios; recipient Gerald Loeb award, 2005. Office: NY Times 229 W 43rd St New York NY 10036 Office Phone: 212-556-7395. Office Fax: 212-556-1967. E-mail: sorkin@nytimes.com.*

**SORKIN, DAVID JAMES,** lawyer; b. NYC, June 26, 1959; BA, Williams Coll., 1981; JD, Harvard U., 1984. Bar: NY 1985. Law clk. judge Charles M. Merrill U.S. Ct. Appeals 9th Cir., San Francisco, 1984-85; assoc. Simpson Thacher & Bartlett, N.Y.C., 1985-92, ptnr., 1993—. Office: Simpson Thacher & Bartlett 425 Lexington Ave Fl 15 New York NY 10017-3954 Office Phone: 212-455-3387. Business E-Mail: DSorkin@stblaw.com.

**SORKIN, IRA LEE,** lawyer; b. NYC, May 30, 1943; s. Nathan and Rosalie (Cohen) S.; m. Ellen M. Sorkin, Aug. 24, 1969; children: Roger David, Peter Neil. BA, Tulane U., 1965; JD, George Washington U., 1968. Trial atty. SEC, N.Y.C., 1968-71, administr., 1984-86; asst. U.S. atty. U.S. Atty.'s Office (so. dist.) N.Y., 1971-76, dep. chief, criminal divsn., 1976; ptnr. Squadron Ellenoff Plesent & Lehrer, N.Y.C., 1977-84, Squadron Ellenoff Plesent & Sheinfeld, N.Y.C., 1986—95, Squadron, Ellenoff, Plesent & Sheinfeld LLP, N.Y.C., 1997—2002; chief legal officer Nomura Securities Internat. Inc., N.Y.C., 1995-97; ptnr. Carter, Ledyard & Milburn LLP, N.Y.C., 2002—. Lectr. Nat. Inst. Trial Advocacy, N.Y.C., 1981-91, Securities Industry Assn. Contbr. articles to profl. jours. Tutor inner city students N.Y.C. Sch. Sys., 1996-97. Mem. ABA, N.Y. Coun. Def. Lawyers, Assn. of the Bar for the City of N.Y. Avocations: golf, reading, skiing. Office: Carter Ledyard & Milburn LLP 2 Wall St New York NY 10005 E-mail: sorkin@clm.com.

**SORKIN, JENNI,** curator, critic; b. Chgo. BFA, Sch. of Art Inst. of Chgo., 1999; MA, Bard Coll., 2002; student PhD program in History of Art, Yale U., 2004—. Former curatorial rsch. asst., project coord. Mus. Contemporary Art, LA; former rsch. asst. Dept. Contemporary Programs and Rsch. Getty Rsch. Inst. Curator (exhibitions include) High Performance: The First Five Years, 1978-1982, Bard Coll., 2002, LA Contemporary Exhibitions, 2003, Judy Chicago: Minimalism, 1965-1973, LewAllen Contemporary, Santa Fe, 2004. Recipient Art Jour. Award for article Envisioning High Performance, Coll. Art Assn., 2004. Mem.: Queer Caucus for Art (co-chair 2004—). Office: Yale U Hist of Art Dept 56 High St New Haven CT 06520

**SORKIN, LAURENCE TRUMAN,** lawyer; b. Bklyn., Oct. 20, 1942; s. Sidney and Lilly (Kowensky) S.; m. Joan Carol Ross, June 25, 1972; children: Andrew Ross, Suzanne Ross. AB summa cum laude, Brown U., 1964; LLB, Yale U., 1967; LLM, London Sch. Econs./Polit. Sci., 1968. Law clk. to Judge J. Joseph Smith U.S. Ct. Appeals (2d cir.), 1968-69; assoc. Cahill Gordon & Reindel, N.Y.C., 1969-75, ptnr., 1975—. Vis. lectr. Yale U., 1972, 73; lectr. various profl. orgns.; rsch. asst. to Lester and Bindman for book Race and Law in Great Britain, 1972. Contbr. to State Antitrust Law (Lifland), 1984; author: (with Lifland, Sorkin and Van Cise) Understanding the Antitrust Laws, 1986; mem. bd. editors Antitrust Report, 2004—. Bd. dirs. Legal Aid Soc., N.Y.C., 1988-94, N.Y. Lawyers for Pub. Interest, 1990-93. Fulbright scholar, 1967-68. Mem. ABA (antitrust law sect. 1978—), N.Y. State Bar Assn. (antitrust sect., chmn. com. on legislation 1978-79, sect. sec. 1979-80, chmn. com. on mergers 1987-89, chmn. Clayton Act com. 1989-94, exec. com. 1989-94, council and fed. litigation sect. chmn. com. antitrust 1996-98), Assn. Bar City N.Y. (com. trade regulation 1974-77, 95-98, com. on electric funds transfer 1979-80), Yale Law Sch. Assn. (exec. com. 1994—), Phi Beta Kappa. Office: Cahill Gordon & Reindel 80 Pine St Fl 17 New York NY 10005-1702 Office Phone: 212-701-3209. E-mail: lsorkin@cahill.com.

**SORLEY, REBECCA ELLEN,** music educator; b. Indpls., June 25, 1964; d. Robert Joe and Carolyn McKinney; m. Darin Scott Sorley, June 7, 1986; children: Allegra Virginia, Alexander Michael, Adam Benjamin. MusB in Piano Performance, Butler U., 1986; MusM in Piano Performance, Ind. U., 1988; ArtsD in Piano Performance, Ball State U., Muncie, Ind., 1996. Adj. instr. Earlham Coll., Richmond, Ind., 1994—96, Ind. U. Sch. Music, Indpls., 1996—97; asst. prof. U. Indpls., 1993—. dir. Cmty. Music Ctr., 1999—. Founder Piano Camp U. Indpls., 1994; founder Music Children Concert Series, 1999—; founder, dir. Chamber Music Inst., 2001—; presenter in field. Benefit recitals participant Riley Hosp. Children, Indpls., 2002, Spl. Olympics, Indpls., 2003—, Easter Seals, Indpls., 2003, Indpls. Symphony Orch., 2005, Music Acad. Scholarship, Greenwood, 2005; organist, choir dir. Wallace St. Presbyn. Ch., Indpls., 1991—2001; dir. worhsip and music Ctr. Grove Presbyn. Ch., Greenwood, Ind., 2002—04, dir. Music Acad., 2002—. Grantee, Target Corp., 2002, 2003. Mem.: Indpls. Piano Tchrs. Assn., Internat. Alliance Women in Music, Coll. Music Soc. (campus rep. 2002—), Mu Phi Epsilon (pres. Kappa chpt 1993—96, prov. alumni chpt. 2001—03). Avocations: running, bicycling, reading. Office: U Indpls Music Dept 1400 E Hanna Ave Indianapolis IN 46227

**SOROKO, JOHN J.,** lawyer; b. NYC, May 13, 1951; AB, Haverford Coll., 1973; JD, NYU, 1977. Bar: Pa. 1977, U.S. Ct. Appeals 3rd Cir., US Ct. Appeals 4th Cir., US Dist. Ct. Ea. Dist. Pa. Assoc. Duane Morris LLP, Phila., 1977—84, ptnr., 1985—, mem. firm partners bd., 1996—, chair trial dept., 2002—. Arbitrator Phila. Stock Exchange; mem. editl. bd. The Legal Intelligencer. Mem. Phila. Vol. Lawyers for the Arts. Mem.: ABA, The Federalist Soc. for Law & Pub. Policy Studies (co-founder & chmn. Phila. Lawyers' Chpt.), Phila. Bar Assn., Pa. Bar Assn.

**SOROKOWSKI, ANDREW DENNIS,** lawyer, researcher; b. Hartford, Conn., Aug. 29, 1950; s. George Wsewolod and Nadia Sorokowski; m. Oksana Bachynska, Mar. 5, 1993. BA, U. Calif., Berkeley, 1972; MA, Harvard U., 1975; JD, Hastings Coll., 1979; PhD, U. London, 1991. Bar: Calif. 1980. Mem. rsch. staff Keston Coll., Kent, U.K., 1984—87; dir. rsch. and documentation Archdiocese of L'viv, Rome, 1989—90; atty. Jaffe, Trutanich, Scatena & Blum, San Francisco, 1990—93; mng. editor, rsch. assoc. Harvard Ukrainian Rsch. Inst., Cambridge, Mass., 1993—97; instr. St. Basil Coll., Stamford, Conn., 1998—99; adj. lectr. U. Mass., Boston, 1999—2000; hist. rsch. specialist U.S. Dept. Justice, Washington, 2000—. Dir. Ukrainian Patrirchal Soc. Jour. Found., N.Y.C., 2005—. Editor: A Millennium of Christian Culture in Ukraine, 1988; co-editor: A Thousand Years of Christianity in Ukraine, 1988. Sec. Shevchenko Sci. Soc., Washington, 2001; bd. dirs. The Washington Group, 2001. Grantee, Internat. Rsch. Exchg Bd., Poland, 1988. Mem.: Am. Cath. Hist. Assn., Am. Ukrainian Studies. Office: US Dept Justice NNRD-EDS PO Box 23986 Washington DC 20026-3986

**SOROS, GEORGE,** pension fund administrator; b. Budapest, Hungary, Aug. 12, 1930; came to U.S., 1956; s. Tivadar and Elisabeth (Szucs) S.; m. Annaliese Witschak, Sept. 17, 1960 (div. June 1983); children: Robert, Andrea, Jonathan; m. Susan Weber, June 19, 1983; children: Alexander, Gregory. BS, London Sch. Econs., 1952; LLD (hon.), New Sch. for Social

Rsch., 1990; D. Civil Law, U. Oxford, Eng., 1990; LHD (hon.), Yale U., 1991. Arbitrage trader F.M. Mayer, NYC, 1956-59; analyst Wertheim & Co., NYC, 1959-63; v.p. Arnhold and S. Bleichroeder, NYC, 1963-73; sole proprietor Soros Fund Mgmt., NYC, 1973—; chmn. Soros Fund Mgmt., LLC, NYC, 1996—. Author: The Alchemy of Finance, 1987, 2nd edit., 1994, Opening the Soviet System, 1990, Underwriting Democracy, 1991, Soros on Soros: Staying Ahead of the Curve, 1995, The Crisis of Global Capitalism: Open Society Endangered, 1998, Open Society: Reforming Global Capitalism, 2000, George Soros on Globalization, 2002, The Bubble of America Supremacy: Correcting the Misuse of American Power, 2004, The Age of Fallibility: Consequences of the War on Terror, 2006; contbr. articles to mags. and newspapers Mem. Coun. on Fgn. Rels., N.Y.C., 1988—; Royal Inst. Internat. Affairs, London, 1990—; Bretton Woods Com., Washington, 1989; mem. exec. com. Helsinki Watch, N.Y.C., 1982—; mem. com. Americas Watch, N.Y.C., 1982—; chmn., founding pres. Ctrl. European U., Budapest, 1991; chmn. Open Soc. Fund, 1981, Open Soc. Inst., 1993, founds. in Albania, Belarus, Bosnia and Herzegovina, Bulgaria, Croatia, Czech Republic, Estonia, Georgia, Hungary, Kazakhstan, Kyrgyestan, Latvia, Lithuania, Macedonia, Moldova, Poland, Romania, Russia, Slovakia, Slovenia, South Africa, Rroma, Ukraine, Yugoslavia. Recipient honor Lawyers Co.for Human Rights, N.Y.C., 1990; named one of World's Richest People, Forbes mag., 2005, Forbes Richest Americans, 2006. Avocations: tennis, skiing, chess, backgammon. Office: Soros Fund Mgmt 888 7th Ave Ste 3300 New York NY 10106-0001*

**SORRELL, MICHAEL E.,** consulting company executive, hospitality executive; b. Pasadena, Calif., Mar. 31, 1945; s. James Hendrick Sorrell and Marie Vivian Bristow. AA, Normandale C.C.; BA, Concordia Coll. Pres., CEO, owner Daggers/La. Inc., Metairie, 1987-89, Mesa Cons. Svcs./MN/Inc., Mpls., 1989-94, Mesa Cons. Svcs., Inc., Las Vegas, 1994—; pres., CEO, majority ptnr. S&W Hospitality Group, Inc., Las Vegas, 1999—; ptnr., dir. Sr. Owl Inc., 1999—; chmn., CEO Bristow-Norwich Internat. Corp., 2000—. With USAF, 1963-69, USN, 74-89. Mem. VFW, Nat. Rifle Assn. Small Bus., Nat. Lic. Beverage Assn., Inst. Mgmt. Cons., Soc. Human Resources Mgmt., Soc. Hospitality Cons., Am. Legion, Fleet Res. Assn., Navy League US, U.S. Naval Inst., Amateur Athletic Union of U.S., Marines' Meml. Club, Victory Svcs. Club Roman Catholic. Avocations: golf, hiking, tennis. Office: Bristow-Norwich Internat Corp 3888 W Sahara Ave Ste 33 Las Vegas NV 89102-0505 Office Phone: 702-364-0989. Business E-Mail: mesaconsultant@aol.com, bristownorwich1@aol.com.

**SORRELL, ROZLYN,** singer, actress, educator, theater director; b. Bklyn. d. Nathaniel Otis and Cupid Viola (Logan) S. BA in Theatre, CUNY, 1976, MS in Edn., 1985. Cert. tchr. Calif., N.Y. Tchr. LA Unified Sch. Dist., 1997, Sylvan Learning Ctr., LA, 1998, Westmark Sch., Encino, Calif., 2000, Achievement Sch., Raleigh, NC, 2002, Easter Seals UCP, NC, 2006. Bus. cons., LA, 1989—; voice tchr., LA, 1992—; mem. Albert McNeil Jubilee Singers, LA, 1994—2000. Actress various TV programs, commls., stage prodn. and films, 1986—; soloist Temple of Music and Art, Tucson, 1990, El San Juan (PR) Hotel, 1985, Hour of Power, Glory of Christmas, Glory of Easter, Garden Grove, Calif., 1994—, Miyazaki Civic Culture Hall, Japan, 1996, Anaheim Pond, Calif., 1997, Honolulu Symphony, 1998, Hollywood Bowl, Calif., 1998, Gospel Recording Artist, 2000, Harris Teeter Harvest Festival, Raleigh Conv. Ctr., 2004, Carolina Theatre, Durham, NC, 2005, Spiritual Awakening, WRAL-TV, NC, 2004, Pops in the Park, Regency Theatre, Cary, NC, 2004, 05, 06, African Am. Cultural Ctr., Raleigh, NC, 2004, Greensboro Coliseum, 2005, Progress Energy Ctr. Performing Arts, Meymandi Concert Hall, Raleigh, NC, 2006, N.C. Fairgrounds, 2006; guest artist, soloist N.C. Symphony, 2006; dir. Storms of Life, 2005. Mem. AFTRA, SAG, Actors Equity Assn. Avocations: dance, walking, theater, exercise. Office Phone: 866-686-0713. Personal E-mail: rozlyn@rozlynsorrell.com. Business E-Mail: sorrell@sorrel-intl.com.

**SORRELL, WILLIAM H.,** state attorney general; b. Burlington, Vt., Mar. 9, 1947; s. Marshal Thomas and Esther Sorrell; children: McKenzie, Thomas. AB, U. Notre Dame, 1970; JD, Cornell U., 1974. Dep. state's atty. Chittenden County State of Vt., 1975—77, state's atty. Chittenden County, 1977—78, 1989—92; ptnr. McNeil, Murray & Sorrell, 1978—89, sec. adminstrn., 1992—97; atty. gen. State of Vt., 1997—. Pres. United Cerebral Palsy Vt.; sec. Vt. Coalition Handicapped; bd. dirs Winooski Valley Pk. Dist., Am. Legacy Found. Mem.: Nat. Assn. Attys. Gen. (chmn., past pres.). Democrat. Office: Office Atty Gen 109 State St Montpelier VT 05609-0001 Office Phone: 802-828-0269. Business E-Mail: rhooker@atg.state.vt.us.

**SORRELLS, NANCY TAYLOR,** publishing executive, writer, historian; b. Washington, Mar. 23, 1959; d. John A. and Clara Tepfer Taylor; m. William (Randy) R. Sorrells, Jr., Aug. 1, 1981. BA in History summa cum laude, Bridgewater Coll., Va., 1981; MA in Local, Regional and State History, James Madison U., 1995, cert. in Secondary Edn. Tchg., 1988. Asst. sports editor Daily News Leader, Staunton, Va., 1981—88; rsch. historian Mus. Am. Frontier Culture, Staunton, 1988—98; head volleyball coach Stuarts Draft H.S., Stuarts Draft, Va., 1988—90; editor Va. Native Plant Soc., Boyce, Va., 1993—; ptnr. Lot's Wife Pub., Staunton, 1995—; bd. supr. Augusta County (Va.) Govt., 2004—. Chmn. comprehensive plan steering com. Augusta County Govt., Verona, Va., 2005—06; vice chmn. Augusta County Bd. Suprs., Verona, Va., 2006; mem. edn. and interpretation com. Shenandoah Valley Battlefields Found., New Market, Va., 1998—. Author (co-author): 11 Books; contbr. to newspapers and mags. (finalist Sportswriting award in 1988, Va. Press Assn. award, 1989). Mem. com. project impact disaster mitigation com. Ctrl. Shenandoah Planning Dist., Staunton, Va., 2002—; sec. Save Our Common Cons., Greenville, Va., 1998—. Scholar, George C. Marshall Libr., Va. Mil Inst. 1980. Mem.: Augusta County Hist. Soc. (bd. dirs 1990—, pres. 1998—99), Outdoor Writers Assn. Am., Va. Outdoor Writers Assn. (pres. 1994—2006, chmn. bd. 1999—2001, 7 awards), Rotary (exchange mem. to Japan 1998, newsletter editor 1998—, Paul Harris fellow 2005), Middlebrook Ruritan Club (assoc.), Alpha Theta, Alpha Chi. Avocations: bicycling, photography, travel, history, outdoor recreation. Home: 3419 Cold Springs Rd Greenville VA 24440 Office: Lot's Wife Publishing PO Box 1844 Staunton VA 24402 Office Phone: 540-377-6390. Business E-Mail: lotswife@adelphia.net.

**SORRIN, MARY LOUISE,** artist; b. Woodward, Okla., Mar. 9, 1946; d. Harland Ralph and Mary Elizabeth McCurdy; m. Bruce Michael Sorrin, Oct. 31, 1969; children: Aimee Lynn, Sean David, Keri Leigh. Diploma in nursing, St. John's Hosp., 1967; AA, Ulster County C.C., 1979. Exhbns. include Women Creating-A Celebration of Cape Cod Women, 1996-98, Leo Diehl Exhbn., 1996-98, Midwest Pastel Soc. Nat., 1996, Cape Cod Art Assn., 1997, 99 (1st pl. 1999), Newport Art Mus., 1998, Northwest Pastel Soc., 1998, Creative Arts Ctr., 1998, Internat. Assn. Pastel Soc., 1999, Northern Colo. Artist Assn., 1999, La Fond Galleries, 1999, Conn. Pastel Soc. (Bd. Dirs award 2000), Cape Cod Mus. Art, 2005, Truro Hist. Soc. and Mus., 2006, Pastel Soc. West Coast, Hudson Valley Art Assn., Pastel Soc. No. Fla., Pastel Painters Soc. Cape Cod, Pastel Soc. Southwest (Merit award), Pastel Soc. (Mountain High award 2001). Pres. chpt. Vietnam Veterans Am., 1985; treas. West Hurley (N.Y.) Libr. Assn. 1st lt. Army Nurse Corps, 1967-69. Mem. Pastel Painters Soc. Cape Cod (treas. 1994-98), Okla. Pastel Soc., Pastel Soc. Conn., Woodstock Artists Assn., Art Soc. Kingston. Democrat. Roman Catholic. Avocations: reading, movies, gardening. Office Phone: 845-331-2932. E-mail: mlouart@yahoo.com.

**SORSBY, JAMES LARRY,** home building company executive; b. Houston, May 31, 1955; s. J.B. Jr. and Viola (Lueckemeyer) S.; m. Terry Prince, July 28, 1984; children: Carson Drew, Cameron Brent. BBA, Stephen F. Austin State U., 1977. Loan officer 1st Mortgage Co. Tex., Houston, 1977-82; pres. The MortgageBanque, Inc., Houston, 1982-88; sr. v.p., treas. Hovnanian Enterprises, Inc., Red Bank, N.J., 1988-2000, CFO, treas., 2000—. Bd. dirs. Am. S.W. Fin. Corp., Phoenix. Office: Hovnanian Enterprises Inc 10 Highway 35 PO Box 500 Red Bank NJ 07701

**SORSTOKKE, ELLEN KATHLEEN,** marketing executive, educator; b. Seattle, Mar. 31, 1954; d. Harold William and Carrol Jean (Russ) Sorstokke. MusB with distinction, U. Ariz., 1976; postgrad., UCLA Extension, 1979-83, L.A. Valley Coll., 1984-85, Juilliard Extension, fall 1987, U. Calif. Berkeley Extension, 1992-93. Pvt. practice music tchr., Tucson, 1975—77, Whiteriver, Ariz., 1977—78, L.A., 1980—85, S.I., N.Y.C., 1986—89; music tchr. Eloy (Ariz.) Elem. Schs., 1976-77, Whiteriver (Ariz.) Pub. Schs., 1977-78; svc. writer, asst. svc. mgr. Alfa of Santa Monica, Calif., 1978-79; purchasing agt. Advance Machine Corp., L.A., 1979-80; asst. mgr. Atlantic Nuclear Svcs., Gardena, Calif., 1980-81; mgr. Blue Lady's World Music Ctr., L.A., 1981-83; instrument specialist Baxter-Northup Music Co., Sherman Oaks, Calif., 1983-85; dir. mktg. Mandolin Bros., Ltd., S.I., 1985-89; product mgr. Gibson Guitar Corp., Nashville, 1989; sales mgr. Saga Musical Instruments, South San Francisco, Calif., 1990-91, mktg. dir., 1991-95, mktg. analyst, 2002—. Freelance mktg. cons., S.I., Foster City, Atlanta, 1986—; freelance cons. www.fussycats.com, 2002; music cons. 20th Century Fox, L.A., 1984; freelance music copyist and orchestrator, Tucson, L.A., N.Y.C., 1972-89; freelance graphic designer and advt., S.I., Foster City, Atlanta, 1986—. Contbr. articles to profl. jours. Campaign worker Richard Jones for Supr., Tucson, 1972; mem., program book designer Marina Del Rey-Westchester Symphony Orch., L.A., 1981-83. Scholar U. Ariz., 1973-76, ASCAP scholar UCLA, 1980-81. Mem. Tucson Flute Club (publicity chmn. 1974-75, v.p. 1975-76). Republican. Personal E-mail: esorstok@bellsouth.net.

**SORSTOKKE, SUSAN EILEEN,** systems engineer; b. Seattle, May 2, 1955, d. Harold William and Carrol Jean (Russ) Sorstokke. BS in Systems Engring., U. Ariz., 1976; MBA, U. Wash., Richland, 1983. Warehouse team mgr. Procter and Gamble Paper Products, Modesto, Calif., 1976-78; quality assurance engr. Westinghouse Hanford Co., Richland, Wash., 1978-80, supr. engring. document ctr., 1980-81; mgr. data control and adminstrn. Westinghouse Electric Corp., Madison, Pa., 1981-82, mgr. data control and records mgmt., 1982-84; prin. engr. Westinghouse Elevator Co., Morristown, NJ, 1984-87, region adminstrn. mgr. Arleta, Calif., 1987-90; ops. rsch. analyst Am. Honda Motor Co. Inc., Torrance, Calif., 1990-95; project leader parts sys. Am. Honda Motor Co., Inc., Torrance, Calif., 1995-96, mgr. parts systems and part number adminstrn., 1996-97, mgr. parts systems, 1997-2000, mgr. supply chain mgmt., 2000—02, mgr. process control and regulatory issues, 2002—. Adj. prof. U. LaVerne, Calif., 1991—92; pres. Fussy Cuts Inc., Torrance, Calif., 2000—05. Advisor Jr. Achievement, 1982—83; literacy tutor Westmoreland Literacy Coun., 1983—84; host parent EF Found., Saugus, Calif., 1987—88, Am. Edn. Connection, Saugus, 1988—89, 1991; instr. Excell, L.A., 1991—92; mem. Calif. Acad. Math. and Sci., 1996—97. Mem.: Am. Inst. Indsl. Engrs., Soc. Women Engrs., Optomists Charities Inc. (bd. dirs. Acton, Calif. 1991—94). Republican. Methodist. Home: 2567 Plaza Del Amo Unit 205 Torrance CA 90503-8962 Office: Am Honda Motor Co Inc Dept Parts 100 5C 3B 1919 Torrance Blvd Torrance CA 90501-2722 Office Phone: 310-783-2854. Personal E-mail: ssorstokke@msn.com.

**SORTE, JOHN FOLLETT,** investment firm executive; b. Boston, June 30, 1947; s. Martin Eugene and Elizabeth Foster (Bradley) S.; m. Colleen Sarah Costello, July 28, 1979; children: Bradley Follett, Laura Elizabeth, Kathryn Clare. BAChemE, Rice U., 1969, M in Chem. Engring., 1970; MBA, Harvard U., 1972. Assoc. Shearson Hammill & Co., Inc., N.Y.C., 1972-74; v.p. Shearson Hayden Stone, Inc., N.Y.C., 1974-79; 1st v.p. Shearson Loeb Rhoades, Inc., N.Y.C., 1979-80, Drexel Burnham Lambert, Inc., N.Y.C., 1980-82, mng. dir., 1982-88, exec. v.p., 1989-90, pres., CEO, dir., 1990-92; pres., CEO New Street Capital Corp., N.Y.C., 1992-94; pres. New Street Advisors L.P., N.Y.C., 1994—2001; pres., CEO, dir. Morgan Joseph & Co Inc., N.Y.C., 2001—. Chmn. NY Media Group, Inc., 1995-2001; bd. dirs. Vail Resorts, Inc. Office: Morgan Joseph & Co Inc 600 Fifth Ave 19th Fl New York NY 10020-2302 E-mail: jsorte@morganjoseph.com.

**SORTER, BRUCE WILBUR,** federal program administrator, educator, consultant; b. Willoughby, Ohio, Sept. 1, 1931; s. Wilbur David and Margaret Louise (Palmer) S.; m. Martha Ann Weirich, Sept. 2,1960 (div. 1967); 1 child, David Robert. BA, U. Mich., 1967; MCP, Howard U., 1969; PhD, U. Md., 1972. Cert. community developer. Commd. USAFR, 1967, advanced through grades to lt. col.; 1964; sr. planner, cons. Md. Nat. Capital Park and Planning Com., 1968-71; instr. psychology, sociology Howard and P.G. C.C., Columbia and Largo, Md., 1971-72; cmty. resource devel. dept. Md. Coop. Extension Svc., U. Md., College Park, Md., 1972-92 coord. rural info. ctr. Md. Coop. Ext. Svc., U. Md., College Park, 1989-92; affiliate prof. U. Md., 1985-92, ret., 1996. Ext. advisor USDA Internat. Programs, Washington, 1991-96; co-author, co-dir. Dept. Edn. Coun. Effectiveness Tng. Program, 1979-81; author First County Energy Conservation Plan, Prince George's County, 1978-85. Author, co-author 12 books; contbr. articles to profl. publs., chpts. to books. Developer. Dir. teamwork tng. programs U.S. Dept. Edn., U.S. Dept. Agriculture, Brazil, Poland, Nat. Grange, 1972-92; cons. Fed. Power Commn. U.S., 1973-75, State Dept. Natural Resources, Md., 1978-79, Dept. Edn., Brazil, 1981-82, Nat. Grange, 1987, Edn. Ext. Svcs., Poland, 1991-92. Urban Planning fellow Howard U., 1968, Human Devel. fellow U. Md., 1970; recipient Meritorious Svc. award Dept. Def., 1983, Disting. Community Svc. award Md. Community Resource Devel. Assn., 1983, Citation for Outstanding Svc., Ptnrs. of Am., 1983, Excellence in Ednl. Programs award Am. Express, 1984, Project of Yr. award Am. Psychol. Assn., 1976, Award of Yr. Am. Vol. Assn., 1976, Achievement award Nat. Assn. of Counties, 1980, Outstanding Profl. award, U. Md., 2005. Mem. Internat. Cmty. Devel. Soc. (bd. dirs., Achievement award for outstanding contbn. to cmty. devel. 1985, Disting. Svc. award 1990), Md. Cmty. Resource Devel. Assn. (sec.-treas. 1979, pres. 1980, 88-89). Avocations: volunteer work, tennis, sailing, skiing. *Do the where you want to go. Ask yourself, is it worth the cost? If the answer is yes, then go with determination for time is in short supply.*

**SORTER, GEORGE HANS,** accounting and law educator, consultant; b. Vienna, Dec. 2, 1927; came to U.S., 1938; s. Alfred and Hertha (Kohn) S.; m. Dorienne Lachman, Aug. 18, 1966; children: David, Ivan, Adrienne. Ph.B., U. Chgo., 1953, MBA, 1955, PhD, 1963. C.P.A.; N.Y. Instr. U. Chgo., 1955-58, asst. prof., 1959-63, assoc. prof., 1963-65, prof., 1966-74; Vincent C. Ross prof. acctg., prof. of law NYU, 1974—2003, prof. emeritus, 2003— Arthur Young prof. U. Kans., 1969; Coopers & Lybrand prof. Tuck Sch. Dartmouth Coll., 1982; bd. dirs. NYU Credit Union, 1982-85; dir. Greater N.Y. Savs. Bank, N.Y.C., 1983-97; audit com. City of N.Y., 1985-94. Author: Accounting Theory, 1963, Accounting Thoughts of W.W. Werntz, Boundaries of Accounting Universe, 1978, Relevant Financial Statements, 1978, Financial Accounting: An Events and Cash Flow Approach, 1990, The Mix-Max Co., 1990. Mem. Ill. Sch. Bd. Dist. 233, Flossmoor, 1970-74; bd. dirs. Sch. Emotionally Disturbed Children, Chgo., 1974-76, Renaissance Soc., 1956-74, Found. Acctg. Edn., N.Y.C., 1975-79. Erskine fellow U. Canterbury, 1979 Mem. Am. Acctg. Assn. (v.p 1980-81 Outstanding Acctg. Educator), N.Y. State Soc. C.P.A.s (dir. 1980-82), Am. Inst. C.P.A.s, Fin. Acctg. Standard Adv. Com. Home: 375 S End Ave Apt 15E New York NY 10280 Office: NYU Tisch Hall 40 W 4th St New York NY 10012-1106

**SORTLAND, PAUL ALLAN,** lawyer; b. Powers Lake, ND, July 30, 1953; s. Allan Berdette and Eunice Elizabeth (Nystuen) S.; m. Carolyn Faye Anderson, June 23, 1979; children: Joseph Paul, Martha Marie, Nicholas John, Benjamin David. BA, St. Olaf Coll., 1975; JD, U. Minn., 1978. Bar: Minn. 1978, N.D. 1981, U.S. Dist. Ct. Minn. 1979, U.S. Dist. Ct. N.D. 1980, U.S. Ct. Appeals (8th cir.) 1987, U.S. Supreme Ct. 1991. Assoc. Alderson & Ondov, Austin, Minn., 1978-80, Qualley, Larson & Jones, Fargo, N.D., 1980-83; ptnr. Holand, Lochow & Sortland, Fargo, 1983-85; pres. Sortland Law Office, Fargo, 1985-88; ptnr. Messerli & Kramer, Mpls., 1988-92; pres. Sortland Law Office, Mpls., 1993—. Adj. prof. bus. law Moorhead State U., 1987. Mem. ATLA, ND Bar Assn., Minn. Bar Assn. (cert. civil trial specialist), Kiwanis, Million Dollar Advocates Forum, Upper Lake Minnetonka Yacht Club, Gamma Eta Gamma. Lutheran. Home: 120 Quebec Ave S Minneapolis MN 55426-1509 Office Phone: 612-375-0400. Business E-Mail: sortland@sortland.com.

**SORTORE, JEREMY,** vocalist, educator; b. Denver, Nov. 29, 1979; s. Sam Sortore and Lori Hermanson. MusB with high honors, U. of Colo., 2002, MusM, 2004. Instr. U. of Colo. Divsn. of Continuing Edn., Boulder, 2002—04; lectr. U. of Colo. at Denver, 2005. Translator: (opera titles) Italian and French libretti. Mem.: Nat. Assn. of Tchrs. of Singing. Personal E-mail: tenor@jeremysortore.com.

**SORTUN, ANA,** food service executive; b. Seattle; Fluency degree, L'Ecole Francais; grand diplome, La Varenne Ecole de Cuisine, Paris; diploma in Wine Studies, L'Academie du Vin. Pastry asst. and rounds cook with chef Tom Douglas Café Sport, Seattle; exec. chef Aigo Bistro, Concord, Mass., 1990; co-opener with Moncef Medeb 8 Holyoke, Cambridge, Mass.; exec. chef Casablanca, Cambridge; chef, owner Oleana, Cambridge, 2001—. Nominee Best New Restaurant, James Beard, 2002, Best Chef, Northeast, 2003, 2004; named Best New Chef, Boston Mag., Rising Star in the city's restaurant cmty., Esquire Mag.; recipient Best Chef, Northeast, 2005. Avocation: travel. Office: Oleana 134 Hampshire St Cambridge MA 02139 Office Phone: 617-661-0505. Business E-Mail: oleanarestaurant@earthlink.net.*

**SORUM, MATT,** drummer; b. Venice Beach, Calif., Nov. 19, 1960; Drummer The Cult, 1988—90, Guns N' Roses, 1990—96, The Cult, 1996—2002, Velvet Revolver, 2002. Musician: (albums) (with The Cult) Sonic Temple, 1989, (with Guns N' Roses) Use Your Illusion I, 1991, Use Your Illusion II, 1991, The Spaghetti Incident?, 1993, (with Slash's Snakepit) It's Five O' Clock Somewhere, 1995, (with Neurotic Outsiders) Neurotic Outsiders, 1996, (with Velvet Revolver) Contraband, 2004, (songs) (with The Cult) Fire Woman, 1989, (with Guns N' Roses) November Rain, 1991 (MTV Video Music awards Best Cinematography, 1992, one of 100 Greatest Videos Ever Made, MTV, 1999, one of 100 Greatest Videos, VH1, 2001); contbr. (albums) Y Can't Tori Read, 1988, (films) Interview with the Vampire, Grosse Point Blank, The Last Marshal, 1999, Me & Will, 1999, Fish in a Barrel, 2001, Now You Know, 2002, Pauly Shore Is Dead, 2003, Hulk, 2003; actor: (films) Bitter End, 1993, Soundman, 1998. Named Favorite Hard Rock Artist, Am. Music awards, 1992, World's Best Selling Hard Rock Artist of Yr., World Music awards, 1993; named an Top Pop Artists of Past 25 Yrs., VH1, 2004; named one of 100 Greatest Artists of Hard Rock, 2001, Sexiest Artists, 2002; recipient Video Vanguard award, MTV Video Music awards, 1992. Office: RCA Records 1540 Broadway New York NY 10036*

**SORVINO, MIRA,** actress; b. Tenafly, N.J., Sept. 28, 1967; d. Paul Sorvino and Lorraine Davis; m. Christopher Backus, June 11, 2004, children: Mattea Angel, Johnny BA in Asian Studies, Harvard U., 1990. Actor (films) New York Cop, 1993, The Obit Writer, 1993, Barcelone, 1994, Quiz Show, 1994, The Dutch Master, 1994, Mighty Aphrodite, 1995 (Acad. award for Best Supporting Actress), Blue in the Face, 1995, Beautiful Girls, 1996, Tarantella, 1996, Sweet Nothing, 1996, Tales of Erotica, 1996, New York Cop, 1996, Romy and Michele's High School Reunion, 1997, Mimic, 1997 The Replacement Killers, 1998, Too Tired to Die, 1998, Lulu on the Bridge, 1998, Free Money, 1998, Summer of Sam, 1999, At First Sight, 1999, Joan of Arc: The Virgin Warrior, 2000, Triumph of Love, 2001, The Grey Zone, 2001, Wise Girls, 2002, Semana Santa, 2002, Between Strangers, 2002, Gods and Generals, 2003, The Final Cut, 2003; actor, assoc. prodr., Amongst Friends, 1993; actor (TV movies) Parallel Lives, 1994, The Second Greatest Story Ever Told, 1994, Jake's Women, 1996, Norma Jean and Marilyn, 1996, The Great Gatsby, 2001, Human Tafficking, 2005; (TV mini-series) The Buccaneers, 1995, Covert One: The Hades Factor, 2006; (TV appearances) The Guiding Light, 1991, The Swans Crossing, 1992, 1995, Will & Grace, 2003; prodr. (films) Famous, 2000 Office: The William Morris Agy 151 El Camino Dr Beverly Hills CA 90212*

**SORVINO, PAUL,** actor; b. N.Y.C., 1939; Attended, Am. Musical and Dramatic Acad. Artistic dir. Am. Stage Co., Teaneck, NJ 1986-90. N.Y.C. stage debut in Bajour, 1964; actor in (plays) including The Baker's Wife, Mating Dance, Skyscraper, That Championship Season, King Lear, An American Millionaire, For My Last Number, We'll Get By, Philemon, (films) The Gambler, 1970, Where's Poppa, 1970, Panic in Needle Park, 1971, Cry Uncle, Made for Each Other, 1971, The Day of the Dolphin, 1973, A Touch of Class, 1973, I Will, I Will...For Now, 1976, Oh God!, 1977, The Brink's Job, 1978, Shoot It, Black, Shoot It, Blue, Slow Dancing in the Big City, 1978, The Bloodbrothers, 1979, Lost and Found, 1979, Cruising, 1980, Reds, 1981, That Championship Season, 1982, I, The Jury, 1982, Off the Wall, Turk 182, A Fine Mess, 1985, The Stuff, 1986, Vasectomy, 1986, Dick Tracy, 1990, Goodfellas, 1990, The Rocketeer, 1991, The Firm, 1993, Nixon, 1995, Romeo and Juliet, 1996, Love Is All There Is, 1996, Escape Clause, 1996, Dog Watch, 1996, Love is All There Is, 1996, Romeo and Juliet, 1996, Men with Guns, 1997, Money Talks, 1997, American Perfekt, 1997, Most Wanted, 1997, Bulworth, 1998, Knock Off, 1998, Ringside, 1999, That Championship Season, 1999, Prince of Central Park, 1999, Harlem Aria, 1999, Goodnight Joseph Parker, 1999, Dead Broke, 1999, Amati Girls, 2000, Family Man, 2000, Longshot, 2000, Perfume, 2001, See Spot Run, 2001, Plan B, 2001, Witches to the North, 2001, Rhode Island Blue, 2001, Irishman: The Legend of Danny Greene, 2001, Ciao America, 2002, Hey Arnold! (voice), 2002, The Cooler, 2003, Mambo Italiano, 2002, Goodnight, Joseph Parker, 2004, Mr. 3000, 2004; (TV miniseries) Seventh Avenue, 1977, (TV movies) Tell Me Where it Hurts, 1974, It Couldn't Happen to a Nicer Guy, 1974, Dummy, 1979, A Question of Honor, 1982, Chiefs, 1983, My Mother's Secret Life, 1984, With Intent to Kill, 1984, Surviving, 1985, Betrayed by Innocence, 1986, Don't Touch My Daughter, 1991, Perry Mason: The Case of the Wicked Wives, 1993, Parallel Lives, 1994, The Art of the Cigar (host), 1996, Joe Torre: Curveballs Along the Way, 1997, That Championship Season, 1999, The Thin Blue Lie, 2000, Mafia Doctor, 2003; (TV series) We'll Get By, 1975, Bert D'Angelo/Superstar, 1976, The Oldest Rookie, 1987, Law and Order, 1991-92, Star Trek: The Next Generation (guest appearance), 1994, That's Life, 2000-02. Office: Gersh Agy c/o Larry Taube 232 N Canon Dr Beverly Hills CA 90210-5302

**SOSA, ERNEST,** philosopher, educator; b. Cardenas, Cuba, June 17, 1940; s. Ernesto and Maria (Garriga) S.; m. Sara Mercedes, Dec. 21, 1961; children: E. David, Adrian J. BA, U. Miami, 1961; MA, U. Pitts., 1962, PhD, 1964. Instr. U. Western Ontario, London, Ont., Canada, 1963-64, U. Pitts., 1964; postdoctoral fellow Brown U., Providence, 1964-66; asst. prof. U. Western Ontario, London, Ont., 1966-67; asst. prof. to full prof. Brown U., Providence, 1967-74, chmn. of philosophy, 1970-76, full prof., 1974—; Romeo Elton prof., 1981—. Vis. prof. U. Miami, 1970, Nat. U. Mexico, 1979, 80, 81, Harvard U., Cambridge, Mass., 1982, U. Salamanca, 1995, 98, Oxford U., 1997; disting. vis. prof. Rutgers U., 1998—; John Locke lectr. Oxford U., 2004; co-chair program com. 20th World Congress of Philosophy, 1998. Author: Knowledge in Perspective, 1991; gen. editor book series, Cambridge Univ. Press, 1990—2002, Blackwell Publishers, 1991—; editor Philosophy and Phenomenol. Rsch.; co-editor: Nous; contbr. numerous articles to profl. jours. Grantee NSF, 1970-72, Exxon Ednl. Found., 1980-82; recipient Sr. fellowship NEH, 1988-89. Mem. Am. Acad. Arts and Scis., Am. Philos. Assn. (sec.-treas. 1974-82, chair internat. coop. com. 1984-89, ea. divsn. rep. 1995-98, pres. ea. divsn. 2004-05, v.p. ea. divsn. 2003-04 bd. chair 2005—), Am. Coun. Learned Socs./Soviet Acad. Commn., Internat. Fedn. Philos. Soc. (steering com. 1988-98, v.p. 1988-93), Institut Internat. de Philosophie (exec. com. 1993-96). Avocations: running, travel. Office: Brown U Dept Philosophy Providence RI 02912-0001 Business E-Mail: sosa@brown.edu.

**SOSA, FRANCISCO JAVIER,** music educator, consultant; b. Laredo, Tex., Sept. 16, 1963; s. Francisco and Elizabeth Morales Sosa; m. Patricia Ramirez, June 13, 1987; children: Elizabeth Marie, Francisco Javier III, Gerardo Reynaldo. BS in Music Edn., Tex. A&I U., 1985. Cert. all-level instrumental music edn. Tex., 1981. Student dir. Tex. A&I U. Mariachi Javelina, Kingsville, 1983—85; dir. bands Cotulla (Tex.) Ind. Sch. Dist., 1986—90; dir. band/fine arts master tchr. Raymond & Tirza Martin H.S., Laredo, Tex., 1990—. Condr./clinician Tulsa Sch. Districts All City Band, 2002; clinician Summer Mariachi Camp McAllen (Tex.) Ind. Sch. Dist., 2005. Dir. Kingsville (Tex.) Youth Mariachi, 1985; youth choir asst. dir. Our Lady of Guadalupe Ch., Laredo, 1999—2006; assoc. musical dir. San Martin de Porres Cath. Ch.,

Laredo, 1993—99. Mem.: Tex. Music Adjudicators Assn. (licentiate), Tex. Bandmasters Assn. (assoc.), Tex. Music Educators Assn. (assoc.; clinician/dir. group II Region XIV Mariachi 2005, condr./clinician jr. high concer band Region XV 2000), Phi Beta Mu. Democrat. Roman Catholic. Avocations: fishing, racquetball, guitar. Office: Raymond & Tirza Martin High School Band 2002 San Bernardo Ave Laredo TX 78040 Office Phone: 956-795-3880. Office Fax: 956-795-3860. Personal E-Mail: fjsosa2@yahoo.com. Business E-Mail: fsosa@elisd.org.

**SOSA, JORGE LUIS,** surgeon; s. Eduardo and Elsa Sosa; children: Sarah Elizabeth, Gladys Michelle. MD, U. South Fla., Tampa, 1987. Board Certified in Surgical Critical Care Am. Bd. of Surgery, 1994. Asst. prof. of surgery U. Miami Jackson Meml. Hosp., Fla., 1993—95; trauma attending Delray Hosp., Delray Beach, Fla., 1995—2002; surgeon, pres. Laparoscopic Inst. of South Fla., Hialeah, 1995—. Dir. bariatric surgery Hialeah Hosp., Fla., 2002—05, Palmetto Gen. Hosp., Hialeah, Fla., 2005—. Fellow: Am. Coll. Surgeons; mem.: Am. Soc. for Bariatric Surgery. Conservative. Office: Laparoscopic Inst S Fla 3499 W 4th Ave Ste 201 Hialeah FL 33012 Office Phone: 305-558-0411. Office Fax: 305-863-3802.

**SOSA, JOSEPH F.,** pharmaceutical executive; b. San Juan, Puerto Rico; BS, Drexel U., 1975. Various positions SmithKline Beecham Pharmaceuticals; mayor Burlington County cmty., Mt. Holly, NJ, 1990—92; rep. 7th legis. dist. NJ Gen. Assembly, 1992—94; dir. Johnson & Johnson, New Brunswick, NJ. Named one of Top 10 Latinos in Healthcare, LatinoLeaders mag., 2004. Office: Johnson & Johnson 1 Johnson & Johnson Plz New Brunswick NJ 08933*

**SOSA, LIONEL,** advertising executive; Co-founder Sosa, Bromley, Aguilar & Assoc.; chmn. DMB&B Americas, 1991—95; head Garcia LKS, 1995—2000. Media consultant Rep. presdl. campaigns, 1980—2004; fellow Inst. of Politics, Harvard Univ., 2001. Author: The Americano Dream: How Latinos Can Achieve Success in Business and in Life, 1998. Mem. bd. regents Tex. A&M Univ. Sys., 1999—2005; bd. mem. Am. Coll. Testing, AVANCE, Hispanic Scholarship Fund; mem. diversity adv. panel Eastman Kodak; past bd. vice chmn. Univ. of Incarnate Word; past chmn. San Antonio Symphony, United Way of San Antonio. Named one of 25 Most Influential Texans, Texas Monthly mag., 25 Most Influential Hispanics, Time Mag., 2005, 100 Most Influential Hispanics, Hispanic Bus. Mag.; named to Tex. Bus. Hall of Fame. Mailing: Texas A&M University System A&M System Bldg Ste 2043 200 Technology Way College Station TX 77845-3424

**SOSA, SAMMY (SAMUEL SOSA),** retired professional baseball player; b. San Pedro de Macoris, Dominican Republic, Nov. 12, 1968; With Tex. Rangers, 1989, Chgo. Cubs, 1992—2004, Balt. Orioles, 2005. Selected to N.L All-Star Team, 1995, 98-2002, 2004; led Nat. League in runs, 1998, 2001-2002; led Nat. League in home runs, 2000, 2002; led Nat. League in RBI's 1998, 2001; record for new major league baseball record for homeruns in a single month (21), 1998; single season club record of 35 homeruns at Wrigley Field, 1998; winner Roberto Clemente award for outstanding svc. to cmty. Major League Baseball, 1998. Achievements include hit 500th career home run, April 4, 2003.*

**SOSEMAN, ELEANOR DOUGLASS,** volunteer; b. Creston, Iowa, May 7, 1930; d. John Wayne and Ruby Neill Douglass; m. Floyd William Soseman, Jr., Aug. 17, 1952 (dec. Aug. 2003); children: Douglass John, Amy Lynn Stover, Elizabeth Kistenmacher, Thomas William. BA, Grinnell Coll., Iowa, 1952. Past mem. We. Iowa Tech. Adv. Bd., Sioux City. Co-editor: Holstein Centennial Book, 1982. Acative Girl Scouts USA, 1938—; trustee Stubbs Meml. Libr., Holstein, 1959—94; vol. Holstein Cmty. Betterment, 1984—87. Recipient Gov.'s Leadership award, Planning Coun., Holstein, 1982, Gov.'s Vol. award, Gov.'s Office, Des Moines, 2002. Mem.: AAUW, United Meth. Women, Gen. Fedn. Women Clubs, Philanthropic Ednl. Orgn. Sisterhood. Democrat. United Methodist. Avocations: reading, doll collecting, travel. Home: 510 E 2nd Box 470 Holstein IA 51025 Office: Agnew-Soseman Ins Holstein IA 51025

**SOSKIN, WILLIAM H.,** lawyer, accountant; m. Marian R. Penn; children: Joshua Penn, David Penn. Law, U. of Chgo. Cert. Pub. Accountant, Calif. Pvt. practice atty., Monterey, Calif. Bd. mem. Arkay Found., Carmel, Calif.; trustee Big Sur Land Trust, Carmel, Calif., 2002—05. Recipient AV Rating, Martindale-Hubbell Law Directory, Best Lawyer, The Best Lawyers in Am., Super Lawyer, No. Calif. Super Lawyers; fellow, Am. Coll. of Trust and Estate Counsel. Mem.: Monterey County Bar Assn., Calif. State Bar Assn. Office: Law Offices of William H Soskin 2100 Garden Rd Ste F Monterey CA 93940 Office Phone: 831-649-8006. Office Fax: 831-655-3432.

**SOSMAN, MARTHA B.,** state supreme court justice; b. Boston, Oct. 20, 1950; BA Middlebury Coll, JD U. Mich. Assoc. Foley, Hoag & Eliot, Boston, 1979—84; with U.S. Atty.'s office, Boston, 1984—89; founding ptnr. Kern, Sosman, Hagerty, Roach & Carpenter, Boston, 1989—93; apptd. judge Superior Ct., Concord, 1993—2000; assoc. justice Mass. Supreme Jud. Ct., 2000—. Mem. bd. directors Planned Parenthood League of Mass. Mem.: Mass. Bar Assn., Mass. Women's Bar Assn. Office: Supreme Judicial Court 1 Pemberton Sq Ste 2-500 Boston MA 02108-1717*

**SOSNA, MORTON PHILIP,** historian, academic administrator; b. Chgo., Apr. 26, 1945; s. Aaron and Rose Sosna; m. Barbara M. Moe, Dec. 17, 1971; children: Rachel Elizabeth Good, Emily Marie. BA, U. Ill., Chgo., 1967; MA, U. Wis., 1967, PhD, 1973. Program officer NEH, Washington, 1973—82; assoc. dir. humanities ctr. Stanford (Calif.) U., 1982—91, lectr. Am. studies, 1983—90; dir. found. rels. Cornell U., Ithaca, NY, 1992—. Vis. asst. prof. history U. Mo., Columbia, 1979—80; lectr. history George Mason U., Fairfax, Va., 1981. Author: In Search of the Silent South: Southern Liberals and the Race Issue, 1977; editor: Reconstructing Individualism: Autonomy, Individuality, and the Self in Western Throught, 2006; editor, contbr.: The Boundaries of Humanity: Humans Animals, Machines, 1990; contbr. articles to profl. publs. (William B. Hesseltine award for best article, 1971). Bd. dirs. Ctr. for Religion, Ethics, and Social Policy, Ithaca, 1993—2000. With USAR, 1969. Fellow, U. Wis., 1968—70. Mem.: Soc. Hist. Assn. (assoc.), Orgn. Am. Historians (assoc.). Avocations: tennis, basketball. Office: Cornell U 130 E Seneca St Ste 400 Ithaca NY 14850-4353 Office Phone: 607-254-7160. Office Fax: 607-254-7166. Business E-Mail: ms25@cornell.edu.

**SOSNICK, STEPHEN HOWARD,** economics educator; b. Portland, Oreg., Feb. 24, 1930; s. Benjamin and Natalie (Schmulowitz) S.; m. Galya Chernow, July 14, 1951; children:—Beryl, Elika, Randall, Tobin. A.B., U. Calif.-Berkeley, 1950, Ph.D., 1954. Instr. Princeton U., N.J., 1954-57; mem. faculty U. Calif., Davis, from 1957, now prof. emeritus, agrl. econs. Author: Hired Hands, 1978; Budget's New Clothes, 1971; also articles. Office: U Calif-Davis Dept Agrl Econs Davis CA 95616*

**SOSOKA, JOHN RICHARD,** consulting firm executive, engineer; b. LA, Nov. 30, 1929; s. John and Mary (Kovach) S.; m. Audrey T. Trezona, Apr. 26, 1952; children: John Richard Jr., Cathie Ann, Karen Elizabeth. BS in Gen. Engring., UCLA, 1952; MBA, CSULB, 1975. Registered mech., elec., fire protection, metallurgy, control systems and civil engr., Calif. Project engr. Stathem Instrument, L.A., 1954-55; staff engr. Aerojet Gen., Azusa, Calif., 1955-60; tech. dir. Unitek Corp., Monrovia, Calif., 1960-65; staff engr. TRW Systems, Redondo Beach, Calif., 1965-69; engr. mgr. AiResearch, Los Alamitos, Calif., 1969-70; sect. head City of Long Beach, Calif., 1970-79; pres. Sosoka & Assocs., Los Alamitos, Calif., 1990-91; exec. v.p. Sparvan, Inc., Long Beach, Calif., 1990-91; pres., CEO P2S Engring., Inc., Long Beach, Calif., 1991—2005; ret. Fellow ASHRAE (dir. and regional chair 1990-93, Disting. Svc. award 1988), Inst. Advancement Engring., L.A. Coun. Engrs. and Scientists (Disting. Engr. award); mem. Assn. Energy Engrs. (v.p. 1980-81, Energy Engr. of Yr. award 1985). Republican. Episcopalian. Achievements include patent in Welding. Home: 848 Roxanne Ave Long Beach CA 90815-5013 E-mail: john.sosoka@p2seng.com.

**SOSS, DANIEL LEE,** social work educator; b. Spokane, Wash., May 30, 1931; s. Walter Lee and Ethelyn F. (Daniel) S.; m. Dorine C., June 17, 1955; children: Nancy Lee, Mark Daniel, Shari Lee, Michael Wayne. BA, Ea. Wash. U., 1955; MSW, U. Wash., 1963. Asst. prof. emeritus Wash. State U., Pullman; adminstr. juvenile ct. Whitman County Superior Ct., Colfax, Wash.; pub. health adminstr. Thurston-Mason Health Dist., Olympia, Wash. Dir. social svcs. Nursing Home and Retirement Ctr. Mem. Nat. Eagle Scout Assn. Home: 2087 W Jester Way Post Falls ID 83854 Personal E-mail: dandee@adelphia.net.

**SOSTARIC, JOE ZELJKO,** research scientist; b. Carlton, Victoria, Australia, Aug. 16, 1970; s. Vinko and Milka Sostaric; m. Eri Miyagi, Nov. 30, 2002; 1 child, Emma Jewel. BSc with honors, U. Melbourne, Parkville, Victoria, Australia, 1993, PhD in Sci., 1999. Vis. fellow Nat. Cancer Inst., NIH, Bethesda, Md., 2000—2004; rschr. Ohio State U., Columbus, 2005—. Vis. fellow Fogarty Internat. Ctr., NIH, 1999—2004. Recipient Fellows award for rsch. excellence, Nat. Cancer Inst., NIH, 2004; Spl. Postgraduate studentship, U. Melbourne, 1994—99. Mem.: Soc. Free Radicals in Medicine and Biology, Internat. Soc. Therapeutic Ultrasound, European Soc. Sonochemistry, Am. Chem. Soc. Achievements include patents pending for methods and compositions for protecting cells from ultrasound mediated cytolysis; discovery of non-cytotoxic concentrations of n-alkyl glucopyranosides completely inhibit cytolysis induced by high intensity ultrasonic waves; dynamic accumulation of surfactants at the gas/solution interface of cavitation bubbles dictate the maximum attainable interfacial concentration; a frequency effect in sonochemistry that was independent of the ultrasound intensity. Office: Ohio State U DHLRI 420 W 12th Ave TMRF 184 Columbus OH 43212 Office Phone: 614-247-5020. Business E-Mail: sostaric.2@osu.edu.

**SOSTARICH, MARK EDWARD,** lawyer; b. Milw., Apr. 10, 1953; s. Edward Michael and Sophia (Hibler) S.; m. Karen Sue Baranek, June 12, 1976; children: Samantha Nicole, Alex Edward. BA with distinction, U. Wis., Madison, 1975, JD cum laude, 1978. Bar: Wis. 1978, U.S. Dist. Ct. (ea. and we. dists.) Wis. 1978, U.S. Trademark Trial and Appeal Bd. 1995. Assoc. Godfrey & Kahn, Milw., 1978-84, ptnr., 1984-96, Petrie & Stocking SC, Milw., 1997—2004; pvt. practice Elkhorn, 2004—. Editor-in-chief U. Wis. Law Rev., 1978, mem., 1977. Mem. bd. visitors U. Wis., Madison, 1983-88; commr. South Milw. Housing Authority, 1985-86; mem. South Milw. Fire and Police Commn., 1986-92, sec., 1987-91, pres., 1991-92; mem. Wis. Elections Bd., 1987-95, vice chmn., 1990, chmn., 1991; mem. Dem. Nat. Com., 1993, 1995-97; mem. platform and resolutions com. Wis. Dem. Party, 1984-97, 1st vice chmn., 1984, chmn., 1985-97; chmn. Wis. Dem. Party, 1995-97; mem. Assn. State Dem. Chairs., 1995-97; chmn. Milw. County Dem. Party, 1986-97, v.p., 2001, pres., 2001-04; mem., usher, HS Sunday sch. tchr., chmn. organ fundraising com. Trinity Luth. Ch., South Milw.; mem. bd. dirs. Arthritis Found. Wis., 2000-03. Mem.: ABA, Walworth County Bar Assn., 7th Cir. Ct. Appeals Bar Assn., Milw. Bar Assn., Wis. Bar Assn. Avocations: politics, photography, art. Home: 1785 Tamarack St South Milwaukee WI 53172-1048 Office: Law Offices Mark E Sostarich 6 South Church St Elkhorn WI 53121 Office Phone: 262-725-5041. Personal E-mail: msostarich@wi.rr.com. E-mail: msostarich@charterinternet.com.

**SOSTILIO, ROBERT FRANCIS,** office equipment maintenance consultant; b. Boston, Nov. 17, 1942; s. Natale J. and Louise Sostilio; m. Gail Marie McGuinness, Apr. 17, 1966. Student, U. Maine, 1960—61, Broward Jr. Coll., Ft. Lauderdale, 1967—70, Miami-Dade Jr. Coll., 1979. Product assurance engr. Saxon Copystatics, Miami, Fla., 1970-77; internat. svc. mgr. Saxon Export Corp., Miami, 1977-80; nat. svc. mgr. Cybernet Internat., Warren, N.J., 1980-81; mgr. nat. copier svc. Monroe Systems for Bus., Morris Plains, N.J., 1981-82; nat. OEM mgr. Panasonic Indsl. Co., Secaucus, N.J., 1982-86; assoc. dir. copier rsch. Dataquest, San Jose, Calif., 1987-90; mgr. product program Ricoh Corp., West Caldwell, N.J., 1986-87, dir. copier mktg., 1990-94, dir. strategic planning, 1994-96; group svc. dir. converging digital peripherals Cap Ventures, 1996—2000; pres., CEO Sostilio and Assocs. Internat. Inc., Ocala, Fla., 2002—. Editor: (newsletter) Multifunctionality, 1987, Color Copiers, 1989. Block capt. Meadow Ridge Civic Assn., Basking Ridge, NJ, 1985—87; sgt.-at-arms UNICO Nat., San Jose, 1990. With USN, 1964—67. Roman Catholic. Avocations: woodworking, home remodeling, dog breeding, travel, cooking. Office: Sostilio & Assocs Internat PO Box 830190 Ocala FL 34483 Office Phone: 352-624-2625. E-mail: sostilio@flash.net.

**SOSTMAN, DIRK,** medical educator; b. NYC, Nov. 20, 1948; s. Henry and Theodora (Slokker) S.; m. Maria Preka, Sept. 1, 2003. MD, Yale University, New Haven, 1977. Diplomate Am. Bd. Radiology, Nat. Bd. Med. Examiners. Intern and resident Yale-New Haven Hosp., 1977—82; prof., chair Weill Med. Coll. Cornell U., NYC, 1995—2005, exec. vice dean, 2003—; exec. v.p. The Meth. Hosp., Houston, 2005—; CEO Meth. Physician Orgn., 2006—. Mem. lung scan interpretation panel and nuclear medicine working group Prospective Investigation of Pulmonary Embolism Diagnosis Study, Nat. Heart, Lung and Blood Inst., 1984-88; cons. Fluoromed Pharms, 1988, Am. Cancer Soc., 1992; mem. Duke Comprehensive Cancer Ctr., 1993—; program dir. Duke Winter Imaging Course, 1993-94; vis. prof. U. Pisa, 1993, U. Milan, 1993; dir. Imaging Rsch. Lab. Yale U. Sch. Medicine, 1981-84, dir. MR Imaging, 1983-87; mem. numerous adv. panels. Assoc. editor: Yearbook of Nuclear Medicine, 1984-92; mem. editorial bd.: Investigative Radiology, 1984—, Magnetic Resonance Imaging, 1985—, Jour. Thoracic Imaging, 1985—; manuscript referee; contbr. chpts. to books and numerous articles to profl. jours. Recipient Fales prize Rutgers U., 1972, Dolgan Meml. award Yale U., 1972; Yale U. summer fellowship, 1975, Lamport Biomed. Rsch. award, 1976; Winchester Chest fellow in radiology; grantee in field. Fellow Am. Coll. Chest Physicians, Am. Coll. Radiology; mem. Soc. Body Computed Tomography/Magnetic Resonance, Am. Coll. Radiology, Fleischner Soc. (George Simon Meml. award 1982, exec. com. 1987-90, mem. Simon award com. 1991—), Soc. MRI (edn. com. 1984-86), Assn. Univ. Radiologists (Pres. 2001, Stauffer award 1988, Stauffer award com. 1983), Radiol. Soc. N.Am., Soc. Thoracic Radiology (founding mem.), Am. Roentgen Ray Soc., Soc. Nuclear Medicine, Sigma Xi, Phi Beta Kappa, others. Office: Dunn 200 6565 Fannin St Houston TX 77030 Office Phone: 713-441-2192. Business E-Mail: dsostman@tmh.tmc.edu.

**SOTELINO, GABINO,** chef; b. Vigo, Spain; Mem. staff Hotel Ritz, Madrid, Plaza Athanee, Paris, Koons Hotel, Switzerland, Hilton Internat. Hotels, Montreal Expo., Madison Hotel, Washington; exec. chef Capitol Hill Restaurants, Washington, Le Perrouquet, Chgo.; head chef The Pump Room, Chgo., 1980; owner, chef Ambria, Chgo., 1980—, Un Grande Cafe, Chgo., 1981—, Cafe Ba-Ba-Reeba!, Chgo., 1985—, Mon Ami, Chgo., 1998—. Named Chef of Yr., Chefs of Am., 1990; recipient Perrier-Jouet Chef of Midwest award, James Beard Found., 1997, Medalla Merito Nacional os Fpain, 1990, Academie Culinaire de France. Mem.: Euro-Toque Inc. (pres. U.S. chpt.), Grand Master Chefs Assn. (nat. chmn.), Commanderie des Corden Bleus de France. Office: Ambria 2300 N Lincoln Park W Chicago IL 60614

**SOTELO, EDUARDO (EL PIOLÍN),** radio personality; b. Ocotlán, Jalisco, Mexico, 1971; arrived in US. 1986, permanent resident, 1996; Broadcaster local radio stations, Calif. 1991—2003, KSCA FM101.9, LA, 2003—; with Univision Radio, LA, 2003—. Host (radio shows) Piolín por la Mañana, 2003—. Achievements include support and organization of demonstrations for immigrants' rights through radio broadcasts. Office: La Nueva #2500 655 N Central Ave Glendale CA 91203 Office Phone: 818-500-4500. Office Fax: 818-500-4550. E-mail: elshowdepiolin@univision.com.*

**SOTELO-DYNEGA, MARLENE,** psychologist; b. Flushing, NY, Sept. 16, 1976; d. Mary and Manuel Sotelo; m. David Dynega, May 26, 2002. BS, Iona Coll., NY, 1998, MA, 2001; D of Psychology, St. John's U., NY, 2002—. Cert. sch. psychologist NY, 2003, Bilingual Ext. (Spanish) Sch. Psychologist NY. Sch. psychologist LMT Sch. for Child Devel., Riverdale, NY, 2001—02; bilingual sch. psychologist Port Chester-Rye Union Free Sch. Dist., Port

Chester, NY, 2002—. Mem.: NASP. Office: Thomas A Edison Sch 132 Rectory St Port Chester NY 10573 Office Phone: 914-934-2997. Business E-Mail: marlene.sotelo.dynega@gmail.com.

**SOTER, GEORGE NICHOLAS,** advertising executive; b. Chgo., May 16, 1924; s. Nicholas A. and Emily (Damascus) S.; m. Effie Hartocollis, Feb. 7, 1949; children: Nicholas, Thomas, Peter. Student, U. Chgo., 1947-51. Writer McCann-Erickson, Chgo., 1951-53; with Needham, Louis & Brorby, Chgo., 1954-62, v.p., creative dir. N.Y.C., 1958-62; v.p., assoc. creative dir. Lennen & Newell Inc., N.Y.C., 1962-67; v.p., co-dir. creative svcs., mgmt. supr. Kenyon & Eckhardt Inc., N.Y.C., 1968-73; exec. v.p., creative dir. Pampuzac-Soter Assocs. Inc., N.Y.C., 1974-76; sr. writer Marsteller Inc., N.Y.C., 1980-82; v.p., creative Lord, Geller, Federico, Einstein, Inc., N.Y.C., 1982-87; sr. v.p., creative dir. Great Scott Advt. Co. Inc., N.Y.C., 1987-93; dir. Soter Advt. & Mktg. Consulting Svcs., N.Y.C., 1993—; copy editor Am. Mgmt. Assn., N.Y.C., 1995—. Founder, pres. Greek Island Ltd., N.Y.C., 1963—86; dir. Interpub. Product Devel. Workshop, N.Y.C., 1967. With U.S. Army, 1943-47, ETO. Home and Office: 468 Riverside Dr # 71 New York NY 10027 Personal E-Mail: gsoter@nyc.rr.com.

**SOTH, ALEC,** photographer; b. 1969; BA, Sarah Lawrence Coll., NY. Prof. photography Mpls. Coll. Art & Design; photographer NY Times Mag., Fortune, Newsweek. One-man shows include The Middle Night, Mpls. Photographer's Gallery, 1993, Art at the Bar, Icebox Gallery, Mpls., 1995—96, Minn. Ctr. Photography, 1998, Portraits (From Here to There), Central Lakes Coll. Gallery, 2001, Sleeping By the Miss., Weitman Gallery of Photography, Wash. U., St. Louis, Mo., 2003, exhibited in group shows at Campus as Place, Photographing Carleton, Carleton Coll. Art Gallery, Minn., 2002, Dog Days, Gallery 1, Mpls., 2003, Summer Life, Alice Austen House Mus., Staten Island, NY, 2003, Picturing Bill - Portraits of William Eggleston, John Stinson Fine Arts, New Orleans, 2003, Sao Paulo Biennial, Sao Paul, Brazil, 2004, Whitney Biennial, Whitney Mus. Am. Art, 2004, Represented in permanent collections, San Francisco Mus. Modern Art, LA County Mus. Art, Mus. Fine Arts, Houston, Walker Art Ctr., Mpls., Mpls. Inst. Arts, Odged Mus. Southern Art, New Orleans, Carleton Coll., Minn., ND Mus. Art; author: (book) Sleeping by the Miss., 2004. Recipient Santa Fe Prize Photography, 2003; McKnight Photography Fellowship, 1999, 2004, Jerome Travel & Study Grant, 2001, Minn. State Arts Bd. Grant, 2001, Jerome Grant, 2001. Office: Yossi Milo Gallery 525 W 25th St New York NY 10001-5501 also: Alec Soth Photography 856 Raymond Ave Unit 3 Saint Paul MN 55114 Office Phone: 651-646-1678. Office Fax: 651-646-2255. E-mail: alec@alecsoth.com.

**SOTIRHOS, MICHAEL,** ambassador; b. N.Y.C., Nov. 12, 1928; m. Estelle Manos; 2 children BBA, CCNY, 1950. Ptnr. Ariston Sales Co., Ltd., 1948, founder, chmn., 1958—; chmn. bd. Ariston Interior Designers, Inc., 1973-85; U.S. amb. to Jamaica, 1985-89; U.S. amb. to Greece Athens, 1989-93. Bd. dirs. Alexander S. Onassis Found.; cons. various internat. shipping ad pharm. firms. Former mem. Nat. Vol. Service Adv. Council; former chmn. Internat. Ops. Com., Peace Corps; mem. nat. adv. council SBA, 1976; former chmn. Nat. Republican Heritage Groups Council Decorated comdr. Order of Distinction (Jamaica); recipient Man of Yr. award Nat. Rep. Heritage Groups Coun. Republican.

**SOTO, ANGELA C.,** elementary school educator; b. Tucson, Ariz., Feb. 17, 1966; d. Gustavo and Maria C. Soto; 1 child, Vicente S. Rodriguez III. BA in Edn., U. Ariz., Tucson, 1998, M of LRC, 2006. Air force dept. clk. Hughes Aircraft, Tucson, 1984—86; legal clk. State of Ariz., Tucson, 1987—88, legal sec., office supr., 1988—97; tchr. Bracker Elem., Nogales, Ariz., 1998—2000, Los Niños Elem., Tucson, 2000—. Democrat. Roman Catholic. Avocations: walking, aerobics, gardening. Office: Los Niños Elem 5445 S Alvernon Way Tucson AZ 85706

**SOTO, GARY,** poet, writer; b. Fresno, Calif., Apr. 12, 1952; s. Manuel Soto and Angie (Trevino) Oftedal; m. Carolyn Sadako Oda, May 24, 1975; children: Mariko Heidi. BA in English, Calif. State U., Fresno, 1974; MFA in Creative Writing, U. Calif., Irvine, 1976. Lectr. Chicano Studies U. Calif., Berkeley, 1977-81, asst. prof. English and Chicano Studies, 1981-85, assoc. prof. English and Chicano Studies, 1985-95. Bd. dirs. Coordinating Council of Literary Mags., N.Y.C., 1985—. Books for Adults and High School Students: The Elements of San Joaquin, 1977 (U.S. Internat. Poetry Forum award), The Tale of Sunlight, 1978 (Where Sparrows Work Hard, 1981, Black Hair, 1985, Living Up the Street, 1985 (Am. Book award 1985), Small Faces, 1986, A Fire in my Hands: A Book of Poems, 1990, A Summer Life, 1990, Jesse, 1994, Off and Running, 1996, Junior College, 1997, Buried Onions, 1997, Natural Man, Nickel and Dime, 2000, The Effects of Knut Hamsun on a Fresno Boy, 2000, Poetry Lover, 2001, The Afterlife, 2003, One Kind of Faith, 2003, Amnesia in a Republican Country; Novels for Children: Taking Sides, 1991, Pacific Crossing, 1992, Crazy Weekends, 2003; Poetry Collections for Children: Neighborhood Odes, 1992, Canto Familiar, 1995, Fearless Fernie, 2002, Worlds Apart: Traveling With Fernie and Me, 2005; Short Story Collections: Baseball in April and other stories, 1990, Help Wanted, Local News, Petty Crimes, 1998 (Lit. award, Hispanic Heritage Found., the Author-Illustrator Civil Rights award, Nat. Education Assn., and PEN Ctr. West Book award, 1999); Chapter Books: The Skirt, 1992, The Cat's Meow, 1995, Marisol; Picture Books: Too Many Tamales, 1993, Chato's Kitchen, 1995, Old Man and His Door, 1996, Snapshots From the Wedding, 1996, If the Shoe Fits, 2002, Chato and the Party Animals, 2000; Biographies: Jessie de La Cruz: A profile of a United Farm Worker, Cesar Chavez: A Hero for Everyone, 2003; Film producer, The Pool Party (Andrew Carnegie Medal, 1993). Young People's Ambassador, Calif. Rural Legal Assistance, United Farm Workers of Am. Fellow Nat. Endowment for Arts, 1981, Gueggenheim, 1980; recipient Acad. Am. Poets Prize, 1975, The Discovery-The Nation Prize, 1975, Levinson award Poetry, 1984. Avocation: Karate. Home: 43 The Cres Berkeley CA 94708-1701

**SOTO, GILBERTO D.,** music educator; b. Torreon, Mex., May 9, 1961; arrived in U.S., 1983; s. Enrique Soto-Ruiz and Maria Martinez; m. Blanc C. Ramirez, Aug. 23, 1986; children: Daney, Erika. BA in Edn., U. del Noreste, Torreon, 1983; BA in Music, Abilene Christian U., 1986; MusM, U. So. Miss., 1988, PhD in Music Edn., 1995. Music instr. Miss. Coast Coll., 1986—90; prof., chair Laredo CC, Tex., 1990—2001; assoc. prof., chair Tex. A&M U., Laredo, 2001—05. Tchr. asst. U. So. Miss., Hattiesburg, 1981—90. Co-author: Spotlight on Music, 2005; author: Fiesta De Canciones, 2005. Mem.: Music Educators Nat. Conf., Tex. Music Edn. Assn. Roman Catholic. Home: 8627 Northridge Loop Laredo TX 78045 Office: Tex A&M Univ 5201 Universary Blvd Laredo TX 78041 Office Phone: 956-326-3046.

**SOTO, NELL,** state senator; b. Pomona, Calif., June 16, 1926; children: Philip, Robert, Michael, Patrick, Anna, Tom. Grad. Pomona High Sch., 1944; student, Mt. San Antonio Jr. Coll., 1944—47, UCLA. Govt. affairs rep. Equal Opportunity Agy., 1971—73; commr. status of women L.A. County, 1972—74; pers. dir. Rest Haven Hosp., 1973—76; govt. affairs rep. Health Sys. Agy., 1976—80; commr. cmty. life commn. City of Pomona, 1979—83, mem. city coun., 1987—98; govt. affairs rep. Rapid Transit Dist., 1984—94; mem., dist. 61 Calif. State Assembly, 1998—2000; mem., dist. 32 Calif. State Senate, 2000—. Mem. Air Quality Mgmt. Dist., 1993—99, Vets. Affairs Com., Transp. Com., Local Govt. Com., Ins. Com., Govtl. Org. Com. chair Pub. Employment and Retirement Com. Mem. PTA St. Joseph Sch. and Giano Sch., Nogales HS, La Puente, 1975—78. Democrat. Roman Catholic. Mailing: State Capitol Rm 4074 Sacramento CA 95814 Office: 82 N Euclid Ave Ontario CA 91762

**SOTOMAYOR, SONIA,** federal judge; b. Bronx, June 25, 1954; d. Sonia and Celina (Baez) Sotomayor; m. Kevin Edward Noonan, Aug. 14, 1976 (div. 1983). BA summa cum laude, Princeton U., 1976; JD, Yale U., 1979; LLD honoris causa (hon.), 1999, JD (hon.) honoris causa, 2001. Bar: N.Y. 1980, U.S. Dist. Ct. (ea. and so. dists.) N.Y. 1984. Asst. dist. atty. Office of Dist.

Atty. County of NY, NYC, 1979—84; assoc., ptnr. Pavia & Harcourt, NYC, 1984—92; fed. judge US Dist. Ct. (so. dist.) NY, NYC, 1992—98; cir. judge US Ct. Appeals (2d Cir.), NYC, 1998—. Adj. prof. NYU Sch. Law, 1998; lectr. law Columbia Law Sch., 1999. Editor: Yale U. Law Rev., 1979. Mem. State Adv. Panel on Inter-Group Rels., N.Y.C., 1990—92, 1990—91; bd. dirs. P.R. Legal Def. and Edn. Fund, N.Y.C., 1980—92, State of N.Y. Mortgage Agy., N.Y.C., 1987—92, N.Y.C. Campaign Fin. Bd., 1988—92. Mem.: ABA, Assn. Hispanic Judges, Am. Philos. Soc., NY Women's Bar Assn., P.R. Bar Assn., Hispanic Bar Assn., Phi Beta Kappa. Office: US Courthouse 40 Foley Sq Rm 401 New York NY 10007*

**SOTOMORA-VON AHN, RICARDO FEDERICO,** pediatrician, educator; b. Guatemala City, Guatemala, Oct. 22, 1947; s. Ricardo and Evelyn (von Ahn) S.; m. Eileen Marie Holcomb, May 9, 1990; m. Victoria Monzon, Nov. 26, 1971; children: Marisol, Clarisa, Ricardo III, Charlotte Marie. MD, San Carlos U., 1972; MS in Physiology, U. Minn., 1978. Diplomate Am. Bd. Pediats., Am. Bd. Pediat. Cardiology, Am. Bd. Neonatology-Perinatal Medicine. Rotating intern Gen. Hosp., Guatemala, 1971-72; pediat. intern U. Ark., 1972-73, resident, 1973-75; fellow in pediat. cardiology U. Minn., 1975-78; rsch. assoc. in cardiovasc. pathology United Hosps., St. Paul, 1976; fellow in neonatal-perinatal medicine St. Paul's Children's Hosp., 1977-78, U. Ark., 1981-82; instr. pediats. U. Minn., 1978-79; pediat. cardiologist, unit cardiovasc. surg. Roosevelt Hosp., Guatemala City, 1979-81; asst. prof. pediats. cardiology and neonatology U. Ark., Little Rock, 1981-83; pvt. practice Little Rock, 1983—. Fellow: Am. Coll. Angiology, Am. Coll. Chest Physicians, Am. Coll. Cardiology, Am. Acad. Pediat.; mem.: AAAS, ABA, Soc. Critical Care Medicine, So. Soc. Pediat. Rsch., Ctrl. Ark. Pediat. Soc., Guatemala Coll. Physicians and Surgeons, Soc. Pediat. Echocardiology, Am. Heart Assn., N.Y. Acad. Scis., Ark. Med. Soc., Soc. Genealogists London, Guatemala Acad. Genealogy, Heraldry and Hist. Studies (corr.), The Little Rock Club, The Country Club of Little Rock. Home: 25 River Ridge Cir Little Rock AR 72227-1523 Office: Evergreen Pl 1100 N Univ Ste 142 Little Rock AR 72207 E-mail: rfsotomora@aol.com.

**SOTT, JANNY,** journalist; BA, Harvard Univ., 1977. Medicine and pub. Health reporter LA Times, 1985—94; reporter NY Times, 1994—. Author: (articles) Life at the Top in America Isn't Just Better, It's Longer (Newswomen's Club of Am. Front Page award, 2005); co-editor: (Book) Portraits: 9/11/01: The Collected Portraits of Grief from The New York Times. Office: The New York Times 229 W 43rd St New York NY 10036 Office Phone: 212-561-1251. Office Fax: 212-556-3690.*

**SOTTILE, JOSEPH JAMES,** elementary school educator, poet; b. Queens, NY; s. Anthony and Mary Sottile; m. Marilyn Dufford, June 24, 1967; children: Mary Lou, April. AA, Suffolk County CC, Selden, NY, 1964; BS, SUNY, Plattsburgh, 1967; postgrad., SUNY, Brockport, 1971. Tchr. Gates Chili Sch. Dist., Rochester, NY, 1967—2000, tutor out of sch. suspension program, 2001—. Adj. faculty Rochester Inst. Tech., 1980—90; presenter in field. Author: Bathroom Vacation, 1998, Picture Poetry on Parade!, 2004, numerous poems; contbr. articles to popular mags., local newspapers. Mem.: Ret. Tchrs. Orgn. Rochester and Vicinity, Rochester Writers and Books, Rochester Area Children's Writers and Illustrators, Soc. Children's Book Writers and Illustrators. Avocations: bicycling, golf, tennis, racquetball, reading. Home: 152 Brooklea Dr Rochester NY 14624 Personal E-Mail: jsottile@frontiernet.net.

**SOUCH, MARY PAULINE,** gifted and talented educator; b. Columbus, Ohio, Jan. 31, 1945; d. Peter Souch Suciu and Mary Savko Souch; children: Sarah Louise Scurlock, Lawrence Daniel Scurlock. BE, Old Dominion U., 1968; MEd, OH State U., 1991. Cert. OH Dept. Edn., Elem. K-8 Gifted Talented OH Pub. Sch., Reading K-12 OH Pub. Sch. Tchr. Norfolk Pub. Sch., 1968—69, Indian Harbor Beach Pub. Sch., Fla., 1969, Archdiocese Cin., Springfield, Ohio, 1969—72, Archdiocese Cleve., 1972—75, Columbus Pub. Sch., 1986—89, 1991—2000, reading specialist, 1989—91, gifted talented specialist, 2000—05. Sr. faculty rep. Columbus Edn. Assn., 1996—98, 2000—01; svc. lectr. gifted edn., 2000—05. Author: Curriculum Guide in Gifted Reading Extensions, 2000. Ch. organist St. Peter and St. John Baptist Ch. Mem.: Nat. Assoc. Gifted Children, Columbus Edn. Assoc., OH Edn. Assoc., Nat. Edn. Assoc. Roman Catholic. Avocations: music, piano, travel, voice. Home: 2361 Sutter Pkwy Dublin OH 43016

**SOUCY, ROBERT JOSEPH,** historian; b. Topeka, June 25, 1933; s. William Joseph and Bernice Winefred (Riley) S.; m. Barbara Stone, May 10, 1960 (div. 1979); children: Anne Marie, Alissa Bernice; m. Sharon Fairchild, Jan. 2, 1986. AB, Washburn U., 1955; MA, Kans U., 1956; student, U. Dijon, France, 1956-57; PhD, U. Wis., 1963. Instr. Harvard U., Cambridge, Mass., 1963-64; asst. prof. Kent (Ohio) State U., 1964-66; assoc. prof. Oberlin (Ohio) Coll., 1966-69, prof., 1969—98; ret., 1998. Author: Fascism in France: The Case of Maurice Barrés, 1972, Fascist Intellectual: Drieu Le Rochelle, 1979, French Fascism, 1924-33, 1986, French Fascism, 1933-39, 1995, Fascismes Français?, 2004, France in the Era of Fascism, 2005; mem. editl. bd. French Hist. Studies, 1986-88. 1st lt. USAF, 1957-60. Fullbright scholar, 1956-57; grantee NEH, 1969, 88, ACLS, 1969, 89, Am. Philos. Soc., 1969, 73. Mem. Am. Hist. Soc., French Hist. Soc. (mem. editorial bd. 1986-88). Avocation: tennis. Home: 143 E College St Oberlin OH 44074-1774 Personal E-mail: bobsoucy@earthlink.net.

**SOUDER, MARK EDWARD,** congressman; b. Ft. Wayne, Ind., July 18, 1950; s. Edward Getz and Irma (Fahling) S.; m. Diane Kay Zimmer, July 28; children: Brooke Diane, Nathan Elias, Zachary. BS, Ind. U., Ft. Wayne, 1972; MBA, U. Notre Dame, 1974. Mgmt. trainee Crossroads Furniture Co., Houston, 1974; mktg. mgr. Gabberts Furniture & Studio, Mpls., 1971-76; mktg. mgr., exec. v.p. Souder's Furniture & Studio, Grabill, Ind., 1976-80, pres., 1981-84; econ. devel. liaison for U.S. Rep. Dan Coats, from 1983; mem. U.S. Congress from Ind. 3rd Dist. (formerly 4th), 1995—, Ho. Select Com. on Homeland Security. Mem. edn. and workforce com., govt. reform and oversight com., small bus. com., natural resources com. Publicity chmn. Grabill County Fair, 1977—; advisor Dan Coats for Congress Com., 1980-81; mem. Ind. Area Devel. Coun.; mem. bus. alumni adv. com. Ind. U.-Ft. Wayne. Mem. Midwest Home Furnishings Assn. (dir. 1976-84, past treas., exec. v.p.), Ft. Wayne, Grabill C. of C., Allen County Hist. Soc., Alumni Assn. Ind. U. at Ft. Wayne (dir., past pres.), Alumni Assn. U. Notre Dame. Republican. Mem. Apostolic Christian Ch. Home: 13733 Ridgeview Ct Grabill IN 46741 Office: US Ho Reps 2231 Rayburn Ho Office Bldg Washington DC 20515-1403 Office Phone: 202-225-4436. Office Fax: 202-225-3479. E-mail: souder@mail.house.gov.*

**SOUKUP, VICTOR GERALD,** chemist; b. Chgo., July 29, 1924; s. Joseph Victor Soukup and Antoinette None Schalansky; m. Shirley Marian White, May 26, 1946; children: Ann Elizabeth Dombos, Thomas Victor, Paul Gerald, Mark White. Student, Kalamazoo Coll., Mich., 1942—43, Western Mich. U., Kalamazoo, 1943—44; BS in Physics, U. Mich., Ann Arbor, 1945; MS in Chemistry, U. Wis., Madison, 1951, PhD in Chemistry, 1953. Rsch. chemist Procter & Gamble Co., Cin., 1953—55; dir. chem. rsch. Cin. Milacron, 1955—73; rsch. cons. Vic Soukup & Assocs., 1973—77; adj. prof. U. Cin., 1979—. US del. Internat. Stds. Orgn. Tech. Com. T31 (Plastics), 1964—72. Contbr. scientific papers. Pres. Ohio Native Plant Soc., Cin., 1961—2003. With USN, 1945—46. Achievements include patents for plastics processing and composition of matter. Avocations: tennis, badminton, bridge, photography. Office: U Cin Clifton Ave Cincinnati OH 45221-0006 Business E-Mail: soukupvg@email.uc.edu.

**SOULE, GEORGE ALAN,** literature educator; b. Fargo, ND, Mar. 3, 1930; s. George Alan and Ruth Georgia (Knudsen) S.; m. Carolyn Richards, Nov. 24, 1961; 1 child, Katherine. BA, Carleton Coll., 1951; postgrad., Corpus Christi Coll., Cambridge (Eng.) U., 1951-52; MA, Yale U., 1956, PhD, 1960. Instr. English lit. Oberlin (Ohio) Coll., 1958-60; asst. prof. U. Wis., Madison, 1960-62; from asst. prof. to prof. Carleton Coll., Northfield, Minn., 1962-95, prof. emeritus, 1995—, chair English dept., 1980—83; tchr. Cannon Valley

Elder Collegium, 1998—, vice chair, 2003—05, chair, 2005—, also bd. dirs. Cons. Ednl. Testing Svc., Princeton, NJ, 1967-84, 94-97; lectr. Wordsworth Winter Sch., Grasmere, UK, 2003-. Author: Four British Women Novelists: An Annotated and Critical Secondary Bibliography, 1998; editor: Theatre of the Mind, 1974; contbr. articles to profl. jours. Mem. libr. bd. City of Northfield, 1997-2000; bd. dirs. Northfield Area Found., 2001-02. With U.S. Army, 1954-55. Internat. fellow Rotary, 1952-53, Sterling pre-doctoral fellow Yale U., 1957-58. Mem.: Anthony Powell Soc., The Iris Murdoch Soc., Friends of Dove Cottge, Boswell Soc. of Auchinleck, Johnson Soc. of Lichfield, Mayflower Soc., Oxford and Cambridge Club, Rotary, Phi Beta Kappa. Episcopalian. Avocations: cooking, travel, Jeopardy (Champion Sr. Tournament 1990). Home: 313 Nevada St Northfield MN 55057-2346 Fax: 507-645-5099. Office Phone: 507-646-4322.

**SOULE, JEREMY,** composer; Founder Artistry Entertainment. Composer: Ecstasy, Storyeum, (video games) Secret of Evermore, 1995, Total Annihilation, 1997 (Gamespot Best Music award, 1997), Forgotten Realms: Icewind Dale, 2000 (Gamespot Best Music award, 2000), Giants: Citizen Kabuto, 2000, Forgotten Realms: Icewind Dale - Heart of Winter, 2001, Final Four 2002, 2001, Harry Potter & the Sorcerer's Stone, 2001, Azurik: Rise of Perathia, 2001, Forgotten Realms: Baldur's Gate - Dark Alliance, 2001, Harry Potter & the Chamber of Secrets, 2002 (BAFTA award for Best Game Score), The Elder Scrolls III: Morrowind, 2002, Dungeon Siege, 2002, Neverwinter Nights, 2002, Impossible Creatures, 2002, SOCOM: US Navy SEALs, 2002, Unreal II: The Awakening, 2003, Star Wars: Knights of the Old Republic, 2003, Harry Potter: Quidditch World Cup, 2003, Dungeon Siege: Legends of Aranna, 2003, Harry Potter & the Prisoner of Azkaban, 2004, Armies of Exigo, Warhammer 40,000: Dawn of War, 2004, Lemony Snicket's A Series of Unfortunate Events, 2004, Guild Wars, 2005, Dungeon Siege II, 2005, Harry Potter & the Goblet of Fire, 2005, Guild Wars: Factions, 2006, The Elder Scrolls IV: Oblivion, 2006 (MTV Video Music award for best Video Game Score, 2006), Prey, 2006, (films) Journey Toward Creation, 2003, (TV films) C.S. Lewis: Beyond Narnia, 2005.*

**SOULTOUKIS, DONNA ZOCCOLA,** library director; b. Princeton, N.J., July 28, 1949; d. Peter Joseph and Josephine (Taraschi) Zoccola; m. Dimitrios Athanasios Soultoukis, July 26, 1980. AB, Georgian Ct. Coll., Lakewood, N.J., 1971; MS, Drexel U., 1976; Cert., Italian U. for Foreigners, Perugia, 1974. Libr. asst. Georgia Cibr. Princeton U., 1971-73; libr. Friends Hosp., Phila., 1976-86, dir. libr. svcs., 1986-98; head libr. Temple U., Sch. Podiatric, 1998-99; ref. libr. MCP/Hahnemann U., Phila., 1999-2000; sr. info. scientist Bristol-Myers Squibb Pharm. Rsch. Inst., Hopewell, N.J., N.J., 2000; libr. Our Lady of Lourdes Sch. Nursing, Camden, NJ, 2001—. Cons. Lower Bucks Hosp., Bristol, Pa., 1991-95. Vol. outreach program Old St. Joseph's Ch., Phila., 1992-95, sanctuary min., 1993—, pastoral coun., 1995-98, 2001—05, website adminstr., 2003—, coord. altar ministers, 2004—, sec. parish coun., 2005—, co-chmn. parish life com., 2006—. Mem. Med. Libr. Assn. (chair mental librs. divsn. 1991-93, chair rsch. com. 1996—), Spl. Librs. Assn. (Phila. chpt. bd. dirs. 1985-88, pres. 1982-84, chmn. long-range planning 1993, mem. adv. bd. 1995-2001, sec. solo divsn. 2000-01, devel. com. 2003-). Avocations: travel, cooking. Home: 290 Cinnabar Ln Yardley PA 19067-5717 Office Phone: 856-757-3722.

**SOUPATA, LEA N.,** human resources specialist; b. NYC; With UPS, Atlanta, 1969—, various positions in human resources and customer service, dist. mgr. NY, 1990—94, mem. mgmt. com. Atlanta, 1995—, v.p. to sr. v.p. human resources. Bd. dirs. UPS. Chair UPS Found.; trustee Annie E. Casey Found.; bd. dirs. Jr. Achievement Ga., St. Basil's Acad. Recipient Human Capital award, Hunt-Scanlon Advisors, 2005. Fellow: Nat. Human Resources Acad.; mem.: Human Resources Policy Assn. (bd. dirs.). Office: UPS 55 Glenlake Pkwy NE Atlanta GA 30328

**SOURIAN, EVE POCQUET,** French educator; b. N.Y.C., June 9, 1932; d. Albert and Elsa (Puschendorf) Pocquet; m. Peter Sourian, Sept. 25, 1971; children: Mark Zareh, Delphine Elsa. Licence in German, Sorbonne, Paris, 1960; MA in English, Bucknell U., 1962; PhD in French, U. Colo., 1971. Instr. French Fairleigh Dickinson U., Rutherford, N.J., 1963-65; asst. prof., assoc. prof., prof. French Grad. Ctr. CUNY, 1982—. Dir. Women Studies Program CUNY, 1985-89. Author: Mme de Staël et Henri Heine: Les Deux Allemagnes, 1974; editor: Nouvelles (George Sand), 1986, Isidora (George Sand), 1990, Impressions et souvenirs (George Sand), 2005, Nouvelles lettres d'un voyageur (George Sand), 2005; contbr. articles to profl. jours. Decorated Chevalier dans l'Ordre des Palmes Academiques, France, 2006; recipient 3 French Govt. Tchg. Assistantships, Eng., Germany, 1957-58; Fulbright Traveling fellow, 1960-62; Inst. on Contemporary French Culture grantee Nat. Endowment for the Humanities, 1982. Mem.: MLA, Soc. French Tchrs. and French Spkrs. in Am. (mem. exec. bd.), Am. Assn. Tchrs. French. Home: 30 E 70th St New York NY 10021-4942 Office: City Coll CUNY 137 Convent Ave New York NY 10031-9126 Office Phone: 212-650-6731. Business E-Mail: esourian@ccny.cuny.edu.

**SOURIAN, PETER,** writer, language educator, educator; b. Boston, Apr. 7, 1933; s. Zareh Missak and Zabelle (Bayentz) S.; m. Eve Jeanne Pocquet, Sept. 25, 1971; children: Mark, Delphine. BA, Harvard U., 1955. Lectr. eng. divsn. NYU, N.Y.C., 1963-65; from instr. English to prof. Bard Coll., Annandale-on-Hudson, NY, 1965—75, prof., 1975—, co-dir. Writing Program, 1980—. Faculty New Sch. Social Rsch., NYC, 1975-2000; TV critic Nation mag., NYC, 1975-81; mem. Anahit Prize Com., 1988—; nat. adv. panel George Polk Awards Com., 1979-92. Author: Miri, 1957, The Best and Worst of Times, 1961, The Gate, 1965, (essays and criticism) At The French Embassy in Sofia, 1992; mem. editl. bd. Ararat Quar., 1975—; contbr. articles to popular mags, profl. jours. Bd. dirs. Armenian Ctr. Columbia U., N.Y.C., 1988-97; mem. Clemente Course Humanities Adv. Bd., 1999—. With U.S. Army, 1957-59. Recipient Bardian award Bard Coll. Alumni, 2000; Lilly Endowment grant, 1976, Kellogg Found. grant, 1977. Mem. MLA, PEN, Nat. Book Critics Circle, Century Assn. Home: 30 E 70th St New York NY 10021-4942 Office: Bard Coll Annandale on Hudson Annandale On Hudson NY 12504 Office Phone: 845-758-6822.

**SOURKES, THEODORE LIONEL,** biochemistry professor; b. Montreal, Que., Can., Feb. 21, 1919; s. Irving and Fannie (Golt) S.; m. Shena Rosenblatt, Jan. 17, 1943; children: Barbara, Myra. B.Sc., McGill U., 1939, M.Sc. magna cum laude, 1946; PhD, Cornell U., 1948; D.U. honoris causa, U. Ottawa, Can., 1990. Asst. prof. pharmacology Georgetown U. Med. Sch., 1948-50; research asso. dept. enzyme chemistry Merck Inst. Therapeutic Research, Rahway, NJ, 1950-53; sr. research biochemist Allan Meml. Inst., Montreal, 1953-65; dir. lab. neurochemistry Allan Meml. Inst. Psychiatry, 1965—91; mem. faculty McGill U., Montreal, 1954—, prof. biochemistry, 1965—, prof. psychiatry, assoc. dean of medicine for research Faculty Medicine, 1972-75; prof. pharmacology, 1990—; emeritus, 1991. Mem. Que. Med. Rsch. Coun., 1971-77; sr. fellow Parkinson's Disease Found., N.Y.C., 1963-66. Author: Biochemistry of Mental Disease, 1962, Nobel Prize Winners in Medicine and Physiology, 1901-1965, 1967, Life and Work of J.L.W. Thudichum, 1829-1901, 2003; sect. editor Internat. Jour. of the History of Neuroscis., 1996—. Decorated officer Order of Canada, Venezuelan Order Andrés Bello; laureate of the Wilder Penfield Prix du Que. for Biomed. Sci., 1998. Fellow Royal Soc. Can.; mem. Canadian Biochem. Soc., Pharmacol. Soc. Can., Canadian Coll. Neuropsychopharmacology (Heinz Lehmann award 1982, medal 1990), Am. Soc. Biol. Chemists, Am. Soc. Pharmacology and Exptl. Therapeutics, Am. Soc. Neurochemistry, Internat. Soc. History of Neurosis. (medal 2001), Internat. Soc. Neurochemistry, Internat. Brain Research Orgn., Sigma Xi. Achievements include research and discoveries on drugs for treatment high blood pressure; 1st basic research on methyldopa; elucidation of role of dopamine and other monamines in nervous system; first trials of L-dopa in Parkinson's disease, biochemistry of mental depression, pathways of stress in the nervous system, imaging serotonin in brain, history of biochemistry. Home: 3033 Sherbrooke St W # 303 Montreal PQ Canada H3Z 1A3 Office: McGill U 1033 Pine Ave W Montreal PQ Canada H3A 1A1 E-mail: theodore.sourkes@mcgill.ca.

**SOUSSLOFF, ANDREW D.,** lawyer; b. Providence, Sept. 21, 1953; s. Dimitri Gregory and Barbara Lucy (Farr) S.; m. Patricia James, June 7, 1986. BA, MA, U. Pa., 1975, JD cum laude, 1979. Bar: NY 1980, Calif. 1987. Assoc. Cadwalader Wickersham & Taft, NYC, 1979-80, Sullivan & Cromwell, NYC, 1981-86, ptnr., 1986—, now co-mng. gen. practice group. Mem.: Internat. Bar Assn. (vice-chmn., capital mkts. forum, co-chmn., securities law com. 2000—03). Office: Sullivan & Cromwell 125 Broad St Fl 28 New York NY 10004-2489 Office Phone: 212-558-4000. Office Fax: 212-558-3588. Business E-Mail: soussloffa@sullcrom.com.

**SOUTAS-LITTLE, ROBERT WILLIAM,** mechanical engineer, educator; b. Oklahoma City, Feb. 25, 1933; s. Harry Glenn and Mary Evelyn (Miller) Little; m. Patricia Soutas, Sept. 3, 1982; children: Deborah, Catherine, Colleen, Jennifer, Karen. BS in Mech. Engring, Duke U., 1955; MS, U. Wis., 1959, PhD, 1962. Design engr. Allis Chalmers Mfg. Co., Milw., 1955-57; instr. mech. engring. Marquette U., 1957-59; instr. U. Wis., Madison, 1959-62, asst. prof., 1962-63, Okla. State U., 1963-65; prof. Mich. State U., 1965—2001, chmn. dept. mech. engring., 1972-77, chmn. dept. biomechanics, 1977-90; dir. biomechanics evaluation lab., 1989—; prof. emeritus Mich. State U., Lansing, 2001—. Cons. A. C. Electronics Co., Ford Motor Co., CBS Research Lab., B.F. Goodrich Co.; lectr. AID, India, 1965 Author: Elasticity, 1973, Engineering Mechanics: Statics, 1999, Engineering Mechanics: Dynamics, 1999; contbr. articles to profl. jours. Vice pres. Okemos (Mich.) Sch. Bd., 1967-72; mem. Meridian Twp. (Mich.) Charter Commn., 1969-70, Meridian Twp. Zoning Bd. Appeals, 1969-71. Recipient award for excellence in instrn. engring. students Western Electric Co., 1970-71, Disting. Faculty award, 1996; NSF grantee, 1964-69, 79, NIH grantee, 1973-75, 79—. Fellow ASME; mem. Soc. Engring. Sci., Am. Soc. Biomechanics, Internat. Soc. Biomechanics, N.Am. Soc. Clin. Gait and Movement Analysis, Sigma Xi, Pi Tau Sigma, Ta Beta Pi. Home: 187 S Highland Dr Leland MI 49654-1143 Office: PO Box 1143 Leland MI 49654-1143 Office Phone: 231-256-7646. Business E-Mail: soutas@egr.msu.edu.

**SOUTER, DAVID HACKETT,** United States Supreme Court Justice; b. Melrose, Mass., Sept. 17, 1939; s. Joseph Alexander and Helen Adams (Hackett) Souter. BA, Harvard U., 1961, LLB, 1966; BA, MA in Jurisprudence, Oxford U., 1989. Bar: N.H. 1967. Assoc. Orr & Reno, Concord, NH, 1966—68, Lowell Ho., Harvard Coll.; asst. atty. gen. State of NH, 1968—71, dep. atty. gen., 1971—76, atty. gen., 1976—78; assoc. justice NH Superior Ct., 1978—83, NH Supreme Ct., 1983—90, US Supreme Ct., Washington, 1990—; judge US Ct. Appeals (1st cir.), NH, 1990. Mem. Maine-NH Interstate Boundary Commn., 1971, NH Police Stds. and Training Coun., 1976—78, NH Jud. Coun., 1976—78, NH Gov.'s Commn. Crime and Delinquency, 1976—78, 1979—83. Trustee Concord Hosp., 1972—85, pres., 1978—84; trustee NH Hist. Soc., 1976—85; v.p., 1980—85; overseer Dartmouth Med. Sch., 1981—87. Rhodes scholar, Magdalen Coll. Oxford U., 1963, Hon. fellow. Master: Gray's Inn (London) (hon.); fellow: Am. Acad. Arts and Scis., Mass. Hist. Soc., Am. Coll. Trial Lawyers (hon.), Am. Bar Found. (hon.); mem.: ABA, Am. Antiquarian Soc., Am. Philos. Soc., Pilgrim Soc. (hon.), New Eng. Hist. Geneal. Soc. (hon.), Merrimack County Bar Assn., Merrimack County Bar Assn., NH Bar Assn., NH Hist. Soc. (v.p. 1980—85, trustee 1976—85), Appalachian Mtn. Club, Phi Beta Kappa. Republican. Episcopalian. Office: US Supreme Ct One First St NE Washington DC 20543*

**SOUTER, PHILIP FRANK,** research scientist; Scientist Procter & Gamble Co., Cin. Co-recipient Nat. Inventor of Yr. award, Intellectual Property Owners Edn. Found., 2006. Achievements include development of PuR Purifier of Water Sachets, which are capable of purifying 10 liters of water by pulling contaminants out of non-drinkable water; patents in field. Office: Health Scis Inst Proctor & Gamble Co 1 P&G Plaza Cincinnati OH 45202*

**SOUTH, RUTH EADES,** reference librarian; b. Inglewood, Calif., Nov. 23, 1928; d. Ted and Ruth Eden (Houltram) Eades; m. Donald Drager South, Sept. 24, 1950 (dec. Apr. 1985); children: Andrew, Carolyn, Barbara. BA, U. Oreg., 1950, MLS, 1971, MA, 1980. Reference libr. U. Oreg., Eugene, 1973-75, instr. Sch. Librarianship, 1975-78, reference libr., assoc. prof., bibliographer Libr., 1979-94; ret., 1994. Part-time traffic petitions officer U. Oreg., 1994—. Author: (bibliography) Citizen Action and the Neighborhood Movement, 1987. Organizer Muscular Dystrophy-Amyotrophic Laterial Sclerosis Support Group, Eugene, 1986; pres. Neighborhood Assn., Eugene, 1990. Mem. Sigma Delta Pi, Beta Phi Mu. Home: 697 Crest Dr Eugene OR 97405-2793 Office: U Oreg Dept Pub Safety Eugene OR 97403

**SOUTH, STEPHEN A.,** academic administrator; Pres. South Coll., Knoxville, Tenn., 1989—. Home: South Coll 200 Hayfield Rd Knoxville TN 37922-2303 Office Phone: 865-251-1800. E-mail: ssouth@southcollegetn.edu.

**SOUTHARD, WILLIAM G.,** lawyer; b. Toledo, May 6, 1953; s. James Theodore and Dorothy (Fergusson) S.; m. Martha Donelan, Aug. 14, 1976. BA, Williams Coll., 1975; JD, Columbia U., 1978. Bar: U.S. Dist. Ct. Ill. 1979, Mass. 1981, U.S. Dist. Ct. Mass. 1981, U.S. Ct. Appeals (1st cir.) 1985. Assoc. Schiff Hardin & Waite, Chgo., 1978-81, Bingham, Dana & Gould LLP, Boston, 1981-85, ptnr., 1985—2002, dep. chmn. litig., 1994-2000, chmn. litig., 2000—02; ptnr. Bingham McCutchen LLP, Boston, 2002—. Assoc. editor Columbia Jour. Transnat. Law, 1978; contbr. articles to profl. jours. Mem. ABA, ASTM, Boston Bar Assn. Office: Bingham McCutchen LLP 150 Federal St Fl 15 Boston MA 02110-1745 Office Phone: 617-951-8232. Business E-Mail: william.southard@bingham.com.

**SOUTHBY, RICHARD MCKELLAR FAIRFAX,** health services educator, consultant; b. Melbourne, Victoria, Australia, Feb. 3, 1940; arrived in U.S., 1979, naturalized, 1985; s. Robert and Marie Heywood (Whyte) Southby; m. Janet Sue Rexrode, June 9, 1979. B.Com., U. Melbourne, 1965; M.P.A. Cornell U., 1967; PhD, Monash U., Clayton, Victoria, Australia, 1973. Rsch. asst. Inst. Applied Econ. Research U. Melbourne, 1965; Sloan scholar in hosp. and med. care administrn. Cornell U., Ithaca, NY, 1965—67; tchg. fellow Monash U., 1967—70, sr. tchg. fellow dept. social and preventive medicine Faculty of Medicine, Monash U., 1970, lectr. in social and preventive medicine, 1971—75, sr. lectr., 1975—78; commr. Australian Hosps. and Health Services Commn., Canberra, Australian Capital Territory, 1975; dir. pub. health services research and tchg. Sch. Pub. Health and Tropical Medicine U. Sydney, New South Wales, Australia, 1978—79; from assoc. prof. to prof., chmn. dept. health svcs., mgmt. and policy The George Washington U. Med. Sch., Washington, 1979—97, assoc. dean health svcs., Friesen prof. internat. health and health policy, prof. health care sics., 1997—2001; dean, Ross prof. internat. health, sch. pub. health and health svcs The George Washington U. Med. Ctr., Washington, 2001—03, exec. dean. disting. prof. global health, 2003—. Adj. prof. dept. preventive medicine and biometrics Sch. Medicine Uniformed Services U. Health Scis. Dept. Def., Bethesda, Md., 1979—; dir. Interagy.-Inst. for Fed. Health Care Execs., 1984—; cons. in hosp. administrn. Walter Reed Army Med. Ctr., Washington, 1983—. Author (with E. Chesterman): Australia: Health Facts, 1979; editor (with others): Health Care Technology Under Financial Constraints, 1987, Health Care Law and Ethics, 1989, AIDS and Long Term Care: A New Dimension, 1989; contbr. articles to profl. jours. Decorated knight of grace Order St. Lazarus of Jerusalem, officer brother Order Hosp. of St. John of Jerusalem. Fellow: Royal Inst. Pub. Health, Royal Soc. Medicine (U.K.), Australian Coll. Health Svc. Execs., Am. Coll. Legal Medicine (hon.); mem.: APHA, Assn. Mil. Surgeons U.S. Internat. Epidemiol. Assn., Cosmos Club (Washington), Wallaby Club. Anglican. Avocations: tennis, gardening, hiking. Office: George Washington U Med Ctr Office Provost and VP Health Affairs 2175 K St NW Ste 810H Washington DC 20037 Office Phone: 202-416-0429.

**SOUTHERLAND, HENRY DELEON, JR.,** retired lawyer, civil engineer; b. Birmingham, Ala., Sept. 8, 1911; s. Henry DeLeon and Edwina (Williams) Southerland; m. Helen Ash (div.); 1 child, Mary Neill 1 stepchild, Carolyn Wilson Long; m. Louise Harris Wilson, Jan. 22, 1955. Student, Ga. Tech. U.,

1929—31; BS, U. Ga., 1934; MS, U. Tenn., 1941; JD, Columbia U., 1948; MA, Samford U., 1983. Registered profl. engr., Tenn., 1942; bar: Ala. 1949. Engring. aide to hydraulic engr. water control planning TVA, Knoxville, Tenn., 1934—48; tax acct. US Steel Corp., Fairfield, Ala., 1948—51, staff asst. land dept., 1951—56, asst. mgr. land dept., 1956—68, mgr. so. lands timber, 1968—71; comml. agt. Birmingham So. RR Co., Fairfield, 1956—71; ret. Co-author: The Federal Road through Georgia, the Creek Nation, and Alabama, 1806-1836, 1949 (Best non-fiction award Ala. Hist. Assn., Best non-fiction award Ala. Libr. Assn.). Mem. Mountain Brook City Coun., Ala., 1976—80, pres. pro tem, 1980; chmn. planning commn. City of Mountain Brook, 1957—76. Lt. col. U.S. Army, 1946, col. U.S. Army, 1954. Mem.: SR (v.p. emeritus), Newcomen Soc., Soc. War of 1812 (past grand marshall), Soc. Colonial Wars (past dep. gov. gen.), St. Andrews Soc. Mid. South (founder), Soc. of Cin. Episcopalian. Avocations: genealogy, gardening, fishing, history. Home: 47 Greenway Rd Mountain Brook AL 35213

**SOUTHERLAND, S. DUANE,** manufacturing executive; b. Durham, N.C., Apr. 24, 1949; s. Sydney Duane and Beatrice Marie (Carver) S.; m. Linda F. Lewis, Jan. 5, 1974, 1 child, S. Duane III. BSE, Duke U., 1971, MS in Engring., 1973, MBA, 1974. Ops. analyst Cooper Group Div. Cooper Industries, Apex, NC, 1974-78, planning analyst Houston, 1978-81, dir. fin. Cooper Electronics Div. Nashua, NH, 1981-83, gen. mgr. Conn. ops. Kirsch Div. Beacon Falls, Conn., 1983-87, pres. Kirsch Div. Sturgis, Mich., 1987-94; pres., CEO Conso Products Co., Union, SC, 1995-98; pres., CEO, dir. Equality Specialties, Inc., N.Y.C., 1999—2001; pres., CEO Conso Products, Union, SC, 2002—, Taos, LLC, Spartanburg, 2005—. Republican. Baptist.

**SOUTHERN, DAVID,** history professor; b. Great Bend, Kans., Feb. 19, 1938; s. Arnett D. Southern and Maxine Loretto Windon; m. Judith Marie Jarvis (div.); 1 child, Sheri Lee. BA, Alderson-Boraddus Coll., W.Va., 1964; MA, Wake Forest U., N.C., 1965; PhD, Emory U., Atlanta, 1971. Instr. N.C. Wesleyan Coll., Rocky Mount, NC, 1965—66; prof. Westminster Coll., Fulton, Md., 1970—2005. Author: The Malignant Heritage: Yankee Progressives and the Negro Question, 1901-1914, 1968, Gunnar Myrdal and Black-White Relations, 1987, John LaFarge and the Limits of Catholic Interracialism, 1911-1963, 1996, The Progressive Era and Race: Reaction and Reform, 1900-1917, 2005; contbr. book revs. to jours., articles to profl. jours. With USAF, 1956—60. Recipient Gustavus Myers award, U. Ark., 1987, 1996; fellow, NEH, 1982—83; Grant, ACLS, APS, CUSHWA. Mem.: So. Hist. Assn., Orgn. Am. Historians. Democrat. Avocations: tennis, basketball, running, gardening, jazz. Home: 116 Merino Canonsburg PA 15317

**SOUTHERN, HUGH,** retired performing arts manager; b. Newcastle-on-Tyne, Eng., Mar. 20, 1932; came to U.S., 1955; s. Norman and Phyllis Margaret (Hiller) S.; m. Jane Rosemary Llewellyn, Dec. 18, 1954 (div.); children: Hilary, William Norman; m. Kathy Ayers Dwyer, Dec. 10, 1988; 1 child, Jaime Andres. BA, King's Coll., Cambridge, Eng., 1956. Assoc. account exec. Fuller & Smith & Ross, N.Y.C., 1956-58; treas. Westport Country Playhouse Conn., 1958; adminstrv. mgr. Theatre Guild-Am. Theatre Soc., N.Y.C., 1959-62; asst. dir. Repertory Theatre, Lincoln Ctr., N.Y.C., 1962-65; gen. mgr. Nat. Repertory Theatre, N.Y.C., 1965-67; mgmt. assoc. San Francisco Opera, 1967-68; exec. dir. Theatre Devel. Fund, N.Y.C., 1968-82; dep. chmn. programs Nat. Endowment for Arts, Washington, 1982-89, acting chmn., 1989; gen. mgr. Met. Opera Assn. Inc., N.Y.C., 1989-90; dir. Va. Festival of Am. Film, Charlottesville, Va., 1995-96. Acting dir. performing arts program N.Y. State Council on Arts, N.Y.C., 1974-75, acting exec. dir., 1976; dir. New Dramatists, N.Y.C., 1978-82, Film Forum, N.Y.C., 1978-82; trustee Actor's Fund Am., N.Y.C., 1978-85 Trustee Manhattan Country Sch., N.Y.C., 1970-82, chmn., 1971-74; mem. Mayor's Com. on Cultural Policy, N.Y.C., 1974-75. Home: 3406 18th St N Arlington VA 22207 E-mail: hsouth2@aol.com.

**SOUTHERN, NANCY C.,** utilities executive; Co-chmn., CEO ATCO Ltd. and Can. Utilities, Calgary, Alba., Canada, 2000—02, pres., CEO, 2003—; bd. dirs. Exec. v.p. Spruce Meadows; bd. dirs. Shell Can. Ltd., Akita Drilling Ltd., Sentgraf Enterprises Ltd. Former mem. Can. Equestrian Team. Office: ATCO Ltd 1500/1600 909 11th Ave SW Calgary AB Canada T2R 1N6

**SOUTHERN, ROBERT ALLEN,** lawyer; b. Independence, Mo., July 17, 1930; s. James Allen and Josephine (Ragland) S.; m. Cynthia Agnes Drews, May 17, 1952; children: David D., William A., James M., Kathryn S. O'Brien. BS in Polit. Sci., Northwestern U., 1952, LL.B., 1954. Bar: Ill. 1955. Assoc. Mayer, Brown & Platt (now Mayer, Brown, Rowe & Maw), Chgo., 1954-64, ptnr., 1965-96, mng. ptnr., 1978-91, L.A., 1991-96; CEO So. Assocs., Grayslake, Ill., 1997—, Chapel Hill, NC, 2004—. Editor in chief Northwestern U. Law Rev., 1953-54. Trustee, v.p. gen. counsel LaRabida Children's Hosp. and Rsch. Ctr., Chgo., 1974-89; trustee Kenilworth (Ill.) Union Ch., 1980-88; pres. Joseph Sears Sch. Bd., 1977-79; trustee Rush U. Med. Ctr., 1983-91; life trustee, 1991—; bd. dirs. Boys and Girls Clubs Chgo., 1986-91; governing mem. Orchestral Assn. Chgo., 1988-93. With U.S. Army, 1955-57. Mem. Chgo. Bar Assn., Lawyers Club Chgo., Order of Coif, Govs. Club (Chapel Hill, N.C.), Chgo. Club. Home: 60116 Davie Chapel Hill NC 27517-8466 Office Phone: 919-969-8292. Personal E-mail: rsouthern@nc.rr.com.

**SOUTHGATE, RICHARD W.,** lawyer, director; b. Chgo., May 6, 1929; m. Anna Fisher Hart, Aug. 25, 1951; children— Richard W., Sarah B., Rebecca W. C., John P. AB cum laude, Harvard U., 1951, LL.B. cum laude, 1954. Bar: Mass. 1954. Assoc. Covington & Burling, Washington, 1956-58; assoc., then ptnr., chmn. policy com. Ropes & Gray, Boston, 1958-94; vol. atty. Greater Boston Legal Svcs., 1995—. Mem. Mass. Commn. on Anti-Takeover Laws; adj. prof. Northeastern U. Sch. Law, Boston, 1996-97. Author: (with Donald W. Glazer) Massachusetts Corporation Law and Practice, 1991. Moderator, Town of Manchester, Mass., 1976-94. Served as sgt. U.S. Army, 1954-56 Mem. Boston Bar Assn., ABA, Mass. Bar Assn. Clubs: Essex County, Somerset; Harvard (Boston). Office: Greater Boston Legal Svcs 197 Friend St Boston MA 02114-1802 Home: 824 Hale St Beverly MA 01915-2214

**SOUTHWELL, DONALD G.,** insurance company executive; Grad., We. Mich. U. Mgmt. positions through pres. in. & fin. svcs. Prudential Ins. Co. Am., 1974—96; pres. life & health ins. group Unitrin, Inc., Chgo., 1996—99, v.p., 1998—99, sr. v.p., pres. ins. group, 1999—2002, pres., COO, 2002—06, pres., CEO, 2006—. Bd. dirs. Unitrin, Inc., 2002—. Office: Unitrin Inc One E Wacker Dr Chicago IL 60601*

**SOUTHWICK, CHARLES HENRY,** zoologist, educator; b. Wooster, Ohio, Aug. 28, 1928; s. Arthur F. and Faye (Motz) S.; m. Heather Milne Beck, July 12, 1952; children: Steven, Karen. BA, Coll. Wooster, 1949; MS, U. Wis., 1951, PhD, 1953. NIH fellow, 1951-53; asst. prof. biology Hamilton Coll., 1953-54; NSF fellow Oxford U., England, 1954-55; faculty Ohio U., 1955-61; assoc. prof. pathobiology Johns Hopkins Sch. Hygiene and Pub. Health, Balt., 1961-68, prof., 1968-79; assoc. dir. Johns Hopkins Internat. Ctr. for Med. Rsch. and Tng., Calcutta, India, 1964-65; chmn. dept. environ., population and organismic biology U. Colo., Boulder, 1979-82, prof. biology, 1979—, prof. emeritus, 1993—. Rschr. and author publs. on animal social behavior and population dynamics, influences animal social behavior on demographic characteristic mammal populations, primate ecology and behavior, estuarine ecology and environ. quality; mem. primate adv. com. Nat. Acad. Sci.-NRC, 1963-75, com. primate conservation, 1974-75; mem. Gov.'s Sci. Adv. Com. State of Md., 1967-68; mem. com. on rsch. and exploration Nat. Geog. Soc., 1979-2000; mem. adv. bd. Caribbean Primate Rsch. Ctr., 1987-99, Wis. Primate Rsch. Ctr. Steer, 1990-98; mem. Integrated Conservation Rsch., 1989-2002; mem. or leader of more than 85 rsch. expdns. on five continents. Editor, author: Primate Social Behavior, 1963, Animal Aggression, 1970, Nonhuman Primates in Biomedical Research, 1975, Ecology and the Quality of Our Environment, 1976, Global Ecology, 1985; Ecology and Behavior of Food-Enhanced Primate Groups, 1988; author: Global Ecology in Human Perspective, 1996. Recipient Fulbright Rsch. award, India, 1959—60, Tchg. Excellence award, U. Colo., 1993. Fellow AAAS, Acad.

Zoology, Animal Behavior Soc.; mem. Am. Soc. Zoologists, Ecol. Soc. Am., Am. Soc. Mammalogists, Am. Soc. Primatology (Disting. Primatologist award 1994), Internat. Primatology Soc., Am. Inst. Biol. Scis. Home: 6507 Baseline Rd Boulder CO 80303-3065

**SOUTHWICK, PAUL,** retired public relations executive; b. West Newton, Mass., Mar. 27, 1920; s. Alfred and Pauline (Winkler) S.; m. Susan Barbara Heider, Feb. 24, 1947; children: Thomas Paul, Peter Alfred, Linda Susan. AB in Econs. cum laude, Harvard Coll., 1943. Coor. AP, Concord, NH, 1947-49; UP UPI, Washington, 1949-57; mem. profl. staff govt. info. subcom. U.S. Ho. Reps., 1957-59; legis. asst., adminstrv. asst. U.S. Senator Long of Hawaii, 1959-62; dep. adminstr. charge accelerated pub. works program Area Redevel. Adminstrn., 1962-63; spl. asst. The White House, 1963-65; spl. asst. for congl. rels. Office of U.S. Sec. Commerce, 1965-67; v.p. Newmyer Assocs., Inc., Washington, 1967-87; ind. cons., 1987-93; ret., 1993. With USNR, 1941-45, PTO. Democrat. Home: 16 Green St Danvers MA 01923

**SOUTHWORTH, ROBERT ALEXANDER, JR.,** education researcher, educator; b. NYC, Jan. 6, 1959; s. Robert Alexander Southworth, Sr. and Katherine Hobson Southworth; m. Linda Estelle Fischl, Sept. 11, 1994; children: Ekaterina Sophia, Anna Natalya, Robert Alexander III. AB, Dartmouth Coll., 1981; EdM, Tufts U., 1983; EdD, Columbia U. Tchrs. Coll., 1999. Secondary sch. tchg. cert. Mass., 1983, cert. advanced study. Apprentice tchr. Shady Hill Sch., Cambridge, Mass., 1982—83; theater tech dir. Colo. Acad., Denver, 1983—86; asst. dir. Denver Ctr. Performing Arts, 1986—87, Am. Conservatory Theater, San Francisco, 1988—89; asst. rschr. Nat. Ctr. for Restructuring Edn., Schools and Tchg., Teachers Coll., NYC, 1993—96; pres. The SchoolWorks Lab, Inc., NYC, 2002—. Cons. Fenway Mid. Coll. H.S., Boston, 1990—92; adj. prof. Adelphi U. Grad. Sch. Edn., NYC, 1996—99, Bank St. Coll. Edn., NYC, 1998—2002; adj. asst. prof. Teachers Coll. Columbia U., NYC, 1998—2005. Named Bus. Man of Yr., US Congress, 2003. Mem.: Nat. Soc. Study of Edn., Am. Evaluation Assn., Am. Edn. Rsch. Assn., Phi Delta Kappa (v.p. 1997—2000), Kappa Delta Pi. Achievements include research in the positive effect on student scores in Music, ELA and Math due to music; development of a new website to help the public understand school reform; a process to improve teacher learning called Assessment Data Gathering; statewide system of accountability for 84 funded arts partnerships in New York. Home: 340 West 87 St Apt 8A New York NY 10024 Office: The SchoolWorks Lab Inc 28 West 44th St Ste 1509 New York NY 10036-6600 Office Phone: 212-768-7800. Office Fax: 212-768-8700. Business E-Mail: rasouth@edspeak.org.

**SOUTHWORTH, WILLIAM DIXON,** retired education educator; b. Union City, Tenn., Dec. 28, 1918; s. Thomas and Gertrude (Dyer) S.; m. Violet Kuehn, July 22, 1944; children: Geoffrey Scott, Linda Jean. PhB, Marquette U., 1948, MEd, 1950; PhD, NYU, 1961. Tchr., coach La Follette Sch., Milwaukee County, Wis., 1948-51; teaching dist. prin. Grand View Sch., Milwaukee County, 1951-56; supervising dist. prin. Maple Dale Sch., Milwaukee County, 1956-58; bldg. prin. Main St. Sch., Port Washington, N.Y., 1958-65; asst. supt. for elem. edn. Huntington (N.Y.) pub. schs., 1965-67; assoc. prof., acting head dept. adminstrn. and supervision St. John's U., Jamaica, N.Y., 1967, chmn. dept., 1968-73, prof., 1968-84. Parliamentarian for 35 internat., nat. regional orgns., expert witness, pub. moderator, and workshop leader. Author: Care and Nurture of the Doctoral Candidate, 1968, 74, Q The Story of Captain Quimby Scott, U.S. Navy WWII, 1997, The Art of Successful Meetings, 1997, Murder on the Flagship, 1998, Corpsman!, 1998, Murder Impossible, 2002, The Wonderful World of Words: How to Build and Retain a Superior Vocabulary, 2002, The Sensual Sailor, 2003, Murders in Old Main, 2004; contbr. over 270 articles to ednl. jours., condomition and parliamentary publs. With USN, 1938—44. Lutheran. Home: 411 First Ave N #811 Saint Petersburg FL 33701 Personal E-mail: vibilfid1@juno.com, williamsouthworth@aol.com. *In the conflicting demands of self and society, one must strike a balance by retaining the uniqueness of one's individuality while serving the society that nurtured that uniqueness. It is in the balance thus struck that the complete person evolves self-esteeming, and socially involved.*

**SOUTTER, THOMAS DOUGLAS,** retired lawyer; b. NYC, Nov. 1, 1934; s. Thomas G. and Hildreth H. (Callanan) S.; m. Virginia Hovenden; children: Alexander D., Christopher A., Hadley H. BA, U. Va., 1955, LL.B., 1962; postgrad., Advanced Mgmt. Program, Harvard U., 1980. Bar: N.Y. 1962, R.I. 1969. Atty. Breed, Abbott & Morgan, N.Y.C., 1962-68; with Textron Inc., Providence, 1968-95, gen. counsel, 1970-95, v.p., 1971-80, sr. v.p., 1980-85, exec. v.p., gen. counsel, 1985-95; cons., 1995-97. Mem. adv. bd. Internat. and Comparative Law Ctr., 1975-95; mem. Assn. Gen. Counsel; bd. dirs. Avco Fin. Svcs., Inc., 1985-95, Paul Revere Corp. 1993-95; trustee New England Legal Found. Nat. chmn. ann. giving campaign U. Va. Law Sch., 1992-94, mem. exec. com. campaign, 1995-2000; former trustee Providence Preservation Soc., Providence Performing Arts Ctr.; mem. U. Va. Arts and Scis. Alumni Coun.; mem. Narragansett coun. Boy Scouts Am. Lt. USNR, 1955-59. Mem. ABA, N.Y. State Bar Assn., R.I. Bar Assn., Internat. Bar Assn. Office: 2 White Birch Ln Barrington RI 02806-4932 E-mail: tdsout@aol.com.

**SOUVEROFF, VERNON WILLIAM, JR.,** corporate financial executive; b. L.A., Aug. 12, 1934; s. Vernon William Sr. and Aileen (Young) S.; m. Aileen Patricia Robinson; children: Gail Kathleen, Michael William, Kirk Laron BS in E.E., Stanford U., 1957; postgrad., Ohio State U., 1958-59. With Litton Industries, Beverly Hills, Calif., 1960-75; with ITT Corp., N.Y.C., 1975-87; prin. Bus. Acquisitions and Investments, 1988—; corp. v.p. ITT Corp., N.Y.C., 1983-84, sr. v.p., 1984-87; pres. ITT Gilfillan, 1979-83; group exec. ITT Def. Space Group, 1983-84; CEO ITT Telecom and Electronics N.Am., 1984-86; pres., chief exec. officer ITT Def. Tech. Corp., 1986-87. Mem. U.S. Def. Policy Adv. Com. on Trade, Washington, 1984-88; bd. advisors, investor Venture Resources, Venture Capital, 1988-92; bd. dirs. Elanix, Inc., Formida Holdings Ltd., Australia; chmn. bd. dirs. Formida Software Corp., San Jose, Calif Author books on def. downsizing Served as officer USAF, 1957-60 Recipient Exec. Salute award Los Angeles C. of C., 1981 Mem. IEEE (life), Nat. Contracts Mgmt. Assn., Electronics Industries Assn., Am. Def. Preparedness Assn. (former dir.), Nat. Security Indsl. Assn., Air Force Assn., Navy League, Assn. U.S. Army, Alamo Town Assn. (bd. mem.), S.R. Valley YMCA (chmn.) Presbyterian.

**SOUZA, DIANE D,** corporate financial executive; BS in acctg. with high honors, U. Mass.; AS in dental hygiene, Forsyth Sch. at Northeastern U. CPA. Dir. northeast ins. Price Waterhouse; sr. mgr. Deloitte Haskins & Sells; asst. v.p. Aetna Inc., 1994—96; v.p., CFO Large Case Pensions divsn. of Aetna Inc., 1996—98; v.p., dir. of internal audit Aetna Inc., 1998—2001, v.p., nat. customer ops., 2001—. Mem.: Conn. Soc. of CPA's (mem. ins. com.), Am. Inst. Cert. Pub. Accountants. Office: Aetna Inc 151 Farmington Ave Hartford CT 06156

**SOUZA, GILVAN CASTRO,** operations and management educator; b. Goiania, Brazil; BS in Aero. Engring., Tech. Inst. Aeronautics, Sao Jose dos Campos, Brazil, 1990; MBA, Clemson U., 1995; PhD, U. of N.C., 2000. Product devel. engr. Volkswagen, Sao Paulo, Brazil, 1991—94; asst. prof. U. of Md., Coll. Pk., Md., 2000—. Contbr. articles to profl. jours. Recipient Outstanding Grad. Student Rsch. award, Kenan Inst., U. of NC, 1998, Summer Rsch. award, U. of Md., 2001; scholar, Technol. Inst. of Aeronautics, Brazil, 1986—90. Mem.: Decision Sciences Inst., Prodn. and Ops. Mgmt. Soc., Inst. for Ops. Rsch. and Mgmt. Sci. Office: University of Maryland Smith School of Business College Park MD 20742

**SOUZA, JONATHAN RAYMOND,** music educator, conductor; b. Ceres, Calif., Mar. 12, 1978; s. Raymond Lee and Elizabeth Anne Souza; m. Christina Ann Stanard, Dec. 29, 2001; children: Cecilia, Nigel. BA in Music Edn. and Vocal Performance, Humboldt State U.; MA in Music Choral Conducting, San Jose State U. Music educator Santa Cruz (Calif.) Waldorf Sch., 2001—02, Branham H.S., San Jose, Calif., 2002—04; dir. music 1st Congl. Ch. San Jose, 2003—05; music educator Spring Hill Elem. Sch., Santa

Cruz, 2004—05, Georgiana Bruce Kirby Prep. Sch., Santa Cruz, 2004—05. Fortuna (Calif.) Union H.S., 2005—. Pvt. music instr. Studio Souza, Fortuna, 1996—2006; tenor soloist, Calif., 1999—2006; music dir. Humboldt Light Opera Co., Arcata, 1999—2001; artist dir., condr. Arcata (Calif.) Choral Artists, 2004—; adjudicator Internat. Championship Collegiate A Cappella, Calif., 2005—05. Composer: (choral composition) For You, Sing Joyfully!, (band composition) Curious. Mem.: No. Calif. Band Dirs. Assn., Calif. Band Dirs. Assn., Am. Choral Dirs. Assn., Calif. Music Educators Assn., Music Educators Nat. Conf. Democrat. Avocations: travel, movies, hiking. Office: Fortuna Union High School 379 12th St Fortuna CA 95540 E-mail: jon@studiosouza.com.

**SOUZA, LAWRENCE M.,** health facility administrator; AB in Bacteriology, U. Calif., Berkeley, 1975; PhD in Molecular Biology, UCLA, 1980. With Amgen, Thousand Oaks, Calif., 1981—, v.p. molecular and cellular biology, dir. exploratory programs, sr. v.p. rsch., 1997—. Adj. prof. dept. microbiology and immunology UCLA.

**SOUZA, THOMAS A.,** music educator; b. Taunton, Mass., July 13, 1977; s. Thomas Joseph and Carol Ann Souza; m. Julie Souza, Aug. 7, 2004. MB, U. Mass., 2001. Cert. music tchr. Mass. Music tchr. Ayer H.S., Mass., 2004—05. Mem. MMEA.

**SOUZA, VALERIE M.,** research scientist; b. Waltham, Mass., Apr. 22, 1980; BA in Portuguese Studies, U. of Mass., North Dartmouth, 2004, MA in Portuguese Studies, 2006. Rsch. asst. U. of Mass., North Dartmouth, 2004—. Part-time lectr. U. Mass., North Dartmouth, 2004—06.

**SOVERN, MICHAEL IRA,** law educator; b. NYC, Dec. 1, 1931; s. Julius and Lillian (Arnstein) S.; m. Lenore Goodman, Feb. 21, 1952 (div. Apr. 1963); children: Jeffrey Austin, Elizabeth Ann, Douglas Todd; m. Eleanor Leen, Aug. 25, 1963 (div. Feb. 1974); 1 child, Julie Danielle; m. Joan Wit, Mar. 9, 1974 (dec. Sept. 1993); m. Patricia Walsh, Nov. 12, 1995. AB summa cum laude, Columbia U., 1953, LLB (James Ordronaux prize), 1955, LLD (hon.), 1980; PhD (hon.), Tel Aviv U., 1982; LLD (hon.), U. So. Calif., 1989. Bar: N.Y. 1956, U.S. Supreme Ct. 1976. Asst. prof., then assoc. prof. law U. Minn. Law Sch., 1955-58; mem. faculty Columbia Law Sch., 1957—, prof. law, 1960—, Chancellor Kent prof., 1977—, dean Law Sch., 1970-79; chmn. exec. com. faculty Columbia U., 1968-69, provost, exec. v.p., 1979-80, univ. pres., 1980-93, pres. emeritus, 1993. Rsch. dir. Legal Restraints on Racial Discrimination in Employment, Twentieth Century Fund, 1962-66; spl. counsel to gov. N.J., 1974-77; cons. Time Mag., 1965-80; mem. panel of arbitrators N.J. Bd. Mediation, Fed. Mediation and Conciliation Svc.; bd. dirs. Sequa, Asian Cultural Coun., Shubert Orgn., Comcast Corp., Sta. WNET-TV, NAACP Legal Def. Fund, 1976-97, Freedom Forum Newseum; chmn. N.Y.C. Charter Revision Commn., 1982-83; co-chmn. 2d Cir. Commn. on Reduction of Burdens and Costs in Civil Litigation, 1977-80; chmn. Commn. on Integrity in Govt., 1986; pres. Italian Acad. Advanced Studies in Am., 1991-93, Shubert Found., 1996—; chmn. Japan Soc., 1993-2004, hon. chmn., 2004—; chmn. Am. Acad. Rome, 1993-2005, chmn. emeritus, 2005—; chmn. Sotheby's, 2000—; chmn. nat. adv. coun. Freedom Forum Media Studies Ctr., 1993-2001. Author: Legal Restraints on Racial Discrimination in Employment, 1966, Law and Poverty, 1969, Of Boundless Domains, 1994; host Sta. WNET-TV series Leading Questions. Mem. Pulitzer Prize Bd., 1980-93, chmn. pro tem, 1986-87; trustee Kaiser Family Found., 1994-2002, Presdl. Legal Expense Trust, 1994-98; chmn. Sotheby's, 2000. Decorated commendatore Order of Merit (Italy), Order of the Rising Sun, Gold and Silver Star (Japan); recipient Alexander Hamilton medal Columbia Coll., 1993, Citizens Union Civic Leadership award, 1993, Town Hall Friend of the Arts award, 2001, Centennial medal Am. Acad. Rome, 2006. Fellow Am. Acad. Arts and Scis.; mem. ABA, Coun. Fgn. Rels., Assn. Bar City N.Y., Am. Philos. Soc., Am. Arbitration Assn. (panel arbitrators), Am. Law Inst., Econ. Club, Nat. Acad. Arbitrators. Office: Columbia U Sch Law 435 W 116th St New York NY 10027-7297 Office Phone: 212-854-7848. Business E-Mail: mem1@columbia.edu. E-mail: msovern@law.columbia.edu.

**SOVIK, EDWARD ANDERS,** architect, consultant; b. Honan, China, June 9, 1918; s. Edward Anderson and Anna (Tenwick) S.; m. Genevieve Elaine Hendrickson, June 29, 1946 (dec.); m. Anne Running, Mar. 25, 2001; children: Rolf, Martin, Peter. Ba. St. Olaf Coll., 1939; student, Art Students League N.Y., 1939-40, Luther Theol. Sem., 1940—41; MArch, Yale U., 1949; DFA (hon.), Concordia Coll., 1981. Ret. chmn. SMSQ, Architects and predecessors, Northfield, Minn.; prof. art emeritus St. Olaf Coll., Northfield. Lectr. on ch. design at various confs., schs., univs.; participant, planner, del. numerous domestic and fgn. confs. on religion and architecture; mem., officer various profl., religious and pub. bds. and comms. Author: Architecture for Worship; Contbr. numerous articles to mags., anthologies.; works include chs., coll. and univ. bldgs., instns. With USMC, 1942-45; maj. Res. Decorated D.F.C., Purple Heart, Air medals; recipient Diekmann award, N.Am. Acad. Liturgy, 2003. Fellow AIA; mem. AIA Minn. (pres. 1977, Gold medal 1981), Phi Beta Kappa. Democrat. Lutheran. Home: 711 Summit Ave Northfield MN 55057-1568 E-mail: sovik@rconnect.com.

**SOWA, ARTUR,** mathematician, researcher; b. Poland, Oct. 27, 1965; came to U.S., 1992; s. Witold and Lucyna Sowa; m. Jolanta Sowa, Aug. 15, 1987; children: Izaak, Oliver. MS in Math., Warsaw U., 1990; PhD in Math., CUNY, 1995. Postdoctoral asst. CUNY, N.Y.C., 1995-97; postdoctoral rsch. assoc. Yale U., New Haven, 1997-2000, lectr., 2000; scientist Pegasus Imaging Corp., Tampa, Fla., 2000—02; online instr. U. Phoenix, 2003—, math. area co-chair, 2006. Collaborator, nano tech. program Utopia Compression Corp., LA, 2005. Contbr. articles to profl. jours. Recipient 1st prize, The Marcinkiewicz Competition, Poland, 1990, Rsch. Associateship award, NRC, 2001. Mem.: IEEE. Achievements include research in mesoscopic physics spectrum of correlated systems of electrons and the mesoscopic mechanics. Home: 109 Snow Crest Trl Durham NC 27707-6102 E-mail: ArturSowa@mesoscopia.com.

**SOWALD, HEATHER GAY,** lawyer; b. Columbus, Ohio, Dec. 26, 1954; d. Martin M. and Beatrice (Kronick) S.; m. Robert Marc Kaplan, June 12, 1977; children: Andrew Scott, Alexis Beth. BA, Case Western Res. U., 1976; JD, Capital U., 1979. Bar: Ohio 1979, U.S. Dist. Ct. (so. dist.) Ohio 1980, U.S. Ct. Appeals (6th cir.) 1981, U.S. Supreme Ct., 1987. Ptnr. Sowald & Sowald, Columbus, 1979-85, Sowald & Daneman, Columbus, 1985-1987, Sowald, Sowald & Mas, Columbus, 1988, Sowald, Sowald & Clouse, Columbus. Hearing officer Cert. Need Rev. Bd. State of Ohio, 1982—; Dept. Adminstrv. Services, 1982—; Dept. Mental Health, 1986—; Dept. Mental Retardation, 1986-88, Dept. Health, 1986-89, Ohio Dept. Liquor Control, 1989—; Bd. dirs. Wilderness Bond, Inc., Franklin County, Ohio, 1982-86, Youth Svcs. Adv. Bd., Franklin County, 1984—, chmn. 1987—, Ohio Bd. of Nursing, 1988—; legal advisor United Way League Against Child Abuse, Franklin County, 1986-87. Mem. Ohio State Bar Assn. (council of dels. 1986, pres. 2004, mem. family law com.), Columbus Bar Assn. (chmn. juvenile law com. 1982-84, chmn. admissions to bar 1984-86, chmn. publications com., 1987-88, chmn. family law com. 1988—, ethics com. 1988—), Franklin County Trial Lawyers Assn. (trustee 1985-88, treas. 1988-89. pres.-elect 1989—, pres. 1989-90), Women Lawyers of Franklin County (pres. 1984-85), Capital U. Law Sch. Alumni Assn. (pres. 1984-86). Democrat. Jewish. Office: Sowald Sowald & Clouse One Americana 400 S 5th St Ste 101 Columbus OH 43215

**SOWANDE, BEVERLY FOLASADE,** lawyer, educator; d. Olufela Charles and Mildred Bernice (Marshall) Sowande. BA, CUNY, 1963, MS, 1966; PhD, NYU, 1974; JD, Yeshiva U., 1980. Bar: N.Y., U.S. Dist. Ct. (so. dist., ea. dist.), U.S. Ct. Appeals (2d cir.), U.S. Supreme Ct. Pvt. practice, N.Y.C., 1986—88, 1990—; assoc. counsel Office Gen. Counsel CUNY, 1988—90; 1st dep. gen. counsel Human Resources Adminstrn., N.Y.C., 1990—92. From lectr. to assoc. prof. Hunter Coll. CUNY, 1970—93, adj. assoc. prof. women's studies program and dept. polit. sci., 1982—86, N.Y.C., 1995—96, adj. assoc. prof. Consortium for Worker Edn., 1987—88, adj. assoc. prof. dept. comm.,

1995—96; panel mem. departmental disciplinary com. 1st Jud. Dept., 1993—98; presenter in field. Pro bono atty. for indigent and abused women and men Coun. N.Y. Law Assocs. and NYU Law Project for Battered Women, 1986—88; adv. bd. Sanctuary Families Legal Advocacy Ctr., N.Y.C., 1988—90; coord. pro bono domestic violence panel Family Ct. Project, Victim Svcs. Agy., 1989—93; mem. N.Y.C. Conditional Release Commn., 1989—96; bd. dirs. Lenox Hill Neighborhood Assn., Inc., N.Y.C., 1993—96; trustee Urban Resource Inst., Bklyn., 1994—97, sec. bd. trustees, 1997—98; adv. bd. Rosen Scholars Program, N.Y.C., 1996—97; cert. rape crisis counselor, sexual assault and violence intervention program Mt. Sinai Med. Ctr., N.Y.C., 2004—. Named to Hunter Coll. Hall of Fame, CUNY, 1987; recipient Cert. Appreciation, Urban Women's Retreat, 1991; Univ. Founder's scholar, NYU, 1974, Danforth Found. fellow, 1974. Mem.: N.Y. State Bar Assn. (Pres.'s Pro Bono Svc. award 1989, Merit award 1990), Assn. Bar City of N.Y. (crime victims com. 1992, matrimonial law com. 1992—93, dir. lawyer's com. violence 1994—96, com. profl. responsibility 1997—98), N.Y. Women's Bar Assn. (chair com. battered women 1987—91, coord. pro bono domestic violence project 1987—93, bd. dirs. 1988—92, chair continuing legal edn. com. 1991—94, corr. sec. 1992—93, rec. sec. 1993—94), N.Y. County Lawyers Assn. (com. minorities 1992), Coun. N.Y. Law Assocs. (bd. dirs. 1988—92, chair bd. mem. not-for-profit law project 1988—92, Cert. of Appreciation for Pro Bono Activities 1988), Wistarians Alumni Hunter Coll. CUNY (v.p. 1986—88, pres. 1988—90), Alumni Assn. Hunter Coll. CUNY (bd. dirs. 1977—78, sec. 1978—81, 2d v.p. 1981—84, 4th v.p. 1984—87, 2d v.p. 1987—90, chair bylaws revision com. 1987—93, 1st v.p. 1990—93, pres. 1993—96). Personal E-mail: bsowande@aol.com.

**SOWDER, FRED ALLEN,** foundation administrator, alphabet specialist; b. Cin., July 17, 1940; s. William Franklin and Lucille (Estes) Sowder; m. Sandra Ann Siegman, July 15, 1961 (div. Sept. 1963); 1 child, William. Student, Cin. Sch. Ct. Reporting, 1975; diploma Self-Health Insts., Sch. of Med. Masso-Therapy, 1985; diploma, Cin. Sch. Hypnosis, 1989. Founder World Union Universal Alphabet, Cin., 1981—; Internat. Assn. Sch. Massage, Cin., 1988—. Inventor of hundreds of published and unpublished alphabets and writing systems, including light wave, color and musical tone systems and tactile systems for the blind; author: Sowder Shorthand, 1980, Universal Alphabet: What and Why, 1981, Your Intimacy Quotient: The Symptoms, Causes & Consequences of Intimacy Deprivation, 1996; contbr. numerous articles to mags. State dir. Soc. Separationists, Cin., 1967-70; bd. dirs. ACLU of Ohio, ACLU Found., 1984-89, sec., Cin. chpt., 1984-89. Mem. AAAS, Amnesty Internat., Ohio Com. to Abolish Capital Punishment, No. Ky. Right to Life, Urban Appalachian Coun. Home: PO Box 252 Cincinnati OH 45201-0252 Office: World Union Universal Alphabet PO Box 252 Cincinnati OH 45201-0252

**SOWDER, KATHLEEN ADAMS,** marketing executive; b. Person county, N.C., Feb. 9, 1951; d. George W. and Mary W. (Woody) Adams; m. Angelo R. LoMascolo, Apr. 11, 1980 (div.); 1 child, Mary Jennifer. BS, Radford Coll., 1976, MBA, Va. Poly. Inst., 1977. Bd. cert. in security mgmt. Cert. Protection Profl. Asst. product mgr. GTE Sylvania, Waltham, Mass., 1978—79, product mgr. video products, 1979—80; comml. mktg. mgr. Am. Dist. Telegraph, N.Y.C., 1980—87; v.p. mktg. ESL, Hingham, Mass., 1987—91; exec. v.p. Falcon Detection Techs., Inc., Plymouth, Mass., 1991—94; gen. mgr. Westec Bus. Security, Irvine, Calif., 1995—2000; CEO Nova Security Sys., Fullerton, Calif., 2000—. Mem.: Am. Soc. Indsl. Security (past chair standing com. on phys. security); Am. Mktg. Assn. Republican. Office: Nova Security Systems 819 Pueblo Fullerton CA 92835 Home: 10473 La Sombra Ave Fountain Valley CA 92708-5210 E-mail: ksowder@novasecuritysystems.com.

**SOWDER, ROBERT ROBERTSON,** architect; b. Kansas City, Kans., Dec. 29, 1928; s. James Robert and Agnes (Robertson) S.; m. Joan Goddard, July 26, 1954; 1 dau., Lisa Robertson Lee. BA, U. Wash., 1953; B.Arch., U. Va., 1958; grad. diploma in Architecture, Ecole Des Beaux Arts, Fontainebleau, France, 1952. Designer Architects Collaborative, Boston, 1958-59, Peirce & Pierce (architects), Boston, 1959-63; asso. Fred. Bassetti & Co. (architects), Seattle, 1963-67; partner Naramore, Bain, Brady & Johanson (architects), Seattle, 1967-81; pres. NBBJ Internat., 1976-81; architect TRA, Seattle, 1981-83; v.p. Daniel, Mann, Johnson & Mendenhall, San Francisco, 1983-93; prin. RRS Consulting, 1993—. Archtl. design critic Boston Archtl. Ctr., 1961-62. Important works include Ridgeway III Dormitories, Bellingham, Wash. (Dept. Housing and Urban Devel. Honor award), Seattle Rapid Transit (HUD Excellence award), Safeco Ins. Co. Home Office Complex, Seattle, King County Stadium, Balt. Conv. Ctr., Oreg. Conv. Ctr., San Francisco (Moscone) Conv. Ctr. Expansion, Honolulu Conv. Ctr., Wilmington (Del.) Conv. Ctr. Mem. Redmond (Wash.) Design Rev. Bd., 1996-2000. Served with CIC U.S. Army, 1954-56. Recipient Premier Prix D'Architecture Ecole Des Beaux Arts, Fontainebleau, 1951, 52, Prix D'Remondet Fontainebleau, 1952 Mem. AIA (emeritus), Internat. Assn. Assembly Mgrs., Seattle Tennis Club, Seattle Rainier Club, Scarab, Sigma Chi. Episcopalian. Home and Office: 17032 NE 135th Ct Redmond WA 98052-1715

**SOWELL, LAVEN,** retired music educator; b. Wewoka, Okla., Jan. 9, 1933; s. Vestal Laven and Viola Jane Sowell. MusB, U. Okla., 1955; MA, Columbia U., 1964; postgrad., Manhattan Sch. Music, 1956—57, Conservatoire de Musique de Fontainebleau, France, 1966; studied with Clark Snell, Martial Singher, Joseph Benton, John Brownlee, Samuel Margolis, Nadia Boulanger, studied choral conducting with Harry Robert Wilson. Choral condr. Edison H.S., Tulsa, 1961—70; chorus master Tulsa Opera, 1962—94, chorus master emeritus, 1994—; dir. music 1st Presbyn. Ch., Tulsa, 1969—85; prof. music U. Tulsa, 1970—91. Vocal adjudicator various mus. orgns.; tchr. pvt. voice lessons. Co-author: Tulsa Opera Chronicles, 1992; author: My Music Notebook, 2000. Bd. dirs. Tulsa Opera. Recipient Gov.'s Arts award State of Okla., 1991. Mem.: Tulsa Accredited Music Teacher's Assn., Okla. Music Teacher's Assn. Democrat. Presbyterian. Avocations: travel, reading, opera. Home: 3800 W 71st Apt 2312 Tulsa OK 74132-2153 Office Phone: 918-388-4461.

**SOWELL, THOMAS,** economist, syndicated columnist; b. Gastonia, NC, June 30, 1930; AB, Harvard U. 1958; A.M., Columbia U., 1959; PhD, U. Chgo., 1968. Economist Dept. Labor, 1961-62; instr. econs. Douglass Coll., Rutgers U., 1962-63; lectr. econs. Howard U., 1963-64; econ. analyst AT&T, 1964-65; asst. prof. Cornell U., 1965-69; assoc. prof. Brandeis U., 1969-70; assoc. prof. econs. UCLA, 1970-74, prof., 1974-80; project dir. Urban Inst., Washington, 1972-74; fellow Hoover Inst., 1977, 80—, 1980—. Vis. prof. Amherst Coll., 1977 Author: Ethnic America, 1981, A Conflict of Visions, 1987, Inside American Education, 1993, Race and Culture, 1994, The Vision of the Anointed, 1995, Basic Economics, 2000, Black Rednecks and White Liberals, 2005, On Classical Economics, 2006; contbr. articles to profl. publs, syndicated columnist. Served with USMC, 1951-53. Mem. Am. Econ. Assn., Nat. Acad. Edn. Office: Stanford Univ Hoover Instn Stanford CA 94305 also: Creators Syndicate 5777 W Century Blvd Los Angeles CA 90045 Business E-Mail: sowell@stanford.edu.

**SOWELL, THORNWELL F. (BIFF),** lawyer; b. Wadesboro, NC, Nov. 7, 1950; BA, Clemson Univ., 1973; JD, Univ. SC, 1976. Bar: SC 1976, US Dist. Ct. (SC) 1977, US Ct. Appeals (4th cir. 1977, Fed. cir. 1999), US Ct. Fed. Claims 1992, US Supreme Ct. 1980. Mem., comml. litigation Sowell Gray Stepp & Lafitte LLC, Columbia, SC. Fellow: SC Bar Found.; mem.: ABA, Am. Bd. Trial Advocates, Fedn. Def. & Corp. Counsel, SC Bar (mem. Ho. Del.), Richland County Bar Assn. Office: Sowell Gray Stepp & Lafitte LLC PO Box 11449 1310 Gadsden St Columbia SC 29211 Office Phone: 803-231-7835. Office Fax: 803-231-7885. Business E-Mail: bsowell@sowell.com.

**SOWER, MILENE A.,** nursing educator; b. LaCrosse, Wis., Oct. 14, 1939; d. Miles Marcus and Dorethea Rose (Cox) Morrison; children: Karlene A. Mrosko, Paula B. Utley. BSN, Coll. St. Scholastica, Duluth, Minn., 1961; MA, U. Iowa, 1972, PhD, 1980. Dir. nursing edn. Moline (Ill.) Pub. Hosp.

Sch. Nursing; dir. nursing administn. grad. prog. U. S.C., Columbia; dean nursing Coastal Carolina Coll., Conway, S.C.; exec. sec. N.Y. State Bd. for Nursing, N.Y. State Edn. Dept., Albany; ret. 2001. Contbr. articles to profl. jours. Mem. Am. Nurses Assn., Am. Bus. Women's Assn. Home: 1960 Bell Rd Crossville TN 38571-7476

**SOWER, VICTOR EDMUND,** management educator; b. Roanoke, Va., Sept. 3, 1946; s. Hammond Edmundson and Daphne Muriel (Dymond) S.; m. Judith Lynn Carroll, June 17, 1967; children: Diane C. Sower Fuller, Christopher Hammond. BS in Chemistry, Va. Poly. Inst. and State U., 1968; MBA, Auburn U., Ala., 1980; PhD, U. North Tex., Denton, 1990. Cert. quality engr., Am. Soc. Quality. Process engr. Radford Army Ammunition Plant, Va., 1968—69; mgr. process devel. engring. Ampex Corp., Opelika, Ala., 1971—80; gen. mgr. Tandy Magnetics, Ft. Worth, 1980—87; mfg. cons. Tandy Corp., Ft. Worth, 1987—90; prof. dept. mgmt. and mktg. Sam Houston State U., Huntsville, Tex., 1990—, Piper prof., 2005—. Mem. steering com. Ctr. Bus. and Econ. Rsch., Huntsville, 1990—; mem. editl. review bd. of Jour. Operations Mgmt., Jour. Bus. Strategies; cons. various mfg. and svc. orgns. Author: Time Study for the Small Business, 1979, Classic Readings in Operations Management, 1995, An Introduction to Quality Management and Engineering, 1999; mem. editl. rev. bd. Jour. Bus. Strategies, Huntsville, 1990—, Jour. Ops. Mgmt., 1995—; contbr. articles to profl. jours. Mem. dist. com. Bedford (Tex.) area Boy Scouts Am., 1987-90, dist. advancement chmn., 1988-89. Lt. U.S. Army, 1969-71 (Army Commendation medal). Named Piper Prof., Minnie Stevens Piper Found. Tex., 2005; recipient Excellence in Tchg. award, Sam Houston State U., 1996, Excellence in Rsch. award, 2001. Mem. AIChE (sr.), Inst. Supply Mgmt., Am. Chem. Soc., Am. Soc. Quality Control (sr. cert.), Prodn. and Inventory Control Soc., Decision Scis. Inst., Acad. Mgmt Roman Catholic. Office: Sam Houston State U Dept Mgmt and Mktg Huntsville TX 77341-2056 Business E-Mail: sowerv@shsu.edu.

**SOWERS, AMELIA BARNET,** speech and language pathologist; b. Houston, Mar. 13, 1952; d. Albert Glenn and Helen June (Meador) Barnet; m. George Vernon Sowers Jr., Aug. 23, 1975; children: George Vernon III, Adam Glenn. BA, U. Houston, 1975, MA, 1993. Lic. and cert. speech-lang. pathologist, Tex. Speech-lang. pathologist Aldine Ind. Sch. Dist., Houston, 1976-78, Tomball (Tex.) Ind. Sch. Dist., 1978-83, Conroe (Tex.) Ind. Sch. Dist., 1984-96; pvt. practice, 1996—. Mem. Crighton Players; organizer Crighton Kidz, Crighton Players Performing Arts Sch. for Youth, exec. dir.; apptd. to City of Conroe Commn. on Arts & Culture; pres. Crighton Theatre Found. 1999-2001; clin. supr. Grad. Sch., Tex. Women's U. 1997-98 Mem. NEA, Am. Speech, Lang. and Hearing Assn., Tex. Speech and Hearing Assn., Tex. Tchrs. Assn., Houston Assn. Comm. Disorders, Montgomery County Performing Arts Soc. (com.), Conroe Svc. League (v.p. 2004-2005, pres. 2005-06) Methodist. Avocations: reading, crafts, dance, theater. Home and Office: 25 Village Hill Dr Conroe TX 77304-3525

**SOWERS, MARILYN RAE,** librarian; b. Gary, Ind., Jan. 5, 1943; d. Terzo Paul and Mary Saveria (DeNicola) Amidei; m. George Maxton Sowers, Aug. 27, 1966; children: George, Joseph, John, Michael. AB in History, Ind. U., 1964, MAT in Social Studies, 1966, MLS, 1970. Tchr. Gary Pub. Schs., 1966, libr., 1969-70, MicIntire Pub. Libr., Charlottesville, Va., 1966-69; reference libr. Indpls. Pub. Libr., 1970; asst. libr. Centerville (Ind.) Pub. Libr., 1976-79; interim libr. Ind. U. East, Richmond, Ind., 1978-79; substitute tchr. Richmond (Ind.) Community Schs., 1984-87; media supervisor Union County Sch. Corp., Liberty, Ind., 1987—. Bd. dirs. Ind. Cooperative Libr. Svcs. Authority. Bd. dirs., sec. Wayne Twp. Bd., Richmond, 1985—; mem. Gov.'s Select Commn. for Primary and Secondary Edn., Ind., 1982-84; mem. State Student's Assistance Commn. of Ind., 1988-90. Mem. ALA, NEA, ASCD, Am. Assn. Sch. Librs., Ind. Media Educators, Ind. State Tchrs. Assn., Assn. Ednl. Comm. and Tech. Avocations: ballroom dancing, camping, running. Office: Union County High Sch 410 Patriot Blvd Liberty IN 47353-1213 Office Phone: 765-458-5136. E-mail: msowers@uc.k12.in.us.

**SOWERS, WESLEY HOYT,** lawyer, management consultant; b. Whiting, Ind., Aug. 26, 1905; s. Samuel Walter and Bertha E. (Spurrier) S.; m. Gladys Krueger, Jan. 21, 1929; children: Penny (Mrs. David Buxton), Wesley Hoyt Jr. BS, Purdue U., 1926, MS, 1927; JD, DePaul U., 1941; grad., Advanced Mgmt. Program, Harvard, 1960. Bar: Ill. 1940; registered patent atty. and practitioner ICC. Chemist Shell Oil Co., East Chicago, Ind., 1927-29; sales engr. Nat. Lead Co., St. Louis, 1929-31; lab. supr. patent atty. Pure Oil Co., Chgo., 1932-42; v.p. Bay Chem. Co., New Orleans, 1942-50, Frontier Chem. Co., Wichita, Kans., 1950-57; pres. Frontier Chem. div. Vulcan Materials Co., 1957-65; exec. v.p., dir. Vulcan Materials Co., Birmingham, 1958-65; mgmt. counsel, 1965—. Mem. health professions vis. com. Wichita State U. Patentee in field. Past chmn. Met. Planning Commn., Wichita and Sedgwick County, 1958; commr. Kans. Econ. Devel. Bd.; chmn. Kansas Com. for Constitutional Revision, Sedgwick County U.S. Savs. Bonds Sales; past chmn. Kans. Radio Free Europe; past mem. adv. coun. Kans. Geol. Survey; mem. Kans. Senate, 1970-81; former mem. engring. adv. council Sch. Engring. and Architecture, Kans. State U.; regent trustee Wichita State U., HCA/Wesley Med. Ctr., Wichita; bd. dirs. Health Systems Agy. of Southeast Kans., Bd. of Health Sedgwick County, Inst. Logopedics, Quivira council Boy Scouts Am., YMCA, Health Systems Agy. S.E. Kans.; past trustee Midwest Research Inst.; mem. adv. bd. Kans. U. Bus. Sch.; vis. com. Coll. Health Profession, Wichita State U.; chmn. Kans. Health Care Providers Malpractice Commn.; mem. Kans. Health Care Costs Commn., Kans. Health Coordinating Council, Wichita/Sedgwick County Bd. Health; mem. gov.'s adv. commn. Kans. Dept. Health and Environment Mem. AAAS, Kans. C. of C. (past pres., past dir.), Wichita C. of C. (past pres. 1959, past dir., Uncommon Citizen award 1988), Kans. Assn. Commerce and Industry (past pres., dir.), Am. Chem. Soc., AAAS, Smithsonian Assocs., Boo. Chem. Industry, Ill. Bar Assn., Wichita Bar Assn., Phi Delta Theta. Lodges: Rotary. Home and Office: 600 W Arapaho Rd Apt 1034 Richardson TX 75080 Office Phone: 972-907-8857.

**SOWMAN, HAROLD GENE,** ceramics engineer, researcher; b. Murphysboro, Ill., July 21, 1923; s. Harold Thomas and Thelma (Crombar) S.; m. Gladys May Wright, Dec. 8, 1945; children— Letitia Ann, Daniel Patrick BS in Ceramic Engring., U. Ill., 1948, MS in Ceramic Engring., 1949, PhD in Ceramic Engring., 1951. Assoc. ceramist Titanium Alloy, Niagara Falls, NY, 1951-52; research assoc. Knolls Atomic Power Lab., Gen. Electric Co., Schenectady, 1952-57; various supervisory and mgmt. positions in nuclear materials research and devel. 3M Co., St. Paul, 1957-65, research specialist, 1965-67, sr. research specialist, 1967-70, corp. scientist, 1970-87. Friedberg Meml. lectr. Nat. Inst. Ceramic Engrs., 1988. Author articles, govt. reports on research and devel. of ceramic and nuclear materials; patentee in field Served to 2d lt. AUS, 1943-46 Recipient Hon. Alumni award for disting. service in engring. U. Ill. Coll. Engring. 1983 Fellow Am. Ceramic Soc. (John Jeppson medal 1985, Samuel Geijsbeek award 1989); mem. Nat. Acad. Engring., Acad. of Ceramics, 3M Carlton Soc., Tau Beta Pi (chpt. Eminent Engr. award 1983). Home: 4770 Aston Gardens Way Unit 304 Naples FL 34109

**SOX, HAROLD CARLETON, JR.,** physician, educator, editor; b. Palo Alto, Calif., Aug. 18, 1939; s. Harold Carleton and Mary (Griffiths) Sox; m. Carol Helen Hill, Aug. 26, 1962; children: Colin Montgomery, Lara Katherine. BS, Stanford U., 1961; MD cum laude, Harvard U., 1966. Diplomate Am. Bd. Internal Medicine. Intern and resident Mass. Gen. Hosp., Boston, 1966—68; clin. assoc. Nat. Cancer Inst., Bethesda, Md., 1968—70; instr. Dartmouth Med. Sch., Hanover, NH, 1970—73; asst. prof. medicine to prof. clin. medicine Stanford U. Sch. Medicine, Calif., 1973—88; Joseph Huber prof., chmn. dept. medicine Dartmouth Med. Sch., 1988—2001; editor Annals of Internal Medicine ACP, Phila., 2001—. Pretest writing com. Am. Bd. Internal Medicine, 1992—94; panel mem. Nat. Bd. Med. Examiners, Physician Assts. Nat. Certifying Exam., 1973—76; chair com. on prioritysetting for health tech. assessment Inst. Medicine, 1990—91, U.S. preventive svcs. task force chair, 1990—95, mem., 1998—2001; chair Inst. Medicine com. on HIV and U.S. blood supply 1994—95; chair task force to revise internal medicine residency curriculum Federated Coun. Internal Medicine, 1993—97; chair Inst. Medicine Com. Health Effects Persian Gulf War Svc.,

1998—2000; nat. adv. com. generalist physician Scholars Program Robert Wood Johnson Found., 1992—, chmn., nat. adv. com. physician Faculty Scholar Program, 2005—; physician Leaders Nat. Drug Policy, 1997—; founding chair exec. com. Medicare Coverage Adv. Com., 1999—2003; report rev. com. NRC, 2000—05. Author: Medical Decision Making, 1988; editor: Common Diagnostic Tests, 1987, Common Diagnostic Tests, 2d edit., 1990; mem. editl. bd.: Med. Decision Making, 1980—87, Jour. Gen. Internal Medicine, 1985—87, New Eng. Jour. Medicine, 1990—97, cons. assoc. editor: Am. Jour. Medicine, 1988—95, assoc. editor: Sci. Am. Medicine, 1995—2001; contbr. chapters to books, articles to profl. jours. Bd. dirs. Found. Informed Med. Decision Making, 2002—; internat. adv. bd. Clin. Trial Registration Platform program WHO, 2005—. Master: ACP (clin. efficacy assessment subcom. 1989—92, bd. regents 1991—2000, chmn. ednl. policy com. 1994—97, pres. 1998—99); fellow: AAAS, Coll. Physicians Phila. (bd. trustees 2000—), Royal Australasian Coll. Physicians (hon.); mem.: Internat. Com. Med. Jour. Editors, Inst. Medicine Nat. Acads., Assn. Am. Physicians, Soc. Med. Decision Making (trustee 1980—83, pres. 1983—84, 4th Career Achievement award 1998), Soc. Gen. Internal Medicine (coun. 1980—83, Robert J. Glaser Career Achievement award 2000), Alpha Omega Alpha. Home: 232 Philip Pl Philadelphia PA 19106 Office: Am Coll Physicians 190 N Independence Mall W Philadelphia PA 19106-1572 Office Phone: 215-351-2620. Personal E-mail: hsox@mail.acponline.org.

**SOYER, DAVID**, cellist, music educator; b. Phila., Feb. 24, 1923; s. Samson and Esther (Faggin) Soyer; m. Janet Putnam, June 23, 1957; children: Daniel, Jeffrey. Student pub. schs., N.Y.C.; DFA (hon.), U. South Fla., 1976, SUNY, 1983. Prof. cello Curtis Inst. Music, 1967; prof. music U. Md.; prof. Manhattan Sch. Music Boston U.; prof. Juilliard Sch. Music, N.Y.C. Musician (cellist): Bach Aria Group, 1948—49, Guilet Quartet, 1949—51, New Music Quartet, 1954—55, Guarneri String Quartet, 1964— (5 Grammy awards for Guarneri Quartet recs.). With USNR, 1942—46. Mem.: Century Assn. Jewish. Home: 6 W 77th St New York NY 10024-5125 Office: Herbert Barrett Mgmt 266 W 37th St Fl 20 New York NY 10018-6648

**SOYFER, VALERY NIKOLAYEVICH**, geneticist, biophysicist; b. Gorky, RSFSR, USSR, Oct. 16, 1936; came to U.S., 1988; s. Nikolay Ilya Soyfer and Anna A. Kuznetsova; m. Nina I. Yakovleva, Aug. 12, 1961; children: Marina, Vladimir. BS in Agronomy, Timiryazev Agrl. Acad., Moscow, 1957; MS in Biophysics, Lomonosov State U., Moscow, 1961; PhD in Molecular Genetics, Kurchatov Inst. Atomic Energy, Moscow, 1964; D Phys. and Math. Scis., Moscow, 1994. Head Group Inst. Gen. Genetics, Moscow, 1966-70; dir. Lab. Molecular Genetics, Moscow, 1970-79; sci. dir. USSR Inst. Applied Molecular Biology and Genetics, Moscow, 1974-76; pres. Moscow Ind. U., 1985-88; disting. prof. Ohio State U., Columbus, 1988-90; Robinson prof. George Mason U., Fairfax, Va., 1990-93, disting. prof. molecular genetics, 1993—. Sci. sec. Coun. on Molecular Biology and Genetics, Moscow, 1972-80; mem. USSR Govtl. Coun. on Molecular Biology and Molecular Genetics, 1974-80; invited lectr. Halle-Wittenberg U., German Democratic Republic, 1975; prin. investigator USSR State Com. on Sci., 1972, 74, 78, NIH, 1990, Dept. of Energy, 1992, Open Soc. Inst., 1995-98. Author: Molecular Mechanisms of Mutagenesis, 1969, History of Molecular Genetics, 1970, Molekulare Mechanismen der Mutagenese und Reparatur, 1976, Power and Science, History of the Crushing of Soviet Genetics, 1989, Lysenko and the Tragedy of Soviet Science, 1994, Triple Helical Nuclec Acids, 1995; contbr. more than 200 articles on molecular genetics, biophysics and history of sci. to Nature, Science Mutation Rsch., Nucleic Acids Rsch., others. Chmn. bd. Friends of St. Petersburg Ind. U., N.Y., 1990—; pres. USSR Amnesty Internat. Group, Moscow, 1983-88. Recipient Gregor Mendel gold medals of Czech Nat. Acad. Scis. and Czech Soc. History Scis., 1995, 96, N. Vavilov silver medal, Russian Acad. Natural Scis., 2002. Mem. USSR Soc. Geneticists and Breeders (founding), Gt. Britain Genetical Soc., USSR Biochem. and Microbiol. Soc., Internat. Soc. for History, Philosophy and Social Studies of Biology (charter), European Culture Club (charter), Internat. Sci. Fedn. (bd. dirs. 1992-95, chmn. bd. Internat. Soros Sci. Edn. program), Nat. Acad. Scis. Ukraine, Russian Acad. Natural Sci., Am. Soc. of Biochemistry and Molecular Biology, others. Achievements include discovery of DNA Repair in higher plants; establishment of correlation between structural damages in DNA and mitagenesis rate in higher plants; co-development of the method of photofootprinting of DNA triplexes, the role of environmental contamination in mutagenesis of organisms. Office: George Mason U Ste 3024 D King Hall Fairfax VA 22030

**SOYSTER, MARGARET BLAIR**, lawyer; b. Washington, Aug. 5, 1951; d. Peter and Eliza (Shumaker) S. AB magna cum laude, Smith Coll., 1973; JD, U. Va., 1976. Bar: N.Y. 1977, U.S. Dist. Ct. (so. and ea. dists.) N.Y. 1977, U.S. Ct. Appeals (2nd cir.) 1979, U.S. Supreme Ct. 1981, U.S. Ct. Appeals (4th cir.) 1982, U.S. Ct. Appeals (11th cir.) 1987, U.S. Ct. Appeals (7th cir.) 1991, U.S. Ct. Appeals (3d cir.) 1992. Assoc. Rogers & Wells, N.Y., 1976-84, ptnr., 1984-99, Clifford Chance US LLP, N.Y.C., 2000—. Mem. ABA, Assn. of Bar of City of N.Y., Lake Placid Club, Union Club and Univ. Attys., Phi Beta Kappa. Office: Clifford Chance US LLP 31 W 52nd St New York NY 10019 Office Phone: 212-878-8479. Business E-mail: blair.soyster@cliffordchance.com.

**SPACE, THEODORE MAXWELL**, lawyer; b. Binghamton, NY, Apr. 3, 1938; s. Maxwell Evans and Dorothy Marie (Boone) Space; m. Susan Shultz, Aug. 18, 1962 (div. Apr. 1979); children: William Schuyler, Susanna; m. Martha Collins, Apr. 6, 1991. AB, Harvard U., 1960; LLB, Yale U., 1966. Bar: Conn., 1966, U.S. Dist. Ct. Conn. 1966, U.S. Supreme Ct. 1970, U.S. Tax Ct. 1989, U.S. Ct. Appeals (2nd cir.) 1967, U.S. Ct. Appeals (6th cir.) 1992, U.S. Ct. Appeals (11th cir.) 1994, U.S. Dist. Ct. (ea. dist.) Mich. 1997. Assoc. Shipman & Goodwin LLP, Hartford, Conn., 1966—71, ptnr., 1971—2005, mng. ptnr., 1984—87, adminstv. ptnr., 1988—91, of counsel, 2006—. Mem. Bloomfield (Conn.) Bd. Edn., 1973-85, chmn., 1975-85; treas. Citizens Scholarship Found., Bloomfield, 1971-73, bd. dirs., 1973-91; mem. Bloomfield Human Rels. Commn., 1973-75; mem. Bloomfield Town Dem. Com., 1976-83; corporator Hartford Pub. Libr., 1976—; trustee Conn. Hist. Soc., 1997-2003, mem. libr. com., 1990—, chair, 1993-2000. Unitarian. Pvt. com., coun. mem. Unitarian Soc. Hartford, 1988-91; dir. Old State House Assn., 2003. Lt. (j.g.) USN, 1960-63. Mem. ABA, Conn. Bar Assn. (mem. exec. com. adminstrv. law sect. 1980—), Hartford County Bar Assn., Am. Law Inst., Am. Health Lawyers Assn., Conn. Health Lawyers Assn., Swift's Inn, Hartford Club, 1892 Club. Democrat. Unitarian Universalist. Avocations: reading, classical music. Home: 59 Prospect St Bloomfield CT 06002-3038 Office: Shipman & Goodwin LLP One Constitution Plz Hartford CT 06103-1919

**SPACEK, SISSY (MARY ELIZABETH SPACEK)**, actress; b. Quitman, Tex., Dec. 25, 1949; d. Edwin S. and Virginia S.; m. Jack Fisk, 1974; children: Schuyler Elizabeth, Virginia Madison. Attended, Lee Strasberg Theatrical Inst. Motion picture appearances include Prime Cut, 1972, Badlands, 1974, Carrie, 1976 (Acad. award nomination for best actress 1976), Three Women, 1977 (Best Supporting Actress 1977), Welcome to L.A., 1977, Heartbeat, 1980, Coal Miner's Daughter, 1980 (Acad. award best actress 1980, Golden Globe best actress 1980, Brit. Acad. award nomination best actress 1980, L.A. Film Critics for best actress 1980, Nat. Soc. Film Critics best actress 1980), Raggedy Man (Golden Globe nomination best actress 1981), 1981, Missing, 1982 (Acad. award nomination best actress, Golden Globe nomination best actress 1982), The River, 1984 (Acad. award nomination best actress), Marie, 1985, Night Mother, 1986, Crimes of the Heart, 1986 (Acad. award nomination best actress, Golden Globe best actress 1986), Violets Are Blue, 1986, JFK, 1991, The Long Walk Home, 1990, Hard Promises, 1992, Trading Mom, 1994, The Grass Harp, 1995, Affliction, 1997, Blast From the Past, 1998, Songs in Ordinary Time, 2000, In the Bedroom, 2001 (Best Actress in Drama Golden Globe 2001, Am. Film Inst. award, Broadcast Critics award, Chgo. Film Critics award, Fla. Film Critics award, Golden Satellite award, Sundance Film Festival award, Southeastern Film award, N.Y. Film Critics award, L.A. Film Critics award 2001), Last Call, 2002 (nominee Outstanding Supporting Actress in Miniseries or Movie Emmy award) Tuck Everlasting,

2002, A Home at the End of the World, 2004, Nine Lives, 2005, The Ring Two, 2005, Summer Racing: The Race to Cure Breast Cancer, 2005, North Country, 2005, An American Hauntig, 2006; TV movie appearances include Straight Story, 1999, In the Bedroom, 2001 (Acad. award nomination best actress 2001, Brit. Acad. award nomination best actress 2001, Brit. Film Critics Choice award best actress 2001, Sundance Film Festival Spl. prize 2001, Golden Globe best actress 2001, Ind. Spirit award best felmale lead 2001,AFI, Actress of Yr. 2001, L.A. Film Critics best actress 2001, N.Y. Film Critics best actress 2001, SAG nomination best actress 2001, nominee Best Actress Acad. award 2001), The Migrants, 1973, Katherine, 1975, Verna: USO Girl, 1978, A Private Matter, 1992, A Place for Annie, 1994, The Good Old Boys, 1995, Streets of Laredo, 1995, If These Walls Could Talk, 1996, Beyond the Call, 1996, Songs in Ordinary Time, 2000, Midwives (SAG nomination best actress 2001), 2001; guest host TV show Saturday Night Live, 1977; appeared in episode TV show The Waltons. Office: care Creative Artists Agy LLC c/o Steve Tellez 9830 Wilshire Blvd Beverly Hills CA 90212-1804*

**SPACEY, KEVIN**, actor; b. South Orange, N.J., July 26, 1959; s. Thomas and Kathleen Fowler. Student, Juilliard Sch., 1979-81. Actor Old Vic Theatre, England, 2003—, artistic dir., 2004—. Artistic dir. Old Vic Theatre, London, 2003—. Stage appearances include Henry IV, part I, 1981, Barbarians, 1982, Hurlyburly, 1985, Long Days Journey into Night, 1986, National Anthems, 1988, Lost in Yonkers, 1991 (Tony award for Best Featured Actor, 1991, Drama Desk award, 1991), Playland, 1993, The Iceman Cometh, 1997 (Tony award Best Male Performance/Drama 1999), The Philadelphia Story, 2005, Richard II, 2005; (TV series) Wiseguy, 1987-88, Nat. Anthems, 2005; (TV films) The Murder of Mary Phagan, 1988, Fall From Grace, 1990, When You Remember Me, 1990, Darrow, 1991, Doomsday Gun, 1994; (films) Heartburn, 1986, Working Girl, 1988, Rocket Gibraltar, 1988, Dad, 1989, See No Evil, Hear No Evil, 1989, A Show of Force, 1990, Henry and June, 1990, Glengarry Glen Ross, 1992, Consenting Adults, 1992, Iron Will, 1994, The Ref, 1994, Outbreak, 1995, The Usual Suspects, 1995 (Acad. award for best supporting actor, 1996), Seven, 1995, A Time to Kill, 1996, Looking for Richard, 1996, Midnight in the Garden of Good and Evil, 1997, L.A. Confidential, 1997, Hurlyburly, 1998, The Negotiator, 1998, A Bug's Life (voice), 1998, American Beauty, 1999 (Acad. award for best actor, 2000)., Its Tough to Be a Bug (voice), 1999, Ordinary Decent Criminals, 2000, Pay It Forward, 2000, K-PAX, 2001, The Shipping News. 2001, The Tower of Babble (voice only), 2001, The Life of David Gale, 2003, Edison, 2005, Superman Returns, 2006; actor, writer, prodr., dir. Beyond the Sea, 2004; actor, prodr. Swimming With Sharks, 1994, The Big Kahuna, 1999, The United States of Leland, 2003; dir. Albino Alligator, 1997; prodr. Triggerstreet.com, 2004, The Sasquatch Dumpling Gang, 2006, Mini's First Time, 2006; exec. prodr. Interstate 88, 2000, Uncle Frank, 2002, Mr. Gibb, 2006. Address: William Morris Agy 151 S. El Camino Dr Beverly Hills CA 90212-2704 Office: Old Vic The Cut London SE1 8NB England*

**SPACH, JULE CHRISTIAN**, church executive; b. Winston-Salem, N.C., Dec. 21, 1923; s. Jule Christian and Margaret Stockton (Coyner) S.; m. Nancy Clendenin, Sept. 18, 1948; children: Nancy Lynn Lane, Margaret Cuningham, Ann Thomerson, Cecelia Welborn, Robert Spach. Student, Va. Mil. Inst., 1942-43; BSChemE, Ga. Inst. Tech., 1949; postgrad., Union Theol. Sem., Richmond, Va., 1951-52, Duke U., 1955-56; MA in Ednl. Adminstrn., U. N.C., Greensboro, 1976; LHD (hon.), Stillman Coll., Tuscaloosa, Ala., 1977; LittD (hon.), Belhaven Coll., Jackson, Miss., 1977; LLD, King Coll., Bristol, Tenn., 1977. Salesman Mengle Corp. subs. Internat. Container Corp., Winston-Salem, 1950-52; from prof. scis., athletic dir. to pres. Quinze de Novembro Coll., Garanhuns, Pernambuco, Brazil, 1952-64; edn. dir. Cruzada ABC-Recife, Pernambuco, 1965-70, pres., 1969-70; exec. sec. Parliamentary Christian Leadership, Brasilia, Fed. Dist., Brazil, 1970-73; exec. dir. Presbyn. Mission in Brazil, Campinas, Sao Paulo, 1973-75; moderator Gen. Assembly of Presbyn. Ch. in U.S., Atlanta, 1976-77; exec. dir. Triad United Meth. Home, Inc., Winston-Salem, 1977—. Bd. dirs. First Home Fed. Savs. and Loan. Author: (biography) Every Road Leads Home, 1997. Bd. dirs. Instituto Gammon, Presbyn. Ch. U.S., Forsyth County Coun. on Aging Forsyth County Sr. Svcs. Forsyth County, Covenent Fellowship of Presbyns., William Black Lodge, Synod of N.C., Presbyn. Ch. U.S.A.; bd. visitors Lee's McRae Coll., Montreat Anderson Coll.; mem. cabinet United Way, 1987; chmn. Winston-Salem Forsyth County Coun. on Svcs. to Homeless; chmn. bd. dirs. Sr. Svcs., Inc., Winston-Salem, Missionary Family Counseling Svc. With USAAF, 1943-45, prisoner of war, Poland. Decorated Purple Heart; recipient Jefferson award, 1991; named Hon. Citizen of of Garanhuas, Brazil. Mem. Sertoma Club (3 Svc. awards), Lions, Rotary. Republican. Home: Arbor Acres 1244 Arbor Rd Apt 197 Winston Salem NC 27104-1199 Office: 1240 Arbor Rd Winston Salem NC 27104-1106 Business E-Mail: jspach1@triad.rr.com. *The Christian faith teaches us that the greatest of all gifts is love. This gift comes from God, and it is ours through the presence of His spirit dwelling in us. This love gives man peace within and with his fellow man.*

**SPACKMAN, THOMAS JAMES**, radiologist; b. Oak Park, Ill., Apr. 24, 1937; s. Thomas Frederick and Louise Mary (Kaiser) Spackman; m. Donna S. Stewart, June 25, 1960; children: Kirsten, Thomas James, Victoria. BA, DePauw U., 1959; MD, Western Res. U., 1964; diploma in bus. studies, London Sch. Econs., 1987. Intern, then resident in internal medicine Yale-New Haven Med. Ctr., 1964-66, resident in diagnostic radiology, 1966-68, fellow clin. rsch. tng. unit, 1968-69; instr., then asst. prof. radiology Yale U. Med. Sch., New Haven, 1969-74; assoc. prof. U. Pa. Med. Sch., 1974-78; prof. radiology U. Conn. Med. Sch., Farmington, 1978—, head dept., 1978-90; dir. radiology St. Francis Hosp. and Med. Ctr., Hartford, Conn., 1992-93; pres. Elscint, Inc., Hackensack, NJ, 1993-97; sr. v.p. Elscint Ltd., Haifa, Israel, 1993-97; pres. Spackman Assocs., Vero Beach, Fla., 1997—; chmn. Xicon Technologies LLC, Vero Beach, 1997-98; v.p. physician affairs Quorum Health Resources, 2000—02, Cambio Health Solutions LLC, 2002—05; chmn. Navix Diagnostix, Inc., 2002—; mng. dir. FTI Cabmrio Health Solutions, 2005—. Mem. Conn. Med. Exam. Bd., 1980—86; bd. dirs. Elscint, Inc. Mem. editl. adv. bd. Diagnostic Imaging, 1989—92; contbr. articles to profl. jours., chapters to books. Fellow: Am. Coll. Radiology; mem.: Soc. Pediatric Radiology, Assn. U. Radiolgoists. Business E-Mail: thomas.spackman@fticambiohealth.com.

**SPADA, ALFRED THOMAS**, publishing executive; b. Fairfax, Va., July 8, 1974; s. Alfred Thomas and Barbara Ann Spada; m. Beth Marie Johnson, Aug. 22, 1997; children: Alyssa Marie, Abigail Ann. BS in Comm., Northwestern U., Evanston, Illinois, 1996; MBA, U. Colo., 2003. Pub., editor in chief Modern Casting & Engineered Casting Solutions, Schaumburg, Ill., 1997—2006; dir. mktg. and pub. rels. Am. Foundry Soc., 1997—2006. Recipient award, Soc. Automotive Engrs., 2001—05, Am. Foundry Soc., 2001—05, Soc. Mech. Engrs., 2001—05. Office: Am Foundry Soc Inc 1695 N Penny Ln Schaumburg IL 60173 Office Phone: 847-824-0181. Office Fax: 847-824-7848. E-mail: aspada@afsinc.org.

**SPADA, DOMINICK**, pharmacist; b. Bklyn., Oct. 21, 1969; s. Vito and Maria A. (Palazzo) S. BS in Pharmacy, L.I. U., 1992; MS in Health Adminstrn., Kennedy Western U.; DPharm, Broadmore U. Registered pharmacist, N.Y.; cert. orthotic fitter. Staff pharmacist Cobble Court Pharmacy, Bklyn., 1992-94; dir. pharmacy, corp. bus. officer Ocean Breeze Infusion Care, S.I., 2000—; dir. pharmacy svcs. NYU Hosp., N.Y.C., 1998-2000; dir. pharmacy/supervising pharmacist Ocean Breeze Infusion Care, S.I., 1994-98, CEO, 2002—06; v.p. clin. affairs Ocean Breeze Assocs., LLC, 2006—; cons. pharmacist Hunt Lung and Surgery, Staten Island NY, 1999—. Bd. dirs. Cmty. Bd. #3, Staten Island, 1996-97, 99—; mem. Rocco Laurie Patrolmen's Scholarship Fund, Staten Island, 1995—. Named Drug Topics Pharmacist of Yr., Homecare divsn., 2001; recipient Anderson gold medal, L.I. U. Schwartz Coll. Pharmacy, 1992, PSSNY, Innovative Pharmacist award, 2002. Mem. Nat. Assn. Retail Druggists, Am. Pharm. Assn., Pharm. Soc. State NY (Innovative Pharmacist award 2002), Am. Soc. Health Sys. Pharmacists, Nat. Hospice Orgn. Roman Catholic. Avocations: travel, computers, career-

oriented activities, fishing. Home: 193 Connecticut St Staten Island NY 10307-1521 Office: Heart Lung and Surgery 501 Seaview Ave Ste 100 Staten Island NY 10305 Office Phone: 718-663-7055. Business E-mail: dspada@si.rr.com.

**SPADA, JAMES**, writer, photographer, publishing executive; b. S.I., N.Y., Jan. 23, 1950; s. Joseph Vincent and Mary Ruberto Spada. Student, Wagner Coll., 1968-71, Calif. State U., 1979-80. Pres. Spada Publs., L.A.; pub. Barbra Quar., L.A., 1980-83. Author: Barbra: The First Decade - The Films and Career of Barbra Streisand, 1974, The Films of Robert Redford, 1977, The Spada Report, 1979, Streisand - The Woman and the Legend, 1981, Monroe - Her Life in Pictures, 1982, Judy and Liza, 1983, Hepburn: Her Life in Pictures, 1984, The Divine Bette Midler, 1984, Fonda: Her Life in Pictures, 1985, Shirley and Warren, 1985, Grace: The Secret Lives of a Princess, 1987, Peter Lawford: The Man Who Kept the Secrets, 1991, More than a Woman: An Intimate Biography of Bette Davis, 1993, Streisand: Her Life, 1995, Jackie: Her Life in Pictures, 2000; photographer, pub.: Black & White Men, 2000, Ronald Reagan: His Life in Pictures, 2001, John and Caroline: Their Lives in Pictures, 2001, Edwardian Men, 2004, Julia: Her Life, 2004, The Bush Family, 2004; book packager The 1984 Marilyn Monroe Pin-Up Calendar, 1983, The Telephone Book, 1984, Elizabeth Taylor: A Biography in Photographs, 1984, Bette Davis: A Biography in Photographs, 1985, Natalie Wood: A Biography in Photographs, 1986; one-man shows include Against the Grain Gallery, Cape Cod, 1998, Gallery One, Boston, 2000, Radiant Light Gallery, Portland, Maine, 2001. Democrat. Personal E-mail: jamesspada1@verizon.net.

**SPADE, DAVID (DAVID WAYNE SPADE)**, actor; b. Birmingham, Mich., July 22, 1964; s. Wayne Spade and Judy Todd. BBA, Ariz. State U., 1986. Comml. spokesperson Sierra Mist soda, Capital One credit cards. Cast mem. & writer, Saturday Night Live, 1990; actor (TV series), (voice) Beavis and Butt-Head, 1994-97, Just Shoot Me, 1997-2003, 8 Simple Rules...For Dating My Teenage Daugher, 2004-05; (TV host) The Showbiz Show With David Spade, 2005-; appeared in films: Police Academy 4: Citizen on Patrol, 1987, Coneheads, 1993, PCU, 1994, Tommy Boy, 1995, Black Sheep, 1996, A Very Brady Sequel, 1996, Eight Heads in a Duffel Bag, 1997, Senseless, 1998, The Rugrats Movie (voice), 1998, Lost & Found (also writer, exec. prodr.), 1999, Little Nicky, 2000, The Emperor's New Groove (voice), 2000, Joe Dirt, 2001, Dickie Roberts: Former Child Star, 2003, (voice) Racing Stripes, 2005, Grandma's Boy, 2006, The Benchwarmers, 2006; actor, writer, exec. prodr. David Spade: Take the Hit (TV), 1998; exec. prodr. Jerome, 1999; appeared on TV shows The Facts of Life, ALF, The Larry Sanders Show, The Dennis Miller Show, Beavis and Butt-head (voice), The Daily Show, BioRhythm, Comedy Central Roast of Pamela Anderson, 2005. Named to Hollywood Walk of Fame, 2003.*

**SPADE, KATE (KATHERINE NOEL SPADE)**, apparel designer; b. Kansas City, Mo., 1962; m. Andy Spade, 1994. BA in journalism and broadcasting, Arizona State U., 1985. From asst. to accessories editor Mademoiselle mag., 1985—92; co-founder, designer Kate Spade Inc., N.Y.C., 1993—; designer Kate Spade paper and social stationary, 1998—, Kate Spade shoe collection, 1999—, Kate Spade glasses, 2001, Kate Spade beauty, 2002—; co-founder Jack Spade, 1999—, Kate Spade Home, 2002—. Designer (uniforms) Song Airlines (subs. Delta Airlines), 2004. Recipient Perry Ellis award, New Fashion Talent, Coun. Fashion Designers of Am., 1996, Accessory Designer of the Year, 1998, FiFi award for Bath & Body Star of the Year, U.S. Fragrance Found., 2003, FiFi award for Best Fragrance in Ltd. Distribution, U.K. Fragrance Found., 2003. Achievements include stores opening in N.Y.C. in 1996, Boston and LA in 1998, and Chicago and San Francisco in 2000. Office: Kate Spade Inc 48 W 25th St New York NY 10010

**SPADER, JAMES**, actor; b. Boston, Mass., Feb. 7, 1960; s. Jean and Todd Spader; m. Victoria Kheel, 1979; children: Sebastian, Elijah. Student, Phillips Acad., Michael Chekhov Studio. Appeared in pictures Endless Love (debut 1981), The New Kids, 1985, Tuff Turf, 1985, Pretty in Pink, 1986, Mannequin, 1987, Wall Street, 1987, Less Than Zero, 1987, Baby Boom, 1987, Jack's Back, 1988, The Rachel Papers, 1989, Sex, Lies and Videotape (Best actor award Cannes Festival 1989), 1989, Bad Influence, 1990, White Palace, 1990, True Colors, 1991, Storyville, 1992, Bob Roberts, 1992, Music of Chance, 1993, Dream Lover, 1994, Wolf, 1994, Stargate, 1994, Two Days in the Valley, 1996, Crash, 1997, Keys to Tulsa, 1997, Critical Care, 1997, Curtain Call, 1999, Curtain Call, 1999, Supernova, 2000, The Watcher, 2000, Slow Burn, 2000, The Stickup, 2001, Speaking of Sex, 2001, Secretary, 2002, I Witness, 2003, Alien Hunter, 2003; TV movies, Cocaine: One Man's Seduction, 1983, Diner, 1983, A Killer in the Family, 1983, Family Secrets, 1984, Starcrossed, 1985, The Pentagon Papers, 2003; TV series The Family Tree, 1983, The Practice, 2003-2004 (Emmy award Outstanding Lead Actor in a Drama Seriesm, 2004), Boston Legal, 2004-(Emmy award for outstanding lead actor in a drama series, 2005); TV guest appearances Frasier, 1994, Seinfeld, 1997. Office: care Toni Howard/ICM 8942 Wilshire Blvd Beverly Hills CA 90211-1934

**SPADE-SHENKER, GEORGE LAWRENCE (GEORGE SHENKER)**, research scientist; b. Sioux City, Iowa, Dec. 14, 1945; s. Walter Charles and LaVancha May (Green) S.; m. Carol Margaret Deaton, Mar. 14, 1966 (div. June 1985); children: Aaron Michael, Margaret. Mem. earthquake study group for China, U.S. Citizen Amb. Programs, 1989. Contbr. articles to profl. jours. Mem. AAAS, Internat. Soc. Philos. Enquiry, Am. Math. Soc., Math. Assn. Am., N.Y. Acad. Scis., Mensa. Avocations: poetry, painting, music. Home and Office: PO Box 2260 Columbia Falls MT 59912-2260

**SPAEDER, ROGER CAMPBELL**, lawyer; b. Cleve., Dec. 20, 1943; s. Fred N. and Luceil (Campbell) S.; m. Frances DeSales Sutherland, Sept. 7, 1968; chidlren: Michael, Matthew. BS, Bowling Green U., 1965; JD with honors, George Washington U., 1970. Bar: D.C. 1971, U.S. Dist. Ct. D.C. 1971, U.S. Ct. Appeals (D.C. cir.) 1971, U.S. Ct. Claims 1979, U.S. Dist. Ct. Md. 1984, U.S. Ct. Appeals (2d and 4th cirs.) 1985, U.S. Supreme Ct. 1976. Asst. U.S. atty. D.C., Washington, 1971-76; ptnr. Zuckerman Spaeder LLP, Washington, 1976—. Faculty Atty. Gen. Advocacy Inst., 1974-76, Nat. Inst. Trial Adv., 1978-79; adj. faculty Georgetown U. Law Ctr., 1979-80, Am. U. Ctr. Adminstrn. Justice, 1976-79; lectr. D.C. Bar Continuing Legal Edn. Programs, 1980-90; Cardozo Prize judge Yale Law Sch., 1992; master Edward Bennett Williams Inn of Ct., 1996—; mem. D.C. Cir. Jud. Conf., 1991. Contbr. articles to profl. jours. and chpts. to books. Recipient Spl. Achievement award Dept. Justice, 1971. Fellow Am. Coll. Trial Lawyers; Mem. ATLA, ABA (co-chair com. on complex crimes litigation 1989-92, divsn. co-dir. sect. litigation 1992-94), Bar Assn. D.C. (lectr. Criminal Practice Inst. 1977-80), D.C. Bar (com. criminal jury instrns. 1972, divsn. cts. lawyers, adminstrn. of justice 1976-78; adv. com. continuing legal edn. 1986), Def. Rsch. Inst., Assn. Plaintiffs' Trial Attys., Nat. Assn. Criminal Def. Lawyers, Omicron Delta Kappa. Home: 7624 Georgetown Pike Mc Lean VA 22102-1412 Office: Zuckerman Spaeder LLP 1800 M St NW Ste 1000 Washington DC 20036-5802 Office Phone: 202-778-1806.

**SPAEPEN, FRANS AUGUST**, physicist, educator; b. Mechelen, Belgium, Oct. 29, 1948; arrived in U.S., 1971; s. Jozef F. M. and Ursula (Roppe) Spaepen; m. Moniek Steemans, Aug. 21, 1973; children: Geertrui M., Elizabet L., Hendrik J. L. Burgerlijk Metaalkundig Ingenieur, U. Leuven, Belgium, 1971; PhD, Harvard U., 1975. IBM postdoctoral fellow Harvard U., Cambridge, Mass., 1975-77, asst. prof. applied physics, 1977-81, assoc. prof., 1981-83, Gordon McKay prof. applied physics, 1983—2002, Franklin prof. applied physics, 2002—, dir. Materials Rsch. Lab., 1990—98, dir. Rowland Inst., 2002—. Vis. prof. U. Leuven, 1984, Deutsches Zentrum für Luft-und Raumfahrt-Köln, 2000, Forschungszentrum Jülich, 2001; chmn. Gordon Conf. on Phys. Metallurgy, 1988; NRC com. on solid state scis., 1992—93; NRC com. on condensed matter and materials physics, 1996—98; Krengel lectr. Technion, Israel, 1994; mem. summer rsch. group Los Alamos Nat. Lab., 1986—99; mem. sci. and tech. steering com. Brookhaven Nat. Lab.; chmn. scientific adv. bd. Netherlands Inst. for Metals Rsch.; J.B. Cohen lectr. Northwestern U., 2004. Co-editor: (series) Solid State Physics; mem. editl.

bd. Jour. Applied Physics, Applied Physics Letters, 1990—93, 1999—2001, Applied Physics Revs., 1991—97, Phys. Rev., 1994—99, Jour. Non-Crystalline Solids, 1990—94; editor (prin. editor): Jour. Materials Rsch., 2001—; contbr. articles to profl. jours., chpts. to books. Recipient Best Paper award, Acta Metallurgica, 1994, Humboldt award, 1999, R.F. Mehl award, TMS Inst. Metals, 2002, Heyn medal, German Soc. Materials Sci., 2005. Fellow: AIME-The Metall. Soc., Am. Phys. Soc. (chmn. divsn. materials physics 1992); mem.: Max Planck Soc. (external mem.), Vlaamse Academie voor Wetenschappen en Kunsten, Orde van den Prince, Vlaamse Ingenieurs Vereniging, Materials Rsch. Soc. (councilor 1986—88, co-chmn. fall meeting Boston 1990, councillor 1990—92, chmn. program com. 1993—2000, Woody award 1998), Am. Soc. Metals. Office: Harvard Univ Divsn Engring and Applied Scis 29 Oxford St Cambridge MA 02138-2901 Business E-Mail: spaepen@deas.harvard.edu.

**SPAETH, EDMUND BENJAMIN, JR.,** retired lawyer, retired law educator, former judge; b. Washington, June 10, 1920; s. Edmund B. and Lena (Link) S. AB magna cum laude, Harvard U., Cambridge, Mass., 1942; LLB, Harvard U., 1948. Bar: Pa. 1949. Judge Ct. of Common Pleas, Phila., 1964-73, Superior Ct of Pa., 1973-86, pres. judge, 1983-86; of counsel Pepper Hamilton LLP, Phila., 1986—2002. Adj. prof. U. Pa. Law Sch., 1976-97; chair Pennsylvanians for Modern Cts., 1987-2000. Fellow Am. Bar Found. (life); mem. Am. Law Inst. (life), Am. Judicature soc., Order of Coif, Phi Beta Kappa. Home: Cathedral Village Apt L-206 600 E Cathedral Rd Philadelphia PA 19128-1933

**SPAETH, GEORGE LINK,** ophthalmologist, educator, writer; b. Phila., Mar. 3, 1932; s. Edmund Benjamin and Lena Marie (Link) S.; m. Ann Ward, May 17, 1958; children: Kristin Lea Crowley, George Link Jr., Eric Edmund. BA magna cum laude, Yale U., 1954; MD cum laude, Harvard U., 1959; postgrad., U. Mich., 1960, U. Pa., 1961. Resident surgeon Wills Eye Hosp., Phila., 1961-63, attending surgeon, 1970—, dir. glaucoma svc., 1968—; clin. fellow NIH, Bethesda, Md., 1963-65; instr. U. Pa., Phila., 1965-68; pvt. practice Phila., 1965-68; prof. ophthalmology Temple U. Med. Sch., Phila., 1968-75, Jefferson Med. Coll., Phila., 1975—, Louis Esposito glaucoma rsch. prof., 2000—. Ophthalmologist Chestnut Hill Hosp., Phila., 1975—; attending surgeon, Graduate Hosp.; cons., Bryn Mawr Hosp., Wills Eye Hosp., Hosp. Jefferson Med. Coll. Author: 19 books in ophthalmology, surgery, and med. ethics, 1970—; contbr. over 500 articles to profl. jours.; editor Ophthalmic Surgery jour., 1985-96; editl. editor Ophthalmic Surgery and Lasers; mem. editl. bd. Jour., Ocular Surgery News, Glaucoma Abstracts; manuscript reviewer, New Eng. Jour. Medicine, Med. Letter Drugs and Therapy, others; patentee differometer, tonometer tip cover. Pres. Chestnut Hill Cmty. Assn., Phila., 1970-72; founder, CEO Internat. Soc. Spaeth Fellows, 1975—; trustee, founder, pres. E.B. Spaeth and Glaucoma Svcs. Found., 1978—; Profls. for Nuclear Army Control, 1985-88; tustee, treas. Thomas Skelton Harrison Found., Inc., 1984—; interviewer Yale Alumni Schs. Com., Phila., 1965—; Yale Class coun., 1968—, Yale Assn. Alumni Reps., 1996-2002; trustee Recording for the Blind and Dyslexia, 1996-2002, Internat. Arts-Medicine Assn., Pa. Ballet, 2002—, Bach Festival of Phila., 2002—, Squirrel Island Chapel, Maine; curriculum com. Jefferson Med. Coll., 1987-90; institutional review bd. Jefferson Med. Coll., 1990-95; pres. Phila. Glaucoma Inst., 1997—. Lt. comdr. USPHS, 1963-68. NIH grantee, 1968—; recipient Pub. Svc. medal Chestnut Hill Coll., 1972, Sir Stuart Duke Elder Glaucoma award Internat. Glaucoma Soc., 1986, Newberg award Lawyers Alliance for World Security, 1995, Derrick Vail award Internat. Soc. Prevention Blindness, 1996, Trantas award Greek Ophthalmol. Soc., 2000, Frominopolous prize Greek Glaucoma Soc., 2003, Large Flower and Vegetable Garden 1st Pl. award Pa. Horticultural Soc., 2004, Nizankowska award Polish Glaucoma Soc., 2006; named Ophthalmic Visionary, Ocular Surgery News, 2003, Bausch & Lomb, 2005. Fellow Am. Acad. Ophthalmology (chmn. ethics com. San Francisco 1987-95, coun. 1980-93, vice chmn. residency rev. com. Chgo. 1982-88, Sr. honor award 1988, life time achievement award 1999), Am. Assn. Rsch. in Vision and Ophthalmology, Royal Coll. Ophthalmologists U.K., Danish Ophthalmol. Soc., Ind. Soc. of Ophthalmology; mem. Am. Glaucoma Soc. (pres. 1983-85), Coll. Physicians Phila. (sec. 1976-84), Phila. County Med. Soc., Pa. Acad. Ophthalmology (pres. coun.), German Ophthalmol. Congress, Physicians for Social Responsibility (pres. emeritus Phila. chpt.), ACS (bd. govs., chmn. emeritus adv. coun. for ophthalmology), Phila. Club, Phila. Cricket Club, Phi Beta Kappa, Alpha Omega Alpha. Democrat. Avocations: composing music, piano, sports, photography, gardening. Office: Wills Eye Hosp 11th Fl 840 Walnut St Philadelphia PA 19107-5109 Office Phone: 215-928-3960. Business E-Mail: gspaeth@willseye.org.

**SPAETH, JAN MILLS,** jury consultant; b. Grinnell, Iowa, July 17, 1951; d. Paul Herbert and Joyce Carol Broadwell; m. Paul Vincent Spaeth, May 26, 1988. BA with honors, U. Wis., 1973; MA, U. Ariz., 1996; PhD, Calif. Coast U., 1999. Social worker Cass County Dept. Social Svcs., Walker, Minn., 1973—75; dir. rsch. Lakehead Social Planning Coun., Thunder Bay, Ont., Canada, 1975—76; social worker Thunder Bay Social Svcs. Dept., 1976—78; free-lance workshop coord. Duluth, Minn., 1979; freelance litig. cons. Tucson, 1980—. Educator Tucson Free U., 1980, Pima County Jail, Tucson, 1981, Pima County Juvenile Ct. Ctr., Tuscon, 1981; instr. U. Ariz., Tuscon, 1980—94, Pima C.C., Tucson, 1990—94, Cochise C.C., Sierra Vista, Ariz., 1991; supplemental juror questionnaire subcom. Supreme Ct. Ariz., Phoenix, 1995; spkr. in field. Contbr. articles to profl. jours. Recipient Appreciation award, Pima County Juvenile Ct. Ctr., 1982. Mem.: APA, Ariz. Attys. for Criminial Justice, Am. Coll. Forensic Examiners, Am. Soc. Trial Cons. Avocations: hiking, travel, golf, research, writing. Office: Ariz Jury Rsch PO Box 91410 Tucson AZ 85752 Office Phone: 520-297-4131.

**SPAETH, KARL HENRY,** retired chemicals executive, lawyer; b. Phila., Mar. 17, 1929; s. Edmund Benjamin and Lena Marie (Link) S.; m. Ann Dashiell Wieland, Sept. 14, 1963; children: Karl Henry, Edmund Alexander, Christopher Philip. AB, Haverford Coll., 1951; postgrad., Oxford U., 1955; JD, Harvard U., 1958. Bar: Pa. 1959, U.S. Ct. (ea. dist.) Pa. 1959, U.S. Ct. Appeals (3d cir.) 1959. Assoc. MacCoy, Evans & Lewis, Phila., 1959-62; counsel for fgn. ops. Scott Paper Co., Phila., 1962-69; v.p., corp. sec. Quaker Chem. Corp., Conshohocken, Pa., 1969-95, ret. v.p., 1995, ret. corp. sec., 1998. Bd. dirs. Greater Phila. Devel. Corp., 1991-98; bd. dirs., sec.-treas. Edmund B. Spaeth Clin. Rsch. Found., 1982—; chmn. bd. dirs. Pa. Chem. Industry Coun., 1984-86. Chmn. bd. trustees Quaker Chem. Found., 1982-2003; bd. overseers Univ. Mus., U. Pa., Phila., 1983-89, 90-96; bd. dirs. Opera Co. Phila., 1988-2003; bd. dirs. Chestnut Hill Acad., Phila., 1976-83, pres. 1979-83; mem. Whitemarsh Twp. Bd. Suprs. Pa., 1969-75, chmn., 1972-74; mem. Com. of Seventy, Phila., 1984-96. Comdr USNR, 1952-55, ret. Mem. Pa. Bar Assn. (chmn. sect. on internat. and comparative law 1980-92), Phila. Com. on Fgn. Rels. (exec. com. sec. 1984-94, chmn. 2001-04), Phila. Club. Phila. Athenaeum, Libr. Co. of Phila., Phila. Cricket Club, Oxford Union Club, Univ. Barge (sec. 1988-94), Mil. Order Fgn. Wars (registrar 1989-91, vice commdr. 1991-93). Republican. Anglican. Home: 2129 Harts Ln Conshohocken PA 19428-2416 E-mail: khspaeth@comcast.net.

**SPAETH, NICHOLAS JOHN,** lawyer, former state attorney general; b. Mahnomen, Minn., Jan. 27, 1950; m. Cindy Spaeth; children: Gawain Kevin, Carl Wilson, William James, Elizabeth Bedont. AB, Stanford U., 1972, JD, 1977; BA, Oxford U., Eng., 1974. Bar: Minn. 1979, US Dist. Ct. Dist. Minn. 1979, US Ct. Appeals 8th cir. 1979, ND 1980, US Dist. Ct. Dist. ND 1980, US Supreme Ct. 1984, Calif. 1999, US Dist. Ct. Calif. 1999, Mo. 2005. Law clk. US Ct. Appeals 8th cir., Fargo, ND, 1977-78; law clk. to Justice Byron White US Supreme Ct., Washington, 1978-79; atty. pvt. practice, 1979-84; atty. gen. State of ND, Bismarck, 1985—93; ptnr. Dorsey & Whitney, Fargo, ND, 1993-99; Oppenheimer Wolff & Donnelly, Mpls., 1999, Cooley Godward, Palo Alto, Calif., 1999—2000; sr v.p., gen. counsel, sec. GE Employers Reinsurance Corp., Overland Park, Kans., 2000—03, Intuit Inc., Mountain View, Calif., 2003—04; sr. v.p., chief legal officer H&R Block Inc., Kansas

City, Mo., 2004—. Adj. prof. law U. Minn., 1980-83. Rhodes scholar, 1972-74. Democrat. Roman Catholic. Office: H&R Block Inc 4400 Main St Kansas City MO 64111 Business E-Mail: nspaeth@hrblock.com.

**SPAFFORD, MICHAEL CHARLES,** artist; b. Palm Springs, Calif., Nov. 6, 1935; BA, Pomona Coll., 1959; MA, Harvard U., 1960. One man shows include Seattle Art Mus., 1982, 86, Reed Coll., 1984, Whtcom county Mus., 1987, U. Puget Sound, Tacoma, Wash., 1973, Tacoma Art Mus., 1975, 86, Utah Mus. Fine Arts, Salt Lake City, 1975, Francine Seders Gallery, Seattle, 1965—, Bellevue Art Mus., 1991, Cheney-Cowles Mus., Spokane, Wash., 1994, Hallie Ford Mus. Art, Willamette U., Salem, Oreg., 1999; exhibited in group shows at Wilcox Gallery, Swarthmore Coll., Pa., 1977, Seattle Art Mus., 1977, 80, 84, Am. Acad. and Inst. Arts and Letters, N.Y.C., 1980, 83, 89, 95, Kobe, Japan, 1981, Eastern Wash. U., 1982, Henry Art Gallery, 1982, 86, Bellevue Art Mus., 1987, 95, Cheney Cowles Mus., 1988, Holter Mus. of Art, Helena, Mont. Recipient Rome Prize Am. Acad. in Rome, 1967-69, award Am. Acad. and Inst. Arts and Letters, 1983, Lifetime Achievement in Arts award Corp. Coun. Arts, Seattle, 1999; Louis Comfort Tiffany Found. grantee, 1965-66; Neddy fellow, 1996. Address: c/o Francine Seders Gallery 6701 Greenwood Ave N Seattle WA 98103-5225

**SPAGNOLETTI, ROBERT J.,** attorney general; BS, Lafayette Coll.; JD, Georgetown Univ. Bar: NJ, NY, Washington, DC. Litig. assoc. Mayor Day Caldwell & Keaton, Houston, Skadden, Arps, Salte, Meagher & Flom, NY & DC; Chief of Domestic Violence Unit Office of U.S. Atty., Washington, DC, 1995, Chief of Sex Offence and Domestic Violence Sec., 1998—2003; Attn. Gen. Washington, DC, 2003—. Prof. law Georgetown Univ. Law Ctr. Recipient Young Lawyer of Year award, Bar Assn. of DC, 1997, Sullivan Award, Asst. US Atty. Assn., 2002. Democrat. Office: Office of Atty General John A Wilson Bldg 1350 Pennsylvania Ave NW Ste 409 Washington DC 20004 Office Phone: 202-727-3400.*

**SPAGNOLO, MARK F.,** telecommunications industry executive; BS, Newark Coll. Engring. With Data Sys.; pres., CEO UUNET; CEO Broadwing Comms., Austin, Tex., 2001—; pres., CEO SiteSmith, Metromedia Fiber Network, 2001; prin., owner The Spagnolo Group, LP, 2002—.

**SPAGNOLO, SAMUEL VINCENT,** internist, educator, pulmonary specialist; b. Pitts., Sept. 3, 1939; s. Vincent Anthony and Mary Grace (Culotta) S.; children: Samuel, Brad, Gregg; m. Dorcas R. Hardy, Sept. 29, 1996. BA, Washington & Jefferson Coll., 1961; MD, Temple U., 1965. Diplomate Am. Bd. Internal Medicine, Bd. Pulmonary Disease, lic. physician Fla., Calif., Md., D.C., Va., Ariz., Pa., Mass. Sr. resident in medicine VA Med. Ctr., Boston, 1969-70, chief resident in medicine, 1970-71; Harvard Clin. and Rsch. fellow in pulmonary diseases Mass. Gen. Hosp., Boston, 1971-72; asst. chief med. svc. VA Med. Ctr., Washington, 1972-75, acting chief med. svc., 1975-76, chief pulmonary disease sect., 1976-94, chief of staff, 1998-99, dir. respiratory care & sr. attending in pulmonary diseases, 1999—; instr. in medicine Boston U. Sch. of Medicine, Tufts U. Sch. Medicine, Boston, 1970-71; clin. and rsch. fellow in pulmonary diseases Harvard U. Sch. of Medicine, Mass. Gen. Hosp., Boston, 1971-72; attending physician George Washington U. Med. Ctr., 1972—; clin. asst. prof. medicine Georgetown U., Washington, 1975-77; asst. clin. prof. medicine George Washington U. Sch. of Medicine and Health Scis., Washington, 1972-75, assoc. prof., 1975-81, prof. medicine, 1981—, dir. divsn. pulmonary diseases and allergy, 1978-93; assoc. chmn. dept. medicine George Washington U. Med. Ctr., Washington, 1986-89. Cons. in pulmonary diseases The Washington Hosp. Ctr., Washington, DC, 1977—, Will Rogers Inst., White Plains, NY, 1980—, US Dept. Labor, Washington, 1980—, Walter Reed Army Med. Ctr., Washington, 1987-90; rep. Am. Coll. Chest Physicians to Am. Registry Pathology, Washington, 1981-92; numerous radio tv appearances on Health Oriented Programs; invited lectr. in U.S., Russia, Jordan; chmn., mem. many coms. George Washington U. Sch. of Medicine, George Washington Med. Ctr., VA Med. Ctr., Washington; med. chest cons. in attempted assasination of former Pres. Regan. Author: Clinical Assessment of Patients with Pulmonary Disease, 1986; co-author: (with A.E. Medinger) Handbook of Pulmonary Emergencies, 1986, Handbook of Pulmonary Drug Therapy, 1993, (with Witorsch, P.) Air Pollution and Lung Disease in Adults, 1994; mem. editl. bd. CHEST Jour., 2002-06; mem. editl. bd. Chest, 2006—; contbr. numerous articles to profl jours. including Med. Clin. N.Am., Chest, So. Med. Jour., Am. Jour. Cardiology, Jour. Am. Med. Assn., Clin. Rsch., Am. Rev. Respiratory Disease, Am. Lung Assn. Bull., Clin. Notes on Respiratory Diseases, Jour. Nuclear Medicine, Drug Therapy; presenter abstracts at profl. meetings. Pres., chmn. Found. Vets. Health Care, 1998—. Lt. comdr. USPHS, 1966-68. Decorated cavaliere Order of Merit, Republic of Italy; nominated for Golden Apple award by med. students George Washington Sch. Medicine, Phila., 1977; recipient cert. appreciation D.C. Lung Assn., 1983. Fellow ACP (coun. critical care 1983-85), Am. Coll. Chest Physicians (gov. DC, coun. of govs. 1989-96); mem. Am. Thoracic Soc. (exec. com. DC chpt. 1978-85, 89, mem. adv. com. Tb control, 1978-84, pres. DC chpt. 1981-83), Nat. Assn. VA Physicians (sec. 1987-89, v.p. 1989-91, pres. 1992-98), Internat. Lung Found. (pres. 1991—). Achievements include first major review of patient outcome during early history of intensive care units; an analysis of mechanisms of hypoxemia in patients with chronic liver disease; first report of Pneumocystis Carinii Pneumonitis in patients with lung cancer; first prospective evaluation of short course therapy reported in U.S. using Isoniazid and Rifampin; first American report using laser through fiberoptic bronchoscope to treat lung cancer; first report to evaluate continuous intravenous morphine to control pain in cancer patients; description of a simple technique to measure the total lung volume non-invasively using the routing chest x-ray. Office: George Washington U 5-425 2150 Pennsylvania Ave NW Washington DC 20037-3201 Office Phone: 202-741-2237. Personal E-mail: drspagnolo@att.net.

**SPAGNUOLO, MARIO,** physician; b. Naples, Italy, Apr. 14, 1930; s. Vincent Spagnuolo and Ronca Julia; m. Kathryn Birchall, July 10, 1962; children: Mario, Sandra, Peter, Eugene. MD, U. Naples (Italy), 1954. Diplomate Am. Bd. Internal Medicine. Instr. of medicine NYU Med. Sch., NYC, 1961—73, asst. prof. to assoc. prof., 1961—73; dir. Irvington House Inst. for Rheumatic Diseases, 1963—70, Juvenile Rheumatoid Arthritis Clinic, Bellevue Hosp., 1966—78; sr. attending St. John's Riverside Hosp., Yonkers, 1974—. Cons. St. Joseph's Hosp., 1982—90; pres. Western Westchester Network Inc.; chief of medicine St. John's Riverside Hosp., 1984—92, chief of staff, 1997—2000, trustee, 1997—. Contbr. over 60 articles in med. textbooks, profl. jours. Named Man of the Yr., Italian Assn. Hosps., 2000. Avocation: painting. Office: 944 N Broadway Ste 201 Yonkers NY 10701 E-mail: mariospa@optonline.net.

**SPAHN, GARY JOSEPH,** lawyer; b. N.Y.C., July 23, 1949; s. Harry G. and Mary (Hopkins) S.; m. Lois Luttinger, Aug. 9, 1975; children: Gary J. Jr., Lori J. BA, LI U., 1971, MA, 1976; JD, U. Richmond, 1975. Bar: Va. 1975, U.S. Ct. Appeals (4th cir.) 1975, U.S. Supreme Ct. 1980. Law clk. to Hon. Judge Dortch U.S. Dist. Ct. (ea. dist.) Va., Richmond, 1975—77; from assoc. to ptnr. Troutman Sanders LLP (formerly Mays & Valentine), Richmond, 1977—; now ptnr. Troutman Sanders LLP, Richmond, past chmn. products liability and ins. sect. Lectr. in field, 1980—; mem. jud. conf. U.S. Ct. Appeals (4th cir.). Co-author: Virginia Law of Products Liability, 2000 Pres. Southhampton Citizens Assn., Richmond, 1982-85; bd. dirs. Southhampton Recreation Assn., Richmond, 1983, Chesterfield County Crime Solvers. With USAF, 1967-73. Mem. ABA (litig. and tort and ins. sects.), Internat. Assn. Def. Counsel (co-chair litig. sect. Products Liability com.), Am. Assn. Ins. Attys., Assoc. Def. Trial Attys., Def. Rsch. Inst., Va. Assn. Def. Attys., Va. Mfrs. Assn., Products Liability Adv. Counsel, Va. Power Boat Assn. (commodore). Avocations: boating, basketball, racquetball. Office: Troutman Sanders LLP PO Box 1122 1001 Haxall Point Richmond VA 23218-1132 Office Phone: 804-697-1400.

**SPAHR, CLINTON S., JR.,** retired elementary school educator; b. Bayshore, N.Y., Feb. 3, 1942; s. Clinton Smith and Averil Witona (Courier) S. BS, Hofstra U., 1967, MA, 1972. Tchr. Brentwood (N.Y.) Pub. Schs., 1966-97.

Mem. Am. Philatelic Soc., Brentwood Tchrs. Assn., Internat. Soc. World Stamp Collectors. Avocations: collecting stamps, tapes, cds, books. Home: 1408 Sara Cir Port Jefferson Station NY 11776

**SPAHR, ELIZABETH,** environmental research administrator; b. Warren, Ohio, Nov. 12, 1930; d. Sullivan and Elizabeth (St. Clair) Spahr; children: Gretchen, Carolyn. BS, Case Western Res. U., 1952, MS, 1954, PhD, 1957, MBA, 1973. Sr. rsch. scientist NASA, Cleve., 1956-71; mgr. internat. ops., mgr. spl. projects The Std. Oil Co., Cleve., 1973-86; v.p. strategic planning Ameritrust Corp., Cleve., 1987-92; dir. fin. & adminstrn. AAUW, Washington, 1993-98; CEO Technol. Exec. Inst., 1998—2002; pres. AcromaTech Group, Inc., 1999—2002; assoc. dir. U. Md. Ctr. for Environ. Scis. Horn Point Lab., Cambridge, 2002—. Dir. supply emergency team Internat. Energy Agy., Paris, 1984-86; chair fed. women's program Fed. Exec. Bd., Cleve., 1969-71. Trustee Case Western Res. U., Cleve., 1988-92, chair ann. fund, 1989-93; pres. bd. dirs. Cuyahoga City Hosp. Found., Cleve., 1983-85. Grantee USPHS, 1952-56. Mem. Women in Tech., Arlington C. of C., Strategic Alliance Va. Employers, Strategic Alliance Md. Employers. Office: Univ Md Ctr Environ Sci Horn Point Lab PO Box 775 Cambridge MD 21613-0775 Home: PO Box 352 Trappe MD 21673-0352 E-mail: espahr@hpl.umces.edu.

**SPAID, GREGORY P.,** academic administrator, art educator; b. Mishawaka, Ind. m. Susan R. Spaid. BA in Art, Kenyon Coll., 1969; MFA, Ind. U., 1976. Mem. faculty Berea (Ky.) Coll., 1976—79; prof. art Kenyon Coll., Gambier, Ohio, 1979—, chair art dept., 1984—88, assoc. provost, 1999—2002, acting provost, 2002—03, provost, 2003—; Tchr summer programs Kenyon Coll., Gambier, Ohio, Santa Fe, Bozeman, Mont., Nantucket Island Sch. Design Art. Photography published in books, The Man Who Created Paradise, 2001, On Nantucket, 2002, Represented in permanent collections Mus. Modern Art, N.Y.C., J. Paul Getty Mus., L.A., Santa Barbara (Calif.) Mus. Art, Smithsonian Instn., Nat. Mus. Am. Art, Washington, Dayton (Ohio) Art Inst., Chase Manhattan Bank, N.Y.C. Fellow Photo Educators fellow, Eastman Kodak, 1993; Individual Artist's fellow, Ohio Arts Coun., 1984, 1986, 1995, 2000, Fulbright Rsch. fellow, Italy, 1987, Profl. Devel. Assistance grantee, Ohio Arts Coun., 1990, Artist Project grantee, 1995. Office: Ransom Hall 21 Kenyon College Gambier OH 43022-9623

**SPAIN, JAMES DORRIS, JR.,** biochemist, educator; b. Washington, Feb. 3, 1929; s. James Dorris and Frances (Pitkin) S.; m. Patricia Mann, Oct. 3, 1952; children: James Williamson, Caryn Ann, Mary Alisa. Student, Tulane U., 1947-48; BS, Mich. Technol. U., 1951; MS, Med. Coll. Va., 1953; PhD, Stanford, 1956. Research fellow biochemistry U. Tex.-M.D. Anderson Hosp. and Tumor Inst., 1955-56; assoc. prof. dept. chemistry Mich. Technol. U., Houghton, 1956-62, head dept. biol. scis., 1962-68, prof. biochemistry, 1962-84, prof. emeritus, 1985—. Dir. Ctr. for Instrnl. Computing, Ea. Mich. U., Ypsilanti, 1984-85; vis. prof. Clemson U., S.C., 1985-94; pres. Electronic Homework Sys., Inc., 1994—; cons. Computer Applications in Biology and Chemistry; dir. SUMIT Courseware Devel. Project, 1979-82. Author: Some Computer Programs for Biology, 1970, Biological Simulation Techniques, 1972, Lake Superior Basin Bibliography, 1976, BASIC Computer Models in Biology, 1978, Basic Microcomputer Models in Biology, 1982, Developing Chemical Skills with Computerized Instruction, 1990, Computer Simulation in Biology: A Basic Introduction, 1992, Chemi-Skill-Bildr Electronic Homework System, 1994, ChemSkill Builder for Windows, 1997, ChemSkill Foundations, 1998, Chem Skill Builder/2000, 1999, GOB-ChemSkills, 2002, ChemSkill Builder/3000, 2005; contbr. articles to profl. jours. Chmn. adv. council St. Josephs Hosp. Sch. Nursing, 1967; Trustee, pres. Portage Twp. Sch. Bd., 1968-76; trustee Copper Country Intermediate Sch. Dist., 1975-78. Recipient Faculty Research award Mich. Technol. U., 1965 Mem. Am. Chem. Soc. (past sect. v.p., chmn.), Rotary, Sigma Xi, Phi Lambda Upsilon. Clubs: Miscowaubik (gov. 1971-74, 79-82), Boscobel Country. Episcopalian. Home: 42498 Lakeshore Dr Chassell MI 49916-9006 also: 129 Leslie Ln Pendleton SC 29670 Personal E-mail: jspain.chemskil@prodigy.net.

**SPAIN, JAMES WILLIAM,** political scientist, writer; b. Chgo., July 22, 1926; s. Patrick Joseph and Mary Ellen (Forristal) S.; m. Edith Burke James, Feb. 21, 1951; children: Patrick, Sikandra, Stephen, William. MA, U. Chgo., 1949; PhD, Columbia U., 1959. Cons. sec. army, 1949—50; with U.S. Fgn. Svc., 1951—53; rschr., lectr. Columbia, 1955—62; mem. policy planning coun. State Dept., 1963—64; dir. Office Rsch. and Analysis for Near East and South Asia, 1964—66; country dir. Pakistan and Afghanistan, 1966—69; charge d'affaires Am. Embassy, Rawapindi, 1969; consul gen. Istanbul, Turkey, 1970-72; minister Am. embassy, Ankara, 1972-74; diplomat-in-residence, vis. prof. history and govt. Fla. State U., Tallahassee, 1974-75; amb. to Tanzania Dar es Salaam, 1975-79; amb., dep. permanent rep. UN, N.Y.C., 1979; amb. to Turkey, Ankara, 1980-81; amb. to Sri Lanka, Colombo, 1985-89; fgn. affairs fellow Carnegie Endowment for Internat. Peace and Rand Corp., Washington, 1982-84; guest resident investor Colombo, Sri Lanka, 1991—. Chmn. Lanka Infrastructure Ltd.; bd. dirs. Hawk Mountain Fed. Express, Ltd.; adj. prof. polit. sci. Am. U., Washington, 1965-67 Author: The Way of the Pathans, 1962, The Pathan Borderland, 1963, American Diplomacy in Turkey, 1984, Pathans of the Latter Day, 1995, Innocents of the Latter Day, 1997, In Those Days: A Diplomat Remembers, 1998, Holding Out in the Eternal City, 2000, The Emperor's Medallion, 2000, The Devils' Mountain, 2000, Digging the Desert, 2000, The Tribsmen's Treasure, 2000, The Monks; Secret, 2000, The Islands' Quota, 2000, Holy Ireland, 2001, Out Beyond, 2002, Innocents, 2002, To Boil a Stew, 2002. Trustee Joseph Frazer Meml. Hosp. With U.S. Army, 1946-47. Fellow Ford Found., 1953-55; recipient Presdl. Exec. award, 1983, Wilbur I. Carr award for Disting. Diplomacy, 1989. Mem. Coun. Fgn. Rels., Washington Inst. Fgn. Affairs, Assn. Diplomatic Studies and Tng., Cosmos Club Home: Galle Face Ct # 42 Colombo 3 Sri Lanka Office Phone: 94-11-243-7179. Personal E-mail: jwspain@sltnet.lk.

**SPAIN, MARY ANN,** realtor, educator, historian, writer; b. Nashville, May 31, 1950; d. James Ivan Spain and Mary Lou Crocker; m. Don Quitman Reynolds II (div.); m. James Clifford Miller, Oct. 15, 1988 (dec. Aug. 10, 1990). BS, Mid. Tenn. State U., 1972; postgrad., U. Ark., 1982; MAT, Mid. Tenn. State U., 1975, MAT, 1977. Lic. realtor Tenn. Counselor State of Tenn. Dept. Human Svcs., 1972—76; grad. tchng. asst. Mid. Tenn. State U., Murfreesboro, 1974—77; instr. Vol. State C.C., Gallatin, Tenn., 1974—92; grad. tchng. fellow U. Ark., Fayetteville, 1977—82; staff sgt. Chem. Corps, I Corp., 2d Infantry Divsn. U.S. Army, 1983—87; realtor Folk-Jordan Better Homes and Gardens, Nashville, 1987—99; instr. State of Tenn. Real Estate Commn., Nashville, 1995—; realtor Crye-Leike Realtors, Nashville, 1999—. Editor: U.S. Mil. Manuals on Chem. Warfare, Chem. Def., Chem. Ops. Newsletter. Charter mem., founder U.S. Army Nat. Mus., 2004. Decorated Army Commendation medal, Good Conduct medal, Army Achievement medal, Overseas medal; recipient Best Article in State or Local Publ. award, Ark. Hist. Commn., 1981. Mem.: PETA, ASPCA, VFW, Sumner County Realtors Assn. (edn. com. dir., Excellence in Real Estate award 1992—2004, nominee Realtor of Yr. 2003), Tenn. Assn. Realtors, Nat. Assn. Realtors, Women in Mil. Svc. for Am. Meml. Found. (charter), Realtors Polit. Action Group Tenn. Avocations: gardening, fishing, animals, travel, reading. Office: Crye-Leike Realtors 383 Johnny Cash Pky Hendersonville TN 37075 Office Phone: 615-824-8008. E-mail: spainma@realtracs.com.

**SPAIN, RICHARD COLBY,** lawyer; b. Evanston, Ill., Nov. 17, 1950; s. Richard Francis and Anne Louise (Brinckerhoff) S.; m. Nancy Lynn Mavec, Aug. 3, 1974; children: Catherine Day, Sarah Colby. BA cum laude, Lawrence U., 1972; JD, Case Western Reserve U., 1975; LLM in taxation, John Marshall Law Sch., 1985. Bar: Ohio 1975, Ill. 1982, U.S. Dist. Ct. (no. dist.) Ohio 1977, U.S. Dist. Ct. (no. dist.) Ill. 1982, Mass. 1996. Ptnr. Spain & Spain, Cleve., 1975-82, Whitted & Spain, PC, Chgo., 1985-89, Spain, Spain & Varnet PC, Chgo., Northborough, Mass., 1989—; assoc. Canel Whitted & Whitted, Chgo., 1982-85. Dir., sec. Stone Perforating Co., Chgo., 1988—, Chgo. EDM, Inc., Chgo., Wheeling, Ill., 1994—. Contbr. articles to profl. jours. Treas. ARC Ill., 1993-2003; dir. Chgo. Youth Symphony Orch., 1983-2002. Mem.: Carlton Club (Chgo.), Chikaming Country Club (dir.

1992—94). Home: 1320 N State Pkwy Chicago IL 60610-2118 Office: Spain Spain & Varnet PC 33 N Dearborn St Ste 2220 Chicago IL 60602-3118 E-mail: rspain@spainspainvarnet.com

**SPAIN, SHERYL SCARBROUGH,** school counselor, educator; b. Columbus, Ohio, Feb. 13, 1944; d. Ernest James and Martha Adams Scarbrough; m. C. Michael Spain, Aug. 6, 1965; children: Christopher Charles, Todd Michael. BS, Ga. State U., 1970, MS, 1987. Cert. sch. counselor K-12 Ga. Instr. Winsalem Jr. Coll., Winston Salem, NC, 1975—78; instr., dept. head Herzing Inst., Birmingham, Ala., 1981—84; tchr. Cobb County Schs., Marietta, Ga., 1984—87, sch. counselor, 1987—2004. Workshop presenter, coord. Bells Ferry Elem., Marietta, 1992—; coord. sheriff's awards Cobb County Sheriff, 1995—; mem. crisis response team Cobb County Schs., Marietta, 2000—. Mem. Citizen's Adv. Counsel, Marietta, 1993—95. Presbyterian. Avocations: reading, tennis, travel. Home: 2492 St James Dr Southport NC 28461

**SPAIN, THOMAS B.,** retired state supreme court justice; Justice Ky. Supreme Ct, Frankfort, 1991-95; ret., 1995; of counsel Whitfield & Cox P.S.C. Office: Whitfield & Cox PSC 29 E Center St Madisonville KY 42431-2037 Office Phone: 270-821-0656.

**SPAINHOUR, J. PATRICK,** outsourcing company executive, former apparel executive; B, Miss. State Univ., 1972. Positions through v.p. fin. & adminstrn. Kellwood Co., 1972—83; exec. v.p. fin. & ops. Seminole Mfg. Co., 1983; sr. v.p. sourcing Gap Inc.; exec. v.p. fin. & ops. Stride Rite Corp.; exec. v.p., CFO Donna Karen Co.; pres., COO Ann Taylor Stores Corp., 1996, chmn., CEO, 1996—2005; interim chmn., CEO Servicemaster Co., Downers Grove, Ill., 2006—. Bd. dir. Tupperware Corp., Circuit City Stores Inc., 2004—, Servicemaster Co., 2005—. Office: Servicemaster Co Ste 600 3250 Lacey Rd Downers Grove IL 60515*

**SPAINHOWER, JAMES IVAN,** retired college president; b. Stanberry, Mo., Aug. 3, 1928; s. Elmer Enoch and Stella Irene (Cox) S.; m. Joanne Steanson, June 10, 1950; children: Janet Dovell, James Jeffrey. BA, Phillips U., Enid, Okla., 1950, LLD (hon.), 1967; BD, Lexington Theol. Sem., Ky., 1953; MA in Polit. Sci., U. Mo., Columbia, 1967, PhD, 1971, U. Ark., 1954; diploma, U. Pacific Sch. Religion, Berkeley, Calif., 1958; DPA (hon.), Culver-Stockton Coll., 1973; LL.D. (hon.), Maryville Coll., St. Louis, 1976; Litt.D. (hon.), Kirksville Coll. Osteo. Medicine, Mo., 1977; D.H.L. (hon.), Mo. Valley Coll., 1984; LLD (hon.), Eureka Coll., 1989, Lynchburg Coll., 1993. Ordained to ministry Christian Ch. (Disciples of Christ), 1950; pastor chs. in Ark. and Mo., 1953-70; mem. Mo. Ho. of Reps. from, Saline County, 1963-70; pres. Asso. Med. Schs. Mo., Jefferson City, 1970-72; part-time prof. polit. sci. Lincoln U., Jefferson City, 1970-72; treas. State of Mo., 1973-80; pres. Sch. of Ozarks, Point Lookout, Mo., 1981-82, Lindenwood Coll., St. Charles, Mo., 1983-89; pres. divsn. higher edn. Christian Ch. (Disciples of Christ), 1989-93. Author: Pulpit, Pew and Politics, 1979. Chmn. Mo. del. Dem. Nat. Conv., 1976; elected mem. Acad. Squires, 1981; 1st chmn. Mo. Children's Trust Fund, 1984-86. Recipient Mental Health award Mo. Mental Health Assn., 1967, Meritorious Service award St. Louis Globe Dem., 1968, Harry S. Truman award Saline County Young Democrats, 1970, citation of merit Alumni Assn. U. Mo., 1975; named Mo. Lay Educator of Year Mo. chpt. Phi Delta Kappa, 1968 Home and Office: 8067 Old White River Rd Rogers AR 72756-7662 E-mail: spainy@cox-internet.com.

**SPAKE, MARY BARBARA,** music educator; b. Mpls., Apr. 7, 1919; d. Donald Nivison Ferguson and Arline Calista (Folsom); m. Virgil F. Spake, July 2, 1978. BS, U. Minn., 1942, M. Music Edn., 1949. Tchr. Grand Marais (Minn.) Pub. Schs., 1942-43, Litchfield (Minn.) Pub. Schs., 1943-45, Mpls. Pub. Schs., 1945-79, Mpls. Coll. Music, 1949-55, Macalester Coll., St. Paul, 1950-56; pvt. music tchr. Golden Valley, Minn., 1949—. Asst. choir dir. Cen. Luth. Ch., Mpls., 1946-56; choir dir. Grace U. Luth. Ch., Mpls., 1950-55. Mem. Retired Tchrs. Mpls., Music Educators Nat. Conf., Nat. Assn. Tchrs. of Singing, Sigma Alpha Iota. Avocation: dress making. Home and Office: Apt C227 5800 Saint Croix Ave N Golden Valley MN 55422-4763

**SPAKE, REUBEN MICHAEL,** mathematics professor, researcher; b. Spokane, Wash., Mar. 20, 1957; s. William Jack and Georgia Geraldine (Christensen) S.; m. Cynthia Spake. BS, U. Calif., Davis, 1978, MA, 1984, PhD, 1986. Mathematician, Edwards AFB, Calif., 1976-79; computer programmer analyst Mgmt. Info. Svcs., Fairfield, Calif., 1979—83; math. teaching asst. U. Calif., Davis, 1983-86; prof. Coll. Charleston, SC, 1987—93; prof. math. Solano CC, Fairfield, Calif., 1993—, Consumnes River Coll., Sacramento, 1994—, San Jacquin Delta Coll., Stockton, Calif., 1994—, Los Medanos Coll., Pitts., 1994—. Pub. power semigroup rsch., 1985—. Recipient Math. Achievement award Bank Am., 1974; Kraft scholar U. Calif., Davis, 1975. Mem. AAAS, SAR, Am. Math. Soc., Math. Assn. Am., NY Acad. Scis., Hereditary Order of First Families Mass., Sons and Daus. of Pilgrims, Sons of the Am. Revolution, Magna Charta Barons, Pi Mu Epsilon, Mu Alpha Theta. Avocations: guitar, music, travel. Office: Solano CC 4000 Suisun Valley Rd Fairfield CA 94534 Personal E-mail: rmspake@yahoo.com.

**SPALDING, ANDREW FREEMAN,** lawyer; b. Toledo, Ohio, June 24, 1951; s. Dean and Shirley Louise (Maitland) S.; m. Adele Talcott. BA, U. Calif., Berkeley, 1973; JD, So. Meth. U., 1977. Bar: Tex. 1977, U.S. Dist. Ct. (so., ea. and we. dists.) Tex. 1978, U.S. Ct. Appeals (5th cir.) 1978; bd. cert. civil trial law, personal injury trial law. Assoc. Bracewell & Giuliani, LLP, Houston, 1977-84, ptnr., 1985—. Notes and comments editor So. Meth. U. Law Jour., Dallas, 1976-77. Fellow Tex Bar Found.; Houston Bar Found.; mem. State Bar Tex., Houston Bar Assn., Tex. Assn. Def. Counsel, Def. Rsch. Inst., Knights Momus, Krewe Maximilian, Pan Tex. Assembly, Houston Country Club. Office: Bracewell & Giuliani LLP 2300 S Tower Pennzoil Pla 711 Louisiana St Ste 2300 Houston TX 77002-2770 Office                    713-221-1220.              Business                E-Mail: Andrew.Spalding@bracewellgiuliani.com.

**SPALDING, JAMES STUART,** retired telecommunications industry executive; b. Edinburgh, Scotland, Nov. 23, 1934; arrived in Can., 1957, permanent resident, 1962; Student, Edinburgh U., 1951-52, Glasgow U., 1953. Gen. mgr., dir. United Corps. Ltd., Montreal, Que., Canada, 1970-72; from pension fund mgr. to exec. v.p. fin. BCE, Inc., Montreal, 1972-90. Mem. Inst. Chartered Accts. Scotland, Order Chartered Accounts Que., Fin. Execs. Inst. Can. (past chmn.), Montreal Soc. Fin. Analysts (past pres.). Home: 126 King St   E   Brockville   ON   Canada   K6V   1B9   Personal   E-mail: stuart231134@aol.com.

**SPALTY, EDWARD ROBERT,** lawyer; b. New Haven, Oct. 1, 1946; s. Kermit and Elinor Turgeon; m. Suzy Clune; children: Thomas John, Kathleen Tess. BA, Emory U., 1968; JD, Columbia U., 1973. Bar: Mo. 1975, Nebr. 1997, Kans. 1998, Colo. 2003, U.S. Dist. Ct. (we. dist.) Mo. 1975, U.S. Ct. Claims 1977, U.S. Ct. Appeals (8th cir.) 1984, U.S. Ct. Appeals (10th cir.) 1999, U.S. Supreme Ct. 1994, U.S. Dist. Ct. (ea. dist.) Wis. 2004. Assoc. Webster & Sheffield, N.Y.C., 1973-74; mng. ptnr. Armstrong Teasdale LLP, Kansas City, Mo., 1991-2001, ptnr., 1980—. Contbr. articles to profl. jours. Chmn. bd. dirs. Mo. Easter Seals, 1990—92; founding mem. Heartland Franchise Assn.; bd. dirs., mem. exec. com. Nat. Easter Seal Soc.; bd. dirs. Mo. Easter Seals, 1984—. With U.S. Army, 1968—70. Named Best of the Bar, Kans. City Bus. Jour., 2006, Superlawyer, Mo., 2006, Kans., 2006; named one of Best Lawyers in Am., Woodward White, 1995—. Mem.: ABA (litigation sect, franchising forum comt), Intern. Rels. Coun. Kansas City, Def. Rsch. Inst., Mo. Orgn. Def. Attys., Lawyers Assn. Kansas City, Kansas City Met. Bar Assn. (chmn antitrust and franchise law comt, co-chair 14th and 16h ann Nat Franchise Law Inst), Mo. Bar Assn. (civil rules and procedures comt) Lex Mundi (regional vice chair N.Am. dispute resolution, antitrust practice group), German-Am C. of C. (v.p. Kansas City chpt), Nat. Golf Club Kansas City (founder), Phi Delta, Pi Sigma Alpha, Sigma Nu. Home: 13703

---

NW 73rd St Parkville MO 64152-1120 Office: Armstrong Teasdale LLP 2345 Grand Blvd Ste 2000 Kansas City MO 64108-2617 Office Phone: 816-221-3420. Business E-Mail: espalty@armstrongteasdale.com.

**SPALVINS, JANIS GUNARS,** steamship company executive; b. Riga, Latvia, May 26, 1936; arrived in Australia, 1949; s. Peter Spalvins and Hilda (Dritmanis) Blumentals; m. Cecily Westall Rymill, Dec. 16, 1961; children: John Rymill and Richard Rymill. B in Econ. Group sec., dir. Camelec Group of Cos., South Australia, 1955-73; asst. gen. mgr. The Adelaide Steamship Co. Ltd., South Australia, 1973-77, chief gen. mgr., dir., 1977-81, mng. dir., 1981-90; dir., chief exec. David Jones Ltd., Australia, 1980, 1988—91; dir. Macmahon Holdings, Ltd., 1987—92; chmn., dir. Galufo Pty. Ltd., 1991—. Fellow Australian Inst. Mgmt., Australian Soc. CPAs, Inst. Chartered Accts., Inst. Dirs., Chartered Inst. Secs., Cruising Yacht of SA, Mt. Osmond Golf Club. Avocations: sailing, tennis, snow and water skiing. Home: 2 Brookside Rd Springfield SA 5061 Australia Office Phone: 618 83792965. Personal E-mail: jgspalvins@bigpond.com.

**SPANBOCK, MAURICE SAMUEL,** lawyer; b. NYC, Jan. 6, 1924; s. Benjamin and Belle (Ward) S.; m. Marion Rita Heyman, Nov. 21, 1954; children: Jonathan H., Betsy W. BA, Columbia U., N.Y.C., 1944; LLB, Harvard U., 1950. Bar: N.Y. 1950. Ptnr. Carro and Spanbock (name changed to Carro, Spanbock, Kaster et al), N.Y.C., 1952-94; of counsel Kleinberg Kaplan Wolff & Cohen, N.Y.C., 1994—. Trustee Carnegie Coun. on Ethics and Internat. Affairs, N.Y.C., 1980-86, 93-2000, hon. trustee, 2002--, chmn. bd., 1987-92; hon. pres. Lincoln Square Synagogue, N.Y.C.; sec. Ohr Torah Stone Instns. Israel. Cpl. AUS, 1943-46, ETO. Mem. ABA (chmn. com. on taxation, patent, trademark and copyright law sect. 1979-81), Assn. of Bar of City of N.Y. (com. on copyright 1965-67, art law com. 1977-80, 86-88), Fed. Bar Coun., Nat. Panel Arbitrators, Am. Abitration Assn., Practising Law Inst. (panel on copyrights, 1979). Jewish. Home: 88 Central Park W New York NY 10023-5209 Office: Kleinberg Kaplan Wolff & Cohen 551 5th Ave Fl 18 New York NY 10176-1800 Office Phone: 212-986-6000.

**SPANDER, DEBORAH L.,** lawyer; b. 1969; BA in polit. sci. with honors and distinction, Stanford U., 1991; JD, UCLA Sch. Law, 1995. Bar: Calif. 1995. Mgr. bus. and legal affairs BLT Prodn., Inc., LA, 1994—96; assoc. Law Offices of Maidie E. Oliveaa, 1996—97; dir. bus. and legal affairs Fox Sports Network, LA, 1998—2001; v.p. bus. and legal affairs Fox Cable Networks Group, LA, 2002—. Guest lectr. UCLA Sch. Law, 1999—2001; adv. bd. mem. Nat. Sports Law Inst., Marquette U. Law Sch. Vol. Friends of Break The Cycle, LA, 1996—. Mem.: Stanford West LA Club, Westcoast Sports Assoc., Women's Entertainment Network, Sports Lawyers Assn. Guest lectr., mem. program com., moderator and spkr. Nat. Conf. 2003—04, spkr. Nat. Conf. 1997—2002). Avocations: tennis, swimming, skiing, travel, cooking. Office: 12100 Sunset Hills Rd Ste 130 Reston VA 20190 Office Phone: 703-437-4377. Business E-Mail: debspander1@yahoo.com.

**SPANDORFER, MERLE SUE,** artist, educator, writer; b. Balt., Sept. 4, 1934; d. Simon Louis and Bernice P. (Jacobson) S.; m. Lester M. Spandorfer, June 17, 1956; children: Cathy, John. Student, Syracuse U., 1952-54; BS, U. Md., 1956. Mem. faculty Cheltenham (Pa.) Sch. Fine Arts, 1969—; instr. printmaking Tyler Sch. Art Temple U., 1980-84; faculty Pratt Graphics Ctr., N.Y.C., 1985-86. One woman shows include Richard Feigen Gallery, N.Y.C., 1970, U. Pa., 1974, Phila. Coll. Textiles and Sci., 1977, Ericson Gallery, N.Y.C., 1978, 79, R.I. Sch. Design, 1980, Syracuse U., 1981, Marian Locks Gallery, Phila., 1973, 78, 82, Temple U., 1984, Tyler Sch. Art, 1985, University City Sci. Ctr., 1987, Gov.'s Residence, 1988, Wenninger Graphics Gallery, Provinceton, Mass.. 1989, Widener U. Art Mus., 1995, Gloucester County Coll., 1996, Mangel Gallery, 1992, 97, 2000, 03, 06, Cabrini Coll., 1999, Mangel Gallery, 2000; group shows Bklyn. Mus. Art, 1973, San Francisco Mus. Art, 1973, Balt. Mus. Art, 1970, 71, 74, Phila. Mus. Art, 1972, 77, Fundacio Joan Miro. Barcelona, Spain, 1977, Del. Mus. Art, Wilmington, 1978, Carlsberg Glyptotek Mus., Copenhagen, 1980, Moore Coll. Art, Phila., 1982, Tyler Sch. Art, 1983, William Penn Meml. Mus., Harrisburg, Pa., 1984, Ariz. State U., 1985, Tiajin Fine Arts Coll., China, 1986, Beaver Coll., Phila., 1988, The Port of History Mus., Phils., 1987, Sichuan Fine Arts Inst., Chong Qing, China, 1988, Glynn Vivian Mus., Swansea, Wales, 1989, Phila. Mus. Art, 1990, Fgn. Mus., Riga, Latvia, 1995, Woodmere Art Mus., Phila., 1996, Am. Coll., 1997, Cheltenham Ctr. for the Arts, Phila., 1997, Rowan Coll., 1997, Villanova U., 1998, U. Pa., 1999, U. of the Arts, 2001, others; represented in permanent collections Met. Mus. Art, N.Y.C., Whitney Mus. Am. Art, N.Y.C., Mus. Modern Art, N.Y.C., The Israel Mus., Balt. Mus. (gov.'s prize and purchase award 1970), Phila. Mus. Art (purchase award 1977), Toyoh Bijutsu Gakko, Tokyo, Library of Congress, Temple U.; co-author: Making Art Safely, 1993 Recipient award Balt. Mus. Art/Md. Inst. Art, 1971, Govs. prize and Purchase award Balt. Mus. Art, 1970, Outstanding Art Educators award Pa. Art Edn. Assn., 1982, Purchase award Berman Mus., 1995, Artist Equity award, 1996; grantee Pa. Coun. Arts, 1989. Mem. Am. Color Print Soc., Pa. Art Edn. Assn. Jewish. Office: 307 E Gowen Ave Philadelphia PA 19119-1023 E-mail: lesspand@home.com.

**SPANEL, HARRIET,** state legislator; b. Audubon, Iowa, Jan. 15, 1939; 3 children. BS in Math., Iowa State U., 1961. Mem. Wash. Ho. of Reps., 1987-93, Wash. Senate, Dist. 40, Olympia, 1993—. Cath. Office: Wash Senate PO Box 40440 Olympia WA 98504-0440

**SPANFELLER, JAMES JOHN, JR.,** publishing executive; b. Phila., Aug. 25, 1956; s. James John Sr. and Patricia Ann (Durkin) S. BA, Union Coll., Schenectedy, N.Y., 1979. Assoc. pub. Soho News, N.Y.C., 1979-81; dir. Alan Western Communications, N.Y.C., 1981-83; pub. Newsweek on Campus, N.Y.C., 1983-86; nat. sales mgr. Newsweek, N.Y.C., 1986—, sales dir. 1987-89; assoc. pub., v.p. Playboy Mag., 1989-93; pub. Inc. mag., 1993—96, Ziff-Davis Yahoo! Internet Life, 1996—98; v.p. Yahoo! Internet Life, 1998-2000, 1998—2000; pres., CEO Forbes.com, 2001—. Mem. mktg. com. Mag. Pub. Assoc.; bd. dirs. Am. Bus. Media, 2004—. Author: The Fantastic Airplane, 1979. Mem.: N.Y. Athletic. Office: Forbes com 24 W 23rd St 11th Fl New York NY 10010 Office Phone: 212-366-8999. Office Fax: 212-366-8801.

**SPANGLER, ARNOLD EUGENE,** investment banker; b. Ft. Dodge, Iowa, Aug. 1, 1948; s. Kermit Charles and Cora (Buroos) Spangler; m. Penelope Angell, Nov. 8, 1980; children: Christopher Paul, Allison Elizabeth. BS, Iowa State U., 1970; MBA, Harvard U., 1972. Assoc. Hornblower & Weeks-Hemphill, Noyes, N.Y.C., 1972—74; product officer Citibank, 1974—76, Lazard Freres & Co. LLC, 1976—89, gen. ptnr., 1983—89; mng. dir. mergers and acquisitions Paine Webber Inc. (now UBS), 1989—91; sr. advisor Bentley Assocs., L.P., 1992—93; mng. dir. Mancuso & Co., 1993—2005; dir. Patient Safety Techs., 2006—. Home: 1165 Park Ave New York NY 10128-1210 Office Phone: 917-670-4873.

**SPANGLER, ARTHUR STEPHENSON, JR.,** psychologist; b. Boston, June 20, 1949; s. Arthur Stephenson and Barbara Louise (Fellows) Spangler; m. Deborah A. Kauders, Nov. 27, 1971; children: Heather Anita, Rebecca Haley. BS, Hobart Coll., 1971; MEd, Boston Coll., 1974; ScD, Boston U., 1985. Diplomate Am. Acad. Pain Mgmt.; lic. psychologist, Mass., clin. social worker, Mass.; bd. cert. rehab. counselor, Mass. Mass. counselor Met. State Hosp., Waltham, 1971-73; rehab. counselor J.T. Berry Rehab. Ctr., North Reading, Mass., 1974-75; program coord. Shore Collaborative, Medford, Mass., 1975-76; dir. instl. sch. programs South Shore Collaborative, North Weymouth, Mass., 1976-79; dir. mental retardation program South Shore Mental Health Ctr., Quincy, Mass., 1979-85; coord. outpatient clinic Boston Pain Ctr., Spaulding Rehab. Hosp., 1985-86; v.p., dir. behavioral medicine svcs. Mass. Bay Counseling, Quincy, Mass., 1985—; dir. indsl. disability mgmt. svcs., psychologist chronic pain program Miriam Hosp., Providence, 1987-88; psychologist John Graham Headache Ctr. Faulkner Hosp., Boston, 1992-94. Adj. prof. Sargent Coll., Boston U., 1990—99. Vol. counselor Multi-Svc. Ctr., Newton, Mass., 1973-75; bd. dirs. Newton-Wellesley-

---

Weston-Needham Cmty. Mental Health and Mental Retardation Ctr., Newton, 1976-80, pres. 1979-80; mem. Boston Symphony Assn. Vols. Recipient award Nat. Assn. Retarded Citizens, 1974. Mem.: ACA, APA (assoc.), New Eng. Pain Assn., Soc. Behavioral Medicine, Internat. Assn. for Study of Pain, Assn. for Study of Pain. Episcopalian. Home: 151 Tremont St # 11P Boston MA 02111-1110 Office: 36 Weston Ave Quincy MA 02170-1833 Office Phone: 617-786-0137. Personal E-mail: sspanglermbc@verizon.net.

**SPANGLER, CLEMMIE DIXON, JR.,** construction company executive; b. Charlotte, N.C., Apr. 5, 1932; s. Clemmie Dixon and Veva C. (Yelton) S.; m. Meredith Jane Riggs, June 25, 1960; children: Anna Wildy, Abigail Riggs. BS, U. N.C., 1954; MBA, Harvard U., 1956; LHD (hon.), Queens Coll., 1985; LLD (hon.), Davidson Coll., 1986, Furman U., 1993; LLD U. N. Carolina (hon.), 2003. Pres. C.D. Spangler Constrn. Co., Charlotte, 1958-86, Golden Eagle Industries, Inc., 1968-86; chmn. bd. Bank of N.C., Raleigh, 1973-82; dir. NCNB Corp., 1983-86; chmn. N.C. Bd. Edn., 1982-86; pres. U. N.C., Chapel Hill, 1986-97; CEO, chmn. C.D. Spangler Constrn. Co., Charlotte, 1997—. Bd. dirs. BellSouth Corp., Atlanta; chmn. bd. dirs. Nat. Gypsum Co., Charlotte. Past deacon Myers Park Bapt. Ch., vice-chmn. Charlotte-Mecklenburg Bd. Edn., Charlotte, 1972-76; past trustee Charlotte Symphony Orch., Crozer Theol. Sem.; past chmn. Charlotte adv. bd. Salvation Army; past bd. dirs. YMCA, Equitable Life Assurance Soc., Jefferson-Pilot Corp.; pres. bd. trustees Mint Mus. Art; bd. dirs. Union Theol. Sem., 1985-90, Assocs. Harvard Bus. Sch.; pres. bd. overseers Harvard Coll., 2003. With U.S. Army, 1956-58. Recipient Liberty Bell award Mecklenburg County Bar Assn., 1985, Alumni Achievement award Harvard Bus. Sch., 1988; named one of Forbes' Richest Americans, 2006. Mem. Assn. Am. Univs., Bus. Higher Edn. Forum, Harvard Club (N.Y.C.), Univ. Club (N.Y.C.), Quail Hollow Country Club (Charlotte). Office: CD Spangler Constrn Co Office of Chmn Box 36007 Charlotte NC 28236-6007*

**SPANGLER, DAVID ROBERT,** academic administrator, educator, engineer; b. Flint, Mich., Aug. 17, 1940; s. John Solomon and Margaret Inger (McKinley) S.; m. Sally Jeanne Henry, Aug. 28, 1965; children: Timothy David, Megan Marie. BS, U.S. Mil. Acad., 1962; MS in Engring., U. Ill., 1966, PhD in Structural Dynamics, 1977. Registered profl. engr. Commd. 2d lt. U.S. Army, 1962, advanced through grades to lt. col., 1979, prof. math. U.S. Mil. Acad. West Point, N.Y., 1968-71, engr. Korea Support Command, 1972-73, dep. dist. engr. C.E. Walla Walla, Wash., 1973-74, research coordinator Def. Nuclear Agy. Washington, 1976-79, bn. comdr. Hawaii, 1979-81, inspector C.E. San Francisco, 1981-82, ret., 1982; prof. engring. St. Martin's Coll., Lacey, Wash., 1982-84, pres., 1984—. Mem. Nat. Com. for Tunnelling Tech., Washington, 1977-79; cons. Thurston County, Olympia, Wash., 1982-84. Contbr. articles to profl. jours. Bd. dirs. Econ. Devel. Coun., Thurston County, 1985-88, Wash. State Capitol Mus., 1988-91. Decorated Bronze Star with 2 oak leaf clusters, Meritorious Service medal, Def. Nuclear Agy. Joint Service medal. Mem. Soc. Mil. Engrs. (v.p. 1980-81, pres. 1973-74), Nat. Assn. Ind. Colls. and Univs. (bd. dirs. 1992-95, treas. 1994), Ind. Colls. Wash. (bd. dirs.), Assn. Benedictine Colls. and Univs. (pres. 1994-95), Rotary (mem. gov.'s oversight com. on tech. 1996—). Roman Catholic. Avocation: running. Office: St Martins Coll Office of Pres Lacey WA 98503

**SPANGLER, DENNIS LEE,** physician; b. Akron, Ohio, Nov. 8, 1947; s. Wesley Daniel and Florence Adele (Smith) S.; m. July 7, 1972; children: Mathew Brian, Adam Christopher. BS, U. Akron, 1969; MD, Ohio State Med. Sch., 1973. Diplomate Am. Bd. Pediatrics, Am. Bd. Allergy and Immunology. Intern U. Fla. Med. Sch., Gainesville, 1973-74, resident, 1974-75, fellow allergy and clin. immunology, 1975-77; pvt. practice Atlanta Allergy Clinic, P.A., 1977—; chief med. officer Atlanta Allergy and Asthma Clinic, 1995—. Dir. chronic lung clinic Ga. Bur. Crippled Children, 1984-97; asst. clin. prof. pediatrics Med. Coll. of Ga., 1980-2001; vice chair divsn. of allergy Children's Healthcare of Atlanta, 2000—. Past pres., bd. dirs. midwest branch Ga. Lung Assn., Atlanta, 1981-82, med. adv. com., 1978-97; pres. Fla. Pediatric Alumni Assn., Gainesville, 1985-86. Fellow Am. Acad. Pediatrics, Am. Acad. Allergy and Immunology, Am. Coll. Allergy, Asthma and Immunology (therapeutics com. 1983-88, chmn. drug and anaphylaxis com. 1988-2003, chmn. com. 1987-2004, bd. regents 1996-99), Am. Assn. Cert. Allergists (bd. govs. 1988—, bd. sec. 1997, v.p. 1998, pres. elect 1999, pres. 2000); mem. Am. Thoracic Soc., Ga. Med. Assn., Cobb County Med. Soc., Southeastern Allergy Assn., Cherokee Country Club. Roman Catholic. Avocations: scuba diving, creating stain glass windows. Office: Atlanta Allergy Asthma Clinic 1965 N Park Pl Atlanta GA 30339-2012

**SPANGLER, JOHN I., III,** lawyer; b. York, Pa., Jan. 6, 1956; AB, Univ. Ill., 1977; JD, Washington Univ., 1980. Bar: Ga. 1980. Ptnr., head, construction law group Alston & Bird LLP, Atlanta. Editl.bd. Georgia Bar Jour., contbr. Georgia Appellate Practice Handbook. (Amicus Curiae award, Ga. Supreme Ct. for his work, 1986), frequent spkr. on construction law. Mem.: ABA, Atlanta Bar Assn. (chmn. construction law com. 1994—1995). Office: Alston & Bird LLP One Atlantic Plz 1201 W Peachtree St NW Atlanta GA 30309-3424 Office Phone: 404-881-7146. Office Fax: 404-881-7777. Business E-Mail: jspangler@alston.com.

**SPANGLER, NITA REIFSCHNEIDER,** volunteer; b. Ukiah, Calif., Apr. 17, 1923; d. John Charles and Olga Augusta (Wuertz) Reifschneider; m. Raymond Luper Spangler, Sept. 22, 1946 (dec.); children: Jon Martin, Mary Raymond, Thor Raymond. BA, Univ. Nev., 1944. News reporter Redwood (Calif.) City Tribune, 1944-46, Country Almanac, Woodside, Calif., 1969-77. Mem. bd. dirs. San Mateo (Calif.) County Hist. Assn., 1961-68, pres., 1964-66; founder, 1st pres. Portolá Expedition Bicentennial Found., 1966-70; chmn. San Mateo County Scenic Rds. Com., 1967-76; mem. San Mateo County Hist. Resource Adv.; mem. commn. San Mateo County Parks and Recreation, 1983-97, past chmn.; cons. hwy. aesthetics Cal Trans., 1981-83; mem. sch. coms. Recipient Commendation, County Bd. Suprs., 1968, 1977, 92. Mem. Sierra Club, Western History Assn., Mormon History Assn., Nev. State Hist. Soc. (life), San Mateo County Hist. Assn. (life), Resolution of Thanks 1968, 76, 94), Friends Redwood City, Kappa Alpha Theta. Democrat. Episcopalian. Avocation: historic preservation. Home: 970 Edgewood Rd Redwood City CA 94062-1818

**SPANGLER, RONALD LEROY,** retired television executive, aircraft executive, automobile consultant; b. York, Pa., Mar. 5, 1937; s. Ivan L. and Sevilla (Senft) S.; m. Svetlana Gavrilova; children: Kathleen, Ronald Jr., Beth Anne, Pavel. Student, U. Miami, 1955-59. Radio announcer Sta. WSBA, York, 1955-59; TV prodr. Sta. WBAL-TV, Balt. and NBC TV, 1958-65; pres., chmn. bd. LewRon Television, N.Y.C., Hollywood, Calif., 1965-78, Spanair Inc.; distbr. Rockwell bus. aircraft, 1975-85. Owner Prancing Horse Farm; dealer vintage and modern Ferrari automobiles; racer numerous courses including LeMans, Daytona, Sebring; racer vintage and modern Ferrari automobiles; Ferrari cons. (PBS show) Motorweek; cons. Bentley Motor Cars, Pininfarina S.P.A.; North Am. rep. Pinin Farina Automotive Design, 2005—. Mem. Video Tape Producers Assn. N.Y.C., Rolls Royce Owners Club, Ferrari Clubs Am. and Italia, Mercedes Benz Club Am., Porsche Club Am. Avocation: antique automobile collector. Home: Prancing Horse Farm 3710 Ady Rd Street MD 21154-1432 Office Phone: 410-452-5500. Personal E-mail: PHFarmFerrari@aol.com.

**SPANGLER, STANLEY EUGENE,** international relations educator; b. Billings, Mont., Apr. 7, 1929; s. John Harold Spangler and Winifred Watt; m. Addie Belle Moore, Sept. 21, 1968; children: John Wayland Spangler, Julia Watt Spangler Garlatz. BA, U. Mont., 1952; MA, Columbia U., 1958; PhD, U. N.C., 1978. Program officer Asia Found., San Francisco, 1963-65; assoc. regional dir. Fgn. Policy Assn., Atlanta, 1965-69; dir. Office Pub. and Internat. Affairs U. N.C. Extension Divsn., Chapel Hill, 1969-73; exec. dir. World Affairs Coun. Boston, 1973-81; internat. program advisor Fletcher Sch. Law and Diplomacy, Medford, Mass., 1983-84; sr. fellow Air Univ. USAF, 1984-89; Sec. of Navy sr. fellow U.S. Naval War Coll., Newport, R.I., 1989-92, sr. fellow, prof. strategy, 1993—. Prof. govt. and fgn. affairs Bentley Coll., Waltham, Mass., 1995—; commr. U.S. Nat. Commn. for UNESCO,

Washington, 1976-81; pres. Nat. Coun. World Affairs Orgns., Washington, 1977-80; mem. editl. adv. bd. Fgn. Policy Assn., N.Y.c., 1975-78; exec. mem. Nat. Def. Exec. Res., Washington, 1980-97. Author: Force and Accommodation in World Politics, 1991; contbr. articles to profl. jours. Dir. Curtis-Saval Internat. Ctr., Boston, 1976-81; mem. exec. com., bd. dirs. Ala. World Affairs Coun., Montgomery, 1986-89; bd. dirs. Ctr. for Internat. Visitors, Boston, 1978-81; mem. African studies adv. com. Boston U., 1978-80. Capt. USAF, 1954-56. Johns Hopkins U. fellow, 1952-53; Columbia U. scholar, 1957-58. Mem. AAUP, Am. Polit. Sci. Assn., Boston Com. on Fgn. Rels., Phi Beta Delta. Democrat. Methodist. Avocations: hiking, writing, travel, reading. Home: 17 Kings Way Scituate MA 02066-2609 E-mail: s.spangler@bentley.edu.

**SPANIER, GRAHAM BASIL,** academic administrator; b. Capetown, South Africa, July 18, 1948; s. Fred and Rosadele (Lurie) Spanier; m. Sandra Kay Whipple, Sept. 11, 1971; children: Brian Lockwood, Hadley Alison. BS, Iowa State U., 1969, MS, 1971, Doctorate (hon.), 2006; PhD, Northwestern U., 1973. Assoc. dean, prof. in charge Pa. State U., University Park, 1973—82, pres., 1995—; vice-provost, prof. SUNY, Stony Brook, 1982—86; provost, v.p. for acad. affairs Oreg. State U., 1986—91; chancellor U. Nebr., Lincoln, 1991—95. Chmn. Presdl. Adv. Group on Info. Tech., 1997—99, Kellogg Commn. on Future of State and Land-Grant Univs., 1997—2000; bd. dirs. Univ. Corp. for Advanced Internet Devel., U.S. Dept. Edn. Commn. on Opportunity in Athletics, 2002—03; host TV and radio programs, 1973—; bd. dirs. Citizens Bank Pa., Jr. Achievement Worldwide; trustee Univs. Rsch. Assn., 2001—05; vice-chmn. Worldwide Univ. Network, 2003—; chair Nat. Security Higher Edn. Adv. Bd., 2005—. Founding editor: Jour. Family Issues. Del. White House Conf. on Families, Washington, 1980; pres., chmn. bd. dirs. Christian Children's Fund, Richmond, Va., 1985—94; bd. dirs. Nat. 4H Coun., 1997—2000. Named Outstanding Young Alumnus, Iowa State U., 1982, Disting. Alumnus, 2005; Woodrow Wilson fellow, 1972. Mem.: Assn. Am. Univs. (com. intellectual property 1997—), Acad. Health Ctrs. (commn. on future of acad. health ctrs. 1996—98), Am. Assn. State Colls. and Univs. (joint commn. on accountability report 1993—95), Nat. Collegiate Athletic Assn. (pres. commn. 1995—97, bd. dirs., exec. com. 1997—2001, divsn. I bd. dirs., chmn. 1998—2001), Am. Coun. on Edn. (commn. on women 1992—95), Nat. Assn. State Univs. and Land Grant Univs. (exec. com. coun. on acad. affairs 1990—91, bd. pres. commn. on info. technologies 1993—99, chmn. 1996—99, bd. dirs. 1997—, chmn. coun. of pres. 1999—2000, bd. chair 2002), Am. Assn. Family and Consumer Scis. (Moran award 1972), Am. Sociol. Assn. (family sect. chmn. 1983—84), Population Assn. Am. (bd. dirs.), Nat. Coun. Family Rels. (pres. 1987—88, Outstanding Grad. Student award 1972), Am. Assn. for Marriage and Family Therapy, Worldwide Univs. Network (vice chair 2003—). Democrat. Avocations: aviation, magic, athletics, public broadcasting. Office: Pa State Univ Office of Pres 201 Old Main University Park PA 16802-1503

**SPANJOL, JELENA,** finance educator; d. Petar and Svetlana Spanjol; m. Adade A. Deganus, May 1, 2004; 1 child, Mihajlo-Joshua Foali Deganus. PhD, U. Ill., Champaign-Urbana, 1997—2002. Internat. mktg. coord./bus. devel. mgr. Wolfram Rsch., Champaign, 1996—97; asst. prof. Tex. A&M U., College Station, 2002—. Faculty advisor Am. Mktg. Assn., Tex. A&M U. Student Chpt., 2003—. Contbr. articles to profl. jours., chapters to books. Grantee Richard D. Irwin fellowship, U. Ill., 2001; Mays Bus. Sch. Summer Rsch. grant, Tex. A&M U., 2004. Mem.: Product Devel. & Mgmt. Assn., Acad. Mgmt., Am. Mktg. Assn. Office: Texas A&M U 220 Wehner Bldg College Station TX 77429 Business E-Mail: jspanjol@tamu.edu.

**SPANN, GEORGE WILLIAM,** management consultant; b. Cuthbert, Ga., July 21, 1946; s. Glinn Linwood and Mary Grace (Hiller) S.; m. Laura Jeanne Nason, June 10, 1967; children: Tanya Lynne, Stephen William. BS in Physics with honors, Ga. Inst. Tech., 1968, MS, 1970, MS in Indsl. Mgmt., 1973. Engr. Martin Marietta Corp., Orlando, Fla., 1968-70; rsch. scientist Engring. Exptl. Sta., Ga. Inst. Tech., 1970-75; v.p., dir. Metrics, Inc., mgmt. and engring. cons., Atlanta, 1973-78, pres., dir., 1978—; v.p., dir. Exec. Data Sys., Inc., 1981—. Mem. Ga. Energy Policy Coun., Ga. Metrication Coun., NASA applications survey group for Landsat follow-on; mem. com. on practical applications of remote sensing from space Space Applications Bd. NRC; market rsch. cons. NOAA, NASA, pvt. cos. Contbr. articles to profl. jours. Regents scholar, 1964. Mem. Am. Soc. Photogrammetry, Urban and Regional Info. Sys. Assn., Atlanta Jaycees, Tau Beta Pi, Phi Kappa Phi, Sigma Pi Sigma. Home: 3475 Clubland Dr Marietta GA 30068-2509 Office: Bldg 14 1640 Powers Ferry Rd SE Marietta GA 30067-5491

**SPANNINGER, BETH ANNE,** lawyer; b. Bucks County, Pa., July 3, 1950; d. Feryl Louis and Nancy Elizabeth (Hendricks) S. AB magna cum laude, Muhlenberg Coll., 1972; MA, MEd, Lehigh U., 1975; JD, Temple U., 1979. Bar: Pa. 1979. Asst. dist. atty. Phila. Dist. Atty.'s Office, 1979-81; assoc. Bolger, Picker, Hankin & Tannenbaum, Phila., 1981-86, ptnr., 1986-88; sr. counsel SmithKline Beecham Corp., Phila., 1988-96; v.p., assoc. gen. counsel Glaxosmithkline, Phila., 1996—. Mem. ABA, Pa. Bar Assn., Phila. Bar Assn. (law com. 1992—), Phi Beta Kappa. Avocations: literature, jogging, theater, piano. E-mail: beth.a.spanninger@gsk.com.

**SPANO, JOSEPH,** actor; b. San Francisco, July 7, 1946; s. Vincent D. and Virginia Jean Spano; m. Joan Zerrien; 2 children. BA, U. Calif., Berkeley, 1967. Actor stage, founding mem. Berkeley (Calif.) Repertory, 1968-78, The Wing, San Francisco, 1968-78, Magic Theatre, L.A. Actor's Theatre, South Coast Repertory Theatre. Star TV series Hill Street Blues, 1981-87 (Emmy award nomination 1983), Amazing Grace, 1995, Murder One, 1995-96, Mercy Point, 1998; appeared in films American Graffiti, 1973, The Enforcer, 1976, Roadie, 1980, The Incredible Shrinking Woman, 1981, Terminal Choice, 1985, Northern Lights, Apollo 13, 1993, Rave Review, 1995, Primal Fear, 1996, In Quiet Night, 1998, Break Up, 1998, Blessed Art Thou, 2000, Texas Rangers, 2001, Ticker, 2001, Hart's War, 2002, Fortunate Son, 2004, Hollywoodland, 2006; plays American Buffalo, 1989 (LADCC award 1989), School for Scandal, 1988, Chorus of Disapproval, 1989, Speed the Plow, 1990, The Price, 1992; numerous TV films and TV series guest appearances including Midnight Caller, 1988 (Emmy award 1989), Disaster at Silo 7, 1988, Cast the First Stone, 1989, Blind Faith, 1990, The Girl Who Came Between Them, 1990, For the Very First Time, 1991, Fever, 1991, Bloodiness: Murder in the Family, 1993, Her Costly Affair, 1996, A Call to Remember, 1997, Logan's War: Bound by Honor, 1998, A.T.F., 1999, (voice) Batman Beyond: The Movie, 1999; prodr., actor (stage prodn.) Dracula, A Musical Nightmare, Los Angeles, N.C., San Francisco; rec. Ed McBain novels for Simon Schuster.*

**SPANO, ROBERT,** conductor, music director; b. Conneaut, Ohio, May 7, 1961; Grad., Oberlin Conservatory Music; student, Curtis Inst. Music; D (hon.), Bowling Green State U., 2004. Faculty Oberlin (Ohio) Conservatory of Music, 1989—; asst. conduct. Boston Symphony Orch., 1990—93; music dir. Bklyn. Philharm. Orch., 1996—2004; musical dir., Robert Reid Topping chair Atlanta Symphony Orch., Atlanta, 1997—. Faculty mem. Tanglewood Music Ctr., head conducting fellowship program, 1998—2000, dir. of Festival of Contemporary Music, 2003—04; guest condr. Chgo. Symphony Orch., Boston Symphony Orch., Houston Symphony Orch., San Francisco Symphony Orch., Cleve. Orch., L.A. Philharm., Nat. Symphony Orch., Phila. Orch., Royal Opera Covent Gardens, Welsh Nat. Opera, Orch. Filharmonica della Scala, City of Birmingham Symphony. Musician (piano): (chamber concerts) Atlanta Symphony, Brooklyn Philharm, Boston Symphony, Oberlin Conservatory; recordings include Rimsky-Korsakov: Scheherazade and Vaughan Williams: A Sea Symphony, Del Tredici: Paul Revere's Ride and Theofanidis: The Here and Now, Berlioz Requiem, Atlanta Symphony Orch. (Grammy award for Best Choral Performance, 2005), featured on (TV series) City Arts, PBS, Breakfast with the Arts, A&E, Late Show with David Letterman, CBS, Sunday Morning, (TV special) Sound Choices - Inside the ASO with Monica Kaufman, WSB-TV. Office: Atlanta Symphony Orch 1293 Peachtree St NE Ste 300 Atlanta GA 30309-3552*

**SPANOGLE, ROBERT WILLIAM,** marketing and advertising company executive, association administrator; b. Lansing, Mich., Nov. 13, 1942; s. William P. and Mary A. (Lenneman) S.; m. Ruth Ann Long, Jan. 14, 1967; children: John Paul Stephen Donald, Amy Lynn. AA, Lansing C.C., 1969; BA, Mich. State U., 1971; postgrad., U. Pa., 1985. Cons. Nat. League Cities, Washington, 1971-72, Am. Legion, Indpls., 1972-75, dir. membership, 1975-79, exec. dir. Washington, 1975-81, nat. adjutant, 1981—; chmn. HP Direct, Inc., Indpls., 1985—, chmn. exec. com. Washington, 1989—. Mem. individual investors com. N.Y. Stock Exch., N.Y.C., 1989-92. Bd. govs. USO, Washington, 1986-92, Childrens Miracle Network, 2001—; trustee St. Mary of the Woods Coll., Terre Haute, Ind., 1991-2001; treas. Civil War Battle Flags Commn. State of Ind., Indpls., 1994—; sec. 500 Festival Assocs., Indpls., 1985-91; mem. Vet.'s Day Coun., Indpls., 1989; bd. dirs. Indpls. Athletic Club, 1989-93, Crossroads Coun. Boy Scouts Am., 1985-92; civilian aide Sec. Army India, 2003-. With U.S. Army, 1962-65. Recipient Silver Buffalo award, Nat. Council Boy Scouts Am., 2004. Mem. Am. Legion of Mich. (Hon. Comdr. 1985), Kiwanis (exec. com. 1989-92). Roman Catholic. Avocations: golf, hunting, reading. Home: 7420 Killarney Dr Indianapolis IN 46217-5472 Office: Am Legion 700 N Pennsylvania St Indianapolis IN 46204-1129

**SPANOS, ALEXANDER GUS,** construction executive, professional sports team executive; b. Stockton, Calif., Sept. 28, 1923; m. Faye Spanos; children: Dean, Dea Spanos Berberian, Alexis Spanos Ruhl, Michael. LLD (hon.), U. Pacific, 1984, Eureka Coll., 1984; DHL (hon.), Wayne State Coll., 2003, Calif. Polytechnic State U., 2004, Anatolia Coll., Thessaloniki, Greece, 2004; HHD (hon.), Hellenic Coll., 2004, Holy Cross Greek Orthodox Sch. Theology, 2004. Chmn. bd. dirs. A.G. Spanos Constrn. Inc., Stockton, Calif., 1960—, chmn. bd. dirs. A.G. Spanos Mgmt, Inc., Stockton, Calif., 1967—, A.G. Spanos Enterprises Inc., Stockton, Calif., 1971—, A.G. Spanos Devel. Inc., Stockton, Calif., 1973—, A.G. Spanos Realty Inc., Stockton, Calif., 1978—, A.G.S. Fin. Corp., Stockton, Calif., 1980—, A.G. Spanos Securities Corp., Stockton, Calif., 1981—, San Diego Chargers, 1984—. Chmn. bd. dirs. AGS Internat. Corp., Stockton, Calif., The Spanos Corp., Stockton, A.G. Spanos Ventures, Stockton, AGS Comms., LLC, Stockton. Former trustee Children's Hosp., San Francisco, San Francisco Fine Arts Mus.; trustee Eisenhower Med. Ctr., Rancho Mirage, Calif., John F. Kennedy Ctr. Performing Arts; hon. regent U. Pacific, Stockton, 1972-82; gov. USO, Washington, 1982—; former gov. Ronald Reagan Presdl. Found.; chmn. U.S. chpt. U.S. Greece bus. coun. Served with USAF, 1942-46. Recipient Albert Gallatin award Zurich-Am. Ins. Co., 1973, Horatio Alger award Horatio Alger Found., 1982, medal of Honor Statue of Liberty-Ellis Islan Found., 1982; named one of Forbes' Richest Americans, 2006. Mem. Am. Hellenic Ednl. Progressive Assn., Calif. C. of C. (bd. dirs. 1980-85). Republican. Greek Orthodox. Avocation: golf. Office: San Diego Chargers Qualcomm Stadium PO Box 609609 San Diego CA 92160-9609 also: A G Spanyos Cos 10100 Trinity Pkwy 5th Fl Stockton CA 95219 Business E-Mail: agspr@agspanos.com.*

**SPANOS, DEAN A.,** professional sports team executive; b. Stockton, Calif., May 26, 1950; s. Alex G. Spanos; m. Susan Spanos; children: Alexander Gus, John Dean. BBA, U. Pacific, 1972. Pres., vice-chmn. San Diego Chargers, 1984—; pres. Spanos corp. entities; vice-chmn. AGS Fin. Corp. Mem. winning team in Sr.'s Reunion Tournament, Dallas, 1985. Past bd. regents U. Pacific. Named co-winner, Bing Crosby Nat. Pro-Am. Golf Tournament, 1985, winner, Bob Hope Chrysler Classic, 1990, 1991, AT&T Nat. Pro-Am. Golf Tournament, 1990; recipient Most Valuable Amateur trophy. Avocation: golf. Office: San Diego Chargers 4020 Murphy Canyon Rd San Diego CA 92123-4407

**SPANOS, POL DIMITRIOS,** engineering educator; b. Messini, Peloponnesus, Greece, Feb. 27, 1950; came to U.S., 1973; s. Dimitrios Constandin Spanos and Aicaterine Polychronis Bonaros; children: Demetri, Eudokia. Diploma in mech. engring., Nat. Tech. U., Athens, 1973; MSCE, Calif. Inst. Tech., 1974, PhD in Applied Mechanics, 1976. Registered profl. engr., Tex., Greece. Rsch. asst. Calif. Inst. Tech., Pasadena, 1973-76, rsch. fellow, 1976-77; from asst. prof. to assoc. prof. U. Tex.-Austin, 1981-84, P.D. Henderson assoc. prof. engring., 1983-84; prof. mech. engring. and civil engring. Rice U., Houston, 1984-88, L.B. Ryon endowed chair in engring., 1988—. Cons. on analytical and numerical applications of theory of dynamics and vibrations, worldwide. Author: Random Vibrations, Probabilistic Offshore Mechanics, Probabilistic Methods in Civil Engineering, Random Vibration and Statistical Linearization, Dynamic Analysis of Non-Linear Structures by the Method of Statistical Quadratization, Stochastic Finite Elements: A Spectral Approach, Computational Stochastic Mechanics, Probabilistic Structural Mechanics: Advances in Structural Reliability Methods, Random Vibrations: A Broad Perspective; contbr. to profl. jour. issues devoted to dynamics and vibrations; mem. editl. bd. 8 jours.; editor-in chief or co-editor 2 primary jours. on mechanics. Recipient European award of sci. N.V. Phillips Co., Eindhoven, Netherlands, 1969, Presdl. Young Investigator award in earthquake engring. NSF, 1984-89, Cert. merit McDonnell Douglas Astronautics Co., Houston, 1987, G.R. Brown award for superior tchg. Rice U., 1995, 96, Newmark medal for lifetime contbns. to dynamics and vibrations ASCE, 1999; named hon. citizen, Messini, Greece, 1987; inducted into The Acad. of Athens, Greece, 2003. Fellow ASCE, AAM, ASME (participant tech. confs. and coms., Pi Tau Sigma Gold medal 1982, W.L. Huber Civil Engring. Rsch. prize 1989, G.L. Larson Meml. award 1991, Alfred M. Freudenthal medal 1992, Humboldt Rsch. award 1995, Disting. Lectr. 1997—, Newmark medal 1999, Theodore Von Karman medal 2003); mem. NAE, Acad. Athens, Am. Acad. Mechanics, Earthquake Engring. Rsch. Inst., Internat. Assn. for Structural Safety and Reliability (rsch. prize in the area of stochastic dynamics 1997), Hellenic Profl. Soc. (sponsor scholarship com.), A. von Humboldt Assn. (life), Nat. Acad. Engring. Fax: (713) 348-5191. E-mail: spanos@rice.edu.

**SPANOVICH, MILAN,** retired civil engineer; b. Steubenville, Ohio, Feb. 19, 1929; s. Stanley and Katherine (Komazec) S.; m. Sylvia J. Tomko, Apr. 16, 1971. BS Civil Engring, Carnegie-Mellon U., 1956, MS Civil Engring., 1957. Registered profl. engr., Pa., Ohio, Va., W.Va., Mich., Ky., N.J. Instr. Carnegie-Mellon U., 1957-60; charter assoc., v.p. E. D'Appolonia Assocs., 1957-61; mem. civil engring. staff U. N.Mex., 1961-63; founder, sr. cons. Engring. Mechs., Inc., Pitts., 1963-96. Contbr. articles on soil mechs. to tech. jours.; patentee found. systems. Bd. dirs. Carnegie Mellon U. Andrew Carnegie Soc. Recipient Pitts. Young Civil Engr. of Yr. award, 1969 Fellow ASCE (Pitts. Civil Engr. of the Yr. 1987, chmn. numerous coms.), Am. Cons. Engrs. Council; mem. Cons. Engrs. Council Greater Pitts. (pres. 1972-74), Engring. Soc. Western Pa. (dir. 1972, 77-83), Nat. Soc. Profl. Engrs., Pa. Soc. Profl. Engrs. (pres. Pitts. chpt. 1971, Hornfeck award Pitts. chpt. 1979, state dir. 1976-79, Disting. Service award Pitts. chpt. 1985, Pa. Engr. of the Yr. 1988, Profl. Devel. award 2009, Outstanding Svc. award Pitts. chpt. 1993), ASTM (chmn. task com. on relative density of granular soils 1959-63), Am. Concrete Inst., Hwy. Research Bd., Internat. Soc. Soil Mechs. and Found. Engring., Pitts. Geol. Soc., Am. Arbitration Assn., Profl. Engrs. in Pvt. Practice (chmn. 1970-71), Pitts. Builders Exchange, Soc. Explosives Engrs., Am. Soc. Hwy. Engrs., Carnegie-Mellon U. Alumni Assn. (mem. planning com.), Chi Epsilon Nat. Civil Engring. Honor Soc.

**SPARBERG, MARSHALL STUART,** gastroenterologist, educator; b. Chgo., May 20, 1936; s. Max Shane and Mildred Rose (Haffron) S.; m. Eve Gaymont Enda, Mar. 15, 1987. BA, Northwestern U., 1957, MD, 1960. Intern Evanston Hosp., Ill., 1960-61; resident in internal medicine Barnes Hosp., St. Louis, 1961-63; fellow U. Chgo., 1963-65; practice medicine specializing in gastroenterology Chgo., 1967—; asst. prof. medicine Northwestern U., 1967-72, assoc. prof., 1972-80, prof. medicine 1980—; instr. Wash. U., St. Louis, 1961-63, U. Chgo., 1963-65. Author: Ileostomy Care, 1969, Primer of Clinical Diagnosis, 1972, Ulcerative Colitis, 1978, Inflammatory Bowel Disease, 1982; contbr. numerous articles to profl. jours. Pres. Fine Arts Music Found., 1974-97; bd. dirs. Lyric Opera Guild, 1974-94, Chamber Music Soc. North Shore Chgo., 1984—; physician to Chgo. Symphony Orch., 1981-97. With USAF, 1965-67. Named Outstanding Tchr. Northwestern U. Med. Sch., 1972

Mem. AMA, ACP, Am. Gastroent. Assn., Am. Coll. Gastroent. (bd. govs.), Chgo. Med. Soc., Chgo. Soc. Internal Medicine, Chgo. Soc. Gastroenterology (pres.), Chgo. Soc. Gastrointestinal Endoscopy (pres.) Office: 676 N Saint Clair St Ste 1525 Chicago IL 60611-2862 Office Phone: 312-944-7080.

**SPARKMAN, BARRY STEVEN,** artist, art educator, museum administrator; b. McMinnville, Fla., May 19, 1962; s. Charles Leroy Sparkman and Susie Sparkman Martha; life ptnr. Daniel Louis Childers, Oct. 1, 1961. BFA in Painting and Sculpture, Mid. Tenn. State, 1984; MFA, La. State U., 1989. Painting, printmaking, Painting. Artist Access grantee, Miami-Dade County Dept. of Cultural Affairs, 2004. Home: 5841 SW 52 Terrace Miami FL 33155-6330 Office: Lowe Art Museum University of Miami 1301 Stanford Drive Miami FL 33155-6330 Office Phone: 305-284-6757. Home Fax: 305-284-2024; Office Fax: 305-284-2024. Personal E-mail: bsparkman@miami.edu.

**SPARKMAN, BRANDON BUSTER,** secondary school educator, consultant, writer; b. Hartselle, Ala., Sept. 5, 1926; s. George Olan and Mary Louise (Jones) S.; m. Wanda Phillips, Sept. 13, 1952; children—Ricky Brandon, Rita Sharon, Robert Lee. BS, U. North Ala., 1952; MA, U. Ala., 1958, EdS, 1961; EdD, Auburn U., Ala., 1970. Tchr., asst. prin. Phlips High Sch., Bear Creek, Ala., 1954-57; prin. Tuscumbia, Ala., 1957-65; asst. supt., 1965-69; ednl. cons. Auburn Center, 1969-70; mem. faculty dept. sch. adminstrn. Auburn U., 1970; asst. supt. for staff personnel devel. Jackson (Miss.) Pub. Schs., 1970-71, supt., 1971-73; sch. supt. Richland County Sch. Dist. 1, Columbia, SC, 1973-75; asst. supt. instruction Hartselle (Ala.) City Schs., 1975-80; supt. Guntersville (Ala.) City Schs. 1980-88; CEO The Right Combination Pub. & Ednl. Svcs. Corp., Guntersville, Ala., 1984-93. Adj. prof. U. Ala., Birmingham, 1998-2000; writer, cons. in field. Sr. author: Blueprint for a Brighter Child, 1973, STEPS (System for Teacher Evaluation of Pre-reading Skills), 1974; co-author: Preparing Your Preschooler for Reading, 1977, Competency Tests for Basic Reading Skills, 1978, Soaring High with Science, 1985, Soaring High with Social Studies, 1985; author: How Well Does Your Child Read, 1979, Writing Composition Made Easy, 1991, Blueprint for Expository Writing, 1993, Reading Skills Competency Tests, 1999; editor: The In-Between Years, 1979; creator: CORE (Program Management Through Computer Systems), 1975; editor, contbg. author: The Advantaged, A Preschool Program for the Disadvantaged, 1969; contbr. articles to profl. jours. Bd. dirs. Morgan County chpt. ARC, United Givers Fund, Colbert-Lauderdale Child Study Center, Sheffield-Tuscumbia Credit Union; bd. govs. Jackson Symphony Orch.; adv. bd. Jackson Mental Health Center. Served with AUS, 1952-54. Recipient Human Relations award Jackson. Mem. Am., Ala. assns. sch. adminstrs. (past pres.), Ala. Council Sch. Adminstrn. and Supervision (past pres.), Assn. Supervision and Curriculum Devel., Ala. Assn. Supervision and Curriculum Devel. (past pres.), Florence State U. Alumni Assn. (past pres.) Methodist (ch. sch. tchr., supt., vice chmn. ofcl. bd., chmn. commn. edn.). Home and Office: 2304 Northfield Dr Jasper AL 35504

**SPARKMAN, LYLE BRUCE,** academic administrator, education educator; b. Springfield, Mo., Sept. 2, 1947; s. Etsyl J. and Rayma LaVern Sparkman; m. Martha Margaret Rosalie Rothrock, Mar. 17, 1984; 1 child, Sarah Anne. BA in English Philosophy, Drury Univ., Springfield, Mo., 1972; MEd Instructional Adminstrn., Univ. Ark., Fayetteville, Ark., 1985, EdS Ednl. Specialist, 1999. Cert. tchg., adminstrn. Mo., Ark. News dir. KMTC TV (channel 27), Springfield, Mo., 1973—74; tchr. 3rd grade Kana. City Mo. Schs., Kans. City, South West R-5, Washburn, 1978—83; prin. Rose Bud Elem., Ark., 1984—88, Green Forest Sch., 1988—2002; asst. supt. East newton R.V.I, Granby, Mo., 2002—. Adj. prof. Lindenwood Univ., Granby, 2002—; grant reader USDE Office Migrant Edn, Washington, 2000, Washington, 04; v.p. Crowder Coll. Admin. Adv. Coun., Mo., 2004—06; nat. pilot leader AIM Project Migrant Families, 1997—2002. Co-author: The Heritage of the Ozarks, 1984; prodr.: (plays) The Toby Show, 1972;, performer folk music. Pub. info. officer Am. Legion post 163, Neosho, 2005—06; patron Wilson's Creek Nat. Found., Springfield, 1991—2006, Nat. Mil. Pk. Found., Pea Ridge, Ark., 2005—06. Specialist 5th class U.S. Army, 1969—71. Grantee Documentaries the Past grant, U.S. Dept. Edn., 2005—. Mem.: Assn. Supervision of Cirriculm Devel., Mo. Archl. Soc. (v.p., Cert. of Appreciation 2005), Phi Delta Kappa. Southern Baptist. Avocations: archaeology, music, comparative folklore. Home: 1905 Cash St Neosho MO 64850 Office: E Newton R VI 22808 F Hwy 86 Granby MO 64844 Business E-Mail: sparkmanl@enr6.k12.mo.us.

**SPARKMAN, STEVEN LEONARD,** lawyer; b. Sarasota, Fla., May 30, 1947; s. Simeon Clarence and Ursula (Wahlstrom) S.; m. Terry Jeanne Gibbs, Aug. 23, 1969; children: Joanna Jeanne, Kevin Leonard. BA, Fla. State U., 1969, JD, 1972. Bar: Fla. 1972, U.S. Dist. Ct. (mid. dist.) Fla. 1974, U.S. Ct. Appeals (5th cir.) 1975. Legal rsch. asst. Office Gen. Counsel, Fla. Dept. Revenue, Tallahassee, 1971; legis. intern com. on cmty. affairs Fla. Ho. of Reps., Tallahassee, 1971-72; jud. rsch. aide Fla. 2d Dist. Ct. Appeals, Lakeland, 1972-73; asst. county atty. Hillsborough County, Tampa, Fla., 1973-75; assoc. Carlton, Fields, Ward, Emmanuel, Smith & Cutler, P.A., Tampa, 1975-80, sr. atty., 1980-2001; pvt. practice Plant City, Fla., 2001—. Mem. bd. visitors Fla. State U. Coll. Law, 1994—2000. Trustee Fla. Bapt. Children's Homes, Inc., 2004—; deacon 1st Bapt. Ch., Plant City, 1980—; sec., bd. dirs. Bapt. Towers Plant City, Inc., 1981—84; bd. dirs. Tampa Kiwanis Found., 1997—2000. 1st lt. USAFR, 1973. Mem.: ABA, Plant City Bar Assn. (sec. treas 2003—05, treas. 2005—), Fla. Bar Assn. (exec. coun. local govt. law sect. 1978—79), Kiwanis (bd. dirs. 2003—06, Plant City). Democrat. Office: Steven L Sparkman PA 212 N Collins St Ste 1 Plant City FL 33563 Business E-Mail: sls@sparklaw.com.

**SPARKS, BENNETT SHER,** military officer; b. Pitts, Oct. 10, 1922, s. Julius and Anna K. Sparks, m. Betty Sparks, May 8, 1943 (dec. Nov. 2005); children: Bennett Sher Jr., James Robert, Richard T.(dec.), John N., Julieann, Donna Beth(dec.). Diploma, Naval War Coll., 1973, Armed Forces Staff Coll., 1978, Nat. War Coll., 1978, The Army War Coll., 1988, The Nat. Def. U., The Indsl. Coll. Armed Forces; PhD in Philosophy (hon.), Sampson U., Oxford, Eng., 1986. Lic. aircraft pilot. Commd. ensign USCG, 1957, advanced through grades to rear admiral, 1985, res. inspector 11th Coast Guard Dist., sr. res. officer Pacific Area San Francisco, sr. res. officer Atlantic Area NYC, comdr. Navy's No. Calif. Maritime Def. Zone San Francisco, civilian aviator; comdr. Navy's Maritime Def. Zone USCG, sector 6, Charleston, SC; ret. USCG, 1993. Aviator Geodetic Survey, Alaska; chief US Del. to Confedn. Res. Officers (CIOR), NATO Hdqrs., Belgium, 1985-86; internat. sec.-gen. Inter-Allied Confedn. Res. Officers, Brussels, 1992-94. Mem. Calif. Vets. Bd., 1995—, chmn., 1998—99; bd. dirs. Sonoma County Area Agy. of Aging, Calif., 2002—; mem. legis. com., 2002—; bd. dirs. North Bay chpt. Alzheimer's Assn. No. Calif. and Nev., 2002—; bd. dirs. Bank of Hollywood. Decorated Legion of Merit, Coast Guard Commendation medals (2), Coast Guard Achievement medal, The Humanitarian Svc. medal, Arctic Svc. medal, Coast Guard Combat Air Crew Wings with three stars, knight Sovereign Mil. Order Temple of Jerusalem, the NATO Grand Priory, 1983, knight comdr., 1987, Meritorious Svc. medal and the Coast Guard Commmand Ashore Device medal; recipient Navy Disting. Pub. Svc. medal Sec. of Navy, 1983, Coast Guard Disting. Pub. Svc. medal Comdt. of Coast Guard, 1983, 93. Mem. DAV, VFW, Am. Legion, Sonoma County United Vets. Coun., Navy League, Naval Res. Assn., Res. Officers Assn. US (pres. 1982-83, nat. dep. exec. dir., dir. adminstrn. and dir. fin. 1988-91, chmn. bd. trustees, bd. dirs.) Home: 573 Pistachio Pl Windsor CA 95492-8168

**SPARKS, BILLY SCHLEY,** lawyer; b. Marshall, Mo., Mar. 1, 1923; s. John and Clarinda (Schley) Sparks; m. Dorothy O. Stone, May 14, 1946; children: Stephen Stone, Susan Lee Sparks Raben Taylor, John David. AB, Harvard U., 1945, LLB, 1949. Bar: Mo. 1949. Ptnr. Langworthy, Matz & Linde, Kansas City, Mo., 1949-62, Linde, Thomason, Fairchild, Langworthy, Kohn & Van Dyke, Kansas City, 1962-91; ret., 1991. Mem. Mission (Kans.) Planning Coun., 1954—63, Dist. 100 Sch. Bd., 1964—68, pres., 1967—69; mem. Dist. 512 Sch. Bd., 1969—73, pres., 1971—72; mem. Kans. Civil Svc. Commn., 1975—90; del. Dem. Nat. Conv., 1964; treas. Johnson County Dem. Ctrl. Com., Kans., 1958—64; candidate rep. 10th Dist., Kans., 1956, 3d Dist.,

Kans., 1962. Lt. USAAF, 1944—46. Mem.: ABA, Nat. Assn. Sch. Bds. (mem. legis. com. 1968—73), Law Assn. Kansas City, Kansas City Bar Assn., Mo. Bar Assn., Kansas City C. of C. (mem. legis. com. 1956—82), Harvard Law Sch. Assn. Mo. (past dir.), Milburn Golf and Country Club, Kansas City (Mo.) Club, Harvard Club (v.p. 1953—54), Am. Legion, St. Andrews Soc. Home and Office: 8517 W 90th Ter Shawnee Mission KS 66212-3053 Office Phone: 913-642-2443.

**SPARKS, CHARLES EDWARD,** pathologist, educator; b. Peoria, Ill., July 29, 1940; s. William Joseph and Meredith (Pleasants) S.; m. Janet Lindsay Dehoff, Aug. 18, 1977; children: William, Debra, Robert. BS in Biology, MIT, 1963; MD, Thomas Jefferson U., 1968. Diplomate Am. Bd. Pathology, Am. Bd. Clin. Chemistry. Rsch. asst. Mass. Gen. Hosp., Boston, 1963; intern NY Hosp., Cornell Naval Hosp., St. Albans, 1968-69; resident in clin. pathology Hosp. of U. Pa., 1972-75; fellow in cardiopulmonary medicine U. Pa., Phila., 1975-76, asst. instr., 1972-75; fellow in biochemistry Med. Coll. Pa., Phila., 1976-77, instr., 1976-77, asst. to assoc. prof. biochemistry and physiology, 1977-82; assoc. prof. pathology U. Rochester (NY), 1982-88, prof. pathology, 1988—. Advisor med. scientist tng. program U. Rochester, 1984-92; attending pathologist, dir. clin. chemistry unit Strong Meml. Hosp., 1982—, chair rsc. adv. com., assoc. chair pathology, 1994—, dir. grad. studies in Integrative Biomed. Scis., 1998—. Contbr. articles to profl. jours.; patentee in field. Chairperson Endocrinology VA Merit Rev. Study Sect., 2000—. Lt. comdr. USN, 1969—72. Postdoctoral fellow NIH, 1975-77. Mem. AAAS, Am. Diabetes Assn. (co-chmn. nat. symposium meeting 1988), Acad. Clin. Lab. Physicians and Scientists, Am. Heart Assn. (fellow coun. on arteriosclerosis, mem. nominating com.). Office: Dept Pathology U Rochester 601 Elmwood Ave Rochester NY 14642-0001 Office Phone: 585-275-8236.

**SPARKS, DALE BOYD,** allergist, health facility administrator; b. Springfield, Mo., July 14, 1929; s. Roscoe R. and Ruby V. (Boyd) S.; children: Susan L., Laura A., Lisa M., Jennifer G.; m. Leeanna M. Molccyk Priboy, Apr. 21, 2001. AB, Southwest Mo. State U., 1951; BS in Medicine, U. Mo., 1953; MD, St. Louis U., 1955. Diplomate Am. Bd. Allergy and Immunology. Intern Kansas City (Mo.) Gen. Hosp. U. Med. Ctr., 1955-56; resident U. Mo. Hosp., 1958-60; fellow in allergy and immunology Northwestern U., 1960-61; mem. cons. staff Parkview Meth. Hosp., 1961—; mem. med. staff Riverside County Regional Med. Ctr., 1961-2000, dir. respiratory therapy, 1968-85, dir. respiratory therapy and diagnostic svcs., 1965—, chmn. dept. medicine, 1978-98, chief med. staff, 1990-98; acting dir., health officer Riverside Pub. Health Dept., 1991-93; ret., 1993. Clin. prof. medicine Loma Linda U. Mem. editl. bd. Immunology and Allergy in Practice, 1980—. Lt. USNR. Fellow ACP (coun. subsplty. socs. 1988—), Am. Coll. Allergy and Immunology (disting., bd. regents 1989-93, pres. 1990-91, chmn. fin. com., treas. 1990-93, recert. com.), Coll. Allergy, Asthma and Immunology; mem. AMA, Am. Lung Assn. (bd. dirs. 1990-95), Am. Heart Assn. (bd. dirs. 1964-70, pres. 1966), Joint Coun. Am. Allergy and Immunology (bd. dirs. 1985-90), Calif. Med. Assn., Calif. Soc. Allergy, Inland Soc. Internal Medicine, Riverside County Med. Assn. (bd. councilors 1980-99, del. CMA 1988-99), Riverside County Found. Med. Care (sec., past pres.). Home and Office: 29368 Big Range Rd Canyon Lake CA 92587 Office Phone: 951-244-7311. Personal E-mail: dsparksmd@aol.com.

**SPARKS, DALE W.,** biologist, research scientist; s. David B. and Dorothy G. Sparks; m. Jodi K. Farrell, May 17, 2003. BS, Murray State U., Ky., 1989—93; MS, Ft. Hays State U., Ky., 1993—97; PhD, Ind. State U., Terre Haute, Ind., 1997—2003. Rsch. scientist Ind. State U., 2003—. Asst. dir. Ctr. N.Am. Bat Rsch. & Conservation, Terre Haute, 2005—. Contbr. articles to profl. jours., chapters to books. Mem.: Am. Soc. Mammalogists (life). Achievements include research in impacts of urbanization on wildlife. Home: 9397 N Grandturn Rd Marshall IL 62441 Office: Ind State Univ 600 N Chestnut Terre Haute IN 47809 Office Fax: 812-237-2526. Business E-Mail: dsparks@isugw.indstate.edu.

**SPARKS, DAVID STANLEY,** academic administrator; b. Phila., Dec. 8, 1922; s. Richard Frederick and Grace Dorothy (Tuttle) S.; m. Phyllis Ann Bate, June 12, 1949; children: E. F. Anne. AB, Grinnell Coll., Iowa, 1944; MA, U. Chgo., 1945, PhD, 1951. Instr., asst. prof., assoc. prof. U. Md., College Park, 1947-65, prof. history, 1965—, assoc. dean grad. studies and research, 1967-70, dean, 1970-77, acting vice chancellor for acad. affairs, 1976-77, acting v. for v.p. grad. studies and research, 1978-79, v.p. grad. studies and research, 1979-87, acting v.p. for acad. affairs, 1982-83, v.p. acad. affairs, grad. studies and research, 1987-88, vice chancellor for acad. affairs, 1988-91, vice chancellor emeritus, 1991. Vis. professorial lectr. dept. history Johns Hopkins, 1965; mem., chair Grad. Record Examinations Bd., 1979-85. Co-editor, author: American Civilization: A History of the United States, 1960, The Making of American Democracy, Readings and Documents, 2 vols, 1962; Editor: Inside Lincoln's Army: The Diary of General Marsena Rudolph Patrick, 1964. Recipient research awards Am. Philos. Soc., 1958, Social Sci. Research Council, 1957 Mem. Am., So. hist. assns., Orgn. Am. Historians, Am. Assn. U. Profs. (pres. U. Md. chpt.), Nat. Acad. Univ. Research Administrs., Phi Kappa Phi. Clubs: Cosmos (Washington). Home: 10500 Rockville Pike Apt 1309 Rockville MD 20852-3350

**SPARKS, DON BERTRAND,** retired geophysicist; b. Somerville, Tex., Oct. 4, 1930; s. Bunyan F. and Daisy B. Sparks; m. Wanda F. Kinsala, July 30, 1952 (div. Mar. 1990); m. Lou Kimball Sparks, Mar. 15, 1991; children: Neva Dione, Don B. Jr. BA in Math. & Physics, Tex. A&M U., 1951; grad., Air War Coll., 1978. Geophysicist various oil cos., Tex.; commd. 2d lt. USAF, 1952, advanced through grades to lt. col.; sr. flight test engr. B-58 plane Convair, Ft. Worth; ops. mgr. space flight ops. facility, data sys. engr. mariner 2/venus, data sys. engr. mariner/mars Calif. Tech./NASA, Pasadena, Calif., 1961—80, ret., 1990, USAF, 1980. Advisor AF Civil Air Patrol, Pasadena, 1970—80. Avocation: fishing. Address: PO Box 291958 Kerrville TX 78029

**SPARKS, HARVEY VISE, JR.,** physiologist; b. Flint, Mich., June 22, 1938; s. Harvey Vise and Ellen Louise (Paschall) S.; m. Barbara M. Taylor, Jan. 17, 1969; children— Matthew Taylor, Catherine Elliott, Wendy Sue, Harvey Vise. Student, U. Mich., 1956-59, MD, 1963. Postdoctoral fellow dept. physiology Harvard Med. Sch., Boston and; U. Goteborg, Sweden; instr. U. Mich., 1966-67, asst. prof. physiology, 1967-70, assoc. prof., 1970-74, prof., 1974-78; asst. to dean U. Mich. (Med. Sch.), 1970-71, asst. dean, 1971-72; prof. physiology Mich. State U., East Lansing, 1978—, chmn. dept., 1978-89, vice provost human health programs, 1989-93, univ. disting. prof., 1997—. Fulbright lectr. U. Zimbabwe, 1986-87; vis. prof. U. Zimbabwe, 1995; mem. survey team, liaison com. on med. edn. AMA Am. Assn. Med. Colls.; mem. rev. teams NIH. Author: Casebook of Physiology, 1973, Essentials of Cardiovascular Physiology, 1987; contbr. numerous articles to profl. jours.; editor: (with others) Handbook of Physiology, 1979. Recipient Meritorious Service award Mich. Heart Assn., 1962, Borden award for med. student research, 1963, Merit award NIH, 1988; Mich. Heart Assn. student fellow, 1962-63; John and Mary Markle scholar, 1967-72; USPHS postdoctoral fellow, 1963-66; U. Mich. student research fellow, 1960-61; USPHS grantee, 1963— Fellow Royal Soc. Medicine; mem. AAAS, Am. Physiol. Soc. (pres. 1987-88, editl. bd. Am. Jour. Physiology 1974-88), Microcirculatory Soc., Am. Heart Assn. (coun. on circulation, editl. bd. Circulation Rsch.), Mich. Pub. Health Inst. (bd. dirs. 1989-94), Internat. Union Physiol. Scis. (treas. 1990—), Coun. Internat. Exch. Scholars (Africa area com. 1988-91), Russian Acad. Sci. (fgn.), Victor Vaughn Soc., Alpha Omega Alpha, Phi Kappa Phi, Phi Zeta. Home: 8122 W Lovejoy Rd Perry MI 48872-8902 Office: Mich State U Dept Physiology East Lansing MI 48824*

**SPARKS, JACK NORMAN,** dean; b. Lebanon, Ind., Dec. 3, 1928; s. Oakley and Geraldine Ruth (Edrington) S.; m. Esther Lois Bowen, Apr. 11, 1953; children: Stephen Michael, Robert Norman, Ruth Ann, Jonathan Russell. BS, Purdue U., 1950; MA, U. Iowa, 1951, PhD, 1960. Tchr. math. Leyden Cmty. H.S., Franklin Park, Ill., 1954—58; rsch. asst. U. Iowa, Iowa City, 1958—60; assoc. prof. applied stats., dir. bur. of rsch. U. No. Colo., Greeley, 1960—65; assoc. prof. ednl. psychology Pa. State U., State College, 1965—68; dir. corr. Campus Crusade for Christ, San Bernardino, Calif., 1968—69; dir. Christian

World Liberation Front, Berkeley, Calif., 1969—75; pastor, ch. overseer New Covenant Apostolic Order, Berkeley, 1975—77; dean St. Athanasius Acad. Orthodox Theology, Santa Barbara, Calif., 1977—87, St. Athanasius Coll., Santa Barbara, 1987—93, St. Athanasius Acad. Orthodox Theology, Elk Grove, Calif., 1996—2005, St. John's Orthodox Cathedral, Eagle River, Alaska, 2005—. Cons. Measurement Rsch. Ctr., Iowa City, 1959-60, We. States Small Schs. Project, Greeley, 1962-65, Colo. Coun. Ednl. Rsch., Denver, 1963-65; project dir. Orthodox Study Bible Old Testament, 1998—. Author: Letters to Street Christians, 1971, The Mind Benders, 1977, 79, The Resurrection Letters, 1978, The Preaching of the Apostles, 1987, Victory in the Unseen Warfare, 1993; editor: Apostolic Fathers, 1978, 88; gen. editor: The Orthodox Study Bible, 1993, Virtue in the Unseen Warfare, 1995, Prayer in the Unseen Warfare, 1996, Christ Is Our Holiness, 1996, The Coming of the Prince, 1997, Tradition in the Early Church, 1997, The Letters of St. Ignatius, 1998, Faith and Godliness, 1999, Pentecost: A Homily of St. John Chrysostom, 2000, No Graven Image, 2000, The Valley of the Shadow of Death, 2000, Death, Fear of Death, Hope of Resurrection, 2000, Kindling the Fire Within, 2000, How Can Jesus Be Both God and Man, 2001, The Annunciation, 2001, The Bride of Christ, 2001, The Boundless Beauty, 2001, Walking Through the Night, 2001, Out of the Depths, 2002, Redemption and Reconciliation, 2002, A Family Baptized, 2003, Zeal and Patience, 2003, The Biblical Story of Esther, 2006. Trustee Rock Mont Coll., Denver, 1962-77, Thomas Nelson Co., Nashville, 1977-78. 1st lt. U.S. Army, 1952-54 Mem. Am. Sci. Affiliation, Assn. Orthodox Theologians, Conf. on Faith and History, Phi Delta Kappa (pres. Epsilon chpt. 1959-60) Republican. Orthodox Christian. Home: 19042 Monastery Dr Eagle River AK 99577 Office: St Johns Orthodox Cathedral PO Box 1108 Eagle River AK 99577 Office Phone: 907-696-2002. Business E-Mail: frjack@saoot.edu.

**SPARKS, JANET LINDSAY DEHOFF,** pathologist, educator; b. Lawrence, Mass., Sept. 13, 1950; d. Ronald Lee and Barbara Isabelle (Platt) DeHoff; m. Charles Edward Sparks, Aug. 18, 1977; 1 child, Robert. BA in Biology, BS in Med. Tech., U. Pa., 1972, PhD in Pathology, 1980. Cert. med. technologist Am. Soc. Clin. Pathologists. Instr. clin. chemistry U. Pa., Phila., 1974-76; fellow Wistar Inst. Anatomy and Biology, Phila., 1975-80; postdoctoral fellow U. Rochester (N.Y.), 1983-85, scientist, 1985-94, asst. prof. pathology and lab. medicine, 1994-96, assoc. prof. pathology and lab. medicine, 1996—. Cons. NIH, Indpls., 1994-96. Contbr. numerous articles to profl. jours.; patentee in field. Nat. NIDDK RO1 grantee, 1995—. Fellow Coun. on Arteriosclerosis Thrombosis and Vascular Biology; mem. AAAS, Am. Soc. Clin. Pathologists, Am. Diabetes Assn., Am. Heart Assn. (coun. on arteriosclerosis, coun. on clin. cardiology), N.Y. Lipid Club, N.Y. Acad. Scis. Office: U Rochester Dept Pathology 601 Elmwood Ave # 626 Rochester NY 14642-0001 E-mail: janet_sparks@ume.rochester.edu.

**SPARKS, JOHN EDWARD,** lawyer; b. Rochester, Ind., July 3, 1930; s. Russell Leo and Pauline Anna (Whittenberger) S.; m. Margaret Joan Snyder, Sept. 4, 1954; children: Thomas Edward, William Russell, Kathryn Chapman McCarthy. AB, Ind. U., 1952; LL.B., U. Calif., Berkeley, 1957; postgrad., London Sch. Econs., 1957-58. Bar: Calif. 1958, U.S. Supreme Ct., 1968. Assoc. Brobeck, Phleger & Harrison, San Francisco, 1958-66, ptnr., 1967-95, of counsel, 1996—2003; ret., 2003. Adj. prof. law U. San Francisco, 1967-69; pres. Legal Aid Soc. San Francisco, 1978-79, dir., 1971-81. Editor U. Calif. Law Rev., 1956-57. Served to 1st lt. Q.M.C. U.S. Army, 1952-54, Korea. Recipient Wheeler Oak Meritorious award U. Calif., Berkeley, 1986. Fellow Am. Bar Found., Am. Coll. Trial Lawyers; mem. ABA, State Bar Calif., Bar Assn. San Francisco (bd. dirs. 1974-75), Boalt Hall Alumni Assn. (pres. 1983-84). Democrat. E-mail: jsparks458@aol.com.

**SPARKS, KENNETH R.,** association executive; b. Mar. 26, 1934; BS, Syracuse U., 1956, MS, 1961, PhD, 1964; JD, George Washington U., 1967. Dir. rsch. Voice of Am. USIA, Washington, 1964-67; dep. dir. pub. affairs U.S. Office Econ. Opportunity, Washington, 1967-68 dir., 1968-69; pres. U.S. Cultural and Trade Ctr. Commn., Washington, 1988—90; dep. dir. Fed. City Coun., Washington, 1970-72, exec. v.p., 1972—2004, ret., 2004; dir. Fed. Res. Bank of Richmond, 2004—; pres. Sparks Assocs., 2004—. Adj. faculty Coll. William and Mary Law Sch., 2005—. Mem.: Econ. Club Washington (sec. 1985—2005). Office: PO Box 1202 White Stone VA 22578 Personal E-mail: krsparks@aol.com.

**SPARKS, MILDRED THOMAS,** state agency administrator, educator; b. Montgomery, Ala., Oct. 2, 1942; d. Leon and Annie Lee (Johnson) Thomas; m. John H. Sparks, Aug. 29, 1964; children: Melanie J. Thomas Bosak, Jennifer L. Gerhartz, Reginald F. BS, Ala. State U., 1964; MS, Pepperdine U., 1978; postgrad., Claremont Coll., Calif. State U., Boston Coll. Cert. reading specialist, contract mgmt., U. Phoenix, U. Wyo. Tchr. Dayton (Ohio) Schs., 1964-66, Oxon Hill (Md.) Schs., 1966-70; technician Reading Lab. Grambling (La.) State U., 1972; reading lab. aide Calif. City (Calif.) Schs., 1975; reading instr. Cerro Coso So. Outreach, Edwards AFB, Calif., 1976-78; substitute tchr. San Bernardino City Schs., 1979, Aquinas H.S., San Bernardino, 1978-79; reading lab. tchr. San Bernardino H.S., 1979; instr. reading lab. San Bernardino Valley Coll., 1980-81, assoc. prof. reading, dept. head, 1981-86; contract adminstr. Hercules Missile Ordinance and Space Group, Magna, Utah, 1986, Alliant Techsys. (formerly Hercules Missile Ordinance and Space Group), 1987-97; dir. Office of Black Affairs State of Utah, 1997—2000; assoc. prof. Salt Lake CC, Salt Lake City, 2003—. Mem. Pres.'s Diversity Coun. Tchg. Cnr. - Courage Teach Salt Lake City (Utah) C.C., 2003—, mem. gen. edn. com. Mem. State Black Adv. Coun., Office of Black Affairs, AARP (mem. Utah bd., safety program instr.); presenter workshops, cmty. events; troop vol. Girl Scouts U.S.; vol. The March of Dimes, Am. Heart Assn., Visitation of the Elderly Homebound, Am. Cancer Soc. and Marriage and Family Workshop for Teens, Cath. Cmty. Svcs.; civil rights movement participant Ala. Bus Boycott; mem. minority health adv. bd. Utah Health Dept.; mem. Cath. Women League, Black Caths. Utah, Salt Lake City, African Am. Task Force, Gov.'s Initiative on Family Today, Anti-Discrimination Com.; planning com. United Way Greater Salt Lake, vol.; past pres. Salt Lake Diocesan Pastoral Coun., vol.; mem. Americorp Legacy program, Salt Lake County, Utah State Bd. Aging and Adult Svcs. Mem. Cath Tchrs. Assn., Nat. Coun. Tchrs. English, Assn. Supervision and Curriculum Devel., Western Coll. Reading Assn., Bus. and Profl. Women's Club, Link's, Jack and Jill of Am. Inc., Delta Kappa Gamma, Alpha Kappa Alpha. Roman Catholic (Norton lav lector). Avocations: reading, writing, gardening, cross country skiing. Home: 3790 Becky Cir Salt Lake City UT 84109-3302 Office: Salt Lake CC Coll Devel Edn 4600 S Redwood Rd Salt Lake City UT 84123

**SPARKS, NICHOLAS,** writer; b. Omaha, Dec. 31, 1965; s. Patrick Michael and Jill Emma Marie (Thoene) Sparks; m. Catherine Sparks, 1989; children: Miles, Ryan, Landon, Lexie, Savannah. BBA with high honors, U. Notre Dame, 1988. Author: (novels) The Notebook, 1996 (Publishers Weekly paperback bestseller list), Message In a Bottle, 1998, A Walk To Remember, 1999, The Rescue, 2000, A Bend in the Road, 2001, Nights in Rodanthe, 2002, The Guardian, 2003, The Wedding, 2003 (Publishers Weekly paperback bestseller list), Three Weeks With My Brother, 2004, True Believer, 2005 (Publishers Weekly hardover bestseller), At First Sight, 2005 (Publishers Weekly hardover bestseller).*

**SPARKS, ROBERT DEAN,** medical administrator, gastroenterologist; b. Newton, Iowa, May 6, 1932; s. Albert John and Josephine Emma (Kleinendorst) S.; children: Steven Robert, Ann Louise, John James. BA, U. Iowa, 1955, MD, 1957; D of Humanitarian Svc. (hon.), Creighton U., 1978. Diplomate Am. Bd. Internal Medicine. Intern Charity Hosp. of La., New Orleans, 1957-58, resident in internal medicine, 1958-59, asst. in medicine, 1958-59; fellow in gen. medicine and gastroenterology Tulane U. Sch. Medicine, 1959-62, instr. medicine, 1959-63, asst. prof., 1963-64, assoc. prof., 1964-68, prof., 1968-76, asst. dean, 1964-67, assoc. dean, acting dean, 1967-68, vice dean, 1968-69, dean, 1969-72, chief sect. gastroenterology, 1968-72; chancellor Med. Ctr. U. Nebr., 1972-76, prof. medicine, 1972-76; v.p. U. Nebr. System, 1972-76; health program dir. W.K. Kellogg Found., Battle Creek, Mich., 1976-81, v.p. programming, 1981-82, sr. v.ps., 1982, pres., chief programming officer, 1982-86, pres., 1982-88, trustee, 1988, pres.

emeritus, cons., 1988-92; pres., CEO, Calif. Med. Assn. Found., Sacramento, 1995-98, sr. assoc., 1998—. Cons. U. Tenn. Health Sci. Ctr., 1988-90, Boston U. Health Policy Inst., 1989-90; mem. sci., compensation and trust rev. coms. Syntex Corp., Palo Alto, Calif., 1987-91, v.p. product safety and compliance, 1991-93; mem. overseers com. to visit Harvard U. Med. and Dental Schs., 1984-90; mem. vis. com. U. Miami Sch. Medicine, 1982-86; assoc. med. dir. for addiction treatment svcs., dir. for edn. and rsch., Battle Creek Adventist Hosp., 1990-91; v.p. Howe-Lewis Internat Inc., Menlo Park, N.Y., 1993-94, cons., 1994-95; mem. adv. coun. to dean Tulane U. Sch. Medicine, 2004—. Mem. editl. bd. Alcoholism Treatment Quar., 1985--; contbr. articles to profl. jours. Bd. dirs. Nat. Coun. on Alcoholism and Drug Dependence, NYC, 1982-93, treas. 1986-88, chmn., 1989-90, past chmn., 1991-92; bd. dirs. Battle Creek Symphony Orch., 1981-88, Lakeview Sch. Dist., Battle Creek, 1979-83, 88-91, Omni Med, 2001-; trustee Monsour Med. Found., Jeannette, Pa., 1976-90, interim pres. 1989, chmn. bd., pres., 1989-90; mem. President's Adv. Bd. on Pvt. Sector Initiatives, Washington, 1986-89; chmn. bd. dirs. Bard Coll. Health Policy and Practice Inst., 1988-96, Consumer Health Info. Rsch. Inst., 1990-95, Chelsea-Arbor Treatment Ctr., 1990-91; bd. dirs. Calhoun County Bd. Health, 1988-91, chmn., 1989-91; mem., bd. dirs. Mental Health and Addictions Found. Mich., Battle Creek, 1991-93; mem. adv. coun. CMA Found., 2004-; mem. cmty. adv. com., Taser Found., Scottsdale, Ariz., 2005—, bd. trustees 2006—, chair 2006—. Recipient Harvard Dental award Harvard U. Sch. Dental Medicine, 1992, Disting. Alumni award for achievement U. Iowa Coll. Medicine, 1998, annual Robert D. Sparks Cmty. Health Leadership Achievement award CMA Found., 1997— Fellow ACP; mem. AMA, Nat. Acad. Scis. Inst. Medicine (com. study of treatment and rehab. svcs. for alcoholism and alcohol abuse, bd. mental health and behavioral medicine), Coun. Mich. Founds. (trustee 1986-88), Assn. Am. Med. Colls. (disting. svc. mem. 1975—), Phi Eta Sigma, Alpha Omega Alpha, Ph Kappa Psi. Republican. Methodist. Avocations: tennis, bridge, reading, travel. Home and Office: 5004 Gresham Dr El Dorado Hills CA 95762-7703 Office Phone: 916-230-0719. Personal E-mail: rdsparksmd1@earthlink.net.

**SPARKS, ROBERT RONOLD, JR.,** lawyer; b. Bklyn., Dec. 4, 1946; s. Robert Ronold Sr. and Marjorie Anne (Boehm) S. BA, Va. Mil. Inst., 1969; JD, U. Va., 1972. Bar: U.S. Dist. Ct. (D.C. cir.) 1979, U.S. Dist. Ct. (ea. dist.) Va. 1979, U.S. Ct. Appeals (2d cir.) 1986, U.S. Ct. Appeals (D.C. cir.) 1975, Va. 1972, U.S. Ct. Appeals (4th cir.) 1982, U.S. Ct. Mil. Appeals 1976, U.S. Tax Ct. 1978, U.S. Supreme Ct. 1981, U.S. Dist. Ct. Md. 1993. From assoc. to ptnr. Sedam & Herge, McLean, Va., 1977-85; ptnr. Herge, Sparks & Christopher, McLean, Va., 1985—. Mem. Bd. Regents James Monroe Law Office Mus. and Meml. Library, Fredericksburg, Va., 1983-86. Mem. Fairfax County Redevel. and Housing Authority, Fairfax, 1981-82; commr. Fairfax County Indsl. Devel. Authority, 1980-81, Fairfax County Planning Commn., 1983-89. Lt. USNR, 1972-77, Philippines. Mem. Va. Bar Assn., D.C. Bar Assn., Rotary (treas., bd. dirs. 1978-80). Roman Catholic. Home: 6448 Spring Ter Falls Church VA 22042-3141 Office: Herge Sparks Christopher 6862 Elm St Ste 360 Mc Lean VA 22101-3867

**SPARKS, ROBERT WILLIAM,** retired publishing executive; b. Seattle, Dec. 30, 1925; s. James Donald and Gladys (Simmons) S. Student, U. Wash., 1947-50; BA, U. Hawaii, 1954, MA, 1965. Editor, various publs., 1947-64; mng. editor U. Hawaii Press, 1964-66, dir., 1967-87. Cons. East-West Ctr. Jour. Hawaiian History, Japanese and Chinese book pubs., 1987-92; advisor New World Press, Beijing, 1986; mem. adv. bd. to pres. Kamehameha Schs. Author: Seattle, Sitka, San Francisco, 1955, Letters From an Island, 1962, New Endings, 1989, Riding Backwards, 2002; contbr. articles to internat. pub. jours. Served with AUS, 1944-46, PTO. Recipient McInerny editorship, 1953; Pacific House citation Pacific and Asian Affairs Council, 1974 Mem. Assn. Am. Univ. Presses, Assn. Am. Publishers, Internat. Assn. Scholarly Publishers, Soc. for Scholarly Pub., Hawaiian Hist. Soc., Hawaii Found. History and Humanities, Honolulu Acad. Arts, Bishop Mus. Assn. Home: 66 Queen St PH4102 Honolulu HI 96813-4449 Personal E-mail: nihipali@hawaii.rr.com.

**SPARKS, SAM,** federal judge; b. 1939; BA, U. Tex., 1961, LLB, 1963. Aide Rep. Homer Thornberry, 1963; law clk. to Hon. Homer Thornberry U.S. Dist. Ct. (we. dist.) Tex., 1963-65; assoc. to ptnr., shareholder Hardie, Grambling, Sims & Galatzan (and successor firms), El Paso, Tex., 1965-91; dist. judge U.S. Dist. Ct. (we. dist.) Tex., 1991—. Fellow Am. Coll. Trial Lawyers, Tex. Bar Found. (life); mem. Am. Bd. Trial Advocates (advocate), State Bar Tex Office: US Dist Ct Judge 200 W 8th St Ste 100 Austin TX 78701-2333 Office Phone: 512-916-5230.

**SPARKS, THOMAS E., JR.,** lawyer; b. Little Rock, Jan. 11, 1942; children: Thomas Gunnar, Eric Richard, Andrew Pal. BS, Washington and Lee U., 1963; JD, U. Ark., 1968; LLM, Harvard U., 1970. Bar: Ark. 1968, Calif. 1970. Assoc. Pillsbury Madison & Sutro, San Francisco, 1970-76; ptnr. Pillsbury, Madison & Sutro, San Francisco, 1977-84, Baker & McKenzie, San Francisco, 1984-87, Pillsbury Madison & Sutro, San Francisco, 1987-2000, Pillsbury Winthrop, San Francisco, 2001—. Trustee Grace Cathedral, San Francisco. 1st lt. U.S. Army, 1965. Mem. ABA, Calif. Bar Assn., Olympic Club (San Francisco), Calif. Tennis Club (pres. 2000). Office: Pillsbury Winthrop LLP 50 Fremont St San Francisco CA 94105-2230

**SPARKS, WILLIAM B., JR.,** consumer products company executive; BA, U of Notre Dame; MBA, Cornell U. Pres. Down River Internat., Greif Bros. Corp, 1978—80, chmn., CEO, 1980—95; mem. bd. dir. Greif Bros. Corp., 1995—, Pres., COO, 1995—. Office: 425 Winter Rd Delaware OH 43015

**SPARKS, WILLIAM SHERAL,** retired librarian; b. Alden Bridge, La., Oct. 30, 1924; s. Fred DeWitt and Truda (Bradford) S.; m. Joy Eleanor Young, Aug. 8, 1947; 1 child, David Frederick. AB, Phillips U., 1946; MDiv, Christian Theol. Sem., 1949; ThM, Iliff Sch. of Theology, 1955, ThD, 1957; MA, U. Denver, 1962. Pastor chs., 1950-60; asst. libr. Kans. Wesleyan U., Salina, 1962-66; dir. libr. and info. svcs. St. Paul Sch. of Theology, Kansas City, Mo., 1966-93, ret., 1993. Horowitz Found. fellow Hebrew Union Coll.-Jewish Inst. of Religion, Cin., 1949-52. Mem. Am. Theol. Libr. Assn.

**SPARROW, HERBERT GEORGE, III,** lawyer, educator; b. Ft. Bragg, N.C., May 26, 1936; s. Herbert George and Virginia (Monroe) S.; m. Nancy Woodruff, Mar. 4, 1962; children: Amy Winslow, Edward Harrison, Herbert G. IV, Alison Kidder. AB cum laude, Princeton U., 1958; JD, U. Mich., 1961. Bar: Mich. 1961, Calif. 1964, D.C. 1979, U.S. Ct. Claims 1982, U.S. Tax Ct. 1983, U.S. Ct. Mil. Appeals 1962, U.S. Supreme Ct. 1959. Assoc. Dickinson Wright PLLC, Detroit, 1965-70, ptnr., 1970—. Adj. prof. Detroit Coll. Law, Mich. State U., 1977-99. Author numerous articles environ. law.; speaker in field. Bd. dirs. Family Life Edn. Coun., Grosse Pointe, Mich., 1982-88, Adult Well-Being Svcs., Inc., Detroit, 1995-2001; cons. Adult Well-Being Svcs. Inc., 2001—. Capt. JAGC, U.S. Army, 1962-65. Mem. Mich. Bar Assn. (rep. assembly 1979-85, environ. law sect. coun. 1985-91), Calif. Bar Assn., Detroit Bar Assn., Am. Arbitration Assn. (panel arbitrators 1975—), Mich. State Bar Found. (fellow 1989-93), Environment Law Inst. (former assoc.). Phi Delta Phi (pres. Kent Inn Assn., Ann Arbor 1985-97). Office: Dickinson Wright PLLC 500 Woodward Ave Ste 4000 Detroit MI 48226-3416

**SPARROW, JOSHUA D.,** child psychiatrist; married; 2 children. BA, Wesleyan U.; MD, Yale Med. Sch. Assoc. prof. psychiatry Univ. Marseille Sch. Med., France; asst. prof. psychiatry Harvard Med. Sch., Boston, clin. prof. pediat. emeritus; supr. inpatient psychiatry unit Children's Hospital, Boston, founder Child Devel. Unit; assoc. dir. Brazelton Touchpoints Ctr., dir. spl. initiatives. Cons. Harlem Children's Zone, NYC, Am. Indian Early Head Start Programs, Careplus HMO, NYC; mem. adv. bd. Ready, Set, Learn, 2005—. Co-author (with Dr. T. Berry Brazelton): (NY Times syndicated column) Families Today, 1999—, (books) Touchpoints: Three to Six, 2001, Brazelton Way book series, 2004—; cons. (TV series) Brazelton on Parenting, 2000, Ready, Set, Learn, 2005—; contbr. Family Circle mag., Family & Child mag. Coach girls' soccer team, Brookline, Mass. Office: Children's Hospital Ste 320 1295 Boylston St Boston MA 02215 also: Children's Hospital 300

Longwood Ave Boston MA 02215 also: NY Times Syndication Sales Corp 14th Fl 122 E 42nd St New York NY 10168 Office Phone: 617-355-7639. Office Fax: 617-859-7215, 212-499-3382. E-mail: joshua.sparrow@tch.harvard.edu, nytsyn-families@nytimes.com.*

**SPATAFORE, ANTHONY R.,** financial executive; b. Bklyn., Nov. 15, 1952; s. Anthony C. and Mercedes (Santiago) S; m. Deborah Spatafore. Student, Bklyn. Coll.; Cert. Fin. Planning, Adelphi U., 1982. Registered fin. planner; registered investment advisor, SEC. Asst. Paul Revere Ins. Co., N.Y.C., 1974-76; ins. cons. M.O.N.Y., N.Y.C., 1976-79; fin. planner Home Life Ins. Co., N.Y.C., 1979-82; pres., fin. planner ARS Fin. Svcs., Inc., Valley Stream, N.Y., 1982—. Contbr. articles to profl. jours. Mem. Internat. Assn. Registered Fin. Planners (bd. govs. 1987-89), Internat. Assn. Fin. Planning, Inst. Cert. Fin. Planners (local bd. dirs. 1987—, pres. L.I. Soc.), Nat. Assn. Securities Dealers. Republican. Roman Catholic. Avocation: tennis. Office: Jericho Atrium 500 N Broadway Jericho NY 11753 Office Phone: 516-932-5130.

**SPATARO, JANIE DEMPSEY WATTS,** freelance/self-employed writer; b. Chattanooga, May 17, 1951; d. Ray Dean and Anne America (Dempsey) Watts; m. Stephen Anthony Spataro, June 18, 1977; children: Anthony Dempsey, Stephen Jackson. BS in Journalism, U. Calif., Berkeley, 1974; MA in Broadcast Journalism, U. So. Calif., 1982. Writer, editor McGiffin Newspapers, South Gate, Calif., 1976; news bur. mgr. Loyola Marymount U., Westchester, Calif., 1976; asst. dir. pub. relations Hawthorne Cmty. Hosp., Calif., 1977—78; pub. rels. cons. Security Pacific Bank, LA, 1978—82; writer Cable Card, Inc., Marina del Rey, Calif., 1983—86; pres. Write Path, Inc., 1997—. Writer, prodr., editor (TV documentary) Who's Minding the Children?, 1983, screenwriter, Monkey Doll, Fireworks, Oatmania, Soft Shoe, Hard World; author: (novels) Moon Over Taylor's Ridge; contbr. chapters to books. Office: 100 Wilshire Blvd Ste 200 Santa Monica CA 90401-1111 Business E-Mail: janie@spataro.com.

**SPATT, ARTHUR DONALD,** federal judge; b. 1925; Student, Ohio State U., 1943-44, 46-47; LLB cum laude, Bklyn. Law Sch., 1949. Assoc. Davidson & Davidson, N.Y.C., 1949, Lane, Winard, Robinson & Schorr, N.Y.C., 1950, Alfred S. Julien, N.Y.C., 1950-52, Florea & Florea, N.Y.C., 1953; pvt. practice N.Y.C., 1953-67, Spatt & Bauman, N.Y.C., 1967-78; justice 10th judicial cir. N.Y. State Supreme Ct., 1979-82; adminstrv. judge Nassau County, 1982-86; assoc. justice appellate div. Second Judicial Dept., 1986-89; dist. judge U.S. Dist. Ct. (ea. dist.) N.Y., Bklyn., 1989-90, Uniondale, NY, 1990-2000, Central Islip, NY, 2000—. Book review editor Bklyn. Law Review, 1948—49. Active Jewish War Vets. With USN, 1944—46. Mem. ABA, Assn. Supreme Ct. Justices State of N.Y., Bar Assn. Nassau County, Jewish Lawyers Assn. Nassau County, Long Beach Lawyers Assn. Office: Long Island Courthouse 1024 Federal Plaza Central Islip NY 11722-4445 Office Phone: 631-712-5620.

**SPATT, HARTLEY STEVEN,** humanities educator; b. Bklyn., Nov. 21, 1947; s. Milton E. and Blanche S. (Bakstansky) S.; m. Wendy Doroshkin, June 13, 1971; children: Martin, Samantha. BA summa cum laude, Colgate U., 1970; MA, NYU, 1971, Johns Hopkins U., 1973, PhD, 1975. Asst. prof. Towson State U., Balt., 1974-76, SUNY Maritime Coll., Bronx, 1976-81, assoc. prof., 1981-87, prof., 1987—, Disting. Tchg. prof., 2004—, assoc. v.p. for acad. affairs, 1999—2002. Writer, editor A.L. Fierst, Greatneck, N.Y., 1977-80, Reference Works, 1993-2001; bus. mgr. Victorian Studies Bull., N.Y.C., 1983—; writer Chernow Editl. Svcs., N.Y.C., 1985-90. Contbr. articles to Victorian Poetry, Walt Whitman Rev., other profl. jours. NEH fellow, 1979, 82, 86, 2004. Mem. MLA, N.E. Victorian Studies Assn. (chair nominations 1989—), William Morris Soc. U.S. (sec.-treas. 1984—), Phi Beta Kappa. Republican. Jewish. Office: Maritime Coll Suny Bronx NY 10465 Office Phone: 718-409-7250. E-mail: hspatt@sunymaritime.edu.

**SPATT, ROBERT EDWARD,** lawyer; b. Bklyn., Mar. 26, 1956; s. Milton E. and Blanche S. (Bakstansky) S.; m. Lisa B. Malkin, Aug. 11, 1979; 1 child, Mark Eric. AB, Brown U., 1977; JD magna cum laude, U. Mich., 1980. Bar: N.Y. 1981. Assoc. Simpson Thacher & Bartlett, N.Y.C., 1980-87, ptnr., 1987—. Mem. ABA, N.Y. State Bar Assn., City of N.Y. Bar Assn., Order of Coif. Avocations: photography, boating, reading. Office: Simpson Thacher & Bartlett 425 Lexington Ave New York NY 10017-3954 Office Phone: 212-455-2685. E-mail: RSpatt@stblaw.com.

**SPATZ, ANDRE,** international organization executive; M in electronics and elec. engring., Swiss Fed. Inst. Tech., Lausanne. Sr. mgmt. positions with Brown Boveri & Cie, Switzerland, Digital Equipment Corp., Landis & Gyr Energy Mgmt. Corp.; chief info. officer, mng. dir. domestic/Swiss divsn. Swiss Bank Corp., Bazel; chief info. officer UNICEF, NYC, 1997—. Named one of Premier 100 IT Leaders, Computerworld, 2005. Office: UNICEF 3 United Nations Plz New York NY 10017 Office Phone: 212-326-7000.*

**SPAULDING, DAN,** public relations executive; BA, MA, U. Mich. Lt. USN; aide, pub. affairs officer to comdr. Tng. Command U.S. Pacific Fleet, San Diego, 1969-72; news anchor/prodr./reporter Staf. WFRV-TV, Green Bay, Wis., Sta. WEYI-TV, Flint-Saginaw, Mich.; mem. faculty U. Wis., Green Bay; news dir. Sta. KOMU-TV, Columbia, Mo., Sta. WOTV-TV 8; with Seyferth & Assocs., Inc., Grand Rapids, Mich., 1989-94, exec. v.p., 1994—. Active West Mich. Environ. Action Coun. Mem. Pub. Rels. Soc. Am. (accredited). Office: Seyferth Spaulding Tennyson 40 Monroe Center NW, Suite 202 Grand Rapids MI 49503-3003 Business E-Mail: info@seyferthpr.com.

**SPAULDING, HELEN BOWDOIN,** former foundation administrator; m. Josiah Augustus Spaulding. HHD (hon.), Rocky Mt. Coll, Pres. and chair New England Aquarium, mem. The Boston Found., 1992-2002, chair, 1997—2002; dir. emeritus Mus. Trustee Assn. Bd. dirs. Georgetown U., Boston U., Mus. Sci., Huntington Theatre, Wang Ctr. Performing Arts, United Way Mass. Bay, World Wildlife Found., Nat. Conf. Christians and Jews, Children's Hosp. Med. Ctr., Spaulding Rehabilitation Hosp.; adv. coun. Malcolm Weiner Sch. Social Policy; adv. coun. Hauser Ctr. for Non-profits Kennedy Sch. Govt., Harvard U. Recipient Disting. Citizen award, Greater Boston C. of C., Lifetime Achievement award, Arthritis Found. Fellow: Am. Acad. Arts and Sciences.*

**SPAULDING, LILA BERNICE,** marriage and family counselor; b. Lake Waccamaw, NC, Mar. 3, 1931; d. Samuel Leslie and Mary Elease (Graham) Mitchell; m. Lloyd Leslie Spaulding, June 24, 1972 (dec. July 1982). BA in Psychology, Molloy Coll., 1985; MA, Hofstra U., 1987. LPN, N.Y., N.C., N.J. Nurse, oper. tech. Burdette Tomlin Hosp., Cape May, N.J., 1963-80; oper. rm. tech. Lydia E. Hall Hosp., Freeport, N.Y., 1980-87; marriage and family counselor North Shore Mental Health, Wantaugh, N.Y., 1987-89; marriage and family counselor in pvt. practice Lake Waccamaw, 1989—; owner, operator Live Christmas Farm, Lake Waccamaw, 1994—, Wacca Country Gift Shop, Lake Waccamaw, 1995—. Mem. health and human svcs. bd. N.C. Comm., Raleigh, 1993—; mem. adv. bd. Columbus County Med. Ctr., Whiteville, N.C.; mem. Columbus County Med. Clinic. Author: Waccamaw Siouan Cooking, 1994, (postcards) Native Am. Scenes, 1994. Bd. dirs., sec., treas., mem. econ. devel. N.C. Cmty. Affairs, Raleigh, 1993—; vol. State of N.C., 1996, pres. of the Concerned Citizens, Inc. of Lake Waccamaw, chmn., Homemade Handmade Festival, 1997. Mem. N.Y. State Psychol. Assn., N.C. Ind. Bus. Assn. (treas. 1994—), Waccamaw Siquan Devel. Assn. (chair fin. com. 1993—). Democrat. Baptist. Avocations: yoga, church activities, organist, crafts, doll collecting. Home and Office: PO Box 170 #555 Carver Moore Rd Lake Waccamaw NC 28450 E-mail: bern@intrstar.net.

**SPAULDING, MAR,** retired special education educator; b. Bellevue, Ky., Oct. 16, 1933; d. Mickey and Blanche Harris; m. Stan Lee Spaulding; children: Karla, Julie Underwood, Lisa Williams, Gregory. MA, Ea. Mich. U., 1978; BS, George Mason U., 1973. Cert. educator Emotionally/Neurologically Impaired, Pre-primary Impaired 1978. Head tchr. in nursery sch., Ann Arbor, Mich., 1973—75; intern Ypsilanti State Mental Instn., Mich., 1975—76; tchr. emotionally impaired and pre-primary impaired Monroe County Intermediate Dist., Monroe, Mich., 1978—93. Leader of groups of parents of handicapped children Monroe County Intermediate Sch. Dist., Monroe, Mich., 1978—93, mem. of grant com., 1980—96, tester on child find com., 1979—85. Author: (children's educational book) Kate Lynn's Fantastic Dream, 1999 (Spl. Edn. Tchr. of the Yr. in Monroe County, Mich., 1995), (companion book) Activities to use with Kate Lynn's Fantastic Dream. Includes cognitive, speech and language, fine motor, gross motor and behavioral, emotional skill areas for teachers and parents., 1999. Story lady Head Start, Baker Devel. Ctr., Punta Gorda, Fla., 1996—2002; tutor Continuing Edn. Ctr. and Even Start, Port Charlotte and Punta Gorda, 1996—2003; membership involvement chairperson Peace River Power Squadron, Punta Gorda, 1996—2003; pub. spkr. topics concerning early childhood edn. Early Childhood Edn. Assn. of SW Fla., Punta Gorda, 1999—2003. Recipient Writer's Award, US Power Squadrons, 2001. Mem.: AAUW (Ft. Myers, Fla. chpt.), U.S. Sail and Power Squadrons, Thomas Paine Nat. Hist. Soc., Nat. Honor Soc., Phi Kappa Phi. Liberal. Avocations: travel, sailing, swimming, bicycling, piano. Home: 1536 Islamorada Blvd Punta Gorda FL 33955 Personal E-mail: marstan@nut-n-but.net.

**SPAULDING, NORMAN W., III,** law educator; b. 1971; BA magna cum laude, Williams Coll., 1993; JD, Stanford U., 1997. Bar: Calif. 1997. Assoc. Skadden, Arps, Slate, Meagher & Flom, San Francisco, 1997—98; law clk. to Judge Thelton E. Henderson US Dist. Ct. No. Dist. Calif., 1998—99; law clk. to Judge Betty B. Fletcher US Ct. Appeals 9th Cir., 1999—2000; acting prof. law Boalt Hall Sch. Law, U. Calif., Berkeley, 2000—05, prof., 2005, Stanford Law Sch., 2005—, John A. Wilson disting. faculty scholar, 2005—. Vis. prof. Stanford Law Sch., 2004—05. Office: Stanford Sch Law Crown Quadrangle 559 Nathan Abbott Way Stanford CA 94305-8610 Office Phone: 650-736-1854. E-mail: nspaulding@law.stanford.edu.

**SPAULDING, WALLACE HOLMES,** retired federal agency professional; b. Oakland, Calif., Sept. 3, 1928; s. Wallace Holmes and May Gibbons (Alves) S.; m. Dorothy Anne Wollon, Jan. 30, 1960; children: James Wallace, Anne Catherine Bridger. AB, U. Calif., Berkeley, 1950; MA, Johns Hopkins U., 1951; PhD, U. Pa., 1969. Rschr. CIA, McLean, Va., 1952-91; ret., 1991. Author: Is the Comintern Coming Back?, 1998; contbr. chpts. to books and articles to profl. jours. Pres. Fellowship of Concerned Churchmen, Mpls., Found. for Christian Theology, Washington; Am. regional sec. Soc. of Mary, McLean. Col. (ret.) USAR, 1950—81. Decorated Meritorious Svc. medal U.S. Army; Fulbright scholar, The Philippines, 1951-52. Mem.: Phi Beta Kappa, Pan Xenia, Alpha Delta Phi. Avocations: walking, domestic and foreign travel. Home: 1206 Buchanan St Mc Lean VA 22101-2943 Personal E-mail: whsdws@verizon.net.

**SPEAKES, LARRY MELVIN,** public relations executive, writer; b. Cleveland, Miss., Sept. 13, 1939; s. Harry Earl and Ethlyn Frances (Fincher) Speakes; m. Aleta Merkel, Oct. 5, 2001; children from previous marriage: Sondra LaNell, Barry Scott, Jeremy Stephen. Student, U. Miss., 1957-61; Litt. D. (hon.), Ind. Central U., 1982, BA in Journalism, 2001. News editor Oxford (Miss.) Eagle, 1961-62; news editor Bolivar Commi., Cleveland, 1962-63, mng. editor, 1965-66; dep. dir. Bolivar County Civil Def., 1963-65; gen. mgr. Progress Pubs., Leland, Miss., 1966-68; editor Leland Progress, Hollandale Herald, Bolivar County Democrat, Sunflower County News; press sec. U.S. Senator J.O. Eastland of Miss., 1968-74; staff asst. Exec. Office of Pres., Mar.-May 1974; press asst. to spl. counsel to Pres., May-Aug. 1974; asst. White House press sec., 1974-76, asst. press sec. to Pres., 1976-77; press sec. to Gerald R. Ford, 1977; v.p. Hill & Knowlton, Inc., internat. pub. relations and pub. affairs counsel, Washington, 1977-81; prin. dep. press sec. and asst. to Pres. of U.S., Washington, 1981-87; sr. v.p. Merrill Lynch & Co., Inc., N.Y.C., 1987-88; v.p. comm. No. Telecom Ltd., Washington and Toronto, Ont., Can., 1991-93; sr. v.p. corp. rels. U.S. Postal Svc., Washington, 1994-98, sr. advisor to postmaster gen., 1998—, mgr. of advt., 2001—. Corp. comm. cons., lectr. on press and politics, 1988-91. Author: Speaking Out: The Reagan Presidency From Inside the White House; contbr. Crisis Repsponse: Inside Stories on Managing Image Under Siege. Recipient Presdl. Citizens medal, 1987, Gen. Excellence award Miss. Press Assn., 1988, Disting. Journalism Alumni award U. Miss., 1981, Hall of Fame, 1985, Silver Em. Miss. Scholastic Press Assn., 1988, Spl. Achievement award Nat. Assn. Govt. Communicators, 1983, Silver Anvil award Pub. Rels. Soc. Am., 1988, NY Addy Gold TV comml. award; named to Top 100 PR Proflls. of Century, PR Week mag., 1999, Pub. Rels. Hall of Fame, D.C. chpt. PRSA, 1999. Mem. Arthur Page Soc. (trustee), Pub. Rels. Seminar, Sigma Delta Chi, Kappa Sigma (Man of Yr. 1982), Lambda Sigma, Omicron Delta Kappa. Methodist.

**SPEAKMAN, ROBERT J.,** archaeologist, chemist, researcher; b. Virginia Beach, Va., Dec. 29, 1970; s. Harry H. and Patricia K. Speakman; m. LuElla M. Parks Speakman, July 18, 1998. AA in Anthropology, Cochise Coll., Sierra Vista, Ariz., 1993—95; BA in Anthropology, No. Ariz. U., Flagstaff, 1996; MA in Anthropology, U. Mo., Columbia, 2002, postgrad. in Anthropology, 2003—. Sr. rsch. specialist U. Mo. Rsch. Reactor, Columbia, 1997—. Office: U Mo Rsch Reactor 1513 Research Park Dr Columbia MO 65211 Office Phone: 573-882-5241.

**SPEAR, ALLAN HENRY,** state legislator, historian, educator; b. Michigan City, Ind., June 24, 1937; s. Irving S. and Esther (Lieber) S. BA, Oberlin Coll., 1958, LLD (hon.), 1997; MA, Yale U., 1960, PhD, 1965. Lectr. history U. Minn., Mpls., 1964-65, assoc. prof., 1965-67, assoc. prof., 1967-2000; mem. Minn. State Senate, St. Paul, 1973-2000, chmn. jud. com., 1983-93; chmn. crime prevention com., 1993-2000; pres. Minn. State Senate, 1993—2000; vice-chair Minn. Campaign Fin. and Pub. Disclosure Bd., 2001—03. Vis. prof. Carleton Coll., Northfield, Minn., 1970, Stanford U., Palo Alto, Calif., 1970. Author: Black Chicago, 1967. Mem. Internat. Network Gay and Lesbian Ofcls. Avocations: cooking, travel, reading, classical music. Home: 2429 Colfax Ave S Minneapolis MN 55405-2942

**SPEAR, HARVEY M.,** lawyer; b. Providence, May 24, 1922; s. Alfred and Esther S.; m. Ruth Abramson, June 27, 1965; children: Jessica, Elizabeth Anne. AB, Brown U., 1942; LL.B., Harvard, 1948; MA, George Washington U., 1949, LL.M., 1952, S.JD, 1955. Bar: Mass. 1948, D.C. 1948, N.Y. 1954, U.S. Supreme Ct. 1954; CPA, Md. Asst. U.S. atty. D.C., 1945; legal asst. to chmn., asst. to vice chmn. SEC, 1944—50; spl. asst. to atty. gen. Dept. Justice, 1951—54; pvt. practice law N.Y.C. and Washington, 1956—; counsel Cadwalader Wickersham & Taft, N.Y.C., 1996—. Contbr. articles to profl. jours. Mem.: ABA, Assn. of Bar of City of NY. Home: 765 Park Ave New York NY 10021-4254 also: 78 Hither Ln East Hampton NY 11937 Office: One World Fin Ctr New York NY 10281 Business E-Mail: harvey.spear@cwt.com.

**SPEAR, LAURINDA HOPE,** architect; m. Bernardo Fort-Brescia. BFA, Brown U., 1972; MArch, Columbia U., 1975. Registered architect, Fla., N.Y.; cert. Nat. Coun. Archtl. Registration. Founding prin. Arquitectonica (ARQ) Miami, Fla., 1977—. Lectr. in field. Prin. works include Pink No., Miami, Fla., 1978, The Palace, Miami, 1982 (Honor award Miami chpt. AIA 1982), The Atlantis, Miami, 1982 (Miami chpt. AIA award 1983), The Imperial, Miami, 1983, Casa los Andes (Record Hos. award Archtl. Record 1986), North Dade Justice Ctr., Miami, 1987 (Honor award Miami chpt. AIA 1989), Rio, Atlanta, 1988 (Honor award AIA 1989), Banco de Credito del Peru, Lima, 1988 (Honor award Miami chpt. AIA 1989), The Ctr. Innovative Tech., Herndon, Va., 1988 (Honor award Va. chpt. AIA 1989, Honor award Miami chpt. 1990, Merit award Fairfax, Va., County Exceptional Design Awards Program 1990), Sawgrass Mills (Merit award Miami chpt. AIA 1990, Honor award Fla. chpt. 1991), Miracle Ctr. (Honor award Miami chpt. AIA 1989), Internat. Swimming Hall of Fame, Ft. Lauderdale, Fla., 1991, Banque de Luxembourg, 1993, Disney All-Star Resorts, Orlando, Fla., 1994, U.S. Embassy, Lima, 1994, USCG Family Housing, Bayamon, P.R., 1994, Altamira Ctr., Caracas, Venezuela, 1994, Festival Walk, Hong Kong, 1998, Miami Fed. Courthouse, Am. Airlines Arena, Miami, 1999, Philips Arena, Atlanta, 1999, Miami Internat. Airport D-E-F Wrap. Mem. beaux arts support group Lowe Art Mus., Miami; bd. dirs. Miami Youth Mus.

Recipient Design Awards citation Progressive Architecture, 1975, 80, Rome Prize in Architecture, 1978, Award of Excellence, Atlanta Urban Design Commn., 1989; inductee Interior Design Hall of Fame, 1999. Fellow AIA (Silver medal for design 1998); mem. Internat. Womens Forum, NAD (academician, 1994-). Office: Arquitectonica International Corp 801 Brickell Ave Ste 1100 Miami FL 33131-2945 Office Phone: 305-372-1812. Office Fax: 305-372-1175. Business E-Mail: lspear@arqintl.com.

**SPEAR, PETER D.,** retired academic administrator; BA, Rutgers U., 1966; PhD in Physiol. Psychology, Yale U., 1970. Postdoctoral fellow dept. neurology Stanford U. Sch. Medicine, Calif., 1970—72; asst. prof. psychology Kans. State U., 1972, U. Wis., Madison, 1976—78, assoc. prof., 1978—81, prof., 1981, chair dept. psychology, 1990—94, assoc. dean social sci. Coll. Letters and Sci., 1994—96, provost, vice chancellor for acad. affairs, 2001—05; dean Coll. Arts and Scis. U. Colo., Boulder, 1996—2001. Co-author: Psychology: Perspectives on Behavior. Office: Univ Wis Madison 150 Bascom Hall 500 Lincoln Dr Madison WI 53706

**SPEAR, TERRY M,** education educator, consultant; b. Butte, Mont., June 23, 1952; s. William P. Spear; m. Sally Seymour, May 28, 1982; children: Trenton S., Tessa E. BA in Microbiology, U. Mont., 1975; MS in Indsl. Hygiene, U.Minn., 1980, PhD in Indsl. Hygiene, 1996. Sr. engr. EG&G Idaho, Inc., Idaho Falls, Idaho, 1980—83; prof. Mont. Tech of The U. of Mont., Butte, 1983—. Contbr. scientific papers. Reviewer Brit. Occupl. Hygiene Soc., England, 1995, Nat. Inst. of Environ. Health Sciences, Rsch. Triangle Park, NC, 1996; mem. EPA, Las Vegas, Nev., 2001—03. Mem.: Am. Sect., Internat. Soc. for Respiratory Protection (assoc.), Brit. Occupl. Hygiene Soc. (assoc.), Am. Indsl. Hygiene Assn. (assoc.). Democrat-Npl. Cath. Home: 110 S Hauser Anaconda MT 59711 Office: Mont Tech of the Univ of Mont 1300 West Park Butte MT 59701 Office Phone: 406-496-4445. Home Fax: 406-496-4650; Office Fax: 406-496-4650. Personal E-mail: tspear@mtech.edu.

**SPEARING, ANTHONY COLIN,** English literature educator; b. London, Jan. 31, 1936; came to U.S., 1987; s. Frederick and Gertrude (Calnin) S. MA, Cambridge U., Eng., 1960. W.M. Tapp rsch. fellow Gonville-Caius Coll. Cambridge U., 1959-60, asst. lectr. in English, 1960-64, official fellow Queens' Coll., 1960-87, life fellow, 1987—, dir. studies in English, 1967-85, lectr. in English, 1964-85, reader in medieval English lit., 1985-87; vis. prof. English U. Va., Charlottesville, 1979-80, 84, prof. English, 1987-89, Kenan prof. English, 1989—. William Matthews lectr. Birkbeck Coll., London, 1983—84; invited lectr. numerous colls. and univs. Eng., Europe, Can., U.S.; Lansdowne vis. fellow U. Victoria, 1993; Benjamin Meaker vis. prof. U. Bristol, 2003. Author: Criticism and Medieval Poetry, 1964, rev. edit., 1972; (with Maurice Hussey and James Winny) An Introduction to Chaucer, 1965; The Gawain-Poet: A Critical Study, 1970, Chaucer: Troilus and Criseyde, 1976, Medieval Dream-Poetry, 1976, Medieval to Renaissance in English Poetry, 1985, Readings in Medieval Poetry, 1987, The Medieval Poet as Voyeur, 1993, Textual Subjectivity, 2005; editor: The Pardoner's Prologue and Tale (Chaucer), 1965, rev. edit., 1994, The Knight's Tale (Chaucer), 1966, rev. edit., 1995, The Franklin's Prologue and Tale (Chaucer), 1966, rev. edit., 1994; co-editor: (with Elizabeth Spearing) Shakespeare: The Tempest, 1971, Poetry of the Age of Chaucer, 1974, The Reeve's Prologue and Tale (Chaucer), 1979, Julian of Norwich: Revelations of Divine Love, 1998; translator: The Cloud of Unknowing and Other Works, 2001; contbr. numerous articles to profl. jours. Mem. Medieval Acad. Am., Internat. Assn. U. Profs. English, New Chaucer Soc. (trustee 1986-90). Office: Univ Va Dept English 219 Bryan Hall PO Box 400121 Charlottesville VA 22904-4121 Business E-Mail: acs4j@virginia.edu.

**SPEARING, SIMON MARK,** aeronautical engineer, educator; b. Brentwood, Essex, England, Dec. 17, 1964; s. Simon Alan and Alison Jean Spearing; m. Elnor Lucy Clare Allhusen, Sept. 7, 2002. BA in Engring., Cambridge U., 1986, PhD, 1989. Grad. student Cambridge U., Cambridgeshire, England, 1986—89; rsch. engr. U. Calif., Santa Barbara, 1990—92; engring. specialist BP Rsch., Carborundum, Cleveland, Ohio, 1992—94; prof., aeronautics and astronautics MIT, Cambridge, Mass., 1994—2004; vis. prof. of aeronautics and astronautics MIT, Cambridge, Mass., 2004—; Dept. editor Acta Materialia, 1996—2003; chmn. AIAA Materials Tech. Com., 1997—99; editor Jour. of Microelectromechanical Sys., 2003—. Contbr. articles various profl. jours. 2nd lt. Royal Arty., 1983—83, Munster, Germany. Recipient Wolfson Rsch. Merit award, Royal Soc. of London, 2004-2009; grantee Career award, NSF, 1997-2001; Assoc. fellow, AIAA, 2002. Fellow: AIAA (assoc.; chmn. materials tech. com. 1997—99); mem.: Materials Rsch. Soc., Am. Ceramic Soc., Am. Soc. of Mech. Engring. Anglican/Episcopalean. Achievements include patents for Unmanned Aerial Vehicles and MEMS. Office: University U Highfield Hampshire Southampton SO17 1BJ England Fax: 44 (0) 23 8059 3016. Personal E-mail: spearing@soton.ac.uk.

**SPEARMAN, MAXIE ANN,** financial analyst, administrator; b. Piedmont, SC, Sept. 14, 1942; d. J. Mac and Margaret Cecille S. BS, U. SC, 1965; postgrad., Ga. State U., 1985, U. Ga. Acct. Shell Oil Co., Atlanta, 1965-66; internal auditor Sears, Roebuck & Co., Atlanta, 1966-67; acct. Econ. Opportunity Atlanta, Atlanta, 1967-68, City of Atlanta, 1968-78, fin. analyst, 1978-89, sr. fin. analyst planner, 1989—. Investment cons., Atlanta, Conyers, Ga., 1980—. Mem. Rep. Presdl. Task Force, 1985—, U.S. Senatorial Club, Rep. Nat. Com., 1988—, Ga. Rep. Party, 1990—, Atlanta Safety Com., 1985—, Mayor's Spl. Events Task Force, 1990; charter founder Ronald Reagan Rep. Ctr., 1988; del.-at-large Rep. Platform Planning Com., 1992, 94. Recipient safety award Atlanta City Com., 1990, Presdl. Commn. Exec. Com. of Republican Party award, 1992, Order of Merit award Nat. Rep. Senatorial Com., 1996. Mem. AAUW, NAFE, Am. Mgmt. Assn., Ga. Assn. Med. Victims, Inc. (sec., treas. 1985—), Nat. Trust for Historic Preservation. Methodist. Avocations: writing, tennis, decorating, investing. Home: 1280 Vineyard Dr SE Conyers GA 30013-2466

**SPEARMAN, ROBERT WORTHINGTON,** lawyer; b. Durham, NC, Jan. 24, 1943; s. Walter and Mary Elizabeth (Dale) S.; m. Patricia Hinds, June 2, 1973; children: Madolyn Marschall, Dorothy Marschall. BA in Polit. Sci., U. N.C., 1965; MA in Philosophy/Econs., Oxford U., 1967; LLB, Yale U., 1970. Bar: NC 1971, DC 1979, US Dist. Ct. (ea., mid. and w. dists. NC), U.S. Ct. Appeals (4th and 5th cirs.), U.S. Supreme Ct. Law clk. to Justice Hugo L. Black U.S. Supreme Ct., Washington, 1971; assoc. Adams, McCullough & Beard, Raleigh, 1971-75, ptnr., 1975—90; ptnr. litig., antitrust & bus. torts practice group leader Parker Poe Adams & Bernstein LLP, Raleigh, 1990—. Adj. prof. Law Sch., U. N.C., Chapel Hill, 1982-83. Vice chmn. corrections planning com. N.C. Crime Control Commn., 1979-81; chmn. Wake County Democratic Com., 1979-81, N.C. Elections Bd., 1981-85. Vice chmn. corrections planning com. N.C. Crime Control Commn., 1979-81; chmn. Wake County Dem. Com., 1979-81, N.C. Elections Bd., 1981-85. Morehead Found. scholar, 1961; Rhodes scholar, 1965; Razor Walker award, 2002. Fellow Am. Coll. Trial Lawyers; mem. NC State Com. 2003-05; mem. ABA, N.C. Bar Assn. (chmn. comml. litigation com. 1982-83), Phi Beta Kappa. Presbyterian. Office: Parker Poe Adams & Bernstein LLP Ste 1400 150 Fayetteville St Mall PO Box 389 Raleigh NC 27602-0389 Office Phone: 919-828-0564. Office Fax: 919-835-4560. Business E-Mail: bobspearman@parkerpoe.com.

**SPEARS, BRITNEY,** singer; b. McComb, Miss., Dec. 2, 1981; d. Jamie and Lynne Spears; m. Jason Alexander, Jan. 2, 2004 (annulled Jan. 5, 2004); m. Kevin Federline, Sept. 18, 2004; children: Sean Preston, Sutton Pierce stepchildren: Kori, Kaleb. Released signature fragrance Curious BRITNEY SPEARS, 2004, Britney Spears: Fantasy, 2005; release of fragrance In Control, 2006. Singer: (albums) Baby One More Time, 1999, Oops! I Did It Again, 2000 (Billboard Album artist of the Year, 2000), Britney, 2001, In the Zone, 2003, Britney Spears, Greatest Hits My Prerogative, 2004; actor- (voice): (TV films) Hooves of Fire, 1999, Legends of the Lost Tribe, 2002,: (films) Longshot, 2000, Crossroads, 2002, (TV reality show) Britney And

Kevin: Chaotic, 2005—; guest appearance with husband (reading a top 10 list on The Late Show with David Letterman), 2005; composer: (songs) (for film Drive Me Crazy) You Drive Me Crazy, 1999, (for film Pokémon the First Movie: Mewtwo Strikes Back) Soda Pop, 1999, (for film On The Line) Let Me Be, 2001, (for film Jimmy Neutron: Boy Genius) Intimidated, 2001, (for film Austin Powers in Goldmember) Boys, 2002. Britney Spears Found. Recipient Female Artist of the Year, Billboard, 1999, New Artist of the Year, 1999, Hot Dance Sales Single of Yr. for "Me Against the Music" featuring Madonna, 2004, Choice Music Single "Baby One More Time", Teen Choice award, 1999, Choice Hottie Female & Choice Female Artist, 2000, 2002, Choice Female Artist, 2001, Choice Music Single "Toxic", 2004, Best New Artist, Am. Music Awards, 2000, Grammy for Best Dance Recording for Toxic, 2005. Mailing: Jive Records 137 W 25th St New York NY 10001-7216

SPEARS, BURL JUNIOR, computer technology educator; b. Stigler, Okla., Mar. 27, 1952; s. Burl Herbert and Mabel Lee Spears; m. Sarah Beth Singleton, Mar. 21, 1959; children: Sabrina Elizabeth Dyer, Alisha Christine, Gwendolyn Ruth Sullivan. B of Music Edn., U. of Okla., 1975; MEd, East Cen. U., Ada, Okla., 1980. Cert. A+ CompTIA, network assoc. Cisco Corp., I-Net+ CompTIA, Network+ CompTIA, Server+ CompTIA, 3.1x netware adminstr.(CNA) Novell; Nat. Bd. of Tchr. Certs. Min. of music Immanuel Bapt. Ch., Poteau, Okla., 1980—; computer tech instr. Kiamichi Tech. Ctr., Poteau, 1984—. Singer, songwriter: Burl Spears & Family Album. Sch. bd. mem. Poteau Pub. Schs., 1993—2003. Mem.: Okla. Vocat. Assn. (Outstanding S.E. Regional Mem. 1999), Am. Career Tech Assn. (assoc.). Democrat. Southern Baptist. Avocations: music, travel. Home: 302 Crest Poteau OK 74953 Office: Kiamichi Tech Ctr 1509 S McKenna Poteau OK 74953 Office Phone: 918-647-4525. Office Fax: 918-647-4525. Personal E-mail: bspears@okktc.org.

SPEARS, DIANE SHIELDS, art director, elementary school educator; b. Seattle, May 21, 1942; d. Richard Keene McKinney and Dorothy Jean (Shields) Thacker; m. Howard Truman Spears, Sept. 3, 1977; 1 child, Truman Eugene. BA in Art, English, Edn., Trinity U., 1964; MA in Christian Counseling, San Antonio Theol. Sem., 1986, D of Christian Edn., 1988. Cert. tchr. secondary edn., elem. edn., indi. supervision, Tex. Instr. ESL Dliel-Geb (Def. Lang. Inst.), San Antonio, 1973-74, Ceta/Ace Bexar County Sch. Bd., San Antonio, 1975-78; tchr. elem. edn., art, music New Covenant Faith Acad., San Antonio, 1983-89; instr. ESL Jewish Family Svc., San Antonio, 1991; from tchr. elem. art to dir. visual arts Edgewood Ind. Sch. Dist., San Antonio, 1992—2002, dir. visual arts, 2002—04; tchr. Pipe Creek Christian Sch., Tex., 2004—06. Owner, operator Art For Kings, San Antonio, 1985—2004, Spears Art Studio, Inco., 2004—05. Illustrator teacher-created materials-lit. activities for young children, 1989-90; author: (art curriculum) Art for Kings, 1987; editor: (art curriculum) Edgewood Ind. Sch. Dist. Elem. Art Curriculum, 1993; exhibited in group shows at Charles and Emma Frye Mus., Seattle, 1966, 68, Centro Cultural Aztlan Galerie Expression, 1998 (Best of Show 1998). Dir. intercessory prayer New Covenant Fellowship, San Antonio, 1980-90. Recipient award for painting and graphics, San Antonio, 1996-98. Mem.: San Antonio Art Edn. Assn. (1st pl. 1995), Tex. Art Edn. Assn. (1st pl. graphics divsn. 1995), Nat. Mus. for Women in Arts (charter). Republican. Avocations: water-skiing, motorcycle riding, sewing, writing. Home: 264 Mountain Dr Lakehills TX 78063-6725 Office Phone: 830-612-2585. E-mail: shieldsandspears@earthlink.net.

SPEARS, JAE, state legislator; b. Latonia, Ky. d. James and Sylvia (Fox) Marshall; m. Lawrence E. Spears; children: Katherine Spears Cooper, Marsha Spears-Duncan, Lawrence M., James W. Student, U. Ky. Reporter Cin. Post, Cin. Enquirer newspapers; rschr. Stas. WLW-WSAI, Cin.; tchr. Jiya Gakuen Sch., Japan; lectr. U.S. Mil. installations East Anglia, England; del. State of W.Va., Charleston, 1974-80; mem. W.Va. Senate, Charleston, 1980-1993. Mem. vis. com. W.Va. Extension and Continuing Edn., Morgantown, 1993-2000, W.Va. U. Sch. Medicine, 1992—; with state sen., 1980-93; apptd. to Jud. Hearing Bd., 1993-2000. Chmn. adv bd. Sta. WNPB, 1992-94; congl. liaison Am. Pub. TV Stas. and Sta. WNPB-TV, 1992-97; mem. coun. W.Va. Autism Task Force, Huntington, 1981-90; mem. W.Va. exec. bd. Literacy Vols. Am., 1986-90, 94—, pres., 1990-92; mem. Gov.'s State Literacy Coun., 1991-97; bd. dirs. Found. Ind. Colls. W.Va., 1986—; mem. regional adv. com. W.Va. Gov.'s Task Force for Children, Youth and Family, 1989; mem. USS W.Va. Commn., 1989; mem. exec. com. W.Va. Employer Support Group for Guard and Res., 1989; mem. steering com., 1990-92. Decorated Purple Heart (hon.); recipient Susan B. Anthony award NOW, 1982, edn. award Profl. Educators Assn. W.Va., 1986, ann. award W.Va. Assn. Ret. Sch. Employees, 1985, Meritorious Svc. award W.Va. State Vets. Commn., 1984, Vets. Employment and Tng. Svc. award U.S. Dept. Labor, 1984, award W.Va. Vets. Coun., 1984; named Admiral in N.C. Navy, Gov. of N.C., 1982, hon. Brigadier Gen. W.Va. N.G., 1984, One of 11 Women Pioneers of W.Va. Legislature, W.Va. U. Inst. for Pub. Affairs, 1997, Disting. West Virginian, Gov. W.Va., 2005, Comm. award W.Va. Womens Comm., 2006. Mem. DAR, VFW (aux.), Bus. and Profl. Women (Woman of Yr. award 1978), Nat. League Am. Pen Women (Pen Woman of Yr. 1984), Nat. Order Women Legislators, Am. Legion (aux.), Delta Kappa Gamma, Alpha Xi Delta. Democrat. Home and Office: PO Box 98 Shinnston WV 26431 Office Phone: 304-558-0070.

SPEARS, JAMES GRADY, small business owner; b. Port Arthur, Tex., July 20, 1941; s. John Grady and Dorothy Nell (Haney) S. Grad. high sch., Port Arthur. Adminstr. Child Health & Devel. Studies, Oakland, Calif., 1962—69; sales mgr. Sunshine Biscuits Inc., Houston, 1969—75; owner, pres. S.W. Tookie Inc./Tookie's Restaurant, Seabrook, Tex., 1975—. Mem. Greater Houston Conv. and Visitors Bur., Clear Lake Conv. Visitors Bur. Mem. with USN, 1959-62. Mem. Tex. Restaurant Assn., Houston Restaurant Assn., Seabrook Assn., Old Seabrook Assn. Republican. Roman Catholic. Avocations: collectibles, fine art, antiques, listening to records, self improvement. Home: 16310 Hickory Knoll Dr Houston TX 77059-5311 Office: SW Tookie Inc/Tookie's Restaurant 1202 Bayport Blvd Seabrook TX 77586-3406

SPEARS, JAMES M(IT), lawyer; b. San Benito, Tex., Dec. 1, 1952; BA, Tex. Tech. Univ., 1975; JD, Univ. Tex., 1978. Bar: Tex. 1978, D.C. 1998. Dep. asst. atty. gen. Lands & Natural Resources div., U.S. Dept. Justice, Washington, 1983—84, Civil div., U.S. Dept. Justice, Washington, 1985—88; gen. counsel FTC, Washington, 1993—94; ptnr. litigation dept. & head antitrust & trade litigation practice group Ropes & Gray, Washington. Contbr. articles to profl. jours. Office: Ropes & Gray One Metro Ctr Suite 900 700 12th St NW Washington DC 20005-3948 Office Phone: 202-508-4681. Office Fax: 202-508-4650. Business E-mail: mit.spears@ropesgray.com.

SPEARS, LOUISE ELIZABETH, minister, secondary school educator; b. Liberty, Miss., Feb. 2, 1945; d. Willie and Alice Gray Spears; 1 child, Guy Alice. BSc, Alcorn State U., 1966; MSc, Ind. U., 1969; PhD, U. N. Colo., 1975; MDiv, Garrett-Evang. Theol. Sem., 1983. Cert. African Meth. Episcopal Ch., 90; Tchr. Ga. Tchr. Hazlehurst H.S., Hazlehurst, Miss., 1967—68; tchg. asst. Ind. U., Bloomington, Ind., 1968—70; tchr. Ala. State U., Montgomery, Ala., 1970—72, Ky. State U., Frankfort, Ky., 1972—75, Jackson State U., Jackson, Miss., 1975—81; pastor United Meth. Ch., Keosauqua, Iowa, 1983—85, Detroit, 1985—88; tchr. Clarke County Sch. Dist., Athens, Ga., 1998—2004; pastor African Meth. Episcopal Ch., various, Ga., 2000—. Reach Out Real Estate, Atlanta, 1989—92; academic adminstr. Emmanuel Bible Coll., Macon, Ga., 1992—93; substitute tchr. Atlanta Pub. Sch., Atlanta, 1994—98; co-chmn. Augusta Ga. Conf., Augusta & Edn., 2001, mem. stewardship commn.; fin. coord. Reach Out and Touch Club, Inc., 2002—03; mem. Athens-Clarke County Commn. on Disability, 2003; mem. career and tech. edn. exec. adv. bd. Athens-Clarke County Commn. on Disability; mem. career and tech. edn. adv. bd. Tech. Prep Awareness, 2003, mem. sub-com., 03. Co-author: National Poetry Book, 1995; featured cover story: Zebra Mag., 2001. Bd. dir. Reach Out & Touch Club, Inc., Athens, 2001—. Recipient Cmty. Svc. award, Reach Out & Touch Club, Inc., Georgia. Mem.: NEA, Nat. Assn. Social Studies, Reach Out and Touch Club (fin. coord.). Democrat. African Meth. Episcopal. Avocations: reading, travel, writing. Home: 10 Huntington Ln Crawford GA 30630-2333

SPEARS, ROBERT FIELDS, lawyer; b. Tulsa, Aug. 1, 1943; s. James Ward and Berneice (Fields) S.; m. Jacquelyn Castle, May 10, 1961; children: Jeff, Sally. BBA, Tex. Tech. U., 1965; JD, U. Tex., 1968. Bar: Tex. 1968. Assoc. Rain, Harrell, Emery, Young & Doke, Dallas, 1968-73, ptnr., 1974-87, Locke Purnell Rain Harrell, Dallas, 1987-91; gen. counsel Fin. Industries Corp., Austin, Tex., 1991-96; gen. counsel, sec. Lone Star Techn. Inc., Dallas, 1996—. Pres. Sr. Citizens of Greater Dallas, 1988. Mem. ABA, Tex. Bar Assn., Dallas Bar Assn., Dallas County Club, Phi Delta Phi. Republican. Baptist. Avocation: tennis. Office: Lone Star Technologies Inc PO Box 803546 Dallas TX 75380-3546 Office Phone: 972-770-6419. E-mail: speers@lonestartech.com.

SPEARS, SALLY, lawyer; b. San Antonio, Aug. 29, 1938; d. Adrian Anthony and Elizabeth (Wylie) S.; m. Tor Hultgreen, July 15, 1961 (div. Jan. 1983); children: Dagny Elizabeth, Sara Kirsten, Kara Spears. BA, U. Tex., 1960, LLB, 1965. Bar: Tex. 1961, Ill. 1971. Practice law, Stamford, Conn., 1966-67, Chgo., 1970-71, Northbrook, Ill., 1972-73, Toronto, Ont., Canada, 1973-81; assoc. firm Cummings & Lockwood, Stamford, 1966-67, Kirkland & Ellis, Chgo., 1970-71; sr. atty. Allstate Ins. Co., Northbrook, Ill., 1971-73; gen. counsel, sec. Reed Paper Ltd., Reed Ltd., Toronto, 1973-78, Denison Mines Ltd., Toronto, 1978-81; pvt. practice law San Antonio, 1981—. Apptd. by Sec. of Def. to serve on Def. Adv. Com., Women in the Svcs., 1997—99. Author: Call Sign Revlon: The Life and Death of Navy Fighter Pilot Kara Hultgreen, 1998. Mem. Tex. Bar Assn., San Antonio Bar Assn., Bankruptcy Bar Assn., Bexar County Women's Bar Assn., San Antonio Country Club, The Club at Sonterra. Home: 433 Evans Ave San Antonio TX 78209-3725 Office: Ste 106 8151 Broadway San Antonio TX 78209-1938 Office Phone: 210-826-7020. Personal E-mail: sespears@swbell.net.

SPEAS, BRUCE ORBURN, theater educator; b. Orburn Lee Speas. BA, U. Richmond; MFA, Va. Commonwealth U.; MA, Bowling Green U. Mng. dir. Raft Theatre, N.Y.C., 1981—89; instr. Longwood U., Farmville, Va., 1996—99; asst. prof. U. Tenn., Knoxville, 2000—; resident dir. Clarence Brown Theatre, Knoxville, Tenn., 2000—. Author: (theatrical play) Stitch & Yubie (Dramalogue Award, Outstanding Writing, 1990), Goodbye Henry (Barn Playwright Festival, NJ, 1988), Summer Storm (NY and LA Prodn.). Mem. panel Knoxville Arts Coun. Mem.: Southeastern Theatre Conf. (assoc.), Theatre Comm. Group (assoc.), Alpha Psi Omega, Pi Kappa Phi. Office: U Tenn 206 McClung Tower Knoxville TN 37996

SPECA, VIVIAN E., music educator, researcher; b. Gilbertsville, Pa., Nov. 25, 1937; d. William Z. and Mary J. Emery; m. Rocco J. Cotellese (dec.); children: Cara Schollenberger, Christopher Cotellese; m. John A. Speca, July 4, 1989. MusB in Edn., U. Rochester, 1959, performer's cert. in percussion, 1959. Elem. sch. tchr. Twin Valley Sch. Dist., Morgantown, Pa., 1959—63, Boyertown Sch. Dist., Pa., 1987—2001; ret., 2000. Mem. sr. choir, New Hanover, Pa., 1959—; dir. Rinder Choir, New Hanover, Pa., 2001—. Cons. Douglas '76, Gilbertsville, Pa., 1970—80. Democrat. Lutheran. Avocations: gardening, crocheting, bowling. Home: 2461 E High St N 4 Pottstown PA 19464

SPECHT, ALICE WILSON, university libraries dean; b. Caracas, Venezuela, Apr. 3, 1948; (parents Am. citizens); d. Ned and Helen (Lockwood) Wilson; m. Joe W. Specht, Dec. 30, 1972; 1 child, Mary Helen. BA, U. Pacific, 1969; MLS, Emory U., 1970; MBA, Hardin-Simmons U., 1983. Libr. social scis. North Tex. State U., Denton, 1971-73; reference libr. Lubbock (Tex.) City and County Libr., 1974-75; system coord. Big Country Libr. System, Abilene, 1975-79; assoc. dir. Hardin-Simmons U., 1981-88, dir. univ. librs., 1988—, dean univ. librs., 2002—. Apptd. Mayor's Task Force Libr. Svcs., 1995-96. Author abbliog. instrn. aids, 1981-90; editor; The College Man, For Pilots Eyes Only. Mem. mayor's task force Abilene Pub. Libr., 1995—96; mem. Libr. Sci. Art. Bd. for Tx. Recipient Boss of Yr., Am. Bus. Women's Assn., 1994. Mem.: ALA, Abilene Libr. Consortium (chair adminstrv. coun. 1990, coord. nat. conf. 1991, 1993, chair adminstrv. coun. 1994, 1998, 2002, coord. nat. conf. 2002, chair adminstrv. coun. 2006, 2006), Tex. Libr. Assn. (chair com. 1978—84, sec.-treas. coll. and univ. librs. divsn. 1993—94, legis. coun. 1994—), Texshare Ednl. Working Group (chair 1999, libr. systems act adv. bd. mem 2001—, chair 2002). Home: 918 Grand Ave Abilene TX 79605-3233 Office: Hardin-Simmons U PO Box 16195 2341 Hickory St Abilene TX 79698-6195 Business E-Mail: aspecht@hsutx.edu.

SPECHT-JARVIS, ROLAND HUBERT, fine arts educator, humanities educator, dean; b. Dortmund, Germany, Oct. 31, 1954; came to U.S., 1982; s. Otto and Waltraud Specht; m. Shawn Cecilia Jarvis, June 15, 1982; children: Alex Jarvis, Elly Jarvis. Staatsexamen in German and pedagogy, Ruhr U. Bochum, Germany, 1982, Staatsexamen in Law and German, 1982, PhD, 1988. Instr. German St. Cloud (Minn.) State U., 1982-87, asst. prof. German, 1987-89, assoc. prof. German, 1989-92, prof. German, 1992—, dir. Intigualt program dept. fgn. langs. and lit., 1984-97, chmn. and dir. fgn. langs., 1988-94, dir. quality enhancement programs State Minn., 1994-97, dean Coll. Fine Arts & Humanities, 1997—. Author: (with H. Walbruck) Deutsch Gestern und Heute, 1986, tchrs. annotated edit., 1986, audio tape program and manual, 1987, workbook, 1987, test series, 1988, Deutsch Aktuell 3 tchrs. edit., 1993, 4th edit. workbook, 1999, Compendium College of Fine Arts and Humanities, 1998, 2000, student edit., 1993, workbook, 1993, tape program manual, 1993, Microsoft Word. Textverarbeitung mit dem Macintosh, 1990, Die Ausbildung des Literarischen Diskurses Friedrich Schlegels zur Zeit der Herausgabe des Athenaeums, 1994, (with Shawn C. Jarvis and Isolde Mueller) Deutsch Aktuell 3, 1998, 5th edit., 2003. V.p., founder Förderverein Ingolstadt-St. Cloud, 1985; bd. dirs. Alexandria-St. Cloud Performing Arts Found., 1997—, St. Cloud State U. Alumni Assn., 1995, Theatre L'Homme Dieu, 1997—, St. Cloud Symphony Orch., 1998-2002, Herberger Coll. Bus., 2000—; mem. coun. Coll. of Arts and Scis., 1995. Mem. St. Cloud Rotary (sec. 1998-99, v.p. 2001-02, pres. 2002-03), Amnesty Internat. Avocations: outdoors, chess, racquetball, motorcycles. Home: 1922 9th Ave SE Saint Cloud MN 56304-2118 Office: St Cloud State Univ 720 4th Ave S Saint Cloud MN 56301-4498 Office Phone: 320-308-3093. E-mail: roland@stcloudstate.edu.

SPECK, EUGENE LEWIS, internist; b. Boston, Dec. 17, 1936; s. Robert A. and Anne (Rosenberg) S.; m. Rachel Shoshana; children: Michael Robert, Keren Sara. AB, Brandeis U., Waltham, Mass., 1958; MS, U. Mass., 1961; PhD, George Washington U., 1966, MD, 1969. Diplomate Am. Bd. Internal Medicine with subspecialty in infectious diseases. Intern N.Y. Hosp.-Cornell, 1969-70; rsch. assoc. NIH, Bethesda, Md., 1970-72; resident Barnes Hosp.-Washington U., 1972-73; instr. medicine Washington U., St. Louis, 1972-73; fellow Strong Meml. Hosp.-U. Rochester, 1973-75; instr. medicine U. Rochester, N.Y., 1973-75, asst. prof. medicine N.Y., 1975-80, U. Nev., Las Vegas, 1980-85, assoc. prof., 1985-95, prof. medicine, 1995—; dir./co-dir. infectious disease unit U. Med. Ctr. of So. Nev., Las Vegas, 1980—; ptnr. Infectious Diseases Consultants, 1983—. Cons. Clark County Health Dept., Las Vegas, 1980—, U. Med. Ctr. So. Nev., Las Vegas, 1980—, Sunrise Hosp., Las Vegas, 1980—, Valley Hosp., Las Vegas, 1980—; Am. coll. physicians gov., State Nev. Contbr. articles to profl. jours., chpts. to books. Recipient Disting. Physician award, State of Nev., 2002. Fellow ACP (elected gov. Nev.); mem. Am. Soc. Microbiology, Infectious Disease Soc. Am., Alpha Omega Alpha. Avocations: tennis, skiing, racquetball. Home: 2228 Chatsworth Ct Henderson NV 89074-5309 Office: Infectious Diseases Cons 3006 S Maryland Pkwy Ste 780 Las Vegas NV 89109-2292 Office Phone: 702-737-0740. Personal E-mail: drsduc@aol.com.

SPECK, LAWRENCE W., architect, educator; b. Houston, Apr. 22, 1949; s. H.K. and Esther (Elliot) S.; m. Cynthia Alexander, Jan. 2, 1971 (div. 1988); children: Sloan Garret, Harrison Alexander; m. Amanda Mayhew Dealey, Oct. 3, 1992. BS in Mgmt., MIT, 1971, BS in Art and Design, 1971, MArch, 1972. Registered architect, Mass. Tx. Instr. MIT, Boston, 1972-75; asst. prof. U. Tex., Austin, 1975-79, assoc. prof., 1979-84, prof., 1984—; dean U. Tex. Sch. Arch., Austin, 1993—; prin. Lawrence W. Speck Assocs., Austin, 1975—. Dir. Ctr. Study Am. Architecture U. Tex., Austin; adj. curator architecture Dallas Mus. Art, 1985-87. Editor: Architecture for the Emerging American City, 1985; author: Landmarks of Texas Architecture, 1986; co-editor: New Regionalism, 1987. Bd. dirs. Buell Ctr. Columbia U., N.Y.C., 1985-87. Fulbright Sr. scholar Council for Internat. Exchange Scholars, 1978. Fellow AIA (5 design awards Austin chpt. 1984-87); mem. Tex. Soc. of Architects (3 design awards 1986), Soc. Arch. Historians, Sigma Chi. Avocations: athletics, children's literature.

SPECK, SAMUEL WALLACE, JR., state official; b. Canton, Ohio, Jan. 31, 1937; s. Samuel Wallace Sr. and Lois Ione (Schneider) S.; m. Sharon Jane Anderson, Jan. 20, 1962; children: Samuel Wallace III, Derek Charles. BA, Muskingum Coll., 1959; postgrad., U. Zimbabwe, 1961; MA, Harvard U., 1963, PhD, 1968. Prof. polit. sci. Muskingum Coll., New Concord, Ohio, 1964-83, asst. to pres., 1986-87, exec. v.p., 1987, acting pres., 1987, 1988-99; assoc. dir. Fed. Emergency Mgmt. Agy., 1983-86; mem. Ohio Ho. of Reps., 1971-76; state senator from Ohio 20th Dist., 1977-83; dir. Dept. Natural Resources, mem. Gov.'s cabinet State of Ohio, 1999—. Bd. dirs. Camco Fin. Corp., Cambridge, Ohio, Advantage Savs. Bank; pres. Eastern Ohio Devel. Alliance, 1990-92; Fund for Improvement of Postsecondary Edn., 1990-92, chmn. 1991. Contbr. numerous articles on African and Am. govt. and pub. policy. Bd. dirs. Ohio Tuition Trust Authority, 1991-93, Internat. Ctr. for Preservation Wild Animals, 1988-99, Lake Erie Commn., 1999—; bd. dirs., chmn. Ohio Water Resources Coun. 1999-2005; mem. Great Lakes Commn., 1999—, chmn., 2002-04; mem. Ohio Power Siting Bd., 1999—; mem. Ohio Pub. Works Commn., 2003—; chmn. coun. Great Lakes water mgmt. working group, Govt. Mich., 2002-05. Recipient Outstanding Legislator award VFW/DAV/Am. Legion, Conservation Achievement award State of Ohio, Disting. Svc. award, Nat. Gov. Conf., 2004, Conservation Leadership award, Ohio Nature Conservancy. Republican. Home: 240 Greenbriar Ct Worthington OH 43085-3055 Office: Dir OH Dept of Natural Resources 2045 Morse Rd Bldg D3 Columbus OH 43229-6605

SPECK, WILLIAM T., former physician, health facility administrator; BS, Rutgers U.; MD, Wake Forest U. Sch. Medicine, 1968. Resident Columbia U., NYC, fellow, with dept. pediat. and microbiology; with dept. pediat. Case Western Reserve U., Cleve., prof., dept. pediat., chmn., dir., dept. pediat.; CEO Rainbow Babies and Children's Hosp., Cleve., 1982—92; pres., CEO Presbyn. Hosp. in NYC/Columbia-Presbyn. Med. Ctr., 1992—99; interim dir., CEO Marine Biol. Lab., Woods Hole, Mass., 2000—01, chmn., CEO, 2001—. Bd. trustees Marine Biol. Lab., 1994—; mem. MBL Corp. Office: Marine Biol Lab 7 MBL St Woods Hole MA 02543

SPECKERT, ROBERT E., engineering educator; b. Cin., July 28, 1952; s. Robert O. and Esther E. Speckert; m. Karen L. Bonno, Oct. 26, 1952; children: Robert C., Adam E., Bradley B., Alexander R. AAS, Cin. State Tech. and C.C., 1973; BS, Miami U., Oxford, Ohio, 1975; MBA, U. Cin., 1980. Cert. mfg. engr., Soc. of Mfg. Engrs. Faculty and program coord. Cin. State Tech. and C.C., 1975—85; prof. and dept. chair Miami U., Oxford, 1985—. Cons. Speckert Cons., Cin., 1975—2006. Author: (software development) LINK-UP/BCX Manufacturing Simulation. Mem.: Cin. Area Bd. of Realtors, Soc. of Mfg. Engr., Epsilon Pi Tau, Tau Alpha Pi. Office: Miami University 1601 University Blvd Hamilton OH 45011-3399 Office Phone: 513-785-3250. Office Fax: 513-785-3183. Business E-Mail: speckere@muohio.edu.

SPECKHART, DAWN SEIDNER, bone marrow transplant/leukemia psychologist; b. Miami, Fla., Mar. 8, 1971; d. Jack Edward and Judith Naomi Seidner; m. Michael Alan Speckhart, June 25, 1995; children: Logan Shay, Jordan Elizabeth. BA, Ind. U., 1989—93; MS, 1993—95, PhD, 1995—99. Licensed Psychologist Ga. 2000. Clin. psychologist Medlin Treatment Ctr., Stockbridge, Ga., 2000—02; bone marrow transplant/leukemia psychologist Northside Hosp., Atlanta, 2002—. Rsch. psychologist Northside Hosp., Atlanta, 2004—. Mem.: APA, Southeastern Psychol. Assn., Am. Psychosocial Oncology Soc., Alpha Chi Omega (social chair 1991—92, Alumni). Office: Northside Hosp 1000 Johnson Ferry Rd BMT Unit Atlanta GA 30342 Office Phone: 404-255-1930. Office Fax: 404-255-1939. E-mail: dawn.speckhart@northside.com.

SPECKMANN, GAIL ELIZABETH, artist; b. Ft. Dodge, Iowa, Sept. 29, 1951; d. Stanley Charles and Joanne Pearl (Mol) Johnson; m. Richard Thomas Speckmann, Aug. 31, 1974; children: Katherine Linnea, Benjamin Ryan BFA, Gustavus Adolphus Coll., 1973. With display dept. Wickes Furniture, Mpls., 1973; dept. mgr., asst. buyer Donaldson's Dept. Store, Mpls., 1973—74; shop mgr. European Flower Markets, West St. Paul, Minn., 1974—76, Bachman's Inc., Mpls., 1976—80, asst. store mgr. St. Paul, 1990; watercolor artist St. Paul, 1981—91, Mpls., 1991—. Artist Graphique de France, Boston, 1990—; instr. watercolor workshop, U.S. and Can., 1995—; leader painting and photography tours, Eng., 1996, 98, Scotland, 1999, Netherlands and Belgium, 2002, 2004, Netherlands, Belgium, Luxembourg, France, Germany, 2005; judge state, regional and nat. art shows Exhibited in shows at Dakota Ctr. for Arts, St. Paul, 1983, 86, Inver Hills (Minn.) C.C., 1984, Bloomington (Minn.) Art Ctr., 1989, J. Michaels Galleries, Edina, Minn., 1991, Vern Carver Gallery, Mpls., 1993, 127th internat. exhbn. Am. Watercolor Soc., 1994, Nat. Irving Shapiro Meml. Watercolor Competition, Chgo., 1995, Watercolor West Nat. Juried Exhbn., 1991, 93, 97, 2000, Arts in Harmony Nat. Juried Competition (award of Excellence, 1997, 98, Merit award 2002), Artists Minn. Ann. Exhbn., 2003, Artists del Norte, 2003, Minn. State Fair (watercolor divsn.), 2003, Extremely Minn., 2003, St. Anthony Cmty. Art Show, 2005, Creative Arts Ctr. Mentors Show, Cape Cod, 2005; author: Wet-into-Wet Watercolor: The Complete Guide to an Essential Watercolor Technique, 1995, 2d printing paperback edit., 2001 Mem. arts task force City of Maplewood (Minn.), 1987, City of Plymouth Arts Coun., 2001-02 Recipient Grumbacher award Dakota Ctr. for Arts, 1989, Grumbacher Gold Medallion award, 1997 Mem. Watercolor West (signature, 2d pl. award 1991, Brand Libr. award 1993, juried assoc. 1991—), Minn. Artists Assn. (Best of Show award 1992, 93, 96, 97), Twin Cities Watercolor Soc. (program chair 1994-96), Northstar Watercolor Soc. (bd. dirs. 1985-91, program chair 1989-91, Recognition of Svc. award 1991, Excellence award 2003), Nat. League Am. Pen Women Democrat. Lutheran. Avocations: photography, yoga, choir, reading, poetry. E-mail: gaile_speckmann@hotmail.com.

SPECTER, ARLEN, senator; b. Wichita, Kans., Feb. 12, 1930; s. Harry and Lillie (Shanin) S.; m. Joan L. Levy, June 14, 1953; children: Shanin, Stephen. Student, U. Okla., 1947-48; BA Internat. Rels., U. Pa., 1951; LLB, Yale U. 1956. Asst. counsel Warren Commn., Washington, 1964; magisterial investigator Commn. of Pa., 1965; asst. dist. atty. City of Phila., 1959-63, dist. atty., 1966-74; ptnr. Dechert Price & Rhoads, Phila., 1956-66, 74-80; US senator from Pa., 1981—. Chmn. Senate judiciary com., 2005-, Appropriations Subcom. on Labor, Health and Human Svcs. and Edn. and Related Agys., Subcom. on Agr., Rural Deve. and Related Agys., Subcom. on Transp., Subcom. on Def., Subcom. on Fgn. Opers., Jud. Subcom. on Antitrusts, Bus. Rights, and Competition, Subcom. on Immigration, Subcom. on Terrorism, Tech. and Govt. Info., Govtl. Affairs Subcom. on Internat. Security, Proliferation and Fed. Svcs., Permanent Subcom. on Investigations, Subcom. on Oversight of Govt. Mgmt., Restructuring and Svcs.; asst. counsel, Pres. Commn. on the Assassination of President Kennedy (Warren Commn.), 1964; lectr. Temple U. Law Sch., 1972-75, U. Pa. Law Sch., 1968-72 Author: Police Guide to Search and Seizure, Interrogation, and Confession, 1967, (with Charles Robins) Passion for Truth: From Finding JFK's Single Bullet to Questioning Anita Hill to Impeaching Bill Clinton, 2000; contbr. articls to profl. jours. 1st lt. USAF, 1951—53. Recipient Youth Svcs. award B'nai B'rith, 1966; recipient Sons of Italy award, 1968, Community Humanitarian award Bapt. Ch., 1969, man of Yr. award, Temple Beth Ami, 1971, N.E. Cath. High Sch. Outstanding Achievement award, 1973, Congl. award, Am. Soc. of Nephrology, 1998, Legis. of the Year award Nat. Assn. of Alcoholism & Drug Abuse Counselors, 1999, Pub. Policy Leadership award, Am. Cancer Soc., 2000, Spl. Recognition award, Am. Heart Assn., 2003, Lead On! award, Nat. Org. on Disability, 2004. Mem. ABA, Pa. Bar Assn., Phila. Bar Assn., Phi

Beta Kappa. Republican. Jewish. Office: US Senate 711 Hart Senate Office Bldg Washington DC 20510-0001 also: District Office Ste 9400 600 Arch St Philadelphia PA 19106 Office Phone: 202-224-4254, 215-597-7200. Office Fax: 202-228-1229, 215-597-0406.*

**SPECTER, RICHARD BRUCE,** lawyer; b. Phila., Sept. 6, 1952; s. Jacob E. and Marilyn B. (Kron) S.; m. Jill Ossenfort, May 30, 1981; children: Lauren Elizabeth, Lindsey Anne, Allison Lee. BA cum laude, Washington U., St. Louis, 1974; JD, George Washington U., 1977. Bar: Mo. 1977, U.S. Dist. Ct. (ea. and we. dists.) Mo. 1977, U.S. Ct. Appeals (8th cir.) 1977, Ill. 1978, Pa. 1978, U.S. Dist. Ct. (ea. dist.) Ill. 1979, U.S. Ct. Appeals (7th cir.) Cir. 1984, U.S. Dist. Ct. (cen. dist.) Calif. 1985, U.S. Ct. Appeals (9th cir.) 1986, U.S. Dist. Ct. (so. dist.) Calif. 1987, U.S. Dist. Ct. (no. dist.) Calif. 1988, U.S. Supreme Ct. 1999. Assoc. Coburn, Croft, Shepherd, Herzog & Putzell, St. Louis, 1977-79; ptnr. Herzog, Kral, Burroughs & Specter, St. Louis, 1979-82; exec. v.p. Uniqey Internat., Santa Ana, Calif., 1982-84; pvt. practice law L.A. and Irvine, Calif., 1984-87; ptnr. Corbett, Steelman, & Specter, Irvine, 1987—. Instr. Nat. Law Ctr. George Washington U. 1975. Mem. ABA, Ill. Bar Assn., Mo. Bar Assn., Pa. Bar Assn., Calif. Bar Assn. Jewish. Home: 37 Bull Run Irvine CA 92620-2510 Office: 18200 Von Karman Ave Ste 900 Irvine CA 92612-1086 Office Phone: 949-553-9266. E-mail: rspecter@corbsteel.com.

**SPECTOR, ANITA FROHMANN,** buyer; b. N.Y.C., Apr. 26, 1943; d. Ira and Minnie (Glazer) Friedman; m. Robert Frohmann, Dec. 24, 1961; 1 child, Edward Frohmann; m. Boris Spector, Apr. 21, 1985; stepchildren: Jeffrey Spector, Lori Spector Krein. BS, Adelphi U., 1984; MA, SUNY, 1992; PhD, Walden U., 1997. Buyer furniture-furnishings Colgate Palmolive Co., N.Y.C., 1983-87, buyer office supplies-forms, 1987-90, buyer fabric care packaging-household surface care packaging, 1990-95, materials sourcing project analyst, 1995-97, oral care buyer point of sale and packaging, 1997—. Mem. Colgate-Palmolive Sys. Applications Products in Data Processing (SAP) core team, 1997—, ergonomics team, 1997—, comml. print team, 2001-02, indirect materials, 2003-05; mem. adv. bd. Adelphi U.; adj. prof. Keller Grad. Sch. Mgmt., N.Y.C., 2005—, DeVry U., 2005—. Mem. adv. bd. Adelphi U. Named Disting. Alumni Adelphi U. U. Coll., 1998. Mem. AAUW, The Doctorate Assn. N.Y. Educators. Avocations: reading, travel, bicycling, music, interior decorating. Home: 4 Park Ave Apt 16C New York NY 10016-5311 Office: Colgate Palmolive Co 300 Park Ave Fl 4 New York NY 10022-7402 Office Phone: 212-310-2801. E-mail: anitaspector@aol.com.

**SPECTOR, DANIEL EARL,** historian, educator; b. Pensacola, Fla., Dec. 19, 1942; s. Joseph and Dorothy Margaret (Givens) S.; m. Esta Gelda Rappaport, Aug. 9, 1964; children: Warren Leigh, Susan Artemis (dec.). BA, George Washington U., 1963; postgrad., U. Fla., 1963-64; MA, U. Tex., 1972, PhD, 1975. Adj. instr. Jacksonville (Ala.) State U., 1975-77; chief skill qualification test br. U.S. Army Mil. Police Sch., Ft. McClellan, Ala., 1975-80; supr. edn. specialist U.S. Army Chem. Sch., Ft. McClellan, 1980-82; chief U.S. Army Chem. Sch. Standardization & Analysis Div., Ft. McClellan, 1982-84; dep. dir. U.S. Army Chem. Sch. Directorate of Tng. & Doctrine, Ft. McClellan, 1984-88; adj. prof. U. Ala., Birmingham, 1986—2001; chem. corps historian U.S. Army Chem. Sch., Ft. McClellan, 1988-94; adj. prof. Troy State U., Ft. Benning, Ga., 2003—05. Accreditation coord. U.S. Army Chem. Sch., Ft. McClellan, 1984-90; accreditation team chief So. Assn. Colls. and Schs., Atlanta, 1985-90; U.S. Army rep. EURO-NATO nuc., biol. and chem. workgroups, 1984-90. Author: Chemical School Annual Historical Reviews, 1988—90; contbr. numerous revs., articles and ency. entries to pubs. Mem. Jacksonville Kiwanis, 1959-63; NDEA fellow U. Fla., 1963-64, NDFL fellow U. Tex. 1972-73. Mem. Middle Eastern Studies Assn., Middle East Inst., Am. Hist. Assn., Soc. Mil. History, Ala. Assn. Historians, MENSA, Temple Beth-El, Scottish Rite, Hiram Lodge, Ala. Master Gardener, Legion of Honor, Chapel of Four Chaplains, Phi Alpha Theta. Democrat. Jewish. Avocations: gardening, fishing. Home: 1317 7th Ave NE Jacksonville AL 36265-1174 Personal E-mail: drspector@cableone.net.

**SPECTOR, DAVID M.,** lawyer; b. Rock Island, Ill., Dec. 20, 1946; s. Louis and Ruth (Vinikour) S.; m. Laraine Fingold, Jan. 15, 1972; children: Rachel, Laurence. BA, Northwestern U., 1968; JD magna cum laude, U. Mich., 1971. Bar: Ill. 1971, U.S. Dist. Ct. (no. dist.) Ill. 1971, U.S. Ct. Appeals (7th cir.) 1977, U.S. Ct. Appeals (4th cir.) 1984, U.S. Dist. Ct. (cen. dist.) Ill. 1984, U.S. Supreme Ct. 1999, N.Y. 2002, U.S. Ct. Appeals (2d cir.) 2002. Clk. Ill. Supreme Ct., Chgo., 1971-72; ptnr., assoc. Isham, Lincoln & Beale, Chgo., 1972-87; ptnr. Mayer, Brown & Platt, Chgo., 1987-97, Hopkins & Sutter, Chgo., 1997-2001, Schiff, Hardin LLP, Chgo., 2001—. Chmn. ABA Nat. Inst. on Ins. Co. Insolvency, Boston, 1986; co-chmn. ABA Nat. Inst. on Internat. Reins.: Collections and Insolvency, NY, 1988; chmn. ABA Nat. Inst. on Life Ins. Co. Insolvency, Chgo., 1993; spkr. in field. Editor: Law and Practice of Insurance Company Insolvency, 1986, Law and Practice of Life Insurer Insolvency, 1993; co-editor: Law and Practice of International Reinsurance Collections and Insolvency, 1988; contbr. articles to profl. jour. Mem. ABA (chair Nat. Inst. on Life Insurer Insolvency 1993), Chgo. Bar Assn., Lawyer's Club of Chgo. Office: Schiff Hardin LLP 6600 Sears Tower Chicago IL 60606 Home: 1418 N Lake Shore Dr Chicago IL 60610-1642 E-mail: dspector@schiffhardin.com.

**SPECTOR, ELEANOR RUTH,** manufacturing executive; b. NYC, Dec. 2, 1943; d. Sidney and Helen Lebost; m. Mel Alan Spector, Dec. 10, 1966; children: Nancy, Kenneth. BA, Barnard Coll., 1964; postgrad. sch. pub. adminstrn., George Washington U., 1965-67; postgrad sch. edn., Nazareth Coll., 1974. Indsl. investigator N.Y. State Dept. Labor, White Plains, 1964-65; mgmt. intern Navy Dept., Washington, 1965, contract negotiator, 1965-68, contract specialist, 1975-78, contracting officer/br. head, 1978-82, dir. div cost estimating, 1982-84 dep. asst. sec. def. for procurement Washington, 1984-91; dir. Def. Procurement, Washington, 1991-2000; v.p. contracts Lockheed Martin Corp., Bethesda, Md., 2000—. Advisor Nat. Contract Mgmt. Assn., 1984—. Recipient Def. Meritorious Civilian Svc. medal, 1986, 93, 96, Meritorious Svc. Presdl. award, 1989, 94, Disting. Civilian Svc. Presdl. award, 1990, 97, Def. Disting. Civilian Svc. medal, 1991, 94, 2000, Nat. Pub. Svc. award, 1998, Sec. Def. award for Excellence, 1997. Office: Lockheed Martin Corp MP 110 6801 Rockledge Dr Bethesda MD 20817-1877

**SPECTOR, GERSHON JERRY,** otolaryngologist, educator, researcher; b. Rovno, Poland, Oct. 20, 1937; came to U.S., 1949; naturalized, 1956; m. Patsy Carol Tanenbaum, Aug. 28, 1965. BA, Johns Hopkins U., 1960; MD cum laude, U. Md., 1964. Intern Beth Israel Hosp., Boston, 1964-65; resident in surgery Sinai Hosp., Balt., 1965-66; resident in otolaryngology Mass. Eye and Ear Infirmary, Boston, 1966-69, Peter Bent Brigham Hosp., Boston, 1968-69; teaching fellow in otolaryngology Harvard U. Med. Sch., Boston, 1968-69; assoc. physician Ill. Crippled Children's Svc., Carbondale, 1971; mem. faculty Washington U. Med. Sch., St. Louis, 1971—, assoc. prof. otolaryngology, 1974-76, prof., 1976—; chief dept. otolaryngology St. Louis County Hosp., 1971-77. Mem. staff Washington U. Med. Ctr., Barnes Hosp.; dir. temporal bone bank, 1971-81; guest examiner Am. Bd. Otolaryngology, 1975-77; rsch. cons. neurosci. group, G.D. Searle Pharm. Corp. Mem. editl. bd. Laryngoscope, 1978, editor-in-chief, 1984-94; contbr. articles to med. jours. With U.S. Army, 1969-71. Hancock scholar, 1962. Fellow ACS; mem. AAAS, AMA, Am. Acad. Ophthalmology and Otolaryngology (Honor award 1979), St. Louis Med. Soc., St. Louis County Med. Soc., Am. Coun. Otolaryngology, St. Louis Ear, Nose and Throat Club (pres. 1986), So. Med. Assn., Deafness Rsch. Found., Pan. Am. Assn. Otorhinolaryngology and Broncho Esophagology, Am. Soc. Head and Neck Surgery, Am. Univ. Otolaryngologists, Am. Laryngol., Rhinol. and Otol. Soc. (Edmund Prince Fowler award 1974), Am. Soc. Cell Biology, Electron Microscopy Soc., N.Y. Acad. Scis., Am. Assn. Anatomists, Am. Acad. Facial Plastic and Reconstructive Surgery, Am. Neuro-Otology Soc., Gesellschaft fur Neurootologie und Aequilibriometrie A.V., Barany Soc., Am. Radium Soc., Am. Assn. Acad. Surgery, Am. Fedn. Clin. Oncologic Socs., Am Otol. Soc., Acoustical Soc. Am., Am. Soc. for Neurosci., Internat. Skull Base Soc. (founding), Brazilian Skull Base Soc.

(hon.), Centurion Club, Alpha Omega Alpha, Psi Chi. Home: 7365 Westmoreland Dr Saint Louis MO 63130-4241 Office: Washington U Med Sch Saint Louis MO 63110 Office Phone: 314-362-7252. Business E-mail: spectorg@wustl.edu.

**SPECTOR, JOHANNA LICHTENBERG,** ethnomusicologist, former educator; b. Libau, Latvia; came to U.S., 1947, naturalized, 1954; d. Jacob C. and Anna (Meyer) Lichtenberg; m. Robert Spector, Nov. 20, 1939 (dec. Dec. 1941). DHS, Hebrew Union Coll.; MA, Columbia U., 1960. Rsch. fellow Hebrew U., Jerusalem, 1951-53; faculty Jewish Theol. Sem. Am., N.Y.C., 1954—, dir., founder dept. ethnomusicology, 1962-85, assoc. prof. musicology, 1966-70, Sem. prof., 1970-85, prof. emeritus, 1985—. Author: Ghetto-und Kzlieder, 1947, Samaritan Chant, 1965, Musical Tradition and Innovation in Central Asia, 1966, Bridal Songs from Sana Yemen, 1960, Jewish Music in a Changing World Vol. 1, 2001; documentary films The Samaritans, 1971, Chicago International, 1973, Middle Eastern Music, 1973, About the Jews of India: Cochin, 1976 (Cine Golden Eagle 1979), The Shanwar Telis or Bene Israel of India, 1978 (Cine Golden Eagle 1979), About the Jews of Yemen, A Vanishing Culture, 1986 (Cine Golden Eagle 1986, Blue Ribbon, Am. Film Festival 1986), 2000 Years of Freedom and Honor: The Cochin Jews of India, 1992, Margaret Mead, 1992, Columbus International, 1993; religious and folk recs. number over 10,000; contbr. articles to encys., various jours.; editorial bd. Asian Music. Fellow Am. Anthrop. Assn.; mem. Am. Ethnol. Soc., Am. Musicol. Soc., Internat. Folks Music Coun., World Assn. Jewish Studies, Yivo, Asian Mus. Soc. (v.p. 1964—, pres. 1974-78), Soc. Ethnomusicology (sec.-treas. N.Y.C. chpt. 1960-64). Home: 400 W 119th St New York NY 10027-7125

**SPECTOR, MARTIN WOLF,** lawyer; b. Phila., 1938; BA, Pa. State U., 1959; JD, U. Pa., 1962. Bar: Pa. 1962. Judge U.S. Dist. Ct., until 1967; asst. gen. counsel ARA Services, Phila., assoc. gen. counsel, 1969-76, v.p., 1976-83, gen. counsel, 1983—, formerly sr. v.p., assoc. v.p. ARAMARK, Phila., 1985—. Served to lt. USN, 1953-56. Office: ARAMARK 1101 Market St Ste 45 Philadelphia PA 19107-2988

**SPECTOR, MELBOURNE LOUIS,** retired foreign service officer; b. Pueblo, Colo., May 7, 1918; s. Joseph E. and Dora (Bernstein) S.; m. Louise Vincent, Nov. 23, 1948; 1 son, Stephen David. BA with honors, U. N.Mex., 1941. Intern U.S. Bur. Indian Affairs, 1941, Nat. Inst. Pub. Affairs, 1941; personnel asst. Office Emergency Mgmt., 1941-42; chief classification div. War Relocation Authority, 1942-43, Hdqrs. USAAF, 1943-45; employment officer UNRRA, 1945-46; pvt. employment, 1946-47; personnel officer Dept. State, 1947-49; detail Econ. Coop. Adminstrn., 1948; dep. dir. personnel Econ. Coop. Adminstrn., Marshall Plan, Paris, 1949-51; dep. dir., acting dir. personnel Econ. Coop. Adminstrn., Mut. Security Adminstrn., FOA, 1951-54; asst., dep. dir. Mission to Mexico, ICA, 1954-57, acting dir., 1957-59; chief C. Am., Mex. and Caribbean div. ICA, 1959-61; dir. Office Personnel Mgmt., AID, 1961-62; exec. dir. Bur. Inter-Am. Affairs, Dept. State, 1962-64; commd. consul gen., sec., 1964; counselor for adminstrv. affairs Am. embassy, New Delhi, India, 1964-66; seminarian Sr. Seminar Fgn. Policy, Dept. State, 1966-67; exec. dir. U.S.-Mex. Commn. for Border Devel. and Friendship, 1967-69; Am. Revolution Bicentennial Commn., 1969-71; mem. mgmt., policy and coordination staffs Dept. State, 1971-73; ret., 1973; cons., 1973—. Mem. Fgn. Svc. Grievance Bd., 1976-77; advisor Peace Corps Dir., 1979-80; exec. dir. Am. Consortium for Internat. Pub. Adminstrn., 1980-84, 93-94, dir. Marshall Plan Oral History Project, 1987-97. Mem. Cosmos Club, Am. Soc. Pub. Adminstrn., Pi Kappa Alpha, Phi Kappa Phi. Home: 5111 Connecticut Ave NW # 407 Washington DC 20008-2004

**SPECTOR, MICHAEL JOSEPH,** agribusiness executive; b. N.Y.C., Feb. 13, 1947; s. Martin Wilson and Dorothy (Miller) S.; m. Margaret Dickson, Sept. 14, 1977. BS in Chemistry, Washington and Lee U., 1968. Rsch. chemist Am. Viscose, Phila., 1968-69; pres. MJS Entertainment Co., Miami, Fla., 1970-84; also MJS Internat., Inc.; ptnr. Old Town Key West Devel. Ltd., Fla., 1977—2002. Pres. MJS Entertainment of Can., Inc., Toronto, Margo Farms, MJS Prodns., Inc., N.Y.C.; chmn., CEO Margo Caribe, Inc., Dorado, PR, 1981—, bd. dir.; pres. Costa Del Norte Devel., Inc., Dorado, 1998—; bd. dir. Goodwill Industries So. Fla., v.p. fin., 1980; bd. dir. Plz. Bank of Miami; hon. Consul Belgium in P.R., U.S. V.I., Turks & Caicos Islands, West Indies, 2000—; dir. Consular Corp. of P.R., 2002, vice-dean, 2003—04, dean, PR, 2004. Internat. judge The Floralies Exhbn., Gent, Belgium, 1995, 2000, 05; knight Sociedad Heraldica Espanola, 2003—. With AUS, 1969-70. Robert E. Lee rsch. grantee Washington and Lee U., 1967-68; named Agri-bus. Exec. of Yr., Govt. of P.R., 1999; knighted Order of King Leopold II, King of Belgium, 2005. Mem. Nat. Assn. Record Merchandisers (dir. Nova divsn., chmn. one-stop distbn. com. 1982-83), Country Music Assn., Dorado Beach Golf and Tennis Club, Bankers Club P.R., Ocean Reef Club (Key Largo, Fla.), Grove Isle Club (Coconut Grove, Fla.). Achievements include patent for synthetic stretching process. Home: Call Box 1370 Dorado PR 00646-1370 Business E-mail: mspector@margocaribe.com.

**SPECTOR, PHIL,** record company executive; b. Bronx, N.Y., Dec. 25, 1940; m. Veronica Bennett, 1968 (div. 1974); children: Gary Phillip and Louis Phillip (twins), Donte Phillip, Nicole and Phillip (twins). Student, UCLA. Producer with Atlantic Records, 1960-61; founder Philles Records, 1962; now pres. Warner-Spector Records, 1974—; also Mother Bertha Music. Mem. mus. group: Teddy Bears, 1958-59; producer records for Gene Pitney, Ike and Tina Turner, Ben E. King, the Beatles, Righteous Bros., Checkmates, Crystals, Ronettes, John Lennon, George Harrison, The Ramones, Yoko Ono, others; producer album A Concert for Bangladesh (Grammy award); composer songs including You've Lost That Lovin' Feelin' (2 million performances; named most performed song in U.S. broadcasting history 1997); others; appeared in films Tami, Easy Rider; prod., TV documentary film A Giant Stands 5 Ft. 7 In.; prod. film That Was Rock. Named to Rock and Roll Hall of Fame, 1989; named Country Music Song of Yr. Songwriter and Pub. for To Know Him Is To Love Him, 1989; recipient lifetime achievement award U. Calif., Berkeley, 1994, Phila. award Phila. Music Alliance, 1994 (includes star on Phila.'s Walk of Fame), Trustees award (Grammy) NARAS, 2000; inducted into Songwriters Hall of Fame, 1996. Office: c/o Warner-Spector Records Inc 686 S Arroyo Pky Pasadena CA 91105-3233 E-mail: phillesrecords@earthlink.net.

**SPECTOR, PHILLIP LOUIS,** lawyer; b. LA, July 15, 1950; s. Everett L. Spector and Rebecca (Horn) Newman; m. Carole Sue Lebbin, May 11, 1980; children: Adam, David. Student, U. Birmingham, Eng., 1970—71; BA with highest honors, U. Calif., Santa Barbara, 1972; M in Pub. Policy, Harvard U., 1976, JD magna cum laude, 1976. Bar: Calif. 1976, D.C. 1978, U.S. Ct. Appeals (D.C. cir.) 1983, U.S. Supreme Ct. 1983, U.S. Dist. Ct. D.C. 1985. Law clk. U.S. Ct. Appeals (2d cir.), Brattleboro, Vt., 1976-77; law clk. to U.S. Supreme Ct., 1977-78; assoc. asst. to Pres. U.S., 1978-80; assoc. Verner, Liipfert, Bernhard & McPherson, 1980-83; ptnr. Goldberg & Spector, 1983-92, Paul, Weiss, Rifkind, Wharton & Garrison, Washington, 1992—2005, mng. ptnr. Washington office, 2001—05; exec. v.p., gen. counsel Intelsat Holdings, Ltd., 2005—. Bd. dirs. Global Relief Techs., LLC, Appleseed Found. Co-author: Communications Law and Practice, 1995, Communications and Techology Alliances: Business and Legal Issues, 1996; contbr. articles to profl. jours. Mem. Coun. on Fgn. Rels., N.Y.C., 1980-85; moot ct. judge Nat. Assn. Attys. Gen., Washington, 1987—; adviser Dem. caucus U.S. Ho. Reps., Washington, 1981-83; speechwriter, podium prodr. Dem. Nat. Convs., N.Y.C., 1980, Phila., 1982, San Francisco, 1984, Atlanta, 1988, N.Y.C., 1992, Chgo., 1996, L.A., 2000, Boston, 2004. Recipient Disting. Achievement in Pub. Svc. medal U. Calif., Santa Barbara, 1981, Close-Up Found. awards Via Satellite Mag., Vol. Recognition award Nat. Assn. Attys. Gen., 1993; named Leading Satellite Specialist in Washington, European Counsel, 2000. Mem. ABA (former chair internat. comm. law com.), Fed. Commns. Bar Assn., Bethesda Country Club, Addison Res. Country Club, Phi Beta Kappa. Jewish. Office: Intelsat 3400 International Dr Washington DC 20008-3006 Office Phone: 202-944-7340. Business E-mail: phil.spector@intelsat.com.

**SPECTOR, ROBERT DONALD,** language educator; b. N.Y.C., Sept. 21, 1922; s. Morris and Helen (Spiegel) S.; m. Eleanor Helen Luskin, Aug. 19, 1945; children: Stephen Brett, Eric Charles. BA, L.I. U., 1948, DHL, 1994; MA, NYU, 1949; PhD, Columbia U., 1962. Instr. L.I. U., Bklyn., 1948-59, asst. prof., 1959-62, asso. prof., 1962-65, prof. English, 1965-94, chmn. senate, 1966-67, 69-70, chmn. dept., 1970-75, dir. humanities and comm. arts, 1975-84, coord. div. of humanities and div. of comms. and performing arts, 1990—, dir. humanities, 1984-90, prof. emeritus, 1993—. Editor, cons. Johnson Reprint Corp., 1967-84 Author: English Literary Periodicals, 1966, Tobias George Smollett, 1968, updated edit., 1989, Pär Lagerkvist, 1973, Arthur Murphy, 1979, Tobias Smollett: A Reference Guide, 1980, The English Gothic, 1983, Backgrounds to Restoration and Eighteenth-Century English Literature, 1989, Political Controversy, 1992, Smollett's Women, 1994, Samuel Johnson and the Essay, 1997, Love Poems & Others, 1998, Mélange a Deux, 1999, Nature's Bounty in Brooklyn, 2000, Poems of Love and Laughter, 2003, New Poems, 2003; editor: Essays on the Eighteenth Century Novel, 1965, Great British Short Novels, 1970, 9 other vols. English and Am. lit., revs. and articles, poetry, fiction. Trustee L.I. U., 1969-70; chmn. George Polk Award Com., 1977—. Served with USCGR, 1942-46. Recipient L.I. U. Trustee award for scholarly achievement, 1978, Tristram Walker Metcalfe Alumnus of Year, 1981; Swedish Govt. travel and research grantee, 1966; fellow Huntington Library, 1974; fellow Folger Library, 1975; fellow Newberry Library, 1976 Mem. MLA, Am.-Scandinavian Found. (publs. com. 1962-84), P.E.N., Acad. Am. Poets. Home: 1761 E 26th St Brooklyn NY 11229-2405

**SPECTOR, ROSE,** former state supreme court justice; BA, Columbia U.; JD, St. Mary's Law, 1965. Judge County Ct. at Law 5, 1975-80, 131st Dist. Ct., 1981-92; justice Tex. Supreme Ct., 1993-98; atty. Bickerstaff, Heath, Pollan, Kever & McDaniel, L.L.P., Austin, Tex., 1998—. Office Phone: 512-404-7867.

**SPECTOR, WARREN J.,** investment company executive; m. Margaret Whitton. Grad., Duke U. Exec. v.p., head fixed income group The Bear Stearns Companies, Inc., N.Y.C., 1997—; pres., co-COO The Bear Stearns Companies, N.Y.C., 2001—. Vol. Gift of Life Bone Marrow Registry; chmn., Wall Street div. United Jewish Appeal; bd. dirs. New York Shakespeare Festival. Named a Forty Under Forty, Crain's NY Business, 1996. Achievements include youngest Life Master in contract bridge, 1974. Avocations: golf, bridge. Office: 383 Madison Ave New York NY 10179

**SPEECE, RICHARD EUGENE,** civil engineer, educator; b. Marion, Ohio, Aug. 23, 1933; s. Irvin Ward S. and Desta May (Speece); m. Jean Margaret Edscorn, Nov. 15, 1969; children: Eric Jordan, Lincoln Dana. BCE, Fenn. Coll., 1956; M of Engring., Yale U., 1958; PhD, MIT, 1961. Assoc. prof. civil engring. U. Ill., Urbana, 1961-65; prof. N.Mex. State U., 1965-70, U. Tex., Austin, 1970-74; Betz chair prof. environ. engring. Drexel U., Phila., 1974-88; Centennial prof. Vanderbilt U., Nashville, 1988—. Vis. scholar Cambridge (Eng.) U., 1994; cons. to govt., industry. Contbr. articles to profl. jours.; patentee in field. Recipient hon. mention for best paper Trans. Am. Fisheries Soc., 1973, Founders award Assn. Environ. Engrs. and Sci. Profs., 2005. Mem. ASCE (J. James Cross medal 1983), Assn. Environ. Engring. and Sci. Profs. (disting. lectr. 1978, trustee 1981-83, Disting. Faculty award 1970, Engring. Sci. award 1982, Founders award 2005, 06), Am. Soc. Microbiologists, Water Environ. Fedn. (Harrison Prescott Eddy medal 1966), U.S. ANC (Founders award 1991), Internat. Assn. on Water Pollution Rsch. and Control. Office: Vanderbilt U Dept Civil Engring Nashville TN 37235 Office Phone: 615-343-6328. E-mail: dick.speece@vanderbilt.edu.

**SPEED, CYNTHIA AGNES,** retired mathematics professor; d. Carter Coleman and Lillian Jeannette Speed. BA, Calif. State U., Sacramento, 1962; MA, Stanford U., 1967. C.C. Supr. credential Calif., 1980, C.C. Instr. credential Calif., 1973, gen. secondary tchg. credential Calif., 1963. Tchg. asst. in ednl. stats. U. of Calif., Berkeley, Calif., 1963; math. instr. Hiram W. Johnson Sr. H.S., Sacramento, 1963—67, John F. Kennedy Sr. H.S., Sacramento, 1967—69; math. lectr. Calif. State U., Sacramento, 1969—69, Calif. Poly. State U., San Luis Obispo, Calif., 1969—71; math. instr. Santa Rosa Jr. Coll., Calif., 1973—73; math. instr. and dept. chair Mendocino Coll., Ukiah, Calif., 1973—2003; ret., 2003. Exec. com. mem. Tech. in the Redwoods Conf., Ukiah, Calif., 1988—89; course descriptors com. mem. Calif. Articulation Number Sys., Sacramento, 1986—88; chairperson, creator, and organizer Math. Contest for Jr. and Sr. H.S. Students in Mendocino and Lake Counties, Ukiah, Calif., 1975—79. Author: (computer program) Technology in the Redwoods Computer Contest Prize Winners, Lake View Water Co. Billing Program, Black Bart Trail Rd. Assn. Dues Assessment Program. V.p. and mem. Lake View Mut. Water Co., Redwood Valley, Calif., 1977—; treas. and mem. Black Bart Trail Rd. Assn., Redwood Valley, Calif., 1977—. Mem.: AAUW, NEA, Cath. Alumni Club Sacramento (treas. 2005—), Calif. Ret. Tchrs. Assn., Calif. Teachers Assn., Nat. Coun. of Teachers of Math., Calif. Math. Coun. (pres. found.), Math. Assn. of Am., Calif. Math. Coun., Cmty. Colls. Found. (pres. 2005—), Calif. State U. Sacramento Alumni Assn., Stanford Alumni Assn., Delta Kappa Gamma. Roman Catholic. Avocations: piano, swimming, golf, dance, travel. Home: 1232 43rd St Sacramento CA 95819 Office: 4949 Black Bart Trail Redwood Valley CA 95470 Office Phone: 916-448-1519. Personal E-mail: sac67449@saclink.csus.edu. Business E-mail: cspeed@mendocino.edu.

**SPEEGLE, LAURA ANN,** elementary school educator; d. James William and Mary Lou Speegle; 1 child, Kimberly Lynn Akers. MA in Edn., Wayne State U., 2003. Cert. tchr. Mich. Educator Detroit Pub. Schs., 1993—. Sch. improvement com. Carl T. Rowan Elem., Detroit, 1994—2001; team leader NASA Explorer Schs., 2005—; sci. adv. com. Mich Dept Edn. Lansing, 2001 . Constrn. com. vol. Habitat for Humanity, Detroit, 1998—2005; tutor Macomb (Mich.) Reading Ptnrs., 2001—02. Recipient Educator Achievement award, Booker T. Washington Bus. Assn., 1998; Target Tchr. scholar, Target Inc., 1999, Detroit Urban Systemic Initiative grantee, Detroit Pub. Schs., 1999—2000, Explorer Sch. grantee, NASA, 2005—. Mem.: Nat. Assn. for Edn. of Young Child, Mich. Sci. Tchr. Assn., Courville Girls Running Club (leader 2004—05). Democrat. Avocations: running, volleyball, weightlifting. Office: Detroit Pub Schs Courville Elem 18040 St Aubin Detroit MI 48234 Office Phone: 313-866-3000. Home Fax: 313-754-4106; Office Fax: 313-866-3011. Personal E-mail: lauraspeegle@sbcglobal.net.

**SPEER, BROWNLOW MAIN,** lawyer; b. Delhi, N.Y., Aug. 24, 1938; s. James Robert and Elizabeth Main Speer; m. Doris Pulver Speer, Jan. 22, 1965; children: James, Andrew(dec.). BA, Haverford Coll., Pa., 1960, Oxford U., Eng., 1962, MA, 1969; JD, Harvard Law Sch., Cambridge, 1970. Bar: Mass. 1970, U.S. Dist. Ct., Dist. Mass. 1971, U.S. Ct. Appeals, 1st Circuit 1974, U.S. Supreme Ct. 1995. Assoc. Palmer & Dodge, Boston, 1970—72; staff atty. Lawyers' Com. for Civil Rights, Boston, 1974—74; dir. of tng. Com. for Pub. Counsel Svcs., 1984—. Co-author (with Blumenson and Kanstroom): Massachusetts Criminal Practice, 2001; co-author: (with Herrmann) (jour. publ.) Facing the Accuser: Ancient and Medieval Precursors of the Confrontation Clause, 2003—. Pres., bd. mgrs. First Parish in Waltham (Mass.) U-U, 1995—97; bd. dirs. Waltham (Mass.) Alliance to Create Housing, 2003—; publicity com. Cmty. Works, Boston, 2003—; with Otto M. Stanfield Law Scholarship Com., 2005—. With U.S. Army, 1962—66. Recipient Mass. Super Lawyer, 2005, Kutak-Dodds Defender prize, Nat. Legal Aid and Defender Assn., 2005. Mem.: Boston Bar Assn. (mem. coun. 1986—89, John G. Brooks award 1996), ABA, Mass. Bar Assn., Nat. Assn. Criminal Def. Lawyers, Mass. Assn. Criminal Def. Lawyers. Democrat. Unitarian Universalist. Avocations: legal history, language study. Home: 141 Barbara Rd Waltham MA 02453 Office: Com for Pub Coun Svcs 44 Bromfield St Boston MA 02108 Office Fax: 617-988-8485. Business E-mail: bspeer@publiccounsel.net.

**SPEER, DAVID BLAKENEY,** industrial executive; b. Sault Ste. Marie, Ont., Apr. 6, 1951; s. Richard Norwood and Mary (Davis) S.; m. Barbara Ann Brugenhemre, June 22, 1974; children: Blake, Sarah. BS in Indsl. Engring.,

Iowa State U., 1973; MBA, Northwestern U., 1977. Sales engr. Precision Paper, Wheeling, Ind., 1976-78, sales mgr., 1976-78; regional sales mgr. ITW Buildex, Itasca, Ill., 1978-81, nat. sales mktg. mgr., 1981-84, v.p., gen. mgr., 1984-92, ITW Paslode, Lincolnshire, Ill., 1992; group v.p., constrn. products Illinois Tool Works Inc. (ITW), 1994—95, exec. v.p. global construction products bus. Glenview, Ill., 1995—2004, exec. v.p. finishing systems bus. 1997—2004, exec. v.p. global Wilsonart laminate bus. unit 2003—04, pres., 2004—, CEO, 2005—, chmn., 2006—. Bd. dirs. Rockwell Automation, Inc. Advisory bd. Northwestern U. Master of Mgmt. and Mfg. program. Mem. Am. Mgmt. Assn., Am. Mktg. Assn., Am. Soc. Indsl. Engrs., Midwest Indsl. Mfg. Assn. Office: Ill Tool Works Inc 3600 W Lake Ave Glenview IL 60025-5811*

**SPEER, JACK ATKESON,** publisher; b. Wichita, Kans., July 3, 1941; s. Jack Shelley and Shannon C. Speer; m. Judith Ann Fuller, Aug. 5,1967; children: Martin Fuller, Elizabeth Speer Goodwin. BS in Bus. Adminstrn., Kansas. State U., 1966, ML, 1967; postgrad., U. Mo., 1967, U. So. Calif., 1969; IBM Pres.'s Class, Harvard U., 1980. Mem. advt., editorial, mech. staffs Wichita Eagle-Beacon, 1954-64; editorial asst. Emporia (Kans.) Gazette, 1964-65; supr. libr. data processing Kans. State U., Emporia, 1965-67, mgr. data processing ctr. Manhattan, 1967-69; mgr. systems and programming John Wiley Inc.-Becker & Hayes Inc., Bethesda, Md., 1969-72; dir. libr. info. systems Informatics Inc. Info. Systems Group, Rockville, Md., 1972-77; v.p. ops. Arcata Real Estate Data Inc., Miami, Fla., 1977-79; mgr. electronic info. systems Arcata Publs. Group, Norwalk, Conn., 1979-83; v.p. mktg./sales, data imaging group The William Byrd Press, Richmond, Va., 1983-84; sr. v.p. ops. NewsBank Inc., New Canaan, Conn., 1984-85; pres., pub. Buckmaster Pub., Mineral, Va., 1986—. Mem. faculty Cath. U. Am. Libr. Sch., Kans. State U. Libr. Sch.; customer adv. coun. U.S. Postal Svc., 1996—. Author: Amateur Radio Call Directory, 1982—, Buckmaster's Ann. Stockholder Reports, 1986—, Front-Page-News (CD-ROM and Internet), 1989, HamCall (CD-ROM and Internet), 1988—; compiler Libraries and Automation: A Bibliography, 1967, The Living Bible Concordance, 1972. Trustee Jefferson-Madison Regional Libr., 1990-91; commr. Louisa County Planning Commn. 1992-; pres. Louisa County Libr. Found. 2003- Mem. ALA, NRA, Am. Radio Relay League, Nat. Info. Standards Orgn. (CD-ROM com), D.C. Libr. Assn. (pres.), Rotary, Sigma Tau Gamma. Office: Buckmaster Pub 6196 Jefferson Hwy Mineral VA 23117-3425 E-mail: speerj@buck.com.

**SPEER, KEVIN PAUL,** surgeon; b. Evansville, Ind., June 8, 1959; m. Marcy Carlson Speer, Mar. 24, 1984; children: Casey, Kira. MD, Johns Hopkins U., 1985. Lic. physician N.C., 1992. Assoc. prof. orthopedics Duke U. Med. Ctr., Durham, NC, 1992—2000; pvt. practice Southeastern Orthopedics, Raleigh, NC, 2000—. Fellow, Am. Orthop. Assn., 1992. Fellow: AAOS. Office: Southeastern Orthopedics 3404 Wake Forest Rd Ste 201 Raleigh NC 27609 Business E-Mail: kspeer@nc.rr.com.

**SPEER, NANCY GIROUARD,** health facility administrator; b. Mankato, Minn., Sept. 14, 1941; d. Jared and Katherine (Schmitt) How; m. Robert L. Girouard, Aug. 29, 1964 (dec. Mar. 1983); children: Robert James Girouard, Mark Jared Girouard; m. David J. Speer, Dec. 21, 1985 (dec. Aug. 1999). BA, Wellesley Coll., 1963; MA in Tchg., Wesleyan U., 1965; cert. mgmt., Smith Coll., 1985. Tchr. secondary sch. Bunnell H.S., Stratford, Conn., 1964-65; tchr., class advisor Lincoln Sch., Providence, 1965-69; substitute tchr. Mankato, 1972-74; pub. info. dir. City of Mankato, 1974-78; univ. editor, dir. pub. affairs forum Mankato State U., 1978-79; comms. mgr. Humphrey Inst., U. Minn., Mpls., 1980-83, dir. external rels., 1983-87, dir. devel. and external rels., 1987-95; dir. devel. Breck Sch., Mpls., 1996-2000; v.p. Abbott Northwestern Hosp., Mpls., 2000—02, Planned Parenthood of Minn. and S.D., 2002—. Steering com. Minn. Meeting, Mpls., 1990-96. Contbr. articles to mag. and periodicals; photographer for publ. and newspapers. Bd. dir. Minn. Newspaper Found., St. Paul, 1985-91, chair, 1990-91, bd. dir., vice-chair Cabrini House, Mpls., 1993-97; bd. dir., sec. Minn. Ctr. for Book Arts, Mpls., 1990-97; bd. dir. Minn. Landmark Ctr., St. Paul, 1994-2000; dir. Minn. Women's Campaign Fund, Mpls., 1994-2000, co-pres. bd., 1997; vice chair, bd. dir. Loft Lit. Ctr., 2000—; vice-chair Met. Airport Commn., 1999-2003; trustee Lake Forest Acad.; bd. mem. Minn. Advocates Human Rights. Bush Leader fellow, 1985-87, Ferry Hall Woman of Distinction, 2006. Avocations: literature, nature, books.

**SPEER, RICHARD JOHN,** security consultant; b. Oxnard, Calif., Aug. 21, 1958; s. Richard McCord Speer and Betty Jean Wilson. Grad. H.S., Las Vegas, Nev. Enlisted U.S. Army, 1976, advanced through grades to sgt. first class, 1990, infantryman 82nd Airborne Divsn. Ft. Bragg, NC, 1976—81, infantry squad leader, 1981—87, infantry squad leader 4th Infantry Divsn. Ft. Carson, Colo., 1987—88, heavy weapons specialist Spl. Forces Ft. Bragg, 1988—94, project mgr. spl. projects, 1995—98, ret., 1998; ops. support mgr., nuclear security cons. Securitas Security Svcs., NJ, 1998—. Life mem. Rep. Nat. Com., Washington, 1994-, Nat. Rep. Congl. Com., 2003-, Nat. Rep. Senatorial Com., 2003-, Rep. Presdl. Task Force, 2005—. Decorated Army Commendation medal 3rd award U.S. Army, 1984, Meritorious Svcs. medals U.S. Army, 1991, 96, 98. Mem. Heritage Found., N.Am. Hunting Club (life), Am. Legion. Avocation: amateur philatelist. E-mail: rspeersecuritas@aol.com.

**SPEERS, ROLAND ROOT, II,** lawyer; b. Jacksonville, Fla., Oct. 8, 1933; s. Roland Root and Alice (Calkins) S.; m. Florence Briscoe, Dec. 18, 1954; children: Kirsten, Guy, Gina Marie. BA cum laude, UCLA, 1955, JD, 1958. Bar: Calif. 1958, D.C. 1978. Dep. commr. corps. Calif. Dept. Corps., Los Angeles, 1958-59; sec., gen. counsel Suburban Cos.. Pomona, Calif., 1959-64; sec. Amcord, Inc., Los Angeles, 1964-66, asst. to pres., 1968, v.p. corp. devel., 1969, v.p., gen. counsel Newport Beach, Calif., 1970, sr. v.p., 1971, exec. v.p., 1972-75, pres., 1975-94; ptnr. Speers, Dana, Teal Balfour & MacDonald, Costa Mesa, Calif., 1977-97. Dir. Logicon, Inc., Torrance, Calif., Twelve Eleven Press, Newport Beach, Calif. Co-author: The Malloy Chronicles: The Hidden Empire, 2003, The Malloy Chronicles: The Rheingold Legacy, 2006, The Malloy Chronicles: The Catalyst, 2006, Trustee Pitzer Coll., Pomona, 1975-80; bd. councillors Center Pub. Affairs U. So. Calif., 1976-81; bd. dirs. Newport Harbor Art Mus., 1977-82; sr. warden St. James Episcopal Ch., 1993; mem rectors counsel St. James Anglican Ch., 2004—. Mem. D.C. Bar Assn., State Bar Assn. Calif., UCLA Alumni Assn., UCLA Law Sch. Alumni Assn., Phi Alpha Delta. Clubs: Big Canyon Country (Newport Beach).

**SPEERSTRA, KAREN M.,** former publishing executive; b. Toledo, Ohio, July 25, 1940; BA, U. Wis., 1962. Dir. music & art acquisition William C. Brown Pub., Debuke, Ill., 1981-87; tech. pub. dir. Focal Press Digitals Press Newnes & Butterworth Heinemann, Woburn, Mass., 1991-00, ret., 2000—.

**SPEERT, ARNOLD,** academic administrator, chemistry educator; b. Bronx, N.Y., June 19, 1945; s. David Jack and Dorothy Bernice (Feldman) S.; m. Myrna Goldstein, June 11, 1967; children: Alan Michael, Debra Beth. BS, CCNY, 1966; PhD, Princeton U., 1971. Asst. to dean grad. and rsch. program William Paterson Coll., Wayne, N.J., 1970-71, from asst. to assoc. prof. chemistry, 1970-80, prof., 1980-85, asst. to v.p. acad. affairs, 1971-78, assoc. dean acad. affairs, 1978-79, v.p. acad. affairs, 1979-85; pres. William Paterson U., Wayne, N.J., 1985—. Bd. dirs. State Farm Indemnity Co. Trustee Barnert Hosp., Paterson, 1986—, chmn. bd. trustees, 1998—; trustee Jewish Fedn. North Jersey, Wayne, 1986-96, YM & YWHA No. N.J., Wayne, 1988—, Respiratory Health Assn., 1990-93; bd. dirs. William Paterson Univ. Found., 1985—. Mem. Am. Assn. State Colls. and Univs. (bd. dirs. 1993-95), Tri-County C. of C. (bd. dirs. 1986-94), N.J. State Bd. Examiners, N.J. Pres.'s Coun. (chair 1996—). Home: 48 Brandon Ave Wayne NJ 07470-6032 Office: William Paterson Univ 300 Pompton Rd Wayne NJ 07470-2152

**SPEESE, MARK E.,** rental company executive; Student, We. Mich. U. Regional mgr. Thorn Americas, 1979—86; from v.p. N.J. Ops. to chmn., CEO Rent A Center, Plano, Tex., 1986—2001; chmn. Rent A Ctr., 2001—, CEO, 2001—. Bd. dirs. Rent A Ctr. Office: Rent A Center 5700 Tennyson Pkwy Plano TX 75024*

**SPEICHER, CARL EUGENE,** pathologist; b. Carbondale, Pa., Mar. 21, 1933; s. William Joseph and Elizabeth Marcella (Connolly) S.; m. Mary Louise Walsh, June 21, 1958; children: Carl E. Jr., Gregory, Erik. BS in Biology, King's Coll., 1954; MD, U. Pa., 1958; student, Sch. of Aerospace Medicine, Brooks AFB, Tex., 1969. Diplomate Am. Bd. Pathology. Intern U. Pa. Hosp., Phila., 1958-59, resident, 1959-63; chief lab. svcs. USAF Hosp., London, Eng., 1963-66, USAF Med. Ctr. Wright Patterson, Dayton, Ohio, 1966-70; dir. clin. labs. and chmn. dept. pathology Wilford Hall USAF Med. Ctr., San Antonio, 1971-77; prof. pathology Ohio State U., Columbus, 1977—2000, vice chair dept. pathology, 1992—2000, prof. emeritus dept. pathology, 2000—; dir. clin. svcs. Ohio State U. Med. Ctr., Columbus, 1977—2000; dir. clin. lab. Stoneridge Med. Ctr., Ohio State U., 2000—. Co-author: Choosing Effective Laboratory Tests, 1983; author: The Right Test, 1990, 3d edit., 1998. Col. USAF, 1956-77. Decorated Legion of Merit; fellow in med. chemistry SUNY, Syracuse, 1970-71. Mem. AMA, Ohio Soc. Pathologists, Ctrl. Ohio Soc. Pathologists, Am. Assn. for Clin. Chemistry, Assn. Clin. Scientists, Coll. Am. Pathologists, Am. Soc. Clin. Pathologists, Alpha Omega Alpha.

**SPEIDEL, JOHN JOSEPH,** public health professional, educator; b. Iowa City, Iowa, Sept. 17, 1937; s. Thomas Dennis and Edna (Warweg) Speidel; m. Melissa Jane Webster, Oct. 7, 2001; 1 child from previous marriage, Sabrina Brett. AB cum laude, Harvard U., 1959, MD, 1963, MPH, 1965. Diplomate Nat. Bd. Med. Examiners, Am. Bd. Preventive Medicine. Intern St. Luke's Hosp., N.Y.C., 1963-64; resident N.Y.C. Dept. Health, 1965-67, dep. dir. maternal and infant care project, 1966-67; chief rsch. divsn. Office Population, AID, Dept. of State, Washington, 1969-76, assoc. dir., 1977, dep. dir., acting dir. office, 1978-83; v.p. Population Action Internat. (formerly Population Crisis Com.), 1983-87, pres., 1987-95; program dir. population Hewlett Found., 1995—2003; adj. prof. Bixby Ctr. Reproductive Health Rsch. and Policy U. Calif., San Francisco, 2003—. Lectr. population and family planning Georgetown U., 1973—75. Editor (with others): (book) Female Sterilization, 1971, Hysteroscopic Sterilization, 1974, Intrauterine Devices, 1974, Control of Male Fertility, 1975, Advances in Female Sterilization Technology, 1976, Risks, Benefits and Controversies in Fertility Control, 1978, Reversal of Sterilization, 1978, Pregnancy Termination, 1979, Vaginal Contraception, 1979; contbr. articles to profl. jours. Served to maj. U.S. Army, 1967—69. Recipient Meritorious Unit citation, Office of Population, 1969—71, Arthur S. Flemming award, Washington Downtown Jaycees, 1972. Mem.: Population Assn. Am., Am. Pub. Health Assn. (Carl S. Shultz award 1982). Office: U Calif San Francisco CRHRP Dept Ob Gyn 3333 California St Ste 335 San Francisco CA 94118 Office Phone: 415-502-3928. Business E-Mail: speidelj@obgyn.ucsf.edu.

**SPEIGEL, BRENNAN MASON ROSS,** internist, gastroenterologist, researcher; b. L.A., Apr. 28, 1972; BA, Tufts U., 1994; MD, N.Y. Med. Coll., 1998; MSHS, UCLA, 2004. Asst. prof. medicine David Geffen Sch. Medicine, UCLA, 2004—. Clin. rsch. physician David Geffen Sch. Medicine, UCLA/VA Greater L.A. Healthcare Sys., 2004. Contbr. articles to profl. jours. Recipient Regal award for excellence in rsch., Janssen Esai, 2003, HSR&D Rsch. Career Devel. award, VA, 2004—; Tng. grant, NIH, 2002—04. Mem.: Am. Gastroenterol. Assn., Am. Coll. Gastroenterology, Alpha Omega Alpha, Golden Key. Office: VA/UCLA Bldg 115 Rm 215E 11301 Wilshire Blvd Los Angeles CA 90073 Business E-Mail: bspiegel@mednet.ucla.edu.

**SPEIR, WILLIAM ARTHUR, JR.,** critical care physician; b. Macon, Ga., July 18, 1939; s. William Arthur Speir and Esther Marie Garland; m. Mary Hazelton Lehmann, June 8, 1963; 1 child, Mary-Butler S. Mathieson. BS in Chemistry, U. Ga., 1961; MD, Med. Coll. Ga., 1965. Asst. prof. pulmonary medicine Med. Coll. Ga., Augusta, 1971-75, assoc. prof. pulmonary medicine, 1975-80, prof. medicine pulmonary/critical care medicine, 1980-2000, prof. emeritus medicine, 2000—, med. dir. med. ICU, 1977-79, 91-00, chief sect. pulmonary diseases, 1979-92; clin. prof. medicine Mercer U. Sch. Medicine, Macon, Ga., 2000—. Contbr. over 170 articles, abstracts to profl. jours., 4 chpts. to books. Bd. dirs. Augusta Opera Assn., 1973-80. Lt. comdr., surgeon USPHS, 1966-68. Recipient Pulmonary Acad. award Nat. Heart, Lung and Blood Inst., 1974-79, Order of St. Obscurus award RTH Laennec Assn., 1983; named Ky. Col. Fellow Am. Coll. Chest Physicians (gov. for Ga. 1998-2002, bylaws com. 1993-99, steering com. sect. on respiratory disease physiology 1984-86, com. undergrad. med. edn. 1976-79, pres. So. chpt. 1980-81, 93-94, Disting. Faculty award 1991), Am. Coll. Critical Care Medicine; mem. Am. Thoracic Soc. (edn. com. 1977-81, councilor-at-large 1980, Disting. Educator award 1972), So. Med. Assn. (chmn. sec. chest diseases 1980-81, 93-94, Paul A. Turner Meml. Lectr. award 1983, 86), Soc. Critical Care Medicine (mem. grad. med. fellowship com. 2004—), Sovereign Mil. Order Temple Jerusalem, Phi Rho Sigma Med. Soc. Episcopalian. Avocations: painting, writing, cooking, music, gardening. Office Phone: 706-738-7953. Personal E-mail: bandmspeir@comcast.net

**SPEIRN, STERLING K.,** foundation administrator; married; children: Paolo, Daniel. BA in Polit. Sci., Stanford U., 1970; JD, U. Mich., 1973. Tchr., counselor Univ. Sch., Shaker Heights, Ohio, 1974-76; law clk. to Judge Paul Merlin Office Hearings and Appeals U.S. Dept. Interior, Washington, 1977-78; staff atty. North Ctrl. Legal Assistance Program, Durham, NC, 1979-81; dep. dir. Humboldt Open Door Clinic Cmty. Health Ctr., Arcata, Calif., 1982-85; intern Peninsula Cmty. Found., Burlingame, Calif., 1986; program officer cmty. leagal affairs dept. Apple Computer, Inc., Cupertino, Calif., 1986-90; program officer Peninsula Cmty. Found., San Mateo, Calif., 1990, acting exec. dir., 1991, sr. v.p., 1991-92, pres., CEO, 1992—2005; CEO W.K. Kellogg Found., Battle Creek, Mich., 2006—. Chmn. steering com. Peninsula Grantmakers, San Jose, 1987-90; presenter in field; mem. planning com. Coun. on Founds., Washington, 1991, 92. Founding co-chmn. Peninsula Partnership for Children, Youth and Families, 1994—; bd. dirs. Am. Leadership Forum of Silicon Valley, Driscoll Family Found.; bd. advisors Silicon Valley Cmty. Ventures, Entrepreneurs' Found.; mem. program com. No. Calif. Grantmakers, San Francisco, 1989-90. Fellow Am. Leadership Forum Silicon Valley. Mem. League Calif. Cmty. Founds. (chmn.), Pvt. Industry Coun. San Mateo County. Avocations: hiking, gardening, running, swimming, camping. Office: WK Kellogg Found One Michigan Ave E Battle Creek MI 49017-4012*

**SPEIRS, DEREK JAMES,** diversified financial services company executive; b. Montreal, Que., Can., Dec. 21, 1933; s. James B. and Marie C. (Hunt) S.; m. Carol Alice Cumming, Dec. 8, 1967 (div. Feb. 1989); children: Lara Marie, Gregory Ross, Scott Lawrence Gordon. B. Commerce with honors in Econs., McGill U., 1954, MBA, 1959. Chartered acct., Can., chartered corp. sec. Devel. dir. fine papers, corp. acctg. dir. Domtar, Inc., Montreal, 1970-72, dir. corp. devel., 1976-78, v.p. fin., corp. devel., 1978-89, sr. v.p. fin. and corp. devel., 1989-91; v.p., sec. fin. Consoltex, Montreal, 1972-76, bus. cons., 1991—; pres. Speirs Fin. Inc., Speirs Cons. Inc., Speirs Capital Inc. Mem. Can. Inst. Chartered Accts., Fin. Execs. Inst., C.D. Howe Inst., Lac Marois Country Club, St. James Club, Montreal Amateur Athletic Assn. Avocations: travel, skiing. Home: 365 Stanstead Ave Mont-Royal Montreal PQ Canada H3R 1X5 Office: Ste 1100 2 Pl Alexis Nihon Montreal PQ Canada H3Z 3C1 Office Phone: 514-342-3857. E-mail: speirsco@videotron.ca.

**SPEIRS, GREG,** artist; Art dir. Grooves Mag., N.Y.C., 1977—79, Changes, Inc., 1980—85. Artwork, Panther Dream Ski for K-2 Corp., 1992, Original Lithuanian Olympic Basketball Jerseys, Am. Eagle Artwork U.S. Olympic Team Bobsleds, 2002, prin. works include for Prince Albert of Monaco Monaco Olympic Bobsled Team. Named to Soc. Illustrators, N.Y., N.Y., 1975, 1976. Achievements include created first 'Extreme Sports' licensed property character, Scully. Owner: 'Scully' and 'Skullman' trademarks; artist's 'Scully' character is enshrined in Basketball Hall of Fame, Spring-

field, Mass. on Dec 07, 1993; trademarked slam dunking skeleton' image, Skullman, first seen on Lithuanian Olympic Tie Dye, Basketball Jerseys. Office: No Rules Graphics and Slammin Sports Box #125 Yonkers NY 10710 Office Phone: 800-362-1886. Personal E-mail: skully77@cloud9.net. E-mail: pdgart@cloud9.net.

**SPEIZER, FRANK E.,** physician, researcher; BA, Stanford U., 1957, MD, 1960. Prof. environ. sci. Harvard Sch. Pub. Health; Edward H. Kass prof. medicine Harvard Med. Sch., mem. environ. epidemiology program dept. environ. health, co-dir. Channing Lab. dept. medicine; sr. physician Brigham & Women's Hosp. Prin. investigator Nurses Health Study, Brigham and Women's Hosp., Harvard Med. Sch. Contbr. articles to profl. jours. Recipient Charles S. Mott prize, 2001. Mem.: Inst. Medicine. Achievements include research in the natural history of respiratory diseases, environmental risks for chronic diseases including risks for cancer and cardiorespiratory diseases. Office: Channing Lab 181 Longwood Ave Boston MA 02115 Business E-Mail: frank.speizer@channing.harvard.edu.*

**SPEJEWSKI, EUGENE HENRY,** physicist, consultant; b. East Chicago, Ind., Sept. 15, 1938; s. Henry Louis and Carrie Jane (Fuss) S.; m. Norma Beverly Seekins, June 8, 1963; children: Maria Suzanne, Beverly Anne, Andrew John, Jeannette Michelle. BS, U. Notre Dame, 1960; PhD, Ind. U., 1966. Research assoc. Ind. U., Bloomington, 1965-67, Princeton U., 1967-69, instr., 1969-71; asst. prof. Oberlin Coll., Ohio, 1971-72; dir. UNISOR, Oak Ridge Assoc. Univs., 1972-85, mgr. SDS program, 1985-86, chmn. spl. projects div., 1986-89; v.p., dir. tng. and mgmt. systems div. Oak Ridge Inst. for Sci. and Edn., 1989-95, v.p., assoc. dir. for edn. and tng. group, 1995-98; cons. Oak Ridge Nat. Lab., 1999—. Vis. prof. physics U. Tenn., Knoxville, 1981-84, adj. prof.; mem., chmn. HHIRF Users Exec. Com., Oak Ridge Nat. Lab., 1982-84; referee U.S. Dept. Energy, various profl. jours. Co-editor: Future Directions in Studies of Nuclei Far from Stability, 1980; contbr. articles to profl. jours. Referee U.S. Soccer Fedn.; bd. dirs. Oak Ridge Community Playhouse, 1985-88, 95—. Mem. AAAS, Am. Phys. Soc., Am. Mgmt. Assn., Oak Ridge Sertoma Club (sec., treas., pres., chair bd. dirs.), Sigma Xi. Office Phone: 865-241-1514. E-mail: gene@mail.phy.ornl.gov.

**SPELBRING, AARON PAUL,** archivist; b. Terre Haute, Ind., June 15, 1976; s. Sheldon Dale Spelbring and Legatha Faye Hayes, Randy Lee Hayes (Stepfather). MSIS, U. Tex., Austin, 2003. Cert. archivist Acad. Cert. Archivists, Ill., 2005. Archivist, reference libr. McConnell Libr., Radford U., Va., 2004—. Mem.: ALA, Va. Libr. Assn., Soc. Am. Archivists. Office Phone: 540-831-5107. Business E-Mail: aspelbrin@radford.edu.

**SPELFOGEL, EVAN J.,** lawyer, educator; b. Boston, Jan. 28, 1936; s. Morris R. and Helen S. (Steinberg) S.; m. Beverly Kolenberg; children: Scott, Douglas, Karen. AB, Harvard U., 1956; JD, Columbia U., 1959. Bar: Mass. 1959, N.Y. 1964, U.S. Supreme Ct. 1969. Atty. Office of Solicitor, U.S. Dept. Labor, Washington, Boston, 1959-60, NLRB, Boston, N.Y.C., 1960-64; assoc. Simpson, Thacher & Bartlett, N.Y.C., 1964-69, Dewey, Ballantine, N.Y.C., 1969-77; ptnr. Fellner, Rovins & Gallay, N.Y.C., 1977-80, Summit, Rovins & Feldesman, N.Y.C., 1981-91, Epstein Becker and Green, P.C., N.Y.C., 1991—. Adj. prof. law Baruch Coll., CCNY. Bd. editors Developing Labor Law: The Board, The Courts and the National Labor Relations Act, also co-editor-in-chief Supplements; bd. sr. editors Employee Benefits Law; contbr. articles to profl. jours. Fellow Coll. Labor and Employment Lawyers; mem. ABA (sect. on labor and employment law, exec. coun. 1978-86, co-editor sect. newsletter 1976-92, editl. bd. The Labor Lawyer 1986—, mem. ho. dels. 1987-90, sect. dispute resolution 1992—), FBA (coun. on labor law), N.Y. State Bar Assn. (chmn. labor and employment law sect. 1977-78, exec. coun. 1975—, ho. dels. 1978-79, com. on profl. discipline 1987-90), Assn. of Bar of City of N.Y. (labor com. 1968-71, 87-90, employee benefits com. 1992-96), Indsl. Resl. Rsch. Assn. (sec. N.Y. chpt. 1999-2000, pres. 2000-01), Am. Arbitration Assn. (nat. panel labor arbitrators), Harvard Varsity Club, Phi Alpha Delta. Home: 17 Parkside Dr Great Neck NY 11021-1042 Office: Epstein Becker & Green, PC 250 Park Ave New York NY 10177-0001 Office Phone: 212-351-4539. Business E-Mail: espelfogel@ebglaw.com.

**SPELL, DERRICK W.,** oncologist, educator; MD, La. State U., New Orleans, 1997. Diplomate internal medicine ABIM, 2000, oncology ABIM, 2002. Clin. asst. prof. medicine La. State U. Health Scis. Ctr., Baton Rouge, 2002—06; physician La. Hematology Oncology Assn., Baton Rouge, 2004—. Chief hematology and oncology Earl K. Long Med. Ctr. - La. State U. Health Svcs. Ctr., 2002—. Co-chair, health initiatives action team Am. Cancer Soc., Baton Rouge, 2002—04; health svcs. adv. com. E. Baton Rouge Parish Schs., 2005—06; mem. Assn. of Retarded Citizens, Baton Rouge, 2004—06, Hospice Found., Baton Rouge, 2004—05, Children's Charter Sch., Baton Rouge, 2004—04. T. H. Harris scholarship, State of La., 1989-1993, LA State Bd. of Trustees scholarship, 1989-1993, scholarship, Nat. Honor Soc., 1989, scholarship, Wal-Mart Found., 1989, Cecil Vaughn scholarship in medicine, McNeese State U., 1993, Kushner Meml. scholarship, 1993. Mem.: ACP (assoc.), Am. Soc. Clin. Oncology (assoc.). Achievements include research in use of red blood cell distribution width for colon cancer screening. Office: La Hematology Oncology Assoc 4950 Essen Ln Ste 500 Baton Rouge LA 70809 Office Phone: 225-767-1311. Office Fax: 225-767-1335. E-mail: derricks@marybird.com

**SPELLACY, WILLIAM NELSON,** obstetrician, gynecologist, educator; b. St. Paul, May 10, 1934; s. Jack F. and Elmyra L. (Nelson) Spellacy; m. Lynn Larsen; children: Kathleen Ann, Kimberly Joan, William Nelson. BA, U. Minn., 1955, BS, 1956, MD, 1959. Diplomate subsplty. cert. in maternal and fetal medicine Am. Bd.-Ob-Gyn. Intern Hennepin County Gen. Hosp., Mpls., 1959—60; resident U. Minn., Mpls., 1960—63; practice medicine specializing in ob-gyn. Mpls., 1963—67, Miami, Fla., 1967—73, Gainesville, Fla., 1973—79, Chgo., 1979—88; prof., head dept. U. Ill. Coll. Medicine, Chgo., 1979—88; prof., chmn. dept. U. So. Fla. Coll. Medicine, Tampa, 1988—. Prof. dept. ob-gyn. U. Miami, 1967—73; prof., chmn. dept. U. Fla., 1973—79. Contbr. articles to med. jours. Mem.: ACOG, AMA, Inst. Medicine, Ill. Med. Soc., Soc. Perinatal Obstetricians, Ctrl. Assn. Obstetrics and Gynecology, South Atlantic Soc. Obstetrics and Gynecology, Perinatal Rsch. Soc., Am. Diabetes Assn., Assn. Profs. Gynecology and Obstetrics, Am. Fertility Soc., Endocrine Soc., Am. Assn. Obstetricians and Gynecologists, Soc. Gynecol. Investigation, Am. Gynecol. and Obstet. Soc., Am. Gynecol. Soc., Rotary. Episcopalian. Home: 845 Seddon Cove Way Tampa FL 33602-5704 Office: U South Fla Coll Medicine Dept OBGYN 4 Columbia Dr Ste 514 Tampa FL 33606-3589

**SPELLER, KERSTIN G. RINTA,** psychologist; b. Washington, Nov. 18, 1949; d. Eugene and Saga (Lindberg) Rinta; Thomas Hughes Speller, Sept. 4, 1971; five children. AB, Ohio U., 1971, MS, 1972; PhD, SUNY, Buffalo, 1983. Cert. sch. psychologist. Sch. psychologist Iroquois Ctrl. Schs., Elma, N.Y., 1974-78; cons. psychologist Amherst, N.Y., 1979-84; program dir. Child's Play Preschool Program, Amherst, 1986-95; sch. psychologist Holland (N.Y.) Schs., 1995—2004. Project dir. ISO-9001 GEMCOR, Buffalo, 1993-2004, corp. dir. human rels., 1998-2002. Bd. dirs. Heritage Ctrs. (Assn. Retarded Children), Erie County, N.Y., 1983-2000, govt. affairs com. chair, 1995-2000. Mem. Nat. Assn. Sch. Psychologists, USTA (ea. mgmt. bd., regional v.p. western region 1996-2003, nat. awards com. 1999-2002), Country Club Buffalo, Buffalo Tennis and Squash Club, East Aurora Pony Club, Village Glen Tennis and Fitness Club. Home: 5 Preston Beach Rd Marblehead MA 01945-2005

**SPELLER, ROBERT ERNEST BLAKEFIELD, JR.,** choreographer; b. N.Y.C., Feb. 5, 1936; s. Robert E.B. and Flora Maxine Elliott (Watkins) S. Student, Duke U., 1954-56, NYU, 1958-59, New Sch. for Social Rsch., 1967-68. English lang. sec. Prince Felix Youssoupoff, Paris, 1961—63; v.p. Robert Speller & Sons, Publishers, N.Y.C., 1963—2006, pres., 2006—; coordinator models New School Soc. Rsch., Parsons, N.Y.C., 1972-2001; instr. Baruch Coll., N.Y.C., 1980—83. Choreographer many shows including

Toulouse, 1981, The Ritz, 1983, Let's Misbehave, 1985-86; dir. I Died Yesterday, 1983; translator: The Mime (by Jean Dorcy), 1961. Mem. SAG, AFTRA, Actors' Equity Assn. (councillor, 1967-73), Am. Guild Variety Artists, Soc. Stage Dirs. and Choreographers N.Y., N.Y. Geneal. and Biog. Soc. Episcopal. Office: Robert Speller and Sons 115 E 9th St New York NY 10003-5414 Office Phone: 212-473-0333.

**SPELLER-BROWN, BARBARA JEAN,** pediatric nurse practitioner; b. Windsor, N.C., Feb. 8, 1958; d. Thomas Franklin and Esther Lee (Bond) Speller; children: Samuel, Shaun, Shea, Shanele, Samara. BSN, Howard U., 1981; MSN, U. Utah, 1993. Cert. PNP. Charge nurse Rosebud (S.D.) Indian Health Facility, 1981-82, Carl Albert Indian Health Facility, 1982-83; asst. head nurse Pitt County Meml. Hosp., Greenville, N.C., 1984-85; staff nurse St. Bernardine's Hosp., San Bernardino, Calif., 1986, San Bernardino Cmty. Hosp., 1986-87; staff nurse/charge nurse Gorgas Army Hosp., Panama, 1987-90; charge nurse Humana Hosp. Davis North, Layton, Utah, 1990-93; staff nurse Primary Children's Med. Ctr., Salt Lake City, 1990-93; clin. preceptor, PNP Cmty. Health Care Inc., Capital Heights, Md., 1994-95; faculty PNP Our Kids Ctr. Vanderbilt U. Med. Ctr., Nashville, 1995-2000; CPNP pediat. Walter Reed Army Med. Ctr., 2001, Army Med. Ctr., 2001—02; pediat. nurse practitioner hematology/oncology Children's Nat. Med. Ctr., 2002—. Mem. Gospel choir The Word of God Bapt. Ch.; scholarship chairperson Watchcare. 1st lt. USPHS, 1981—83. Named Outstanding Young Woman Am. Delta Sigma Theta. Mem. ANA, Nat. Assn. PNPs, Sigma Theta Tau, Phi Kappa Phi. Home: 11020 Lake Victoria Ln Bowie MD 20720 Personal E-mail: workingmom04@aol.com.

**SPELLING, IAN,** columnist; b 1965; BA, SUNY Albany. Writer Albany Student Press, Starlog mag.; freelance columnist NY Times Syndication Sales Corp., 1991—93, syndicated columnist, 1993—. Author: (syndicated columns) Inside Trek & Sci-Fi (title changed to Strange Worlds: Inside Sci-Fi & Fantasy), 1993—. Office: NY Times Syndication Sales Corp 14th Fl 122 E 42nd St New York NY 10168 Office Phone: 212-661-9122. Office Fax: 212-499-3382.*

**SPELLING, TORI (VICTORIA DAVEY SPELLING),** actress; b. LA, May 16, 1973; d. Aaron and Carol Jean Spelling; m. Charlie Shanian, July 2004 (div. Sept. 2005); m. Dean McDermott, May 7, 2006. Actor: (TV films) Shooting Stars, 1983, The Three Kings, 1987, A Friend to Die For, 1994, Awake to Danger, 1995, Deadly Pursuits, 1996, Co-ed Call Girl, 1996, Mother, May I Sleep with Danger?, 1996, The Alibi, 1997, Way Downtown, 2002, A Carol Christmas, 2003, Hush, 2005, The Family Plan, 2005, Mind Over Murder, 2006; (TV series) Beverly Hills, 90210, 1990—2000, So Downtown, 2003, The Help, 2004, So noTORIous (also co-exec. prodr.), 2006—; (films) Troop Beverly Hills, 1989, The House of Yes, 1997, Scream 2, 1997, Perpetrators of the Crime, 1998, Trick, 1999, Sol Goode, 2001, Scary Movie 2, 2001, Evil Alien Conquerors, 2002, 50 Ways to Leave Your Lover, 2004, Cthulhu, 2006. Office: c/o United Talent Agy Ste 500 9560 Wilshire Blvd Beverly Hills CA 90212-2401*

**SPELLINGS, MARGARET LAMONTAGNE,** secretary of education; b. Ann Arbor, Mich., Nov. 30, 1957; d. John and Peg Dudar; m. Robert Spellings, 2001; children: Mary, Grace. BA in polit. sci. & jornalism, U. Houston, 1979. Worked for Tex. Gov. William P. Clements; assoc. exec. dir. Tex. Assn. Sch. Bds.; polit. dir. Gov. George W. Bush gubernatorial campaign, Tex., 1994; sr. advisor to Gov. George W. Bush State of Tex., 1994—2000; asst. to Pres. for domestic policy The White House, Washington, 2001—05; sec. US Dept. Edn., Washington, 2005—. Host online interactive forum Ask the White House. Named one of 100 Most Powerful Women in Wash., Washingtonian mag., 2001. Achievements include one of the principal authors of the No Child Left Behind Act, 2001. Office: US Dept Edn 400 Maryland Ave SW Washington DC 20202*

**SPELLMAN, DOUGLAS TOBY,** advertising executive; b. Bronx, NY, May 12, 1942; s. Sydney M. and Leah B.S.; m. Ronni I. Epstein, Jan. 16, 1966 (div. Mar. 1985); children: Laurel Nicole, Daren Scott; m. Michelle Ward, Dec. 31, 1986; 1 child, Dallas Ward Spellman. Media buyer Doyle, Dane, Bernbach, Inc., NYC, 1964-66; various postions, 1966-72; media supr. Ogilvy & Mather, Inc., LA, 1973-74; media dir. VW Media Internat., Inc., LA, 1973-74; v.p., dir. West Coast ops. Ind. Media Svcs., Inc., LA, 1974-75; owner Douglas T. Spellman, Inc., LA, 1975-77, pres., chmn. bd., 1977-82; pres., COO Douglas T. Spellman Co. div. Ad Mktg., Inc., 1982-85; pres., CEO, chmn. bd. Spellbound Prodns. and Spellman Media divs. Spellbound Comms, 1984-86; gen. ptnr. Faso & Spellman, 1984-86; COO, pres. Yacht Mgmt. Internat., Ltd., 1984-86; v.p. media Snyder, Longino Advt. div. Snyder Advt., 1986-91; advt./media cons., 1986-90; gen. ptnr. Nucleus Nuance, LA, 1987-88, Conv. Photos Unltd., Hawaii, 1988-89; v.p. mktg. Pacific Med. Products, Inc., LA, 1990-91. Media dir. Kennedy-Wilson Inc., LA, 1991-94; dir. media and advt. svcs. Goddard & Claussen/First Tuesday, LA, 1994-97; v.p. advt. and mktg. Cosmetic Tech. Internat., Inc., LA, 1997-98; mng. dir. Med. Mktg. and Advt., LA, 1998-99; dir. media svcs., Publicis Dialog-FusionDM, San Francisco, 1999-2000; mgr. media, promotions and direct mktg. Pleasant Holidays, LLC, LA, 2001—; guest lectr. Sch. Bus. UCLA, 1964-69. Served with USAR N.G., 1964-69. Mem. Aircraft Owner and Pilots Assn., NRA, Calif. Pistol and Rifle Assn., Rolls Royce Owners, Mercedes Benz Am., Aston Martin Owners, Phi Zeta Kappa, Phi Omega Epsilon. Personal E-mail: spellman.doug@att.net.

**SPELLMAN, MITCHELL WRIGHT,** surgeon, academic administrator, educator; b. Alexandria, La., Dec. 1, 1919; s. Frank Jackson and Altonette Beulah (Mitchell) S.; m. Billie Rita Rhodes, June 27, 1947 (dec.); children: Frank A., Michael A. (dec.), Mitchell A., Maria S. Weaver, Melva A., Mark A., Manly A. (dec.), Rita S. Parks; m. Adrienne Foster Williams, Feb. 14, 2001 (dec.). AB magna cum laude, Dillard U., 1940, LLD (hon.) 1983; MD, Howard U., 1944; PhD in Surgery, U. Minn., Mpls., 1955; DSc (hon.), Georgetown U., 1974, U. Fla., 1977. Intern Cleve. Met. Gen. Hosp., 1944-45, asst. resident in surgery, 1945-46, Howard U. and Freedmen's Hosp., Washington, 1946-47, chief resident in thoracic surgery, 1947-48, tchg. asst. in physiology, 1948-49, chief resident in surgery, 1949-50, tchg. asst. in surgery, 1950-51; asst. prof. surgery Howard U., 1954-56, assoc. prof., 1956-60, prof., 1960-68; dir. Howard surgery svc. at DC Gen. Hosp., 1961-68; fellow in surgery U. Minn., 1951-54; sr. resident in surgery U. Minn. Med. Sch. and Hosp., 1951—54; dean Charles R. Drew Postgrad. Med. Sch., LA, 1969-77, prof. surgery, 1969-78; asst. dean, prof. surgery Sch. Medicine, UCLA, 1969-78; clin. prof. surgery Sch. Med., U. So. Calif., 1969-78; dean for med. svcs., prof. surgery Harvard Med. Sch., Boston, 1978-90, dean emeritus for med. svcs., 1990—, dean emeritus for internat. projects, 1990—, prof. surgery emeritus, 1990—; dir. internat. exch. programs Harvard Med. Internat., 1995—; exec. v.p. Harvard Med. Ctr., 1978-90. Fellow Ctr. for Advanced Study in Behavioral Scis.; vis. prof. Stanford U., 1975-76; bd. dirs. Kaiser Found. Hosps., Kaiser Found. Health Plan, 1971-89; mem. DC Bd. Examiners in Medicine and Osteopathy, 1955-68; mem. Nat. Rev. Com. for Regional Med. Programs, 1968-70; spl. med. adv. group, nat. surg. cons. VA, 1969-73; mem. Commn. for Study Accreditation of Selected Health Ednl. Programs, 1970-72; chmn. adv. com. med. devices Nat. Heart and Lung Inst., 1972; Am. health del. to visit People's Republic of China, 1973; hon. dir. State Mut. Cos., 1990—; mem. commn. mandatory retirement in higher edn. NAS/NRC, 1989-91; panel on internat. programs Nat. Libr. Medicine, 1996-97; adv. bd. faculty medicine and health scis. United Arab Emirates U., 2004—. Mem. editl. bd.: Jour. Medicine and Philosophy, 1977-90; contbr. articles on cardiovasc. physiology and surgery, measurement of blood volume, and radiation biology to profl. jours. Past bd. dirs. Sun Valley Forum on Nat. Health; mem. ethics adv. bd. HEW, 1977-81; bd. dirs. Harvard Cmty. Health Plan, 1979-84; former trustee Occidental Coll.; former bd. overseers com. to visit univ. health svc. Harvard, bd. overseers Harvard Cmty. Health Plan, 1984-95; former regent Georgetown U. bd. dirs., 1986-92; former visitor U. Mass. Med. Ctr.; mem. bd. visitors UCLA Sch. Medicine; mem. corp. MIT; adv. bd. PEW Scholars Program in Biomed. Scis., 1984-86; bd. dirs. Med. Edn. for South African Blacks, 1985—; adv. bd. United Arab Emirates U. Faculty of Medicine and Health Scis. 2004-. Recipient Disting. Alumnus award Dillard U., 1963, Disting. Postgrad.

Achievement award Howard U., 1974, Outstanding Achievement award U. Minn., 1979, Surg. Alumnus of Yr. award U. Minn., 1991, Disting. Support citation Charles R. Drew U. of Medicine, 2002; named U. Minn. Dept. Surgery Alumnus of Yr., 1991; Markle scholar in med. scis., 1954-59; Commonwealth Fund fellow, U. Minn., Mpls., 1955. Mem. AMA, AAAS, AAUP, ACS, Nat. Med. Assn. (William A. Sinkler Surgery award 1968), Soc. Univ. Surgeons, Am. Coll. Cardiology, Am. Surg. Assn., Inst. Medicine of NAS (chmn. program com. 1977-79, governing coun. 1978-80), Nat. Acad. Practice in Medicine, Am. Assn. Sovereign Mil. Order of Malta (Knights and Dames of Malta), Soc. Black Acad. Surgeons, MIT Corp. (life mem. emeritus), Cosmos Club. Roman Catholic. Office: Harvard Med Internat 1135 Tremont St Ste 900 Boston MA 02120 Office Phone: 617-535-6400.

**SPELLMAN SWEET, JULIA T.,** lawyer; b. Orange, Calif., Oct. 11, 1967; BA, Claremont McKenna Coll., 1989; JD, Columbia Univ., 1992. Bar: NY 1993. Assoc. Cravath Swaine & Moore LLP, NYC, 1992—2000, ptnr., corp., 2000—. Bd. trustees Claremont McKenna Coll.; dir. Drew Found. Mem.: NY Lawyers for the Pub. Interest, Disability Rights Task Force, Phi Beta Kappa. Fluent in Mandarin Chinese. Office: Cravath Swaine & Moore LLP Worldwide Plz 825 Eighth Ave New York NY 10019-7475 Office Phone: 212-474-1572. Office Fax: 212-474-3700. Business E-Mail: jspellman@cravath.com.

**SPELLMIRE, GEORGE W.,** lawyer; b. Oak Park, Ill., June 10, 1948; Student, Brown U.; BA, Ohio State U., 1970; JD, De Paul U., 1974. Bar: Ill. 1974, US Dist. Ct. (no. dist.) Ill. 1974, US Tax Ct. 1984, US Ct. Appeals (7th cir.) 1984, US Supreme Ct. 1994. Ptnr. Hinshaw & Culbertson, Chgo., 1982 98, D'Ancona & Pflaum, Chgo., 1998—2003, Spellmire & Sommer, Chgo., 2003—. Author: Attorney Malpractice: Prevention and Defense, 1988, supplemental edit., 1990; co-author: Accounting, Auditing and Financial Malpractice, 1998, supplemental edit., 2000, Accountants' Legal Liability Guide, 1990, Illinois Handbook on Legal Malpractice, 1982, Associates Primer for the Prevention of Malpractice, 1987. Mem. ABA, Am. Coll. Trial Lawyers, Soc. Trial Lawyers, Fed. Trial Bar, Internat. Assn. Def. Counsel (legal malpractice com., def. counsel practice mgmt. com.), Ill. State Bar Assn. Office: 77 W Wacker Dr Ste 4800 Chicago IL 60601-1664 Office Phone: 312-606-8722. Business E-mail: gws@spellmireSommer.com.

**SPELMAN, LUCY H.,** zoological park administrator; b. Bridgeport, Conn. BS in Biology, Brown U., 1985; DVM, U. Calif., Davis, 1990. Intern in small animal medicine and cardiology Dr. S. Ettinger and Assocs., L.A., 1990—91; resident in zool. medicine NC State Coll. Vet. Medicine/NC State Zool. Park, Asheboro, 1991—94; assoc. vet. med. officer Nat. Zool. Pk., Washington, 1995—99, sr. vet. med. officer, 1999—2000, dir., 2000—. Vet. advisor giant panda species survival plan Am. Zoo and Aquarium Assn., 1998—. Editor: Jour. Zoo and Wildlife Medicine, 1994—. Mem.: Am. Coll. Zool. Medicine (mem. exam. com. 1995—). Office: Nat Zool Park 3001 Connecticut Ave NW Washington DC 20008

**SPELTS, RICHARD JOHN,** lawyer; b. Yuma, Colo., July 29, 1939; s. Richard Clark and Barbara Eve (Pletcher) S.; children: Melinda, Meghan, Richard John Jr.; m. Gayle Merves, Nov. 14, 1992. BS cum laude, U. Colo., 1961, JD, 1964. Bar: Colo. 1964, U.S. Dist. Ct. 1964, U.S. Ct. Appeals (10th cir.) 1970, U.S. Dist. Ct. (ea. dist.) Mich. 1986. With Ford Motor Internat., Cologne, Germany, 1964-65; legis. counsel to U.S. Senator, 89th and 90th Congresses, 1967-68; minority counsel U.S. Senate Subcom., 90th and 91st Congresses, 1968-70; asst. U.S. atty., 1st asst. U.S. atty. Fed. Dist. of Colo., 1970-77; pvt. practice Denver, 1977-89; risk mgr. sheriff's dept. Jefferson County, Golden, Colo., 1990-91. Selected for Leadership Denver, 1977; recipient cert. for outstanding contbns. in drug law enforcement U.S. Drug Enforcement Adminstrn., 1977, spl. commendation for criminal prosecution U.S. Dept. Justice, 1973, spl. commendation for civil prosecution U.S. Dept. Justice, 1976. Mem. Fed. Bar Assn. (chmn. govt. torts seminar 1980), Colo. Bar Assn. (bd. govs. 1976-78), Denver Bar Assn., Colo. Trial Lawyers Assn., Denver Law Club, Order of Coif. Republican. Methodist. Home and Office: 9715 Sunset Hill Cir Lone Tree CO 80124-6716

**SPENCE, ANDREW,** artist, painter; b. Bryn Mawr, Pa., Oct. 4, 1947; s. Thomas and Elizabeth Spence; m. Mary Stewart Stoll, June 24, 1977. BFA, Temple U., 1969; MFA, U. Calif., Santa Barbara, 1971. One-man shows include TransAvant Garde Gallery, Austin, Tex., 1989, Barbara Krakow Gallery, Boston, 1989, Barbara Toll Fine Arts, NYC, 1982-83, 85, 87-88, 90, Compass Rose Gallery, Chgo., 1990, James Corcoran Gallery, LA, 1990, Max. Protetch Gallery, NYC, 1992-93, Barbara Scott Gallery, Miami, 1993, 96, Worcester Art Mus., Mass., 1991, Morris Healy Gallery, NYC, 1996, Art Resources Transfer, NYC, 2000, Edward Thorp Gallery, NYC, 2001, 02, Ulrich Mus. Art, Wichita, Kans., 2005, Edward Thorpe Gallery, NYC, 2006; exhibited in group shows including Corcoran Gallery of Art, Washington, 1987, Hirshhorn Mus. and Sculpture Garden, Smithsonian Instn., Washington, 1989, 04, Whitney Mus. Am. Art, NY, 1989, 91-92, Met. Mus. Art, NYC, 1993, Am. Acad. Arts and Letters, NYC, 1994, Wall Street Rising, NYC, 2002, Wayne State U., Detroit, 2004, Andrew Kreps Gallery, NYC, 2006; represented in permanent collections including Addison Gallery Am. Art, Albright Knox Art Gallery, Balt. Mus. Art, Carnegie Mus. Art, Pitts., Cleve. Mus. Art, Cin. Art Mus., Hirshhorn Mus. and Sculpture Garden, Austin Mus. Art, Mus. Modern Art, NY, Met. Mus. Art, NYC, San Diego Mus. Contemporary Art, Walker Art Ctr., Whitney Mus. Am. Art, NYC. Painting grantee Nat. Endowment for Arts, 1987; Guggenheim fellow, 1994.

**SPENCE, ANDREW MICHAEL (A. MICHAEL SPENCE),** former dean, finance educator; b. Montclair, NJ, 1943; m. Ann Bennett (div.); children: Graham, Catherine, Marya; m. Monica Spence. BA in Philosophy summa cum laude. Princeton U. 1966, BA, MA in Mathis., Oxford U., 1968, PhD in Econs. with honors, Harvard U., 1972. Asst. prof. polit. econ. Kennedy Sch. Govt. Harvard U., Cambridge, Mass., 1971-75, min. rsch. fellow, 1975—76, vis. prof. econs. dept., 1976-77, prof. econs., 1977-83, prof. bus. adminstrn., 1979-83, George Gund prof. econs. and bus. adminstrn., 1983-86, chmn. bus. econs. PhD program, 1981-83, chmn. econs. dept., 1983-84, dean Faculty Arts and Scis., 1984-90; assoc. prof. dept. econs. Stanford U., Calif., 1973-75, Philip H. Knight Prof., dean Grad. Sch. Bus. Calif., 1990-99, Philip H. Knight Prof. Emeritus, prof. mgmt. Calif., 1999—; ptnr. Oak Hill Venture Ptnrs. and Oak Hill Capital Ptnrs., Menlo Park, Calif., 1999—. Bd. dirs. Gen. Mills, Inc., Nike, Inc., Exult Inc., Siebel Syss. Inc., Blue Martini Software, Torstar Corp., ITI Edn.; mem. econs. adv. panel NSF, 1977-79; chmn. Nat. Rsch. Coun. Bd. on Sci., Tech. and Econ., Policy, 1990-97. Author: Market Signaling: Informational Transfer in Hiring and Related Processes, 1974; Co-author: Industrial Organization in an Open Economy, 1980, Competitive Structure in Investment Banking, 1983; past mem. editl. bd. Am. Econs. Rev., Bell. Jour. Econs., Jour. Econ. Theory and Pub. Policy; contbr. over 50 articles to profl. jours. Mem. econs. adv. com. Sloan Found., 1979—. Recipient J.K. Galbraith prize for excellence in tchg., 1978, Nobel prize in econ. scis., 2001; Danforth fellow, 1966, Rhodes scholar, 1966. Fellow Am. Acad. Arts & Scis., 1983-, Econometric Soc.; mem. Am. Econ. Assn. (John Bates Clark medal 1981). Office: Stanford U Grad Sch Bus Bldg 350 Memorial Way Stanford CA 94305-5015 also: Oak Hill Venture Partnership 2775 Sand Hill Rd Ste 220 Menlo Park CA 94025-7085*

**SPENCE, GERRY (GERALD LEONARD SPENCE),** lawyer, writer; b. Laramie, Wyo., Jan. 8, 1929; s. Gerald M. and Esther Sophie (Pfleeger) S.; m. Anna Wilson, June 20, 1947; children: Kip, Kerry, Kent, Katy; m. LaNelle Hampton Peterson, Nov. 18, 1969. BSL, U. Wyo., 1949, LLB, 1952, LLD (hon.), 1990. Bar: Wyo. 1952, U.S. Ct. Claims 1952, U.S. Supreme Ct. 1982. Sole practice, Riverton, Wyo., 1952-54; county and pros. atty. Fremont County, Wyo., 1954-62; ptnr. various law firms, Riverton and Casper, Wyo., 1962-78; sr. ptnr. Spence, Moriarity & Schuster, Jackson, Wyo., 1978—2002, Spence, Moriarity & Shockey, 2002—03, Spence Law Firm, 2004—. Lectr. legal orgns. and law schs. Author: (with others) Gunning for Justice, 1982, Of Murder and Madness, 1983, Trial by Fire, 1986, With Justice for None, 1989, From Freedom to Slavery, 1993, How To Argue and Win Every Time, 1995, The Making of a Country Lawyer, 1996, O.J.: The Last Word, 1997, Give Me

Liberty, 1998, A Boy's Summer, 2000, Gerry Spence's Wyoming: The Landscapes, 2000, Half Moon and Empty Stars, 2001, Seven Simple Steps to Personal Freedom, 2001, The Smoking Gun, 2003, Win Your Case, 2005 Mem. ABA, Wyo. Bar Assn., Wyo. Trial Lawyers Assn., Assn. Trial Lawyers Am., Nat. Assn. Criminal Def. Lawyers Office: The Spence Law Firm LLC PO Box 548 Jackson WY 83001-0548 Office Phone: 307-733-7290. Office Fax: 307-733-5248. Business E-Mail: infointake@spencelawyers.com.

**SPENCE, JAMES ROBERT, JR.,** broadcast executive, educator; b. Bronxville, N.Y., Dec. 20, 1936; s. James Robert and Mary Jeffrey (Grant) Spence; m. Betsy Jo Viener, June 16, 1992. BA, Dartmouth Coll., 1958. Prodn. asst. ABC Sports, Inc. (known as Sports Programs, Inc. through 1966), N.Y.C., 1960-63; asst. to exec. prodr. ABC's Wide World of Sports, 1963-66, coordinating prodr., 1966-70; v.p. program planning ABC Sports, Inc., 1970-78, sr. v.p., 1978-86; pres. Sports TV Internat. Inc., N.Y.C., 1986—. Adj. assoc. prof. broadcasting NYU Sch. Continuing and Profl. Studies, N.Y.C., 1999—2003; vis. scholar Coll. William and Mary, Williamsburg, Va., 2004—. Author: Up Close and Personal - The Inside Story of Network Television Sports, 1988. With U.S. Army, 1958—60. Mem.: Two Rivers Country Club (Williamsburg, Va.), Westchester Country Club (Rye, N.Y.). Office Phone: 212-758-9020.

**SPENCE, JONATHAN DERMOT,** historian, educator; b. Surrey, Eng., Aug. 11, 1936; came to U.S., 1959; s. Dermot Gordon Chesson and Muriel (Crailsham); m. Helen Alexander, Sept. 15, 1962 (div. 1993); children: Colin Chesson, Ian Alexander; m. Chin Annping, Aug. 12, 1993. BA, Cambridge U., Eng., 1959; PhD, Yale U., 1965; LHD (hon.) Knox Coll., 1984, U. New Haven, 1989; DLitt. (hon.), Wheeling Coll., 1985, Chinese U. Hong Kong, 1996, Gettysburg Coll., 1996, Quinnipiac Coll., 1998, Union Coll., 2000, Beloit Coll., 2000, Conn. Coll., 2000; DLitt. (hon.), Oxford U., 2003. Asst. prof. history Yale U., New Haven, 1966-71, prof., 1971—, chmn. dept. history, 1983-90, dir. div. humanities., Sterling prof. history. Wiles lectr. Queens's U., Belfast, 1985; Gauss lectr. Princeton U., 1987; vis. prof. Peking U., 1987; chmn. Council on East Asian Studies; bd. govs. Yale U. Press, 1988—; hon. prof. Nanjing U., 1993, Wuhan U., 1999. Author: Ts' Ao Yin and the K'Ang-Hsi Emperor, 1966, To Change China, 1969, Emperor of China, 1974, The Death of Woman Wang, 1978, The Gate of Heavenly Peace, 1981, The Memory Palace of Matteo Ricci, 1984, The Question of Hu, 1988, The Search for Modern China, 1990, Chinese Roundabout, 1992, God's Chinese Son, 1996, The Chan's Great Continent, 1998, Mao Zedong, 1999, Treason By the Book, 2001; editor: Ch'ing-Shih We'T'I, 1965-73, (with others) From Ming to Ch'ing, 1979; mem. editorial bd. Am. Hist. Rev., 1990-93, Yale Jour. Criticism, 1989, Yale Rev., 1991, China Quar., 1992, Revista Española del Pacifico, 2000. Served with Brit. Army, 1954-56. Recipient John Adison Porter prize, 1965, Christopher award, 1975, Devane teaching medal, 1978, L.A. Times book award, 1982, Vursell prize Am. Acad. and Inst. Arts and Letters, 1983, Comisso prize (Italy), 1987, Gelber prize (Can.), 1990; named to Coun. of Scholars, Libr. of Congress, 1988—; Yale fellow in East Asian Studies, 1962-65, 68-70, Guggenheim fellow, 1979-80, John D. and Catherine T. MacArthur Found. fellow, 1988-93. Fellow Brit. Acad.; mem. Am. Acad. Arts and Scis., Am. Philos. Soc., Am. Hist. Assn. (pres. 2004), Assn. Asian Studies, Order of St. Michael and St. George (companion). Home: 691 Forest Rd West Haven CT 06516-7932 Office: Yale U History Dept PO Box 208324 New Haven CT 06520-8324

**SPENCE, KENNETH F., III,** lawyer; b. Balt., Apr. 18, 1955; BA summa cum laude, Dickinson Coll., 1977; JD with honors, U. Md., 1982. Bar: Md. 1982, US Fed. Ct. 1982. Mem. litig. dept. Miles & Stockbridge, Balt., 1983—96, ptnr., 1990—96; with USF&G (merged with St. Paul Companies Inc.), 1996—98; v.p. corp. litig. St. Paul Companies Inc. (merged with Travelers Property Casualty Corp.), 1998—2004; v.p. legal services divsn., dep. gen. counsel St. Paul Travelers Companies Inc., 2004, exec. v.p., gen. counsel, 2004—. Mem.: Md. State Bar, Minn. State Bar. Office: St Paul Travelers Companies Inc 385 Wash St Saint Paul MN 55102

**SPENCE, NANCY ELIZABETH,** psychologist, educator, literature educator, writer; d. Frederick Richard and Elizabeth M. R. (Harter) Spence; m. Earl Arthur Crossland, Mar. 14, 1970 (div. 1985); children: Catherine Elise Spence Crossland Davison, Susannah Elizabeth Spence Crossland-Dwyer; m. Benjamin Lee Hemingway, Aug. 5, 1991. BA in English Lang. and Lit., Pa. State U., 1970; MA in Libr. Sci., U. Mich., 1973, MA in Am. Culture, 1974; PhD in East/West Psychology, Union Inst., Cin., 1994. Adj. instr. English School-craft C.C., Livonia, Mich., 1974—77; ethnic studies bibliographer U. Cin., 1977—78, office women's programs and svcs., 1985—98, adj. instr. counseling Ohio, 1987—97; adj. asst. prof. English Xavier U., Cin., 1978—82; freelance spkr., writer, editor, workshop developer Cin., 1998—. Chief writer, editor, cons. Pro-Ohio, Cin., 1998—; co-founder Ikigai; adj. prof. Union Inst. U., Cin., 1999—. Editor: Life Medicine: Wisdom for Extraordinary Living, 1997, 4th edit., 2006. Recipient Margaret Mann award, U. Mich., 1973, Golden Rule award, Greater Cin. United Way, 1993, U.S. Presdl. citation, Point of Light Found., 1994. Mem.: Am. Coll. Pers. Assn., Beta Phi Mu, Phi Beta Kappa (life). Avocations: international travel and volunteer work, travel writing;. reading, bicycling, yoga, writing. Office Phone: 513-321-6345.

**SPENCE, PAUL HERBERT,** librarian; b. Geraldine, Ala., Dec. 25, 1923; s. John Clardy and Leila (Carrell) S.; m. Ruth Schmidt, May 9, 1954 (dec. Aug. 2003); children— John Carrell, Peter Schmidt, Robert McCollough AB, Emory U., 1948, MA, 1956; PhD, U. Ill., 1969. Asst. reference librarian Emory U., Atlanta, 1950-53; periodical reference librarian Air U., Maxwell AFB, 1953-56; dir. library Air Force Inst. of Tech., Wright-Patterson AFB, Ohio, 1957-58; asst. dir. social studies U. Notre Dame, South Bend, Ind., 1959 60, U. Nebr., Lincoln, 1960-63, history and polit. sci. librarian U. Ill., Urbana, 1963-66; assoc. dir. libraries U. Ga., Athens, 1966-70; dir. libraries U. Ala., Birmingham, 1970-84, collection devel. librarian, 1985-89, prof. emeritus, 1989—, libr. cons., 1990—. Bd. dirs. Southeastern Library Network, Atlanta, 1973-75. Served with U.S. Army, 1943-46, ETO Mem. ALA (council mem. 1976-78), Ala. Library Assn. (treas. 1975-76), Southeastern Library Assn. (pres. 1980-82) Democrat. Presbyterian. Home: 614 Warwick Rd Birmingham AL 35209-4426 Office: U Ala at Birmingham 172 Sterne Libr Birmingham AL 35294-0001 Business E-Mail: pspence@beowulf.mhsl.uab.edu.

**SPENCE, ROBERT LEROY,** publishing executive; b. Carlisle, Pa., Sept. 13, 1931; s. Leroy Oliver and Esther Helen (Lau) S.; m. Barbara Amelia Hunter, Sept. 1, 1954 (div. Sept. 1978); children— Robert Roy, Bonnie Leigh; m. 2d, Maryanne Elizabeth Yacono, Jan. 10, 1979 BA, Dickinson Coll., 1953; postgrad, Temple U., 1955-57, Rutgers U., 1956, 59-60, U. Pa., 1960. Cert. tchr., N.J. Pub. schs. math. Haddon Heights High Sch., NJ, 1954-62; sr. editor Silver Burdett Co., Morristown, NJ, 1962-64; editor-in-chief Harcourt Brace Jovanovich, Inc., N.Y.C., 1964-81; v.p., pub. Harper & Row Publishers, Inc., N.Y.C., 1981-85, Scribner Ednl. Pubs. div. Macmillan, Inc., N.Y.C., 1985; pres. R&M Spence, Inc., Sparta, NJ, 1985—. Author textbook series: Growth in Mathematics, 1978, Excel in Mathematics, 1989-90, Mathematics Plus: Multicultural Projects, 1993; editor: Financial Planning for The Baby Boomer Client, 2000, 2d edit., 2004, Money Forever, 2002. Mem. Assn. Am. Pubs. (mem. exec. com. 1981-84), Nat. Council Tchrs. Math., Internat. Reading Assn., Am. Numismatic Assn. Avocations: rare coin collecting, coin newsletter author and publisher, artist, investor, writer. Home and Office: 37 Heather Ln Sparta NJ 07871-3538 E-mail: rlsmys@tellurian.net.

**SPENCE, RODNEY GLEN,** education educator, coach; b. West Plains, Mo., May 13, 1951; s. Glen Oscar and Margaret Carolyn Spence; m. Barbara Ellen Faulkenberg, Nov. 21, 1970; 1 child, Kelli Amanda. BS, Oakland City U., Ind., 1973; MEd, Ind. U., Bloomington, 1976. Cert. tchr. Ind. Tchr., coach Paoli Cmty. Schs., Ind., 1973—75. Salem Cmty. Schs., Ind., 1975—84, Perry Ctrl. Cmty. Schs., Leopold, Ind., 1984—. Coach varsity track, jr. high football Paoli Jr-Sr HS, 1973—75; football/basketball/track coach Salem HS, 1975—84; football/basketball/track/golf coach Perry Ctrl. HS, 1984—2004; football coach Forest Pk. H.S., Ferdinand, Ind., 2006—. Named Tchr. of Yr.,

Perry County C. of C., 1999, Walmart-Tell City Region, 2004. Mem.: NEA, Ind. Football Coaches Assn., Ind. State Tchrs. Assn. (governance com. 2004—06), Perry Ctrl.Tchrs. Assn. (pres. 2004—06). Home: 621 Meadowlark Ln Ferdinand IN 47532 Office: Perry Ctrl Jr-Sr HS 18677 Old State Rd 37 Leopold IN 47551 Office Phone: 812-843-5121. Office Fax: 812-843-4198. E-mail: spencr@pccs.k12.in.us.

**SPENCE, ROY MILAM, JR.,** advertising executive; b. Brownwood, Tex., Oct. 10, 1948; BA in Govt., U. Tex., 1971. Founder, pres. GSD&M Advt., Austin, Tex., 1971—. Office: GSD&M Advertising 828 W 6th St Austin TX 78703-5420

**SPENCE, SANDRA,** retired professional society administrator; b. McKeesport, Pa., Mar. 25, 1941; d. Cedric Leroy and Suzanne (Haudenshield) S. BA, Allegheny Coll., 1963; MA, Rutgers U., 1964. With Pa. State Govt., Harrisburg, 1964-68, Appalachian Regional Commn., Washington, 1968-75; legis. rep. Nat. Assn. Counties, Washington, 1975-77; fed. rep. Calif. Dept. Transp., Washington, 1977-78; dir. congl. affairs Amtrak, Washington, 1978-81, corp. sec., 1981-83; dir. computer svcs. Nat. R.R. Passenger Corp., Washington, 1983-84; co-owner Parkhurst-Spence Inc., 1985; owner The Spence Group, 1986-90; v.p. Bostrom Corp., Washington, 1990-92; exec. dir. Soc. Glass and Ceramic Decorators, 1992-2000. Chmn. legis. com. Womens Transp. Seminar, 1977-79, dir., 1982-83, v.p., 1983-84, chmn. edn. com., 1982-83; com. on edn. and tng. Transp. Rsch. Bd., 1982-85; mng. ptnr. Cambio Capital Club, 1996. Contbr. articles to profl. jours. Commnr. DC Commn. for Women, 1983—88; pres. Found. for Work of Laity, 2001—; del. Ward III Dem. Com., 1982—90, 1st vice chmn., 1987—88; bd. dir. DC Habitat for Humanity, 1998—2002, chmn. devel. com., 1998—2000, sec., 2000—01, Sussex County (Del.) Habitat for Humanity, 2003—05, bd. dirs., 2003—, treas., 2005—. Fellow Eagleton Inst. Politics, 1963-64; recipient Achievement award Transp. Seminar, 1982, 83 Mem. Greater Washington Soc. Assn. Execs. (vice-chair law and legis.com. 1989-90, chmn. 1990-91, chmn. scholarship com. 1992-93, bd. dirs. 1993-96, Rising Star award 1989, Chmn.'s award for Govt. Rels. 1991), Am. Soc. Assn. Execs. (mgmt. cert. 1987), Phi Beta Kappa. Home: 18471 Seashell Blvd Lewes DE 19958 Personal E-mail: sandy_s@juno.com.

**SPENCE, SIQUE (MARY STEWART SPENCE),** art dealer; b. Balt., Aug. 16, 1946; d. Joseph Adolphus and Nell Orum (Jones) Stoll; m. Ronald A. Kuchta, Nov. 2, 1969 (div. 1975); m. Andrew R. Spence, June 24, 1977. Dir. Galeria del Sol/Fairtree Fine Crafts Inst., Santa Barbara, Calif., 1970-75; asst. to dir. Arco Ctr. for the Visual Arts, L.A., 1975-77; registrar Droll/Kolbert Gallery, N.Y.C., 1977-78; gallery asst. Nancy Hoffman Gallery, N.Y.C., 1978-81, dir., 1981—. Office: Nancy Hoffman Gallery 429 W Broadway New York NY 10012-3799 Fax: 212-334-5078.

**SPENCE, TERRY R.,** state legislator; b. Wilmington, Del., Nov. 30, 1941; m. Nancy Spence; children: Terry Jr., Mark, Greg, Laura. AS, Goldey Beacom Coll.; BBA, Wilmington Coll. Mem. Dist. 18 Del. Ho. of Reps., spkr. of house, 1987—, ethics and adminstrv. coms., legis. coun.; acct. exec. Brooks Courier Svc. Co., Wilmington, Del. Hon. mem. Wilmington Manor Vol. Fire Co. Recipient Disting. Legis. award MADD, 1987, Disting. Legis. Svc. award Del. Bar Assn., 1986. Mem. NRA, Del. Assn. Retarded Citizens, Del. Assn. Blind Athletes, Lions. Home: 26 Freeport Rd New Castle DE 19720-3019 Office: PO Box 1401 Dover DE 19903-1401 Business E-Mail: terry.spence@state.de.us.

**SPENCER, ALLISON ANN,** biology educator; b. Cin., Mar. 8, 1957; d. James John and Laurette Christine Blair; children: Kelsey B., Keith R. BS in Biology, Bucknell U., Lewisburg, Pa., 1979. Cert. tchr. Pa. Biology tchr. Berwick Area Sch. Dist., Pa., 1979—. Coach Sci. Olympiad team Berwick Area HS, 1997—. Stephen ministry leader Trinity United Meth. Ch., Danville, Pa., 2003—, chair coun. on ministries, 2005—06. Home: 101 N Glenbrook Ave Danville PA 17821 Office: Berwick Area HS 1100 Fowler Ave Berwick PA 18603 Office Phone: 570-759-6400 ext 2032. E-mail: aspencer@berwicksd.org.

**SPENCER, CAROL BROWN,** retired educational association administrator; b. Normal, Ill., Aug. 26, 1936; d. Fred William and Sorado (Gross) B.; m. James Calvin Spencer, Dec. 18, 1965 (div. July 1978); children: James Calvin Jr., Anne Elizabeth. BA English, Calif. State U., L.A., 1964, MA Pub. Adminstrn., 1986. Cert. secondary edn. tchr., Calif. Tchr. English Seneca Vocat. H.S., Buffalo, 1966—70; pub. info. officer City of Pasadena, Calif., 1979—90, City of Mountain View, Calif., 1990—93; exec. dir. Calif. Assn. for Gifted, 1993—98; ret., 1998. Owner PR to Go, 1994— Sec., bd. dirs. Calif. Music Theatre, 1987-90; bd. dirs. Pasadena Beautiful Found., 1984-90, Pasadena Cultural Festival Found., 1983-86, Palo Alto-Stanford Heritage, 1990-93, Mountain View Libr. Found., 1997-98; mayoral appointee Strategic Planning Adv. Com., Pasadena, 1985-86; active Nev. Arts Advocates; trainer Clark County Election Dept., 1975-2004; centennial com. City of Las Vegas, 2004-06 Mem. NOW, Pub. Rels. Soc. Am., Calif. Assn. Pub. Info. Ofcls. (Paul Clark Achievement award 1986, Mktg. award 1990), City/County Comm. and Mktg. Assn. (bd. dirs. 1988-90, Savvy award for mktg. 1990), Las Vegas Art Mus Democrat. Episcopalian. Home: 7915 Laurena Ave Las Vegas NV 89147-5064

**SPENCER, CATHERINE ELLEN,** academic administrator; b. Englewood, N.J., Apr. 17, 1959; d. Donald Mansfield and Lois Anne Spencer. BS in edn., U. of Steubenville (Ohio), 1981; MS in edn. adminstrn., Franciscan U. of Steubenville (Ohio), 1996. Tchr. St. Francis Cath. Sch., Toronto, Ohio, 1981—82, St. Peter Sch., Steubenville, Ohio, 1982—92; tchr., asst. prin. Lincoln Internat. Acad., Managua, Nicaragua, 1992—93; residence dir. Franciscan U. of Steubenville (Ohio), 1993—96; prin. All Saints Sch., Steubenville, Ohio, 1996—2004; asst. supt. Diocese of Wheeling-Charleston, Wheeling, W.Va., 2004—. Mem. bd. trustees North Ctrl. Assn. Commn. on Accreditation and Sch. Improvement, Tempe, Ariz., 2004—; bd. of dirs. Holy Family Child Care and Devel. Ctr., Wheeling, W.Va. Missionary Dene Indian Reservation, Assumption, Canada, 1990—90. Recipient John Vaughn award, North Ctrl. Assn. Commn. on Accreditation and Sch. Improvement, 2006. Mem.: Chief Administrs. of Cath. Edn., Ohio Geneal. Soc., Kappa Delta Pi (life), Alpha Chi (life), Delta Zeta Sorority (life; pres. 1980—81). Home: 2012 Oregon Ave Steubenville OH 43952 Office: Diocese of Wheeling-Charleston 11 - 13th St Wheeling WV 26003 Office Phone: 304-233-0880. Business E-Mail: cspencer@dwc.org.

**SPENCER, CHARLES S.,** anthropologist; BA in Anthropology, Rice U., 1972; MA in Anthropology, U. Mich., 1976, PhD in Anthropology, 1981. Assoc. prof. anthropology U. Conn.; assoc. curator divsn. anthropology Am. Mus. Natural Hist., NYC, 1991—94, chair, curator, 1994—. Adj. assoc. prof. anthropology dept. Columbia U., adj. sr. rsch. scientist Ctr. Environ. Rsch. and Conservation. Contbr. articles to profl. jours., chapters to books. Fellow: Am. Acad. Arts & Scis.; mem.: Sigma Xi, AAAS, Soc. Am. Archaeology. Office: Divsn Anthropology Am Mus Natural Hist Ctrl Pk West at 79th St New York NY 10024-5192 E-mail: cspencer@amnh.org.*

**SPENCER, CHRISTOPHER S.,** lawyer, insurance company executive; b. Boston, Mass., Apr. 29, 1946; BA, Beloit Coll., 1969; JD, Univ. Wis., Madison, 1972. Bar: Wis. 1972. V.p., legal Am. Family Ins. Group, Madison, Wis. Office: American Family Insurance Group Legal Dept 6000 American Pkwy Madison WI 53783-0001 Office Phone: 608-249-2111. Office Fax: 608-243-4917.

**SPENCER, DAVID ANTHONY,** geologist, researcher, educator; b. London, Nov. 7, 1963; s. Henry William George and Veronica Clair (Bonanno) S. BSc in Geology with honors, U. Exeter, Eng., 1986; Diploma, U. London, 1988, MSc in Structural Geology, 1988; Dr Natural Sci., Swiss Fed. Inst. Tech., Zurich, 1993. Chartered geologist, European geologist. Ins. claims broker Winchester Bowring Ltd., London, 1982-83; platinum exploration geologist Eastern Bushveld Complex, South Africa, 1986-87; rsch. fellow Swiss Fed. Inst. Tech., Zürich, 1988-89, rsch. and tchr. asst., 1989-92, vis. ETH rsch. fellow, 1992-93, vis. rsch. fellow, 1993-94, rsch. fellow in tectonics Zurich, 1994-97; vis. lectr. U. of the Punjab, Lahore, Pakistan, 1995; vis. scientist Tokyo Inst. Tech., Zurich, 1996; rsch. asst. prof., lectr. in structural geology U. Maine, Orono, 1997-98; geologist Saga Petroleum ASA, Norway, 1998—99; project mgr. numerous rsch. projects; founder Spencer Structural Cons., 2000; sr. reservoir geologist Roxar Software Solutions, 2003—. Vis. scientist U. Beijing, 1986; vis. prof. U. of the Punjab, Lahore, 1997—; Himalayan regional coordinating com. Internat. Lithosphere Program, 1992-96, com. tectonic map of Himalaya, 1995; organizer com. in field; founder, moderator, coord. HimNet, 2000-90; presenter, cons., lectr. in field. Contbr. numerous articles to profl. jours.; European regional editor Himalayan Notes, 1994-97; reviewer numerous internat. jours. in field; assoc. editor The Professional Geologist. Found. gov. Raine's Found. Sch., 2002—; trustee The Raine's Found., 2002—. Sir John Cass Found. scholar, 1987-88, travel award, 1988; recipient travel award Swiss Geol. Soc., 1991, 93, Huber-Kudlich Found., 1992, Swiss Acad. Natural Scis., 1992, Pub. award Staub Fund, 1992, Educational Tng. award Saga Petroleum ASA; rsch. fellow Swiss Nat. Sci. Found., 1994-97; recipient Duke of Edinburgh Gold award, 1987. Fellow Geol. Soc., Royal Geog. Soc., Royal Soc. Arts, Am. Geog. Soc., Geol. Assn. of Can.; mem. AAAS, Inst. Petroleum, Royal Instn. of Gt. Britain, Royal Scottish Geog. Soc. (profl. assoc.), Order of Internat. Fellowship, Internat. Assn. Structural/Tectonic Geologists, Mineral. Soc., European Assn. Geoscientists and Engrs., Soc. for Sedimentary Geology, Geosci. Info. Soc., Computer Oriented Geol. Soc., European Union Geoscis., Am. Geophys. Union, Assn. Geoscientists for Internat. Devel., Geol. Soc. Am., Geol. Soc. Switzerland, Geol. Soc. Pakistan, Geol. Soc. Punjab, Geol. Soc. Nepal, Swiss Mineral. and Petrological Soc., Soc. for Mining, Metallurgy and Exploration, Geochem. Soc., Am. Chem. Soc., Petroleum Exploration Soc. of Gt. Britain, Am. Assn. Petroleum Geologists, Nat. Geog. Soc., Assn. Geographers, Can. Assn. Geographers, Brit. Assn. for Advancement of Sci., Sci. Exploration Soc., N.Y. Acad. Scis., Nat. Earth Sci. Tchrs. Assn., Nat. Assn. Geosci. Tchrs., Assn. for Sci. Edn., Himalayan Found., Himalayan Club, Himalayan Explorers Club, Nepal Studies Assn., Internat. Assn. for Ladakh Studies, Integrated Mountain Rsch. Soc., Internat. Mountain Soc., Brit. Mountaineering Coun., Sigma Xi. Avocations: mountain climbing, guitar, long distance walking, sports. Address: PO Box 2827 Reading RE1 9EN England

**SPENCER, DAWN JOYCE,** animal advocate; b. St. Louis, Nov. 7, 1938; d. Leslie Sylvan II and Iris Nunn (Burdick) S. AB, Syracuse U., 1964, MA, 1967, MA, 1995. Cert. secondary education educator, N.Y., Calif. Exec. sec. to permanent observer Rep. Korea to UN UN, N.Y.C., 1964-65; secondary level social studies tchr. Bd. Edn., Utica, N.Y., 1966-69; mgr. apt. complex Oakland, Calif., 1969-75; lectr. Fukushima (Japan) U., Fukushima Med. Coll., Sakura no Seibo Women's Coll., Kennedy Internat. Coll., 1975-94; dir. Bowerston (Ohio) Pub. Libr., 1996—2001; animal advocate Farm Sanctuary, Watkins Glen, NY, 2002—. English fluency instr. to migrant workers N.Y. Dept. Edn., Clinton, summers 1967-68; sr. lectr. Fukushima Women's Coll., 1982-94. Pres. Syracuse-in-Asia, 1962-64; advisor U.S. Mil. Svc. Recruitment, Utica, N.Y., 1966-69; active Humane Soc. U.S., Animal Protective League, 1969-75, Fukushima Organic Farm Cooperative, 1982-94, Japan Animal Welfare Soc., Tokyo, 1993-94, African Wildlife Found., Am. Rivers, Best Friends Animal Sanctuary, Ctr. Marine Conservation, Defenders of Wildlife, numerous others. Mem. ASPCA, Am. Legal Def. Fund, Greenpeace, Animal Legal Def. Fund, Animal Protection Inst., The Ark Trust, The Fund for Animals, Humane Soc. U.S., Human Soc. Schuyler Co., Last Chance for Animals, Progressive Animal Welfare Soc., People for the Ethical Treatment Animals, Farm Sanctuary, In Defense of Animals, United Poultry Concerts, Fund for Animals. Green Party. Avocations: skiing, jazz, computers. Home: 121 Havana Glen Rd Lot 19 Montour Falls NY 14865 Office: Farm Sanctuary 3150 Aikens Rd Watkins Glen NY 14891 Personal E-mail: djspence@localnet.com. Business E-Mail: dspencer@farmsanctuary.org. E-mail: djspence@tusco.net.

**SPENCER, DENNIS DEE,** medical educator, director; b. Bedford, Iowa, Apr. 1, 1945; s. George and Wilma Spencer; m. Susan S. Spencer; children: Andrea, Joanna; children: Christopher, Kathleen. Grad., Grinnell Coll.; MD, Wash. U., St. Louis, 1971. Intern Barnes Hosp., St. Louis, 1971—72; resident in neurological surgery Yale-New Haven Hosp., 1972—76, assoc. neurosurgeon, 1977—80, attending neurosurgeon, 1980—87; prof. neurosurgery Yale U. Sch. Medicine, 1985—, chief neurosurgery, Nixdorff-German Prof., 1987—97, chmn. dept. neurosurgery, Harvey and Kate Cushing Prof., 1997—, dir. epilepsy program, acting dean, 2003—04. Mem.: Am. Epilepsy Soc. (bd. dirs.), Milken Family Found. Clin. Investigator Award 1999), Am. Bd. Neurol. Surgeons (past chair), Am. Assn. Neurol. Surgeons, Soc. Neurol. Surgeons. Achievements include pioneer in sterotaxic cellular replacement therapy for patients with parkinson's desease. Office: Yale Neurosurgery Yale Physicians Bldg 3rd Fl 800 Howard Ave New Haven CT 06519*

**SPENCER, DONALD SPURGEON,** historian, academic administrator; b. Anderson, Ind., Jan. 29, 1945; s. Thomas E. and Josephine (Litz) S.; m. Pamela Sue Roberts, June 19, 1965; 1 child, Jennifer Wynne. BA, Ill. Coll., 1967; PhD, U. Va., 1973. Asst. prof. history Westminster Coll., Fulton, Mo., 1973-76, Ohio U., Athens, 1976-77; from asst., assoc. to full prof., assoc. dean, asst. provost U. Mont., Missoula, 1977-90; provost SUNY, Geneseo, 1990-93; pres. Western Ill. U., Macomb, 1994—. Author: Louis Kossuth and Young America, 1978, The Carter Implosion: Jimmy Carter and the Amateur Style of Diplomacy,1989; contbr. articles to jours. in field. With U.S. Army, 1968-71, Korea. Woodrow Wilson Found. fellow, 1968; Danforth Found. univ. teaching fellow, 1971. Mem. Phi Alpha Theta, Phi Beta Kappa. Congregationalist. Home: 124 Links Of Leith Williamsburg VA 23188-7461

**SPENCER, EDGAR WINSTON,** geology educator; b. Monticello, Ark., May 27, 1931; s. Terrel Ford and Allie Belle (Shelton) S.; m. Elizabeth Penn Humphries, Nov. 26, 1958; children: Elizabeth Shawn, Kristen Shannon. Student, Vanderbilt U., 1957; BS, Washington and Lee U., 1953; PhD, Columbia U., 1957. Lectr. Hunter Coll., 1954-57; mem. faculty Washington and Lee U., 1957—, prof. geology, head dept., 1965-75, Ruth Parmly prof. Pres. Rockbridge Area Conservation Coun., 1978-79, co-pres. 1992-98; NSF sci. faculty fellow, New Zealand and Australia; dir. grant for humanities and pub. policy on land use planning Va. Found., 1975; dir. grant Petroleum Rsch. Fund, 1981-82; leader field trip Ctrl. Appalachian Mts. Internat. Geol. Congress, 1989. Author: Basic Concepts of Physical Geology, 1962, Basic Concepts of Historical Geology, 1962, Geology: A Survey of Earth Science, 1965, Introduction to the Structure of the Earth, 1969, 3d edit., 1988, The Dynamics of the Earth, 1972, Physical Geology, 1983, Geologic Maps, 1993, 2nd edit., 2000, Earth Science-Understanding Environmental Systems, 2003; co-author: Geologic Map and Report on the Geology of Rockbridge County, Virginia, 2006. Recipient Va. Outstanding Faculty award Va. Coun. of Higher Edn., 1990. Fellow Geol. Soc. Am., AAAS; mem. Am. Assn. Petroleum Geologists (dir. field seminar on fold and thrust belts 1987, 88-91), Am. Inst. Profl. Geologists, Am. Geophys. Union, Nat. Assn. Geology Tchrs., Yellowstone-Bighorn Rsch. Assn., Phi Beta Kappa (hon.), Omicron Delta Kappa (hon.), Sigma Xi. Home: PO Box 1055 Lexington VA 24450-1055 Office Phone: 540-458-8866. E-mail: spencere@wlu.edu.

**SPENCER, ELIZABETH,** writer; b. Carrollton, Miss., 1921; d. James Luther and Mary James (McCain) S.; m. John Arthur Blackwood Rusher, Sept. 29, 1956. BA, Belhaven Coll., 1942; MA, Vanderbilt U., 1943; LittD (hon.), Southwestern U. at Memphis, 1968; LLD (hon.), Concordia U. at Montreal, 1988; LittD (hon.), U. of the South, 1992; DLitt (hon.), U. NC, Chapel Hill, 1998, Belhaven Coll., 1999. Instr. N.W. Miss. Jr. Coll., 1943-44, Ward-Belmont, Nashville, 1944-45; reporter The Nashville Tennessean, 1945-46; instr. U. Miss., Oxford, 1948-51, 52-53. Vis. prof. Concordia U., Montreal, Que., Can., 1976-81, adj. prof., 1981-86; vis. prof. U. NC, Chapel Hill, 1986-92. Author: Fire in the Morning, 1948, This Crooked Way, 1952, The Voice in the Back Door, 1956, The Light in the Piazza, 1960, Knights and Dragons, 1965, No Place for an Angel, 1967, Ship Island and Other Stories, 1968, The Snare, 1972, The Stories of Elizabeth Spencer, 1981, Marilee, 1981, The Salt Line, 1984, Jack of Diamonds and Other Stories, 1988, (play) For Lease or Sale, 1989, On the Gulf, 1991, The Night Travellers, 1991, (memoir) Landscapes of the Heart, 1998, The Southern Woman, 2001; contbr. short stories to mags. and anthologies. Named to NC Hall of Fame, 2002; recipient Women's Dem. Com. award, 1949, recognition award, Nat. Inst. Arts and Letters, 1952, Richard and Hinda Rosenthal Found. award, Am. Acad. Arts and Letters, 1957, Fortner award for lit., 1998, Award of Merit medal for the short story, 1983, 1st McGraw-Hill Fiction award, 1960, Henry Bellamann award for creative writing, 1968, Salem award for lit., 1992, Dos Passos award for fiction, 1992, NC Gov.'s award for lit., 1994, Corrington award for lit., 1997, Richard Wright award for lit., 1997, award for non-fiction, Miss. Libr. Assn., 1999, Brooks medal, Fellowship of So. Writers, 2001, Thomas Wolfe award for lit., 2002, William Faulkner award for lit. excellence, 2002, Miss. Gov.'s award for excellence in the arts, 2006; fellow, Guggenheim Found., 1953; Kenyon Rev. fellow in fiction, 1957, Bryn Mawr Coll. Donnelly fellow, 1962, Nat. Endowment for Arts grantee in lit., 1983, Sr. Arts Award grantee, Nat. Endowment for the Arts, 1988. Mem. Am. Acad. Arts and Letters, Fellowship of So. Writers (charter; vice chancellor 1993-97). Home: 402 Longleaf Dr Chapel Hill NC 27517-3042 Office Phone: 919-929-2115. E-mail: elizabeth0222@earthlink.net.

**SPENCER, FRANK COLE,** medical educator; b. Haskell, Tex., 1925; MD, Vanderbilt U., 1947. Intern Johns Hopkins U., Balt., 1947-48, fellow in surgery, 1947-48, asst. resident in surgery, 1953-54; resident in gen. and cardiothoracic surgery Johns Hopkins Sch. Medicine, Balt., 1954-55; surgeon, outpatient dept. Johns Hopkins Hosp., 1955; resident in surgery Wadsworth VA Ctr. Hosp., 1949—51; asst. prof. surgery Johns Hopkins U., 1955-59, assoc. prof., 1959-61; prof. surgery U. Ky., 1961—66; chmn. dept. surgery, George David Steward prof. surgery NYU, 1966—98, dir. patient safety. Served to lt. M.C., USN, 1951-53. John and Mary R. Markle scholar in med. sci. Johns Hopkins U., 1956. Office: NYU Sch Medicine HCC 1508 550 1st Ave New York NY 10016

**SPENCER, GEORGE HENRY,** lawyer; b. Vienna; s. Frank Henry and Lillian (Godin) S.; m. Joan Betty Spencer, Sept. 16, 1956 (dec.); children: Lucy, Margaret, Robert, Nancy; m. Mollie Cole Sabol, Oct. 31, 1987; stepchildren: Jeanne, Marta. BE, Yale U., 1948; JD, Cornell U., 1952. Bar: D.C., N.Y. Examiner U.S. Patent Office, 1952-54; sole practice N.Y.C., Washington, 1954-62; ptnr. Spencer & Frank, Washington, 1962-98, Venable, LLP, Attys. at Law, Washington, 1998—2003; counsel Fitch, Even, Tabin & Flannery, Washington, 2003—05, Stein, McEwen & Bui, LLP, Washington, 2006—. Master of bench Prettyman-Leventhal Am. Inn of Ct.; lectr. World Trade Inst. Served to capt. JAGC, U.S. Army, 1956-62. Mem. ABA, Am. Patent Law Assn., Lawyer-Pilots Bar Assn., World Intellectual Property Orgn. (panel of arbitrators and mediators), Cosmos Club (Washington). Avocations: aviation, music, German and French language studies, poetry. Home: 1102 Flor Ln Mc Lean Va 22102-1737 Office: Stein McEwen & Bui 1400 I St NW Ste 300 Washington DC 20005 Office Phone: 202-216-9505 ext. 227. Personal E-mail: specole@aol.com. Business E-Mail: gspencer@smbiplaw.com.

**SPENCER, HERBERT HARRY,** structural engineer, researcher, computer analyst; b. Vienna, Jan. 2, 1928; arrived in US, 1953; s. Ingenieur Oskar and Bronia (Steinberger) Schnabel; m. Margot Goldrei (div.); m. Sara Slomka, July 24, 1992. BSc, U. London, 1948; MS, Poly. Inst. Bklyn., 1955; PhD, U. London, 1976. Asst. jr. engr. Tarmac Ltd., Coventry, England, 1944—45, George Wimpey & Co., Coventry, 1945—46, Kershaw & Kaufman, London, 1946—48; engr. William Halcrow & Ptnrs., London, 1948—49, Hydraulic Dept., Nazareth, Israel, 1949—50, Quibuts Eyn Hashofet, Galilee, Israel, 1950—51, Rendel Palmer & Tritton, London, 1951—53; rsch. asst. Poly. Inst. Bklyn., 1953—55; instr. Yale U., New Haven, 1955—56; rsch. asst., lectr. Columbia U., N.Y.C., 1956—59; asst. prof. San Diego State Coll., 1959—61; rsch. assoc. Caltech, Pasedena, Calif., 1961—62; asst. prof. U. So. Calif., L.A., 1961—65; sr. scientist Ford Instrument Co., Sperry Gyro, L.I. City, NY, 1965—66, Tech. Rsch. Group, Melville, NY, 1966—67; engr. cons. Spencer Rsch., N.Y.C. and London, 1967—77; sr. lectr. Hatfield Poly., England, 1970—77; vis. assoc. prof. U. Pitts., 1976—77; assoc. prof. La. State U., Baton Rouge, 1977—79; vis. rsch. cons. Columbia U., N.Y.C., 1979; asst. prof. Rutgers U., New Brunswick, NJ, 1979—82. Pres. Spencer Sci. Computing, New Brunswick, 1982—; vis. prof. Aero Lab., Technion, Haifa, Israel, 1988, Rutgers U., Piscataway, NJ, 1998-2003 Contbr. articles to profl. jours. Mem. ASCE, ASME, Israeli Soc. Engrs. and Architects, Gesellschaft für Angewandte Mathematik und Mechanik, Structural Rsch. Coun., Mensa, Intertel. Home: 10-8M Landing Ln New Brunswick NJ 08901 Office: Spencer Sci Comp PO Box 4191 Highland Park NJ 08904-4191 Office Phone: 732-246-0499. Business E-Mail: sscc@isp.com.

**SPENCER, JEAN,** retired business executive; b. Bklyn., Oct. 26, 1946; d. Frederic R. and Lucy Anne Spencer. BBA cum laude, Adelphi U., 1973, MBA, 1989; MS in Human Nutrition. U. Bridgeport, 1998. Notary public, 1986—. Exec. adminstrv. mgmt. Underwriters Labs., Inc., Melville, NY, 1966—2003, ret., 2003; pres., CEO All Natural Health Corp., Seaford, NY, 1990—2002; ret. Vol., life mem. Nat. Ski Patrol, Colo. Recipient NASTAR, Bronze medal, Silver medal. Mem. Am. Coll. Nutrition, Am. Soc. Quality Control, Nat. Nutritional Foods Assn., Nat. Ctr. for Homeopathy. Avocations: skiing, bicycle riding, physical fitness, opera, theater. Office: All Natural Health Inc 3830 Sunrise Hwy Seaford NY 11783-2634 Office Phone: 516-785-5521.

**SPENCER, JEFF,** biologist, educator; b. Akron, Ohio, Apr. 23, 1965; s. Robert and Kayrn Spencer; m. Ronda Spencer, Apr. 13, 1969. MS, U. Akron, 1997. Instr./lab coord. U. Akron, 1997—. Office: University of Akron Akron OH 44325 Office Phone: 330-972-7996. E-mail: spence6@uakron.edu.

**SPENCER, JOHN HEDLEY,** biochemistry educator; b. Stapleford, Eng., Apr. 10, 1933; emigrated to Can., 1956; s. Thomas and Eva (Johnson) S.; m. Magdeliene Vera Kulin, Sept. 16, 1958; children: Robin Anne, David Thomas, Mark Stewart. BSc, U. St. Andrews, Scotland, 1955, BSc with honors, 1956; student, Montreal Cancer Rsch. Soc., 1956-59; PhD, McGill U., 1960. Damon Runyon Meml. Fund postdoctoral fellow Columbia U., N.Y.C., 1959-61; mem. faculty McGill U., Montreal, 1961-78, assoc. prof. biochemistry, 1966-71, prof., 1971-78; prof. biochemistry Queen's U., Kingston, Ont., 1978-98, head biochemistry, 1978-90, prof. emeritus, 1998—. Vis. scientist NICHHD/NIH, Bethesda, Md., 1987-88; vis. prof. U. Montreal, 1992-93. Author: The Physics and Chemistry of DNA and RNA, 1972; co-editor: Planet Earth: Problems and Prospects, 1995. Recipient Ayerst award Can. Biochem. Soc., 1972 Fellow Royal Soc. Can.; mem. Can. Biochem. Soc. (treas. 1966-69, pres. 1979-80), Can. Fedn. Biol. Socs. (pres. 1981-82), Canadians for Health Rsch. (bd. dirs. 2001—), Biochem. Soc., Am. Soc. Biochemistry and Molecular Biology, Royal Soc. Can., Sigma Xi. Home: 36 Kenwoods Cir Kingston ON Canada K7K 6Y1 E-mail: spencerj@post.queensu.ca

**SPENCER, KIMBERLY ANN,** psychologist; b. Towson, Md., Nov. 2, 1979; BA in Psychology, Deaf Studies, Towson U., 2001, MA in Sch. Psychology, 2004. Cert. sch. psychologist 2004. Sch. psychologist Carroll County Pub. Schs., Westminster, Md., 2004—. Mem.: Nat. Assn. Sch. Psychologists. Office: Carroll County Pub Schs 125 N Court St Westminster MD 21157 Personal E-mail: kspencer1005@yahoo.com. Business E-Mail: kaspenc@k12.carr.org.

**SPENCER, LARA,** television personality, journalist; married; 1 child. BA in Journalism, Pa. State U. Reporter WDEF-TV, Chattanooga, News 12, L.I., NY, WABC, NY Eyewitness News, 1995—99; nat. corr. ABC News' Good Morning Am., 1999—2001; corr., 2001—04; host Antiques Roadshow, WGBH-PBS, 2004—; co-host, NY anchor Paramount TV The Insider, NYC, 2004—. Office: Antiques Roadshow-WGBH 125 Western Ave Allston MA 02134 Studio: Paramount Studios 5555 Melrose Ave Los Angeles CA 90038

**SPENCER, LISA ANN,** special education educator; d. Jack and Betty Jean Spencer. BS, Bowie State Coll., 1983; M, Howard U., 1989, George Wash. U., 2004. Tchr. PGCPS, Mitchellville, Md., 1988—90, spl. edn. tchr. Bowie, Md., 1990—97, tech. coord. Hyattsville, Md., 1997—99, regional tech. coord. Oxon Hill, Md., 1999—2004, tng. and support mgr. Upper Marlboro, Md., 2004—. Mem.: NEA, Internat. Soc. Tech. Edn., Assn. Info. Tech. Profls. Democrat. Office Phone: 301-952-6251. Business E-Mail: lspencer@pgcps.org.

**SPENCER, LONABELLE (KAPPIE SPENCER),** political agency administrator, lobbyist; b. Owatonna, Minn., Aug. 3, 1925; d. Reuben Alvin and Florence Elizabeth (Wells) Kaplan; m. Mark Rodney Spencer, Sept. 14, 1947 (dec. May 1986); children: Gregory Mark, Gary Alan, Carol Ann, Dane Kaplan. BA, Grinnell Coll., 1947. State bd. legis. chair Am. Assn. Univ. Women, Iowa, 1978-82, nat. legis. com. Washington, 1980-83, nat. bd. legis. chair, 1982-83, nat. legis. and program coms., 1985-89, nat. bd. dir. for women's issues, 1985-89; founder, dir. Nat. Gender Balance Project, Sarasota, Fla., 1988—; bd. dirs., nat. steering com. Nat. Women's Political Caucus, Washington, 1992-97. Lobbyist, cmty. activist state legis. and congress, Fla. Iowa, Washington, 1974—; rep. Fla. women's pol. caucus ERA summit, Washington, 1992—; cons., presenter in field. Author: (manuals) Don't Leave It All to the Experts, 1981, Take An Unratified State to Launch, 1981, I Think We Need a Woman, 1982, It's a Man's World Unless Women Vote, 1983, Woman Power: It's a Capitol Idea, 1995, Gender Balance Project-USA: Politics and Decision Making, 1995, Whose Money Is It Anyway: Wills and Trusts for Women, 1999. U.S. rep. World Assn. Girl Guides Girl Scouts U.S., Acapulco, Mex., 1965, bd. dirs. Moingona Coun. Girl Scouts U.S., 1965-75; Rep. candidate Iowa Senate, Des Moines, 1976; del. Internat. Fedn. U. Women, Netherlands, New Zealand, Finland, Sweden, 1983, 86, 89; trustee Grinnell (Iowa) Coll., 1993—; Iowa del. to Nat. Women's Conf., 1977; founder Fla. Women's Consortium, 1989; active People to People Internat.; tour leader Mission in Understanding to Cuba, 2001. Recipient Girl Scout awards Moingona Girl Scout Coun., Des Moines, 1969, 73, 78, Christine Wilson medal for Equality and Justice, Iowa Women's Hall of Fame, Des Moines, 1990; named gift honoree Am. Assn. Univ. Women, Des Moines and Sarasota, Fla. branches, Iowa and Vt. divsns., 1980, 82, 87, 92; named in National Women's Hall of Fame Book of Lives and Legacies, 2002. Mem. AAUW (leader corps, com. mem. 1975—89), UN Fund for Women (UNIFEM), Nat. Assoc. Commns. for Women, Vet. Feminists of Am. (Medal of Honor 2000), Women in Senate and House WISH-LIST (founder 1992). Republican. Avocation: travel.

**SPENCER, MARGARET GILLIAM,** lawyer; b. Spokane, Wash., Aug. 30, 1951; d. Jackson Earl and Margaret Kathleen (Hindley) Gilliam; m. John Bernard Spencer, Feb. 21, 1993. BA in Sociology, U. Mont., 1974, MA in Sociology, 1978, JD, 1982. Bar: Mont. 1982, Colo. 1982. Assoc. Holland & Hart, Denver, 1982-84, Roath & Brega, P.C., Denver, 1984-88, shareholder, dir., 1988-89; spl. counsel Brega & Winters, P.C., Denver, 1989; corp. counsel CH2M Hill, Inc., Denver, 1989—. Democrat. Episcopalian. Avocations: skiing, scuba diving. Office: CH2M Hill Inc 9191 S Jamaica St Englewood CO 80112 Business E-Mail: pspencer01@msn.com.

**SPENCER, MARK WILLIAM,** music educator, minister, announcer; b. Binghamton, NY, Apr. 11, 1955; s. James Walter and Beulah Augusta (Wormuth) S.; m. Cathy Jean Tinkham, Aug. 1, 1981; children: Scott, Cheryl, Ann. AA, Broome CC, 1975; BA, Judson Coll., 1981; MusM, Southwestern Sem., Ft. Worth, 1984, MusD in Art, 1992. Announcer Sta. WNBF/WQYT, Binghamton, 1974-78, Sta. WSKG FM-TV, Binghamton, 1979; min. of music Trinity So. Bapt. Ch., Kaufman, Tex., 1982-84, St. Timothy Cumberland Presbyn. Ch., Bedford, Tex., 1984-86; instr. of music Golden Gate Bapt. Theol. Sem., Mill Valley, Calif., 1986-88; reader Christian Edn. for the Blind, Ft. Worth, 1988-89; assoc. prof. Calif. Bapt. U., Riverside, 1989—93; min. of music 1st Bapt. Ch., Riverside, Calif., 1989—93; assoc. prof. Cedarville U., Ohio, 1993—. Adj. prof. Golden Gate Sem., So. Calif. extension, Brea, 1990-93. Soloist oratorios in Riverside/San Bernardino area, 1989—; Dodger Stadium, L.A., 1991, choral tours U.S. and abroad. Mem. Nat. Assn. Tchrs. Singing. Avocations: home video, classic film collection, swimming. Home: 678 White Oak Dr Springfield OH 45504-4171 Office: Cedarville Univ 251 N Main St Cedarville OH 45314 E-mail: spencerm@cedarville.edu.

**SPENCER, MARY MILLER,** civic worker; b. Comanche, Tex., May 25, 1924; d. Aaron Gaynor and Alma (Grissom) Miller; 1 child, Mara Lynn. BS, U. North Tex., 1943. Cafeteria dir. Mercedes (Tex.) Pub. Schs., 1943-46; home economist coord. All-Orange Dessert Contest Fla. Citrus Commn., Lakeland, 1959-62, 64; tchr. purchasing sch. lunch dept. Fla. Dept. Edn. 1960. Clothing judge Polk County (Fla.) Youth Fair, 1951-68, Polk County Federated Women's Clubs, 1964-66; pres. Dixieland Elem. Sch. PTA, 1955-57, Polk County Coun. PTA's, 1958-60; chmn. pub. edn. com. Polk County unit Am. Cancer Soc., 1959-60, bd. dirs., 1962-70; charter mem., bd. dirs. Lakeland YMCA, 1962-72; sec. Greater Lakeland Cmty. Nursing Coun., 1965-72; trustee, vice-chmn. Polk County Eye Clinic, Inc., 1962-64, pres., 1964-82; bd. dirs. Polk County Scholarship and Loan Fund, 1962-70; mem. exec. com. West Polk County (Fla.) Cmty. Welfare Coun., 1962-65, 65-68; mem. budget and audit com. Greater Lakeland United Fund, 1960-62, bd. dirs., 1967-70; residential chmn. fund drive, 1968; mem. adv. bd. Polk County Juvenile and Domestic Rels. Ct., 1960-69; sec. bd. dirs. Fla. West Coast Ednl. TV, 1976-81; mem. Polk County Home Econs. Adv. Com., 1965-71; mem. exec. com. Suncoast Health Coun., 1968-71; worker children's svcs. divsn. family svcs. Dept. Health and Rehab. Svcs., State of Fla., 1969-70, social worker, 1970-72, 74-82, social worker Overpayment Fraud Recoupment unit, 1977-81, with other pers. svcs., 1981-82, supr. Overpayment Fraud Recoupment unit, 1982-83, pub. assistance specialist IV, 1984-89; bd. dirs. Lake Region United Way, Winter Haven, 1976-81; mem. Polk County Cmty. Svcs. Coun., 1978-88; with other pers. Trust in p'l Fin. Assistance Housing Program, 1990-96. Mem. AAUW (pres. Lakeland br. 1960-61), Nat. Welfare Fraud Assn., Fla. Congress Parents and Tchrs. (hon. life, pres. dist. 7 1961-63, chmn. pub. rels. 1962-66), Fla. Health and Welfare Coun., Fla. Health and Social Svc. Coun., Polk County Mental Health Assn., U. North Tex. Alumni Assn., Order Ea. Star. Democrat. Methodist. Home: 1639 Crystal Lake Dr Lakeland FL 33801-5915

**SPENCER, MELISSA JOHANNA,** psychotherapist, special education educator; b. Durham, NC, Sept. 13, 1951; d. Joseph Whitney and Regina Colleen (Barnett) Spencer; m. Charles Ray Barrow, Aug. 21, 1972; children: Matthew R. Barrow, Christine N. Gonzales, Charlotte D. Barrow. Attended, U. Hawaii-Manoa, 1986—88; BA in Psychology, Tex. Tech. U., Lubbock, 1990, MEd in Counseling, 1994, EdD in Counselor Edn., 1999. Lic. profl. counselor NC, 2000. Dir. vols. Rappahannock Coun. Domestic Violence, Fredericksburg, Va., 1999—2000; asst. prof. U. NC-Pembroke, 2000—02; pvt. practice psychotherapy Southeastern Psychol. Svcs., Fairmont, NC, 2002—; tchr. exceptional children with autism Seventy-First HS, Fayetteville, NC, 2003—06, Magnolia Sch., Lumberton, NC. Adv. bd. Substance Abuse & Traumatic Brain Injury Linking Svcs., Fairmont, 2005—06. Recipient Tchg. Excellence award, Jiffy Lube, 2005. Mem.: Assn. Counselor Edn. and Supervision, Assn. Specialists Group Work, Internat. Assn. Marriage & Family Counselors, Am. Counseling Assn. Office: Southeastern Psychol Svcs 302 N Main Fairmont NC 28340 Personal E-mail: dr_melissajspencer@yahoo.com.

**SPENCER, MELVIN JOE,** retired health facility administrator, retired lawyer, retired consultant; b. Buffalo Center, Iowa, Jan. 2, 1923; s. Kenos W. and Jennie (Michaelson) S.; m. Dena Joyce Butterfield, Mar. 1, 1952; children: Dennis Norman, Gregory Melvin, Shelly Lynn Spencer Goodnight. AB, U. Mich., 1948, JD, 1950. Bar: Iowa 1950, Mo. 1950, Okla. 1961. Practiced in, Kansas City, Mo., 1950-61, Oklahoma City, 1961—; assoc., then ptnr. Watson, Ess, Marshall & Enggas, 1950-61; ptnr. Miller & Spencer (and predecessor firm), 1961-75, of counsel, 1975-80; adminstr. Deaconess Hosp., 1975-92, cons., 1992-93; ret., 1993. Dir. Union Bank & Trust Co., Oklahoma City, 1977-88, 89-96, adv. dir., 1996-99; dir., sec. Hosp. Casualty Co., 1977-92; dir. VHA Okla., Inc., 1986-92 Assoc. editor Mich. Law Rev.,

1949-50. Mcpl. judge City of Roeland Park, Kans., 1952, city coun., 1954; area Rep. precinct chmn., 1968-69; del. Rep. State Conv., 1968, 96; bd. dir. Deaconess Hosp., Oklahoma City, 1966-2005, Christian Counseling Ctr., 1973-75, Witteman Corp., 2005-, Butterfield Meml. Found., 2005—; trustee Okla. Hosp. Assn., 1978-84, chmn. bd. trustees, 1983, trustee Okla. Co. Med. Soc. Found., 2002—; trustee, vice chmn. bd. dir. Ctrl. Coll., McPherson, Kans., 1972-86; trustee Okla. Ambulance Trust, 1984-87; adv. bd. Okla. State U. Tech. Inst., 1980-92; bd. dir. Emergency Med. Svcs. Ctrl. Okla., 1975-78, FMC Ministries, Inc.; const. coun. Free Meth. Ch. World Fellowship, 1975-95; chmn. Free Meth. Found., 1988-99; gen. counsel Free Meth. Ch. N.Am., 1969-95, bd. adminstrn., 1969-99, sec., 1985-95, investment com., 1976-88, chmn. investment com., 1988-88. Capt. USAAF, 1943-46 Named Layman of Yr., Free Meth. Ch. N.Am., 1984; recipient W. Cleveland Rodgers Disting. Svc. award Okla. Hosp. Assn., 1985; fellow Cen. Coll. Acad. of Achievers, 1990. Mem. Okla. Bar Assn., Oklahoma County Bar Assn., Order of Coif, Phi Beta Kappa, Phi Kappa Phi Home: 5910 N Shawnee Ave Oklahoma City OK 73112-1627

**SPENCER, REX LEROY,** retired secondary school educator; b. Kendallville, Ind., Jan. 29, 1944; s. Richard Donald and Mildred Francis (Fourman) Spencer; m. Diana Carole Land, Nov. 21, 1981; children: Katie Jo, Emily Paige. BS, Defiance Coll., 1966, MA, Ball State U., 1970. Cert. tchr. Ohio. Tchr. Ansonia (Ohio) HS, 1966-80, 1986—2003, Ansonia Mid. Sch., 1982-86; ret., 2003. Instr. Edison CC, Piqua, Ohio, 1983—88, Defiance (Ohio) Coll., 1989—92. Named Outstanding Am. History Tchr., Darke County DAR, 1992. Mem.: NEA, Ohio Coun. Social Studies, Nat. Coun. Social Studies, Ansonia Edn. Assn. (pres. 1976—77, treas. 1991—98), Ohio Edn. Assn. (Ohio Ret. Tchrs. Assn. (life) Defiance Coll. Alumni Assn. (bd. dirs. 1976—79, v.p. 1979—80, pres. 1980—82). Methodist. Avocations: golf, bicycling, walking, antiques. Personal E-mail: spencerclan@adelphia.net.

**SPENCER, RICHARD HENRY,** lawyer; b. Kansas City, Mo., Nov. 29, 1926; s. Byron Spencer and Helen Elizabeth (McCune) Hockaday; m. Barbara G. Rau, Aug. 2, 1952 (div. 1955); 1 chlid, Christina G. Cuevas; m. Katherine Graham, Dec. 28, 1957; children: Elisabeth M., Katherine S. Rivard. BS in Engring., Princeton U., 1949; LLB, U. Mo., 1952. Bar: Mo. 1952, U.S. Dist. Ct (we. dist.) Mo. 1952. assoc. Spencer, Fane, Britt & Browne, Kansas City, 1952-59, ptnr., 1959-94; ret. ptnr., 1995—. Sec., bd. dirs. Met. Performing Arts Fund, Kansas City, 1984—; trustee Barstow Sch., Kansas City, 2002—; dir. Kansas City Symphony, 2004—. Mem. ABA, Mo. Bar Assn., Kansas City Club (pres. 1974), Kansas City Country Club (pres. 1986). Episcopalian. Avocations: hunting, golf, travel. Home: 77 Le Mans Ct Shawnee Mission KS 66208-5230 Office: Spencer Fane Britt & Browne 1400 Commerce Bank Bldg 1000 Walnut St Kansas City MO 64106-2140 Office Phone: 816-474-8100. E-mail: rhs@spencertone.com.

**SPENCER, RICHARD PAUL,** biochemist, educator, physician; b. NYC, June 7, 1929; s. David E. and Frances (Fried) S.; m. Gwendolyn Enid Williams, Apr. 7, 1956; children: Carolyn Roberts, Jennifer Holt, Priscilla James. AB, Dartmouth Coll., 1951; MD, U. So. Calif., 1954; MA (NSF fellow, Helen Hay Whitney fellow), Harvard U., 1958, PhD, 1961. Intern Beth Israel Hosp., Boston, 1954-55; practice medicine specializing in nuclear medicine; mem. faculty biophysics U. Buffalo, 1961-63; chief radioisotope service VA Hosp., Buffalo, 1961-63; asso. prof. nuclear medicine Yale Sch. Medicine, 1963-68, prof., 1968-74; prof., chmn. dept. nuclear medicine U. Conn. Health Center, 1974-97, prof., vice chmn. Dept. Diagnostic Imaging, 1997—2000, residency dir. nuclear medicine, 2000—. Author: The Intestinal Tract, 1960, (with others) Biophysical Principles, 1965, Radionuclide Studies of the Spleen, 1975, Clinical Focus on Nuclear Medicine, 1977, Handbook of Nuclear Medicine, 1977, Therapy in Nuclear Medicine, 1978, Radiopharmaceuticals: Structure-Activity Relationships, 1981, Interventional Nuclear Medicine, 1984, New Procedures In Nuclear Medicine, 1988; contbr. (with others) articles to profl. jours. Mem. Am. Physiol. Soc., AAAS, Soc. Nuclear Medicine, Biophys. Soc. Achievements include co-discovery of functional asplenia; developed first complete description of relationship of food intake to reproductive success and to longevity in a species. Office: U Conn Health Ctr Farmington CT 06030-2804 Business E-Mail: rspencer@adp.uchc.edu.

**SPENCER, RICHARD THOMAS, III,** health products executive; b. Oak Park, Ill., Mar. 18, 1936; s. Richard Thomas Spencer Jr. and Lois Anne (Pollock) Spencer; m. Andrea B. Schlickeiser, June 26, 1962; 1 child, Richard Thomas IV. BA, U. Mich., 1959; postgrad., U. Pa., 1976, Stanford U., 1984, Clemson U., 1985. Mktg. group Mobil Oil Co., Detroit, 1962; internat. trade specialist U.S. Dept. Commerce, Detroit, 1963—64; account exec. J. Walter Thompson Co., Detroit, 1965—66; sales mgr. Sarns Inc., Ann Arbor, Mich., 1967—69; v.p. mktg. Cordis Dow Corp., Miami, Fla., 1970—81; pres. mktg. divsn. Cordis Corp., Miami, 1982—87; pres., CEO Uni-Med Internat. Corp., Miami, 1988—2000; exec. v.p., COO Bd. dirs. World Med. Mfg. Corp., Sunrise, Fla., 1995—2000. Bd. dirs. Viacor Corp., Wilmington, Mass. Bioheart, Inc., Weston, Fla., Hyperion, Inc., Miami; cons. in field. Contbr. articles to profl. jours. With CIC U.S. Army, 1959—61. Republican. Avocations: skiing, golf, running, stereo equipment, geopolits. Home and Office: 3641 N 47th Ave Hollywood FL 33021-2211 Home: 811 E Hill Rd North Troy VT 05859 Office Phone: 954-558-3689.

**SPENCER, ROGER FELIX,** psychiatrist, educator; b. Apr. 19, 1934; came to U.S., 1941; s. Eugene S. Spitzer and Santa Spencer; m. Barbara Ann Houser, Aug. 18, 1958; children: Geoffrey, Jennifer, Rebecca. BS, Yale Coll., 1956; MD, Harvard Med. Sch., 1959. Diplomate Am. Bd. Psychiatry. Intern N.C. Meml. Hosp., Chapel Hill, 1959-60, resident in psychiatry, 1960-63; instr. U. N.C. Sch. Medicine, Chapel Hill, 1963-66, asst. prof., 1966-69, assoc. prof., 1969-76, prof., 1976—. Dir. of liaison and cons., U. N.C., 1967-77, dir. out patient psychiatry, 1977-95 Contbr more than 25 articles and short stories to profl. jours. and lit. mags. Recipient Career Tchr. award NIMH, 1965-67. Fellow Am. Psychiat. Assn. (life), Am. Psychoanalytic Assn.; mem. N.C. Psychoanalytic Soc. (past pres.), N.C. Psychiat. Assn. (past pres.). Office: UNC Hosps Dept Psychiatry CB 7160 Chapel Hill NC 27599-7160 Office Phone: 919-966-5772. Business E-mail: roger_spencer@med.unc.edu.

**SPENCER, SHIRLEY ANN,** secondary school educator, speech educator, literature educator; b. Dayton, Ohio, Mar. 8, 1953; d. Omar and Bertha Keg (Spencer) Whitaker; m. Donald Eugene Lebkisher, Nov. 27, 1977 (div. Nov. 1986); children: Laura Ann, Lindsey Marie; m. William Daniel Burkhalter, Dec. 12, 1987 (div. Aug. 2000). BS in English, Speech & Theatre Edn. Wright State U., 1976; MA in Interpersonal Comm., Ctrl. Mich. U., 1977; Ednl. Specialist in English, Ga. So. U., 1993. Cert. tchg. in Eng., speech and theatre Ga. Tchr. speech Ctrl. Mich. U., Mt. Pleasant, Mich., 1976-77; tchr. ESL and speech Ctrl. Tex. Coll., Killeen, 1978; tchr. speech European divsn. U. Md., Heidelberg, Germany, 1979-81; tchr. Baker H.S., Columbus, Ga., 1982-83, Brookstone, Columbus, Ga., 1983-84; tchr. speech Columbus (Ga.) Coll., 1986; tchr. English Shaw H.S., 1985-86, Jonesboro (Ga.) H.S., 1986-89; tchr. speech, English and theater Glynn Acad. H.S., Brunswick, Ga., 1989—. Instr. for workshops Communications Unltd., Columbus, 1985. Co-author: (textbook) Tools for the Speaker, 1985; contbr. articles to profl. jours. Recipient Teaching assistantship Ctrl. Mich. U., 1976-77; named Tchr. of Yr., Glynn Acad. H.S., 1994-95. Mem. Nat. Coun. Tchr. English, Ednl. Theater Assn., Ga. Theatre Conf. (sec. 2000-2003), Internat. Thespian Soc. Sponsor. Methodist. Avocations: play directing, the Glynn Academy Players, dance. Office: Glynn Acad H S 1001 Mansfield St Brunswick GA 31520-7349

**SPENCER, WILLIAM EDWIN,** retired telecommunications industry executive, engineer; b. Mar. 22, 1926; s. Erwin Blanc and Edith Marie (Peterson) S.; m. Ferne Arlene Nieder, Nov. 14, 1952; children: Elizabeth Ann, Gary William, James Richard, Catherine Sue. Student, U. Kansas City, 1942; AS, Kansas City Jr. Coll., 1945; BSEE, U. Mo., 1948; postgrad., Iowa State U., 1969. Registered profl. engr., Kans. With Southwestern Bell Telephone Co., Kansas City, Mo., 1948-50, Topeka, 1952-61, sr. engr., 1966-69, equipment maintenance engr., 1967-76, engring. ops. mgr., 1976-79, dist. mgr., 1979—86, ret., 1986. Mem. tech. staff Bell Telephone Labs.,

N.Y.C., 1961-62, Holmdel, N.J., 1962-66; pres., owner W.E. Spencer Co.; mem. U.S. Senatorial Club, 1985—. Patentee in field. Mem. Rep. Presdl. Task Force, 1984—; supervising judge Shawnee County Election Comm.; trustee, bd. dirs. Brookwood Covenant Ch., also pres. Joy Sr. Group. With AUS, Pentagon, Washington, 1950-52. Recipient Best Kans. Idea award Southwestern Bell Telephone Co., 1972, cert. of appreciation Kans. Miss Teen Pageant, 1984, Rep. Presdl. League of Merit, 1992—. Mem. IEEE, NSPE, Kans. Engring. Soc., Topeka Engrs. Club (pres.), Telephone Pioneers Assn. (life mem., rep., Sunflower and Heartland chpt.), Topeka life mem., coun. pres. and club pres.), Nat. Geog. Soc., Kans. Hist. Soc., Am. Assn. Ret. Persons, U. Mo.-Columbia Alumni Assn., Nat. Travel Club, Topeka Geog. Soc., Active Prime Timer (historian). Republican. Home: 3201 SW Macvicar Ct Topeka KS 66611-1800 Office: 220 SE 6th Ave Topeka KS 66603-3507 Personal E-mail: wespenc@attglobal.net.

**SPENCER, WILLIAM H.,** farming executive; b. 1945; Pres. Spencer Farms, 1964—, Plants of Ruskin (Fla.) Inc., 1979—; v.p. DiMare Ruskin Inc., Ruskin, 1968-79; owner Spencer Farms Inc., Ruskin. Home: 1187 Skye Ln Palm Harbor FL 34683-1460

**SPENCER-FLEMING, JULIA,** writer; married; 3 children. Graduate, Ithaca Coll., George Washington Univ.; JD, Univ. Maine. Former atty. Portland, Maine. Author: (novels) In the Bleak Midwinter, 2003 (St. Martin's/Malice Domestic award, 2001, Dilys award, Independent Mystery Booksellers Assn., Agatha, Anthony, Macavity, Barry awards for Best First Novel), A Fountain Filled with Blood, 2004 (Borders Original Voices selection, nominee Barry award for Best Mystery Novel, Deadly Pleasures Mag.), Out of the Deep I Cry, 2004 (St. Martin's Minotaur's lead title, nominee Reviewers' Choice award, Romantic Times Book Club, 2005, nominee Edgar award for Best Mystery, 2004, nominee Anthony award for Best Mystery, 2004), To Darkness and to Death, 2005. Episcopalian. Mailing: c/o Jimmy Vines The Vines Agy Ste 901 648 Broadway New York NY 10012

**SPENGLER, DAN MICHAEL,** orthopedic surgery educator, surgeon; b. Defiance, Ohio, Feb. 25, 1941; s. Harold A. and Wilhelmina Spengler; m. Cynthia Niswonger; children: Christina, Craig. BS, Baldwin-Wallace Coll., 1962; MD, U. Mich., 1966. Diplomate Am. Bd. Orthopaedic Surgery (bd. dirs. 1988-97). Rotating intern King County Hosp., Seattle, 1966-67; resident in orthopedics U. Mich., Ann Arbor, 1970-73; asst. prof. U. Wash., Seattle, 1974-78, assoc. prof., 1978-83. Author: Low Back Pain, 1982. Bd. dirs. Musculoskeletal Transplant Found.; bd. trustees Jour. of Bone and Joint Surgery, 2004—. Fellow: Am. Acad. Orthopaedic Surgeons; mem.: ACS, Internat. Soc. for Study of Lumbar Pain, Assn. Bone and Joint Surgeons, Am. Bd. Orthopaedic Surgeons (pres. 1993—94), Am. Orthopaedic Assn. (pres. 2003—04), U. Nashville Club. Avocations: flying, golf, running, skiing. Office: Vanderbilt Ortho Inst Med Ctr E S Tower Rm 4200 Nashville TN 37232-8774 Office Phone: 615-343-6364. Business E-Mail: dan.m.spengler@vanderbilt.edu.

**SPENGLER, PAUL ALBERT,** grants and foundation administrator; b. Buffalo, Feb. 18, 1947; s. Albert Henry and Hazel Mae Spengler; m. Cheryl Ann Spengler, June 22, 1985; stepchildren: Jennifer Ann MacFarlane, Mara Elizabeth Sroczyk. BS, SUNY, Buffalo, 1969, MA, 1973; PhD, U. Del., 1977. Dep. commr. Erie County Dept. Youth Svcs., Buffalo, 1984-87; dir. cmty. svcs. Salvation Army, Buffalo, 1988-93; dir. grants Niagara County C.C., Sanborn, N.Y., 1993-99; dir. found. giving Roswell Pk. Cancer Inst., Buffalo, 2000—. Cons. Edn. Devel. Ctr., Newton, Mass., 1978, Erie C.C., Buffalo, 1999-00, Genesee C.C., Batavia, N.Y., 1999, Adirondack C.C., Queensbury, N.Y., 1999; adj. instr. D'Youville Coll., Buffalo, 1988-90. Author: Yankee Swedish and Italian Acculturization and Economic Mobility in Jamestown New York from 1860 to 1920, 1980; contbr. articles to profl. jours. Sec. standing com. Episcopal Diocese Western N.Y., Buffalo, 1998-2002; vestryman Episcopal Ch. Good Shepherd, Buffalo, 1998—2001, 04-05; mem. legis. commn. homelessness Erie County Legis., Buffalo, 1991-93. N.Y. State Regents scholar, 1965-69; Andelot fellow U. Del., 1973-74, 75-76, 76-77. Democrat. Avocations: reading, gardening, classical music. Home: 26 Groveland St Buffalo NY 14214-1012 Office: Roswell Pk Alliance Elm And Carlton Sts Buffalo NY 14267-0001 Office Phone: 716-845-7719. Business E-Mail: paul.spengler@roswellpark.org.

**SPENGLER-MILLER, JANET TAYLOR,** retired music educator, choral director; b. Wilmington, Del., Jan. 11, 1941; d. Arthur Holt and Dorothy (Price) Taylor; m. Gary Kenneth Spengler (div. 1990); 1 child, Kristin Spengler Zerbe; m. Richard Stanley Miller, Oct. 15, 2005. BSc in Music Edn., Lebanon Valley Coll., 1963; postgrad., U. N.Mex., 1966—67, Westminster Choir Coll., 1986—89; MSc in Music Edn., Towson State U., 1991. Cert. Orff/Kodaly/Daleroze music edn. Towson U., music tchr. K-12 Del., nat. tchr. piano Music Tchrs. Nat. Assn. Tchr. music, choral dir. Kennett Jr./Sr. HS, Kennett Square, Pa., 1963—64, Cornwall Elem. Sch., NY, 1964—66; piano instr. Wesley Coll., Dover, Del., 1970—81; tchr. music, choral dir. Caesar Rodney Sch. Dist., Camden, Del., 1981—84; tchr. music William Henry Middle Sch., Dover, 1984—85; tchr. music, choral dir. Seaford Sch. Dist., Del., 1985—2002; ret. 2002. Pres. So. Del. Music Tchrs., Kent County, 1975—80, Del. Music Educators Assn., 1996—98; accompanist, piano recitalist, music workshop presenter, 1987—; mem. edn. bd. Del. Symphony Orch., Wilmington, 2004—. Chair state standards commn. for visual and performing arts Del. Dept. Edn., 1994—97; conductor cmty. chorus Diamond State Chorlaiers, Dover, 1986—92; dir. music Wesley United Meth. Ch., Dover, 1993—. Named State Music Tchr. of Yr., Del. Music Educators, 1990; recipient Jesse Ball duPont Educator award, Del. Symphony Orch., 2002, Lifetime Disting. Svc. award, Del. Music Educators, 2002. Mem.: Am. Choral Dirs. Assn., Music Tchrs. Nat. Conf. (mem. Ea. Divsns. bd. 1994—2000), Sigma Alpha Iota (past chpt. 1962—63, Sword of Honor 1963), Delta Alpha. Republican. United Methodist. Achievements include frequent performer at Delaware All-State Chorus. Personal E-mail: JTMillerMusic@aol.com.

**SPENSER, IAN DANIEL,** chemistry professor; b. Vienna, June 17, 1924; m. Anita Fuchs, Sept. 5, 1951; children: Helen Ruth, Paul Andrew. BSc with honors, U. Birmingham, Eng., 1948; PhD in Biochemistry, U. London, 1952, DSc in Organic and Biochemistry, 1969; DSc (hon.), McMaster U., 2004. Demonstrator in biochemistry King's Coll., U. London, 1948-52, asst. lectr. in biochemistry Med. Coll. St. Bartholomew's Hosp., 1952-54, lectr., 1954-57; postdoctoral fellow div. pure chemistry NRC Can., Ottawa, Ont., 1953-54; asst. prof. biochemistry McMaster U., Hamilton, Ont., Can., 1957-59, assoc.prof., 1959-64, prof., 1964-68, prof. chemistry, 1968-89, prof. emeritus, 1989—; Akademischer Gast Laboratorium für Organische Chemie/Eidgenössische Technische Hochschule, Zürich, Switzerland, 1971, 89; vis. prof. Inst. Organic Chemistry, Tech. U. Denmark, Lyngby, 1977, Inst. Organische Chemie/Univ. Karlsruhe, Fed. Republic Germany, 1981, Institut für Pharmazeutische Biologie, Universität Bonn, Federal Republic of Germany, 1989. Research in biosynthesis of alkaloids, biosynthesis of vitamin B1 and vitamin B6 Recipient Sr. Scientist award NATO, 1980; recipient Can.-Japan Exchange award, 1982-83, Univ. Club of Hamilton award, 1990. Fellow Royal Soc. Can., Chem. Inst. Can. (John Labatt Ltd. award 1982-83, R.U. Lemieux award 2005), Royal Soc. Chemistry (U.K.); mem. Biochem. Soc., Am. Soc. Biochemistry Molecular Biology, Am. Soc. Pharmacognosy, Phytochem. Soc. N. Am. Office: McMaster U Dept Chemistry Hamilton ON Canada L8S 4M1 E-mail: spenser@mcmaster.ca.

**SPERA, DOMINIC GREGORIO,** music educator, writer; b. Kenosha, Wis., Apr. 18, 1932; s. Costanzo and Anita Spera; m. Patty Jean Graber, Jan. 22, 1956; children: Gregory Allen, Mark Christopher. MusB in Educ., Ind. U., 1967, MusB in Trumpet, 1967, MusM in Educ., 1968. Bandsman U.S. Army, Fort Sheridan, Ill., 1953—56; profl. musician N.Y.C., 1957—67; dir. of instrumental music U. Jr. and Sr. HS, Bloomington, Ind., 1967—68; prof. of music U. of Wis., Eau Claire, Wis., 1968—77; prof. of music Sch. Music Ind. U., Bloomington, 1977—97, prof. emeritus Sch. Music, 1997—. Profl. trumpet player various TV shows, N.Y.C., 1958—66, Radio City, N.Y.C., 1958—66, City and Roxy Theaters, Bands of Lionel Hampton, Charlie Barnet, Benny Goodman, Tito Puente, Tommy Dorsey Bands, N.Y.C.,

1958—66; profl. trumpet player with Burt Bacharach, Johnny Mathis, Henry Mancini, Andy Williams, Frank Sinatra, International Locations, 1966—92. Composer: (songs) more than 100 pub. compositions; author: Blues and the Basics, Making the Changes, 1973, Take the Lead, 1981, Stretching Out, 1985; trumpet soloist and composer (albums) Yamaha Trumpet Series, trumpet soloist, composer, producer Make a Joyful Noise, Chops Don't Fail Me Now; trumpet soloist, composer, producer: albums Dominic Spera Big Band, soloist, condr., edn. dir.: Hawaii Internat. Jazz Festival, 1997—2000, guest soloist, clinician: Jazz Festival, 2003; composer: Dominic Spera Writes for the Brass Quintet, 2005; arranger: CD Dominic Spera Presents the American Popular Songbook for Brass Quintet, 2006. Dir. Eau Claire (Wis.) Jazz Festival, 1968—77; founder, dir. U. Alta. Summer Jazz Camp-, Edmonton, Alberta, Canada, 1979—2002, Bloomington (Ind.) Jazz Festival, 1981—2002. Pvt. first class U.S. Army, 1953—56. Recipient awards, 19 US States, Can., and Australia, 1968—2002, Outstanding Svc. award, Internat. Assn. of Jazz Educators, 1974, 1982; grantee, NEA, 1976. Mem. Internat. Trumpet Guild (life), Internat. Assn. of Jazz Educators (life), Music Educators Nat. Conf. (life). Achievements include first to publish jazz composition utilizing the 12 tone system of composition introduction and allegro for jazz ensemble and percussion; publish theme and variations for jazz ensemble. Avocations: painting, travel. Home and Office: 3704 Grasstree Ct Bloomington IN 47401 Office Phone: 812-339-3210.

**SPERAKIS, NICHOLAS GEORGE,** artist; b. NYC, June 8, 1943; s. George and Cathren (Cokatas) S.; m. Yolanda de Carmen Mesa, Feb. 1, 1983. Student, Pratt Inst., 1960, NAD, 1960—61, Art Students League N.Y., Pratt Graphic Art Center, 1961—63. Instr. Sumitt (N.J.) Art Center, 1971, New Sch. Social Research, N.Y.C., 1972—; Fashion Inst. Tech., N.Y.C., 1977—. Exhibited one-man shows at Paul Kessler Gallery, 1963, 64, Provincetown, Mass., Hinckley and Brohel Art Gallery, Washington, 1964, N.Y.C., 1965, Mari Galleries, Woodstock, N.Y., 1966, 67, 68, Larchmont, N.Y., 1967, Eric Schindler Galleries, 1965, Richmond (Va.) Art Gallery, N.Y. U. Student Loeb Center, 1969, L.I. U., 1971, Pratt Inst., 1971, Bienville Gallery, New Orleans, 1972, 74, Pace U., N.Y.C., 1972, Lerner-Heller Gallery, N.Y.C., 1975, 76, Daedal Gallery, Balt., 1976, Reading Mus. Art, (Pa.), 1977, Bklyn. Mus., 1977, Washington Irving Gallery, N.Y.C., 1982, Museo Universitario Del Chopo, Mexico City, 1984, Forum Gallery, N.Y.C., Mus. Universitario art, Bogota, The Atler Gallery, Munich, 1989, Galerieverein Blankenese, Hamburg, Fed. Republic Germany, 1988, Galeria Sextante, Bogota, 1989, La Francia, Centro de Arte, Medellin, Colombia, 1989, various woodcut exhbns., Alexander S. Onassis Ctr. N.Y.U., 1995, Claudia Carr Gallery, N.Y.C., 1997-98, The Old Print Shop, N.Y.C., 1998, Stephen Gang Gallery, N.Y.C., 2000, Andrew Edlin Fine Arts, N.Y.C., 2003, others; exhibited group shows, Mercy Hurst Coll., Erie, Pa., 1963, 64, Bklyn. Mus., 1964, 77, Jewish Mus., 1964, Chrysler Mus., 1964, 65, Assoc. Am. Artists Galleries, N.Y.C., 1965, Norfolk (Va.) Mus. Arts Scis., 1965, Long Beach (Calif.) Coll., 1969, Am. Acad. and Nat. Inst. Arts and Letters, 1969, 75, Mid West Mus-Am-Art, 1981, numerous others, print exhbns., France, Italy, Spain, other European Countries, Far East, 1970-71, Lerner-Heller Gallery, 1973, 76, Amherst Coll., 1974, Worcester (Mass.) Mus. Fine Art, 1977, Reading (Pa.) Mus. Art, 1977, Galeria El Museo Santate de Bogota, Colombia, 1992, Mus. Modern Art, Rio de Janeiro, Brazil, 1992, travel Ams., Europe, 1992, Rhino Horn, N.Y.C., 1994, WhiteHall, N.Y.C., 1993, 94, Barnard/Biderman Fine Art, N.Y.C., 1994, 10th Ann. Art Miami 2000, 2000, Siron Studios, N.Y.C., 2001; represented in permanent collections Bklyn. Mus., Walter P. Chrysler Mus., Norfolk, Va., Norfolk Mus. Arts and Scis., N.Y.C. Public Library, Phila. Mus. Fine Arts, Worcester Mus. Fine Art, Flint (Mich.) Art Inst., Boston Mus. Art, N.Y.C., U. Conn., Storrs, Amherst Coll., Okla. Fine Arts Center Mus., Am. Acad. and Nat. Inst. Arts and Letters, Detroit Inst. Fine Art, Corcoran Gallery of Art, Midwest Mus. Am. Art, Exeter Acad., Conn., Mus. Modern Art N.Y.C., print collections Nat. Mus. Am. Art Smithsonian Instn., DeHunter Mus. Art, Chattanooga, Libr. of Congress, Washington, High Mus. Art, Atlanta, Free Libr., Phila., Kunst Mus., Fine Arts Mus. Bern Switzerland, Australian Nat. Gallery, Canberra, Snite Mus. Art, U. Notre Dame, Ind., Bibliotheque Royale Albert/ER, Bruxelles, Belgium, Museo Rayo, Roldanillo, Colombia, Stedelijk Mus., Amsterdam, The Netherlands, Hirshhorn Mus., Washington, Mus. Modern Art Santa Fe de Bogota, Nordjyllands Kunstmus., Aalborg, Denmark, Banco Bozano Simonsen, Rio de Janeiro, Mus. Modern Art, Bogota, Rose Art Mus. Brandeis U., Conn.; organized (with others), Rhino Horn artist group, N.Y.C., 1970. Recipient First Prize Purchase award Mercy Hurst Coll., 1964; Lawrence and Hinda Rosenthal award Am. Acad. and Nat. Inst. Arts and Letters, 1969; Guggenheim graphics fellow, 1970; McDowell Colony summer residency, 1976 Mem. Soc. Am. Graphic Artists. Address: 245 W 29th St Fl 12A New York NY 10001-5208 Office Phone: 212-695-5770. *Art doesn't bring out the voters for candidates X or Z. Art brings forth an experience and enters the knowledge of the viewer, so it helps the individual consider new channels and modes of behavior. One of the reasons there is so much censorship of art is due to the power art has to transform people at the roots not into some action but in a more generalized manner in terms of understanding institutions and traditions for what they really are. I think art changes emotions more than it changes specific ideas.*

**SPERATI, CARLETON ANGELO,** retired chemist; b. Fergus Falls, Minn., Sept. 1, 1918; s. Carsten Emmanuel S. and Martha Eline Johnson; m. Eloise Morris, June 1, 1941; children: Charles Robert, William Eller, Solveig Sperati Korte. AB, Luther Coll., Decorah. Iowa, 1934—38; MA in Chemistry, U. Ill., Urbana, 1939, PhD in Organic Chemistry, 1941. Lab. asst. Union Oil Calif., San Pedro, Calif., 1940; rsch. chemist E. I. DuPont de Nemours, Inc., Arlington, 1941—50; supr. E. I. DuPont de Nemours & Co., Wilmington, Del., 1952—55; sr. supr. E. I. DuPont de Nemours & Co, 1955—60, rsch assoc., 1960—69; rsch. fellow E. I. DuPont de Nemours & Co., Parkersburg, W.Va.; cons. E. I. DuPont de Nemours & Co, 1979—98; C. Paul Stocker prof. of engring. (first appointee to the position) Ohio U., Athens, Ohio, 1979—81, Stocker adj. prof. of chem. engring., 1981—. Cmn. U.S.A. tech. adv. group tech. com. 37 on terminology Internat. Orgn. Standardization, Geneva, 1989—98; presenter in field. Contbr. articles to profl. jours. Fellow: ASTM Internat. (Frank W. Reinhart award in terminology 1991, Award of Merit 1998); mem.: Am. Chem. Soc. (life Best Paper of Yr. 1986). Lutheran. Achievements include patents in field. Avocations: music, travel, reading, white water canoeing, skiing. Home: 23 Mustang Acres Parkersburg WV 26104-8040 Office Phone: 304-485-2374. Personal E-mail: pka00099@alpha.wvup.wvnet.edu.

**SPERBER, DANIEL,** physicist; b. Vienna, May 8, 1930; came to U.S., 1955, naturalized, 1967; s. Emanuel and Nelly (Lieberman) S.; m. Ora Yuval, Nov. 29, 1963; 1 son, Ron Emanuel. M.Sc., Hebrew U., 1954; PhD, Princeton U., 1960. Tng. and asst. Israel Inst. Tech., Haifa, 1954-55, Princeton U., 1955-60; sr. scientist, rsch. adviser Ill. Inst. Tech. Rsch. Inst., Chgo., 1960-67; assoc. prof. physics Ill. Inst. Tech., 1964-67, Rensselaer Poly. Inst., Troy NY, 1967-72, prof., 1972—. Nordita prof. Niels Bohr Inst., Copenhagen, 1973-74, NATO research fellow, vis., prof., 1974-77; vis. prof. G.S.I., Darmstadt, Fed. Republic Germany, 1983; sr. Fulbright research scholar, Saha Inst. Nuclear Physics, Calcutta, India, 1987-88. Contbr. over 100 sci. papers to profl. jours. Served to capt. Israeli Army, 1948-51. Fellow Am. Phys. Soc.; mem.: Israel Phys. Soc., N.Y. Acad. Scis., Sigma Xi. Jewish. Home: 1 Taylor Ln Troy NY 12180-7162 Office: Rensselaer Poly Inst 110 8th St Dept Physics Troy NY 12180-3522 Business E-Mail: sperbd@rpi.edu. *My goals are to further an understanding of nature by basic research in nuclear theory and to introduce a new generation to this research.*

**SPERDUTO, MICHAEL A.,** corporate financial executive; From sr. acct. to treas. Engelhard, Iselin, NJ, 1983—92, treas., 1993, corp. contr., 1999, v.p., 2001—, CFO, 2001—. Office: Engelhard 101 Wood Ave PO Box 770 Iselin NJ 08830-0770

**SPERELAKIS, NICHOLAS, SR.,** physiology and biophysics educator, researcher; b. Joliet, Ill., Mar. 3, 1930; s. James and Aristea (Kayaidakis) S.; m. Dolores Martinis, Jan. 28, 1960; children: Nicholas Jr., Mark (dec.), Christine, Sophia, Thomas, Anthony. BS in Chemistry, U. Ill., 1951, MS in Physiology, 1955, PhD in Physiology, 1957. Tchg. asst. U. Ill., Urbana, 1954-57; instr. Case Western Res. U., Cleve., 1957-59, asst. prof., 1959-66, assoc. prof., 1966; prof. U. Va., Charlottesville, 1966-83; Joseph Eichberg prof. physiology Coll. Medicine U. Cin., 1983-96, chmn. dept., 1983-93, Eichberg prof. emeritus, 1996—. Cons. NPS Pharm., Inc., Salt Lake City, 1988-95, Carter Wallace, Inc. Cranbury, N.J., 1988-91; vis. prof. U. St. Andrews, Scotland, 1972-73, U. San Luis Potosi, Mex., 1986, U. Athens, Greece, 1994; Rosenblueth prof. Centro de Investigacion y Avanzades, Mex., 1972; mem. sci. adv. com. several internat. meetings, editl. bds. numerous sci. jours. Co-editor: Handbook of Physiology: Heart, 1979; editor: Physiology and Pathophysiology of the Heart, 1984, 2d edit., 1988, 3rd edit., 1994, 4th edit., 2000, Calcium Antagonists: Mechanisms of Action on Cardiac Muscle and Vascular Smooth Muscle, 1984, Cell Interactions and Gap Junctions, vols. I and II, 1989, Frontiers in Smooth Muscle Research, 1990, Ion Channels in Vascular Smooth Muscle and Endothelial Cells, 1991, Essentials of Physiology, 1993, 2d edit., 1996, Cell Physiology Source Book, 1995 (Outstanding Acad. Book, Choice Am. Libr. Assn. 1996, 98), 3d edit., 2001, Electrogenesis of Biopotentials, 1995; assoc. editor Circulation Rsch., 1970-75, 75-80, Molecular Cellular Cardiology; regional editor Current Drug Targets, 2000-02; contbr. more than 500 articles to profl. jours. Lectr. Project Hope, Peru, 1962. Sgt. USMC, 1951-53, Res., 1953-59. Recipient Disting. Alumnus award Rockdale (Ill.) Pub. Schs., 1958, Rsch. Excellence award Am. Heart Assn. Ohio, 1995, Visionary award Am. Heart Assn., S.W. Ohio, 1996; U. Cin. Grad. fellow, 1989; NIH grantee, 1959-99. Mem. IEEE, Engring. in Medicine and Biology, Am. Physiol. Soc. (chair steering com. sect. 1981-82), Biophys. Soc. (coun. 1990-93), Am. Soc. Pharmacology and Exptl. Therapeutics, Internat. Soc. Heart Rsch. (coun. 1980-89, 92-98), Am. Hellenic Ednl. Progressive Assn. (pres. Charlottesville chpt. 1980-82), Ohio Physiol. Soc. (pres. 1990-91), Phi Kappa Phi. Independent. Greek Orthodox. Avocations: ancient Greek coins, stamp collecting/philately. Personal E-mail: nicksperel@aol.com.

**SPERGEL, IRVING ABRAHAM,** social worker, researcher; b. N.Y.C., Jan. 17, 1924; s. Julius and Frieda Mann Spergel; m. Bertha Jampol Spergel, June 27, 1949 (dec. Nov. 1989); children: Barry Alexander, Mark Jonathan, Daniel Jeremy; m. Annot Mary McGiffin, Oct. 5, 1996. BSS, CCNY, 1946; MA, Columbia U., 1948, PhD in Social Work, 1960; MSW, U. Ill., 1952. Program asst. YM-YWHA, Wilmington, Del., 1948—49; gang worker, supr. N.Y.C., 1950, 1952; ct. rep. Youth Bd., N.Y.C., 1954, 1958, 1960; dir. Neighbors United St. Club project Lenox Hill Neighborhood House, N.Y.C., NY, 1954—57; from asst. to assoc. prof. U. Chgo., 1960—66, prof., 1967—92, George Herbert Jones prof., 1993—2002, George Herbert Jones prof. emeritus, 2002—. UN youth adv. Hong Kong Govt., 1970—71; external examiner social work Chung Chi Coll., 1978—97; cons. Hong Kong Coun. Social Svc., 1978—97; cons., rschr. in field. Author: Racketville, Slumtown, Haulberg, 1964, Street Gang Work, 1966, Community Problem Solving, 1969, The Youth Gang Problem: A Community Approach, 1995, Reducing Youth Gang Violence, 2006. Mem. Ill. Gov.'s Commn. on Gangs, 1995—96, Nat. Youth Gang Adv. Com., Boys and Girls Clubs Am., 1989—91; mem. acad. adv. com. Ill. Criminal Justice Info. Authority, 1989—. With U.S. Army, 1943—46, ETO. Grantee, Ford Found., 1960, NIMH, 1960—61, U.S. Dept. Justice, 1987—2003. Jewish. Office: U Chgo Sch Social Svc Adminstrn 969 E 60th St Chicago IL 60637 Office Phone: 773-702-1134. E-mail: iasperge@uchicago.edu.

**SPERGEL, JONATHAN MICHAEL,** pediatrician, researcher, allergist; immunologist, researcher; married. MD, PhD, Mt. Sinai Sch. Medicine, N.Y.C., 1992. Diplomate Am. Bd. Pediatrics, Am. Bd. Allergy and Immunology. Asst. prof. U. Pa. Sch. of Medicine, Phila., 1998—. Contbr. articles to profl. jours. Fellow: Am. Acad. Allergy, Asthma and Immunology, Am. Coll. Allergy; mem.: Am. Acad. Pediatrics. Office: Children's Hosp Phila 34th St and Civic Ctr Blvd Philadelphia PA 18977

**SPERLIK, ROBERT VAL, JR.,** music educator, musician; b. Oak Park, Ill., Dec. 15, 1959; s. Robert Val and Dorothy J. Sperlik. BS in Music Edn., U. of Ill., Champaign-Urbana, 1982; MA in Music Performance, DePaul U., Chgo., 1986. Cert. Tchr. Ill., 1982. Dir. of percussion J. S. Morton HS, Berwyn-Cicero, Ill., 1983—96; dir. of percussion Morton Coll., Cicero, Ill., 1984—2000; band dir. Sch. Dist. 100, Berwyn, Ill., 1987—. Percussion cons. Shorewood H.S. Band, Shorewood, 1999—; founder-director Take-Ten Percussion Ensemble, Berwyn, Ill., 1996—; prin. percussionist Lake Shore Symphony, Chgo.; jazz band dir. Dist. 100 Heritage Mid. Sch., Berwyn, Ill., 1999—; prin. percussionist Classical Symphony Orch., Chgo., 1985—2001, Lincolnwood Chamber Orch., Lincolnwood, Ill., Salt Creek Ballet Co., Chgo., Chgo. Symphonic Wind Ensemble, Ill.; theatre percussionist Cir. Theatre, Forest Park, Ill.; percussionist Chgo. Chamber Orch., Beijing Opera Orch., Kumamoto Youth Symphony, Festival Marimba Orch. Musician: (percussion soloist) The World of Percussion, 1995, (marimba soloist) DePonte Concertino for Marimba, 2002. Recipient Ill. State Scholarship, State of Ill., 1984 through 1986, First Pl. Percussion Ensemble, Ill. H.S. Music Assn., 1983 through 1996, Divsn. 1 State Band Contest, Ill. Grade Sch. Music Assn., 1989, 1993, 1997, 1999, Dist. 100 Honor Band Day, City of Berwyn, 1997. Mem.: NEA, Chgo. Fedn. of Musicians, Percussive Arts Soc., Music Educators Nat. Conf. Ill. Edn. Assn. Episcopalian. Avocations: performing, bicycling, reading, sports, travel.

**SPERLING, ALLAN GEORGE,** lawyer; b. NYC, Dec. 10, 1942; s. Saul and Gertrude (Lober) Sperling; m. Susan Kelz, 1965 (div. 2001); children: Matthew Laurence, Jasper Jane Kendra; m. Ferne Goldberg, 2001. AB, Columbia U., 1964; LLB, Yale U., 1967. Bar: N.Y. 1969, U.S. Ct. Appeals (2d cir.) 1975. Law clk. to Hon. William H. Timbers U.S. Dist Ct., New Haven, 1967-68; assoc. Cleary, Gottlieb, Steen & Hamilton, N.Y.C., 1968-75, ptnr., 1976—. Editor Yale Law Jour. Bd. dirs. Vol. Lawyers for the Arts, 1998—, Merce Cunningham Dance Found., NYC, 1985-98, 2000—, chmn. bd., 1992-98; chmn. bd. Rye (NY) Arts Ctr. Inc., 1985-88, bd. dirs., 1990-94; bd. dirs. Friends of the Neuberger Mus. Art, Purchase, NY, 1989-2004, chmn. bd., 1997-2000. Mem.: N.Y. State Bar Assn., Phi Beta Kappa, Order of the Coif. Home: 2 Fifth Ave New York NY 10011 Office: Cleary Gottlieb Steen & Hamilton 1 Liberty Plz Fl 43 New York NY 10006-1470 Office Phone: 212-225-2260. Office Fax: 212-225-3999. Business E-Mail: asperling@cgsh.com.

**SPERLING, GEORGE,** psychologist, educator; s. Otto and Melitta Sperling BS in Math., U. Mich., 1955; MA in Psychology, Columbia U., 1956; PhD in Psychology, Harvard U., 1959. Rsch. asst. in biophysics Brookhaven Nat. Labs., Upton, NY, summer 1955; rsch. asst. in psychology Harvard U., Cambridge, Mass., 1957-59; mem. tech. rsch. staff Acoustical and Behavioral Rsch. Ctr., AT&T Bell Labs., Murray Hill, NJ, 1958-86; prof. psychology and neural sci. NYU, N.Y.C., 1970-92; disting. prof. cognitive scis., neurobiology and behavior U. Calif., Irvine, 1992—. Instr. psychology Washington Sq. Coll., NYU, 1962-63; vis. assoc. prof. psychology Duke U., spring 1964; adj. assoc. prof. psychology Columbia U., 1964-65; acting assoc. prof. psychology UCLA, 1967-68; hon. rsch. assoc. Univ. Coll., U. London, 1969-70; vis. prof. psychology U. Western Australia, Perth, 1972, U. Wash., Seattle, 1977; vis. scholar Stanford (Calif.) U., 1984; mem. sci. adv. bd. USAF, 1988-92. Recipient Meritorious Civilian Svc. medal USAF, 1993; Gomberg scholar U. Mich., 1953-54; Guggenheim fellow, 1969-70, APS fellow. Fellow: APA (Disting. Sci. Contbn. award 1988), AAAS, Am. Psychol. Soc. (William James fellow), Optical Soc. Am. (Tillyer award 2002), Am. Acad. Arts and Sci.; mem.: NAS, Soc. Math. Psychology (chmn. 1983—84, exec. bd. 1979—85), Soc. Exptl. Psychologists (Warren medal 1996), Psychonomic Soc., Soc. Computers in Psychology (steering com. 1974—78), Eastern Psychol. Assn. (bd. dirs. 1982—85), Am. Interdisciplinary Conf. (founder, organizer 1975—), Assn. Rsch. in Vision and Ophthalmology, Sigma Xi, Phi Beta Kappa. Office: U Calif SS Plz A Dept Cognitive Scis Irvine CA 92697-5100 E-mail: sperling@uci.edu.

**SPERLING, GODFREY, JR.,** retired journalist; b. Long Beach, Calif., Sept. 25, 1915; s. Godfrey and Ida (Bailey) Sperling; m. Betty Louise Feldmann, June 22, 1942; children: Mary McAuliffe, John Godfrey. BS, U. Ill., 1937; JD, U. Okla., 1940. Bar: Ill. 1940. Pvt. practice, Urbana, Ill.; reporter Champaign-Urbana News-Gazette, 1940-41; mem. staff Christian Sci. Monitor, 1946—2005, Midwest bur. chief, 1957-62, N.Y. bur. chief, 1962-65, news mgr., asst. chief Washington bur., 1965-73, nat. polit. corr., 1970-83, chief Washington Bur., 1973-83, sr. Washington columnist, 1971—2005; ret. Woodrow Wilson vis. fellow, 1976—; cons., lectr. Served to maj. USAF, 1941—46, col. USAF Res., 1960—. Recipient Alumni Achievement award, U. Ill., 1987, Spl. citation, Nat. Press Found. for unique contbns. to Am. journalism, 1994; Sperling Journalism fellow, U. Ill., 2003. Mem.: Fort Myer Officers Club, Overseas Writers Club (Washington), Nat. Press Club (Washington), White House Press Corr. Assn., Congl. Press Corr. Assn., Mass. Bar Assn., Ill. Bar Assn., Okla. Bar Assn., Sperling Breakfast Group (host 1966—2001), Cosmos Club (Washington), Gridiron Club Washington (pres. 1991), Sigma Delta Chi. Christian Scientist. Home: 8101 Connecticut Ave Apt N500 Chevy Chase MD 20815-2827

**SPERLING, IRENE R.,** publishing executive; Asst. mktg. coord. seminars and trade shows Security World Publ., 1979—80; asst. show mgr. Cahners Expn. Group Kitchen and Bath and Office Product Shows, 1980—83, co-pub., 1983—86, v.p. sales and mktg., 1986—2000, publ., 2000—; publisher Tradeshow Week, LA, 2000—02; v.p. spl. projects and internat. sales Trade Show Exec. Mag., 2003—05, v.p., assoc. pub., 2005—. Office: Trade Show Exec 701 Palomar Airport Rd #300 Carlsbad CA 92009 Office Phone: 818-990-1050. E-mail: irenesperling@tradeshowexecutive.com.

**SPERLING, JOHN GLEN,** education company executive, educator; b. Willow Springs, Mo., Jan. 9, 1921; s. Leon Birchfield and Lena (McNama) S.; m. Virginia Vandergrift, June 1951 (div. 1965); 1 child, Peter Vandegrift. BA, Reed Coll., 1948; MA, U. Calif., 1952; PhD, U. Cambridge, Eng., 1955. Mem. faculty Northern Ill. U.; instr. U. Md., Europe, 1955-57; asst. professor Ohio State U., Columbus, 1957—61; prof. Humanities San Jose (Calif.) State U., 1961—73, dir., Right to Read Project, dir., NSF Cooperative Coll.-Sch. Sci. Prog in Econ.; pres. Inst. Profl. Devel., San Jose, 1972-76; founder, pres. U. Phoenix, 1976-80; founder, dir. Apollo Group Inc., Phoenix, 1973—, pres., 1973—98, CEO, 1973—2001, chmn. bd. dir., 1973—2004, acting exec. chmn., 2006—. Author: The South Sea Company, 1964, Great Depressions: 1837, 1893, and 1929, 1966, Against All Odds, 1989; co-author: (with Peter Dixon) War Finance 1698-1714, (with Suzanne Helburn) Economic Concepts and Institutions, 1974, Industry Performance, 1974, National Economic Policies, 1974, Social and Economic Priorities, 1974, Communist Economics, 1974, Third World Economics, 1974, (with Robert Tucker) For Profit Higher Education: Developing a World Class Workforce, 1997; contbr. articles to profl. jours. including Hist. Jour., Econ. History Rev., Bull. NASSP, Rule Mag., among others. Cons. Combating Juvenile Delinquency, Sunnyvale, Calif., 1972-75. Recipient Ehrman Studentship, Kings Coll., Cambridge U., 1953-55, Acad. Freedom award Calif. Fedn. Tchrs., L.A., 1988; named of Forbes Richest Americans, 2006. Mem. Arizona Club. Democrat. Founder the U. Phoenix, which has established itself as a leading provider of higher education programs for working adults by focusing on servicing the needs of the working adult; Primary investor in Genetic Savings and Clone, Inc., "Missyplicity Project" (cloned dog) and "Operation CC" (cloned cat that was created was called CopyCat), made first sale: a cloned male kitten, for $50,000 in December, 2004; latest quest: to research, develop, and sell the new science of longevity; opponent of drug prohibition and is actively financing initiatives to legalize medical marijuana in the US. Office: Apollo Group Inc 4615 E Elwood St Phoenix AZ 85040-1958 Office Phone: 480-921-5394.*

**SPERLING, SHELDON J.,** prosecutor; m. Marvetta Sperling; 2 children, BA, Northeastern State Coll., 1971; JD, U. Tulsa, 1979. Pvt. practice, Tulsa, 1979—82; asst. dist. atty. Okla. Dist. Atty.'s Office, 1983—85; asst. US atty. (ea. dist.) Okla. US Dist. Justice, 1985—89, 1st asst. US atty., criminal chief, 1989—2000, US atty. (ea. dist.) Okla., 2000—. Mem. Tulsa County Bar Assn., 1979—82, Am. Bar Assn., 1979—86, Okla. Dist. Atty.'s Assn., 1983—85, Nat. Dist. Atty.'s Assn., 1984, Nat. Assn. Asst. US Attorneys, 1994—2001, exec. dir., regional dir., del. Recipient Special Commendations, FBI Dir. William S. Sessions, 1993, FBI Dir. Louis J. Freech, 1998, FBI Dir. Robert S. Mueller III, 2002, Dept. Justice Dir. award, 1994. Mem.: Bar of Northern Dist. Okla., Bar of Eastern Dist. Okla., Phi Rho Pi, Rho Theta Sigma, Delta Theta Phi. Office: US Attys Office 1200 W Okmulgee St Muskogee OK 74401*

**SPERO, BARRY MELVIN,** retired health facility administrator; b. Richmond, Va., July 13, 1937; s. Stanley Leo and Jean (Marmorstein) Spero; m. Merle Burns, May 29, 1960; children: Amy, Robin, Melissa. BA, U. Richmond, 1959; MHA, Med. Coll. Va., 1961. Asst. adminstr. Bapt. Hosp., Nashville, 1963-66, adminstrv. dir., 1966-68; v.p., dir. hosp. adminstrn. Hosp. Affiliates, Inc., Nashville, 1968-71; exec. dir. Bon Secours Hosp., Grosse Pointe, Mich., 1971-77; pres. The Mt. Sinai Med. Ctr., Cleve., 1977-85; pres., pres. NeWell Health Care System Newton-Wellesley Hosp., 1985-90; pres. Maimonides Med. Ctr., Bklyn., 1990-95; pres., CEO Masonicare, Wallingford, Conn., 1995—2005; ret., 2005. Mem. pers. practice com. Combined Jewish Philanthropies; chmn. United Way West Suburban Hosp. divsn.; regional bd. mem. Bay Bank Middlesex; mem. Perpetual Benevolent Fund Com., Blue Print 2000, Commonwealth Mass.; bd. dirs. Premier Health Alliance, chmn., 1981—84; bd. dirs. Premier Preferred Care, Healthfirst; trustee Villa Maria Nursing Ctr./Bon Secours Hosp., 1974—94, chmn., bd. dirs., 1988—94; bd. dirs. Assn. Not-for-Profit Providers for the Aging, League Vol. Hosps. and Homes, 1991—95, chmn.-elect, 1992—95; mem. State of Ohio Gov.'s Commn. on Health Care Cost, 1984—85; various coms. Coun. Tchg. Hosps., 1992—95; treas. Vol. Hosps. Am., Mass., 1986—90; chmn. hosp. adv. com. Blue Cross N.E. Ohio, 1983—85; trustee Med. Instrumentation Sys., 1978—84; bd. dirs. Am. Assn. Homes and Svcs. for the Aging, 1998—; adv. bd. Gateway Cmty. Coll. Fellow: Am. Coll. Healthcare Execs.; mem.: Greater New Haven C. of C. (bd. dirs.), Ohio Hosp. Assn. (bd. trustees 1981—85, exec. coun.), Mass. Hosp. Assn. (com. on health sys. 1986—90, bd. trustees 1987—90, com. on Medicare payment for outpatient svcs. 1989—90), Met. Boston Hosp. Coun. (chmn. 1988—90), New Eng. Healthcare Assembly (Blue Ribbon com. 1985—90), Greater Cleve. Hosp. Assn. (bd. trustees 1981—85, exec. coun.), Greater N.Y. Hosp. Assn. (bd. govs. 1992—94), Am. Assn. Homes Svcs. Aging (bd. dirs. 1997—,), Conn. Hosp. Assn. (bd. dirs. 1997—2000), Coun. Tchg. Hosps. (various coms. 1992—94), Am. Hosp. Assn. (com. on Medicare payment for outpatient svcs. 1989—90). Jewish. Avocation: Avocations: golf, tennis, scuba diving. Home: 112 Acadia Dr Poinciana FL 34759

**SPERO, JOAN EDELMAN,** foundation administrator; b. Davenport, Iowa, Oct. 2, 1944; d. Samuel and Sylvia (Halpern) Edelman; m. C. Michael Spero, Nov. 9, 1969; children: Jason, Benjamin. Student, L'Inst. d'Etudes Politiques, Paris, 1964-65; BA in Internat. Rels. with honors, U. Wis., 1966; MA, Columbia U., 1968, PhD, 1973; LLD (hon.), Amherst Coll., 1997. Asst. prof. Columbia U., N.Y.C., 1973-79; amb. of U.S. to UN Econ. and Social Coun., N.Y.C., 1980-81; v.p. Am. Express Co., N.Y.C., 1981-83, sr. v.p. internat. corp. affairs, 1983-89; treas., sr. v.p., 1989-91; exec. v.p. corp. affairs and communications Am. Express Co., 1991-93; under sec. for econ., bus. and agrl. affairs Dept. of State, Washington, 1993-97; pres. Doris Duke Charitable Found., N.Y.C., 1997—. Vis. scholar Fed. Res. Bank NY, 1976—77; bd. dirs IBM Corp., 1st Data Corp.; hon. trustee The Brookings Inst. Author: The Politics of International Economic Relations, 6th edit., 2003, The Failure of the Franklin National Bank, 1980; contbr. articles to profl. jours. Trustee Wis. Alumni Rsch. Found., 1997—, Columbia U., 1998; trustee emeritus Amherst Coll.; mem. Coun. Am. Ambs. Named to Acad. Women Achievers, YWCA, 1983; named Fin. Woman of Yr., Fin. Women's Assn., 1990; recipient George Washington U. Disting. Statesperson award, 1994; Woodrow Wilson fellow. Mem. Am. Acad. Diplomacy, Coun. on Fgn. Rels. (bd. dirs.), Am. Philos. Soc., Phi Beta Kappa. Democrat. Jewish. Avocations: writing, swimming. Office: Doris Duke Charitable Found 650 5th Ave 19th Fl New York NY 10019-6108 Office Phone: 212-974-7000.

**SPERO, MORTON BERTRAM,** retired lawyer; b. NYC, Dec. 6, 1920; s. Adolph and Julia (Strasburger) S.; m. Louise Thacker, May 1, 1943 (dec. Dec. 2003); children: Donald S., Carol S. Flynn. BA, U. Va., 1942, LLB, 1946. Bar: Va. 1946, U.S. Dist. Ct. (ea. dist.) Va., U.S. Ct. Appeals (4th cir.), U.S. Supreme Ct. 1961. Mem. legal staff NLRB, Washington, 1946-48; pvt. practice Petersburg, Va., 1948—2001; sr. ptnr. Spero & Levinson, Petersburg, 1970-75, Spero & Diehl, Petersburg, 1975-85; ret., 2001. Chmn. The Community Bank, Petersburg, 1976-79, dir., 1976-91. Chmn. United Fund Drive, 1960, bd. dirs., 1999-2003; pres. Dist. IV Petersburg Coun. Social Welfare, Southside Sheltered Workshop, 1965, pres. Congregation B'rith Achim, 1973. Lt. USNR, 1942-45, WWII. Recipient Outstanding Mem. award Petersburg chpt. B'nai B'rith, 1966; Svc. to Law Enforcement award Petersburg Police Dept., 1965. Fellow Am. Acad. Matrimonial Lawyers; mem. Va. Bar Assn., Petersburg Bar Assn. (pres. 1981-82), Va. State Bar (coun. 1981-84, chmn. criminal law sect. 1972, chmn. family law sect. 1979, bd. dirs. litigation sect. 1983-86, Lifetime Achievement award for family law sect. 1995), Va. Trial Lawyers Assn. (v.p. 1972), Civitan Club (hon.), Rotary, Elks (exalted ruler 1968). Democrat. Jewish. Home: 9706 Bunker Ct Petersburg VA 23805-9125

**SPERONE, KENNETH J.,** transportation executive; s. Joseph Nicholas and Thelma Margaret Sperone; m. Terri Jo Ebert; 1 child, Nicholas. BS in Mgmt., Ind. Wesleyan U., 2001; MS in Mgmt., IIT, 2003. Wood pattern maker Allen Pattern Works, Ft. Wayne, 1975—79, Std. Pattern, Ft. Wayne, 1979—98, Internat. Truck & Engine, Ft. Wayne, 1998—2000, mgr. rapid prototype lab, 2000—. Mem.: Soc. Manf. Engrs. (mem. panel experts 2005). Avocations: golf, collecting diecasts cars. Office: Internat Truck and Engine 2911 Meyer Rd Fort Wayne IN 46803

**SPEROS, JAMES DEMITRIOS,** advertising executive; b. NYC, Jan. 15, 1954; s. George and Liberty (Stikardis) S.; m. Noreen Mary McKenna, Oct. 29, 1977; children: Keri Melissa, Lindsay Ann. BBA, Bernard M. Baruch Coll., 1976; postgrad., Duke U., 1987. Media planner Benton and Bowles, NYC, 1976; asst. media dir. SSC and B, NYC, 1976-78; group media supr. N.W. Ayer, NYC, 1978-79; advt. dir. AT&T, 1979—98; chief mktg. officer Ernst & Young LLP, 1998—2006; sr. v.p., chief mktg. officer Marsh & McLennan Companies., Inc., NYC, 2006—. Chmn. Assn. Nat. Advertisers, 2002—04. Recipient Print Powerhouse award Inside Print Mag., 1986, Communicator of the Yr. award Bus. Wire, 2001; named one of 100 Best and Brightest Ad Clients Advt. Age mag., 1986; named to the Am. Advertising Fedn. Hall of Achievement, 1993 Mem. Mktg. Media Fedn., Assn. of Nat. Advertisers (chmn. print com. 1986-89, mgmt. com. 1989—), Consumer Audit Adv. Com. (BPA 1987-88). Greek Orthodox. Republican. Avocations: caligraphy, playing guitar, platform tennis, pen collection. Office: Marsh & McLennan Companies Inc 1166 Ave Americas New York NY 10036*

**SPERRIN, GRAHAM FREDERICK,** marketing professional; b. London, Eng., Aug. 22, 1956; s. Frank Reginold and Joyce Ivy Sperrin; m. Kim Julie Hollox; children: Luke, Justin. Degree in Elec. & Electronic Engring., Thames Poly., London, 1979. Sr. design engr. Marconi Comm., Chelmsford, Essex, 1979—83; prin. design engr. Electro Optic Develop., Basildon, Essex, 1983—86; European product mktg. mgr. Anritsu Co., Luton, Bedfordshire, 1987—98, mktg. mgr. Richardson, Tex., 1998—. Contbr. articles to profl. jours. Mem.: IEEE, Inst. Elec. Engineers (chartered engr. 1980), Inst. Mgmt. (assoc.). Office: Anritsu Co 1155 E Collins Blvd Richardson TX 75081

**SPERRY, LEN THOMAS,** psychiatrist and preventive medicine educator; b. Milw., Dec. 1, 1943; s. Leonard V. and Wanda R. (Sadowski) S.; m. Patricia L. Garcia, June 11, 1977; children: Tracey, Christen, L. Timothy, Steven, Jonathon. BA, St. Mary's U. Minn., Winona, Minn., 1966; PhD, Northwestern U., 1970; MD, U. Cen. Technol. Studies, Dominican Republic, 1981. Diplomate Am. Bd. Profl. Psychology, Am. Bd. Psychiatry and Neurology, Am. Bd. Preventive Medicine. Asst. prof. Marquette U., Milw., 1971-74; assoc. prof. U. Wis., Milw., 1974-75, U.S. Internat. U., San Diego, 1976-78; resident in psychiatry and preventive medicine Med. Coll. Wis., Milw., 1982-85; fellow in behavioral medicine U. Wis. Med. Sch., Milw., 1984-85; assoc. prof. psychiatry, preventive medicine Med. Coll. Wis., Milw., 1992-2000, prof., 1992-2000, prof. cmty. and family medicine, 1998-2000, vice chair dept. psychiatry, 1997-2000, clin. prof. psychiatry, 2000—; prof. health adminstrn., prof. psychology Barry U., Miami Shores, Fla., 2000—02, dir. doctoral program in counseling, 2003; prof., dir. doctoral program in counseling Fla. Atlantic U., 2002—. Author: Learning Performance and Individual Differences, 1972, Contract Counseling, 1974, You Can Make It Happen: Self-Actualization and Organization, 1977, Together Experience, 1978, Aderian Counseling and Psychotherapy, 1987, Psychiatric Case Formulations, 1992, Psychopathology and Psychotherapy, 1993, 2d edit., 1996, Psychiatric Consultation in the Workplace, 1993, Handbook of Diagnosis and Treatment of DSM-IV Personality Disorders, 1995, Psychopharmacology and Psychotherapy, 1995, Treatment Outcomes in Psychotherapy and Psychiatric Interventions, 1996, Aging in the 21st Century, 1996, Family Therapy: Ensuring Treatment Efficacy, 1997, The Disordered Couple, 1997, The Intimate Couple, 1998, Brief Therapy Strategies with Individuals and Couples, 2000, Ministry and Community, 2000, Integrative and Biopsychosocial Therapies, 2000, Spirituality in Clinical Practice, 2001, Transforming Self and Community, 2002, Effective Leader, 2002, Becoming an Effective Therapist, 2003, Becoming an Effective Health Care Manager, 2003, Sex, Priestly Ministry and the Church, 2003, Executive Coaching, 2004, Spiritually-Oriented Psychotherapy, 2005, Couple and Family Assessment, 2005, Health Promotion and Health Counseling, Couples Therapy (2d edit.), 2005, Family Therapy Techniques, 2005, The Ethical and Professional Practice of Counseling and Psychotherapy, 2006, Cognitive Behavior Therapy of DSM-TR Pesonality Disorders, 2006, Psychological Treatment of Chromic Illness, 2006; contbr. articles to profl. jours. Bd. dirs. Am. Coun. on Sci. and Health, Nat. Acad. for Certified Family Therapists, St. Camillus Health Ctr., 1996-2000, Cath. Health Svcs., 2001—; cons. dir. Staff Devel. Am. Appraisal Assn., Milw., 1972-76. Northwestern U. fellow, 1969, Med. Coll. Wis. grantee, 1981. Fellow APA (Harry Levinson award 1998), Am. Psychiat. Assn. (chair com. on psychiatry in workplace 1998—,disting. fellow 1998-2001), Am. Coll. Preventive Medicine, Am. Coll. Psychiatrists, Am. Bd. Profl. Psychology, Am. Bd. Psychiatry and Neurology, Acad. Orgnl. and Occupational Psychiatry (v.p. 1993-96, Alan McLean lifetime achievement award 2000), Group for Advancement of Psychiatry, Coalition for Family Diagnosis. Avocations: reading, racquet sports, music. Office: Fla Atlantic Univ 777 Glades Rd Boca Raton FL 33431 E-mail: lsperry@fau.edu.

**SPERZEL, GEORGE E., JR.,** former personal care industry executive; b. 1951; BS in Bus. Adminstrn./Mgmt., U. Louisville, 1977. With General Electric Co., 1977-93; v.p., CFO Andrew Jergens Co., Cin., 1993-2000, Kao Am. Inc., Wilmington, Del., 1995-2000; svp and CFO Alliant Exchange, Inc., 2000—. Office: Alliant Food Service 9933 Woods Dr Skokie IL 60077-1057

**SPETH, GERALD LENNUS,** educational consultant, management consultant; b. Logan, Utah, July 14, 1934; s. Fredrick William and Elizabeth LaVern (Nuttall) Speth; m. Dora Goff, Aug. 11, 1955; children: Camille, Michael Gerald, Mark Alan, Janell, Doreen. BS, Utah State U., 1956; MBA, Ind. U., 1969; EdD, Ball State U., 1988. Auditor Ernst & Ernst, Salt Lake City, 1956, 58-59; officer 1st and 2d lt. U.S. Army, 1956-58, officer capt. to col., 1959-82; contr. Columbia Club, Indpls., 1982-83; sr. v.p. Allied Fidelity Corp., Indpls., 1983-85; adj. faculty Ind. Cen U., Indpls., 1982-85; prof., dir. grad. bus. progs. U. Indpls., 1985—2001, prof. emeritus, 2001—. Cons. in field. Counselor in stake presidency, bishop, area welfare dir., mission pres., high councilor LDS Ch., 1965—. Decorated Legion of Merit, Bronze Star medal. Mem.: U.S. Govt. Accts. Assn., Am. Soc. Mil. Comptrs., Delta Mu Delta, Kappa Delta Psi, Alpha Kappa Psi, Sigma Iota Epsilon, Beta Gamma Sigma. Home: 8337 Goldfinch Cir Indianapolis IN 46256-1629 Office: U Indpls 1400 E Hanna Ave Indianapolis IN 46227-3630 Business E-mail: speth@uindy.edu.

**SPETH, JAMES GUSTAVE,** dean, environmental studies educator, lawyer; b. Orangeburg, S.C., Mar. 4, 1942; s. James Gustave and Amelia St. Clair (Albergotti) S.; m. Caroline Cameron Council, July 3, 1965; children: Catherine Council, James Gustave, Charles Council. BA summa cum laude, Yale U., 1964, LLB, 1969; MLitt, Oxford U., 1966; LLD (hon.), Clark U., 1995; MSE (hon.), Coll. of the Atlantic, 2001; LLD (hon.), Vt. Law Sch. 2005. Bar: D.C. 1969. Law clk. to Justice Hugo L. Black U.S. Supreme Ct., 1969-70; sr. staff atty. Natural Resources Def. Council, Washington, 1970-77; mem. Council Environ. Quality, Washington, 1977-79, chmn., 1979-81; prof. law Georgetown U. Law Ctr., Washington, 1981-82; pres. World Resources Inst., Washington, 1982-93; adminstr. UN Devel. Program, N.Y.C., 1993-99; dean, prof. Yale Sch. Forestry and Environ. Studies Yale U., 1999—. Founded World Resources Inst.; organized Western Hemisphere Dialogue environ. and devel., 1990; chaired U.S. Task Force internat. devel. and environ. security. Contbr. articles to profl. jours.; speaker in field. Bd. dirs. World Resources Inst., Nat. Resources Def. Coun., Woods Hole Rsch. Ctr., Keystone Ctr., Leadership award 1994. Recipient Resources Def. award Nat. Wildlife Fedn., 1976, Barbara Swain award of honor Nat. Resources Coun. Am., 1992, Environ. Law Inst. Lifetime Achievement award, 1999, Blue Planet prize, 2002; named to Global 500 Honor Role UN Environ. Program, 1988; Rhodes scholar, 1964-66. Mem. Coun. on Fgn. Rels. (N.Y.C.). Episcopalian. Home: 88 Mulberry Farms Rd Guilford CT 06437-3215 E-mail: gus.speth@yale.edu.

**SPEVACK, MARVIN,** language educator; b. N.Y.C., Dec. 17, 1927; s. Nathan and Miriam (Propper) S.; m. Helga Massmann, May 28, 1962; 1 child, Edmund Daniel (dec.). BA, CCNY, 1948; MA, Harvard U., 1950, PhD, 1953. Instr. English CCNY, 1955-61; asst. prof. City Coll. N.Y., 1961-63; prof. English, U. Muenster, Germany, 1963-89, dir. English seminar, 1964-89, dir. Inst. Erasmianum, 1974-89; Fulbright lectr. U. Münster, Germany, 1961-62. Vis. prof. U. Munich, 1962-63, NYU, summer 1966, Harvard U., summer 1973, U. N.Mex., 1985-86, Bowling Green State U., fall 1989; fellow Folger Shakespeare Libr., 1970, 98; hon. rsch. fellow Univ. Coll., London, 1980-81, 94—; vis. fellow Wolfson Coll., Cambridge (Eng.) U., 1984; scholar-in-residence Ctr. for Renaissance and Baroque Studies, U. Md., spring 1989; vis. rsch. fellow Inst. for Advanced Studies in Humanities, U. Edinburgh, Scotland, 1991. Author: Harvard Concordance to Shakespeare, 1973, A Complete and Systematic Concordance to the Works of Shakespeare, 9 vols., 1968-80, Robert Burton, Philosophaster, 1984, Shakespeare: The second, Third, and Fourth Folios, 1985, New Cambridge Julius Caesar, 1988, Shakespeare-Text, Language and Criticism: Essays in Honor of Marvin Spevack, 1988, New Variorum Antony and Cleopatra, 1990, A Shakespeare Thesaurus, 1993, James Orchard Halliwell- Phillipps: A Classified Bibliography, 1997, A Victorian Chronicle: The Diary of Henrietta Halliwell-Phillipps, 1999, James Orchard Halliwell-Phillipps: The Life and Works of the Shakespearean Scholar and Bookman, 2001, Isaac D'Israeli on Books: Pre-Victorian Essays on the History of Literature, 2004; also articles and editions. Served with AUS, 1953-55. Guggenheim fellow, 1973-74, Andrew W. Mellon Found. fellow Huntington Libr., 1992, Ctr. for Book fellow Brit. Libr., London, 1994-95. Mem. MLA, Internat. Assn. Univ. Profs. English, Internat. Shakespeare Assn., The Bibliog. Soc., Deutsche Shakespeare Gesellschaft W., Shakespeare Assn., Soc. Textual Scholarship, Harvard Club (N.Y.C.), Harvard of Rhein-Ruhr Club (Germany), Phi Beta Kappa. Home: 14 Potstiege 48161 Münster Germany Office: 12-20 Johannisstrasse 48143 Münster Germany

**SPEYER, JAMES L.,** oncologist; b. Flushing, NY, July 26, 1948; MD, Johns Hopkins U., 1974. Cert. Internal Medicine 1977, Hematology 1978, Med. Oncology 1979. Intern NY Presbyn. Hosp., N.Y.C., 1974—75, resident in medicine, 1975—76, resident in hematology, 1976—77; fellow Nat. Cancer Inst., Bethesda, Md., 1977—79; assoc. dir. clin. affairs NYU Cancer Inst., N.Y.C., 1998—, assoc. dir. clin. and hosp. ops., 2003—; prof. clin. medicine NYU, N.Y.C., 1980—, prof. medicine, 2002—. Office: NYU Cancer Inst 160 E 34th St New York NY 10016-6402 Office Phone: 212-731-5432. Business E-Mail: james.speyer@nyumc.org.

**SPEYER, JERRY I.,** real estate company executive; b. June 23, 1940; m. Lynne Tishman (div.); 3 children; m. Katherine G. Farley, 1991; 1 child. BA, Columbia Coll., 1962; MBA, Columbia U., 1964. Co-founder, pres., CEO Tishman Speyer Properties, N.Y.C., 1978—. Dep. chair Federal Reserve Bank of NY; chmn. emeritus Columbia U., Real Estate Board of NY; bd. mem. Siemens AG, Yankees Global Enterprises, Real Estate Roundtable, Urban Land Inst.; mem. Council on Foreign Relations. Vice chmn. Museum of Modern Art, N.Y.C., NY Presbyterian Hospital; co-chair NYC Partnership. Named one of Top 200 Collectors, ARTnews Mag., 2004, 2005, 2006. Mem.: Economic Club of NY. Avocation: Collector of Contemporary Art. Office: Tishmanspeyer Properties 45 Rockefeller Plz Fl 12 New York NY 10111-1299 Office Phone: 212-715-0300.*

**SPEZIALE, RICHARD SALVATORE,** financial executive; b. N.Y.C., Jan. 27, 1957; s. Vito Anthony and Sally Ann (Buccheri) S.; m. Linda Candida Scro, May 31, 1986; children: Derek Joseph, Chiara Rose, Deanna Caterina. BSBA, L.I. U., 1983, MBA, 1988. Account exec. Dreyfus Corp., Garden City, N.Y., 1983-85; fin. advisor Home Life, Hauppauge, N.Y., 1985-86; br. chief SEC, N.Y.C., 1986-91; 1st v.p., dept. mgr. Prudential Securities, N.Y.C., 1991-94; mng. dir. Citigroup Corp. and Investment Bank, N.Y.C., 1994—. Instr. NYU, N.Y.C., 1989-91, Securities Tng. Corp., N.Y.C., 1989-91. Cpl. U.S. Army, 1975-78. Mem. Securities Industry Assn. (mem. capital com. 1994-03), Bond Market Assn. (mem. capital com. 1995-2003). Avocations: diving, bicycling, weightlifting. Home: 143 Tahlulah Ln West Islip NY 11795-5219 Office: Citigroup Corp and Investment Bank 388 Greenwich St New York NY 10013-2320

**SPHEERIS, PENELOPE,** film director; b. New Orleans, Dec. 2, 1945; MFA, UCLA Film Sch. Film dir. The Gersh Agy. Inc., 1993—. Producer: TV series of shorts for Saturday Night Live; films include: Real Life, 1979; dir. The Decline of Western Civilization, 1981, The Boys Next Door, 1985, Hollywood Vice Squad, 1986, Dudes, 1987, Wayne's World, 1992, Black Sheep, 1996, The Thing in Bob's Garage, 1998, The Decline of Western Civilization Part II, 1998, Senseless, 1998, Hollywierd, 1999, Posers, 2001, (TV series) Danger Theater, 1993; dir., prodr. The Beverly Hillbillies, 1993, The Kid & I, 2005; dir., writer, prodr. The Decline of Western Civilization, 1981; dir., writer Suburbia, 1984, The Little Rascals, 1994; screenwriter: Summer Camp Nightmare, 1987; actress: Wedding Band, 1990; TV films directed include: Prison Stories: Women on the Inside, 1991, Applewood 911, 1998, Dear Doughboy, 2000, The Crooked E: The Unshredded Truth About Enron, 2003. Office: The Gersh Agency Inc 232 N Canon Dr Beverly Hills CA 90210-5302*

**SPHIRE, RAYMOND DANIEL,** anesthesiologist, educator; b. Detroit, Feb. 12, 1927; s. Samuel Raymond and Nora Mae (Allen) S.; m. Joan Lois Baker, Sept. 5, 1953; children— Suzanne M., Raymond Daniel, Catherine J. BS, U. Detroit, 1948; MD, Loyola U., Chgo., 1952. Diplomate Am. Bd. Anesthesiology. Intern Grace Hosp., Detroit, 1952-53; resident Harvard Anesthesia Lab.-Mass. Gen. Hosp., 1953-55; attending anesthesiologist Grace Hosp., Detroit, 1955-72, dir. dept. inhalation therapy, 1968-70; sr. attending anesthesiologist, dir. dept., dir. dept. respiratory therapy Detroit-Macomb Hosps. Assn., 1970—, trustee, 1978—; chief of staff, 1980—. Clin. asst. prof. Wayne State U. Sch. Medicine, 1967—; clin. prof. respiratory therapy Macomb Community Coll., Mount Clemens, Mich., 1971—; examiner Am. Registry Respiratory Therapists, 1972—; insp. Joint Rev. Com. Respiratory Therapy Edn., 1972— Co-author: Operative Neurosurgery, 1970, First Aid Guide for the Small Business or Industry, 1978 With AUS, 1944-45; 1st lt. M.C., USAF, 1952 Fellow Am. Coll. Anesthesiologists, Am. Coll. Chest Physicians; mem. AMA, Am. Soc. Anesthesiologists, Wayne County Soc. Anesthesiologists (pres. 1967-69), Am. Assn. Respiratory Therapists, Soc. Critical Care Medicine, Country Club of Detroit, Grosse Pointe Club, Cumberland Club (Portland, Maine), Severance Lodge. Roman Catholic. Home and Office: 688 Morningside Ln Grosse Pointe MI 48236-1403

**SPICE, DENNIS DEAN,** financial consultant; b. Rochester, Ind., Feb. 7, 1950; s. Donnelly Dean and Lorene (Rhodes) S.; m. Linda Kay Buehler, Oct. 1, 1971; children: Kristie Lorene, Danielle Deanne. AA, SUNY, Albany, 1974; BA, Ea. Ill. U., 1978; MBA, U. Ill., Urbana, 1985. Employee benefits mgr. Ea. Ill. U., Charleston, 1977-80; disbursements officer State U. Retirement Sys., Champaign, Ill., 1980-81, asst. dir. adminstrn., 1981-85, assoc. exec. dir., 1985-90, exec. dir., 1991-95; pres., chmn. Instnl. Advisors, Ltd., Champaign, 1995—. Mng. mem., founding ptnr. Open Prairie Ventures, Champaign, 1997—2006; chmn. Sch. Tech. Ea. Ill. U.; bd. dirs. Employee's Credit Union, U. Ill. Staff sgt. USMC, 1968-77, Vietnam. Paul Harris fellow. Mem.: Champaign West Rotary Club. Office: Institutional Advisors Ltd 5008 W Bluebill Rd Ste 200 Champaign IL 61822 Business E-Mail: dspice@ia-ltd.com.

**SPICER, BARBARA JEAN WENTZ,** elementary school educator; b. Hanover, Pa., Mar. 27, 1951; d. Elwood Frederick and Viola Grace (Wantz) Wentz; m. Edwin Franklin Spicer, June 16, 2001. BS, Shippensburg U., 1972, MEd, 1976. Substitute tchr. various schs. South Western Sch. Dist., Hanover, Pa., 1973, Littlestown (Pa.) Sch. Dist., 1973, Title I reading instr., tutor, 1973-74; elem. supr., tchr. New Freedom (Pa.) Christian Schs., 1974—. Vol. Landis Valley Mus., Lancaster, Pa., 1994, 95. Avocations: writing and directing school plays, sightseeing, sewing, reading. Office: New Freedom Christian Schs PO Box 519 851 Campbell Rd New Freedom PA 17349-0519 Office Phone: 717-235-6877.

**SPICER, HAROLD OTIS,** retired English language educator, communications educator; b. Gosport, Ind., Dec. 10, 1921; s. Otis R. and Hattie Grace (Wampler) S.; m. Hilda Jane Templeton, June 21, 1946 (dec. Nov. 1994); children: Sherry Lynne (dec. May 1987), Sylvia Jean, Stephen Michael, Zachary Ian. BA, DePauw U., 1947, MA, 1949; PhD, Ind. U., 1962. Instr. English DePauw U., Greencastle, Ind., 1947-49, asst. prof. English, 1957-63; from instr. to prof. English We. Ill. U., Macomb, 1949-57; adj. prof. English Ind. U., Indpls., 1960-63; assoc. prof. to prof. English Ind. State U., Terre Haute, 1963-85; ret., 1985. Sec. Main Street, Greencastle, 1993-95. Author: Covered Bridges of Putnam County, 1989, Organizational Handbook for Council on Aging, 1989 (Ameritech Tchr. Vol. award, 1989), James Whitcomb Riley: Hoosier Poet, 1993; co-author: DePauw: Pictorial History, 1987; editor: Ten O'Clock News, a museum newsletter, 2003—05; author, narrator, interviewer: 20th Century Golden Memories, 2001—02. Pres. Ret. Tchrs. Putnam County, Greencastle, 1988-90, 2005-06, Putnam County Coun. on Aging, 1990-96 (Man of Yr. award 1994); bd. dirs. Heritage Preservation Soc., Greencastle, 1993—, Putnam County Found., 1995-02 sec., 2000-03; pres. West Ctrl. Ind. Area Agy. on Aging, 2000, 06. Recipient Danforth Tchr. grant, 1959, Man of Yr. award Area 7 Agy. on Aging West Ctrl. Ind. Econ. Devel. Dist., Terre Haute, 1994; named Older Hoosier of Yr. Ind. Gov.'s Conf., Indpls., 1994, RSVP Vol. of Yr., 1995, Ameritech Vol. Tchr. of Yr., 1989, Martin H. Miller Vol. of Yr. award Ind. Family and Social Svcs. Adminstrn., 1999, Outstanding Leadership award in area/agy. on aging Ind. Assn. Area Agys. on Aging, 2000. Mem.: VFW (life), Am. Assn. Ret. Persons (pres. Putnam County chpt. 1995—96, 1999—2002, 2005—06), Kiwanis Club Greencastle, West Ctrl. Ind. Civil War Roundtable (v.p. 1998—2000), Greencastle C. of C. (bd. dirs. 1995—99, Putnam County Citizen of Yr. 1996), Am. Legion. Avocations: music, writing, travel. Home: PO Box 892 Greencastle IN 46135-0892 Personal E-mail: h.spicer@insightbb.com

**SPICER, HOLT VANDERCOOK,** retired theater educator; b. Pasadena, Calif., Feb. 1, 1928; s. John Lovely and Dorothy Eleanor (Clause) S.; m. Marion Arel Gibson, Aug. 16, 1952; children: Mary Ellen, Susan Leah, Laura Alice, John Millard. BA, U. Redlands, 1952, MA, 1957; PhD, U. Okla., 1964. From instr. speech and theatre to prof. S.W. Mo. State Coll., 1952-93, emeritus prof., 1993—, head dept. speech and theatre, 1967-71, dean Sch. Arts and Humanities, 1971-85. Chmn. Dist. 4 Nat. Debate Tournament Com., 1955, 58, 64, 68 Vestryman Episcopalian Ch., 1981—85, 1998—2001; bd. dirs. Springfield (Mo.) Cmty. Ctr., 1981—. Named Debate Coach of Decade U.S. Air Force Acad., 1965, Holt V. Spicer Debate Forum, 1988; recipient Alumni Achievement award in Speech and Debate U. Redlands, 1991, Alumni award of appreciation S.W. Mo. State U., 1996; team won CEDA Nat. Debate championship, 1992. Mem.: AAUP, Am. Forensic Assn., Speech Communication Assn. Episcopalian. Home: 2232 E Langston St Springfield MO 65804-2646 E-mail: holtspicer9@mchsi.com.

**SPICER, MICHAEL E.,** lab administrator; BS in Acctg., U. Va.; MBA, Harvard U. CPA. Fin. and acctg. White River Corp., The Chinet Co., Kraft Gen. Foods, Deloitte & Touche; v.p., fin. Orchid BioScis., Inc., Princeton, NJ, 2001, v.p., fin., CFO. Office: Orchid BioScis Inc 4390 US Rte 1 Princeton NJ 08540

**SPICER, S. GARY (SAMUEL GARY SPICER),** lawyer, writer, educator; b. Dickson, Tenn., Jan. 8, 1942; s. Clark and E. Maybelle (Hogin) S.; children: Victoria, S. Gary Jr., Matthew, Katy, Mark, David. BA, Adrian Coll., 1964; MBA, Wayne State U., 1965; JD, Detroit Coll. Law, 1969; LLD (hon.), Adrian Coll., 2002. Bar: Mich. 1969, Tenn. 1969. With pers. dept. GM Truck & Coach, Detroit, 1964-66; with trust dept. Nat. Bank Detroit, 1966-69; acct. Price Waterhouse & Co., Detroit, 1969-71; propr. Law Firm of S. Gary Spicer, Detroit, 1971—. Adj. prof. law, sports and entertainment Mich. State U., Lansing, 2002—; adj. prof. law, sports U. Detroit, 2006—. Author: Surviving Success, 1990. Co-chmn. endowment com. Adrian (Mich.) Coll., 1982-94, Don and Dolly Smith Found., Detroit, 1981—; trustee Grosse Pointe Acad., 1983-95, Joseph Sloan Bonsall and Mary Ann Bonsall Found., 1988—, Don Baylor Found., 1995—, JoAnne Nicolay Found., 1996—, Richard A. and Donna L. Stornan Found., 1997, Pam Lewis Found., 1997—, Detroit Tch. Arts, 2004—; Detroit Tigers Players Home Clubhouse Scholarship Fund, Doris and Don Duchene, Sr. Found., Mary I. McLeod Found.; former elder, treas., Fort St. Presbyn. Ch.; memorabilia cons. Ernie Harwell Libr. Sports. With USAR, 1965-71 Recipient Young Alumni Achievement award Adrian Coll. Alumni Assn., 1987; named to Athletic Hall of Fame, Adrian Coll., 1996. Mem. Detroit Athletic Club Avocations: Russian literature, squash. Office Phone: 313-884-9700. Personal E-Mail: sgspicer@aol.com.

**SPICER, SHIRLENE,** history curator; b. Wilmington, NC, Dec. 17, 1966; d. George Andrew and Irene Henderson Foyles Spicer. BA, U. NC, Greensboro, 1989; MA, Hampton U., Va., 1996. Tng. supr. Am. Express Travel Related Svcs., Greensboro, 1990—94; vol. coord. Greensboro Hist. Mus., 1991—93; edn. cons. The Mariners' Mus., Newport News, Va., 1995; asst. curator of mus. edn. Abby Aldrich Rockefeller Folk Art Ctr., Colonial Williamsburg, Va., 1995—98; edn. dir., registrar Mus. of the Albemarle, Elizabeth City, NC, 1998—2002; adj. prof. mus. studies Elizabeth City State U., NC, 1999—2002; curator of cmty. history NC Mus. of History, Raleigh, 2002—. Adj. faculty pub. history NC Ctrl. U., Durham, 2006. Vol. Spl. Olympics NC, Raleigh, 1999—; mem. Somerset Pl. State Hist. Site, Creswell, NC, 2000—. Fellow Smithsonian Ctr. Edn. and Mus. Studies, 2001. Mem.: Am. Assn. Museums (adv. bd. com. for diversity 2005—), Assn. African Am. Museums (sec. 2005—). Avocations: travel, rare/antique book collector.

**SPIEGEL, ALLEN MICHAEL,** dean, internist; b. Lundsberg, Germany, May 18, 1946; BA summa cum laude, Columbia U., 1967; MD cum laude, Harvard U., 1971. Intern and resident in internal medicine Mass. Gen. Hosp., Boston, 1971—73; mem. Endocrinology Rsch. Tng. Program Nat. Inst. Diabetes and Digestive and Kidney Disease, NIH, 1973—76, sr. investigator Metabolic Diseases Branch, 1977—84, chief molecular pathophysiology sect. Metabolic Diseases Br., 1985—, chief Metabolic Diseases Br., 1988, sci. dir., 1990—99, dir., 1999—2006; dean Albert Einstein Coll. Medicine Yeshiva U., 2006—. Recipient Jacobaeus Prize, Novo Nordisk Insulin Found., 1990, Komrower Meml. Lecture Award, Soc. for the Study of Inborn Errors of Metabolism, 1996, Edwin B. Astwood Lecture Award, Endocrine Soc., 1998. Mem.: Inst. Medicine, Assn. Am. Physicians, Am. Soc. Clin. Investigation. Office: Albert Einstein Coll Medicine Jack and Pearl Resnick Campus 1300 Morris Park Ave Bronx NY 10461

**SPIEGEL, ANDREA,** marketing executive; Mktg. and advt. mgr. Avis Rent A Car; dir. mktg. Virgin Atlantic Airways; v.p. mktg. Cunard Line; owner AKS Comms.; marketing. cons. Virgin USA; chief mktg. officer JetBlue Airways, Forest Hills, NY, 2005—. Office: JetBlue Airways 118-29 Queens Blvd Forest Hills NY 11375*

**SPIEGEL, DANIEL LEONARD,** lawyer; b. Balt., Sept. 5, 1945; s. William and Anna (Stiffman) S.; m. Marianne Albertson; 1 child, Anna. BA magna cum laude, Washington U. St. Louis, 1967; MPA, Harvard U., 1969; JD, Georgetown U., Washington, 1979. Legis. asst. to Sen. Alan Cranston U.S. Senate, Washington, 1969-76, legis. asst. to Sen. Hubert Humphrey, 1971—76; spl. asst. to sec. Cyrus Vance US Dept. State, Washington, 1977-78, mem. policy planning staff, 1978-79; ptnr. Akin Gump Strauss Hauer & Feld LLP, Washington, 1983—93, dir. internat. practice, 1991-93, ptnr., pub. law & policy, mem. mgmt. com., 1996—; vice chmn. AG Global Solutions (joint venture between Akin Gump and First Internat. Resources Inc.); amb., permanent rep. US Mission to UN, Geneva, 1993-96. Sr. advisor Clinton-Gore transition Dept. of State, Washington, 1992-93. Office: Akin Gump Strauss Hauer & Feld LLP Ste 400 1333 New Hampshire Ave NW Washington DC 20036-1532 Office Phone: 202-887-4000. Office Fax: 202-887-4288. Business E-Mail: dspiegel@akingump.com.

**SPIEGEL, ELWYN,** advertising executive, art director; b. N.Y.C., Apr. 26, 1926; s. Morris and Rose Ann (Nemetzky) S.; m. Doris Kay, Apr. 25, 1954 (dec.); children: Elizabeth Ann Simendinger, Susan Gail Ambrose, Laura Faith Ciecierski. BSEE, N.C. State U., 1945; BS in Econs., Columbia U., 1950. Pres. Ad Infinitum, Inc., Hackensack, NJ, 1954-63; exec. v.p. Alden Advt. Agy., N.Y.C., 1964-81; pres. Spiegel/Labatt-Simon, Inc., N.Y.C., 1981-88, Compris, Inc., N.Y.C., 1989-96, Elwyn Spiegel & Ptnrs., N.Y.C., 1996—. Cons. in field. Creative dir. TV commls. including Colorforms, 1976 (Clio award, 1976), creative dir. (mag.) Russell Fabrics, 1981; author: Get a New Life, The Jacknife Gypsies. Judge, Clio Awards, N.Y.C., 1975. Recipient Silver award, Neographics 1977, Addy (4), Am. Advt. Fedn., 1977-80, Desi (3), Graphics Design USA, 1981-82, Clio (3), Clio Adv. Bd., 1981. Mem. Nat. Trust for Hist. Preservation, Kiwanis (pres. 1954-55), Alpha Delta Sigma. Avocations: photography, music, sports cars, literature, writing. Address: 41 Park Ave New York NY 10016-3400 Office Phone: 212-490-1991. Business E-Mail: espiegel@ix.netcom.com.

**SPIEGEL, HERBERT,** psychiatrist, educator; b. McKeesport, Pa., June 29, 1914; s. Samuel and Lena (Mendlowitz) S.; m. Natalie Shainess, Apr. 24, 1944 (div. Apr. 1965); children: David, Ann; m. Marcia Greenleaf, Jan. 29, 1989. BS, U. Md., 1936, MD, 1939. Diplomate Am. Bd. Psychiatry. Intern St. Francis Hosp., Pitts., 1939-40; resident in psychiatry St. Elizabeth's Hosp., Washington, 1940-42; practice medicine specializing in psychiatry N.Y.C., 1946—; attending psychiatrist Columbia-Presbyn. Hosp., N.Y.C., 1960—; faculty psychiatry Columbia U. Coll. Physicians and Surgeons, 1960—. Adj. prof. psychology John Jay Coll. Criminal Justice, CUNY, 1983-; mem. faculty Sch. Mil. Neuropsychiatry, Mason Gen. Hosp., Brentwood, N.Y., 1944-46. Author: (with A. Kardiner) War Stress and Neurotic Illness, 1947, (with D. Spiegel) Trance and Treatment: Clinical Uses of Hypnosis, 1978, 2d edit., 2004; subject of book: (by Donald S. Connery) The Inner Source: Exploring Hypnosis with Herbert Spiegel, M.D.; mem. edit. bd.: Preventive Medicine, 1972; Contbr. articles to profl. jours. Profl. advisory com. Am. Health Found.; pub. edn. com., smoking and health com. N.Y.C. div. Am. Cancer Soc.; advr. com. Nat. Aid to Visually Handicapped. Served with M.C. AUS, 1942-46. Decorated Purple Heart. Fellow Am. Psychiat. Assn., Am. Coll. Psychiatrists, Am. Soc. Clin. Hypnosis, Am. Acad. Psychoanalysis, Internat. Soc. Clin. and Exptl. Hypnosis, William A. White Psychoanalytic Soc., N.Y. Acad. Medicine, N.Y. Acad. Scis.; mem. Am. Orthopsychiat. Assn., Am. Psychosomatic Soc., AAAS, AMA, N.Y. County Med. Soc. Office: 19 E 88th St New York NY 10128-0557 Office Phone: 212-534-8877.

**SPIEGEL, HERMAN D.J.,** architecture and structural engineering educator; b. Boston, Dec. 31, 1924; s. Harry and Annie (Gittleman) S.; m. Sally Peery, June 2, 1957; children: Robert Stewart, William Steven. BS in Arch., RISD, 1953; M Structural Engring., Yale U., 1955. Registered profl. engr., Calif., Mass., R.I., D.C., Ky., Md., Va., Conn. Dean Sch. Arch. Yale U., New Haven, 1971—76, from instr. archtl. engring. to prof. emeritus, 1955—93, prof. emeritus arch. engring., 1992—; founder, prin. Spiegel Zamecnik & Shah Cons. Structural Engrs., New Haven, 1966—, Washington, 1971—. Lectr. in field. With U.S. Army, 1943-46, WW II, ETO and PTO. Recipient Alumni Gold medal, RISD, 1972. Fellow ASCE, Yale Eng. and Sci. Soc.; mem. AIA (hon.), ASTM, Amigos de Gaudi (hon.), Assn. Collegiate Schs. Arch., Am. Concrete Inst., Am. Inst. Steel Constrn., Conn. Soc. Architects (hon.), Conn. bldg. Congress, Yale Engring. Soc., Army and Navy Club of Washington, Mory's Assn. Inc., Yale Club of N.Y.C., Yale Club of New Haven.

**SPIEGEL, JAYSON LESLIE,** lawyer, educator, professional society administrator; b. N.Y.C., Mar. 1, 1959; s. Jack and Frieda Rhoda (Michaelson) S.; m. Deborah Marie Scott, Nov. 1, 1986; children: Kyle Reid, Alicia Jean. AB, Georgetown U., 1980; JD, U. Va., 1983; postgrad., USMC Command and Staff Coll., 1991, Army Comd. & Gen. Staff Coll., 1996. Bar: Md. 1984, D.C. 1985, U.S. Ct. Appeals (D.C. cir.) 1986, U.S. Ct. Mil. Appeals 1987, U.S. Ct. Appeals (4th cir.) 1987, U.S. Supreme Ct. 1988, U.S. Ct. Claims 1990. Law clk. to assoc. judge Md. Ct. Appeals, Balt., 1983—84; assoc. Jordan, Coyne, Savits & Lopata, Washington, 1985—91, ptnr., 1991—94; dep. asst. sec. U.S. Army, 1994—99, acting asst. sec., 1997—99; exec. dir. Res. Officers Assn., 1999—2003; sr. nat. def. counsel Ball Janik, LLP, 2003—05; prin. tech. dir. Anteon Corp., 2005—. Lectr. law and transfusion medicine NIH, 1989, 91-94. Contbr. articles to profl. jours. Mem. recreation adv. bd. Montgomery County, Md., 1989-93. With USAR, 1981—. Desert Shield/Desert Storm, 1990-91. Mem.: ABA (young lawyers mem. com. on law and nat. security, vice chair internat. criminal law com. 1991—94), Conf. of Def. Assn. (Can.), Nat. Def. Indsl. Assn., Md. Bar Assn., D.C. Bar Assn. (founder, chmn. com. on law and nat. security 0197—1994, Com. Chmn. of Yr. 1988, 1991), U.S. C. of C. (com. of 100 assn. execs. 2000—03), Mil. Coalition (bd. dirs. 1999—2003), Res. Officers Assn. (life), Army and Navy club. Avocations: running, tennis. Office Phone: 202-777-1399. Personal E-mail: jayson_spiegel@yahoo.com. Business E-Mail: jspiegel@anteon.com.

**SPIEGEL, JENNIFER,** language educator; d. Francis A. and Dawn L. Markovich; m. Thomas F. Spiegel, June 20, 1998. BA in Comm. and Secondary Edn., Point Park Coll., Pitts., 1997; MA in Libr. Sci., U. Pitts, 2005. Cert. tchr. comm. level II Pa., libr. sci. level II Pa. Tchr. English Elizabeth Forward Sch. Dist., Elizabeth, Pa., 1999—. Yearbook advisor Elizabeth Forward Sch. Dist., 1999—. Named 1st pl. Yearbook, Pa. Sch. Publs. Assn., 2002, 2003, Keystone award, 2003, 2d pl. Yearbook, 2004, 1st pl. Yearbook, Am. Sch. Publs. Assn., 2002, 2003, 2004; recipient Bronze cert., Columbia Scholastic Press, 2004. Mem.: Pa. State Edn. Assn., Pa. Scholastic Press Assn. Presbyterian. Avocations: reading, piano, gardening, scrapbooks.

**SPIEGEL, JOAN ELIZABETH,** anesthesiologist, educator; b. Buffalo, N.Y., May 4, 1967; d. David Isaac and Sally Bogolub Fand; m. Jeffrey Howard Spiegel, Apr. 9, 1995 (div. May 2002); 1 child, Jacob Harris. BS, MIT, Cambridge, Mass., 1990; MD, U. Mich., Ann Arbor, 1995. Diplomate Am. Bd. Anesthesiology, Am. Bd. Internal Medicine. Clinician Beth Israel Deaconess Med. Ctr., Boston, 2002—, dir. post anesthesia care unit, 2003—. Course dir. surg. airway mgmt. Surg. Ctr. Beth Israel Deaconess Med. Ctr., Boston; instr. Harvard Med. Sch., Boston, 2002—; cons. MedaCorp Consulting, Boston, 2006—. Author, editor: Anesthesia: Key Words Defined, 2006, cons. editor: Med. Sci. Monitor, 2005—; contbr. articles to profl. jours. Recipient Rsch. award, STARR Found. of MIT, 1990, Am. Heart Saver award, Am. Heart Assn., 2002; grantee, Portex, Inc., 2003. Mem.: Am. Soc. Anesthesiologists. Achievements include patents pending for endotracheal tube pressure device. Avocations: bicycling, gardening, inventing. Office: BIDMC Dept Anesthesia 330 Brookline Ave ST-308 Boston MA 02215 Business E-mail: jspiegel@bidnc.harvard.edu.

**SPIEGEL, LAWRENCE HOWARD,** advertising executive; b. NYC, Oct. 9, 1942; s. Melvin Arthur and Rose (Black) S.; m. Christy Mansfield; children from previous marriage: Robert, David. BA, NYU, 1963. Print buyer William Esty Co., N.Y.C., 1964-65, broadcast buyer, 1965-66; media planner Batten, Barton, Durstine & Osborn, Inc., N.Y.C., 1966-67, media supr., 1967-68, assoc. media dir., 1969-72, v.p., 1972-74; media group head Jack Tinker & Ptnrs., N.Y.C., 1968-69; v.p. Tracy-Locke, Dallas, 1974-80, sr. v.p., 1980-84, exec. v.p., 1984-89; prin. The Richards Group, Dallas, 1989—. Pres. Tex. Coun. Advt., 1991-97, Leading Agy. Network, 1997—; dir. Dream Fund, 1999—; charter mem. broadband video adv. bd. AOL. Guest editor Mktg. and Media Decision mag., June 1982. Mem. Dallas Cable Bd., 1983-86; chmn. mktg. com. U. Tex., Dallas, 1984-89; pres. Cable Access Dallas, Inc., 1985-86; trustee Dallas Symphony Assn., 1978—; bd. dirs. Equest Inc., 1991-92, DREAM Fund, 1999—. Mem. Assn. Broadcasting Execs. Tex. (pres. 1975-76), Am. Women in Radio and TV, Inc. (bd. dirs. 1992-93). Republican. Avocations: skiing, sailing. Office: The Richards Group 8750 N Central Expy Ste 1200 Dallas TX 75231-6436 Office Phone: 214-891-5843. Business E-Mail: Larry_Spiegel@richards.com.

**SPIEGEL, MARCIA COHN,** writer; b. Chgo., Oct. 16, 1927; d. Alfred and Helen Cohn; m. Sidney L. Spiegel; children: Linda Allen, Randi, Judy, Edward, Steven. BA in Psychology, Rockford (Ill.) Coll., 1949; MA in Communal Svc., Hebrew Union Coll., L.A., 1979; Cert. Beyond Classroom, U. So.Calif, L.A., 1980. Instr. U. Judaism, L.A., 1979-91, UCLA Ext., 1980-81. Cons. in vol. devel., 1979-92; lectr., workshop facilitator in women's studies and spirituality, 1980—. Co-author: Women Speak to God, 1987, Jewish Women's Awareness Guide, 1992, Chemical Dependency: Catholic-Jewish Relfections, 1987; author: The Jewish Woman: A Portrait in Her Own Words, 1978, The Heritage of Noah: Alcoholism in the Jewish Community Today, 1980, Women in the Bible: A Study Course, 1983; contbr. articles to books, mags. and periodicals. Co-founder Jr. Great Books, Palos Verdes, Calif., 1960-75; co-founder, later pres. Alcoholism Coun. South Bay, Torrance, Calif., 1968-80; co-founder, pres. Women Writers West, L.A., 1980; commr. L.A. County Commn. on Alcohol, 1980-83; founder Jewish Arts Assocs., 1981—, Creative Jewish Women's Alliance, 1979, Alcohol/Drug Action Program, 1983-98; mem. Bnot Eish Spiritual Cmty., 1981—; mem. Jewish task force Ctr. for Prevention of Sexual and Domestic Violence, 1993-2005, sec. Project Kesher, 1996—; dr. Jewish Communal Svc., Hebrew Union Coll./Jewish Theol. Sem., 2004. Recipient Award of Distinction, Rockford Coll., 1984, Frances Henry award Hebrew Union Coll., L.A., 1978, Cmty. award Jewish Fedn. South Bay, 1992, Achievement award Nat. Fedn. Temple Sisterhoods, 1978, Alumni of Yr. award Hebrew Union Coll./Jewish Inst. Religion, 1994; named L.A. County Woman of Yr., 1997; named one of Living Feminists Who Changed Soc., Am. Jewish Women's Archive, 2005. Democrat. Avocations: photography, travel.

**SPIEGEL, MELVIN,** retired biology professor; s. Philip Edward and Sadie (Friedman) S.; m. Evelyn Sclufer, Apr. 16, 1955; children: Judith Ellen, Rebecca Ann. BS, U. Ill., 1948; PhD, U. Rochester, 1952; MA (hon.), Dartmouth Coll. Research fellow U. Rochester, 1952-53, Calif. Inst. Tech., 1953-55, 64-65; asst. prof. Colby Coll., 1955-59; mem. faculty Dartmouth Coll., Hanover, NH, 1959—, prof. biology, 1966-93; prof. emeritus Dartmouth Coll, Hanover, NH; chmn. dept. biol. scis. Dartmouth Coll., Hanover, NH, 1972-74. Summer investigator Marine Biol. Lab., Woods Hole, Mass., 1954—; sr. rsch. biologist U. Calif.-San Diego, 1970-71; vis. prof. biochemistry Nat. Inst. Med. Rsch., Mill Hill, London, 1971; vis. prof. Biocenter, U. Basel, 1979-82, 85; Wilson Meml. lectr. U. N.C., 1975; program dir. developmental biology NSF, 1975-76; mem. cell biology study sect. NIH, 1966-70 Editl. bd.: Biol. Bull., 1966-70, 71-75, Cell Differentiation, 1979-88; contbr. articles to profl. jours. Trustee Marine Biol. Lab. Corp.; mem. exec. com., trustee Marine Biol. Lab., 1976-80. Fellow AAAS; mem. Am. Soc. Cell Biology, Am. Soc. Devel. Biology, Internat. Soc. Devel. Biologists (sec.-treas. 1977-81, bd. dirs. 1981-85). E-mail: melvin.spiegel@dartmouth.edu.

**SPIEGEL, PHYLLIS,** public relations consultant, journalist; b. Bronx, N.Y. d. Bernard and Lillian (Horowitz) Finkelberg; m. Stanley Spiegel, Sept. 20, 1959 (div. 1981); children: Mark, Adam. BA, NYU. Feature writer various newspapers, pubs., 1960's-70's; dir. pub. rels. Mort Barish Assocs., Princeton, NJ, 1975-80; account exec. pub. rels. Keyes Martin, Springfield, NJ, 1980-84; pres. Phyllis Spiegel Assocs., Plainsboro, NJ, 1984—. Pub. rels. dir., founder Red Oak Coop. Nursery Sch., Middletown, N.J., 1960's, Matawan (N.J.) Student Enrichment Program, 1960s-70s; pub. rels. cons., event organizer New Philharm. of N.J., Morristown, 1991-93; mem. Child Placement Rev. Bd. of Family Ct., Mercer County, N.J., 1994-98. Recipient Commendation from Gov. N.J. for U. Med. and Dentistry of N.J. campaign, 1983, Commendation for N.J. Pharm. Assn. campaign Pub. Rels. News Assn., 1979. Mem.: Soc. Humanistic Judaism (bd. dir. 1983—85). Avocations: film and theatre, classical music, reading, travel, walks. Office: Phyllis Spiegel Assocs PO Box 243 Plainsboro NJ 08536-0243

**SPIEGEL, SIEGMUND,** architect; b. Gera, Germany, Nov. 13, 1919; came to U.S., 1938, naturalized, 1941. s. Jakob and Sara (Precker) S.; m. Ruth Josias, Apr. 13, 1945; children: Sandra Renee, Deborah Jean. Student, Colll. City N.Y., 1939—40, Columbia U., 1945—50; DHL (hon.), Hofstra U., 1993. Registered arch., N.Y., N.J., Mass., Md., Va., Pa., Conn., Ga., Vt., Tenn., N.H., Fla.; lic. profl. planner, N.J. Draftsman Mayer & Whittlesey, Archs., N.Y.C., 1941-47, office mgr., 1947-55; pvt. practice arch. East Meadow, N.Y., 1956—. Author: The Spiegel Plan; contbr. articles to Progressive Arch.; prin. works include Syosset (N.Y.) Hosp., 1962, Reliance Fed. Savs. and Loan Assn. Bank, Queens, N.Y., 1961, Louden Hall Psychiat. Hosp., 1963, Human Resources Sch., Albertson, N.Y., 1964, Nassau Ctr. for Emotionally Disturbed Children, 1968, Harbor Club Apt., Babylon, N.Y., 1968, Reliance Fed. Bank, Albertson, 1967, North Isle Club and Apt. Cmty., Coram, N.Y., 1972, County Fed. Savs. & Loan Assn., Commack, N.Y., 1972, Birchwood Glen Apt. Cmty., Holtsville, N.Y., 1972, Bayside Fed. Savs. & Loan Bank Plaza, Patchogue, N.Y., 1973, L.E. Woodward Sch. for Emotionally Disturbed Children, Freeport, N.Y., 1974, Birchwood Sagamore Hills, Blue Ridge and Bretton Woods Condominium Cmtys., Coram, N.Y., 1975, Maple Arms Condos, Westbury, N.Y., 1982, Dept. Pub. Works, Freeport, N.Y., Nuc. Molecular Resonance Bldg., 1983. Served with AUS, 1941-45, ETO. Decorated Purple Heart, Bronze Star, Croix de Guerre with palme (Belgium); recipient grand prize for instnl. bldgs. (for Syosset Hosp.), L.I. Assn., 1963, grand prize Human Resources Sch., 1966, grand prize Stony Brook Profl. Bldg., 1966, Beautification award, Town Hempstead, N.Y., 1969, Archi award for Harbour Club Apts., L.I. Assn., 1970, for Birchwood Blue Ridge Condominiums, 1974, Dr. Martin Luther King Jr. award Nassau County, 1986, Louise E. Yavner award N.Y. State Bd. Regents, 1992; fellow Acad. Mktg. Sci., L.I.U. 1971. Mem. AIA, N.Y. State Assn. Archs., East Meadow C. of C. (pres. 1966), Kiwanis Club. Home: Carlton Terr 6-D 10245 Collins Ave Bal Harbour FL 33154-1407 E-mail: sigaia@aol.com.

**SPIEGELBERG, EMMA JO,** business education educator, academic administrator; b. Mt. View, Wyo., Nov. 22, 1936; d. Joseph Clyde and Dorcas (Reese) Hatch; m. James Walter Spiegelberg, June 22, 1957; children: William L., Emory Walter, Joseph John. BA with honors, U. Wyo., 1958, MEd, 1985; EdD, Boston U., 1990. Tchr. bus. edn. Laramie H.S., Wyo., 1960—61, 1965—93, adminstr., 1993—97; prin. McCormick Jr. H.S., Cheyenne, 1997—2002; exec. dir. Wyo. Assn. Secondary Sch. Prins., 2001— Author: Branigan's Accounting Simulation, 1986, London & Co. II, 1993; co-author: Glencoe Computerized Accounting, 1993, 2d edit., 1995, Microcomputer Accounting: Daceasy, 1994, Microcomputer Accounting: Peachtree, 1994, 3d edit., 2000, Microcomputer Accounting: Accpac, 1994, Computerized Accounting with Peachtree, 1995, 2000, 02. Bd. dir. Cathedral Home for Children, Laramie, 1967-70, 72—, pres., 1985-88, Laramie Plains Mus., 1970-79. Named Wyo. Bus. Tchr. of Yr., 1982, Wyo. Asst. Prin. of Yr., 1997. Mem.: NASSP, NEA, Wyo. Edn. Assn. Secondary Sch. Prins. (sec., treas. 1997—2001), Albany County Edn. Assn. (sec. 1970—71), Wyo. Edn. Assn., Wyo. Bus. Edn. Assn. (pres. 1979—80), Internat. Soc. Bus. Edn. (rep. Mt. Plains chpt. 2006—), Mt. Plains Bus. Edn. Assn. (Wyo. rep. to bd. dirs. 1982—85, pres. 1987—88, Sec. Tchr. of Yr. 1991 Leadership award 1992),

Nat. Bus. Edn. Assn. (bd. dir. 1987—88, 1991—96, Sec. Tchr. of Yr. 1991) Wyo. Vocat. Assn. (exec. bd. 1978—80, pres. 1981—82, exec. sec. 1986—89, Outstanding Contbns. to Vocat. Edn. award 1983, Tchr. of Yr. 1985), Am. Vocat. Assn. (policy com. region V 1984—87, region V Tchr. of Yr. 1986), U. Wyo. Alumni Assn. (bd. dir. 1985—90, pres. 1988—89), Laramie C. of C. (bd. dir. 1985—88), Zonta Internat. (Laramie) (v.p. 2002—03, pres. 2003—04, dist. 12 parliamentarian 2004—06), Delta Pi Epsilon, Pi Lambda Theta, Chi Omega, Alpha Delta Kappa (state pres. 1978—82), Phi Delta Kappa, Kappa Delta Pi. Episcopalian. Home: 3301 Grays Gable Rd Laramie WY 82072-5031 Office Phone: 307-745-5468. Personal E-mail: jwejspigelberg@aol.com.

**SPIEGELBERG, HARRY LESTER,** retired paper company executive; b. New London, Wis., Apr. 24, 1936; s. Harry Henry and Gladys Louise (Kalt) Spiegelberg; m. Bonnie Faye Ludden, Jan. 23, 1960; children: Susan Faye Spiegelberg Schuldes, Sharon Louise Spiegelberg Kozlowski, Stephen Harry, Scott Charles. BSChemE, U. Wis., 1959; MS, Inst. Paper Chemistry, Appleton, Wis., 1963, PhD, 1966; MBA, U. Chgo., 1980. Tchg. asst. U. Wis. Coll. Engring., Madison, 1957-59; engr. Kimberly-Clark Corp., Neenah, Wis., 1959-61, rsch. scientist, 1965-68, mgr. new concepts, 1968-73, dir. R & D, 1973-84, v.p. consumer tissue rsch., 1985-92, v.p. tech. and patent strategy, 1992-93, v.p. tech. transfer, 1993-96; ret., 1996. Mem., past chmn. indsl. liaison coun. Coll. Engring., 1987—93; founder, chmn. Paper Industry Internat. Hall of Fame; past pres. Ctr. Project Inc. Paper industry bus. columnist:; contbr. chapters to books; patentee in nonwovens and tissue fields. Mem. U. Wis. Found. Capt. C.E. USAR, 1959—67. Recipient Disting. Svc. citation, U. Wis., 1986. Congregationalist. Avocations: bicycling, backpacking, kayaking, antique farm equipment. Home: 3624 S Barker Ln Appleton WI 54915-7038 E-mail: hspiegel@athenet.net.

**SPIEGELMAN, ART,** writer, cartoonist; b. Stockholm, Feb. 15, 1948; s. Wladek and Andzia (Zylberberg) S.; m. Francoise Mouly, July 12, 1977; children: Nadja, Dashiell. Student, Harpur Coll. (now SUNY), Binghamton, N.Y. Creative cons., artist, designer, editor, writer Topps Chewing Gum, Inc., Bklyn., 1966-88; editor Douglas Comix, 1972; contbg. editor Arcade, the Comics Revue, 1975-76; founding editor Raw, 1980—; artist, contbg. editor New Yorker, 1992—2003. Instr. San Francisco Acad. Art, 1974-75, N.Y. Sch. Visual Arts, 1979-87. Author, illustrator: The Complete Mr. Infinity, 1970, The Viper Vicar of Vice, Villainy, and Vickedness, 1972, Ace Hole, Midge Detective, 1974, The Language of Comics, 1974, Breakdowns: From Maus to Now: An Anthology of Strips, 1977, Work and Turn, 1979, Every Day Has Its Dog, 1979, Two-Fisted Painters Action Adventure, 1980, Maus: A Survivor's Tale, 1986 (Joel M. Cavior award for Jewish Writing 1986, Nat. Book Critics Cir. nomination 1986, Pulitzer prize 1992), Maus, Part Two, 1992 (Nat. Book Critics Cir. nomination 1992, Pulitzer prize 1992), Open Me.I'm a Dog!, 1997; (with J.M. March) The Wild Party, 1994, Kisses from New York; (with F. Mouly) Read Yourself Raw, 1987, In the Shadow of No Towers, 2004 (named one of the 100 Notable Books of 2004, NY Times Book Review); contbr. The Apex Treasury of Underground Comics, 1974; compiling editor (with B. Schneider) Whole Grains: A Book of Quotations, 1972; creator (with composer Phillip Johnston) Drawn to Death: A Three Panel Opera, Am. Repertory Theatre Co., Cambridge, Mass.; editor (comic series) Little Lit; exhbns. include N.Y. Cultural Ctr., Inst. Contemporary Art, London, Seibu Gallery, Tokyo, Mus. Modern Art, N.Y.C., 1991, Galerie St. Etienne, N.Y.C., 1992, Ft. Lauderdale Mus. Art, 1993; creator Wacky Packages, Garbage Pail Kids and other novelties; contbr. to numerous underground comics. Recipient Playboy Editorial award for best comic strip, 1982, Yellow Kid award for best comic strip author, 1982, Regional Design award Print mag., 1983, 84, 85, Inkpot award San Diego Comics Conv., 1987, Stripschappening award for best fgn. comics album, 1987, Alpha Art award Angouleme, France, 1993; Named one of Time Mag. 100 Most Influential People, 2005. Office: c/o The Steven Barclay Agency 321 Pleasant St Petaluma CA 94952-2648 Office Phone: 888-965-7323.

**SPIELBERG, STEPHEN PAUL,** dean, educator; b. 1945; m. Laurel A. Spielbery. AB, Princeton U., 1966; PhD in pharmacology, U. Chgo., 1971; MD, U. Chgo. Pritzker Sch. Medicine, 1973. Pediat. resident Children's Hosp. Med. Ctr., Boston, 1974—75; instr. to asst. prof. pediat. & pharmacology Johns Hopkins U. Sch. Medicine, 1971—81; assoc. prof. to prof. pediat. & pharmacology U. Toronto, 1981—92, dir. Ctr. for Drug Safety Rsch., 1988—92; sr. scientist rsch. inst. Hosp. for Sick Children, Toronto, established & headed div. pediat. clin. pharmacology and toxicology, 1987—92; exec. dir. exploratory biochemical toxicology and clin. and regulatory develop. Merck Labs., 1992—97; v.p. pediat. drug develop. Johnson & Johnson Pharm. Rsch. & Develop., Titusville, NJ, 1997—2003, established dept. of pediat. drug develop.; v.p. health affairs Dartmouth Coll., 2003—; dean & prof. pediat. and pharmacology and taxicology Dartmouth Med. Sch., 2003—. Adj. prof. pediat., medicine and pharmacology Thomas Jefferson U.; adj. prof. pediat. Robert Wood Johnson Med. Sch.; mem. adv. bd. PediaLink; mem. Fed. Adv. Com., Nat. Children's Study, Nat. Inst. of Child Health and Human Develop.; chair Pediat. Task Force, Pharm. Rsch. and Mfr. of Am.; bd. dirs. Found. for NIH; mem. panel on ethics and pediat. clin. trials Inst. Medicine; mem. pediat. adv. subcom. FDA; mem. sci. adv. bd. Elizabeth Glaser Pediat. Rsch. Network. Recipient Rawls-Palmer Award, Am. Soc. for Clin. Pharmacology and Therapeutics, 1992, Werner Kalow Award for Pharmacogenetics and Drug Safety, 1995, William B. Abrams Award and Lectureship, FDA & Am. Soc. for Clin. Pharmacology and Therapeutics, 2001, Exceptional Service Award, Pharm. Rsch. and Mfr. of Am., 2003. Fellow: Nat. Inst. of Child Health and Human Develop. Office: Dartmouth Med Sch 1 Rope Ferry Rd Hanover NH 03755*

**SPIELBERG, STEVEN (STEVEN ALLAN SPIELBERG),** film director, film producer; b. Cin., Dec. 18, 1946; m. Amy Irving, Nov. 27, 1985 (div. Feb. 2, 1989); 1 child: Max Samuel; m. Kate Capshaw Oct. 12, 1991; children: Theo (adopted), Sasha, Sawyer, Mikaela (adopted), Destry, Jessica (stepchild). BA, Calif. State U., Long Beach; D of creative arts (hon.), Brandeis U., 1986; DHL (hon.), Yale U., 2002. Founder Amblin Entertainment, 1984—; co-founder (with Jeffrey Katzenberg & David Geffen), ptnr. DreamWorks SKG, Universal City, 1994—. Co-founder DreamWorks SKG, 1995—2005; co-creator of concept, story and design of new game franchises EA Games, LA, 2005—. Dir.: (films) The Last Gun, 1959, Jaws, 1975, 1941, 1979, Raiders of the Lost Ark, 1981 (Acad. Award nomination for best dir., 1982), Indiana Jones and the Temple of Doom, 1984, Indiana Jones and the Last Crusade, 1989, Hook, 1991, Jurassic Park, 1993, The Lost World: Jurassic Park, 1997, Minority Report, 2002, War of the Worlds, 2005; (TV films) Columbo: Murder by the Book, 1971, Duel, 1971, Something Evil, 1972, Savage, 1973, (episodes for TV series) The Name of the Game, 1968, Marcus Welby, M.D., 1969, Night Gallery, 1970, The Psychiatrist, 1971, Owen Marshall: Counselor at Law, 1971; exec. prodr.: (films) I Wanna Hold Your Hand, 1978, Used Cars, 1980, Continental Divide, 1981, Gremlins, 1984, Back to the Future, 1985, Young Sherlock Holmes, 1985, The Money Pit, 1986, An American Tail, 1986, Innerspace, 1987, *batteries not included, 1987, Who Framed Roger Rabbit, 1988, The Land Before Time, 1988, Tummy Trouble, 1989, Dad, 1989, Back to the Future Part II, 1989, Joe Versus the Volcano, 1990, Yume, 1990, Back to the Future Part III, 1990, Roller Coaster Rabbit, 1990, Gremlins 2: The New Batch, 1990, Arachnophobia, 1990, Trail Mix-Up, 1993, We're Back! A Dinosaur's Story, 1993, I'm Mad, 1994, The Flintstones, 1994, Casper, 1995, Balto, 1995, Twister, 1996, The Lost Children of Berlin, 1997, Men in Black, 1997, Deep Impact, 1998, The Mask of Zorro, 1998, The Last Days, 1998, The Haunting, 1999, Eyes of the Holocaust, 2000, Jurassic Park III, 2001, Price for Peace, 2002, Men in Black II, 2002, The Legend of Zorro, 2005, Monster House, 2006; (TV films) Class of '61, 1993, Survivors of the Holocaust, 1996, Shooting War, 2000, Semper Fi, 2001, We Stand Alone Together, 2001, Burma Bridge Busters, 2003, Dan Finnerty & the Dan Band: I Am Women, 2005; (TV miniseries) Band of Brothers, 2001 (Emmy for outstanding miniseries, 2002), Broken Silence, 2002, Taken, 2002 (Emmy for outstanding miniseries, 2003), Into the West, 2005; (TV series) The Plucky Duck Show, 1992, Family Dog, 1992, SeaQuest DSV, 1993—96, ER, 1994, Pinky and the Brain, 1995—98, Freakazoid!, 1995—97, Toonsylvania, 1998—2000, Pinky, Elmyra & the

Brain, 1998; prodr.: (films) An American Tail: Fievel Goes West, 1991; writer (films) Ace Eli and Rodger of the Skies, 1973, dir., prodr. E.T. the Extra-Terrestrial, 1982 (Acad. Award nomination for best dir., 1983, Acad. Award nomination for best picture, 1983), Twilight Zone: The Movie, 1983, The Color Purple, 1985 (Acad. Award nomination for best picture, 1986), Empire of the Sun, 1987, Always, 1989, Schindler's List, 1993 (Acad. Award for best dir., 1994, Acad. Award for best picture, 1994, Golden Globe for best dir., 1994), Amistad, 1997, Saving Private Ryan, 1998 (Acad. Award for best dir., 1999, Acad. Award nomination for best picture, 1999, Golden Globe for best dir., 1999, Disting. Pub. Svc. Award USN, 1999), Catch Me If You Can, 2002, The Terminal, 2004, Munich, 2005, dir., writer Fighter Squad, 1961, Escape to Nowhere, 1961, Firelight, 1964, Slipstream, 1967, Amblin', 1968, The Sugarland Express, 1974, Close Encounters of the Third Kind, 1977 (Acad. Award nomination for best dir., 1978); prodr.: (films) Memoirs of a Geisha, 2005; prodr., writer (films) Poltergeist, 1982, exec. prodr., writer The Goonies, 1985, (TV series) Amazing Stories, 1985—87, Tiny Toon Adventures, 1990—92, Animaniacs, 1993—98, dir., prodr., writer Artificial Intelligence: AI, 2001, asst. dir. action scenes (films) Star Wars III: Revenge of the Sith, 2005. Mem. adv. bd. Sci. Fiction Mus. and Hall of Fame. Recipient Man of Yr. award Hasty Pudding Theater, Harvard U., 1983, Outstanding Directorial Achievement award for feature films Dirs. Guild Am., 1985, Film award Brit. Acad. Film and TV Arts, 1986, Irving Thalberg Mem. award Acad. Motion Picture Arts and Scis., 1987, Golden Lion award for career achievement Venice Film Festival, 1993, Life Achievement award Am. Film Inst., 1995, John Huston award Artists Rights Found., 1995, Kennedy Ctr. Honor, John F. Kennedy Center for Performing Arts, 2006; named Entertainment Weekly's Most Powerful Person in Entertainment, 1997, Lifetime Achievement award, Dir. Guild Am., 2000; named one of 50 Most Powerful People in Hollywood Premiere mag., 2004-06, Forbes' Richest Americans, 2006; knighted Order of British Empire, 2001. Fellow Brit. Acad. Film and TV Arts. Achievements include winning film contest with 40-minute war movie, Escape to Nowhere, at age 13; made film Firelight at age 16, and made 5 films while in coll.; became TV dir. at Universal Pictures at age 20. Office: Creative Artists Agy 9830 Wilshire Blvd Beverly Hills CA 90212-1804*

**SPIELBERGER, CHARLES DONALD,** psychologist, educator; b. Atlanta, Mar. 28, 1927; s. A.R. and Eleanor (Wachman) S.; m. Carol Lee, June 4, 1971. BS, Ga. Inst. Tech., 1949; BA, U. Iowa, 1951, MA, 1953, PhD, 1954. Asst. prof. med. psychology Duke U., Durham, N.C., 1955-58, from asst. prof. to assoc. prof. psychology, 1955-63; prof. psychology Vanderbilt U., Nashville, 1963-66; tng. specialist in psychology NIMH, Bethesda, Md., 1965-67; prof. psychology, dir. clin. training program Fla. State U., Tallahassee, 1967-72; prof. psychology U. South Fla., Tampa, 1972—85, dir. clin. tng., 1972—78, disting. univ. rsch. prof., 1985—. Fellow Netherlands Inst. for Advanced Study, Wassenaar, 1979-80, 85-86; cons. FAA, NIMH, VA, USAF, others. Author: Anxiety and Behavior, 1966, Understanding Stress and Anxiety, 1979, Anxiety in Sports, 1989, Test Anxiety: Theory, Assessment and Treatment, 1995; editor: Stress and Anxiety Series, 1975; editor: (gen.) Centennial Psychology Series, 1979—; editor: (in-chief) Encyclopedia of Applied Psychology, 2004—. Named Disting. scholar U. South Fla., 1973, Disting. Sci. Contbr., Fla. Psychol. Assn., 1977, 88, Outstanding Faculty Rschr., U. South Fla., 1985. Fellow APA (pres. 1991-92, nat. treas. 1987-90, nat. coun. v.p. 1994-99, 2001-, pres. divsn. clin. psychology 1989, pres. divsn. cmty. psychol. 1975-76, pres. divsn. internat. psychol., 2002, Disting. Sci. Contbr. to Cmty. Psychology 1982, Disting. Sci. and Prof. Contbr. Clin. Psychology 1989, Disting. Contbr. Edn. Psychology 1992, Disting. Contbr. Profl. Practice 1993, APA/APF Gold Medal Disting. Contbr., 2003, Disting. Contbr. Internat. Psychology, 2005 pres. divsn. media psychol., 2005); mem. Southeastern Psychol. Assn. (pres. 1975-76), Soc. for Personality Assessment (pres. 1986-89, Disting. Sci. Contbr. 1990), Nat. Coun. Sci. Soc. Presidents (chair 1996-2000), Internat. Stress Mgmt. Assn. (pres. 1992-2000), Internat. Coun. Psychologists (pres. 1986-87), Internat. Assn. Applied Psychology (pres. 1998-2002, Wundt James Disting. Contbr. award), Stars & Anxiety Rsch. Soc. (pres. 1980-84), Psi Chi (nat. pres. 1980-83). Home: 11313 Carrollwood Dr Tampa FL 33618-3703 Office: U South Fla Dept Psychology Tampa FL 33620 Office Phone: 813-974-2342.

**SPIELER, EMILY A.,** dean, law educator; AB, Radcliffe Coll., Harvard U., 1969; JD, Yale U., 1973. Ptnr. Women's Law Collective, Cambridge, Mass.; spl. asst. atty. gen. Mass. Dept. Pub. Health's Lead Poisoning Prevention Div.; commr. W.Va. Workers' Compensation Fund; first dep. atty. gen. for civil rights Govt. W.Va., mem. Human Rights Commn.; Hale J. and Roscoe P. Posten Prof. Law W.Va. U., 1990—2002; dean Northeastern U. Sch. Law, 2002—. Com. mem. U.S. Department of Energy, Nat. Inst. Occupl. Safety and Health. Contbr. articles to law jours. Recipient Fulbright award, 2001, Martin Luther King Jr. Advocacy of Justice Award. Mem.: NAS, Nat. Acad. Soc. Insurance. Office: Northeastern U Sch Law 120 Knowles Ctr 400 Huntington Ave Boston MA 02115 Office Phone: 617-373-3307. Office Fax: 617-373-8793. Business E-Mail: e.spieler@neu.edu.

**SPIELER, RICHARD EARL,** oceanographer, educator; b. Washington, Mar. 11, 1942; s. Ernst Henry Spieler and Gladys Gnegy; m. Janice Schact (div.); children: Lara L., Lisel R. BA, U. Md., 1963; BS, Ark. State U., 1970, MS, 1971; PhD, La. State U., 1975. Curator fishies Milw. Pub. Mus., 1975—91; assoc. prof. Nova S.E. U., Ft. Lauderdale, Fla., 1991—96, prof., 1996—, dir. Guy Harvey Rsch. Inst., 1999—2002. Cons. fish ecology, 1991—. Contbr. articles to profl. jours. Lt. col. USAFR, 1963—92. Avocations: sailing, scuba diving, reading, hiking. Office: Nova Southeastern Univ Oceanographic Ctr 8000 N Ocean Dr Dania Beach FL 33004 Office Phone: 954-262-3613.

**SPIELMAN, CHRIS,** former professional football player; b. Canton, Ohio, Oct. 11, 1965; Student, Ohio State U. With Detroit Lions, 1988-95, Buffalo Bills, 1996—99; coach Columbus Destroyers; coll. football analyst ESPN. Co-founder Stefanie Spielman Fund for Breast Cancer Rsch. Recipient Lombardi award, 1987; named to Sporting News Coll. All-Am. team, 1986, 87, Pro Bowl team, 1989-91.*

**SPIELVOGEL, DAVID,** thoracic surgeon; b. Washington, July 30, 1960; s. Bertrum and Sally Spielvogel; m. Lisa Anne Spielvogel, June 25, 1988; children: Julia, Bertram. BS, Pa. State U., State College, 1982; MD, SUNY, Bklyn., 1990. Diplomate Am. Bd. Surgery, Am. Bd. Thoracic Surgery. Asst. prof. Mt. Sinai Hosp., N.Y.C., 1999—2005; assoc. prof. N.Y. Med. Coll., Valhalla, 2005—. Author: Adult Cardiac Surgery, 2004. Mem.: N.Y. Thoracic Soc., Soc. Thoracic Surgeons, Internat. Soc. Heart/Lung Transplant. Avocations: woodworking, drawing, skiing. Office: NY Cardiothoracic Group Westchester Med Ctr Valhalla NY 10595 Office Phone: 914-493-8793.

**SPIELVOGEL, SIDNEY MEYER,** investment banker; b. NYC, July 14, 1925; s. Hyman and Rae (Mandel) S.; m. Beverly Anne Gold, Dec. 18, 1960; 1 son, Peter James. BSS., CCNY, 1944; A.M., Harvard U., Cambridge, Mass., 1946, MBA, 1949. Economist Treasury Dept., Washington, 1946-47; assoc. dept. mgr. Alexander's Dept. Stores, 1949-53; asst. to mdse. mgr., dept. mgr. Bloomingdale's Dept. Store, 1953-56; with Prudential-Bache Securities Inc., 1956-88, 1st v.p., 1971-75, sr. v.p., 1975-85, mng. dir., 1986-88. Dir. MoneyMart Assets Inc., 1976-96, pres., 1981-87; lectr. Hunter Coll., N.Y.C., 1963-68, The New Sch., 1993-96. Bd. dirs. Emanu-el Midtown YM-YWHA, N.Y.C., 1975-91; mem. Harvard Grad. Soc. Coun., 1983-88, 89-92, 94—, chmn., 1985-87. Mem. Phi Beta Kappa. Clubs: Harvard (N.Y.C.), Harvard Bus. Sch. (N.Y.C.), World Trade Center (N.Y.C.). Home: 245 E 19th St New York NY 10003-2639 Office: Corp Capital Cons Inc 730 Fifth Ave New York NY 10019

**SPIERER, ROBERT,** family practice physician; b. S.I., N.Y., June 26, 1945; s. Efram and Regina (Stern) Spierer; m. Marilyn J Borak, July 7, 1968; children: Sharon, Henry, Eric. BA, Columbia U., 1967; MD, Albert Einstein Coll. Medicine, 1971. Diplomate Am Bd. Family Medicine, Am. Bd. Pediatrics, Am. Bd. Emergency Medicine. Intern Montefiore Med. Ctr., Bronx, NY, 1971-72, resident in pediatrics, 1972-73, 1975-76; resident in internal medicine U. Medicine and Dentistry of N.J., Newark, 1976-77;

physician Edison (N.J.) Med. Group, 1977-98, Monroe Medical Group, 1999—. With USPHS, 1973—75. Office: Monroe Med Group 369 Applegarth Rd Monroe Township NJ 08831-3732

**SPIERINGS, EGILIUS LEONARDUS HENDRICUS,** pharmacologist, neurologist, headache specialist; b. Helmond, The Netherlands, Aug. 16, 1953; came to U.S., 1986; s. Egilius L.H. and Johanna A. (Schellekens) S.; m. Maria K.B. Zarska, Dec. 27, 1976; children: Sven E.J., Natalia M.K. BS cum laude, Erasmus U., Rotterdam, The Netherlands, 1974, MD, 1978, PhD in Experimental Pharmacology, 1980. Registered in medicine, cert. in neurology The Netherlands; lic. physician Mass. Intern in neurosurgery Univ. Hosp., Rotterdam, Netherlands, 1980-81, resident in neurology, 1982—; fellow in headache mgmt. Headache Rsch. Found., Boston, 1981-82; resident in psychiatry Hippolytus Hosp., Delft, Netherlands, 1985; asst. prof. neurology Tufts U. Sch. Medicine, Boston, 1986-90; dir. Headache Rsch. Found., 1986—89, John R. Graham Headache Ctr., 1987—90; dir. headache sect. dept. neurology Brigham & Women's Hosp., 1990—94, dir. headache rsch. dept. neurology, 1994—96; dir. Boston Clin. Rsch. Ctr., Wellesley Hills, 1996—2003, Medvadis Rsch., 2003—. Lectr. neurology Harvard Med. Sch., 1990-99, assoc. clin. prof. neurology, 1999—; spkr. in field. Author: The Pathophysiology of the Migraine Attack, 1980, Migraine, 1986, Migraine Questions & Answers, 1995, 2d edit., 2001, Management of Migraine, 1996, Headache, 1998; co-author: Hoofdpijn, 1984; sect. editor Office Practice of Neurology, 1996, 2003; editor: De Pathogenese van Migraine, 1982; contbr. numerous articles to profl. jours. and chpts. to books, over 40 radio and TV appearances. Edn. dir. Headache Coop. New Eng., 1991-2003. Fellow Am. Assn. Study of Headache (bd. dirs. 1991-93); mem. Netherlands Migraine Found. (bd. dirs. 1980-85), Netherlands Soc. Migraine Patients (bd. dirs. 1982-86), Internat. Headache Soc. (bd. dirs. 1985-86, assoc. editor Cephalagia, 1986-89). Home: 24 Algonquian Dr Natick MA 01760-6095 Office: 25 Walnut St Ste 400 Wellesley Hills MA 02481-2106 Office Phone: 781-431-1113. Business E-Mail: spierings@medvadis.com.

**SPIERKEL, GREGORY M.,** information technology executive; b. 1957; BA, Carleton U., Ottawa, Can.; MBA, Georgetown U.; attended, Advanced Manufacturing Program at INSEAD, Fontainebleau, France. Mng. dir. Mitel Telecom, United Kingdom, 1986—89; gen. mgr. Mitel Far East Ltd., Hong Kong, 1989—90; pres., CEO, N. Am. Mitel Inc., Reston, Va., 1992—96, v.p., global sales and marketing Canada, 1996—97; sr. v.p., pres. Ingram Micro Inc., Santa Ana, Calif., 1997—99; pres. Ingram Micro Asia-Pacific, 1997—99; exec. v.p. Ingram Micro Inc., 1999—2004, officer, 1997—, pres., 2004—05, CEO, 2005—; pres. Ingram Micro Europe, 1999—2004. Bd. mem. Sch. Bus., U. Calif., Irvine. Office: Ingram Micro Inc 1600 E St Andrew Pl Santa Ana CA 92705-4931 Office Phone: 714-566-1000. Office Fax: 714-566-7900.*

**SPIERS, RONALD IAN,** diplomat; b. Orange, N.J., July 9, 1925; s. Thomas Hoskins and Blanca (De Ponthier) S.; m. Patience Baker, June 11, 1949; children: Deborah Wood, Peter, Martha, Sarah. BA, Dartmouth Coll., 1948; M in Pub. Affairs, Princeton U., 1950. With AEC, 1950-54; officer-in-charge disarmament and arms control Dept. State, Washington, 1955-61, dir. NATO affairs, 1962-66; polit. counselor Am. Embassy, London, 1966-69; asst. sec. for Politico-Mil. Affairs U.S. Dept. State, 1969-73; amb. to Bahamas, Am. Embassy, Nassau, 1973-74, dep. chief of mission London, 1974-77; U.S. permanent rep. to CENTO Coun., 1977-79; amb. to Turkey, Am. Embassy, Ankara, 1977-80; asst. sec. for intelligence and rsch., mem. U.S. Intelligence Bd. U.S. Dept. State, Washington, 1980-81; amb. to Pakistan, Am. Embassy, Islamabad, 1981-83; under-sec. for mgmt. U.S. Dept. State, 1983-89; under-sec. gen. for polit. affairs UN, N.Y.C., 1989-92; internat. affairs cons. Dept. State, 1992—. Career ambassador U.S. Fgn. Svc., 1984. Served to lt. (j.g.) USN, 1943-46, PTO. Woodrow Wilson fellow Princeton U., 1948. Fellow Nat. Acad. of Pub. Adminstrn.; mem. Am. Fgn. Svc. Assn., Internat. Inst. Strategic Studies, Coun. on Fgn. Rels., Am. Acad. of Diplomacy, Washington Inst. Fgn. Affairs. Home: 1320 Middletown Rd South Londonderry VT 05155-9145 E-mail: embassy@adelphia.net.

**SPIES, JAMES B.,** radiologist, educator; MD, Georgetown U., Washington, D.C., 1980. Diplomate in vascular and interventional radiology Am. Bd. Radiology, 2005. Prof. Dept. Radiology Georgetown U., 2004—, chmn. Dept. Radiology, 2004—. Maj. USAF, 1985—89. Fellow: Am. Coll. Radiology, Soc. Interventional Radiology (chmn. found. 2005—). Achievements include research in uterine fibroid embolization, uterine fibroids. Office: Georgetown University Hospital 3800 Reservoir Rd NW CG 201 Washington DC 20007-2113 Office Phone: 202-444-3450.

**SPIES, KAREN BORNEMANN,** writer, educational consultant; b. Renton, Wash., Sept. 5, 1949; d. William Edward and Aina Jeanette (Johnson) Bornemann; m. Allan Roy Spies, July 18, 1970; children: Karsten, Astrid. BA, Calif. Luth. U., 1970; MEd, U. Wash., 1974. Vice prin., tchr. Lake Washington Sch. Dist., Kirkland, 1971—79; tchr. various pub. schs. NJ, 1979—82; tchr. kindergarten Mt. Park Sch., Lake Oswego, Oreg., 1982—84; writer, seminar leader, cons. Wash., 1984—87. Lectr. Arapahoe C.C., Littleton, 1988-98; ski instr. various locations, 1974—; curriculum writer Augsburg-Fortress Pubs.; lectr. in field. Author: Family Activities for the Christmas Season, 1988, Denver, 1988, Raffi: The Children's Voice, 1989, Visiting in the Global Village, Vol. I, 1990, Vol. II, 1991, Vol. III, 1992, Vol. IV, 1993, Vol. V, 1994, Everything You Need to Know About Grieving, 1990, Competitiveness, 1991, Barbara Bush, 1991, George Bush, 1991, Everything You Need to Know About Incest, 1992, Our National Holidays, 1992, Our Money, 1992, The American Family: Can It Survive?, 1993, Everything You Need to Know About Diet Fads, 1993, Our Folk Heroes, 1994, Earthquakes, 1994, Our Presidency, 1994, Isolation vs. Intervention, 1995, Buffalo Bill Cody: Western Legend, 1998, Franklin D. Roosevelt, 1999, John F. Kennedy, 1999, Heroes in Greek Mythology, 2002, The Iliad and Odyssey in Greek Mythology, 2002, Pan Am Flight 103: Terrorism over Lockerbie, 2003. Bd. Regents Calif. Luth. Univ.; organist Wooden Cross Luth. Ch., 1977—79; bd. dirs. Parent Pathways. Recipient Notable Social Studies Trade Books for Young People, 2000; Title III grantee, 1974. Mem. AAUW, Soc. Children's Book Writers and Illustrators, Mensa, Profl. Ski Instrs. Am., Colo. Authors' League, Pi Lambda Theta. Republican. Lutheran. Avocations: tennis, reading, sewing, skiing, golf. Personal E-mail: buddyspies@msn.com.

**SPIGARELLI, JAMES L.,** science administrator; BA in Chemistry, MS in Chemistry, PhD in Chemistry, Kans. State Coll. Various positions Midwest Rsch. Inst., Kansas City, Mo., 1961—68, v.p., 1978—91, sr. v.p., 1991—97, exec. v.p., 1997—98, COO, 1998—99, pres., CEO, 1999—. Bd. dirs. Sci. City at Union Sta., Kansas City Mus., KCCatalyst, Brush Creek Cmty. Ptnrs., Sci. Pioneers; founding bd. mem. Kansas City Area Life Sci. Inst., Inc., 2000; trustee Univ. Mo.-KC Avila Coll., Rockhurst Univ. R&D task force Kansas City Area Life Scis. Inst., 1999; trustee U. Mo., Kansas city, Avila Coll., Rockhurst U.; bd. dirs. Kansas City Area Life Scis. Inst., 2000. Lt. Chemical Corps U.S. Army, Rocky Mt. Arsenal. Named Tech. Leader of Yr., Silicon Prairie Tech. Assn., 2000; recipient Meritorious Achievement award, Pitts. State U., 1993. Fellow: Coll. Arts and Scis. Alumni, Kans. State U. Office: Midwest Rsch Inst 425 Volker Blvd Kansas City MO 64110

**SPIKES, PATRICIA WHITE,** medical technologist; b. Houston, Nov. 30, 1951; d. Matthew and Myrtle Mae (Sneed) White; m. Herbert Charles Pete, May 24, 1980 (div.); 1 dau., Sheatri Denise; m. John Ray Spikes, Sept. 7, 1991; 1 child, John Ray II. BS Tex. Christian U., Ft. Worth, 1974. Med. technologist, edn. coordinator Riverside Gen. Hosp., Houston, 1974-76; chief lab. technologist Almeda Med. Lab., Houston, 1976-80; med. technologist Jefferson Davis Hosp., Harris County Hosp. Dist., Houston, 1980—, Lyndon B. Johnson Hosp., Harris City Hosp. Dist. Founder Coalition of Pre-Sch. Dirs., 1982—; dir. Parents Calling Parents, Houston, 1980—; and 3 v.p. Vols. in Pub. Sch. Adv. Bd., Houston, 1981, 2d v.p., 1983, pres. 1986-89, v.p. tng. chair, 1990-92, v.p. community coalitions, 1993; mem. Tex. State Bd. for Vols. in Pub. Sch., 1982—, sec., 1988—, 1st v.p., 1985, pres., 1986, sec. 1987—; chairperson Bucks for Belts Coalition for Sch. Bus Seat Belts, 1985; chair awards com. Salute to Sch. Vols.; mem. Mayor's Task Force on Edn.,

Houston, Mayor's Com. on Child Abuse Prevention; panelist Regional IV Svc. Ctr. State Seminar; mem. adv. bd. Blueridge Health Dept., Attucks Community Coll.; pres. Reynolds Elem. Parent Tchr. Orgn., 1982, treas., 1984; sec. Pershing Middle Sch., PTO, 1985, Class of 1969 Worthing High Sch. Reunion; candidate for Houston Ind. Sch. Dist. Bd. Edn., 1989; pres. Kings Row Child Care Parent Tchrs. Orgn., 1978; mem. Nat. Sch. Vol. Program 1982—, Mo. City Space; panelist Houston Area Black Sch. Educators, 1987; bd. dirs. Women in Action, 1984-85; mediator Dispute Resolution Ctr., 1984—, Women of Vision, Chs. Interested in Premature Parentage; city wide adv. com. Houston Ind. Sch. Dist., 1988; edn. adv. com. Family Life; pres. adv. com. Inner City 4-H, 1989—; chmn. adult leaders adv. bd. Harris County 4-H, 1989-91, treas. 1890 program, 1991-93; chmn. Northeast Adolescent Program, 1990-92; computer maintenance adv. com. Reagan High Sch., 1988—; chair Salute to Sch. Vols., 1984-86; speaker career day Houston Ind. Sch. Dist., 1989—; chmn. adv. bd. Sunnyside Multi-Svc. Ctr./Health Ctr., 1991—; mem. steering com. Tex. Cancer Coun., 1992—; spkr. screen Test Health Symposium Prairie View Adminstrn. 1980 4-H Program, 1992, 93; coord. baby buddy program Sunnyside Clinic City of Houston Health Dept., 1989—; chmn. S.E. br. adv. bd. ARC, 2004—, mem. member svcs. com. Greater Houston coun.; mem. membership com. Nat. Healthy Start Assn., 1974—; consortium chmn. Sunny Futures Healthy Start Program, Houston, 1998-2003; coord. Girls Rite of Passage, 2000-02; chmn. Prairie View A&M Coll. Cooperative Extension Project H.O.P.E., 2001—; cons. Families Under Urban and Social Attack Non Profit Devel., 2002—; CEO, founder S & J Literary Works, 2003, Rewriting the Script Through Connections, 2005; mem. Syphilis Elimination Adv. Task Force, 2003—; chair Syphilis Elimination Bd., Am. Red Cross, 2004-06; mem. program svcs. com., mem. Sunnyside Pride, 2005; mem. African Am. Healthy Marriage Initiative, 2006; mem. City of Houston HIV/AIDS Task Force, 2003—; presenter, cons., spkr. in field. Recipient Vols. in Pub. Sch. Spl. Service cert., 1984; recipient numerous certs. of appreciation. Mem. NAACP, Delta Sigma Theta. Recipient Cert. of Appreciation, Vols. Am., 1980, Vols. in Pub. Schs., 1986, 87, Houston Ind. Sch. Dist., 1981, 82, 83, pres.' award Vols. in Pub. Schs., 1986-95; Outstanding Service award Reynolds Sch., 1982, cert. recognition Training Tchrs. and Adminstrs. for Parent Involvment, 1986, Kay On-going Edn. Ctr., Pershing Mid. Schs., 1987, Neighborhood Ctrs. Crystal House award for Cmty. Svc., 2005, vol. award Prairie View A&M U. project H.O.P.E. Democrat. Baptist. Club: Top Ladies of Distinction. Home: 3134 Sunbeam St Houston TX 77051-3526 Personal E-mail: pspikes30@aol.com.

**SPIKES, TAKEO GERARD,** professional football player; b. Sandersville, Ga, Dec. 17, 1976; Student, Auburn U. Player Cincinnati Bengals, 1998—2002, Buffalo Bills, 2003—. Named to NFL Pro-Bowl Team, 2003—04. Office: c/o Buffalo Bills 1 Bills Dr Orchard Park NY 14127*

**SPIKOL, EILEEN,** artist; b. Sarasota, Fla. 1 child, Hannah. BA in Fine Arts, Fordham U., 1975; MFA in Sculpture, City Coll., N.Y., 1977. Supr. reproduction studio Am. Mus. Natural History, N.Y.C., 1971-78; tchr. painting and drawing grades 7-12 Fieldston Sch., Riverdale, N.Y., 1977-79; tchr. molding, casting, patina workshop Children's Mus. Manhattan, N.Y.C., 1979-80; tchr. art spl. edn. Sch. Visual Arts, N.Y.C., 1982; tchr. drawing, painting, sculpture, printmaking Studio in a Sch., N.Y.C., 1987-90; instr. Bronx (N.Y.) Mus. Arts, 1990-91. Tchr. sculpture Md. Ctr. Arts Goucher Coll., Towson, 1986; adj. prof. art edn., spl. edn. Bkyln. (N.Y.) Coll., 1979-85, field supr.; adj. prof. fine arts St. Johns U., Queens, N.Y., 1991-93; artist in residence Found. Michel Karolyi, Vence, France, 1989, Domiciliary Care Program for Homeless Vets., St. Albans (N.Y.) Va Ctr., 1997—; adj. prof. in art edn., spl. edn. Nat. History N.Y.C., 1979-85; lectr. in field. One woman exhbns. include Soho 20 Gallery, N.Y.C., 1974, 75, 77, 78, Maples Gallery Fairleigh Dickinson U., Teaneck, N.J., 1980, 84, Islip Art Mus., E. Islip, N.Y., 1986, Bronx (N.Y.) Mus. Arts, 1988; group exhbns. include One Hundred Acres Gallery, N.Y.C., 1972, Aldrich Mus., Ridgefield, Conn., 1974, New Britain (Conn.) Mus., 1974, Hera Gallery, Wakefield, R.I., 1976, Bronx (N.Y.) Mus. Arts, 1979, 1980, Landmark Gallery, N.Y.C., 1979, Nobe' Gallery, N.Y.C., 1979, Walnut St. Galleries, Phila., 1979, Blaffer Gallery U. Houston, 1980, Mus. Natural History, N.Y.C., 1982, The Fine Arts Ctr. SUNY, Stony Brook, 1982, Fed. Plz., N.Y.C., 1982, Freedman Gallery Albright Coll., Reading, Pa., 1982, The New Mus., N.Y.C., 1984, Henry Street Settlement, N.Y.C., 1986, Artspace Gallery, New Haven, Conn., 1992, Leopold-Hoesch-Mus., Duren, Ger., 1992, B4A Gallery, N.Y.C., 1993; featured in Arts Mag., Soho Weekly News, Womanart, The Nation, The Village Voice, Coll. Art Jour., N.Y. Times, Newsday, New Haven Register. Home: 175 W 72nd St New York NY 10023-3203

**SPILHAUS, ATHELSTAN FREDERICK, JR.,** oceanographer, director; b. Boston, May 21, 1938; s. Athelstan F. and Mary (Atkins) S.; m. Sharon Brown, June 11, 1960; children— Athelstan F. III, Ruth Emily, Mary Christina S.B. in chem. Engring., MIT, 1959, S.M. in Geology and Geophysics, 1960, PhD in Oceanography, 1965. Cert. meeting profl. Phys. scientist U.S. Govt., Washington, 1965-67; asst. exec. dir. Am. Geophys. Union, Washington, 1967-70, exec. dir., 1970—. Bd. dirs. Renewable Natural Resources Found., Washington. Editor newspaper EOS. Chmn. Conv. Liaison Council, Washington, 1981-82. Fellow AAAS, Washington Acad. Sci., Am. Geophys. Union (hon.), Indian Geophys. Union, Geol. Soc. Am., Royal Astonomical Soc.; mem. Am. Soc. Limnology and Oceanography, Council Biology Editors, Am. Inst. Physics (mem. gov. bd. 1988—), Philos. Soc. Washington (pres. 1982-83), Geol. Soc. Can., Geol. Soc. Washington (2d v.p. 1975), Am. Soc. Assn. Execs., Assn. Am. Pubs. (div. exec. com. 1980-82, 94-97), Assn. Earth Sci. Editors (dir. 1972-78, pres. 1977), Coun. Engring. and Scientific Soc. Execs. (dir. 1976-82, pres. 1980-81), Internat. Union Geodesy Geophysics (fin. com. 1987—2003, chmn. 1999-2003), Canadian Geophys. Union, European Geophys. Soc., Cosmos Club (Washington, pres. 1992-93), Chesapeake Yacht Club (Md.). Home: 10900 Picasso Ln Rockville MD 20854-1710 Office: Am Geophys Union 2000 Florida Ave NW Washington DC 20009-1231

**SPILIOTES, NICHOLAS JAMES,** lawyer; b. Blue Point, N.Y., Nov. 1, 1955; s. James Nicholas and Constance (Greven) S.; m. Lauren Talner, June 3, 1984; children: Alexander, Ariana. BA, Williams Coll., 1977; MIA, Columbia U., 1979, JD, 1985. Bar: N.Y., 1985, D.C. 1989. Jr. staff mem. NSC, Washington, 1979-81; special assts. Office of the U.S. Rep., U.S. Mission to the UN, N.Y.C., 1981; research assoc. Ctr. Strategic and Internat. Studies, Washington, 1981-82; assoc. Morrison & Foerster, Washington, 1988-92, ptnr., 1992—, mng. ptnr. ops., 1997—2000, exec. com., bus. dept. chmn., 2004—, leader project fin. & devel. practice group, 2001—04. Mem. ABA (vice chmn. African law com. 1991-93), Am. Hist. Assn. Democrat. Office: Morrison & Foerster 2000 Pennsylvania Ave NW Washington DC 20006-1812 Office Phone: 202-887-1579. Business E-Mail: nspiliotes@mofo.com.

**SPILKER, LINDA JOYCE,** aerospace scientist; b. Mpls., Apr. 26, 1955; d. Arthur Elzear and Bonnie Joy (Jansen) Bies; m. John Leonard Horn Jr., July 31, 1976 (div.); children: Jennifer, Jessica; m. Thomas Richard Spilker, 1997. BA in Physics, Calif. State U., Fullerton, 1977; MS in Physics, Calif. State U., L.A., 1983; PhD in Geophysics and Space Physics, UCLA, 1992. Rep. Voyager Infrared Radiometer and Spectrometer expt. Jet Propulsion Lab., Pasadena, Calif., 1977-90, sci. assoc. Voyager Photopolarimeter, 1984-90, sc. assoc. Voyager Infrared Radiometer and Spectrometer, 1988-90, study scientist Cassini asst., 1988-90, co-investigator Cassini Composite Infrared Spectrometer, 1990—, dep. project scientist Cassini mission, 1990—, prin. investigator planetary geology and geophysics, 1993—. Mem. planetary sci. data steering group NASA, Washington, 1991-95, adv. coun. for planetary data sys. ring node, Moffett Field, Calif., 1990—. Contbr. chpt. Van Nostrand Encyclopedia of Planetary Science, 1994; contbr. jour. articles Icarus. Pres. North San Gabriel Valley Dem. Club, Monrovia, Calif., 1992-94. Named one of Hottest 25 in Orange County, Orange County Metro mag., 2004; named to Hall of Fame, Placentia-Yorba Linda Unified Sch. Dist., 1998—99; recipient Exceptional Svc. medal, NASA, 1990, Sci. Achievement award, 1992, Disting. Alumna award, Calif. State U., L.A., 1996, Calif. State U., Fullerton, 2005. Mem. AAAS, AAUW, Divsn. of Planetary Sci. Democrat. Presbyterian.

Avocations: hiking, astronomical observing, piano, jogging. Home: 457 Granite Ave Monrovia CA 91016-2324 Office: Jet Propulsion Lab MS 230-205 4800 Oak Grove Dr Pasadena CA 91109-8001 Business E-Mail: Linda.J.Spilker@jpl.nasa.gov.

**SPILLANE, DENNIS KEVIN,** lawyer; b. N.Y.C., Sept. 15, 1953; s. Denis Joseph and Mary Kate (Sullivan) S. BA magna cum laude, Manhattan Coll., 1974; JD, N.Y. Law Sch., 1978; MS in Taxation, Pace U., 1986, post-masters cert. in bus., 1992. Bar: N.Y. 1979, U.S. Dist. Ct. (ea. and so. dists.) N.Y. 1979, U.S. Tax Ct. 1986, D.C. 1988, U.S. Ct. Appeals (2d cir.) 1988, U.S. Supreme Ct. 1989. Asst. dist. atty. Borough of Bronx, N.Y.C., 1978-85; prin. atty. N.Y. State Tax Dept., N.Y.C., 1985-87; supervising atty. Office of Profl. Discipline, N.Y. State Edn. Dept., 1987—. Prof. law and taxation Pace U., 1987—. Contbr. articles to profl. jours. Mem. Conn. Bar Assn, N.Y. State Bar Assn., D.C. Bar Assn. Conservative. Roman Catholic. Office: NY State Edn Dept 475 Park Ave S Front 3 New York NY 10016-6901 Business E-Mail: dspillan@mail.nysed.gov.

**SPILLANE, MARY CATHERINE,** television producer; b. S.I., N.Y., Nov. 30, 1956; d. Joseph Bernard and Mary Catherine (Minoque) Spillane. BA, U. Hartford, 1978. Exec. sec. CBS Evening News, N.Y.C., 1978-80, asst. to prodr., 1980; weekend prodr./E.N.G. coord. Sta. KTVI-TV, St. Louis, 1981-82, spl. projects prodr., 1982-83, asst. news dir., 1983-86; assoc. prodr. CBS News, Detroit, 1986, N.Y.C., 1986-87; sr. prodr., 1987-89, Washington, 1989-93, prodr., 1993-99, CBS Weekend News, London, 1999—2006, CBS Evening News, London, 2006—. Avocations: reading, travel, cooking, gardening. Office: CBS News 1st Fl Bldg 10 Chiswick Park Chiswick High Rd London W4 5XS England Office Phone: 44 207 887 3000. E-mail: msx@cbsnews.com.

**SPILLER, EBERHARD ADOLF,** physicist, researcher; b. Halbendorf, Ger., Apr. 16, 1933; came to U.S., 1968; s. Walter Richard and Ruth Elfriede Spiller; children: Michael, Bettina. Diploma, U. Frankfurt, Ger., 1960, PhD, 1964. With U. Frankfurt, 1960-68; physicist IBM Research Center, Yorktown Heights, NY, 1968-93; emeritus physicist IBM, 1993-97; owner Spiller X-Ray Optics, 1996—. Guest prof. Tech. U. Denmark, 1994—95, U. Ctrl. Fla., 1996; vis. scientist European Synchrotron Radiation Facility Nat. Inst. Stds. and Tech., 1996—97; vis. scientist Lawrence Livermore Lab., Calif., 1997—. Author: Soft X-Ray Optics, 1994. Fellow AAAS, Am. Optical Soc., Photo-Optic Instrumentation Soc.; mem. German Phys. Soc. Achievements include research in solid state physics, laser and coherence optics, nonlinear optics, thin films, soft x-rays, x-ray microscopy, lithography; inventor multilayer x-ray optics, x-ray astronomy, x-ray lithography. Office: Lawrence Livermore Nat Lab MS-L210 Livermore CA 94551 Office Phone: 925-423-4938. E-mail: spiller@llnl.gov.

**SPILLER, GENE ALAN,** nutritionist, health facility administrator; b. Milan, Feb. 19, 1927; came to U.S., 1950, naturalized, 1962; s. Silvio and Beatrice (Galli) S. D of Chemistry, U. Milan, 1949; MS, U. Calif., Berkeley, 1968, PhD in Nutrition, 1972. Cert. nutrition specialist. Cons. nutrition rsch. and edn., L.A., 1952-65; rsch. chemist U. Calif., Berkeley, 1966-67, assoc. specialist physiology dept., 1968-72; prin. scientist, head nutritional physiology Syntex Rsch., Palo Alto, Calif., 1972-80; cons. clin. nutrition rsch. Los Altos, Calif., 1981—; head Health Rsch. and Studies Ctr., 1988—. Lectr. Mills Coll., Oakland, Calif., 1971-81; Foothill Coll., Los Altos, 1974—. Co-author: The Last Puff, 1990; editor: Fiber in Human Nutrition, 1976, Topics in Dietary Fiber, 1978, Medical Aspects of Dietary Fiber, 1980, Nutritional Pharmacology, 1981, The Methylxanthine Beverages and Foods, 1984, CRC Handbook of Dietary Fiber in Human Nutrition, 1986, 3d edit., 2001, New Protective Roles for Selected Nutrients, 1989, The Mediterranean Diets in Health and Disease, 1991, The Superpyramid Eating Program, 1993, CRC Handbook of Lipids, 1995, Nutrition Secrets of the Ancients, 1996, Cancer Survivor's Nutrition & Health Guide, 1996—, Caffeine, 1997, Healthy Nuts, 2000, Calcium Power, 2000, Diagnosis Heart Disease, 2000, CRC Handbook of Dietary Fiber, 2001, What's With Fiber, 2006; rev. Jour. Am. Coll. Nutrition, 1976—95. Pres. SPHERA Found., 1990—. Mem. Am. Inst. Nutrition, Am. Soc. Clin. Nutrition, Brit. Nutrition Soc., Am. Assn. Cereal Chemists, Am. Diabetes Assn., Am. Coll. Nutrition, Alpine Hills Club. Achievements include research on human nutrition; prin. investigator in human nutrition studies; dietary fibers, lipids, and carbohydrates effect on humna health; role of lesser known food components in nutrition; effect of whole foods vs. single nutrients; food antioxidants. Office: Health Rsch and Studies Ctr 340 2nd St Los Altos CA 94022-3624 E-mail: spiller@sphera.org.

**SPILLERS, WILLIAM RUSSELL,** civil engineering educator; b. Fresno, Calif., Aug. 4, 1934; s. William Horton and Marguerite Ester (Johnson) S.; m. Priscilla Watson, Sept. 10, 1960 (div. 1981); children: Sarah, William, Lars; m. Sandra Lynn Newsome, July 15, 1983 (div. 1995); m. Joy Bechard, Mar. 13, 2000. Student, Fresno State Coll., 1951-53; BS, U. Calif., Berkeley, 1955, MS, 1956; PhD, Columbia U., 1961. Registered profl. engr., N.Y., N.J. Structural engr. John Blume Assocs., San Francisco, 1956-57; teaching asst. Columbia U., N.Y.C., 1957-61, prof. civil engring. and engring. mechanics, 1961-76; prof. civil engring. Rensellaer Poly. Inst., Troy, NY, 1976-90; prof., chmn. civil and environ. engring. N.J. Inst. Tech., Newark, 1990—, disting. prof. civil and environ. engring., 1995—. Cons. Weidlinger Assoc., N.Y.C., 1957-76, Geiger Berger Assoc., N.Y.C., 1957-76, DeLeuw Oh Eocha, Manchester, Eng., 1974, Parsons Hawaii, L.A., 1983, Horst Berger Ptnrs., N.Y.C., 1980; organizer NSF workshop on design theory, Troy, N.Y., 1988. Author: Automated Structural Analysis, 1972, Iterative Structural Design, 1975, Intro Structures, 1985; (with R. Levy) Analysis of Geometrically Nonlinear Structures, 1995, 2d edit., 2003, Introduction to Structures, 2002; editor 4 books including Design Theory, 1988; contbr. over 140 articles to profl. jours. Named Educator of Yr. award, Cons. Engrs. Coun. N.J., 1998; NSF fellow, 1976, Guggenheim fellow, 1968. Mem. ASCE (numerous coms., chmn. exec. com. TCCP, 1987), Internat. Assn. Bridge & Structural Engrs. Democrat. Achievements include contribution to the development of fabric structures; initiated the science of design theory; participated in development of applications of digital computers to large structural systems. Home: 7 Oak Ave West Orange NJ 07052-2409 Office: NJ Inst Tech Dept Civil & Environ Engring Newark NJ 07102 Office Phone: 973-596-2479. E-mail: spillers@njit.edu.

**SPILLETT, ROXANNE,** social services administrator; 1 son, Keith. BA in Edn., SUNY; postgrad., St. Lawrence U., Hunter Coll., N.Y. Tchr., curriculum writer NY State Schs., 1971-73; program specialist Girl Scouts USA, 1973; dir. nat. health project Boys & Girls Clubs Am., Atlanta, 1978-79, dir. program svcs., 1979-91, asst. nat. dir. program svcs., 1991-1995, v.p. N.E. regional office, 1995, acting pres., 1995-96, pres., 1996—. Vice chair bd. dirs. Assembly of Health and Human Svc. Orgns. Office: Boys & Girls Clubs Am 1230 W Peachtree St NW Atlanta GA 30309-3404*

**SPILLMAN, JANE SHADEL,** curator, writer, researcher; b. Huntsville, Ala., Apr. 30, 1942; d. Marvin and Elizabeth (Russell) Shadel; m. Don Lewis Spillman, Feb. 18, 1973 (dec. Jan. 1999); children: K. Elizabeth, Samuel Shadel. AB, Vassar Coll., 1964; MA, SUNY, 1965. Rsch. asst. Corning (N.Y.) Mus. Glass, 1965-70, asst. curator, 1971-73, assoc. curator Am. glass, 1974-77, curator, 1978—, head of curatorial dept., 1994-99, dep. dir. collections, 1999—2004. Cons. The White House Curator's Office, Washington, 1987-90, other museums. Author: Complete Cut and Engraved Glass of Corning, 1979, rev. edit. 1997, Knopf Collectors Guide to Glass, Vol. 1, 1982, Vol. 2, 1983, White House Glassware, 1989, Masterpieces of American Glass, 1990, The American Cut Glass Industry: T.G. Hawkes and His Competitors, 1996, Glass of the Maharajahs: European Cut Glass Furnishings for Eastern Palaces, 2006, also 6 other books, numerous articles; editor The Glass Club Bull., 1999—. Mem. Am. Assn. Mus. (chair curators com. 1989-93), Nat. Early Am. Glass Club (bd. dirs. 1989-95), Glass Circle of London, Internat. Assn. for the History of Glass (gen. sec. 2003—). Office: Corning Mus Glass 1 Museum Way Corning NY 14830-2253

**SPILLMAN, ROBERT ARNOLD,** architect; b. Bethlehem, Pa., May 21, 1931; s. Otto Henry and Ruth Meredith (Miller) S.; m. Cidney Jane Brandon, July 7, 1956; children: Catherine, Sarah, Peter. BArch, Cornell U., 1954. Registered arch., Pa., N.J. Archtl. designer Office Douglass Orr, New Haven, 1956-58; ptnr. Lovelace & Spillman, Archs., Bethlehem, 1959-70; sr. ptnr. Spillman Farmer Archs., Bethlehem, 1971-82; pres. Spillman Farmer Shoemaker Pell Whildin, P.C., Bethlehem, 1983—96, sr. prin., 1997—. Trustee Laros Found., Bethlehem, 1970—; pres. Bethlehem Libr. Bd., 1970-74, United Way Northampton and Warren Counties, 1979-81, Lehigh River Found. Lehigh Valley Indsl. Parks bd., 1985-96, pres., 1996-2001; chmn. Bethlehem Bd. Hist. Archtl. Rev., 1961-82; mem. pres.'s coun. Lehigh Valley Partnership, 2001—; bd. dirs. KidsPeace, 2003—; Olympic torchbearer, 1996. 1st lt. USAF, 1954-56. Fellow AIA (pres. Ea. Pa. chpt. 1969-70); mem. Pa. Soc. Archs. (disting. bldg. awards 1971, 76, 78, 94, 2001, 02, 04, 05), Soc. Coll. and Univ. Planners, Bay Head Yacht Club (N.J.) (rear commodore 1985-87, vice commodore 1999-2001, commodore 2001-03). Democrat. Episcopalian. Office: Spillman Farmer Shoemaker Pell Whildin 1 W Broad St Bethlehem PA 18018-5704 Business E-Mail: rspillman@spillmanfarmer.com.

**SPILMAN, JANET LYNNE,** special education educator; b. Marysville, Calif., Nov. 29, 1957; d. Mary Elizabeth and James Maurice Spilman. BA in Hist. and Polit. Sci., Jamestown Coll., ND, 1980; BS in Spl. Edn., Moorhead State U., Minn., 1983; MEd, U. La Verne, Calif., 2004. Specialist Instrn. Credential: Learning Handicapped Commn. on Tchr. Credentialing, Calif., 1989, Single Subject Tchg. Credential: Soc.Sci. Commn. on Tchr. Credentialing, Calif., 1989, Resource Specialist Cert. Commn. on Tchr. Credentialing, Calif., 2000, Nat. Cert. In Assistive Tech. Calif. State U. Northridge, 2000. Case mgr., behavior analyist Fraser Hall, Inc, Fargo, ND, 1983—85; spl. edn. tchr. Yuma Union H.S. Dist. - Kofa H.S., Yuma, Ariz., 1985—89; job coord. Job Tng. Partnership Act - Summer Youth Program, 1986—88; tchr. (govt.) Yuma Union H.S. Dist., Migrant Edn. Dept., Yuma, Ariz., 1987—89; resource specialist Live Oak Unified Sch. Dist., Calif., 1989—94; ind. living instr. Cmty. Resource Svcs., Marysville, Calif., 1994—96; spl. day class tchr., emotionally disturbed program Milhous Sch., Inc., Sacramento, 1996—97; resource specialist Wash. Unified Sch. Dist., West Sacramento, Calif. 1997—2002, Sacramento City Unified Sch. Dist., Sacramento, 2002—. Mem.: ASCD, Vocat. Evaluation and Work Adjustment Assn., Nat. Rehab. Assn., Assn. for Children and Adults with Learning Disabilities, Coun. for Children with Behavioral Disorders, Calif. Assn. for Resource Specialists, Phi Delta Kappa, Assn. Calif. Sch. Adminstrs., Am. Assn. Sch. Adminstrs., Prader Willi Assn., Coun. For Exceptional Children. Avocations: working cattle, packing (horse and burro), hiking, photography, gardening, horseback riding. Home: 9524 North Butte Rd Live Oak CA 95953 Personal E-mail: spilmanrsp@comcast.net.

**SPILMAN, ROBERT HENKEL,** furniture company executive; b. Knoxville, Tenn., Sept. 27, 1927; s. Robert Redd and Lila (Henkel) S.; m. Jane Bassett, Apr. 2, 1955; children: Robert Henkel Jr., Virginia Perrin, Vance Henkel. BS, N.C. State U., 1950. With Cannon Mills, 1950-57; with Bassett Table Co., Va., 1957-60; dir. Bassett Furniture Industries Inc., 1960—97, exec. v.p., 1966, pres., 1966-89, CEO, 1979—97, chmn., 1982—97, ret., 1997. Bd. dir. Internat. Home Furnishing Ctr., High Point, N.C.; adv. bd. Liberty Mut. Ins. Co Trustee Va. Found. Ind. Colls.; bd. dir. Blue Ridge Airport Authority. Lt. U.S. Army, WWII and Korea. Named Humanitarian of Yr., City of Hope, 1982; named to Furniture Hall of Fame, 2005; recipient Best CEO Home Furnishing Industry award, Wall Street Transcript, 1981, 1982. Mem. Am. Furniture Mfrs. Assn. (James T. Ryan award 1984), Nat. Furniture Mfrs. Assn. (bd. dir., past pres.), Furniture Factories Mktg. Assn. (past chmn., bd. dirs.), Va. Mfrs. Assn. (past dir. exec. com.), Bassett Country Club, Commonwealth Club, Kinloch Golf Club, Linville Golf Club, Grandfather Golf and Country Club (Linville, N.C.), The Country Club Va., Olde Farm (Bristol, Va.). Episcopalian. Avocation: fishing. Office: Spilman Properties PO Box 880 Bassett VA 24055 Personal E-Mail: bspilman@sitestar.net.

**SPINA, ANTHONY FERDINAND,** lawyer; b. Chgo., Aug. 15, 1937; s. John Dominic and Nancy Maria (Ponzio) S.; m. Anita Phyllis De Orio, Jan. 28, 1961; children: Nancy M. Spina Okal, John D., Catherine M. Spina Samatas, Maria J. Spina Samatas, Felicia M. Spina DiGiovanni. BS in Social Sci., Loyola U., Chgo., 1959; JD, DePaul U., 1962. Bar: Ill. 1962; U.S. Supreme Ct. 2005. Assoc. Epton, Scott, McCarthy & Bohling, Chgo., 1962-64; pvt. practice Elmwood Park, Ill., 1964-71; pres. Anthony & Spina, PC, 1971-84; arbitrator Circuit Ct. of Cook County, 1990—98; pres. Spina, McGuire & Okal, PC, Elmwood Park, 1985—. Codifier Rosemont Village Ordinances, 1971, Elmwood Park Bldg. Code, 1975, Leyden Twp. Codified Ordinances, 1987. Mem. Elmwood Pk. Bldg. Code Planning Commn. Bd. Appeals; bd. dirs. Sheridan Carrol Charitable Works Fund, 1994—; atty. Leyden Twp., Ill., 1969—89, Village of Rosemont, Ill., 1971; counsel for Pres. and dir. Cook County Twp. Ofcls Ill., 1975—96; counsel for exec. dir. Ill. State Assn. Twp. Ofcls., 1975—96; counsel Elmwood Park Village Bd., 1967—89, Norwood Park St. Lighting Dist., 1988—, various Cook County Twps. including DuPage, 1980—82, Maine, 1981—97, Norwood Park, 1982—, Wayne, 1982—84, Berwyn Twp., 1997—99, Hanover Twp., 1997, Cook County Hwy. Commrs. Traffic Fine Litigation, 1974—96, 1999—2001, Hanover Twp. Mental Health Bd., 1991—2002, Glen Edens Assn., 1994—99, Berwyn Twp. Mental Health Bd., 1997—2002. Recipient Lacodaire medal Deans Key Loyola U., Loyola U. Housing awards, 1965, 71, 76; Appreciation award Cook County Twp. Ofcls., B. Scidmore award Ill. Twp. Attys. Assn., 2002. Mem. ABA, Ill. Bar Assn., Chgo. Bar Assn., West Suburban Bar Assn. Cook County (past chmn. unauthorized practice law sect.), Am. Judicature Soc., Justinian Soc. Lawyers, Ill. State Twp. Attys. Assn. (past v.p., pres. 1982-86, dir. 1996-99, dir. emeritus 1999—., B. Scidmore award 2002), Nat. Inst. Town and Twp. Attys. (past v.p., pres. 1993-95, Ill. del.), Montclare/Leyden C. of C., Edgebrook C. of C. (past bd. dirs.), Nat. Assn. Italian Am. Lawyers, Joint Civic Com. Chgo. (exec. com.), World Bocce Assn. (dir. 1994--), St. Rocco Soc. Simbario, KC (scribe, trustee, past Grand Knight, bldg. com. dir. 1967-99), Calabresi in Am. Orgn. (bd. dirs. 1991—), Fra Noi Ethnic Publ. (dir. 1995—), Blue Key, Delta Theta Phi, Tau Kappa Epsilon, Pi Gamma Mu. Roman Catholic. Office: 7610 W North Ave Elmwood Park IL 60707-4100 Office Phone: 708-453-2800. Personal E-Mail: spinalaw@aol.com, Speens1@sbcglobal.net.

**SPINA, DOUGLAS JOHN,** priest, educator; b. Providence, R.I., Apr. 27, 1949; s. Angelo and Gilda (Petrucci) Spina. BA, Our Lady of Providence Sem. Coll., Warwick, R.I., 1971, Cath. U. Louvain, Belgium, 1973, MA, 1974, MA in Moral and Religious Scis., 1975, PhD, 1979. Ordained Roman Cath. priest, Diocese Providence, 1976. Instr. Italian grammar and lit. Ursuline Convent Sch., Tildonc, Belgium, 1972—75; assoc. pastor St. Clement Ch., Warwick, RI, 1976—78, St. Mary's Ch., Newport, RI 1979—81; Catholic chaplain Roger Williams U., Bristol, RI, 1979—81; instr. religion Our Lady of Providence Prep. Sem., Providence, 1981—82; from asst. to assoc. prof. religious studies Salve Regina U., Newport, RI, 1982—87; assoc. pastor St. Joan of Arc Ch., Cumberland, RI, 1987—90; chaplain, adj. prof. Bryant Coll., Smithfield, RI, 1990—96; pastor St. Anthony's Ch., Woonsocket, RI, 1992—97; adj. prof. religious studies Calif. State U., Long Beach, Calif., 1996—97; pastor Our Lady of Grace Ch., Johnston, RI, 1997—2004; chaplain Johnston Police Dept., 1998—2004, Johnston Fire Dept., 1999—2004, KC, North Providence, RI, 2001—; chaplain RI chpt. Am. Guild Organists, 2003—; pastor St. Martha's Ch., East Providence, RI, 2004—. Mem. nat. bd. dirs. Nat. Religious Studies/Theology Honor Soc., N.Y.C., 1986—88; mem. Humanities Forum of R.I., 1986; bd. dirs. Lucy's Hearth, Middletown, RI, 1986—87; mem. Bishop's Task Force on AIDS, Roman Cath. Diocese, Providence, 1988—89. Author: (plays) Could've Been, 1988 (First Place award R.I. Cable TV. Video Prodn. Competition Ednl., Instrn. Category, 1989), (Book) Reaching Across the Table: Meditations on the Journey towards Common Ground, 2001; contbr. articles short stories, poetry to various publications. Recipient Citation, Mayor, Cranston, R.I., 1976, Citation, Key to City, Mayor of Warwick, R.I., 1978, Citation, Mayor of Woonsocket, R.I., 1992, R.I. State Senate, 2001, R.I. Gov.'s Office, 2001, Mayor, Johnston, R.I., 2001. Mem.: Coll. Theology Soc., Cath. Campus Ministry Assn., R.I. Philos. Soc., Cath. Theol. Soc. Am.

Avocation: collector Victorian period. Home and Office: St Marthas Rectory 2595 Pawtucket Ave East Providence RI 02914 Office Phone: 401-434-4060. Personal E-mail: Bd0521111@aol.com.

**SPINA, FRANCIS X.,** state supreme court justice; b. Pittsfield, Mass., Nov. 13, 1946; m. Sally O'Donnell; 2 children. BA, Amherst Coll.; JD, Boston Coll. Law Sch. With Western Mass. Legal Services, 1972—74; asst. city solicitor Pittsfield Law Dept., 1975—77; second asst. dist. atty. Berkshire County Dist. Attorney's Office, Mass., 1979—83; atty. Reder, Whalen, and Spina, 1983—87, Katz, Lapointe, and Spina, 1987—93; judge Mass. Superior Ct., 1993-97, Appeals Ct., Pittsfield, 1997-99; assoc. justice Mass. Supreme Jud. Ct., Boston, 1999—. Mem. Mass. Standing Com. on Pro Bono Legal Services. Mem.: Boston Bar Assn., Mass. Bar Assn. Office: Supreme Judicial Court 1 Pemberton Sq Ste 2-500 Boston MA 02108-1717*

**SPINAK, JANE M.,** law educator; BA, Smith Coll., 1974; JD, NYU, 1979. Staff atty. Juvenile Rights Div., Legal Aid Soc. of NY, 1980—82, atty.-incharge, 1995—98; co-founder Child Advocacy Clinic Columbia Law Sch., NYC, 1982—, Edward Ross Aranow Clin. Prof. of Law, dir., clin. progs. Steering com. Columbia U. Inst. on Child and Family Policy. Contbr. articles to law jours. Mem.: NY State Permanent Judicial Commn. on Justice for Children. Office: Columbia Law Sch 435 W 116th St New York NY 10027 E-mail: spinak@law.columbia.edu.

**SPINDEL, ROBERT CHARLES,** electrical engineering educator; b. NYC, Sept. 5, 1944; s. Morris Tayson and Isabel (Glazer) S.; m. Barbara June Sullivan, June 12, 1966; children: Jennifer Susan, Miranda Ellen BSEE, Cooper Union, 1965; MS, Yale U., 1966, MPhil, 1968, PhD, 1971. Postdoctoral fellow Woods Hole Oceanographic Instn., Mass., 1971-72, asst. scientist Mass., 1972-76, assoc. scientist Mass., 1976-82, sr. scientist Mass., 1982-87, chmn. dept. ocean engring. Mass., 1982-87; dir. applied physics lab. U. Wash., Seattle, 1987—. Mem. naval studies bd. NRC, 1987-99; mem. Naval Rsch. Adv. Com., 1998—. Contbr. articles to profl. jours.; patentee on underwater nav. Recipient A.B. Wood medal Brit. Inst. Acoustics, 1981, Gano Dunn medal The Cooper Union, 1989, Ocean Engr. Soc. Tech. Achievement award, 1990. Fellow IEEE (assoc. editor jour. 1982—), Acoustical Soc. Am., Marine Tech. Soc. (pres. elect 1991-93, pres 1993-95), Oceanography Soc. (Munk award 2001). Independent. Jewish. Avocations: auto restoration, hiking. Home: 14859 SE 51st St Bellevue WA 98006-3515 Office: U Wash Applied Physics Lab 1013 NE 40th St Seattle WA 98105-6606 E-mail: spindel@APL.Washington.edu.

**SPINDLER, GEORGE DEARBORN,** anthropologist, educator, writer; b. Stevens Point, Wis., Feb. 28, 1920; s. Frank Nicholas and Winifred (Hatch) S.; m. Louise Schaubel, May 29, 1942 (dec. Feb. 1997); 1 dau., Sue Carol Spindler Coleman. BS, Central State Tchrs. Coll., Wis., 1940; MA, U. Wis. 1947; PhD, U. Calif. at Los Angeles, 1952. Tchr. sch. in, Wis., 1940-42; rsch. assoc. Stanford U., 1950-51, mem. faculty, 1951—85, prof. anthropology and edn., 1960-78, exec. head dept., 1963-67, 84; ret., 1985. Cons. editor Holt, Rinehart & Winston, 1965-91, Harcourt, 1991-99, Wadsworth-Thomson, 2002-; vis. prof. U. Wis., 1979-85, U. Calif., Santa Barbara, 1986-91, Harvard U., 1999. Author: Menomini Acculturation, 1955, (with A. Beals and L. Spindler) Culture in Process, 1967, rev. edit., 1973, Transmission of American Culture, 1959, (with L. Spindler) Dreamers Without Power, 1971, rev. edit., 1984, Burgbach: Urbanization and Identity in a German Village, 1973, (with Louise Spindler) The American Cultural Dialogue and its Transmission, 1990, (with Lorie Hammond) Innovations in Educational Ethnography, 2006; editor: Education and Anthropology, 1955, (with Louise Spindler) Case Studies in Cultural Anthropology, 1960—, Am. Anthropologist, 1962-66, Methods in Cultural Anthropology, 1965-71, Case Studies in Education and Culture, 1966-72, Basic Units in Anthropology, 1970, (with Janice Stockard) Globalization and Utilization in Fifteen Cultures-Born in One World, Living in Another, 2006; editor, contbr.: Education and Culture, 1963, Being An Anthropologist, 1970, Education and Cultural Process, 1974, rev. edit., 1997, 97, The Making of Psychological Anthropology, 1978, 2nd edit., 1994, Doing the Ethnography of Schooling, 1982, Interpretive Ethnography of Schooling at Home and Abroad, 1987, Pathways to Cultural Awareness: Cultural Therapy with Students and Teachers, 1994, Fifty Years of Anthropology and Education: A Spindler Anthology, 2000. Pres. Peninsula Sch. Bd., Menlo Park, Calif., 1954-56. Served with AUS, 1942-45. Recipient Lloyd W. Dinkelspeil award Stanford U., 1978, Disting. Svc. award Soc. Internat. Diplomacy and Third World Anthropologists, 1984, Disting. Career Contbn. award Com. on Role and Status of Minorities, Am. Edn. Rsch. Assn., Nat. Acad. Edn., 1994, Father of Ednl. Ethnography award Nat. Ednl. Ethnography Conf., 2000, George and Louise Spindler award for Excellence in Anthropology Stanford U., 2001; fellow Ctr. Advanced Study of Behavioral Scis., 1956-57; subject of Vol. 17 Psychoanalytic Study of Soc. essays, 1992. Fellow Am. Anthrop. Assn.; mem. Southwestern Anthrop. Assn. (pres. 1962-63), Coun. for Anthropology and Edn. (pres. 1982, George and Louise Spindler award for outstanding contbns. to ednl. anthropology 1987, disting. Scholar award 1998), Nat. Acad. Edn. Office: Ethnographics 1247 Alice St Davis CA 95616-2174 Office Phone: 530-753-5690. E-mail: geospinner@aol.com. *My major aims as a professional observer and interpreter of human behavior are to acquire knowledge by research and disseminate understanding to others by teaching, writing, and editing. As a person I try to keep love, work, play in balanced relationship to each other, and strive for tolerance at least, and hopefully appreciation for others who are different than myself.*

**SPINDLER, GEORGE S.,** lawyer, retired oil industry executive; BCE, Ga. Inst. Tech., 1961; JD, DePaul U., 1966. Bar: Ill. 1966. Asst. gen. counsel, patents and licensing Amoco Corp., Chgo., 1979-81, gen. mgr. info. svcs., 1981-85, v.p. planning and adminstrn., 1985-87, assoc. gen. counsel, 1987-88, dep. gen. counsel, 1988-89, v.p., gen. counsel, 1989-92, sr. v.p., gen. counsel, 1992-95, sr. v.p. law and corporate affairs, 1995-99; ret., 1999. Dir. Methode Electronics Inc, 2004—. Office: Methodde Electronics 7401 W Wilson Ave Chicago IL 60706

**SPINDLER, JAMES ANDREW,** not-for-profit executive; b. Morgantown, W.Va., Oct. 20, 1950; s. Garold Ralph and Elizabeth (Carroll) Spindler; m. Ann Bailie Trautman; 2 children; James Andrew, Jr. AB, Harvard Coll., Cambridge, Mass., 1972; MPA, Princeton U., 1975; PhD, 1983. Bus. fellow The Brookings Instn., Washington, 1980—82; v.p. Continental Ill. Nat. Bank., Chgo., 1984—85, Fed. Res. Bank of N.Y., N.Y.C., 1985—89, sr. v.p., 1989—93; mng. dir. Fin. Svcs. Vol. Corps, N.Y.C., 1993—95, exec. dir., 1995—2005, pres., CEO, 2005—. Mem. Basle Com. on Banking Supervision, Switzerland, 1991—93, G10 Com. on Payment and Settlement Sys., Basle, 1991—93; prin. investigator Russia Initiative Project of the Carnegie Corp. of NY, NYC, 2000—01; mem. bd. dirs. Dubai Fin. Svc. Authority, United Arab Emirates, 2004—. Author: The Politics of International Credit: Private Finance and Foreign Policy in Germany and Japan, 1984, (Op-Ed Pieces) International Herald Tribune, San Francisco Chronicle, and The Jakarta Post, 2001. Recipient Medal of Svc. for assistance in developing Russian fin. mkts., Ctrl. Bank of Russia and the Russian Finance Ministry, 1996. Mem.: Am. Coun. on Germany (Bretton Woods com.), Coun. on Fgn. Relations. Presbyterian. Avocations: classical music, travel, opera, running. Office: Financial Services Volunteer Corps 800 3d Ave 11th Fl New York NY 10022 Office Phone: 212-771-1412. Business E-Mail: jspindler@fsvc.org.

**SPINDLER, JUDITH TARLETON,** elementary school educator; b. Dayton, Tenn., Mar. 4, 1932; d. Frank Willson and Julia Elizabeth (Venable) S. BS in Edn., Longwood Coll., 1953; MA in Edn., Va. Commonwealth U., 1976. Tchr. Oceana, King's Grant Sch., Virginia Beach, Va., 1953-66, Ginter Park Elem. Sch., Richmond, Va., 1966-67, Bon Air Elem. Sch., Chesterfield County, Va., 1967-87; ret., 1987. Founder, Web of Hope, 2000, St. Mary's Knitters, 2006. Recipient 86 ribbons for 1st, 2nd and 3rd pl. awards various knitting competitions, 5 Best in Show awards rosette competition, including blue ribbons State Fair Va., 1998, 6 ribbons Best in Show rosette Chesterfield Fair, 1998, 2 Best in Show Chesterfield County Fair, 1 Best in Show State Fair of Va., 3 Blue ribbons Chesterfield County Fair, 2000, 2 Red

Ribbons, 1 White Ribbon Va. State Fair, 2000, 3 Blue ribbons Chesterfield County Fair, 2 Red ribbons, 1 White ribbon 1 Blue, 5 in Va. State Fair, 2002, 1 Blue ribbon, 1 Red Ribbon, 3 Blue ribbons State Fair Va., 2004, Humanitarian award ARC. Mem. NEA, Va. Edn. Assn., Knitting Guild Am. (qualified tchr.), Knit Wit Guild (founding mem.), West End Web of Hope and St. Mary's Knitters. Avocations: knitting, reading, travel. Home: 10201 Navarre Ct Richmond VA 23238-5543

**SPINDLER, PAUL,** communications executive, consultant; b. Chgo., May 2, 1931; s. Isaac Edward and Sophie (Stein) Spindler; m. Gail Klynn; children from previous marriage: Kevin, Makayla, Sydney, Jeffrey. BA in Journalism, Temple U., 1952. Reporter Akron Beacon Jour., Akron, Ohio, 1955-58, San Francisco Examiner, 1958-59; editor Santa Clara (Calif.) Daily Jour., 1959-63; dir. pub. affairs Litton Industries, Inc., Beverly Hills, Calif., 1963-68; dir. pub. relations Internat. Industries, Beverly Hills, 1968-70; pres. Paul Spindler & Co., L.A., 1970-75; exec. v.p. Manning Selvage & Lee, Inc. N.Y.C., 1975-85; pres. The Spindler Co., L.A., 1985-87; pres. Western div. GCI Group, L.A., 1987-91; pres. GCI Spindler, L.A., 1991-96; chmn. Bristol Retail Solutions, Inc., Newport Beach, Calif., 1996-98; pres. Paul Spindler Co., L.A., 1998—. Bd. dirs. Phoenix House Calif.; bd. visitors, Temple U. Sch. Comm. and Theatre; co-pres., dir., The Partnership Scholars, 2004—. Bd. dirs. Bright Future Adoption Found. Cpl. U.S. Army, 1952—54. Mem. Mountain Gate Country Club (L.A.). Democrat. Jewish. Office: Paul Spindler Co 1901 Ave of the Stars 2nd Flr Los Angeles CA 90067 Office Phone: 310-286-0102. Business E-mail: paul@spindlercompany.com

**SPINDLER, TIMOTHY JAMES,** school librarian; b. Rock Hill, SC, Jan. 7, 1967; s. James Raymond Richard and Nancy Louise Spindler; m. Sandra Ann Tremblay, July 22, 2000. BA in History, U. Wis., Milw., 1988, MA in Libr. & Info. Sci., 1992; MA in History, U. Wis., Eau Claire, 1990. Reference libr., info. tech. coord. RI Coll., Providence, 1999—2005; user svcs. sys. libr. Roger Williams U., Bristol, RI, 2005. Recipient award, Reference & User Svcs Assn., 2004. Mem.: ALA (RUSA Press award 2004), Am. Soc. Info. Sci. & Tech., RI Libr. Assn. Office Phone: 401-254-3225.

**SPINETTA, JEAN-CYRIL,** airline executive; b. Paris, Oct. 4, 1943; s. Adrien Spinetta and Antoinette Brignoli; m. Nicole Ricquebourg, Nov. 22, 1969; children: Eric, Isabelle, Cécile, Adrien. Student, Paris Law Sch.; diploma, Inst. Internat. Politics, Paris; graduate, Ecole Nationale d'Administration. Ctrl. adminstrv. attache, 1969-70; nat. adminstr. Paris Higher Edn. Secondary Schs., 1970-72; bur. chief dept. investments and planning Nat. Edn. Ministry, 1972-76; spl. prosecutor State Coun. Govt., 1976-78; sec. gen. French Govt., 1978-81; info. svc. chief Prime Min. of France, 1981-83; dir. colls. Ministry Nat. Edn., 1983-84; cabinet dir. Min. Labour, Employment and Profl. Devel., 1984-86; inspector gen. Nat. Edn. Adminstrn., 1986-88; cabinet dir. Min. Social Affairs and Employment, Min. Overseas Transport, 1988-90; chair, CEO Air Inter, 1990-93; indsl. advisor Presidency of the Republic, 1994-95; adminstr. to 1st mission pub. svc. relevant to govt., 1995; chmn., CEO Air France, 1997—; CEO Air France-KLM Group, 2004—. Decorated officer Legion of Honor, officer Nat. Order of Merit (France), Officier des Palmes Académiques, bar Nat. Edn. Ministry. Mem.: IATA (chmn. 2004), Assn. European Airlines (pres. 2001). Avocations: tennis, skiing. Office: Air France 125 W 55th St New York NY 10019-5369 also: 45 Rue de Paris 95747 Roissy France Office Phone: 33-1-41-56-63-82. Office Fax: 33-1-41-56-63-89.

**SPINKA, WILLIAM J.,** art educator; b. Bridgeport, Conn., Oct. 3, 1920; s. Jacob J. Spinka and Anna M. Syrotiak; m. Valerie A. Lauten, June 19, 1943; children: Kenneth W., Caryl V. BS in Edn., CCNY, 1942, MS in Edn., 1945. Tchr., phys. edn. dir. Birch Wathen Sch., N.Y.C., 1942—44; instr. marine engring. U.S. Mcht. Marine Acad., Kings Point, NY, 1944—45; instr. art CCNY, 1946—60, asst. prof. art, 1961—66, assoc. prof., 1967—81, prof., 1981—85, prof. emeritus, 1986—. Edn. affiliate Am. Soc. Interior Design, N.Y.C., 1976—88; profl. mem. Nat. Soc. Interior Designers, 1960—75; sculptor; painter. Exhibitions include Salmagundi Club, Nat. Arts Club, Nat. Acad., NY, 1976—99, Corcoran Gallery, 1946, Lever House Gallery, 1986—95, one-man shows include Canton Artists Guild, Conn., 1979, works pub. in mags. Ensign US Maritime Svc., 1944—46. Mem.: Audubon Artists Inc. (v.p. sculpture 1987—93, sr. v.p. 1994—98, Gold medal of honor 1988, Silver medal of honor 1992). Avocations: construction, landscape design, athletics.

**SPINNER, LEE LOUIS,** accountant; b. Hillsboro, Ill., Nov. 9, 1948; s. John Louis and Clara Mae (Brown) Spinner; m. Rosemary T. Dean, Mar. 2, 2002. BS in Acctg., U. Ill., 1971, MAS in Acctg., 1972; MS in Taxation, DePaul U., 1983. CPA, Ill. Sr. tax acct. Ernst & Young, Chgo., 1972-78; dir. tax returns and audits Sunbeam Corp., Chgo., 1978-82; dir. tax compliance Sara Lee Corp., Chgo., 1982-83; mgr. tax compliance AM Internat., Inc., Chgo., 1983-85; mgr. taxes Household Mfg., Inc., Prospect Heights, Ill., 1985-89; mgr. internat. taxes Pittway Corp., Chgo., 1990-2000; dir. taxes Methode Electronics, Inc., Harwood Heights, Ill., 2000—. Instr. tax tng. program Ernst & Young, 1975-78; tax advisor Sta. WIND, Call Your Acct., Chgo., 1977-78. Sec. Grant Park Accts. Softball League, Chgo., 1976-77. Mem. AICPA, Ill. CPA Soc., U. Ill. Alumni Assn. (bd. assoc., audit com. 1997—), Top Social Athletic Club, Moose, KC. Democrat. Roman Catholic. Home: 435 W Wilshire Dr Palatine IL 60067-4788

**SPINNER, STEVEN L.,** food products executive; With AFI Foodservice Distributors Performance Food Group, Richmond, Va., 1985—89; v.p. AFI Foodservice Distributors, 1989—97, pres., 1997—2000; regional pres. Broadline div. Performance Food Group, Richmond, Va., 2000—01, pres. Broadline div., 2001—02, sr. v.p., CEO Broadline div., 2002—05, pres., COO, 2005—06, pres., CEO, 2006—. Office: Performance Food Group 12500 West Creek Pkwy Richmond VA 23238*

**SPINNEY, CAROLL,** entertainer, educator; b. Waltham, Mass., Dec. 26, 1933; s. Chester and Margaret Spinney; m. Janice Spinney (div. 1971); children: Jessica, Melissa, Ben; m. Debra Spinney. Studied Comml. Art, Art Inst. Boston; LHD (hon.), Villanova U., 2004. Illustrator, full time puppeteer Bozo's Big Top, 1960, performed Big Bird and Oscar (TV series) Sesame Street, 1969—(Lifetime Acheivement award, Daytime Emmy Awards, 2006); author (with J. Milligan): The Wisdom of Big Bird and the Dark Genius of Oscar the Grouch): Lessons Learned From a Life in Feathers. Served USAF, Las Vegas. Recipient 5 Emmy awards, 2 Grammy awards, Star on the Hollywood Walk of Fame, Living Legend award, Library of Congress, 2000. Achievements include performing in the White House for every president since Nixon. Office: Sesame Street One Lincoln Plaza New York NY 10023*

**SPINRAD, RICHARD WILLIAM,** former federal agency administrator, oceanographer; b. N.Y.C., Apr. 6, 1954; s. Leonard William and Thelma (Zipkin) S.; m. Alanna Wynn Thompson, June 1, 1980; 1 child, Gary Brian. BA, Johns Hopkins U., 1975; MS, Oreg. State U., 1978, PhD, 1982. Rsch. asst. Oreg. State U., Corvallis, 1975-82; rsch. scientist Bigelow Lab. for Ocean Sci., West Boothbay Harbor, Maine, 1982-86, prin. investigator, 1986—99; pres. Sea Tech., Inc., Corvallis, 1986-87; program mgr. optical oceanography Office of Naval Research, Arlington, Va., 1987-89; div. dir. Office of Naval Rsch., Arlington, Va., 1989-94; dir. Consortium for Oceanographic Rsch. & Edn., 1994—99; tech. dir. Oceanographer of the Navy, 1999—2003; asst. adminstr. Nat. Ocean Svc. Nat. Oceanic and Atmospheric Adminstrn., Washington, 2003—05. Adj. faculty George Mason U., 1994-97, U.S. Naval Acad., 1997-99; trustee Bigelow Lab. for Ocean Scis., 1995—. Editor: Oceanography; contbr. scis. articles to profl. jours. Mem. AAAS, Am. Soc. Limnology and Oceanography, Am. Geophys. Union, The Oceanography Soc., Optical Soc. Am. (Johns Hopkins U. Schs. com.), Oceanography Soc. (coun. 1994-97). Democrat. Avocations: banjo, outdoor activities, woodworking.

**SPINRAD, ROBERT JOSEPH,** computer scientist; b. N.Y.C., Mar. 20, 1932; s. Sidney and Isabel (Reiff) S.; m. Verna Winderman, June 27, 1954; children: Susan Irene, Paul Reiff. BS, Columbia U., 1953, MS (Bridgham

fellow), 1954; PhD (Whitney fellow), MIT, 1963. Registered profl. engr., N.Y. Project engr. Bulova Research & Devel. Lab. N.Y.C., 1953-55; sr. scientist Brookhaven Nat. Lab., Upton, NY, 1955-68; v.p. Sci. Data Systems, Santa Monica, Calif., 1968-69; v.p. programming Xerox Corp., El Segundo, Calif., 1969-71; dir. info. scis., 1971-76; v.p. systems devel., 1976-78, v.p. research Palo Alto Rsch. Ctr., 1978-83, dir. systems tech., 1983-87, dir. corp. tech., 1987-92, v.p. tech. analysis and devel., 1992-94, v.p. technology strategy, 1994-98; cons. in field, Palo Alto, Calif., 1998—. Contbr. articles to profl. jours. Mem. Nat. Acad. Engring., Calif. Coun. on Sci. and Tech., Sigma Xi, Tau Beta Pi. Achievements include patents in field. E-mail: robert@spinrad.com.

**SPIRA, MELVIN,** plastic surgeon; b. Chgo., July 3, 1925; s. Samuel and Jessie (Tivin) S.; m. Rita Silver, Nov. 27, 1952; children— Mary Ann, Joel Bennett, Pamela Beth Student, Wright Jr. Coll, Chgo., 1942-43, Franklin and Marshall Coll. Lancaster, Pa., 1943-44; DDS, Northwestern U., 1947, MSD, 1951; MD, Med. Coll. of Ga., 1956. Diplomate Am. Bd. Plastic Surgery (chmn. 1984-85). Intern Duke U. Hosp., Durham, NC, 1956-57, jr. asst. resident, 1958-59, asst. resident, 1959-60; resident Jefferson Davis Hosp, Houston, 1960-61, asst. in surgery and plastic surgery; sr. attending physician Ben Taub Gen. Hosp, Houston, attending physician, Tex. Children's Hosp., Houston, St. Lukes Episcopal Hosp., Houston; prof. Baylor Coll. Medicine, Houston, past head divsn. plastic surgery. Past chmn. Am. Bd. Plastic Surgery. Served with USN, 1943-45, 48-50 Fellow ACS; mem. Houston Surg. Soc., Am. Soc. Maxillofacial Surgeons (pres. 1974-75), Am. Soc. Plastic and Reconstructive Surgeons, Harris County Med. Soc., Plastic Surgery Research Council, So. Med. Assn., Tex. Med. Assn., Am. Trauma Soc., G V Black Soc., Internat. Soc. for Burn Injuries, Am. Burn Assn., Am. Cleft Palate Assn., Am. Assn. Plastic Surgeons (pres. 1992-93), Acad. Plastic Surgery Forum, Internat. Soc. Reconstructive Microsurgery, Tex. Surg. Soc., Michael E. DeBakey Internat. Cardiovascular Soc., Baron Hardy Soc., Am. Soc. for Aesthetic Plastic Surgery, Alpha Omega Alpha, Sigma Xi Avocations: skiing, photography, painting, tennis, golf. Office: Baylor College of Medicine Div Of Plas 1709 Dryden Rd Ste 1600 Houston TX 77030-2414 Personal E-mail: rmspira@comcast.net.

**SPIRO, HERBERT JOHN,** political scientist, ambassador; b. Hamburg, Germany, Sept. 7, 1924; came to U.S. 1938, naturalized, 1944; s. Albert John and Marianne (Stiefel) S.; m. Elizabeth Anna Petersen, June 7, 1958 (div.); children: Peter John, Alexander Charles Stiefel; m. Marion Ballin, July 22, 1985. Student, San Antonio Jr. Coll., 1942-43; AB summa cum laude, Harvard U., 1949, MA, 1950, PhD, 1953; MA (hon.), U. Pa., 1971. Adminstrv. asst. U.S. War Dept., Vienna, 1945-46; mem. faculty Harvard U., Cambridge, Mass., 1950-61, asst. prof., 1957-61; assoc. prof. polit. sci. Amherst (Mass.) Coll., 1961-65; prof. polit. sci. U. Pa., Phila., 1965-73; mem. policy planning staff Dept. State, Washington, 1970-75; ambassador to Cameroon, 1975-77; amb. to Equatorial Guinea, 1975-76; fellow Woodrow Wilson Internat. Ctr. for Scholars, Smithsonian Instn., Washington, 1978; vis. prof. polit. sci. John F. Kennedy Inst. for N.Am. Studies, Free U. Berlin, 1980-89. Fulbright sr. rsch. prof. U. Coll. Rhodesia and Nyasaland, 1959-60; cons. Brit. Commn. to Rev. Constn., Fedn. Rhodesia and Nyasaland, 1960, Japanese Commn. on Revision Constn., 1962; vis. assoc. prof. U. Chgo., 1961, Stanford (Calif.) U., 1963; chmn. Asian and African Studies program, Amherst-Smith-Mt. Holyoke Colls., U. Mass., 1964-65; vis. prof. internat. affairs Woodrow Wilson Sch., Princeton (N.J.) U., 1966; adv. coun. polit. sci. Haverford Coll., 1966-71; affiliated with Nuffield Coll., Oxford (Eng.) U., 1967-68; resident scholar Rockefeller Found. Study Ctr., Bellagio, Italy, 1968, 78; vis. prof. govt., guest scholar Ctr. for Internat. Affairs, Harvard U., 1983; vis. scholar U. Tex., Austin, 1984-89; life mem. Brit. studies faculty seminar U. Tex., Austin, 1983—; rschr. Lyndon Baines Johnson Presdl. Libr., 1985-86; fellow Aspen (Colo.) Inst. Humanistic Studies, 1986; adj. prof. govt. U. Tex., Austin, 1989-91; participant internat scholarly and diplomatic confs.; founder Brackenridge H.S.-Wilhelm Gymnasium Exchange; lectr. in field. Author: Politics of German Codetermination, 1958, (with others) Patterns of Government, 1958, 2d edit., 1962, Government by Constitution, 1959, Politics in Africa, 1962, 2d edit., 1975, Five African States, 1963, World Politics: The Global System, 1966, (with others) Authority, Nomos I, 1958, Responsibility, Nomos III, 1960, Privacy Nomos XIII, 1971, Why Federations Fail, 1968, Responsibility in Government, 1969, The Dialectic of Representation 1619-1969, 1969, Politics as the Master Science: From Plato to Mao, 1970 (with others), Theory and Politics, 1971 (with others), Between Sovereignty and Integration, 1974, A New Foreign Policy Consensus?, 1979, (with others) The Legacy of the Constitution, 1987, (with others) Anti-Americanism, 1988; editor, contbr.: (with others) Africa: The Primacy of Politics, 1966, Patterns of African Development, 1967, 'Privatization' of U.S. Foreign Relations, 1995; contbr.: World Book Ency., Ency. Britannica, Intern. Ency. of the Social Scis.; host Spiro's Conversations, Austin Community TV, 1992-97, San Antonio TimeWarner Access TV channel 20, 1999—; contbr. articles to profl. jours. Del. Tex. State Rep. Conv., 1990-92; precinct chmn. Travis County; Rep. cand. for Tex. Ho. of Reps., 1991, U.S. House of Reps., 1992, 94, U.S. Senate, 1993. Decorated Bronze Star medal with oak leaf cluster, Purple Heart; grand officer Legion of Valor Cameroon, 1977; recipient Detur prize Harvard Coll., 1948, Bowdoin prize, 1952; John Harvard scholar, 1949-51, Holzer scholar, 1949-51; Guggenheim fellow, 1959-60, Social Sci. Research Council faculty fellow, 1962, 67-68, Rockefeller Found. fellow, 1958, Sheldon travelling fellow Harvard U., also Fulbright fellow, 1953-54; Moody grantee Lyndon Baines Johnson Found., 1985. Fellow Assn. for Diplomatic Studies; mem. African Studies Assn., Am. Polit. Sci. Assn. (coun. 1968-70, chmn. election com. 1969), Internat. Polit. Sci. Assn., Am. Soc. Polit. and Legal Philosophy, Coun. Fgn. Rels., Coun. Am. Ambs., Am. Fgn. Svc. Assn., Mil. Order Purple Heart, San Antonio World Affairs Coun., Harvard Alumni Assn. (unpd. regional dir. Tx., 1994-97), San Antonio Coll. Alumni Assn. (dir. 1999—), Disting. Former Student award 2000), Wissenschaftliche Gesellschaft Berlin, Signet Soc., Harvard U. Faculty Club, Harvard Club (N.Y.C., del. to Tex.), Harvard Club Berlin (pres. 1989-89), Harvard Club Austin (pres. 1990-92), Harvard Club San Antonio, Phi Beta Kappa. Republican. Address: Apt 713 1 Towers Park Ln San Antonio TX 78209-6423 Personal E-mail: octospiro@sbcglobal.net.

**SPIRO, ROBERT HARRY, JR.,** foundation and business executive, educator; b. Asheville, Dec. 5, 1920; s. Robert Harry and Eoline Peterson (Shaw) S.; m. Juanita T. Henderson, June 25, 2006; children by previous marriage: Robert Timothy, Elizabeth Susan, James Monroe. BS, Wheaton Coll., Ill., 1941; postgrad. Navy Supply Sch., Harvard U., 1943; postgrad., U. N.C., 1945-46; PhD, U. Edinburgh, Scotland, 1950; student, Union Theol. Sem., summers 1951-53; postdoctoral, Duke U., summer 1956; ScD (hon.), Fla. Inst. Tech. Assoc. prof. King Coll., Bristol, Tenn., 1946-50; prof. history Miss. Coll., 1950-57; pres. Blue Ridge Assembly, Black Mountain, NC, 1957-60; dean Coll. Liberal Arts Mercer U., prof. history, 1960-64; pres. Jacksonville U., Fla., 1964-79; under sec. of Army, 1980-81; cons. to bus., 1981-84, 86-99; nat. exec. dir. Res. Officers Assn., U.S., 1984-86; chmn. RHS Imprinted Products Inc., 1988-99; past bd. mgrs. Voyager Variable Annuity of Fla., 1972-79. V.p. Am. Security Coun. Found., 1991-99, chmn., 2002—; pres. Nat. Security Caucus Found., 1997—2002; past pres. Fla. Assn. Colls. and Univs.; past chmn. Ind. Colls. and Univs., 1964—79, chmn, 1967; sec.-treas. Assn. Urban Univs., 1968—76; past mem. Fla.-Columbia Ptnrs.; gen. chmn. Jacksonville Sesquicentennial Commn., 1970—72; past mem. adv. coun. Robert A. Taft Inst. Govt., Inst. Internat. Edn. Editor (with D.F. Winkler and J.C. Reilly Jr.) Destroyer Squadron Two From Leyte Gulf Through Okinawa, 2002; contbr. articles to profl. publs. and encys. Trustee Southwestern Bapt. Theol. Sem., 1968—78; chmn. bd. Bapt. Coll. and Sem., Washington, 1989—2001. Ensign to lt. USNR, 1941—45, PTO, ret. rear adm. USNR, 1978. Decorated Palmes Academique (France); recipient Disting. Civilian Svc. award, Dept. of Army, 1981, Disting. Alumnus award, Navy Supply Corps Sch., 2000, Disting. Svc. award, Mil. Order Carabao, 2005. Mem. Navy League U.S. (former pres. Jacksonville coun.). Naval Res. Assn. (nat. adv. coun.), Res. Officers Assn. U.S. Naval Inst., Ret. Officers Assn., Am. Legion, Kiwanis (pres. Clinton, Miss. 1956-57; pres. Georgetown, D.C. Club 1991-92), Army-Navy Country

Club (Arlington, Va.), Phi Delta Kappa, Alpha Kappa Psi, Phi Alpha Theta, Phi Kappa Phi. Home: 904 Cherokee Rd Charlotte NC 28207 *Esse Quam Videre "To Be Rather than to Seem" is an eloquent apothegm I learned in high school Latin classes. For me it has been a demanding goal for daily living, a worthy aspiration for each task in life and a challenging vision of what I wish and ought to be.*

**SPIRO, ROSANN LEE,** marketing professional, educator; b. Fort Wayne, Ind., Oct. 13, 1945; d. Samuel G. and Vivian Marie Spiro; m. Rockney G. Walters, June 10, 1990; children: Samantha G., Jennifer Lauren Walters, Christi Marie Walters. AB, Ind. U., 1967, MBA, 1969; PhD, U. of Ga., 1976. Prof. and chairperson Dept. of Mktg., Kelley Sch. of Bus., Ind. U., Bloomington, Ind., 1992—; vis. prof. Insitute of Mgmt., U. of Aarhus, Aarhus, Denmark, 1991—92, I.E.S.E., Barcelona, 2000. Author: (textbook) Management of a Salesforce, 11th edition; contbr. articles to profl. jours. Recipient Outstanding Article award, Pi Sigma Epsilon, 1981, 1996. Mem.: Am. Mktg. Assn. (chairperson of the bd. 1994—95, Ann. Excellence in Rsch. award 2002). Office: Kelley Sch of Business Indiana University Bloomington IN 47405

**SPISAK, JOHN FRANCIS,** management consultant executive; b. Cleve., Mar. 27, 1950; s. Ernest Lawrence and Adele Marie (Chipko) S.; m. Barbara Ann Heisman, June 10, 1972; children: John Stefan, Theresa Rose. BS in Chemistry, Purdue U., 1972, BS in Biology with honors, 1972. Rsch. engr. Anaconda Minerals, Tucson, 1972-79; chief metallurgist Fed. Am. Uranium, Riverton, Wyo., 1979-80; v.p. ops. Anschutz Mining Corp., Denver, 1980-87; chmn. bd. dirs. Newmont Refining (subs. of Anschutz Corp.), Denver, 1987-89; dir., owner BE&K/Terranext, Inc., Denver, 1989—; pres. Continental Supply, Woodland, Calif., 2003—; with Exegesis, Lone Tree, Colo., 2005—. Mem. Western States-U.S. Senate Coalition for Superfund Reform; CEO, Am. Purificaion Corp., Newport Beach, Calif., 1998-02, pres. Prosonic Corp., Marietta, Ohio, 2002-03; CEO, Exegesis--Mgmt. Cons., Exec. Coaching, 2003—. Contbr. articles to profl. publs.; patentee sequential flotation of sulfide ores. Named One of Fifty Colo. Top Bus. Leaders, Colo. Assn. Commerce and Industry. Mem. AIME, Soc. Mining, Metallurgy and Exploration, Nat. Assn. Environ. Mgrs. (co-founder, bd. dirs. Washington chpt., co-chmn. govt. liaison and advocacy com.), Denver Petroleum Club, Elks. Republican. Roman Catholic. Avocations: classical piano, bicycling, model railroads. Home: 9384 Oakbrush Way Lone Tree CO 80124-3070 Office: Exegesis 10475 Park Meadows Dr Ste 600 Lone Tree CO 80124 Office Phone: 303-810-6602. Personal E-mail: tnxtceo@aol.com.

**SPITLER, KENNETH F.,** wholesale distribution executive; b. 1949; BA in Philosophy, Univ. of Tulsa, 1971. With Sysco Corp. 1986—, exec. v.p. Dallas, 1986—92, pres. Detroit, 1992—95, pres., CEO Houston, 1995—2000, sr. v.p. operations, northeast region, 2000—02, exec. v.p., redistribution and northeast region, 2002—03, exec. v.p. foodservice operations, 2003—. Office: Sysco Corp 1395 Enclave Pkwy Houston TX 77077

**SPITZ, BARBARA SALOMON,** artist; b. Chgo., Jan. 8, 1926; d. Fred B. and Sadie (Lorch) Salomon; m. Lawrence S. Spitz, Mar. 19, 1949; children— Thomas R., Linda J., Joanne L. Student, Art Inst. Chgo., 1942—43, R.I. Sch. Design, 1945; AB, Brown U., 1947. One-woman exhbns. include Benjamin Galleries, Chgo., 1971, 73, Kunsthaus Buhler, Stuttgart, Germany, 1973, Van Straaten Gallery, Chgo., 1976, 80, Elca London Studio, Montreal, Que., Can., 1977, Loyola U. Chgo., 1988, Schneider, Bluhm, Loeb gallery, Chgo., 1993, Newport Beach Pub. Lib., 2002, The Ctr. Gallery, 1994; group exhibitions include Am. Acad. Arts and Letters, Library of Congress traveling print exhbn., Tokyo Cen. Mus. Arts, Nat. Acad. Design, NYC, Pratt Graphic Ctr., Honolulu Acad. Arts, Wadsworth Atheneum, Nat. Aperture, 1986—, Laguna Art Mus., others; represented in permanent collections Phila. Mus. Art, DeCordova Mus., Okla. Art Ctr., Milw. Art Ctr., Los Angeles County Mus. Art, Art Inst. Chgo., Portland Mus. Art, Wadsworth Atheneum, med. arts programs UCLA, Block Mus./Northwestern U., Smart Mus./U. Chgo. Vicechmn. Chgo. area Brown U. Bicentennial Drive; treas. Hearing and Speech Rehab. Ctr., Michael Reese Hosp., 1960; fine arts patron bd. Newport Harbor Art Mus. Mem. Print Club Phila., Boston Printmakers, Arts Club of Chgo., Soc. Am. Graphic Artists. Address: 1106 Somerset Ln Newport Beach CA 92660-5629 Personal E-mail: bsslss@adelphia.net.

**SPITZ, MARGARET R.,** epidemiologist, researcher; Grad., U. Witwatersrand Med. Sch.; M in pub. health, U. Tex. Prof. divsn. cancer prevention MD Anderson Cancer Ctr., U. Tex., Houston, chmn. dept. epidemiology, 1998—. Bd. sci. advisors Nat. Cancer Inst., cons.; professorship in cancer prevention Mesa Petroleum Co.; served on study sections NIH. Contbr. articles to profl. jour. Recipient Am. Cancer Soc. award for rsch. excellence in cancer epidemiology and prevention, Am. Assn. Cancer Rsch., 2002. Mem.: Am. Soc. Preventive Oncology (past pres.). Achievements include research in genetic susceptibility to cancer devel; discovery of possible hereditary component to nicotine addiciton. Office: U Tex MD Anderson Cancer Ctr 1515 Holcombe Blvd Houston TX 77030 Office Phone: 713-792-3020. Office Fax: 713-792-0807. Business E-Mail: mspitz@mail.mdanderson.com.

**SPITZ, MARK,** Olympic athlete; b. Modesto, Calif., Feb. 10, 1950; m. Suzy Weiner; 2 children. BS, Ind. U, 1972. Mem. U.S. swimming team Olympic Games, 1968, 72, guest T V swimming commentator. Former owner Beverly Hills Real Estate Co. Author: (novels) The Mark Spitz complete book of swimming, 1976, Seven Golds: Mark Spitz Own Story, 1987. Inducted as Honor Swimmer to Internat. Swimming Hall of Fame, 1977; Sullivan award for top athlete in any sport AAU, 1971; named World Swimmer of Yr., 1969, 1971, 1972. won total of 9 Olympic Gold medals, 4x100m freestyle, 4x200m freestyle, 1968, 1972, 100m freestyle, 200m freestyle, 100m butterfly, 200m butterfly, 4x100m medley, 1972; only Olympian in history to win 7 Gold medals (all World Records) in a single Olympics, Munich Olympic Games, 1972, Silver Medal, 100m butterfly, Bronze Medal, 100m freestyle, Mexico City Olympic Games, 1968, 5 Gold medals Pan-Am. Games, 1967, held 32 world records, 1967-1972; 4 times Champion NCAA, 1969-72.

**SPITZ, SEYMOUR JAMES, JR.,** retired fragrance company executive; b. Milw., Nov. 17, 1921; s. Seymour James and Marie (Spinette) S.; m. Elizabeth Taylor Parks, Feb. 7, 1948 (div. Aug. 1967); children: William Taylor, Elizabeth Seymour, Anne Bellin; m. Ellen C. Flynn, July 25, 1969; 1 dau., Ellen Christina. SB, MIT, 1943. With Newport Industries div. Heyden Newport Chem. Corp., Pensacola, Fla., 1946-65; asst. chief engr., 1955-57; asst. v.p., 1957-58; v.p. Newport Industries div. Heyden Newport Chem. Corp., 1959-60, exec. v.p., 1960-61, pres., 1961-65; v.p. parent co. Heyden Newport Chem. Corp., 1962-65, became group v.p., 1965; exec. v.p. Heyden Newport Chem. Corp. (renamed Tenneco Chems., Inc.), 1966; pres. Tenneco Chems., Inc., 1967-69; sr. v.p. parent co. Tenneco Inc.; pres. and dir. Internat. Flavors & Fragrances Inc., N.Y.C., 1970-85. Mem. MIT Corp. Devel. Com., 1977-86; trustee Spence Sch., 1982-88, Savannah (Ga.) Symphony, 1990-95, 98, Telfair Mus. Art, Savannah, 1993-96; MBA adv. bd. Ga. Southern U., 1998—. USN ENS-LCDR, 1943-46. Mem. Univ. Club (N.Y.C.), Larchmont Yacht Club (N.Y., trustee 1986-89), Landings Club, Oglethorpe Club (Savannah, bd. dirs. 1995-99). Home: 6 Brandenberry Rd Savannah GA 31411-2201 E-mail: sjstennis@aol.com.

**SPITZBERG, IRVING JOSEPH, JR.,** lawyer; b. Little Rock, Feb. 9, 1942; s. Irving Joseph and Marie Betty (Seeman) S.; m. Roberta Frances Alprin, Aug. 21, 1966 (div. 1988); children: Edward Storm, David Adam; m. Virginia V. Thorndike, Dec. 24, 1988. BA, Columbia U., 1964; B.Phil., Oxford U., 1966; JD, Yale U., 1969. Bar: Calif. 1969, DC 1985, Va. 1991. Asst. prof. Pitzer Coll., Claremont, Calif., 1969-71; fellow Inst. Current World Affairs, NYC, 1971-74; vis. lectr. Brown U., Providence, 1973; assoc prof. SUNY, Buffalo, 1974-80, dean of coll., 1974-78; gen. sec. AAUP, Washington, 1980-84; exec. dir. Coun. for Liberal Learning of Assn. Am. Colls., Washington, 1985-89; pres. The Knowledge Co., Fairfax, Va., 1985-2001; ptnr. Spitzberg & Drew, Washington, 1990-92; of counsel Spirer & Goldberg, Washington, 1993—; pvt. practice, 1993—. Coord. Alvan Ikoku Coll.,

Nigeria, 1979-80; cons. Bd. Adult Edn., Kenya, 1973-74, Philander Smith Coll., Little Rock, 1978-80; co-dir. nat. study on campus life for Carnegie Found. for Advancement Teaching, 1989-90. Author and editor: Exchange of Expertise, 1978, Universities and the New International Order, 1979, Universities and the International Exchange of Knowledge, 1980; author: Campus Programs on Leadership, 1986, Racial Politics in Little Rock, 1987; co-author: (with Berdahl and Moodie), Quality and Access in Higher Education, 1991, (with Virginia Thorndike) Creating Community on College Campuses, 1992; polit. columnist Prince William Times, 2001-02. Founder Coalition for Ednl. Excellence, Western NY, 1978-80, Advocates for the Rural Crescent, Va., 1999-2002, Coun. Liberal Learning; founding mem. Alliance for Leadership Devel., Washington, 1985; counsel GASP, Pomona, Calif., 1969-71; Dem. Committeeman, Erie County, NY, 1978-80; founding pres. Internat. Found. for St. Catherine's Coll., Oxford, 1986-91; v.p. Sparks-Glencoe Cmty. Coun., 2004-05; pres. North County Preservation, Inc., 2004—. Nat. winner Westinghouse Sci. Talent Search, 1960; Kellett scholar Trustees of Columbia U., 1964-66. Mem. Am. Immigration Lawyers Assn., Nat. Acad. Elder Law Attys., Washington Ethical Soc. (adj. leader 2002—), Ethical Culture Soc., Columbia Club, Yale Club (Washington), Rotary Internat. Jewish. Avocation: the internet. Personal E-mail: ijs@aol.com.

SPITZE, GLENYS SMITH, retired teacher and counselor; b. Rozel, Kans., May 20, 1919; d. Harry H. and Mary Louisa (Mishler) Smith; m. LeRoy A. Spitze, Dec. 31, 1942 (dec. Nov. 1995); children: Randall LeRoy, Kevin Lance, Kimett Alvin, Terril Christian, Shawn Smith; 1 fosterchild, Theo Ritz-Spitze. Cert. tchg., U. Kans., 1939; AA, San Jose (Calif.) City Coll., 1963; BA in Psychology, San Jose State U., 1965, MA in Child Devel., 1968. Cert. tchr., counselor, Calif. Elem. sch. tchr. Topeka County Schs., Richland, Kans., 1939-40, Kinsley (Kans.) Pub. Schs., 1940-42; presch. substitute tchr. AAUW Kindergarten, Newark, Ohio, 1945—46; presch. tchr. Meth. Ch. Facility, Campbell, Calif., 1956-58; guest lectr. Govt. Sch. Social Work, Colombo, Sri Lanka, 1965-66; instr. woman-woman relationship San Jose State Free U., 1966-67; child devel. lab. psychol. examiner Child Labs San Jose State U., 1967-68; pvt. informal practice tchr., counselor, cons. San Jose, Kailua-Kona, Hawaii. Vocal music dir. grades 1-3 Southside Sch., 1940-41; 6th dist. Calif. Congress Parent-Tchrs. Social Welfare dir., officer 6th dist. com. Calif. Coun. on Crime and Delinquency, San Jose, 1956-62; mem. kindergarten com. AAUW, Newark, Ohio, 1945-46; coord. Sangha Symposium, Asian Philosophy Club, San Jose State U., 1964-65; lectr. in field. Contbr. articles, poems to profl. publs. Hon. del. Gov. Brown's Conf. on Prevention of Juvenile Delinquency, Sacramento, 1963; co-organizer Post Polio Support Group, Kailua-Kona, HI, 2000. Mem.: Psi Chi. Avocations: writing, reading, swimming, snorkeling, anthropology. Home: 78-6800 Alii Dr KKSRC 5-103 Kailua Kona HI 96740-4421 Home (Summer): 311 E Bowman Woodland Park CO 80863 also: PO Gen Delivery Woodland Park CO 80863 Personal E-mail: gmglenys@webtv.net.

SPITZE, ROBERT GEORGE FREDERICK, agricultural studies educator; b. Berryville, Ark., Oct. 12, 1922; s. Wesley Henry and Nora Catherine (Stullken) Spitze; m. Hazel Cleo Taylor, Mar. 4, 1944; children: Glenna Dean, Ken Rollin. Student, Columbia U., 1944; BS (Sears Roebuck nat. fellow), U. Ark., 1947; PhD (Knapp research fellow), U. Wis., 1954. Instr. U. Wis., Madison, 1950; asst. prof. to prof. U. Tenn., Knoxville, 1951-60; prof. agrl. econs. U. Ill., Urbana, 1960-93. Vis. prof. Wye Coll., U. London, 1967-68; vis. research prof. policy U.S. Dept. Agr., Washington, 1975; vis. lectr. various univs., U.S. and Eng.; cons. Fed. Intermediate Credit Bank, 1958-59, Ill. Gen. Assembly Commn. on Revenue, 1963, Tex. A&M U., 1970, Am. Farm Bur. Fedn., Chgo., 1971, Ill. Gov.'s Commn. on Farm Income, 1972, Nat. Agrl. Research Policy Adv. Com., 1975, U.S. Dept. Agr. Econs. Research Service, 1976, Wharton Econometric Forecasting Inc., 1977, Nat. Rural Center, Washington, 1979-80, Nat. Public Policy Com., 1980, Okla. State U., 1986; mem. Ill. Gov.'s Council Econ. Advisers, 1974-76 Co-author: Food and Agricultural Policy, Economics and Politics, 1994; co-editor Policy Rsch. Notes, 1975-92, Food, Agriculture, and Rural Policy into the Twenty-first Century, 1994; editor: Agricultural and Food Policy: Issues and Alternatives for the 1990s, 1990; contbr. articles to profl. jours., chpts. to books Lt. USNR, 1943—47. Recipient Funk recognition award, 1973, Excellence in Teaching award U. Ill., 1977, Outstanding Agr. Coll. Alumni award U. Ark., 1994; co-recipient Outstanding Philanthropist Award Nat. Agrl. Alumni Devel. Assn., 2004 Mem. AAAS, Am. Econ. Assn., Am. Agrl. Econs. Assn. (Disting. Policy award 1981, Disting. Teaching award 1972, travel study grantee to France 1964), Internat. Assn. Agrl. Econs., Agrl. Econs. Soc. (U.K.), AAUP, Blue Key, Sigma Xi, Omicron Delta Kappa, Gamma Sigma Delta, Phi Eta Sigma, Alpha Zeta, Phi Sigma Office: U Ill Dept Agr Econ 1301 W Gregory Dr Dept Agr Urbana IL 61801-9015

SPITZER, ADRIAN, pediatrician, educator; b. Bucharest, Rumania, Dec. 21, 1927; came to U.S., 1963, naturalized, 1968; s. Osias and Sophia S. S.; m. Carole Zelter, Oct. 31, 1951; 1 son, Vlad. BS, Med. Sch. Bucharest, 1946; MD, Med. Sch. Bucharest, 1952. Diplomate: Am. Bd. Pediatrics. Intern White Plains (N.Y.) Hosp., 1964; resident Hosp. Med. Coll. Pa., 1965-66; postdoctoral fellow pediatric nephrology Albert Einstein Coll. Medicine, 1966-67; postdoctoral fellow in renal physiology Cornell U. Med. Sch., 1967-68; practice medicine specializing in pediatric nephrology Bronx, NY, 1968—; asst. prof. pediatrics Albert Einstein Coll. Medicine, 1968-72, assoc. prof., 1972-76, prof., 1976—; dir. div. nephrology, 1973-99; mem. staff Bronx Mcpl. Hosp. Ctr., Hosp. Albert Einstein Coll. Medicine/Montefiore Med. Ctr.; mem. Medicine B Study sect.-NIH, 1976-80. Prof. C. Donders rotating chmn. U. Utrecht, The Netherlands, 1990-91; Christiansen vis. fellow St. Catherine's Coll.; vis. fellow dept. biochemistry Oxford U., 1981-82; internat. Study Kidney Disease in Children; chmn. organizing com. 1st-7th Internat. Workshop on Devel. Renal Physiology, 1980-98, pres. 2001; mem. renal adv. com. N.Y.C. Dept. Health; sci. adv. bd. rsch. and grant com. Nat. Kidney Found., 1982; chmn. pediatric nephrology bd. Am. Bd. Pediat., 1982-83. Mem. editorial bd.: Pediatric Nephrology, Seminars in Nephrology; assoc. editor: Pediatric Renal Disease, 1979, 2d edit., 1992; editor: The Kidney Development, 1982. NIH spl fellow, 1967; John E. Fogarty Sr. Internat. fellow, 1981-82; grantee NIH, N.Y. State Health Research Council, Nat. Kidney Found.; recipient Bela Schick medal for extraordinary achievements in acad. and clin. pediatrics; The Scientific Advancement award of the Internat. Pediatr. Nephrol. Assn Mem.: Intersoc. Coun. for Kidney and Urinary Tract Rsch. (sec.-treas. 1984—89), Am. Pediat. Soc., Am. Acad. Pediat. (Henry L. Barnett award for pediat. nephrology 2005), Soc. Pediatric Rsch., Am. Physiol. Soc., Am. Fedn. Clin. Rsch., Am. Soc. Pediatric Nephrology (coun. 1977—80, pres. 1981—82, Founder's award 2006), Am. Soc. Nephrology (com. on govtl. rels. 1999—2001). Office: Albert Einstein Coll Medicine Montefiore Med Ctr 111 E 210th St Bronx NY 10467-2401 Office Phone: 718-655-1120. Business E-Mail: spitzer@aecom.yu.edu.

SPITZER, CARY REDFORD, avionics consultant, electrical engineer; b. New Hope, Va., July 31, 1937; s. Clyde Burke and Marion Jeanette (Redford) S.; m. Carrie Laura Ruth Logan, June 18, 1960; 1 child, Stiegel Logan. BSEE, Va. Poly. Inst. & State U., 1959; MS in Engring. Mgmt., George Washington U., 1970. Rsch. engr., engring. mgr. Langley Rsch Ctr., NASA, Hampton, Va., 1962-94; founder, pres. AvioniCon, Inc., 1993—. Lectr. UCLA, 1989—, George Washington U., 1994. Author: Viking Orbiter Views of Mars, 1981, Digital Avionics Systems, 1987, 2d edit., 1993, Avionics Handbook, 2000, Digital Avionics Handbook, 2006; contbr. articles to sci. publs. 1st lt. USAF, 1959-62. Recipient Volare award Airline Avionics Inst., 1988; named Va. Peninsula Engr. of Yr., 1993; recipient Digital Avionics award Am. Inst. of Aeronautics and Astronautics, 1994; nominated Collier Trophy, 1991. Fellow: IEEE (Centennial medal 1984, Millennium medal 2000), AIAA (assoc.); mem.: Aerospace and Electronic Systems Soc. of IEEE (pres. 1973—74, editor-in-chief Trans. 1996—99, chmn. IEEE-USA aerospace policy com. 1997—2000), Exch. Club (pres. Williamsburg 1985). Methodist. Avocations: kite flying, car mechanics. Home and Office: 3409 Foxridge Rd Williamsburg VA 23188-2499 Office Phone: 757-221-8031.

SPITZER, ELIOT LAURENCE, state attorney general; b. Bronx, June 10, 1959; s. Bernard and Anne Spitzer; m. Silda A. Wall, Oct. 17, 1987; children: Elyssa, Sarabeth, Jenna. BA, Princeton U., 1981; JD, Harvard U., 1984. Law clk. to Hon. Robert W. Sweet US Dist. Ct., NYC, 1984—85; assoc. Paul, Weiss, Rifkind, Wharton & Garrison, 1985—86, Skadden Arps Slate Meagher & Flom, 1992—94; ptnr. Constantine & Ptnrs., NYC, 1994—98; asst. dist. atty. NYC, 1986—92, chief, Labor Racketeering unit, 1991—92; atty. gen. State of NY, Albany, 1999—. Analyst, commentator on nat. news programs including NBC's Today Show, CNN's Burden of Proof, CNBC, Court TV; pro bono counsel N.Y. State Commn. for the Study of Youth Crime and Violence, 1993—94. Editor: Harvard Law Rev.; contbr. articles in leading newspapers and legal jours. Founder Ctr. for Cmty. Interest; trustee Montifiore Med. Ctr. Named Crusader of the Yr., TIME mag., 2002; named one of 100 Most Influential People, Time Mag., 2005; recipient Pub. Svc. award, NY mag., Paul H. Douglas Ethics in Govt. award, 2004. Democrat. Office: The Capitol Dept of Law 2nd Fl Albany NY 12224 Office Phone: 518-474-7330.*

SPITZER, HUGH D., lawyer; b. Seattle, Feb. 14, 1949; s. George Frederick and Dorothy Lea (Davidson) S.; m. Ann Scales, Oct. 14, 1983; children: Johanna Spitzer, Claudia Spitzer, Jenny Spitzer. BA, Yale U., 1970; JD, U. Wash., 1974; LLM, U. Calif., 1982. Bar: Wash. 1974, U.S. Dist/ Ct. (ea. and we. dists.) Wash. 1975, U.S. Ct. Appeals (9th and D.C. cirs.) 1975, U.S. Supreme Ct. 1980. Program analyst N.Y.C. Health and Hosp. Corp., 1970-71; labor lawyer Hafer, Cassidy & Price, Seattle, 1974-76; legis. asst. Seattle City Coun., 1976-77; legal counsel to mayor City of Seattle, 1977-81; mcpl. bond lawyer Foster Pepper & Shefelman, PLLC, Seattle, 1982—. Affiliate prof. sch. law U. Wash. Contbr. articles to profl. jours. Chair Seattle Law Income Housing Levy Oversight com., 1988-96, Wash. State Affordable Housing Adv. Bd., 2000—; vice chair Puget Sound Water Quality Authority Wash. State, 1989-96, State Tax Structure Com., 2001-02. Mem. Nat. Assn. Bond Lawyers, Am. Judicature Soc. (mem. exec. com. Coun. on Pub. Legal Edn.). Democrat. Avocations: piano, hiking, skiing. Office: Foster Pepper & Shefelman PLLC 1111 3rd Ave Bldg Ste 3400 Seattle WA 98101-3292 Office Phone: 206-447-8965. E-mail: spith@foster.com.

SPITZER, JOHN BRUMBACK, lawyer; b. Toledo, Mar. 6, 1918; s. Lyman and Blanche (Brumback) S.; m. Lucy Ohlinger, May 10, 1941 (dec. Oct. 13, 1971); children: John B., Molly (Mrs. Edmund Frost), Lyman, Adelbert L.; m. Vondah D. Thornbury, July 3, 1972 (dec. Nov. 2001); stepchildren: Vondah, Barbara, James R. Thornbury. Grad., Phillips Andover Acad., 1935; BA, Yale U., 1939, LLB, 1947. Bar: Ohio 1947. Law clk. to U.S. Supreme Ct. Justice Stanley Reed, 1947-48; ptnr. Marshall, Melhorn, Cole, Hummer & Spitzer, Toledo, 1955-86, Hummer & Spitzer, Toledo, 1986-89; with Hummer Legal Svcs. Corp., 1990—2002; ptnr. Spitzer and Hummer, 2002—. Pres. Spitzer Paper Box Co., 1955-63; v.p. Spitzer Bldg. Co., 1960-91, pres. 1992—. Pres. Toledo Symphony Orch., 1956-58, v.p., sec., 1958-86, trustee, 1986—. Maj. AUS, World War II. Mem.: Belmont Country Club. Congregationalist. Home: 29620 Gleneagles Rd Perrysburg OH 43551-3530 Office: Spitzer Bldg Co Rm 430 Spitzer Bldg 520 Madison Ave Toledo OH 43604 Office Phone: 419-255-1440. Personal E-mail: info@winelandlegal.com

SPITZER, MARC LEE, commissioner, former state legislator; b. Pitts., Sept. 12, 1957; s. Richard A. and Edith (Brodie) S., m. Jacque, one child. BA in History and Polit. Sci. summa cum laude, Dickinson Coll., 1979; JD cum laude, U. Mich., 1982. Bar: Ariz. 1982, U.S. Dist. Ct. Ariz. 1982, U.S. Tax Ct. 1982, U.S. Ct. Appeals (9th cir.) 1985. Dir. KPMG Peat Marwick, Phoenix, 1982—; mem. Ariz. State Legislature, Phoenix, 1992—2000, majority leader, 1997—2000; commr. Ariz. Corp. Commn., Phoenix, 2000—06, chmn., 2003—05; commr. Fed. Energy Regulatory Commn., Washington, 2006—. Bd. dirs. Ariz. Acad., 1990; mem. devel. com. Dickinson Coll., 1985-86; dir. Arizonans for Cultural Devel.; vice-chmn. Ariz. 18th Dist., 1986—; alternate del. 1988 Rep. Nat. Conv. GOP; legal counsel Ariz. Rep. Party. Recipient awards for legis. svc. from 32 non-profit orgns. Mem. ABA (vice-chmn., tax legis. sect.), State Bar Ariz. (cert. specialist taxation), Ariz. Tax Research Found. (bd. dirs. 1984—), Ariz. Tax Research Assn., Maricopa County Bar Assn., Phoenix 100 Rotary, Heritage Found., Ariz. Club, Phi Beta Kappa, Sigma Alpha Epsilon. Jewish. Avocations: fishing, prospecting, classical music, racquetball. Office: Fed Energy Regulatory Commn 888 First St NE Washington DC 20426

SPITZER, MATTHEW LAWRENCE, retired retail store executive; b. Pitts., June 20, 1929; s. Martin and Ruth G. S.; children: Mark, Edward, Eric, Joseph. Student, U. Buffalo, 1948-50. Lic. airline transport pilot. Product line mgr. Gen. Dynamics, Rochester, NY, 1962-67; dir. contracts Friden divsn. Singer, San Leandro, Calif., 1969; asst. v.p. Talcott Computer Leasing, San Francisco, 1970-71; pres. Spitzer Music Mgmt. Co., Hayward, Calif., 1972-95, Spitzer Helicopter Leasing Co., Hayward. Chmn. bd. Leo's Audio and Music Techs., Oakland, Calif. Mem. Masons, Mensa. Personal E-mail: mspitz6685@aol.com

SPITZER, MORTON EDWARD, management consultant; b. N.Y.C., Jan. 3, 1937; s. Henry Lawrence and Martha (Michel) S.; m. Nancy Dinetz, Oct. 10, 1965; children: Matthew, Douglas. BA, Bklyn. Coll., 1957; MS, N.C. State U., 1959; PhD, N.Y. U., 1964. Dir./mgr. planning and analysis The Prudential Ins. Co. Am., Newark, 1964-74, v.p. S.W. ops. Houston, 1975-79, v.p. ordinary agys. Newark, 1979-87, pres. North Ctrl. ops. Mpls., 1988, sr. v.p. dist. agys. Newark, 1989, Woodland Hills, Calif., 1990-91; COO Liberty Life Assurance Co. Boston, Dover, NH, 1992—2002, ret., 2002. Bd. dirs. Liberty Life Assurance Co., Boston, Liberty Assignment Co., Liberty Life Distbrs. LLC, Liberty Life Securities LLC, BARCO Lto, Barbados, Limra Internat., N.Am. Life and Health of N.Y.; bd. govs. ACLI Forum 500; bd. dirs. N. Am. Co., NY, N.Am. Life and Health Ins. Co. N.Y. Co-author: The Law and Personnel Testing, 1971. Bd. dirs. Nat. Soc. to Prevent Blindness, N.J., 1986-89, nat. bd. dirs., Chgo., 1989. Mem. APA, Am. Psychol. Soc., Ea. Psychol. Assn., Sigma Xi. Avocations: tennis, art. Home: 449 E Deering Rd Deering NH 03244 Personal E-mail: morts@optonline.net.

SPITZER, ROBERT J., academic administrator; BBA, Gonzaga U.; MPhil, St. Louis U.; STB, Gregorian U., Rome; ThM, Weston Sch. Theology, Cambridge, Mass.; PhD in Philosophy, Cath. U. of Am. Tchr. Georgetown U., 1984-90, Seattle U., 1978-80, 90-98; pres. Gonzaga U., 1998—. Co-founder U. Faculty for Life; founder, adv. Life Principles. Office: Gonzaga U 502 E Boone Ave Spokane WA 99258-0001

SPITZLI, DONALD HAWKES, JR., lawyer; b. Newark, Mar. 19, 1934; s. Donald Hawkes and Beatrice (Banister) S.; children: Donald Hawkes III, Peter Gilbert, Seth Armstrong. AB, Dartmouth Coll., 1956; LL.B., U. Va., 1963. Bar: Va. 1963. Assoc. Willcox, Savage, Lawrence, Dickson & Spindle, Norfolk, Va., 1964-67, 68-70, ptnr., 1971-77; atty. Eastman Kodak Co., Rochester, N.Y., 1967-68; pres. Marine Hydraulics Internat., Inc., Chesapeake, Va., 1978-80; sole practice Virginia Beach, Va., 1980—. Owner Chieftain Motor Inn, Hanover, N.H., 1980-87. Comdr. USNR, 1956-70. Episcopalian. Office: 4460 Corporation Ln Ste 180 Virginia Beach VA 23462 Office Phone: 757-499-1191. Personal E-mail: airbuzzard24@aol.com.

SPITZNAGEL, JOHN KEITH, retired microbiologist, immunologist, physician; b. Peoria, Ill., Apr. 11, 1923; s. Elmer Florian and Anna S. (Kolb) S.; m. Anne Moulton Sirch, Feb. 2, 1947; children: John, Jean, Margaret, Elizabeth, Paul. BA, Columbia U., 1943, MD, 1946. Diplomate Nat. Bd. Med. Examiners, Am. Bd. Internal Medicine. Intern Johns Hopkins Hosp., Balt., 1946-47; resident in internal medicine Barnes Hosp., St. Louis, 1949-51; vis. investigator Rockefeller Inst., N.Y.C., 1952-53, Nat. Inst. Med. Research, London, 1967-68; mem. faculty U. N.C., Chapel Hill, 1957-79, prof. microbiology and infectious diseases, prof. medicine, 1957-79; mem. N.C. Meml. Hosp., Chapel Hill, 1974-79; ad hoc adviser NIH, 1971—; prof. microbiology and immunology, chmn. dept. Emory U., Atlanta, 1979-93, prof. emeritus microbiology and immunology, 1993—, assoc. dean rsch., 1997-98; attending physician, vol. and co-founder Good Samaritan Health and Wellness Ctr., Jasper, Ga., 2002—, chmn. exec. bd., CEO, 2004-06. Mem. study sect. bacteriology and mycology NIH, 1975-79, 85-89, chmn., 1977-79. Editor: Infection and Immunity, 1970-80, Jour. Immunology, 1973-80, Jour. Reticuloendothelial Soc, 1973-80. Served with M.C. AUS, 1947-57. Recipient Research Career Devel. award USPHS, 1957-67, Disting. Service award Sch. Medicine U. N.C., Chapel Hill, 1987; USPHS postdoctoral fellow, 1968; USPHS and AEC grantee; lectureship named in his honor, Spitznagel Lectureship on Host Antimicrobial Def., Emory U., 1998. Fellow ACP, Infectious Disease Soc.; mem. AAAS (life), Am. Soc. Microbiology (div. group councilor 1977-79), Am. Assn. Immunologists, Reticuloendothelial Soc. (pres. 1982), Infectious Disease Soc., So. Soc. Clin. Rsch., Assn. Am. Med. Sch. Microbiology and Immunology Chmn. (pres. 1990-91), Sigma Xi. Achievements include research on cell biology of human neutrophil polymorphonuclear leukocytes, and oxygen ind. mechanisms of antimicrobial phagocytoses; first to demonstrate cationic antimicrobial proteins of polymorphonuclear leukocytes granules; co-discoverer of a cationic protein of polymorph granules with antimicrobial action and a powerful attractant for mononuclear phagocytes. Home: 95 Starcross Ln # 20804 Jasper GA 30143-7883 Office: 1510 Clifton Rd NE Atlanta GA 30322-4218 E-mail: spitzna@mac.com.

SPIVAK, ALVIN A., retired public relations executive; b. Phila., Nov. 30, 1927; s. Herman and Bella (Haimovitz) S.; m. Martha Barry, Dec. 21, 1964; 1 dau., Denise. BS, Temple U., 1949. With I.N.S., 1949-58, Senate reporter, also mem. gen. staff Washington, 1951-58; with U.P.I., 1958-67, White House reporter, 1960-67; pub. affairs dir. Nat. Adv. Commn. on Civil Disorders, 1967-68, Democratic Nat. Com., 1968-70; corp. pub. affairs dir. Gen. Dynamics Corp., 1970-94, ret., 1994. Served with USAAF, 1946-47. Mem. Mil. Order of Carabao, Nat. Press Club, Beta Gamma Sigma. Home: 5726 W 1st Sq SW Vero Beach FL 32968-2256

SPIVAK, JOAN CAROL, communications executive; b. Phila., May 12, 1950; d. Jack and Evelyn Lee (Copelman) S.; m. John D. Goldman, May 17, 1980; children: Jesse, Marcus. AB, Barnard Coll., 1972; M of Health Scis., Johns Hopkins U., 1980. Freelance writer, N.Y.C., 1980-84; project dir. Impact Med. Communication, N.Y.C., 1984-87; exec. v.p., gen. mgr. health and sci. strategies Edelman Worldwide, N.Y.C., 1987—2002; pres. Prime Medica, Inc., 2002—. Co-author: (pamphlet) Lead: New Perspectives on an Old Problem, 1978; contbr. The Book of Health, 1981, articles to profl. jours. Bd. dirs. May O'Donnell Dance Co., N.Y.C., 1983-85, Chamber Ballet U.S.A., N.Y.C., 1985-87, Nat. Child Labor Commn., 1991-2000, Cases, 1995-2001, Learning Through an Expanded Arts Program, 2004—. Mem. N.Y. Acad. Sci. Democrat. Jewish. Avocations: pottery, boating. Office Phone: 212-921-1250. E-mail: joan.spivak@prime-medica.com.

SPIVAK, LEONARD A., lawyer; b. N.Y.C., July 11, 1943; s. Jack and Esther (Peckolick) S.; children: Kate, Allison, Jon, Gabrielle. B.A. with honors, SUNY-Stony Brook, 1964; LLB cum laude, Columbia U., 1967. Bar: N.Y. 1967, U.S. Dist. Ct. (so. and ea. dists.) N.Y., U.S. Ct. Appeals (2d, 3d, 5th, 7th, 9th and 10th cirs.), U.S. Supreme Ct. Assoc., Gilbert, Segal & Young, N.Y.C., 1967-68; assoc. Cahill, Gordon & Reindel LLP, N.Y.C., 1968-75, ptnr., 1975—. Bd. dirs. Stony Brook Found., Raby Peck Found. Mem. Alumni Assn. SUNY-Stony Brook (past pres.). Democrat. Office: Cahill Gordon & Reindel LLP 80 Pine St Fl 17 New York NY 10005-1790 E-mail: LSpivak@cahill.com.*

SPIVAK, MARK R., lawyer; b. NYC, Nov. 5, 1958; BA magna cum laude, Muhlenberg Coll., 1980; JD, Georgetown U., 1983. Bar: NJ 1983, DC 1984. Ptnr., co-head Bus. & Internat. Sect. Vinson & Elkins LLP, Washington, DC. Assoc. editor The Tax Lawyer, 1982—83. Office: Vinson & Elkins LLP Willard Office Bldg 1455 Pennsylvania Ave, Ste 600 Washington DC 20004 Office Phone: 202-639-6664. E-mail: mspivak@velaw.com

SPIVAK, MAURICE SIDNEY, civil engineer, consultant; b. Milford, Mass., Jan. 5, 1926; s. Phillip None and Esther Sarah Spivak; m. Annette Charlotte Mann; children: Michelle Melinger, Myra Runge, Jonah. BS, The Citadel, Charleston, S.C., 1950; MS, W. Va. U., Mogantown, 1955; PhD (hon.), U.of Berkley, Southhill, Mich. Registered Profl. Engr., Wis., 1976. Biochemical asst. Mass. Gen. Hosp., Boston, 1950—53; Biochemist Worcester Found., Shrewsbury, Mass., 1955—56; chem. engr. U.S.Army, Springfield, Mass., 1956—67; project engr. U.S.Army Arsenal, Edgewood, Md., 1967—73; chief project mgmt. engring. U.S. Army Corps of Engrs., Norfolk, Va., 1973—86. Cons. U.S. Army Corps of Engrs., Norfolk, Va., 1986—99. Author: (Engineering Papers) Published in Govt. and Jour.Biolog. Chemistry, 1960 (Numerous awards, 1977). Direct commr. USNR; First V.P. B'rith Sholom, Norfolk, Va. Pvt. First Class U.S. Army, 1944—46, European Theater. Decorated Bronze Star Medal US Army, Combat Infantry badge; recipient Several Civilian Awards, Springfield Armory, 1956-1966, Numerous Awards, Edgewood Arsenal, 1967-1973, US Army Corps of Engineers, 1973-1986; fellow, Worcester Found., 1955, W. Va. U., 1955. Mem.: ASCE. Home: 821 Jennings St Virginia Beach VA 23464 Personal E-mail: MSpivak650@aol.com.

SPIVEY, BRUCE E., ophthalmologist, educator, health facility administrator; b. Cedar Rapids, Iowa, Aug. 39, 1934; s. William Loranzy and Grace Loretta (Barber) S.; children: Lisa, Eric; m. Patti Amanda Birge, Dec. 20, 1987. BA, Coe Coll., 1956; MD, U. Iowa, 1959, MS, 1964; MEd, U. Ill., 1969; DSc (hon.), Coe Coll., 1978. Diplomate Am. Bd. Ophthalmology (fellow, bd. dirs. 1975-83, chmn. oral exam 1976-81). Asst. prof. U. Iowa Coll. Medicine, Iowa City, 1966, assoc. prof., 1968—71; dean Sch. Med. Scis. U. Pacific, San Francisco, 1971—76; prof., chmn. dept. ophthalmology Pacific Med. Ctr. (now Calif. Pacific Med. Ctr.), San Francisco, 1971—87; pres., CEO Calif. Pacific Med. Ctr., San Francisco, 1976—91; exec. v.p., CEO Am. Acad. Ophthalmology, San Francisco, 1977—93; pres., CEO Calif. Healthcare Sys., Bay area, 1986—92; CEO Northwestern Healthcare Network, Chgo., 1992—97, Columbia Cornell Care, N.Y.C., 1997—2000, Columbia Cornell Network Physicians, N.Y.C., 1999—2000. Bd. dirs. Reliance Group Holdings Inc., N.Y.C.; trustee, bd. dirs., sec. bd. MedEx, Balt., 1999—; v.p. Am. Bd. Med. Spltys., 1978—80, pres., 1980—82, Coun. Med. Splty. Socs., 2000—02, dep. exec. v.p., 2002—; chmn. bd. dirs. Vol. Hosps. of Am.-No. Calif., 1985—87, nat. bd. dirs., 1991—96; nat. adv. coun. NEI/NIH, 1987—92; spl. med. adv. group Dept. Vets Affairs, 1987—93; trustee, bd. dirs., sec. bd. Ophthal. Mut. Ins. Co., 1988—; trustee, sec. bd. PrimeSight, San Francisco, 1996—99; bd. dirs., chmn MedBiquitous, Balt., 2001—. Contbr. over 115 articles to profl. jours.; inventor instruments for eye surgery. Bd. dirs. Pacific Vision Found., San Francisco, 1978—, U.S.-China Ednl. Inst., 1979—; trustee Coe Coll., 1985—, Found. AAO, 1981—, Internat. Coun. Ophthalmology, 1985—, Helen Keller Internat., 1999—; trustee Medbiquitous, 2000—, chmn, 2001—06. Served to capt. U.S. Army, 1964-66. Decorated Bronze Star; recipient Emile Javal Gold medal Internat. Contact Lens Council, San Francisco, 1982, Gradle medal Pan-Am. Assn. Ophthalmol., Disting. Alumni award U. Iowa, 2003, others. Fellow ACS, Am. Acad. Ophthalmology (Disting. Svc. award 1972, Sr. Honor award 1986, Guest of Honor 1996, Lifetime Achievement award, 2002); mem. AMA, Am. Ophthal. Soc. (Howe medal 1993, bd. dirs. 1986-91, pres. 1994-95), Academia Ophthal. Internat. (founder internat. (Bernardo Streiff Gold medal 2002), Soc. Med. Adminstrs. (pres. 1999-2001), Internat. Congress Ophthalmology (sec.-gen. 1978-82), Internat. Coun. Ophthalmology (sec.-gen. 1994—2006, trustee 1986—, pres. 2006—, Jules Francois Gold medal 2000), Pacific-Union Club, Chevy Chase Club, Knickerbocker Club, Cosmos Club. Presbyterian. Office: 945 Green St San Francisco CA 94133 Business E-Mail: bruce@spivey.org.

SPIVEY, TED RAY, language educator; b. Fort Pierce, Fla., July 1, 1927; s. Theodore Roosevelt and Etty Pearl (Sumner) S.; m. Julia Brannon Douglass, June 30, 1962; children— Mary Leta, John Andrew. AB, Emory U., 1949; MA, U. Minn., 1951, PhD, 1954. Reporter Greenville Reporter, SC, 1949-50; instr. Emory U., Atlanta, 1954-56; mem. faculty Ga. State U., Atlanta, 1956-89, assoc. prof. English, 1960-64, prof., 1964-89, Regents' prof., 1984-89, emeritus, 1989—. Author: (with Kenneth M. England) A Manual of Style, 1960, The Renewed Quest, 1969, The Coming of the New Man, 1971, The Journey Beyond Tragedy, 1980, Revival: Southern Writers in the Modern

City, 1986, The Writer as Shaman: The Pilgrimages of Conrad Aiken and Walker Percy, 1986, To Die in Atlanta: Poems of the Civil War and After, 1987, Beyond Modernism: Toward a New Myth Criticism, 1988, A City Observed: Poems of the New Age, 1988, (with Arthur Waterman) Conrad Aiken: A Priest of Consciousness, 1989, Flannery O'Connor: The Woman, The Thinker, the Visionary, 1995, Airport: America Rediscovered, 1997, Time's Stop in Savannah: Conrad Aiken's Inner Journey, 1997, Bridges of Light: Four Poets of the Golden Isles, 2001. Served with USN, 1945-46. Urban Life Center grantee, 1977-80. Mem. So. Atlantic MLA, Brittany Club. Democrat. Episcopalian. Home: 104 Plemmons Dr Saint Simons Island GA 31522-9767

**SPIWAK, LAWRENCE J.,** legal association administrator; married; 1 child. BA with hons, George Washington U., 1986; JD, 1989. Bar: N.Y., Mass., D.C., U.S. Ct. Appeals (D.C. cir.). Sr. atty. Fed. Energy Regulatory Commn., 1992—94; sr. atty. Competition Divsn. Office Gen. Counsel FCC, 1994—98; pres. Phoenix Ctr. Advanced Legal and Econ. Pub. Policy Studies, Washington, 1998—. Spkr. in field; vis. prof. law U. Toulouse, France. Contbr. articles to profl. jours. Office: Phoenix Ctr Advanced Legal and Econ Public Policy Studies 5335 Wisconsin Ave NW Ste 440 Washington DC 20015-2034

**SPLAKE, T. KILGORE See SMITH, THOMAS**

**SPLANE, RICHARD BEVERLEY,** social work educator; b. Calgary, Alta., Can., Sept. 25, 1916; s. Alfred William and Clara Jane (Allyn) S.; m. Verna Marie Huffman, Feb. 22, 1971. BA, McMaster U., 1940, LLD (hon.), 1990; cert. social sci. and administrn., London Sch. Econs., 1947; MA, U. Toronto, 1948, MSW, 1951, PhD, 1961, LLD (hon.), 2005, Wilfrid Laurier U., 1988, U. B.C., 1996. Exec. dir. Children's Aid Soc., Cornwall, Ont., Canada, 1948—50; with Health and Welfare Can., Ottawa, 1951—72, exec. asst. to dep. min. nat. welfare, 1959—60, dir. unemployment assistance, 1960—62, dir. gen. welfare assistance and svcs., 1960—70, asst. dep. min. social allowances and svcs., 1970—72; vis. prof. U. Alta., Edmonton, 1972—73; prof. social policy Sch. Social Work, U. B.C., Vancouver, 1973—82. Cons. Govt. Can., Govt. Alta., UNICEF. Author: The Development of Social Welfare in Ontario, 1965; (with Verna Huffman Splane) Chief Nursing Officers in National Ministries of Health, 1994, 75 Years of Community Service to Canada: Canadian Council on Social Development, 1920-1995, George Davidson Social Policy and Public Policy Exemplar, 2003 Served with RCAF, 1942-45. Recipient Centennial medal Govt. Can., 1967, Charles E. Hendry award U. Toronto, 1981, Commemorative medal for 125th anniversary of Confedn. of Can., 1992, Disting. Svc. award Internat. Coun. on Social Welfare, 1996, Queen's Golden Jubilee medal, 2002. Mem. Can. Assn. Social Workers (Outstanding Nat. Svc. award 1985, Touzel award 2002, Queens Golden medal 2002), Can. Inst. Pub. Adminstrn., Can. Hist. Assn., Can. Coun. on Social Devel. (Lifetime Achievement award 1995), Internat. Assn. Schs. Social Work, Internat. Confs. Social Devel. (prof. emeritus U. BC 1991-06), World Federalists Can., UN Assn. Can. (bd. dirs. Vancouver br.), Vancouver Club, Officer Order Can. Mem. United Ch. Can.

**SPLANSKY, SANDRA J.,** director; b. Chgo., Sept. 4, 1958; d. Joseph Carl and Marilyn (Lesser) Splansky; children: Charles K. Kuchynka, Mara Jean Kuchynka. BS in Merchandising, No. Ill. U., 1980, MS in Resources and Svcs., 1983, EdS in Counseling, 1992. Acad. advisor dept. family, consumer, nutrition scis. No. Ill. U., DeKalb, 1983—86, dir., acad. advising Coll. Health and Human Svcs., 1986—. Coord. freshmen connections No. Ill. U., DeKalb, 1991—97, faculty coord. health professions ho., 2001—. Contbr. articles to profl. jours.; presenter profl. confs. Bd. dirs. Congregation Beth Shalom, DeKalb. Recipient Presdl. Supportive Profl. Staff award, No. Ill. U., 1992, Student Svcs. Recognition award, Student Affairs, No. Ill. U., 1999, Outstanding 1st yr. Student Adv. award, First Yr. Experience SC, 2000; Faculty Devel. grantee, No. Ill. U., 1990, 2000. Mem.: Nat. Acad. Advising Assn. (Outstanding Acad. Advising cert. of merit 1988), Am. Coll. Pers. Assn. (sec. commn. XVI 1999—2003, Outstanding Svc. award 2002). Office: No Ill Univ Coll Health and Human Scis Dekalb IL 60115 Personal E-mail: ssplansky@niu.edu.

**SPLETE, ALLEN PETERJOHN,** educational association administrator, educator; b. Carthage, NY, June 24, 1938; s. Howard Henry and Minnie Bertha (Peterjohn) S.; m. Marilyn Lois Detweiler, June 18, 1966; children: Heidi, Michael. BA, St. Lawrence U., 1960; MA with distinction, Colgate U., 1962; PhD, Syracuse U., 1968; LHD, Campbellsville Coll., 1990; LLD, Davis and Elkins Coll., 1990; LHD, Mt. Union Coll., 1992, St. Thomas Aquinas Coll., 1992, U. Indpls., 1994, Juniata Coll., 1994, Hastings Coll., 1994; EdD, Marywood Coll., 1995; LHD, Holy Family Coll., 1996, Wesley Coll., 1996, Bluffton Coll., 2003. Adminstrv. asst. to v.p. acad. affairs Syracuse (NY) U., 1965-68, assoc. dean, exec. asst. to provost, 1968-70; v.p. for acad. planning St. Lawrence U., Canton, NY, 1970-82; pres. Westminster Coll., New Wilmington, Pa., 1982-85; exec. v.p. Coun. Ind. Colls., Washington, 1985-86, pres., 1986-2000; dir., pres. Consulting Svc., 2002—05; pres. emeritus Coun. Ind. Colls., Washington, 2000—. Dir. Nat. Prepaid Tuition Plan, 1988-91; cons. York Coll., Pa., 1974; mem. planning and rsch. com. N.Y. State Coun. on Ind. Colls. and Univs., 1975-82; statewide higher edn. adv. com. N.Y. State Senate Com. on Higher Edn., 1979-82; nat. adv. bd. Flaming Rainbow U., 1989-96; mem. advisory bd. Assn. Gov. Bds. Presdl. Search Consultation Svc., 1987-94, Academic Search Consultation Svc., 1989—, mem. Harvard Sem. for new pres. adv. bd., 1990—; bd. dirs. Tchr. Edn. Accreditation Coun., 1998—, chair, 2001—; oversight and rev. com. leadership and orgnl. devel. program United Negro Coll. Fund, 1991-96, SCT adv. coun., 1996-2001; adv. bd. Eric Nat., 1996-03, Boyer Ctr. for Advanced Studies, 1998-2005; UAW/Ford U. Help Steering Com., 1997-01; mem. exec. bd. Project Pericles, 1999-05 (nat. adv. bd. 2005), CIC Pres. Consulting Svc., 2003-05. Co-author: Frederic Remington-Selected Letters, 1988, A Good Place To Work: Sourcebook for the Academic Workplace, 1991, Presidential Transitions in Private Colleges, 2005; editor: (with others) Confs. on Adirondack Park, 1972-82, Can.-Am. Relations, 1974-75, Presidential Essays — Success Stories, 2000; contbr. articles to profl. jours. Chmn. planning bd. Village of Canton, 1974-81; elder Neelsville Presbyn. Ch., 1986-89; trustee Adirondack Conservancy, Wilsboro, N.Y., 1980-82; trustee Millikin U., 2000—; mem. adv. bd. Sage Scholars, 2000—. Served to 1st lt. U.S. Army, 1960-62. Recipient Alumni citation, St. Lawrence U., 1987, Algernon Sydney Sullivan award, 1997, CIC Acad. Leadership award, 2000, Henry D. Paley award, Nat. Assn. Ind. Colls. and Univs., 2001, Partnership award, Assn. Presbyn. Colls. and Univs., 2000; grantee, John Ben Snow Found., 1981. Mem. Pa. Assn. Colls. and Univs. (govt. rels. com. 1983-85), Mid. States Assn. (team chmn. com. on higher edn. 1976-78, 81), Assn. Am. Colls. (project rev. cons. 1981-82), Soc. Educators and Scholars (bd. editors), Assn. Am. Colls. (pres. adv. com. 1977-78, reviewer Quill project 1978-79), St. Lawrence County Hist. Assn. (pres. 1977-82), Frederic Remington Mus. Assn., Beta Theta Pi (v.p. 1980-83). Republican. Home: 10821 Longmeadow Dr Damascus MD 20872-2240 Office: Coun Ind Colls 1 Dupont Cir NW Ste 320 Washington DC 20036-1137 Office Phone: 301-253-1274. Personal E-mail: splete@earthlink.net.

**SPLETE, MARILYN DETWEILER,** retired secondary school educator; b. Abington, Pa., Mar. 7, 1942; d. Russell Stover and Mabel Haring (Clymer) Detweiler; m. Allen Peterjohn Splete, June 18, 1966; children: Heidi, Michael. BA, Dickinson Coll., 1964; MS, Syracuse U., 1970. Asst. dean admissions Dickinson Coll., Carlisle, Pa., 1964—66; tchr. Jordan Elbridge Ctrl. Sch., Elbridge, NY, 1966—70; dir. administr. Canton C. of C., NY, 1979—82; tchr. Howard County Pub. Schs., Ellicott City, Md., 1986—2003; ret., 2003. Editor, author (with others): Frederic Remington: Selected Letters, 1989 Pres. Ctrl. N.Y. Health Sys. Agy., Syracuse, 1980-82; deacon Neelsville Presbyn. Ch., 1987-90, elder, 1991-93, 1999-2002 Mem. NEA, Md. State Tchrs. Assn., Nat. Coun. Social Studies Republican. Avocations: reading, knitting, cross country skiing, travel, photography. Home: 10821 Longmeadow Dr Damascus MD 20872-2240

**SPLICHAL, JOACHIM,** chef, restaurant owner; b. Spaichingen, Germany; Chef La Bonne Auberge, Antibes, L'Oasis, La Napoule; sous chef Chantecler Restaurant, Nice, France; exec. chef Regency Club, L.A., 1981, Seventh St. Bistro, L.A.; owner Max Au Triangle, L.A., 1984; chef, founder Patina Group, L.A., 1989—, Patina, 1989—, Kendall's Brasserie, Calif., Zucca Ristorante, L.A., Nick & Stef's Steakhouse, L.A., Cafe Pinot, L.A., Pinot Provence, L.A., Pinot Brasserie, L.A., Catal Restaurant, L.A., Naples Ristorante, L.A., Tortilla Joe's, L.A. Author: (book) Spuds, Truffles and Wild Gnocchi and Feeding Baby. Named Best California Chef, James Beard Found., 1991, 1995, Treasure of L.A., L.A. Mayor Richard Riordan and Ctrl. City Assn., 1996, Restaurateur of the Yr., Calif. Restaurant Writers Assn., 1997, So. Calif. Restaurant Writers, 1999, Legendary Chef, Bon Appetit mag., 2002. Office: The Patina Group 400 S Hope St Los Angeles CA 90071 Office Phone: 213-239-2520.

**SPLINTER, MICHAEL R.,** manufacturing executive; BEE, Univ. of Wis., Madison, Wis., 1972, MEE, 1974. Gen. mgr., exec. v.p. Intel Corp., Santa Clara, Calif., 1984—96; v.p. and asst. Gen. mgr. Tech. and Mfg. Group, Intel Corp., Santa Clara, Calif., 1996—98, v.p. and Gen. mgr., 1998—99, sr. v.p. and Gen. mgr., 1999—2001, exec. v.p. and Gen. mgr., 2001, exec. v.p. and dir., Sales and Mktg. group, 2001—03; pres. and CEO Applied Materials, Inc., Santa Clara, Calif., 2003—. Mem. Computer Sys. Policy Project; bd. dir. Semiconductor Equipment and Materials'Intern., Silicon Valley Leadership Group. Named to, Jr. Achievement Hall of Fame; recipient Intern. Partnership Award, Calif.-Israel C. of C., Disting. Alumni Award, U. Wis. Mem.: Governors' Coun. of World Econ. Forum, Applied Materials (bd. dir. 2003). Office: Applied Materials Inc 3050 Bowers Ave Santa Clara CA 95054*

**SPLINTER, WILLIAM ELDON,** agricultural engineering educator; b. North Platte, Nebr., Nov. 24, 1925; s. William John and Minnie (Calhoun) Splinter; m. Eleanor Love Peterson, Jan. 10, 1952 (dec. Jan. 1999); children: Kathryn Love, William John, Karen Ann, Robert Marvin; m. Elizabeth Butters Calhoun, Feb. 9, 2002. BS in Agrl. Engring., U. Nebr., 1950; MS in Agrl. Engring., Mich. State U., 1951, PhD in Agrl. Engring., 1955. Instr. agrl. engring. Mich. State U., East Lansing, 1953-54; assoc. prof. biology and agrl. engring. N.C. State U., Raleigh, 1954-60, prof. biology and agrl. engring., 1960-68; head agrl. engring. dept. U. Nebr., Lincoln, 1968—88, vice chancellor rsch., 1988—93; interim dean Coll. Engring. & Tech. U., 1994—95, 2001—02; interim dir. Nebr. State Mus., 2002—. Cons. engr.; exec. bd. Am. Assn. Engring. Socs.; hon. prof. Shengyang (People's Republic of China) Agrl. U. Contbr. articles to tech. jours.; patentee in field. Vol. dir. L.F. Larsen Tractor Mus. Served with USNR, 1946-51. Recipient Massey Ferguson Gold medal, 1978, John Deere Gold medal, 1995, Disting. Svc. award Kiwanis, 1994, George Howard-Loiuse Pound award, 2001; named to Nebr. Hall of Agrl. Achievement; named Disting. Alumni, U. Nebr., Lincoln, 2000, Mich. State U., 2005; named U. Nebr. Splinter Rsch. Lab. in his honor, 2004. Fellow AAAS, NSPE, Am. Soc. Agrl. Engrs. (pres., adminstrv. council, found. pres., Presdl. citation 1999); mem. Nat. Acad. Engring., Soc. Automotive Engrs., Am. Soc. Engring. Edn., Sigma Xi, Sigma Tau, Sigma Pi Sigma, Pi Mu Epsilon, Gamma Sigma Delta, Phi Kappa Phi, Beta Sigma Psi. Home: 4801 Bridle Ln Lincoln NE 68516-3436 Office: U Nebr Lincoln PO Box 830833 Lincoln NE 68583-0833 Office Phone: 402-472-8389. Business E-Mail: wsplinter1@unl.edu.

**SPLITTSTOESSER, WALTER EMIL,** botanist, educator; b. Claremont, Minn., Aug. 27, 1937; s. Waldemar Theodore and Opal Mae (Young) S.; m. Shirley Anne O'Connor, July 2, 1960; children: Pamela, Sheryl, Riley. BS with distinction (univ. fellow), U. Minn., 1958; MS, S.D. State U., 1960; PhD, Purdue U., 1963. Plant breeder U. Minn., 1956-58; weed scientist S.D. State U., 1958-60; plant physiologist Purdue U., 1960-63, Shell Oil Co., Modesto, Calif., 1963-64; biochemist U. Calif., Davis, 1964-65; mem. faculty U. Ill., Urbana, 1965-97, prof. plant physiology, 1974-97, head vegetable crops div., 1972-82. Vis. prof., biotechnologist Univ. Coll., Dublin, Ireland, 1987; vis. prof. Univ. Coll., London, 1972, La Trobe U., Melbourne, Australia, 1995; biologist Parkland Coll., Champaign, Ill., 1974; vis. rsch. assoc. Rothamsted Exptl. Sta., Herpenden, England, 1980; disting. vis. prof. Nagoya (Japan) U., 1982. Author: Vegetable Growing Handbook, 1979, 3d edit., 1990; contbr. articles to profl. jours.; rev. editor: Analytical Biochemistry, 1969-78, NSF, 1978-79; others. Recipient J.H. Gourley award Am. Fruit Grower-Am. Soc. Hort. Sci., 1974, Outstanding Grad. Educator award, 1990; NIH fellow, 1964-65. Fellow Am. Soc. Hort. Sci. (rev. editor jour. 1969-98), Japanese Soc. Promotion of Sci.; mem. Am. Soc. Hort. Sci., Plant Growth Reg. Soc. Am., Sigma Xi (pres. 1990-91), Alpha Zeta, Gamma Sigma Delta, Delta Theta Sigma, Phi Kappa Phi. Home: 2006 Cureton Dr Urbana IL 61801-6226 Personal E-mail: splittst@uiuc.edu.

**SPODAK, MICHAEL KENNETH,** forensic psychiatrist; b. Bklyn., Nov. 5, 1944; s. Harry and Betty (Rahn) S.; children: Lisa Beth, Brett David. BS, Union Coll., 1966; MD, SUNY-Syracuse, 1970. Diplomate: Nat. Bd. Med. Examiners, Am. Bd. Neurology and Psychiatry. Intern Mary Imogene Bassett Hosp., Cooperstown, NY, 1970-71; resident John Hopkins Hosp., Balt., 1974-77; practice medicine specializing in civil and criminal forensic psychiatry Towson, Md., 1977—; chief dept. psychiatry Balt. County Gen. Hosp., Randallstown, 1978-85; mem. staff Clifton T. Perkins Hosp. Ctr., Jessup, Md., 1977-92; clin. asst. prof. psychiatry U. Md. Hosp., Balt., 1983-97; psychiat. cons. Bur. Disability Ins., Social Security Adminstrn., Workmen's compensation Commn., Balt., 1981—; dir. community forensic services Mental Hygiene Adminstrn., Md., 1982-92; faculty Nat. Jud. Coll., 1988—. Mem. Md. Task Force on Somatic Therapies Contbr. numerous articles on forensic psychiatry to profl. jours.; chpt. to book. Served with M.C. USN, 1972-74. Mem. Am. Acad. Psychiatry and Law, Am. Psychiat. Assn., Md. Psychiat. Soc. (chmn. peer rev. com. 2001), Md. Med. Soc. (chmn. occupational health com. 1987-90), Baltimore County Med. Soc. Office: 26 W Pennsylvania Ave Towson MD 21204-5001 Office Phone: 410-337-0343. E-mail: mkspodak@yahoo.com.

**SPODEK, BERNARD,** early childhood educator; b. Bklyn., Sept. 17, 1931; s. David and Esther (Lebenbaum) S.; m. Prudence Debb, June 21, 1957; children: Esther Yin-ling, Jonathan Chou. BA, Bklyn. Coll., 1952; MA, Columbia U., 1955, EdD, 1962. Cert. early childhood edn. tchr., N.Y. Tchr. Beth Hayeled Sch., N.Y.C., 1952-56, N.Y. City Pub. Schs., Bklyn., 1956-57, Early Childhood Ctr., Bklyn. Coll., 1957-60; asst. prof. elem. edn. U. Wis.-Milw., 1961-65; assoc. prof. early childhood edn. U. Ill., Champaign, 1965-68, prof. dept. curriculum and instrn., 1968-97, dir. dept. grad. programs, 1986-87, chair dept., 1987-89; dir. hons. program, Coll. Edn., 1984-86, mem. faculty Bur. Ednl. Rsch., 1981-85, prof. emeritus, 1997—; adv. prof. Hong Kong Inst. of Edn., 1999-2001. Dir. insts. Nat. Def. Edn. Act, 1965-67, dir. experienced tchr. fellowship program, 1967-69, co-dir. program for tchr. trainers in early childhood edn., 1969-74; vis. prof. Western Wash. State U., 1974, U. Wis., Madison, 1980, Kobe Shinwa Women's U., Japan, 2004; vis. scholar Sch. Early Childhood Studies, Brisbane (Australia) Coll. Advanced Edn., Delissa Inst. Early Childhood Studies, S. Australia Coll. Advanced Edn., 1985, Beijing Normal U., Nanjing Normal U., East China Normal U., Shangai, People's Republic China, 1986; rsch. fellow Kobe U., Japan, 1996; adj. prof. Queensland (Australia) U. Tech., 2000. Author or co-author 42 books including: (with others) A Black Studies Curriculum for Early Childhood Education, 1972, 2d edit., 1976, Teaching in the Early Years, 1972, 3d edit., 1985, Early Childhood Education, 1973, Studies in Open Education, 1975 (Japanese trans.), Early Childhood Education: Issues and Perspectives, 1977, (with Nir-Janiv and Steg) International Perspectives on Early Childhood Education, 1982 (Hebrew trans.), (with Saracho and Lee (Mainstreaming Young Children, 1984, (with Saracho and Davis) Foundations of Early Childhood Education, 1987, 2d edit. (Japanese trans.), 1991, (with Saracho) Right from the Start, 1994 (Chinese and Korean translations), Dealing with Individual Differences in the Early Childhood Classroom, 1994; editor: Handbook of Research in Early Childhood Education, 1982, revised edit., 2005, Today's Kindergarten, 1986, (with Saracho and Peters) Professionalism and the Early Childhood Practitioner, 1988, (with Saracho) Early Childhood Teacher Education, 1990, Issues in Early Childhood Curriculum, 1991, Educationally Appropriate Kindergarten Practices, 1991, Issues in Childcare, 1992, Handbook of Research on the Education of Young Children (Portuguese tranls.), 1993, revised edit., 2005, (with Saracho), Language and Literacy in Early Childhood Education, 1993; (with Safford and Saracho) Early Childhood Special Education, 1994; (with Garcia, McLaughlin & Saracho) Meeting the Challenge of Cultural and Linguistic Diversity, 1995, (with Saracho) Issues in Early Childhood Educational Evaluation and Assessment, 1996, (with Saracho) Multiple Perspectives on Play in Early Childhood Education, 1998, (with Saracho and Pellegrini) Issues in Early Childhood Educational Research, 1998, (with Saracho) Contemporary Perspectives in Early Childhood Curriculum, 2002, (with Saracho) Contemporary Perspectives in Early Childhood Education, 2002, (with Saracho) Contemporary Perspectives on Play in Early Childhood Education, 2003, (with Saracho) Studying Teachers in Early Childhood Settings, 2003, (with Saracho) Contemporary Perspectives on Language Policy and Literacy Instruction, 2004, (with Saracho) Contemporary Perspectives on Families, Communities, and Schools for Young Children, 2005, (with Saracho) International Perspectives on Research in Early Childhood Education, 2005, (with Saracho) Handbook of Research on the Education of Young Children, 2d edit., 2006; series editor Research in Early Childhood Education, early childhood edn. publs., 1990-00; series co-editor: Contemporary Perspectives in Early Childhood Education, 2002—; guest editor Studies in Ednl. Evaluation, 1982, Early Education and Child Development, 1995; also contbr. chpts to books, articles to profl. jours. Mem. Am. Ednl. Rsch. Assn. (chair early childhood and child devel. spl. interest group 1983-84, publs. com. 1984-86), Nat. Assn. Edn. Young Children (sec. 1965-68, bd. govs. 1968-72, pres. 1976-78, editorial adv. bd. 1972-76, book rev. editor, 1972-74, cons. editor, 1985-87 Young Children jour., mem. tchr. edn. commn. 1981-88, chair commn. on appropriate edn. 4-5 yr. old children, 1984-85, cons. editor Early Childhood Rsch. Quar. 1987-90), Nat. Soc. for Study of Edn. (1972 yearbook com.), Pacific Early Childhood Edn. Rsch. Assn. (pres. 2000—). Office: U Ill Dept Curriculum & Instrn 1310 S 6th St Champaign IL 61820-6925 Business E-Mail: b-spodek@uiuc.edu.

**SPODICK, PEARL BLEGEN,** counselor, medical psychotherapist; b. Mpls., June 4, 1927; d. Harry Cornelius and Vera Maude (Kidder) Blegen; m. Robert Casper Spodick, Nov. 1, 1955; children: Michael, Peter, Russell, Edward, Rebecca. BA, Albertus Magnus Coll., 1978; MA in Psychology and Art Therapy, Goddard Coll., 1980; postgrad., Simmon's Coll., 1977. Cert. Am. Bd. Behavioral Therapists; cert. med. psychotherapist, clin. mental health counselor; nat. cert. counselor; CHAMPUS (Civilian Health and Med. Program for Uniformed Svcs.) authorized marriage and family therapist, Conn.; lic. mental health counselor, R.I.; lic. profl. counselor, Conn., nat. cert. addictions prevention specialist; diplomate Nat. Bd. Cert. Clin. Hypnotherapists. Cons., art psychotherapist Conn. D.C.Y.S., 1978—, Conn. Sexual Trauma Tratment Program, 1978-79, Arden House Long Term Care Facility, Hamden, Conn., 1979-82, Ctr. for Study of Normative Behavior, Hamden, 1982-85, Curtis Home Children's Residential Treatment Ctr., Meriden, Conn., 1982-93; instr. psychology Albertus Magnus Coll., Hamden, 1988-90; med. psychotherapist, counselor The Psychotherapy Ctr., Woodbridge, Conn., 1980-93, Hamden, Conn., 1993—, Art Psychotherapy and Counseling Ctr., Woodbridge, 1980-93, Hamden, 1993—. Cons. in field. Fellow Am. Bd. Med. Psychotherapists (diplomate); mem. ACA (cert.), Am. Art Therapy Assn. (ATR, legis. rep. 1983-89), Am. Assn. Study Mental Imagery, Am. Assn. Cert. Clin. Mental Health Counselors (cert.), Am. Mental Health Counselors Assn., Conn. Assn. Marriage and Family Counselors (pres. 1997-99, treas. 1999-2002). Democrat. Jewish. Avocations: painting, drawing, sculpture, crocheting, reading. Home: Oronoque Village 108B Seminole Ln Stratford CT 06614-8147 also: 108B Seminole Ln Stratford CT 06614-8147 E-mail: pb.spodick@snet.net.

**SPOERI, RANDALL KEITH,** healthcare company executive; b. Cleve., June 12, 1946; s. Theodore Warren and Marion (Barrick) S.; m. Kathleen Loma Bryden Hayes, Aug. 31, 1968 (div. Mar. 1981); 1 child, Jennifer Anne; m. Deborah Jean Hammett, June 20, 1981 (div. Nov. 1998); 1 child, Jason Randall; m. Laura Joan Lenhardt, Apr. 24, 1999. BS, Calif. Polytech. State U., 1968; MS, Tex. A&M U., 1970, PhD, 1976. Math. statistician U.S. Bur. of the Census, Suitland, Md., 1976-80; assoc. prof. U.S. Naval Acad., Annapolis, 1980-83; assoc. exec. dir. Am. Statis. Assn., Alexandria, Va., 1983-88; sr. corp. statistician Humana, Inc., Louisville, 1988-92; chief program coord. info. branch Health Care Fin. Adminstrn., Balt., 1993; asst. v.p. Nat. Com. for Quality Assurance, Washington, 1994-95; adminstrv. v.p. health care analysis NYLCare Health Plans, Inc., N.Y.C., 1995-98; v.p. med. and quality informatics HIP Health Plans, N.Y.C., 1998—2004; dir. Health Analytics, Cerner Corp., Kans. City, Mo., 2005—. Author: Quantitative Methods In Quality Management, 1991; contbr. articles to profl. jours. Mem. adv. com. Health Care Fin. Adminstrn., Balt., 1990-92, bur. dir. citation, 1993, adv. bd. Juran Inst., Wilton, Conn., 1995-98. 1st lt. U.S. Army, 1970-72. Recipient Svc. award Am. Statis. Assoc., Alexandria, 1994. Fellow AAAS, Am. Soc. for Quality (health care divsn. chair 1995-96); mem. Am. Statis Assn., Inst. Indsl. Engring., Inst. for Ops. Rsch. and the Mgmt. Scis. Avocations: sports, music. Home: 148 Top Of The World Way Green Brook NJ 08812-1839

**SPOERRY, ROBERT F.,** manufacturing executive; B Mech. Engring., Fed. Inst. Tech., Zurich Switzerland; MBA, Univ. Chgo. Mgmt. positions with Mettler-Toledo Internat., 1983—87, head. indsl. & retail (Europe), 1987—93, pres., CEO, 1993—98, chmn., pres., CEO, 1998—. Bd. dir. Phonak Group. Bd. dir. Swiss-Am. C. of C. Office: Mettler-Toledo Internat 1900 Polaris Pkwy Columbus OH 43240 Office Phone: 614-438-4511.*

**SPOFFORD, SALLY (SALLY HYSLOP),** artist; b. N.Y.C., Aug. 20, 1929; d. George Hall and Esther (McNaul) Hyslop; m. Gavin Spofford, Mar. 11, 1950 (dec. Jan. 1976); children: Lizabeth Spofford Smith, Leslie Spofford Russell Baldwin, Tita China Inst., N.Y.C., The Art Students League, 1950; BA with high honors, Swarthmore Coll., 1952. Instr. Somerset Art Assn., Peapack, N.J., 1978-95, Hunterdon Mus. Art, Clinton, N.J., 1985—; adv. bd., lectr. Apollo Muses, Inc., Gladstone, N.J.; trustee Artshowcase, Inc. One-woman shows include Riverside Studio, Pottersville, N.J., 1985, Morris Mus., Morristown, N.J. 1989, Schering-Plough Gallery, Madison, N.J., 1989, Phoenix Gallery, N.Y.C., 1990, Robin Hutchins Gallery, Maplewood, N.J., 1992, Berlex Labs. Corp. Office, Wayne, N.J., 1992, Hunterdon Mus. Art, Clinton, 1993, 2003, Newark Acad., Livingston, N.J., 1997, Simon Gallery, Morristown, 2004; exhibited in group shows at Hickory (N.C.) Mus., 1983, Purdue U., 1983, Monmouth (N.J.), 1984, Nabisco Brands Gallery, East Hanover, N.J., 1985, 89, Hunterdon Mus. Art, 1988, 93, 99, Schering-Plough Gallery, Madison, 1988, Morris Mus., Morristown, 1989, Montclair (N.J.) State U., 1995, Williams Gallery, Princeton, N.J., 1997, Monmouth Mus., Lincroft, N.J., 1998, Newark Acad., Livingston, 2000, Bristol-Myers Squibb Gallery, Princeton, N.J., 2005; represented in permanent collections N.J. State Mus., Trenton, Newark Mus., Morris Mus., Morristown. Painting residency fellow Vt. Studio Ctr., 1992. Mem. Assoc. Artists N.J. (pres. 1985-87), N.J. Watercolor Soc., Federated Art Assns. of N.J. (panel mem. 1985, demonstrator 1991). Home: PO Box 443 Bernardsville NJ 07924-0443 Office Phone: 908-766-1219.

**SPOGLI, RONALD P.,** ambassador; m. Georgia Beth Caudle; 2 children. AB in History, Stanford U., 1970; MBA, Harvard U., 1975. V.p. corp. fin. dept. Dean Witter Reynolds, Inc., LA, 1978—82, mng. dir. investment banking divsn.; ptnr. Freeman Spogli & Co., L.A., 1983—; US amb. to Italy US Dept. State, Rome, 2005—. Lead rschr. Stanford Univ. Labor Migration Project, Milan. Bd. dir. (presdl. appointee) J. William Fulbright Fgn. Scholarship Bd., 2002—. Recipient J. William Fulbright Foreign Scholarship, 2002. Address: American Embassy Rome Italy Via Vittorio Veneto 119/A-00187 Rome Italy Office: American Embassy Rome Italy PSC 59 Box 100 F APO AE 09624 Italy Office Phone: 39-06-46741. Office Fax: 39-06-488-2672. E-mail: webteam@usembassy.it.*

**SPOHN, HERBERT EMIL,** psychologist; b. Berlin, June 10, 1923; s. Herbert F. and Bertha S.; m. Billie M. Powell, July 28, 1973; children: Jessica, Madeleine. BSS., CCNY, 1949; PhD, Columbia U., 1955. Research psychologist VA Hosp., Montrose, NY, 1955-60, chief research sect., 1960-64; sr.

research psychologist Menninger Found., Topeka, 1965-80, dir. hosp. research, 1979-94, dir. research dept., 1981-94; ret., prof. emeritus for rsch. 1994—. Mem. mental health small grant com. NIMH, 1972-76, mem. treatment assessment rev. com., 1983-86, chmn. 1986-87. Author: (with Gardner Murphy) Encounter with Reality, 1968; assoc. editor: Schizophrenia Bull, 1974-87, 91—; contbr. articles to profl. jours. Served with AUS, World War II. USPHS grantee, 1964—Fellow Am. Psychopath. Assn.; mem. AAAS, N.Y. Acad. Sci., Soc. Psychopath. Research, Phi Beta Kappa, Sigma Xi. Office: 1906 SW Village Dr Topeka KS 66604-3714 E-mail: hspohn@prodigy.net.

**SPOHN, WILLIAM GIDEON, JR.,** mathematician, retired musician; b. Lancaster, Pa., Mar. 8, 1923; s. William Gideon and Inza Mae (Huber) S.; m. Alice Liane Bailey, Sept. 13, 1946 (div.); children: Susan Jeannine Grochowina (dec.), William Gideon III (dec.), Peter Jonathan, Kathleen Anne Precht, Mary Louise; m. Evelyn Walsh Moreland, June 15, 1963 (div. Oct. 1978); m. Claire Louise Burgstahler, Dec. 19, 1987 (div. Sept. 1999). BA, St. Johns Coll., 1947; MA, U. Calif., Berkeley, 1950; PhD, U. Pa., 1962. Instr. math. Temple U., Phila., 1952-54, U. Del., Newark, 1954-56; mathematician Aberdeen Proving Ground, Md., 1954-55; instr. math. Bowling Green (Ohio) State U., 1956-59; mathematician, sr. staff Johns Hopkins U. Applied Physics Lab., Laurel, Md., 1959-84; singer, prodr. Spohn Music Co., Columbia, Md., 1981-99. Contbr. articles to profl. jours. Served to lt. USNR, 1943-46, PTO. Johns Hopkins U. Applied Physics Lab. fellow, 1966-67. Mem. Math. Assn. Am. Home: 1 Heritage Farm Dr Mount Airy MD 21771-5783

**SPOHR, EARL CLYDE,** retired investment advisor, retired military officer; b. Washington, Jan. 15, 1931; s. Earl Clyde and Helen Ruth Spohr; m. Gloria Sue Crabtree, June 19, 1962. Diploma, Cal-Aero Tech. Inst., Calif., 1951. Aircraft maintenance USAF, 1950—69, advisor air nat. guard, 1964—68, aircraft maintenance supt. Vietnam, 1968—69, sr. enlisted advisor Rhine AFB, Germany, 1969—74, aircraft maintenance supt. March AFB, Calif., 1974—75, Thule AFB, Greenland, 1975—76, sr. enlisted advisor Ramstein AFB, Germany, 1976—79, Malstrom AFB, Mont., 1979—81; ret. Chmn. Ill. Am. Diabetes Assn., 1986—89; dir. Iowa Found. for Wealth Care, Iowa, 1988—, Ill., 1988—. Pres. Co. Hist. Soc., Mt. Vernon, Ill., 1986—87; pres., exec. dir. ARC, Jefferson Co., Ill., 1984—86; pres. Crossroads Cmty. Hosp. Aux., Mt. Vernon, Ill., 2005—; v.p. Jefferson Co. C. of C., 1985—88; com. chmn. Crosswalk Cmty. Action Agy., 1987—; state legislative chmn. AARP, Ill., 1984—87. Comdr. sgt. USAF, 1950—81. Recipient Purple Cross, Masonic Bodies, 1988. Mem.: Air Force Assn., Internat. Soc. Phil. Rsch., MENSA. Republican. Avocations: travel, reading, volunteering. Home: 108 Mockingbird Ln Woodlawn IL 62898 Office: Ill Found for Quality Health Care 2625 Butterfield Rd Oak Brook IL 60521

**SPOKANE, ROBERT BRUCE,** biophysical chemist; b. Cleve., Aug. 5, 1952; s. Herbert Norman and Marjorie Ellen (Firsten) S.; m. Linda Carol Wright, June 20, 1976; children: Lea, Hannah, Tara. BS in Chemistry, Ohio U., 1975; MS in Biophys. Chemistry, U. Colo., 1978, PhD in Biophys. Chemistry, 1981. Cert. full cave diver. Tchg. asst. dept. chemistry U. Colo., Boulder, 1975-77, rsch. asst. dept. chemistry, 1977-81; staff scientist Procter & Gamble Co., Cin., 1981-84; rsch. scientist dept. neurophysiology Children's Hosp., Cin., 1984-90; sr. scientist, product mgr. YSI Co., Yellow Springs, Ohio, 1990—. Cons. Synthetic Blood Internat., Yellow Springs, 1992. Contbr. articles to profl. jours. Rescuer, treas. Boulder Emergency Squad, 1980; rescue diver Kitty Hawk Scuba, Dayton, Ohio, 1992. Recipient Merck Index award Ohio U., 1975. Mem. Am. Chem. Soc., N.Y. Acad. Sci., Am. Physiol. Soc., Nat. Speleological Soc. (cave diving sect.), Sigma Xi. Achievements include research in implantable glucose sensors; oxygen tonometer for peritoneal oxygen measurements; interferant removal system for biosensors for methanol, ethanol, glutamate, and glutamine, optical carbon dioxide sensor, water chemistry in submerged caves. Home: 1715 Garry Dr Bellbrook OH 45305-1362 Office: Co 1725 Brannum Ln Yellow Springs OH 45387-1107 Office Phone: 937-767-7241. Business E-Mail: rspokane@ysi.com.

**SPOLAN, HARMON SAMUEL,** lawyer; b. Phila., Dec. 12, 1935; s. Jay and Edythe (Greenberg) S.; m. Betty Jane Evnitz, Mar. 30, 1958; children: Michael, Suzanne. AB, Temple U., 1957, LLB, 1959; postgrad., Oxford U., 1966. Bar: Pa. 1960. Ptnr. Ravetz & Shuchman, Phila., 1960-68, Blair & Co., N.Y.C., 1968-72; v.p. Butcher & Singer, Phila., 1972-74; pres. Capital First Corp., Phila., 1974-75, State Nat. Bank, Rockville, Md., 1975-78, Jefferson Bank, Phila., 1978-99; pres., bd. dirs. JeffBanks, Inc., Phila., 1986-99; sr. mem. Cozen O'Connor, Phila., 1999—. Lectr. law U. Pa., Phila., 1964-68. Author: Federal Aids to Financing, 1970; contbr. articles to profl. jours. Former chmn. bd. Huntingdon Hosp., Willow Grove, Pa., 1982—89; bd. dirs. YMHA, Phila., 1978—95. Anti-Defamation League, 1982. Named Man of Yr., Nat. Assn. Women Bus. Owners, 1978, Disting. Alumnus, Central H.S., 1975. Mem. ABA, Phila. Bar Assn. Democrat. Jewish. Office: 1900 Market St Philadelphia PA 19103-3527 Business E-Mail: hspolan@cozen.com.

**SPOLAORE, ENRICO,** economist; b. Rovigo, Italy, Oct. 11, 1964; s. Antonio Spolaore and Rosanna Meneguzzo; m. Deborah Menegotto, Oct. 15, 1993; 1 child, Edoardo. BA in Econs., U. Rome La Sapienza, 1987; PhD in Econs., Harvard U., Cambridge, Mass., 1993. Asst. prof. econs. and polit. sci. OH State U., Columbus, 1996—97; asst. prof. econs. Boston Coll., Chestnut Hill, Mass., 1997—98; Kutayba Alghanim asst. prof. polit. economy Brown U., Providence, 1998—2004; prof. econs. Tufts U., Medford, Mass., 2004—, chair, econs. dept., 2006—. Contbr. articles to profl. jours. Grantee Democratization, Secessions and Fiscal Institutions, NSF, 1994—97; Marco Fanno fellow, Mediocredito Centrale, 1989—90, Luciano Jona fellow, Instituto San Paolo, 1990—92, Harvard/MIT Doctoral fellow in Positive Polit. Economy, NSF, 1992—93, Human Capital and Mobility fellow, European Commn. Fellow: CES-Ifo, Ente Luigi Einaudi. Home: 244 East St Lexington MA 02420 Office: Tufts University Econs Dept 8 Upper Campus Rd Medford MA 02155 Office Phone: 617-627-4068. Business E-Mail: enrico.spolaore@tufts.edu.

**SPONG, JOHN SHELBY,** retired bishop, writer, columnist; b. Charlotte, NC, June 16, 1931; s. John Shelby and Doolie Boyce (Griffith) S.; m. Joan Lydia Ketner, Sept. 5, 1952 (dec. 1988); children: Ellen Elizabeth, Mary Katharine, Jaquelin Ketner; m. Christine Mary Bridger, Jan. 1, 1990. AB, U. N.C., 1952; M.Div., Va. Theol. Sem., 1955; D.D., St. Paul's Coll., 1976, Va. Theol. Sem., 1977; DHL (hon.), Muhlenberg Coll., 1998, Holmes Inst. Chgo., 2003, Lehigh U., 2006, U. NC, 2006. Ordained to ministry Episcopal Ch., 1955, bishop, 1976; rector St. Joseph's Ch., Durham, NC, 1955-57, Calvary Ch., Tarboro, NC, 1957-65, St. John's Ch., Lynchburg, Va., 1965-69, St. Paul's Ch., Richmond, Va., 1969-76; bishop Diocese of Newark, 1976-2000, ret., 2000. Mem. governing body Nat. Episc. Ch., 1973-76; vis. lectr., Harvard U. Div. Sch., 2000, U. Pacific, Stockton, Calif., 2003; mem. faculty Grad. Theol. Union, Berkeley, Calif., 1997, 99, 2001, 03, 05. Author: Honest Prayer, 1973, This Hebrew Lord, 1974, Dialogue--In Search of Jewish-Christian Understanding, 1975, Christpower, 1976, The Living Commandments, 1977, The Easter Moment, 1980, Into the Whirlwind: The Future of the Church, 1983, Beyond Moralism, 1986, Survival and Consciousness, 1987, Living in Sin? A Bishop Rethinks Human Sexuality, 1988, Rescuing the Bible from Fundamentalism--A Biship Rethinks the Meaning of Scripture, 1991, Born of a Woman, 1992, Resurrection: Myth or Reality?, 1994, Liberating the Gospels, Reading the Bible with Jewish Eyes, 1996, Why Christianity Must Change or Die, 1998, Here I Stand: My Struggle for a Christianity of Integrity, Love and Equality, 2000, A New Christianity for a New World, 2001, The Sins of Scripture-Exploring the Bible's Texts of Hate to Discover The God of Love, 2005; columnist Beliefnet.com, 2000—02, Waterfront Media, 2002—. Elected Quartercentury Scholar Emmanuel Coll., Cambridge, Eng., 1992, named Humanist of Yr., 1999, William Belden Noble lectr. Harvard U., 2000. Mem.: Rotary. Episcopalian. Home: 24 Puddingstone Rd Morris Plains NJ 07950-1114

**SPONGBERG, ANDREW K.,** otolaryngologist, law educator; b. Wichita, Kans., Aug. 17, 1941; s. Lyle Curtis Spongberg and Beluha Beatris Kent; m. Sarah Randolph Benham, May 30, 1964; 1 child, Sarah Lyerly. MD, Tulane U., 1964; JD, So. New England Sch. Law, 1996. Bar: Mass. 96; diplomate Am. Bd. Otolaryngology. Physician New Eng. Ear Nose and Throat, New Bedford, Mass., 1971—96, Hawthorn Med. Assocs. LLC, Dartmouth, Mass., 1990—; adj. prof. law So. New England Sch. Law, Dartmouth, 1996—2000; clin. instr. Tufts Med. Sch., Boston, 1996—; intern U.S. Pub. Health Svc. Hosp., New Orleans, 1996—97, resident gen. surgeon, 1997—98; resident in otolaryngology Tulane U., 1998. Cons. in health law, 1996—; bd. dirs. Hawthorn Med. Assocs. Lt. comdr. USPHS, 1967—71. Fellow: Am. AcademyNeurology, Am. Bd. Otolaryngology; mem.: Am. Health Lawyers Assn. Avocations: fishing, farming, motorcycle touring. Home: 849 Rock O'Dundee Rd South Dartmouth MA 02748 Office: Hawthorn Med Assocs 35 Arnold St New Bedford MA 02740 Office Phone: 508-956-3951.

**SPONSLER, GEORGE CURTIS, III,** science administrator, lawyer; b. Collingswood, NJ, Dec. 2, 1927; s. George Curtis and Mary Grace (Hollinberger) S.; m. Bridget Ruth Butcher, Sept. 3, 1955; children: Freda Grace, Naomi Margaret Bride, Curtis Alexander. BS in Engring. Physics, Princeton U., 1949, MA, 1951, PhD, 1952; JD, George Washington U., 1981. Bar: Md. 1981, D.C. 1982, U.S. Ct. Appeals (4th cir.) 1982, U.S. Ct. Appeals (fed. cir.) 1984. U.S. Supreme Ct. 1986. With Lincoln Lab., MIT, 1952-56; liaison officer Office Naval Research, London, 1956-58, head spl. projects for Washington, 1958-59; sr. scientist Hoffman Sci. Center, Santa Barbara, Calif., 1959-60; chief sci., dir. tech. analysis and ops. research U.S. Navy Bur. Ships, 1960-63; dir. advanced planning, fed. systems div. IBM, 1963-66, dir. center exploratory studies, 1966-68; exec. sec. div. engring. Nat. Acad. Sci.-NRC, 1968-70; pres. Law Math. and Tech. Inc., 1970—2002; semi-ret. On leave, Congl. fellow U.S. Senate, Washington, 1987-88; mem. adv. com. to Office Emergency Planning, Nat. Acad. Sci., 1967-72, chmn. subcom. automation, 1966-68, mem. joint adv. com. on electromagnetic pulse, 1970-74; cons. Exec. Office of Pres., 1971-73 Contbr.: Tech. Innovation, Harper Ency. of Sci.; author articles in field. Fellow AAAS (electorate nominating com. 1980-83, chmn.-elect sect. X, 1983-84, chmn. 1984-85, mem. coun. 1985-86), Am. Physics Soc.; mem. IEEE (life, sr., chmn. subcom. on privacy of communications and info. policy com. 1982-85, aerospace R&D policy com. 1990-92), Phi Beta Kappa, Sigma Xi. Democrat. Episcopalian. Personal E-mail: sponsler@worldnet.att.net.

**SPONZILLI, EDWARD GEORGE,** lawyer; b. Newark, Mar. 30, 1948; s. Edward James and Dorothy Maria (Murillo) Sponzilli. BA in History with high honors, Rutgers U., 1971, JD, 1975; summer diploma, Cath. Inst. of Paris, 1971; MA, Columbia U., 1972. Bar: N.J. 1975, U.S. Dist. Ct. N.J. 1975, U.S. Ct. Appeals (3d cir.) 1976, U.S. Supreme Ct. 1979, D.C. 1979, N.Y. 1981, U.S. Ct. Appeals (2d cir.) 1992, U.S. Dist. Ct. (so. dist.) N.Y. 1991, U.S. Dist. Ct. (ea. dist.) N.Y. 1991. Law clk. to judge U.S. Dist. Ct. NJ, Newark, 1975—77; assoc. Pitney, Hardin & Kipp, Morristown, NJ, 1975—81, Dunn, Pashman, Sponzilli, Swick & Finnerty (formerly Cummins, Dunn & Pashman), Hackensack, NJ, 1982—, ptnr., 1984—95, Norris, McLaughlin & Marcus, P.A., 1995—. Co-adj. prof. Rutgers U., New Brunswick, NJ, 1980—81, 1994, 98, mcpl. pros., 1981—, mem. Jessup Internat. Law Moot Ct. Team, 1975, coach Mock Trial Team, 1994—97; counsel Judo of NJ Inc., Cranford, 1983—; judge law sch. moot ct. competition Seton Hall, 1977—79, 1981, 81, 86; cert. civil trial atty. NJ Supreme Ct., 1997—; mem. faculty Nat. Inst. Trial Advocacy, 1995—; faculty N.J. Atty. Gens. Trial Advocacy Inst., 2002—. Contbr. articles to profl. jours. Active Rutgers U. Found., 1987—. Named Superlawyer, N.J. Mag., 2005; recipient Nancy Higgenson Dorr award, Rutgers U., 1971, Disting. Svc. award, Animals Need You-Kindness Corp., NJ, 1981, Client Protection award, NJ Supreme Ct. Fund for Client Protection, 1999; Henry Rutgers scholar. Master: Am. Inns of Ct (pres. 2000—01); mem.: ATLA, ABA (trial practice com. of litigation sect.), N.J. State Ct. Mediator (fed. arbitrator), Nat. Assn. Coll. and Univ. Attys., N.J. Def. Assn., Def. Rsch. Inst., Middlesex County Bar Assn., Essex County Bar Assn., Bergen County Bar Assn., Trial Attys. NJ (trustee 1987—), NJ Trial Lawyers Assn., Assn. Fed. Bar NJ, Fed. Bar Assn., NJ State Bar Assn. (higher edn. com.), Columbia Grad. Faculties Alumni Assn., Civil War History Assn., So. Hist. Assn., Am. Hist. Assn., Orgn. Am. Historians, Rutgers U. Law Sch. Alumni Assn. (nominating com. 1982, program dir. 1982, treas. 1991—92, sec. 1992—93, v.p. 1993—94, pres. 1994—95, exec. counsel, alumni fedn. rep.), Scarlet R Round Table Alumni Assn., Phi Alpha Delta, Kappa Sigma (sec. 1978—79, alumnus advisor 1978—99, v.p. 1979—82, pres. 1982—86, dist. grand master 1986—2000, pres. 1994—2001, chmn. nat. legal commn. 1995—97, trustee Gamma Upsilon chpt.), Phi Beta Kappa. Home: 37 Brookside Ave Caldwell NJ 07006-5603 Office: Norris McLaughlin & Marcus PA 721 Rt 202-206 PO Box 1018 Somerville NJ 08876-1018 Office Phone: 908-252-4166. Business E-Mail: egsponzilli@mmlaw.com.

**SPOOLSTRA, LINDA CAROL,** minister, educator, religious organization administrator; b. Hillsdale, Mich., July 11, 1947; d. Jay Carroll and Carol Elsa (Linstrom) Lehmann; m. Gerald William Spoolstra, Feb. 17, 1973. BA, Bethel Coll., 1969; MA, Fla. State U., 1970; M of Div., McCormick Theol. Sem., Chgo., 1978; DD (hon.), Cen Bapt. Theol. Sem., Kansas City, Kans., 1988. Ordained Am. Bapt. Clergywoman. Tchr. Dade County Pub. Schs., Miami, Fla., 1970-71; ins. claims adjustor Safeco Ins. Co., Chgo., 1971-72; dir. of community outreach and edn. N. Shore Bapt. Ch., Chgo., 1972-78, assoc. pastor, 1978; pastor First Bapt. Ch., Swansea, Mass., 1978-84; exec. dir. commn. on the ministry Am. Bapt. Chs. U.S.A., Valley Forge, Pa., 1984-90; exec. minister Am. Bapt. Chs. Mass., Dedham, 1990—2003; pastor Calvary Bapt. Ch., Providence, 2003—. Mem. Nat. Coun. Chs. Profl. Ch. Leadership, N.Y.C., 1984-90; mem. commn. on pastoral leadership Bapt. World Alliance, McLean, Va., 1986-90; mem. gen. bd. Nat. Coun. Chs. of Christ, 1990-96. Trustee Andover-Newton Theol. Sch., 1990—2003. Avocations: sailing, reading, travel, classical music. Office: Calvary Bapt Ch 747 Broad St Providence RI 02907 Personal E-mail: spoolstra@msn.com.

**SPOON, ALAN GARY,** venture capital company executive; b. Detroit, June 4, 1951; s. Harry and Mildred (Rudman) S.; m. Terri Alper, June 3, 1975; children: Ryan, Leigh, Randi. BS, MS, MIT, 1973; JD, Harvard U. 1976. Cons. The Boston Cons. Group, 1976-79, mgr., 1979-81, v.p., 1981, The Washington Post Co., 1982-84; v.p., contr. Washington Post, 1985-86, v.p. mktg., 1986-87; v.p. fin., CFO The Washington Post Co., 1987-89; pres. Newsweek mag., 1989-91; COO The Washington Post Co., 1991-2000, pres., 1993-2000; mng. gen. ptnr. Polaris Venture Ptnrs., Waltham, Mass., 2000—. Dir. Info. Industry Assn., Washington, 1982-83, 88-89; bd. dirs Danaher Corp. Washington, Interactive Corp., N.Y.C.; regent Smithsonian Instn., Washington; mem. corp. MIT. Bd. dirs. Norwood Sch., 1989-93, chmn., 1993-95; bd. dirs. Smithsonian Nat. Mus. Natural History, Washington, 1994-99; trustee WETA-Pub. Broadcasting, 1986-92. Recipient award for scholarship and athletics Ea. Coll. Athletic Conf. and MIT, 1973. Office: Polaris Venture Partners 1000 Winter St Ste 3350 Waltham MA 02451-1476

**SPOONER, DAVID M.,** federal agency administrator, lawyer; BA, U. Va., 1991; JD, Coll. William and Mary, 1994. Legal counsel to Rep. Wes Cooley US Ho. of Reps, Washington, comm. dir. Com. on Agr., assoc. Com. on Rules; adminstrv. asst. Office of Rep. Sue Myrick, US Ho. of Reps, Washington, press sec., legis. dir.; transition coord. Office of US Trade Rep. Exec. Office of the Pres., Washington, spl. textile negotiator Office of US Trade Rep., 2002—05; asst. sec. import adminstrn. Internat. Trade Adminstrn. US Dept. Commerce, Washington, 2005—. Office: US Dept Commerce Herbert Clark Hoover Bldg 1401 Constitution Ave NW Washington DC 20230 Office Phone: 202-482-1780. Office Fax: 202-482-0947.*

**SPOONER, JOHN D.,** financial planner, writer; b. Boston, July 25, 1937; s. Herbert M. and Helen F. Spooner; m. Susan Farnsworth, June 15, 1966; children: Scott Fabyan, Nicholas Monroe, Amanda Davis. AB, Harvard U., Cambridge, Mass., 1959. Dir. investments Smith Barney, Boston, 1961—. Chmn. dirs. coun. Shearson, N.Y.C., 1978, Smith, Barney, N.Y.C., 1994—95. Contbr. articles to Atlantic Mag., Playboy, Town & Country. Bd. dirs. Boys and Girls Club, Boston, 1953—, Mass. Cystic Fibrosis Found., 1980—, Mass.

Cultural Coun., 1993—; vis. com. Harvard Coll., Cambridge, 1997—. Sgt Med. Corps U.S. Army, 1960—65. Recipient Literary Lights award, Boston Pub. Libr., 1993. Mem.: Harvard Club (Boston), St. Boltoph Club, The Country Club, Belmont Country Club. Achievements include co-founder and trustee The Curious George Found. Avocations: golf, painting, squash. Home: 101 Chestnut St Boston MA 02108 Office: Smith Barney Inc Boston MA 02109 E-mail: spoonersmtpeople@compus.nc.com.

**SPOOR, RHYS,** dentist; Grad., U. Wash., 1983. With Aesthetic & Restorative Dentistry, Seattle. Fellow: Pierre Fauchard Acad., Acad. Gen. Dentistry; mem.: Am. Acad. Cosmetic Dentistry. Office: Aesthetic & Restorative Dentistry 701 5th Ave Ste 4660 Seattle WA 98104 Office Phone: 206-682-8200. E-mail: info@rhysspoor.com.

**SPOOR, WILLIAM HOWARD,** food products executive; b. Pueblo, Colo., Jan. 16, 1923; s. Charles Hinchman and Doris Field (Slaughter) S.; m. Janet Spain, Sept. 23, 1950; children: Melanie G., Cynthia F., William Lincoln. BA, Dartmouth Coll., 1949; postgrad., Denver U., 1949, Stanford U., 1965. Asst. sales mgr. N.Y. Export divsn. Pillsbury Co., 1949-53; mgr. N.Y. office Pillsbury Co., 1953-62, v.p. export divsn. Mpls., 1962-68, v.p., gen. mgr. internat. ops., 1968-73, CEO, 1973-85, also bd. dirs., chmn. exec. com., 1987, pres., CEO, 1988, past chmn. bd. dirs. Bd. dirs. Coleman Co. Mem. regional export expansion coun. Dept. Commerce, 1966-74; bd. dirs. exec. Coun. Fgn. Diplomats, 1976-78; mem. bd. visitors Nelson A. Rockefeller Ctr., Dartmouth Coll., 1992-95; Minn. Orchestral Assn., United Negro Coll. Fund, 1973-75; chmn. Capitol City Renaissance Task Force, 1985; trustee Mpls. Found., 1985-92; mem. sr. campaign cabinet Carlson Com. U. Minn., 1985; mem. corps. rels. com. Nature Conservancy, 1985; mem. Nat. Cambodia Crisis Com., pres. pvt. sector Dept. Treas. coord. 1983; chmn. YWCA Tribute to Wonwn in Internat. Industry. 2d lt. inf. U.S. Army, 1943-46. Recipient Golden Plate award, Am. Acad. Achievement, Disting. Bus. Leadership award, St. Cloud State U., Miss. Valley World Trade award, Outstanding Achievement award, Dartmouth Coll., Horatio Alger award, 1986, Medal of Merit, U.S. Savs. Bond Program; honored with William H. Spoor Dialogues on Leadership, Dartmouth Coll., honored Fair Player Minn. Women's Polit. Caucus, 1989. Mem. Grocery Mfrs. Am. (treas. 1973-84), Nat. Fgn. Trade Coun., Minn. Hist. Soc. (mem. exec. com. 1983, bd. dirs.), Minn. Bus. Partnership, River Club N.Y.C., Woodhill Country Club, Lafayette Club, Mpls. Club (bd. govs. 1985, pres. 1986), Gulf Stream Bath and Tennis Club, The Country Club Salt Lake City, Gulf Stream Golf Club, Old Baldy Club, Alta Club, Phi Beta Kappa. Home: 1173 Oak Forest Rd Salt Lake City UT 84103 Office: 4900 IDS Ctr Minneapolis MN 55402 Office Phone: 612-330-4621.

**SPORE, KEITH KENT,** newspaper executive; b. Milw., May 29, 1942; s. G. Keith and Evelyn A. (Morgan) S.; divorced; children: Bradley, Julie, Justine; m. Kathy Stokebrand. BS in Journalism, U. Wis., 1967. City editor Milw. Sentinel, 1977-81; asst. mng. editor/news Milw. Jour. Sentinel, 1981-89, mng. editor, 1989-91, editor, 1991-95, editl. page editor, 1995, pres., 1995—, pub., 1996—. Author: (novels) The Hell Masters, 1977, Death of a Scavenger, 1980. With U.S. Army, 1961-64. Recipient Freedom of Info. award Soc. Profl. Journalists, 1995; named Mass Comms. Alumnus of Yr., U. Wis.-Milw., 1994. Mem. Greater Milw. Com. Office: Milw Jour Sentinel PO Box 661 Milwaukee WI 53201-0661 E-mail: kspore@onwis.com.

**SPORLEDER, THOMAS LYNN,** economist, researcher; b. Perrysburg, Ohio, Apr. 2, 1942; s. John Loren Sporleder, Ruth Cordelia Westrick; m. Marjorie Jean Stout; children: Thomas James, Candace Lynn. BS, Ohio State U., 1964, MS, 1965, PhD, 1968. Mgr. Agrl. Grading Sta. Campbell Soup Co., Napoleon, Ohio, 1961—64; prof. agrl. econs. Tex. A&M U., College Station, 1968—89; prof. agribus., income enhancement endowed chair Ohio State U., Columbus, 1989—. Vis. scholar USDA, Washington, 1974—75; rsch. economist Office Tech. Assessment, U.S. Congress, Washington, 1976—77; bd. dirs. Internat. Food and Agribusiness Mgmt. Assn., Washington, Heartland Agdeavor Assn., Columbus. Contbr. articles to profl. jours. Mem.: Am. Agrl. Econs. Assn. (pres. agribus. econs. and mgmt. sect. 2002—03). Roman Catholic. Home: 4518 Elderberry Ct Upper Arlington OH 43220-3020 Office: Ohio State Univ 2120 Fyffe Rd Columbus OH 43210-1066 Office Phone: 614-292-0286. Business E-Mail: sporleder.1@osu.edu.

**SPORN, AARON ADOLPH,** physician, educator; b. NYC, Nov. 5, 1953; s. Herbert and Eunice (Aron) S.; m. Beverly Sporn; children: Hunter, Melanie. BS, SUNY, Stony Brook, 1974; MD, Columbia U., 1978. Diplomate Am. Bd. Orthopaedic Surgery. Intern. gen. surgery Roosevelt Hosp., N.Y.C., 1978-79, resident gen. surgery, 1979-80; resident, chief resident in orthopaedic surgery NYU and Bellevue Hosp., N.Y.C., 1980-83; fellow Midwest Inst. for Orthopaedics, Cin., 1983-84; v.p. medical affairs Inst. for Medicine in Sports, Trenton, NJ, 1984-85; clin. sr. instr. Hahnemann U. Med. Sch., Phila., 1986—; 1991clin. instr. Rutgers U. Med. Sch., New Brunswick, NJ, 1986—91; chief, dept. orthopaedic surgery Robert Wood Johnson U. Hosp. at Hamilton, 1994—2004, vice chmn., dept. surgery, 1993-95, chmn. dept. surgery, 1995—98. Vis. clin. fellow Columbia U., N.Y.C., 1978-80, teaching asst. NYU, N.Y.C., 1982-83; com. mem. Arthroscopy Bd. N.Am. Exam Com., 1989-90; cons. N.J. State Police, Trenton, 1987-92; fundraising com. orthopaedics wing Hamilton Hosp., Trenton, 1989. Contbr. articles to profl. jours. Ind. Rsch. Project grantee NIMH, 1975, 88. Fellow Am. Acad. Orthopaedic Surgery, Arthroscopy Bd. N.Am.; mem. Phi Beta Kappa. Office: Med Arts Bldg 8 Quakerbridge Plz Hamilton NJ 08619-1255

**SPORN, MICHAEL V.,** producer, director; b. NYC, Apr. 23, 1946; s. Mario and Amy (Young) Rosco. BFA, N.Y. Inst. Tech., 1967. Asst. dir. Hubley Studio, N.Y.C., 1972-76; supr., coord. R. Williams Animation, N.Y.C., 1976-77; asst. dir. R.O. Blechman Prodns., N.Y.C., 1977-79; founder, owner, dir. Michael Sporn Animation Inc., N.Y.C., 1980—. Prodr., dir.: Doctor DeSoto, 1984 (Oscar nomination 1985), Abel's Island, 1988 (Emmy nomination 1988), Red Shoes, Dancing Frog, Ira Sleeps Over, dir.: The Man Who Walked Between the Towers, 2005 (Am. Libr. Assn. Carnegie Medal, 2006), 30 other animated films. Recipient Ace awards Acad. Cable Arts, 1990-92. Mem. ASIFA East (bd. dirs. 1974—, 23 awards 1972—), Acad. Motion Picture Arts and Scis. Office: Michael Sporn Animation Inc 35 Bedford St New York NY 10014 Office Phone: 212-242-0647.*

**SPORTY, LAWRENCE DOUGLAS,** psychiatrist; b. June 17, 1943; BA in Chemistry and Biology, Queens Coll., CUNY, 1964; MD, SUNY, Bklyn., 1968. Diplomate Am. Bd. Psychiatry and Neurology. Attending psychiatrist SUNY, Bklyn., 1972—74; adminstrv. and clin. dir. South Beach Psychol. Ctr, NY, 1972—74, chief of svc. NY, 1974—75; asst. chief prof. SUNY-Downstate Med. Ctr., Bklyn., 1975—76; med. dir. Met. State Hosp., Norwalk, Calif., 1978—79; assoc. prof. clin. psychiatry U. So. Calif., L.A., 1978—79, chief adult in-patient svcs., 1979; acting chmn. dept. psychiatry U. Calif.-Irvine Med. Ctr., Orange, 1979—82, vice chmn. clin. svcs., 1982—, assoc. clin. prof., 1979, clin. prof., 1979—83, prof. clin. psychiatry, 1983—. Cons., lectr. in field. Contbr. articles to profl. jours. Fellow: Am. Psychiat. Assn. (disting. life); mem.: So. Calif. Psychiat. Soc. (exec. coun. 1982—), Alpha Omega Alpha. Office: U Calif-Irvine Med Ctr 2021 E 4th St Ste 118 Santa Ana CA 92705 Office Phone: 714-285-0870.

**SPOTNITZ, ALAN JEFFREY,** cardiothoracic surgeon; b. NYC, May 31, 1944; s. Hyman and Miriam (Berkman) S. BA, Harvard U., 1966; MD, Columbia U., 1970. Intern gen. surgery Beth Israel Hosp., Boston, 1970-71; rsch. fellow Columbia U., 1973-74; resident gen. surgery Beth Israel Hosp., Boston, 1971-75; thoracic resident thoracic surgery Presbyn., N.Y., 1978-79; assoc. prof. clin. surgery Robert Wood Johnson Med. Sch., New Brunswick, NJ, 1982—87, chief sect. cardiac surgery, 1988—2001. Dir. surg. clerkship program Robert Wood Johnson Med. Sch., New Brunswick, 1982—, assoc. dir. thoracic surgery residency program U. Medicine and Dentistry N.J., 1991-2001. Author: (with others) Homograft Valve Durability:

Host or Donor Influence, Heart Vessels, 1990; contbr. articles to profl. jours. Maj. USAF, 1975—77. Office: Robert Wood Johnson Med Sch 125 Paterson St New Brunswick NJ 08901 Office Phone: 908-235-7805. Business E-Mail: spotnitz@umdnj.edu.

**SPOTO, CARL ALEXANDER, JR.,** history educator; b. Saranac Lake, NY, Mar. 14, 1972; s. Katherine Schaffer; m. Sarah Jean Cudzilo, July 5, 2003. BA, SUNY Cortland; M, Nazareth Coll. of Rochester. Cert. tchr. NY State. Tchr. Honeoye Falls-Lima CSD, NY, 1994—96, Midlakes CSD, Clifton Springs, NY, 1996—. Coach Midlakes H.S., Clifton Springs, NY. Mem.: NYS Coun. for the Social Studies (corr.). Democrat. Home: 8 Larkspur Lane Fairport NY 14450 Office: Midlakes HS 1554 State Route 488 Clifton Springs NY 14432 Office Phone: 315-548-6300. Business E-Mail: cspoto@midlakes.org.

**SPOTO, DONALD,** writer, educator; b. New Rochelle, N.Y., June 28, 1941; s. Michael George and Anne Hortense (Werden) S. BA summa cum laude, Iona Coll., New Rochelle, 1963; MA, Fordham U., 1966, PhD, 1970. Instr. Fairfield U., Conn., 1966-68; prof. Coll. New Rochelle, 1968-74; mem. faculty CUNY, N.Y.C., 1974-75, New Sch. for Social Rsch., N.Y.C., 1975-86; adj. prof. U. So. Calif., L.A., 1987-89. Vis. lectr. Brit. Film Inst., Nat. Film Theatre, London, 1980-86; nat. lectr. Am. Film Inst., Washington, 1979-82. Author: The Art of Alfred Hitchcock, 1976, 2d edit., rev., 1992, Camerado, 1978, Stanley Kramer: Film Maker, 1978, The Dark Side of Genius: The Life of Alfred Hitchcock, 1983 (Edgar award Mystery Writers Guild 1984), The Kindness of Strangers: The Life of Tennessee Williams, 1985, Falling In Love Again, 1985, Lenya: A Life, 1989, Madcap: The Life of Preston Sturges, 1990, Laurence Olivier: A Biography, 1991, Blue Angel: The Life of Marlene Dietrich, 1992, Marilyn Monroe: The Biography, 1993, A Passion for Life: The Biography of Elizabeth Taylor, 1995, The Decline and Fall of the House of Windsor, 1995, Rebel: The Life and Legend of James Dean, 1996, Notorious: The Life of Ingrid Bergman, 1997, Diana, The Last Year, 1997, The Hidden Jesus: A New Life, 1999, Jacqueline Bouvier Kennedy Onassis: A Life, 2000, In Silence: Why We Pray, 2004; author numerous revs., essays; contbr. articles to mags. and newpapers. Mem. Authors Guild Am., Writers Guild Am. Roman Catholic. Office: care Elaine Markson Literary Agy 44 Greenwich Ave New York NY 10011-8347

**SPOUTZ, ERIC I.,** art dealer, conservator, curator, investor, consultant; s. Carl and Rosemary (Hornak) Spoutz. Degree in mktg., Wayne State U., 2003. Art brokerage rep. Holy See, Vatican City, 2003; dir., curator, founder in field. Home: 2560 S Ocean Blvd Ste 518 Palm Beach FL 33480 Office: Fisher Bldg 3011 W Grand Blvd Ste 216 Detroit MI 48202 Personal E-mail: slaenterprises@yahoo.com.

**SPRAGGINS, JOHNNIE DAVID,** sociology and cultural studies educator; b. Opelika, Ala., Oct. 13, 1954; s. John David and Alma Jean McCormick Spraggins; 1 child, Jada Ruth. BA, Auburn U., 1978, MA, 1988, U. Mich., 1993, PhD, 1995. Rsch. assoc. Auburn U., 1981-90; prof. Madonna U., U. Mich.-Ann Arbor, 1990—96; prof. sociology Asian divsn. U. Md., Tokyo, 1996—99; prof. Randolph-Macon Coll., Ashland, Va., 1999—2001; asst. prof. Our Lady of the Lake U., San Antonio, 2001—. Advisor Woman's Studies Coun., Randolph-Macon Coll., 1999—; vis. asst. prof. SUNY, Geneseo; vis. asst. prof. Asian divsn. U. Md., Sagamihara-shi, Japan; prof. Kitasato U., Sagamihara-shi, Kanagawa-ken, 1996-98. Contbr. articles to profl. jours. Mem. Ctr. for Rsch. on Social Orgn., Am. Sociological Assn., Soc. Applied Sociology. Democrat. Buddhist. Avocations: gardening, travel. Office: 411 SW 24th St San Antonio TX 78207 E-mail: spraj@lake.ollusa.edu.

**SPRAGUE, ANN LOUISE,** aerospace scientist; b. Bellfonte, Pa., Feb. 25, 1946; d. David Carpenter and Opal (Wheat) S.; m. Donald M. Hunten, 1995. BA Geology, Syracuse U., 1969; MA, Boston U., 1980; PhD, U. Ariz., 1990. Tchr. sci. Selinsgrove Mid. Sch., 1970—79; space scientist Lunar and Planetary Lab. U. Ariz., Tucson, 1990—. Mem. Lunar and Planetary Exploration com. NRC, 2000—. Contbg. author: Caloris Basin: An Enhanced Source for Potassium in Mercury's Atmosphere, 1990, Sulfur at Mercury, Elemental at the Poles and Sulfides in the Regolith, 1995, Water Brought In to Jupiter's Atmosphere by Fragments R and W of Comet SL-9, 1996, Distribution and Abundance of Sodium in Mercury's Atmosphere, 1985-1988, 1997, Exploring Mercury: The Iron Planet, 2003; editl. bd. ICARUS Mem. AAAS, Internat. Astron. Union, Am. Astron. Soc. (com. divsn. planetary scis.), Am. Geophys. Union Office: U Ariz Lunar & Planetary Lab Tucson AZ 85721-0001 Business E-Mail: sprague@lpl.arizona.edu.

**SPRAGUE, BILLY MICHAEL,** aerospace transportation executive; b. Wichita Falls, Tex., Nov. 22, 1953; s. Billy Meryl Sprague and Virginia Maxine Vines; m. Stella Renee Schaefer, Aug. 15, 1987; children: Patricia Noel children: Billy Michael Jr., Jonathan Christian, Elizabeth Kathryn. B in Phys. sci., U. Calif., Irvine, 1979, BS in Physics/Engring., 1979; AAS in Phys. sci., Ft. Steilacoom, 1975. Cert. Sys. Engring. Mgmt., Martin Marietta Aerospace, Colo., 1985, Engring. Mgmt. and Supervision, Martin Marietta Aerospace, Colo., 1986. Rocket propulsion engring. R&D Boeing, Martin Marietta, Gen. Dynamics, Rockwell, Thiokol, United Technologies, 1976—95; sr. prin. scientist McDonnell Douglas Aerospace, Huntington Beach, Calif., 1995—97; mgr. advanced systems lab. Intel Corp., San Diego, 1997—99; v.p., engring. Truax Engring., Inc., Vista, Calif., 1999—2001; pres. and chief scientist Am. Astronautics Corp., Lake Tahoe, Nev., 2001—. Lectr., sys. engring. and mgmt. Maj. Aerospace Companies, 1985—95. Fellow, Emily Peasley, 1975—76. Mem.: AIAA, Phi Theta Kappa. Republican. Protestant. Achievements include development of reusable liquid propellant launch vehicle for commercial space tourism. Office: American Astronautics Corporation 276 Kinsbury Sq Ste 104 Stateline NV 89449 E-mail [illegible]@cox.net.

**SPRAGUE, CHARLES WARREN,** geologist; b. Berlin, Nov. 29, 1955; s. Kenneth Manchester Sprague and Ingrid Emma Marie Albrecht; m. Penni Marie O'Brien, May 2, 1998; 1 child, Charles Wilfred. BS, U. of Fla., 1978—80, MS, 1980—83. Professional Geoscientist Tex., 2003, Professional Geologist Tenn., 1990. Geologist Chevron USA, Inc., New Orleans, 1983—85; geologist/lead geologist Groundwater Tech., Inc., Mandeville, La., 1989—92; project geologist/hydrogeologist Fugro-McClelland (SW) Inc., Dallas, 1992—93; project/sr. hydrogeologist Law Engring. and Environ. Services, Inc., Dallas, 1993—96; sr. hydrogeologist LCA Environ., Inc., Dallas, 1996—98; v.p.ops. Dougherty Sprague Environ., Inc., Richardson, Tex., 1998—. Bd. mem. Ellison Miles Geotechnology Inst. Earth Sci. Tchr. Enhancement Adv. Bd., Farmers Branch, Tex., 1999—2000; student/boy scout trainer and/or advisor Ellison Miles Geotechnology Inst. Cmty. Outreach Program, Farmers Branch, Tex., 2001—. Commr. Planning and Zoning Commn., Sachse, Tex., 2000—06; judge Dallas Morning News Regional Sci. Fair, 1995—2006; leadership sachse class no. 1 Econ. Devel. Corp./Sachse C of C., 2005—. Mem.: Am. Planning Assn., Am. Mil. Engineers, Assn. Engring. Geologists, Nat. Ground Water Assn., Geol. Soc. Am., Tex. Assn. Profl. Geoscientists (bd. advisors 2001—04, pres. 2002—03), Sachse Hist. Soc., Leadership Sachse Class 1. Avocations: gourmet cooking, genealogy. Office: Dougherty Sprague Environ Inc 1236 Executive Dr West Richardson TX 75081 Office Phone: 972-907-8666. Office Fax: 972-907-8633. E-mail: cwsprague@dsei.com.

**SPRAGUE, EDWARD AUCHINCLOSS,** retired professional society administrator, economist; b. N.Y.C., Oct. 9, 1932; s. Irvin Auchincloss and Maude Browning (Fisher) S.; m. Patricia Ivy Cannon, Apr. 27, 1957; children: James Edward, Elizabeth Mary, Jennifer Ann. BA, Princeton U., 1954; MA, NYU, 1961. Rsch. analyst N.J. State C. of C., Newark, 1957-59; assoc. economist F.W. Dodge Corp., N.Y.C., 1959-62; economist Lehman Bros., N.Y.C., 1962-67; v.p. Nat. Assn. Mfrs., N.Y.C. and Washington, 1967-77; dir. tax policy The Tax Found., Washington, 1977-82, sr. v.p., 1985-89; exec. dir. Tax Exec. Inst. 1982-85; v.p., exec. dir. The Tax Coun., 1979-82, 86-91, cons., 1991-92, Employers Coun. on Flexible Compensation, Washington,

1992-93; ret., 1993. Editor: Building Business, 1961-62; jour. The Tax Executive, 1983-85. With U.S. Army, 1955-57. Mem. Nat. Tax Assn. Republican. Home: 2850 Prism Ct Lusby MD 20657

**SPRAGUE, JOHN LOUIS,** management consultant; b. Boston, 1930; s. Robert Chapman and Florence Antoinette (van Zelm) S.; m. Mary-Jane Whitney, June 19, 1952; children: John Louis, William Whitney, Catherine van Zelm, David Hyatt. AB, Princeton, 1952; PhD, Stanford, 1959. With Sprague Electric Co., North Adams, Mass., 1959-87, co-dir. engring. labs., sr. v.p. engring., 1964-65, v.p. research and devel., 1965-66, sr. v.p. semi-condr. div., 1967-76, pres., 1976-87, chief exec. officer, 1981-87; pres. John L. Sprague Assocs. Inc., 1988—2003; self-employed, 2003—. Bd. dirs. MRA Labs., Inc., Calif. Micro Devices. Chmn. Williamstown United Fund-ARC Campaign, 1961; trustee Pine Cobble Sch., 1978, Middlesex Sch., 1994-96. Lt. (j.g.) USNR, 1952-55. Mem. IEEE, Electrochem. Soc., Am. Chem. Soc., Sci. Research Soc. Am., Confrerie des Chevaliers du Tastevin, Confrerie de la Chaine des Rotisseurs, Princeton Club (N.Y.C.), Sigma Xi, Phi Lambda Upsilon. Home: 175 Bee Hill Rd Williamstown MA 01267-2703 Office Phone: 413-743-9454. E-mail: beehilljon@aol.com.

**SPRAGUE, MARY GABRIELLE,** lawyer; b. Phila., Pa., Oct. 7, 1957; AB summa cum laude, Harvard U., 1979; JD, Yale U., 1983. Bar: Colo. 1984, D.C. 1992. Law clk. to Hon. Jim R. Carrigan US Dist. Ct. Colo., 1984-85; law clk. to Hon. Byron R. White US Supreme Ct., Washington, 1986-87; ptnr. Arnold & Porter, Washington. Mem. Phi Beta Kappa. Office: Arnold & Porter 555 12th St NW Washington DC 20004-1206 Office Phone: 202-942-5773. Office Fax: 202-942-5999. E-mail: Mary.Gay.Sprague@aporter.com.

**SPRAGUE, PETER JULIAN,** software company executive, lecturer; b. Detroit, Apr. 29, 1939; s. Julian K. and Helene (Coughlin) S.; m. Tjasa Krofta, Dec. 19, 1959; children: Carl, Steven, Kevin, Michael. Student, Yale U., 1961, MIT, 1961, Columbia U., 1962-66. Chmn. Wave Sys., Inc.; bd. dirs. Enlighten Software Inc. Bd. dirs. vwink.com, Inc. Trustee Strang Clinic. Mem. Yale Club. Office: Wave Systems Corp 1 Penn Plz Ste 2420 New York NY 10119

**SPRAGUE, RAYMOND,** music educator; b. Yonkers, N.Y., Nov. 28, 1947; s. Raymond Arthur and Rosemary (Lockwood) S.; m. Kathleen Jane Turner, May 30, 1981. BA in Music, Williams Coll., Williamstown, Mass., 1969; MMus, U.N.Mex., 1973; DMA, U. Colo., 1979. Tchr. cert. music/choral-gen. k-12 Ind., 1985. Instr. Albuquerque Acad., 1969-71; grad. asst. U. N.Mex., Aubuquerque, 1972-73; instr., grad. asst. U. Colo., Boulder, 1973-77; dir. music King of Glory Luth. Ch., Arvada, Colo., 1974-77; asst. prof., dir. choral activities St. Mary's Coll., South Bend, Ind., 1977-84; assoc. prof., dir. choral activities U. New Orleans, 1985-95, prof., 1995—99; dir. music St. Charles Ave. Bapt. Ch., New Orleans, 1986-91; artistic dir., conductor La. Vocal Arts Chorale, New Orleans, 1992—99; prof. and dir. choral activities Davidson (NC) Coll., 1999—, chmn. music dept., 2000—06. Clinician, adjudicator, guest conductor high sch. and colls. Musical debut Carnegie Hall, 1999, Return Engagement, 2006; Mus. and book reviewer The Choral Jour., 1977—; editor Treble Choir Music, 1985—. Mem. Am. Choral Dirs. Assn. (state pres. La. chpt. 1989, state pres. Ind. choral dirs. 1983), Chorus Am., Coll. Music Soc. Episcopalian. Avocations: hiking, camping, fishing, golf, sports. Office: Davidson Coll Dept Music Davidson NC 28035 Office Phone: 704-894-2591. Business E-Mail: rasprague@davidson.edu.

**SPRAGUE, RICHARD A.,** lawyer; b. Balt., Sept. 22, 1925; s. George Sidney and Marian (Barsel) S.; divorced; children: Thomas Andrew, Barbara Anne. BS, Temple U., 1949; LLB, U. Pa., 1953. Bar: Pa., 1954, NY, 2002, U.S. Dist. Ct. (ea. dist.) Pa., 1971, U.S. Ct. Appeals (Fed. cir.), U.S. Supreme Ct., 2003. Asst. vol. defender Defender Assn., Phila., 1954—57; asst. dist. atty. Dist. Atty.'s Office, Phila., 1958—65, 1st asst. dist. atty., 1966—74; counsel Berger & Montague, Phila., 1975—79; sr. ptnr. Sprague & Sprague, Phila., 1979—; pres. judge ct. of jud. discipline Commonwealth Pa. Former chief counsel Select Com. on Assassinations, U.S. Ho. of Reps.; spl. prosecutor for Washington County, Pa., 1970-85, for Delaware County, Pa., 1971-74, for Phila. County dist. atty., 2000-; spl. asst. to U.S. atty. gen., 1973-74; spl. counsel to Pa. Supreme Ct. Jud. Inquiry and Rev. Bd., 1981-83; spl. investigator for Allegheny County, Pa., 1999—; vol. defender Defender's Assn. Phila.; lectr. Temple U. Sch. Law, Phila., 1972-; mem. faculty ATLA; mem. Phila. Criminal Justice Coordinating Commn., U.S. Senate Jud. Nominating Commn.; former treas. Phila. Regional Planning Coun. Gov.'s Justice Commn.; bd. dirs. Biotech. Found., Inc. With USN, 1943-45, WWII. Mem. ABA (antitrust law sect., criminal justice sect.), Pa. Bar Assn., Phila. Bar Assn. (bd. govs. 1971-74), Nat. Dist. Attys. Assn., Assn. Trial Lawyers Am. Office: Sprague & Sprague 135 S 19th St Ste 400 Philadelphia PA 19103-4912

**SPRAGUE, WILLIAM DOUGLAS,** lawyer; b. Houston, Dec. 23, 1941; s. William Douglas and Helen (Mims) S.; m. Marilyn Wells, Aug. 7, 1965; children: William Douglas III, Anne W., Robert L. BS, U. Wis., 1964; JD, Harvard U., 1967. Bar: Mich. 1972, Ind. 1978, Pa. 1991. Assoc. Reinhart, Boerner, Van Deuren, Norris & Rieselbach, Milw., 1967-71; lawyer Ford Motor Credit Co., Dearborn, Mich., 1971-77; various legal positions to sr. v.p. adminstrn. AMAX Coal Co., Indpls., 1977-87; assoc. gen. counsel Alumax Inc., San Mateo, Calif., 1987-88; v.p., gen. counsel Lukens Inc., Coatesville, Pa., 1988; v.p., gen. counsel, sec. AmeriSource; sr. v.p., gen. counsel, sec. AmerisourceBergen (from merger of Bergen Brunswig and AmeriSource Health), Valley Forge, Pa., 2001—05, sr. v.p., gen. counsel, 2005—. Chmn. bd. dirs. United Way Chester County, Exton, Pa., 1992-94. Mem. ABA, Phi Kappa Phi, Phi Eta Sigma. Avocations: golf, bridge. Office: AmerisourceBergen PO Box 959 Valley Forge PA 19482 Office Phone: 610-727-7159.

**SPRANG, MILTON LEROY,** obstetrician, gynecologist, educator; b. Chgo., Jan. 15, 1944; s. Eugene and Carmella (Bruno) S.; m. Sandra Lee Karabelas, July 16, 1966; children: David, Christina, Michael. Student, St. Mary's Coll., 1962-65; MD, Loyola U., 1969. Diplomate Am. Bd. Ob-gyn; Nat. Bd. Med. Examiners; CME accreditation. Intern St. Francis Hosp., Evanston, Ill., 1969-70, resident, 1972-75, sr. attending physician, 1985—; assoc. attending phsycian Evanston Hosp., 1975-79, attending physician, 1980-84, sr. attending physician, 1985—, v.p. med. staff, 1990-91, pres.-elect, 1991-92, pres., 1992-93; also bd. dirs., 1991-94; sec. exec. com. Evanston Hosp., 1993-94; chmn. ob-gyn Cook County Grad. Sch. Medicine, Chgo., 1983-91. Instr. Northwestern U. Med. Sch., Chgo., 1975-78, asst. prof., 1984-95, assoc. prof., 1995-04, prof., 2004—; pres. Northwestern Healthcare Network Physician Leadership, 1994; lectr. acad. and civic groups Ob-Gyn. med. advisors Nat. Adv. Med. Edn., 1991—; bd. dirs. Ill. Found. Med. Rev.; bd. trustees Ill. State Ins. Svcs., 1992—, chair, 1998-00, chair rates and res., 2002—; bd. govs. Ill. State Med. Inter-Inst. Exch., 1987-92; adv. bd. practicing physicians Sec. Health and Human Svc., 2005—. Editor: Profl, Staff News, 1992-93; chmn. editorial bd. Jour. Chgo. Medicine, 1986-91; contbr. articles to profl. jours. Bd. dirs. Am. Cancer Soc., chmn. profl. edn. com. North Shore unit, 1982-85; bd. dirs. Chgo. Community Info. Network, 1994-95; mem. Nat. Rep. Congrl. Com., 1981—, Ill. Med. Polit. Action Com.; bd. advisors Nat. Youth Leadership Forum on Medicine, Chgo., 1998—; trustee Midwest Ctr. Women's Healthcare, 2002—, pres., 2002—; adv. patients and med. profession. With USN, 1970-72. Fellow: ACOG (chmn. Ill. sect. 1975—76), ACS, Inst. Medicine Chgo.; mem.: AMA (com. to select pub. mem. 2003—, Physician Recognition award 1977, 1980, 1983), Gt. Lakes States Coalition of Dels. to AMA (chmn. 2003—), Orgn. State Med. Assn. Presidents (steering com. 2003—06, sec. 2006—), Chgo. Found. Med. Care (med. care evaluation and edn. com. 1980—83, nominating com. 1980—84, practice guidelines com. 1984), Ednl. and Scientific Found. (bd. dirs. 1994—98), Chgo. Med. Soc. (adv. com. advt. stds. 1978—84, physician's rev. com. 1980—85, trustee ins. bd. 1982—, nominating com. 1985—, treas. 1986—89, chmn. fin. com. 1986—89, trustee 1986—92, sec. 1989—90, pres.-elect 1990—91, chmn. bd. trustees 1990—91, pres. 1991—92, chmn. ethical rels. com. 1994—), Ill. Med. Soc. (del. to AMA 1987—, govt. affairs com. 1988—, chmn. reference com. 1989, chmn. fin. com. 1992—94, sec.-treas. 1994—96, chmn. bd. trustees 1996—98, chmn.

bylaws com. 1998—99, pres. 2000—01), Physician Benefit Trust (chmn. fin. com. 1993—2004, chmn. 2004—, adv. coun. 2005—). Roman Catholic. Avocations: reading, swimming. Home: 4442 Concord Ln Skokie IL 60076-2606 Office: AGSO 1000 Central St Evanston IL 60201-1777 Office Phone: 847-869-3300. E-mail: sprangml@aol.com.

**SPRANKEL, SHANE TYLER,** music educator; b. Zanesville, Ohio, July 13, 1976; s. Thomas Eugene and Judith Lynn Sprankel. MusB in Music Edn., Capital U., 1998, MusM in Music Edn. with Kodaly Emphasis, 2001. Cert. profl. edn. Ohio, 2002, Orgn. Am. Kodaly Educators, 2001. Asst. dir. bands Sidney (Ohio) City Sch. Dist., 1999—. Contbr. articles to profl. jours. Nominating com. chair Sidney Dance Co., 2002—06; pres. Sock and Buskin Cmty. Theatre, Sidney, 2004—06. Mem.: Midwest Kodaly Music Edn. Assn. (member-at-large 2002—06), Music Educator's Nat. Conf., Orgn. Am. Kodaly Educators (secondary music task force), Sidney Edn. Assn. (treas. 2001—03, Do-er's Award 2002), Ohio Edn. assn., NEA, Ohio Music Edn. Assn., Phi Mu Alpha Sinfonia. Avocations: sewing, ballet. Office Phone: 937-497-2238.

**SPRANSY, JOSEPH WILLIAM,** corporate lawyer; b. Durham, N.C., July 17, 1946; s. George Brower and Marion Elizabeth (Dibble) S.; m. Lillian Drew Darden, Aug. 8, 1970; children: Katherine Leigh, Joseph William II. AB in Math., King Coll., Bristol, Tenn., 1968; JD, U. N.C., 1973. Bar: Ala. 1973, U.S. Dist. Ct. (no. dist.) Ala. 1973, U.S. Ct. Appeals (5th cir.) 1976, U.S. Supreme Ct. 1980, U.S. Ct. Appeals (11th cir.) 1981. Math. tchr. Castlewood (Va.) High Sch., 1968-70; program dir. Camp Monroe, Laurel Hill, NC, 1968-70; assoc. Bradley, Arant, Rose & White, Birmingham, Ala., 1973-79; corp. counsel U.S. Pipe and Foundry Co., 1979—2003, v.p., 1999—2003; atty. pvt. practice, 2003—. Vice moderator Birmingham Presbytery, Presbyn. Ch. USA, 1986, moderator, 1987; elder Mountain Brook Presbyn. Ch., 1982-84, 1986-88, 91-94, 98-2000; asst. scoutmaster, Boy Scouts Am., 1994—, troop 320 com. chair, 1994-97. Mem. ABA, Ala. State Bar Assn. (chair labor and employment sect. 1992-93, chair bus. law sect. 1999-2000), Birmingham Bar Assn. (chair mem. com. 1999—2000, 2001-2003), Assn. Corp. Counsel in Am. (bd. dirs. Ala. chpt. 1985-91, 1998-2003, sec.-treas. 2002), U. N.C. Alumni Assn. (pres. Ala. chpt. 1983-84, 95), Phi Alpha Delta. Clubs: Birmingham Sailing, Birmingham Tip Off Club (bd. dirs. 1992-96), Ruffner Mountain Nature Ctr (bd. dirs. 2004—, treas. 2005). Avocations: woodworking, sailing. Home: 4000 Hunters Ln Birmingham AL 35243-5820 Office: Law Office Joseph W Spransy PO Box 430093 Birmingham AL 35243 Office Phone: 205-930-9800. Business E-Mail: jwspransy@spransylaw.com.

**SPRATLAN, LEWIS,** composer, educator; b. Miami, Sept. 5, 1940; m. Melinda Spratlan. BA, Yale U., 1962, MusM, 1965. Faculty mem. Pa. State U., 1967—70, Amherst Coll., Mass., 1970—, prof. music. Mass., 1980—, chmn. music dept. Mass., 1977—94. Composer: Missa Brevis, 1965, Cantate Domine, 1968, Serenade for 6 instruments, 1970, Moonsong, 1970, Two Pieces for orch., 1971, Woodwind quintet, 1971, Fantasy, 1973, Ben Jonson Songs, 1974, Coils for ensemble, 1980, String Quartet, 1982, When Crows Gather, 1986, Hung Monophonies, 1990, Night Music, 1991, In Memorian, 1993, A Barred Owl, 1994, Concertino, 1994, Psalm 42, 1996, Apollo and Daphne Variations, Vocalise with Duck, 1998, Sojourner, 2000, Life is a Dream, 2000 (Pulitzer prize for music, 2000), Mayflies, 2000, Of Time and the Seasons, 2001, Peeves, 2001, (chamber opera) Earthrise, 2002, Zoom, 2003, The Manatees at Blue Springs, 2003, Streaming, 2004, Mega-Ditty, 2004, Piccolosophy, 2005, Wonderer, 2005, Shadow, 2006. Guggenheim fellowship, NEA fellowship, Mass. Artists Found. fellowship, MacDowell fellowship. Office: Music Dept Amherst Coll PO Box 5000 Amherst MA 01002-5000 Business E-Mail: mlspratlan@amherst.edu.

**SPRATT, JOHN MCKEE, JR.,** congressman, lawyer; b. Charlotte, NC, Nov. 1, 1942; s. John McKee and Jane Love (Bratton) Spratt; m. Jane Stacy, May 31, 1968; children: Susan Elizabeth, Sarah Stacy, Catherine Bratton. AB, Davidson Coll., 1964; MA, Corpus Christi Coll., Oxford U., 1966; LL.B., Yale U., 1969. Ops. analyst Office of Asst. Sec. Def., 1969-71; ptnr. Spratt, McKeown & Spratt, York, SC, 1973-82; pres. Spratt Ins. Agy., Ft. Mill, SC, 1973-82, Bank of Ft. Mill, SC, 1973-82; mem. US Congress from 5th SC dist., 1983—, ranking Dem. budget com., mem. armed svcs. com. Chmn. bd. visitors Winthrop Coll., 1976; bd. dirs. Piedmont Legal Svcs., Inc., 1978-83; bd. visitors Davidson Coll., 1978-80; chmn. bd. trustees Divine Saviour Hosp., York, 1980-82 Positions up to capt. JAGC U.S. Army, 1969—71. Decorated Meritorious Svc. medal. Mem. SC Bar Assn. (ho. dels.), ABA. Democrat. Presbyterian. Office: US Ho Reps 1401 Longworth Ho Office Bldg Washington DC 20515-4005 Office Phone: 202-225-5501.*

**SPRATT, RANDALL N.,** health products executive; BS in Biology, U. Utah. Exec. positions to COO Advanced Lab. Systems; chief process officer McKesson Provider Technologies, Alpharetta, Ga.; exec. v.p. chief info. officer McKesson Corpn., San Francisco, 2005—. Office: McKesson Corpn 1 Post St San Francisco CA 94104*

**SPRAY, PAUL ELLSWORTH,** retired surgeon; b. Wilkinsburg, Pa., Apr. 9, 1921; s. Lester E. and Phoebe Gertrude (Hull) S.; m. Mary Louise Conover, Nov. 28, 1943; children: David C., Thomas L., Mary Lynn (Mrs. Thomas Branham). BS, U. Pitts., 1942; MD, George Washington U., 1944; MS, U. Minn., 1950. Diplomate Am. Bd. Orthop. Surgery. Intern U.S. Marine Hosp., S.I., 1944-45; resident Mayo Found., Rochester, Minn., 1945-46, 48-50; practice medicine specializing in orthop. surgery Oak Ridge, Tenn., 1950-98; ret., 1998; vol. physician Knoxville Interfaith Clinic, 1998—. Mem. active staff Oak Ridge Hosp., 1950-98, hon. staff, 98-2000, 01—, emeritus staff, 2000-01; courtesy staff Harriman Hosp, Tenn. ret. 1990 and vis. com. CARE Medico, Jordan, 1959, Nigeria, 1962, 65, Algeria, 1963, Afghanistan, 1970, Bangladesh, 1975, 77, 79, Peru, 1980; U. Ghana, 1982; AMA vol. physician, Vietnam, 1967, 72; vis. assoc. prof. U. Nairobi, 1973; mem. tchg. team Internat. Coll. Surgeons to Peru, 1979, 84; vis. prof. orthop. surgery U. Khartoum, 1976; hon. prof. San Luis Gonzaga U., Ica, Peru, 1979; AmDoc vol. cons. U. Biafra Tchg. Hosp., 1969; vis. prof. Mayo Clinic, 1988; sec. orthops. overseas divsn. CARE Medico, 1971-76, sec. Medico adv. bd., 1974-76, vice chmn., 1976, chmn., 1977-79, v.p. CARE, Inc., 1977-79, pub. mem. CARE bd. dirs., 1980-90, mem. bd. overseers, 1991-99; chmn. Orthops. Overseas, Inc., 1982-86, treas., 1986-88, emeritus mem., 1994; mem. U.S. organizing com. 1st Internat. Acad. Symposium on Orthops., Tianjin, China, 1983; mem. CUPP Internat. Adv. Coun., 1986-99; invited guest spkr. Japan Orthop. Assn., 1994; mem. curriculum com. Oak Ridge Inst. Continual Learning, 1999—, chmn. med. programs subcom.; bd. dirs. MMC Oak Ridge Found., chmn., 2003-04. Mem. editl. bd. Contemporary Orthopedics, 1984-96. V.p. Anderson County Health Coun., 1975, pres., 1976—77, hon. bd. dirs.; pres. health commn. Coun. So. Mountains, 1958—65, sec., bd. dirs., 1965—66; Tenn. pres. UN Assn., 1966—67; vice-chmn. bd. Camelot Care Ctr., Tenn., 1979—82, chmn. Tenn., 1982—86; hon. mem. World Orthopedic Concern, 1990; with del. to Vietnam People to People, citizen amb. to Vietnam, 1993; del. to Oak Ridge's Sister City, Obninsk, Russia Obninsk, Russia, 1993; trustee Vietnam Am. Scholarship Fund, 1992; 93; Rotary vol. orthopaedic surgeon Kikuyu Hosp. Rehab. Ctr. of East Africa Presbyn. Ch., 1998; vol. Habitat for Humanity, 2004; vol. surgeon Interpaita Health Clinic, Knoxville, Tenn., 1990—; bd. dirs. Meth. Hosp. Oak Ridge Found., 2000—, chmn., 2003—04; bd. dirs. Hope of East Tenn. 2002—06, Clinch Valley Home Health Assn., 2005—. Recipient Svc. to Mankind award, Serotoma, 1967, Humanitarian award, Lions Club, 1968, Freedom Citation, Serotoma, 1978, award, Amb. Goodwill Lions Club, 1979, Medico Disting. Svc. award, 1990, 1st Ann. Vocat. Svc. award, Oak Ridge Rotary, 1979, Tech. Comm. award, East Tenn. chpt. Soc. for Tech. Comm., 1983, Individual Achievement award, Meth. Med. Ctr. of Oak Ridge, 1991, Humanitarian award, Orthopaedics Overseas, 1992, Biographic Exhibit recognition, Mus. Appalachia Hall of Fame, Norris, Tenn.; fellow Melvin Jones fellow, Lions Club, 1993. Fellow ACS, Internat. Coll. Surgeons (Tenn. regent 1976-80, bd. councilors 1980-84, hon. chmn. bd. trustees 1981-83, trustee 1983-84, v.p. U.S. sect. 1982-83, mem. surg. teams com. 1983-90, Humanitarian award 1992); mem. AMA (Humanitarian Svc. award 1967, 72), Société International Chirurgie

Orthopèdique et de Traumauatologie, So. Orthop. Assn., Western Pacific Orthop. Assn., Am. Fracture Assn., Am. Acad. Orthop. Surgeons (mem. com. on injuries 1980-86), Tenn. Med. Assn. (com. on emergency med. svcs. 1978-97), Peru Acad. Surgery (corr.), Peruvian Soc. Orthop. Surgery and Traumatology (corr.), Clin. Orthop. Soc., Mid-Am. Orthop. Soc., Rotary Club (Oak Ridge chpt., chmn. cmty. and world svc. com. 2000-04, Paul Harris fellow). Home: 507 Delaware Ave Oak Ridge TN 37830-3902 Home Fax: 865-483-8657. Personal E-mail: spray507@aol.com.

**SPRAYREGEN, JAMES H.M.,** diversified financial services company executive, lawyer; b. Dec. 2, 1959; BA cum laude, U. Mich., 1982; JD cum laude, U. Ill. 1985. Bar: Ill. 1985, N.Y. 1985, U.S. Dist. Ct. no. dist Ill. 1985, U.S. Dist. Ct. ea. dist Wis. 1988, U.S. Dist. Ct. so. & ea. dist. N.Y. 1992, U.S. Dist. Ct. we. dist Mich. 1992, U.S. Dist Ct. Ariz. 1992, U.S. Dist. Ct. Del. 1992. Atty. Lord Bissell & Brook, 1985—89, Rudnick & Wolfe, 1989—90; ptnr., mem. firm mgmt. com. Kirkland & Ellis LLP, Chgo., 1990—2006; mng. dir. investment banking divsn. The Goldman Sachs Group, Inc., NYC, 2006—. Co-chmn. Comml. Am. Bankruptcy Inst., bd. dir.; Chicago region bd. dir. Anti-Defamation League; vice chmn. Chicago region Am. Comm. Weizman Inst. Sci. Named Top Debtor Lawyer by active assignments, Deal's Bankrupcty Insider newsletter, 2004; named one of 12 Dealmakers of Year, Am. Lawyer, 2004, 45 Under Forty: Rising Stars Pvt. Bar, 2003. Mem.: Seventh Circuit Bar Assn. (Ill. chmn. Comml. Bankruptcy Law & Procedure), Chicago Bar Assn., Ill. Bar Assn., Comml. Law League Am., ABA. Office: The Goldman Sachs Group Inc 85 Broad St New York NY 10004*

**SPRECHER, BARON WILLIAM GUNTHER,** musician, cinematographer, conductor, diplomat; b. Saarbrucken, Germany, Jan. 20, 1924; arrived in U.S., 1952; s. Wolf and Karoline (Jung) Sprecher; m. Blossom Tag, Aug. 6, 1952. Studied piano with Prof. Wittels, Tel Aviv; studied piano with Madame Vengerova, NYC; studied composition with Paul Ben-Haim, Tel Aviv, studied conducting with Georg Singer; degree (hon.), Inst. Vocal Arts, 1957; D in Philosophy Music (hon.), World U. Roundtable, 1988; Mus D (hon.), London Inst. Applied Rsch., 1991, DFA, HHD, London Inst. Applied Rsch., 1993; Mus D (hon.), Australian Inst. Coord. Rsch., 1991; diploma, Gran Premio Am., 1990, Paladino del Tricolore, 1990; D Musicology, Somerset U.; D Music (hon.), Atlantic Southeastern U.; Diploma, Acad. Argentina de Diplomacia; Assoc. (hon.), Inst. Affairs Internat., Paris, 1993; DD (hon.), The Christian Congregation; D rerum politicarum, LittD (hon.), U. Aeterna Lucina Vitama, 1991; DD LittD (hon.), Eng., 1994; PhD (hon.), Germany, 1994. Korrepetitor Israel Folk Opera, Tel-Aviv, 1940-43; piano soloist Israel Philharm. Orch., Tel-Aviv, 1946-48; music dir. Temple Anshe Chesed, N.Y.C., 1966—69, Temple Sholom, Greenwich, Conn., 1976—82; pres., music dir. Bronx Philharm., N.Y.C., 1971-83; music dir. Sta. WEVD, N.Y.C., 1969-85; asst. pianist accompanying Lotte Lenya, Richard Tucker, Jan Peerce, Itzhak Perlman, Jan Kiepura, Ilona Massey; prof. Inst. Hautes Etudes Economiques et Sociales, Rsch. prof. Alliance Universelle Paix Connaissance, Paris, 1991; prof. Haute Ecole de Recherche, Inst. des Hautes Etudes Economiques et Sociales; mem. coun. Inst. de Documentation et D'Etudes Europeennes; dep. mem., diplomat State Parliament; dep. mem. assembly Internat. Parliament for Safety and Peace. Composer: (song book) Yinglish, piano soloist 1st performance of Gershwin's Concerto in F in Israel; composer Piano Sonata, 1945, Jerusalem Concerto for Piano and Orch., 1967, (TV) Great is Thy Faith, 1970; pianist-condr. 24 record albums; mem. The First Piano Quartet (Acad. award nomination, Peabody award). Consul Sovereign State Aeterna Lucina for State and City of NY; comdr. fgn. rels. Island Du Caricom, 1995; diplomat World Jewish Congress; senator Coun. of States for Protection of Life and Human Rights, Palermo, Italy; del. at large Rep. Presdl. Task Force, nat. rep. senatorial com.; active Nat. Com. to Preserve Social Security and Medicare, Ctr. for Am. Values, Sr. Coalition, Common Cause; founding sponsor Disabled Vets. Life Meml. Gold Medal Merit Soc., Washington, 2004; Reagan Presdl. Libr. supporter USS Ronald Reagan, Air Force One. Decorated noble knight Noble House of Amena, knight order Knight Templars of Jerusalem, knight comdr. Lofsensis Ursinius Order, baron Order of Bohemian Crown, comdr. Order of Golden Lance (Australia), Capt. Légion de L'Aigle Mer, Baron of Montsalvat, knight Holy Grail, count San Ciriaco, comdr. fgn. rels. Island du Caricom, 1995, Sen Maison Internat. Des Intellectuels, Sen European Parliament, Internat. Parliament for Safety and Peace, diplomat World Jewish Congress, Laird-Lord of Camster, Caithness, Scotland, 1995; recipient Diplomatic medal Internat. Parliament for Safety and Peace, 1995, Gold Cross of Honour, Albert Schweitzer Soc. Austria, Albert Einstein medal, Circulo Nobiliario Caballeros U., 1992, Swan Knight (Chevalier du Cygne), Order of the Swan, Congl. Order of Merit, 2006; named Knight of Yr., Internat. Writers and Artists Assn., 1995; recipient Medal of Merit, Rep. Presdl. Task Force, 1998, Noble Conquistador, Internat. Chivalric Order of the Knights of Justice, Music and Humanity award, 2003, Hall of Fame Music and Humanity award ABI, 2003, Disting. Leader Gold medal, 2003, Rep. Senatorial Gold medal of Freedom, 2004; Ronald Reagan Ranch Trailblazer, Name on Freedom Wall, Rep. Presidential Task Force (Life), name on Wall of Freedom, Rep. Ctr., Washington, Cert. of Appreciation, Pres. Bush and V.P. Dick Cheney, others. Fellow United Writers' Assn. India; mem. ASCAP, Maison Internat. des Intellectuels, Internat. Parliament for Safety and Peace, World Parliament Confedn. of Chivalry (Grand Coun.), World Acad. Assn. of the Universe (life), Bronx Philharm. Symphony Soc., Inc. (founder, pres.), Internat. Platform Assn., Am. Fedn. Musicians, Robert Stolz Soc. Gt. Britain, World Univ. Roundtable (trustee, founder), Internat. Cultural Corr. Inst., Circulo Nobiliario de los Caballeros Universales (grandmaster U.S.), Lègion de L'Aigle de Mer (capt.), USA United Srs. Assn. Inc. Avocations: walking, music, coin collecting/numismatics, antique coptic ethiopian crosses.

**SPRENGER, GORDON M.,** hospital administrator; b. Albert Lea, Minn., Apr. 30, 1937; Bachelors degree, St. Olaf Coll., 1959; masters degree, U. Minn., 1961. Registrar USAF Hosp., Hamilton AFB, Calif., 1961-64; with St. Luke's Hosp., Milw., 1964-67, Northwestern Hosp., Mpls., 1967-71; exec. v.p. Abbott-Northwestern Hosp., Mpls., 1971-75, pres. ceo., 1975-88, LifeSpan, 1982-92; exec ofcr HealthSpan, 1992-94; chief exec. ofcr Allina Health, 1994—. Prof. U. Minn., 1976—; acad. lectureship; preceptor. Mem. ACHE and AHA; Affiliated Hosp. Srvs: Past Sec. Bd mem., 1971-74; Council of Community Hosp., chair. 1980-81; Governor's Task Force on Nursing, 1981; Health Political Action Comm. of Minn., chair. 1981; Minn. Hosp. Assoc. Governmntl Relations Comm., chair. 1979, bd mem, 1978-81, exec. comm. treas., 1981; chair. elect, Minn. Hosp. Assoc., 1982; MMI Cos bd mem, currently vice chair., preceptor and faculty mem., U of Minn. Hosp. and Health Care Admin., 1982 bd of Minnehaha Acad.; disting. alumnus, St. Olaf Coll., mem. bd of regents; Voluntary Hosp. of Amer., past chair., mem. Medtronics, Inc., bd of dirs., 1991-; mem. St. Paul Cos., bd of dirs. Office: Allina Health System 5601 Smetana Dr PO Box 9310 Minneapolis MN 55440-9310 Home: 6244 Ridge Rd Chanhassen MN 55317-9438

**SPREWELL, LATRELL FONTAINE,** professional basketball player; b. Milw., Sept. 8, 1970; s. Latoska Fields and Pamela Sprewell; children: Aquilla, Page, Latrell II. Student, Three Rivers C.C., Poplar Bluff, Mo., 1988—90, Ala. U., 1990—92. Profl. basketball player Golden State Warriors, Oakland, Calif., 1992—98; profl. basketball Player New York Knicks, N.Y.C., 1998—2003, Minnesota Timberwolves, 2003—. Named an NBA All-star, 1994, 1995, 1997, 2001. Avocations: music, repairing stereo equipment. Office: c/o Minn Timberwolves 600 First Ave N Minneapolis MN 55403

**SPRIESER, JUDITH A.,** former software company executive; BA in Linguistics, Northwestern U., MBA in Fin. CPA, Ill., 1982. Comml. banker Harris Bank, Chgo., 1974-81; dir. treasury ops. Esmark, 1981-84; asst. treas. internat. Nalco Chem. Co., 1984-87; asst. treas. corp. fin. Sara Lee Corp., 1987-90; sr. v.p., CFO Sara Lee Bakery N.Am., 1990-93, pres., CEO, 1993-94; sr. v.p., CFO Sara Lee Corp., 1994-99, CEO, Foods and Food Svc., 2000-2001; CEO Transora, Chgo., 2001—05. Bd. dirs. USG Corp., Reckitt Benckiser, Allstate Corp., 1999-; Kohl's Corp., 2003-; CBS Corp., 2005- Bd.

dirs. Hinsdale Hosp. Found.; trustee Northwestern U. Mem. AICPA, Chgo. Network, Young Pres. Orgn., Chgo. coun. Fgn. Rels., Econ. Club, Conf. Bd. Coun. Fin. Execs. Mailing: Bd Dir Allstate Corp 2775 Sanders Rd Northbrook IL 60062-6127*

**SPRIESTERSBACH, DUANE CARYL,** academic administrator, speech pathology/audiology services professional, educator; b. Pine Island, Minn., Sept. 5, 1916; s. Merle Lee and Esther Lucille (Stucky) Spriestersbach; m. Bette Rae Bartell, Aug. 31, 1946; children: Michael Lee, Ann. BEd, Winona State Tchrs. Coll., 1939; MA, U. Iowa, 1940, PhD, 1948. Asst. dir. pers. rels. Pacific Portland Cement Co., San Francisco, 1946-47; prof. speech pathology U. Iowa, Iowa City, 1948-89, prof. emeritus, 1989—, dean. Grad. Coll., v.p. ednl. devel. and rsch., 1965-89, v. pres. and dean emeritus, 1989—, acting pres., 1981-82; v.p. ops. Breakthrough, Inc., Oakdale, Iowa, 1993-94; freelance cons., 1994—2006. Com. mem. Nat. Inst. Neurol. Disease and Blindess; chmn. dental tng. com. Nat. Inst. Dental Rsch., 1967—72, chmn. spl. grants rev., 1978—82; chmn. bd. dirs. Midwest Univs. Cons. Internat. Activities, Columbus, 1978—87. Author: (book) Psychosocial Aspects of Cleft Palate, 1973; author: (with others) Diagnostic Methods in Speech Pathology, 1978; co-editor: Cleft Palate and Communication, 1968, Diagnosis in Speech Language Pathology, rev. edit., 1999, The Way It Was: The University of Iowa 1964-1989, 1999. Pres. Iowa City Cmty. Theater, 1964, 1977, 1983. Served to lt. col. U.S. Army, 1941—46, ETO. Decorated Bronze Star; fellow Nat. Inst. Dental Rsch., 1971. Fellow: AAAS; mem.: Midwestern Assn. Grad. Schs. (chmn. 1979—80), Am. Cleft Palate Assn. (pres. 1961—62, disting. svc. award), Am. Speech and Hearing Assn. (pres. 1965, honor award), Assn. Grad. Schs. (pres. 1979—80), Cosmos Clug (Washington), Mortar Bd., Sigma Xi. Home: 2 Longview Knoll NE Iowa City IA 52240-9148 Office: Univ Iowa M212 Oakdale Hall Iowa City IA 52242-5000 Office Phone: 319-335-4012. Business E-mail: duane-spriestersbach@uiowa.edu.

**SPRIGGS, RICHARD MOORE,** ceramics engineer, science administrator, researcher; b. Washington, Pa., May 8, 1931; s. Lucian Alexander and Kathryn (Aber) S.; m. Patricia Anne Blaney, Aug. 1, 1953 (dec. 2002); children: Carolyn Elizabeth Spriggs Muchna, Richard Moore, Alan David; m. Brenda L. Ferrier, May 5, 2005. BS in Ceramics, Pa. State U., 1952; MS in Ceramic Engring., U. Ill., 1956, PhD, 1958. Sr. research engr. Ferro Corp., Cleve., 1958-59; sr. staff scientist, group leader, ceramics rsch. AVCO Corp., Wilmington, Mass., 1959-64; assoc. prof. metall. engring. Lehigh U., Bethlehem, Pa., 1964-67, prof. metallurgy and materials sci. and engring., 1967-80, adminstrv. asst. to pres., 1970-71, asst. v.p. for adminstrn., 1971-72, v.p. for adminstrn., 1972-78, dir. phys. ceramics lab., 1964-70, assoc. dir. Materials Research Ctr., 1964-70; vis. sr. staff assoc. Nat. Materials Adv. Bd. NRC, Washington, 1979-80, sr. staff officer, staff scientist, 1980-87, staff dir. bd. on assessment of NBS programs, 1984-87; J.F. McMahon prof. ceramic engring., dir. NYS Ctr. Advanced Ceramic Tech. N.Y. State Coll. Ceramics, Alfred (N.Y.) U., 1987-97, dir. office of sponsored programs, 1988-97, prof. emeritus, 1997—. Affiliate staff scientist Pacific Northwest Lab., 1994—. Contbr. articles to profl. publs. Co-patentee in field Pres., bd. dirs. YMCA, Bethlehem, Pa., 1978-79. Served to lt. USNR, 1952-56 Fellow Armco Steel Corp., 1956-58, Am. Coun. on Edn., 1970-71; Centennial fellow Coll. Earth and Mineral Scis., Pa. State U., 1996, Alumni Achievement award, 1999, 30th Ann. SHS Medal of Honor, 1997, Disting. Engring. Alumnus awrd U. Ill., 1988. Fellow: Brit. Inst. Materials, Ceramic Soc. Japan (Centennial medal 1991), Am. Ceramic Soc. (trustee pension trust fund 1979—84, pres. 1984—85, coord. programs and meetings 1991—92, Ross Coffin Purdy award 1965, Hobard M. Kraner award Lehigh Valley sect. 1980, Orton lectr. 1988, McMahon lectr. 1988, Mueller lectr. 1996, Albert Victor Bleininger award Pitts. sect. 2000, disting. life); mem.: Serbian Acad. Scis. and Arts (fgn.), Ceramic Assn. N.Y. (sec.-treas. 1988—99), Fed. Materials Socs. (trustee 1978—84), Materials Rsch. Soc., Materials Rsch. Soc. Japan (hon.), World Acad. Ceramics (trustee 1988—96, 2006—), Brit. Ceramic Soc., Ceramic Ednl. Coun., Nat. Inst. Ceramic Engrs., Internat. Inst. for Sci. of Sintering, Rotary (dir. 1982—87, pres. 1985—86). Office Phone: 607-587-8557. Personal E-mail: rmspriggs@excite.com.

**SPRINCE, LEILA JOY,** retired librarian; b. Toronto, Ont., Can., July 10, 1936; came to U.S., 1981; d. Harry and Anna Helen Caller; children: Alan Rosenthal, Joel Rosenthal; m. Arnold Joel Sprince, Feb. 16, 1982 BA, U. Toronto, 1957, B of Edn., 1962; MA, U. South Fla., 1987. Cert. tchr., Ont. Ballet dancer Volkoff Can. Ballet, Toronto, 1953-54; tchr. h.s. North York Bd. Edn., Toronto, 1958-60; libr. Broward County Libr. Sys., Plantation, Fla., 1987-88, 91-93, Margate, Fla., 1988-91, head youth svcs. Coconut Creek, Fla., 1996—2001; ret., 2001. Advisor Omnigraphics Pub., Detroit, 1993—; cons. Gale/U*X*L* Pubs., N.Y.C., 1996—; state facilitator summer programs State Libr. Fla., 1993. Contbr. articles to profl. jours. Mem. nat. children and youth membership orgns. outreach com. ALA/ALSC, 2001—; mem. adv. bd. Broward County Libr., 2006—. Mem. ALA (Best Books for Young Adult Cmty. spkr. 1989, 90), Fla. Libr. Assn. (spkr.), B'nai B'rith Women (fin. sec. 1983, pres. 1984, 85), Phi Kappa Phi, Beta Phi Mu. Democrat. Jewish. Avocations: music/dance, computers, travel, history. Personal E-mail: ajsprince@aol.com.

**SPRING, BONNIE JOAN,** psychology professor; b. Hackensack, N.J., Oct. 9, 1949; d. John Edwin and Sonja Joan (Litwinowich) S. BA, Bucknell U., 1971; MA, Harvard U., 1975, PhD, 1977. Diplomate Am. Bd. Health Psychology, Am. Bd. Profl. Psychology; lic. psychologist, Mass., Ill. Rsch. scientist Biometrics Rsch., N.Y.C., 1975-78; instr. psychology Harvard U., Cambridge, Mass., 1977, asst. prof., 1977-82, assoc. prof., 1982-84; prof. psychology Tex. Tech U., Lubbock, 1984-88, dir. clin. tng., 1986-88; prof. U. Health Scis.-Chgo. Med. Sch., 1988-98, U. Ill., Chgo., 1998—2005; prof. preventive medicine, dir. behavioral medicine, co-dir. cancedr prevention Feinberg Sch. Medicine, Northwestern U., Chgo., 2005—. Lectr. psychiatry Columbia Coll. Physicians and Surgeons, N.Y.C., 1979-86; vis. lectr. nutrition MIT, Cambridge, 1979-80; staff psychologist Mass. Mental Health, Boston, 1981-84; rsch. assoc. prof. psychiatry U. Md. Med. Sch., Balt., 1984-90. Author: Psychology, 1988; editor: Attentin in Schizophrenia, 1979, Psychopharmacology, 1986-95; mem. editl. bd. Jour. Social and Clin. Psychology, 1985—, Psychopharmacology, 1995-2000, Jour. Cons. and Clin. Psychology, 1996—; contbr. articles to profl. jours. Mem. com. on status of women Harvard U., 1979-81; panel mem. com. on nat. needs for behavioral rsch. pers. Inst. Medicine, NAS, Washington, 1984086; panel mem. nat. plan for rsch. on schizophrenia NIMH, 1987; mem. behavioral medicine study sect. NIH, 1994-98. Nutrition grantee Ctr. for Brain Scis., 1980-81, Ford Found., 1981-82, VA, 1989—, schizophrenia grantee NIMH, 1980-84, grantee NIH, 1995—. Fellow APA; mem. AAAS, Am. Psychol. Soc., Soc. for Biol. Medicine, Am. Psychopath. Assn., Soc. for Biol. Psychiatry, Am. Coll. Neuropsychopharmacology (chair evidence-based b ehavioral medicine com.). Avocations: travel, running. Office: Northwestern U Feinberg Sch ·Medicine Behavioral Medicine 680 N Lakeshore Dr Ste 1102 Chicago IL 60611 E-mail: bspring@northwestern.edu.

**SPRING, CARL CHAFFEE, JR.,** writer; b. L.A., Nov. 17, 1936; s. Carl C. Spring, Sr. and Emilie Temple Spring; m. Alice Waters, Oct. 7, 1967. BA, Calif. State U., LA, 1960, MA, 1968. Writer, news editor, L.A., 1960—68; med. writer, sr. editor Audio-Digest Found., Glendale, Calif., 1968—. Melvin Jones fellow, 2002, 2006. Mem.: Am. Med. Writers Assn. (v.p. 1973—74), Lions Club (editor of bull. 1994—, program chmn. 1994—, LA Internat., pres. 2004—05), Bay Cities Shrine Club (pres. 2001—02). Republican. Episcopalian. Avocations: beach walks, swimming, travel, meteorology. Home: 3490 Wade St Los Angeles CA 90066 Office: Audio-Digest Found 1577 E Chevy Chase Dr Glendale CA 91206 Office Phone: 818-240-7500. Personal E-mail: ccspring55@earthlink.net.

**SPRING, KATHLEEN,** writer; b. Mich. d. Edward and Mary Broilo; m. Samuel Taylor (div. 1984); 1 child, Justin; m. Paul Riethmeier (div. 1991) AD summa cum laude, Oakland C.C., 1990; BA cum laude, Wayne State U., 1993. Cert. holistic health profl. Adminstr. comm. dept. Wayne State U., Detroit, 1990-95; stringer The Daily Tribune, Royal Oak, Mich., 1992-98;

writer, photographer Spring Times, Detroit, 1992-98; pub. rels. mktg., editor Fanclub Found. for Arts, Southfield, Mich., 1993-98; writer, tchr. Spring Times, Lyons, Colo., 1998—; travel cons. holistic svcs. Rocky Mt. Retreats, 1998—; cdir. Integrated Healers Assn., Boulder, Colo., 2004—05. Author: Small Towns, Detroits Crown, 1997, WRITERS Birthing of Creative Writing and Capturing Random Memories, 2002; dir., author, exec. prodr.: (documentaries) Sandstone Quarry History: Our Stones Gather Moss, 2001; Lyons Geology, 2002; Come Stay Awhile, 2003. Vol. PBS-Detroit, 1982-95. Named Journalist of Yr., Wayne State U., 1992; scholar numerous acad. scholarships. Mem.: Colo. Press Women (three journalism awards 2003), Denver Film Soc., Colo. Authors League, Film and Video Assn., Women in Comm., Soc. Profl. Journalists (1st v.p. 1993—98, Howard Dubin Outstanding Pro Chpt. Mem. 1996, Cir. of Excellence-Newsletter 1996). Avocations: travel, books, films, photography. Office: Spring Times PO Box 512 Lyons CO 80540-0512

**SPRING, MICHAEL,** editor, writer; b. NYC, Oct. 14, 1941; s. Sol and Muriel (Roth) S.; m. Marjorie Hornblower Bauer, Mar. 1965 (div 1980); children: Declan, Evan; m. Janis Abrahms, 1993. BA, Haverford Coll., Pa., 1964; MA, Columbia U., N.Y.C., 1970. Reporter Bergen Record, Hackensack, NJ, 1969-71; editor Scholastic Inc., N.Y.C., 1971-87; editorial dir. Fodor's Travel Publs., 1987-94, v.p., 1989-94; pub. Macmillan Travel, N.Y.C., 1994-99; pub. Frommer's Travel Guides John Wiley & Sons, N.Y.C., 1999—2001; pub. Wiley Travel, 2001—. Broadcaster, writer WNCN-FM, N.Y.C., 1983-84. Author: Great Weekend Escape Book, 1982, 4th rev. edit. 1990, Student's Guide to Julius Caesar, 1984; editor: American Way of Working, 1980, 50 vol. Barron's Book Notes series, 1984, Scholastic Literature Anthologies, 4 vols., 1985, 87, Great European Itineraries, 1987, Touring Europe, 1990, 3d edit. 1994; contbg. editor Conde Nast's Traveler, 1987—; travel expert CNN Travel Show, 1991-94, WCBS Radio daily travel show, 1998—. Democrat. Jewish. Home: 20 Country Rd Westport CT 06880-2525 Office: John Wiley & Sons 111 River St Hoboken NJ 07030-5774 Office Phone: 201-748-5662. Business E-Mail: mspring@wiley.com.

**SPRINGER, DAVID WILLIAM,** dean, social sciences educator; b. NYC, Sept. 1, 1968; s. Paul David and Elizabeth Springer; m. Sarah Eagle Smith, Dec. 8, 2001; 1 child, Aidan David. BA, Fla. State U., 1990, MSW, 1992, PhD, 1997. LCSW Tex., ACSW. Clin. social worker Univ. Behavioral Ctr., Orlando, Fla., 1992—94; rsch. assoc. Fla. State U., Tallahassee, 1994—97; asst. prof. U. Tex., Austin, 1997—2000, assoc. prof., 2000—02, assoc. dean, 2002—, assoc. disting. tchg. prof., 2005—. Author: Substance Abuse Treatment for Criminal Offenders, 2003. Fundraiser Leukemia and Lymphoma Soc., Austin, 2000; bd. dirs. Austin Child Guidance Ctr., 1998—2003. Named to Acad. Disting. Tchrs., U. Tex. at Austin, 2005, Who'w Who in Social Scis. Higher Edn., 2004; recipient Outstanding Grad. Tchg. award, U. Tex. at Austin, 2003. Mem.: NASW, Tex. Assn. Social Work Deans and Dirs. (pres. 2005—), Coun. Social Work Edn., Soc. Social Work and Rsch. Democrat. Avocations: running, guitar, photography, camping, hiking. Office: U Tex at Austin Sch Social Work Austin TX 78712 Office Phone: 512-471-0512. Office Fax: 512-471-7268. Business E-Mail: dwspringer@mail.utexas.edu.

**SPRINGER, DOUGLAS HYDE,** retired food products executive, lawyer; b. Englewood, N.J., Jan. 31, 1927; s. Arthur Hyde and Melicent Katherine (Messenger) S.; m. Virginia Helen Chouinard, Nov. 23, 1949; children: Susan Compton, Debora Lee. Student, Wesleyan U., 1944-45; AB, Yale U., 1947; LLB, Columbia U., 1950. Bar: N.Y. 1950. Atty. Port of N.Y. Authority, 1950-52; legal counsel Worthington Corp., Harrison, N.J., 1953-61, asst. sec., 1956-61; asst. counsel Campbell Soup Co., Camden, N.J., 1961-65, asst. sec., 1965, spl. assignments, 1966, dir. spl. studies, corp. planning, 1966-69, dir. corp. planning frozen foods, 1969-70, asst. treas., 1970-71, treas., 1971-73, v.p. fin. planning, 1973-75, v.p., controller, 1975-78, v.p., treas., 1978-88, v.p. investment mgmt., 1988-90. Trustee Meml. Health Alliance, 1981-99; trustee, treas. Virtua Health Hosp., 2000—, Meml. Hosp. Found., 1990-2002, Virtua Health Found., 2003—; mem. adv. bd. Pa. Liberty Mut. Ins. Co., 1971-88, Eastern regional adv. bd. Arkwright-Boston Mfrs. Mut. Ins. Co., 1985-90; exec. sec. Gov.'s Interstate Adv. Com., 1966; asst. to mem. Pres.'s Commn. on Postal Orgn., 1967-68; spl. asst. to chmn South Jersey Port Corp., 1969-71; mem. N.J. Econ. Devel. Council, 1972-76; mem. adv. coun. Tax Found., 1980-89. Trustee Nat. Food Processors Assn. Retirement Plan and Trust Indenture Fund, 1976-89, Perkins Ctr. for Arts, 1979-88, Ind. Coll. Fund, N.J., 1982-88, The Estaugh, 2004—; mem. exec. bd., v.p. fin. Camden County coun. Boy Scouts Am., 1978-90; bd. dir. Family "Y" of Burlington County, 1995—, exec. 2000—, Yale Alumni Fund, 1996-2002, exec. com. 1998-2002. With USNR, 1944-46. Mem. Nat. Assn. Corp. Treas. (bd. dirs. 1982-88), Phila. Treas. Club, Internat. Bus. Forum (bd. dirs. 1980-88), Phi Nu Theta, Phi Delta Phi, N.J. Soc. Pa. (pres. 1992-93, treas. 1994—). Clubs: Yale (Phila., N.Y.C.); Nassau (Princeton, N.J.), Laurel Creek (Mt. Laurel, N.J.), Y's Men's Club (v.p., 1992-94, pres., 1994-95). Home: 670 Medford Leas Medford NJ 08055

**SPRINGER, GEORGE STEPHEN,** mechanical engineering educator; b. Budapest, Hungary, Dec. 12, 1933; came to U.S., 1959; s. Joseph and Susan (Grausz) S.; m. Susan Martha Flory, Sept. 15, 1963; children: Elizabeth Anne, Mary Katherine. B in Engring., U. Sydney, Australia, 1959; M in Engring., Yale U., 1960, MSc in Engring., 1961, PhD, 1962; D (hon.), Tech. U. Budapest, 2000. Registered profl. engr., Mass. Asst. prof. mech. engring. MIT, Cambridge, 1962-67; prof. mech. engring. U. Mich., Ann Arbor, 1967-83; Paul Pigott prof. Stanford (Calif.) U., 1983—, chmn. dept. aeronautics and astronautics, 1990—2001. Author: Erosion by Liquid Impact, 1975; co-author, co-editor 14 books; contbr. over 200 articles to scholarly and profl. jours. Recipient Pub. Svc. Group Achievement award, NASA, 1988, Medal of Excellence in Composite Materials U. Del., 1999. Fellow AIAA (Engr. of Yr. 1995, Structures Structural Dynamics and Materials award 2000), ASME (Worcester Reed Warner medal 1994), Soc. Advancement Materials and Process Engring. (Delmonte award 1991); mem. Am. Phys. Soc., Soc. Automotive Engrs. (Ralph Teetor award 1978), NAE, Hungarian Nat. Acad. Sci. (fgn. mem.), Am. Soc. Composites (Outstanding Rschr. award 1997). Achievements include patents in field. Office: Stanford U Dept Aeronautics & Astronautics Stanford CA 94305 Office Phone: 650-723-4135. Business E-Mail: gspringer@stanford.edu.

**SPRINGER, JERRY,** television talk show host, radio personality; b. London, 1944; BA in Polit. Sci., Tulane U.; JD, Northwestern U., 1968. Presdl. campaign aide Sen. Robert F. Kennedy; elected mem. at large Cin. Coun., 1971-77; elected mayor Cin., 1977; polit. reporter, commentator WLWT-TV, Cin., 1982-84, anchor, mng. editor, 1984-93; host The Jerry Springer Show, 1991—, Springer on the Radio, Air Am. Radio, 2005—. Author Ringmaster, 1998; video collection Jerry Springer: Too Hot for TV; actor: (films) A Fair to Remember, 1998, Citizen Verdict, 2003, The Defender, 2004, (TV films) Since You've Been Gone, 1998, Talking to Americans, 2001; actor, prodr.: (films) Ringmaster, 1998; performer, Dancing With the Stars, 2006 On-site reporter Cin. Reaches Out; mem. adv. bd. Audrey Hepburn Hollywood for Children Fund; co-host Stars Across America Muscular Dystrophy Labor Day Telethon; v.p. bd. Nat. Muscular Dystrophy Assn.; founder scholarship fund Kellman Sch., Chgo. Recipient 7 Emmy awards for nightly news commentaries; named Best Anchor Cin. Mag. 5 times. Achievements include top rated daytime talk show series in the U.S. Office: Jerry Springer Show 454 N Columbus Dr Fl 2 Chicago IL 60611-5514 also: Air America Radio 641 Avenue Of The Americas Fl 4 New York NY 10011-2038

**SPRINGER, LINDA M.,** federal official; BS, Ursinus Coll., 1977. Staff assoc. Coopers and Lybrand, 1977—79; actuary Penn Mut. Life Ins. Co., Phila., 1979—86, exec. asst. to pres., 1986—87, asst. v.p. & prod. mgr., 1987—90, v.p & prod. mgr., 1990—92; actuary Provident Mut. Life Ins. Co., Berwyn, Pa., 1992—95, asst. v.p. & actuary, 1995—96, v.p. and contr., 1996—2000, sr. v.p. & contr., 2001—02; counselor to the dep. dir. for mgmt. Office Fed. Fin. Mgmt., Office Mgmt. & Budget, Washington, 2002—03, contr., 2003—05; dir. US Office Pers. Mgmt., Washington, 2005—. Avocations: golf, gardening, cello. Office: US Office Pers Mgmt Theodore Roosevelt Fed Bldg 1900 E St NW Rm 5A09 Washington DC 20415*

**SPRINGER, MARLENE,** university administrator, educator; b. Murfreesboro, Tenn., Nov. 16, 1937; d. Foster V. and Josephine Jones; children: Ann Springer, Rebecca Springer. BA in English and Bus. Adminstrn., Centre Coll. 1959; MA in Am. Lit., Ind. U., 1963, PhD in English Lit., 1969. Chair English dept. U. Mo., Kansas City, 1980-81, acting assoc. dean grad. sch., 1982; Am. Coun. of Edn. Adminstrn. fellow U. Kans., Lawrence, 1982-83; dean of grad. sch. U. Mo., Kansas City, 1983-84, assoc. vice chancellor for acad. affairs and grad. studies, 1985-89; vice chancellor for acad. affairs East Carolina U., Greenville, NC, 1989-94; pres. CUNY Coll., Staten Island, 1994—. Author: Edith Wharton and Kate Chopin: A Reference Guide, 1976; What Manner of Woman: Essays, 1977, Thomas Hardy's Use of Allusion, 1983, Plains Woman: The Diary of Martha Farnsworth, 1986 (Choice award 1986), Ethan Frome: A Nightmare of Need, 1993. Huntington Libr. fellow, 1988. Mem.: Coun. Grad. Schs. (chair 1986—88), Assn. Tchr. Educators (chair 1992), Acad. Leadership Acad. (exec. com. 1992—94), Am. Assn. State Colls. and Univs., Am. Coun. on Edn. (profl. devel. com. 1991—, invited participant Nat. Forum 1984, bd. dirs. 2001—). Office: Coll Staten Island 2800 Victory Blvd Rm 1a-404 Staten Island NY 10314-6609

**SPRINGER, PAUL DAVID,** lawyer, film company executive; b. NYC, Apr. 27, 1942; s. William W. and Alma (Markowitz) S.; m. Marian Frankfurt, Aug. 16, 1964; children: Rob, Will. BA, U. Bridgeport, 1963; JD, Bklyn. Law Sch., 1967. Bar: N.Y. 1968, U.S. Dist. Ct. (so. and ea. dists.) N.Y. 1968, U.S. Ct. Appeals (2d cir.) 1970, U.S. Supreme Ct. 1973, Calif. 1989. Assoc. Johnson & Tannenbaum, N.Y.C., 1968—70; assoc. counsel Columbia Pictures, N.Y.C., 1970, Paramount Pictures, N.Y.C., 1970—79, v.p., theatrical distbn. counsel, 1979—85, sr. v.p., chief resident counsel East Coast, 1985—87, sr. v.p., asst. gen. counsel L.A., 1987—. Bar: N.Y. 1968, U.S. Dist. Ct. (so. and ea. dists.) N.Y. 1968, U.S. Ct. Appeals (2d cir.) 1970, U.S. Supreme Ct. 1973, Calif. 1989. Trustee West Cunningham Park Civic Assn., Fresh Meadows, N.Y., 1978—. Mem. ABA, Assn. of Bar of City of N.Y., L.A. Copyright Soc., Acad. Motion Picture Arts and Scis., Motion Picture Pioneers. Business E-Mail: paul_springer@paramount.com.

**SPRINGER, ROBERT DALE,** retired air force officer, consultant, lecturer; b. Millheim, Pa., Jan. 17, 1933; s. Simon Peter and Ruth Olive (McCool) S.; m. Bonnie Joan Brubaker, Aug. 30, 1953; children: Robert Dale Jr., Debra K. Springer Miller, Curtis A., Michele L. Becker, Tania. BA in Social Sci., George Washington U., 1964, MS in Internat. Affairs, 1969. Cert. command pilot. Commd. 2d lt. USAF; advanced through grades to lt. gen.; comdr. 435th Tactical Airlift Wing, Rhein-Main Air Base, Federal Republic Germany, 1978-80, 322d Airlift Divsn., Ramstein Air Base, Federal Republic Germany, 1980-81, Air Force Manpower and Pers. Ctr., Randolph AFB, Tex., 1982-84, 21 A.F., McGuire AFB, NJ, 1984-85; insp. gen. USAF, Washington, 1985-87; with DCS-pers. Mil. Airlift Command, Scott AFB, Ill., 1981-82, vice comdr.-in-chief, 1987-88; ret., 1988; pres. bsone, Inc., 1999—, NovaLogic Sys., 1999—. Media cons., lectr., 1989—; dir. Air Force Commissary Svc., San Antonio, 1982-84, Army-Air Force Exch. Svc., Dallas, 1982-84; chmn. bd. dirs. Air Force Welfare Bd., San Antonio, 1982-84; mem. adv. bd. First Bank; bd. dirs. NovaLogic, Inc. Exec. dir Air Force Meml. Found., 1992-96, pres. 1996-98, vice chmn., 1998—; trustee Aerospace Edn. Found., 1992-94, The Falcon Found., 1996—. Mem. Air Force Assn. (Presdl. Citation 1984), Airlift-Tanker Assn. (life mem., sr. v.p. 1989-94), Arnold Air Soc. (exec. dir 1990-93, trustee 1993-2001), Ret. Officers Assn. (life), Daedalians (life), Masons (33 deg.). Lutheran. Avocations: golf, reading. Personal E-mail: bsone@nc.rr.com.

**SPRINGER, ROBERT WADE,** music educator; BS in Music Edn., Indiana U. Pa., 1999. Music tchr. Southeastern Greene Sch. Dist., Greensboro, Pa., 2000—. Marching band instr., mem. staff Southmoreland Marching Band, Alverton, Pa., 2000—. Mem. troop com. Boy Scouts Am., New Stanton, Pa.; mem. Scottdale (Pa.) Cmty. Band, 2000—. Mem.: Pa. Music Educators Assn. Avocations: backpacking, auto repair, music. Home: PO Box 4 Hunker PA 15639

**SPRINGER, SALLY PEARL,** university administrator; b. Bklyn., Mar. 19, 1947; d. Nathaniel Margulies and Fanny (Schoen) S.; m. Hakon Hope; children: Erik Jacob Hope, Mollie Liv Hope. BS, Bklyn. Coll., 1967; PhD, Stanford U., 1971. Postdoctoral fellow Stanford U. Med. Sch., Calif., 1971-73; asst. prof. SUNY, Stony Brook, 1973-78, assoc. provost, 1981-85, assoc. prof., 1978-87; exec. asst. to chancellor U. Calif., Davis, 1987-92, asst. chancellor, 1982-2001, assoc. chancellor, 2001—. Author: (with others) Left Brain, Right Brain, 1981 (Am. Psychol. Found. Disting. Contbr. award 1981), 5th rev. edit., 1998, How to Succeed in College, 1982, Admission Matters: What Students and Parents Need to Know About Getting Into College, 2005; contbr. articles to profl. jours Mem. Internat. Neuropsychol. Soc., Psychonomic Soc. Office: Univ Calif Office Chancellor Davis CA 95616 Office Phone: 530-752-2068. Business E-Mail: spspringer@ucdavis.edu.

**SPRINGER, TIMOTHY ALAN,** health researcher, immunology educator; b. Ft. Benning, Ga., Feb. 23, 1948; BA in Biochemistry, U. Calif., Berkeley, 1971; PhD in Biochemistry & Molecular Biology, Harvard U., 1976. NIH rsch. fellow U. Cambridge (Eng.)/MRC Lab. Molecular Biology, 1976-77; asst. prof. Med. Sch., Harvard U., 1977-83, assoc. prof., 1983-89, Latham family prof., 1989—. Chief lab. membrane immunochemistry Dana-Farber Cancer Inst., Boston, 1981-88; v.p. Ctr. Blood Resch. Inst. Biomed. Rsch., Boston, 1989—; organizer Juan March Found. Workshop, Madrid. 1991 Assoc. editor Jour. Immunology, 1981-85; adv. editor Jour. Exptl. Medicine, 1981-85; mem. editl. bd. Hybridoma, 1981-, Jour. Clin. Immunology, 1988-92, Cellular Immunology, 1988-93, Cell Regulation, 1989-92, New Biologist, 1989—; contbr. numerous articles to profl. jours. NIH grantee, 1988, basic Rsch. prize, Am. Heart Assn., 1993, William B. Coley Medal for Disting. Rsch. in Fundamental Immunology, Cancer Rsch. Inst., 1995, Marie T. Bonazinga award for Excellence in Leukocyte Biology Rsch, Society for Leukocyte Biology, 1995, Crafoord prize, 2004. Mem. Am. Assn. Immunologists, Reticuloendothelial Soc. (membership chair 1986—, chair 1989), Am. Soc. Biol. Chemists, Am. Assn. Immunologists (block chmn. macrophages and natural killer cells 1985-86), Am. Assn. Pathologists, Nat. Acad. Scis. (chair biophysics and computational biology sect. 29 2004-), Am. Acad. Arts and Sciences, Phi Beta Kappa. Office: Ctr for Blood Resch Inst for Biomedical Rsch Harvard Med Sch Warren Alpert Bldg Rm251 200 Longwood Ave Boston MA 02115 Office Fax: 617-278-3200, 617-278-3232. Business E-Mail: springer@cbr.med.harvard.edu.

**SPRINGER, WAYNE GILBERT,** computer company executive; b. El Paso, Tex., Oct. 6, 1951; s. Wayne Gill and Constance A. (Courtney) S.; m. Dianne Louise Slaydon, Jan. 3, 1981; children: Courtney Lee, Carol Jeanne, Kent Slaydon. BS in Engring., U.S. Mil. Acad., 1973; MBA, So. Meth. U., Dallas, 1979, MSCE, 1980. Registered profl. engr. Commd. 2d lt. U.S. Army, C.E., 1973, advanced through grades to capt., 1977, resigned, 1978; grad. sch. instr. So. Meth. U., 1978-80; engr. Fluor Corp., Irvine, Calif. and Houston, 1980-82; coord. project devel. United Energy Resources, Houston, 1982-83; founder Computer Leasing Exch. Corp., Houston, 1983—. Founder Computer Helpline, Houston, 1984—, Network Systems Tech. Corp., 1993—; pres., founder Laser Express Corp., 1991; pres. Atiwa Computing, Inc., 1995—; ptnr. Springer Cons., Houston and Whittier, Calif., 1980-86. Author: Your Road Map to E-Commerce Success, 2000; contbr. articles to profl. jours.; inventor mech. devices. Home: Kansas Houston Conv. and Visitors Coun., 1983—; mem. technology com. United Way. Mem. MIT Enterprise Forum, West Point Alumni Assn., Houston C. of C., Computer and Audio Visual Execs. Assn. (founder 1989), Nat. Speakers Assn. (pres.), Rotary Club, Mensa, Plaza Oaks Club. Avocations: skiing, tennis. Office: Atiwa Computing Inc STE 125 2500 City West Blvd Houston TX 77042-3037

**SPRINGER, WILMA MARIE,** retired elementary school educator; b. Goshen, Ind., Jan. 13, 1933; d. Noah A. and Laura D. (Miller) Kaufman; m. Walter Frederick Springer, May 25, 1957; children: Anita Daniel, Timothy, Mark. BA, Goshen Coll., 1956; MS, Bradley U., 1960. Tchr. Topeka Elem. Sch., Ind., 1956—57, Metamora Grade Sch., Ill., 1957—59, Bellflower Unified Sch. Dist., Calif., 1960—61, 1968—2001, Lindstrom Elem. Sch., 1970—89, Jefferson Elem. Sch., Bellflower, 1989—92, Woodruff Elem., 1992—93, Williams Elem. Sch., Lakewood, Calif., 1993—96, Baxter Elem. Sch., Bellflower, 1996—2001; ret., 2001. Chmn. gifted and talented edn. Lindstrom Elem. Sch., Lakewood, 1986—89, Jefferson Elem. Sch., Bellflower, 1989—91, Baxter Elem., 1996—2001; stage mgr. Hour of Power TV Crystal Cathedral, 1983—; mem. program quality rev. team State of Calif., 1989—91; mem. adv. bd. Weekly Reader, 1989—96. Contbr. articles to profl. jours. Active sch. bd. campaign, 1984, Bellflower City Coun., 1988, state senator and assemblyman campaigns, 1986-87; petition circulator various state initiatives, 1987-88; bd. dirs. Women's Ministries of Crystal Cathedral, Garden Grove, Calif., 1978-88; educator del. People to People Ambassadors Program, South Africa, 2003, Russia, 2004. Instructional Improvement Program grantee State of Calif., 1986-87; recipient Recognition award Regional Ednl. TV Adv. Coun., 1986, Cathedral Star award Women's Ministries of Crystal Cathedral, 1985. Mem.: AAUW, NEA (del. nat. conv. 1986, 1987, 1990, 1992, 1993, 1994, 1995), Calif. Tchrs. Assn. (del. 1986, 1994), Bellflower Edn. Assn. (elem. dir. 1986—88, treas. 1988—89, v.p. 1989—91, pres. 1991—95), Toastmasters (Founder's Dist. Gov. 2001—02, Disting. Toastmaster, Disting. Dist.), Delta Kappa Gamma. Republican. Mem. Reformed Churches of Am. Avocations: quilting, painting. Home: 3180 Marna Ave Long Beach CA 90808-3246 Personal E-mail: wmspr@aol.com.

**SPRINGFIELD, JAMES FRANCIS,** retired lawyer, banker; b. Memphis, Nov. 5, 1929; s. C.L. and Mildred (White) S.; m. Shirley Burdick, June 1, 1951 (div.); children: Sidney, Susan, James Francis; m. Nancy Hardwick Ragan, Feb. 8, 1987 (dec. Jan. 1988); m. Donna Thomas Moore, Feb. 22, 1989. BA with distinction in econs., Southwestern at Memphis (now Rhodes Coll.), 1951; LLB, U. Memphis, 1960. Bar: Tenn. 1960. With Union Planters Nat. Bank, Memphis, 1951-94, exec. v.p., sr. trust officer, head trust dept., 1968-85, gen. counsel, sec. bd., 1985-94; sec. bd., exec. v.p., gen. counsel Union Planters Corp., 1985-94; ret., 1994. Adv. bd. Memphis Alzheimer's Assn., 1999-2001; president's coun. Rhodes Coll., Memphis, chmn., 1991-92, internat. chmn. ann. fund, 1995-96; chmn. bd. trustees So. Coll. Optometry, 1978-80; trustee Plough Found., Memphis Conf. United Meth. Ch. Found., 1978-85, U. Tenn. Med. Units Found., 1975-82, MidSouth Pub. Comm. Found., 1985-87, sec. bd., 2002-; chmn. fin. com. Hutchinson Sch.; sec. bd. trustees Vision Edn. Found., 1977-78; bd. regents Tenn. Trust Sch., chmn., 1977; mem. pres.'s adv. coun. Lambuth Coll., 1982-85; exec. bd. Chickasaw coun. Boy Scouts Am., 1983-87; bd. visitors Memphis State U. Cecil C. Humphreys Sch. Law, treas. Balmoral Civic Club, 1987-68; pres., bd. dir. Village of Bailey Station Homeowners Assn., Inc., 2000-01; dir. Shoreline Towers Condominium Assn. Inc., 2004—. Lt. (j.g.) USNR, 1951-54. Mem. Tenn. Bar Assn. (chmn. interprofl. rels. com. 1976), Memphis and Shelby County Bar assn. (chmn. moral fitness com. 1972), Tenn. Bankers Assn. (chmn. legis.com. trust div. 1976-77, treas. 1972-73, pres. 1976-77, bd. dir. 1976-77), Bank Adminstrn. Inst. (chmn. trust commn. 1981-82), Estate Planning Coun. Memphis (pres. 1973-74), Sigma Nu (div. comdr. 1967-68, treas., bd. dir. House Corp. 1966-81), Omicron Delta Kappa (Rhodes Coll. chpt., pres. ODK Assocs. 2002-03). Republican. Home: 1692 Village Ridge Rd Collierville TN 38017-9793 Personal E-mail: jimmyspringfield@msn.com.

**SPRINGFIELD, SANYA A.,** federal agency administrator; BS in zoology, Howard U., PhD in physiology and biophysics. Fellow Dept. Pharmacology Robert Wood Johnson Sch. Medicine, Piscataway, NJ; asst. prof. to assoc. prof. Dept. Biology CCNY, 1985—95; program dir. Divsn. Integrative Biology and Neurosciences NSF; participant NIH Grants Assoc. Program; sci. rev. adminstr. Grants Rev. Br. Nat. Cancer Inst., dir. Comprehensive Minority Biomedical Br., 1999—, acting dir. Ctr. to Reduce Cancer Health Disparities. Office: Comprehensive Minority Biomedical Br Nat Cancer Inst 6116 Executive Blvd Ste 7028 Bethesda MD 20892-8350 also: Ctr to Reduce Cancer Health Disparities Nat Cancer Inst 6116 Executive Blvd Ste 602 MSC 8341 Bethesda MD 20892 Office Phone: 301-496-7344. Office Fax: 301-402-4551. E-mail: springfs@mail.nih.gov.

**SPRINGGATE, CLARK FRANKLIN,** physician, researcher; b. Champaign, Ill., Nov. 14, 1946; s. William F. and Marjorie E. (Fitch) S.; children from a previous marriage: Elizabeth, Benjamin; m. Diane Louise Rotnem, Oct. 19, 1991. AB in Biology, Boston U., 1967; PhD in Biochemistry, Boston Coll., 1972; MD, U. Miami, 1983. Diplomate Nat. Bd. Med. Examiners, Am. Bd. Pathology. Med. dir. Richardson Vicks Pharm., Shelton, Conn., 1989-91; v.p., med. dir. TSI Biomed. Rsch. Group, Medford, Mass., 1992-94. V.p. Scicor, Indpls., 1988-89; pres. Springgate Biotech, Guilford, Conn., 1991—, Biotech Regular Cons., Guilford, 1994—; designer/executor Phase I, Phase II, Phase III and Phase IV clin. trials in oncology, cardiology, rheumatology, endocrinology, infectious diseases, neurology. Contbr. articles to jours. Heart Transplant, Am. Soc. Hist. Immunogcy. Bd. dirs. AIDS Protect New Haven, 1994-95; funding bd. Leap Youth Program, New Haven, 1991-92 Leukemia Soc. Am. fellow, 1972-74. Mem. AAAS, ACP Execs., Conn. State Med. Soc. Achievements include research in immune monitoring of heart transplant patients to prevent rejection and infection, diagnostic flow cytometry-oncology, gene therapy for cancer, heart disease, autoimmune disease and infectious disease. Home: 1320 Little Meadow Rd Guilford CT 06437-1659 E-mail: clarkmd@tx.netcom.com.

**SPRINGSTEEN, BRUCE (BRUCE FREDERICK JOSEPH SPRINGS-TEEN),** musician, singer, lyricist; b. Freehold, N.J., Sept. 23, 1949; s. Douglas and Adele Springsteen; m. Julianne Phillips, May 13, 1985 (div. 1988); m. Patti Scialfa, June 8, 1991; children: Evan James, Jessica Rae, Sam Ryan. Student, Ocean County CC, 1967. Performer: N.Y. and N.J. nightclubs, Jazz & Heritage Festival, New Orleans, 2006; signed with Columbia Records, 1972, nationwide concert tours with The E-Street Band, 1974—92, albums include Greetings from Asbury Park, 1973, The Wild, The Innocent and the E-Street Shuffle, 1973, Born to Run, 1975 (Gold Record award, 1975), Darkness on the Edge of Town, 1978, The River, 1980, Nebraska, 1982, Born in the U.S.A., 1984 (Best Pop/Rock Album of Yr., Downbeat Readers Poll, 1984), Bruce Springsteen and the E-Street Band Live/1975-1985, 1986, Tunnel of Love, 1987, Chimes of Freedom, 1988, Human Touch, 1992, Lucky Town, 1992, Bruce Springsteen Greatest Hit, 1995, The Ghost of Tom Joad, 1995, Bruce Springsteen Plugged (from MTV Live), 1997, 18 Tracks (compilation with unreleased tracks), 1998, The Rising, 2002 (Grammy award best male rock vocal performance, 2003, Grammy award best rock song, 2003, Grammy award best rock album, 2003), Devils and Dust, 2005 (Grammy award, Best Solo Rock Vocal Performance, 2006), We Shall Overcome: The Pete Seeger Sessions, 2006; composer: (songs) Growing Up, Rosalita, Prove It All Night, Promised Land, Born to Run, Thunder Road, Hungry Heart, Atlantic City, Dancing in the Dark, Born in the USA, Glory Days, Brilliant Disguise, Pink Cadillac, Jersey Girl, Streets of Philadelphia, 1994 (Golden Globe award for Best Original Song in a Film, 1994, Acad. award for best original song in a film, 1994, MTV Best Video from a Film award, 1994, Grammy, Song of Yr., 1994), Dead Man Walking, 1996 (Acad. award nominee for best original song in a film, 1996); appears on: albums Rumble Doll with Patti Scialfa, 1993, The Wind with Warren Zevon, 2003 (Grammy award, Best Rock Performance By A Duo Or Group With Vocal for song "Disorder in the House", 2003). Recipient Grammy award for best male rock vocalist, 1984, 1987, 1994. Achievements include being inducted into Rock and Roll Hall of Fame, 1999.*

**SPRINKEL, BERYL WAYNE,** economist, consultant; b. Richmond, Mo., Nov. 20, 1923; s. Clarence and Emma (Schooley) S.; m. Lory Kiefer, Aug. 29, 1993; children: Gary L., Kevin G. Student, N.W. Mo. State U., 1941-43, U. Oreg., 1943-44; BS, U. Mo., 1947; MBA, U. Chgo., 1948, PhD, 1952; LHD (hon.), DePaul U., 1975; LLD (hon.), St. Michael's Coll., 1981, U. Mo., 1985, U. Rochester, 1985, Govs. State U., 1988, U. Nebr., 1988; Doctor of Pub.

Adminstrn., Marion Coll., 1988. Instr. econs. and fin. U. Mo., Columbia, 1948-49, U. Chgo., 1950-52; with Harris Trust & Savs. Bank, Chgo., 1952-81, v.p., economist 1960-68, dir. rsch., 1963-69, sr. v.p., 1968-74, economist, 1968-81, exec. v.p., economist, 1974-81; undersec. monetary affairs Dept. Treasury, Washington, 1981-85; chmn. Coun. Econ. Advisers, The White House, Washington, 1985-89, mem. Pres.'s Cabinet, 1987-89; pvt. cons. economist, 1989—. Cons. Fed. Res. Bd., 1955-59, Bur. of Census, 1962-70, Joint Econ. Com. U.S. Congress, 1958, 62, 67, 71, Ho. of Reps. Banking and Currency Com., 1963, Senate Banking Com., 1975; econ. adv. bd. to sec. commerce, 1967-69; bd. economists Time mag., 1968-80. Author: Money and Stock Prices, 1964, Money and Markets-A Monetarist View, 1971; co-author: Winning with Money, 1977 Pres. Homewood-Flossmoor (Ill.) Community High Sch., 1959-60. With AUS, 1943-45. Recipient Hamilton Bolton award Fin. Analysts Assn., 1968, Alexander Hamilton award U.S. Treasury, 1985, Disting. Alumnus award U. Chgo., 1986, Disting. Alumnus award U. Mo., 2000. Fellow Nat. Assn. Bus. Economists; mem. Nat. Assn. Bus. Economists, Beta Gamma Sigma. Home (Winter): 16625 Waters Edge Fort Myers FL 33908 Personal E-mail: sprinkelec@comcast.net.

**SPRINKLE, MARTHA CLARE,** elementary school educator; b. Tehachapi, Calif., Oct. 17, 1944; d. William Foote and Mildred Sprinkle; BA, U. Calif., Santa Barbara, 1966; MA in Orgn. Mgmt., U. Phoenix, 2000. Cert. tchr. Calif., water aerobics instr. 1986. Tchr. Muroc Unified Sch. Dist., Edwards, Calif., 1966—71, Elk Hills Sch., Tupman, Calif., 1971—79, Tehachapi Valley Recreation and Pks., 1979—, So. Kern Unified Sch., Rosamond, Calif. 1984—2003. Planning commr. City of Tehachapi, Calif., 1984— Home: PO Box 852 Tehachapi CA 93581

**SPRINKLE, ROBERT LEE, JR.,** podiatrist; b. Winston-Salem, N.C., July 13, 1932; s. Robert Lee and Elton Elizabeth Sprinkle; children: Robert III, Karen, Ralph, Richard, Roy, Randy, Drouin; m. Nancy House Dixon. Student, Salem Coll., 1952; BS, Ohio Coll. Podiatry, 1956; DPM, Pa. Coll. Podiatry, 1970. Diplomate Am. Bd. Disability Analysts, Am. Coun. Cert. Podiatric Phys. and Surgeons, Sr. Acad. Ambulatory Podiatric Surgeons. Pvt. practice, Winston-Salem, 1957—. Chmn. N.C. Bd. Podiatry Examiners, 1968-74; clin. assoc. prof. Dr. William M. School Coll. Podiatric Medicine; researcher reconstructive surgery human foot and ankle; bd. dirs. Cmty. Gen. Hosp. Found., Thomasville, N.C.; bd. dirs. Am. Coun. Cert. Podiatric Phys. and Surgeons. Chmn. Mayor's Com. on Hiring the Handicapped, 1963-64; commr. Old Hickory Coun., Boy Scouts Am., 1970-71, v.p., 1973-74, Silver Beaver award, 1969, mem. adv. bd. Old North State Coun.; pres. St. Leo's Parochial Sch. PTA, 1969-70; dir. Halfway House, 1965-66; chmn. Bishop McGuiness PTA, 1976. Recipient St. George medal Charlotte Diocese, Roman Cath. Ch., 1971; Schering grantee, 1972-74. Mem. APHA, Am. Podiatric Med. Assn. (life mem.), N.C. Podiatry Assn. (past pres., Podiatrist of Yr. 1976), Piedmont Podiatry Assn., Acad. Ambulatory Podiatric Surgeons (life mem.), Internat. Analgesia Soc., Forsyth Country Club, Colonial Country Club, Twin City Club, KC (4th degree), SAR (life; N.C. state registrar, past pres. Bethabara chpt., N.C. state pres. 2002—, mem. George Washington Found.), SCV, NRA (life), Rotary (Paul Harris fellow, dist. gov. 1976-77), St. Andrew's Soc., Sons of the Revolution (life; state chpt. sec. pres. NCSSR). Republican. Roman Catholic. Home: 10 Mock St Thomasville NC 27360-4622 Office: ABC Family Foot and Ankle Clinic PO Box 366 17 W Main St Thomasville NC 27360-3934 Office Phone: 336-472-7543. Business E-Mail: foot1@northstate.net.

**SPRINKLE, WILLIAM MELVIN,** acoustical engineer, engineering executive; b. Washington, Sept. 2, 1945; s. Melvin Cline and Gladys Virginia (Miller) S.; div.; children: Timothy William, Allison Anne; m. Theresa Torregrossa Ellis, June, 2004. BS in Chemistry, Randolph-Macon Coll., 1967; M in Engring. Adminstrn., Va. Poly. Inst. & State U., 1990. Registered profl. engr., Va. Sr. cons. Sprinkle & Assocs., Kensington, Md., 1973-76; audio systems engr. Robertshaw Controls Co., Richmond, Va., 1976-80; sr. engr. TDFB-Engrs. & Archs., Richmond, 1980-85; property mgmt. officer Signet Bank, Richmond, 1985-87; asst. dir. engring. Va. Dept. Corrections, Richmond, 1987—. Mem. summer adj. faculty Eastman Sch. Music, Rochester, NY, 1974-83; bd. assocs. Randolph Macon Coll., 2005—. Editor newsletter Richmond Area Bicycling Assn.; contbr. Time Saver Standards for Architectural Design Data, 1982. Scoutmaster Boy Scouts Am., 1970-72, unit commr., 1990-92. Named Eagle Scout Boy Scouts Am. Mem. Acoustical Soc. Am., Pi Delta Epsilon (v.p.), Pres.'s Soc. Randolph Macon Coll. Baptist. Office: Dept of Corrections 6900 Atmore Dr Richmond VA 23225-5646

**SPRINTHALL, NORMAN ARTHUR,** psychology educator; b. Attleboro, Mass., Aug. 19, 1931; s. William Archie and Edith Jarvis (Clark) S.; m. Lois May Thies; children: Douglas, Jane, Carolyn. AB magna cum laude, Brown U., 1954, MA, 1959; EdD, Harvard U., 1963. Dir. fin. aid Brown U., 1955-60; asst. prof., then assoc. prof. psychology, program chmn. counseling Harvard U., 1963-72; mem. faculty U. Minn., Mpls., 1972-82, prof. ednl. psychology, 1973-82, program chmn. counseling, 1972-74; prof. psychology, head counselor edn. program N.C. State U., Raleigh, 1982-87, prof., counselor, 1987-95, prof. emeritus, 1995—. Co-dir. Ethical Reasoning Project in Pub. Adminstrn., U.S. and Poland, 1993-95, Russia, 1998-99. Author: Educational Psychology: Readings, 1969, Guidance for Human Growth, 1971, Educational Psychology: A Developmental Approach, 7th edit., 1998, Value Development as the Aim of Education, 2d edit., 1981, Adolescent Psychology: A Developmental View, 1984, 2d rev. edit., 1998, 3d edit., 1995; co-author: Stewart-Sprinthall Management Survey (SSMS) Ethics and Public Administration, others; mem. editl. bd. profl. jours. Bd. dirs. Josephson Inst. Advancement of Ethics, 1986-90, mem. bd. advisors Character Counts Coalition, 1994—2004. Fellow APA (Disting. Sr. Contbr. award): mem. Phi Beta Kappa. Office: Phone: 919-278-7899.

**SPRITZER, RALPH SIMON,** lawyer, educator; b. NYC, Apr. 27, 1917; s. Harry and Stella (Theuman) S.; m. Lorraine Nelson, Dec. 23, 1950; children: Ronald, Pamela. BS, Columbia U., 1937, LL.B., 1940. Bar: N.Y. bar 1941, U.S. Supreme Ct. bar 1950. Atty. Office Alien Property, Dept. Justice, 1946-51; anti-trust div. Dept. Justice, 1951-54, Office Solicitor Gen., 1954-61; gen. counsel FPC, 1961-62; 1st asst. to solicitor gen. U.S., 1962-68; prof. law U. Pa., Phila., 1968-86, Ariz. State U., Tempe, 1986—; gen. counsel AAUP, 1983-84. Adj. prof. law George Wasington U., 1967; cons. Adminstrv. Conf. U.S., Ford Found., Pa. Gov.'s Justice Commn. Served with AUS, 1941-46. Recipient Superior Service award Dept. Justice, 1960; Tom C. Clark award Fed. Bar. Assn., 1968 Mem. Am. Law Inst. Home: 1024 E Gemini Dr Tempe AZ 85283-3004 Office: Ariz State Univ Coll Law Tempe AZ 85287 Office Phone: 480-965-7419.

**SPRIZZO, JOHN EMILIO,** federal judge; b. Bklyn., Dec. 23, 1934; s. Vincent James and Esther Nancy S.; children— Ann Esther, Johna Emily, Matthew John. BA summa cum laude, St. John's U., Jamaica, N.Y., 1956; LLB summa cum laude, St. John's U., 1959. Bar: N.Y. 1960. Atty. U.S. Dept. Justice, 1959-63; asst. U.S. atty. so. dist. N.Y. Dept. Justice, N.Y.C., 1963-68; chief appellate atty., 1965-66, asst. chief criminal div., 1966-68; assoc. prof. Fordham U. Law Sch., N.Y.C., 1968-72; prtnr. Curtis, Mallet-Prevost, N.Y.C., 1972-81; judge U.S. Dist. Ct. (So. Dist.), N.Y., 1981—2000, sr. judge NY, 2000—. Cons. Nat. Com. for Reform of Criminal Laws, N.Y.C., 1971-72; mem. Knapp Commn., 1971-72; assoc. atty. Com. on Judiciary, N.Y., 1971-72 Co-contbr. articles to profl. law revs. Mem. ABA, D.C. Bar Assn., Assn. of Bar of City of N.Y. Office: US Dist Ct US Courthouse 500 Pearl St Rm 730 New York NY 10007-1502

**SPROAT, EDWARD F., III, (WARD SPROAT),** federal agency administrator; b. Sept. 12, 1951; With Gas Cooled Reactor Assocs., La Jolla, Calif.; mgr.-nuc. group bus. unit, mgr. projects Limerick Engring. Station PECO Energy, sect. mgr. computer engring., mgr. elec. engring. nuc. generation br., dir. quality mgmt. Phila. Electric, 1991—94, dir. engring. PECO Nuc., dir. engring and maintenance Limerick Nuc. Generating Station, dir. strategic programs PECO Nuc.; v.p. internat. projects Exelon Generation, bd. dirs., COO Board of Pebble Bed Modular Reactor Pty. Ltd. South Africa, 2002;

mng. ptnr. McNeill, Sproat & Assocs., LLC, Berwyn, Pa.; dir. Office Civilian Radioactive Waste Mgmt. US Dept. Energy, Washington, 2006—. Office: US Dept Energy 1000 Independence Ave SW Washington DC 20585*

**SPROAT, JOHN GERALD,** historian, educator; b. LA, Apr. 1, 1921; s. John Gerald and Grace (Elwell) Drummond S.; m. Ruth Christensen, Mar. 18, 1967; 1 child from previous marriage, Barbara BA, San Jose State Coll., 1950; MA, U. Calif.-Berkeley, 1952, PhD, 1959. Instr. Mich. State U., 1956-57; asst. prof. Williams Coll., 1957-63; prof. Lake Forest Coll., Ill., 1963-74; prof. history U. S.C., Columbia, 1974-92, chmn. dept., 1974-83; dist. prof. emeritus, 1992—; sr. fellow Inst. for So. Studies, 1992—. Fulbright prof. Hamburg U., Fed. Republic Germany, 1961-62; vis. fellow Cambridge U., Eng., 1970; vis. prof. U. Calif., Berkeley, 1972; Fulbright prof. U. Munich, Fed. Republic Germany, 1982, Indonesia, 1993-94; Am. participant lectr. USIA, India, Pakistan, 1987; mem. S.C. Commn. Archives and History, 1974-83, chmn., 1979-83; mem. S.C. Bd. Rev. Hist. Places, 1974-86, chmn., 1978-83; del. Am. Council Learned Socs. Author: The Best Men: Liberal Reformers in the Gilded Age, 1968, 3d edit., 1972; (with others) The Shaping of America, 1972, Making Change: South Carolina Banking in the 20th Century, 1990; contbr. chpts. to books; exec. producer A Bond of Iron, S.C. ETV, 1979; gen. editor So. Classics Series. Past pres., trustee Columbia Mus. Art; pres. Historic Columbia Found., 1997-99. With USAAF, 1941-45. Grantee, NEH, 1976-77, 1979, 1985, Shell Found., 1967, 1970, 1973, Lilly Endowment, 1966—67. Mem. Am. Hist. Assn., Orgn. Am. Historians, So. Hist. Assn., Summit Club. Home: 1686 Woodlake Dr Columbia SC 29206-4647 Office: U SC Inst For So Studies Columbia SC 29208-0001 Office Phone: 803-777-4477. Personal E-mail: jgsproat@sc.rr.com.

**SPROAT, RUTH C.,** retired director, consultant; b. Lake Forest, Ill., Aug. 22, 1930; d. Christian Peter and Anna Elsa Christensen; m. Robert M. Volpe (div.); m. John Gerald Sproat, Mar. 18, 1967; 1 stepchild, Barbara Jeanne. BA in History, Lake Forest Coll., 1952; MA in History, Northwestern U., 1962. Registrar, admissions counselor Lake Forest Coll., 1948—68, dir. alumni affairs, 1972—74; dir. Master's Degree Program, asst. to pres. Lake Forest Coll. Grad. Sch. Mgmt., 1968—70, asst. to pres., 1971—72; dir. higher edn. SC Ednl. TV Network, Columbia, 1974—80, asst. dir. programming, exec. prodr., prodr., 1980—82, dir. higher edn., project dir., prodr., exec. prodr., 1982—87, asst. to pres. for devel. Satellite Ednl. Resources Consortium, 1988—92, exec. staff, dir. planning, grants and rsch., project dir., exec. prodr., 1992—97, cons. and asst. to pres., 2000—02; dir. devel. U. SC, Columbia, 1997—99; ret., 2002; cons. in field, 2002—. V.p. S.C. chpt. Am. Women in Radio and TV, 1983; co-prodr. with Am. Film Inst. Am. TV and Video Festival, India, 1985, prodr., presenter, India, 1986—91. Project dir., grant writer (PBS TV series) Voices and Visions; U.S. project dir. Spaceship Earth; coordinating prodr. Cinematic Eye (Day Time Emmy award). Mentor to devel. staff Columbia Mus. Art, 2002. Recipient Alumni Disting. Svc. citation, Lake Forest Coll., 1987. Mem.: Hist. Columbia Found., Ill. Assn. Coll. Registrars and Admissions Officers (hon.; pres. 1965), Am. Assn. Collegiate Registrars and Admissions Officers (hon. sec. 1966—68), Riverbanks Zoo Soc., Friends of U. S.C. Sch. Music (sec. 2001—03, dir. publicity for ann. fundraiser 2002—03, 2003—04, v.p. 2005—), State Mus. S.C., Sierra Club. Democrat. Avocations: gardening, writing, photography, travel. Home: 1686 Woodlake Dr Columbia SC 29206 E-mail: rcsproat@sc.rr.com.

**SPROGER, CHARLES EDMUND,** retired lawyer; b. Chgo., Feb. 18, 1933; s. William and Minnette (Weiss) Sproger. BA (David Himmelblau scholar), Northwestern U., 1954, JD, 1957. Bar: Ill. 1957. Assoc. Ehrlich & Cohn, 1958-63, Ehrlich, Bundesen, Friedman & Ross, 1963-72; partner Ehrlich, Bundesen, Broecker & Sproger, 1972-77; pvt. practice, 1977—2000; ret., 2000. Mem. adv. com. curriculum Ill. Inst. Continuing Legal Edn., Chgo., 1976—90; v.p. Mediation Coun. of Ill., 1986-87; arbitration panelist for Cir. Ct. Cook County, 1990—. Editor: Family Lawyer, 1962-63; contbr. articles to legal publs. Mediator Pastoral Psychotherapy Inst., 1982-86, vol. Coun. for Jewish Elderly, Chgo., 2002-. Recipient Vol. of Yr. award, Coun. for Jewish Elderly, 2004. Fellow Am. Acad. Matrimonial Lawyers (bd. examiners 1972-86, chmn. Law Day U.S.A. 1975); mem. ABA, Ill. Bar Assn. (chmn. coun. family law 1970-71), Chgo. Bar Assn. (matrimonial law com. 1958-2000), Am. Arbitration Assn. (divorce mediation com. 1983-92), Decalogue Soc., U. Mich. Club Chgo. (pres. 1988-89, bd. dirs. 1987-2004), Phi Alpha Delta. Address: 2800 W Birchwood Ave Chicago IL 60645-1218

**SPROLE, FRANK ARNOTT,** retired pharmaceutical executive, lawyer; b. Bklyn., Sept. 13, 1918; s. Frank Newland and Eleanor Arnott (Greenberg) S.; m. Sarah Louise Knapp, Sept. 23, 1944; children— Wendy Sprole Bangs, Frank J., Anne Sprole Mauk, Jonathan K., Sarah Sprole Obregon. BA, Yale U., 1942; LLB. Columbia U., 1949. Bar: N.Y. 1949. Assoc. firm Winthrop Stimson, Putnam & Roberts, N.Y.C., 1949-50; atty. Bristol-Myers Co. N.Y.C., 1950-52, asst. sec., 1952-55, sec., 1955-67, v.p., 1965-73, sr. v.p., 1973-77, vice-chmn. bd., 1977-84; ret., 1984. Officer Proprietary Assn., Washington, 1978-84; dir., officer Knapp Fund, N.Y.C., 1960-93. Pres. bd. trustees Hotchkiss Sch., Lakeville, Conn., 1980-85; trustee Internat. Inst. Rural Reconstrn., N.Y.C., and Manila, 1983-87. Lt. comdr. USNR, 1942-45, PTO. Mem. Assn. of Bar of City of N.Y., Yale Club of N.Y.C., Wee Burn Country Club, Bohemian Club, John's Island Club, Riomar Country Club. Republican. Episcopalian. Home: 394 Mansfield Ave Darien CT 06820-2112

**SPROSTY, JOSEPH PATRICK,** film producer, writer, motion picture weapons specialist; b. Cleve., Aug. 25, 1947; s. Joseph Patrick and Anna Margret (Louchka) S. Grad.. Maphard H.S., Middleburgh, Ohio, 1965; student, San Diego City Coll., 1972—73. Class 2 firearms lic. Prop builder The Goulardi Show WJW-TV8, Cleve., 1962-65; sub-agent Internat. Artists Agy., San Diego and L.A., 1982-83; casting dir. Cinemode Films, 1982; operator, owner Actors Artists Agy., L.A., 1983-87; founder, prodr., dir. Magnum Prodns., 1985; founder Sprosty Prodns., 1990. Demonstrator weapons and handling of weapons, Propmaster TV Co., Van Nuys, Calif., 1992; expert witness Laser Weapon Scam, 1984; vis. lectr. firearms safety, handling, rules and regulations governing use of firearms in motion picture, TV prodn. U. So. Calif., 1996—; animal wrangler specializing in opossums, Hollywood: (films) Vanishing Point II, The Apartment Manager, The Big House, Rambo III (optioned), Rambo IV (revised), Boneyard, Mister Ed - Talking Again, Mister Ed - Radio Talk, Brick, Life Plus One, Gun Slave, Fixation, Last Chance (renamed Terminal Virus), You're So Beautiful, Home Dead Home, Kung Fu Cop, The Fisherman, numerous others; prodr., dir. (video) Break Disc, 1985; location mgr., armorer, weapons splst.: (film) Heat from Another Sun (retitled Malediction), 1988; armorer, 2nd asst. dir., assoc. prodr., weapons splst.: (film) Provoked, 1989; weapons splst.: (film) Big City, 1990; co-prodr., animal wrangler, weapons splst.: (film) Opossum de Oro, 1996; weapons splst.: (tv shows) Jake and the Fat Man, Black's Magic, Hill Street Blues, Murder, She Wrote, On the Edge of Death, Emerald Point N.A.S., (7 episodes) America's Most Wanted, (3 episodes) FBI: The Untold Stories, prodr., numerous others, (films) Revolt, Body IV, Streets of Fire, Walk in the Sun, Cloak & Dagger, One Man's Poison, Killing Zoe, Desert Storm, The Movie, Live Shot, Outer Heat, Zipperhead, Four Minute Warning, The Robbery, Spirit, Texas Payback, High Adventure, The Waterfront, The Philadelphia Experiment II, Opossum de Oro, Harlem Nights, Tango & Cash, Die Hard, Provoked, Beverly Hills Cop II, Big City, prodr., weapons splst. Big Bruce's Ballistic Babes, Girls Gone Ballistic, 2004, numerous others. Spkr. Veterans Day Calif. State U., Dominguez Hills, 1993. Served with USN, 1965-67 (hon. discharge). Mem. AFTRA, SAG (charter mem. San Diego br.). Home: 337 W Maple St Glendale CA 91204-2014 Office Phone: 818-244-9214.

**SPROTT, RICHARD LAWRENCE,** foundation administrator, researcher; b. Tampa, Fla., Aug. 9, 1940; s. Joseph Albert and Marie Marguerite (Goaper) S.; m. Margaret Ann Weidel, June 19, 1965; children: Lynn Marie, Deborah Ann. Student, Franklin and Marshall Coll., 1958—60; BA, U. N.C., 1962, MA in Psychology, 1964; PhD in Psychology, 1965. Asst. prof. Bowdoin Coll., Brunswick, Maine, 1965-67; assoc. prof. Clark U., Worcester, Mich., 1967-69; assoc. staff scientist Jackson Lab., Bar Barbor, Maine, 1969-71; staff scientist, 1971-80; health scientist adminstr. Divsn. Rsch. Resources, NIH, Bethesda, Md., 1980-81; br. chief Nat. Inst. on Aging,

Bethesda, 1981-84, assoc. dir., 1984-98; exec. dir. Ellison Med. Found., Bethesda, 1998—. Editor: Hormonal Correlates of Behavior, 1975, Age, Learning Ability and Intelligence, 1980; mem. editl. bd. Exptl. Aging Rsch. Jour., 1978-; contbr. articles to profl. jours. Mem. Bar Harbor Town Coun. 1975-79, chmn., 1978-79; mem. bd. appeals Town of Bar Harbor, 1972-75, mem. warrant com., 1972-75. NIH fellow, 1965-67; NIH grantee, 1969-79; recipient Kent award Gerontologic Soc. Am., 1997. Fellow Am. Psychol. Assn., Gerontol. Soc. Am.; mem. Behavior Genetics Assn. (membership chmn. 1979). Home: 11514 Regency Dr Potomac MD 20854-3733 Office: Ellison Med Found 4710 Bethesda Ave Ste 204 Bethesda MD 20814-5226 Office Phone: 301-657-1830. E-mail: rsprott@ellisonfoundation.org.

**SPROUL, JOHN ALLAN,** retired utilities executive; b. Oakland, Calif., Mar. 28, 1924; s. Robert Gordon and Ida Amelia (Wittschen) S.; m. Marjorie Ann Hauck, June 20, 1945; children: John Allan, Malcolm J., Richard O., Catherine E. AB, U. Calif., Berkeley, 1947, LL.B., 1949. Bar: Calif. 1950. Atty. Pacific Gas & Electric Co., San Francisco, 1949-52, 56-62, sr. atty., 1962-70, asst. gen. counsel, 1970-71, v.p. gas supply, 1971-76, sr. v.p., 1976-77, exec. v.p., 1977-89; ret.; gen. counsel Pacific Gas Transmission Co., 1970-73, v.p., 1973-79, chmn. bd., 1979-89, also bd. dirs. Atty. Johnson & Stanton, San Francisco, 1952-56. Bd. dirs. emeritus Hastings Coll. Law. Served to 1st lt. USAAF, 1943-46. Mem. Calif. Bar Assn. (inactive), Pacific Coast Gas Assn., Pacific-Union Club, Orinda Country Club. Home: 8413 Buckingham Dr El Cerrito CA 94530-2531 Office: Pacific Gas & Electric Co Mail Code B26 PO Box 770000 San Francisco CA 94177-0001 also: Pacific Gas & Electric Co 77 Beale St Rm 2680 San Francisco CA 94105-1814 Office Phone: 415-973-2693. Office Fax: 415-973-8808. Personal E-mail: johnsprawl@comcast.net.

**SPROULE, JAMES MICHAEL,** dean, communications educator; b. Dayton, Ohio, Feb. 8, 1949; s. John Harper and Katherine Veronica Sproule; m. Betty Ann Mathis, Mar. 3, 1973; children: John Harold, Kevin William. BA, MA, Ohio State U., Columbus, 1971, PhD, 1973. Asst. prof. U. of Tex. of Permian Basin, Odessa, 1973—77; assoc. prof. Ind. U. S.E., New Albany, 1977—86; vis. lectr. U. of Calif., Berkeley, 1986—87; prof. San Jose (Calif.) State U., 1987—2001; prof., dir. Bowling Green (Ohio) State U., 2001—04; prof., dean St. Louis U., 2004—. Author: (book) The Rhetoric of Western Thought, Propaganda and Democracy, Channels of Propaganda, Speechmaking, Communication Today, Argument: Language and Its Influence. Recipient Golden Anniversary Monograph award, Nat. Comm. Assn., 1988; fellow, NEH, 1983. Mem.: Western States Comm. Assn., Internat. Soc. for the History of Rhetoric, Author's Guild, Nat. Comm. Assn. (pres. 2006—). Home: 3655 Flora Pl Saint Louis MO 63110-3703 Office: St Louis Univ Saint Louis MO 63108 Personal E-mail: sproulej@slu.edu.

**SPROULE, MICHAEL E.,** insurance company executive; b. Toronto, Canada; m. Doreen Sproule; 3 children. BA in Math, Physics, U. Toronto, MBA in Fin., Mktg. Cons. Tillinghast; various positions MetLife; former sr. v.p., CFO Alper Holdings USA, Inc., NYC; exec. v.p., CFO AmerUs Group; sr. v.p. New York Life, 1999—2001, 2002—03, acting CFO, 2001, CFO, 2002—, exec. v.p., 2003—. Fellow: Soc. Actuaries; mem.: Am. Acad. Actuaries. Office: New York Life 51 Madison Ave New York NY 10010*

**SPROULL, ROBERT FLETCHER,** research and development company executive; b. Ithaca, N.Y., June 6, 1947; s. Robert L. and Mary L. Sproull; m. Lee Sonastine, June 26, 1971; 1 child, Katherine. AB in Physics, Harvard U., 1968; MS in Computer Sci., Stanford U., 1970, PhD in Computer Sci., 1977. Mem. rsch. staff Xerox Palo Alto Rsch. Ctr., 1973—77; asst. prof. Carnegie Mellon U., Pitts., 1977-80, assoc. prof., 1980-83; v.p. Sutherland, Sproull & Assoc., Pitts., 1980-90, Sun Microsystems Lab., Burlington, Mass., 1990—2006, fellow, 1990—, interim dir., 2000—06, dir., 2006—. Venture ptnr. Advanced Tech. Ventures, 1981—; mem. tech. adv. coun. R. F. Donnelley & Sons, Chgo., 1981—89; mem. adv. com. NSF, Washington, 1990—97; bd. dirs. Alphatech, Inc., 2000—04. Co-author: (book) Principles of Interactive Computer Graphics, 1979, Logical Effort: Designing Fast CMOS Circuits (The Morgan Kaufmann Series in Computer Architecture and Design). Mem. sci. adv. bd. USAF, 1997—99. Sr. asst. health svcs. officer USPHS, 1970—72. Fellow: Am. Acad. Arts & Scis.; mem.: NAE (councillor 2006—). Achievements include patents in field. Office: SUN Microsystems Lab ubur02-311 1 Network Dr Burlington MA 01803-2757 Office Phone: 781-442-0353. Personal E-mail: bob.sproull@sun.com.

**SPROULL, ROBERT LAMB,** retired academic administrator, physicist, director; b. Lacon, Ill., Aug. 16, 1918; s. John Steele and Chloe Velma (Lamb) S.; m. Mary Louise Knickerbocker, June 27, 1942; children: Robert F., Nancy M. Sproull Highbarger. AB, Cornell U., 1940, PhD, 1943; LLD (hon.), Nazareth Coll., 1983; DMusic (hon.), New Eng. Conservatory, 1997. Research physicist RCA labs., 1943-46; faculty Cornell U., 1946-63, 65-68, prof. physics, 1956-63, dir. lab. atomic and solid state physics, 1959-60, dir. materials sci. center, 1960-63, v.p for acad. affairs, 1965-68; dir. Advanced Research Projects Agy., Dept. Def., Washington, 1963-65; v.p., provost U. Rochester, NY, 1968-70, pres., 1970-84, pres. emeritus, 1984—. Prin. physicist Oak Ridge Nat. Lab., 1952; physicist European Rsch. Assoc., Brussels, 1958-59; lectr. NATO, 1958-59; pres. Environ. Literacy Coun., 1997-99, chmn. 1999—; past bd. dirs., John Wiley & Sons, Charles River Labs., United Technols. Corp., Xerox Corp., Bausch & Lomb; mem. sci. adv. com. GM Corp., 1971-80, chmn., 1973-80; mem. Def. Sci. Bd., Home-26-70, chmn., 1968-70; mem. naval Rsch. Adv. Coun., 1974-76, Sloan Commn. Higher Edn., 1977-79, N.Y. Regents Commn. Higher Edn., 1992-93. Author: Modern Physics, 1956, A Scientist's Tools for Business, 1997; Editor: Jour. Applied Physics, 1954-57. Trustee Deep Springs Coll., 1967—75, 1983—87, Cornell U., 1972—77. Ctr. for Advanced Study in Behavioral Scis. fellow, 1973; Meritorious Civilian Svc. medal Sec. of Def., 1970. Fellow Am. Acad. Arts and Scis.; mem. Telluride Assn. (pres. 1945-47), Inst. of Def. Analysis (trustee 1984-92). Home: 6 Eliot Circle Pittsford NY 14534 Personal E-mail: lambspr@aol.com.

**SPROUSE, JAMES EDWARD,** lawyer; b. Clarksville, Tenn., July 11, 1943; s. James Edward Sprouse and Grace Pratt (Stacker) Cunningham; m. Sharon Dow, July 10, 1965; children: Kathleen, Shannon, Barbara. BS in Indsl. Mgmt., Ga. Inst. Tech., 1965; JD cum laude, U. Ga., 1971. Bar: Ga. 1971. Chem. sales profl. Dow Chem. Co., Midland, Mich., 1965-68; assoc. Bouhan, Williams & Levy, Savannah, Ga., 1971-72, Arnall, Golden & Gregory, Atlanta, 1972-74; ptnr. Sprouse, Tucker & Ford, PC, Columbus, Ga., 1974-77; prin. Sprouse, Tucker & Ford, PC, Columbus, 1977-96, Page, Scranton, Sprouse, Tucker & Ford, Columbus, 1996—. Mem. Trinity Episcopal Ch., 1974—, vestry mem., 1977-79, 83-85, Sunday sch. tchr., 1978-79, co-chmn. every member canvas, 1981; bd. dirs. Ctrl. YMCA, 1975-78, Met. Boys Club Columbus, 1976-82, Country Club Columbus, Inc., 1985-88; trustee Hist. Columbus Found., Inc., 1976—, pres., 1983-85, exec. com., 1983—, chmn. bd. trustees, 1986—; bd. dirs. Anne Elizabeth Shepherd Home, Inc., 1978-81, treas., 1979-81; trustee St. Francis Hosp., 1980-2001, chmn. bd. trustees, 1995-97; chmn. legal divsn. United Way Campaigns, 1982, 94; trustee Columbus Mus. Arts & Scis., Inc., 1983-88, 94-96; vice chmn., trustee Hughston Sports Medicine Found., Inc., 1983-86; trustee, mem. exec. com. Uptown Columbus, Inc., 1988-2000, bd. trustees, 1994-95; mem. bd. dirs., exec. com. Big Eddy Club, Inc., 1986-88; mem. Columbus Tech. Coll. Found., 2000-, chmn. 2004-05; mem. Muscogee Edn. Excellence Found., 2000-, chmn 2005. Mem. ABA (tax sect., corp. law sect., com. on banking), State Bar Ga. (corp. and bus. law sect., tax sect., real property law sect., lectr. CLE, corp. code revision com., co-chmn. basic lawyers handbook program young lawyers sect. 1973-76), Columbus Lawyers Club, Columbus Rotary Club (bd. dirs. 1988-91, 2004—, pres. 2005—, trustee Rotary Ednl. Fund), Greater Columbus C. of C. (bd. dirs. 1982-84, exec. com. 1996-98, chmn. bd. dirs. 1988), Candun Club, Omicron Delta Kappa, Sigma Alpha Epsilon, Phi Kappa Phi, Phi Beta Kappa, Phi Delta Phi. Office: Page Scrantom Sprouse Tucker & Ford 1111 Bay Ave Third Flr Columbus GA 31901-2501 Office Phone: 706-243-5603.

**SPROVIERI, BRIDGETTE ANN,** social worker, school system administrator; b. Oaklawn, Ill., Jan. 19, 1976; d. Timothy Fenton and Claudette Ann Bernatowicz; m. Paul Richard Sprovieri, Aug. 26, 1975. BSW, Quincy U., Ill., 1994—98; MSW, Aurora U. Ill., 1999—2001; MA in Spl. Edn., Lewis U., Romeoville, Ill., 2002—06. Lic. Social Worker Ill., 2003. Sch. social worker Christ Hosp., Oaklawn, Ill., 1999—2006; dean of students Valley View Sch. Dist., Romeoville, 2002—. Office: Valley View Sch Dist 755 Luther Dr Romeoville IL 60446 Office Phone: 815-886-6100. Office Fax: 815-886-7824. Personal E-mail: bridgettesprovieri@sbcglobal.net.

**SPROW, FRANK BARKER,** oil company executive; b. Council Bluffs, Iowa, Nov. 20, 1939; s. Dwight Barker and Lucille (Tuttle) S.; m. Ann Bledsoe, Aug. 24, 1962; children: John, Diane. BS in Chem. Engring., MIT, 1962, MS in Chem. Engring., 1963; PhD in Chem. Engring., U. Calif., Berkeley, 1965. Jr. engr. Humble Oil and Refining Co., Baytown, Tex., 1962, sr. analyst long range supply Houston, 1971-75; sr. rsch. chem. engr./Sp/Sh Esso Rsch. and Engr. Co., Baytown, 1965-71; tech. mgr. Bayway Ref. Exxon Co. U.S.A., Linden, N.J., 1975-77, ops. mgr. Bayway Ref., 1977-79; gr. mgr. petroleum programs Exxon Rsch. and Engring. Co., Florham Park, N.J., 1979-80, v.p. synthetic fuels rsch., 1980-82, v.p. tech. support Annandale, N.J., 1982-86, v.p. corp. rsch., 1986—93, v.p. petroleum & synthetic fuels rsch., 1993—95; v.p., environment & safety ExxonMobil Corp. (formerly Exxon Corp.), 1995—. Mem. governing bd. Coun. for Chem. Rsch., Washington, 1984—; bd. dirs. Exxon Edn. Found., Dallas, 1986—. Contbr. articles to jours. in field. Bd. dirs. R & D Coun. N.J., Parsippany, 1985—, N.J. Safety Coun., Newark, 1983—; campaign officer Republican Party, various elections, Mercer County, N.J. Recipient award in computing Max Planck Soc., Fed. Republic Germany, 1988. Mem. Am. Inst. Chem. Engrs., Soc. Automotive Engrs., Nassau Club (Princeton, N.J.).

**SPROWL, CHARLES RIGGS,** lawyer; b. Lansing, Mich., Aug. 22, 1910; s. Charles Orr and Hazel (Allen) S.; m. Virginia Lee Graham, Jan. 15, 1938; children: Charles R., Robert A., Susan G., Sandra D. AB, U. Mich., 1932, JD, 1934. Bar: Ill. 1935. Pvt. practice, 1934—; of counsel Taylor, Miller, Sprowl, Hoffnagle & Merletti, 1986—. Dir. Simmons Engring. Corp., Petersen Aluminum Corp. Mem. Bd. Edn., New Trier Twp. High Sch., 1959-65, pres. 1962-65; mem. Glencoe Zoning Bd. Appeals, 1956-76, chmn., 1966-76; mem Glencoe Plan Commn., 1962-65; bd. dirs. Glencoe Pub. Libr., 1953-65, pres. 1955-56; trustee Highland Park Hosp., 1959-69; bd. dirs. Cradle Soc., 1968-92. Fellow Am. Coll. Trial Lawyers; mem. Chgo. Bar Assn. (bd. mgrs. 1949-51), Ill. Bar Assn., ABA, Juvenile Protective Assn. (dir. 1943-53), Northwestern U. Settlement (pres. 1963-70, dir.), Soc. Trial Lawyers, Law Club (pres. 1969-70), Legal Club (pres. 1953-54), Skokie Country Club, Delta Theta Phi, Alpha Chi Rho. Presbyterian. Home: 380 Green Bay Rd Apt 2A Winnetka IL 60093-4051 Office: 33 N La Salle St Chicago IL 60602-2603

**SPRUILL, W. MURRAY,** lawyer; b. Columbia, NC, Mar. 24, 1954; BS in Biology, E. Carolina Univ., 1976; PhD in Genetics, Molecular Biology, NC State Univ., 1981; JD, George Washington Univ., 1992. Bar: Va. 1992, NC 1996, registered: US Patent and Trademark Off. Sr. atty. Ciba-Geigy Corp.; patent examiner US Patent and Trademark Office, Washington; ptnr., chmn., biotech., pharmaceutical patent group, Research Triangle Alston & Bird LLP, Raleigh, NC. Frequent lectr. and author on biotech. and pharmaceutical patent law. Office: Alston & Bird LLP Ste 600 3201 Beechleaf Ct Raleigh NC 27604-1062 Office Phone: 919-862-2202. Office Fax: 919-862-2260. Business E-mail: mspruill@alston.com.

**SPRUNG, DONALD WHITFIELD LOYAL,** physics professor; s. Lyall MacCaulay and Doreene Bishop (Price) S.; m. Hannah Sueko Nagai, Dec. 12, 1958; children: Anne Elizabeth, Carol Hanako. BA, U. Toronto, Ont., 1957; PhD, U. Birmingham, Eng., 1961, DSc, 1970. Asst lectr. U. Birmingham, England, 1960-61; instr. Cornell U., Ithaca, NY, 1961-62; rsch. staff lab. nuclear sci. MIT, 1964-65; asst. prof. McMaster U., Hamilton, Ont., 1962-66, assoc. prof., 1966-71, physics prof., 1971—, dean faculty sci., 1975-84, 89, mem. bd. govs., 1986-90, chair dept. physics and astronomy, 1991-97. Vis. prof. U. Barcelona, Spain, 1991-92, 95, McMaster Cmty. Homes Corp. (pres. 2004-). Contbr. articles to profl. jours. C.D. Howe fellow, 1969-70, Rotary Found. fellow, 1957-58. Fellow Royal Soc. Can.; mem. Can. Assn. Physicists (Herzberg medal 1972, medal for outstanding achievement 1997), Am. Phys. Soc.; mem. Inst. Physics. Avocations: bicycling, cabinet making. Office: McMaster Univ Dept Physics and Astronomy 1280 Main St W Hamilton ON Canada L8S 4M1

**SPRUNG, WILLIAM,** school system administrator; s. Bill Sprung; m. Judi Sprung, June 19, 1982; children: Allison, Matthew. AA, ND State Sch. Sci., 1979; BA, Moorhead State U., 1982; MA, ND State U., 1988. Lic. tchr. Minn., 1982. Tchr. Sydney Pub. Schools, Mont., 1982—84, Killdeer Pub. Schools, ND, 1984—88; elem. prin. Norman County West Pub. Schools, Hendrum, Minn., 1988—90, Lidgerwood Pub. Schools, ND, 1990—94; dir. ednl. services New Ulm Pub. Schools, Minn., 1994—. Dir., coach New Ulm Basketball Assn., 1994—98, New Ulm Football Assn., 1998—2000; asst. scout master, dist. chair Boy Scouts of Am., New Ulm, 1998—2005; eucharistic min., lector St. Mary's Cath. Ch., New Ulm, 1994; dir. New Ulm Cable Commn., 2006. Recipient Bell Ringer award, ND Assn. Elem. Sch. Principals, 1994. Mem.: New Ulm C of C (bd. mem. 2001—04), Minn. Rural Edn. Assn. (legislative action com. 2003), Minn. Assn. Sch. Administrators, Sioux Valley Supt. Org. (dir. 2004), Sertoma (dir. 2004—05). Office: New Ulm Pub Schools 400 South Payne St New Ulm MN 56073

**SPRUNGER, KEITH L.,** historian, educator; b. Berne, Ind., Mar. 16, 1935; s. Arley and Lillian (Mettler) S.; m. Aldine Mary Slagell, June 13, 1959; children: David, Mary, Philip. BA, Wheaton Coll., 1957; MA, U. Ill., 1958, PhD, 1963. Tchr. Berne (Ind.) High Sch., 1958-60; Oswald H. Wedel prof. history Bethel Coll., N. Newton, Kans., 1963—2001. Author: Dutch Puritanism, 1982, The Learned Doctor William Ames, 1972, Voices against War, 1973, Auction Catalogue of The Library of William Ames, 1988, Trumpets From The Tower, 1994, Campus, Congregation, and Community, 1997. Mem. Newton Historic Preservation Commn.; bd. dirs. Germantown Mennonite Historic Trust. Recipient Harbison award for gifted teaching Danforth Found., 1972; fellow Social Sci. Rsch. Coun., 1969, Am. Coun. Learned Soc. fellow, 1976, Huntington Libr. fellow, 1982, 90; grantee Am. Philos. Soc., 1967, 1969, 83, The Netherlands Orgn. for Advancement of Pure Rsch., 1983. Fellow Pilgrim Soc.; m.em. AAUP, Am. Hist. Assn., Am. Soc. Ch. History (coun. 1974-76), Conf. on Faith and History. Mennonite. Avocation: book collecting. Home: 2412 Clg Ave North Newton KS 67117 Office: Bethel Coll 300 E 27th St North Newton KS 67117 Office Phone: 316-283-2500. Business E-mail: sprunger@bethelks.edu.

**SPRUNGER, LESLIE KAREN,** physiologist, educator; b. Palo Alto, Calif., Aug. 29, 1961; d. Richard Marmion and Patricia Joann (Sprunger) Oldacre; 1 child, Katherine Elyse Traynor. BS, U. Alaska, 1983; DVM, Wash. State U., 1987; PhD, U. Minn., 1995. Vet. Alder Trail Animal Hosp., Bremerton, Wash., 1987-88; vet. med. assoc. U. Minn. Dept. Vet. Pathobiology, St. Paul, 1988-94; rsch. assoc. U. Minn. Dept. Physiology, Mpls., 1994-95; rsch. investigator human genetics U. Mich., Ann Arbor, 1995—2000; asst. prof. Wash. State U., 2000—. Howard Huges Med. Inst. cons., 2003—. Contbr. articles to profl. jours. including Jour. Vet. Med. Edn., Jour. Comparative Neurology, Neuron, Jour. Neurosci. Cell & Tissue Rsch., Human Molecular Genetics. Tutor ESL Project Literacy, Mpls., 1988-89. Grantee NIH, 1994-2000; Howard Hughes Med. Inst. fellow, 1989-94. Mem. Am. Assn. Anatomists, Soc. Gen. Physiologists, Soc. for Neurosci., Internat. Mouse Genome Soc., Sigma Xi, Phi Zeta. Democrat. Avocations: reading, music, exercise. Office: Dept of Veterinary and Comparative Anatomy Pharmacology and Physiology Wash State U 205 Wegner Hall Pullman WA 99164-6520 Office Phone: 509-335-7071. Business E-mail: lsprunger@wsu.edu.

**SPRY, DONALD FRANCIS, II,** lawyer; b. Bethlehem, Pa., Nov. 17, 1947; s. Donald Francis and Carol Annette (Bolger) S.; m. Mary Frances, June 20, 1981; stepchildren: Michael Matlaga, Michelle Fehnel. BA, Moravian Coll.,

1969; JD, U. Pitts., 1972. Bar: Pa. 1972, U.S. Dist. Ct. (ea. dist.) Pa. 1975. Assoc. Law Offices of Edmund P. Turtzo, Bangor, Pa., 1973—76; ptnr. Turtzo, Spry, Powlette & Sbrocchi, P.C., Bangor, 1976—83, Turtzo, Spry, Powlette, Sbrocchi & Faul, P.C., Bangor and Stroudsburg, Pa., 1983—90, Turtzo, Spry, Sbrocchi, Faul & LaBarre, P.C., Bangor and Stroudsburg, 1990—2000; mem. King, Spry, Herman, Freund & Faul, LLC, Bethlehem, 2001—. Capt. USAR, 1979-80. Mem. ABA (family law sect.), Pa. Bar Assn. (chmn. family law sect. edn. law com.) Northampton County Bar Assn. (family law com.), North County Bar Assn. (pres.-elect 1989, pres. 1990), Pa. Sch. Bds. Assn., Nat. Sch. Bds. Assn., ACLU, Edn. Law Assn., Pomfret Club. Republican. Methodist. Office: King Spry Herman Freund & Faul LLC 1 W Broad St Bethlehem PA 18018 Office Phone: 610-332-0390. Business E-Mail: dfs@kingspry.com.

**SPUDICH, JAMES A.,** biology professor; b. Collinsville, Ill., Jan. 7, 1942; married, 1964; 2 children. BS, U. Ill., 1963; PhD in Biochemistry, Stanford U., 1968. Asst. prof. biochemistry U. Calif., San Francisco 1971-74, assoc. prof., 1974-76; prof. structural biology, biochemistry and devel. biology Stanford U. Sch. Medicine, 1977—92. Editor: Annual Rev. Cell Biology, 1987-1998. Recipient Lewis S. Rosentiel award for disting. work in basic med. rsch., 1996, Repligen Corp. award, 1997. Mem. Am. Soc. Cell Biologists (pres. 1989), Nat. Acad. of Sci., 1991, Am. Acad. of Arts and Scis., 1997. Achievements include research in molecular basis of cytokinesis amoeboid movement and other forms of cell motility. Office: Stanford U Sch Medicine Dept Biochemistry Stanford Med Ctr Beckman Ctr B400 Stanford CA 94305-5307

**SPUNT, AVERY L.,** pharmacist; b. Chgo. m Janet Spunt, Sept. 2, 1984; children: Marc, Sarah, Katie. BS in Pharmacy, U. Ill., Chgo., 1970, MEd, 1984. Lic. pharmacist Ill. Staff pharmacist U. Ill. Chgo., 1973—74, mem. staff Eye and Ear Infirmary, 1974—76, clin. asst. prof. dept. neurology, 1978—2002, asst. head acad. programs, clin. assoc. prof. dept. pharmacy practice, 1992—2002, pharmacy supr., clin. specialist Coll. Medicine, 1976—84; competency assessment dir. Nat. Assn. Bds. Pharmacy, Park Ridge, Ill., 2002—05; asst. dean Midwestern U. Chgo. Coll. Pharmacy, Downers Grove, Ill., 2005—. Cons. in field; v.p. Clin. Pharmacy Cons., Inc., 1975—90; lectr. at confs. in field. Contbr. articles to profl. jours., chpts. to books. Sgt. USMC, 1970—72. Fellow, Buehler Ctr. on Aging, McGaw Med. Ctr. of Northwestern U., 1990. Fellow: Am. Soc. Health-Sys. Pharmacists (mem. student adv. panel 1985—96, ednl. programming assoc. 1989); mem.: ASCD, No. Ill. Soc. Hosp. Pharmacists, Ill. Coun. Health-Sys. Pharmacists (mem. edn. com. 1996—), Ill. Pharmacists Assn. (bd. dirs. 1988—89, mem. continuing edn. com. 1985—89, ho. del. 1983—88, mem. pub. rels. com. 1984—88, Pharmacist of Yr. 1991), Am. Coll. Clin. Pharmacy, Am. Assn. Colls. Pharmacy (chmn. spl. interest group on exptl. edn. 1985—86, ho. dels. 1989, 1991, 1994), Am. Pharmacists Assn., U. Ill. Coll. Pharmacy Alumni Assn. (v.p. 1988—89, pres. 1989—90, pres. bd. dirs. 1989—90), Rho Pi Phi (1st vice chancellor 1995—96). Avocation: photography. Home: 1724 Mundelein Rd Naperville IL 60565 Office Phone: 630-515-6100. Business E-Mail: aspunt@midwestern.edu.

**SPUNT, SHEPARD ARMIN,** real estate company executive, management and financial consultant; b. Cambridge, Mass., Feb. 3, 1931; s. Harry and Naomi (Drooker) S.; m. Joan Murray Fooshee, Aug. 6, 1961 (dec. June 1969); children: Erica Frieda and Andrew Murray (twins). BS, U. Pa., 1952, MBA, 1956. Owner Colonial Realty Co., Brookline, Mass., 1953—, Cambridge, 1960—; mgr. Colonial Realty LLC, 2002—. Sr. assoc. Gen. Solids Assocs., 1956—; chmn. bd. Gen. Solids Sys. Corp., 1971-74; trustee Union Capital Trust, Boston; incorporator Liberty Bank & Trust Co., Boston; dir., clk. The Computer Co., Inc., Cambridge, 1986—, treas., 1997—; author, sponsor consumer protection, election law and pub. safety legislation Mass. Gen. Ct., 1969—, pub. safety U.S. Congress, 1998. Co-author: A Business Data Processing Service for Small Business Practitioners, 1956, A Business Data Processing Service for Medical Practitioners, 1956, rev. edit., 1959; patentee in field of automation, lasers, dieelectric bonding. Chmn. Com. for Fair Urban Renewal Laws, Mass., 1965—; treas. Ten Men of Mass., 1980; pres. New Eng. Coun. Young Reps., 1964-67, 69-71; vice chmn. Young Rep. Nat. Fedn., 1967-69, dir. region I, 1964-67, 69-71; mem. Brookline Rep. Town Com., 1960—, treas., 1996—; del. Atlantic Conf. Young Polit. Leaders, Brussels, 1973; bd. dirs. Brookline Taxpayers Assn., 1964—, v.p., 1971-72, pres., 1972—; dep. sheriff Norfolk County, 1998-99. Mem. Nat. Soc. Profl. Engrs., Rental Housing Assn., Greater Boston Real Estate Bd., Navy League, Boston Athenaeum, Copley Soc. Boston, Collector's Club N.Y., Masons, Shriners. Home: 177 Reservoir Rd Chestnut Hill MA 02467-1426 Office: 21 Elmer St Cambridge MA 02138-6107

**SPURCK, RICHARD FRANCIS,** materials engineer; b. Schenectady, NY, Sept. 2, 1922; s. Robert M. and Gertrude Veronica Spurck; m. Greta Elizabeth Nelson, Aug. 28, 1954; 1 child, Robert M. BS in Ceramics, Pa. State U., 1943. Devel. engr. Electron Tube divsn. GE, Schenectady, 1946—53; devel. engr. Coors Porcelain Co., Golden, Colo., 1953—55, project devel. engr., 1963—74; electron tube design engr. Machlett Labs., Springdale, Conn., 1955—63; project engr. Kyocera Internat., San Diego, 1975—77; cons. RFS Assocs., Golden, 1977—81; materials engr. Martin-Marietta, Denver, 1981—89. Ceramic head Office of Mil. Govt. of Bavaria, 1945—46. Contbr. articles to profl. jours. Staff sgt. U.S. Army, 1944—46, ETO. Recipient Nepcon award, Nat. Electronic Packaging and Prodn. Conf., 1966. Fellow: Am. Ceramic Soc.; mem.: IEEE, Internat. Soc. Hybrid Microelectronics, Nat. Inst. Ceramic Engrs. Achievements include patents for electron tube structure; electron tube with flexible grid connector; electroplating rack; electrical component package. Office: RFS Assocs 2001 Table Dr Golden CO 80401

**SPURGEON, DENNIS RAY,** federal agency administrator, former manufacturing executive; b. Lake City, Iowa, Oct. 21, 1943; s. Merle Donald and Dorothy (Gidel) S.; m. Carrol Ann Malanoski, Feb. 19, 1966; children: Dennis Jr., Scott, Kimberly. BS, U.S. Naval Acad., 1965; SM in Nuclear Engring., MIT, 1969. Regional mgr. Gen. Atomic Co., Washington, 1973-75, exec. asst. to pres. San Diego, 1975-76; asst. dir. U.S. Energy Rsch. and Devel. Adminstrn., Washington, 1976-77; v.p. UNC Naval Products Div., Montville, Conn., 1977-78; pres. UNC Nuclear Industries, Richland, Wash. 1978-80; group v.p. UNC Inc., Falls Church, Va., 1980-85; chmn., CEO Swift Group LLC, Potomac, Md.; exec. v.p., COO USEC, Inc., 2001—03; asst. sec. for nuclear energy US Dept. Energy, Washington, 2006—. Chmn. Normco Contractors Inc., Morgan City, La., 1985—, NGS Enterprises Inc., Morgan City, 1985—. With USN, 1965-73. Office: US Dept Energy Forrestal Bldg 1000 Independence Ave SW Washington DC 20585*

**SPURGEON, EDWARD DUTCHER,** lawyer, educator, foundation administrator; b. Newton, N.J., June 2, 1939; s. Dorsett Larew and Mary (Dutcher) S.; m. Carol Jean Forbes, June 17, 1963; children: Michael Larew, Stephen Edward. AB, Princeton U., 1961; LLB, Stanford U., 1964; LLM in Taxation, NYU, 1968. Bar: Calif. 1965. Assoc. atty. Stammer McKnight et al, Fresno, Calif., 1964-67, Paul Hastings Janofsky and Walker, L.A., 1968-70, ptnr., 1971-80; prof. law U. Utah Coll. Law, Salt Lake City, 1980-90, Wm. H. Leary prof. law and policy, 1990-93, assoc. dean acad. affairs Coll. Law, 1982-83, dean Coll. Law, 1983-90, clin. prof., 2002—; dean Sch. Law U. Ga., Athens, 1993-98, prof., 1993—2002; ptnr. Moyle & Draper, Salt Lake City, 2000—03, of counsel, 2003—05. Vis. prof. law NYU, 1985, Univ. Coll. London, fall 1990, Stanford U. Law Sch., spring 1991, dist. vis. prof. law UOP-McGeorge Sch. of Law, 2003-; ex-officio mem. Utah State Bar Commn., 1984-90. Co-author: Federal Taxation of Trusts, Grantors and Beneficiaries, 1st edit., 1978, 2d edit., 1989, 3d edit., 1997. Mem. Utah Gov.'s Task Force Officers and Dirs. Liability Ins., 1985-87, Utah Dist. Ct. Reorgn. Commn., 1986-87, Justice in 21st Century Commn., 1989-91; bd. visitors, exec. com. Stanford U. Law Sch., 1988-93; pres., dir. Albert and Elaine Borchard Found., 1983—; dir. Nat. Sr. Citizens Law Ctr., 1990—. Mem. ABA (Commn. on Legal Problems of the Elderly 1991-95, spl. advisor 1995-2003), Am. Bar Found. Mailing: 1414 E 4500 S # 2 Salt Lake City UT 84117 Office Phone: 801-578-3205.

**SPURLING, TERESA PHILLIPS,** education educator; b. Campbellsville, Ky., May 2, 1946; d. Floyd Elwin and Pearl Mae (Benningfield) P.; m. Jimmie Ray Spurling, Jan 18, 1963; children: Mark Anthony, David Alan, Ronald Dale, Aaron Ray. BS, Campbellsville Coll., 1970; MA, Western Ky. U., 1973, MA, 1979; PhD, Capella U., 2006—. Cert. elem. tchr., adminstr. and supr. Ky., early adolescent/generalist Nat. Bd. for Profl. Tchg. Standards, 1998. Sales clk. Wilson's-Blue Bunny, Campbellsville, 1962-63; tchr. Taylor County Bd. Edn., Campbellsville, 1971—2001; cons. Ky. Dept. of Edn., Office of Acad. & Profl. Devel., Divsn of Cirruculm, 1998—2001; Ky. lt. gov. Taskforce for Childhood Nutrition & Physical Fitness, 2000—03; asst. prof. Campbellsville Univ., 2001—; project dir. for outdoor classroom Clayhill Meml. Forest and Environ. Edn. Ctr., 2002—; mid. sch. educator, 1971—98. Resource tchr. Ky. Intern Tchr. Program, Campbellsville, 1986-97; rep. tech. conf. Ky. Ednl. Tech. Conf., 1992-96; instrnl. tech. leader Ptnrs. in Reform Initiatives in Sci. and Math., 1993-96. Leader 4-H, Campbellsville, 1975-88; dir. Vacation Bible Sch., Spurlington, Ky., 1986, 88; ptnr. Ky.-Ecuador Ptnrs. in Edn., Campbellsville, 1986—; rep. Am. Interdependence Inst., Louisville, 1986-87; mem. Taylor County Bicentennial Com., 1991-92. Recipient cert. of honor Ky. Treasury, 1984, tchg. award Ashland Oil Co., 1983, Excellence in Tchg. award Campbellsville Coll., 1989; grantee Ky. Arts Coun., 1987, NASA, 1991. Mem. NEA (life), ASCD, NSTA, Ky. Edn. Assn., Taylor County Edn. Assn. (sec. 1975-76, pres. 1987-88), Ky. Sci. Tchrs. Assn. (rep. 1993, 95), Ky. Hist. Soc., Taylor County Hist. Soc., DAR (sr. soc. pres. David Allen chpt. Children Am. Revolution 1996). Democrat. Methodist. Avocations: genealogy, reading, sewing, quilt-making, gardening. Home: 354 Hidden Meadows Dr Campbellsville KY 42718-3323 Office: Campbellsville Univ Sch Edn UPO 885 Campbellsville KY 42718-1500 Office Phone: 270-789-5345. Personal E-mail: spurling4403@comcast.net. Business E-Mail: tspurling@campbellsville.edu.

**SPURLOCK, MORGAN,** television producer, film producer; b. Parkersburg, W.Va., Nov. 7, 1970; m. Alexandra Jamieson, May 3, 2006. BFA, NYU, 1993. Prodr.: (TV series) I Bet You Will, 2002; exec. prodr.: 30 Days, 2005—; (films) Class Act, 2006; prodr., dir., writer: Super Size Me, 2004; actor: Drive-Thru, 2006; author: (book) Don't Eat This Book: Fast Food and the Supersizing of America, 2006. Mem.: ACLU.*

**SPURRIER, STEVE (STEVEN ORR SPURRIER),** college football coach; b. Miami Beach, Apr. 20, 1945; m. Jerrie Spurrier. Quarterback San Francisco 49'ers, 1967-75, Tampa Bay Buccaneers, 1976; head coach Tampa Bay Bandits, USFL, 1983—85, Duke U., 1987—90, U. Fla., Gainesville, 1990—2002, Wash. Redskins, 2002—03, U. South Carolina, Columbia, 2004—. Winner Heisman Trophy, U. Fla., 1966. Office: Rex Enright Athletic Center 1300 Rosewood Drive Columbia SC 29208*

**SPUSTEK, MARIA S.,** lawyer; d. John A. Spustek, Sr. and Marguerite H. Spustek; m. Bertram J. Rodgers, III, Jan. 1, 2005. BA, La. State U., 1988; JD, Emory U., 1991. Bar: Calif. 1993, Ga. 1991. Law clk. to Hon. Louis M. Phillips U.S. Bankruptcy Ct. (mid. dist.) La., Baton Rouge, 1991—93; assoc. Murphy Weir & Butler, San Francisco, 1993—94, Skjerven Morrill MacPherson, San Jose, 1995—2000, Condert Bros. LLP, San Francisco, 2000—04; ptnr. Schnader Harrison Segal & Lewis LLP, San Francisco, 2004—. Invited spkr. tech. and e-commerce com. mid-yr. conf. Internat. Bar Assn., Istanbul, Turkey, 2006. Contbr. articles to legal jours.; exec. editor: Bankruptcy Devels. Jour. Mem.: ABA, Licensing Execs. Soc., Internat. Bar Assn., Olympic Club. Avocations: swimming, tennis, golf, opera, walking. Home: 630 17th Ave San Francisco CA 94121 Office: Shnader Harrison Segal & Lewis LLP # 2200 1 Montgomery St San Francisco CA 94104

**SPYERS-DURAN, PETER,** librarian, educator; b. Budapest, Hungary, Jan. 26, 1932; came to U.S., 1956, naturalized, 1964; s. Alfred and Maria (Almasi-Balogh) S-D; m. Jane F. Cumber, Mar. 21, 1964; children: Kimberly, Hilary, Peter. Certificate, Free U. Budapest, 1955; MA in L.S, U. Chgo., 1960; Ed.D., Nova S. Ea. U., 1975. Profl. asst. libr. adminstrn. div. ALA, Chgo., 1961-62; assoc. dir. librs., assoc. prof. U. Wis., 1962-67; dir. librs., prof. Western Mich. U., 1967-70; dir. librs., prof. libr. sci. Fla. Atlantic U., 1970-76; dir. libr. Calif. State U., Long Beach, 1976-83; prof. libr. and info. sci., dir. libr. Wayne State U., Detroit, 1983-86, dean, prof. libr. and info. sci. program, 1986-95, dean and prof. emeritus, 1995—; cons. Spyers-Duran Assocs., 1995—; acting univ. libr. Nova Southeastern U., Ft. Lauderdale, Fla., 1996-97. Vis. prof. State U. N.Y. at Geneseo, summers 1969-70; cons. publs., libr. and info. scis.-related enterprises; chmn. bd. internat. confs., 1970—. Author: Moving Library Materials, 1965, Public Libraries - A Comparative Survey of Basic Fringe Benefits, 1967; editor: Approval and Gathering Plans in Academic Libraries, 1969, Advances in Understanding Approval Plans in Academic Libraries, 1970, Economics of Approval Plans in Research Libraries, 1972, Management Problems in Serials Work, 1973, Prediction of Resource Needs, 1975, Requiem for the Card Catalog: Management Issues in Automated Cataloging, 1979, Shaping Library Collections for the 1980's, 1981, Austerity Management in Academic Libraries, 1984, Financing Information Systems, 1985, Issues in Academic Libraries, 1985; mem. editorial bd. Jour. of Library Adminstration, 1989-95. Mem. Kalamazoo County Library Bd., 1969-70; Bd. dirs. United Fund. Reciient G. Flint Purdy award for outstanding contbns. Wayne State U., 1999. Mem. ALA, Mich. Libr. Assn., Internat. Fed. Libr. Assns., Assn. Info. Sci., Fla. Libr. Assn., Calif. Libr. Assn., Fla. Assn. Community Colls., Boca Raton C. of C., U. Chgo. Grad. Libr. Sch. Alumni Club (pres. 1973-75), Solinet Mich. Libr. Consortium (founder charter bd. mem 1973—, bd. dirs. 1973-76), Detroit Area Libr. Network (pres. bd. dirs. 1985-95), Mich. Ctr. for Book (pres. 1988-89), Am. Soc. Info. Sci., Assn. Libr. and Info. Sci. Edn., Sago Point Homeowners Assn. (pres., bd. dirs. 2001-05), Bayou Club Cmty. Assn. (pres., bd. dirs. 2005—). Home: 7295 Maidencane Ct Largo FL 33777 1900 Office: Wayne State Univ Libr Detroit MI 48202 Business E-Mail: spyers-duran@wayne.edu, ae8249@wayne.edu.

**SPYKER, HARRY A., III,** music educator; b. Dayton, Ohio, Feb. 12, 1945; s. Donna M. Spyker; m. Renee' A. Arcella; 1 child, Kelsey Justine. BS in Music Edn., Ctrl. State U. Wilberforce, Ohio, 1966; MusM, Ohio State U., 1972. Band dir. Fairborn Pub. Schs., Ohio, 1966—68, Springfield North H.S., Ohio, 1968—72, Deerfield Beach H.S./Middle Schs., Fla., 1973—86, Fla. Atlantic U., Boca Raton, 1986—87, Boca Raton Cmty. H.S., Fla., 1986—91, Santaluces H.S., Lantana, Fla., 1991—94, Congress Cmty. Middle Sch., Boynton Beach, Fla., 1994—. Clarinet player Springfield Symphony Orch., 1967—71; All-County Honor Band clinician/condr. 1991 and 1996 Broward County Pub. Schs., Ft.Lauderdale, Fla.; All-District Honor Band condr./clinician Palm Beach County Dist. 14, West Palm Beach, Fla. Music curriculum writing team Palm Beach County Schools, West Palm Beach, 1987—89. Mem.: Fla. Music Educators Assn., Music Educators Nat. Conf., Am. Sch. Band Dirs. Assn. (nat. chmn. for marching bands 1983—85), Fla. Bandmasters Assn. (life; Fla. adjudicator for dist. band evaluations 1977—, dist. chmn., sec. 1978—82, Twenty Five Yr. award 1998). Roman Catholic. Avocations: jogging, golf, tennis, travel, music. Home: 2036 SW 36th Ave Delray Beach FL 33445-6651 Personal E-mail: hspyker@bellsouth.net.

**SPYKER, LEOLA EDITH,** missionary; b. Wallace, Mich., Mar. 15, 1925; d. Oscar Eugene Anderson and Edith Ragnhild Nelson; m. George Spyker, Feb. 16, 1951 (div. June 1967); children: Marilyn Joy, John George, Thomas Oscar, Sandra Lee. AA, N. Park U., Chgo., 1944; BA, Bob Jones U., Greenville, S.C., 1947; postgrad. in Counseling, Seattle Pacific U., Seattle, Wash., 1969—70. Cert. in ESL Upton Coll., Pasadena, Calif., 1961, in French and Italian, Academia Uruapan, Michoacan, Mex. 1965, in Secondary Edn. Mich., Wis., Wash., Tex. Instr. King's Garden Sch., Seattle, 1969—71; lectr. Seminario El Calvario, El Carmen, Nuevo Leon, Mexico, 1971—74, 1977—80; lectr. in missionary outreach, anthropology, history, comparative religions Inst. Misionera Morelia, Michoacan, 1983—92; prof. U. Michoacan, Uruapan, Michoacan, Mexico, 1975—77, Mexico, 1982—84. Founder, dir. Casa Hogar La Esparanza, Uruapan, Michoacda, Mexico, Hogar la Esperanza, Utuapan, 1953—93; conf. spkr. Vida Abundante, Morelia, Mexico, 1980—2003; coord. student groups to Honduras, Nicaragua and Spain, 1995,

99, 2002; Spanish translator internat. conf. for Billy Graham, Amsterdam, Netherlands, 1996; worker refugee rehab. and outreach, Honduras, Nicaragua, 84, Honduras, Nicaragua, 86, Honduras, Nicaragua, 87. Contbr. 40 articles in profl. publications. Avocations: painting, travel, reading, ornithology. Home: PO Box 2050 2021 Harvey Dr Mcallen TX 78501 Office Phone: 956-682-6774. Personal E-mail: leolas@juno.com.

**SQUATRITO, DOMINIC J.,** judge; BA, Wesleyan U., 1961; JD, Yale U., 1965. Judge U.S. Dist. Ct. Conn., 1994—. Office: US Dist Court 450 Main St Fl 2 Hartford CT 06103-3010 Office Phone: 860-240-3873.

**SQUIBB, SAMUEL DEXTER,** chemistry professor; b. Limestone, Tenn., June 20, 1931; s. Benjamin Bowman and Lou Pearl S.; m. JoAnn Kyker, Dec. 15, 1951; children: Sandra Lavanne, Kevin Dexter. BS, E. Tenn. State U., 1952; PhD, U. Fla., 1956. Assoc. prof., dir. chemistry Western Carolina U., Cullowhee, NC, 1956-60; asst. prof., dir. chemistry Eckerd Coll., St. Petersburg, Fla., 1960-63, asso. prof., 1963-64; prof. chemistry U. N.C., Asheville, 1964-84, chmn. dept., 1964-94. Vis. prof. U. NC, Chapel Hill, 1976-81, 83-87, 92-95, Clemson U., SC, 1982; cons. So. Assn. Colls. and Schs. State of W.Va. Author: Experimental Organic Chemistry, 1972, Understanding Chemistry One, 1979, rev. 1990, Two, 1981, rev. 1991, Three, 1981, rev. 1992, Four, 1981, rev. 1992, Five, 1981, rev. 1989, Six, 1984, Chemistry One, 1976, rev. 1987, Two, 1980, rev. 1990, Experimental Chemistry One, 1976, rev. 1988, Two, 1981, rev. 1991; contbr. articles to profl. jours. Mem. Grose United Meth. Ch. Disting. Tchr. award U. N.C.-Asheville, 1983; S.D. Squibb Disting. Chemistry Lectureship U. N.C., Asheville, established 1997; named to We. Carolina Fedn. Square and Round Dancing Hall of Fame, 2001; recipient Pres.'s Svc. award, Folk, Round and Square Dancing Fedn. N.C., 2001. Fellow Am. Inst. Chemists (life, nat. publs. bd. 1988-92); mem. Am. Chem. Soc. (Charles H. Stone award Carolina Piedmont sect. 1979, Disting. Chemist award Western Carolinas sect. 1993, chmn. Tampa Bay subsect. 1963, Western Carolina sect. 1981, editor Periodic News Western Carolina sect. 1980—), NC Inst. Chemists (pres. 1977-79, sec. 1975-77, 85-91, Disting. Chemist award 1986), Skyland Twirlers Square Dance Club, Silver Spurs Advanced Square Dance Club, Jerry's Kids Advanced Square Dance Club, Skylarks Round Dance Club, Phi Beta Kappa.

**SQUIER, DAVID LOUIS,** manufacturing executive; b. Buffalo, Oct. 30, 1945; s. Clayton L. and Ruth H. Squier; m. Sue Sampson, Aug. 12, 1967; children: Jennifer, Allison. BS in Mech. Engring., Lehigh U., 1967; MBA, Wharton Sch., U. Pa., 1971. With mfg. mgmt. program GE, various cities, 1967-70; mgr. corp. planning Howmet Corp., Greenwich, Conn., 1971-73, mgr. corp. and bus. planning Muskegon, Mich., 1973-75, plant mgr. Hampton, Va., 1976-78, gen. mgr. Wichita Falls, Tex., 1979-82, v.p. Greenwich, 1983-87, sr. v.p., 1987-89, exec. v.p., 1989-91, COO, 1991-92, pres., CEO, 1992-2000, also bd. dirs., advisor, 2000—. Mem. rev. and prioritization bd. Iacocca Inst., Bethlehem, Pa., 1990—. Office: Howmet Corp 1 Misco Dr C Whitehall MI 49461-1755

**SQUIER, JACK LESLIE,** sculptor, educator; b. Dixon, Ill., Feb. 27, 1927; s. Leslie Lee and Ruth (Barnes) S.; m. Jane Bugg, June 9, 1950. Student, Oberlin Coll., 1945-46; BS, Ind. U., 1950; M)F.A., Cornell U., 1952. Instr. Cornell U., 1952, asst. prof. art, 1958-61, assoc. prof., 1961-65, prof., 1965—. Designer Howatt Pottery Co., N.Y.C., 1953; account exec. Jamian Advt. Co., N.Y.C., 1954-58; asst. prof. U. Calif., Berkeley, 1960; mem. Internat. Assn. Art, UNESCO, 1964-72, mem. exec. com., 1966-69, v.p., 1969-72 One-man shows include Alan Gallery, N.Y.C., 1956, 59, 62, 64, White Mus., Cornell U., 1959, 68, Instituto de Arte Contemporaneo, Lima, Peru, 1963, Landau-Alan Gallery, N.Y.C., 1966, 69, Herbert F. Johnson Mus., Cornell Univ. (retrospective of work, 1953-93); exhibited in group shows at Mus. Modern Art, N.Y.C., 1957, Whitney Mus., N.Y.C., 1952, 54, 56, 58, 62, 67, 78, Hirshhorn Mus., Washington, 1978, Mus. Fine Arts, Boston, 1958, Chgo. Art Inst., 1960, Brussel's Worlds Fair, 1956, competition, Auschwitz, Poland, 1957, Albright-Knox Mus., Buffalo, 1968, Claude Bernard Gallery, Paris, 1957, Hanover Gallery, London, 1958; represented in permanent collections Mus. Modern Art, N.Y.C., Whitney Mus. Art, Hirshhorn Mus., Instituto de Arte Contemporaneo, Everson Mus., Syracuse, N.Y., Stanford U. Mus., St. Lawrence U. Mus., SUNY at Potsdam, Ithaca Coll., Johnson Mus. at Cornell U., Houston Mus., Hamilton Coll. Mus., Hood Mus.-Dartmouth (N.H.) U., Castellani Mus., Niagara U., N.Y., Fogg Mus., Harvard U., Cambridge; bronze garden piece at Fogg Mus./Harvard U., Conn. Conservancy; retrospective exhbn. Herbert F. Johnson Mus. Cornell U., 1993; work pub. in various, books, mags., newspapers, slide collections, catalogs. Served with AC USN, 1945-47. Office: Cornell U Dept Art 100 Tjaden Hall Ithaca NY 14853-7301

**SQUIER, VICTORIA (VICKI) J.,** mathematics educator; d. Erwin M. and Betty Jean Ohlendorf; m. Steven D. Squier, Nov. 8, 1975; children: Clint P., Leah M. BA, Ill. Wesleyan U., 1973. Cert. 6-12 tchr. Ill., 1973. Tchr. math Beecher H.S., Ill., 1973—. Mcpl. treas. Village of Beecher, Ill., 1988—2003. Mem.: NEA, Ill. Edn. Assn., Ill. Coun. Tchrs. of Math., Beecher Part-Time Players, Beecher Women's Club. Office: Beecher HS PO Box 338 538 Miller St Beecher IL 60401 Office Phone: 708-946-2266. Office Fax: 708-946-3403. Business E-Mail: vsquier@beecher.will.k12.il.us.

**SQUIRE, ALEXANDER,** management consultant; b. Dumfrieshire, Scotland, Sept. 29, 1917; s. Frederick John and Lillian (Ferguson) S.; m. Isabelle L. Kerr, June 23, 1945; children: Jonathan, David, Deborah, Stephen, Philip, Martha, Timothy, Rebecca, Elizabeth. BS, MIT, 1939. Research metallurgist Handy and Harman, Fairfield, Conn., 1939-41; devel. metallurgist Sullivan Machinery Co., Michigan City, Ind., 1941-42; head powder metallurgy br. Watertown Arsenal Lab., Mass., 1942-45; mgr. metall. devel. Westinghouse Electric Corp., Pitts., 1945-50; project mgr. Bettis Atomic Power Lab., Pitts., 1950-62; gen. mgr. plant apparatus div. Westinghouse, 1962-69; dir. purchases and traffic Westinghouse Electric Corp., 1969-71; pres. Westinghouse Hanford Co., Richland, Wash., 1971-79; bus. cons. Richland, 1979-80; dep. mng. dir. Wash. Public Power Supply System, 1980-85, cons., 1985—. Mem. Nat. Acad. Engring., Am. Nuclear Soc., Am. Soc. Metals, AIME, Am. Def. Preparedness Assn. Address: Pittsboro Christian Village 1825 East St Pittsboro NC 27312

**SQUIRE, ANNE MARGUERITE,** retired humanities educator; b. Amherstburg, Ont., Can. Oct. 17, 1920; d. Alexander Samuel and Coral Marguerite Park; m. William Robert Squire, June 24, 1943; children: Frances, Laura, Margaret. BA, Carleton U., Ottawa, 1972, BA with honors, 1974, MA, 1975; LLD (hon.), Carleton U., 1988; DD (hon.), United Theol. Coll., 1979, Queen's U., 1985. Cert. tchr., Ont. Adj. prof. Carleton U., 1975-82; sec. div. ministry personnel and edn. United Ch. Can., Toronto, 1982-85, moderator, 1986-88; ret., 1988. Author curriculum materials, 1959—; contbr. articles to profl. jours. Mem. bd. mgmt. St. Andrew's Coll., Saskatoon, Sask., 1982, Queens Theol. Coll., Kingston, Ont., 1999-2005; founding mem. Muslim-Christian Dialogue Group; patron MultiFaith Housing Initiative; hon. advisor Can. Ctr. for Progressive Christianity. Recipient Senate medal Carleton U., 1972. Mem. Can. Research Inst. for Advancement Women, Delta Kappa Gamma (pres. 1978-79). Mem. United Ch. Can. Office: 731 Weston Dr Ottawa ON Canada K1G 1W1 E-mail: a.squire@sympatico.ca.

**SQUIRE, LARRY RYAN,** neuroscientist, psychologist, educator; b. Cherokee, Iowa, May 4, 1941; s. Harold Walter and Jean (Ryan) S.; children: Ryan, Luke. BA, Oberlin Coll., 1963; PhD in Psychology, MIT, 1968; postgrad., Albert Einstein Med. Coll., 1968-70. With U. Calif. San Diego (UCSD), 1970—, prof., 1981—; rsch. career scientist VA Med. Ctr., San Diego, 1980—; mem. faculty U. Calif. Irvine Ctr. Neurobiology of Learning & Memory, 1981—. Lectr. in field. Editor, author: Memory and Brain, 1987; co-author: Memory: From Mind to Molecules, 1999; editor Behavioral Neuroscience, 1990-95; mem. editl. adv. bd. numerous profl. jours.; contbr. articles to profl. jours., chpts. to books. Recipient Charles A. Dana Award for Pioneering Achievements in Health and Education, 1993, Disting. Sci. Contbn. award APA, Lashley prize Am. Philosophical Soc., McGovern award

AAAS; William James fellow Am. Psychol. Soc. Mem. Nat. Acad. Scis., Am. Acad. Arts and Scis., Soc. Neurosci. (pres. 1994), Am. Philos. Soc., Inst. Medicine. Office: UCSD SDVAMC 3350 La Jolla Village Dr San Diego CA 92161 Office Fax: 858-552-7457. E-mail: lsquire@ucsd.edu.*

**SQUIRE, WALTER CHARLES,** lawyer; b. NYC, Aug. 5, 1945; s. Sidney and Helen (Friedman) S.; m. Sara Jane Abamson; children: Harrison, Russell, Zachary, andrew. BA, Yale U., 1967; JD, Columbia U., 1971. Bar: N.Y. 1971, U.S. Dist. Ct. (so. and ea. dists.) N.Y. 1975, U.S. Ct. Appeals (2d cir.) 1974, U.S. Supreme Ct. 1977. Ptnr. Jones Hirsch Connors & Bull P.C., NYC, 1986-98, Jacobson, Mermelstein & Squire, LLP, NYC, 1998—; prin. Squire & Co., LLC, NYC, 1998—. Bd. govs. Arthritis Found. N.Y., Inc., 1993-99; bd. dirs. MedicAlert Found., N.Y., 1990-99. Mem. ABA, N.Y. State Bar Assn., Assn. of Bar of City of N.Y., Internat. Bar Assn., Licensing Execs. Soc., Chartered Inst. Arbitrators (London), Am. Arbitration Assn. (arbitrator 1975-2000, mediator 1993—), Am. Acad. Hosp. Attys., Risk Ins. Mgmt. Soc. (lectr. 1983-84), AIDA Reinsurance & Ins. Arbitration Soc. (cert.). Office: Jacobson Mermelstein et al 52 Vanderbilt Ave New York NY 10017-3808 Office Phone: 212-697-1420.

**SQUIRES, ALLISON P.,** nursing educator; b. Pitts., June 24, 1973; d. David A. and Maureen M. Squires. BSN, U. Pa., Phila., 1995; MSN, Duquesne U., Pitts., 1999; postgrad., Yale U., New Haven, Conn., 2002—. Clin. staff nurse U. Pitts. Med. Ctr., 1996—99; clin. devel. specialist Lewistown Hosp., Lewistown, 1999—2000; unit based educator, staff nurse Yale-New Haven Hosp., 2001—06; clin. instr. cmty. health nursing Yale U. Sch. Nursing, 2003—05; health policy advisor Scott Kleeb Congress, Kearney, Nebr., 2006—. Cons. Tri-County Hosp., Lexington, Nebr., 2006—; bd. mem. New Immigrant Welcome Ctr., Lexington, Nebr., 2006—; adj. asst. prof. nursing Quinnipiac U. Sch. Nursing, Hamden, Conn., 2001—06. Fellow, Yale U., 2003; scholar, Nurses Ednl. Funds, 2000—04. Mem.: Latin Am. Studies Assn., Global Health Coun., Sigma Theta Tau (grantee 2006), Phi Sigma Pi (life; alumni liaison rush chair 1993—94, Outstanding Alumni Rels. Program 1995). Liberal. Avocations: travel, dance. Home: 1919 West 39th St #B11 Kearney NE 68845 Personal E-mail: asquires@earthlink.net.

**SQUIRES, ARTHUR MORTON,** chemical engineer, educator; b. Neodesha, Kans., Mar. 21, 1916; s. Charles Loren and Vera Amber (Moore) S. AB with distinction in Chemistry, U. Mo., 1938; PhD, Cornell U., 1947. Design engr. M.W. Kellogg Co., N.Y.C., 1942-46; asst. dir. process devel. Hydrocarbon Research, Inc., N.Y.C., 1946-51, dir. process devel., 1951-59; cons. chem. process industries N.Y.C., 1959-67; prof. chem. engring. CUNY, 1967-74, disting. prof., 1974-76, chmn. dept. chem. engring., 1970-73; Vilbrandt prof. chem. engring. Va. Poly. Inst. and State U., Blacksburg, 1976-82, disting. prof., 1978-86, disting. prof. emeritus, 1986—. Author: The Tender Ship, 1986; editor: (with D.A. Berkowitz) Power Generation and Environmental Change, 1971; contbr. articles to profl. jours.; patentee in field Mem. N.Y. Pro Musica, 1953-60 Fellow Am. Acad. Arts and Scis., AAAS; mem. ASME, NAE, AIChE (dist. lectr.), Am. Chem. Soc. (Henry H. Storch award 1973), Internat. Soc. for Human Ethology, Human Behavior and Evolution Soc., Sigma Xi, Tau Beta Pi Avocation: performing medieval and renaissance music. Home: 2710 Quincy Ct Blacksburg VA 24060-4124 Office: Va Poly Inst and State U Dept Chem Engring Blacksburg VA 24061 Business E-mail: verasqu@vt.edu.

**SQUIRES, JAMES RALPH,** development company executive; b. Jan. 2, 1940; s. William Guilford and Ruby Alice (Whittington) S.; m. Ann Newton, Apr. 17, 1965; children: Samuel Guilford, James Drew. Student, pub. schs., Charlotte, N.C. With Squires Constrn. Co., 1959-62; pres. SBS Builders, Inc., Charlotte, 1968-70, Ralph Squires Homes, Charlotte, 1970-88, Squires & Assocs., Realtors, 1975-88. Bd. dirs., mem. exec. com. Park Meridian Bank, 1991, Dover Mortgage, First Landmark; chmn. Squires Enterprises, Inc. Mem. Charlotte Tree Commrn., 1977; bd. dirs. Athletic Found. U. N.C., Charlotte, 1979-84, Better Bus. Bur., 1983, MMAES Inn 1983-87, Charlotte Symphony; pub. mem. N.C. State Bar, 1980-85; pres. Metrolina Home Owners, 1982, bd. dirs., 1983; bd. govs. Polit. Action Com. for Bldg. Industry; mem. bd. visitors Mercy Hosp., Charlotte, 1986; bd. dirs. Mercy Hosp. Found., chmn., 1993—; chmn. new bldg. fund United Cerebral Palsy; mem. exec. coun. Mecklenburg County coun. Boy Scouts Am., 1986-90; mem. exec. coun. Muscular Dystrophy Assn., Charlotte, 1987; mem. N.C. Wildlife Resources Commn., 1995-98 bd. dirs. Harris YMCA, N.C. March of Dimes, 1997. Recipient Profile award N.C. Blue Cross/Blue Shield, 1974, Albert Gallatin merit cert., 1974; named Charlotte Builder of Yr., 1977. Mem. Nat. Homebuilders Assn., N.C. Homebuilders Assn. (v.p. 1975), Charlotte Homebuilders Assn. (pres. 1974), Charlotte Bd. Realtors, Carolina Ambs., Quail Hollow Country Club, Old North State Country Club, Grandfather Golf and Country Club, Brays Island Plantation. Republican. Baptist. Home: 6828 Phillips Place Ct Charlotte NC 28210-2715

**SQUIRES, JOHN,** publishing executive; b. Pocatelllo, Idaho; Degree, U. Washington. From asst. circulation dir. People Mag. to pres. Entertainment Weekly Time Inc., N.Y.C., 1989—98, pres. Entertainment Weekly, 1998—2002, exec. v.p., 2002—04, pres., sports & leisure, 2004, and co-COO, 2005—. Office: Sports Illustrated 1271 Avenue of the Americas New York NY 10020-1300*

**SQUIRES, JOHN HENRY,** judge; b. Oct. 21, 1946; married; five children. AB cum laude, U. Ill., 1968, JD, 1971. Bar: Ill. 1971, U.S. Dist. Ct. (cen. dist.) Ill. 1972, U.S. Tax Ct. 1978. Assoc. Brown, Hay & Stephens, Springfield, Ill., 1971-76, ptnr., 1977-87; judge U.S. Bankruptcy Ct. No. Dist. Ill. ea. divsn., 1988—2001, reappointed, 2002—. Trustee in bankruptcy, 1984-87; adj. prof. law John Marshall Law Sch., Chgo., 1994, DePaul U., Chgo., 1995-96; lectr. Am. Bankruptcy Inst., Sangamon County Bar Assn., Winnebago County Bar Assn., Chgo. Bar Assn., Ill. Inst. CLE, Comml. Law League Am., DuPage County (Ill.) Bar Assn. Mem. Nat. Conf. Bankruptcy Judges, Am. Bankruptcy Inst., Fed. Bar Assn., Am. Bus. Club, Union League Club Chgo.

**SQUIRES, RICHARD FELT,** research scientist; b. Sparta, Mich., Jan. 15, 1933; s. Moses Nathan and Dorothy Lois (Felt) S.; m. Else Saederup, 1 child, Iben. BS, Mich. State U., 1958; postgrad., Calif. Inst. Tech., 1958-61. Rsch. biochemist Pasadena Found. for Med. Rsch., 1961-62; chief biochemistry sect. rsch. dept. A/S Ferrosan, Soeborg, Denmark, 1963-78; neurochemistry group leader CNS Biology sect. Lederle Labs. div. Am. Cyanamid Co., Pearl River, NY, 1978-79; prin. rsch. scientist The Nathan S. Kline Inst. for Psychiat. Rsch., Orangeburg, NY, 1979-2000, ret., 2000. Contbr. over 85 articles to profl. jours.; patentee in field. Nat. Inst. Neurol. and Communication Disorders and Stroke grantee, 1981-84. Mem. Soc. Neurosci., Collegium Internat. Neuro-Psychopharmacologicum, Internat. Soc. Neurochemistry, Am. Soc. Neurochemistry, Am. Soc. Biochemistry and Molecular Biology, Am. Soc. Pharmacology and Exptl. Therapeutics. Home: 861 Laugenour Ct Woodland CA 95776-4911 Personal E-mail: else_dick@hotmail.com.

**SQUIRES, ROBERT H.,** pediatrician, educator; b. Houston, Sept. 17, 1951; s. Robert H. and Elizabeth Cunningham Squires; m. Janet E. Endress, June 2, 1979; children: Gregory Robert, James Eugene, Elizabeth Mary. BA, Austin Coll., Sherman, Tex., 1973; MD, U. Tex., Galveston, 1977. Lic. Tex., 1982, Pa., 2003. Pvt. medial practice, Ft. Worth, 1982—87; prof. pediat. U. Pitts., 2003—; prof. pediat., clin. dir. pediat. gastroenterology, 2003—; prof. pediat. U. Tex. Southwestern Med. Sch., Dallas, 1987—2003. Recipient Spl. Achievement award, Am. Acad. Pediat., 2001. Mem.: Am. Pediat. Soc., N.Am. Soc. Pediat. Gastroenterology Hepatology and Nutrition, Am. Assn Study of Liver Disease, Am. Acad. Pediat. Office: Children's Hospital Pittsburgh 3705 Fifth Ave Pittsburgh PA 15213 Office Phone: 412-692-8181. Office Fax: 412-692-7355. Personal E-mail: rhsjunior@aol.com. Business E-Mail: robert.squires@chp.edu.

**SQUIRES, WILLIAM ALLEN,** distribution company executive; b. Springfield, Mass., May 30, 1949; s. Robert P. and Irma Ruth (Alpert) Squires; m. Nancy Faye Weiner, Nov. 15, 1981; children: Maxine Rhea, Sarah Jill,

Michelle Anne. BA, U. Pa., 1971; postgrad., Temple U., 1971-74. Cert. CPR, first aid, sports safety tng. instr. ARC. V.p. Esquire Gas Products Co., Enfield, Conn., 1972-87, pres., 1987—. Mem. assoc. bd. Enfield Nat. Bank, Enfield, Conn., 1989—91. Singer: Spl. Olympic World Games Opening Ceremony, 1995, Makhela Choral Group; soloist for nat. anthem: numerous minor league baseball and hockey games, New Eng. Revolution Soccer. Mem. local emergency planning com. Town of Enfield, 1988—; bd. dirs. Jewish Family Svc. Greater Springfield, Mass., 1983—86, Goodwill Industries Springfield-Hartford Area, Inc., 1997—2003; life mem. Friends of Storrowton; torchbearer Olympic Torch Relay, 1996; mem. distbn. com. Springfield Jewish Endowment Found., 2006; bd. dirs. Congregation Kodimoh; mem. Kodimoh Brotherhood, v.p., 2001—02; mem. we. Mass. athletic recruiting com. U. Pa., chmn. we. Mass. athletic recruiting com., 1974—2005, mem. We. Mass. Secondary Sch. Com., chmn. We. Mass. Secondary Sch. com., 1974—84, mem. N.E. regional adv. bd., bd. assoc. alumni trustees. Finalist Family Bus. of Yr. award, U. Conn. Sch. Bus., 2003. Mem.: U. Pa. Alumni Assn. (pres. We. Mass. Club 1974—2005, pres. We. New Eng. Club 1974—2005, v.p. class 1971 1981—), Nat. Wildlife Fedn. (life), Nat. Audubon Soc. (life), Enfield Rotary Club (pres. 1982—83), Rotary Internat. (dist. sec. 1984—85, dist. gov.'s area rep. 1995—96, Paul Harris fellow 1988, 2000), Delta Upsilon Alumni (treas. U. Mass. chpt. 1979—82). Jewish. Home: 33 Willow Cir Longmeadow MA 01106-2152 Office: Esquire Gas Products Co PO Box 281 156 Spring St Enfield CT 06082-3431

**SQUIRES, WILLIAM RANDOLPH, III,** lawyer; b. Providence, Sept. 6, 1947; s. William Randolph and Mary Louise (Gress) S.; m. Elisabeth Dale McAnulty, June 23, 1984; children: Shannon, William R. IV, Mayre Elisabeth, James Robert. BA in Econs., Stanford U., 1969; JD, U. Tex., 1972. Bar: Wash. 1973, U.S. Dist. Ct. (we. dist.) Wash. 1973, U.S. Dist. Ct. (ea. dist.) Wash. 1976, U.S. Ct. Appeals (9th cir.) 1976, U.S. Supreme Ct. 1976, U.S. Ct. Fed. Claims 1982. Assoc. Oles, Morrison, Rinker, Stanislaw & Ashbaugh, Seattle, 1973-78; ptnr., chmn. litig. group Davis Wright Tremaine, Seattle, 1978-97; mem. Summit Law Group, Seattle, 1997—, chmn., 2005—. Fellow Am. Coll. Trial Lawyers; mem. ABA, Internat. Bar Assn., Wash. State Bar Assn., King County Bar Assn., Wash. Athletic Club, Rainier Club (Seattle). Episcopalian. Home: 5554 NE Penrith Rd Seattle WA 98105-2845 Office: Summit Law Group 315 Fifth Ave S Ste 1000 Seattle WA 98104 Office Phone: 206-676-7054. E-mail: randys@summitlaw.com.

**SQUYRES, STEVEN WELDON,** astronomy educator, planetary geology researcher; b. Woodbury, NJ, Jan. 9, 1956; m. Mary Squyres; children: Katie, Nicole. BA, Cornell U., 1978, PhD in Geology, 1981. Assoc. Voyager imaging sci. team, 1978—81; radar investigator Magellan mission to Venus; mem. Mars Observer gamma-ray spectrometer flight investigation team; co-investigator Russian Mars '96 Mission; assoc. NRC, Ames Rsch. Ctr., NASA, 1981—86; assoc. prof. dept. astronomy Cornell U., 1986—; mem. Planetary Geol. Working Group, NASA, 1982—; scientific principal investigator Mars Exploration Rover Project, twin rovers, Spirit and Opportunity; co-investigator Mars Express Mission, Mars Reconnaissance Orbiter's High Resolution Imaging Science Experiment; mem. Gamma-Ray Spectrometer Flight Investigation Team, Mars Odyssey mission; mem. imaging team Cassini mission to Saturn. Author: Roving Mars: Spirit, Opportunity, and the Exploration of the Red Planet, 2005; contbr. articles to profl. jours. Recipient Rave Award in Science, WIRED, 2005. Mem. AAAS, Am. Geophys. Union. Office: Cornell U 428 Space Sciences Bldg Ithaca NY 14853 Office Phone: 607-255-3508. E-mail: squyres@astro.cornell.edu.*

**SRAON, DILBER S.,** dentist; b. London; BA in Biology, U. Calif. Irvine; DDS, Northwestern U. Dental Sch. Assoc. San Joaquin Valley Dental Group, Calif., dental dir. Calif., 1999. Mem.: ADA, Am. Acad. Implants Dentistry, Santa Clara County Dental Soc., Calif. Dental Soc., Am. Dental Soc. Office: 6105 Snell Ave Ste 100 San Jose CA 95123 Office Phone: 408-227-1404.

**SREDNICKI, RICHARD J.,** diversified financial services company executive; With Colgate Palmolive Co., 1975—83, Citibank, 1983—96; pres., CEO AT&T Universal Card Svcs., 1997—98; pres. Sears Home Svcs., 1998; exec. v.p. Chase Corpn., CEO; officer J.P. Morgan Chase & Co., mgr. credit card bus., exec. v.p. Chase cardmember svcs., 0199—2004, CEO card svcs., 2004—. Chmn. US Region Bd. MasterCard, 2004. Office: JP Morgan Chase & Co 270 Park Ave New York NY 10017-2070*

**SREEBNY, LEO M.,** oral biology and pathology professor; b. NYC, Jan. 8, 1922; s. Morris and Lillie (Bogdanoff) S.; m. Mathilda L. Sternfeld, Mar. 9, 1945; children— Oren, Daniel. BA, U. Ill., 1942, D.D.S., 1945, MS, 1950, PhD, 1954; MD (hon.), Semmelweis Med. U., 2001. With dept. periodontics U. Ill., 1948-57, asso. prof., 1956-57; assoc. prof., chmn. dept. oral biology U. Wash., Seattle, 1957-60, prof., 1960-75; dir. U. Wash. (Center for Research Oral Biology), 1967-75; dean Sch. Dental Medicine, SUNY-Stony Brook, 1975-79, prof. dept. oral biology and pathology, 1979—. Cons. VA Hosp., Seattle, 1960—; mem. dental study sect. NIH, 1964-68, chmn., 1967-68; mem. com. on sci. policy Nat. Acad. Sci., 1973-74; mem. med. adv. coun. Internat. Conf. on Integrative Medicine, 1998-99. Author: (with Julia Meyer) Secretory Mechanisms in Salivary Glands, 1963, The Salivary System, 1987, (with I. Van der Waal) Diseases of the Salivary Glands, 1997; contbr. numerous articles to sci., biol. jours. Mem. med. adv. bd. Sjogren's Syndrome Found., 1997, bd. govs. 1998—. Served with AUS, 1942-45; with USNR, 1946-48. Recipient Internat. Assn. for Dental Research Sci. award, 1969; Silver medal for contbns. to dental sci. and art City of Paris, 1979; Salivary Research Group Award, 1987. Mem. Fedn. Dentaire Internat. (chmn. sci. assembly com. 1973—, rep. UN Conf. on Youth 1983-84), Internat. Assn. Dental Research (bd. govs. 1981), Fedn. Dentaire Internat. (list of honor 1988), Am. Assn. Dental Research, ADA. Home: 35 Gnarled Hollow Rd East Setauket NY 11733-2929 Office: SUNY Stony Brook Sch Dental Medicine Stony Brook NY 11794-0001 E-mail: lsreebny@usa.net.

**SREENIVASAN, RAMAVARAPU S.,** mathematics professor; b. Madras, Tamilnadu, India, Apr. 6, 1963; s. Ramavarapu Ramji Rao and Suseela Ramavarapu; m. Manjula V. Tekal; children: Vikram P. Ramavarapu, Maya G. Ramavarapu. PhD, Carnegie Mellon U., Pitts., 1985—90. Post-doctoral fellow Harvard U., Cambridge, Mass., 1990—92; assoc. prof. U. Ill., Urbana, Ill., 1992—. Office: Univ Ill 117 TB 104 S Mathews Ave Urbana IL 61801 Business E-Mail: rsree@uiuc.edu.

**SREENIVASAN, KATEPALLI RAJU,** mechanical engineering educator; b. Kolar, India, Sept. 30, 1947; married 1980; 2 children. BE, Bangalore U., 1968; ME, Indian Inst. Sci., 1970, PhD in Aeronautical Engring., 1975. JRD Tata fellow Indian Inst. Sci., 1972-74, project asst., 1974-75; fellow U. Sydney, Australia, 1975, U. Newcastle, 1976-77; rsch. assoc. Johns Hopkins U., Balt., 1977-79; from asst. prof. to assoc. prof. Yale U., New Haven, 1982-85, prof. mech. engring., 1985—2002, Harold W. Cheel prof. mech. engring., 1988—2002, prof. physics, 1990—2002, prof. applied physics, 1993—2002; Disting. Univ. prof., dir. Inst. Phys. Sci. and Tech., U. Md., College Park, 2002; Abdus Salam hon. prof., dir. Internat. Ctr. for Theoretical Physics, Trieste, Italy. Vis. scientist Indian Inst. Sci., 1979, vis. prof., 1982, Calif. Inst. Tech., Pasadena, 1986, Rockefeller U., 1989, Jawaharlala Nehru Ctr. Advancement Sci. Studies, 1992, chmn. mech. engring. dept.; 1987-92; vis. sci. DFVLR, Gottingen, Germany, 1983; mem. Inst. for Advanced Study, Princeton, N.J., 1995. Contbr. articles to Physics World and other profl. jours. Recipient Narayana Gold medal Indian Inst. Sci., 1975, Disting. Alumnus award, 1992; Humboldt Found. fellow, 1983, Guggenheim fellow, 1989. Fellow AAAS, ASME, Am. Phys. Soc. (Otto Laporte award 1995), AIAA (assoc.), Am. Acad. Arts and Sci., Third World Acad. Scis. (Engring. Sci. medal 2003), Conn. Acad. Arts and Scis.; mem. NAE, Am. Math. Soc., Conn. Acad. Sci. and Engring., Sigma Xi. Achievements include research in origin and dynamics of turbulence; control of turbulent flows; chaotic dynamics; fractals. Office Phone: 39-040-224-0250. E-mail: krs@ictp.trieste.it.*

**SRERE, BENSON M(ORTIMER),** communications executive, consultant; b. Rock Island, Ill., Aug. 13, 1928; s. Jacob H. and Margaret (Weinstein) S.; m. Betty Ann Cerruti, June 20, 1957; children: David Benson, Anne Michele, Peter John. BA magna cum laude, U. So. Calif., 1949. Newsman U.P., L.A., 1948-56; assoc. editor Good Housekeeping mag., N.Y.C., 1956-59, sr. editor, 1959-67, asst. mng. editor, dir. spl. publs. div., 1967-68, mng. editor, 1968-72, exec. editor, v.p., 1972-75, v.p., editorial dir., 1975-76; v.p., gen. mgr. King Features Syndicate, 1976-81; v.p. Hearst Metrotone News, 1976-81; exec. asst. to pres. Hearst Corp., 1981—, v.p., 1983-94. Dir. Hearst/ABC Video Svcs., Hearst/ABC Viacom Entertainment Svcs., A&E Cable Network, Lifetime Cable Network, 1980-94. Trustee Optometric Center of NY Found., 1978-79. Served with U.S. Army, 1950-52. Mem. Soc. Profl. Journalists, Phi Beta Kappa, Phi Kappa Phi, Phi Eta Sigma. Home: 11 Lafayette Ct Greenwich CT 06830-5324

**SRIDHARA, VINAY,** computer scientist; b. Mandya, Karnataka, India, Feb. 20, 1978; arrived in US, 2000; s. Sridhara Keshavamurthy Saligame and Vinoda Venkatasubbaiah Bidare; m. Vasuki Manicka, Sept. 29, 2006. B in Engring., Computer Engring., R. V. Coll. Engring., Bangalore, India, 1999; MS in Computer Sci., U. So. Calif., 2002; PhD in Elec. and Computer Engring., U. Del., 2003—. Software engr. Siemens Comm. Software, Banaglore, Karnataka, 1999—2000; rsch. asst. U of So Calif., L.A., 2000—02, U. of Del., Newark, 2003—06; sys. engring. intern Qualcomm Inc, San Diego, 2006—. Contbr. articles to profl. jours. Named one of Best Undergraduate Rschr. for state, Karnataka, India, 1999; recipient undergrad. rsch. scholarship, Bangalore U., 1999, rsch. scholarship, U. So. Calif., 2000—02, U. Del., 2003—. Mem.: IEEE. Hindu. Achievements include research in methodologies for building and evaluating community wireless mesh networks; development of propagation and mobility simulators which produce results that are close to reality; new methodologies for performance evaluation and planning of Urban Wireless Mesh Networks; new protocols for wireless communication in Urban Mesh Networks; new handoff and system selection protocols for cellular and wireless LAN systems; patents pending for. Avocations: philosophy, sociology, travel, hiking.

**SRIKANT, R.,** electrical and computer engineering professor; B Tech., Indian Inst. Tech., Madras, 1985; MS, U. Ill., Urbana, 1988, PhD, 1991. Mem. tech. staff Bell Labs., Holmdel, NJ, 1991—95; prof. U. Ill., 1995—. Author: Mathematics of Internet Congestion Control; contbr. more than 150 articles to profl. jours. and confs. Fellow: IEEE. Achievements include patents for communications network algorithms. Business E-Mail: rsrikant@uiuc.edu.

**SRINIVASA, VEMURU R.,** engineering educator, researcher; arrived in U.S., 1986; s. Prabhakara R. and Nirmala Vemuru; m. Lakshmi G. Gali, July 12, 1965; children: Lekha S. Vemuru, Priyanka S. Vemuru. BSEE, Indian Inst. Tech., Madras, India, 1984, MSEE, 1986; PhD, U. Toledo, 1991. Asst. prof. City Coll., CUNY, N.Y.C., 1991—2001. Cons. Anadigics, Inc, Warren, NJ, 1996—2001. Home: 25969 Wood Creek Ct Perrysburg OH 43551 Office: Ohio Northern University Dept ECE & CS 525 S Main St Ada OH 45810 Office Phone: 419-772-2388. Office Fax: 419-772-2404. Business E-Mail: s-vemuru@onu.edu.

**SRINIVASAN, PURUSHOTHAMAN,** electrical engineer, researcher; s. Srinivasan Vengadabalagurumoorthy and Vijayalakshmi Srinivasan. PhD, IMEC/N.J. Inst. Tech., 2003—. Sr. design engr. Whirlpool Corp., St. Joseph, Mich., 1994—2002; rschr. N.J. Inst. Tech., University Heights, 2002—. Cons. InPHot Inc., Princeton, NJ, 2004. Contbr. articles to profl. jours. Vol. www.rosevzw.org, Heverlee, Belgium, 2004—06. Recipient Recognition, Whirlpool Corp., 2001, Electronic Design Ctr. Excellence award, 2001, Best Innovator, 2002; grantee, N.J. Inst. Tech., 2003—, U. Md., 2003; Hashimoto fellow, N.J. Inst. Tech., 2005—06, Internat. scholar, Interuniversity Microelectronics Ctr., 2004—05. Mem.: IEEE, Electrochem. Soc. (Travel grantee 2003, 2004, 2005). Achievements include research in High-k dielectrics. Home: 4 Jersey St Fl 2 Harrison NJ 07029 Office Phone: 973-596-6509. Personal E-mail: purushothaman@ieee.org.

**SRINIVASAN, RANGASWAMY,** chemical physicist; b. Madras, India, Feb. 28, 1929; came to U.S., 1953; s. K. Rangaswamy. BSc with honors, Madras U., India, 1949; PhD, U. So. Calif., 1956. Mgr., rsch. T.J. Watson Rsch. Ctr. IBM, Yorktown Heights, NY, 1961-90; chief exec. officer UV Tech Assocs., Ossining, NY, 1990—. Vis. rsch. prof. chemistry Ohio State U., Columbus, 1966-67, Wellman Lab., Mass. Gen. Hosp., Boston, 1987-89, Columbia-Presbyn. Med. Ctr., N.Y.C., 1984-90. Editor: (books) Organic Photochemical Syntheses, Vol. 1, 1972, Vol. 2, 1976; contbr. over 200 articles to profl. jours. Guggenheim fellow, 1966; recipient award for creative invention Am. Chem. Soc., 1997, Essalen award for chemistry in the pub. interest, 1997. Fellow AAAS, Am. Physical Soc. (Biol. Physics prize 1998), NY Acad. Scis., Am. Soc. Laser Medicine and Surgery; mem. NAE (Inventor's Hall of Fame 2002), Am. Inst. Physics (Indsl. Applications prize 2004), Optical Soc. Am. (Wood prize 2004). Achievements include invention of Ablative Photodecomposition, a laser technique for removal of microscopic thickness of organic matter such as plastics (of use in microelectronics) or tissue (of use in LASIK eye surgery).

**SRINIVASAN, SHANKAR PATTAMADAI,** materials scientist, researcher; s. Srinivasan Pattamadai Somaskandan and Bhagavathy Subramanian; m. Shweta Srinivasan, Sept. 16, 2004. BS in Metall. Engring., Regional Engring. Coll., Durgapur, India, 1993; MS in Metall. Engring., Indian Inst. Sci., Bangalore, 1997; PhD in Metall. Engring., U. Utah, Salt Lake City, 2002. Fellow Argonne Nat. Lab., Ill., 2002—. Grantee, Argonne Nat. Lab., 2005. Mem.: Materials Rsch. Soc., ASM Internat., Minerals, Metals and Materials Soc. Office: Argonne National Laboratory 9700 S Cass Ave Argonne IL 60439 Office Phone: 630-252-5111. Office Fax: 630-252-3604. E-mail: shankar@anl.gov.

**SRINIVASAN, VENKATARAMAN,** marketing and management educator; b. Pudukkottai, Tamil Nadu, India, June 5, 1944; came to U.S., 1969; s. Annaswamy and Jambagalakshmi Venkataraman; m. Sitalakshmi Subrahmanyam, June 30, 1972; children: Ramesh, Mahesh. B Tech., Indian Inst. Tech., Madras, India, 1966; MS, Carnegie-Mellon U., 1970, PhD, 1971. Asst. engr. Larsen & Toubro, Bombay, 1966-68; asst. prof. mgmt. and mktg. U. Rochester, NY, 1971-73, assoc. prof. NY, 1973-74, Stanford (Calif.) U., 1974-76, prof., 1976-82, dir. PhD program in bus., 1982-85, Ernest C. Arbuckle prof. mktg. and mgmt. sci., 1982—2003, Adams disting. prof. mgmt., 2003—; mktg. area coord. Stanford U., 1976—78, 1988—93, 2000—03. Mem. bd. acad. trustees Mktg. Sci. Inst., 2004—; cons. in field. Mem. editl. bd. Jour. Mktg. Rsch., 1988—, Mktg. Sci., 1980—, Mgmt. Sci., 1974-91; contbr. articles to profl. jours. Mem. Am. Mktg. Assn., Inst. Ops. Rsch./Mgmt. Scis. Hindu. Avocation: classical music.

**SRIRANGARAJAN, SESHAN,** electrical engineer, researcher; arrived in US, 2001; s. Srirangarajan H.R. and Vathsala Srirangarajan. B of Engring. in Electronics, U. Mumbai, India, 2001; MSEE, U. Minn., Mpls., 2005, postgrad. in electrical engring., 2001—. Tchg. asst. U. Minn., 2002—04, rsch. asst., 2004—; internship Honeywell Internat., Mpls., 2006—. Recipient Cert. Appreciation award, Royal Commonwealth Soc., 1995, Outstanding Tchg. Asst. award, U. Minn., 2002—04, Technical award, Honeywell Tech. Ctr., 2006; grantee Golden Jubilee Scholarship, Tata Chem. Found., 2001. Mem.: IEEE. Hindu. Achievements include patents pending for installation procedure for anchor location information in people and asset localization. Home: 921 24th Ave S Apt # 7 Minneapolis MN 55406 Office: U Minn 200 Union St SE 4-174 EE/CSci Bldg Minneapolis MN 55455 Home Fax: 612-625-4583; Office Fax: 612-625-4583, Business E-Mail: seshan@umn.edu.

**SRIVASTAVA, ANURAG K.,** research scientist; b. Azamgarh, Uttar Pradesh, India, June 30, 1976; s. Suresh C. Sinha and Kamla Srivastava. B Tech., Harcourt Butler Tech. Inst., Kanpur, India, 1997; M Tech., BHU, Varanasi, India, 1999; PhD, Ill. Inst. Tech., 2005. Sr. rsch. assoc. Indian Inst. Tech., Kanpur, 1999—2000; tchg. asst. Ill. Inst. Tech., Chgo., 2001—05, rsch.

assoc., 2001—. Rsch. fellow Asian Inst. Tech., Bangkok, 2000—01. Coord. Nat. Svc. Scheme, Kanpur, Uttar Pradesh, 1996—97. Named Dean's scholar, Ill. Inst. Tech., 2001; scholar, Univ. Grant Commn., 1998—99. Mem.: IEEE (mem. editl. bd. Transactions on Power Sys. 2002), Student Employee Assn. IIT (pres. 2005), IEEE Power Engring. Soc., IEEE Computer Soc., Eta Kappa Nu, Sigma Xi. Office: Ill Inst Tech 3301 S Dearborn St 136 Chicago IL 60616 Home: 60 E 32d St Apt 902 Chicago IL 60616 Personal E-mail: anurags@ieee.org. Business E-Mail: srivanu@iit.edu.

**SRIVASTAVA, ASHOK NARAIN,** computer scientist, consultant; s. Jagdish Narain and Usha Srivastava; m. Lynn Clare Waelde. PhD, U. Colo., Boulder, 1996. Sr. cons. IBM, San Jose, Calif., 1996—2000; sr. dir. Blue Martini Software, San Mateo, Calif., 2000—02; leader intelligent data understanding group Rsch. Inst. Advanced Computer Sci., Moffett Field, Calif., 2002—04; dep. tech. area, mgr. NASA Ames Rsch. Ctr., Moffett Field, 2004—. Program mgr. vulnerability discovery from distributed databases NASA, Moffett Field, 2004—06. Editor: (jour. special issue) Data Mining in Fin. Acharya SGRY, Boulder, 2001—06. Recipient Golden Cir. award, IBM, 1996, Profl. Svcs. award, Blue Martini Software, 2001, Performance award, Rsch. Inst. Advanced Computer Sci., 2003, Disting. Achievement award, NASA, 2005, Group Achievement award, 2005. Mem.: IEEE. Achievements include patents for attributing forecasts to specific variables: a new method to understand why forecasts are made using nearest neighbor methods; symbol extraction from time series: a new method to convert time series into symbolic representations; patents pending for system and method for comparing populations of entities using nearest neighbor methods: a method to compare arbitrary groups of entities using naive Naïve Bayes methods; COLAP database and interactive visualization: a method to develop clickstream online analytical processing cubes with automatic clickstream pattern recognition; research in text mining, data mining, and machine learning. Office: NASA Ames Rsch Ctr Intelligent Systems Divsn Moffett Field CA 94035

**SRIVASTAVA, RAJENDRA PRASAD,** finance educator, researcher; b. Baradih, India, Jan. 1, 1944; s. Ram Dhani Lal and Yashoda Devi; m. Madhuri Srivastava; children: Priti, Alok Kumar. BSc, U. Gorakhpur, India, 1959—61, MSc, 1961—63; MS in Physics, Oreg. State U., Corvallis, 1968—71, PhD in Physics, 1968—72; PhD in Acctg., U. Okla., Norman, 1979—82. Lectr. Birla Inst. Tech., Pilani, India, 1963—68; tchg. asst., physics Oreg. State U., 1968—72, post doctoral fellow, physics, 1972—73; post doctoral fellow, instr. U. N.B., Fredericton, Canada, 1973—76, sr. instr. in physics, 1976—79; tchg. asst. U. Okla., 1979—82; asst. prof. U. Kans., Lawrence, 1982—87, assoc. prof., 1987—93, prof., acctg. & info. systems, 1993—95, Ernst & Young prof. acctg. & info. systems, 1995—. Pres., pres. elect, AI/ET sect. Am. Acctg. Assn., Sarasota, Fla., 1993—95, chair, best dissertation award, AI/ET sect., 2001—02; vis. prof. Inst. Internat. Bus. Studies, Pordenone, Italy, 1993—94; dir. Ernst & Young Ctr. Auditing Rsch. & Advanced Tech., U. Kans., 1995—; vis. prof. Deakin U., Geelong, 1998, U. Fla., Gainesville, 1998; mem. rev. panel NSF, 2000; vis. prof. U. Sydney, 2003, Australian Nat. U., Canberra, 2003, U. Ctrl. Fla., Orlando, 2005; spkr. in field. Assoc. editor Journal of Emerging Technologies in Accounting; author: (internet, xbrl, and online business) The Chartered Accountant. Vol. 51, No. 12, 2003: 1251-1226.; guest co-editor: Info. Sys. Frontier; contbr. papers to profl. jours. and pubs. Active Internat. MBA Program, Pordenone, Italy, 1995—97. Recipient Rsch. Excellence award, U. Kans., 1996—97, Outstanding Mentor award, 1996, Maybry Rsch. award, 1996, Outstanding Grad.& Profl. Mentor Award, 2002, Outstanding Mentor award, 2202, 2004, 2005, 2006; fellow, Am. Acctg. Assn., 1980—81; grantee Post Doctoral fellowship, U. N.B., 1974—75, U. Kans., 1982—2006, Peat Marwick Main & Co., 1986—87, Faculty in Residence, Arthur Andersen & Co., 1987, Peat Marwick Main & Co., 1988—89, 1989—90, Ernst & Young LLP, 1999—2001, Ernst & Young LLP & CIBER, 2003—05, Ernst & Young LLP, 2006, CIBER, 1999—2000, 2001—03, XBRL.org, 2001. Mem.: Am. Acctg. Assn. (assoc.; chmn., nomination com. 1996—97, regional program dir. 1998—2000, mem. IT com. 2000—00). Achievements include patents pending for FRAANK: Financial Reporting and Auditing Agent with Net Knowledge. Office Phone: 785-864-7590.

**SRIVASTAVA, SANJAY K.,** medical researcher; b. Lucknow, India; m. Rekha Srivastava; children: Sameer, Suyash. PhD, Indsl. Toxicology Rsch. Ctr., India, 1992. Prin. investigator U. Pitts. Cancer Inst., 2000—. Achievements include patents pending for use of dietary agents against treating cancer. Home: 8922 Highland Rd Pittsburgh PA 15237 Office: U Pitts Cancer Inst 5117 Centre Ave Pittsburgh PA 15213 E-mail: srivastavask@upmc.edu.

**SROKA, JOHN WALTER,** trade association executive; b. Perth Amboy, N.J., July 24, 1946; s. John and Mary (Teliszewski) S.; m. Paula J. Devitt, Aug. 17, 1968; children: Amanda, Alexandra. BA in Psychology, Fairleigh Dickinson U., 1968, postgrad., 1968-69; postgrad. in law, Am. U., 1972-73. Asst. exec. dir. Associated Gen. Contractors of Am., Washington, 1973-87; exec. v.p. Nat. Assn. Sheet Metal and Air Conditioning Contractors, Chantilly, Va., 1987—. Sgt. U.S. Army, 1969-71. Mem. Am. Soc. Assn. Execs. Roman Catholic. Office: SMACNA 4201 Lafayette Center Dr Chantilly VA 20151-1219 Office Phone: 703-803-2980. Business E-Mail: jsroka@smacna.org.

**SROKA, KAREN JEAN,** clinical director; b. Warwick, RI, Feb. 6, 1967; d. John Adolph and Vivian Joy Sroka. MSN, Georgetown U., Washington, 1996. Cert. geriatric nurse practitioner, ANCC. Nurse practitioner Elder Health Mid-Atlantic, Balt., 1998—2003, clin. dir., 2003—. Bd. mem. Exec. Women's Golf Assn., Washington, 1998. Roman Catholic. Avocation: golf. Office: Elder Health Mid-Atlantic 3601 O'Donnell St Baltimore MD 21224 Office Phone: 410-864-4493, Office Fax: 410-361-1572 Personal E-mail: ohccpr@verizon.net. E-mail: karen.sroka@elderhealth.com.

**SRULOWITZ, MARVIN,** lawyer; b. NYC, Dec. 16, 1948; BA, AA, Yeshiva U., 1969; JD, NYU, 1972. Bar: N.Y. 1973, U.S. Dist. Ct. (ea. and so. dists.) N.Y. 1973, U.S. Ct. Appeals (2d cir.) 1974, U.S. Ct. Internat. Trade 1976, U.S. Supreme Ct. 1976. Assoc. Delson & Gordon, N.Y.C., 1972-77, Mayer Nussbaum Katz & Baker, P.C., N.Y.C., 1977-80; sole practice N.Y.C., 1981—. Mem. New York County Lawyers Assn., Am. Arbitration Assn. Office: 16 E 34th St 16th Fl New York NY 10016-4359 Office Phone: 212-686-1224. E-mail: marvinlaw@aol.com.

**STAAB, DIANE D.,** lawyer; BA, CUNY Hunter Coll., 1977; JD, Yeshiva U., 1980. Bar: N.Y. 1981. Assoc. atty. Hall, McNicol, Hamilton & Clark, 1980-84, Patterson, Belknap, Webb & Tyler, 1984-87; corp. counsel Internat. Paper Co., 1987—95; v.p., gen. counsel, corp. ethics/environ. compliance officer Ariz. Chem., Panama City, 1996—2001; gen. counsel Internat. Paper Europe, 2001—. Mem. ABA (mem. bus. law sect. fed. ref. of securities com. 1988-2001, vice-chmn. com. on corp. & bus. legis. subcom. on corp. governance 1992-98), Assn. of the Bar of the City of N.Y. (mem. spl. com. on election law 1987-89, mem. com. 1989-92, sec. com. on corp. law dept. 1992-93). Office: Internat Paper 400 Atlantic St Stamford CT 06921 Office Phone: 32 02 774 1254.

**STAAB, THOMAS ROBERT,** consumer product company financial executive; b. Beaver Falls, Pa., Apr. 23, 1942; s. Henry Louis and Margaret Constance (Clarke) S.; m. Angela Maria Simon, Aug. 6, 1965; children: Thomas II, Jennifer, Thea. BBA, U. Pitts., 1964, MBA, 1965. CPA, Pa. Sr. audit mgr. Price Waterhouse & Co., 1970-77; practice fellow Fin. Acctg. Standards Bd., Stamford, Conn., 1978-80; fin. corp. acctg. and taxes Fieldcrest Cannon Inc., Eden, NC, 1981-84, asst. contr., 1985, contr., 1986-91, v.p. fin., 1992-93, CFO, 1994-97; bd. dirs., sr. v.p., CFO Lorillard Inc., Greensboro, NC, 1998—. Served to lt. USN, 1966-70. Mem. AICPA, Pa. Inst. CPAs. Republican. Roman Catholic. Home: 3726 NC # 65 Reidsville NC 27320 Office: Lorillard Inc PO Box 10529 714 Green Valley Rd Greensboro NC 27404-0529

**STAAL, ERIC,** professional hockey player; b. Thunder Bay, Ont., Can., Oct. 29, 1984; Center Carolina Hurricanes, 2003—. Player NHL YoungStars Game, 2004. Achievements include being a member of Stanley Cup Champion Carolina Hurricanes, 2006. Office: Carolina Hurricanes RBC Ctr2 1400 Edwards Mill Rd Raleigh NC 27607*

**STAATS, ARTHUR W.,** psychology professor; b. Jan. 17, 1924; BA in Psychology, UCLA, 1949, MA in Psychology, 1953, PhD in Gen. Exptl. and Clin. Psychology, 1956. Psychologist UCLA Counseling Ctr., Los Angeles, 1950-53; clin. trainee VA Hosps., Los Angeles, 1953-55; instr. psychology Ariz. State U., Tempe, 1955-56, asst. prof., 1956-58, assoc. prof., 1958-60, prof., 1960-64; NSF faculty fellow U. London, 1961-62; vis. prof. U. Calif., Berkeley, 1964-65; prof. ednl. psychology and research U. Wis. Research and Devel. Ctr. Cognitive Learning, Madison, 1965-67; vis. prof. U. Hawaii, Honolulu, 1966-67, prof. psychology and ednl. psychology, 1967—. *Mr. Staats was one of several founders of the fields of behavior therapy and behavior analysis and invented the "time out" and token reinforcement methods for training children. His larger career program involves constructing a broad, unified learning-behavior theory of human behavior, known as psychological behaviorism, with numerous possibilities for research and application. This program led to his philosophy of science, the major tenet of which is that all sciences begin in disunity. Phenomena are studied as unrelated, then relationships are found and sought, and sciences become unified. Psychology and behavioral science are currently in disunity and greatly need to be unified.* Author Complex Human Behavior, 1963, Learning, Language and Cognition, 1968, Child Learning, Intelligence, and Personality: A Behavioral Interaction Approach, 1971, Social Behaviorism, 1975, Psychology's Crisis of Disunity: Philosophy and Method for a Unified Science, 1983, Behavior and Personality: Psychological Behaviorism, 1996; editor Human Learning, 1964, Current Issues in Theoretical Psychology, 1987, Annals of Theoretical Psychology, Vol. 5, 1987; contbr. over 80 articles to profl. jours. and 61 chpts. to books; editl. bd. 9 Am. and internat. jours. Named in his honor, Arthur W. Staats Unifying Psychology lectr. (annually). Fellow AAAS, Am. Psychol. Soc.; mem. APA (gen. psychology divsn.), exptl. psychology divsn., devel. psychology divsn., personality and social psychology divs., clin. psychology divsn., ednl. psychology divsn., theoretical and philos. psychology divsn., exptl. analysis of behavior divsn.), Sociedad Interamericana de Psicologia, Psychonomic Soc., Assn. Latinoamericana del Analisis y Modificacion del Comportamiento, Soc. for Exptl. Social Psychology. Home: 1460 Kamole St Honolulu HI 96821-1422 Office: U Hawaii Dept Psychology Honolulu HI 96822 Office Phone: 808-377-3195. E-mail: staats@aloha.com.

**STAATS, DEAN ROY,** retired reinsurance executive; b. Somerville, N.J., Sept. 18, 1924; s. Roy Theodore and Mabel Ellen (Rhodes) S.; m. Marilyn Ann Hockenbury, 1947 (div. 1956; 1 child, Barry Clinton; m. Marilyn Lee Truitt, Dec. 16, 1961 B.Sc., Brown U., 1946, MA, 1948. Asst. actuary N.Am. Reassurance Co., N.Y.C., 1959-67, data processing officer, 1967-69, v.p., actuary, 1969-71, sr. v.p., 1971-84, exec. v.p., 1984-86; pres., dir. NARe Life Mgmt. Co., N.Y.C., 1985-86; rep. Life Ins. Guaranty Corp, 1977-86; U.S. mgr. Can. Reassurance Co., 1984-86; cons. actuary, 1986-89. Served to lt. (j.g.), USN, 1943-46, PTO Fellow Soc. Actuaries; mem. Am. Acad. Actuaries N.Y. Jr. Actuaries Club (pres. 1960-61), Soc. Actuaries (reins. adminstrn. com. 1984-85) Clubs: Anchor and Saber (pres. 1959-60). Republican. Avocations: art, tennis, gardening, travel. Home and Office: 3 Post Run Newtown Square PA 19073-3014 Office Phone: 610-356-5236.

**STABENOW, DEBORAH ANN,** senator, former congresswoman; b. Gladwin, Mich., Apr. 29, 1950; d. Robert Lee and Anna Merle (Hallmark) Greer; m. Tom Athans; children: Todd Dennis, Michelle Deborah. BS magna cum laude, Mich. State U., 1972, MSW magna cum laude, 1975. With spl. svcs. Lansing (Mich.) Sch. Dist., 1972-73; county commr. Ingham County, Mason, Mich., 1975-78; state rep. State of Mich., Lansing, 1979—91, state senator, 1991—94; mem. 103rd-106th Congress from Mich. 8th dist. U.S. Ho. Reps., 1997—2001; US Senator from Mich., 2001—. Founder Ingham County Women's Commn.; co-founder Council Against Domestic Assault. Recipient Service to Children award Council for Prevention of Child Abuse and Neglect, 1983, Service to Mich. Families award Mich. Council Family Relations, 1983, Outstanding Leadership award Nat. Council Community Mental Health Ctrs., 1983, Snyder-Kok award Mental Health Assn. Mich., Awareness Leader of Yr. award Awareness Communications Team Developmentally Disabled, 1984, Communicator of Yr. award Woman in Communications, 1984, Lawmaker of Yr. award Nat. Child Support Enforcement Assn., 1985, Disting. Service award Lansing Jaycees, 1985, Disting. Service in Govt. award Retarded Citizens of Mich., 1986, Cmty. award Mich. Mental Health, 1988, Boxing Glove award Nat. Com. to Preserve Social Security and Medicare, 1999, Home Health Hero Nat. Assn. for Home Care, 1999, Friend of Farm Bur. Mich. Farm Bur., 1999, Leadership award Nat. Coun. of Space Grant Dirs., 1998, Outstanding Achievement Nat. Farmers Union, 1998, Legislator of Yr. award Nat. Multiple Sclerosis Soc., 1992, Assn. for Children's Mental Health, 1991, Mich. Assn. of Vol. Adminstrs., 1989, Citizens Alliance to Uphold Spl. Edn., 1989, Recognition award State 4-H Alumni, 1991, Public. Elected Ofcl. award Nat. Assn. Social Workers, 2004, Congressional Support for Sci. award Inst. Food Technologists, 2004, Cmty. Health Defender award Nat. Assn. Cmty. Health Centers, 2005; named One of Ten Outstanding Young Ams. Jaycees, 1986. Mem. NAACP, Nat. Assn. Social Workers, Lansing Regional C. of C., Delta Kappa Gamma. Democrat. Meth. Office: US Senate 702 Hart Senate Office Bldg Washington DC 20510 also: District Office Ste 100 221 W Lake Lansing Rd East Lansing MI 48823-8661 Office Phone: 202-224-4822, 517-203-1760. Office Fax: 202-228-0325, 517-203-1778. E-mail: senator@stabenow.senate.gov.*

**STABILE, BRUCE EDWARD,** surgeon; b. Monterey Park, California Apr 14, 1944; s. Edward Emilio and Angela (Cramanuzzi) S.; m. Caroline Graston, Sept. 18, 1967; children: Jessica, Drew. BA, UCLA, 1966; MD, U. Calif., San Francisco, 1970. Diplomate Am. Bd. Surgery. From assoc. prof. to prof. vice chmn. dept. surgery Sch. Medicine U. Calif., San Diego, 1985—93, from asst. prof. to assoc. prof. Sch. Medicine, 1977-85, vice chmn. dept. surgery Sch. Medicine, 1993—. Chmn. dept. surgery Harbor UCLA Med. Ctr., Torrance, 1993—, acting med. dir. 1997-98; interim assoc. dean UCLA Sch. Medicine, 1997-98; med. expert Med. Bd. Calif., 1980—; bd. dirs. Am. Bd. Surgery, 1998-2004. Mem. editl. bd.: Jour. Surg. Rsch., 1993—97, Archives of Surgery, 1991—2004. Fellow ACS (gov. 2001—, pres. So. Calif. chpt. 2005-06), Am. Surg. Assn.; mem. Soc. Univ. Surgeons, Assn. Acad. Surgery, Am. Gastroenterol. Assn., San Diego Soc. Gen. Surgeons (pres. 1992-93), L.A. Surg. Soc. (pres. 2000-01), Pacific Coast Surg. Assn. (pres.-elect 2005-2007). Office: Harbor U Calif at L A Med Ctr 1000 W Carson St Torrance CA 90502-2004 Office Phone: 310-222-2701.

**STABLER, LEWIS VASTINE, JR.,** lawyer; b. Greenville, Ala., Nov. 5, 1936; s. Lewis Vastine and Dorothy Daisy Stabler; m. Monteray Scott, Sept. 5, 1958; children: Dorothy Monteray Scott, Andrew Vastine, Monteray Scott Smith, Margaret Langston. BA, Vanderbilt U., 1958; JD with distinction, U. Mich., 1961. Bar: Ala. 1961. Assoc. Cabaniss & Johnston, Birmingham, Ala., 1961-67; assoc. prof. law U. Ala., 1967-70; ptnr. Cabaniss, Johnston, Gardner, Dumas & O'Neal (and predecessor firms), Birmingham, 1970-91, Walston, Stabler, Wells, Anderson and Bains, Birmingham, 1991-97; pvt. practice, Birmingham, 1997—. Mem. com. of 100 Candler Sch. Theology, Emory U. Bd. editors: Mich. Law Rev, 1960-61. Fellow Am. Bar Found. (life); mem. Am. Law Inst. (life), Ala. Law Inst. (mem. coun., dir. 1968-70), ABA, Ala. Bar Assn., Birmingham Bar Assn., Am. Judicature Soc., Am. Assn. R.R. Trial Counsel, Order of Coif. Methodist (tchr. lay leader). Clubs: Country of Birmingham, Rotary. Home: 3538 Victoria Rd Birmingham AL 35223-1404 Office: PO Box 53-1161 Birmingham AL 35253-1161 Office Phone: 205-802-7290. Business E-Mail: vstabler@networktel.net.

**STABY, DOROTHY LOUISE,** elementary school educator; b. Washington, July 26, 1932; d. Charles Pemberton and Eleanor (Thompson) Sheffield; m. Jack Bradford Staby, Oct. 27, 1956; children: John Bradford, Robert Stanford, Mary Katherine. BS in Edn. with honors, James Madison U., 1954; MA, State

U. Iowa, 1955; postgrad., Columbia U., 1957, Bklyn. Coll., 1957, SUNY, New Paltz, 1962, SUNY, Binghamton, 1993. Cert. elem., health and phys. edn. tchr., N.Y. Tchr. phys. edn. Garden City (N.Y.) High Sch., 1955-58; substitute tchr.1st-12th grades Amityville Sch., Capaigue Sch., Massapeque Sch., L.I., N.Y., 1958-63; tchr. 1st and 2d grades St. Patricks Elem. Sch., Owego, N.Y., 1969-70; tchr. 5th grade Glenwood Elem. Sch., Vestal, N.Y., 1970-83; tchr. 2d grade Clayton Ave. Elem. Sch., Vestal, NY, 1983—97. Head, counselor Coll. Settlement Farm Camp, Willow Grove, Pa., 1954-55; instr. Iowa City Recreation Dept., 1955; counselor Garden City Recreation Dept., 1956-57, Country Day Camp, Plainedge, N.Y., 1960-62; tchr. computer Vestal Schs., 1983-87, Vestal Recreation Dept., Vestal, 1989-90, health tchr. Vestal H.S., 1988. Reading vol. Clayton Ave Elem. Sch., 1997—. State U. Iowa scholar, 1954-55. Mem. NEA, AAUW, N.Y. Edn. Assn., Vestal Ret. Tchrs. Assn. Democrat. Methodist. Avocations: computers, reading, sports. Home: PO Box 475 Little Meadows PA 18830-0475 E-mail: jds56@cableracer.com.

**STACEY, JAMES HENRY,** writer, columnist; b. Chgo., July 26, 1935; s. John James and Mary (Hollister) S.; m. Lelia West, Feb. 4, 1956 (div. Mar. 1978); children: Nicole, Michelle; m. Carol Ann Levenson, Apr. 26, 1980. BA, Grinnell Coll., 1957; MA, Grinnell State U., 1960. Asst. editor Bus. Week, Chgo., 1966-68; lectr. Northwestern U., Evanston, Ill., 1968-71; writer, devel. officer U. Chgo., 1972-76; nat. affairs editor Am. Med. News, Chgo., 1976-83, sci. news editor, 1983-86, dir. media rels., 1986-99; freelance writer Chgo., 1999—. Author: Inside the New Temple, 1993, A Wounded Name, 2001, The Medicine Men, 2006; co-author: Severed Trust, 2001; contbr. articles to mags. Avocations: theater, travel, literature. Home: Apt 3006 260 E Chestnut St Chicago IL 60611-2464 Personal E-mail: j.stacey@rcn.com.

**STACEY, SUSAN STEPHANIE,** education administrator; b. N.Y.C., Feb. 9, 1953; d. William John and Margaret Elke Stacey. BFA, Pratt Inst., 1974; MS, Northwestern U., 1975; MA, Columbia U., 1985. Freelance editor N.Y.C., 1975-76; head publs. dept. Christie's, 1976-77; editor Newsbank, New Canaan, Conn., 1977-80; editor Columbia Sch. Press Assn., 1983; tchr. art history and fine arts King Sch., Stamford, Conn., 1980-85, adj. faculty mem., 1987—; adminstr., dir. pub. rels./devel., St. Mary's High Sch., New Haven, 1987-89. Mem. Am. Film Inst., Am. Assn. Museums, Nat. Mus. of Women in the Arts (charter), Friends of Ferguson Library (dir.), Stamford Art Assn. (dir.), Columbia Scholastic Press. Adv. Assn., Assn. Tchrs. in Ind. Schs. (dir.), AAUW, Coll. Art Assn., Am. Soc. for Aesthetics, Northwestern U. Alumni Admissions Council, Kappa Delta Pi. Republican. Episcopalian.

**STACEY, TRUMAN,** journalist, consultant; b. Port Arthur, Tex., Dec. 8, 1916; s. James Harrison and Billie (Davis) S.; m. Dorothy Mary Piboin, May 25, 1963 (dec.); m. Norma Elaine Trahan, Feb. 2, 1980 (dec.). B in Philosophy, U. Detroit, 1946, MA, 1954. Reporter Beaumont (Tex.) Enterprise, 1937-42, Oklahoma City Daily Oklahoman, 1943-44, Detroit Free Press, 1944-45; dir. pub. rels. U. Detroit, 1945-49; reporter Washington Times Herald, 1949-50; sports editor Lake Charles (La.) Am. Press, 1950-60, editor-in-chief, 1961-82; dir. communications Diocese Lake Charles, 1982-90, pres. Coun. of Cath. Men, 1990-92 Author: Louisiana's French Heritage, 1990, The Church Visible, 2000. Mem. Calcasieu Parish (La.) Family Svc. Agy., 1979-82; coord. SW La. Citizens for Ednl. Freedom, 1968-70; bd. dirs. La. Clean. Music and Performing Arts, 1967-79, Calcasieu Citizens for Decency, 1967-69, Lake Charles Symphony Orch., 1967-69. Sgt. U.S. Army, 1942-43; mem. Mayor's Armed Forces Commn., 2003—. Decorated chevalier Order of Merit France; named to La. Sports Writers Hall of Fame, 1982, Columbian Hall of Fame, 1987; recipient Merit award, Sociedad Española de La., 1978, Silver Antelope award, Boy Scouts Am., 1979, George Washington medal of Honor, Freedom Found., 1980, Faith and Freedom award, Religious Heritage Am., Inc., 1980, Harry J. O'Haire Meml. award, Serra Internat. Found., 1987, John Donahue award, 2003, Pilgrim's Shell award, Latin Patriarch Jerusalem, 1988, Nat. Silver Merit medal, Knights of Peter Claver, 1992, Gold medal of merit, 2003, Stephen T. Victory Meml. award, La. Bar Assn, 1992, Past State Deputies award, La. K.C, 1994, Spes Mundi-O'Connell award, Internat. Cath. Com. on Scouting, 2000, Donald Millet Meml. award, S.W. La. Hist. Assn., 2001, Silver St. George emblem, Nat. Cath. Com. on Scouting, 2002, Silver medal of Merit, Sacred Mil. Constantinian Order St. George, 2002, Bishop Charles Pascal Greco Lifetime Achievement award, KC, 2004, St. Christopher emblem, Tex. KC, 2005. Mem.: NCCJ (Brotherhood award 1975), La. Press Assn. (bd. dirs. 1976—79), S.W. La. Hist. Assn. (pres. 2000—02), Inst. de la Maison Royale de France, Lake Charles C. of C. (Man of Yr. 1971), Am. Soc. Newspaper Editors, AP Mng. Editors Assn., La.-Miss. AP Assn. (mem. 1962—63, Merit citation 30 Yrs. Cmty. Svc. 1980), La. Sports Writers Assn., Order St. Lazarus of Jerusalem (officer). Avocations: reading, classical music, stamp collecting/philately. Home: 1802 2nd Ave Lake Charles LA 70601-6432

**STACEY, WESTON MONROE, JR.,** nuclear engineer, physicist, educator; b. Birmingham, Ala., July 23, 1937; s. Weston Monroe and Dorothy (Toole) S.; m. Penny Smith; children: Helen Lee, Weston Monroe III, Lucia Katherine. BS in Physics, Ga. Inst. Tech., 1959, MS in Nuc. Sci., 1963; PhD in Nuc. Engring., MIT, 1966. Nuc. engr. Knolls Atomic Power Lab., Schenectady, NY, 1962-64, 66-69; assoc. dir. applied physics divsn. and dir. fusion program Argonne Nat. Lab., Chgo., 1969-77; Callaway Regents prof. Ga. Inst. Tech., Atlanta, 1977—. Author: Modal Approximation in Reactor Physics, 1967, Space-Time Nuclear Reactor Kinetics, 1969, Variational Methods in Nuclear Reactor Physics, 1972, Fusion Plasma Analysis, 1981, Fusion, 1984, Nuclear Reactor Physics, 2001, 2nd edit., 2006, Fusion Plasma Physics, 2005; contbr. over 250 articles to profl. jours. Recipient Cert. Appreciation Dept. Energy, 1981, 88, Disting. Assoc. award Dept. Energy, 1990, Rsch. award Sigma XI, 1998. Fellow. Am. Nuc. Soc. (bd. dirs. 1974—77, Outstanding Achievement award 1981, 1996, Seaborg medal 2001, Wigner award 2003), Am. Phys. Soc.; mem.: AAAS, Am. Soc. Engring. Edn. Office: Ga Inst Tech Nuclear Engring Dept 0425 Atlanta GA 30332-0425 Office Phone: 404-894-3714. Business E-Mail: weston.stacey@nre.gatech.edu.

**STACHEL, JOHN JAY,** physicist, researcher; b. NYC, Mar. 29, 1928; s. Jacob Abraham and Bertha Z. Stachel; m. Evelyn Lenore Wassermann, Feb. 8, 1953; children: Robert, Laura, Deborah. BS, CCNY, 1956; MS, Stevens Inst. Tech., 1959, PhD, 1962. Instr. physics Lehigh U., Bethlehem, Pa., 1959-61; instr. physics U. Pitts., 1961-62, research assoc., 1962-64; asst. prof. physics Boston U., 1964-69, assoc. prof., 1969-72, prof., 1972-96; dir. Ctr. for Einstein Studies, Boston U., 1985—, prof. emeritus, 1996—. Vis. rsch. assoc. Inst. Theoretical Physics, Warsaw, 1962; vis. prof. King's Coll., U. London, 1970-71, U. Paris, 1990-91, Max Planck Inst. for History of Sci., Berlin, 1994—, Calif. Inst. Tech., 1998; vis. sr. rsch. fellow Dept. Physics, Princeton U., 1977-84; rsch. assoc. U. Calif., Berkeley, 1994. Author: Einstein from B to Z, 2002; editor: Selected Papers Leon Rosenfeld, 1979, Foundations of Space-Time Theories, 1977, Einstein Studies, 1989—, Collected Papers of Albert Einstein, 1978-88, Einstein's Miraculous Year, 1998, 2d edit., 2005. Office: Boston U Ctr Enstein Studies 745 Commonwealth Ave Boston MA 02215-1401 Business E-Mail: stachel@bu.edu.

**STACHIW, JAROSLAW (JERRY) DRAHOMYR,** mechanical engineer, consultant; b. Lviv, Ukraine, May 23, 1931; arrived in U.S., 1949; s. Mathew and Frances Stachiw; m. Joan Lee Atkerson, June 5, 1955; children: Michael, Mark. BSME, Okla. State U., 1955; MS in Engring. Mechs., Pa. State U., 1961, DEd in Higher Edn., 1963. Cert. profl. engr. Rsch. engr. Ordnance Rsch. Lab., State College, Pa., 1959—64, Naval Civil Engring. Lab., Port Hueneme, Calif., 1964—70; sr. engr., program mgr., staff scientist for materials Naval Undersea Ctr., Naval Command Control and Ocean Surveillance, San Diego, 1970—94; cons. Stachiw Assocs., Rockport, Tex., 1972—. Author: Acrylic Plastic Viewports, 1982, Handbook of Acrylics for Submersibles, Hyperbaric Chambers and Aquaria, 2003; contbr. articles to profl. jours. 1st lt. U.S. Army, 1957—59, Redstone Arsenal, Ala. Recipient Lauritsen Bennet award, U.S. Naval Systems Ctr., 1991. Fellow: ASME (chmn. ocean engring. divsn. 1972—73, chmn. subcom. pressure vessels for human occupancy 1972—87, hon. mem. pressure vessels for human occupancy 1987, Centennial medal 1990, Mil. Oceanographer award 1970, Pressure Tech. Codes Dedicated Svc. award 1989); mem.: Marine Tech. Soc., N.Y. Acad. Scis., Sigma Xi. Achievements include patents in field. Home and Office: Mountain Springs Ranch 2057 Holland Spring Canyon Lake TX 78133 E-mail: j.stachiw@hydroports.com.

STACK, BRENDAN CURRAN, JR., head and neck surgeon, researcher, educator; b. New Orleans, Mar. 25, 1963; s. Brendan Curran and Marailyn Kay (Snyder) S.; m. Cynthia Louise Albright, Jan. 28, 1989; children: Brendan Curran III, Mallory Corbin, Cameron Elliott, Madison Hailey. BS, Brigham Young U., 1985; MD, Ea. Va. Med. Sch., 1989. Diplomate Am. Bd. Otolaryngology, Nat. Bd. Med. Examiners. Intern U. South Fla., Tampa, 1989-90, resident, 1990-95; fellow U. Wash., Seattle, 1995-97, instr., 1995-97; asst. prof. St. Louis U., 1997—. Investigator LDF monitoring of regional tissue flaps, Otolaryngology—Head & Neck Surgery, 1995 (Resident rsch. award 1995); mem. editl. rev. bd. Otolaryngology HNS, 1995—; editor Internat. Online Jour. ORL-HNS. Fellow Am. Acad. Otolaryngology—Head and Neck Surgery. Republican. Mem. Lds Ch. Office: St Louis Univ Sch Med Dept ORL-H&NS 3635 Vista Ave # Saint Louis MO 63110-2539

STACK, EDWARD W., retail executive; Mdse. mgr., store mgr., pres. Dick's Sporting Goods Inc., Pitts., 1977—84, chmn., CEO, 1984—. Office: Dick's Sporting Goods Inc RIDC Park W 300 Industry Dr Pittsburgh PA 15275*

STACK, EDWARD WILLIAM, diversified financial services company executive; b. Rockville Centre, NY, Feb. 1, 1931; s. Edward Henry and Helen Margaret (Leitner) S.; m. Christina Carol Hunt, Aug. 19, 1967; children: Amy Alison, Kimberly Anne, Suzanne Gail. BBA, Pace U., 1956; LLD (hon.), Hartwick Coll., 1982; LHD (hon.), Pace U., 1991, L.I. U., 1994. With Clark Estates, Inc., N.Y.C., 1956-2000, pres., bd. dirs., 1990-2000. Trustee NY State Hist. Assn., Cooperstown, 1975—2002, Mary Imogene Bassett Hosp., 1973—; vice chmn. NY State Trooper Found.; emeritus trustee Hartwick Coll., Oneonta, NY; sec. Nat. Baseball Hall of Fame and Mus., Inc., Cooperstown, 1961—77, pres., chmn., 1977—93, chmn., 1993—2000, dir. 1977—; mem. adv. bd. Salvation Army Nassau County and Greater N.Y., Ctr. for Family Life, Sunset Pk., Bklyn.; trustee United Meth. Ch., Sea Cliff, NY; bd. dirs. Farmers' Mus., Inc., Cooperstown, The Clark Found., NYC, The Scriven Found., NYC, SCO Family of Svcs., Glen Cove, NY, Mental Health Assn. Nassau County, Baseball Assistance Team; hon. dir. United Meth. City Soc. Mem. Mohican Club (Cooperstown, N.Y.). Republican. Home: 25 Waverly St Glen Head NY 11545-1004 Personal E-mail: ewstack@aol.com.

STACK, FRANK HUNTINGTON, painter, retired art educator; b. Houston, Oct. 31, 1937; s. Maurice Z. and Norma Rose (Huntington) S.; m. Mildred Roberta Powell, June 12, 1959; children: Joan Elaine, Robert Huntington. BFA, U. Tex., 1959; postgrad., Sch. Art Inst. Chgo., 1960-61; MA, U. Wyo., 1963. Assoc. art editor Houston Chronicle, 1959-60; instr. U. Mo., Columbia, 1963-69, prof., art, 1969-95, Catherine P. Middlebush prof. humanities, 1995-2000, prof. emeritus, 2000—. Mem. regional adv. bd. Mo. Arts Coun., Columbia, 1979-80; mem. exec. bd. U. Mo. Art and Archaeology Mus., Columbia, 1983-84; mem. art dept. U. Mo., Columbia, 1981-83; mem. pers. com. U. Mo. Columbia Arts and Sci. Coll., Columbia, 1976-80; vis. artist W.Va. Arts Coun. and Exxon, Shepherd Coll., Shepherdstown, W.Va., 1983. Artist, author: (cartoons) The New Adventures of Jesus, 1963-95, (book of cartoons) Dorman's Doggie, 1990; illustrator artist: (graphic novel) Our Cancer Year, 1994 (Best Graphic Novel Harvey award 1995), Naked Glory: erotic art of Frank Stack. 1997; artist traveling exhibit Watercolors by Frank Stack, 1977-79; editor: (collection of comic strips) Alley Oop, 3 vols. 1946-47, 47-48, 48-49, 1990, 93, 95 (nominated Best Reprint 1991, 94, 96), Alley Oop mag., 1997—; mem. dv. bd. Jour. Cartoon and Comic Art, 1984—; contbg. writer The Comics Jour., 1989—. Mem. mus. rev. bd. U. Mo., 4 campus sys., Columbia, 1989. With U.S. Army, 1960—62. Recipient Rsch. Grants, U. Mo. Rsch. Coun., Columbia, 1969, 85, 93, 98, Gov.'s Arts awards Artist of Yr. Mo. Arts Coun., St. Louis, 1986. Mem, Kans. Watercolor Soc. (awards 1992, 96), Columbia Art League (adv. bd. 1978-82), Mo. Watercolor Soc. (award 2003). Avocations: historical research, art history, newspaper comics of 1930's and 40's, collector of master prints. Home: 409 Thilly Ave Columbia MO 65203-3458 Office Phone: 573-442-3009. Personal E-mail: stackf@missouri.edu.

STACK, GEOFFREY LAWRENCE, real estate developer; b. Trinidad, Brit. West Indies, Sept. 16, 1943; s. Gerald Francis and V. Louise (Bell) S.; m. Victoria Hammack, 1970 (div. 1986); 1 child, Kathryn; m. Nancy J. Haarer, Apr. 19, 1987; children: Alexandra, Natalie. BA, Georgetown U., 1965; MBA, U. Pa., 1972. Dir. acquisitions J.H. Snyder Co., L.A., 1972-75; from project mgr. to exec. v.p. Richards West, Newport Beach, Calif., 1975-77; pres. Regis Homes Corp., Newport Beach, 1977-93; mng. dir. Sares-Regis Group, Irvine, Calif., 1993—. Bd. dirs. Arral & Ptnrs., Hong Kong, Caalif. Housing Coun., Sacramento, Tejon Ranch Co. Chmn. bd. dirs. Nat. Multihousing Coun., 1987—; trustee Urban Land Inst., Marine Corps Scholarship Found., 2005. Capt. USMC, 1967—70. Decorated 2 Bronze Stars, 21 Air medals, Navy Commendation medal, Purple Heart. Mem. Young Pres. Orgn., Calif. Club, Big Canyon Country Club, Pacific Club, Olympic Club. Democrat. Roman Catholic. Office: SARES REGIS Group 18802 Bardeen Ave Irvine CA 92612-1521 Office Phone: 949-756-5959. Business E-Mail: jstack@saresregis.com.

STACK, GEORGE JOSEPH, philosopher, writer; b. NYC; m. Mary K. Di Maria, 1997; children: Diane, Christopher, stepchildren: Jena, Shelley. BA, Pace U., 1960; MA, Pa. State U., 1962, PhD, 1964. Instr. humanities Pa. State U., 1962-63; instr. philosophy L.I. U., 1963-64, asst. prof., 1964-67, SUNY, Brockport, 1967-68, asso. prof., 1968-70, prof., chmn., 1970-77, 1985—94, prof., 1994—95, prof. emeritus 1995—, also advisor Center for Philosophic Exchange, 1970-82. Author: Berkeley's Analysis of Perception, 1970, re-printed, 1991, On Kierkegaard: Philosophical Fragments, 1976, Kierkeg-aard's Existential Ethics, 1977;: 2d edit., 1992, Japanese transl., 1985, Sartre's Philosophy of Social Existence, 1978, reprinted, 1992, Lange and Nietzsche, 1983, Nietzsche and Emerson, 1992, Nietzsche's Anthropic Circle, 2005; contbg. author Nietzsche and Modern German Thought, 1991, Emerson/Nietzsche, 1998, The Emerson Enigma, 2003; contbr. numerous articles and reviews to profl. jours. Office: PO Box 92 Grapevine TX 76099-0092

STACK, KEVIN J., lawyer; b. NYC, Aug. 12, 1951; BA cum laude, UCLA, 1973; JD cum laude, Loyola U., L.A., 1976. Bar: Calif. 1976, U.S. Dist. Ct. (ctrl. dist.) Calif. 1977. Ptnr. Knapp, Petersen & Clarke, Glendale, Calif., 1984—. Office: Knapp Petersen & Clarke 500 N Brand Blvd Fl 20 Glendale CA 91203-1923

STACK, MAY ELIZABETH, retired library director; b. Jackson, Miss. Nov. 10, 1940; d. James William and Irene Thelma (Baldwin) Garrett; m. Richard Gardiner, Apr. 15, 1962; children: Elinor, Harley David. BS, Miss. State Coll. for Women, 1962; MBA, Western New Eng. Coll., 1981; MLS, So. Conn. State U., 1989. Clk. Western New Eng. Coll., Springfield, Mass., 1965-66, acquisitions staff, 1966-72, cataloger, 1972-84, asst. dir., 1984-89, acting dir., 1989-92, dir., 1990—2005. Chair Ctrl./Western Mass. Automated Resource Sharing Collection Devel. Com., Paxton, Mass., 1993-95, exec. bd., 1993-96. Mem. East Longmeadow (Mass.) Hist. Soc., 1989-92. Mem. ALA, Mass. Libr. Assn., Assn. Coll. and Rsch. Librs., Libr. and Mgmt. Assn., Libr. Info. and Technology Assn. Methodist. Avocations: horseback riding, show dogs. Office: Western New Eng Coll D'Amour Libr 1215 Wilbraham Rd Springfield MA 01119-2612 Business E-Mail: mstack@wnec.edu.

STACK, MICHAEL, artist; b. Chgo., Oct. 30, 1941; life ptnr. Alice Lyn Rudolph; children: Paul, Timothy, Erin Kelly. MFA, U. Fla., Gainesville, 1966. Artist STACKART, Inc., Chgo., 1996—. Office: STACKART Inc 2023 W Carroll Ave Chicago IL 60612 Office Phone: 312-415-0768. Business E-Mail: michael@stackart.com.

STACK, PAUL FRANCIS, lawyer; b. Chgo., July 21, 1946; s. Frank Louis and Dorothy Louise Stack; m. Nea Waterman, July 8, 1972; children: Nea Elizabeth, Sera Waterman. BS, U. Ariz., 1968; JD, Georgetown U., 1971. Bar: Ill. 1971, U.S. Ct. Claims 1975, U.S. Tax Ct. 1974, U.S. Ct. Internat. Trade 1977, U.S. Supreme Ct. 1975. Law clk. U.S. Dist. Ct., Chgo., 1971-72; asst. U.S. atty. No. Dist. Ill., Chgo., 1972-75; mng. dir. Stack & Filpi, Chgo., 1976—. Bd. dirs. Riverside (Ill.) Pub. Libr., 1977-83, Suburban Libr. Sys., Burr Ridge, Ill., 1979-82; mem. Mayor's ad hoc adv. com. on Ctrl. Libr., Chgo., Ill., 1987-88; mem. bd. edn. Twp. H.S. Dist. 208, Riverside, Ill., 1989-97; pres. Village of Riverside, Ill., 1997-2001; mem. exec. com. Chgo. Area Transp. Study, 1999-2001. Mem. Chgo. Zool. Soc. (gov. 1980—, planned giving adv. com. 1996-99), Chgo. Bar Assn., Union League Club of Chgo. (bd. dirs. 1986-89). Home: 238 N Delaplaine Rd Riverside IL 60546-2035 Office: 140 S Dearborn St Ste 411 Chicago IL 60603-5201

STACK, ROBERT B., lawyer; b. Feb. 9, 1955; MA, NYU, 1980; MSFS, Georgetown Univ., 1984, JD magna cum laude, 1984. Bar: NY 1987, DC 1988. Law clk. Judge Thomas A, Flannery, US Dist. Ct. (DC dist.), Justice Potter Stewart, US Supreme Ct., 1985; ptnr., co-chmn. Tax dept. Wilmer Cutler Pickering Hale & Dorr, Washington. Editor (in chief): Georgetown Law Jour. Mem.: US Council on Internat. Bus. (mem. Tax com.), Internat. Fiscal Assn. Office: Wilmer Cutler Pickering Hale & Dorr 1899 Pennsylvania Ave NW Washington DC 20006 Mailing: Wilmer Cutler Pickering Hale & Dorr 2445 M St NW Washington DC 20037 Office Phone: 202-663-6272. Office Fax: 202-663-6363. Business E-mail: robert.stack@wilmerhale.com.

STACK, ROBERT TIMOTHY, health facility administrator; b. Pitts., 1952; m. Mary Stack; 3 children. BA, Bethany (W.Va.) Coll., 1952; MA, Med. Coll. Va., 1977. Asst. adminstr. Southside Hosp., Pitts., 1977-79; sr. v.p., COO Cen. Med. Ctr., Pitts., 1980-81; pres., CEO Southside Hosp., Pitts., 1981-87, Borgess Health Alliance Inc., Kalamazoo, 1987—2001, Piedmont Med. Ctr., Atlanta, 2001—03, MedQuist Inc., Marlton, NJ, 2003—. Mem.: bd. dirs. MedQuist Inc., 1997-2000, 2003-, bd., American Hosp. Assoc., 1999-2001, bd. dirs., Piedmont Med. Ctr., 1997-2000.

STACK, ROBERT VERNON, dean, mathematics professor; b. Hastings, Nebr., Sept. 12, 1967; s. Philip and Fe Stack; m. Jill Marie Rausch, July 7, 1990; children: Kennady, Kiya, Riley, Cassin, Jayden, Brooklyn. BA in Edn., U. S.D., 1990, MA in Math., 1991, EdD, 1998. Assoc. prof. math. Chadron (Nebr.) State Coll., 1998—2004, dean students, 2004—. Recipient Nebr. State Coll. Tchg. Excellence award, Nebr. State Coll. Sys., 2004. Mem.: Nebr. Assn. Tchrs. Math. (pres. 2005—05), Nat. Coun. Tchrs. Math. Office: Chadron State College 1000 Main St Chadron NE 69337 Office Phone: 308-432-6280. Business E-Mail: rstack@csc.edu.

STACK, STEPHEN S., manufacturing executive; b. DuPont, Pa., Apr. 25, 1934; s. Steve and Sophie (Baranowski) Stasenko; m. Lois Sims Agnew, May 25, 1996. BSME, Case Western Res. U., 1956; postgrad., Syracuse Univ. registered profl engr., Ill. Mech. engr. Kaiser Aluminum, Erie, Pa., 1956-58; instr. Gannon Univ., Erie, Pa., 1958-60, Syracuse U., NY, 1960-61; engrg. supr. A.O. Smith Corp., Erie and Los Angeles, 1961-66; gen. mgr. Am. Elec. Fusion, Chgo., 1966-67; mgr.new products Maremont Corp., Chgo., 1967-69; dir. market planning Gulf and Western Ind., Bellwood, Ill., 1969-71; mgmt. and fin. cons. Stack & Assocs., Chgo., 1971-76; pres. Seamcraft, Inc., Chgo., 1976—. Mem. Ill. Legis. Small Bus. Conf., 1980, Gov.'s Small Bus. Adv. Commn., 1984-94, Ill. State House Conf. on Small Bus., 1984, 86, 99; chmn. West Cell, 1988-2000; chmn., founder Bridge Pers. Svcs. Corp., 1989—; vice pres., founder Ind. Bus. Assn. Ill., 1993-94; small bus. adv. coun. Fed. Res. Bank Chgo., 1989-91, Nat. Fedn. Ind. Bus., 1980—, mem. Ill. State. Leadership Coun. 1999-, del. White House Conf. on Small Bus., 1986, Nat. Small Bus. Attitudes Rsch. Panel, 1987-, pres. Chgo. Marine Heritage Soc., 1999—, mem. Navy League of the US, 1991-2001, del. Congl. Small Bus. Summit, 1998, 2000, 02, 04, 06; with Ill. Small Bus. Leadership Coun., 2000—. Treas. Sem. Townhouse Assn., 1993-94; active Lincoln Park Conservation Assn., Sheffield Neighbors Assn.; mem. adv. coun., DePaul U. Coll. Commerce, 2000—. Recipient Am. Legion awd., 1948, Case Western Res. U. Honor key, 1956, Easgle Scout awd., 1949. Mem. Ill. Mfrs. Assoc. (bd. dirs. 1986-98, vice chmn. 1995-98), Small Mfrs. Action Couns. (chmn. 1986-87, chmn. 1988-89), Mfrs. Polit. Action Com. (exec. com. 1987-98, vice chmn. 1993-95, chmn. 1995-98), Am. Mgmt. Assn., Pres. Assn., Blue Key, Beta Theta Pi, Theta Thau, Pi Delta Epsilon. Chgo. Yacht Club, East Bank Club, Fullerton Tennis Club (pres. 1971-79, treas. 1979-83, bd. dirs 1983-86), Lake Shore Ski Club (v.p. 1982, 91), Lincoln Park Tennis Assn. Patentee in liquid control and metering fields. Office: 932 W Dakin St Chicago IL 60613-2922

STACKELBERG, JOHN RODERICK, history professor; b. Munich, May 8, 1935; came to U.S., 1946; s. Curt Freiherr and Ellen (Biddle) von Stackelberg; m. Steffi Heuss, Oct. 10, 1963 (div. Apr. 1983); m. Sally Winkle, Mar. 30, 1991; children: Katherine Ellen, Nicholas Olaf, Emmet Winkle. AB, Harvard U., 1956; MA, U. Vt., 1972; PhD, U. Mass., 1974. Reading instr. Baldridge Reading Svcs., Greenwich, Conn., 1957-62; lang. tchr. Hartnack-schule, Berlin, 1963-67; English and social studies tchr. Lake Region Union High Sch., Orleans, Vt., 1967-70; lectr. history San Diego State U., 1974-76; asst. prof. history U. Oreg., Eugene, 1976-77, U. S.D., Vermillion, 1977-78, Gonzaga U., Spokane, Wash., 1978-81, assoc. prof. history, 1981-88, prof. history, 1988—, Powers prof. of humanities, 1997—. Author: Idealism Debased, 1981, Hitler's Germany: Origins, Interpretations, Legacies, 1999, (with Sally A. Winkle) The Nazi Germany Sourcebook: An Anthology of Texts, 2002; contbr. articles to profl. jours. Pres. Spokane chpt. UN Assn., 1986-90. With U.S. Army, 1958-60. Leadership Devel. fellow Ford Found., 1969-70. Avocations: chess, tennis. Home: 530 W 24th Ave Spokane WA 99203 Office: Gonzaga U Dept History Spokane WA 99258-0001 Office Phone: 509-747-2077. Personal E-mail: rodstackelberg@comcast.net.

STACKHOUSE, JERRY, professional basketball player; b. Kinston, N.C., Nov. 5, 1974; Student, N.C. U., 1997. Basketball player Phila. 76ers, 1995—98, Det. Pistons, 1997—2002, Washington Wizards, 2002—04, Dallas Mavericks, 2004—. Named to NBA All-Rookie Team, 1995—96, NBA All-Star Game, 2000, 2001. Office: c/o Dallas Mavericks The Pavillion 2909 Taylor St Dallas TX 75226*

STACKHOUSE, MAX LYNN, religious studies educator; b. Ft. Wayne, Ind., July 29, 1935; s. C. Dale and Naomi Elizabeth (Graham) S.; m. N. Jean Hostetler, Aug. 19, 1959; children: Dale Emil, David Graham, Sara Elizabeth. BA, De Pauw U., Greencastle, Ind., 1957, LHD (hon.), 1995; cert., Nijenrode U., Breukelen, The Netherlands, 1958; BD, MDiv, Harvard U., Cambridge, Mass., 1961, PhD, 1966. Ordained to ministry United Ch. of Christ, 1961. Lectr. Harvard Divinity Sch., Cambridge, Mass., 1964-66; asst. prof. Andover-Newton Theol. Sch., Mass., 1966-69, assoc. prof. Mass., 1969-73, prof. Mass., 1973-78, Herbert Gezork prof. Mass., 1978-93; Stephen Colwell prof. Princeton Theol. Sem., NJ, 1993—2004, Rimmer and Ruth de Vries prof. theology and pub. life NJ, 2004—. Vis. prof. United Theol. Coll., Bangalore, India, 1973, 76, 82, 87, 2000, Pacific Theol. Coll., Suva, Fiji, 1982, Das Sprachenkonvikt, East Berlin, 1983; pres. joint doctoral program Boston Coll. and Andover Newton Theol. Sch., 1988-89, chmn. rels. and soc. dept., 1975-93; dir. Kuyper Ctr. for Pub. Theology, 1994—; pres. Berkshire Inst. Theology and Arts, 1991—. Author: Creeds, Society and Human Rights, 1984, Public Theology and Political Economy, 1987, Apologia, 1988 (Best Booklist Internat. Bull. Missiology 1988), On Moral Business, 1994, Christian Ethics in a Global Era, 1996, Covenant and Commitments, 1998, God and Globalization, vol. 1, 2000, vol. 2, 2001, vol. 3, 2002; author, editor 24 books; mem. editl. bd. Jour. Religious Ethics, Christian Century, Jour. Polit. Theology; contbr. articles to profl. jours. Investigation team Am. Com. for Human Rights, Philippines, 1987-93; exec. sect. Am. Com. for Higher Edn. in India, 1986-91. Rsch. grantee Ctr. for Urban Studies, Harvard U., 1965-66, Assn. Theol. Schs., 1986-87, Lilly Endowment, Indpls., 1989, 91, Pew Charitable Trusts, 1993, 98; recipient Outstanding Alumnus award DePauw U., 1988. Fellow Soc. for Sci. Study of Religion (bd. dirs. 1980-84), Soc. for Values in Higher Edn.; mem. NAACP.

Amnesty Internat., Am. Theol. Assn., Soc. Christian Ethics (past pres., past exec. sec.), Stockbridge Club. Democrat. Office: Princeton Theol Sem PO Box 821 Princeton NJ 08542-0803 Office Phone: 609-497-7898.

STACKPOLE, KERRY CLIFFORD, association executive; b. Putnam, Conn., Feb. 24, 1955; s. Howard Thompson Stackpole and Shyrlee Gladys Burr; m. Miriam Weisberg, July 29, 1984. MEd, Cambridge Coll., 1983. Gen. mgr. E.J. Ardon Co., Boston, 1978-82; ops. mgr. Fotobeam/Brookside, Waltham, Mass., 1982-83; assoc. dir. Printing Industries of New Eng., Natick, Mass., 1983—, v.p., 1989-91; exec. dir. Smaller Bus. Assn. New Eng., Waltham, Mass., 1991-93; pres., CEO The Assn. for Work Process Improvement, Inc., 1993-97, Electronic Messaging Assn., 1997—2000, chmn. CEO Neoterica Ptnrs., LLP, McLean, Va., 2000—; exec. dir., CEO Nat. Assn. Catering Execs., Inc., Columbia, Md., 2003—09. Bd. dirs. Mass. Cert. Devel. Corp., EC Inst., Denver, Conv. Industry Coun.; mem. U.S. C. of C. Com. of 100, 2000—. Recipient HIRE Trust Fund award Graphic Arts Employers of Am., 1987, 2000. Fellow Am. Soc. Assn. Execs. (cert., mem. ann. meeting adv. com. 1996-97, mem. edn. com., 1996-99, chmn., exec. mgmt. sect. coun., 1997-98, bd. dirs., 1997-98, mem. key industries assn. com. 2000—); mem. Assocs. Advance Am. Com. (chmn. 1999-2000), New Eng. Soc. Assn. Execs. (committeeman 1983-84, membership devel. com. 1989-91, chmn. edn. com. 1991-93, bd. dirs. 1991—, treas.-sec. 1994-95, chmn.-elect 1995, chmn. bd. dirs. 1996—, immediate past chmn, 1997-98, Ralph Louis Towne award 1986). Avocations: reading, cross country skiing, ocean kayaking, jazz music buff. Office: Neoterica Ptnrs LLP PO Box 7763 Mc Lean VA 22106 Personal E-mail: kerry.stackpole@neoterica.com.

STACKS, KAREN BETH, music educator; b. Springfield, Mo., Apr. 27, 1970; d. Roy Lee and Grace Chandler Woodall; m. Eric Ray Stacks, Dec. 21, 1991; children: Tyler Isaac, Morgan Elise, Macy Danielle. MusB, SW Bapt. U., 1992; M, So. Bapt. Theol. Sem., 1995. Teaching Certification SW Mo. State U., 2001. Music tchr. Neosho R-V Schools, Mo., 1998—2000, Adams 12 Five Star Schools, Thornton, Colo., 2001—. Honors choir clinician Adams 12 Five Star Schools, Thornton, Colo., 2002, Adams 50 Schools, Westminster, Colo., 2005; reading session clinician Flesher Hinton Music Corp., Denver, 2005. Music scholarship, SW Bapt. U., 1992—95. Mem.: Internat. Assn. of Jazz Educators (assoc.), Music Educators Nat. Conf. (assoc.), Am. Choral Directors Assn (assoc.; membership chair 2005—06). Avocations: golf, reading, music, travel, musical theater. Home: 13945 Jasmine Thornton CO 80602 Office: Legacy HS 2701 W 136th Ave Broomfield CO 80020 Office Phone: 720-972-6795. E-mail: karen.stacks@adams12.org.

STACY, BILL WAYNE, academic administrator; b. Bristol, Va., July 26, 1938; s. Charles Frank and Louise Nelson (Altwater) S.; m. Sue Varnon; children: Mark, Sara, James. BSEd., S.E. Mo. State U., 1960; MS, So. Ill. U., 1965, PhD, 1968. Tchr. Malden High Sch., Mo., 1960-64; faculty Southeast Mo. State U., Cape Girardeau, 1967-89, dean Grad. Sch., 1976-79, interim pres., 1979, pres., 1980-89, Calif. State U., San Marcos, 1989-97; chancellor U. Tenn., Chattanooga, 1997—2004; headmaster Baylor Sch., Chattanooga, 2004—. Bd. dirs. River Valley Ptnrs. Bd. dirs. United Way; mem. Allied Arts Bd. Mem. Am. Assn. Higer Edn., Chattanooga C. of C. (bd. dirs.). Presby-terian. Office: Baylor Sch PO Box 1337 Chattanooga TN 37401

STACY, DENNIS WILLIAM, architect; b. Council Bluffs, Iowa, Sept. 22, 1945; s. William L. and Mildred Glee (Carlsen) S.; m. Judy Annette Long, Dec. 28, 1968; 1 child: Stephanie. BArch, Iowa State U., 1969; postgrad., U. Nebr., 1972. Registered arch., Iowa, Tex., Colu., Mo. Designer Troy & Stalder Archs., Omaha, 1967, Archs. Assocs., Des Moines, 1968-69, Logsdon & Voelter Archs., Temple, Tex., 1970; project arch. Roger Schutte & Assocs., Omaha, 1972-73; arch., assoc. Robert H. Burgin & Assocs., Council Bluffs, 1973-75, Neil Astle & Assocs., Omaha, 1975-78; owner, prin. Dennis W. Stacy, AIA, Arch., Glenwood, Iowa, 1978-81; pres. Stacy Archs., Inc., Dallas, 1981—2001, Stacy Archtl. Studio, PLLC, 2002—. Mem. organizing com. symposium Tex. A&M U., 1991—2006. Archtl. works include: Davies Amphitheater, 1980, Addison Nat. Bank Bldg., 1985, Villa Roma, 1988, C.U. Performing Arts Ctr., 1989, Mercedes-Benz Distbn. Ctr., 1987, Dallas Chpt. AIA Offices, 1990, Janadria Festival Arena, 1994, Physicians Consultants Clinic, 1994, Horizon Pain Mgmt. Ctr., 1995, Rheumatology Assoc. Clinic, 1996, Addison Nat. Br. Bank, 1996, Cummins So. Plains Distbn., Fabrication and Corp. Offices Ctr., 1998, Arthur Murray Dance Studios, 2001, 05, Tatum Residence, 2001, Big Glee Office Plz., 2005. Mem. City of Dallas Urban Design Adv. Coun., 1992-96, chmn., 1995-96; dir. Greater Dallas Planning Coun., 1997-05; chmn. Glenwood Zoning Bd. Adjustment, 1979-81; chmn. Mills County Plant Iowa Program, 1979-81; mem. S.W. Iowa Citizen's Adv. Com., Iowa State Dept. Transp., 1977-81; regional screening chmn. Am. Field Svc. Internat./Intercultural Programs, 1974-79, Iowa-Nebr. rep., 1978-80. With U.S. Army, 1969-71. Decorated Nat. Def. Svc. medal, Vietnam Svc. medal, Vietnam Campaign medal, Army Commendation medal, Disting. Alumnus Design Achievement award Iowa State U., 1999. Fellow AIA (chmn. nat. conv. 2000, Iowa Design Honor award 1981, Dallas AIA commendation awards (2) 1990, 92, 95, 96, 97, 98, Citation of Honor award 1991, 92, 01, Dallas Design awards (2) 1991, 96, 97, Tex. Design Honor award 1992, Dallas AIA Firm of Yr. award 1992, Nat. Presdl. Citation 2000, Dallas commnr. design 1991, chmn. Dallas design awards 1992, pres. Dallas AIA 1996), Tex. Soc. Archs. (environ. resource com. 1994-95, chmn., Tex. arch. pub. com., 1992-98, chmn. 1997, 98), Nat. Coun. Archtl. Registration Bds., Iowa State U. Adv. Coun. (1997-00, 05-06, chmn. 1999-00), The 500 Inc. (Outstanding mem. 1985), Glenwood Optimist Club (Disting. Svc. award 1982, pres. 1980-81), Masons. Home and Office: 4148 Cobblers Ln Dallas TX 75287-6725 Office Phone: 972-250-1909. Personal E-mail: dstacyarch@aol.com.

STACY, FRANCES H., federal judge; b. 1955; BA, Baylor Univ., 1977; JD, Baylor Law Sch., 1979. With U.S. Atty.'s Office (Tex. so. dist.) Criminal Divsn., 1980, Civil Rights Divsn., 1980-81, Land and Resources Divsn., 1981-87, Civil Divsn., 1987-88, Appelate Divsn., 1988-90; magistrate judge U.S. Dist. Ct. (Tex. so. dist.), 5th circuit, Houston, 1990—. Author: Federal Civil Procedure Before Trial, Lawyers Cooperative Practice Guide. Mem. Tex. Bar Found.

STACZEK, JOHN JOSEPH, academic administrator, consultant; b. Toledo, Mar. 1, 1943; s. John Louis and Marilyn Kosnikowski Staczek; m. Camille Mikulak Mikulak, June 16, 1965; children: Jason Luis, Eric Jon. AB, Ohio State U., 1965; MS, Georgetown U., 1970, PhD, 1973. Dir. applied linguistics Georgetown U., Washington, 1990—97; chmn. modern langs. Thunderbird, Glendale, Ariz., 1997—2000, v.p. for faculty, 1999—2001, dir. global svcs., 2001—. Cons. Kuwait U., 1980—92. Editor: (academic research) On Spanish, Portuguese, and Catalan Linguistics, Perspectives on Bilingualism and Bilingual Education. NSF Traineeship, Georgetown U., 1970—72, Sr. Fulbright Professorship, Nicaragua, Coun. for Internat. Ednl. Exch., 1971—72, Sr. Fulbright Professorship, Colombia, 1975, Sr. Fulbright Rsch. Professorship, Poland, 1994. Mem.: Am. Dialect Soc. Democrat. Roman Catholic. Avocations: golf, travel, hiking. Home: 36 E Paint Your Wagon Trail Phoenix AZ 85085 Office: Thunderbird Am Grad Sch Internat Mgmt 15249 N 59th Ave Glendale AZ 85306-6000 Business E-Mail: staczekj@t-bird.edu.

STADDON, JOHN ERIC RAYNER, psychology professor, neurobiology professor, zoology professor; b. Grayshott, Hampshire, Eng. came to U.S., 1960; s. Leonard John and Dulce Norine (Rayner) S.; m. Lucinda Paris. BSc, Univ. Coll. London, 1960; PhD, Harvard U., 1964. Asst. prof. psychology U. Toronto, Ont., Canada, 1964-67; from asst. prof. to prof. Duke U., Durham, NC, 1967-72, prof., 1972-83, J.B. Duke prof. psychology, prof. neurobiology and biology, 1983—. Author: Adaptive Behavior and Learning, 1983, The New Behaviorism, 2001, Adaptive Dynamics, 2001; editor Behavioural Processes, 1970-2001, Behavior and Philosophy, 1993-2004; mem. editl. bd. Jour. Exptl. Analysis of Behavior, 1979-82. Recipient von Humboldt prize, 1985. Fellow AAAS, N.Y. Acad. Scis., Soc. Exptl. Psychologists; mem. Phi Beta Kappa (hon.), Sigma Xi. Avocations: history, philosophy of science, public policy. Office: Duke U Dept Psychol and Brain Scis PO Box 91050 Durham NC 27708 Business E-Mail: staddon@psych.duke.edu.

**STADE, GEORGE GUSTAV,** humanities educator; b. NYC, Nov. 25, 1933; s. Kurt Herman and Eva Bergit (Aronson) S.; m. Dorothy Louise Fletcher, Dec. 16, 1957; children: Bjorn, Eric, Nancy, Kirsten. BA, St. Lawrence U., 1955; MA, Columbia U., 1958, PhD, 1965. Tchr. Collegiate Sch., NYC, 1957-58; instr. Bernard Baruch Sch. Bus., NYC, 1958-59, Bklyn. Poly. Inst., 1959-60, Rutgers U.-Newark, 1960-62, Columbia U., NYC, 1962, asst. prof., 1965, assoc. prof., 1968, prof. English, 1971—. Cons. various law firms, NYC, 1960—; author: Robert Graves, 1967, Confessions of a Lady-Killer, 1979; editor: European Writers, Selected Letters of E.E. Cummings, 1968, Six Modern British Writers, 1974, Six Contemporary British Writers, 1976, European Writers: Selected Authors, 1992, British Writers Supplement II, 1992, British Writers Supplement III, 1995, British Writers Supplement IV, 1997; cons. editl. dir.: Barnes and Nobles Classics; contbr. over 100 articles and reviews; author: Sex and Violence, a Love Story, 2005. Mem. PEN, NY Book Critics Circle, Popular Culture Assn., MLA Home: 430 W 116th St New York NY 10027-7220 Office: Columbia U 604 Philosophy Hall New York NY 10027 Office Phone: 212-854-6410. Business E-Mail: ggs3@columbia.edu.

**STADELMAN, WILLIAM RALPH,** chemicals executive; b. Ont., Can., July 18, 1919; s. John Joseph and Lillian (Trachsell) S.; m. Jean MacLaren, Nov. 2, 1951; 1 child, Mary Laren. BASc, U. Toronto, 1941; MBA, U. Pa., 1949. Chief process engr. Can. Synthetic Rubber, Ltd., 1943-47; lectr. mktg. U. Pa., 1948-49; asst. to mgr. Pa. Salt Mfg. Co., 1950; sec.-treas. Ont. Research Found., Mississauga, 1950-64, pres., 1964-84, WRS Assocs., 1984—; dir. sr. exec. Inst. Chem. Sci. and Tech., 1985-89. Dir. Med. Tech. Investment Corp. Fellow World Acad. Art and Sci.; mem. Assn. Profl. Engrs. Ont., Innovation Mgmt. Assn. Can., Bd. Trade Met. Toronto, Club of Rome, Caledon Ski Club. Home and Office: WRS Assocs 31 Rykert Crescent Toronto ON Canada M4G 2T1 Office Phone: 416-425-4126.

**STADELMANN, EDUARD JOSEPH,** retired plant physiologist, educator, researcher; b. Graz, Austria, Sept. 24, 1920; s. Eduard Joseph and Josefa (Eigner) S.; m. Ok Young Lee, Mar. 22, 1975 (dec. 2005). BS, Bundesreal-gymnasium, Graz, Austria, 1939; PhD, U. Innsbruck, Austria, 1953; Pvt. Docent, U. Freiburg, Switzerland, 1957; PhD (hon.), Agrl. U. Vienna, 1989. Sr. asst. U. Freiburg, 1962-63; rsch. assoc. U. Minn., Mpls., 1963, asst. prof., 1964-66, assoc. prof., 1966-72, prof. hort. sci., 1972-91, prof. emeritus, 1991—. Muellhaupt Scholar in Biology, Ohio State U., 1958-59; Humboldt Found. awardee, 1974-75; Fulbright award, Coun. Internat. Exchange, 1979-80, 87-88. Mem. Am. Inst. Biology, Am. Soc. Plant Biologists, German Bot. Soc., Swiss Bot. Soc., Sigma Xi. Roman Catholic. Office: Univ Minn Dept Hort Sci 1970 Folwell Ave Saint Paul MN 55108-6007 Office Phone: 612-624-3267. Business E-Mail: estadelm@umn.edu.

**STADLER, CRAIG ROBERT,** professional golfer; b. San Diego, June 2, 1953; s. Donald Edwin and Betty M. (Adams) S.; m. Susan Barrett, Jan. 6, 1979; children: Kevin Craig, Christopher Barrett. Student, U. So. Calif. Profl. golfer PGA, Palm Beach Gardens, Fla., 1975—; winner Hope Classic, 1980, Greater Greensboro Open, 1980, Kemper Open, 1981-82, Tucson Open, 1982, Masters, 1982, World Series of Golf, 1982, 92, Canon European Masters, 1985, Dunlop Phoenix, Japan, 1987, Scandinavian Enterprise Open, 1990, Tour Championship, 1991, NEC World Series of Golf, 1992, Argentine Open, 1992, Buick Invitational Calif., 1994, Nissan Open, 1996. U.S. amateur champion, 1973; mem. (nat. teams) U.S. Walker Cup, 1975, U.S. vs. Japan, 1982, Ryder Cup, 1983, 85; mem. PGA Tour Charity Team, Nissan Open, 1999; leading money winner PGA Tour, 1982; inductee Breithard Hall of Fame, San Diego, 1996. Mem. Golf Mag. (Player of Yr. 1982) Avocations: skiing, hunting.

**STADLER, GERALD P.,** transportation executive; b. 1937; married. Student, Loyola U. Chmn. S&M Moving Sys., Santa Fe, Calif.; sec. United Van Lines, Fenton, Mo., 1982—84, vice chmn., 1984—2001, also bd. dirs., 1978—, chmn., 2001—; chmn., CEO UniGroup Inc., 2001—. Mem.: American Moving Storage Assn. (bd. dirs.). Office: United Van Lines Inc 1 United Dr Fenton MO 63026-2578

**STADTHER, MICHAEL JON,** entrepreneur, writer, publisher; b. Mobile, Ala. m. Helen Demetrios. BS in Math., Tulane U., 1973. Software developer, NYC; prin. GDK Systems Inc., NYC; co-owner, pres. The Frustum Group, White Plains, 1991—96; now owner publ. co. Treasure Trove Inc., Pound Ridge, NY. Author, illustrator, publisher A Treasure's Trove: A Fairy Tale About Real Treasure for Parents and Children of All Ages, 2004, A Treasure's Trove Puzzle Book Companion, 2004. Trustee Caramoor Ctr. for the Arts, Katonah, NY; supporter Music Conservatory of Westchester, White Plains, NY. Office: Treasure Trove Inc 161 Cherry St New Canaan CT 06840

**STADTHERR, MARK A.,** chemical engineer, educator; B in Chem. Engring., U. Minn., 1972; PhD in Chem. Engring., U. Wis., 1976. Faculty U. Ill., Urbana-Champaign, 1976-95; chem. engring. faculty U. Notre Dame, Ind., 1996—. Presenter in field. Contbr. articles to profl. jours. Recipient Xerox award for engring. rsch., 1982, Computing in Chem. Engring. award AIChE, 1998; named GTE Emerging scholar lectr. U. Notre Dame, 1986. Achievements include research on advanced computational strategies for process engineering, application of interval analysis to chemical engineering problems, environmentally conscious process design. Office: Dept Chem Engring Univ Notre Dame Notre Dame IN 46556 Fax: 574-631-8366. E-mail: markst@nd.edu.

**STADTLER, WALTER EDWARD,** diplomat; b. NYC, Apr. 4, 1936; s. Walter Henry and Paula (Nagl) S.; m. Maida Maria Macdonald, Mar. 4, 1937; children: Fiona, Walter Jr., Catriona. Student, Sorbonne U., Paris, 1955-56; AB, Fordham U., 1957; postgrad., Columbia U., 1957-58. With Dept. State, 1962—91; vice consul Am. Consulate, Southampton, Eng., 1962-63, third sec. Am. Embassy, London, 1963-64, econ. officer, second sec. Bonn, Fed. Republic of Germany, 1966-69; personnel officer Dept. State, Washington, 1966-69; second sec. Am. Embassy, Pretoria, South Africa, 1969-72, charge' d'affaires then dep. chief of mission, 1982-85, first sec. Addis Ababa, Ethiopia, 1972-75, Stockholm, 1975-78; European affairs advisor U.S. Mission UN, N.Y.C., 1978; mem. Royal Coll. Def. Studies, London, 1979; counselor Am. Embassy, Bonn, Fed. Republic of Germany, 1980-82; mem. Sr. Seminar, Washington, 1985-86; ambassador Am. Embassy, Cotonou, Benin, 1986-90; v.p. Nat. Def. U., Ft. McNair; sr. fellow Office of the Sec. of Def., 1992—94; U.S. mem. Internat. Def. Adv. Bd. for the Baltic Republics, 1995—2000; prof. and dir. program on peacekeeping policy George Mason U., Fairfax, Va., 1995—2000; bd. chair Geodata Systems, Inc., 1999—. Bd. mem. Nat. Def. U. Found., Coop. Housing Found.; mem. Coun. on Standards for Internat. Edn. Travel; councillor Atlantic Coun. of the U.S. Served to capt. U.S. Army, 1958-62. Mem. Am. Fgn. Service Assn., Army and Navy Club. Roman Catholic. Avocations: music, travel, fgn. policy and polit. mil. hist. Office: 7063 Wyndale St NW Washington DC 20015-1428 Office Phone: 202-363-9894. E-mail: walter.stadtler@digicola.com.

**STADTMAN, EARL REECE,** biochemist, researcher; b. Carrizozo, N.Mex., Nov. 15, 1919; s. Walter William and Minnie Ethyl (Reece) Stadtman; m. Thressa Campbell, Oct. 19, 1943. BS, U. Calif., Berkeley, 1942, PhD, 1949. With Alcan Hwy. survey Pub. Rds. Adminstrn., 1942—43; rsch. asst. U. Calif., Berkeley, 1938—49; sr. lab. technician, 1949; AEC fellow Mass. Gen. Hosp., Boston, 1949—50; chemist lab. cellular physiology Nat. Heart Inst., 1950—58, chief enzyme sect., 1958—62, section chief lab. biochemistry, 1962—. Biochemist Max Planck Inst., Munich, Pasteur Inst., Paris, 1959—60; faculty dept. microbiology U. Md.; prof. biochemistry grad. program dept. biology Johns Hopkins U.; adv. com. Life Scis. Rsch. Office, Am. Fedn. Biol. Sci., 1974—77; chmn. dept. biochemistry Found. Advanced Edn. Scis., 1966—68; biochem. study sect. rsch. grants NIH, 1959—63; Julius Schultz Meml. vis. prof. U. Miami, 2002. Editor: Jour. Biol. Chemistry, 1960—65, Current Topics in Cellular Regulation, 1968—, Circulation Rsch., 1968—70; exec. editor: Archives Biochemistry and Biophysics, 1960—2001, Life Scis., 1973—75, Procs. NAS, 1975—81, Trends in Biochem. Rsch., 1975—78; mem. editl. bd. Biochemistry, 1969—76, 1981—. Recipient

medallion, Soc. de Chemie Biologique, 1955, U. Pisa, 1966, Presdl. Rank award as Disting. Sr. Exec., 1981, Rsch. award, Am. Aging Assn., 1992, Lifetime Achievement and Mentoring award, NIH, 1998, Sci. and Humanity prize, Oxygen Club Calif., 2002, Trevor Slater award, Soc. for Free Rabical Rsch., 2002. Mem.: NAS (award in microbiology 1970), Washington Acad. Scis. (award biol. chemistry 1957, Nat. medal sci. 1979, meritorious exec. award 1980, Robert A. Welch award in chemistry 1991, Paul Glenn award in aging 1993), Am. Soc. Microbiology, Am. Acad. Arts and Scis., Am. Soc. Biol. Chemists (publs. com. 1966—70, coun. 1974—77, pres. 1983—, Merck award 1983), Am. Chem. Soc. (exec. com. biol. div 1959—64, chmn. div. 1963—64, Paul Lewis Lab, award in enzyme chemistry 1952, Hillebrand award 1969). Office: Nat Heart and Lung Inst 9000 Rockville Pike Bethesda MD 20892-0001 Office Phone: 301-496-4096. Business E-Mail: erstadtman@nih.gov.

**STADTMAN, THRESSA CAMPBELL,** biochemist; b. Sterling, NY, Feb. 12, 1920; d. Earl and Bessie (Waldron) Campbell; m. Earl Reece Stadtman, Oct. 19, 1943. BS, Cornell U., 1940, MS, 1942; PhD, U. Calif., Berkeley, 1949. Rsch. assoc. U. Calif., Berkeley, 1942-47, Harvard U. Med. Sch., Boston, 1949-50; biochemist Nat. Heart, Lung and Blood Inst. NIH, USPHS, HHS, Bethesda, Md., 1950—. Mem. Burroughs-Wellcome Fund Toxicology Adv. Commn., 1994-97; pres. Internat. Soc. Vitamins and Related BioFactors, 1998-2001. Editor Jour. Biol. Chemistry, Archives Biochemistry and Bio-physics, Molecular and Cellular Biochemistry; editor-in-chief Bio Factors, 1991-95; contbr. articles on amino acid metabolism, methane biosynthesis, vitamin B12 biochemistry, selenium biochemistry to profl. jours. Helen Haye Whitney fellow Oxford U., Eng., 1954-55; Rockefeller Found. grantee U. Munich, 1959-60; recipient Rose award, 1987, Klaus Schwarz medal, 1988, Life Achievement Women in Sci. award L'Oreal-UNESCO, 2000, Bertrand medal and prize Assn. European Trace Elements and Metals in Biology and Medicine, Venice, 2001. Mem. NAS, Am. Soc. Microbiology, Biochem. Soc., Soc. Am. Biochemists, Am. Chem. Soc., Am. Acad. Arts and Scis., Sigma Delta Epsilon (hon.). Home: 16907 Redland Rd Derwood MD 20855-1954 Office Phone: 301-496-3002. Business E-Mail: tcstadtman@nih.gov.

**STADTMUELLER, CLAIRE LOUISE,** soprano, performing arts educator; 1 child, Alexis Wyrofsky. MusB, New Eng. Conservatory, Boston, 1981; MusM, U. of R.I., 2004. Soloist Carnegie Hall, N.Y.C., 1998—2004; vis. lectr. Assumption Coll., Worcester, Mass., 2004—. Singer (creator of concept: (cd) Sweet Peace. Avocation: practioner of reconnective healing. Home: 963 Seven Mile Rd Hope RI 02831 Personal E-mail: cstadtmueller@earthlink.net.

**STAEHELIN, LUCAS ANDREW,** cell biology professor; b. Sydney, Australia, Feb. 10, 1939; came to U.S., 1969; s. Lucas Eduard and Isobel (Malloch) S.; m. Margrit Weibel, Sept. 17, 1965; children: Daniel Thomas, Philip Roland, Marcel Felix. Dipl. Natw., Swiss Fed. Inst. Tech. Zurich, 1963, PhD in Biology, 1966. Research scientist N.Z. Dept. Sci. and Indsl. Research, 1966-69; research fellow in cell biology Harvard U., Cambridge, Mass., 1969-70; asst. prof. cell biology U. Colo., Boulder, 1970-73, assoc. prof., 1973-79, prof., 1979—. Vis. prof. U. Freiburg, 1978, Swiss Fed. Inst. Tech., 1984, 92, U. Melbourne, Australia, 1998; mem. cellular biology and physiology study sect. NIH, Bethesda, Md., 1980-84; mem. DOE panel on rsch. directions for the energy bioscis., 1988, 92; mem. NSF adv. panel for cellular orgn., 1994-96; mem. plant biology panel NASA. Editl. bd. Jour. Cell Biology, 1977-81, European Jour. Cell Biology, 1981-90, Plant Physiology, 1986-92, Plant Jour., 1991-97, Biology of the Cell, 1996-99, Planta, 2003—; Current Opion in Plant Biology, 2003—; editor: (with C.J. Antzen) Encyclopedia of Plant Physiology, Vol. 19, Photosynthesis III, 1986; contbr. numerous articles to sci. jours. Recipient Humboldt award Humboldt Found., 1978, Sci. Tchr. award U. Colo., 1984, Outstanding Faculty award U. Colo.-Boulder Parents Assn., 2001, Highly Cited Rschr. ISI, 2004, Haselkorn Scholar award, U. Chgo., 2006; grantee NIH, 1971-, USDA, 1994-, NASA, 1997-; hon. sr. fellow U. Melbourne, Australia, 1998, Am. Assn. Adv. Sci., 2004. Mem. AAAS, Am. Soc. Cell Biology, Am. Soc. Plant Physiology, German Acad. Natural Scis. Leopoldina. Home: 2855 Dover Dr Boulder CO 80305-5305 Office: Dept Molecular Cell U Colo 347 UCB Boulder CO 80309-0347 Office Phone: 303-492-8843. E-mail: staeheli@colorado.edu.

**STAEHLE, ROBERT L.,** foundation executive; b. Rochester, NY, Apr. 22, 1955; s. Henry Carl and Isabel Montgomery S. BS in Aero. and Astronautic Engring., Purdue U., 1977. Prin. investigator Skylab Expt. ED-31 (bacteria aboard Skylab), NASA/Marshall Space Flight Center, Huntsville, Ala., 1972-74, student trainee engring., 1974-77; sci. observation analyst Caltech/Jet Propulsion Lab., Pasadena, Calif., 1977-78, engr. advanced projects group, 1978-83, mem. tech. staff system integration sect. of Space Sta., 1983-87, mem. tech. staff and space sta., user ops. team leader, 1987-88; from tech. mgr. to dep. mgr.various positions Jet Propulsion Lab., Pasadena, Calif., 1988—2004, dep. mgr. Space Experiments Sys. Sect., 2004—. Prin. founder, pres. World Space Found., South Pasadena, Calif., 1979—; founding dir. So. Calif. Space Bus. Roundtable, 1987-95; bd. dirs. Altadena Foothills Conservancy, 2000—. Co-author: Project Solar Sail, New Am. Libr., 1990; contbr. articles to profl. jours. Mem. Cmty. Leaders Adv. Bd. for Irvine Scholars, Occidental Coll., L.A., 1996-97; bd. dirs. Caltech Y, 1987-93. Nat. Space Club Goddard scholar, 1977; Charles A. Lindbergh Fund grantee, 1986. Fellow Brit. Interplanetary Soc.; mem. AIAA, Tau Beta Pi, Sigma Gamma Tau. Avocations: photography, hiking, mountain biking. Office: Jet Propulsion Lab Pasadena CA 91109 Business E-Mail: robert.l.staehle@jpl.nasa.gov.

**STAELIN, DAVID HUDSON,** electrical engineering educator, consultant; b. Toledo, May 25, 1938; s. Carl Gustav and Margaret E. (Hudson) S.; m. Ellen Mahoney, June 16, 1962; children: Carl H., Katharine E., Paul H. SB, MIT, 1960, SM, 1961, ScD in Elec. Engring., 1965. instr. elec. engring. MIT, Cambridge, 1965, asst. prof., 1965—69, assoc. prof., 1969—76, prof., 1976—, asst. dir. Lincoln Lab. Lexington, 1990—2001. Vis. asst. scientist Nat. Radio Astronomy Obs., Charlottesville, Va., 1968-69; cons. Jet Propulsion Lab., Pasadena, Calif., 1969, Wellesley, Mass., 1965—; dir. Environ. Rsch. and Tech., Inc., Concord, Mass., 1969-78; co-founder, chmn. PictureTel Corp., Peabody, Mass., 1984-87; mem. com. on radio frequency requirements for rsch., NAS, Washington, 1980-86, chmn. 1983-86; chmn. advanced microwave sounder working group NASA, Washington, 1981-82, mem. space applications adv. com., 1983-86; mem. adv. com. info. tech. Pres. U.S., Washington, D.C., 2003-05. Co-author: Made in America, 1989, Electromagnetic Waves, 1994; contbr. articles to profl. jours. Fellow: IEEE, AAAS; mem.: Am. Geophys. Union, Am. Meteorl. Soc., Internat. Union for Radio Sci. Achievements include patents for grinding and polishing sheet glass, display of dynamic images, ribbon-beam cathode ray tube. Office: MIT Rm 26-341 Cambridge MA 02139

**STAFEIL, JEFF,** corporate financial executive; BS in Acctg., Ind. U.; MBA, Duke U. CPA. Various positions Mobil Corp.; acct. Peterson Consulting, Ernst & Young; cons. Boz, Allen & Hamilton; v.p., corp. controller Heartland Indsl. Ptnrs.; v.p. Metaldyne, Plymouth, Mich., 2001, CFO, 2001—

**STAFF, JOEL V.,** energy executive; BA, U. Tex., Austin; MBA, Tex. A&M U., Kingsville. Various fin. and gen. mgmt. positions Baker Hughes, Inc., 1976—93; chmn., pres., CEO Nat. Oilwell, Inc., 1993—2001; chmn., CEO Reliant Resources, Inc., Houston, 2003—; also bd. dirs. Bd. dirs. Nat. Oilwell, Inc., Enceco Internat., Inc.; adv. dir. King Chapman & Broussard; devel. bd. U. Tex. Health Sci. Ctr., Houston. Adv. dir. Boys and Girls Club, Houston. Office: Reliant Energy Exec Offices PO Box 2286 Houston TX 77252-2286*

**STAFF, VIRGIL CLINTON,** retired history educator; b. South Haven, Minn., Apr. 2, 1928; s. Herman Theodore Staff and Eva Mae Holm; m. Katie Velma LaVada Falkner. BA, Atlantic Union Coll., 1951; MA, U. Calif., Berkeley, 1954. Cert. gen. secondary Calif. Mgr. Blue Chip Co., Richmond, 1957, Alta Employment Agy., Oakland, Calif., 1957—58; staff James Lick Sch., San Francisco, 1958—68; instr. Am. history Balboa H.S., San Fran-

cisco, 1968—89; ret. 1989. *Virgil Staff joined the Board of Directors of the Mutual UFO Network in 1999. Also, transportation negatives for the AT&SF, WP, SP, and the Magma Copper Company are held in the collection of the California Railroad Museum in Sacramento, California. Transportation magnetic audio tapes of NdeM have been accepted into the collections of the Museum of Transportation in Mexico City, and into the "Musee de los Ferrocarriles de Yucatan."* Author: D-Day on the Western Pacific, 1982; contbr. articles to profl. jours. With U.S. Army, 1954—56. Mem.: Am. Hist. Assn., Mutual UFO Network (state sect. dir. 1980—90, dir. No. Calif. chpt. 1990—99, dir. We. Region 1999—, bd. dirs. 1999—), Feather River Rail Soc., Pacific Locomotive Assn., Railway and Locomotive Hist. Soc., Calif. State Sheriffs' Assn. (assoc.), Lexington Group, Friends of Cal History Dept., Bay Area Electric RR Assn., Am. Legion. Avocation: philately. Home: 1700 Sonoma Ave Berkeley CA 94707 Personal E-mail: sbx120@earthlink.net.

**STAFFIER, PAMELA MOORMAN,** psychologist; b. Passaic, NJ, Dec. 7, 1942; d. Wynant Clair and Jeannette Frances (Rentzsch) Moorman; m. John Staffier, Jr., Apr. 5, 1975; children: M. Anthony, C. Matthew. BA, Bucknell U., 1964; MA in Psychology, Assumption Coll., Worcester, Mass., 1970, CAGS, 1977; PhD, Union Inst., 1978. Psychologist Westboro (Mass.) State Hosp., 1965, prin. psychologist, asst. to supt., 1973—76; rsch. psychologist Wrentham (Mass.) State Sch., 1966, Cushing Hosp., Framingham, Mass., 1967; prin. psychologist, asst. to supt. Grafton (Mass.) State Hosp., 1967—72; dir. Staffier Clinic, 1978—; psychologist Moriarty Mental Health Clinic; psychiat. cons. local gen. hosp. Mem.: APA (assoc.), Nat. Register Health Svc. Providers Psychology, Mass. Psychol. Assn., Am. Psychol. Practitioners Assn. (founding mem.) Achievements include research in state hospital closings; biochemical basis of schizophrenia. Home: 68 Adams St Westborough MA 01581 Office: 57 E Main St Westborough MA 01581-1464 Office Phone: 508-366-0406. E-mail: johnstaffier@charter.net.

**STAFFIERI, VICTOR A.,** energy executive; BA, Yale U., 1977; JD, Fordham U., 1980. From atty. to gen. counsel L.I. Lighting Co., Hicksville, NY, 1980-92; sr. v.p., gen. counsel, corp. sec. LG&E Energy Corp., Louisville, 1992, sr. v.p. pub. policy, gen. counsel, 1992-93, pres. Louisville Gas and Electric Co., 1993-97, pres. distbn. svcs. divsn., 1995-97, CFO, 1997-99, pres., COO, 1999—2001, chmn., CEO, 2001—. Bd. trustees Bellarmine Coll., 1995—; co-chair Jefferson County-Louisville Area C. of C. Family Bus. Partnership, 1996-97; bd. dirs. Ky. Country Day, 1996—, Metro United Way, 1998—. Mem. Louisville Area C. of C. (bd. dirs. 1994-97). Office: LG&E Energy Corp Dept Corp Comm 220 W Main St Louisville KY 40202*

**STAFFORD, ARTHUR CHARLES,** medical association administrator; b. Cleve., May 10, 1947; s. Charles Arthur and Florence Mildred (Hovey) S.; m. Patricia Anne Cz, Dec. 20, 1991. BS, Kent State U., 1977; MBA, Lake Erie Coll., 1984. Med. tech. VA, Cleve., 1977-81, supr. med. tech., 1981-97; lab. mgr. Univ. Hosps. Health System Meml. Hosp. of Geneva, Ohio, 1998-99; instr. Lake Erie Coll., Painesville, Ohio, 1980-82; mgr. customer svc. Giant Eagle Supermarket, Madison, Ohio, 2001—02; instr. Cuyahoga C.C., Cleve., 1988-91, 2003—; customer svc. Progressive Ins. Co., Mayfield Heights, 2004—. Pres. Kent State U. Veterans Assn., 1974, mem. Kent State U Budget Review Com., 1975. Contbr. articles to profl. jour. Mem. Am. Legion, 1974, VFW, 1973. With USN, 1968-72. Mem.: Rock and Roll Hall of Fame, Founders Club. Republican. Avocations: genealogy, computers, antiques, chess, cooking. Home: 2193 Chimney Ridge Dr Madison OH 44057-2588 E-mail: czstafford@ncweb.com.

**STAFFORD, BONNIE,** social studies educator; b. Fargo, ND, July 20, 1976; d. Wayne and Jeanne Ingersoll; m. Thad Stafford, May 22, 1998; children: Ryan Wayne, Kate Elizabeth, Olivia Grace. Degree in Social Studies Secondary Edn., Moorhead State U., Minn., 1998; EdM in Curriculum and Instrn., St. Thomas U., Mpls., 2002. Social studies tchr. Moorhead H.S., 1999—. Home: 2048 33 St South Moorhead MN 56560 Office: Moorhead High School 2300 4 Ave South Moorhead MN 56560 Office Phone: 218-284-2300. Personal E-mail: bstafford@moorhead.k12.mn.us.

**STAFFORD, C. STEWART,** educational consultant, educator; b. Bluefield, W.Va., Aug. 25, 1939; s. John Roy Stafford and Virginia Walker O'Rourke Stafford. BA, Flora MacDonald Coll. Cert. Teacher NC Dept. of Pub. Instrn., 1961. Tchr. Robeson County Pub. Schs., Lumberton, NC, 1961—66; tchr. of gifted/talented Cumberland County Pub. Schs., Fayetteville, NC, 1963—75, asst. prin., 1967—75, coord. of fed. project, 1975—78, resouce tchr. for gifted/talented, 1979—83; vice chmn. adv. com. NC State Bd. Edns. Title IV, 1976—80; resource tchr. for gifted/talented Ft. Bragg Dependents Schs., NC, 1983—99; acting dir. career develop. program Ft. Bragg Schs., 1986, ednl. technologist, 1999—. Cons. and trainer NC Dept. Pub. Instrn., Raleigh, NC, 1967—90; US rep. World Confederation Profl. Tchrs., 1977; pres., nc assn. of educators NC Assn. Educators, 1978—79; trainer NC Tchr. Acad., Durham, 1994—. Contbr. booklet, training manual. Adv. dir. North Carolina State Bd. Educations, 1977—82. Recipient Outstanding Tchr. Yr., NC Assn. Gifted and Talented, 1986. Spl. Services award NC Assn. of Educators, 1974 - 1983, Disting. Svc., Nat. Edn. Assns. First Am. Caucus, 1977. Mem.: NEA (life), Assn. Supervision and Curriculum Develop., Phi Delta Kappa (assoc.), ASCD (assoc.), NC Assn. for the Gifted,Talented (life), NC Assn. of Educators (life). Achievements include research in Mainstreaming the Gifted and Talented: Grades 7-12; Integrating Schools in the 1960s; Effective Instructional Methods for Gifted/Talented Students; Construction of the North Carolina Association of Educators State Headquarters. Avocations: reading, travel. Home: P O Box 53024 Fayetteville NC 28305-3024 Office: Fort Bragg Schs P O Box 70089 Fort Bragg NC 28307-0089 Office Phone: 910-436-4666 222.

**STAFFORD, DONALD GENE,** chemistry professor; b. Valliant, Okla., Oct. 9, 1930; s. Otto Lewis and Rose Lavelle (Osterdock) S.; m. Jane Wright, July 5, 1951; children— Michael Royce, Robert Gene, Joel Dan. BS, U. Okla., 1957, PhD, 1969; MS, Okla. State U., 1961. Prof. sci. edn. East Cen. U., Ada, Okla., 1961-73, prof. chemistry, 1973—. Adj. prof. U. Okla., Norman, 1970—. Author: The Improvement of Science in Oklahoma (7-12), 1970, Guidelines and Successful Practices in Elementary Edn, 1970, Wings for a Dinosaur, 1972, Early Childhood Resource Book, 1972, Teaching Science in the Elementary School, 1973, 3d edit., 1979, Teaching Science in the Secondary School, 1973, Research, Teaching, and Learning with the Piaget Model, 1976, Investigations in Physical Science, 1976, The Learning Science Program K-6 (7 children's books and 7 tchr.'s guides), 1976, TOP, The Oklahoma Project, Chemistry, 1987, The Learning Cycle, 1988, The Lost City of Balee, A Novel for Young Teenagers, 2000, Don's Rhymes, A Book of Poetry, 2000. Served with AUS, 1948-53. Mem. Am. Chem. Soc., Nat. Sci. Tchrs. Assn., Okla. Sci. Tchrs. (pres. 1973-74, 78-79), Sigma Xi. Home: 2202 Fullview Dr Ada OK 74820-4436 Personal E-mail: donjane@cableone.net.

**STAFFORD, FRANK PETER, JR.,** economics professor, consultant; b. Chgo., Sept. 17, 1940; s. Frank Peter and Ida Gustava (Tormala) S.; m. Lilian Elisabeth Lundin, Aug. 8, 1964; children: Craig Peter, Jennifer Elisabeth, Christine Anna BA, Northwestern U., 1962; MBA, U. Chgo., 1964, PhD, 1968. Asst. prof. econs. U. Mich., 1966-71, assoc. prof. 1971-73, 74-75, prof., 1976—, chmn. dept. econs., 1980—, rsch. scientist Inst. Social Rsch., 1995—, chair budget study com., 1993-76; vis. prof. dept. econs. U. Saarlandes, Fed. Republic Germany, 1986; faculty rsch. assoc. Inst. Social Rsch., Ann Arbor, 1979—; vis. scholar Indsl. Inst. for Econs. and Social Rsch., Stockholm, 1979, 83, 90, Worklife Study Ctr., Stockholm, 1988, 90; Tinbergen Found. prof. U. Amsterdam, 1992, 94; panel mem. Social Sci. Rsch. Coun., N.Y.C., 1979—; rsch. assoc. Nat. Bur. Econ. Rsch., Cambridge, Mass., 1983—; prof. econs. Tinbsrgne Found. U. Amsterdam, 1992; vis. scholar U. Stockholm, 1994. Author, editor: Time Use Goods and Well Being, 1986, Studies in Labor Market Behavior: Sweden and the United States, 1981; mem. editorial bd.: Am. Econ. Rev., 1976-78; contbr. articles to profl. jours. Dir. Panel Study of Income Dynamics, 1995—. Grantee NSF, 1973, 80,

95—, 2002—, NICHD, 1995—, Nat. Ins. on Aging, 1999—. Mem. Am. Econs. Assn. Home: 3535 Daleview Dr Ann Arbor MI 48105-9686 Office: U Mich Dept Econs Lorch Hall Rm 312 Ann Arbor MI 48105 Business E-Mail: fstafford@umich.edu.

**STAFFORD, J. FRANCIS CARDINAL,** archbishop; b. Balt., July 26, 1932; s. F. Emmett and Mary Dorothy Stafford. Student, Loyola Coll. Balt. 1950—52; BA, St. Mary's Sem., Balt., 1954; STB, STL, Gregorian U., Rome, 1958; MSW, Cath. U., 1964; postgrad., Rutgers U., 1963, St. Mary's Sem. and Univ., Balt., 1973—75. Spiritual moderator Ladies of Charity Ch., Balt., 1966—76; spiritual moderator Soc. St. Vincent de Paul, Balt., 1965—76; urban vicar Archdiocese of Balt., 1966—76, monsignor, 1970, vicar gen., auxiliary bishop, 1976—82; bishop Diocese of Memphis, 1982—86; archbishop Archdiocese of Denver, 1986—96; pres. Pontifical Coun. Laity, 1996—2003; elevated to cardinal, 1998—; mem. Major Penitentiary, Apostolic Penitentiary, 2003—; Archdiocesan liaison Md. Cath. Conf., Balt., 1975—78; Oriental Orthodox/Roman Cath. cons. Nat. Cath. Conf. Bishops, 1977—85, com. on doctrine, 1978—82, chmn. ecumenical and interreligious affairs com., 1987—90; co-chmn. bilateral dialogue Roman Cath./World Meth. Coun., 1977—86; co-chmn. U.S. Roman Cath.-Luth. Dialogue, 1986—; chmn. Bishops' com. marriage and family life U.S. Cath. Conf., 1978—84; mem. gen. Synod Bishops, Vatican City, 1980. Contbr. articles to profl. jours. Trustee Good Samaritan Hosp., Balt., 1973—77, Cath. U. Am., 1990—, Blue Cross of Md., Inc., 1973—76, Balt. Urban Coalition, 1970—75; trustee, chmn. St. Thomas Theol. Sem., 1987—; bd. dirs. Assn. Cath. Charities, Balt., 1966—76, U. Md. Sch. Social Work and Planning, 1973—76. Recipient Father Kelly Alumni award, Loyola H.S., 1978, Alumni Laureate, Loyola Coll., 1979. Mem.: Oriental Orthodox Roman Cath. Consultation, World Meth. Conf. Roman Cath. Dialogue (co-chmn. 1977—86), Congregation for Doctrine of Faith, Luth. Roman Cath. Dialogue, Nat. Conf. Cath. Bishops. Office: Penitenziere Maggiore Penitenzieria Apostolica 00120 Vatican City Italy Office Phone: 066 9837625. Business E-Mail: vati877@apostpnt.va.

**STAFFORD, JAMES FRANCIS,** cardinal; Ordained priest, Balt., 1957; aux. bishop, 1976; bishop Memphis, 1982—86; archibishop Denver, 1986—96; pres. Pontifical Coun. for Laity, Vatican, 1996—; elevated to cardinal, 1998; Major Penitentiary Apostolic Penitentiary, Vatican City, 2003—. Office: Tribunale della Penitenzieria Apostolica Palazzo della Cancelleria 00120 Vatican City Italy Office Phone: 39 06 69887625.

**STAFFORD, JOHN DAVID,** director, consultant; b. Roanoke, Va., Jan. 28, 1967; s. George Oakley, Jr and Edna Lee White Stafford. BA, Lenoir-Rhyne Coll., Hickory, N.C., 1990; MS, Radford U., Va., 1996. Area coord. Roanoke Coll., Salem, Va., 1992—97; asst. dir. residence life Rider U., Lawrenceville, NJ, 1997—2000, acting dir. residence life, 2000—01; dir. residential and cmty. devel. Coll. NJ., Ewing, 2001—04. Cons., Bensalem, Pa., 1999; mgr. box office Mill Mountain Theatre, Roanoke, Va.; com. co-chair NJ Com. Residence Life Educators, 1999; treas. Mid-Atlantic Assn. Univ. and Housing Officers, Pa., 2001—02; mng. editor newsletter, Pa., 2003; cons.-in-residence MACUHO, Pa., 2004; spkr. and presenter on orgnl. change and leadership, pub. spkg. coach. Contbr. articles to websites, to profl. jours. Vol. Roanoke County chpt. ARC, Va., 1991—96, mem. Lower Bucks County Levittown, Pa., 2001—02; vol. youth leader Va. ELCA Ch., Salem, Va., 1993—96; mem. ch. coun. St. Paul Luth. Ch., Roanoke, 1992, youth dir., 1992—95. Recipient Vol. Recognition award, Roanoke chpt. ARC, 1992, Regions Best award, MACUHO, 1999; grantee Multimedia, ACUHO-I, 1995; Adminstrv. Edn. grant, ELCA/Roanoke Coll., 1995, 1996. Mem.: MACUHO (treas. 2001—02), Am. Coll. Pers. Assn. Lutheran. Avocations: public speaking, reading, bicycling, outdoors.

**STAFFORD, JOHN H., II,** composer, music educator; b. Danville, Ill., Feb. 7, 1978; s. Andrew and Joy C. Stafford. MB, Millikin U., 2000; MusM, Bowling Green State U., 2003. Adj. prof. music theory and composition Millikin U., Decatur, Ill., 2004—. Composer: numerous works performed in U.S. and abroad. Mem.: Soc. Composers, Inc., Am. Soc. Composers, Authors and Pubs. Office: Millikin Univ PMC201 1184 W Main St Decatur IL 62522 Personal E-mail: johnstafford@hotmail.com. Business E-Mail: jstafford@mail.millikin.edu.

**STAFFORD, MARK SMITH,** anesthesiologist, researcher, education educator; m. Gillian Ann Aylward; children: Lauren Stafford Smith, Kristian Stafford Smith, Bethany Stafford Smith. Med. Sch., McGill U., Montreal; Anesthesiology Residency, Dalhousie U., Nova Scotia, 1991; Cardiac Anesthesia Clin. and Rsch. Fellowship, Duke U., Durham, N.C., 1994. Cert. Anesthesiology Am. Bd. Anesthesiologists, 1994, diplomate Perioperative Transesophageal Echocardiography Nat. Bd. Echocardiography, 2000. Cardiovasc. and gen. anesthesiologist Maritime Heart Ctr., Halifax, Canada, 1994—96; cardiothoracic anesthesiologist Duke U. Med. Ctr., Durham, NC, 1996—. Dir., cardiothoracic anesthesiology and critical care fellowship Duke U. Med. Ctr., Durham, NC, 1997—; assoc. prof. anesthesiology Dept. of Anesthesiology, Duke U. Med. Ctr., Durham, NC, 2003—; dir. fellowship edn., 2006—. Fellow, Royal Coll. Physicians and Surgeons, Can., 1991. Mem.: Internat. Anesthesia Rsch. Soc. (assoc. editor 2006—), Assn. U. Anesthesiologists. Achievements include research in First reports of a genetic basis for acute renal injury after cardiac surgery. Office: Dept of Anesthesiology Box 3094 Duke Univ Med Ctr Durham NC 27710 Office Phone: 919-681-6944. Business E-Mail: staff002@mc.duke.edu.

**STAFFORD, REBECCA,** retired academic administrator, sociologist, consultant; b. Topeka, July 9, 1936; d. Frank C. and Anne Elizabeth (Larrick) S.; m. Willard Van Hazel. AB magna cum laude, Radcliffe Coll., 1958, MA, 1961; PhD, Harvard U., 1964. Sociology lectr., dept. social rels. Sch. Edn., Harvard U., Cambridge, Mass., 1964-70, mem. vis. com. bd. overseers, 1973-79; assoc. prof. sociology U. Nev., Reno, 1970-74, prof., 1973-80, chmn. dept. sociology, 1974-77, dean Coll. Arts and Scis., 1977-80; pres. Bemidji (Minn.) State U., 1980-82; exec. v.p., prof. sociology Colo. State U., Ft. Collins, 1982-83; pres. Chatham Coll., Pitts., 1983-91, prof. sociology, 1992-93; pres. Monmouth U., West Long Branch, NJ, 1993—2003. Cons. higher edn., 1992—, U.S. Internat. U. on Acad. Planning, 1992-94, USDA, 1992-93, Integra Bank, 1992-93, Millsaps Coll, Jackson, Miss., 1991, U. Pitts. Med. Sch., 1992-93; co-dir. acad. leadership inst. Carnegie Mellon U., 1991-93, U. Tenn., Knoxville, 1992-93; vis. scholar dept. sociology Harvard U., 1991; mem. faculty coll. mgmt. program. Carnegie Mellon U., Pitts., 1984-93; cons. adult devel. grant Harvard U. Health Svcs., Cambridge, 1979, rsch. sociologist, 1964-69; dir. ednl. enrichment project Harvard Sch. Edn., 1966-67, 69-70. Mem. editl. bd. Sociometry, 1974-77, Sociol. Focus., 1974-77; contbr. articles to profl. jours.; presenter papers at profl. confs. Trustee Monmouth Med. Ctr., 1993—, Winchester-Thurston Sch., Pitts., 1986-91, Montefiore Hosp., Pitts., 1990-93; trustee Presbyn.-Univ. Hosp., Pitts., 1984-93, exec. planning com., 1986-89, fin. com., 1989-93; pres. Coun. Higher Edn., 1990; mem. Found. Ind. Colls. Pa., 1984-91, sec., 1986; mem. Colo. Commn. Higher Edn. Task Force on Quality, 1981; mem. adv. bd. Animal Rescue League, Pitts., 1989-93; founder Bemidji Area Women's Network, Minn., 1980-82; mem. intergovtl. planning steering com. Bemidji, 1980-82; mem. cmty. rels. com. Girl Scouts Southwestern Pa., 1983-86; mem. brotherhood dinner coun. Nat. Conf. Christians and Jews, 1985; mem. hon. centennial com. Pa. Sch. Blind Children, Pitts., 1986; mem. citizens sponsoring com. Allegheny Conf. Cmty. Devel., Pitts., 1983-91; mem. five state regional bd. First Union Nat. Bank, 1996—; bd. dirs. Pitts. Symphony, 1984-93, First Fidelity Bank, N.A., N.J., 1993-95, Integra Bank, Pitts., 1987-97, Urban League, Pitts., 1984-87, Women's Ctr., Ft. Collins, Colo., 1982-83, Coun. Colls. Arts and Scis., 1978-81; chmn. Harvard U. Grad. Soc. Coun., 1987-93. Recipient McCurdy-Rinkle prize for rsch. Eastern Psychiat. Assn., 1970; named Woman of Yr. in Edn., City of Pitts., 1986, Vectors/Pitts., 1987, Woman of Yr. in Edn., YWCA Tribute to Women, 1989, Women of Distinction award Muscular Dystrophy Assn., 1999, Women of Leadership award Monmouth County Girl Scouts Am., 1995, Woman of Achievement in Edn. award Monmouth County Adv. Commn. on Status of Women, 1994, Salute to Policymakers award Exec. Women in N.J., 1994;

grantee Am. Coun. Edn. Inst. Acad. Deans, 1979, Inst. Ednl. Mgmt., Harvard U., 1984. Mem. Assn. Ind. Colls. and Univs. of N.J. (v.p. 1999—, sec. 1998-99, treas. 1994-98, pres. northeastern conf. 1995-99, bd. dirs. 1993—), Am. Coun. on Edn., Assn. Am. Colls., Soc. for Coll. and Univ. Planning (mem. instl. decision making and resource planning acad. 1994—), Ind. Coll. Fund (treas 1995-96, bd. dirs. 1993—), Nat. Coun. Family Rels., Harvard U. Alumni Assn. (bd. dirs. 1985-87), Phi Beta Kappa, Phi Kappa Phi. Business E-Mail: Becky@monmouth.edu.

**STAFFORD, ROBERT THEODORE,** lawyer, retired senator; b. Rutland, Vt., Aug. 8, 1913; s. Bert L. and Mable R. (Stratton) S.; m. Helen C. Kelley, Oct. 15, 1938; children— Madelyn, Susan, Barbara, Dianne. BS, Middlebury Coll., 1935, LL.D. 1960; postgrad., U. Mich., 1936; LL.D., Boston U., 1938, LL.D., 1959, Norwich U., 1960, St. Michaels Coll., 1967, U. Vt., 1970. Bar: Vt. bar 1938. City prosecutor, Rutland, 1939-42; state's atty. Rutland County, 1947-51; dep. atty. gen. Vt., 1953-54; atty. gen. Vt., 1954-56; lt. gov. Vt., 1957-58; gov. Vt., 1959-60; mem. 87th to 92d Congresses, Vt.-at-large; apptd. U.S. Senate, 1971, mem., 1972-89, chmn. com. on environment and public works, 1981-87, chmn. edn. subcom., 1981-87, ranking mem., 1987-89; ptnr. Stafford, Abiatell & Stafford, 1938-46; sr. ptnr. Stafford & LaBrake, 1946-51. Chmn. UN-U.S.A. Assn. Panel UNESCO, 1989—. Lt. comdr. USNR, 1942-46, 51-52; capt. Res. Named Disting. Scholar U. Vt., 1989, Disting. Prof. Pub. Affairs Castleton State Coll., 1989. Mem. V.F.W., Am. Legion. Clubs: Elk. Home and Office: 108 Gables Pl Rutland VT 05701-9448 Office: Castleton Coll Coolidge Libr Bldg Castleton VT 05735

**STAFFORD, WILLIAM FRANKLIN,** veterinarian, educator; b. Loudon, Tenn., Mar. 18, 1955; s. Gene Franklin and Martha Catherine Stafford; m. Jody Ann Rudd, Sept. 1, 1979; children: William Brent, Emily Ann. DVM, U. Tenn., Knoxville, 1980. Cert. secondary edn. tchr. Veterinarian Bilderback Animal Clinic, Sweetwater, Tenn., 1980—85; farmer Loudon, 1982—2004; tchr. Knoxville Th.S., 2005—. Deacon and master min. Stockton Valley Bapt. Ch., Loudon, 2000—. Named New Tchr. of Yr., London County Edn. Found., 2005—06; named one of Young Dairymen, Dairymen, Inc., 1990. Mem.: Lions. Home: 1622 Stafford Rd Loudon TN 37774 Fax: 865-458-4536. Personal E-mail: volvolvolv@aol.com.

**STAFFORD, WILLIAM HENRY, JR.,** federal judge; b. Masury, Ohio, May 11, 1931; s. William Henry and Frieda Gertrude (Nau) S.; m. Nancy Marie Helman, July 11, 1959; children: William Henry, Donald Helman, David Harrold. BS, Temple U., 1953, LL.B., 1956; JD, 1968. Bar: Fla. 1961, U.S. Ct. Appeals (5th cir.) 1969, U.S. Supreme Ct. 1970. Assoc. firm Robinson & Roark, Pensacola, 1961-64; individual practice law Pensacola, 1964-67; state atty., 1967-69; U.S. atty., 1969-75; U.S. dist. judge U.S. Dist. Ct. for No. Dist. Fla., Tallahassee, 1975—, chief judge, 1981-93, sr. judge, 1996—, Fgn. Intelligence Surveillance Ct., 1996—. Instr. Pensacola Jr. Coll., 1964, 68; mem. judicial council U.S. Ct. Appeals (11th cir.), 1986-89; apptd. com. on intercircuit assignments, 1987-92, subcom. on fed. jurisdiction, 1983-87; adj. prof. Fla. State U. Coll. Law, 1992-97. Lt. (j.g.) USN, 1957-60. Mem. Fla. Bar (mem. numerous coms., bench/bar commn. 1991-92, bench/bar implementation commn. 1993), Dist. Judges Assn. 11th Cir. (pres. 1984-85), State Fed. Judicial Council Fla., Am. Inns of Ct., Tallahassee Bar Assn., Tallahassee Inn (founding pres. 1989-91), Mason (33d degree), Rotary, Sigma Phi Epsilon, Phi Delta Phi. Republican. Episcopalian.

**STAGE, THOMAS BENTON,** psychiatrist; b. Marietta, Ohio, July 23, 1926; s. John Douglas and Grace (Shawhan) S.; m. Doris Jeane Weinstock, Dec. 22, 1951; children: Samuel Ray, Amy Elizabeth, James Robert; m. Alicia Anderson Marsh, June 7, 1993. BA cum laude, Marietta Coll., 1949; MD, Ohio State U., 1952. Diplomate: Am. Bd. Psychiatry and Neurology. Intern Detroit Receiving Hosp., 1952-53; psychiat. resident, fellow Menninger Sch. Psychiatry, Topeka, 1953-56; sect. chief psychiatry VA Hosp., Topeka, 1956-62, adminstr. Sheridan, Wyo., 1962-66; dir. Salem, Va., 1967-72; dep. asst. chief med. dir. for ambulatory care VA Central Office, Washington, 1972-74; dir. No. Va. Mental Health Inst., Falls Church, 1974-78; asst. commr. for mental health State of Va., Richmond, 1978-79; dir. clin. svcs. Fairfax-Falls Ch. Cmty. Svcs. Bd., Vienna, Va., 1979-82, psychiat. cons. for med. affairs, 1982-99, med. dir. Fairfax, 1999—2002, cons. quality improvements, 2002—. Instr. Menninger Sch. Psychiatry, 1958-62, U. Wyo. Sch. Nursing, 1963-66; assoc. prof. U. Va. Med. Sch., 1972-74; cons. surveyor Joint Commn. on Accreditation of Hosps., 1976-2004; cons. Crow-No. Cheyenne USPHS Hosp., 1963-66, Ala. Dept. Mental Health (Wyatt Com.), 1986-91; psychiatric cons. on accreditation Commonwealth of Va. Dept. Mental Health, Mental Retardation and Substance Abuse, 1982-2002; mem. Comprehensive Mental Health Ctr. Com., 1968-73, Gov.'s Adv. Commn. on Mental Health, 1971-74; chmn. Drug Abuse Rehab. Com., 1970-73; cons. adminstrv. psychiatry NIMH, 1975-78; chmn. steering com. Asso. Faculties Program Community Psychiatry, Washington, 1975-77; mem. State Health Coordinating Coun., 1976-89. Contbr. articles to profl. jours. Served wtih USNR, 1944-46, PTO. Fellow Am. Psychiat. Assn. (life, disting.); mem. Am. Assn. Psychiat. Adminstrs., Washington Psychiat. Soc., Psychiat. Soc. Va., Am. Assn. Community Psychiatrists. Office: Fairfax-Falls Ch Comty Svcs Bd 11410 Hollow Timber Way Reston VA 20194-1906 Office: Fairfax-Falls Ch Comty Svcs Ste 800 12011 Government Center Pkwy Fairfax VA 22035-1100

**STAGEBERG, ROGER V.,** lawyer; B of Math. with distinction, U. Minn., 1963, JD cum laude, 1966; MA in History and Theology, Luther Seminary, 2006. Assoc. Mackall, Crounse & Moore, Mpls., 1966-70, ptnr., 1970-86; shareholder and officer Lommen, Abdo, Cole, King & Stageberg, P.A., Mpls., 1986—. Co-chmn. joint legal svcs. funding com. Minn. Supreme Ct., 1995-96. Mem. U. Minn. Law Rev. Bd. dirs. Mpls. Legal Aid Soc., 1970-2003, treas., 1973, pres., 1977, dir. of fund, 1980—, chmn. of fund, 1998-2000; chmn. bd. trustees Colonial Ch. of Edina, 1975, chmn. congregation, 1976, pres. found., 1978; officer, trustee Mpls. Found., 1983-88. Mem. Minn. State Bar Assn. (numerous offices and coms., pres. 1994), Hennepin County Bar Assn. (chmn. securities law sect. 1979, chmn. attys. referral svc. com. 1980, sec. 1980, treas. 1981, pres. 1983), Order of Coif. Office: Lommen Abdo Cole King & Stageberg PA 80 S 8th St Ste 2000 Minneapolis MN 55402-2119 Office Phone: 612-336-9335. Business E-Mail: roger@lommen.com.

**STAGER, DONALD K.,** retired construction company executive; Chmn., pres., CEO Dillingham Constrn. Holdings Inc., Pleasanton, Calif., 1982-99; with Guy F. Atkinson Co., 1952—82; ret., 1999. Recipient, Roebling award Am. Soc. of Civil Engineers, 1995, Golden Beaver award for Mgmt Beavers, Inc., 1998. Office: 957 Wapato Way Manson WA 98831-9595

**STAGER, JOHN C.,** information scientist, educator; b. Johnstown, Pa., June 28, 1955; s. John A. and Lillian R. Stager; m. Joanne F. Burke, Nov. 1, 1986; children: Jessica, Cassidy Boyd. AA, Riverside C.C., 1995; BA in Environ. Studies, U. Redlands, 2000, M in Mgmt., 2001; MS in Mgmt. of Info. Systems, Claremont Grad. U., 2004, PhD in Mgmt. of Info. Systems, 2006. Programmer US Nat. Bank, Johnstown, Pa., 1974—77, Carnegie Mellon U., Pitts., 1976—77; programmer analyst North Am. Van Lines, Ft. Wayne, Ind., 1977; sr. programmer Philips Industries Inc., Dayton, Ohio, 1977—79; programmer, analyst Kaufman and Broad, L.A., 1979; sr. computer analyst/dba Beckman Instruments Inc., Brea, Calif., 1979—80; sr. staff cons. Yourdon, Inc., N.Y.C., 1980—81; sr. computer analyst/dba Beckman Instruments, Brea, Calif., 1981—82; data administr. Shiley Inc., Irvine, Calif., 1982—83; account systems engr. IBM, L.A., Calif., 1983—84; systems mgr. Colonial Ins. Co., Anaheim, Calif., 1984—86; sr. cons. Carter, Hawley, Hale Stores, Anaheim, Calif., 1986—89; database administr. No. Ariz. U., Flagstaff, Ariz., 1989—90; pres./prin. cons. Acorn Design Consultants, Inc., Norco, Calif., 1999—2006; sr. cons. Compuware, Irvine, Calif., 1990—2004; adj. prof. U. Redlands, Calif., 2004—06, Chapman U., Orange, Calif., 2005—06; dir. Pemco Technologies, Seattle, 2006—. Author: (book chapter) Geographical Information Systems in Business; contbr. articles to prof. jours. Fellow, Claremont Grad. U., Sch. Info. Sci., 2002—04; Whitehead Leadership Soc.

fellow, U. Redlands, 2000. Mem.: Western History Assn., Am. Soc. Environ. History, Western Social Sci. Assn. (sect. coord. geography 2004—06), Assn. Am. Geographers, Assn. Info. Systems. Personal E-mail: jcstager@earthlink.net.

**STAGER, LAWRENCE E.,** archaeologist, educator; b. Kenton, Ohio, Jan. 5, 1943; married; 2 children. BA, Harvard U., 1965, MA, 1972, PhD in Syro-Palestinian Archeology and History, 1975. Instr. Oriental Inst., U. Chgo., 1973-74, asst. prof., 1974-75, assoc. prof. Syro-Palestinian archaeology, 1976-87; Dorot prof. archeology of Israel, Dept. Near Eastern Langs. and Civilizations and Anthropology Harvard U., Cambridge, Mass., 1986—, dir. Semite Mus. Fellow Inst. for Advanced Study, Hebrew U., 1983-84; co-dir. Am. Expdn., Idalion, Cyprus, 1972-74; dir. UNESCO Save Carthage Project, Am. Punic Archaeol. Expdn., 1975-80, Harvard Semitic Mus., 1987—, Leon Levy Expdn. to Ashkelon, Israel, 1985—; dir. Harvard Semitic Mus., Cambridge, 1987—. Author: Ashkelon Discovered, 1991, A Heap of Broken Images: Essays in Biblical Archaeology, 2005; co-author: Idalion I, Idalion II, Life in Biblical Israel, 2001; contbr. articles to profl. jours. Recipient Levi-Salla prize, Ben Gurion U., Bibl. Archaeology Soc. prize. Mem. Am. Schs. Oriental Rsch. (editor newsletter 1975-76, assoc. trustee 1977-80, trustee 1987-90, assoc. editor bull. 1978—), Archaeol. Inst. Am. (v.p. 1986-88, trustee 1989-91), Am. Orient Soc., Soc. Bibl. Lit. Achievements include rsch. in economy, society and religion of ancient Israel; archaeology of Philistines, Canaanites and Phoenicians. Office: Harvard U Semitic Mus Dept Near Ea Langs/Civil Cambridge MA 02138-2091 Office Phone: 617-495-5756. Business E-Mail: stager@fas.harvard.edu.

**STAGG, LOUIS CHARLES,** English language and literature educator; b. Jan. 3, 1933; s. Louis Anatol and Gladys (Andrews) S.; m. Mary Casner, June 5, 1959; children: Robert Charles, Helen Marie. BA in English, La. Coll., 1955; MA in English, U. Ark., 1957, PhD in English, 1963. Tchg. asst. English U. Ark., 1955-59; asst. prof. William Jewell Coll., 1959-60; instr. Stephen F. Austin State U., 1960-62; asst. prof. Memphis State U. (now U. Memphis), 1962-69, assoc. prof., 1969-77, prof. English lang. and lit., 1977-98, prof. emeritus, 1998—, dir. grad. studies in English, 1985-88, dir. English Drama Players, 1968-92, dir. undergrad. advising for English, 1970-80, 88-91, chair policies and procedures com. for English, 1983-95, cons. for 2001 program. Chmn. acad. policies com. Memphis State U. Senate, 1981-82, 88-90, 93-96, exec. com. senate, 1987-91, 93-96, parliamentarian of senate, 1987-88, 90-91, 94-96, humanities rep. budget adv. com. dean Coll. Arts and Scis., 1992-93, adv. bd. Acad. Exch. Quar., 1997-2000, steering com., chair of schedules, originator Alliance Creative Theatre, Edn. and Rsch. series, 1986, 89-90, 92, 94, 96, 98; cons. NEH, 1975-76, 78, Ohio State U. Press, 1985-86, U. Jordan, Amman, 1985; chair policies and procedures subdivsn. Eng. dept. so. assn. colls., schs. self study, steering com. 1992-93; cons. Memphis State U. Learning Media-Ctrs. catalogue Shakespeare holdings, 1992-93, rev., 1993-95. Author: (with J. Lasley Dameron) Poe's Critical Vocabulary, 1966; author series: Index to the Figurative Language of John Webster's Tragedies, 1967, of Ben Jonson's Tragedies, 1967, of Thomas Heywood's Tragedies, 1967, of George Chapman's Tragedies, 1970, of Thomas Middleton's Tragedies, 1970, of Cyril Tourneur's Tragedies, 2d edit., all 7 under title Index to the Figurative Language of the Tragedies of Shakespeare's Chief 17th Century Contemporaries, 1977, 3d edit., 1982, Index to the Figurative Language of the Tragedies of Shakespeare's Chief 18th Century Contemporaries, 1984; contbr. to Great Writers of the English Language Dramatists, 1979, 87; circulation editor Interpretations, 1976-80, Libraries of the World Series for U. Memphis Libr. Jour. (series 1-9); contbr. articles to profl. jours. Mem. Memphis Oratorio Soc. Chorus, 1969-92, diction coach, 1987; active Memphis Symphony Chorus, 1993-2004, newsletter com., 1999-2000; active Memphis in May Sunset Symphony Choir, 1996, Martin Luther King Tribute Concert Choir, 1995-96, 1999-2004, City of Memphis Faure Requiem Concert, 2001, Memphis Symphony Chorus and Orch. prodn. Rolling Requiem for 9/11/02; lay reader Episcopal Ch.; program chair Friends of Univ. Librs., 2000-02, v.p., 2002-03, pres. 2003—05, exec. coun., 2005—, vice chmn. pub. programs, 2005—; mem. at large exec. com. U. Memphis Assn. Retirees, 2003-. Grantee NEH, 1967, Memphis State U., 1965, Travel grant to U.S. Libr. Congress, 1971. Mem. MLA (life), So. Humanities Coun. (sec.-treas. 1974-76, exec. com. 1976-83, 94-96, chmn coun. 1993-94, chmn. sect. humanities in pluralistic soc. 1984, ad hoc com. on crisis in tchg. humanities 1977, chmn. local arrangements for convs. 1975, 94, chmn. sect. on Thomas Hardy 1996), Tenn. Philol. Assn. (pres. 1976-77, exec. com. 1977, local arrangements chmn. 1965, 69, 75, 87, chmn. Shakespeare sect. 1996), Marlowe Soc. Am. (book reviewer 1984, 86-88, 93), Am. Soc. for Theatre Rsch., Samuel Beckett Soc., Conf. on Christianity and Lit., South Cen. Conf. on Christianity and Lit. Soc. for Study of Works of Harold Pinter (life, asst. constn. revision 1988, asst. with planning 1992, treas. 1994-98, exec. com. 1994-98), Ark. Philol. Assn., Shakespeare Assn. Am. (local arrangements host com. 1985). Stratford-upon-Avon Shakespeare Festival (Eng.), Eugene O'Neill Soc., Alliance for Creative Theatre, Edn. and Rsch. (chmn. schedules com., originator of proposal 1986, 89-90, 92, 94, 96, 98, cons. residency S.E. Mo. State U. 1997), Internat. Shakespeare Assn., Am. Soc. Theatre Rsch., Internat. Soc. Theatre Rsch., Medieval and Renaissance Drama Soc., Renaissance Soc. Am., South Cen. Renaissance Conf. (life, chmn. nominations 1976, exec. com. 1978-80, program com. 1981-83, chmn. sect. Shakespeare 1981, 85, 95, 99, 2002-04, chair non dramatic lit., 2005, chair Renaissance drama sect. 2006, chair renaissance poetry sect., 16th Century lit. 1982, chmn. local arrangements 1983, symposium on humanism 1984, chmn. Shakespeare on film and the tchg. Brit. drama 1986, chmn. music in Shakespeare's plays, 1987, chmn. sect. Thematic Approaches to Tudor/Stuart Drama 1988, chmn. sect. Medieval Influences on Renaissance drama 1993, chmn. Shakespeare's Villains: Stage and Page 1995, Adaptions of Renaissance Drama 1993, chmn. local arrangements for conv. 1990, chmn. spl. session 1989, 95, Shakespeare II sect. 1996, chair Renaissance Drama Sect. 1999, 2001, chmn. Performing Rennaissance Drama 2001), South Cen. MLA (life, assoc. editor for English, South Cen. Bull. 1982-84, nominations com. 1985-86, 95-96, book reviewer South Cen. Rev. 1983, 85-86, sec. English I.B. Renaissance, 1986, chair, 1987, sec. spl. sect. Renaissance Drama, 1988, chair Shakespeare's Tragi-comedies and tragi-comic romances, 1989, co-chair local arrangements, 1999, chair panel on renaissance drama criticism 1995, sec. renaissance drama sect. 1997, sect. chmn. 1998, mem. com. Conv., Memphis, 1999, sec. renaissance non-dramatic lit. 2005), South Atlantic MLA, South Ctrl. Coll. English Assn. (sec.-treas. 1980-81, v.p. 1981-82, pres. 1982-83, exec. com. 1983-90, co-host 1982, com. constitution revision 1989), Coll. English Assn., Internat. Patristic Medieval and Renaissance Conf. (sect. chmn. Medieval drama 1977, chair Shakespeare session 1994, chmn. Renaissance drama section 1995, chmn. 17th century Brit. lit. sect. 1996, chmn. Milton sect. 1996), Am. Theatre Assn. (chmn. sect. combining Brit. lit. and theatre in teaching of drama 1983, chmn. Shakespeare sect. 1994), Marlowe Soc. Am., Eugene O'Neill Soc., Stratford Can. Shakespeare Festival, AAUP (sec. treas. Memphis State U. chpt. 1982-86, v.p. 1986-88, pres. 1988-90), Phi Beta Kappa (pres. memphis alumni assn. 1985-88, spl. panel Soc. and New Scholarship at 37th triennial coun. 1994), Humanities Tenn., Alpha Chi. Democrat. Home: 5219 Mason Rd Memphis TN 38117-2104 Personal E-mail: mlcshake@aol.com.

**STAGG, TOM,** federal judge; b. Shreveport, La., Jan. 19, 1923; s. Thomas Eaton and Beulah (Meyer) S.; m. Margaret Mary O'Brien, Aug. 21, 1946; children: Julie, Margaret Mary. BA, La. State U., 1943, JD, 1949. Bar: La. 1949. With firm Hargrove, Guyton, Van Hook & Hargrove, Shreveport, 1949-53; pvt. practice law Shreveport, 1953-58; sr. ptnr. firm Stagg, Cady & Beard, Shreveport, 1958-74; judge U.S. Dist. Ct. No. La., 1974-84, 91-92, chief judge, 1984-90, sr. judge, 1992—. Mem. Shreveport Airport Authority, 1967-73, chmn., 1970-73; chmn. Gov.'s Tidelands Adv. Council, 1969-70; del. La. Constl. Conv., 1973-74; chmn. rules com., com. on exec. dept.; mem. Gov.'s Adv. Com on Offshore Revenues, 1972-74 Active Republican party, 1950-74, del. convs., 1956, 60, 64, 68; mem. exec. com. for La., 1964-72, mem. exec. com., 1964-68; Pres. Shreveport Jr. C. of C., 1955-56; v.p. La. Jr. C. of C., 1956-57. Served to capt., inf. AUS, 1943-46, ETO. Decorated Bronze Star, Purple Heart with oak leaf cluster, Combat Inf.

badge. Mem. Am., La., Shreveport bar assns. Office: US Dist Ct 300 Fannin St Ste 4100 Shreveport LA 71101-3123 Office Phone: 318-676-3260. Business E-Mail: tom_stagg@lawd.uscourts.gov.

**STAGGERS, KERMIT LEMOYNE, II,** history professor, political science professor, state legislator, municipal official; b. Washington, Pa., Nov. 2, 1947; s. Kermit LeMoyne and Christine Ruby (Scherich) S.; m. June Ann Wenda, Aug. 22, 1970; children: Ayn Kristen Staggers Bird, Kyle Lee Staggers. BS, U. Idaho, 1969, MA, 1975; PhD, Claremont Grad. U., 1986. Instr. history Troy (Ala.) State U., 1975-76, U. Idaho, Moscow, 1977, Northwestern Coll., Orange City, Iowa, 1979-80, Coll. Lake County, Grayslake, Ill., 1981-82; lectr. history Chapman Univ., Orange, Calif., 1979, U. Md.-Europe, Heidelberg, Germany, 1988-89; vis. instr. history Trinity Internat. U., Deerfield, Ill., 1980; adj. instr. history U. St. Francis, Joliet, Ill., 1982; prof. history and polit. sci. U. Sioux Falls (S.D.), 1982—; mem. S.D. Senate, Pierre, 1995—2002, Sioux Falls City Coun., 2002—. Lectr. Diplomatic Acad. Ukrainian Fgn. Ministry and Nat. U. Kiev-Mohyla Acad., 2001; expert analyst on polit. and social issues for local radio and TV. Contbr. to profl. publs. Chair Senate Transp. Com., 1997-99. Capt. USAF, 1970-76. Recipient Guardian Small Bus. award Nat. Fedn. Ind. Bus., 1996; Malone Faculty fellow, 1993. Mem. Orgn. Am. Historians, Great Plains Polit. Sci Assn. (pres. 2000-01), Conf. on Faith and History, Federalist Soc., Fulbright Assn., Hist. Soc., Kiwanis, Phi Alpha Theta, Phi Kappa Phi. Republican. Avocations: book collecting, travel. Home: 616 E Wiswall Pl Sioux Falls SD 57105-2030 Office: U Sioux Falls Dept History/Polit Sci 1101 W 22nd St Sioux Falls SD 57105-1699 Office Phone: 605-331-6754. Business E-Mail: kermit.staggers@usiouxfalls.edu.

**STAGGERS, MARY E.,** minister; b. Rocky Mount, N.C., Sept. 28, 1923; d. John and Emma Jane White; m. Calvin Staggers, Jr., May 18, 1938; children: Luther, Gervis, Earlie Mae, Curtis, Herbert, Betty Joann, Yvonne. BA, Coll. New Rochelle, 1983; M in Profl. Studies, N.Y. Theol. Sem., 1985; M in Humanities, Ctr. Humanities N.Y., 1985; D of Theology of Bible, Internat. Sem. Fla., 1990; DD, Balt. Coll. Bible, 1988. Pastor Holy Redeemer Bapt. Ch., Bklyn., 1961—. Family therapist Beth Israel Hosp., N.Y.C., 1980—98; min. N.Y.C. World's Fair. Author: It's Seed Time, 1999, The Spirit Supercedes Nature, 2003. Liaison N.Y.C. Cmty. Bd. Dist. 16; v.p. Women's Nat. Evang. and Missionary Conf., 1996—2001; pres. World Conf. Gospel Explosion, 1994—, United Ladies Ministers Counsel, 1978—99; pres. Ea. N.Y. br. Women's Nat. Evang. and Missionary Conf., 1997—2001; pres. Mother's Bd. Cedar Grove Bapt. Ch., 1940—51. Mem.: N.Y.C. Clergy Conf., Ea. Bapt. Conf., So. Bapt. Conf., Nat. Bapt. Conf. Democrat. Avocations: cooking, reading, writing. Office Phone: 718-816-5181.

**STAGGS, BARBARA ANNETTE,** state representative; b. Hulbert, Okla., July 18, 1940; d. Truman and Veleria (Trapp) Masterson; m. Ross Staggs; children: Rick, Matt. BA in Edn., Northeastern U., 1963; MA, U. Tulsa, 1968, EdD, 1987. Tchr., adminstr.; mem. Okla. Ho. of Reps., 1995—. Named Outstanding Adminstr., Okla. Schs. Adhoc Coun., 1993, Woman of Distinction, Muskogee Soroptimist's, 1996. Democrat. Office: State Capitol 2300 N Lincoln Blvd Rm 302 Oklahoma City OK 73105 Home: PO Box 1545 Muskogee OK 74402 Office Phone: 405-557-7310.

**STAGGS, TERESA LAVERNE,** special education educator; b. Flora, Ill., June 26, 1950; d. Jasper LaVerne and Frieda Lee Feather; m. Kent DeWayne Staggs, Feb. 22, 2002; children: Tyrell, Erin, Shayna. BS, So. Ill. U., Carbondale, 1974, MS, 1980. Elem. tchr. Wayne City Unit #100, Ill., 1974—81, spl. edn. tchr., 1981—. Mem. 708 mental health bd. Wayne County, Ill., 1997—2000; mem. REACH, Wayne City, 2002—. Author: (poetry) Good Job (Famous Poets Shakespeare award, 2003). Group leader Kids Without Barriers, Wayne City, 2003—; youth group mission participant First Christian Ch. Wayne City, Mexico, 1995—96. Mem.: Ruritan Club (rummage sale chmn. 2002—), Delta Kappa Gamma (Gamma Upsilon chpt. sec. 2002—04, v.p. 1993—, 1st v.p. 2004—, Book Bearing Bunny award 1997—2001, Everybody Reads award 2003). Avocation: reading. Home: RR1 Box 103 Wayne City IL 62895 Office Phone: 618-895-3103.

**STAGGS, THOMAS O.,** entertainment company executive; Mgr. strategic planning Walt Disney Co., Burbank, Calif., 1990—94, v.p. planning & development, 1995—97, exec. v.p., CFO, 1998—99, sr. exec. v.p., CFO, 2000—. Office: Walt Disney Co 500 S Buena Vista St Burbank CA 91521-0006 Office Phone: 818-560-1000.*

**STAGINNUS, ULF,** pharmaceutical executive, health economist; b. Eilenburg, Germany, Dec. 27, 1970; s. Lothar Fritz and Hermine Staginnus; m. Libia Marina Naranjo Cruzatty, Aug. 11, 2004; 1 child, Julien Staginnus Naranjo. MS in Econs. with hon., U. Bayreuth, Germany, 1996; degree in pharm. mktg. and strategic mgmt. Cons., health econs. & outcomes rsch. HealthEcon Ltd., Basel, Switzerland, 1997—98; sr. mgr. health econs., new product devel. Glaxo Smith Kline Biologicals, Brussels, 1998—2001; assoc. dir. global health econs. and competitive intelligence Baxter Healthcare, Madrid, 2001—04; sr. mgr. worldwide outcomes rsch. Pfizer Inc., N.Y., 2004—05; mng. dir. European Health Econs., Madrid, 2005—06; assoc. dir. outcomes rsch. Bristol-Myers Squibb, Madrid, 2006—. Mng. dir. ptnr. Premor Assocs. Madrid and N.Y.C., 2005—06. Mem. editl. bd.: Spanish Jour. Health Econs.; contbr. chapters to books, articles to profl. jours. Mem.: Internat. Soc. of Pharmacoeconomics & Outcomes Rsch. Business E-Mail: ulf.staginnus@healtheconomics.es. E-mail: ustaginnus@hotmail.com.

**STAGLIANO, VITO ALEXANDER,** federal agency administrator, utilities executive; b. Catanzaro, Calabria, Italy, May 13, 1942; arrived in U.S., 1956; s. Filippo and Maria Stagliano; m. Julie Ann Werth, Sept. 30, 1967; children: Jason Vito, Carlo Oxford. Program analyst U.S. Office Econ. Opportunity, Washington, 1968-69; exec. dir. Palau Cmty. Devel. Agy., 1969-71; program officer U.S. Peace Corps, Ghana, 1971-73, dir. Mauritania, 1973-74, dir. West Africa Washington, 1974-77; counselor Interstate Commn. on Drought Control, Ouagadougou, Bourkina Faso, 1977-79; staff asst. Sec. of Energy, Washington, 1979-81; dir. River Basins Devel. Office, Dakar, Senegal, 1981-85; dir. Office of Energy Demand Policy, U.S. Dept. Energy, Washington, 1986-89, assoc. dep. undersec. of energy, 1990-91, dep. asst. sec. energy for policy planning, 1991-93; vis. scholar Resources for Future, 1993-95; dir. Energy Security Analysis, Inc., Washington, 1996-98; v.p. Commonwealth Edison Co., Chgo., 1998-2000, Calpine Corp., 2001—06; rsch. dir. Nat. Commn. Energy Policy, Washington, 2006—. Guest lectr. Harvard U., Boston, Tufts U., Medford, Nat. Def. U., Washington, Va. Mil. Inst., Lexington, École Nationale Superieure, France. Author: A Policy of Discontent: The Making of a National Energy Strategy, 2001; co-author: Energy and National Security in the 21st Century, 1995, A Shock to the System: Restructuring America's Electricity Industry, 1996. Founder Micronesia Legal Svcs. Program, 1971; mem. Theodore Thomas Soc. of Chgo. Symphony Orch. Recipient rank of meritorious Sr. Exec., Pres. George Bush; Ampart fellow, USIA, 1981. Mem.: U.S. Assn. for Energy Econs., Internat. Assn. Energy Econs., So. Poverty Law Ctr., Am. Poetry Soc. Avocations: poetry, history. E-mail: vstagliano@aol.com.

**STAGLIN, GAREN KENT,** computer company executive, venture capitalist; b. Lincoln, Nebr., Dec. 22, 1944; s. Ramon and Darlene (Guilliams) S.; m. Sharalyn King, June 8, 1968; children: Brandon Kent, Shannon King. BS in Engring. with honors, UCLA, 1966; MBA, Stanford U., 1968. Assoc. Carr Mgmt. Co., NYC, 1971-75; v.p. Crocker Nat. Bank, San Francisco, 1975-76; dir. fin. Itel Corp., San Francisco, 1976-77, pres. ins. services divsn., 1977-79; corp. v.p., gen. mgr. ADP Automotive Svcs. Group, San Ramon, Calif., 1978-91; chmn., CEO Safelite Glass Corp., Columbus, Ohio, 1991-97, chmn., 1998-2000; owner Staglin Family Vineyard, Rutherford, Calif., 1985—; pres., CEO eOne Global L.L.C., Napa, Calif., 2000—05; sr. advisor FT Ventures, San Francisco, 2005—. Bd. dir. Certive Corp., Specialized Bicycle Corp., Global Document Solutions, Inc., Solera, Inc. Bd. dir. Peralta Hosp. Cancer Inst., 1977-78, Berkeley Reportory Theatre, 1979-85; trustee

Justin Sienna H.S., Napa, Calif., 1995-20; chmn. major gifts program East Bay region Stanford (Calif.) U., 1989-92; mem. adv. bd. Stanford Bus. Sch., 1995-00, Judge Inst. Mgmt. Cambridge U., Eng., 2004-; chmn. 75th anniversary campaign Stanford Grad. Sch. Bus., 1998-00; capital campaign UCLA Coll. Letters Sci., 2004-; pres. bd. trustees Am. Ctr. Wine, Food and Arts, Napa, Calif., 1998-03. Lt. USN, 1968-71. Recipient Gold Spike award, Stanford U., 2000. Mem. Stanford Assocs. (bd. govs. 1985-92), World Pres. Orgn., Internat. Inst. Soc. (bd. govs. 1985-92). Democrat. Lutheran. Home: PO Box 680 1570 Bella Oaks Ln Rutherford CA 94573 Office Phone: 707-280-5374. E-mail: gstaglin@eoneglobal.com.

**STAHL, ALICE SLATER,** retired psychiatrist; b. Vienna, Jan. 28, 1913; came to U.S., 1938; d. Sam and Helen (Bluman) Slater; widowed; children: Kenneth Lee, June Audrey. Baccalaureate, Gymnasium, Vienna, 1932; Med. Dr., U. Vienna Med. Sch., 1938. Intern Williamsport (Pa.) Gen. Hosp., 1939-40; resident in psychiatry Gallinger Mcpl. Hosp., Washington, 1940-41, Independence State Hosp., 1941-42, Bellevue Hosp., N.Y.C., 1942-43, attending psychiatrist, 1945-48; staff psychiatrist Jewish Bd. of Guardians, N.Y.C., 1943-45; attending psychiatrist Jamaica Hosp., Queens, NY, 1948-52; dir. adolescent pavilion Hillside Hosp., Glen Oaks, NY, 1954-96, staff psychiatrist, 1982—95; supervising psychiatrist Bergen Regional Hosp., Paramus, NJ, 1987—2002. Asst. prof. clin. psychiatry Yeshiva U. Med. Sch., 1978-96. Fellow AMA (life), Am. Psychiat. Assn. (life); mem. Am. Psychoanalytic Assn. (life), Am. Soc. for Adolescent Psychiatry (life) Avocations: swimming, hiking, gardening. Home and Office: 305 Joan Pl Wyckoff NJ 07481-2818

**STAHL, CRAIG L.,** lawyer; b. Riverside, NJ, Jan. 14, 1959; s. George W. Stahl III and Judy R. (Collins) Stahl; m. Donna J. Jacobs, Aug. 18, 1984; 1 child, Bryan T. AB cum laude, Princeton U., 1981; JD, So. Meth. U., 1984. Bar: Tex. 1984, admitted to practice: US Dist. Ct. (No. Dist.) Tex., US Dist. Ct. (So. Dist.) Tex., US Dist. Ct. (We. Dist.) Tex., US Dist. Ct. (Ea. Dist.) Tex., US Ct. Appeals (5th Cir.). Assoc. Bracewell & Patterson, Houston, 1984—, Sifford & Pezzulli, Dallas, 1986; ptnr., Energy Litig. Andrews Kurth LLP, The Woodlands, Tex. Elected mem., Rep. Com. Burlington County, NJ, 1979—81. Mem.: Tex. Bar Found., Houston Bar Found., State Bar Tex., Houston Young Lawyers Assn., Houston Bar Assn., ABA, NJ Assn. Soccer Coaches (All-State award 1977). Republican. Methodist. Avocations: jogging, golf, soccer, tennis. Office: Andrews Kurth LLP 1001 Woodloch Forest Dr Ste 200 The Woodlands TX 77380 Office Phone: 713-220-4834. Office Fax: 713-238-7478. Business E-Mail: cstahl@andrewskurth.com.

**STAHL, FRANK LUDWIG,** civil engineer; b. Fuerth, Germany; came to U.S., 1946, naturalized, 1949; s. Leo E. and Anna (Regensburger) S.; m. Edith Cosmann, Aug. 31, 1947; children: David, Robert. BSCE, Tech. Inst. Zurich, Switzerland, 1945. With Ammann & Whitney, Cons. Engrs., N.Y.C., 1946-93, project engr., 1955-67, assoc., 1968-76, sr. assoc., 1977-81, chief engr. Transp. div., 1982-93; pvt. cons., 1994—. Expert in field. Prin. works include Verrazano-Narrows Bridge, Throgs Neck Bridge, Walt Whitman Bridge, improvements to Golden Gate Bridge, rehab. of Williamsburg Bridge, N.Y.C., Royal Gorge Bridge, Colo., Interstate-10 Deck Tunnel, Phoenix; author: Cable Corrosion in Bridges and Other Structures; co-author: Golden Gate Bridge, Report of the Chief Engineer to the Board of Directors, Vol. II; contbr. articles to profl. jours. on bridge design and constrn. Recipient Gold award The James F. Lincoln Arc Welding Found., 1986, John A. Roebling medal Internat. Bridge Conf., 1992. Fellow ASCE (Thomas Fitch Rowland prize 1967, Innovation in Civil Engring. award of mert 1983, Metro. Civil Engr. of Yr. award 1987, Roebling award 1990), ASTM (vice chmn. com. A-1 on steel, stainless steel and related alloys 1978-83, chmn. steel reinforce-subcom. 1971-82, award of merit 1982); mem. Am. Inst. Steel Constrn. (Prize Bridge award 1986), Engring. Found. (rsch. coun. on structural connections), Internat. Assn. Bridge and Structural Engring., Internat. Bridge Tunnel and Turnpike Assn. Home: 20911 28th Rd Flushing NY 11360-2412 Personal E-mail: bridgfrank@aol.com.

**STAHL, FRIEDA AXELROD,** physicist, researcher, physics professor; b. Bklyn., May 27, 1922; d. Benjamin and Gertrude Fagen Axelrod; m. Joseph I. Stahl, June 19, 1942 (div. 1980); children: Linda Beverly Stahl Cofsky, Richard Cary. BA, Hunter Coll., 1942; MA, Hofstra U., 1957; PhD, Claremont Grad. U., 1969. Jr. physicist U. S. Army Signal Corps Labs., Belmar, N.J., Mobile, Ala., 1942-44, Petty Geophys. Labs., San Antonio, 1944-46, Hillyer Instrument Co., N.Y.C., 1946-48; from physicist to sr. physicist Sylvania Rsch. Labs., Bayside, N.Y., 1948-52; grad. teaching asst. in physics Hofstra U., Hempstead, N.Y., 1954-56; cons. physicist Gen. Instruments, Jamaica, N.Y., 1956-57; lectr. physics Calif. State U., L.A., 1958-59, asst. prof. physics, 1959-69, assoc prof., 1969-73, prof., 1973-92, prof. emeritus, 1992—, assoc. dean, 1970-75, chmn. Acad. Senate, 1981-83. Rsch. assoc. in physics Harvey Mudd Coll., Claremont, Calif., 1969-79, 90-91. Contbr. articles to scientific jours. NSF sci. faculty fellow, 1966-67. Fellow: Am. Phys. Soc.; mem.: AAUP, Union Concerned Scientists, Assn. for Women in Sci., Am. Assn. Physics Tchrs., Sigma Xi, Sigma Pi Sigma, Sigma Delta Epsilon, Phi Kappa Phi. Avocations: art, classical music, linguistics. Office: Calif State U LA 5151 State University Dr Los Angeles CA 90032-8206 Business E-Mail: fstahl@calstatela.edu.

**STAHL, JACK LELAND,** real estate company executive; b. Lincoln, Ill., June 28, 1934; s. Edwin R. and Edna M. (Burns) S.; m. Carol Anne Townsend, June 23, 1956; children: Cheryl, Nancy, Kellea BS in Edn., U. N.Mex., 1957. Tchr. Albuquerque Pub. Schs., 1956-59; pres. House Finders, Inc., Albuquerque, 1959-65; v.p. N.Mex. Savs. & Loan Assn., Albuquerque, 1965-67; chmn. bd. Hooten-Stahl, Inc., Albuquerque, 1967-77; mem. N.Mex. Ho. of Reps., 1969-70; pres. The Jack Stahl Co., Albuquerque, 1977—; mem. N.Mex. Senate, 1981-86; lt. gov. State of N.Mex., 1987-90. Mem, N. Mex Ho of Reps, 1969 70, exec 1st Ch S.W. Coun. Boy Scouts Am, 1982-89; bd. dirs. BBB N. Mex., 1968-82, pres. 1975-76; trustee Univ Heights. Hosp.,1980-85; vice chmn. N. Mex. Bd. Fin., 1987-90, N. Mex. Cmty. Devel. Coun., 1987-90; bd. dirs. Ctr. for Entrepreneurship and Econ. Devel., 1994-96; mem. Gov.'s Bus. Adv. Coun., 1995-97. Named Realtor of Yr., Albuquerque Bd. Realtors, 1972. Mem. Nat. Assn. Realtors, Nat. Homebuilders Assn., N.Mex. Amigos, 20-30 Club (pres. 1963-64), Rotary. Republican. Methodist. Office: 1911 Wyoming Blvd NE Albuquerque NM 87112-2865 Office Phone: 505-292-6635.

**STAHL, LADDIE L.,** engineering company executive; b. Terre Haute, Ind., Dec. 23, 1921; s. Edgar Allen and Martha (Llewellyn) S.; m. Thelma Mae Beasley, Dec. 11, 1942; children: Stephanie, Laddie L., Craig. BSCE, Purdue U., 1942; MS in Engring., Johns Hopkins U., 1950. With GE, 1954-90, mgr. planning and resources, electronics sci. and engring., corp. research and devel. Schenectady, NY, 1974-76, mgr. electronics systems programs ops., elec. sci. and engring., 1976-84, mgr. spl. programs and project devel. operation, 1984-90; dir. tech. transfer program Data Storage Systems Ctr. Carnegie Mellon U., Pitts., 1990—. Chmn. adv. group U.S. Army Electronics Command, 1971-74; mem. U.S. Army Sci. Bd., 1978-87; cons. in field. Contbr. articles to profl. publs. Mem. alumni bd. dirs. Purdue U., 1979-82. Served with U.S. Army, 1942-54, ETO; maj. gen. Res. (ret.), 1954-77. Decorated D.S.M., Legion of Merit. Mem. AIAA (sr.), IEEE (life), Am. Def. Preparedness Assn., Army and Navy Club (Washington), Tau Beta Pi, Chi Epsilon. Home: 29 Fairway Ln Rexford NY 12148-1213 Office: Carnegie Mellon U Data Storage Sys Ctr ECE Dept 5000 Forbes Ave Pittsburgh PA 15213-3815 Office Phone: 518-399-0451. E-mail: lstahlz@nycap.rr.com.

**STAHL, LESLEY R.,** news correspondent; b. Lynn, Mass., Dec. 16, 1941; d. Louis and Dorothy J. (Tishler) Stahl; m. Aaron Latham; 1 child, Taylor. BA cum laude, Wheaton Coll., Norton, Mass., 1963. Asst. to speechwriter Mayor Lindsay's Office, N.Y.C., 1966—67; rschr. N.Y. Election unit CBS News, 1967—68; rschr. London-Huntley Brinkley Report, NBC News, 1969; prodr., reporter WHDH-TV, Boston, 1970—72; news corr. CBS News, Washington, 1972—; co-anchor CBS Morning News, 1977—79; White House corr. CBS News, 1979-91; moderator Face The Nation, 1983-91; anchor America Tonight, 1990—91; co-editor, corr. CBS News, 60 Minutes, 1991—; host 48

Hours, 2002—04. Notable TV appearances include: Murphy Brown, 1993, 1995; Frasier, 1997. Trustee Wheaton Coll. Named Best White House Corr., Washington Journalism Rev., 1991; named to Broadcasting Mag. Hall of Fame, 1992; recipient Tex. Headliners award, 1973, Dennis Kauff award for lifetime achievement in journalism, Fifth Estate award, Fred Friendly First Amendment award, 1996.

**STAHL, NANETTE,** librarian, biblicist; b. Brooklyn, N.Y., July 23, 1941; d. David and Hannah Stahl; m. William W. Hallo, Oct. 18, 1998. BA, Brooklyn Coll., Brooklyn, N.Y., 1964; MLIS, Pratt Univ., Brooklyn, N.Y., 1966; PhD, Univ. Calif., Berkeley, Calif., 1993. Judaica Bibliographer Univ. Calif., Sch. of Law, Berkeley, Calif., 1970—80; head libr. Bureau of Jewish Edn., San Francisco, 1980—89; Judaica curator Yale Univ. Libr., New Haven, 1993—. Author: Law and Liminality in the Bible, 1996; editor: (book) Sholem Asch Reconsidered, 2004. Mem.: Assn. Jewish Studies, Assn. of Jewish Libr. Office: Yale Univ Libr Box 208240 130 Wall St New Haven CT 06520

**STAHL, NICK,** actor; b. Harlingen, Tex., Dec. 5, 1979; Actor: (TV miniseries) Seasons of Love, 1999; (TV series) Carnivàle, 2003—05; (TV films) Stranger at My Door, 1991, Woman with a Past, 1992, Incident in a Small Town, 1994, Blue River, 1995, My Son Is Innocent, 1996, Wasted, 2002; (films) The Man Without a Face, 1993, Safe Passage, 1994, Tall Tale, 1995, Eye of God, 1997, Disturbing Behavior, 1998, Soundman, 1998, The Thin Red Line, 1998, All Forgotten, 2000, Sunset Strip, 2000, In the Bedroom, 2001, The Sleepy Time Gal, 2001, Bully, 2001, Taboo, 2002, Bookies, 2003, Terminator 3: Rise of the Machines, 2003, Twist, 2003, Sin City, 2005. Office: ICM 8942 Wilshire Blvd Beverly Hills CA 90211

**STAHL, NORMAN H.,** judge; b. Manchester, NH, 1931; BA, Tufts U., 1952; LLB, Harvard U., 1955. Law clk. to Hon. John V. Spalding Mass. Supreme Ct., 1955—56; assoc. Devine, Millimet, Stahl & Branch, Manchester, NH, 1956—59, ptnr., 1959—90; dist. judge U.S. Dist. Ct. (N.H. dist.), 1990—92; cir. judge U.S. Ct. Appeals (1st cir.), Concord, NH, 1992—. Del to Rep. Nat. Conv., 1988. Mem.: N.H. Bar Assn. Office: US Courthouse Ste 8730 1 Courthouse Way Boston MA 02210*

**STAHL, PETER WILLIAM,** archaeologist, educator; b. Val D'Or, Canada, Dec. 10, 1953; s. Ernst Helmut and Hildegard Ingeborg Stahl; m. Ann Brower; children: Christina Mary, Emma Rebecca. BA, U. of Toronto, 1973—75; MA, U. of Calgary, 1976—78; PhD, U. of Ill., 1978—84. Assoc. prof. Binghamton U., 2004—. Contbr. articles to profl. jours. Sr. Investigator, NSF, 1995, 2002. Mem.: Internat. Coun. Archaeozoology, Soc. for Archaeological Sci., Soc. of Ethnobiology, Soc. for Am. Archaeology. Office: Binghamton Univ Vestal Parkway East Binghamton NY 13902-6000 Office Phone: 607-777-2557. Office Fax: 607-777-2477. E-mail: pstahl@binghamton.edu.

**STAHL, PHILIP ANTHONY,** physicist, educator; b. Milw., July 6, 1946; s. Curtis Philip and Magdalen Mary (Polacheck) S.; m. Janice Anne Johnson, Aug. 9, 1975. BA in Astronomy, U. South Fla., 1971; MPhil in Physics, U. W.I., St. Michael, Barbados, 1984. Sci. tchr. U.S. Peace Corps, Barbados, W.I., 1971-75; head sci. dept. West St. Joseph Secondary, Barbados, 1975-77, Garrison Secondary, St. Michael, Barbados, 1977-82; asst. tutor Barbados C.C., St. Michael, 1982-83; lectr. physics Harrison Coll., St. Michael, 1985-91; tech. writer Nucletron Corp., Columbia, Md., 1993-96. Dir. Solar Rsch. Sect., Harry Bayley Observatory, St. Michael, 1984-91; tech. writer, cons. in field. Author: Metacosmos: Cosmic Connections and Self-Actualizing Universe, 1997, The Atheist's Handbook to Modern Materialism, 2000; contbr. articles to profl. jours. Mem. Barbados Environ. Assn., St. Michael, 1987—, Barbados Cancer Soc., St. Michael, 1986—, Barbados and Latin Am. Mus. Soc., 1988— Recipient Studentship award Solar Physics Div. Am. Astron. Soc., 1984, Postgrad. Rsch. grant, 1980-84. Mem.: Intertel, Am. Astron. Soc. (Dynamical Astron. divsn., Solar Physics divsn.), Barbados Astron. Soc. (pres. 1977—80), Am. Geophys. Union, Am. Math. Soc., Intertel, Mensa, Top One Percent Soc. Achievements include development of first astronomy syllabus used at secondary level by Caribbean Examination Coun.; discovery of basic relationship between sudden ionospheric disturbances and specific types of H-alpha flare assoc. with sunspot. Home and Office: 2720 Nogal Ct Colorado Springs CO 80917 E-mail: jpstahl@msn.com.

**STAHL, RICHARD SHELDON,** surgeon; b. Chattanooga, Tenn., Dec. 8, 1950; s. Paul and Alena S. BA in Physics, Emory U., 1972; MD, Vanderbilt U., 1976; MBA, U. New Haven, 1994. Diplomate Nat. Bd. Med. Examiners, Am. Bd. Surgery, Am. Bd. Plastic Surgery. Intern, asst. resident dept. surgery Yale U. Sch. Medicine, New Haven, Conn., 1976-80, chief resident, 1980-81; resident plastic and reconstructive surgery Emory U. Sch. Medicine, 1981-82, chief resident, 1982-83; instr. surgery Yale U. Sch. Medicine, 1980-81, asst. prof. plastic surgery, 1983-89, assoc. prof. plastic surgery, 1989-90, assoc. clin. prof. plastic surgery, 1991-95, clin. prof. plastic surgery, 1995—; attending physician Yale Vascular Ctr., 1986-90, chmn. telemedicine com., 1998—; attending physician dept. surgery Yale-New Haven Hosp., 1980-81, 83—, asst. med. dir. surgery emergency svcs., 1983-90, attending physician surg. ICU, 1986-88, dir. internat. ops. dept. surgery, 1995—, assoc. chief dept. surgery, 1994—; attending physician Hosp. St. Raphael, 1983—, West Haven VA Hosp., 1983—. Founding co-dir. Yale Breast Care Ctr., 1989-90; cons. physicians assoc. surg. residency program Yale U.-Norwalk Hosp., 1978-81; resident surgeon Hospital Albert Schweitzer, Deschapelles, Haiti, 1980; med. mgmt. cons. Yale-New Haven Health Sys., 1997-98; program dir. of clin. telemedicine of NASA Comml. Space Ctr. at yale, 1997—; spkr. in field. Sports reporter The Chattanooga Times, 1967-69; contbr. over 40 articles to profl jours; Pres. Kingswood Homeowner's Assn., 1987-93; mem. Charter Oak Bassett Hound Club, 1981—. Recipient Rsch. grant Charles W. Ohse Fund, Rsch. grant Smith Kline and French Labs., Rsch. grant Kendall Co. Fellow Am. Coll. Surgeons (mem. Conn. chpt.); mem. APHA, AMA, Am. Assn. Plastic Surgeons, Am. Soc. Plastic and Reconstructive Surgeons, Am. Coll. Physician Execs., Am. Coll. Med. Quality, Am. Burn Assn., Soc. for Critical Care Medicine, New Eng. Soc. Plastic and Reconstructive Surgeons (v.p. 1998-99), New Haven County Med. Soc., Conn. Soc. Am. Bd. Surgeons, Conn. State Med. Soc., Sigma Xi. Office: Yale New Haven Hosp Assoc Chief Dept Surg CB228 20 York St New Haven CT 06504

**STAHL, WILLIAM MARTIN,** retired surgeon; b. Danbury, Conn., Nov. 6, 1922; s. William Martin and Sarah Stahl; m. Patricia Ann Maloney, Aug. 8, 1988; m. Betty Barrett, May 6, 1944 (div. June 3, 1966); children: Matyas Sebastian, William Martin, Elizabet Cordelia, Katherine Anne, Sarah Elizabeth, Jonathan Barrett, Elizabeth Parkinson; m. Alice Miller, June 12, 1968 (dec. Aug. 12, 1986). BA, Dartmouth Coll., Hanover, N.H., 1943; MD, Harvard U., Boston, Mass., 1946. Diplomate Am. Bd. of Surgery, 1956, cert. critical care Coll. Critical Care Medicine, 1987. Intern Mary Hitchcock Meml. Hosp., Hanover, NH, 1946—47; gen. practice medicine Danbury, Conn., 1947—51; surg. resident, 1953—57; pvt. practice surgery Danbury, 1957—62; chief of surgery Danbury (Conn.) Hosp., 1960—62; assoc. prof. surgery Coll. Medicine U. Vt., Burlington, Vt., 1962—66; prof. surgery NYU, N.Y., 1966—77, N.Y. Med. Coll., Valhalla, NY, 1977—97, ret., 1997. Dir. surgery Met. Hosp., N.Y., 1977—82, Lincoln Med. and Mental Health Ctr., N.Y., 1980—97. Contbr. 19 chapters to books, over 175 articles to profl. jours. Capt. med. corps. U.S. Army, 1951—52. Home: 145 Rockland Avenue Larchmont NY 10538 Personal E-mail: mdreedman@aol.com.

**STAHLECKER, BARBARA JEAN,** marketing professional, consultant; b. Stamford, Conn., Jan. 22, 1958; d. Roger Francis and Lillian Ann Beauleau; m. Richard Walter Stahlecker; children: Shannon Lee Banks, Brande Lauren Beach; children: Cori, Cara. Grad., Brien McMahon H.S., Norwalk, Conn., 1975. New bus. adminstr. Mutual of Omaha Ins. Co., L.A., 1983—85; ind. ins. agt. L.A., 1985—88; mktg. coordt. LifeCare Assurance Corp., Canoga Park, Calif., 1988—96; v.p. nat. mktg. dir. Centrelink Ins. & Fin. Svcs., Woodland, Calif., 1996—. Author: (Continuing Education Courses) Everything You've Always Wanted to Know about LTC - and Then Some, 1998,

(Continuing Education Course) The Nuts and Bolts of Long Term Care Insurance, 2000, TQ vs. NTQ LTCi, 2001; contbr. articles to profl. jours., 2001. Recipient Million Dollar Prodr. award, UNUM/Provident, 2001. Mem.: Soc. Cert. Sr. Advisors (cert. sr. advisor), Long-Term Care Profl., Am. Assn. Long-Term Care Ins. (Top Prodr. award 2000, 2001, BRAMCO Million Dollar Club award 2002), Nat. Assn. Health Underwriters (cons. 1999—). Office: Centrelink Ins & Fin Svc 20750 Ventura Blvd #300 Woodland Hills CA 91364 Business E-Mail: barbara@centrelink.com.

**STAHLER, JOYCE ANN,** history educator; b. Salt Lake City, Dec. 21, 1957; d. Lawrence and Verna Marie Rotvold; m. David Stahler, July 30, 1995; children: Nicholas, Eric. BA, U. Colo., Boulder, 1995; MA in Edn., U. Phoenix, Denver, 2005. Tchr. Boulder Valley Sch. Dist., Louisville, Colo., 1995—. Coach volleyball Boulder Valley Sch. Dist., Louisville, 1998—2001. Mem.: NEA, Colo. Tchrs. Assn. Avocations: hiking, piano, cooking, learning Italian language. Office: Boulder Valley Sch Dist 329 Campus Dr Louisville CO 80027

**STAHLMAN, MILDRED THORNTON,** pediatrician, pathologist, educator, medical researcher; b. Nashville, July 31, 1922; d. James Geddes and Mildred (Thornton) Stahlman. AB, Vanderbilt U., 1943, MD, 1946; MD (hon.), U. Goteborg, Sweden, 1973, U. Nancy, France, 1982. Diplomate Am. Bd. Pediat., Am. Bd. Neonatology. Intern Boston Children's Hosp., 1947—48; resident Vanderbilt Univ. Hosp., 1948—49; fellow Royal Caroline Inst. Medicine, Sweden, 1949—50; cardiac resident La Rabida Sanitarium, Chgo., 1951; instr. pediat. Vanderbilt U., Nashville, 1951—58, instr. physiology, 1954—60, asst. prof. pediat., 1959—64, asst. prof. physiology, 1960—62, assoc. prof. pediat., 1964—70, prof., 1970—, prof. pathology, 1982—, Harvie Branscomb Disting. prof., 1984, dir. divsn. neonatology, 1961—89, prof. pediat. and pathology. Editor: Respiratory Distress Syndromes, 1989; contbr. over 175 articles to profl. publs., chpts. to books. Recipient Apgar award, Am. Acad. Pediat., 1987; grantee NIH, 1954—. Mem.: AAAS, Inst. Medicine NAS, Royal Swedish Acad. Scis., So. Soc. Pediatric Rsch. (pres. 1961—62), Am. Physiology Soc., Soc. Pediatric Rsch., Am. Pediatric Soc. (pres. 1984, John Howland award 1996). Episcopalian. Home: 538 Beech Creek Rd S Brentwood TN 37027-3421 Office: Vanderbilt Univ Med Ctr 2215 B Garland Ave 1125 MRB IV LH Nashville TN 37232-0656 E-mail: mildred.stahlman@vanderbilt.edu.

**STAHLY, G. PATRICK,** chemist; b. Washington, Jan. 24, 1953; s. Glenn F. and Alice M. Stahly; m. Barbara C. Clack, July 12, 1975; children: Christopher P., Brian C. PhD, U. Md., College Park, 1979. Rsch. chemist, sr. rsch. specialist Ethyl Corp, Baton Rouge, 1980—88, mgr., r&d, 1988—91; r&d advisor Albemarle Corp, Baton Rouge, 1991—92; sr. r&d advisor Albemarle Corp., 1992—95; v.p. r&d SSCI, Inc., West Lafayette, Ind., 1995—97, COO, 1997—. Adj. prof. Purdue U., West Lafayette; topic editor Crystal Growth & Design. Contbr. articles to profl. jours. Fire fighter Hillandale Vol. Fire Dept., Md., 1970—75, EMT, 1970—75. Mem.: NRA (life), Am. Assn. Pharm. Scientists, Am. Chem. Soc. Achievements include patents for 43 US patents. Avocations: shooting, hunting, scuba diving. Home: 3908 Sunnycroft Pl West Lafayette IN 47906 Office: SSCI Inc 3065 Kent Ave West Lafayette IN 47906 Office Fax: 765-463-0112. Office Fax: 765-497-2649. E-mail: pstahly@ssci-inc.com.

**STAHR, BETH A.,** librarian; b. Elmhurst, Ill., June 13, 1951; d. John H. Pohlmann and Mary Anne Price; m. Charles Ward Stahr, Aug. 25, 1973; children: Margaret L., Andrew J. BS Engring., Purdue U., 1973; MLS, Syracuse U., 1999. Environ. specialist Owens Corning Fiberglas, Toledo, 1973—78; genealogical rschr. pvt. practice, Wausau, Wis., 1988—98; libr. Southeastern La. U., Hammond, La., 1999—, asst. prof., 2000—05, assoc. prof., 2006—. V.p., trustee Wis. Genealogical Coun., 1992—98; treas., trustee Assn. Profl. Genealogists, Washington, 1994—95, Bd. Cert. Genealogists, Washington, 1998—, pres., 2004—05. Vol. Birch Trails coun. Girl Scouts Am., Tomahawk, Wis., 1980—91; v.p., trustee La. Genealogical and Hist. Soc., La., 2001—. Mem.: ALA, La. Geneal. and Hist. Soc. (v.p. 2001—05), ACRL. Episcopalian. Home: 55 Dogwood Ln Covington LA 70435 E-mail: bstahr@selu.edu.

**STAHR, CURTIS BRENT,** photographer, art association administrator, educator; b. West Union, Iowa; s. Freman H. and Lucile M. (Schreiner) S. AA, Ellsworth Coll., 1966; BFA, Peru (Nebr.) State U., 1968. Cert. tchr., Iowa, Colo., Ariz. Art dir. Iowa Falls (Iowa) High Sch., 1968-70, Wiley (Colo.) Schs., 1971-72, Judson Sch., Scottsdale, Ariz., 1973-79; freelance graphic artist, photographer and mktg. dir., 1979-88; prof. photography, photography dir. Des Moines Area C.C., 1988—; art dir. Homestead Assn., Des Moines, 1993-98. Bd. dirs. Homestead Corp., Alpha Inst., Unoged Corp., v.p., 1999; v.p. Young Masters Photographic Art Collection, 1998—; pres. Interpretive Photography, 1999; art dir. Starland Design Band Group, 1979-86, graphic effects dept. Bischoff's, 1987-88; photographic dir. ednl. exchange trip to China. Exhibited in 16 one-man art shows, in 34 invited/juried art shows; represented in numerous pvt. collections; photographer numerous field trips including migration of Am. eagle from Alaska to Fla., all 99 Iowa County Courthouses, Yellowstone Nat. Park, Grand Teton Nat. Park, Waterton-Glacier Internat. Peace Park (U.S. and Can.), Isle Royale Nat. Park, Grand Canyon Nat. Park, Denali Nat. Park, Arctic Nat. Park & Preserve, Canyon de Chelly Nat. Monument, Rainbow Bridge Nat. Monument, Devils Tower Nat. Monument, Effigy Mounts Nat. Monument, Yosemite Nat. Park, Sequoia Nat. Park, Kings Canyon Nat. Park, Japser Nat. Park (Can.), Glacier Nat. Park (Can.), Banff (Can.) Nat. Park, Terra Nova Nat. Park (Newfoundland), Boundary Waters Canoe Area Wilderness, Quetico Provincial Park, Can., North Magnetic Pole, Can., Canyonlands (Utah), Auyuittuq Nat. Park Res., Can., Ellesmere Island Nat. Park Res, Can. Yoho Nat. Park, Can., Kootenay Nat. Park, Can., Angel Falls, Venezuela, Machu Picchu, Peru, Atacama Desert, Chile, Queen Charlotte Islands, Can.,Nahanni Nat. Pk. Res., Yukom, Lake Titicac, Bolivia and Peru, North Baffin Nat. Pk., Baffin Islands, Can., Hells Canyon, U.S.A., Sand Hills, Nebr., U.S.A., Seeley-Swan Valley, Mont., U.S.A., Iwavik Nat. Pk., Yukon Terr.; numerous cross country trips to U.S., Can., Mex., Cen. Am., S.Am., Yukon Territory and Arctic Cir. Speaker Ariz.-Calif. Lecture Series, 1982-84; chairperson art evaluation com. State of Iowa, 1970; bd. dirs. Ariz. Arts Festival, 1974-79, Muscular Dystrophy Assn. Fund Drive, Ariz., 1982-85. Recipient 14 purchase awards. Democrat. Office: Des Moines Area CC 2006 S Ankeny Blvd Ankeny IA 50021-8995

**STAIK, IRENE MCVAY,** psychology professor; d. Hugh and Irene Yeilding McVay; m. John Reed Staik, Mar. 11, 1980 (dec.); 1 child, Susan Wu Onizuka. BA, Ga. Coll. and State U., Milledgeville, 1965; MS, U. Ga., Athens, 1966; PhD, U. Ala., Tuscaloosa, 1982. Therapist Chilton-Shelby Mental Health, Calera, Ala., 1979—81; prof. psychology U. Montevallo, Ala., 1981—. Office: U Montevallo Sta 6440 Montevallo AL 35115 Office Phone: 205-665-6446. E-mail: staiki@montevallo.edu.

**STAINES, DAVID MCKENZIE,** language educator; b. Toronto, Aug. 8, 1946; s. Ralph McKenzie and Mary Rita (Hayes) S. BA, U. Toronto, 1967; AM, Harvard U., 1968, PhD, 1973. Asst. prof. English Harvard U., Cambridge, Mass., 1973-78, vis. assoc. prof., summers 1980, 82; assoc. prof. English U. Ottawa, Ont., 1978-85, prof. 1985—, vice-dean faculty of Arts Ont., 1994-95, dean faculty of arts Ont., 1995—2003. Author: Tennyson's Camelot, 1982, Beyond the Provinces: Literary Canada at Century's End, 1995; contbr. articles to profl. jours.; editor: The Canadian Imagination, 1977, The Forty-ninth and Other Parallels, 1986, Margaret Laurence: Critical Reflections, 2001, The Letters of Stephen Leacock, 2006; editor Jour. Can. Poetry, 1984—; gen. editor New Can. Libr., 1988—; translator The Complete Romances of Chrétien de Troyes, 1990; co-editor Elements of Literature, 1987, 90, 04, The Short Story in English, 1991, Northrop Frye on Canada, 2003, Marshall McLuhan's Understanding Me, 2003. Recipient Lorne Pierce medal, 1998; Ind. study fellow NEH, London, 1977-78, fellow Huntington Libr., San Marino, Calif., 1979. Fellow Royal Soc. Can.; mem. Medieval Acad. Am. (chmn. com. on ctrs. and regional assn. 1981-87), MLA, Internat.

Arthurian Soc., Assn. Can. Univ. Tchrs. English. Roman Catholic. Avocations: theater, bridge. Home: 222 Clemow Ave Ottawa ON Canada K1S 2B6 Business E-Mail: dstaines@uottawa.ca.

**STAINES, MAVIS AVRIL,** performing company executive; b. Cowansville, Que., Can., Apr. 9, 1954; d. David Russell and Betty (Knott) S.; m. Jyrki Virsunen, Feb. 4, 1988. Student, Nat. Ballet Sch., 1968-73, 81-83. Dancer Nat. Ballet of Can., 1973-78, 1st soloist, 1975-78; dancer Dutch Nat. Ballet, 1978-81; artistic dir. The Nat. Ballet Sch., Toronto, Ont., Canada, 1989—. Mem. artistic staff Nat. Ballet Sch., 1982; assoc. artistic dir., 1984; juror Prix de Lausanne, Switzerland, 1993, 94, 95, pres. jury 1998, 99; guest spkr., 1997; presenter Prix de Lausanne Internat. Symposium, 1997; mem. task force on classicl ballet tng. DANCE/USA, Phila., 1994; pres. Prix de Lausanne, 1998, 99; artistic pres. designate, 2001; artistic pres., 2001-; bd. dirs. Kala Nidhi Fine Arts of Can. Recipient Toronto Arts award for performing arts, 1998. Office: The Nat Ballet Sch 400 Jarvis St Toronto ON Canada M4Y 2G6 Business E-Mail: mavis-assist@nbs-enb.ca.

**STAINROOK, HARRY RICHARD,** photographer, retired bank executive; b. Phila., Jan. 11, 1937; s. Millward M. and Janet S.; m. Judith Anne, May 21, 1966; children: Jennifer, Eric. BA, Rutgers U., 1970. Mgr. bank ops. First Pa. Bank, Phila., 1956-61, asst. v.p. br. dept., 1964-73, v.p., mgr. London office, 1973-75, v.p. internat. dept., 1975-78, sr. v.p. comml. group, 1978-81, exec. v.p., trust and investments, 1981-85; exec. v.p. trust and investments Mfrs. and Traders Trust Co., Buffalo, 1985-97; ret., 1997. Past chmn., bd. dirs. Greater Buffalo Opera Co.; past pres. Buffalo Philharm. Orch., Acad. Vocal Arts, Phila. With U.S. Army, 1961—64. Mem. The NY Artists Group, World Future Soc., Inst. Noetic Scis., Saturn Club. Lutheran. Home: 150 Columbus Ave Apt 4A New York NY 10023-5964 Office Phone: 646-228-7290. Personal E-mail: hstainrook@nyc.rr.com.

**STAIR, THOMAS OSBORNE,** physician, educator; b. Richmond, Va., Jan. 10, 1950; s. Frederick Rogers Jr. and Martha (Osborne) S.; m. Lucy Caldwell, Dec. 28, 1973; children: Rebecca Caldwell, Peter Caldwell. AB, U. N.C., 1971; MD, Harvard U., 1975. Diplomate Am. Bd. Emergency Medicine (examiner 1982-88). Residency dir. emergency dept. Georgetown U. Sch. Medicine, Washington, 1979-85, asst. dir. emergency dept., 1979-89, asst. dean for continuing med. edn., 1985-89, chair dept. emergency medicine, 1989-95; prof. U. Md., Balt., 1995-98; assoc. prof. Harvard Med. Sch., 1998—; attending emergency physician Brigham and Women's Hosp., Boston, 1998—. Co-author: Common Simple Emergencies, 1985, Emergency Medicine, 1997, Minor Emergencies, 1999. Recipient Excellence in Teaching award Emergency Medicine Residents Assn., 1986. Fellow Am. Coll. Emergency Physicians; mem. Soc. Acad. Emergency Medicine, Am. Med. Informatics Assn. Home: 46 Woodcliff Rd Newton MA 02461-1825 Office: 75 Francis St Boston MA 02115-6110 Office Phone: 617-732-5640. Business E-Mail: tstair@partners.org.

**STAIRS, DENIS WINFIELD,** political science professor, department chairman; b. Halifax, N.S., Can., Sept. 6, 1939; s. Henry Gerald and Freda (Winfield) S.; m. Valerie Downing Street, Aug. 10, 1963 (div. Dec. 1986); children: Robert Woodliffe, Christopher Winfield; m. Jennifer Smith, July 18, 1987. BA, Dalhousie U., 1961, Oxford U., 1964, MA, 1968; PhD, U. Toronto, 1969. Asst. prof. dept. polit. sci. Dalhousie U., 1964-70, assoc. prof., 1970-75, dir. Centre Fgn. Policy Studies, 1971-75, prof. polit. sci., 1975—, McCulloch prof., 1995—2005, chmn. dept., 1980-85, v.p. acad. and rsch., 1988-93; prof. emeritus 2005—. Bd. dirs. Atlantic Coun. Can., 1979—, Inst. Rsch. Pub. Policy, 1989-97, 98-06; mem. coun. Social Sci. and Humanities Rsch. Coun. Can., 1981-87; mem. rsch. coun. Can. Inst. Advanced Rsch., 1986-97; bd. dirs. Orgn. for Study of Nat. History of Can., 1995-98; bd. vis. Can. Forces Coll., 2002—, chair, 2006—; fellow, mem. adv. com. Can. Def. and Fgn. Affairs Inst., 2002—. Author: The Diplomacy of Constraint: Canada, the Korean War, and the United States, 1974; editl. bd. Internat. Jour., 1997—. Rhodes scholar, 1961; J.W. Dafoe postgrad. fellow internat. studies, 1965-66; Can. Coun. leave fellow, 1972-73; Social Scis. and Humanities Rsch. Coun. Can. leave fellow, 1979-80; recipient Disting. Writing award, Marcel Cadieux, 2000, 2003. Fellow Royal Soc. Can., Order of Can. (officer 2006-); mem. Can. Polit. Sci. Assn. (pres.), Can. Inst. Internat. Affairs, Internat. Studies Assn. Clubs: Royal N.S. Yacht Squadron. Office: Dalhousie U Dept Polit Sci Halifax NS Canada B3H 4H6 Office Phone: 902-494-2396.

**STAIVISKY, JEANNE LOUISE,** counselor, alcohol/drug abuse services professional; b. Hughesville, Pa., Dec. 30, 1947; d. Charlotte Bowen and John Staivisky. AA in Psychology, Palm Beach Jr. Coll., 1981; BS in Gen. Psychology, Nova U., 1984, M in Sci. in Counseling Psychology, 1987. Lic. profl. counselor Ill., 2003, nat. cert. psychologist Psychology Profl. Bd., 2000, lic. mental health counselor Ind., 1999, cert. Nat. Bd. Cert. Counselors, 1996, Am. Acad. Health Providers Addictive Disorders, 1995. Program mgr., counselor Hugs Not Drugs Treatment Program, Boca Raton, Fla., 1987—87; clin. supr., counselor The Starting Pl., Hollywood, Fla., 1987—89; counselor, clin. supr. Adolescent Substance Abuse Counseling Svc., Kaiserslautern and Hanau, Army Military Bases, Germany, 1987—89, clin. supr., counselor Kaiserslautern and Hanau, 1989—97, counselor, acting clin. supr. Camp Zama, 1997—2002, counselor Schofield Barracks/Wahiawa, Hawaii, 2002—. Cons. Crisis Intervention Team, Kaiserslautern; sponsor Teen Peer Facilitator Programs, Kaiserslautern; chair Character Edn. Program in Schools, Camp Zama, Japan, 2000—02; team mem. Camp Zama HS Crisis Intervention Team, 1997—2002; yean mem. WMS Crisis Intervention Team Wheeler Army Airfield Middle School, 2002—; youth 2 youth group Youth 2 Youth Internat. Group Camp Zama, 1998—2002; sponsor S.A.D.D., Kaiserslautern and Camp Zama, 1987—2002; chairperson Jorney Into Adulthood for Teens Risk, 1996—97; sponsor ASACS Role Model Club, Wheeler Army Air Base/WMS, Hawaii, 2002—05, Teen Panell educationg parents on teen issues, Schofield Barracks/Wahiawa, 2002—. Author: Looking For The Pot of Gold at The End of The Rainbow, poems; contbr. articles to profl. jours. Sponsoring mem. So. Law Poverty-Wall of Tolerance Civil Rights, Alabama, Ga., 2004—05. Mem.: Nat. Assn. Master Psychologists, Nat. Alcohol and Drug Abuse Counselors, Hawaii Alcohol and Drug Abuse Counselors, Am. Mental Health Counselors, Am. Assn. Counseling. Achievements include 1990 letter of Commendation from Gerneral Crosbie E. Saint; SAIC 1990 Environmental Achievement Award for Single Superior Performance; 1997 415th Base Support Battalion Community Coin; SAIC 2000 Founders Award; Y2Y group nominated to represent the Army in the first DoD Youth Alcohol and Drug Awareness Program Award; 2002 Legendary Service Award for the Army Military Community in Hawaii. Avocations: needlecrafts, stamp'in up-making cards, designing clothes, collecting porcelain dolls from all over the world. Home: 226 Cullom Way Clarksville TN 37043 Personal E-mail: jeanne123047@yahoo.com.

**STAKE, PETER,** art educator, artist; BFA, Ariz. State U.; MFA, Calif. State U., Long Beach. Chmn. art & art hist. dept. Skidmore Coll., Saratoga Springs, Calif. Exhibitions include, Ctr. Art & Design, U. Wales Inst. Bd. trustees Hyde Collection. Office: Skidmore College- Art Dept 815 North Broadway Sasselin 200 Saratoga Springs NY 12866 Office Phone: 518-580-5032. E-mail: pskake@skidmore.edu.

**STAKER, ROBERT JACKSON,** retired judge; b. Kermit, W.Va., Feb. 14, 1925; s. Frederick George and Nada (Frazier) S.; m. Sue Blankenship Poore, July 16, 1955; 1 child, Donald Seth; 1 stepson, John Timothy Poore. Student, Marshall U., Huntington, W.Va., W.Va. U., Morgantown, U. Ky., Lexington; LL.B, W.Va. U., 1952. Bar: W.Va. 1952. Practiced in, Williamson, 1952-68; judge Mingo County Circuit Ct., Williamson, 1969-79; U.S. dist. judge So. Dist. W.Va., Huntington, 1979-95, sr. U.S. dist. judge, 1995—2005. Served with USN, 1943-46. Democrat. Presbyterian. Office: robert_staker@wvsd.uscourts.gov.

**STALCUP, JOE ALAN,** lawyer, dean; b. Hooker, Okla., Feb. 13, 1931; s. Herbert I. and Ruby (Gantt) S.; m. Nancy Jo Vaughn, Sept. 3, 1950; children: Melinda, Sondra Jo, Cheri Ann. BBA cum laude, So. Methodist U., 1951, JD

magna cum laude, 1959, M.Th. magna cum laude, 1978. Bar: Tex. 1959. Tchr. Dallas Ind. Sch. Dist., 1951-57; assoc. atty. firm Locke, Purnell, Boren, Laney & Neely, Dallas, 1959-66; assoc. atty., partner firm Geary, Brice & Lewis, Dallas, 1966-67; founder, sr. partner firm Stalcup, Johnson, Meyers & Miller (and predecessor firm), Dallas, 1968-75; dean Sch. Theology for the Laity, 1978—80, 1992—96, 2003—06. Pres. Dallas County Young Democrats, 1952-54; Bd. dirs., mem. exec. com. N. Tex. Christian Communications Commn., 1972-78; bd. dirs., v.p. Greater Dallas Council Chs., 1972-75; bd. dirs., chmn. Christian Ch. Found., 1976-84, 86-91, Christian Bd. Publ., 1991-98. Mem. ABA, Tex. Bar Assn., Dallas Bar Assn., Am. Judicature Soc., Phi Alpha Delta. Mem. Disciples of Christ (minister). Home: 7594 Benedict Dr Dallas TX 75214-1903 Office: 6510 Abrams Rd Dallas TX 75231-7217

**STALEY, ALVIN,** artist, educator; b. Phila., Jan. 27, 1955; s. Albert Mungo and Elease Staley; m. Bretta Reed, Feb. 1, 1977; children: Altroy Willie, Kizzi Alicia Staley Gibson. BA, Claflin U., Orangeburg, S.C., 1976; MFA, Am. U., Washington, D.C., 1981. Instr. art Morris Coll., Orangeburg, SC, 1984—85; chmn. Dept. Art Claflin U., Orangeburg, 1985—87; artist-in-residence Orangeburg-Wilkinson H.S., 1987—. Coord. visual arts, instr. Orangeburg-Calhoun Consortium for Arts, 1989—2004; instr. drawing Gov.'s Sch. for Arts and Humanities, Greenville, SC, 1988—2003; adj. prof. art Claflin U. Exhibitions include Hofp Gallery, Annual Oil Painters Open Invitational, NBSC, 2002 (First Pl. Best in Show award, 2002), Arthur Rose Mus., Piccolo Spoleto Art Festival, 2005 (Second Pl. award, 2005), 2006 (Second Pl. award, 2006), Burwell Gallery, S.C. State Fair, 2003 (Best in Show award, 2003), Spartanburg County Mus. Nominee Distinguished Tchrs. in Arts, Coca Cola Co.; recipient Star Tchr. Award, Time Warner Cable. Mem.: Nat. Art Edn. Assn. Home: 153 Harvey lane Orangeburg SC 29118 Office: Orangeburg-Wilkinson High 601 Bruin Parkway Orangeburg SC 29118 Office Phone: 803-516-6062. Personal E-mail: as577@aol.com.

**STALEY, BRETTA,** artist, educator; b. Orangeburg, S.C., Sept. 1, 1955; d. Willie and Sadie Reed; m. Alvin Staley, Feb. 1, 1977; children: Altroy Willie, Kizzi Alicia Gibson. BA in Art Edn., Claflin U., 1977; MEd in Divergent Learning/Emphasis Art, Columbia Coll., S.C., 2005. Lic. tchr. art S.C. Dept. Edn., 1980. Tchr. art Calhoun County Schs., St. Matthews, SC, 1985—94, Orangeburg-Wilkinson (S.C.) H.S., 1994—. Coord. fine arts Upward Bound Claflin U., Orangeburg, 1983—2000. Exhibitions include S.C. State Fair, 2000 (Artists for Art award Drawing, 2000), 2002 (First prize Drawing, 2002), 2003 (Merit award Drawing, 2003), 2004 (First prize Sculpture, 2004), Florence Mus., 2005 (Hon. Mention, 2005). Finalist Recognition and Talent Search award, Nat. Found. Advancement In The Arts, 2003, 2004; nominee Presdl. Visual Arts scholar, Us Dept. Edn., 2004, 2005, Disting. Tchrs. In Arts, Coca-cola Co. and Nat. Fine Arts Assn., 2004, 2005; recipient Nat. Gold award, Scholastic Art And Writing Awards, 1999—2004, Tchr. of U.S Congl. H.S. ART COMPETITION winner, U.s Congl. H.s. Art Competition, 1996 - 2004. Mem.: Nat. Art Edn. Assn. (assoc.), S.C. Art Edn. Assn. (assoc.). Home: 153 Harvey lane Orangeburg SC 29118 Office: Orangeburg-Wilkinson High School 601 Bruin Parkway Orangeburg SC 29118 Office Phone: 803-516-6062. Personal E-mail: as577@aol.com.

**STALEY, DAWN MICHELLE,** professional basketball player; b. Phila., May 4, 1970; d. Estelle. Grad., U. Va., 1992. Profl. basketball player Brazil, France, Italy, Spain, Richmond Rage, ABL, 1996—98, Charlotte Sting, WNBA, 1999—; head women's basketball coach Temple U., 2000—. Mem. USA Basketball Teams, 1989—. Founder Dawn Staley Found. Named USA Basketball Female Athlete of Yr., 1994, MVP, Goodwill Games, 1994, Phila. Big Five Coach of Yr., 2002, Atlantic 10 Coach of Yr., 2004; named to First Team All-ABL, 1997, WNBA All-Star Team, 2001, 2002, 2003; recipient Spectrum Award, ARC, 1998, Entrepreneurial Spirit Award, WNBA, 1999, Sportsmanship Award, 1999. Achievements include being a member of US Women's Basketball gold medal team, Atlanta, 1996; being a member of US Women's Basketball gold medal team, Sydney Olympics, 2000; being a member of US Women's Basketball Team, Athens Olympics, 2004; having her number retired at U. Va; being the first women in professional basketball history to record 1,000 career assists; serving as Olympic Flag bearer, Athens Olympic Games, 2004. Office: 100 Hive Dr Charlotte NC 28208-7707

**STALEY, GREG,** retail executive; Former pres., CEO Toys 'R' Us, USA; former dir., consultant KB Toy Stores, now pres., CEO, 2005—. Office: KB Toys 100 West St Pittsfield MA 01201*

**STALEY, HENRY MUELLER,** manufacturing executive; b. Decatur, Ill., June 3, 1932; s. Augustus Eugene, Jr. and Lenore (Mueller) S.; m. Violet Lucas, Feb. 4, 1955; children: Mark Eugene, Grant Spencer. Grad., Governor Dummer Acad., 1950; BS in Psychology, Northwestern U., 1954, MBA in Finance, 1956. Salesman Field Enterprises, Chgo., 1953; salesman A.E. Staley Mfg. Co., 1951, mgmt. trainee, 1956-57, ins. mgr., 1957-59, asst. treas., 1959-65, treas., asst. sec., 1965-73, v.p., treas., asst. sec., 1973-77, v.p. bus. and econ. analysis, 1977-87, also dir., 1969-85; pvt. investor Decatur, 1987—. Dir. Staley Continental, Inc., 1985-88. Crusade chmn. Macon County unit Am. Cancer Soc., 1964-65, mem. bd. dirs., 1965-71, vice chmn. bd., 1965-66, chmn. bd., 1966-69; bd. dirs. United Way Decatur and Macon County, 1972-74; mem. adv. council Millikin U., 1968-91, chmn. adv. coun., 1970-71; mem. Decatur Meml. Hosp. Devel. Council, 1969-71, mem. finan. com., bd. dirs., 1970-79, mem. long-range planning com., 1976-77, mem. devel. and community relations com., 1977-78. Mem. Decatur C. of C. (dir. 1967-72), Sigma Nu, Decatur Country.Club. Home and Office: 276 N Park Pl Decatur IL 62522-1952

**STALEY, JAMES E.,** diversified financial services company executive; Officer J.P. Morgan Chase & Co., head Pvt. Bank, mng. dir. asset & wealth mgmt., mem. exec. com., 2001—. Office: JP Morgan Chase & Co 270 Park Ave New York NY 10017-2070*

**STALEY, JOHN FREDRIC,** lawyer; b. Sidney, Ohio, Sept. 26, 1943; s. Harry Virgil and Fredericka May (McMillin) S.; m. Sue Ann Bolin, June 11, 1966; children: Ian McMillin, Erik Bolin. AB in History, Fresno State Coll., 1965; postgrad., Calif. State U., Hayward, 1967-68; JD, U. Calif., San Francisco, 1972. Bar: Calif. 1972. Ptnr. Staley, Jobson & Ford, Pleasanton, Calif., 1972—. Lectr. U. Calif. Hastings Coll. Law, San Francisco, 1973-74; founding mem. Bank of Livermore (now U.S. Bank); del. U.S.-China Joint Conf. on Law, Beijing, 1987. Co-author: (book) California Child Custody Litigation Practice, 2006. Mem. Livermore City Coun., 1975-82, vice mayor, 1978-82; bd. dirs. Alameda County Tng. and Employment Bd., Alameda-Contra Costa Emergency Med. Svcs. Agy., Valley Vol. Ctr. With M.I., U.S. Army, 1966-67. Fellow Am. Acad. Matrimonial Lawyers; mem. ABA, Calif. State Bar, Alameda Bar Assn., Amador Valley Bar Assn., Calif. Assn. Cert. Family Law Specialists (pres. 1988-89, Hall of Fame award 1994), Hastings Coll. Law Alumni Assn. (bd. dirs.). Personal E-mail: jstaley@sjf-familylaw.com.

**STALEY, KENNETH BERNARD,** civil engineer; b. Dec. 31, 1948; s. Kinzy and Bernice Florence (Williams) S.; m. Sheila Ruth Keeys, Apr. 26, 1975; children: Tabbatha, Christina, Harrison. ThM, Villanova U., 1971, MA, 1976, DD, 1978. Registerd profl. engr.; ordained to ministry Bapt. Ch., 1978. Cost estimator Joseph A. McCollum Inc., Marlton, N.J., 1967-69; expeditor R. V. Rulon Inc., Riverton, N.J., 1971; field engr. United Engrs., Phila., 1971-72; civil engr., v.p., dir. Kinzy Staley & Sons, Inc., Phila., 1972—. Vol. Aid Sickle Cell Anemia, 1974, Mendenhall Ministries, Miss.; asst. pastor Christian Stronghold Bapt. Ch., Phila., 1978—; bd. dirs. Christian R&D, Phila., Germantown Cmty. Devel., Phila.; bd. advisors Manna Bible Inst., Phila.; trustee Ctr. Urban Theol. Studies, Conservative Bapt. Sem., Phila. Prison Sys. Mem. Nat. Soc. Profl. Engrs., Assn. Cost Engrs., Am. Arbitration Assn., Am. Ceramic Soc., Am. Concrete Inst., Phila. Engrs. Club, Alpha Phi Alpha. Democrat. Home: 1130 Lakeside Ave Philadelphia PA 19126-2308 Office: Covenant Cons Group PO Box 698 Bala Cynwyd PA 19004-0698

**STALEY, LYNN,** literature educator; b. Madisonville, Ky., Dec. 24, 1947; d. James Mulford and Florine (Hurt) Staley. AB, U. Ky., 1969; MA, PhD, Princeton U., 1973. Grad. asst. Princeton (N.J.) U., 1971-73; instr. English Colgate U., Hamilton, NY, 1974-75, from asst. to assoc. prof., 1975-86, prof., 1986—. Author: The Voice of the Gawain-Poet, 1984, The Shepheardes Calendar: An Introduction, 1990, Margery Kempe's Dissenting Fictions, 1994; author: (with David Aers) The Powers of the Holy: Religion, Politics and Gender in, 1996;, 1996; editor: The Book of Margery Kempe, 1996; translator, 2001, Dictionary of the Middle Ages, 2004, Languages of Power in the Age of Richard II, 2005; contbr. articles to profl. jours. NEH fellow, 2003—04, Guggenheim fellow, 2003—04. Mem. MLA, Medieval Acad. Am., Renaissance Soc. Am., New Chaucer Soc., Spenser Soc. Office: Colgate U Dept English 13 Oak Dr Dept English Hamilton NY 13346-1383 Office Phone: 315-228-7667. Business E-Mail: lstaley@mail.colgate.edu.

**STALEY, THOMAS FABIAN,** language professional, academic administrator; b. Pitts., Aug. 13, 1935; s. Fabian Richard and Mary (McNulty) S.; m. Carolyn O'Brien, Sept. 3, 1960; children: Thomas Fabian, Caroline Ann, Mary Elizabeth, Timothy X. AB, BS, Regis Coll., 1957; MA, U. Tulsa, 1958; PhD, U. Pitts., 1962; D.H.L., Regis Coll. Asst. prof. English Rollins Coll., 1961-62; mem. faculty U. Tulsa, 1962-88, prof. English, 1969-88, dean Grad. Sch., 1969, dean Coll. Arts and Scis., 1981-83, provost, v.p. acad. affairs, 1983-88, McFarlin prof. modern lit., 1988; prof. English, dir. Ransom Humanities Rsch. Ctr. U. Tex., Austin, 1988—, Chancellor's Centennial prof. of the Book, 1989—92, Harry Huntt Ransom chair liberal arts, 1992—; Fulbright prof., Italy, 1966-67; Fulbright lectr., 1971; Danforth assoc., 1962-67; chmn. Internat. James Joyce Symposium; dir. Grad. Inst. Modern Letters, 1970-81. Author: James Joyce Today, 1966, James Joyce's Portrait of the Artist, 1968, Italo Svevo: Essays on His Work, 1969, (with H.J. Mooney) The Shapeless God: Essays on the Modern Novel, 1968, (with B. Benstock) Approaches to Ulysses: Ten Essays, 1970, Approaches to Joyce's Portrait: Ten Essays, Jean Rhys: A Critical Study; editor: Il Punto Su Joyce, 1973, Dorothy Richardson, Ulysses: Fifty Years, 1974, Twentieth-Century Women Novelists, 1982, British Novelists, 1890-1929, Traditionalists, Dictionary of Lit. Biography, Vols. 34, 36, 70, 77, An Annotated Critical Bibliography of James Joyce, 1989, Joyce Studies: An Annual edit., 1990-2003, Studies in Modern Literature Series, 1990—, Reflections on James Joyce: Stuart Gilbert's Paris Journal, 1993, Writing the Lives of Writers, 1998, James Joyce Quar., 1963-89; adv. editor Twentieth-Century Lit., 1966—, Jean Rhys Rev., 1986—; bd. dirs. Eighteenth-Century Short Title Catalogue/North America, 1990; editl. bd. Tulsa Studies in Women's Literature, Jour. Modern Lit., 1989—; contbr. articles to profl. jours. Bd. dirs. Tulsa Arts Coun., 1969-76, NCCJ, 1979—, Christopher Isherwood Found.; pres. James Joyce Found., 1968-72; chmn. bd. Undercroft Montessori Sch., 1968-70, Marquette Sch., 1969-70; bd. dirs. Cascia Hall Prep. Sch.; chmn. disting. authors com. Tulsa Libr. Trust, 1984; mem. bd. commrs. Tulsa City-County Libr., chmn., 1980-82; mem. adv. coun. Tex. Inst. for Humanities; trustee Regis U., 1992—; bd. dirs. Libr. of Am., 1994—, Harlick Trust, 1994—; mem. symposium com. Lyndon Baines Johnson Presdl. Libr., 1993—. Recipient Am. Council Learned Socs. award, 1969, 80 Mem. MLA, Internat. Assn. Univ. Profs. English, Anglo-Irish Studies Assn., Am. Com. for Irish Studies, Assn. Internat. de Bibliophilie, James Joyce Soc., Hopkins Soc., Tex. Philos. Soc. (bd. dirs. 1991—), Internat. James Joyce Found. (hon. trustee), U.S. Tennis Assn., Tulsa Tennis Club, Westwood Country Club, The Athenaeum Club (London), Grolier Club (N.Y.), Edgecomb Tennis Club (Kennebunk, Maine), Tarry House, Phi Beta Kappa. Home: 2528 Tanglewood Trl Austin TX 78703-1540 also: 4 Surf Ln Kennebunk ME 04043 Business E-Mail: TFS@mail.utexas.edu.

**STALEY, WARREN R.,** agricultural products and diversified services company executive; b. Springfield, Ill., May 14, 1942; BS in Elec. Engring., Kans. State U., 1965; MS in Bus. Adminstrn., Cornell U., 1967. With Cargill, Inc., Mpls., 1969—, gen. mgr., European corn milling bus., 1978—82, gen. mgr., Argentine ops., 1983—87, pres. for N.Am. and Latin Am., to 1998, pres., COO, 1998—2000, CEO, 1999—, chmn., 2000—. Apptd. mem. President's Export Coun. (PEC), 2003, chmn. Cargill Found. Bd. dirs. U.S. Bancorp, Target Corp., Greater Twin Cities United Way, Minn. Pvt. Coll. Coun. Office: Cargill Inc 15407 McGinty Rd, W Wayzata MN 55391

**STALKER, JACQUELINE D'AOUST,** academic administrator, educator; b. Penetang, Ont., Can., Oct. 16, 1933; d. Phillip and Rose (Eaton) D'Aoust; m. Robert Stalker; children: Patricia, Lynn, Roberta. Teaching cert., U. Ottawa, 1952; tchr. music, Royal Toronto Conservatory Music, 1952; teaching cert., Lakeshore Tchrs. Coll., 1958; BEd with honors, U. Manitoba, 1977, MEd, 1979; EdD, Nova U., 1985. Cert. tchr. Ont., Man., Can. Adminstr., tchr., prin. various schs., Ont. and Que., 1952-65; area commr. Girl Guides of Can., throughout Europe, 1965-69; administr., tchr. Algonquin Community Coll., Ottawa, Ont., 1970-74; tchr., program devel. Frontenac County Bd. Edn., Kingston, Ont., 1974-75; lectr., faculty advisor dept. curriculum, edn. U. Man., Can., 1977-79; lectr. U. Winnipeg, Man., Can., 1977-79; cons. colls. div. Man. Dept. Edn., 1980-81, sr. cons. programming br., 1981-84, sr. cons. post secondary, adult and continuing edn. div., 1985-88, dir. post secondary career devel. br. and adult and continuing edn. br., 1989; asst. prof. higher edn., coord. grad. program in higher edn. U. Man., 1989-92, assoc. prof., coord. grad. program in higher edn., 1992-95. Cons. lectures, seminars, workshops throughout Can. Contbr. articles to profl. jours.; mng. editor Can. Jour. of Higher Edn., 1989-93. Mem. U. Man. Senate, 1976-81, 86-89, bd. govs., 1979-82; Can. rep. Internat. Youth Conf., Garmisch, Fed. Republic of Germany, 1968; vol. Can. Cancer Soc.; mem. Assn. RN Accreditation Coun., 1980-85; chair Child Care Accreditation Com., Man., 1983-90; chair Task Force Post-Secondary Accessibility, Man., 1983; vol. United Way Planning and Allocations; provincial dir., mem. nat. bd. Can. Congress for Learning Opportunities for Women. Recipient Award for enhancing the Outreach activities of the univ. U. Man., 1994. Mem. Can. Soc. Study Higher Edn., Man. Tchrs Soc., U. Man. Alumni Assn., Women & Legal Edn. and Action Fund.

**STALKER, JAMES RAGHI,** meteorologist, environmental services administrator; b. Papaiahpet, Andhra Pradesh, India, Sept. 4, 1963; arrived in U.S., 1989; s. R V Krishna Rao and Sarojini Raghi; m. Karen Ann Caldwell, Oct. 30, 2000; 1 child, Charlotte. BSME, JNTU, Hyderabad, India, 1986; MSME, U. Ala., Huntsville, 1992, MS in Atmospheric Scis., 1995, PhD in Atmospheric Scis., 1997. Postdoctoral fellow Los Alamos (N.Mex) Nat. Lab., 1997—99, tech. staff mem., 1999—2003; pres., CEO Respr, Inc., Santa Fe, 2002—. Contbr. articles to profl. jours. Mem.: AAAS, ASME, Am. Phys. Soc., Am. Math. Soc., Am. Geophys. Union, Am. Meteorol. Soc. Avocations: travel, national parks, hiking, Karate, computers. Office: Respr Inc 5 Bisbee Ct Santa Fe NM 87508-1398 E-mail: jrstalker@respr.com.

**STALL, ALAN DAVID,** packaging company executive; b. Moose Jaw, Sask., Can., June 14, 1951; arrived in US, 1982; s. Joel and Evelyn (Schwartz) S.; m. Carol I. Johnston; children: Jeffrey, Jennifer, Michael, Timothy. BSME, U. Sask., 1973; MBA, Lewis U., 1986. Registered profl. engr., Ont. Devel. engr. DuPont Can., North Bay, Ont., 1973-76; project engr. Union Carbide Corp. Can., Lindsay, 1976-79, engring. mgr., 1979-82; mgr. shirring rsch. Union Carbide Corp., Chgo., 1982-85; dir. engring. tech. Viskase Corp., Chgo., 1985-90, v.p. engring. 1990-95; gen. mgr. Kuko Corp., Gross-Gerau, Germany, 1995-98; pres. Films Casings Tech. Inc., Woodridge, Ill., 1996—; gen. mgr. Alfacel Inc., Woodridge, 1998—; v.p. Teepak de Mex., 2003—; CEO Stratek Plastics, Wallingford, Conn., 2006—. Patentee breathable plastic, shirring apparatus, sausage stuffing machine, cellulose casings, cellulose regeneration. Rotary bus. exchange fellow, London, 1982. Mem. Engring. Inst. Can., Can. Soc. Mech. Engrs., Soc. Plastics Engrs., Assn. Profl. Engrs., Ont., Am. Mensa, Can. Club Chgo. Home: 23W540 James Way Naperville IL 60540-9552 Office: FCT Inc PO Box 5415 Woodridge IL 60517-0415 Personal E-mail: astall@msn.com.

**STALL, WILLIAM READ,** retired newswriter; b. Phila., Feb. 21, 1937; s. Sidney Joseph and Helen (Read) S.; m. Carolee Ramsey, July, 1961 (div. 1979); children: Tracy Stall Roll, Erica Stall Wiggins; m. Anne Elizabeth Baker, Dec. 8, 1979. BS, U. Wyo., 1959. Reporter Laramie (Wyo.) Boomerang, 1956-59, Associated Press, Cheyenne, Wyo., 1960-63, corres. Reno, 1963-66, bur. chief, polit. writer Sacramento, 1966-74; press sec. Edmund G. Brown Jr., Sacramento, 1975-76; staff writer, asst. met. editor, corres. L.A. Times, 1976-81, editorial writer, 1984-90, polit. writer, 1990-96, editl. writer, 1997—2006; bur. chief Hartford Courant, Washington, 1981-84; ret., 2006. Sr. lectr. journalism dept. U. So. Calif., 1985-94. With U.S. Air N.G., 1960-67. Named Disting. Alumni, U. Wyo., 2005; recipient Pulitzer prize for editl. writing, 2004. Mem. Am. Alpine Club (dir. 1992-98). Episcopalian. Avocations: rock climbing, mountain climbing, sailing. Personal E-mail: billstall@aol.com. E-mail: bill.stall@latimes.com.

**STALLER, JOHN EDWARD,** archaeologist, anthropologist, educator; b. Grosseraming, Austria, Jan. 28, 1951; s. John Staller and Elizabeth Pokorny; m. Margaret Mary Tentler, Jan. 20, 1973. PhD, So. Meth. U., Dallas, 1994. Vis. asst. prof. U. of Ill., Chgo., 1999—2001; rsch. assoc. The Field Mus., Chgo., 1998—. Bd. mem. Fulbright Assn., Chgo., 1999—; vis. faculty in Summer Inst. MIT Workshop, 2001. Editor (senior editor): Histories of Maize: Multidisciplinary Approaches to the Prehistory, Biogeography, Domestication, and Evolution of Maize. Elsevier/Academic Press (forthcoming).; contbr. articles to profl. jours. Fellow Fulbright scholar, Fulbright Hays, 1988—89. Office: The Field Museum Dept of Anthropology 1400 S Lake Shore Dr Chicago IL 60605

**STALLINGS, CHARLES HENRY,** retired physicist; b. Durham, NC, Dec. 28, 1941; s. Henry Harroll and Dorothy (Powers) S.; m. Elizabeth Bright, Sept. 4, 1965; children: Deborah, Sharon. BS, N.C. State U., 1963, MS, 1964; PhD, U. Wis., 1970. Sr. physicist Physics Internat. Co. (now Maxwell Physics Internat.), San Leandro, Calif., 1970-73, dep. dept. mgr., 1974-76, dept. mgr., 1976-79, dir. satellite x-ray test facility office, 1979-81, dir. bus. devel., 1981-83, v.p., dir. rsch. devel., v.p., gen. mgr., 1983—2001; ret., 2001. Contbr. articles to tech. jours. Mem. Gen. Plan Rev. Com., Pleasanton, Calif. 1983. Mem. Am. Phys. Soc., IEEE (mem. pulsed power sci. and tech. com. 1996—, chmn. 12th internat. pulsed power conf. 1999). Home: 3608 Fieldview Ct Pleasanton CA 94588

**STALLINGS, FRANK, JR.,** realtor, director; b. Concord, NC, Aug. 21, 1954; s. Frank and Theresa Ann Stallings BS in Indsl. Engring., N.C. State U., 1976; MS in Adminstrn., George Washington U., 1979. Lic. real estate agt. Tex. Jr. indsl. engr. Naval Air Rework Facility, Norfolk, Va., 1974—75; indsl. engr. Babcock & Wilcox, Lynchburg, Va., 1977—79; sr. prin. engr. NCR Corp., Columbia, SC, 1979—82; mgr. indsl. engring. Mars Electronics, Ltd., Reading, England, 1987—88; liaison between European/U.S. mfg. divsn., sr. indsl. engr. M&M/MARS, Inc., Waco, Tex., 1982—84, mgr. quality assurance, 1984—87, mgr. indsl. engring., 1988—96, inbound logistics mgr., 1996—97; mng. prin. Oracle Corp., 1998—2001, practice mgr., 2001; mgmt. cons., 2001—05; dir. indsl. engring. Minyards, Inc., 2005—. Coach Heart of Tex. Soccer League, Waco, 1985-87; Sunday sch. tchr. Columbus Ave. Bapt. Ch., Waco, 1988-97, mem. Missions com., 1991-96, Bapt. Youth leader, 1990-97, mem. ch. singles coun., 1989-91; Sunday sch. tchr. First Bapt. Hartsville (S.C.) Ch., 1998-2000; exec. mem. singles coun. Waco Bapt. Assn.; counselor Royal Ambs., 1990-96; children's leader Bible Study Fellowship, 1995-97; v.p. DFW Aquatic Plant Club, 2006-, Chaucer Estates Howmeowners Assn., 2006-. Mem. Inst. Indsl. Engrs. (sr.), Am. Soc. Quality Control, Am. Prodn. and Inventory Control Socl., Am. Radio Relay League, Project Mgmt. Inst. (cert.), Radio Amateurs Civil Emergency Svcs., Amateur Radio Emergency Svcs., Ten-10 Internat. Amateur Radio Network, Waco Amateur TV Soc. (bd. dirs. 1995-96), Appalachian Trail Soc. (life). Democrat. Avocations: camping, boating, running, bicycling, radio operator. Home: PO Box 89 Argyle TX 76226-0089 Business E-Mail: frank@stallings.com.

**STALLINGS, NORMAN (CHARLES NORMAN STALLINGS),** lawyer; b. Tampa, Fla., Apr. 3, 1914; s. Otto Pyromus and Minnie Henderson (Mitchell) S.; m. Mary Phillips Powell, Feb. 6, 1943 (dec. 1999); children: Charles Norman, Jean Katherine (dec.), Mary Anne. AB, U. Fla., 1935; JD, Harvard U., 1938, LL.M., 1940. Bar: Mo. 1939, Fla. 1940, D.C. 1941, Ga. 1946. Asso. firm Ryland, Stinson, Mag & Thomson, Kansas City, Mo., 1938-39, Sutherland, Tuttle & Brennan, Washington, 1940-41, Atlanta, 1946-49; mem. firm Shackleford, Farrior, Stallings & Evans, Tampa, Fla., 1949-84, of counsel, 1984—2002, Gray & Robinson, 2003—. Vice chmn. Hillsborough County (Fla.) Aviation Authority, 1955-61. Served to lt. col. U.S. Army, 1941-46, ETO. Decorated Bronze Star; Croix de Guerre avec Palme, Belgium. Fellow Am. Coll. Trial Lawyers; mem. ABA, Hillsborough County Bar Assn. (past pres.), Fla. Bar (past gov.), Univ. Club (past pres.), Tampa Yacht and Country Club (past gov.), Ye Mystic Krewe of Gasparilla (past capt. and king), Phi Delta Phi, Kappa Alpha. Republican. Episcopalian. Home: 3501 Bayshore Blvd Apt 805 Tampa FL 33629 Office: PO Box 3324 Tampa FL 33601-3324

**STALLINGS, VALERIE A.,** physician, state agency administrator; b. N.Y.C., Nov. 27, 1943; BS in Zoology, Duke U., 1964; MD, U. N.C., 1968, MPH, 1988. Intern, resident Pediat. Med. Coll. Va., 1968-71; physician Va. Dept. Health Bur. Crippled Children, Norfolk, 1972—75, Portsmouth (Va.) Health Dept., 1972—77; dir. Tidewater Child Devel. Clin., Norfolk, 1977-82; dep. dir. Norfolk Dept. Pub. Health, 1982-89, dir., 1989—. Office: Norfolk Dept Pub Health 830 Southampton Ave Norfolk VA 23510-1001

**STALLINGS, VIRGINIA A.,** pediatric gastroenterologist; BS, Auburn U.; MS, Cornell U.; MD, U. Ala. Cert. pediatrics, clin. nutrition. Pediat. resident U. Va.; nutrition fellow Hosp. for Sick Children, Toronto; prof. pediatrics U. Pa. Sch. Med., Phila.; with Children's Hosp. Phila., 1985, attending physician, div. gastroenterology & nutrition, chief of nutrition sect., prof. pediatrics, Jean Cortner Endowed Chair in Pediat. Gastroenterology, dir. Nutrition Ctr., dep. dir. Joseph Stokes Rsch. Inst. Mem.: APA, Inst. Medicine (chair food & nutrition bd. 2000—). Office: Children's Hosp of Philadelphia 34th St & Civic Ctr Blvd Philadelphia PA 19104*

**STALLMAN, BOB,** farmer, farm bureau executive; m. Stacey Lynne Bryan; children: Kimberly Willingham, Angela Kulhanek. Grad. with honors, Univ. Tex., 1974. Family farm operator, Tex., 1975—; past dir. & pres. Colorado County Farm Bureau; pres. Tex. Farm Bureau, 1993—2000; dir. Am. Farm Bureau Fedn., 1994—, pres., 2000—. Mem. Commn. 21st Century Production Agr., US Ho. Rep., 1996; bd. dir. Am. Council for Capital Formation, 2002—; mem. Agrl. Policy Adv. Com. for US Sec. Agr. & US Trade Rep., 2001, Adv. Com. on Internat. Economic Policy, US State Dept., 2001; trustee Farm Found., 2001—; mem. adv. bd. World Economic Forum; mem. Tex. Citizens Com. Property Tax Relief, 1996; mem. develop. council Tex. A&M Coll. Agr.; co-chmn. Tex. Agrl. Summit; mem. exec. com. Tex. Rice Task Force. Named Man of the Year in Agriculture, Columbus Tex. Rotary Club, 1986; recipient Friend of Agriculture award, Tex. A&M Univ., 1999. Lutheran. Office: American Farm Bureau Federation Ste 800 600 Maryland Ave SW Washington DC 20024

**STALLMAN, DONALD LEE,** environmental executive; b. Rochester, NY, Feb. 20, 1930; s. William F. and Clara Elizabeth (Boulle) S.; m. Dolores Anita Putney, Nov. 8, 1958; stepchildren: Nancy, Terri, Jeff. Student, Hobart Coll., Geneva, NY, 1948-49, U. Rochester, 1953-54. V.p. Kolstad Assocs., Inc., Rochester, NY, 1954—2002; pres. Water Treatment Assocs., Latham, NY, 1975—, KB Fabrications, Latham, 1977—. Chmn. bd. Water Treatment Assocs.; vice chmn. bd. KB Fabrications; adv. bd., pres. Bruner Corp., Milw., 1982-83. Designer Chock-o-Lette Spl. Aircraft Wheel Chock, 1978, Water Treatment Skid for Oil Field Applications, 1980; inventor in field. Cons. Capital Dist. Planning Commn., Albany, 1980-81. With U.S. Army, 1951-53. Decorated Bronze Star medal, Silver Star medal, Purple Hearts (2). Mem. Am. Soc. Plumbing Engrs., Quiet Birdman Assn., Sigma Chi. Republican. Roman Catholic. Avocations: flying, boating, golf. Home (Winter): 111 Royal Park Dr Fort Lauderdale FL 33309-5893 Office: Water Treatment Assocs PO Box 367 Latham NY 12110-0367 Home: 16 Hillcrest Rd Latham NY 12110-4133 Office Phone: 518-785-5654. Personal E-mail: alboff@aol.com.

**STALLMAN, RICHARD MATTHEW,** software developer; b. NYC. 1953; BA in Physics, Harvard U., 1974; PhD (hon.), Royal Inst. Tech., Stockholm, 1996, U. Glasgow, 2001, Free U. Brussels, 2003, U. Nacional de Salta, Argentina, 2004. Software developer MIT, Cambridge, 1971-83. Chief GNUisance, GNU Project, 1984—; founder, pres. Free Software Found., Boston, 1985—; hon. prof. Universidad Nacional de Ingeniería de Perú, 2003. Author: Free Software, Free Society, 2002; (software) EMACS, 1975, GNU EMACS, 1984, GNU C Compiler, 1988. Bd. dirs. League Programming Freedom, 1989-95, pres., 1989-92. Recipient Grace Hopper award Assn. Computing, 1990, MacArthur prize fellowship MacArthur Found., 1990, Pioneer award Electronic Frontier Found., 1998, Yuri Rubinski Insight Found. award, 1999, Takeda prize for social/econ. betterment, 2001, Fondazione Pistoletto prize, 2005. Mem.: NAE, Am. Acad. Arts and Scis. Avocations: balkan folk dance, balinese and javanese gamelan music, reading, eating. Office: Free Software Found 51 Franklin St 5th Fl Boston MA 02111 Office Phone: 617-542-5942.

**STALLMAN, ROBERT,** flutist, editor, recording artist, arranger; b. Boston, June 12, 1946; s. Robert Wooster and Virginia (Blume) S.; m. Hannah Day Woods, Sept. 26, 1981. MusB, New Eng. Conservatory Music, 1968, MusM, 1971; studied with James Pappoutsakis, Boston, Alain Marion, Gaston Crunelle, J.P. Rampal, Paris. Debut Merkin Concert Hall, N.Y.C., 1980. Tchr. New Eng. Conservatory Music, 1978—82, CUNY Queens Coll., 1980—, Nat. Conservatory of Mex., 1982, Nat. U. Mex., 1999—2001, Domaine Forget, Que., Canada, 1982—85, Académie Internationale d'Eté, Nice, France, 1985, Boston Conservatory, 1986—90, Hochschule für Musik Mannheim, Germany, 2000, Shanghai Conservatory, China, 2004; founder, artistic dir. Cambridge Chamber Players & Marblehead Music Festival, 1976—96. Musician: Libr. of Congress, Carnegie Hall, Alice Tully Hall, Avery Fisher Hall, Symphony Hall, Phila. Acad. Music, Wigmore Hall, Salle Pleyel, Suntory Hall, Am. Symphony, Mostly Mozart Festival, Netherlands Chamber Orch., Royal Philharm. Orch., No. Sinfonia, Suk Chamber Orch., Czech Chamber Orch., Odessa Philharmonic, Lincoln Ctr. Chamber Music Soc., Mendelssohn, Orion, Alexander, Muir, Martinu, St. Lawrence String Quartets, festivals in Can., Spain, Czech Republic, Holland, Finland, France, Mex., Japan, Brazil, China, U.S.; editor: Internat. Music Co., 1984—, G. Schirmer, 1996—, Kalmus Music, 2005—; creator: Flute Workout: Melodic Studies for Technical Mastery, 1995; musician: (albums) American Flute, The Lyric Flute, Gypsy Flute, The Nightingale in Love, Incantations, Bach Sonatas, Leclair Sonatas, —, Blavet Sonatas, Handel Sonatas, Schubert Sonatas, Mozart Sonatas, —, Telemann Concertos, Vivaldi Concertos, Dodgson Concerto, McKinley Concerto; contbr. articles to profl. jours. Fulbright grantee, 1968-69, Arcadia Found. grantee, 1994; Koussevitzky fellow, 1970; recipient Chadwick medal, 1968, C.D. Jackson prize, Tanglewood, 1970, 1st prize USA Nat. Assn. Collegiate Artists Competition, 1971; NEA Solo Recitalist grantee, 1983. Avocations: travel, swimming, French culture, Mozart research. Address: 1530 Locust St Philadelphia PA 19102-4415 Office Phone: 215-893-9030.

**STALLONE, SYLVESTER ENZIO,** actor, film director, scriptwriter; b. NYC, July 6, 1946; s. Frank and Jacquline (Labofish) S.; m. Sasha Czack, Dec. 28, 1974 (div. 1985); children: Sage, Seth; m. Brigitte Nielsen, Dec. 15, 1985 (div. 1987); m. Jennifer Flavin, May 17, 1997; children: Sophia, Sistine, Scarlet. Student, Am. Coll. of Switzerland, 1965-67, U. Miami, 1967-69. Formerly, usher, fish salesman, horse trainer, delicatessen worker, truck driver, bouncer, zoo attendant, short order cook, pizza demonstrator, phys. edn. tchr., motel supt., bookstore detective Appeared in motion pictures No Place to Hide, 1970, The Party at Kitty and Stud's, 1970, Lords of Flatbush, 1973, The Prisoner of Second Avenue, 1975, Capone, 1975, Farewell, My Lovely, 1975, Death Race 2000, 1975, Cannonball, 1976, Rocky, 1976, (Oscar for Best Picture 1976, Golden Globe award for best picture 1976, Donatello award for best actor in Europe 1976, Christopher Religious award 1976, Bell Ringer award Scholastic Mag. 1976, Nat. Theatre Owners award 1976) F.I.S.T, 1978, Paradise Alley, 1978, Rocky II, 1979, Nighthawks, 1981, Victory, 1981, Rocky III, 1982, First Blood, 1982, Rhinestone, 1984, Rambo: First Blood Part II, 1985, Rocky IV, 1985, Cobra, 1986, Over the Top, 1987, Rambo III, 1988, Lock Up, 1989, Tango and Cash, 1989, Rocky V, 1990, Oscar, 1991, Stop! Or My Mom Will Shoot, 1992, Cliffhanger, 1993, Demolition Man, 1993, The Specialist, 1994, Judge Dredd, 1995, Assassins, 1995, Firestorm, 1996, Daylight, 1996, Copland, 1997, An Alan Smithee Film: Burn Hollywood Burn, 1998, Antz (voice only), 1998, Get Carter, 2000, Driven (also prod.), 2001, D-Tox, 2002, Avenging Angelo, 2002, My Little Hollywood, 2002, Taxi 3, 2003, Shade, 2003, Spy Kids 3-D: Game Over, 2003; dir. film Paradise Alley, 1978, Rocky II, 1979, Nighthawks, 1981, Rocky III, 1982, Staying Alive (also prod.), 1983, Rocky IV, 1985; author: The Lords of Flatbush, 1974, Rocky, 1976, F.I.S.T., 1978, Paradise Alley, 1977, The Rocky Scrapbook, 1977, Rocky II, 1979, Rocky III, 1982, First Blood, 1982, Staying Alive, 1983, Rhinestone (screenplay), 1984, Rambo: First Blood Part II, 1985, Rocky IV, 1985, Cobra, 1986, Over the Top, 1987, Rambo III, 1988, Rocky V, 1990, Cliffhanger (screenplay), 1993, Driven (screenplay), 2001; exec. prod.: Heart of a Champion: The Ray Mancini Story, 1985; exec. prodr., host (TV Series) The Contender, 2005. Recipient Star of the Year award 1977, named Show West actor of the year 1979, Artistic Achievement award Nat. Italian Am. Found., 1991, Order of Arts and Letters, French Ministry, 1992, Caesar award for Career Achievement, 1992. Mem. Screen Actors Guild, Writers Guild, Stuntmans Assn. (hon.), Dirs. Guild. Achievements include being nominated for two Oscars (acting and writing) in same year (1976); occurred for only 3d time in history. *Once in one's life, for one mortal moment, one must make a grab for immortality; if not, one has not lived.*

**STALLONES, JARED REUEL,** education educator; s. Reuel Arthur and (Eliza) Joyce Graves Stallones; m. Janis Hosack Hosack, June 22, 1980; children: Lindsay Erin Marshall, Cameron Jared. BA in Plan II, U. Tex., 1979, MA in Curriculum and Instrn., 1992, PhD in Curriculum Studies, 1999. Cert. life tchr. in social studies State of Tex., 1980. Tchr., dir. student svcs. The Perry Sch., Austin, Tex., 1981—83; tchr., social studies dept. chair Hyde Pk. Bapt. H.S., Austin, 1983—99; rsch. asst., asst. instr. U. Tex., Austin, 1994—99; asst. prof. history Calif. State U., Fresno, 1999—2000; acad. dir. Grace Covenant Christian Sch., Austin, 2000—02; assoc. prof. edn. Calif. State Poly. U., Pomona, Calif., 2002—, coord. secondary tchg. credential, 2002—. Prin. investigator, project dir. CPP-HLPUSD Tchg. Am. History Grant, Hacienda Heights, Calif., 2004—. Author: (biography) Paul Robert Hanna: A Life of Expanding Communities, (history) Zebulon Pike and the Explorers of the American Southwest. Treas., v.p. North Austin Mcpl. Utility Dist. #1, Austin, 1988—96. Recipient Disting. Svc. award, YMCA of Austin, 1991; David G. Bruton, Jr. Grad. fellow, U. Tex., Coll. Edn., 1991, Alexander Caswell Ellis scholar in edn., 1994. Mem.: Calif. Coun. for Social Studies (chair com. profl. standards and awards 2004—06), Nat. Coun. for Social Studies (mem. com. curriculum 2004—06). Office: Calif State Polytechnic Univ 3801 W Temple Ave Pomona CA 91768 Office Phone: 909-869-2086. E-mail: jrstallones@csupomona.edu.

**STALLWORK-CLARK, ROSEMARIE,** education educator; b. Repton, Ala., Sept. 14, 1943; d. Thomas Nettles Stallworth and Eva Mae Turnipseed; m. James Hubert Clark; 1 child, Rosemary Clark Kitashima. BS, Huntington Coll., 1965; MEd, Ga. So. U., 1982; PhD, U. Ga., 1996. Tchr. Ensley Elem. Sch., Pensacola, Fla., 1964—65, Emma P. Flowers Elem. Sch., Ozark, Ala., 1965—66, Ft. Rucker Elem. Sch., Ft. Rucker, Ala., 1966—68, Beatrice H.S., Ala., 1969—70, Julia P. Bryant Elem. Sch., Statesboro, Ga., 1980; assoc.prof. ednl. psychology Ga.So. U., 1981—. Co-chair, nat. youth rsch conf. Ga. So U.; program chair Am.Ednl. Rsch.; edn. cons. Newsweek Corp., 1990—98. Singer: (albums) Little Children Rejoice, 1977; author: Strategies for Regents' Reading Exams, 2003, (TV) Learning to Learn, 1991. Supporter/blood donor Am. Red Cross, 2002—. Recipient Award for excellence in instrn., Ga. So. U., 1997. Mem.: Am. Ednl. Rsch.Assn. (pres.), Ga. Ednl Rsch. Assn., Phi Kappa Phi. Democrat. Avocations: singing, writing, reading, exercise. Office Phone: 912-681-5715.

**STALLWORTH, CHARLES DEROTHA, JR.,** psychologist; b. Riderwood, Ala., July 4, 1940; s. Charles D. and Annie (Horn) S. BS, Tenn. State U., Nashville, 1963; MS, Tenn. State U., 1966; postgrad., Calif. Sch. Profl. Psychology, 1977-79, U. South Ala., 1967, Tuskegee Inst., 1968, U. Ky., 1980; PhD in Psychology, Internat. Coll., 1983; cert. in mental disability law, N.Y. Law Sch., 2001. Diplomate Am. Bd. Psychotherapy, Am. Psychotherapy Assn., Am. Coll. Mental Health Practitioners, Am. Coll., Forensic Counselors, Acad. Cert. Neurotherapists. Psychiat. asst. Hubbard Hosp., Nashville, 1964-66; counselor, tchr. North Ctrl. H.S., Chatom, Ala., 1966-68; tchr. Washington County H.S., 1968-70; supr. adult edn. Washington County Bd. Edn., Chatom, 1968-70; dir. counseling ctr. Albany State Coll., Ga., 1970—91; pvt. practice, 1993—. Mem. staff Auburn U., summer 1969; counselor Spl. Svc. program Albany State Coll., 1992-93; cons. Peace Corps, 1979-81; dep. dir. gen. Internat. Biographical Ctr., Cambridge, Eng., 2004. Contbr. articles to profl. jours. Bd. dirs. Dougherty County CODAC, Inc., Albany, 1973-77; hon. mem. Ga. Sheriff's Assn. Named Best Poems & Poets, Internat. Libr. Poetry, 2003; recipient Internat. Poet of Merit award, Internat. Soc. Poets, 2003, Internat. Peace prize, United Cultural Consortium, 2002, Outstanding Scientist of the 20th Century, 2000, DaVinci Diamond, Internat. Biog. Centre, Cambridge, Eng., 2004; grantee HEW, 1970—77, U.S. Office Edn., 1972. Mem. APA, Am. Psychotherapy Assn., Nat. Assn. Cognitive-Behavioral Therapists, Ga. Psychol. Assn., Alpha Phi Alpha. Democrat. Baptist. Achievements include research on impact of affective domain on learning outcomes and on application of cognitive therapies as a means of controlling negative effects. Home: 805 E 4th Ave Albany GA 31705-1203 Personal E-mail: charlesd260@yahoo.com.

**STALLWORTH, STANLEY B,** lawyer; b. 1963; BS summa cum laude, Ala. Agrl. and Mech. Univ., 1985; JD, Univ. Wis., 1990. Bar: Ala. 1990, Ill. 1990, Wis. 1990. Joined Sidley Austin Brown & Wood, Chgo., 1990—, now ptnr. real estate practice, and co-chmn. com. on racial and ethnic diversity. Articles editor Univ. Wis. Multi-Cultural Law Jour., 1989—90. Bd. trustees Univ. Wis. Law Alumni Assn.; chmn. bd. trustees Chgo. Acad. for Arts. Mem.: Chgo. Coun. of Lawyers (bd. dir.). Nat. Bar Assn., ABA, Cook County Bar Assn. (past mem. exec. bd. dir.). Office: Sidley Austin Brown & Wood LLP Bank One Plz 10 S Dearborn St Chicago IL 60603 Office Phone: 312-853-4715. Office Fax: 312-853-7036. Business E-mail: sstallworth@sidley.com.

**STALLWORTH, TERRESA LOUISE,** psychiatrist, educator; b. Tuscaloosa, Ala. d. William Wesley and Louise Catherine (Goodrich) S. Student, Va. Intermont Coll., Bristol, 1954—55; MusB, U. Tenn., 1959, MD, 1963. Diplomate Am. Bd. Psychiatry and Neurology, Am. Bd. Adminstrv. Psychiatry. Intern U. Tenn. Meml. Hosp. and Rsch. Ctr., 1963-64; resident in neurology Univ. of Memphis Hosp., 1964-65; resident in psychiatry U. Mo., St.Louis, 1966-68, chief resident, 1968; clin. dir. asst. supt., acting supt. Lakeshore Mental Health Inst., Knoxville, Tenn., 1969-74; dir. cmty. programs and splty. units San Antonio State Hosp., 1974—, clin. dir., 1997—. Dir. Camino Real State Operated Cmty. Mental Health Ctr., 1993-95; exec. dir. Camino Real Cmty. MH/MR Svcs., 1995-97; assoc. prof. psychiatry U. Tex. Health Scis. Ctr. San Antonio, 1974—, clin. prof. psychiatry, 1995—; chmn. profl. adv. bd. Bexar County Mental Health/Mental Retardation Ctr., 1979-81; mem. med. coun. Tex. Dept. State Health Svcs Concert pianist Trinity U., St. Mary's U., Incarnate Word Coll., 1975—, San Antonio Symphony, San Antonio State Hosp., U. Tenn., Knoxville, 1989, Austrian Embassy, Washington, 1996; premier performance own Piano Sonata, 1980; commd. Yellow Rose of Tex., 1997. Mem. San Antonio Internat. Piano Boar, 2002—. Recipient 1st prize Memphis and Mid-South Piano Contest, 1958, Disting. Svc. award U. Tex. Health Sci. Ctr. San Antonio, 1997, Spl. Svc. award Soc. Psychiat. Physicians, 2004, Bob Polunski award, 2002, Spl. Svc. award Tex. Soc. Psychiat. Physicians, 2004; selected to play in 1st Ann. Van Cliburn Internat. Piano Competition for Outstanding Amateurs, 1999. Fellow Am. Psychiat. Assn.; mem. AMA, NOW, Tex. Psychiat. Assn. (com. on women), Bexar County Psychiat. Soc. (pres.-elect 1996—), Tex. Med. Assn., Bexar County Med. Soc. (chmn. bd. censors 2003-04, bd. dirs. 2003-04), Chopin Found. U.S.A., Tuesday Music Club, Alpha Omega Alpha, Sigma Kappa Alumnae. Office: San Antonion State Hosp Ste 100 6711 S New Braunfels Ave San Antonio TX 78223 Office Phone: 210-531-7715.

**STALNAKER, LANCE KUEBLER,** lawyer; b. Tampa, Fla., Jan. 2, 1948; s. Leo Jr. and June Esther Stalnaker. BS in Journalism, U. Fla., 1970, JD, 1973. Bar: Fla. 1973, U.S. Dist. Ct. (mid. dist.) Fla. 1974, U.S. Ct. Appeals (5th cir.) 1974, U.S. Ct. Appeals (11th cir.) 1981. Ptnr. Stalnaker & Stalnaker, Tampa, 1973-75; pvt. practice Tampa, 1975-83, 91—; staff atty. Legal Aid Bur. of Hillsborough County, Tampa, 1983-85, interim exec. dir., atty., 1985-86, exec. dir., atty., 1986-90. Asst. cir. ct. commr. 13th Jud. Cir., Tampa, 1981-82. Pres. St. John's Luth. Ch., 1997-99, mem. bd. dirs., 1999—; of counsel St. John Luth. Ch. Learning Ctr., 2002—; mem. steering com. Pregnancy Care Ctr. Ministries, Tampa, 1999-2000. Capt. U.S. Army Res. to 1978. Mem. Hillsborough County Bar Assn. (family law sect.), Fla. Bar (family law sect.). Office: 1319 W Fletcher Ave Tampa FL 33612-3310

**STALOFF, ARNOLD FRED,** financial executive, trade association administrator; b. Dover, N.J., Dec. 12, 1944; s. William and Ida (Greenberg) S.; m. Sharon Marcia Teplitsky, June 10, 1967; children: Kimberly, Lindsay. BBA, U. Miami, 1967. Statistician U.S. Census Bur., Washington, 1967-68; fin. analyst SEC, Washington, 1968-71; sr. v.p. Phila. Stock Exch., 1971-78; v.p. Securities Industry Automation Corp., N.Y.C., 1978-80; pres. Fin. Automation Corp., Phila., 1980-83, Phila. Bd. Trade, 1983-89; pres., CEO Commodity Exch., Inc. (COMEX), N.Y.C., 1989-90; CEO Bloom Staloff Corp., Phila., 1991—2003; chmn. SFB Market Sys., Inc., 2005—. Bd. dirs. Lehman Bros. Fin. Products, Inc.; bd. govs. Phila. Stock Exch., 1991-97. Bd. dirs. Variety Club for Handicapped Children, Phila., 1987-92; mem. adv. bd. Phila. Internat. Airport, 1988—; mem. U. Miami Pres.'s Cir. Mem. Nat. Futures Assn. (bd. dirs. 1987-90). Avocations: fly fishing, golf, skiing. Office Phone: 856-853-1800. Business E-mail: staloff@staloff.com.

**STAM, DAVID HARRY,** librarian; b. Paterson, N.J., July 11, 1935; s. Jacob and Deana B. (Bowman) S.; m. Deirdre Corcoran, May 15, 1963; children—Julian, Wendell, Kathryn. AB, Wheaton Coll., 1955; postgrad., New Coll., U. Edinburgh, 1955-56; MLS, Rutgers U., 1962; postgrad., CUNY, 1963-64; PhD, Northwestern U., 1978. Asst. editor library publs., reference librarian, manuscript cataloguer New York Pub. Library, 1959-64; librarian Marlboro (Vt.) Coll., 1964-67; head tech. services dept. Newberry Library, Chgo., 1967-71, assoc. librarian; 1969-73; librarian Milton S. Eisenhower Library, Johns Hopkins U., Balt., 1973-78; Andrew W. Mellon dir. rsch. libraries N.Y. Pub. Library, N.Y.C., 1978-86; Univ. librarian Syracuse U., 1986-98, sr. scholar, History Dept., 1998—. Trustee Gladys K. Delmas Found. Author: Wordsworthian Criticism, 1974, International Dictionary of Library Histories, 2001; co-author (with Rissa Yachnin): Turgenev in English: A Checklist of Works by and about Him, 1960; contbr. articles to profl. jours. Served with USNR, 1956-58. Brit. Acad. Overseas fellow, 1975, Brit. Libr. fellow, 1995-96. Mem.: Am. Antiquarian Soc., Am. Hist. Assn., Groller Club (N.Y.C.), Princeton Club N.Y. Office: Syracuse U History Dept Eggers Hall Syracuse NY 13244 E-mail: dhstam@syr.edu.

**STAMATAKIS, CAROL MARIE,** lawyer, former state legislator; m. Michael Shklar. BA in Criminology and Criminal Justice, Ohio State U., 1982; JD, Case Western Res., 1985. Bar: N.H. 1985, U.S. Dist. Ct. N.H. 1985. Atty. Elliott, Jasper & Stamatakis, Newport, NH, 1990-93; state rep. N.H. State Legislature, 1988-94; atty. N.H. Dept. Health and Human Svcs., Concord, 1994—. Instr. Am. Inst. Banking, Claremont, 1987-88, 91-92, 95. Treas., mem. Town of Lempster N.H. Conservation Commn., 1987—; town chair N.H. Dem. Party, 1987—. Mem. N.H. Bar Assn., Sierra Club, Upper Valley Group (former vice chair and solid waste chair). Avocations: drawing, painting. Home: PO Box 807 Newport NH 03773-0807

**STAMATOYANNOPOULOS, GEORGE,** internal medicine educator; b. Athens, Greece, Mar. 11, 1934; came to U.S., 1964; s. John and Demetra (Fraginea) S.; m. Thalia Papayannopoulou, Nov. 19, 1964; children: John, Alexis. MD, U. Athens, 1958, DSc in Medicine, 1960, DSc in Biology (hon.),

1989, PhD (hon.), U. Thessaloniki, U. Patras. Asst. prof. medicine U. Wash., Seattle, 1966-68, assoc. prof. medicine, 1969—73, rsch. prof. medicine, 1973—75, prof. medicine, 1975—, dir. molecular med. prog., 1987—, head med. genetics, 1989—, adjunct prof. pathology, 1989—, dir. Markey Molecular Medicine Ctr., 1990—, prof. genetics, 1992—, prof. genome sciences, 2001—, Arno G. Motulsky endowed prof. medicine, 2003—. Fellow Royal Hellenic Rsch. Inst., Athens, 1960-64; editorial bd. mem. Jour Clinical Investigation, 1993-98, Gene Therapy, 1993-, Experimental Hematology, 1994-98, Blood Cells, Molecules & Diseases, 1994-, Current Opinion in Molecular Therapeutics, 1998-, Expert Reviews in Molecular Medicine, 1998-, Haematologica, 1998-, Haema, 1999-, Physiological Genomics, 1999-2004, Molecular Therapy, 1999-. Author: Molecular Basis of Blood Disease, 1987, others; editor 7 conf. proc.; contbr. over 250 articles to med. jours. Lt. Greek Air Force, 1958-60. Recipient merit award NIH, 1987. Fellow, Am. Acad. Arts & Sci.; mem. Assn. Am. Physicians, Am. Soc. Clin. Investigation, Am. Soc. Hematology (v.p. 1989-90, pres.-elect 1990-91, pres. 1991-92, Dameshek award 1990), Am. Bd. Medical Genetics, Am. Soc. Human Genetics, Am. Federation Clinical Rsch., Western Soc. Clinical Investigation, Am. Soc. Microbiology, Am. Soc. Gene Therapy, AAAS, Internat. Soc. Hematology. Office: U Wash Div Med Genetics Box 357720 Seattle WA 98195

**STAMATY, MARK ALAN,** cartoonist, writer, artist; b. Bklyn., Aug. 1, 1947; s. Stanley and Clara Gee Stamaty. B.F.A., The Cooper Union, 1969. Mem. faculty Parson's Sch. Design, N.Y.C., 1977-81. Author-illustrator: (children's books) Who Needs Donuts?, 1973 (Bklyn. Art Books For Children award 1974), Small in the Saddle, 1975, Minnie Maloney & Macaroni, 1976, Where's My Hippopotamus?, 1977, Too Many Time Machines, 1999, Alia's Mission, 2004, (comic strip collections) Macdoodle St., 1981, Washington, 1983; cartoonist: Macdoodle St. Village Voice newspaper, 1978-79, Carrrttoooonnn, Village Voice newspaper, 1980-81, (Washington Post and syndication) Washingtoon, 1981-94, Boox, N.Y. Times Book Review, 2001—; polit. cartoonist TIME mag., 1994-96, Doodlennium, 1996-98; contbr.: The New Yorker mag., 1992—, Slate Mag., 1996—; illustrator various publs., including: (children's book) Yellow Yellow, 1971, (Bklyn. Art Books for Children award); cartoon coverage of Milan fashion show for GQ Mag., 2000—. Recipient Purchase award, N.J. State Mus., 1969, Gold medal, Soc. Illustrators, 1974, Silver medal, 2005, Gold medal cert., 2005, Forte Dei Marmi, Museo-Premio Satira Politica, 2005. Mem. PEN Am. Ctr. Avocations: impersonating Elvis Presley, softball, swimming. Office Phone: 212-396-0744. E-mail: markstamaty@earthlink.net.

**STAMBAUGH, JOHN EDGAR,** oncologist, hematologist, educator, pharmacologist; b. Everrett, Pa., Apr. 30, 1940; s. John Edgar and Rhoda Irene (Becker) S.; m. Shirley Louise Fultz, June 24, 1961; 4 children. BS in Chemistry cum laude, Dickinson Coll., 1962; MD, Jefferson Med. Coll., 1966, PhD, 1968. Intern Thomas Jefferson U. Hosp., Phila., 1968-69, resident, 1968-69; oncology fellow Jefferson Med. Coll., 1970-72, instr. pharmacology, 1969-70, asst. prof., 1970-74, assoc. prof., 1974-82, prof., 1982—. Pvt. practice med. oncology, hematology and cancer pain, Woodbury, N.J.; staff physician Underwood Meml. Hosp., Woodbury, 1972—2004, West Jersey Hosp., 1973—. Contbr. articles to profl. jours. Fellow: Am. Soc. Pain Mgmt., Am. Acad. Pain Mgmt., Am. Coll. Clin. Pharmacology; mem.: Am. Assn. Clin. Rsch., Am. Pain Soc., Internat. Assn. for Study of Pain, Am. Assn. for Cancer Rsch., Am. Soc. Clin. Oncology, Am. Soc. for Pharmacology and Exptl. Therapeutics, Camden County Med. Soc., Gloucester County Med. Soc., N.J. Med. Soc. (bd. del.), Am. Soc. Clin. Pharmacology, AMA, ABA, Sigma Xi. Office: 17 W Red Bank Ave Ste 101 Woodbury NJ 08096-1630 Office Phone: 856-848-9292.

**STAMBAUGH, LARRY G.,** finance company executive; b. Topeka, Feb. 1, 1947; s. Merle J. and Eileen M. (Denslow) S.; m. Sallie M. Underwood, Jan. 18, 1969 (div. Oct. 1981); children: Matt, Julie; m. Suzanne Van Slyke, May 14, 1982 (div. Oct. 2006); children: Todd, Scott, Andy. BBA, Washburn U., 1969. CPA, Kans. Mgr. KPMG Peat, Marwick, Mitchell Co., Kansas City, Mo., 1969-76; co-owner Automotive Investment & Devel. Co., Olathe, Kans., 1976-82; chief fin. officer CNB Fin. Corp., Kansas City, Kans., 1983-90, ABC Labs., Columbia, Mo., 1990, pres., chief exec. officer, 1990-92; chmn., pres., CEO Maxim Pharms., San Diego, 1993—2006; prin. Apercu Cons., 2006—. Bd. dirs. BioCom; mem. adv. bd. U. Calif. San Diego Rady Sch. Bus. Chmn. bd. dirs. Forum for Corp. Dirs., 1996-99. Recipient Dir. of Yr. award, Forum for Corp. Dirs., 2002, 2006. Mem. Am. Mgmt. Assn., Nat. Assn. Corp. Dirs. Avocations: photography, golf. Home: 645 Front St 314 San Diego CA 92101 Office Phone: 619-955-8204. Personal E-mail: lgstambaugh@gmail.com.

**STAMBAUGH, REGINALD JACK,** ophthalmologist; b. West Palm Beach, Fla., Jan. 1, 1930; s. Gleason Noah and Marjorie (Hilton) S.; m. Carolyn Stroupe, Nov. 24, 1965; children— Melanie, Joette, Valerie, Reginald Giles. A.B., U. Fla., 1952; M.D., U. Miami, 1959. Diplomate Am. Bd. Ophthalmology, Nat. Bd. Med. Examiners. Intern, Grady Meml. Hosp., Atlanta, 1959-60, resident 1960-64; practice medicine specializing in ophthalmology, West Palm Beach, 1963—; chief ophthalmology Good Samaritan Hosp., West Palm Beach, 1966-74; lectr. Bascom Palmer Eye Inst., U. Miami Sch. Medicine, 1964-73; mem. med. adv. bd. Fla. Soc. for Prevention of Blindness, 1972-77, Crippled Children's Soc. Palm Beach, 1965-82; pres., chmn. bd. Ophthalmic mutual Ins. Co., 1987—. Contbr. numerous articles, papers in field. Bd. dirs. Fla. Med. Polit. Action Com., 1975-81, Palm Beach County Hall of Fame, 1977-80, Health Planning Council, 1979-81; bd. dirs. Found. Med. Care, 1979-82, pres., 1980; mem. vestry Bethesda by the Sea Ch. Palm Beach, 1981—. Served with USAF, 1952-54. Decorated Korean Presdl. citation. Mem. AMA, Am. Acad. Ophthalmology (bd. councilors 1981—87, chmn. bd. councilors 1986-87, com. eye care for Am. people 1985-86, state affairs com. 1981-83, long range planning com. 1983-86), Fla. Soc. Ophthalmology (sec.-treas. 1975-77, pres. 1980-81), Palm Beach County Med. Soc. (pres. 1977, trustee 1977). Democrat. Episcopalian. Clubs: Sailfish of Fla. (bd. govs. 1976-78); Bath and Tennis (Palm Beach). Home: 272 Queens Ln Palm Beach FL 33480-3240

**STAMBERG, SUSAN LEVITT,** radio personality; b. Newark, Sept. 7, 1938; d. Robert I. and Anne (Rosenberg) Levitt; m. Louis Collins Stamberg, Apr. 14, 1962; 1 child, Joshua Collins BA, Barnard Coll., 1959; DHL (hon.), Gettysburg Coll., 1982, Dartmouth Coll., 1984, Knox Coll., U.H. SUNY, Brockport. Editorial asst. Daedalus, Cambridge, Mass., 1960-62; editorial asst. The New Republic, Washington, 1962-63; host, producer, mgr., program dir. Sta. WAMU-FM, Washington, 1963-69; host All Things Considered Washington, 1971-86; host Weekend Edition Nat Pub. Radio, Washington, 1987-89; spl. corr. Nat. Pub. Radio, 1990—. Bd. dirs. AIA, Washington, 1983-85, PEN/Faulkner Fiction Award Found., 1985—. Author: Every Night at Five, 1982, The Wedding Cake in the Middle of the Road, 1992, Talk: NPR's Susan Stamberg Considers All Things, 1993. Recipient Honor award Ohio U., 1977, Edward R. Murrow award Corp. for Pub. Broadcasting, 1980; named Woman of Yr., Barnard Coll., 1984; fellow Silliman Coll. Yale U., 1984—; inducted Broadcasting Hall of Fame, 1994, Radio Hall of Fame, 1996. Avocations: drawing, piano, knitting. Office: Nat Pub Radio 635 Massachusetts Ave NW Washington DC 20001-3753 Office Phone: 202-513-2000.

**ŠTAMBUK, NIKOLA,** research scientist; b. Varaždin, Croatia, Mar. 25, 1959; s. Ranko and Vjera (Mrakovčić) Š.; m. Ana Lazić, Nov. 12, 1988; children: Albert, Danijel. MD, Zagreb (Croatia) U., 1984, MS, 1988; PhD, Inst. Med. Rsch. Occup. Health, Zagreb, 1991. Intern Sisters of Mercy Clin. Hosp., Zagreb, 1984-85; resident Railway Health Ctr., Zagreb, 1986-88; postdoctoral fellow Mc Gill U., Montreal, Can., 1991-92; rschr. Rugjer Bošković Inst., Zagreb, 1994—. Sci. com. Internat. Conf. on Math. and Computer Modelling and Sci. Computing, Berkeley, Calif., 1993, Boston, 1995, Washington, 1997. Contbr. articles to profl. jours. Mem. Internat. Assn. for Math. and Computer Modelling, Internat. Ocular Inflammation Soc., Internat. Soc. for Thymology and Immunotherapy. Achievements include the discovery of necklace model, I Ching and horseshoe map representation of the genetic code (SCA procedure), rsch. in models of artificial barriers

constrn., protein transfer and molecular recognition, computer-aided drug design, compartmental volume-pressure relationships. Home: Šubićeva 16 HR-10000 Zagreb Croatia Office: Rugjer Bošković Inst Bijenička 54 HR-10000 Zagreb Croatia Office Phone: +3851 4680 193. E-mail: stambuk@irb.hr.

**STAMELMAN, RICHARD HOWARD,** French and humanities educator; b. Newark, Mar. 7, 1942; s. Louis Robert and Golda (Senzer) S.; children: Emily, Gibson, Jeremy White. BA, Hamilton Coll.; PhD, Duke U. Asst. prof. French and humanities Wesleyan U., Middletown, Conn., 1967-74, assoc. prof., 1974-79, prof., 1979-93, William R. Kenan Jr. prof. humanities, 1983-92, dean humanities, 1986-89, dir. Ctr. for the Humanities, 1976-82, dir. humanities devel., 1982-85; dir. Weston Ctr. for Fgn. Langs., Lits. and Cultures Williams Coll., Williamstown, Mass., 1992-97, prof. Romance langs., lit. studies, 1992—; chmn. dept. French and Italian U. Colo., Boulder, 1991-92. Organizer (study group) Ecrire le Livre: Autour d'Edmond Jabès, Cerisy-la-Salle, France, 1987; co-dir. Edouard Morot-Sir Summer Inst. for French Cultural Studies, Hanover, N.H., 1994. Author: The Drama of Self in Guillaume Apollinaire's Alcools, 1976, Claude Garache: Prints, 1965-85, 1985, Lost Beyond Telling: Representations of Death and Absence in Modern French Poetry, 1990; editor: Contemporary French Poetry, Studies in 20th Century Literature, 1989, Ecrire le Livre: Autour d'Edmond Jabès, 1989, Italian transl., 1991, French Poetry since the War, L'Esprit Créateur, 1992; editor, prin. translator: The Lure and the Truth of Painting, Selected Essays by Yves Bonnefoy, 1995; translator: The Grapes of Zeuxis and Other Fables by Yves Bonnefoy, 1987, Once More the Grapes of Zeuxis by Yves Bonnefoy, 1989, The Last Grapes of Zeuxis by Yves Bonnefoy, 1993, Transmorphoses by Yves Bonnefoy, 1998; mem. editorial bd. French Forum; contbr. articles to profl. jours. Recipient Chevalier dans l'ordre des Palmes Académiques award French Govt., 1993; NEH fellow, 1973, John Simon Guggenheim Meml. Found. fellow, 1999; Am. Council Learned Socs. grantee, 1983 Mem. MLA (regional del. 1987-90, mem. program com. 1996-99), Societe Francaise des Parfumeurs. Home: PO Box 1624 Norwich VT 05055 Office: Williams Coll Weston Ctr Fgn Langs Lits Culture 995 Main St Williamstown MA 01267-2615 Business E-mail: Richard.H.Stamelman@dartmouth.edu, rstamelm@williams.edu.

**STAMEY, THOMAS ALEXANDER,** urologist, educator; b. Rutherfordton, NC, Apr. 26, 1928; s. Owen and Virginia (Link) S.; m. Kathryn Simmons Dec. 1, 1973; children: Fred M., Charline, Thomas A. III, Allison, Theron. BA, Vanderbilt U., 1948; MD, Johns Hopkins U., 1952. Diplomate Am. Bd. Urology. Intern, then resident Johns Hopkins Hosp., 1952-56; asst. prof. urology Johns Hopkins U. Sch. Medicine, Balt., 1958-60, assoc. prof., 1960-61; assoc. prof., chmn. divsn. urology Stanford (Calif.) U., 1961-64, assoc. prof., 1964-90, 1991—, chmn. dept., 1964-95. Author: Renovascular Hypertension, 1967, Pathogenesis and Treatment of Urinary Tract Infections, 1980, Urinalysis and Urinary Sediment: A Practical Guide for the Health Science Professional, 1985; editor: Campbell's Urology, edits. 4-6, 1978-92, Monographs in Urology, 1980-99. Capt. M.C., USAF, 1956-58. Recipient Sheen award ACS, 1990, Ferdinand C. Valentine award N.Y. Acad. Medicine, 1991. Mem. Am. Urol. Assn. (Ramon Guiteras award 1995, John K. Lattimer award 2000, Eugene Fuller Triennial Prostate award 2001), Am. Surg. Assn. (sr.), Inst. Medicine of NAS. Avocations: fishing, astronomy. Office: Stanford U Med Ctr Dept Urology S 287 300 Pasteur Dr Stanford CA 94305-5118 Business E-mail: tstamey@stanford.edu.

**STAMM, ALAN,** lawyer; b. Galesburg, Ill., Nov. 22, 1931; s. Gustave Frederick and Miriam (Simon) S.; m. Shelley Lynn Ramage, Mar. 19, 1978; 1 child, Lucinda Anne. Student, Universidad Nacional de Mex., summer 1950; AB, Yale U., 1952; JD, Harvard U., 1957. Bar: Calif. 1957, U.S. Supreme Ct. 1963. Assoc. Thelen, Marrin, Johnson & Bridges, San Francisco, 1957-60; staff atty. Litton Industries Inc., Beverly Hills, Calif., 1960-66, asst. sec., 1963-66; sec., gen. counsel Rectifier Corp., L.A., 1966-69, v.p., 1968-69; v.p., gen. counsel Republic Corp., L.A., 1969-71, also bd. dirs., 1970-71; v.p., gen. counsel Star. Industries, N.Y.C., 1971-72, Mattel Inc., Hawthorne, Calif., 1972-74, staff cons., 1974-75; of counsel Long & Levit, L.A., 1975-82, O'Donnell & Gordon, L.A., 1983-87, Hedges, Powe & Caldwell, L.A., 1988-90; pvt. practice L.A., 1990—. Judge pro tem Mcpl. Ct. L.A. Jud. Dist., 1977—; arbitrator L.A. Superior Ct. 1979—, judge pro tem L.A. Superior Ct. 1989—, arbitrator Nat. Assn. Securities Dealers, 1981—. Founding trustee Ctr. for Law in the Pub. Interest; former trustee Marlborough Sch., L.A.; former mem. bd. govs. Century City Hosp., L.A.; counsel bus. and profl. com. L.A. Philharm.; former bd. dirs. Yale Alumni Fund. Lt. (j.g.) USNR, 1952-54; lt. comdr. Res. ret. Mem. ABA, Calif. Bar Assn., L.A. Bar Assn., Harvard Law Sch. Assn., L.A. County Art Mus., Am. Arbitration Assn. (nat. panel arbitrators 1968—), NAACP, Sierra Club, Nat. Assn. Yale Alumni (former bd. govs.), Yale Club of So. Calif. (former dir.), Harvard Club of So. Calif., Phi Beta Kappa. Home: 422 Denslow Ave Los Angeles CA 90049-3507 Office: 1950 Pelham Ave Unit 1 Los Angeles CA 90025-5835

**STAMM, CAROL ANN,** obstetrician, gynecologist; b. Denver, Aug. 8, 1959; d. Robert L. and Mary Ellen Stamm. BA in Biology cum laude, U. Colo., 1981, cert. in elem. tchg., 1985; MD with honors, U. Colo., Denver, 1991. Diplomate Am. Bd. Ob-Gyn. Bilingual elem. tchr. Denver Pub. Schs., 1986—87; intern in ob-gyn U. Colo. Sch. Medicine, Denver, 1991—92, resident in ob-gyn, 1992—95, asst. prof., 1997—2003; staff ob-gyn, asst. prof. Denver Health Med. Ctr., 1995—2003; dir. women's health rotation Colo. Health Found. (formerly High St. Primary Care Clinic), Denver, 2003—, asst. prof. clin. medicine, 2003—, dir. women's svcs., 2004—. Mem. Patient and Family Edn. Work Group, 1996—97; mem. ob-gyn edn. com. U. Colo. Health Scis. Ctr., 1997—2003; dir. ob-gyn Grand Rounds, 1997—2001; provider design team Lifetime Clin. Record Project, 1998—2001; alt. mem. Colo. Multiple Instl. Rev. Bd., 1998—2003; presenter in field. Co-author: (book) Management of High-Risk Pregnancy, 4th edit., 1999, Medical Care of the Pregnant Patient, 2000, The Female Athlete, 2002, Contemporary Therapy in Obstetrics and Gynecology, 2002; contbr. articles to profl. jours.; peer reviewer Jour. Obstetrics and Gynecology, 1999—, Am. Jour. Obstetrics and Gynecology, 1999—. Recipient Richard Whitehead award, Phi Rho Sigma, 1989; grantee, March of Dimes, 2000—01; Trust fellow, Am. Cancer Soc. Brooks, 1988, Acad. Enrichment grantee, U. Colo. Health Scis. Ctr., 1993—95, NIH subcontract grantee, U. Pitts., 2000—03, NIH grantee, IBBEX, 2002. Fellow: ACOG (History fellow 2006); mem.: N.Am. Menopause Soc, Golden Key, Phi Beta Kappa (mem. mortar bd.). Avocations: reading, running, pilates, symphony, opera. Home: 155 S Jackson St Unit C Denver CO 80209 Office: Health One Alliance/High St Primary Care Clinic 1801 High St Denver CO 80218 Office Phone: 303-869-2158. Business E-Mail: cstamm@health1.org.

**STAMM, JOHN WILLIAM RANDOLPH,** dentist, educator; b. Germany, Nov. 3, 1942; naturalized, Can., naturalized, US; married; 2 children. DDS, U. Alta., Can., 1967; DDPH, U. Toronto, Can., 1969, MScD, 1971. Diplomate Am. Bd. Dental Pub. Health. Dental dir. Baffin region Nat. Health & Welfare, 1967; pvt. dental practice Fort Saskatchewan, Alta., 1968; rsch. asst. & biometrics Sch. Hygiene & Faculty Dentistry U. Toronto, 1968—71; asst. prof. Faculty Dentistry McGill U., 1971—74, assoc. prof., 1974—80, chmn., 1974—84, prof., 1980—84; dir. Dental Rsch. Ctr. U. N.C., 1985—89; prof. U. N.C. Sch. Dentistry, 1985—, asst. dean, 1985—89, dean, 1989—2005. Vis. prof. U. Riyadh, Saudi Arabia, 1980; mem. expert adv. panel oral health WHO, 1984—90; mem. study sect. oral biology and medicine NIH, 1988—90; cons. Que. Min. Social Affairs, 1974—76, Alta. Health Unit Assn., 1977—79, Can. Electrolytic Zinc, 1978—82, Can. Dental Assn., 1980, Am. Fund Dental Health, 1980—83, Dental Health St. Regis Indians N.Y. State Dept. Health, 1980; pres. Can. Div. of the Internat. Assn. for Dental Rsch., 1984. Mem. editl. bd. Jour. Dental Edn., 1980—83, Jour. Cmty. Dentistry and Oral Epidemiology, 1988—, Oral Diseases, 1994, assoc. editor Caries Rsch., 1995—; contbr. articles to profl. jours. Grantee, Ont. Dept. Health, 1969, McGill U., 1973, Que. Health Sci. Rsch. Coun., 1973, Min. Social Affairs Que., 1972—74, Nat. Inst. Dental Rsch., 1976—78, 1985, Med. Rsch. Coun., 1981—84, Nat. Health and Welfare, 1982—85, NIH, 1985—, Robert Wood Johnson Found., 1986—91. Fellow: AAAS, Am. Assn. for the Advancement for the Sci., Japanese Soc. for Promotion of Sci., Acad. Dentistry Internat., Royal Coll. Dentists of Can. (chief examiner 1980—82), Internat. Coll. Dentists, Am. Coll. Dentists; mem.: Internat. Assn. Dental Rsch. (treas. 1997—2001), Can. Soc. Pub. Health Dentists (pres. 1979—81), Can. Dental Assn., Am. Assn. Dental Rsch., Am. Assn. Pub. Health Dentists, Am. Assn. Dental Schs., Omicron Kappa Upsilon. Office: U NC Sch Dentistry Cb 7450 105 Dental Research Center Chapel Hill NC 27599-7450 Office Phone: 919-966-3415.*

**STAMM, KEITH G.,** energy executive; BS in mech. engring., U. Mo.-Columbia; MBA in fin., Rockhurst Coll. Lic. Staff Aquila's Mo. Pub. Svc.; CEO Aquila Merchant Svcs.; chmn., CEO United Energy Ltd.; pres., COO Aquila Global Networks Group; sr. v.p., COO Aquila, Kans. City, Mo., 2002—. Former bd. mem. Alinta Ltd., Uecomm. Office: Aquila 20 W 9th St Kansas City MO 64105-1711

**STAMOS, JOHN,** actor; b. Orange County, Calif., Aug. 19, 1963; s. Bill and Loretta Stamos; m. Rebecca Romijn, Sept. 19, 1998 (div. Mar. 1, 2005). Drummer with various bands. Actor: (TV series) General Hospital, 1982-84 (Emmy award, 2 Soap Opera Digest awards), Dreams, 1984, You Again?, 1986-87, Full House, 1987-95, ER, 2006- (TV movies) Daughter of the Streets, 1990, Captive, 1991, The Disappearance of Christina, 1993, Fatal Vows: The Alexandra O'Hara Story, 1996, A Match Made in Heaven, 1997, Sealed with a Kiss, 1999, How to Marry a Billionaire: A Christmas Tale, 2000, Fortunate Son, 2000, The Reagans, 2003; (films) Never Too Young to Die, 1986, Born to Ride, 1991, Private Parts, 1998, The Marriage Fool, 1998, Dropping Out, 2000, Party Monster, 2003, I Am Stamos, 2004; actor, assoc. prodr. (films) My Best Friend's Wife, 2001, actor, prodr. (TV series) Theives, Jake in Progress, 2005; exec. prodr. (TV series) Virgin Chronicles, 2002, (TV films) The Beach Boys: An American Family, 2000; TV appearances include Hangin' with Mr. Cooper, 1992, Tales from the Crypt, 1993, Step by Step, 1994, Baywatch, 1995, Clone High, 2003, Friends, 2003. Recipient Youth in Film award. Mem. AFTRA, Child Help U.S.A. (nat. spokesperson). Office: William Morris Agy care Les Stollman 151 El Camino Dr Beverly Hills CA 90212-2775*

**STAMP, TERENCE HENRY,** actor; b. London, July 22, 1938; s. Thomas and Ethel Esther (Perrott) S. ArtsD, U. East London, 1993. Actor: (films) include Billy Budd (Oscar nomination, Golden Globe award), 1960; Term of Trial, 1962, The Collector (Cannes Best Actor award), 1964, Alfie, 1964, Modesty Blaise, 1966, Far From the Madding Crowd, 1966, Poor Cow, 1967, Blue, 1967, Tales of Mystery, 1967, Theorem, 1968, The Mind of Mr. Soames, 1969, A Season in Hell, 1971, Hu-man, 1975, The Divine Creature, 1976, Black-OUt, 1977, Striptease, 1977, Meetings With Remarkable Men, 1978, Superman, 1978, Superman II, 1979, I Love You, I Love You Not, 1979, Death in the Vatican, 1980, Monster Island, 1981, The Bloody Chamber, 1982, The Company of Wolves, 1984, The Hit, 1984, Link, 1985, Hud, 1986, Legal Eagles, 1986, The Sicilian, 1987, Wall Street, 1987, Alien Nation, 1988, Young Guns, 1988, Genuine Risk, 1990, Beltenebros, 1991, Prince of Shadows, 1991, The Real McCoy, 1993, The Adventures of Priscilla, Queen of the Desert, 1994, Mindbender, 1995, Tire a Part, 1997, Bliss, 1997, The Bitter End, 1997, Tiré à part, 1997, Love Walked In, 1998, Kiss the Sky, 1999, The Limey, 1999, Star Wars: Episode I-The Phantom Menace, 1999, Bowfinger, 1999, Red Planet, 2000, My Wife Is an Actress, 2001, Revelation, 2001, Full Frontal, 2002, My Boss's Daughter, 2003, The Kiss, 2003, The Haunted Mansion, 2003, Dead Fish, 2004, Elektra, 2005; (TV films) The Thief of Baghdad, 1978, Deadly Recruits, 1986, Cold War Killers, 1986, The Alamut Ambush, 1986; (TV series) Chessgame, 1983, The Hunger, 1997-98; TV appearances include Smallville, 2003, 04, Static Shock, 2003; (plays) Dracula, The Lady From the Sea; author: Stamp Alan, 1987, Coming Attractions, 1988, Double Feature, 1989, The Night, 1992. Mem. Brook's Club (London), Manchester. Office: IFA 8730 W Sunset Blvd Ste 490 Los Angeles CA 90069-2248

**STAMPER, EWA SZUMOTALSKA,** psychologist; b. Warsaw, Sept. 8, 1954; came to U.S., 1984; d. Tadeusz and Regina S.Szumotalska MA in Clin. Psychology, U. Warsaw, Poland, 1978; PhD in Psychology, New Sch. U., N.Y.C., 1992. Staff therapist Marital Therapy Counseling Ctr., Warsaw, 1978—79, Ctr. for Psychotherapy and Personality Growth, Warsaw, 1978—80; sr. staff therapist Lab. for Psychoedn. Polish Psychol. Assn., Warsaw, 1981—85; postgrad. affiliate Washington Sq. Inst. for Psychotherapy, N.Y.C., 1990—92; police psychologist Honolulu Police Dept., 1993—98; pvt. practice, Honolulu, 1994—. With Tng. Ctr. for Family Therapy, Warsaw, 1976—78, Stuyvesant Poly., N.Y.C., 1988—89, North Ctrl. Bronx (N.Y.) Hosp., 1988—89, Yale Psychiat. Inst., 1989—90, Castle Med. Ctr., Kailua, Hawaii, 1993—94; co-chmn. Crystal Methampetamine Forum, Honolulu, 1996—99. Mem. APA, Am. Acad. Experts in Traumatic Stress, Hawaii Psychol. Assn. (clin. divsn. rep. 1998-99, coord. for Disaster Response Network 2005—). Avocations: horseback riding, raising German Shorthaired Pointers and Siamese cats, gardening, fiction and poetry writing, running. Office: 30 Aulike St Ste 306 Kailua HI 96734 Office Phone: 808-261-5555. E-mail: ewastamper@aol.com.

**STAMPER, JOHN W.,** architecture educator, academic administrator; b. Mishawaka, Ind., Dec. 18, 1950; s. Clay V. and Hazel M. Stamper; m. Erika Pistorius, June 28, 1986; 1 child, Alessandra Marie. Mar., U. Ill., Champaign-Urbana, 1973—75; MA, Williams Coll., Williamstown, Mass., 1975—77; PhD, Northwestern U., Evanston, Ill., 1981—85. Lic. architect, Ill., 1981. Assoc. prof. U. Notre Dame, Ind., 1984—; assoc. dean, 2004—. Author: (scholarly books) The Architecture of Roman Temples: The Republic to the Middle Empire, Chicago's North Michigan Avenue: Planning and Development, 1900-1930. Com. mem. Mayor's Civic Alliance, South Bend, Ind., 2003—06. Grantee Fontainebleau Traveling Fellowship, U. Ill., Dept. Architecture, 1978. Mem. AIA, Soc. Archit. Historians. Democrat-Npl. Roman Catholic. Achievements include proposing a radically new reconstruction of the Temple of Capitoline Jupiter in Rome. Avocations: travel, photography. Home: 228 N Esther St South Bend IN 46617 Office: Univ Notre Dame Sch Architecture Notre Dame IN 46556 Home Fax: 574-631-8486; Office Fax: 574-631-8486. Business E-Mail: stamper.1@nd.edu.

**STAMPER, NORMAN H.,** protective services official; BS, MS in Criminal Justice Adminstrn., San Diego State U.; PhD in Leadership and Human Behavior, U.S. Internat. U. Chief of police Seattle Police Dept., 1994—. Exec. dir. Mayor Pete Wilson's Crime Control Commn.; apptd. (by U.S. Atty. Gen. and Sec. Health and Human Svcs.) Adv. Coun. Violence Against Women; mem. adv. panel on Excessive Force by Police, Police Exec. Rsch. Forum, Major Cities Chiefs; mem. steering com. Seattle Equal Justice Coalition; co-chair Ptnr's. in Pub. Edn's. Urban Scholar's Program; mem. bd. dirs. Leadership Tomorrow; trustee Ctr. for Ethical Leadership. Author: Removing Managerial Barriers to Effective Police Leadership, 1992; tchnical adv. Municipal Police Administration, 1992. Named to Alumni Hall of Fame Boys and Girls Club of Am.; recipient Katharine M. Bullitt award for Leadership Ptnrs. in Pub. Edn. Mem. Internat. Assn. Chiefs of Police. Office: Seattle Police PO Box 34986 Seattle WA 98124-4986

**STAMPER, ROBERT LEWIS,** ophthalmologist, educator; b. NYC, July 27, 1939; m. Naomi T. Belson, June 23, 1963; children: Juliet, Marjorie, Alison. BA, Cornell U., 1961; MD, SUNY-Downstate, 1965. Diplomate Am. Bd. Ophthalmology (assoc. examiner 1976-92, bd. dirs. 1992-99). Intern Mt. Sinai Hosp., N.Y.C., 1965-66; resident in ophthalmology Washington U.-Barnes Hosp., St. Louis, 1968-71; Nat. Eye Inst.-NIH fellow dept. ophthalmology Washington U., St. Louis, 1971-72, from instr. ophthalmology to asst. prof. dept. ophthalmology, 1971-72; asst. prof. dept. ophthalmology Pacific Presbyn. Med. Ctr., San Francisco, 1972-76, assoc. prof. ophthalmology, 1976-87; chmn. dept. ophthalmology Calif. Pacific Med. Ctr. (formerly Pacific Presbyn. Med. Ctr.), San Francisco, 1987-96; vice-chmn. dept. ophthalmology U. Calif. San Francisco 2003—2003, prof. clin. ophthalmology, dir. glaucoma, 1999—. Asst. opthalmologist Barnes Hosp., St. Louis, 1971-72, Harkness Hosp., San Francisco, 1973-74; dir. ophthalmic photography and fluorescin angiography, dept. ophthalmology Washington U., St.

Louis, 1969-72; dir. resident tng. Pacific Presbyn. Med. Ctr., 1972-89, dir. glaucoma svc., vice-chmn. dept. ophthalmology, 1974-87; chief ophthalmology svc. Highland Hosp., Oakland, Calif., 1974-76; clin. instr. dept. ophthalmology U. Calif., San Francisco, 1974-77, prof. clin. ophthalmology, 1998—; clin. asst. prof. ophthalmology U. Calif., Berkeley, 1974-78, asst. clin. prof. ophthalmology, 1978-85; sr. rsch. assoc. Smith-Kettlewell Inst. Visual Scis., San Francisco, 1972-89; project co-dir. ophthalmic curriculum for med. students Nat. Libr. Medicine, 1973-75; commr. Joint Commn. on Allied Health Pers. in Ophthalmology, 1975-87, bd. dirs., 1978-88, sec., 1980, v.p., 1982-83, pres., 1984-85; provisional asst. chief dept. ophthalmology Mt. Zion Hosp., San Francisco, 1976-87, assoc. chief dept. ophthalmology, 1982-86; ophthalmic cons. Ft. Ord, Calif., 1976-1984, Oakland Naval Hosp., 1978-83; instr. Stanford U., Calif., 1977—; glaucoma cons. U. Calif., Davis, 1978-84; vis. lectr. dept. ophthalmology Hadassah Hebrew U. Med. Ctr., Jerusalem, 1978, Oxford U. Eye Hosp., Eng., 1986; ind. med. examiner State of Calif., 1979—; mem. appeals hearing panel Accreditation Coun. for Grad. Med. Edn., 1986-93; mem. residency rev. com. for ophthalmology, 1993-98; mem. provisional courtesy staff Peralta Hosp., Oakland, 1988-92; mem. ophthalmic devices adv. panel USFDA, 1989-92; presenter, lectr. in field. Co-author: Update in Glaucoma, 2004; editor Ophthalmology Clinics of North Am., 1988-2004, 06; mem. editl. adv. com. Ophthalmology, 1982-89, mem. editl. bd., 1983-94; co-author: Becker and Shaffer's Diagnosis and Management of the Glaucomas, 7th edit., 1999; co-editor Essentials in Ophthalmology: Glaucoma, 2004; contbr. articles to profl. jours. Chmn. bd. Agy. for Jewish Edn., Oakland, 1986-89; bd. dirs. Jewish Fedn. Greater East Bay, Oakland, 1992-94; bd. dirs. Found. for Glaucoma Rsch.; mem. glaucoma adv. com. Nat. Soc. to Prevent Blindness; mem. Am. Diabetes Assn. Surgeon USPHS, 1966-68. Recipient Self-Instrnl. Material in Ophthalmology award Nat. Soc. for Performance and Instrn., 1975, Honor award Am. Acad. Ophthalmology, 1982, Sr. Honor award, 1992, Statesmanship award Joint Commn. on Allied Health Pers. in Ophthalmology, 1989, Disting. Alumnus award Wash. U. Sch. Medicine, 2004; named Troutman Master Tchr. in Ophthalmology, 2000; Regents scholar NY State, 1961, scholar NY State, 1965; Blalock fellow UCLA Sch. Medicine, 1961, Fight for Sight fellow Dept. Ophthalmology NY Hosp. and Cornell Med. Ctr., 1962, 63, 64. Fellow Am. Acad. Ophthalmology and Otolaryngology (rep. to joint commn. on allied health pers., faculty home study course sect. X, chmn. sect. VIII 1983-85, bd. councilors, editl. adv. com. Opthalmology jour. 1982-89, editl. bd. Ophthalmology jour. 1983-94, and many others), ACS; mem. AMA (Physician's Recognition award 1989), Am. Ophthalmologic Soc., Assn. for Rsch. in Vision and Ophthalmology, Calif. Med. Assn. (asst. sec. sect. ophthalmology, chmn., sci. bd. rep. adv. panel on ophthalmology 1985-91), Nat. Soc. Prevent Blindness (mem. glaucoma adv. com. 1981-2004), No. Calif. Soc. Prevent Blindness (bd. dirs. 1986—, pres.-elect 2006—), Calif. Assn. Ophthalmology, Pan Am. Ophthal. (bd. dirs. 1992—), Soc., NY Acad. Scis., Las Vegas Ophthal. Soc. (hon.), Am. Glaucoma Soc. (v.p. 1997-99, pres. 1999-2000), Glaucoma Rsch. Found. (bd. dirs.). Office: Dept Opht UCSF Med Ctr 8 Koret Way San Francisco CA 94143-0730 Office Phone: 415-476-3717. Business E-Mail: stamper@itsa.ucsf.edu.

**STAMPFER, MEIR JONATHAN,** epidemiologist, nutritionist, educator; b. Lincoln, Nebr., Mar. 1, 1950; s. Joshua and Goldie Stampfer; m. Claire Diane Blum, Dec. 30, 1975; children: Samuel, Eliane, Orly. AB, Columbia Coll., 1973; MD, NYU, 1977; MPH, Harvard U., 1980, DPH, 1985. Diplomate Am. Bd. Med. Examiners. Instr. medicine Harvard Med. Sch., Boston, 1982-85, asst. prof. medicine, 1985-88; assoc. prof. Harvard Sch. Pub. Health, Boston, 1988-93, prof. nutrition and epidemiology, 1993—, chair Dept. Epidemiology, 2000—; assoc. physician Brigham & Women's Hosp., Boston, 1982-92; physician Brigham and Women's Hosp., Boston, 1992—. Lectr. in field. Contbr. numerous articles to profl. jours. Recipient Nat. Rsch. Svc. award NIH, 1977-82; NIH grantee, 1982—. Fellow Am. Heart Assn., Am. Coll. Nutrition; mem. Internat. Soc. Cardiology, Soc. Epidemiologic Rsch. Democrat Jewish. Office: Dept Epidemiology Kresge Bldg, 9th Fl 667 Huntington Ave Boston MA 02115 also: Channing Lab 181 Longwood Ave Boston MA 02115-5804 Office Phone: 617-432-6477. Office Fax: 617-566-7805. Business E-Mail: mstampfe@hsph.harvard.edu.

**STAMPKE, STUART REH,** physicist, researcher; b. Burbank, Calif., Apr. 20, 1950; BS in Physics summa cum laude, Calif. State U., Northridge, 1973; PhD in Physics, Calif. Inst. Tech., Pasadena, 1982. Rsch. fellow in physics Calif. Inst. Tech., Pasadena, 1982; rsch. assoc. Mich. State U., East Lansing, 1982-86; scientist I Superconducting Super Collider Lab., Waxahachie, Tex., 1989-94; sr. scientist Aura Sys., Inc., El Segundo, Calif., 1996—2003. From vis. asst. prof. to vis. assoc. prof. U. Notre Dame, Ind., 1986-88; mem. part-time faculty Calif. State U., Northridge, 1994-96. Contbr. articles to profl. jours. on particle physics, detectors, and accelerator physics. Mem. IEEE, Am. Phys. Soc., Am. Solar Energy Soc. Home: 17803 Superior St Apt 215 Northridge CA 91325-4795 E-mail: s.stampke@ieee.org.

**STAMPS, LAURA ANNE,** writer, poet; b. Indpls., Apr. 2, 1957; d. James Oliver and Isabelle Anne (Holland) Smith; m. Carl Thomas Stamps, Jr., June 30, 1979. Student, Dalton (Ga.) Jr. Coll., 1977, Coll. of Charleston, S.C., 1979. Owner Kittyfeather Press, Columbia, SC, 1985—. Author: Art Marketing Manual, 1988, How to Create the Life You Desire, 1995, How to Become a Prosperous Woman, 1995, Songs of Power, 1996, (fiction) Earth Lessons, 1995, Tuning Out, 1996, The Way of Love, 1998, I Can Do Anything, vol. 1, 2000, vol. 2, 2000, Restore my Soul, 2002, In the Company of Cats, 2002, Joy Unspeakable, 2003, Evergreen, 2003, Cat Daze, 2004, Angel, 2004, In the Garden, 2004, Cats and Chrysanthemums: New and Collected Poems 1987-2005, 2005, The Year of the Cat, 2005 (nominated Pulitzer Prize), The Cat Lady, 2006, (novellas) The Tarot Cats, 2006, Blue Moon, 2006, The Cat Lady, 2006; editor The Artist's Forum, 1989-94, Laura's Letter for Women, 1996-97 Avocations: gardening, cats. Office: Kittyfeather Press PO Box 212534 Columbia SC 29221-2534 E-mail: laurastamps@mindspring.com.

**STAMSTA, JEAN F.,** artist; b. Sheboygan, Wis., Nov. 2, 1936; d. Herbert R. and Lucile Caroline (Malwitz) Nagel; m. Duane R. Stamsta, Aug. 18, 1956; children: Marc, David. BS, BA, U. Wis., 1958. Guest curator Milw. Art Mus., 1986; resident artist Leighton Artist Colony, Banff, Alta., Can., 1987. One-woman shows include Am. Craft Mus., N.Y.C., 1971, Winona (Minn.) State U., 1986, Lawrence U., Appleton, Wis., 1990, Walkers Point Ctr. Arts, Milw., 1990, U. Wis. Ctr., Sheboygan, 1998, Wis. Luth. Coll., Milw., 1999, Carroll Coll., Waukesha, Wis., 2006, exhibited in group shows at Cleve. Mus. Art, 1977, Milw. Art Mus., 1986, 1988, Nat. Air and Space Mus., Smithsonian Instn., Washington, 1986, Madison (Wis.) Art Ctr., 1987, 1990, Paper Press Gallery, Chgo., 1988, North Arts Ctr., Atlanta, 1990, Dairy Barn Cultural Arts Ctr., Athens, Ohio, 1991, Paper Arts Festival, Appleton, 1992, Fine Arts Mus., Budapest, Hungary, 1992, Tilburg Textile Mus., Netherlands, 1993, U. Wis. Union Gallery, 1994, Holland Area Arts Coun. Gallery, U. Mich., Ann Arbor, 1996, Charles Allis Art Mus., Milw., 1996, Bergstrom-Mahler Mus., Neenah, Wis., 1998, West Bend Mus. Art, Wis., 2000, Three Rivers Arts Festival, Pitts., 2001, U. Wis. Alumni Assn., Milw., 2002, Racine (Wis.) Art Mus., 2003, 2005, Rochester Art Ctr., 2004. Fellow Craftsman fellow, NEA, 1974. Avocations: swimming, travel. Home: 9313 Center Oak Rd Hartland WI 53029 E-mail: jstamsta@aol.com.

**STANALAJCZO, GREG CHARLES,** computer company executive; b. 1959; Degree, Oakland U. With CDI Computer Svc., Inc., Troy, Mich., 1986-95, pres., 1993-95; exec. v.p., COO, co-owner Trillium Teamologies, Inc., Royal Oak, Mich., 1996—; pres., owner Stano Enterprises, LLC, Stano Transp. Svcs., LLC, Stano Electronics & Tech., LLC; owner, ptnr. Sullivan Investment Group, 3rd St. Properties; ptnr. Heritage Pewter LLC; founder, pres. Trillium Charities, Inc.; owner, pres. Stano Electronics and Tech., LLC; co-owner, sec. and v.p. i-mdo.USA, Inc.; COO, co-owner, co-founder i-mob USA, Inc. Office: Trillium Teamologies Inc 219 S Main St Ste 300 Royal Oak MI 48067-2611 Office Phone: 248-584-2080. E-mail: greg_stano@compuserve.com.

**STANBERRY, D(OSI) ELAINE,** English literature educator, writer; b. Elk Park, N.C. m. Earl Stanberry; 1 child, Anita St. Lawrence. Student in Bus. Edn., Steed Coll. Tech., 1956; BS in Bus. and English, East Tenn. State U., 1961, MA in Shakespearean Lit., 1962; PhD, Tex. A&M U., 1975; postgrad., North Tex. State U., U. South Fla., NYU, Duke U., U. N.C. Prof. Manatee Jr. Coll., Bradenton, Fla., 1964-67; Disting. prof. English Dickinson State U., ND, 1967-81; retired, 1981. Author: Poetic Heartstrings, Mountain Echoes, Love's Perplexing Obsession Experienced by Heinrich Heine and Percy Bysshe Shelley, Poetry from the Ancients to Moderns: A Critical Anthology, Finley Forest, Chapel Hill's Tree-lined Tuck, (plays) The Big Toe, The Funeral Factory; contbr. articles, poetry to jours., mags. Recipient Editor's Choice award Nat. Libr. Poetry, 1988, 95, Distinguished Professor of English Award, Dickinson State U., 1981; included in Best Poems of 1995. Mem. Acad. Am. Poets, N.C. Writers Network, N.C. Poetry Soc. (Carl Sandburg Poetry award 1988), Poetic Page, Writers Jour., Poets and Writers, Friday-Noon Poets, Delta Kappa Gamma. Home: 1840 Crawford Rd Graham NC 27253-9204

**STANBRIDGE, ERIC JOHN,** biology professor; b. London, May 28, 1942; came to U.S., 1965; BS, Brunel U., 1964; PhD, Stanford U., 1971. Rsch. asst. Wistar Inst., Phila., 1965—67; mem. sci. staff Nat. Inst. Med. Research, London, 1968-69; research assoc. med. microbiology Stanford (Calif.) U., 1972-73, instr. med. microbiology, 1973-75; asst. prof., dept. microbiology U. Calif., Irvine, 1975-78, assoc. prof., dept. microbiology, 1978-82, prof., dept. microbiology and molecular genetics, 1982—, disting. prof., dept. microbiology and molecular genetics, 2002—. Chmn. Gordon Conf. Cancer Biology, 1985; advisor Office of Tech. Assessment, 1986; co-organizer UCLA-Triton Bioscis. Symposium, 1986; mem. external adv. bd., U. Calif. San Francisco Comprehensive Cancer Ctr., 2000-; bd. sci. advisors, Norwegian Inst. Gene Ecology, 2002-; coll. reviewers, Can. Rsch. Chairs Program, 2003-;lectr. in the field. Editorial bd. mem. Microbiol. Revs., 1985-, In Vitro, 1987-, J. Cellular Biochemistry, 1990-, Oncology Rsch., 1992-, Geno Methods, 1993-, Cancer Rsch. Ency., 1999-, Cancer Letters, 1998-; assoc. editor Cancer Research, 1985-, J. Cellular Physiology, 1989-, Molecular and Cellular Differentation, 1992-, Cancer Sci. (Japan), 2004-; contbr. articles to profl. jours. and chpts. to books; 4 US patents in the field. Fellow Leukemia Soc., 1976-1978, Internat. Union Against Cancer, 1979, Eleanor Roosevelt Internat., 1983-84, Am. Acad. Microbiology, 1986, AAAS, 1993; recipient Research Career Devel. award, NIH, 1978-83, NIH Merit award, 1987-96, Phi Kappa Phi Biology Colloquium award, Oregon State U., 1988; named one of Outstanding Young Men of Am., Jaycees, 1979. Mem. AAAS, NY Acad. Scis., Internat. Orgn. Mycoplasmologists, Am. Soc. Microbiology, Sigma Xi, Tissue Culture Assn., Internat. Orgn. Mycoplplasmologist, Am. Assn. for Cancer Rsch., Internat. Soc. for Differentiation, UICC Acad. Fellows Office: U Calif Irvine B235/B210 Med Sciences Mail Code 4025 Irvine CA 92697-4025 Office Phone: 949-824-7042, 949-824-5259. Office Fax: 949-824-8598. Business E-Mail: ejstanbr@uci.edu.

**STANBURY, JOHN BRUTON,** retired pharmacologist, educator; b. Clinton, N.C., May 15, 1915; s. Walter A. and Zula (Bruton) S.; m. Jean F. Cook, Jan. 6, 1945; children: John Bruton, Martha Jean, Sarah Katherine, David McNeill, Pamela Cook. AB, Duke U., 1935; MD, Harvard U., 1939; Doctor honoris causa, U. Leiden, Netherlands, 1975, U. Pisa, Italy, 1994, U. Cuyo, Argentina, 2005. House officer Mass. Gen. Hosp., 1940-41, asst. resident, 1946, chief med. resident, 1948, mem. med. staff, 1949—; research fellow pharmacology Harvard Med. Sch., 1947; vis. prof. medicine U. Leiden, 1955; prof. exptl. medicine MIT, Cambridge, 1966-80, emeritus, 1980—. Cons. Pan Am. Health Orgn., WHO, UNICEF, U.S. AEC. Author: Endemic Goiter: The adaptation of man to iodine deficiency, 1954, Metabolic Basis of Inherited Disease, 5th edit., 1984, The Thyroid and Its Diseases, 5th edit., 1984, Endemic Goiter, 1969, Human Development and the Thyroid, 1972, Endemic Goiter and Endemic Cretinism, 1980, Prevention and Control of Iodine Deficiency Disorders, 1987, A Constant Ferment, 1991, The Damaged Brain of Iodine Deficiency, 1994, The Inborn Errors of the Thyroid System, 1994, Iodine in Pregnancy, 1998. Served from lt. (j.g.) to comdr. USNR, 1941-45. Decorated gran oficial Ordenar Hipoloitio Unanue (Peru); recipient Delmar S. Fahrney medal Franklin Inst., 1993, Prince Mahidol award, Thailand, 1994. Mem. Am. Assn. Physicians, Soc. Clin. Investigation, Am. Thyroid Assn. (pres. 1969), Am. Acad. Arts and Scis., Endocrine Soc., Endocrine Socs. Finland, Colombia, Peru, Ecuador and Argentina, Internat. Coun. for Control of Iodine Deficiency Disorders (chair emeritus). Democrat. Episcopalian. Home: 43 Circuit Rd Chestnut Hill MA 02467-1802 E-mail: john_stanbury@hms.harvard.edu, JohnBStanbury@aol.com.

**STANCEU, TIMOTHY CHARLES,** federal judge; b. Canton, Ohio, July 31, 1951; s. Charles and Marian Kathryn (Coman) S. AB, Colgate U., 1973; JD, Georgetown U., 1979. Bar: D.C. 1980, U.S. Ct. Appeals (fed. cir.) 1991, U.S. Ct. Internat. Trade, 1991. Environ. protection specialist U.S. EPA, Washington, 1974-82; spl. asst. to asst sec. U.S. Dept. Treasury, Washington, 1982-85, dep. dir. Office of Trade and Tariff Affairs, 1985-89; atty. Hogan & Hartson, Washington, 1990—2003; judge US Ct. Internat. Trade, NYC, 2003—. Mem. Nat. Assn. Fgn. Trade Zones (dir. 1994—). Republican. Office: US Ct Internat Trade One Federal Plz New York NY 10278-0001

**STANCIL, IRENE MACK,** family counselor; b. St. Helena Island, Sept. 29, 1938; d. Rufus and Irene (Wilson) Mack; m. Nesby Stancil, Dec. 29, 1968; 1 child, Steve Lamar. BA, Benedict Coll., 1960, CUNY, 1983; MA, New World Bible Coll., 1984; SSD, United Christian Coll., 1985; cert., Mercy Coll., 1993. Supr. City of New York; tchr. local bd. edn., SC; supr. case worker, counselor City of New York. Mem. Am. Ctr. for Law & Justice.

**STANCILL, JAMES MCNEILL,** finance educator, consultant; b. Orange, NJ, July 30, 1932; s. James Sr. and Anne Jeanne (Sauter) S.; m. Catherine Jackson, Sept. 25, 1954; children: Martha A., Mary C., Christine E. AB, George Washington U., 1954, MBA, 1957; PhD in Fin. and Econs., U. Pa., 1965. Buyer Melpar Inc., Falls Church, Va., 1954-59; instr., adminstrv. officer U. Pa., Phila., 1959-64; prof. fin. U. So. Calif., L.A., 1964—. Prin. Stancill & Assocs., Pasadena, Calif., 1964—. The McNeill Bush Co. Ltd.; chmn. S.W. Products Co., 1991—97. Author: Management of Working Capital, 1970, Entrepreneurial Finance: for New and Emerging Businesses, 2004; contbr. numerous articles to Harvard Bus. Rev., 1977—. Avocations: genealogy, sailing, travel. Office: U So Calif Marshall Sch Bus Los Angeles CA 90089-1427

**STANCZAK, JULIAN,** artist, educator; b. Borownica, Poland, Nov. 5, 1928; came to U.S., 1950, naturalized, 1957; s. Victor and Elizabeth (Cwynar) S.; m. Barbara M. Meerpohl, June 10, 1963; children: Danuta M., Christopher. B.F.A., Cleve. Inst. Art, 1954; M.F.A., Yale U., 1956. Tchr. Art Acad. Cin., 1957-64, Cleve. Inst. Art, 1965—. One-man shows include Dayton Art Inst., 1964, Martha Jackson Gallery, N.Y.C., 1964, 65, 68, 71, 72, 75, 77, 79, Miami U., Oxford, Ohio, 1965, Feingarten Galleries, Los Angeles, 1966, Kent State U., 1968, Dartmouth, 1968, Akron (Ohio) Art Inst., 1969, Cleve. Inst. Art, 1971, London Arts Gallery, 1971, Cin. Art Mus., 1972, 80, Corcoran Gallery Art, Washington, 1972, Canton (Ohio) Art Inst., 1974, Pollack Gallery, Toronto, 1975, Ohio State U., 1976, IMF and CARE, Washington, 1978, Butler Inst. Am. Art, Youngstown, Ohio, 1980, Nat. Mus., Warsaw, Poland, 1981, Alice Simsar Gallery, Ann Arbor, Mich., 1982, 88, New Gallery, Cleve., 1983, Charles Foley Gallery, Columbus, Ohio, 1984, 88, Walker Gallery, Chgo., 1986, Carl Solway Gallery, Cin., Jane Haslem Gallery, Washington, 1986, Standard Oil Co. Hdqrs., Cleve., 1987, Alice Simsar Gallery, Ann Arbor, Mich., Boca Raton Mus. Art, Fla., 1989, Carl Solway Gallery, Cin., Charles Foley Gallery, Columbus, Ohio, Ctr. for Contemporary Art, Cleve., 1990; one man retrospective David Anderson Gallery, Buffalo, N.Y., Dennos Mus.,Traverse City, Mich., Butler Inst. of Am. Art, Youngstown, Ohio, 2000, /Columbus Mus. of Art, 2001, Ashville Mus. of Art, N.C., 2001, Lowe Art Mus Univ. Miami, Fla., 2001; many others; exhibited in group shows: Mus. Modern Art, N.Y.C., 1965, Albright Knox Art Gallery, Buffalo, 1965, 68, Detroit Art Inst., 1965, Larry Alrich Mus., 1965, U. Ill., 1965, Gallery Moos, Toronto, 1965, Kranert Art Mus., Urbana, Ill., 1965, San Francisco Mus. Art, 1965, Flint (Mich.) Inst. Art, 1966, Carnegie Inst., Pitts., 1967, Japan Cultural

Forum, 1967, Smithsonian Instn., Washington, 1967, 69, 85, Dept. State, Washington, 1968, Cin. Art Mus., 1968, 83, Del. Art Ctr., 1970, Seibu, Tokyo, 1971, Mansfield (Ohio) Art Ctr., 1973, Butler Art Inst., Youngstown, Ohio, 1973, Minn. Art Mus., Mpls., 1973, Akron Art Inst., 1975, Indpls. Mus. Art, 1976, Bklyn. Mus. Art, 1976, 80, Cleve. Mus. Art, 1976, 77, 83, Memphis Acad. Art, 1981, Nat. Gallery Art, 1981, 85, Hirshhorn Mus. Art, 1981, Montclair Art Mus., N.J., 1982, Art Acad. Cin., 1986, Embassies Travelling Exhbn., Madrid, 1987, Warsaw, Poland, 1991; represented in permanent collections: Nat. Mus. Am. Art, Albright Knox Art Gallery, Larry Aldrich Mus., Mus. Modern Art, Dayton Art Inst., Hirshhorn Mus., Washington, Butler Inst. Am. Art, Youngstown, Ohio, Rufino Tomajo Mus., Mex., Cleve. Art Assn., Milw. Art Inst., Canton (Ohio) Art Inst., USIA, N.Y.C., Balt. Mus. Art, San Francisco Mus. Art, Herron Mus. Art, Indpls., Okla. Art Ctr., Oklahoma City, Pa. Acad. Fine Arts, Phila., Carnegie Inst., Pitts., Cleve. Mus. Art, Cin. Art Mus., Tulsa Mus. Fine Arts, Columbus (Ohio) Art Mus., Akron Art Inst., Corcoran Art Mus., Nat. Gallery, Washington, Lowe Art Mus., Coral Gables, Fla., Contemporary Art Mus., Houston, Winnipeg Fine Arts Ctr., Man., Can., Dracket Fine Art Collection, Cin., Kalamazoo Inst. Arts, Worcester Art Mus., Phoenix Art Mus., Indpls. Mus. Art, Wasserman Devel. Corp., Cambridge, Dartmouth Coll., Hanover, N.H., Etzold Sammlung, Cologne, Fed. Republic Germany, Johnson & Johnson Fine Art Collection, Conn., Nelson Rockefeller Collection, N.Y., Chase Manhattan Bank, N.Y., Mus. Fine Arts, Los Angeles, Newport Harbor Mus., Newport Beach, Calif., N.Y. State U. at Buffalo; mus. collections include Aldrich Mus. Cotemporary Art, ridgefield, Conn., Akron Art Inst., Ohio, Asheville Mus. Art, Asheville, N.C., Albright Knox Art Gallery, Buffalo, Ball State U. Mus. Art, Muncie, Ind., Balt. Mus. Art, Boca Raton, Fla., Butler Inst. Am. Art, Youngstown, Ohio, Canton Art Inst., Ohio, Carnegie Inst., Pitts., Mus. Modern Art; others; represented in permanent collections at Air Products & Chems., Alcoa, Am. greetings, Cleve., Ameritrust Bank, Cleve., David Anderson Collection, Buffalo, Am. Republic Ins. Co., Des Moines, Atlantic ridgefield Com., N.Y., The Art Collection First Nat. Bank Chgo., Balt. Gas & Electric, Balt., Bank N.Y.; others; monographs include Gene Baro Corcoran Gallery Art, Washington, Rudolf Arnheim, Harry Rand, Robert Bertholf, Poetry and Rare Book Collection, SUNY Buffalo, 20 Tectronic Images and Poetry Barbara Stanczak Clev., (color and form Vibrations of Geometrical Space) Dennos Mus. ctr. Northwestern Mich. Coll., Traverse City, Mich. Recipient 1st prize Dayton Art Inst., 1964; recipient Butler Inst. Am. Art award, 1966, Cleve. Fine Arts prize, 1970, Ohio Arts Council award, 1972, Best of Show award Internat. Platform Assn., 1973-76 Mem. Abstract Artists Am., Internat. Platform Assn. Achievements include being a pioneer in optical art. Address: 6229 Cabrini Ln Seven Hills OH 44131-2848 Business E-Mail: bstanczak@gate.cia.edu.

**STANDARD, KENNETH G.,** lawyer; b. Sept. 4, 1936; AB, Harvard Coll., 1958, LLB, 1962; LLM, NYU, 1971. Former v.p. and sr. counsel products divsn. Bristol-Myers Co.; dir. Office Legal Svcs. N.Y.C. Sch. Sys., 1985—89; gen. counsel labor rels. Environ. and Benefits Plans ConEd, N.Y.C., 1989—2000; spl. counsel labor and employment practice group Morgan Lewis & Bockius LLP, 2000—04; ptnr. Epstein Becker & Green PC, 2004—; pres. N.Y. State Bar Assn., Albany, 2004—. Named one of 100 Most Powerful Minority Bus. Leaders in N.Y., N.Y. Bus., 2003. Mem.: Harvard Club (v.p. 1997—99, pres. 1999—2002). Office: Epstein Becker & Green PC 250 Pk Ave New York NY 10177 also: NY State Bar Assn One Elk St Albany NY 12207

**STANDBERRY, HERMAN LEE,** school system administrator, educational consultant; b. Oran, Mo., Feb. 22, 1945; s. Willie Standberry and Bettie Mae (Thompson) Standberry-Taylor; m. Barbara Irene Palmer, July 1, 1942; children: Donna, Debra, Nina, Miriam, Miranda, Gretchen, Charles, Mary, Dwayne, Helena, Regina, Lakesha. BS, So. Ill. U., 1968; MA, Newport U., 1981, LHD (hon.), 1990; EdD, Walden U., 1992; DMin, Am. Christian Coll. and Sem., 1992; MEd, Ind. Wesleyan U., 1997. Cert. supt., gen. adminstr., curriculum, tchr., sch. counselor; approved profl. devel. provider Ill. State Bd. Edn. and Ill. State Tchr. Cert. Bd. Tchr. Community H.S. Dist. 428, Blue Island, Ill., 1968-70; exec. dir., dep. dir. program planner, HeadStart dir. Kane County Coun. for Econ. Opportunity, Batavia, Ill., 1970—75; case mgr., youth supr., educator State of Ill., Dept. Pub. Aid., Dept. Corrections, Chgo., Joliet and St. Charles, Ill., 1975—85; adminstrv. asst. to prin. Bloom High Sch. Dist. 206, Chicago Heights, Ill., 1993—94; asst. prin. Rogers High Sch. Michigan City, Ind., 1994-95; prin. Mich. City (Ind.) Area Alternative H.S., 1993—2000; chmn. bd./CEO Dr. Herman Standberry and Assocs., 2000—; interim supt. LaPorte Cmty. Schs., asst. supt. personnel, asst. supt. curriculum-instruction; prof. curriculum instruction Indiana Wesleyn U., 1997—2005; supt. United Ednl. Cultural Acad., 2000, principal, 2000. Chmn. bd. dirs. Greater Chgo. Coun. of Religious Orgns., 1985-89; mem. George Bush's Rep. Presdl. Task Force, Washington, 1989; nominated mem. U.S. Rep. Senatorial Inner Cir., Washington, 1989; hon. chmn., Bus. Advisory Coun. Rep. Nat. Advisory Coun.; faculty advisor, mentor, Indiana Wesleyan U.; NCATE Accreditation, Indiana Wesleyan U., Valparaiso U. Author (curriculum) Business Law I & II, 1968, Career Counseling and Survival, 1978, Accelerated Learning, 1993, Recovery from Academic Deficiency, 2000, Pastoral Counseling and Organizational Compliance, 2005. Bd. dirs. United Way, Elgin, Ill, 1972, City of Elgin-Fremont Youth Orgn., 1971-72; host agy. rep. Dept. Human Svcs., Chgo., 1985-90; sustaining mem. Ill. Rep. Party, Springfield, 1989; host agy. Percy Julian High Sch., Chgo., 1989-90, 2000—, Ill. Dept. Pub. Aid, Chgo., 1987. Recipient NBC 5/Chgo. and AT&T Jefferson award; grantee Ill. Dept. Pub. Aid, 1984-87, hon. award Christian World Affairs Conf., 1985-86. Mem. Internat. Assn. Police and Community Rel. Officers, United Evangelistic Consulting Assn. (chmn. bd. dirs., pres. 1985-93, 2000-), Assn. Christian Schs. Internat. Administrator, 2005, Internat. Assn. Christian Sch. Bds., 2005, S Suburban Ministerial Conf., 2006. Avocation: hunting. Home: 803 E 193rd St Glenwood IL 60425-2011 Office: United Evangelistic Assn 1236 W 103rd St Chicago IL 60643-2361 Office Phone: 773-238-2707. Personal E-mail: drstandberry@yahoo.com.

**STANDIFORD, RONALD DAWSON,** minister, educator; b. Balt., July 2, 1949; s. Howard William and Rosalie Burton Standiford; m. Darby Shaver, Sept. 7, 1985; children: Leah Dawson, Emily Ashmore. BA in Polit. Sci., Am. U., 1971; MA in Religion, Westminster Sem., 1979, MDiv, 1980. Ordained minister Presbyn. Ch. Am., 1981. Law clk. Law Office Saunders M. Almond, Jr., Towson, Md., 1974—77; assoc. pastor Timonium (Md.) Presbyn. Ch., 1981—88; pastor Redeemer Presbyn. Ch., Kingsville, Md., 1988—. Bd. mem. Presbyn. Home Md., Towson, Md.; program com. Md. Hist. Soc., Baltimore, Md., 1989—92; adj. faculty Redeemer Classical Christian Sch., Kingsville, Md., 1996—, founder, 1996; pres. Beachmont Christian Camp, 1984—94. Co-author: Villages; Baltimore County, MD, 1994; exhibites include various local shows. Mem. campaign com. Md. Ho. Dels., 1994, 1998. Recipient award, Am. U., 1971. Achievements include first to founder, 1st K-12 classical christian school in Maryland. Avocations: gardening, racquetball, tennis. Home: Beachmont Farm 6415 Mt Vista Road Kingsville MD 21087 Office Phone: 410-592-9625. Personal E-mail: classicdadman@yahoo.com.

**STANDING BEAR, ZUGGUELGERES GALAFACH,** criminologist, educator, forensic specialist; b. Boston, Jan. 10, 1941; m. Nancy Lee Karlovic, July 13, 1978 (div. Aug. 1985); m. Virginia Anne Red Hawk, Mar. 22, 1988. BS, U. Nebr., 1971; MS in Forensic Sci., George Washington U., 1974; postgrad. cert. in forensic medicine, Armed Forces Inst. Pathology, 1974; MSEd, U. So. Calif., 1976; MPA, Jacksonville State U., 1981; PhD in Criminology, Fla. State U., 1986. Diplomate Am. Bd. Forensic Examiners, Am. Bd. Forensic Medicine, chmn. 2002-03; cert. coroner, Ga., 1988-92; cert. criminal justice instr., Calif., Ga. Criminal investigator U.S. Army, 1965; dist. comdr. 7th region U.S. Army Criminal Investigation Command, Seoul, 1974-77; course mgr. U.S. Army Mil. Police Sch., Ft. McClellan, Ala., 1978-81; ret. U.S. Army, 1981; instr. Fla. State U., Tallahassee, 1981-85; asst. prof. No. Ariz. U., Flagstaff, 1985-86; program coord., prof. Valdosta (Ga.) State U., 1986-95; assoc. prof. Colo. State U., Ft. Collins, 1995—2001, U Colo., 2001—; adminstr. The Flash and Thelma Meml. Hedgehog Rescue of N.Am., Inc., 1998—. V.p Bearhawk Cons. Group, Ft. Collins, 1986—; chair

Am. Bd. Forensic Examiners. Editor Jour. Contemporary Criminal Justice, 1992. Mem., task group coord. Com. for Sexual Assault Evidence Stds., ASTM, 1993— Com. Colo State U.; mem. leadership coun. Cmty. Policing Project, Valdosta, Ga., 1993-95; treas. and v.p. edn. and rsch. No. Colo. WOLF rescue, edn., and rsch. project, LaPorte, Colo., 1995—; mem. Nat. Am. lang. preservation com. Colo. State Univ. Decorated Bronze Star medal, Meritorious Svc. medal (with oak leaf cluster). Fellow Am. Acad. Forensic Scis. (gen. sec. 1987-88, gen. chmn. 1988-90, gen. program co-chair 1995-96, Gen. Sec. Meritorious Svc. award 1996), Am. Coll. Forensic Examiners, Internat. Assn. Forensic Nurses (disting. fellow, mem. exec. bd. dirs., cons. and permissions exec., chmn. ethics com.); mem. ASTM (co-coord. sexual assault evidence stds. task group), Am. Sociol. Assn., Acad. Polit. Sci., Am. Soc. Criminology, Acad. Criminal Justice Scis. (program com. 1996-97), So. Criminal Justice Assn., Am. Assn. of U. Profs., Harley Owners Group, Internat. Hedgehog Assn., (treas.). Haudenosaunee (Native Am.). Avocations: hedgehog and wolf behavior, traditional Native American religious counseling, motorcycling. Office: Forensic Health Sci Programs Beth-El Coll Nursing and Health Scis U Colo Colorado Springs CO 80918 Home: 514 Hopi Circle Divide CO 80814

**STANDISH, JOHN SPENCER,** textile manufacturing company executive; b. Albany, N.Y., Apr. 17, 1925; s. John Carver and Florence (Spencer) S.; m. Elaine Joan Ritchie, Oct. 20, 1962 (div. 1984); children: John Carver, Christine Louise; m. Patricia Hunter, Nov. 9, 1985. BS, MIT, 1945. Asst. to prodn. mgr. Forstmann Woolen Co., Passaic, NJ, 1945-52; various positions Albany Internat. Corp., 1952-72, v.p. 1972-74, exec. v.p., 1974-76, vice chmn., 1976-84, chmn., 1984-98, also bd. dirs., 1958-98, chmn. emeritus, 1998—. Bd. dirs. Albany chpt. ARC, 1966-92, chpt. chmn., 1971-74, bd. govs., Washington, 1980-86; bd. dirs. United Way Northeastern N.Y., Albany, 1980-97, pres., 1984-85; trustee Albany Med. Coll. and Ctr., 1984-93, Siena Coll., Loudonville, N.Y., 1987-2003; chmn. U. Albany Found, 1982-87, 89-92; pres. U. Albany Found., 1992-98. Sgt. U.S. Army, 1945-46. Mem.: Ft. Orange Club, Schuyler Meadows Country Club, John's Island Club (Fla.). Republican. Episcopalian. Avocations: bridge, tennis, golf. Home: 395 Llwyd's Ln Vero Beach FL 32963

**STANDISH, WILLIAM LLOYD,** judge; b. Pitts., Feb. 16, 1930; s. William Lloyd and Eleanor (McCargo) S.; m. Marguerite Oliver, June 12, 1963; children: Baird M., N. Graham, James H., Constance S. BA, Yale U., 1953; LLB, U. Va., 1956. Bar: Pa. 1957, U.S. Supreme Ct. 1967. Assoc. Reed, Smith, Shaw & McClay, Pitts., 1957-63; ptnr., 1963-80; judge Ct. Common Pleas Allegheny County (Pa.), 1980-87, U.S. Dist. Ct. (we. dist.) Pa., 1987—. Solicitor Edgeworth Borough Sch. Dist., 1963-66. Bd. dirs. Sewickley (Pa.) Cmty. Ctr., 1981-83, Staunton Farms Found., mem., 1984-2002, trustee, 1984-92; corporator Sewickley Cemetery, 1971-87; trustee Mary and Alexander Laughlin Children's Ctr., 1972-90, Leukemia Soc. Am., 1978-80, We. Pa. chpt., 1972-80, We. Pa. Sch. Deaf, 1983—, YMCA of Sewickley, 1996—; bd. dirs. Pitts. Theol. Sem., 2001—. Recipient Pres. award, Leukemia Soc. Am., 1980. Mem. ABA, Pa. Bar Assn., Allegheny County Bar Assn., Am. Judicature Soc., Acad. Trial Lawyers Allegheny County (treas. 1977-78, bd. dirs. 1979-80), Am. Inn of Ct. (Pitts. chpt. 1993—). Office: US Dist Ct 6170 US Post Office & Ct House 700 Grant St Pittsburgh PA 15219-1906 Office Phone: 412-208-7430. Business E-Mail: Judge_William_Standish@pawd.uscourts.gov.

**STANDLEY, JOHN T.,** food market executive; married; 2 children. BS in Acctg., Pepperdine U. Audit mgr. retail and fin. industry groups Arthur Andersen LLP, LA; v.p. fin. Food 4 Less Supermarkets, Inc., Compton, Calif., 1991—94; sr. v.p. admin. Smith's Food & Drug, Salt Lake City; CFO Smitty's Supervalu Inc., Phoenix; sr. v.p., CFO Ralphs Grocery Co., 1996—98, Fred Meyer, Inc., Portland, Oreg., 1998—99; exec. v.p., CFO Fleming Co. Inc., Oklahoma City, 1999, Rite Aid Corp., Camp Hill, Pa., 1999—2002, sr. exec. v.p., chief adminstrv. officer, 2002, CFO, 2003—05; CEO Pathmark Stores, Inc., 2005—. Office: Pathmark Stores Inc 200 Milik St Carteret NJ 07008*

**STANDRING, JAMES DOUGLAS,** real estate developer; b. Fresno, Calif., Dec. 2, 1951; s. James Robert Pusey and Jacquelin (Moore); m. Patricia Ann Standring; children: Craig Douglas, Ryan Scott, Melinda Jean, Kevin Paul. BS, Calif. State U., Fresno, 1975. Pres. Westland Industries, Inc., Portland, Oreg., 1976—; ptnr. Aloha Land and Cattle, Inc., Portland, 1982— Bd. dirs. Tualitin Valley Econ. Devel. Corp., Portland, 1988-95; co-founder, bd. dirs. People for Washington County Charities, Beaverton, Oreg., 1985-88; mem. Westside Econ. Alliance, 1000 Friends of Oreg.; mem. steering com. Oreg. Med. Laser Ctr., 1995—. Named Portland Metro. Builder of Yr., 1992, Oreg. Builder of Yr., 1992; named to Oreg. Housing Hall of Fame, 2000. Mem. Homebuilders Assn. Metro Portland (v.p. 1988-90, pres. 1990-91), Oreg. Bldg. Industry Assn. (v.p. 1993-96, pres. 1996-97), Nat. Assn. Homebuilders, BUILD-PAC (Oreg. trustee 1992-2002, exec. com. 1994-2000). Republican. Episcopalian. Home: Oregon Yacht Club Slip F Portland OR 97202 Office: Westland 12670 SW 68th Ave Ste 400 Portland OR 97223-8370 Office Phone: 503-639-3104, Personal E-mail: jswestland@aol.com.

**STANFIELD, BRENT B.,** federal agency administrator; BS in Biol. Sciences, U. Calif., Irvine, 1973; PhD in Neurobiology, Washington U., St. Louis, 1978. Post-doctoral trainee Washington U., St. Louis, Salk Inst. for Biol. Studies, mem. faculty Devel. Neurobiology Lab., 1981; dir. unit on devel. neuroanatomy Lab. Neurophysiology NIMH, 1987—96, acting dep. dir. Divsn. Intramural Rsch., 1996—97, dir. Office Sci. Policy and Program Planning, 1998—2000; dep. dir. Ctr. Sci. Rev., NIH, 2000—03, acting dir., 2003—05; dir. Divsn. Extramural Activities Nat. Inst. Diabetes and Digestive and Kidney Diseases, NIH, 2005—. Asst. adj. prof. dept. neurosciences U. Calif. Sch. Medicine, San Diego, 1982. Office: Nat Inst Diabetes and Digestive and Kidney Diseases 2 Democracy Plz Rm 715 6707 Democracy Blvd Bethesda MD 20892 Office Phone: 301-594-8843. Office Fax: 301-480-3965. E-mail: stanfbr@niddk.nih.gov.*

**STANFIELD, JEFFREY L.,** lawyer; b. Suffolk, Va. BA, Old Dominion Univ., 1971; JD, Vanderbilt Univ., Nashville, 1974. Bar: Tenn. 1974, DC 1979. Asst. to gen. counsel Fed. Energy Adminstrn., Washington, 1977; energy policy and planning staff Exec. Office of Pres., Washington, 1977; asst. to sec. US Dept. of Energy, Washington, 1977—79, assoc. under-sec., 1979—80; founding and mng. ptnr. Cutler & Stanfield LLP (merged with Akin Gump), Washington, 1988—2000; ptnr., chair project and infrastructure devel. dept. and mem. mgmt. com. Akin Gump Strauss Hauer & Feld LLP, Washington, 2000—. Mem. ABA, Tenn. Bar Assn., DC Bar Assn. Office: Akin Gump Strauss Hauer & Feld LLP Robert S Strauss Bldg 1333 New Hampshire Ave NW Washington DC 20036-1564 Office Phone: 202-887-4250. Office Fax: 202-955-7716. Business E-Mail: jstanfield@akingump.com.

**STANFILL, DENNIS CAROTHERS,** corporate financial executive; b. Centerville, Tenn., Apr. 1, 1927; s. Sam Broome and Hattie (Carothers) S.; m. Therese Olivieri, June 29, 1951; children: Francesca, Sara, Dennis Carothers. BS, U.S. Naval Acad., 1949; MA (Rhodes scholar), Oxford U., 1953; LHD (hon.), U. S. C. Corporate finance specialist Lehman Bros., N.Y.C., 1959-65; v.p. finance Times Mirror Co., Los Angeles, 1965-69; exec. v.p. 20th Century-Fox Film Corp., 1969-71, pres., 1971, chmn. bd., chief exec. officer, 1971-81; pres. Stanfill, Bowen & Co., 1981-90; chmn. bd. dirs., chief exec. officer AME, Inc., 1990-91; co-chmn., co-CEO Metro-Goldwyn-Mayer, Inc., 1992-93; sr. advisor Credit Lyonnais, 1993-95; pres. Dennis Stanfill Co., 1995—. Trustee Calif. Inst. Tech.; bd. dirs. Weingart Found., 1987-2002. Served to lt. USN, 1949-59; politico-mil. policy div. Office Chief Naval Ops., 1956-59.

**STANFORD, HENRY KING,** college president; b. Atlanta, Apr. 22, 1916; s. Henry King and Annie Belle (Callaway) S.; m. Laurie Ruth King, Sept. 19, 1936; children: Henry, Lowry, Rhoda, Peyton. AB, Emory U., 1936, MA, 1940, LLD, 1961; postgrad., U. Heidelberg, Germany, 1936—37; MS in

Govt. Mgmt., U. Denver, 1943, LLD, 1962; PhD, NYU, 1949; DCL, Jacksonville U., Fla., 1963; LLD, Loyola U., New Orleans, 1968, U. Akron, Kyung Hee U., Seoul, Korea, 1968, Rollins Coll., 1977, Barry Coll., 1979; DHL, U. Tampa, 1969; DLitt, U. R.I., 1970, U. Chile, Santiago, 1980; D in Higher Edn., U. Miami, 1981; DHL, Birmingham-So. Coll., 1987. Instr. Emory U., 1937-40; asst. prof. Ga. State. Coll. Tech., 1940-41; instr. NYU, 1943-46; prof. pub. administrn., also dir. sch. pub. administrn. U. Denver, 1946-48; pres. Ga. Southwestern Coll., Americus, 1948-50; dir. U. Ctr. in Ga., 1950-52; asst. chancellor U. Sys. of Ga., 1952-53; pres. Ga. State Coll. for Women, Milledgeville, 1953-56; chief of party NYU-Internat. Cooperation Adminstrn. Contract, Ankara, Turkey, 1956-57; pres. Birmingham-So. Coll., 1957-62, U. Miami, Fla., 1962-81, pres. emeritus, 1981—; interim pres. U. Ga., 1986-87, pres. emeritus, 1987—. Rsch. asst. Tax Found., N.Y.C., 1943-44; staff N.A.M. com. exec., 1944-46; chmn. Fed. Res. Bank Atlanta, 1969, 72. Trustee Knight Found., 1982-97; vice chmn. Invest-in-Am., 1984-86, chmn. 1986-87; pres. Dade County Cmty. Rels. Bd., 1969-71; bd. visitors Air U., Maxwell AFB, Ala., 1963-66; trustee Caribbean Resources Devel. Found., 1978-85, pres., 1978-83, chmn., 1983-84; chmn. Jimmy Carter Nat. Site Adv. Commn., 1990-2001. Decorated Star of Africa medal Liberia, 1971; officer Order of Merit Fed. Republic of Germany, 1972; recipient Eleanor Roosevelt-Israel Humanitarian award, 1965, Outstanding Civilian Svc. award U.S. Army, 1966, Silver Medallion Fla. Region NCCJ, 1968, Ga. Region, 1987, Disting. Svc. award Ga. Coll., 1979, hon. alumnus, 1996, C.H.I.E.F. award Ind. Colls. and Univs. Fla., 1983, Sibley award Ga. Mil. Coll., 1991, Emory medal, 1991, Adrian Dominican Ednl. Leadership award Barry U., 1991, Atlanta Boys' High Alumnus award, 1992, James Blair Humanitarian award Americus, 1993, Westmeyer award pub. svc. NYU, 1993. Mem. So. Assn. Colls. and Schs. (chmn. commn. colls. 1960-62, pres. 1972-73), Nat. Assn. Ind. Colls. and Univs. (dir. 1976-80), Assn. Caribbean Univs. and Rsch. Insts. (v.p. 1965-79), Golden Key Honor Soc. (bd. dirs. 1982-91), Internat. Assn. Univ. Pres. (exec. com. 1977-81), Delta Phi Alpha, Phi Beta Kappa, Omicron Delta Kappa, Phi Sigma Iota, Alpha Kappa Psi, Phi Mu Alpha, Phi Kappa Phi, Rotary Club (pres. Americus club 1984-85). Methodist. Office: PO Box 1065 Americus GA 31709-1065 E-mail: hksumuga@bellsouth.net. *The greatest literary influence on my life has been Goethe's Faust, Part I. Reading it in the original German as a college student, I was struck immediately with the demands Faust made of himself in concluding the contract with Mephistopheles: he would lose his soul if he ever chose a "bed of ease," succumbed to flattery, opted for pleasure alone, or said to any one moment, "Linger awhile; you are so nice!" In other words, whenever he ceased striving, he was lost.*

**STANFORD, (FRANCES) JANE HERRING,** management consultant, educator, writer; b. Lockhart, Tex., Dec. 17, 1939; d. John William and Frances Argyra (Cheatham) Jr.; m. Rube V. Stanford; children: Steven Scott, Lisa Ann. BS, Texas A&M U., Kingsville; MS in Counseling, Texas A&M U., Corpus Christi; MBA, Texas A&M U., Kingsville; PhD in Orgn. Theory and Strategic Mgmt., U. North Tex. Tchg. fellow U. North Tex., Denton; prof. bus. policy and strategic mgmt., pres. faculty senate Texas A&M U., Kingsville, 1990—, grad. rsch. advisor, MBA/MPA program, Coll. Bus., 1992-98, 2004—, asst. v.p. Acad. Affairs, 1997—99, ret., 1999, vis. assoc. prof. mgmt. Corpus Christi, Tex., 2000—04, Kingsville, 2004—, chair dept. mgmt. and mktg. Coll. Bus., 1993—97, current mem. grad. faculty, Coll. Bus. grad. rsch. advisor; mgmt. cons. Strategic Mgmt. Solutions, Inc., 1999—. Chair univ. assessment, budgeting and planning com. Tex. A&M U., 1997—98; internat. lectr. strategic mgmt. within internat. context, Colombia, Argentina; workshop leader and participant in acad. issues. Author: Building Competitiveness: U.S. Expatriate Management Strategies in Mexico, 1995; contbr. articles to profl. jours. and conf. procs. Apptd. to water resources adv. com. City of Corpus Christi, 2003—. Named Leadership Corpus Christi Class of XXX, 2001—02; fellow Sys. Chancellor's fellow in leadership in higher edn. program, Tex. A&M U., 1997. Mem.: Univ. Grad. Faculty, Soc. Advancement Mgmt., Acad. Mgmt., Inst. Mgmt. Cons., Strategic Mgmt. Soc., Delta Signa Pi, Kappa Delta Pi (life). Presbyterian. Avocations: book collecting, photography, travel. Home: 13526 Carlos Fifth Ct Corpus Christi TX 78418 Office: 212 Coll Bus Admin TAMUK Kingsville TX 78363 Office Phone: 361-593-3939. E-mail: jhstanford@aol.com.

**STANFORD, JOSEPH STEPHEN,** diplomat, lawyer, educator; b. Montreal, Que., Can., May 7, 1934; s. Walter Albert and Geraldine (O'Loghlin) S.; m. Agnes Mabelle Walker, Nov. 16, 1957; children: Kevin, Karen, Michael. BA, U. Montreal, 1953; LLB, U. Alta., Edmonton, Can., 1956. Bar: Alta. 1957; called to Queen's Counsel 1984. Mem. Greenan, Cooney & Stanford, Calgary, Alta., Canada, 1957-60; joined Fgn. Svc., Dept. External Affairs, Govt. of Can., 1960; amb. to Israel Tel Aviv, 1979-82; also Can. high commr. to Cyprus; asst. dep. min. for Africa and Mid. East Dept. External Affairs, Ottawa, Ont., 1983-85, asst. dep. min. for Europe, 1985-87, assoc. undersec. of state for external affairs, 1987-88; dep. solicitor gen. Govt. of Can., Ottawa, 1988-93; ret., 1994; sr fellow, conflict mgr. Canadian Center Mgmt. Devel., Ottawa, 1993-96; assoc., bd. dirs. Conflict Mgmt. Group, Cambridge, Mass., 1994—97, 2002—04, chmn. bd. dirs., 1997-99. Cons. Conflict Mgmt. Group, Cambridge, Mass., 1994—97. Contbr. articles on internat. law, fgn. investment and conflict resolution to profl. jours. Roman Catholic. Avocations: canoeing, skiing. Home: 58 Amberwood Cres Ottawa ON Canada K2E 7C3 Office Phone: 613-226-1328. E-mail: joseph.stanford066@sympatico.ca.

**STANFORD, KATHLEEN THERESA,** secondary school educator; b. Belize City, Belize, Sept. 28, 1933; d. Frederick Gill and Ila Mae (Cherrington) Hyde; m. Herman Emanuel Stanford., Oct. 3, 1970 (dec. Feb., 1989). Student (summer), S. We. La. U., Lafayette, 1958; BA Seton Hill Coll., 1962; student (summer), Xavier U., New Orleans, 1956, 68; postgrad., Southern U. and A&M Coll., 1962, 67, Adelphi U., 1988, C.W. Post, N.Y., 1988. Cert. sci. tchr., La. (life). Tchr. Mem. Sisters of Holy Family Order, various cities, U.S. & Belize, 1953-69; sci. tchr., moderator Sisters of Holy Family, Grand Coteau, La., 1967-68, Lafayette, La., 1968-70; laicized, 1970; sci. tchr., sponsor of sci. fair N.Y.C. Bd. of Edn., Bklyn., 1981—. Sci. coord. La. Sci. Acad., Lafayette, 1968-70; mem. U.F.T. /IHS sci. com., N.Y.C., 1984-85. Contbr. poetry to Poetry Mags., 1974—. Hon. mem. Pres. Clinton's 2d Term Com., Washington, 1997; sci. sponsor Ford Future Scientists of Am., 1968, Dist. Sci. Fair, Bklyn., 1984; sec. Belize Parkfest of N.Y., Inc., 1990-92 Recipient Commendation for pupils 20th Internat. Sci. Fair, 1969, poetry awards Am. Poetry Assn., 1989, 90, cert. for leadership, Dem. Nat. Com., Washington, 1997. Mem. Belize Cosmopolitan Benevolent Assn. (v.p.). Democrat. Avocations: poetry, photography, bird watching, swimming, walking, singing.

**STANG, ARNOLD,** actor, writer, film director; b. N.Y.C., Sept. 28, 1928; s. Harold Louis and Anna (Chest) S.; m. JoAnne Taggart, Sept. 21, 1949; children: David Donald, Deborah Jane Stang-Healy. Ind. actor, dir., writer, N.Y.C., 1936—. Actor: (Broadway prodns.) Front Page, A Funny Thing Happened On the Way to the Forum, Wallflower, All in Favor, (TV shows) Bonanza, Ed Sullivan Show, McHale's Navy, Bewitched, Milton Berle Show, Jack Benny Show, Jackie Gleason Show, Top Cat, Emergency, Robert Klein Show, Playhouse 90, Frank Sinatra Spls., Bob Hope Spls., What's My Line, Bill Cosby Show, Tales From The Dark Side, numerous others, (stock theatrical prodns.) Don't Drink the Water, Death Knocks, Charley's Aunt, Finian's Rainbow, Three Men on a Horse, The Gazebo, Wish You Were Here, Pajama Game, Let 'Em Eat Cake, Anything Goes, Luv, Tobacco Road, Play It Again, Sam, Annie Get Your Gun, (starring film roles) Double for Della, Arnold the Benedict, Honorable Myrtle, The Expectant Father, Dondi, The Wonderful World of the Brothers Grimm, The Aristocats, Hello Down There, Alakazam the Great, The Man With the Golden Arm, The Cottonwood, Hercules in New York, Skidoo, My Sister Eileen, Seven Days Leave, Let's Go Steady, It's A Mad, Mad, Mad World, Dennis the Menace, numerous featured roles; rec. artist numerous albums including Winnie & Baby Pooh, Winnie the Pooh, Peter and the Wolf, Arnold Stang Meets Gus Edwards, Beezy the Sneezy Bee, The Hippy Hippo, Chester the Chimp, Further Adventures of Harry the Horse. Mem. Screen Actors Guild, Acad. Motion Picture Arts and Scis., Actors Equity Assn., AFTRA. Clubs: Players (N.Y.C.). Avocations: gardening, poetry, carpentry, social work. Office: 257 Park Ave S 9th Fl New York NY 10010

**STANG, PETER JOHN,** organic chemist; b. Nürnberg, Germany, Nov. 17, 1941; came to U.S., 1956; s. John Stang and Margaret Stang Pollman; m. Christine Schirmer, 1969; children: Antonia, Alexandra. BA, DePaul U., Chgo., 1963; PhD, U. Calif., Berkeley, 1966; degree (hon.), Moscow State Lomonossov U., 1992, Russian Acad. Scis., 1992. Instr. Princeton (N.J.) U., 1967-68; from asst. to assoc. prof. U. Utah, Salt Lake City, 1969-79, prof., 1979-92, Disting. prof. chemistry, 1992—. Co-author: Organic Spectroscopy, 1971; author: (with others) Vinyl Cations, 1979; editor: (with F. Diederich) Modern Acetylene Chemistry, 1995, Metal Catalyzed Cross Coupling Reactions, 1998, (with Z. Rappaport) Dicoordinated Carbocations, 1997; editor-in-chief Jour. Organic Chemistry, 2000-01; contbr. numerous articles to sci. publs. Recipient Humboldt-Forschungspreis, 1977; JSPS fellow, 1985; Fulbright-Hays sr. scholar, 1988. Fellow AAAS; mem. NAS, Am. Acad. Arts and Scis., Am. Chem. Soc. (assoc. editor jour. 1982-99, editor 2002-), Chinese Acad. Scis. (fgn. mem.). Office: U Utah Dept Chemistry 315 South 1400 East Salt Lake City UT 84112-0850 Office Phone: 801-581-8329. E-mail: stang@chemistry.utah.edu.

**STANG, ROLF KRISTIAN,** vocalist, educator, actor, advertising executive, writer; b. Rockford, Ill., Sept. 19, 1939; s. Trygve Ingvald and Kirsten (Anfinsen-Kristiansen) S. BA, Augustana Coll., 1961; MA, Columbia U., 1963; performance/repertoire cert., opera div., Musikhochschule, Hamburg, Germany, 1964. Vocal soloist Christoph-Weber-Barock Ensemble, Hamburg, 1965-67; German and music faculty Coll. of White Plains, N.Y., 1968-73; sec. Internat. Percy Grainger Soc., White Plains, N.Y., 1974-79, pres., 1979—. Music critic Norway Times, NYC, 1970—; advt. exec. The Frank Vos Co AS/VP, 1973-83; lectr., recital Songs of Frederick Delius, Cambridge U., 1984—; multimedia lectr. on career of Wagnerian singer Kirsten Flagstad, 1995—; lectr. on English composer Frederick Delius, 1966—. Translator Songs of Grieg, Collected Works of Grieg, 1993; composer (for solo voice, chorus and orchestra) Backward Tracings, 1974; (for soprano/15 stringed instruments) Train Window Thoughts; (for chorus/6 instruments) Hymns in Praise of Night/Nietzschean Nocturnes; Lied/Romanse Art Song and opera rep. (Am., English, German, Norwegian, Swedish) 1963—; concert vocalist numerous states and countries, 1963—; author, actor touring with one-man play on Norwegian composer Edvard Grieg, US, Norway, Eng., 1993—; Millennium characterization of Viking-age voyager Icelander Leif Eriksson, 2000—; touring as Danish author Hans Christian Andersen, 1994—, as Askeladden telling Norwegian fairytales and singing traditional songs, 1995—. Vol. Cath. Ctr. for Deaf, N.Y.C., 1975-79, Children to the Beach prog., N.Y.C., 1978-83, Reaching Out to the Homeless, N.Y.C., 1988—. Decorated knight (Norway), St. Olav medal King Harald V of Norway, 1997; named to Scandinavian-Am. Hall of Fame, 1998; recipient Leif Eriksson citation, 2000. Mem. SAG, Am. Choral Dirs. Assn. (life), Nordmanns Forbundet/Norsemen's Fedn. (hon., life), Delius Assn. of Fla. (life), Delius Soc. of Great Britain, Sons of Norway Internat., Delius Soc. of Phila. (life), Am.-Scandinavian Soc. of N.Y., Soc. for Advancement of Scandinavian Studies (life), Edvard Grieg Soc. Great Britain (hon., life). Lutheran. Avocations: furniture making, carpentry, gardening, promoting Nordic culture and music. Home: The Monks Cell 29 W 65th St New York NY 10023-6630 E-mail: rolf_k_stang@hotmail.com.

**STANGE, JAMES HENRY,** architect; b. Davenport, Iowa, May 25, 1930; s. Henry Claus and Norma (Ballhorn) S.; m. Mary Suanne Peterson, Dec. 12, 1954; children: Wade Weston, Drew Dayton, Grant Owen. BArch, Iowa State U., 1954. Registered architect, Iowa, Nebr., Kans., Mo., Okla. Designer Davis & Wilson, Lincoln, Nebr., 1954-62, v.p., 1962-68; v.p., sec. Davis, Fenton, Stange, Darling, Lincoln, Nebr., 1977-92, pres., 1976—93, chmn., 1978—94. Mem. State Bd. Examiners for Engrs. and Architects, 1989-92, chmn. region V NCARB, 1991. Prin. works include Dorsey Labs., 1960, East H.S., Lincoln, 1966, Lincoln Gen. Hosp., 1967, Lincoln Airport Terminal, Sq. D Mfg. Plant, Lincoln, Bryan Meml. Hosp. (masterplans and additions), 1970, 80, 90, Bryan Ambulatory Care Ctr. Med. Office Bldg., Same Day Surgery Conf. Ctr., Parking Garage, 1993-95, Nebr. Wesleyan Theatre, Lincoln, Hasting (Nebr.) YMCA, various structures U. Nebr., Lincoln, ctr. and br. offices Am. Charter Fed. Savs. & Loan, S.E. H.S. (addition), 1984, U. Nebr. Animal Sci. Bldg., 1987, Beadle Ctr., UNL, 1991, Carriage Park Parking Garage, 1995. V.p. Nebr. Jazz Orch., 1995, 2000—, pres., 1997, Nebr. Art Assn., 1996—99; deacon 1st Presbyn. Ch., 1960, chmn. bd. trustees, 1968—90, elder, 1972—87, 1997—99, chmn. property com., 1998—2000, found. bd. trustees, 2005—; bd. dirs. Capitol Assn. Retarded Citizens, 1968—72, 1994—, pres., 1970; chmn. United Way Campaign, 1986, chmn. bd., 1988; chmn. endowment com. Bryan Hosp. Found., 1988—90; bd. dirs. Delta Dental, 1987—92, Downtown Lincoln Assn., 1985—94, mem. steering com., 1989; mem. mayor's com. Study Downtown Redevel., 1989, pub. bldg. commn., masterplan rev. com., 1994; pres. Lincoln Ctr. Assn., 1979. Recipient Honor award Conf. on Religious Architecture-First Plymouth Ch. Addition, 1969, also numerous state and nat. awards from archtl. orgns.; inducted into Hall of Fame, Iowa H.S. Athletic Assn., 2001. Mem. AIA (Nebr. bd. dirs. 1964-65, treas. 1965, sec. 1966, v.p. 1967, pres. Nebr. 1968, mem. com. on architecture for health 1980-94, Regional Design award 1976, 88, 96), Am. Assn. Health Planners, Interfaith Forum on Religion, Art, Architecture, Lincoln C. of C. (bd. dirs. 1982), Exec. Club (pres. 1972), Crucible Club, 12 Club, Hillcrest Country Club (pres. 1977), Lincoln U. Club (sec. 1992, bd. dirs. 1991-97, pres. 1995, 96, teammates mentor 1990—). Avocations: travel, photography, golf. Home: 3545 Calvert St Lincoln NE 68506-5744 Office: Davis Design 211 N 14th St Lincoln NE 68508-1616 Personal E-mail: jh3545@aol.com.

**STANGE, SHARON (SHERRI),** science educator; d. Edwin and Thelma Lowry; life intnr. Donald Domenigoni; children: Brian, Karla Sluis. AA, Mt. San Jacinto Coll., 1972—77; BSc, U. of Calif., 1978—81; M, LaVerne U., 1995—96, Teaching Credential Calif. Strn. U., San Bernardino, 1982. Tchg. asst. Kiddie Korners Preschool, Hemet, Calif., 1972—74; biology lab asst. Mt. San Jacinto Coll., San Jacinto, Calif., 1973—82; sci. tchr. San Jacinto Unified Sch. Dist., Calif., 1982—; sub. tchr. Hemet Unified Sch. Dist., Calif., 1979—82; environ. sci. tchr. Mt. San Jacinto Coll., 1989—90. Mentor tchr. San Jacinto Unified Sch. Dist., 1998—, green schools coord., 2004—; profl. affairs/scholarship chair Delta Kappa Gamma/Gamma Theta chpt., 1999—; scholarship chair Gene Lombard Meml. Scholarship, 2001—; sci. club advisor Monte Vista and North Mountain Mid. Sch., San Jacinto, 1982—98; cheerleading advisor Monte Vista Mid. Sch., San Jacinto, 1984—92; sci. fair coord. Monte Vista Mid. Sch./North Mountain Mid. Sch., San Jacinto, 1982—2001; sci. dept. chair Monte Vista and North Mountain Mid. Sch., San Jacinto, 1982—. Co-founder Valley Youth Task Force, Hemet/San Jacinto, Calif., 1991—93; leader Neighborhood Watch, Hemet/San Jacinto, 1991—98; mem. PTA, Hemet/San Jacinto, 1973—2005, Friends of the No. San Jacinto Valley, 1995—2005. Recipient Calif. Environ. Edn. award, State of Calif., 1995, Inland Empire Environ. Educator of the Yr., Calif. Environ. Edn. Coll., 1976, Environ. Edn. award, Nat. Audubon Soc., 1991, We Honor Ours award, Calif. Teachers Assn., 1992, 1994; Audubon Naturalist grant, Hemet Valley Women's Club, 1995. Mem.: NSTA, San Jacinto Teachers Assn./CTA/NEA (pres., v.p., site rep, San Gorgonia coun. rep 1983—2005), Mt. San Jacinto Coll. Alumni Assn. (life; v.p.), Living Desert Assn., Nat. Audubon Soc./San Bernardino Valley chpt. (v.p./edn. chair/idyllwild christmas bird count compiler 1980—2005). Avocations: fishing, camping, travel, birdwatching. Office: North Mountain Middle Sch 1202 E 7th St San Jacinto CA 92583 Office Phone: 951-487-7797.

**STANGER, ILA,** editor-in-chief; b. NYC; d. Jack Simon and Shirley Ruth (Nadelson) S. BA, Bklyn. Coll., 1961. Feature and creative editor Harpers Bazaar, N.Y.C., 1969-75; exec. editor Travel and Leisure mag., N.Y.C., 1975-85; editor in chief Food and Wine Mag., N.Y.C., 1985-89, Travel and Leisure mag., N.Y.C., 1990-93; mng. editor More mag., N.Y.C., 1999—. Writer on arts, features and travel. Mem. Am. Soc. Mag. Editors Office: More Magazine 375 Lexington New York NY 10017 Business E-Mail: ila.stanger@meredith.com.

**STANGER, JOHN GOODMAN,** literature and language professor, archivist; b. Chgo., Mar. 16, 1940; s. Julius John and Rosamond Fixmer Stanger; m. Carol Jean Lenling, June 27, 1965; children: John, Jeanne, Jennifer. BA, Ill. Coll., Jacksonville, 1961; Cert., Atlanta Law Coll., 1964; MA, Concordia U., River Forest, Ill., 1967. Cert. tchr. grades 13-14 Ill. Tchr. English and history Sch. Dist. 89, Maywood, Ill., 1966—2000; instr. English Triton Coll., River Grove, 1968—77; instr. reading Concodia U., River Forest, 1977—79, instr. English, 1999, Morton Coll., Cicero, 2000—01, Wright Coll., Chgo., 2000—01; prof. English Elmhurst Coll., 2001—. Hisory fair sponsor Melrose Pk. Sch., Ill., 1990—2000, supr. student tchrs. history, 1990—97, sponsor sch. newspaper, 1975—91. Editor: English: Argumentation, 2003, English Composition I, 2004, Prominent Pen Pals, 2005, English, 2006. Mem. econ. com. Village of Oak Park, Ill., 1983; archivist Grace Luth. Ch., River Forest, 2005—; mem. reunion planning com. Oak Park-River Forest H.S., 2005—. Capt. Ill. Nat. Guard, 1964—65. Mem.: ROMEOS, Soc. Am. Archivists, Kappa Delta Pi, Alpha Phi Sigma, Pi Gamma Mu, Phi Alpha Theta. Republican. Lutheran. Avocations: reading, sports, writing. Office: Elmhurst Coll 190 Prospect Ave Elmhurst IL 60126-3296 Home: 727 Gunderson Ave Oak Park IL 60304 Office Phone: 630-617-3475. Business E-Mail: stangerj@elmhurst.edu.

**STANGL, PETER E.,** transportation executive; BA, MA, Univ. Conn. With Met. Transp. Authority, NY, 1980—95; pres. Metro North Railroad, NY, 1983—91; chmn., CEO Met. Transp. Authority, NY, 1991—95; pres. Bombardier Transit Corp., 1995—2000, Bombardier Transp. US, 2000—03; non-exec. chmn. Laidlaw Internat., Naperville, Ill., 2003—. Past vice chmn. Am. Public Transit Assn. Office: Laidlaw International Ste 400 55 Shuman Blvd Naperville IL 60563*

**STANGROOM, TOM M.,** non-profit organization administrator; BS in bus. adminstrn./mgmt. info. systems, George Mason U., 1982. V.p., chief info. officer Nat. Rural Electric Coop. Assn. (NRECA). Named one of Premier 100 IT Leaders, Computerworld, 2005. Office: Nat Rural Electric Coop Assn 4301 Wilson Blvd Arlington VA 22203 Office Phone: 703-907-5500.*

**STANHAUS, JAMES STEVEN,** lawyer; b. Evergreen Park, Ill., Oct. 22, 1945; s. Wilfrid Xavier and Mary (Komanecky) S.; m. Naomi Evelyn Miller, June 27, 1971; 1 child, Heather. AB magna cum laude, Georgetown U., 1966; JD magna cum laude, Harvard U., 1970. Bar: Ill. 1970, U.S. Dist. Ct. (no. dist.) Ill. 1970. Assoc. Mayer, Brown, Rowe & Maw LLP, Chgo., 1971-76, ptnr., 1977—2005, sr. counsel, 2005—. Mem. ABA, Ill. Bar Assn., Chgo. Bar Assn., Chgo. Coun. Lawyers, Chgo. Estate Planning Coun., Met. Club, Riverpark Club (Chgo.), Phi Beta Kappa. Avocations: computers, tennis, racquetball. Office: Mayer Brown Rowe & Maw LLP 71 S Wacker Dr Ste 3300 Chicago IL 60606-4639 Office Phone: 312-701-7135. Business E-Mail: jstanhaus@mayerbrownrowe.com.

**STANISH, CHARLES,** anthropologist, educator; BA, Pa. State U., 1979; AM, U. Chgo., 1983, PhD, 1985. Postdoctoral rsch. fellow, vis. asst. prof. dept. anthropology U. Ill., Chgo., 1986—87; asst. curator dept. anthropology Field Mus. Natural Hist., 1988—92, assoc. curator, 1993—97; assoc. prof. dept. anthropology UCLA, 1998—2000, prof., 2001—; interim dir. Cotsen Inst. Archaeology, 2001—03, dir. Cotsen Inst. Archaeology, 2003—; rsch. assoc. dept. anthropology LA County Mus. Natural Hist., 2001—. Adj. assoc. prof. grad. coll. dept. anthropology U. Ill., Chgo., 1988—97; adj. prof. dept. anthropology U. Chgo., 1990—97; vice chair dept. anthropology Field Mus. Natural Hist., 1993—95, chair, 1995—97. Contbr. articles to profl. jours., chapters to books; co-editor: Ecology, Settlement and Hist. in the Osmore Drainage, 1989, Archaeol. Rsch. on the Islands of the Sun and Moon, Lake Titicaca Bolivia: Final Results from the Proyecto Tiksi Kjarka, 2004; author: Ancient Andean Polit. Economy, 1992, Ancient Titicaca: The Evolution of Complex Soc. in Southern Peru and Northern Bolivia, 2003; co-author: Archaeol. Rsch. at the Site of Tumatumani Juli, Peru, 1994, Archaeol. Survey in the Juli-Desaguadero Area, Lake Titicaca Basin, Peru, 1997, Ritual and Pilgrimage in the Ancient Andes, The Islands of the Sun and Moon, 2001; mem. editl. bd.: Latin Am. Antiquity, 1998—. Fellow: Am. Acad. Arts & Scis. Office: Dept Anthropology UCLA 341 Haines Hall Los Angeles CA 90095-7553 E-mail: stanish@anthro.ucla.edu.*

**STANISLAO, JOSEPH,** engineering educator, consultant; b. Manchester, Conn., Nov. 21, 1928; s. Eduardo and Rose (Zaccaro) S.; m. Bettie Chloe Carter, Sept. 6, 1960. BS, Tex. Tech. U., 1957; MS, Pa. State U., 1959; Eng.ScD, Columbia U., 1970. Registered profl. engr., Mass., Mont. Asst. engr. Naval Ordnance Research, University Park, Pa., 1958-59; asst. prof. N.C. State U., Raleigh, 1959-61; dir. research Darlington Fabrics Corp., Pawtucket, RI, 1961-62; from asst. prof. to prof. U. R.I., Kingston, 1962-71; prof., chmn. dept. Cleve. State U., 1971-75; prof., dean N.D. State U., Fargo, 1975-94, acting v.p. agrl. affairs 1983-85, asst. to pres., 1983—, dir. Engring. Computer Ctr., 1984—, prof. emeritus indsl. engring. and mgmt. Fargo, 1994—; pres. XOX Corp., 1984-90; chmn. bd., chief exec. officer ATSCO, 1989-94, chief engr., 1993—; prof. emeritus N.D. State U., 1994. Adj. prof. Mont. State U., 1994—, dir. indsl. and mgmt. engring. program, 1996—, mfg. rsch., sponsored by Nat. Sci. Found. 1997—; pres., CEO J&B Inc., 1996—2006; v.p., co-owner, bd. dirs. D.T.&J. Inc., Fargo, N.D., 1999-2006, London, 1999—; v.p. engring. Roll-A-Ramp, Rolla-A-Latter, and Rolla-A-conveyor, 2000-05; cons. to healthcare sys., 1999-2005. Contbr. chpts. to books, articles to profl. jours.; inventor Handicap Loading Dock, 2005. Served to sgt. USMC, 1948-51. Recipient Sigma Xi award, 1968; Order of the Iron Ring award N.D. State U., 1972, Econ. Devel. award, 1991; USAF recognition award, 1979, ROTC appreciation award, 1982. Mem. Am. Inst. Indsl. Engrs. (sr.; v.p. 1964-65), ASME, Am. Soc. Engring. Edn. (campus coord. 1979-81), Acad. Indsl. Engrs. Tex. Tech U., Lions, Elks, Am. Legion, Phi Kappa Phi, Tau Beta Pi (advisor 1978-79). Roman Catholic. Achievements include patents for pump apparatus, jump fluid housing, roll-conveyer, and handicap loading dock; roll-a-ramp. Home: 8 Park Plaza Dr Bozeman MT 59715-9343 Business E-Mail: jstanslo@ie.montana.edu.

**STANKE, JACLYN,** history professor; d. Gerald John Stanke and Dolores M. Lasecke. BA in Polit. Sci. summa cum laude, Wash. State U., 1988, BA in Fgn. Langs. and Lits. summa cum laude, 1988; MA in History, Emory U., 1994, PhD in Am. History, 2001. Tchg. asst. Emory U., Atlanta, 1992, tchg. assoc., 1994, 1997; adj. lectr. history Carroll Coll., Waukesha, Wis., 1998—99; instr. history Campbell U., Bluies Creek, NC, 1999—2001, asst. prof. history, 2001—. Advanced placement reader in U.S. history Ednl. Testing Svcs., 2003—; social studies outside content reviewer State N.C. Social Studies Assessment Test in U.S. History, N.C. Dept. Pub. Instrn., 2003—; presenter in field. Contbr. book reviews to publs. Rsch./Travel grantee, Inst. Internat. Edn., 1994, English Speaking Union US-Atlanta Br., 1994, 1995, Univ. Summer Rsch. grantee, Campbell U., 2004, Doctoral fellow history dept., Emory U., 1990—94, Fgn. Lang. and Area Studies Fellowship in Russian, Ctr. for Russian and East European Studies, 1994, 1995, 1995—96, 1996—97, George Comegy scholar, Wash. State U., 1984—84, Kenneth Vanderford scholar, 1985—86, Richard G. Kappler Meml. scholar, 1985—86, 1986—87, Arne O. Lindberg scholar, 1986—87. Mem.: AAUW, Soc. for Historians Am. Fgn. Rels. (Myrna Bernath Rsch. fellow 1995), Orgn. Am. Historians, N.C. Assn. Historians, Assn. for Women in Slavic Studies (profl. issues com. 1997—99), Am. Hist. Assn., Am. Assn. for the Advancement Slavic Studies, Pi Gamma Mu, Phi Kappa Phi, Phi Beta Kappa, Pi Sigma Alpha, Phi Alpha Theta. Democrat. Roman Catholic. Office: Campbell Univ Dep Govt History & Justice PO Box 356 Buies Creek NC 27506

**STANKIEWICZ, JAMES A.,** otolaryngologist; b. Chgo., Ill., Oct. 30, 1948; Attended, U. Chgo., Ill., 1966—70, MD, 1974. Cert. Otolaryngology. Resident, basic surgery U. Chgo., Ill., 1974—75, resident, otolaryngology Ill., 1975—78; team physician Ill. HS, 1975—76; otolaryngology cons., student and employee health clinic U. Chgo., 1976—78; lectr. U. Chgo. Med. Sch., 1977—78; otology clerk Pub. Health Svc., 1977; asst. chief otology US Navy-Navy Regional Med. Ctr., Oakland, Calif., 1978—79, otolaryngology staff, chief otology, 1979—80; clin. assoc., dept otolaryngology U. Calif., San Francisco, 1979—80; asst. prof., dept. otolaryngology-head and neck surgery Loyola U. Med. Ctr., Stritch Sch. Medicine, 1980—85, assoc. prof.-tenure, dept. otolaryngology-head and neck surgery, 1986—90, prof., dept. otolaryngology-head and neck surgery, 1990—, vice-chmn., dept. otolaryngology-head and neck surgery, 1987—, chmn. dept. otolaryngology-head and neck surgery, 2005, attending physician-full time, dept. otolaryngology-head and neck surgery, 1980—; attending physician, dept. otolaryngology-head and neck surgery, cons. Hines Veterans Hosp., Hines, Ill., 1980—; attending physician (courtesy staff) Children's Meml. Hosp. Chgo., Ill., 1984—; residency program dir., dept. otolaryngology-head and neck surgery Stritch Sch. Medicine, 1995—. Co-dir., Loyola U. Health Sys. Nasal Sinus Ctr.; cert. occupational hearing conservationist, 1977—; presenter in field. Contbr. chapters to books, articles to profl. jours.; mem. editl. bd. Operative Techniques in Head and Neck Surgery, Sinus Newsletter, Vanderbilt U., Ear, Nose, Throat Jour., St. Louis, Mo., Otolaryngology-Head and Neck Surgery, 2005—, mem. internat. editl. bd., 2004—07, reviewer for several profl. jours. Fellow: Am. Coll. Surgeons, Am. Acad. Otolaryngology-Head and Neck Surgery (Honors award, New Orleans, La. 1989, First Place Poster President's award, San Diego, Calif. 1990); mem.: Am. Acad. Otolaryngology Allergy, Sinus and Allergy Health Partnership, Soc. Univ. Otolaryngologists-Head and Neck Surgeons, Parmly Hearing Inst.-Loyola U., Am. Cleft Palate-Craniofacial Assn., Am. Rhinologic Soc. (chmn., CME com. 1994—2005, cons. 1995—96, bd. dir. 1997—2001, 2005—06, 2nd v.p. 2005—06), Am. Broncho-Esophagological Assn., Am. Acad. Pediatrics-Specialty Divsn., Pan American Head and Neck Soc., Pacific Coast Oto-Ophthalmological Soc., Chgo. Laryngological and Otological Soc. (pres. 1994—95), Ill. State Med. Soc., Chgo, Med Soc., AMA. Office: Loyola U Med Cir Stritch Sch Medicine 2160 S First Ave Maywood IL 60153 Office Phone: 708-216-9183. Office Fax: 708-216-3835.*

**STANKO, SUSAN G.,** librarian; b. Tucson, Ariz., Sept. 20, 1971; d. Ivan and Anna Stanko. BA in Sociology, U. W. Stevens Point, 1997; degree, U. Milw., 2000. Asst. reference libr. Chgo. Heights Publ. Libr., 2000—. Home: 17 Olympic Vlg Apt 2D Chicago Heights IL 60411 Office: Chgo Heights Publ Libr 25 W 15t St Chicago Heights IL 60411 Office Phone: 708-754-0323. E-mail: cosmicbimbo@sbcglobal.com.

**STANKRAUFF, ALISON HARPER,** archivist; b. Ann Arbor, Mich., Oct. 17, 1974; d. Jack Bogue and Constance Davis Stankrauff. B in History, Antioch Coll., 1996; MLS, Wayne State U., 2002. Archives asst. Wayne State U., Detroit, 2001—02; ref. archivist Am. Jewish Archives, Cin., 2002—04; archivist, libr. Ind. U., 2004—. Mem. Soc. Indiana Archivists (bd. mem. 2005—), Midwest Archives Conf., Soc. Am. Archivists. Avocations: bicycling, travel. Home: 1236 1/2 Lincoln St East South Bend IN 46601 Office: Schurz Libr South Bend Indiana U 1700 Mishawaka Ave P O Box 9111 South Bend IN 46601

**STANLEY, ALESSANDRA,** critic; Corr. NY Times, Moscow, co-chief Moscow bur., chief Rome bur., chief TV critic NYC. Office: NY Times Culture Desk 229 W 43rd St New York NY 10036 Office Phone: 212-556-8892. Office Fax: 212-556-1516.*

**STANLEY, AMY DRU,** history professor; b. Trenton, NJ, June 25, 1956; d. Lewis Charles and Sylvia (Gelernter) Stanley; m. Craig Becker, Aug. 1, 1982; children: Tom Stanley-Becker, Isaac Stanley-Becker. AB, Princeton U., 1978; PhD, Yale U., 1990. Lectr. Howard U., Washington, 1987; asst. prof. U. Calif., Irvine, 1989—94, U. Chgo., 1994—97, assoc. prof., 1997—. Author: From Bondage to Contact: Labor, Marriage and the Market in the Age of Slave Manpower, 1998 (Frederick Jackson Turner award, 1999, Avery Craven award, 1999, Morris D. Forkasch award, 1999). Mem.: Am. Studies Assn., Orgn. Am. Historians, Am. Hist. Assn. Avocations: drawing, tennis, swimming, gardening. Office: U Chgo 1125 E 59th St Chicago IL 60637

**STANLEY, CHARLES L.,** alcohol/drug abuse services professional; b. Clinton, Okla., May 9, 1946; s. Charles Elmo and Lillie Stanley; m. Linda L. Stanley; children: Kristina Sheetz, Kathena Sheetz; m. Ruth Eva McBath (div.); children: Ruth Ellen, Diana Lynn. AA, Ctrl. Ariz. Coll., Coolidge, 1983; BSW, Ariz. State U., Tempe, 1985. Substance abuse counselor Behavioral Health Counseling, Coolidge, 1982—93; counselor Pinal Hispanic, Eloy, Ariz., 1993—94, Horizon Human Svcs., Casa Grande, Ariz., 1994—2004, clinician I, 2004—05, clinician II, 2006—. Named Employee of the Yr., Horizon Human Svc., 2005. Fellow: Am. Group Psychotherapy Assn. Republican. Pentecostal. Avocation: gardening. Home: 120 W Main St Casa Grande AZ 85222-4820

**STANLEY, (MALCHAN) CRAIG,** school system administrator, consultant, psychologist, researcher; b. Boston, Nov. 19, 1948; s. Harry Eugene and Ruth (Shultz) S.; 1 child, Jessica. BA in Psychology, Antioch Coll., Yellow Springs, Oh., 1971; MEd, Boston State Coll., 1975; EdD, Boston Coll., 1992. Counselor Fernald Sch., Waltham, Mass., 1970-71, psychologist, 1975; tchr. Boston Pub. Schs., 1972-74; sch. psychologist EdCo, Inc., Brookline, Mass., 1975-76, Greater Lawrence Ednl. Collaborative, Lawrence, Mass., 1976-77, exec. dir., 1977—2004; ref., exec. 2004; ednl. cons., 2004—. Sec. adv. commn. Mass. Dept. Edn., 1981-84; treas. Mass. Orgn. Ednl. Collaboratives, 1988-93, pres., 1993-95. Chmn. Greater Lawrence Interagy. Task Force, 1980—83; clk. Middleton Planning Bd., 1991—96; trustee Middleton Congl. Ch., 2001—04. Recipient Ednl. Excellence award, Pioneer Inst., 2003, E. Robert Stephens Rsch. award, AESA, 2003. Mem.: USCG Aux., Assn. Ednl. Svc. Agys. (exec. coun. 1997—2000). Home: 19 Gates Rd Middleton MA 01949-1924 Office Phone: 978-777-4775. E-mail: craig77@comcast.net.

**STANLEY, DANIEL RAYMOND, SR.,** federal agency administrator; b. Kansas City, Kans., Sept. 29, 1951; s. Winfield Scott and Irene May (Flint) S.; m. Kay Carrol Armstead, Jan. 4, 1970; children: Elizabeth Kay, Daniel Raymond Jr. Student, U. Kans., 1970-73; BS in Nuclear Tech., SUNY, Albany, 1979. Enlisted USN, 1973, advanced through grades to lt., weapons officer, 1980-83; officer Office Joint Chiefs of Staff, Washington, 1983-85; resigned, 1985; mgr. strategic and space systems Washington Studies and Analysis Group, Arlington, Va., 1985-87; mgr. bus. planning McDonnell Douglas Corp., St. Louis, 1987; adminstrv. asst. Office of Senator Robert J. Dole, Kans.; commr. Postal Rate Commn., 1990—2000; prin. dep. asst. sec., manpower, reserve affairs, Dept. Army, US Dept. Def., dep. asst. sec., Senate affairs, prin. dep. asst. sec., legis. affairs, acting asst. sec. legis. affairs, 2005, asst. sec., legis. affairs, 2005—. Contbr. articles to profl. jours. Mem., analyst Stanton Group, Washington, 1986, Dole for Pres. Def. Policy, Washington, 1987; cubmaster Boy Scouts Am., Springfield, Va., 1987. Mem. Assn. of Army, Armed Forces Communication and Electronics Assn., Submarine League. Clubs: Army-Navy Country (Arlington). Avocation: golf. Office: Asst Sec Legis Affairs Rm 3E966 Dept Defense 1300 Defense Pentagon Washington DC 20301-1300 Office Phone: 703-697-6210.

**STANLEY, DEIRDRE,** lawyer; b. Huntsville, Ala. BA, Duke U.; JD, Harvard U., 1989. With Cravath, Swaine & Moore, NYC and London, 1990—97; assoc. gen. counsel, head mergers and acquisitions group GTE Corp., 1997—99; dep. gen. counsel USA Networks, Inc. (now InterActive Corp.), 1999—2002; sr. v.p., gen. counsel The Thomson Corp., 2002—. Office: The Thomson Corp Toronto-Dominion Bank Tower 66 Wellington St W Toronto Canada M5K 1A1*

**STANLEY, DUFFY B.,** architect, planner; b. Midland, Tex., Feb. 14, 1923; s. Benjamin M. and Mary L. (White) S.; m. Irene M. Muller, July 31, 1948; children: Sheila, Lars, Brock, Sonya, Sharon. BArch, Tex. A&M U., 1948; diploma (hon.), U. Autonoma de Cd. Juarez, Mex., 1977. Registered architect, Tex., N.Mex.; cert. Nat. Coun. Archtl. Registration Bds. Draftsman, designer J.J. Black, Architect, Midland, 1948-51; job capt. Carroll & Daeuble Architects, El Paso, Tex., 1951-57; pvt. practice El Paso, 1957—. Lectr. in field. Author: Open Space in the El Paso Region, 1970. Vice chmn. Citizens Environ. Coun. of El Paso, 1972—73; chmn. GARC com. West Tex. Coun. Govts., El Paso, 1977; chmn. El Paso County Hist. Commn., 1978, Zoning

Bd. of Adjustment, El Paso, 1959—70; mem. Open Space Com., El Paso, 1970—71; bd. dirs. Mission Heritage Assn. of El Paso, 1977—84. Capt. U.S. Army, 1943—46, ETO. Decorated Combat Inf. badge, Bronze Star, Silver Star; recipient Caudill award, Tex. Assn. Sch. Bds. and AIA Tex., 1996. Fellow AIA (chpt. pres. 1964, Design award 1995, Service to Profession award 1991, Lifetime Achievement award El Paso chpt. 2004). Avocations: reading, travel. Office: 303 Texas Ave Ste 704 El Paso TX 79901-1452 Business E-mail: ivolta@zianet.com.

**STANLEY, E. RICHARD,** biomedical researcher; b. Sydney, NSW, Australia, Sept. 28, 1944; came to US 1977; s. Neville Fenton and Muriel (MacDonald) S.; m. Pamela Mary Fetherstonhaugh, Feb. 6, 1970; children: Damian Alexander, Robert Fenton. BSc with honors, U. Western Australia, 1967; PhD in Med. Biology, U. Melbourne, Australia, 1970. Mem. sr. sci. staff Ont. Cancer Inst., Toronto, 1972-77; lectr. dept. medicine and biophysics U. Toronto, 1972-73, asst. prof., 1973-77; asst. prof. dept. microbiol. and Immunology, cell biology Albert Einstein Coll. Medicine, Bronx, 1977-79, assoc. prof., 1979-84, prof., 1984-87, Renee and Robert A. Belfer prof. devel. biology, chair dept. devel. and molecular biology, 1987—. Cons. Cetus Corpn., Emeryville, Calif., 1983; sci. adv. bd. Internat. Coun. for Coordination Cancer Rsch., NYC, 1989. Contbr. articles to profl. jours. Named to Roll of Honor, Internat. Union Against Cancer; recipient Scholar award, Leukemia Soc. Am., 1977, Irma T. Hirschl Career Scientist award, 1983, Marie T. Bonazinga Rsch. award, Soc. Leukocyte Biology, 1989, Method to Extend Rsch. in Time (MERIT) award, NIH, 1989, 2002, E. Donnall Thomas prize, Am. Soc. Hematology, 2006. Achievements include isolation and characterisation of growth factor, colony stimulating factor-1 and its receptor; cloning CSF-1 gene; establishment of the biological importance of CSF-1 in regulation of white cell production and placental function. Office: Dept Devel and Molecular Biology Albert Einstein Coll Med 1300 Morris Park Ave Bronx NY 10461-1926 E-mail: rstanley@aecom.yu.edu.*

**STANLEY, EDWARD ALEXANDER,** geologist, researcher, retired director, forensic specialist; b. NYC, Apr. 7, 1929; s. Frank and Elizabeth (Wolf) S.; m. Elizabeth Ann Allison, June 7, 1958; children: Karen (dec.), Scott. BS, Rutgers U., 1954; MS, Pa. State U., 1956, PhD, 1960. Rsch. geologist Amoco Petroleum Co., Tulsa, Okla., 1960-62; prof. U. Del., 1962-64, U. Ga., 1964-77; assoc. dean rsch., chmn. geology dept. Indiana (Pa.) U., 1977-81; supr. Phillips Petroleum Co., Bartlesvill, Okla., 1981-86; dir., comdg. officer NYC Police Dept. Crime Lab., 1986—94; pvt. practice, 1994—97; assoc. Internat. Environ. Svcs., 1997—. Cons. in field. Contbr. articles to profl. jours. Served to sgt. U.S. Army Air Corps/USAF, 1947—50. Grantee NSF, 1965-68, 74, Rsch. grant Office Water Resources, 1965-68; NAS exch. prof. Soviet Union, 1968-69, 73; invited guest Moscow Police Dept. Forensic Labs., 1990; invited speaker FBI Internat. Symposium on Forensic Trace Evidence, 1991, 98; recipient Commemorative medal of the lab. Dept. Botany, Jozsef Attila U., Szeged, Hungary, 2000, Millenium medal, 2000. Fellow: AAAS, Geol. Soc. Am.; mem.: Am. Soc. Crime Lab. Dirs., Am. Acad. Forensic Sci., Am. Assn. Petroleum Geologists, Sigma Xi. Presbyterian. Avocations: photography, music, firearms. Home: 578 Myrtle Ct Harrisburg PA 17112-2255 Personal E-mail: eas.aquila7@verizon.net.

**STANLEY, ELIOT HUNGERFORD,** small business owner, writer, lawyer; b. Baton Rouge, Jan. 4, 1942; s. Allan John Stanley and Ruth Ristine Moore; m. Julia Frances Adams, Aug. 29, 1981. BA in History, Harvard U., 1963; JD, George Washington U., 1972. Legis. asst. U.S. Sen. Fred Harris, Washington, 1964—65; mem. congl. liaison staff Office of Sec. HUD, Washington, 1965—66; staff dir., adminstrv. asst. Hon. Chet Holifield, Washington, 1967—69; assoc. dir. Citizens Advocate Ctr., Washington, 1970—72; acting regional counsel U.S. Commn. Civil Rights, N.Y.C., 1973—76, legal cons. Washington, 1977—81; owner, CEO New Eng. Antigenics, Portland, Maine, 1982—2003; cons., 2003—. Mem. Gov. of Maine's Trade Mission to Brazil and Argentina, 1997; mem. seminar on def. and nat. security Brookings Inst., Washington, 1967; mem. advance staff Hubert Humphrey Campaign for Pres., 1968. Author: (short stories) River Coffee and Five Others, 1995; editor: The Jewel (by Rockwell Kent), 1990 (1st pl. graphic arts award, 91); author: Nat. Report on Police Practices, U.S. Commn. on Civil Rights, 1981. Commr. Portland Civil Svc. Commn., 2003—05; mem. Maine Regulatory Fairness Bd., 2006—; speech writer Sargent Shriver Campaign for V.P. U.S., 1972. Recipient Disting. Svc. award, U.S. Commn. on Civil Rights, 1975. Mem.: Linnaean Soc. N.Y., Baxter Soc. Maine (founder, 1st pres.), Caxton Club of Chgo., Book Club of Calif. Democrat. Unitarian. Avocations: lecturing, book arts, ornithology, natural history. Office: PO Box 1822 Portland ME 04104 Office Phone: 207-773-2597. Personal E-mail: jaes15@maine.rr.com.

**STANLEY, ELLEN MAY,** historian, consultant; b. Dighton, Kans., Feb. 3, 1921; d. Delmar Orange and Lena May (Bobb) Durr; m. Max Neal Stanley, Nov. 5, 1939; children: Ann Y. Stanley Epps, Janet M. Stanley Horsky, Gail L. Stanley Peck, Kenneth D., Neal M., Mary E. Stanley McEniry. BA in English and Journalism, Ft. Hays State U., Kans., 1972, MA in History, 1984. Pvt. practice local/state historian, cons., writer local history, Dighton, 1973—; cons. genealogy, 1980—. Vice chmn. State Preservation Bd. Rev., Kans., 1980-87; area rep. Kans. State Mus. Assn., 1978-84. Author: Early Lane County History: 12,000 B.C.-A.D. 1884, 1993 (Cert. of Commendation, Am. Assn. for State and Local History, 1994), Cowboy Josh: Adventures of a Real Cowboy, 1996, Early Lane County Development, 1993, Golden Age, Great Depression and Dust Bowl, 2001 (Ferguson Kans. History Book award Kans. Author Club, 2002); contbr. articles to profl. jours. Recipient woman com. Alamota Township, Kans., 1962-86; mem. Dem. State Affirmative Action Com., 1975. Recipient hon. mention for photography Ann. Christian Arts Festival, 1974, Artist of Month award Dane G. Hansen Mus., 1975. Mem. Kans. State Hist. Soc. (pres. 1990-91), Lane County Hist. Soc. (sec. 1970-78). Methodist. Avocations: fossil hunting, walking, photography, antiques. Home: 100 N 4th Dighton KS 67839 Office: 110 E Pearl St Dighton KS 67839

**STANLEY, GEORGE JOEL,** social services administrator, advocate; b. Wethersfield, Vt., Sept. 1, 1947; s. George and Lucretia (Lincoln) Stanley. BA, U. Mass., 1990, MEd, 1997. Lic. real estate agt. Mass. Min., missionary Watchtower Soc. Bklyn., 1960-81; founder, dir. Carefree Living Ctrs., Springfield, Mass., 1970—, Networks, Springfield, 1980—, Cult Busters, Springfield, 1981—, Free at Last, Springfield, 1981—, Caring Cmty., Vt., N.H. and Mass., 1980—, Essential Svcs., New Eng. area, 1972—, Live Free or Die, Keene, N.H., 1997—. Owner, operator thrift shops and drop-in ctrs., 1972—; bd. dirs., founder Valley Singles, Northampton, 1985—, Paradise Coalition, Northampton, Mass., 1990—97. Author: The Patriarch and Prodigal Son, 1981; contbr. articles to profl. publs. Past guardian ad litem, conservator for homeless, indigent, disabled; candidate for Mass. Senate People's Party, Springfield, 1995; vol. Michael Dukakis for Pres., 1975—83. Mem.: APA, Artists Alliance Against Violence, Nat. Artists for Mental Health. Unitarian/Episcopalian. Avocations: naturism, spirituality, community building, anything experimental.

**STANLEY, GERARD FRANCIS,** language educator; b. Phila., Pa., Apr. 21, 1950; s. Frank and Stella Stanley; m. Candace Ruth Thomas, July 5, 1980; 1 child, Thomas Russell. BA in English Edn., LaSalle U., Phila., 1972; MA in Theatre, Villanova U., Pa., 1978. Tchr. English NJ Dept. of Edn., 1982, Pa. Dept. of Edn., 1972—81; tchr. of mid. and h.s. English Bristol Twp. Sch. Dist., Pa., 1972—81; tchr. of h.s. English Pemberton Twp. Sch. Dist., Pemberton, NJ, 1982—. Faculty trainer Pemberton Twp. Sch. Dist., Pemberton, NJ, 2003—04, selected mem. - summer leadership inst., 2003—03, initiator faculty peer coaching program, 2003—03, initiator faculty idea sharing program, 2002—03, advisor, dir. drama club, 1983—86, elected mem. and chmn., bldg. adv. com., 1985—90, mem. needs assessment com., 2002—03; advisor/dir. - drama club Bristol Twp. Sch. Dist., Pa., 1979—81. Author/editor/presenter (public lecture, slide presentation) Time Capsule: Henry David Thoreau's Cape Cod. Record keeper Boy Scouts of Am., Lower Makefield, Pa., 1995—98; co-den leader Cub Scouts, 1992—93; coach Yardley, Morrisville Soccer, Pa., 1992—96; mem., discussion leader - men's group Luth. Ch. of the Resurrection, 1994—2005, lector, 1995—2005,

communion asst., 2005. Mem.: NEA, Pennsbury Athletic Assn., Pemberton Twp. Ednl. Assn., Burlington County Edn. Assn., NJ Edn. Assn., Lakeside Kayak Club. Lutheran. Achievements include founder, director - The Chancel Players - Lutheran Church of the Resurrection. Avocations: reading, kayaking, travel, dogs, church related activities. Home: 362 Saly Rd Yardley PA 19067 Personal E-mail: jerrycand@comcast.net.

**STANLEY, GWEN G.,** elementary school educator; b. Abbington, Pa., Feb. 11, 1954; d. Richard A. and Doris K. Guba; m. Ray L. Stanley, June 6, 1976; children: R. L., Sarah Rae. BA, Maryville Coll., 1977; MA in Edn., State U., 2002, D of Edn., 2003. Nat. Bd. Cert. Tchr. US, 2001, cert. asst. tchr. 2005. Libr. educator Whittier County Schs., Calif., 1976—79; tchr. Montessori Sch. of Ligonier, Ligonier, Pa., 1981—83, Ligonier Bd. of Edn., 1985—88, Perston Ridge Monetssori Sch., Alpharetta, Ga., 1990—92, Forsyth County Bd. of Edn., Cumming, Ga., 1992—, Ga. State U., Atlanta, 2004—. Presentor Internat. Reading Assn., Reno, 2003—04; standards and benchmarks contbr. Forsyth County Schs., Ga., 2000—01. Contbr. seminar on literacy. Recipient Tchr. of Yr., 2002. Office: Forsyth County Schs 1670 James Burgess Rd Suwanee GA 30024 Home: 434 Winfield Blf Dawsonville GA 30534-8634 Office Phone: 770-888-7511. Personal E-mail: gstanley@forsyth.k12.ga.us.

**STANLEY, HARRY EUGENE,** physicist, researcher; b. Norman, Okla., Mar. 28, 1941; s. Harry Eugene and Ruth S.; m. Idahlia (Dessauer), June 2, 1967 (dec. Mar. 2003); children: Jannah, Michael, Rachel. BA in Physics, Wesleyan U., 1962; postgrad., U. Cologne, Germany, 1962—63; PhD in Physics, Harvard U., 1967; PhD (hon.), Bar Ilan U., Ramat Gan, Israel, 1994, Roland Eötvös U., Budapest, Hungary, 1997, U. Liege, 2001, U. Dortmund, 2001, U. Wroclaw, 2004. NSF pre-doctoral rsch. fellow Harvard U., Mass., 1963—67; mem. staff Lincoln lab. MIT, Cambridge, 1967—68, asst. prof. physics, 1969—71, assoc. prof., 1971—73; Miller rsch. fellow U. Calif., Berkeley, 1968—69; Hermann von Helmholtz assoc. prof. health sci. and tech. Health Sci. and Tech. Program Harvard U., MIT, 1973—76; vis. prof. Osaka U., Japan, 1975; prof. physics, physiology Sch. Medicine, dir. ctr. polymer studies Boston U., 1976. Joliot-Curie vis. prof. Ecole Superieure de Physique et Chimie, Paris, 1979; vis. prof. Peking U., 1981, Seoul Nat. U., 1982; hon. prof. U. Pavia; 30th Ann. Saha Meml. Lecture, 1992; Sigma Xi nat. lectr., 2002-03; dir. NATO Advanced Study Inst., Cargese, Corsica, 1985, 88, 90, IUPAP Internat. Conf. on Thermodynamics and Statis. Mechanics, 1986, Enrico Fermi Sch., Varenna, Italy, 1996, 2003, Gordon Rsch. Conf. on Water and Aqueous Solutions, 1998, NATO advanced rsch. workshop, 1999, 2001; cons. Sandia Nat. Lab., 1983-94, Dowell Schlumberger Co., 1982-92, Elscint Co., 1983-85; nat. co-chmn. Com. of Concerned Scientists, 1974-76; Disting. prof. U. Paris, 2004. Author: Introduction to Phase Transitions and Critical Phenomena, 1971, From Newton to Mandelbrot: A Primer in Theoretical Physics, 1990, Fractal Forms, 1991, Fractal Concepts in Surface Growth, 1995, Cours de physique, 1999, Introduction to Econophysics: Correlations and Complexity in Finance, 2000; editor: Biomedical Physics and Biomaterials Science, 1972, Cooperative Phenomena Near Phase Transitions, 1973, On Growth and Form: Fractal and Non-Fractal Patterns in Physics, 1985, Statis. Physics, 1986, Random Fluctuation and Pattern Growth, 1988, Correlations and Connectivity: Geometric Aspects of Physics, Chemistry and Biology, 1990, Fractals in Science, 1994, Disordered Materials and Interfaces, 1996, Physics of Complex Systems, 1997, Statis. Mechanics in the Physical Biological and Social Sciences, 1997, Application of Statis. Mechanics to Practical Problems, 1999, Structure and Function of Biological Systems under Extreme Conditions, 2002, Statis. Physics, 2000, Statis. Mechanics: From Rigorous Results to Applications, 2000, Scaling in Disordered Systems, 2002, New Kinds of Phase Transitions, 2002; editor Physica A., 1988—. Recipient Choice award, Am. Assn. Book Pubs., 1972, Macdonald award, 1986, Venture Rsch. award, Brit. Petroleum, 1989, Mass. Prof. of Yr. award, Coun. Advancement and Support of Edn., 1992, Floyd K. Richtmyer prize, 1997, Turnbull prize, 1998, Memory Ride prize, 2001, NSF Disting. Tchr. Scholar prize, 2001, Nicholson medal, 2003, Boltzmann medal, 2004, Teresiana medal, 2004; Nat. Merit scholar, Wesleyan U., 1962, Fulbright scholar, U. Cologne, 1962—63, John Simon Guggenheim Meml. fellow, 1979—80. Fellow AAAS, NAS, am. Phys. Soc. (chmn. New Eng. sect. 1982-83, Centennial lectr. 1999); mem. NAS (non-linear sci. panel), Hungarian Phys. Soc. (hon.), Brazilian Acad. Sci. (hon.). Home: 50 Metacomet Rd Waban MA 02468-1465 Office: Boston U Ctr for Polymer Studies Boston MA 02215 Office Phone: 617-353-2617. Business E-mail: hes@bu.edu. *The greatest joy of my prof. life is to share in the excitement of learning something new, however minor about the workings of nature. The greatest joy of my personal life is to be able to imagine that I've done my very best to meet the needs of my family and my co-workers. The greatest obstacle to happiness is the persistent feeling that it is impossible to find that tortuous path whereby both joys may occasionally be experienced.*

**STANLEY, HELEN CAMILLE,** composer, musician; b. Tampa, Fla. d. Edward and Lucy Gage (Crehore) S.; widowed; 1 child, Helen Marjorie. MusB, Cin. Conservatory Music, 1951; MusM, Fla. State U., 1954; BS, Muskingum Coll., 1961. Instr. music and fine arts Jacksonville (Fla.) U., 1962-67; instr. music in communications Jones Coll., Jacksonville, 1965-66; composer, condr. St. Paul's by-the-Sea, Jacksonville Beach, Fla., 1976; composer-in-residence, pianist Fla. Contemporary Ensemble, Jacksonville, 1986; ind. composer, lectr., pianist, 1963—. Cons. Beaches Fine Arts Series, Neptune Beach, Fla., 1973—. Composer Rhapsody for Electronic Tape and Orchestra, 1972 (Composition Commn. award), Allegro, Passacaglia, Sonata for trombone and piano, various instrumental and vocal works, Evocation I for piano; orchestral works on CD include: Fanfare for Orchestra (Warsaw Nat. Philharmonic Orch. and Owensboro Symphony), 1994, Passacaglia (St. Petersburg Philharmonic), Concerto Romantico, Prague, 1997, Fanfare for Orchestra (All American Celebration by Owensboro Symphony), 1999; composer website theme music The Living Music Found.; composer Dorian Diversion in Functional Chromaticism, 2003, Phrygiana for Piano, 2005, Concerto Romantico, 2006. Mem. Soc. Mayflower Descs., 1987—. Recipient Pogner Music Composition award, Cin., 1950, C. Hugo Ensemble Composition award, Cin., 1951, Anthem Descant award St. Paul's-by-the-Sea, 1980, Art Ventures Fund award, 1992, Jacksonville Comty. Found. award, 1994; named Outstanding Achievements Classical Music, Jacksonville, 1997. Mem. ASCAP, Am. Music Ctr., Am. Keyboard Artists, Performing Arts Directory, Pi Kappa Lambda. Avocations: art, walking, dance. Address: 1768 Emory Cir S Jacksonville FL 32207-7707 Home and Studio: Aladdin Farm 12047 Aladdin Rd Jacksonville FL 32223-3201 Office Phone: 904-268-5475. E-mail: hscomposer@aol.com.

**STANLEY, HUGH MONROE, JR.,** lawyer; b. Ft. Lewis, Wash., Oct. 25, 1944; s. Hugh Monroe Sr. and Rita (McHugh) S.; m. Patricia Page, Aug. 17, 1968; children: Allison Michelle, Matthew Monroe, Trevor Marshall. BA magna cum laude, U. Dayton, 1966; JD, Georgetown U., 1969. Bar: Ohio 1969, U.S. Ct. Appeals (6th cir.) 1983, U.S. Supreme Ct. 1979. Assoc. Arter & Hadden, Cleve., 1969-76, prtnr., 1976—2003, chmn. litigation dept., 1983-96; prtnr. Tucker Ellis & West LLP, 2003—. Fellow Am. Bar Found., Bar Assn. Greater Cleve., Am. Coll. Trial Lawyers, Internat. Acad. Trial Lawyers, Internat. Soc. Barristers, Nat. Assn. R.R. Trial Counsel; mem. ABA, Fed. Bar Assn., Def. Rsch. Inst., Cleve. Assn. Civil Trial Attys., Ohio Assn. Civil Trial Attys. Republican. Roman Catholic. Avocation: reading. Office: Tucker Ellis & West 1150 Huntington Bldg 925 Euclid Ave Ste 1100 Cleveland OH 44115-1475 Office Phone: 216-696-3934. Business E-mail: hstanley@tuckerellis.com.

**STANLEY, JASON,** education educator; b. Syracuse, N.Y., Oct. 12, 1969; s. Manfred Intrator and Sara Stanley, Mary Breya Stanley (Stepmother) and William Rivera (Stepfather); m. Njeri Thande, Aug. 18, 2001. BA, SUNY at Stony Brook, 1990; PhD, MIT, Cambridge, 1995. Lectr. U. Coll., Oxford, England; assoc. prof. philosophy Cornell U., Ithaca, NY, 1995—2000; assoc. prof. philosophy U. of Mich., Ann Arbor, 2000—04; prof. philosophy Rutgers U., New Brunswick, NJ, 2004—. Author: (book) Knowledge and Practical Interests (OUP), (article) Knowing How; editor: Stanford Encyclopedia of Philosophy, 2002—; mem. editl. bd. Philosopher's Imprint, 2002—, assoc. editor Nous, 2004—. Recipient H. Lee Dennison Valedictorian, SUNY at

Stony Brook, 1990; Vis. Fellow, New Coll., Oxford U., 2003, Australian Nat. U., 2003. Jewish. Avocation: blogging. Office: Dept of Philosophy Rutgers Univ 26 Nichol Rd New Brunswick NJ 08901 Office Phone: 732-932-9861.

**STANLEY, JEAN-DANIEL,** geological oceanographer; b. Metz, France, Apr. 14, 1934; came to U.S. 1941, naturalized, 1946; s. Paul Emile and Madeleine (Simon) Streisguth; m. Adrienne N. Ellis, Mar. 5, 1988; children: Marc Michel, Eric Paul, Brian Northrop, Natalie Anne, Susan N. B.Sc., Cornell U., 1956; M.Sc., Brown U., 1958; D.Sc., U. Grenoble, France, 1961. Rsch. geologist French Petroleum Inst., Paris, 1958-61; asst. to dir. U.S. Waterways Expt. Sta., Vicksburg, Miss., 1961-63; asst. prof. geology Ottawa U., Ont., Canada, 1963-64; rsch. assoc. prof. Dalhousie U., Halifax, N.S., Canada, 1964-66; sr. scientist, oceanographer, dir. Geoarchaeology-Global Change Program, NMNH Smithsonian Instn., Washington, 1966—; adj. prof. U. Québec, 1992—2001. Cons. to govts. Mediterranean countries; sci. expert Internat. Ct. Justice, 1981—. Editor: New Concepts of Continental Margin Sedimentation, 1969, Mediterranean Sea: A Natural Sedimentation Laboratory, 1972, Marine Sediment Transport and Environmental Management, 1976, Sedimentation in Submarine Canyons, Fans and Trenches, 1978, The Shelfbreak: A Critical Interface on Continental Margins, 1983, Geological Evolution of the Mediterranean Basin, 1985, Nile Delta, A Geological Excursion, 1997; contbr. chpts to books, articles to profl. jours. Bd. dirs. Geoarchaeology and Deltas Programs. Served to capt. C.E., U.S. Army, 1961-63. Recipient médaille Alpes Maritimes, France, 1976, F.P. Shepard medal Soc. for Sedimentary Geology, 1990, Gold Trident medal Italian Acad., 1998; named Hon. Prof., East China U., 1995; grantee in field. Fellow Geol. Soc. Am., AAAS, Geol. Soc. Belgium; mem. Internat. Assn. Sedimentologists, Am. Assn. Petroleum Geologists, Soc. Econ. Paleontologists and Mineralogists, Geol. Soc. Washington, Cosmos Club (Washington), Sigma Xi. Clubs: Cosmos (Washington). Office: Smithsonian Instn E205 Nl Mus Natural History Washington DC 20013-7012 Business E-mail: stanleyd@si.edu.

**STANLEY, MARGARET KING,** performing arts association administrator; b. San Antonio, Dec. 11, 1929; d. Creston Alexander and Margaret (Haymore) King; children: Torrey Margaret, Jean Cullen. Student, Mary Baldwin Coll., 1948-50; BA, U. Tex., Austin, 1952; MA, U. Incarnate Word, 1959. Cert. elem. tchr. Tex. Elem. tchr. San Antonio Ind. Sch. Dist., 1953-54, 55-56, Arlington County Schs., Va., 1954-55, Ft. Sam Houston Schs., San Antonio, 1956—58; art and art history tchr. St. Pius X Sch., San Antonio, 1959-60; originator, founding chairwoman Student Music Fair, San Antonio, 1963; English tchr. Trinity U., 1963-65; designer-mfr., owner CrisStan Clothes, Inc., San Antonio, 1967-73; founder, exec. dir. San Antonio Performing Arts Assn., 1976-92; founding chmn. Joffrey Workshop, San Antonio, 1979; host On Stage with Margaret Stanley Sta. KTRU-FM, San Antonio, 1983-98. Orginator (with the Joffrey Ballet) Jamboree, 1984. Mem. Met. Opera Nat. Coun., 1969—80; founder Arts Coun. San Antonio, 1962, v.p., 1975; pres. San Antonio Symphony League, 1971—74; v.p., founder San Antonio Opera Guild, 1974—, pres., 2002—05; bd. govs. Artists Alliance San Antonio, 1982; founder San Antonio Early Music Festival, 1990—92; artistic advisor, dir. presentation, dir. devel. San Antonio Symphony, 1992—94; founding organizer Musica San Antonio, 1997—98; v.p. Instnl. Devel. Carver Cultural Ctr., 1998—2000; adv. bd. Hertzberg Circus Collection, San Antonio Dance Umbrella, Houston Early Music, Morgan-Scott Ballet; pres. Univ. Roundtable, 1995—97. Named to Women's Hall of Fame, San Antonio, 1984, Disting. Alumnae, St. Mary's Hall, 1990; recipient Outstanding Tchr. award, Arlington County Sch. Dist., 1954, Emily Smith award for outstanding alumni, Mary Baldwin Coll., 1973, Today's Woman award, San Antonio Light Newspaper, 1980, Woman of the Yr. in Arts award, San Antonio Express News, 1983, Erasmus medal, Dutch Consulate, 1992, Mary Baldwin Sesquicentennial medallion, 1992, Opera Guild Founder's award, 2000, Vol. award, Opera Vols. Internat., 2005, Music Support award, Cactus Pear Festival, 2006; Tchg. fellow, Trinity U., San Antonio, 1964—66. Mem.: S.W. Performing Arts Presenters (chmn. 1988—92), Battle Flowers Assn., Jr. League San Antonio (Vol. Extraodinaire 2001), Women in Comm. (Headliner award 1982), Assn. Performing Arts Presenters (award for commn.of Jamboree 1984), Internat. Soc. for Performing Arts (hon.; regional rep. 1982—85, bd. dirs. 1991—97). Avocations: travel, reading, cooking, music, dance.

**STANLEY, MARIANNE,** professional athletics coach; 1 child, Michelle. BS in Sociology, Immaculata Coll., 1976. Asst. coach women's basketball Old Dominion U., Norfolk, Va., 1976—77, head coach, 1977—87; coach women's basketball U. Pa., 1987—89, U. So. Calif., 1989—93, Stanford U., Calif., 1995—96, U. Calif., Berkeley, 1996—2000; asst. L.A. Sparks, 2000—01; asst. coach Washington Mystics, Washington, 2001—02, head coach, 2002—. Mem. coaching staff US Nat. Team, 1981—93. Named Coach of the Yr., Nat. Coach of the Yr.; named to Women's Basketball Hall of Fame, 2002. Office: Washington Mystics MCI Ctr 601 F St NW Washington DC 20004

**STANLEY, MARY ELIZABETH,** judge; AB, Mt. Holyoke Coll., 1970; JD, Univ. of Va., 1973. Bar: W.Va., U.S. Dist. Ct. (so. dist.) W.Va., U.S. Ct. Appeals (4th cir.). Atty. Columbia Gas Transmission Corp., 1973-76; law clk. to Judge Dennis R. Knapp, 1976-77; asst. U.S. atty. Charleston, W. Va., 1977-92; magistrate judge U.S. Dist. Ct. (so. dist.) W. Va., Bluefield, W. Va., 1992-01, Charleston, W. Va., 2001—. Office: Robert C Byrd US Courthouse Rm 5408 300 Virginia St E Charleston WV 25301

**STANLEY, PAMELA AURELIA,** state legislator; b. Mar. 13, 1956; 2 children. Student, Ga. Inst. Tech., Ga. State, Morris Brown Coll. Former clk. U.S. Postal Svc.; mem. Ga. Ho. of Reps., 1992—. Mem. game, fish & parks, ins. and state planning and cmty. affairs coms. Democrat. Baptist. Home: 706 Foundry St NW Atlanta GA 30314-4004 Office: Ga Ho of Reps 512 Legislative Office Bldg Atlanta GA 30334

**STANLEY, PETER WILLIAM,** former academic administrator; b. Bronxville, NY, Feb. 17, 1940; s. Arnold and Mildred Jeanette (Pattison) Stanley; m. Mary-Jane Cullen Cosgrove, Sept. 2, 1978; 1 child, Laura. BA magna cum laude, Harvard U., 1962, MA, 1964, PhD, 1970; LHD (hon.), Occidental Coll., 1994, Rhodes Coll., 2001. Asst. prof. history U. Ill., Chgo., 1970—72, Harvard U., 1972—78, lectr. history, 1978—79; dean of coll. Carleton Coll., Northfield, Minn., 1979—84; program officer in charge edn. and culture program Ford Found., 1984—87, dir. edn. and culture program, 1987—91; pres. Pomona Coll., Claremont, Calif., 1991—2003, pres. emeritus, 2003—; v.p. Isaacson, Miller, Boston, 2004—. Lectr. Fgn. Service Inst., Arlington, Va., 1977—89. Author: A Nation in the Making: The Philippines and the United States, 1974; co-author: Sentimental Imperialists: The American Experience in East Asia, 1981; editor: Reappraising an Empire: New Perspectives on Philippine-American History, 1984; contbr. articles to profl. jours. Trustee The Coll. Bd., 1991—99, vice-chmn. 1993—94, chmn., 1994—96, Barnard Coll., 2000—06; humanities and scis. coun. Stanford U., 1986—2002; nat. adv. coun. Nat. Fgn. Lang. Ctr., 1991—2002; bd. dirs. The James Irvine Found., 1997—2006, chmn., 2003—06; bd. dirs. The Pacific Basin Inst. 1998—, chmn., 1998—2003; bd. dirs. The Hitachi Found., 1993—2000, Assn. Am. Colls. and Univs. 1995—2001, vice-chmn. 1998—99, chmn., 1999—2000; bd. fellows Claremont Grad. U. and Claremont U. Consortium, 1991—2003; bd. overseers Nat. Bd. Ednl. Testing and Pub. Policy, 2000—. Fellow Frank Knox Meml. fellow, Harvard U., 1962—63, Charles Warren Ctr. for Studies in Am. History fellow, 1975—76. Mem.: Coun. on Fgn. Rels., Assn. Asian Studies, Am. Hist. Assn., Phi Beta Kappa. Home: 65 Knollwood Dr Old Saybrook CT 06475 Office: Pomona Coll Pres Office Claremont CA 91711-6301

**STANLEY, RICHARD HOLT,** consulting engineer; b. Muscatine, Iowa, Oct. 20, 1932; s. Claude Maxwell and Elizabeth Mabel (Holthues) S.; m. Mary Jo Kennedy, Dec. 20, 1953; children: Lynne Elizabeth, Sarah Catherine, Joseph Holt. BSEE, BSME, Iowa State U., 1955; MS in Sanitary Engring., U. Iowa, 1963. Registered profl. engr., Iowa. With Stanley Cons. Inc., Muscatine, Iowa, 1955—, pres., 1971-87, chmn., 1984—. Vice chmn. HNI Corp., 1979-05; chmn Nat. Constrn. Industry Coun., 1978, Com. Fed. Procurement

Archtl.-Engring. Svcs., 1979; pres. Ea. Iowa CC, Bettendorf, 1966-68; mem. indsl. adv. coun. Iowa State U. Coll. Engring., Ames, 1969-97, chmn. 1979-81; bd. dirs. Stanley Cons. Inc., Muscatine, Iowa. Contbr. articles to profl. jours. Bd. dirs. N.E.-Midwest Inst., 1989-95, treas., 1991-93, chmn., 1993-95; bd. dirs. Stanley Found., 1956—, pres., 1984—, chmn., 1995—; bd. dirs. Muscatine Health Support Found., pres., 1984—; bd. dirs. Muscatine United Way, 1969-75, Iowa State U. Meml. Union, 1968-83, U. Dubuque, Iowa, 1977-93, Inst. Social and Econ. Devel., 1992-2001, Unity Healthcare, 1999-2005, chmn. 1999-2002; bd. govs. Iowa State U. Found., 1982-96. Recipient Young Alumnus award Iowa State U. Alumni Assn., 1966, Disting. Svc. award Muscatine Jaycees, 1967, Profl. Achievement citation Coll. Engring., Iowa State U., 1977, Anson Marston medal Iowa State U., 1991, Harry S. Truman disting. svc. award Am. Assn. C.C., 1998; Disting. Alumni Achievement award U. Iowa Alumni Assn., 1999, award for Citizen Diplomacy, Nat. Coun. for Internat. Visitors, 2000, Hoover medal, 2001, Order of Knoll Cardinal and Gold award Iowa State U., 2004; named Sr. Engr. of Yr., Joint Engring. Com. Quint Cities, 1973; named to Disting. Engring. Alumni Acad., U. Iowa, 1998; named to Muscatine H.S. Hall of Honor, 2000. Fellow ASCE, Am. Cons. Engrs. Cos. (pres. 1976-77, chmn. 1976-77, Cmty. Svc. award 1997, Disting. Award of Merit 1998), Iowa Acad. Sci.; mem. IEEE (sr.), ASME, Am. Soc. Engring. Edn., Nat. Soc. Profl. Engrs., Cons. Engrs. Coun. Iowa (pres. 1967), Iowa Engring. Soc. (pres. 1973-74, John Dunlap-Sherman Woodward award 1967, Disting. Svc. award 1980, Voice of Engr. award 1987, Herbert Hoover Centennial award 1989), Muscatine C. of C. (pres. 1972-73), C. of C. of U.S. (constrn. action coun. 1976-91), Rotary, Tau Beta Pi, Phi Kappa Phi, Pi Tau Sigma, Eta Kappa Nu. Presbyterian (elder). Home: 516 Hogan Ct Muscatine IA 52761-2740 Office: Stanley Cons Inc Stanley Bldg Muscatine IA 52761

**STANLEY, RICHARD P.,** mathematics professor; b. NYC, June 23, 1944; s. Alan and Shirley (Silver) S.; m. Doris S. Skulsky, July 4, 1971; children: Kenneth, Sharon. BS, Calif. Inst. Technology, 1966; PhD, Harvard U., 1971. Math. instr. MIT, Cambridge, Mass., 1970-71; Miller research fellow Miller Inst., Berkeley, Calif., 1971-73; asst. prof. applied math. MIT, Cambridge, 1973-75, assoc. prof. applied math., 1975-79, prof. applied math., 1979-2000, Norman Levinson prof. applied math., 2000—. Cons. in field. Author: Combinatorics and Commutative Algebra, 1983, 2d edit., 1996, Enumerative Combinatorics, Vol. 1, 1986, Vol. 2, 1999. Recipient SIAM Polya Prize Soc. Indsl. and Applied Math., Guggenheim Fellowship, Guggenheim Found., 1983-84, Steele prize for math. exposition, 2001, Rolf Schock prize in math Royal Swedish Acad. Scis., 2003. Fellow Am. Acad. Arts and Scis.; mem. Nat. Acad. Scis., Am. Math. Soc., Math. Assn. Am. Office: MIT Dept Math 2-375 77 Massachusetts Ave Cambridge MA 02139-4307 E-mail: rstan@math.mit.edu.

**STANLEY, SCOTT, JR.,** editor; b. Kansas City, July 11, 1938; s. Winfield Scott and Irene Mae (Flint) S.; m. Janice Johns, Aug. 30, 1959 (dec. July 1992); children: Leslie, Scott, Margaret; m. Cynthia Ward, Dec. 30, 1995; 1 child, Elizabeth. BA, Earlham Coll., 1960. Mng. editor Am. Opinion mag., Boston, 1961-85; editor Rev. of The News mag., Boston, 1965-85; editor-in-chief Conservative Digest, Washington, 1985-88, Am. Press Internat., Washington, 1987—; pres. USA Tech., 1991-92; mng. editor Nutrition and Healing, 1994-2000; dep. editor Insight on the News, Washington, 1995–2005. Mem. nat. bd. dirs. Young Ams. for Freedom, 1960-62; public speaker and univ. lectr., 1962—Keynote speaker Am. Party Nat. Conv., 1976; pres. Ams. Legal Def. Fund, 1977—; bd. govs. Council for Nat. Policy, 1981—; bd. dirs. Free Congress Polit. Action Com., 1985-88, Conservative Caucus Found., 2006—; pres. Scott Stanley Real Estate Trust, 1988—Recipient award of merit Young Ams. for Freedom, Freedom award Nat. Congress for Freedom. Mem.: Nat. Press, Meganset Yacht. Episcopalian. Personal E-mail: cwardstanley@cox.net.

**STANLEY, SHERRY A.,** lawyer; b. Buffalo, Oct. 17, 1955; d. Arthur A. and Irene S. Stanley. BA, U. West Fla., 1975; JD, U. Fla., 1978. Bar: Fla. 1978. Assoc. Mahoney, Hadlow & Adams, Miami, Fla., 1978-80; ptnr. Steel, Hector & Davis, Miami, 1980-87, Weil, Gotshal & Manges, Miami, 1987-92; sr. counsel Barnett Banks, Inc., Miami, 1992-94; ptnr. Coll, Davidson, Carter, Smith, Salter & Barkett, P.A./Shook, Hardy Bacon, Miami, Fla., 1994—2000; exec. v.p., gen. counsel Greenstreet Ptnrs., 2001—; dir. Semeo Energy, Inc., 2004—05. Dir. SEMCO Energy, Inc., 2004—05. Mem.: Fla. Bar, Order of Coif, Phi Theta Kappa. Republican. Roman Catholic. Office: 2601 S Bayshore Dr Ste 800 Miami FL 33133 Office Phone: 305-858-8119. Business E-Mail: sas@greenstreetpartners.com.

**STANLEY, STEVEN MITCHELL,** paleontologist, educator; b. Detroit, Nov. 2, 1941; s. William Thomas and Mildred Elizabeth (Baker) S.; m. Nell Williams Gilmore, Oct. 11, 1969. AB with highest honors, Princeton U., 1963; PhD, Yale U., 1968. Asst. prof. U. Rochester, 1967-69; asst. prof. paleobiology Johns Hopkins U., 1969-71, assoc. prof., 1971-74, prof., 1974, chmn. dept. Earth and planetary Scis., 1987-88, chmn. MS program in environ. scis. and policy. Assoc. in rsch. Smithsonian Instn., 1972—; mem. bd. earth scis. NRC, 1985—, vice chmn., 1988, mem. bd. earth scis. resources, 1988-88, com. on solid earth scis., exec. and steering com., 1988, 2004—, com. on geoscis., environ. and resources, 1990-96. Author: Relation of Shell Form to Life Habits in the Bivalvia, 1970, (with D.M. Raup) Principles of Paleontology, 1971, Macroevolution: Pattern and Process, 1979, The New Evolutionary Timetable: Fossils, Genes, and the Origin of species, 1981, Earth and Life Through Time, 1986, Extinction, 1987, Exploring Earth and Life Through Time, 1992, Children of the Ice Age: How a Global Catastrophe Allowed Humans to Evolve, 1996, Earth System History, 1999; mem. editl. bd. Am. Jour. Sci., 1975—, Paleobiology, 1975-82, 88—, Evolutionary Theory, 1973—. Recipient Outstanding Paper award Jour. Paleontology, 1968, Allan C. Davis medal Md. Acad. Scis., 1973 Outstanding 100h. Paper award Washington Geol. Soc., 1986, Bownocker medal Ohio State U., 1997; Guggenheim fellow, 1981 Fellow NAS (Mary Clark Thompson Medal, 2006), Am. Acad. Arts and Scis., Geol. Soc. Am. (chmn. Penrose com. 1978, councilor 2002—); mem. Paleontol. Soc. (councilor 1976-77, sr. councilor 1991-93, pres. 1993-94, Charles Schuchert award 1977), Soc. for Study Evolution (councilor 1982-84), Am. Geophys. Union (pub. affairs com.), Paleontol. Rsch. Inst., Am. Geol. Inst. (mem. exec. com. 1996-99, pres. 2001—). Office: Johns Hopkins U Dept Earth Planetary Sciences Baltimore MD 21218 E-mail: stanley@jhu.edu.*

**STANLEY, TIM,** information technology executive; BS in Engring., U. Wash.; degree in Internat. Bus. and Tech. Mgmt., Thunderbird U., Ariz. State U. With Intel Corp., Optima/KPMG, Innova Tech, Kimberly-Clark Corp.; v.p. info. sys. Nat. Airlines, chief info. officer; ptnr. USWeb (now marchFIRST); v.p., info. tech. devel. Harrah's Entertainment, Las Vegas, 2001—03, sr. v.p., chief info. officer, 2003—. With USAF. Named one of the Top 25 Unsung Heroes of the Internet, Interactive Week Mag. Office: Harrahs Entertainment Inc One Harrahs Ct Las Vegas NV 89119*

**STANN, JOHN ANTHONY,** investment banker; b. San Francisco, Nov. 10, 1947; s. John Peter and Mary Jane (Erny) S.; m. Judith Darlene Knapp, Apr. 27, 1973; children: John Andrew, Theodore Joseph, Rebecca Marie. BA in Econs. and Math., U. Mo., 1969. Cost acct. Monsanto Co., St. Louis, 1971-73, acctg. supr., 1973-76, salesman Brighton, Mo., 1976-79, market mgr. St. Louis, 1979-81; mfr's. rep. Farbenfabriken, Bayer, Davos & Others, St. Louis, 1981-82; A.G. Edwards & Sons, Inc., St. Louis, 1982-2000; pres. Stann Fin., St. Louis, 2000—. Investment banking advisor to numerous pvt. cos.; Dev. Comm. of Nerinx Hall H.S., 1994-97. Fundraiser Archdiocese of St. Louis, 1981-84, 87-92, YMCA, St. Louis, 1987; chmn. fin. com. St. Clare Parish, St. Louis, 1982-84; mem. Assumption Parish Coun., 1988-90, chmn., 1989-90; youth baseball mgr. Arbor Athletic Assn., St. Louis, 1985-86; coun. mem. St. Louis Parish, 2001-03, campaign chmn., 2003; bd. trustees Chaminade Coll. Prep., 2002—. Lt. USNR, 1969-71. Named Man of Yr. St. John's Men's Club, 1988. Roman Catholic. Avocations: basketball, golf. Home: 9148 Fox Bridge Dr Saint Louis MO 63127-1362 Office: Stann Financial LLC PO Box 270001 Saint Louis MO 63127 E-mail: john@stannfinancial.com.

**STANNARD, NATALIE MARIE,** secondary school educator; b. Vinton, Iowa, Mar. 9, 1969; d. Edward John and Jacqueline Marie Rhinehart; life ptnr. Raymond Michel Saunders; children: Samantha Marie, Leslie Marie. BA, U. No. Iowa, Cedar Falls, Iowa, 1992. Tchr. English and theatre Clear Creek Amana Sch., Tiffin, Iowa, 1992—98, Ottumwa H.S., Iowa, 1998—. Mem.: Iowa H.S. Speech Assn. (dist. officer 2005—), Internat. Thespian Soc. (adult sponsor Iowa chpt. 1998—). Luth. Home: 127 E Pennsylvania Ottumwa IA 52501 Office: Ottumwa High School 501 East Second Street Ottumwa IA 52501 Office Phone: 641-683-4444 306. Office Fax: 641-682-7528. Personal E-mail: stannardnatalie@hotmail.com. Business E-Mail: stannardn@aea15.k12.ia.us.

**STANO, SISTER DIANA,** academic administrator; AB, Ursuline Coll.; PhD, Ohio State U. Prof. edn. Ursuline Coll., Pepper Pike, Ohio, chair edn. dept., dir. grad. program in non-pub. sch. adminstrn., dir. master's degree program, dean of grad. studies, dir. of instl. rsch., pres., 1996—. Bd. trustees Coll. of New Rochelle; sec. bd. trustees Ohio Found. Ind. Coll.; cons. in field. Recipient YWCA Women of Profl. Excellence award, No. Ohio Live Rainmaker in Edn. award. Mem.: In Counsel With Women, Exec. Women's Leadership Forum. Office: Ursuline Coll 2550 Lander Rd Pepper Pike OH 44124-4398

**STANSBERRY, JAMES WESLEY,** air force officer; b. Grafton, W.Va., Dec. 29, 1927; s. William Adrian and Phyllis Gay (Robinson) S.; m. Audrey Mildred Heinz, May 7, 1950; children: Nora G., Amy G. Stansberry Goodhand, Lisa Porten. BS, U.S. Mil. Acad., 1949; MBA with hons., Air Force Inst. Tech., 1956. Advanced through grades from pvt. to lt. gen. USAF; chief prodn. (Kawasaki Gifu Contract Facility), Gifu, Japan, 1956-57; dep. asst. to Sec. of Def. for atomic energy Washington, 1970-71; dep. dir. procurement policy U.S. Air Force, 1972-73; dep. chief staff contracting and mfg. (Hdqrs. Air Force Systems Command), Andrews AFB, Md., 1977-81; comdr. Electronic Systems Div. Hanscom AFB, Mass., 1981-84; pres. Stansberry Assocs. Inc., 1984—. Bd. dirs. Griffon Corp., Kidde Techs., Inc., Triton. Decorated DSM with oak leaf cluster, Legion of Merit with oak leaf cluster; named Disting. grad. Lancaster (N.Y.) H.S., award, Wall St. Jour., 1956, Mervin E. Gross award, USAF, 1956. Mem.: Order of Sword. Methodist. Home: 1117 Vera Cruz Ct Virginia Beach VA 23454 Office Phone: 757-716-2804. Personal E-mail: us49@aol.com. *The real secrets are enthusiasm, competence and good luck; and it helps immensely to marry a good woman. Work and persistence define us, accomodating various levels of talent and intelligence. Work and persistence prevail, buttressed by discipline and determination, and perhaps supported by a good sense of humor.*

**STANSBURY, HARRY CASE,** state commissioner; BS in Gen. Studies, La. State U., 1968; JD, Loyola U., New Orleans, 1971; student, Oxford (Eng.) U., 1985, Harvard U., 1988; MBA, U. New Orleans, 1998; MA, Columbia U., 2000. Bar: La., N.Y., D.C., U.S. Supreme Ct., U.S. Ct. Appeals (1st-11th cirs., D.C. cir., fed. cir.), U.S. Ct. Mil. Appeals, U.S. Ct. Fed. Claims, U.S. Ct. Internat. Trade, U.S. Tax Ct., U.S. Dist. Ct. (ea., mid. and we. dists.) La., U.S. Dist. Ct. (ea., no., so. and we. dists.) N.Y., U.S. Dist. Ct. D.C. Staff atty. La. Securities Commn., New Orleans, 1971-75, dep. commr. securities, 1975-?. Mem. liaison com. fed. securities code project Am. Law Inst.-ABA, 1974-80; speaker, expert witness in field. Contbr. articles to profl. jours. Mem.: ABA (mem. subcom. derivative instruments fed. regulation securities com. 1993—, sect. bus. law, sect. internat. law and practice, sect. legal edn. and admissions to bar), Harvard Law Sch. Assn., Loyola Law Alumni Assn., La. State U. Alumni Assn., Internat. Bar Assn. (mem. issues and trading in securities com. 1991—, sect. bus. law), Fed. Bar Assn. (fin. instms. and economy sect.), New Orleans Bar Assn. (vice chair corps. and bus.law com. 1992—94, chair 1994—96), Assn. Bar City of D.C., Assn. Bar City of N.Y., D.C. Bar Assn. (corp., fin. and securities law divsn.), N.Y. State Bar Assn., La. State Bar Assn. (sect. corp. and bus. law, mem. internat. law com. 1991—92), N.Am. Securities Adminstrs. Assn. (mem. registration exemption com. 1991—94), Am. Friends Rewley House, Supreme Ct. Hist. Soc. Address: 10001 Lake Forest Blvd Ste 803 New Orleans LA 70127 Office Phone: 504-248-3000. E-mail: hstans@msn.com.

**STANSELL, LELAND EDWIN, JR.,** lawyer, mediator, educator; b. Central, SC, July 13, 1934; s. Leland Edwin and Hettie Katherine (Hollis) S.; children: James Leland, Susan. BS, Fla. So. Coll., 1957; LLB, U. Miami, Fla., 1961, JD, 1968. Bar: Fla. 1961; cert. civil mediator Fla. Supreme Ct., U.S. Dist. Ct. Fla. Assoc. Wicker & Smith, Miami, 1961-62, ptnr., 1962-75; pvt. practice, Miami, 1975-99, Leland E. Stansell, Jr., P.A., Miami, 1995—. Chmn. Appellate Jud. Nominating Com., Dade County (Fla.), 1983-87; mem. adv. com. Am. Arbitration Assn., 1975-90. Served with U.S. Army, 1957. Mem. ABA (ho. of dels. 1982-86), Fla. Bar (bd. govs. 1966-70, 70-80), Dade County Bar Assn. (dir. 1969-72, exec. com. 1974-75, pres. 1975-76), U. Miami Law Alumni Assn. (dir., officer, pres. 1968-69), Fla. Criminal Def. Attys. Assn. (treas. 1964-66), Am. Judicature Soc., Am. Bd. Trial Advs., Internat. Assn. Def. Counsel, Fla. Acad. Profl. Mediators, Fedn. Ins. Counsel, Miami Beach Rod and Reel Club (pres.), Coral Reef Yacht Club, Miami City Club, Ocean Reef Yacht Club, Delta Theta Phi (pres. Miami alumni chpt. 1966, regional dir. 1968. Office: 19 W Flagler St Miami FL 33130-4400

**STANSELL, RONALD BRUCE,** retired investment banker; b. Hammond, Ind., Apr. 9, 1945; s. Herman Bruce and Helen Rose Stansell; m. Kathie Van Atta, Oct. 2, 1976; children: Kelsey, Kymberlie. BA, Wittenberg U., 1967; MA, Miami U., Oxford, Ohio, 1969. Investment officer First Nat. Bank, Chgo., 1969-73; mgr. investments Chrysler Corp., Detroit, 1973; asst. v.p. A.G. Becker, Chgo., 1973-76; v.p. Blyth Eastman Dillon, Chgo., 1976-79, Dean Witter Reynolds Inc., Chgo., 1979-82, First Boston Corp., 1982-88; sr. v.p. Prudential-Bache Securities, Chgo., 1988-90; ptnr. William Blair & Co., 1991-99, jnrs Oakwood of Carolina, 1999-2001. Mem. McHawa (Ill.) Zoning Bd., 1978-80; treas. Village of Mettawa, 1977-78, trustee, 1980-91. With USMCR, 1968-74. Mem. Bond Club Chgo., Investment Analyst Soc., Fixed Income Group, Grandfather Golf Club, Forest Creek Golf Club, Belfair Golf Club, Berkeley Hall Club, Old Chatham Club, Diamond Creek Golf Club, Univ. Club.

**STANSFIELD, CHARLES W.,** educational administrator; m. Charlene Rivera, Sept. 6, 1989. BA in Spanish, Fla. State U., 1968, MA in Fgn. Lang. Edn., 1969, MS in Teaching English as Second Lang., 1970, PhD in Fgn. and Second Lang. Edn., 1973. Tchr. English, Centro Colombo-Americano, Bogota, Colombia, 1966; 2jr. high sch. tchr. Spanish Fla. State U. Demonstration Sch., 1968-69; instr. Spanish, U. Colo., Boulder, 1970-73, asst. prof., 1973-80, assoc. prof., 1980-81; assoc. program dir. lang. programs Ednl. Testing Svc., Princeton, NJ, 1981-86; dir. fgn. lang. and testing div. Ctr. for Applied Linguistics, Washington, 1986-94, dir. ERIC Clearinghouse Lang. and Linguistics, 1986-94; pres. Second Lang. Testing, Inc., Bethesda, Md., 1994—. Dir. Peace Corps Tng. Ctr., Managua, Nicaragua, 1987-88; com. Joint Nat. Com. on Langs., 1988-93; conf. coord. Interagy. Lang. Roundtable Invitational Symposium on Lang. Aptitude Testing, Rosslyn, Va., 1988; mem. adv. bd. Nat. Fgn. Lang. Resources Ctr., U. Hawaii, 1991-93; numerous presentations at profl. meetings, 1970—. Author: Cuaderno de ejercicios, 1976, rev. edit., 1981; co-author: Manual de laboratorio, 2d rev. edit., 1981, The Test of Spoken English as a Measure of Communicative Ability in the Health Professions,: Validation and Standard Setting, 1983, (with others) Multiple-Choice Cloze Items and the Test of English as a Foreign Language, 1988; co-editor: Second Language Proficiency Assessment: Current Issues, 1988, Language Aptitude Reconsidered, 1990; also numerous articles. Named Outstanding Alumnus Fla. State U., 1994; Colo. Congress Fgn. Lang. Tchrs. scholar, 1981. Mem. Am. Assn. Tchrs. Spanish and Portuguese (life), Am. Coun. on Teaching Fgn. Langs. (Paul Pinsleur award 1984), Am. Ednl. Rsch. Assn., Internat. Assn. Applied Linguistics, Nat. Assn. for Bilingual Edn., Nat. Coun. on Measurement in Edn., Internat. Lang. Testing Assn. (pres. 1992-93), Tchrs. English to Speakers Other Langs., Washington Area Tchrs. English to Speakers Other Langs., Colo. Tchrs. English to Speakers Other Langs. (Gladys Doty award 1987). Office: 6135 Executive Blvd Rockville MD 20852-3437 Office Phone: 301-231-6046. Business E-Mail: cstansfield@2LTI.com.

**STANSFIELD, CLAIRE,** apparel designer; b. London, Aug. 27, 1964; Co-founder C&C California, 2003—. Actor: (films) The Doors, 1991, Nervous Ticks, 1992, Best of the Best II, 1993, The Swordsman, 1993, The Favor, 1994, Drop Zone, 1994, Gladiator Cop, 1994, Sensation, 1995, Red Shoe Diaries 5: Weekend Pass, 1995, The Outpost, 1995, Darkdrive, 1996, Steel, 1997, Sweepers, 1999; (TV series) Xena The Warrior Princess, Fraiser, Twin Peaks. Office: c/o Lela Tillem #705 127 E 9th St Los Angeles CA 90015

**STANSFIELD, WILLIAM DONALD,** retired education educator; b. L.A., Feb. 7, 1930; m. Janis Rae Doty, July 25, 1953; children: Lorraine, Lynn, William Jr. BS in Agriculture, Calif. Polytech. State Coll., San Luis Obispo, 1959, MA in Agrl. Edn., 1960; MS in Genetics, U. Calif.-Davis, 1962, PhD in Genetics, 1963. Prof. Calif. Polytech. State U., 1963—92, prof. emeritus, 1992—. Author: (book) Death of a Rat: Understandings and Appreciations of Science, 2000; co-author: Theory and Problems of Genetics, 4th edit., 2002, A Dictionary of Genetics, 4th edit., 2002. Lt. USNR, 1953—57. Mem.: Am. Genetics Soc., Am. Assn. for the Advancement of Sci., Sigma Xi. E-mail: wstansfi@calpoly.edu.

**STANSKY, PETER DAVID LYMAN,** historian, writer, retired history professor; b. NYC, Jan. 18, 1932; s. Lyman and Ruth (Macow) Stansky. BA, Yale U., 1953, King's Coll., Cambridge U., Eng., 1955, MA, 1959; PhD, Harvard U., 1961; DL (hon.), Wittenberg U., 1984. Tchg. fellow history and lit. Harvard U., 1957-61, from instr. to asst. prof. history, 1961-68; assoc. prof. Stanford (Calif.) U., 1968-73, prof., 1973-74, Frances and Charles Field prof., 1974—2004, Frances and Charles Field prof. emeritus, 2004—, chmn. dept. history, 1975-78, 79-82, 89 90, assoc. dean humanities and scis., 1985-88. Chmn. publs. com. Conf. Brit. Studies, 1970—78; vis. fellow Wesleyan Ctr. Humanities, Middletown, 1972; pres. Pacific Coast Conf. Brit. Studies, 1974—76, N.Am. Conf. Brit. Studies, 1983—85; vis. fellow All Soul's Coll. Oxford (Eng.) U., 1979, vis. fellow St. Catherine's Coll., 83. Author: Ambitions and Strategies, 1964, England Since 1867, 1973, Gladstone, 1979, William Morris, 1983, Redesigning the World, 1985, On or About December 1910, 1996, Another Book that Never Was, 1998, From William Morris to Sergeant Pepper, 1999, Sassoon: The Worlds of Philip and Sybil, 2003; co-author: Journey to the Frontier, 1966, The Unknown Orwell, 1972, Orwell: The Transformation, 1979, London's Burning, 1994. Guggenheim fellow, 1966—67, 1973—74, Am. Coun. Learned Socs. fellow, 1978—79, NEH fellow, 1983, 1998—99, Royal Hist. Soc. fellow, Ctr. Advanced Study Behavioral Scis., 1988—89. Fellow: Am. Acad. Arts and Scis. (coun. 1994—98, 2002—05); mem.: AAUP, Century Assn., William Morris Soc., Victorian Soc., Conf. Brit. Studies, Am. Hist. Assn. Home: 375 Pinehill Rd Hillsborough CA 94010-6612 Office: Stanford U Dept History Stanford CA 94305-2024 Office Phone: 650-723-2663. Business E-Mail: stansky@stanford.edu.

**STANTON, AMY,** marketing executive; BA; M in Mktg., U. Pa. Account dir. Bartle Bogle Hegarty, NYC; dir. mktg. & comm. NYC2012; chief mktg. officer, sr. v.p. Martha Stewart Living Omnimedia, 2005—. Office: Martha Steward Living Omnimedia 11 W 42nd St New York NY 10036 Office Phone: 212-827-8000.*

**STANTON, DONALD SHELDON,** academic administrator; b. Balt., June 8, 1932; s. Kenneth Gladstone and Dorothy Erma (Hetrick) S.; m. Barbara Mae Hoot, June 25, 1955; children: Dale Richard, Debra Carol, Diane Karen. AB, Western Md. Coll., 1953, LittD, Oglethorpe U., 1999; LLD, Western Md. Coll., 1981; MDiv magna cum laude, Wesley Theol. Sem., 1956; MA, Am. U., 1960; Ed.D., U. Va., 1965; L.H.D., Columbia Coll., 1979; Litt.D., Albion Coll., 1983. Ordained to ministry United Methodist Ch., 1956; pastor Balt. and Va. confs. United Meth. Ch., 1953-59; dir. Richmond (Va.) Area Wesley Found., 1959-63; chaplain, dean of students Greensboro Coll., 1963-65; chaplain Wofford Coll., 1965-69; dir. office coll. services United Meth. Div. Higher Edn., Nashville, 1969-75; v.p. for devel. Wesleyan Coll., 1975-78; pres. Adrian Coll., 1978-88, Oglethorpe U., Atlanta, 1988-99, pres. emeritus, 1999—; interim pres. Haywood Cmty. Coll., 2005—06. Adminstr., prof. European internat. ednl. programs, summers 1960, 69-71, 73; chmn. pres.'s assn. Mich. Intercollegiate Athletic Assn., 1986-87. Contbr. articles, revs. to profl. publs. in U.S., Japan, Argentina, chpts. to books; editor: Faculty Forum, 1972-74; bass-baritone soloist. Bd. dirs. Toledo (Ohio) Symphony, 1980-83, Lewanee County Jr. Achievement, 1980-83, Found. Ind. Higher Edn., 1996-99, Nat. Conf. for Cmty. and Justice, Atlanta Region, Atlanta Area Coun. Boy Scouts Am.; chair bd. trustees U. Ctr. Ga., 1994-96; chair So. Collegiate Athletic Conf., 1994-95. Adminstrn. bldg. at Adrian Coll. named in honor of Stanton and his wife, 1988. Mem. Am. Assn. Univ. Adminstrs. (bd. dirs. 1990-93), Ga. Assn. Colls. (pres. 1992), Soc. Wesley (Disting. Alumni Recognition award 1988), Ga. Found. for Ind. Colls. (vice chair 1992), Nat. Assn. Ind. Colls. and Univs. (past mem. pub. rels. com.), Assn. Pvt. Colls. and Univs. Ga. (treas. 1996-97), Rotary, Omicron Delta Kappa, Order of Omega, Tau Kappa Epsilon, Psi Chi, Phi Eta Sigma. Home: 312 Tillman Rd Lake Junaluska NC 28745-9779 E-mail: stantons2@earthlink.net.

**STANTON, GEORGE PATRICK, JR.,** lawyer; b. Fairmont, W.Va., Nov. 21, 1933; s. George Patrick and Wilma Roberta (Everson) S.; m. Shirley Jean Champ, Sept. 3, 1956; children: George Patrick, Edward Scott. BS in Bus. Adminstrn., Fairmont Coll., 1956; MBA in Fin., U. Dayton, 1971; JD, U. Balt., 1977. Bar: Md. 1978, U.S. Dist. Ct. Md. 1978, W.Va. 1979, U.S. Dist. Ct. (so. dist.) W.Va. 1979, U.S. Dist. Ct. (no. dist.) W.Va. 1980, U.S. Ct. Appeals (4th cir.) 1985. Auditor 1st Nat. Bank Fairmont, 1955-61; asst. cashier S.C. Nat. Bank, Columbia, 1961-64; sr. sys. analyst Chase Manhattan Bank, N.Y.C., 1964-65; asst. v.p. Winters Nat. Bank, Dayton, Ohio, 1965-69, Md. Nat. Bank, Balt., 1969-74; v.p. Equitable Trust Co., Balt., 1974-79; gen. ptnr. Stanton & Stanton Attys at Law, Fairmont, W.Va., 1979 2005; dir. Office Consumer Advocacy, State of W.Va., 2005—. Asst. pros. atty. Marion Co., W.Va., 2003—; staff sect. leader, faculty Sch. for Bank Adminstrn. U. Wis., Madison, 1978-89. Treas. Montaineer Area coun. Boy Scouts Am., Fairmont, 1982-90; pres. Three Rivers Coal Festival, Inc., Fairmont, 1984-85, pres., 1985-86, bd. dirs., 1982-86; pres. Appalachian Coal Festival, 1985-86, bd. dirs., 1985—; adv. bd. Inst. for Living, Fairmont, 1983-85; pres. Firemans' CSC, Fairmont, W.Va., 1992-96; elder Christ Cmty. Ch., 2003. Mem. W.Va. Bar Assn. (Kaufman award 1997), Marion County Bar Assn. (pres.), Md. Bar Assn., W.Va. Trial Lawyers Assn., Marion County C. of C. (bd. dirs. 1983—), Fairmont State Coll. Alumni Assn. (bd. dirs. 1982—, pres. 1992-94, Alumnus of Yr. 2002), Fairmont Field Club, Rotary, Masons. Home: 12 Pheasant Dr Fairmont WV 26554 Office: WVa Ins Commr PO Box 50540 Charleston WV 25305-0540 Office Phone: 304-558-3864. Home Fax: 304-342-3021. E-mail: patstanton@wvinsurance.gov.

**STANTON, HARRY DEAN,** actor; b. West Irvine, Ky., July 14, 1926; Actor: (feature films) Tomahawk Trail, 1957, The Proud Rebel, 1958, Pork Chop Hill, 1959, A Dog's Best Friend, 1959, Cool Hand Luke, 1967, Kelly's Heroes, 1970, Two-Lane Blacktop, 1971, Pat Garrett and Billy the Kid, 1971, Dillinger, 1973, Zandy's Bride, 1974, The Godfather, Part II, 1974, Rancho Deluxe, 1974, Farewell, My Lovely, 1975, The Missouri Breaks, 1976, 92 in the Shade, 1976, Renaldo and Clara, 1977, Straight Time, 1977, The Rose, 1979, Wise Blood, 1979, Alien, 1979, Deathwatch, 1979, The Black Marble, 1980, UFOria, 1980, Private Benjamin, 1980, Escape from New York, 1981, Young Doctors in Love, 1982, One From the Heart, 1982, Tough Enough, 1983, Christine, 1983, Repo Man, 1984, The Bear, 1984, Red Dawn, 1984, Paris, Texas, 1984, One Magic Christmas, 1985, Pretty in Pink, 1986, Fool for Love, 1986, The Last Temptation of Christ, 1988, Dream A Little Dream, 1989, Twister, 1989, The Fourth War, 1990, Wild at Heart, 1990, Man Trouble, 1992, Twin Peaks: Fire Walk With Me, 1992, Cent et une nuits, 1995, Never Talk to Strangers, 1995, Midnight Blue, 1996, Down Periscope, 1996, Ben Johnson: Third Cowboy on the Right, 1996, She's So Lovely, 1997, Fire Down Below, 1997, The Mighty, 1998, Ballad of the Nightingale, 1998, Fear and Loathing in Las Vegas, 1998, The Straight Story, 1999, The Green Mile, 1999, The Man Who Cried, 2000, The Pledge, 2001 Ginostra, 2002, Chrystal, 2004, The Wendell Baker Story, 2005, Alpha Dog, 2006, Alien Autopsy, 2006, others; (TV spl.) Faerie Tale Theatre, Showtime, 1987; (TV film) Flatbed Annie and Sweetie Pie: Lady Truckers, 1979, I Want to

Live, 1983, Payoff, 1992, Hostages, 1993, Hotel Room, 1993, (mini-series) Dead Man's Walk, 1996. Mem. Screen Actors Guild. Office: Bresler Kelly & Assocs 11500 W Olympic Blvd Ste 510 Los Angeles CA 90064-1578*

**STANTON, JOHN JEFFREY,** editor, director, journalist, government agency administrator, educator; b. Wichita Falls, Tex., July 19, 1956; s. John Joseph Jr. and Joan (Marley) S.; m. Scylla Maria Silva, Jan. 6, 1981; 1 child, Damien Kristian. BS in Pub. Adminstrn. and Bus. Adminstrn., Nichols Coll., 1978; M in Pub. Adminstrn., U. Detroit, 1980. Rsch. asst. Am. Enterprise Inst., Washington, 1977; rep. aide R.I. Ho. of Reps., Providence, 1977-78; mng. editor Am. Politics, Washington, 1982, assoc. editor, 1983, corp. advisor, 1984, sr. editor, 1985-87; editor, govt. programs mgr. ENTEK, Alexandria, Va., 1988-90; govt. programs dir., cons. Tuckerman Group, Springfield, Va., 1991; analyst, writer Nat. Security Issues, Arlington, Va., 1991—; program dir. TeleStrategies, McLean, Va., 1991-93; Washington corr., mem. editl. bd. Tech. Transfer Jour., 1994-98; editor Tech. Transfer Newsletter; asst. to pres., info. transfer specialist Am. Def. Preparedness Assn., Arlington, 1994-97; contbg. writer Nat. Def. Mag., 1996—; adminstrn. dir. Nat. Def. Indsl. Assn., Arlington, 1997—2004; Washington corr. Australian Def. Mag., 1998-99; editor Voice of the Indsl. Base NDIA, 1998—2000; tchr., facilitator St. Stephens & Agnes, 2005—. Creator, co-host (radio) Power Breakfast, Sta. WNTR, Washington, 1987, Am. Politics Radio, 1987; commentator WAMU-NPR, WBAL, KPFA, Am. Talk Live, NYC, Radio 101, Croatia, Radio Adelaide, KCMO, Kansas City, WNTR, WAMU, WBAC, Balt.; campaign mgr. Madsen for Congress, 8th dist., Va., 2004; polit.-mil. analyst CBS News, CNN, ABC, 2001—. Co-author: America's Nightmare, 2003; author: A Power But Not Super, 2004; contbr. articles to profl. jours., popular mags. Polit. campaign cons. to Glenn Tenney, 1992—; commr. Arlington Little League Baseball, 1993, coach 1997—; mentor Arlington County Ct. Sys., 1997; varsity football coach Wakefield H.S., Arlington, Va., 1998-2002, St. Stephen's Agnes, 2003—. Recipient Doers Honoree The Washington Times, 1988. Avocation: coaching youth sports programs. Personal E-mail: cioran123@yahoo.com.

**STANTON, JOHN W.,** communications executive; b. Seattle; BA in Polit. Sci., Whitman Coll.; MBA, Harvard U. Chmn., CEO Western Wireless (now Alltel Corp.), Bellevue, Wash., 1992—2005; chmn. Telocator, 1986—95; chmn., CEO VoiceStream Wireless, 1992—2002; cons. cellular and long-distance bus.; v.p. McCaw Comms., 1983; exec. v.p., COO McCaw Cellular, 1985—88, vice-chmn., 1988—91; dir. McCaw and LIN Broadcasting, 1991—94; co-founder Stanton Comms., 1988; founder, chmn., CEO (now Western Wireless) Pacific N.W. Cellular, 1992; dir. Columbia Sportswear Co., 1997—. Bd. dirs. Advanced Digital Info. Corp., Columbia Sportswear, Pacific Sci. Ctr.; trustee Whitman Coll. Mem.: Cellular Telecomms. Industry Assn. (chmn. emeritus). Office: c/o Columbia Sportswear 14375 NW Science Park Drive Portland OR 97229*

**STANTON, KATHRYN,** retail executive; b. Nov. 29, 1954; BS in Acctg., U. Ill., 1976; MBA, U. Chgo., 1996. CPA, Ill. From auditor to mgr. Arthur Anderson, Chgo., 1976-81, mgr., 1981-86; from controller to v.p. finance, CFO Follett Corp., Chgo., River Grove, Ill., 1986-97, v.p. finance, CFO River Grove, Ill., 1997—. Bd. dirs. Mus. Sci. and Industry, Chgo. Mem. Am. Inst. CPAs, Financial Exec. Inst., Ill. CPA Soc., Chgo. Council Foreign Rels. Office: Follett Corp 2233 N West St River Grove IL 60171-1895 Fax: 708-452-9347.

**STANTON, LOUIS LEE,** federal judge; b. NYC, Oct. 1, 1927; s. Louis Lee and Helen Parsons (La Fétra) S.; m. Berit Eleonora Rask; children: L. Lee, Susan Helen Benedict, Gordon R., Fredrik S. BA, Yale U., 1950; JD, U. Va., 1955. Assoc. Davis Polk Wardwell Sunderland & Kiendl, N.Y.C., 1955-66, Carter, Ledyard & Milburn, N.Y.C., 1966-67, ptnr., 1967-85; judge U.S. Dist. Ct. (So. Dist.) NY, 1985—96, sr. judge NY, 1996—. Served to 1st lt. USMCR, 1950-52. Fellow Am. Coll. Trial Lawyers, N.Y. Bar Found.; mem. Va. Bar Assn. Office Phone: 212-805-0252.

**STANTON, M(ORRIS) DUNCAN,** psychologist, researcher, dean; b. Lockport, N.Y. Forebears came from England, Scotland, Wales, the Netherlands, France, Ireland, Germany, and Lithuania. Ancestors include a country doctor, several clergy, Canada's first female medical school graduate, a civil engineer who helped build the Panama Canal, artists, teachers, writers, an attorney, two superintendents of schools, and a registered nurse. Related to: Sir Francis Drake, President Grover Cleveland, Alexander Graham Bell, Lincoln's Secretary of War Edwin M. Stanton, and Elizabeth Cady Stanton's husband, New York anti-slavery journalist, attorney and political lecturer Henry Stanton. BA in Psychology, Alfred U., 1962; MA in Clin. Psychology, George Washington U., 1964; PhD in Clin. and Cmty. Psychology, U. Md., 1968. Lic. psychologist NY, Ky., bd. cert. diplomate in clin. psychology Am. Bd. Profl. Psychology, bd. cert. diplomate in family psychology Am. Bd. Profl. Psychology, approved supr. Am. Assn. Marriage Family Therapy, cert. in treatment of alcohol and other psychoactive substance abuse disorders APA. Commd. 2d lt. US Army, 1962, advanced through grades to capt., 1966; intern Walter Reed Gen. Hosp., Washington, 1966—67; lectr. U. Md., 1969—72; from asst. prof. to assoc. prof. psychology in psychiatry U. Pa. Sch. Medicine, Phila., 1972—83; assoc. clin. dir. Penn Psychiatry Phila. Gen. Hosp., 1972—74; dir., addicts and families prog. Phila. Child Guidance Clinic, 1974—83; dir., family therapy tng. program Drug Dependence Treatment Ctr., Phila. VA Med. Ctr., 1974—79; faculty mem. family therapy tng. ctr. Phila. Child Guidance Clinic, 1977—83; tchg. faculty Family Inst. of Phila., 1977—83; instr. Wilmington Med. Ctr., Del., 1978—79; dir., rsch. Phila. Child Guidance Clinic, Pa., 1982—83; prof., psychiatry (psychology) U. Rochester Sch. Medicine and Dentistry, 1983—97; dir., div. family programs, dept. psychiatry U. Rochester Med. Ctr., 1983—93; dir., rsch. div. family programs, dept. of psychiatry U. of Rochester Med. Ctr., 1993—97; prof., dean Sch. Profl. Psychology and Social Work Spalding U., Louisville, 1997—99, v.p., acad. rsch., 1999, prof. emeritus psychology, 1999—. Vis. scholar Fulbright Found., USIA, Argentina, 1991; cons. White House Office of Drug Abuse Policy, 1977—81, USIA, 1987—96, Inst. Medicine Nat. Acad. Scis., 1988, 1991—92; chair, mem. various rev. comms., task forces, site visit teams NIDA, NIMH, NIAAA, 1975—; mem. 16 editl. bds., including Am. Jour. Drug Alcohol Abuse, Family Process, Psychosocial Stress, 1980—; bd Family Process Press, NYC, 1982—99; spkr., presenter invited lectrs., workshops in 27 countries. Conducted an anonymous survey of drug use among 2,372 Army servicemen in Vietnam which, via testimony before the U.S. Senate Special Subcommittee on Alcoholism and Narcotics, received considerable attention in the national media. Consultant/advisory board member to over 90 government agencies, universities, medical centers, and organizations across five continents. Published reviews of the outcome studies on family and couples therapy for drug abuse (meta-analysis, 1997), and the methods for getting reluctant substance abusers to enter treatment or self-help (2004). Author of a recent, brief, and at times humorous book on how America can cure its health care system. Contbr. more than 150 works to sci., profl. publs.; author: monographs and books in field, 1977—. Mem. dept. def. task group on alcoholism The Pentagon, Washington, 1971—72; ad hoc com. mem. special action office on drug abuse policy The White House, Washington, 1974; mem. advisory group family therapy prevention rsch. project Nat. Inst. Drug Abuse, 1981—82; chair, moderator family rsch. conf. Alcohol, Drug Abuse and Mental Health Adminstrn., 1981; cons. Family Health Plan, 1985—88; cons., sponsor, supr. Fulbright Commn., 1987—92. Decorated Bronze Star Medal; recipient Plaque of Appreciation, Found. for Parents in Action (Argentina), 1991, Shield of Police of Salta Province (Argentina), 1991, Cert. of Appreciation for Svc. on Mayor's Drug, Alcohol Planning Com., City of Louisville, 1998; grantee, NIH (NIDA/NIAAA), 1974—84, 1995—; Ann. Disting. fellow, Pikes Peak Mental Health Ctr., 1980. Fellow: APA (Pres. Citation 2001), Acad. Family Psychology, Nat. Coun. Family Rels. (Award Appreciation for dedication to the enhancement of family life 1988, Recognition cert. for longstanding svc. 1988, Legacy Circle award 1999), Am. Assoc. Marriage and Family Therapy (Outstanding Rsch. Contbn. in Marital and Family Therapy 1980, Cumulative Contbn. Family Therapy Rsch. award 2003, Ky. Divsn. award of Appreciation 2004); mem.: Internat. Family Therapy Assn., Am. Family Therapy Acad. (chair

alcohol and drug interest group 1982—87, Disting. Contbn. Family Systems Rsch. 1997), Associacion Sistemica de Buenos Aires (hon.), South African Inst. Marital and Family Therapy (hon.). Office: The Morton Center 1028 Barret Ave Louisville KY 40204

**STANTON, PAMELA FREEMAN,** interior designer, writer; b. Jacksonville, Tex., July 18, 1941; d. William Thomas and Ruth Ethel (Branton) Freeman; m. Karl F. Edmonds, Jr., Jan. 28, 1961 (div. 1966); m. Charles Calvin Stanton, Sept. 1, 1973; 1 child, Julie Anne. AA in Bus., Kilgore Coll., 1961. Design cons., Denver, Boston and Salem, Oreg., 1963-69; exec. sec. Alexander: Alexander of Tex. Inc., Dallas, 1967-69; interior designer Milmac Furniture, Dallas, 1969-73, Homestead House, Denver, 1973-76; case aide counselor Eliot Cmty. Mental Health Ctr., Concord, Mass., 1980-82; pres., owner Stancom Designs, Virginia Beach, Va., 1990-2000; interior designer Willis Furniture Co., 2000—. Author: I Am That I Am, 1994 (Best Book of Yr. N.Am. Bookdealers Exch., 1995). Recipient Cert. of Appreciation for vol. work Emerson Hosp., Concord, 1981; named Internat. Writer of Yr., 2003. Republican. Avocations: collecting art, travel, gardening, theatre-plays, entertaining. Home and Office: 4401 Leatherwood Dr Virginia Beach VA 23462-5704 Office Phone: 757-499-3432.

**STANTON, PATRICK MICHAEL,** lawyer; b. Phila., Sept. 8, 1947; s. Edward Joseph and Helen Marie (Coghlan) S.; m. Kathleen Ann Fama, Aug. 22, 1970; children: Cheryl Marie, Susan Elizabeth. BS in History, St. Joseph's U., 1969; JD, U. Va., 1972; MBA, Fairleigh Dickinson, 1984. Bar: Ohio 1972 (inactive), N.J. 1982, N.Y. 1985, U.S. Dist. Ct. (so. dist.) Ohio 1972, U.S. Dist. Ct. (ea. dist.) N.J. 1982, U.S. Dist. Ct. (so. dist.) N.Y. 1984. Assoc. Taft, Stettinius & Hollister, Cin., 1972—80; labor counsel Union Camp Corp., Wayne, NJ, 1980—83; dir. labor rels., equal employment opportunity programs W.R. Grace & Co., N.Y.C., 1983—86; of counsel Shanley & Fisher, P.C., Morristown, NJ, 1986—89, ptnr., chmn. labor and employment group, 1989—95; dir. Stanton, Hughes, Diana, Cerra, Mariani & Margello, P.C., Morristown, 1995—2003; atty., shareholder Ogletree, Deakins, Nash, Smoak & Stewart, P.C., Morristown, 2004—. Adj. prof. bus. law Fairleigh Dickinson U. 1984-92; pres. Sidney Reitman employment law Am. Inn. Ct., 1997-2001. Pres., bd. dirs. N.Y. State Adv. Coun. on Employment Law, Inc., N.Y.C., 1985-86. DuPont Schooldist U. Va., 1970. Mem. ABA, N.J. State Bar Assn. (exec. com. labor employment law sect. 1989—, rec. sec. 1995-97, treas. 1997-99, 2d vice chair 1999-2001, 1st vice chair 2001-03, chair 2003-05, immediate past chmn. 2005—), Phi Alpha Theta, Delta Mu Delta. Roman Catholic. Home: 292 Forest Ave Glen Ridge NJ 07028-1808 Office: Ogletree Deakins Nash Smoak & Stewart PC 10 Madison Ave Ste 402 Morristown NJ 07960-7303 Office Phone: 973-656-1600. Office Fax: 973-656-1611. Business E-Mail: patrick.stanton@ogletreedeakins.com.

**STANTON, R. THOMAS,** lawyer; b. Moline, Ill., 1943; BA, Knox Coll., 1965; postgrad., Harvard U., 1966—67; JD, Northwestern U., 1969. Bar: Ohio 1969, N.Y. 1982. Mng. ptnr. Squire Sanders & Dempsey LLP, chmn. Cleve., 1990—, chmn. mgmt. com. Bd. editors Northwestern U. Law Review, 1969. Bd. chair Leadership Cleve., Univ. Circle, Inc.; trustee The Musical Arts Assn./The Cleve. Orchestra, Ohio Bus. Roundtable; mem. law bd. Northwestern Univ.; mem. Dean's Adv. Coun. Case Western Reserve Law Sch. Mem. Order of Coif. (chmn. mgmt. com.). Office: Squire Sanders & Dempsey LLP 4900 Key Tower 127 Public Sq Cleveland OH 44114-1304 Fax: 216-479-8780. Office Phone: 216-479-8728. Business E-Mail: rstanton@ssd.com.

**STANTON, ROBERT JAMES, JR.,** geologist, educator; b. LA, June 17, 1931; s. Robert James and Audrey (Franke) S.; m. Patricia Ann Burns, Sept. 13, 1953; children— John, Carol. BS, Calif. Inst. Tech., 1953, PhD, 1960; MA, Harvard U., 1956. Research geologist Shell Devel. Co., Houston, 1959-67; mem. faculty Tex. A&M U., 1967—, prof. geology, 1972-86, Ray C. Fish prof. geology, 1986-98, head dept., 1979-83, prof. geology emeritus, 1998—. Vis. prof. U. Nuremburg-Erlangen, Germany, 1984; rsch. assoc. invertebrate paleontology Natural History Mus. L.A. County. Co-author: Paleoecology: Principles and Applications, 1981, 2d edit., 1990. Served with AUS, 1953-55. Fellow Geol. Soc. Am.; mem. Internat. Paleontol. Union, Paleontol. Soc., Paleontol. Research Inst., Soc. Econ. Paleontologists and Mineralogists (Outstanding Paper award 1970), Sigma Xi, Tau Beta Pi. Home: 2297 Valleyfield Ave Thousand Oaks CA 91360 Office: Nat Hist Mus LA County Dept Invertebrate Paleontol 900 Exposition Blvd Los Angeles CA 90007 Business E-Mail: robertstanton@adelphia.net.

**STANTON, ROBERT JOHN, JR.,** language educator; b. N.Y.C., July 7, 1942; s. Robert John Stanton and Mary McGinty; m. Felicia Lena Giancola, Nov. 15, 1959; children: Robert III, Sharon. BA, Hofstra U., 1970; MA, U. Mass., Amherst, 1972, postgrad., 1974-79. Instr. English Flagler Coll., St. Augustine, Fla., 1972-74; tchg. asst. U. Mass., Amherst, 1974-77, lectr. in rhetoric, 1979-81; English tchr. Bishop Kenny H.S., Jacksonville, Fla., 1982-83, Duval County Pub. Schs., Jacksonville, 1984-87; asst. prof. English Jacksonville U., 1987-91, assoc. prof. English, 1992—2006, chmn. divsn. humanities, 1993-97. Author: Seventeen British Novelists, 1978, Gore Vidal, 1978, Truman Capote, 1980, Views From A Window: Conversations with Gore Vidal, 1980; (poems) Collected Word Paintings, 2000; co-author: Beneath Mad River Mansion, 1992, Noah's Orbella, 1994, The Devil's Reed, 1996, Dangerous Words, 2003. Mem. MLA, Nat. Assn. Tchrs. English, Fla. Assn. Depts. English (pres. 1996), Swift River Hist. Soc. Democrat. Avocations: astronomy, reading, writing, observing the universe. Home: 614 15th Ave S Jacksonville Beach FL 32250 Office: Jacksonville Univ English FL 32211 Office Phone: 904-256-7106. Business E-Mail: bstanto@ju.edu.

**STANTON, ROGER D.,** lawyer; b. Oct. 4, 1938; s. George W. and Helen V. (Peterson) S.; m. Judith L. Duncan, Jan. 27, 1962; children: Jeffrey B., Brady D., Todd A. AB, U. Kans., 1960, JD, 1963. Bar: Kans. 1963, U.S. Dist. Ct. Kans. 1963, U.S. Ct. Appeals (10th cir.) 1972, U.S. Supreme Ct. 1973. Assoc. Stanley, Schroeder, Weeks, Thomas & Lysaught, Kansas City, 1963—68; ptnr. Weeks, Thomas & Lysaught, Kansas City, 1969—81, also bd. dirs., chmn. exec. com., 1981-82; ptnr. Stinson, Mag & Fizzell, Kansas City, 1983-96, chmn. products practice group, also bd. dirs., 1993-95; ptnr. litig. practice Berkowitz Stanton Brandt Williams & Shaw LLP, Prairie Village, Kans., 1997—2005; pvt. practice Overland Pk., Kans., 2005—. Chmn. bd. editors Jour. Kans. Bar Assn., 1975-83; contbr. articles to profl. jours. Active Boy Scouts Am., 1973-79; pres. YMCA Youth Football Club, 1980-82; co-chmn. Civil Justice Reform Act com. Dist. of Kans., 1991-95; bd. dirs. Kans. Appleseed Found., 2000—. Fellow: Am. Coll. Trial Lawyers (state SRSC Com. 1983—88, state chmn. 1984—86, state SRSC Com. 2001—); mem.: Hist. Soc. Tenth Cir. (bd.dirs. 2005—), Earl O'Conner Inn of Ct. bd. dirs. 1972—75, founding mem. 1991—), Kans. Assn. Def. Counsel (pres. 1977—78), Johnson County Bar Assn. (chmn. bench, bd. dirs. bar com.), Johnson County Bar Found. (pres., trustee), Kans. Bar Assn. (Pres.'s award 1982), Def. Rsch. Inst. (state co-chmn. 1979—90, Exceptional Performance award 1979), Am. Bd. Trial Adv. (exec. com. East Kans./West Miss. chpt. 1994—99), Internat. Assn. Def. Counsel, U. Kans. Kansas City Alumni (bd. dirs. 2001—), U. Kans. Sch. Law Alumni Assn. (bd. dirs. 1975—76, 1985—86), Phi Delta Phi. Office: Ste 500 Bldg 51 9393 W 110th St Overland Park KS 66210 Office Phone: 913-451-6958. Business E-Mail: rstanton@stanton-law.com.

**STANTON, RONALD P.,** export company executive; b. 1928; Grad., City College of NY; PhD (hon.), Yeshiva U., 1982. Chmn. Transammonia, Inc., N.Y.C., 1965—. Mem. bd. of trustees Yeshiva U., New York, 1976—, vice chmn bd. of trustees, 1992—2002, chmn. bd. of trustees, 2002—; bd. mem. Lincoln Center, New York, NY Presbyterian Hospital, New York; chmn. Ministerial Commt. Office: Transammonia Inc 350 Park Ave New York NY 10022*

**STANTON, SYLVIA DOUCET,** artist, art gallery owner; b. New Orleans, Sept. 21, 1935; d. Clifton Leo Sr. and Maria Delbert (Alfonso Swiber) Doucet; m. Robert Elmer Stanton, Jan. 3, 1953; children: Robert, Sylvia,

Barbara, Richard, Laura, Cheri. Grad. high sch., New Orleans, 1952. Real estate agt. Century 21, Slidell, La., 1982-88; ptnr. Doucet's Jewelry, Slidell, 1969-82; owner Plantation Antiques, Slidell, 1974-88, Magnolia Plantation, Slidell, 1988-97, Doucet-Stanton Ltd., Slidell, 1988-97, Gallery at Milbrook, Picayune, Miss., 2001—05; co-owner Lott Stanton Gallery, Jackson, Miss., 2006—. Appraiser jewelry, antiques, real estate, 1969—; artist, painter, 1950—. Exhibited in group shows at Montserrat Gallery, N.Y.C., Abita Gallery, Abita Springs, La., The Gallery at Milbrook, Picayune, Miss., Serenity Gallery, Bay St. Louis, Miss., Sterling Art Gallery, New Orleans, Represented in permanent collections Montserrat Salon, NY. Founder Le cotillion, Slidell, 1975; founding chmn. Pres. Coun. of Le Cotillion, 1987. Recieved title of nobility Countess De Miron Delbert, Greece, 1988. Mem.: Allied Artists of Am., New Orleans Art Assn., Inner Wheel (dist chmn. 6840 1990—91, founding pres. Slidell 1989), World Trade Ctr., Albuquerque Art League, Bayou Liberty Garden Club (sec. 1988—), Picayune Garden Club, Ozone Camellia Club. Republican. Roman Catholic. Avocations: art, antiques, gardening, interior decorating. Home: 615 E Lakeshore Dr Carriere MS 39426 Office: Lott Stanton Gallery 1800 N State St Jackson MS 39202 Personal E-mail: stanfam2@bellsouth.net. Business E-Mail: lottstantongallery@homestead.com.

**STANTON, WILLIAM ANTHONY,** diplomat; b. Jersey City, Jan. 17, 1947; s. Harold Arthur Stanton and Armen Katherine Kharajian; m. Karen Clark Stanton, Sept. 14, 1984; children: Katherine Ruth, Elizabeth Armen. BA, Fordham U., 1968; MA, U. N.C., 1970, PhD, 1978. Fgn. svc. officer, 1978—; consular Embassy Beirut, 1979—81; staff asst. Sec. NE S Asian Affairs, 1982—83; polit. officer U.S. Embassy, Beijing, 1987-90; sr. tng. Hoover Instn., Stanford, Calif., 1990-91; polit.-mil. affairs officer U.S. Embassy, Islamabad, Pakistan, 1991-93; spl. asst. for East Asian affairs Office Under Sec. for Polit. Affairs, U.S. Dept. State, Washington, 1993-94; dep. dir. office Chinese and Mongolian affairs U.S. Dept. State, Washington, 1994-95; min. counselor for polit. affairs U.S. Embassy, Beijing, 1995-98; sr. seminar U.S. Dept. State, Washington, 1998-99, dir. Office of UN Polit. Affairs, 1999-2001, dir. Office of Egyptian and No. African Affairs, 2001—03; dep. chief of mission, US Embassy in Canberra US Dept. State, Washington, 2003—, chargé d'affaires ad interim, US Embassy in Canberra, 2005—06. Mem. Am. Fgn. Svc. Assn., Phi Beta Kappa. E-mail: stantonwa@state.gov.

**STANTON, WILLIAM F.,** retired elementary school educator, retail executive; b. Chgo., June 30, 1950; s. Robert Crawford and Margaret Virginia Stanton. BA, MacMurray Coll., 1978; MA, U. Ill., 1983. Tchr. grade 6 Glen Oaks Sch., Hickory Hills, Ill., 1977—81; tchr. grades 3, 4, 6 Knox Elem. Sch., Chandler, Ariz., 1981—2005; retail supr. J.C. Penney, Mesa, Ariz., 1991—. Mem. oversight com. SANTAN Credit Union, Chandler, 1995—. Mem.: ASCD, NEA, Ariz. Geog. Alliance, Internat. Reading Assn. Avocations: travel, reading, photography.

**STANTON, WILLIAM JOHN, JR.,** marketing educator, author; b. Chgo., Dec. 15, 1919; s. William John and Winifred (McGann) S.; m. Imma Mair, Sept. 14, 1978; children by previous marriage: Kathleen Louise, William John III. BS, Ill. Inst. Tech., 1940; MBA, Northwestern U., 1941, PhD, 1948; D (hon.), Cath. U. Santo Domingo, Dominican Republic, 2003. Mgmt. trainee Sears Roebuck & Co., 1940-41; instr. U. Ala., 1941-44; auditor Olan Mills Portrait Studios, Chattanooga, 1944-46; asst. prof., assoc. prof. U. Wash., 1948-55; prof. U. Colo., Boulder, 1955-90; prof. emeritus, 1990—; head mktg. dept. U. Colo., 1955-71, acting dean, 1963-64; assoc. dean U. Colo. (Sch. Bus.), 1964-67; ret. Author: Economic Aspects of Recreation in Alaska, 1953; author: (with others) Challenge of Business, 1975; author: (with M. Etzel and B. Walker) Marketing, 14th edit., Spanish, Chinese, Portuguese, Indonesian and Korean transl., 2003; author: (with R. Varaldo) Italian Edition, 2d edit., 1989; author: (with others) South African Edition, 1992; author: (with M.S. Sommers and J.G. Barnes) Canadian Edition Fundamentals of Marketing, 11th edit., 2004; author: (with K. Miller and R. Layton) Australian Edition, 4th edit., 2004; author: (with Rosann Spiro and G.A. Rich) Management of a Sales Force, 11th edit., Spanish, Portuguese, Chinese, and Russian transl., 2003; contbr. articles to profl. jour. Mem. Am. Mktg. Assn., Mktg. Educators Assn., Beta Gamma Sigma. Roman Catholic. Home: 1445 Sierra Dr Boulder CO 80302-7846

**STANTON-HICKS, MICHAEL D'ARCY,** anesthesiologist, pain medicine specialist; b. Adelaide, Australia, June 3, 1931; arrived in U.S.A., 1972; s. Cedric Stanton-Hicks and Florence (Haggett) Perrin; m. Kristina Litsmark, Aug. 4, 1969 (div. Aug. 1984); children: Erik Michael, Leif Neal; m. Ursula Koch, Aug. 27, 1985. MB, BChir, Adelaide U., 1962; Dr. med., U. Dusseldorf, 1984. Bd. equivalent Am. Bd. Anesthesiology; diplomate Am. Bd. Pain Medicine, Interventional Pain Practice, 2002. Intern Queen Elizabeth Hosp., Adelaide, 1961-62, tutor, staff anesthesiologist, 1970-72; resident Royal Postgrad. Med. Sch., London and Lasarettet Köping, 1966-68; asst. dir. anesthesiology intensive care Södersjükhuset, Stockholm, 1968-69; instr. anesthesiology U. Wash. Med. Sch., Seattle, 1969-70, asst. prof., 1972-75; prof., chmn. dept. U. Mass. Med. Sch., Worcester, 1975-83; prof. U. Colo. Health Scis. Ctr., Denver, 1983-86, vice chmn. dept., 1983-85, acting chmn., 1985-86; prof., dir. pain clinic and rsch. Johannes Gutenberg U., Mainz, Germany, 1986-88, prof., 1986—97; dir. pain mgmt. ctr. Cleve. Clinic Found., 1988-98, vice chmn. pain mgmt. and rsch. divsn. anesthesia, 1998—; prof. Lerner Coll. Medicine, Case Western Res. U., Cleve., 2004—. Med. examiner Indsl. Commn. Ohio; mem. Ohio Pain Adv. Com., Dept. Health; mem. liaison com. med. bd. Ohio Pain Com.; advisor Am. Acad. Disability Evaluating Physicians, 2000-02; appt. to gov.'s task force on compassionate care, Dept. of Health, Ohio; bd. dirs. World Inst. Pain; sci. advisor Reflex Sympathetic Dystrophy Assn., 2006. Author, editor Regional Anesthesia: Advances and Selected Topics, 1978, (with Boas) Chronic Low Back Pain, 1982; author, editor: (with Wilson and Harden) CRPS: Current Diagnosis and Therapy, 2005; co-author: (with Raj and Nolte) Illustrated Manual of Regional Anesthesia, 1988 (Most Beautiful Book of Yr. award Frankfurt, Fed. Republic Germany Pubs. Book Conv., 1989), (with Janig and Boas) Reflex Sympathetic Dystrophy, 1989, (with Janig) Reflex Sympathetic Dystrophy: A Reappraisal, 1996; author: Pain and Sympathetic Nervous System, 1989; exec. editor Pain Practice Jour., 2001—, sect. editor Complex Regional Pain Syndrome, 2002, mem. editl. bd. Pain Physician, 2002—; editor (with Dulson and Harden): CRPS: Current Diagnose and Therapy, 2005. Squadron leader res. Royal Australian Air Force, 1962-65. Recipient Disting. Scientist award Reflex Sympathetic Dystrophy Assn., 2002; named Top Doc Good Housekeeping Mag., 2003, Disting. Svc. award European Soc. Regional Anesthesia, 2003; named Scientist of Yr. Am. Herschel Soc., 1991-92; Australian Univs. Commn. mature age scholar, 1953-60. Fellow Royal Coll. Surgeons (faculty anesthetists), Royal Coll. Anesthetists, Am. Acad. Pain Medicine, Interventional Pain Practice; mem. Internat. Assn. Study Pain (chmn. spl. interest group pain and sympathetic nervous sys. 1990—), World Inst. Pain (bd. dirs. 1995—), Am. Soc. Regional Anesthesia (bd. dirs. 1979-91, pres. 1989-90, Disting. Svc. award, 1998), Assn. Anesthetists Gt. Britain and Ireland, Ohio State Med. Assn., Cleve. Acad. Medicine, Am. Acad. Med. Infrared Imaging (bd. dirs. 1991-95, pres. 1994-95, William Hobbins Rsch. award 1993), Am. Acad. Disability Evaluating Physicians (adv. com. mem. complex regional pain syndrome 2000—02), Am. Pain Soc., Am. Acad. Pain Medicine, Am. Neuromodulation Soc. (pres. 1994-98, bd. dirs. 1998-2000), Reflex Sympathetic Dystrophy Assn. (sci. adv. bd. 2000-05), Army-Navy-Air Force Club. Republican. Anglican. Avocations: skiing, photography, travel, flying. Home: 11405 Clearfield Lane Chardon OH 44024 Office: Cleve Clinic Found 9500 Euclid Ave Cleveland OH 44195-0001 Office Phone: 216-445-9559. Business E-Mail: stantom@ccf.org.

**STANZIANO, STEPHEN,** music educator; b. Cleve., Apr. 11, 1955; s. E. Joseph and Adrianna Angelina (Buccili) Stanziano. MusB magna cum laude, Cleve. State U., 1996; MA, Kent State U., 1998, PhD Music Theory and Composition, 2004. Tchg. asst. Kent State U., 1996—2000; lectr. music Cleve. State U., 1999—2000; adj. faculty Hiram Coll., Ohio, 2000—01, Lakeland C.C., Kirtland, Ohio, 2001—. Lectr. music Cleve. State U., 2002—; sr. lectr. music U. Akron, Ohio, 2004—; program annotator Kent Blossom Music, 2000—, Suburban Symphony Orch., Beachwood, Ohio, 2004—;

reviewer Wadsworth Pub. Co., Belmont, Calif., 2004—. Co-author: Learning To Listen, 1998; musician: Suburban Symphony Orch., 2004—. Fellow, Kent (Ohio) State U., 2000—01. Mem.: Am. Soc. Composers, Authors and Pubs., Golden Key, Pi Kappa Lambda. Republican. Roman Catholic. Avocations: jogging, gardening, reading, woodworking, collectable sheet music and books. Office: Cleveland State Univ 2001 Euclid Ave Cleveland OH 44115

**STANZIONE, DANIEL C.,** communications company executive; b. Yonkers, N.Y. BSEE, Clemson U., 1967, MS in Envirion. Systems Engring., 1968, PhD in Elec. and Computer Engring., 1972. Former pres. Bell Labs, Network Sys. Group, 1995-99; former exec. v.p., COO Lucent Technologies, Inc., Murray Hill, N.J., chief network architect, 1999—. Bd. dirs. Quest Diagnostics, Inc., Zhone Technologies, Inc., Flavion Techs., Avaya, Inc. Contbr. articles to profl. jours. and publs.; patentee in field. Bd. overseers N.J. Inst. of Technology; chmn. engring. adv. bd. Hampton U. Fellow IEEE.

**STAPLES, BRENT,** writer, reporter; b. Chester, Pa., 1951; BA, Widener Univ., 1973; PhD in Psychology, Univ. Chgo., 1977. Tchr. psychology; reporter Chgo. Sun-Times; editor NY Times Book Rev.; reporter NY Times, asst. editor met. news, editl. bd. mem., 1990—. Author: (essays) Just Walk On By: A Black Man Ponders His Power to Alter Public Space, 1986, (memoir) Parallel Time: Growing Up in Black and White, 1994 (Anisfield-Wolf Book award, 1995, LA Times Book prize finalist). Grantee Danfort Fellowship. Office: Editl Bd NY Times 229 W 43rd St New York NY 10036 Office Phone: 212-556-7407. Office Fax: 212-556-3815.

**STAPLES, DAVID M.,** corporate financial executive; B in Acctg., Mich. State U. Audit and bus. adv. practice Arthur Andersen LLP, 1985—96; divisional v.p., strategic planning and reporting Kmart Corp., 1996—2000; v.p. fin. Spartan Stores, Grand Rapids, Mich., 2000, exec. v.p., CRO, 2000—. Office: Spartan Stores PO Box 8700 Grand Rapids MI 49518-8700

**STAPLES, GEORGE MCDADE,** federal agency administrator, former ambassador; b. 1947; m. Jo Ann; 1 child, Catherine. BA, U. So. Calif., 1970; MS, Ctrl. Mich. U. With U.S. Fgn. Svc., El Salvador, Uruguay, Equatorial Guinea, Bahamas, Zimbabwe, 1961-81, sr. Turkey desk officer Bur. European Affairs Washington, sr. watch officer State's Ops. Ctr., dep. chief of mission Bahrain; US amb. to Rwanda US Dept. State, Kigali, Rwanda, 1999—2001, US amb. to Equatorial Guinea & Cameroon, 2001—04; nat. security affairs fellow Hoover Instn., Stanford U., 1995-96; polit. advisor to Supreme Allied Comdr. NATO, Brussels, 2004—06; dir. US Fgn. Svc. US Dept. State, Washington, 2006—, dir. human resources, 2006—. Officer USAF, 1970-78. Office: US Dept State Harry S Truman Bldg 2201 C St NW Rm 6218 Washington DC 20520 E-mail: rwandaamb@yahoo.com.*

**STAPLES, RICHARD FARNSWORTH,** lawyer; b. Providence, Nov. 24, 1919; s. Harold E. and Margaret (Smith) S.; m. Mary Kingsbury, June 20, 1942; children: Richard Farnsworth, Jr., Benjamin T., Edward K. AB, Harvard U., 1941, LLB, 1949. Bar: R.I. 1949. Ptnr. Tillinghast, Collins & Graham, Providence, 1949-81, Hinckley, Allen & Snyder, Providence, 1981-87, of counsel, 1987—. Mem. commn. on jud. tenure and discipline, 1987-93; mem. ethics adv. panel R.I. Supreme Ct., 1995-97. Chmn. sch. com. Town of Barrington (R.I.), 1957-62; mem., 1956-62; mem. State Bd. Edn., Providence, 1964-69, chmn., 1968-69; pres. R.I. Hist. Soc., 1981-83. Served to 1st lt. U.S. Army, 1943-46. Decorated Bronze Star Mem. ABA, R.I. Bar Assn., Soc. Colonial Wars, Providence Art Club, Harvard Club. Home: 229 Medway St # 104 Providence RI 02903-5300 also: 79 Loon Lake Rd Freedom NH 03836-0298 Office Phone: 401-274-2000.

**STAPLETON, BENJAMIN F., III,** lawyer; b. Newport News, Va., 1943; BA, Harvard U., 1965; LLB, Yale U., 1969. Bar: NY 1972. Assoc. Sullivan & Cromwell, NYC, 1969—77, ptnr., 1977—, mem. mergers & acquisitions group, 1978—; sr. ptnr. Bd. trustees Amon Carter Mus., Ft. Worth. Office: Sullivan & Cromwell 125 Broad St New York NY 10004-2498

**STAPLETON, BEVERLY COOPER,** aerospace executive; b. Birmingham, Ala., June 4, 1933; d. Herston MacAger and Virginia (Averyt) Cooper; m. John Parker Stapleton, Aug. 31, 1959 (div. July 1981); children: Lisa Karen, Lawrence Cooper BBA magna cum laude, U. Miami, 1954; MA, U. Ala. 1960. Tchr. Miami Beach H.S. Dade County Pub. Schs., Fla., 1956—59; mem. behavior R & D program U. Ala., Tuscaloosa, 1959—61; contracts adminstr. Houghton Mifflin Co., Palo Alto, Calif., 1974—78; Calif. sales rep. Prentice-Hall Inc., San Jose, 1978; contract adminstr., cost analyst United Techs., Sunnyvale, Calif., 1978—82; mgr. contract adminstrn. Echo Sci. Corp., Mountain View, Calif., 1982; contracts mgr. Lockheed Martin Corp. Missiles & Space, Sunnyvale, 1982—98; ret., 1998. Instr. master's program in contracts and material mgmt. St. Mary's Coll., Moraga, Calif., 1984—86; mem. adv. bd. grad. program in contracts and acquisition mgmt. Golden Gate U., San Francisco, 1984—85; contracts mgr. Hubble Space Telescope Program, 1983—85. Fellow polit. sci. U. Ala., 1954-55; recipient Women of Achievement award Santa Clara County Commn. on Status of Women, 1985 Fellow Nat. Contract Mgmt. Assn. (cert., pres. San Francisco area chpt. 1984-85, nat. coun. fellows 1983—, nat. exec. com. 1986-88, nat. bd. dirs. 1985-86, 97-98, nat. v.p. 1987-88), Mgmt. Assn. (treas. Chem. Systems divsn., 1981), Beta Gamma Sigma, Delta Delta Delta Democrat. Presbyterian. Home: 3728 Rhoda Dr San Jose CA 95117-3421

**STAPLETON, BILL,** sports and entertainment agent; b. St. Louis; s. Bill and Brooke Stapleton; m. Laura Stapleton, 1995 (div.); 2 children; m. Patty Stapleton, 2005. BA in Biology, U. of Tex. at Austin, 1987, MBA, 1991, JD, 1994. Atty., sports agent Brown McCarroll & Oaks Hartline; represented Lance Armstrong, 1995—; founder, principal Capital Sports & Entertainment, Austin, Tex., 1998—. Chmn. athletes advisory coun. US Olympic Com 1997, v.p., mem. ... com., bd. dirs., co-chair governance and ethics task force, 2003. Promoter, producer Lance 6 (to celebrate Lance Armstrong's sixth Tour de France victory). Achievements include member of 1988 US Olympic Swimming Team; double Gold Medallist 1987 Pan-Am Games; US Champion and four-time NCAA All-American; work on behalf of Lance Armstrong includes numerous Fortune 500 endorsement partnerships, publication of two NY Times bestsellers, and development of the Lance Armstrong Foundation for cancer. Office: Capital Sports & Entertainment 98 San Jacinto Blvd Ste 430 Austin TX 78701 Office Phone: 512-478-7211. Office Fax: 512-476-0611.*

**STAPLETON, COREY,** financial planner; b. Seattle, Sept. 17, 1967; BS, U.S. Naval Acad., 1992; MA, Temple U., 1995. Commd. officer USN, 1986, advanced through grades, 1997; fin. planner Prudential Ind. Fin. Svcs., 1997—. Mem. Midland Empire Pachyderm Club, 1998—; campaign aide Bob Dole for Pres. Campaign, 1996; campaign mgr. Norm Mills, Mont. State House Dist. 19, 1998; chair Yellowstone County Young Reps., 1999-2000. Mem. Am. Legion, Billings C. of C., Rotary. Office: 2015 Eastridge Dr Billings MT 59102-7904 E-mail: stapletonct@aol.com.

**STAPLETON, CRAIG ROBERTS,** ambassador; b. Kansas City, Mo. m. Dorothy Walker, 1971; children: Walker, Wendy Reyes. BA magna cum laude, Harvard U., 1967, MBA. Real estate exec., pres. Marsh and McLennan Real Estate Advisors, Inc., N.Y., NY, 1982—2001; US amb. to Czech Republic US Dept. State, Prague, 2001—03, US amb. to France Paris, 2005—. Ptnr. with George W. Bush Texas Rangers Baseball Team, 1989—98; chmn. Conn. State Re-Election Campaign George W. Bush, 2004; pres. Vaclav Havel Found.; dir. cos. Allegheny Properties, Metro PCS, TB Woods and Winston Ptnrs. Former bd. dirs. Peace Corps; pres. Vaclav Havel Found.; trustee Brunswick Sch., Greenwich, Conn.; vis. com. other coms. Harvard Univ. Recipient Jan Masaryk Medal for Service to Czech Republic. Office: US Dept State 9200 Paris Pl Washington DC 20521

**STAPLETON, HARVEY JAMES,** physics professor; b. Kalamazoo, Dec. 22, 1934; s. Herbert James and Viola Delia (Early) S.; m. Joan Eileen Sylvander, June 22, 1957; children: Patricia Lynne, Susan Joan, Jeffrey Denis.

BS, U. Mich., 1957; PhD, U. Calif., Berkeley, 1961. Faculty physics U. Ill. Urbana, 1961—, prof., 1969-95, prof. emeritus, 1995—, assoc. dean Grad. Coll., 1980-95, assoc. vice chancellor for rsch., 1987-95; interim dean Grad. Coll., 1992; interim vice chancellor for rsch. U. Ill., 1992. Alfred P. Sloan fellow, 1962-64 Contbr. articles to profl. jours. Fellow Am. Phys. Soc.; mem. Phi Beta Kappa, Sigma Xi, Phi Sigma Kappa, Phi Kappa Phi, Phi Eta Sigma. Roman Catholic. Home: 3806 Gulf Of Mexico Dr Unit 310 Longboat Key FL 34228-2733 Personal E-mail: hjstapleton@earthlink.net.

**STAPLETON, JAMES FRANCIS,** lawyer; b. Bridgeport, Conn., June 30, 1932; s. James M. and Lucy V. (Moran) S.; m. Margaret M. Daly, July 13, 1957; children: James F., Mark T., Paul and Kathleen. BSS, Fairfield U., 1954; LLB, Boston Coll., 1957; LLM, Georgetown U., 1958. Bar: Conn. 1957, U.S. Dist. Ct. (ea. and so. dists.) N.Y. 1979, U.S. Ct. Appeals (2d cir.) 1966, U.S. Dist. Ct. Conn. 1961, Mass. 1957, U.S. Supreme Ct. 1965, U.S. Ct. Appeals (D.C. cir.) 1958. Atty.; Appellate Sect., Antitrust Divsn. U.S. Dept. Justice, 1957-58; assoc., ptnr. Marsh, Day & Calhoun, Bridgeport, 1958-73; city atty. City of Bridgeport, 1971-73; legis. counsel Conn. Bankers Assn., 1971-73; judge Conn. Superior Ct., 1973-78; chmn. Criminal Justice Commn. State of Conn., 1991-95; ptnr. Day, Berry & Howard, Stamford, Conn., 1978—2002, of coun., 2003—. Active Bridgeport Bd. Edn., 1960—69. Fellow Am. Bar Found.; Am. Coll. Trial Lawyers (chmn. state com. 1994-96, regent 1996-2000); mem. ABA (ho. of dels. 1984-88), Am. Bd. Trial Advocates, Conn. Bar Assn. (bd. govs., ho. of dels., v.p., pres.), Fed. Bar Coun. Found. for 2d Cir. (v.p., chmn.). Home: 6 Winding Way Trumbull CT 06611 Office: Day Berry & Howard One AudubonSt New Haven CT 06511 Office Phone: 203-752-5019. Personal E-mail: jfstapleton@dbh.com.

**STAPLETON, JAMES HALL,** statistician, educator; b. Royal Oak, Mich., Feb. 8, 1931; s. James Leo and Dorothy May (Hall) S.; m. Alicia M. Brown, Apr. 3, 1963; children: James, Lara, Sara. BA, Eastern Mich. U., 1952; MS, Purdue U., 1954, PhD, 1957. Statistician Gen. Electric Co., 1957-58; asst. prof. stats. and probability Mich. State U., East Lansing, 1958-63, assoc. prof., 1963-72, prof., 1972—, chmn. dept., 1968-75, grad. dir., 1985—. Cons. Gen. Telephone Co. of Ind.; vis. prof. U. Philippines, 1978-79 Mem. USS-Mich. Swim Com., AAU, 1976-84, chmn., 1976-78; mem. Mich. AAU Exec. Bd., 1976-81. NSF fellow, 1956-67 Mem. Inst. Math. Stats., Am. Statis. Assn. Office: Mich State U Dept Statistics East Lansing MI 48823 Office Phone: 517-355-9678. E-mail: stapleton@stt.msu.edu, staplet5@aol.com.

**STAPLETON, JAMES JAY,** agricultural scientist, consultant; b. Santa Monica, Calif. BS, U. Calif., Davis, 1978, MS, 1981, PhD, 1983. Rsch. plant pathologist USDA Agrl. Rsch. Svc., Beltsville, Md., 1983-87; vis. plant pathologist U. Calif., Davis, 1986-87, area IPM adv. Modesto, 1987-90, integrated pest plant pathologist Parlier, 1991—. Collaborator USDA Animal and Plant Health Inspection Svc., Hyattsville, Md., 1986—; agrl. cons., Oakdale, Calif., 1993—; lectr. Calif. State U., Fresno, 1995—; chair Internat. Workgroup Soil Solarization, 1997. Editor profl. jours. With USA, 1969-70, Vietnam. Host Scientist, Postdoctoral Fellow USA-Israel BARD Found., 1991-92; Fulbright scholar J. Wm. Fulbright Bd., 1995-96; Recipient disting. svc. award U. Calif., 1991; keynote address 2d Internat. Conf. Soil Solarization, 1997. Mem. Am. Phytopath. Soc., Orgn. Nematologists of Tropical Am. Office: U Calif Kearney Agrl Ctr Parlier CA 93648

**STAPLETON, JEAN (JEANNE MURRAY),** actress; b. N.Y.C., Jan. 19, 1923; d. Joseph E. and Marie (Stapleton) Murray; m. William H. Putch (dec.); 2 children. Student, Hunter Coll., NYC, Am. Apprentice Theatre, Am. Actors Co., Am. Theatre Wing; studied with Harold Clurman; LHD (hon.), Emerson Coll.; degree (hon.), Hood Coll., Monmouth Coll. Opera debut in Candide with Balt. Opera Co.; appeared in The Italian Lesson with Balt. Opera; first N.Y. stage role in The Corn is Green, Equity Library Theatre; starred as mother in Am. Gothic, Circle-in-the-Sq.; Broadway debut with Judith Anderson In The Summer House; also appeared on Broadway in Damn Yankees, Bells Are Ringing, Juno, Rhinoceros and Funny Girl, Arsenic & Old Lace, Bwax & On Tour; first major break in comic ingenue role as Myrtle Mae with Frank Fay in Harvey on-tour; played with nat. tour of Come Back, Little Sheba starring Shirley Booth; starred in tour of Morning's at Seven, The Show-Off, Daisy Mayme; (Films) Damn Yankees, 1958, Bells Are Ringin, 1960, Something Wild, 1961, Up the Down Staircase, 1967, Cold Turkey, 1971, Klute, 1971, The Buddy System, 1984, Michael, 1996, You've Got Mail, 1998, Pursuit of Happiness, 2001; (TV series) All in the Family, 1968-79, Archie Buncker's Place, 1979, Beakman's World, 1995-96; (TV Films) Tail Gunner Joe, 1977, You Can't Take It With You, 1979, Aunt Mary, 1979, Angel Dusted, 1981, Isabel's Choice, 1981, Eleanor, First Lady of the World, 1982, Something Afoot, 1984, A Matter of Sex, 1984, Grown-Ups, 1985, Dead Man's Folly, 1986, Tender Places, 1987, Mother Goose Rock 'n' Rhyme, 1990, Fire in the Dark, 1991, The Habitation of Dragons, 1992, The Parallax Garage, 1993, Ghost Mom, 1993, Lily Dale, 1996, Chance of a Lifetime, 1998, Baby, 2000, Like Mother Like Son: The Strange Story of Sante and Kenny Kimes, 2001; (guest appearances) Robert Montgomery Presents, 1952, Women with a Past, 1954, The Phileo TV Playhouse, Dr. Kildare, 1961, Dennis the Menace, 1962, The Nurses, 1962, The Defenders, 1962, Car 54, Where Are You?, 1962, Studio One, Naked City, 1963, Armstrong Circle Theatre, Jackie Gleason Show, The Eleventh Hour, 1963, Route 55, 1963, My Three Sons, 1964, The Patty Duke Show, 1965, Scarecrow and Mrs. King, 1984, Faerie Tale Theatre, 1983, 1985, The Love Boat, 1986, Shelley Duvall's Bedtime Stories, 1992, Ray Bradbury Theatre, Grace Under Fire, 1994 (Emmy nomination), Caroline in the City, 1995, Murphy Brown, 1996, Everybody Loves Raymond, 1996, Style and Substance, 1998, Touched by an Angel, 2000; performances include The Matchmaker at A.C.T., San Francisco, Trying Times Shakespeare Co. D.C., 1994, Night Seasons, Signature Theatre N.Y., 1994, Blithe Spirit, Costa Mesa, Calif., Mrs. Piggle-Wiggle on Showtime, stepmother in N Y C Opera'n Cinh n th, 1993, On Tour: Eleanor: Her Secret Journey, 1998-99, Indian Ink by Tom Stoppard, A.C.T., Geary Theater, San Francisco, 1999, The Habitation of Dragon's on TNT, Roads to Home, Night Seasons, The Birthday Party, Mountain Language, Classic Stage Co., N.Y.C., The Death of Papa, Hartford Stage, 1999, Eleanor: Her Secret Journey, Coconut Grove Playhouse, Miami, Fla., 1999, Canon Theatre, L.A., Royal Poinciana, Palm Beach, Fla., Spreckles Theatre, San Diego, Paramount Theatre, Austin, Tex., Marines Meml. Theatre, San Francisco, 2000, Smithsonian Inst., Washington, 2000, Hartford (Conn.) Stage, 2000, Syracuse (N.Y.) Stage, 2000; CD-Rom Grandma Ollie's Morphabet Soup, 1996. U.S. commr. to Internat. Woman's Yr. Commn. and Nat. Conf. Women, Houston, 1977; bd. dirs. Women's Rsch. and Edn. Inst.; trustee Actors' Fund Am. Recipient Emmy award for best performance in comedy series All in the Family 1970-71, 71-72, 78, Golden Globe awards Hollywood Fgn. Press Assn. 1972, 73, Obie award, 1990, Cable Ace award. Mem. AFTRA, SAG, Actors Equity Assn. Office: care Bauman & Assocs 5757 Wilshire Blvd Los Angeles CA 90036-3635*

**STAPLETON, JEAN,** journalism educator; b. Albuquerque, June 24, 1942; d. James L. and Mary (Behrman) S.; m. John Clegg, Apr. 15, 1965 (dec. Sept. 1972); m. Richard Bright, Jan. 13, 1973 (div. 1985); children: Lynn, Paul Bright; m. William Walter Farran, Nov. 9, 1996. BA, U. N.Mex., 1964; MS in Journalism, Northwestern U., 1968. Reporter Glenview (Ill.) Announcements, 1967-68, Angeles Mesa News Advertiser, L.A., 1968-69, City News Svc., Radio News West, L.A., 1969-71; press sec. polit. campaign, 1972; instr. journalism East L.A. Coll., 1973-75, prof., dept. chair, 1975—. Author: Equal Marriage, 1975, Equal Dating, 1979. Recipient Lifetime Achievement award, Journalism Edn. Exhbn., 2006. Mem. NOW (pres. L.A. chpt. 1973-74), Assn. Women in Comm., Soc. Profl. Journalists, Ninety Nines, L.A. Poets Writers Collective. Democrat. Methodist. Home: 3232 Philo St Los Angeles CA 90064-4719 Office: East LA Coll 1301 Avenida Cesar Chavez Monterey Park CA 91754-6001 Office Phone: 323-265-8875.

**STAPLETON, KATHARINE HALL (KATIE STAPLETON),** commentator, writer; m. Benjamin Franklin Stapleton; children: Benjamin Franklin III, Craig Roberts, Katharine Hall. BA, Vassar Coll., 1941. Prodr., writer, host Cooking with Katie Sta. KOA, 1979—89. Author: Denver Delicious, 1980, 3d edit., 1983, High Notes, 1985. Chmn. women's divsn. United Fund,

1955-56; founder, chmn. Denver Debutante Ball, 1955, 56; hon. chmn. Nat. Travelers Aid Assn., 1952-56 95-; commr. Denver Centennial Authority, 1958-60; trustee Washington Cathedral, regional v.p., 1967-73; trustee Colo. Women's Coll., 1975-80; sole trustee Harmes C. Fishback Found., 1989-; hon. chmn. Le Bal à Versailles, 2000, 02, 04, Rocky Mountain Planned Parenthood Campaign, 2006. Decorated chevalier de L'Étoile Noire (France); recipient People-to-People citations, 1960, 66, Beautiful Activist award, Colo.-Wyo. Restaurant Assn. award, 1981, Humanitarian of Yr. award Arthritis Found., 1995, Arts award Colo. Symphony, 1998; Outstanding Vol. Fundraiser, Nat. Philanthropy Day, 1995, Outstanding Alumna, Barstow Sch., 2003, Girl Scout award, 2006. Mem. Denver Country Club. Republican. Episcopalian. Home: 8 Village Rd Cherry Hills Village CO 80113-4908 E-mail: kties8@aol.com.

**STAPLETON, MARYLYN ALECIA,** diplomat; b. St. Thomas, V.I., Sept. 25, 1936; d. Lambert George and Aletha C. (Callendar) John; m. Frank Stapleton, Oct. 22, 1967 (div. Apr. 1983); 1 child, Linda E. Student, Washington Bus. Inst., 1959. Reservations agt. Caribair Airlines, St. Thomas, 1954-56; sales clk. Macy's Dept. Store, N.Y.C., 1956-57, Gift Shop, N.Y.C., 1957-63; supr. Ea. Airlines, Inc., N.Y.C. and St. Thomas, 1964-86; travel cons. Caribbean Travel Agy., St. Thomas, 1986-87; asst. commr. Dept. Licensing and Consumer Affairs, Govt. of V.I., St. Thomas, 1987-95, dep. of planning and natural resources, 1995—, small bus. tech. assistance program coord., 1995—; state exec. dir. Internat. Assn. Plumbing Mech. Officials, 1999—; environ. program mgr. Dept. Planning and Natural Resources, 2004. Owner, pres. Stapleton Enterprises, St. Thomas, 1989—. Pub. rels. officer Nevis Benevolent Soc., St. Thomas, 1966-85; state chair Dem party V.I., 1986—, dist. chair, 1984-86; small bus. ombudsman Clean Air Act of 1990, 1998—. Recipient Legis. Resolution V.I. Legislature, St. Thomas, 1986. Mem. Internat. Assn. Plumbing and Mech. Ofcls., Nat. Assn. Plumbing, Heating and Cooling Contrs., St. Thomas/St. John Plumbing Assn. (pres. 1995—), St. Thomas Lioness Club (treas. 1985-86, pagent chair 1986-87, pres. 1987-88, mem. chair 1988-89, Melvin Jones fellow 1989), Lions Club of Charlotte Amalie (bd. dirs.). Democrat. Anglican. Home: 148-87 Est Annas Retreat PO Box 303739 St Thomas VI 00803-3739 Office: Democratic Party of Virgin Islns PO Box 3739 Saint Thomas Charlotte Amalie VI 00801 Office Phone: 340-774-3320.

**STAPLETON, WALTER KING,** federal judge; b. Cuthbert, Ga., June 2, 1934; s. Theodore Newton and Elizabeth Grantland (King) Stapleton; m. Georgianna Duross Stapleton; children: Russell K., Theodore N., Teryl J. BA, Princeton, 1956; LLB, Harvard, 1959; LLM, U. Va., 1984. Bar: Del. Assoc. Morris, Nichols, Arsht & Tunnell, Wilmington, Del., 1959—65; dep. atty. gen. State of Del., 1963—64; ptnr. Morris, Nichols, Arsht & Tunnell, 1966—70; judge U.S. Dist. Ct., Wilmington, Del., 1970—85, chief judge, 1983—85; judge U.S. Ct. Appeals (3d cir.), 1985—99, sr. judge, 1999—. Mem. Jud. Conf. US, 1984—85. Bd. dirs. Am. Bapt. Chs., 1978. Mem.: ABA, Del. Bar Assn., Am. Jud. Soc., Am. Bar. Baptist. Office: US Ct Appeals Lockbox 33 5323 Fedl Bldg 844 N King St Wilmington DE 19801-3519*

**STAPP, DAN ERNEST,** retired lawyer, utilities executive; b. New Orleans, July 1, 1934; s. James Frank Stapp Jr. and Marguerite Edna (Joubert) Stapp; m. Barbara Allan Wilmot, June 10, 1961; children: Marguerite Wilmot(dec.), Mary Darby, Paul Wilmot(dec.), James Andrew. BBA, Loyola U., New Orleans, 1955, LL.B., 1957. Bar: La. 1957. With New Orleans Pub. Service Inc., 1958-68, asst. to v.p., 1965-68; with Entergy Svcs. (formerly MSU System Svcs. Inc.), New Orleans, 1968-92; v.p., sec., asst. treas. Entergy Svcs., 1968-80, sr. v.p., 1980-92. Sec. System Fuels, Inc., New Orleans, 1972-92, Entergy Corp. (formerly Middle South Utilities, Inc.), New Orleans, 1974-92, Systems Entergy Resources, Inc., Jackson, Miss., 1974-91, Electec, Inc., 1984-91; Entergy Ops., Inc., 1990-91, Entergy Power, Inc., 1990-92. Trustee Mercy Hosp., New Orleans, 1973-80, pres., 1975, chmn. bd. devel. 1971-72; mem. pres.'s coun. Loyola U., 1975-85, chmn., 1980-82; adv. coun. Archbishop's Annual Appeal, 1969-70; mem. adv. bd. Asso. Cath. Charities, 1979-82; gen. chmn. United Way Greater New Orleans, 1978, trustee, 1978-84; mem. exec. bd. New Orleans Area coun. Boy Scouts Am. 1980-85, pres., 1984-85. 2d lt. AUS, 1957. Mem. ABA, La. Bar Assn., New Orleans Country Club, Blue Key (past chpt. pres.), Alpha Sigma Nu, Delta Theta Phi. Republican. Roman Catholic. Home: 19415 Kelly Wood Ct Baton Rouge LA 70809

**STAPRANS, ARMAND,** electronics executive; b. Riga, Latvia, Feb. 28, 1931; s. Theodore and Elvira (Ulmanis) S.; m. Vija Spalvins, Sept. 25, 1955; children: Silvija, Armin, Erik. Student, Willamette U., 1949-52; BSEE, U. Calif., Berkeley, 1954, MSEE, 1955, PhDEE, 1959. Rsch. asst. dept. elec. engring. U. Calif., 1955-57; engr. microwave tube div. Varian Assocs., Palo Alto, Calif., 1957-60, engring. mgr., 1960-68, ops. mgr., 1978-78, 86-89, chief engr., 1978-86, gen. mgr. coupled cavity tube divsn., 1989-92, v.p., 1990-95; gen. mgr. microwave power tube products, 1992-95; pres. microwave power tube products divsn. Comms. and Power Inds., Palo Alto, Calif., 1995-98; mgmt. cons., 1999—. Contbr. articles to profl. jours., chpt. to book; patentee microwave tubes field. Fellow IEEE (electron device adminstrv. com. 1983-88). Home: 445 Knoll Dr Los Altos CA 94024-4732 Office: Comm & Power Inds M S B 100 Microwave Power Tube Prod Divsn PO Box 50750 Palo Alto CA 94303-0665

**STARCHER, LARRY VICTOR,** state supreme court justice; b. Rocksdale, W.Va., Sept. 25, 1942; m. Rebecca Wiles; children: Mollianne, Victor, Amy. AB cum laude, W.Va. U., 1964, JD, 1967. Bar: W.Va. 1967. Judge and chief judge W.Va. Ct. (17th jud. cir.), 1977—96; justice W.Va. Supreme Ct. Appeals, 1997—, chief justice, 1999, 2003. Pvt. practice, Morgantown, 1976—; dir. North Ctrl. W.Va. Legal Aid Soc., 1969-76: former instr, law, statistics and history W.Va. U., contract adminstr. W.Va. U., 1966-67, asst. to v.p., 1967-69. Editor W.Va. Law Rev.; contbr. articles to profl. jours. Mem. City Coun. Morgantown, 1971-72; mem. W.Va. Martin Luther King, Jr. Holiday Commn. Fellow Harvard U., summer 1978. Mem. ATLA, Am. Correctional Assn., W.Va. Jud. Assn., W.Va. State Bar, Monongalia County Bar Assn., Kanawha County Bar Assn., Conf. Chief Justices, Beta Theta Pi, Phi Delta Phi, Phi Alpha Theta, Pi Sigma Alpha. Avocations: carpentry, gardening. Office: Supreme Ct Appeals State Capitol Rm E 307 Charleston WV 25305 Office Phone: 304-558-2604. Business E-Mail: larrystarcher@courtswv.org.*

**STARCK, CHRISTIAN WALTER,** judge, retired law educator; b. Breslau, Germany, Jan. 9, 1937; s. Walter and Ruth (Hubrich) S.; m. Brigitte Edelmann, Aug. 31, 1965; children: Annette, Johannes, Marie-Christine. Student, U. Kiel, 1957, U. Freiburg, 1958-59; Dr. iur., U. Würzburg, 1963, Habil., 1969. Clk. Fed. Constl. Ct., 1964-67; govt. ofcl., 1968-69; lectr. U. Würzburg, 1969-71; prof. pub. law U. Göttingen, Germany, 1971; prof. emeritus; rector U. Göttingen, 1976-77; judge Constl. Ct. Lower Saxony, Germany, 1991—2006. Vis. prof. U. Paris-Sorbonne, 1972. TV bd. Zweites Deutsches Fernsehen, 1978-92; pres. TV bd. ARTE, 1991-2000. Author: Der Gesetzesbegriff des Grundgesetzes, 1970, Spanish edit., 1979, Das Bundesverfassungsgericht im politischen Prozess, 1976, Japanese edit., 1978, Der demokratische Verfassungsstaat, 1995, La Constitution, cadre et mesure du droit, 1994, Praxis der Verfassungs auslegung, 1994, 2d edit., 2006, Grundgesetz Kommentar, 5th edit., 3 vols., 2005, Freiheit und Institutionen, 2002; editor: Studien und Materialien zur Verfassungsgerichtsbarkeit, 1973—; co-editor: Juristenzeitung, 1978—2006; contbr. over 300 articles to law jours. and festschriften, —. Fellow, Inst. for Advanced Study, Berlin, 1990—91. Mem. Internat. Assn. Constl. Law (exec. com. 1981-2004, hon. pres. 2004-), Acad. Scis. Göttingen, Assn. German Profs. Pub. Law (exec. com. 1988-89, pres. 1998-99), German Assn. Comparative Law (exec. com. 1986-), Soc. Juris Publicis Europaei (pres. 2003-). Home: Schlegelweg 10 D-37075 Göttingen Germany Business E-Mail: c.starck@gwdg.de

**STARER, BRIAN DOUGLAS,** lawyer; b. Utica, NY, 1945; BS, U.S. Merchant Marine Acad., 1967; JD, Union U., 1972. Bar: NY 1972, US Dist. Ct. (no., so. and ea. dists.) NY, US Ct. Appeals (2nd, 3rd and 5th cirs.) 1973, US Ct. Appeals (9th cir.) 1976, US Supreme Ct. 1977, US Ct. Internat. Trade

1977, US Ct. Customs and Patent Appeals 1980. Mem. Haight Gardner Holland & Knight, NYC; ptnr., maritime law, dir., mem. mgmt. com. Holland & Knight, NYC, 1997—. Mng. editor Albany Law Rev., 1971-72; contbr. articles to profl. jours. Named to Internat. Maritime Hall of Fame, 2002. Mem. ABA, Maritime Law Assn. US, Internat. Bar Assn., NY State Bar Assn. Office: Holland & Knight 195 Broadway Fl 24 New York NY 10007-3189 Office Phone: 212-513-3200. Business E-Mail: brian.starer@hklaw.com.

**STARFIELD, BARBARA HELEN,** pediatrician, educator; b. Bklyn., Dec. 18, 1932; d. Martin and Eva (Illions) Starfield; m. Neil A. Holtzman, June 12, 1955; children: Robert, Jon, Steven, Deborah. AB, Swarthmore Coll., 1954; MD, SUNY, 1959; MPH, Johns Hopkins U., 1963. Tchg. asst. in anatomy Downstate Med. Ctr., N.Y.C., 1955—57; intern in pediat. Johns Hopkins U., 1959—60, resident, 1960—62, dir. pediatric med. care clinic, 1963—66, dir. cmty. staff comprehensive child care project, 1966—67, dir. pediatric clin. scholars program, 1971—76, prof. health policy, joint appointment in pediat., 1975—, disting. univ. prof., 1994—. Mem. Nat. Com. Vital Stats., 1994—2002; cons. DHHS; mem. nat. adv. coun. Agy. for Health Care Policy and Rsch., 1990—94; adv. subcom. on Health Systems and Svcs. Rsch. Pan Am. Health Orgn., 1988—92, 1995—; cons. Health Care Fin. Adminstrn., 1980—. Editl. bd. Med. Care, 1977—79, Pediat., 1977—82, Internat. Jour. Health Svcs., 1990—. Med. Care Rev., 1980—84, Health Svc. Rsch., 1996—, assoc. editor Ann. Rev. Pub. Health, 1996—2001; contbr. articles to profl. jours. Recipient Dave Luckman Meml. award, 1958, HEW Career Devel. award, 1970—75, Disting. Investigator award, Assn. Health Svcs. Rsch., 1995, 1st Primary Care Achievement award, Pew Charitable Trust Fund, 1994, 1st Ann. Rsch. award, Ambulatory Pediatric Assn., 1990, Baxter prize, 2004. Fellow: Am. Acad. Pediat.; mem.: APHA (Martha May Eliot award 1995), Internat. Soc. for Equity in Health (pres. 2000—02), Ambulatory Pediatric Assn. (pres. 1980), Internat. Epidemiologic Assn., Soc. Pediatric Rsch., Inst. Medicine of NAS (governing coun. 1981—83), Alpha Omega Alpha, Sigma Xi. Office: Johns Hopkins Sch Hygiene 624 N Broadway Baltimore MD 21205-1900 Business E-Mail: bstarfie@jhsph.edu.

**STARGATT, BRUCE M.,** lawyer; b. NYC, July 8, 1930; s. Sydney S. and Janet (Feldman) S.; m. Barbara Hirschfield, Aug. 21, 1954; children: Linda, Daniel, Deborah. AB, U. Vt., 1951; LLB, Yale U., 1954. Bar: D.C. 1955, N.Y. 1955, D.C. 1956. Assoc. Arnold Fortas & Porter, Washington, 1954; ptnr. Young, Conaway, Stargatt & Taylor, Wilmington, Del., 1956—. Lawyer chmn. Del. Appellate Ct. Handbook comm., 1984—95; chmn. Del. Supreme Ct. Rules Lawyers Adv. Comm., 1986—93. 1st Lt. USAF, 1954—56. Recipient Herbert Harley award Am. Judicature Soc., 1993. Fellow Am. Bar Found., Am. Coll. Trial Lawyers; mem. ABA (ho. of dels., bd. gov. 2003-), Am. Law Inst., Del. State Bar Assn. (pres. 1981-82, 1st State Disting. Svc. award 1992), Del. Bar Found. (pres. 1995-2000). Office: Young Conaway Stargatt & Taylor 17th Fl 1000 West St PO Box 391 Wilmington DE 19899-0391

**STARING, GRAYDON SHAW,** lawyer; b. Deansboro, N.Y., Apr. 9, 1923; s. William Luther and Eleanor Mary (Shaw) S.; m. Joyce Lydia Allum-Poon, Sept. 1, 1949; children: Diana Hilary Agnes, Christopher Paul Norman. AB, Hamilton Coll., 1947; JD, U. Calif., Berkeley, 1951. Bar: Calif. 1952, U.S. Supreme Ct. 1958. Atty. Office Gen. Counsel, Navy Dept., San Francisco, 1952-53; atty. admiralty and shipping sect. U.S. Dept. Justice, San Francisco, 1953-60; assoc. Lillick & Charles (now Nixon Peabody), San Francisco, 1960-64, ptnr., 1965—88, of counsel, 1989—. Titulary mem. Internat. Maritime Com.; bd. dirs. Marine Exch. at San Francisco, 1984-88, pres. 1986-88; instr. pub. speaking Hamilton Coll., 1947-48; adj. prof. Hastings Coll. Law, 1996-97, Boalt Hall, U. Calif., 1999. Author: Law of Reinsurance, 1993; assoc. editor Am. Maritime Cases, 1966-92, editor, 1992—; contbr. articles to legal jours. Mem. San Francisco Lawyers Com. for Urban Affairs, 1972-90; bd. dirs. Legal Aid Soc., San Francisco, 1974-90, v.p., 1975-80, pres., 1980-82. With USN, 1943-46, comdr. USNR. Fellow Am. Bar Found., Am. Coll. Trial Lawyers; mem. ABA (chmn. maritime com. 1975-76, mem. standing com. admiralty law 1976-82, 86-90, chmn. 1990, ho. dels. 1986-90), Fed. Bar Assn. (pres. San Francisco chpt. 1968), Bar Assn. San Francisco (sec. 1972, treas. 1973), Calif. Acad. Appellate Lawyers, Maritime Law Assn. U.S. (exec. com. 1977-88, v.p. 1980-84, pres. 1984-86), Brit.-Am. C. of C. (bd. dirs. 1987-2001), World Trade Club San Francisco, Tulane Admiralty Inst. (permanent adv. bd.), Assoc. Maritime Mus. Libr. (dir. 1990-2001, pres. 1992-94). Office: 2 Embarcadero Ctr Ste 2700 San Francisco CA 94111-3900 Office Phone: 415-984-8310. Personal E-mail: Starlaw@att.net. Business E-Mail: gstaring@nixonpeabody.com. *"How small, of all that human hearts endure,/That part which laws or kings can cause or cure!".*

**STARK, ALTRECA,** admissions counselor; d. Allen and Joann Stark. BA, Loyola U., 2002; MEd, U. New Orleans, 2004. Admissions counselor Hollins U., Roanoke, Va., 2004—. Adviser Hollins U. Black Student Alliance, Roanoke, 2005—; mentor Hollins U. Adopt a Half Staff/Faculty Mentoring Program, Roanoke; admissions search process asst. Hollins U. Office Admissions, Roanoke, student affairs liaison, 2005—. Mem. NAACP, Roanoke. Mem.: So. Assn. for Coll. Admissions Counseling, Am. Coll. Pers. Assn., Nat. Assn. Student Pers. Adminstrs., Kappa Delta Pi, Zeta Phi Beta (chpt. pres. 2001—02). Avocations: reading, travel, fashion.

**STARK, BRUCE GUNSTEN,** artist; b. Queens, NY, Feb. 17, 1933; s. Richard M. and Karen (Gunsten) S.; m. Joan Patricia Lauer, Nov. 19, 1960; children: Robert, Ronald. Student, Sch. Visual Arts, N.Y.C., 1955-58. Artist, cartoonist NY Daily News, NYC, 1961—82. One-man shows Art Inst., Pitts., 1968, U. Kutztown, Pa., 1970, N.Y. Bank for Savs., N.Y.C., 1971; group shows Nat. Art Mus. Sport, N.Y.C., 1971; represented in permanent collections Everett Dirksen Library, L.D. Johnson Library, Baseball Hall Fame, Cooperstown, N.Y., Basketball Hall Fame, Mass. Served with USN, 1952-54. Recipient Nat. Cartoonist Soc.'s Rueben Catagory awards for sports, 1966, 75, spl. features, 1968; Page One award for best sports cartoon, 1970, 73 N.Y.C., 71; 3d, 4th, 6th prizes Internat. Salon de Caricatures Montreal, 1966, 68, 69; Most Outstanding Achievement award Sch. Visual Arts, 1982 Achievements include having original cartoons requested by Pres. Nixon, Johnson; 1st color cartoon appearing on front page of N.Y. Daily News. Home: 3139 Stonewater Dr Lakeland FL 33803-2572 *My goals, ideas, principles and standards of conduct are all helpfully outlined for me by God in His holy word— the Bible. I really need no other source. Whatever success has come to me, I think, is because of this, and what God has done for me, through His Son, Jesus Christ.*

**STARK, DENNIS EDWIN,** private investigator, retired bank executive; b. Springfield, Ill., Dec. 24, 1937; s. Edwin C. and Ida (Fentem) S. BS, Ill. Wesleyan U., 1959; Sanxay fellow practical ethics, Princeton U., 1959-60; MBA, Harvard U., 1962. Adminstrv. asst. to chmn. bd. Industrial Valley Bank, Phila., 1962-64; fin. analyst E.I. DuPont de Nemours, Wilmington, Del., 1964-65; asst. treas. Old Stone Bank, Providence, 1965-68, treas., 1968-71; sr. v.p., treas., sec. Old Stone Bank and Old Stone Corp., Providence, 1971-76; exec. v.p., chief fin. officer Old Stone Corp., Old Stone Bank, 1976-86, Dime Bank, N.Y.C., 1986-88; ptnr. Bank Mgmt. Ptnrs., N.Y.C., 1988-90; sr. v.p., CFO, corp. sec. Cen Fed Bank, Pasadena, Calif., 1990-92; exec. v.p., CFO, corp. sec. Ea. Bank, Lynn, Mass., 1992-96; ptnr. Fin. Mgmt. Ptnrs., Pawtucket, RI, 1996-99; v.p. bus. and fin., CFO U. R.I. Kingston, 1999—2003; bank dir., exec. v.p., CFO, corp. sec. Ind. Bank, East Greenwich, RI, 2003—05; ret., 2005. Bd. dirs., chmn. fin. com. Preservation Soc. Pawtucket; mem. bd. visitors Ill. Wesleyan U., Bloomington; trustee, chmn. Preserve R.I.; mem. Diocesan Coun. Episcopal Diocese; mem. audit com. RISD; vestry, treas. St. Martins Episcopal Ch., Providence; dep. to gen. conv. Episcopal Ch. USA, mem. exec. coun.; bd. dirs. exec. com. Art and culture, Chorus of Westerly. Mem. Fin. Execs. Inst., Harvard Bus. Sch. Assn. of R.I., Acacia (co-founder Ill. Wesleyan U. chpt.), Providence Art Club, Hope Club, Univ. Club (R.I.), Harvard Club (N.Y.C.), Agawam Hunt, Dunes Club, Brown

Faculty Club, U. R.I. Univ. Club (treas.). Republican. Episcopalian. Avocations: stamp collecting/philately, coin collecting/numismatics. Home (Summer): 41 Courtway St Narragansett RI 02882-3610 E-mail: destark@cox.net.

**STARK, DIANA,** public relations executive; b. NYC, July 01; d. Benjamin and Sara (Zelasny) S. BA, Hunter Coll. Promotion mgr. TV Guide mag., N.Y.C., 1950-61, Show Bus. Illustrated, N.Y.C., 1961-62; broadcast specialist Young & Rubicam, N.Y.C., 1962-69; pres. Stark Comms. Inc., N.Y.C., 1969-76; pub. svc. publicity account exec. Y & R E, N.Y.C., 1976-77; pres. Stark Comms. Internat., N.Y.C., 1978—. Pub. rels. workshop leader Chgo. Econ. Devel. Corp., 1973-76; cons. to Asahi Shimbun for English Language Newsletter. 1991-92, columnist Host mag., 1960-65; writer, producer programs for women's TV shows, 1962—. Book developer Ellis Island: The First Experience With Liberty, 1991. Coord. We Have Arrived, Portraits at Ellis Island, Augustus Sherman Photographs, 1992-24. Mem. NATAS (trustee 1974-78, publicity com., chmn., chpt. gov. 1972-76, 82-86, 87-91, editor N.Y. TV Directory 1987-90). Office Phone: 212-582-5619. Office Fax: 212-765-3670. Personal E-mail: dstarkny@aol.com.

**STARK, EVELYN BRILL,** poet, musician; b. N.Y.C., Sept. 12, 1913; d. Henry Brill and Rae Hessberg; m. Morton W. Stark, Apr. 27, 1933; 1 child, Henry. BA, Barnard Coll., 1933; artist student of Edouard Dethier, Juilliard Sch. Music, 1933-40. Bd. dirs., violinist Nat. Found. Mus. Therapy, N.Y.C., 1940-50; violinist ARC Hosp. Music Unit, N.Y.C., 1950-70, Hosp. Music Unit, Protestant Coun. Chs., N.Y.C., 1950-70; bd. dirs., violinist Music Therapy Ctr., N.Y.C., 1960-80; founder, sponsor Nora Hellen Music Friends, N.Y.C., 1970-80; ret., 1980. Author: My Search for the Infinite, 2002; mem. editl. bd. Music Jour., 1969-70; recorded tapes with original programs; author: (poetry) Never Apart, 1992, 2003; (autobiography) Life is a Poem, 1999; dramatic presentations of Life is a Poem, Hartford, Conn., 2000, Essex, Conn., 2000, Brooklyn, Conn., East Haddam, Conn., Middleton, Conn.; performer (record) All About the Violin, 1969; (CD) Journey of a Soul in Music via the Infinite Way, 2003; contbr. articles to profl. jours.; author numerous poems. Donated 3 violins (Amati, Carcassi, Gragnani) to the Met. Mus. Art, N.Y.C., 1974, 80, 97. Recipient 1st prize poetry award Altrusa Internat. Middletown, Conn., 1997-98; named Poet Laureate of Conn. Gilbert and Sullivan Soc., 1998; named to Internat. Poetry Hall of Fame, 1998. Mem. Internat. Soc. Poets. Address: 317 W Main St Chester CT 06412-1057

**STARK, FORTNEY HILLMAN (PETE STARK),** congressman; b. Milw., Nov. 11, 1931; s. Fortney Hillman Sr. and Dorothy M. (Mueller) S.; children: Jeffrey Peter, Beatrice Ann, Thekla Brumder, Sarah Gallun, Fortney Hillman Stark III; m. Deborah Roderick; children: Hannah Marie, Andrew Peter. BS In Engring., MIT, 1953; MBA, U. Calif. Berkeley, 1960. Teaching asst. MIT, Cambridge, 1953-54; prin. Skaife & Co., Berkeley, Calif., 1957-61; founder Beacon Savs. & Loan Assn., Antioch, Calif., 1961; pres., founder Security Nat. Bank, Walnut Creek, Calif., 1963-72; mem. U.S. Congress from 13th (formerly 9th) Calif. dist., 1973—; mem. ways and means com., formerly chmn., now ranking minority mem. health subcom.; mem.joint econ. com. Bd. dirs. ACLU, 1971, Common Cause, 1971, Starr King Sch.; del. Dem. State Cen. Com.; trustee Calif. Dem. Coun. Capt. USAF, 1955-57. Mem. Delta Kappa Epsilon. Democrat. Unitarian. Office: US Ho Reps 239 Cannon Ho Office Bldg Washington DC 20515-0513

**STARK, JOAN SCISM,** education educator; b. Hudson, N.Y., Jan. 6, 1937; d. Ormonde F. and Myrtle Margaret (Kirkey) S.; m. William L. Stark, June 28, 1958 (dec.); children: Eugene William, Susan Elizabeth, Linda Anne, Ellen Scism; m. Malcolm A. Lowther, Jan. 31, 1981. BS, Syracuse U., 1957; MA (Hoadly fellow), Columbia U., 1960; Ed.D., SUNY, Albany, 1971. Tchr. Ossining (N.Y.) High Sch., 1957-59; free-lance editor Holt, Rinehart & Winston, Harcourt, Brace & World, 1960-70; lectr. Ulster County Community Coll., Stone Ridge, NY, 1968-70; asst. dean Goucher Coll., Balt., 1970-73, asso. dean, 1973-74; assoc. prof., chmn. dept. higher postsecondary edn. Syracuse (N.Y.) U., 1974-78; dean Sch. Edn. U. Mich., Ann Arbor, 1978-83, prof., 1983-2001, prof. and dean emeritus, 2001—; dir. Nat. Ctr. for Improving Postsecondary Teaching and Learning, 1986—91. Editor: Rev. of Higher Edn., 1991-96; contbr. articles to various pubs. Leader Girl Scouts U.S.A., Cub Scouts Am.; coach girls Little League; dist. officer PTA, intermittently, 1968-80; mem. adv. com. Gerald R. Ford Library, U. Mich. 1980-83; trustee Kalamazoo Coll., 1979-85; mem. exec. com. Inst. Social Research, U. Mich., 1979-81; bd. dirs. Mich. Assn. Colls. Tchr. Edn., 1979-81. Mem. Am. Assn. for Higher Edn., Am. Ednl. Rsch. Assn. (Div. J Rsch. award 1998), Assn. Study Higher Edn. (dir. 1977-79, v.p. 1983, pres. 1984, Rsch. Achievement award 1992, svc. award 1998, Disting. Career award 1999), Assn. Innovation Higher Edn. (nat. chmn. 1974-75), Assn. Instl. Rsch. (disting. mem., Sidney Suslow award 1999), Assn. Colls. and Schs. Edn. State Univs. and Land Grant Colls. (dir. 1981-83), Acctg. Edn. Change Commn., Phi Beta Kappa, Phi Kappa Phi, Sigma Pi Sigma, Eta Pi Upsilon, Lambda Sigma Sigma, Phi Delta Kappa, Pi Lambda Theta.

**STARK, LE A., JR.,** music educator; b. Houston, Jan. 3, 1931; s. Levi Alvin, Sr. and Sarah (Vining) Stark. MusB, N. Tex. U., 1953; MusM, Sam Houston U., 1983. Permanent tchr. cert. Tex. Tutor Dr. Isabel Scionti Studio, Denton, Tex., 1951—54; pvt. piano tchr. Houston, 1954—; head piano tchr. Houston Bapt. U., 1969—72; instr. piano & music theory San Jacinto Jr. Coll., Houston, 1972—74; instr. piano, music theory & history U. Houston, 1974—96. Founder Houston Music Tchr.'s Forum, 1961. Mem. Ecumenical Coun. Religious Music, Houston, 1955—57. With U.S. Army, 1954—56. Mem.: Phi Mu Alpha (life), Pi Kappa Lambda (life). Independent. Avocations: gardening, travel, reading, history.

**STARK, MARTIN J.,** management consultant; b. NYC, May 29, 1941; s. Nathan and Lola (Belmont) S.; m. Shigemi Matsumoto, Apr. 27, 1967. AA, Glendale Coll., 1960; BA, Calif. State U., 1966; postgrad., San Fernando Valley Coll. Law, 1967—70. Sys. analyst Indsl. Electronic Engrs., Van Nuys, Calif., 1969—71, sales mgr. 1971—73; sales rep. Columbia Artists Mgmt., Inc., N.Y.C., 1973—78, sales mgr., 1978—79, v.p. bus. affairs, mgr. data processing, 1979—82; dir. corp. affairs Kolmar-Luth Entertainment, Inc., N.Y.C., 1982—84; pres. Oryx & Corp., N.Y.C., 1984—85; exec. v.p. Asco Aerospace Products, Inc., El Segundo, Calif., 1985—87, Internat. Engine Parts, Inc., Chatsworth, Calif., 1987—92; pres. Stark & Assocs., Northridge, Calif., 1985—91; owner Mail Boxes Etc., 1992—. Lectr. Calif. State U. Long Beach, U. So. Calif.; cons. City of N.Y., Memory Data Software, IEPO, Inc.; advisor Thornton Protégé Program Thornton Sch. Music U. So. Calif.; bd. dirs. Holy Cross Hosp.; mentor Thornton Sch. Music, U. So. Calif. Mem.: Calabas C. of C., Classical Singer's Assn., Dista Upsilon. Avocations: sports cars, antiques, travel. Home: 18342 Chatham Ln Northridge CA 91326-3603 Office: 23679 Calabasas Rd Calabasas CA 91302-1502 Office Phone: 818-591-1086. E-mail: mbe1047@aol.com.

**STARK, NELLIE MAY,** forester, ecologist, educator; b. Norwich, Conn., Nov. 20, 1933; d. Theodore Benjamin and Dorothy Josephine (Pendleton) Beetham; m. Oscar Elder Stark, Oct. 1962 (dec.). BA, Conn. Coll., 1956; AM, Duke U., 1958, PhD, 1962. Botanist Exptl. Sta., U.S. Forest Svc., Old Strawberry, Calif., 1958-66; botanist, ecologist Desert Rsch. Inst., Reno, 1966-72; prof. forest ecology Sch. Forestry, U. Mont., Missoula, 1972-92; pvt. cons. Philomath, Oreg. Pres. Camas Analytical Lab., Inc., Missoula, 1987—92. Author: Will Your Family Survive the 21st Century, 1997, Memories of Wren, Oregon, 1998, So You Want to Build a Little Log Cabin in the Woods, 2002, Thirteen Days of Christmas, 2005; contbr. articles to profl. jours. Named Disting. Dau. Norwich, Conn., 1985; recipient Conn. award Conn. Coll., 1986, 54 grants. Mem. Ecol. Soc. Am. (chair ethics com. 1974, 76), Soc. Am. Foresters (taskforce 1987-88).

**STARK, PATRICIA ANN,** psychologist; b. Ames, Iowa, Apr. 21, 1937; d. Keith C. and Mary L. (Johnston) Moore. BS, So. Ill. U., Edwardsville, 1970, MS, 1972; PhD, St. Louis U., 1976. Counselor to alcoholics Bapt. Rescue Mission, East St. Louis, Ill., 1969; rschr. alcoholics Gateway Rehab. Ctr., East St. Louis, 1972; psychologist intern Henry-Stark Counties Spl. Edn. Dist., and

Galesburg State Rsch. Hosp., Ill., 1972—73; instr. Lewis and Clark C.C., Godfrey, Ill. 1973—76, asst. prof., 1976—84, assoc. prof., 1994, coord. child care svcs., 1974—84; mem. staff dept. psychiatry Meml. Hosp., St. Elizabeth's Hosp., 1979—2001; supr. students interns, 1974—94. Dir. child and family svc. Collinsville Counseling Ctr., 1977-82; clin. dir., owner Empas-Complete Family Psychol. and Hypnosis Svcs., Collinsville, 1982—; cons. cmty. agys., 1974—; mem. adv. bd. Madison County Coun. on Alcoholism and Drug Dependency, 1977-80. Mem. APA, Ill. Psychol. Assn., Midwestern Psychol. Assn., Am. Soc. Clin. Hypnosis, Internat. Soc. Hypnosis. Office: 2802 Maryville Rd Maryville IL 62062 Office Phone: 618-345-6632.

**STARK, RICHARD BOIES,** surgeon, artist; b. Conrad, Iowa, Mar. 31, 1915; s. Eugene and Hazel (Carson) S.; m. Judy Thornton, Oct. 31, 1967 AB, Stanford U., 1936; postgrad., U. Heidelberg, 1936—37; MD, Cornell U. 1941. Diplomate Am. Bd. Plastic Surgery (pres. 1967-68). Intern Peter Bent Brigham Hosp., Boston, 1941-42; asst. resident surgery Childrens Hosp., Boston, 1942; plastic surgeon Northington Gen. Hosp., Ala., 1945-46, Percy Jones Gen. Hosp., Mich., 1946; postwar fellow anatomy and embryology Stanford U., 1946-47; from asst. resident to resident in head and neck surgery VA Hosp., Bronx, NY, 1947-50; asst. resident, resident surgery, plastic, head and neck and gen. surgery N.Y. Hosp., NY, 1947-50; instr. surgery Cornell U., 1950-52, asst. prof., 1952-55, assoc. prof., 1955; asst. attending surgeon N.Y. Hosp., 1950-55; asst. prof. surgery Columbia U., 1955-58, assoc. prof., 1958-73, prof. clin. surgery, 1973—; assoc. attending surgeon St. Luke's Hosp., N.Y.C., 1955-58, founding attending surgeon dept. plastic surgery, 1958—; founder dept. plastic surgery, 1955. Cons. Walter Reed Med. Ctr., 1970-77 Author: Plastic Surgery at the New York Hospital 100 Years Ago, 1952, Plastic Surgery, 1962, Cleft Palate, 1968, Aesthetic Plastic Surgery, 1980, Total Facial Reconstruction, 1985, Plastic Surgery of the Head and Neck, 1986; founding editor: Annals Plastic Surgery, 1978-81; assoc. editor: Plastic Reconstructive Surgery, 1977-82; contbr. 51 chpts. to books, more than 210 articles to profl. jours.; 25 one-man art shows, 1946—; rep. in permanent art exhibits, NY Hosp., St. Lukes Hosp., Army Med. Mus. Chmn. Medico Adv. Bd., 1976-77; mem.; v.p. CARE Bd.; v.p. Wellborn Found., N.Y.C. Served to maj. M.C., AUS, 1943-46. Decorated Bronze Star (U.S.); Medal of Honor (2) (Vietnam); cavallero Order of San Carlos (Colombia), Dieffenbach medal (Berlin), Gold medal Nat. Inst. Social Scis.; named Disting. Alumnus, St. Lukes-Roosevelt Hosp. Fellow ACS; mem. Am. Assn. Plastic Surgeons, Am. Soc. Plastic and Reconstructive Surgery (pres. 1966, Spl. Achievement award), Found. Am. Soc. Plastic and Reconstructive Surgery (pres. 1961-65), Am. Surg. Assn., Soc. Univ. Surgeons, French Soc. Plastic Surgeons, Brasilian Soc. Plastic Surgeons, Colombian Soc. Plastic Surgeons, Argentina Soc. Plastic Surgeons, Brit. Assn. Plastic Surgery, Peruvian Acad. Surgeons, N.Y. Surg. Soc., N.Y. Acad. Medicine (pres. Friends Rare Book Room), Plastic and Reconstructive Surgery (sec., pres. 1966), N.Y. State Med. Soc. (pres., sec., med. history), N.Y. Regional Soc. Plastic and Reconstructive Surgery (pres. 1064-65), Halsted Soc. (pres. 1973-74), James IV Assn. Surgeons, Am. Soc. Aesthetic Plastic Surgery (pres. 1974-75), Nat. Arts Club (exhibiting mem.), Century Club (profl. artist), Artist Fellowship, Lotos Club. Home: 3744 SE Old St Lucie Blvd Stuart FL 34996

**STARK, ROBERT J.,** lawyer; b. Middletown, N.Y., July 16, 1970; s. Jeffrey and Patricia Stark. BA, Lafayette Coll., Easton, Pa., 1992; JD, Vanderbilt U., Nashville, Tenn., 1995. Bar: N.J. 1995, N.Y. 1996, U.S. Dist. Ct. N.J. 1995, U.S. Dist. Ct. (So. Dist.) N.Y. 1996, U.S. Dist. Ct. (Ea. Dist.) N.Y. 1996. Panelist and bankruptcy confs. Contbr. articles to law jours. Recipient Jessup Internat. Moot Ct. Team, Vanderbilt U. Law Sch., 1994-1995; scholar McKnight-Black Scholarship, Lafayette Coll., 1992. Mem.: Turnaround Mgmt. Assn., Bar Assn. of City of N.Y. E-mail: rstark@akingump.com.

**STARK, ROBERT MARTIN,** mathematician, civil engineer, educator; b. N.Y.C., Feb. 6, 1930; s. Alexander and Julia (Gross) S.; m. Carol LaSage, Jan. 13, 1955 (dec. Mar. 1988); children: Bradley R., Timothy D., Steven M., Candice B. AB, Johns Hopkins U., 1951; MA, U. Mich., 1952; PhD, U. Del., 1965. Rsch. scientist Bausch and Lomb, Rochester, NY, 1955; instr. Rochester Inst. Tech., 1956-57; asst. dean engring., asst. prof. math. Cleve. State U., 1957-62; instr. U. Del., 1962-64, asst. prof. civil and environ. engring., math. scis., 1964-68, assoc. prof., 1968-76, prof., 1976—2002, prof. emeritus, 2002—; pres., cons. applied sci. R.M. Stark & Co., Inc., 2003—. Vis. assoc. prof. MIT, 1972—73; chmn. grad. program in ops. rsch.; cons. in field. Author: (with R.L. Nicholls) Mathematical Foundations for Design: Civil Engineering Systems, 1972, reprint 2005, (with R.H. Mayer, Jr.) Quantitative Construction Management: Uses of Linear Optimization, 1983, (with R. Engelbrecht-Wiggans and M. Shubik) Auctioning, Bidding and Contracting, 1983, (with C. Sloyer, et al) Contemporary Applied Mathematics Series, 1987, Mathagrams, 1996. Mem. Del. Heritage Commn., 1990—, treas., 2005—; bd. dirs. Generations Home Care, Inc., 1989—, Wilmington Sr. Ctr., 1994—2006, Meals on Wheels, Del., 1990—2003; bd. dirs., v.p. White Clay Watershed Assn., 1992—97; mem. cmty. adv. bd. WHYY Pub. Broadcasting Corp., 2002—. Recipient Outstanding Alumnus award, U. Del. Dept. Civil and Environ. Engring., 1999; grantee, Office Naval Rsch., 1974—81, NSF, 1969—70, U.S. Army Rsch. Office, 1966—68. Mem. AAAS, ASCE, Nat. Coun. Tchrs. Math., Inst. Mgmt. Sci., Ops. Rsch. Soc. Am., Phila. Ops. Rsch. Soc. (pres. 1970), U. Del. Assn. Ret. Faculty (pres. 2003—), Del. Acad. Sci. (bd. dirs. 1990—, pres. 1994-96, 2005—), Rotary. Home: One Fox Ln Newark DE 19711 Personal E-mail: rstark@udel.edu.

**STARK, S. DANIEL, JR.,** diversified financial services company executive; b. Port Hueneme, Calif., Mar. 26, 1953; s. S. Daniel and Eloise Marie (Fisher) S.; m. Pauline Laube Finley, June 7, 1997; 1 child, Kaitlyn Elizabeth. BS, Calif. Poly. U., Pomona, 1981; cert. in exec. mgmt., Claremont Grad. U., 1989, MA in Mgmt., 1992. Driver-guide San Diego Wild Animal Pk./Zool. Soc. San Diego, Escondido, Calif., 1974—76; attractions host Disneyland divsn. The Walt Disney Co., Anaheim, Calif., 1976—80, mgmt. intern, 1981, supr. ops., 0981—1982, area supr. ops., dept. mgr., 1982—87; mgmt. cons. S.D. Stark, Jr., Las Vegas, 1985—; dir. mktg. Ramada Express Hotel & Casino, Laughlin, Nev., 1988—89; exec. dir. San Bernardino (Calif.) Conv. and Visitors Bur., 1989—95; pres. CEO Panama City Beach Conv. & Visitors Bur., 1998—99; exec. dir. Bay County (Fla.) Tourist Devel. Coun. 1998—99; dir. corp. mktg. Boyd Gaming Corp., Las Vegas, 1999—2005, v.p. corp. mktg., 2006—. Part-time instr. mgmt. and mktg. So. Calif. campus U. Phoenix, 1997-98, Nev. campus, 1999—, area chair for mktg., 2001-04; cons. Hemmeter Devel. Corp., Honolulu, 1985, Calif. Authority Racing Fairs, Sacramento, 1987-88, USIA for Latvian Ministry Transp., tourism divsn., 1992, U.S. Bur. Land Mgmt., tourism mgmt. project U. Alaska Sch. Mgmt.; adj. prof. Sch. Bus. and Pub. Adminstrn., Calif. State U., San Bernardino, 1992-93 Bd. dirs. Leadership So. Calif., 1993-98, grad. pub. affairs tng., 1993; congl. appointee del. White House Com. on Travel and Tourism, 1995; mem. regional econ. strategies consortium Soc. Calif. Assn. Govts., 1996-98; mem. Visit Fla. Mktg. Com., 1998-99; bd. dirs. Fla. Assn. Conv. and Visitors Burs., 1998-99, Speedway Childrens Charities Las Vegas Chpt., 1999—, treas., 2000-01, chmn., 2001-2002; v.p. Cops Helping Kids, 2002-2003, pres., 2003-04; mem. spl. events com. Las Vegas Centennial Comm.; bd. trustees Crime Stoppers of Nev., Inc., 2004—. Recipient resolution Calif. Assembly, 1989, 98, San Bernardino County Bd. Suprs., 1989, City of San Bernardino Mayor and Coun., 1989, 98, Calif. Senate, 1989, 98; selected as one of 1991 Up and Coming Young Bus. Leaders in San Bernardino County; named one of Inland Empire Bus. All Stars, 1991; recipient World Champion Trail Horse award Am. Jr. Quarter Horse Assn., 1972, Calif. Tourism award for Best Spl. Event-Kt. 66 Rendezvous, 1997. Mem. U.S. Equestrian Fedn. (life), Am. Quarter Horse Assn (life), Assn. Travel Mktg. Execs., Internat. Assn. Conv. and Visitors Burs. (cert. comm., conv. mktg., tourism mktg.), Pub. Rels. Soc. Am. (bd. dirs. Calif. Inland Empire chpt. 1990-95, Polaris award 1997), Calif. and Nev. Festivals and Events Assn. (pres. 1997-98, bd. dirs. 1994-98, 2002—), Inland Empire Tourism Coun. (bd. dirs. 1996-98, exec. com. 1996-98, treas. 1997-98), Calif. Travel Industry Assn., Tourism Assn. So. Calif. (bd. dirs. 1990-95, vice chair 1992-95), Western Assn. Convs. and Vis. Bur. (chmn. Calif. coun. 1992-94), E Clampus Vitus Inc (bd. proctors

2005—), FarmHouse Fraternity (internat. bd. dirs. 1986-94, v.p. 1990-92, Snyder Alumni award 1984). Avocations: boating, fishing, films, equestrian competition. Office: 2950 Industrial Rd Las Vegas NV 89109-1150 Personal E-mail: sdsjr@aol.com.

**STARKE, HAROLD EUGENE, JR.,** lawyer; b. Richmond, Va., Aug. 1, 1944; BA, Randolph-Macon Coll., 1967; JD, U. Richmond, 1971; LLM in Taxation, NYU, 1973. Bar: Va. 1971, D.C. 1981. Ptnr. Troutman Sanders LLP, Richmond. Editor U. Richmond Law Rev., 1970-71. Bd. trustees Randolph-Macon Coll., 1983-85, 95-97, 99—. Fellow Am. Coll. Tax Counsel; mem. ABA (taxation sect.), Va. State Bar (chmn. taxation sect. 1985-86), D.C. Bar, Richmond Estate Planning Coun., McNeill Honor Soc., Phi Delta Phi. Office: Troutman Sanders LLP Troutman Sanders Bldg 1001 Haxall Point PO Box 1122 Richmond VA 23218-1122 Office Phone: 804-697-1287.

**STARKEY, CLIFF,** musician; b. Phila., Pa., Mar. 19, 1963; Recording artist Capitol Records; mem. Emeril Live Band, 1997—, The Groovemasters. Composer: (songs) Phila. Conv. Bd. promotional video; musician: (music video projects) NFL Studios. Achievements include touring with the Three Degrees, the Temptations, and Pieces of a Dream. Office Phone: 323-462-6252.*

**STARKEY, JERRY L.,** real estate developer; BBA, N. Tex. State Univ., Denton; JD, Tex. Tech. Univ., Lubbock. Bar: Tex. Pres., secy. Fla. Design Communities, 1994—2005; pres., sec. Ashton Care Sys. Inc., 1996—98; pres. Watermark Communities LP (WCI), Bonita Springs, Fla., 1998—, COO, 1998—2005, CEO, 2005—. Bd. trustees Fla. Gulf Coast Univ., 2001—. Office: WCI 24301 Waldon Ctr Dr Bonita Springs FL 34134

**STARKEY, RICHARD See STARR, RINGO**

**STARKEY, RUSSELL BRUCE, JR.,** energy executive; b. Lumberport, W.Va., July 20, 1942; s. Russell Bruce and Dorotha Mable (Field) S.; m. Joan McClellan, May 27, 1966; children: Christine, Pamela, Joanne. BS, Miami U., Oxford, Ohio, 1964; grad. student, U. New Haven, 1972—73, N.C. State U., 1974—75; postgrad., U.S. Navy Schs., 1964—66, postgrad., 1968. From sr. engr. nuc. generation sect. to prin. engr. Carolina Power & Light Co., Raleigh, NC, 1973—75; supr. quality assurance, supt. tech. and administrn. Brunswick Steam Electric Plant, Southport, NC, 1975—77; plant mgr. H. B. Robinson Steam Electric Plant, Hartsville, SC, 1977—83; mgr. environ. svcs. Carolina Power & Light Co., Raleigh, 1984—85, mgr. nuc. safety and environ. svcs. dept., 1985—88; mgr. Brunswick Nuc. Project Dept., 1988—89, v.p., 1989—92, v.p. Nuc. Svc. Dept., 1992—93; exec. v.p. energy mgmt. divsn. Hesco, Inc., 1993; from dir. indsl. electrotech. lab. to v.p. gen. tech. mgr. Advanced Energy Corp., 1993—97; cons. U.S. Enrichment Corp., Paducah, Ky., 1997—98, tng. mgr., 1998—2001, plant gen. mgr., 2001—05, v.p. ops., 2005—. With USN, 1964-73. Named Hon. Ky. Col. Mem.: Am. Nuc. Soc. Home: 6613 Belle Chase Ct Gaithersburg MD 20882 Office: 6903 Rockledge Dr Bethesda MD 20817

**STARKMAN, GARY LEE,** lawyer; b. Chgo., Sept. 2, 1946; s. Oscar and Sara (Ordman) Starkman. AB, U. Ill., 1968; JD cum laude, Northwestern U., 1971. Bar: Ill. 1971, U.S. Dist. Ct. (no. dist.) Ill. 1972, U.S. Ct. Appeals (7th cir.) 1972, U.S. Supreme Ct. 1974, Trial Bar U.S. Dist. Ct. (no. dist.) Ill. 1982, U.S. Ct. Appeals (3d cir.) 1984, U.S. Ct. Appeals (D.C. cir.) 1984. Asst. U.S. Atty. No. Dist. Ill., 1971-75; gen. counsel, dir. rsch. Citizens for Thompson Campaign Com., 1975-77; counsel to Gov. of Ill., 1977-81; admissions com. U.S. Dist. Ct. (no. dist.) Ill., 1982-90; ptnr. Ross & Hardies, Chgo., 1990—2003, McGuire Woods LLP, Chgo., 2003—. Co-author: (textbook) Cases and Comments on Criminal Procedure, 1974, 6th edit., 2003; contbr. articles to profl. jours.; reviewer in field. Chmn. state agys. divsn. Jewish United Fund Met. Chgo., 1978-81; chmn. Ill. Racing Bd., 1991-96; bd. dirs. Internat. Assn. Racing Commn., 1992-94; cmty. adv. bd. Jr. League Chgo., 1979-83. Named one of Ten Outstanding Young Citizens, Chgo. Jr. C. of C., 1978; recipient John Marshall award for appellate litigation, Atty. Gen. U.S., 1974, Nat. Svc. award, Tau Epsilon Pi, 1968. Mem.: ABA (litigation sect.), Chgo. Bar Assn. (constl. law com.), Decalogue Soc., Northwestern U. Law Alumni Assn. Office: McGuire Woods LLP 77 W Walker Dr Ste 4100 Chicago IL 60601-1681 Office Phone: 312-750-2788. Business E-Mail: gstarkman@mcguirewoods.com.

**STARKS, CAROL ELIZABETH,** retired principal; b. Elizabeth, N.J., Oct. 16, 1941; d. Arthur E. and Argetha P. (Henderson) Starks. AA, Graceland Coll., 1961; BA in Elem. Edn., Mich. State U., 1963; MA in Elem. Adminstrn., San Jose State U., 1972. Cert. elem. sch. tchr. Calif., life diploma for elem. edn. Calif., specialist tchr. in reading Calif., std. svc. credential in supervision Calif., elem. sch. tchr. N.J., elem. adm. N.J., early childhood edn. Mo. Tchr. grade 3 Hayes Sch., Monterey, Calif., 1963—65; tchr. grade 2 Woodruff Sch., Berkeley Heights, NJ, 1965—67; tchr. remedial reading and educationally handicapped Ord Terrace Sch., Monterey, 1967—68, asst. prin., 1975—77, prin., 1984—88; tchr. grade 3 Manzanita Sch., Monterey, 1968—73; asst. prin. La Mesa Sch., Monterey, 1973—74, tchr. grade 6, 1974—75; prin. Foothill Sch., Monterey, 1977—80, Olson Sch., Monterey, 1980—84, Highland Sch., Monterey, 1988—95, Bay View Sch., Monterey, 1995—99; career ladder asst. Kansas City Sch. Dist., Mo., 2000—. Interviewed as representative of elementary principals Calif. Commn. on the Tchg. Profession, 1984—85. Mem. world ch. pubs. com. Remnant Ch. Jesus Christ of Latter Day Saints, 2001—05, music dir. Blue Springs congregation, 2001—05, mem. world ch. hymnbook com., 2003—. Recipient Calif. Disting. Sch. Prin.'s award, 1989, 1993, Proclamation for profl. accomplishments and 19 yrs. of svc., City of Seaside (Calif.), 1995. Mem.: AAUW (sec. Independence br. 2003—05), Monterey Bay Sch. Adminstr. Assn. (pres. 1997—99), Assn Calif Sch Adminstr. (pres./treas Monterey Peninsula chapter 1977—70, v.p. 1978—79, pres. 1979—80, treas. region X 1979—81, pres. region X 1981—82, elem. adminstrn. com. 1982—86, del. to Nat. Assn. Elem. Sch.Prins. Convention 1983—84, state facilitator Elem. Adminstrn. Acad. North 1984—85, state dir. Elem. Adminstrn. Acad. North 1985—86, state del. to rep. assembly 1986—91, Region X Blanche Montague award for Outstanding Sch. Administr. 1987), Delta Kappa Gamma (pres. Delta Lambda chpt. 1990—92, Calif. membership task force 1991—93, Calif. personal growth and svcs. com. 1993—95, dir. area V Calif. 1995—97, state chair comms. com. 1997—99, scholarship com. Kansas City coun. 2000—01, pres. Phi chpt. 2000—02, state comm. com. 2001—03, treas. Kansas City coun. 2002—, chair state comm. com. 2003—05). Republican. Avocations: travel, reading, music, computers, quilting. Home: 3341 S Cochise Ave Independence MO 64057

**STARKS, DANIEL J.,** medical technology and services executive; BA, Shimer Coll., Waukegan, Ill.; JD magna cum laude, U. Minn. Law Sch., 1979. Comml. litigation atty. Nichols, Starks, Carruthers and Kaster, 1979—85; gen. counsel to pres., CEO Daig Corp. (bought by St. Jude Medical Inc.), 1985—96; pres., CEO, Daig Corp. St. Jude Medical Inc., St. Paul, 1996—98, dir., 1996—, pres., CEO Cardiac Rhythm Mgmt. div., 1998—2001, pres., COO, 2001—04, chmn., pres., CEO, 2004—, dir. Urologix Inc. Office: St Jude Medical Inc 1 Lillehei Plz Saint Paul MN 55117-9913

**STARKS, DORIS N.,** retired nursing educator, retired administrator; b. Conecuh County, Ala., July 30, 1937; m. Wilbert L. Starks Sr., Dec. 25, 1961; children: Wilbert L. Jr., Garrick Edward. BS in Nursing, Tuskegee U., 1958; MS in Nursing, The Cath. U. of Am., 1965; PhD, Union Grad. Sch., 1978. Lic. nurse, Md. Staff nurse VA Hosp. Ctr., Tuskegee, Ala., 1958-61, insvc. edn. instr., 1965-66; staff nurse Washington Hosp. Ctr., 1963-65; asst. prof. med./surg. nursing Tuskegee U., 1966-68; prof. Community Coll. Balt. 1968, asst. chair dept. nursing, 1980-84, chair, 1984-86, chair dept. nursing and health scis., 1986-89, dir. nursing and program 1989; asst. dean, prof. nursing St. Coppin State Coll., Balt., 1990-91, dean nursing, div. nursing, 1991-98; ret., 1998. Item writer Nat. State Bd. Exam. Test Pool. Author bi-weekly health issues column Christian World, 1976-77. Mem. adv. coun. on vocat. edn. City of Balt. 1nd lt. US Army Nurse Corps., 1959-62. Recipient plaque and

commendation Tuskegee Inst. Alumni Assn., 1983, Leadership in Nursing award Md. Found. for Nursing, 1994, Strong Blacks in Health Care award, Balt., 1995; honoree Black Nurses Assn., 1984; inducted Tuskegee U. Sch. Nursing Hall of Fame, 1992. Fellow Am. Acad. Nursing; mem. ANA, Tuskegee U. Nurses Alumni Assn. (Balt. met. area chpt.), Nat. Coalition of 100 Black Women, Alpha Kappa Alpha, Sigma Theta Tau, Chi Eta Phi. Home: 318 Bullskin St Charles Town WV 25414

**STARKS, FLORENCE ELIZABETH,** retired special education educator; b. Summit, N.J., Dec. 6, 1932; d. Edward and Winnie (Morris) S. BA, Morgan State U., 1956; MS in Edn., CUNY, 1962; postgrad., Fairleigh Dickinson U., 1962—63, Seton Hall U., 1963, Newark State Coll. Cert. blind and visually handicapped and social studies tchr., N.J. Tchr. adult edn. Newark Bd. of Edn.; ret., 1995; tchr. N.Y. Inst. for Edn. of the Blind, Bronx. Developer first class for multiple handicapped blind children in pub. sch. system, Newark, 1960; ptnr. World Vision Internat. Mem. ASCD, AFL-CIO, AAUW, Coun. Exceptional Children, Am. Assn. U. Women, Nat. Assn. Negro Bus. and Profl. Women's Club Inc., N.J. Edn. Assn., Newark Tchrs. Assn., Newark Tchrs. Union-Am. Fedn. Tchrs., World Vision Internat. (ptnr.). Home: 4 Park Ave Summit NJ 07901-3942

**STARKS, FRED WILLIAM,** chemicals executive; b. Millford, Ill., Aug. 16, 1921; s. Otis Earl and Evelyn Viola Starks; m. Minnie Jane Reynolds, Sept. 4, 1946; children: David F., Steven J., Daniel J. BS, U. Ill., 1943, MS, 1947; PhD, U. Nebr., 1950. Supr. US Rubber Co., Torrance, Calif., 1943—44, DuPont, Niagara Falls, NY, 1950—57; pres. Starks Assocs., Inc., Buffalo, 1957—89, chmn., 1989—. Spl. lectr. U. Buffalo, 1959—63. Lt. (j.g.) USNR, 1944—46. Avery fellow, 1948—49, USPHS fellow, 1949—50. Mem.: Am. Inst. Chemists, NY Acad. Sci., Am. Chem. Soc., Chemists Club, Buffalo Club, Cosmos, Sigma Xi. Achievements include patents in field. Home: 742 Highland Ave Buffalo NY 14223-1645 Office: Starks Assocs Inc 1280 Niagara St Buffalo NY 14213-1592

**STARKWEATHER, FREDERICK THOMAS,** retired data processing executive; b. Sioux City, Iowa, Feb. 24, 1933; s. Fred Ervin and Gertrude Faye (Madden) S.; m. Margot Glassen, Nov. 19, 1959; children: Thomas Frederick, Jerry Russell, Michael Glassen. BA in Math. and Physics, U. Nebr., Omaha, 1955. Mathematician Flight Determination Lab., White Sands Missile Range, N.Mex., 1955-56; supervisory mathematician Analysis & Computation, White Sands Missile Range, 1956-81; chief data scis. divsn. Nat. Range Ops., White Sands Missile Range, 1981—93; co-owner B and T Managed Care, LLC, 2001—; owner The Spotlight Restaurant, 2002—. Nat. coun. rep. Am. Def. Preparedness Assn., Washington, 1980-93; pres. White Sands Pioneer Group, White Sands Missile Range, 1983-86; bd. dirs. Assn. U.S. Army, Washington. Author hist. and geneal. books; contbr. book revs. and articles to newspapers and mags. Chmn. El Paso (Tex.) City Planning Commn., 1980-84; bd. dirs. El Paso County Hist. Soc., 1983-87; mem. El Paso County Hist. Commn., 1983-2000. With USAR, 1955-63. Recipient Profl. Secs. Internat. Exec. of Yr. award, 1987, Conquistador award City of El Paso, 1980; named Disting. Alumnus U. Nebr., Omaha, 1985; named to Hon. Order of St. Barbara U.S. Field Arty. Assn., 1988; cited for svcs. to mankind El Paso chpt. Sertoma, 1985. Mem. Fed. Mgrs. Assn. (bd. dirs.), Freedom Found. at Valley Forge (pres. El Paso chpt., George Washington Hon. medal 1982), El Paso C. of C. (assoc. dir. 1984-92, bd. dirs.), Toastmasters (dist. gov. 1970-71), Masons, Tau Kappa Epsilon (Hall of Fame 1986). Avocations: coin collecting/numismatics, genealogy, books, weaponry.

**STARNER, DON EDWARD,** radiologist, educator; b. Zanesville, Ohio, June 28, 1959; s. Larry and Sara Ann Starner; m. Carla Marcote, Aug. 31, 1991; 1 child, Ryan. BS, The Ohio State U., 1982. Cert. Radiographer Am. Registry of Radiologic Technologists, 1982, Quality Mgmt. Radiographer Am. Registry of Radiologic Technologists 2002, lic. Radiologic Technologist Fla. Dept. Health, 1988. X-ray technologist The Ohio State U. Hospitals, Columbus, Ohio, 1982—88; from clin. instr. to program dir. West Boca Med. Ctr. Sch. of Radiography, Boca Raton, Fla., 1988—91, program dir., 1991—96; dir. of clin. radiography edn. Indian River CC, Ft. Pierce, Fla., 1996—. Contbr. chapters to books Web-Based Training, 2001; author: (films) Brubaker, 1980. Mem.: AAUP, Fla. Assn. of C.C., Am. Soc. of Radiologic Technologists, Am. Registry of Radiologic Technologists. Home: 6717 NW Dorothy St Port Saint Lucie FL 34983 Office: Indian River Community College 3209 Virginia Ave Fort Pierce FL 34981

**STARNES, EARL MAXWELL,** retired urban and regional planner, retired architect, retired educator; b. Winter Haven, Fla., Sept. 14, 1926; s. Thomas Lowe and Kathryn Maxwell (Gates) Starnes; m. Dorothy Jean Prather, Aug. 21, 1949; children: Tom, Will, Janet, Patricia. Student, Fla. So. Coll., 1946—48; BArch cum laude, U. Fla., 1951; MS in Urban and Regional Planning, Fla. State U., 1973, PhD, 1977. Registered arch., Fla. Assoc. Courtney Stewart, Ft. Lauderdale, Fla., 1951-52, William Bigoney, Ft. Lauderdale, 1952-53, William T. Vaughn, Ft. Lauderdale, 1953, Alfred B. Parker, Miami, Fla., 1953-55, Rufus Nims, Miami, 1955-57; ptnr. Starnes & Rentscher, Miami, 1957-63, Starnes, Rentscher & Assocs., Miami, 1963-71; dir. divsn. mass transp. Fla. Dept. Transp., Tallahassee, 1971-72; dir. divsn. state planning Fla. Dept. Adminstrn., 1972-75; engaged in rsch. and cons. svc. Tallahassee, 1975; prof., chmn. urban and regional planning Coll. Architecture U. Fla., Gainesville, 1976-88, prof. urban and regional plan coord., doctoral studies, 1989-93, prof. emeritus, 1993—. Instr. architecture U. Miami, 1953; adj. asst. prof. dept. urban and regional planning Coll. Social Scis., Fla. State U., 1971—74; mem. adv. panel B8-15 Nat. Coop. Hwy. Rsch. Program, Transp. Rsch. Bd., NRC-Nat. Acad. Scis., 1974—; mem. adv. bd. Pub. Tech., Inc., 1974—; mem. N. Central Fla. Regional Planning Com., 1980—85, Fla. Substate Dist. Com., 1985—87; co-chmn. Joint Liaison Com. Divsn Responsibility Urban Systs, Dade County, Fla. 1963—71 chmn. joint policy com. U. Miami-Dade County Jackson Med. Ctr., 1966—71; chmn. Cape Fla. State Pk. Adv. Coun., 1966—69, Dade County Landscape Ordinance Study Com., 1967—70, S. Fla. Everglades Area Planning Coun., 1969—71; vis. lectr. Calif. Poly. State U. San Luis Obispo, 1988—89; cons. Urban Planning Fla. and Caribbean. Prin. works include 1st Unitarian Ch., Miami; co-author: Growth Management, 1992, Rural Sustainability in America, 1996; contbr. articles to profl. jours., chapters to books. Active Nat. Task Force Natural Resources and Land Use Info. and Tech., 1973—74, Cape Fla. Acquisition Com., 1966, South Dade Mental Health Soc., 1967—68, Dade County Downtown Govtl. Ctr. Com., 1967—71, Miami Downtown Devel. Authority, 1970, Gov.'s Task Force Resource Mgmt., 1971—72, Fla. Gov.'s Commn. Property Rights, 1993—94, Fla. Greenway's Commn., 1991—93, Fla. Greenway Coordinating Coun., 1998—99; bd. dirs., chmn. retirement and compensation com. State Assn. County Commrs., 1968—71; mem. Alachua County Budget Study Com., 1978, Fla. Land Use Adv. Com. Phosphate Lands, 1978—80, Suwanee River Water Mgmt. Bd., 1982—87, 1991—98, chmn., 1987—88, Fla. Inst. Phosphate Rsch., 1984—87; bd. dirs. 1000 Friends Fla., 1986—2003; mem. gov.'s adv. commn. coastal mgmt., 1997; county commr. Dist. 7 Dade County, 1964—71; vice mayor, 1964, 1968. With USCG, 1944—46. Fellow: AIA (urban design com. 1976—80), Assn. Collegiate Schs. Planning (bd. dirs. 1986—88), Nat. Inst. Bldg. Scis. (steering com. for rsch. 1979—80), Am. Inst. Cert. Planners, Gargoyle Soc.; mem.: Phi Kappa Phi. Democrat. Unitarian Universalist. Office: PO Box 234 Cedar Key FL 32625-0234 Personal E-mail: estarnes@inetw2.net.

**STARNES, WILLIAM HERBERT, JR.,** chemist, educator; b. Knoxville, Tenn., Dec. 2, 1934; s. William Herbert and Edna Margaret (Osborne) Starnes; m. Maria Sofia Molina, Mar. 4, 1986. BS with honors, Va. Poly. Inst., 1955; PhD, Ga. Inst. Tech., 1960. Rsch. chemist Esso Rsch. & Engring. Co. Baytown, Tex., 1960—62, sr. rsch. chemist, 1962—64, polymer additives sect. head, 1964—65, rsch. specialist, 1965—67, rsch. assoc., 1967—71; instr. and rsch. assoc. dept. chemistry U. Tex., Austin, 1971—73; mem. tech. staff AT&T Bell Labs., Murray Hill, NJ, 1973—85; prof. chemistry Poly. U., Bklyn., 1985—89, head dept. chemistry and life scis., 1985—88, assoc. dir. polymer durability ctr., 1987—89; prof. chemistry Coll. William and Mary, Williamsburg, Va., 1989—2006, Floyd Dewey Gottwald Sr. prof. chemistry emeritus, 2006—, prof. applied sci., 1990—2006. Invited lectr. several fgn.

countries and U.S.; ofcl. guest USSR Acad. Scis., 1990, Russian Acad. Scis., 1992; disting. vis. prof. Beijing Inst. Tech., 1996; vis. scientist Tex. Acad. Scis., 1964—67; mem. bd. doctoral thesis examiners Indian Inst. Tech., New Delhi, 1988, McGill U., Montreal, 1989, MacQuarie U., Sydney, Australia, 1991, McMaster U., Hamilton, Canada, 1994; panelist, reviewer NSF Acad. Rsch. Facilities Modernization Program, 1990; channel program mentor U. Cairo, 1994—95; mem. opinion leader panel Wall St. Jour., 1995—; charter mem. dept. chemistry adv. coun. Va. Poly. Inst. and State U., 1996—; vis. advisor European Multinational Environ. Rsch. Project on PVC in Soil and Landfills, 1995—99; cons. numerous indsl. cos., govtl. and pvt. agys.; course dir. continuing edn. Editor-in-chief: Jour. Vinyl and Additive Tech., 1998—; mem. adv. bd., bd. reviewers: Jour. Vinyl Tech., 1981—83, mem. editl. bd.: Jour. Chem. and Biochem. Kinetics, 1992—, Polymer Degradation and Stability, 1997—, Internat. Jour. Coatings Sci., 2001—; mem. editl. bd. The Chemist, 2003—; contbr. chapters to books, articles to profl. jours. Named honoree Plastics History and Artifacts Program, Plastics Pioneers Assn., 2001; recipient Profl. Progress award, Soc. Profl. Chemists and Engrs., 1968, Disting. Tech. Staff award, AT&T Bell Labs., 1982, Polymer Sci. Pioneer award, Polymer News, 1988, Honor Scroll award, N.J. Inst. Chemists, 1989, Excellence in Innovation award, Hampton Rds. Tech. Coun., 2004; fellow, NSF, 1958—60, grantee, 1989—, Nat. Bur. Stds. Ctr. Fire Rsch., Internat. Copper Rsch. Assn., Va. Ctr. Innovative Tech., GenCorp Found., several indsl. cos. Fellow: AAAS (Project 2061 1985—86, chmn. chemistry subpanel 1985—86, mem. panel on phys. scis. and engring. 1985—86), Soc. Plastics Engrs. (nat. publs. com. 1998—2001, thesis advisor nat. award of vinyl plastics divsn. 1996, 1998), N.Y. Acad. Scis., Am. Inst. Chemists (life); mem. Soc. Chem. Industry, Va. Acad. Sci., Am. Chem. Soc. (bd. dirs. southeastern Tex. sect. 1970, spkrs. bur. divsn. polymer chemistry 1976—, mem.-at-large exec. com. Va. sect. 1995), N.Am. Thermal Analysis Soc., Phi Lambda Upsilon (pres. Va. Poly. Inst. chpt. 1954—55), Sigma Xi (M. A. Ferst award Ga. Inst. Tech. chpt. 1960), Phi Kappa Phi (life). Achievements include patents in field; invention of ester thiol stabilization technology for poly(vinyl chloride); research in degradation, stabilization, flammability, microstructures and polymerization mechanisms of synthetic polymers, especially poly(vinyl chloride); free radical chemistry; carbon-13 nuclear magnetic resonance and organic synthesis; subspecialities include organic chemistry, polymer chemistry. Office: Coll William and Mary Dept Chemistry PO Box 8795 Williamsburg VA 23187-8795 Business E-Mail: whstar@wm.edu.

**STAROSELSKY, ALEXANDER,** mechanical engineer, materials scientist; b. Moscow, Apr. 18, 1962; s. Vladimir Staroselsky and Maria Khayn; m. Svetlana Staroselsky; children: Maxim, Michael, Benjamin. MSc, Moscow Inst. Electronics and Math., 1989; ScD, Russian Acad. Sci., Moscow, 1991; PhD, MIT, 1997. Rsch. scientist Skochinsky Inst. of Mining, Moscow, 1987—92; vis. scientist Courant Inst. of Math. Scis., N.Y.C., 1993; staff scientist United Techs. Rsch. Ctr., East Hartford, Conn., 1997—2004, Pratt and Whitney, 2004—. Adj. prof. Hartford U., Conn., 1998—. Contbr. articles to profl. jours. Grantee, Office of Naval Rsch., 2001-2003. Fellow: NY. Acad. Sci.; mem.: ASME, Soc. for Computational Engring. and Sci. Achievements include research in brittle and elastic-plastic, thermal-mechanical fracture, mechanics of advanced alloys; large deformation plasticity; surfactant assisted fracture; acoustics, vibration; mass transport in non-saturated porous media. Home: 80 Fox Hollow Avon CT 06001 Office: Pratt and Whitney 400 Main St MS 165-16 East Hartford CT 06108 Office Phone: 860-565-2751. Personal E-Mail: starosel@alum.mit.edu.

**STARR, DAVID,** editor, publisher; b. NYC, Aug. 1, 1922; s. Aaron and Helen (Simon) S.; m. Marjorie Giffen, Aug. 3, 1943; children: Pamela, Peter. BA, Queens Coll., 1942. Reporter, rewriteman L.I. Daily Press, 1942-50; exec. editor Nassau Daily Rev. Star, 1950-53; asst. editor Newark Star-Ledger, 1954-56; asso. editor L.I. Press, 1953-54, 56-62, mng. editor, 1962-69, editor, 1969-77; sr. editor Newhouse Newspapers, 1971—; pub. Springfield Republican, 1977-99, pres., 1999—. Pres. Springfield Ctrl., Inc., 1978-88, chmn., 1989-95. Trustee Nassau C.C., SUNY, 1959-66; bd. dirs. Springfield Libr. and Mus. Assn., chmn., 1988-90; mem. Mass. Cultural Coun., 1980—; bd. dirs. Am. Arts Alliance, 1988-92, chmn., 1989-92. Mem. Am. Soc. Newspaper Editors, Am. Newspaper Pubs. Assn. Office: The Republican Co 1860 Main St Springfield MA 01103-1000 E-mail: dstarr@repub.com.

**STARR, EDWARD H., JR.,** lawyer; b. Greenwich, Conn., 1953; BA cum laude, Duke Univ., 1975; JD, Univ. Richmond, 1975. Bar: Va. 1979. Ptnr., tort liability, product liability, insurance coverage Troutman Sanders LLP, Richmond, Va. Editor: Va. Insurance Law Digest, 1992—. Mem.: ABA, Va. Assn. Def. Attys., Fedn. Def. & Corp. Counsel, Va. Bar Assn., Richmond Bar Assn., Def. Rsch. Inst. Office: Troutman Sanders LLP Bank Am Ctr 1111 E Main St PO Box 1122 Richmond VA 23218-1122 Office Phone: 804-697-1268. Office Fax: 804-698-5137. Business E-Mail: ed.starr@trtoutmansanders.com.

**STARR, JUDSON WILMARTH,** lawyer; b. Boulder, Colo., July 18, 1945; s. Wilmarth Holt and Eva Jones Starr; 1 child, Alexander. BA, Washington and Jefferson Coll., 1968; JD, Georgetown U., 1975. Bar: D.C. 1975, Va. 1978. Staff Office of the Adminstr. U.S. EPA, Washington, 1972—73; asst. editor Environ. Law Inst., Washington, 1973—75; assoc. Price Grove, Washington, 1975—78; dir. environ. crimes unit Dept. Justice, Washington, 1982—87, chief environ. crimes sect., 1987—88; ptnr., Environ., Corp. Def. & White Collar practices Venable LLP, Washington, 1988—. Adv. mem. U.S. Sentencing Commn. on Corp. Sentencing; co-chair Annual ALI-ABA Conf. on Environ. Crimes; chair Environ. Crimes Subcom. Bus. law sect. Corp. Counsel Inst., Georgetown Univ. Contbr. articles to profl. jours.; editor: Georgetown Rev. Law & Pub. Interest; co-author: Environmental Crimes Deskbook, 1995, Environmental Criminal Liability: Avoiding & Defending Enforcement Actions, 1995; author: The Knock on the Door: Preparing for and Responding to a Criminal Investigation, 1999. Founding mem., pres. Bethesda (Md.)/Chevy Chase Baseball League, 1995—99. Capt. U.S. Army, 1968—70. Decorated Bronze Star; named a Top Washington Lawyer, Washingtonian Mag., 2004; named one of Nation's Top White Collar Crime Experts, Nat. Law Jour., Corp. Counsel's Best Lawyers, Criminal Def. Law, 2004; named to Best Lawyers in Am., 2003—04, 2005—06. Mem.: Barristers. Avocations: baseball, golf, sailing. Office: Venable LLP 575 7th St NW Washington DC 20004 Office Phone: 202-344-4886. Office Fax: 202-344-8300. Business E-Mail: jwstarr@venable.com.

**STARR, KENNETH WINSTON,** dean, lawyer; b. Vernon, Tex., July 21, 1946; s. W. D. and Vannie Maude (Trimble) Starr; m. Alice Jean Mendell, Aug. 23, 1970; children: Randall Postley, Carolyn Marie, Cynthia Anne. BA, George Washington U., 1968; MA, Brown U., 1969; JD, Duke U., 1973; LLD (hon.), Hampden Sydney Coll., 1992, Shenandoah U., 1993, John Marshall Coll. Law, 1993, Pepperdine U., 1996. Bar: Calif. 1973, D.C. 1979, Va. 1979. Law clk. to Judge David Dyer U.S. Ct. Appeals (5th cir.), Miami, Fla., 1973—74; assoc. Gibson, Dunn & Crutcher, Los Angeles, 1974—75; law clk. to Chief Justice Warren E. Burger U.S. Supreme Ct., Washington, 1975—77; assoc., ptnr. Gibson, Dunn & Crutcher, Washington, 1977—81; counselor to atty. gen. U.S. Dept. Justice, Washington, 1981—83; judge U.S. Ct. Appeals (D.C. circuit), Washington, 1983—89; solicitor gen. US Dept. Justice, Washington, 1989—93; ptnr. Kirkland & Ellis LLP, Washington, 1993—2005, of counsel LA, 2005—; ind. counsel for Whitewater, Washington, 1994—99; dean Pepperdine U. Sch. of Law, Malibu, Calif., 2004—. Author: First Among Equals: The Supreme Court in American Life, 2002; contbr. articles to legal jours. Legal advisor CAB transition team office of pres.-elect, 1980—81, SEC transition team, 1980—81; bd. adv. Duke Law Jour. Named one of 75 Best Lawyers In Washington, Washingtonian survey mag., 2002; recipient Disting. Alumni awards, George Washington U., Duke U., Atty. Gen.'s award for disting. svc., 1993, Am. Values award, U.S. Indsl. Coun. Ednl. Found., 1993. Fellow: Am. Bar Found. (jud. fellows com., jud. conf. com. on bicentennial of U.S. constn.); mem.: ABA, Am. Inns of Court, Va. Bar Assn., D.C. Bar Assn., Calif. Bar Assn., Supreme Ct. Hist. Soc., Inst. Jud.

Adminstrn. (pres.), Am. Judicature Soc., Am. Law Inst., Phi Delta Phi (Hughes chpt. Man of Yr. 1973), Order of Coif. Republican. Office: Pepperdine U Sch of Law 24255 Pacific Coast Hwy Malibu CA 90263 Fax: 310-506-4266.

**STARR, KEVIN,** librarian, educator; BA, U. San Francisco, 1962; MA, Harvard U., 1965, PhD, 1969; MLS, U. Calif., Berkeley, 1974; postgrad., Ch. Div. Sch. Pacific, Berkeley, 1983-84. From asst. to assoc. prof. Am. lit. Harvard U., Cambridge, Mass., 1969-74; city libr. San Francisco, 1973-76; prin. Kevin Starr Assocs., San Francisco, 1983-85; prof. comm. arts U. San Francisco, 1981-89; prof. Sch. Planning and Devel. U. So. Cavalir., 1989—; state libr. Calif., 1994—. Allston Burr sr. tutor Eliot House Harvard U., Cambridge, 1970-73; cons. Beyl and Boyd, Inc., San Francisco, 1979-83; sr. cons. Hill and Knowlton USA, San Francisco, 1983-84; vis. assoc. prof. English U. Calif., Berkely, 1974, vis. lectr. polit. sci., 1976, lectr. librarianship, 1978; adj. prof. humanities San Francisco State U., 1975-76; Regent's lectr. polit. sci. U. Calif., Riverside, 1977; adj. prof. English Santa Clara (Calif.) U., 1977-78; vis. prof. history U. Calif., Davis, 1985-86; vis. scholar, media fellow Hoover Inst., 1986-88; vis. fellow Ctr. Humanistic Studies, Claremont McKenna Coll., 1987; faculty master Embassy Residential Coll., 1990-94. Sr. editor New West Mag., 1977; vatican corr. Hearst Newspapers, Rome, 1978; columnist Examiner, San Francisco, 1977-83; contbng. editor L.A. Times, 1994—; contbr. articles to profl. jours., chpts. to books. Exec. aide to mayor San Francisco, 1973; bd. trustees Am. Issues Forum, 1975-76, Calif. Hist. Soc., 1992—; co-chmn. sister city com., San Francisco and Sydney, Australia, 1981-86; advisor Jr. League San Francisco, 1982-84; canidate San Francisco Bd. Suprs., 1984; councilor Am. Antiquarian Soc., 1996—; mem. Calif. Coun. Humanities, 1996—; regent Cathedral St. Mary Assumption, San Francisco, 1996—. Lt. German Army, 1962-64. Office: Calif State Lib PO Box 942837 Sacramento CA 94237-0001

**STARR, LEON,** retired chemical research company executive; b. Bronx, NY, May 2, 1937; s. Michael and Bella (Foux) S.; m. Joan Gail Linett, June 19, 1960; children— Michael Jason, Jennifer Nicole BS, Poly. Inst., Bklyn., 1958; PhD, U. Mo., 1962. Teaching asst. U. Mo., Columbia, 1958-62; chem. rschr. Mobil Chem. Co., Edison, N.J., 1962-67; various mgmt. positions then dir. tech. Celanese Corp., N.Y.C., 1967-83; corp. v.p. tech., 1983-86; pres. Celanese Rsch. Co., N.Y.C., 1983-90; pres., corp. v.p. tech. Hoechst Celanese Corp., Chatham, N.J., 1986-90, ret., 1990; pres. Lee Starr Assocs., 1991—. Adv. bd. U. Pa. 1988-90; adv. coun. Hampton U., 1988-97; nat. adv. coun. Synthesis Coalition on Engring. Edn. 1991-96; ptnr. Internat. Think-Tank Group, 1995-97; bd. dirs Internat. Fibers Corp., 2000—. Contbr. chpt. to book; patentee in field. Chmn. conservation commn. Town of Westport, 1996-, chmn., 2001—; chmn. Land Acquisition Com., Westport, 1998—. Fellow Phillips Corp., U. Mo., 1961-62, Poly. Inst. N.Y., 1985. Mem. AAAS, Assn. Rsch. Dirs. (bd. dirs. 1995-97), Am. Chem. Soc. (corp. assoc. 1983-90, bd. govs.), Natural Sci. Assn., N.Y. Acad. Scis., Soc. Chem. Industry, Chem. Mfrs. Assn. (chmn. chem. regulations and adv. com. 1977-82), Am. Inst. Chemists, Sales and Mktd. Execs. Internat. (v.p 1972-73), STAR Residential (bd. dirs. 1994-98), Sigma Xi. Avocations: tennis, golf, sailing, collecting antique scientific instruments. Personal E-mail: lstarr112@aol.com.

**STARR, MARTIN KENNETH,** management educator; b. N.Y.C., May 21, 1927; s. Harry and Melanie (Krauss) S.; m. Polly Exner, Apr. 3, 1955; children: Christopher Herschel, Loren Michael. BS, MIT, 1948; MS, Columbia U., 1951, PhD, 1953. Ptnr., dir. M.K. Starr Assocs., 1956-61; prof. mgmt. sci. Columbia U., N.Y.C., 1961-96, dir. Ctr. for the Study of Ops., 1980-95, dir. Ctr. for Enterprise Mgmt., 1995-96, vice dean Grad. Sch. Bus., 1974-75; Disting. prof. ops. mgmt. Crummer Grad. Sch. Bus. Rollins Coll., Winter Park, Fla., 1996—2003, prof. emeritus, 2003—, dir. Ctr. for Enterprise Mgmt., 1996—2001; prof. emeritus Columbia U., 1996—. Lectr. in field; cons. in field. Author: (with David W. Miller) The Structure of Human Decisions, 1967, Inventory Control-Theory and Practice, 1972, Product Design and Decision Theory, 1963, (with David W. Miller) Executive Decisions and Operations Research, 2d edit., 1969, Systems Management of Operations, 1971, Management: A Modern Approach, 1971, Production Management: Systems and Synthesis, 2d edit., 1972, (with Irving Stein) The Practice of Management Science, 1976, Operations Management, 1978, (with David G. Dannebring) Management Science: An Introduction, 1981, (with Earl K. Bowen) Statistics for Business and Economics, 1982, (with Marion Sobol) Statistics for Business and Economics: An Action Learning Approach, 1983, Managing Production and Operations, 1989, Global Corporate Alliances and the Competitive Edge, 1991, (with Marion Sobol) Introduction to Statistics for Executives, 1993, Operations Management: A Systems Approach, 1996, ED-text rev., 2000, Production and Operations Management, 2004; editor: Executive Readings in Management Science, 1965, (with Milan Zeleny) Multiple Criteria Decision Making, 1977, Global Competitiveness: Getting the U.S. Back on Track, 1988; editor-in-chief Mgmt. Sci., 1967-82; mem. editl. bd. Behavioral Sci., 1970—, Internat. Jour. Flexible Mfg. Sys., 1989—; mem. editl. adv. bd. Jour. Ops. Mgmt., 1983—; editl. adviser Operational Rsch. Quar., 1970-85; cons. editor: Columbia Jour. World Business: Focus: Decision Making, fall, 1977, Quantitative Methods in Mgmt.; contbr. articles to profl. jours. Fellow Inst. for Ops. Rsch. and the Mgmt. Scis.; mem. Inst. Mgmt. Scis. (pres. 1974-75), Prodn. and Ops. Mgmt. Soc. (pres.-elect 1994—, pres. 1995, past pres., bd. dirs. 1996—, chair Coun. of Pres. 1999—), fellow Prodn. and Operations Mgmt. Soc., Beta Gamma Sigma. Home: 100 S Interlachen Ave Winter Park FL 32789-4450 Office: Rollins Coll 120 Crummer Grad Sch Bus Winter Park FL 32789 Office Phone: 407-383-4264. Business E-Mail: mstarr@cfl.rr.com. *The ability to manage complex systems, to maximize societal benefits under conditions of safety and security, has become the most pressing requirement in the decade 2006-2015. Remarkable growth of strong systems interdependencies has occurred since 2000. Global connectivity through the Internet is altering established patterns for living and doing business. Management science using the systems approach combines art and logic with advancing computer-linked technology to rationalize transitions to achieve social benefit. Perhaps a new name is needed to describe this effort. By whatever name it is called, the impact of systems-oriented management science will determine the character of the 21st century and will, in turn, be changed by it.*

**STARR, PAUL ELLIOT,** sociologist, educator, editor, writer; b. NYC, May 12, 1949; s. Saul and Sarah Marion (Buzen) S.; m. Sandra Lurie Stein, Apr. 12, 1981 (dec.); m. Ann Baynes Coiro, June 9, 2000. BA, Columbia U., 1970; PhD, Harvard U., 1978. Jr. fellow Harvard Soc. Fellows, 1975-78; asst. prof. Harvard U., Cambridge, Mass., 1978-82; assoc. prof., 1982-85; prof. sociology Princeton (NJ) U., 1985—. Stuart Prof. Comm., Pub. Affairs, Woodrow Wilson Sch.; founder, co-editor The Am. Prospect. Author: The Discarded Army: Veterans After Vietnam, 1974, The Social Transformation of American Medicine, 1983 (C. Wright Mills award 1983, Pulitzer prize for nonfiction 1984, Bancroft award 1984), The Logic of Health-Care Reform, 1992, The Creation of the Media: Political Origins of Modern Communications, 2004 (Goldsmith Book prize 2005). Guggenheim Found. fellow, 1981-82. Democrat. Office: Dept of Sociology Wallace Hall Princeton U Princeton NJ 08544-1010*

**STARR, RINGO (RICHARD STARKEY),** musician, actor; b. Liverpool, Eng., July 7, 1940; s. Richard and Elsie (Gleave) Starkey; m. Maureen Cox, Feb. 11, 1965 (div. 1975); children: Zak, Jason, Lee; m. Barbara Bach, Apr. 27, 1981. Drummer Ed Clayton Skiffle Group, 1959; drummer & singer Rory Storm's Hurricanes, 1959—62; The Beatles, 1962—69; solo performer, 1970—. Formed Pumpkinhead Records (with Mark Hudson). Musician: (albums) (with The Beatles) Please, Please Me, 1963, With the Beatles, 1963, Meet the Beatles, 1964, Beatles for Sale, 1964, A Hard Day's Night, 1964 (Grammy award best performance by a group, 1964, Grammy award best new artists, 1964), Help!, 1965, Yesterday & Today, 1966, Rubber Soul, 1966, Revolver, 1966, Sergeant Pepper's Lonely Hearts Club Band, 1967 (Grammy award album of the yr., 1967, Grammy award best contemporary album, 1967), Magical Mystery Tour, 1967, The Beatles (The White Album), 1968, Yellow Submarine, 1968, Abbey Road, 1969, Let It Be, 1970 (Grammy award best original score, 1970), Beatles Anthology, 1995 (Grammy award best long

form music video, 1996, Grammy awards best pop performance & best short form music video for Free As A Bird single, 1996); film appearances (with The Beatles) A Hard Day's Night, 1964, Help!, 1965, Yellow Submarine (voice), 1968, Let It Be (also co-exec. prodr.), 1970, TV film appearances Magical Mystery Tour (also co-prodr., co-dir.), 1967; musician: (solo albums) Sentimental Journey, 1970, Beaucoups of Blues, 1970, Ringo, 1973, Goodnight Vienna, 1974, Blast from Your Past, 1975, Ringo's Rotogravure, 1976, Ringo the Fourth, 1977, Scouse the Mouse, 1977, Bad Boy, 1978, Stop and Smell the Roses, 1981, Old Wave, 1983, Starr Struck, 1989, Time Takes Time, 1992, Vertical Man, 1998, I Wanna Be Santa Claus, 1999, Ringo Rama, 2003, Tour 2003, Choose Love, 2005, Ringo Starr & Friends, 2006, (with All-Starr Band) Ringo Starr and His All-Starr Band, 1989, Ringo Starr and His All-Starr Band: Live From Montreux, 1992, Ringo Starr and His Third All-Starr Band, 1997, Ringo & His New All-Starr Band, 2002; musician: (with George Harrison, Ravi Shankar and others) (albums) The Concert For Bangla Desh, 1972 (Grammy award album of the yr., 1972); actor: (films) Candy, 1968, The Magic Christian, 1969, Commonwealth, 1970, 200 Motels, 1971, Blindman (also known as Il Cieco and Il Pistolero Cieco), 1972, That'll Be the Day, 1974, Lisztomania, 1975, Sextette, 1978, Caveman, 1981, Give My Regards to Broad Street, 1984, To the North of Katmandu, 1986; actor, prodr., dir. (films) Born to Boogie, 1972, actor, prodr Son of Dracula, 1974; actor: (TV films) Ringo, 1978, The Cooler, 1982, Princess Daisy, 1983, Alice in Wonderland, 1985, Shining Time Station Christmas: 'Tis a Gift, 1990; (TV series) Thomas the Tank Engine & Friends (voice), 1985—91, Shining Time Station, 1990—91. Decorated Order Brit. Empire; inducted with The Beatles into Rock and Roll Hall of Fame, 1988. Office: c/o KOCH Entertainment 22 Harbor Park Dr Port Washington NY 11050

**STARR, ROSS MARC,** economist, educator; b. Oak Ridge, Nov. 14, 1945; s. Chauncey and Doris E. S.; m. Susan S. Strauss, July 2, 1967; children: Daniel, Diana. BS, Stanford U., 1966, PhD, 1972. Cons. Rand Corp., summers 1966, 67, Western Mgmt. Sci. Inst., Grad. Sch. Mgmt., UCLA, summers 1967, 71; Cowles Found. staff rsch. economist Yale U., New Haven, 1970, faculty, 1970-74; assoc. prof. econs., 1974, U. Calif., Davis, 1975-76, prof. econs., 1976-80, San Diego, 1980—, chmn. dept., 1987-90. Vis. lectr. London Sch. Econs., 1973-74, Peoples U. China, Beijing, 1987; vis. scholar U. Calif., Berkeley, 1978-80, vis. prof., 1997. Author: General Equilibrium Theory: An Introduction, 1997; co-editor: Essays in Honor of Kenneth J. Arrow, 1986: v.1, Social Choice and Public Decision Making, v.2, Equilibrium Analysis, v.3, Uncertainty, Information and Communication; editor: Gen. Equilibrium Models of Monetary Economies, 1989; contbr. articles to profl. jours. NDEA fellow, 1966-69, Yale jr. faculty fellow, 1973-74, Guggenheim fellow, 1978-79; NSF grant, 1979-81, 83-85. Office: U Calif San Diego Dept Econs 0508 9500 Gilman Dr La Jolla CA 92093-0508 Office Phone: 858-534-3879. Business E-Mail: rstarr@ucsd.edu.

**STARR, STEPHEN,** restaurant owner; Grad., Temple U., 1977. Owner Grand Mom Minnie's, Phila.; owner cabaret, comedy club Stars, Phila.; owner Ripley Music Hall, Phila., The Concert Co. (acquired by Electric Factory Concerts in 1990), Phila., Shake, Burger and Roll, Phila., The Bank, Phila., Cafe Republic, Phila.; founder, owner Starr Restaurant Org., Phila., 1995—, Continental Restaurant and Martini Bar, Phila., 1995—, Buddakan, Phila., Tangerine, Phila., Pod, Phila., Alma de Cuba, Phila., Morimoto, Phila., Jones, Phila., Angelina, Phila., El Vez, Phila., Striped Bass, Phila., Washington Square, Phila., Barclay Prime, Phila., Morimoto, NYC, 2006—, Buddakan, NYC, 2006—. Named Restaurateur of the Year, Bon Appetit mag., 2005. Office: Starr Restaurant Org 134 Market St Philadelphia PA 19106*

**STARR, STEVEN DAWSON,** photographer; b. Albuquerque, Sept. 6, 1944; s. Richard Vernon and Carol (Harley) S.; m. Marilynne Sue Anderson, Aug. 6, 1965; 1 child, Stephen Richard. Student, Antioch Coll., 1962-63, Bethel Coll., 1963-64; BA, San Jose State Coll., 1967. Photographer San Jose Mercury-News, Calif., 1966-67; photographer, picture editor A.P., 1968-73; audiovisual producer Starr Productions, Inc., Coral Gables, Fla., 1974-85; photographer Picture Group Agy., 1986-88, Saba Press, N.Y.C., 1988—2000, Corbis, 2000—. Recipient Pulitzer prize for spot news photography, 1970, Nat. Headliners award, 1970, George Polk Meml. award, 1970, Pictures of Year hon. mention, 1970 Office: Corbis 902 Broadway 4th Fl New York NY 10010 E-mail: steve@stevestarr.com.

**STARREN, JUSTIN BRUCE,** medical educator; b. San Diego, Jan. 4, 1959; s. Byron and Geneva Graves Willis Starren; m. Jeanne Rene Valente, Sept. 21, 1991; children: Genevieve Dane, Quinten Dana. AB summa cum laude, Wash. U., St. Louis, 1980, MA, MD, Wash. U., St. Louis, 1987; PhD, Columbia U., 1997. Lic. N.Y., 1996. Intern UCLA Sepulveda Med. Ctr., 1987—88; resident Columbia Presbyn. Hosp., N.Y.C., 1988—90; med. dir. PA Consulting Group, Princeton, NJ, 1990—92; assoc. rsch. scientist Columbia U., N.Y.C., 1996—98, asst. prof. med. informatics and radiology, 1998—. Nsf summer rsch. program com. Columbia U., 2000—; sci. program com. Am. Med. Informatics Symposium, 1998; faculty coun. Columbia U., 1999—. Contbr. articles to profl. jours. Recipient Hugh Wilson award for Radiology Rsch., Wash. U. Sch. Medicine, 1987, Best Electronic Poster, Symposium on Computer Applications in Med. Care, 1995, Martin Epstein award, Am. Med. Informatics Symposium, 1996, Top Ten IT Innovation award, Healthcare Informatics Mag., 2002; fellow, nat. Libr. Medicine, 1992—95; grantee, N.Y. State Ctr. Advanced Tech., 1995—97, 1997—2000, Lifescan Corp., 2001, N.Y. State Ctr. Advanced Tech., 2002—03. Mem.: Am. Telemedicine Assn., Assn. for Computing Machines, Am. Med. Informatics Assn. (chair fin. 1998—2001), Wash. U. Ballroom Dance Club (founding pres. 1977—80), Pi Mu Epsilon. Achievements include patents pending for A Method and System for Voice Activating Web Pages. Avocations: ballroom dancing, gardening. Office: Columbia U 622 W 168th St VC-5 New York NY 10032

**STARRETT, FREDERICK KENT,** lawyer; b. Lincoln, Nebr., May 23, 1947; s. Clyde Frederick and Helen Virginia (Meyers) Starrett; m. Linda Lee Jensen, Jan. 19, 1969; children: Courtney, Kathryn, Scott. BA, U. Nebr., 1969; JD, Creighton U., 1976. Bar: Nebr 1976, Kans 1977, US Dist Ct Nebr 1976, US Dist Ct Kans 1977, US Ct Appeals (8th and 10th cirs) 1983, Mo 1987, US Dist Ct (we dit) Mo 1987, US Supreme Ct 1993. Pvt. practice law, Gt. Bend, Kans., 1976-77, Topeka, 1977-86; with Miller, Bash & Starrett, P.C., Kans. City, Mo., 1986-90; ptnr. Lathrop Norquist & Miller, 1990-91, Lathrop and Norquist, Overland Pk., Kans., 1991-95, Lathrop & Gage L.C., Overland Pk., Kans., 1996—. Judicial nominating commr 10th Judicial Dist, 2000—04. Lt (jg) USNR, 1969—72. Mem.: ABA, Kans. Assn. of Defense Counsel, Mo. Orgn. Def. Lawyers, Def. Rsch. Inst. (state rep. Kans. 1998—2001, bd. dirs. 2002—05), Am. Bd. Trial Advs. (pres. Kans. chpt. 1997), Kans. Bar Assn. (pres. litig. sect. 1985—86), Civitan Club (pres. 1985—86, Disting. Pres. award 1985—86). Democrat. Presbyterian. Avocations: aviation, scuba diving, sailing. Office: Lathrop & Gage LC 10851 Mastin Blvd Bldg 82 Ste 1000 Shawnee Mission KS 66210-1669 Office Phone: 913-451-5140. Business E-Mail: fstarrett@lathropgage.com.

**STARRETT, LUCINDA,** lawyer; b. Washington, June 21, 1957; BA magna cum laude, Princeton U., 1979; student, U. Nigeria, 1980-84; JD cum laude, U. Pa., 1984. Bar: Calif. 1986. Law clerk to Hon. Dorothy W. Nelson U.S. Ct. Appeals (9th cir), 1984-85; ptnr. Latham & Watkins, L.A., 1991—. Chief comment editor Jour. Capital Markets and Securities Regulation, 1983. Mem. bd. alternative dispute resolution Western Justice Ctr. Fulbright scholar, Nigeria, 1980—81. Mem. ABA, L.A. County Bar Assn. Office: Latham & Watkins 633 W 5th St Ste 4000 Los Angeles CA 90071-2005 E-mail: cindy.starrett@lw.com.

**STARRETT, WILLIAM,** dancer, artistic director; b. Indio, Calif., Oct. 18, 1959; s. George Lester and Arleen (LaDroute) S. Soloist Royal Winnipeg (Can.) Ballet, 1974-76, Eglevsky Ballet, N.Y.C., 1977; mem. Am. Ballet Theater, 1977; prin. Joffrey Ballet, N.Y.C., 1978-81; guest artist Ballet West, Salt Lake City, 1981, Atlanta Ballet, 1982, No. Ballet Theatre, Manchester, England, 1983; artistic dir. Columbia (S.C.) City Ballet, 1986—. Named Sr.

Medalist Jackson (Miss.) U.S. Ballet Competition, 1979; recipient Key to City, Singapore, 1985. Mem. Leadership Columbia. Office: Columbia City Ballet PO Box 11898 Columbia SC 29211-1898

**STARRY, DONN ALBERT,** retired aerospace corporate executive, retired military officer; b. N.Y.C., May 31, 1925; s. Don Albert and Edith (Sortor) S.; m. Leatrice Hope Gibbs, June 15, 1948; children: Michael, Paul, Melissa, Melanie. BS, U.S. Mil. Acad., 1948; MS in Internat. Affairs, George Washington U., 1966. Commd. 2d lt. U.S. Army, 1948, advanced through grades to gen., 1977; svc. in Europe, Korea and Vietnam; comdr. 11th armored cavalry rgt. Vietnam, Cambodia, 1969-70; assigned Dept. Army Staff, 1970-72; comdr. Armor Center and Ft. Knox, Ky., 1973-76, V Corps, Europe, 1976-77; comdr. Tng. and Doctrine Command Ft. Monroe, Va., 1977-81; comdr. in chief U.S. Readiness Command, 1981-83, ret., 1983; v.p. mission analysis and tech. affairs Ford Aerospace and Communications Corp., Detroit, 1983-84, v.p., gen. mgr. space missions group, 1984-86; exec. v.p. Ford Aerospace Corp., Arlington, Va., 1987-90; spl. asst. to pres. BDM Internat., McLean, Va., 1988-90. Chmn. bd. Maxwell Techs. Inc., San Diego, 1995-97, Universal Voltronics, Brookfield, Conn., 1998—; author, lectr., counselor to govt. and industry. Mem. Def. Sci. Bd., 1985—93, Order of Aaron and Hur, Friends of Fifth of May; mem. bd. Eisenhower Found., 1995—; chmn. bd. U.S. Cavalry Meml. Found., 1995—2003; mem. bd. Army Hist. Found., 2000—; mem. Army Sci. Bd., 2002—. Decorated Def. D.S.M., Army D.S.M. with oak leaf cluster, Silver Star, Bronze Star with V, Soldier's medal, Purple Heart, Legion of Merit with 2 oak leaf clusters, French Ordre Nationale du Merite, German Knight Commdr.'s Cross of Order of Merit with Badge and Star, Disting. Flying Cross, Air Medal with 9 oak leaf clusters; named to U.S. Army Ft. Leavenworth Command and Gen. Staff Coll. Hall of Fame, 1993; recipient Gold medal The Order of St. George. Mem.: Assn. U.S. Army, U.S. Armor Assn. Episcopalian. Address: 3003 Downing St Williamsburg VA 23185 Personal E-mail: dastarry@cox.net.

**STARSHAK, JAMES L.,** lawyer; b. Chgo., Feb. 3, 1945; s. Norbert Phillip and Enda (Reiter) S.; m. Susanne M. Smith, Oct. 25, 1969; children: Lesle M., Phillip E. BBA, U. Notre Dame, 1966, JD, 1969. Bar: Ill. 1969, Hawaii 1972, U.S. Dist. Ct. (no. dist.) Ill. 1973, U.S. Tax Ct., U.S. Supreme Ct. Atty. estate tax IRS, Chgo., 1969-71, Honolulu, 1971-77; ptnr. Steiner & Starshak, Honolulu, 1971-79; assoc. Conahan & Conahan, Honolulu, 1979-86; ptnr. Carlsmith, Ball et al, Honolulu, 1986—. Office: Carlsmith Ball Pacific Tower 22d Fl 1001 Bishop St Honolulu HI 96813-3429

**STARTIN, W. LANE,** insurance agent; b. Coeur d'Alene, Idaho, July 15, 1973; s. Wesley Ralph and Diana Lynn Startin; m. Amber Jeanette Schneiter, Mar. 22, 2003; 1 child, Evelyn Ruth. BA, Idaho State U., Pocatello, Idaho, 1996. Support mgr. Shift4 Corp., Las Vegas, 2001—05; ins. agt. Farm Bur. Idaho, Twin Falls, Idaho, 2005—. Editor: From Bordello to Ballot Box. Mem.: Spring Mountain Ranch Homeowners Assn. (bd. dirs 2004—05), Twin Falls Lodge No. 45 AF&AM. Unitarian. Home: 282 Dubois Avenue Twin Falls ID 83301-4611 Office: Farm Bureau PO Box 1788 Twin Falls ID 83303-1788 Office Phone: 208-733-7212. Office Fax: 208-733-6586. Personal E-mail: lane@lanestartin.org. Business E-Mail: lstartin@idfbins.com.

**STARTT, JAMES DILL,** history educator; b. Balt., July 26, 1932; s. William Andrew Jr. and Viola (Dill) S.; m. Catherine Louise Felten, Apr. 10, 1960; children: James Nelson, Jennifer Leigh. BA, U. Md., 1957, MA, 1961, PhD, 1965. Asst. prof. history Murray State U., Ky., 1964-66; assoc. prof. Valparaiso U., 1966-71, prof., 1971-97, sr. rsch. prof., 1997—. Author: Journalists for Empire, 1991, Journalism's Unofficial Ambassador: A Biography of Edward Price Bell, 1980; co-author: Hist. Methods in Mass Comm., 2003; co-editor: The Significance of the Media in American History, 1994, The Media in Am.: A History, 1996; author: Woodrow Wilson and the Press: Prelude to the Presidency, 2004; contbr. articles to profl. jours. Active adminstrv. bd. First United Meth. Ch., Valparaiso, 1976-86. With U.S. Army, 1953-55. Endowment grantee Eli Lilly Co., 1983. Mem. Am. Hist. Assn., Am. Journalism Historians Assn. (bd. dir. 1985-88, 90-93, 98-2000, v.p. 1995-97, pres. 1997-98), Valparaiso Rotary Club. Avocations: classical music, walking, travel. Home: 1121 North Waverly Pl Milwaukee WI 53202-3412 Office: Valparaiso U History Dept Huegli Hall Valparaiso IN 46383 Office Phone: 219-241-6682.

**STARYK, STEVEN SAM,** violinist, concertmaster, educator; b. Toronto, Ont., Can., Apr. 28, 1932; s. Peter and Mary Staryk; m. Ida Elisabeth Busch, May 17, 1963; 1 child, Natalie. Student, Royal Conservatory of Music, Toronto, 1942-48, Harbord Collegiate Inst., 1945-48; LittD (hon.), York U., Toronto, 1980. Soloist, concertmaster CBC-Radio Can., Toronto, 1951-55, Royal Philharmonic Orch., London, 1956-59; 1st concertmaster, tchr. Concertgebouw Orch. and Amsterdam Conservatory, 1960-63; concertmaster Chgo. Symphony Orch., 1963-67; prof. of violin Oberlin (Ohio) Coll. Conservatory, 1968-72, Acad. of Music, Vancouver, B.C., Canada, 1972-75, Royal Conservatory of Music, Toronto, 1975-87; concertmaster Toronto Symphony, 1982-87; prof. of violin, chair string div. U. Wash. Sch. Music, Seattle, 1987-97, prof. emeritus, 1997—. Faculty music U. Toronto, 1980-87; vis. prof. U. Victoria, 1972, U. Ottawa, 1975, Northwestern U., 1965-66; founding mem. Quartet Can., 1975-80. Soloist, recitalist, N.Am., Europe and the Far East; recording artist on EMI-HMV, CBC, Everest, Orion, other labels; biography (by Thane Lewis) Fiddling with Life, 2000. Recipient 2 Arts awards Can. Coun., Ottawa, 1968, 75, Queen's Silver Jubilee medal Govt. of Can., Toronto, Shevchenko medal, Winnipeg, Man., Can.; biography "Fiddling with Life" by T. Lewis and S. Staryk, 2002. Home: 12068 E Bella Vista Cir Scottsdale AZ 85259-6034 Office: U Wash Sch Music Mail Stop DN-10 PO Box 353450 Seattle WA 98195-3450

**STARZ, MARY HELEN,** language educator; b. May 9, 1945; BS in Linguistics, U. Tex., El Paso, 1990; PhD in Fgn. Lang. Edn., U. Tex., Austin, 1996. ESL instr. S.W. Tex. State U., San Marcos, Tex., 1995-97; GED instr. Harris County Adult Edn., Houston, 1997-98; chmn. Tex. So. U., Houston, 1998—2005, assoc. prof., 1998—2005; dir. Dual Lang. Inst. U. St. Thomas, Houston, 2005—, assoc. prof., 2005—. Home: 5021 Scenic Dr Dickinson TX 77539 Office: U St Thomas 3800 Montrose Blvd Houston TX 77006 Office Phone: 713-525-3549. Personal E-mail: starzmaryh@earthlink.net.

**STARZINGER, VINCENT EVANS,** political scientist, educator; b. Des Moines, Jan. 12, 1929; s. Vincent and Genevieve (Evans) Starzinger; m. Mildred Hippee Hill, June 16, 1953; children: Page Hill, Evans. AB summa cum laude, Harvard U., 1950, LLB, 1954, PhD, 1959; AM (hon.), Dartmouth Coll., 1968. Bar: Iowa 1954. Practice with firm Bannister, Carpenter, Ahlers & Cooney, Des Moines, 1954; tchg. fellow, instr. govt. Harvard U., 1957—60; mem. faculty dept. govt. Dartmouth U., 1960—94, chmn. dept. govt., 1972—77, 1983—85, Joel Parker prof. law polit. sci., 1976—94, prof. emeritus, 1994—. Author: Middlingness: Juste Milieu Political Theory in England and France, 1815-48, 1965, republished as The Politics of the Center, 1991; contbr. articles to profl. jours. Recipient award, Am. Philos. Soc.; fellow, Earhart Found., 1970—71; Sheldon Traveling fellow, 1950—51, Social Sci. Rsch. Coun. fellow, 1958—59, Faculty fellow, Dartmouth U., 1963—64. Mem.: ABA, Iowa Bar Assn., Am. Polit. Sci. Assn., Cambridge (Mass.) Boat Club, Am. Alpine Club, Phi Beta Kappa. Home: Elm St Norwich VT 05055 Office: PO Box 981 Hanover NH 03755-0981 Office Phone: 603-643-6016.

**STASEK, LORRAINE ANNE,** elementary school educator; b. East Chgo., Ind., July 12, 1932; m. Charles R. Stasek; children: Diane, Charles R., John Charles, Ruthanne. AA in Social Work, 1976; BA in Sociology, Calumet Coll., 1978, BS in Elem. Edn., 1980; BA in Theology, Cal Coll., 1984; M Elem. Edn., Purdue U., Hammond, Ind., 1990. Lic. life elem. Lic. and Substitute tchr. East Chgo. (Ind.) Pub. Sch. System; tchr. Ind. Harbor Cath. Elem. Sch., East Chgo. Task force Grand Cal, bd. pres., citizen of yr. award. Leadership roles Roman Cath. Ch.; mem. Citizens in Action, Operation Hope

Inc.(pres.). Recipient Silver Beaver medal Boy Scouts Am., St. Anne medal Cath. Diocese of Gary, Vol. in Action award State of Ind., Hoosier Environ. Coun. award. Mem. NSTA, ASCD, Nat. Coun. Tchrs. Math.

**STASH, SUSAN MICHELE,** critical care nurse; b. Inglewood, Calif., Mar. 28, 1965; d. Michael Paul and JoAnn Patricia (Margan) S. BSN, Westminster Coll., Salt Lake City, 1987. RN, Calif.; cert. med.-surg. nurse ANCC. Staff nurse gen. surg. unit St. Joseph Hosp., Orange, Calif., 1987-91; staff nurse gen. med. surg. unit Castle Med. Ctr., Kailua, Hawaii, 1992-94; staff nurse renal/pulmonary/telemetry unit Mary Washington Hosp., Fredericksburg, Va., 1994-95; intermediate med. care unit staff nurse Onslow Meml. Hosp., Jacksonville, NC, 1995-97; staff nurse progressive care unit Swedish Med. Ctr., Englewood, Colo., 1998—; staff nurse subacute ICU Hoag Meml. Hosp. Presbyn., Newport Beach, Calif., 1999—. Mem. ANA, AACN, Am. Assn. Cert. Nurses, Sigma Theta Tau.

**STASHOWER, DANIEL MEYER,** writer; b. Cleve., Sept. 21, 1960; s. David L. and Sally (Weiss) S.; m. Alison Corbett, May 18, 1996. BA, Northwestern U., 1982; MFA, Columbia U., 1984. Magician, 1978—; author, 1986—. Author: The Ectoplasmic Man, 1985, Elephants in the Distance, 1989, Teller of Tales: The Life of Arthur Conan Doyle, 1999 (Edgar Allan Poe award Mystery Writers Am., 2000), The Dime Museum Murders, 1999, The Floating Lady Murder, 2000, The Houdini Specter, 2001, The Boy Genius and the Mogul, 2002, The Beautiful Cigar Girl, 2006. Raymond Chandler Fulbright fellow, 1992-93. Business E-mail: daniel@stashower.com.

**STASIO, MARILYN LOUISE,** columnist; b. Boston, Aug. 20, 1943; d. Joseph Louis and Margaret Martha (Crivello) S.; m. Richard Joseph Hummler, Apr. 24, 1971 (dec. Oct. 1990). BA, Regis Coll., 1964; MA, Columbia U., 1966. Theater critic CUE Mag., NYC, 1968-78; columnist Penthouse, NYC, 1975-80, Politicks, NYC, 1977-78; theater critic The Trib, NYC, 1978, After Dark, NYC, 1981-82, Entertainment Weekly, NYC, 1988-90, NY Post, NYC, 1978-88; book critic NY Times, NYC, 1988—, mystery reviewer. Adj. theater prof. NYU, The New Sch.; teaching residencies Va. Tech., Emerson Coll.; vis. lectr. Carnegie Mellon, Columbia U., Hunter, Bennington Coll., SUNY (Buffalo and Albany), Howard U., Mich. U., U. Ala., Dallas Theater Ctr.; seminar participant Leage Profl. Theater Women, 1993, Naples Lit. Seminar, 1991, Key West Lit. Seminar, 1988, Conn. Lit. Coun. Seminar, 1986, ATA Conf.: Women in Can. Theater, Montreal, 1985, World Affairs Conf. at Boulder U., 1984. Co-author: "Showtune" Memoir with Jerry Herman, 1996; author: The Lily Room, Broadway's Beautiful Losers. Mem.: Am. Soc. Journalists and Authors, Nat. Writers Union, Authors Guild, Lit. Mgrs. and Dramaturgs of the Americas, NY Drama Critics Cir., Nat. Book Critics Cir. Democrat. Office: NY Times 229 West 43rd St New York NY 10036*

**STASSEN, JOHN HENRY,** lawyer; b. Joliet, Ill., Mar. 22, 1943; s. John H. and Florence C. (McCarthy) S.; m. Sara A. Gaw, July 6, 1968; children: John C., David A. BS, Northwestern U., 1965, JD, Harvard U., 1968. Bar: Ill. 1968. Assoc. Kirkland & Ellis, LLP, Chgo., 1968, 73-76, ptnr. 1977—. Contbr. articles to legal jours. Mem. bd. govs. Northwestern U. Libr., chmn., 2003—; bd. dirs. Landmark Preservation Coun. Ill., chmn., 2001-03. Lt. comdr., JAGC, USNR, 1969-72. Mem. ABA (past chmn. com. on futures regulation), Ill. Bar Assn., Chgo. Bar Assn., Phila. Soc., Mid America Club. Home: 1310 N Astor St Chicago IL 60610-2114 Office: Kirkland & Ellis 200 E Randolph St Ste 5900 Chicago IL 60601-6436 Office Phone: 312-861-2238. Business E-Mail: jstassen@kirkland.com.

**STASSINOPOULOS, ARIANNA See HUFFINGTON, ARIANNA**

**STASTNY, JOHN ANTON,** real estate executive; b. Chgo., June 30, 1921; s. John Joseph and Bozena (Brezina) S.; m. Elizabeth Regina Ossowski, Jan. 2, 1943; children: Mary Elizabeth, John Bernard. Grad. high sch., Chgo. Owner, pres. Stastny Builders, Berwyn, Ill., 1945—; founder, pres. John A. Stastny & Co., Inc., Berwyn, 1954—, Care Ctr. Profls. Inc., Berwyn, 1961-95, Fairfax Health Care Ctr., LaGrange Park, Ill., 1975-95; chmn. bd. Fairview Health Care Ctr., LaGrange Park, Ill., 1983-95. Pres., adv. bd. Fed. Nat. Mortgage Assn., Washington, 1971-73; chmn. bd. Home Loan Bank, Chgo., 1972-78. Contbr. articles to profl. jours.; co-founder (tech. jour.): Compendium of Multi-Family Housing, 1965. Bd. dirs. Avery Coonley Sch., Downers Grove, Ill., 1956-60, MacNeal Meml. Hosp., Berwyn, 1978-95; founding gov. West Towns Cmty. Nursing Svc., Berwyn, 1968, Washington Sq. retirement housing, Hinsdale, Ill., 1986; elected del. Cmty. Caucus, Hinsdale, 1955. With U.S. Army, 1942-43. Named Presdl. Appointee Constrn. Industry Collective Bargaining Com., Washington, 1969-71, advisor to U.S. Del. to Econ. Commn. for Europe, U.S. State Dept., Geneva, Switzerland, 1971; named to Housing Hall of Fame, Washington, 1980. Mem. Chgo. Home Builders Assn. (life mem., bd. dirs., pres. 1964-65, Award of Merit 1961), Nat. Assn. Home Builders (life bd. dirs., pres. 1971, numerous disting. service awards 1965-78), Nat. Housing Ctr. (gov., chmn. 1974), Lambda Alpha Internat. (Key award 1964). Clubs: Edgewood Valley Country (LaGrange, Ill.). Republican. Avocations: fishing, golf. Home: 3231 Golfside Dr Naples FL 34110-7006

**STASZESKY, FRANCIS MYRON,** electric power industry executive, consultant; b. Wilmington, Del., Apr. 16, 1918; s. Frank J. and Ruth (Jones) S.; m. Barbara F. Kearney, May 30, 1943; children: Francis Myron, John B., Barbara J., Faith A., Paul D. BSME, MIT, 1943; MSME, Mass. Inst. Tech., 1943. Mech. engr. Union Oil Co. Calif., L.A., 1943-45; with E.I. duPont de Nemours Co., Wilmington, Del., 1946-48; joined Boston Edison Co., 1948, supervising engr. design and constrn., 1948-57, supt. engring. and constrn. dept., 1957-64, v.p., asst. to pres., 1964-67, exec. v.p., 1967-79, pres., chief operating officer, 1979-83; cons., 1983—; dir. Boston Edison Co., 1968-83. Fellow ASME (life); mem. IEEE (sr. life), Nat. Acad. Engring., Engring. Soc. New Eng. (pres. 1961-62). Address: 166 Bank St Harwich Port MA 02646-1321

**STATHAM, JASON,** actor; b. London, Sept. 12, 1972; Former Olympic diver British Nat. Diving Team. Actor: (films) Lock, Stock and Two Smoking Barrels, 1998, Snatch, 2000, Turn It Up, 2000, Ghosts of Mars, 2001, The One, 2001, Mean Machine, 2001, The Transporter, 2002, The Italian Job, 2003, Collateral, 2004, Cellular, 2004, Transporter II, 2005, London, 2005, Revolver, 2005, Chaos, 2006, The Pink Panther, 2006, Crank, 2006. Office: Creative Artists Agy 9830 Wilshire Blvd Beverly Hills CA 90212*

**STATHIS, NICHOLAS JOHN,** lawyer; b. Calchi, Greece, Feb. 27, 1924; Republican. s. John and Sylvia (Koutsonouris) S. Student, Columbia U., 1942-43, 44-48, AB, 1946, JD, 1948. Bar: NY 1949. Assoc. James Maxwell Fassett, NYC, 1948—50; asst. counsel to spl. com. to investigate organized crime in interstate commerce U.S. Senate, Washington, 1951; trial atty. Fidelity & Casualty Co., NYC, 1952; law sec. to Harold R. Medina Judge U.S. Ct. Appeals (2d cir.), NYC, 1952—54; spl. dep. atty. gen. N.Y. State Election Frauds Bur., Dept. Law, N.Y.C., 1956; assoc. Watson, Leavenworth, Kelton & Taggart, NYC, 1954—60, ptnr., 1961—81, Hopgood, Calimafde, Kalil, Blaustein & Judlowe, NYC, 1981—84, Botein, Hays & Sklar, NYC, 1984—89; of counsel White & Case, NYC, 1989—93; corp. coun., dir. intellectual property Aphton Corp., NYC, 1993—. Lectr. Practising Law Inst. N.Y.C., 1968-69. Contbr. articles to profl. jours. on trademarks. Pres., exec. dir., chmn., bd. dirs. Found. Classic Theatre and Acad., 1973—; bd. dirs. Concert Artists Guild, 1974-91, Pirandello Soc., 1976—, Bklyn. Philharm. Orch., 1986-91, Orpheon, Inc., 1986-98, Friends of Young Musicians, 1998—. With AUS, 1943-44. Mem. ABA, Assn. of Bar of City of N.Y., N.Y. State Bar Assn., Fed. Bar Coun., Am. Intellectual Property Law Assn., N.Y. Intellectual Property Law Assn. Greek Orthodox. Office: 515 Madison Ave Ste 2511 New York NY 10022-5403 Home: 2700 John F Kennedy Blvd Apt 402 Jersey City NJ 07306-5751

**STATHOPOULOS, PETER,** internist; b. Hackensack, N.J., Mar. 24, 1952; s. Anastasios and Vasiliki S.; m. Diane Menichella. MD, U. Thessaloniki, 1981. Diplomate Am. Bd. Internal Medicine. Intern St. Vincent's Med. Ctr., S.I., 1981-82, resident in internal medicine, 1982-84, attending physician, 1985—. Office: 856 Castleton Ave Staten Island NY 10310-1809 Office Phone: 718-720-6300.

**STATLER, IRVING CARL,** aerospace engineer; b. Buffalo, Nov. 23, 1923; s. Samuel William and Sarah (Strauss) S.; m. Renee Roll, Aug. 23, 1953; children: William Scott, Thomas Stuart BS in Aero. Engring., U. Mich., 1945, BS in Engring. Math., 1945; PhD, Calif. Inst. Tech., 1956. Research engr. flight research dept. Cornell Aero. Lab., Inc., Buffalo, 1946-53, prin. engr. flight research dept., 1956-57, asst. head aero-mechanics dept., 1957-63, head applied mechanics dept., 1963-70, sr. staff scientist aeroscis., 1970-71; research scientist U.S. Army Air Mobility Research and Devel. Lab., Moffett Field, Calif., 1971-73, dir. Aeromechanics Lab., 1973-85, dir. AGARD, 1985-88; sr. staff scientist NASA Ames Rsch. Ctr., 1988-92, chief Human Factors Rsch. Divsn., 1992—. Research scientist research analysis group Jet Propulsion Lab., Pasadena, Calif., 1953-55; chmn. flight mechanics panel adv. group aerospace research and devel. NATO, 1974-76; lectr. U. Buffalo, Millard-Fillmore Coll., Buffalo, 1957-58 Served with USAAF, 1945-46 Fellow AIAA (Internat. Cooperation in Space Sci. medal 1992), AAAS, German Aerospace Soc., Royal Aero Soc.; mem. Am. Helicoptor Soc., Sigma Xi. Home: 1362 Cuernavaca Circulo Mountain View CA 94040-3571 Office: NASA Ames Rsch Ctr MS 262-7 Moffett Field CA 94035 Office Phone: 650-690-6003. E-mail: irving.c.statler@nasa.gov.

**STATMAN, JAN B.,** artist; b. N.Y.C., July 27; d. Saul Berliner and Sylvia Charlotte (Rose) Berliner; m. Max Statman; children: Charles Barry, Louis Craig, Sherry, Michelle. BA in Art, Hunter Coll., N.Y.C. Works in prt. mus. collections, including Mus. of Contemporary Art, Saso Ferrato, Italy, Alto Aragon En Huesca, Spain, Longview (Tex.) Art Mus., various pvt. collections; one-woman shows include Milam Gallery, Dallas, Tex., Longview (Tex.) Art Mus., Art Gallery, 1000, Longview, McAllen (Tex.) Internat. Mus., Barnwell Art Ctr., Shreveport, La., Kilgore (Tex.) Coll., Vandersen Gallery, N.Y.C., Guild Gallery, Houston, Marshal Visual Arts Ctr., Marshall, Tex.; author: (book) Battered Woman's Survival Guide, 1990; co-author: Living With Environmental Illness, 1998, Raisins & Almonds & Texas Oil, 2004; contbr. articles to profl. jours Mem. Longview Women's Commn., 1995—99. Named to Outstanding Young Women of Am., 1976, Artist-in-Residence, Tex. Commn. on the Arts, Austin, 1986, 94; recipient various awards Tex. Press Women, 1972-90. Mem. Nat. Assn. Women Artists, Zonta. Home: 461 Country Pl Longview TX 75605-9707

**STATON, CECIL POPE, JR.,** writer, educator, broadcast executive; b. Greenville, S.C., Jan. 26, 1958; s. Cecil Pope and Shirley Ann (Hughes); m. Catherine Lynn Davidson, Aug. 23, 1986. BA, Furman U., 1980; MDiv, Southeastern Bapt. Theol. Sem., 1982, ThM, 1983; DPhil, U. Oxford, 1988. Assoc. minister Washington Ave. Bapt. Ch., Greenville, SC, 1977—79; pastor Maple Heights Bapt. Ch., Greenville, SC, 1979—80, Trinity Bapt. Ch., Arcadia, NC, 1983—85; prof. Christianity Brewton-Parker Coll., Mount Vernon, Ga., 1989—91; pub., pres. Smyth & Helwys, Macon, Ga., 1990—, bd. dirs.; pres. Sta. Broadcasting, Macon, 2003—, Stroud & Hall Pubs. Macon, 2004—. Assoc. provost, 1996-2004, pub. Mercer U. Press, Macon, 1991-2003; assoc. prof. Coll. Liberal Arts, Mercer U., 1991-2004. Author: A Sturdy American Hybrid: Associated New American Colleges, 2003; editor: Interpreting Isaiah for Preaching and Teaching, 1991, Interpreting Hosea for Preaching and Teaching, 1993, Interpreting Amos for Preaching and Teaching, 1995, Why I Am a Baptist: Preserving the Baptist Heritage for the 21st Century, 1999; contbr. articles to profl. jours. Recipient Am. scholarship Regent's Park Coll., 1986-87, G. Henton Davies Prize in Hebrew, 1985, R.T. Daniel award in Old Testament, 1983, Baggott award Furman U., 1980, Richard Furman Bapt. Heritage award Furman U., 2000. Mem. Soc. Biblical Lit., Am. Acad. Religion, Nat. Assn. Bapt. Profs. Religion, Rotary (local chpt.). Baptist. Home: 103 Plantation Oaks Dr Macon GA 31220-8757 Office: 6316 Peake Rd Macon GA 31210-3960

**STATZ, OLGA,** law educator; b. NYC, May 2, 1965; d. Jean and Cléomie Simon; m. Klaus-Peter Statz, Jan. 3, 1997; 1 child, Anna. BA, CCNY, NYC, 1984; JD, NYU, NYC, 1987; LLM, Cardozo Sch. Law, NYC, 2001. Asst. corp. counsel NYC Law Dept., 1987—90; dep. dir. Legal Outreach Inc., NYC, 1990—91; atty., pvt. practice Law Office Olga Simon, NYC, 1991—97; adj. prof. law Cardozo Sch. Law, 2000—. Sr. editor: jour. Cardozo Studies in Law and Lit., 2001.

**STAUB, AUGUST WILLIAM,** theater producer, educator; b. New Orleans, Oct. 9, 1931; s. August Harry and Laurel (Elfer) S.; m. Patricia Gebhardt, Nov. 22, 1952; 1 child, Laurel Melicent. BA, La. State U., 1952, MA, 1956, PhD, 1960. Instr., tech. dir. La. State U., 1955; instr. Ea. Mich. U., 1956-58; assoc. dir. Dunes Summer Theatre, Michigan City, Ind., summers 1957-60; asst. prof., assoc. dir. univ. theatre U. Fla., 1960-64; assoc. prof. U. New Orleans, 1964-66, prof., chmn. dept. drama and communications, 1966-76; prof., head drama dept. U. Ga., 1976-95, prof. emeritus, 1996—. Exec. producer Jekyll Island Mus. Comedy Festival, 1984-88, Highlands (N.C.) Playhouse, 1989-2000, Ga. Repertory Theatre, 1991-95; staff dir. Theatre in the Square, Marietta, Ga., 1996—; exec. sec. Theatres of La.; v.p. New Orleans Internat. Jazz Festival, 1967-69; pres. S.W. Theatre Conf., 1973-74. Author: Lysistrata, 1968, The Social Climber, 1969, A Small Bare Space, 1970, Introduction to Theatrical Arts, 1971, Creating Theatre, 1973, Varieties of Theatrical Arts, 1980, 83, 94; gen. editor: Artists and Ideas in the Theatre (Peter Lang), 1989—; contbr. articles over 100 titles including Speech Tchr., 1966-68, So Speech Comm. Jour. 1974-77, Quar. Jour. Speech. 1977-79. Bd. dirs. Friends Ga. Mus., Athens, Ga. Symphony, Coun. Arts for Children, New Orleans, New Orleans Ctr. Creative Arts, Athens Arts. Commn., Ga. Alliance Arts Edn. Lt. AUS, 1952-54. Recipient Creativity in Rsch. medallion U. Ga., 1987, Disting. Svc. award S.W. Theater Conf., 1985; La. State U. Found. Disting. Faculty fellow, 1970-71. Fellow Coll. of Fellows of Am. Theatre (bd. dirs. 1999-2001), Coll. of Fellows of the S.W. Theatre Assn.; mem. Am. Theatre Assn. (pres. 1985-86, bd. dirs.), Univ. and Coll. Theatre Assn. (pres. 1974-75), Nat. Assn. Schs. Theatre (pres. 1981-83), Univ. Resident Theatre Assn. (bd. dirs. 1976-79), Inst. European Theatre, Nat. Theatre Conf., Am. Soc. Theatre Rsch., Internat. Fedn. Theatre Rsch., Soc. Lit., Sci. and Arts Home: 190 Ravenwood Ct Athens GA 30605-3340 Personal E-mail: pastaub@bellsouth.net. *How good it is to be able to spend a lifetime doing what one loves to do.*

**STAUB, CAROL ANNE,** artist; b. Milford, Del., Jan. 30, 1948; d. Charles Edward and Isabelle Gill; m. William Edward Staub, July 23, 1977; children: William Knapp, Denise Casalino. Instr., Port St. Lucie, Fla., 2003, Elliott Mus., Stuart, Fla., 2004. One-woman shows include Town of South Palm Beach, Fla., 2005, Represented in permanent collections U. Fla., Ft. Pierce, Fla., Elliott Mus., Stuart, Fla., Arcolle, Sergines, France, Museo De Collage, Mexico, Assn. Promotion Social Artetica, Rome, Italy, Country Arts Found., Ingram, Tex., Real Tart Gallery, Taranaki, New Zealand; contbr. articles to newspapers; numerous group shows including most recently, exhibited in group shows at Somerset Art Assn., Pluckemin, NJ, 2006, Cornell Mus. Art, Delray Beach, Fla., 2006, Vero Beach Mus. Art, Fla., 2006, Morris Pub. Libr., Whippany, NJ, 2006, Elliott Mus., Stuart, Fla., 2006. Finalist, The Artist's Mag., 2002; recipient Merit award, A.E. Bean Backus Mus., 2005, award, Nat. Collage Soc., 2005, Best in Show award, Somerset Art Assn., 2006, Ana Drobnies award, San Diego Watercolor Soc., 2004, East West Arts Frames award, 2005, numerous others. Mem.: NJ Watercolor Soc. (Excellence award 2005, Beall Rodgers Meml. award 2005), The Fla. Watercolor Soc. (assoc.), The Palm Beach Watercolor Soc., Fla. (assoc.), The Exptl. Artists Ala. (assoc.), The Nat. Watercolor Soc. (assoc.), The Nat. Collage Soc. (assoc.), The Am. Watercolor Soc. (assoc.), The Internat. Soc. Exptl. Artists (assoc.), Allied Artists Am. (assoc.), Women In The Visual Arts (life), Garden State Watercolor Soc. (life), Internat. Soc. Acrylic Painters (life Savoir-Faire award 2006), The Nat. Assn. Women Artists (life; bd. dirs., treas. Fla. chpt.), The

Audabon Soc. (assoc.), The Boca Raton Mus. Art Artists Guild (life). Home (Winter): 10316 Crosby Place Port Saint Lucie FL 34986 Home (Summer): 531 Elizabeth Ave Somerset NJ 08873 Home Fax: 772-466-2982. Personal E-mail: carolcando@aol.com.

**STAUB, W. ARTHUR,** health care products executive; b. Detroit, Dec. 25, 1923; s. Edward Elmer and Emma Josephine (Fleury) S.; m. Alla Elizabeth Edwards, June 26, 1948; children: James Randall, Sally Ann, David Scott. BS, Dartmouth Coll., 1944; MD, Temple U., 1947. Intern Muhlenberg Hosp., Plainfield, NJ, 1947-48; resident in pediatrics Abington (Pa.) Meml. Hosp., 1950-51; practice medicine specializing in pediatrics Westfield (N.J.) Med. Group, 1948-63; assoc. med. dir. Ciba Pharm. Co., Summit, NJ, 1963-66; med. dir., v.p. life sci. div. Becton-Dickinson and Co., Rutherford, NJ, 1966-70; v.p. med. affairs C. R. Bard Co., Murray Hill, NJ, 1970-88, also bd. dirs. Bd. dirs. Crestmont Fed. Savs. and Loan Assn., Edison, N.J., Colonial Trust Nat. Bank, North Palm Beach, Fla.; cons. Children's Specialized Hosp., Westfield, 1948-88, Overlook Hosp., Summit, 1948-88. Contbr. articles to profl. jours. Deacon Presbyn. Ch., Westfield, 1959—. Ensign USNR, 1944—50, to capt. USAF, 1950—53. Fellow Am. Coll. Physician Execs.; mem. AAAS, Assn. Advancement Med. Instrumentation, Health Industry Mfrs. Assn. (chmn. med. and sci. steering com.). Clubs: Echo Lake Country (Westfield) (bd. trustees 1984-88); Lost Tree (North Palm Beach, Fla., bd. govs. 1989-94, sec. 1989-94); Skytop (Pa.). Republican. Presbyterian. Avocations: golf, physical fitness, reading, sailing, travel. Home: 3330 Devonshire Way Palm Beach Gardens FL 33418 E-mail: DoctorWAS@aol.com.

**STAUBACH, ROGER THOMAS,** real estate executive, former professional football player; b. Cin., Feb. 5, 1942; s. Robert Joseph and Elizabeth (Smyth) S.; m. Marianne Jeanne Hoobler, Sept. 4, 1965; children: Jennifer Anne, Michelle Elizabeth, Stephanie Marie, Jeffrey, Amy Lynn. Student, Roswell Mil. Inst., N.Mex., 1960-61; BS, US Naval Acad., 1965. Quarterback Dallas Cowboy Football Team, 1969-79; pres. Holloway-Staubach Co. (name now Staubach Co.), 1980-92; chmn., CEO, pres. Staubach Co., Dallas, 1993—; former announcer CBS Football. Author: First Down, Lifetime to Go, 1974, Time Enough to Win, 1981. Bd. dirs. Halliburton Co., Gibson Greetings, Salvation Army; active Pres. Coun. on Phys. Fitness, 1981-83. Lt. USNR, 1965-69. Recipient Heisman Trophy, 1963; played Pro Bowl, 1971, 76, 78; inducted into Nat. Football League Hall of Fame, 1985. Mem. Fellowship of Christian Athletes. Roman Catholic. Office: Staubach Co 15601 Dallas Parkway Ste 400 Addison TX 75001

**STAUBER, KARL NEILL,** foundation administrator; b. Statesville, N.C., Jan. 4, 1951; s. Van G. and Dorthea (Mills) S.; m. Hollis Scott, Aug. 14, 1971. BA, U. N.C., 1973; Program for Mgmt. Devel., Harvard U., 1983; PhD, Union Inst., Cin., 1993. Asst. dir. Reynolds Babcock Found., Winston-Salem, N.C., 1974-79; exec. dir. Needmor Found., Toledo, 1979-83; pres. Econ. Devel., Inc., Boulder, Colo., 1983-86; v.p. program N.W. Area Found., St. Paul, 1986-93; dep. under sec. rsch., edn., and econ. USDA, Washington, 1993-94, under sec. rsch., edn., and econ., 1994—; CEO and pres. N.W. Area Found., St. Paul, 1996—. Contbr. editorials to newspapers. Adv. bd. mem. Found. Mid South, Jackson, Miss., 1988-93, Mpls. Found., 1991-93. Avocations: furniture building, tractor restoration. Office: Northwest Area Found 60 Plato Blvd East Ste 400 Saint Paul MN 55107*

**STAUBER-JOHNSON, ELIZABETH JANE,** retired elementary school educator; b. Duluth, Minn., Apr. 7, 1950; d. Edward James and Kathleen Mary (LeBlanc) Stauber; m. A(lden) Ronald Johnson, July 26, 1975; children: Todd Alden, Heidi Ann, Dean Edward, Shane Ronald. BS summa cum laude, Coll. St. Scholastica, 1972; MEd summa cum laude, U. Minn., Duluth, 1982; PhD in Curric./Instrn. Elem. Math. Edn., U. Minn., 1996. Cert. tchr., Minn. Tchr. Ind. Sch. Dist. 709/Duluth Pub. Schs., 1972-88; tchr. elem. math. Nettleton Math./Sci./Computer Magnet Sch., Duluth, 1988-93; asst. prof. math. edn. U. Wis., Superior, 1993-97; instr., 1997. Pres. Equine Attire, Inc., 2004—; trainer Success Understanding Math. Project, Des Moines, gender-ethnic excellence student achievement GESA, 1991—; instr. tchr. Family Math., Mpls., 1988—; mem. project for reforming and improving math. edn. com. Minn. Dept. Edn., math. framework team, 1992—; com. mem. Gov.'s Nat. Sci. Found. Statewide Systemic Initiative, 1991—, Coll. of St. Scholastica Ctr. for Promotion of Underrepresented in Sci., 1990—; desegregation adv. com. Duluth Schs., 1987—; initiative com. Gov.'s Nat. Sci. Found.; past mem. Minn. Dept. Edn. Math. Frameworks; presenter in field Trustee Coll. St. Scholastica, Duluth, chair acad. affairs; bd. dirs. Marshal Coll. Prep. Sch., 2003—, v.p., 2004—; pres. Equine Allies, Inc., 2004—. Mem. Minn. Coun. Tchrs. Math., Nat. Assn. Tchrs. Math., Minn. Reading Assn., Arrowhead Reading Coun. (bd. dirs. 1984—, pres. 1988-89), Assn. Childhood Edn. (pres. Duluth chpt. 1980-81, state bd. dirs. 1982-83), Phi Kappa Phi, Alpha Delta Kappa (pres. 1982-84), Phi Delta Kappa. Avocations: reading, children's pop-up books, orchid collecting/growing, showing and breeding quarter horses. Home: 2400 Minnesota Ave Duluth MN 55802-2518

**STAUBITZ, ARTHUR FREDERICK,** retired lawyer, retired health products executive; b. Omaha, Mar. 14, 1939; s. Herbert Frederick Staubitz and Barbara Eileen (Dallas) Alderson; m. Linda Medora Miller, Aug. 18, 1962; children: Michael, Melissa, Peter. AB cum laude, Wesleyan U., Middletown, Conn., 1961; JD cum laude, U. Pa., 1964. Bar: Ill. 1964, U.S. Dist. Ct. (no. dist.) Ill. 1964, U.S. Ct. Appeals (7th cir.) 1964, Pa. 1972. Assoc. Sidley & Austin, Chgo., 1964-71; sr. internat. atty., asst. gen. counsel, dir. Japanese ops. Sperry Univac, Blue Bell, Pa., 1971-78; from assoc. to dep. gen. counsel Baxter Internat. Inc., Deerfield, Ill., 1978—85, v.p., dep. gen. counsel, 1985—90; v.p. Baxter Diagnostics, 1990—91; sr. v.p., sec., gen. counsel Amgen, Inc., Thousand Oaks, Calif., 1991—92; v.p., gen. mgr. Ventures Group Baxter World Trade Corp., Deerfield, Ill., 1992—93, v.p., sec., gen. counsel Baxter Internat. Inc., Deerfield, 1993, sr. v.p., gen. counsel, 1993—97, sr. v.p. portfolio strategy, 1997—98; ret., 1998. Mem. Planning Commn., Springfield Twp., Montgomery County, Pa., 1973-74, mem. Zoning Hearing Bd., 1974-78; bd. dirs. Twp. H.S. Dist. 113, Deerfield and Highland Park, Ill., 1983-91, pres., 1989-91; trustee Food and Drug Law Inst., 1991-92, 93-96, Carthage Coll., Kenosha, Wis., 1996—, exec. com., 1999—; bd. dirs. Music of the Baroque, 1994-2001, vice-chmn.; mem. adv. bd. Ariz. Cancer Ctr. Episcopalian. Home: 6251 E Placita Aspecto Tucson AZ 85750 Office Phone: 520-529-2331. Personal E-mail: staubitz@msn.com.

**STAUBUS, GEORGE JOSEPH,** finance educator; b. Brunswick, Mo., Apr. 26, 1926; s. George Washington and Florence Lidwina (Pittman) S.; m. Sarah Mayer, Apr. 11, 1949; children: Lindsay, Martin, Paul, Janette. BS, U. Mo., 1947; MBA, U. Chgo., 1949, PhD, 1954. C.P.A., Ill. Instr. U. Buffalo, 1947-49, U. Chgo., 1950-52; asst. prof. then prof. acctg. U. Calif.-Berkeley, from 1952, now Michael N. Chetkovich prof. emeritus. Vis. prof. NYU, 1965, London Bus. Sch., 1966-67, U. Kans., 1969-70; Erskine lectr. U. Canterbury, New Zealand, 1972, 91. Author: A Theory of Accounting to Investors, 1961, Activity Costing and Input-Output Accounting, 1971, Making Accounting Decisions, 1977, An Accounting Concept of Revenue, 1980, Activity Costing for Decisions, 1988, Economic Influences on the Development of Accounting in Firms, 1996, The Decision-Usefulness Theory of Accounting: A Limited History, 2000. Served with USN, 1944-46. Recipient Disting. prof. Calif. Soc. C.P.A.s, 1981 Mem. Am. Acctg. Assn. (disting. internat. lectr. 1982), AICPA, Fin. Execs. Inst. Office: UC Berkeley Haas Sch Bus Berkeley CA 94720-0001

**STAUDENMEIER, WILLIAM JOHN, JR.,** academic administrator, sociology professor; b. Wilmington, Del., Oct. 28, 1950; s. William John and Virginia Arlene Staudenmeier; m. Elizabeth Robin Medina, May 28, 1978; children: William Francis, Thomas Maxim. BS, U.S. Mil. Acad., West Point, N.Y., 1972; MA in Mgmt. and Human Rels., Webster Coll., St. Louis, Mo., 1978; PhD in Sociology, Washington U., St. Louis, Mo., 1985. Chief drug and alcohol edn. and rehab. Travis AFB, Fairfield, Calif., 1972—75; chief drug/alcohol abuse control Clark AFB, Angeles, Philippines, 1975—76, Hdqs. Mil. Airlift Command, Scott AFB, Ill., 1976—78; acting asst. prof. sociology Drake U., Des Moines, 1985—87; asst. prof. sociology Eureka Coll., Ill., 1987—90, chaired prof. sociology, 1990—95, prof. sociology, 1995—, v.p. acad. affairs, dean, 2005—. Divsn. chair social scis. and bus.

divsn. Eureka Coll., 1991—94; manuscript referee jours., 1987—2005; instr. cmty. orgn. sect. Nat. Alcoholism Tng. Program for Profls., St. Louis, 1976—78; cons. and instr. alcohol studies cert. program, employee assistance program Continuing Edn. Washington U., St. Louis, 1980—84; cons. Harbor Ho., St. Louis, 1983—84; cons. employee assistance edn. and rsch. program Sch. of Indsl. and Labor Rels., Cornell U., Ithaca, NY, 1987; cons. medicalization of substance abuse treatment in the workplace Inst. for Behavioral Rsch., U. of Ga., Athens, 1987; faculty rep. to bd. of trustees Eureka Coll., 1988—90, chair coll. strategic planning, 1989—91, founder, dir., faculty colloquia series, 1988—94; vis. scientist U. Edinburgh, Scotland, 1994; vis. fellow Sch. Indsl. and Labor Rels., Cornell U., NY, 1992. V.p. Eureka Area United Way, 1989—91; charter chpt. faculty adviser Eureka Coll. Nat. Charter Campus Chpt. of Habitat for Humanity, 1988—92; bd. dirs. Solano County Mental Health Adv. Bd., Vallejo, Calif., 1974—75. Capt. USAF, 1972—78. Named pioneering EAP practioner for oral history project, Prof. Harrison M. Trice, Cornell U., 1987, Dean's Lectr., Office of the Dean, Eureka Coll., 1988, 1995; recipient PhD tuition scholarship, Washington U., 1980—85, Helen B. Cleaver Disting. Tchg. award, Eureka Coll., 1989—90; fellow, Nat. Inst. on Alcohol Abuse and Alcoholism, 1979—80. Mem.: Kettil Bruun Soc. for Social and Epidemiol. Rsch. on Alcohol, Midwest Sociol. Soc. (soc. bd. of dirs. 2004—06, sec. 1999—2001), Ill. Sociol. Assn. (governing bd. 1995—2001, pres. 1998—99), Alpha Chi (life). Achievements include first to early social actions drug/alcohol education/rehabilitation in the USAF. Avocations: hiking, reading, chess, soccer. Office: Eureka Coll 300 E College Ave Eureka IL 61530 Office Phone: 309-467-6301.

**STAUDERMAN, ALBERT PHILIP, JR.,** media consultant; b. Englewood, N.J., Dec. 14, 1936; s. Albert Philip Stauderman and Martha Louise (Dodd) Williamson; m. Helen MacKenzie Layton, Dec. 27, 1958; children: Elizabeth, Sarah, Edward (Ted). BSc, Syracuse U., 1958. Audio-visual prodn. supr. Luth. Ch. in Am., Phila., 1960-64; TV commit. prodn. supr. Procter & Gamble, Cin., 1964-71, assoc. mgr., 1971-82; dir. advt. prodn. Richardson-Vicks, Wilton, Conn., 1982-85; CEO Bird Bonette Stauderman Inc., Westport, Conn., 1985—; co-chmn., dir. Bird Bonette Stauderman Europe Ltd., London, 1996-2000, chmn., dir., 2000—, founder Sao Paulo, Brazil, 2001—; ptnr. Stauderman/Petray, LLC, Westport, Conn., 2001—. Pres. Dikaia Found., Inc., 1995—2001. Author: TV Commercial Production Cost Trends, 1985, 2d edit., 1986; writer, dir. various pub. svc. TV Commls., 1970-82; actor Golden Age TV programs, 1949-56. Commr. Wilton (Conn.) various land use Commns., 1988—; founding pres. Syracuse U. Newhouse Sch. Alumni Assn., 1985—87; mgmt. comm. vice chmn. office for comms. Luth. Ch. in Am., NY, 1978—86; chmn. comms. unit Ohio Synod of Luth. Ch. in Am., Columbus, 1978—82; pres. congregation and coun. St. Michael's Luth. Ch., New Canaan, Conn., 1999—2001. Recipient Alumni Svc. award Syracuse U., 1981. Mem. Sprite Island Yacht Club (chmn. race com. 1993-98), Williams Club (N.Y.C.), Delta Upsilon. Republican. Avocation: sailing race management official. Office Phone: 203-454-8781.

**STAUDERMAN, BRUCE FORD,** advertising executive, writer; b. Jersey City, Mar. 17, 1919; b. Herbert Henry and Helen Ann (Jacobus) S.; m. Claude Outhier, Mar. 23; 1946. Student, Syracuse U., 1936-38, TV Workshop, N.Y.C., 1949-50, Sch. TV Technique, 1950. V.p. TV, radio, films Meldrum & Fewsmith, Inc., Cleve., 1954-62, exec. v.p., chmn. plans bd., exec. creative dir., 1973-79; v.p., creative dir. Ogilvy & Mather, N.Y.C., 1962-63; Kenyon & Eckhardt, Inc., N.Y.C., 1979-83, Barnhart & Co., Denver, 1983-84; pres. Stauderman Advt., 1984—; v.p., creative dir. Mktg. Resources Group, 1985-88. Dir. TV, Intermarco-Elvinger (advt. co.), Paris, 1969-73; TV cons. gov., Ohio, 1958; mem. coun., judge C.L.I.O. Festival, 1960—; chmn. Paris jury, 1969-73; jury mem. Internat. Advt. Film Festival, Cannes, Venice, 1976— Author: The England Book, 2006; radio, TV program writer: House of Mystery, The Big Story, Columbia Workshop, 1946-51; writer, producer, dir., WXEL-TV, Cleve., 1951-54. Mem. men's com. Cleve. Playhouse, 1958-62; chmn. TV com. Cleve. United Fund, 1958-59. Served from pvt. to 2d lt. AUS, 1941-46; to 1st lt. N.G. Essex Troop AUS, 1948-50. Mem. Am. Assn. Advt. Agys. (TV and radio adminstrs. com. 1963-62), Am. Fedn. TV and Radio Artists, Naval Club (London). Home: 8647 Falcon Green Dr West Palm Beach FL 33412-1576 E-mail: bfswriter@aol.com.

**STAUDOHAR, PAUL DAVID,** economics professor, labor arbitrator; b. Duluth, Minn., Dec. 3, 1940; s. Matthew Paul Staudohar and Patricia Constance Landell. BA, U. Minn., 1962; MBA, U. So. Calif., L.A., 1966, MA, 1968, PhD, 1969. Adminstrv. officer United Calif. Bank, L.A. 1964—66; instr. econ. U. So. Calif., L.A., 1967—69; asst. prof. bus. adminstrn. Calif. State, Hayward, 1969—72, assoc. prof. bus. adminstrn., 1972, prof. bus. adminstrn., 1977—. Pres. Internat. Assn. of Sports Economists, France, 1999—2002; bd. editors Jour. of Individual Employment Rights, 1992—; co-founder Jour. of Sports Econs., bd. editors, 2000—. Author: Labor Econ. and Indsl. Rels., 1994, Playing for Dollars, 1996; author, editor: Diamond Mines: Baseball and Labor, 2000, More Sports Best Short Stories, 2004. Recipient disting. svc. award, Omicron Delta Epsilon, 1981. Mem.: Labor and Employment Rels. Assn., Am. Arbitration Assn., Am. Econ. Assn., Nat. Acad. Arbitrators, Beta Gamma Sigma (hon.). Office: Calif State U East Bay 25800 Carlos Bee Blvd Hayward CA 94542 Office Phone: 510-885-3080.

**STAUFFER, ERIC P.,** lawyer; b. Tucson, Feb. 1, 1948; s. Robert D. and Jeanne E. (Catlin) S.; m. Jane F. Snyder, Aug. 2, 1969; children: Curtis Austen, Marcus Elias, Laura Afton. BA, New Coll. of Fla., 1969; JD, Yale U., 1972. Bar: Ariz. 1972, Maine 1974, D.C. 1979. Spl. asst. to gov., fed. state coord. State of Maine, 1973-75; Maine alt. New England Regional Commn., 1973-75; gen. counsel Maine State Housing Auth., 1976-77; adminstrv. asst. to chmn. Dem. Nat. Com., 1977-78; mem. Preti, Flaherty, Beliveau & Pachios, LLP, Portland, Maine, 1978—. Bd. dirs. Jr. Achievement Maine, Inc., 1995-98; pres. Goodwill Industries No. New Eng., 1981-82, bd. dirs., 1979-93, 1999-2005. Fellow Am. Coll. Mortgage Attys.; mem. Am. Health Lawyers Assn., Maine State Bar Assn., Ariz. State Bar, D.C. Bar, Maine Real Estate Devel. Assn. (bd. dirs. 1991—, Pub. Svc. award 1992, Founder's award 2002). Office: Preti Flaherty Beliveau & Pachios LLP PO Box 9546 One City Ctr Portland ME 04112-9546 Office Phone: 207-791-3000. Business E-Mail: estauffe@preti.com.

**STAUFFER, GEORGE B.,** dean, music historian, musician, consultant; b. Hershey, Pa., Feb. 18, 1947; s. Howard Hamilton and Elizabeth Boyer Stauffer; 1 child, Matthew. BA, Dartmouth Coll., Hanover, NH, 1969; MA, Bryn Mawr Coll., Pa., 1971; PhD, Columbia U., NYC, 1978. Adj. asst. prof. Yeshiva U., NYC, 1978—79; asst. to prof. music CUNY, NYC, 1979—2000; dean, prof. music Mason Gross Sch. Arts, Rutgers U., New Brunswick, NJ, 2000—. U. organist, chapel music dir. Columbia U., 1977—99; bd. trustees Keewaydin Found., Salisbury, Vt., 1981—2000. Author: (books) The Organ Preludes of J.S. Bach, 1980, Bach: The Mass in B-Minor, 1997; co-author: Organ Technique: Modern & Early, 2002; editor: J.S. Bach as Organist, 1986, The World Of Baroque Music, 2006; gen. editor: Yale Music Masterworks Series, 2002—. Fellowship, Guggenheim Found., NYC, 1985—86, Fulbright Commn., DC. 1999—2000, Am. Coun. Learned Societies, NYC, 1999—2000. Mem.: Coll. Music Soc., Am. Bach Soc. (adv. bd. mem. 2000—, pres. 1996—2000), Am. Musicological Soc. Avocation: canoeing. Home: 1050 George St 15G New Brunswick NJ 08901 Office: Office of Dean Mason Gross Sch 33 Livingston Ave New Brunswick NJ 08901 Office Phone: 732-932-9360. Business E-Mail: stauffer@masongross.rutgers.edu.

**STAUFFER, JOHN WILLIAM,** cultural historian; b. Lincoln, Nebr. s. William Albert and Jean Stanley Stauffer; m. Deborah Cunningham MALS in Humanities, Wesleyan U., 1991; MA in Am. Studies, Purdue U., 1993; PhD in Am. Studies, Yale U., 1999. Asst. prof. Harvard U. Cambridge, Mass., 1999-2001, assoc. prof., 2001—03, prof. 2003—. Spkr. in field. Author: The Black Hearts of Men, 2002 (Frederick Douglass Book prize 2002, Lincoln priz, 2d pl. winner, 2003), The Meteor of War: The John Brown Story; editor: My Bondage and My Freedom; contbr. articles to profl. jour. Newhouse fellow in writing Yale U., 1996-97, Rsch. fellow, 1994-95, History and Am. Studies Rsch. fellow, 1996, Charlotte Newcombe fellow Woodrow Wilson

Nat. Fellowship Found., 1997-98; grantee NEH, 1999; recipient Ralph Henry Gabriel prize, 1999, Jan Thaddeus Tchg. award Harvard U., 2002, Frederick Douglass Book prize 2002, Avery Craven pize, 2003, Lincoln prize, 2003, Everett Mendelsohn Excellence in Mentoring award, 2005. Mem. Soc. for Values in Higher Edn., Orgn. of Am. Historians (presenter 1998), Am. Studies Assn. (Ralph Henry Gabriel prize 1999), Daguerreian Soc., Phi Kappa Phi. Avocations: photography, tennis, ballet, dance (jazz). Office: Harvard U Dept English Barker Ctr 12 Quincy St Cambridge MA 02138-3804 Home: 1 Amory Pl Cambridge MA 02139 E-mail: stauffer@fas.harvard.edu.

**STAUFFER, SCOTT WILLIAM,** lawyer, accountant; b. Oshkosh, Wis., Aug. 17, 1954; s. Robert Edward and Shirley Lydia (Wrasse) S.; m. Debralee Bowland, Nov. 14, 1987. BBA in Acctg., U. Wis., 1975; JD, U. Denver, 1979. Bar: Colo. 1979; CPA, Colo. Tax acct. Arthur Andersen & Co., Denver, 1979-82; tax mgr. Gary-Williams Oil, Englewood, Colo., 1982-85; pvt. practice Aurora, Colo., 1986—. Active Colo. Chorale, Denver, 1977—, pres., 1984-85, 92-93 Mem. ABA, AICPA, Colo. Bar Assn. (multidisciplinary practice taskforce 2000-02, ethics com. 1997-99, exec. coun. solo and small firm sect. 2002-06, chair 2004-05), Denver Bar Assn. (chmn. law office mgmt. com. 1993-95, chmn. intraprofl. com. 1997-04), Colo. Soc. CPA (chmn. fed. tax com. 1994-96, bd. dirs. 2000-02), Am. Assn. Atty.-CPA., Denver Tax Assn. (chair 2003), Bethany Luth. Ch. Found. (pres. 2002-04). Lutheran. Avocations: singing, golf, travel, reading, computer. Home: 8147 W Frost Pl Littleton CO 80128-4325 Office: 2851 S Parker Rd Ste 720 Aurora CO 80014-2728 Office Phone: 303-337-2323. Business E-Mail: sstauffer@staufferlawcpa.com.

**STAUFFER, THOMAS GEORGE,** retired hotel executive; b. Akron, Ohio, Mar. 4, 1932; s. Caldwell E. and Rose C. (Ortscheidt) S.; m. Lois Campsey, June 18, 1960. BS, Case Western Res. U., 1954. Cert. hotel adminstr. Pres. Renaissance Hotels Internat. (Ams.), 1954-98; ret., 1998. Trustee Cleve. Bot. Garden. Recipient Legion of Honor, Order of DeMolay. Mem. Am. Hotel and Motel Assn., Urban Land Inst., Nat. Restaurant Assn. (pres.); Rolling Rock Club, Lakewood Country Club, Masons, Scottish Rite, Sigma Chi (Significant Sigma Chi). Home: 19 Warwick Ln Cleveland OH 44116-2305 Office: Renaissance Hotels Internat Marriott Dr Washington DC 20058-0001 E-mail: tomgstau@aol.com.

**STAUFFER, THOMAS MICHAEL,** former university president; b. Harrisburg, Pa., Dec. 5, 1941; s. John Nisley and Louise Lee Stauffer; children: Amity Juliet, Courtney Amanda, Winston Thomas; life ptnr. Susie Heller. BA cum laude, Wittenberg U., Ohio, 1963; Cert. in E. European Politics, Freie U. Berlin, 1964; MA, PhD, U. Denver, 1973; Doctorate (hon.), Jackson State U., 2002. Asst. dean coll. Keene State Coll., 1968—72; dir. office leadership devel., v.p., external rels. Am. Coun. on Edn., 1972—82; pres., prof. pub. policy U. Houston-Clear Lake, 1982—91; spl. asst. to adminstr. NASA, 1991—92; pres., prof. pub. policy and internat. rels. Golden Gate U., 1992—99; CEO Mgmt. Cons. Internat., 1985—, Young Pres. Orgn. Internat., 1999—2001, Family Bus. Internat. Consultation, 2001—; exec. dir. Lincoln Ctr. for Ethics in Internat. Mgmt., prof. global bus. Thunderbird--The Garvin Sch. of Internat. Mgmt., 2003—05. Exec. sec. Fedn. Assn. of Acad. Health Care Profls.; chmn. task force Am. Coun. Edn.; exec. dir. Bus. Higher Edn. Forum, Nat. Com. Higher Edn. Issues, 1975—82. Exec. editor Ednl. Record and Higher Edn. and Nat. Affairs; contbr. articles to profl. jours. and newspapers. Chair Challenger Ctr. for Space Sci. Edn.; chair nat. bd. Ctr. for Advanced Space Studies; adv. com. advanced tech. Tex. Econ. Devel.; chmn. com. advanced tech. Houston Com. on Econ. Diversification Planning, Houston World Trade Ctr. Task Force, Clear Lake Area Econ. Devel. Found.; co-chair Tex. Sci. and Tech. Coun.; pres. St. John Hosp.; co-chair San Francisco World Trade Assn.; chair San Francisco Consortium on Higher Edn., San Francisco Mayor's Blue Ribbon Com. on Econ. Devel.; mem. steering com. Silicon Valley Mfrs. Group; bd. dirs. San Francisco C. of C., San Francisco YMCA, Acad. of Art U. Recipient Disting. Alumni award Grad. Sch. Internat. Studies U. Denver, 1989, Tex. Senate Resolution of Commendation, 1991, Challenger Ctr. Nat. award, 1990, ACE Fellow Anniversary award, 1990, 05, Leadership HS Do the Right Thing award, 1998; Am. Coun. on Edn. fellow in acad. adminstrn., 1971, Ford Found. and Social Sci. Rsch., 1963-68, sr. fellow Am. Leadership Forum. Home: 3080 Coombsville Rd Napa CA 94558 Office: 1806 Green St San Francisco CA 94123 Office Phone: 415-516-8767. Business E-Mail: globalconsultation@gmail.com.

**STAUFFER, VALERIE VILAS,** civic volunteer; b. N.Y.C., Aug. 29, 1935; d. Frank Jay and Kathleen Vilas Brown; m. John Eugene Stauffer, June 5, 1956; children: Jill Stauffer Cobbs, Karen Stauffer Murphy, John Christian, Peter Eugene. BA, Wellesley Coll., 1956. V.p. Stauffer Tech., Greenwich, Conn., 1985—. Contbr. Greenwich Rev. mag.; editor: Quality Assurance of Food, 1988, Round Hill Association Newsletter, 1991—92; mng. editor: Inkwell mag., 2004—. Chmn. dist. 7 Rep. Town Meeting, Greenwich, Conn., 1984—, chmn. social svcs. com., 1997; chmn. Friends of Greenwich Libr., 1997—99; trustee, exec. com., sec. bd. trustees Greenwich Libr., 1999—. Mem. Greenwich Garden Club (pres. 1999-2001). Home: 6 Pecksland Rd Greenwich CT 06831-3738 Office: Stauffer Tech 6 Pecksland Rd Greenwich CT 06831-3738 Personal E-Mail: stauftek@aol.com.

**STAUNTON, IMELDA (IMELDA MARY PHILOMENA BERNADETTE STAUNTON),** actress; b. London, Jan. 9, 1956; d. Joseph and Bridie (McNicolas) Staunton; m. Jim Carter, 1985; 1 child. Grad., Royal Acad. Dramatic Art. Actress (TV series) The Singing Detective, 1986, Thompson, 1988, Izzy, 1990, Up the Garden Path, 1990, Muriel Spry, 1993, If You See God, Tell Him, 1993, Stella Pingles, 1995, Is It Legal?, 1995, Mrs. Twit, 2003, Let's Write a Story, 2003, (films) Comrades, 1987, They Never Sleep, 1990, Antonia and Jane, 1991, Peter's Friends, 1992, Much Ado About Nothing, 1993, Deadly Advice, 1993, Sense and Sensibility, 1995, Twelfth Night: Or What You Will, 1996, Remember Me?, 1997, Shakespeare in Love, 1998, Rat, 2000, Another Life, 2001, Crush, 2001, Ready, 2002, The Virgin of Liverpool, 2003, Bright Young Things, 2003, Blackball, 2003, I'll Be There, 2003, Vera Drake, 2004 (Coppa Volpi award, Venice Film Festival, 2004, Gold Lion award, Venice Film Festival, 2004, Best Actress, NY Film Critic Circle award, 2004, Los Angeles Film Critics Assn. award, 2004, Washington, DC Film Critics, 2004), 3 & 3, 2005, Nanny McPhee, 2005, (TV) A Sleeping Life, 1989, Yellowbacks, 1990, The Englishman's Wife, 1990, The Heat of the Day, 1990, A Masculine Ending, 1992, Don't Leave Me This Way, 1993, Woodcock, 1994, Mole's Christmas, 1994, Citizen X, 1995, The Adventures of Mole, 1995, David Copperfield, 1999, Murder, 2002, Cambridge Spies, 2003, Fingersmith, 2005, A Midsummer Night's Dream, 2005, My Family and Other Animals, 2005, (TV miniseries) Look at the State We're In, 1995, Cambridge Spies, 2003;, performer repertory productions, (stage appearances) Guys and Dolls, 1982, 1996, The Beggar's Opera, 1985, A Chorus of Disapproval, 1985 (Laurence Olivier award, Soc. of West End Theatre, Best Supporting Actress, 1985, London Critics Circle award, Best Supporting Actress, 1985, Laurence Olivier award, 1986), The Corn is Green, 1985 (Laurence Olivier award, 1986), The Wizard of Oz, 1986, Fair Maid of the West, 1986, Uncle Vanya, 1988 (Plays and Players London Theatre Critics award, Best Supporting Actress, 1988), Into the Woods, 1990 (Olivier award, Best Actress in a Musical, 1991), Phoenix, 1990 (Laurence Olivier award, Best Actress in a Musical, 1990); voice The Snow Queen's Revenge, 1996, The Ugly Duckling, 1997, The Canterbury Tales, 1998, The Chicken Run, 2000, Jack and the Beanstalk, 2000, guest appearances (TV) A Sleeping Life, 1989, Charity, 1993, "Local Government," Look at the State We're In!, 1995, A Bit of Fry and Laurie, 1995, Midsomer Murders, 1999, Incubus, 2003. Assoc. mem. Royal Acad. Dramatic Art. Address: Peters Fraser & Dunlap Ltd Drury House 34-43 Russell St London WC2B 5HA England Office Phone: 44 (0) 207 344 1041. Office Fax: 44 (0) 207 836 9543.*

**STAUTBERG, SUSAN SCHIFFER,** communications executive; b. Nov. 9, 1945; d. Herbert F. and Margaret (Berwind) Schiffer; m. T. Aubrey Stautberg, Jr., Dec. 10, 1979. BA, Wheaton Coll., 1967; MA, George Washington U., 1970. Nat. TV corr., Washington, 1970-74; fellow White Ho., Washington, 1974-75; mem. U.S. Consumer Products Safety Commn., Washington, 1976-78, McNeil Consumer Products Co., 1978-80; v.p. Fraser Assocs.,

Washingron, 1980; exec. asst. to pres. Morgan Stanley & Co., NYC, 1980-82; dir. comm. Deloitte & Touche, NYC, 1982; pres. MasterMedia Ltd., 1986—, PartnerCom, NYC. Bd. dirs. States Inc. Author: Making It in Less Than an Hour, 1976, Pregnancy Nine to Five: The Career Woman's Guide to Pregnancy and Motherhood, 1985, The Pregnancy and Motherhood Diary: Planning the First Year of Your Second Career, 1988, Managing It All, 1989, Balancing Act, 1992. Mem. nat. chmn. adv. coun. Ctr. Study Presidency, 1976—; mem. Phila. Regional Panel Selection White Ho. Fellows; bd. dirs. Schiffer Pub., Berwind Found.; mem. Reagan-Bush Presdl. Transition Team; mem. Commn. Presdl. Scholars; State Dept. spkr. Selected One of Wheaton's 10 Most Oustanding Grads. Alumnea Assn. Wheaton Coll., 1982. Mem. Pub. Rels. Soc. Am. (bd. dirs.), Pub. Affairs Profls., Nat. Soc. Colonial Dames, Acorn Club, City Tavern Club, Cosmopolitan Club, Colony Club, Radnor Hunt Club. Office: PartnerCom 17 E 89th St Ste 7D New York NY 10128-0615

**STAVELY, KEITH WILLIAMS FITZGERALD,** librarian; b. New Brunswick, N.J., May 13, 1942; s. Homer Eaton and Elizabeth (Williams) S.; m. Kathleen Fitzgerald, Aug. 19, 1978; 1 child, Jonathan Keith. BA, Yale U., 1964, PhD, 1969; MLS, Simmons Coll., 1980. Asst. prof. English Boston U., 1963—74, Ohio State U., 1990—91; lectr. in English Boston Coll. 1975—80; adult svcs. libr. Watertown Free Pub. Libr., Mass., 1979—89, br. libr., 1984—89, head adult svcs., 1989—90; reference libr. Somerville Pub. Libr., Mass., 1991—92; asst. adminstr. Fall River Pub. Libr., Mass., 1992—99, adminstr., 1999—. Author: Puritan Legacies: Paradise Lost and the New England Tradition, 1630-1890, 1987, paperback edit., 1990, The Politics of Milton's Prose Style, 1975; co-author: Family Man: What Men Feel About Their Wives, Their Children, Their Parents, and Themselves, 1978, America's Founding Food: The Story of New England Cooking, 2004; contbr. articles and revs. to profl. publs. Fellow Fulbright Found., India, 1964-65, Am. Coun. Learned Socs., 1988-89, John Simon Guggenheim Meml. Found., 1989. Mem. MLA (Prize for Ind. Scholars 1987), ALA, Mass. Libr. Assn., Phi Beta Kappa. E-mail: kstavely@sailsinc.org, kstavely@cox.net.

**STAVERT, ALEXANDER BRUCE,** archbishop; b. Montreal, Apr. 1, 1940; s. R. Ewart and Kathleen H. (Rosamond) S.; m. Diana Greig, June 26, 1982; children: Kathleen, Rosamond, Timothy. Student, Lower Can. Coll., Montreal, 1957; BA, Bishop's U., 1961; STB, U. Toronto, Ont., Can., 1964, ThM, 1976, DD (hon.), 1986. Ordained to ministry Anglican Ch. as deacon, 1964, as priest, 1965. With Mission of Schefferville, Que., 1964-69; fellow, tutor in div. Trinity Coll., U. Toronto, 1969-70, chaplain, 1970-76; with St. Clement's Mission East, St. Paul's River, Que., 1976-81; chaplain Champlain Regional Coll., Bishop's U., 1981-84; dean, rector St. Alban's Cathedral, Prince Albert, Sask., Canada, 1984-91; consecrated bishop Anglican Diocese of Que., Quebec, 1991—; metropolitan Province of Can., 2004—; archbishop Quebec, 2004—. Address: Diocese of Que 31 rue des Jardins Quebec City PQ Canada G1R 4L6 Office Phone: 418-692-3858. Business E-Mail: archbishop@quebec.anglican.ca.

**STAVES, SUSAN,** humanities educator; b. N.Y.C., Oct. 5, 1942; d. Henry Tracy and Margaret (McClemon) Staves. AB, U. Chgo., 1963; MA, U. Va., 1964, PhD, 1967. Woodrow Wilson intern Bennett Coll., Greensboro, NC, 1965-66; from assoc. prof. to prof. Brandeis U., Waltham, Mass., 1967-93, Paul Proswimmer prof. of Humanities, 1993—2001, dept. chair, 1986-89, 95-98, prof. emerita, 2001—. Clark prof. UCLA, 1989—90. Author: Players' Scepters: Fictions of Authority in the Restoration, 1979, Married Women's Separate Property in England, 1660-1833, 1990, A Literary History of Women's Writing in Britain, 2005, Studies on Voltaire and the 18th Century, (essays) Fetter'd or Free?: Collected Essays on 18th Century Women Novelists, 1986, History, Gender, and 18th Century Literature, 1994, Woman and Political Writing, 1998, Enchanted Ground: Reimagining John Dryden, 2004, Cambridge Companion to Aphra Behn, 2004; co-author (with John Brewer): Early Modern Conceptions of Property, 1994; co-editor (with Cynthia Ricciardi): Elizabeth Griffith's Delicate Distress, 1997; contbr. articles to profl. jours. Mem. ACLU, 1967—; assoc. mem. Belmont Dem. Town Com., Belmont, Mass. Woodrow Wilson fellow, 1963—64, Woodrow Wilson Dissertation fellow, 1966—67, Harvard Liberal Arts fellow, 1980—81, John Simon Guggenheim fellow, 1981—82. Mem.: AAUP, MLA (exec. com. divsn. on late 18th century English lit. 1984—86), English Inst., Am. Soc. for 18th Century Studies (exec. bd. 1987—90). Episcopalian. Avocations: hiking, harpsichord. Office: Brandeis U Dept English MS 023 Waltham MA 02454 Office Phone: 781-736-2161. Business E-Mail: staves@brandeis.edu.

**STAVIG, MARK LUTHER,** language educator; b. Northfield, Minn., Jan. 20, 1935; s. Lawrence Melvin and Cora (Hjertaas) S.; m. Donna Mae Ring, July 3, 1957; children— Anne Ragnhild, Thomas Edward, Rolf Lawrence BA, Augustana Coll., 1956, Oxford U., 1958, MA, 1962; PhD, Princeton U., 1961. Instr. to asst. prof. English U. Wis., Madison, 1961-68; from assoc. prof. to prof. English Colo. Coll., Colorado Springs, 1968—2001; ret., 2001—. Author: John Ford and the Traditional Moral Order, 1968, The Forms of Things Unknown: Renaissance Metaphor in Romeo and Juliet and A Midsummer Night's Dream, 1995; editor: Ford, 'Tis Pity She's a Whore, 1966. Fellow Danforth Found., 1956-61, Woodrow Wilson Found., 1956-57; Fulbright scholar Oxford U., 1956-58 Mem.: Shakespeare Assn. Am. Democrat. Home: 1409 Wood Ave Colorado Springs CO 80907-7348

**STAVISKY, TOBY ANN,** state legislator; b. NYC; m. Leonard Stavisky, 1964 (dec. 1999); 1 child, Evan. BA, Syracuse U.; Grad. Degree, Hunter Coll., Queens Coll. Social studies tchr. N.Y.C. Pub. High Schs.; dist. mgr. N.E. Queens 1980 Census; mem. N.Y. Senate from 16th Dist., Albany, 1999—, asst. minority whip, 2003—. Mem. legis. commns. fin., tourism, recreation and sports devel. N.Y. State Sen. 16th Dist., ranking minority mem., mem. aging com., mem. civil svc. and pensions com., mem. edn. com. Founder North Flushing Sr. Ctr., bd. dirs.; trustee Whitestone Hebrew Ctr. Named Worthy Woman of Forest Hills; recipient Claire Shulman award, Top 10 Women in Bus., 2004, award, Neurol. Impaired Brain Injured Children, 2002, Counseling, Admissions and Fin. Aid Legis. Consortium, 2003, Flushing C. of C. and Bus. Assn., Taiwanese Assn. Am., CUNY, Korean-Am. Assn. Flushing. Democrat. Office: Rm 504 Legislative Office Bldg Albany NY 12247 also: 14436 Willets Point Blvd Flushing NY 11357-3411 Office Phone: 718-445-0004. Business E-Mail: stavisky@senate.state.ny.us.

**STAVITSKY, ABRAM BENJAMIN,** immunologist, educator; b. Newark, May 14, 1919; s. Nathan and Ida (Novak) S.; m. Ruth Bernice Okney, Dec. 6, 1942; children: Ellen Barbara, Gail Beth. AB, U. Mich., 1939, MS, 1940; PhD, U. Minn., 1943; VMD, U. Pa., 1946. Research fellow Calif. Inst. Tech., 1946-47; faculty Case Western Res. U., 1947—, prof. microbiology, 1962—, prof. molecular biology and microbiology, 1983-89, emeritus, 1989; mem. expert com. immunochemistry WHO, 1963-83; mem. microbiology fellowship com. NIH, 1963-66; mem. microbiology test com. Nat. Bd. Med. Examiners, 1970-73; chmn. microbiology test com. Nat. Bd. Podiatry Examiners, 1978-82. Mem. editl. bd. Jour. Immunological Methods, 1979-88, Immunopharmacology, 1983-96. Vice pres. Ludlow Community Assn., 1964-66. Fellow AAAS; mem. Am. Assn. Immunologists, Am. Soc. Microbiology, Sigma Xi. Home: 14604 Onaway Rd Shaker Heights OH 44120-2845 Office: 2119 Abington Rd Cleveland OH 44106-2333 Business E-Mail: abs7@case.edu.

**STAVOLE, JANET M.,** librarian, library director; b. Cleve., Ohio, Nov. 25, 1949; d. Frank A and Gertrude E Stavole. BA, Kent State U., 1972, MLS, 1972—79. Children's libr. Kent Free Libr., Ohio, 1973—78, Main Children's Rm. Akron-Summit County Pub. Libr., Akron, Ohio, 1979—85; br. mgr. & early childhood libr. Nordonia Hills Br. Akron-Summit County Pub. Libr., Northfield Ctr., Ohio, 1985—. Pres. Akron-Summit Pub. Libr. Staff Assn., 1984—85. Mem.: Ohio Libr. Coun. Avocations: reading, gardening, art. Office: Akron-Summit County Pub Libr 9458 Olde Eight Rd Northfield OH 44067 Office Phone: 330-467-8595. Office Fax: 330-467-4332. E-mail: jstavole@akronlibrary.org.

**STAVREV, KRASSIMIR K.,** chemist, researcher; b. Shumen, Bulgaria, Nov. 11, 1958; s. Kolio K. Stavrev and Penka P. Iovcheva; m. Galina N. Nikolova, Sept. 24, 1978 (div. Jan. 1983); 1 child, Nikolay; m. Galina I. Georgieva, Feb. 3, 1985 (div. July 2001); children: Lidia, Jordan; m. Antonia M. Smillova, May 7, 2002. PhD, Sofia U., Bulgaria, 1988. Asst. prof. Sofia U., 1988-92; postdoctoral fellow Scuola Normale Superiore, Pisa, Italy, 1992-94, U. Fla., Gainesville, 1994-97; dir. sci. support Hypercube, Inc., Gainesville, 1997-98; asst. dir. U. Fla. Coll. Medicine, 1998—2003; rschr. ProQuest, 2003—. Office Phone: 772-220-4410. Fax: 772-220-4420. Business E-Mail: krassimir.stavrev@proquestalison.com.

**STAVROPOULOS, ROSE MARY GRANT,** community activist, volunteer; b. Decatur, Ill. d. Walter Edwin and Ora Lenore (Kepler) Grant; m. Stan Stavropoulos; children: Becky Ann Stavropoulos Betian, Stephanie Diane. BS, Ea. Ill. U. Cert. elem. edn. Tchr. 2nd grade Garfield Sch., Decatur; bd. dirs. Wilmot Sch. Bd. PTA, Deerfield, Moraine Girl Scout Coun., Deerfield, also bd. dirs.; chmn. Human Rels. Commn., Deerfield; mem. sr. citizen adv. com. Deerfield Park Dist.; pres. Lake County (Ill.) LWV; chmn. Deerfield Village Caucus; pres. Caring For Others, Inc., Deerfield, Deerfield Area LWV; bd. mem., pres. Deerfield Area United Way, pres. Mem. Deerfield Village Caucus Adv. Coun. Recipient Deerfield Human Rels. Humanitarian award, Lerner Life's Citizen of Month. Mem. Deerfield Area Hist. Soc., Highland Park Hosp. Aux, Legacy at Bryant Ranch Home Assn. (bd. dirs., treas., sec.), Delta Zeta. Home: 23959 Sanctuary Pkwy Yorba Linda CA 92887 Personal E-mail: jjjjgrandma@aol.com.

**STAVROPOULOS, WILLIAM S.,** retired chemical company executive; b. Bridgehampton, NY, May 12, 1939; m. Linda Stavropoulos; children: S. William, Angela E. BS in Pharm. Chemistry, Fordham U.; PhD in Medicinal Chemistry, U. Washington; LLD (hon.), Northwood U., 1998. Rsch. chemist in pharm. rsch. Dow Chem. Co., Midland, Mich., 1967, rsch. chemist for diagnostics product rsch., 1970, rsch. mgr. diagnostics product rsch., 1973, bus. mgr. diagnostics product rsch., 1976, bus. mgr. polyolefins, 1977, dir. mktg. plastics dept., 1979; comml. v.p. Dow Chem. Co. Latin Am., Coral Gables, Fla., 1980; pres. Dow Latin Am., 1984; comml. v.p., basics and hydrocarbons Dow Chem. Co. U.S.A., Midland, 1985-87, group v.p., 1987-90; pres. Dow U.S.A., 1990; v.p. The Dow Chem. Co., 1990, sr. v.p., 1991, pres., COO, 1993—95, CEO Midland, 1995—2000, 2002—04, chmn. 2001—06. bd. dirs. Dow Corning Corp., The Dow Chem. Co., Marion Merrel Dow Inc., BellSouth Corp., Chem. Financial Corp., Maersk Inc., NCR Corp.; trustee, Fidelity Group of Funds; bd. Am Enterprise Inst. Public Policy Rsch.; CEO Essex Chem Corp., 1988-92. Recipient Ellis Island Medal of Honor, 1998, Man of the Year award, Hellenic Am. C. of C., 2000, Palladium Medal award, Societe de Chimie Industrielle, 2001, Annual Bus. Mgmt. award, Society of Plastic Engineers, 2003. Mem.: Society of Chem. Industry (Chem. Industry Medal award 2003).*

**STAWICKI, JOSEPH JOHN, JR.,** marketing executive; b. New Haven, Conn., Nov. 27, 1944; s. Joseph J. Sr. and Tonya (Bolash) S.; m. Barbara Jean Schneider, Jan. 19, 1968, children: Kevin, Dennis. BS, St. Joseph Coll., 1966; MBA, No. Ill. U., 1968. Investment adminstr. Phoenix Equity Planning Corp., Hartford, Conn., 1971—74; asst. prof. Ctrl. Conn. State U., New Britain, 1975—81; trade officer New Eng. Trade Assistance Ctr., Boston, 1981—83; dir. ops. Multimate Internat. Corp., East Hartford, Conn., 1983—84; pres. Mercor Resources Corp., Winsted, Conn., 1985—, also bd. dirs.; pres. Stawicki Realty, Winsted, 1988—. Mem. Wyantenuck Country Club, Elks, Sigma Iota Epsilon. Roman Catholic. Home: PO Box 416 Winsted CT 06098-0416 Office: Mercor Resources Corp 135 W Wakefield Blvd Winsted CT 06098-2929 Office Phone: 860-379-5028. Personal E-mail: joseph.stawicki@snet.net.

**STAWNYCHY, ZORIANA MARIA,** financial executive; b. NYC, May 31, 1953; d. Walter and Eugenia (Hanuszczak) Salak; m. Yuri Andrij Stawnychy, Oct. 26, 1985. BA, Fordham U., 1975. Cert. fin. planner, registered investment advisor. Fin. planner Cigna, N.Y.C., 1978—83, 1985—90; mgr. Bruce Raines Assocs., N.Y.C., 1983—84; sr. fin. counselor Ind. Fin. Services, White Plains, NY, 1984—85; owner Stawnychy Fin. Svcs., Inc., Butler, NJ, 1991—. Mem. Fin. Planning Assn. Avocation: tennis. Office Phone: 973-283-0024.

**STAY, BARBARA,** zoologist, educator; b. Cleve., Aug. 31, 1926; d. Theron David and Florence (Finley) S. AB, Vassar Coll., 1947; MA, Radcliffe Coll., 1949, PhD, 1953. Entomological Army Research Center, Natick, Mass., 1954-60; vis. asst. prof. Pomona Coll., 1960; asst. prof. biology U. Pa., 1961-67; asso. prof. zoology U. Iowa, Iowa City, 1967-77, prof., 1977—. Fulbright fellow to Australia, 1953; Lalor fellow Harvard U., 1960 Fellow AAAS, Entomol. Soc. Am.; mem. Soc. Comparative and Integrative Biology, Am. Inst. Biol. Scis., Am. Soc. Cell Biology, Iowa Acad. Scis., Sigma Xi. Office: U Iowa Dept Biological Scis Iowa City IA 52242 E-mail: barbara-stay@uiowa.edu.

**STAYIN, RANDOLPH JOHN,** lawyer; b. Cin., Oct. 30, 1942; s. Jack and Viola (Tomin) S.; children: Gregory S., Todd R., Elizabeth J. BA, Dartmouth Coll., 1964; JD, U. Cin., 1967. Bar: Ohio 1967, U.S. Dist. Ct. (so. dist.) Ohio 1968, U.S. Dist. Ct. D.C. 1977, U.S. Ct. Appeals (6th cir.) 1968, U.S. Ct. Appeals (fed. cir.) 1986, U.S. Supreme Ct. 1974, U.S. Ct. Appeals (D.C. cir.) 1976, U.S. Ct. Internat. Trade, 1985. Assoc. Frost & Jacobs, Cin., 1967-72; exec. asst., dir. of legislation U.S. Sen. Robert Taft, Jr., Washington, 1973-74, chief of staff, 1975-76; assoc. Taft, Stettinius & Hollister, Washington, 1977, ptnr., 1978-88, Barnes & Thornburg, Washington, 1988—. Mem. adv. coun. U.S. and FGN. Comml. Svc., U.S. Dept. Commerce. Chmn., mem. numerous coms., chmn., worker campaigns for local politicians Rep. Party state and local orgns.; mem. Citizens to Save WCET-TV, 1967-72, Fine Arts Fund, 1970-72, Cancer Soc. 1970-72; chmn. adv. info. com. Hamilton County Mental Health and Mental Retardation Bd., 1969-71, vice chmn., 1971, chmn., 1971-72; v.p. Recreation Commn., City of Cin., 1970-72; mem. funds mgmt. com. Westwood 1st Presbyn. Ch., 1968, v.p., 1969, pres., 1970, trustee, 1970, elder, 1971-72; bd. dirs. Evans Mill Pond Owners Assn., v.p., 1986, pres., 1987; chmn. Washington Nat. Cathedral Fund Com., mem. devel. com.; co-chair 1907 Soc. Mem.: ABA (sect. on internat. law and practice, vice chmn.com.on nat. legislation 1977—79, internat. sect., anti-trust sect.), D.C. Bar Assn. (com. on internat. law), Internat. Bar Assn., Am. Soc. Assn. Execs. (legal sect., internat. sect.). Avocations: theater, tennis, skiing, travel, boating. Office: Barnes & Thornbury 750 17th St NW Ste 900 Washington DC 20006-2225 Office Phone: 202-289-1313.

**STAYTON, JAMES MICHAEL,** music educator; b. Phila., Mar. 1, 1975; s. Norman J. and Mary J. Stayton; m. Catherine A. Padovano, July 20, 2002. BA in Music, Fla. Atlantic U., 2001—01, MA in Music, 2005. Dir. music ministry Our Lady Queen of Heaven Ch., North Lauderdale, Fla., 1994—2002; dir. omusic ministry St. Pius X Ch., Ft. Lauderdale, Fla., 2002—; music tchr. St. Helen Sch., Lauderdale Lakes, Fla., 1996—2001; tchr., dir. choral activities Cardinal Gibbons H.S., Ft. Lauderdale, 2003—; Composer choral art songs and contemporary music. Mem.: Am. Guild Organists, Am. Choral Dir.'s Assn., Nat. Cath. Educator's Assn., Fla. Music Educator's Assn., Music Educator's Nat. Conv., Sigma Alpha Mu (pres., edn. chmn. 1996—99, Brother of the Yr. 1998). Roman Catholic. Avocations: golf, travel, cooking. Home: 9124 SW 22nd St Boca Raton FL 33428 Office: Cardinal Gibbons HS 2900 NE 47th St Fort Lauderdale FL 33308 Office Phone: 954-491-2900. Office Fax: 954-772-1025. Personal E-mail: stayton@cghsfl.org.

**STAYTON, THOMAS GEORGE,** lawyer; b. Rochester, Minn., May 1, 1948; m. Barbara Joan Feck, Aug. 8, 1970; children: Ryan, Megan. BS, Miami U., Oxford, Ohio, 1970; JD, U. Mich., 1973. Bar: Ind. 1973, U.S. Dist. Ct. (so. dist.) Ind. 1973, U.S. Ct. Appeals (7th cir.) 1977. Ptnr. Baker & Daniels, Indpls., 1973—. Sustaining mem. Product Liability Adv. Coun. Recipient Sagamore of the Wabash Gov. of Ind., 1988. Mem. ABA, Ind. State Bar Assn., Indpls. Bar Assn. Office: Baker & Daniels 300 N Meridian St Ste 2700 Indianapolis IN 46204-1782 Office Phone: 317-237-1260. E-mail: tstayton@bakerd.com.

**STAYTON, WILLIAM RALPH,** psychologist, educator; b. Kelso, Wash., Dec. 25, 1933; s. Ralph Willard and Marguerite (Hunter) S.; m. Kathleen Boucher, Sept. 4, 1954; children: Mark, John, Cheryl, Paul. BA, U. Redlands, 1956; MDiv, Andover Newton Theol. Sem., 1960; ThD, Boston U., 1967; PhD, Inst. Advanced Study of Human Sexuality, 2002. Ordained to ministry Am. Bapt. Ch., 1959. Assoc. min. 1st Bapt. Ch. in Newton, Mass., 1956-61; min. 1st Bapt. Ch., Gloucester, Mass., 1961-68; chaplain New Eng. Bapt. Hosp., Boston, 1968-71; asst. prof. U. Pa. Sch. Medicine, Phila., 1971—78; adj. assoc. prof. U. Pa. Grad. Sch. Edn., Phila., lectr., faculty, 1982—2004; asst. prof. Jefferson Med. Coll./Thomas Jefferson U., 1978-83; marriage and family therapist Wm R. Stayton & Assocs., Ltd., P.C., Phila., 1978—. Mem. faculty La Salle U., Phila., 1983-2002; prof. and coord., human sexuality program Widener U., Chester, Pa., 1999—. Editor spl. issue Topics in Clin. Nursing, 1980; contbr. articles to profl. jours., chpts. to books. Pres. Cmty. Svcs. for Human Growth, Paoli, Pa., 1989-91, bd. dirs., 1981-97. Named Man of Yr., B'nai B'rith, Gloucester, Mass., 1968; recipient Outstanding Svc. award Community Svcs. for Human Growth, 1990, Richard J. Cross award U. Medicine and Dentistry N.J., 1997, Dean's award Sch Human Svc. Professions Widener U., 2002, Tchr. Excellence award Kappa Delta Pi, 2006. Mem. APA, Am. Assn. Marriage and Family Therapists, Am. Assn. Sex Educators, Counselors and Therapists (bd. dirs. 1982-86, 88-90, 2005—, chmn. dist. VI 1982-86, pres. 1996-98, Outstanding Svc. award 1978-87, 87, Disting. Svc. award 2000), Sex Info. and Edn. Coun. U.S. (pres. 1985-87, sec. 1990-92), Soc. for Sci. Study Sex (chmn. ann. meeting 1983), Pa. Assn. Marriage and Family Therapists (continuing edn. com. 1985-90), Planned Parenthood Southeastern Pa. (bd. dir. 1999—, first vice chmn. 2001-04, chmn. 2004—), Phi Kappa Phi. Democrat. Home: 81 Andover Ct Wayne PA 19087-5616 Office: 987 Old Eagle School Rd Ste 719 Wayne PA 19087-1708 Office Phone: 610-971-0700. Business E-Mail: william.r.stayton@widener.edu. E-mail: wmstayton@cs.com.

**STEAD, JAMES JOSEPH, JR.,** securities company executive; b. Chgo., Sept. 13, 1930; s. James Joseph and Irene (Jennings) S.; m. Edith Pearson, Feb. 13, 1954; children: James, Diane, Robert, Caroline. BS, DePaul U., 1957, MBA, 1959. Asst. sec. C. F. Childs & Co., Chgo., 1957-62; exec. v.p., sec. Koenig, Keating & Stead, Inc., Chgo., 1962-66; 2d v.p., mgr. midwest mcpl. bond dept. Hayden, Stone Inc., Chgo., 1966-69; sr. v.p., nat. sales mgr. Ill. Co. Inc., 1969-70; mgr. instl. sales dept. Reynolds and Co., Chgo., 1970-72; partner Edwards & Hanly, 1972-74; v.p., instnl. sales mgr. Paine, Webber, Jackson & Curtis, 1974-76; v.p., regional instl. sales mgr. Reynolds Securities, Inc., 1976-78; sr. v.p., regional mgr. Oppenheimer & Co., Inc., 1978-88; sr. v.p., regional mgr. fixed income Tucker Anthony, 1988—; instr. Mcpl. Bond Sch., Chgo., 1967—. With AUS, 1951-53. Mem. Security Traders Assn. Chgo., Nat. Security Traders Assn.; Am. Mgmt. Assn., Mcpl. Fin. Forum Washington. Clubs: Execs., Union League, Mcpl. Bond, Bond (Chgo.); Olympia Fields Country (Ill.); Wall Street (N.Y.C.). Home: 1005 Hickory Ridge Ct Frankfort IL 60423-2114 Office: 1 S Wacker Dr Chicago IL 60606-4614

**STEAD, WILLIAM WALLACE,** medical educator, researcher, department chairman; b. Durham, NC, Aug. 23, 1948; s. Eugene Anson Jr. and Evelyn Emogene S.; m. Janet Louise Mackey, Aug. 13, 1977; 1 child, Elizabeth Mackey. BA in Chemistry, Duke U., 1970, MD, 1973. Diplomate Am. Bd. Internal Medicine, Am. Bd. Nephrology. Intern in medicine Duke U., Durham, 1973, resident in medicine, 1974, fellow in nephrology, 1975-76, assoc. medicine, 1977-80, asst. prof. medicine, 1980-83, assoc. prof. medicine, 1984-90; prof. medicine and biomed. informatics Vanderbilt U., Nashville, 1991—, assoc. vice chancellor health affairs Med. Ctr. Office chief info. officer, 1991, dir. Informatics Ctr., 1991, prof. biomed. informatics, chief info. arch., 1994—, univ. info. arch., 1999—2000, asst. to chancellor informatics, 2000—, chmn. Vanderbilt Ctr. Better Health, 2002—. Dir. HealthStream, Inc., Nashville, 1998—; mem. com. nat. quality report on health care delivery Inst. Medicine Nat. Acads., Washington, 2000-01, com. rapid advance demonstration projects, 2002, computer sci. and telecom. bd. Nat. Rsch. Coun., 2002-; bd. regents Nat. Libr. Medicine, Bethesda, 2001-05; mem. commn. systemic interoperability, 2004-05. Editor in chief: Jour. Am. Med. Informatics Assn., 1993-2002; editor: Proceedings of Eleventh Annual Symposium on Computer Applications in Medical Care, 1987. Recipient Healthcare Pioneer award Computers in Healthcare, 1991; grant of fast track provision of IAIMS Nat. Libr. Medicine, 1995-99. Fellow Am. Coll. Med. Informatics (founding fellow), Am. Inst. Med. and Biol. Engring. (founding fellow); mem. Am. Med. Informatics Assn. (bd. dirs. 1999—, pres.'s award 1997), Inst. Medicine of NAS, Engle Soc., Sigma Xi, Alpha Omega Alpha. Office: Vanderbilt U Vanderbilt Ctr Better Health 3401 W End Ave Ste 290 Vanderbilt Campus Mail Stop 8670 Nashville TN 37203-6866 Business E-Mail: bill.stead@vanderbilt.edu.

**STEADHAM, RICHARD LYNN,** magazine art director; b. Sacramento, Calif., Sept. 3, 1951; s. Lyndell Harvey and Dorothy Mae (Dennis) S.; m. Karen Jean Stoner, May 2, 1971; children: Taylor Ryan, Erin Danielle, Nathan Lynn. Book designer/staff illustrator Rev. and Herald Pub. Assn., Hagerstown, Md., 1982-87; art dir. Governing Mag./Congrl. Quarterly, Washington, 1987—. Freelance illustrator, Hagerstown, Md., 1982-88, Woodbridge, Va., 1988—. Editor and designer Art Dirs. Club Newsletter, Halfbleed, 1995. Recipient Merit award Soc. Illustrators, N.Y., 1985, Comm. Arts Illustration Ann., 1994. Mem. Art Dirs. Club of Met. Washington (v.p. publs. 1994-96, Merit award 1993, editor, designer newsletter Halfbleed 1995), Soc. Pub. Designers (Merit award 1994), Va. State Soc. (George Washington chpt.), Nat. Soc. of SAR (editor, designer newsletter The Surveyor, George Washington chpt. 1988-2000, Timen Stiddem Soc. (founding officer, editor, designer of the award-winning newsletter NGS 1998 99 2000) Avocations: travel, gardening, family history. Office: Gov Mag-Congrl Quarterly 1100 Connecticut Ave NW Washington DC 20036-4101 E-mail: rsteadham@governing.com.

**STEAD LEE, POLLY JAE See LEE, PALI**

**STEADMAN, DAVID ROSSLYN AYTON,** corporate financial executive, director; b. Wembley, Eng., June 7, 1937; came to U.S., 1980; s. Eric and Iris Sina (Smith) S.; m. Beryl Ellen Giles, Jan. 5, 1963 (div.); children: Michael, Christopher, Timothy; m. Sharon Ruatto, Apr. 9, 2001 B.Sc. in Engring. with honors, City U., London, 1960. Mng. dir. Cossor Electronics, Harlow, England, 1974-78; chmn. EMI med. Electronics, London, 1978-80; pres. Raytheon Data Systems, Norwood Mass., 1980—84, Raytheon Ventures, Lexington, 1985-87; chmn., CEO GCA Corp., Andover, Mass., 1987-88; pres. Atlantic Mgmt. Assocs., Inc., Bedford, NH, 1988—; chmn. Brookwood Cos., Inc., 1989—, Visibility, Inc., 1996-2000, CEO, 1999-2000; chmn. Visaer, Inc., 2000—05. Chmn. Tech/Ops-Sevcon, Inc.; bd. dirs. Aavid Thermal Techs., Inc., Telequip Corp., Express Point Tech. Svcs., Inc., Sterling Constrn. Co. Inc. Fellow Instn. Elec. Engrs. (U.K.); mem. Inst. Mgmt. (U.K.; companion), Inst. Mech. Engrs. (U.K.). Avocations: music, sailing. Office: Atlantic Mgmt Assocs Inc PO Box 10670 Bedford NH 03110 Personal E-mail: drsteadman@aol.com.

**STEADMAN, DAVID WILTON,** retired museum director, deacon; b. Honolulu, Oct. 24, 1936; s. Alva Edgar and Martha (Cooke) S.; m. Kathleen Carroll Reilly, Aug. 1, 1964; children: Alexander Carroll, Kate Montague. BA, Harvard U., Cambridge, Mass., 1960, MAT., 1961; MA, U. Calif.-Berkeley, 1966; PhD, Princeton U., N.J., 1974; M Theol. Studies, Ch. Divinity Sch. of Pacific, 2002. Ordained deacon Episcopal Ch., 2004. Lectr. Frick Collection, N.Y.C., 1970-71; asst. dir., acting dir., assoc. dir. Princeton U. Art Mus., 1971-73; dir. galleries Claremont Colls., Calif., 1974-80; art cons. Archtl. Digest, L.A., 1974-77; rsch. curator Norton Simon Mus., Pasadena, Calif., 1977-80; dir. Chrysler Mus., Norfolk, Va., 1980-89, Toledo Mus. Art, Ohio, 1989-99; ret., 2000. Author: Graphic Art of Francisco Goya, 1975, Works on Paper 1960-1960, 1977, Abraham van Diepenbeeck, 1982. Chester Dale fellow Nat. Gallery Art, Washington, 1969-70 Episcopalian. Personal E-mail: punto31157@aol.com.

**STEADMAN, JOHN MARCELLUS, III,** retired language educator; b. Spartanburg, SC, Nov. 25, 1918; s. John Marcellus and Medora Rice (Rembert) S. AB, Emory U., 1940, MA, 1941, DHL (hon.), 1976; MA (T.W. Hunt scholar), Princeton U., 1948, PhD, 1949; DHL (hon.), St. Bonaventure U., 1989. Instr. English Ga. Inst. Tech., 1941-42; asst. prof. U. N.C., 1949-51; ind. study and rsch. in English lit., 1953-61; from rsch. assoc.to sr. rsch. assoc. Henry E. Huntington Libr., San Marino, Calif., 1962—2002; mem. faculty U. Calif., Riverside, 1966—2002, prof. English, 1967—2002, faculty rsch. lectr., 1977, prof. emeritus, 1989—. Vis. disting. prof. CUNY, fall, 1974 Author numerous books including Milton and the Renaissance Hero, 1967, Milton's Epic Characters, 1968, The Myth of Asia, 1970, Disembodied Laughter: Troilus and the Apotheosis Tradition, 1972, The Lamb and The Elephant: Ideal Imitation and the Context of Renaissance Allegory, 1974, Epic and Tragic Structure in Paradise Lost, 1976, Nature into Myth: Medieval and Renaissance Moral Symbols, 1979, Milton's Biblical and Classical Imagery, 1984, The Hill and the Labyrinth: Discourse and Certitude in Milton and His Near-Contemporaries, 1984, The Wall of Paradise: Essays on Milton's Poetics, 1985, Milton and the Paradoxes of Renaissance Heroism, 1987, Redefining a Period Style: "Renaissance," "Mannerist," and "Baroque" in Literature, 1990, Ryoanji Temple and Other Poems, 1993, Moral Fiction in Milton and Spenser, 1995, Reconnaissances: Poems, 1995, Winter Harvest, A Retrospective, 1996, In Earnest or Game: A Seriocomic Medley. Verses Early or Late, 1998, Siege of Contraries: Rumors of Wars Real or Metaphorical, Stories and Sketches, 1998; co-editor latest being A Milton Ency., vols. I-IX, 1978-83; editor: latest being Huntington Libr. Quar., 1962-81; mem. numerous editl. and advisory bds.; contbr. articles to profl. jours. Served to capt. USAAF, 1942-46; capt. AUS, 1951-52. Grantee Huntington Libr., 1961-62; Procter fellow Princeton U., 1949, Guggenheim fellow, 1979. Mem. Milton Soc. Am. (pres. 1973, honored scholar 1976), So. Calif. Renaissance Conf., Phi Beta Kappa, Chi Phi, Fine Arts Club. Democrat. Home: Care Atria Regency 4720 Morrison Dr Apt 220 Mobile AL 36609-3345

**STEADMAN, JOHN MONTAGUE,** judge; b. Honolulu, Aug. 8, 1930; s. Alva Edgar and Martha (Cooke) S.; m. Alison Storer Lunt, Apr. 8, 1961; children—Catharine N., Juliette M., Eric C. Grad., Phillips Acad., Andover, Mass., 1948; BA summa cum laude, Yale U., 1952; LLB magna cum laude, Harvard U., 1955. Bar: D.C. 1955, Calif. 1956, U.S. Supreme Ct. 1964, Hawaii 1977. Assoc. Pillsbury, Madison & Sutro, San Francisco, 1956-63; atty. US Dept. Justice, 1963-64; dep. under sec. for internat. affairs US Army, 1964-65; spl. asst. to sec. & dep. sec. US Dept. Def., 1965-68; gen. counsel USAF, 1968-70; vis. prof. law U. Pa. Law Sch., 1970-72; prof. law Georgetown U. Law Ctr., Washington, 1972-85, assoc. dean, 1979-84; assoc. judge DC Ct. Appeals, 1985—2004, sr. judge, 2004—. Instr. Lincoln Law Sch., San Francisco, 1961-63; San Francisco Law Sch., 1962-63; vis. prof. U. Mich. Law Sch., 1976, U. Hawaii Sch. Law, 1977; of counsel firm Pillsbury, Madison & Sutro, Washington, 1979-85 Editor: Harvard Law Rev, 1953-55. Sinclair-Kennedy Traveling fellow, 1955-56 Mem. Am. Law Inst., Cosmos Club, Phi Beta Kappa, Delta Sigma Rho, Zeta Psi. Episcopalian. Office: DC Ct Appeals 500 Indiana Ave NW Washington DC 20001-2131 Office Phone: 202-879-2765. Business E-Mail: jsteadman@dcca.state.dc.us.

**STEADMAN, PAUL WILLIS,** insurance company executive; b. Walterboro, SC, Apr. 29, 1961; s. Morris Eugene and Annie Fripp Steadman; m. Cheryl May Hawkins, Dec. 20, 1986; children: Chelsea Elizabeth, Palmer Maybank. Degree in bus. adminstrn., Coll. Charleston, SC, 1979—83. Cert. insurance counselor Soc. CIC, 1992, assoc. risk mgmt. Ins. Inst. Am., 1990, cert. underwriting Ins. Inst. Am., 1996, accredited insurance adviser Ins. Inst. Am., 1996. Exec. v.p. Steadman Agcy., Inc., Walterboro, SC, 1986—2001, pres., CEO, 2001—. Bd. mem. Ind. Ins. Agents SC, Columbia, 1997—99, Med. U. SC Children's Hosp., Charleston, 1998—, Coll. Charleston Sch. Bus. & Economics Bd. Govs., 2004—. Chmn. Colleton Rep. Party, Walterboro. Mem.: IIABSC (Young Agt. of Yr. award 1995), Rotary Club Walterboro (pres.), Yeaman's Hall Club, Country Club Charleston, Kiawah Island Club. R-Consevative. Episcopal.

**STEADMAN, ROBERT K.,** oral surgeon; s. Henry K. and Helen S.; m. Susan E. Hoffman; children: Andrea, Darcy, Richard, Michael BS, U. Wash., Seattle, 1969, DDS, 1974; MD, Grace U., 2002. Diplomate Am. Bd. Oral and Maxillofacial Surgery, 1983, Am. Dental Bd. Anesthesia, 2005. Resident USAF, Elgin AFB, Fla., 1974—75; resident oral and maxillofacial surgery U. Okla., 1977—80, La. State U., Shreveport, 1980—81; pvt. practice Spokane Wash., 1981—. Cons. Group Health Coop., 1989—. Fellow Am. Acad. Cosmetic Surgery, Internat. Assn. Oral and Maxillofacial Surgery, Am. Coll. Oral and Maxillofacial Surgery, Am. Soc. Oral and Maxillofacial Surgery, Acad. Gen. Dentistry; mem. Delta Sigma Delta (pres. 1987-88) Office: 801 W 5th Ave Ste 212 Spokane WA 99204-2800

**STEADMAN, STEPHEN GEOFFREY,** physicist; b. Rochester, NY, June 28, 1942; s. Luville T. and Elizabeth (Genung) S.; m. Brigitte M. Kreuzer, Aug. 1, 1975; children: Claudia, Mark, William. BS, U. Rochester, 1964; MS, Rutgers U., 1966, PhD, 1969. Asst. Univ. Freiburg, Germany, 1971-72; vis. scientist Univ. Erlangen-Nürnberg, Erlangen, Germany, 1969-71; sr. rsch. assoc. MIT, Cambridge, 1972-74, asst. prof., 1975-79, assoc. prof., 1979-82, sr. rsch. scientist, 1982-98, asst. dir. sci. adminstrn. lab. nuc. sci., 2004—06, assoc. dir., 2006—; guest scientist Max Planck Inst., Heidelberg, Germany, 1974-75, program mgr., 1998—2001; sr. nuc. physics advisor US Dept. Energy, Washington, 2001—04. Program dir. nuc. physics NSF, Arlington, Va., 1994—97; E866 co-spokesman Brookhaven Nat. Lab., Upton, NY, 1992—98. Contbr. articles to profl. jours. Watertown provincial guard, 1998—; mem. Amateur Reuse Com., Watertown, Mass., 1992—97. Fellow: Am. Phys. Soc.; mem.: AAAS. Episcopalian. Avocations: piano, tropical fish. Office: MIT Lab for Nuclear Sci RM 26-505 Cambridge MA 02139 Office Phone: 617-250-0078. Business E Mail: steadman@mit.edu.

**STEAMER, ROBERT JULIUS,** political science professor; b. Rochester, N.Y., Oct. 14, 1920; s. William August and Lotte (Becker) S.; m. Jean Worden, Apr. 12, 1947; children: Gregg Robert, James Worden. BA in Social Sci., Bucknell U., 1947; MA in Polit. Sci., U. Va., 1952; PhD, Cornell U. 1954; postgrad. law, Oxford U., Eng., 1968-69. Asst. prof. Oglethorpe U., 1952-55, U. Mass., 1955-56; assoc. prof. La. State U., 1956-62; prof. polit. sci., chmn. dept. Lake Forest (Ill.) Coll., 1962-72; prof. U. Mass., Boston, 1972-88, dean Coll. II, 1974-78, vice chancellor for acad. affairs, provost, 1976-79. Vis. summer prof. Tulane U., 1958, Cornell U., 1960, UCLA, 1965; staff cons. La. sect. U.S. Commn. Civil Rights, 1961 Author: The Constitution: Cases and Comments, 1959, The Supreme Court in Crisis, 1971, The Supreme Court: Constitutional Revision and the New Strict Constructionism, 1973, Chief Justice: Leadership and the Supreme Court, 1986; sr. co-author: American Constitutional Law: Cases and Commentary, 1991; contbr. articles to profl. jours. Served with USAAF, 1942-46. Recipient Gt. Tchr. award Lake Forest Coll., 1965; Lilly Found. Research award, 1967; Major Research award Project 87, 1981; hon. research fellow U. Exeter, Eng., 1981 Mem. Am. Polit. Sci. Assn., Midwest Polit. Sci. Assn. (v.p. 1970-71), New Eng. Polit. Sci. Assn. (pres. 1979-80) Home: 1 Sinclair Dr Apt 101 Pittsford NY 14534-1735 Office Phone: 585-248-1388.

**STEARLEY, ROBERT JAY,** retired packaging company executive; b. Brazil, Ind., Sept. 6, 1929; s. Melvin George and Hila Mona (Bolin) S.; m. Helen Louise Dellacca, Rose Hulman Inst. Tech., 1957; postgrad., Harvard U., 1979. Gen. mgr. Poly Tech Corp., Mpls., 1961-63; gen. mgr. plastics Gt. Plains Bag Corp., Stamford, Conn., 1963-66, v.p., 1966-71, v.p. ops., 1971-75, pres., 1975-84, dir., 1966-84; v.p. Jefferson Smurfit Corp., Alton, Ill., 1984—. Mem. Paper Shipping Sack Mfg. Assn. (dir. 1980-82), Am. Legion Clubs: Norwood Hills Country (St. Louis). Lodges: Elks. Republican. Methodist. Home: 2 Country Estates Pl Saint Louis MO 63131-3411

**STEARNS, CLIFFORD BUNDY,** congressman, diversified financial services company executive; b. Washington, Apr. 16, 1941; s. Clifford Robert and Emily Elizabeth (Newlin) Stearns; m. Joan Bette Moore, 1973; children: Douglas Moore, Clifford Bundy Jr., Scott Newlin. BSEE, George Washington

U., 1963. Mgr. Control Data Sys., Inc., LA, 1967-69; sr. contract adminstr. CBS, Inc., Stamford, Conn., 1969; account exec. Kutola Advt. Agy., Greenwich, Conn., 1970-71, Images 70/Wilson Haight Welch, Inc., Greenwich, 1971-72; motel owner Hatfield, Mass., 1972-77; pres., motel mgr. Stearns House, Inc., Silver Springs, Fla., 1972—88; mem. U.S. Congress from 6th Fla. dist., 1989—, mem. vets. affairs com., mem. energy and commerce com., chmn. subcom., commerce, trade, consumer protection chmn., others. Broker Silver Springs (Fla.) Real Estate, 1981—88. Bd. dirs. Boys Club Ocala, 1980—84; trustee, vice chmn. Monroe Regional Hosp., Ocala, Fla., 1984—89; pres. Toastmaster Club, LA, 1962. Capt. USAF, 1963—67. Mem: Marion County Motel Assn. (pres. 1979), Fla. Assn. Realtors, Am. Assn. Realtors, Fla. Hotel/Motel Assn., Am. Hotel/Motel Assn., Marion C. of C. (bd. dirs. 1987—), Kiwanis (pres. Ocala club 1984). Republican. Presbyterian. Avocations: basketball, swimming, computers. Office: US House of Reps 2370 Rayburn House Office Bldg Washington DC 20515-0906 also: 115 SE 25th Ave Ocala FL 34471-9179

**STEARNS, NEELE EDWARD, JR.,** investment company executive; b. Chgo., Apr. 2, 1936; s. Neele Edward Sr. and Grace (Kessler) S.; m. Bonnie Ann Evans; children: Katherine Stearns Sprenger, Kendra Stearns Drozd. BA magna cum laude, Carleton Coll., 1958; MBA with distinction, Harvard U., 1960. Audit staff Arthur Andersen Co., 1962-66, audit mgr., 1966-67; asst. gen. mgr. internat. divsn. Imperial-Eastman Corp., 1967-68; asst. treas. Allied Products Corp., 1968-69, treas., 1969-72; v.p. Henry Crown (Ill.) and Co., 1972-75, v.p., controller, 1975-79; exec. v.p., COO Henry Crown and Co., 1979—86; pres., CEO, CC Industries, Inc., Chgo., 1986-95; chmn. exec. com. Barnes Internat., Inc., Northbrook, Ill., 1996-99; chmn. Wallace Computer Svcs., Inc., 2000, Fin. Investments Corp., Chgo., 2001—. Bd. dir. Click Commerce, Inc. Trustee Evanston Northwestern Healthcare; bd. dir. Presbyn. Homes. Mem. Comml. Club Chgo., Econ. Club Chgo., Country Club Fla., Chgo. Club, Old Elm Club, Skokie Country Club, Phi Beta Kappa. Office: Fin Investments Corp 405 N Wabash River Plz 2E Chicago IL 60611 Office Phone: 312-494-4513. Business E-Mail: nstearns@fic-sff.com.

**STEARNS, PETER NATHANIEL,** history professor; b. London, Mar. 3, 1936; (parents Am. citizens); s. Raymond P. and Elizabeth (Scott) S.; children: Duncan, Deborah; m. Carol Zisowitz, Mar. 26, 1978 (div. 1999); children: Clio Elizabeth, Cordelia Raymond. AB, Harvard U., 1957, MA, 1959, PhD, 1963. From instr. to assoc. prof. U. Chgo., 1962-65; prof., chmn. history dept. Rutgers U., New Brunswick, NJ, 1965-74; Heinz prof. history Carnegie Mellon U., Pitts., 1974—, chmn. dept. history, 1986-92, dean Coll. Humanities and Social Scis., 1992-2000; provost George Mason U., 2000—. Co-dir. Pitts. Ctr. for Social History, 1986-92; chmn. acad. adv. coun. NYC Coll. Bd., 1982-85; chmn. Pacesetter World History commn., Coll. Bd., 1992-95, Coll. Bd. Advanced Placement World History, 1997-2006; adv. bd. Liberal Edn., 2001— Author: The Working Classes and the Rise of Socialism, 1971, European Society in Upheaval: Social History since 1800, 1967, Swedish transl., rev. edit., 1975, 3rd edit., 1991, Priest and Revolutionary: Lamennais and the Dilemma of French Catholicism, 1967, Polish tranl., 1967, Modern Europe 1789-1914, 1969, Revolutionary Syndicalism and French Labor: a cause without rebels, 1971; author: (with Harvey Mitchell) Workers and Protest: The European Labor Movement, The Working Classes and the Rise of Socialism, 1890—1914; author: The European Experience since 1815, 1972, 1848: The Revolutionary Tide in Europe, 1974, (publ. in England) The Revolutions of 1848, Lives of Labor: Work in Maturing Industrial Society, 1975, German tranl., 1975, Old Age in European Society, 1977, Face of Europe, 1977, Paths to Authority: Toward the Formation of Middle Class Consciousness, 1978, Be A Man! Males in Modern Society, 1979, rev. edit., 1990; author: (with Linda Rosenzweig) Themes in Modern Social History, 1985; author: (with Carol Stearns) Anger: The Struggle for Emotional Control in America's History, 1986; author: World History: Patterns of Change and Continuity, 1987, 6th edit., 2006; author: (with others) Makers of Modern Europe, 1987-; rev. edit., 1994-; author: (with others) Documents in World History, Vol.1: The Great Tradition and Vol. 2: The Modern Centuries, 1987; author: Life and Society in the West, The Modern Centuries, 1987, Expanding the Past: A Reader in Social History, 1988, Life and Society in the West, The Modern Centuries, 1988; author: (with C. Stearns) Emotion and Social Change, Toward a New Psychohistory, 1988; author: (with Andrew Barnes) Social History and Issues in Consciousness and Cognition, 1989; author: Jealousy: Evolution of an Emotion in American History, 1989, Interpreting the Industrial Revolution, 1991; author: (with Michael Adas and Stuart Schwartz) World Civilizations, 1991, 4th edit., 2003; author: Meaning Over Memory: Issues in Humanities Education, 1993, The Industrial Revolution in World History, 1993, 3rd edit., 2006, Swedish tranl., American Cool: Developing a 20th Century Emotional Style, 1994, Turbulent Passage: A Global History of the 20th Century, 1994, rev. edit., 2003, 3rd edit., 2005; author: (with Ron Harre) Discursive Psychology in Practice, 1995; author: Millenium III, Century XXI, 1996; author: (with Hinshaw) Encyclopedia of the Industrial Revolution, 1996, with Hinshaw: rev. edit., 1998;; author: Fat History: Bodies and Beauty in the West, 1997, rev. edit., 2002, Schools and Students in Industrial Society: Japan and the West, 1997, History in Documents, 1998; author: (with Lewis) Emotional History of the U.S., 1998; author: World History in Documents: and Comparative Analysis in World History, 1998, Battleground of Desire: The Struggle for Self-Control in Modern America, 1999, Experiencing World History, 2000, Teaching, Learning and Knowing History, 2000, Gender in World History, 2000, Consumerism in World History, 2001;: rev. edit., 2006;; author: (with Brindle) Facing Up to Management Faddism, 2001; author: Cultures in Motion, 2001, Anxious Parents: History of Modern American Child Rearing, 2003, Western Civilization in World History, 2003, A Day in the Life, 2005, Behavioral History, 2005, Childhood in World History, 2005, Global Outrage: Evolutuion and Impact of World Opinion, 2005, American Fear, 2006; editor: Century for Debate, 1969, The Impact of the Industrial Revolution, 1972; editor: (with Walkowitz) Workers in the Industrial Revolution, 1974; editor: The Other Side of Western Civilization, 1979, rev. edit., 1984, 4th edit., 1991, The Rise of Modern Women, 1977; editor: (with Michael Weber) The Spencers of Amberson Avenue: A Turn-of-the-Century Memoir, 1983; editor: (with Van Tassel) Old Age in a Bureaucratic Society, 1986; editor: Encyclopedia World History, 2000, Encyclopedia of European Social History, 1999; editor in chief Jour. Social History, 1967—; contbg. editor: History of Emotions, Thinking History, 2004; contbr. articles to prof. jours. Bd. dirs. Ctr. for Arts and Culture, 2005—, Toynbee Soc., 2004—. Guggenheim Found. fellow, 1973-74; NEH grantee, 1981-84, 86, 90, Rockefeller Found. grantee, 1982-83. Fellow Internat. Soc. for Rsch. on Emotion; mem. Am. Hist. Soc., World History Assn., Am. Hist. Assn. (v.p., head teaching div. 1995-98), Nat. Bd. Profl. Tchg. Standards. Democrat. Avocations: racquet sports, travel. Home: 7750 Wyckland Ct Clifton VA 20124 Office: George Mason Univ Fairfax VA 22030 Office Phone: 703-993-8776. Business E-Mail: pstearns@gmu.edu.

**STEARNS, RICHARD GAYLORE,** judge; b. LA, June 27, 1944; s. Gaylore Rhodes and Jeannetta Viola (Hofheinz) S.; m. Patricia Ann McElligott, Dec. 21, 1975. BA, Stanford U., 1968; MLitt, Oxford U., Eng., 1971; JD, Harvard U., 1976. Bar: Mass. Dep. campaign mgr. McGovern for Pres., Washington, 1970-72; spl. asst. U.S. Senate, Washington, 1972-73; asst. dist. atty. Norfolk County, Dedham, 1976-79, 80-82; del. dir. Kennedy for Pres., Washington, 1979-80; asst. U.S. atty. U.S. Dept. Justice, Boston, 1982-90; assoc. justice Superior Ct. Mass., Boston, 1990-94; U.S. dist. judge U.S. Dist. Ct. Mass., Boston, 1994—. Author: Massachusetts Criminal Law: A Prosecutor's Guide, 24st edit., 2004. Trustee Vincent Meml. Hosp., Boston. Rhodes scholar, 1968. Mem. ABA, Mass. Bar Assn., Phi Beta Kappa. Office: US Courthouse 1 Courthouse Way Ste 7130 Boston MA 02210-3009

**STEARNS, ROBERT LELAND,** curator; b. L.A., Aug. 28, 1947; s. Edward Van Buren and Harriett Ann (Hauck) S.; m. Sheri Roseanne Lucas, Oct. 2, 1982 (div. 1994); children: Marissa Hauck, Caroline Lucas. Student, U. Calif., San Diego, 1965-68, BFA, 1970; student, Calif. Poly. State U., San Luis Obispo, 1968. Asst. dir. Paula Cooper Gallery, N.Y.C., 1970-72; prodn. asst. Avalanche Mag., N.Y.C., 1972; dir. Kitchen Ctr. for Video/Music, N.Y.C., 1972-77, Contemporary Arts Ctr., Cin., 1977-82; dir. performing arts Walker Art Ctr., Mpls., 1982-88; dir. Wexner Ctr. for Arts, Columbus, Ohio,

1988-92; mem. Wexner Ctr. Found., Columbus, 1990-92; dir. Stearns & Assocs./Contemporary Exhbn. Svcs., Columbus, Ohio, 1992—2000; sr. prgm. dir. Arts Midwest, Mpls., 1998—2005; cons. curator Franklin Park Conservatory, Columbus, Ohio, 2005—. Adj. prof. dept. art, assoc. dean Coll. Art, Ohio State U., Columbus, 1988-92; lectr. Sch. of the Art Inst. Chgo., 2002; cons. McKnight Found., St. Paul, 1978, Jerome Found., 1978-79; chmn. Artists TV Workshop, N.Y.C., 1976-77; bd. dirs., chmn. Minn. Dance Alliance, Mpls., 1983-88; bd. dirs. Haleakala, Inc. N.Y.C.; mem. various panels Nat. Endowment for Arts, Washington, 1977-91; mem. pub. arts policy Greater Columbus Arts Coun., 1988-90; adv. coun. Bklyn. Acad. Music, 1982-84, Houston Grand Opera, 1991-93; fundraising cons. Art for Life Columbus AIDS Task Force, 2000-; mem. Advocacy Com. Ballet Met, Columbus, 2003-. Author, editor: Robert Wilson: Theater of Images, 1980, Photography and Beyond in Japan, 1995; author: Mexico Now: Point of Departure, 1997, Robert Wilson: Scenografie e Installazioni, 1997, Illusions of Eden: Visions of the American Heartland, 2000, Aspirations: Toward a Future in the Middle East, 2001, The View from Here: Recent Pictures from Central Europe and the American Midwest, 2002, Russel Wright: Living with Good Design, 2006; editor: Dimensions of Black, 1970; exec. editor: Breakthroughs: Avant Garde Art in Europe and America 1950-1990, 1991; author and editor numerous catalogues. Mem. gov.'s residence com. State of Ohio, 2004—. Decorated chevalier Order of Arts and Letters (France); Travel grantee Jerome Found., 1986, Japan Found., 1991, Can. Cultural Ministry, 2004. Office Phone: 614-268-8603. E-mail: arts2020@aol.com.

**STEARNS, SALLY CLARK,** education educator; b. Lakewood, Ohio, Mar. 14, 1955; d. David Pyott Stearns and Catherine Arnold Clark; m. Raymond Edward Thomas, May 27, 1990; children: Rachel Samira Clark Thomas, Erica Eleanor Stearns Thomas. PhD, U. Wis., Madison, 1987. Assoc. prof. U. N.C., Chapel Hill, 1989—. Achievements include research in health economics. Office: Univ NC Pittsboro St Chapel Hill NC 27599-7411 Office Phone: 919-843-2590.

**STEARNS, SHEILA MACDONALD,** academic administrator; b. Ft. Snelling, Minn., Aug. 30, 1946; d. Alexander Colin and Marie Kristine (Peterson) MacD.; m. Hal Stearns, June 22, 1968; children: Scott, Malin. BA, Univ. Mont., Missoula, 1968, MA, 1969, EdD, 1983. English and history tchr. Wiesbaden (Germany) Jr. High Sch., 1969-72; libr. media specialist Missoula Pub. Schs., 1975-77; dir. alumni rels. Univ. Mont., Missoula, 1983-87, v.p. univ. rels., 1987-93; chancellor Univ. Mont. Western, Dillon, 1993—99; pres. Wayne State Coll., Mich., 1999—2003; commr. higher ed. State of Mont., Helena, 2003—. Contbr. articles to profl. publs. Chair gov. bd. dirs. St. Patrick Hosp., Missoula, 1991-93; mem. Mayor's Adv. Bd., Missoula; nat. chair NAIA Coun. of Pres., 1996-97; chair NAIA Gender Equity com. Mem. Missoula C. of C. (v.p. exec. com.), Rotary (bd. dirs.) Alpha Phi (Chi chpt.), Phi Delta Kappa. Roman Catholic. Avocations: golf, reading, writing. Office: Commissioner Of Higher Education 46 N Last Chance Gulch St Helena MT 59601-4122 Office Phone: 406-444-0311.

**STEARNS, STEWART WARREN,** charitable association executive; b. Denver, Apr. 8, 1947; s. Vinton H. and Marjorie L. (Tedro) S.; m. Marjorie L. Fuller, Jan. 25, 1969; children: Theresa Lyn, Gregory Robert. BS, Ea. N.Mex. U., 1970; MA, No. Ill. U., 1973; postgrad., SUNY, Albany, 1974—. Mng. editor Studies in Linguistics, DeKalb, Ill., 1972-73; instr. No. Ill. U., DeKalb, 1972-73; cons. AID, Guatemala, 1973-74; instr. Skidmore Coll., Saratoga Springs, N.Y., 1975; OAS fellow Guatemala, 1976-77; asst. dir. Chaves County Cmty. Action Program, Roswell, N.Mex., 1977-78; exec. dir. United Way Chaves County, Roswell, 1978-83, Levi Strauss Found., Dallas, 1983-85, Cmty. Trust Met. Tarrant County, Ft. Worth, 1985-88; pres., CEO, Cmty. Found., Sarasota County, 1989—. NDEA fellow, Dallas, 1970-71. Office Phone: 941-955-3000. Business E-Mail: stewart@sarasota-foundation.org.

**STEARNS, SUSAN TRACEY,** lighting design company executive; lawyer; b. Seattle, Oct. 28, 1957; d. Arthur Thomas and Roberta Jane (Arrowood) S.; m. Ross Alan De Alessi, Aug. 11, 1990; 1 child, Chase Arthur. AA, Stephens Coll., 1977, BA, 1979; JD, U. Wash., Seattle, 1990. Bar: Calif. 1990, U.S. Ct. Appeals (9th cir.) 1990, U.S. Dist. Ct. (no. dist.) Calif 1990, U.S. Dist. Ct. (we. dist.) Wash. 1991, Wash. 1991. TV news prodr. KOMO, Seattle, 1980-86; atty. Brobeck, Phleger & Harrison, San Francisco, 1990-92; pres. Ross De Alessi Lighting Design, Seattle, 1993—. Author periodicals in field. Alumnae Assn. Coun. Stephens Coll., Columbia, Mo., 1995—. Named Nat. Order of Barristers, U. Washington, Seattle, 1990. Mem. ABA (mem. state labor and employment law subcom.), Wash. State Bar Assn. (mem. benchbar-press com.), State Bar Calif., King County Bar Assn., Bar Assn.San Francisco, Wash. Athletic Club. Avocations: travel, dance. Office: Ross De Alessi Lighting Des 2330 Magnolia Blvd W Seattle WA 98199-3813

**STEARNS, TIMOTHY P.,** biology professor, geneticist; BS in Genetics, Cornell U.; PhD in Biology, MIT. Postdoc. fellow Stanford U., Palo Alto, Calif., faculty, 1993—, assoc. prof. dept. biol. sci.; assoc. prof. dept. genetics Stanford U. Sch. Medicine, Palo Alto. Rsch. prof. Howard Hughes Med. Inst., 2002—. Howard Hughes Med. Inst. grantee, 2002. Office: Biol Sci Lokey 136 Stanford Univ Stanford CA 94305-5020 Office Phone: 650-752-6934. Office Fax: 650-724-9945. Business E-Mail: stearns@stanford.edu.

**STEBBINS, DONALD J.,** car parts manufacturing company executive; BS in Fin., Miami U., Ohio; MBA, U. Mich. With Citibank, Bankers Trust Co.; v.p., treas., asst. sec. Lear Corp., Southfield, Mich., 1992; sr v.p., CFO, treas., 1997, pres., COO Americas, pres., COO Europe, Asia and Africa; pres., COO Visteon Corp., 2005—. Office: Visteon Corp One Village Center Dr Belleville MI 48111

**STEBBINS, PAUL H.,** energy executive; b. 1965; 3 children. BA Govt., Georgetown Univ., 1979. Bunker broker Gary Bunkering Services, Inc.; with Trans-Tec Services, 1985, World Fuel Services Corp., 1995—, sr. vice-pres, 1995—97, exec. vice-pres., 1997—2000, pres. and COO, 2000—02, chmn. and CEO, 2002—. Planning coord. Internat. Energy Corp. Office: World Fuel Services Ste 400 9800 NW 41st St Miami FL 33178*

**STEBBINS, ROBERT ALAN,** sociology educator; b. Rhinelander, Wis., June 22, 1938; s. William Nelson and Dorothy May (Guy) S.; m. Karin Yvonne Olson, Jan. 11, 1964; children: Paul, Lisa, Christi. BA, Macalester Coll., 1961; MA, U. Minn., 1962, PhD, 1964. Assoc. prof. Presbyterian Coll., Clinton, SC, 1964-65; assoc. prof.to prof. Meml. U. Nfld., St. John's, Canada, 1965-73; prof. U. Tex.-Arlington, 1973-76; prof. sociology U. Calgary, Alta., Canada, 1976-96, faculty prof. social scis. Alta., 2000—, dept. head Alta., 1976-82; head dept. sociology and anthropology Meml. U. Nfld., 1968-71. Author: Commitment to Deviance, 1971, The Disorderly Classroom: Its Physical and Temporal Conditions, 1974, Teachers and Meaning, 1975, Amateurs, 1979, The Magician, 1984, Sociology: The Study of Society, 2d edit., 1990, Canadian Football: The View from the Helmet, 1987, Deviance: Tolerable Differences, 1988, The Laugh-Makers: Stand-Up Comedy as Art, Business, and Life-Style, 1990, Amateurs, Professionals and Serious Leisure, 1992; co-editor: Fieldwork Experience, 1980, The Sociology of Deviance, 1982, Experiencing Fieldwork, 1991, Career, Culture, and Social Psychology in a Variety Art, 1993, Predicaments: Moral Difficulty in Everyday Life, 1993, The Franco-Calgarians: French Language, Leisure and Linguistic Lifestyle in an Anglophone City, 1994, The Connoisseur's New Orleans, 1995, The Barbershop Singer: Inside the Social World of a Musical Hobby, 1996, Tolerable Differences: Living with Deviance, 2d edit., 1996; After Work: The Search for an Optimal Leisure Lifestyle, 1998, The Urban Francophone Volunteer: Searching for Personal Meaning and Community Growth in a Linguistic Minority, 1998, The French Enigma: Survival and Development of Canada's Francophone Societies, 2000, Exploratory Research in the Social Sciences, 2001, New Directions in the Theory and Research of Serions Leisure, 2001, The Organizational Basis of Leisure Participation: A Motivational Exploration, 2002, Francophonie et langue dans un monde diverse en évolution: contacts interlinguistiques socioculturels, 2003, Volunteering as Leisure/Leisure as Volunteering: An International Assessment, 2004, Between

Work and Leisure: A Study of the Common Ground of Two Separate Worlds, 2004, Challenging Mountain Nature: Risk, Motive, and Lifestyle in Three Hobbyist Sports, 2005, Serious Leisure: A Perspective for our Own Time, 2006, A Dictionary of Nonprofit Terms and Concepts, 2006. Pres. St. John's Orch., 1967-68; mem. Dallas Civic Symphony, 1973-76, Orch. Soc. of Calgary, 1978-97. Can. Coun. Sabbatical Leave fellow, 1972-72, Calgary Inst. for Humanities fellow, 1987-88, Killam resident fellow, 1990; NEH summer stipend, 1976; Acad. Leisure Scis. fellow, 1996—, Royal Soc. Can. fellow, 1999—. Mem. Leisure Studies Assn., Can. Sociology and Anthropology Assn. (pres. 1988-89), Internat. Sociol. Assn., Assn. for Can. Studies, World Leisure and Recreation Assn. (bd. dirs. 1997-2002), Social Sci. Fedn. Can. (pres. 1991-92), Can. Assn. for Leisure Studies (v.p. 1993-96). Home: 144 Edgemont Estates Dr NW Calgary AB Canada T3A 2M3 Office: U Calgary Dept Sociology 2500 University Dr NW Calgary AB Canada T2N 1N4 Office Phone: 403-220-5827. E-mail: stebbins@ucalgary.ca.

**STEBER, JOHN H.,** information technology executive; With Aetna US Healthcare; exec. v.p. ops. & chief info. officer HIP Health Plan of Greater NY, 1997—. Office: EVP & CIO HIP Health Plan of NY 7 W 34th St New York NY 10001

**STEBLETON, MICHELLE MARIE,** music educator, musician; b. Midland, Mich., Apr. 10, 1966; d. Leo Frederick and Sally Joanne (Brosman) Stebleton. MusB in Horn Performance, U. Mich., 1988, MusM in Horn Performance, 1989; diploma, European Mozart Found., Prague, Czech Republic, 1993. Third horn Ann Arbor (Mich.) Symphony, 1986-89, Saginaw (Mich.) Symphony, 1988-89; hornist Lone Star Brass Quintet, Midland, Tex., 1989-90; prin. horn Midland (Tex.)/Odessa Symphony, 1989-90; adj. prof. horn Odessa (Tex.) Coll., 1990; assoc. prof. horn Fla. State U., Tallahassee, 1990—. Clinician First Internat. Swiss Horn Workshop, 1994, Nove Straseci Internat. Interpreters Course, 1996, 2001; bd. dirs., co. pres. RM Williams Pub., Tallahassee, 1997—; chair faculty senate profl. devel. and welfare com. Fla. State U., Tallahassee, 1999—; lectr. in field. Performer Internat. Mozart Festival, 1991, Orquesta Filarmonica de la UNAM, Mexico City, 1992, Vienna Philharm. Chamber Players, Sapporo, Japan, 1994, 95, Pacific Music Festival, Sapporo, Tokyo, 1994, Sapporo, Hiroshima, Tokyo, 1995, Vienna Chamber Players, Santo Domingo, Dominican Republic, 1997, Internat. Orch. Festival Santo Domingo, 1997, 99, others; soloist (concert tour Vietnam) Fla. State U. Singers, 1999. Fin. advisor Sigma Alpha Iota, Fla. State U., Tallahassee, 1994—; performer Peace Concert, Pacific Music Festival, Hiroshima, Japan, 1995; coord. dept. fundraising United Way Big Bend, Tallahassee, 1998. Recipient second prize Am. Horn Competition-Natural Horn Divsn., 1989, second prize Am. Horn Competition-Profl. Divsn., 1994, 99, Tchg. Incentive Program award State of Fla., Fla. State U., 1996; com. on faculty rsch. support grantee Fla. State U., 1992, 97. Mem. Internat. Horn Soc. (life, co-host, lectr., bd. mem. S.E. region conf. adv. bd. 1991—, first prize solo competition 1987), Nat. Assn. Coll. Wind and Percussion Instrs., Music Educators Nat. Conf., Music Tchrs. Nat. Assn., Pi Kappa Lambda. Avocations: travel, photography, T'ai chi teaching. Home: 2519 Prest Ct Tallahassee FL 32301-3386 Office: Fla State Univ HMU 127 Tallahassee FL 32306-1180

**STEC, JOHN ZYGMUNT,** retired real estate company officer; b. Stalowawola, Poland, Jan. 21, 1925; Came to U.S.A. 1947. s. Valenty and Maria (Madej) S. m. Amanda G. Baca, Oct. 13, 1956; children: David, Maria, Monica. Student, Poland, 1941-44, Kent State U., Ohio, 1965-66, student, 1966-67. Cert. Master of Corporate Real Estate. With The Singer Co., Cleve., 1952-54, dis. mgr., 1954-60, sales supr., 1960-67, dir. real estate Detroit and Chgo., 1967-73; v.p. Fabri Center of Am., Beachwood, Ohio, 1973—; sr. v.p. real estate Fabri-Centers of Am., Beachwood, Ohio, 1987—2005, spl. counsel to pres., 2005—; ret., 2005. With U.S. Army 1950-52 With U.S. Army, 1950-52. Mem. Nat. Assoc. of Corporate Real Estate (speaker, organizer 1974-77, audit Com. 1977-79, bd. dirs. 1970-82, Outstanding Achievement award 1982). Chagrin Valley Club. Republican. Roman Catholic. Avocations: swimming, hiking, reading. Home: 725 Sagewood Dr Chagrin Falls OH 44023-6733 Office: JoAnn Stores Inc 5555 Darrow Rd Hudson OH 44236-4011 Office Phone: 440-543-4154. Business E-Mail: johnstec@joannstores.com. *Personal philosophy: Think success and you'll be successful. Perseverence of any goal leads to achievement. Learning is knowledge. Knowledge is the most powerful key that leads to greatness and opens any door.*

**STECCATO, CARL L.,** lawyer; b. Bronx, NY, Mar. 18, 1954; BA, York Coll., CUNY; JD, NY Law Sch., 1985. Bar: NY 1987, NJ 1987, US Dist. Ct. So., Ea., No. & We. Districts NY. Ptnr. Wilson, Elser, Moskowitz, Edelman & Dicker LLP, White Plains, NYC. Mem.: ABA (torts & ins. practice sect.), Am. Corp. Counsel Assn. (portfolio mem.), Assn. of the Bar of the City of NY, NY State Bar Assn. (ins. sect.), Nat. Fire Protection Assn., Am. Boat & Yacht Coun. Office: Wilson Elser Moskowitz Edelman & Dicker LLP 3 Gannett Dr White Plains NY 10604 Office Phone: 914-323-7000 ext. 4269. Office Fax: 914-323-7001. Business E-Mail: steccatoc@wemed.com.

**STECHER, KENNETH W.,** financial corporation executive; With Inter-Ocean Life Ins. Co. (acquired by Cin. Fin. Corp.); joined Cin. Fin. Corp., 1973—, sr. v.p., treas., co. sec., 1997—, CFO, 2001—. Office: 6200 S Gilmore Rd Fairfield OH 45014-5141

**STECHER, PAULINE,** painter, educator; b. Bklyn. d. Helen Solomon; m. Bernard Stecher; children: Martin Alan, David Joseph. Attended, pvt. studio instrn. with Paul Puzinas, NYC, 1961—63. Oil painting instr., Bellerose, Bellerose Village, Little Neck, New Hyde Park, NY, 1965—85. Judge, lecture demonstrator American Pen Women, Floral Park Art League, Flushing Art League, Ind. Art Soc., Island Art Guild, Rockville Ctr. Art Club, Tri-County Artists, Queens Alliance Artists, Suburban Art League, 1978—. *Ms. Stecher's articles and paintings appeared in Palette Talk magazine in 1983 as featured teacher, in 1987 including the cover, and in 1990. She exhibited extensively in galleries throughout Long Island's East End, in Boca Raton, and Naples, Florida. Ms. Stecher's painting of a cyclist on a wooded road appeared in the Literary Cyclist, Great Bicycling Scenes in Literature in 1997, which was edited with introductions by Professor James E. Starrs and had a foreword by William Saroyan. Professor Starrs, one of America's leading professors of Law and Forensic Science and an avid cyclist, owned a print of the painting. She felt honored when he requested permission to reproduce her painting in this anthology.* Exhibitions include Newington-Cropsey Found. Gallery Art, Hastings-on-Hudson, NY, Westchester County Ctr., NY, Salmagundi Club, NYC, Nat. Arts Club, N.Y.C., N.Y., Nassau County Mus. Art, Roslyn, N.Y., Roslyn, NY; contbr. articles to mags. and books. Recipient Jane Peterson Meml. First Pl. Still Life award, 2004, John R. Grabach Meml. award, 1994, Helen De Cozen award, 1997. Fellow: Hudson Valley Art Assn. (Dumond Meml. award Best Light and Atmospheric Effect, First prize 1998, Georgie Read Barton Meml. award 2002, Jane Peterson Still Life Meml. award, First Pl. Still-Life award 2004), Am. Artists Profl. League (bd. dirs. 1985—2002, Dir.'s award 1997, John R. Grabach Meml. award 1994, Helen De Cozen award 1997, Pres.'s award 1999, 2001); mem.: Coun. Am. Artists Soc. (Painting award 1993), Nat. Art League (Gold medal 1973), Art. League Nassau County (Coun. Am. Artists Soc. Painting award 1993). Avocation: painting. Home: 80 30 250th St Bellerose NY 11426

**STECKEL, RICHARD J.,** retired radiologist, educator, academic administrator; b. Scranton, Pa., Apr. 17, 1936; s. Morris Leo and Lucille (Yellin) Steckel; m. Julie Raskin, June 16, 1960; children: Jan Marie, David Matthew. BS magna cum laude, Harvard U., 1957, MD cum laude, 1961. Diplomate Am. Bd. Radiology. Intern UCLA Hosp., 1961-62; resident in radiology Mass. Gen. Hosp., Boston, 1962-65; clin., rsch. assoc. Nat. Cancer Inst., 1965-67; faculty UCLA Med. Sch., 1967—, profl. radiol. scis. and radiation oncology, 1974—2000; chmn. dept. radiol. scis. UCLA Med. Ctr., 1994-2000, prof. emeritus, 2000—; pres. Assn. Am. Cancer Insts., 1981. Dir. Jonsson Comprehensive Cancer Ctr., 1974—94; mem. staff UCLA Med. Ctr., Cottage

Hosp., Santa Barbara, Calif. Author, editor 3 books; contbr. more than 130 articles to profl. jours. Fellow: Am. Coll. Radiology; mem.: Assn. Univ. Radiologists, Am. Roentgen Ray Soc., Radiol. Soc. N.Am.

**STECKELBERG, JAMES,** epidemiologist, educator; MD, Mayo Med. Sch., Rochester, Minn. Diplomate infectious diseases and internal medicine Am. Bd. Internal Medicine. Prof. medicine Mayo Clinic Coll. Medicine, Rochester, Minn.; chair divsn. infectious diseases Mayo Clinic. Contbr. scientific papers. Rhodes Scholar. Fellow: ACP, Infectious Disease Soc. Am. Achievements include research in antimicrobial agents and chemotherapy; epidemiology of infectious diseases. Office: Mayo Clinic and Found 200 2d St SW Rochester MN 55906 Office Phone: 507-284-2511.

**STECKLER, LARRY,** publishing executive, writer; b. Bklyn., Nov. 3, 1933; s. Morris and Ida (Beekman) S.; m. Catherine Coccozza, June 6, 1959 (div. June 1999); children: Gail Denise, Glenn Eric, Kerri Lynn, Adria Lauren; m. Lorraine Mary Rubsamen, Oct. 16, 1999. Student, CCNY, 1951. Lic. realtor Ariz., 2005. Assoc. editor Radio-Electronics mag., NYC, 1957-62, editor, 1967-85; pub., editor-in-chief Radio Electronics mag., NYC, 1985-92; electronics editor Popular Mechanics mag., NYC, 1962-65; assoc. editor Electronic Products mag., Garden City, NY, 1965-67; editl. dir. Merchandising 2-Way Radio mag., NYC, 1975-77; v.p., dir. Gernsback Publs., NYC, 1975-84, pres., dir. 1984—2003; pub., editl. dir. Spl. Projects mag., 1980-84, Radio-Electronics Ann., 1982-84; pub., editor-in-chief Hands-On Electronics, 1984-88, Computer Digest, 1985-90, Experimenters Handbook, 1986-96, Modern Short Stories, 1987-90, Video/Stereo Digest, 1989-91, Popular Electronics Mag., 1988-99, GIZMO, 1988-99, Hobbyists Handbook, 1989-96, Sci. Probe! mag., 1989-93, StoryMasters, 1989—2001, Electronics Shopper, 1990-99, Electronics Market Ctr. 1991-99, Electronics Now Mag., 1992-99, Radio Craft, 1993-96, Poptronix Handbook, 1996—2003; pres. Claggk, Inc., 1986—2003, Silicon Chip, 1993-94, Sci. Probe Inc., 1989-93, Poptronix Inc., 1997—2005; realtor Long Realty Co., Tucson, 2005—. Mem. electronics adv. bd. Bd. Coop. Ednl. Svcs., Nassau County, NY, 1975—77; pres. Electronics Industry Hall of Fame, 1985—2001; bd. dirs. Pub. Hall of Fame, 1987—89. Author books, handbooks, pub., editor-in-chief Poptronics, 2000-03, Poptronics Shopper, 2000-03, PC Tech, 2000-03; co-editor The Shofar, 1998-2002; contbr. articles to profl. jours. Bd. dirs. Nassau County coun. Camp Fire Girls, 1971-72; 1st v.p. bd. dirs. Temple Beth Am, Las Vegas, 1998-2002 pres. 2001-02; apptd. bd. adjusters, Marana, Ariz., 2005; apptd. sec.-treas. Dove Mt. Civic Assn., Marana, 2005—. With U.S. Army, 1953-56. Recipient Coop. award Nat. Alliance TV and Electronic Svcs. Assns., 1974, 75; inducted into Electronics Industry Hall of Fame, 1985; ISCET Gov's. award, 1998, FESA Pres. award, 1998. Mem.: IEEE, LA Press, Soc. Profl. Journalists, Internat. Performing Magicians (exec. dir.), Internat. Underwater Explorers Soc., Am. Mgmt. Assn., Nat. Electronics Sales and Svc. Dealers Assn. (rec. sec. NY State 1976—78, treas. 1991—94, Man of Yr. award 1975, 1985, M.L. Finneyberg Excellence award 1994), Internat. Soc. Cert. electronic Technicians (chmn. 1974—76, 1979—81, dir.-at-large 1991—93, rep. to NESDA bd. 1991—93, chmn. 1993—95, Region 9 dir. 1995—97, chmn. 1999—2001, Chmn.'s award 1985), Am. Soc. Bus. Press Editors (sr.), Radio Club Am. Home: 12317 N Fallen Shadows Dr Marana AZ 85653 Office Phone: 520-918-5761. Personal E-mail: lartronics@aol.com, larrysteckler@aol.com. *Do not be afraid to try the unaccepted. Do not be afraid to do the undesirable. Do what you enjoy...do it well...and after it is done...never regret having done it...only regret what you have not yet done.*

**STECKLER, PHYLLIS BETTY,** publishing consultant; b. NYC; d. Irwin H. and Bertha (Fellner) Schwartzbard; m. Stuart J. Steckler; children: Randall, Sharon Steckler-Slotky. BA, Hunter Coll.; MA, NYU. Editl. dir. R.R. Bowker Co., NYC, Crowell Collier Macmillan Info. Pub. Co., NYC, Holt Rinehart & Winston Info. Systems, NYC; pres., CEO Oryx Press, Scottsdale, Ariz., 1973-76, Phoenix, 1976—2000, Zephyr Info., Phoenix, 2001—; publ. cons., 2001—. Adj. prof. mktg. scholarly publs. Grad. History dept., Ariz. State U., Tempe; mem. dean's coun. Coll. of Extended Edn., Ariz. State U., Phoenix. Past chmn. Info. Industry Assn.; past chair Ariz. Ctr. for the Book; past pres. Contemporary Forum of Phoenix Art Mus.; founding mem. Nat. Edn. Network, U.S. Dept. Edn.; past pres. Friends of the Libr., U.S.A.; mem. Ariz. Women's Forum; bd. dirs. Ariz. region Com. for the Weizmann Inst. Sci. Recipient Women Who Make a Difference award The Internat. Women's Forum, 1995, Excellence in Pub. award Ariz. Book Pub. Assn., 1997, The Pub. History Program Ariz. State U. Founding Friend award 2000; elected to Hunter Coll. Hall of Fame. Mem.: ALA, Ariz. Libr. Assn., Univ. Club of Phoenix. Home and Office: 6446 N 28th St Phoenix AZ 85016-8946 E-mail: pbs.zephyr@cox.net.

**STECKO, PAUL T.,** packaging company executive; With Internat. Paper Co.; pres., CEO Tenneco Packing, 1993-96, COO, 1997-98, pres., COO, 1998-99; CEO, chmn. bd. Packaging Corp. of Am., Lake Forest, Ill., 1999—. Bd. dirs. Tenneco Inc. Forest and Paper Assn., State Farm Mut. Ins. Co. Office: Packaging Corp of Am 1900 W Field Ct Lake Forest IL 60045-4828*

**STECKROAT, PATRICIA A.,** special education educator; b. Bristol, Pa., July 27, 1970; d. James J. and Joann D. Klein; m. Thomas F. Steckroat, June 20, 1998; children: Payton, Ryan. BS, Millersville U., 1992; M, Arcadia U., 1998; postgrad., Gwynedd Mercy Coll., 2006. Cert. adminstr. Learning support tchr. Pennsbury H.S., Fairless Hills, Pa., 1994—2003, reading specialist, 2003—. Spl. edn. chmn. Pennsbury H.S., 2006—. Avocations: reading, travel. Office: Pennsbury Sch Dist 608 S Olds Blvd Fairless Hills PA 19030

**STEDGE-FOWLER, JOYCE,** retired clergywoman; b. Spring Valley, N.Y., Mar. 2, 1926; d. Sidney and Lila Mae (Joyce) Kearsing; m. Leland Stedge, Sept. 4, 1948 (div. Apr. 1978); children: Leland Jr., Deborah Stedge-Stroud, David, Donald, Claudia, Douglas; m. Joseph Charles Fowler, June 23, 1983. BA in Liberal Arts, U. Iowa, 1947; MDiv, Union Theol. Sem., N.Y.C., 1973. Ordained to ministry Ref. Ch. in Am., 1973; cert. eslem. tchr., N.Y. Elem. tchr. Ramapo I Sch. Dist., Suffern, N.Y., 1966-68, Ramapo II Sch. Dist., Spring Valley, 1968-69; pastor Rochester Ref. Ch., Accord, N.Y., 1973-76; NIMH clin. pastoral intern in mental health St. Elizabeths Hosp., Washington, D.C., 1976-77, clin. pastoral resident in supervision and consultation, 1977-79; pastor-at-large New Castle Presbytery, Wilmington, Del., 1979-82; interim pastor Coop. Parish St. George's, Port Penn, Del. City, Pencader Presbyn. chs., 1980; interim pastor 1st and Olivet Presbyn. Ch., Wilmington, 1980, Hanover Presbyn. Ch., Wilmington, 1981, Ocean City (Md.) Presbyn. Ch., 1982; pastor Christ Presbyn. Ch., Martinsville, N.J., 1982-85; min. to elderly United Presbyn. Ch., Plainfield, N.J., 1985-91; ret., 1991. Chaplain Robert Wood Johnson Health Care Ctr., Plainfield, 1985-91; cons., clin. pastoral educator and therapist, 1975-95; mem. task force on abortion Nat. Coun. Chs., 1970-73, mem. Commn. on Women in Ministry, 1973-80, mem. women's ecumenical coordinating group, 1973-79; mem. justice for women com. Elizabeth Presbytery, 1982—, mem. social issues com., 1986-91, moderator, 1991-92, mem. gen. coun., 1990-91, mem. pers. com., 1991-95; del. to Gen. Assembly, Presbyn. Ch. (U.S.A.), 1985, 91. Former leader Rockland County coun. Girl Scouts U.S.A.; former treas., fin. chmn., bd. dirs. LWV; com. mem. Water, Sewer and Fgn. Policy Rockland County Study, 1955-73; former program chmn. Women's Assn.; former adult edn. chmn. Spring Valley Ref. Ch.; former mem. coun. and edn. chmn. Ctrl. Rockland Ecumenical Witness, Spring Valley; bd. dirs. Somerset Chaplaincy to Elderly, 1985-91, Somerset Chaplaincy to Ex-Offenders, 1982-86, NAMI-Familya, 1999—. Democrat. Achievements include becoming the 1st woman ordained in the Reformed Church in America by Rockland-Westchester Classis. Home: 10 Summit Park Rd Spring Valley NY 10977-1510

**STEDMAN, RICHARD RALPH,** retired lawyer; b. Columbus, Ohio, July 18, 1936; s. Ralph Dale and Kathleen (Smith) S.; m. Elizabeth Ann Witchey, Dec. 18, 1965; children: Gretchen Kathleen, Richard Ralph II, Patrick Christopher Raymond. BBA, Ohio State U., 1958, JD, 1964. Bar: Ohio 1964; CPA, Ohio. Staff acct. Price Waterhouse & Co., Columbus, 1958-60; salesman Royal McBee Co., Columbus, 1960; assoc. Vorys, Sater, Seymour & Pease, Columbus, 1964-69, ptnr., 1970-99. Contbr. articles to profl. jours.

Trustee Found. Cath. Diocese of Columbus, 1985-2000; trustee Ohio Dominican Coll., 1990-96, St. Charles Prep. Sch., 1990—, Edward Orton, Jr. Ceramic Found., 1994—. Merson fellow Ohio State U., 1963-64. Mem. Athletic Club Columbus, Columbus Club, Brookside Golf and Country Club, Zanesfield Rod and Gun Club, Equestrian Order of Knights Holy Sepulchre of Jerusalem, Order of St. Gregory the Great. Republican. Avocations: golf, fishing, photography.

**STEED, AIRICA DANITA,** medical/surgical nurse, consultant; b. Chgo., Dec. 31, 1977; d. Earl Dempsey and Mary Lynn Powell; m. Charles Edward Steed, Aug. 21, 2005; 1 child, Eryk Juwan Holcomb. BSN, Rush U., 2000; MBA, Governors State U., 2006. RN Ill. RN U. So. Calif. U. Hosp., L.A., 1999—2001; healthcare cons./liaison VITAS Hospice, Matteson, Ill., 2001—03; rN St. James Hosp., Olympia Fields, Ill., 2001—04; RN implementation cons./sr. project mgr. Piicis, Inc, Rosemont, Ill., 2003—05; sr. assoc./healthcare adv. practice PricewaterhouseCoopers LLP, Chgo., 2005—. Ministry New Faith Bapt. Ch., Matteson, Ill., 2005—06; vol. Nat. Lymphoma and Leukemia Soc., 2001—06, ARC, Ill., 2005—06; donor United Way Found., Ill., 2005—06. Mem.: Nat. Black MBA Assn. (assoc.), AMIA (assoc.), HIMSS (assoc.), Graduation MBA Honor Soc. (assoc.). Baptist. Avocations: reading, travel, writing, volunteering. Office Phone: 312-298-3168. Personal E-mail: airica26@comcast.net.

**STEED, THERESA JEAN,** manufacturing executive; b. Grapeland, Tex., Mar. 10, 1932; d. Robert Tresband and Alma Inez (Denson) Bobbitt; m. Jarvis Lacy Steed, July 8, 1950; children: Judy Karen, Pamela Kay, Kim Lacy. Grad., Elliott Bus. Sch., Houston, 1949; BMus. Edn., So. Coll. Fine Arts, Houston, 1956; postgrad., U. Tex. 1961, Sul Ross U., Alpine, Tex., 1962, U. Wis., 1962; M Rhymes (hon.), Duke U., 1961. Exec. sec. various cos., Houston, 1950—57; tchr. elem. sch. Rosenburg Ind. Sch. Dist., Tex. 1957—58; tchr. kindergarten/music edn. Sonora Ind. Sch. Dist., Tex., 1959—65; tchr. elem. sch. Houston Ind. Sch. Dist., 1965—67, Conroe Ind. Sch. Dist., Tex., 1968—70; co-founder, co-owner Steed Tile & Mfg. Co., Conroe, 1965—. Author: Audio-Visual Curriculums for Music Education: Kindergarten Through Eighth Grade, 1962 Mem. Dem. Nat. Com., Washington, 1993—, Dem. Senatorial Campaign Com., Washington, 1996 Recipient Presdl. Letter of Commendation, Pres. Lyndon B. Johnson, 1969. Mem.: Am.'s Nat. World War II Mus. (charter), Nat. Women's History Mus. (charter), Nat. Trust for Hist. Preservation, Order Ea. Star (assoc. matron 1963), Women in Constrn. (charter) (reporter 1970—75, publicity chmn.), Nat. Federated Music Clubs Am., Pilot Club, Delta Kappa Gamma (publicity chmn. 1962—65). Methodist. Avocations: cooking, gardening, politicking. Home: 452 Lexington Ct Conroe TX 77302-3050 E-mail: quechick007@yahoo.com.

**STEEDMAN, DORIA LYNNE SILBERBERG,** foundation administrator; b. LA; d. Mendel B. and Dorothy H. (Howell) Silberberg; m. Richard Cantey Steedman, Feb. 19, 1966; 1 child, Alexandra Loren. BA summa cum laude, UCLA. Producer EUE/Screen Gems, N.Y.C., 1963-66, Jack Tinker & Ptnrs., N.Y.C., 1966-68, Telpac Mgmt., N.Y.C., 1968-72; v.p. broadcast prodn. Geer DuBois Advt., N.Y.C., 1973-78, account mgr., dir. ops., 1979-92; exec. v.p., creative dir. Partnership for a Drug-Free America, N.Y.C., 1992—. Bd. dirs. Friends of the Earth. Recipient Andy award Art Dirs. Club, 1968, 71; named one of 100 Best and Brightest Women in Advt., Advt. Age mag.; named Advt. Woman of Yr., 1996. Mem. Advt. Women N.Y. (pres. 1993-95), Advt. Women N.Y. Found. (pres. 1995-97), Phi Beta Kappa. Office: Partnership for a Drug-Free Am 405 Lexington Ave New York NY 10174-0002 Business E-Mail: doria_steedman@drugfree.org.

**STEEFEL, DAVID SIMON,** lawyer; b. Mpls., June 27, 1951; s. Lawrence D. Jr. and Marion (Charlson) S.; m. Mary Ann Moody, May 24, 1981; children: Emily, Daniel, Katherine. BA, Carleton Coll., 1973; JD, U. Colo., 1978. Bar: Colo. 1978, U.S. Dist. Ct. Colo. 1978, U.S. Ct. Appeals (10th cir.) 1978. Assoc. Gorsuch, Kirgis, Denver, 1978-80, Holme Roberts & Owen, Denver, 1980-84, ptnr., 1984—, litig. practice group leader, 1994—. Instr. U. Colo. Law Sch., Boulder, 1978, 91. Home: 1300 Green Oaks Dr Littleton CO 80121-1331 Office: Holme Roberts & Owen 1700 Lincoln St Ste 4100 Denver CO 80203-4541 Office Phone: 303-866-0348. Business E-Mail: david.steefel@hro.com.

**STEEL, DANIELLE FERNANDE,** author; b. NYC, Aug. 14, 1947; d. John and Norma Schuelein-Steel; 9 children. Student, Parsons Sch. Design, 1963, NYU, 1963-67. Vice pres. pub. relations and new bus. Supergirls Ltd., NYC, 1968-71; copywriter Grey Advt., San Francisco, 1973-74; founder Steel Gallery of Contemporary Art, San Francisco, 2003—. Author novels Going Home, 1973, Passion's Promise, 1977, Now and Forever, 1978, The Promise, 1978, Season of Passion, 1979, Summers End, 1979, To Love Again, 1980, Loving, 1980, The Ring, 1981, Love, 1981, Remembrance, 1981, Palomino, 1981, Once in a Lifetime, 1982, Crossings, 1982, A Perfect Stranger, 1982, Thurston House, 1983, Changes, 1983, Full Circle, 1984, (non-fiction) Having A Baby, 1984, Family Album, 1985, Secrets, 1985, Wanderlust, 1986, Fine Things, 1987, Kaleidoscope, 1987, Zoya, 1988, Star, 1988, Daddy, 1989, Message from Nam, 1990, Heartbeat, 1991, No Greater Love, 1991, Jewels, 1992, Mixed Blessings, 1992, Vanished, 1993, Accident, 1994, The Gift, 1994, Wings, 1994, Lightning, 1995, Five Days in Paris, 1995, Malice, 1996, The Ghost, 1997, The Ranch, 1998, The Long Road Home, 1998, The Klone & I, 1998, Silent Honor, 1997, His Bright Light, 1998, Mirror Image, 1998, Bittersweet, 1999, Granny Dan, 1999, Irresistible Forces, 1999, The Wedding, 2000, The House on Hope Street, 2000, Journey, 2000, Lone Eagle, 2001, Leap of Faith, 2001, The Kiss, 2001, The Cottage, 2002, Sunset in St. Tropez, 2002, Answered Prayers, 2002, Dating Game, 2003, Johnny Angel, 2003, Safe Harbour, 2003, Ransom, 2004, Second Chance, 2004, Echoes, 2004, Impossible, 2005, Miracle, 2005, Toxic Bachelors, 2005; (children's) Martha's Best Friend, Martha's New School, Martha's New Daddy, Max's New Daddy, Max and The Babysitter, Max's Daddy Goes To The Hospital; contbr. poetry to mags., including Cosmopolitan, McCall's, Ladies Home Jour., Good Housekeeping. Chevalier of the distinguished Order of Arts and Letters, France. Home: PO Box 1637 New York NY 10156-1637 Office: care Dell Publishing 1540 Broadway New York NY 10036-4039*

**STEEL, DUNCAN GREGORY,** engineering educator; b. Cleve., Jan. 11, 1951; s. Robert John and Mildred (Graham) S.; children: Adam, Benjamin. BA, U. N.C., 1972; MS, U. Mich., 1973, 75, PhD, 1976. Physicist Exxon Rsch. and Engring., Linden, NJ, 1977-78, Hughes Rsch. Labs., Malibu, Calif., 1975-85; prof. U. Mich., Ann Arbor, 1985—; sr. rsch. scientist Inst. Gerontology Sch. Medicine, U. Mich., Ann Arbor, 1986—; sr. rsch. scientist biophys. rsch. divsn., 1992—, area chair optical scis., dir. optical scis. lab., 1989—, Robert J. Hiller prof., 2005—, Peter S. Fuss prof., 2001—05. Topical editor Jour. Optical Soc., Washington, 1986—92. Contbr. articles to profl. jours. Guggenheim fellow, 1990. Fellow IEEE, Optical Soc. Am., Am. Phys. Soc. Achievements include development of first phase conjugate laser; first high resolution nonlinear laser spectroscopy of semiconductor heterostructures; research in collision induced resonances in atoms; low noise (below the standard quantum limit) room temperature semiconductor lasers; of first demonstration of coherence optical control and wave function engineering in quantum dots; of first demonstration of wave function engineering; first deimonstration quantum entanglement in a single quantum dot; demonstration of in vitro tryptophan phosphorescence for studies of protein structure in solution; discovery of structural annealing in proteins during protein folding. Office: U Mich Physics Dept 500 E University Ave Ann Arbor MI 48109-1120 Home: 11516 Waters Rd Chelsea MI 48118-9615 Business E-Mail: dst@umich.edu.

**STEEL, KUNIKO JUNE,** retired artist; b. San Francisco, June 3, 1929; d. Jirohei and Moriyo (Shiraishi) Nakamura; m. John Schuelein-Steel, Jan. 26, 1963 (dec. May 1978). Student, U. Calif., 1948-49; diploma, Am. Acad. Art, Chgo., 1951; student, Academic Julian, Paris, 1952-53, Art Inst. Chgo., 1954-55, Art Students League, N.Y.C., 1959-62, 79-85. Exhibited in group shows at Rafilson Gallery, Chgo., 1954, Arts of N.E., Silvermine, Conn., 1966, 79, 90, 92, Modern Maturity Traveling Exhibit, 1990-92, Schoharie

Exhibit, Cobleskill, N.Y., 1993-94, Mus. of Modern Art, Miami, Coral Gables, Fla., 1993, 37th Chautaqua Nat. Exhibit of Am. Art, 1994, Montclair State U., 1994, 95. Vol., crafts tchr. Hosp. for Spl. Surgery, N.Y.C., 1967-84; vol. Japanese Gallery Met. Mus., 1994; past vol. costume conservation Met. Mus., N.Y.C., 1979-94. Recipient scholarship Palo Alto Quota Club, 1948, Art Students League, 1960. Avocations: designing arts and crafts, painting.

**STEEL, MICHAEL J.,** lawyer; b. Marysville, Calif., May 9, 1955; BA, Univ. Calif., Davis, 1977; JD, Univ. Calif., Hastings, 1982. Bar: Calif. 1982. Ptnr., co-leader Environ. Litigation practice Pillsbury Winthrop Shaw Pittman, San Francisco. Office: Pillsbury Winthrop Shaw Pittman 50 Fremont St San Francisco CA 94105 Office Phone: 415-983-7320. Office Fax: 415-983-1200. Business E-Mail: michael.steel@pillsburylaw.com.

**STEEL, ROBERT K.,** former diversified financial services company executive; married; 3 children. BA in History & Polit. Sci., Duke U., 1973; MBA, U. Chgo., 1984. Joined Goldman Sachs Group, Inc., 1976, head equities divsn. Europe N.Y.C., 1988—94, head instnl. equities U.S., 1994—98, co-head equities divsn., 1998—2001, head equities divsn., 2001—02, vice chmn., 2002—04, adv. dir., non-exec. chmn., securities divsn., 2004—; sr. fellow, Ctr. Bus. & Govt. John F. Kennedy Sch. Govt., Harvard U., Cambridge, Mass., 2004—. Chmn. The After School Corp., 2004—. Vice chmn. bd. trustees Duke U.; chmn. Duke U. Mgmt. Co. Mem.: NYSE (mem. various coms.), Securities Industry Assn. (bd. dirs.). Office: JFK Sch Govt Harvard U 79 John F Kennedy St Cambridge MA 02138*

**STEELBERG, CHAD,** broadcast advertising company executive; Attended, U. So. Calif. Co-founder, chief tech. officer, CEO AdForce (acquired by CMGI), 1995—99; co-founder, chief tech. officer, CEO, chmn. Winfire (purchased by Broadband Digital Group), 1999—2000; CEO Broadband Digital Group, 2000—; chmn., CEO dMarc Broadcasting, Inc. (purchased by Google), Newport Beach, Calif., 2002—06. Spkr. in field. Recipient Smithsonian award for develop. of the best tech. in information services, 2000. Office: dMarc Broadcasting Inc 537 Newport Ctr Ste 355 Newport Beach CA 92660*

**STEELBERG, RYAN,** broadcasting advertising company executive; Co-founder, head sales and mktg. AdForce (acquired by CMGI), 1995—99; founder, CEO 2CAN Media (AdSmart) (acquired by CMGI, 1999; co-founder, dir. Winfire (purchased by Broadband Digital Group), 1999—2000; pres. Broadband Digital Group, 2000—, dMarc Broadcasting, Inc. (purchased by Google), Newport Beach, Calif., 2002—06. Finalist Entrepreneur of Yr., Ernst & Young, 2000; named one of 50 Most Influential Businesspeople, Orange County Bus. Jour. Office: dMarc Broadcasting Inc 537 Newport Ctr Ste 355 Newport Beach CA 92660*

**STEELE, ANA MERCEDES,** retired federal agency administrator; b. Jan. 18, 1939; d. Sydney and Mercedes (Hernandez) S.; m. John Hunter Clark, June 2, 1979. AB magna cum laude, Marywood Coll., 1958. Actress, 1959-64; sec. Nat. Endowment for Arts, Washington, 1965-67, dir. budget and rsch., 1968-75, dir. planning, 1976-78, dir. program coordination, sr. exec. svc., 1979-81, assoc. dep. chmn. programs, dir. program coordination, 1982-93, acting chmn., acting sr. dep. chmn., 1993, sr. dep. chmn., sr. exec. svc., 1993-96, dep. chmn. mgmt. and budget, sr. exec. svc., 1996-98; ret., 1998. Guest lectr. George Washington U., 1987; trustee Marywood Coll., 1989-96, Marywood U., 1997-98. Author, editor report: History of the National Council on the Arts and National Endowment for the Arts During the Johnson Administration, 1968; editor: Museums USA (Fed. Design Coun. award of Excellence 1975), 1974, National Endowment Arts, 1965-85: A Brief Chronology of Federal Involvement in the Arts, 1985. Former reader Rec. for the Blind, N.Y.C.; former tutor Future for Jimmy, Washington; judge Helen Hayes Awards, 2003—. Named Disting. Grad. in Field of Arts, Marywood Coll., 1976; recipient Sustained Superior Performance award Nat. Endowment for Arts, 1980, Disting. Svc. award, 1983-85, 89, 92, 96, Presdl. medal Marywood U., 2000; named to Disting. Alumnae Hall of Fame, Ursuline Acad., 2001. Mem. Actors' Equity Assn., Screen Actors Guild, Delta Epsilon Sigma, Kappa Gamma Pi. Home: 2475 Virginia Ave NW Apt 604 Washington DC 20037-2639

**STEELE, ANITA MARTIN (MARGARET ANNE MARTIN),** law librarian, law educator; b. Haines City, Fla., Dec. 30, 1927; d. Emmett Edward and Esther Majulia (Phifer) Martin; m. Thomas Dinsmore Steele, June 10, 1947 (div. 1969); children: Linda Frances, Roger Dinsmore, Thomas Garrick, Carolyn Ann; m. James E. Beaver, Mar. 1980 (dec. Feb. 1996). BA, Radcliffe Coll., 1948; JD, U. VA., 1971; M in Law Librarianship, U. Wash., 1972. Asst. prof. law U. Puget Sound, Tacoma, 1972—74, assoc. prof. law, 1974—79, prof. law, 1979—94, dir. law libr., 1972—94; prof. law, dir. law libr. Seattle U., Tacoma, 1994—98, prof. law emeritus, 1998—. Author: (book) Martin and Carmichael Descendants in Ga., 1811-1994, 1994; contbr. articles to profl. jours.; mem. editorial adv. bd.: various law book pubs. Treas. Congl. Campaign Orgn., Tacoma, 1978, 1980; mem. adv. bd. Clover Pk. Vocat.-Tech. Sch., Tacoma, 1980—82. Mem.: DAR, Collectors' Cir. of Art Mus. Va., Am. Soc. Internat. Law, Internat. Assn. Law Librs., Am. Assn. Law Librs., Colonial Dames XVII Century. Republican. Home: 4434 Pheasant Ridge Rd Condo # 303 Roanoke VA 24014-5280 E-mail: ams145@cox.net.

**STEELE, CARL LAVERN,** academic administrator; b. Patoka, Ill., Aug. 22, 1934; s. Boyd Alfa and Effie Jane (Corson) S.; m. Lula Irene Saliba, June 11, 1961; children: Jeffrey Van, Gregory Michael, Douglas Alan. BEd, So. Ill. U., 1956, MEd, 1960; MLS, No. Ill. U., 1971. Tchr. Shawneetown (Ill.) Community High. Sch., 1956-57; GED instr., U.S, Army Ti [Itool], Tex. and Uim, Fed. Republic of Germany, 1957-59; tchr. Forrest-Strawn-Wing Unit Dist., Forrest, Ill., 1959-61, Richwoods Community High Sch., Peoria, Ill., 1961-66; asst. dir. instructional materials Sauk Valley Coll., Dixon, Ill., 1966-68; dir. Ednl. Resources Ctr., Rock Valley Coll., Rockford, Ill., 1968-93; ret., 1993. Part-time traffic safety instr. Rock Valley Coll., 1992—. Asst. World Record sec. Nat. Fresh Water Fishing Hall of Fame, Hayward, Wisc., 1977-79. Served with U.S. Army, 1954-56. Mem. ALA, Assn. Ednl. Communications and Technology, Ill. Assn. Ednl. Communications and Technology (conv. chmn. 1976), No. Ill. Media Assn. (conv. chmn.), Learning Resource Commn. ICCCA (chmn. 1981). Democrat. Presbyterian. Avocations: fishing, travel, reading, woodworking, gardening. Home: 5758 Weymouth Dr Rockford IL 61114-5569 Personal E-mail: lsteele@steele.com.

**STEELE, CHARLES, JR.,** civil rights association executive, former state legislator; b. Tuscaloosa, Ala., Aug. 3, 1946; m. Cathelean Annette; children: LeKeisha, Charla. Student, Miss. Valley State, Oakland U.; BA, Am. Internat. U.; LHD (hon.), Stillman Coll.; Ph.D (hon.), Am. Internat. U. Co-owner Van Hoose and Steele Funeral Home; former mem. Tuscaloosa City Coun.; senator Ala. State Senate, Montgomery, 1995—2004; pres., CEO SCLC, Atlanta, 2004—. Mem. Local Legis. No. 1 Com., Fiscal Responsibility and Accountability Com., Fin. and Taxation Gen. Fund Com., Fin. and Taxation Edn. Com., Agr. and Forestry Com., Health and Human Resources Com., Oil and Gas subcom. Commerce, Transp., and Utilities Com., Indsl. Devel. and Recruitment Com., Small Bus. and Rural Devel. Com., Constitution, Campaign Fin., Ethics, and Elections Com., Postsecondary and Higher Edn. subcom. Edn. Com., Law Enforcement and Victims Rights subcom., Violence in Schs. subcom. Judiciary Com.; chairperson Rural Devel. Com. Small Bus. and Rural Devel. Com., Mental Health subcom. Health and Human Resources Com. Named one of Most Influential Black Americans, Ebony mag., 2006. Mem. Nat. Assn. Funeral Dirs. and Morticians, Ala. Funeral Dirs. and Morticians Assn. Democrat. Avocations: walking, reading. Office: SCLC PO Box 89128 Atlanta GA 30312*

**STEELE, CHARLES GLEN,** retired accountant; b. Faulkton, SD, July 24, 1925; s. Clifford D. and Emily O. (Hanson) S.; m. Shirley June Ferguson, Nov. 9, 1947; children: Richard Alan (dec.), Deborah Ann Steele Host (dec.). BBA, Golden Gate U., San Francisco, 1951, MBA, 1962. With Deloitte Haskins & Sells, 1951-86, partner, 1963-86, partner charge Chgo. office,

1973-76, partner charge personnel and adminstrn. N.Y.C., 1976-78, chmn., chief exec. officer, 1978-86. Instr. evening program Golden Gate U., 1952-58. Served with USNR, 1943-48, aircraft carrier fighter pilot, 1946-48. Recipient Elijah Watts Sells Gold medal for highest grade in U.S. for C.P.A. exam., 1951 Mem. AICPA. Home and Office: 5 Stonecrest Circle Rancho Mirage CA 92270

**STEELE, ERIC HENRY,** sculptor, lawyer; b. Chgo., Mar. 5, 1941; s. Henry Bernard and Ivy (Newman) S.; m. Talmage Mullen, Oct. 17, 1970; children: Margaret Ivy, Henry Donnan. AB, Yale U., 1963; JD, Harvard U., 1967; postgrad., Northwestern U., 1991. Bar: Ill. 1967. Assoc. Aaron, Aaron, Schimberg & Hess, Chgo., 1967-70, Sonnenschein, Carlin, Nath & Rosenthal, Chgo., 1970-72; sr. rsch. atty., project dir. Am. Bar Found., Chgo., 1972-86; v.p., dir. planning R & D Merchandise Mart Properties, Inc., Chgo., 1986-90; prin. Steele, Scharbach Assoc. LLC, 1991—; now metal sculpture. Adam Posner Ctr. Study Criminal Justice, U. Chgo. Law Sch., 1973-75. Exhibitions include Evanston + Vicinity Biennial, Evanston Art Ctr., 2006, Chgo. Sculpture Internat. Biennale, Flatfile Galleries, 2006. Dir. MAP 2000 study Met. Housing and Planning Coun., Chgo., 1999-2000. Mem. ABA, Chgo. Bar Assns., Inspired Partnerships (bd. dirs., sec. bd.). Phi Beta Kappa, Chgo. Artists' Coalition, Chgo. Sculpture Internat., Contemporary Arts Coun., Evanston Art Ctr. (bd. dirs.), Internat. Sculpture Ctr. Home: 2124 N Dayton St Chicago IL 60614-4302 Office Phone: 773-327-0806. E-mail: Eric@EricHSteele.com.*

**STEELE, ERNEST CLYDE,** retired insurance company executive; b. Corbin, Ky., May 11, 1925; s. J. Fred and Leona (McFarland) S.; m. Cora Jones, June 17, 1944 (dec. Nov. 1988); children: Gerald R., David P.; m. Helen LeCoultre, July 7, 1990. BS with honors, U. Ky., 1948, MS, 1950. Asst. actuary Peninsular Life Ins. Co., Jacksonville, Fla., 1950-54; actuary Pioneer Life & Casualty Co., Gadsden, Ala., 1955; v.p., actuary Guaranty Savs. Life Ins. Co., Montgomery, Ala., 1956-57; exec. v.p., actuary Am. Investment Life Ins. Co., Nashville, 1958-59; pres., actuary Appalachian Nat. Life Ins. Co., Knoxville, Tenn., 1959-67; sr. v.p., chief investment officer, ops. analyst Coastal States Life Ins. Co., Atlanta, 1968-71, exec. v.p., dir., 1971-74, pres., dir., 1974-79; pres. Occidental Life Ins. Co. of N.C., 1979-85, chmn., 1986-88; pres., dir. Peninsular Life Ins. Co., 1981-83, chmn., 1986-88; exec. v.p. investments MCM Corp., 1985-88; ret., 1988. Past pres. Ga. Assn. Life Inst. Cos., 1976-77. Mem. devel. coun. U. Ky.; past pres. Gt. Smoky Mountain Coun. Boy Scouts Am., 1965—66. Served to 2d lt. U.S. Army, 1943—45. Fellow Life Mgmt. Inst.; mem. Life Office Mgmt. Assn. (past chmn. bd.), Am. Council Life Ins. (past dir.), U. Ky. Alumni Assn. (past bd. dirs.), Am. Acad. Actuaries, Pi Mu Epsilon. Republican. Baptist. Home: 103 Newell Village Cir Seymour TN 37865-5931 *My success in life is measured by the success of those with whom I have been associated.*

**STEELE, HOWARD L.,** psychology professor; b. Vancouver, B.C., Can., Oct. 16, 1959; arrived in Eng., 1986. s. Arnold J. and Goldie R. (Karsh) S.; m. Miriam N. Blum, Sept. 2, 1984; children: Gabriella, Joseph, Michael. BA, U. B.C., 1981, MA, 1983, Columbia U., 1986; PhD, U. Coll., London, 1991. Lectr. U. Coll., London, 1991-99, sr. lectr., 1999—, hon. sr. lectr.; lectr. New Sch. for Social Rsch., N.Y.C. Editor: (jour.) Attachment and Human Devel., 1999; founding editor Attachment and Human Devel., 1999, exiting editor; cons. editor: Infant Mental Health Jour., 1998. Recipient Overseas Rsch. Scholar award Com. of Vice-Chancellors and Prins. of Univs. of U.K., 1986-87; Commonwealth scholar, Brit. Coun., 1987-90; rsch. grantee Econ. and Social Rsch. Coun., 1992-94, 98-99. Mem. Soc. for Rsch. in Child Devel. Office: New Sch Univ Grad Faculty Polit and Social Sci New York NY 10003

**STEELE, HOWARD LOUCKS,** economic development consultant, author; b. Pitts., Jan. 27, 1929; s. Howard Bennington and Ruby Alberta (Loucks) S.; m. Sally E. Funk, June 6, 1952 (div. 1977); children: John F., David A., Patricia A.; m. Jane R. Cornelius, July 30, 1977 (div. 1996); 1 child, Jennifer L.; m. Elaine Haddock, Aug. 23, 1997. BS, Washington and Lee U., 1950; MS, Pa. State U., 1952; PhD, U. Ky., 1962. Sales mgr. Greenville (Pa.) Dairy Co., 1952-56; owner H.L. Steele Bulk Milk Hauling, Greenville, 1955-60; asst. prof. Clemson (S.C.) U., 1956-57, assoc. prof., 1957-64, Ohio State U., Columbus, 1964-71; with Fgn. Agrl. Svc./Internat. Coop. and Devel. U.S., Dept. Agr., Washington, 1971-97; ret.; econ. devel. cons., 1997—. Project mgr. AID, Guatemala, 1976-77, Bolivia, 1977-80, Honduras, 1980-82, Sri Lanka, 1982-84, Bur. L.Am. and Caribbean USAID, Washington, 1984-88, office of the dir. tech. assistance divsn., 1988-90, with office of dep. adminstr., 1990-97; USDA liaison officer Inter-Am. Inst. Coop. in Agr., 1993-97; instr. U. Md., College Park, 1974-76; vis. prof. U. Sao Paulo, Piracicaba, Brazil, 1964-66; ptnr. Kingwood Acres Farm, Rockwood, Pa., 1966-98. Author: Commercializacao Agricola, 1971, A 200 Year History of Some Descendents of the Pioneer James Steel of Castleblaney, Ireland and Mt. Pleasant, Pennsylvania, 1994, Your Tax Dollars at Work (I'd Rather Have Gone Business Class!), 1998, Food Soldier, 2002, Food Soldier: Training—Troubles--Triumphs, 2005; contbr. articles to profl. jours. Recipient Nat. Forensic Union award; named One of Outstanding Young Men U.S., U.S. Jaycees, 1965; cert. of merit Dept. Agr., 1975, 92. Mem.: SAR, Masons, Internat. Assn. Agrl. Economists, Am. Agrl. Econs. Assn., Shriners, Sigma Nu, Gamma Sigma Delta. Home: 5204 Holden St Fairfax VA 22032-3418 Office Phone: 703-978-4066. Personal E-mail: ehsteele@juno.com.

**STEELE, JAMES EUGENE,** retired school system administrator; b. South Norfolk, Va. s. James Edward and Blanche Eugenia (Munden) S. BS in Music Edn., Coll. William and Mary, 1961; MEd in Ednl. Adminstrn. and Supervision, Temple U., 1972; EdD in Ednl. Adminstrn., Nova U., 1976. Cert. tchr. Va. Piccoloist Va. Symphony Orch., 1951-73; dir. choral music Hampton (Va.) City Schs., 1960-65, supr. music, 1965—2003; ret., 2003. Guest flute soloist Music Tchrs. Assn., Great Britain, 1962. Dir. fine arts division Hampton Assn. Arts Humanities, 1970—. Mem. NEA, Va. Edn. Assn., Hampton Edn. Assn., Va. Assn. Sch. Execs., Hampton Instrnl. Suprs. Assn., Tidewater Regional Suprs., Va. Assn. Sch. Curriculum Devel., Va. Music Suprs. Assn., Va. Music Educators Assn., Music Educators Nat. Conf., Va. Choral Dirs. Assn., Va. Band and Orch. Dirs. Assn., Va. String Tchrs. Assn. Home: 132 Fayton Ave Norfolk VA 23505-4428

**STEELE, JAMES HARLAN,** retired veterinarian; b. Chgo., Apr. 3, 1913; s. James Hahn and Lydia (Nordquist) S.; m. Aina Oberg, 1941 (dec. 1969); children: James Harlan, David, Michael; m. Maria-Brigitte Meyer. DVM, Mich. State Coll., 1941; MPH, Harvard U., 1942. With Ohio Dept. Health, 1942-43; with USPHS, 1943-71; advancing through grades to asst. surgeon gen. for vet. affairs and chief vet. officer; chief vet. pub. health activities Communicable Disease Center, Atlanta, 1947-71; prof. environ. health U. Tex. Sch. Pub. Health, Houston, 1971-83, prof. emeritus, 1983—. Cons. WHO, 1950-2005, Pan-Am. Health Orgn., 1945—, FAO, UN, 1960, German Health Svc., 1986-93; vis. prof. Tex. A&M U., 1976—, all univ. prof., 1981-82; spkr. in field. Author: (with J. Arthur Myer) Bovine Tuberculosis Control in Man and Animals, 1969, 95, (with Charles Thoen), Mycobacterium Bovis Infections, revised edit., 2005, (with James Steele) Hendrik Stafseth and Public Health Veterinarians Ole Stalheim, 2005; editor-in-chief CRC Zoonoses Handbooks, 1979-84, cons. editor, 1994, 8 vols. transl. into Russian and Farsi, Bacterial & Viral Zoonoses, 2 vols. rev. by Beran; mem. editl. cons. bd. APHA Control Communicable Disease, 1960-2000, Merck Vet. Manual, 1955-2005; contbr. articles to profl. jours. and sects. to books on food hygiene and irradiation. Recipient Carlos Finlay medal, 1952, Mich. State U. Centennial award, 1955, Mich. State U. Alumni award, 1958, USPHS Order of Merit, 1963, Karl F. Meyer Gold Head Cane award, 1966, Disting. Svc. award USPHS, 1971, Mich. State U. Coll. Vet. Medicine award, 1972, hon. mem. Epidemic Intelligence Svc., 1975, James Law award Cornell U., 1983, Centennial award U. Pa., 1984, Am. Vet. Med. Assn. Internat. Vet. award, 1984, Pub. Svc. award, 1993; James H. Steele Vet. Pub. Health award World Vet. Epidemiology Soc., 1975, Disting. Svc. award Am. Vet. History Soc., 1995, James H. Steele award Ctr. for Disease Control, 1998, Disting. Alumni award Mich. State U., 2001, Lifetime Achievement award Assn. Tchrs. VPH and Preventive Medicine, 2005, Calvin Schwabe Lifetime Achievement award, 2005, James McCallam award Mil. Surgeons, 2005, Surgeon Gen.'s

medallion USPHS, 2005, Pahs Horwitz award Pub. Health Leadership, 2006; named James H. Steele ann. lectr. in his honor U. Tex. Health Sci. Ctr., 1993, James H. Steele Epidemiology Professorship in his honor, 1996. Fellow APHA (emeritus, 1984; Bronfman award 1971, Centennial award 1972), Am. Coll. Epidemiology (founding fellow); mem. Am. Soc. Tropical Medicine (emeritus), Am. Coll. Vet. Preventive Medicine (founder, hon. diploma 1983, Pres.'s award 1994), Nat. Acad. Health Practiioners, World Vet. Epidemiology Soc. (founder, pres. 1971), Am. Vet. Epidemiology Soc. (pres. 1986-88), World Vet. Assn. (hon.), Philippines Vet. Med. Assn. (hon.), Peru Vet. Med. Assn. (hon.), Hellenic Vet. Soc. (Athens Greece, hon. diploma, 1977), U.S. Animal Health Assn. (life), U.S.-Mex. Pub. Health Assn. (hon., life, Border award 2003), Mil. Surgeons Assn. (hon. life), Infectious Disease Soc. Am. (emeritus), Internat. Epidemiology Soc. (emeritus), XXI World Vet. Congress (Moscow, hon. diploma 1979), German Health Svc. (hon. diploma, 1988, Order of Merit 1993), Harvard U. Alumni Assn. (Alumni award 1998), Alpha Psi. Episcopalian. Home: 10722 Riverview Houston TX 77042-1121 Personal E-mail: drjameshsteele@houston.rr.com. *I have believed firmly throughout my career that I should share my knowledge and expertise with my fellow man, be he American or citizen of the world. Those of us who are more fortunate to be endowed with intellectual advantages have an even greater responsibility to share.*

**STEELE, JAMIE KEYS,** social services executive, consultant; b. Greeneville, Tenn., Feb. 16, 1965; d. James Franklin and Joyce Annette Keys; m. Dwayne Steele, Aug. 17, 1984; 1 child, James William Jordan. BS in Criminal Justice and Criminology, East Tenn. State U., 1988, BSW, 1989; MA in Orgnl. Mgmt., Tusculum Coll., Greeneville, Tennessee, 2002. Ct. apptd. spl. adv. CASA, Johnson City, Tenn., 1986—88; residential life supr. Holston Home for Children, Greeneville, Tenn., 1992—94, dir. Wiley Ctr. Residential Treatment Ctr., 1994—97; dir. in home svcs. Holston United Meth. Home for Children, Inc., Greeneville, Tenn., 1997—2000, coord. continuous quality improvement, 2000—03; v.p. program svcs. Family Ministries, Inc., Greeneville, Tenn., 2003—. Cons. Social Svc. Strategies, Limestone, Tenn., 2000—. Presenter (over 47 workshops); contbr. articles to profl. jours. Mem. Clear Springs Ruritan, Limestone, Tenn., 2003—, PTO, Afton, Tenn., 2004—, Overlook Dr. FWB Ladies Aux., Greeneville, Tenn., 1998—. Mem.: ASTD, Va. Alliance for Children and Families, Child Welfare League of Am., Tenn. Conf. on Social Welfare, Tenn. Assn. of Child Care. Free Will Baptist. Achievements include development of Proactive Behavior Management Planning; research in Effects of Physical Restraint on Children and Youth; Resistance to Change in Organizational Settings; Restraint Reduction Strategies and Outcome Study; Risk Factors Associated with Youth Runaways. Avocations: reading, scrapbooks, auto restoration. Office Phone: 423-639-9449.

**STEELE, JOHN HYSLOP,** marine scientist, oceanographic institute administrator; b. Edinburgh, Scotland, Nov. 15, 1926; s. Adam and Annie H.; m. Margaret Evelyn Travis, Mar. 2, 1956; 1 son, Hugh. B.Sc., Univ. Coll., London U., 1946, D.Sc., 1964. Marine scientist Marine Lab., Aberdeen, Scotland, 1951-66, sr. prin. sci. officer, 1966-73, dep. dir., 1973-77; dir. Woods Hole Oceanographic Instn., Mass., 1977-89, pres. Mass., 1986-91. Mem. NAS/NRC Ocean Sci. Bd., 1978-88, chmn., 1986-88; mem. rsch. and exploration com. Nat. Geog. Soc.; mem. Arctic Rsch. Commmn., 1988-92; trustee U. Corp. Atmospheric Rsch., 1987-91, Bermuda Biol. Sta., R.W. Johnson Found.; del. Internat. Coun. Exploration Sea; hon. prof. U. Aberdeen. Author: The Structure of Marine Ecosystems, 1974; Contbr. articles to profl. jours. Served with Brit. Royal Air Force, 1947-49. Recipient Alexander Agassiz medal Nat. Acad. Sci., 1973 Fellow Royal Soc. London, AAAS, Royal Soc. Edinburgh, Am. Acad. Arts and Scis. Home: PO Box 25 Woods Hole MA 02543-0025 Office: Woods Hole Oceanographic Inst Woods Hole MA 02543 E-mail: jsteele@whoi.edu.

**STEELE, JOHN M.,** human resources specialist; b. Sept. 21, 1955; m. Joanna Steele; 1 child. BA, Ea. Mich. U., 1977. Various positions in staffing orgn. Elec. Data Sys., 1985—94; mgr. recruitment Alcon Labs., 1994—95; asst. v.p. recruitment Hosp. Corp. Am. Inc. (HCA), Nashville, 1995—97, v.p. recruitment and compensation, orgnl. effectiveness and exec. devel., 1997—2003, sr. v.p. human resources, 2003—. Bd. dirs. Inst. Diversity in Health Mgmt. Office: HCA Inc One Park Plz Nashville TN 37203 Office Phone: 615-344-9551.

**STEELE, JUDITH MCCONNELL,** writer; b. Lamar, Colo., Oct. 5, 1945; d. Taylor and Elva June (Buchtel) McC.; m. Richard M. Steele, Nov. 14, 1975. BA, Cornell Coll., 1967; MA, Northwestern U., 1972. Vol. Peace Corps, Sergipe, Brazil, 1968-70; translator office Project Hope, Rio Grande do Norte, Brazil, 1972; reporter, columnist The Idaho Statesman, Boise, 1978-93; freelance writer fiction, poetry Boise, 1993—. Chair young writers competition IJA Prodns., Boise, 1994. Author: Stories From Home, 1989, More Stories From Home, 1993, (anthology) Family, 1998, Woven on the Wind, 2001; collaborative work with Sun Valley Ctr. Arts, 1999, Balance Dance Co., 2003, Dance Forum, 2003; group exhibits with Chris Binion, 1999-99; poetry duet, 2000-2002. Mem. Snake River Writers, Log Cabin Literary Ctr., Treas. Valley Pub. Access TV, Acad. Am. Poets.

**STEELE, KAREN DORN,** journalist; b. Portland, Oreg., Oct. 27, 1943; d. Ronald and Margaret Elizabeth (Cates) Moxness; m. Charles Stuart Dorn, Oct. 30, 1965 (div. Oct. 1982); children: Trilby Constance Elizabeth Dorn, Blythe Estella Dorn; m. Richard Donald Steele, July 4, 1983. BA, Stanford U., 1965; MA, U. Calif., Berkeley, 1967. Prodr. Sta. KSPS-TV, Spokane, Wash., 1970—72, dir. news and pub. affairs, 1972—82; reporter Spokesman-Rev., Spokane, 1982—87, environ./spl. projects reporter, 1987—. Contbr. articles to sci. publs. (Olive Br. award NYU Ctr. War, Peace & The Media, 1989). Bd. dirs. Women Helping Women, Spokane, 1994; trustee St. George's Sch., Spokane, 1988-92. Mid-career fellow Stanford Knight Fellowship Program, 1986-87, Arms Control fellow Ctr. for Internat. Security and Arms Control, Stanford U., 1986-87; Japan Travel grant Japan Press Found., Tokyo, 1987, Rsch. grantee John D. and Catherine T. MacArthur Found., 1992; recipient Gerald Loeb award Anderson Sch. Mgmt. UCLA, 1995, George Polk award L.I. U., 1995, William Stokes award U. Mo., 1988, Nat. Headliner award, Excellence in Legal Journalism award Wash. State Bar Assn., 2000; named to State Hall of Journalistic Achievement, Wash. State U., Pullman, 1995. Unitarian Universalist. Office: Spokesman Review 999 W Riverside Ave Spokane WA 99210-2160 Office Phone: 509-459-5462. Business E-Mail: karend@spokesman.com.

**STEELE, KATHRYN ANN,** social studies educator, gifted and talented educator; b. Manitowoc, Wis., May 9, 1950; d. Edward and Dorothy Rose Hecker; m. Bruce Conrad Steele, Aug. 5, 1972; children: Jennifer Steele Thomas, Jordan Conrad. BS in Edn., U. Pitts., 1972 MS in Gifted Edn., Ashland U., Ohio, 1998. Cert. elem. edn. K-8 Ohio, gifted edn. K-12 Ohio. Tchr. grade 1 Pitts. City Schs., 1972—75; tchr. grade 6 Massillon (Ohio) City Schs., 1980—81; tchr. grade 5 Jackson Local Schs., 1983—90; tchr. gifted and talented social studies grade 6-9 Perry Local Schs., 1996—. Modell UN advisor Perry H.S., Edison Jr. H.S. and Pfeiffer Mid. Sch., 1997—; academic challenge coach Pfeiffer Mid. Sch., 1996—, student adv. coun. advisor, 2003—, lead tchr., 2003—05. Contbr. articles to profl. jours. Nominee Disney Tchr. award, 2006; recipient Golden Apple award, Ashland Oil, 1998, Top 25 award, Massillon Schs., 2000, 2001, 2002, 2003, 2006; grantee, Martha Holden Jennings Found., Nat. Coun. Social Studies. Mem.: Delta Kappa Gamma (v.p. 2001—02). Democrat. Presbyterian. Avocations: swimming, travel, quilting, reading, U.S. Civil War. Home: 8600 Glenridge Ave Clinton OH 44216 Office: Perry Local Schs 4315 13th St SW Massillon OH 44646 Office Phone: 330-478-6163.

**STEELE, KENNETH FRANKLIN, JR.,** hydrologist; b. Statesville, N.C., Jan. 16, 1944; s. Kenneth Franklin and Ruth Virginia (Wilhelm) Steele; m. Sheila Kay Stumpf, Sept. 3, 1966 (dec.); children: Krista Robin, Celisa Anne; m. Beth Vaughan-Wrobel, Sept. 24, 2005. BS in Chemistry, U. N.C., 1966, PhD in Geology, 1971. Registered profl. geologist, Ark.; registered hydrogeologist. From instr. to assoc. prof. geology U. Ark., Fayetteville, 1970-83, dir.

Ark. Water Resources Ctr., 1988—2001, prof., 1983—. Mem. State Bd. Registration for Profl. Geologists, 1992-96, 2000-2004, chmn., 1996, 2002-03, vice chmn., 2001-02; cons. in field. Contbr. numerous articles to profl. jour., chpts. to books; editor: Animal Waste and the Land-Water Interface. Mem. Internat. Order St. Luke the Physician. Summer faculty fellow Oak Ridge Associated Univ., 1981, 83, 85. Mem. Nat. Ground-Water Assn., Internat. Assn. Hydrologists, Am. Inst Hydrology, Assn. Applied Geochemists, Soc. Environ. Geology & Health, Geol. Soc. Am. (regional bd. dir. 1980-82, 84-86), Am. Water Resources Assn. (bd. dirs. 1991-94), Ark. Ground Water Assn. (bd. dir. 1988-90, 93-95, v.p. 1991, pres. 1992), Nat. Assn. Water Inst. Dirs. (counselor 1990-93), Nat. Inst. Water Resources (bd. dir. 1998-2001). Achievements include research on the importance of rainstorms on ground and surface water chemistry in karstic terrain, nitrate and pesticide contamination of ground water, and evolution of ground water chemistry with emphasis on iron and arsenic. Office: U Ark Dept Geoscis 113 Ozark Hall U Ark Fayetteville AR 72701-4040 Home: PO Box 1065 Fayetteville AR 72702 Office Phone: 479-575-7937. E-mail: ksteele@uark.edu.

**STEELE, MICHAEL,** lieutenant governor; b. Oct. 19, 1958; m. Andrea Steele; children: Michael, Drew. Grad., Johns Hopkins U.; JD, Georgetown U., 1991; student, Augustinian Friars Sem. Pvt. law practice; assoc. internat. law firm Cleary, Gottlieb, Steen & Hamilton, Wash., DC, 1991—97; chmn. Republican Ctrl. Com. for Prince George's County, Md., 1994—2000; cand. Md. State Comptroller, 1998; chmn. Md. Republican Party, 2000—02; lt. gov. State of Md., Annapolis, 2003—. Advisor to campaigns of fellow politicians; treas., advisor Michele Dyson for Congress, 1994. Host (hour long radio program) WOLB 1010AM, Balt., Md., appeared (numerous radio and TV programs including) Politically Incorrect with Bill Maher, Metro Talk, That Show With Those Black Guys, The Joe Madison Show, Extra, Capitol Sunday, BET Tonight; contbr. columns in newspapers including The Washington Times, The Washington Post, The Baltimore Sun, The Jour. Newspapers. Bd. visitors U.S. Naval Acad., 2002; commr. Nat. Fed. Election Reform Commn.; mem. St. Mary's Cath. Ch., Landover Hills, Md. Named Md. State Republican Man of Yr., Man. of Yr., Ch. cmty., 1998. Mem.: NAACP (served blue ribbon panel on election reform, bd. dirs. hospice of nat. capital area, Prince George's County chpt.), Johns Hopkins U. (bd. trustees), Johns Hopkins Soc. Black Alumni, Term Limits Coalition (chmn. 2000), Truth iN Taxation Com. (hon. co-chmn. 1996), Republican Nat. Convention Phila., Pa. (del. 2000), Republican Nat. Convention San Diego, Calif. (alt. del. 1996), Md. State Minority Outreach Task Force (chmn. 1995—97), Md. State Republican Party Victory Campaigns, Prince George's County Md. Black Republican Coun., Republican Nat. Com. (mem. exec. com.), Knights of Columbus. Republican. Catholic. Office: Office of Lt Governor State House Annapolis MD 21401 Business E-Mail: info@mdgop.org.*

**STEELE, MYRON THOMAS,** state supreme court chief justice; b. Taunton, Mass., July 28, 1945; s. Myron Thetus and Coleen Amelia (Polk) Steele; m. Beverly June Heaps, Feb. 4, 1967; children: Clayton Carter, Jenness Farnham. BA, U. Va., 1967, JD, 1970. Bar: Va. 1970, Del. 1970, U.S. Dist. Ct. Del. 1970, U.S. Ct. Appeals (3d cir.) 1974. Assoc. Prickett, Ward, Burt & Sanders, Dover, Del., 1970, 1973, ptnr., 1974; dep. atty. gen. State of Del., 1971—72; v.p., dir. Prickett, Jones, Elliott, Kristol & Schnee, Dover, 1974—88; assoc. judge Superior Ct., 1988—90, res. judge, 1990—94; vice chancellor Ct. Chancery, Del., 1994—2000; justice Del. Supreme Ct., 2000—, chief justice, 2004—. Mem. exec. com. Del. Democratic State Com., 1974—88; bd. dirs. Childrens Bur. Del., Del. News Coun.; chmn. Consumer Affairs Bd., 1974—88, Ctrl. Del. Health Care Corp., 1990—93. Served to 1st. lt. U.S. Army, 1970, col. ret. Del. N.G., 1974—97. Mem.: ABA (mem. jud. liaison comml. and bus. litig. com., bus. sect.), Del-Vets, Commn. on Ct. 2000 (Del.), Kent County Bar Assn. (past pres.), Va. State Bar, Del. Bar Assn. (past v.p.), Kiwanis (past pres.), Rehoboth Beach Country Club, Wilmington Club, Masons. Episcopalian. Office: Del Supreme Ct Carvel State Office Bldg 820 N French St Fl 11 Wilmington DE 19801*

**STEELE, PATRICIA ANN,** dean, librarian; b. Columbus, Ohio, Mar. 28, 1943; d. Gerald Henry and June Eileen (McCullough) Costlow; m. Charles Nolan Steele, Aug. 31, 1963; children: Kelly Colleen, Ryan Charles. AB in English, Ind. U., 1966, MLS, 1981. Cert. tchr., Mich. Tchr. Chippewa Valley Schs., Mt. Clemens, Mich., 1966-67; br. head, extension asst. Lansing Pub. Library, Mich., 1967-74; head librarian, Atomic Energy Commn. plant research lab. Mich. State U., East Lansing, 1969-73; head librarian, Health, Physical Edn. and Recreation Library Ind. U., Bloomington, 1979-81, head librarian sch. of library and info. sci., 1981, exec. assoc. dean, head customer and access svcs., coord. academic info. and customer svc., Ruth Lilly interim dean of univ. libraries, 2005—. Chmn. faculty council ednl. task force on pornography Ind. U., 1985—; cons., specialist conspectus Research Libraries Group, 1985-86. Editor Library Sci. Nat. Newsletter, 1984-86; columnist Library Bookshelf, 1981—, InULA Innuendo, 1984—. Mem. ALA (v. chmn. library sci. librarians discussion group 1984-86), Ind. Library Assn. (chmn. exec. com. div. on women 1983-86), Ind. U. Librarian's Assn., Stone Hills Area Library Sci. Authority. Avocations: swimming, jogging, hiking. Home: 4791 N Benton Dr Bloomington IN 47408-9503 Office: Herman B Wells Libr Ind U 1320 E Tenth St Bloomington IN 47405*

**STEELE, RICHARD J.,** management consultant; b. Elkhart, Ind., Sept. 27, 1925; s. Cornelius H. and Harriett (Poel) S.; m. Shirley P. Ballard, Sept. 28, 2001; children: Barbara, Cheryl, Patricia, Thomas, Richard Jr., Marjorie, Gregory, Susan, Kathleen. SB, MIT, 1946; MBA, Ind. U., 1949. Cert. mgmt. cons. V.p. Fry Cons.'s, Inc., Chgo., 1950-70; pres. Richard Steele and Ptnrs., Inc., N.Y.C., 1970-72, Richard Steele Cons.'s, Inc., Columbia, Md., 1978-96; group v.p. Macro Systems, Inc., Silver Spring, Md., 1972-78; sr. v.p. Birch & Davis Assocs., Inc., Silver Spring, 1979-94. Counselor Nat. Health Coun., N.Y.C., 1971-94. Author: (with others) Determinants of HMO Success, 1988. Trustee Village of Riverwoods, Ill., 1967. Lt. USNR, 1943-75, WWII, Korea. Recipient Award of Merit Am. Heart Assn., 1974. Mem. Inst. Mgmt. Cons. Unitarian Universalist. Home and Office: Unit 201 20918 Island Sound Cir Estero FL 33928-8951 Business E-Mail: rjsteele@alum.mit.edu.

**STEELE, ROBERT EDWIN,** orthopedic surgeon; b. Kansas City, Mo., Jan. 8, 1937; s. Robert Edwin and Margaret Jane (Levens) S.; m. Emily Wells Stephens, May 9, 1964; children: Edward Stephen, Thomas McKewon, Linda Katherine. AB, U. Mo., 1959; MD cum laude, Harvard U., 1963. Diplomate Am. Bd. Orthopedic Surgery; cert. Am. Acad. Orthopedic Surgeons, Assn. Arthritic Hip and Knee Surgery. Intern Mass. Gen. Hosp., Boston, 1963-64; resident in orthopedics Harvard U., 1966-71; instr. in orthopedic surgery Harvard Med. Sch., Boston, 1971; mem. med. staff Good Samaritan Hosp., Corvallis, Oreg., 1971—. Bd. Good Samaritan Hosp., 1984-88, pres. med. staff, 1985, chmn. peer rev. com., 1994. Author: Studies on Osteonecrusis, 1979. Lt. USNR, 1964-66, Vietnam. Recipient Kappa Delta award for Outstanding Orthopedic Rsch., Am. Acad. Orthopedic Surgeons, 1978. Mem. Corvallis Orthopedic Surgeons (pres. 1990). Achievements include performance of total knee replacement. Address: 560 NW Tyler Ave Corvallis OR 97330

**STEELE, RODNEY REDFEARN,** judge; b. Selma, Ala., May 22, 1930; s. C. Parker and Miriam Lera (Redfearn) S.; m. Frances Marion Blair, Aug. 1, 1964; children: Marion Scott, Claudia Redfearn, Parker Blair. AB, U. Ala., 1950, MA, 1951; LLB, U. Mich., 1954. Bar: Ala. 1954, U.S. Dist. Ct. (mid. dist.) Ala. 1959, U.S. Ct. Appeals (5th cir., now 11th cir.) 1981. Law clk. Ala. Ct. Appeals, 1956-57; assoc. Knabe & Nachman, Montgomery, Ala., 1957-61; asst. U.S. atty. Dept. Justice, Montgomery, 1961-66; staff atty. Soc. Bell T&T Co., Atlanta, 1966-67; judge U.S. Bankruptcy Ct., Mid. dist. Ala., Montgomery, 1967—, chief judge, 1985-99; ret., 1999—. Served with U.S. Army, 1954-56, Korea. Mem. ABA, Ala. State Bar, Montgomery County Bar Assn. Democrat. Episcopalian. Home: 1227 Magnolia Curv Montgomery AL 36106-2136

**STEELE, RUSSELL LOREN,** football coach; b. Westminster, Calif., May 9, 1967; s. Loren Duane and Lois Lyn Steele; m. Patricia Alice Rees, Dec. 13, 1962; 1 child, Alexandria Eden. BA in Bus. Mgmt., Northrop U., LA, 1985—89. Running back, spl. teams coach LA Cobras, 1988; spl. teams coach Toronto Agonauts, 1989—92; asst. head coach San Diego Mesa Coll. 1993—95; spl. teams coach Anaheim Piranhas, Calif., 1996—97; gen. mgr. Biltmore Agy., Biltmore Lake, NC 2000—. Recipient Grey Cup Championship, CFL, 1991, Spl. Teams Coach of Yr., Am. Football League, 1996. Mem.: Am. Football Coaches Assn. (assoc.). Methodist. Avocation: football. Home: 223 Fennel Dun Cir Biltmore Lake NC 28715

**STEELE, SHARI,** think-tank executive; Grad., Widener U.; LLM in Advocacy, Georgetown U.; MS in Instrnl. Media, West Chester U. Legal dir. Electronic Frontier Found., San Francisco, 1992—2000, exec. dir., pres., 2000—. Spkr. in field; tchg. fellow Georgetown U. Law Ctr. Office: Electronic Frontier Found 454 Shotwell St San Francisco CA 94110-1914

**STEELE, SHELBY,** writer, educator; b. Chgo., 1946; s. Shelby Sr. and Ruth S. Grad., Coe Loll., 1968; M in Sociology, So. Ill. U., 1971; PhD in English, U. Utah, 1974. Prof. dept English Calif. State U., San Jose; rsch. fellow Hoover Instn., Stanford, Calif. Author: The Content of Our Character: A New Vision of Race in America, 1991 (Nat. Book Critics Circle award 1991), A Dream Deferred: The Second Betrayal of Black Freedom in America, 1998, (TV documentary) Seven Days in Bensonhurst (Emmy award, San Francisco Film Festival award); contbr. essays to profl. jours. Mem.: Ctr. for New Am. Cmty. at Manhattan Inst. (nat. bd.), Univ. Accreditation Assn., Am. Acad. Liberal Edn. (nat. bd.), Nat. Assn. Scholars. Office: Hoover Inst Pub Affairs Stanford Univ Stanford CA 94305-6010

**STEELE, THOMAS MCKNIGHT,** law educator; b. Bartlesville, Okla., June 4, 1948; s. James Robert and Erma Blanche (McKnight) S.; m. Barbara Van Curen, Mar. 23, 1973 (div. 1985); children: James Robert, Ryan Thomas, David Christopher Joyce, Justin Daniel Joyce; m. Martha Bolling Swann, Apr. 1985 (div. 1990); m. LeAnn P. Joyce, Jan. 1995. BA in History, Okla. State U., 1969; MLS, U. Oreg., 1974; JD, U. Tex., 1977. Administrv. asst. Tarlton Law Libr. U. Tex., Austin, 1975-77; acting law librarian Underwood Law Libr. So. Meth. U., Dallas, 1977-78, asst. law librarian, 1978-79; assoc. prof. law, dir. Franklin Pierce Law Ctr., Concord, N.H., 1979-82; asst. prof., dir. U. Miss. Law Libr., University, 1982-85; assoc. prof., dir. Wake Forest U. Sch. Law Libr., Winston-Salem, N.C., 1985-91; dir. Profl. Ctr. Libr. Wake Forest U., Winston-Salem, NC, 1991—99, prof. law, 1991—. Cons. in field; exec. dir. SCRIBES, Am. Soc. Writers on Legal Subjects, 1988—97, bd. dirs., 2002—. Editor (newsletter) Scrivener, 1986-88; mng. editor Scribes Jour. Legal Writing, 1989-91; editor Pub. Librs. and Pub. Laws, 1986-88; compiler bibliography IDEA, 1981-83, Jour. Air Law and Commerce, 1977-81; co-author: A Law Library Move: Planning Preparation and Execution, 1994, Materials and Cases on Law Practice Management: A Learning Tool for Law Students, 2003. With U.S. Army. Mem.: Legal Mkrg. Assn., Assn. Legal Administrs. Democrat. Baptist. Office: Wake Forest U Sch Law PO Box 7206 Winston Salem NC 27109-7206

**STEELE-GOETEMANN, JUDITH ANN,** artist, educator, art gallery owner; b. Gloucester, Mass., June 11, 1935; d. Owen Eldred Steele and Elizabeth Verna LAwson; m. Gordon George Goetemann, Dec. 27, 1958; children: Elisabeth, David, Mark, Christopher. AA, Sullins Coll., 1955; student, Boston Mus. Sch., 1956, Romano Sch. Art, 1954—55, Evanston Arts Ctr., 1966—69; BA in Art and Secondary Edn., Coll. St. Benedict, 1974. Instr. spl. art labs. Kennedy Sch., St. Joseph, Minn., 1972—73, tchr. grades 1-3, 1974—75; tchr. grades 9-12 Apollo High Sch., St. Cloud, 1976—77; co-dir. European studies St. John's U., St. Joseph, 1983, 1988, 1989, Upper Mid-West Assn. Ind. Colls., St. Paul, 1983, 1984, 1988, 1990. Adj. prof. art Coll. St. Benedict, St. Joseph, 1980—90, St. Johns U., Collegeville, Minn.; lectr. in field. One-woman shows include St. John's U., 1976, 1989, Blaisdell Pl., Mpls., 1982, Coll. St. Benedict, 1984, 1991, Meridian Hotel, Boston, 1988, Hammond Castle, Gloucester, 1989, U. St. Thomas, 1995, exhibited in group shows at Marshall Field and Co. Gallery, Chgo., 1976, U. Minn., St. Paul, 1977, Augsburg Coll., 1978, Bergen County Mus., N.J., 1980, North Hennepin C.C., Bklyn. Pk., Minn., 1981—82, Women's ARt Reg. Minn., Mpls., 1982, BFM Gallery, N.Y.C., 1983, 1985, Gallery 702, St. Cloud, 1993, Coll. St. Benedict/St. John's U., 1993, Rockport Art Assn., Mass., 1994 (Excellence in Watercolor award), Nat. Weavers Symposium, Mpls., 1994, exhibitions include Am. Craft Coun., Rhinebeck, N.Y., 1978, 1980, Notre Dame U., South Bend, Ind., 2005, Bryan Gallery, Rocky, Mass., 2005, 2006, Rocky Neck, 2005, Gloucester Stage Co., 2006. Critic Oddessy of the Mind, St. Cloud, 1996—98; critic, juror various schs. and assns., 1976—2000. Recipient Cerino Meml. prize, 1996, Harriet Wengenroth award, 1996, Cereno Meml. prize, 1997, G.O. Davis award, 1998, W.J. Hibbard Meml. award, 1999, Marguerite Pearson Gold medal, 2006. Mem.: Cape Am Artisans, Soc. Encouragement of Arts (charter mem.), Rocky Neck Art Colony. Democrat. Roman Catholic. Office: Goetemann Gallery 37 Rocky Neck Ave Gloucester MA 01930 Office Phone: 978-281-6128. Personal E-mail: goetemann.gallery@verizon.net.

**STEELMAN, LALA CARR,** sociologist, educator; d. Joseph Flake and Lala Carr Steelman; m. Carl Albert Ek, June 22, 1986; 1 child, Lala Christina Ek. BA in Sociology and Polit. Sci., U. N.C., Chapel Hill, 1973; PhD, Emory U., 1980. Prof. U. S.C., Columbia, SC, 1981—. Mem. editl. bd.: Am. Sociol. Rev., Social Forces, Sociology of Edn. Recipient Ednl. Found. Excellence in Rsch. award, U. SC. Mem.: So. Sociol. Soc., Am. Sociol. Assn. (publications com., presider, presenter). Avocations: pilates, bicycling, writing. Office Phone: 803-77-3123. Business E-Mail: steelman@sc.edu.

**STEELMAN, SARA GERLING,** retired art association administrator; b. Wichita Kans., Apr. 24, 1946; d. Paul Henry and Amy (Gessner) Gerling; m. John Henry Steelman; 1 child, Amy. BS in Zoology, U. Chgo., 1967; PhD in Behavior Genetics, Stanford U., 1976. Instr. dept. psychology No. Ill. U., DeKalb, 1974-75; instr. Fullerton (Calif.) Jr. Coll., 1976-80; postdoctoral fellow dept. psychobiology U. Calif., Irvine, 1976-80; asst. prof. dept. biology Skidmore Coll., Saratoga Springs, NY, 1980-83; staff writer Saratogian, Saratoga Springs, 1983-86; contbg. writer Indiana Gazette, 1987-93; elected mem. Pa. Ho. of Reps., Harrisburg, 1990—2002; administr. Indiana Arts Coun., Indiana, Pa., 2002—06; ret. Contbr. articles to sci. publs. Co-chair com. women in politics Pitts. Inst. Politics, 1993—2002; mem. bd. dirs. First Unitarian Universalist Ch. Ind. Rsch. fellow, Nat. Inst. Aging, 1979—80. Mem.: LWV, AAUW (Notable Woman 1991), Common Cause (state chairperson). Democrat. Avocations: gardening, music, horseback riding.

**STEELY, ALLEN MERLE,** secondary school educator; b. Geneva, Ill., Apr. 5, 1952; s. Merle Ashel and Vera Mae S.; m. Marcia Anne Limkeman, May 30, 1981; children: Rachel Anne, Joshua Allen, Jonathan David, Kathryn Elizabeth. BA in Psychology, Wheaton (Ill.) Coll., 1974. Lic. stationary engr. City of Elgin, Ill. Psychology tchr. Igbaja (Nigeria) Theol. Sem., 1974; info. officer for famine relief program Soc. Internat. Ministries, Ethiopia, 1975; sci. tchr. Bingham Acad., Addis Ababa, Ethiopia, 1975-76; stationary engr. Indeck Power Equipment Co., Wheeling, Ill., 1976-77; sci. tchr. Rockford (Ill.) Christian Jr. H.S., 1977—, sci. dept. chmn., 1996—. Soccer coach Rockford (Ill.) Christian Schs., 1978—; sch. coord. Invent Am., Rockford, 1993-96. Author: A God-Centered View of Salvation: A Theocentric Perspective of the Gospel. Bd. dirs First Evangelical Free Ch., Rockford, 1986-90, Rockford Reachout Jail Ministry; chmn. First Free Ch. Social Concerns Com., Rockford, 1989. Recipient Excellence in Sci. Tchg. award Ill. Math. and Sci. Acad., Aurora, 1988; nominee for Presidential award sci. and math. tchg., Washington, 1991. Mem. Nat. Fedn. Interscholastic Ofcls. Assn. (cert. soccer referee), Nat. Sci. Tchrs. Assn. Republican. Mem. Evangelical Free Ch. Avocations: pairs dance skating, soccer, rock climbing. Home: 420 Laurel Dr Rockford IL 61107-4829 Office: Rockford Christian Schs 1401 N Bell School Rd Rockford IL 61107-2872 Office Phone: 815-399-3465. Personal E-mail: amsteely@juno.com.

**STEELY, MELVIN T.,** language educator; b. Atlanta, May 9, 1939; s. Henry Thomas and Katherine Patrick Steely; m. Judy E. Pipes, Sept. 1, 1960 (div. June 1982); children: Bonnie Lynn Vernon, Karen Elizabeth Campbell; m. Nancy Gail Kunz, Dec. 31, 1987. BA, Carson-Newman Coll., Jefferson City, Tenn., 1961; MA, Vanderbilt U., Nashville, 1963; PhD, Vanderbilt U., 1971. Asst. prof. history Lambuth Coll., Jackson, Tenn., 1963—64; prof. history State U. of West Ga., Carrollton, 1964—. Author: (book) Gentleman from Georgia, 2000. Com. mem. Boy Scouts Am., 1998—; adminstrv. aide Rep. Newt Gingrich, 6th Dist. Ga., 1979—93. Mem.: AAUP (state pres. 1979—80, lobbyist 1976—96, AKIN award 1996, Sumberg award 1998), The Hist. Soc. (regional pres. 2000—), Kiwanis (disting. mem.). Methodist. Avocations: stamp collecting/philately, politics. Home: 60 S Greenwood Dr Carrollton GA 30117 Office: State Univ of West Georgia Dept History Carrollton GA 30118

**STEELY, ROBERT LEE,** plastic surgeon; b. Houston, Sept. 6, 1966; s. Robert Lee and Yvonne Brulet Steely; m. Katherine Anne DeLaune, Nov. 8, 2003; 1 child, Ava DeLaune. BS, Tulane U., 1988; MD, U. Tex., Galveston, 1993. Diplomate Am. Bd. Gen. Surgery, Am. Bd. Plastic Surgery. Resident in gen. surgery St. Joseph Hosp., Houston, 1993—98, resident in plastic surgery, 1998—2000. Contbr. articles to profl. jours. Participating surgeon Operation San Jose, Mexico, 2000, Peru, 2001; supporter Plastic Surgery Polit. Action Com., 2000—. Fellow: Am. Coll. Surgeons; mem.: Am. Soc. Plastic Surgeons. Office: Box 22780 Houston TX 77227 Office Phone: 713-622-6500.

**STEEMERS, FRANK J.,** research scientist; s. W. J. Steemers. PhD, U. Twente, 1996. Scientist Illumina, San Diego, 2000—02, sr. scientist, 2002—. Grantee, STW, 1999—2000. Mem.: ASHG. Achievements include research in Genotyping, whole genome genotyping, biosensors Office: Illumina 9885 Towne Centre Dr San Diego CA 92121 Office Phone: 858-202-4615. E-mail: fsteemers@illumina.com.

**STEEN, CARLTON DUANE,** private investor, retired food products executive; b. Walnut Grove, Minn., June 12, 1932; s. Conrad Wendell and Hilda (Eng) S.; m. Dorothy Corinne Sorknes, Aug. 16, 1953; children: James, Craig, Jennifer. BA in Econs. cum laude, St. Olaf Coll., 1954; MA in Indsl. Relations, U. Minn., 1957. Job analyst Exxon Corp., Roselle, NJ, 1958-59; personnel adminstr. Kraft Inc., Chgo., 1959-65, compensation mgr., 1965-69, plant mgr. Decatur, Ga., 1969-70, Champaign, Ill., 1971-74, v.p. prodn. Chgo., 1974-76; pres. Indsl. Foods div., Memphis, 1976-82, Indsl. Foods Group, 1982-87. Served to capt. USAF, 1955-57. Republican. Lutheran.

**STEEN, JOHN,** health policy executive, consultant; b. Bklyn., Dec. 14, 1941; m. Carol Nolde, June 3, 1978 (div. Nov. 2001); 1 child, Thoa Flaherty; m. Karen Kauffeld, June 20, 2004. BA, NYU, 1962, MA, 1964, PhD, 1965. Cert. of Need. Asst. dir. Health Systems Agy. of N.Y.C., 1976-86; mgr. C.O.N./planning Munns & Dobbins, CPAs, Scarsdale, N.Y., 1986-92; exec. dir. Essex & Union Adv. Bd. for Health Planning, Inc., South Orange, N.J., 1992-95; rsch. assst. prof. Seton Hall U., South Orange, 1992-95; dir. regulatory compliance State Health Planning Agy., Atlanta, 1996-97; prin. John Steen & Assocs., Meadville, Pa., 2004—. Vis. prof., lectr 7 colls. and univs.; pres. Am. Health Planning Assn., 2006-07. Contbr. articles to profl. jours. Mem. health task force Cmty. Coun. of Greater N.Y., 1971-74, chmn. state health issues com., 1974-76; chmn. project rev. com. Comprehensive Health Planning Agy. of N.Y.C., 1974-76; officer, chmn. health and hosps. com. Cmty. Bd. #2, Staten Island, N.Y., 1973-76; chmn. landmarks com. Borough Coun., Mountain Lakes, N.J., 1984-92, borough historian, 1993-97; bd. dirs. Morris County Trust for Historic Preservation, Morristown, 1998-2000. Mem. APHA, Am. Health Planning Assn. (bd. dirs., chair pub. policy), Am. Coll. Med. Quality, Mensa. Office: John Steen & Assocs 18254 Southwood Dr Meadville PA 16335-9292 E-mail: jwsteen@expedient.net.

**STEEN, JOHN THOMAS, JR.,** lawyer; b. San Antonio, Dec. 27, 1949; s. John Thomas and Nell (Donnell) S.; m. Ida Louise Clement, May 12, 1979; children: John T. III, Ida Louise Larkin, James Higbie Clement. AB cum laude, Princeton U., 1971; JD, U. Tex., 1974; degree with honors, U.S. Army Mil. Police Sch., 1974. Bar: Tex. 1974, U.S. Dist. Ct. (we. dist.) Tex. 1976, U.S. Ct. Appeals (5th cir.) 1989. Assoc. Matthews & Branscomb, San Antonio, 1977—82; ptnr. Soules, Cliffe & Reed, San Antonio, 1982—83; sr. v.p., gen. counsel, dir. Commerce Savs. Assn., San Antonio, 1983—88; pvt. practice San Antonio, 1988—. Trustee San Antonio Acad., 1976-81, 87-93, chmn. bd., 1989-91, adv. coun., 1991—; v.p. Bexar County Easter Seal Soc., San Antonio, 1976-77; trustee, vice-chmn. San Antonio C.C. Dist., 1977-82; bd. dirs. Tex. Easter Seal Soc., Dallas, 1977-80, San Antonio Rsch. and Planning Coun., 1978-81, Cmty. Guidance Ctr., 1983-84, Accord Med. Found., 1987-92; vice-chmn. Leadership San Antonio, 1978-79; dir. Fiesta San Antonio Commn., 1982-83, 93-96, 98-2001, 2003—, v.p., 2004-06, pres.-elect 2006—; commr. Bexar County, San Antonio, 1982, Tex. Commn. on Economy and Efficiency in State Govt., 1985-89; adv. bd. Freeman Coliseum, 1985-91, chmn. bd. 1990-91; pres. San Antonio Performing Arts Assn., 1984-85; trustee World Affairs Coun. San Antonio, 1982—, chmn. bd., 1984-86; trustee United Way, San Antonio, 1985-92, Tex. Cavaliers Charitable Found., 1994-97, 2003-05, Austin Coll., 1996-2001; bd. dirs. Houston Livestock Show and Rodeo; mem. adv. bd. U. Tex., San Antonio, 1987—, exec. com. mem. chancellor's coun. U. Tex. Sys., 2005—, active Pan-Tex. Assembly, 1985-2002; commr. Tex. Alcoholic Beverage Commn., 1998—, chmn., 2002—; exec. com. mem. Rep. Eagles, 2000—; hon. dir. San Antonio Livestock Exposition, Inc.; bd. dirs. Fiesta Commn. Charitable Corp. 2004-06. 1st lt. USAR. Named Chevalier Confrérie de Chevaliers du Tastevin, Sous-Commanderie de So. Tex., 1994—. Fellow San Antonio Bar Found., Tex. Bar Found. (life); mem. Tex. Bar Assn., San Antonio Acad. Alumni Assn. (pres. 1976-77), Ivy Club (Princeton, N.J.), San Antonio German Club (pres. 1982-83), Order of Alamo, Tex. Cavaliers (bd. dirs. 1989-92, 94-97, comdr. 1994-95, King Antonio LXXIV 1996-97, Kings coun, 1997—, vice chmn. 2003-04, chmn. 2004-05), San Antonio Country Club (bd. govs. 1990-93, v.p. 1992-93), Argyle Club, Conopus Club (bd. dirs. 1989-90), Princeton Club San Antonio and South Tex. (pres. 1980-81), Maclean Soc. at Princeton U., Phi Delta Phi. Republican. Home: 601 Garraty Rd San Antonio TX 78209-6148 Office: 300 Convent St Ste 2440 San Antonio TX 78205-3722 Office Phone: 210-224-7700.

**STEEN, LOWELL HARRISON,** retired physician; b. Kenosha, Wis., Nov. 27, 1923; s. Joseph Arthur and Camilla Marie (Henriksen) S.; m. Cheryl Ann Rectanus, Nov. 20, 1969; children: Linda C., Laura A., Lowell Harrison Jr., Heather J., Kirsten M. BS, Ind. U., Bloomington, 1945; MD, Ind. U., 1948. Intern Mercy Hosp.-Loyola U. Clinics, Chgo., 1948-49; resident in internal medicine VA Hosp., Hines, Ill., 1950-53; pvt. practice Highland, Ind., 1953—; ret., 1999. Pres., CEO Whiting Clinic, 1960-85; mem. hon. staff St. Catherine Hosp., East Chicago, Ind.; hon. staff Cmty. Hosp., Munster, Ind.; bd. commrs. Joint Commn. Accreditation of Hosps. With M.C., AUS, 1949-50, 55-56 Recipient Disting. Svc. award Ind. U., 1983 Fellow ACP; mem. AMA (trustee 1975, chmn. bd. trustees 1979-81), Ind. Med. Assn. (pres. 1970, chmn. bd. 1968-70), World Med. Assn. (dir. 1978-82, chmn. 1981-82, del. world assembly), Ind. Soc. Internal Medicine (pres. 1963), Am. Soc. Internal Medicine (Disting. Internist award 1981), Lake County Med. Soc., Ind. U. Sch. Medicine Alumni Assn. (pres. 1989-90, Disting. Alumnus award 1981). Presbyterian. Home: 1580 Parkway Dr Highland IN 46322-1520 Personal E-mail: candlsteen@comcast.net.

**STEEN, LYNN ARTHUR,** mathematician, educator; b. Chgo., Jan. 1, 1941; s. Sigvart J. and Margery (Mayer) S.; m. Mary Elizabeth Frost, July 7, 1940; children: Margaret, Catherine. BA, Luther Coll., 1961; PhD, MIT, 1965; DSc (hon.), Luther Coll., 1986, Wittenberg U., 1991, Concordia Coll., Minn., 1996. Prof. math. St. Olaf Coll., Northfield, Minn., 1965—. Vis. scholar Inst. Mittag-Leffler, Djursholm, Sweden, 1970-71; writing fellow Conf. Bd. Math. Sci., Washington, 1974-75; exec. dir. Math. Sci. Edn. Bd., Washington, 1992-95. Author: Counterexamples in Topology, 1970, Everybody Counts, 1989; editor: Mathematics Today, 1978, On the Shoulders of Giants, 1990, Math. Mag., 1976-80, Why Numbers Count, 1997, Mathematics and Democracy, 2001, Achieving Quantitative Literacy, 2004, Math and Biology 2010, 2005; contbg. editor: Sci. News, 1976-82. NSF Sci. faculty fellow, 1970-71,

Danforth Found. grad. fellow, 1961-65. Fellow AAAS (sec. math. sect. 1982-88); mem. Am. Math. Soc., Math. Assn. Am. (pres. 1985-86, Disting. Svc. award 1992), Coun. Sci. Soc. Pres. (chmn. 1989), Sigma Xi (Bd. Dirs. Spl. award 1989). Home: 716 Saint Olaf Ave Northfield MN 55057-1523 Office: St Olaf Coll Dept of Math Northfield MN 55057 E-mail: steen@stolaf.edu.

**STEEN, MORRIS GRISSOM, JR.,** academic administrator, retired military officer; b. Mosely Hall, Fla., Apr. 8, 1941; s. Morris Grissom and Sarah Helen (Hendry) Steen; m. Judy Gilliam Steen, July 30, 1970; children: Hayne Addison, Heath Ashley, Brittany Alwyn. BS, U. Fla., 1965; MS, George Washinton U., 1977. Commd. ensign USN, 1965, advanced through grades to capt., 1992; fin. svcs. Mass. Mutual, Jacksonville, Fla., 1992—97; dir. tech. programs North Fla. CC, Madison, 1997—2001, pres., 2001—. Chmn. Fla. Easter Seal Soc., Jacksonville, 1997, Daniel Meml. Inc., Jacksonville, 1997, Daniel Meml. Hosp., Jacksonville, 1996. Named Outstanding Profl. Adv., Fla. Easter Seal Soc., 1996, Outstanding Alumni, North Fla. CC, 1998. Mem.: Madison County Devel. Coun., Coun. Pres., Rotary (pres.-elect Madison chpt. 2006). Methodist. Avocations: farming, hunting, travel, reading. Home: PO Box 604 Shady Grove FL 32357 Office: North Fla Cmty Coll Turner Davis Dr Madison FL 32340

**STEEN, PAUL JOSEPH,** retired broadcasting executive; b. Williston, ND, July 4, 1932; s. Ernest B. and Inez (Ingebrigtson) S.; m. Judith Smith; children— Michael M., Melanie. BA, Pacific Luth. U., 1954; MS, Syracuse U., 1957. Producer, dir. Sta. KNTV, San Jose, Calif., 1957-58, Sta. KVIF, Sacramento, 1958-60; asst. prof. telecommunications Pacific Luth. U., Tacoma, 1960-67; dir. ops. Sta. KPBS San Diego State U., 1967-74; gen. mgr., 1974-93; prof. telecommunications and film, 1974-93; dir. univ. telecommunications. Co-chmn. Office of New Tech. Initiatives. Dir. (tel. program) Troubled Waters (winner Nat. Ednl. TV award of excellence 1970). With AUS. Named Danforth Assoc. Mem. Pacific Mountain Network (bd. dirs., chmn., bd. of govs. award 1993), NATAS, Assn. Calif. Pub. TV Stas. (pres.), San Diego County Sr. Golf Assn., (pres.), Pi Kappa Delta. Home: 6068 Caminito De La Taza San Diego CA 92120-5323 Personal E-mail: psteen@mail.sdsu.edu.

**STEENBERGEN, JUDITH N.,** research scientist; d. Steenbergen; m. Michael S. Cohen, July 8, 2001; children: Gabriella Cohen, David Cohen. PhD, Albert Einstein Coll. of Medicine, Bronx, N.Y., 2003. Rsch. scientist II Cubist Pharms., Lexington, Mass., 2002—. Office Phone: 781-860-8434.

**STEENBURGEN, MARY,** actress; b. Newport, Ark., Feb. 8, 1953; m. Malcolm McDowell, 1980 (div. 1990); children: Lilly, Charlie; m. Ted. Danson, Oct. 7, 1995. Student, Neighborhood Playhouse. Films: Goin' South, 1978, Time After Time, 1979, Melvin and Howard, 1980 (Academy award best supporting actress 1981), Ragtime, 1981, A Midsummer Night's Sex Comedy, 1982, Cross Creek, 1983, Romantic Comedy, 1983, One Magic Christmas, 1985, Dead of Winter, 1987, End of the Line, 1987 (also exec. prodr.), The Whales of August, 1987, Miss Firecracker, 1989, Parenthood, 1989, Back to the Future III, 1990, The Long Walk Home, 1990 (narrator), The Butcher's Wife, 1991, Philadelphia, 1993, What's Eating Gilbert Grape, 1993, Clifford, 1994, It Runs in the Family, 1994, Pontiac Moon, 1994, Powder, 1995, Nixon, 1995, My Family, 1995, The Grass Harp, 1995, About Sarah, 1995, Trumpet of the Swan (voice), 1999, Life as a House, 2001, I Am Sam, 2001, Sunshine State, 2002, Wish You Were Dead, 2002, Hope Springs, 2003, Casa de los babys, 2003, Elf, 2003; appeared in Showtime TV's Faerie Tale Theatre prodn. of Little Red Riding Hood and (miniseries) Tender Is the Night, 1985, Gulliver's Travels, 1996;, (miniseries) Noah's Ark, 1999, Living with the Dead, 2002; TV series: Ink, 1996, Joan of Arcadia, 2003-; TV films: The Attic: The Hiding of Anne Frank, 1988, About Sarah, 1998, Picnic, 2000, Nobody's Baby, 2001, It Must Be Love, 2004, Capital City, 2004; theater appearances include: Holiday, Old Vic, London, 1987, Candida, Broadway, 1993. Nat. spokesperson Elizabeth Glaser Pediatric AIDS Found. Office: The Gersh Agency 232 N Canon Dr Beverly Hills CA 90210

**STEENBURGH, FRANK D.,** consumer products company executive; b. Johnstown, NY, Jan. 23, 1943; BSME, General Motors Inst., 1966; MBA, Rensselaer Poly. Inst., 1967. Sr. v.p. bus. growth Xerox Corp., Stamford, Conn., 2003—. Bd. dirs. Nat. Tech. Inst. for Deaf Found. Recipient Power of Communicatons Award, Assn. Graphic Comm., print-on-demand award, Cygnus Bus. Media. Office: Xerox Corp 800 Long Ridge Rd Stamford CT 06904

**STEENHAGEN, ROBERT LEWIS,** landscape architect, consultant; b. Grand Rapids, Mich., July 11, 1922; s. Abraham and Rena (Vanden Broek) S.; m. Doris Brisentine, Aug. 2, 1952; children: Deborah, Cynthia, James. A.S., Grand Rapids Jr. Coll., 1942; BS, Mich. State U., 1949. Chief landscape design Eastern design office Nat. Park Service, Phila., 1963-66; capt. planning team Nat. Park Service, Washington, 1966-70, asst. mgr. N.E. area Design Office Denver, 1971-77, assoc. mgr., 1978-80; cons. landscape architecture Lakewood, Colo., 1980—. Served to sgt. U.S. Army, 1942-45, PTO. Recipient Meritorious Service award Nat. Park Service, 1971; recipient Performance award for Nat. Bicentennial Program, 1976 Fellow Am. Soc. Landscape Architects Home: 2473 S Carr Ct Denver CO 80227-3104

**STEEN-HINDERLIE, DIANE EVELYN,** social worker, musician; b. Duluth, Minn., June 13, 1947; d. Julian Sem and Evelyn Synnove (Helgaas) Steen; m. John Peter Hinderlie, June 27, 1971 (div. Sept. 1987); children: Peder Donald, Erik Steen; m. John Richard Olson, July 21, 1989. BA in Asian Studies/Social Psychology cum laude, St. Olaf Coll. 1969; postgrad, U. Minn. and other instns., 1991 Hamline U., 1989—91. Lic. social worker, Minn.; cert. music tchr. Music Tchrs. Nat. Assn. Social worker child care licensing Hennepin County Welfare Dept., Mpls., 1970—73; mem. clergy team exch. program Luth. World Fedn., Göppingen, Germany, 1973—77; mem. clergy team, music dir. Jubilation Singers Bethel Luth. Ch., Rochester, Minn., 1978—83; mem. clergy team, music dir. youth choir First Luth. Ch., St. Louis Park, Minn., 1983—86; administr. Family Child Care facility, St. Louis Park, 1986—90; faculty, tchr. Stenson Suzuki Studios and Home Studio, St. Louis Park, 1988—92; small group leader, tchr. vol. Mt. Olive Ch., Children's Hosp., Mpls., 1993, 1996—98; workshop and children's ministry Augsburg Coll. Youth and Family Inst., Trinity Cong., 1998—; founding dir. Fair Pay Inst., Mpls., 1995—; trainer United for a Fair Economy, 1997—; Founder orgn. and curriculum Early Childhood Orgn. for Edn. with Singing, 1993—, co-leader German-Am. youth group exch., 1979-82; co-founder Family DayCare Cert. Program and Babygarten (B-12 edn.) classes, 1970-73; bd. dirs. Midwest Coun., Nat. Peace Inst. Found., Grinnell, Iowa, 1991; presenter in field.; mem. root causes of violence action team Initiative for Violence-Free Families, 4th Jud. Dist. Minn., 1997—. Author: (tng. manual) Mother Tongue Singing/Voice Method, 1998, (study packet) School Start Time/Teen Sleep Deprivation, 1996-97, A+=Baby Church School, 2002; rec. artist, mem. ensemble record/cassettes Nowell Sing We, 1986; performer Nordic Am. Psalmodikon Forbundet, 1997—. Vol. People of Faith Peacemakers, Feminists in Faith/ReImagining and Jewish Cmty. Rels. Coun., 1992-2003, Muslim-Christian Rels. Coun., Joint Religious Legis. Coalition, Bread for the World; founder People for Reforming Early Start Time for Teens Orgn., Mpls., 1993—; mem. steering com. Progressive Cmty. and FairVote, Minn., 1994-99; local host youth com. NAACP Conv., Mpls., 1995; vol. Common Cause, St. Paul and Washington; charter mem. U.S. Holocaust Mus., 1993; cofounder antitorture com. Women Against Mil. Madness, 2005. Recipient appreciation plaque Christian Boy/Girl Scouts Germany; Svc. pin Am. Luth. Ch. Women; listed in Minn. Profiles, Minn. Hist. Soc. A Tribute to Outstanding Minn. Women by Marilyn Chelstrom, 2001; named Asset Builder of Month, St. Louis Park Children First Initiative, 1997; named to Honor Roll, Mendota Mdewakanton Dakota Cmty., 1999. Mem.: MADD, Minn. Music Tchrs. Assn. (first early childhood music chair 2001—03), Assn. Pre- and Perinatal Psychology and Health, Wash. Nat. Cathedral, Soc. for Psychol. Studies of Social Issues, Interfaith Alliance Minn., Nat. Luth. Choir Acad., Suzuki Assn. Americas (study area co-organizer, editl. adviser), Internat. Suzuki Assn., Nat. Assn. Tchrs. Singing and VoiceCare Network, UN

Assn., Sojourner Project, Inc., Am.'s Jr. Miss. Coun., Germanic-Am. Inst., Nat. Peace Found., Amnesty Internat., Minn. Parenting Assn., Ctr. for Victims of Torture, World Wildlife Fund, Sons of Norway (lodge trustee 1991—), Phi Beta Kappa, Am. Mensa. Green. Lutheran. Avocations: reading, political activism, concerts, travel, memory albums. Office: Fair Pay Inst PO Box 16031 Minneapolis MN 55416-0031

**STEENLAND, DOUGLAS M.,** air transportation executive; married; 2 children. BA in History, Calvin Coll.; JD, George Washington U., 1976. Sr. ptnr. Verner, Liipfert, Bernhard, McPherson and Hand, Washington; v.p., dep. gen. counsel Northwest Airlines Corp., Eagan, Minn., 1991—94, sr. v.p., gen. counsel Minn., 1994—98, exec. v.p., gen. counsel and alliances Minn., 1998—99, exec. v.p., chief corp. officer Minn., 1999—2001, pres. Minn., 2001—, also bd. dirs. Minn., 2001—, CEO, 2004—. Mem. bd. dirs. MAIR Holdings, Inc., The Guthrie Theater, The Minn. Symphony Orch.; mem. Super Bowl XL-Detroit 2006 Host Com. Office: Northwest Airlines Corp 2700 Lone Oak Pkwy Eagan MN 55121*

**STEENSGAARD, ANTHONY HARVEY,** federal agency administrator; b. Rapid City, S.D., Mar. 21, 1963; s. Harvey Hans and Dorothy Lorraine (Hansen) S. Student, Ft. Mead Vocat. Inst., 1974—75, U. S.D., 1978—80, Anchorage C.C., 1983—84; BSCE, U. Alaska, 1985; student, Northwestern U., 1986; AAS in Indsl. Security, C.C. Air Force, 1989; BS in Criminal Justice, Wayland U., 1989; MS in Computer Systems Engring., U. Calif., San Diego, 1996; LLD in Criminal Law, U. Trinity Coll., 2000, PhD in Computer Engring., 2000; BSc in Criminological Psychology, Rusland Coll., 2003. Lic. pilot, amateur radio operator; cert. hostage negotiator FBI, FBI Nat. Acad., Va., 1987; Fed. Air Marshall Sch., FAA; cert. Instr. Am. Soc. Protection Profls., 1986—, fed. emergency mgmt. agy. level III incident comdr., security specialist, 2001—, info. security specialist, intelligence and surveillance profl., 2001—. Bookseller B. Dalton Bookseller, Rapid City, 1978—81, Anchorage, 1981—83; warehouseman Sears, Roebuck & Co., Anchorage, 1983—85; air res. technician Alaska Air N.G., Anchorage, 1985—88; agt., draftsman, engring. cons., asst. intelligence officer U.S. Border Patrol, El Centro, Calif., 1988—. Fed. counter terrorism cons., 2001—; fed. info. warfare cons., 2001—; computer crime cons., 1994-2000; computer criminal investigator, 1999—; CEO Totalwarfare.com webzine, 1997—; founding assoc. Amazon.com.; technical support working group, technical support officer Dept. Homeland Security, 2002—; intelligence officer U.S. Coast Guard Auxiliary, 2003—; founding mem. U.S. Dept. Homeland, 2003. Author: Unit Security Manager's Guide Book, 1988. Vol. Spl. Olympics, Rapid City, 1981; navigator, observer Civil Air Patrol, Anchorage, 1981; mentor Municipality Anchorage Sch. Dist., 1983—84; sr. pilot Civil Air Patrol, Rapid City, 1996, pub. affairs officer, 1996—98, aerospace edn. officer, 1998—2000, wing dir. aerospace edn., 2000—04; aircraft navigator US Coast Guard Aux., 2003—; Vol. U.S. Senator George McGovern's Campaign, Rapid City, 1980, Senator Tom Daschle's Campaign, Rapid City, 1980. With USNR, 1980—81, With USMCR, 1981—85, With USAF, 1985—98, with, 1990, Operation Desert Shield, with, 1991, Operation Desert Strom, with, 1991, Operation Provide Comfort, with, 2002, Operation Liberty Shield. Recipient Hon. Sci. award Bausch and Lomb, 1984, commendation State of Alaska, 1987, 2d commendation, 1988, Brigadier Gen. Charles E. Yeager Aerospace Achievement award, 2000, Blanchard trophy, 1990, Afghanistan royal Oder Almara el Ala, 2003. Fellow N.Am. Acad. Arts and Sci.; mem. U.S. Cavalry Assn. (heritage mem.), HTML Writer's Guild, Am. Legion, Air Force Assn., VFW, Fraternal Order Eagles, S.D. Sheriff's Assn., Fraternal Order of Police, Virtual Geog. League, WWII Meml. Soc. (charter mem.), US Naval Inst., US Coast Guard Inst., Nat. D-Day Mus. Found., Adventurer's Club. Avocations: reading, flight simulations, aviation, history, wargaming. Office: US Border Patrol 1111 N Imperial Ave El Centro CA 92243-1795 Personal E-mail: ahsteensgaard@juno.com.

**STEENSLAND, RONALD PAUL,** librarian; b. Dothan, Ala., Dec. 16, 1946; s. Maurice John and Claire Folkes S.; m. Nancy Hollister, Dec. 20, 1970; 1 child, Ronald Paul. BA, Fla. State U., Miss. 96, 1970; postgrad., Miami U., Ohio, 1972, U. Md., 1980, US Army War Coll., 1995. Dir. Davidson County Pub. Libr., Lexington, N.C., 1970-73, Hidalgo County Libr. System, McAllen, Tex., 1973-76, Los Alamos County Libr., 1976-77, Lexington (Ky.) Pub. Libr., 1977—. Chmn. John Cotton Dana Library Public Relations Awards, 1977 Treas. Hildago County chpt. ARC, 1975. Served to col. USAR, 1969-70. Recipient Service award United Way. Mem. ALA, Res. Officers Assn. (sec.-treas. chpt. 100), Assn. U.S. Army (sec. Bluegrass chpt.), U.S. Chess Fedn., Southeastern Library Assn., Ky. Library Assn., Lexington C. of C., Alpha Tau Omega. Clubs: Lafayette, Pres.'s, Lexington Chess, Rotary. Baptist. Office: Lexington Pub Libr 140 E Main St Lexington KY 40507-1318 E-mail: ron2085@yahoo.com.

**STEEPLES, DOUGLAS WAYNE,** retired university dean, consultant, researcher; b. Great Bend, Kans. Mar. 30, 1935; s. Marion Wayne and Dorothy Augusta (King) S.; children from previous marriage: Donald Bruce, John Douglas, Sheila Margaret; m. Christine Marie MacKinnes, Dec. 8, 1990. BA summa cum laude, U. Redlands, 1957; MA, U.N.C., 1958, PhD, 1961; cert., Inst. Ednl. Mgmt., Harvard U., 1981. Asst. prof. history Calir. State U., North Ridge, 1961—64; prof. history Earlham Coll., Richmond, Ind., 1963-80; acad. v.p. Wartburg Coll., Waverly, Iowa, 1979-80; exec. v.p. Westminster Coll., Salt Lake City, 1980-83; provost Ohio U., Delaware, Ohio, 1983-85, acting pres., winter 1984; dean Coll. Liberal and Fine Arts, U. So. Colo., Pueblo, Colo., 1985-89; v.p. for acad. affairs Aurora U., Ill., 1989—93, v.p. acad. planning, 1993—94; dean, prof. history Coll. Liberal Arts, Mercer U., Macon, Ga., 1994-2000, ret., 2000; proctor, participant clin. practice program Mercer U. Med. Sch., Macon, 2005—. Cons. higher edn. mgmt.; cons., reader advanced placement program Ednl. Testing Svc., Princeton, NJ, 1976-93; cons., evaluator North Ctrl. Assn. Sch. and Coll., Chgo., 1985-1994; mem. Accreditation Rev. Commn., 1992-94; bd. dirs. Western Ind. Coll. Fund, Salt Lake City, 1980-83; bd. dirs. Am. Conf. Acad. Deans, 1995-2000, sec.-treas., 1998-99; trustee Econ. and Bus. Hist. Soc., 1995-2000, pres., 1998-99; bd. dirs. Associated New Am. Colls., 1994-00. Editor, contbg. author: Institutional Revival: Case Histories, 1986, Successful Strategic Planning Case Studies, 1989, Mng. Change in Higher Ed., 1990, Treasure from the Painted Hills: Calico Calif., 1882-1907, 1999; (with David O. Whitten) Democracy in Desperation: The Depression in the 1890s, 1998 (Choice Mag. Acad. Book of Yr. award); editor John Randolph Spears, Illustrated Sketches of Death Valley, 2000, Advocate for Am. Enterprise: William Buck Dana and the Commercial and Fin. Chronicle, 1865-1910, 2001; assoc. editor Bus. Libr. Rev., 1996-2001; occational columnist for Macon Telegraph; contbr. over 45 articles and 80 book revs. to profl. jour. Adv. bd. Pueblo Symphony Orch., 1987—89; allocations com. United Way, Richmond, 1976—79, Pueblo, 1988—89, Aurora, 1990—94; vol. in svc., spl. cons. to pres. Ho-Chunk Wis. Winnebago Nation, 2001; mem. Mayor's Commn. on Restoration of Ft. Hawkins, Macon, Ga., 1997—; pipe maj. Mercer U. Pipes and Drums, 2002—06, pipe sgt., 2006—; pres. Luth. Inter-parish Coun., Richmond, 1975—78; bd. dir. Soc. for Use and Preservation of Resources, Richmond, 1974-79. Scholar U. Redlands, Calif., 1953-57; Danforth fellow, 1957-61; Woodrow Wilson fellow, 1957-58; Found. for Econ. Edn. fellow in bus., 1963; Am. Philos. Soc. grantee, 1966 Mem. Am. Hist. Assn., Orgn. Am. Hist., U.S. Hist. Assn., Soc. for Values in Higher Edn., Sierra Club, Rotary (bd. dirs. 1983-84), Palaver Club, Phi Beta Kappa (senator united chpt. 1973-79, sec.-treas. mid-Ga. alumni assoc. 1996-2000, pres. 2003-04), Omicron Delta Kappa, Phi Kappa Phi. Republican. Avocations: mountain climbing. running, bagpiping. Office: 656 River North Blvd Macon GA 31211-6340 Office Phone: 478-750-1051. E-mail: steeplesmcn@aol.com.

**STEER, JOHN RICHARD,** lawyer; b. Greenwood, S.C., Sept. 9, 1949; s. Robert Lindley and Evelyn (Patterson) S.; m. Mary-Lynne Sever, July 29, 1979; children: Meredith, Derrison. BS, Clemson U., 1971, MS, 1975; JD, U. S.C., 1978. Bar: S.C. 1979, U.S. Ct. Appeals (4th cir.) 1982, U.S. Ct. Appeals and D.C. cirs.) 1988, U.S. Ct. Mil. Appeals, 1989, U.S. Supreme Ct. 1988. Instr., regional specialist Clemson (S.C.) U. Extension Svc., 1973; legis. asst. U.S. Senator Strom Thurmond, Washington, 1974-76, state office

staff asst. Columbia, SC, 1976-79, legis. dir. Washington, 1979-85, adminstrv. asst., 1985-86; chief dep. gen. counsel U.S. Sentencing Commn., Washington, 1986-87, gen. counsel, 1987—, vice chair, 1999—. Contbr. articles to law rev. Active Springfield United Meth. Ch., Va. Mem. Clemson U. DC Area Alumni Assn. Home: 8413 Lake Crest Ter Fairfax Station VA 22039-2678 Office: US Sentencing Commn 1 Columbus Cir NE Ste 2-500 Washington DC 20002-8040 Office Phone: 202-502-4500, 202-502-4592. Business E-Mail: jsteer@ussc.gov.

**STEER, REGINALD DAVID,** lawyer; b. NYC, July 16, 1945; s. Joseph D. and Rozica (Yusim) S.; m. Marianne Spizzy, July 22, 1983; children: Derek B., Trevor A. BA, U. Minn., 1966, JD, 1969. Bar: Minn. 1969, Calif. 1973, U.S. Dist. Ct. (no., ea. so. and ctrl. dists.) Calif., U.S. Ct. Mil. Appeals 1969, U.S. Ct. Appeals (9th cir.), U.S. Ct. Appeals (11th cir.), U.S. Supreme Ct. 1981, U.S. Ct. Internat. Trade, 1994. Ptnr. Akin Gump Strauss Hauer & Feld, LLP, San Francisco. Capt. U.S. Army, 1969—73. Fellow Am. Coll. Trial Lawyers; mem. ABA (antitrust and litigation sects.), San Francisco (Calif.) Bar Assn. Office: Akin Gump Strauss Hauer & Feld LLP 580 California St Ste 1500 San Francisco CA 94104 Office Phone: 415-765-9520. E-mail: rsteer@akingump.com.

**STEERE, ALLEN CARUTHERS, JR.,** physician, educator; b. Apr. 11, 1943; m. Margaret Mercer; children: Allen Caruthers III, Margaret Hamilton, Samuel Mercer, John Summers. BA, Columbia U., 1965, MD, 1969; DSc. (hon.), Indiana U., 1992, SUNY, 1997; M (hon.), Harvard Med. Sch., 2002. Diplomate Am. Bd. Internal Medicine; lic. rheumatologist, N.Y., Ga., Ct., Mass. Intern St. Luke's Hosp., N.Y.C., 1969-70, asst., s. resident, 1970-72, chief resident, instr. medicine, 1972-73; chief resident, instr. medicine Coll. Physicians and Surgeons Columbia U., N.Y.C., 1972-73; clin. fellow in rheumatology Yale U., New Haven, 1975-77, asst. prof. medicine, epidemiology and pub. health, 1977-81, assoc. prof. medicine, 1981-87; prof. medicine, chief rheumatology and immunology New Eng. Med. Ctr. Tufts U., Boston, 1987—2002, Natalie V. & Milton O. Zucker prof. rheumatology/immunology, 1998—2002; prof. medicine Harvard Med. Sch., Boston, 2002—; dir. rheumatology Mass. Gen. Hosp., 2002—06, dir. clin. rsch. in rheumatology, 2006—. With USPHS, 1973-75. Recipient Citation for Elucidation of Lyme disease, Infectious Diseases Soc. Am., 1984, Ciba-Geigy Rheumatology prize, Internat. League Against Rheumatism, 1985, award for discovery of Lyme disease, Nat. Inst. Arthritis and Musculoskeletal Skin Diseases, 1988, Richard and Hinda Rosenthal award, ACP, 1990, Joseph Mather Smith prize, Coll. Physicians and Surgeons, Columbia U., 1990, Zucker Faculty prize, Tufts U., 1990, award for studies Lyme disease, Nat. Health Coun., 1990, Lee C. Howley Sr. prize, Arthritis Found., 1993, Gold medal, Albert Sabin Vaccine Inst., 1998, Astute Clinician award, NIH, 1999, award, Am. Lyme Disease Found., 2000, Columbia Coll. of Phys. and Surgeon's Alumni award for Disting. Acad. Accomplishment, 2001. Mem. Am. Soc. Clin. Investigation, Am. Fedn. Clin. Rsch., Am. Coll. Rheumatology (Howard and Martha Holley rsch. prize in rheumatology 1995), Assn. Am. Physicians, Clin. Immunology Soc. Office: Mass Gen Hosp 55 Fruit St CNY 149/8301 Boston MA 02114

**STEERE, PETER LAWSON,** archaeologist, historian; b. Bryn Mawr, Pa., Feb. 3, 1948; s. David Trueblood Steere and Margaret deVeaux Lawson; m. Susan Leicht, Dec. 29, 1979; children: Bretton Thomas, Amy DeVeaux, Megan Helene. BA, U. Mont., 1970, MA, 1972; MLS, U. Ariz., 1987. Cert. hist. photographer. Archaeologist, historian Helena Nat. Forest, Helena, Mont., 1977, Deerlodge Nat. Forest, Butte, Mont., 1978—79, Mineral Rsch. Ctr., Butte, Mont., 1978—83, Coronado Nat. Forest, Tucson, 1983; archaeologist, mgr. Cultural and Environ. Systems, Tucson, 1983—87; congl. archivist U. Ariz., Tucson, 1987—97; archaeologist, mgr. Tohono O'odham Nation, Sells, Ariz., 1997—. Archival and archaeol. cons., Tucson, 1983—. Author: San Xavier Survey, 7 vols., 1987, Cultural Resources and Excavation Reports, 1978—2006. Vol. Dem. Party, Ga., 1975—76. Recipient Best Paper award, Mont. Psychol. Assn., 1972. Mem.: Soc. S.W. Archivists (com. chair 1987—97), Ariz. Hist. Soc., Ariz. Archaeol. Soc. Democrat. Episcopalina/Quaker. Avocations: photography, hiking, fishing. Home: PO Box 1279 Sells AZ 85634 Office: Tohono O'odham Nation PO Box 837 Sells AZ 85634 E-mail: psteere@tona.net.

**STEERE, WILLIAM CAMPBELL, JR.,** pharmaceutical executive; b. Ann Arbor, Mich., June 17, 1936; s. William Campbell and Dorothy (Osborne) S.; m. Lynda Gay Powers, Jan. 29, 1957; children: William, Mark, Christopher. BS, Stanford U., 1959. Sales rep. Pfizer & Co., Modesto, Calif., 1970-72; v.p., dir. ops. Pfizer Labs, N.Y.C., 1982-84; sr. v.p., dir. ops. Pfizer Pharms., N.Y.C., 1982-84, exec. v.p., 1984-86, pres., 1986-91; pres., CEO Pfizer Inc., 1991-92, CEO, 1991—2000, chmn., 1992—2001, chmn. emeritus, 2001—. Bd. dirs. NYU Med. Ctr., Health Mgmt. Assocs. (HMA), Met Life, Dow Jones. Bd. dirs. N.Y. Bot. Garden; bd. overseers Meml. Sloan-Kettering Cancer Ctr. Mem. Bus. Coun. (bd. dirs.), Univ. Club, N.Y. Yacht Club. Avocations: sailing, skiing. Office: Pfizer Inc 235 E 42nd St New York NY 10017-5755 Office Phone: 212-573-3116. Office Fax: 212-573-2200.

**STEEVES, JOHN G. (JACK STEEVES),** science educator, consultant; BS, Northwestern U.; MS, U. Minn.; D in engring. tech. (hon.), Wentworth Inst. Tech., 1996. Instr. Wentworth Inst. Tech., 1958—95, prof. emeritus, 1995—. Cons. Advanced Integrated Mfg. Ctr., Dayton, Ohio. Machinist U.S. Army, Korea, Japan. Mem.: Soc. Mfg. Engrs. (chmn. Boston chpt. 33 1985, chmn. region 5 1993, former mem. edn. com., proposal reviewer mfg. edn. plan, former dir. nom. com., Joseph A. Siegal Svc. award 2002).

**STEFAN, TODD ROBERT,** music educator; b. Pitts., Nov. 3, 1973; s. Robert James and Linda Stefan; m. Kristen Leigh Fox, July 20, 2002; 1 child, Tyler. B Music Edn., Youngstown State U., 1997. Cert. tchr. Pa. Dir. bands Sharpsville (Pa.) Area HS, 1997—2000, Cumberland Valley HS, Mechanicsburg, Pa., 2000—02, Thomas Jefferson HS, Jefferson Hills, Pa., 2002—03, North Allegheny HS, Wexford, Pa., 2003—. Percussion instr. Grove City (Pa.) Coll., 1998—2000. Mem.: Pa. Music Educators Assn. (assoc.), Percussive Arts Soc. (assoc.). Office: North Allegheny Sr HS 13075 Perry Hwy Wexford PA 15090

**STEFANELLI, JOSEPH JAMES (JOE STEFANELLI),** artist; b. Phila., Mar. 20, 1921; s. Alessandro and Carmela (Leone) S. Student, Graphic Sketch Club, 1934-38, Phila. Mus. Coll. Art, 1938-40, Pa. Acad. Fine Arts, 1940-41, New Sch. for Social Research, 1949-50, Art Students League, 1951, 1950-51, Hans Hoffman Sch. Painting, 1951-52. Faculty U. Calif., Berkeley, summers 1960, 63; vis. critic Cornell U., U. Ark., U. Iowa, U. W.Va., U. Wis., U. N.Mex.; artist in residence Princeton U., 1963-66; faculty Columbia U., 1966-74, New Sch. for Social Research, 1966—, Bklyn. Coll., from 1974. One-man shows, Artists Gallery, 1950, New Gallery, 1952, Artists Gallery, 1954, Poindexter Gallery, 1957, 58, 60, Hacker Gallery, 1962, Thibaut Gallery, 1963, Princeton U., 1964, U. Ark., 1965, Westbeth Galleries, 1971, Bertha Schaeffer Gallery, 1973, 74, Andre Zarre Gallery, 1977, R.H. Love Gallery, Chgo., 1989, Randall Gallery, St. Louis, 1989, Penna Acad. Fine Arts, 1989, M13 Gallery N.Y.C., 1991, Benson Gallery, Southampton, N.Y., 1992, Olaf Clasen Gallery, 1992; group shows include, Stable Gallery, Kootz Gallery, Poindexter Gallery, Tanager Gallery, Mus. Modern Art, Whitney Mus., Andre Zarre Gallery, ann. shows, Whitney Mus., Pa. Acad., Corcoran Gallery, Carnegie Internat., U. Ill., Albright Mus., Walker Art Center, Chgo. Art Inst., Mus. Modern Art; represented in permanent collections, Balt. Mus., Sarah Lawrence Coll., N.Y. U., Cornell U., U. Calif. Mus., Geigy-Ciba collection, Chase Manhattan Bank, Union Carbide Co., J. Mass. U. Mont., Norfolk Art Mus., Walker Art Center, Whitney Mus., also pvt. collections; murals include, pub. schs., Bklyn., Manhattan Community Coll.; War artist for: Yank, Army weekly. Recipient Fulbright award for Rome, 1958-59, Spear Rsch. Fund award Princeton U. for Rome, summer 1965; fellow Am. Rsch. Ctr. in Egypt, 1966-67, Esther and Adolph Gottlieb Found., 1986, 88, Krasner/Pollock Found., 1991. Mem.: NAD (academician 1995—). Studio: 463 West St Apt D1006 New York NY 10014-2039

**STEFANI, GWEN RENEE,** singer; b. Anaheim, Calif., Oct. 3, 1969; d. Dennis and Patti Stefani; m. Gavin McGregor Rossdale, Sept. 14, 2002; 1 child, Kingston James McGregor. Student, Calif. State U., Fullerton. Musician No Doubt, 1987—. Designer, creator fashion line L.A.M.B. (Love. Angel. Music. Baby.), 2004—; launched toy doll line (8 dolls) Love. Angel. Music. Baby. Fashion Dolls, 2006. Singer: (albums) No Doubt, 1992, Tragic Kingdom, 1995, Beacon Street Collection, 1995, Collector's Orange Crate, 1997, Return of Saturn, 2000, Rock Steady, 2001 (Grammy award: Best Pop Performance By A Duo Or Group With Vocal for song "Hey Baby", 2002, Best Pop Performance By A Duo Or Group With Vocal for song "Underneath it All", 2003), The Singles 1992-2003, 2004, Love, Angel, Music, Baby, 2004, Everything In Time, 2005, (songs) Let Me Blow Your Mind (with Eve), 2001 (Grammy award, Best Rap/Song Collaboration, 2001), It's My Life (MTV Video Music award Best Group Video, 2004, MTV Video Music award Best Pop Video, 2004), Hollaback Girl, 2005 (Billboard awards, Digital Song of Yr., 2005); actor: (voice) Malice; A Kat's Tale, 2002, (film) Zoolander, 2001, (TV guest appearances) Saturday Night Live, 1996, 2001, Mad TV, 2000, Dawson's Creek, 2002, (voice) King of the Hill, 2001; (films) The Aviator, 2004. Recipient Best Choreography In a Video for Hollaback Girl, MTV Video Music Awards, 2005, Best Art Direction In a Video for What You Waiting For?, Favorite Female Artist, Am. Music Awards, 2005, New Artist of Yr., Billboard Music Awards, 2005, Best-Selling New Female Artist, World Music Awards, 2005.*

**STEFANICK, MARCIA LYNN,** medical educator, researcher; d. John Edward and Doris Marie Stefanick; m. Robert Neil Horowitz. PhD, Stanford U., 1982. Rsch. asst. Oreg. Regional Primate Rsch. Ctr., Beaverton, 1974—75; sr. rsch. scientist Stanford U., Calif., 1987—97, prof. medicine, 2003—. Steering and exec. com. chair Women's Health Initiative, Stanford, 1998—. Contbr. articles to profl. jours. Democrat. Office: Stanford U Hoover Pavilion 211 Quarry Rd Stanford CA 94305 Office Phone: 650-725-5041.

**STEFANO, KENNETH,** psychologist, psychotherapist; b. Pitts., May 28, 1964; s. Vincent Anthony Stefano and Marietta Bruno-Stefano; life ptnr. Kevin Richard Lawlor. BS in Psychology and Comm., U. Pitts., 1987; MA in Clin. Psychology, Ind. U. Pa., 1990, D in Psychology, 1992. Lic. psychologist Md., 1995. Psychologist Regional Inst. for Children & Adolescents, Rockville, Md., 1993—99; dir. of psychology internship tng. John L. Gildner Regional Inst. Children and Adolescents, 1999—2004, clin. dir., evaluation unit, 2004—; ptnr., gen. mgr. Child & Family Psychol. Svcs., Gaithersburg, Md., 1999—. Mem. adv. bd. Dept. Juvenile Svcs., Noyes Children's Ctr., Rockville, 2005—. Mem.: APA, Md. Psychol. Assn., Nat. Register Health Svc. Providers in Psychology (licentiate). Avocations: egyptology, cooking, community theater. Home: 3012 Sanctuary Ln Frederick MD 21701 Office: Regional Inst Children & Adololescents 15000 Broscharf Rd Rockville MD 20850 Office Phone: 301-471-8405. Personal E-mail: kstefano@erols.com.

**STEFANO, TONI AMANDA,** voice educator; b. Bedford, Ohio, June 11, 1970; d. Patrick Paul and Charlotte France Stefano; m. Matthew G. Hartman; 1 child, Alexander Hartman. Voice tchr. McDonogh Sch., Reisterstown, Md. Singer: Anne Truelove, The Rake's Progress, Countess Maria Luisa, With Blood, With Ink, Ulia Henriton, Where Angels Fear to Head, Depuna Cosi Pantutti, Magnet, Lucy, The Telephone, Lauretta, Gianni Schicchi, Papagena, Die Zauberflote, Christine, The Crucible. Office: McDonogh School 7 Bensmill Ct Reisterstown MD 21136

**STEFANOV, IVANKA,** music educator; d. Miodrag and Jozefa Zivkovic; m. Petar Stefanov; 1 child, Emi. B, Acad. of Musical Art, 1967—71. Treas. Jr. Friday Morning Musicale Club, Tampa, Fla., 1997—2004. Ch. pianist and choir dir. Presbyn. Ch. of Seffner, Seffner, Fla., 1992—98. Recipient Honor Roll, Nat. Guild of Piano Tchr., 2004. Mem.: Nat. Guild of Piano Teachers (assoc.), Nat. Fedn. of Musical Clubs (assoc.), Music Tchr. Nat. Assn (assoc.). Home: 9005 Bana Villa Ct Tampa FL 33635

**STEFANOV, STEFAN MINEV,** mathematics professor, researcher; b. Sevlievo, Bulgaria, Aug. 8, 1964; s. Minio Stefanov and Nedka Marinova (Kadieva) Minevi. BS, Sofia U., Bulgaria, 1988, MEd, MS, Sofia U., Bulgaria, 1989, PhD in Ops. Rsch., 1991, DSc in Math., 1996. Asst. prof. Neofit Rilski U., Blagoevgrad, Bulgaria, 1991-96, assoc. prof., 1996-97, prof., 1997—. Extraordinary prof. and rsch. fellow U. Limerick, Ireland, spring 1998; mem. rsch. group in math. inequalities and applications, Melbourne, Aus.; editor: Jour. of Inequalities in Pure and Applied Mathematics, Melbourne. Contbr. numerous articles on math. programming and numerical analysis to profl. jours.; textbooks and monographs; reviewer many internat. math. jours. Mem. Nat. Acad. Syndicate, Bulgaria, 1992—. Recipient medal Ministry of Edn., Bulgaria, 1982, contbg. to science, engring. and computer science for the monograph Separable Programming, Open Soc. Fund, 2001. Fellow Nat. Acad. Scis.; mem. Royal London Math. Soc., European Math. Soc., Am. Math. Soc. (reviewer, editor Math. Revs. Jour. 1997—), Math. Programming Soc. Phila., Soc. Indsl. and Applied Math., Union Bulgarian Mathematicians, Union Bulgarian Scientists (contbn. award 1996, 98), Activity Group on Optimization Phila., Ops. Rsch. Soc. Bulgaria, Can. Math. Soc., Can. Applied and Indsl. Math. Soc. Avocations: history, philosophy, fiction, fine arts. Home: 4 Ilio Vlaev Str 5400 Sevlievo Bulgaria Office: Neofit Rilski U 66 Ivan Mihailov Str 2700 Blagoevgrad Bulgaria E-mail: stefm@aix.swu.bg.

**STEFANOVIC, VICTOR R,** electrical engineer, consultant; b. Belgrade, Yugoslavia, Aug. 2, 1940; arrived in US, 1979; s. Ratimir and Milica Mihailovic Stefanovic; m. Dragana Kotarlic Stefanovic, July 16, 2003. MSc, McGill U., 1969, PhD, 1975. Prof. Concordia U., Montreal, Canada, 1969—79, U. Mo., Columbia, Mo., 1979—81; mgr. motion control Gen. Electric, Charlottesville, Va., 1981—85; v.p., gen. mgr. electronic sys. divsn. Electro-Craft, Mpls., 1985—86; v.p., mgr. engring. Electronic Speed Control divsn. Emerson Electric, St. Louis, 1986—89; dir. drives divsn. Vickers, Milan, 1989—92; cons. V-S Drives, Afton, Va., 1992—. Adj. prof. U. Bologna, Italy, 1990, U. Torino, Italy, 1991—92, Va. Tech., Blacksburg, 1995—; invited keynote spkr. Several Profl. Conf. Contbr. articles to tech. publs. Fellow: Inst. Elec. and Electronic Engring. Achievements include patents in field; one international patent. Avocations: sailing, skiing, tennis. Home office: 8540 Taylor Creek Rd Afton VA 22920

**STEFANYSHYN-PIPER, HEIDEMARIE M.,** astronaut; b. St. Paul, Minn., Feb. 7, 1963; d. Michael and Adelheid Stefanyshyn; m. Glenn A. Piper; 1 child. BS in Mech. Engring., MIT, 1984, MS in Mech. Engring., 1985. Tng. as Navy basic diving officer and salvage officer Naval Diving and Salvage Tng. Ctr., Panama City, Fla.; several tours of duty as an engring. duty officer in area of ship repair and maintenance; underwater ship husbandry ops. officer for the supr. of salvage and diving Naval Sea Systems Command; astronaut, mission specialist NASA Johnson Space Ctr., 1996—. Crew mem., will perform spacewalks Space Shuttle Atlantis (STS-115), 2006. Recipient Meritorious Svc. medal, Navy Commendation medal (2), Navy Achievement medal (2). Mem.: Am. Soc. Mech. Engineers. Avocations: scuba diving, swimming, running, rollerblading, ice skating. Office: Astronaut Office CB NASA Lyndon B Johnson Space Ctr Houston TX 77058*

**STEFFAN, JUDY MAE,** medical/surgical nurse; b. Beatrice, Nebr., Apr. 6, 1949; d. Wilke J. and Mary Elizabeth (Shultz) Duitsman; m. William Arthur Steffan, Apr. 22, 1967; 1 child, Rodney Alan. RN, Lincoln Gen. Hosp. Sch. Nursing, 1973. Nurse Beatrice (Nebr.) Cmty. Hosp., 1973—80, Luth. Hosp., Beatice, 1980—83; pvt. duty nurse various nursing agencies, Omaha. Bus. adviser to Frank Sinatra; polit. advisor to Sen. Ted Kennedy, 1988—96, Pres. Bill Clinton, 1992—96. Author: A Presidential Story, 1996. Mem. St. Joseph's Cath. Ch., Beatrice. Recipient Bausch and Lomb Honoary Sci. award, 1966. Democrat. Roman Catholic. Achievements include discovery of re-creation and the partitioning effect. Avocations: piano, reading. Home: 420 N 86th St Lincoln NE 68505 Office Phone: 402-488-7776.

**STEFFE, CYNTHIA,** fashion designer; m. Richard Roberts. Grad., Parsons Sch. of Design, 1981. Asst. to Donna Karan and Louis Dell'Olio Anne Klein & Co., 1981—83; designed sportswear line Spitalnick & Co., 1983—88; prin., owner Cynthia Steffe Collection, 1988—, Francess & Rita, Cynthia's Closet. Featured as one of the "New Majors" Women's Wear Daily, one of "Fifty Most Beautiful People" People Mag. Avocations: auctions, tennis, gardening. Office: 550 7th Ave Fl 21 New York NY 10018-3203*

**STEFFEN, LLOYD HOWARD,** minister, religious studies educator; b. Racine, Wis., Nov. 27, 1951; s. Howard C. and Ruth L. (Rode) S.; m. Emmajane S. Finney, Feb. 14, 1981; children: Nathan, Samuel, William. BA, New Coll., 1973; MA, Andover Newton Theol. Sch., 1978; MDiv, Yale U., 1978; PhD, Brown U., 1984. Ordained to ministry United Ch. of Christ, 1983. Chaplain Northland Coll., Ashland, Wis., 1983-90, assoc. prof., 1982-90, Lehigh U., Bethlehem, Pa., 1990-97, chaplain, 1990—, prof., 1997—; co-dir. Mellon Global Citizenship, 2003—04; chair dept. religion studies Lehigh U., Bethlehem, Pa., 2000—06. Mem. theol. comn. Wis. Conf. United Ch. of Christ, Madison, 1985—87; mem. div. ofc. and ministry NW assn. Wis. Conf., Eau Claire, 1987—90; mem. ecumenical commn. Penn N.E. Conf., 1994—96; mem. Common Ground, Bethlehem, Pa., 1994—97, chair, 1995—97; mem. ch. and ministry com. Pa. Northeast Conf., 1997—2000; mem. ethics com. St. Luke's Hosp., Bethlehem, Pa., 1998—; mem., sec., vice chair, bd. dirs. Religious Coalition for Reproductive Choice, 2002—; non-govtl. orgn. rep. UN, 2002—, sec., 2005—; 10th Curtis Lectr. Sacred Heart Univ., 1999; Frederick C. Wood Lectr. Cornell U., 2002; mem. instl. rev. bd. Haverford Coll., 2005—. Author: Self-Deception and the Common Life, 1986, Life/Choice: The Theory of Just Abortion, 1994, Abortion: A Reader, 1996, Executing Justice: The Moral Meaning of the Death Penalty, 1998, The Demonic Turn: The Power of Religion to Inspire or Restrain Violence, 2003; contbr. articles to profl. jours. Town supr. Town of La Pointe, Wis., 1988-90. Recipient 1st Pilgrim Press Church and Soc. Book award, 2001, NEH Inst. award, Harvard U., 1988, East-West Ctr., 1995; fellow, Brown U., 1982; faculty devel. grant, Northland Coll., 1986, faculty devel. grantee, 1990, Lehigh U., 1994, 1998, 2003, Travel grant, Ford Found., 2004, Mellon Global Citizenship grant, Japan, 2003. Mem. Soc. Christian Ethics, Am. Acad. Religion, Assocs. for Religion and Intellectual Life, Assn. for Coordination of Univ. Religious Affairs. Home: 1349 Woodland Cir Bethlehem PA 18017-1636 Office: Lehigh U Johnson Hall # 36 Bethlehem PA 18015 Office Phone: 610-758-3877. Business E-Mail: lhs1@lehigh.edu.

**STEFFEN, PATRICK RUSSELL,** psychology professor, researcher; s. Robert Frederick and Joann Hastings Steffen; m. Monica Cecilia Pacheco, Aug. 2, 1996; children: Alexander Robert, Cecilia Joann, William Michael. PhD, U. Miami, Coral Gables, Fla., 1998. Lic. psychologist Utah, 2000. Postdoctoral fellow Duke U. Med. Ctr., Durham, NC, 1998—2000; assoc. prof. of clin. psychology Brigham Young U., Provo, Utah, 2000—. Grantee, Am. Heart Assn., 2004—. Mem.: APA, Am. Psychosomatic Soc., Soc. of Behavioral Medicine. Office Phone: 801-422-7757. E-mail: steffen@byu.edu.

**STEFFEN, TINA MARIE,** journalist, home economist, elementary school educator; b. Amarillo, Tex., Apr. 10, 1958; d. Lynn Troy and Mary Lou (Odell) Bavousett; m. Gary Edgar Steffen, June 6, 1981; children: Christopher Michael, Erin Marie. Student, Sam Houston State U., 1976-78; BS in Home Econs., Tex. Tech U., 1981; student, U. Tex., Arlington, 2000—02. Cert. home economist, in family and consumer sci., tchr. in elem. edn., early childhood edn. and ESL. Lifestyle writer Big Spring (Tex.) Herald, 1981-82, lifestyle editor, 1982-85, dir. creative svcs., 1985-86; reporter edn. beat Daily Ardmoreite, Ardmore, Okla., 1987; freelance writer home econs. reference books and curriculum guides Tex. Edn. Agy. and Tex. Tech U. Home Econs. Curriculum Ctr., Lubbock, Tex., 1987-89; feature writer, fashion editor, Lifestyle writer Lubbock Avalanche-Jour., 1989-91; communications writer Ft. Worth Ind. Sch. Dist., 1991-92; asst. editor spl. features Fort Worth Star-Telegram, 1992-98; editor Abode mag. Impact Publs., Ft. Worth, 1993-94; spl. features editor Fort Worth Star-Telegram, 1998—2000; substitute tchr. Hurst-Euless-Bedford Sch. Dist. and Grapevine-Colleyville Ind. Sch. Dist., 2002—05; tchr. St. Peter the Apostle Cath. Sch., 2005—. Author: Hospitality Services, 1990; co-author: Apparel and Textiles Production, Management and Services, 1990; contbr. numerous articles to newspapers and mags. Mem.: Assn. Tex. Profl. Educators, Women in Comms., Inc. (chair freedom of info. com. 1990—91, Communicator of Yr. 1991), Nat. Fedn. Press Women (1st Pl. Writing award 1990), Tex. Profl. Comm. (treas. dist. 14 1990—91, state scholarship dir. 1991—93, numerous writing awards), Soc. Profl. Journalists, Am. Assn. Family and Consumer Scis., Smocking Arts Guild Am., Lone Star Smocking Guild. Mem. Christian Ch. Avocations: sewing, photography, travel, reading, needlecrafts. Home: 2403 Amber Hill Ln Euless TX 76039-8002

**STEFFENS, BRIAN DOUGLAS,** elementary school educator, director; b. Elizabeth, N.J., Mar. 25, 1958; s. Herbert Gustave and Billie Virginia Steffens; m. Kyle Marie Gullery, July 14, 1984; children: Daryl Ginger, Jaimeson Douglas. MusB Edn. magna cum laude, SUNY, 1980; MusM Edn. Ithaca Coll., 1984. Cert. elem., secondary tchr. Va. Dir. band Madrid-Waddinton Sr. H.S., NY, 1981—82, Monroe-Woodbury Sr. H.S., Central Valley, NY, 1984—87, Langley H.S., McLean, Va., 1987—2000, Farmwell Sta. Mid. Sch., Ashburn, Va., 2000—02, River Bend Mid. Sch., Sterling, Va., 2002—. Composer: Sunrise on the River's Bend. Moderator, bd. deacons Ashburn Presbyn. Ch., Va., 2003—05. Named Tchr. of Yr., Langley H.S., 1996; recipient Music Dept. Blue Ribbon, Va. Music Educators Assn., 2005. Mem.: Music Educators Nat. Conf. (licentiate). Presbyterian. Home: 21065 View Glass Terr Sterling VA 20164 Office: River Bend Mid Sch 46240 Algonkian Pkwy Sterling VA 20165 Office Phone: 703-444-7574. Office Fax: 703-444-7578. Personal E-mail: bksteffens@aol.com. Business E-Mail: bsteffen@loudoun.k12.va.us.

**STEFFENSEN, DWIGHT A.,** former medical products and data processing services executive; b. Fresno, Calif., 1943; BA, Stanford U., 1965. Corp. contr. Synergex Corp. (merged with Bergen Brunswig Corp. 1985), Orange, Calif., 1969-72, chief fin. officer, v.p., 1972-80, chief oper. officer, chief fin. officer, exec. v.p., treas., 1980-83, pres., chief exec. officer, 1983-85, exec. v.p., 1985—; pres. Drug Service Inc., 1975-80; pres., coo, dir. Bergen Brunswig Corp.; chmn. & CEO Merisel, Inc., El Segundo, Calif., 1996—2000.

**STEFFER, ROBERT WESLEY,** clergyman; b. Spokane, Wash., June 24, 1934; s. Harold Wesley and Kathryne (Trumble) S.; m. Diane DeMoisey, Aug. 19, 1960; children: Erika Kirsten, Beauregard Gregory Robert. BA, Whitworth Coll., 1956; BD, Lexington Theol. Sem., 1959; MA, Ind. U., 1966, PhD, 1967. Ordained to ministry Christian Ch. (Disciples of Christ), 1959. Civilian dir. religious edn. U.S. Army Armor Ctr., Ft. Knox, Ky., 1960-64; assoc. regional min. Christian Ch. (Disciples of Christ), Oklahoma City, 1967-71; prof. Phillips U., Enid, Okla., 1971-76; fraternal worker div. overseas ministries Christian Ch. (Disciples of Christ), Barrow-in-Furness, Cumbria, Eng., 1976-79; Lilly vis. prof. religious edn. Christian Theol. Sem., Indpls., 1979-81; dir. edn. for mission Christian Ch. (Disciples of Christ), Indpls., 1981-87; exec. regional min. Christian Ch. (Disciples of Christ) in Can., Guelph, Ont., 1987-97; interim sr. minister Eureka (Ill.) Christian Ch., 1997-98; curator Cane Ridge Hist. Preservation Project, 1998—. Sec. Coll. Chs. of Christ in Can., Guelph, 1987-97. Editor Cane Ridge Bull., 1999—; contbr. articles to religious publs. and ency. Col., chaplain USAR ret., 1964—. Lilly Found. fellow in adult edn. Ind. U., 1964-66. Mem. Disciples of Christ Hist. Soc. (life, trustee 1990-94), Religious Edn. Assn. (bd. dirs. 1994-97), Conf. Regional Mins. and Moderators (2nd v.p.), Ch. Fin. Coun. (bd. dirs. 1995-96, exec. com. 1995), Phi Delta Kappa, Theta Phi. Democrat. Avocations: gardening, reading, travel, music. Office: PO Box 26 Paris KY 40362-0026 Mailing: PO Box 5226 Paris KY 40362-5226 Office Phone: 859-987-5350. E-mail: canerdgmtg@aol.com.

**STEFFEY, FRED H.,** retired lawyer; b. Wilmington, N.C., July 8, 1931; s. Fred L. and Leila Newman Steffey; m. Betty Stimpson Steffey, Sept. 9, 1951; children: Cynthia, Eric. BA, Duke U., 1952, LLB, 1955. Instr. Duke U.,

Durham, NC, 1955—56; trial atty. IRS Office Chief Counsel, Atlanta, 1956—62, Jacksonville, Fla., 1956—62; ptnr. Mahoney, Hadlow & Adams, Jacksonville, 1962—82; pvt. practice Jacksonville, 1982—2005. Dir. Hope Haven Childrens Clinic, Jacksonville, 1975—95. Mem.: ABA, Fla. Bar, N.C. State Bar, Rotary Internat.

**STEFFY, JOHN RICHARD,** nautical archaeologist, educator; b. Lancaster, Pa., May 1, 1924; s. Milton Grill and Zoe Minerva (Fry) S.; m. Esther Lucille Koch, Oct. 20, 1951; children: David Alan, Loren Craig. Student, Pa. Area Coll., Lancaster, 1946—47, Milw. Sch. Engring., 1947—49. Ptnr. M.G. Steffy & Sons, Denver, Pa., 1950-72; ship reconstructor Kyrenia Ship Project, Cyprus, 1972-73, Inst. Nautical Archaeology, College Station, Tex., 1973—; from lectr. to prof. anthropology Tex. A&M U., College Station, 1976-88, Sara W. and George O. Yamani prof. nautical archaeology, 1989-90, prof. emeritus, 1990—. Lectr. on ship constrn. Author: Wooden Shipbuilding and the Interpretation of Shipwrecks, 1994; co-editor: The Athlit Ram, 1991; contbr. chpts. to books and articles to profl. jours. Sec. Denver Borough Authority, Pa., 1962-72. With USN, 1942—45. MacArthur Found. fellow, 1985. Republican. Meth. Office: Tex A&M U Inst Nautical Archaeology College Station TX 77845 Business E-Mail: rsteffy@neo.tamu.edu.

**STEGALL, MARK D.,** surgeon, medical educator; b. Lubbock, Tex., June 24, 1957; BA, Harvard Coll., 1979; postgrad., Trinity Coll., Oxford (Eng.), 1979; MD, Columbia U., 1984. Diplomate Am. Bd. Surgery. Resident in surgery Presbyn. Hosp., N.Y.C., 1984-91; post-doctoral rsch. scientist Columbia U., N.Y.C., 1987-89; fellow in transplantation U. Wis., Madison, 1991-93; asst. prof. surgery, dir. pancreas and islet transplantation U. Colo., Denver, 1993-98; dir. kidney and pancreas transplantation surgery Mayo Clinic, Rochester, Minn., 1998—, chmn. divsn. transplantation surgery, 2002—; assoc. prof. surgery Mayo Med. Sch., Rochester, 1998—. Post-Doctoral Rsch. fellow N.Y. State Diabetes Fund, 1987-88; recipient NIH-NIAID Individual Nat. Rsch. Svc. award, 1988-89, Upjohn prize N.Y. State Transplantation Soc., 1988. Mem. Am. Soc. Transplant Surgeons (Upjohn award 1989, Ortho Faculty Devel. award 1995), Soc. Univ. Surgeons, Assn. Acad. Surgery. Office: Mayo Clinic Campus Box C-318 200 1st St SW Rochester MN 55905-0002

**STEGENGA, JAMES JAY,** bank examiner, director; b. Berea, Ky., May 1, 1954; s. Preston Jay and Marcia J Stegenga. BA, Hope Coll., Holland, Mich., 1976; MA, U. So. Calif., L.A., 1978; MBA, San Diego State U., 1982. Cert. regulatory compliance mgr. Inst. Cert. Bankers, Washington, 1999, bank examiner FDIC, 1990. Asst. examiner FDIC, Seattle, 1986—88, bank examiner Sacramento, 1990—98, sr. bank compliance examiner Grand Rapids, Mich., 1998—. Mem.: Inst. Cert. Bankers (licentiate), Mensa. Mem. Reformed Church In America. Office Phone: 616-942-8391.

**STEGER, CHARLES WILLIAM,** academic administrator; b. Richmond, Va., June 16, 1947; s. Charles William and Virginia Belle (Garrett) S.; m. Janet Grey Baird, Sept. 13, 1969; children: Christopher B., David C. BArch, Va. Poly. Inst. & State U., 1970, MArch, 1971, PhD, 1978. Registered architect, Va. Project planner, architect Wiley & Wilson Inc., Lynchburg, Va., 1971-72, mgr. urban planning dept., 1973-74; dir. Environ. Design Consortium Inc., Blacksburg, Va., 1974-85; inst. grad. urban design program Coll. Architecture and Urban Studies, Va. Poly. Inst. and State U., Blacksburg, 1974-76, chmn. grad. urban design program, 1976-81; dean Coll. Architecture and Urban Studies, Va. Poly. Inst. and State U., Blacksburg, 1981-93; acting v.p. for pub. svc. Va. Poly. Inst. and State U., Blacksburg, 1990-93, v.p. for devel. and univ. rels., 1993-99; pres. Va. Tech. U., 2000—. Bd. dirs. Va. Found. Architecture, Richmond, Innovative Tech. Authority; mem. Gov.'s Secure Va. Tech. Initiative, 2001-02; mem. Gov.'s Va. Preparedness and Security Panel, 2001-02; bd. mem. Va. Advanced Shipbuilding and Carrier Integration Ctr., 2001—. Contbr. articles to jours. in field. Bd. dirs. Hollins Coll., Roanoke, Va., 1987-96, Boswil (Switzerland) Found., 1986—. Ct. in the Square, Roanoke, 1993-99; v.p. Va. Tech. Found., Inc., 1993-99; adv. coun. Va. Ctr. on Rural Devel., 1992—; commr. Govs. Commn. on Population Growth and Devel., Richmond, 1989-94. Fellow AIA, bd. dirs. ACSA Health Facilities Rsch. Program, Washington 1989—, ACSA Coun. on Arch. Rsch., 1987—); mem. Am. Planning Assn., Am. Inst. Cert. Planners, Commonwealth Club (Richmond, Va.), Shenandoah Club (Roanoke, Va.). Avocations: cattle farming, golf, canoeing. Office: Va Tech (0131) Pres 210 Burruss Hall Blacksburg VA 24061

**STEGER, EDWARD HERMAN,** retired chemist; b. New Orleans, Dec. 11, 1936; s. Herman Christoph and Katherine (Walther) S.; m. Amy Patricia Duvall, July 29, 1960; children: David B., Sandra E. BS, Tulane U., 1958. Analytical chemist Absuit Rsch. Corp., Gainesville, Va., 1960-64; head control lab., 1964—2004, ret., 2004. Presenter at profl. confs. Contbr. articles to Fine Particle Soc. Jour. Lt. USNR, 1958—60. Mem.: NY Acad. Scis., Am. Chem. Soc., Alpha Chi Sigma, Phi Eta Sigma, Phi Beta Kappa. Baptist. Home: 4311 Alta Vista Dr Fairfax VA 22030-5302

**STEGER, RALPH JAMES,** chemist; b. Meridian, Okla., Jan. 24, 1940; s. Daniel Bose and Opal Creola (Brothers) S. BS in Chemistry and Math., Langston U., 1962. Cartographer Aeronautical Chart and Info. Ctr. ACIC USAF, St. Louis, 1962-63; lab. technician Sigma Chem. Co., St. Louis, 1963; phys. scientist U.S. Army Chem. Corps, Edgewood Arsenal, Md., 1963-65; rsch. chemist Chem. Rsch., Devel. and Engring. Ctr. SMCCR Rsch. Lab. Analytical Div., Aberdeen Proving Ground, Md., 1965-86; chemist Chem. Rsch., Devel. and Engring. Ctr. SMCCR-Detection, Detection Technology, Aberdeen Proving Ground, 1986-97. Adv. com. Garrison Gents, Balt., 1980—; ACOR monitoring govt. contracts, Balt., 1987—. Contbr. articles to profl. jours, Mem. AAAS, NY Acad. Scis, Okla. Hist. Soc., Omwel CBDCOM-RTE Aberdeen Proving Ground MD 21010-5423 Personal E-mail: rjsteger@erols.com.

**STEGMAYER, JOSEPH HENRY,** housing industry executive; b. Teaneck, NJ, Jan. 4, 1951; s. Arthur Harry and Alicia (Ward) S.; m. Delene Russell. BS in Fin., U. Louisville, 1973. Spl. projects Worthington Industries Inc., Columbus, Ohio, 1973-75; dir. investor rels., 1975-77, dir. corp. rels., 1977-80, v.p. corp. devel., 1980-82, v.p., CFO, treas., 1982-93, also bd. dirs.; pres., vice chmn. Clayton Homes, Inc., Knoxville, Tenn., 1995—98, also bd. dirs.; pres. retail & CFO Champion Enterprises, Inc., Auburn Hills, Mich., 1998-2000; chmn., CEO Centex Mfg. Housing Group, Dallas, 2000—03; chmn., pres., CEO Cavco Industries, 2003—. Editor: We've Only Scratched the Surface, 1981. Chmn. YMCA, Columbus, 1981-83; pres. Columbus Zoo, 1987-90, chmn., 1990-93; bd. dirs. Muskingum Coll., 1984-93, Knoxville Zoo, Found. of Diocese of Columbus, United Way Knoxville; fin. chmn. Ronald McDonald House, Columbus; mem. chancellor's assocs. bd. U. Tenn.; dir. Desert Voices Oral Learning Ctr. Named Citizen of Yr., Columbus Jaycees, 1984; recipient Outstanding Achievement in Fin. award Phi Beta Kappa, 1984. Roman Catholic. Avocations: scuba diving, travel, investing. Office: CAVCO 1001 N Central Ave Phoenix AZ 85004 Office Phone: 602-256-6263.

**STEHLE, EDWARD RAYMOND,** secondary education educator, school system administrator; b. Pitts., May 30, 1942; s. Edward August and Mary Josephine (Veverka) S.; m. Alberta McConnell; 1 child, Christian Dollison (dec.). BA, U. Pitts., 1964; MA, Columbia U., 1966, doctoral student, 1966-68. Instr. European history C.W. Post Coll., Long Island U., Greenvale, N.Y., 1967-68, Middlebury (Vt.) Coll., 1968-69; history master The Lawrenceville (N.J.) Sch., Lawrenceville, N.J., 1969—, dir. day students, 1978-83, asst. dir. coll. counseling, 1983-88, chmn. history dept., 1988-94; asst. dir. The N.J. Scholars Program, Lawrenceville, N.J., 1982-91, chmn. bd., 1988-96, bd. dirs., 1988—. Cons. U. Del. Sea Grant Coll., Newark, 1981-82; cons. on history of migrations Statue of Liberty-Ellis Island Found., N.Y.C., 1985-88; mem. selection com. Morris County (N.J.) Summer Opportunities for Tchrs. Program, Morristown, 1985-86; trustee Craftsbury Chamber Players, Greensboro, Vt., 1985-89; N.E.H. Coun. for Basic Edn. fellowship ind. study in the humanities, 1997. Co-author: A Guide to Programming

in Basic Plus, 1975; contbr. Harper's Encyclopedia of the Modern World, 1972. Vice pres. Assoc. Mems., Ch. of Christ, Greensboro, 1974-76, pres., 1976-78. Vis. scholar Cambridge (Eng.) U., 1996. Mem. Am. Hist. Assn., Nassau Club (Princeton, N.J.), Mountainview Country Club (Greensboro, Vt.), N. Am. Conf. British Studies. Democrat. Episcopalian. Avocation: painting. Home: 2810 Main St Lawrenceville NJ 08648-1017 Office: The Lawrenceville Sch Main St Lawrenceville NJ 08620-2310 E-mail: estehle@lawrenceville.org.

**STEHMAN, FREDERICK BATES,** gynecologic oncologist, educator; b. Washington, July 20, 1946; s. Vernon Andrew and Elizabeth Coats (Bates) S.; m. Helen Sellinger, July 17, 1971; children— Christine Renee, Eileen Patricia, Andrea Kathleen, Lara Michelle. A.B., U. Mich., 1968, M.D., 1972. Diplomate Am. Bd. Ob-gyn. Resident in ob-gyn. U. Kans. Med. Ctr., Kansas City, 1972-75, resident in surgery, 1975-77; fellow in gynecol. oncology UCLA, 1977-79; asst. prof., attending staff Ind. U. Med. Ctr., Indpls., 1979-83, assoc. prof., 1983-87, prof., 1987—, chief gynecol. oncology, 1984-88, interim chmn., 1992-94, chair 1994—; chief ob-gyn service Wishard Meml. Hosp., Indpls., 1987-95. Author: (with B.J. Masterson and R.P. Carter) Gynecologic Oncology for Medical Students, 1975; also articles. Nat. Cancer Inst. grantee, 1981-89. Fellow Am. Coll. Obstetricians and Gynecologists, ACS (chpt. dir. 1984-92); mem. AMA, Am. Soc. Clin. Oncology, Am. Cancer Soc., Am. Gynecology and Obstetrics Soc., Int. Med. Assn., Assn. Profs. Gynecology and Obstetrics, Central Assn. Obstetricians and Gynecologists, Gynecol. Oncology Group, K.E. Krantz Soc., Marion County Med. Soc., Soc. Gynecol. Oncologists, Western Assn Gynecol. Oncologists, Phi Chi. Office. Ind U Med Ctr 550 University Blvd # 2440 Indianapolis IN 46202-5149

**STEHNEY, ANN KATHRYN,** academic administrator, mathematician, educator; b. Oak Ridge, Tenn., June 30, 1946; d. Andrew F. and Virginia Allen Stehney; m. Philip J. Heyman, Aug. 2, 2004; children: Jessica S. Charlap, Emily Elizabeth S. Charlap. AB, Bryn Mawr Coll., 1967; PhD, SUNY, Stony Brook, 1971. Math. prof. Wellesley (Mass.) Coll., 1971—85; rsch. staff mem. IDA Ctr. Comm. Rsch., Princeton, NJ, 1983—94; assoc. dean Douglass Coll. Rutgers U., New Brunswick, NJ, 1994—2000; v.p. academic affairs, dean faculty Cedar Crest Coll., Allentown, Pa., 2000—01; sr. lectr. math. Moravian Coll., Bethlehem, Pa., 2001—; v.p. planning and rsch. Moravian Coll. and Moravian Theol. Sem., Bethlehem, 2002—. Vis. scholar Enrico Fermi Inst., U. Chgo., 1974—75; vis. assoc. prof. SUNY, Stony Brook, 1981—82; faculty assoc. math. dept. Rutgers U., 1994—2000. Co-editor (book) Selected Papers in Geometry, 1979; contbr. articles to profl. publs., book revs. Mem. edn. com. DaVinci Discovery Ctr. Sci. and Tech., Allentown, 2004; bd. dirs. Congregation Brith Sholom, Bethlehem, 2004, Coalition Jewish Edn. in Lehigh Valley, Allentown, 2004. Mem.: Math. Assn. Am. NJ, Commn. Profls. Sci. and Tech. (mem. com. representing Am. Math. Soc. 1990—96), Am. Math. Assn. (mem. various coms. 1983), Math Assoc Am. (life; mem. various coms. 1975), Sigma Xi, Pi Mu Epsilon. Achievements include research in differential geometry, general relativity, cryptology, applied mathematics. Office: Moravian Coll 1200 Main St Bethlehem PA 18018 Office Phone: 610-861-1555. Office Fax: 610-861-1445. Business E-Mail: stehney@moravian.edu.

**STEIB, JAMES TERRY,** bishop; b. May 17, 1940; Ordained priest Roman Cath. Ch., 1967. Titular bishop, Fallaba, 1983; aux. bishop St. Louis, 1983; consecrated bishop, 1984; bishop Diocese of Memphis, 1993—. Address: Diocese of Memphis PO Box 341669 Memphis TN 38184-1669

**STEICHEN, RANDALL R.,** lawyer; b. 1952; BA cum laude, Northwestern Coll., 1976; JD with distinction, Univ. Iowa, 1980. Bar: Iowa 1981, Colo. 1982, Wash. 1989. Law clerk, Hon. Louis W. Schultz Iowa Supreme Ct., 1980—82; ptnr., trial practice group Dorsey & Whitney LLP, Seattle, and co-chair, construction and design law group. Arbitrator Am. Arbitration Assn. Mng. editor Iowa Law Rev., 1979—80, lectr., writer in field. Named a Super Lawyer, Wash. Law & Politics, 2003. Mem.: ABA, Associated Builders and Contractors of Western Wash. (v.p., bd. dir.), Ct. Fed. Claims Bar Assn., Board of Contract Appeals Bar Assn., Seattle-King County Bar Assn., Wash. State Bar Assn. Office: Dorsey & Whitney LLP Ste 3400 US Bank Ctr 1420 Fifth Ave Seattle WA 98101-4010 Office Phone: 206-903-8857. Office Fax: 206-903-8820. Business E-Mail: steichen.randall@dorsey.com.

**STEIDEL, CHARLES C.,** astronomy educator; b. Ithaca, NY, Oct. 14, 1962; married. AB in Astrophys. Scis., Princeton U., NJ, 1984; PhD in Astronomy, Calif. Inst. Tech., Pasadena, 1990. Parisot fellow U. Calif., Berkeley, 1989—90, Hubble fellow 1990—93; asst. prof. physics MIT, Cambridge, Mass., 1993—95; asst. prof. astronomy Calif. Inst. Tech., 1995—97, assoc. prof., 1997—98, prof., 1998—. Mem. telescope allocation com. Cerro Tololo Inter-Am. Obs., 1994—97; mem. sci. steering com. Keck Obs., 1996—2003, co-chair sci. steering com. 1997—2003; mem. Hubble space telescope second decade com., 1998—99; mem. external sci. rev. panel Next Generation Space Telescope, 1998—99; mem. space scis. origins sub-com. NASA, 1998—2000; chair sci. working grp. Calif. Extremely Large Telescope, 1999—2002, co-chair steering com., 2000—02; mem. Hubble fellowship selection com., 2000; chair sci. adv. com. Thirty Meter Telescope (formerly Calif. Extremely Large Telescope), 2003—. Contbr. articles to sci. jours. Recipient Young Investigator award, NSF, 1994—99, Helen B. Warner prize, Am. Astron. Soc., 1997; fellow Alfred P. Sloan Found., 1994—96, David and Lucile Packard Found., 1997—2002, MacArthur Found., 2002. Mem.: NAS (US/Japan Frontiers in Sci. organizing com. 1997—98). Office: Calif Inst Tech Dept Astronomy 1201 E Calif Blvd Pasadena CA 91125-0001 Home: 230 S Arroyo Blvd Pasadena CA 91105*

**STEIDER, DORIS,** artist; b. Decatur, Ill., Apr. 10, 1924; d. Rudy C. and Helen (Regan) Sleeter; m. Robert E. Steider, Nov. 16, 1944 (div.); children: Kristen (Mrs. Gerald Latham), Robert S., Tim D; m. Carroll B. McCampbell, May 19, 1972. BS, Purdue U.; MA, U. N.Mex. Exhibited in more than 190 maj. juried shows including Smithsonian Instn., Washington, Gilcrease Inst., Tulsa, Army Traveling Print Shows, 1963, 64, Witte Mus. Western Art, San Antonio, Mont. State Hist. Soc. Mus., Helena, Mus. N.Mex. Biennials, N.Mex. State Fair Profl. Show, Nat. Art Shows, La Junta, Colo., 1978, 81, 83, Nebraskaland Days Invitational Art Exbhn., 1976—; exhibited in over 100 one-woman shows; represented in permanent collections Holt Rinehart and Winston, Purdue U. Galleries, Time Inc., Loewen Group British Columbia, West Tex. Mus., U. N.Mex. Art Mus., N.Mex. State Fair Collection, Albuquerque Pub. Libr., over 2500 in pvt. collections; Book (by Mary Carroll Nelson) A Vision of Silence: The Egg Tempera Landscapes of Doris Steider, 1997. Mem. Albuquerque Fine Arts Adv. Bd., 1966-72; chmn. standards com. N.Mex. Arts and Crafts Bd., 1964-70; chmn. invitational rev. bd. SW Arts and Crafts Fair, 1977-78. Doris Steider St. named in her honor Albuquerque, 1989; recipient over 85 local, regional, nat. and internat. awards, Disting. Alumni honor Purdue U., 2000. Mem.: Soc. of Layerists in Multi-Media. Home: 12905 Sunrise Trail Pl NE Albuquerque NM 87111-8194 Personal E-mail: steiderart@cs.com.

**STEIDLEY, JUAN DWAYNE,** lawyer, judge; b. Claremore, Okla., Mar. 8, 1959; s. J.D. and Gwendolyn Ann (Barnes) S.; m. Teresa Ann Brim, July 31, 1987; 1 child, Terrence. BA, Okla. State U., 1981; JD, Tulsa U., 1984. Bar: Okla. 1985. Judge, 1999—. Mem. Ho. of Rep. Okla. Assn. Okla. Claremore City, 1986-98; past chmn. Sequoyah Dist. Boy Scouts Am. Methodist. Home: 2710 Highwood Ct Claremore OK 74017-4872 Office: Rogers County Court House 219 S Miss Divs II Claremore OK 74017

**STEIER, JEFFREY DAVID,** neurologist; b. Queens, N.Y., Mar. 21, 1952; s. Morton and Ruth Steier; m. Elizabeth Schleeter, Aug. 6, 1983; children: Nathan, Julia, Emma. BA, U. Del., 1973; MD, SUNY, Buffalo, 1978. Diplomate Am. Acad. Neurology, Am. Bd. Elective Medicine, cert. Clin. Neurophysiology. Resident U. Minn. Mayo Clinic, Mpls., 1978—84; mem. staff Scottsdale Neurol. Cons., Ariz., 1984—. Mem. nat. bd. Myasthenia Gravis, Phoenix, mem. Ariz. bd.; mem. Stroke Coun., 2000—. Mem.: Am.

Clinic Neurophysiology Soc., Am. Assn. Sleep Medicine, Am. Assn. Neurology, Am. Assn. Electrodiagnostic Medicine, Am. Epilepsy Soc. Avocations: astrophotography, astronomy. Office: Scottsdale Neurological Cons 10210 N 92d St 352 Scottsdale AZ 85258

**STEIER, MICHAEL EDWARD,** cardiac surgeon; b. N.Y.C., Mar. 22, 1942; s. Philip (deceased) and Gertrude S.; m. Sheila Elaine Finkelstein, June 9, 1963; children: Douglas, James, Lauren. BA, Long Island U., 1964; MD, Univ. Health Scis., Chgo., 1968. Diplomate Am. Bd. Surgery, Am. Bd. Thoracic Surgery. Resident in gen. surgery St. Vincent's Hosp., N.Y.C., 1969-73; resident in thoracic surgery Mayo Clinic, Rochester, Minn., 1973-75; cardiac surgeon S.W. Fla. Regional Med. Ctr., Ft. Myers, Fla., 1975—; Lee Meml. Hosp., Ft. Myers, 1975—, Cape Coral (Fla.) Hosp., 1977—; Naples (Fla.) Cmty. Hosp., 1996—; pres. Cardiac Surg. Assocs. West Fla., Ft. Myers; ret. Chief surgery, S.W. Fla. Regional Med. Ctr., Ft. Myers, 1980-82, pres. med. staff, 1982; cons. Naples Cmty. Hosp., 1996—. Capt., USAR, 1969-78. Fellow ACS, Am. Coll. Chest Physicians, Am. Coll. Cardiology; mem. Soc. for Thoracic Surgeons, N.Y. Acad. Scis., Cardiac Surg. Assn. S.W. Fla. (pres. 1993-99), Explorers Club. Office: Cardiac Surgical Assocs SW Fla 2675 Winkler Ave Fort Myers FL 33901-9342

**STEIGBIGEL, ROY THEODORE,** epidemiologist, educator, research scientist; b. Bklyn., Nov. 23, 1941; s. Samuel and Lillian I. (Parker) S.; m. Julia Ann Enterline, June 10, 1967 (div. 1983); children: Keith D., Glenn N.; m. Sidonie Ann Morrison, Oct. 15, 1985; 1 child, Andrew M. BA, Carleton Coll., 1962; MD, U. Rochester, 1966. Diplomate Am. Bd. Internal Medicine, Am. Bd. Infectious Disease. Resident U. Rochester, NY, 1966-68, Stanford U., Palo Alto, Calif., 1970-71, fellow, 1971-73; from asst. to assoc. prof. U. Rochester, NY, 1973-83; prof. SUNY, Stony Brook, 1983—. Mem. adv. bd. infectious disease U.S. Pharmacopea, Rockville, Md., 1980—; mem. adv. panels NIH, Bethesda, Md., 1985-87. Contbr. over 15 chpts. to books and over 100 articles to profl. jours. Served in USPHS, 1968-70. Fellow NIH, 1971-73, grantee, 1985—. Fellow ACP, Infectious Disease Soc. Am. Office: SUNY Stony Brook Sch Medicine hsc T 15 080 Stony Brook NY 11794-8153 Office Phone: 631-444-3490. Business E-mail: roy.steigbigel@stonybrook.edu.

**STEIGER, PAUL ERNEST,** editor, journalist; b. NYC, Aug. 15, 1942; s. Ernest and Mary Agnes (Walsh) Steiger; m. Heidi Brine, Nov. 23, 1985 (div.); children: Isabelle Amanda, William Ernest; m. Wendy Brandes, July 22, 2001; children from previous marriage: Erika Maren, Laura Arlene. BA in economics, Yale U., 1964. Staff reporter Wall Street Jour., San Francisco, 1966-68, asst. mng. editor NYC, 1983-85, dep. mng. editor, 1985—91, mng. editor, 1991—, v.p., 1992—; staff writer LA Times, 1968-71, econ. corr. Washington, DC bur., 1971-78, bus. editor LA, 1978-83. Mem. Pulitzer Prize Bd., 1999—; rep., Dow Jones SmartMoney Bd., Wall Street Journal Mag., SmartMoney.com. co-author: (book) The 70's Crash and How to Survive It, 1970. Chmn. Com. to Protect Journalists, 2005—. Recipient G.M. Loeb Award, UCLA, 1971, 1974, 1978, John Hancock Award, 1971, George Beveridge Editor of Yr. Award, Nat. Press Found., 2001, Leadership Award, Am. Soc. Newspaper Editors, 2002, Lifetime Achievement, John E. Anderson Sch. Mgmt., UCLA, 2002, Columbia Journalism Award, Columbia U. Sch. Journalism, 2002, Decade of Excellence Award, World Leadership Forum, 2005, Mo. Honor medal, Mo. Sch. Journalism, 2005; Poynter Fellow, Yale U., 2001—02. Office: Wall Street Journal Dow Jones & Co Inc 200 Liberty St New York NY 10281-1003*

**STEIGER, RANDI JANINE,** English educator; b. New Rochelle, N.Y., Oct. 30, 1953; m. Justin E. Steiger, Nov. 2, 1986. BA magna cum laude, SUNY, Albany, 1975; MS in Edn., Fordham U., 1993. Cert. English tchr., N.Y. English tchr. Monticello (N.Y.) High Sch., 1975-86, Susan E. Wagner High Sch., Staten Island, N.Y., 1986-88, Humanities H.S., N.Y.C., 1988—, acad. adviser, 1989—95, guidance program office liaison, 1995—. Mem. parent adv. coun. Humanities High Sch., 1988—, mem. portfolio adv. coun., 1991—; conflict mediator N.Y.C. Bd. Edn., 1992. Mem. N.Y. State Reading Assn., N.Y. State English Coun. (Educator of Excellence 1997). Avocations: skiing, tennis, reading, movies. Home: 305 E 24th St Apt 8D New York NY 10010-4024 Office Phone: 212-675-5350 108. E-mail: steiger30@yahoo.com.

**STEIGERWALD, LOUIS JOHN, III,** corporate executive; b. Syracuse, NY, Dec. 24, 1953; s. Louis John Jr. and Virginia (Irving) S.; m. Mary Rescorl, May 31, 1980; children: Amy Elizabeth, Louis John IV. BS, St. Lawrence U., 1976. Salesperson Cathedral Candle Co., Syracuse, 1976-80, v.p., 1980-2001, pres., 2001—, also bd. dirs. Account exec. United Way Ctrl. NY, Syracuse, 1982-83, sect. chmn., 1984-85; active Boy Scouts Am., 1992-2003. Mem. Nat. Ch. Goods Assn. (bd. dirs. 1990-2000, pres. 1997, 98), Nat. Candle Assn. (bd. dirs. 1989-99, 2005—), Ea. Ch. Goods Guild, Onondaga Hist. Assn. (bd. dirs. 2004—). Avocations: golf, tennis, woodworking, skiing, music. Office: Cathedral Candle Co 510 Kirkpatrick St Syracuse NY 13208-2100

**STEIKER, CAROL S.,** law educator; b. Phila., May 31, 1961; AB in History and Lit., Harvard-Radcliffe, 1982; JD, Harvard U., 1986. Bar: NY 1987, DC 1988. Law clk. to Judge J. Skelly Wright US Ct. Appeals DC Cir.; law clk. to Justice Thurgood Marshall US Supreme Ct.; asst. prof. law Harvard Law Sch., Cambridge, Mass., 1992—98, prof., 1998—, assoc. dean academic affairs, 1998—2001. Office: Harvard Law Sch 1563 Massachusetts Ave Cambridge MA 02138 Office Phone: 617-496-5457. Office Fax: 617-496-5156. Business E-mail: steiker@law.harvard.edu.

**STEIL, GEORGE KENNETH, SR.,** lawyer; b. Darlington, Wis., Dec. 16, 1924; s. George John and Laura (Donahoe) S.; m. Mavis Elaine Andrews, May 24, 1947; children: George Kenneth, John R., MIchelle Steil Bryski, Marcelaine Steil-Zimmermann. Student, Platteville State Tchrs. Coll., 1942-43; JD, U. Wis., Madison, 1950. Bar: Wis. 1950, U.S. Tax Ct. 1971, U.S. Dist. Ct. (western dist.) Wis. 1950. Assoc. J. G. McWilliams, Janesville, 1950-53; ptnr. McWilliams and Steil, Janesville, 1954-60, Brennan, Steil, Basting & MacDougall, Janesville, 1960-72; pres. Brennan, Steil & Basting (S.C., and predecessor), Janesville, 1972—. Lectr. law U. Wis., 1974; bd. dirs. Acuity Ins. Co., Sheboygan, Wis., Acuity Bank, SSB, Tomah, Wis., chmn. 2000—; trustee, bd. dirs. Roman Cath. Diocese of Madison; mem. Wis. Supreme Ct. Bd. Atty. Profl. Responsibility, 1982-87, chmn., 1984-87; chmn. gov.'s adv. coun. jud. selection State of Wis., 1987-92; chmn. Wis. Lottery Bd., 1987-90. Bd. dirs. St. Coletta Sch. for Exceptional Children, Jefferson, Wis., 1972-76, 78-84, 86-89, chmn., 1982-83; bd. regents U. Wis., 1990-97, pres., 1992-94; bd. dirs. U. Wis. Hosp. Authority, 1996—2004, chmn., 2002-04; bd. dirs. chair U. Wis. Med. Found., 1996-99. Recipient Disting. Svc. award U. Wis. Law Alumni, 1991, Cath. Leadership awrd Diocese of Madison, 1998; named Knight of St. Gregory, Pope John Paul II, 1997. Fellow Am. Bar Found. (life); Am. Coll. Trust and Estate Counsel; mem. ABA, Jamesville Area C. of C. (pres. 1970-71), State Bar Wis. (pres. 1977-78), Wis. Bar Found. (bd. dirs. 1976-2003, Charles L. Goldberg Disting. Svc. award 1990). Roman Catholic. Home: 2818 Cambridge Ct Janesville WI 53548-2797 Office: PO Box 1148 1 E Milwaukee St Janesville WI 53545 Office Phone: 608-756-4141. Business E-Mail: gsteilsr@brennansteil.com.

**STEIMAN, H. ROBERT,** dean, dental educator; BS, ND State U., 1964; MS, Wayne State U., 1967, PhD in physiology, 1969; DDS, U. Detroit, 1973; MS in endodontics. Ind. U., 1979. Diplomate Am. Bd. Endodontics. Chmn. dept. physiology, dept. basic scis. U. Detroit-Mercy Sch. Dentistry, named chmn. dept. endodontics, 1980, interim dean, 2000—01, dean, 2001—. Office: 8200 W Outer Dr Box 98 Detroit MI 48219 Office Phone: 313-494-6621. Office Fax: 313-484-6627. Business E-Mail: steimanr@udmercy.edu.*

**STEIN, ALVIN,** surgeon; b. Paterson, N.J., Oct. 16, 1936; s. David and Minnie (Bochner) S.; B.A., NYU, 1957; M.D., Chgo. Med. Sch., 1961; m. Leona L. Greenbaum, June 22, 1958; children— Eileen Gale, Randy Sue, David. Diplomate Am. Bd. Orthopedic Surgery. Intern, Hosp. for Joint Diseases, N.Y.C., 1961-62, resident, 1962-63; resident Met. Hosp. and Flower-Fifth Ave. Hosp., N.Y.C., 1963-64, 65-66, Hosp. for Crippled Chil-

dren, Newark, 1964-65; practice medicine, specializing in orthopedic surgery, Bronx, N.Y., 1966-73, Ft. Lauderdale area, Fla., 1973—; chief Children's Orthopedic Service and Bronx Lebanon Hosp., 1960-73; chief staff Fla. Med. Center, 1974-75; mem. staff Westside Regional Med. Ctr. Bennett, Plantation, Fla., Plantation Gen. Hosp., Univ. Community Hosp., Tamarac, Fla., Cypress Community Hosp., 1973-77, Pompano Beach, Fla.; expert witness, State Fla. Dept. Profl. Regulations, 1991—; dir. Pointe Fed. Savs. Bank, Boca Raton, Fla., 1984-97. Bd. dirs. Miami Hebrew Acad., 1973-81, mem. exec. com. bd., 1975-81; bd. dirs. Moriah Sch., Englewood, N.J., 1968-75, Yeshiva Torah Vodaath and Mesifta, Bklyn., 1965—; v.p. Hebrew Acad. Greater Miami, 1977-80; trustee Finch U. Health Scis. The Chgo. Med. Sch. 1990-2001. Fellow ACS, Am. Acad. Orthopedic Surgeons, Internat. Coll. Surgeons, Am. Bd. Quality Assurance Utilization Rev. Physicians; mem. Am. Assn. Orthopedic Medicine, Am. Acad. Pain Mgmt., Am. Coll. for Advancement in Medicine, Fla. Orthopedic Assn., Eastern Orthopedic Assn., Broward County Orthopedic Soc., Internat. Arthroscopy Soc., Chgo. Med. Sch. Alumni Assn. (nat. exec. com. 1975—, 1st v.p. 1981-85, nat. pres. 1985-87, bd. govs.), Disting. Alumnus award 1988), Am. Acad. Neuromuscular Thermography (cert.), Biofeedback Soc. Am., Masons, Shriners. Home: 3650 N 45th Ave Hollywood FL 33021-2449 Office: 4101 NW 4th St Ste 401 Plantation FL 33317-2836 Office Phone: 954-581-8585. Personal E-mail: nobones@aol.com.

**STEIN, ANDY,** musician, composer; b. N.Y.C., Aug. 31, 1948; s. Ernest and Doris Stein; m. Cecilia de Wolf (div.); 1 child, Louis. MB, U. Mich., 1971. Musician Comdr. Cody and His Lost Planet, Ann Arbor, 1968—, Asleep at the Wheel, Oakland, Calif., 1971—80, Emmy Lou Harris, L.A., 1975, Bob Dylan, L.A., 1978, Vince Giordano's Nighthawks, N.Y., 1979—, A Prairie Home Companion with Garrison Keller, N.Y.C. and St. Paul, 1989—. Arranger: symphony Symphony in d Minor, Death of the Maiden, 2000, piano concerto Fantasie Concertante, 2001, composer, arranger: opera Mr. and Mrs. Olson, 2002. Recipient Grammy award for country instrumental, Asleep at the Wheel, 1978, Oscar for mus. arranger, prodr. animated short, Sundae in N.Y., 1984. Mem.: N.Y. Musician's Club.

**STEIN, ARLAND THOMAS,** lawyer; b. Pitts., Nov. 19, 1938; s. Thomas Edward and Josephine Cecelia (Kiedaisch) Stein; m. Helen Marie Horin, Aug. 14, 1965; children: Thomas Arland, John Andrew, Christian Michael. BS in Engring. Sci., Purdue U., 1961, postgraduate student, 1960-62; LLB, U. Va., 1965. Bar: Pa. 1965, Ohio 1966, US Patent Office 1967, US Supreme Ct. 1969. Assoc. Blenko, Leonard & Buell, Pitts., 1965-71; ptnr. Yeager, Stein & Wettach, Pitts., 1971-74; Reed Smith Shaw & McClay, Pitts., 1974-1999, Barnes & Thornburg, Indianapolis, 1999-2005, Hahn, Loeser and Parks, 2005-. Mem. ABA, Allegheny County Bar Assn., Am. Patent Law Assn., Pitts. Patent Law Assn., Lic. Execs. Soc., Tau Beta Pi, Omicron Delta Kappa (charter, Purdue chpt.), Rose Ade Found., life mem. Rep. Lutheran. Clubs: Masons, KT, Duquesne Club, Columbia Club. Office: Hahn Loeser and Parks 65 E State St Ste 1400 Columbus OH 43215 E-mail: astein@hahnlaw.com.*

**STEIN, BARRY EDWARD,** medical educator; BA, CUNY, Queens, 1966, MA, 1969; PhD, CUNY, 1971. Prof. dept. physiology Med. Coll. Va.-Va. Commonwealth U., Richmond, 1982-94, affil. prof., 1994—; prof., chair dept. neurobiology and anatomy Wake Forest U Sch. Medicine, Winston-Salem, NC, 1994—. Bd. trustees The Gwendolyn Hardy Williams and Oliver Williams Found., Inc., 1992—; lectr. in field. Co-author: The Merging of the Senses, 1993; contbr. chpts. to books including The Cognitive Neurosciences, 1995, 99, Electrophysiology of Vision, 1991, The Development of Intersensory Perception: Comparative Perspectives, 1994, others; co-editor: The Handbook of Multisensory Processes, 2004; mem. editl. bd. Jour. Cognitive Neuroscience, The Behavioral and Brain Sciences; contbr. numerous articles to profl. pubs. including Jour. Neurophysiology, Jour. Neurosci., Sci., Jour. Comparative Neurology, others. Home: 1825 Georgia Ave Winston Salem NC 27104-3101 Office: Wake Forest Sch Medicine Med Ctr Blvd Winston Salem NC 27157-0001 Business E-Mail: bestein@wfubmc.edu.

**STEIN, BEN (BENJAMIN JEREMY STEIN),** television personality, writer, lawyer, economist; b. Washington, Nov. 25, 1944; s. Herbert and Mildred (Fishman) S.; m. Alexandra Denman, June 22, 1968 (div. 1974); m. Alexandra Denman, 1977; 1 child, Thomas. BA, Columbia U., 1966; LLB, Yale U., 1970. Bar: Conn. Trial lawyer FTC, Washington, 1970-72; speech writer The White House, Washington, 1973-74; columnist Wall St. Jour., NYC, 1974-76; writer, commentator, columnist LA Herald-Examiner, 1978-87; TV personality Win Ben Stein's Money, Comedy Ctrl., 1997—; host Turn Ben Stein On Comedy Ctrl., 1999—2001. Fin. cons. LAACO, Inc., LA; contbg. editor Am. Spectator, 1980—; law and econs. tchr. Pepperdine, Malibu, 1992—; adj. prof. Am. U., Washington, U. Calif. Santa Cruz; spokesperson Clear Eyes eye drops. Author: On The Brink, 1977, The View from Sunset Boulevard, 1978, DREEMZ, 1978, Moneypower, 1980, 'Ludes, 1981, Financial Passages, 1986, A License to Steal, 1992, Tommy and Me, 1999, How To Ruin Your Life, 2002, How to Ruin Your Love Life, 2003, How to Ruin Your Financial Life, 2004, (with Phil DeMuth) You Can Time the Market!, 2003, Can America Survive? The Rage of the Left, the Truth, and What to Do about It, 2004, Yes, You Can Be a Successful Income Investor: Reaching for Yield in Today's Market, 2005, (with Philip De Muth) Mechanical and Electrical Equipment for Buildings, 1999; author numerous articles on leveraged buy-outs and other fin. frauds for Barrons, 1984—; syndicated columnist King Features Syndicate; regular columnist LA Mag., NY Mag., E! Online, N.Y. Times (Everybody's Money) SundayBusiness; contbr. Wash. Post, Wall St. Jour.; guest speaker on fin. Fox News Channel; co-creater: (TV series) Fernwood Tonight; actor: (films) The Wild Life, 1984, Ferris Bueller's Day Off, 1986 (ranked as one of 50 most famous scenes in Am. films), Planes, Trains, and Automobiles, 1987, Ghostbusters II, 1989, Soapdish, 1991, Honeymoon in Vegas, 1992, Dennis the Menace, 1993, My Girl 2, 1994, North, 1994, The Mask, 1994, Richie Rich, 1994, Miami Rhapsody, 1995, Casper, 1995; (TV series) The Wonder Years, 1988-91, (voice) Animaniacs, 1993, (voice) Freakazoid, 1995, (voice) Earthworm Jim, 1995, (voice) The Mask, 1995, (voice) Bruno the Kid, 1996, (voice) The Secret Files of the SpyDogs, 1998; (TV films) Mastergate, 1992, The Day My Parents Ran Away, 1993, (voice) Santa vs. the Snowman, 1997, Breakfast with Einstein, 1998; exec. prodr. Turn Ben Stein On, 1999; host: (TV series) Win Ben Stein's Money, 1997-2002 (Daytime Emmy award Outstanding Game Show Host, 1999); TV appearances include Charles in Charge, 1987, 88, 90, MacGyver, 1991, Melrose Place, 1993, Full House, 1993, Hearts Afire, 1993, 94, Tales from the Crypt, 1995, Lois & Clark: The New Adventures of Superman, 1995, Married...With Children, 1995, The Marshal, 1995, (voice) Duckman, 1996, 97, Seinfeld, 1997, Murphy Brown, 1997, Muppets Tonight!, 1998, (voice) Rugrats, 1998, The Drew Carey Show, 2001, (voice) The Adventures of Jimmy Neutron: Boy Genius, 2002, (voice) Family Guy, 2003, (voice) The Fairly Odd Parents, 2004; contbr. CBS TV News Mem. Writers Guild Am., Screen Actors' Guild, Am. Fedn. TV and Radio Actors, Yale Club NYC, Friars, LA Athletic Club, Calif. Yacht Club, Morningside Country Club. Republican. Jewish. Office: 8787 Shoreham Dr West Hollywood CA 90069-2231 Office Phone: 310-652-9406. Personal E-mail: benstein@aol.com.*

**STEIN, BERNARD ALVIN,** retail executive, consultant; b. Winnipeg, Can., June 4, 1923; s. Herman Louis and Rebecca (Harris) S.; m. Dorothy Lock, Jan. 1, 1942; 1 dau., Marilynn Stein Lakein. Vice-pres. food drug div. Giant Food, Inc., Washington, 1951-69; v.p., gen. mgr. Read Drug Stores, Balt., 1969-70; pres. Scotty Stores div. Sav-A-Stop, Jacksonville, Fla., 1970-71; pres., gen. mgr. Liberal Markets, Dayton, Ohio, 1971-72; pres. Pueblo Supermarkets, San Juan, P.R., 1972-74, Hills Supermarkets, Brentwood, NY, 1974-75, Allied Supermarkets, Detroit, 1976-78, Chatham Supermarkets, Detroit, 1978-81; CEO Network Assocs., Chgo., 1981-92; bus. cons. Balt., 1992—; pres. Jewelry Markdowns, Inc., 2003—. Pres. Jewelry website business, 2003—. Mem. Presdl. Com. for Emergency Food Controls, 1969; mem. scholarship com. Am. Indian Edn. Found., 2004—. Served with USAAF, 1943-45. Decorated Air medal. Home: 7902 Brynmor Ct # 104 Pikesville MD 21208-4351 Office Phone: 410-486-8431. Personal E-mail: bernie230@comcast.net. E-mail: jewelrymd@comcast.net.

**STEIN, BERNARD L.,** journalist; b. Cleve. m. Marguerite Adams; 1 child, Anna. BA in Lit., Columbia U., 1963; postgrad., U. Calif., Berkeley, 1964—66; DHL (hon.), Manhattan Coll., 1999. Editor Riverdale Press, 1978—2005, co-pub., 1980—. Mem. team of scholars editing Mark Twain's writing for pub. U. Calif. Press; James H. Ottaway Disting. vis. prof. SUNY, New Paltz, NY, 2002; prof. journalism Hunter Coll. CUNY, 2005—. Named Writer of the Yr., N.Y. Press Assn., 1986; recipient First Amendment award, Soc. Profl. Journalists, 1989, Pulitzer Prize for editl. writing, 1998. Office: c/o Riverdale Press 6155 Broadway Bronx NY 10471-3136 Office Phone: 718-543-6065. Business E-Mail: bstein@riverdalepress.com.

**STEIN, CHRIS,** musician; b. Bklyn., Jan. 5, 1950; m. Barbara Sicuranza, 1999; 1 child, Akira. Co-founder, guitarist Blondie, 1974—82, 1997—. Musician: (albums) Blondie, 1976, Plastic Letters, 1977, Parallel Lines, 1978, Eat to the Beat, 1979, Autoamerican, 1980, The Hunter, 1982, No Exit, 1999, Livid, 2000, The Curse of Blondie, 2004, Live, 2004, Best Live, 2005. Named to Rock and Roll Hall of Fame, 2006. Office: c/o 10th St Entertainment Ste G410 700 San Vicente Blvd West Hollywood CA 90069*

**STEIN, DANIEL ALAN,** lawyer; b. Washington, Mar. 9, 1955; s. Edward Seymour and Ann Rose Stein; m. Sharon McCloe, Oct. 18, 1986; children: Claire, Corrieanne. BA, Ind. U., 1977; JD, Cath. U. Am., 1984. Bar: D.C. 1984, U.S. Dist. Ct. D.C. 1985, U.S. Ct. Appeals (D.C. cir.) 1987, U.S. Tax Ct. 1987, Md. 2002, U.S. Dist. Ct. Md. 2003. Profl. staff mem. select com. on narcotics abuse and control U.S. Ho. of Reps., Washington, 1977—81; pvt. practice Washington, 1984—89; exec. dir. Immigration Reform Law Inst., Washington, 1986—88, Fedn. for Am. Immigration Reform, Washington, 1982—86, 1989—2004, pres., 2004—. Mem. adv. bd. Social Contract periodical, Petosky, Mich., 1990—. Mem. Capitol Hill Club, Nat. Press Club. Republican. Avocations: trombone, american history, western civilization, jazz, antique books. Office: Fedn for Am Immigration Reform 1666 Connecticut Ave NW Ste 400 Washington DC 20009-1039 Office Phone: 202-328-7004.

**STEIN, DAVID BERNARD,** psychology professor; b. NYC, Oct. 15, 1943; s. Abe and Evelyn Stein; children: Alex, Kevin. BA, Bklyn. Coll., 1961; MS, Va. Commonwealth U., 1972, PhD, 1978. Diplomate Am. Coll. Forensic Examiners, cert. psychologist Va. Prof. psychology Langwood U., Farmville, Va., 1985—, asst. prof., 1976-78, assoc. prof., 1990—2000; clin. asst. prof. U. Tenn. Ctr. Health Scis., Knoxville, 1980—85. Psychology resident U. Miss. Med. Ctr., 1973—74; mental health ctr. staff psychologist St. Dominic's Hosp., 1974—76; pvt. practice clin. psychology, 1974—; dir. psychol. svcs. Dogwood Village, 1978—79; staff psychologist Memphis Mental Health Inst., 1979—81; dep. sheriff Prince Edward County, 2005—; cons. Va. State Police, Richmond, 2002—; disting. prof. U. Teeside, Middlesbrough, England, 2000; appearances on numerous TV and radio programs; spkr., presenter, lectr. in field. Contbr. articles to profl. jours. V.p. Hinds County Mental Health Assn., Jackson, Miss., 1979—86; mem. adv. bd. Lakeside Psychiat. Hosp., Memphis, 1982—85. Named one of Va. Outstanding Scholars, Pub. Broadcast Radio, 1999; recipient Exceptional Merit Scholarship award, Longwood Coll., 1999, Marie Bristow Starke award, 2000, Outstanding Achievement award, Internat. Ctr. Psychiatry and Psychology, 2005. Mem.: Am. Assn. Behavior Therapists, Va. Psychology Assn. (mem. task force 2000—05), Am. Assn. Cognitive Behavior Therapists, Internat. Ctr. for Study of Psychiatry and Psychology (bd. dirs. 2002, mem. adv. coun. 1998—), Am. Soc. Criminology, Am. Criminal Justice Assn., So. Criminal Justice Assn., Acad. Crminal Justice Scis., Psi Chi (pres. 1972). Achievements include research in operational definition for disease in psychology and psychiatry; methods of behavioral treatment for adolescents; analysis of adolescent treatment; effectiveness of hospital treatment for adolescents; improving freshman performance; outpatient treatment of attentional disorders without medication. Office: Longwood U High St Farmville VA 23909

**STEIN, DAVID ERIC,** physicist, defense analyst, futurist, retired military officer; b. Jacksonville, Fla., Jan. 13, 1950; s. Stanley Wolfe and Dorothy Jean (Lilley) S. BS with high honors, U. Fla., 1971, postgrad., 1971-72, MS in Physics, 1977; grad., Air Command and Staff Coll., 1982, Naval War Coll., 1995, Air War Coll., 1996. Instr. dept. physics U. Fla., Gainesville, 1971-74, NSF rsch. asst., 1974-76; commd. 1st lt. U.S. Army, 1977, advanced through grades to lt. col., 1994; maj. USAF HQ Air Force Systems Command, Andrews AFB, Md., 1992; lt. col. Air Force Sci. adv. bd., 1994-95; project engr. advanced surveillance concepts Rome Air Devel. Ctr., 1979-81; field engr. radar systems test and evaluation Rome Air Devel. Ctr. and MIT Lincoln Lab., 1981-83; radar data and imagery analyst 6585th Test Group, Holloman AFB, N.Mex., 1983-87; elec. engr. specialist LTV Aircraft Products Group, 1987-90; fellow engr. Westinghouse Electric Corp., 1990-91; ops. rsch. analyst CSCI, 1992-94, Office of Asst. Sec. of Air Force, 1995, 96-97, Joint Staff, 1996, 98-99, Army Digitization Office, 1999-2000, CACI, 2000—03, Northrop Grumman Info. Tech., 2003—. Part-time coll. faculty, 1982-84; short course instr. radar techs. George Washington U., 1991-97; adv. assoc. editor NATO Advanced Rsch. Workshop, Bad Windsheim, Germany, 1988; cons., 1994—. Editor-in-chief Applied Computational Electromagnetics Soc. Jour., 1987-93, FUTURETakes, 2003-; assoc. sci. editor Frontier Perspectives, 2000—; contbr. articles to profl. jours.; patentee in field. With USAF Res., 1992, 94-99. Recipient Disting. Svc. award Applied Computational Electromagnetics Soc., 1994; fellow Alpha Found.'s Inst. for Advanced Study; J. Hillis Miller Meml. scholar U. Fla., Ford Found. fellow. Mem. Am. Phys. Soc., Am. Assn. Physics Tchrs., World Affairs Coun., World Future Soc., Army-Navy Club, Philos. Soc. Washington, Fla. Blue Key, Phi Beta Kappa, Sigma Pi Sigma, Omicron Delta Kappa, Phi Kappa Phi. Achievements include identification of new atmospheric refractivity effects on low-altitude radar propagation, extended quantum-mech. computational technique to electromagnetic scattering, co-pioneered new acquisition sizing methodology for next-generation fighter aircraft; co-authored section of Defense Critical Technologies Plan for the Executive Office of the President; key advisor to Air Force Requirements Oversight Council; mem. U.S. delegation to NATO Y2K integrated process team; identified non-Y2K compliant NATO command and control systems and possible impact to interconnected U.S. systems; identified systems acquisition implications of alternative geostrategic futures, asymmetric-capable adversaries, new concepts in warfare, futuristic techs; co-pioneered modeling and simulation as a technology investment planning tool for an uncertain and rapidly changing national security environment. Home: PO Box 169 Linthicum Heights MD 21090-0169 Office Phone: 202-452-5592. Home Fax: 410-385-3315. Personal E-mail: futuretakes@cs.com.

**STEIN, DAVID FRED,** investment company executive; b. NYC, May 17, 1940; s. William Howard and Phoebe Louise (Hockstader) S.; m. Susan Vail Berresford, June 17, 1963 (div. 1970); 1 child, Jeremy Vail; m. Ellen Gail Cohen, Sept. 16, 1973; children: Katharine Ellen, Nicholas David. BA, Harvard U., 1962; MBA, Harvard Grad. Sch. Bus. Adminstrn., 1965. Assoc. Bache & Co., N.Y.C., 1965-68; assoc., then gen. ptnr. Kuhn Loeb & Co., N.Y.C., 1969-77; mng. dir. Lehman Brothers Kuhn Loeb, N.Y.C., 1977-83, Shearson Lehman Am. Express, N.Y.C., 1983-86; sr. exec. v.p., dir. Am. Express Bank, N.Y.C., 1986-87; mng. dir. Shearson Lehman Hutton, N.Y.C., 1987-89; mng. dir., mem. exec. com. The Stamford Co., N.Y.C., 1989-90; mng. dir. J & W Seligman & Co., N.Y.C., 1990-96, vice chmn., 1997—; co-chmn. Seligman Henderson Co., N.Y.C., 1991-98. Bd. dirs. Griffin Land & Nurseries Inc. Trustee P.R. Traveling Theatre, NYC, 1970-72, Altro Health and Rehab. Ctr., Bronx, NY, 1975-82, Montefiore Med. Ctr., Bronx, 1990—, Montefiore Health Svcs., 2006—, Our Lady of Mercy Hosp., 2006—, Children's Aid Soc., 2000—; trustee Blythedale Children's Hosp., Valhalla, NY, 1977-2001, hon. trustee, 2001—; trustee Riverdale Country Sch., Bronx, 1988-2000, chmn. bd. trustees, 1997-2000, trustee emeritus, 2005—; active Coun. on Fgn. Rels. With U.S. Army, 1962-63. Mem. Nat. Assn. Security Dealers (internat. com. 1970-85), Century Country Club (Purchase, N.Y.), River Club (NYC), Harvard Club (NYC), Edgartown (Mass.) Yacht Club, Mill Reef Club (Antigua, Brit. V.I.), Chappaquiddick Beach Club (Edgartown), Reading Room Club (Edgartown). Democrat. Avocations: reading, sailing, bicycling, fishing, skiing. Home: 875 Park Ave New York NY 10021-0341 Office: J & W Seligman 100 Park Ave Fl 8 New York NY 10017-5516

**STEIN, ELEANOR BANKOFF**, retired judge; b. N.Y.C., Jan. 24, 1923; d. Jacob and Sarah Rashkin Bankoff; m. Frank S. Stein, May 27, 1947; children: Robert B., Joan Jenkins, William M. Student, Barnard Coll., 1940—42; BS in Econ., Columbia U., N.Y.C., 1944; LLB, N.Y. U., N.Y.C., 1949; grad., Ind. Jud. Coll., 1986. Bar: N.Y. 1950, Ind. 1976, U.S. Supreme Ct. 1980. Atty. Hillis & Button, Kokomo, Ind., 1975—76, Paul Hillis, 1976—78, Bayliff, Harrigan, 1978—80; judge Howard County Ct., 1981—89; ret., 1989. Co-referee Howard County Juvenile Ct., Kokomo, 1976—78. Mem. Rep. Women's Assn. Kokomo, 1980—; bd. dir. Kokomo Human Rels. Commn., Ind., 1967—70, Howard County Legal Aid Soc., 1976—80; bd. advisors St. Joseph Hosp., 1979—2000; bd. dir. Howard County Children's Ctr., 1993—98. Mem.: ABA, Howard County Bar Assn., Ind. Bar Assn., Nat. Assn. Women Judges, Ind. Jud. Assn., Am. Judicature Soc., Kokomo Country Club. Jewish. Home: 3204 Tally Ho Dr Kokomo IN 46902 Personal E-mail: eleanorbstein@aol.com.

**STEIN, ELIAS M.**, mathematician, educator; b. Antwerp, Belgium, Jan. 13, 1931; arrived in US, 1941; s. Elkan and Chana (Goldman) S.; m. Elly Intrator, Mar. 21, 1959; children— Jeremy, Karen AB, U. Chgo., 1951, MA, 1953, PhD, 1955; degree (hon.), Peking U., 1988, U. Chgo., 1992. Instr. MIT, Cambridge, 1956-58; asst. prof., then assoc. prof. U. Chgo., 1958-63; mem. Inst. for Advanced Study, Princeton, N.J., 1962-63, 1984-85; prof. dept. math. Princeton U., N.J., 1963—, chmn. dept. math N.J., 1968-70, N.J., 1985-87. Author: Singular Integrals and Differentiability Properties of Functions, 1970 (Am. Math. Soc. Steele prize 1984), Topics in Harmonic Analysis Related to the Littlewood-Paley Theory; co-author: (with G. Weiss) Introduction to Fourier Analysis on Euclidean Spaces, Harmonic Analysis, 1993; contbr. articles to profl. jours. NSF fellow, 1955-56, sr. post-doctoral fellow, 1962-63, 71-72; Sloan Found. fellow, 1961-63; Guggenheim Found. fellow, 1976-77, 1984-85, Wolf prize in math., Wolf Found., Israel, 1999, Nat. Medal of Sci., 2002. Mem. NAS, Am. Acad. Arts and Scis., Am. Math. Soc., Swedish Acad. of Scis. (Schock prize 1993). Home: 132 Dodds Ln Princeton NJ 08540-4106 Office: Princeton U Dept Math 802 Fine Hall Washintgon Rd Princeton NJ 08544-0001 Office Phone: 609-258-6463. Business E-Mail: stein@math.princeton.edu.*

**STEIN, ELLEN GAIL**, information technology manager; b. N.Y.C., May 19, 1951; d. Manuel W. and Bella (Skutel) Stein. BA, SUNY, Stony Brook, 1972; M of Urban Planning, Hunter Coll., 1976; cert. program execs. state/local govt., Harvard U., 1985. Sr. rsch. assoc. Nassau Suffolk (N.Y.) Regional Med. Program, 1976-77; sr. planner N.Y.C. Dept. Correction, 1977—79; group leader criminal justice Mayor's Office, Dept. Ops., NY, 1979—81, dep. asst. dir. citywide spl. projects, 1981, dir. citywide audit implementation, 1981—84; administr. Bur. Supplied N.Y.C. Bd. Edn., N.Y.C., NY, 1984—90; mgmt. cons. Project Provide Hope, Russia, Citizen's Budget Commn., 1990-94; pres., CEO FEDVentures Inc., 1994-99; assoc. commr. Office of CIO N.Y.C. Dept. Tech. and Telecomm., 1999—. Mem. Nat. Assn. Purchasing Mgmt., Am. Women Econ. Devel., Ctrl. Women's Focus, Gov.'s Procurement Coun. (N.Y.), Human Svcs. Coun. (contracting com.). Home: 67 Park Ter E New York NY 10034-1445 Office: 75 Park Pl Fl 9 New York NY 10007-2146 Office Phone: 212-788-2345. Personal E-mail: egstein@hotmail.com. Business E-Mail: estein@doitt.nyc.gov.

**STEIN, ELLIOT, JR.**, business executive; b. St. Louis, Jan. 31, 1949; s. Elliot and Mary Ann (Bleiweiss) S.; m. Pamela Sztybel, Oct. 4, 1997. BA, Claremont McKenna Coll., 1971. Assoc. Lehman Bros., NYC, 1972-79; chmn. Caribbean Internat. News Corp., San Juan, PR, 1985—; ptnr. Commonwealth Capital Ptnrs., NYC, 1988—. Bd. dirs. Apollo Investment Corp., VTG Holdings, Inc., Cloud Solutions LLC, Bargain Shop Holdings, LLC; adv. bd. Investigative Group Internat., 1998—. Trustee Claremont Grad. U., 1980—, New Sch. U., 1990—; bd. councillors Annenberg Sch. Comm., U. So. Calif., 1998—. Democrat. Office: Commonwealth Capital Ptnrs 509 Madison Ave Ste 604 New York NY 10022

**STEIN, ERIC**, retired law educator; b. Holice, Czechoslovakia, July 8, 1913; came to U.S., 1940, naturalized, 1943; s. Zikmund and Hermina (Zalud) S.; m. Virginia Elizabeth Rhine, July 30, 1955. JUD, Charles U., Prague, Czechoslovakia, 1937; JD, U. Mich., 1942; Dr. honoris causa, Vrije U., Brussels, 1978, U. Libre, 1979, West-Bohemian U., Pilsen, Czech Republic, 1997. Bar: Ill. 1946, D.C. 1953. Practiced law, Prague, 1937; with State Dept., 1946-55; acting dep. dir. Office UN Polit. Affairs, 1955; mem. faculty U. Mich. Law Sch., Ann Arbor, 1956, prof. internat. law and orgn., 1958-76, Hessel E. Yntema prof. law, 1976-83, emeritus prof., 1983—; co-dir. internat. legal studies, 1958-76; dir., 1976-81. Vis. prof. Stanford Law Sch., 1956, 77, Law Faculties, Stockholm, Uppsala and Lund, Sweden, 1969, Inst. Advanced Legal Studies U. London, 1975, U. Ariz., 1991, 92; lectr. Hague Acad. Internat. Law, summer 1971; vis. lectr. European U. Inst., Florence, Italy, 1983, Beijing, Shanghai, Wuhan, 1986, U. Tokyo, Kyoto, 1986, Coll. of Europe, Bruges, Pontificia, Madrid, 1988; Jean Monnet prof. European U. Inst., Florence, Italy, 1991, Henry Morris lectr. Kent Coll. of Law, Chgo., 1992, Jeanne Kiewit Taylor disting. vis. lectr. U. Ariz., winter 1993; adviser U.S. delegation UN Gen. Assembly, 1947-55; mem. adv. panel, cons. Bur. European Affairs, State Dept., 1966-73; cons. U.S. rep. for trade negotiations, 1979; vice chmn. com. Atlantic studies Atlantic Inst., 1966-68; mem. adv. council inst. European Studies, Free U., Brussels, Belgium, 1965-70; mem. U.S. Com. for Legal Edn. Exchange with China, 1983-91; lectr. Acad. of European Law, Florence, Italy 1990. Author: (with others) American Enterprise in the European Common Market-A Legal Profile, vols. I, II, 1960, (with H.K. Jacobson) Diplomats, Scientists and Politicians, The United States and the Nuclear Test Ban Negotiations, 1966 (U. Mich. Press Best Book of Yr. award), Harmonization of European Company Law: National Reform and Transnational Coordination, 1971, Impact of New Weapons Technology on International Law-Selected Aspects, 1971, Un Nuovo Diritto per l'Europa, 1991, Czecho Slovakia: Ethnic Conflict, Constitutional Fissure, Negotiated Breakup, 1997, Czech translation, 2000, Thoughts From a Bridge: A Retrospective of Writings on New Europe and American Federalism, 2000 (U. Mich. Press Best Book of Yr. award); editor: (with Peter Hay) Law and Institutions in the Atlantic Area Readings, Cases and Problems, 1967, (with Peter Hay and Michel Waelbrock) European Community Law and Institutions in Perspective, 1976; co-author, co-editor: Courts and Free Markets-Perspectives From the United States and Europe, 1982; bd. editors: Am. Jour. Internat. Law, 1965—; mem. adv. bd. Common Market Law Rev., 1964—, Legal Issues of European Integration, 1974—, Rivista di Diritto Europeo, 1978—, Columbia Jour. East European Law, 1994—, Columbia Jour. European Law, 1994—; contbr. articles to profl. jours. Mem. Internat. Com. for Revision Czechoslovak Constn., 1990-92. With AUS, 1943-46. Decorated Bronze Star, Order Italian Crown, Italian Mil. Cross; Guggenheim fellow, 1962-63; Social Sci. Rsch. Coun. grantee; Rockefeller Found. scholar-in-residence, 1965, 73; Alexander von Humboldt Stiftung awardee, 1982; fellow Inst. Advanced Study, Berlin, 1984-85, Rsch. grant IREX, 1995; recipient Lifetime Achievement award Am. Soc. Comparative Law, 2004, Lifetime Contbn. prize European Union Studies Assn., 2005, First Degree Outstanding Scholarly Achievement Medal Pres. Czech Republic, 2001, Gold medal Charles U., Prague, 2005; named Hon. Citizen of Czech Republic, 2001. Mem. ABA (co-chmn. European law com. 1982, mem. coun. sect. on internat. law and practice 1983-84), Internat. Law Assn., Coun. Fgn. Rels., European Studies Assn., Am. Soc. Internat. Law (exec. coun. 1954-57, bd. rev. and devel. 1965-67, 70-75, hon. v.p. 1982-2000), Brit. Inst. Internat. and Comparative Law, Internat. Acad. Comparative Law. Home: 2649 Heather Way Ann Arbor MI 48104-2850 Office Phone: 734-764-0541. E-mail: steine@umich.edu.

**STEIN, FRANKLIN JOSEPH**, music educator; b. Eau Claire, Wis., Mar. 26, 1945; s. Herbert Charles Stein and Gwenn Marie Lassek. BS in Secondary Edn., U. Wis., 1968; BS in Computer Sci., Coleman Coll., La Mesa, Calif.,

1989, MIS in Info. Systems, 1995. Cert. tchr. Wis. Biology, sci., Spanish tchr. Stanley-Boyd HS, Stanley, Wis., 1968-71; salesman Jerry's Hammond Organ & Piano Studios, Eau Claire, Wis., 1971—72; dept. mgr. Day Music Co., Eau Claire, 1973—74; store mgr. Tropic Waters Pet Store, Eau Claire, 1975-76, Thearle Music Co., San Diego, 1977—82; 6th grade tchr. St. Paul's Luth. Sch., Pacific Beach, Calif., 1977-78; profl. theatre organist Organ Power Pizza Restaurants, San Diego, 1977-85; store mgr. Organ Stop Inc., San Diego, 1982—89; computer programmer analyst Health Examinetics, Rancho Bernardo, Calif., 1989-91; clin. computer systems specialist SHARP Health Care, San Diego, 1991—97; systems programmer/clin. analyst U. Calif., San Diego, 1997—2002; counselor emotionally disturbed youth New Alternatives, Inc. Comprehensive Adolescent Treatment Ctr., San Diego, 2003—04. Profl. musician, 1965—. Author: Technician's Manual of Thermography, 1987, IDXrad User's Manual & Annual Updates, 1991-97; editor: Manual of Thermography, 1988. Music dir., organist Airman Meml. Chapel US Marine Corps Air Sta., Miramar, Calif., 1996—; sponsor PLAN USA/Childreach, 2000—. Recipient Silver medal Piano Performance Wis. Music Educators, 1962, 63, Cert. of Merit for Excellence in Sci., Wis. Jr. Acad. of Sci., 1963. Democrat. Buddhist. Avocations: martial arts, Judo, classical music, travel, cooking. Home: 10227 Kamwood Pl San Diego CA 92126-5139

**STEIN, GARY S.**, retired judge, lawyer; b. Newark, June 13, 1933; s. Morris J. and Mollie (Goldfarb) S.; married, July 1, 1956; children— Jill, Carrie, Michael, Terri, Jo; m. Et Tilchin, July 1, 1956 AB, Duke U., 1954, LL.B. with distinction, 1956; D.H.L. (hon.), N.J. Inst. Tech., 1985. Bar: D.C. 1956, Ohio 1957, N.Y. 1958, N.J. 1963. Research asst. U.S. Senate AntiTrust and Monopoly Subcom., Washington, 1955; assoc. Kramer, Marx, Greenlee & Backus, N.Y.C., 1956-65; sole practice Paramus, NJ, 1966-72; ptnr. Stein & Kurland, Esquires, Paramus, NJ, 1972-82; dir. Gov.'s Office of Policy and Planning, Trenton, NJ, 1982-85; assoc. justice Supreme Ct. N.J., Hackensack, 1985—2002, ret., 2002; counsel Pashman Stein, Hackensack, 2002—. Mcpl. atty., Paramus, 1967-71; counsel N.J. Election Law Revision Commn., 1970; atty. Bd. Adjustment, Teaneck, N.J., 1973-82 Mem. editl. bd. Duke Law Jour., 1954-56, assoc. editor, 1955-56. Mem. Dist. Ethics Com. for Bergen County, N.J., 1977-80, chmn. 1981. Served with U.S. Army, 1957-58, 61-62 Mem. ABA, N.J. State Bar Assn. (com. on state legislation 1973-79, chmn. 1973-76, jud. selection com. 1976-81, Constl. amendment com. 1977-79, court modernization com. 1976-79), Bergen County Bar Assn., Order of Coif. Jewish. Avocation: tennis. Office: Pashman Stein Ct Plaza South 21 Main St Hackensack NJ 07601 Office Phone: 201-488-8200. Business E-Mail: gstein@pashmanstein.com.

**STEIN, GEORGE HENRY**, historian, educator, administrator; b. Vienna, May 18, 1934; came to U.S., 1939, naturalized, 1948. m. Dorothy Ann Lahm, Nov. 22, 1963; 1 child, Kenneth. BA with honors (State Regents scholar), Bklyn. Coll., 1959; MA in History (Regents fellow), Columbia U., 1960, PhD in History (Pres.'s fellow), 1964. Lectr. history City Coll., CUNY, 1962-63; instr. dept. history Columbia U., N.Y.C., 1963-65, asst. prof., 1965-66; assoc. prof. dept. history SUNY-Binghamton, 1966-70, prof., 1970-73, disting. teaching prof., 1973-98, emeritus, 1998—, vice chmn. grad. affairs, 1974-76, v.p. acad. affairs, 1976-87, provost, 1985-87, acting pres., 1986-87. Manuscript evaluator and cons. to numerous publishers, 1964—. Author: The Waffen SS: Hitler's Elite Guard at War, 1939-45, 1966, paperback edit., 1984 (transl. into German, 1967, French, 1967, Spanish, 1973, Portuguese, 1970, Japanese, 2002, Finnish, 2004); contbr. articles on modern European history to scholarly pubs.; editor: Hitler, 1968; contbr. book revs. to hist. jours. Served with USAF, 1953-57. NEH fellow, 1970-71 Mem. Am. Hist. Assn. (mem. conf. group on cen. European history, conf. group for use of psychology in history), Acad. Polit. Sci., Assn. of Contemporary Historians, Am. Assn. Higher Edn., Nat. Assn. State Univs. and Land Grant Colls. (mem. council acad. affairs 1976-87), Am. Counc. Edn. (exec. com. nat. coun. chief acad. officers 1983-85), Com. Internat. d'Histoire de la Deuxieme Guerre Mondiale, WWII Studies Assn. Home: 2300 Hemlock Ln Vestal NY 13850-2633 Office: SUNY Dept History Binghamton NY 13902-6000

**STEIN, GRANT T.**, lawyer; b. Chgo., Aug. 4, 1956; BBA cum laude, Emory Univ., 1978; JD cum laude, Univ. Ga., 1981. Bar: Ga. 1981. Law clk., Hon. W. Homer Drake US Bankruptcy Ct. (no. dist.), Georgia; ptnr., head, Bankruptcy, Reorganization and Workouts Group Alston & Bird, LLP, Atlanta. Exec. com. Emory Univ. Bd. Visitors. Fellow: Am. Coll. Bankruptcy; mem.: Southeastern Bankruptcy Law Inst. (dir.), Assn. of Insolvency and Restructuring Advisors (dir., v.p.). Office: Alston & Bird LLP One Atlantic Ctr 1201 W Peachtree St NW Atlanta GA 30309-3424 Office Phone: 404-881-7285. Office Fax: 404-881-7777. Business E-Mail: gstein@alston.com.

**STEIN, HOWARD**, humanities educator, economics professor; b. Toronto, Ont., Can., Aug. 4, 1952; came to U.S., 1977; s. David Solomon and Beulah (Tanner) S.; m. Alisa Erika Koch, June 19, 1988; children: Joshua Walter, Daniel Nathan. BA, U. Toronto, 1975; MA, U. Ottawa, Can., 1977; PhD, U. Calif., Riverside, 1983. Lectr. Dept. Econs. U. Dar es Salaam, Tanzania, 1980-82; prof. dept. econs. Roosevelt U., Chgo., 1983—2004; prof. Am. and African studies U. Mich., 2006—. Vis. scholar Ctr. Rsch. on Econ. Devel., U. Mich., Ann Arbor, 1990-91, Sch. Internat. Svc., Am. Univ., Washington, 1995, Sch. Oriental and African Studies, U. London, 1998; vis. prof. Inst. Econ. Rsch., Hitotsubashi U., Tokyo, 1995-96, 06, Ctr. African Am. and African studies, Dept. Epidemiology, U. Mich., 2003—. Co-author: Supporting Ownership: Swedish Development Cooperation with Kenya, Tanzania and Uganda, 2 vols., 2003; co-editor: Tanzania and the IMF: The Dynamics of Liberalization, 1992, Deregulation and the Banking Crisis in Nigeria: A Comparative Study, 2002; editor: Asian Industrialization and Africa: Studies in Policy Alternatives to Structural Adjustments, 1995. Doctoral fellow Soc. Social Sci. and Humanities Rsch. Coun. Can., 1979, Nat. Endowment for Humanities grantee, 1985; recipient U.S. Info. Agy. Spkr. and Specialist award, 1999, 2002. Mem. Am. Econ. Assn., African Studies Assn. Avocations: ice hockey, gardening. Home: 4002 Calgary Ct Ann Arbor MI 48108 Office: U Mich CAAS 4700 Haven Hall 505 S State St Ann Arbor MI 48109-1045 Office Phone: 734-763-5519. E-mail: howstein@umich.edu.

**STEIN, HOWARD S.**, retired banker, investment advisor, consultant; b. NYC, Dec. 27, 1939; s. J. Zachary and Adele (Epstein) S. BA, U. Mich., 1961; MBA, Harvard U., 1963. Mem. treas.'s staff Gen. Motors Corp., N.Y.C., 1963-69; dep. dir., dir. fiscal ops. Human Resources Adminstrn., City of N.Y., 1969-71; dep. adminstr., 1972-74, 1st dep. adminstr., 1974-78; asst. commr. Manpower and Career Devel. Agy., N.Y.C., 1971-72; dep. commr. rent and housing maintenance Housing and Devel. Adminstrn., City of N.Y., 1972; v.p. Citicorp Credit Services Inc., N.Y.C., 1979-86; sr. v.p. Citicorp Retail Services Inc., N.Y.C., 1986-87; exec. dir. Landmark Mut. Funds Group of Citibank, N.A., N.Y.C., 1987-88; v.p. br. banking sect. devel. div. Citibank NA, 1989-91, sr. credit officer worldwide securities svcs. div. Fin. Instns. Group N.Y.C., 1991-94; group risk mgr. Global Transaction Svcs., N.Y.C., 1995—2001, head operational risk mgmt., emerging markets and transaction svcs., 2002—03; mng. dir., head operational risk mgmt. Global Corp. and Investment Bank, 2003—04; ret., 2004; treas., bd. dirs. Applecore Ptnrs., 1999—; sr. advisor Fortent (formerly Searchpace Corp.), 2005—; chmn. adv. com. Risk Bus., 2006—. Lectr. human resources policy Nova U., Ft. Lauderdale, Fla., 1973-74; field instr. adminstrn. specialization NYU Sch. Social Work, 1976-77; mem. risk mgmt. com. Participants Trust Co., 1995-99. Past Bd. dirs., chmn. program com. Vol. Urban Corp. Group, Inc.; past chmn. bd. dirs. Nova Inst; past treas.; past pres., bd. dirs. Child Study Assn. Am./Wel-Met, Inc., 1963-85; past treas., bd. dirs. Career Center for Social Services Greater N.Y., Inc.; past treas., past pres. bd. dirs. Cavalier King Charles Spaniel Club U.S.A., Inc.; past bd. dirs., past sec. Child Welfare Info. Services; treas., bd. dirs., chmn. fin. com. WNYC Radio; bd. dirs. Senate Residence Owners Inc., New Goddard-Riverside Housing Devel. Fund Co., N.Y.C. Health and Hosps., Corp., 1976-; past bd. dirs. Homes for the Homeless; past mem. corp. Children's Mus., Boston; bd. dirs., treas., chair fin. com. Goddard Riverside Neighborhood House; trustee, chair fin. com. Pratt Inst.; treas., bd. dirs. Applecore Ptnrs., 1999—; past mem. Dept. Disciplinary com. Supreme Ct. State N.Y. Appellate Divsn. 1st Jud. Dept.;

past mem. corp. adv. com. U. Mich., Coll. Lit., Sci and the Arts, treas.; bd. dirs. The Childrens' Cause for Cancer Advocacy, 2003—; mem. risk mgmt. adv. com., Fin. Svcs. Vol. Corp, 2006—. Mem.: Risk Mgmt. Assn. (co-chmn. operational risk coun. 2002—03, chair 2004), Inst. Internat. Fin. (mem. working group on operational risk 2001—04), Harvard (N.Y.C., past mem. admissions com.). Home: 1158 5th Ave New York NY 10029-6917 Office Phone: 212-378-1415. Personal E-mail: owardstein@aol.com.

**STEIN, JAMES ERIC**, pediatric surgeon; b. NYC, Mar. 25, 1959; children: Stephanie, Dylan. Bachelor's degree, Brown U., Providence, RI, 1981; MD, Tufts U. Sch. Medicine, Boston, 1986. Cert. Surgery, 1995, Pediatric Surgery, 1998. Intern, dept. surgery Tufts-New England Med. Ctr., 1986—87, resident, dept. surgery, 1987—89, 1991—92, chief surgical resident; rsch. fellow, pediatric surgery Boston Children's Hosp., 1989—91; pediatric surgery fellow Royal Children's Hosp., Melbourne, Australia, 1993—94, Babies and Children's Hosp., NYC, 1994—96; attending pediatric surgeon, divsn. surgery Children's Hosp., LA, 1996—, dir., Extra Corporeal Membrane Oxygenation program, mem., cancer com.; attending pediatric surgeon Huntington Meml. Hosp., Pasadena, Calif., 1996, Pomona Valley, Calif., 1996; asst. prof. surgery Keck Sch. Medicine, U. So. Calif., 1996—. Contbr. articles to peer-reviewed publications. Office: Childrens Hosp LA 4650 Sunset Blvd Los Angeles CA 90027*

**STEIN, JAMES HOWARD**, medical educator, researcher; b. Milw., Wis., Aug. 17, 1964; Bachelor's degree with honors, U. Wis.; MD, Yale U., 1990. Diplomate Am. Bd. Echocardiography in Comprehensive Adult Echocardiography, cert. Internal Medicine, 1993, Cardiovascular Disease, 1997. Intern, internal medicine U. Chgo. Pritzker Sch. Med. Ctr., 1990—91, resident, cardiology, 1991—93; fellow in cardiology Rush-Presbyterian-St. Luke Med. Ctr., Chgo., 1994—96; assoc. prof. cardiovascular medicine U. Wis. Med. Sch., Madison, Wis., 1996—. Dir. atherosclerosis imaging rsch. program U. Wis.; assoc. dir., preventative cardiology program U. Wis. Hosp. and Clinics, dir., vascular health screening program; dir. Outpatient Cardiovascular Medicine Services; assoc. dir. Adult Echocardiography Lab.; mem. Complications of HIV Therapy Subcommittee Rsch. Adv. Com., Adult AIDS Clin. Trial Group Divsn. AIDS, Nat. Inst. Allergy and Infectious Diseases; ad hoc reviewer for two NIH study sessions. Co-author: Am. Soc. Echocardiography Recommendations for Use Echocardiography in Clinical Trials; contbr. articles to peer-reviewed jours. Named one of Top Docs in Cardiology, Madison Mag. Fellow: Am. Coll. Cardiology (co-chmn. ann. scientific sessions 2006, rep. to Nat. Cholesterol Edn. program, mem. clin. expert and consensus documents task force, W. Proctor Harvey Young Tchr. award for Excellence in Tchg.); mem.: Am. Coll. Physicians, Am. Soc. Echocardiography (mem. Carotid IMT task force), Am. Heart Assn., Alpha Omega Alpha. Office: Sect Cardiovascular Medicine U Wis Med Sch G7/341 CSC 600 Highland Avenue H6-315 MC 3248 Madison WI 53792-3248 Office Phone: 608-263-9648. Office Fax: 608-263-0405. Business E-Mail: jhs@medicine.wisc.edu.*

**STEIN, JANE WALLISON**, lawyer; b. Mar. 23, 1947; AB, Barnard Coll., 1968; MA, NYU, 1969; JD magna cum laude, Bklyn. Law Sch., 1974. Bar: NY 1975. Ptnr., co-leader Project Fin. practice Pillsbury Wiinthrop Shaw Pittman, NYC. Editor (in chief): Bklyn. Law Rev. Mem.: Nat. Assn. Bond Lawyers, NY State Bar Assn., Assn. Bar City of NY (chmn. com. on Project Fin. 2002—). Office: Pillsbury Winthrop Shaw Pittman 1540 Broadway New York NY 10036 Office Phone: 212-858-1225. Office Fax: 212-858-1500. Business E-Mail: jane.stein@pillsburylaw.com.

**STEIN, JAY**, retail executive; 2 children. With Stein Mart, Inc., Greenville, Miss., 1966-79, pres., 1979-89, chmn. Jacksonville, Fla., 1989—. Bd. dirs. Promus Hotel Corp., Nations Bank Jacksonville, Bolles Sch., Nat. Conf. Christians and Jews, Am. Heritage Life Ins. Co.; trustee, mem. exec. com. John F. Kennedy Ctr. for Performing Arts; vice chmn. bd. govs. Hebrew Union Coll.; founding mem. The Holocaust Mus., Washington. Pres. Jacksonville Symphony Orch.; past mem. Mayor's Select Com. on Ethics in City Govt.; bd. mem. Peres Ctr. for Peace, Tel Aviv. Recipient Humanitarian award Nat. Conf. Christians and Jews, 1993. Office: 1200 Riverplace Blvd Jacksonville FL 32207-9046

**STEIN, JEROME LEON**, economist, educator; b. Bklyn., Nov. 14, 1928; s. Meyer and Ida (Shapiro) S.; m. Hadassah Levow, Aug. 27, 1950; children: Seth, Gil, Ilana. BA summa cum laude, Bklyn. Coll., 1949; MA, Yale U., 1950, PhD, 1955; Docteur honoris causa, U. de la Méditerranée, 1997. Instr. Brown U., Providence, 1953-56, asst. prof., 1956-60, assoc. prof., 1960-62, prof., 1962-70, Eastman prof. polit. economy, 1970-94, prof. emeritus Providence, 1994—. Vis. prof. Hebrew U., Jerusalem, 1965-66, 72-73, 78; Ford Found. rsch. prof. econs. U. Calif., Berkeley, 1979-80, Sorbonne, U. Paris, 1982, Tohoku U., Sendai, Japan, 1983, Haute Etudes Comml., France, 1987, Monash U., Melbourne U., Australia, 1989, U. Aix-en-Provence, Marseille, France, 1992, 95, 96, 97, 98, France, 1992, U. Munich, 1994, La Sapienza, Rome, 1994; vis. prof. applied math. Brown U., 1996—. Author: Essays in International Finance, 1962, (with G.M. Borts) Economic Growth in a Free Market, 1964, Money and Capacity Growth, 1971, Monetarism, 1976, Monetarist, Keynesian and New Classical Economics, 1982, Economics of Futures Markets, 1986, International Finance Markets, 1991, Fundamental Determinants of Exchange Rates, 1995, Stochastic Optimal Control-International Finance and Debt Crises, 2006; bd. editors Am. Econ. Rev., 1974-80; assoc. editor Jour. Fin., 1964-70, Jour. Banking Fin., 1986-. Ford Found. faculty fellow, 1961-62; Social Sci. Research Council grantee, 1965-66; Guggenheim fellow, 1972-73 Mem. Am. Econ. Assn. Home: 77 Elton St Providence RI 02906-4505 Office: Brown U 183 George St Providence RI 02912-9036 Fax: 401-863-1355. Office Phone: 401-863-2143. Business E-Mail: Jerome_Stein@brown.edu.

**STEIN, JOHN C.**, lawyer; b. Flint, Mich., May 8, 1939; s. Joseph Aloyosius and Gertrude (Carlin) S.; m. Dorothea Ruel, Nov. 20, 1965; children: John Jr., Christian, Peter, Thea. BA, U. San Francisco, 1963; JD, U. Calif. Hastings, San Francisco, 1966; cert., Mil. Justice Sch., Newport, R.I., 1968. Bar: Calif. 1966, U.S. Dist. Ct. (no., ctrl. and so. dists.) Calif. 1969. Dep. city atty. City of San Francisco, Office of City Atty., 1969-71; with The Boccardo Law Firm, San Jose, Calif., 1971—; mng. ptnr., 1981-99. Judge pro tem San Francisco County Superior Ct., 1978—, Santa Clara County Superior Ct., 1981—; lectr. U. Santa Clara Law Sch., 1985—, Hastings Coll. of Law, U. C. San Francisco. Bd. dirs. Katherine Delmar Burke Sch. Girls, San Francisco, 1988-92, Planning Orgn. for The Richmond, San Francisco, 1985-88. Capt. USMC, 1966-69. Fellow Am. Coll. Trial Lawyers; mem. ATLA, Consumer Attys. of Calif. (Trial Lawyer of Yr. San Jose), Am. Bd. Trial Advocates. Democrat. Roman Catholic. Avocations: golf, skiing, scuba diving. Office: Boccardo Law Firm 111 W Saint John St Ste 400 San Jose CA 95113-1107 Office Phone: 408-298-5678. Business E-Mail: jstein@boccardo.com.

**STEIN, KARL N.**, plastic and reconstructive surgeon; b. Phila., July 1, 1940; BA in Chemistry, Temple U., 1962, MD, 1966. Diplomate Am. Bd. Plastic Surgery. Intern U. Pa. Grad. Hosp., 1966-67; resident in surgery Abington Meml. Hosp., 1967-68, SUNY Up-State Med. Ctr., 1970-71, instr. in surgery, 1970—; resident in plastic surgery Hosp. Albert Einstein Coll. Medicine, Bronx Mcpl. Hosp. Ctr., 1971-74, asst. instr. plastic surgery and hand surgery, 1974; pvt. practice in plastic surgery, 1974—. Surgeon Sherman Oaks (Calif.) Burn Ctr., 1975—; cons. L.A. Dept. Water and Power; med. legal expert for burns and plastic surgery; med. legal cons. Author (patent) Treatment of Tar Burns, 1980. Capt. USAF, 1969-71. Fellow Am. Coll. Surgeons; mem. AMA, Am. Soc. Plastic and Reconstructive Surgeons, Am. Burn Assn., Am. Soc. Aesthetic Plastic Surgery, Calif. Soc. Plastic Surgeons, Calif. Med. Assn., L.A. County Med. Assn. Office: PO Box 220340 Newhall CA 91322-0340 Office Phone: 661-255-5451.

**STEIN, LAURA**, food products executive; b. 1961; children: Amanda, Christopher. BA, Dartmouth Coll., 1983; JD, Harvard Law Sch., 1987; MA, Dartmouth Coll. Bar: Calif., 1987. Tracsactional corp. lawyer Morrison &

Foerster, San Francisco; asst. gen. counsel, regulatory affairs The Clorox Co., 1992—99; sr. v.p., gen. counsel The Heinz Co., Pittsburgh, Pa., 2000—. Mem. ABA (chmn. Commn. on Domestic Violence), Calif. State Bar, Assn. Am. Corp. Counsel Assn., Am. Soc. Corp. Sect. Office: H J Heinz Co 600 Grant St Ste 6000 Pittsburgh PA 15219-2857

**STEIN, LAURENCE JAY,** lawyer; b. West Hartford, Conn., Mar. 20, 1961; s. Milton and Selma (Roth) S.; m. Miriam Beth Siegel, Aug. 17, 1986. AB magna cum laude, Harvard Coll., 1982; JD, Stanford U., 1985. Bar: Ill. 1986, Calif. 1989. Clk. to Chief Judge Walter J. Cummings U.S. Ct. Appeals (7th cir.), Chgo., 1985-86; assoc. Latham & Watkins, Chgo., 1986-92, partner, 1993-97, L.A., 1997—; global chmn. Tax Dept., 2000—. Recipient Urban A. Sontheimer award Stanford U., 1985, John Harvard Scholarships, Harvard Coll., 1979-82. Mem. ABA, Calif. Bar Assn., Order of the Coif, Phi Beta Kappa Avocation: golf. Office: Latham & Watkins 633 W 5th St # 4000 Los Angeles CA 90071-2005

**STEIN, LAWRENCE A.,** lawyer; b. Balt., Mar. 18, 1965; s. Hersh and Ellen (Hart) S.; m. Diane Wells, June 23, 1991; children: Joshua A., Julie E. AB, U. Chgo., 1988; JD, No. Ill. U., 1993. Bar: Ill. 1993, U.S. Dist. Ct. (no. dist.) Ill. 1993, U.S. Dist. Ct. Md. 1994, U.S. Dist. Ct. (we. and ea. dists.) Wis. 2001, U.S. Ct. Appeals (7th cir.) 1993, Md. 1994, U.S. Supreme Ct. 1997. Shareholder Huck Bouma PC, Wheaton, Ill., 1993—. Advisor Prairie State Legal Svcs., Carol Stream, Ill., 1993—. Commr. Glen Ellyn (Ill.) Architecture Review Commn., 1994-97; pres. Friends of the No. Ill. U. Librs., 2003-04; mem. Law Sch. Alumni Coun., No. Ill. U., 2003—; sec. Glen Ellyn Libr. Found., Ill., 2006—. Recipient Am. Jurisprudence award for excellence in appellate advocacy Lawyers Coop., 1991. Mem.: ABA, Am. Inns Ct., Ill. State Bar Assn., DuPage County Bar Assn., U. Chgo. Club of Met. Chgo. (bd. dirs. 2003—04), Phi Delta Phi. Republican. Jewish. Home: 300 Lorraine St Glen Ellyn IL 60137-5632 Office: Huck Bouma PC 1755 S Naperville Rd Wheaton IL 60187-8144 Office Phone: 630-221-1755. Business E-Mail: lstein@huckbouma.com.

**STEIN, LAWRENCE V.,** lawyer; b. Newark, Feb. 10, 1950; m. Donna Baier; children: Jonathan, Sarah. AB cum laude, Columbia Coll., 1971; MA, Cornell U., 1974; JD magna cum laude, U. Pa. Law Sch., 1976. Atty. Arnold & Porter, 1976—84, ptnr., 1984—92; sr. v.p., gen. counsel, sec. Genetics Inst., 1992—97; sr. v.p., chief legal counsel Wyeth-Ayerst Global Pharmaceuticals and Genetics Inst., 1997—2001; sr. v.p., dep. gen. counsel Wyeth, 2001—03, sr. v.p., gen. counsel Madison, NJ, 2003—. Comment editor U. Penn Law Review, 1975—76. Avocation: golf. Office: Wyeth 5 Giralda Farms Madison NJ 07940-0874 Office Phone: 973-660-6138. E-mail: steinl@wyeth.com.

**STEIN, MARK RODGER,** allergist; b. Phila., Apr. 24, 1943; s. Eli and Norma Stein; m. Phyllis Feinstein, Dec. 27, 1964; children: Amy Lynn, Philip Warren. BA, LaSalle Coll., Phila., 1964; MD, Jefferson Med. Coll., Phila., 1968. Diplomate Nat. Bd. Med. Examiners, Am. Bd. Internal Medicine, Am. Bd. Allergy and Immunology. Intern Abington (Pa.) Meml. Hosp., 1968-69; resident internal medicine Letterman Army Med. Ctr., San Francisco, 1972-75; fellow allergy and clin. immunology Fitzsimons Army Med. Ctr., Denver, 1975-77; pvt. practice West Palm Beach, Fla., 1979—. Asst. prof. depts. medicine and pediatrics William F. Health Scis. Sch. Medicine, Bethesda, Md., 1978—79; clin. asst. prof. dept. internal medicine U. South Fla. Coll. Medicine, Tampa, 1979—83, Tampa, 1997—2000; clin. care cons. Clin. Ctr., NIH, Bethesda, 1978—79; mem. active staff Good Samaritan Hosp., West Palm Beach, Fla., chief svc. dept. allergy, 1990—98, chief svc. allergy, 2001—; chief dept. allergy St. Mary's Hosp., West Palm Beach, 1985—98; mem. active staff Palm Beach Gardens Med Ctr.; chief allergy svc. Intracostal Health Sys., 2000—01. Editor Gastroesophageal Reflux Disease and Airway Disease, 1999; contr. articles to profl. jours. Trustee Am. Lung Assn., West Palm Beach, 1984-93, 95—. Fellow ACP, Am. Acad. Allergy, Asthma and Immunology, Am. Coll. Allergy, Asthma and Immunology (chmn. geriat. com. 1988-90), Am. Assn. Cert. Allergists, Am. Coll. Chest Physicians; mem. Am. Thoracic Soc., Mil. Allergists, Fla. Med. Assn., Palm Beach County Med. Assn., Asthma and Allergy Found. Am., Fla. Allergy and Immunology Soc. (pres. 1987-88), Southeastern Allergy Assn. Jewish. Avocations: tennis, golf. Office: 840 Us Highway 1 North Palm Beach FL 33408-3830 Office Phone: 561-626-2006. E-mail: latallergy@aol.com.

**STEIN, MARTIN MATTHEW,** management consultant; b. Bad Gastein, Austria, Feb. 21, 1946; arrived in U.S., 1949, naturalized, 1956; s. Leon and Bess (Kicis) Stein; children: Joshua, Michelle, Claudia, Stephen, William. BS in Econs., U. Md., 1967, MA in Econs., 1975; DES in Info. Sys. and Applied Math., U. Paris VI Sorbonne, 1976, DSc, 1979. Econ. U.S. Dept. Commerce and U.S. Dept. Transp., Washington, 1967—73; petroleum allocation officer Exec. Office of Pres., Washington, 1973; mgr. socio-econ. group Md. Dept. Transp., Balt., 1973—78; dir. transp. and automotive cons. dept. Abt Assocs., Inc., Cambridge, Mass., 1978—89; sr. cons. Forum Corp., Boston, Frankfurt and London, 1989—91; v.p. Circadian Techs., Inc., Cambridge, 1992; dep. dir. Ctr. for Transp. Studies MIT, Cambridge, 1992—93; dir. process reengring. and logistics mgmt. strategies; v.p. Competitive Capabilities Internat., Newport Beach, Calif. and Capetown, South Africa, 2005—. Program chmn. conf. in N.Y. and Brussels Am. Productivity and Quality Ctr., Houston; pres. Martin Stein Assocs., Needham, Mass., 1991—; program dir. JIT II Edn. and Rsch. Ctr., Framingham, Mass., 1995—; sr. econ. cons. Booz-Allen & Hamilton; asst. prof. econs. Sch. Bus. U. Balt.; lectr. Johns Hopkins U., Balt.; lectr. MBA program Babson Coll., Wellesley, Mass.; mem. adj. faculty U. Phoenix; v.p. Internat. Policy Inst., Washington; sr. tech. advisor energy and transport UN Dept. Tech. Coop. and Devel., N.Y.C., Slovenia, UN Devel. Programme Ctr. for Water and Transport, Geneva; mem. adv. com. Def. Econ. Analysis Coun., U.S. Dept. Def.; cons. macrologistics, strategy adaptation design and implementation, benchmarking, just-in-time techniques for automotive and transp. industries, total quality mgmt.; strategic implementation processes and customer communication programs; spkr. to industry and trade assns.; v.p. Competitive Capabilities Internat., Newport Beach, Calif., Capetown, South Africa. Mem. retail trade study exec. com. Greater Balt. Com., 1976, Econ. Devel. Coun., Regional Planning Coun., 1977—78. Fellow: Internat. Inst. Social Econs.; mem.: Transp. Rsch. Forum, Transp. Rsch. Bd., Internat. Inst. Forecasting, Internat. Soc. Logistics Execs. (chmn. exec. adv. coun. 1994—), Internat. Assn. Energy Economists, Am. Econ. Assn., Balt. Econ. Soc. (founder, pres.), Nat. Coun. Assns. for Policy Scis. (co-founder, v.p.), Soc. Automotive Analysts (pres., founder, hon. lifetime mem., Pres. award), Soc. Govt. Economists (founder, pres., chmn. bd., award 1972), U. Md. Alumni Assn. (coun., chpt. v.p., pres. 1973—77), John Marshall Soc., U.S. C. of C. (coord. coll. bus. symposium 1966), Delta Sigma Pi, Omicron Delta Epsilon. Home: 52 Cranberry Ln Needham MA 02492-1422 Office Phone: 781-444-0213. E-mail: martin.stein@comcast.net.

**STEIN, MARVIN,** psychiatrist, historian; b. St. Louis, Dec. 8, 1923; s. Samuel G. and Dora (Kline) S.; m. Ann Hackman, May 5, 1950; children: Leslie, David, Lisa. BS, MD, Washington U., St. Louis, 1949; grad., Phila. Psychoanalytic Inst., 1959. Intern St. Louis City Hosp., 1949-50; asst. resident in psychiatry Barnes Hosp., St. Louis, 1950-51; fellow in psychiatry Hosp. U. Pa., 1953-55; asst. prof., then assoc. prof. psychiatry U. Pa. Med. Sch., 1956-63; prof. psychiatry Cornell U. Med. Sch., N.Y.C., 1963-66; prof. Med. Sch., 1956-63; prof. psychiatry Cornell U. Med. Sch., N.Y.C., 1963-66; prof. chmn. dept. psychiatry SUNY Downstate Med. Ctr., Bklyn., 1966-71; chmn. dept. psychiatry Mt. Sinai Sch. Medicine, N.Y.C., 1971-87, Esther and Joseph Klingenstein prof., 1971-94, Esther and Joseph Klingenstein prof. emeritus, 1994—. Mem. fellowships rev. panel NIMH, 1961-64, chmn. mental health extramural rsch. adv. com., 1968-71, chmn. rev. com. Mental Health Aspects of AIDS, 1988-90; mem. rsch. adv. com. VA, 1965-68, mem. rsch. svc. merit rev. bd. in behavioral sci., 1972-75; chmn. Mental Health Rsch. Career Award Com., 1963-67; chmn. bd. dirs. Founds. Fund for Rsch. in Psychiatry, 1967-70; mem. behavioral medicine study sect. NIH, 1981-83, geriatric rev. com., 1986-88. Contbr. articles on brain and behavior and immune function and history of psychiatry to med. and history jours. USPHS postdoctoral fellow, 1951-53; mental health career investigator, 1956-61; sr. fellow grantee, 1961-63. Mem. Am. Psychiat. Assn. (chmn. rsch. coun. 1981-84),

N.Y. Acad. Medicine (Salmon com. 1984—), Alpha Omega Alpha. Home: 5700 Arlington Ave Bronx NY 10471-1503 Office: Mt Sinai Sch Medicine 1 Gustave L Levy Pl New York NY 10029-6500 Business E-Mail: marvin.stein@mssm.edu.

**STEIN, MELVIN A.,** accountant; b. N.Y.C., Sept. 7, 1932; s. William H. and Lillian (Goldberg) S.; m. Barbara Blumencranz, Dec. 17, 1955 (dec.); children: Susan, Karen; m. Marie Sacco, Nov. 1, 1992. BS, N.Y. U., 1953. Pvt. practice acctg., Jericho, NY, 1961-75; pres. Stein & Stein, P.C., Hicksville, 1975-81, Stein, Stein & Feit, P.C., 1982—. Bd. dir. Stern Sch. Bus. N.Y. U., treas. bd. dir., 1991—92, v.p. bd. dir., 1995—, alumni bd. dir., mem. dean adv. coun., 2002—, pres. exec. forum, 2002—, dir. entrepreneurship conf., 2000—. Recipient NYU Alumni Meritorious Svc. award, 2005. Mem. AICPA, N.Y. State Soc. CPAs, N.J. Soc. CPAs, C.W. Post Tax Inst., NYU Club, Princeton Club, The Exec. Forum (pres.). Jewish. Home: 7 Ingleside Ln White Plains NY 10605-5009 Office: 1 Frederick Pl Hicksville NY 11801-4205 also: Buccaneer Mall St Thomas VI 00801 Office Phone: 516-938-2100. Personal E-Mail: cpa35@aol.com.

**STEIN, M(EYER) L(EWIS),** journalist, editor, writer; b. Escanaba, Mich., July 30, 1920; s. Alexander and Fannie Stein; m. Romana Susan Paal, Apr. 15, 1981 (dec. Feb. 1994); children: Andrea, Jeannine; stepchildren: Adam Paal, Edith Paal; m. Barbara Betlejewska, May 15, 2001 BJ, U. Mo., 1942; MA, Stanford U., 1961. Reporter, telegraph editor Daily Tribune, Royal Oak, Mich., 1946—51; reporter San Francisco Examiner, 1951—60; prof., chair dept. journalism and mass comm. NYU, 1961—74; prof., chair dept. journalism Calif. State U., Long Beach, 1974—87; west coast editor Editor & Publ. mag., Palo Alto, Calif., 1981—89. Lectr. in field. Author 17 books including: Freedom of the Press, 1970, Reporting Today, 1971, How to Write Plain English, 1976, Shaping the News, 1974, When Presidents Meet the Press, 1969, Under Fire: Story of American War Correspondents, 1995, (with Susan Paterno) Introduction to Journalism, 1998, 2d edit., 2006, (with Susan Paterno) Talk Straight, Listen Carefully: The Art of Interviewing, 2001; lit. cons.; contbr. over 500 articles to newspapers and mags. Sgt. U.S. Army, 1942-45, Africa, Italy. Gannett fellow, 1980. Mem. Assn. Edn. in Journalism and Mass Comm. (chmn. freedom and responsibility com. 1964), Am. Soc. Journalists and Authors. Avocation: travel. Home and Office: 10 Bella Rosa Irvine CA 92602 Office Phone: 714-838-8149. E-mail: mlsteinav@aol.com.

**STEIN, MILTON MICHAEL,** retired lawyer; b. NYC, Sept. 18, 1936; s. Isidore and Sadie (Lefkowitz) S.; m. Jacqueline Martin, June 17, 1962; children: April, Alicia. AB, Columbia U., 1958, LLB, 1961. Bar: N.Y. 1962, Pa. 1971, U.S. Supreme Ct. 1971. Asst. dist. atty. N.Y. County, 1962-67; sr. counsel Nat. Commn. for Reform of Fed. Criminal Law, Washington, 1967-70; asst. dist. atty., chief of appeals City of Phila., 1970-73; asst. dir. Nat. Wire Tapping Commn., Washington, 1973-75; dir. D.C. Law Revision, Washington, 1975-77; spl. assst. HUD, Washington, 1977-79; asst. gen. counsel U.S. Commodity Futures Trading Commn., Washington, 1979-83; v.p. N.Y. Futures Exch., N.Y.C., 1983-89, N.Y. Stock Exch., N.Y.C., 1989—2005; ret., 2005; arbitrator, 2005—. Democrat. Jewish. Home: Hudson House PO Box 286 Ardsley On Hudson NY 10503-0286 Personal E-Mail: thejamis@aol.com.

**STEIN, PAUL DAVID,** cardiologist; b. Cin., Apr. 13, 1934; s. Simon and Sadie (Friedman) S.; m. Janet Louise Tucker, Aug. 14, 1966; children: Simon, Douglas, Rebecca. BS, U. Cin., 1955, MD, 1959. Intern Jewish Hosp., Cin., 1959-60, med. resident, 1961-62, Gorgas Hosp., C.Z., 1960-61; fellow in cardiology U. Cin., 1962-63, Mt. Sinai Hosp., N.Y.C., 1963-64; rsch. fellow Harvard Med. Sch., Boston, 1964-66; asst. dir. cardiac catheterization lab. Baylor U. Med. Ctr., Dallas, 1966-67; asst. prof. medicine Creighton U., Omaha, 1967-69; assoc. prof. medicine U. Okla., Oklahoma City, 1969-73; prof. rsch. medicine U. Okla. Coll. Medicine, Oklahoma City, 1973-76; dir. cardiovascular rsch. Henry Ford Hosp., Detroit, 1976-94, med. dir. cardiovascular rehab., 1994-2000; dir. rsch. St. Joseph Mercy Oakland Hosp., Pontiac, Mich., 2000—04; Henry Ford prof. medicine Case Western Res. U., Cleve., 1994—2000; prof. medicine Wayne State U., Detroit, 2003—. Adj. prof. physics Oakland U., Rochester, Mich., 1985— Author: A Physical and Physiological Basis for the Interpretation of Cardiac Ausculation: Evaluations Based Primarily on Second Sound and Ejection Murmurs, 1981, Pulmonary Embolism, 1996; contbr. articles to profl. jours. Coun. on Clin. Cardiology fellow Am. Heart Assn., 1971, Coun. on Circulation fellow, 1972. Recipient Lifetime Achievement award, Am. Heart Assn., Mich. chpt., 2002. Master Am. Coll. Chest Physicians (pres. 1993); fellow ACP (Laureate award, Mich. chpt. 2003), ASME, Am. Coll. Cardiology. Office Phone: 248-858-6772, 248-858-6772. E-mail: steinp@trinity-health.org.

**STEIN, PAULA JEAN ANNE BARTON,** hotel real estate company executive, real estate broker; b. Chgo., July 29, 1929; m. Marshall L. Stein; children: Guy G., George L.; guardian of Bradley Stein, Gregory Stein. BA, Lake Forest (Ill.) U., 1951; postgrad., Roosevelt U., Chgo., 1955—77, UCLA, 1978—79. Administrv. asst. publicity Kefauver for Pres., Chgo., 1951; administrv. asst. Wells Orgns., Chgo., 1952; rschr., writer Employers Assn. Am., Chgo., 1951-52; writer Woodworking Jobbers Assn., Chgo., 1953; cons. L.A., 1978-80; pres., broker Steinvest, Inc., Chgo., 1980—; freelance writer, 1996—. Cons., hotels Nat. Diversified Svcs., Inc., Chgo., 1990—, Beach Hotel, Inc., Monterey, Calif., IBA Women's Adv. Bd., 1999; advocate for learning disorder solutions. Script for first TV bus. prog. on WGN-TV, 1951-52. Mem. Ragdale Found., Lake Forest, Ill. IBA fellow, 1990. Mem. World Future Soc. (profl.), Sisters in Crime, Mystery Writers, So. Poverty Law Ctr., others. Avocations: painting, writing. Home and Office: Steinvest Inc 2291 Hybernia Dr Highland Park IL 60035-5509 Office Fax: 847-748-8349. Personal E-Mail: steinvest@msn.com.

**STEIN, PHYLLIS KRAVET,** research scientist; d. Charles and Helen Kravet; m. Valerian Titus D'Souza, June 20, 1995; children: Daniel Arthur Katz-Stein(dec.), Jonah Gordon. AB, Barnard Coll., N.Y., 1962; MEd, U. Va., Charlottesville, Va., 1985, PhD, 1990, PhD, 2000. Dir. heart rate variability lab. Washington U. Sch. of Medicine, St. Louis, 1997—, rsch. assoc. prof. medicine, 2005—. Contbr. articles pub. to over 60 profl. jour. grantee R0-3, R01, NIH-NHBLI, 1997-2007. Office: Wash Univ Sch Medicine 660 S Euclid St Saint Louis MO 63110 Home Fax: 314-286-1394; Office Fax: 314-286-1394. Personal E-Mail: pstein@im.wustl.edu.

**STEIN, RICHARD LOUIS,** chemist, educator; b. Washington, July 7, 1944; s. Edward John and Margaret Ann (Hickey) S.; m. J. Teresa Taylor, Apr. 12, 1968. BS in Chemistry, George Washington U., 1966; PhD in Medicinal Chemistry, Med. Coll. Va., 1970. Rsch. asst. Med. Coll. Va., Richmond, 1966-70; asst. prof. chemistry Germanna C.C., Locust Grove, Va., 1970-72, assoc. prof., 1973-75, prof. chemistry, 1975—, program head dept. natural sci., 1970-84. Vis. scientist Va. Acad. Sci., Richmond, 1980—; com. sci. curricula Va. C.C. System, Richmond, 1976; design cons. J. Sargent Reynolds C.C., Richmond, 1974. Author: Experiments in Chemistry, 1985; contbr. articles to chem. publs. including Jour. Medicinal Chemistry, Jour. Chem. Edn. Bd. dirs. Am. Cancer Soc., Culpeper, Va., 1972; drug abuse cons. Rappahannock Regional Coun. Drug Abuse, Culpeper, 1974; judge Rappahannock Sci. Fair, Orange, Va., 1978 Grantee Inst. Instrn. Excellence, 1985; summer faculty fellow Oak Ridge (Tenn.) Nat. Atomic Rsch. Lab., 1982; grantee Autodesk, Inc., Sausalito, Calif., 1992. Fellow AICE; mem. AAAS, Am. Chem. Soc., Sigma Xi. Office: Germanna Community College 2130 Germanna Hwy Locust Grove VA 22508-2102

**STEIN, ROBERT A.,** writer, educator, military officer; b. Duluth, Minn., Aug. 5, 1933; s. A. A. and Grace (Wichterman) Stein; m. Betty Lou Pavlak, 1955; children: Robert Jr., David K., Steven J. BS in Commerce, U. Iowa, 1956; degree with hons. in Academic Instr. Sch., USAF, 1966; MA in Counselor Edn., U. Iowa, 1968, MA in Writing, 1986; degree with honors, Indsl. Coll. Armed Forces, 1973. Cert. tchr. Iowa, 1991; profl. counselor. Commd. 2d lt. USAF, 1956, advanced through grades to col., 1977, pilot trainee Goodfellow AFB, Tex., 1957, pilot 345th Squadron Sewart AFB, Tenn.,

1957—61, instr. pilot 1602nd Wing Chateauroux AB, France, 1961—64; asst. prof. aerospace studies U. Iowa, Iowa City, 1964-66, assoc. prof., 1966-68, prof., 1975-77; dir., safety and security U. Iowa Hosps./Clinics, Iowa City, 1977-85; mem. faculty divsn. writing Kirkwood CC, Iowa City, Cedar Rapids, 1984-89; writer, tchr. Iowa City, 1985—. Writer, tchr. Iowa City/Johnson County Sr. Citizens Ctr., 1994—; sports announcer U. Iowa. Author: (novels) Apollyon: A Novel, 1985, The Chase, 1988, The Black Samaritan, 1997, 2d edit., 2000, The Vengeance Equation, 2000, hardcover edit., 2001, Death Defied (Internat. Lit. award, 1988); co-author: (screenplays) WGAW-Registered, 2001. Decorated Bronze Star; recipient Outstanding Faculty award, U. Iowa, 1968. Mem.: Authors League Am., Authors Guild, Mil. Affairs Assn. (charter), Air Force Assn. (life), Nat. Iowa Varsity Club (exec. bd., pres. 2002—03, Lifetime Achievement award 1990), Nat. Iowa Lettermen's Club (past pres.), Rotary (Paul Harris fellow), Daedalians, Phi Delta Kappa. Avocations: flying, travel, reading, swimming. Home and Office: 2020 Ridgeway Dr Iowa City IA 52245-3238

**STEIN, ROBERT ALAN,** electronics executive; b. Chgo., Oct. 18, 1930; s. Manfred and Mildred (Rosenfield) S.; m. Frances Roslyn Berger, Dec. 25, 1960; 1 dau., Marcia Beth. BA, U. Chgo., 1950, MBA, 1953. C.P.A., Ill. Sr. auditor Scovell, Wellington & Co., Chgo., 1955—63; supr. corp. acctg. Mack Trucks, Inc., Montvale, NJ, 1963—65; v.p. fin., treas. Lionel Corp., N.Y.C., 1965—82; pres. ITI Electronics, Inc., Fairfield, NJ, 1982—. Served with U.S. Army, 1953-55. Mem. Am. Inst. CPAs. Home: 32 Stonewall Dr Livingston NJ 07039-1822 Office: 214 Little Falls Rd Fairfield NJ 07004 Personal E-Mail: itielect@aol.com.

**STEIN, ROBERT ALLEN,** legal association administrator, law educator; b. Mpls., Sept. 16, 1938; s. Lawrence E. and Agnes T. (Brynildson) S.; m. Sandra H. Stein; children: Linda Stein Routh, Laura Stein Conrad, Karin Stein O'Boyle. BS in Law, U. Minn., 1960, JD summa cum laude, 1961; LLD (hon.), Uppsala U., Sweden, 1993. Bar: Wis. 1961, Minn. 1967. Assoc. Foley, Sammond & Lardner, Milw., 1961-64; prof. U. Minn. Law Sch., Mpls., 1964-77; assoc. dean U. Minn., 1976-77, v.p. adminstrn. and planning, 1978-80; dean U. Minn. Law Sch., 1979-94; faculty rep. men's intercollegiate athletics U. Minn., 1981-94; of counsel Mullin, Weinberg & Daly, PA, Mpls., 1970-80, Gray, Plant, Mooty, Mooty & Bennett, Mpls., 1980-94. Vis. prof. UCLA, 1969-70, U. Chgo., 1975-76; commr. Uniform State Laws Commn. Minn., 1973—; v.p. Nat. Uniform Laws Com., 1991-93, exec. comm., 1991—, sec., 1997—; acad. fellow Am. Coll. Trusts and Estates Counsel, 1975—; vis. scholar Am. Bar Found., Chgo., 1975-76; trustee Gt. No. Iron Ore Properties, 1982—, Uniform Laws Found., 1992—; advisor Restatement of Law Second, Property, 1977—, Restatement of Law Trusts (Prudent Investor Rule), 1989-90, Restatement of Law Third, Trusts, 1993—; chmn. bd. dirs. Ednl. Credit Mgmt. Corp., 1993—; bd. dirs. Fiduciary Counselling Inc. Author: Stein on Probate, 1976, 3d edit., 1995, How to Study Law and Take Law Exams, 1996, Estate Planning Under the Tax Reform Act of 1976, 2d edit, 1978, In Pursuit of Excellence: A History of the University of Minnesota Law School, 1980, contbr. articles to profl. jours. Founding bd. dirs. Park Ridge Ctr., 1985-95; co-chair Gov.'s Task Force on Ctr. for Treatment of Torture Victims, 1985, bd. dirs., 1985-87. Fellow Am. Bar Found (bd. dirs. 1987-94), Am. Coll. Tax Counsel; mem. ABA (coun. sect. of legal edn. and admission to bar 1986-91, vice chairperson 1991-92, chair-elect 1992-93, chair 1993-94, exec. dir., 1994-2006), Internat. Acad. Estate and Trust Law (academician), Am. Judicature Soc. (bd. dirs. 1984-88), Am. Law Inst. (coun. mem. 1987—, exec. com. 1993—), Minn. Bar Assn. (bd. govs. 1979-94, exec. coun., probate and trust law sect. 1973-77), Hennepin County Bar Assn.

**STEIN, ROBERT BENJAMIN,** biomedical researcher, physician; b. Buffalo, Oct. 28, 1950; s. Frank and Eleanor (Bankoff) S.; m. Marcia Joan Lieberman, Aug. 10, 1975 (div.); children: Rebecca Anne, Joshua David; m. Sophia Anne Rose, Dec. 29, 1989 (div.); children: Susan Claire, Stephanie Michelle; m. Faye Elizabeth Sutherland, Aug. 2, 2000. BS, Ind. U., 1972; MD, PhD, Duke U., 1979. Diplomate Am. Bd. Anatomic and Clin. Pathology. House staff Duke U. Med. Ctr., Durham, N.C., 1980-83; sr. rsch. fellow Dept Virus and Cell Biology Merck Sharp & Dohme Rsch. Labs, West Point, Pa., 1983-87, assoc. dir. molecular and cardiovascular pharmacology, 1987-89, sr. dir., head dept. pharmacology, 1989-90; v.p. rsch. Ligand Pharms., Inc., San Diego, 1990-92, v.p. rsch. and preclin. devel., 1992-93, sr. v.p., CSO, 1993-96; exec. v.p., rsch. and preclin. devel. DuPont Merck, Wilmington, Del., 1996-98; exec. v.p. rsch. and preclin. DuPont Pharms., Wilmington, 1998—. Contbr. articles to profl. jours., chpts. to books. Ins. Med. scholar, 1977-79; James B. Duke scholar, 1976-78; Lang Med. Pub. award, 1979; NIH grantee, 1974-75. Fellow Am. Soc. Clin. Pathologists, N.Y. Acad. Scis., Am. Physiol. Soc., AAAS, Sigma Xi, Phi Beta Kappa, Alpha Omega Alpha. Avocations: piano, history, literature. E-mail: Robert.B.Stein@dupontpharma.com.

**STEIN, RONALD J.,** lawyer; b. NYC, 1935; AB, Columbia Univ., 1956; LLB cum laude, Harvard Univ., 1959; LLM, Georgetown Univ., 1962. Bar: NY 1959, DC 1959. Fla. 1975. Adminstrv. ptnr., labor, employment practice area Stroock & Stroock & Lavan LLP. NYC. Bd. dir. City Parks Found. NYC, 92nd St. YMCA, NYC. Bd. of editors Harvard Law Rev., 1958—59. Mem.: NY State Bar Assn., Assn. Bar City NY. Office: Stroock & Stroock & Lavan LLP 180 Maiden Ln New York NY 10038-4982 Office Phone: 212-806-6018. Office Fax: 212-806-6006. Business E-Mail: rstein@stoock.com.

**STEIN, RUTH ELIZABETH KLEIN,** physician; b. NYC, Nov. 2, 1941; d. Theodore and Mimi (Foges) Klein; m. H. David Stein, June 9, 1963; children: Lynn Andrea Stein Melnick, Sharon Lisa, Deborah Michelle. AB, Barnard Coll., 1962; MD, Albert Einstein Coll. Medicine, 1966. Diplomate Am. Bd. Pediat. Intern, then resident Bronx Mcpl. Hosp. Ctr., 1966—68; sr. resident, fellow; 1968instr. dept. pediats. George Washington U., Washington, 1968—70; with Albert Einstein Coll. of Medicine, Bronx, 1970—77, assoc. prof. pediats., 1977—83, prof., 1983—; vice-chmn. dept. pediats. Albert Einstein Coll., 1992—2002, dir. office of acad. affairs, dept. pediats., 1997—2002; pediatrician-in-chief, dir. pediats. Jacobi Med. Ctr. (formerly Bronx Mcpl. Hosp. Ctr.), 1992—97. Vis. prof. pub. health dept. epidemiology Yale U. Sch. Medicine, New Haven, 1986-87; scholar-in-residence United Hosp. Fund, NY, 1995-97; dir., prin. investigator Preventive Intervention Rsch. Ctr. for Child Health, NY, 1983-94, Nat. Child Health Assessment Planning Project, NY, Behavioral Pediatric Tng. Program, NY; dir. gen. pediatrics Pediat. Divsn., NY, 1992-97; apptd. to Montefiore Med. Ctr., North Ctrl. Bronx Hosp., Jacobi Med. Ctr.; bd. dirs. Ctr. for Child Health Rsch. of Am. Acad. Pediatrics, mem. exec. com., 1999-2004; co-chmn. com. on evaluation of child health 2002-04, NRC/Inst. Medicine, 1999-2005; bd. sci. counselors Nat. Ctr. Health Stats. of CDC, 2006-. Editor: Caring for Children with Chronic Illness: Issues and Strategies, 1989, Health Care for Children: What's Right, What's Wrong, What's Next, 1997. mem. editorial bd. Jour. Behavioral and Devel. Pediatrics; contbr. articles to profl. jours. Fellow Am. Acad. Pediats.; mem. APHA, Am. Pediatric Soc., Soc. for Pediat. Rsch., Ambulatory Pediat. Assn. (bd. dirs. 1982-89, pres. 1987-88, rsch. award 1995, Ray Helfer award 1999), NY Acad. Medicine (chmn. NY forum on child health 2001-05), Soc. for Devel. and Behavioral Pediats., Alpha Omega Alpha. Jewish. Home: 91 Larchmont Ave Larchmont NY 10538-3748 Office: Albert Einstein Coll Med Montefiore Med Ctr Dept Pediat 111 E 210 St Bronx NY 10467-2804 Office Phone: 718-920-7932. Business E-Mail: rstein@aecom.yu.edu.

**STEIN, SAM LEE,** lawyer; b. Cherokee, Okla., Nov. 19, 1958; s. Leroy Clark and Rosevelyn Edith (Peterson) Stein; m. Kelly Lee Pelter, Dec. 27, 1980; children: Patrick Leroy, Kelsy Lee. BS in Agr., Okla. State U., 1981; JD with honors, U. Okla., 1987. Bar: Okla. 1987, U.S. Dist. Ct. (we. dist.) Okla. 1987, U.S. Dist. Ct. (no. dist.) Tex. 1987, Tex. 1988, U.S. Dist. Ct. (we. dist.) Tex. 1989, U.S. Ct. Appeals (5th cir.) 1993, cert.: Tex. Bd. Legal Specialization (civil trial and consumer and comml. lawl) 1994. Assoc. Morris, Moore, Dalrymple, et. al., Amarillo, Tex., 1987—89, Templeton & Garner, PC, Amarillo, 1989—90; shareholder Garner, Stone & Lovell, Amarillo,

1990—94; mng. shareholder Garner, Lovell & Stein, PC, Amarillo, 1994—97; prin. Garner & Stein, LLP, Cherokee, Okla., 1997—2001, Garner, Stein & Dean, LLP, Cherokee, 2001—04, Whittenburg, Whittenburg, Garner & Stein, P.C., Cherokee, 2004—. Asst. scoutmaster Troop 335 Boy Scouts Am., Cherokee, 1997—; bd. dirs. Cimarron Coun. Enid, Okla., 1999—. Recipient Profl. Responsibility award U. Okla., 1987. Mem.: ATLA, ABA, Okla. Trial Lawyers Assn., Okla. Bar Assn., State Bar Tex. Office: Whittenburg Whittenburg Garner & Stein PC 305 S Grand Cherokee OK 73728 Office Phone: 580-596-3000. E-mail: sstein@akslc.net.

STEIN, SANDRA LOU, educational psychology professor; b. Freeport, Ill., Oct. 6, 1942; d. William Kenneth and Marien Elizabeth Stein. BS, U. Wis., Madison, 1964; MS Edn., No. Ill. U., 1967, EdD, 1969. Tchr. English Rockford Sch. Dist., Ill., 1964—65; tchr. Russian Jefferson County Sch. Dist., Lakewood, Colo., 1966—67; asst. prof. edn. U. S.C., Columbia, 1969—71, No. Ill. U., DeKalb, 1971—72, Rider U. Lawrenceville, NJ, 1972—75, assoc. prof. edn., 1975—81; prof. edn. Rider Coll., Lawrenceville, 1981—; dept. chair, 1983—91, 2003—06. Cons. on measurement and evaluation, women's edn., 1973— Contbr. articles to ednl. publs Deacon Presbyn. Ch. Lawrenceville, 1984—87. Recipient Disting. Tchg. award Rider Coll. and Lindback Found., 1981 Mem. APA, AAUP (chpt. pres. 2000-01, negotiating team 2002, Outstanding Achievement award Rider Coll. chpt. 1988), Am. Ednl. Rsch. Assn., Phi Delta Kappa (chpt. pres. 1986-87, Svc. Key award 1991, faculty advisor 1994—99) Office: Rider U 2083 Lawrenceville Rd Lawrenceville NJ 08648-3099 Office Phone: 609-896-5348. E-mail: stein@rider.edu.

STEIN, SHERYL E., lawyer; b. Bklyn., Apr. 20, 1952; BA cum laude, Univ. Miami, 1974; JD, Southwestern Univ., 1978. Bar: Calif. 1979. Ptnr., office mng. ptnr., leader office Corp. & Securities practice sect. Pillsbury Winthrop Shaw Pittman, LA. Mem.: LA County Bar Found. (bd. mem.), LA County Bar Assn., Org. Women Exec. Office: Pillsbury Winthrop Shaw Pittman Suite 2800 725 S Figueroa St Los Angeles CA 90017 Office Phone: 213-488-7194. Office Fax: 213-629-1033. Business E-Mail: sheryl.stein@pillsburylaw.com.

STEIN, SOL, publishing executive, writer; b. Chgo. Oct. 13, 1926; s. Louis and Zelda (Zam) S.; m. Patricia Day, Mar. 31, 1962 (div. Oct. 1997); children: Kevin David, Jeffrey Lewelyn, Leland Dana, Robert Bruce, Andrew Charles, David Day, Elizabeth Day; m. Edith Tennenbaum Shapiro, Nov. 25, 2000. BSS, CCNY, 1948; MA, Columbia U., 1949, postgrad., 1949-51. Lectr. social studies CCNY, 1948-51; sr. editor, ideological adv. staff Voice of Am., US State Dept., 1951-53; exec. dir. Am. Com. for Cultural Freedom, 1953—56; gen. editor, originator Beacon Press Paperbacks, Boston, 1954—; mng. editor Rsch. Inst. Am., 1956—58; cons. to pres. Harcourt, Brace, Jovanovich, NYC, 1958-59; exec. v.p. The Mid-Century Book Soc., NYC, 1959-62; pres., editor in chief Stein & Day Pubs., Briarcliff Manor, NY, 1962-89; pres. The Colophon Corp., Scarborough, NY, 1983-95, The WritePro Corp., 1989—2001, The Stein Software Corp., 1993—. Lectr., playwright Columbia U., 1958-60, Dialogue for Writers, Pub., U. Calif., Irvine, 1990-93; treas. The Forensic Found., N.Y.C., 1959-62; founding mem. Playwrights Group, The Actors Studio, 1957. Author: (plays) The Illegitimist, 1953 (1st prize Dramatists Alliance), A Shadow of My Enemy, 1957, (novels) The Husband, 1969, The Magician, 1971. Living Room, 1974, The Childkeeper, 1975, Other People, 1979, The Resort, 1980, The Touch of Treason, 1985, A Deniable Man, 1989, The Best Revenge, 1991 (computer software) WritePro, The Stein Creative Writing Program, 1989—, FirstAid for Writers, 1991, FictionMaster, 1993, WritePro for Business, 1996; (non-fiction) A Feast for Lawyers, 1989, Stein on Writing, 1995, How to Grow a Novel, 1999, (with James Baldwin) Native Sons, 2004; also articles, revs. poetry. Mem. exec. com. Am. Friends of Captive Nations. Served to 1st lt. AUS, 1945-47. Fellow Yaddo Found., 1952, MacDowell Colony, 1952-56. Recipient Disting. Instr. award U. Calif. at Irvine, 1992. Mem. New Dramatists Com. (coun. mem.), Internat. Brotherhood Magicians (hon. life), Writers Guild Am. East, Authors Guild, Phi Beta Kappa. Avocations: tennis, inventing computer software programs. Office: 277 E South Broadway Tarrytown NY 10591-5322 Personal E-mail: solstein@aol.com.

STEIN, STANLEY RICHARD, lawyer, fast food company executive; b. Boston, Apr. 17, 1942; s. Frederick J. and Minnie L. (Gilette) S.; m. Ann Debra Stein, July 2, 1967; children: Jason, Jamie. BA, Boston U., 1964; JD, Boston Coll., 1967. Bar: Mass., Ohio. Supervisory atty. NLRB, 1967-72; head labor rels. dept. Schottenstein, Garel & Zox, Columbus, Ohio, 1972-74; labor rels. counsel McDonald's Corp., Oak Brook, Ill., 1974-78, v.p. labor rels., 1978-81, v.p. pers. and labor rels., 1981—. Mem. ABA.

STEIN, STEPHEN WILLIAM, lawyer; b. NYC, Apr. 12, 1937; s. Melvin S. and Cornelia (Jacobowitz) S.; m. Judith N., Jan. 22, 1966. AB, Princeton U., 1959; LLB, Columbia U., 1962; LLM, NYU, 1963. Bar: NY 1962. Assoc. White & Case, N.Y.C., 1963-67; atty. advisor U.S. Agy. Internat. Devel., Washington, 1967-69, regional legal advisor Mission to India New Delhi, 1969-71, asst. gen. counsel Washington, 1971-73; assoc. ptnr. Delson & Gordon, N.Y.C., 1973-87; ptnr. Kelley Drye & Warren, N.Y.C., 1987—. U.S. exec. com. Internat. Trade, Tourism & Investment Promotion Program, 1990-92; mem. U.S.-Indonesia Trade & Investment Adv. Com., 1989-92; vis. instr. Internat. Devel. Law Inst., 1993; lectr. Internat. Law Inst., Washington, 1984, 85; spkr. in field. Mem. ABA (mem. sect. internat. law, co-chair African law com. 1999-2002), Assn. Bar of City of N.Y. (mem. com. project fin. 1997-2003, mem. com. Asian affairs 1992—2004, former mem. others), Am. Indonesian C. of C. (bd. dirs. 1986—, pres. 1989-96). Home: 320 Central Park W New York NY 10025-7659 Office: Kelley Drye & Warren 101 Park Ave New York NY 10178-0062 Office Phone: 212-808-7794. Business E-Mail: sstein@kelleydrye.com.

STEIN, STEVEN H., pharmaceutical research scientist; b. Johannesburg, Nov. 10, 1966; m. Debbie Stein, Jan. 19, 1992; children: Joshua, David, Jacob, Noah. MB, BCh, U. Witwatersrand, Johannesburg, 1992. Diplomate Am. Bd. Internal Medicine, Am. Bd. Hematology, Am. Bd. Oncology. Group dir. GSK, Collegeville, Pa., 2004—. Asst. prof. Hosp. U. Pa., Phila., 2001—. Mem.: Am. Soc. Hemotology, Am. Coll. Physicians, Am. Soc. Clin.Oncology. Achievements include research in novel molecules for breast cancer. Office: GlaxoSmithKline 1250 S Collegeville Rd Collegeville PA 19426 Office Phone: 610-917-4733. E-mail: steven.h.stein@gsk.com.

STEIN, THOMAS HENRY, social sciences educator; b. Elmhurst, Ill., May 17, 1949; s. Peter Leonard and Marion Edith (Zirbel) S.; m. Alberta Piazza, July 10, 1971; 1 child, Heather. BA in Polit. Sci., Loyola U., Chgo., 1971; postgrad., Loyola U., 1972-76; MS in Edn., Pacific Western U., 1988, PhD in Edn., 1989. Cert. tchr., Ill. Budget analyst, dean global studies divsn. U.S. Dept. Def., Gt. Lakes Naval Sta., Ill., 1971—72; global studies dean, tchr. social sci., coach bowling, softball Mother Guerin High Sch., River Grove, Ill., 1972—; tchr. Highland Park (Ill.) High Sch., 1981-84. Instr. Franklin Park (Ill.) Park Dist., 1977—; tchr. Triton Coll., River Grove, 1990-91; evaluator Chgo. Met. History Fair, 1980-89; faculty adviser Scholastic Inc., N.Y.C., 1990—; dir. Students Against Animal Cruelty, River Grove, 1991—; moderator Nat. Honor Soc., 1993—; adj. faculty St. Mary's U., 2003--. With Ill. N.G., 1971-77. Recipient Outstanding Achievement award Am. Express/Assn. Am. Geographers, 1989, Heart of the Sch. award for Peace and Justice, Archdiocese of Chgo. Fellow Acad. Polit. Sci.; mem. ASCD, Nat. Coun. Social Studies, Nat. Hist. Soc., Ctr. Study of the Presidency, Nat. Cath. Edn. Assn., Orgn. History Tchrs., Am. Polit. Sci. Assn. Democrat. Roman Catholic. Home: 3601 Emerson St Franklin Park IL 60131-1713 Office: Guerin Coll Prep HS 8001 W Belmont Ave River Grove IL 60171-1096 Office Phone: 708-453-6233 ext 91. Business E-Mail: tstein@guerinprep.org.

STEIN, ZENA A., retired epidemiologist, retired educator; b. Durban, South Africa, July 7, 1922; married; 3 children. BA in History, U. Capetown, 1941, MA in History with honors, 1942; MB, BChir, U. Witwatersrand, 1950, DSc (hon.), 1993. Med. officer Alexandra Health Ctr. & U. Clinic, Johannesburg, 1952—55; registrar psychiatry Shenley Mental Hosp., England, 1956; rsch.

assoc. Dept. Social & Preventive Medicine U. Manchester, 1959—62, sr. rsch. fellow Mental Health Rsch. Fund, Dept. Social & Preventive Medicine, 1959—62, rsch. fellow, Medical Rsch. Coun., Dept. Social & Preventive Medicine, 1962—65; rsch. assoc. Assn. for Aid Crippled Children, NYC, 1965—66; assoc. prof. epidemiology Columbia U. Sch. Pub. Health, NYC, 1966—73, prof. pub. health epidemiology, 1973—92, prof. pub. health epidemiology, Gertrude H. Sergievsky Ctr., 1977—, assoc. dir. rsch. and acad. affairs N.Y.C., 1986—; dir. epidemiology of brain disorders rsch. dept. NY State Psychiat. Inst., NYC, 1968—98, co-dir. HIV Ctr. for Clin. and Behavioral Studies, 1987—; co-dir. HIV Ctr. for Clin. and Behavioral Studies, NY State Psychiatric Inst. Columbia U., NYC, 1987—, prof. psychiatry dept. psychiatry, 1991—92, acting chair divsn. epidemiology, sch. pub. health, 1993—95, prof. emerita dept. epidemiology & psychiatry, sch. pub. health, 1993—. Cons. Pan Am. Health Orgn., 1972, WHO, 1978, 83, 86, 91, UNICEF, South African Med. Rsch. Coun., 1992-93, Robert Wood Johnson Found., 1993-94; vis. prof. U. Sydney, 1975, Nat. Inst. Mental Health, Lima, Peru, 1988, Inst. Sukperiore de Sanita, Rome, 1989; hon. prof. Nat. Sch. Pub. Health, Madrid, Spain, 1999; co-dir. Africa Ctr. Population Studies & Reproductive Health, Mtubatuba, South Africa, 1999; spkr. in field. Co-editor: (with Hatch, M.) Reproduction at the Workplace, 1986, (with M. Wright, J. Scandlyn) Women's Health and Apartheid: The Health of Women and Children and the Future of Progressive Health Care in Southern Africa, 1988, (with A. Zwi) Action on AIDS in Southern Africa: Maputo Conference on Health in Transition in Southern Africa, 1990; co-author: (with Kline, J.) Conception to Birth: Epidemiology of Prenatal Development, 1989; editl. bd. Am. Journal of Public Health, Genetic Epidemiology, Teratogenesis, Carcinogenesis & Mutagenesis, Reproductive Toxicology, American Journal of Human Genetics; contbr. chpts. to books and articles to profl. jours. Lt. South African Defense Force, 1943—45. Recipient Physicians & Surgeons Disting. Svc. award, Coll. Physicians & Surgeons, Columbia U., 1994, 75th Jubilee medal, U. Witwatersrand Med. Sch., 1997, Tribute to Zena Stein award, Internat. Conf. Microbicides Organizing Com., 2002; grantee Fogarty Ctr., NIMH. Mem.: NAS, NIMH (mem. study sects.), Joint Commn. Internat. Aspects Mental Retardation, Am. Soc. Human Genetics, Am. Epidemiological Soc., Soc. Study of Social Biology, Soc. Life History Rsch. Psychiatric Epidemiology, Internat. Epidemiological Assn., Soc. Epidemiologic Rsch., Am. Pub. Health Assn. (Wade Hampton Frost award & lecture 1992, John Snow award 1999), Am. Assn. Mental Deficiency, Inst. Medicine (sr. mem. 1998), Nat. Inst. Child Health & Human Devel., Nat. Inst. Occupl. Safety & Health, Nat. Inst. Environ. Health Scis. Office: HIV Ctr NY State Psychiat Inst 722 W 168th St New York NY 10032-2603 Business E-Mail: zas2@columbia.edu.

STEINAGLE, MARTIN GENE, contractor, paralegal, poet, writer; b. Buffalo, N.Y., Aug. 27, 1951; s. Raymond George and Dorothy Jean (Martin) Steinagle. Cert.: So. Career Inst., Boca Raton, Fla. (paralegal) 1987; comml. art illustrated design Wesport, Conn., 1971, electromechanicl Tech. Advanced Tng. Ctr., Kenmore, N.Y., 1983, firearms N. Am. Sch. of Firearms, Scranton, Pa., 1982. Carpenter Barden Homes, Middleport, NY, 1974—77; grademan Lockport Excavating Inc., Lockport, NY, 1978—81; illustrator Thencan, Lockport, NY, 1985—2002; owner New Day Constrn., Lockport, NY, 1988—. Author: Everyday, But Not Common Poems and Quotes, 2001, More, but Not Common Poems and Quotes, 2004, Common Poems and Quotes to Read, 2005, (songs) Please, Why, 1974, Every Bus on the Street, 1974, (poem) Love is Two, 1982, You're Like a Candle, 1973. Mem.: Improved Order of Red Men, Loyal Order of Moose. Democrat. Judaic Christian. Avocations: art, reading, writing, music, computers. Home and Office: 284 Willow St Apt 24 Lockport NY 14094

STEINBACH, FALKO, pianist, composer, educator; b. Aachen, Germany, Sept. 30, 1957; arrived in U.S., 1999; s. Hans Horst Steinbach and Marthel Gawellek; children: Tankred, Ronja. B in Piano/Theory, Musikhochschule, Cologne, Germany, 1983, MusM, 1984, D in Piano Performance, 1986; cert. in advanced studies, Guildhall Sch. Music and Drama, London, 1987. Instr. Musikschule, Lohmar, Germany, 1987—88; Lehrauftrag U. Cologne, 1989—99; asst. prof. piano U. N.Mex., Albuquerque, 1999—2005, assoc. prof., 2005—, head Keyboard Area, 1999—. Compendium of Piano Technique, 1995;, performer more than 500 concerts in Europea, U.S. and Asia, composer of more than 80 compositions mostly for piano, 11 CD's. Grantee, Endowment of the Arts NRW, 1997; Deutscher Akademischer Austauschdienst grant, German Dept. State, 1986. Mem.: Komponistenverband-Gesellschaft für Musikalische Aufführungs-und Mechanische Verfielfältigungsrechte-Gesellschaft zur Verwertung von Leistungsschutz, Deutscher Ton Künstlerverband, Profl. Music Tchrs. N.Mex. (bd. dirs. 1999—), Kiwanis Club Albuquerque. Roman Catholic. Avocations: music, theater, dance, literature. Home: 1712 Notre Dame NE Albuquerque NM 87106 Office: Univ NMex Albuquerque NM 87131-1411 Office Phone: 505-277-4925.

STEINBACH, LYNNE SUSAN, radiologist, educator; b. San Francisco, Dec. 28, 1953; d. Howard Lynne and Ilse (Rosengarten) S.; m. Eric Franklin Tepper, Aug. 14, 1977; 1 child, Mark Evan. Student, Vassar Coll.; BA, Stanford U., 1975; MD, Med. Coll. Pa., 1979. Intern Coll. Medicine and Dentistry N.J., Newark, 1979—80; resident radiologie N.Y. Hosp.-Cornell Med. Ctr., N.Y.C., 1980—83; fellow musculoskeletal radiology Hosp. Spl. Surgery Cornell Med. Ctr., N.Y.C., 1983—84; asst. prof. radiology U. Calif., San Francisco, 1984—92, assoc. prof., 1992—98, prof., 1998—. Chief musculoskeletal imaging U. Calif. San Francisco. Editor 4 books; contbr. articles 130 on radiology, chpts. on musculoskeletal radiology to profl. publs. Fellow Am. Coll. Radiology; mem. Internat. Skeletal Soc. (mem.-at-large 2002-03, asst. sec. 2003-04, Pres. medal), San Francisco Radiol. Soc. (sec. treas. 1994, pres. 1996), Radiol. Soc. N.Am., Am. Assn. Women Radiologists (mem. at large 1987 88, sec. 1989-91, 91, pres. elect 1992-93, pres. 1993-94), Am. Roentgen Ray Soc., Assn. U. Radiologists, Soc. Skeletal Radiology. Avocations: swimming, piano, travel, gardening. E-mail: lynne.steinbach@radiology.ucsf.edu.

STEINBACH, MEREDITH LYNN, writer, educator; b. Ames, Iowa, Mar. 18, 1949; d. Christopher Gene and Joy Janice (Johnson) Steinbach; m. Charles Ossian Hartman, May 5, 1979 (div. Dec. 1991); 1 child Zachary Steinbach Hartman BGS, U. Iowa, 1973, MFA, 1976. Teaching fellow U. Iowa, Iowa City, 1975-76; writer in residence Antioch Coll., Yellow Springs, Ohio, 1976-77; lectr. in fiction Northwestern U., Evanston, Ill., 1977-79; vis. asst. prof. U. Washington, 1979-82; Bunting fellow Harvard-Radcliffe, Cambridge, Mass., 1982-83; asst. prof. Brown U., Providence, R.I., 1983-97, prof. English, 1997—. Author: Zara, 1982, Here Lies the Water, 1990, Reliable Light, 1990, The Birth of the World As We Know It, Or, Teiresias, 1996. In the Realm of Which There Is No Sign, 1995. Recipient Pushcart prize Best of the Small Presses, 1976, R.I. award for Excellence in Lit., R.I. Coun. on Arts, 1986-87, O'Henry award for short story, 1990, creative writing fellow in fiction Nat. Endowment for Arts; 1978; Travel grant Thomas J. Watson Inst. for Internat. Study, France and Greece, 1993-94. Mem.: PEN, Assoc. Writing Programs, Amnesty Internat. Office: Brown U Dept of English Grad Program Literary Arts Box 1923 Providence RI 02912 E-mail: Meredith_Steinbach@Brown.edu.

STEINBAUGH, ROBERT P., management and finance educator; b. Mineral City, Ohio, Aug. 25, 1927; s. Paul W. and Blanche (Lechner) Steinbaugh; m. Carolyn Ann Gates, Nov. 24, 1967. BS, Ohio State U., 1950, MA, 1952, PhD, 1957. Instr. Miami U., Oxford, Ohio, 1953-55, Ohio State U., Columbus, 1955-57; asst. prof. mgmt. and fin. Ind. State U., Terre Haute, 1957-60, assoc. prof., 1960-63, prof. bus. adminstrn., 1963—. Mem. Acad. Mgmt. Am. Mgmt. Assn., Ohio State Alumni Assn., Beta Gamma Sigma, Delta Sigma Pi, Delta Pi Epsilon, Phi Delta Kappa, Phi Kappa Phi. Lodges: Rotary. Republican. Episcopalian. Home: 675 Woodlawn St Terre Haute IN 47803-4253

STEINBAUM, BERNICE, art dealer; b. Flushing, NY, Jan. 3, 1941; d. Julius Dov and Sarah (Lasker) Aptowitz; m. Harold Steinbaum; children: Jeremy, Sara, Carrie. BA, Queens Coll., 1961; MA. Hofstra U., 1965; PhD in Art Edn., Columbia U., 1977. Tchr. Iowa Pub. Sch. System; assoc. prof.

Drake U., Iowa; prof. Hofstra U., N.Y.C.; gallery dir. Bernice Steinbaum Gallery, N.Y.C. Curator numerous exhbns. and traveling mus. shows; speaker in field; juror numerous art shows. Host: Art Time with Mrs. Steinbaum, Iowa; contbr. articles to profl. publs., mags., and newspapers; author: The Rocker, 1992. Named Woman of Yr. NOW, 1988. Office: Bernice Steinbaum Gallery 3550 N Miami Ave Miami FL 33127-3112 Office Phone: 305-573-2700. Business E-Mail: info@berniesteinbaumgallery.com.

STEINBAUM, ROBERT S., publishing executive, lawyer; b. Englewood, NJ, Oct. 13, 1951; s. Paul S. and Esther R. (Rosenberg) S.; m. Rosemary Konner, May 26, 1982; children: Marshall, Elliot. BA, Yale U., 1973; JD, Georgetown U., 1976. Bar: D.C. 1976, N.J. 1980, N.Y. 1982. Atty. Cole & Groner P.C., Washington, 1976—79; asst. U.S. atty. U.S. Atty.'s Office, Newark, 1979—84; atty. Scarpone & Edelson, Newark, 1984—87; pub. N.J. Law Jour., Newark, 1987—. Trustee N.J. Jewish News, Whippany, 1990-95, 96—, pres. 2002-04, Blood Ctr. N.J., East Orange, 1987-93, Leadership N.J., 1990; trustee Leadership Newark, 1997—, United Jewish Cmtys. MetroWest, N.J., 2002—, N.J. Vol. Lawyers for Arts, 2004—. Office: NJ Law Jour PO Box 20081 238 Mulberry St Newark NJ 07101-6081 Business E-Mail: rsteinbaum@alm.com.

STEINBERG, ALAN WOLFE, investment company executive; b. Bklyn., Oct. 26, 1927; s. Benjamin F. and Gertrude (Wolfe) S.; m. Suzanne Nichols, Oct. 12, 1958; children: Carol Albanese, Laura Frohman, Benjamin T. AB with honors and spl. distinction in math, Columbia U., 1947, MS, 1950. Indsl. engr. USDA, Washington, 1948—50; ops. rschr. Port N.Y. Authority, 1950—55; prof. engring. NYU, 1956—63; pres. Am. Computing Ctrs., N.Y.C., 1962—66; v.p., dir. TBS Computer Ctrs., N.Y.C., 1967—76; mng. ptnr. Alan W. Steinberg Partnership, N.Y.C. and Coral Gables, 1974—. Contbr. articles to profl. jours. Nat. advisor automation United Jewish Appeal, N.Y.C., 1965-75; trustee Fla. Nature Conservancy, Winter Park, 1990—, treas., 1990-2004; bd. dirs., treas. Fla. Audubon Soc., Casselberry, 1984-95, Defenders of Wildlife, Washington, 1985-95, chmn. bd. dirs. 1990-98, treas., 2000—; 1st v.p. Tropical Audubon Soc., South Miami, 1983-93; trustee Stiltsville Trust, Miami, 2004—. Recipient Chmn.'s award Fla. Audubon Soc., 1989, 93; funded named scholarship Columbia Coll. Fellow Fairchild Tropical Garden; mem. Columbia Coll. Alumni Assn. (bd. dirs. 1992-93), Phi Beta Kappa. Home: 5522 Riviera Dr Coral Gables FL 33146-2747 Office: 1501 Venera Ave Ste 205 Coral Gables FL 33146-3052 Personal E-mail: SteinbergX@aol.com.

STEINBERG, ANDREW B., lawyer; b. 1958; m. Roxann Steinberg; 2 children. BA magna cum laude, Princeton U., 1980; JD cum laude, Harvard Law Sch., 1984. Jud. law clk. to Hon. Richard A. Gadbois, Jr. US Dist. Ct., Calif.; associate Gibson, Dunn and Crutcher LLP, 1986—90; assoc. gen. counsel & sr. atty. for antitrust Am. Airlines, Inc., 1990—96; sr. v.p. to exec. v.p., gen. counsel, and sec. Sabre, Inc., 1996—2000; exec. v.p. administrn., gen. counsel & corp. sec. Travelocity.com, Inc., 2000—02; v.p., gen. counsel & corp. sec. Church & Dwight Co., Inc., 2002—03; chief counsel FAA, Washington, 2003—. Office: FAA 800 Independence Ave SW Washington DC 20591 Office Phone: 202-267-3222. Office Fax: 202-267-3227. Business E-Mail: andrewbsteinberg@yahoo.com.

STEINBERG, ARTHUR IRWIN, periodontist, educator; b. Pitts., Sept. 16, 1935; s. Ben and Sylvia (Jacobs) S.; m. Barbara Fay Ehrenkranz, May 23, 1959; chldren: Sharon Jill, Mindy Ruth, Michael Eli. BS in Microbiology, U. Pitts., 1957, DMD cum laude, 1963, postgrad. in radiobiology, 1957-59; diploma in periodontology-immunology, Harvard U., 1966. Asst. prof. periodontology SUNY, Buffalo, 1966-67; assoc. prof. periodontology Temple U., Phila., 1967-68, assoc. prof. grad. periodontology, 1968-70; attending periodontist Phoenixville (Pa.) Hosp., 1971—95; clin. assoc. prof. U. Pa. Sch. Dental Medicine, 1981—2002, clin. prof. of gen. restorative dentistry, 2002—. Mem. infections control com., by-laws com., religious affairs com., 1977—, credentials com., 1982—; mem. staff Suburban Gen. Hosp. Norristown, Pa., 1971-80, Phoenixville Hosp., 1968-95; asst. prof. periodontics U. Pa., 1973-82, clin. assoc. prof. 1982-2002, clin. prof. of general restorative dentistry, 2000—, admissions interviewer Sch. Dental Medicine, 2002—; lectr. continuing edn., off-campus program U. Pitts., 1973-93; Fulbright-Hays lectr. Nat. U. Ireland, Cork, 1970-71; vis. prof. Cork Dental Sch. and Hosp., 1971—; lectr. Periodontology Soc. Madrid, 1980, 5th Region Soc. Periodontology Viña Del Mar, Chile, 1985; dentist in pediatrics Charlestown (Mass.) Boys Club, 1965-66; spkr. Periodontists Conv., Chgo., 1966, N.J. Coll. Medicine and Dentistry, Conn. Dental Assn., 1967, U. Ind. Schs. Dentistry and Medicine, Phila. Ann. Dental Sci. Session, 1969, N.J. Dental Assn., 1970, Wilmington chpt. Sigma Epsilon Delta, 1974, Lehigh Valley Dental Soc.m 1974, Inst. Medicine, Bucharest, Romania, 1976, Irish Dental Assn., 1992, other confs., and convs.; participant Project Head Start, Childrens Hosp., Boston, 1966; mem. fund-raising subcom. Harvard U. Sch. Dental Medicine, 1980—; mem. faculty U. Pitts., 1988-93; commencement spkr. U. Pa. Sch. Dental Medicine, 1988, Harcum Coll. Dental Hygiene Program, 1994-95, C.C. of Phila. Dental Hygiene Program, 2002; presenter Phila. County Dental Soc., Ann. Meeting Liberty Dental Conf., 1988, 90, Acad. Gen. Dentistry Ann. Meeting, 1988; judge divsn. medicine and healthcare Del. Valley Sci. Fair, 1997; clin. prof. gen. restorative dentistry U. Pa., 2002; admissions interviewer U. Pa. Sch. Dental Medicine, 2002—. Contbg. author: The Fulbright Experience, 1987, Dentistry and the Allergic Patient, 1973; contbr. numerous articles to profl. jours. Named to Phoenixville Hosp. Hall of Honor, 1996; USPHS fellow; reipient Dean J.L.T. Appleton Excellence in CLin. Tchg. award U. Pa., 2003. Fellow Acad. Dentistry Internat., Internat. Acad. Dental Studies, Am. Coll. Dentists, Coll. Physicians Phila., Pierre Fouchard Acad.; mem. AMA, AAUP, Harvard Dental Alumni Assn., Harvard Odontological Soc. Fulbright Assn., Nat. Fulbright Alumni Assn. (a founder 1976, v.p.fin. affairs 1976-79), Am. Acad. Periodontology (ins. com. 1969, hosp. care com. 1973-74, continuing edn. spkr. 1976 conv., 1983 conv., nominating com. chmn. Pa. region to exec. coun. 1975, nat. clin. affairs com. 1984), Am. Coll. Clin. Pharmacology, Northea. Soc. Periodontists, Acad. Stomatology Phila., Phila. Acad. Scis., Sigma Xi, Omicron Kappa Upsilon (life, pres. 2004—), Psi Omega (dep. councillor Zeta chpt. 1977-79, 2004—), Masons (32 degree Shriner), Legion Honor Chapel Four Chaplains, Rotary (dir. 1973-76, chmn. found. com., chmn. internat. svc. 1974-76), B'nai B'rith, Hadassah (assoc. mem.), Harvard of Phila., 25 Yr. Club U. Pa., Area Study (pres. 1976-79), Harvard Assn. Soc. Ret. Dentists, Omicron Kappa Upsilon (svc. chpt. 2005-06). Home and Office: 1681 Pheasant Ln Norristown PA 19403-3331 Office Phone: 215-898-4778. Business E-Mail: arthurst@pobox.upenn.edu.

STEINBERG, ARTHUR JAY, lawyer; b. Bklyn., Sept. 25, 1955; s. Eugene and Estelle (Bzezensky) S.; m. Ninette Zavelson, Oct. 19, 1980; children: Jaclyn, Lauren, Alyx. BA in Econs. cum laude, Columbia Coll., 1976; JD, NYU, 1979. Bar: NY 1980, US Dist. Ct. (so., ea. and no. dists.) NY, US Cir. Ct. (2d cir.) 1986, US Cir. Ct. (4th cir.) 1991. With Kay, Scholer LLP, NYC, 1979-87, ptnr., 1988—. Mem. ABA, Am. Banks Inst., NYC Bar Assn. Democrat. Jewish. Office: Kaye Scholer LLP 425 Park Ave New York NY 10022-3506 Office Phone: 212-836-8564. E-mail: asteinberg@kayescholer.com.

STEINBERG, DANIEL, preventive medicine physician, educator; b. Windsor, Ont., Can., July 21, 1922; came to U.S., 1922; s. Maxwell Robert and Bess (Krupp) S.; m. Sara Murdock, Nov. 30, 1946 (dec. July 1986); children: Jonathan Henry, Ann Ballard, David Ethan; m. Mary Ellen Stratthaus, Aug. 11, 1991; 1 stepchild: Katrin Seifert. BS with highest distinction, Wayne State U., 1941, MD with highest distinction, 1944; PhD with distinction (fellow Am. Cancer Soc. 1950-51), Harvard U., 1951; MD (hon.), U. Gothenburg, 1991. Intern Boston City Hosp., 1944-45; physician Detroit Receiving Hosp., 1945-46; instr. physiology Boston U. Sch. Medicine, 1947-48; joined USPHS, 1951, med. dir., 1959; research staff lab. cellular physiology and metabolism Nat. Heart Inst., 1951-53, chief sect. metabolism, 1956-61, chief of lab. metabolism, 1962-68; lectr. grad. program NIH, 1955, mem. sci. adv. com. ednl. activities, 1955-61, com. chmn., 1955-60; mem. metabolism study sect. USPHS, 1959-61; chmn. heart and lung research rev. com. B Nat. Heart,

Lung and Blood Inst., 1977-79; vis. scientist Carlsberg Labs., Copenhagen, 1952-53, Nat. Inst. Med. Research, London, 1960-61, Rockefeller U., 1981; pres. Lipid Research Inc., 1961-64, adv. bd., 1964-73; prof. medicine Sch. Medicine, U. Calif., San Diego, 1968—. Former editor Jour. Lipid Research; mem. editorial bd. Jour Clin. Investigation, 1969-74, Jour. Biol. Chemistry, 1980-84, Arteriosclerosis, 1980—; ed. editor Analytical Biochemistry, 1978-80; contbr. articles to profl. jours. Bd. dirs. Found. Advanced Edn. in Scis., 1959-68, pres., 1956-62, 65-67. Served to capt. M.C. AUS, World War II. Mem. Nat. Acad. Scis., AAAS, Am. Acad. Arts and Scis., Am. Heart Assn. (mem. exec. com. coun. on arteriosclerosis 1960-63, 65-73, chmn. coun. arteriosclerosis 1967-69), Fedn. Am. Scientists (exec. com. 1957-58), Am. Soc. Biol. Chemists, Am. Soc. Clin. Investigation, Assn. Am. Physicians, Am. Fedn. Clin. Rsch., Inst. Medicine, European Atherosclerosis Discussion Group, Alpha Omega Alpha. Home: 7742 Whitefield Pl La Jolla CA 92037-3810 Office: U Calif San Diego Dept Medicine 9500 Gilman Dr La Jolla CA 92093-0682 Office Phone: 858-534-0569. Personal E-mail: dsteinb1@san.rr.com. Business E-Mail: dsteinberg@ucsd.edu.

**STEINBERG, DAVID ISAAC,** social sciences educator, consultant; b. Cambridge, Mass., Nov. 26, 1928; s. Naaman and Miriam (Goldberg) S.; m. Isabel Maxwell, 1951 (div. 1962); 1 child, Christopher; m. Ann Myongsook Lee, May 15, 1964; children: Alexander L., Eric D. BA, Dartmouth Coll., 1950; MA, Harvard U., 1955; DLitt (hon.), Sungkunkwan U., Seoul, Republic of Korea. Analyst Nat. Security Coun., Washington, 1951-53; program officer Asia Found., N.Y.C., 1956-58, asst. rep. Burma, 1958-62, Hong Kong, 1962-63, rep. Republic of Korea, 1963-68, Washington, 1968-69; cons., sr. fgn. svc. officer AID, Washington and Bangkok (Thailand), 1969-86; ret., 1986; pres. Mansfield Ctr. for Pacific Affairs, Helena, Mont., 1986-87, Sr. Resources Internat., 1989-94; disting. prof. Korea Studies Georgetown U., Washington, 1990-94; rep. The Asia Found., Seoul, Republic of Korea, 1994-97; dir. Asian studies Sch. Fgn. Svc. Georgetown U., Washington, 1997—, Disting. prof. and dir. Asian studies, 1997—. Pvt. cons. Washington, 1987—, World Bank, 1987—; Woodrow Wilson Ctr. for Scholars of the Smithsonian Instn., Dept. of State and the Agy. for Internat. Devel., the Can. Internat. Devel. Agy., Devel. Assocs., Inc., and others; founding mem. Burma Studies Found., De Kalb, Ill., 1987. Author: Burma's Road Toward Development, 1981, Burma, 1982, The Republic of Korea Economic Transformation and Social Change, 1988, The Future of Burma, 1990, Burma: The State of Myanmar, 2001, Stone Mirror: Reflections on Contemporary Korea, 2003; co-editor Georgetown Southeast Asia Survey 2002-05. 1st lt. U.S. Army, 1953-55. Fellow Lingnan U., Canton, China, 1948, Dartmouth Coll., 1950; named Disting. Prof. of Korea Studies, Georgetown U. Mem. Assn. Asian Studies, Oriental Ceramic Soc., Asia Devel. Roundtable (chmn. 1984-86, 87—), Siam Soc., Royal Asiatic Soc. (life Korea br.), Burma Rsch. Soc. (life), Asia Soc. (cons. 1988—), Cosmos Club, Royal Bangkok (Thailand) Sports Club. Home: 6207 Goodview St Bethesda MD 20817-6101 Office: Georgetown U Sch Fgn Svc Washington DC 20057 Office Phone: 202-687-0251. Business E-Mail: steinbdi@georgetown.edu. E-mail: DSteinb620@aol.com.

**STEINBERG, DAVID JOEL,** academic administrator, historian, educator; b. N.Y.C., Apr. 5, 1937; s. Milton and Edith (Alpert) S.; m. Sally Levitt (div. Dec., 1986); children: Noah, Jonah; m. Joan Diamond, Aug. 28, 1987. BA magna cum laude, Harvard U., 1959, MA, 1963, PhD, 1964; LittD, Kyung Hee U., Seoul, Korea, 1989; LLD (hon), Keimyung U., Daegu, Korea. Prof. history U. Mich., 1964-73; exec. asst. to pres. Brandeis U., Waltham, Mass., 1973-77, v.p., univ. sec., 1977-83; pres. L.I. U., Brookville, NY, 1985—. Testified before Com. on Fgn. Affairs, U.S. Ho. of Reps., Fgn. Affairs Com. of U.S. Senate; cons. The Ford Found., UN Fund for Population Activities. Author: Philippine Collaboration in World War II, 1967 (Univ. Press award, 1969), The Philippines: A Singular and a Plural Place, 1982, 1987, Asia in Western and World History: A Guide for Tchg., 1993; co-author: The Emergence of Modern Southeast Asia: A New History, 2004, Religion and Religiosity in the Philippines and Indonesia: Essays on State, Society and Public Creeds, 2005. Chmn. Commn. Ind. Colls. and Univs.; past pres. Cambridge (Mass.) Ctr. for Adult Edn., chmn. L.I. Group; bd. trustee Nat. Commn. Coop. Edn. English Speaking Union Exch. scholar, Malvern Coll., NDEA scholar, Fulbright Found. exch. scholar. Mem. Coun. Fgn. Rels., Assn. Asian Studies (chmn. fin. com.), Harvard Club (N.Y.C.), Century Club (N.Y.C.). Democrat. Jewish. Office: LI Univ Off Pres 700 Northern Blvd Greenvale NY 11548-1320 Business E-Mail: pres@liu.edu.

**STEINBERG, DONALD R.,** lawyer; b. 1962; BSE magna cum laude, Princeton Univ., 1984; JD cum laude, Harvard Univ., 1988. Bar: Mass. 1988, U.S. Patent & Trademark Office. Ptnr., vice chmn. Intellectual Property dept. Wilmer Cutler Pickering Hale & Dorr, Boston, 1994—. Adj. faculty mem. New Eng. Sch. Law. Mem.: Intellectual Property Owners Assn. (mem. Trademark Law Com.), Phi Beta Kappa. Office: Wilmer Cutler Pickering Hale & Dorr 60 State St Boston MA 02109 Office Phone: 617-526-6453. Office Fax: 617-526-5000. Business E-Mail: donald.steinberg@wilmerhale.com.

**STEINBERG, GREGG MARTIN,** financial and management consultant, investment banker; b. Columbus, Ind., Mar. 26, 1962; s. Jerry H. and Sharla C. (Waitzman) S.; m. Stacy A. Schneider, Nov. 6, 1988; 2 children. BSBA, U. Ariz., 1982; M in Mgmt., Am. Grad. Sch. Internat. Mgmt., Glendale, Ariz., 1984. V.p. fin. Bera Hotels Ltd., Phoenix, 1984-85; gen. mgr. Les Jardains Hotel, Phoenix, 1985-87; asst. dir., sr. negotiator GVA Mergers & Acquisitions, Phoenix, 1987-88; pres. Gregg M. Steinberg Ltd., Phoenix and Chgo., 1987—89; prin. Berger, Goldstein Capital Group, Inc., Chgo., 1989-91; joined Internat. Profit Assocs. and Integrated Bus. Analysis (IPA-IBA), Buffalo Grove, Ill., 1992, CFO, 1995—97, pres., 1997—. Chmn., Midwestern region Am. Com. for Weizmann Inst. Sci., 2005—. Bd. dirs., chmn. N.W. com. Jewish Coun. for Youth Svcs., Chgo., 1989-92; bd. dirs. J.C.C., 1997—. Avocations: golf, squash.*

**STEINBERG, HOWARD,** chemical company executive, consultant; b. Chgo., Aug. 23, 1926; s. Leo and Hattie (Seskind) Steinberg; m. Eve Taubman, Feb. 10, 1946; children: Lisa Beth Leonard, Gary Robert, Erik Jon. BS, U. Ill., Urbana, 1946—48; PhD, UCLA, 1948—51. Rsch. chemist Aerojet Gen. Corp., Azusa, Calif., 1952—52; rsch. assoc. UCLA, 1952—53; collaborator USDA, Pasadena, Calif., 1953—54; mgr. organic rsch. U.S. Borax Rsch., Anaheim, Calif., 1954—58, asst. dir., 1958—59, assoc. dir., 1959—61, dir. chem. rsch., 1961—63, v.p., 1963—69, pres., 1969-90; v.p. US Borax and Chem. Corp., LA, 1969—90, dir., 1973—90, cons., 1990—92; dir. Ireco Chem. Co., Salt Lake City, 1970—75. Author: (book) Organoboron Chemistry; co-author (book (treatise); editor: (books) Progress in Boron Chemistry; contbr. numerous research papers; numerous US and foreign patents in field of organoboron chemistry. Mem. Sci. and Engring. Adv. Coun., Calif. State Univ., Fullerton, 1964—90; dir. Orange County Cultural Groups Found., Fullerton, Calif., 1970—71. Pre-aviation cadet Air Corp U.S. Army, 1945—45. Named to Am. Men Sci., Adv. Com. apptd. by the NAS, 1961, Leading Men in the USA, 1965; AEC Fellow, UCLA, 1950—51, AEC Postdoctoral Fellow, MIT, 1951—52. Mem.: AIME, Am. Chem. Soc., Brit. Chem. Soc., Indsl. Rsch. Inst., Soc. Chem. Industry, Phi Lambda Upsilon, Pi Mu Epsilon, Sigma Xi. Achievements include researcher and coauthor with Professor Donald J. Cram in the first two papers of his seminal work (Host-Guest chemistry) leading to his 1987 Nobel Prize in Chemistry. Avocations: woodworking, golf, fiction writing. Home and Office: 16 Corte Sevilla San Clemente CA 92673 Office Phone: 949-661-9009.

**STEINBERG, HOWARD ELI,** lawyer, diversified financial services company executive; b. NYC, Nov. 19, 1944; s. Herman and Anne Steinberg; m. Judith Ann Schucart, Jan. 28, 1968; children: Henry Robert, Kathryn Jill. AB, U. Pa., 1965; JD, Georgetown U., 1969. Bar: N.Y. 1970, U.S. Dist. Ct. (so. and ea. dists.) N.Y. 1973, U.S. Ct. Appeals (2d cir.) 1976. Assoc. Dewey, Ballantine, Bushby, Palmer & Wood, NYC, 1969-76, ptnr., 1977-83; exec. v.p., gen. counsel Reliance Group Holdings, Inc., NYC, 1983-2000, exec. v.p., chief corp. ops., 2000—01; exec. v.p., gen. counsel Prudential Securities, Inc., NYC, 2001—03, Prudential Equity Group, NYC, 2003—05; ptnr. McDermott Will & Emery LLP, NYC, 2005—. Chmn. N.Y. State Thruway

Authority, 1996—99; dep. chmn. L.I. Power Authority, 1999—. Editor: Georgetown Law Jour., 1968—69. Bd. dirs. Puerto Rican Legal Def. and Edn. Fund, Inc., 1993—95, Sheltering Arms Children's Svc., 1997—2005; bd. overseers U. Pa. Sch. Arts and Scis., 1989—2002; bd. regents Georgetown U., 1999—2005. Capt. JAGC USAR, 1972—74. Mem.: ABA, Securities Industry Assn. (co-chair, mem. fed. regulation com. 2001—05, mem. exec. compliance and legal divsn. 2001—05), Assn. Bar City of N.Y. (mem. com. scurities regulation 1984—87, mem. com. corp. law 1987—90, mem. com. fed. legis. 1990—93, chair ad hoc com. Senate Confirmation Process 1991—92), N.Y. State Bar Assn., Univ Club. Office: McDermott Will Emery 340 Madison Ave New York NY 10017 Office Phone: 212-547-5415. Business E-Mail: hsteinberg@mwe.com.

**STEINBERG, JEFFREY MARK,** obstetrician, gynecologist, medical researcher; b. Phila., Oct. 7, 1953; BS, UCLA, 1973; MD, U. Guadalajara, Mex., 1977; MS, U. Saskatchewan, Can., 1978. Diplomate Am. Bd. Ob-Gyn, Am. Bd. Med. Reproductive Endocrinology. Advanced infertility tng. Bourne Hall Clinic, Cambridge U., England; intern, obstetrics and gynecology U. Saskatchewan. Regina, 1977—78; resident, endocrinology Rush Presbyterian St. Lukes Hosp., Chgo., 1979—81; dir. InVitro Fertilization program Northridge Hosp. Med. Ctr., Calif., 1981-83; dir. fertility InVitro Fertilization program Glendale Adventist Med. Ctr., Calif., 1986; fellow reproductive endocrinology and infertility U. Calif.-San Diego, La Jolla, 1986—88; med. dir. Fertility Inst. (LA, Calif. and Las Vegas, Nev.), 1986—. Hosp. appt. Northridge Hosp. Med. Ctr., Calif.; hosp. appt., dept. reproductive medicine U. Calif. San Diego. Contbr. articles to profl. jours.; featured on 60 Minutes and several other news programs and documentaries in the field of infertility and related disorders. NIH grantee, 1986. Fellow Am. Coll. Obstetricians and Gynelcologists; mem. Am. Fertility Soc., Am. Assn. Gynecologic Laprnascopists, Pacific Coast Fertility Soc. Avocations: music, recording and sound engring. Office: The Fertility Inst 18370 Burbank Blvd Ste 414 Tarzana CA 91356 Office Phone: 818-776-8700.*

**STEINBERG, JONATHAN S.,** cardiologist, educator; BA, Queens Coll., 1976; MD, Mt. Sinai Sch. Medicine, 1980. Diplomate Am. Bd. Internal Medicine with subspecialty cardiovasc. disease and clin. electrophysiology. Resident NYU Med Ctr., chief resident NY VA, 1981-84; fellow critical cardiology George Washington U. Med. Ctr., 1984-86; fellow electrophysiology Columbia Presbyn. Hosp., 1986-88; chief divsn. cardiology, dir. arrhythmia svc. St. Luke's-Roosevelt Hosp. Ctr. Prof. medicine Columbia U., Coll. Physicians and Surgeons. Office: St Lukes-Roosevelt Hosp Ctr 1111 Amsterdam Ave New York NY 10025-1716 Fax: 212-523-3915.

**STEINBERG, KENNETH PAUL,** medical educator; b. Bklyn., July 8, 1959; s. David Herman Steinberg and Lorraine Godlin; m. Laura Drange Drange, Aug. 14, 1993; children: Haley Rose, Annika Lea. MD, NY Med. Coll., Valhalla, 1985. Asst. prof. medicine U. Wash., Seattle, 1994—2000, assoc. prof. medicine, 2000—. Assoc. med. dir., critical care svcs. Harborview Med. Ctr., Seattle, 1998—. Exec. com. LifeCenter NW, Bellevue, Wash., 2000—06; mem. Am. Lung Assn. Wash., Seattle, 2003—06. Recipient Paul B. Beeson Faculty Tchr. award, U. Wash., 2000. Fellow: Am. Coll. Chest Physicians; mem.: Alpha Omega Alpha. Achievements include research in acute lung injury and acute respiratory distress syndrome. Office: Harborview Med Ctr Box 359762 325 Ninth Ave Seattle WA 98104 Office Phone: 206-731-3356. Office Fax: 206-731-8584.

**STEINBERG, LAURA,** lawyer; b. Phila., Feb. 3, 1948; d. Leonard and Pearl (Zeid) S.; children: Seth, Adam, Bree. BA magna cum laude with honors, Bryn Mawr Coll., 1968; JD cum laude, Harvard U., 1972. Bar: Mass. 1972, U.S. Dist. Ct. Mass. 1972, U.S. Dist. Ct. R.I. 1974, U.S. Ct. Appeals (1st cir.) 1973, U.S. Ct. Appeals (10th and D.C. cirs.) 1986, U.S. Ct. Appeals (4th cir.) 1988, U.S. Claims Ct. 1979, U.S. Supreme Ct. 1988. Assoc. Sullivan & Worcester, Boston, 1972-79, ptnr., 1979—, mem. mgmt. com., 1988-2000, head litigation dept., 1987—99, chair complex bus. fiduciary litigation group, 2004—. Dir. Greater Boston Legal Svcs., 1987-90. Bd. dirs. Law Firm Resources Project, Boston, 1980-86, Lawyers Com. for Civil Rights Under Law, 1998—; pres. Peirce Extended Day Program, Inc., West Newton, Mass., 1983-86. Spl. career fellow U. Calif., Berkeley, 1968-69; Fulbright scholar, 1968. Mem. Boston Bar Assn. (vice-chmn. litigation sect. 1992-94, chmn. 1994-95). Avocations: reading, tennis. Office: Sullivan & Worcester LLP One Post Office Sq Ste 2100 Boston MA 02109-2129 Office Phone: 617-338-2800. E-mail: lsteinberg@sandw.com.

**STEINBERG, LAWRENCE EDWARD,** lawyer; b. Dallas, Nov. 25, 1935; s. Oscar J. and Pearl L. (Soloman) S.; children: Adam Joseph, Ilana Sara, Oliver David. BBA, U. Tex., 1958; JD, So. Meth. U., 1960. Bar: Tex. 1960. Since practiced in, Dallas; ptnr. firm Steinberg Soloman & Meer, 1971-88, Johnson & Steinberg, Dallas, 1988-93; chmn., CEO Eagle Equity, Inc., Dallas, 1991—; of counsel Jenkins & Gilchrist, Dallas, 1993—98. Active Urban Rehab. Stds. Bd., Dallas, 1975-76; adv. com. affirmative action program Dallas Ind. Sch. Dist., 1974-76; regional bd. chmn. Anti-Defamation League of B'nai Brith, 1974-77, nat. exec. com., 1977—, nat. law com., 1974-87; trustee Edna Gladney Home, 1975-92; v.p., trustee Shelton Sch., 1987-90; trustee Temple Emanu-El, 1992-94, Dallas Jewish Cmty. Found., 1990-2001, 2005—; pres. U. Tex. Hillel Found., 2001-2003, mem. exec. com., 2001—; bd. dirs. Jewish Fedn. Greater Dallas, 1984-87, 91-94, Dallas Coun. on World Affairs, 1998—, Stephen Wise, Acad., 1998-2002, Dallas Holocaust Ctr., 1998—, Jewish Hist. Inst. Securities Affairs, 1999—, Dallas Furniture Found., 2003—; v.p. Am. Jewish Commn., 2003—; regional bd. chmn. Am. Israel Pub. Affairs Com., 1997-2001, nat. exec. com., 1998—; mem. Dallas Com. Fgn. Rels. 2d lt. U.S. Army, 1959-60. Mem. Columbian Club, Masons, Shriners, Zeta Beta Tau, Phi Delta Phi, Beta Gamma Sigma, Pi Tau Pi (nat. pres. 1964-66). Home: 10131 Hollow Way Rd Dallas TX 75229-6634 Office: 5430 LBJ Fwy Ste 1575 Dallas TX 75240

**STEINBERG, LEIGH WILLIAM,** sports agent; b. LA, 1949; m. Lucy Steinberg; 3 children. BA in Polit. Sci., UCLA, 1970; JD, U. Calif., Berkeley, 1973. Founder, ptnr. Steinberg, Moorad & Dunn, 1975—99; CEO Assante Sports Mgmt. Group, 1999—2003; founder, ptnr. Steinberg, Tollner & Moon, Newport Beach, Calif., 2003—. Co-author (with Michael D'Orso): Winning with Integrity: Getting What You Want Without Selling Your Soul, 1998. Office: 660 Newport Ctr Dr Ste 1000 Newport Beach CA 92660

**STEINBERG, LEO,** art historian, educator; b. Moscow, July 9, 1920; arrived in U.S., 1945; s. Isaac N. and Anna (Esselson) S. PhD, NYU Inst Fine Arts, 1960; PhD (hon.), Phila. Coll. Art, 1981, Parsons Sch. Design, 1986, Mass. Coll. Art, 1987, Bowdoin Coll., 1995, Columbia U., 2004, Harvard U., 2006. Freelance writer, translator, life-drawing instr. Parsons Sch. Design; assoc. prof. art history Hunter Coll., CUNY, N.Y.C., 1962—66, prof., 1966-75; prof. Grad. Ctr. CUNY, 1969-75, co-founder art history dept., 1972; Benjamin Franklin prof. art. history U. Pa., Phila., 1975-91, prof. emeritus, 1991—. A.W. Mellon lectr. in Fine Arts, Nat. Gallery Art, Washington, D.C., 1981-82; Gauss Lectures, Princeton U., NJ, 1985; Charles Eliot Norton lectr. Harvard U., Cambridge, Mass., 1995-96; Meyer Schapiro Chair, Columbia U., N.Y., 1991; spkr. in field. Author: Jasper Johns, 1963, Other Criteria: Confrontations with Twentieth-century Art, 1972, Michelangelo's Last Paintings, the Conversion of St. Paul and the Crucifixion of St. Peter in the Cappella Paolina, Vatican Palace, 1975, Borromini's San Carlo alle Quattro Fontane: A Study in Multiple Form and Architectural Symbolism, 1977, The Sexuality of Christ in Renaissance Art and in Modern Oblivion, 1983, 2nd revised and enlarged edit., 1996, Encounters with Rauschenberg, 1999, Leonardo's Incessant Last Supper, 2001. Recipient award in lit. Am. Acad. and Inst. Arts and Letters, 1983; fellow Am. Acad. Arts and Scis., 1978, Univ. Coll., London U., 1979, MacArthur Found., 1986; resident scholar, Am. Acad. in Rome, Getty Ctr. for History of Art and the Humanities, Santa Monica, Calif. Mem. Coll. Art Assn. Am. (bd. mem. 1969-71, recipent Frank Jewett Mather award for Distinction in Criticism, 1956, 84, Disting. Scholar award 2002). Home: 165 W 66th St New York NY 10023-6508

**STEINBERG, MARTY,** lawyer; b. Balt., May 13, 1945; BS cum laude in Pharmacy, U. Pitts., 1968; JD cum laude, Ohio State U., 1971. Bar: Ohio 1971, Fla. 1974; U.S. Supreme Ct. 1981; Registered Pharmacist Ohio 1968. Atty. U.S. Dept. Justice, Washington, Miami, 1972-78, atty. in charge N.Y. regional offices Washington, 1978-79; chief counsel, permanent subcommittee on investigations U.S. Senate, Washington, 1979-82; ptnr. Holland & Knight, Miami, Fla.; mng. ptnr., litig., intellectual property, antitrust Hunton & Williams LLP, Miami, 1999—. Inst. Canisius Coll. Buffalo, N.Y. 1978-79, SUNY Buffalo 1978-79, Am. U. Washington D.C. 1980-81. Contbr. articles to profl. jours. Bd. dirs. Miami Citizens Against Crime. Recipient Am. Jurisprudence award. Mem. ABA, Fla. Bar Assn., Ohio State Bar Assn., Am. Law Inst. (chmn. civic justice adv. com.), Fellow, Am. Coll. Trial Lawyers, Am. Bar Found., Am. Pharm. Assn., Am. Corporate Counsel. Office: Hunton & Williams LLP 1111 Brickell Ave Miami FL 33131 Office Phone: 305-810-2500. Office Fax: 305-810-2460. Business E-Mail: msteinborg@hunton.com.

**STEINBERG, MEYER,** chemical engineer; b. Phila., July 10, 1924; s. Jacob Louis and Freda Leah S.; m. Ruth Margot Elias, Dec. 24, 1950; children: David Martin, Jay Louis. BSChemE, Cooper Union, 1944; MSChemE, Bklyn. Poly. Inst., 1949. Registered profl. engr. N.Y. Jr. chem. engr. Manhattan dist., Kellex Corp., Oak Ridge, Los Alamos, 1944-46; asst. chem. engr. Deutsch & Loonam, 1947-50; chem. engr. Guggenheim Brothers, Mineola, NY, 1950-57; head process sci. div. Brookhaven Nat. Lab., Upton, NY, 1957—. Expert in fossil and nuclear energy; v.p. HCE LLC on coal conversion energy and environment. Author: (with Martin Hallman) Carbon Dioxide Greenhouse Gas Mitigation Technologies, 1999; contbr. articles to profl. jours. Served with AUS, 1944-46. Recipient IR-100 award, 1970; Wasson award Am. Concrete Inst., 1972, Engr. of Year award, 1985, Ind. award Quest, 1985, Greenman award, Internat. Energy Agy., London UK, IEA Greenhouse Program, 1996. Fellow Am. Nuclear Soc., Am. Inst. Chem. Engrs. (dir. L.I. sect.); mem. Am. Chem. Soc., AAAS, Am. Concrete Inst. Inst. Assos. Hydrogen Energy, Sigma Xi. Democrat. Jewish. Achievements include research on nuclear and fossil energy. Home: 15 Alderfield Ln Melville NY 11747-1724 Office: Brookhaven Nat Lab Upton NY 11973 Office Phone: 631-427-0768. Office Fax: 631-427-0590. Personal E-Mail: mrsteinb@optonline.net.

**STEINBERG, MICHAEL,** music critic, educator; b. Breslau, Germany, Oct. 4, 1928; came to U.S., 1943, naturalized, 1950; s. Siegfried and Margarethe (Cohn) S.; m. Jane Bonacker, July 26, 1953 (div. 1983); children: Peter Sebastian, Adam Gregory; m. Jorja Fleezanis, July, 1983. AB, Princeton U., 1949, M.F.A., 1951; Mus. D. (hon.), New Eng. Conservatory Music, 1966. Free-lance writer, 1952—; head history dept. Manhattan Sch. Music, N.Y.C., 1957-64; music critic Boston Globe, 1964-76; dir. publs. Boston Symphony Orch., 1976-79; artistic adviser San Francisco Symphony, 1979-89, program annotator, lectr., 1989-99; artistic adviser Minn. Orch., 1989-92; artistic dir. Minn. Sommerfest, 1990-92; program annotator, lectr. N.Y. Philharmonic, 1995-2000. Vis. mem. faculty Hunter Coll., 1954, U. Sask. (Can.), 1959, Smith Coll., 1964, Brandeis U., 1964-65; faculty New Eng. Conservatory Music, 1968-71, Wellesley Coll., 1971-72, Brandeis U., 1971-72, Mass. Inst. Tech., 1973; disting. vis. prof. McMaster U., Hamilton, Ont., 1982; cons. NEH, Nat. Endowment for Arts, Mass. Council of Arts and Humanities, Calif. Arts Council, Rockefeller Found.; free-lance writer, lectr. Author: The Symphony: A Listener's Guide, 1995, The Concerto: A Listener's Guide, 1998, Choral Masterworks: A Listener's Guide, 2005, (with Larry Rothe) For the Love of Music, 2006. Served with U.S. Army, 1955-57. Recipient Sang prize for criticism in arts, 1969; citation for Excellence in Criticism Am. Guild Organists, 1972 Mem. Am, Internat. musicological socs. Home: 750 2d St South # 701 Minneapolis MN 55401-2375 Personal E-Mail: fleeberg@earthlink.net.

**STEINBERG, MICHAEL PHILIP,** history professor; PhD, U. Chgo., 1985. Instr. Humanities Divsn., Columbia Coll., Chgo., 1981—82; lectr. Social Sciences Collegiate Divsn. and Dept. History, U. Chgo., 1983—85; William Rainey Harper instr. U. Chgo., 1985—86; asst. prof. history Colgate U., 1986—89, Cornell U., 1989—93, prof. modern European history, 1989—. Dir. European Cultural Studies work group, Princeton U., 1983—85; faculty mem. Salzburg Seminar, Salzburg, Austria, 1987; vis. asst. prof. of history Cornell U., 1988; assoc. prof. Ecole des Hautes Etudes en Sciences Sociales, Paris, 1991; faculty fellow for the Humanities Cornell U., 1994; vis. prof. Inst. of Lit., Nat. Tsignhua U., Taiwan, 1994; vis. assoc. prof. Divinity Sch., U. of Chgo., 1995. Author: The Meaning of Salzburg Festival: Austra as Theater and Ideology, 1890-1938, 1990; assoc. editor The Musical Quarterly. Fellowship, John Simon Guggenheim Meml. Found., 2003. Office: Dept of History Cornell U 450 McGraw Hill Ithaca NY 14853 Home: 574 Angell St Providence RI 02906-4409*

**STEINBERG, MORTON M.,** lawyer; b. Chgo., Feb. 13, 1945; m. Miriam C. Bernstein, Aug. 25, 1974; children: Adam Michael, Shira Judith. AB with honors, U. Ill., 1967; JD, Northwestern U., 1971. Bar: Ill. 1971, DC 1994, Colo. 1995, NY, 2003, US Dist. Ct. (no. dist.) Ill. 1971, US Dist. Ct. Colo. 1998, US Ct. Appeals (7th cir.) 1971, US Supreme Ct. 1974. Assoc. Caffarelli & Wiczer, Chgo., 1971-73, Arnstein, Gluck, Lehr, Barron & Milligan, Chgo., 1974-76, ptnr., 1977-86, DLA Piper Rudnick Gray Cary US, LLP (and predecessor firms), 1986—. Spkr. in field. Sr. editor Jour. Criminal Law and Criminology, Northwestern U., 1969-71. Chmn. Chgo. region Leaders Tng. Fellowship, 1962-63; bd. dirs. Camp Ramah in Wis., Inc., Chgo., 1974—, sr. v.p., 1992-94, pres. 1994-2003, chmn. bd. trustees, 2003-; bd. dirs., pres. The Ramah Day Camp, Inc., Chgo., 2001-03; bd. dirs., v.p. Camp Ramah in Wis. Endowment Corp., 1993-2003, pres. 2003-; bd. dirs. North Suburban Synagogue Beth-El, Highland Park, Ill., 1978—, corp. sec., 1983-87, pres., 1989-91, chmn. bd. trustees, 1991-93, trustee, 1991—; mem. Nat. Ramah Commn., Jewish Theol. Sem., 1987—, v.p., 1994-2003, pres., 2003—; mem. bd. overseers Albert A. List Coll., 2004—; mem. Leadership Coun. Conservative Judaism, 2004—; bd. dirs. Found. Conservative Judaism in Israel, 1985-90; Midwest region bd. dirs. United Synagogue of Conservative Judaism, 1989-91, 94-2003; mem. editor's cir. Jewish Forward Newspaper, 1997-2000; trustee Am. Jewish Hist. Soc., 1998—; charter mem. US Holocaust Meml. Mus., 1992; pro bono counsel Frank Lloyd Wright Preservation Trust, Oak Park, Ill., 1996—. Served with USAR, 1969-75. Recipient Youth Leadership award Nat. Fedn. Jewish Men's Clubs, NYC, 1963; cert. of merit U.S. Dist. Ct. Fed. Defender Program, Chgo., 1969; named Ill. Super Lawyer, Chgo. (Ill.) Mag., 2005 Mem. ABA, DC Bar, N.Y. State Bar Assn., Ill. State Bar Assn., Chgo. Bar Assn., Profl. Assn. Diving Instrs. (cert. scuba open water diver 2005), Standard Club. Jewish. Home: 1320 Lincoln Ave S Highland Park IL 60035-3459 Office: DLA Piper Rudnick Gray Cary US LLP Ste 1900 203 N La Salle St Chicago IL 60601-1225

**STEINBERG, ROBERT PHILIP,** lawyer; b. Danville, Ill., Apr. 4, 1931; s. Frederick Philip and Beulah Iona (Olmsted) S.; m. Doris Elizabeth Blank, May 10, 1958; children: Susan Elizabeth, Mary Louise. BA, DePauw U., 1953; LLB, N.Y. U., 1956. Bar: N.Y. 1956, Pa. 1959. Assoc. Shearman & Sterling, N.Y.C., 1956, Drinker Biddle & Reath, Phila., 1958-65, ptnr. 1965-97, chmn., 1992-94, of counsel, 1997-98; ptnr. Commons & Commons LLP, Phila., 1998—2004, of counsel, 2004—. V.p. Germantown Hist. Soc., Phila., 1991-95, The Phila. Theatre Co., 1992-96; pres. E. Falls Cmty. Coun., 1997-2000. Mem. Phila. Bar Assn. (treas. 1970-72). Home: 3906 W Netherfield Rd Philadelphia PA 19129-1014 Office: Commons & Commons LLP 6377 Germantown Ave Philadelphia PA 19144 Office Phone: 215-849-4400. E-mail: psteinberg@commonslaw.com.

**STEINBERG, ROY BENNETT,** television producer, director, educator; b. N.Y.C., Mar. 24, 1951; s. Seymour and Flora Joyce (Matthews) S.; m. Marlena Lustik, Sept. 8, 1984, 1 child, Alexa Catherine. BA, Tufts U., 1973; MFA, Yale U., 1978. Guest artist various univs., 1978-87; dir. Circle Repertory Co. Lab., N.Y.C., 1985-90; artistic dir. John Michael Kohler Arts Ctr., Sheboygan, Wis., 1988; prodr. Guiding Light, CBS-TV, N.Y.C., 1990-98; dir. One Life To Live, 1999; prodr., dir. Days of Our Lives, NBC, 1999—. Freelance drama coach, N.Y.C., 1978—; script cons. Circle Repertory Co. Lab., N.Y.C., 1985-90; casting dir. Theatre Matrix, N.Y.C., 1981-83; adv. bd. Sch. Film & TV, N.Y.C., 1995—. Actor: (play) Wings, 1979 (Tony nomination 1979), (TV spl.) The Wall, 1980, (soap opera) Another World, 1985, (film) The Man Who Envied Women, 1986; dir. (play) Private Lives, 1987, Absent Friends, 1987, Broadway Bound, 1988, The Miser, 1989, The Learned Ladies, 1989, The Marriage Fool, 1989, Othello, 1989, Children, 1996, Blithe Spirit, 1997, Intuition, 1997. Five Towns Music & Art Found. scholar, 1969, 4 Emmy nominations, 1990-93. Mem. AFTRA (nat. del. 1988), Actors Equity Assn. (dep.), Soc. Stage Dirs. and Choreographers, Dirs. Guild Am., Screen Actors Guild. Avocations: travel, cooking, movies, sports, reading. Home: 3821 Berry Drive Studio City CA 91604 Office Phone: 818-840-2816. Business E-Mail: rsteinberg@dool.net.

**STEINBERG, RUBIN**, retired art educator, artist; b. Chgo., May 31, 1934; s. Louis Steinberg and Tanya Zelmanov; m. Marcia Kay Mann, 1960. B in Edn., Chgo. Tchrs. Coll., 1957; M in Edn., Roosevelt U., 1961; MFA, Art Inst. Chgo., 1968. Art tchr. Curie HS for the Performing and Creative Arts, Chgo., 1960—95. One-man shows include Bernard Horwich Jewish Cmty. Ctr., Chgo., 4 Arts Assocs., Evanston, Ill., One Ill. Ctr., Chgo., Monroe Gallery, Oak Park Libr., Park Forest Art Ctr., Northbrook Racquet Club # 2, Deerfield HS, Mayer Kaplan Jewish Cmty. Ctr., Skokie, Ill., Krochs & Brentanos, Chgo., Bonwit Teller, Suburban Fine Arts Ctr., Highland Park, Ill., A.R.C. Gallery, Chgo., Chgo. Cultural Ctr., Renaissance Ct. exhibited in group shows at Chgo. Soc. Artists Retrospective, 1983, Mus. Sci. and Industry, Chgo., Ill. State Mus., Springfield, So. Ohio Mus., Portsmouth, 1982, Oakbrook Invitational Crafts Exhbn., 1979—80, 1987—91, North Shore Art League, 1979, Chgo. Soc. Artists, 1977—, Am. Jewish Artists Club Exhbns., 1970—, Midwest Craft Festival, —, North Shore Art League, 1974—, 1978 , 1986, Art Inst. Chgo., 1968, 1973 (Mcpl. Art League award, 1973), Suburban Fine Arts Festeival, Highland Park (award for excellence, 1973), Old Orchard Art Festival, North Shore Art League, 1991—96, Gold Coast Assn., 1967—89, Mcpl. Art League (award for excellence, 1990), Blue Moon Gallery, Skokie, 1996, 2000, Batzekas Mus., Chgo., 1996, Loyola U., 1997, Taipei Fine Arts Mus., Taiwan, 1999, Time Life Bldg., Chgo., 1999, Spertus Mus., Represented in permanent collections So. Ohio Mus., Ill. State Mus., Spertus Mus. Judaica, Kraziai Mus. Contemporary Art, Lithuania, Sudler & Co., Chgo., McDonald's Corp., Oakbrook, Ill., Continental Bank, Chgo., Borg Warner, JJ Barrett, Inc. Comm., Slotowski Sausage Co., Malow Cordage Corp., Mt. Prospect, Ill., Morgan, Madison Steel Co., Skokie, Dance Fashions, Chgo., Aval Corp., P&R Mfg. Co., Lyric Opera Chgo., Peat, Marwick & Mitchell, Accts., Chgo., Marshall Field's Home Store, Schaumburg, Ill., Binney & Smith Co., Easton, Pa., Sanford Co., Bellwood, Ill., Sakura of Am., Hayward, Calif., Emily Oaks Nature Ctr., Skokie. Served with U.S. Army, 1958—60. Address: 3127 W Jerome St Chicago IL 60645

**STEINBERG, SALME ELIZABETH HARJU**, academic administrator, historian; b. N.Y.C. d. Johan Edward and Jenny Lydia (Peltonen) Harju; m. Michael Stephen Steinberg, Sept. 15, 1963; children: William, Katharine Lovisa. BA, Hunter Coll., 1960; MA, CCNY, 1962; PhD, Johns Hopkins U., 1971. Lectr. history Goucher Coll., Towson, Md., 1971—72; asst. prof. history Northwestern U., Evanston, Ill., 1972—75; prof. Northeastern Ill. U., Chgo., 1975—83, chmn. dept., 1983—87, assoc. provost then acting provost, 1987—92, provost, v.p. for acad. affairs 1992—95, pres. 1995—. Author: Reformer in the Marketplace: Edward W. Bok and The Ladies' Home Journal, 1979; contbr. articles to profl. jours. Named to. Hunter Coll. Hall of Fame, 1997; recipient 14th Ann. award Appreciation, Asian Am. Coalition Chgo., 1997; grantee, Danforth Found., 1967—68. Episcopalian. Avocations: opera, theater. Office: Northeastern Ill U Office of President 5500 N Saint Louis Ave Chicago IL 60625-4679

**STEINBERG, WILLIAM MARK**, physician; b. NYC, Apr. 16, 1945; s. Louis and Florence (Weisberger) S.; m. Leah Stern, 1970; 3 children. BA, Columbia Coll., 1966; MD, NYU, 1970. Intern Kings County/Downstate, N.Y.C., 1970-71; resident in medicine Boston U., 1973-74, U. Conn., Hartford, 1974-75; fellow in gastroenterology U. Fla., Gainesville, 1976-79; asst. prof. gastroenterology George Washington U., Washington, 1979-83, assoc. prof. medicine, 1983-90, prof. gastroenterology, 1990—. Dir. William M. Steinberg bd. rev., Balt., 1999—. Fellow ACP, Am. Coll. Gastroenterology; mem. Am. Pancreatic Assn. (pres. 1995-96), Am. Gastroent. Assn. Achievements include research in diagnosis and therapy of pancreatic disorders. Office: 1201 Seven Locks Rd Ste 111 Rockville MD 20854

**STEINBERGER, JACK**, physicist, researcher; b. Bad Kissingen, Germany, May 25, 1921; came to U.S., 1935; s. Ludwig Lazarus and Berta (May) S.; m. Joan Beauregard, 1943, (div. 1962); children: Joseph, Richard Ned; m. Cynthia Eva Alff; children: Julia Karen, John Paul. BS in Chemistry, U. Chgo., 1942, PhD in Physics, 1948; degree (hon.), Ill. Inst. Tech., 1989, U. Glasgow, 1990, Dortmund U., 1990. Columbia U., 1990, U. Autonoma de Barcelona, Spain, 1992, U. Blaise Pascal, Clermont-Ferrand, France, 1995, U. Würzburg, 1997. Mem. Inst. for Advanced Study, Princeton, NJ, 1948-49; asst. U. Calif., Berkeley, 1949-50; prof. Columbia U., N.Y.C., 1950-68, Higgins prof., 1968-72; staff mem. European Orgn. for Nuclear Research, Geneva, 1968-86, dir., 1969-72; prof. physics Scuola Normale, Pisa, Italy, 1986—. Pfc. U.S. Army, 1943-46. Co-recipient Nobel prize in physics, 1988; recipient Nat. Medal of Sci., 1988, Mateuzzi medal Societa Italiane delle Scienze, 1991; fellow Guggenheim Found., Sloan Found. Mem. Am. Acad. Arts and Scis., Heidelberg Acad. Scis., Academia Europea, Academia Nationale dei Lincei. Avocations: tennis, sailing. Home: 25 Chemin des Merles CH 1213 Onex Switzerland Office: European Ctr for Nuclear Rsch CH 1211 Geneva 23 Switzerland E-mail: jack.steinberger@cern.ch.

**STEINBOCK, JOHN THOMAS**, bishop; b. L.A., July 16, 1937; Student, L.A. Diocesan sems. Ordained to ministry Cath. Ch., 1963. Aux. bishop Diocese of Orange, Calif. 1984—87, bishop Diocese of Santa Rosa, 1987—91; Titular Bishop of Midila, 1984; bishop Diocese of Fresno, Calif., 1991—. Roman Catholic. Office: Diocese of Fresno 1550 N Fresno St Fresno CA 93703-3788 Fax: 559-488-7464. Office Phone: 559-488-7400. E-mail: malanis@dioceseoffresno.org.

**STEINBRENNER, GEORGE MICHAEL, III**, professional baseball team executive, shipbuilding company executive; b. Rocky River, Ohio, July 4, 1930; s. Henry G. and Rita (Haley) Steinbrenner; m. Elizabeth Joan Zieg, May 12, 1956; children: Henry G. III, Jennifer Lynn, Jessica Joan, Harold Zeig. BA, Williams Coll., 1952; postgrad., Ohio State U., 1954—55. Asst. football coach Northwestern U., 1955, Purdue U., 1956—57; treas. Kinsman Transit Co., Cleve., 1957—63; pres. Kinsman Marine Transit Co., Cleve., 1963—67, dir., 1965; pres., chmn. bd. Am. Ship Bldg. Co., Cleve., 1967—78, chmn. bd., 1978—; prin. owner NY Yankees, Bronx, 1973—90, 1993—, limited ptnr., 1990—93; owner Bay Harbor Inn, Tampa, Fla., 1988—. Bd. dirs. Gt. Lakes Internat. Corp., Gt. Lakes Assocs., Cin. Sheet Metal & Roofing Co., Nashville Bridge Co., Nederlander-Steinbrenner Prodns. Chmn. Olympic Overview Commn.; v.p. US Olympic Com., 1989; mem. Cleve. Little Hoover Com., group chmn., 1966; chmn. Cleve. Urban Coalition; vice chmn. Greater Cleve. Growth Corp., Greater Cleve. Jr. Olympic Found.; founder Silver Shield Found., NYC. 1st lt. USAF, 1952—54. Named Outstanding Young Man of Yr., Ohio Jr. C. of C., 1960, Cleve. Jr. C. of C., 1960, Chief Town Crier, Cleve., 1962, New Yorker of Yr. Mem. Press Club, 1968; recipient General Douglas MacArthur award, US Olympic Com., 2002, New Yorker of Yr. Mem.: Greater Cleve. Growth Assn. (bd. dirs.). Avocation: owns racehorse Bellamy Road trained by Nick Zito. Office: NY Yankees Yankee Stadium E 161st St & River Ave Bronx NY 10451

**STEINDL, FRANK GEORGE**, economist, educator; b. Chgo., Aug. 26, 1935; s. Frank and Anna (Bumeder) S.; m. Joyce Ann Becker, Aug. 26, 1961; children: David F., Andrew M., Peter E., Matthew T. BA, DePaul U., Chgo., 1957; AM, U. Ill., 1958; PhD, U. Iowa, 1963. Asst. prof. Okla. State U., Stillwater, 1962-65, assoc. prof., 1965-70, prof., 1970-89, regents prof. of econ., 1989—, Ardmore prof. bus. administrn., 1994—. Economist Fed. Res. Bank Cleve., 1966-67; economist, counselor budget com. U.S. Senate, Washington, 1976; vis. prof. U. Munich, 1986—; Konrad Zuse guest prof. U.

Bamberg, Germany, 1991; vis. scholar London Sch. Econs. Brown U., 1993-94, U. Iowa, 2000-01. Author: Monetary Interpretations of the Gt. Depression, 1995, Understanding Econ. Recovery in the 1930s: Endogenous Propagation in the Gt. Depression, 2004; contbr. articles to profl. jour. Mem. sch. bd. St. Francis Sch., Stillwater, 1973-77; scoutmaster Boy Scouts Am., 1984-86. Named Disting. Lectr., Mid-Am. State Univs. Assn., 1981-82. Mem. Am. Econ. Assn., So. Econ. Assn (trustee 1989-91), Midwest Econs. Assn. (v.p. 1974), Southwestern Econ. Assn. (pres. 1974). Avocations: gardening, walking, opera. Home: 2206 Tanglewood Cir Stillwater OK 74074-1713 Office: Okla State Univ Dept Econs Stillwater OK 74078-1104 Business E-Mail: steindl@okstate.edu.

**STEINDLER, HOWARD ALLEN**, lawyer; b. Cleve., June 12, 1942; s. Sidney and Lois Jean (Rosenberg) S.; m. Terri Cowan Steindler; c. Rebecca, Allison, Daniel. BS, Miami U., Oxford, Ohio, 1964; JD, Ohio State U., 1967. Bar: Ohio 1967. Mem. firm Benesch, Friedlander, Coplan & Aronoff, Cleve., 1967—. Pres. bd. trustees Cleve. Scholarship Program, 1987-97, trustee, 1997—; trustee Downtown Cleve. Partnership, Inc., The Ratner Sch. Office: Benesch Friedlander Coplan & Aronoff 2300 BP Tower 200 Public Sq Cleveland OH 44114-2378 E-mail: hsteindler@bfca.com.

**STEINDLER, MARTIN JOSEPH**, chemist; b. Vienna, Jan. 3, 1928; came to U.S., 1938; s. J.P. and M.G. S.; m. Joan Long, Aug. 16, 1952; children: M.H., T.P. PhB, U. Chgo., 1947, BS, 1948, MS, 1949, PhD, 1952. Chemist Argonne (Ill.) Nat. Lab., 1953-74, sr. chemist, 1974—, assoc. dir. div. chem. engring., 1978-84, dir. chem. tech. div., 1984-93, sr. tech. advisor, 1993—. Mem adv com on nuclear waste NRC, Washington, 1988-96, chmn. 1995; adminstrv. judge ASLBP, 1973-90. Contbr. articles to profl. publs.; patentee in field. Pres. Matteson-Park Forest (Ill.) Sch. Bd., 1959-78. Recipient Disting. Performance medal U. Chgo., 1992, Meritorious Svc. award for Scientific Excellence, U.S. NRC, 1996, Lawroski award, ANL Chem. Tech. Divsn., 2002. Mem. AAAS, Am. Nuclear Soc., Am. Inst. Chem. Engrs. (Robert E. Wilson award 1990). Office: Argonne Nat Lab 9700 Cass Ave Argonne IL 60439-4803

**STEINDLER, WALTER G.**, retired lawyer; b. N.Y.C., Dec. 2, 1927; s. Mortimer B. and Ray (Feingold) S.; m. Carol A. Halpin, June 28, 1969; children: Michael, Morty, Melissa, Amy, Ellen. BA, Queens Coll., 1950; JD, NYU, 1953. Bar: N.Y. 1953, U.S. Supreme Ct. 1965, U.S. Dist. Ct. (ea. dist.) N.Y. 1972, U.S. Dist. Ct. (so. dist.) 1974, U.S. Ct. Appeals (2d cir.) 1974. Ptnr. Borden Skidell Fleck & Steindler, Jamaica, NY, 1955-62; pvt. practice law Babylon, NY, 1962-67; town atty. Town of Babylon, 1967-69; asst. county atty. Suffolk County, NY, 1970-71; ptnr. Sarisohn, Carner, Steindler, Lebow, Braun & Castrovinci, Commack, NY, 1976-93; ret., 1993. Capt., judge adv. 2d area command N.Y. Guard, N.Y.C., 1965-70; guardian ad litem 20th Jud. Cir. Lee County, Fla., 1995-98. With U.S. Army, 1946—47. Mem.: Free Sons Israel (pres. 1953), Masons. Office: 350 Veterans Memorial Hwy Commack NY 11725-4330 Office Phone: 631-543-7667.

**STEINEM, GLORIA**, writer, editor, advocate; b. Toledo, Mar. 25, 1934; d. Leo and Ruth (Nuneviller) S.; granddaughter of suffragette Pauline Steinem; m. David Bale, Sept. 3, 2000 (dec. Dec. 30, 2003); step-son Christian Bale. BA in Govt., magna cum laude (hon.), Smith Coll., 1956; postgrad. (Chester Bowles Asian fellow), India, 1957-58; D. Human Justice, Simmons Coll., 1973, PhD (hon.). Co-dir., dir. ednl. found. Ind. Rsch. Svc., Cambridge, Mass. and N.Y.C., 1959-60; contbg. editor Glamour Mag., N.Y.C., 1962-69; co-founder, contbg. editor New York Mag., 1968-72; feminist lectr., 1969—; co-founder, editor Ms. Mag., 1971-87, columnist, 1980-87, cons. editor, 1987—. Active various civil rights and peace campaigns including United Farmworkers, Vietnam War Tax Protest, Com. for the Legal Def. of Angela Davis (treas., 1971-72); active polit. campaigns of Adlai Stevenson, Robert Kennedy, Eugene McCarthy, Shirley Chisholm, George McGovern; Co-founder, bd. dirs. Women's Action Alliance, 1970-2001, (now Feminist Majority Found.); co-founder, convenor, mem. nat. adv. com. Nat. Women's Polit. Caucus, 1971; co-founder, pres. bd. dirs. Ms. Found. for Women, 1972-1990; founding mem. Coalition of Labor Union Women, 1974, Pres. Voters for Choice, 1979; mem. Internat. Women's Year Commn., 1977, pres. Choice USA, co-founder, chmn. Liberty Media for Women, 1998 (current owner and operator Ms. mag); editorial cons., Conde Nast Publications, 1962-69, Curtis Publishing, 1964-65, Random House Publishing, 1988-, McCall Publishing. Author: The Thousand Indias, 1957, The Beach Book, 1963, Wonder Woman, 1972, Outrageous Acts and Everyday Rebellions, 1982, Marilyn: Norma Jeane, 1986, Revolution from Within: A Book of Self-Esteem, 1992; contbg. contr. NBC Today Show, 1987—88; author: Moving Beyond Words: Age, Rage, Sex, Power, Money, Muscles - Breaking the Boundaries of Gender, 1994; contbr. to various anthologies. Named Woman of Yr., McCall's mag., 1972; named to Nat. Women's Hall of Fame, 1993; recipient Penney-Missouri Journalism award, 1970, Award for Journalism, Gov. Ohio, 1972, Bill of Rights award, ACLU of So. Calif., 1975, Mo. Honor Medal for Disting. Svc. in Journalism, U. Mo. Sch. Journalism, 2005; Woodrow Wilson Internat. Ctr. for Scholars Fellow, 1977. Mem.: Author's Guild, Soc. Mag. Writers, Nat. Press Club, AFTRA, NOW, Phi Beta Kappa. Coined phrase "reproductive freedom" during 1972 nat. abortion debate. Office: MS Magazine 433 S Beverly Dr Beverly Hills CA 90212-4401 also: Choice USA 712 Hershey Ave Monterey Park CA 91755-1473

**STEINER, BENJAMIN M.**, criminologist, researcher; s. Stanley F. and Kathy M. (Jarolimek) Steiner. BSc, N.D. State U., Fargo, 1997; MA, Boise State U., Idaho, 2002. Juvenile probation officer Canyon County Juvenile Probation, Caldwell, Idaho, 1998—2003, rsch. assoc. U. Cin., 2003—. Author: (book) Juvenile Justice Casebriefs, articles in profl. jours. Recipient 3d Pl. Gene Carte Student Paper Competition, Am. Soc. Criminology, 2006, academic excellance scholarship, Boise State U., 2001—02, scholarship, U. Cin., 2003—06; grantee, Am. Statis. Assn., 2005. Mem.: Acad. Criminal Justice Scis., Am. Soc. Criminology. Office: Divsn of Criminal Justice Univ Cincinnati PO Box 210389 Cincinnati OH 45221-0389 Office Phone: 513-556-9956. Office Fax: 513-556-3303. Business E-Mail: benjamin.steiner@uc.edu.

**STEINER, CHARLES K.**, museum director, painter; b. Champaign, Ill., Apr. 27, 1951; s. Gilbert Y. and Louise (King) S.; m. Mary B. Shepard; children: Frances Shepard, Hope Bradley. BFA, Cornell U., 1973; MFA, George Washington U., 1976. Aide, educator Percou, St. Prex, Switzerland, 1973-74; Rockefeller Found. fellow Met. Mus. Art, NYC, 1976-77, asst. and assoc. mus. educator, 1977-86; asst. dir. The Art Mus., Princeton U., NJ, 1986—90, assoc. dir. NJ, 1990—2000; dir. Wichita Art Mus., Kans., 2000—. Bd. dirs. Save Outdoor Sculpture, NJ, 1994-95, Arts Coun. Princeton, 1972-76; mem. art bd. Bellevue Hosp., N.Y.C., 1983-86; vis. painter Edward Albee Found., Montauk, N.Y., 1977-78. Exhibited in solo shows in N.Y.C. and Princeton; group shows at George Washington U., Washington, 1982, Delphine Gallery, Santa Barbara, Calif., 1987, Braithwaite Fine Arts Gallery/So. Utah U., Cedar City, 1993, Lexington Gallery, Lawrenceville, N.J., 1993, others; represented in collections at 3M, Mpls., N.Y. Health and Hosp. Corp., Montgomery County (Md.) Collection; author publis. in field. Spears travel grantee Princeton U., 1995; Met. Mus. Art travel grantee, Europe, 1981. Office: Wichita Art Mus 1400 West Museum Blvd Wichita KS 67203-3296

**STEINER, DAVID M.**, dean; BA, MA, Oxford U.; PhD, Harvard U. Assoc. prof. Sch. Edn. Boston U., chmn. Edn. Policy; dir. Arts Edn. Nat. Endowment of Arts, Washington, DC, 2004—05; dean Sch. Edn. Hunter Coll., CUNY, NYC, 2005—. Vis. prof. Cambridge U.; sr. rsch. assoc. Mass. State Edn. Policy. Contbr. articles to profl. jours. Mem.: Clare Hall Coll. (life). Office: Hunter Coll Sch Edn Rm W1000 695 Park Avenue New York NY 10021 Office Phone: 212-772-4622, 212-772-4621. E-mail: David.Steiner@hunter.cuny.edu.

**STEINER, DAVID P.**, waste management executive; BS in Acctg., La. State U., 1982; JD with honors, UCLA, 1986. Formerly with Gibson, Dunn & Crutcher, San Jose; former ptnr. Phelps Dunbar, New Orleans; v.p., dep. gen. counsel Waste Mgmt., Inc., Houston, 2000—01, sr. v.p., gen. counsel, corp. sec., 2001—03, exec. v.p., CFO, 2003—04, CEO, 2004—. Mem.: ABA, Calif. Bar Assn., La. Bar Assn. Office: Waste Mgmt Inc 1001 Fannin St Ste 4000 Houston TX 77002*

**STEINER, DONALD FREDERICK**, biochemist, physician, educator; b. Lima, Ohio, July 15, 1930; s. Willis A. and Katherine (Hoegner) S. BS in Chemistry and Zoology, U. Cin., 1952; MS in Biochemistry, U. Chgo., 1956, MD, 1956; D Med. Sci. (hon.), U. Umea, 1973, U. Ill., 1984, Technische Hochschule, Aachen, 1993, U. Uppsala, 1993, Mt. Sinai Sch. Medicine, N.Y.C., 1998. Intern King County Hosp., Seattle, 1956-57; USPHS postdoctoral research fellow, asst. medicine U. Wash. Med. Sch., 1957-60; mem. faculty med. sch. U. Chgo., 1960—, chmn. dept. biochemistry, 1973-79, A.N. Pritzker prof. biochemistry, molecular biology and medicine, 1985—, sr. investigator Howard Hughes Med. Inst., 1986—. Jacobaeus lectr., Oslo, 1970; Luft lectr., Stockholm, 1984. Co-editor: The Endocrine Pancreas, 1972, discoverer proinsulin. Recipient Gairdner award Toronto, 1971, Hans Christian Hagedorn medal Steensen Meml. Hosp., Copenhagen, 1970, Lilly award, 1969, Ernst Oppenheimer award, 1970, Diaz-Cristobal award Internat. Diabetes Fedn., 1973, Banting medal Am. Diabetes Assn., 1976, Banting medal Brit. Diabetes Assn., 1981, Passano award, 1979, Wolf prize in medicine, 1985, Frederick Conrad Koch award Endocrine Soc., 1990. Mem. AAAS, Nat. Acad. Scis., Am. Soc. Biochemists and Molecular Biologists, Am. Phllos. Soc., Am. Diabetes Assn. (50th Anniversary medallion 1972), European Assn. Study Diabetes, Am. Acad. Arts and Scis., Am. Philos. Soc., Sigma Xi, Alpha Omega Alpha. Home: 2626 N Lakeview Ave Apt 2508 Chicago IL 60614-1821 Business E-Mail: dfsteine@midway.uchicago.edu.

**STEINER, GEORGE (FRANCIS STEINER)**, author, educator; b. Paris, Apr. 23, 1929; s. Frederick George and Elsie (Franzos) S.; m. Zara Shakow, 1955; children: David Milton, Deborah Tarn. BA, U. Chgo., 1949; MA, Harvard U., 1950; PhD, Oxford U., 1955; DLitt (hon.), Trinity Coll., Dublin, 1996; LittD (hon.), Louvain U., 1980, Mount Holyoke Coll., 1983, Durham U., 1995; D honoris causa, U. Bristol, 1989; DLitt (hon.), U. Glasgow, 1990, U. Liége, 1990, U. Ulster, 1993, U. Durham, 1995, Kenyon Coll., 1996, U. Rome, 1998, U. Sorbonne, 1998, U. Salamanca, 2002, U. London, 2006, U. Bologna, 2006. Mem. staff Economist, London, 1952-56; mem. staff Inst. Advanced Study Princeton (N.J.) U., NJ, 1956-58, Gauss lectr. NJ, 1959-60; Massey lectr., 1974; First Lord Weidenfeld prof. Comp. Lit. Oxford U., 1994—; Charles Eliot Norton prof. poetry Harvard U., 2001—. Cons. and lectr. in field; Maurice lectr. U. London, 1984, Leslie Stephen lectr. Cambridge U., 1985, W.P. Ker lectr. U. Glasgow, 1986; lectr. Page-Barbour Lectures U. Va., 1987, Gifford lectr., 1990; vis. prof. Coll. France, 1992; First Lord Weidenfeld vis. prof. comparative lit., Oxford U., 1994—. Author: Tolstoy or Dostoevsky, 1958, The Death of Tragedy, 1960, Anno Domini, 1964, Language and Silence, 1967, Extraterritorial, 1971, In Bluebeard's Castle, 1971, The Sporting Scene: White Knights in Reykjavik, 1973, After Babel, 1975 (adapted for TV as The Tongues of Men, 1977), Heidegger, 1978, On Difficulty and Other Essays, 1978, The Portage to San Cristobal of A.H., 1981, Antigones, 1984, George Steiner: A Reader, 1984, Real Presences, 1989, Proofs and Three Parables, 1992, Homer in English, 1996, No Passion Spent, 1996, The Deeps of the Sea, 1996, Errata, An Examined Life, 1997, Grammars of Creation, 2001, Lessons of the Masters, 2003; editor: The Penguin Book of Modern Verse Translation, 1966, Homer: A Collection of Critical Essays (with Robert Flagles), 1962. Decorated chevalier de la Legion d'Honneur (France); Churchill Coll. fellow, 1961—; Hon. Royal Academician (London), Commandeur dans l'Ordre des Arts et des Lettres (Paris); hon. fellow Balliol Coll., Oxford, Eng., 1995, St. Anne's Coll., Oxford; Fulbright prof., 1958-69; recipient O. Henry Short Story award, 1958, Guggenheim fellowship, 1971-72, Zabel award Nat. Inst. Arts and Letters, U.S., 1970, King Albert medal Royal Belgian Acad., 1982, P.E.N. Internat. Fiction prize, 1993; Faulkner Fiction grantee P.E.N., 1983; Le Prix du Souvenir, 1974, Truman Capite Lifetime award for Lit., 1999, Prince of Asturias prize in humanities, 2001, Ludwig-Börne prize, Germany, 2003; named Hon. Royal Academician, London. Fellow British Acad.; mem. Am. Acad. Arts and Scis. (hon.), English Assn. (pres. 1975), German Acad. Lit. (corr.). Office: Churchill Coll Cambridge England

**STEINER, HENRY JACOB**, law and human rights educator; b. Mt. Vernon, NY, June 14, 1930; s. Meier and Bluma (Henigson) S.; m. Pamela Pomerance, Aug. 1, 1982; stepchildren: Duff, Jacoba. BA magna cum laude, Harvard U., 1951, MA, 1955, LLB magna cum laude, 1955. Bar: N.Y. 1956, Mass. 1963. Law clk. to Hon. John M. Harlan U.S. Supreme Ct., 1957-58; assoc. Sullivan and Cromwell, N.Y.C., 1958-62; asst. prof. sch. law Harvard U., Cambridge, Mass., 1962-65, prof., 1965—, Jeremiah Smith Jr. prof. law, 1986—2005; prof. emeritus, 2005—. Founder, dir. Law Sch. Human Rights Program, 1984—2005; chair univ. com. on human rights studies Harvard U., 1994—2002; bd. dirs. U. Middle East project, 1996—99, chair bd. dirs., 2000—; vis. prof. Yale U., 1972—73, Stanford U., 1965; cons. AID, 1962—64, Ford Found., 1966—69. Co-author: (textbook) Transnational Legal Problems, 4th edit., 1994, Tort and Accident Law, 2d edit., 1989, International Human Rights in Context: Law, Politics, Morals, 2d edit., 2000; author: Moral Argument and Social Vision in the Courts, 1987, Diverse Partners: Non-Governmental Organizations in the Human Rights Movement, 1991; former devels. editor Harvard Law Rev.; contbr. articles to profl. jours. Office: Harvard U Law Sch Cambridge MA 02138 Home: 28 Madison St Cambridge MA 02138 Business E-Mail: hsteiner@law.harvard.edu.

**STEINER, HERBERT MAX**, physics professor; b. Goeppingen, Germany, Dec. 8, 1927; came to U.S., 1939, naturalized, 1944; s. Albert and Martha (Epstein) S. BS, U. Calif., Berkeley, 1951, PhD, 1956. Physicist Lawrence Berkeley Lab., Berkeley, Calif., 1956—; mem. faculty U. Calif., Berkeley, 1958—, prof. physics, 1966-2000, prof. emeritus, 2000—, William H. McAdams prof. physics, chmn. dept., 1992-95; vis. scientist European Center Nuclear Research, 1960-61, 64, 68-69, 82-83, Max Planck Inst. Physics and Astrophysics, Munich, 1976-77; vis. prof. Japanese Soc. Promotion Sci., 1978. Vis. prof. physics U. Paris, 1989-90; vis. scientist Deutsches Electron Synchrotron Lab., 1995-96. Author articles in field. Served with AUS, 1946-47. Recipient Sr. Am. Scientist award Alexander von Humboldt Found., 1976-77; Guggenheim fellow, 1960-61 Fellow Am. Phys. Soc. Office: U Calif Berkeley Dept Physics 7300 Berkeley CA 94720-0001 Office Phone: 510-486-6805. Business E-Mail: steiner@lbl.gov.

**STEINER, JEFFREY JOSEF**, manufacturing executive; b. Vienna, Apr. 3, 1937; came to U.S., 1958; s. Beno and Paula (Bornstein) S.; m. Claude Angel, Apr. 11, 1957 (div. 1972); children: Eric, Natalia, Thierry; m. Linda Schaller, Mar. 6, 1976 (div. June 1983); children: Benjamin, Alexandra. Student textile design, U. London, 1956; student textile mfg., Bradford Inst. Tech., London, 1957; HHD (hon.), Yeshiva U., 1996. Mgmt. trainee Metals and Controls div. Tex. Instruments, Attleborough, Mass., 1958-59, mgr. internat., 1959-60, pres. Argentina, Brazil, Mex., Switzerland, France, 1960-66, Burlington Tapis, Paris, 1967-72; chmn., pres. Cedec S.A. Engring. Co., Paris, 1973-84; chmn., CEO Fairchild Corp., N.Y.C., 1985—, Banner Aerospace, 1993—. Bd. dirs. Copley Fund, Fall River, Mass., Comms. Intelligence Corp., Cyber Express, Inc. Trustee Montefiore Med. Ctr. N.Y.C.; bd. dirs. Israel Mus., Yeshiva U. Bus. Sch. Decorated Knight of Arts (France), knight Indsl. Merit of France, chevalier de L'Ordre des Arts et des Lettres, 1990, chevalier de L'order National du Merite (France), commandatore de la Republica (Italy); recipient mayor's medal City of Paris, 1990; named one of Top 200 Collectors, ARTnews Mag., 2004, 2005, 2006. Mem. City Athletic Club, Racing Club, Polo Club. Jewish. Avocations: tennis, sailing, collector of Impressionism, modern & contemporary art. Office: The Fairchild Corp 110 E 59th St New York NY 10022 Office Phone: 212-308-6700. E-mail: jsteiner@fairchild.com.

**STEINER, JOHN MICHAEL,** sociologist, educator; b. Prague, Czech Republic, Aug. 3, 1925; arrived in U.S., 1958; s. Kurt John and Ilse (Ornstein) Steiner; 1 child, Ingmar Michael Augustus. BA, U. Melbourne, 1952; MA, U. Mo., 1955; PhD, U. Alberto-Ludovica, 1968. Liaison officer United Relief and Rehab. Adminstrn. Mission, Prague, 1946—48; immigration officer Dept. Immigration, Canberra, Melbourne, Australia, 1949—52; indsl. therapist Hosp. No. 1, Fulton, Mo., 1955—56; lectr. speech U. Calif., Berkeley, 1956—59; rsch. social psychologist USAF, Wright-Patterson AFB, Ohio, 1959—61; rsch. assoc. Inst. World Civilization, Freiburg, Germany, 1963—64; vis. asst. prof. Dept. Criminology, 1964—65; prof. sociology Sonoma State U., Rohnert Park, Calif., 1968—92, sr. scholar in residence, 1993—, prof. emeritus, 1992. Founding dir. Sonoma State Holocaust Studies Ctr., 1984—92. Author: Power Politics and Social Change in National Socialist Germany, 1975; author: (with Joel E. Dimsdale) Survivors, Victims, and Perpetrators Essays on the Nazi Holocaust, 1980; author: Graig, Haney, Curtis Banks and Philip Zimbarado, Das Stanford Gefoganis Experiment, 1984; contbr. articles to profl. jours., books, chpts. to books on polit. crime. Co-founder, v.p. Ams. Dem. Action, Berkeley, 1960. Recipient Disting. cross Svc. and Valor, Czech Republic, 1948, cert. recognition, Calif. State Assembly, 1994, Order Merit, Pres. Germany, 2002; fellow, Fulbright Found., 1974—75, 1981—82; Alexander Von Humboldt rsch. fellow, U. Freiburg, 1964—67, 1990. Mem.: Fulbright Assn., Czechoslovak Acad. Arts and Scis., Acad. Criminal Justice Scis., Alexander Von Humbodt Assn., Am. Sociol. Assn., Alpha Pi Zeta. Democrat. Achievements include studies on the authoritarian personality based on SS (Nazi) perpetrators; studies on the role margin as the site of moral and social intelligence; studies on the case of Germany and national socialism; studies on Hitler's exemptions from the Nuremberg Racial Laws; genocide, holocaust and perpetrator studies on price-tag switching. Avocations: art, antiques, swimming, photography. Home: 65 Sotelo Way Novato CA 94945 Office: Sonoma State U Dept Sociology Rohnert Park CA 94928 Business E-Mail: john.stener@sonoma.edu.

**STEINER, JOHN WILLIAM,** retired biophysicist; b. Chgo., Feb. 3, 1934; s. John Deacon Steiner and Bernice Marguerite Taylor; m. Phyllis Irene Rendell, July 12, 1958; children: John Alfred, Jay William. BA in Chemistry, Boston U., 1964. Analytical chemist MIT Nuc. Reactor, Cambridge, Mass., 1965—66; rsch. biophysicist biophysics dept. Boston U. Med. Ctr., Boston, 1967—99; ret., 1999. Contbr. Handbook of Liquid Research, vol. 4, 1986. Vestryman, mem. various coms. Ch. of Our Redeemer, Lexington, Mass., 1985—. Col. USAR, 1952—86. Mem.: Employer Support of Guard/Res., Res. Officers Assn. (Mass. state pres. 1999—2000). Republican. Episcopalian. Avocations: stamp collecting/philately, coin collecting/numismatics, genealogy. Home: 22 Estabrook Rd Lexington MA 02421-7540

**STEINER, JOSEPH FRANCIS,** pharmacy educator; b. Toledo, Ohio, July 4, 1949; s. Joseph Francis and Carmel Louise (D'Agostino) S.; m. Susan Day Haake, Aug. 26, 1972; children: Katharine Day, Josephine Susan. BS Zoology, U. Mich., 1971, BS Pharmacy, 1973, PharmD, 1974. Resident U. Mich. Med. Ctr., Ann Arbor, 1973-75; from asst. prof. to prof. U. Wyo., Laramie, 1975—, dir. pharmacy practice, 1997—. Mem. Am. Coll. Clin. Pharmacy, Am. Assn. Colls. Pharmacy, Am. Soc. Health-Svcs. Pharmacists, Am. Soc. Microbiology, Casper (Wyo.) Lions Club (pres. 1996-97). Avocations: skiing, fly fishing, boating. Office: U Wyo Sch Pharmacy PO Box 3375 Laramie WY 82071-3375 Home: 1485 Cedar Lake Rd Pocatello ID 83204-4949

**STEINER, ROBERT ALAN,** neuroendocrinologist, educator; b. Chgo., Mar. 9, 1947; s. Alan Dale and Elizabeth Ann (Smith); m. Sally Jean Hewett, Mar. 19, 1983. BA, U. Pacific, 1969; PhD in Physiology, Oreg. Health & Sci. U., 1975. Sr. fellow Regional Primate Rsch. Ctr. U. Wash., Seattle, 1974—78, asst. prof. ob-gyn., physiology and biophysics, 1978—83, assoc. prof., 1983, prof. Adj. prof. biology U. Wash. Contbr. articles to profl. jours.; mem. editl. bd.: Biology of Reproduction, 1986—90, Endocrinology, 1986—90, 1994—98, 2001—04, Am. Jour. Physiology, 1993—98, Neuroendocrinology, 2000—; editor: Molecular and Cellular Neurosciences, 1991—94. Recipient Nat. Human Growth Found. award, 1977; grantee, Nat. Inst. Child Health and Human Devel., 1978—. Mem.: Soc. Behavioral Neuroendocrinology, Internat. Soc. Neuroendocrinology, Internat. Neuropeptide Soc., Am. Physiol. Soc., Soc. Study Reproduction, AAAS, Soc. Neuroscience, Endocrine Soc. Democrat. Office: Dept Physiology and Biophysics U Wash Box 357290 Seattle WA 98195-7290 E-mail: steiner@u.washington.edu.*

**STEINER, ROBERT FRANK,** biochemist; b. Manila, Philippines, Sept. 29, 1926; came to U.S., 1933; s. Frank and Clara Nell (Weems) S.; m. Ethel Mae Fisher, Nov. 3, 1956; children: Victoria, Laura. AB, Princeton U., 1947; PhD, Harvard U., 1950. Chemist Naval Med. Research Inst., Bethesda, Md., 1950-70, chief lab. phys. biochemistry, 1965-70; prof. chemistry U. Md., Balt., 1970—, chmn. dept. chemistry, 1974—; prof. emeritus, 1996—; dir. grad. program in biochemistry U. Md., Balt., 1985. Biophysics study sect. NIH, 1976. Author: Life Chemistry, 1968, Excited States of Proteins and Nucleic Acids, 1971, The Chemistry of Living Systems, 1981, Excited States of Biopolymers, 1983, A Pilot's Tale and Other Stories, 1998, The Decoy and Other Stories, 1999, The Student Pilot and Other Stories, 2000, The Beauty Contest and Other Stories, 2002, Dreamtime, 2004; editor Jour. Biophys. Chemistry, 1972—, Jour. Fluorescence, 1991; contbr. over 160 articles to profl. jours. Served with AUS, 1945-47. Recipient Superior Civilian Achievement award Dept. Def., 1966; NSF rsch. grantee, 1971-77, NIH, 1973-93. Fellow Washington Acad. Sci., Japan Soc. for Promotion Sci.; mem. Am. Soc. Biol. Chemists. Clubs: Princeton (Washington). Achievements include development of fluorescence techniques for studying proteins. Home: 2609 Turf Valley Rd Ellicott City MD 21042-2021 Office: 5401 Wilkens Ave Baltimore MD 21250-1000 Office Phone: 410-465-0987. Personal E-mail: xuxw63A@aol.com.

**STEINER, ROBERT LISLE,** retired language educator; b. Tehran, Iran, May 21, 1921; s. Robert Lisle and Lois (Foresman) S.; m. Margaret S. Sherrard, June 4, 1944; children: Patricia Jean, Robert Lisle III, William Sherrard, John Scott. BA, Wooster Coll., Ohio; MA, Columbia U., 1948. Cons. Commn. Chs. on Internat. Affairs, 1948-49; cultural attache Am. embassy, Iran, 1950-52; educationist U.S. Office Edn., 1952-54; program dir. Am. Friends of Mid. East, 1954-59; v.p. Vershire Co., Vt., 1959-62; dir. Peace Corps, Kabul, Afghanistan, 1962-66; regional dir. North Africa, Near East and South Asia, 1966-69; dir. Washington office Devel. & Resources Corp., 1969-70; dir. Ctr. for Cross-Cultural Tng. and Rsch., adviser to univ. press on internat. affairs U. Hawaii, Honolulu, 1971-72; dir., gen. mgr. Hawaii Pub. Broadcasting Authority, 1972-73; exec. dir. N.J. Edn. Consortium, Princeton, 1973-78; pres. InterLink Lang. Ctrs., Princeton, 1979-91, chmn., 1992—; Tchr. U. Kansas City, Mo., 1957, Bradford (Vt.) Acad., 1961; poultry cons. Mid. East Tech. U., Ankara, Turkey, 1963. Councilman, v.p. Shanks Village Assn., Orangeburg, N.Y., 1948; chmn. Kabul Sch. Bd., 1965. Served as pilot USNR, 1943-46. Mem. Princeton Mid. East Soc. (sec. 1986-88, treas. 1993-95). Democrat. Presbyterian. Home: 1898 Villa Ct Lancaster PA 17603-2386 Office: Interlink Lang Ctrs 1898 Villa Ct Lancaster PA 17603-2386

**STEINER, ROGER JACOB,** linguistics educator, writer, researcher; b. South Byron, Wis., Mar. 27, 1924; s. Jakob Robert and Alice Mildred (Cowles) S.; m. Ida Kathryn Posey, Aug. 7, 1954 (dec. May 1992); children: David Posey, Andrew Posey, Anthony Wright. BA cum laude, Franklin & Marshall Coll., 1945; MDiv, Union Theol. Sem., 1947; MA, U. Pa., 1958, PhD, 1963. Ordained to ministry, Meth. Ch., 1947. Clergyman United Meth. Ch., N.Y., Wis., Pa., 1945-61; lectr. U. Bordeaux, France, 1961-63; instr. fgn. langs. & lit. U. Del., Newark, 1963-64, asst. prof., 1964-71, assoc. prof., 1971-80, prof., 1980-85, dept. linguistics U. Del., Newark, 1985-96, prof. emeritus, 1998—. Cons. Charles Scribner's Sons, N.Y.C., 1972-75, Larousse, N.Y.C., 1981-84, Houghton-Mifflin, Boston, 1981-84, Macmillan, 1994-99. Author: Two Centuries of Spanish and English Bilingual Lexicography (1590-1800), 1970, New College French and English Dictionary, 1972, 3d edit., 2004; editor: Simon & Schuster's International Spanish Dictionary, 2d

edit., 1997, Cuyás Spanish and English Dictionary, 3d edit., 1999, New College Spanish and English Dictionary, 3d edit., 2003; contbr. articles to profl. jours., chpts. to books. Recipient fellowship Am. Philos. Soc., Phila., 1971, Lilly Found., Phila., 1979-81. Mem. MLA (founder lexicography group 1974-75, chmn. 1976, 77, 80, 85), Dictionary Soc. N.Am., Phi Beta Kappa (pres. chpt. 1975-76). Republican. Avocation: languages. Office: U Del Dept Linguistics Newark DE 19716-2551 E-mail: jacobjoos@aol.com.

**STEINER, RUTH,** music educator, educator; b. Oak Park, Ill., Feb. 2, 1931; d. Eugene and Ruth Piette; children: Jonathan, Miriam. BA, Wellesley Coll., Mass., 1952; MA, U. Calif., Berkeley, 1958; PhD, Cath. U. of Am., Washington, DC, 1964. Prof. of music Cath. U. of Am., Washington, 1966—2000; ret., 2000. Author: (book) Studies in Gregorian Chant, 1999; contbr. articles to profl. jours. Grant, Nat. Endowment for the Humanities, 1989, 1992, 1994, 1982, 1985, 1988. Mem.: Am. Musicological Soc. (sec. 1984—89), Medieval Acad. of Am. Home: 6624 Barnaby St NW Washington DC 20015 Personal E-mail: steiner@cua.edu.

**STEINER, STUART,** college president; b. Balt., July 24, 1937; s. Louis and Lillian (Block) S.; m. Rosalie Weiner, Sept. 12, 1962; children: Lisa, Susan, David, Robyn. AA, Balt. Jr. Coll., 1957; BS, U. Md., 1959; grad. cert., Fla. State U., 1962; MSW., U. Pa., 1963; JD, U. Balt., 1967; MA, Tchrs. Coll., Columbia U., 1972; EdD, Columbia U., 1987. Caseworker, then supr. and dir. juvenile ct. services Balt. Dept. Social Services, 1960-64; dir. info. and referral ctr. Healt and Welfare Coun. Met. Balt., 1964; dir. admissions and placement Harford Jr. Coll., Bel Air, Md., 1965-67; dean of students Genesee Community Coll., Batavia, NY, 1967-68, dean of coll., 1968-75, pres., 1975—. Pres. SUNY West, acting dep. to chancellor for community colls., 1985, pres. of assn. Pres. of Pub. Community Colls., 1987-89; acting pres. Fashion Inst. Tech., N.Y.C., 1997-98; CEO Ednl. Found. Fashion Industries, 1997-98; bd. dirs. Workforce Investment Bd.; commr. Commn. of Higher Edn., Mid. States Assn., 1999—. Contbr. chpts. to art books and articles to profl. jours. Bd. dirs. St. Jerome Hosp., Genesee County Community Chest, campaign chmn.; bd. dirs. Health Sci. Agy., Western N.Y.; trustee Villa Maria Coll.; trustee, v.p. N.Y. Chiropractic Coll.; bd. dirs. St. Jerome Hosp., Genesee Mercy Healthcare, United Meml. Med Ctr.; pres. Genesee County United Way, Community Coll. of Balt. Hall of Fame. Sigma Delta scholar U. Md., 1958-59, Heuisler scholar U. Balt. Law Sch., 1960-61, Kellogg fellow, 1971-72; recipient CEO award Assn. of C.C. Trustees (N.E. region) 1997. Mem. Pvt. Indsl. Coun. (bd. dirs. 1998—2000, workforce investment bd. 2000-02). Home: 33 Woodcrest Dr Batavia NY 14020-2721 Office: Genesee Community Coll 1 College Rd Batavia NY 14020-9703 Office Phone: 585-345-6812. E-mail: ssteiner@genesee.edu.

**STEINERT-THRELKELD, THOMAS MILLER,** editor, journalist; b. Glen Ridge, N.J., June 20, 1954; s. Aubrey Miller and Elizabeth (Morgan) Threlkeld; m. Kayte Steinert, Aug. 16, 1983; children: Zachary and Shane. BJ, U. Mo., 1976; MBA, Harvard U., 1979. Bus. writer Ft. Worth Star-Telegram, 1979-82, bus. columnist, 1987-88; rsch. dir. electronic pub. Capital Cities Comm., Ft. Worth, 1980-81, dir. new tech., 1981-82; owner, pres. The Info. Companies, Azle, Tex., 1982-86; editor-in-chief Interactive Week, Garden City, NY, 1995—99, editl. dir., 1999—2001; v.p. enterprise group, founding editor Baseline mag. Ziff Davis, 2001—05; editor-in-chief Multichannel News (subs. Reed Elsevier Inc.), 2005—. Recipient John Hancock award for excellence in bus. journalism, 1982, AP Mng. Editors award for bus. writing, 1989, Headliners award, Headliners Club, 1990. Avocation: long distance cycling. Office: Multichannel News 360 Park Avenue New York NY 10022*

**STEINES, JOHN P., JR.,** law educator; b. 1948; BIE, Gen. Motors Inst., 1971; JD, Ohio State U., 1974; LLM in taxation, NYU, 1978. Bar: Mich. 1974, NY 1981. Assoc. Miller, Johnson, Snell & Cummiskey, Grand Rapids, Mich., 1974—78; instr. in taxation NYU Sch. Law, 1978—80, asst. prof., 1980—83, assoc. prof., 1983—85, prof., 1985—; counsel Weil, Gotshal & Manges, 1984—2001, Kronish, Leib, Weiner & Hellman, 2004—. Office: NYU Sch Law Vanderbilt Hall Rm 430J 40 Washington Sq S New York NY 10012-1099 Office Phone: 212-998-6167. E-mail: john.steines@nyu.edu.

**STEINFELD, ALLAN,** sports association administrator; B, City College, NY, 1969; M in Elec. Enging. and Radio Astronomy, Cornell U., 1971. Staff mem. NY Road Runners Club, NYC, 1978-92, pres., 1992—. Chief referee of men's and women's marathons, 1984 LA Olympics; adviser several TV broadcasts; race dir. Fifth Ave Mile, the Advil Mini Marathon, the Trevira Twosome, NY Games; mem. exec. com. TAF's Men's Long Distance Running Com.; tech. dir.; NYC Marathon, 1981-94; race dir., 1994-; adv. bd. mem., Nat. Distance Running Hall of Fame, Utica, NY. Achievements include winner, NY Roadrunner Club 8-mile Handicap Race, 1966. Office: NY Road Runners Club 9 E 89th St New York NY 10128-0602

**STEINFELD, JEFFREY IRWIN,** chemistry professor, educator, writer; b. Bklyn., July 2, 1940; s. Paul and Ann (Ravin) S. B.Sc., MIT, 1962; PhD, Harvard U., 1965. Postdoctoral fellow U. Sheffield, Yorkshire, England, 1965-66; asst. prof. chemistry MIT, Cambridge, 1966-70, assoc. prof., 1970-79, prof., 1980—. Author: Molecules & Radiation, 1974; co-author: Chemical Kinetics and Dynamics, 1989, 2d edit., 1999; editor: Laser and Coherence Spectroscopy, 1977, Laser-Induced Chemical Processes, 1981; co-editor: Spectrochimica Acta, 1983-98; contbr. articles to profl. jours. Treas. Ward 2 Democratic Com., Cambridge, 1972-73 NSF fellow Harvard U., Cambridge, 1962-65; NSF fellow Sheffield U., 1965-66; Alfred P. Sloan Found. research fellow MIT, 1969-71; Guggenheim fellow, 1972-73 Fellow Am. Phys. Soc.; mem. AAAS, Union Concerned Scientists, Fedn. Am. Scientists, Sigma Xi, Phi Lambda Upsilon. Jewish. Office: MIT Room 2-221 Cambridge MA 02139

**STEINFELD, MANFRED,** furniture manufacturing executive; b. Josbach, Germany, Apr. 29, 1924; s. Abraham and Paula (Katten) Steinfeld; m. Fern Goldman, Nov. 13, 1949; children: Michael, Paul, Jill. Student, U. Ill., 1942; BS in Commerce, Roosevelt U., 1948, LLH (hon.), 1997. Rsch. analyst State of Ill., 1948-50; v.p. Shelby Williams Industries, Inc., Chgo., 1954-63, pres., 1964-72, chmn. bd., 1973-96, chmn. exec. com., 1996—99. Bd. dirs. Amalgamated Trust & Savs. Bank; founder Daniel Paul Chairs LLC, 2004. Mem. adv. bd. Sch. Human Ecology U. Tenn., 1981—87, devel. coun., 1982—87; mem. adv. bd. dept. interior design Fla. Internat. U., 1981—85; life trustee Roosevelt U., Chgo.; past pres. Roosevelt U. Bus. Sch. Alumni Coun.; hon. governing mem. Art Inst. Chgo., mem. com. 20th century decorative art, endowed gallery on 20th century decorative art, 1984; established Manfred Steinfeld Hospitality Mgmt. Program at Roosevelt U., 1988; endowed Fern and Manfred Steinfeld Chair Judaic Studies, U. Tenn., Knoxville, 1995; endowed Danny Cunniff Leukemia Rsch. Lab., Hadassah Hosp., Jerusalem; mem. U. Tenn. Devel. Coun., 1985—2005; nat. vice chmn. Jewish United Fund, 1988—94, bd. dirs., 1987, 1997; chmn. bd. dirs. Jewish Fedn. Chgo., 1988—2000. Staff sgt. AUS, 1942—45, 1st lt. AUS, 1950—52. Decorated Bronze Star, Purple Heart; named Small Bus. Man of Yr., Ctrl. Region, 1967, Vol. of Yr., U. Tenn., 1998; recipient Horatio Alger award of disting. Ams., 1981, Outstanding Bus. Leader award, Northwood Inst., 1983, Lifetime Achievement award, Hospitality Design Mag., 1999, Julius Rosenwald award, 2000. Mem.: Horatio Alger Assn., Bocaire Country Club (Boca Raton, Fla.), Bryn Mawr Country Club (Chgo.), Std. Club (Chgo.), Beta Gamma Sigma. Home: 1300 N Lake Shore Dr Apt 34D Chicago IL 60610-5165 E-mail: manfern@aol.com.

**STEINFELD, PHILIP SHELDON,** pediatrician; b. Bronx, Mar. 4, 1932; s. Samuel and Sarah (Frishman) S.; m. Ruth L. Hyman, Aug., 1961 (div. June 1977); children: Andrea, Melissa, David; m. Sherry Lynn Rubinroit, Jan. 15, 1978; 1 child, Sara. BS, Queens Coll., 1953; MD, U. Basle, Switzerland, 1960. Diplomate Am. Bd. Pediatrics. Rotating intern Kings County Hosp. Ctr., Bklyn., 1960-61; resident pediatrics Mt. Sinai Hosp., N.Y., 1961-63, jr. clin. asst. pediatrics 1963-65; sr. clin. asst., 1965-68; attending pediatrician L.I. Jewish Hosp., 1968—, North Shore Univ. Hosp., 1970—; clin. instr.

pediatrics Cornell U., N.Y.C., 1986-90, clin. asst. prof. pediatrics, 1991—. Mem. adv. bd. TEMPO, Woodmere, N.Y., 1975-92, Five Town Adolescent Ctr., Woodmere, 1975-93. Fellow Am. Acad. Pediatrics. Office: 1573 Broadway Hewlett NY 11557-1428 Office Phone: 516-374-3322. Business E-Mail: philsteinfeld@pol.net.

**STEINFINK, HUGO,** chemical engineering professor; b. Vienna, May 22, 1924; s. Mendel and Malwina (Fiderer) S.; m. Cele Intrator, Mar. 21, 1948; children: Dan E., Susan D. BS, CCNY, 1947; MS, Columbia U., 1948; PhD, Bklyn. Poly. Inst., 1954. Rsch. chemist Shell Devel. Co., Houston, 1948-51, 53-60; T. Brockett Hudson prof. chem. engring. U. Tex., Austin, 1960-2000, prof. emeritus, 2000. Contbr. articles to profl. jours. With AUS, 1944-46. Fellow Am. Mineral Soc.; mem. AIChE, Am. Chem. Soc., Am. Crystallographic Assn. (pres.-elect 1994, pres. 1995, past pres. 1996), Materials Rsch. Soc., Phi Beta Kappa, Sigma Xi, Phi Lambda Epsilon. Home: 3811 Walnut Clay Dr Austin TX 78731-4011 Office Phone: 512-471-5233. E-mail: steinfink@che.utexas.edu.

**STEINGASS, SUSAN R.,** lawyer; b. Cambridge, Mass., Dec. 18, 1941; BA in English Lit., Denison U., 1963; MA in English Lit. with honors, Northwestern U., 1965; JD with honors, U. Wis., 1976. Bar: Wis. 1976, U.S. Dist. Ct. Wis. 1976. Instr. dept. English La. State U., 1965—66, Calif. State Coll., L.A., 1966—68, U. Wis., Stevens Point, 1968—72; law clk. Hon. Nathan S. Heffernan Wis. Supreme Ct., 1976—77; ptnr. Stafford, Rosenbaum, Reiser and Hansen, 1977—85; judge Dane County Cir. Ct., Wis., 1985—93; ptnr. Habush, Habush & Rottier, S.C., Madison, Wis., 1993—. Lectr. civil procedure, environ. law, evidence, trial advocacy Law Sch., U. Wis., 1981—; dir. comm. and advocacy programs, 2003—; instr. Nat. Inst. for Trial Advocacy, 1987—, trustee, 2002—; instr. Nat. Jud. Coll., 1993—. Note and comment editor Wis. Law Rev., 1974-76; co-editor: Wisconsin Civil Procedure Before Trial, 1994, The Wisconsin Rules of Evidence: A Courtroom Handbook, 1998—. Chair Wis. Equal Justice Task Force, 1989—91, Wis. Sentencing Commn., 2003—; mem., chair Wis. Jud. Selection Com., 2003—. Recipient Disting. Svc. award Am. Assn. Mediators, 1991, Presdl. award of excellence State Bar Wis., 2000; named Wis. Trial Judge of Yr. Am. Bd. Trial Advocates, 1992. Fellow Wis. Bar Found.; mem. ATLA, ABA (ho. dels. 2000—), Am. Bar Found., Am. Law Inst., Wis. Bar Assn. (pres. 1998-99), Wis. Law Alumni Assn. (bd. dirs., pres. 2001-05), Wis. Acad. Trial Lawyers, Wis. Equal Justice Fund (pres. 2000-05), Dane County Bar Assn., Wis. Trust Account Found. (bd. dirs. 1999), Order of the Coif (Marygold Melli Achievement award 2001). Office: Habush Habush Davis & Rottier SC 150 E Gilman St Ste 2000 Madison WI 53703-1481 also: Univ Wis Law School 975 Bascom Mall Madison WI 53706 Business E-Mail: ssteingass@habush.com.

**STEINGRABER, FREDERICK GEORGE,** management consultant; b. Mpls., July 7, 1938; s. Frederick F. and Evelyn (Luger) S.; m. Veronika Agnes Wagner, Aug. 9, 1974; children: Karla, Frederick. BS, Ind. U., 1960; MBA, U. Chgo., 1964. Cert. mgmt. cons. Internat. banker Harris Trust, Chgo., 1960-61; with commcl. loan and credit No. Trust Co., Chgo., 1963—68; assoc. A.T. Kearney, Chgo., 1969—72, prin., 1972—, officer/ptnr., 1972—, pres., COO, 1981—82, CEO, chmn. bd., 1983—2000, chmn. emeritus, 2002, chmn., bd. advs., 2002, also bd. dirs.; mem. adv. bd. L.L.C., 1999—. Bd. dirs. Continental AG, 1989—, John Hancock Fin. Trend Funds3, PLC, 2001—, Maytag Corp., 2004—, Elkay Mfg., 2004—, Chgo. Stock Exch.; mem. Talent Intelligence Adv. Bd., Global Bus. Coun. Adv. Bd. Chief crusader United Way Crusade of Mercy, Chgo., 1983—90; divsn.chmn., bd. dirs.l Ill. Coalition, 1989; fin. rsch. aand adv. coun. City of Chgo., 1989—; mem., past chmn. dean's adv. coun. Ind. U. Bus. Sch., Bloomington, 1985—; bd. dirs. Ind. U. Found.; mem. bd. dirs. Grad. Sch. Bus. U. Chgo.; mem. Northwestern U. Assocs., Evanston, Ill.; exec. com. Mid. Am. Com., 1985—; mem. Chgo. Com., 1994—; bd. dirs. Northwestern Healtcare Network, 1989—96, Children's Meml. Hosp., Chgo., 1985—. Recipient Disting. Alumnus award U. Chgo., 1996, Disting. Corp. Exec. award U. Chgo., 1996, Disting. Corp. and Comm. Leadership award Am. Jewish Com., 1998, Disting. Alumnus award Ind. U., 2000. Mem. NAM (bd. dirs.), Chgo. Coun. Fgn. Rels. (bd. dirs., exec. com.), Ill. State C of C. (bd. dirs. 1982-88, exec. com. 1984-88, chmn. Ill. Alliance for Econ. Initiatives), Coun. Grad. Sch. Bus. (life), Pres.'s Cir., Exec. Club Chgo., Acad. Alumni Fellows Ind. U. (award), Chgo. Club, Econ. Club (bd. dirs.), Commcl. Club, Met. Club, Glenview Club, Beta Gamma Sigma, others. Office: Bd Advisors LLC 615 Warwick Rd Kenilworth IL 60043 Office Phone: 847-251-5386. Business E-Mail: fgs@brad-advisors.com.

**STEINHAFEL, GREGG W,** retail executive; BBA, Carroll Coll., 1977; MBA, Northwestern Univ., 1979. With Target Corp., Mpls., 1979—, sr. v.p., gen. mdse. mgr., 1987—94, exec. v.p. merchandising, 1994—99, pres. Target Stores, 1999—. Mem. bd. dir. Toro Co. Dir. Walker Art Ctr. Office: Target Corp 1000 Nicollet Mall Minneapolis MN 55403-2467*

**STEINHARDT, MICHAEL H.,** diversified financial services company executive; b. Bklyn., 1940; s. Sol Frank Steinhardt; m. Judy Steinhardt; children: Jacob, Joshua, Kira. BS, U. Pa. Wharton Sch. Fin., 1960. Rsch. assoc.; staff writer; securities analyst; founding ptnr. Steinhardt Ptnrs. L.P., 1967—95; mng. mem. Steinhardt Mgmt. LLC, 1996—. Author: No Bull: My Life In and Out of the Markets, 2001. Chmn. Jewish Life Network/Steinhardt Found., NYC, 1994—; Jewish Media Renaissance, Birthright Israel; trustee & chmn. investment com. NYU, 1995—; trustee Brandeis U., Bklyn. Bot. Garden, Wildlife Conservation Soc., Mus. Jewish Heritage; mem. vis. com., dept. Greek & Roman art Met. Mus. Art, NYC. Named one of Top 200 Collectors, ARTnews Mag., 2003—06; recipient Medallion, U. Albany, 2004. Jewish. Avocation: collector of classical antiquities & modern art, especially drawings. Mailing: Jewish Life Network 10th Fl 6 E 39th St New York NY 10016

**STEINHART, JESSICA,** lawyer; BA, U. Mich., Ann Arbor, 1992; JD, Fordham U., N.Y.C. 1996. Tax assoc. Coopers & Lybrand LLC, N.Y.C., 1996—98; assoc. Greenberg Traurig LLC, N.Y.C., 1998—2000; sr. counsel Pfizer Inc., N.Y.C., 2000—02; asst. gen. counsel Sanofi-Aventis, Bridgewater, NJ, 2002—. Contbr. articles to profl. jours. Recipient Archibald Murray Pub. Svc. award, Fordham U. Sch. Law, 1995—96. Mem.: N.J. Assn.Corp. Counsel, N.Y. State Bar Assn., Phi Psi. Office: Sanofi-Aventis 300 Somerset Corporate Blvd Bridgewater NJ 08807

**STEINHAUER, GILLIAN,** lawyer; b. Aylesbury, Bucks, Eng., Oct. 6, 1938; d. Eric Frederick and Maisie Kathleen (Yeates) Pearson; m. Bruce William Steinhauer, Jan. 2, 1960; children: Alison (Humphrey) Eric, John, Elspeth. AB cum laude, Bryn Mawr (Pa.) Coll., 1959; JD cum laude, U. Mich., 1976. Bar: Tenn. 1998, U.S. Dist. Ct. (ea. dist.) Mich. 1976, U.S. Ct. Appeals (6th cir.) 1982. From assoc. to sr. ptnr. Miller, Canfield, Paddock & Stone, Detroit, 1976-92; dir. Commonwealth of Mass. Workers' Compensation Litigation Unit, Boston, 1992—2002; atty. U.S. Postal Svc., 2002—. Chancellor Cath. Ch. St. Paul, Detroit, 1976-83, 91; pres. bd. trustees Cath. Cmty. Svcs. Inc., 1989-92; bd. dirs. Spaulding for Children, 1991-92, Davenport House, 1992-96, chair 1995-96, vestry mem. St. Michael's Ch., Marblehead, Mass., 1994-97; chpt. mem. St. Mary's Cathedral, Memphis, 2005—. Mem. Mich. State Bar Found. (life), Fed. Jud. Conf. 6th Cir. (life). Home: 4010 S Galloway Dr Memphis TN 38111-6842

**STEINHAUER, SHERRI,** professional golfer; b. Madison, Wis., Dec. 27, 1962; Student, U. Tex. Mem. Futures Tour, LPGA Tour, 1986—; mem. US Team Solheim Cup, 1994, 1998, 2000. Achievements include winning LPGA Tour events including du Maurier Ltd. Classic, 1992, Sprint Championship, 1994, Weetabix Women's British Open, 1999, Japan Airlines Big Apple Classic, 1999, Sybase Classic Presented by Lincoln Mercury, Women's British Open, 2006; 4 LPGA career holes-in-one. Office: c/o LPGA 100 Internat Golf Dr Daytona Beach FL 32124-1092*

**STEINHAUS, JOHN EDWARD,** retired anesthesiologist, educator; b. Omaha, Feb. 23, 1917; s. Emil F. and Pearl (Haynie) S.; m. Mila Jean Pinkerton, Feb. 21, 1943; children: Kathryn, Carolyn, Barbara, William, Elizabeth. BA, U. Neb., 1940, MA, 1941; MD, U. Wis., 1945, PhD, 1950. Diplomate: Am. Bd. Anesthesiologists. Pvt. practice specializing in anesthesiology, Madison, Wis., 1951-58, Atlanta, 1958—; faculty U. Wis., 1951-58; mem. faculty Emory U., Atlanta, 1958—, prof. anesthesiology, 1959-87, prof. emeritus, 1987—, chmn. dept., 1959-85; chief anesthesiology service Grady Meml. Hosp., 1959-77, Emory U. Hosp., 1958-85; ret., 1987. Author: Medical Care Divided; contbr. articles to profl. jours. Past pres. Anesthesia Found. Mem. Am. Soc. Anesthesiologists (past pres., Disting. Service award 1982), So. Soc. Anesthesiologists (past pres.), AMA, AAAS, Assn. U. Anesthetists (past pres.), Anesthesiology History Assn. (past pres.), Soc. Pharm. Exptl. Therapeutics, Phi Beta Kappa, Sigma Xi, Alpha Omega Alpha. Home and Office: 836 Castle Falls Dr NE Atlanta GA 30329-4114 Personal E-mail: jsteinh@emory.edu.

**STEINHAUSE, MITCHELL,** former mercantile exchange executive; BA, U. Pitts.; MBA, St. John's U., NY. Mem. NY Mercantile Exch., Inc., NYC, 1975—, bd. dirs., 1992—2006, mem. exec. com., 1994—2006, vice chmn., 2000—04, chmn., 2004—06.*

**STEINHAUSER, JOHN WILLIAM,** retired lawyer; b. Akron, Ohio, June 25, 1924; s. John Hugo and Francis Lillian (Pearson) S.; m. Patricia E. Mooney, Dec.1, 1956; children: John, Christian, Mark, Sharon. BSBA, Ohio State U., 1949; JD, U. Mich., 1950. Bar: Mich. 1950, Colo. 1972. Atty., dir. L.Am., dir. export sales, gen mgr. Africa-Far E. Chrysler Corp., dir. Chrysler Internat., dir. Africa Far East, 1950-71; atty. Denver, 1971—; founder, dir., pres. Pearson Energy Corp., 1977—. Founder, chmn. Sharon Energy, Ltd., Denver, 1980, also dir., 1980-97. Active Colo. Rep. Com.; sponsor Denver Symphony; pres. John and Patricia Steinhauser Found. With USNR, 1943—46. Mem. ABA, SAR, Colo. Bar Assn., Mich. Bar Assn., Soc. Internat. Law, Rocky Mountain Mineral Law Found., Cherry Hills Country Club, Royal Poinciana Golf Club, Rotary. Home: 46 Charlou Cir Englewood CO 80111-1103 Personal E-mail: jwsteinhauser@sbcglobal.net.

**STEINHOFF, RAYMOND O(AKLEY),** consulting geologist; b. Hart, Mich., Apr. 22, 1925; m. Anne M. Steinhoff, 1952; 1 child, Kirk O. BS, MS, So. Meth. U., 1948; PhD in Geology, Tex. A&M, 1965. Instr. geology Tex. A&M U., Coll. Sta., Tex., 1948-51; geologist Atlantic Rich., Wichita, Kans., 1951-53, Humble Oil and Refining Co., New Orleans, 1953-57; asst. prof. geology Tulane U., New Orleans, 1957-65, assoc. prof., 1965-70, chmn. dept., 1969-70; prof. and dept. head geology Stephen F. Austin State U., Nacogdoches, Tex., 1970-78; divsn. geologist Buttes, New Orleans, 1978-79; cons. geologist Graham, New Orleans, 1979-83. Cons. Trinexco, New Orleans, 1964-69. Sgt. U.S. Army, 1944—46, WWII, 1st lt. USAF, 1952—53, Korea. Mem. Am. Assn. Petroleum Geologists (emeritus), New Orleans Geol. Soc. (emeritus), Phi Kappa Phi (emeritus). Home: 6 North H St Pensacola FL 32501

**STEINHORN, CHARLES IRA,** mathematician, educator; b. N.Y.C., July 31, 1952; s. Paul and Adele Steinhorn; m. Elizabeth M. Frankel, July 15, 1989; children: Sarah E., Maureen R. BA, Wesleyan U., 1973; MA in Math., U. Wis., 1975, MA in Philosophy, 1978, PhD, 1980. Asst. prof. Lehigh U., Bethlehem, Pa., 1980—81, Vassar Coll., Poughkeepsie, NY, 1981—88, assoc. prof., 1988—93, prof. math., 1993—, chair dept. math., 1995—2000, assoc. dean of faculty, 1989—92, acting dean of faculty, 1992—92. Dir., founder Vassar Sci. Scholars Program, Poughkeepsie, 1995—; vis. asst. prof. U. Notre Dame, Ind., 1987; vis. rsch. fellow Merton Coll., U. Oxford, England, 1993. Author: Calculus with Discrete Mathematics, 1991; editor: Logic: From Foundations to Applications, 1996, Model Theory, Algebra, and Geometry, 2000; contbr. articles to profl. jours. Bd. mem. Chappaqua (N.Y.) AYSO, 2002—05. Grantee, NSF, 1984—90, 1994—2003; postdoctoral fellow, McGill U., Montreal, Que., Can., 1982—83, vis. fellow, Sci. and Engring. Rsch. Coun., 1993. Mem.: Math. Assn., Am. Math. Soc. Avocation: travel. Office: Vassar College Dept Math 124 Raymond Ave Poughkeepsie NY 12604 Office Phone: 845-437-5524. Office Fax: 845-437-7065. Personal E-mail: steinhorn@vassar.edu.

**STEINHORN, IRWIN HARRY,** lawyer, educator, corporate financial executive; b. Dallas, Aug. 13, 1940; s. Raymond and Libby L. (Miller) Steinhorn; m. Deborah Kelley Steinhorn, Apr. 7, 2002; 1 child, Leslie Robin. BBA, U. Tex., 1961, LLB, 1964. Bar: Tex. 1964, U.S. Dist. Ct. (no. dist.) Tex. 1965, Okla. 1970, U.S. Dist. Ct. (we. dist.) Okla. 1972. Assoc. Oster & Kaufman, Dallas, 1964-67; ptnr. Parness, McQuire & Lewis, Dallas, 1967-70; sr. v.p., gen. counsel LSB Industries, Inc., Oklahoma City, 1970-87; v.p., gen. counsel USPCI, Inc., Oklahoma City, 1987-88; ptnr. Hastie & Steinhorn, Oklahoma City, 1988-95; mem., officer, dir. Conner & Winters, Oklahoma City, 1995—. Adj. prof. law Oklahoma City U. Sch. Law, 1979—; lectr. in field. Mem. adv. com. Okla. Securities Commn., 1986—; mem. exec. adv. bd. Oklahoma City U. Sch. Law, 2000—; bd. dirs. Okla. Venture Forum, 2000—. Served to capt. USAR, 1964-70. Mem.: ABA, Com. to Revise Okla. Bus. Corp. Act, Okla. Bar Assn. (bus. assn. sect., sec., treas. 1986—87, chmn. 1988—89), Tex. Bar Assn., Rotary, Phi Alpha Delta. Republican. Jewish. Home: 224 NW 18th St Oklahoma City OK 73103 Office: Conner & Winters One Leadership Sq 211 N Robinson Ave Ste 1700 Oklahoma City OK 73102-7136 Office Phone: 405-272-5711. Business E-mail: isteinhorn@cwlaw.com.

**STEINHORN, ROBIN H.,** neonatologist, educator; b. Akron, Ohio, June 12, 1956; d. Paul Henry and Marion Robinson Steinhorn; m. David Marc Steinhorn; children: Rachel, Benjamin. BS, U. Akron, 1976; MD, Washington U., 1980, Bd. cert. pediat., Am. Bd. Pediat., bd. cert. neonatal-perinatal medicine. Neonatologist Children's Hosp. Buffalo, 1991—99; chief neonatology Children's Meml. Hosp., Chgo., 1999—; intern Wash. U., St. Louis, 1980—81; resident, fellow U. Minn., 1982—88. Assoc. prof. pediat. SUNY, Buffalo, 1991—99; prof. pediat. Northwestern U., Chgo., 1999—. Editor: (book) Extracorporeal Cardiopulmonary Support in Critical Care, 2000; contbr. articles to profl. jours. Grantee, NIH, 1995—. Mem.: Soc. for Pediat. Rsch., Am. Thoracic Soc., Am. Acad. Pediat., Am. Heart Assn. (Established Investigator award 1998). Office: Childrens Meml Hosp Neonatology #45 2300 Childrens Plaza Chicago IL 60614 Office Phone: 773-880-4142. Business E-mail: r-steinhorn@northwestern.edu.

**STEINKEN, WILLIAM THEODORE, JR.,** military officer, secondary school educator; b. June 16, 1928; s. William Theodore Steinken and Mary Webic; m. Keiko-Sakaki Steinken, Sept. 11, 1961; 1 child, Deborah Kay. A in Liberal Arts, Santa Ana Coll., Calif., A in History, Liberal Arts (hon.), 1976. Seaman fireman Merchant Marine, Great Lakes, 1944—45; seaman sea bees USN, Pacific Theatre, 1945—46; pvt. infantry sgt. 1st class U.S. Army, Japan, 1947—50; capt. USMC, Korea, 1951—71; inst. El Rancho HS, Pico Rivera, Calif., 1972—91. Capt. USMC, with U.S. Army, with USN, 1945—71, PTO. Decorated Disting Flying Cross, Air Medal with 5 Silver Stars, Combat Action Ribbon, Naval Flight Officer Wings. Mem.: Mil. Officers Assn. Am. (bd. dirs. Rio Hondo chptr. 1998—), Disting. Flying Cross Soc. Avocation: golf. Home: 3515 W Lehnhardt Santa Ana CA 92704

**STEINMAN, LISA MALINOWSKI,** English literature educator, writer; b. Willimantic, Conn., Apr. 8, 1950; d. Zenon Stanislaus and Shirley Belle Malinowski; m. James A. Shugrue. Apr. 1968 (div 1980); m. James L. Shugrue, July 23, 1984. BA, Cornell U., 1971, MFA, 1973, PhD, 1976. Asst. prof. English Reed Coll., Portland, Oreg., 1976-82, assoc. prof., 1982-90, prof., 1990—, Kenan prof. English lit. and humanities, 1993—. Cons. NEH, Washington, 1984—85. Author: Lost Poems, 1976, Made in America, 1987, All That Comes to Light, 1989, A Book of Other Days, 1992, Ordinary Songs, 1996, Masters of Repetition, 1998, Carslaw's Sequences, 2003; editor: Hubbub Mag., 1983—; mem. editl. bd. Williams Rev., 1991—, Stevens Jour., 1994—; contbr. articles to profl. jours. Appt. adv. com. Publ. of the Modern Lang. Assn., 2006—. Fellow Danforth Found., 1971-75, NEH, 1983, 96,

---

2006, Oreg. Arts Commn., 1983, Nat. Endowment for Arts, 1984; Rockefeller Found. scholar, 1987-88; recipient Pablo Neruda award, 1987, Oreg. Inst. Lit. Arts award, 1993. Mem. MLA, Poets and Writers, PEN (N.W. chpt., co-founder, officer 1989-93). Home: 5344 SE 38th Ave Portland OR 97202-4208 Office: Reed Coll Dept English 3203 SE Woodstock Blvd Portland OR 97202-8138 Business E-mail: lisa.steinman@reed.edu.

**STEINMANN, JOHN COLBURN,** architect; b. Monroe, Wis., Oct. 24, 1941; s. John Wilbur and Irene Marie (Steil) S.; m. Susan Koslosky, Aug. 12, 1978 (div. July 1989); m. Genevieve Sim, Aug. 29, 1998. BArch, U. Ill., 1964; postgrad., Ill. Inst. Tech., 1970-71. Registered architect, Wash., Oreg., Calif., N.Mex., Ariz., Utah, Alaska, Wis., Ill., Hawaii. Project designer C.F. Murphy Assocs., Chgo., 1968-71, Steinmann Architects, Monticello, Wis., 1971-73; design chief, chief project architect State of Alaska, Juneau, 1973-78; project designer Mithun Assos., architects, Bellevue, Wash., 1978-80; owner, prin. John C. Steinmann Assos., Architect, Kirkland, Wash., 1980-94; supr. head facilities sect. divsn. fin. Dept. Edn. State of Alaska, Juneau, 1994-96; docs. mgr. Loschky Marquardt and Nesholm, Architects, Seattle, 1996-98; project mgr. Dept. Gen. Adminstrn. Divsn. Engring. and Archtl. Svsc., State of Wash.. Olympia, 1998-99; project mgr. URS Architects, Seattle, 2000—. Bd. dirs. Storytell Internat.; lectr. Ill. Inst. Tech., 1971-72. Prin. works include Grant Park Music Bowl, Chgo., 1971, Menomonee Falls (Wis.) Med. Clinic, 1972, Hidden Valley Office Bldg., Bellevue, 1978, Kezner Office Bldg., Bellevue, 1979, The Pines at Sunriver, Oreg., 1980, also Phase II, 1984, Phase III, 1986, The Pines at Sunriver Lodge Bldg., 1986, 2d and Lenora highrise, Seattle, 1981, Bob Hope Cardiovascular Rsch. Inst. lab animal facility, Seattle, 1982, Wash. Ct., Bellevue, 1982, Anchorage Bus. Pk., 1982, Garden Townhouses, Anchorage, 1983, Canterwood Townhouses, Anchorage, 1983, Vallarta Torres III, Puerto Vallarta, Mex., 1987, Torres Mazatlan (Mex.) II, 1988, Canterwood Townhouses, Gig Harbor Wash., 1988, Inn at Ceres (Calif.), 1989, Woodard Creek Inn, Olympia, Wash., 1989, Northgate Corp. Ctr., Seattle, 1990, Icicle Creek Hotel and Restaurant, Leavenworth, Wash., 1990, Bellingham (Wash.), Market Pl., 1990, Boeing Hot Gas Test Facility, Renton, Wash., 1991, Boeing Longacres Customer Svc. Tng. Ctr. Support Facilities, Renton, 1992, Boeing Comml. Airplane Group Hdqs., Renton, 1996, U. Wash./Cascade C.C., Bothell, 1999, Wash. State U., Pullman, Wash., Sea-Tac Airport Comm. Control Ctr., Seattle, 2000, McCarty, Internet Cafe and Residence Hall Renovation, U. Wash., Seattle, 2001, K'ima Med. Ctr. Dental Clinic, Hoopa, Calif., 2001, Sea-Tac Airport Flight Info. Mgmt. Sys., 2002; 600 Bed student housing, classroom, parking mixed use project, U. Idaho, Moscow, The Vegetable Bin, Seattle, 2004, Kona Coffee and Tea Plantation Visitors Ctr., Hawaii; also pvt. residences. Served to 1st lt. C.E., USAR, 1964-66, Vietnam. Decorated Bronze Star. Mem. AIA, Am. Mgmt. Assn., Nat. Coun. Archtl. Registration Bds., U. Wash. Yacht Club, Columbia Athletic Club, Alpha Rho Chi. Republican. Roman Catholic. Address: 4316 106th Pl NE Kirkland WA 98033-7919

**STEINMETZ, DAVID CURTIS,** religious studies educator; b. Columbus, Ohio, June 12, 1936; s. Walter Curtis and Lucy Margaret (Binderbasen) S.; m. Virginia Ruth Verploegh, June 20, 1959; children: Claire Elise, Matthew Eliot. BA (hon.), Wheaton Coll., Wheaton, IL, 1954—58; BD (hon.), Drew U., Madison, NJ, 1958—61; ThD, Harvard U., Cambridge, MA, 1961—66. Ordained to ministry United Meth. Ch., 1959. Asst. and assoc. prof. Lancaster Theol. Sem., Lancaster, Pa., 1966—71; Amos Ragan Kearns prof. of the history of christianity Duke U., Durham, NC. Vis. prof. Harvard U., 1977; adv. coun. Interpretation, Richmond, Va., 1979-84, 87-92. Author: Misericordia dei, 1968, Reformers in the Wings, 1971, Luther and Staupitz, 1980, Luther in Context, 1986, Calvin in Context, 1995; editor Oxford Studies in Historical Theology; mem. editorial bd. Archiv für Reformationsgeschichte, 1977-93, Duke U. Monographs in Medieval and Renaissance Studies, 1972-98, Brill Studies in Medieval and Reformation Thought, Leiden, Netherlands, 1981-99. Pres. Am. Friends of the Herzog Aug. Libr., St. Louis, Mo., 1996—2002; mem., governing bd. Meeter Ctr. for Calvin Studies, Grand Rapids, Mich., 1993—99; pub. The Labyrinth Press, Durham, NC, 1981—95. Named Scholar-Tchr. of Yr. Duke U., 1986; Rockefeller doctoral fellow Rockefeller Found., 1964-66, faculty Assn. Theol. Schs., 1970, 77-78, Guggenheim fellow Guggenheim Found., 1977-78, NEH summer fellow, 1990. Mem. Medieval Acad. Am., Am. Soc. Ch. History (pres. 1985), Renaissance Soc. Am., Soc. for Reformation Rsch., Am. Friends of the Herzog August Bibliothek (founding pres.). United Methodist. Achievements include research in History of Biblical Interpretation in Reformation Europe. Office: Duke University The Divinity School Durham NC 27708-0967 Personal E-mail: dsteinmtz@nc.rr.com. E-mail: steinmtz@acpub.duke.edu.

**STEINMETZ, JON DAVID,** health facility administrator, psychologist; b. N.Y.C., June 4, 1940; s. Lewis I. and Rose (Josefsberg) S.; m. Jane Audrey Hilton, Dec. 24, 1964; children: Jonna Lynn, Jay Daniel. BA, NYU, 1962; MA, Bradley U., 1963. Lic. psychologist, Ill. Intern in psychology Galesburg (Ill.) State Rsch. Hosp., 1963-64; staff psychologist Manteno (Ill.) State Hosp., 1964-68, program dir., 1968-70, asst. dir., 1970-72; dep. dir. Manteno Mental Health Ctr., 1972-80, Tinley Park (Ill.) Mental Health Ctr., 1980-88; dir. Chgo. Read Mental Health Ctr., 1988-91; ret., 1991. Clin. dir. Jane Addams Hull House Assn., 1992-98. Trustee Village of Park Forest, Cook and Will Counties, Ill.; officer, bd. dirs. various civic orgns., Park Forest; dir. SOS Children's Village Ill., Lockport, 2004—05. Home: 200 Hickory St Park Forest IL 60466-1016

**STEINMETZ, RICHARD BIRD, JR.,** lawyer; b. Orange, N.J., Mar. 27, 1929; s. Richard Bird and Charlotte (Quinby) S.; m. Merriam Holly Miller, June 9, 1956; children: Richard Blair, Jonathan Bird, Edward Quinby. BA, Yale U., 1951; JD, Harvard U., 1955. Bar: N.Y. 1955. Assoc. Chadbourne and Parke, N.Y.C., 1955-59; with Anaconda Co., N.Y.C., 1959-79, v.p., gen. counsel, 1971-79; v.p. Colt Industries Inc., N.Y.C., 1979-82; v.p., gen. counsel Pittston Co., Greenwich, Conn., 1982-84; exec. v.p. Case, Pomeroy and Co., N.Y.C., 1984-94. Bd. dirs. Case, Pomeroy and Co. Served to capt. USMC, 1950-52. Mem. ABA, Assn. of Gen. Counsel. Republican. Episcopalian. Home: 275C Park St New Canaan CT 06840-5739

**STEINMEYER, ROBERT JAY,** retired lawyer; b. Aug. 10, 1921; s. William F. and Willie (Davis) Steinmeyer; m. Susie (Levicki), Dec. 23, 1948; children: William Bruce, James Jay, Sharon Sue. BS, U. Nebr., 1943; post grad., Albany Law Sch., 1947—48; LLB, George Washington U., 1949. Bar: D.C. 1950, Calif. 1958. Devel. engr. G.E. Co., Schenectady, NY, 1943—46, patent atty., 1947—53, patent counsel, 1953—57, Beckman Instruments, Inc., Fullerton, Calif., 1957—63, resident counsel, 1963—71, v.p., legal, 1971—85, dir., 1984—85; sole practice Fullerton, Calif., 1985—86; of counsel Karon, Morrison and Savikas Ltd., Fullerton, Calif., 1986—88; ret., 1988. Mem.: ABA, Assn. Corp. Patent Counsel (pres. 1975—76), Am. Patent Law Assn., Pi Mu Epsilon, Sigma Tau, Order of Coif. Home: 813 Morningside Dr Fullerton CA 92835 Personal E-mail: steinfull21@gmail.com.

**STEINMILLER, JANET L.,** literature and language educator; b. Pitts., June 11, 1954; d. Eunice C Kravec and Louis W Steinmiller; children: Justin D Ingala, Kevin D Ingala. MLS, U. Pitts., 1998. Professional Certificate Commonwealth of Pa., 1998. Tchr. English grades 9 - 12 Booker Wash. Inst. Tech., Kakata, Liberia, 1976—77; tchr. English and Reading grades 7 - 12 Forest Area Sch. Dist., Tionesta, Pa., 1978—81; libr. elem.,mid. sch., tchr. English and Reading S.A. Escuela Campo Alegre, Caracas, Venezuela, 1981—. Presenter (conference paper) The Plagiarism Problem, Dancing with Databases (Cert. of Achievement, 2003). Recipient Hon. Membership in the Nat. Honor Soc., Araguaney Chpt. of Escuela Campo Alegre, 1991—

**STEINMILLER, JOHN F.,** professional basketball team executive; b. Mt. Prospect, Ill. m. Corinne Steinmiller; children: John Henry, Mary Kate. V.p. bus. ops. Milw. Bucks, 1977—. Bd. dirs. M.W. Athletes Against Childhood Cancer Fund, Metro Milw. YMCA; chmn. Milw. Conve. and Visitors Bur. VISIT Milw.; mem. Greater Milw. Com. Recipient Contardi Commitment

---

award MACC Fund, 1991, Vol. of Yr. award YMCA, 1996. Office: Milw Bucks 1001 N 4th St Milwaukee WI 53203-1314 Office Phone: 414-227-0500. E-mail: jsteinmiller@milwaukeebucks.com.

**STEINSMITH, WILLIAM,** internist, research scientist; b. NYC, July 31, 1933; s. David Steinsmith and Dorothy Burtoff. BS, U. Calif., San Francisco, 1965, MD, 1968. Lic. physician and surgeon Calif. Med. Bd., Va. Bd. Medicine. Freelance polit. journalist, 1960—; postdoctoral scholar in pharmacology and pharmacokinetics dept. pharmacology U. Calif.-San Francisco, 1969—74; pvt. practice internist San Francisco, 1970—2004; asst. chief of medicine St. Joseph's Hosp., San Francisco, 1973—76; ind. rsch. in math. biology, 1974—; med. staff internist Veterans Home of Calif., Yountville, Calif., 1989—91. Author: (polit. history/analysis) Lenin, Inter-Imperialism, and National-Colonial Revolution, 1979. Recipient Owen D. Young Prize in Internat. Rels., U. Calif.- Berkeley, 1963. Mem.: San Francisco Med. Soc./U. Calif.-San Francisco Health Care Fedn. (bd. trustees, exec. com. 1973—75). Home and Office: 108 Alexander Walker Williamsburg VA 23185 Personal E-mail: bbhaywood@aol.com.

**STEINWURTZEL, RICHARD A.,** lawyer; b. Newark, Jan. 1, 1950; BA cum laude, Union Coll., 1972; JD with honors, George Washington U., 1975. Bar: D.C. 1975. Ptnr. Fried, Frank, Harris, Shriver & Jacobson, Washington. Mem. ABA (sect. corp., banking and bus. law), N.Y. State Bar Assn., D.C. Bar, Securities Industry Assn. (mem. legal and compliance divsn. 1985—). Office: Fried Frank Harris Shriver & Jacobson 1001 Pennsylvania Ave NW Washington DC 20004-2505

**STEITZ, JOAN ARGETSINGER,** biochemistry professor; b. Mpls., Jan. 26, 1941; d. Glenn D. and Elaine (Magnusson) Argetsinger; m. Thomas A. Steitz, Aug. 20, 1966; 1 child, Jon. BS, Antioch Coll., 1963; PhD, Harvard U., 1967; DSc (hon.), Lawrence U., Appleton, Wis., 1981, Rochester U. Sch. Medicine, 1984, Mt. Sinai Sch. Medicine, 1989, Bates Coll., 1990, Trinity Coll., 1992, Harvard U., 1992, Brandeis U., 2002, Brown U., 2003, Princeton U., 2003, Watson Sch. Biol. Sciences, Cold Spring Harbor Lab., 2004. NSF postdoctoral fellow, Andorra, 1967—69; Jane Coffin Childs Meml. Fund Fellow, Divsn. Cell Biology Med. Rsch. Coun. Lab. Molecular Biology, Cambridge, England, 1967—70; asst. prof. molecular biophysics and biochemistry Yale U., New Haven, 1970-74, assoc. prof., molecular biophysics and biochemistry, 1974-78, prof., molecular biophysics and biochemistry, 1978—92, Henry Ford II prof. molecular biophysics and biochemistry, 1992—98, chmn. dept. molecular biophysics and biochemistry, 1996—99, dir. molecular genetics program Boyer Ctr. Molecular Medicine, Sterling prof. molecular biophysics and biochemistry, 1998—. Josiah Macy Scholar Max Planck Inst. fur Biophysikalische Chemie (Göttingen), Germany and Med. Coun. Ctr., Lab. of Molecular Biology, Cambridge, England, 1976—77; Fairchild Disting. Fellow Calif. Inst. Technology, Pasadena, Calif., 1984—85; investigator Howard Hughes Med. Inst, Yale Univ., 1986—; scientific dir. Jane Coffin Child Fund for Med. Rsch., 1991—2002; dir. molecular genetics program Boyer Center for Molecular Medicine; mem. vis. com. for biology divsn. Caltech, Calif. Inst. Technology, 1999—; mem. basic sciences scientific adv. bd. Fred Hutchinson Cancer Ctr., 2001—; mem. scientific adv. bd., biology divsn. Molecular Biology Dept., Princeton Univ., Max Planck Inst. for Biophysical Chemistry (Göttingen), 1999—; mem. Lasker Awards Jury, 2001—, Jury for L'Oréal UNESCO award, 2001—; mem. scientific adv. com. Sci. Found. Ireland, 2002—. Mem. editl. bd. Genes and Development, 1994—, assoc. editor RNA, 1994—; bd. reviewing editors Science, 2004—. Bd. overseers Harvard Univ., 2003—. Co-recipient (with Thomas R. Cech) Warren Triennial Prize, Mass. Gen. Hosp., 1989; named Fritz Lipmann Lectr. Am. Soc. for Biochemistry and Molecular Biology, 1989, 11th Ann. Keith Porter Lectr. on Cell Biology, Am. Soc. for Cell Biology, 1992; recipient Young Scientist award, Passano Found., 1975, Eli Lilly Award in Biol. Chemistry, 1976, U.S. Steel Found. Award in Molecular Biology, 1982, Lee Hawley, Sr. Award for Arthritis Rsch., 1983, Nat. Medal Sci., 1986, Radcliffe Grad. Soc. Medal for Disting. Achievement, 1987, Dickson Prize for Sci., Carnegie-Mellon U., 1988, Christopher Columbus Discovery Award in Biomed. Rsch., 1992, Rebecca Rice award for Disting. Achievement, Antioch Coll. Alumni Assn., 1993, Weizmann Women and Sci. Award, 1994, City of Medicine Award, 1996, Disting. Svc. award, Miami Bio/Technology Winter Symposium, 1996, Novartis Drew Award in Biomed. Rsch., 1999, UNESCO-L'Oreal Women in Sci. Award, 2001, Lewis S. Rosenstiel for Distinguished Work in Basic Medical Rsch. Award, 2002, FASEB Excellence in Sci. Award, 2003, Howard Taylor Ricketts Award, U. Chgo., 2004, Caledonian Rsch. Found. Prize Lectureship, Royal Soc. Edinburgh, 2004, The RNA Soc. Lifetime Achievement Award, 2004, Gairdner award for achievement in med. rsch., Gairdner Found., 2006. Fellow: AAAS, Am. Acad. Microbiology; mem.: NAS, Inst. Medicine, Academia Europaea, Japanese Biochemical Soc. (hon.), European Molecular Biology Orgn. (assoc.), Conn. Acad. Sciences and Engring., Am. Philos. Soc., Am. Acad. Arts and Sciences. Office: Yale Univ Rm BCMM 136E Dept Mol Biophys & Biochem 189 Elm St New Haven CT 06520 Office Phone: 203-737-4418. Business E-mail: joan.steitz@yale.edu.*

**STELCK, CHARLES RICHARD,** geology educator; b. Edmonton, Alta., Can., May 20, 1917; s. Robert Ferdinand and Florella Maud (Stanbury) S.; m. Frances Gertrude McDowell, Apr. 24, 1945; children: David, Brian, Leland, John (dec.). BSc, U. Alta., 1937, MSc, 1941, DSc (hon.), 2003; PhD, Stanford U., 1951. Registered profl. geologist Alta. Field geologist B.C. Dept. Mines, Victoria, Canada, 1939-41, Consol Project, Norman Wells, N.W.T., Canada, 1941-43, Imperial Oil Co., Calgary, Alta., 1943-49; from lectr. to prof. emeritus geology U. Alta., Edmonton, 1946—. Contbr. numerous articles principally on biostratigraphy of Cretaceous to sci. publs. Decorated officer Order of Can.; recipient Disting. Educator award Am. Assn. Petroleum Geologists, 2001, Queen's Golden Jubilee medal, 2002, Alberta Centennial medal, 2005; named to Can. Petroleum Hall Fame, 2005. Fellow Royal Soc. Can.; mem. Assn. Profl. Engrs., Geologists and Geophysicists Alta. (Centennial award 1979), Geol. Assn. Can. (Logan medal 1982), Geol. Soc. Am., Can. Soc. Petroleum Geologists (Douglas medal 1994, Stanley Slipper gold medal 2002), Order of Can. (officer 1997). Conservative. Office: U Alta Dept Earth & Atmospheric Scis Edmonton AB Canada T6G 2E3

**STELLA, FRANK PHILIP,** artist; b. Malden, Mass., May 12, 1936; s. Frank and Constance Aida (Santonelli) S.; m. Barbara Rose, 1961 (div.); children: Rachel, Michael, Laura; m. Harriet McGurk, 1978; children: Peter, Patrick. AB in History, Princeton U., 1958, DFA (hon.), 1984; degree (hon.), Mpls. Coll. Art Design, 1974, Brandeis U., 1985, Dartmouth Coll., 1985. Represented by Leo Castelli Gallery, 1959; artist-in-residence Dartmouth Coll., 1963; instr. Brandeis U., 1969; Charles Eliot Norton prof. poetry Harvard U., Cambridge, Mass., 1983. Lectr. Pratt Inst., Bklyn., 1960, Yale U., 1965, Cornell U., 1965, Seattle Art Mus., 1967, Detroit Inst. Arts, 1967, Art Inst. Chgo., 1968, 85, Bezalel Acad. Arts and Design, Jerusalem, 1981, Whitney Mus., Mus. Fine Art, Boston, 1982, San Antonio Art Inst., 1983, Harvard U., 1983-84, Musee Nat. d'Art Moderne, Paris, 1984, Coun. for U.S. and Italy, N.Y., 1984, Frick Collection, N.Y., 1985, Dartmouth Coll., 1985; instr. art U. Saskatchewan, 1967, Brandeis U., 1968; vis. critic dept. art, Cornell U., 1965. One-man shows Leo Castelli Gallery, N.Y.C., 1960, 62, 64, 66, 69, 73, 75, 79, 82, Galerie Lawrence, Paris, 1961, 64, Ferus Gallery, L.A., 1963, 65, Kasmin Ltd., London, 1964, 66, 68, M. Knoedler & Co., 1976, 77, 85, David Mirvish Gallery, London, 1966, Pasadena (Calif.) Art Mus., 1966, Seattle Art Mus., 1967, Galerie Bischofsberger, Zurich, Switzerland, 1967, Gallery Modern Art, Washington, 1968, Irving Blum Gallery, L.A., 1968, 69, 71, 73, Mus. Modern Art, N.Y.C., 1970, 1987 (restrospective); touring show Stella, since 1970, 1978, Galerie Daniel Templon, Paris, 1975, Andre Emmerich, Zurich, 1976, Galerie M Bochum, Fed. Republic Germany, 1977, Mus. Modern Art, Oxford, Eng., 1977, Galerie Valeur, Nagoya, Japan, 1978, 79, Getler/Pall Gallery, N.Y.C., 1980, Akira Ikeda Gallery, Nagoya, Japan, 1980, 81, 82, 83, 85, 86, 87, 88, 89, Koh Gallery, Tokyo, 1980, Knoedler Gallery, 1977, 80, 82, 85, 87, Galerie Hans Strelow, Dusseldorf, Fed. Republic Germany, 1981-82, 87, Mus. Modern Art, San Francisco, 1983, Inst. Contemporary Arts, London, 1985, Greenberg Gallery, St. Louis, 1985-86, Laumeier Sculpture Pk., St. Louis, 1986, Gagosian Gallery, N.Y.C., 1987,

Nat. Mus. Art, Osaka, Japan, 1988, Staatsgalerie Stuttgart, Fed. Republic Germany, 1988-89, Kawamura Mem. Museum of Art, Japan, 1991; numerous group shows throughout U.S., Europe, 1959—, including 37th Corcoran Gallery Art Bienniale, Washington, 1981; included in permanent collections, Bernard Jacobson Gallery, London, Addison Gallery Am. Art, Phillips Acad., Andover, Mass., Art Gallery Ont., Toronto, Can., Balt. Mus., Rose Art Mus., Brandeis U., Waltham, Mass., Bklyn. Mus., List Art Ctr., Brown U., Providence, Cleve. Art Mus., Contemporary Art Mus., Houston, Dallas Mus. Fine Art, Denver Mus. Art, Des Moines Art Ctr., 1st Nat. Bank Houston, Fogg Art Mus., Boston, Guggenheim Mus., High Mus., Atlanta, Hirshhorn Mus. and Sculpture Garden, Washington, Ind. U. Art Mus., Bloomington, Inst. Contemporary Art, Phila., Jacksonville (Fla.) Art Mus. Inc., Kitakyushu (Japan) Mcpl. Mus., Kunstmuseum, Basel, Switzerland, Stedelijk Mus., Amsterdam, Art Inst., Chgo., Detroit Inst. Art, L.A. County Mus. Art, Walker Art Center, Mpls., Mus. Modern Art, N.Y.C., San Francisco Mus. Art, Whitney Mus. Am. Art, N.Y.C., Albright-Knox Gallery, Buffalo, La. Mus., Humlebaek, Denmark, Met. Mus. Art, N.Y.C., Milw. Art Ctr., Mpls. Inst. Arts, Modern Art Mus. Ft. Worth, Moderna Museet, Stockholm, Musee Nat. d'Art moderne, Paris, Mus. Bochum, Fed. Republic Germany, Mus. Boymans von Beuningen, Rotterdam, The Netherlands, Mus. Contemporary Art, Chgo., Mus. Contemporary Art, L.A., Mus. Fine Arts, Houston, Nagoaka (Japan) Mus. Art, Smithsonian Instn., Washington, Nat. Gallery Art, Washington, Nationalgalerie, Berlin, Nat. Mus. Am. Art, Washington, Nelson-Atkins Mus. Art, Kansas City, Mo., Phila. Mus., Phillips Collection, Washington, Portland (Oreg.) Ctr. Visual Arts, St. Louis Art Mus., Seattle Art Mus., Seibu Art Mus., Tate Gallery, London, Toledo Mus. Art, Vancouver (B.C.) Art Mus., Can., Wadsworth Atheneum, Hartford, Conn., Wallraf-Richartz Mus., Cologne, Fed. Republic Germany; author: Frank Stella: Illustrations after El Lissitzky's Had Gadya 1982-84, 1985, Working Space, 1986; work subject of numerous monographs and publs.; subject of film Frank Stella at the Fogg 1984, 1985. Bd. dirs. Coun. for U.S. and Italy. Recipient 1st prize Tokyo Internat. Biennale, 1967, Claude M. Fuess award Phillips Acad., 1979, Skowhegan Medal for Painting, 1981, Mayor's Award of Honor Mayor of N.Y.C., 1982, Award of Am. Art Pa. Acad. Fine Arts, 1985, Creative Arts award Brandeis U., 1968; hon. fellow Bezalel Acad. Arts and Design, 1981, Am. Acad. Arts and Letters, 1982-83. Fellow Soc. Fellows (NYU). Office: Bernard Jacobson Gallery 6 Cork St London W1S 3EE England

**STELLA, GEORGE,** chef; b. 1959; m. Rachel Stella; children: Anthony, Christian. Exec. chef Windows on the Green, Pier 66 Hotel, Ft. Lauderdale, Café Max; founder Stella Foods, The Low Carb Chefs!; chef Victoria and Albert's, Grand Floridian Hotel, Orlando, Citricos, Grand Floridian Hotel, Orlando. Founder Cooking Magic, food product line. Host Low Carb and Lovin' It, Food Network; author: Livin' Low Carb Family Recipes Stella Style, 2005, Eating Stella Style: Low Carb Recipes for Healthy Living, 2006; appearances on The View, Fox and Friends, FOX News, CNN, CBS TV Nightly News, Orlando, 48 Hours special, The Low Carb Revolution, Food Network. Home: PO Box 31 Norwalk CT 06852*

**STELLA, JOHN ANTHONY,** financial executive; b. Jessup, Pa., Feb. 3, 1938; s. John Anthony and Alda (Parri) S.; m. Aurelia M. Arre, Feb. 20, 1965; children— John C., Matthew A., Krista R. BS, U. Detroit, 1960; MBA, NYU, 1965. Bus. evaluation cons. Allied Chem. Co., N.Y.C., 1965-70; treas. Spinnerin Yarn Co., Hackensack, NJ, 1970-72, Penn-Dixie Cement Corp., N.Y.C., 1972-74; v.p. finance Halecrest Co., 1974-76; treas. Rsch.-Cottrell, 1976-84, v.p., contr./treas., 1984-88; pres. John A. Stella & Assocs., Plainfield, NJ, 1988-91; sr. v.p. Investment Support Systems, Inc., Bloomfield, NJ, 1991-95. Pres. State Tax Auditing and Rsch., Inc., Bethlehem, 1993—. Served with AUS, 1960. Office: State Tax Auditing & Rsch Inc 1775 Arden Ln Bethlehem PA 18015-5829

**STELLA, MARIE VITA,** engineer, consultant; b. Bklyn., N.Y., Mar. 27, 1943; d. Joseph Domenico and Maria (Savino) Stella. BA, CCNY, 1965—70; MS, U. of Colo. Sch. of Engring., 1978—80. Cert. info. sys. security profl. Cons. IBM, White Plains, NY, 1980—82; telecommunication engr. Port Authority of NY and NJ, NYC, 1982—84; dep. dir. govt. systems Network Mgmt., Fairfax, Va., 1984—85; lead engr., group leader MITRE Corp, McLean, Va., 1985—90; dep. dir. Network Strategies, Fairfax, Va., 1990—91; lead security engr. FAA, Washington, 1991—2005; sr. rsch. fellow Ctr. For Tech. and Nat. Security Policy, Nat. Def. U., Washington, 2003—04; cons. in field. Vol. Ct. Apptd. Spl. Adv. (CASA), Spotsylvania, Va., 1998—2004. Office Phone: 804-744-1420. Personal E-mail: mvstella_99@yahoo.com

**STELLA, VALENTINO JOHN,** chemistry professor; b. Melbourne, Victoria, Australia, Oct. 27, 1946; came to U.S., 1968; s. Giobatta and Mary Katherine (Sartori) S.; m. Mary Elizabeth Roeder, Aug. 16, 1969; children: Catherine Marie, Anne Elizabeth, Elise Valentina. B of Pharmacy, Victorian Coll. Pharmacy, Melbourne, 1967; PhD, U. Kans., 1971. Lic. pharmacist, Victoria. Pharmacist Bendigo (Victoria) Base Hosp., 1967-68; asst. prof. Coll. Pharmacy U. Ill., Chgo., 1971-73; from asst. prof. to assoc. prof. to prof. Sch. Pharmacy U. Kans., Lawrence, 1973-90, Univ. disting. prof., 1990—. Dir. Ctr. for Drug Delivery Rsch.; cons. to 15 pharm. cos., U.S., Japan, Europe. Co-author: Chemical Stability of Pharmaceuticals, 2d edit., 1986; co-editor: Prodrugs as Novel Drug Delivery Systems, 1976, Directed Drug Delivery, 1985, Lymphatic Transport of Drugs, 1992; author numerous papers, revs., abstracts. Fellow AAAS, Am. Assn. Pharm. Scientists, Am. Acad. Pharm. Scientists. Roman Catholic. Achievements include 6 U.S. patents; rsch. in application of drug./organic chemistry to the solution of pharm. problems. Office: U Kans West Campus Dept Pharm Chemistry 2095 Constant Ave Lawrence KS 66047-3729 Home: 1135 W Campus Rd Lawrence KS 66044-3115

**STELLAR, ARTHUR WAYNE,** educational association administrator; b. Columbus, Ohio, Apr. 12, 1947; s. Fredrick and Bonnie Jean (Clark) S. BS, Ohio U., 1969, MA, 1970, PhD, 1973. Tchr. Athens (Ohio) City Schs., 1969-71; curriculum coord., tchr. Belpre (Ohio) City Schs., 1971-72; prin. elem. schs., head tchr. learning disabilities South-Western City Schs., Grove City, Ohio, 1972-76; dir. elem. edn. Beverly (Mass.) Pub. Schs., 1976-78; coord. spl. projects and systemwide planning Montgomery County Pub. Schs., Rockville, Md., 1978-80; asst. supt. Shaker Heights (Ohio), 1980-83; supt. schs. Mercer County Pub. Schs., Princeton, W.Va., 1983-85, Oklahoma City Pub. Schs., 1985-92, Cobb County, Ga., 1992-93, Kingston (N.Y.) Sch. Dist., 1996—2001, Taunton Pub. Schs., Mass., 2005—; dep. supt. Boston Pub. Schs., 1993-95, acting supt., 1995-96; pres, CEO High/Scope Ednl. Rsch. Found., Ypsilanti, Mich., 2001—03; v.p., chief edn. officer Renaissance Learning, Madison, Wis., 2003—04; sr. assoc. Proact Search, Inc., Milw., 2004—; rep. Docufide, Inc., L.A., 2004—05, also adv. bd. dirs., 2004—05; supt. Taunton (Mass.) Pub. Schs., 2005—. Cons., mem. ednl. adv. bd. Tchrs. Support Network, 2004—; adj. faculty Harvard U., 1992-93; assoc. Sch. Match, Ohio, 2004—. Author: Educational Planning for Educational Success, Effective Schools Research: Practice and Promise; editor: Effective Instructional Management; cons. editor, book rev. editor Jour. Ednl. Pub. Rels.; mem. editl. bd. Jour. Curriculum & Supervision, Reading Today's Youth; contbr. articles to profl. jours. Mem. Urban Ctr. Ednl. Adv. Bd., U.S. Dept. Edn. Urban Supt. Network, Coun. Great City Schs. Bd., Urban Edn. Clearing House Adv. com., U. Okla. Administrn. cert. program com., Cmty. Literacy Coun. Bd.; chmn. bd. dirs. Langston U.; bd. dirs. Oklahoma County chpt. ARC, Jr. Achievement Greater Oklahoma City Bd., Okla. State Fair Bd., Horace Mann League, 1993-2000, v.p. 2000-01, pres.-elect, 2001-02, pres. 2002-03, past pres. 2003-04, mem. found. com. 2003—; v.p. Last Frontier Coun. Bd., v.p. NY State PTA, 1996-2000, Kingston chpt. Rip Van Winkle Coun.; v.p. Boy Scouts Am., 1996-2001, membership chmn., 1996-97; exec. bd. Nat. Dropout Prevention Ctr. Network, 1998—, chmn. 2003—; curriculum com. NY State Coun. Sch. Supts., 1996-2001; bd. dirs. Friends Historic Kingston, 1996-2001, Friends Senate House, Kingston, 1996-2001,Project Contemporary Competitiveness, Inc., 2005—. Named to Linden McKinley H.S. Acad. Hall of Fame, 2003; recipient Silver Beaver award, Boy Scouts Am., 1990, Am. award, Horace Mann League, 1995—2005; fellow, Charles Kettering Found. IDEA, 1976, 1978, 1980, NEH, Danforth Found., 1987—88. Mem. ASCD

(life, exec. coun., pres. 1994-95, rev. coun. 1997-2002), Mich. ASCD, Mass. ASCD, Ohio ASCD, Okla. ASCD (Publ. award 1989), N.Y. ASCD, Wis. ASCD, Internat. Soc. Ednl. Planning, Internat. Reading Assn. (govt. rels. com. 2003-04), Nat. Soc. Study Edn., Nat. Planning Assn., Nat. Assn. Gifted Children (life), Nat. Assn. Edn. Young Children (life), Nat. Coun. Tchrs. English (life), Music Educators Nat. Conf. (life), Nat. Orgn. Legal Problems Edn., Nat. Policy Bd. Ednl. Adminstrn., Am. Assn. Sch. Adminstrs. (life, Leadership for Learning award 1991), Coll. Bd. Advanced Placement Spl. Recognition award 1991, Nat. Assn. Elem. Sch. Prins. (life), Am. Edn. Fin. Assn., Nat. Assn. Edn. Young Children (life), Nat. Sch. Pub. Rels. Assn. (Honor award 1991), Am. Assn. Sch. Adminstrs. (assoc.), Mass. Assn. for Sch. Supts., Mass. Assn. for Edn. of Young Children, Harvard U. Roundtable of Supts., Mass. Urban Supts., Nat. Sch. Pub. Rels. Assn., Taunton Area C. of C., World Coun. Curriculum and Instrn. (life, bd. dirs. N.Am. chpt. 1996-2000, pres. 2000-02), Coun. Basic Edn., Ohio Assn. Elem. Sch. Adminstrs., Buckeye Assn. Sch. Adminstrs., Ohio U. Coll. Edn. (disting. alumnus award 1991), Okla. Assn. Sch. Adminstrs., Mass. Assn. Sch. Adminstrs., Okla. Coalition Pub. Edn., Okla. Commn. Ednl. Leadership, Urban Area Supts. (Okla. br.), Ohio U. Alumni Assn. (nat. dir. 1975-78, pres. Ctrl. Ohio chpt. 1975-76, pres. Mass. chpt. 1976-78, life mem. trustees acad.), World Future Soc. (life) Greater Oklahoma City C. of C. (bd. dirs.), Okla. Heritage Assn., Heritage Hills Assn. (bd. dirs.), Victorian Soc. (New England chpt.), Nat. Eagle Scout Assn. (life), Aerospace Found. (hon. bd. dirs.), PLATO, Learning, Inc. (bd. dirs. 2000-03), Tchrs. Support Network (adv. bd. dirs. 2004—), Am. Bus. Card Club, Coca Cola Collectors Club, Internat. Club, Mgmt. Consortium (bd. advisors),Fulbright Alumni Assn. (life), Tau Kappa Epsilon Alumni Assn. (regional officer Mass. 1976-78, named Alumni Nat. Hall of Fame 1986, Nat. Alumnus of Yr. 1993, Excellence in Edn. award 1993), Kappa Delta Pi (advisor Ctrl. Okla. chpt., nat. publs. com.), Phi Delta Kappa. Methodist. Office Phone: 508-821-1201. Business E-Mail: astellar@tauntonschools.com

**STELLATO, LOUIS EUGENE,** lawyer; b. Bethlehem, Pa., 1950; BBA, U. Tex., 1972; JD, U. Pitts., 1977; LLM, Temple U., 1979. Bar: PA. 1977. With Touche Ross & Co., 1977-79; with tax dept. Sherwin-Williams Co., 1981-87; sr. corp. counsel The Sherwin-Williams Co., 1987-90, asst. secy. and corp. dir. of taxes, 1990-91, v.p., gen. counsel, sec., 1991—. Office: Sherwin Williams Co 101 Prospect Ave NW Cleveland OH 44115-1075

**STELLE, KELLOGG SHEFFIELD,** physicist; b. Washington, Mar. 11, 1948; s. Charles Clarkson and Jane Elizabeth (Kellogg) S. AB, Harvard Coll., 1970; PhD, Brandeis U., 1977. Field observer Bartol Research Found., South Pole, Antarctica, 1970-72; lectr. math. King's Coll., U. London, Eng., 1977-78; sci. assoc. Cern, Geneva, 1980-81, 87, 97-98; rsch. fellow Imperial Coll., London, 1978-80, advanced fellow, 1982-87, lectr. then reader, 1987-95, prof. physics, 1995—, head theoretical physics group, 2002—. Mem. Inst. for Advanced Study, Princeton, N.J., 1986; vis. fellow Ecole Normale Supérieure, Paris, 1981-82; program dir. Inst. Henri Poincaré, Paris, 2000. Editor Classical and Quantum Gravity, 1984-93; contbr. articles to profl. jours. Fellow Inst. of Physics, Am. Phys. Soc.; mem. AAAS, Fedn. Am. Scientists. Office: Blackett Lab Imperial Coll Prince Consort Rd London SW7 2AZ England

**STELLE, ROBERT E.,** physician, retired educator; b. Kalamazoo, Mich., Feb. 7, 1930; s. Earl Clarkson and Norma Lillian Stelle; m. Barbara Lutz, Apr. 29, 1955; children: Amy, Mark, Nancy. BA, Kalamazoo Coll., 1955; MD, U. Mich., 1959. Diplomate Am. Bd. Family Practice (charter). Intern Toledo Hosp., 1959-60; mng. ptnr. Falls Clinic P.C., Crystal Falls, Mich., 1960-79; assoc. prof. Mich. State U., Lansing, 1974-79, U. Wis., Madison, 1979-81; prof., vice chmn. dept. U. Mo., Kansas City, 1981-82, U. Colo., Denver, 1982-85; med. dir. Hertzler Clinic, Wichita, Kans., 1985-86; cons. Locum Tenens Contractors Inc., Colorado City, Colo., 1986—99. Home and Office: PO Box 19051 7710 Charles Colorado City CO 81019

**STELLMACHER, JON MICHAEL,** corporate financial executive; b. Green Bay, Wis., Feb. 25, 1956; s. Leroy Frederick and Helen Mae (Koss) S.; m. Rebecca Jean Hein, Aug. 20, 1976; children: James Michael, Paul Frederick, Abigail Joy. BBA with honors, U. Wis. Underwriting clk. State Life Insur. Fund, Madison, Wis., 1977-78; actuarial student Aid Assn. for Luths., Appleton, Wis., 1978-79, actuarial asst., 1979-83, asst. actuary, 1983-85, assoc. actuary, 1985-87, 2nd v.p., actuary, 1987—97, v.p., 1997—99, sr. v.p., 1999—2002; exec. v.p. Thrivent Fin. for Luths., Appleton, 2002—05, exec. v.p., chief adminstrv. officer, 2005—. Chpt. reviewer Health Ins. Textbook, Soc. Actuaries, 1984-85; cmnts. actuaries sect. Health Workshop Nat. Fraternal Congress Am., 1986, 88; mem. actuarial adv. com. Wis. Health Ins. Risk Sharing Pool, 1987—92; co-chmn. workshop, spring meeting Soc. Actuaries, 1989, 91, Loma Ins. Comm., 1999-2000. Acting pres., v.p. coun. 1st English Luth. Ch., Appleton, 1984; mission interpreter Am. Luth. Ch., Appleton area, 1985-87, Sunday Sch. tchr., 1984-2006, stewardship com., 1981-90, social concerns com. 1994-97, Elderly Housing Task Force, 1990-91, Benevolence Task Force, 1994; co-chair Capital Appeal, 2000; asst. den leader Cub Scouts, Boy Scouts Am., Appleton, 1989-91; asst. coach Appleton Soccer Club, 1990-93, Odyssey of the Mind, 1990-93; coach Appleton Park and Recreation Dept., 1990-98; vice chmn. Arthur Krempin Sch. Music and Art, 2003-04; bd. dirs. Appleton Boychoir, 1994—, pres., 1999—; bd. dirs. Appleton Med. Ctr. Found., 2000—, sec., 2001—; bd. dirs. United Way Fox Cities, 2001—, co-chmn. campaign com., 2002, vice-chair, 2006; mem. sr. adv. bd. J.T. Achievement, 2001—; bd. dirs. YMCA of the Fox Cities, 2002—, vice-chair, 2006, co-chair capital campaign, 2006—; bd. dirs. Fox Cities Performing Arts Ctr., 2003—, ThedaCare, 2006—, Wis. Mfrs. and Commerce, 2006—; mem. Theda Care Quality Coun., 2003—, Cmty. Health Action Team, 2005—; co-chair Emergency Shelter Endowment Campaign, 2005-06. Fellow Soc. Actuaries; mem. Am. Acad. Actuaries. Office: Thrivent Fin for Luths 4321 N Ballard Rd Appleton WI 54919 Home: 3124 E Sandpiper Ln Appleton WI 54913-7771 Office Phone: 920-628-2002. Business E-Mail: jon.stellmacher@thrivent.com

**STELLMAN, KEITH M.,** meteorologist, researcher; s. Terry A. and Theresa J. Stellman; m. Karen C. Conly, Dec. 19, 1998; 1 child, Zachary T.; 1 child, Zoey R. Degree in Atmospheric Scis., N.E. U., Monroe, La., 1996; MS in Meteorology, Fla. State U., Tallahassee, 1999. Hydrometeorologist Nat. Weather Svc., Slidell, La., 1999—2003, techniques devel. meteorologist Ft. Worth, 2004—06. Named to Acad. All-Conf., Southland Conf. Athletics, 1996; recipient Athletic Scholarship award, dept. baseball U. New Orleans, 1991—94, Bronze medal, Dept. of Commerce, 2002, Nat. Isaac Cline award, Nat. Weather Svc., 2004. Mem.: Nat. Weather Assn. (assoc.; mem. broadcast com. 2004—06), Am. Meteorol. Soc. (assoc.), Lions Club. Office Phone: 817-978-1100. Business E-Mail: keith.stellman@noaa.gov.

**STELLUTO, SHARON RENEE,** apparel designer, painter; b. West Trenton, NJ, Apr. 17, 1981; d. Joseph Fernando and Barbara Ann Stelluto. BFA, SUNY, New Paltz, 2003. Asst. to profl. artist Andrew Braitman Art Studio, Charlotte, NC, 1995—98; server, barista, hostess Xando's Coffee, Bar, Bryn Mawr, Pa., 1999—2000; display designer, sales assoc. Illuminations, King of Prussia, Pa., 2001—01; sales assoc. Health and Nutrition Ctr., New Paltz, 2002—02; customer serv. rep. Certa Pro Painters, Oaks, Pa., 2003—03; handbag designer, office mgr., pub. rels. Debbie Brooks Designs, Gardiner, NY, 2003—04; asst. designer of handbags, quality supr., office mgr. L'egent Internat., Newburgh, NY, 2004. Fashion vendor Accessories Show at Jacob Javitts Ctr., Manhattan, NY, 2004—04; invitation Internat. Biennial of Contemporary Art, Ferrara, Italy, 2004—04. Official 2004 olympics pop art, Splash To Victory, one-woman show include Living Seed Gallery, exhibitions include Samual Dorsky Mus., Backstage Studio Productions, Kingston Libr., online art exhibit, www. projekt30.com. Avocations: steel welder, piano, hiking, oil painting. Personal E-mail: sstelluto@yahoo.com.

**STELLWAGEN, ROBERT HARWOOD,** biochemistry professor; b. Joliet, Ill., Jan. 6, 1941; s. Harwood John and Alma Dorothy (Handorf) S.; m. Joanne Kovacs, June 15, 1963; children: Robert Harwood, Alise Anne. AB, Harvard U., 1963; PhD, U. Calif., Berkeley, 1968. Staff fellow NIH, Bethesda, Md.,

1968-69; postdoctoral scholar U. Calif., San Francisco, 1969-70; asst. prof. biochemistry, molecular biology U. So. Calif., L.A., 1970-74, assoc. prof., 1974-80, prof., 1980—, chmn. dept., 1981-86, vice chmn. dept., 1993—. Vis. scientist Nat. Inst. for Med. Rsch., Mill Hill, Eng., 1979. Contbr. articles to profl. jours. Recipient Henderson prize Harvard U., 1963; NSF fellow, 1963-67; NIH grantee, 1971-84. Mem. Sierra Club, Phi Beta Kappa. Democrat. Office: U So Calif Keck Sch Medicine 1333 San Pablo St Los Angeles CA 90089-9151 Office Phone: 323-442-1149. E-mail: stellwag@usc.edu.

**STELPSTRA, WILLIAM JOHN,** minister; b. Paterson, N.J., Nov. 1, 1934; s. Duke and Nellie (Stapert) S.; m. Anna Rizkovsky, Sept. 6, 1958; 1 child, Linda Mae. BA, Alma White Coll., 1957; B. of Religion, Zarephath Bible Sem., 1958. Ordained to ministry Pillar of Fire Ch., 1954. Pastor Pillar of Fire Ch., Little Falls, N.J., 1956-60; evangelist Wesleyan Meth. Ch., 1960-64; founder, dir. Bethel Children's Home, Paterson, N.J., 1964-71, Bethel Ranch Rehab. for Men, West Milford, N.J., 1971—; founder, pres. World for Christ Crusade, Inc., N.J., Fla., 1960—, dir. fgn. missions Haiti, Ghana, India, 1980—; adminstr. Fellowship House, Bloomfield, N.J., 1979—, Bright Side Manor, Teaneck, N.J., 1978—. Mem. Ocean Grove C. of C. Republican. Wesleyan Ch. Avocations: painting with oils, swimming, boating, travel, gardening. Home: 1005 Union Valley Rd West Milford NJ 07480-1220 Office Phone: 973-728-3267. E-mail: reustelpstra@aol.com.

**STELTZLEN, JANELLE HICKS,** lawyer; b. Atlanta, Sept. 18, 1937; d. William Duard and Mary Evelyn (Embrey) Hicks; divorced; children: Gerald William III, Christa Diane. BS, Okla. State U., 1958; MS, Kans. State U., 1961; JD, U. Tulsa, 1981. Bar: Okla. 1981, U.S. Dist. Ct. (no., ea. and we. dists.) Okla. 1981, U.S. Tax Ct. 1982, U.S. Ct. Claims 1982, U.S. Ct. Appeals (10th cir.) 1983, U.S. Ct. Appeals (Fed. cir.) 1984, U.S. Supreme Ct. 1986; lic. real estate broker. Pvt. practice, Tulsa, 1981-97. Lectr. Coll. of DuPage, Glen Ellyn, Ill., 1976, Tulsa Jr. Coll., 1981-88; dietitian, Tulsa; res. dep. for Tulsa County Sheriff's Office; 2d dep., legal Tulsa County Clk., 1997-2000. Christian counselor 1st United Meth. Ch., Tulsa, 1986—, coord. legal counseling ministry, 1985—, lay pastor, 1987—; mem. Tulsa County Bd. Equalization and Excise Tax Bd., 1989-90; mem. Leadership Tulsa XX, 1993—; recipient of Leadership Tulsa Paragon award, 1996; bd. dirs. Sister Cities Tulsa/San Luis Potosi, 1988—, South Peoria Neighborhood Connection Found., 1991—, pres., 1995-96; active Tulsa County Tax Oversight Com., 1994—, Tulsa Home Rule Charter Com., 1994—. Recipient Okla. Sr. Olympics medal. Mem. Okla. Bar Assn., Tulsa County Bar Assn., Vol. Lawyers Assn. (bd. dirs.), Am. Dietetic Assn., Tulsa Dist. Dietetic Assn., Kiwanis Internat., Mensa, DAR, Delta Zeta. Republican. Avocations: swimming, scuba diving, jogging, bicycling, reading. Home: 6636 S Jamestown Pl Tulsa OK 74136-2615

**STELZER, GUSTAV R.,** retired automotive executive; b. St. Louis, June 1, 1915; s. Martin J. Stelzer and Alma Mangelsdorf; m. Lorraine Louise Sueme, Feb. 3, 1940; children: Gail Messett, John J. Stelzer. Grad. in acctg. and comml. law, Mo. Bus. Sch., St. Louis, 1929. Acct. Craig Furniture Co., St. Louis, 1930-32; sales rep. Newsom & Stelzer, St. Louis, 1933-34; various positions GM Corp., various cities, 1935-66, sr. exec. regional mgr. Chevrolet Motor Divsn. Kansas City, Mo., 1966-76; ret., 1976. Author: Free Trade and the Constitution, 1987, 89, 94, The Nightmare of Camelot, An Expose of Free Trade, 1994, The State Against Religion, The Case for Equal Protection, 2001; contbr. over 130 articles to profl. publs.; appeared numerous radio and TV talk shows. Mem. World Affairs Coun., San Diego, 1981-85, Inst. of the Ams., San Diego, 1982-86; mem. adv. coun., U. San Diego Sch. Edn., 1983-85. Avocations: golf, travel, writing. Home: 1836 163d Pl SE Mill Creek WA 98012 E-mail: gusstelzer@aol.com.

**STELZER, IRWIN MARK,** economist; b. NYC, May 22, 1932; s. Abraham and Fanny (Dolgins) S.; m. Marian Faris Stuntz, 1981. BA cum laude, NYU, 1951, MA, 1952; PhD, Cornell U., 1954. Fin. analyst Econometric Inst., 1952; tchg. fellow Cornell U., 1953-54; instr. U. Conn., 1954-55; rschr. Twentieth Century Fund, 1953-55; economist W.J. Levy, Inc., 1955-56; sr. cons., v.p. Boni, Watkins, Jason & Co., Inc., 1956-61; rschr. Brookings Instn., 1956-57; pres. Nat. Econ. Rsch. Assocs., Inc., 1961-85, I.M. Stelzer Assocs. Inc., 1986—; dir. Energy and Environmental Ctr., Harvard U., 1987-90. Dir. econ. policy studies Am. Enterprise Inst., 1990-98; bd. dirs. Econs. Policy Inst., Oxford U.; dir. econ. policy studies Hudson Inst., 1998—; adv. coun. Electric Power Rsch. Inst.; adv. com. revision of rules of practice and procedure FERC; chmn. com. on adequate power supply FPC; bd. dirs. The Energy Adv. Group of the Keystone Ctr; mng. dir. Rothschild, Inc.; mem. trade and environment policy adv. com. U.S. Trade Rep.; vis. fellow Nuffield Coll., Oxford U.; adv. bd. Am. Antitrust Inst.; lectr. in field. Author: Selected Antitrust Cases: Landmark Decisions, 1955, The Antitrust Laws: A Primer, 1993, 4th edit., 2001, Neoconservatism, 2004, The NEOCON Reader, 2004; econ. columnist The Sunday Times, London, 1986—; contbg. editor The Weekly Standard; columnist Courier Mail, Australia; contbr. articles to econs. field. Mem. Mayor's Energy Policy Adv. Group for NYC; adv. panel Pres.'s Nat. Commn. for Rev. of Antitrust Laws and Procedures; mem. Gov.'s Adv. Panel on Telecom.; bd. governing trustees Am. Ballet Theatre; bd. dirs. U.S. Nat. Com., World Energy Conf., Regulatory Policy Inst., Oxford U.; mem. Fed. Energy Regulatory Com. Task Force on Pipeline Competition; pres. appointee advisor to U.S. Trade Rep. Mem. Am. Econ. Assn., Reform Club, Cosmos Club, Phi Beta Kappa. Home: PO Box 1008 Aspen CO 81612-1008 Office: 1150 17th St NW Ste 502 Washington DC 20036 Personal E-mail: stelzer@aol.com.

**STELZER, PAUL,** cardiac surgeon, educator; MD, Columbia U., 1972. Diplomate Am. Bd. Surgery, Am. Bd. Thoracic Surgery. Resident gen. surgery Roosevelt Hosp., N.Y.C., 1972-77; resident thoracic surgery N.Y. Hosp.-Cornell Med. Ctr., 1979-81; attending surgery Beth Israel Med. Ctr., 1981—. Assoc. prof. surgery Albert Einstein Coll. Medicine. Office: Beth Israel Med Ctr 317 E 17th St New York NY 10003-3804 Office Phone: 212-420-2584. Office Fax: 212-420-2321. E-mail: pstelzer@bethisraelny.org.

**STELZNER, PAUL BURKE,** textile company executive; b. Iowa City, Iowa, Jan. 1, 1935; s. Glenn W. and Ruth (Schroder) S.; m. Martha Jane Schneeberger, Aug. 23, 1958; children: Martha Elizabeth Beuke and Barbara Jane Lubbering. BS, Muskingum Coll., 1960; postgrad., Akron U., 1961-65. Tech. dir. Buckeye Fabric Finishing Co., Coshocton, Ohio, 1963-74; sec., sales mgr. Excello Fabric Finishers Inc., Coshocton, 1966-74; gen. mgr. Mineral Fiber Mfg. Corp., Coshocton, 1974-76, 1998—; v.p., gen. mgr. Kellwood Co. Recreation Group, 1976-85; v.p. Am. Recreation Products, Inc., New Haven, Mo., 1985-88; v.p., gen. mgr. John Boyle & Co., Statesville, NC, 1989-93, pres., CEO, 1993—2004, dir., 1999—. Bd. dirs. Indsl. Fabrics Found., 1998-2002. Served with USN, 1953-57. Mem. Indsl. Fabrics Assn. Internat. (dir. 1973-74, 82-88, 94-99). Presbyterian. Office: John Boyle & Co Inc 1803 Salisbury Rd Statesville NC 28677-6219 Home: 843 Scenic Ridge Dr Washington MO 63090 E-mail: pstelz@yhti.net.

**STEM, CARL HERBERT,** business educator; b. Eagleville, Tenn., Jan. 30, 1935; s. Marion Ogilvie and Sara Elizabeth (Jones) Stem; m. Linda Marlene Wheeler, Dec. 28, 1963; children: Anna Elizabeth, Susan Kathleen, John Carl, David Leslie. *Great-great-great-great-grandfather Jacob Stem of Pennsylvania Dutch ancestry-migrated from the Philadelphia region after the Revolutionary War to Granville County, N.C., where there is still a farming village named Stem. In the 1830s several sons migrated to Middle Tennessee. Great-great-grandfather John Richard Stem was a lieutenant in the 55th (McKoins) Tennessee Infantry (CSA). Great-grandfather Marion Luther Stem was the first to "leave the farm", owning general merchandise stores. Grandfather Charles R. Stem practiced country dentistry for more than 50 years. Father Marion Ogilvie Stem died at the age of 28 in 1941.* BA, Vanderbilt U., 1957; AM (Woodrow Wilson fellow, Harvard scholar), Harvard U., 1960, PhD, 1969. Internat. fin. economist, bd. govs. Fed. Res. System, Washington, 1963—70; from assoc. prof. to prof. econ. Tex. Tech. U., Lubbock, 1970—75; from assoc. prof. to prof. internat. fin. Tex. Tech U., Lubbock, 1970—2001; prof. emeritus Tex. Tech. U., Lubbock, 2001—; from chmn. fin., adminstr. grad. programs, exec. assoc. dean to dean Tex. Tech U. Coll. Bus. Adminstrn., Lubbock, 1971—97, dean emeritus, 1997—. Sr. econ. adviser Office Fgn. Direct Investments, U.S. Dept. Commerce, Washington, 1973-74; cons. U.S. Dept. Treasury, 1974-75; mem. faculty Grad. Sch. Credit and Fin. Mgmt., Lake Success, N.Y., 1974-87; adj. scholar Am. Enterprise Inst. Pub. Policy Rsch., Washington, 1974-88; treas. Mission Jour., Inc., 1969-88. Editor (with Makin and Logue): Eurocurrencies and The International Monetary System; contbr. articles to profl. jours. Trustee St. Mary Plains Hosp., Lubbock, Tex., 1987-92, chmn., 1992; v.p. Tex. Coun. Collegiate Edn. Bus., 1977-78, pres., 1978-79; mem. acad. adv. bd. United Arab Emirates U., Al Ain, 1996-03; mem. Coun. on Podiat. Med. Edn., Washington, 1998—; bd. visitors Abilene Christian U., 1998-2006; elder Broadway Ch. of Christ, Lubbock, 2001-04. Capt. Security Agy. AUS, 1961-62. Fulbright scholar, U. Reading, Eng., 1957—58. Fellow Phi Beta Kappa; mem. Southwestern Bus. Adminstrn. Assn. (pres. 1982-83), Nat. Assn. for Bus. Econs., So. Bus. Adminstrn. Assn. (v.p. 1985-86, pres. 1986-87), Lubbock Econ. Coun. (pres. 1973), Am. Assembly Collegiate Schs. Bus. (stds. com. 1981-84, bd. dirs. 1993-96), Lubbock Club (pres. 1986-87), Omicron Delta Kappa, Phi Kappa Phi, Beta Gamma Sigma, Tau Kappa Alpha, Phi Beta Kappa. Home: 12508 W 123rd St Overland Park KS 66213 Personal E-mail: cstem@sbcglobal.net. *Most important to me are the ever timely values of our Judeo-Christian heritage- faith in God and a deep appreciation for the inherent value of man. These values have underpinned my aspirations and sustained me through disappointments. They have generated the perseverance and continual hope so vital to me as I have worked for self-growth and to make a contribution to the institutions and people with which I have been associated in various periods of my life.*

**STEMERMAN, DAVID H.,** radiologist; b. Elmira, N.Y., Aug. 2, 1966; BA, Emory U., 1988; MD, Boston U., 1992. Diplomate Nat. Bd. Med. Examiners; bd. cert. Am. Bd. Radiology. Intern Mass. Gen. Hosp., Boston, 1992-93; resident Temple U., Phila., 1993-97; fellow NYU, N.Y.C., 1997-98; assoc. radiologist Abington (Pa.) Meml. Hosp., 1998-99, St. Joseph's Med. Ctr., 1999—2000, St. Barnabas Hosp., 2000—01; pres. GDS Imaging PC, Larchmont, NY, 2001—. Fax: (914) 722-9409.

**STEMMER, EDWARD ALAN,** surgeon, educator; b. Cin., Jan. 20, 1930; s. Edward Purcell and Helen Marie (Smith) S.; m. Lois Jean Moss, May 1, 1954; children: Susan Helen, Linda Diane, Paul Frederick, Nancy Joan, Carol Jean. BA, U. Chgo., 1949, MD, 1953. Diplomate Am. Bd. Surgery, Am. Bd. Thoracic Surgery. Resident in surgery U. Chgo., 1953-60; chief resident in surgery Stanford U., Palo Alto, Calif., 1960-62, instr. surgery, 1962-64; asst. prof. surgery U. Utah, Salt Lake City, 1964-65; from asst. prof. surgery to prof. surgery U. Calif., Irvine, 1966—. Acting chmn. surgery U. Calif., Irvine, 1978-80; chief surg. svc. VA Hosp., Long Beach, Calif., 1965—. Editor: Vascular Disease in the Elderly, 1997; contbr. articles to profl. jours., chpts. to books. Capt. USAF, 1955-57, maj. USAFR, 1957-72. Grantee NIH, Am. Heart Assn., 1962-72; recipient disting. svc. award Am. Heart Assn., 1971. Mem. Am. Am. Thoracic Surgery, Assn. VA Surgeons (pres. 1979-80, disting. svc. award 1995), Am. Surg. Assn., Am. Coll. Surgeons (pres. So. Calif. chpt. 1974-75), L.A. Surg. Soc. (pres. 1986-87), Sigma Xi. Avocations: carpentry, gardening, electronics. Home: 136 College Park Dr Seal Beach CA 90740-2527 Office: VA Med Ctr 5901 E 7th St Long Beach CA 90822-5201 Business E-Mail: edward.stemmer@med.va.gov.

**STEMMLER, EDWARD JOSEPH,** physician, retired health facility administrator, dean; b. Phila., Feb. 15, 1929; s. Edward C. and Josephine (Heitzmann) Stemmler; m. Joan C. Koster, Dec. 27, 1958; children: Elizabeth, Margaret, Edward C., Catherine, Joan. BA, La Salle Coll., Phila., 1950, ScD (hon.), 1983; MD, U. Pa., 1960; ScD (hon.), Ursinus Coll., 1977, Phila. Coll. Pharmacy and Sci., 1989; LHD (hon.), Rush U., 1986, Med. Coll. Pa., 1994; ScD (hon.), SUNY, Syracuse, 1994; ScD, Georgetown U., 1998. Diplomate Am. Bd. Internal Medicine. Intern U. Pa. Hosp., 1960—61, resident in internal medicine, 1961—63, fellow in cardiology, 1963—64, chief med. resident, 1964—65, chief med. outpatient dept., 1966—67; chief of medicine U. Pa. Med. Svc., VA Hosp., Phila., 1967—73; deans com. VA Hosp., 1974—88; instr. medicine grad. divsn. medicine U. Pa., 1964—66, NIH postdoctoral rsch. trainee, dept. physiology, grad. divsn. medicine, 1965—67, assoc. in medicine grad. divsn. medicine, 1966—67; assoc. in physiology Grad. Div. Medicine, 1967—72, from asst. prof. medicine to prof., 1967—91, Robert G. Dunlop prof., 1981—91, prof. emeritus, 1991—; assoc. dean Univ. Hosp. Sch. Medicine, 1973, assoc. dean student affairs, 1973—75, from acting dean to dean, 1974—88, dean emeritus, 1989—; exec. v.p. U. Pa. Med. Ctr., 1986—89, Assn. Am. Med. Colls., 1990—94, sr. adv. to pres., 1994—95. Nominating and ad hoc governance coms. Nat. Bd. Med. Examiners, 1985, exec. com., 1986—99, vice-chmn., 1987—89, treas., 1989—91, chmn., 1991—95; editl. policy com. Nat. Fund for Med. Edn., 1975—77; deans com. VA Hosp., 1974—89; chmn. Pa. Deans Com., 1976—87, Mid-Ea. Regional Med. Libr. Svcs., 1978—81; adv. com. dept. medicine U. Ala., Birmingham, 1985—89; vis. com. Tufts U. Sch. Medicine, 1990—94, Med. U. S.C., 1990—99, U. Calif., Davis, 1993—. Contbr. articles to profl. jours. Trustee Dorothy Rider Pool Healthcare Trust, 1991—2000, Ursinus Coll., 1991—2006, Wintergreen Nature Found., 1996—2001, Saw Cmty. Found., 2000—04, AHC Cmty. Found., 2002—; mem. opbd. U. Va. Med. Ctr., 2004—. Recipient Frederick A. Packard award, 1960, Albert Einstein Med. Ctr. staff award, 1960, Roche award, 1960, Disting. Svc. award, Nat. Bd. Med. Examiners, 1999. Master: ACP (treas., chmn. investment com. 1975—80, Laureate award Ea. Pa. region 1986, Disting. Svc. award); mem. AMA, Am. Clin. and Climatological Soc. (pres. 1997—98), Coll. of Physicians of Phila. (bd. censors, coun. 1979—85, coun. 1990—92), Assn. Am. Med. Colls. (ad hoc external exam. rev. coun. 1980—82, exec. coun., coun. of deans adminstrv. bd. 1980—85, chmn. 1983—85, nat. chmn.-elect 1985—86, chmn. assembly 1986—87), Inst. Medicine Alpha Omega Alpha, Republican. Mem. Christian Ch. Home: RR 1 Box 676 Roseland VA 22967-9209 Personal E-mail: ejstemmler@aol.com.

**STEMPEL, ERNEST EDWARD,** insurance executive; b. N.Y.C., May 10, 1916; s. Frederick Christian and Leah Lillian S.; m. Phyllis Brooks (dec. Mar. 1993); children: Diana Brooks Bergquist, Calvin Pinkcomb, Neil Frederick, Robert Russell. AB, Manhattan Coll., 1938; LL.B., Fordham U., 1946; LL.M., NYU, 1949, D.J.S., 1951; LL.D. (hon.), Manhattan Coll., 1986. Bar: N.Y. 1946. With Am. Internat. Underwriters Corp., N.Y.C., 1938-53; v.p., dir. Am. Internat. Co. Ltd., Hamilton, Bermuda, 1953-63, chmn. bd., from 1963; ret. Chmn., dir. Am. Internat. Assurance Co. (Bermuda) Ltd., Am. Internat. Reins. Co. Ltd., Bermuda, Philippine Am. Life Ins. Co., Manila, Australian Am. Assurance Co., Ltd., Am. Internat. Assurance Co., Ltd., Hong Kong, AIG Life Ins. Co., Del. Am. Life Ins. Co., Wilmington, Del., Am. Internat. Life Assurance Co. of N.Y.; pres., dir. Starr Internat. Co. Inc.; sr. advisor Am. Internat. Group Inc.; dir. C.V. Starr & Co. Inc., N.Y.C., Am. Life Ins. Co., Wilmington, Seguros Interamericana (S.A.), Mexico, Mt. Mansfield Co., Inc., Stowe, Vt., Seguros Venezuela (C.A.), Caracas, dir. Am. Internat. Underwriters (Latin Am.), Inc., Bermuda, Am. Internat. Underwriters Mediterranean, Inc., Bermuda, Pacific Union Assurance Co., Calif., Underwriters Adjustment Co., Panama. Served to lt. (s.g.) USNR, 1942-46. Named one of Forbes' Richest Americans, 2006. Mem. Am. Bar Assn., N.Y. State Bar. Clubs: Marco Polo (N.Y.C.), Royal Bermuda Yacht (Bermuda), Mid-Ocean (Bermuda), Coral Beach & Tennis Club (Bermuda), Riddell's Bay Golf and Country (Bermuda). Office: Am Internat Co Ltd Am Internt Bldg Richmond Rd Pembroke HM 08 Bermuda*

**STEMPEL, GUIDO HERMANN, III,** journalism educator; b. Bloomington, Ind., Aug. 13, 1928; s. Guido Hermann Jr. and Alice Margaret (Menninger) S.; m. Anne Elliott, Aug. 30, 1952; children: Ralph Warren, Carl William, Jane Louise. Student, Carnegie Tech., 1945-46; AB in Journalism, Ind. U., 1949, AM in Journalism, 1951; PhD in Mass Communication, U. Wis., 1954. Sports editor Frankfort (Ind.) Times, 1949-50; instr., asst. prof. Sch. Journalism, Pa. State U., University Park, 1955-57; from assoc. prof. to prof. Dept. Journalism, Cen. Mich. U., Mt. Pleasant, 1957-65; assoc. prof. Sch. Journalism, Ohio U., Athens, 1965-68, prof., 1968-82, Disting. prof., 1982—96, Disting. prof. emeritus, 1996—, dir., 1972-79. Rsch. cons. Ohio

Newspaper Assn., Columbus, 1985—; chmn. rsch. com. Coll. Media Advisors, 1963-69, 79-84; mem. adv. bd. dept. comm. arts U. West Fla., 1987-00; survey coord. Scripps Howard News Svc., 1992—; dir. Scripps Survey Rsch. Ctr., 2002—. Co-author: The Media in the 1984 and 1988 Presidential Campaigns, 1991; assoc. editor, Newspaper Rsch. Jour., 1992-2001; co-editor Web Jour. of Mass Comm. Rsch., 1997—; editor, co-author: The Practice of Political Communication, 1994; co-editor, co-author: Research Methods in Mass Communications, 1981, 2d edit., 1989, The Media in the 1984 and 1988 Presidential Campaigns, 1991, Historical Dictionary of Political Communication in the United States, 1999, Mass Communication Research and Theory, 2003; author: Media and Politics in America, 2003; editor: Journalism Quar., 1972-89; sr. rsch. editor Newspaper Research Jour., 2000—; contbr. articles to profl. jours. Mem. bd. visitors Def. Info. Sch., Ft. Meade, 1985-96. Named to Ctrl. Mich. Journalism Hall of Fame, 2004; recipient Chancellor's award, U. Wis., 1977, Francis Asbury award, West Ohio Meth. Conf., 2004, Harold C. Nelson award, U. Wis., 2004. Mem. Assn. for Edn. in Journalism and Mass Comm. (chmn. rsch. com. 1968-71; Eleanor Blum award 1989, Trayes Tchr. of Yr. 1997, Disting. Svc. award 1999, award for excellence in contbns. to journalism 2005), Soc. Profl. Journalists, Kappa Tau Alpha (nat unit 1984-85). Democrat. Methodist. Home: 7 Lamar Dr Athens OH 45701-3730 Office: Ohio Univ Sch of Journalism Athens OH 45701 Office Phone: 740-593-2609. Business E-Mail: stempel@ohio.edu.

**STEMPEL, JOHN DALLAS,** international studies educator; b. Easton, Pa., July 26, 1938; s. John Emmert and Mary Roberts (Farmer) S.; m. Nancy A. Dean, Feb. 11, 1961 (div. Jan. 1990); m. Susan Hodgetts, May 18, 1991; children: Amy, Alix, Jill. AB cum laude, Princeton U., 1960; MA with distinction, U. Calif., Berkeley, 1963, PhD, 1965. Jr. officer U.S. Embassy U.S. Fgn. Svc., Conakry, Guinea, 1966, acting dep. chief mission U.S. Embassy Bujumbura, Burundi, 1966-68, watch officer State Dept. Ops. Ctr. Washington, 1968-70, staff asst. to dep. sec. state, 1968-70, Ghana desk officer, 1970-72, polit.-econ. officer U.S. Embassy Lusaka, Zambia, 1972-74, from sr. internal polit. reporter to dep. chief sect. to acting polit. counselor U.S. Embassy Tehran, Iran, 1975-79; diplomat-in-residence, mem. faculty U.S. Naval Acad., Annapolis, Md., 1979-81; dir. ops. ctr. Dept. State U.S. Fgn. Svc., Washington, 1981-83, dir. Office Near East and South Asian Affairs Bur. Internat. Security Affairs Dept. Def., 1983-84; spl. asst. Persian Gulf affairs U.S. Dept. State, Washington, 1984-85; consul gen. U.S. Fgn. Svc., Madras, India, 1985-88; prof. internat. studies, assoc. dir. Patterson Sch. Diplomacy and Internat. Commerce U. Ky., Lexington, 1988-93, prof. internat. studies, dir. Patterson Sch. Diplomacy, 1993—2003, sr. prof. internat. studies Patterson Sch. Diplomacy, 2003—. Adj. prof. George Washington U., Washington, 1968-72, 80-85, Am. U. Washington, 1975; prof. Regional Coop. and Devel. Coll., Tehran, 1975-78; rsch. assoc. Mershon Ctr. Ohio State U., 1972. Author: Inside the Iranian Revolution, 1981, Faith, Diplomacy and the International System, 2000; (monograph) Theory and Practice in Foreign Affairs: Why Two Worlds Seldom Meet, 1972; contbr. articles to profl. jours. Mem. exec. coun. Episcopal Diocese of Lexington, Ky. With USN, 1960-62, lt. USNR, 1962-70. Mem. Internat. Studies Assn., N.Y. Coun. on Fgn. Rels. (mem. U.S. Dept. Commerce Export Coun. Ky.). Avocations: tennis, reading, railroads, philosophy. Office: U Ky Patterson Sch Diplomacy Patterson Tower Rm 455 Lexington KY 40506-0027 Office Phone: 859-257-4666.

**STEMPER, BRIAN D.,** biomedical engineer; b. Fond du Lac, Wis., Oct. 30, 1974; s. Gerald A. and Judith M. Stemper; m. Julie M Rumpf, June 28, 2003. PhD, Marquette U., 2003; BS in Biomed. Engring., Milw. Sch. Engring., 1998. Biomedical rschr. Milw. Sch. Engring. Rapid Prototyping Ctr., 1996—98; asst. prof. dept. neurosurgery Med. Coll. of Wis., Milw., 1998—. Author: articles in peer-reviewed jours. Bd. mem. Rocky Mountain Bioengring. Symposium, Inc. Recipient Best of Session, Rocky Mountain Bioengring. Symposium, 2000, Best Paper by a Young Rschr., Internat. IRCOBI Conf. Biomechanics of Impact, 2005. Mem.: Soc. Automotive Engrs., Assn. for the Advancement of Automotive Medicine, ASME, Cervical Spine Rsch. Soc. R-Consevative. Roman Catholic. Office: Med Coll of Wis 5000 W National Ave Research 151 Milwaukee WI 53295 Office Phone: 414-384-2000 41525. Business E-Mail: stemps@mcw.edu.

**STEMPIEN, JOSEPH JEFFREY,** music educator; b. Lewistown, Pa., Aug. 13, 1952; s. Joseph Victor and Thelma Elizabeth Stempien; m. Eleanor Jane Lurwick, Nov. 22, 1975; children: Heather Lynne, Aimee Leigh. MusM in Music Edn., Ithaca Coll., N.Y., 1983. Instrumental music tchr. Penn Yan Mid. Sch., Penn Yan, NY, 1978—, Hobart & William Smith Colls., Geneva, NY, 1989—; band dir. Keuka Coll., Keuka Park, NY, 2002—; choral and band dir. Penn Yan United Meth. Ch., Penn Yan, NY, 1992—; prin. trumpet Orch. of the So. Fingers Lakes, Corning-Elmira, NY, 1982—; trumpet player So. Tier All Star Jazz Band, Finger Lakes Area, NY, 1990—; mechanic Marbles Automotive, Penn Yan, NY, 2002—. Condr. Penn Yan Area Cmty. Band, Penn Yan, NY, 1991—2004. Mem.: ITG (assoc.), NYSSMA (assoc.), MENC (assoc.), Kappa Kappa Psi (life), Phi Mu Alpha (life). Home: 519 Assembly Ave PO Box 475 Keuka Park NY 14478 Office: Penn Yan Central School District 515 Liberty St Penn Yan NY 14527 Office Phone: 315-536-3366. Personal E-mail: stempien@usadatanet.net.

**STEMPLER, JACK LEON,** aerospace executive; b. Newark, Oct. 30, 1920; s. Morris and Ida (Friedman) S.; m. J. Adelaide Williams, Oct. 28, 1950; children: Mark N., Sandra J., Carrie B. BA, Montclair State U., NJ, 1943; LL.B., Cornell U., 1948. Bar: NY 1949, DC 1949. Atty. com. uniform code mil. justice Dept. Def., 1948-49, atty. adviser legis. div., 1949-50; asst. counsel Munitions Bd., 1950-51; counsel Armed Forces Housing Agy., 1952-54, Advanced Research Projects Agy., 1958-65; asst. gen. counsel logistics Dept. Def., 1953-65, asst. to sec. def. for legislative affairs, 1965-70; gen. counsel Dept. Air Force, 1970-77; asst. to sec. of def. for legis. affairs, 1977-81; v.p. legis. affairs LTV Aerospace, Washington, 1982-92; ret., 1992. Cons. in field. Served to 1st lt. USMCR, 1942-46, PTO. Recipient Outstanding Civilian Performance award Dept. Def., 1959, Distinguished Civilian Service award, 1965, Distinguished Civilian Service award with palm, 1969, with 2d bronze palm, 1970; Exceptional Civilian Service award USAF, 1973, 75, 77; awarded Presdl. rank of Disting. Exec., 1980; recipient Disting. Public Service award Dept. Def., 1981 Mem. Fed. Bar Assn., D.C. Bar Assn., Cornell Law Sch. Assn. Home: 4701 Newcomb Pl Alexandria VA 22304-1506

**STENBERG, CARL W., III,** public administration educator, dean; b. Pitts., July 8, 1943; s. Carl W. and Mildred (Baggs) S.; m. Kirstin D. Thompson; children: Erik Anders, Kerry Cathryn, Kaameran Baird. BA, Allegheny Coll., 1965; MPA, SUNY, Albany, 1966, PhD, 1970. Research asst. N.Y. State Div. Budget, Albany, 1967; analyst, then sr. analyst U.S. Adv. Commn. on Intergovtl. Relations, Washington, 1968-77, asst. dir. for policy implementation, 1977-83, acting exec. dir., 1982; exec. dir. Council of State Govts., Lexington, Ky., 1983-89; prof., dir. Weldon Cooper Ctr. for Pub. Svc. U. Va., Charlottesville, 1989-95, Disting. prof. pub. svc., 1991-95; prof., dean Yale Gordon Coll. Liberal Arts U. Balt., 1995—2003; prof. Sch. Govt. U. N.C., Chapel Hill, 2003—. Mem. Am. Part Program USIA, 1987; adj. prof. George Washington U., 1971, 81, Am. U., 1972-80, 82, U. Md., 1976, U. So. Calif., 1984-87; v.p. Bureaucrat Inc., Washington, 1973-77, mng. editor, 1973-77. Feature editor Pub. Mgmt. Forum Pub. Adminstrn. Rev., 1977-83, editor U. of Va. newsletter, 1994-95; co-editor-in-chief The Regionalist, 1997-2002. Pres. Reston Home Owners' Assn., Va., 1973-74; mem. U.S. del. Ad Hoc Group on Urban Problems, OECD, 1980-82. Vivien Stewart vis. fellow Cambridge U., Eng., 1980; recipient Disting. Alumni award Polit. Sci. Dept. Rockefeller Coll., 1985. Fellow: Nat. Acad. Pub. Adminstrn. (chair bd. dirs. 2002—04); mem.: Va. Alliance for Pub. Svc. (pres. 1991—92), Am. Soc. Pub. Adminstrn. (pres. 1990—91, Marshall E. Dimock award, Louis Brownlow award, Donald Stone award). Home: 301 Madera Ln Chapel Hill NC 27517-8356 Office: U NC Sch Govt CB # 3330 Knapp Bldg Chapel Hill NC 27599-3330 Office Phone: 919-962-2377. E-mail: stenberg@sog.unc.edu.

**STENBERG, DONALD B.,** lawyer; b. David City, Nebr., Sept. 30, 1948; s. Eugene A. and Alice (Kasal) Stenberg; m. Susan K. Hoegemeyer, June 9, 1971; children: Julie A., Donald B. Jr., Joseph L., Abby E. BA, U. Nebr., 1970; MBA, Harvard U., 1974, JD cum laude, 1974. Bar: Nebr. 1974, U.S. Dist. Ct. Nebr. 1974, U.S. Ct. Appeals (fed. cir.) 1984, U.S. Ct. Claims 1989, U.S. Ct. Appeals (8th cir.) 1989, U.S. Supreme Ct. 1991. Assoc. Barlow, Watson & Johnson, Lincoln, Nebr., 1974—75; ptnr. Stenberg and Stenberg, Lincoln, 1976—78; legal counsel Gov. of Nebr., Lincoln, 1979—82; prin. Erickson & Sederstrom, Lincoln, 1983—85, of counsel, 2003—; pvt. practice Lincoln, 1985—90; atty. gen. State of Nebr., Lincoln, 1991—2002. Mem.: Phi Beta Kappa. Republican. Office: Erickson & Sederstrom Regency Westpointe 10330 Regency Pkwy Dr Ste 100 Omaha NE 68114-3761 Office Phone: 402-397-7120. Business E-Mail: donstenberg@eslaw.com.

**STENBIT, JOHN PAUL,** former federal agency administrator; b. Oakland, Calif., June 1, 1940; s. Paul Charles and Antoinette (Inguglia) S.; m. Albertine Heederik, Aug. 19, 1966; children: Elisabeth Francesca, Antine Elaine. BS, Calif. Inst. Tech., 1961, MS, 1962; postgrad., Stanford U., 1981. Rsch. fellow Technische Hogesch., Eindhoven, The Netherlands, 1962-63, 65-67; engr. Aerospace Corp., El Segundo, Calif., 1962-68; prin. dep. dir. Office of Sec. US Dept. Def., Washington, 1973-77; engr. TRW, Redondo Beach, Calif., 1968—73, Fairfax, Va., 1977—2001; asst. sec. def. networks & info. integration (formerly command, control, comm. & intelligence) US Dept. Def., Washington, 2001—04. Mem. adv. bd. Dir. Naval Intelligence, Washington, 1982-91; mem. sci. adv. group Def. Communications Agy., Arlington, Va., 1989—; bd. dirs., Cogent Systems, 2004-, Loral Space & Communications Inc., 2006-; cons. Def. Sci. Bd., Washington. Chmn. Internat. Children's Festival, Fairfax, 1991-92. Recipient medal for outstanding pub. svc. Sec. Def., 1977; Fulbright fellow, The Netherlands, 1962-63, Aerospace Corp., The Netherlands, 1965-67. Mem. NAE, AIAA, Security Affairs Support Assn. (bd. dirs. 1990—), Electronic Industries Assn. (bd. dirs. 1991—), Armed Forces Communications and Electronics Assn., Va. Bus. Coun., Korean-Am. Bus. Coun., Met. Club (Washington). Republican.*

**STENCHEVER, MORTON ALBERT,** obstetrician, gynecologist; b. Paterson, NJ, Jan. 25, 1931; s. Harold and Lena (Suresky) Stenchever; m. Diane Bilsky, June 19, 1955 (dec. 1999); children: Michael A., Marc R., Douglas A.; m. Luba Kane, Sept. 8, 2001. AB, NYU, 1951; MD, U. Buffalo, 1956. Diplomate Am. Bd. Ob-gyn., 1965. Intern Mt. Sinai Hosp., 1956-57; resident obstetrics and gynecology Columbia-Presbyn. Med. Center, N.Y.C., 1957-60; asst. prof., Oglebey research fellow Case-Western Res. U., Cleve., 1962-66, asso. prof. dept. reproductive biology, 1967-70, dir. Tissue Culture Lab., 1965-70, coordinator Phase II Med. Sch. program, 1969-70; prof., chmn. dept. obstetrics-gynecology U. Utah Med. Sch., Salt Lake City, 1970-77; prof. ob-gyn. U. Wash. Sch. Medicine, Seattle, 1977-98; prof. emeritus, 1998—; chmn. dept. U. Wash. Sch. Medicine, Seattle, 1977-96. Chmn. test com. for ob-gyn. Nat. Bd. Med. Examiners, 1979-82; cons. in urogynecology Fedn. Internat. for Gynecology & Obstetrics, 1998—. Author: Labor: Workbook in Obstetrics, 1968, Labor: Workbook in Obstetrics, 2d edit., 1993, Human Sexual Behavior: A Workbook in Reproductive Biology, 1970, Human Cytogenics: A Workbook in Reproductive Biology, 1973, Introductory Gynecology: A Workbook in Reproductive Biology, 1974; co-author: Comprehensive Gynecology, 1987, Comprehensive Gynecology, 4th edit., 2001, Caring for the Older Woman, 1991, Health Care for the Older Woman, 1996, Office Gynecology, 1992, Office Gynecology, 2d edit., 1996, Good Health, Great Sex After 40: A Woman's Guide, 1997; sr. editor: Atlas of Gynecology, 5 vols., 1997—99, assoc. editor: Ob-Gyn., 1986—2001, Ob-Gyn. Survey; editor: Clinical Updates in Women's Health Care, 2001—, ACOG Clin. Review, 2001—; mem. editl. bd.: Western Jour. Medicine; contbr. articles to profl. jours. Served to capt. USAF, 1960-62. Fellow Am. Coll. Obstetricians and Gynecologists (com. on residency edn. 1974-80, learning resource commn. 1980-86, vice chmn. 1982-83, chmn. prolog self-assessment program 1982-86, vice chair com. health care for the underserved women 1995-97), Am. Assn. Obstetricians and Gynecologists, Am. Gynecol. Soc., Am. Gyencol. and Obstetrical Soc., Pacific Coast Ob-Gyn. Soc.; mem. AAAS, AMA, Am. Bd. Ob-Gyn. (bd. dir. 1988-2004, v.p. 1990-92, treas. 1992-96, chmn. 1996-98, mem. resident rev. com. 1993-97, chmn. divsn. female pelvic medicine/reconstructive surgery), Assn. Profs. Gynecology and Obstetrics (chmn. steering com. teaching methods in ob-gyn. 1970-79, v.p. 1975-76, pres. 1983-84, v.p. Found. 1986-87, pres. Found. 1987-91), Pacific N.W. Ob-Gyn. Soc., Wash. State Med. Assn., Seattle Gynec. Soc. (v.p. 1981, pres.-elect 1982, pres. 1982-83), Am. Soc. Human Genetics, Ctrl. Assn. Ob-Gyn., Soc. Gynecologic Investigation, Wash. State Obstet. Soc., Tissue Culture Assn., N.Y. Acad. Sci., Utah Ob-Gyn. Soc., Utah Med. Assn., Teratology Soc., Am. Fertility Soc., Internat. Pelvic Floor Dysfunction Soc. Home: 8301 SE 83rd St Mercer Island WA 98040-5644 Office: Ob-Gyn 130 Knickerson St Ste 211 Seattle WA 98109 Office Phone: 206-286-1775.

**STENDAHL, BRITA KRISTINA,** humanities educator, social studies educator; b. Stockholm, Jan. 10, 1925; came to U.S., 1954; d. Johan Victor and Ingeborg (Normann) Johnsson; m. Krister Stendahl, Sept. 7, 1946; children: Johan, Anna, Dan. Cand. Theology, Uppsala U., Sweden, 1949, cand. Philosophy, 1954, PhD (hon.), 1981. Hist. and lit. tchr. Gymnasium, Uppsala, Sweden, 1949-54; hist. and lit. tchr. extension program Harvard U., Cambridge, Mass., 1956-59, hist. and lit. tchr. freshman program, 1964-74; hist. and lit. tchr. seminar program Radcliffe Coll., Cambridge, 1976-84; cultural sec. Ch. of Sweden, Stockholm, 1984-88. Mem. Govt. Coun. for Coord. and Planning of Rsch., Stockholm, 1985-88. Author: (monographs) Søren Kierkegaard, 1976, The Force of Tradition, 1984, The Education of a Self-Made Woman, Fredrika Bremer, 1801-1865, 1994, (autobiography) Sabbatical Reflections, 1978; contbr. Multicultural Writers from Antiquity to 1945, 2002; book reviewer. Co-chair Fellowship in Israel for Arab-Jewish Youth, Boston, 1972-84, 88-95; bd. dirs. The Abraham Fund, N.Y.C., 1996—. Bunting fellow, Radcliffe Coll., Cambridge, Mass., 1961-63; assoc. fellow Henry A. Murray Ctr. at Radcliffe, 1981-82; recipient Myron B. Bloy award The Assn. for Religion and Intellectual Life, 1993. Mem. Arstasallskapet for Fredrika Bremer-Studier (chmn. 1985—89). Democrat. Lutheran. Avocations: walking, Tai Chi.

**STENDER, JULIA MAE,** mathematics educator; b. Greenfield, Iowa, Feb. 11, 1952; d. Virgil Clarence Boos and Grace Arlene Chapman; m. Kent Edwin Stender, Apr. 1, 1972; children: Kevin, Tamela, Rachel, Rana. BA, Buena Vista U., Council Bluffs, Iowa, 1993. H.S. math tchr. Cumberland-Massena Cmty., Iowa, 1995—2005, Anita Cmty. Sch., Iowa, 2005—. Mem.: NEA. Avocations: antiques, sewing, reading. Home: 72142 Tucson Rd Massena IA 50853 Office: Anita Cmty Sch 1000 Victory Park Anita IA 50020

**STENEHJEM, WAYNE KEVIN,** state attorney general, lawyer; b. Mohall, ND, Feb. 5, 1953; s. Martin Edward and Marguerite Mae (Peg) (McMaster) Stenehjem; m. Tama Lou Smith, June 19 (div. Apr. 1984); 1 child, Andrew; m. Beth D. Bakke, June 30, 1995. AA, Bismarck Jr. Coll., ND, 1972; BA, U. ND, 1974, JD, 1977. Bar: ND 1977. Ptnr. Kuchera & Stenehjem, Grand Forks, ND, 1977—2000; spl. asst. atty. gen. State of ND, 1983—87, atty. gen., 2000—; mem. ND Indsl. Commn., 2001—; chair RAGA, 2001—02; mem. ND Ho. Reps., 1976—80, ND State Senate, 1980—2000, pres. pro tempore, 1998—99; bd. Univ. and Sch. Lands, 2001—. Chmn. Senate Com. on Social Svcs., 1985—86, Senate Com. on Judiciary, 1995—2000, Interim Legis. Judiciary Commrs., 1995—2000, Legis. Coun., 1995—2000; mem. ND Legis. Coun. Commrs. on Uniform State Laws, 1995—2000, Gov.'s Com. on Juvenile Justice. Exec. bd. dirs. Northern Lights coun. Boy Scouts Am., 2005—; chmn. Dist. 42 Reps., Grand Forks, 1986—88; bd. dirs. Christus Rex Luth. Ch., pres., 1985—86; bd. dirs. no. lights coun. Boy Scouts Am., 2005—; bd. ND Spl. Olympics, 1985—89, Bismarck (N.D.) Mandan Big Bros. Big Sisters, 2001—. Named Champion of People's Right to Know, Sigma Delta Chi, 1979, ND Friend of Psychology, ND Psychol. Assn., 1990, Outstanding Young Man of ND, Jaycees, 1985; recipient Excellence in County Govt. award, ND Assn. Counties, 1991, Love Without Fear award, Bismarck Abused Adult Resource Ctr., 2003, Lone Eagle award, N.D. Peace Officers Assn., 2005, Public Svc. award, Lignite Energy

Coun., 2005. Mem.: Grand Forks County Bar Assn., N.D. State Bar Assn. (Legis. Svc. award 1995). Republican. Home: 1216 Crestview Ln Bismarck ND 58501 Office: Office of the Atty Gen State Capitol Bldg 600 E Boulevard Ave Bismarck ND 58505

**STENGEL, RICHARD,** editor; b. NYC, May 2, 1955; m. Mary Pfaff; 2 children. BA magna cum laude, Princeton U., 1977; student in English and History, Christ Church Oxford U., 1981. Staff writer Time Mag., NYC, 1981—83, assoc. ed., 1984—88, sr. writer, essayist, contbr., 1989—, mng. ed. Time.com, 2000, culture ed., nat. ed., mng. ed. 2006—; pres., CEO Nat. Constitution Ctr., Phila., 2004—06. Ferris prof. journalism, instr. course Politics and the Press Princeton U., 1998—99; senior adviser, chief speechwriter presidential candidate Bill Bradley, 1999. Author: January Sun: One Day, Three Lives, a South African Town, 1990; author: (with Nelson Mandela) Long Walk to Freedom, 1993; author: You're Too Kind: A Brief History of Flattery, 2000; co-prodr.: (documentaries) Mandela, 1995; writer (articles) The New Yorker, The New Republic, NY Times, and many other publications, TV commentator MSNBC, CNN. Rhodes Scholar. Office: Time Mag One Time Warner Ctr New York NY 10019-8016*

**STENGEL, ROBERT FRANK,** engineering and applied science educator; b. Orange, N.J., Sept. 1, 1938; s. Frank John and Ruth Emma (Geidel) S.; m. Margaret Robertson Ewing, Apr. 8, 1961; children: Brooke Alexandra, Christopher Ewing. SB, MIT, 1960; MS in Engring., Princeton U., 1965, MA, 1966, PhD, 1968. Aerospace technologist NASA, Wallops Island, Va., 1960-63; tech. staff group leader C.S. Draper Lab., Cambridge, Mass., 1968-73, Analytic Scis. Corp., Reading, Mass., 1973-77; assoc. prof. Princeton (N.J.) U., 1977-82, prof. engring. and applied sci., 1982—, assoc. dean engring., 1994-97. Cons. GM, Warren, Mich., 1985-94; mem. com. strategic tech. U.S. Army NRC, 1989-92; vice chmn. Congl. Aero. Adv. Com., Washington, 1986-89; mem. com. on trans-atmospheric vehicles USAF Sci. Adv. Bd., 1984-85; mem. com. on low altitude wind shear and its hazard to aviation Nat. Rsch. Coun., 1983, Navy Theater Missile Defense com. NRC, 2000-01. Author: Stochastic Optimal Control: Theory and Application, 1986, reprinted as Optimal Control and Estimation, 1994, Flight Dynamics, 2004; N.Am. editor Cambridge Aerospace Series, 1993—98; contbr. over 200 tech. papers to profl. publs.; patentee wind probing device. Lt. USAF, 1960—63. Recipient Apollo Achievement award NASA, 1969, Cert. of Commendation, MIT, 1969, Excellence in Aviation award FAA, 1997, John R. Ragazzini Edn. award, AACC, 2002. Fellow IEEE, AIAA (Mechanics and Control of Flight award 1997); mem. Inst. Advanced Study. Home: 329 Prospect Ave Princeton NJ 08540-5330 Office: Princeton U D202 Engineering Quadrangle Princeton NJ 08544-0001 Office Phone: 609-258-5103. Office Fax: 609-258-6109. Business E-Mail: stengel@princeton.edu.

**STENGEL, RONALD FRANCIS,** management consultant; b. Lock Haven, Pa., Oct. 18, 1947; s. Elmer S. and Elizabeth (Heivley) S.; m. Margaret Linda Dezack, Aug. 23, 1969. BSME, U. Pa., 1969, MBA, 1976. Mfg. engr. Control Data Corp., Valley Forge, Pa., 1969-70; mgr. mfg. svcs. Knoll Internat., East Greenville, Pa., 1970-75; ptnr. mgmt. cons. Touche Ross & Co., Phila., 1976-85; pres. RF Stengel & Co. Inc., Valley Forge, 1985—. Office Phone: 610-296-8950.

**STENHOUSE, EVERETT RAY,** clergy administrator; b. Minco, Okla., May 15, 1931; s. George E. and Jessie Loraine (Dean) S.; m. Alice Irene English, Aug. 22, 1948; children: Brenda Jones, Judy Lundberg, Stephen, Andrew. Student, U. Calif. Berkeley, U. Athens, 1969-71. Ordained to ministry Assemblies of God, 1955. Pastor Wayside Chapel, Bakersfield, Calif., 1955-59, Bethel Temple, Bakersfield, 1960-63; dist. dir. youth So. Calif. Dist. Assemblies of God, Costa Mesa, Calif., 1963-67; assoc. pastor 1st Assembly of God, San Diego, 1968-69; missionary Assemblies of God Fgn. Missions, Athens, Greece, 1969-73; pastor Bethany Ch., Alhambra, Calif., 1974-79; supt. So. Calif. Dist., Assemblies of God, Costa Mesa, 1979-85; asst. gen. supt. Gen. Coun. Assemblies of God, Springfield, Mo., 1986-94. Bd. adminstrn. Nat. Assn. Evangs., Wheaton, Ill., 1986-94, Pentecostal Fellowship of No. Am., Ont., Can., 1986-94; chmn., bd. dirs Assemblies of God Theol. Sem., Springfield, 1991-94, Ministers Benefit Assn., Springfield, 1986-94; bd. mem. Evangel L., 1986-94. Contbr. articles to various mags. Mem. Assemblies Of God Ch. Home: 77696 Westbrook Ct Palm Desert CA 92211-0416 Personal E-mail: erevev@aol.com.

**STENITZER, GEORGE IGNATIUS,** corporate communications specialist; b. Granite City, Ill., June 30, 1956; s. George Ignatius and Beatrice Marie (Cuenca) S.; m. Donna Dwyer, Jan. 16, 1982; children: Jody Bea, Jonathan Jacob. BA in English, Quincy Coll., 1977. Editor Alton (Ill.) Citizen, 1978-80; writer Sverdrup Corp., St. Louis, 1980-84; advt. mgr. Consol. Aluminum, St. Louis, 1984-85; mgr. advt. Southwestern Bell Telecom, St. Louis, 1985-90; corp. mgr. news rels. Southwestern Bell Corp., St. Louis, 1990-94; dir. corp. positioning Ameritech Corp., Chgo., 1994-99; v.p. corp. comm. R.R. Donnelley & Sons., Chgo., 1999-2000, Tellabs, Chgo., 2000—. Mem.: Bus. Mktg. Assn. (dir. Chgo. chpt. 2001—03, exec. v.p. 2002—03, pres. 2003—04), Pub. Rels. Soc. Am. (dir. Chgo. chpt. 2000—04), Nat. Investor Rels. Inst. (dir. Chgo. chpt. 2000—01), Bus. Profl. Advt. Assn. (mess. 1985—87, v.p. profl. devel. 1987—88, pres. 1988—89, pub. The St. Louis Bus. Profl. Advt. Assn. Communicator 1989—90). Roman Catholic. Business E-Mail: george.stenitzer@tellabs.com. E-mail: geo4747@yahoo.com.

**STENNETT, WILLIAM CLINTON (CLINT STENNETT),** television station executive, state legislator; b. Winona, Minn., Oct. 1, 1956; s. William Jessie and Carole Lee Stennett. BA in Journalism, Idaho State U., 1979. Gen. mgr. Wood River Jour., Hailey, Idaho, 1979-85, pres., pub.. 1985-87; pres. Sta. KSVT-TV, Ketchum, Idaho. Sta. KSKI-FM, Sun Valley, Idaho; mem. Idaho Ho. of Reps., Boise, 1990-94; mem., minority leader Idaho Senate, Dist. 25, Boise, 1996—. Named Legislator of Yr., Idaho Soil Conservation Dists., 1994, Idaho Wildlife Found., 1996, Idaho Assn. Recyclers, 2002, Idaho Profl. Firefighters Assn., 2002; recipient Gen. Excellence award, Idaho Newspaper Assn., 1985, 1986—87. Mem.: Idaho Broadcasters (bd. dirs.), Ketchum Sun Valley C. of C. (bd. dirs. 1990—95), Rotary. Democrat. Office Phone: 208-332-1000.

**STENT, ANGELA E.,** political scientist, educator, director; b. London, Feb. 24, 1947; arrived in U.S., 1970; d. Ronald Walter and Gabriele Stent; m. Daniel H. Yergin, Aug. 10, 1975; children: Alexander Yergin, Rebecca Yergin. BA in Econs. and History with honors, Cambridge U., Eng., 1969; MSc with distinction, London Sch. Econs., 1970; AM in Soviet Studies, Harvard U., 1972, PhD in Govt., 1977. Assoc. prof. dept. govt. Georgetown U., Washington, 1983—, prof. dept. govt. and Sch. Fgn. Svc., 1998—, dir. Ctr. for Eurasian, Russian and East European Studies, 2001—; nat. intelligence officer for Russia and Eurasia, Nat. Intelligence Coun., Washington, 2004—05. Sr. policy advisor Office Policy Planning U.S. Dept. State, Washington, 1999—2001; adv. bd. U.S.-Russia Bus. Coun., Women in Internat. Security, Am. Inst. for Contemporary German Studies. Author: From Embargo to Ostpolitik, 1981, Russia and Germany Reborn, 1999; contbr. articles to profl. jours. Mem.: Coun. Fg. Rels. N.Y., Cosmos Club. Office: Ctr for Eurasian Russian and East European Studies Georgetown Univ Washington DC 20057

**STENT, GUNTHER SIEGMUND,** molecular biologist, educator; b. Berlin, Mar. 28, 1924; came to U.S., 1940, naturalized, 1945; s. George and Elizabeth (Karfunkelstein) S.; m. Inga Loftsdottir, Oct. 21, 1951; 1 son, Stefan Loftur. BS, U. Ill., 1945, PhD, 1948; DSc (hon.), York U., 1984. Research asst. U. Ill., 1945-48; research fellow Calif. Inst. Tech., 1948-50, U. Copenhagen, Denmark, 1950-51, Pasteur Inst. Paris, France, 1951-52; asst. research biochemist U. Calif., Berkeley, 1952-56, faculty, 1956—, prof. molecular biology, 1959-94; prof. emeritus, 1994—; prof. arts and scis. U. Calif., 1967-68, chmn. molecular biology, 1980-86, chmn. molecular and cell biology, 1987-92, dir. virus lab., 1980-86. Document analyst U.S. Field Info. Agy. Tech., 1946-47; mem. genetics panel NIH, 1959-64, NSF, 1965-68; fellow Inst. Advanced Studies, Berlin, 1985-90. Author: Papers On Bacterial Viruses, 2d edit., 1966, Molecular Biology of Bacterial Viruses, 1963, Phage and the Origin of Molecular Biology, 1966, The Coming of the Golden Age, 1969, Function and Formation of Neural Systems, 1977, Morality as a Biological Phenomenon, 1978, Paradoxes of Progress, 1978, Molecular Genetics, 2d edit., 1978, Nazis, Women and Molecular Biology, 1998, Paradoxes of Free Will, 2002; mem. editl. bd. Jour. Molecular Biology, 1965-68, Genetics, 1963-68, Zeitschrift für Vererbungslehre, 1962-68, Ann. Revs. Genetics, 1965-69, Ann. Revs. Microbiology, 1966-70, Jour. Neurosci., 1988-96; contbr. aricles to profl. jours. Merck fellow NRC, 1948-54; sr. fellow NSF, 1960-61; Guggenheim fellow, 1969-70; Fogarty Resident scholar NIH, 1990-92. Mem. NAS, Am. Acad. Arts and Scis., Soc. Neurosci., Am. Philos. Soc., Acad. Scis. and Lit. of Mainz (Germany), European Acad. Scis. and Arts. Home: 145 Purdue Ave Kensington CA 94708-1032 Office Phone: 510-642-5214. Business E-Mail: stent@berkeley.edu.

**STENT, TERRY,** pilot, art collector; m. Margaret Stent. BA, Yale Univ., 1961; MBA, Harvard Univ., 1968. Pilot Delta Air Lines, 1970—97. Dir. Callanwolde Fine Arts Ctr., Atlanta, 1983—86; mem. bd. commr. & Art Forum Smithsonian Am. Art Mus., Washington, chmn. bd. commr., 1999—2003; mem. Art Collectors group High Mus. Art, Atlanta, 1993—, dir., 1997—, chmn. collections com., 1999—2001, bd. chmn., 2001—. Fighter pilot USS Coral Sea USN, Vietnam. Decorated nine Air Combat medals; named one of Top 200 Collectors, ARTnews Mag., 2004. Avocation: collector of 19th & 20th century art, especially Hudson River School, Ashcan School & American Realism. Mailing: High Museum of Art 1280 Peachtree St NE Atlanta GA 30309

**STENWICK, MICHAEL WILLIAM,** retired internist, geriatrician, consultant; b. Red Wing, Minn., Nov. 12, 1941; s. Vincent Ferdinand and Geraldine Frances (Veith) S.; m. Judith Ann Nelson, June 10, 1961; children: Scott Michael, Gregg William. BS cum laude, Hamline U., 1963; MD, U. Minn., 1969. Diplomate Am. Bd. Internal Medicine. Fellow dept. pharmacology U. Minn., Mpls., 1966-68; intern in internal medicine Northwestern Hosp., Mpls., 1969-70, resident in internal medicine, 1970-73; sr. internist internal medicine sect. Bloomington Lake Clinic, Mpls., 1973—2000; ret., 2000. Bd. dirs. Bloomington Lake Clinic, Mpls., pres. 1977, v.p. 1989-97, fin. com., 1987—, chmn. properties, 1984—, chmn. trustees profit sharing; med. adviser Kimberly Quality Care, St. Paul, 1990-94; internal medicine cons. Fairview Multiple Sclerosis Ctr. and Rehab. Unit, Mpls., 1986-91; informal adviser internal medicine sect. Minn. Relative Value Index, Mpls., 1971; mem. task force Riverside Med. Ctr., Mpls., 1988-91, chmn. critical care com., 1986-91; reviewer quality assurance subcom., 1989-90. Contbr. articles to profl. jours. Mem., co-organizer, 1st pres. Cyrus Barnum Soc., U. Minn. Med. Sch., Mpls.; bd. dirs. Signal Inn Beach and Racquetball Club, Sanibel Island, Fla., 1983-84, 89-98, Signal Inn Condominium Assn., Sanibel Island, 1983-84, 89-98; co-emcee Nursing Talent Show, Northwestern Hosp., Mpls., 1969; 1st med. dir. Beltrami Health Ctr., Mpls., 1970-72. Recipient scholarship Charles and Alora Allis Found., 1960-63, Walter Kenyon award, 1963, grant U. Minn., 1963. Fellow ACP; mem. AMA, Am. Soc. Internal Medicine, Minn. Med. Assn., Hennepin County Med. Assn., Mpls. Soc. Internal Medicine, Minn. Acad. Medicine. Republican. Lutheran. Achievements include research in drug specificity that could be defined even in an alkylating agent; providing evidence for an active role of the choroid plexus in distributing and concentrating morphine in the brain. Office: Bloomington Lake Clinic 3017 Bloomington Ave Minneapolis MN 55407-1771

**STENZ, LISA ANN,** reading specialist; b. Windham, Conn., Mar. 4, 1971; d. Arnie and Cindy Bubucis; m. Greg Stenz, Aug. 7, 1999. BS in Spl. Edn., West Chester U., 1993, MS in Edn., 2001; cert. K-12 prin., Immaculata U., 2005. Cert. reading specialist 2001. Elem. learning support tchg. Vanguard Sch., Paoli, Pa., 1994—96, Child and Career Devel. Ctr., Chester County Intermediate Unit, Downingtown, Pa., 1996—2001, reading specialist, 2001—. Adj. instr. Immaculata (Pa.) U., 2005; trainer the trainer cert. Project Read Lang. Cir. PHonology Strand, Minn. Recipient Outstanding Svc. award, Chester County Intermediate Unit, 2001. Mem.: ASCD. Home: 120 Irwin Dr Lincoln University PA 19352 Office: Child and Career Devel Ctr 1525 E Lincoln Hwy Coatesville PA 19320

**STENZEL, MARY FRANCIS,** social worker; b. Milw., Apr. 9, 1960; d. Joseph Edward and Betty Josephine (Andracki) Gronowski; m. Paul Anthony Stenzel, Oct. 17, 1997. BSW, Marian Coll., 1982; MBA, Cardinal Stritch Coll. U., 1992. Geriatric social worker various nursing homes, Milw., 1984—86; youth care specialist Child and Adolescent Treatment Ctr., Milw. County, 1988—94. Pres. Milw. Area Self Help W. Milw., 1997—. Cpl. USMC, 1976—80. Mem.: Brain Injury Assn. (mem. Brain Injury Support Group). Roman Catholic. Avocations: crafts, gardening, scrapbooks, woodworking. Home: 3115 W Plaza Dr Franklin WI 53132 Office Phone: 414-761-3186.

**STEP, EUGENE LEE,** retired pharmaceutical executive; b. Sioux City, Iowa, Feb. 19, 1929; s. Harry and Ann (Keiser) S.; m. Hannah Scheuermann, Dec. 27, 1953; children: Steven Harry, Michael David, Jonathan Allen. BA in Econs., U. Nebr., 1951; MS in Acctg. and Fin., U. Ill., 1952. With Eli Lilly Internat. Corp., London and Paris, 1964-69, dir. Elanco Internat. Indpls., 1969-70, v.p. marketing, 1970-72, v.p Europe, 1972; v.p. mktg. Eli Lilly and Co., Indpls., 1972-73, pres. pharm. div., 1973-86, exec. v.p., 1986—. Bd. dirs. Ceregene, Cell-Genesys. 1st lt. U.S. Army, 1953-56. Mem. Pharm. Mfrs. Assn. (bd. dirs. 1980-92, chmn. 1989-90), Internat. Pharm. Mfrs. Assn. (pres. 1991-92). Home: PO Box 8997 Rancho Santa Fe CA 92067-8997 Office Phone: 858-759-8958.

**STEPAK, ASA MARTIN,** writer, linguist; b. Bklyn., Nov. 23, 1950; s. Louis and Anna (Leyter) S. BA cum laude, NYU, 1973. Author: Southern Rhapsody, 1995, Southern Heritage Potpourri, 1995, Southern Heritage Revisited: A Compendium of Behind the Scene E-mail's, 2000, Music: Primordial Birdsong, 2001, Linguistics: Oral Metaphor Construct, Knowledge Inheritance, 2002, Fundamental Basis of Sentence Competency and Word Order, 2003, Symbiotic Competiveness, 2003, A Recipe for Peace, 2003-04, Frequency Value Grammar, 2004, Entropy as a Formal Method, 2005.

**STEPAN, FRANK QUINN,** chemicals executive; b. Chgo., Oct. 24, 1937; s. Alfred Charles and Mary Louise (Quinn) S.; m. Jean Finn, Aug. 23, 1958; children: Jeanne, Frank Quinn, Todd, Jennifer, Lisa, Colleen, Alfred, Richard. AB, U. Notre Dame, 1959; MBA, U. Chgo., 1963. Salesman Indsl. Chems. div. Stepan Chem. Co., Northfield, Ill., 1961-63, mgr. internat. dept., 1964-66, v.p. corporate planning, 1967-69, v.p., gen. mgr., 1970-73, pres., 1973-84; pres., chmn., CEO Stepan Co., Northfield, Ill., 1984-99, chmn., CEO, 1999—2005, chmn., 2006—. Bd. dirs. Am. Chemistry Coun. Mem. liberal arts coun. Notre Dame U., 1972—; bd. dirs. Big Shoulders, Chgo. 1st lt. AUS, 1959-61. Mem. Soap and Detergent Assn. (bd. dirs., exec. com., chmn.), Ill. Bus. Roundtable (policy com., sec.), Econ. Club Chgo., Exmoor Country Club, Bob O'Link Golf Club, Everglades Club, Sailfish Club Fla. Home: 200 Linden St Winnetka IL 60093-3862 Office: Stepan Co Edens & Winnetka Rds Northfield IL 60093

**STEPAN, FRANK QUINN, JR., (F. QUINN STEPAN JR.),** chemical company executive; b. 1960; married; 3 children. BA, U. Notre Dame, 1982; MBA, U. Chgo., 1988. With Monsanto Co., 1983—87, Stepan Co., Northfield, Ill., 1987—, v.p., gen. mgr. Surfactant dept., 1999—2005, CEO, 2005—. Dir. Follett Corp.; bd. dirs. Soap and Detergent Assn., Am. Chem Coun. Office: Stepan Co 22 W Frontage Rd Northfield IL 60093 Office Phone: 847-446-7500, 847-501-2100.*

**STEPANEK, CURTIS E,** electrical engineer; s. Leroy B. and Shirley B. Stepanek; m. Edna P. Stepanek, June 2, 1980; children: Tara K., Mark E. BSEE, U. Mo., Columbia, 1979, MSEE, 1980. Lic. Profl. Engr. (PE), Mo., 1984. Subtransmission bulk substitution planning engr. Union Electric Co., Saint Louis, 1980—87, transmission interconnections planning engr., 1987—96; supervising transmission planning engr. Ameren Svcs. Co., Saint Louis, 1996—98, prin. transmission planning engr., 1998—. Chmn. expansion planning working group Midwest Ind. Sys. Operator, Carmel, Ind., 2004—05. Chmn. Maryland Heights Stormwater Com., Mo., 1996—. Named Vol. of Yr., City of Maryland Heights, Mo., 1998. Mem.: IEEE, Tau Beta Pi. Avocations: baseball, music. Home: 11914 Glenridge Dr Maryland Heights MO 63043 Office: Ameren Services Co One Ameren Plz Saint Louis MO 63166

**STEPANEK, DAVID LESLIE,** financial services company executive; b. Atchison, Kans., Oct. 1, 1929; s. Henry William and Helen Louise (Howarth) S.; m. Carmen Mercedes Comez, Aug. 22, 1960; children: Karen L. Barrow, James W. BS in Petroleum Engring., U. Calif., Berkeley, 1952; MBA in Fin., UCLA, 1962. CFP, registered investment advisor. Petroleum engr. Creole Petroleum Corp., Venezuela, 1952—64, mgr. budget dept., 1964—66, mgr. planning sect., 1966—69; sr. advisor in prodn. dept. Exxon Corp., N.Y.C., 1969—77, sr. advisor in coal dept. Coral Gables, Fla., 1977—82, mgr. planning dept. Abu Dhabi, United Arab Emirates, 1983—87; pres. DLS Tax Preparation, Inc. and DLS Fin. Planning, Inc., Thomasville, Ga., 1989—; franchise owner H & R Block franchises, Thomasville, Quitman, Cairo, 1991—. Republican. Avocations: tennis, golf. Home: 225 Primo Dr Fort Myers Beach FL 33931-2732 Office: H R Block 15036 US Highway 19 S Thomasville GA 31757-4819 E-mail: dlstepanek@netscape.net.

**STEPANEK, JOSEPH EDWARD,** real estate developer, consultant; b. Ellinwood, Kans., Oct. 29, 1917; s. Joseph August and Leona Mae (Wilson) S.; m. Antoinette Farnham, June 10, 1942; children: Joseph F., James B., Antoinette L., Debra L. BSChemE, U. Colo., 1939; DEng in Chem. Engring., Yale U., 1942. Registered profl. engr., Colo. Engr. Stearns-Roger Mfg., Denver, 1939-45; from asst. to assoc. prof. U. Colo., Boulder, 1945-47; from cons. to dir. UN, various countries, 1947-73; cons. internat. indsl devel., U.S.-China bus. relations Boulder, 1973—. Bd. dirs. 12 corps., 1973—. Author 3 books on indsl. devel.; contbr. 50 articles to profl. jours. Exec. dir. Boulder Tomorrow, 1965-67. Recipient Yale Engring. award Yale Engring. Assn., 1957, Norlin award U. Colo. 1978, Annual award India League of Am., 1982. Mem. AAAS. Democrat. Unitarian Universalist. Avocation: ranching. Home: 11679 Gold Hill Rd Boulder CO 80302-9789 Personal E-mail: jestepanek@worldnet.att.net.

**ŠTĚPÁNEK, PETR,** computer science educator; b. Pardubice, Czech Republic, Jan. 24, 1943; s. Otakar and Ludmila (Brabcová) Š.; m. Olga Burešová, Dec. 19, 1970; children: Kateřina Barbora. Promovaný matematik, Charles U., Prague, 1965, RNDr, 1968, postgrad., 1973, DSc in Logic, 1991. Asst. prof. computer sci. Charles U., Prague, 1965-87, assoc. prof., 1987-98, prof., 1998—, head dept. theoretical computer sci. and math. logic, 2000—. Free-lance cons., Prague, 1992—. Author: Mathematical Logic Set Theory, 1982. Mem. Fed. Assembly, Prague, 1992; chmn. Dist. Orgn. Civic Dem. Party, Prague, 1993-95. Rsch. grantee Ministry Edn., Prague, 1993, Czech Grant Agy., Prague, 1996—. Mem. Am. Math. Soc., Assn. Symbolic Logic, Assn. Logic Programming (hon.), Info. Soc. (Czech forum 2000—). Mem. Civic Democratic party. Office Phone: 420 221 914 243. Business E-Mail: petr.stepanek@mff.cuni.cz.

**STEPANSKI, ANTHONY FRANCIS, JR.,** computer company executive; b. Jersey City, June 29, 1941; s. Anthony Francis and Georgette Stepanski; m. Jane Ellen Schuler, Sept. 5, 1965; children: Matthew A.W., Melinda Kate. BA in Physics, Clark U., 1963. Sales rep. IBM Corp., NYC, 1964-68; from sales rep. to sr. v.p. AGS Computers, Inc., NYC, 1968-82, Mountainside, NJ, 1968—82, exec. v.p., 1982-93; pres., CEO AGS Info. Services, Inc., Mountainside, 1986-93; also bd. dirs. AGS Computers, Inc., a NYNEX Co., Mountainside; pres., CEO Origin Tech., N.A. (subs. Orign BV/Amsterdam, Netherlands), 1994—97; mng. dir. Melmatt Ptnrs., LLP, 1998; CEO, bd. mem. IZODIA, plc, London, 2001—02. Trustee Clark U., Worcester, Mass., 1987-99, Children's Specialized Hosp. Found., Mountainside, 1989-96; bd. dirs. Westchester Artificial Kidney Ctr., Valhalla, N.Y., 1982-97, Westfield Symphony Orch., N.J., 1983-96. Served with USAR, 1964-70.

**STEPEHENS, J.T. See STEPHENS, JAMES**

**STEPHAN, ALEXANDER FRIEDRICH,** German language and literature educator; b. Lüdenscheid, Fed. Republic Germany, Aug. 16, 1946; arrived in US, 1968; s. Eberhard and Ingeborg (Hörnig) S.; m. Halina Konopacka, Dec. 15, 1969; 1 child, Michael. MA, U. Mich., 1969; PhD, Princeton U., 1973. Instr. German Princeton (NJ) U., 1972-73; from asst. prof. to prof. German UCLA, 1973-85; prof. German U. Fla., Gainesville, 1985-2000, chmn., 1985-93; prof. German, Ohio Eminent scholar, sr. fellow Mershon Ctr., Ohio State U., 2000—. Author: Christa Wolf, 1976, Die deutsche Exilliteratur, 1979, Christa Wolf (Forschungsbericht), 1981, Max Frisch, 1983, Anna Seghers im Exil, 1993, Im Visier des FBI, 1995, paperback edit. 1998, English transl. Communazis, 2000, Anna Seghers: Das sieben Kreuz. Welt und Wirkung eines Romans, 1997; editor: Peter Weiss: Die Ästhetik des Widerstands, 1983, 3d edit., 1990, Exil. Literatur und die Künste, 1990, Exil-Studien, 1993—, Christa Wolf: The Author's Dimension, 1993, 2d edit., 1995, Themes and Structures, 1997, Uwe Johnson: Speculations about Jakob and Other Writings, 2000, Early 20th Century German Fiction, 2003, Anna Seghers, Die Entscheidung, 2003, Americanism and Anti-Americanism. The German Encounter with American Culture after 1945, 2004, Exile and Otherness: New Approaches to the Experience of the Nazi Refugees, 2005, The Americanization of Europe: Culture, Diplomacy, and Anti-Americanism After 1945, 2006; co-editor: Studies in GDR Culture and Society, 1981—90, Schreiben im Exil, 1985, The New Sufferings of Young Werther and Other Stories from the GDR, 1997, Rot=Braun? Brecht Dialog, 2000, Nationalsozialismus und Stalinismus bei Brecht und Zeitgenossen, 2000, Jeans, Rock und Vietnam. Amerikanische Kultur in der DDR, 2002, Refuge and Reality: Feuchtwanger and the European Emigres in California, 2005, Das Amerika der Autoren von Kafka bis, 2006; co-prodr.: (TV films) Im Visier des FBI, 1995, Das FBI und Marlene Dietrich, 2000, Das FBI und Brechts Telephon, 2002, Exilanten und das OSS, 2002, Thomas Mann und der CIA, 2002. Grantee, NEH, 1974, 1984, 1997, Am. Coun. Learned Socs., 1976, 1977, 1984, Am. Philos. Soc., 1979, 1981, 1992, Humboldt Found., 1988, 1994, 1998—99, 2002—03, Guggenheim Found., 1989, German Acad. Exch. Svcs., 1993, 1997, Feuchtwanger Meml. Libr., 1998, Weichmann Stiftung, 1998, Transcoop/AvH, 2002—04; Fulbright Sr. Specialist, 2005—. Mem.: German PEN, German Assn. for Am. Studies, German Studies Assn., Internat. Anna Seghers Soc., Soc. Exile Studies. Office: Ohio State U Dept Germanic Lang Lit 498 Hagerty Columbus OH 43210-1340 Office Phone: 614-247-6068. Business E-Mail: stephan.30@osu.edu.

**STEPHAN, JOHN JASON,** historian, educator; b. Chgo., Mar. 8, 1941; s. John Walter and Ruth (Walgreen) S.; m. Barbara Ann Brooks, June 22, 1963. BA. Harvard U., MA, 1964; PhD, U. London, 1969. Rsch. assoc. Social Sci. Ctr., Waseda U., Tokyo, 1969—70; mem. faculty U. Hawaii, Honolulu, 1970—, prof. history, 1977—2001, emeritus prof. history, 2001—, chmn. East Asian studies program, 1973—74, dir. program on Soviet Union in Pacific-Asia region, 1986—88. Rsch. prof. Japan Found.; fellow U. Hokkaido, 1976-77; vis. prof. Inst. of Far East, Moscow, 1982, Inst. Econ. Rsch., Khabarovsk, USSR, 1982-83, Stanford U., 1986, Kennan Inst. for Advanced Studies, 1987; adj. rsch. assoc. East-West Ctr., 1988-92; Sanwa disting. lectr. Tufts U. Fletcher Sch. Law and Diplomacy, 1989. Author: Sakhalin: A History, 1971, The Kuril Islands: Russo-Japanese Frontier in the Pacific, 1974, The Russian Fascists, 1978, Hawaii Under the Rising Sun, 1984, Soviet-American Horizons on the Pacific, 1986, The Russian Far East, 1994. Sr. assoc. mem. St. Antony's Coll., Oxford (Eng.) U., 1977; Bd. dirs. Library Internat. Relations, Chgo., 1976-87; Hawaii rep. U.S.-Japan Friendship Commn., 1980-83. Recipient Kenneth W. Baldridge prize Hawaii chpt. Phi Alpha Theta, 1996; Fulbright fellow, 1967-68; Asia Found. grantee, 1974. Mem. AAUP, Am. Hist. Assn., Am. Assn. Advancement Slavic Studies, Assn. Asian Studies, Authors Guild, Internat. House of Japan, Can. Hist. Assn.

Home: 4334 Round Top Dr Honolulu HI 96822-5021 Office: U Hawaii Dept History 2530 Dole St Honolulu HI 96822-2303 Office Phone: 808-956-9600. Business E-Mail: stephan@hawaii.edu.

**STEPHAN, KENNETH C.,** state supreme court justice; b. Omaha, Oct. 8, 1946; m. Sharon Ross, Apr. 19, 1969; 3 children. BA, U. Nebr., 1968, JD with high distinction, 1972. Bar: Nebr. Atty. pvt. practice, 1973-97; judge Nebr. Supreme Ct., Lincoln, 1997—. With U.S. Army, 1969—71. Mem.: Am. Coll. Trial Lawyers (jud. fellow). Office: Nebr Supreme Ct State Capitol Bldg Rm 2211 PO Box 98910 Lincoln NE 68509-8910 Office Phone: 402-471-3737. E-mail: kstephan@nsc.state.ne.us.

**STEPHAN, PAUL BROOKE, III,** law educator; b. Somerville, NJ, 1950; BA, Yale U., 1973, MA, 1974; JD, U. Va., 1977. Bar: DC 1979, Va. 1982. Law clk. to Hon. Levin H. Campbell US Ct. Appeals 1st Cir., Boston, 1977—78; law clk. to Hon. Lewis F. Powell, Jr. US Supreme Ct., Washington, 1978—79; asst. prof. U. Va. Sch. Law, 1979—83, assoc. prof., 1983—85, prof., 1985—91, Percy Brown, Jr. prof., 1991—2003, Barron F. Black rsch. prof., 1996—99, now Lewis F. Powell, Jr. prof. law, also Hunton & Williams rsch. prof. Vis. prof. U. Vienna, 1998, Lausanne U., 2001, U. Pantheon-Assas, Paris, 2004; vis. lectr. Melbourne U., 2002, 04. Co-editor (with B. Klimenko): International Law and International Security: Military and Political Dimensions: A US-Soviet Dialogue, 1991; co-editor: (with S. Frankowski) Legal Reform in Post-Communist Europe: The View from Within, 1995; co-author (with D. Wallace, Jr. and J. Roin): International Business and Economics: Law and Policy, 1993, 1996; co-author: (with F. Parisi and B. DePoorter) The Law and Economics of the European Union, 2003. Office: U Va Sch Law 580 Massie Rd Charlottesville VA 22903-1789 Office Phone: 434-924-7098. E-mail: pbs@virginia.edu.

**STEPHANI, NANCY JEAN,** social worker, journalist; b. Garden City, Mich., Feb. 19, 1955; d. Ernest Helmut Schulz and Margaret Mary Fowler Thompson; m. Edward Jeffrey Stephani, Aug. 29, 1975; children: Edward J., Margaret J., James E. AA, Northwood Inst., Midland, Mich., 1975; student in theology, Boston Coll., 1991; BS summa cum laude, Lourdes Coll., Sylvania, Ohio, 1992; MSW, Ohio State U., 1995. Lic. ind. social worker; cert. cognitive behavioral therapist, master addictions counselor. Profl. facilitator Parents United, Findlay, Ohio, 1989-94; contbg. writer Cath. Chronicle, Toledo, 1988-95; mem. ministry formation faculty Cath. Diocese of Toledo, 1992-96; crisis intervention specialist John C. Hutson Ctr., 1994-98; contbg. writer Sunset Gazette, Findlay, Ohio, 1996-98; mgr. Century Health Svcs., Findlay, Ohio, 1998, dir. emergency mental health svcs., 1998—, co-chair strategic planning action team, 1999-00; prof., field coord. MSW program Ohio State U., Lima, 2000—. Social work clinician Family Svc. Hancock County, coord. clin. svcs. Family Svc., 1997—98, Blanchard Valley Home Health Social Svc.; trustee, bd. dirs. Hope House for Homeless, Findlay, 1990—99, v.p., 1996—97, pres., 1997—99; mem. Hancock County Cluster on Elderly; v.p., pres. parish coun. St. Michael Parish, Findlay, 1985—89, adult edn. coord., 1986—93, mem. strategic plan core com., 1989—91; program planning com. Family Life Conf., Cath. Diocese, 1994—95, mem. accreditation com. ministry formation dept.; profl. facilitator Hope Plus Program through Hancock County Common Pleas Ct., 1996—; coord. critical incident stress mgmt. team Hancock County, 1997—; profl. facilitator Hancock County Survivors of Suicide group, 1997—2000; coord. Hancock County Survivors of Suicide Group, 1997—; field instr. dept. social work U. Findlay, Ohio, 1996—, mem. social work adv. coun., 1998—, adj. faculty, 2003—; field instr. Capital U., Bowling Green State U., Heidelberg U., 1997—98; mem. adj. faculty Owens Tech. Coll., Findlay; trustee City Mission, 2000—04; co-program coord., field edn. coord. MSW program Ohio State U., Lima, 2001—; profl. facilitator Persons Affected by a Loved one's Suicide, 2002—. Founder Food Coop., MPBA, Findlay, 1981; founding mem. Chopin Hall, Findlay, 1983; mem. Hancock County AIDS Task Force, 1994-98; strategic planning com. mem., co-chair goal setting com. Findlay Pub. Schs., 1994, steering com., Call to Action Northwest Ohio, 1997—; trustee City Mission, 1999—; clin. dir. Hancock County CISM Team; mem. Red Cross Disaster Svcs. Team. Nat. Inst. Food Svcs. grantee, 1974; Diocese of Toledo grantee, 1991; Ohio State U. Coll. Social Work grantee, 1994. Mem. NOW, NASW (ethics com. Ohio 1997—, v.p. bd. trustees 2000-02, nat. com. on nominations and leadership 2001—, region VII rep. nat. leadership identification com. 2001-04, treas.-elect 2003—, program planning com., Social Worker of Yr. Region 1, 2000), AAUW (legis. chair Findlay chpt.), Internat. Critical Incident Stress Found., Am. Assn. on Child Abuse, Transpsychol. Assn., Friends of Creation Spirituality, Cognitive/Behavioral Profl. Soc., Call to Action, Pax Christi, Women in Ch. Leadership, Green Cross (clin. mem.). Avocations: jogging, hiking, cooking, travel. Home: 2615 Goldenrod Ln Findlay OH 45840-1025 Office Phone: 419-422-3711. E-mail: NancyStephani@hotmail.com.

**STEPHANOPOULOS, GEORGE ROBERT,** political reporter; b. Fall River, Mass., Feb. 10, 1961; s. Robert and Nikki C. Stephanopolous; m. Alexandra Wentworth, Nov. 20, 2001; children: Elliott Anastasia, Harper Andrea. BA in Polit. Sci. summa cum laude, Columbia U., 1982; MA in Theology, Oxford U., 1986. Adminstrv. asst. rep. Edward Feighan, Washington; dep. comm. dir. Dukakis Bentsen campaign, 1988; exec. floor mgr. to House Majority leader Gephardt, Washington; dir. Clinton/Gore campaign, Little Rock, 1992, The White House, Washington, 1992—96, sr. advisor to the Pres. of U.S., 1993-96; vis. prof. polit. sci. Columbia U., NYC, 1997; contbr. & corr. ABC News, 1997—, chief Washington corr., 2005—; host This Week with George Stephanopoulos, 2002—. Author: All Too Human, 1999. Recipient Medal of Excellence, Columbia U., 1993; Rhodes Scholar, Oxford U. Mem.: Phi Beta Kappa. Democrat. Greek Orthodox. Address: 1717 DeSales St NW Washington DC 20036*

**STEPHEN, RALPH ARCHIBALD,** geophysicist, researcher; b. Toronto, Ontario, Canada, Feb. 18, 1951; s. James Alexander and Carrie Patricia (Taylor) Stephen; m. Mary Ellen Moffett, May 25, 1974; children: Moffett Alexander, Emily Patricia. BASc, U. Toronto, Canada, 1974; PhD, U. Cambridge, England, 1978. Asst. scientist Woods Hole Oceanog. Instn., Mass., 1978—82, assoc. scientist, 1982—86, assoc. scientist with tenure, 1986—90, sr. scientist, 1990—. Pres. and CEO RASCON Assocs., West Falmouth, Mass., 1982—. Contbr. scientific papers to field. Fellow: Acoustical Soc. Am.; mem.: Royal Astron. Soc., Soc. Exploration Geophysicists, Seismol. Soc. Am., Am. Geophys. Union, Hawks Club. Office: Woods Hole Oceanographic Instn MS#24 360 Woods Hole Rd Woods Hole MA 02543-1542 Office Phone: 508-289-2583. Office Fax: 508-457-2150. E-mail: rstephen@whoi.edu.

**STEPHENS, ANNA JO,** finance educator; d. Roy Leonis and Peggy Jo Stephens. BA, Lyon Coll., Batesville, 1987; MBA, Ark. State U., Jonesboro, 1996. Master certified internet webmaster designer Prosoft Learning Corp., Ariz., 2001, cert. CIW instr. Prosoft Learning Corp., Ariz., 2001, MOUS master cert. Microsoft, Wash., 2000, cert. MOUS master instr. Microsoft, Wash., 2000. Asst. instr. U. Ark. C.C., Batesville, 1993—96, computer specialist, 1996—2000, bus. instr., 2000—. Mem. student affairs com. U. Ark. C.C., Batesville, 2000—02, mem. curriculum com., 2004—04, mem. faculty affairs com., 2004—, v.p. faculty senate, 2005—. Mem. Lebanon Missionary Bapt. Ch., Smithville, Ark., 1993—2006. Home: 58 Stanfield Rd Smithville AR 72466 Office: University of Arkansas Community College 2005 White Dr Batesville AR 72501 Office Phone: 870-793-7581.

**STEPHENS, ANNE CATHERINE,** special education educator; b. Miles City, Mont., Sept. 23, 1979; d. James Donley and Connie Hecker Stephens; 1 child, Hayden James. B in Elem. Edn., No. Ariz U., Flagstaff, 2001, B in Spl. Edn., 2001, M in Elem. Edn., 2002. Spl. edn. tchr. Kingman Acad. Learning, Ariz., 2001—. Mem. child study team KADL, Kingman, Ariz., 2001—; guest spkr. psychology class No. Ariz. U., Kingman, 2001—. Office: Kingman Acad Learning 2299 Beverly Ave Kingman AZ 86401

**STEPHENS, B. CONSUELA,** minister, consultant; b. Bklyn., May 12, 1947; d. Montiphus (Mortimer King) DeReyes and Bernadine Whitley. PhD Religion, Clayton Theol. Inst., 1983. Pastor Chenaniah Missionary Ch., Hollis, NY, 1986—. Cons. Chenaniah Missionary Ch., Hollis, United States, 1986—. Author: (book) Behold, I Shew You A Mystery, 1998. Dir. CASE Group, Inc., 2003—. Avocation: gardening. Home: 515 Mount Prospect Ave Newark NJ 07104-2964 E-mail: consuelastephens@yahoo.com.

**STEPHENS, BART NELSON,** former foreign service officer; b. Norfolk, Va., May 29, 1922; s. Bart Dannelly and Lura Lee (Cannon) S.; m. Barrett Krausz, Jan. 7, 1950; children: Tracey Rainier, Schuyler Barrett, Holly Cannon, Sinah Kendall Lee. AB, Duke, 1943; grad., USNR Midshipman Sch., Notre Dame, 1944; AM, Harvard, 1947. Divisional asst. Greece-Turkey-Iran sect., pub. affairs overseas program staff Dept. State, 1948-49; asst. pub. affairs officer Thessaloniki, Greece, 1950; asst. info. officer Athens, 1950-51; pub. affairs officer Patras, Greece, 1951-54 and Thessaloniki, 1954; dir. Amerika Haus, Nuernberg, Germany, 1955-59; mem. cultural council City of Nuernberg, 1958-59; mgmt. analyst USIA, Washington, 1959-61; cultural attache Am. Embassy, Warsaw, Poland, 1963-65; dir. Am. Cultural Center, Saigon, Vietnam, 1967-68; 1st sec., regional projects officer Am. Embassy, Vienna, Austria, 1968-70; consul, pub. affairs officer Am. consulate gen. Stuttgart, Germany, 1970-73; area coordinator (Europe) USIA, Washington, 1973, seminar-conf. Programming officer, 1973-74; dep. dir. Office Internat. Arts Affairs, Dept. State, 1974-76; counselor cultural affairs officer Am. Embassy, Bangkok, 1977-82; counselor Sr. Fgn. Service. Contbr. articles to profl. jours. Vice chmn., bd. dirs. Thailand-U.S. Ednl. Found., 1977-82; bd. dirs. John F. Kennedy Found., Thailand, 1977-82, John E. Peurifoy Found., 1979-82, Lynchburg Symphony Orch., 1992-93; exec. sec. Eisenhower Exch. Fellowship Selection Com., Thailand, 1977-82; mem. winter forums com. Sweet Briar Coll., 1990-96. Lt. (j.g.) USNR, 1944-46, PTO. Decorated Bronze Star with combat V, Purple Heart.; recipient Meritorious Svc. award USIA, 1956, medal for civilian service in Vietnam, 1968, Civilian award U.S. European Command, 1973. Mem. Am. Fgn. Svc. Assn., Soc. Lees of Va., Siam Soc., Phi Beta Kappa, Omicron Delta Kappa, Phi Eta Sigma, Pi Kappa Phi. Home: 501 V E S Rd Apt C210 Lynchburg VA 24503 *Personal responsibility should be an essential principle for all of us, in the family, job and community. My 34 years in the U.S. Foreign Service gave me a wonderfully stimulating and rewarding career and a profound belief: the diplomatic service is America's first line of defense.*

**STEPHENS, BILLIE LOWELL,** quality assurance professional, writer; b. Eunice, N.Mex., Apr. 4, 1950; children: Michael, David. BS in Mgmt., Calif. Coast U., 1994, MBA, 1997. Microsoft cert. engr. Chief network engr. Def. Info. Security Agy., Washington, 1999—2000; instr. nat. learning ctr. IRS, Austin, Tex., 2000—01; info. assurance mgr. SAIC, Columbia, Md., 2001—. Author: Coastal Del Rey and Mesa De Lagrimas, 2001, The Dome, 2002. Bd. dirs. Writers League Tex., Austin, 2001—01. With U.S. Army, 1969—81. Mem.: Writers League of Tex. (bd. dirs., v.p. 2002—), Tex. Assn. for Hist. Preservation (pres. 2001—02). Baptist. Avocations: golf, writing, travel, history. Home: 701 Bond St Copperas Cove TX 76522-3080 Personal E-mail: sierrav8@hotmail.com.

**STEPHENS, BOBBY GENE,** college administrator, consultant; b. Glendale, SC, Mar. 8, 1935; s. Dewey and Bertha Cordelia (Mott) S.; m. Sandra Elizabeth White, June 27, 1957; children: Elaine, Ward, Todd, Adam. BS, Wofford Coll., 1957; MS, Clemson U., 1961, PhD, 1964; LHD (hon.), MacMurray Coll., 1987. Textile chemist Reeves Bros., Fairforest, SC, 1957-58; grad. asst. Clemson (S.C.) U., 1960-63; instr. chemistry Wofford Coll., Spartanburg, SC, 1963-64, asst. prof., 1964-67, assoc. prof., 1967-72, prof., v.p. acad. affairs, 1972-80; pres. MacMurray Coll., Jacksonville, Ill., 1980-86; v.p. research and enrollment Wofford Coll., Spartanburg, SC, 1986-91, v.p. sci. and tech., 1991—, prof. chemistry emeritus, 2000—. Project dir. Howard Hughes Med. Inst., 1992—; pres. BGS Cons.; cons. in field Contbr. articles to sci. jours.; inventor extractions with propylene carbonate, 1975; producer: TV series The Psychology of Interpersonal Behavior, 1974. Co-chmn. Daniel Morgan Restoration Com., 1986-88; vice chmn. Spartanburg County Pollution Control Authority, 1970-74; bd. dirs. SC Lung Assn., Spartanburg, 1970-75; sect. maj. United Way, 1975-77; chair SC State Libr. Bd., 2004—. 1st lt. U.S. Army, 1958-60. Recipient Jefferson award S.C. Acad. Sci., 1969; recipient 1st prize graphics div. 2d Edit. Art Contest, 1971, 2d and 3d prizes Lawson's Fork Creek Photography Contest, 1978, Alumni Disting. Svc. award Wofford Coll., 2001; USPHS grantee; NSF grantee Mem. Am. Chem. Soc. (chair Western Carolinas sect. 2003), Nat. Assn. Gifted Children, Assn. Ednl. Communications and Tech., Phi Beta Kappa. Methodist. Home: 460 S Fairview Ave Spartanburg SC 29302 Office: Wofford College 429 N Church St Spartanburg SC 29303-3663 Personal E-mail: bgsphd@bellsouth.net. E-mail: stephensbg@wofford.edu.

**STEPHENS, D. RICHARD,** manufacturing executive; married; 2 children. BS in chem. engring., U. Akron, 1972; MBA, Bowling Green U., 1990; grad. advanced mgmt. program, Harvard Bus. Sch., 1997. Pres. Cooper Tire & Rubber Co., Findlay, Ohio, 2001—, truck devel. chemist, 1978—79, compound devel. mgr., 1979—85, product devel. mgr., 1985—90, dir. tech., 1990—94, v.p. tech., 1994—2000, v.p. tech. and comm. tire oper., 2000; pres. Cooper Tire & Rubber Co., Internat. Tire Dvsn., 2000—01. Mem. bd. trustees U. Findlay, 2000—; mem. Findlay-Hancock County C. of C., 1992; mem. bd. trustees Vennard Coll. Fin. Com., 1994—96. Office: Cooper Tire Rubber Co 701 Lima Ave Findlay OH 45840

**STEPHENS, DAVID CHRISTOPHER,** mathematics professor; b. Knoxville, Tenn., Nov. 22, 1976; s. David Leon and Carol Ruth Stephens; m. Heather Leiann Waggoner, July 22, 2000; children: Christopher, Nicholas, Abigail, Brandon. PhD in Math., Vanderbilt U., Nashville, Tenn., 2004. Math. prof. Mid. Tenn. State U., Murfreesboro. Recipient B. F. Bryant prize for Excellence in Tchg., Dept. Math., Vanderbilt U., 2003, Summer Rsch. award, Coll. Arts and Scis., Vanderbilt U., 2003, grantee, Mid. Tenn. State U., 2005; Harold Stirling Vanderbilt fellow, Vanderbilt U., 1999—2003. Mem.: Am. Math. Soc. Achievements include solution of problem of nonorientable genus of the complete tripartite graph. Home: 319 Kirtley Ct Murfreesboro TN 37130 Office: Middle Tenn State U PO Box 34 Murfreesboro TN 37132 Office Phone: 615-494-8957. Business E-Mail: cstephen@mtsu.edu.

**STEPHENS, DIANA L.,** counselor, educator; d. Arthur Lee Frazier and Wynonah Irene Sullivan; m. Edward K. Stephens, Jan. 11, 1969; 1 child, Stacie Ann Karl. MA in Edn., U. of Redlands, Calif., 1999; postgrad., Fielding Grad. U. Cert. family life educator Nat. Coun. on Family Rels., 1996, pupil pers. svcs. Calif. Comm. on Tchr. Credentialing, 1999. Counselor/supr. Lan Jordan Inst. of Counseling and Psychotherapy, Beverly Hills, Calif., 1975—91; clin. prof. U. of Redlands, Redlands, Calif., 1998—; counselor/family life educator ed, Redlands, Calif., 1991—. Author: (seminar for parents/adolescents) Growing in God's Love. Mem.: Nat. Coun. of Family Rels., Calif. Assn. of Counseling and Devel., ACA, Am. Sch. Counseling Assn. Avocations: boating, hiking, poetry, creative writing, natural mysticism. Home: PO Box 2788 Camarillo CA 93011 Office: Calif Luth Univ Thousand Oaks CA E-mail: diana_stephens@redlands.edu, dstephens@clu.net.

**STEPHENS, DONALD R(ICHARDS),** investor; b. San Francisco, June 28, 1938; s. Donald Lewis and Anona Marie (O'Leary) S.; m. Christina Brinkman, Sept. 11, 1971 (div. 1996); m. Patricia Hamilton, Oct. 21, 2000; children: Lane B., Justin H., Nicholas W., Adam H. BS, U. So. Calif., 1961; JD, Hastings Coll., 1969. Pres. Campodonico & Stephens, San Francisco, 1963-65; pres., owner Union Investment Co., San Francisco, 1966-69; assoc. Law Offices of Louis O. Kelso, 1969-72; pres. D.R. Stephens & Co., San Francisco, 1972—; mng. ptnr. Stephens & Stephens, San Francisco, 1999—. Chmn., bd. dirs., CEO Bank of San Francisco Group, 1978-91; chmn., bd. dirs. N.Am. Trust REIT; bd. dirs. Am. Inst. for Fgn. Study, Charles Schwab Family of Funds Inc. Bd. dirs. Bay Area Coun.; trustee St. Francis Meml. Hosp., San Francisco, 1976-82; mem. policy adv. bd. U. Calif., 1985—. Mem. Urban

Land Inst., World Bus. Coun., Bohemian Club, Reserve Palm Desert, Napa Valley Reserve. Republican. Presbyterian. Avocations: tennis, bridge. Office Phone: 415-781-8000. Business E-Mail: info@drstephens.net.

**STEPHENS, EARNEST B.,** academic administrator; s. Genello Stephens and O'neal Bean (Stepfather), Louis Henry Gordon. AA, Itawamba C.C., Fulton, Miss., 1990; BBA, U. of Miss., University, 1993, M of Higher Edn., 1995, PhD, 2002. Wellness programming specialist U. Counseling Svcs., Universtiy, 1995—97; coord. of wellness programming Student Health Svcs., University, 1997—98; site coord. AmeriCorp - Campus Link, Oxford, Miss., 1998—2000; coord. of grad. sch. sponored programs U. of Miss., University, 2001—. Substitute tchr. Oxford Sch. Dist., 2000—01. Mem. of friends North Miss. Retardation Ctr., Oxford, 2004—06; vol. Miss. Red Cross, Oxford, 2005—06; supporter Boys and Girls Club, Oxford, 2005—06; co-youth dir. Mays Chapel Bapt. Ch., Houlka, Miss., 2002—06; spkr. Oxford/Holly Springs CME Dist. Edn. Conf., Holly Springs, Miss., 2003—04. Recipient Miss. Hwy. Safety grant, Miss. Dept. of Hwy. Safety, 1996. Mem.: NASPA (assoc.), Kappa Delta Pi. Achievements include research in effectiveness of a program on cultural tolerance and diversity for teacher education candidates; preceptions of African American Ph.D. students in Mississippi on their graduate school experiences. Office: U Miss 108 Somerville University MS 38677 Office Phone: 662-915-1211. Office Fax: 662-915-3177. Business E-Mail: estephen@olemiss.edu.

**STEPHENS, EDWARD CARL,** communications educator, writer; b. LA, July 27, 1924; s. Carl Edward and Helen Mildred (Kerner) S.; children: Edward, Sarah, Matthew. AB, Occidental Coll., 1947; MS, Northwestern U., 1955. Advt. exec. Dancer-Fitzgerald-Sample Inc., N.Y.C., 1955-64; prof. Medill Sch. Journalism, Northwestern U., Evanston, Ill., 1964-76; prof., chmn. dept. advt. S.I. Newhouse Sch. Pub. Communications, Syracuse U., NY, 1976-80, dean, 1980—89; prof. comms. S.I. Newhouse Sch. Pub. Comms. Syracuse U., 1990-92, prof. emeritus, 1992—. Cons. Foote, Cone & Belding Communications Author: (novels) A Twist of Lemon, 1958, One More Summer, 1960, Blow Negative!, 1962, Roman Joy, 1965, A Turn in the Dark Wood, 1968, The Submariner, 1974, (nonfiction) Submarines, 1960. Mem. George Polk Awards Com. With USN, 1943-46, 1950-53. Capt. USNR (ret.). Decorated Purple Heart Mem. Am. Acad. Advt. (pres. 1976-77), Assn. Edn. Journalism and Mass Communication, The Army and Navy Club, Authors League, Century Club of Syracuse, Alpha Tau Omega. Episcopalian. Personal E-mail: stephens@dreamscape.com.

**STEPHENS, ELISA,** college president; d. Richard A. Stephens. Pres. Acad. of Art Coll., San Francisco, 1992—. Office: 79 New Montgomery St 6th Fl San Francisco CA 94105-3410*

**STEPHENS, GEORGE EDWARD, JR.,** lawyer; b. Lawrence, Kans., Mar. 26, 1936; s. George Edward and Mary Helen (Houghton) Stephens; m. Gretel Geiser, Dec. 31, 1965; children: Thaddeus Edward, Edward Houghton, Mary Schoentgen. Student, U. Colo., Boulder, 1954-57, U. Colo., Denver, 1957-59; LLB, Stanford U., 1962. Bar: Calif. 1963, U.S. Dist. Ct. (cen. dist.) Calif. 1963, U.S. Ct. Appeals (9th cir.) 1971. Law clk. to judge U.S. Dist. Ct., L.A., 1962-64; assoc. ptnr. Pollock & Palmer, L.A., 1964-69; ptnr. Gates, Morris, Merrill & Stephens, L.A., 1969-72, Paul, Hastings, Janofsky & Walker LLP, L.A., 1972—. Mem. Coordinating Com. on Lawyer Competence, Conf. Chief Justices, 1983-86; chmn. probate sect. L.A. County Bar Assn., 1979-80. Nat. chmn. Stanford (Calif.) U. Law Fund Quad Program, 1980-87; mem. bd. visitors Stanford Law Sch., 1982-85; founder mus. Contemporary Art, L.A., 1982; bd. dirs. Pacific Oaks Coll., 1990-94. Recipient Stanford Assocs. award, 1982. Fellow: Fellows of Contemporary Art (bd. dirs. 1991—92), Internat. Acad. Probate and Trust Law, Am. Coll. Trust and Estates Counsel, Am. Bar Found.; mem.: Stanford Law Soc. (pres. 1972—73, chmn. 1998—99), ABA (chmn. standing com. specialization 1979—82, standing com. lawyer referral svcs. 1969—76, consortium delivery legal svcs. and the pub. 1979—82), The Athenaeum, Valley Hunt (Pasadena, Calif.), Annandale Golf (Pasadena, Calif.), Chancery (L.A.). Episcopalian. Office: Paul Hastings Janofsky & Walker LLP 515 S Flower St 25th Fl Los Angeles CA 90071-2300 Office Phone: 213-683-6211. Business E-Mail: georgestephens@paulhastings.com.

**STEPHENS, JACK EDWARD,** civil engineer, consultant; b. Eaton, Ohio, Aug. 17, 1923; s. Harry M. and Mary Elizabeth (Galloway) S.; m. Virginia May Ives, June 19, 1948; children: Jay Edward, Jerry Edward, Jill Louise, Jana Lynn. BS in Engring., U. Conn., Storrs, 1947; MS in Engring., Purdue U., 1955, PhD, 1959. Registered profl. engr., Conn. Jr. hwy. engr. Conn. Dept. Hwys., New Haven, 1949-50; instr. U. Conn., Storrs, 1947-48, asst. prof., then assoc. prof. civil engring., 1950-62, prof. civil engring., 1962-88, head civil engring. dept., 1965-72, prof. emeritus, 1989—, dir. Conn. Advanced Pavement Lab., 1995—2004; sr. rsch. advisor Conn. Advanced Pavement Lab., 2004—. Soils cons. A.J. Macchi Engrs., Hartford, Conn., 1958-65; pavement cons. Conn. Dept. Hwys., Hartford, 1962-63, Consumers Union Auto Test Facility, Colchester, Conn., 1991—; prin. Jack E. Stephens Soil and Materials Test Lab., Storrs, 1958—. Contbr. jour. articles to Procs. Assn. Asphalt Paving Tech., Transp. Rsch. Bd., others. Cpl. U.S. Army, 1943-46, ETO. Fellow Automobile Safety Found., Washington, 1958-59; recipient citation for tchg. excellence Western Electric Fund, Washington, 1974. Mem. ASCE (life, B. Wright award Conn. sect. 1989), NSPE, AAUP, Assn. Asphalt Paving Tech. (life), Conn. Acad. Sci. and Engring. (chmn. transp. com. 1984-94), Conn. Soc. Profl. Engrs., Am. Rd. and Transp. Builders Assn., Transp. Rsch. Bd., Am. Assn. Engring. Edn., Am. Soc. for Photogrammetry and Remote Sensing, Sigma Xi. Office: U Conn Transp Inst Box U 202 Glenn Mansfield CT 06269-3202 Office Phone: 860-429-7600. E-mail: jack.stephens@uconn.edu.

**STEPHENS, JAMES T. (J.T. STEPHENS),** publishing executive; b. 1939; married. BA in Bus. Adminstrn., Yale U., 1961; MBA, Harvard U., 1964. With Ebsco Industries Inc., Birmingham, Ala., 1961—, asst. v.p., 1966-67, v.p., 1967-70, exec. v.p., 1970—71, pres., also bd. dirs., 1971—2005, chmn. Office: EBSCO Industries Inc 5724 Highway 280 E Birmingham AL 35242-6818 also: PO Box 1943 Birmingham AL 35201-1943*

**STEPHENS, JAY B.,** lawyer, manufacturing executive; b. Akron, Iowa, Nov. 5, 1946; s. Lyle R. and Marie (Borchers) S. BA magna cum laude, Harvard U., 1968, JD cum laude, 1973. Bar: D.C. 1973, U.S. Supreme Ct., 1979. Assoc. Wilmer, Cutler & Pickering, Washington, 1973-74; asst. spl. prosecutor Watergate Spl. Prosecution Force, Washington, 1974-75; assoc. gen. counsel Overseas Pvt. Investment Corp., Washington, 1976-77; asst. U.S. atty. Dept. Justice, Washington, 1977-81, spl. counsel to asst. atty. gen., 1981-83, dep. assoc. atty. gen., 1983-85, assoc. dep. atty. gen., 1985-86; dep. counsel to Pres. Reagan, 1986-88; U.S. atty. for D.C. Office U.S. Atty., 1988-93; ptnr. Pillsbury Madison & Sutro, Washington, 1993-97; v.p. and dep. gen. counsel Honeywell, Morristown, NJ, 1997—2001; assoc. atty. gen. U.S. Dept. Justice, Washington, 2001—02; sr. v.p. gen. counsel Raytheon Co., Lexington, Mass., 2002—. Dir. Nat. Legal Ctr. for Pub. Interest, New Eng. Legal Found. Contbr. articles to profl. jours. Knox fellow Oxford, Eng., 1968-69. Mem. D.C. Bar Assn., Assn. U.S. Atty. Assn., Nat. Assn. Former U.S. Attys. Republican. Presbyterian. Office: Raytheon Co 870 Winter St Waltham MA 02451 Office Phone: 781-522-5096. Office Fax: 781-522-6471.

**STEPHENS, JERRY WAYNE,** librarian, director; b. Birmingham, Ala., Sept. 10, 1949; s. William Larkin and Odell (Kerr) S.; m. Lisa Brown, June 2, 1972; children— Jeramy Wayne, Elizabeth Ashley. John Larkin BS in Acctg., U. Ala.-Birmingham, 1974, MBA, 1976; M.L.S., U. Ala., 1977, PhD in Adminstrn. Higher Edn., 1982. Svc. mgr. Hammond Organ Studios, Birmingham, 1973-74; acct. Mervyn Sterne Libr., U. Ala., Birmingham, 1974-75, asst. to dir., 1975-76, asst. dir., 1976-85, libr. dir., 1985—; interim fiscal officer Univ. Coll. U. Ala., Birmingham, 1982, interim asst. v.p. for acad. affairs, 1989-91. Vice chmn. Network Acad. Librs., 1985-86, 95-96, chmn., 1986-88, 96, 2000-01; cons. Birmingham Pub. Libr., 1977—; cons. Southeastern Libr. Assn., Atlanta, 1979-80; bd. dirs. Southeastern Libr. Network, treas., 1992-93, chmn., 1993-94; mem. user's coun. Online Computer Libr. Ctr., 1997—, pres.-elect, 2000-01, pres., 2001-2002, bd. trustees, 2002—. Contbr. articles to profl. publs. Sponsored exec. United Way, Birmingham, 1978, sr. exec., 1982; foster parent Dept. Pensions and Securities, Birmingham, 1982-83; elder Homewood Cumberland Presbyn. Ch., Birmingham, 1982-84, 88-90. With USN, 1972-73 Named one of Outstanding Young Men Am., U.S. Jaycees, 1978, 79 Mem. ALA, SE Libr. Assn., Ala. Libr. Assn. (treas. 1977-78), Am Mgmt. Assn. Avocations: camping, softball. Office: U Ala-Birmingham Mervyn H Sterne Libr 1530 3d Ave South Birmingham AL 35294-0014 Home: 470 Renaissance Dr Birmingham AL 35226-4155 Office Phone: 205-934-6360. E-mail: jerry@beowulf.mhsl.uab.edu, jerryw@uab.edu.

**STEPHENS, JOE ALAN,** investigative reporter; b. Mariemont, Ohio, July 26, 1959; s. Ken and Wilma (Vanover) S. Student, De Pauw U., 1977-78; BA in English, Miami U., Oxford, Ohio, 1981. Editor-in-chief Clermont Sun, Batavia, Ohio, 1981-83; investigative reporter State Jour.-Register, Springfield, Ill., 1983-87; investigative & spl. projects reporter Kansas City (Mo.) Star, 1987—99; spl. projects desk reporter Washington Post, 1999—. Co-recipient George Polk award for fgn. reporting, 2006; recipient George Polk award for polit. reporting, 1994, Fred Moen Sweepstakes award Mo. Assoc. Press Mng. Editors Assn., Columbia, 1994, Pub. Svc. award Kansas City Soc. Profl. Journalists, 1993. Mem. Investigative Reporters and Editors. Office: Washington Post 1150 15th St NW Washington DC 20071-0070 Home: # Lawr 1523 T St NW Washington DC 20009-3909 Office Phone: 202-334-6723. Office Fax: 202-334-6581. E-mail: stephensj@washpost.com.

**STEPHENS, JOHN JOSEPH, JR.,** materials engineer; s. John J. and Ann L. S.; m. Linda J. Brown, July 19, 1986. BA in Physics, Cornell U., 1977; MS in Metallurgical Engring., Stevens Tech. Inst., Hoboken, N.J., 1980; PhD in Materials Sci. and Engring., Stanford U., 1985. Rsch. technician Exxon Rsch. & Engring. Co., Linden, NJ, 1977-80; grad. rsch. asst. Stanford U., Palo Alto, Calif., 1980-84; prin mem. tech. staff Sandia Nat. Labs., Albuquerque, 1985-87, 88—; mem. tech. staff Lockheed Missiles & Space, Palo Alto, 1987-88. Inventor in field. Recipient Best Tech. Paper award Internat. Metallographic Soc., 1987, AWS Peasley award for best paper in brazing, 1999, 2000. Fellow: ASM Internat. (mem. chpt. devel. task force 1992—94); mem.: TMS (chmn. refractory metals com. 1989—92), ASTM (co-chair subcom. F1.03 1993—, chair F1 electronics com. 2004—, Charles Marsden award 1995), Am. Welding Soc. (C3 brazing and A5 filler metals coms.).

**STEPHENS, JOSEPH,** psychiatrist, researcher; b. Frederick, Md., Apr. 9, 1927; s. Joseph Snyder and Mazie Naomi Stephens. BA, Johns Hopkins U., 1948, MD, 1952, MusM, 1959. Assoc. prof. psychiatry Johns Hopkins U., 1967. Contbr. articles to profl. jours. Lt. USNR, 1954—56. Recipient Honorary Denison Strong Fellow, 1952. Fellow: Am. Psychiat. Assn. (life); mem.: Parlovian Soc., Am. Psychopathology Assn. Avocation: music. Home: 1616 Bolton St Baltimore MD 21217

**STEPHENS, KAREN LORENE,** librarian; b. Detroit; BA, Mich. State U., 1969; MSLS, Wayne State U., 1973. Tchr. econs. Warren (Mich.) Consol. Schs., 1972-73, media specialist, 1973-82; libr. transp. rsch. GM, Warren, 1982—83, libr. econ. info. ctr. Detroit, 1983—93; sys. operator, media specialist, libr., tchr. Warren Con. Schs., Mich., 1993—. Mich. rep. Home Owners Against Def. Dwellings, Home Owners for Better Bldgs. Mem.: Mich. Assn. for Media in Edn., Mich. Assn. for Computer Users in Learning. Avocations: travel, reading, swimming. Office: Carleton MS 8900 E 15 Mile Rd Sterling Heights MI 48312

**STEPHENS, LAURENCE DAVID, JR.,** linguist, investor, oil industry executive; b. Dallas, July 26, 1947; s. Laurence D. Sr. and Amy Belle (Schickram) S.; m. Susan Leigh Foutz, Apr. 16, 1988; 1 child, Laurence David III. MA, Stanford U., 1972, PhD, 1976. Cert. materials mgr. Nat. Assn. Royalty Owners, 2003. Vis. fellow Yale U., New Haven, summer 1979; rsch. fellow U. SC, Columbia, 1980; asst. prof. U. NC, Chapel Hill, 1982-88, assoc. prof., 1989—; pres. Colgate Mgmt. Co., Inc., Dallas, 1997—; gen. ptnr. Moorman, Schickram & Stephens, Ltd., Dallas, 1997—; mgr. Stephens Resources, LLC, 2004—; v.p., mgr. 4025 Colgate LLC, 2004—05, 3712 Wentwood, LLC, 2004—05. Co-author: Two Studies in Latin Phonology, 1977, Language and Metre, 1984, The Prosody of Greek Speech, 1994, Discontinuous Syntax, 1999, Latin Word-Order: Structured Meaning and Information, 2006; editor ann. vol. L'Année Philologique, 1987-92; contbr. numerous articles to profl. jours. Mem. University Park Cmty. League, Park Cities Hist. Soc., Nat. Trust for Hist. Preservation, Washington, 1989—, The Dallas Symphony Assn. Ann. Fund, Metro. Opera Guild, N.Y.C., 1992—, Wythe County VA Hist. Soc., 1998—. Grantee L'Année Philologique, NEH, 1987-89, 89-91, 91-93. Mem. Am. Philol. Assn., Greek and Latin Linguistic Assn. (chmn. 1987-92), N.Y. Acad. Scis., Indogermanische Gesellschaft, Internat. Soc. Bibliographie Classique, Arabian Horse Assn., Nat. Assn. Royalty Owners, Sigma Xi. Achievements include discovery of language universal regularities concerning labiovelar phonemes, laws of palatalization, the law of catathesis in Greek (pitch lowering), and grammatical, semantic, pragmatic (information structure) regularities of discontinuous constituency and nonconfigurational syntactic structures in Greek and Latin; co-developer of Justeson-Stephens probability distribution for cognates between unrelated languages, Justeson-Stephens probability distribution of the numbers of vowels, consonants, and total phonological inventory size in the languages of the world; research on the law of the quantitative form of diachronic polysemy growth, semantic universals of aspect and modality, universals of writing systems and their evolution. Office: Univ NC Chapel Hill Dept Classics Cb 3145 212 Murphey Hl Chapel Hill NC 27599-0001 Home: 2785 Turnpike Rd Lexington VA 24450 also: 3319 Greenbrier Dr Dallas TX 75225 Office Phone: 276-228-1276. Personal E-mail: lsteph8694@aol.com.

**STEPHENS, LOREN M.,** publishing executive, writer; b. NYC, Mar. 8, 1944; d. Seymour and Carol Meyer; m. Dana Miyoshi; 1 child, Joshua. BA, Cornell U., 1965; MA in Internat. Affairs, Columbia U., 1967. Editor Houghton Mifflin, Boston, 1969—71; assoc. Berg & Co./Mortgage Bankes, Boston, 1971—73, sr. v.p., 1973-80; asst. v.p. Nat. Med. Enterprises, LA, 1980—82; prin. Stephens & Hyde, LA, 1982—84, One Step Prodns., Studio City, 1984—97; asst. devel. officer Anti Defamation League, LA, 1990—94, dir. devel., 1994—2000, dir. planned giving & endowments, 2000—05; dir. devel. U. Judaism, 2005—06. Pres. Write Wisdom, Inc.; founder, owner Provenance Press, 2000—. Exec. prodr.: (documentaries) Legacy of the Hollywood Black List, 1985 (Cine Gold Eagle, 1985), Sojourner Truth: Ain't I a Woman, 1987 (Golden Apple, 1987), Los Pastores (Cine Gold Eagle, 1997). Alice Stetton Fellow, Columbia U., 1966, 1967. Avocations: skiing, hiking, teaching writing classes. Home: 847 S Bundy Dr Los Angeles CA 90049 Office Phone: 310-820-2052. Business E-mail: loren@writewisdom.com.

**STEPHENS, NORRIS LYNN,** school librarian; b. Charleroi, Pa., Dec. 14, 1930; BFA, Carnegie-Mellon U., 1954, MFA, 1957; M in Sacred Music, Union Theol. Sem., NY, 1956; MLS, U. Pitts., 1966, PhD, 1968. Sales clk. Wagner-Bund Music Co., Pitts., 1957—62; assoc. organist E. Liberty Presbyn. Ch., Pitts., 1962—83, First Bapt. Ch., Pitts., 1983—98. Sr. libr. U. Pitts., 1966—98, adj. asst. prof., 1972—82. Co-author: Collected Editions, Historical Series and Sets-Monuments of Music, 1997; contbr. chapters to books, articles to profl. jours. Grantee, NEH, 1984. Mem.: Am. Guild Organists, Am. Musicological Soc. (chpt. chair 1982—84), Internat. Music Libr. Assn., Music Libr. Assn. (chpt. chair 1982—84) Avocations: gardening, model railroading, stamp collecting/philately, coin collecting/numismatics.

**STEPHENS, NORVAL BLAIR, JR.,** marketing consultant; b. Chgo. Nov. 20, 1928; s. Norval Blair and Ethel Margaret (Lewis) S.; m. Diane Forst, Sept. 29, 1951; children: Jill E., John G., Sandra J. (dec.), Katherine B., James N.

---

BA, DePauw U., 1951; MBA, U. Chgo., 1959. Asst. to v.p. ops. Walgreen Drug Co., Chgo., 1953-56; with Needham, Harper Worldwide (formerly Needham, Harper & Steers), Chgo., 1956-86, v.p., 1964-70, sr. v.p., 1970-72, exec. v.p. internat., 1972-74, exec. v.p., mng. dir. N.Y.C., 1974-75; exec. v.p. Chgo. office Needham, Harper & Steers, 1975-82, exec. v.p. internat., 1982-86; also dir.; pres. Deltacom, N.Y.C., 1971-76; pres. Norval Stephens Co., 1987—2000; exec. dir. Internat. Comms. Agy. Network, 1988-98; founder, dir., pres. Barrington Area Cmty. Found., 1998—. Trustee DePauw U., 1979—. Recipient Rector award DePauw U., 1976, Old Gold Goblet award for outstanding svc. DePauw U., 1994, Outstanding Greek Vol. award N.Am. Interfraternity Conf.: 2001, Carol Beese award Barrington Area C. of C., 2004; named Young Man of Yr., Arlington Heights Jaycees, 1964, Barrington Area Citizen of Yr., 1999; named to Sr. Hall of Fame, Barrington, Ill., 2002. Mem. DePauw Alumni Assn. (pres. 1977-79), Phi Beta Kappa, Delta Tau Delta (bd. dirs. edn. found. 1987—, vice chmn. 1994-95, chmn. 1995—, 2d v.p. Arch chpt. 1988-90, 1st v.p. 1990-92, pres. 1992-94). Republican. Methodist. Home: 3400 Garlands Lane Barrington IL 60010 Office Phone: 847-382-1588. Personal E-mail: norval@norvalstephens.com. *I view my life not as a passage but a daily renewing challenge: to be better; to be a better father, husband, brother, son; to return each day an honest day's work; to bear witness to my beliefs and my faith; to serve my fellowman. I seek a whole life and a life of rewarding parts, each a lesson and an experience.*

**STEPHENS, OTIS HAMMOND, JR.,** political science professor, law educator; b. East Point, Ga., Sept. 20, 1936; s. Otis Hammond and Mary Margaret (Fisher) S.; m. Linda Duren, June 18, 1960 (dec. July 1988); children: Ann S. Henderson, Carol S. Frazier; m. Mary Torpey Ballard, Oct. 21, 1989. AB cum laude, U. Ga., 1957, MA, 1958; PhD, Johns Hopkins U., 1963; JD with high honors, U. Tenn., 1983. Bar: Tenn. 1984. Grad. rsch. asst. U. Ga., 1957-58; jr. instr. Johns Hopkins U., 1959-61; asst. prof. to prof. Ga. So. Coll., 1962-67; assoc. prof. U. Tenn., Knoxville, 1967-71, prof., 1971—, Lindsay young prof., 1981-82, alumni disting. svc. prof. polit. sci., 1983—, acting head dept., 1986-88; Russell Sage Found. resident in law and social sci. Harvard Law Sch., 1975-76; assoc. dean Coll. of Arts and Scis. Univ. Tenn., 1996—2000; resident scholar of Constitutional Law Coll. Law, Univ. Tenn., 2000—. Lectr. U.S. Govt. Mgmt. Devel. Ctr., 1972-96; panel mem., chmn. various assns. Author: The Supreme Court and Confessions of Guilt, 1973; co-author: (with Gregory J. Rathjen) The Supreme Court and the Allocation of Constitutional Power, 1980; (with John M. Scheb, II) American Constitutional Law: Essays and Cases, 1988, American Constitutional Law, 1993, 3d edit., 2003, (with Richard A. Glenn) Unreasonable Searches and Seizures: Rights and Liberties Under the Law, 2006; contbr. articles to profl. jours., chpts. to books. Pres. Nat. Accreditation Coun. for Agys. Serving the Blind and Visually Handicapped, 1979-83; pres. Am. Coun. of Blind, 1987-89; trustee Am. Found. for Blind, 1987-99, exec. com., 1992-99; mem. Gov.'s Adv.Com. on Fair Employment Opportunity, State of Tenn., 1987-95. Ford Found. pub. affairs grantee, 1961, faculty rsch. grantee summers 1968, 69, 70, 74, 91, Coll. of Law, 2003, 04; recipient Migel medal Am. Found. Blind, 2001; grad. fellow Am. Found. Blind, 1962, Johns Hopkins U., 1958-62; liberal arts fellow law and polit. sci. Harvard Law Sch., 1975-76; recipient Acad. Achievement award Recording for the Blind, Inc., 1962, Alumni Assn. Outstanding Teaching award U. Tenn., 1977, 84, L.R. Hesler award, 1998-99, Macebearer, 2001-02. Mem. AAUP (pres. U. Tenn. chpt. 1985-86), ABA, Am. Polit. Sci. Assn. (exec. coun. pub. law sect. 1990-92), Tenn. Polit. Sci. Assn. (pres. 1991-92), So. Polit. Sci. Assn., Tenn. Bar Assn., Knoxville Bar Assn., Phi Beta Kappa (pres. Epsilon of Tenn. chpt. 1981-82), Golden Key, Order of Coif, Omicron Delta Kappa, Phi Kappa Phi, Pi Sigma Alpha. Home: 1141 Southgate Rd Knoxville TN 37919-7647 Office: U Tenn Coll of Law Ste 377 1505 W Cumberland Ave Knoxville TN 37996

**STEPHENS, PAUL ALFRED,** dentist; b. Muskogee, Okla., Feb. 28, 1921; s. Lonny and Maudie Janie (Wynn) S.; m. Lola Helena Byrd, May 7, 1950; children: Marsha Stephens Wilson, Paul Alfred Jr., Derek M. BS cum laude, Howard U., 1942, DDS, 1945. Instr. dentistry Howard U., Washington, 1945-46; gen practice dentistry Gary, Ind., 1947—; chmn. bd. Assocs. Med. Ctr., Inc., Gary. Sec. Gary Ind. Sch. Bldg. Corp., 1967-85; pres. Bd. Health, 1973-81; Ind. State Bd. Dental Examiners, 1975-83. Mem. adv. bd. Ind. U.-Purdue U. Calumet Campus, 1973; bd. dirs. Urban League Northwest Ind.; pres. Gary Ednl. Devel. Found., 1990—. With AUS, 1942-44. Fellow Internat. Coll. Dentists, Acad. Dentistry Internat., Acad. Gen. Dentistry (pres. chpt. 1973, nat. chmn. dental care com. 1977, Midwestern v.p., nat. bd. dirs. 1984-89, v.p. 1990-91, pres. 1992-93), Am. Coll. Dentists; mem. ADA, Nat. Dental Assn., N.W. Ind. Dental Assn. (bd. dirs., pres. 1976-77, Disting. Svc. award 1993), Am. Soc. Anesthesia in Dentistry, Am. Acad. Radiology, Gary C. of C., Alpha Phi Alpha (pres. Gary Ednl. Found. 1988, pres. Gary Ednl. Devel. Found. 1990—), Acad. Gen. Dentistry (pres. 1992-93). Baptist. Home: 1901 Taft St Gary IN 46404-2759 Office: 2200 Grant St Gary IN 46404-3439

**STEPHENS, RALPH RENNE,** massage therapy educator; b. Vinton, Iowa, Apr. 19, 1948; s. E.O. and Carrie D. S.; m. Sara Ann Beckley. BS in Indsl. Edn., Iowa State U., 1971; Natural Therapeutics Splst., N.Mex. Sch. Natural Therapeutics, 1986. Lic. massage therapist Iowa, N.Mex., massage therapy instr. N.Mex., cert. therapeutic massage and bodywork Nat. Cert. Bd. Therapeutic Massage and Bodywork, St. John method neuromuscular therapy. Pvt. practice Helping Hands Body Therapy Ctr., Iowa City, 1986-92; staff instr. Carlson Coll. Massage Therapy, Cedar Rapids, Iowa, 1987-92; instr. St. John Neuromuscular Therapy Seminars, 1991-99; pvt. practice Ralph Stephens Seminars, Cedar Rapids, 1992—; mem. tchng. staff Himalayan Inst. Yoga Sci. and Philosophy of U.S.A., Honesdale, Pa., 2001—. Dir. sports massage Iowa City Annual Hospice Road Race Com., 1986-88; cons., sys. engr., equipment supplier to workshop and seminar presenters Helping Hands Audio/Video, 1989-94; chairperson Iowa Bd. Examiners Massage Therapy, Des Moines, 1995-2000; sec. Iowa Bd. Examiners Massage Therapy, Des Moines, 1992-95; presenter in field. Author: Massage Therapy Principles and Practice, 1999, 2d edit., 2003, Therapeutic Chair Massage, 2005; contbr. articles to profl. jours.; prodr. videos Seated Therapeutic Massage, Vol. 1, Back and Neck, 1995, Vol. 2, Shoulder, 1996, Vol. 3, Forearm, Wrist and Hand, 1996, Feel Great Hands on Health Series (4 tapes) Feel Great Every Day, Posture Yourself and Move Right, Massage Made Easy, Stretching that Works, 1998, Event Sports Massage, 1998, Side-Lying Therapeutic Massage, 1999, Therapeutic Sports Massage for the Lower Extremity, 1999, Anatomy of the Lower Extremity, 1999, Medical Massage for the Cervical Region, 2001, Medical Massage for the Lumbar Region, 2002, Golf-Flexology, 2003; monthly editl. columnist Massage Today, 2000-, quar. columnist Up Close and Personal Newsletter, 2002-. Trustee Am. Massage Therapy Assn. Found., 1990-93, 95-96; chairperson Walford (Iowa) Disaster Preparedness Com., 1999. Mem. Am. Massage Therapy Assn. (cert. sports massage therapist, registered massage therapist cert., organizer, chair Iowa sports massage team 1986-88, 1st v.p., convention coord. Iowa chpt. 1988-89, edn. chair Iowa chpt. 1988-89, pres. Iowa chpt. 1989, ctrl. dist. mgr. 1990-93, media spokesperson nat. media rels. team 1991-96, nat. nominating com. 1994, mem.-at-large nat. bd. dirs. 1995-96, nat. nominating comm. 1998-99, Disting. Nat. Officer award 1993, 96, Meritorious award Iowa chpt. 1997, Nat. Meritorious award 1997), Himalayan Inst. Yoga Sci. and Philosophy, tchg. staff, 2000. Independent. Avocations: golf, yoga, meditation. Home: PO Box 8267 Cedar Rapids IA 52408-8267 Office: Ralph Stephens Seminars LLC PO Box 8267 Cedar Rapids IA 52408-8267 Office Phone: 319-350-1590. Business E-mail: ralph@ralphstephens.com.

**STEPHENS, ROBERT,** horticulturist; m. Julie Packard Grad. in Computer Sci., UCSC. Former pres. Santa Cruz Natural History Museum; owner, gen. mgr. Elkhorn Native Plant Nursery. Former chmn. Audubon Calif. Bd. dirs. David and Lucile Packard Found.; adv. bd. mem. O'Neill Sea Odyssey, Elkhorn Slough Found.; trustee Future of Children, Los Altos. Named Man of the Yr., Santa Cruz Chamber of Commerce, 1999. Office: Elkhorn Native Plant Nursery 3621 N Main St Soquel CA 95073*

---

**STEPHENS, ROBERT DAVID,** environmental engineering executive; b. La Follette, Tenn., Nov. 8, 1949; s. Robert Oscar and Billie Jean (Maples) S.; m. Donna Jean Reece, July 11, 1970 (div. Apr. 1984), m. Mary Nasca, Sept.; children: Jaclyn-Marie, Svetlana, robert Igor. BA in Biology, Berea Coll., Ky., 1971; postgrad., U. Cin., 1973-74. Cert. environ. assessor Fla.; environ. trainer, registered environ. property assessor, environ. mgr. Environ. specialist Ky. Dept. Health, Ludlow, 1971-74; project mgr. Pedco Environ. Specialists, Cin., 1974-77; environ. control mgr. Mobil Chem. Corp., Richmond, Va., 1978-84; v.p. Environ. Analysis Corp., Richmond, 1984-85; mgr. Environ. Rsch. and Tech. Group GSX Corp., Greensboro, N.C., 1985-86; mgr. regulatory affairs and cmty. rels. Internat. Tech. Corp., Knoxville, Tenn., 1986-88, mgr. environ. studies Tampa, Fla., 1988-90; gen. mgr. First Environment, Inc., Tampa, 1990-91; co-owner Bruder Stephens, Inc., Tampa, 1991—2004; pres. Environ. Evaluations Inc., 2004—. Faculty Fla. C. of C. Environ. Seminars, 1988—; adj. faculty U. South Fla. Coll. Pub. Health; expert witness in environ. mgmt., sampling and analysis, environ. risk, indoor air quality, mold & mildew. Contbr. articles to profl. jours. Co-founder Berea Cmty. Theater, 1970; bd. dirs. So. Waste Info. Exch., Inc.; mem. adv. bd. Ctr. for Environ./Occup. Risk Analysis and Mgmt., 1998-2004, U. South Fla. Coll. Pub. Health, 1998-2004. Mem. Fla. Bar Assn. (assoc., environ and land use sect.), Fla. Environ. Assessors Assn. (pres. 1996-97, bd. dirs. 1993—), Internat. Soc. Tech. & Environ. Profls. (exec. dir.), Va. Orchid Soc. (pres. 1980-85, del. World Orchid Congress, Miami 1984), Ridge Orchid Soc., Tampa Club (bd. dirs. 1999-2002), Outback Bowl (bd. dirs. 2001—). Republican. Avocations: horticulture, guitar. Home: PO Box 145 Mango FL 33550-0145 Office: 717 W Wheeler Rd Brandon FL 33510 Office Phone: 813-684-8049. Business E-mail: robert@environmentalevaluations.com

**STEPHENS, SHAND SCOTT,** lawyer; b. Pasadena, Calif., Mar. 25, 1949; s. Elmer Shand and Gladys Joy (Baker) S.; m. Marcia Pizzo, July 25, 1982 (div. Dec. 1985); m. Kieran Candy, Feb. 6, 1999; children: Sofia, Shannon, Shand BA, Yale U., 1971; JD, U. Calif., San Francisco, 1975. Bar: Calif. 1975, U.S. Dist. Ct. (no., so., ea. and cen. dists.) Calif. 1975, U.S. Ct. Appeals (8th, 9th, 11th cir.) 1975. Assoc. Bronson, Bronson & McKinnon, San Francisco, 1978-82, ptnr., 1982—93; counsel Aon Corp., Nat. Litigation, 1993—2004; ptnr. DLA Piper Rudnick Gray Cary US, LLP, 2004—. Gen. counsel San Francisco State U. Found., 1987-93; gen. counsel Westamerica Bank, San Rafael, Calif., 1987-93; bd. dirs. Russian Art Found., Kydsncars. Named No. Calif. Super Lawyer, 2005, So. Bay Area Best Lawyer, 2005; recipient Calif. Lawyer of Yr. award, 1998. Mem. ABA, Calif. Bar Assn., Order of Coif. Avocations: american civil war history and archaeology, skiing, tennis. Office: DLA Piper Rudnick Gray Cary US LLP 153 Townsend St Ste 800 San Francisco CA 94107 Office Phone: 415-615-6028. Business E-Mail: shand.stephens@dlapiper.com.

**STEPHENS, SHIRLEY LYNNE,** writer, editor; b. Glendale, Ariz., Mar. 11, 1934; d. Burrell G. and Kathryn Sullivan Anderson; m. William H. Stephens; children: Laura, Paula Baker, Greg, Carol. BA, Grand Canyon U., Phoenix, AZ, 1958; MDiv, So. Bapt. Theol. Sem., Ft. Worth, TX, 1967. Contract writer, editor Lifeway Christian Resources, Nashville, 1968—94; writer self-employed, Nashville, 1968—2002; v.p. Authors Book Nook, Brentwood. Co-author Under the SS Shadow, 1976; author: A New Testament View of Women, 1980, Breaking Crime's Vicious Cycle, 1993, From the Cell to the Cross, 1999, (book) My Daughter Susan Smith, 2000, Great Truths from Jesus' Conversations With Women, 2003. Avocations: sports, movies, esl teaching. Office: Authors Book Nook PO Box 513 Brentwood TN 37024-0513 Office Phone: 615-370-4936. Business E-Mail: authorsbooknook@bellsouth.net.

**STEPHENS, SIDNEY DEE,** human resources specialist, retired chemical manufacturing company executive; b. St. Joseph, Mo., Apr. 26, 1945; s. Lindsay Caldwell and Edith May (Thompson) S.; m. Ellen Marie Boeh, June 15, 1968 (div. 1973); m. Elizabeth Ann Harris, Sept. 22, 1973; 1 child, Laura Nicole. BS, Mo. Western State U., 1971; MA, U. Houston, 1980; advanced cert. employment law, Inst. Applied Mgmt. and Law, 1998. Cert. Stephen Covey programs facilitator, 1997. Assoc. urban planner Met. Planning Commn., St. Joseph, 1967-71; prodn. acctg. assoc. Quaker Oats Co., St. Joseph, 1971-72, office mgr., pers. rep. Rosemont, Ill., 1972-73, employee and cmty. rels. mgr. New Brunswick, NJ, 1973-75, Pasadena, Tex., 1975-80; mgmt. cons., Houston, 1981—; regional mgr. human resources Syngenta Crop Protection Inc., 2001—, nat., 2004—; pvt. advisor fin. adminstrn. Ross Estates Investments, Ltd., Houston, 2004—. Contbr. articles to profl. jours. With USNR, 1963-65. Mem. ASTD, Nat. Soc. for Human Resources Mgmt., Houston Human Resources Mgmt. Assn. (cmty. and govtl. affairs com. 1984-85, 85-86). Republican. Methodist. Home and Office: 16446 Longvale Dr Houston TX 77059-5420 Office Phone: 281-488-8330. Fax: 281-488-8912. E-mail: elsid45@aol.com.

**STEPHENS, STEVE ARNOLD,** real estate broker; b. Irby, Cheshire, Eng., May 25, 1945; came to U.S., 1983; s. Harold Dennis George and Hilda Leonora (Howell) S.; m. Lynn Williams, Apr. 14, 1983. Student, Manchester U., Eng., 1967-69. Lic. pvt. detective, Ill.; cert. comml. investment. From cadet to detective Cheshire Police, England, 1961-69; acting detective sgt. Merseyside Police, England, 1969-75; acting sgt. Hampshire Police, England, 1975-77; retail store owner Horsham, West Sussex, Eng., 1977-79; pvt. detective Carratu Internat., London, 1979-83, D.A.C. Stephens, Aurora, Ill., 1983-86; broker Coldwell Banker Comml.-Primus Realty, Oswego, Ill., 1986-98; broker owner Stephens Comml. Real Estate, Aurora, Ill., 1998—. Bd. dirs. Aurora Crimestoppers, pres., 1995-96. Recipient Rep. Legion of Merit award, Rep. Order of Merit award. Mem. Nat. Assn. Realtors (CCIM), CCIM Inst. (cert., bd. dirs. Ill. CCIM chpt. 1992-97, sec.-treas. 1994, v.p. 1995, pres. 1996, v.p. region 7 1999-2001, nat. bd. dirs. 1999-2005), No. Ill. Comml. Assn. Realtors (dir. 1995-97), Soc. Indsl. and Office Realtors (SIOR), Internat. Assn. Chiefs Police, Ill. Assn. Realtors, Greater Aurora C. of C Avocations: travel, literature, golf. Home: 7 Saddlewood Ct Sugar Grove IL 60554 Office: 518 N Lake St Aurora IL 60506-3105 Office Phone: 630-906-9900. *Work hard. Tell the truth and shame the Devil!.*

**STEPHENS, THEODORE REED,** lawyer; b. Sept. 22, 1966; BA in History, Princeton U., 1988; JD, Stanford U., 1991. Bar: Pa. 1992, DC 1993. Law clk. to Hon. Clifford Scott Green US Dist. Ct. Ea. Dist. Pa.; trial atty. civil fraud sect., civil divsn. US Dept. Justice, 1995—2003; ptnr., litig. & bus. regulation practice Sonnenschein Nath & Rosenthal LLP, Washington, 2003—. Recipient Spl. Commendation Award, US Dept. Justice, 2002. Mem.: ABA (health law sect.), Am. Inns of Ct. (Edward Bennett Williams Chpt.), Am. Health Lawyers Assn., DC Bar Assn. Office: Sonnenschein Nath & Rosenthal LLP Ste 600, E Tower 1301 K St NW Washington DC 20015 Office Phone: 202-408-6434. Office Fax: 202-408-6399. Business E-Mail: rstephens@sonnenschein.com.

**STEPHENS, THOMAS G.,** automotive executive; BS in Mech. Engring., U. Mich., 1971. With General Motors, Mich., 1969—; experimental engr., staff project engr. GM Cadillac Motor Car Div., Detroit, 1971—80, supr. product engring., 1980—82, staff engr. emission, transmissions, 1982—85; sr. staff engr. transmission, powertrain controls GM Buick-Oldsmobile-Cadillac Powertrain Div., 1985—88; plant mgr. GM Buick-Oldsmobile-Cadillac Powertrain Livonia Engine Plant, 1988—90; dir. engring. GM Engine Div., 1990—91; dir. engine engring. GM Powertrain, 1991—93, engring ops gen. mgr. Pontiac, 1993—94; v.p. GM Corp., Detroit, 1994; v.p., group dir. engring. ops. GM Truck Group, 1996—2000; v.p. vehicle integration GM Corp., 2001; group. v.p. GM Powertrain, 2001—. Mem.: U. Mich. Nat. Adv. Coun., Detroit Sci. Ctr. (bd. trustees).

**STEPHENS, THOMAS M(ARON),** education educator; b. Youngstown, Ohio, June 15, 1931; s. Thomas and Mary (Hanna) S.; m. Evelyn Kleshock, July 1, 1955. BS, Youngstown Coll., 1953; MEd, Kent State U., 1957; EdD, U. Pitts., 1966. U.S. psychologist, Ohio. Tchr. Warren (Ohio) public schs., 1955-57, Niles (Ohio) public schs., 1957-58; psychologist Montgomery County, Ohio, 1958-60; dir. gifted edn. Ohio Dept. Edn., Columbus, 1960-66;

assoc. prof. edn. U. Pitts., 1966-70; prof. edn. Ohio State U., 1970—, chmn. dept. exceptional children., 1972-82, chmn. dept. human services edn., 1982-87, assoc. dean Coll. Edn. 1987-92, prof., 1987-92, prof. emeritus, 1992—; clin. prof. edn. U. Dayton, Ohio, 1993—; exec. dir. Sch. Study Coun. Ohio, Columbus, 1993—. Mem. Higher Edn. Consortium for Spl. Edn., chmn., 1976-77; pub., pres. Cedars Press, Inc. Author: Directive Teaching of Children with Learning and Behavioral Handicaps, 2d edit, 1976, Implementing Behavioral Approaches in Elementary and Secondary Schools, 1975, Teaching Skills to Children with Learning and Behavioral Disorders, 1977, Teaching Children Basic Skills: A Curriculum Handbook, 1978, 2d edit. 1983, Social Skills In The Classroom, 1978, 2d edit., 1991, Teaching Mainstreamed Students, 1982, 2d edit., 1988, Social Behavior Assessment Scale, 1991; dir.: Jour. Sch. Psychology, 1965-75, 80—; exec. editor: The Directive Tchr.; assoc. editor: Spl. Edn. and Tchr. Edn., Techniques, Behavioral Disorders, Spl. Edn. and Remedial Edn.; contbr. articles to profl. jours. Named to Ohio State U. Coll. of Edn. Hall of Fame, 1999; U.S. Office of Edn. fellow, 1964-65. Mem. APA, NASP (charter), State Dirs. for Gifted (pres. 1962-63), Coun. for Exceptional Children (gov., Tchr. Educator of Yr. tchr. edn. divsn. 1985), Coun. Children with Behavioral Disorders (pres. 1972-73). Home: 551 E Cooke Rd Columbus OH 43214-2813 Office: Sch Study Coun of Ohio 4795 Evanswood Dr 300 Columbus OH 43229-6294

**STEPHENSON, ALAN CLEMENTS,** lawyer; b. Wilmington, NC, Nov. 7, 1944; s. Abram Clements and Ruth (Smith) Stephenson; m. Shannon Kennedy; children from previous marriage: Edward Taylor, Anne Baldwin. AB in Hist., U. N.C., 1967; JD, U. Va., 1970. Bar: NY 1971. Assoc. Cravath, Swaine & Moore, N.Y.C., 1970-78, ptnr., 1978-88; mng. dir. Wasserstein, Perella and Co. Inc., N.Y.C., 1988-92; ptnr., corp. Cravath, Swaine & Moore, N.Y.C., 1992—. Mem. external adv. bd. undergrad. honors program U. N.C., 1998—. Trustee Cold Spring Harbor Lab., 2003-. Morehead scholar, John M. Morehead Found., 1963. Mem.: NY State Bar Assn., Assn. of Bar of City of NY, Brook Club, Union Club, Farmington Country Club, Meadow Brook Club, Links Club, Phi Beta Kappa. Office: Cravath Swaine & Moore 825 8th Ave 47th Fl New York NY 10019-7475 Office Phone: 212-474-1400. Office Fax: 212-474-3700. Business E-Mail: astephenson@cravath.com.

**STEPHENSON, ARTHUR EMMET, JR.,** investment company executive; b. Bastrop, La., Aug. 29, 1945; s. Arthur Emmet and Edith Louise Stephenson; m. Toni Lyn Edwards, June 17, 1967; 1 child, Tessa. BS in Fin. magna cum laude, La. State U., 1967; MBA (Ralph Thomas Sayles fellow), Harvard U., 1969. Chartered fin. analyst. Adminstrv. aide to U.S. Sen. Russell Long of La., Washington, 1966; security analyst Fidelity Funds, Boston, 1968; chmn. bd., pres. Stephenson & Co., Denver; sr. ptnr. Stephenson Ventures, Stephenson Properties; founder, chmn. Gen. Comm., Inc., Denver; founder, chmn. bd. dirs. StarTek, Inc., 1987–2006. Bd. dirs. Danaher Corp.; founder Charter Bank and Trust, chmn., 1980—91; mem. adv. bd. First Berkshire Fund, 1984–2002, Capital Resources Ptnrs., L.P., 1987–2004; former pub. Law Enforcement Product News, Colo. Book, Pub. Safety Product News, 1990–98, Denver mag., Denver Bus. mag.; bd. dean's adv. Bus. Sch. Harvard U., 2006—. Del. White House conf., 1980; past. nat. trustee Nat. Symphony Orch., John F. Kennedy Ctr. Performing Arts, 1995—98; past mem. nat. steering com. Norman Rockwell Mus., Stockbridge, Mass.; past mem. Colo. Small bus. Coun.; past mem. assocs. coun. Templeton Coll., Oxford (Eng.) U. Named to Hall of Distinction, Coll. Bus. Adminstrn., La. State U., 1999, La. State U., 2006; recipient Hall of Fame award, Inc. mag., 1994, Albert Einstein Tech. medal, 1999. Mem.: Young Pres. Orgn. (chpt. chmn. 1992—93), Colo. Investment Advisors Assn. (treas., bd. dirs. 1975—76), World Pres.'s Orgn., Chief Execs. Orgn., Harvard U. Bus. Sch. Assn. (internat. pres. 1987—88), So. Calif. Harvard Bus. Sch. Club, Jonathan Club (L.A.), Annabel's (London), Colo. Harvard Bus. Sch. Club (pres. 1980—81, chmn. 1981—82), Thunderbird Country Club (Rancho Mirage, Calif.), Delta Sigma Pi, Kappa Sigma, Beta Gamma Sigma, Phi Kappa Phi, Omicron Delta Kappa. Office: 400 Nevada Way Boulder City NV 89005

**STEPHENSON, ARTHUR G.,** aerospace engineer; b. New London, Conn. m. Loa J. Stehenson; 2 children. BS in Elec. Engring., U. Redlands, Calif., 1964; postgrad., UCLA, 1988. Design engr. TRW, Redondo Beach, Calif., 1964-72, mgr. telecomm. dept., 1972-79, mgr. advanced systems, 1979-80, mgr. solar array programs, 1980-82, mgr. space sta. mission and user requirements analysis study, 1982-83, mgr. orbital maneuvering vehicle project, 1983-84, mgr. orbital maneuvering vehicle Phase B study program, 1984-85, mgr. orbital vehicle sys. engring. and integration, 1985-88, mgr. orbital maneuvering vehicle advanced systems, 1988-90, dir. space transp. and servicing advanced programs, 1990-92; v.p., gen. mgr. Oceaneering Space Systems, Houston, 1992-97, pres., 1997-98; dir NASA Marshall Space Flight Ctr., Huntsville, Ala., 1998—2002, with ednl. br., 2002—. Chmn. Bay Area United Way Campaign, 1997. Mem AIAA (mem. space systems, space ops., space automation and robotics), Nat. Contract Mgmt. Assn., Nat. Space Soc. Achievements include management of space craft subsystems, spacecraft and entire launch vehicles. Office: Marshall Space Flight Ctr Mail Code C0-70 Huntsville AL 35812

**STEPHENSON, EDWARD,** psychology professor; b. Black River, Jamaica, W.I., Jan. 17, 1958; s. Leandro Stephenson and Merle Ivadne Ireland. BA, Queens Coll., 1979; PhD, U. Calif., 1987. Assoc. prof. Fla. Meml. U., 1997—. Mem.: Assn. Black Psychol., Am. Psychol. Assn. Office Phone: 954-805-6689. Personal E-Mail: estephen@fmuniv.edu.

**STEPHENSON, HERMAN HOWARD,** retired banker; b. Wichita, Kans., July 15, 1929; s. Herman Horace and Edith May (Wayland) S.; m. Virginia Anne Ross, Dec. 24, 1950, (dec. Sept. 2004); children: Ross Wayland, Neal Bevan, Jann Edith. BA, U. Mich., 1950; JD with distinction, U. Mo., Kansas City, 1958, LLD (hon.), U. Mo., Kansas City, 1981. Bar: Kans. 1958. With City Nat. Bank, Kansas City, Mo., 1952-54 City Bond & Mortgage Co., Kansas City, 1954-59, Bank of Hawaii, Honolulu, 1959-94, CEO, 1989-94, ret. chmn., 1994—. Bd. dirs. Friends of Cancer Rsch. Ctr. Hawaii. With U.S. Army, 1950—52. Mem.: Pacific Forum/CSIS (bd. govs.), Navy League U.S., Waialae Country Club, Oahu Country Club, Eagle Bend Country Club, Rotary, Pi Eta Sigma, Kappa Sigma.

**STEPHENSON, HUGH EDWARD, JR.,** retired surgeon; b. Columbia, Mo., June 1, 1922; s. Hugh Edward and Doris (Pryor) S.; m. Sarah Norfleet Dickinson, Aug. 15, 1964; children: Hugh Edward III, Ann Dunlop. AB, BS, U. Mo., 1943; MD, Washington U., St. Louis, 1945. Diplomate Am. Bd. Surgery, Am. Bd. Thoracic Surgery. Mem. faculty U. Mo. Sch. Medicine, Columbia, 1953—; prof. surgery U. Mo. Hugh E. Stephenson Jr. Dept. Surgery, Columbia, 1956—, chmn. dept. surgery, 1956—60, chief div. gen. surgery, 1976—87, chief staff, 1982—94; John Growdon Disting. prof. surgery emeritus U. Mo. Sch. Medicine, Columbia, 1987—, interim dean, 1988—89, assoc. dean, 1989—92; dist. prof. surgery emeritus, 1993; curator U. Mo. System, 1996—. Pres. bd. curators U. Mo., 2000; Markle scholar acad. medicine, 1954-60. Author: Immediate Care of the Acutely Ill and Injured, 2d edit, 1974, Cardiac Arrest and Resuscitation, 4th edit., 1975, The Kicks That Count; Contbr. articles to profl. jours. Named one of Outstanding Young Men of Nation, Nat. Jr. C. of C., 1956, James IV Surg. Traveler Gt. Britain, 1962, Dist. Faculty award, 1989. Mem. ACS, AMA (del., chmn. coun. on med. edn. 1994-95, co-chmn. liaison com. on med. edn. 1995, pres. surgical caucus 1996), Vascular Surgery Soc., Soc. Thoracic Surgeons, So. Thoracic Surgery Assn., So. Med. Assn. (coun., pres. 2001), Mo. Med. Assn. (chmn. jud. coun. 1986—, v.p. 1986-87), Beta Theta Pi (trustees, pres. gen. frat. 1978-81). Baptist. Home: 5 Danforth Cir Columbia MO 65201-3509 Office: University of Missouri Hugh E Stephenson Jr Dept Surgery 1 Hospital Dr Columbia MO 65201-5276 Office Phone: 573-882-5645.

**STEPHENSON, HUNTER W.,** writing educator; b. Milan, Mo., Aug. 16, 1964; m. Shelley Stephenson. BS in Marine Engring., USCG Acad., New London, Conn., 1986; MA in English, Kent State U., 1998, PhD in Rhetoric and Composition, 2004. Asst. prof. writing U. Houston-Clear Lake, 2004—. Author: Forecasting Opportunity: Kairos, Production and Writing, 2005. Vol. Habitat for Humanity, Houston, 2005, SPCA, League City, Tex., 2004—05.

Lt. USCG, 1986—95. Mem.: Rhetoric Soc. Am., Nat. Coun. Tchrs. of English, Am. Ednl. Rsch. Assn. Office: Univ Houston Clear Lake 2700 Bay Area Blvd Houston TX 77058 Office Phone: 281-283-3403. Business E-Mail: stephenson@cl.uh.edu.

**STEPHENSON, IRENE HAMLEN,** biomedical researcher, consultant, editor, educator; b. Chgo., Oct. 7, 1923; d. Charles Martin and Carolyn Hilda (Hilgers) Hamlin; m. Edgar B. Stephenson, Sr., Aug. 16, 1941 (div. 1946); 1 child, Edgar B. Author biorhythm compatibilities column Nat. Singles Register, Norwalk, Calif., 1979-81; instr. biorhythm Learning Tree Open U., Canoga Park, Calif., 1982-83, instr. biorhythm personality analysis, 1980—, instr. biorhythm compatibility, 1982—; owner, pres. matchmaking svc. Pen Pals Using Biorhythm, Chatsworth, Calif., 1979—. Editor newsletter The Truth, 1979-85, Mini Examiner, Chatsworth, 1985—; rschr. biorhythm personality and compatibility, 1974—, biorhythm columnist Psychic Astrology Horoscope, 1989-94, True Astrology Forecast, 1989-94, Psychic Astrology Predictions, 1990-94, Con Artist Types, 1995, Pedophile (child molester) Types, 1995-2000, Personality Types, 1996, Trouble-Addict (Suicide) Types, 1997, Domineering/Nag Types, 1998, Con Artists, Sweetheart Swindlers, Super Con Artist Types, 1998, Bully types, 2000, Deadly Compatibility Combination, 2000, Fatal Attraction Types, 2000, Sadism, Sadistic, Sadistic Predators, 2000, Salesperson, Practical Joker Types, 2000, Doormat Types, 2000, Famous/Queen Bee/Rescuer Types, 2000, Prostitution, 2000. Author: Learn Biorhythm Personality Analysis, 1980, Do-It-Yourself Biorhythm Compatibilities, 1982; contbr. numerous articles to mags. Office: PO Box 3893 Chatsworth CA 91313-3893

**STEPHENSON, LARRY KIRK,** geography educator, financial planner; b. Seattle, Sept. 22, 1944; s. Norman Eugene and Virginia Dare (Frost) S.; m. Margery Alsever, Aug. 15, 1992; children: Matthew Alan, Leah Anela. BS, Ariz. State U., 1966, MA, 1971; PhD, U. Cin., 1973. Manpower rsch. analyst Employment Security Commn. of Ariz., 1969-70; asst. prof. geography U. Hawaii, Hilo, 1973-76, assoc. prof., 1976-78, chmn. dept. geography, 1975-77; planner Ariz. Dept. Health Svcs., Phoenix, 1978-84; strategic planner City of Glendale, Ariz., 1984-92; pub. health analyst Gila River Indian Comty., Ariz., 1992-98, econ. devel. planner, 1998—. Vis. lectr. dept. geography Ariz. State U., 1978, adj. assoc. prof., 1979—; vis. assoc. prof. dept. geography, area devel. and urban planning U. Ariz., 1978; faculty U. Phoenix, 1979—; adj. prof. Golden Gate U., 1981—, Coll. St. Francis, 1982—; ptnr. Urban Rsch. Assocs., Phoenix, 1981—; faculty Troy State U., 1990—; governing bd. Gila County CC Dist., Ariz., 2004—. Author: Statistics for Health Managers, 1981; co-author: Student Study Guide and Instructor's Manual to accompany Geography: A Modern Synthesis, 4 edits., 1975-83; editor: Kohala keia: Collected Expressions of a Community, 1977; contbr. articles to profl. jours., chpts. to textbooks. Active. Hawaii Island Health Planning Coun., 1974-78, Glendale Cmty. Colls. Pres.'s Coun., 1986-92. With U.S. Army, 1966-68. NDEA fellow 1971-72, Mem. Am. Inst. Cert. Planners, Am Planning Assn., Assn. Am. Geographers, Ariz. Planning Assn. (pres. 1987—), S.W. Profl. Geog. Assn., Lambda Alpha. Unitarian Universalist. Home: HC 4 Box 28K Payson AZ 85541 Office: PO Box 99 Sacaton AZ 85247-0097 Office Phone: 520-562-6014. Personal E-Mail: lstephe739@aol.com.

**STEPHENSON, MASON WILLIAMS,** lawyer; b. Atlanta, May 29, 1946; s. Donald Grier and Katherine Mason (Williams) S.; m. Linda Frances Partee, June 13, 1970; children: Andrew Mason, Walter Martin. AB cum laude, Davidson Coll., 1968; JD, U. Chgo., 1971. Bar: Ga. 1971, U.S. Dist. Ct. (no. dist.) Ga. 1985. Assoc. Alston, Miller & Gaines, Atlanta, 1971-76, ptnr., 1976-77, Trotter, Bondurant, Griffin, Miller & Hishon, Atlanta, 1977-82, Bondurant, Miller, Hishon & Stephenson, Atlanta, 1982-85, King & Spalding, LLP, Atlanta, 1985—, mng. ptnr. Atlanta office, 2001—. Fin. com. Atlanta Olympic Organizing Com., 1988—90. Mem. ABA (sect. bus. law, real property, probate and trust sect.), Am. Coll. Real Estate Lawyers, State Bar Ga. (exec. com., real property law sect. 1989-97, chair intangible rec. tax com. 1994-97), Atlanta Bar Assn. (chair real estate sect. 1981-82), Causeway Club, Capital City Club, Phi Beta Kappa, Phi Delta Phi. Avocations: boating, skiing, jogging. Office: King & Spalding LLP 1180 Peachtree St Atlanta GA 30309 Office Phone: 404-572-4600. Office Fax: 404-572-5100. Business E-Mail: mstephenson@kslaw.com.

**STEPHENSON, PATRICIA ANN,** public health researcher, educator; b. Washington, July 21, 1954; arrived in Sweden, 1990; d. Stanley Edwin and Mary Virginia (Brenneman) S.; m. Marsden Grigg Wagner, Dec. 14, 1990. BS, Calif. State U., Hayward, 1979; ScD, Johns Hopkins U., 1986. RN. Asst. prof. Sch. Pub. Health U. Wash., Seattle, 1986-90, adj. asst. prof. Sch. Nursing, 1987-90; sr. rschr. Ctr. for Pub. Health Rsch., Karlstad, Sweden, 1990-94; cons. health policy analyst, ops. rschr. Copenhagen, 1990-97; sr. advisor health and research USAID, Washington, 1998—. Vis. assoc. prof. Sch. Pub. Health U. Mich., Ann Arbor, 1995-96; cons. WHO, 1989, UNICEF, 1990—, World Bank, 1995-96. Mng. editor, co-founder European Jour. Pub. Health, 1991-94; author, editor: Tough Choices - InVitro Fertilization and the New Reproductive Technologies, 1993; contbr. articles to profl. publs. Women's health policy fellow John D. and Catherine T. MacArthur Found., 1995; recipient Commendation for work in fertility U.K. Parliament/House of Commons, 1989. Mem. APHA, Global Health Council, Delta Omega. Avocations: equestrian sports, dog agility training. Home: 123 Sherman Ave Takoma Park MD 20912 E-mail: pstephenson@usaid.gov.

**STEPHENSON, RANDALL L.,** telecommunications industry executive; BS in acctg., Ctrl. State U., Edmond, Okla.; MS in Acctg., U. Okla., Norman. With Southwestern Bell Tel. Co., Oklahoma City, 1982, area mgr. corp. taxes, 1986—91, dist. mgr. fin analysis, 1991 921 dir fin SBC Comm., Inc., Mexico City, 1992, contr. San Antonio San Antonio, 1996, v.p., contr., 1997, sr. v.p. fin. San Antonio, 1982—2001, exec. v.p., CFO, 2001, COO, 2004—05, AT&T Inc. (merger of SBC Comm. & AT&T Corp.), San Antonio, 2005—; bd. dirs. AT&T Inc., 2005—. Bd. dir. Cingular Wireless, Emerson Electric, 2006—; mem. audit com. H.E. Butt Grocery Co. Mem. nat. exec. bd. Boy Scouts Am.; mem. exec. com., audit com. United Way San Antonio; bd. mem. San Antonio Met. Missions Bd. Mem.: Okla. Soc. CPAs. Office: AT&T Inc 175 E Houston St PO Box 2933 San Antonio TX 78299-2933*

**STEPHENSON, RICHARD ISMERT,** lawyer; b. Augusta, Kans., Oct. 13, 1937; s. Paul Noble and Dorothy May (Ismert) S.; m. Mary Lynn Bryden, July 2, 1967 (div. 1973); 1 child, Richard William; m. Linda Cox, Apr. 5, 1976. BA, U. Kans., 1958; JD, U. Mich., 1965. Bar: Kans. 1965, U.S. Dist. Ct. Kans. 1965, U.S. Ct. Appeals (10th cir.) 1965. Assoc. Fleeson, Gooing, Coulson & Kitch, Wichita, Kans., 1965-72, ptnr., 1973-95; gen. counsel RAGE Inc. and Affiliated Cos., Wichita, 1995—. Lt. (j.g.) USNR, 1959-62. Recipient Hilden Gibson award, U. Kans., 1958. Mem. ABA (forum on franchising), Def. Rsch. Inst., Internat. Assn. Def. Counsel, Kans. Bar Assn., Wichita Bar Assn., Wichita Country Club, Pi Sigma Alpha, Beta Theta Pi. Avocations: golf, fishing. Home: 9203 Killarney Wichita KS 67206-4027 Office: RAGE Inc 1313 N Webb Rd Ste 200 Wichita KS 67206-4077 Office Phone: 316-634-1888. Business E-Mail: dick@rage-inc.com.

**STEPHENSON, ROSCOE BOLAR, JR.,** state supreme court justice; b. Covington, Va., Feb. 22, 1922; AB, Washington and Lee U., 1943, JD, 1947, LL.D. (hon.), 1983. Bar: Va. 1947. Ptnr. Stephenson & Stephenson, Covington, 1947-52; commonwealth's atty. Alleghany County, Va., 1952-64; ptnr. Stephenson, Kostel, Watson, Carson and Snyder, Covington, 1964-73; judge 25th Jud. Cir. Ct. Commonwealth Va., Covington, 1973-81; justice Va. Supreme Ct., Richmond, 1981-97, sr. justice, 1997—. Recipient Covington Citizen of Yr. award, 1973, Outstanding Alumni award Covington H.S., 1973, Disting. Alumnus award Washington and Lee U., 1997. Mem. Am. Coll. Trial Lawyers; mem. Va. State Bar (council 1969-73), Va. Bar Assn., Va. Trial Lawyers Assn., Order of Coif, Omicron Delta Kappa. Home: North Ridge Hot Springs VA 24445 Office: Va Supreme Ct 214 W Main St PO Box 198 Covington VA 24426-0198 also: Va Supreme Court Supreme Court Bldg 100 N 9th St Richmond VA 23219-2335 Office Phone: 540-962-6601.

**STEPHENSON, SHERRY MADELINE,** trade economist; d. Joe Harrell and Bettie Beasley Stephenson; children: Matthew Hector Travis, Corinne Louise Madeline. MA, NYU, 1974; PhD, Grad. Inst. Internat. Studies, Geneva, 1987. Trade specialist UNCTAD, Geneva, 1978—80; trade specialist Gen. Agreement Tariffs and Trade GATT, Geneva, 1980—82; prin. adminstr. Trade Directorate OECD, Paris, 1983—91; advisor Ministry of Trade, Jakarta, Indonesia, 1992—95; prin. trade specialist Trade Unit OAS, Washington, 1995—2000, dep. dir. for trade, 2000—05, dir. dept. trade and competitiveness, 2006—. Cons. Pacific Econ. Cooperation Coun., Singapore, 1993—2000, Asian Devel. Bank, Manila, 1993—96, World Bank, Washington, 1995—97, USAID, 1997—2000. Editor: (academic books) Services Trade in the Western Hemisphere, 2000, Services Trade Liberalization and Facilitation, 2002. Mem.: European Inst., Internat. Trade and Fin. Assn., Pacific Econ. Cooperation Coun., Inter-American Dialogue, Cosmos Club. Office: Orgn Am States 1889 F St NW Washington DC 20006 Office Phone: 202-458-3342. Business E-Mail: sstephenson@oas.org.

**STEPHENSON, TONI EDWARDS,** publishing executive, investment company executive, communications executive; b. Bastrop, La., July 23, 1945; d. Sidney Crawford and Grace Erleene Little; m. Arthur Emmet Stephenson Jr., June 17, 1967; 1 child, Tessa Lyn. Grad. owner/pres. mgmt. program, Harvard Bus. Sch. Pres., dir. Gen. Comm., Inc., Denver; sr. v.p., founder Stephenson & Co., Denver, 1971—; ptnr. Stephenson Properties, Stephenson Ventures. Past. pres. Children's Hosp. Assn. Vols.; past troop leader Girl Scouts Am.; past dir. Anchor Ctr. for Blind Children; dir. bd. dean's advisors Harvard U. Bus. Sch.; past dir. The Children's Hosp., St. Joseph's Hosp.; Cherry Creek H.S. Parent Tchr Conf. Orgn. Mem. Harvard Bus. Sch. Club Colo., DAR, Delta Gamma, Jonathan Club, Annabel's (London), Thunderbird Country Club.

**STEPHENSON, VIVIAN M.,** former retail executive; B Math., NYU; MBA, U. Havana; PhD (hon.), Mills Coll., Oakland. Mgmt. positions Rand Info. Sys., Occidental Petroleum Corp., Assoc. Credit Burs. Svcs., Inc.; dir. info. sys. devel. Mervyn's, 1989-90, v.p. MIS, 1990-94, sr. v.p., 1994-95; sr. v.p., chief info. officer Dayton Hudson Corp., Mpls., 1995-2000; exec. v.p., chief info officer Target Corp., Mpls., —2000; ret., 2000. Bd. dirs. MobiNetrix Sys. Inc.; mem. info. sys. customer adv. coun. IBM; mem. Tandem Americas Customer Coun; mem. bd. dir. Mills Coll. Chair bd. dirs. San Francisco AIDS Found.; mem. Nat. Retail Fedn. Info. Sys. Bd. Mem. Calif. C. of C. Office: Target Corp 1000 Nicollet Mall Minneapolis MN 55403-2467

**STEPNER, DONALD LEON,** lawyer; b. Boston, Apr. 23, 1939; s. Neil and Sadie (Adelman) S.; m. Beth Klass, Aug. 14, 1965 (div. Dec. 1985); children: David, Jeff. AA, Wentworth Inst., Boston, 1958; BA, Ky. Wesleyan Coll., 1963; JD, U. Ky., 1966. Bar: Ky. 1966, U.S. Dist. Ct. Ky. 1966, U.S. Ct. Appeals (6th cir.) 1966, U.S. Supreme Ct. 1971. Assoc. Charles Adams, Covington, Ky., 1966-69; ptnr. Adams, Stepner, Woltermann & Dusing, Covington, 1969—. Pres. Ky. State Ethics Com. Bd. dirs. Boys Club. Recipient Human Rels. award NCCJ, 1986; named in Best Lawyers in Am. Fellow Am. Coll. Trial Lawyers; mem. ABA (ho. delegates 2000-), Ky. Bar Assn. (pres. 1990—2000), No. Ky. Bar Assn., Ky. Def. Rsch. Inst., Kenton County Bar Assn. (pres. 1973-74, Merit award 1973, Gavel award 1973), U.S. Soccer Fedn. (cert. referee, pres. 1980-85), Ky. High Sch. Referees Assn., No. Ky. Soccer Assn. (ofcl. pres. 1980—). Avocations: golf, jogging, bicycling. Office: Adams Stepner Woltermann & Dusing PO Box 861 Covington KY 41012-0861

**STEPNER, MICHAEL JAY,** architect; b. Chgo., Aug. 7, 1940; s. Lester Harry and Florence (Addison) S.; m. Rosemary Reiser, Apr. 2, 1965; children: Rachel, Jessica, Adam, Joshua, Rebekah. Student, U. Minn., 1961-62; BArch, U. Ill., 1964; postgrad., U. Calif., Berkeley, 1971, U.S. Navy Engring. Schs., 1965-66. Registered architect, Calif. Urban designer, planner Crosstown Assocs., Chgo., 1968-71; urban designer, planner planning dept. City of San Diego, 1971-81, asst. planning dir., 1981-88, acting planning dir., 1987-88, city architect, 1988-92, asst. to city mgr., spl. projects coord., 1992-94, city urban design coord., 1984—97; pvt. practice The Stepner Design Group, San Diego; dean New Sch. Arch. and Design, 1997—2001. Vis. critic in urban design U. Ill, Chgo., 1970-71, San Diego State U. Grad. Sch. Planning and Pub. Adminstrn., Urban Design & Site Planning Inst., 1974-85; lectr. Urban Conservation Grad. Sch. History, U. San Diego, 1978, 81, 82, 84; asst. prof., lectr., design critic New Sch. Arch. and Design, San Diego City U., 1988—, prof. arch. and urban design; faculty assoc. for transp. and land use planning Lincoln Inst. Land Policy, Cambridge, Mass., 1993—; former mem. hist. bldg. code bd. State of Calif.; peer profl. Federal Govt. Design Excellence Program, 2002-04; mem., dir. Community Planning and Design Ctr., San Diego, 1971-74; mem. faculty New Sch. Arch. and Design.; mem. post licensure competency task force Calif. Archtl. Registration Bd. Bd. dirs. Citizens Coordinate for Century III, 1991—; mem. Regional Urban Design Assistance Team, Seattle, Washington, and Liverpool, Eng.; past bd. dirs. Californians for Preservation Action; mem. Congress for the New Urbanism; mem. Calif. State Bd. Arch. Exams, 1999; peer profl. Fed. Ct. Fed. Design Excellence Program, 2002-04. Recipient Leadership in Planning award New Sch. Architecture, 1992, Gaslamp Pioneer award San Diego Gaslamp Quarter Found., 1993, Ellen and Roger Revelle award Citizens Coordinate for Century III, 1993. Fellow AIA (co-chair housing assistance team City of Washincton, 1990, bd. dirs. San Diego chpt. 1976-78, 94-95, 97—, pres-elect 2001, mem. nat. urban design com., past mem. Calif. Coun. mem. preservation-urban conservation com., urban design commr. San Diego chpt. 1975-76, Spl. award for Excellence in Govt. 1983), Am. Inst. Cert. Planners, Inst. for Urban Design; mem. Am. Planning Assn. (Disting. Leadership award Calif. chpt. 1991), San Diego Fed. Courthouse Design Team (selection panel), Urban Land Inst., Lambda Alpha. Home: 4760 Hortensia St San Diego CA 92103-1103 Office: 3620 30th St Ste B San Diego CA 92104 Office Phone: 619-234-2112. Business E-Mail: stepner1@pacbell.net.

**STEPONAITIS, VINCAS PETRAS,** archaeologist, anthropologist, educator; b. Boston, Aug. 10, 1953; s. Vincas and Elena (Povydis) S.; m. Laurie Cameron, Dec. 31, 1976; children: Elena Anne, Lillian Kazimiera. AB in Anthropology magna cum laude, Harvard U., 1974; MA in Anthropology, U. Mich., 1975, PhD in Anthropology, 1980. From lectr. to assoc. prof. dept. anthropology SUNY, Binghamton, 1979-87; assoc. prof. U. N.C., Chapel Hill, 1988-94, prof., 1995—, dir. Rsch. Labs. Archaeology, 1988—. Guest worker Nat. Bur. Stds., 1979; adj. lectr. dept. anthropology SUNY, Binghamton, 1979; lectr. and presenter in field. Author: Ceramics, Chronology, and Community Patterns, An Archaeological Study at Moundville, 1983, Archaeology of the Moundville Chiefdom, 1998, (CD-Rom) Excavating Occaneechi Town, 1998; editor Southeastern Archaeology, 1984-87; regional editor Investigations in Am. Archaeology, 1987-91; mem. editl. bd. Prehistory Press, 1990-97, Southern Cultures, 1992—, Am. Archaeology, 1996-2000; contbr. articles to profl. jours. Smithsonian Instn. fellow, 1978-79; grantee NSF, 1978-80, 83, 89-92, 94, 2000, 05, IMLS, 2003, Wenner-Gren Found., 1981, 86-88, Nat. Geographic Soc., 1987-88, Z. Smith Reynolds Found., 1992-94, Alcoa Found. 2005. Fellow Am. Anthrop. Assn.; mem. Soc. Am. Archaeology (Presdl. Recognition award 1993-94, exec. com. 1983-84, mem. 1992-94, pres. 1997-99), Archaeological Conservancy (bd. dirs. 2000—, chmn. 2003—), Ctr. for Maya Rsch. (bd. dirs. 2002-), Southeastern Archaeol. Conf. (editor 1984-87, pres. 1990-92), N.C. Archaeol. Soc. (exec. sec. 1988-91, sec. 1991-96), N.C. Archaeol. Coun. (exec. com. 1988-92), Archaeol. Soc. S.C., Ala. Archaeol. Soc., Miss. Archaeol. Soc., La. Archaeol. Soc. Office: U NC Rsch Labs Archaeology Alumni Bldg Cb 3120 Chapel Hill NC 27599-3120

**STEPP, JAMES MICHAEL,** finance company executive; b. Huntington, W.Va., Apr. 26, 1944; s. James Dial and Helen (Shelton) S.; m. Lilian Arlene Radeker, Jan. 3, 1970; children: James Michael, Scott Adams, John Radeker. BS, U.S. Mil. Acad., 1966; MBA, Stanford U., 1972. Commd. lt. C.E. U.S. Army, 1966, advanced through grades to capt., 1968, served in Vietnam, resigned, 1970; asst. v.p. Bank of Am., San Francisco, 1972-75, v.p. N.Y.C., 1975-81; v.p., treas. Fotomat Corp., Wilton, Conn., 1981-83, Emhart Corp., Hartford, Conn., 1983-89; pres. Am. Corp. Fin. Group Inc., West Hartford, 1989-92; exec. v.p., CFO Purolator Products Co., Tulsa, Okla., 1992—, bd.

dirs. Adv. dir. Conn. Nat. Bank, 1986-92. Bd. dirs. Jr. Achievement, North Cen. Conn., 1986-92. Decorated Silver Star, Bronze Star, Purple Heart, Army Commendation medal, Air medal. Mem. Fin. Execs. Inst., Stanford Bus. Sch. Alumni Assn., West Point Soc. of N.Y. Republican. Episcopalian. Avocations: tennis, fishing, jogging, golf. Home: 7021 Old Dairy Ln Charlotte NC 28211-3562

**STEPPE, STEPHEN,** management consultant; Various positions including v.p., mktg. dir. investment properties Coldwell Banker, 1972—86; prin. RREEF Mgmt. Co., San Francisco, 1986—, sr. v.p., mng. ptnr. Bd. mem., principal Instl. Real Estate,Inc.; chmn. Pension Real Estate Assn. Editl. bd. Instl. Real Estate Letter. Office: RREEF Mgmt Co 26th Fl 101 California St San Francisco CA 94111

**STEPS, BARBARA JILL,** lawyer; b. Springfield, Mo., June 19, 1945; d. Louis Edward and Margaret Pearl (Stiver) Bredeman; m. Robert William Steps, Dec. 21, 1968; children: Rebecca Harper, Aaron Andrew, Jessica Anne. BA in Psychology, St. Louis U., 1966; JD, U. Mo., 1969; MBA, U. Conn., 1983. Atty. Ralston Purina Co., St. Louis, 1969; law clerk U.S. Dist. Ct., St. Louis, 1969-72; assoc. Stone, Keck & Staser, Evansville, Ind., 1973-75, Cline & Callahan, Indpls., 1975-77, Law Office, Herbert V. Camp, Ridgefield, Conn., 1978-81; from comml. counsel to corp. counsel, sec. Framatome Connectors USA, Inc. (now FCI USA, Inc.), Fairfield, Conn., 1981-93; v.p., counsel, sec. FCI USA, Inc. (formerly Framatome Connectors USA, Inc.), Etters, Pa., 1993—2002, sr. v.p. adminstrn., counsel, sec., 2002—. Mem.: ABA, Am. Corp. Counsel Assn. Home: 23 Emlyn Ln Mechanicsburg PA 17055-8017 Office: FCI USA Inc 825 Old Trail Rd Etters PA 17319-9392

**STEPTOE, MARY LOU,** lawyer; b. Washington, July 15, 1949; d. Philip Pendleton and Irene (Hellen) S.; m. Peter E. Carson, Sept. 1986; children: Elizabeth Maud, Julia Grace. BA, Occidental Coll., 1971; JD, U. Va., 1974. Bar: Va., 1974, Supreme Ct., 1987, D.C. 1996. Staff atty., Bur. of Competition FTC, Washington, 1974-79, atty. advisor to commr., 1979-86, exec. asst. to chmn., 1988-89, assoc. dir., Bur. of Competition, 1989-90, dep. dir., 1990-92, acting dir., 1992-95, dep. dir., 1995-96; ptnr. Skadden Arps Slate Meagher & Flom LLP, Washington. Office Phone: 202-371-7020. Business E-Mail: msteptoe@skadden.com.

**STEPTOE, SONJA,** journalist; b. Lutcher, La., June 16, 1960; d. Eldridge Willie and Rosa Jane Steptoe. BA in Econs., U. Mo., 1982, B in Journalism, 1982; JD, Duke U. Law Sch., 1985. Staff reporter Wall St. Jour., N.Y.C., 1985—90; sr. editor Sports Illustrated, N.Y.C., 1990—2001, People Mag., N.Y.C., 2001—02; nat. corr, CNN Sports, N.Y.C., 1999—2001; corr. HBO Sports, 1995—2001; sr. corr. Time Mag., L.A., 2002—. Editl. adv. bd. U. Mo. Alumni Mag., Columbia, Mo., 1991—96; alumni bd. Duke U. Law Sch., Durham, NC, 1996—98; mem. U. Mo. Strategic Develop. Bd., 1988—. Co-author: (book) Guide to Women's Golf, 1993, A Kind of Grace" The Autobiography of the World's Greatest Female Athlete, 1997. Bd. mem. Alvin Ailey Dance Sch., NYC, 2001—02, Assoc. Black Charities, NYC, 1991—97. Recipient Emmy award, Nat. Assn. TV Arts and Sci., 1998, Nat. Headliner award, Press Club of Atlantic City, 1999, Disting. Alumni award, U. Mo., Duke Law Sch. Young Alumni award, 1994, 2000. Mem.: ABA, Nat. Assn. Black Journalists, World Affairs Coun.

**STERBA, JEFFRY E.,** energy executive; BA in Econ. summa cum laude, Washington Univ., St. Louis; post-grad study in Econ., Washington Univ., Univ. N.Mex. Various positions PNM (subs. PNM Resources), Albuquerque, 1977—98, pres., 2000—; now chmn., pres., CEO PNM Resources, Albuquerque; exec. v.p. USEC, Md., 1998—2000. Bd. dir., exec. com. Edison Elec. Inst.; vice chmn. Elec. Power Rsch. Inst. Former campaign chmn. United Way Ctrl. N. Mex.; mem. Gov. Bus. Adv. Coun.; bd. dir. US C of C; co-chmn. Albuquerque Econ. Forum. Mem.: Mortar Board, Omicron Delta Kappa. Office: PNM Resources Alvarado Sq Albuquerque NM 87158-0001 Office Phone: 505-241-2700. Office Fax: 505-241-2367.

**STERBENK-LUND, JACQUELYN MARIE,** chemistry educator, biology educator; m. Peter L. Lund. BA in Biology, Coll. St. Scholastica, Duluth, Minn., 1972—76; M in Sci. Edn., Bemidji State U., Minn., 1984—90. Life sci. tchr. Holy Trinity H.S., Winsted, Minn., 1977—84; biology & chemistry tchr. North Br. HS, Minn., 1984—87, Bemidji HS, 1987—. Bd. mem. Beltrami County Fair, 1990—2006, Beltrami County Ext. Com., 1992—2006; ch. coun. mem. Bethel Luth. Ch., Bemidji, 1990—95. Mem.: NSTA, Delta Kappa Gamma. Office: Bemidji HS 3300 Gillett Dr NW Bemidji MN 56601 Office Phone: 218-444-1600.

**STERKINA, SOFIYA,** writer; b. Neshin, Ukraine, Aug. 5, 1962; arrived in U.S., 1998; d. Aaron Sterkin and Zinaida Gornaya. RN, Med. Coll., Ukraine, 1985. Nurse Kiev Railroad Hosp., 1985—89, Kiev Hosp., 1989—91, Kiev Med. U., 1991—93, Irpen Mil. Hosp., 1993—97; nurse asst. trng., 1998—99; author San Francisco, 2001—. Author: With the Secret for All World, Dragonfly, Baby, Magicians, Circus, Tobik Bobik and Me, The Little Brothers, Unusual Adventure of the Small Duck, On the Children's Ground, Inspiration, Holidays of Jewish Nation, Children's Horoscope, Why Little Noses of the Small Ducks are Flat, The Animals Are Smiling, How I Was Treated, To Las Vegas for the Adventure, The Wineglass of the Champagne, The Girl and the Dragon or The Story of the Broken Hearts, What I Saw, I Knew, I Understood, Master Bob, Master Tom and Master John, Story of the Small Princess of the Lion's Kingdom. Served Irpen Mil. Hosp., 1993—97, Ukraine. Jewess. Avocations: reading, swimming, badminton. Home: 491 31st Ave Apt #518 San Francisco CA 94121 Office Phone: 415-752-2265.

**STERLING, ARTHUR JAMES,** retired legal assistant; b. Pineville, La., July 27, 1944; s. Leon Henry and Dorothy Mae Sterling; children: Hope, Monique, Heather. AA in bus. adminstrn., Compton CC, 1986; student in psychology, U. Southern Calif., 1988—89; AA in bus. paralegal, Cerritos CC, 1994; PhD in counseling, Progressive Univeral Life Ch., 2000. With U.S. Naval Weapons Sta., Seal Beach, Calif., 1979-83, Norwalk Superior Ct., 1991; law clk.; guidance counselor, 2000—02; ret. Dave Holt Meml scholar, K.T. Skula meml. scholar, Johnson Controls, Inc. Fund scholar, Amy Welch Meml. scholar. Mem. Soc. for Advancement of Mgmt. (pres.), Phi Beta Lambda (pres.), Associated Student Body (senator, pres.), The Oxford Club, The Highlander Club. Democrat. Avocations: computers, cooking, reading. Home: 4216 Carlin Ave #C Lynwood CA 90262-5208 Office Phone: 310-631-8774. Personal E-mail: drdoodlebug06@yahoo.com.

**STERLING, COLLEEN,** artist; b. Sterling, Ill., Dec. 17, 1951; d. Gordon Dennis and Ruth Mary (Lendman) McKee. Student, Mundelein Coll., Chgo., 1970—72, Sch. of the Art Inst., 1973—74, U. Cin., 1974. Mass. Coll. Art, Boston, 1980, student, 1985. Mem. staff Mus. of the Art Inst., Chgo., 1973—74, Mus. Fine Arts, Boston, 1974—76; owner, operator Sterling Graphics, Blairsville, Ga., 1989—92; visual artist Blairsville, 1989—. Dir. Studio Epona, Cambridge, 1980—83. One-woman shows include Amarillo (Tex.) Art Ctr. and Mus., 1993, Atlanta Bur. Cultural Affairs, 1996, exhibited in group shows at Riverside (Calif.) Art Mus., 1992, An Art Place, Chgo., 1993, Telfair Mus. Art, Savannah, Ga., 1995, Vanderbilt U., Nashville, 1995, Hunter Mus. Am. Art, Chattanooga, 1998, major commn., Hyatt Roissy, Paris, 1992, Hartsfield Internat. Airport, Atlanta, 1998. Mem. Nat. M us. Women in the Arts, Ga. Citizens for the Arts, Atlanta, 1995—98, Calif. Lawyers for the Arts, San Francisco, 1994—95; bd. dirs. S.A.F.E. House, Blairsville, 1996—98. Recipient 2d pl., Hunter Mus. Am. Art, Donald Kuspit, juror, 1998; grantee individual arts grantee, Ga. Women in the Visual Arts, Ga. Commn. on Women, 1997;, Ga. Coun. for the Arts, Atlanta, 1995. Democrat. Avocations: herb gardening, trout fishing, canoeing, hiking. Home: 3529 Mason Rd Blairsville GA 30512-5256 Office Phone: 706-745-7900. Personal E-mail: csinbville@yahoo.com.

**STERLING, DONALD T.,** real estate mogul, professional basketball team executive; b. Chgo., 1934; m. Shelly Stein, 1957; 3 children. BA, Calif. State U., LA; JD, Southwestern U. Sch. Law, LA. Owner LA (formerly San Diego) Clippers, NBA, 1981—, also chmn. bd. Office: c/o LA Clippers 1111 S Figueroa St Ste 1100 Los Angeles CA 90015

**STERLING, KEIR BROOKS,** historian, educator; b. N.Y.C., Jan. 30, 1934; s. Henry Somers and Louise Noel (de Wetter) S.; m. Anne Cox Diller, Apr. 3, 1961; children: Duncan Diller, Warner Strong, Theodore Craig. BS, Columbia U., 1961, MA, 1963, profl. diploma, 1965, PhD, 1973. Asst. to dean Sch. Gen. Studies Columbia U., N.Y.C., 1959-65; rsch. grantee England, 1965-66; instr. history Pace U., N.Y.C. and Pleasantville, NY, 1966-71, from asst. prof. to assoc. prof., 1971-77, adj. prof., 1977-83; ordnance br. historian U.S Army Ordnance Ctr. and Sch., Aberdeen Proving Ground, Md., 1983-94, Ft. Lee, Va., 1994-98; historian U.S. Army Combined Arms Support Command, Ft. Lee, 1998—. Lectr. gen. counseling Bklyn. Coll., CUNY, 1967-68; asst. acad. dean, adj. asst. prof. history, coord. Am. studies program, dir. summer session Marymount Coll., Tarrytown, N.Y., 1968-71; asst. dean Rockland C.C., SUNY, Suffern, 1971-73; vis. prof. Mercy Coll., Westchester C.C., King's Coll., Nyack Coll., U. Wis., 1971, 75, 78-80, 83, Harford (Md.) C.C., 1987-94; adj. instr. Army Logistics Mgmt. Coll., Ft. Lee, 1995—; co-project dir. Am. Ornithologists Union Centennial Hist., Project, 1976-89; cons. Arno Press, Inc., 1973-78, Coun. State Colls. of N.J., 1984-85, NSF, 1983—, Am. Trust for Brit. Libr., 1986-89; active Columbia U. Seminar on History and Philosophy of Sci., 1976-83; archivist, historian mem. steering com. sect. mammalogy Internat. Union Biol. Scis., 1985—; judge Ann. Nat. History Day Competition U. Md., 1993-; grant reviewer Teaching Am. History Program U.S. Dept. Edn., 2003-. Author: Last of the Naturalists: The Career of C. Hart Merriam, 1974, 77; editor: Notes on the Animals of North America (B.S. Barton), 1974; assoc. editor: Am. Nat. Biog., 1989-98; editor, contbr.: Natural Sciences in America, 1974, 68 vols., 1974, Biologists and Their World, 1978, 77 vols.; gen. editor, contbr.: The International History of Mammalogy, 1987—; sr. editor, contbr. (with R. Harmond, G. Cevasco, and L. Hammond) Biographical Dictionary of American and Canadian Naturalists and Environmentalists, 1997; contbg. author: Ground Warfare: An International Encyclopedia, 2002, Dictionary of Am. History, 3d edit., 2003, Encyclopedia of World Environmental History, 2003; editor, contbr. to numerous works in history, Am. natural scis., and Am. mil. history. With U.S. Army, 1954—56. Grantee Theodore Roosevelt Meml. Fund, Am. Mus. Natural History, 1967, Nat. Geog. Soc., 1977, NSF/Am. Soc. Mammalogists, 1978, Pace U., 1980, 81, NSF, 1981-82, IREX, 1982; recipient Editor's Spcll. Award, Internat. Assn. of Torch Clubs, 2003. Mem.: History of Sci. Soc., Orgn. Am. Historians, Am. Hist. Assn., Assn. Bibliography of History (mem. coun. 1994—), Am. Soc. Environ. History (sec., mem. governing bd., editor newsletter); Am. Ornithologists Union (co-chmn. centennial hist. com., mem. archives com., grantee 1976, 1977), Am. Soc. Mammalogists (mem. archives com., mem. 75th ann. com.), Phi Delta Kappa, Sigma Tau Delta, Phi Alpha Theta. Democrat. Episcopalian. Home: 7104 Wheeler Rd Richmond VA 23229-6939 Office: 3901 A Ave Room 119 Fort Lee VA 23801-1807 Office Phone: 804-734-0082. Business E-Mail: keir.sterling@us.army.mil. E-mail: kbs1934@cs.com.

**STERLING, MARCIA KEMP,** lawyer; b. Texarkana, Ark. m. Nathaniel Sterling. Grad., Vanderbilt U., 1965, Stanford U., 1982. Ptnr. Wilson, Sonsini, Goodrich & Rosati, Palo Alto, Calif.; sr. v.p., gen. counsel, sec. Autodesk, Inc., San Rafael, Calif. Lectr. Calif. Continuing Edn. of the Bar, Practicing Law Inst.; bd. dirs. Bus. Software Alliance. Bd. dirs. Nat. Spasmodic Dysphonia Assn.; mem. advisory coun. program in law sci. and tech. Stanford U.; mem. bd. trustees First United Methodist Ch., Palo Alto, Calif. Mem.: ABA, Santa Clara County Bar Assn., Palo Alto Bar Assn. Office: Autodesk Inc 111 McInnis Pkwy San Rafael CA 94903-2773*

**STERLING, RAYMOND LESLIE,** civil engineering educator, researcher, consultant; b. London, Apr. 19, 1949; came to U.S., 1966; s. Richard Howard and Joan Valeria (Skinner) S.; m. Linda Lee Lundquist, Aug. 8, 1970 (div. Sept. 1982); children: Paul, Juliet, Erika; m. Janet Marie Kjera, Aug. 20, 1983; 1 child, Zoey. B in Civil and Structural Engring. with 1st class honors, U. Sheffield, Eng., 1970; MS in Geol. Engring., U. Minn., 1975, PhDCE, 1977. Registered civil engr., Minn.; chartered structural engr., Eng. Engr. trainee Met. Water Bd., London, 1968; civil engr. Egil Wefald and Assocs., Cons. Engrs., Mpls., 1969-71; structural engr. Husband and Co., Cons. Engrs., Eng., 1971-73; rsch. asst. U. Minn., Mpls., 1973-77, dir. Underground Space Ctr., 1977-95, asst. prof. dept. civil and mineral engring., 1977-83, assoc. prof., 1983-95; project. coord., structural engr. Setter, Leach and Lindstrom, Inc., Mpls., 1976-77; prin. cons. Itasca Cons. Group, Inc., Mpls., 1981-94; prof. civil engring. La. Tech. U., Ruston, 1995—, dir. Trenchless Tech. Ctr., 1995—. Vice-chmn. U.S. Nat. com. on tunneling tech. NRC, NAS, 1990-91, chmn. 1992-94, com. on infrastructure, 1991-93. bd. infrastructure and the constructed environment, 1994-96; acting co-dir. Minn. Cold Climate Bldg. Rsch. Ctr. U. Minn., 1987-89, co-dir. Bldg. Energy Rsch. Ctr., 1986, speaker's bur., other u. coms.; energy adv. com. Legis. Com. on Minn. Resources, 1989-95; com. on moisture control in bldgs. U.S. Bldg. Thermal Envelope Coordinating Coun., 1985-86; program planning com. on bldg. founds. U.S. Dept. Energy, 1995-95; adv. bd. for energy efficient residence demonstration project Nat. Assn. Home Builders, 1980; mem. Gov's. Exxon Oil Overcharge Adv. Task Force, 1986, Mpls. Energy Future Com., 1980-81, Scientist's Inst. for Pub. Info., N.Y.; cons. U.S Army Corps. Engrs., UN, N.Y., Opus Corp., Mpls., Dames & Moore Internat., London, City of Mpls., Larson Engring., White Bear, Minn., Pilsbury Co., Mpls., Colgate Divsn. Sch., Rochester, N.Y., others; adv. prof. Chongqing Jianzhu U., Sichuan, People's Republic China, 1995—; vis. rschr. Nat. Inst. Pollution and Resources MITI, Japan, 1991; vis. prof. U. Mo., Rolla, 1979; Shimizu prof. civil and mineral engring., U. Minn., 1988-95; adv. prof. Tongji U., Shanghai, 1996—; mem. eminent speaker program Instn. Engrs., Australia, 1993; hon. prof. Changsha Rwy. U., China, 1998—, Xian U. Arch. and Tech., China, 1999; lectr., presenter in field. Author: Earth Sheltered Housing Design: Guidelines, Examples and References, 1978, transl. into Chinese, French, Spanish and Russian, 2d edit., 1985, (with others) Earth Sheltered Community Design: The Design of Energy-Efficient Residential Communities, 1980 (award for Best Book in Architecture and Urban Planning Prof. and Scholarly div. Assn. Am. Pubs. 1981), transl. into Spanish, 1981, Underground Building Design, 1983, translated into Japanese and Russian, others, Building Foundation Handbook, 1988, Underground Space Design, 1993, others; editor: (with others) Key Questions in Rock Mechanics: Proc. 29th U.S. Symposium on Rock Mechanics, 1988; contbr. articles to profl. jours. including Jour. Agrl. Engring., Internat. Jour. Rock Mechanics and Mining Scis., Exptl. Mechanics, many others. Named Most Valuable Profl., Gulf Coast Trenchless Assn., 1999; recipient Young Engr. of Yr. award, Minn. Fedn. Engring. Soc., 1982, Applied Rsch. award in rock mechanics, NRC, 1993, elected fgn. mem., Acad. Engring. of Russian Fedn., 1993, Person of Yr. award, Trenchless Tech. mag., 2001, Engring. Faculty Professionalism award, La. Tech. U., 2005; grantee Shimizu Constrn. Co., 1987—93, Nat. Assn. Homebuilders, 1989, U.S. Dept. Energy, 1989—90, NSF, 1991, Minn. Dept. Transp., 1991, ASHRAE, 1991—92, many others. Fellow: Am. Soc. Civil Engrs. (bd. dirs 1985—92, exec. Minn. sect. 1990—91, Young Civil Engr. of Yr. award 1982, Stephen D. Bechtel Pipeline Engring. award 2003), Royal Soc. Arts, Mfrs. & Commerce, Inst. Structural Engrs.; mem. Civil Engrs.; mem.: NSPE, Internat. Soc. Trenchless Tech. (vice chmn. 1999—2002, chmn. 2002—), N. Am. Soc. Trenchless Tech. (bd. dirs. 1996—, treas. 1997, internat. rep. 1998—, vice chmn. 1999, chmn. 2000), Internat. Tunneling Assn. (coordinating editor jour. 1986—95, co-sr. editor 1996—, animateur working group on direct/indirect advantages of underground structures 1997—2000), Am. Underground Constrn. Assn. (Award of Distinction 2000). Achievements include research in underground construction, underground space utilization, trenchless technology, rock mechanics, and energy use in buildings. Office: Trenchless Technology Ctr Louisiana Tech U PO Box 10348 Ruston LA 71272-0046 Office Phone: 318-257-4072. Business E-Mail: sterling@latech.edu.

**STERLING, RICHARD LEROY,** English and foreign language educator; b. Atlantic City, Feb. 18, 1941; s. Richard Leroy and Anne (Bass) S. BA, Am. U., 1968; MA, Cath. U., 1971; PhD, Howard U., 1990. Head Start tchr. DC Pub. Schs., summer 1968, tchr. French and English, adult and continuing edn., 1969-71, 76-83; instr. French Howard U., Washington, 1973-76, grad. tchg. asst., 1983-85; instr., lectr. in French, 1985-89; tchr. English Cmty.-Based Orgns., DC Pub. Schs., 1989-91; asst. prof. French and English Bowie (Md.) State U., 1991-97, assoc. prof. French, 1997—, dir. modern langs. program, 1997—. Tchr. summer enrichment program for gifted children Sch. Edn., Howard U., summers 1985, 86; tchr. ESL, DC Pub. Schs., summer, 1989, 94; asst. coord. Humanities Immersion Program, Project Access for H.S. Students, Bowie State U., summer 1997-98; vice-chmn. World Centennial Conf.; French, Am. and Planetary Dimensions of Saint-John Perse, U. DC, 1987; mem. adv. coun. Northeast Conf. Tchg. Fgn. Langs; NAACP-ACT-SO competition humanities judge 1997-2000; judge Md. French, Southeastern U., Washington, summer 1998—; judge DC Pub. Schs. World Langs. Festival, 2001; presenter, book reviewer in field. Author: The Prose Works of Saint-John Perse: Towards an Understanding of His Poetry, 1994; contbg. editor MaComere Rev., 2003—; contbr. articles to profl. jours. Active Assn. Democratique des Francais a L.Etranger, 1988—, Senegal friendship com. Office Cmty. and Ethnic Affairs, Prince George's County Govt., Md., 1993-94, Inst. for Haitian Cultural and Sci. Affairs, 1992-94, local arrangements com. Conf. Coll. Composition and Communication, Washington, 1995, Friends of the Corcoran, 1999; membership com. and outreach com. St. John's Ch., Washington, 1993, ch. growth com., 1995. With U.S. Army, 1964-66. Mem. MLA, Coll. Lang. Assn., Mid. Atlantic Writers Assn. (chmn. essay contest com. 1995-2000, bd. dirs. 2000—), Samuel Beckett Soc., Societe des Professeurs Francais et Francophones d'Amerique, Zora Neale Hurston Soc., Am. Assn. Tchrs. French (sec.-treas. Washington chpt. 1986-90), Nat. Cathedral Assn., Md. Fgn. Lang. Assn. (bd. dirs. 1997-2001, 2003—), Coun. Internat. d'Etudes Francophones, Friends DC Superior Ct. (bd. dirs. 1996—), Univ. Club (Washington), Md. Fgn. Lang. Assn. (bd. dirs. 1997-2001, 2003—), Pi Delta Phi, Sigma Tau Delta Democrat. Episcopalian. Avocations: classical music, history, travel. Office: Bowie State U Dept English & Modern Langs Bowie MD 20715 Business E-Mail: rsterling@bowiestate.edu.

**STERLING, ROBERT LEE, JR.,** investment company executive; b. Cleve., June 12, 1933; s. Robert Lee and Kathryn (Durell) S.; children from previous marriage: Robert Livingston, William Lee, Cameron Platt; m. Joyce Lanier Milner, June 4, 1994. Student, U. Edinburgh, Scotland, 1955; BA, Brown U., 1956; MBA, Columbia U., 1962. Corp. rsch. analyst Morgan Guaranty Trust, N.Y.C., 1962-63; asst. comptr. Western Hemisphere CPC Internat., N.Y.C., 1963—76; v.p. White, Weld & Co., Inc., N.Y.C., 1976—78, Merrill Lynch Asset Mgmt., 1978-80, Wood, Struthers & Winthrop Mgmt. Corp., N.Y.C., 1980-83; sr. v.p. Shearson Lehman Bros. Asset Mgmt., 1983-88; v.p., sr. portfolio mgr. Chase Manhattan Bank, 1988-93; exec. v.p., sr. portfolio mgr. Melhado, Flynn & Assocs., Inc., N.Y.C., 1993—; mng. ptnr. Winthrop Asset Mgmt., 1995—. Mem. adv. bd. Mus. Modern Art, Oxford U. Eng.; trustee Soc. of the Four Arts, Palm Beach, Preservation Soc., Palm Beach, Game Conservancy, U.S. Mem. New Eng. Soc. (past pres., J.P. Morgan medal), St. Nicholas Soc., Pilgrims, N.Y. State Soc. of Cin. (past pres.), Univ. Club (N.Y.C.), Everglades Club (Palm Beach, Fla.), Bath and Tennis Club (Palm Beach, Fla.), The Bathing Corp.(Southampton, N.Y.), Anabell's (London), Alpha Delta Phi, Alpha Kappa Psi. Home: 200 Regent Park Palm Beach FL 33480 Office: Melhado Flynn & Assocs Inc 530 5th Ave New York NY 10036-5101 Office Phone: 800-333-3610.

**STERMER, DUGALD ROBERT,** designer, writer, consultant, illustrator; b. LA, Dec. 17, 1936; s. Robert Newton and Mary (Blue) S.; children: Dugald, Megan, Chris, Colin, Crystal. BA, UCLA, 1960. Art dir., v.p Ramparts mag., 1965-70; freelance designer, illustrator, writer, cons. San Francisco, 1970—; founder Pub. Interest Communications, San Francisco, 1974; chmn. illustration dept. Calif. Coll. Arts and Crafts, 1994—, disting. prof., 1994—. Bd. dirs. Am. Inst. Graphic Arts, Illustration Partnership Am.; mem. San Francisco Art Commn., 1997—. Cons. editor: Communication Arts mag., 1974-90; designer: Oceans mag., 1976-82; editor: The Environment, 1972, Vanishing Creatures, 1980; author: The Art of Revolution, 1970, Vanishing Creatures, 1980, Vanishing Flora, 1994, Birds and Bees, 1994; illustration exhbn. Calif. Acad. Scis., 1986; one-man show Jernigan Wicker Gallery, San Francisco, 1996 Mem. Grand Jury City and County San Francisco, 1989; bd. dirs. Delancey St. Found., 1990—. Recipient various medals, awards for design and illustration nat. and internat. competitions. Achievements include design of 1984 Olympic medals. Office: 600 The Embarcadero # 204 San Francisco CA 94107-2121 Office Phone: 415-777-0110. Business E-Mail: ds@dugaldstermer.com.

**STERN, ALAN (S. ALAN STERN, SOL ALAN STERN),** astrophysicist, researcher; b. New Orleans, Nov. 22, 1957; s. Leonard Arthur and Joel Strauss (Sugar) S.; m. Carole Ann Jones, Aug. 5, 1982; children: Sarah L., Kate E., Jordan. BS, U. Tex., 1978, MS in Aerospace Engring., 1980, BA, 1981, MS in Planetary Atmospheres, 1981; PhD in Astrophysics and Planetary Sci., U. Colo., 1989. Engr. NASA Johnson Space Ctr., Houston, 1979-80; systems engr. Martin Marietta Aerospace, Denver, 1982-83; spacecraft / instrument engr. Lab. for Atmospheric and Space Physics U. Colo., Boulder, 1983-86, rsch. assoc., 1989—90, asst. dir. Office of Space Sci. and Tech., 1986—87, asst. to v.p. for rsch., 1987—88, rsch. fellow Ctr. for Space & Geosciences Policy, 1989—91, rsch. assoc. Ctr. for Astrophysics and Space Astronomy, 1990—91, prof. adj. Astrophysical and Planetary Sci. Dept., 2002—; prin. scientist Space Science Dept. S.W. Rsch. Inst., 1991-92, sect. mgr., 1992—97, dept. dir., 1998—2005, exec. dir. Space Sci. and Engring. Div., 2004—. Mem. lunar exploration sci. working group NASA, 1992—, discovery program sci. working group, 1989—90, chmn. Neptune/Pluto outer planet sci. working group, 1994—, project scientist Spartan-Halle spacecraft mission; prin. investigator Alice UV spectrometer in ESA/NASA Rosetta mission, Lunar Recon Orbiter Lyman-Alpha Mapping (LAMP) Experiment, Ralph Imager/IR Spectrometer on New Horizons, Alice UV Spectrometer on New Horizons, New Horizons Pluto-Kuiper Belt Mission. Author: The U.S. Space Program After Challenger, 1987, Pluto and Charon, 1997, The Exploration of Pluto, 1997, The Search for Extra-Solar Earthlike Planet: Techniques and Technology, 1997, The Exploration of Pluto, 1997, Pluto and Charion, 1997, Our Worlds, 1998.; editor: Geophysical Research Letters Spl. Issues on Pluto and the Moon, 1989, 91, (U. Ariz. space sci. series volume) Pluto and Cluster; contbr. numerous articles to profl. jours. Recipient Martin Marietta New Design Innovation Award, 1983, Solar Max Repair Mission Recognition Award, 1984, Hale-Bopp Sounding Rocket Campaign Group Achievement Award, NASA, 1998, New Millennium Deep Space-1 Mission Group Achievement Award, 2002, Rosetta Group Achievement Award, 2005; grad. fellow, Colo. Commn. on Higher Edn., 1988—89. Mem. AAAS, AIAA, Internat. Astron. Union, Am. Astron. Soc., Am. Geophys. Union, Aircraft Owners and Pilots Assn. Avocations: flying, scuba diving, photography, skiing, hiking, gardening, writing. Office: SW Rsch Inst 1050 Walnut St No 400 Boulder CO 80302-5150 Office Phone: 303-546-9670. E-mail: astern@swri.edu.*

**STERN, ALEXANDRA MINNA,** education educator; b. San Francisco, May 3, 1966; BA, San Francisco State U., 1990; MA, U. Calif., La Jolla, 1993; PhD, U. Chgo., 2000. Asst. prof. U. Calif., Santa Cruz, 2000—02; assoc. prof. U. Mich., Ann Arbor, Mich., 2002—. Assoc. dir. Ctr. for the History of Medicine, Ann Arbor, 2002—. Author: (book) Eugenic Nation: Faults and Frontiers of Better Breeding in Modern America (Arthur Viseltear award from the APHA, 2006); editor: Formative Years: Children's Health in the United States, 1880-2000; author: (jour. article) Hispanic American Historical Review (Berkshire Women's History Best Article prize, 2000). Recipient Beveridge Rsch. award, Am. Hist. Assn., 1997; fellow Fellowship, Social Sci. Rsch. Coun., 1997—98, Fulbright Hays, 1998, Nat. Endowment for the Humanities, 2005; grantee Contract, Def. Threat Reduction Agy., 2005—06, Publ. Grant, Nat. Libr. of Medicine, 2006—, Rsch. Grant, NIH,

2006—. Liberal. Office: Univ of Mich 100 Simpson 102 Observatory Ann Arbor MI 48103 Office Phone: 734-647-6914. Office Fax: 734-647-6915. Business E-Mail: amstern@umich.edu.

**STERN, ANDREW L.,** labor union administrator; State social svc. worker, mem. Local 668 Svc. Employees Internat. Union (SEIU), 1973—80, mem. internat. exec. bd. Wash., DC, 1980—, org. field svc. programs, 1984—96, internat. pres., 1996—. Bd. dirs. AFL-CIO Housing and Bldg. Investment Trust, Medicare Rights Ctr., Aspen Inst. Bd. dir. Rock the Vote; chmn. Ctr. for Cmty. and Corp. Ethics. Mem.: Am. Hosp.Assn. (commn. on workforce for hosps. and health care), Nat. Acad. Social Ins. (bd. dir.). Office: Svc Employees Internat Union 1313 L St NW Washington DC 20005-4101*

**STERN, ANDREW MILTON,** public relations executive; b. Cleve., Mar. 22, 1947; s. Sidney Harrison Stern, Jr. and Sue (Friedlander) Miller; m. Sabina R. Bobzin, Feb. 28, 1971; children: David Patrick, Eric Thomas. BA, U. Del., 1970. Press sec. to mayor City of Wilmington, Del., 1970-73; dir. pub. affairs Wilmington Med. Ctr., 1973-75; staff asst. to pres. The White House, Washington, 1975-77; dir. pub. relations and advt. Wylain, Inc., Dallas, 1977-80; sr. v.p. Assocs. Corp. N.Am., Dallas, 1980-82; chmn., chief exec. officer Sunwest Communications, Inc., Dallas, 1982—. Founder, dir. Dallas Nat. Bank. Mem. Med. City Dallas Hosp., Dallas County Hist. Found. Mem. Pub. Rels. Soc. Am., North Dallas C. of C. (past chmn.). Clubs: Salesmanship, Prestonwood, Press (Dallas). Republican. Jewish. Home: 5916 Club Oaks Dr Dallas TX 75248-1124 Office: Sunwest Communications Inc 5420 Lyndon B Johnson Pwy 1475 Dallas TX 75240-6265

**STERN, ARTHUR PAUL,** electronics executive; b. Budapest, Hungary, July 20, 1925; arrived in U.S., 1951; s. Leon and Bertha (Frankfurter) Stern; m. Edith M. Samuel; children: Daniel, Claude, Jacqueline. Diploma in Elec. Engring., Swiss Fed. Inst. Tech., Zurich, 1948; MSEE, Syracuse U., 1955. Mgr. electronic devices and applications lab. GE, Syracuse, NY, 1957-61; dir. engring. Martin Marietta Corp., Balt., 1961-64; dir. ops. Bunker Ramo Corp., Canoga Park, Calif., 1964-66; v.p., gen. mgr. advanced products divsn. Magnavox, Torrance, Calif., 1966-79; pres. Magnavox Advanced Products and Systems Co., Torrance, 1980-90; vice chmn., bd. dirs. Magnavox Electronics Systems Co., Ft. Wayne, Ind., 1987—90; pres. Ea. Beverly Hills Corp., 1991—. Pres. Calif.-Israel C. of C., 1994—98, chmn. bd. dirs., 1998—2000; mem. governing coun. Am.-Jewish Congress, 1997—98; bd. dirs. Jewish Coun. Pub. Affairs, 1996—2002; v.p. Progressive Jewish Alliance, 1999—; non-resident staff mem. MIT, 1956—59; instr. GE Bus. Mgmt., 1955—57. Co-author: (book) Transistor Circuit Engineering, 1957, Handbook of Automation, Computation and Control, 1961; contbr. articles to profl. jours. Mem. adv. bd. elec. engring. U. Calif., Santa Barbara, 1980—92; mem. Sch. Engring. Adv. and Devel. Coun. Calif. State U., Long Beach, 1985—90; chmn. bd. dirs. Calif. Humanitarian Found. for Holocaust Survivors, 2000—; regional chair, bd. dirs. Ams. for Peace Now, 2002—; bd. dirs. So. Calif. Ams. for Dem. Action, 2000—; chmn. engring. divsn. United Jewish Appeal, Syracuse, 1955—57; bd. dirs. Bur. Jewish Edn., L.A., 1995—2005, chmn. investment com., 2000—05; vice-chmn. Jewish Cmty. Rels. Com. of Jewish Fedn. of L.A., 1998—2003; bd. dirs. Jewish Fedn. Greater L.A., 2003—05. Recipient Justice-Tzedek award, Labor Zionist Alliance, 2001, Educating for Life award, Bur. Jewish Edn., 2004. Fellow: IEEE (pres. 1975, bd. dirs., officer 1970—77, guest editor spl. issue IEEE Trans. on Circuit Theory 1956, invited guest editor spl. issue Procs. IEEE on Integrated Electronics 1964, Centennial medal 1984, Millennium medal 2000, Haraden Pratt award 2001), AAAS; mem.: Eta Kappa Nu Assn. (eminent mem.). Achievements include patents in field. Personal E-mail: apstern@att.net.

**STERN, CARL LEONARD,** retired news correspondent, federal official; b. NYC, Aug. 7, 1937; s. Hugo and Frances (Taft) S.; m. Joy Elizabeth Nathan, Nov. 27, 1960; children: Lawrence, Theodore. AB, Columbia U., 1958, MS, 1959; JD, Cleve. State U., 1966, JD (hon.), 1975, New Eng. Coll. Law, 1977. Bar: Ohio 1966, D.C. 1968, U.S. Supreme Ct. 1969. Law corr. NBC News, Washington, 1967—93; dir. Office of Pub. Affairs U.S. Dept. Justice, Washington, 1993—96; Shapiro Prof. of Media and Pub. Affairs George Washington U., 1996—. Mem. editl. stds. rev. com. Pub. Broadcasting Svc., 2005; lectr. Nat. Jud. Coll.; adj. prof. George Washington U., Stanford U. Editl. bd. The Dist. Lawyer Mem. Dept. Transp. Task Force on Assistance to Families in Aviation Disasters, 1997; mem. nat. adv. coun. Cleveland-Marshall Law Sch. Recipient Peabody award, 1974, Emmy award, 1974, Gavel award, 1969, 74, Headliner Club award, 1991, Edmond J. Randloph award U.S. Dept. Justice. Mem. ABA (vice chmn. criminal justice sect. com. on criminal justice and media, gov., forum com. on comm. law, working group intelligence requirements and criminal code reform, standing com. on strategic comm.), AFTRA (nat. exec. bd. 1984-86, first v.p. Washington, Balt. chpt. 1985-87) Home: 2956 Davenport St NW Washington DC 20008 Office: George Washington U #400 805 21st St NW Washington DC 20052 Office Phone: 202-994-1464. Personal E-Mail: sterncarl@aol.com. Business E-Mail: cstern@gwu.edu.

**STERN, CARL WILLIAM, JR.,** management consultant; b. San Francisco, Mar. 31, 1946; s. Carl William and Marjorie Aline (Gunst) S.; m. Karen Jaffe, Sept. 7, 1966 (div. Mar. 1972); 1 child, David; m. Holly Drick Hayes, Mar. 21, 1985; children: Kenneth, Matthew. BA, Harvard U., 1968; MBA, Stanford U., 1974. Cons. Boston Cons. Group, Inc., Menlo Park, Calif., 1974-77, mgr., 1977-78, London, 1978-80, v.p. Chgo., 1980-87, sr. v.p., 1987-97, pres., CEO, 1998—2003, co-chmn. bd., 2004—. Lt. USNR, 1968-71. Office: Boston Consulting Group Inc 200 S Wacker Dr Ste 2700 Chicago IL 60606-5846

**STERN, COLIN D.,** lawyer, retail executive; b. Johannesburg, Dec. 3, 1948; BA, U. Witwatersrand, South Africa, 1970; LL.B. cum laude, U. Witwatersrand, 1971; LL.M., Harvard U., 1978; LL.M. in Taxation, Temple U., 1984. Bar: Transvaal, South Africa 1974, Pa. 1979, U.S. Dist. Ct. (ea. dist.) Pa. 1979. Assoc. Morgan, Lewis & Bockius, 1978-80; assoc., ptnr. Cohen, Shapiro, Polisher, Shiekman & Cohen, 1980-89; exec. v.p., gen. counsel Charming Shoppes, Inc., Bensalem, Pa., 1991—. Mem. ABA, Pa. Bar Assn., Phila. Bar Assn. Office: Charming Shoppes Inc 450 Winks Ln Bensalem PA 19020-5993

**STERN, DAVID JOEL,** National Basketball Association Commissioner; b. NYC, Sept. 22, 1942; s. William and Anna (Bronstein) Stern; m. Dianne Bock, Nov. 27, 1963; children: Andrew, Eric. BA, Rutgers U., 1963; LLB, Columbia U., 1966. Bar: N.Y. 1963. Assoc. Proskauer Rose Goetz & Mendelsohn, N.Y.C., 1966—74, ptnr., 1974—78; gen. counsel Nat. Basketball Assn., N.Y.C., 1978—80, exec. v.p. bus. and legal affairs, 1980—84, commr., 1984—. Mem. Martin Luther King Jr. Fed. Holiday Commn., 1988—; White House Conf. for a Drug-Free Am., 1988; bd. dirs. NAACP, 1990—93; trustee Beth Israel Med. Ctr., 1985—; Rutgers U. Found., 1987—; Columbia U., 1992—. Named to Internat. Jewish Sports Hall of Fame, 1998. Mem.: ABA, Assn. Bar City N.Y. (chmn. com. on entertainment and sports 1983—86), N.Y. State Bar Assn. Achievements include assisting in creation of NBA Entertainment Divsn. Office: NBA Olympic Tower 645 5th Ave Fl 10 New York NY 10022-5986*

**STERN, DAVID MARK,** dean, educator; b. Great Neck, NY; s. Robert and Florence Stern; m. Kathleen Shirley Stern; children: Eric David, Alan Robert. BS, Yale U., 1973; MD, Harvard U., 1978. Mem. faculty Coll. Physicians and Surgeons, Columbia U. NYC, 1983—2002, named Gerald & Janet Carrus Prof. of Surg. Sci., 1998, dir. Ctr. Vascular and Lung Pathobiology, dir. Juvenile Diabetes Rsch. Ctr.; dean sch. medicine, sr. v.p. clin. activities Med. Coll. Ga., Augusta, 2002—05, prof. medicine, physiology and grad. studies, 2002—05; Christian R. Holmes prof. medicine U. Cincinnati, 2005—, dean Coll. Medicine, 2005—. Mem.: Am. Assn. Physicians, Am. Soc. Clin. Investigation. Office: Univ Cincinnati Coll Medicine 231 Albert Sabin Way PO Box 670552 Cincinnati OH 45267-0552 Office Phone: 513-558-7334. Business E-Mail: dstern@mail.mcg.edu. E-Mail: david.stern@uc.edu.*

**STERN, DONALD ALLAN,** lawyer; b. N.Y.C., Apr. 13, 1954; s. Robert and Florence S.; m. Antje Mewes, Sept. 14, 1989; children: Elizabeth, Robert. AB, Harvard U., 1976, JD, 1980. Assoc Cleary, Gottlieb, Steen & Hamilton, N.Y.C., 1980-88, ptnr., 1989—. Corp. trustee Jackson Lab., Bar Harbor, Maine, 1986-90, governing trustee, 1990—, chmn. exec. com., chmn. compensation com., 2001-; unit commr. Boy Scouts Am., Nassau County, N.Y., 1992—; commr.-at-large Village of Thomaston, 1998—. Office: Cleary Gottlieb Steen & Hamilton 1 Liberty Plz Fl 38 New York NY 10006-1470 Office Phone: 212-225-2640. E-mail: dstern@cgsh.com.

**STERN, DONALD KENNETH,** lawyer; BA, Hobart Coll., 1966; JD, Georgetown U., 1969; LLM, U. Pa., 1973. Intern Dist. Atty.'s Office, Mineola, NY, 1967, Citizen's Adv. Ctr., Washington, 1968; staff atty. Defender Assn. Phila., Cmty. Legal Svcs., Phila., 1969-71; adj. prof. law, supervising atty. Boston Coll. Law Sch., Boston Coll. Legal Assistance Bur., 1971-73, asst. prof. law, dir. clin. programs, supervising atty., 1973-75; asst. atty. gen., dir. atty. gen. clin. program, Mass. Atty. Gen.'s Office, Boston Coll. Law Sch., 1975-77, asst. prof. law, dir. atty. gen. clin. program, spl. asst. atty. gen., 1977-78, asst. atty. gen., dir. atty. gen. clin. program, 1978-79; chief govt. bur. Mass. Atty. Gen.'s Office, 1979-82; assoc. Hale and Dorr, Boston, 1982-85, jr. ptnr., 1985-87, sr. ptnr., 1987, 91-93, of counsel, 1990-91; chief legal counsel to Gov. Mass., 1987-90; U.S. atty. Dist. Mass., 1993—2001; ptnr. Bingham McCutchen, LLP, 2001—; lectr. Harvard Law Sch., 2002—05. Office: Bingham McCutchen LLP 150 Federal St Boston MA 02210-1726 Office Phone: 617-951-8250. E-mail: donald.stern@bingham.com.

**STERN, EDWARD ABRAHAM,** physics professor; b. Detroit, Sept. 19, 1930; s. Jacob Munich and Rose (Kravitz) S.; m. Sylvia Rita Sidell, Oct. 30, 1955; children: Hilary, Shari, Miri. BS, Calif. Tech., 1951, PhD, 1955. Post-doctoral fellow Calif. Tech., Pasadena, 1955-57; assist. prof. U. Md., College Park, 1957-61, assoc. prof., 1961-64, prof., 1964-65, U. Wash., Seattle, 1965—2000, emeritus, 2000—. Contbr. over 200 articles to profl. jours.; editor: three books. Recipient B. Warren award Am. Crystallography Assn., 1979, Outstanding Achievement award Internat. XAFS Soc., 2000; named Guggenheim fellow, Cambridge, Eng., 1963-64, NSF Sr. Post-doctoral fellow, Haifa, Israel, 1970-71, Fulbright fellow, Jerusalem, Israel, 1985-86. Fellow AAAS, Am. Physical Soc. Achievements include patent for x-ray focusing device; development of x-ray absorption fine structure technique; research on surface plasmons, nonlinear reflection from surfaces, electronic properties of alloys, structural phase transition; named Father of EXAFS. Office: U Wash Dept Physics PO Box 351560 Seattle WA 98195-1560 Office Phone: 206-543-2023. Business E-Mail: stern@phys.washington.edu.

**STERN, ELIZABETH ESPIN,** lawyer; b. Prince Georges County, Md., June 21, 1961; d. Cesar A. and M. Cecilia (Salvador) E.; m. Michael L. Stern, May 16, 1992; 1 child, Alexander. BA magna cum laude, U. Va., 1983; JD, U. Va. Sch. Law, 1986. Bar: Va. 1986, U.S. Dist. Ct. (Ea. Dist.) Va., D.C. 1988, Supreme Ct. U.S., U.S. Ct. Appeals, D.C. Cir. Ptnr. comml. immigration Shaw Pittman LLP (formerly Shaw, Pittman, Potts & Trowbridge), Washington, 1986—2005; (Shaw Pittman LLP merged with Pillsbury Winthrop Shaw Pittman LLP, 2005); ptnr. & head bus. immigration practice group Pillsbury Winthrop Shaw Pittman LLP, Washington, 2005; ptnr., bus. immigration & exec. transfer Baker & McKenzie LLP, Washington, 2005—. Spkr. in field. Named one of Top 30 lawyers in Washington, Washingtonian Mag., 2004; recipient Martin Preis award, Vol. Bar Assn. D.C., 1992. Mem.: Immigration Task Force Internat. Inst. of Human Resources, ABA, U.S.C. of C. (immigration com.), Inst. Internat. Human Resources, Bus. Immigration Bar Assn. D.C., Internat. Sects. Am. Immigration Lawyers Assn., Soc. for Human Resources Mgmt., Immigration Tech. Assn., Am. D.C. Bar Assn. (internat. sec. 1986—, chair young lawyers sect. 1992—93, del. to ABA, Young Lawyer of Yr. 1994), Va. Bar Assn., Am. Immigration Lawyers Assn., Washington Internat. Trade Assn. Republican. Avocation: journalism. Office: Baker & McKenzie LLP 815 Connecticut Ave NW Washington DC 20006-4078 Office Phone: 202-452-7000. Business E-Mail: elizabeth.e.stern@bakernet.com.

**STERN, ERIC L.,** lawyer; b. Dec. 2, 1956; m. Jacqueline S. Stern. BA, Brandeis U., 1978; JD, Boston Coll. Law Sch., 1981. Bar: Pa. 1981, Mass. 1987. Ptnr. Morgan, Lewis & Bockius LLP, Phila., leader firmwide real estate practice. Mem.: Internat. Coun. Shopping Ctrs., Internat. Assn. Attys. and Execs. Corp. Real Estate, Phila. Region Nat. Assn. Indsl. and Office Properties, Samuel Zell and Robert Lurie Real Estate Ctr.-Wharton Sch. U. Pa., Am. Coll. Real Estate Lawyers. Office: Morgan Lewis & Bockius LLP 1701 Market St Philadelphia PA 19103 Office Phone: 215-963-5178. Office Fax: 215-963-5001. Business E-Mail: estern@morganlewis.com.

**STERN, FRITZ RICHARD,** historian, educator; b. Breslau, Germany, Feb. 2, 1926; came to U.S., 1938, naturalized, 1947; s. Rudolf A. and Catherine (Brieger) S.; m. Margaret J. Bassett, Oct. 11, 1947 (div. 1992); children: Frederick P., Katherine Stern Brennan; m. Elisabeth Niebuhr Sifton, Jan. 1, 1996. BA, Columbia U., 1946, MA, 1948, PhD, 1953; DLitt (hon.), Oxford U., 1985; LLD (hon.), New Sch. for Social Rsch., 1997, Columbia U., 1998; LLD (hon.), U. Wroclaw, 2002. Lectr., instr. Columbia U., 1946-51, faculty, 1953—, prof. history, 1963—, Seth Low prof. history, 1967-92, univ. prof., 1992-96, provost, 1980-83; acting assoc. prof. Cornell U., 1951-53; univ. prof. emeritus Columbia U., 1997—; tchr. Free U. Berlin, 1954, Yale U., 1963; permanent vis. prof. U. Konstanz, West Germany, 1966—; sr. adviser U.S. Embassy, Bonn, 1993-94. Élie Halévy prof. U. Paris, spring 1979; Phi Beta Kappa vis. scholar, 1979-80; Tanner lectr. Yale, 1993. Author: The Politics of Cultural Despair, 1961, The Failure of Illiberalism-Essays in the Political Culture of Modern Germany 1972, rev. edit., 1992, Gold and Iron: Bismarck, Bleichroeder and the Bldg. of the German Empire, 1977 (recipient Lionel Trilling award Columbia U.), Dreams and Delusions: The Drama of German History, 1987, rev. edit. 1999, Einstein's German World, 1999; editor: The Varieties of History, 1956, 71, (with I. Krieger) The Responsibility of Power, 1967; mem. editorial bd. Foreign Affairs, 1978-92; contbr. articles to profl. jours.; reviewer Fgn. Affairs, 1963-95. Trustee German Marshall Fund, 1981-99, Aspen Inst. of Berlin, 1983—; senator Deutsche Nationalstiftung, 1994—; mem. Trilateral Commn., 1983-90. Decorated Officer's Cross Order of Merit Fed. Republic of Germany; fellow Center Advanced Behavioral Scis., 1957-58; fellow Social Sci. Research Council, 1960-61; fellow Am. Council Learned Socs., 1966-67; fellow Netherlands Inst. Advanced Study, 1972-73; mem. Nuffield Coll., Oxford, 1966-67, Inst. Advanced Study Princeton, 1969-70; Guggenheim fellow, 1969-70; Ford Found. grantee, 1976-77; vis. scholar Russell Sage Found., 1989, spring 1993; recipient Leopold-Lucas-prize Evang. Faculty U. Tübingen, 1984, Peace prize German Book Trade Frankfurt Book Fair, 1999, Bruno Snell medal U. Hamburg, 2002, Leo Baeck medal, NY, 2004, Nationalpreis, Berlin, 2005. Mem. Am. Hist. Assn., AAAS, Am. Philos. Soc., Coun. Fgn. Rels., Deutsche Akademie für Sprache und Dichtung (corr.), Berlin Brandenburgische Akademie der Wissenschaften (corr.), Orden Pour le Mérite, Germany, Phi Beta Kappa (senator-at-large 1973-78). Clubs: Century (N.Y.). Home: 15 Claremont Ave New York NY 10027-6802 E-mail: fs20@columbia.edu.

**STERN, GARY HILTON,** bank executive; b. San Luis Obispo, Calif., Nov. 3, 1944; s. Robert Earl and Joy Merdis (Shimon) S.; m. Mary Katherine Nelson, Aug. 17, 1969; children: Matthew Stuart, Meredith Faulkner. AB, Washington U., St. Louis, 1967; MA, Rice U., 1970, PhD, 1972. Economist Fed. Res. Bank of N.Y., N.Y.C., 1970-73; mgr. domestic research, 1973-77; mgr. fixed income research Loeb Rhoades, Hornblower, N.Y.C., 1977-78; sr. economist A.G. Shilling & Co., N.Y.C., 1978-81; sr. v.p. Fed. Res. Bank Mpls., 1982-85, CFO, 1983, pres., 1985—. Adj. assoc. prof. NYU, 1980-82; adj. asst. prof. Columbia U., 1976-79. Author: In the Name of Money, 1980. Trustee West Side Montessori Sch., N.Y.C., 1978-79; bd. dirs. Nat. Coun. Econ. Edn., N.W. Area Found.; Carlson Sch. Mgmt. U. Minn.; bd. trustees Hamline U., Mpls. Coll. Art and Design. NDEA fellow, 1969-70; Bache & Co. scholar, 1963-67; univ. scholar Washington U.-St. Louis, 1964-67, Rice U.-Houston, 1967-68. Mem.: Mpls. Club (treas.). Office: Fed Res Bank of Mpls PO Box 291 90 Hennepin Ave Minneapolis MN 55480-0291*

**STERN, GEOFFREY,** lawyer; b. Columbus, Ohio, Nov. 29, 1942; s. Leonard J. and Anastasia (Percin) S.; m. Barbara Shnider; children: Emily Staheli, Elizabeth Leskowyak; stepchildren: Courtney, Jennifer, Brian Feuer. Student, Williams Coll., 1960-63; BA cum laude, Ohio State U., 1965, JD summa cum laude, 1968. Bar: Ohio 1968. Assoc. Alexander, Ebinger, Holschuh & Fisher, Columbus, Ohio, 1968-72; ptnr. Folkerth, Calhoun, Webster & O'Brien, Columbus, Ohio, 1972-80, Arter & Hadden, Columbus, Ohio, 1980-93; disciplinary counsel Supreme Ct. of Ohio, 1993-97; counsel Kegler, Brown, Hill & Ritter, Columbus, 1997-2000, dir., 2000—. Nat. coordinating counsel for asbestos litigation Combustion Engring. Inc. and Basic, Inc., 1985-93; lectr. on legal ethics and profl. responsibility; mem. Spl. Commn. to Review Ohio Ethics Rules, 1995-98, Spl. Commn. on Legal Edn., 1995-98; mem. symposium on ethics and Chinese legal sys., Shanghai, 1998; keynote spkr. Faith and Law Symposium, 1999; spl. investigator Bd. Commrs. Character and Fitness Ohio Supreme Ct., 1998. Sr. editor Ohio State Law Jour., 1967-68. Pres. Bexley (Ohio) City Coun., 1977-80, mem., 1973-80, mem. Bexley Civil Svc. Commn., 1983-85; v.p., trustee Creative Living, Columbus, 1981-89, Ohio Citizens Com. for Arts, Columbus, 1982-88; mem. Nat. Def. Com. on Asbestos in Bldgs. Litigation, 1986-92; pub. mem. Ohio Optical Dispensers Bd., Columbus, 1978-82. Recipient Am. Jurisprudence Evidence award Ohio State U. Coll. Law, 1967. Fellow Am. Bar Found., Columbus Bar Found., Ohio State Bar Found.; mem. Ohio State Bar Assn. (com. on legal ethics and profl. conduct, sec. 1981-90, vice chmn. 1990-92, chmn. 1992-93), Columbus Bar Assn. (profl. ethics com. 1975-86, 90-93, Liberty Bell award for Cmty. and Profl. Svc. 1998), Order of Coif, Phi Beta Kappa, Pi Sigma Alpha. Home: 278 Crossing Crk N Columbus OH 43230-6108 Office: Kegler Brown Hill & Ritter 65 E State St Ste 1800 Columbus OH 43215-4213 Office Phone: 614-462-5400. Business E-Mail: gstern@keglerbrown.com.

**STERN, GERALD MANN,** lawyer; b. Chgo., Apr. 5, 1937; s. Lloyd and Fannye (Wener) S.; m. Linda Stone, Dec. 20, 1969; children: Eric, Jesse, Maia. BS in Econs., U. Pa., 1958; LL.B. cum laude, Harvard, 1961. Bar: D.C. 1961, Calif. 1991, U.S. Supreme Ct. 1971. Trial atty. civil rights div. U.S. Dept. Justice, 1961-64; assoc. firm Arnold & Porter, Washington, 1964-68, ptnr., 1969-76; founding ptnr. Rogovin, Stern & Huge, Washington, 1976-81; exec. v.p., sr. gen. counsel Occidental Petroleum Corp., L.A., 1981—92; spl. counsel fin. instn. fraud and health care fraud U.S. Dept. Justice, Washington, 1993-95; ind. legal cons. pvt. practice, Washington, 1995—; cons. Antitrust divsn. U.S. Dept. Justice, 1998—2001. Bd. dirs. Oceania Cruises, Inc., Pitzer Coll. Author: The Buffalo Creek Disaster, 1976; co-author: Southern Justice, 1965, Outside the Law, 1997. Trustee Facing History and Ourselves, 1996—. Mem. ABA. Home and Office: 3322 Newark St NW Washington DC 20008-3330 Fax: 202-364-2595. Office Phone: 202-253-2257, 202-362-2078. E-mail: GMS37@aol.com.

**STERN, HERBERT JAY,** lawyer; b. NYC, Nov. 8, 1936; s. Samuel and Sophie (Berkowitz) S.; children: Jason Andrew and Jordan Ezekiel (twins), Samuel Abraham, Sarah Katherine. BA, Hobart Coll., 1958; JD (Ford Found. scholar), U. Chgo., 1961; LL.D. (hon.), Seton Hall Law Sch., 1973, Hobart Coll., 1974; L.H.D. (hon.), Newark State Coll., 1973; D.C.L. (hon.), Bloomfield Coll., 1973; Litt.D. (hon.), Montclair State Coll., 1973. Bar: N.Y. 1961, N.J. 1971. Asst. dist. atty., New York County, 1962-65; trial atty. organized crime and racketeering sect. Dept. of Justice, 1965-69; chief asst. U.S. atty. Dist. of N.J., Newark, 1969-70, U.S. atty., 1971-74, U.S. dist. judge, 1974-87; ptnr. Stern & Kilcullen, Roseland, NJ, 1990—. Adv. com. U. Chgo. Law Sch. Author: Judgment in Berlin, 1984 (Valley Forge award Freedoms Found. 1984, Torch of Learning award Am. Friends of Hebrew U. 1987), Trying Cases to Win, Vol. I, 1991, Vol. II, 1992, Vol. III, 1993, Vol. IV, 1995; co-author: Trying Cases to Win, Anatomy of A Trial, 1999, Trying Cases to Win: Evidence Weapons for Winning, Vol. I, 2000, Vol. II, 2003, Vol. III, 2004; subject of book Tiger in the Court, 1973. Trustee Hobart and William Smith Colls. Named One of America's 10 Outstanding Young Men U.S. Jr. C. of C., 1971; Swartzer scholar U. Chgo. Law Sch., 1985; recipient Dean's Club award U. Akron Sch. Law, 1986, medal of excellence Hobart Coll., 1990, Citizen's award N.J. Acad. Medicine, 1997. Fellow ABA, Am. Law Inst. (Clarence Darrow award), Internat. Platform Assn.; mem. ABA, N.J. Bar Assn., Fed. Bar Assn. (past pres. Newark chpt., recipient William J. Brennan, Jr. award 1987), Essex County Bar Assn., Am. Judicature Soc., Phi Alpha Delta. Achievements include being subject of book Tiger in the Court, 1973. Office: 75 Livingston Ave Roseland NJ 07068-3701 E-mail: dpenna@sgklaw.com.

**STERN, HOWARD ALLAN,** radio personality, television show host; b. Jackson Heights, N.Y., Jan. 12, 1954; s. Ben and Ray S.; m. Alison Berns, 1978 (div. 2001); children: Emily, Debra, Ashley Jade. BA in Comm., Boston U., 1976. Disc jockey Sta. WRNW, Briarcliff Manor, NY, 1976-78, Sta. WCCC, Hartford, Conn., 1978-79, Sta. WWWW, Detroit, 1979-80, Sta. WWDC, Washington, 1980-82, Sta. WNBC, NYC, 1982-85, Sta. WXRK, NYC, 1985—2005, numerous other markets, 1986—2005; disc jockey Howard Stern Show Sirius Satellite Radio, 2006—. Author: Private Parts, 1993, Miss America, 1995; TV shows include The Howard Stern Show (WOR-TV), 1990-92, The Howard Stern Interview (E!), 1992-93, The Howard Stern Show (E!), 1994-2005, Howard Stern on Demand, 2005-; actor (films) Private Parts, 1997; writer, exec. prodr. voice Doomsday, 2000; writer, exec. prodr. (TV series) Son of the Beach, 2000-02; recordings include 50 Ways To Rank Your Mother, 1982, Crucified by the FCC, 1991; pay-per-view spls./videos include: Howard Stern's Négligé and Underpants Party, U.S. Open Sores, Butt Bongo Fiesta, The Miss Howard Stern New Year's Eve Pageant. Libertarian candidate for gov. State of NY, 1994. Rest Stop on I-295 in NJ named in his honor, 1995, recipient Rave Awards, Wired Renegade, WIRED, 2005; named one of 100 Most Influential People, Time Mag., 2006 Office. care Don Buchwald & Associates 10 E 44th St New York NY 10017-3601*

**STERN, JACQUELINE,** physician; b. Syracuse, NY, May 2, 1958; d. Arthur Paul and Edith Margerite Stern; m. Howard Bellowe, Sept. 4, 1988; children: Ilana, Gabriel, Nathan. BS, UCLA, 1979; MD, U. San Diego, 1983. Resident Mercy Med. Ctr., Denver, 1983—86; staff physician Colo. Permaneate Med. Ctr., Denver, 1986—89; pvt. practice physician Anderson Family Practice, Aurora, Colo., 1990—2000; faculty UCHSC, 2000—. Office: Rose Family Medicine Residency 2149 S Holly St Denver CO 80222

**STERN, JAMES ANDREW,** investment banker; b. NYC, Oct. 1, 1950; s. Arthur and Lenore (Oppenheimer) S.; m. Jane Yusem, April 13, 1975; children: Peter, David. BS, Tufts U., 1972; MBA, Harvard U., 1974. Assoc. Lehman Bros. Inc., N.Y.C., 1974-79, v.p., 1979-82, mng. dir., 1982-94; chmn. The Cypress Group, N.Y.C., 1994—. Bd. dirs. Lear Corp., Southfield, Mich., Amtrol, Inc., West Warwick, RI, Affinia Group Inc., Medpointe Inc. Trustee Tufts U., Medford, Mass., 1982-, chmn. bd. trustees 2003-, Jewish Mus., N.Y.C.; bd. dirs. Cystic Fibrosis Found. Mem. Quaker Ridge Golf Club (Scarsdale, NY), Beach Point Club (Mamaroneck, NY). Avocations: golf, reading. Office: The Cypress Group Inc 65 E 55th St New York NY 10022-3219 Office Phone: 212-705-0151. Business E-Mail: jstern@cypressgp.com.

**STERN, JAMES COPER,** sales executive; b. N.Y.C., Dec. 12, 1925; s. George Charles and Ruth (Coper) S.; m. Judith Vinson, Oct. 31, 1963 (div. Mar. 1974); children: Hillary Anne, Renee Jean; m. Ruth Nussbacker Szold, Aug. 22, 1982. BA, NYU, 1949. Trainee, exec. asst. Gardner Advt. Co., N.Y.C., 1949-50; advt. mgr. NOPCO Chem. Co., Harrison, N.J., 1950-53; account exec. Ziv TV Programs, N.Y.C., 1954-56; sales rep. United Artists Associated, N.Y.C., 1957-61; v.p., sales mgr. Allied Artists TV, N.Y.C., 1961-70; exec. v.p., gen. sales mgr. ITC Entertainment, Inc., Studio City, Calif., 1970-89; pres. JCS Syndication Svcs., L.A., 1990—. Cpl. U.S. Army, 1944-46, ETO. Mem. Internat. Radio and TV Soc., Nat. Assn. TV Program Execs., Ind. TV Program Execs. Republican. Jewish. Avocations: watercolor painting, skiing, golf, art. Home and Office: JCS Syndication Svcs 1855 Industrial St # 419 Los Angeles CA 90021 Office Phone: 323-654-3487. E-mail: jcssyndication@netscape.net.

**STERN, JAMES D.,** film producer, theater producer; Former hedge fund mgr.; founder, CEO Endgame Entertainment, West Hollywood, Calif. Co-owner Chgo. Bulls. Assoc. prodr.: (films) Jeffrey, 1985; dir., prodr. All the Rage, 1999; Michael Jordan to the Max, 2000; Year of the Yao, 2004; prodr.: 35 Miles from Normal, 1997, Pulse: A Stomp Odyssey, 2002, The Alibi, 2005; co-exec. prodr.: Let the Devil Wear Black, 1999; exec. prodr.: Stage Beauty, 2004, Harold & Kumar Go to White Castle, 2004, Five Children and It, 2004, Rag Tale, 2005, Lord of War, 2005; prodr.: (Broadway plays) The Producers (Tony award), Hairspray (Tony award, 2003), Little Shop of Horrors, Diary of Anne Frank, Sound of Music, (off-Broadway play) Stomp. Named one of 50 Most Powerful People in Hollywood, Premiere mag., 2005.

**STERN, JEAN,** museum director; b. Casablanca, Morocco; arrived in U.S., 1955; s. Frederic and Sultana Stern; m. Linda Susan Stern, Jan. 18, 2004; m. Carol Elizabeth Adams (div.); children: Carrie Dona, Hannah Marie. BA History, Calif. State, Northridge, Calif., 1968; MA Art History, Calif. State, San Diego, Calif., 1972; post graduate, UCLA, L.A. Instr. San Diego State Univ., San Diego, 1974—76; instr. art history Mesa Coll., San Diego, 1975; dir. Petersen Galleries, Beverly Hills, Calif., 1978—91; exec. dir. The Irvine Mus., Irvine, Calif., 1992—. Guest curator San Diego Mus. of Art, San Diego, 1976. Co-author: Enchanted Isle, 2003, California, This Golden Land, 2001; contbr. essays, articles pub. numerous to profl. jour. Mem.: Am. Assn. Mus., Calif. Art Club (Man of the Yr. 1998). Avocation: coin collecting/numismatics. Office: The Irvine Mus 18881 Von Karman #100 Irvine CA 92612 Office Phone: 949-476-0294.

**STERN, JOAN NAOMI,** lawyer; b. Phila., Mar. 7, 1944; d. Clarence J. and Diana D. (Goldberg) S. BA, U. Pa., 1965; JD, Temple U., 1977. Bar: Pa. 1977. Assoc. Blank Rome LLP, Phila., 1977—83, ptnr., 1983—, co-chair pub. fin. group, 1983-92, chair pub. fin. group, 1993, chair pub. fin. dept., 1994—. Cons. counsel Phila. Charter Commn., 1993-94. Contbr. articles to profl. jours. Mem. Sch. Dist. Task Force on Regulatory Reform, Phila., 1987, Tax Policy and Budget Com., Phila., 1989, Phila. Mayor's Fiscal Adv. Com., 1990; chair Sch. Dist. of Phila. Task Force on Alternate Financing Strategies, 1995; bd. mgrs. Moore Coll. Art and Design, Phila., 1993—, vice chair bd. trustees, bd. mgrs., 1995—; bd. dirs. Police Athletic League, Phila., 1994—, Jewish Fedn. of Greater Phila., 2000—, Am. Jewish Congress, 1995—, Urban Tree Connection, 2000-; trustee The Franklin Inst., 2004—. Fellow Am. Bar Found. (life); mem. ABA, Nat. Assn. Bond Lawyers, Phila. Bar Assn., Phila. Bar Assn. (chmn. mcpl. govt. com. 1983-97), Pa. Assn. Bond Lawyers. Office: Blank Rome LLP One Logan Square Philadelphia PA 19103-6998 Office Phone: 215-569-5526. E-mail: stern@blankrome.com.

**STERN, JOSEPH A.,** lawyer; b. Cleve., Dec. 7, 1949; s. Arthur J. and Thelma (Arnold) S. BA, Yale U., 1972, JD, 1976. Assoc. Winthrop Stimson, NYC, 1976-79, Fried Frank Harris Shriver & Jacobson, NYC, London, 1979-84, ptnr., 1984—2005; gen. counsel, v.p. & corp. sec. Dow Jones & Co. 2005—. Vice chair, dir. Mex. Am. Legal Defense and Edn. Fund, L.A. 1991-95; dir. Am. Friend Chamber Music of Europe, N.Y.C., 1986—. Mem. ABA, City Bar N.Y.

**STERN, JOSEPH SMITH, JR.,** former footwear manufacturing company executive; b. Cin., Mar. 31, 1918; s. Joseph S. and Miriam (Haas) S.; m. Mary Stern, June 14, 1942; children: Peter Joseph, William Frederick, Peggy Ann Graeter. AB, Harvard U., 1940, MBA, 1943; HHD (hon.), Xavier U., 1988; DSc (hon.), U. Cin., 1989. With R. H. Macy & Co., N.Y.C., 1940-41; with U.S. Shoe Corp., Cin., 1941-68, v.p., 1951-65, pres., 1965-66, chmn. bd., chief exec. officer, 1966, chmn. exec. com., 1966-68, dir., 1956-70. Prof. bus. policy emeritus U. Cin. Pres. bd. trustees Cin. and Hamilton County Pub. Libr.; chmn. Cin. Bicentennial Com., Greater Cin. Tall Stacks Commn.; trustee Cin. Music Hall Assn., Cin. Hist. Soc., Children's Hosp. Med. Center, Cin. Symphony Orch., Cin Country Day Sch., 1956-72, Family Svc., Cin., 1964-82; trustee, pres. Cin. Mus. Festival Assn.; pres. bd. trustees Children's Convalescent Hosp., Cin., 1972-75; bd. overseers vis. com. univ. libr. Harvard U. Served to lt. USNR, 1943-46. Recipient Disting. Community Svc. award NCCJ, 1986, Great Living Cincinnatian award Cin. C. of C., 1989, Disting. Svc. award U. Cin. Coll. Bus., 1992. Mem. Am. Footwear Industries Assn. (life; dir.) Jewish (past pres. temple). Clubs: Literary (Cin.), Harvard (Cin.) (pres. 1965), Queen City (Cin.), Queen City Optimists, Harvard (N.Y.C.). Home: 3 Grandin Pl Cincinnati OH 45208-3402

**STERN, JUDITH SCHNEIDER,** nutritionist, researcher, educator; b. Bklyn. d. Sidney and Lillian (Rosen) Schneider; m. Richard C. Stern; 1 child, Daniel Arthur. BS, Cornell U., 1964; MS, Harvard U. Sch. Pub. Health, 1966, ScD, 1970. Rsch. asst., dept. food sci. and nutrition MIT, Cambridge, 1964—65; rsch. assoc. dept. human behavior and metabolism The Rockefeller U., NYC, 1968—72, asst. prof. dept. human behavior and metabolism, 1972—74; contbg. editor Vogue Mag., Conde Nast Publs., NYC, 1974; asst. prof. nutrition U. Calif., Davis, 1975—77, assoc. prof. dept. nutrition, 1977—82, dir. food intake lab. group, 1980—2001, prof. dept. nutrition, 1982—, prof. divsn. endocrinology, clin. nutrition and vascular biology, 1988—, disting. prof., 2003—. Mem. editl. bd. Internat. Jour. Obesity, 1976-85, Appetite, 1990, Obesity Rsch., 1993—2002, Nutrition Today, 1999—. Bd. sci. advisors Am. Coun. Sci. and Health, 1980—; mem. U.S. Dept. Agr. Dietary Guidelines Adv. Com., 1983—85; mem. obesity task force NIDDK, 1996—2002, AAAS; mem. expert com. U.S. Pharmacopeia Bioavailability and Nutrient Absorption, 2000—03; mem. adv. bd. USDA Nat. Agrl. Rsch. Ext., Edn. and Econs., 2000—03. Recipient Sec.'s Honor award USDA, 2004; NIH tng. grantee, 1979-2006. Fellow Am. Heart Assoc.; mem. Am. Soc. Clin. Nutrition (pres. 1995-96), Am. Dietetic Assn., Am. Diabetes Assn., Am. Obesity Assn. (co-founder, v.p. 1995-), N.Am. Assn. for Study of Obesity (pres. 1992-93), Inst. Medicine of NAS, Inst. Food Technologists, Am. Soc. Nutrition Sci. (chair pub. info. com. 1992-94), Sigma Xi, Delta Omega. Office: U Calif Dept Nutrition 1 Shields Ave Davis CA 95616-5271 Office Phone: 530-752-6575. Business E-Mail: jsstern@ucdavis.edu.

**STERN, KENNETH P.,** broadcast executive; b. 1963; BA, Haverford Coll.; JD, Yale U. Mgmt. and legal actns. Radio Free Europe/Radio Liberty, Munich and Prague; dep. gen. counsel Clinton/Gore Campaign, 1996; chief counsel 53rd Presdl. Inaugural Com.; sr. adv., cons. to dir., dir. affiliate rels., rsch. & media training US Internat. Broadcasting Bur., Washington, 1996—99; exec. v.p. Nat. Pub. Radio (NPR), 1999—, CEO, 2006—. Recipient Harold Kurzman Prize in Polit. Sci. Mem.: Phi Beta Kappa. Office: NPR 635 Massachusetts Ave, NW Washington DC 20001 Office Phone: 202-513-2000. Office Fax: 202-513-3329.*

**STERN, LEO G.,** lawyer; b. Mpls., Apr. 10, 1945; s. Philip J. and June I. (Monasch) S.; m. Christine E. Lamb, June 29, 1968; children: Alison M., Zachary A. BA, U. Calif., Davis, 1967; JD cum laude, U. Minn., 1970. Bar: Minn. 1970, U.S. Dist. Ct. Minn. 1971, Calif. 1971, U.S. Ct. Appeals (6th, 7th and 8th cirs.) 1985, U.S. Supreme Ct. 1993, Wis. 1999; cert. mediator and arbitrator, Minn. Ptnr. Cox, King & Stern, Mpls., 1970-77, Wright, West & Diessner, Mpls., 1977-84, Fredrikson & Byron, P.A., Mpls., 1984—. Mem. Minn. Bar Assn. (governing coun. environ. and natural resources law sect. 1989-95, governing coun. litigation sect. 1995-99), Am. Arbitration Assn. (arbitrator, mediator). Avocations: sailing, jogging. Home: 206 Central Ave S Wayzata MN 55391-1818 Office: Fredrikson & Byron PA 4000 Pillsbury Ctr 200 S 6th St Minneapolis MN 55402 Office Phone: 612-492-7061. Business E-Mail: lstern@fredlaw.com.

**STERN, LEONARD NORMAN,** real estate developer, former pet supply manufacturing company executive; b. NYC, Mar. 28, 1938; s. Max and Hilda (Lowenthal) Stern; m. Judith Stern (div.); children: Emanuel Theodore, Edward Julius, Andrea Caroline; m. Allison Maher, 1987. BS cum laude, NYU, 1956, MBA, 1957; DHL (hon.), Yeshiva U., 1985; LLD (hon.), Fairleigh Dickinson, 1995. Formerly pres., dir., now chmn., CEO Hartz Group, Inc., 1959—, sold pet div., 1999; chmn., CEO Hartz Mountain Industries Inc., 1966—; founder Stern Pub., 1986—99; owner 667 Madison Ave., NYC, Tribeca Grand Hotel, NYC, SoHo Grand Hotel, NYC, Harmon

Cove, Secaucus, NJ, Lincoln Harbor, Weehawken, NJ, Colgate Ctr., Jersey City, Journal Square, Jersey City. Mem. adv. bd. Chem. Bank, NYC, 1970-; active real estate constrn., devel. Bd. dirs. Manhattan Day Sch., Jewish Ctr. NYC; founder Albert Einstein Coll. Medicine, 1958; mem. NYC Holocaust Meml. Commn.; founder Homes for the Homeless, 1986-; trustee NYU, 1976-1996, former chmn. fin. com. Named Graduate and Undergraduate Schs. of Bus. The Leonard N. Stern Sch. Bus., NYU, 1984; named one of Forbes' Richest Americans, 2006; recipient Albert Gallatin medal, NYU. Office: Hartz Group 667 Madison Ave 26th Floor New York NY 10021

**STERN, LOUIS WILLIAM,** marketing educator, consultant; b. Boston, Sept. 19, 1935; s. Berthold Summerfield Stern and Gladys (Koch) Cohen; m. Rhona L. Grant; children: Beth Ida, Deborah Lynn. AB, Harvard U., 1957; MBA in Mktg., U. Pa., 1959; PhD in Mktg, Northwestern U., 1962. Mem. staff bus. research and consumer mktg. sects. Arthur D. Little, Inc., Cambridge, Mass., 1961-63; from asst. prof. bus. orgn. to prof. Ohio State U., Columbus, Ohio, 1963—70, prof. mktg., 1970—73; from prof. mktg. to A. Montgomery Ward prof. mktg. Northwestern U., 1973—83, John D. Gray disting. prof. mktg., 1983—2001, John D. Gray disting. prof. emeritus mktg., 2001—; on leave as exec. dir. Mktg. Sci. Inst., Cambridge, Mass., 1983-85; Thomas Henry Carroll Ford Found. vis. prof. Harvard U. Grad. Sch. Bus. Adminstrn., 1984-85; Dorinda and Mark Winkelman Disting. Scholar sr. fellow, co-dir. Jay H. Baker Retailing Initiative, The Wharton Sch., U. Pa., 2004—06; mem. bd. trustees Williston Northhampton Sch., Easthampton, Mass. Mem. staff Nat. Commn. on Food Mktg., Washington, 1965-66; vis. assoc. prof. bus. adminstrn. U. Calif., Berkeley, 1969-70; guest lectr. York U., U. Minn., U. Ky., UCLA, Ohio State U., U. N.C., Duke U., U. Wis., U. Pitts., U. Chgo., MIT, U. Mich., U. Pa., Cornell U., U. Mo., Norwegian Sch. Econs. and Bus. Adminstrn.; faculty assoc. Hernstein Inst., Vienna, Austria, 1976-77, Mgmt. Centre Europe, 1988-96; faculty assoc. Gemini Cons. Inc., Montvale, N.J., 1977-96. mem. midwest adv. bd., 1989-94; Xerox rsch. prof. Northwestern U., 1981-82; cons. to FTC, 1973, 80; vis. scholar U. Calif. Berkeley, 1997-2001; mem. faculty adv. bd. CSC Index, 1997-99; co-dir. Jay H. Baker Retailing Initiative Wharton Sch., U. Pa., 2004. Author: Distribution Channels: Behavioral Dimensions, 1969, (with Frederick D. Sturdivant and others) Managerial Analysis in Marketing, 1970, Perspectives in Marketing Management, 1971, (with John R. Grabner, Jr.) Competition in the Marketplace, 1970, (with Anne T. Coughlan, Erin Anderson and Adel I. El-Ansary) Marketing Channels, 6th edit., 2001, (with Thomas L. Eovaldi) Legal Aspects of Marketing Strategy: Antitrust and Consumer Protection Issues, 1984; (with Adel I. El-Ansary and James R. Brown) Management in Marketing Channels, 1989; mem. editl. bd. Jour. Mktg. Rsch., 1976-82, Jour. Mktg., 1979-83, Mktg. Letters, 1988-94; contbr. articles to profl. jours. Mem. exec. com. Northwest Area Coun. on Human Rels., Columbus, 1971—72. Rsch. grantee Ohio State U., 1964-73, Mktg. Sci. Inst., 1976-77, 88-90, 92-94; recipient Harold H. Maynard award best article Jour. Mktg., 1980, Kellogg's Spl. Lifetime Achievement Award for Tchg. Excellence, 1999; named Mktg. Educator of Yr. Sales and Mktg. Execs. Internat., 1989, also Chgo. chpt. 1990, Outstanding Profl. of Yr. award, 1992, and named One of Top 6 Profs. in Kellogg Sch., Northwestern U., Grad. Mgmt. Assocs., 1984-94, (named 6 times Outstanding Prof. Exec. Masters Program), One of Top 12 Tchrs. in U.S., U.S. Bus. Schs., Bus. Week; named Dorinda and Mark Winkelman Disting. scholar, Sr. fellow Wharton Sch., U. Pa., 2004. Mem. AAUP, Am. Mktg. Assn. (mem. program com. educators conf. 1971, chmn. com. 1978, Paul D. Converse award 1986, Richard D. Irwin Disting. Mktg. Educator of Yr. 1994), Hellenic Inst. Mktg., Beta Gamma Sigma. Home: Apt 1401 800 Elgin Rd Evanston IL 60201-5629 Office: Northwestern U Kellogg Sch Mgmt Dept Mktg Evanston IL 60208-2001 Office Phone: 847-491-2718. Business E-Mail: lwstern@kellogg.northwestern.edu.

**STERN, LOUISE,** artist; b. New Haven, Apr. 24, 1921; d. Louis Michael and Bertha (Vorhaus) Gompertz; m. Siegfried Stern, June 30, 1945; children: Frederick, David. Student, Syracuse U., 1939-41; MusB, Boston U., 1943. Art instr., New Rochelle, N.Y.; juror Mamaroneck Artists Guild, Larchmont, N.Y., 2005, New Rochelle Art Assn., 2004. One-woman shows include Ward-Nasse Gallery, NYC, 1978, 80, Hudson River Mus., Yonkers, NY, 1982, Mamaroneck Artists Guild Gallery, Larchmont, NY, 1983, Concordia Coll. Libr. Gallery, Bronxville, NY, 1987, Union Am. Hebrew Congregations, NYC, 1992, Dobbs Ferry (NY) Libr. Gallery, 1993, Banco Popular, NYC, 1993, Silvermine Guild Art Ctr., New Canaan, Conn., 1994, Goldstein Cultural Ctr., Temple Israel, New Rochelle, 2004, Mamaroneck Artists Guild Gallery, Larchmont, NY, 2005; exhibited in group shows Nat. Assn. Women Artists traveling shows, 1978-84-86, 89-90, Hudson River Mus., Ny Carlsberg Glyptokek Mus., Copenhagen, 1980, Fukuoka (Japan) Cultural Ctr., 1981, Bergen Cmty. Mus., Paramus, NJ, 1983, Silvermine Collection Pitney-Bowes, Stamford, Conn., 1987-89, Audubon Artists, NYC, Prints Internat., 1990, 92, Gallery at Hastings, NY, 1992, Adelphi U. Manhattan Ctr., 1991, Westchester Art Coun., Krafts Gen. Foods & Readers Digest, 1993, Broome St. Gallery, 1996, Hurlbust Gallery, Greenwich, Conn., 1997, 2003, Conn. Graphic Arts, Norwalk, 1999, Manhattan (NY) Borough Pres. Virginia Fields Office Gallery, Katonah Mus. Artists, North Westchester Hosp., Mt. Kisco, NY, 2003, Brother Chapman Gallery, Iona Coll., New Rochelle, 2004, Silvermine Guild Galleries, 2005, Mamaroneck Small Works, Larchmont, NY, 2005, Pelham Art Ctr., web page www.louisestern.com, also others; represented in permanent collections Cabrini Med. Ctr., NYC, Morani Art Gallery, Med. Coll. Pa., Gen. Foods, Tarrytown, NY, Simpson, Thacker and Bartlett, NYC, Genesis Hebrew Ctr., Tuckahoe, NY, Pfizer Collection, Westchester MetroMedia Corp., White Plains, Med. Profl. Liability Agy., Mt. Kisco, also pvt. collections and cos. Recipient 1st in graphic award New Rochelle Art Assn., 1983, 2d award for graphics, 1985, 1st in graphics award Serge Hollerbach, 1989, Dr. and Mrs. I.C. Gaynor award, 1990, Dermot Gale award New Rochelle Art Assn., 2002, 2d Pl. award Mamaroneck Artist's Guild, 2002, 1st Pl. award, 2004, 1st pl. award in mixed media New Rochelle Artists Assn., 2004, others. Mem. AAUW, Nat. Assn. Women Artists (chmn. print jury 1988-90, chmn. nominating com. 1990-92, Morris J. Helman award 1984, Stelly Sterling Meml. award 1989, Louise H. Renwick Meml. award 1999), Silvermine Guild of Artists, Mamaroneck Artists Guild, Katonah Mus. Avocations: horseback riding, french conversation. Home: 120 Lakeshore Dr N Eastchester NY 10709-5217

**STERN, MADELEINE BETTINA,** rare book dealer, writer; b. N.Y.C., July 1, 1912; d. Moses Roland and Lillie (Mack) S. BA, Barnard Coll., 1932; MA, Columbia U., 1934. Tchr. English N.Y.C. High Schs., 1934-43; ptnr. Leona Rostenberg Rare Books, N.Y.C., 1945—. Leona Rostenberg and Madeleine B. Stern Rare Books, N.Y.C., 1945—. Lectr. history of book, feminism, pub. history, lt. Author: We Are Taken, 1935, The Life of Margaret Fuller, 1942, Louisa May Alcott, 1950, new edit., 1996, Purple Passage: The Life of Mrs. Frank Leslie, 1953, Imprints on History: Book Publishers and American Frontiers, 1956, We the Women: Career Firsts of Nineteenth Century America, 1962, new edit., 1994, So Much in a Lifetime: The Story of Dr. Isabel Barrows, 1965, Queen of Publishers' Row: Mrs. Frank Leslie, 1966, The Pantarch: A Biography of Stephen Pearl Andrews, 1968, Heads and Headlines: The Phrenological Fowlers, 1971, Books and Book People in 19th-Century America, 1978, Antiquarian Bookselling in the United States: A History from the Origins to the 1940s, 1985, Nicholas Gouin Dufief of Philadelphia Franco-American Bookseller, 1776-1834, 1988, The Life of Margaret Fuller: A Revised Second Edition, 1991, Louisa May Alcott: From Blood & Thunder to Hearth & Home, 1998; (with Leona Rostenberg) Old and Rare: Forty Years in the Book Business, 1974, rev. edit. 1988, Between Boards: New Thoughts on Old Books, 1978, Bookman's Quintet: Five Catalogues about Books, 1980, Quest Book-Guest Book: A Biblio-Folly, 1993, Connections: Our Selves-Our Books, 1994, Old Books in the Old World: Reminiscences of Book Buying Abroad, 1996, Old Books, Rare Friends: Two Literary Sleuths and Their Shared Passion, 1997, New Worlds in Old Books, 1999, Books Have Their Fates, 2001, Bookends: Two Women, One Enduring Friendship, 2001, From Revolution to Revolution: Perspectives on Publishing and Bookselling, 2002; editor: Women on the Move, 4 vols., 1972, Victoria Woodhull Reader, 1974, Louisa's Wonder Book-An Unknown Alcott Juvenile, 1975, Behind a Mask: The Unknown Thrillers of Louisa May Alcott, 1975, new edit., 1995, Plots and Counterplots: More Unknown

Thrillers of Louisa May Alcott, 1976, Publishers for Mass Entertainment in 19th-Century America, 1980, A Phrenological Dictionary of 19th-Century Americans, 1982, Critical Essays on Louisa May Alcott, 1984, A Modern Mephistopheles and Taming a Tartar by Louisa May Alcott, 1987, Louisa May Alcott Unmasked: Collected Thrillers, 1995, Modern Magic by Louisa May Alcott, 1995, The Feminist Alcott: Stories of a Woman's Power, 1996, Louisa May Alcott: Signature of Reform, 2002; co-editor: Selected Letters of Louisa May Alcott, 1987, A Double Life: Newly Discovered Thrillers of Louisa May Alcott, 1988, The Journals of Louisa May Alcott, 1989, Louisa May Alcott: Selected Fiction, 1990, (co-editor) Freaks of Genius: Unknown Thrillers of Louisa May Alcott, 1991, From Jo March's Attic: Stories of Intrigue and Suspense, 1993 (Victorian Soc. award), The Lost Stories of Louisa May Alcott, 1995. Recipient Medalie award, Barnard Coll., 1982, Victorian Soc. award, Disting. Alumna award, 1997; Guggenheim fellow, 1943—45. Mem. Antiquarian Booksellers Assn. Am. (gov. 1966-68, 78-80), Internat. League Antiquarian Booksellers, MLA, Am. Printing History Assn. (co-recipient award 1983), Authors League, Manuscript Soc. (former trustee), Phi Beta Kappa. Jewish. Home: 40 E 88th St New York NY 10128-1176

**STERN, MARCUS A.,** journalist; b. Washington; Grad., UCLA. With San Pedro News-Pilot, Calif., States News Svc., Washington; with Washington Bur. Copley News Svc., 1983—, news editor, Washington bur., 2000—. Recipient Eugene Katz award, Ctr. Immigration Studies, 1998, Edgar A. Poe award, White House Corrs. Assn., 2006, George Polk award for polit. reporting, 2006, Pulitzer Prize for nat. reporting, 2006. Office: Copley News Svc Washington Bur 1100 Nat Press Bldg Washington DC 20045 Business E-Mail: newseditor@copleydc.com

**STERN, MARGARET BASSETT,** retired special education educator, author; b. Bklyn., June 6, 1920; d. Preston Rogers and Jeanne (Mordorf) Bassett; m. Fritz R. Stern Oct. 11, 1947 (div. Dec. 1992); children: Frederick Preston, Katherine Stern Brennan. BA, Wellesley Coll., 1942; MEd, Bank Street Coll. Edn., N.Y.C., 1943, MEd, 1974. Propr. Castle Sch., N.Y.C., 1944-51; dir. Mothers' Coop. Nursery Sch., Ithaca, N.Y., 1952-54; tchr. sci. and math. The Brearley Sch., N.Y.C., 1956-57. Cons., lectr. Head Start, Tuskegee, Ala., 1964; cons. in math. The Gateway Sch., N.Y.C., 1967-90; spl. lectr. Columbia U. Tchrs. Coll., N.Y.C., 1990-94; condr. workshops in Eng., 1960-88. Author: (with Catherine Stern and Toni Gould) Structural Reading Program, Workbooks and Teachers Guides A through E, 1963, 3d edit., 1978, Structural Arithmetic Workbooks and Teachers Guides Grades 1-3, 1965, 2d edit., 1966, (with Stern) Children Discover Arithmetic, 1971, (with Gould) Spotlight on Phonics, Four Workbooks and Teachers Guides, 1980, Sound/Symbol Activities and Decoding Activities, 1980, 2d edit., 1994; Experimenting with Numbers, 1988, 2004, Structural Arithmetic, 1-3, 1992, 2006. Recipient award, Orton Dyslexia Soc. N.Y., 1989, Bank St. Coll. Edn., 1998. Mem.: Nat. Coun. Tchrs. Math., Internat. Dyslexia Assn. Home: 3204 River Crescent Dr Annapolis MD 21401 Personal E-mail: structuralarith@aol.com.

**STERN, MARILYN,** photographer, editor, writer; b. Detroit, Nov. 8, 1953; d. Julian and Phyllis Stern. BA, Brown U., 1976. Photographer's asst., N.Y.C., 1976-82; freelance photographer, 1976—; freelance writer, 1985—; picture editor Across the Board mag., N.Y.C. 1990-96; faculty Internat. Ctr. of Photography, 2001, NYU, 2004—. Photographer, organizer: (book) Masked Culture: The Greenwich Village Halloween Parade, 1994; author, photographer: Kval! Die Walfänger der Lofoten, 1990; solo exhbns. Profil Gallery, Bratislava, 2001, Scandinavia House, N.Y.C., 2003; several group exhbns., 1976—; represented in permanent collection Detroit Inst. Arts, also numerous pvt. collections. Travel Study grantee Royal Norwegian Consulate to Norway in the U.S., 1987, Am.-Scandinavian Found., 1986. E-mail: mstern@sternphoto.com.

**STERN, MARILYN JEAN,** special education educator; b. Akron, Ohio, Oct. 7, 1937; d. Walter Keith Pallage and Betty Jane Freeman-Pallage; m. Robert Stern, June 14, 1974 (dec.); children: John Daily, Anne Tunney, Jane Henault, Andrew Daily. BS in Elem. Edn., U. Akron, 1961, MS in Spl. Edn., 1978. Cert. in tchg. Ohio, 1974, Penn., 1963, in tchg. spl. edn. 1978. Tchr. Phila. Sch. Dist., 1963—64; spl. edn. tchr. Summit County Bd. Mental Health, Tallmadge, Ohio, 1974—78, Girard Sch. Dist., Pa., 1999—2004; spl. edn. Learning Disabilities tchr. NW Tri-County Intermediate Unit, Girard, 1978—88, county computer advisor edn. Erie County, Pa., 1988—90, ret., 2004. Computer cons. NW Tri-County Intermediate Unit, 1985—90; vol. reading tutor Hooked-On-Books, Erie County, 2004—; presenter in field; leader spl. programs 4th grade level. Mem. Lake Erie Ballet Bd., Erie, Pa., 1980—92; polit. action chair Girard Fedn. Tchrs., 2000—04; past pres. Local Ridge Coun., nominating chmn., act 48 hours chairperson, spl. projects chair; vol. Hooked on Books; reader Erie Zoo. Mem.: Keystone State Reading Assn. (exec. bd. mem. 2003—), Internat. Reading Assn. (chair 2000—, del. to conf. 2005), Reading Tchrs. Orgn. (pres. 2003—05). Avocations: reading, gardening, quilting, fiber arts, quilting. Home: 1420 Lord Rd Fairview PA 16415

**STERN, MICHAEL LAWRENCE,** psychologist; b. N.Y.C., July 3, 1948; s. Abraham Isaac and Etta (Silverberg) S.; m. Karen Beth Rivard, July 26, 1981; children: Joshua Ethan, Rachel Lynn. BA, Calif. State U., Long Beach, 1970; PhD, U. Wash., 1977. Diplomate Am. Bd. Med. Psychotherapists; cert. employee assistance profl., sex therapist. Intern St. Elizabeth's Hosp. NIMH, Washington, 1973-74; instr. dept. psychology U. Wash., Seattle, 1975-77; rsch. assoc. dept. psychiatry U. Tenn. Med. Sch., Memphis, 1977-78; clin. dir. drug abuse program Fed. Correction Inst., Danbury, Conn., 1978-85, chief psychologist, 1985-86; dir. outpatient recovery ctr. Briarcliff Manor, N.Y. 1986-88; pvt. practice clin. psychology, 1981-86; cons. Addiction Recovery Corp, Westchester, 1987-88; adj. faculty Fairfield U., 1981-86; dir. OMNI Health Assn. U. Tenn. postdoctoral fellow, 1977-78. Mem. Am. Psychol. Assn. (cert. addictions), Assn. Advancement Behavior Therapy, Am. Assn. Sex Educators, Counselor, and Therapists, Conn. Psychol. Assn. Family Firm Inst. Cons. editor TSA News, 1977-78. Home: Saw Mill Ridge Rd Newtown CT 06470 Office: Green Knoll Profl Ctr 60 Old New Milford Rd Brookfield CT 06804-2430 Office Phone: 203-740-2900.

**STERN, MITCHELL,** broadcast executive; B. U. Pa., 1976; MBA, U. Chgo., 1978. With CBS TV Stas. Divsn., 1978—86, dir. planning and adminstrn. WCBS-TV N.Y.C., dir. planning and adminstrn. WBBM-TV Chgo., fin. analyst corp. office; v.p. CFO Fox TV Stas., L.A., 1986—90, v.p. gen. sta. mgr. KTTV-Fox 11, 1990—92, sr. v.p., 1990—92, exec. v.p., COO, 1992—93, pres., COO, 1993—98, chmn., CEO, 1998—2003, Twentieth TV, L.A., 1998—2003; CEO DirecTV, 2003—05. Office: Fox TV Stas Inc 205 E 67th St New York NY 10021

**STERN, MORT(IMER) P(HILLIP),** communications educator, editor, reporter, consultant; b. New Haven, Conn., Feb. 20, 1926; s. Bernard and Louise Eleanor (Spiro) S.; m. Patricia Ruth Freeman, Jan. 10, 1946; children: Susan C., Margaret L. AB, U. Ark., 1947; MS, Columbia U., 1949; postgrad., Harvard U., 1954—55; PhD, U. Denver, 1969. Reporter S.W.-Am., Ft. Smith, Ark., 1946-47; night bur. mgr. UPI, Little Rock, 1947-48; reporter, polit. writer, state editor Ark. Gazette, Little Rock, 1949-51; reporter, rewrite man Denver Post, 1951-53, night city editor, 1953-54, asst. editor Rocky Mountain Empire sect., 1955-56, mng. editor, 1956-58, assoc. editor, 1958, editl. page editor, 1958-65, asst. to pub., 1965-70, editl. page editor, 1971-73; dean Sch. Pub. Communication U. Ala., 1973-74; dean Sch. Journalism U. Colo., Boulder, 1974-77; lectr. journalism U. Denver, 1953-54, adj. prof., 1970, exec. dir. pub. affairs, 1977-78, exec. asst. to chancellor, 1978-84; prof. chmn. dept. journalism and mass communication U. No. Colo., Greeley 1985-90; pres. P. Paty & Co., Georgetown, Colo., 1989—. Atwood prof. journalism U. Alaska, Anchorage, 1981-82. With USAAF, 1944-45. Mem. Georgetown Bd. of Selectmen, 1997-99; mem. Georgetown Bd. Adjustment, 2001-. Nieman fellow Harvard U., 1954-55; named Disting. Alumnus dept. journalism U. Ark., 1999; inducted to Fulbright Coll. Alumni Acad. U. Ark., 1999. Mem.: Georgetown Libr. Assn. (v.p. 1999, pres. 2001—04, bd. dirs.), Phi Beta Kappa, Sigma Delta Chi, Omicron Delta Kappa. Baptist. Home: PO Box 549 Georgetown CO 80444-0549

**STERN, PAULA,** international trade consultant; b. Chgo., Mar. 31, 1945; d. Lloyd and Fan (Wener) Stern; m. Paul A. London; children: Gabriel Stern London, Genevieve Stern London. BA, Goucher Coll., 1967; MA in Middle Eastern Studies, Harvard U., 1969; MA in Internat. Affairs, Fletcher Sch. of Law and Diplomacy, 1970, MA in Law and Diplomacy, 1970, PhD, 1976; D Comml. Sci. (hon.), Babson Coll.; LLBS; LLD (hon.), Goucher Coll., 1985. From legis. asst. to sr. legis. asst. to U.S. Sen. Gaylord Nelson U.S. Senate, Washington, 1972—74, 1976; guest scholar Brookings Inst., Washington, 1975-76; policy analyst Pres. Carter-V.P. Mondale Transition Team, Washington, 1977-78; internat. affairs fellow Council on Fgn. Rels., Washington, 1977-78; commr. Internat. Trade Commn., Washington, 1978-87, chair, 1984-86; sr. assoc. Carnegie Endowment for Internat. Peace, Washington, 1986-88; sr. fellow Program Policy Inst., 1994—95. Howard W. Aikire chmn. internat. bus. and econs. Hamline U., 1994—2000; chairwoman The Stern Group, Inc., 1988—; bd. dirs. Avaya, Inc., Avon Products, Inc., Hasbro, Inc.; mem., sr. advisor U.S. trade policy coun. Competition Policy Inst., 1991—93; sr. fellow Progressive Policy Inst., 1994—95; pub. vice chairwoman Atlantic Coun. U.S.; trustee Com. Econ. Devel.; mem. Inter-Am. Dialogue, Coun. Fgn. Rels.; past co-chair Internat. Competition Adv. Com.; antitrust divsn. U.S. Dept. Justice; past chmn. US Export-Import Bank; past mem. U.S. Pres. Adv. Com. on Trade Policy and Negotiation; bd. dirs. Carnegie Coun. Ethics and Internat. Affairs. Author: Water's Edge--Domestic Politics and the Making of American Foreign Policy, 1979; contbg. author newspapers; contbr. articles to profl. jours. Recipient Journalism award, Alicia Patterson Fund, 1971, Joseph Papp Award for Racial Harmony, Found. Ethnic Understanding, 2004. Democrat. Jewish. Avocations: sculpting, tennis, dance. Office: 3314 Ross Pl NW Washington DC 20008-3332 Office Phone: 202-966-7894. Business E-Mail: pstern@sterngroup.biz.

**STERN, RICHARD DAVID,** investment company executive; b. New Rochelle, NY, Nov. 5, 1936; s. Leo and Grace Marjorie S.; m. Phyllis Marlene Edelstein, Nov. 20, 1966; children: Marjorie Anne, Andrew Howard. AB, Princeton U., 1958; MBA, Harvard U., 1962. CFA. 1st v.p. Newburger, Loeb & Co., N.Y.C., 1962-74, also bd. dirs., 1969-74; sr. investment officer Ctrl. Trust Co. (now known as PNC Back), Cin., 1974-76, owner bus. valuation cons. co., 1976-78; v.p. Gt. Western Bank & Trust Co. (now Wells Fargo Bank), Phoenix, 1978-84; pres. Stern, Ludke & Co. (now Stellar Capital Mgmt. LLC.), Phoenix, 1984—; mng. mem., 2000—. Co-author: Air Cushion Vehicles, 1962. Trustee endowment trust Phoenix Chamber Music Soc., 1982-91; v.p., 1986-90, bd. dirs., 1982-91, 93-94; pres. Cen. Ariz. chpt. Arthritis Found., 1982-84, chmn. planned giving com., 1986-91, mem. nat. planned giving com., 1987-89; chmn. endowments and trusts com. Temple Beth Israel, Phoenix, 1980-83; dir. investment com. Endowment Found., Temple Solel, Paradise Valley, 1990-92; pres. Am. Jewish Com., Phoenix, 1983-84, bd. dirs., 1980-84, adv. bd., 1985-2005; bd. dirs. Asian Arts Coun., Phoenix Art Mus., 1987-93, v.p., 1989-90, pres., 1990-92; trustee Ariz. Theatre Co., 1990-97, mem. regional nominating com., 1995-97, chmn., 1995-96, asst. treas., 1996-97; grants award panelist Phoenix Office of Arts and Culture, 2002, 05. Mem. CFA Inst., Phoenix CFA Soc. (chmn. profl. conduct com. 1980-83, membership com. 1990-91, bd. dirs.), Anti-Defamation League (dir. Ctrl. Ariz. chpt. 1986—, exec. bd. 1989—, chair nominating com. 1990-94, 2001—, chair bd. devel. 1993-94, treas. 1994-2004, assoc. nat. commr. 1998—), Princeton Alumni Assn. No. Ariz. (alumni schs. com. 1992—, v.p. 2005—), Univ. Club Phoenix (bd. dirs. 1990-92, fin. com. 1990-91), Harvard Bus. Sch. Club Ariz. (bd. dirs. 1991—, pres. 1993-95), Clearwater Hills Improvement Assn. (dir. 2002-, sec. 2006-). Republican. Home: 7547 N Lakeside Ln Paradise Valley AZ 85253-2857 Office: 2200 E Camelback Rd Ste 130 Phoenix AZ 85016-3455 Business E-Mail: rstern@stellarmgt.com.

**STERN, RICHARD GUSTAVE,** writer; b. N.Y.C., Feb. 25, 1928; s. Henry George and Marion (Veit) S.; m. Gay Clark, Mar. 14, 1950 (div. Feb. 1972); children: Christopher Holmes, Kate Macomber, Andrew Henry, Nicholas Clark; m. Alane Rollings, Aug. 9, 1985. BA, U. N.C., 1947; MA, Harvard U., 1950; PhD, State U. Iowa, 1954. Mem. faculty U. Chgo., 1955—, prof. English, 1965—, Helen Regenstein prof. English, 1990—2002, prof. emeritus, 2002. Author: Golk, 1960, Europe and Up and Down with Baggish and Schreiber, 1961, In Any Case, 1962, Teeth, Dying and Other Matters, 1964, Stitch, 1965, 1968: A Short Novel, An Urban Idyll, Five Stories and Two Trade Notes, 1970, The Books in Fred Hampton's Apartment, 1973, Other Men's Daughters, 1973, Natural Shocks, 1978, Packages, 1980, The Invention of the Real, 1982, A Father's Words, 1986, The Position of the Body, 1986, Noble Rot: Stories, 1949-88, 1989 (book of yr. award Chgo. Sun-Times 1990), Shares and Other Fictions, 1992, One Person and Another, 1993, A Sistermony, 1995 (Heartland award, nonfiction book of year), Pacific Tremors, 2001, What Is What Was, 2002, Almonds to the Zhoof: The Collected Stories of Richard Stern, 2005; editor: Honey and Wax, 1966. Recipient Longwood Found. award, 1960, Friends of Lit. award, 1963, fiction award Nat. Inst. Arts and Letters, 1968; Nat. Coun. Arts and Humanities fellow, 1967-68, Carl Sandburg award for fiction, 1979, Arts Coun. awards, 1979, 81, Am. Acad. and Inst. of Arts and Letters medal of Merit for Novel, 1985; Rockefeller fellow, 1965, Guggenheim fellow, 1973-74. Fellow Ctr. Advanced Studies in the Behavioral Scis.; mem. Am. Acad. Arts and Scis. Office: U Chgo Dept English Chicago IL 60637 E-Mail: rstern@uchicago.edu.

**STERN, ROBERT,** psychiatrist; b. Aug. 12, 1928; BS, Swiss Fed. Inst. Tech., Zurich, 1951; MS, Yale U., 1953, PhD, 1956; MD, Case Western Res. U., 1966. Diplomate Am. Bd. Psychiatry and Neurology; lic. physician, Conn. Asst. prof. chemistry Wesleyan U., Middletown, Conn., 1957—58, Conn. Coll., New London, 1959-60; supr. bio-organic chem. rsch. Arthur D. Little, Inc., Cambridge, Mass., 1960-62; vis. fellow medicine Mass. Gen. Hosp., 1964; rsch. assoc. biol. chemistry Harvard Med. sch., Boston, 1964, tchg. fellow psychiatry, 1967-68; intern medicine King County Hosp./U. Wash., Seattle, 1966-67; resident in psychiatry McLean Hosp., Belmont, Mass., 1967-68; jr/sr asst. resident internal medicine Yale-New Haven Hosp., 1968-70, clin. fellow medicine, 1970-71; postdoctoral fellow psychiatry Yale U. Sch. Medicine, 1971-73, asst. clin. prof. psychiatry, 1974-86, assoc. clin. prof. psychiatry, 1986—; pvt. practice New Haven, 1973—. Conn. Child Guidance clinic of Southeastern Conn., New London, 1973-82; cons. CHAMPUS peer reviewer Qualidigm, Inc., Middletown, 1994—; lectr. in field. Contbr. articles to profl. jours. Fellow Am. Psychiat. Assn. (Disting. life fellow); mem. New Haven Individual Practice Assn. (co-chmn. psychiatry panel 1985-98, quality assurance com. 1988-89, 1986-89), Conn. Psychiatry Soc. (councilor-at-large 2001—06, councilor 2000-01, pres. New Haven/Middlesex chpt. 1999-2000, treas. 1996-99), Conn. State Med. Soc., New Haven County Med. Assn., New Haven pvt. practice assn. 1995—. Office: 340 Whitney Ave New Haven CT 06511-2317 Office Phone: 203-562-9110.

**STERN, ROBERT ARTHUR MORTON,** architect, educator, writer; b. NYC, May 23, 1939; s. Sidney S. and Sonya (Cohen) S.; m. Lynn G. Solinger, May 22, 1966 (div. 1977); 1 child. Nicholas S.G. BA, Columbia U., 1960; MArch, Yale U., 1965. Registered architect, Calif., Colo., Conn., Fla., Hawaii, Ill., Ind., Maine, Mass., Mich., N.H., N.J., Ohio, S.C., Tex., N.Y., D.C., Ga. Program dir. Archtl. League N.Y., 1965-66; designer Office Richard Meier, Architect, N.Y.C., 1966; cons. Small Parks Program, Dept. Parks, N.Y.C., 1966-70; urban designer, asst. to asst. administr. housing and devel. adminstrn. N.Y.C., 1967-70; ptnr. Hagmann & Stern & John S. Hagmann, Architects, N.Y.C., 1969-77; prin. Robert A.M. Stern, Architects, 1977-89, sr. ptnr., 1989—. Bd. dirs. Walt Disney Co.; cons. Eye on New York TV documentary, CBS-TV, 1966-67; mem. architecture com. Whitney Mus. Am. Art, 1970-76, adv. commn., archtl. sect. Venice Biennale, 1980; lectr. architecture Columbia U., 1970-72, asst. prof. 1973-77, assoc. prof., 1977-82, prof. 1982—; vis. fellow Inst. for Architecture and Urban Studies, 1974-76, trustee, 1983-85; dir. Temple Hoyne Buell Ctr. for Study Am. Architecture, 1984-88, dir. Hist. Preservation Program, 1991-98; vis. lectr. Yale U., 1972, 73; vis. critic R.I. Sch. Design, 1976, U. Pa., 1977, N.C. State U., Raleigh, 1978; William Henry Bishop vis. prof. architecture Yale U., fall 1978; editorial cons. Archtl. History Found., 1979-83; dean Yale Sch. Arch., 1998—, J.M. Hoppin prof. arch., 2000—. Author: New Directions in American Architecture, 1969, rev. edit., 1977, George Howe: Toward a Modern American Architecture, 1975, (with Deborah Nevins) The Architect's Eye, 1979, (with John M. Massengale) The Anglo-American Suburb, 1981, (with Thomas Catalano) Raymond Hood, 1982, East Hamptons Heritage, 1982, (with John M. Massengale and Gregory Gilmartin) New York 1900, 1983, Pride of Place, 1986, (with Gregory Gilmartin and Thomas Mellins) New York 1930, 1987, (with Raymond Gastil) Modern Classicism, 1988, The House That Bob Built, 1991, The American Houses of Robert A.M. Stern, 1991, (with Thomas Mellins and David Fishman) New York 1960, 1995, (with Thomas Mellins and David Fishman) New York 1880, 1999. Mem. N.Y.C. Mayor's Task Force on Urban Design, 1966-67, architects selection com. N.Y. Conv. Ctr., 1979; trustee Am. Fedn. Arts, 1967-79, Inst. for Architecture and Urban Studies, 1983-85; v.p. Cunningham Dance Found., 1969-73; bd. dirs. Preservation League N.Y., 1984—, Historic Landmarks Preservation Ctr., 1995—; trustee Nat. Bldg. Mus., 1999—, Trust for Historic Preservation, 2000—. Recipient numerous awards for archtl. works including Nat. Hon. awards of AIA, 1980, 85, 90, John Jay award Columbia Coll., 1991. Fellow AIA (bd. dirs. N.Y. chpt. 1976-78, Disting. archtl. award N.Y. chpt. 1982, 84, 85, 87, medal of honor 1984), Soc. Archtl. Historians (bd. dirs. 1975-78), Archtl. League N.Y. (pres. 1973-77, exec. com. 1977—), N.Y. State Assn. Architects (excellence in design cert. 1985), Am. Architecture Found. (bd. regents 1989-91), Skidmore, Owings and Merrill Found. (bd. dirs. 1984-90), Chgo. Inst. for Architecture and Urbanism (bd. dirs. 1990-93), Century Assn., Coffee House Club. Office: 460 W 34th St Fl 18 New York NY 10001-2320

**STERN, ROBERT C.,** pediatrician, medical educator; b. NYC, Dec. 13, 1938; s. Samuel and Lily S. BA, Drew U., 1959; MD, Albert Einstein Coll. Medicine, 1963. Diplomate Nat. Bd. Med. Examiners, Am. Bd. Pediat., Am. Bd. Pediatric Pulmonology. Intern pediat. U. Hosps. Cleve. Babies and Childrens Hosp. Divsn., 1963-64, jr. asst. resident pediat., 1964-65; sr. asst. resident pediat. Bronx Mcpl. Hosp. Ctr., N.Y.C., 1965-66; fellow cystic fibrosis/pediat. pulmonary diseases Case Western Res. U. Sch. Medicine, Cleve., 1968-70; sr. instr. pediat. Case Western Res. U., Cleve., 1970-71, asst. prof., 1971-77, assoc. prof., 1977-83, prof., 1983—. Cons. Cystic Fibrosis Founds. various countries, 1990—, various pharm. and med. tech. cos., 1990—. Author: Treatment of Hospitalized Cystic Fibrosis Patients, 1998, Treatment of Cystic Fibrosis, 2000; contbr. numerous chpts. to Nelson's Textbook of Pediatrics, 1979—, also over 100 articles to med. jours. Pres., CEO, Children's Lung Found., Cleve., 1983—. Capt. USAF, 1966-68. Recipient David Stuckert award Cystic Fibrosis Rsch. Inst., San Francisco, 1997. Mem. Am. Thoracic Soc., Soc. Pediat. Rsch. Achievements include introduction of heparin lock for intermittent administration of intravenous drugs; research in cystic fibrosis. Home: 2300 Overlook Rd Apt 406 Cleveland Heights OH 44106-2391 Office: Univ Hosp Cleve 11100 Euclid Ave Cleveland OH 44106-1736 Office Phone: 216-844-3267. Personal E-mail: rcs1@prodigy.net.

**STERN, ROBERT D.,** publishing executive; b. NYC, Sept. 30, 1929; s. Morris and Jean (Gordon) S.; m. Natalie Greenberg, Sept. 5, 1952 (div. 1978); children: Mitchell, Bradley; m. Roslyne Paige, June 5, 1978. BA, Syracuse U., 1950; JD, NYU, 1953, LLM, 1958. Bar: N.Y. 1955, U.S. Dist. Ct. (D.C. cir.) 1953, U.S. Supreme Ct. 1967. Ptnr. Fink, Weinberger, Levin & Gottschalk, N.Y.C., 1957-59, 1957—72; chmn. Rudor Consol. Industries, 1972—99, Dance Mag., Inc., 1985—2001, AGC/Sedgwick Inc., Princeton, NJ, 1990—2001. Bd. dirs. Ctr. for Graphic Comms. Mgmt. and Tech., NYU, N.Y.C., 1979—; mem. Bd. dirs. AGC Sedgwick, Princeton, N.J., Rudor Consol. Ind. Inc.; pub. Stern's Performing Arts Directory, 1989-98. Bd. dirs. YMCA, N.Y.C., 1987-90 Mem. ABA, N.Y. State Bar Assn., Sheldrake Yacht Club (Mamaroneck, N.Y.), Birchwood Country Club (Westport, Conn.). Avocations: tennis, skiing, sailing. Home: 2 Imperial Lndg Westport CT 06880-4934 Office Phone: 203-454-0752.

**STERN, ROBERT MORRIS,** gastroenterologist, psychologist, researcher; b. NYC, June 18, 1937; s. Irving Dan and Nellie (Wachstetter) S.; m. Wilma Olch, June 19, 1960; children: Jessica Leigh, Alison Rachel. AB, Franklin and Marshall Coll., 1958; MS, Tufts U., 1960; PhD, Ind. U., 1963. Research assoc. dept. psychology Ind. U., 1963-65; asst. prof. psychology Pa. State U., 1965-68, assoc. prof., 1968-73; prof., 1973—2005, emeritus 2005—, disting. prof., 1992—2005; head dept., 1978-87. Author (with W.J. Ray): Biofeedback, 1977; author: (with W.J. Ray and C.M. Davis) Psychophysiological Recording, 1980; author: (with K.L. Koch) Electrogastrography, 1985; author: (with W.J. Ray and K.S. Quigley) Psychophysiological Recording, 2nd edit., 2001; author: (with K.L. Koch) Handbook of Electrogastrography, 2004; contbr. articles. Recipient Nat. Media award Am. Psychol. Found., 1978 Mem. Am. Psychol. Soc., Aerospace Med. Assn., Soc. Psychophysiol. Rsch., Am. Gastroent. Assn., Internat. EGG Soc., Functional Brain-Gut Rsch. Assn., Internat. Brain-Gut Soc. Home: 1360 Greenwood Cir State College PA 16803-3232 Office: Pa State U 512 Moore Bldg University Park PA 16802-3105 Office Phone: 814-865-1712. Business E-Mail: RS3@psu.edu.

**STERN, ROBIN LAURI,** medical physicist; b. Urbana, Ill., Mar. 12, 1959; d. Morris Stern and Myrna (Tanzer) Stern Longenecker; m. Donald Neil Bittner, May 20, 1989. BA in Physics and German Studies, Rice U., 1981; MS in Physics, U. Mich., 1983, PhD in Physics, 1987. Rsch. assoc. Duke U., Durham, N.C., 1987-89; postdoctoral rsch. fellow U. Mich., Ann Arbor, 1989-91; asst. prof. U. Calif.-Davis, San Francisco, 1992-98; assoc. prof. U. Calif., Davis, 1998—2004, prof., 2004—. Cons. Scanditronix, Inc., Livonia, Mich., 1991. Contbr. articles to jours. Rev. of Sci. Instruments, Magnetic Resonance Imaging, Med. Physics. Argonne Nat. Lab. grantee, 1985-86; Nat. Merit scholar, 1977-81. Mem. Am. Assn. Physicists in Medicine, Am. Soc. Therapeutic Radiology and Oncology, Sigma Pi Sigma, Phi Beta Kappa.

**STERN, ROSLYNE PAIGE,** magazine publisher; b. Chgo., May 26, 1926; d. Benjamin Gross and Clara (Sniderman) Roer; m. William E. Weber, May 3, 1944 (div. Mar. 1956); m. Richard S. Paige, June 28, 1958 (div. Apr. 1978); children: Sandra Weber Porr, Barbara Paige Kaplan, Elizabeth Paige (dec.); m. Robert D. Stern, June 5, 1978. Cert., U. Chgo., 1945. Profl. model, singer, 1947-53; account exec. Interstate United, Chgo., 1955-58; sales mgr. Getting To Know You Internat., Great Neck, NY, 1963-71, exec. v.p., 1971-78; pub. After Dark Mag., N.Y.C., 1978-82; assoc. pub. Dance Mag., N.Y.C., 1978-85, pres., pub., 1985—2001, pres. emeritus, 2001—. Bd. dirs. Rudor Consol. Industries, Inc., N.Y.C., AGC/Sedgwick, Inc., Princeton, N.J. Founding pres. Dance Mag. Found., N.Y.C. 1984-86 chair Dance Mag. awards, 1986-2004; life mem. nat. women's com. Brandeis U., Waltham, Mass., 1958—; bd. dirs. Westport Arts Ctr.; The Internation Com. for Dance Libr. of Israel. Recipient Disting. Svc. award Dance Notation Bur., 1996, Am. Coll. Dance Festival award, 1998, Pres.'s award Dance Masters of Am., Inc., 1998, Documents of Dance award Dance Library of Israel 1999. Mem. Pub. Relations Soc. Am., LWV, Am. Theatre Wing, Nat. Arts Club. Democrat. Jewish. Avocations: dance, theater, opera, visual arts, travel. Home: 2 Imperial Lndg Westport CT 06880-4934 Office: 1930 Broadway Ste 25C New York NY 10023 Office Phone: 212-724-4909. Personal E-mail: sterndance@aol.com.

**STERN, SAMUEL ALAN,** lawyer; b. Phila., Jan. 21, 1929; AB, U. Pa., 1949; LLB, Harvard U., 1952. Bar: Mass. 1952, D.C. 1958. Ptnr. Wilmer, Cutler & Pickering, Washington, 1962-88, Dickstein, Shapiro & Morin, Washington, 1988-92; pvt. practice law and bus. Washington and St. Petersburg, Russia, 1992-94; counsel Rogers & Wells, Washington, N.Y.C., 1994-97; pvt. practice law and bus. Washington, 1997-98; ptnr. Hills & Stern LLP, Washington, 1999—; pres. Hills Enterprises, 1999—. Vis. prof. law Harvard Law Sch. Cambridge, Mass., 1976; dir. Internat. Law Inst. Georgetown U., 1971—2004, adj. prof. law, 1979—92; asst. counsel Warren Commn., 1964; cons. UN, 1984—96; bd. dirs. Hills Enterprises, Ltd., Warp Network Corp., Verihealth Internat. Macrobuild.com, Lexsite.com, India, Pan-Asia Pictures, Beijing, VeriPay, Target World Ltd., Commonwealth Shore Power, China Alarm Holdings LTD, Global Dataguard Inc., Precipia, Inc.; lectr. profl. confs. on project fin., privatization, cross-border investment and alternative dispute resolution. Contbr. articles to legal jours. Mem. ABA, Am. Law Inst., Internat. Bar Assn., D.C. Bar Assn. Home: 210 Lee Ct Alexandria VA 22314 Office: 901 15th St NW Washington DC 20005 Office Phone: 202-822-1638. Business E-Mail: sastern@hillsandstern.com.

**STERN, SANDOR,** film director, writer; b. Timmins, Ont., Can., July 13, 1936; s. Stephen Mendel and Ann (Gurevitch) S.; m. Marlene Greenstein, May 19, 1957 (div. 1976); children: Shawn, Mark, Adam, Jamie; m. Kandy Lea Cave, Jan. 26, 1980; children: Lauren, Seth. BA, U. Toronto, 1957, MD, 1961. Intern New Mount Sinai Hosp., Toronto, 1961-62; physician Toronto, Can., 1962-68; writer L.A., 1968—; dir., 1974—. Writer (films) The Amityville Horror, 1978, Fastbreak, 1979 (NAACP Image award); writer, dir. (film) Pin, 1988, (TV films) Web of Deceit, 1990, Deception: A Mother's Secret, 1991, Dangerous Pursuit, 1989, John and Yoko, 1985, Muggable Mary: Street Cop, 1982, (TV miniseries) Woman on the Run: The Lawrencia Bembeneck Story, 1992-93; dir. (TV films) Glitz, 1988, Passions, 1984, Heart of a Child, 1993, The Stranger Beside Me, 1995, Gridlock, 1995, Badge of Betrayal, 1996, In My Sister's Shadow, 1997; co-writer, dir. (TV films) Jericho Fever, 1992, Duplicates, 1992, A Child's Cry for Help, 1994, (episodes for TV shows) Touched by an Angel, 1997, 98, 99, Promised Land, 1997, 98, 99, Early Edition, 2000, Leap Years, 2001. Mem. Writers Guild Am., Dirs. Guild Am., Producers Guild Am. Office: Jamson Prodns Inc 9472 Rembert Ln Beverly Hills CA 90210-1720 E-mail: sandorstern@sbcglobal.net.

**STERN, STANLEY,** psychiatrist; b. NYC, Apr. 5, 1933; s. Frank and Gussie S.; children: Marcus F., David S. BA cum laude, NYU, 1953; MD, SUNY, 1957. Intern Ohio State U. Hosp., Columbus, 1957-58; resident in psychiatry Inst. Living, Hartford, Conn., 1958-60, Austen Riggs Ctr., Stockbridge, Mass., 1960-61; psychoanalytic tng. We. New Eng. Inst. for Psychoanalysis, New Haven, 1965-73; asst. clin. prof. psychiatry Yale U., New Haven, 1975-81; assoc. clin. prof. psychiatry U. Calif., San Diego, 1982-84; pvt. practice New Haven, 1965-82, La Jolla, Calif., 1982-84, Phoenix, 1984—. Mem. faculty San Diego Psychoanalytic Inst., 1980-84; pres. Ariz. Psychoanalytic Study Group, Phoenix, 1986-88, Phoenix Psychoanalytic Study Group, 1986-88; tng. and supervising analyst So. Calif. Psychoanalytic Inst., 1989; chmn. edn. com. Ariz. Pyschoanalytic New Tng. Facility, 1990-91; lectr., presenter, participant seminars and confs. in field. Contbr. article to profl. jours. Trustee, Gesell Inst., New Haven, 1986-88, Ctr. for the Exceptional Patient, New Haven; bd. dirs. ACLU. Capt. USAF, 1961-63. Mem. Am. Coll. Psychoanalysts, Am. Psychoanalytic Assn. (cert.), Am. Psychiat. Assn., Am. Acad. Psychoanalysts, Irene Josselyn Group Advancement of Psychoanalysis, So. Calif. Psychoanalytic Inst. and Soc. (faculty), San Diego Psychoanalytic Inst., Council for the Advancement of Psychoanalysis (treas. 1972-73, pres.-elect 1973-74, pres. 1974-75, councillor 1975-80), Phi Beta Kappa, Beta Lambda Sigma, Psi Chi. Home and Office: 3104 E Camelback Rd # 601 Phoenix AZ 85016 Address: 4438 E Arlington Rd Phoenix AZ 85018-1262 Office Phone: 602-840-5614. *Personal philosophy: "Be a little kinder to each other" Aldous Huxley.*

**STERN, SUSAN TOY,** human resources specialist; BA in Sociology, UCLA, 1974. Chief dep. dir. LA County Dept. Human Resources. Co-chair UCLA Fund; spkr. in field. Mem.: So. Calif. Personnel Mgmt. Assn. Human Resources (past pres.), Internat. Pub. Mgmt. Assn. Human Resources (life; pres. 2001, former mem. exec. coun., former chair Conf. rev. task force). Office: LA County Dept Human Resources 3333 Wilshire Blvd Ste 100 Los Angeles CA 90010

**STERN, T. NOEL,** political science professor; b. Pitts., July 7, 1913; s. Leon Thomas (LeFevre) and Elizabeth Gertrude (Limburg) S.; m. Katherine Frances Kirk, Dec. 28, 1940; children: S. Yolanda, Roland Craig, Ellen Cornog, Joan Thrush. BA with honors, Swarthmore Coll., 1934; postgrad., U. Lyons, France, 1934-35; MA in Polit. Sci., U. Pa., 1940, PhD in Polit. Sci, 1942. Tchr. Lycée des Garçons, Roanne, France, 1934-35; prof., acting chmn. dept. govt. Boston U., 1945-53; Fulbright prof. U. Rennes, U. Strasbourg, 1952; dir. Fondation des Etats-Unis, U. Paris, France, 1953-56; acting chief UN Pub. Adminstrn. Mission to Ethiopia, 1956-57; dir. research and stats. Pa. Dept. Revenue, 1957-60; pres. West Chester State Coll., Pa., 1960-61; research prof. govt. African Studies program Boston U., 1962-63; also chief pub. adminstrn. team Boston U./US Aid, Guinea, West Africa; prof., founding chmn. dept. polit. sci. U. Mass., Dartmouth, 1964-69, prof., 1969-85, prof. emeritus, 1985—, also past chmn. acad. coun. Frequent guest on radio, Boston, 1948-53, New Bedford, Fall River and Providence, 1964-2000. Author: Community Forests in Pennsylvania for U.S. Allegheny Forest Experiment Station, 1941, Secret Family, 1988, Your Guide to Dartmouth Town Government, 1991; past mem. editl. bd. Internat. Rev. History and Polit. Sci., Revue de la Cité, Paris; contbr. to Boston U. Law Rev., Sch. and Society, New Republic, Progressive mag., Christian Sci. Monitor, Friends Jour., Quaker Life, Quaker History, Boston Globe, Providence Jour.-Bull, New Bedford Standard-Times, U. Pa. Gazette, Pitts. Post-Gazette, Indiana (Pa.) Gazette, Johnstown (Pa.) Tribune-Dem., others; collective writings deposited in Archives of Friends Libr., Swarthmore Coll. and Libr. U. Mass., Dartmouth; frequent contbr. to internet discussion groups Quaker-Spectrum and Quaker-List. Past mem. permanent bd. New Eng. Yearly Mtg. of Friends; past mem. exec. com. Friends Gen. Conf., Phila.; past mem. adminstrv. bd. William Penn House, Washington; past clk. North Dartmouth Friends Mtg., past presiding clk. Sandwich Quar. Mtg. of Friends; trustee, chmn. Dartmouth Town Librs., 1992-98; bd. dirs. Cmty. Ctr. for Non-Violence, New Bedford, Mass., 1994-98; mem. governing com. New England Friends Home, Hingham, Mass., 1996-98. Mem. AAUP (past pres. U. Mass.-Dartmouth chpt.), Am. Polit. Sci. Assn., LWV (acting pres. New Bedford-Fall River area 1990-91). Home: The Village House 1155 Indian Springs Rd Indiana PA 15701 E-mail: ltnstern@alphlin.net.

**STERN, WALTER EUGENE,** neurosurgeon, educator; b. Portland, Oreg., Jan. 1, 1920; s. Walter Eugene and Ida May (McCoy) S.; m. Elizabeth Naffziger, May 24, 1946; children: Geoffrey Alexander, Howard Christian, Eugenia Louise, Walter Eugene III. AB cum laude, U. Calif., MD, 1943. Diplomate Am. Bd. Neurol. Surgery (vice chmn. 1975-80). Surg. intern, asst. resident surgeon and neurol. surgery U. Calif. Hosp., 1943-46, asst. resident neurol. surgery and neuropathology, 1948; clin. clk. Nat. Hosp. Paralyzed and Epileptic, London, 1948-49; Nat. Rsch. fellow med. sci. Johns Hopkins, Balt., 1949-50; asst. resident, resident U. Calif. Svc., 1951; clin. instr. U. Calif., 1951; asst. prof. neurosurgery UCLA, 1952-56, assoc. prof., 1956-59, prof., 1959—87, prof. emeritus, 1987—, chief divsn. neurosurgery, 1952-85, chmn. dept. surgery, 1981-87; NIH spl. fellow univ. lab. physiology Oxford (Eng.) U., 1961-62. Cons. neurosurgery Wadsworth VA Hosp. Former mem., chmn. editl. bd. Jour. Neurosurgery; contbr. articles to sci. jours., chpts. to books. Lt. to capt. M.C. AUS, 1946-48. Fellow ACS (sec.); mem. AMA, Am. Surg. Assn., Pacific Coast Surg. Assn., L.A. Surg. Soc. (pres. 1978), Am. Assn. Neurol. Surgeons (pres. 1979-80, Cushing medalist, 1992), James IV Assn. Surgeons, Western Neurosurg. Soc., Soc. Neurol. Surgeons (past pres., Disting. Svc. award 2001), Neurosurg. Soc. Am., Am. Neurol. Assn., Soc. Univ. Surgeons, Soc. Brit. Neurol. Surgeons (hon.), Calif. Assn. Neurol. Surgery (Disting. Svc. award 2004), Phi Beta Kappa, Sigma Xi, Alpha Omega Alpha. Episcopalian. Home: 435 Georgina Ave Santa Monica CA 90402-1909

**STERN, WALTER PHILLIPS,** investment company executive; b. NYC, Sept. 26, 1928; s. Leo and Marjorie (Phillips) S.; m. Elizabeth May, Feb. 12, 1958; children: Sarah May, William May, David May. AB, Williams Coll., 1950; MBA, Harvard U., 1952. With Lazard Freres & Co., N.Y.C., 1953-54; assoc. Burnham & Co., Inc. (predecessor firm to Drexel Burnham Lambert Group, Inc.), N.Y.C., 1954-60, ptnr., 1960-71, sr. exec. v.p., 1972-73; mng. dir. Ea. ops. Capital Rsch. Co., 1973-95; chmn. bd. New Perspective Fund, Inc., 1973—2003, vice chmn., 2003—; chmn. emeritus, 2003—; chmn. Capital Internat. Inc., 1973—2002, vice-chmn., 2002—; chmn. Europacific Growth Fund, Inc., 1984—99; chmn. bd. dirs. Emerging Markets Growth Fund Capital Group Internat., Inc., 1987—2004, chmn., 1984—2004, chmn. emeritus, 2005—; mem. Mcpl. Securities Rulemaking Bd., 1984—87; trustee Fin. Analysts Rsch. Found., 1975—2003; chmn. bd. trustees Hudson Inst., 1983—; instr. investment mgmt. and fin. NYU, 1956—62; mem. adv. bd.

South African Growth Fund, 1996—2002, CyberCity Capital LLC, 1999—2002. Contbr. articles to profl. jours. Mem. Coun. Fgn. Rels.; comm. fin. adv. com. Haddassah, Tel Aviv U., Jaffee Inst. Strategic Studies, Tel Aviv; mem. publ. com. Commentary, 1995—; editl. adv. bd., Moment, 1998—; dir. Am.-Israel Friendship League, 1996—; Rep. Jewish Coalition, 2005—; v.p., mem. exec. com. Washington Inst. Near East Policy; chmn. steering com. Freedom Trade with Israel; adv. bd., dir. Am. Committees on Fgn. Rels. 1998—; bd. visitors Monterrey Inst., 2001—; trustee The Jewish Pol. Ctr.; adv. bd. CFA Ctr. Fin. Mkt. Integrity, 2004— Mem. N.Y. Soc. Security Analysts (bd. dirs.), Fin. Analysts Fedn. (pres. 1971-72, bd. dirs.), Inst. Chartered Fin. Analysts (pres. 1976-77, bd. dirs.), Assn. Investment and Mgmt. Rsch. (bd. dirs., exec. com. 1990-92), Harvard Club, Econ. Club, Sunningdale Country Club, Calif. Club, Phi Beta Kappa. Jewish. Home: 450 Fort Hill Rd Scarsdale NY 10583-2413 Office: Capital Group Inc 630 5th Ave New York NY 10111-0100 also: Capital Group Inc 333 S Hope St Los Angeles CA 90071-1406 Business E-Mail: wps@capgroup.com

**STERN, WALTER WOLF, III,** lawyer; b. Cin., Mar. 25, 1946; s. Walter W. Jr. and Harriet Louise Stern; (div.); 1 child, Rachael Louise. BA, Carthage Coll., 1969; JD, Marquette U., 1974. Bar: Wis. 1974, U.S. Dist. Ct. (ea. and we. dists.) Wis. 1974, U.S. Ct. Appeals (7th cir.) 1981, U.S. Supreme Ct. 1983, U.S. Dist. Ct. (no. dist.) Ill. 1989, U.S. Ct. (no. dist.) Wis. 2000. Pvt. practice, Kenosha, Wis., 1974-82, 85-91; sr. ptnr. Joling Rizzo Willems Stern & Burroughs, Kenosha, 1982-85; pvt. practice Union Grove, Wis., 1991—. Lectr. criminal law Carthage Coll., Kenosha, Wis., 1976—. Educator, Domestic Violence Project, Kenosha, 1983-94; hearing examiner Gen. Relief, Kenosha, 1990-95; candiate Cir. Judge, 2005. Fellow Am. Acad. Forensic Scis. Avocations: fishing, hunting, jogging, reading, creative writing. Home and Office: PO Box 64 Union Grove WI 53182-0064 Office Phone: 262-878-5060. Personal E-mail: walterstern@excite.com.

**STERNBERG, BETTY J.,** school system administrator; b. N.Y., Jan. 30, 1950; d. Julius and Edith Jane (Meyer) Levin; m. Robert Jeffrey Sternberg, June 18, 1972 (div. Jan. 13, 1987); children: Seth, Sara. BA, Brandeis U., 1971; MA, Columbia U., 1972; PhD, Stanford U., 1978. Bur. chief Dept. Edn., Hartford, Conn., 1980-85, divsn. dir., 1985-92, assoc. commr., 1992—2003, commr. edn., 2003—. Cons. Nat. Bd. for Profl. Teaching Standards, Washington, 1992. Co-author: (textbook) Metric Multibase Mathematics, 1973, Attribute Acrobatics, 1973, People Pieces Primer, 1975; (textbook series) Math In Stride, 1987. Mem. bd. dirs. William Benton Mus. of Art U. Conn., 1989—; mem. adv. coun. Ctr. for Ednl. Excellence, 1992-93. Recipient Disting. Managerial Svc. award State of Conn., 1986. Mem. ASCD (sec. 1975-80), Conn. Assn. Suprs. of Curriculum Devel. Avocations: tennis, interior design, gardening. Home: 2 Squirrel Hill Rd West Hartford CT 06107-1036 Office: Conn Dept Edn 165 Capitol Ave Hartford CT 06106-1659

**STERNBERG, PAUL,** ophthalmologist, researcher; b. Chgo., Apr. 30, 1953; s. Doris Feitler and Paul Sternberg; m. Gloria May, Oct. 17, 1987; children: Matthew Gregory, Zachary Ian. BA, Harvard Coll., Cambridge, Mass, 1971—75; MD, U. Chgo., 1975—79. Diplomate Nat. Bd. Med. Examiners, 1980, cert. Am. Bd. Ophthalmology, 1985. Thomas Aabye prof. ophthalmology Emory U. Sch. Medicine, Atlanta, 1985—; G.W. Hale prof., chmn. dept. ophthalmology Vanderbilt U. Sch. Medicine, Nashville, 2003—. Bd. sci. counselors Nat. Eye Inst., Bethesda, Md., 2003—, bd. trustees, Assn. Rsch. in Vision and Ophthalmology, Rockville, Md., 2005—. Bd. trustees Cheekwood Bot. Garden & Mus. of Art, Nashville, 2003—06. Mem.: Am. Acad. Ophthalmology (life; sec. of comm. 2000—05, bd. trustees 2005—). Office: Vanderbilt Eye Inst 1215 21st Ave S Nashville TN 37232-8808 Office Phone: 615-936-1453. Business E-Mail: paul.sternberg@vanderbilt.edu.

**STERNBERG, ROBERT JEFFREY,** dean, psychology professor, researcher; b. Newark, Dec. 8, 1949; s. Joseph Sternberg and Lillian Myriam (Politzer) Weingast; m. Elena Grigorenko, 2003; children from previous marriage: Seth, Sara. BA summa cum laude, Yale U., 1972; PhD in Psychology, Stanford U., 1975; D honoris causa, Complutense U., Madrid, 1994, U. Cyprus, 2000, U. Paris, 2000, U. Leuven, Belgium, 2001, Constantine the Philosopher U., Nitra, Slovakia, 2004, DSc, U. Durham, Eng., 2006, St. Petersburg U., Russia, 2006. Mem. faculty dept. psychology Yale U., New Haven, 1975—2005, asst. prof., 1975—80, assoc. prof., 1980—83, prof. psychology, 1983-86, dir. grad. studies, 1983—88, IBM prof. psychology and edn., 1986—, acting chmn. dept. psychology, 1992, dir. Yale Ctr. Psychology of Abilities, Competencies and Expertise, 2000—05, prof. Sch. Mgmt., 2005; dean Sch. Arts and Scis. Tufts U., Medford, Mass., 2005—, prof. psychology, 2006—; sr. scholar Ctr. for Pub. Leadership, Kennedy Sch. Govt., Harvard U., 2006—. Editor-in-chief Ency. of Human Intelligence, Psychol. Bull., 1991-96, Contemporary Psychology, 1999-2004; cons. editor Learning and Individual Differences, 1992—, Intelligence, 1977—, Devel. Rev., 1987-91, Jour. Personality and Social Psychology, 1989-91, Psychol. Rev., 1989-91; author: Intelligence, Information Processing and Analogical Reasoning, 1977, Beyond IQ, 1985, The Triarchic Mind, 1988, Metaphors of Mind, 1990, In Search of the Human Mind, 1995, 98, (with T. Lubart) Defying the Crowd, 1995, Successful Intelligence, 1997, Pathways to Psychology, 1997, Thinking Styles, 1997, Intelligence, Heredity and Environment, 1997, Love is a Story, 1998, Cupid's Arrow, 1998, Handbook of Intelligence, 2000, Psychology 101-1/2, 2002, Wisdom, Intelligence, and Creativity Synthesized, 2003. Recipient award for Excellence Mensa Edn. and Rsch. Found., 1989, Disting. Lifetime Contbn. to Psychology Conn. Psychology Assn., 1999, Disting. Scientist and Scholar award Positive Psychology Network, 2002, Anton Jurovsky award, Slovak Psychol. Soc., 2004, Interam. Psychologist award Interam. Psychol. Soc., 2005, E. Paul Torrance award 2006; Guggenheim Found. fellow, 1985-86. Fellow AAAS, APA (bd. dirs. 2002-04, pres. 2003, past pres. divsns. 1, 10, 15, 24, trustee ins. trust 2004, McCandless Young Scientist award divsn. devel. psychology 1982, Disting. Sci. award for early career contbn. 1981, pres. 2003, Farnsworth award, Arthur W. Staats award, E.L. Thorndike award 2003, Arnheim award, 2005), Ea. Psychol. Assn. (bd. dirs., pres.-elect 2006—), Am. Psychol. Found. (trustee 2005—), Am. Acad. Arts and Scis., Am. Psychol. Soc., Soc. Exptl. Psychologists; mem. Am. Ednl. Rsch. Assn. (Rsch. Rev. award 1986, Outstanding Book award 1987, Sylvia Scribner award 1996, James McKeen Cattell award 1999), Soc. Multivariate Exptl. Psychology (Cattell award 1982), Nat. Assn. Gifted Children (Disting. Scholar award 1985, E. Paul Torrance award 2006), Phi Beta Kappa, Kappa Delta Pi (Laureate chpt. 2003). Achievements include theory of successful intelligence; balance theory of wisdom; theory of mental self; investment theory of creativity; triangular theory of love; duplex theory of hate. Avocations: exercise, travel, reading, collecting. Office: Tufts U Office Dean Art and Scis Ballou Hall 3d Fl Medford MA 02155 Office Phone: 617-627-3864. Home Fax: 203-432-8317; Office Fax: 617-627-3703. Business E-Mail: robert.sternberg@tufts.edu.

**STERNBERG, SEYMOUR,** insurance company executive; b. Bklyn., June 24, 1943; s. Max and Mollie Sternberg; m. Roslyn Jacobowitz, June 14, 1965 (div.); children: Jodi, Donna; m. Laurette Zolty, Sept. 14, 1980; 1 child, Matthew. BSEE, CCNY, 1965; MSEE in Computer Sci., Northeastern U., 1968. Mgr. Raytheon Co., Bedford, Mass., 1965-73; mgr. Data Architects, Waltham, Mass., 1973-75; dir. info. svcs. Mass. Mut. Life Ins. Co., Springfield, 1975-76, 2d v.p., 1976-77, v.p. info. svcs., 1977-81, sr. v.p. group life and health divsn., 1981-84, exec. v.p. group life and health divsn., 1984-87, sr. exec. v.p., 1987-88; sr. v.p. group ops. N.Y. Life Ins. Co., 1989, exec. v.p., 1991, vice chmn., pres., COO, 1995-97, chmn., pres., CEO, 1997—2002, chmn., CEO, 2002—. Bd. govs. United Way Tri-State; bd. trustees Hackley School, Tarrytown, NY, NY Presbyterian Hosp., Big Bros./ Big Sisters of NYC, Northeastern U., Boston, 2004—; bd. dirs. Express Scripts Inc. Mem.: CUNY Bus. Leadership Coun., NYC Partnership and C. of C. (bd. mem.), BRT, ACLI (bd. dirs.). Avocations: stamp collecting/philately, tennis. Office: NY Life Ins Co 51 Madison Ave Rm 1304 New York NY 10010 Business E-Mail: sy150@newyorklife.com.

**STERNBERGER, LUDWIG AMADEUS,** neurologist, educator; b. Munich, May 26, 1921; s. Hugo and Emy (Welinger) S.; m. Nancy Jeanne Hoy, Dec. 13, 1961. BA, Am. U. Beirut, 1941, MD, 1945. Fellow Sloan Kettering

Meml. Cancer Ctr., N.Y.C., 1948-50; sr. med. biochemist N.Y. State Dept. Health, Albany, 1950-54; asst. prof. medicine Northwestern U., Chgo., 1954-55; chief basic scis. div. Med. Research Labs., Edgewood Arsenal, Md., 1957-78; prof. brain research U. Rochester Med. Ctr. (N.Y.), 1978-86; prof. neurology, pathology and anatomy U. Md., Balt., 1986-92; sci. co-dir., treas. Sternberger Monoclonals, Inc., Balt., 1992—. Author: Immunocytochemistry, 1974, 3d edit, 1986; mem. editoral bd. Cell and Tissue Research, Histochemistry, Jour. Histochemistry and Cytochemistry, Jour. Neurosci. Methods, Jour. Neuroimmunology, Histochem. Jour., Electron Microscopy in Biology. Served to maj. M.C. U.S. Army, 1955—57. Recipient Paul A. Siple prize, 1972; recipient Humboldt prize for sr. U.S. scientists, 1980, Classic Author citation Inst. Sci. Info., 1983; Senator Jacob K. Javits neurosci. investigator award, 1984; 25th most frequently cited author in sci. lit. of 1984; author of one of 17 Newcomer Superstar papers among 100 most cited of all time. Mem. Histochem. Soc. (pres. 1977-78), Am. Soc. Neurochemistry (program com. 1983-84), Am. Assn. Immunologists, Endocrine Soc., Am. Acad. Allergy, Am. Assn. Neuropathologists Lutheran. Home: 10 Burwood Ct Lutherville Timonium MD 21093-3502 Office Phone: 410-821-6719. Personal E-mail: n-l-s@att.net.

**STERNE, JOSEPH ROBERT LIVINGSTON,** editor, educator; b. Phila., Apr. 25, 1928; s. Robert Livingston and Edith Eisner (Heymann) S.; m. Barbara Adele Greene, Feb. 10, 1951; children: Robert Greene, Paul Livingston, Edward Joseph, Adam Heymann, Lee Winslow Greene. BA cum laude, Lehigh U., 1948; MS, Columbia U., 1950. Reporter Salt Lake Telegram, Salt Lake City, 1948-49, Wall Street Jour., N.Y.C., 1950-51, Dallas Morning News, 1951-53; reporter Balt. Sun, 1953-72, editorial page editor, 1972-97; sr. fellow Inst. for Policy Studies Johns Hopkins U., 1997—. Mem. Am. Soc. Newpaper Editors, Hamilton St. Club, Phi Beta Kappa. Home: PO Box 599 Sparks MD 21152-0599 Office: Johns Hopkins U Inst Policy Studies 3400 N Charles St Baltimore MD 21218-2680 E-mail: sterne@jhunix.hcf.jhu.edu.

**STERNER, FRANK MAURICE,** manufacturing executive; b. Lafayette, Ind., Nov. 26, 1935; s. Raymond E. and Maudelene M. (Scipio) S.; m. Elsa Y. Rasmusson, June 29, 1958; children: Mark, Lisa. BS, Purdue U., 1958, MS, 1959, PhD, 1962. Sr. staff specialist Gen. Motors Inst., Flint, Mich., 1962-63; dir. personnel and orgnl. research Delco Electronics, Milw., 1963-66, dir. personnel devel. and research, 1966-68; partner Nourse & Sterner, Inc., Milw., 1968-69; pres., 1969-73; assoc. dean, prof. Krannert Grad. Sch. of Mgmt., Purdue U., West Lafayette, Ind., 1973-79; v.p. strategic mgmt. Johnson Controls, Inc., Milw., 1979-89; pres., chief exec. officer E.R. Wagner Mfg. Co., 1989—; pres., owner Ridgeway Devel. Inc., Milw., 1993—. Bd. dirs. Wausau Homes, Inc., E.R. Wagner Mfg. Co., Ridgeway Devel. Inc., Greenheck Fan Corp. Home: 1440 E Standish Pl Milwaukee WI 53217-1958 Office: ER Wagner Mfg Co 4611 N 32nd St Milwaukee WI 53209-6000 Office Phone: 414-449-8204. Business E-Mail: frank.sterner@erwagner.com.

**STERNFELD, MARC HOWARD,** finance educator; b. N.Y.C., July 12, 1947; s. Joseph and Jeane (Richstein) S.; m. Arleen Estelle Weinreb, Aug. 25, 1968; children: Joshua, Jonathan. BA, Queens Coll., 1968; MS, NYU, 1970; MBA, Columbia U., 1971; student, Jewish Theol. Sem., 2001—. Spacecraft programmer Grumman Aero., 1968-70; fin. analyst CBS, N.Y.C., 1971-72; rsch. asst. Nat. Bur Econ. Rsch., 1970-71; sr. analyst N.Y.C. Police Dept., 1972-75; ptnr. Arthur Andersen & Co., N.Y.C., 1975-88; prin. Morgan Stanley, N.Y.C., 1987-94; mng. dir. Salomon Bros., N.Y.C., 1994-96; pres. Trans-Form L.L.C., N.Y.C., 1995—2001; mng. dir. Deutsche Bank Global Ops. and Tech., 1996—2001; CEO Settlement.com, 2000—01. Asst. prof. Columbia U. Internat. bd. dirs., exec. com. United Synagogue Conservative Judaism; past pres. Marlboro Jewish Ctr.; v.p. World Counsel of Synagogues; dean's coun. Tisch Sch. Arts; bd. dirs. Hillel. Home: 13 Evan Dr Morganville NJ 07751-1062 Personal E-mail: marcsternfeld@hotmail.com.

**STERNHAGEN, FRANCES,** actress; b. Washington, Jan. 13, 1930; Student, Vassar Coll., Perry-Mansfield Sch. Theatre; studied with Sanford Meisner, NY. Tchr. Milton Acad., Cath. U.; actress Arena Stage, Washington, DC, 1953-54. Debut Thieves Carnival, NY, 1955; plays include The Carefree Tree, The Admirable Bashville (Clarence Derwent award, Obie award), Ulysses in Night Town, Red Eye of Love, Misalliance, The Return of Herbert Bracewell, Laughing Stock, The Displaced Person, The Pinter Plays (Obie award); Broadway shows include The Skin of our Teeth, Viva Madison Avenue, Great Day in the Morning, The Right Honorable Gentleman, The Cocktail Party, Cock-a-Doodle Dandy, Playboy of the Western World, The Sign in Sidney Brustein's Window, The Good Doctor (Tony award 1973), Equus (Drama Desk award), Angel, On Golden Pond (Drama League award), The Father, Grownups, Summer, You Can't Take It With You, Home Front, Driving Miss Daisy, Remembrance, A Perfect Ganesh, The Heiress (Tony award 1995), Long Day's Journey into Night, 1998, The Exact Center of the Universe, 1999, Morning's at Seven, 2003, The Foreigner, 2003, Echoes of the War, 2004, Seascape, 2005, Steel Magnolias, 2005; actress (films) Up The Down Staircase, 1967, Starting Over, 1979, Outland, 1981, Independence Day, 1983, Romantic Comedy, 1983, Bright Lights, Big City, 1988, See You in the Morning, 1989, Communion, 1989, Misery, 1990, Doc Hollywood, 1991, Raising Cain, 1992, Curtain Call, Land Fall, 1997, The Rising Place, 1998; (TV series) Love of Life, The Doctors, Secret Storm, Cheers, Golden Years, Under One Roof, The Road Home, E.R., Sex and the City, The Closer; (TV movies) Who Will Save Our Children?, 1978, Prototype, 1982, Resting Place, 1986, Follow Your Heart, 1990, She Woke Up, 1992, Labor of Love: The Arlette Schweitzer Story, 1993, Reunion, 1994, Tales from the Crypt, Outer Limits, Law and Order, 1990, 96, The Con, 1997, To Live Again, 1997, New York: A Documentary Film, 1999, The Laramie Project, 2001. Recipient Edith Oliver Award for Sustained Excellence, 2005.

**STERNICK, JOHN LEWIS,** biology professor; (parents Am. citizens); s. Henry and Jacqueline Sternick; m. Millie Wanda Beran Sternick, Oct. 23, 1972; children: James R., Michele J., Jessica M. BS, Huron Coll., S.D., 1970; MS, S.D. State U., Brookings, 1977; PhD, Marquette U., Milw., 1980. Post doctoral fellow Sloan Kettering Inst., N.Y.C., 1980—82; group leader Unigene, Fairfield, NJ, 1982—86; chief scientist and v.p. R&D Nygene, N.Y.C., 1986—92; prof. Mansfield U., Pa., 1992—. Recipient Nanotechnlogy Motor award, Pa. Sys. Higher Edn. 2006. Mem.: AAAS, Am. Soc. Microbiology, Lions. Achievements include patents in field of molecular tag reader; development of veterinary clinical reference laboratory for infectious diseases. Avocations: painting, reading, Judo. Office: Mansfield Univ Grant Sci Ctr Mansfield PA 16933 Home: 55 Wakefield Ter Mansfield PA 16933 Office Phone: 570-662-4532.

**STERNLICHT, BARRY STUART,** hotel executive; b. Lake Success, NY, Nov. 27, 1960; m. Mimi Sternlicht; 3 children. BA magna cum laude, Brown U., 1982; MBA with distinction, Harvard U., 1986; PhD in bus. adminstrn. (hon.), Johnson & Wales. Pres., CEO Starwood Capital Group, LLC, Phoenix, 1991—2004; chmn., CEO Starwood Hotels and Resorts Trust, Phoenix, 1995—2004; CEO iStar Fin. Inc., 1996—97, chmn., 1996—2000, Starwood Hotels & Resorts Worldwide, Inc., White Plains, NY, 1997—2004, CEO, 1999—2004, exec. chmn., chief design officer, 2004—. Trustee Equity Residential Trust; bd. dirs. Starwood Fin. Trust, U.S. Franchise Systems and Comm.; mem. Urban Land Inst., Nat. Multi-Family Housing Coun, Young Presidents Org., World Travel & Tourism Council, Council for the U.S. and Italy. Bd. dirs. Com. to Encourage Corp. Philanthropy, Bus. Com. for the Arts, Inc., Channel 13/WNET, Nat. Leadership Advocacy Program for Juvenile Diabetes Rsch. Found. Internat. Kids in Crisis, Fairfield County Jr. Achievement, Ctr. for Christian-Jewish Understanding; bd. govs. NAREIT. Named Man of the Year, Juvenile Diabetes Rsch. Found. Internat.; recipient Preston Robert Tisch Disting. Industry Leadership award, NYU Sch. Hospitality, Tourism & Travel Admin. Office: Starwood Hotels and Resorts Worldwide 1111 Westchester Ave White Plains NY 10604-3520

**STERNLICHT, BENO,** research and development company executive; b. Nowy Sacz, Poland; arrived in U.S., 1949, naturalized, 1950; s. Hugo Charles and Helena (Anisfeld) Sternlicht; m. Lisa Spilberg; children: Mark David,

Eric Alan, Joshua Hugh, Aaron Jonathan. BSEE, Union Coll., Schenectady, N.Y., 1950; MS, Columbia U., 1951, PhD, 1954, DSc (hon.), 1970. Staff engr. Thermal Power Sys., gen. engring. lab. GE, 1951-54, specialist applied mechanics, 1954-58, cons. engr., 1958-61; co-founder, 1961; since chmn. bd., tech. dir. Mech. Tech., Inc., Latham, NY; pres. Benjosh Mgmt. Corp., NY, 1983, Ameast, N.Y.C., 1981—, Arben Internat. LLC, N.Y.C., 1994—. Dir. Small Diesels Ltd., India, New Ea. India Ltd., Plub Power LLC; pres. Vols. Internat. Tech. Assistance, 1965—71, chmn. bd. dirs., 1971—73; chmn. com. energy tech. and space propulsion NASA, 1969—72, mem. rsch. adv. coun., 1970—72; mem. Nat. Energy Task Force, 1981; bd. chmn. Comfortex Corp., 1995—; cons. to PRC, Israel. Author: numerous tech. articles on energy, tech., social and ednl. fields., co-author tech. book. Mem. AIPAC, World Jewish Congress, Jewish Fedn., ORT; chmn. Lisbon Charitable Trust; advisor on energy & innovation to Pres. Carter; advisor to Pres. Reagan, Pres. Bush. Fellow: ASME (Machine Design award 1966); mem.: AIAA, Am. Soc. Lubrication Engrs., Nat. Acad. Engring., Navy League, Sigma Xi, Tau Beta Pi. Achievements include patents in field. Address: 123 Partridge Run Schenectady NY 12309-1321 Office Phone: 718-376-0070. Personal E-mail: Lisben26@aol.com.

**STERNLICHT, SANFORD,** literature educator, writer; b. NYC, Sept. 20, 1931; s. Irving Stanley and Sylvia (Hilsenroth) S.; m. Dorothy Hilkert, June 4, 1956 (dec. 1977); children: David, Daniel. BS, SUNY, Oswego, 1953; MA, Colgate U., 1955; PhD, Syracuse U., 1962. Instr. SUNY, Oswego, 1959-60, asst. prof., 1960-62, prof. and dir. grad. studies in English, 1962-72, chmn. dept. theater, 1972-84; adj. prof. English Syracuse (N.Y.) U., 1981—. Leverhulme vis. prof. English, U. York, Eng., 1965-66; Fulbright sr. specialist, vis. prof. English, U. Pecs, Hungary, 2004. Author: Gull's Way, 1961, The Blue Star Commodore, 1961, Love in Pompeii, 1967, John Webster's Imagery and the Webster Canon, 1972, John Masefield, 1977, McKinley's Bulldog, 1977 (Mil. Book Club award, Saturday Evening Post Book Club award), C.S. Forester, 1981, Padraic Colum, 1985; (with E.M. Jameson) The Black Devil of the Bayous, 1971; (with E.M. Jameson) U.S.F. Constellation: Yankee Racehorse, 1981, John Galsworthy, 1986, R.F. Delderfield, 1988, Stevie Smith, 1990, Stephen Spender, 1992, Siegfried Sassoon, 1993, All Things Herriot: James Herriot and His Peaceable Kingdom, 1995, Jean Rhys, 1997, A Reader's Guide to Modern Irish Drama, 1998, C.S. Forester and the Hornblower Saga, 1999, Chaim Potok: A Critical Companion, 2000, A Reader's Guide to Modern American Drama, 2002, A Student Companion to Elie Wiesel, 2003, A Reader's Guide to Modern British Drama, 2004, The Tenement Saga: The Lower East Side and Early Jewish American Writers, 2004, Masterpieces of Modern British and Irish Drama, 2005; editor: The Selected Short Stories of Padraic Colum, 1985, The Selected Plays of Padraic Colum, 1986, The Selected Poems of Padraic Colum, 1988, In Search of Stevie Smith, 1991, New Plays from the Abbey Theatre, 1993-1995, 96, 96-98, 99, 99-2001, 2003. Lt. (j.g.) USN, 1955-59, comdr. USNR, ret. Recipient New Poets award Writer mag., 1960, Chancellor's award SUNY, 1974; fellow Poetry Soc. Am., 1964; rsch. grantee SUNY, 1963-70; named Tchr. of Yr. Syracuse U., 1986. Mem. MLA, PEN, Shakespeare Assn. Am., Am. Conf. Irish Studies. Democrat. Jewish. Home: 128 Dorset Rd Syracuse NY 13210-3048 Office: Syracuse U Dept English Syracuse NY 13244-0001 Office Phone: 315-443-9480. Business E-Mail: svsternl@syr.edu.

**STERNMAN, JOEL W.,** lawyer; b. NYC, Oct. 20, 1943; s. Abraham and Sarah (Simon) S.; children: Mark S., Cheryl A.; m. Barbara E. Shiers, March 31, 1985; children: Matthew S., Julia S. AB, Dartmouth Coll., 1965; LLB, Yale U., 1968. Bar: N.Y. 1970, U.S. Dist. Ct. (so. and ea. dists.) N.Y. 1971, U.S. Ct. Appeals (2d cir.) 1972, U.S. Supreme Ct. 1984, U.S. Ct. Appeals (6th cir.) 1985, U.S. Ct. Appeals (9th cir.) 1994, U.S. Tax Ct. 1996, U.S. Dist. Ct. (ea. dist.) Mich. 1997. Law clk. to judge U.S. Dist. Ct., New Haven, 1968-69; assoc. Rosenman Colin Freund Lewis & Cohen, N.Y.C., 1969-77; ptnr. Rosenman & Colin LLP, N.Y.C., 1977—2002, Katten Muchin Rosenman LLP (formerly Katten Muchin Zavis Rosenman), 2002—. Editor Yale Law Jour., New Haven, 1966-68. Mem. Phi Beta Kappa. Office: Katten Muchin Rosenman LLP 575 Madison Ave New York NY 10022-2585 Office Phone: 212-940-7060. E-mail: j.sternman@kattenlaw.com.

**STERNS, JOEL HENRY,** lawyer; b. NYC, Apr. 13, 1934; s. Barney and Yvetta S.; m. Joanne Glickman, Nov. 19, 1961; children: Rachel, Leslie, David. BS in Journalism, 1956; MPA, Princeton U., 1958; JD, NYU, 1967. Bar: N.J., D.C. Exec. asst. to commr., acting commr. N.J. Dept. Conservation and Econ. Devel., 1958-61; exec. asst. to adminstr. Bur. Security and Consular Affairs, U.S. Dept. State, 1961-62; regional programs coord. Alliance for Progress, 1962-64; exec. asst. to pres. Export-Import Bank U.S., 1964; dep. commr. N.J. Dept. Cmty. Affairs, 1967-68; counsel to gov. N.J., 1968-70; pres. firm Sterns, Herbert & Weinroth (P.A.), Trenton, NJ, 1970-88; mem. exec. com., compensation com. and mktg. com. Sterns, Herbert & Weinroth (merged with Hannoch-Weisman 1988), Roseland, NJ, 1988-91; pres. Hannoch-Weisman, Roseland, 1991-93, Sterns & Weinroth, Trenton, 1994—. Mem. lawyers adv. com. U.S. Dist. Ct. N.J., 1995—. Mem. ABA, Am. Law Inst., Am. Judicature Soc., N.J. Bar Assn. (trustee), Mercer County Bar Assn., Assn. Princeton U. Grad. Alumni (trustee 1975-77), NYU Alumni Assn. N.J. (Disting. Alumni award 1987). Home: 28 Heritage Hills Dr Washington Crossing PA 18977 Office: Sterns & Weinroth PO Box 1298 50 W State St Ste 1400 Trenton NJ 08607 Office Phone: 609-392-2100. E-mail: jsterns@sternslaw.com.

**STERNS, SAMANTHA,** gerontologist, researcher; d. Richard Harold and Gwen Kunken Sterns; m. James Andrew Cole, Sept. 3, 2006. BA, Case Western Res. U., Cleve., 2001, MA, 2004, PhD, 2006. Rsch. asst. Case Western Res. U., Cleve., 2001—03 sr. rsch. asst., 2003—06, rsch. assoc., 2006—. Contbr. articles to profl. jours. Recipient Marie Haug Student award, Case Western Res. U., 2005; fellow, Nat. Inst. Aging, 2001—03. Mem.: Assn. Edn. and Rehab. of Blind and Visually Impaired, N.Y. State Soc. Aging, Gerontol. Soc. Am. (co-convenor interest group 2006—), Golden Key. Avocations: photography, dancing. Home: 39 High County Trail Pittsford NY 14534-9619

**STERNSTEIN, ALLAN J.,** lawyer; b. Chgo., June 7, 1948; s. Milton and Celia (Kaganove) Sternstein; m. Miriam A. Dolgin, July 12, 1970 (div. July 1981); children: Jeffery A., Amy R.; m. Beverly A. Cook, Feb. 8, 1986 (div. 2004); 1 child, Julia S. BS, Ill., 1970; MS, U. Mich., 1972. Bar: Ill. 1977, U.S. Dist. Ct. (no. dist.) Ill. 1977, U.S. Dist. Ct. (no. dist.) Ohio 1977, U.S. Dist. Ct. (ea. dist) Mich. 1986, U.S. Dist. Ct. (we. dist.) Mich. 1990, U.S. Ct. Customs and Patent Appeals 1978, U.S. Ct. Appeals (7th cir.) 1979, U.S. Ct. Appeals (Fed. cir.) 1982, U.S. Dist. Ct. (ea. dist.) Wis. 2003, U.S. Ct. Appeals (5th cir.) 2003. Patent agt. Sunbeam Corp., Oak Brook, Ill., 1972—76; ptnr. Neuman, Williams, Anderson & Olson, Chgo., 1976—84; divsn. patent counsel Abbott Labs., North Chgo., Ill., 1984—87; ptnr. Brinks Hofer Gilson & Lione, Chgo., 1987—2005, mng. ptnr., 1996—99; ptnr., head IP litigation Dykema Gossett, Chgo., 2005—. Adj. prof. law U. Ill., 1992—; lectr. Oxford (Eng.) U., 2003. Co-author: Designing an Effective Intellectual Property Compliance Program; contbr. articles to profl. jours. Legal advisor Legal Aid Soc., Chgo., 1974—76, Pub. Defender's Office, Chgo., 1974. Mem.: ABA, Licensing Execs. Soc., Intellectual Property Law Assn., Patent Law Assn. Chgo. (com. chmn. 1982), Chgo. Bar Assn., Phi Eta Sigma, Sigma Gamma Tau, Sigma Tau, Tau Beta Pi. Jewish. Office: Dykema Gossett 10 S Wacker Dr Ste 2300 Chicago IL 60606 Office Phone: 312-321-4228, 312-627-2143.

**STERRETT, JAMES MELVILLE,** accountant, consultant; b. Chgo., Dec. 25, 1949; s. James McAnlis and Antoinette (Galligan) S.; m. Joyce Mieko Motoda, Sept. 1, 1989; 1 child, Victoria Hanako. BS in Acctg., Chaminade U., Honolulu, 1988; MBA, Chaminade U., 1991. CPA, Hawaii. Cons. Profitability Cons., Honolulu, 1985-87; pres. Sterrett Cons. Group, Honolulu, 1987-88; auditor Deloitte & Touche, Honolulu, 1988-90; acct., cons. pvt. practice, Honolulu, 1990—. Mem. Nat. Soc. Pub. Accts., Nat. Assn. Tax Practitioners, Hawaii Soc. CPA's, Delta Epsilon, Sigma. Office: 1314 S King St Ste 855 Honolulu HI 96814-1979 Office Phone: 808-591-6686.

**STERRETT, SAMUEL BLACK,** lawyer, former judge; b. Washington, Dec. 17, 1922; s. Henry Hatch Dent and Helen (Black) S.; m. Jeane McBride, Aug. 27, 1949; children: Samuel Black, Robin Dent, Douglas McBride. Student, St. Albans Sch., 1933-41; grad., US Mcht. Marine Acad., 1945, BS, 2004; BA, Amherst Coll., 1947; LLB, U. Va., 1950; LLM in Taxation, NYU, 1959. Bar: D.C. 1951, Va. 1950. Atty. Alvord & Alvord, Washington, 1950-56; trial atty. Office Regional Counsel, Internal Revenue Service, N.Y.C., 1956-60; ptnr. Sullivan, Shea & Kenney, Washington, 1960-68; municipal cons. to office vice pres. U.S., 1965-68; judge U.S. Tax Ct., 1968-88, chief judge, 1985-88; ptnr. Myerson, Kuhn & Sterrett, Washington, 1988-89; of counsel Vinson & Elkins, Washington, 1990—; pvt. practice Law Offices of Samuel B. Sterrett, Washington, 2002—. Bd. mgrs. Chevy Chase Village, 1970-74, chmn., 1972-74; 1st v.p. bd. trustees, mem. exec. com. Washington Hosp. Ctr., 1969-79, chmn. bd. trustees, 1979-84, trustee, 1999—; chmn. bd. trustees Washington Healthcare Corp., 1982-87; chmn. bd. trustees Medlantic Healthcare Group, 1987-89; mem. audit com. Medstar Health, 1990—, mem. fin. com., 1998—, chmn., 1999—; mem. governing bd. St. Albans Sch., 1977-81; trustee Louise Home, 1979-89. Served with AUS, 1943, with U.S. Mcht. Marine, 1943-46. Fellow Am. Bar Found. (life); mem. ABA, D.C. Bar Assn.; Am. Coll. Tax Counsel, Soc. of the Cincinnati, Coun. for Future, Am. Inst. of Ct., Chevy Chase Club (bd. govs. 1979-84, pres. 1984), Met. Club, Lawyers Club, Alibi Club, Alfalfa Club, Ch. of N.Y. Club, Beta Theta Pi. Episcopalian. Office: Law Offices of Samuel B Sterrett Ste 600 1455 Pennsylvania Ave NW Fl 7 Washington DC 20004-1013 Office Phone: 202-639-6665. Personal E-mail: csterrett@aol.com. Business E-Mail: ssterrett@velaw.com.

**STERRETT, STEVEN E.,** real estate company officer; Various positions MSA, 1989—93; v.p. Simon Property Group, Inc., 1993—2001, treas., 1993—, exec. v.p., 2001—, CFO, 2001—. Bd. mem. Simon Youth Found. Office: Simon Property Group Inc National City Ctr 115 W Washington St Indianapolis IN 46204

**STERTZ, STEPHEN ALLEN,** historian, educator; b. NYC, Aug. 2, 1944; s. Philip Bernard and Anne (Herman) S. BS, Columbia U., 1968; PhD, U. Mich., 1974. Rschr. Bronx (N.Y.) County Hist. Soc., 1978-82, 83—. Adj. asst. prof. history Rutgers U., Newark, 1980—82, 1986, Dowling Coll., Oakdale, NY, 1991—, Mercy Coll., Bronx, 1996—; vis. asst. prof. classics U. Ill., Urbana, 1982—83; adj. lectr. classics and history St. Peter's Coll., Jersey City, 2000—03, Fordham U., N.Y.C., 2000, Montclair State U., Upper Montclair, NJ, 2002—05, Seton Hall U., South Orange, 2005—06, Met. Coll. NY, 2006—. Author: Jonathan Swift's Gulliver's Travels, 1996; editor: Concordantia in Orationem Quae Aristidis Fertur Eis Basilea, 1996; contbr articles to profl. jours. Candidate N.Y. State Legislature, 1970. Travel to Collections grantee NEH, Washington, 1984; rsch. grantee Wilbur Found., Mecosta, Mich., 1992, Soc. Farsarutul, L.I. City, N.Y., 1992, Richter Found., N.Y.C. 1996. Mem. Am. Hist. Assn., Am. Philol. Assn., Archaeol. Instn. Am. (nat. coun. 1977-78). Avocations: reading, book collecting. Office: Montclair State Univ Dept Classics and Gen Humanities Montclair NJ 07043 E-mail: sstertz@pipemail.mercy.com.

**STERZER, FRED,** research physicist; b. Vienna, Nov. 18, 1929; came to U.S., 1947, naturalized, 1952; s. Karl and Rosa (Trumer) S.; m. Betty Distel, Sept. 5, 1964 (dec.). BS in Physics, CCNY, 1951; MS in Physics, NYU, 1952, PhD in Physics, 1955. With RCA, 1954-87, RCA Labs., David Sarnoff Research Center, Princeton, NJ, 1956-87, dir. microwave tech. center, 1972-87; dir. microwave research lab. David Sarnoff Research Ctr., 1987-88; pres. MMTC, Inc., Princeton, 1988—. Herbert J. Kayser research prof.; City Coll., CUNY, 1986-87. Contbr. numerous articles to profl. publs. Fellow IEEE; mem. Am. Phys. Soc., Nat. Acad. Engring., Sigma Xi, Phi Beta Kappa. Achievements include condr. research on optical components, microwave solid-state devices and circuits, med. microwave tech. Home: 4432 Province Line Rd Princeton NJ 08540-4368 Office: MMTC Inc 12 Roszel Rd Princeton NJ 08540-6234 Office Phone: 609-520-9699. E-mail: sterzer@mmtc.com.

**STETLER, DAVID J.,** lawyer; b. Washington, Sept. 6, 1949; s. C. Joseph and Norine (Delaney) S.; m. Mary Ann Ferguson, Aug. 14, 1971; children: Brian, Christopher, Jennifer. BA, Villanova U., 1971, JD, 1974. Bar: U.S. Supreme Ct. 1978, Ill. 1988, U.S. Ct. Appeals (7th cir.) 1988, U.S. Ct. Appeals (3d cir.) 1992, U.S. Dist. Ct. (ctrl. dist.) 1994, U.S. Ct. Appeals (8th cir.) 1994. Atty. IRS, Washington, 1974-79; spl. atty. tax divsn. Dept. Justice, Washington, 1975-79; asst. U.S. Atty.'s Office, Chgo., 1979-88, dep. chief spl. prosecutions div., 1985-86, chief criminal receiving and appellate divsns., 1986-88; ptnr. McDermott, Will & Emery, Chgo., 1988-98; prin. Stetler & Duffy, Ltd., Chgo., 1998—. Lectr. Atty. Gen. Trial Advocacy Inst., Washington, 1977—. Fellow Internat. Soc. Barristers, Am. Coll. Trial Lawyers; mem. ABA (chmn. midwest subcom. White Collar Crime com. 1991-93), Wong Sun Soc. San Francisco. Office: 11 S LaSalle St Ste 1200 Chicago IL 60603 Office Phone: 312-338-0202. E-mail: dstetler@stetlerandduffy.com.

**STETLER, RUSSELL DEARNLEY, JR.,** investigator; b. Phila., Jan. 15, 1945; s. Russell Dearnley and Martha Eleanor (Schultz) S. BA with honors in Philosophy, Haverford Coll., Pa., 1966; postgrad., New Sch. Social Rsch., 1966-67. Research asst. to Bertrand Russell, 1967; lectr. Hendon Coll., London, 1968-69; pres. Archetype, Inc., Berkeley, Calif., 1971-78; pub. Westworks, Berkeley, 1977-80; pvt. investigator, 1980-90; chief investigator Calif. Appellate Project, 1990-95; dir. of investigation and mitigation N.Y. State Capital Defender Office, N.Y.C., 1995—2005; nat. mitigation coord. Office of the Fed. Pub. Defender, Oakland, Calif., 2005—. Cons., dir. Rampartk Press Palo Alto, 1971-80; editorial cons. Interviews, Berkeley, 1973-78; faculty Caribbean Sch., Ponce, P.R., 1978-80 Author: The Battle of Bogside, 1970; co-editor: The Assassinations: Dallas and Beyond, 1976. Research grantee Atlantic Peace Found., 1969-70 Mem. Calif. Assn. Lic. Investigators, Nat. Assn. Legal Investigators, Calif. Soccer Referees Assn.-North (treas. Marin County chpt. 1982-90), Amigos de las Americas (pres. Marin chpt. 1985-88). Clubs: Mill Valley Soccer (dir. 1981), Albany-Berkeley Soccer (pres. 1977-78). Office: Office of the Fed Pub Defender 555 12th St Ste 650 Oakland CA 94607 E-mail: russell_stetler@fd.org.

**STETLER-STEVENSON, WILLIAM GEORGE,** pathologist; b. Trenton, N.J., Nov. 27, 1953; BS in Biochemistry cum laude, Albright Coll., 1975; PhD in Biochemistry & Molecular Biology, Northwestern U., 1983, MD, 1984. Diplomate Am. Bd. Pathology. Mem. house staff anatomic pathology McGaw Med. Ctr., 1984-87; sr. staff fellow NIH, 1987-91, med. officer, rschr., 1991—, chief extracellular matrix pathology sect., 1993—. Editl. bd. Cancer Rsch. FASEB Jour., Am. Jour. Pathology, Invasion & Metastasis; contbr. articles to profl. jours. Kemper Found. Med. scholar, 1978-79. Mem. Am. Soc. Biochemistry and Molecular Biology, Am. Soc. Investigative Pathology (Warner-Lambert/Parke-Davis award 1996). Office: Nat Cancer Inst Cell & Cancer Biology Extracellular Matrix Pathology Sect 81147 Grovemont Cir Bethesda MD 20892-4605

**STETSON, EUGENE WILLIAM, III,** film producer, environmentalist, consultant; b. Norwalk, Conn., Mar. 31, 1951; s. Eugene William Jr. and Grace Stuart (Richardson) S.; m. Jane White Watson, June 14, 1993. AB, Harvard U., 1982, postgrad. in Sch. Arts and Scis., 1986. Assoc. exec. dir. Conn. River Watershed Coun., Easthampton, Mass., 1978-81; v.p. Fairhill Oil & Gas Corp. (Fairhill Oil Ltd.-Can.), N.Y.C., Calgary, Alta., Canada, 1981-84, pres., 1984-92; film and TV writer and producer, 1991—. Supr. Ottauquechee Conservation Dist., Woodstock, Vt., 1978-82; pres. Boatwright Found., NYC, 1981—; exec. com. Westminster Sch., Simsbury, Conn., 1984-86; trustee Proctor Acad., Andover, NH, 1985-95; co-founder River Watch Network, Montpelier, Vt., 1987—; pres. bd. dirs. Vt. Film Commn., 1996—. Active Vt. Gov.'s Coun. of Environ. Advisors, 1992—; Vt. Gov.'s Coun. on Bus. and the Environment, 1994-96; pres. Vt. Film Commn., 1996—; gov. Smith Richardson Found., NY, 1984—, trustee, 1990—; chmn.

Found. for our Future, 2001—. Mem. Harvard-Radcliffe Club Vt. (v.p. 1994-98), Harvard Club NYC, Hasty Pudding Club, Ocean Reef Club. Home: 139 Elm St Norwich VT 05055-9445 Office Phone: 802-296-2277. E-mail: e.w.stetson@valley.net.

**STETSON, JOHN BATTERSON, IV,** construction executive; b. Phila., Dec. 21, 1936; s. John Batterson Stetson III and Winifred (Walton) Todd; m. Solveig Weiland, Nov. 23, 1963; children: John Batterson V, Eric Weiland, Scott Walton. BA, Yale U., 1959, MArch, 1966; postgrad., U. Pa., 1969-73. Registered architect, Pa., Mass., Fla. Staff architect Bower & Fradley, Architects, Phila., 1966-68, Young & Exley, Architects, Phila., 1968-69; project architect Day & Zimmerman Assocs., Phila., 1969-71, mgr. tech. staff, 1974-76; project mgr. Schnabelbach & Braun, Phila., 1971-74; project exec. Bldg. Scis., Inc., Balt., Kinshasa, Zaire, 1976-77; project mgr. Bldg. Scis., Inc., Balt., 1977-78; sr. cons., v.p., pres. MDC Sys. unit Day and Zimmermann, Inc., Phila., 1978-95, v.p. transp. svcs. unit, 1996-99; cons.-Construction Project, 1999. Active Haverford (Pa.) Civic Assn., 1981-84. Comdr. USNR, 1959-81. Mem. Constrn. Mgmt. Assn. Am. (bd. dirs. 1986—), Am. Arbitration Assn., Constrn. Specifications Inst., Haverford Sch. Alumni Assn. Clubs: Union Cricket (Haverford). Republican. Avocations: music, sailing. Home: 7 Druid Ln Malvern PA 19355-2825

**STETSON, ROBERT FRANCIS,** retired metallurgist; b. N.Y.C., Oct. 20, 1928; s. Ralph Jerome and Margaret Mary Stetson; m. Rita Marie Jubach, Dec. 30, 1950 (dec. May 31, 1991); 1 child, Barbara A.; m. Mary Jane McKinney, June 10, 1999. Cert. in Metallurgy, Pa. State U., 1955. ICET A NSPE. Lab. technologist, insp. Babcock & Wilcox Co., Beaver Falls, Pa., 1949—58; tech. specialist materials sci. Gen. Atomics, San Diego, 1958—86, cons., 1986—98; ret., 1998; cons. NASA Marshall Space Flight Ctr., Huntsville, Ala., 2002—. With AC U.S. Army, 1946—47, ETO. Recipient Nat. Engring. Assocs. Achievement award, Am. Soc. Metals, 1979, James F. Lincoln Arc Welding Found. award, 1979. Fellow: Am. Soc. Metals Internat. (exec. bd. San Diego chpt. 1964—96, chmn. San Diego chpt. 1972—73). Achievements include patents for plasma orifice tip. Avocation: genealogy. Home: 7245 Navajo Rd D-200 San Diego CA 92119 Personal E-mail: robert.stetson@cox.net.

**STETTLER, STEPHEN F.,** performing company executive; b. Phila., May 1, 1952; s. Wallace Frederick and Catherine Sue (Brill) S. AB summa cum laude, Kenyon Coll., 1974; MFA in Directing, Cath. U. Am., 1982; MLitt in Theatre, Lincoln Coll., Oxford, Eng., 1983. Dir. dramatics Westminster Sch., Simsbury, Conn., 1975-80; acting coach Hartke Conservatory Cath. U., Washington, 1982; chair drama dept. St. Albans and Nat. Cathedral Schs., Washington, 1980-84; dir., instr. acting Nat. Theatre Inst. O'Neill Theater Ctr., Waterford, Conn., 1984-93; artistic dir. TNT/New Theatre Bklyn., 1985-90; producing dir. Weston (Vt.) Playhouse, 1988—. Lit. asst. Arena Stage Co., Washington, 1983-84; site evaluator theatres Nat. Endowment for Arts, Washington, 1990—; panelist Vt. Coun. Arts, Montpelier, Vt., NEA, Washington, D.C.; mem. capital grants com. N.Y.C. Dept. Cultural Affairs; guest instr. directing Teatret Vart, Norway. Dir.: Who's Afraid of Virginia Woolf?, Dancing at Lughnasa, Animal Fair, Rough Crossing, Nora, Donkeys' Years, Floyd Collins (Moss Hart award for best prodn. in New Eng.), Sweeney Todd, Six Degrees of Separation, A Midsummer Night's Dream (Best Play award Folger Shakespeare Libr. competition). Mem. Phi Beta Kappa. Office: Weston Playhouse 703 Main St Weston VT 05161 Business E-Mail: sstettler@westonplayhouse.org.

**STETTNER, EDWARD A.,** political science professor; b. NYC, Feb. 18, 1940; s. Frederick Albert and Celia Carolyn S.; m. Laura Gagliardi, July 17, 1966; children: Victoria, Jeffrey, Thomas. BA, Brown U., 1962; MA, Princeton U., 1964, PhD, 1968. Lectr. polit. sci. Rutgers U., New Brunswick, N.J., 1965-66; instr. polit. sci. Wellesley (Mass.) Coll., 1966—68, asst. prof. polit. sci., 1968—74, assoc. prof., 1974—80, prof. polit. sci., 1980-95, Ralph Emerson and Alice Freeman Palmer prof. polit. sci., 1995—, assoc. dean of the coll., 1977-86, dean of the faculty, 1986—88. Author: Shaping Modern Liberalism: Herbert Croly and Progressive Thought, 1993; editor: Perspectives on Europe, 1970. Trustee Mount Ida Coll., Newton, Mass., 2000—. Mem. AAUP (pres. com. 1970-73, pres. Mass. State Conf. 1975-77), Am. Polit. Sci. Assn., New Eng. Polit. Sci. Assn., Phi Beta Kappa. Home: 67 Carriage Hill Cir Southborough MA 01772 Office: Wellesley College 106 Central St Wellesley MA 02481 Office Phone: 781-283-2198. E-mail: estettner@wellesley.edu.

**STETTNER, JERALD WALTER,** retired retail executive; b. Miami, Fla., Mar. 31, 1952; s. Richard A. and LeJean D. (Haberman) S.; m. Linda G. Day, Dec. 22, 1978; children: Kelly R., Jarrod M., Zachary A. BS in Behavioral Mgmt., Ga. Inst. Tech., 1974. Various mgmt. positions Eckerd Drug Co., Clearwater, Fla., 1974-87; regional v.p. Eckerd Corp., Clearwater, Fla., 1987-98, sr. v.p., 1998—2004, ret., 2004. Mem. Ga. Tech. Alumni Assn., Phi Delta Theta. Avocations: tennis, golf, skiing. Personal E-mail: JWStettner@aol.com.

**STETZ, PHIL E.,** management educator, entrepreneur; BS, Rockhurst U., 1969; BA summa cum laude, U. W. Fla., 1975; MBA, Baylor U., 1995; PhD, Tex. Tech. U., 2001. Acct. Cooper's Lybrand, Fort Lauderdale, Fla., 1974—75; CEO Stetz's, Oakley, Kans., 1975—91; prof. strategic mgmnt. and entrepreneurship Stephen F. Austin State U., Nacog Noches, Tex., 2002—, Lavoy Moore entrepreneurship prof. Contbr. articles various profl. jours. Recipient Tchg. award, Tex. Tech Coll. of Bus. Mem. Acad. of Mgmt. Office: Stephen F Austin State U 403 McGee MMIB Nacogdoches TX 75962 Office Phone: 936-468-1474. Office Fax: 936-468-1600.

**STEUBEN, NORTON LESLIE,** lawyer, educator; b. Milw., Feb. 14, 1936; s. Benjamin and Ria (Beerman) S.; m. Judith Ann Dickens, June 21, 1958; children: Sara Ann, Marc Nelson. AB, U. Mich., 1958, JD with distinction, 1961. Bar: N.Y. 1962, Colo. 1975. Assoc., then ptnr. Hodgson, Russ, Andrews, Woods & Goodyear, Buffalo, 1961-68; mem. faculty U. Colo. Law Sch., Boulder, 1968—2002, prof. law, 1974—2002, Nicholas Rosenbaum prof., 1997—2002, Nicholas Rosenbaum prof. emeritus, 2002—; of counsel Ireland, Stapleton, Pryor & Pascoe, Denver, 1980-97, 1999—. Lectr. Law Sch., SUNY, Buffalo, 1961-68; officer Buffalo-Niagara Indsl. Devel. Corp., 1963-68, Buffalo Opportunities Devel. Corp., 1966-68; vis prof. law U. Puget Sound. Sch. Law, 1992-93; resident tax policy advisor to the govt. of Ukraine, Treas. Dept., 1997-99. Author: Cases and Materials on Real Estate Planning, 1974, 4th edit., 2006; co-author: Problems in the Fundamentals of Federal Income Taxation, 1985, 3d edit. 1994, Problems in the Federal Taxation of Business Enterprises, 1985, 3d edit., 1996; co-editor: Bittker, Fundamentals of Federal Income Taxation, 1983; editor Jour. Affordable Housing & Cmty. Devel. Law, 1994-97; contbr. articles to profl. jours. Mem. Boulder Human Rights Commn., 1969-72, chmn., 1972-74; mem. Boulder Landlord-Tenant Com., 1973-74; trustee Boulder Open Space Bd., 1976-81, vice chmn., 1978-79, chmn., 1979-81; trustee Congregation Har Ha-Shem, Boulder, 1978-79, v.p., 1979-81, pres., 1982-84; mem. Boulder Housing Authority, 1982-89, vice chmn., 1984-85, chmn., 1985-88; mem. legal and advocacy com. Am. Tinnitus Assn., 2002—; Cmty. Adv. Panel Roche Colo., 2004—; mem. Boulder County Aging Svcs. Found., 2005—. Recipient S.J. Goldberg award Alpha Epsilon Pi, 1957, Disting. Svc. to Community award Buffalo Area C. of C., 1966, John W. Reed award U. Colo. Law Sch., 1970; Teaching Recognition award U. Colo.-Boulder, 1972, Teaching Excellence award, 1982; Commendation for Exceptional Assistance to Govt. of Ukraine, 1999; Presdl. Tchg. scholar U. Colo., 1989, Fulbright scholar, Ukraine, 2003-04. Mem. ABA, N.Y. State Bar Assn., Colo. Bar Assn., Boulder County Bar Assn., Am. Law Inst., AAUP, Scribes (officer, editor Scrivener 1975-76, dir. 1979-82), Barristers Soc., Order of Coif, Tau Epsilon Rho. Democrat. Home: 845 8th St Boulder CO 80302-7408 Office: 461 Wolf Law Boulder CO 80309 Office Phone: 303-492-7963. E-mail: norton.steuben@colorado.edu.

**STEUER, RICHARD MARC,** lawyer; b. Bklyn., June 19, 1948; s. Harold and Gertrude (Vengar) S.; m. Audrey P. Forchheimer, Sept. 9, 1973; children: Hilary, Jeremy. BA, Hofstra U., 1970; JD, Columbia U., 1973. Bar: NY 1974, US Dist. Ct. (ea. and so. dists.) NY 1974, US Ct. Appeals (2d cir.) 1974, US Supreme Ct. 1979, US Dist. Ct. (no. dist.) NY 1984, US Dist. Ct. (we. dist.) NY 1997, US Ct. Appeals (3d cir.) 1987, US Ct. Appeals (5th cir.) 1995, US Ct. Appeals (10th cir.) 2003, US Ct. Appeals 2004. Ptnr. Kaye Scholer LLP, N.Y.C., 1973—2002, chair antitrust practice group, 1996—2002; ptnr. Mayer, Brown, Rowe and Maw LLP, N.Y.C., 2002—. Adj. assoc. prof. law NYU, 1985; adj. prof. law St. John's U., 2003; lectr. in field; neutral evaluator U.S. Dist. Ct. Ea. Dist., N.Y., 1994-96. Author: A Guide to Marketing Law: Law and Business Inc., 1986; contbr. articles to profl. jours. Fellow: Am. Bar Found.; mem.: ABA (editl. bd. antitrust devel. vol. 1984—86, vice-chmn. program com. 1988—91, coun. sect. antitrust law 1993—96, chmn. publs. com. 1996—98, editl. chmn. Antitrust mag. 1998—2001, coun. sect. antitrust law 2001—04, comms. officer 2004—05, sec. 2004—05, ho. of dels. 2005—), Assn. Bar City N.Y. (chmn. antitrust and trade regulation 1995—98, antitrust and trade regulation, internat. trade, lectures and CLE coms). Office: Mayer Brown Rowe and Maw LLP 1675 Broadway New York NY 10019-5820 Office Phone: 212-506-2530. Business E-Mail: rsteuer@mayerbrownrowe.com.

**STEVANOVIC, MILAN V.,** surgeon; MD, Belgrade Med. Sch., Yugoslavia, 1972; PhD, U. Belgrade Med. Sch., 1987. Internship U. Belgrade, 1972—73, resident, sports medicine, 1973—75, resident, orthopedic surgery, 1975—79; fellowship, hand surgery U. So. Calif. Med. Ctr., 1979—80; fellowship, hand and microvascular surgery Duke U. Med. Ctr., 1983—84; surgeon, dept. orthopedics Children's Hosp., L.A. Asst. prof. clinical orthopedic surgery Keck Sch. Med. U. So. Calif. Mem.: SICOT: The World Orthopedic Orgn., Western Orthopedic Assn., Internat. Orthopedic Assn., Am. Soc. Peripheral Nerve, Am. Soc. Reconstructive Microsurgery, Am. Soc. Surgery of Hand (corr. mem.). Fluent in Serbian. Office: Children's Hosp LA Div Orthopaedic Surgery 1510 San Pablo St #322 Los Angeles CA 90033 Office Phone: 323-442-5860. Office Fax: 323-226-1513. E-mail: stevanov@hsc.usc.edu.

**STEVENS, AILEEN,** retired secondary school educator; b. Delano, Calif., Oct. 9, 1915; d. Floyd Edward Buoy and Melvina Waits; m. James Malcolm Stevens, Nov. 15, 1941; children: Aileen Margaret, James Christopher, Terrance Duane, Eleanor Melaina, Wanda Floriene. AA, Stockton (Calif.) Jr. Coll., 1936; BA, Coll. of Pacific, 1940; MS, U. Calif., Chico, 1968. Tchr. Humphrey's Bus. Coll., Stockton, 1934—40; social worker State Relief Agy., Stockton, 1940; tchr. Angel's Camp, Bret Hart HS, Calif., 1941; English tchr., head dept. Marysville (Calif.) HS, 1960—80. Grantee, Coll. of Pacific, 1939. Mem.: LWV, Literary Guild, Lioness Club. Episcopalian. Avocation: reading. Home: 6277 Marysville Rd Browns Valley CA 95918

**STEVENS, ANNE L.,** retired automotive executive; b. Reading, PA, 1948; BS in mechanical & materials engring., Drexel U., 1980; Grad. Level Business student, Rutgers U. Mktg. specialist plastic products divsn. Ford Motor Co., 1990—92, mgr., Quality Services Dept., 1992—95, mfr. mgr., Automotive Components Divsn., 1995, Plant mgr., Automotive Components Div. Enfield, England, 1995—97, asst. vehicle line dir., Ford Automotive Operations Dunton, England, 1997—99, dir., Manufacturing Business Office, N. Am., 1999—2000, v.p. N. Am. Assembly Ops., 2000—01, v.p. N. Am. Vehicle Ops., 2001—03, group v.p., Canada, Mexico, and S. Am., 2003—05, exec. v.p., COO, The Americas, 2005—06. Bd. dirs. Lockheed Martin Corp., 2002—, Coun. Americas; bd. trustees Drexel U.; trustee Women's Automotive Assn. Internat.; mem. advisory bd. Mexico Inst., Woodrow Wilson Internat. Ctr. for Scholars; mem. exec. advisory bd. Juran Ctr. for Leadership in Quality, U. Minn. Named one of Most Powerful Women in Bus., Fortune mag., 2005; recipient Shingo Leadership award, 2000, Circle of Distinction award, Drexel U. Coll. Engring., 2001, Eli Whitney award, Soc. Mfg. Engineers, 2003. Mem.: NAE.*

**STEVENS, ART,** public relations executive; b. NYC, July 17, 1935; m. Eva Sandberg, Mar. 19, 1972. BA, CCNY, 1957. Pub. relations dir. Prentice Hall, Inc., Englewood Cliffs, NJ; account exec. William L. Safire Public Relations Inc., N.Y.C., 1966-69, v.p., 1967-68, pres., 1968-69, Lobsenz-Stevens Inc., N.Y.C., 1970—99; instr. Fairleigh Dickinson U.; chmn. & CEO Publicis Dialog, N.Y.C., 1999—2002; cons., 2003—; mng. ptnr. Stevens Gould Ptnrs., LLC, 2003—. Weekly humor commentator WINK-TV, Ft. Myers, Fla. Author: The Persuasion Explosion, 1985, Sanibel Shell Shocked, 1992; weekly columnist Sanibel-Captiva (Fla.) Islander; contbr. articles to profl. jours. Bd. dirs. United Way of Putnam County, N.Y.; trustee Gotthelf Lupus Rsch. Inst. Inducted City Coll. N.Y. Comms. Alumni Hall Fame, 2001. Mem.: Public Relations Soc. Am. (sec. 2003, pres. N.Y. chpt. 2006, nat. bd., pub. rels. com., chair-elect tri-state dist., exec. com., chmn. eligibility com., counselors acad. sect.), Publicity Club N.Y. (Disting. Svc. award 1969), Gipsy Trail (pres., chmn. Carmel, N.Y.). Personal E-mail: artstevens@att.net. *Life is not an accident. The events in one's life are not accidents either. When I look back at what I have done and the lives that have been interwined with mine, it's as though it's all been scripted by a higher power.*

**STEVENS, BERTON LOUIS, JR.,** data processing executive; b. Chgo., Apr. 4, 1951; s. Berton Louis Sr. and Mary Cover (Kochavaris) S.; m. Janet Alene Madenberg, May 20, 1990. Student, Ill. Inst. Tech., Chgo., 1969-73. Systems and applications programmer Judge & Dolph, Ltd., Elk Grove Village, Ill., 1978-91, mgr. data processing, 1991-99; bus. sys. coord. Meml. Med. Ctr., Inc., 2000-2001, lead sys. analyst, 2001—02; svc. ctr. mgr. Siemens Health Sys., 2002—04; mgr. applications Province Healthcare, Las Cruces, N.Mex., 2004—. Instr. Adler Planetarium and Astron. Mus., Chgo., 1980-86; dir. Desert Moon Observatory #148; Editor and author newsletter Bett's Bull., 1987-90; editor newsletter No. Lights, 1990-98. Recipient Regional award North Ctrl. Region Astron. League, 1989. Mem. Nat. Assn. Sys. Programmers, Internat. Occulation Timing Assn. (sec. 1975-78), Chgo. Computer Soc., Chgo. Astron. Soc. (pres. 1977, 80, 84), Racine Astron. Soc. (pres. 1979), Astron. League (exec. sec. 1993-95, webmaster 1995-02), Desert Moon Observatory (dir.), Astron. Soc. Las Cruces (pres. 2001). Personal E-mail: bstevens@zianet.com. Business E-Mail: Berton.Stevens@lpnt.net.

**STEVENS, CHARLES THOMAS, SR.,** drafting technology educator; b. Atlanta, Dec. 9, 1944; s. James Thomas and Christeen Bush Stevens; m. Erendira Daphne Aparicio, June 13, 1980; children: Missy Moore, Secundina Angelic Moore, Charles Thomas Jr. AA in Applied Tech., Physics, Chattahoochee Tech. Coll., Marietta, Ga., 2002; diploma in Drafting, 2002, diploma in Drafting Aid, 2002. Cert. engring. technician, 1975, sr. engring. technician, Nat. Inst. for Certification in Engring. Technologies, 1977. Elec. designer TVA, Decatur, Ala., 1990, Oglethorpe Power Corp., Atlanta, 1992, Brown & Caldwell, Inc., Atlanta, 1997, Applied Engring. and Sci., Atlanta, 1997; drafting educator Chattahoochee Tech. Coll., Marietta, 2001—, mem. engring. adv. bd., 2001—; designer Mech. Solutions, Hiram, Ga., 2002—. Mem. engring. adv. bd. Chattahoochee Tech. Coll., 2001—. Mem.: Am. Soc. Cert. Engring. Technicians. Libertarian. Roman Catholic. Office: Mechanical Solutions 65 Lancaster Way Hiram GA 30141-5463 Office Phone: 678-773-1516. Business E-Mail: ctstevens@ctstevens.org. E-mail: ctstevens@studiostevens.com.

**STEVENS, CHERITA WYMAN,** social sciences educator, writer; b. Erick, Okla., Jan. 12, 1938; d. Forrest Clarence and Wilma Peter Wyman; m. Paul Donald Stevens, May 30, 1958 (div. Nov. 10, 1978); children: Paul McDonald, Mark Liu. BA in Social Sci., Phillips U., 1961; MA in Sch. Law and Fin., Calif. State U., LA, 1976; cert. in ESL, U. Calif., LA. Administ. credential K-12 and adult; LA, Calif. Classroom tchr. grades 7-9 South Pasadena (Calif.) Unified, 1961-66; assoc. regional pastor Disciples of Christ, Pacific Southwest, 1976—82; computer store owner Claremont (Calif.) Computer, 1982—87; tchr., prin., grant writer Cabrillo Unified Sch. Dist., Half Moon Bay, Calif., 1987—97; ESL computer lab. media instr. Chapman Edn. Ctr., Garden Grove, Calif., 1997—2005. Legis. intern Calif. State Assembly, Sacramento, 1978—80; NASD registered rep. Primerica

Life/Citigroup, Orange, Calif., 2000—05; grant reviewer U.S. Dept. Edn., Washington, 2002; presenter in field; grant writer Calif. Dept. Edn./Joint Partnership Training Act, Half Moon Bay, 1996. Editor: Direction Newspaper, 1976—82; author: (software) Apartment Maintenance, 1988, Grants Tracking, 1989, Financial Management, 1991, Curriculum and Lesson Plans for the Independent Learning Lab, 1995; designer, lesson plan builder: OTAN Website, 2002—05; contributor KOCE (PBS) Schoolhouse Video Project, 2004; contbr. articles to newspapers and mag. Mem. Ams. for Dem. Action, Pasadena, 1963—80; civil rights activist, 1960—69; organizer first Martin Luther King Jr. celebration in U.S. L.A., 1972; active First Christian Ch., Orange, 1963—2005, Pasadena, Calif. Mem.: Assn. Calif. Sch. Adminstrs. (site rep. 1993—97, state presenter 2005, state workshop presenter). Avocations: golf, photography, genealogy. Home: 401 W La Veta Ave #220 Orange CA 92866-2649 Personal E-mail: cheri1066@msn.com.

**STEVENS, CLAUZELL,** plant pathologist; b. Mobile, Ala., July 16, 1944; s. Clauzell Stevens Sr. and Pearl Robinson Stevens; m. Brenda Crooms, Aug. 18, 1968; 1 child, Clauzell Stevens III. BS in Biology and Chemistry, Ala. State U., Montgomery, Ala., 1968; MS in Biology, Ala. State U., Montgomery, Ala., 1974; PhD in Plant Pathology and Microbiology, Auburn U., Auburn, Ala., 1979. Cert. lay minister Concordia Coll., Selma, Ala. Asst. prof. Ala. A&M U., Normal, Ala., 1979—80; rsch. prof. Tuskegee U., Ala., 1980—. Lectr. in field; spkr. in field. Lay min. Bethlehem Luth., Prattville, Ala. Mem.: Ala. Acad. Sci., So. Nursery Assn., Inc. (assoc.), Pickle Packers Internat., Inc. (assoc.), Am. Soc. Plasticulture (assoc. Past Presidents Found. award 1996), Am. Phytopathological Soc. (assoc.), Nat. Sweetpotato Collaborators Group, Gamma Sigma Delta (assoc.), Sigma XI Sci. Rsch. Soc. (assoc.). Independent. Luth. Achievements include research in characterization of the genus spiroplasma; development of plasticulture research activities centered on the transfer of new technologies such as plastic mulch systems, drip irrigation and soil solarization for the Alabama; isolation spiroplasmas from mosquitoes. Office: Tuskegee Univ Dept of Agriculture Sci 207 Milbank Hall Tuskegee Institute AL 36088 Office Phone: 334-727-8044. Office Fax: 334-727-8552. Business E-Mail: cstevens@tuskegee.edu.

**STEVENS, CONNIE,** actress, singer; b. Bklyn., Aug. 8, 1938; d. Peter and Eleanore (McGinley) Ingolia; m. Maurice Elias; m. Edwin Jack Fisher (div.); children: Joely, Tricia Leigh. Pres. Forever Spring Cosmetics; founder Windfeather Foundation. Show bus. debut as vocalist with, The Three Debs, Hollywood, at age 16; appeared in: Finians Rainbow for Hollywood Repertory Co.; numerous motion pictures, including Way, Way Out, Scorchy, Eighteen and Animals, Young and Dangerous, Drag Strip Riot, Rock-a-bye Baby, Parish, Susan Slade, Palm Springs Weekend, The Grissom Gang, Never Too Late, Grease II, 1983, Back to the Beach, 1987, Bring Me the Head of Dobie Gillis, 1988, Love Is All There Is, 1996; starred in TV series Wendy and Me and TV series Hawaiian Eye, 1959-62, Head Over Heals, 1997, Titus, 2000-02, TV films for ABC-TV Movie-of-the-Week; Call Her Mom, 1972, Playmates, Mister Jericho, Cole Porter in Paris, The Sex Symbol, 1974, Starting From Scratch, 1988, James Dean: Live Fast, Die Young, 1997; guest star on TV with, Bob Hope, Red Skelton, Englebert Humperdinck, Tom Jones, Perry Como and Laugh-In; TV appearance comedy spl. Harry's Battles; headliner at Flamingo Hotel, Las Vegas, also, Hilton Internat., Sands Hotel, Desert Inn, Aladdin, MGM, Sahara, 1969-76; stage appearances include The Wizard of Oz at Carousel Theatre in So. Calif., Any Wednesday at Melodyland, Anaheim, Calif.; made Broadway debut in Star Spangled Girl, 1967; accompanied Bob Hope around world on his Christmas tour, 1969, Persian Gulf Christmas tour, 1987; dir., prodr., writer, editor, cinematographer: A Healing, 1997 (Santa Clarita Internat. Film Festival Award, 1998); created line of cosmetics called Forever Spring and opened the Garden Sanctuary day spa in Los Angeles Bd. dirs. Ctr. for Plastic and Reconstructive Surgery, South Vietnam. Recipient Lady of Humanities Award, Shriners Hospital, 1991, Humanitarian of the Year, Sons of Italy, 2001, Distinguished Civilian Service Medal, 2002.

**STEVENS, CURTIS,** consumer products company executive; BA in Econs., U. Calif., LA, Calif., MBA. Sr. fin. exec. Planar Sys., Inc., 1984—97; v.p., treas. CFO La.-Pacific Corp., Portland, Oreg., 1997—2002, exec. v.p. adminstrn., 2002—, CFO, 2002—. Office: Louisiana Pacific 805 SW Broadway Ste 740 Portland OR 97205-3344

**STEVENS, DAVID ALEC,** medical educator; b. NYC, June 3, 1940; m. Julie Anne Teece, Aug. 15, 1964; children: Joseph John, Emily Beth Stevens Marsh. BA, Cornell U., 1960; MD, U. Rochester, 1965. Diplomate Nat. Bd. Med. Examiners, Am. Bd. Internal Medicine; med. lic. Wis., Calif. Intern, asst. resident dept. medicine U. Wis. Hosps., Madison, 1965-67; rsch. assoc. Nat. Cancer Inst., Bethesda, Md., 1967-69; resident dept. medicine UCLA Med Ctr., 1969-70; fellow divsn. infectious diseases, dept. medicine Stanford U., Calif., 1970-72, asst. prof. divsn. infectious diseases, dept. medicine, 1972-78; chief divsn. infectious diseases Santa Clara County-Valley Med. Ctr., San Jose, Calif., 1972—, assoc. chief dept. medicine, 1972—, epidemiologist, 1972—; assoc. prof. divsn. infectious diseases, dept. medicine Stanford U., 1978-85, assoc. prof. divsn. geographic medicine, dept. medicine, 1984-85, prof., 1985—. Co-dir. microbiology lab. Santa Clara Valley Med. Ctr., 1972—; prin. investigator Infectious Diseases Rsch. Lab., Calif. Inst. Med. Rsch., San Jose, 1973—; bd. regents, 1978-90, 92—, sec.-treas., 1979-81, sci. dir. coun., 1986-88, pres., 1992—; mycology ref. lab. Pub. Health Lab. Svcs. Dept. Microbiology, U. London, 1979. dir. clin. labs. Calif. Inst. Med. Rsch., 1980—; co-dir. AIDS program Santa Clara Valley Med. Ctr., 1986-88, assoc. dir., 1988-98; lectr. fourth ann. O.J. Farness lectr. U. Ariz., Tucson, 1999. Author: (with others) Coccidioidomycosis, 1980; mem. editl. bd. various profl. jours.; contbr. articles to profl. jours, chpt. to books; patentee in field. With USPHS, 1967-69. Ian Murray Meml. lectr. British Soc. Mycopathology, Canterbury, Eng., 1985. Fellow ACP, Am. Soc. Microbiology (chair mycology 1992-93, divsn. lectr. mycology ann. meeting 2001), Infectious Diseases Soc. Am., Am. Acad. Microbiology; mem. AMA, AAUP, AAAS, Am. Fedn. Clin. Rsch., Am. Soc. Clin. Investigation, Fedn. Am. Scientists, Med. Mycology Soc. Ams. (Rhoda Benham medal 1999), Calif. Med. Assn., Western Assn. Physicians, Calif. Collaborative Treatment Group, Santa Clara County Med. Soc. (Outstanding Achievement in Medicine award 2003), Internat. Soc. Human and Animal Mycology (clin. mycology com. 1985-91, Lucille Georg medal 2006). Achievements include patents for antigenic preparation and diagnostic method for identification of Nocardia infections. Avocations: jazz, running, stamp collecting/philately. Home: 19070 Portos Dr Saratoga CA 95070-5169 Office: Santa Clara Valley Med Ctr 751 S Bascom Ave San Jose CA 95128-2699 Office Phone: 408-885-4313.

**STEVENS, DAVID D.,** health products executive; COO So. Health Systems, Inc., 1983; dir. Accredo Health, 1997, chmn., CEO. Mem. bd. dir. Thomas & Betts Corp., Wright Medical Group, Inc. Office: Accredo Health Ste 101 1640 Century Ctr Pkwy Memphis TN 38134 Office Phone: 877-222-7336. Office Fax: 901-385-3689.

**STEVENS, DENNIS MAX,** auditor; b. Jersey City, Sept. 3, 1944; m. Susan Gail Brown, Mar. 15, 1969; children: Julie Ayn, Daniel Ross. BBA, Rutgers U., 1966; MA in Acctg., U. Mo., 1968. CPA Mo. Staff Peat, Marwick, Mitchell and Co., St. Louis, 1968-80, ptnr., 1980-84; sr. v.p., internal auditor Southwestern States Bankcard Assn., Dallas, 1985-86, sr. v.p., CFO, 1986-89; corp. planner NCH Corp., Irving, Tex., 1989-95, dir. corp. audit, 1995—2002; dir. internal audit Alamo Group, Seguin, Tex., 2002—. Contbr. articles to profl. jours. 1st lt. U.S. Army, 1969—70. Mem.: AICPA (mem. electronic data processing auditing stds. com. 1979—84), Inst. Internal Auditors, Beta Gamma Sigma, Beta Alpha Psi. Home: 23711 Legend Gln San Antonio TX 78258-4316 E-mail: den.stevens@attglobal.net.

**STEVENS, DIANA LYNN,** elementary school educator; b. Waterloo, Iowa, Dec. 12, 1950; d. Marcus Henry and Clarissa Ann (Funk) Carr; m. Paul John Stevens; 1 child, Drew Spencer. BS, Mid Am. Nazarene Coll., 1973; M in Liberal Arts, Baker U., 1989. Elem. tchr. Olathe (Kans.) Sch. Dist. #233, 1975—. Artwork appeared in traveling exhibit ARC/Nat. Art Edn. Assn., 1968, Delta Kappa Gamma Bull., 2001. Olathe Sch. Dist. Action grantee,

1996-97; recipient Excellence in Edn. award Olathe Pub. Schs. Found., 2002. Mem. NEA, Kans. Edn. Assn., Olathe Edn. Assn. (social com. Olathe chpt.), Coll. Ch. of the Nazarene, Delta Kappa Gamma (profl. affairs com. mem., chpt. membership chair 2006-, Excellence in Edn. award 2002), Beta Omega (membership chair, 2d v.p. 2006-). Avocations: portrait art, reading, walking. Home: 217 S Montclaire Dr Olathe KS 66061-3828

**STEVENS, DONALD JOHN,** secondary school educator; b. Chgo., Sept. 4, 1944; s. Mitchell Stevens; 1 child, Jacob Stevens Sweet. BA, U. Notre Dame, South Bend, Ind., 1967; MA, Columbia U., N.Y.C., 1969; PhD, Duke U., Durham, N.C., 1978. Master tchr. Northfield Mt. Hermon Sch., Mass., 1979—. Office: Northfield Mt Hermon Sch 206 Main St Northfield MA 01360 Office Phone: 413-498-3000. Business E-Mail: dstevens@nmhschool.org.

**STEVENS, DONALD KING,** retired aeronautical engineer, consultant; b. Danville, Ill., Oct. 27, 1920; s. Douglas Franklin and Ida Harriet (King) S.; m. Adele Carman de Werff, July 11, 1942; children: Charles August, Anne Louise, Alice Jeanne Stevens Kay. BS with high honors in Ceramic Engring., U. Ill., 1942; MS in Aeros. and Guided Missiles, U. So. Calif., 1949; grad., U.S. Army Command and Gen. Staff Coll., 1957, U.S. Army War Coll., 1962. Staff mem. Ill. State Geol. Survey, 1938—40; commd. 2d lt. US Army, 1942; ceramic engr. Harbison-Walker Refractories Co., Pitts., 1945—46; antiaircraft and guided missiles br. The Arty. Sch. US Army, Ft. Bliss, Tex., 1949—52, commdr. 2d battalion 1st guided missile group, 1954—56, mem. weapons sys. evaluation group Office Sec. Def. Washington, 1957—61, chief J2 plans br. UN Command US Forces Republic of Korea, 1962—63, advanced through grades to col., 1963, comdr. Niagara-Buffalo def. 31st arty. brigade Lockport, NY, 1963—65, chief air def. and nuc. br. war plans divsn. Washington, 1965—67, dir. US ballistic missile def. studies DEPEX and X-66 for Sec. Def., 1965—66, chief strategic forces divsn. office dep. chief of staff mil. ops., 1967—69, chief J5 spl. weapons plans U.S. European command Germany, 1969—72, ret., 1972. Guest lectr. U.S. Mil. Acad., 1958-59; mem. Army Air Def. Sys. 1970's, West Calif., 1973-95; U.S. Army Concepts Analysis Agy., Bethesda, Md., 1973-95; cons. on strategy Lulejian & Assocs., Inc., 1974-75; cons. nuc. policy and plans to Office Asst. Sec. of Def., 1975-80, 84-93; cons. Sci. Applications, Inc., 1976-78. Contbr. articles to profl. jours. Asst. camp dir. Piankeshaw Area coun. Boy Scouts Am., 1937; mem. chancel choir, elder First Christian Ch., Falls Church, Va., 1957-61, 65-69, 72-2002, elder emeritus 2004-; elder, trustee Presbyn. Ch., Niagara Falls, NY, 1963-65. Decorated D.S.M., Legion of Merit, Bronze Star. Mem. Am. Ceramic Soc., Assn. U.S. Army, U. Ill. Alumni Assn., U. So. Calif. Alumni Assn., Rotary, Keramos, Niagara Falls Country Club, Ill. Club (Washington), Terrapin Club, Sigma Xi, Sigma Tau, Tau Beta Pi, Phi Kappa Phi, Alpha Phi Omega. Disciples Of Christ. Achievements include pioneer in tactics and deployment plans for Army surface-to-air missiles. Address: 5916 5th St N Arlington VA 22203-1010 Personal E-mail: dkstevens@starpower.net.

**STEVENS, ELISABETH GOSS (MRS. ROBERT SCHLEUSSNER JR.),** journalist, writer, graphic artist; b. Rome, N.Y., Aug. 11, 1929; d. George May and Elisabeth (Stryker) Stevens; m. Robert Schleussner, Jr., Mar. 12, 1966 (dec. 1977); 1 child, Laura Stevens BA, Wellesley Coll., 1951; MA with high honors, Columbia U., 1956. Editl. assoc. Art News Mag., 1964-65; art critic and reporter Washington Post, Washington, 1965-66; freelance art critic and reporter Balt., 1966—; contbg. art critic Wall Street Jour., N.Y.C., 1969-72; art critic Trenton (NJ) Times, 1974-77; art and architecture critic The Balt. Sun, 1978-86; critic-at-large srqradio.com, 2004—; art correspondent Sarasota Herald Tribune, 2005—. Author: Elisabeth Stevens' Guide to Baltimore's Inner Harbor, 1981, Fire and Water: Six Short Stories, 1982, Children of Dust: Portraits and Preludes, 1985, Horse and Cart: Stories from the Country, 1990, The Night Lover: Art & Poetry, 1995, In Foreign Parts, 1997, Household Words, 1999, 2000, Eranos, 2000, Cherry Pie & Other Stories, 2001; one-woman shows include Coll. Notre Dame of Md., 1997, Galerie Francoise, Lutherville, Md., 2000, exhibited in group shows at The Corcoran Gallery of Art, Washington, Towson State U., Balt., Atelier A/E, N.Y.C., Stephen Gang Gallery, Govt. Ho., Annapolis, U. Minn., Morris, Cooperstown (N.Y.) Art Assn., Armory Art Ctr., West Palm Beach, Fla., Venice (Fla.) Art Ctr., Ft. Meyers (Fla.) Alliance for the Art, Katharine Butler Gallery, Sarasota, Fla., 2004, Combined Talents: Fla. Internat., Tallahassee, 2005, Mus. Fine Arts, Tallahassee, 2005; contbr. articles, poetry and short stories to jours., nat. newspapers and popular mags. Recipient A.D. Emmart award for journalism, 1980, Critical Writing citation Balt.-Washington Newspaper Guild, 1980, fiction awards Md. Poetry Rev., 1992, 93, 94, 2d prize Lite Circle, 1994, 1st prize in fiction Lite Circle, 1995, 96, Balt. Writers Alliance Play Writing Contest award, 1994; art critics' fellow NEA, 1973-74, fellow MacDowell Colony, 1981, Va. Ctr. for Creative Arts, 1982-85, 88-90, 92, 93, 95, 97, 2000, Ragdale Found., 1984, 89, Yaddo, 1991, Villa Montalvo, 1995; Work-in-Progress grantee for poetry Md. Art Coun., 1986, Creative Devel. grantee for short fiction collection Balt. Mayor's Com. on Art and Culture, 1986. Mem. Coll. Art Assn., Authors Guild, Fla. Printmakers Assn., Poetry Soc. Am., Am. Soc. Graphic Artists, Nat. Book Critics Circle, Women Contemporary Artists Sarasota. Home: Bards Castle 5353 Creekside Trail Sarasota FL 34243

**STEVENS, ELLIOTT WALKER, JR.,** allergist, cardiologist, pulmonologist; b. Wilmington, N.C., Sept. 13, 1940; s. E. Walker Sr. and Margaret Ardelle (Hester) S.; m. Blanche Bonner, July 10, 1965; children: Elliott W. III, Margaret Baker. AB in French, U. N.C., 1962, MD, 1966. Diplomate Am. Bd. Internal Medicine, Am. Bd. Allergy and Immunology, Am. Bd. Pulmonery Diseases. Intern U. N.C. Hosp., Chapel Hill, N.C., 1966-67; resident Duke U., Durham, N.C., 1969-70, fellow Allergy and pulmonary diseases, 1970-72; allergist and pulmonologist Greensboro Chest Disease and Allergy Associates, Greensboro, N.C., 1972—. Capt. USAF, 1967-69. Fellow Am. Coll. Allergy and Immunology, Am. Coll. Chest Physicians. Republican. Episcopalian. Avocations: skiing, sailing. Home: 4 Round Hill Ct Greensboro NC 27408-3709 Office: Greensboro Chest Diseases and Allergy Assocs and Allergy Assocs 1018 N Elm St Greensboro NC 27401-1488 Office Phone: 336-275-7238. Personal E-mail: wstev7970@aol.com.

**STEVENS, GARY,** retired jockey; Jockey, 1991. Named winner, Breeder's Cup Turf Race, 1990, Breeder's Cup Juvenile, 1993, Breeder's Cup Distaff, 1994. Achievements include being a top money winner, 1991. Office: Jockey's Guild Inc PO Box 150 Monrovia CA 91017-0150

**STEVENS, GARY LEE,** state senator; b. McMinnville, Oreg., Aug. 21, 1941; m. Rita Stevens; children: Anna, Matthew, Natalie. BA, Linfield Coll., 1963; MFA, U. Oreg., 1965, PhD, 1984. Dir. Kodiak Oral History Project; gen. mgr. No. Processors Inc., 1970—75; mayor Kodiak, Kodiak Island Borough; mem. Alaska Ho. of Reps., 2000—02, Alaska Senate, 2003—04. Prof. U. Alaska, Kodiak, Alaska, 1975—2000. Pres. Kodiak Sch. Bd.; presiding officer Borough Assembly; bd. dirs. Alaska Humanities Forum, Alaska Mcpl. League, Alaska Conf. Mayors. 1st lt. U.S. Army, 1966—69. Decorated Army Commendation medal, Nat. Def. medal. Mem.: Nat. Assn. Counties (edn. steering com.), Alaska Hist. Soc. (pres.), Rotary (gov.). Republican. Office: Rm 417 State Capitol Juneau AK 99801-1182 E-mail: senator_gary_stevens@legis.state.ak.us.

**STEVENS, GEORGE ALEXANDER,** real estate broker; b. Loma, Mont., Nov. 10, 1923; s. Otto Oliver and Josephine (Dale) S.; m. Martha Evie Fultz, Sept. 16, 1944 (div. 1978); children: Gary, Kathleen, Arlene, Tina; m. Arleen Dorothea Largent, Nov. 14, 1978. A in Bus Adminstrn., SUNY, 1992. Prin. George Stevens Farm, Loma, Mont., 1946-93, George Stevens, Real Estate Broker, Loma, Mont., 1957-93; pres. George A Stevens Corp., Loma, 1976-93, Gold and Silver Realty, Inc., Great Falls, Mont., 1993—2005, Cowboys n Plowboys, Inc., Great Falls, 2000—05, George Stevens, Broker, Great Falls, 2005—. Trustee Sch. Dist. # 32, Loma, 1947-50; election judge Precinct # 7, Loma, 1953-88. With USN, 1944-46, PTO. Mem.: VFW (life), Eagles Lodge (life), Elks (life), Am. Legion (life). Democrat. Lutheran. Home: 810 8th Ave N Great Falls MT 59401-1036 E-mail: gastevens@montana.com.

**STEVENS, GEORGE RICHARD,** business consultant, public information officer; b. Chgo., Sept. 6, 1932; s. George and Irene (Kaczmarek) S.; m. Jeanne E. Sowden, Aug. 2, 1957; children: Stacey, Samantha, Pamela. BS with honors, Northwestern U., 1954. CPA, Ill. With Arthur Andersen & Co., 1954-78, mng. ptnr. Brussels, 1957—71, ptnr. Chgo., 1971-78; pres. Daubert Industries, Oak Brook, Ill., 1978-80, G.R. Stevens Group, 1981—; founder, pres. Stevens Ctr. for Pub. Policy Studies, 1981—. Commr. Ill. Ednl. Facilities Authority, 1989-04. Commr. Ill. State Scholarship Commn., 1981-87; vice chmn. Ill. Ind. Higher Edn. Loan Authority, 1982-88. Home and Office: 22615 N Las Lomas Ln Sun City West AZ 85375-2022

**STEVENS, GLADSTONE TAYLOR, JR.,** retired industrial engineer, retired educator; b. Brockton, Mass., Dec. 16, 1930; s. Gladstone Taylor and Blanche Ruth S.; m. Jane A. Crouch, July 20, 1953; children— Robert, Bartlett. BSM.E., U. Okla., 1956; MSM.E., Case Inst. Tech., 1962; PhD in Indsl. Engring., Okla. State U., 1966. Registered profl. engr., Tex., Okla. Project engr. E.I. duPont, Orange, Tex., 1956-59; research engr. Thompson-Ramo-Wooldridge, Cleve., 1960-62; asst. prof. mech. and indsl. engring. Lamar U., Beaumont, Tex., 1962-64; asst. prof. to asso. prof. indsl. engring. Okla. State U., Stillwater, 1966-75; prof., chmn. dept. indsl. engring. U. Tex., Arlington, 1975-98; ret., 1998. Author: (with J.E. Shamblin) Operations Research: A Fundamental Approach, 1974, Economic and Financial Analysis of Capital Investments, 1993; Engineering Economy, 1983. Served with AUS, 1948-52. Recipient E.L. Grant award, 1974, AMOCO Teaching award, 1979, Wellington award, 1992. Fellow Am. Inst. Indsl. Engrs.; mem. Sigma Xi, Alpha Pi Mu (nat. pres.), Tau Beta Pi, Sigma Tau, Omicron Delta Kappa. Home: 2501 Spanish Trl Apt 212 Arlington TX 76016-1410 Office: U Tex Indsl Engring Arlington TX 76019-0001

**STEVENS, GLENN H.,** lawyer; Grad., Johns Hopkins U.; JD, NYU. Positions in legal dept. US West Inc., 1979—92; atty. pvt. practice, 1992—94; v.p.; gen. counsel, sec. Maxtor Corp., Milpitas, Calif., 1994—2001, sr. v.p., gen. counsel, sec., 2001—. Mem.: Nebr. State Bar Assn., Colo. Bar Assn. Office: Maxtor Corp 500 McCarthy Blvd Milpitas CA 95035

**STEVENS, GREGORY SCOTT,** information technology manager; b. Albuquerque, N. Mex., Mar. 17, 1962; s. Orlando and Betty Jo Stevens. BA in Theater Design, 2000; MAT in Mus. Edn., George Wash. U., 2001. Outreach coord. San Diego Opera, 1983—87; design asst. Gaslamp Quarter Theater, San Diego, 1983—87; fine arts program designer Kellogg Sch., Chula Vista, Calif., 1989—2000; scenic artist Old Globe Theater, San Diego, 1994—96; edn. specialist Nat. Air and Space Mus. Smithsonian, Wash., DC, 2001—03; program mgr. Mid Atlantic Assn. Mus., Balt., 2003—05; project mgr. for edn. Nat. Mus. of the U.S. Army, Ft. Belvoir, Va., 2005—. Bd. dirs. Mus. Edn. Roundtable, Wash., DC, 2001—03. Bd. dirs. Mus. Edn. Roundtable. Recipient Arts Edn. Achievement award, Calif. Ctr. for the Arts, 1997, Employee of Yr., Chula Vista Elem. Sch. Dist., 1997, Dir's. award of Excellence, Nat. Air and Space Mus., 2002.

**STEVENS, HELEN JEAN,** music educator; b. Nevada, Iowa, July 11, 1934; d. Paul Ellison and Helen Margaret (Ives) Stevens. MusB, U. So. Calif., 1956. Cert. secondary music tchr. Calif. Tchr. San Francisco Sch. Dist., 1956-58; prin. oboist Marin Symphony Orch., San Rafael, Calif., 1956-94, Santa Rosa (Calif.) Symphony, 1956-86; tchr. Santa Venetia Mid. Sch., San Rafael, 1958-83; asst. prof. music Sonoma State Coll., Rohnert Park, Calif., 1963-76; tchr. Davidson Mid. Sch., San Rafael, 1984-89; pvt. tchr. oboe. Oboist Evenings on the Roof Series, LA., 1953—56, Debut TV Show, L.A., 1954—56, Carmel (Calif.) Bach Festival, 1954—82; prin. oboist Light Opera Curren Theatre, San Francisco, 1966—67, Marin Opera Co., San Rafael, 1980—84. Leader Sonoma County 4-H Guide Dog Project Guide Dogs for Blind, Inc., 1974—87; organist, music dir. Korean Meth. Ch., L.A., 1953—56; music dir. United Meth. Ch., St. James, Mo., 2002—. Named Outstanding Tchr., Marin Edn. Found., 1986; recipient Svc. award, PTA, 1974, Golden Bell award, Marin County Office Edn., 1984, Continuing Svc. award, Calif. Congress Parents, Tchrs. and Students, Inc., 1989. Mem.: German Shepherd Dog Club Am. Avocations: computers, animals. Home: 14713 State Rt BB Saint James MO 65559 E-mail: stevfam@fidnet.com.

**STEVENS, HERBERT FRANCIS,** lawyer, educator; b. Phila., Nov. 19, 1948; s. Herbert F. and Lois Marie (Kenna) S.; m. Jane Pickard, 1994; children: Sarah, Ben. SB, MIT, 1970; JD, Catholic U. Am., 1974; ML in Tax, Georgetown U., 1983. Bar: D.C., 1975; U.S. Supreme Ct., 1980. Law clk Md. Ct. of Spl. Appeals, 1974-75; with Morgan, Lewis & Bockius, Washington, 1975-78, Lane & Edson, P.C., Washington, 1979-89, Kelley Drye & Warren, Washington, 1989-93, Nixon Peabody LLP, Washington, 1993—; adj. prof. Georgetown U. Law Ctr., 1983-98. Spkr. in field. Editor: Real Estate Aspects of the 1984 Tax Law, 1984; author: Real Estate Taxation: A Practitioner's Guide, 1986, Developer's Guide to Low Income Housing Tax Credit, 4th edit., 2000. Bd. dirs. Nat. Fund for U.S. Botanic Garden, 1992—, exec. com. Mem. ABA, D.C. Bar Assn. Democrat. Presbyterian. Home: 8301 Hackamore Dr Potomac MD 20854-3877 Office: Nixon Peabody LLP 401 9th St NW Washington DC 20004-2128 Business E-Mail: hstevens@nixonpeabody.com.

**STEVENS, JAMES C.,** chemist; Rsch. fellow performance polymers and chems. R & D Dow Chem. Co. Contbr. articles to profl. jours. Co-recipient US Nat. Inventor of Yr. award, 1994; named one of 50 R & D Stars, Industry Week Mag., 1994; recipient Inventor of Yr. award, Mich. Saginaw Valley Patent Lawyers Assn., 1992, Carothers award, Am. Chem. Soc., Del. sect., 2004, Indsl. Chemistry award, Am. Chem. Soc., 2006, Perkin medal, Soc. Chem. Industry, 2006. Achievements include patents in field. Mailing: Dow Chem Co 2301 N Brazosport Blvd Freeport TX 77541*

**STEVENS, JAMES HERVEY, JR.,** retired financial planner; b. Balt., June 22, 1944; s. James H. and Hilda (Pearce) S.; m. Patricia Carol Donohue, Aug. 27, 1967 (div. Mar. 1983); children: James III, Carol; m. Lisa Gay Landrum, Apr. 29, 1984. BA, Duke U., 1966; MS in Fin. Svcs., Am. Coll., Bryn Mawr, Pa., 1981. CLU; ChFC; CFP; registered health underwriter. Supr. New Eng. Life, Overland Park, Kans., 1969-75, agt., 1969—; v.p., treas. Creative Planning, Inc., Overland Park, 1980-95; pres. Hokanson, Lehman & Stevens, Inc., Overland Park, 1982-95; founder, chmn. Wings Over Mid-Am., Inc., 1995-97, chmn. emeritus, 1997—; chmn. Air Care Alliance, 1997—; chmn. emeritus Wings Over Mid-Am., Inc., 1997—; founder, chmn. legacy fund Angel Flight Ctrl., Inc., Kansas City, Mo. Contbg. editor monthly tax topics Kansas City Bus. Jour.; contbg. editor Pvt. Pilot Mag.; contbr. articles to profl. jours. Bd. dirs. Mo. divsn. Am. Cancer Soc., Kans. and Mo., 1982-84, Ctrl. United Meth. Ch., Kansas City, Mo., 1990-92, North Cross United Meth., 1991—; bd. dirs. Apple Valley Homes Assn., Overland Park, 1990—, pres. 1992; co-founder Kansas City Friends of Gilda's. Recipient Outstanding Young Man award, 1977; named one of Top 200 Fin. Advisors, Money Mag., 1987, Boss of Yr., Kansas City LICOMA, 1983. Mem. Kansas City Life Underwriters (pres. 1980-82, Herbert A. Hedges award 1987), Kansas City CLU & ChFC Soc. (pres. 1981-83), Mo. Life Underwriters (pres. 1984-86), Am. Soc. CLU & ChFC (vice chmn., bd. dirs.). Republican. Avocations: model railroading, collecting post-war "lionel", airline transport pilot, instrument flight instr. Home: 5200 W 98th Ter Shawnee Mission KS 66207-3221 Office: Angel Fly Ctrl Inc 10 Richards Rd Kansas City MO 64113 E-mail: jstevens10@gmail.com.

**STEVENS, JOHN PAUL,** United States Supreme Court Justice; b. Chgo., Apr. 20, 1920; s. Ernest James and Elizabeth (Street) Stevens; m. Elizabeth Jane Sheeren, June 7, 1942 (div. 1979); children: John Joseph(dec.), Kathryn Stevens Jedlicka, Elizabeth Jane Stevens Sesemann, Susan Roberta Stevens Mullen; m. Maryan Mulholland Simon, Dec. 1979. AB, U. Chgo., 1941; JD magna cum laude, Northwestern U., 1947. Bar: Ill. 1949. Practiced in, Chgo.; law clk. to Justice Wiley B. Rutledge U.S. Supreme Ct., Washington, 1947—48; assoc. Poppenhusen, Johnston, Thompson & Raymond, 1949—52; assoc. counsel, sub-com. on study monopoly power, com. on judiciary U.S. Ho. of Reps., Washington, 1951—52; ptnr. Rothschild, Stevens, Barry & Myers, 1952—70; judge U.S. Ct. Appeals (7th cir.), Chgo.,

1970—75; assoc. justice U.S. Supreme Ct., Washington, 1975—. Lectr. anti-trust law Northwestern U. Sch. Law, 1952—54, U. Chgo. Law Sch., 1955—58; mem. Atty. Gen.'s Nat. Com. to Study Anti-Trust Laws, 1953—55; chief counsel to commn. investgating the judgment of People v. Isaacs Ill. Supreme Ct., 1969; appellate judge seminar NYU Sch. Law, 1979. With USNR, 1942—45. Decorated Bronze Star. Mem.: Am. Law Inst., Fed. Bar Assn., Ill. Bar Assn., Am. Bar Assn., Chgo. Bar Assn. (2d v.p. 1970), Order of Coif, Phi Delta Phi, Psi Upsilon, Phi Beta Kappa. Office: US Supreme Ct One First St NE Washington DC 20543*

**STEVENS, JOSEPH CHARLES,** psychology professor; b. Grand Rapids, Mich., Feb. 28, 1929; s. Joseph, Jr. and Anne Katheryn Stevens. AB, Calvin Coll., Grand Rapids, 1950; MA, Mich. State U., 1953; PhD, Harvard U., 1957. Instr., asst. prof. psychology Harvard U., 1957-66; fellow emeritus John B. Pierce Found. Lab., sr. rsch. scientist Yale U., 1966—. Cons. in field. Author: Laboratory Experiments in Psychology, 1965; co-editor: Sensation and Measurement, 1974; mem. editl. bds. profl. jours.; contbr. numerous articles to profl. jours. Grantee NSF; Grantee NIH, Air Force Office Sci. Rsch. Fellow AAAS, Am. Psychol. Soc., NY Acad. Scis.; mem. Acoustical Soc. Am., Optical Soc. Am., Soc. Neuroscience, Ea. Psychol. Assn., Gerontol. Soc. Am. Office: 290 Congress Ave New Haven CT 06519-1403 Business E-Mail: jstevens@jbpierce.org.

**STEVENS, JOYCE WEST,** social worker, educator, researcher; b. Clayton, Mo., Mar. 15, 1936; d. John Lawrence and Gertrude M. West; children: Janet, Melinda Stevens-Ademuyiwa. BS, Loyola U., Chgo., 1960, MSW, 1964, PhD, 1993. LCSW, Acad. Cert. Social Workers. Social worker, counselor Cook County Dept. Pub. Aid, Chgo., 1960—66; project dir. YMCA Met. Chgo., 1969—71; social work counselor, cons. Lake Bluff Chgo. Homes for Children, 1972—73; counselor, psychotherapist U. Ill., Chgo., 1973—74; faculty advisor Chgo. State U., 1974—75; program coord., counselor Michael Reese Hosp. and Med. Ctr., Chgo., 1974—91; field work instr. U. Chgo. Social Svc. Adminstrn., 1979—82; clin. field work instr. DePaul U., Chgo., 1990—91; instr. Loyola U. Chgo., 1990—92; asst. prof. Boston U. Sch. Social Work, 1993—2001, assoc. prof., 2001—; pvt. clin. practice Boston, 1993—. Mem. ETA Creative Arts Found. Aux., 1976—92, Chgo. Urban League Women's Bd., 1977—94; clin. cons. St. Philip Neri Parish, Chgo., 1989—91; adj. prof. Smith Coll. Sch. Social Work, Northampton, Mass., 1991—92; mem. Beethoven Project adv. bd. Ctr. for Successful Child Devel., 1991—94; trustee Family Svc. Greater Boston, 2000—02; rsch. cons. Mass. Dept. Social Svcs. Teen Living Program Network Evaluation Study, Boston; mem. instnl. rev. bd. Family Svc. Grater Boston and Latino Health Inst. Author: Smart and Sassy: The Strengths of Inner City Black Girls, 2002 (Black Adminstrs. Child Welfare Scholars award, 2002); editor, book rev. editor: Child and Adolescent Social Work Jour., 1993, 2002, editor, consulting editor: Social Work Jour., 1999, 2002, Families in Society, 1998, 2002; contbr. chapters to books, articles to profl. jours. Minority Fellow grant, Nat. Inst. Drug Abuse, 1999—; African Am. Women's Study grant, 1999—2002. Avocation: book collecting. Office: Boston Univ Sch Social Work 264 Bay State Rd Boston MA 02215

**STEVENS, KATHERINE,** secondary school educator; b. Ypsilanti, Mich., July 21, 1942; d. Francis Raymond and Eileen Agnes Simkins; m. Jack Alan Stevens, Nov. 11, 1962 (dec.); children: John Alan, Merry Margaret. BS in English and History, U. Dubuque, Iowa, 1974; MA in English, Middlebury Coll., 1985. Cert. tchr., Iowa. Tchr. Dubuque Cmty. Schs., 1976—. Facilitator of planning insts., mem. nat. faculty Expeditionary Learning Outward Bound, Cambridge, Mass., 1993—. Contbr. poetry to publs. Pres., Dubuque Fine Arts Soc., 1988-94, 2000-03; bd. dirs. Dubuque Mus. Arts, 1985-89, 90-93; mem Dubuque Human Rights Commn., 1993-96, 2000-03. Named Dubuque Comty. Schs. Tchr. of Yr., 2004. Mem. Iowa Poetry Assn. (area rep.), Nat. Coun. Tchrs. English. Roman Catholic. Avocations: reading, gardening, writing.

**STEVENS, KENNETH NOBLE,** electrical engineer, educator; b. Toronto, Ont., Can., Mar. 23, 1924; arrived in U.S., 1948, naturalized, 1962; s. Cyril George and Catherine (Noble) Stevens; m. Phyllis Fletcher, Jan. 19, 1957 (div. 1979); children: Rebecca, Andrea, Michael Hugh, John Noble; m. Sharon Manuel, Jan. 14, 1994; children: Kendra Wenyu Manuel, Mackenzie Yin Ying Manuel. BASc., U. Toronto, 1945, MASc., 1948; Sc.D., MIT, 1952. Instr. U. Toronto, 1946—48; faculty MIT, Cambridge, 1948—; prof. elec. engring., 1963—; Clarence J. LeBel prof., 1977—. Vis. fellow Royal INst. Tech., Stockholm, 1962—63; cons. to industry, 1952—; vis. prof. phonetics U. Coll., London, 1969—70; mem. Nat. Adv. Coun. on Neurol. and Communicative Disorders and Stroke, NIH, 1982—86. Author (with A.G. Bose): Introductory Network Theory; author: Acoustic Phonetics, 1998; contbr. articles to profl. jours. Trustee Buckingham Browne and Nichols Sch., 1974—80. Recipient Quintana award, Voice Found., 1992, medal, European Speech Comm. Assn., 1995, Nat. Medal of Sci., 1999; fellow, Guggenheim, 1962. Fellow: IEEE (James L. Flanagan Speech and Audio Processing award 2004), Am. Acad. Arts and Scis., Acoustical Soc. Am. (exec. com. 1963—66, v.p. 1971—72, pres.-elect 1975—76, pres. 1976—77, Gold medal 1995); mem.: NAE, NAS. Home: 7 Larchwood Ln Natick MA 01760 Office: MIT 77 Massachusetts Ave Cambridge MA 02139-4307

**STEVENS, KENNETH T.,** retail executive; b. 1952; Grad., DePauw U., 1974; student, U. Redlands; MBA, U. So. Calif. Former ptnr. McKinsey & Co.; former sr. v.p. and treas. Pepsico; exec. v.p. mktg. Taco Bell divsn. of Pepsico, 1993—94, pres. and COO, 1994—97; chmn. and CEO Bank One Retail Group, 1997—2000; pres. and COO inChord Comm., 2000—01; exec. v.p. and COO Bath & Body Works divsn. of Ltd. Brands, Inc., 2002, pres., 2003—04; CEO Express (subs. Limited Brands), 2004. Office: Express Stores, 2002 ... Office Express One Limited Pkwy Columbus OH 43230

**STEVENS, LAUREN ROGERS,** writer, environmentalist; b. Phila., May 3, 1938; s. Lewis Miller and Elizabeth (Morgan) Stevens; m. Beverly Decker, June 20, 1964 (div. Dec. 1987); children: Rebecca Fasciano, Jeffrey L., Jennifer B.; m. Peggy Brooks, June 26, 2004; 1 adopted child, Tamirat Brooks-Stevens. BA, Princeton U., 1960; MA, U. Iowa, 1962. Tchr. English lang. & environ. studies Williams Coll., Williamstown, Mass., 1963-81, dean of freshmen, 1970-81; founder, pub., editor Advocate Newsweekly, Williamstown, Mass., 1981-83. Writer, freelance, 1983—. Author: The Double Axe, 1961, Skiing: Downhill and Cross Country, 1991; co-author (with Deborah Burns): Most Excellent Majesty, 1988; co-author: (with Richard W. Babcock) Old Barns in the New World: Reconstructing History, 1996; author: The Berkshire Book, 2006; columnist: Berkshire Eagle; author: Hikes and Walks in the Berkshire Hills, 2004; contbr. articles to mags. and newspapers. Founder Hoosic River Watershed Assn., Williamstown, 1986, co-pres., 1994—96, exec. dir., 1997—2002; leader Mahican-Mohawk Trail, N.Y., Vt., Mass., 1992—; co-founder Greylock A Better Chance, Williamstown, 1968; deacon First Congl. Ch., Williamstown, 1985—, moderator, 2000—03. Mem.: The Trustees of Reservations, Phi Beta Kappa. Democrat. Avocations: hiking, canoeing, cross country skiing. Home: 235 Lesure Rd Stamford VT 05352

**STEVENS, LEONARD BERRY,** educational consultant; b. Fall River, Mass., Sept. 19, 1938; s. Henry Bennett and Manetta (Berry) S.; m. Elizabeth Holihen, Aug. 17, 1963; children: Lisa M., Christopher M., Andrew B., Rosa B. A. BS, Boston U., 1960; EdD, U. Mass., 1978. Cert. supt., Mass. Edn. writer Providence Jour.-Bull., 1963—67; sr. editor Cowles Comm., Inc., N.Y.C., 1967—68; exec. editor Change in Higher Edn. Mag., N.Y.C., 1968—70; spl. asst. to Chancellor N.Y.C. Bd. Edn., 1970—73; rsch. asst. U. Mass., Amherst, 1973—76; dir. Greater Cleve. Project, 1976—78; dir. Office Sch. Monitoring and Cmty. Rels. U.S. Dist. Ct. (no. dist.) Ohio, Cleve., 1978—88; dir. Compact for Ednl. Opportunity, Milw., 1988—90; race-related sch. planning cons. Sarasota, Fla., 1990—. Cons. as racial/cultural diversity and sch. desegregation planning expert and analyst to state edn. depts., pub. sch. dists., parties in litigation; expert witness in over 30 sch. desegregation

cases; lectr. in field at univs. and seminars. Co-author: Make Your Schools Work, 1975; contbr. articles to profl. jours. and mass media publs. Trustee Inst. Child Advocacy, Cleve.; bd. dirs. Com. on Cath. Cmty. Action, Cleve., 1981-88. Lt. (j.g.) USN, 1960-63.

**STEVENS, LORETTA MARIE,** special education educator; b. Bethpage, N.Y., Nov. 26, 1955; d. Hamilton Thomas and Evelyn Barbara Pendergast; m. Louis C. Stevens, Apr. 2, 1987; children: Erin Michelle Cook, Megan Colleen Oneill. BS, Shenandoah U., Winchester, Va., 1995; MEd, James Madison U., Harrisonburg, Va., 1997; M of Ednl. Adminstrn., Shenandoah U. Winchester, Va., 2005. Cert. elem. edn. tchr. Va., 1995, spl. edn. tchr. Va., 1997, ednl. adminstr. Va., 2005. Learning disabilities specialist Warren County Pub. Schs., Front Royal, Va., 1995—2004, ednl. diagnostician, 2004—06, supr. spl. edn., 2006—. Lead tchr. for learning disabilities Warren County Pub. Schs., Front Royal, Va., 1996—2004, spl. edn. dept. chairperson, 1997—2004; individual edn. plan coord. Warren County Pub. Schools, Front Royal, Va., 1999—; mentor new spl. educators Old Dominion U., Newport News, Va., 1997—. Pres. PTA, Manassas Park, Va., 1986—89; mem./advisor 4-H Club, Warren County, Va., 2002—04; dir. children's choir St. John the Bapt. Cath. Ch., Front Royal, Va., 1989—93, dir. adult modern music choir, 1993—98. Mem.: ASCD, Therapeutic Riding Assn., Internat. Reading Assn., Learning Disabilities Assn., Coun. for Exceptional Children (Professionall Recognized Spl. Educator 200-2005). Achievements include development of Educational program to improve learning for students who are slow learners. Avocations: horseback riding, hiking. Office: Warren County Public Schs 210 N Commerce Ave Front Royal VA 22630 Office Phone: 540-635-2171 ext. 247.

**STEVENS, LORI ANN LABEAU,** school librarian, educator; b. Yakima, Wash., Dec. 31, 1959; d. Raymond L. and Irene A. LaBeau; m. Mark D. Stevens, Apr. 24, 1981; children: Elisabeth A., Jared S., Mark D., Jonathan R. BMus, Brigham Young U., 1983; MLS, Emporia State U., 1999. Pub. svcs.-media ref. libr. Orem Pub. Libr., Utah, 1991—99; media instrn. libr. Utah Valley State Coll., Orem, 1999—. Contbr. chapters to books. Chair libr. adv. commn. City of Orem, 2002. Recipient Merit award, Utah Humanities Coun., 2001, Trustees award Excellence, Utah Valley State Coll. Bd. Trustees, 2002. Mem.: ALA (assoc.; chair 2001—05), Video Round Table ALA (assoc.; program chair 2004—), Music Libr. Assn., Mountain Plains Chpt. (assoc.; mem. at large 2002—03), Utah Libr. Assn. (assoc.; mem. at large 2002—, Spl. Recognition award 2005), Music Libr. Assn. (assoc.; chair film music roundtable 2005—). Mem. Lds Ch. Avocations: singing, piano, hiking, travel, gardening. Office: Utah Valley State Coll Libr 800 W University Pky Orem UT 84058 Home Fax: 801-863-7065. Personal E-mail: stevenlo@uvsc.edu.

**STEVENS, LYDIA HASTINGS,** community volunteer; b. Highland Park, Ill., Aug. 2, 1918; d. Rolland T.R. and Ruth Shotwell (Beebe) Hastings; m. George Cooke Stevens, Nov. 2, 1940; children: Lydia Stevens Gustin, Priscilla Stevens Goldfarb, Frederick S., Elizabeth Stevens MacLeod, George H., Ruth Stevens Stellard. BA, Vassar Coll., 1939. State rep. 151st Dist. of Conn., Greenwich, 1988-92. Cons. Nat. Exec. Svc. Corps, N.Y.C., 1985. Pres. Greenwich YWCA, 1971-74, Greenwich Housing Coalition, 1982-86; v.p. planning Greenwich United Way, 1973-76; sr. warden Greenwich Christ Episcopal Ch., 1981-86; chmn. rev. commn. Episcopal Diocese of Conn., 1985-87; bd. dirs. Greenwich Libr., 1985-93; chmn. Greenwich Commn. Aging, 1986-88; pres., bd. dirs. Greenwich Broadcasting Corp., 1977-79; bd. dirs. Fairfield County Cmty. Found., 1992, United Way of Greenwich, Save the Sound, 1996—, League Conservation Voters Conn., 1999. Recipient Golden Rule award J.C. Penney, 1987, President's award Greenwich YWCA, 1992, Brava award, 1994, Conn. Assn. for Human Svc. Dirs. award, 1992; named Layperson of Yr., Coun. Chs. and Synagogues, 1995. Republican. Episcopalian. Avocations: sailing, organic gardening. Home: 125 West Ln Guilford CT 06437-3230

**STEVENS, MARK,** banker; b. Chgo., May 24, 1947; s. Joseph K. and Phoebe (Copeland) S.; m. Joyce Sue Skinner, Aug. 22, 1970; children: Mark Benjamin, Katherine Joyce. BA, W.Va. U., 1969, JD, 1972. V.p. Continental Ill. Nat. Bank & Trust Co., Chgo., 1972-79, No. Trust Co., Chgo., 1979-81; pres., CEO, No. Trust Bank Fla., Sarasota, 1984-87, chmn., pres., CEO, 1987-96; exec. v.p. No. Trust Co. & No. Trust Corp., 1996-98, pres. personal fin. svcs., 1998—. Pres. No. Trust Fla. Corp., Miami, 1987-96, chmn., 1996—. Trustee Ctr. Fine Arts, 1988-94, 1988-94, Miami Children's Hosp. Found., 1993-96, South Fla. Performing Arts Ctr. Found., 1993—, U. Miami, 1994, Beacon Coun., 1990—; mem. U. Miami Citizens Bd., 1988-89, Young Pres.'s Orgn., 1988—; bd. dirs. Miami Coalition and Task Force, 1988—, New World Symphony, 1991—; charter mem. Coun. of 100 Fla. Internat. Univ. Found., 1990—; hon. bd. dirs. Audubon House; mem. Orange Bowl Com., 1994. Mem. Young Pres. Orgn., Riviera Country Club, Miami Club. Office: The No Trust Co 50 S Lasalle St Chicago IL 60603-1006

**STEVENS, MARK,** publishing executive; m. Trish Stevens; children: Kyle, Kevin. BS in Commerce, U. Toronto, 1981. With Spicer MacGillivray, 1981—85; mgr. fin. reporting Nabisco Brands Ltd., 1985—88; from asst. controller to pub., CEO Toronto (Can.) Sun, 1988—2000, pub., CEO, 2000—01; v.p., CFO Houston (Tex.) Post, 1991—95; v.p. corp. comms. Sun Media, 1999—2000; group pub. Rogers Pub., Toronto, 2001—04; pub. Press-Telegram, Long Beach, Calif., 2004—.

**STEVENS, MARK WHITNEY,** art critic; b. NYC, Aug. 14, 1951; s. Whitney Stevens and Rhoda (Winton) Kraft; m. Annalyn Swan, June 12, 1977; children: Emmelyn Swan, Julia Philippa. AB, Princeton U., 1973; MA, Cambridge (Eng.), 1975. Art critic Newsweek, NYC, 1977-87, The New Republic, Washington, 1986—94, Vanity Fair, NYC, 1988—92, NY Mag, NYC, 1994—. Author: (art history) Richard Diebenkorn, 1984, (novel) Summer in the City, 1984; co-author (with Annalyn Swan), de Kooning: An American Master, 2004 (Nat. Book Critics Guild prize for biography, 2004, Pulitzer Prize for Biography, 2005); also numerous articles and essays on art. Office: NY Magazine 444 Madison Ave New York NY 10022

**STEVENS, MARTIN BRIAN,** publisher; b. N.Y.C., Dec. 29, 1957; s. David Robert and Shirley Stevens. Grad. high sch. Advt. Unitron Pubs., N.Y.C., 1977, Westchester Publs., Elmsford, 1978; founder, CEO The Composing Rm., N.Y.C., 1979—83; pub. Retailers Forum, Centerport, 1981—, Swap Meet mag., 1990—; founder, CEO Forum Pub. Co., 1981—. Pub. 8 bus. directories; rep. 6 bus. book pubs.; founder Rodeo Dr. Limousine Svc., 1990—93, Mercedes-Benz Limousine Svc., 1990—93; founder, CEO Party Fun House, Inc., 2004—. Named Top Mail Order Dealer, Nat. Mail Dealers Counsel, 1978. Mem. Mail Order Bus. Bd. (pres. 1978-80), Better Bus. Bur., Nat. Assn. Self-Employed, Nat. Assn. Desktop Pub., L.I. Assn., Can. Direct Mail Assn. Avocations: weight training, reading. Office: Forum Pub Co 383 E Main St Centerport NY 11721-1538

**STEVENS, MAY,** artist; b. Boston, June 9, 1924; d. Ralph Stanley and Alice Margaret (Dick) S.; m. Rudolf Baranik, June 5, 1948; 1 child, Steven. BFA, Mass. Coll. Art, 1946; postgrad., Academie Julian, Paris, 1948-49, Art Students League, 1948. Mem. faculty Sch. Visual Arts, N.Y.C., 1964-96, Skowhegan Sch. Painting and Sculpture, 1992, Vt. Studio Ctr., 1997, 2005, Santa Fe Art Inst., 2000, 2003. Lectr. Royal Coll. Art, London, 1981, U. Wis.-Racine, 1973, Coll. Art Assn., Washington, 1975; sole juror Am. Drawing Biennial, Coll. William and Mary, Williamsburg, Va., 2000; lectr. Coll. Santa Fe, 1998, Santa Fe Art Inst., 2003. One-woman shows: Terry Dintenfass Gallery, N.Y.C., 1971, Cornell U., 1973, Douglass Coll., Rutgers U., 1974, Lerner-Heller Gallery, N.Y.C., 1975, 76, 78, 81, Clark U. Libr., 1982, Boston U. Art Gallery, 1984, Frederick S. Wight Gallery, UCLA, 1985, U. Md., College Park, 1985, Real Art Ways, Hartford, 1988, New Mus. Contemporary Art, 1988, Orchard Gallery, Derry, No. Ireland, 1988, Kenyon Coll., Gambier, Ohio, 1988, Greenville County (S.C.) Art Mus., 1991, Herter Gallery, U. Mass., Amherst, 1991, U. Colo., Boulder, 1993, U. N.Mex., Albuquerque, 1996, Mary Ryan Gallery, N.Y.C., 1996, 97, 99, 2001, 2003, 2005, Mus. Fine Arts, Boston, 1999, LewAllen Contemporary, Santa Fe,

1998, Minn. Inst. Art, 2005, Nat. Mus. Women in the Arts, Washington, 2005, Springfield (Mo.) Art Mus., 2006; exhibited in numerous group shows including most recently: Santa Fe Art Inst., 2002, Mus. Fine Art, Santa Fe, 2002, Guild Hall, East Hampton, N.Y., 2002, Hobart & William Smith Colls., 2002, We. Wash. U. Bellingham, 2002, UBS Paine Webber Art Gallery, N.Y.C., 2002, Deutsche Bank, N.Y.C., 2002, Bass Mus. Art, Miami Beach, Fla., 2002, Bklyn. Mus., 2003, Nat. Mus. Women in the Arts, Washington, 2003, Danese Gallery, N.Y.C., 2003, Tamarind Inst., Albuquerque, N.Mex., 2004, Harwood Mus., Taos, N.Mex., 2004, Ctr. Contemporary Arts Warehouse, Santa Fe, N.Mex., 2004, Nat. Acad. Design, N.Y.C., 2004, Evo Gallery, Santa Fe, N.Mex., 2005, Mason Gross Sch. of Arts, Rutgers U., New Brunswick, NJ, 2006; represented in permanent collections: Met. Mus. Art, N.Y.C., Mus. Modern Art, N.Y.C., Moca, L.A., San Francisco Mus. Art, New Mus. Contemporary Art, Whitney Mus., Bklyn. Mus., Herbert F. Johnson Mus., Cornell U., Mus. Fine Arts Boston, De Cordova Mus., Lincoln, Mass., Harwood Mus., Taos, N.Mex., Joslyn Art Mus., Omaha, Nat. Mus. Women in Arts, Washington, Minn. Inst. Art, Mpls., Springfield Mus. Art, Mo., Mcnhy Art Mus., San Antonio, Tex., McCormick Pl. Ctr. Art Coll., Chgo., Jacksonville Art Mus., Fla., Cleve. Mus. Art, Ill., U. Miami, Fla.; contbr. articles to various mags. Recipient Childe Hassam Purchase awards Nat. Inst. Arts and Letters, 1968, 69, 75, N.Y. State Coun. on Arts award, 1974, Disting. Alumna award Mass. Coll. Art, 1997, Disting. Artist award Coll. Art Assn., 2001, Edwin Palmer Meml. prize NAD, 2004; Andy Warhol Found. grantee for project space Headlands Ctr. for Arts, Sausalito, Calif., 2001; MacDowell Colony fellow, 1971, 72, 74, 75, 81, 82, 84, Bunting Inst. fellow Radcliffe Coll., 1988-89; Line Assn. grantee for artists books, 1978; grantee NEA, 1983, Guggenheim, 1986; honoree Women's Caucus for Art, 1990. Mem.: NAT, Coll. Art Assn.

**STEVENS, MICHAEL N.,** lawyer; b. Rockville Centre, NY, Jan. 24, 1949; BA, Temple U., 1971; JD, Bklyn. Law Sch., 1974. Bar: NY 1975, US Dist. Ct. Ea. Dist. NY 1975, US Dist. Ct. So. Dist. NY 1975, US Ct. Appeals 2nd Cir. 1975. Joined Wilson, Elser, Moskowitz, Edelman & Dicker LLP, NYC, 1979, ptnr., 1983—. Mem.: NY State Med. Malpractice Def. Assn., NY State Bar Assn. Office: Wilson Elser Moskowitz Edelman & Dicker LLP 150 E 42nd St 23rd Fl New York NY 10017-5639 Office Phone: 212-490-3000 ext. 2265. Office Fax: 212-490-3038. Business E-Mail: stevensm@wemed.com.

**STEVENS, PAUL SCHOTT,** lawyer; b. New Orleans, Nov. 19, 1952; s. Miles Gordon and Rosemary Louise (Schott) S.; m. Joyce Lynn Pilz, Aug. 18, 1979; Paul Schott Jr., Alexander Holmes, Andrew Colby, Carl Bernard. BA magna cum laude, Yale U., 1974; JD, U. Va., 1978. Bar: D.C. 1979, U.S. Dist. Ct. D.C. 1979, U.S. Ct. Appeals (D.C. cir.) 1979, U.S. Ct. Appeals (fed. cir.) 1983, U.S. Supreme Ct. 1982. Assoc. prin. Dickstein, Shapiro & Morin, Washington, 1978-85, ptnr., 1989-93; dep. dir., gen. counsel Pres.'s Blue Ribbon Commn. on Def. Mgmt., Washington, 1985-86; legal adviser NSC, Washington, 1987, exec. sec., 1987-89; spl. asst. to Pres. for nat. security affairs The White House, Washington, 1987-89; exec. asst. to Sec. of Defense, Washington, 1989; sr. v.p., gen. counsel Investment Co. Inst., Washington, 1993-97; sr. v.p., gen. counsel Mut. Funds and Internat. Enterprise, Charles Schwab & Co., Inc., San Francisco, 1997-99; ptnr. Dechert LLP, Washington, 1999—2004; pres. Investment Co. Inst., 2004—. Bd. dirs. ICI Mut. Ins. Co.; lectr. law Washington Coll. Law, Am. U., Washington, 1980-83; trustee M.G. Stevens Corp., New Orleans, 1978—; quality of markets com. NASDAQ Stock Market, Inc., 1997, investment cos. com. NASD Regulation, Inc., 1999; adv. bd. Ctr. Banking and Fin. Law, Boston U., 1996—. Author: U.S. Armed Forces and Homeland Defense: The Legal Framework, 2001. Chmn. bd. dirs. Student Conservation Assn., Charlestown, N.H., 1986-87, bd. dirs., 1985-91, 94-96, sec., gen. counsel, 1991-93; mem. fin. coun. Cath. Diocese of Arlington, 2006—; mem. Life Guard Soc. of Mt. Vernon, 2005-, mem. bd. trustees, Yale Libr. Assoc., 2006-. Recipient medal for disting. pub. svc. Dept. Def., 1989; Bates fellow Yale U., 1973, Scholar of House, 1973-74; Rotary Internat. Found. grad. fellow, 1978, U.S.-Japan Leadership fellow Japan Soc., 1989-90, assoc. fellow Saybrook Coll., Yale U., 1993—. Mem.: ABA (chmn. standing com. law and nat. security 1995—98), Fed. Bar Assn., Coun. Fgn. Rels., Federalist Soc., Internat. Bar Assn., DC Bar Assn., Soc. of Sons of the Am. Revolution, Soc. War 1812, Soc. of Mayflower Descendants, Jamestowne Soc., Cosmos Club, Elizabethan Club, Yale Club. Met. Club. Republican. Roman Catholic. Office: Investment Co Inst 1401 H St NW Washington DC 20005 Business E-Mail: paul.stevens@ici.org.

**STEVENS, PHYLLIS A.,** conceptual artist; b. Washington, June 14, 1931; d. Carle Wright Stevens and Maybelle Bayley Whiting; 1 child, Karen. Student, Antioch Coll., 1953, Art Students League, Acad. of Realist Art. Self employed free lance artist, 1956—; set designer Eccentric Circles Theater, N.Y.C.; stage sets dir. Theater Genesis, N.Y.C.; designer CBS Network, Shadow Puppet Productions, N.Y.C., Am. Opera Soc., Shadow Puppet Production, N.Y.C. Exhibitions include Salmagundi Club, NYC, Philmont Ranch, N. Mex., Art Expo, NYC, Artist and Artisans, NJ, Hunter Crafts Show, NYC, Living Handcrafts, Mus. of Contemporary Crafts, Mus. of Fine Arts, Del., Bonwit-Teller, N.Y.C., Bratta Gallery, Antioch Coll., Ohio, prin. works include Mural in Lobby, Internat. Longshoreman's Union, Anthony Anastasia Med. Ctr., NY, Four built-in panels, Private home, NY; contbr. articles to profl. jours. Mem.: Writers Guild of Am. East, N.Y. Artists Equity Assn., Graphic Artists Guild, Chatham (N.C.) Plein Air, Salmagundi Club. Home: 214 Weaver Mine Trail Chapel Hill NC 27517 Personal E-mail: phyllisstevens@earthlink.net.

**STEVENS, RICHARD YATES,** state senator; b. Raleigh, NC, Dec. 12, 1948, s. Floyd L. and Luna (Yates) Stevens; m. Jere Ann Gilmore, Sept. 13, 1980; children: Charles Andrew, Katherine Elizabeth. BA in Polit. Sci., U. N.C., 1970, JD, 1974, MPA, 1978. Bar: NC 1974. Asst. dean men U. N.C., Chapel Hill, 1970-71, asst. residence dir., 1971-75, asst. Office Student Affairs, 1973-75; pvt. practice Chapel Hill, 1974-76; adminstrv. asst. City of Durham, NC, 1975-76, budget officer, 1976-78, dir. adminstrn., 1978-79, dir. fin. and program devel., 1979-80; from asst. county mgr. to county mgr. Wake County, NC, 1980—2000; mem. NC State Senate, 2003—. Coord. NC State Govt. intern program, Inst. Govt., 1971; adj. prof. polit. sci. NC State U., 1980, 92, 94; sr. budget advisor NC Gov.'s Transition Team, 2000—01. Bd. visitors U. N.C., Chapel Hill, 1991—95, trustee, 1995—2003, chmn., 1997—99; chmn. bd. dirs. U N.C. Endowment Fund, 1997—99; chmn. U. N.C. Found., 1997—99. Mem.: ASPA (Nat. Pub. Svc. award 2000), N.C. Mus. Natural Scis. Soc. (bd. dirs. 1987—88, treas. 1988—89, pres.-elect 1989—90, pres. 1990—91), N.C. City-County Mgmt. Assn. (bd. dirs. 1991—92, 2d v.p. 1997—98, 1st v.p. 1999—99, pres. 1999—2000), N.C. State Nat. Assn. County Administrs. (bd. dirs. 1989—92), Internat. City-County Mgmt. Assn. (life), Yates Mill Assn. (bd. dirs.), Cary Acad. (bd. dirs.), U. N.C. Gen. Alumni Assn. (dir. 1978—80, 1983—88, chmn. 1998—99, chmn.-elect 1999—2000, chmn. 2000—01, Disting. Svc. medal 1994), U. N.C. Pub. Adminstrn. Alumni Assn. (pres. 1977—79, dir. 1982—84, Disting. Pub. Svc. award 1998), Carolina Club (vice chmn. 1993—94, chmn. 1994—98, 2002—). Home: 132 Lochwood Dr W Cary NC 27511-8301 Office: NC Gen Assembly Rm 406 Legislative Office Bldg Raleigh NC 27601-2808 Office Phone: 919-733-5653.

**STEVENS, RISË,** performing arts association administrator; b. NYC; m. Walter Surovy; 1 child, Nicolas. Student, Juilliard Sch.; Hon. Degree Smith Coll., Coll. of Senecas, Russell Sage Coll., Rider Coll., U. Pa., Baylor U., Rice U., Mercy Coll., Manns Coll Music, Hobart Coll., Cleve. Inst. Music, Va. Commonwealth U. Co-gen. mgr. Met. Opera Nat. Co., N.Y.C. 1965-88; pres. The Mannes Coll. Music, N.Y.C., 1975-78; mng. dir. Met. Opera Bd., N.Y.C. Performer Prague Opera, Vienna State Opera, Royal Opera, NY Met. Opera, 1938-61; starred in films, concerts, TV, and radio. Mem. Nat. Endowment for Arts (co-chair music panel 1981-83), N.Y. State Coun. on Arts (chmn. music panel), Met. Opera Guild (bd. dirs.), Wagnerian Soc. Buenos Aires, Sigma Alpha Iota. Office: Met Opera Assn Lincoln Ctr New York NY 10023

**STEVENS, ROBERT BOCKING,** lawyer; b. U.K., June 8, 1933; naturalized, 1971; s. John Skevington and Enid Dorothy (Bocking) S.; m. Katherine Booth, Dec. 23, 1985; 1 child, Robin; children by previous marriage: Carey, Richard. BA, Oxford U., 1955, BCL, 1956, MA, 1959, DCL, 1984; LLM, Yale U., 1958; LLD (hon.), N.Y. Law Sch., 1984, Villanova U., 1985, U. Pa., 1987; D.Litt. (hon.), Haverford Coll., 1991. Bencher, Gray's Inn, 1999. Barrister-at-law, London, 1956; tutor in law Keble Coll. Oxford U., 1958-59; asst. prof. law Yale U., 1959-61, assoc. prof., 1961-65, prof., 1965-76; provost, prof. law and history Tulane U., 1976-78; pres. Haverford Coll., 1978-87; chancellor, prof. history U. Calif., Santa Cruz, 1987-91; counsel Covington and Burling, Washington and London, 1991—; master Pembroke Coll., Oxford, 1993-2001; mem. Essex Court Chambers, 1966—; sr. rsch. fellow Univ. Coll., London, 2001—. Vis. prof. U. Tex., 1961, U. East Africa, 1962, London Sch. Econs., 1963, Stanford U., 1966, Brookings Instn., 1967-68, U. Coll. London, 1991-94, U. Hong Kong, 1998, Yale U., 1999, George Washington U., 2003, Cardozo Law Sch., 2004; cons. UN, HEW, U.S. Dept. State; fellow, Keble Coll., Oxford U., 1985, Pembroke Coll., Oxford U., 2001. Author: The Restrictive Practices Court, 1965, Lawyers and the Courts, 1967, In Search of Justice, 1968, Income Security, 1970, Welfare Medicine in America, 1974, Law and Politics, 1978, The Law School, 1983, The Independence of the Judiciary, 1993, The English Judges, 2002, 2d edit., 2005, From University to Uni, 2004, 2d edit., 2005. Chair Marshall Memorial Commn., 1994—2001, Sulgrave Manor, 2001—; mem. Nat. Humanities Coun., 1982—86. Fellow, Russell Sage Found., 1967—68, Cromwell Found., 2005; grantee, Rockefeller Found., 1962—64, Ford Found., 1962—64, 1973—74, Nuffield Found., 1975; NEH grantee, 1973—74, 2005. Home: Mill Bank Northleach GL54 3HJ England Office: Covington and Burling 265 Strand London WC2R 1BH England Office Phone: 44-20-7067-2213. Personal E-mail: rstevens@cov.com.

**STEVENS, ROBERT DAVID,** librarian, educator; b. Nashua, NH, Aug. 11, 1921; s. David Philip and Ruth (Ackley) S.; m. Helen Medora Conrad, Jan. 16, 1943; children Ruth Wilson Robertson, Hope Conrad. AB magna cum laude, Syracuse U., 1942; BS in L.S. with honors, Columbia, 1947; MA, Am. U., 1955, PhD, 1965. Employed Libr. Congress, Washington, 1947-64, coord. pub. law, 480 programs, 1962-64; dir. Libr. East West Ctr., Honolulu, 1964-65; dean Grad. Sch. Library Studies U. Hawaii, 1966-75; chief cataloging div. Copyright Office, 1975-80, coordinator copyright collections, 1980; lectr. grad. Sch. Libr. Studies, U. Hawaii, 1981-91; chief exec. officer Molesworth Inst. West, Inc., 1984-91, chmn., 1991-96. Fulbright lectr. U. Indonesia, 1971; US del. Intergovtl. Conf. Planning Nat. Libraries Infrastructures, 1974 Author: Role of the Library of Congress in International Exchange of Government Publications, 1955, Toshokan Kyoryoku, 1970, Documents of International Organizations, 1974, Japanese and US Research Libraries at the Turning Point, 1977, Short History of the School of Library and Information Studies, 1991; contbr. articles to profl. publs. Served to lt. USNR, 1943-46. Mem. Hawaii Library Assn. (pres. 1966-67), ALA (mem. council 1967-70, mem. US, Japan adv. com. 1972-79, chmn. 1974-76, Rlms policy and rsch. com. 1977-81), Assocs. U. Hawaii Library (vice chmn. 1981-84), Japan Library Assn., Hui Dui, Phi Beta Kappa, Pi Sigma Alpha. Clubs: 15 (Honolulu). Democrat. Home: 3-3400 Kuhio Hwy Apt C208 Lihue HI 96766-1084 Personal E-mail: robertds@hawaii.edu.

**STEVENS, ROBERT EDWARD,** engineering company executive; b. Kansas City, Mo., Oct. 30, 1957; s. Kenneth E. and Nina (France) S. BS in Chem. Engring., U. Mo.-Rolla, 1980, MS in Engring. Mgmt., 1985. Process design engr. The Pritchard Corp., Kansas City, Mo., 1981-83; process engr. Procter & Gamble, Cape Girardeau, Mo., 1986-87, tech. mgr., 1987-90; from project engring. mgr. to site mgr. Bechtel, 1990—99, engring. mgr. Mex., 1999-2000, project mgr., 2000-01, resident engring. mgr. Egypt, 2001, sys. engring. mgr. Hanford, 2002—. Contbr. to Properties of Gases and Liquids, 1987. Chmn. bd. dirs. Wesley Found., St. Louis, 1993-98; corp. devel. coun. U. Mo., Rolla, 1995-2003, chair benchmarking com., 1996-2000, chair distance learning com., 2001-03, mem. chem. engring. indsl. adv. bd., 2002—. Recipient Stan Adams Reliability award P & G Paper Div., 1990, Pres.'s award for team excellence Shell Oil Co., 1994; Nat. Merit scholar, 1976. Mem.: AIChE (life), Acad. Chem. Engrs. (bd. dirs. 2006—), Am. Soc. Engring. Mgmt., Project Mgmt. Inst., Nat. Fire Protection Assn., B-Reactor Mus. Assn., Chem. Heritage Found./Robert Boyle Soc, George C. Marshall Inst., Alpha Chi Sigma Ednl. Found. (bd. dir. 2003—), U. Mo. Rolla-Wesley Found. Alumni Assn. (pres. 1988—97, named outstanding contr. 1983, 1988), Order of the Golden Shillelagh, Tau Beta Pi, Alpha Chi Sigma (expansion com 2002—04, N.W. Dist. com. 2004—, cert. appreciation 1991, Hall of Fame Selection Adv. Bd. 2004—, Kuebler award Selection Com. 2006—). Methodist. Home and Office: 11220 W Florissant # 369 Florissant MO 63033-6741

**STEVENS, ROBERT J.,** aerospace transportation executive; b. McKeesport, Pa. BS summa cum laude, Slippery Rock U., 1976; grad., Dept. Def. Sys. Mgmt. Coll.; M in Engring. and Mgmt., Polytechnic N.Y.; M in Bus., Columbia U. With Fairchild Republic Co.; gen. mgr. to v.p., CFO Loral Sys. Manufacturing Co. (acquired by Lockheed Martin), 1987—93; exec. v.p., sr. v.p., CFO, air traffic mgmt. Lockheed Martin, 1993—96; pres., air traffic mgmt. Lookheed Martin, 1996—98; pres., COO energy and environ. bus Lockheed Martin, 1998—99, v.p. strategic devel. Bethesda, Md., 1998—99, exec. v.p., CFO, 1999—2001, pres., COO, 2000—04, pres., CEO, 2004—, chmn. bd. dirs., 2005—. Commr. Commn. Future of US Aerospace Industry, 2001—02; chmn., bd. dirs. Sandia Corp.; presiding dir., bd. dirs. Monsanto Co., 2002—; assoc. fellow Am. Inst. Aeronautics and Astronautics; mem., internat. adv. bd British-American Business Coun. Served USMC. Recipient Disting. Alumni award, Slippery Rock Univ., 2003, Exec. Yr., Nat. Mgmt. Assn., 2004; fellow Fairchild Fellowship, Am. Astronautical Soc. Fellow: Am. Astronautical Soc.; mem.: Aerospace Industries Assn. (mem. exec. com.).*

**STEVENS, ROBERT JAY,** magazine editor; b. Detroit, July 25, 1945; s. Jay Benjamin and Louise Ann (Beyreuther) S.; m. Dahlia Jean Conger, Aug. 15, 1970; children—Sandra Lee, Julie Ann. Student, Huron Coll., SD, 1963-66, Wayne State U., 1968-71. Sr. staff writer Automotive News, Detroit, 1968-71; editor Excavating Contractor mag., Cummins Pub. Co., Oak Park, Mich., 1971-78, Chevrolet's Pro Jour., Sandy Corp., Southfield, Mich., 1978—79, Cars and Parts mag., Cars and Parts Corvette mag. Amos Press, Sidney, Ohio, 1979—; truck editor Automotive Design & Devel. mag., 1971-78. Lectr., speaker in field. Contbr. articles to profl. jours.; author: numerous poems. Served with AUS, 1966-68, Vietnam. Decorated Air medal, Bronze star, Commendation medal; recipient Alphomega Publs. award, 1965—, Robert F. Boger Meml. award for outstanding constrn. journalism, 1975, U.L.C.C. nat. editl. award, Am. Pub. Works Assn., 1978, Moto award for outstanding automotive journalism, Internat. Automotive Media Conf., 1997, 1998, 1999, 2000, 2001, Internal. Automotive Media Conf., 2002, Best of Divsn. award, Internat. Automotive Media Conf., 2001, Folio mag. Editl. Excellence award, 2001. Mem. Detroit Auto Writers (past dir.), Internat. Motor Press Assn., Antique Automobile Club Am. (Lifetime Achievement award 2005. Republican. Presbyterian. Home: 653 Ridgeway Dr Sidney OH 45365-3432 Office: PO Box 482 911 Vandemark Rd Sidney OH 45365 E-mail: bstevens@carsandparts.com.

**STEVENS, ROBYN ANNE,** music educator; d. James Anthony Stevens and Stella Maria Pollard; m. R. Read Woodle (div.); children: Matthew Tobias Woodle, Morgan Maria Woodle. MusB in Voice Performance, U. Cin., 1979; MusM in Voice Performance, Peabody Conservatory Music, Balt., 1988; D in Musical Arts Voice Performance, U. Md., College Park, 2005. Adj. voice faculty, lectr. C.C. Balt., 1994—2004, Morgan State U., Balt., 1988—2003; assoc. prof. voice, coord. vocal studies U. N.C., Pembroke, 2006—. Dir. Arion Gesangverein Chorale, Balt., 1992—94, Catonsville Cmty. Coll. Chorale, C.C. Balt., 1994, 95; guest spkr. Winona State U., Minn., 1992; guest lectr. Balt. Opera Co., 2002—03; featured artist Nat. Conf. United Meth. Ch., Nat. Cathedral, Washington, 2000; founder Music at the Monastery Concert Series St. Joseph's Monastery Ch., Irvington, Md., 2002—. Finalist Friederich Schorr Vocal Competition, Lewaniec, Mich., 1997; named winner, Montpellier Recital Competition, Md., 1995; recipient Met. Opera Nat. Coun. Audition Dist. award, Sarasota Opera Co., Fla., 1982, Zaidee Thomas award,

Peabody Inst., Balt., 1987—88; Career Devel. grantee, 1992. Mem.: Am. Guild Musical Artists, Nat. Assn. Tchrs. Singing, Nat. Scholars Honor Soc. Office: U NC Pembroke Music Dept PO Box 1510 Pembroke NC

**STEVENS, ROGER TEMPLETON,** writer; b. Syracuse, N.Y., Jan. 11, 1927; s. Raymond Alfred and Mabel Eunice Stevens; m. Mildred Lorraine Hasbrouck, June 12, 1948 (dec. Aug. 1978); children: Margaret Ann, David Keith; m. Barbara Ann Wilkinson, July 14, 1979. AB in English, Union Coll., Schenectady, N.Y., 1949; MA in Math., Boston U., 1959; MS in Systems Engring., Va. Inst. Tech., Blacksburg, 1975; PhD in Elec. Engring., Calif. Western U., 1978. Tech. writer Raytheon Mfg. Co., Waltham, Mass., 1950—51; engr. Lab. for Electronics, Boston, 1951—55; sr. engr. Spencer Kennedy Labs., Boston, 1955—56, Avco Mfg. Co., Boston, 1956—57, Electronics Systems, Inc., Boston, 1957—60; supr., video and display Sanders Assocs., Nashua, NH, 1960—65; mem. tech. staff The Mitre Corp., Bedford, Mass., 1965—67, 1983—92, 1970—74; sr. rsch. engr. The Dikewood Corp., Albuquerque, 1967—70, 1974—81; sect. head EG & G Inc., Albuquerque, 1981—83. Author: Operational Test and Evaluation, 1979, Graphics Programming in C, 1988, Fractal Programming with C, 1989, Fractal Programming with Turbo Pascal, 1990, Advanced Fractal Programming in C, 1990, Fractal Programming and Ray Tracing with C++, 1991; author: (with Christopher Watkins) Advanced Graphics Programming in C and C++, 1991, Advanced Graphics Programming with Turbo Pascal, 1991; author: The C Graphics Handbook, 1992, Learning C with Fractals, 1993, Quick Reference Guide to Computer Graphics Terms, 1993, Object Oriented Graphics Programming in C++, 1994, Using PCX Graphics Files, 1995, Understanding Self-Similar Fractals, 1995, The C++ Graphics Handbook, 1996, Graphics Programming with Java, 1997, Computer Graphics Dictionary, 2002, Creating Fractals, 2005. With USN, 1945—46, Pacific. Mem.: AF and AM, Shriners. Avocations: computers, photography. Home: 17 Castle Rock Rd Rio Rancho NM 87124 Personal E-mail: rogerstevens76@msn.com.

**STEVENS, RON A.,** lawyer, advocate, surveyor; b. Indpls., Sept. 4, 1945; s. Granville Thomas and Charlotte May (Wheeler) S.; m. Judy Rohde, June 15, 1968; children: Samuel Thomas, Alison Elizabeth. BA, Okla. State U.; JD with honors, Ill. Inst. Tech., 1976. Bar: Ill. 1976. Staff atty. Legal Assistance Found. Chgo., 1976-79; staff atty., dir. housing agenda Bus. and Profl. People for Pub. Interest, Chgo., 1979-81; chief housing divsn. Office of Cook County State's Atty., Chgo., 1981-82; campaign coord. north lakefront Washington for Mayor, Chgo., 1982-83; program officer The Joyce Found., Chgo., 1983-86; pres. Citizens for a Better Environment, Chgo., 1986-89; pres., CEO United Way Santa Fe County, 1989—2003; dir. cmty. impact svcs. United Way.Am., 2003—. Adv. bd. state support ctr. on environ. hazards Nat. Ctr. for Policy Alternatives, Washington, 1987-89; chair Local Bd. EFSP, 1989—, Santa Fe Affordable Housing Roundtable, 1992-97; chair Exec. Leadership Coun. for Cmty. Schs. 1998—; bd. dirs. No. N.Mex. Grantmakers Assn., v.p., 1999, pres., 2000. Mem. bldg. code enforcement com. Mayor's Transition Team Housing Task Force, Chgo., 1983, steering com. Chgo. Ethics Project, 1986-88; founder, chmn. Progressive Chgo. Area Network, 1981-84; bd. dirs Uptown Recycling Sta., Chgo., 1987-89; mem. South Ctrl. Regional Coun., United Way of Am., 1993-98. Mem. Chgo. Coun. Lawyers (chmn. housing com. 1978-81, bd. govs. 1981-83, bd. dirs. Fund for Justice, 1986-88), Chgo. Area Runners Assn. (founder, v.p. 1977-81). Office: United Way Santa Fe County 440 Cerrillos Rd Santa Fe NM 87501-0261 Home: 7006 Stone Mill Pl Alexandria VA 22306-1329

**STEVENS, ROSEMARY A.,** medicine and public health historian, artist; b. Bourne, Eng. came to U.S., 1961, naturalized, 1968; d. William Edward and Mary Agnes (Tricks) Wallace; m. Robert B. Stevens, Jan. 28, 1961 (div. 1983); children: Carey, Richard; m. Jack D. Barchas, Aug. 9, 1994. BA, Oxford U., Eng., 1957; Diploma in Social Adminstrn., Manchester U., Eng., 1959; MPH, Yale U., 1963, PhD, 1968; LHD (hon.), Hahnemann U., 1988; DSc (hon.), Northeastern Ohio U. Coll. Medicine, 1995; DSc, Rutgers U., 1995. Various hosp. adminstrv. positions, Eng., 1959-61; rsch. assoc. Med. Sch. Yale U., 1962-68, asst. prof. Med. Sch., 1968-71, assoc. prof. Med. Sch., 1971-74, prof. pub. health Med. Sch., 1974-76; master Jonathan Edwards Coll., 1974-75; prof. dept. health systems mgmt. and polit. sci. Tulane U., New Orleans, 1976-78, chmn. dept. health systems mgmt., 1977-78; prof. history and sociology of sci. U. Pa., Phila., 1979—2002, chmn. dept., 1980-83, 86-91, UPS Found. prof., 1990-91, dean Sch. Arts and Scis., Thomas S. Gates prof., 1991-96, Stanley I. Sheerr prof., 1997—2001, prof. emeritus, 2002—. Prof. emeritus U. Pa., Phila., 2002-; vis. lectr. Johns Hopkins U., 1967-68; guest scholar Brookings Instn., Washington, 1967-68; acad. visitor London Sch. Econs., 1962-64, 1973-74; DeWitt Wallace disting. scholar social medicine and pub. policy, dept. psychiatry Weill Cornell Med. Coll., 2005—. Author: Medical Practice in Modern England: The Impact of Specialization and State Medicine, 1966, new edit., 2003, American Medicine and the Public Interest, 1971, rev. edit., 1998, In Sickness and in Wealth: American Hospitals in the Twentieth Century, 1989, rev. edit., 1999, (with others) Foreign Trained Physicians and American Medicine, 1972, Welfare Medicine in America, 1974, new edit., 2003, Alien-Doctors: Foreign Medical Graduates in American Hospitals, 1978. Bd. dirs. Milbank Meml. Fund. Rockefeller Humanities fellow, 1982-83, Guggenheim fellow, 1984-85; Bellagio Study and Conf. scholar, 1984; recipient Frohlich medal Royal Soc. Medicine, London, 1986, Baxter Found. prize distinction in health svcs. rsch., 1990, James A Hamilton Book award Am. Coll. Healthcare Execs. best book, 1990, Welch medal distinction in history of medicine Am. Assn. History Medicine, 1990, Arthur Viseltear award history pub. health Am. Pub. Health Assn., 1990, Nicholas E. Davies award Piedmont Hosp., Atlanta, 1997, Investigator award in health policy rsch. Robert Wood Johnson Found., 1998-2003, Carlson award for extraordinary contbns. to history of medicine Cornell U., Weill Med. Coll, 2000., Lifetime Achievement award Am. Assn. History Medicine, 2002. Fellow Am. Acad. Arts and Scis.; mem. AAAS (chmn. sect. history and philosophy of sci., 2002-03), Inst. Medicine of Nat. Acad. Sci., Am. Sociol. Assn., Am. Assn. for History of Medicine, Coll. Physicians of Phila.Am. Bd. Med. Specialties (pub. mem., bd. dirs.), Cosmopolitan Club. Home: 500 E 77th St Apt 419 New York NY 10162 Office Phone: 212-746-5798. E-mail: ras2023@medcornell.edu.

**STEVENS, ROY W.,** sales and marketing executive; b. Ottumwa, Iowa, Oct. 28, 1924; s. Manley O. and Ruth (Worrell) S.; m. Donna R. Borman, June 7, 1952 (dec. Jan. 1973); children: Katharine Anne Stevens Dillon, Thomas W., John M.; m. Beth A. Murphy, Apr. 20, 1974; children: Carrie Theresa, Elizabeth Mary. BSc, U. Iowa, 1948. With Coca-Cola Co., 1948-54, Gen. Foods Corp., 1954-67; exec. v.p. Riviana Foods, Houston, 1967-73; v.p. mktg. Hiram Walker Inc., Detroit, 1973-75, pres., 1975-80, Maidstone Wine & Spirits Inc., L.A., 1980-91, Kahlua Group (Allied Domecq), 1987-91; exec. v.p. The Century Coun., Los Angeles, 1991-98. Bd. dirs., past chmn. Detroit Met. YMCA; bd. dirs. L.A. Met. YMCA. Lt. (j.g.) USN, 1943-46. Mem. Jonathan Club, Sigma Alpha Epsilon. Episcopalian. Home: 1444 S Marengo Ave Pasadena CA 91106-4228

**STEVENS, ROY W.,** microbiologist, researcher, photographer; BS, State Univ. of N.Y., Albany, 1956, MS, 1958; PhD, Albany Med. Coll., 1965. Diplomate Am. Bd. Med. Microbiology; cert. emeritus Am. Bd. Med. Microbiology, 2002. Rsch. scientist Wadsworth Ctr., N.Y. State Dept. Health, Albany, 1967—70, assoc. rsch. scientist, 1970—73, prin. rsch. scientist, 1973—79, dir. lab. diagnostic immunology 1979—85, dir. retrovirology and immunology lab., 1985—91; adj. prof. microbiology and immunology Albany Med. Coll., 1982—92; assoc. prof. sch. pub health State Univ. N.Y., Albany, 1988—98; pres. Bio-med. Resource Group, Albany, 1991—. Trustee Bender Sci., Albany, 1986-98; chair Bender Sci. Ltd. Cmty. Found., Albany, 2002—; chair Univ. Libr. Devel. Com. State Univ. of N.Y., Albany, 2003-. Fellow Am. Acad. Microbiology (emeritus 2002), Assn. Med. Lab. Immunologists (pres. 1989), Am. Soc. Microbiology (chmn. clin. and diagnostic immunology divsn. 1997-98), Nat. Assn. Photoshop Profls. Home: 507 Acre Dr Schenectady NY 12303-5226

**STEVENS, SCOTT,** retired professional hockey player; b. Kitchener, Ont., Canada, Apr. 1, 1964; Player Washington Capitals, 1982—90, St. Louis Blues, 1990—91; capt. NJ Devils, 1991—2005. Played in NHL All-Star Game, 1985, 89, 91-94, 96; named to NHL All-Rookie Team, 1982-83, Sporting News All-Star Second Team, 1987-88, NHL All-Star First Team, 1987-88, 93-94, 2004, NHL All-Star Second Team, 1991-92, Sporting News All-Star First Team, 1993-94; recipient Conn Smythe Trophy, 2000; set NHL record for games played by a defenseman. Achievements include being a member of Stanley Cup Champion NJ Devils, 1995, 2000, 2003; having his number, 4, retired by NJ Devils, 2006. Office: c/o NJ Devils Continental Airlines Arena PO Box 504 East Rutherford NJ 07073-0504*

**STEVENS, SHANE,** novelist; s. John and Caroline (Royale) S. MA, Columbia U. Mem. numerous writers confs. including Bread Loaf, Santa Barbara Writers Conf. Author: Go Down Dead, Way Uptown in Another World, Dead City, Rat Pack, By Reason of Insanity, The Anvil Chorus; (as J.W. Rider) Jersey Tomatoes (Best Novel award), Hot Tickets; contbr. articles to pubs. including N.Y. Times, Life, Washington Post; screenwriter: By Reason of Insanity, The Me Nobody Knows. Mem. Authors Guild, Writers Guild Am.

**STEVENS, SHEILA MAUREEN,** retired teachers union administrator; b. Glendale, Calif., Nov. 1, 1942; d. Richard Chase and Sheila Mary (Beatty) Flynn; m. Ian Whitney Stevens, Sept. 12, 1964; children: Ian Whitney, Bevin Michelle. AA in Liberal Arts, Monterey Peninsula Coll., Calif., 1963; BA in Anthropology, Calif. State U., Long Beach, 1969; postgrad. studies in Edn., U. Guam, 1976-77. Tchr. U.S. Trust Territory of the Pacific, Koror, Palau Island, 1968-72, Kolonia, Ponape Island, 1972-76, Dept. Edn., Agana, Guam, 1976-79; newspaper editor Pacific Daily News (Gannett), Agana, 1979-83; comm. dir. Guam Fedn. of Tchrs., Agana, 1983-84, exec. dir., 1984-85, Alaska Fedn. Tchrs., Anchorage, 1985-87; labor rels. specialist N.Y. State United Tchrs., Watertown, 1987-93, regional staff dir. Potsdam, 1993—2003; ret., 2003. Mem. Gov.'s Blue Ribbon Panel on Edn., Agana, Guam, 1983-85; leadership devel. coord. Am. Fedn. Tchrs., Washington, 1983—; trainer positive negotiations program Situation Mgmt. Sys., Hanover, Mass., 1988—. Author: editor: Pacific Daily News, 1981-83 (Guam Press Club awards 1981, 82, 83); contbr. articles to mag. and jours. Mem. task force on labor policy, com. on self determination, Govt. of Guam, Agana, 1984-85, Adult Basic Edn. Planning Com., 1985; mem. labor studies adv. bd., Anchorage, Alaska, 1989, regional compact coalition N.Y. State Edn. Dept., Albany, 1994; del. NY State Labor Religion Coalition. Named Friend of Edn., Carthage (N.Y.) Tchrs. Assn., 1990. Mem. NOW, ACLU, ASCD, AAUW, Am. Fedn. Tchrs. Comm. Assn. (Best Editorial award 1984), Indsl. Rels. Rsch. Assn. Democrat. Methodist. Avocations: travel, reading, free-lance writing, cross country skiing. Personal E-mail: seawings49@hotmail.com.

**STEVENS, STANLEY DAVID,** historian, researcher, retired librarian, archivist; b. San Francisco, Nov. 10, 1933; s. David Franklin and Ellen Myrtle (Wixson) S.; m. Carli Ann Lewis, Sept. 3, 1960; adopted children: Alexander Lewis, Nikolas Harriman, Brooke Cayton Stevens. BA, San Jose (Calif.) State U., 1959. Conf. officer polit. and security com. 14th Gen. Assembly, UN, NYC, 1959; map libr. U. Calif., Santa Cruz, 1965-93, ret., 1993, coord. Hihn-Younger Archive, Univ. Libr., 1994—. Mem. Cartographic Users Adv. Coun., 1976-86, chmn., 1982-86; presenter in field; adj. prof. libr. sci. San Jose State U., 1989, 91. Author: Index to Guinn's Biographical Record of Santa Cruz, San Benito, Monterey and San Luis Obispo Counties, Catalog of aerial photos by Fairchild Aerial Surveys, Inc. now in the collections of the Dept. Geography, UCLA, 1982, Correspondence of Charles B. Younger Sr. and Charles B. Younger Jr., Santa Cruz, California Attorneys and Counsellors at Law, vols. 1-13, 1996—, indexed edit. Santa Cruz County, Calif., 1997, Index to Personal Names, Portraits & Illustrations Appearing in California City, County & Regional Histories 1867-1910, 2005; editor, Santa Cruz County History Jour., 1994-96, 98, Index to Sidewalk Companion to Santa Cruz Architecture, 3d edit., 2005; co-author A Legal History of Santa Cruz County: an account of the local bench and bar through the end of the Twentieth Century, 2006; The Rowland West & The Content of the Leon Rowland Collection, 2006; also 10 others related to Hihn-Younger Archive; prodn. editor: Index to Boulder Creek Mountain Echo, 1896-1916, 1999; contbr. over 100 articles to profl. jours Mem. adv. com. archaeol. program Cabrillo Coll., Aptos, Calif., 1985—; bd. dirs. Santa Cruz County Hist. Soc., 1985-94, chmn. publs. com., 1985-96, mem. programs adv. coun., 1994-95; mem. Santa Cruz Orgn. for Progress and Euthenics, 1987—; bd. dirs. Friends of U. Calif.-Santa Cruz Libr., 1994-97; founding mem. Rschr. Anonymous, Santa Cruz, 1993—; mem. U. Calif.-Santa Cruz Emeriti Group, sec.-treas. 1996—; mem. collections adv. com. Santa Cruz City Mus. Natural History, 1995—; mem. publs. com. Mus. Art and History, 2000—; vol. Spl. Collections, Univ. Libr., U. Calif., Santa Cruz, 1994—. With U.S. Army, 1954-56. Recipient honors award geography and map divsn. for outstanding achievement in map librarianship Spl. Librs. Assn., 1981, cert. of commendation Santa Cruz Hist. Soc., 1986, appreciation cert. for svcs. Assn. Info. and Image Mgmt., 1989, Proclamation of Honor, Santa Cruz County Bd. Suprs., 1998, Historian of Yr. award History Forum of Santa Cruz Mus. of Art and History, 2001; grantee Librs. Assn. U. Calif., 1981-82, rsch. grantee Office of Pres., U. Calif., 1985-86. Mem. ALA (publs. com. Map and Geography Round Table 1985-86, editl. bd. Meridian 1989-2000, honors award Map and Geography Round Table 1992), ACLU (mem. bd. dirs. Santa Cruz County chpt. 1962-68, bd. dirs. No. Calif. br. 1973-76), Western Assn. Map Librs. (hon. life, founding pres. 1967-68, treas. 1968-89, editor Info. Bull. 1969-84, Exec. Com. award 1984, Stanley D. Stevens Hon. Map presented at 30th anniversary meeting 1997, Calif. Hist. Soc., Calif. Map Soc., Pajaro Valley Hist. Assn., Santa Cruz County Geneal. Soc., Capitola Hist. Soc., El Paso de Robles Hist. Soc. (life). Democrat. Avocations: researching local history, listening to jazz and classical music. Home: 231 13th Ave Santa Cruz CA 95062-4831 Office: U Calif Dean E McHenry Libr Santa Cruz CA 95064 Business E-Mail: sstevens@library.ucsc.edu.

**STEVENS, STANLEY M.,** lawyer; b. Dec. 21, 1948; m. Kristin Stevens. BA, U. Mo., Columbia, 1970; JD, U. Chgo., 1973. Bar: Ga. 1973, US Dist. Ct. No. Dist. Ga. 1974, Ill. 1976, US. Dist. Ct. No. Dist. Ill. 1977, Fla. 1987, US Dist. Ct. Mid. Dist. Fla. 1987. Exec. v.p., chief legal counsel, sec. Equity Office Properties Trust, Chgo., 1996—. Office: Equity Office Properties Trust 2 N Riverside Plz Ste 2100 Chicago IL 60606

**STEVENS, SUFJAN,** musician; b. Detroit, July 1, 1975; Band mem. Marzuki, Holland, Mich.; solo career, 1999—; co-founder Asthmatic Kitty Records, Mich., 1999—. Musician: (albums) A Sun Came, 2000, Enjoy Your Rabbit, 2001, Greetings from Michigan: The Great Lakes State, 2003, Seven Swans, 2004, Illinois, 2005, The Avalanche, 2006. Recipient New Pantheon award, 2006. Office: Asthmatic Kitty Records PO Box 1282 Lander WY 82520 E-mail: info@asthmatickitty.com.*

**STEVENS, SUSAN SELTENREICH CIRILLO,** special education educator; b. Rockville Centre, NY, Apr. 16, 1962; d. Richard Paul and Estelle Duboise Seltenreich; m. John Stafford Cirillo (div.); children: Adam Cirillo, Jeremy Cirillo, Nicholas Cirillo; m. Peter Stevens, Oct. 4, 2003. AS in Early Childhood Edn., SUNY, Farmingdale, 1982; BS in Edn., SUNY, Geneseo, 1986; MEd, U. North Tex., 1992. Cert. lay min. United Meth. Ch. of N.Y., local lay min. United Meth. Ch. of N.Y.; spl. edn. tchr. N.Y. nursery, kindergarten, grades 1-6 N.Y., spl. edn. tchr. K-12 Wash., tchr. ESL Wash., elem. edn. tchr. Wash., early childhood educator Wash., spl. edn. tchr. Tex., tchr. ESL Tex., elem. edn. tchr. Tex., kindergarten tchr. Tex. Spl. edn. tchr. United Cerebral Palsy of Queens, Jamaica, NY, 1987—88; elem. and ESL educator Herbert Marcus Elem. Sch., Dallas Ind. Sch. Dist., 1988—92; spl. edn. educator Hillcrest H.S., 1994—96; enrichment educator The Huntington Learning Ctr., Issaquah, Wash., 1999—2000; spl. edn. educator Beaver Lake Mid. Sch., Issaquah Sch. Dist., 2000—02; spl. edn. educator Silas Wood 6th Grade Ctr., South Huntington Union Free Sch. Dist., Huntington Sta., NY, 2000—. Author: (poetry) Mellie the Muskrat, 2004. Lay min., mem. edn. com., Sunday sch. educator, children's sermon min. Dix Hills (N.Y.) United Meth. Ch., 2002—05; Sunday sch. educator Faith United Meth. Ch.,

Issaquah, 2000—02, St. John's Luth. Ch., Columbia, Md., 1996—98; Sunday sch. educator, mem. worship and music coun. Preston Meadow Luth. Ch., Plano, Tex., 1988—96. Fellow ednl. grantee, South Huntington Parent Tchr. Ctr., 2004. Mem.: Coun. Exceptional Children (assoc.). Avocations: poetry, travel. Home: 3 Wexford St Huntington NY 11743 Office: Silas Wood 6th Grade Ctr 23 Harding Pl Huntington Station NY 11746 Office Phone: 631-425-5515. Personal E-mail: susanc001@msn.com. E-mail: sstevens@shufsd.org.

**STEVENS, TED (THEODORE FULTON STEVENS),** senator; b. Indpls., Nov. 18, 1923; s. George A. and Gertrude (Chancellor) S.; m. Ann Mary Cherrington, Mar. 29, 1952 (dec. 1978); children: Susan B., Elizabeth H., Walter C., Theodore Fulton, Ben A.; m. Catherine Chandler, 1980; 1 child, Lily Irene. BA, U. Calif. at Los Angeles, 1947; LL.B., Harvard U., 1950. Bar: Calif., Alaska, D.C., U.S. Supreme Ct. bars. Pvt. practice, Washington, 1950-52, Fairbanks, Alaska, 1953; U.S. atty. Dist. Alaska US Dept. Justice, Fairbanks, 1953-56; legis. counsel US Dept. Interior, Washington, 1956—57, asst to sec., 1958—59, solicitor, 1960; pvt. law practice Anchorage, 1961-68; mem. Alaska Ho. of Reps., 1965-68, majority leader, speaker pro tem, 1967-68; US Senator from Alaska, 1968—; asst. Rep. leader, 1977-85; pres. pro tempore, 2003—; chair appropriations com., 1997—2001, 2003—05, commerce com., 2005—; co-chair sci. com., 2005—. Served in USAAF, 1943—46. Decorated Disting. Flying Cross, Air medal, Yuan Hai medal. Mem. ABA, Alaska Bar Assn., Calif. Bar Assn., D.C. Bar Assn., Am. Legion, VFW. Lodges: Rotary, Pioneers of Alaska, Igloo #4. Republican. Episcopalian. Office: US Senate 522 Hart Senate Bldg Washington DC 20510-0001

**STEVENS, THELMA KAPLAN,** artist, educator; b. N.Y.C., Dec. 4, 1932; d. Nathan and Shirley (Laufer) Kaplan; m. Jay P. Stevens, Mar. 17, 1956; children: Wendy, Andrew BS, Pratt Inst., 1954; MS, Queens Coll., 1959; PhD, Fordham U., 1980. Tchr. art pub. schs., NY, 1954—88; instr. Grad. Sch. Fordham U., N.Y.C., 1979; pres. Isis Gallery Ltd., Searingtown, NY, 1982—. Pres. Reunions to Remember, Manhasset, NY, 1996—. Co-author: Super Sculpture, 1974; contbr. numerous articles to profl. jours Mem. Internat. Soc. Edn. Thru Art (N.Y. state rep. 1989—), U.S. Soc. for Edn. Thru Art, N.Y. State Art Tchrs. Assn., Nat. Art Edn. Assn. (dir. ea. region U.S. and Can. secondary art edn. 1986-89, N.Y. State Art Educator of Yr. 1983), James Madison H.S. Alumni Assn. (pres. 1995-2004, bd. dirs.) Avocations: travel, reading, cooking, theater. Studio: Reunions to Remember 565 Plandome Rd # 130 Manhasset NY 11030 Office Phone: 516-944-2240.

**STEVENS, THOMAS CHARLES,** lawyer; b. Auburn, N.Y., Oct. 17, 1949; s. Alice (Kerlin) S.; m. Christine Eleanor Brown, June 2, 1973; children: Erin, Leigh, Timothy. BA, SUNY, Albany, 1971; JD, Duke U., 1974. Bar: Ohio 1974. Mng. ptnr. Thompson, Hine & Flory, Cleve., 1991-96; vice-chmn. KeyCorp., Cleve., 1996—, chief adminstrv. officer, 1996—. Bd. dirs. Key-Corp. Trustee Greater Cleve. Growth Assn., 1993-96, Greater Cleve. Round-table, 1993-2003,(chmn. of bd. trustees), Playhouse Sq. Found., 1998—, Greater Cleve. (Ohio) Partnerships, 2003—; active Leadership Cleve., 1992-93, Young Audiences, 1999—, 1999 United Way Campaign; mem. Fin. Svcs. Roundtable, 1997—. Mem. ABA, Cleve. Bar Assn., Am. Soc. Corp. Secs., N.Y. Bankers Assn., Nisi Prius. Office: KeyCorp 127 Public Sq Cleveland OH 44114-1306 E-mail: thomas_stevens@keybank.com.

**STEVENS, THOMAS D., JR.,** secondary school educator, music educator; b. Newington, N.H., Oct. 6, 1977; s. Thomas Dwight Stevens, Sr. and Carol Ann Stevens; m. Jennifer Rae Comtois, June 22, 2002; 1 child, Raechel Grace. BS in Music Edn. K-12, Plymouth State Coll., 2001. Music tchr. Alton (N.H.) Ctrl. Sch., 2001—04, Prospect Mountain H.S., Alton, 2004—. Facilities asst. Prospect Mountain H.S., Alton, 2004—; class advisor Alton Ctrl. Sch. and Prospect Mountain H.S., 2002—; curriculum leader Alton Ctrl. Sch., 2002—04. Youth pastor Faith Cmty. Bible Ch., Loudon, NH, 2004—, worship leader, 2005. Recipient Eagle Scout, Boy Scouts Am., 1993. Mem.: Music Educator's Nat. Conf. (assoc.). Republican. Office: Prospect Mountain High School 242 Suncook Valley Rd Alton NH 03809 Office Phone: 603-875-3800. Office Fax: 603-875-8200. Business E-Mail: tstevens@pmhschool.com.

**STEVENS, WARREN,** actor; b. Clark's Summit, Pa., Nov. 2, 1919; s. Albert Clifford and Helen Dodd (Blakeslee) S.; m. Barbara Helen Fletcher, Sept. 9, 1969; children—Adam Fletcher, Matthew Dodd; l son by previous marriage, Laurence Blakeslee. Student, U.S. Naval Acad., 1939-40. Appeared on: New York stage in Galileo, 1947, Sundown Beach, 1948, Smile of the World, 1949, Detective Story, 1949; appeared in numerous motion pictures, since 1950, including, Barefoot Contessa, Forbidden Planet; appeared on: numerous television shows, including Richard Boone Rep. With USN, 1937-40; with USAAF, 1942-46. Mem. Actors Studio.

**STEVENS, WILBUR HUNT,** accountant; b. Spencer, Ind., June 20, 1918; s. John Vosburgh and Isabelle Jane (Strawser) S.; m. Maxine Dodge Stevens, Sept. 28, 1941; children: Linda Maxine Piffero, Deborah Anne Augello. BS, MBA, U. Calif., Berkeley, 1949. CPA, Calif.; cert. fraud examiner, fin. svcs. auditor; diplomate Am. Bd. Forensic Acctg. Staff acct. McLaren, Goode, West & Co., San Francisco, 1949-52; mng. ptnr. Wilbur H. Stevens & Co., Salinas, Calif., 1952-70; regional ptnr. Fox & Co., CPAs, Salinas, 1970-73, nat. dir. banking practice Denver, 1973-80; pres., chmn. Wilbur H. Stevens, CPA, PC, Salinas, 1980-94; chmn. Stevens, Sloan & Shah, CPAs, 1994—. Adj. prof. acctg. U. Denver, 1975-78; faculty mem. Assemblies for Bank Dirs., So. Meth. U., Dallas, 1976-81, Nat. Banking Sch., U. Va., Charlottesville, 1979-87; chmn., dir. Valley Nat. Bank, 1963-71, Pacific Ag Credit, Inc., 1997; dir. World Travel, Inc., p., dir. Dirs. Coun. Ind. Banks, Global Uplift, Inc. Editor Issues in CPA Practice, 1975; contbr. articles to profl. jours. Capt. AUS, 1942-53. Decorated Bronze Star; Frank G. Drum fellow U. Calif., Berkeley, 1949. Mem. AICPA (v.p. 1971), Am. Acctg. Assn., Am. Assembly Collegiate Schs. Bus. (accreditation coun. 1975-78, 81-84), Nat. Assn. State Bds. Accountancy (pres. 1976-77, strategic initiatives com. 1997-99), Inst. Internal Auditors (fin. svcs. group), Am. Acad. Cert. Consultants and Experts, Calif. Soc. CPAs (pres. 1968-69, Disting. Svc. award 1988), Acctg. Rsch. Assn. (pres. 1973-75), Acad. Acctg. Historians, Assn. Cert. Fraud Examiners, Am. Coll. Forensic Examiners, Cert. Calif. Past Masters Assn. (pres. 1998), Burma Star Assn., CBI Vets. Assn., 14 AF Assn., Hump Pilots Assn., Salinas C. of C. (pres. 1960), Commonwealth Club Calif., Masons (master 1992, 97, Hiram award 1998, grand lodge com. taxation), Knight Templar (comdr. 2000), Royal Arch (high priest 1998, grand chpt. inspector 1999-2000), Cryptic Masons (illus. master 2000), Knight Masons Am., Royal Order Scotland, 32 degree Scottish Rite, Nat. Sojourners (pres. Monterey Bay chpt. 1996), Heroes of '76 (comdr. John C. Fremont chpt. 1996-97), Fed. for Collingwood Libr. and Mus., Red Cross of Constantine, Salinas High Twelve Club (pres. 1995), Philalethes Soc., QCCC, London, Rotary (dist. gov. 1983, chmn. internat. fellowship accounts 1994-96, Paul Harris fellow 1973), Phi Beta Kappa, Beta Gamma Sigma (v.p. 1949), Beta Alpha Psi. Republican. Methodist. Home: 38 Santa Ana Dr Salinas CA 93901-4136 Office: 975 W Alisal St Ste D Salinas CA 93901-1148

**STEVENS, WILLIAM DOLLARD,** mechanical engineer, consultant; b. Bayonne, NJ, Aug. 4, 1918; s. William B. and Beatrice (Dollard) S.; m. Mary E. King, Oct. 12, 1940; children: Sandra A. (Mrs. Jeffrey N. Melin), Barbara E. (Mrs. Dennis Gallagher), William K. BSME, Rensselaer Poly. Inst., 1940; postgrad., Case Inst. Tech., 1958; DSc (hon.), N.J. Inst. Tech., 1986. Various engring. and mgmt. positions Babcock & Wilcox Co., N.Y.C., 1940-62; v.p. equipment div. Foster Wheeler Corp., Livingston, NJ, 1962-73, sr. v.p., 1972-74, exec. v.p., 1974-78, chmn. bd., 1978-81, dir., 1974-86, dir. emeritus, 1986-90; bd. of dir. Am. Soc. for Macro Engring., 1992—2001. Instr. Pratt Inst., 1946-47; bd. overseers N.J. Inst. Tech., 1978-94. Contbr. articles to profl. jours.; patentee in field Chmn. fund drive ARC, Hackensack, N.J., 1956; planning commr., Hackensack, 1952-58; trustee Bergen County Mental Health Consultation Ctr., 1955-58; bd. dirs. Metals Properties Coun.; mem. coun. Rensselaer Polytech. Inst., 1983—. Lt. USNR, 1943-45. Fellow ASME.

---

mem. Nat. Acad. Engring., Sigma Xi, Tau Beta Pi, Phi Kappa Tau, Pi Tau Sigma. Methodist. Home and Office: 3302 Pointe Gate Rd Livingston NJ 07039 E-mail: wmdstevens3@verizon.net.

**STEVENS, WILLIAM KENNETH,** lawyer; b. Chgo., Apr. 19, 1917; s. Ernest James and Elizabeth (Street) S.; m. Anne Hughes, Jan. 4, 1943; children: Anne Elizabeth Stevens Fishman, William Hughes Stevens, Mary Carol Stevens Williams, Martha Street Stevens Gingrich. AB cum laude, U. Calif., Berkeley, 1938; MA, U. Chgo., 1940; JD, Harvard U., 1948. Bar: Ill. 1948, Fla. 1977. With First Nat. Bank Chgo., 1948-74, asst. v.p., 1958-61, v.p., 1961-74; ptnr. McDermott, Will & Emery, Chgo., 1974-85, Myers Krause & Stevens, Naples, Fla., 1986—2001; of counsel Fowler White Boggs Banker, Naples, Fla., 2001—. Author: Illinois Estate Administration, 1968. Chmn. Ill. Inst. Continuing Legal Edn., 1971-72; pres. Hinsdale (Ill.) Pub. Libr., 1977-79. Lt. USNR, 1941-45. Recipient Disting. Svc. award Chgo. Estate Planning Coun., 1981. Fellow Am. Coll. Trust and Estate Counsel; mem. ABA, Am. Law Inst., Chgo. Bar Assn., Ill. Bar Assn., Fla. Bar Assn. (bd. cert. estate planning and probate lawyer), Internat. Acad. Estate and Trust Law. Clubs: Mid-Day, Hinsdale Golf; Chikaming Country (Lakeside, Mich.), The Club at Pelican Bay (Naples). Office: Ste 600 5811 Pelican Bay Blvd Naples FL 34108-2711 E-mail: wstevens@fowlerwhite.com.

**STEVENS, WILLIAM TALBERT,** financial services executive; b. Houston, Mar. 11, 1952; s. Talbert Maxton and Peggy Elizabeth (Cagle) S.; m. Christine Leslie Treml, May 24, 1975; 1 child, Anne Kathleen. BBA, Pacific Western U., 1988. Mgr. Capital Fin. Svcs. Akron, Ohio, 1975-80, Beneficial Mgmt., Columbus, Ohio, 1980-85; v.p. Mid Am. fed. Savs. and Loan, Columbus, 1985-87, Lender's Svc., Inc., Pitts., 1987-89; pres. Equity Mgmt. Svcs., Inc., Pitts., 1989-90; sr. v.p. CBC Cos., Pitts., 1990—2001, Gen. Am. Corp., Pitts., 2001—. Mem. faculty, bd. govs. Nat. Inst. Consumer Credit Mgmt. Marquette U., Milw., 1988-94. Recipient Pres.'s Disting. Achievement Beneficial Mgmt., 1982, 83. Avocation: golf. Office: Gen Am Corp 700 Grant St Pittsburgh PA 15219 also: CBC Cos 520 E Main St Carnegie PA 15106-2051 Office Phone: 412-261-4791.

**STEVENS, YVETTE MARIE See KHAN, CHAKA**

**STEVENSON, A. BROCKIE,** retired artist; b. Montgomery County, Pa., Sept. 24, 1919; s. Alfred Brockie and Caroline Lansdale (Sill) Stevenson; m. Jane Merriman Mackenzie, Dec. 23, 1978. Student, Pa. Acad. Fine Arts, 1940-41, 46-50, Barnes Found., 1946-48, Skowhegan Sch., Maine, 1950. Instr. Sch. Fine Arts, Washington U., St. Louis, 1960-62; head dept. painting and drawing Corcoran Sch. Art, 1965-81, from assoc. prof. to prof. design, painting, drawing & watercolor, 1965-98; ret., 1998. One-man shows include War Paintings, London and Salisbury, Eng., 1944, Instituto Cultural Peruano-Norteamericano, Lima, Peru, 1953, Art Ctr., Miraflores, Peru, 1958, 1960, Assn. Cultural Peruano-Britanica, Lima, 1959, Mickelson Gallery, Washington, 1970, Pyramid Galleries Ltd., 1973, No. Va. C.C., 1974, Fendrick Gallery, Washington, 1978, 1984, 1988, exhibited in group shows at Nat. Gallery Art, London, 1944, Pa. Acad. Fine Arts, Phila., 1948—51, Sociedad Bellas Artes del Peru, Lima, 1953—56, SUNY, Potsdam and Albany, 1971, Columbia (S.C.) Mus. Art, 1971, EXPO '74, Spokane, Wash., 1974, Corcoran Gallery, Washington, 1980, retrospective, Villanova (Pa.) U., 2002, Strath-more Hall Arts Ctr., Bethesda, Md., 2004, Represented in permanent collections Corcoaran Gallery Art, Washington, Dept. Def., Nat. Mus. Am. Art, Phillips Collection, Fed. Res. Bank, Richmond, Va., Woodward Found., Washington, Ogunquit (Maine) Mus. Art, Brown U. Libr. Milit. Coll., Providence, one-man shows include Villanova U., 2002. With U.S. Army, 1941—45, ETO. Home: 6106 Yale Ave Glen Echo MD 20812-1122

**STEVENSON, ADLAI EWING, III,** lawyer, retired senator; b. Chgo., Oct. 10, 1930; s. Adlai Ewing and Ellen (Borden) S.; m. Nancy L. Anderson, June 25, 1955; children: Adlai Ewing IV, Lucy W., Katherine R., Warwick L. Grad., Milton Acad., 1948; AB, Harvard U., 1952, LL.B., 1957. Bar: Ill. 1957, D.C. 1977. Law clk. Ill. Supreme Ct., 1957-58; assoc. Mayer, Brown & Platt, Chgo., 1958-66, ptnr., 1966-67, 81-83, of counsel, 1983-91; treas. State of Ill., 1967-70; U.S. senator from Ill., 1970-81; chmn. SC&M Internat. Ltd., Chgo., 1991-95, pres., 1995-98, chmn. of bd., 1998—. Mem. Ill. Ho. of Reps., 1965-67; Dem. candidate for gov. of Ill., 1982, 86. Capt. USMCR, 1952-54. Office: Ste 750 20 N Clark St Chicago IL 60602 Office Phone: 773-281-3578.

**STEVENSON, ALEXANDRA,** professional tennis player; b. San Diego, Calif., Dec. 15, 1980; d. Samantha. Student, U. Colo. Mem. U.S. Fed Cup Team, 2003. Winner ITF/Midland, Mich., 1998, 13 of 15 grass court matches, 1999; semifinalist Wimbledon, 1999, U.S. Open, 1999; mem. U.S. Pan Am Games Team, 1999; jr. competition winner U.S. Open Jr., 1997, USTA Nat. Girls' 18s, 1997; jr. competition singles finalist USTA Nat. Girls' 18 Clay Courts, 1996; named Roles Rookie of the Yr., Tennis Mag., 1999. Avocations: singing, ballet, swimming, dance.

**STEVENSON, AMANDA (SANDY STEVENS),** librettist, composer, song-writer; b. Bklyn., Oct. 24, 1943; d. Haakon and Grace Svendsen. Cert. Nat. Bur. Document Examiners. Composer, librettist, Nellie Bly, Victorine, (screenplay) The Last Assignment Mem. Actors Equity Assn., BMI, Song-writers Guild. Democrat. Avocations: chess, art history, song-writing. Home and Office: 35-43 84th St Jackson Heights NY 11372 Office Phone: 718-429-9998.

**STEVENSON, BEN,** artistic director; b. Portsmouth, Eng., Apr. 4, 1936; arrived in U.S., 1968; s. Benjamin John and Florence May (Gundry) S.; m. Joan Tuasdvine, Jan. 6, 1968. Grad., Arts Ednl. Sch., London, 1955. Artistic dir. Harkness Ballet Youth Dancers, 1968—71, Chgo. Ballet, 1974—75, Houston Ballet, 1973—2003, artistic dir. emeritus, 2003—; co-dir. Nat. Ballet, Washington, 1971—74; artistic dir. Tex. Ballet Theater, 2003—. Mem. dance panel Tex. Commn. Arts, 1977; guest tchr. Am. Ballet Theatre, Joffrey Ballet, Royal Ballet, London, Beijing Dance Acad. Dancer Theatre Arts Ballet, London, 1952-54, Sadler's Wells Theatre Ballet, 1955-56, Royal Ballet, 1956-60, London Festival Ballet, 1960-62; appearances in Wedding in Paris, 1954-55, Music Man, London, 1962-63, Half a Sixpence, also, Boys in Syracuse, London, 1964; prin. dancer, ballet master, London Festival Ballet, 1964-68; prin. ballets choreographed include Three Faces of Eve, 1965, Cast Out, 1966, Sleeping Beauty (full length), 1967, 71, 76, 78, Fervor, 1968, Three Preludes, 1968, Forbidden, 1969, Cinderella (full length), 1969, 71, 73, 74, 76, Bartok Concerto, 1970, Nutcracker (full length), 1972, 76, Symphonetta, 1972, Courant, 1973, Swan Lake (full length), 1977, L. 1978, Britten Pas de Deux, 1979, Four Last Songs, 1979, Space City, 1980, Peer Gynt (full length), 1981, Zheng Ban Qiao, 1982, The Prince of Pagodas, 1986 Recipient 1st prize London Choreographic competitions, 1965, 66, 67, modern ballet choreography Internat. Ballet Competition, Varna, Bulgaria, 1972, Gold medal for choreography Internat. Ballet Competition, 1982, Dance mag. award, 2000; named Order of Brit. Empire, 1999. Assoc. mem. Royal Acad. Dancing (Adeline Genee Gold medal 1955) Office: Tex Ballet Theatre 6845 Green Oaks Rd Fort Worth TX 76116 Office Phone: 817-763-0207 817-763-0207. E-mail: bstevenson@texasballettheater.org.*

**STEVENSON, BRYAN ALLEN,** lawyer; b. Milton, Del., Nov. 14, 1959; s. Howard Carlton and Alice Gertrude (Golden) S. BA, Eastern Coll., St. Davids, Pa., 1981; MPP, Kennedy Sch. Govt., Cambridge, Mass., 1985; JD, Harvard U., 1985. Bar: Ga. 1985, Ala. 1987. Staff atty. So. Prisoners Def. Com., Atlanta, 1985-89; exec. dir. Ala. Capital Representation Resource Ctr., Montgomery, 1989-95; dir. Equal Justice Initiative of Ala., Montgomery, 1995—. Vis. prof. law NYU Sch. Law, 1997, U. Mich. Law Sch., 1995. Contbr. articles to publs. Recipient MacArthur Found. award, Thurgood Marshall medal of justice, Nat. Human Rights award Reebol Human Rights Found., 1989, ACLU Medal of Liberty, 1991, ABA Wisdom Award for Pub. Svc., 1991; Harvard Law Sch. Pub. Interest fellow, 1985. Avocations: music, piano and keyboards. Office: Equal LJustice Initiative of Alabama 122 Commerce St Montgomery AL 36104-2538

---

**STEVENSON, DAVID WAYNE,** municipal official; b. Commerce, Tex., Aug. 9, 1957; s. Billy Wayne Stevenson and Constance Marie-Essary Underwood; m. Tami Gail Thomas; children: James David, Ashlei Gail Jones, John Thomas, Amber Michelle. Degree in acctg., Tyler Cornell. Coll., 1976. Office mgr. Fountain & Holdredge CPA, Athens, Tex., 1976—78; brakeman Union Pacific RR, Mineola, Tex., 1978—86; firefighter City of Mineola, 1986—94, city sec., 1994—. Firefighting instr. Tex. A&M, College Station; mem. homeland security adv. bd. East Tex. Coun. of Govts., Kilgore, 2003—; mem. adv. bd. Nat. Coun. Readiness and Preparedness, Washington, 2005—. Chief Mineola Vol. Fire Dept., 1997—. Named Mineola Man of Yr., Mineola C. of C., 1997, Mineola Firefighter of Yr., Mineola Fire Dept., 1990, 1994; named to Leadership Mineola, C. of C., 1997. Mem.: Tex. State Fireman's and Fire Marshal's Assn., Wood County Fire Chiefs Assn. (pres. 1998—99), Kiwanis (pres. 1997). Methodist. Avocations: hunting, golf, reading. Office: City of Mineola 300 Greenville Ave Mineola TX 75773 Office Phone: 903-569-6183. Business E-Mail: dstevenson@mineola.com.

**STEVENSON, DENISE L.,** diversified financial services company executive, consultant, realtor; b. Washington, Sept. 18, 1946; d. Pierre and Alice (Mardrus) D'Auga; m. Walter Henry Stevenson, Oct. 17, 1970 (div. 1990). AA, Montgomery Coll., 1967; BA in Econs./Bus. Mgmt., N.C. State U., 1983; cert. legal asst., Meredith Coll., 1989; cert. in mgmt., Fin. Women Internat., 1990. Lic. ins. agt.; accredited buyer rep. Nat. Assn. of Realtors, grad. Realtor Inst., sr. real estate specialist, e-PRO Coun. of Residential Spleciaists, cert. new home specialist. Savs. counselor Perpetual Bldg. Assn. (now Crestar Bank), Washington, 1968—70; regional asst. v.p 1st Fed. Savs. (now Centura Bank, Rocky Mount), NC, 1971—83; pres. owner Diversified Learning Svcs., Raleigh, 1983—; pres., treas. Daily Life Svcs., Inc., 1994—99; realtor Prudential Carolinas Realty, 2002—. Instr. Inst. Fin. Edn., Raleigh, 1983—89, Am. Inst. Banking, 1986. Mem. Am. Bus. Women's Assn. (Woman of Yr. 1982), Fin. Women Internat. (cert. leader 1987, Mem. of Yr. award 1992, N.C. Woman of Yr. 1992), Laurel Hills Women's Club (pres. 1974-75, Raleigh), Omicron Delta Epsilon, Broker Assoc. Hon. Soc. Avocation: fishing. Office: Diversified Learning Svcs PO Box 33231 Raleigh NC 27636-3231 E-mail: divlrnserv@aol.com.

**STEVENSON, EDWARD WARD,** retired otolaryngologist, surgeon; b. Chester, S.C., Jan. 9, 1926; s. Thomas M. and Annie Lou (Ward) S.; m. Dorothy Giles, Sept. 2, 1947; children: Sally Anne Stevenson Yeilding, Laura Stevenson Healy, Nancy Stevenson Schonbeger (dec.), Molly Stevenson Walker. B in Medicine, Duke U., 1945; MD, U. Md., Balt., 1949. Intern Bapt. Meml. Hosp., Memphis, 1949-50; resident Med. Coll. Va. Hosp., Richmond, 1953-55; fellow Ochsner Found. Hosp., New Orleans, 1955-56; staff oto-laryngologist Ochsner Clinic, 1956-57; pvt. practice Birmingham, 1957-60, 65-94, 1965—94; instr., clin. asst. prof. surgery U. Ala., 1957-94; pvt. practice Decatur, 1960-65; ret., 1994. Faculty Tulane U. Sch. Medicine, 1956-57; staff Bapt. Med. Ctr.-Montclair, Birmingham. Contbr. articles to profl. jours. Bd. dirs. So. Mus. Flight, Birmingham, 1989—, Ala. Aviation Hall of Fame, chmn. pres, 2003, bd. dirs., 2003—; pres. Birmingham Aero Club, 1996. Lt. M.C. USNR, 1949—53. Mem. AMA, ACS, Am. Laryngol., Rhinol. and Otol. Soc. (sec.- treas. so. sect. 1990-93, v.p. so. sect. 1993-94), Am. Soc. Head and Neck Surgery, Am. Acad. Otolary., Jefferson County Med. Soc., Ala. Otolaryn. Soc. (founder, pres. 1971), Med. Assn. State Ala., Morgan County Med. Soc. (pres. 1964-65), Tri-State Otolarynx. Assembly (co-founder), Birmngham Otolaryn. Soc. (pres. 1984), Birmingham Down-town Rotary Club. Methodist. Avocations: aerobatic flying, world travel. Home: 4249 Antietam Dr Birmingham AL 35213-3221 E-mail: edstevenson@bellsouth.net.

**STEVENSON, FRANCES KELLOGG,** museum program director; b. Boston; d. Charles Summers and Alice deGueldry (Stevens) S.; m. James Richard Wein, 1971 (div. 1989). BA, Wells Coll., Aurora, N.Y., 1967; MA, Oxford U., England, 1972; MBA, U. Pa., Phila., 1992. Publs. officer Nat. Portrait Gallery Smithsonian Instn., Washington, 1974—2001, strategic planning officer, 2001—. Bd. mem. Am. Friends of St. Hilda's Coll., Oxford U.; mem. St. John's Episcopal Ch., Georgetown; James E. Webb fellow Smithsonian Instn., 1988-89. Mem. Sulgrave Club, Am. Friends St. Hilda's coll., Oxford U. (bd. mem.). Home: 2724 Ordway St NW Apt 4 Washington DC 20008-5047 Office: Smithsonian Instn Nat Portrait Gallery PO Box 37010 Victor Bldg MRC 973 Washington DC 20013-7012

**STEVENSON, GARTH,** social sciences educator; b. Montreal, Que., Can., Apr. 7, 1943; s. Andrew Archibald Stevenson and Ruth Graham (Scott) Swinton; m. Carol Barbara Krell, Aug. 10, 1968 (div. 1983); children: Colin, Fiona, Moira; m. Yvonne Brown, Aug. 5, 1983 (separated 2005); 1 child, Jacqueline. BA, McGill U., Montreal, 1963, MA, 1965; PhD, Princeton U., 1971. Asst. prof. Carleton U., Ottawa, Ont., 1968—76, assoc. prof., 1976—78, U. Alberta, Edmonton, Alberta, Canada, 1978—82, prof., 1982—87, Brock U., St. Catharines, Ont., Canada, 1987—, chmn. dept. polit. sci., 2003—06. Vis. prof. Duke U., Durham, NC, 1992—93. Author: The Politics of Canada's Airlines, 1987, Ex Uno Plures, 1993, Community Besieged, 1999, Parallel Paths, 2006. Candidate in Canadian Gen. Election New Democratic Party, Edmonton North, Alberta, 1984. Mem.: World Soc. for Protection of Animals, United Nations Assn. in Can., Canadian Railroad Hist. Assn., Amnesty Internat. Canadian Civil Liberties Assn., Internat. Polit. Sci. Assn., Canadian Polit. Sci. Assn. (bd. dirs 1988—2000), Am. Polit. Sci. Assn. Anglican Ch. Of Canada. Office: Brock U 500 Glenridge Ave Saint Catharines ON Canada L2S 3A1 Address: Brock U Polit Sci Dept PO Box 1600 Lewiston NY 14092-5000 Office Phone: 905-688-5550. Business E-Mail: stevensn@brocku.ca.

**STEVENSON, HOWARD HIGGINBOTHAM,** business educator; b. Salt Lake City, June 27, 1941; s. Ralph Shields and Dorothy Dee (Higginbotham) S.; m. Fredericka O'Connell; children: William, Charles, Andrew. BS, Stanford U., 1963; MBA, Harvard U., 1965, DBA, 1969. From asst. prof. to prof. Harvard U., Cambridge, Mass., 1968—82, prof., 1982—, sr. assoc. dean for fin. adminstrn., 1991-94, sr. assoc. dean external rels., 2000—04, faculty chair, sr. assoc. provost resources and planning, 2004—. Owner, pres., mgr. Program in Exec. Edn., 1998—2000; chmn. publs. rev. bd. Harvard Bus. Sch. Press, 1999—2000; faculty chmn. Latin. Am. Adv. Bd., 1999—2001; v.p. Simmons Assocs., Boston, 1970—72; v.p. fin. adminstrn. Preco Corp., Mass., Newton, West Springfield, Mass., 1978—81; bd. dirs. Landmark Comms., Norfolk, Va., Camp Dresser and McKee Inc., Cambridge, The Baupost Group, Inc., Boston, Commonwealth Capital Ptnrs., Boston, Nat. Pub. Radio, Washington. Co-author: Policy Formation and Administration, 1984, New Business Ventures and the Entrepreneur, 1985, 89, 94, 5th edit., 1999, Entrepreneurial Ventures, 1992, 2d edit., 1999, Do Lunch or Be Lunch: The Power of Predictability in Creating Your Future, 1997, (with David Amis) Winning Angels: The Seven Fundamentals of Early Stage Investing, 2001, (with David Amis) Winning Angels: Mentors in a Network of Success, 2003, (with Laura Nash) Just Enough: Tools for Creating Success in Your Work and Life, 2004. Trustee Rural Land Found., Lincoln, Mass., 1973-78, Boston Ballet, 1991-2004, Suffield Land Conservancy, Conn., 1978-82; dir. Sudbury Valley Trustees, 1991-2004, pres. bd. trustees, 1996-2000; trustee Nat. Pub. Radio Found., 1998-2003, Mass. Chpt. Nature Conservancy. IBM Nat. Merit scholar, 1959; Ford Found. fellow, 1965. Mem. Fin. Execs. Inst., Acad. Mgmt., Harvard Club (N.Y.C.). Office: Harvard U 1350 Mass Ave #867 Cambridge MA 02138

**STEVENSON, IAN,** psychiatrist, educator; b. Montreal, Que., Can., Oct. 31, 1918; s. John Alexander and Ruth Cecilia (Preston) m. Octavia Reynolds, Sept. 13, 1947 (dec. Nov. 1983); m. Margaret H. Pertzoff, Nov. 29, 1985. Student, U. St. Andrews, Scotland; BS, McGill U., 1942, MD, CM, 1943. Cert. Am. Bd. Psychiatry, 1952. Asst. prof. medicine La. State U., New Orleans, 1949-52, assoc. prof. psychiatry, 1953-57; prof. psychiatry, chmn. U. Va. Med. Sch., Charlottesville, 1957-67, Carlson prof. psychiatry, head divsn. of personality studies, 1967—2002, rsch. prof. psychiatry, 2001—; assoc. mem. Darwin Coll., U. Cambridge, 1981-96. Author: The Diagnostic Interview, 1960, Twenty Cases Suggestive of Reincarnation, 1966, Reincarnation and Biology, 1997, 10 other books; contbr. 250 articles to profl. jours. Fellow: Am. Psychiat. Assn. (life disting. fellow); mem.: Soc. for Sci.

Exploration (founding com.), Am. Soc. for Psychical Rsch., Soc. for Psychical Rsch. London (coun. and pres. 1988—89), Oxford and Cambridge Club, Colonnade Club. Office: U of Va Health Sys PO Box 800152 Charlottesville VA 22908-0152

**STEVENSON, JAMES LARAWAY,** engineering company executive, electronics engineer, computer engineer, communications engineer, engineering educator; b. Detroit, Oct. 25, 1938; s. Joseph Morley and Kittie Harriet (Laraway) S.; m. Jeanie Lorraine Minkstein, Aug. 7, 1965; children: Amy Jean, Brian Morley. AAS in Electronics Engring., US Armed Forces Staff Coll., 1958; BSEE in Electronics Engring., MIT, 1960, MSEE in Electronics Engring., 1962; DSc in Electronics and Computer Engring., Buxton U., 1994. Cert. master radio and telecom. engr. Nat. Assn. Radio and Telecomm. Engrs., Inc.; 1st class cert. competency Associated Pub. Safety Comm. Officers, Inc.; lic. 1st Class FCC Commercial Radiotelephone, 1964. With USN Mercury Space Project, 1957-63, Office of Naval Rsch. (Naval Rsch. Lab., Naval Air Sta. and Flight Test Ctr., Patuxent River MD/Argonne Nat. Lab.), DC, 1962—63, London, 1962—63; engr. Sta. WBCM-FM, Bay City, Mich., 1964-65; chief engr. Sta. WCRM, Clare, Mich., 1965-66, Sta. WSMA, Marine City, Mich., 1966; engr. Sta. WWJ-AM-FM-TV, Detroit, 1966-79; owner, mgr. Twin Oaks Comms. Engring. now Twin Oaks Comms. Engring. P.C.), North Branch, Mich., 1972—. Charter pilot, flight and ground instr. G. B. DuPont Co., Almont Marlette Aviation Inc., 1977-82; expert legal witness, 1968—; corp. edn. dean's adv. coun. Colls. Bus. Adminstr., Sci., Engring. and Tech., Saginaw Valley State U., 1997—; curriculum adv. com. ITT Tech. Inst., Canton, Mich., 2002—; mem. Intern. Engring. Consortium, 2005-; cons. in field. Mem. editl. advisory panel: eWeek Mag., 2004; contbr. articles to profl. jours. Jury foreman, Lapeer County Circuit Ct, 1974; sr. divsn. judge Detroit Met. Sci. and Engring. Fair, 1975—, Mich. State Sci. and Engring. Fair, 2000—; spl. awards judge Intel Internat. Sci. and Engring. Fair, Detroit, 2000; search and rescue pilot, mission comdr., capt. Mich. wing CAP, 1961-81; cubmaster Boy Scouts Am., North Branch, 1983-85; mich. state chmn. bus. adv. coun. Rep. Congl. Com., 2002—. With USN, 1957—63. Recipient appreciation award CAP, 1980, North Branch Area Schs., 1985, Century award Boy Scouts Am., 1984, Chairman's award, Saginaw Valley Engrg. Coun., 1991, 2001, Intl. Scientist of Yr. award, IBC, Cambridge, 2002. Mem. AIAA, IEEE (sr., chmn. N.E. Mich. sect. 1987-88, 95—, bd. dirs. 1984—), NSPE, Am. Soc. for Engring. Edn. (profl. mem.), Nat. Assn. Radio Telecomm. Engrs. (sr.), Am. Inst. Physics (assoc.), Mich. Soc. Profl. Engrs. (flint chpt.), Network and Sys. Profls. Assn., Saginaw Valley Engring. Coun. (chmn. 1990-91, 2000-01, sec.-treas. 1992-95, Outstanding Leadership award 1991, 2001), Engring. Soc. Detroit (profl.), Profl. Activities Coun. Engrs. (chmn. U.S. activities bd. 1985—), Network and Systems Profls. Assn., Nat. Pilots Assn. (sr. pilot citation, Safe Pilot award 1978), Aircraft Owners and Pilots Assn., Network and Systems Profls. Assn., North Br. C. of C. (charter), Tri-County Econs. Club, Am. Legion, (vice-commander North Br. club 2001-02), Lions (sec. North Br. club 1985-90, pres. 1990-91), Radio Club Am., Tri-County Econs. Club, Sigma Alpha Epsilon. Conservative. Methodist. Avocations: computers, amateur radio, flying. Office: Twin Oaks Comms Engring PC 2465 Johnson Mill Rd PO Box 340 North Branch MI 48461-0340 Office Phone: 810-688-2633. Personal E-mail: stepthe8@aol.com.

**STEVENSON, JAMES RICHARD,** radiologist, educator, lawyer; b. Ft. Dodge, Iowa, May 30, 1937; s. Lester Lawrence and Esther Irene (Johnson) S.; m. Sara Jean Hayman, Sept. 4, 1958; children: Bradford Allen, Tiffany Ann, Jill Renee, Trevor Ashley. BS, U. N.Mex., 1959, JD, 1987; MD, U. Colo., 1963. Diplomate Am. Bd. Radiology, Am. Bd. Nuc. Medicine, Am. Bd. Legal Medicine, 1989: Bar: N.Mex. 1987, U.S. Dist. Ct. N.Mex. 1988. Intern U.S. Gen. Hosp., Tripler, Honolulu, 1963-64, resident radiology Brook, San Antonio, 1964-67; radiologist, ptnr. Van Atta Labs., Albuquerque, 1970-88, Radiology Assocs. of Albuquerque, 1988—, pres., 1994-96. Radiologist, ptnr. Civerolo, Hansen & Wolf, Albuquerque, 1988-89; adj. asst. prof. radiology U. N.Mex., 1970-71; pres. med. staff AT & SF Meml. Hosp., 1979-80, chief of staff, 1980-81, trustee, 1981-83. Author: District Attorney manual, 1987. Participant breast screening Am. Cancer Soc., Albuquerque, 1987-88; dir. profl. divsn. United Way, Albuquerque, 1975. Maj. U.S. Army, 1963-70, Vietnam; col. M.C. USAR, 1988—. Decorated Bronze Star; Allergy fellow, 1960; Med.-Legal Tort scholar, 1987. Fellow Am. Coll. Radiology (councilor 1980-86, mem. med. legal com. 1990-96), Am. Coll. Legal Medicine, Am. Coll. Nuc. Medicine, Am. Coll. Physicians, Radiology Assn. Albuquerque; mem. AMA (Physicians' Recognition award 1969—), Am. Soc. Law & Medicine, Am. Arbitration Assn., Albuquerque Bar Assn., Soc. Nuc. Medicine (v.p. Rocky Mountain chpt. 1975-76), Am. Inst. Ultrasound in Medicine, N.Am. Radiol. Soc. (chmn. med. legal com. 1992-95), N.Mex. Radiol. Soc. (pres. 1978-79), N.Mex. Med. Soc. (chmn. grievance com.), Albuquerque-Bernalillo County Med. Soc. (scholar 1959), Nat. Assn. Health Lawyers, ABA (antitrust sect. 1986—), N.Mex. State Bar, Albuquerque Bar Assn., Sigma Chi, Albuquerque Country Club, Elks, Masons, Shriners. Republican. Methodist. Home: 3333 Santa Clara Ave SE Albuquerque NM 87106-1530 Office: Med Arts Imaging Ctr A6 Med Arts Sq 801 Encino Pl NE Albuquerque NM 87102-2612

**STEVENSON, JOSIAH, IV,** management consultant; b. Jamaica, N.Y., Oct. 4, 1935; s. Josiah and Ruth Lillian (Leech) S.; m. Jane Margaret Kupfer, Sept. 1, 1957; children: Josiah V., Todd Sander. AB, Dartmouth Coll., 1957; MBA, Amos Tuck Sch. Bus., 1958. Lt. U. Md.-Far East, 1959—61; account supr. Benton & Bowles, Inc., N.Y.C., 1961—66; group product mgr., mgr. Japan Chesebrough-Pond's Inc., Greenwich, Conn., 1967—77; dir. devel. Dartmouth Coll., 1977—84, Boston Symphony Orch., 1984—95; v.p. Curtis Inst. Music, Phila., 1995—2003; mng. ptnr. Dover Stevenson & Assocs., 1987—. Trustee Opera North. With USAF, 1958-61. Mem. U.S. C. of C., Assn. Fund Raising Profls. (Mass. chpt. bd. dirs., v.p. 1993-95, Greater Phila. chpt. bd. dirs., v.p. fin. 1996-2003), Dartmouth Club, Tokyo Lawn Tennis Club, Yale-Dartmouth Club (N.Y.C.), Badminton and Tennis Club (Boston). Independent. Presbyterian. Home: 23 Spring Pond Rd PO Box 1810 Norwich VT 05055-1810 E-mail: jstevenson@valley.net.

**STEVENSON, KATHERINE HOLLER,** federal agency administrator; b. Jan. 20, 1948; d. Jacob W. and Sheila Holler; m. Donald Stevenson, aug. 14, 1982; 2 children. BA, Skidmore Coll., 1969; MA, U. Del., 1971. Researcher Nat. portrait Gallery, Smithsonian Inst., Washington, 1971; with Nat. Park Svc., Washington, 1972-80, Denver, 1980-87, Phila., 1987-95, assoc. dir. Washington, 1995—. Co-author: Houses by Mail, 1983. Recipient Meritorious Svc. award Dept. Interior, 1994. Office: Nat Park Svc Cultural Resource 1849 C St NW Washington DC 20240-0001 E-mail: Kate_Stevenson@nps.gov.

**STEVENSON, LAURA CAROLINE,** writer, educator; b. Ann Arbor, Mich., Sept. 8, 1946; d. Charles Leslie and Louise Ellen (Destler) S.; m. Michael William O'Connell, Sept. 27, 1969 (div. July 1981); children: Katharine O'Connell, Margaret O'Connell; m. Franklin D. Reeve, Dec. 22, 1997. AB with highest honors, U. Mich., 1968; MPhil, Yale U., 1971, PhD, 1974. Lectr. history U. Calif., Santa Barbara, 1970-71; prof. humanities Bradford Coll., Haverhill, Mass., 1980-83, Marlboro (Vt.) Coll., 1986—. Author: Praise and Paradox, 1984, 2d edit., 2002, Happily After All, 1990, The Island and the Ring, 1991, All the King's Horses, 2001, A Castle in the Window, 2003. Recipient Grant-in-Aid, Am. Coun. Learned Socs., 1975; Andrew W. Mellon Faculty fellow Harvard U., 1982-83, Rsch. fellow NEH, 1996-97. Mem.: AAUW, Windham County Farm Bur., Vt. Natural Resources Coun., Authors Guild, Royal Oak Found., Beatrix Potter Soc., Assn. Late-Deafened Adults, Phi Beta Kappa. Soc. Of Friends. Avocations: gardening, farming. Home: PO Box 14 Wilmington VT 05363-0014 Office: Marlboro Coll Dept Humanities Marlboro VT 05344 Office Phone: 802-258-9285. Business E-Mail: lsteve@marlboro.edu.

**STEVENSON, MICHAEL KEITH,** elementary school educator; b. Columbus, Jan. 3, 1963; s. John Barnt and Elaine Elizabeth Stevenson; m. Cynthia Ann Paulson, Nov. 10, 1990; children: Dustin, Devin, Dylan. BS in Edn., U. Wis., LaCrosse, 1986; MS in Kinesiology, U. Nev., Las Vegas, 1994. Phys. edn. tchr. Clark County Pub. Schs., Las Vegas, 1986—95, 1998—, Orange County Pub. Schs., Orlando, Fla., 1995—98. Youth coach City of Henderson Parks and Recreation, Nev., 2000—. Named Coach of Yr., City of Henderson Parks and Recreation, 2004, Nat. Coach of Yr., Nat. Youth Sports Coaches Assn., 2005; recipient Disting. Educator award, Clark County Sch. Dist., 2001. Avocations: sports, woodworking.

**STEVENSON, NANCY NELSON,** museum director; b. Annapolis, Md., Oct. 23, 1950; d. Perry Waldemar and Grace Anne Nelson; m. Roger Stevenson Jr., Nov. 18, 1972; children: Jennifer Loren, Matthew Austin. BA, Sarah Lawrence Coll., 1972. Tchr. Montgomery County (Md.) Pub. Schs., 1972—76; bd. dirs. Jr. League of Washington, 1988—89, 1990—92; trustee Nat. Mus. Women in the Arts, Washington, 1996—, sec. bd. of trustees, 1997—98, treas. bd. of trustees, 1998—2002, v.p. bd. trustees, 2002—04, pres. bd. trustees, 2004—. Co-author French immersion curriculum, 1974. Pres. Country Pl. Citizens Assn., Potomac, Md., 1983-84. Office: Nat Mus Women in the Arts 1250 New York Ave NW Washington DC 20005-3970

**STEVENSON, NORMA ANN,** elementary school educator, real estate agent, property manager; b. Detroit, Aug. 10, 1931; d. Austin Sipple and Viola (Anderson) Neeb; m. Thomas J. Stevenson Jr., June 20, 1953 (div. Feb. 1983); children: Mark, Lori Ann Smith, Thomas J. III; m. Gordon E. Sawyers, July 6, 2003. BS, Mich. State U., 1953; MA, Wayne State U., 1972. Tchr. Grosse Pointe Schs., Mich., 1969—87; real estate sales staff Schweitzer, Prudential, Grosse Pointe, 1979—2007; owner, pres., real estate developer Thompson Marlor Fin. Mgmt. Co., Grosse Pointe, 1980—. Bridge dir. Celebrity Cruise Line, 2001—, Norweigian Cruise Line, 2001—; developer condominium conversion Stevenson Condominium, Grosse Pointe, 1995; lectr., spkr. in field. Treas. PTA, Grosse Pointe, 1968; vol. Hospice, Grosse Pointe, 1990—94, Meals on Wheels, Grosse Pointe, 1999—2003; mem. St. James Luth. Ch., Grosse Pointe, 1940—2006. Mem.: PEO, Am. Contract Bridge League (dir.), Delta Kappa Gamma (Woman of Distinction 1980). Republican. Avocations: sailing, bridge, bicycling, travel, exercise. Home (Winter): 16236 W Tuscany Way Surprise AZ 85374 Home (Summer): 225 N Maloney Dr North Platte NE 69101-8901

**STEVENSON, PATRICIA ANN,** elementary educator; b. Longview, Wash., July 12, 1948; d. Richard Marion and Phyllis (Lilley) Barge; m. Clifford Lynn Stevenson, July 13, 1974; 1 child, Sherri Lynlee-Deann. Assoc. in Liberal Arts, Tacoma C.C., 1968; BA in Edn., Ctrl. Wash. U., 1971, cert., 1976; MA in Edn., Heritage Coll., 1993. Substitute tchr. Puyallup (Wash.) Sch. Dist., 1971-73, Tacoma Sch. Dist., 1971-73, Sumner (Wash.) Sch. Dist., 1971-73, North Franklin Sch. Dist., Connell, Wash., 1976—. Custom decorator J. C. Penney, Tacoma, 1972-73; purchasing sales rep. Singer Co., Tacoma, 1973-74, Kennewick, Wash., 1974-81; sales rep. Sterling Recreation Orgn., Richland, Wash., 1981-84. Site coord. Am. Heart Assn., Mesa, Wash., 1988—2006. Ednl. grantee North Franklin Sch. Dist., 1988. Mem. NEA, Wash. Edn. Assn., North Franklin Edn. Assn., Order Ea. Star (Worthy Matron Alma chpt. 2006, mem. Rainbow adv. bd. Kennewick Washington assembly 2005, 06), Sigma Tau Alpha. Mem. Lds Ch. Home: 70 Canal Dr Mesa WA 99343-9520 Office: Basin City Elem 303 Bailie Blvd Mesa WA 99343-9510 Office Phone: 509-269-4224. E-mail: cstevenson@centurytel.net.

**STEVENSON, PAUL MICHAEL,** physics professor, researcher; b. Denham, Eng., Oct. 10, 1954; came to U.S., 1983; s. Jeremy and Jean Helen (Jennings) S. BA, Cambridge (Eng.) U., 1976; PhD, Imperial Coll., London, 1979. Rsch. assoc. U. Wis., Madison, 1979-81, 1983-84; fellow European Orgn. for Nuclear Rsch., Geneva, 1981-83; sr. rsch. assoc. Rice U., Houston, 1984-86, asst. prof. physics, 1986-89, assoc. prof., 1989-93; prof. physics, 1993—. Contbr. articles to profl. jours. Avocation: music. Business E-Mail: stevenson@physics.rice.edu.

**STEVENSON, ROBERT EDWIN,** microbiologist, consultant; b. Columbus, Ohio, Dec. 2, 1926; s. Arthur Edwin and Mary Lucille (Beman) S. BS, Ohio State U., 1947, MS, 1950, PhD, 1954. Cert. Am. Bd. Microbiology. Virologist USPHS, Cin., 1954-58; head cell culture sect., Tissue Bank U.S. Naval Med. Sch., Bethesda, Md., 1958-60; head cell culture and tissue material sect. Nat. Cancer Inst., Bethesda, 1960-63, chief viral carcinogenesis br., 1963-67; mgr. biolog. scis., corp. devel. dept. Union Carbide Corp., Tarrytown, NY, 1967-72; v.p., gen. mgr, Frederick (Md.) div. Litton Bionetics, 1972-80; dir. Am. Type Culture Collection, Rockville, Md., 1980-93; dir. emeritus, 1993. Dir. Large Scale Biology, Inc., Rockville, 1984-90; cons. Am. Assn. Tissue Banks, 1999—; chmn. biotech. adv. com. Dept. Commerce, Washington, 1985-93. With USN, 1944-45. Recipient Hyatt award, AATB, 2004. Fellow Inst. for Soc., Ethics & Life Scis.; mem. Tissue Culture Assn. (pres. 1988-90), World Fedn. Culture Collections, U.S. Fedn. Culture Collections (pres. 1988-90), Am. Soc. Micrbiology, Cosmos Club (Washington). Episcopalian. Avocations: painting, cross country skiing. Home: 27 Evart's Ln Madison CT 06443-2564 Office Phone: 703-827-9582.

**STEVENSON, ROBERT MURRELL,** music educator; b. Melrose, N.Mex., July 3, 1916; s. Robert Emory and Ada (Ross) S. AB, U. Tex., El Paso, 1936; grad., Juilliard Sch. Music, 1938; MusM, Yale, 1939; PhD, U. Rochester, 1942; STB cum laude, Harvard U., 1943; BLitt, Oxford U., Eng.; Th.M., Princeton Theol. Sem.; DMus honoris causa, Cath. U. Am., 1991; LHD honoris causa, Ill. Wesleyan U., 1992; LittD honoris causa, Universidade Nova de Lisboa, 1993. Instr. music U. Tex., 1941-43, 46; faculty Westminster Choir Coll., Princeton, NJ, 1946-49; faculty rsch. lectr. UCLA, 1981, mem. faculty to prof. music, 1949—. Vis. asst. prof. Columbia, 1955-56; vis. prof. Ind. U., Bloomington, 1959-60, U. Chile, 1965-66, Northwestern U., Chgo., 1976, U. Granada, 1992; adj. prof. Cath. U. Am., 1991—; cons. UNESCO, 1977; Louis Charles Elson lectr. Libr. of Congress, Washington, 1969; inaugural prof. musicology Nat. U. Mex., 1996; spkr. Dumbarton Oaks Pre-Columbian Music Workshop, 1998. Internat. Colonial Music Congress, Lima, Peru, 2000; lectr. Tureck Bach Rsch. Found., Oxford U., 2000; hon. prof. Conservatorio Nacional, Peru, 2000, Real Conservatorio Superior, Madrid, 1991-2003; hon. lectr. Royal Conservatory, Madrid, 2004; keynote spkr. Morales Colloquium, Oxford U., 2004. Author: Music in Mexico, 1952, Patterns of Protestant Church Music, 1953, La musica en la catedral de Sevilla, 1954, 85, Music Before the Classic Era, 1955, Shakespeare's Religious Frontier, 1958, The Music of Peru, 1959, Juan Bermudo, 1960, Spanish Music in the Age of Columbus, 1960, Spanish Cathedral Music in the Golden Age, 1961, La musica colonial en Colombia, 1964, Protestant Church Music in America, 1966, Music in Aztec and Inca Territory, 1968, Renaissance and Baroque Musical Sources in the Americas, 1970, Music in El Paso, 1970, Philosophies of American Music History, 1970, Written Sources for Indian Music Until 1882, 1972, Christmas Music From Baroque Mexico, 1974, Foundations of New World Opera, 1973, Seventeenth Century Villancicos, 1974, Latin American Colonial Music Anthology, 1975, Vilancicos Portugueses, 1976, Josquin in the Music of Spain and Portugal, 1977, American Musical Scholarship, Parker to Thayer, 1978, Liszt at Madrid and Lisbon, 1980, Wagner's Latin American Outreach, 1983, Spanish Musical Impact Beyond the Pyrenees, 1250-1500, 1985, La Música en las catedrales españolas del Siglo de Oro, 1993; contbg. editor: Handbook Latin Am. Studies, 1976—; editor Inter-Am. Music Rev., 1978—; contbr. to New Grove Dictionary of Music and Musicians, 17 other internat. encys. Decorated Army Commendation ribbon, 1946; fellow Folger Shakespeare Library, 1950, Ford Found., 1953-54, Gulbenkian Found., 1966, 81, Guggenheim Found., 1962, NEH, 1974, Comité Conjunto Hispano-Norteamericano (Madrid), 1989; recipient Fulbright rsch. awards, 1958-59, 64, 70-71, 88-89, Carnegie Found. tchg. award, 1955-56, Gabriela Mistral award OAS, 1985, Héitor Villa Lobos Jury award OAS, 1988, OAS medal, 1986, Cert. Merit Mexican Consulate San Bernardino, Calif., 1987, Silver medal Spanish Ministry Culture, 1989, Gold medal Real Conservatorio Superior, 1994, 97, 1st Lifetime Achievement award Sonneck Soc., 1999, All-Calif. Constantine Penunzio award, 2004. Mem. Real Academia de Bellas Artes (hon.), Hispanic Soc. Am., Am. Liszt Soc. (cons. editor) Heterofonia (cons. editor), Brazilian Musicol. Soc. (hon.), Portuguese Musicol. Soc. (hon.), Argentinian Musicol. Soc. (hon.), Venezu-elan Musicol. Soc. (hon.), Am. Musicol. Soc. (hon.), Orden Andrés Bello, Primera Clase, Venezuela, 1992. Avocation: playing piano. Office: UCLA Dept Music 405 Hilgard Ave Los Angeles CA 90095-9000 Business E-Mail: info@ericdilauro.com.

**STEVENSON, RUTH CARTER,** art patron; b. Ft. Worth, Oct. 19, 1923; d. Amon Giles and Nenetta (Wiess) Carter; m. J. Lee Johnson III, June 8, 1946 (div. Feb. 1978); children: Sheila Broderick Johnson, J. Lee, Karen Carter Johnson Hixon, Catherine Johnson, Mark Lehane; m. John R. Stevenson, May 21, 1983 BA, Sarah Lawrence Coll., 1945. Pres. Ft. Worth Jr. League, 1954—55, Amon Carter Mus., Ft. Worth, 1961—, Amon G. Carter Found., 1982—, Arts Coun. Greater Ft. Worth, 1963—64; bd. regents U. Tex. Austin, 1963—69; v.p. internat. coun. Mus. Modern Art, 1965—72; bd. dirs. Nat. Trust Hist. Preservation, 1968—74; bd. dirs. Nat. Coll. Fine Arts Smithsonian Instn., Washington, 1966—70; bd. dirs. U. Dallas, 1971—74; trustee Tex. Christian U., 1974—86, Nat. Gallery Art, Washington, 1979—97; bd. dirs. Nat. Trust Hist. Preservation. Pres. Ft. Worth City Art Commn., 1960-80; nat. chmn. collector's com. Nat. Gallery Art, Washington, 1975—97; mem. vis. com. Fogg Mus., Cambridge, Mass., 1978-83 Roman Catholic. Office: Amon Carter Mus 3501 Camp Bowie Blvd Fort Worth TX 76107 Office Phone: 817-989-5095.

**STEVENSON, THOMAS RAY,** plastic surgeon; b. Kansas City, Mo., Jan. 22, 1946; s. John Adolph and Helen Ray (Clarke) S.; m. Judith Ann Hunter, Aug. 17, 1968; children: Anne Hunter, Andrew Thomas. BA, U. Kans., 1968, MD. Diplomate Am. Bd. Plastic and Reconstructive Surgery, Am. Bd. Surgery. Resident in gen. surgery U. Va., Charlottesville, 1972-78; resident in plastic surgery Emory U., Atlanta, 1980-82; asst. prof. surgery U. Mich., 1982-88, assoc. prof. surgery, 1988-89. Chief plastic surgery Ann Arbor VA Hosp., 1982—, U. Calif., Davis, 1989—. Served to maj. USAR, 1978-80. Fellow ACS; mem. Am. Soc. Plastic and Reconstructive Surgery, Am. Bd. Plastic Surgery, chair-elect 2006- Office: UC Davis Divsn Plastic Surg 2221 Stockton Blvd 2d Fl Sacramento CA 95817-2214

**STEVENSON, WILLIAM ALEXANDER,** retired justice of Supreme Court of Canada; b. Edmonton, Alta., Can., May 7, 1934; s. Alexander Lindsay and Eileen Harriet (Burns) S.; m. Patricia Ann Stevenson; children: Catherine, Kevin, Vivian, James. BA, U. Alta., Edmonton, 1956, LLB, 1957; LLD (hon.), U. Alta., 1992. Called to Alta. bar, 1958. Ptnr. Hurlburt Reynolds Stevenson & Agrios, Edmonton, 1957-68; prof. U. Alta., 1968-70; ptnr. Reynolds Stevenson & Agrios, Edmonton, 1970-75; judge Dist. Ct. Alta., Edmonton, 1975-79; justice Ct. of Queens Bench Alta., Edmonton, 1979-80, Ct. of Appeal Alta., Edmonton, 1980-90, Supreme Ct. Can., Ottawa, Ont., 1990-92. Officer Order of Can., 1997. Co-author: Civil Procedure Guide, 1995. Mem. Can. Bar Assn., Can. Inst. for Adminstrn. Justice (pres. 1983-85, hon. dir.), Nat. Jud. Inst. (hon. dir.), Legal Archives Soc. Alta (hon. dir.). Home: 7 Laurier Pl Edmonton AB Canada T5R 5P4 E-mail: wmstevenson@shaw.ca.

**STEVENSON, WILLIAM HENRI,** author; b. London, June 1, 1924; s. William and Alida (Deleporte) S.; m. Glenys Rowe, July 28, 1945; children: Andrew, Jacqueline, Kevin, Sally. Student, Royal Navy Coll., 1942. Fgn. corr. Toronto (Ont., Can.) Star, 1948-58; Toronto Globe & Mail, 1958-63; Ind. TV News, London, Eng., 1964-66; CBC, 1966-77; ind. writer, broadcaster, 1977—. Author: Travels In and Around Red China, 1957, Rebels in Indonesia, 1964, Chronicles of the Israeli Air Force, 1971, A Man Called Intrepid, 1976, Ninety Minutes at Entebbe, 1976, The Ghosts of Africa, 1981; producer: TV documentaries; movie screenplays include The Bushbabies, 1970. Served as aviator Royal Navy, 1942-45. Mem. Assn. Naval Aviation U.S.A., Authors Guild, Royal Overseas League (London). Mem. Progressive Conservative Party Can. Church of England. Clubs: Royal Bermuda Yacht, Royal Hong Kong Yacht. Office: care Paul Gitlin Agy 15th Fl 353 Lexington Ave Fl 15 New York NY 10016-0941 Address: 25 Roxborough E Toronto ON Canada M4W Z2G

**STEVENTON, ROBERT WESLEY,** marketing executive; b. Allentown, Pa., Nov. 2, 1948; s. Robert Wesley and Catherine May (Feineur) S.; m. Deborah Damon Barrett, Aug. 29, 1977 (dec.); m. Gineva Mary Malliot, Nov. 4, 2003; children: Calvin Nathaniel, Alexander MacAuley BA, Pa. State U., 1970; MA, U. Minn., 1975; Cert. Resident, Cambridge U., Eng., 1992. Mktg. specialist U.S. Bur. of Census, Washington, 1975-77; mktg. mgr. Am. Chem. Soc., Washington, 1978-83; account exec. Kreitlow & Assocs., Silver Spring, Md., 1983-84; sr. account exec. Mktg. Gen., Inc., Washington, 1984-85, v.p. Alexandria, Va., 1985-89, sr. v.p. 1989-94; pres. AB&C Mktg., McLean, Va., 1994-2000; mng. ptnr. iMark Comms. Ltd., Fairfax, Va., 2000—02; dir. Somerset Trade Fin. LLC, Washington, 2002—. Dir. Intelmark Corp., 1995-2000, Immedia Corp., 1999-2000, InfoQuest Comms. Corp., 1999-2002; advisor Euro Broadcasting Corp., 1996-99; lectr. Direct Mktg. Assn., Washington, 1988-92, Coun. Engring. and Sci. Socs. Execs., N.Y.C., 1988-98; gen. chmn. Direct Mktg. Days Conv. Com., Washington, 1988 Mem. com. econ. devel. bur. Greater Washington Bd. Trade, 1989-92, bus. mktg. com., 1993-96; mem. Greater Washington Initiative, 1999-2002; vol. Christ House, Alexandria, Va., 1987—. With U.S. Army, 1970-73 Recipient Capital award Nat. Leadership Coun., 1992 Mem. Am. Soc. Assn. Execs. (membership com. 1989-1997), Am.-European Cmty. Assn., Brit. Am. Bus. Assn., Direct Mktg. Assn. Washington (bd. dirs. 1983-85), Soc. for Assn. Mktg. Internat. (pres. 1991-94), Assn. Svcs. Group (chmn. bd. 1996-2000), Order St. Etheldreda (officer 1993), Manorial Soc. Gt. Britain (life), Army and Navy Club Washington, Salisbury Club (U.K.), Kappa Tau Alpha Republican. Episcopalian. Avocations: downhill skiing, bicycling, golf. Office: Somerset Trade Fin LLC Ste 450 1747 Pennsylvania Ave NW Washington DC 20006 Home: 103 Wolfe St Alexandria VA 22314-3831 Office Phone: 202-463-2188. E-mail: bob@stfllc.com.

**STEVER, DONALD WINFRED,** lawyer; b. Altoona, Pa., Jan. 25, 1944; s. Donald Winfred and June Lily (Bargfrede) S.; m. Betsy Jean Seaman, May 28, 1968 (div. Oct. 1975); 1 child, Heather Elene; m. Margo Leaman Taft, July 30, 1976; children: David Whittaker, James Taft. BA, Lehigh U., 1965; JD, U. Pa., 1968. Bar: Conn. 1968, N.H. 1969, D.C. 1983, N.Y. 1983, U.S. Dist. Ct. N.H. 1969, U.S. Dist. Ct. Conn. 1986, U.S. Dist. Ct. (so. dist.) N.Y. 1985, U.S. Dist. Ct. (no. and we. dists.) N.Y. 1990, U.S. Ct. Appeals (1st cir.) 1974, U.S. Ct. Appeals (10th cir.) 1980, U.S. Ct. Appeals (5th, 11th and Fed. cirs.) 1984, U.S. Ct. Appeals (2d cir.) 1990, U.S. Supreme Ct. 1972. Atty. Aetna Life & Casualty co., Hartford, Conn., 1968-69, Office of N.H. Atty. Gen., Concord, 1969-72, asst. atty. gen., chief environ. protection, 1972-77; atty. pollution control sect. U.S. Dept. Justice, Washington, 1978-79, chief pollution control sect., 1979-80, chief environ. def. sect., 1980-82; prof. Pace U. Sch. Law, White Plains, NY, 1982-87, adj. prof. environ. law, 1987-92; ptnr. Sidley and Austin, N.Y.C., 1987-93, Dewey Ballantine, N.Y.C., 1993—2004, Kirkpatrick and Lockhart LLP, 2004—. Bd. dirs. Environ. Law Inst., Washington, chmn., 1996-97, 99-2003; bd. dirs. Hudson Valley Writers Ctr. Inc., Sleepy Hollow, N.Y., Friends of Rockefeller State Park Preserve, Inc. Author: Seabrook and The Nuclear Regulatory Commission, 1980; Law of Chemical Reation and Hazardous Waste, 1986; editor: Environmental Law & Practice, 1992; co-editor Environmental Law & Practice, 1992. Bd. dirs. Biddeford Pool (Maine) Improvement Assn., 1989-93; mem. conservation adv. com. Village of North Tarrytown, N.Y., 1989-93; trustee Village of Sleepy Hollow, 1998-2003. Mem. Biddeford Pool Yacht Club (treas. 1989-92, sec. 1992-2000, rear commodore 2000-02, vice commodore 2002—), Sleepy Hollow Country Club, Abenakee Club, Mill Reef Club. Avocations: golf, tennis, sailboat racing, early music. Home: 157 Millard Ave Sleepy Hollow NY 10591-1412 Office: Kirkpatrick & Lockhart Nicholson Graham LLP 599 Lexington Ave New York NY 10022-6030 Office Phone: 212-536-4861. E-mail: dstever@klng.com.

**STEVER, HORTON GUYFORD,** aerospace scientist, educator, aerospace engineer, consultant; b. Corning, N.Y., Oct. 24, 1916; s. Ralph Raymond and Alma (Matt) Stever; m. Louise Risley Floyd, June 29, 1946; children: Horton Guyford, Sarah, Margarette, Roy. AB, Colgate U., 1938, ScD (hon.), 1958; PhD, Calif. Inst. Tech. 1941; LLD, U. Pitts., 1966, Lehigh U., 1967,

Allegheny Coll., 1968, Ill. Inst. Tech., 1975; DSc, Northwestern U., 1966, Waynesburg Coll., 1967, U. Mo., 1975, Clark U., 1976, Bates Coll., 1977; DH, Seton Hill Coll., 1968; D.Engring., Washington and Jefferson Coll., 1969, Widener Coll., Poly. Inst. N.Y., 1972, Villanova U., 1973, U. Notre Dame, 1974; DPS, George Washington U., 1981. Staff radiation lab. MIT, Cambridge, Mass., 1941—42, asst. prof., 1946—51, assoc. prof. aero. engring., 1951—56, prof. aero. and astro., 1956—65, head depts. mech. engring., naval architecture, marine engring., 1961—65, assoc. dean engring., 1956—59, exec. officer guided missiles program, 1946—48; chief scientist USAF, 1955—56; pres. Carnegie-Mellon U., Pitts., 1965—72; dir. NSF, Washington, 1972—76; sci. adviser, chmn. Fed. Council Sci. and Tech., 1973—76; dir. Office Sci. and Tech. Policy, sci. and tech. adviser to Pres., 1976—77, sci. cons., corp. trustee, 1977—. Secretariat guided missiles com. Joint Chiefs of Staff, 1945; sci. liaison officer London Mission, OSRD, 1942—45; guided missiles tech. evaluation group Rsch. and Devel. Bd., 1946—48; sci. adv. bd. to chief of staff USAF, 1947—69, chmn., 1962—69; steering com. tech. adv panel on aeros. Dept. Def., 1956—62; chmn. spl. com. space tech. NASA, chmn. rsch. adv. com. missile and spacecraft aerodynamics, 1959—65; mem. Nat. Sci. Bd., 1970—72, ex-officio, chmn. exec. com., 1972—75; mem. Def. Sci. Bd., 1962—68; adv. panel U.S. Ho. Reps. Com. Sci. and Astronautics, 1959—72; mem. Pres.'s Commn. on Patent System, 1965—67; chmn. U.S.-USSR Joint Commn. Sci. and Tech. Cooperation, 1973—77, Fed. Council Arts and Humanities, 1972—76; Pres. com. Nat. Sci. medal, 1973—77. Author: Flight, 1965, In War and Peace: My Life in Sci and Tech, 2002; contbr. articles to profl. jours. Past trustee Colgate U., Shady Side Acad., Sarah Mellon Scaife Found., Buckingham Sch; trustee Univ. Rsch Assn., 1977—, pres., 1982—85; trustee Woods Hole Oceanographic Inst., 1980—, Sci. Svc., 1982—, Univ. Corp. for Atmospheric Rsch., 1980—83; bd. dirs. Saudi Arabia Nat. Ctr. for Sci. and Tech., 1978—81; bd. govs. U.S. Israel Binat. Sci. Found. 1977—76, chmn., 1972—73; mem. Carnegie Commn. on Sci., Tech. and Govt., 1988—93. Recipient Pres.'s Cert. of Merit, 1948, Exceptional Civilian Svc. award, USAF, 1956, Scott Gold medal, Am. Ordinance Assn., 1960, Disting. Pub. Svc. medal, award, Dept. Def., 1969, NASA, 1988, Nat. Medal of Sci., 1991. Fellow: AAAS, AIAA (hon.; pres. 1960—62), Am. Phys. Soc., Royal Soc. Arts, Am. Philos. Soc., Am. Acad. Arts and Scis., Royal Aero. Soc.; mem.: NAE (chmn. aero. and space engring. bd., 1967—69, fgn. sec. 1984—88), NAS (chmn. assembly engring. 1979—83, chmn. policy divsn. 1995—97), Royal Acad. of Engring. of Great Britain (fgn. mem.), Acad. of Engring. of Japan (fgn. mem.), Cosmos Club, Phi Beta Kappa, Tau Beta Pi, Sigma Gamma Tau, Sigma Xi. Episcopalian.

**STEVES, GALE C.,** marketing professional, writer, editor-in-chief, publishing executive; b. Mineola, N.Y., Dec. 20, 1942; d. William Harry and Ruth (May) Steves; m. David B. Stocker, Mar. 31, 1972 (div. Apr. 1978); m. Philip L. Perrone, Aug. 14, 1983. BS, Cornell U., 1964; MA, NYU, 1966. Editl. asst. Ladies Home Jour., N.Y.C., 1966-69; seafood consumer specialist U.S. Dept. Commerce, N.Y.C., 1969-73; editor food Homelife mag., N.Y.C., 1973-74; editor food and equipment Co-Ed mag., N.Y.C., 1974-76, Am. Home mag., N.Y.C., 1976-78; editor kitchen design and equipment Woman's Day mag., N.Y.C., 1979-83; editor-in-chief Woman's Day Spls., N.Y.C., 1983-91; v.p., editor-in-chief Home Mag. Group, N.Y.C., 1991—2001; pres. Open House Prodns., N.Y.C., 2001—03, 2005—; v.p., editl. dir., pub. AMI Mini Mags. Group, N.Y.C., 2003—05. Bd. dirs. Les Dames d'Escoffier, Coun. Sr. Ctrs. and Svcs. N.Y.C., Catskill Ctr. Cons. and Econ. Devel. Author: Game Cookery, 1974, The International Cook, 1980, Creative Microwave Cooking, 1981; author: (with Lee M. Elman) Country Weekend Cooking, Home Magazine's Best Little Houses, 1998; mem. editl. bd. Sr. Summary, N.Y.C., 1982—88. Co-chmn. Alder Lake Restoration Soc.; chmn. alumni adv. bd. Coll. Human Ecology, Cornell U., 1993—97, mem. univ. couns., 1996—2000, mem. pres.'s coun. Cornell Women; mem. adv. bd. Cornell Plantations, 1998—2005; bd. mem. Catskill Ctr. Conservation and Econ. Devel. Mem.: Garden Writers Assn. Am., Am. Soc. Mag. Editors, Internat. Furnishings and Design Assn., Acad. Women Achievers YWCA N.Y.C. Address: 185 West End Ave Ste 26C New York NY 10023-5551

**STEWARD, ALETA JOANNA,** fine artist, digital artist; b. Bethpage, N.Y., Dec. 18, 1957; d. John L. and Loretta Rossi; m. Steve M. Steward, June 10, 1978; children: Luke, Bill, Nathan. Student, Art Students League, 1977. Artist, Alturas, Calif., 1979-87, Cape Cod, Mass., 1987—; owner Deco Graphics. One woman show including Trees Place, Orleans, Mass., 1995—, Cape Cod Mus. of Natural History, 1988, 90, Christina Gallery, Martha's Vineyard, Mass., 2006—; exhibited in group exhibitions Schaff Gallery, Cin., 1996, Gallery 503, Klamath Falls, Oreg., 1986-87, Marine Arts Gallery, Salem, Mass., 1996-97. Recipient multiple nat., regional and local art awards, 1985—. Mem. Soc. Animal Artists. Republican. Avocations: astronomy, photography, interior design, digital imaging. Home: 57 Colonial Way Harwich MA 02645-1456 E-mail: decographics@earthlink.net.

**STEWARD, DAVID L.,** technology company executive; b. Clinton, Mo. m. Thelma Steward; children: David, Kimberly. BS, Ctrl. Mo. State U., 1973. Various sales and mktg. positions Wagner Elec., Mo. Pacific Railroad, Fed. Express; founder, chmn. World Wide Tech., Maryland Heights, Mo., 1990—. Bd. dir. St. Louis Cmty. Coll. Found., Civic Progress of St. Louis, St. Louis Regional Chamber and Growth Assn., Mo. Tech. Corp., Webster U., BJC Health Sys., First Banks, Inc., St. Louis Sci. Ctr., United Way of Greater St. Louis Bd., Greater St. Louis Area Coun. of Boy Scouts of Am., Harris-Stowe State Coll. African-Am. Bus. Leadership Coun., RCGA, Barnes-Jewish Hosp.; chaired (with wife) United Way's 2000 African-American Leadership Giving Initiative. Named 14th Best Am. Entrepreneur, Success Mag., 1998, Minority Small Bus. Person of Yr., Small Bus. Adminstrn., 1997—98, Entrepreneur of Yr. in Tech., Ernst & Young, 1998, #1 African-Am.-Owned Bus. in US, Black Enterprise Mag., 2000; named to Small Bus. Adminstrn. Hall of Fame, 2001. Office: World Wide Technology 58 Weldon Pkwy Maryland Heights MO 63043-3237

**STEWARD, JAMES,** museum director, art history educator; BA, U. Va.; MA, NYU; PhD in art hist., Oxford U. Prof. hist. art U. Mich., Ann Arbor; dir. U. Mich. Mus. Art, Ann Arbor. Office: U Mich Mus Art 525 S State St Ann Arbor MI 48109 Office Phone: 734-764-0395. E-mail: jsteward@umich.edu.

**STEWARD, OSWALD,** neuroscience educator, researcher; b. Sept. 12, 1948; m. Kathy L. Pyle; children: Jessica, Oswald IV. BA in Psychology magna cum laude, U. Colo., 1970; PhD in Psychobiology, U. Calif., Irvine, 1974. Asst. prof. neurosurgery and physiology U. Va. Sch. Medicine, Charlottesville, 1974-79, assoc. prof., 1979-84, prof., 1984-86, acting chmn. neurosci. dept., 1986-88, chmn., 1998-99; dir. Reeve Irvine Rsch. Ctr. U. Calif., Irvine, Calif., 1999—. assoc. editor Journal of Comparative Neurology. Author: Principles of Cellular, Molecular, and Developmental Neuroscience, 1989, Functional Neuroscience, 2000; contbr. over 200 articles and revs. to profl. publs. Predoctoral fellow NIMH, Bethesda, Md., 1971-74; rsch. career devel. grantee NIH, 1978-83, Jacob Javitts neurosci. grantee NIH, 1987-94, Disting. Investigator award, Nat. Alliance for Rsch. on Schizophrenia & Depression. Mem. Soc. Neurosci. (chmn. chpts. com. 1985-87), Am. Assn. Anatomists, Am. Soc. Cell Biology, Cajal Club. Office: Reeve-Irvine Rsch Ctr 1105 Gillespie Neurosci Rsch Facility Irvine CA 92697-4292 E-mail: osteward@uci.edu.

**STEWARD, SHERRY ANN,** information technology executive, educator; b. Ft. Campbell, Ky., Aug. 22, 1959; d. Vincent John Nappa and Mary Emma Woodward; m. J.R. Hooper, June 1977 (div. Oct. 1982); children: Amanda Renee Hooper, James Robert Hooper; m. W.H. Steward, Dec. 4, 1992. BA in English, Rollins Coll., 1996; MA in English and Tech. Writing, U. Ctrl. Fla., 1999; MS in Info. Tech., Barry U., 2001; PhD in Texts and Tech., U. Ctrl. Fla., 2004—. Sr. logistics specialist Harris Corp., Palm Bay, Fla., 1981—89; sr. documentation specialist Ea. Test Range, Malabar, Fla., 1989—93; sr. tech. writer DME Corp, Orlando, Fla., 1993—96; program mgr. Dimensions Internat., Inc., Orlando, 1996—2005, Technologist Dimensions Internat., 1996—2005; dir. applied tech. and life cycle support DEI Svcs. Corp., Winter Park, 2005—. Contbr. articles to profl. jours. Mem.: IEEE (adcom 2000—03, 2004—05), Simulation Interoperability Stds. Orgn., Internat. Soc. Logistics.

Army Aviation Assn. Am., Armed Forces Comm. Electronics Assn. (v.p. publicity 2002—03), Nat. Def. Indsl. Assn. Democrat. Roman Catholic. Achievements include 25 years in the acquisition and development of defense technologies and 10 years in flight and weapons simulations; ground-based tactical maintenance training devices; interactive technical documentation. Office: DEI Svcs Corp 7213 Sandscove Ct Winter Park FL 32792 Office Phone: 407-678-3388. E-mail: ssteward@deicorp.net.

**STEWARD, THOMAS JAMES,** school system administrator; b. Wis. Rapids, Wis., July 26, 1954; s. James Edward and Bernice Anne Steward; m. Sandra L. Schulenburg, June 1, 1985; children: Jordan, Rachel. BSc, U. Wis., LaCrosse, 1976; M, U. Wis., River Falls, 1981. Tchr. St. Vincent de Paul Sch., Wis. Rapids, Wis., 1978—80; counselor (grades 9-12) Marshfield Columbus H.S., Wis., 1981—86, Medford Sr. H.S., Wis., 1986—90; counselor (grades K-12) Abbotsford Sch. Dist., Wis., 1990—90; prin. Abbotsford Jr./Sr. H.S., 1996—2000; dir. of instrn., K-5 prin. Clintonville Pub. Sch., Wis., 2000—03; dir. of instrn. Sparta Area Sch. Dist., Wis., 2003—. Ad hoc instr. U. Wis., Eau Claire, Green Bay. Past dir. Colby Libr. Bd., Wis., 1990—96, Abbotsford Housing Authority, 1998—2002. Named Career Educator of Yr., Wis. Ctr. of Edn. and Work, 1999; recipient Nat. Cath. Elem. award, Nat. Cath. Edn. Assn., 1998; Hon. scholar, Target Corp., 2000. Mem.: ASCD, Nat. Coun. for Teachers of Math, Assn. Wis. Sch. Administrators. Avocations: school sports official, travel. Home: 200 W Hickory St Abbotsford WI 54405 Office: Sparta Area Sch Dist 201 E Franklin St Sparta WI 54656

**STEWARD, WELDON CECIL,** architecture educator, architect, consultant; b. Pampa, Tex., Apr. 7, 1934; s. Weldon C. and Lois (Maness) S.; m. Mary Jane Nedbalek, June 9, 1956; children: Karen A., W. Craig. Cert. in architecture and planning, Ecole des Beaux Arts, Fontainebleu, France, 1956; B.Arch., Tex. A&M U, 1957; MS in Architecture, Columbia U., 1961; LHD (hon.), Drury Coll., 1991. Registered architect, Tex. Designer Perkins & Will, Architects, White Plains, NY, 1961-62; asst. prof. architecture Tex. A&M U., College Station, 1962-67, assoc. chmn. Sch. Architecture, 1966-69, assoc. dean, prof. Coll. Environ. Design, 1969-73; dean, prof. Coll. Architecture U. Nebr., Lincoln, 1973-2000, emeritus dean, prof. arch. and planning, 2000—; founding pres. Joslyn Castle Inst. Sustainable Cmtys., Omaha, 1996—; W. Cecil Steward dist. chair sustainable arch. U. Nebr., Lincoln, 2000—02; founding dir. Nebr. Ctr. for Sustainable Constrn., 2003; editor-in-chief Greensource Report, Atlanta, 2002—04; founding mem. UN-Habitat North/North Network Urban Sustainability and Leadership, 2004—. Adj. prof. Sch. Arch. U. Hawaii, 1999—; ednl. cons. People's Republic of China, 1979—; project dir. Imo State U. Planning, Nigeria, 1981-88; vis. prof. Tong ji U., Shanghai, 1984; hon. prof. N.W. Inst. Architects Engrs., Xian, 1989; specialist Design USA, USSR, 1990; co-chmn. nat. coordination com. AIA Nat. Coun. Archtl. Registration Bd. Intership, Washington, 1980-81; bd. visitors Drury Coll., 1980-97, Coll. Arch. U. Miami, Fla., 1993-96, Judson Coll., 1998-2000; mem. nat. design rev. bd. GSA, Washington, 1994—; mem. founding bd. dirs. East/West Pacific Arch., U. Hawaii, 1995—; vice chmn. Design Futures Coun., Reston, Va., 1995—; sr. fellow Design Futures Coun., 1999. Designer, Quinnipiac Elem. Sch., New Haven, Conn., 1961 (Am Assn. Sch. Adminstrs. Exhibit 1969), J.J. Buser Residence, Bryan, Tex., 1969, Steward Urban Residence, Lincoln, Nebr., 1994. Mem. Lincoln Architects, Engrs. Selection Bd., 1979-88; mem. Nat. Com. for U.S.-China Rels., N.Y.C., 1981—, Nebr. Capitol Environ. Commn., 1989-97; bd. dirs. Downtown Lincoln Assn., 1996—, KZUM Pub. Radio, 1997-2001; mem. Lincoln/Lancaster County Planning Commn., 1996-2004, chmn., 2003-04; co-chmn. steering com. City of Lincoln Downtown Master Plan, 2004—; bd. dirs. Lincoln Children's Mus., 1996-2001; profl. adviser nat. design competition Wick Alumni Ctr., Lincoln, 1981; steering com. Internat. Coun. Tall Bldgs., 1992-96. Recipient T.R. Russel award for Newsletters, 2003; named Disting. Alumnus, Tex. A&M U., 1998; Grad. fellow Columbia U., 1960. Mem. AIA (pres. Brazos chpt. 1969, chmn. profl. devel. com. 1979, bd. dirs. 1979-90, dir. Cen. States 1987-90, nat. pres. 1991-92, Coll. of Fellows 1983, Tri-Nat. com. 1991-02, Nebr. Gold medal 1997, nat. AIA/ACSA Topaz award for excellence in architecture 1999, honor award for excellence in urban design 2005, charter award for excellence Congress for New Urbanism 2005); mem. Am. Planning Assn. (chair Dubai Internat. award for sustaining cmty. 2000), Nebr. Soc. Architects (bd. dirs. 1977-2000), Archtl. Found. Nebr. (bd. dirs. 1981-94, treas. 1981-94), Assn. Collegiate Schs. Architecture (bd. dirs. 1975-79), Nat. Archtl. Accrediting Bd. (bd. dirs. 1986-89, pres. 1988-89), Kazakhstan Union Architecture, Assn. Siamese Architects, Royal Inst. Canadian Architects, Fedn. Mexican Achitects, Japan Inst. Architects (hon.), Tau Sigma Delta (medal 1999), Phi Kappa Phi, Phi Beta Delta. Home: 125 N 11th St Lincoln NE 68508-3605 Office: U Nebr Coll Architecture Lincoln NE 68508 Office Phone: 402-472-0087. Business E-Mail: csteward1@sustainabledesign.com. E-mail: csteward1@unl.edu.

**STEWART, ALEC THOMPSON,** physicist, educator; b. Windthorst, Sask., Can., June 18, 1925; s. Arthur and Nelly Blye (Thompson) Stewart; m. Alta Aileen Kennedy, Aug. 4, 1960 (dec. Sept. 2000); children: A. James Kennedy, Hugh D., Duncan R.; m. Annabel C. Wenzel, Apr. 21, 2004. BSc, Dalhousie U., Halifax, N.S., Can., 1946, MSc, 1949; PhD, Cambridge U., Eng., 1952; LLD, Dalhousie U., Halifax, N.S., Can., 1986. Research officer Atomic Energy Can., Chalk River, Ont., Canada, 1952-57; assoc. prof. Dalhousie U., Halifax, 1957-60; assoc. prof. to prof. U. N.C., Chapel Hill, 1960-68; head physics Queen's U., Kingston, Ont., 1968-74, prof. physics, 1968-90, prof. physics emeritus, 1990—. Vis. prof. various univs., Can., Europe, Japan, China, Hong Kong. Author: 2 books; contbr. over 100 articles to profl. jours. Dir. Can. Olympic Tng. Regatta Kingston, 1976—82, Marine Mus. Great Lakes, Kingston, 1988—94. Decorated officer Order of Can.; recipient CAP medal for achievement in physics, 1992, Canada 125 medal, 1992, Queen Elizabeth II Golden Jubilee medal 2002. Fellow Am. Phys. Soc., Royal Soc. Can. (pres. Acad. Sci. 1984-87), Japan Soc. for Promotion Sci.; mem. Can. Assn. Physicists (pres., other offices 1970-74). Achievements include research in solid state physics, behavior of phonons, electrons, positrons and postronium in crystals and liquids, public service: nuclear reactor safety, emergency measures following a nuclear accident, state of nuclear technology in Canada; developed a series of international conferences on positron annihilation and chaired it's international advisory committee for twenty five years. Office: Queens U Dept Physics Kingston ON Canada K7L 3N6

**STEWART, AMY LEE,** lawyer; b. Fla. d. Marshall J. and Patricia R. Stewart; m. David William Bailin; children: Emma S. Bailin children: Patricia C. Bailin, Hannah G. Bailin, Clara L. Bailin, Sarah F. Bailin. BA in Econ., Wellesley Coll., 1981; JD, NYU, 1986. Bar: Ga. 1987, Mass. 1987, Ark. 1988, cert.: (Coll. Mediators); Lex Mundi Coll. Mediators. Jud. clk. US Dist. Ct., Little Rock, 1986—88; assoc. Rose Law Firm, Little Rock, 1988—92, mem., 1992—. Mem. Ark. Supreme Ct. Commn. on Model Jury Instrns.- Civil, 2005—; adj. prof. law U. Ark., Little Rock, 2001—. Mem. Leadership Program, C of C., Little Rock. Named one of 40 Under 40, Ark. Bus., 1999, Mid-South Super Lawyer, 2006. Mem.: Ark. Bar Assn. (mem. ho. dels. 2002—05). Avocations: reading, hiking. Office: Rose Law Firm 120 East Fourth St Little Rock AR 72201 Office Phone: 501-375-9131.

**STEWART, ANNETTE,** judge; b. Paris, Tex., Jan. 1, 1928; d. Ray Bryan and Mary Christene (Plumer) Stewart. BA, U. Tex., Austin, 1949; MEd, U. Tex., 1952; LLB summa cum laude, So. Meth. U., 1966. Bar: Tex. 1966. Assoc. Parnass, McGuire & Handy, 1966-67; ct. reporter Ct. Domestic Rels., Dallas, 1957-66, 67-74, judge, 1975-77, 301st Dist. Ct., Dallas, 1977-83, 305th Dist. Ct., 1985-86, Ct. Appeals, Dallas, 1983-84, 86-92, sr. judge, 1993—. Fellow Tex. Bar Found.; mem. State Bar Tex., Tex. Bar Found., Dallas Bar Assn., P.E.O., Phi Beta Kappa. Democrat. Presbyterian.

**STEWART, ARDEN RUTH,** retired automotive executive; b. Wheeling, W.Va., Sept. 29, 1930; d. Oliver Shaw and Helen (Neitzel) Stewart; children: Mark, Todd. BA, Baldwin Wallace Coll., 1952. Trainee GM, Cleve., 1952—57; tchr. Elyria (Ohio) City Bd. Edn., 1967—85; pres., CEO AAR, Inc., Cleve., 1984—2005. Pres. Elyria Schs. PTA, 1967; treas. Homeowners Assn., North Ridgeville, Ohio, 1988-89; mem. adv. com. bus. and tech.

Cuyahoga C.C. Recipient Weatherhead 100 award Case Western Res. U., 1990, 91, 92, 93, 94, 95. Republican. Episcopalian. Avocations: music, scuba diving, dance. Home: 32889 Brownstone Ln PO Box 39359 North Ridgeville OH 44039-0359 Office: AAR Inc 34999 Mills Rd North Ridgeville OH 44039-1366 Personal E-mail: arden9201@aol.com.

**STEWART, ARTHUR IRVING, III, (ART STEWART),** management consultant; b. Plainfield, N.J., Aug. 1, 1958; s. Arthur Irving Jr. and Audree Claire (Rollerson) S. BS in Mass Comm., Emerson Coll., 1982; Profl. Devel. cert. in Sr. Exec. Leadership, Georgetown U., 2004, postgrad. in Policy Mgmt., 2005—. Intern Sta. KYW Newsradio/TV, Phila., 1977; news anchorman, reporter Sta. WLBR-WUFM-FM, Lebanon, Pa., 1984; ops. mgr. Sta. WMSP-FM, Harrisburg, Pa., 1984-86; sr. account exec. mktg. and sales promotion Sta. WFCC-FM, Chatham, Mass., 1987-88; account mgr. Vizwiz Film-Video, Inc., Brookline, Mass., 1989-90; pub. rels. account exec. The Interface Group, Needham, Mass., 1991-92; sr. account exec. pub. rels. Mullen Advt., 1992-93; pres., sr. counsel Stewart Strategies Group, LLC, Wayne, Pa., 1993—. Dir. mktg. and pub. rels. Cape and Islands Chamber Music Festival, Cape Cod, Mass., 1988; asst. organist The United Parish, Brookline, 1982-84. Producer (radio concert broadcasts) Harrisburg Symphony Orch., 1984-86, documentary on U.S. debut tour of Westminster Cathedral Choir of London, 1985, investigative report on acid rain, 1985 (Excellence in Broadcasting award), documentary on Nat. Cathedral Wash ington, 1986 (Excellence in Broadcasting award). Editor OUTREACH newsletter Trinity Ch., Boston, 1990-94; staff media rels. 72d gen. conv. Episcopal Ch. U.S.A., 1997, Recipient Excellence in Broadcasting award Pa. Assn. Broadcasters; named to Outstanding Young Men in Am., 1996. Mem. Am. Polit. Sci. Assn., Pub. Rels. Soc. Am., Greater Wash. Bd. Trade, Leadership, Inc., Phila., Am. Guild Organists, Edn. Com., Pub. Rels. Com., Anti Defamation League, Washington Ind. WRiters, World Affairs Coun., World Future Soc. Episcopalian. Avocations: running, bicycling, travel, the arts, politics. Office Phone: 610-407-0182. E-mail: results@stewartgrp.com.

**STEWART, BARBARA LYNN,** church administrator; b. Billings, Mont., May 13, 1954; d. Joseph Isacc and Ima Evelyn (Daugherty) Gates; m. Forrest Y. Stewart, Nov. 15, 1997. BS in Elem. Edn., Eastern Mont. Coll., 1976. Cert. tchr. Mont. Tchr. Union Sch., Lindsay, Mont., 1976-79, Greycliff Sch., Mont., 1979-80; supr. Alliance Christian Sch., Lewistown, Mont., 1981-83, prin., supr., 1983-86, Paradise Christian Acad., Lewistown, 1986-91; driver, dispatcher, contracts and svcs. coord. Spl. Transp. Inc., Billings, Mont., 1991-94; in-home caregiver Billings, 1994-97; tax preparer H&R Block, Carbondale, Ill., 1999, Herrin, Ill., 1999—2000; adminstrv. asst. First Presbyn. Ch., Carbondale, 2000—.

**STEWART, BRADLEY MITCHELL,** secondary school educator; b. Youngstown, Ohio, Mar. 8, 1954; s. Ralph Franklin and Donna Mae Stewart; children: Eric A., Jefferson Thomas. BS, Ball State U., Muncie, Ind., 1976, MA, 1981. Lic. Ind., 1977. Tchr. Tri Creek Sch. Corp., Lowell, Ind., 1979—; coach, 1979—. Clinic spkr. Ind. Football Coaches Assn., Richmond, Indpls., and Lafayette, Ind., 1996—06. Named Coach of Yr., Gary Post Tribune, 1992. Mem.: Ind. Football Coaches Assn. (assoc. Region 1 All Star Coach and Coach of Yr. 1992, 2004, 2006). R-Consevative. Methodist. Avocation: travel. Home: 114 Elm St Lowell IN 46356 Office: Tri Creek Sch Corp 2051 E Commercial Lowell IN 46356 Office Phone: 219-696-7733. Office Fax: 219-696-0042. Personal E-mail: stewdef@yahoo.com. E-mail: bstewart@tricreek.k12in.us.

**STEWART, BURTON GLOYDEN, JR.,** retired banker; b. Clayton, N.C., Mar. 14, 1933; s. Burton Gloyden and Evelyn I. (Stallings) S.; m. Patricia Taylor, June 16, 1956; children: Burton Gloyden III, H. Taylor. AB, Duke U., 1955; grad., Sch. Banking of the south, 1970; exec. program, U. N.C., 1975. With Allstate Ins. Co., 1957-66, regional sales mgr. Charlotte, NC, 1964-66; with Branch Banking and Trust Co., Wilson, NC, 1966-98, sr. v.p., mgr. corp. planning and mktg. divsn., 1972-81, dir. investor rels., 1981-98, ret., 1998. Dir. Branch Corp., 1974-82; dir. N.C. Payments System, 1980-89, v.p., 1983-86, chmn. bd. 1986-89; bd. dirs., chmn. Electronic Fin. Svcs., Inc., 1988-90. Bd. dirs., treas. Wilson Arts Coun., 1969-71; bd. dirs. Wilson Heart Assn., 1968, Wilson United Way, 1974-80, 86-89, campaign chmn., 1977, pres., 1979, chmn. strategic planning com., 1986-90; mem. N.C. Gov.'s Efficiency Study Commn., 1985, N.C. Goals and Policy Bd., 1985-93; local com. Cypress Glen Retirement Cmty., 1991—, chmn., 1999-2001; fin. com. trustee United Meth. Ret. Homes, Inc., 1999—, chmn., 2002—; trustee UMRH Found., 1999—, chmn., 2002—. Lt. USNR, 1955-57. Mem. Bank Investor Rels. Assn. (bd. dirs. 1984-98, v.p. 1987-88), Wilson Country Club, Dunes Club. Methodist. Address: 1107 Salem St NW Wilson NC 27893-2139

**STEWART, CARL E.,** federal judge; b. Shreveport, La., 1950; BA magna cum laude, Dillard U., 1971; JD, Loyola U., New Orleans, 1974. Atty. Piper & Brown, Shreveport, La., 1977—78; staff atty. La. Atty. Gen. Office, Shreveport, 1978—79; asst. U.S. atty. Office U.S. Atty. (we. dist.) La., Shreveport, 1979—83; prin. Stewart & Dixon, Shreveport, 1983—85; spl. asst. dist. atty., asst. prosecutor City of Shreveport, 1983—85; judge La. Dist. Ct., 1985—91, La. Ct. Appeals (2d cir.), 1991—94, U.S. Ct. Appeals (5th cir.), 1994—. Bd. trustees Cmty. Found. Shreveport-Bossier, Shreveport, La., 1994—2004, Am. Inns Ct. Found.; chmn. nat. search com. Boy Scouts Am. Capt. JAGC other, 1974—77, Ft. Sam Houston, Tex. Recipient Am. Silver Buffalo awrd, Boy Scouts Am., 2002. Mem.: La. State Bar Assn. (bench/bar liaison com.), La., Conf. Ct. Appeal Judges, Black Lawyers Assn. Shreveport-Bossier, Am. Inns of Ct. (Harry Booth/Henry Politz chpt. Shreveport), Nat. Bar Assn., Omega Psi Phi (Rho Omega chpt.). Office: US Ct Appeals 5th Cir 300 Fannin St Ste 2299 Shreveport LA 71101-3124 Office Phone: 318-676-3765.*

**STEWART, CARLETON M.,** retired bank executive, director; b. Chgo., 1921; s. Carleton Merrill and Margaret (Lyon) S.; m. Alicia Dewar (dec.); 3 children; m. Kathryn White. Student, Stanford U., 1939-42; grad. in indsl. adminstrn., Harvard U., 1943, MBA, 1947. With Citibank, 1947-76, v.p. N.Y.C., 1960-67, sr. v.p. in charge of Asia Pacific area, 1967-69, sr. v.p. in charge of South Asia, Middle East and Africa, 1969-73; sr. officer London, 1973-76; dir. Grindlay's Bank Ltd., London, Banque Internat. pour L'Afrique Occidentale, Paris, 1973-76; chmn. bd., chief exec. officer Am. Security Corp. and Am. Security Bank, Washington, 1976-80; chmn. bd. Internat. Bank Miami, 1983-85; dir. Travelers Asset Mgmt. Internat. Corp., NYC, 1985-87, ret., 1987—. Mayor Longboat Key, Fla., 1987-88, town commr., 1984-90, ethics com., 1990-99, chmn. 1992-94; mem. Planning Commn., Sarasota County, Fla., 1990-92. Capt. AUS, 1943-46.

**STEWART, CHARLES LESLIE,** lawyer; b. Fayetteville, Ark., Aug. 12, 1919; s. Charles Leslie and Ruth (Want) Stewart; m. Edalee Esther Gastrock, Aug. 30, 1941; children: William Paul, Thomas Alan, Katherine Jean, Robert Edward. AB, U. Ill., 1940; MA, La. State U., 1941; student, George Washington U. Law Sch., 1944-45; JD, U. Chgo., 1947. Bar: Ill. 1948, U.S. Supreme Ct. 1954. Economist Dept. Agr., 1941—42; adminstrv. asst. OPA, 1942-43, Bd. Econ. Warfare, 1943; exec. dir. Chgo. divsn. ACLU, 1946—47; assoc. Mayer, Brown, Rowe & Maw, Chgo., 1947-55, ptnr., 1956-67, 70-71, resident ptnr. charge European office, Paris, 1967-70; v.p., sec., gen. counsel, 1974-83, Hartmarx Corp., Chgo., 1983-84, v.p., sec., sr. counsel, 1984, of counsel legal dept., 1985-89; arbitrator Mandatory Arbitration Program Cir. Ct., Cook County, Ill., 1990-2005. Mem. Am. Law Inst., 1983-90. Mem. Glencoe (Ill.) Bd. Edn., 1965-66; mem. planning com. Corp. Counsel Inst., Northwestern U. Sch. Law and Ill. Inst. Continuing Legal Edn., 1978-84, vice-chmn., 1983, chmn., 1984; mem. Glencoe Union Ch.; sec. projects com. Rsch. and Analysis Br., 1944-45. Served with Rsch. and Analysis Br. OSS, AUS, 1943-45. Mem. ABA, Ill. State Bar Assn., Chgo. Bar Assn. (com. devel. of law 1977-91, vice chmn. 1984-85, chmn. 1985-86, corp. law com. 1981-91, corp. law depts. com. 1981-83, sr. lawyers com. 1987-92), Am. Soc. Corp. Secs. (adv. com. Chgo. regional group 1978-83, vice chmn. 1979-80, chmn. 1980-81, nat. dir.

1981-84, exec. com. 1983-84, corp. practices com. 1982-87, assoc. mem. 1986-91), Skokie Country Club, Rotary, Delta Phi. Avocations: genealogy, history, bridge. Home and Office: 2525 Mayapple Ct Northbrook IL 60062-6531

**STEWART, COLIN L.,** biologist, researcher; DPhil, U. Oxford. Staff scientist European Molecular Biology Lab. (EMBL); mem. Roche Inst. Molecular Biology; chief Cancer and Devel. Biology Lab. Ctr. Cancer Rsch. Nat. Cancer Inst., also head Mammalian Devel. Biology Sect., Cancer and Devel. Biology Lab. Office: Cancer and Devel Biology Lab Ctr Cancer Rsch PO Box B Bldg 539 Rm 121 Frederick MD 21702-1201 Office Phone: 301-846-1755. Office Fax: 301-846-7177. E-mail: stewartc@ncifcrf.gov.

**STEWART, CONNIE WARD,** retired academic administrator; b. Athens, Ga., Nov. 19, 1938; d. Fred Tendal and Elsie (Janes) Ward; m. D.G. Stewart, 1960 (div. 1967); 1 child, Sheri Lyn; m. Nick Vista, Apr. 16, 1982. AB in Journalism, U. Ga., 1959, MA, 1968; postgrad., George Washington U., 1979; cert. in ednl. mgmt., Harvard U., 1985. Cert. elem. and secondary tchr., Ga. Promotion-pub. rels. staff Sta. WSB-TV, Atlanta, 1959—61; assoc. dir. Ga. Scholarship Commn., Atlanta, 1967; faculty U. Ga. Journalism Sch., Athens, 1967—70; dir. orientation U. Ga., Athens, 1970—71; project mgr. Planned Mgmt. Corp., Tampa, Fla., 1976—77; dir. policy comm., mem., Carter-Mondale adminstrn. HEW, Washington, 1977—79; orgnl. staff U.S. Dept. Edn., Washington, 1979; v.p. Mich. State U., East Lansing, 1980—87; assoc. v.p. Emory U., Atlanta, 1987—93; ret., 1993. Dir. Cmty. Forum on Children and Families Ga. State U., 1995; mil. acad. screening com. Office USS Senator Donald Riegle, Lansing, Mich., 1984-86. Editor, columnist Oconee Enterprise, l97l-72. Steering com. Carter for Pres. Campaign, Fla., 1975—76; exec. com. Mich. Sesquicentennial Celebratoin, 1985—87; mem. Ga. Scholarship Commn., 1965—67, Ga. Motion Picture-TV Adv. Bd., 1972—76, Ga. Gov.'s Commn. on Edn., 1965—67, Mich. Film and TV Coun., 1984—86; exec. com. Comm. Coun., The Atlanta Project, 1992—94; vol. mentor in pub. schs. Success-by-Six program, 1993—96; trainer vols. United Way, 1993—96, Big Bros./Bis Sisters Teach One program, 1997—99; docent Carter Presdl. Libr./Mus., 1998—; bd. councilors Carter Presdl. Ctr., 2005—; bd. dirs. Olympic Acad., 1987—88, Atlanta Olympics Organizing Com. for Olympic Games, 1991—93. Recipient Outstanding Alumna award Henry W. Grady Coll. of Journalism and Mass Communications, U. Ga., 1993, hon. alumnus award Mich. State U., 1987; disting. svc. award Ga. Edn. Advancement Coun., 1990. Mem. Coun. for Advancement and Support Edn., Nat. Assn. State Univs. and Land Grant Colls. (univ. rels. coun. 1984-87), Atlanta C. of C. (Forward Atlanta 1989), Soc. Profl. Journalists, Nat. Press Club (Washington), Pub. Rels. Soc. Am., Phi Beta Kappa (v.p. Mich. State U. chpt. 1986, pres. 1987), Phi Kappa Phi, Sigma Delta Chi, Theta Sigma Phi, Di Gamma Kappa, Zeta Tau Alpha. Democrat. Avocations: travel, reading, poetry. Home: 2848 Warrington Close Tucker GA 30084-2598

**STEWART, CYNTHIA WILLIS,** minister; b. Friendship, Guyana, Dec. 13, 1944; arrived in U.S., 1985; d. William Nathaniel and Hilloise Isola Willis; m. Ronald Eustace Stewart, June 3, 1990. BSc magna cum laude, Mich. State Univ., 1973; MA in Comm. Arts, Cornell Univ., 1980; MDiv, Hood Theol. Sem., 1983; DD, Drew Univ., 1990. Lic. local preacher 1979, admitted on trial 1981, Deacon's Orders 1982, Elder's Orders 1983; cert. Pub. Rels. Sch. of Pub. Rels., Eng., 1975. Pastor Alleyne A.M.E. Zion Ch., Guyana, South America, 1982—85; bishop's adminstrv. asst., presiding elder, advisor Guyana Conf., 1982—88; bishop's adminstrv. asst., presiding elder, 1992—96, Guyana, Barbados, Trinidad, Tobago Conf., 1996—98; assoc. min. First A.M.E. Zion Ch., Bklyn., 1986—92; pastor Westbury A.M.E. Zion Ch., NY, 1992—2000; presiding elder L.I. Dist., N.Y. Conf., 2000—01, Westchester Dist., N.Y. Conf., 2001—. Editor, design and layout artist, contbg. writer Missionary Seer; contbr. articles pub. to non-profit jours. Bd. dirs. Harriet Tubman Home Inc.; adminstrv. bds. Theol. Sem., Christian Edn. Sch. and Coll.; pres. elder's coun. A.M.E. Zion Ch., first v.p.; chmn. bd. Christian Edn. and Admission Com.; mem. Budget Com., Holy Orders Com., N.Y. Conf.; bd. trustees N.Y. Conf., M. Ardelle Shaw Retreat Ctr. Recipient Excellence in Christian Life and Conduct, GW Griffin Meml. Preaching award, Hood Theol. Sem., Nat. Sojourner Truth Meritorious Svc. award, Nat. Assn. of Negro Bus. and Profl. Women's Club. Mem.: NAACP, Ch. Women United, World Fedn. of Meth. and Uniting Ch. Women, Ministerial Alliance, Nat. Coun. of Negro Women (life), Assn. of Christian Educators (life), A.M.E. Zion Ch. Min. and Lay Assn. (life). Home: 1129 Pembrooke St Uniondale NY 11553-1408

**STEWART, DANIEL CLARK,** lawyer; b. Morristown, N.J., Sept. 23, 1947; BA, Brown U., 1969; JD, Duke U., 1972. Bar: Tex. 1972. Ptnr. Winstead, Sechrest & Minick, P.C., Dallas; ptnr., head Insolvency & Reorganization Sect. Vinson & Elkins LLP, Dallas. Mem. ABA, State Bar Tex. (bankruptcy and reorganization law com. 1979—, bankruptcy adv. comsn. to Tex. Bd. Legal Specialization 1981—), Dallas Bar Assoc. (chmn. ethics com. 1979 and bankruptcy and coml. law sect. 1979-80). Office: Vinson & Elkins LLP Trammell Crow Ctr 2001 Ross Ave, Ste 3700 Dallas TX 75201 also: 26 Fl 666 Fifth Ave New York NY 10103 Office Phone: 214-220-7761. E-mail: dstewart@velaw.com.

**STEWART, DAVID,** history professor, researcher; b. Bethesda, Md., May 14, 1965; m. Carla Elizabeth Barton; children: Alison Jelyane, Arianna Jessica, Justinian Aurelius. BA, BS, Eastern Nazarene Coll., Quincy, Mass., 1987; MA, Ohio State U., Columbus, 1989, PhD, 1993. Lab. technician ARC, Gaithersburg, Md., 1983—87; prof. history Hillsdale Coll., Mich., 1993—; honours program dir., 1999—2004. Fgn. lang. instr. Will Carleton Acad., Hillsdale, 2003—04. Author: (monograph) Assimilation and Acculturation in Early Modern France, Dictionary of the Treaties of the War of the Spanish Succession. Office: Hillsdale Coll 30 E College St Hillsdale MI 49242 Office Phone: 517-437-7341. Business E-mail: david.stewart@hillsdale.edu.

**STEWART, DAVID JAMES,** oncologist, educator; m. Lesley Gayle Carruthers, 2002. MD, Queen's U., Kingston, Ont., 1974. Faculty assoc. med. instr. U. Tex. M.D. Anderson Hosp. and Tumor Inst., Houston, 1978—79, asst. prof. and asst. internist dept. devel. therapeutics, 1979—80; med. oncologist and clin. asst. prof. of medicine Ottawa Regional Cancer Ctr. and U. of Ottawa, Ont., Canada, 1980—84, med. oncologist and prof. of medicine, cellular and molecular medicine (pharmacology), 1988—2003, med. oncologist and assoc. prof. of medicine and pharmacology, 1984—88; chief of the divsn. of med. oncology Ottawa Civic Hosp., Canada, 1989—99; oncologist U. Tex. M.D. Anderson Cancer Ctr., Houston, 2003—, prof. medicine, 2003—, chief exptl. therapeutics dept. thoracic/head and neck med. oncology, 2003—, chair ad-interim dept. thoracic/head and neck med. oncology, 2005—. Contbr. over 500 articles and abstracts to profl. jours., chapters to books. Mem.: Am. Assn. for Cancer Rsch., Am. Soc. of Clin. Oncology. Achievements include research in Of anticancer agents, mechanisms of resistance to chemotherapy and methods of overcoming resistance. Avocations: running, skiing, hiking. Office: UT MD Anderson Cancer Center 1515 Holcombe Blvd Houston TX 77030 Office Phone: 713-792-6363. Personal E-mail: dstewart@mdanderson.org.

**STEWART, DAVID MARSHALL,** librarian; b. Nashville, Aug. 1, 1916; s. David and Mary (Marshall) Stewart; m. Gladys Carroll, June 9, 1947; 1 child, James Marshall. BA, Bethel Coll., 1938; BSLS, George Peabody Coll., 1939. Circulation asst. Vanderbilt U. Library, 1938-39; county librarian Ark. Library Commn., 1939-40; Tenn. supr. WPA library service projects, 1940-42; librarian Memphis State U., 1942-46; spl. asst. to chief card div. Library of Congress, Washington, 1947; librarian CIA, Washington, 1948-60; chief librarian Nashville Pub. Library, 1960-85; Instr. Peabody Library Sch., 1966-80. Bd. dirs. Coun. Cmty. Agys., Nashville, Friends Chamber Music, Nashville, Traverlers Aid, Nashville; v.p. bd. Mid.-E. Tenn. Arthritis Found. Served to lt. comdr. USNR, 1942—46. Mem.: ALA, Pub. Libr. Assn. AM. (chmn. stds. com. 1964—65, pres. 1966—67), Southeastern Libr. Assn. Tenn. Libr. Assn. (chmn. legis. com. 1961—65, v.p. 1965, pres. 1966, Honor award 1983), Alumni Assn. Bethel Coll. (dir., Disting. Alumni award 1992), Coffe House Club (Nashville), Kiwanis. Democrat. Mem. Ch. Of Christ. Home: 6342 Torrington Rd Nashville TN 37205-3157

**STEWART, DAVID PENTLAND,** lawyer, educator; b. Milw., Dec. 24, 1943; s. James Pentland and Frederica (Stockwell) S.; children from previous marriage: Jason, Jonathan; m. Jennifer Kilmer, June 21, 1986; children: Daniel, Mary Elizabeth. AB, Princeton U., 1966; JD, MA, Yale U., 1971; LLM, N.Y.U., 1975. Bar: N.Y. 1972, U.S. Dist. Ct. (ea. and so. dists.) N.Y. 1973, U.S. Ct. Appeals (2d cir.) 1973, D.C. 1976. Assoc. Donovan, Leisure, Newton & Irvine, N.Y.C., 1971-76; atty. adviser, office of legal adviser U.S. Dept. State, Washington, 1976-82, asst. legal adviser, 1982—. Adj. prof. law Georgetown U., Washington, 1984—; Am. U., Washington, 1985—; Johns Hopkins U. Sch. Advanced Internat. Studies, 2000—; vis. lectr. Sch. Law U. Va., 1993-96. Nat. Law Ctr., George Washington U., 1993-99. Co-editor: (ann. vols.) Digest of United States Practice in International Law, 1989—2005; contbr. articles to profl. jours. Served to maj. USAR, 1970-87. Mem. ABA, Am. Law Inst., Am. Soc. Internat. Law., Internat. Law Assn. (adv. coun. procedural aspects internat. law inst.). Office: US Dept State Office Legal Adviser Washington DC 20520-6310 Business E-mail: stewartdp@state.gov.

**STEWART, DAVID WAYNE,** marketing educator, psychologist, consultant; b. Baton Rouge, Oct. 23, 1951; s. Wesley A. Stewart, Jr. and Edith L. (Richhart) Moore; m. Lenora Francois, June 6, 1975; children: Sarah Elizabeth, Rachel Dawn. BA, N.E. La. U., 1972; MA, Baylor U., 1973, PhD, 1974. Rsch. psychologist HHS, La., 1974-76; rsch. mgr. Needham, Harper & Steers Advt., Chgo., 1976-78; assoc. prof. Jacksonville (Ala.) State U., 1978-80, Vanderbilt U. Nashville, 1980-86, sr. assoc. dean, 1984-86; prof. U. So. Calif., L.A., 1986-90, Ernest W. Hahn prof. mktg., 1990-91, Robert Brooker rsch. prof. mktg., 1991—, chmn. dept. mktg., 1995-99, dep. dean faculty, 1999-2001, dep. dean, 2001—04, chmn. dept. mktg., 2006—. Mgmt. cons., 1978—. Author, co-author: Secondary Research: Sources and Methods, Effective Television Advertising: A Study of 1000 Commericals, Consumer Behavior and the Practice of Marketing, Focus Group: Theory and Practice, Attention, Attitude, and Affect in Repsonse to Advertising, Nonverbal Communication and Advertising; editor: Jour. of Mktg., 1999-2002, Jour. Acad. Mktg. Sci., 2006—; contbr. articles to profl. jours.; editor: Jour. of Mktg., 1999-2002; mem. editl. bd. Jour. Pub. Policy and Mktg., Jour. Mktg., Jour. Advt., Jour. Promotion Mgmt., Current Issues and Rsch. in Advt., Jour. Internat. Consumer Mktg., Jour. Managerial Issues, Jour. Promotion Mgmt., Jour. Advt, Rsch., others; past pres. policy bd. Jour. Consumer Rsch., Acad. Mgmt.; editor-in-chief Jour. Acad. Mktg. Sci. Recipient Outstanding Contbn. to Advt. Rsch. award, Am. Acad. Advt., 1998, named Disting. Mktg. Educator, Acad. Mktg. Sci., 2006. Fellow APA (coun. rep.), Am. Psychol. Soc. (charter); mem. Soc. for Consumer Psychology (past pres.), Inst. Mgmt. Scis., Decision Sci. Inst., Am. Mktg. Assn. (pres. acad. coun. 1997-98, v.p. fin. 1998-99), Assn. for Consumer Rsch., Am. Statis. Assn. (chair sect. on stats. in mktg. 1997), Acad. of Mgmt., Acad. Mktg. Sci. (bd. govs. 2004—). Republican. Baptist. Office: U So Calif Marshal Sch Bus Dept Mktg Acc 308B Los Angeles CA 90089-0443 Office Phone: 213-740-5037. Business E-Mail: david.stewart@marshall.usc.edu.

**STEWART, DAVID WITHERINGTON,** business consultant; b. Marion, Ind., Feb. 9, 1939; s. Edgar Allen Jr. and Faye Maxine (Cummings); m. Ruth Ada Valk, Aug. 26, 1961, (div.); m. Annette Louise Witherington, Dec. 17, 1962 (dec. Aug. 1999); children: Edna (dec.) Geoffrey. BS in Physics, U. Fla., Gainesville, 1959. Sr. engr. Atlas Gen. Dynamics/Convair, Cape Canaveral, Fla., 1959—63; lead engr. Gemini-Titan Martin Canaveral, Cape Canaveral, 1963—66; lead engr. Sprint Martin-Orlando, Orlando, Fla., 1966—67; lead engr. Apollo Rockwell Internat., Kennedy Space Center, Fla., 1967—74, lead engr. avionics, 1975—78, prime system integ. engr. shuttle, 1978—79, supr. orbiter software, 1979—81, project mgr. software, 1982—84, project mgr. design, 1984—85, project mgr. adv. programs, 1985—89, mgr. adv. program, 1989—91, project mgr. adv. program and bus. devel., 1991—92, program devel. mgr. Fla. ops. space sys. divsn., 1992—96; owner, pres. L&D Consulting, Titusville, Fla., 1996—; owner, gen. mgr. Coreopsis Publs., 2004—. Author: Edie and the Globe, 1966. Pres. North Brevard Environ. Action Com., Titusville, 1970-73; chmn. Marine Resources Coun. East Fla., 1996-97, 2000—02; pres.-elect Space Coast Devel. Commn. 1995-96; sec. Space Coast Grant Profls. Network, 1997-99; pres. Brevard Adult Literacy Vols., Inc., 2000—04; vol. treas. Brevard Humanity Ctr., Inc, 2000—. Mem. Inst. Cert. Profl. Mgrs. (cert. mgr.), Am. Cons. League (accredited profl. cons.). Republican. Unitarian Universalist. Home: PO Box 5869 Titusville FL 32783-5869 Office: Bus Devel Cons 609 Garden St Titusville FL 32796 Fax: 321-264-1885. Office Phone: 321-223-0830. E-mail: david@coerepsis.gs, david@davidwstewart.com.

**STEWART, DEBRA WEHRLE,** academic administrator; b. Petersburg, Va., May 22, 1943; BA in Philosophy and Govt. Pol. Sci., Marquette U., 1965; MA in Govt., U. Md., 1967; PhD in Polit. Sci., U. N.C., 1975. Instr. polit. sci. European divsn. U. Md., Nuremberg, Germany, 1967-69; instr. polit. sci. and pub. adminstrn. N.C. State U., Raleigh, 1974-75, asst. prof., 1975-78, assoc. prof., 1979-83, prof., 1984—, acting dir. MPA program, 1978, assoc. dean Grad. Sch., 1983-86, interim vice provost and dean Grad. Sch., 1986-88, dean Grad. Sch., 1988-2000, vice provost, 1995-98, vice chancellor, dean Grad. Sch., 1998-2000; pres. Coun. Grad. Schs., Washington, 2000—. Interim chancellor U. N.C., Greensboro, 1994; mem. com. on assessment of rsch. doctorate NRC, 1992-95; mem. Grad. Record Exam. Bd., 1992-96, chmn.-elect, 1994-95, chmn., 1995-96; bd. dirs. Coun. Grad. Schs., 1990—, chmn.-elect,1992-93, chmn., 1993-94; mem. Test Battlash as Fgn. Lang. Bd., 1992-95; councilor Oak Ridge Assoc. Univs., 1988-92, bd. dirs., 1993—, chair-elect 1997—; bd. dirs. Nat. Phys. Scis. Consortium, 1998—; mem. exec. com. Coun. So. Grad. Schs., 1989-91; trustee Triangle U. Ctr. for Advanced Studies, 1989—; mem. Commn. on Peer Rev. and Accreditation, Nat. Assn. of Schs. of Pub. Affairs and Adminstrn., 1997-99. Author: The Women's Movement in Community Politics: The Role of Local Commissions on the Status of Women, 1980, (with G. David Garson) Organizational Behavior and Public Management, 1983, 3d edit. (with Vasu and Garson), 1998; editor: Women in Local Politics, 1980; mem. editl. bd. Rev. Pub. Pres. Adminstrn., 1981-89, Annals Pub. Adminstrn., 1982-84, Women and Politics, 1980-88, Politics and Policy, 1983-86; contbr. articles to profl. jours., chpts. to books. Recipient edn. award YWCA Acad. Women, 1988 Mem. Nat. Assn. State Univs. and Land-Grant Colls. (bd. dirs. 1992-94, exec. com. coun. on rsch. policy and grad. edn. 1989-92, chmn. 1990-91), Am. Soc. for Pub. Adminstrn. (com. on status of women in pub. adminstrn. 1976-78, com. on profl. stds. and ethics 1980-89, chmn. com. on whistle blowing and dissent channels of profl. stds. and ethics com. 1985-86, Burchfield award 1976), So. Polit. Sci. Assn. (nominating com. 1978, coord. pub. adminstrn. sect. 1979), Women's Forum N.C., Phi Kappa Phi, Pi Sigma Alpha, Pi Alpha Alpha. Office: Coun Grad Schs Grad Sch 1 Dupont Cir NW Ste 430 Washington DC 20036-1136 Office Phone: 202-223-3791. Business E-mail: dstewart@cgs.nche.edu.

**STEWART, DONALD GEORGE,** musician, composer, music industry executive; b. Sterling, Ill., Jan. 8, 1935; s. Donald Balmer and Elinore Maud (Denison) S.; m. Susan Ann Trainer, June 13, 1963 (div. 1979); 1 child, Elizabeth Ann. MusB, Ind. U., 1960; postgrad., Manhattan Sch., 1960-62; student, Sch. of Jazz, 1958-60; studied with Roy Harris, Bernhard Heiden, Gunther Schuller. 2d clarinetist Birmingham (Ala.) Symphony, 1954-56, Fla. Symphony, Orlando, 1963; musician with numerous jazz groups including Ornette Coleman, David Baker, Sammy Davis, 1957-65; woodwind player Orch. USA, N.Y.C., 1963-65; libr. Harkness Ballet, N.Y.C., 1967-72; founder, clarinetist Boehm Quintette, N.Y.C., 1968-88; music asst. N.Y. State Coun. on the Arts, N.Y.C., 1972-75; freelance copyist N.Y.C., 1958-88; founder, pres. Trillenium Music Co., 1986—, clarinetist, saxophonist, 1975—; pres. Opera North, Norwich, Vt., 1987-89; musician Sarasota Jazz Ensemble, 2005—. Founder, treas. Chamber Music Am., N.Y.C., 1977-81; panelist Vt. Coun. on the Arts, 1976-78. Composer Piccolo Concerto, 1973, August Lions for Youth Orch., 1978, Song of Arion, 1985 (2d prize Am. Harp Soc.), First Blue Symphony, 1988, Book of Sliding Things, 1989, Green Mountain Christmas Card (opera), 1995, Never Seek to Tell Thy Love (voice and ensemble), 1998, Duo for Violin and Cello, 1999, Flute Quartet, 2003, Third Symphony, 2005; others; transcriber wind chamber music; composer, arranger for G. Schirmer,

Boosey and Hawkes, Carl Fischer, Trillenium Music Co.; recs. for Columbia, Orion, New World, Margun and Marlboro, 1964—; participant Marlboro Festival, Vt., 1966-68, Berkshire Festival, Mass., summer 1965, 68. Vt. Coun. on the Arts fellow, 1985, Nat. Endowment for Arts grant, 1978—. Mem. ASCAP, Am. Fedn. Musicians, Am. Soc. Music Copyists (bd. dirs. 1970-87, treas. 1984-87), Am. Music Ctr., Music Pub.'s Assn. Democrat. Congregationalist. Office: Trillenium Music Co PO Box 51059 Sarasota FL 34232-0329 Office Phone: 941-377-7375. Office Fax: 941-377-9043. Business E-Mail: don@trillmusic.com.

**STEWART, DORIS MAE,** biology professor; b. Sandsprings, Mont., Dec. 12, 1927; d. Virgil E. and Violet M. (Weaver) S.; m. Felix Loren Powell, Oct. 8, 1956; children: Leslie, Loren. BS, Coll. Puget Sound, 1948, MS, 1949; PhD, U. Wash., 1953. Instr. U. Mont., Missoula, 1954-56, asst. prof., 1956-57, U. Puget Sound, Tacoma, 1957-58; head sci. dept. Am. Kiz Lisesi, Istanbul, Turkey, 1958-62; rsch. asst. dept. U. Wash., Seattle, 1963-67, rsch. assoc. prof., 1967-68; assoc. prof. Cen. Mich. U., Mt. Pleasant, 1970-72, U. Balt., 1973-81, prof., 1981-95, prof. emeritus, 1995—. Contbr. numerous articles to profl. jours. Mem. Am. Physiol. Soc., Sigma Xi. Home: 1103 Frederick Rd Baltimore MD 21228-5032

**STEWART, DOROTHY K.,** librarian; b. Bristol, Conn., Sept. 28, 1928; d. Robert and Anna Esther (Schwirtz) Konopask; m. David Benjamin Stewart, Sept. 27, 1952 (div. Nov. 1979); children: Douglas Neil, Diane Alison. BA in Romance Langs. and Lit. cum laude, Boston U., 1950; MSLS, Cath. U. Am., 1959. Children's libr. Brookline (Mass.) Pub. Libr., 1953-55, Takoma Park (Md.) Libr., 1955-57; reference libr. U.S. Geol. Survey, 1961; libr. Washington Internat. Sch., 1979-80, Office Sea Grant NOAA, Rockville, Md., 1980-82; info. specialist Life Ring, Inc., Silver Spring, Md., 1983-84; pub. svc. libr. Urban Inst., Washington, 1984-85; user svcs. coord. ERIC Clearinghouse on Tchg. and Tchr. Edn., Washington, 1985-97; ret., 1997. Active, past pres. PTA, Rockville, Md., 1973-78; chmn., mem. com. Potomac (Md.) Libr. Adv. Com., 1975-85. Mem. Capital PC User Group, French lang. clubs, Phi Beta Kappa, Beta Phi Mu. Democrat. Avocations: travel, hiking, birding, computers. Personal E-mail: dkstewart24@comcast.net.

**STEWART, E(DWARD) NICHOLSON,** investment management executive; b. Bronxville, N.Y., Sept. 28, 1940; s. Edward Nicholson and Helen (Davis) S.; m. Mary Patricia Hunter, Aug. 8, 1964; children: Pamela S. Burke, Wendy S. Leary. Student, Hamilton Coll., 1959-62; BA, New Sch. Social Rsch., 1965. Dir. membership Investment Co. Inst., N.Y.C., 1968; v.p. Lord, Abbett & Co., N.Y.C., 1969-74; pres. Trevor Stewart Burton & Jacobsen Inc., N.Y.C., 1974-95, CEO, 1990—2004, chmn., 1995—. Pres., bd. dirs. Robert Hampton Tapp Found., 1993—. Co-founder, editor Hackley Rev., 1963-68. Trustee Hackley Sch., 1971-87, treas., 1972-87, v.p. 1980-87; pres. Hackley Alumni Assn., Inc., 1967-69. Mem. USN League (Marine Corps com. N.Y. 1986—), Naval War Coll. Found. (life), Marine Corps Univ. Found. (assoc.), U.S. Naval Inst., Nat. Def. Indsl. Assn. (life), Union League Club (bd. govs. 1985-87, 95-97, vice-chmn. 1987, pres. 1989-90), Pendennis Club (Louisville), Sleepy Hollow Country Club (bd. govs. 1993-96, sec. 1995, 2001-2003, asst. sec. 2000, v.p. 2003-2004, pres. 2005—), Econ. Club N.Y., The 200 Club (bd. dirs.), Delta Kappa Epsilon. Republican. Office: 405 Lexington Ave Ste 4700 New York NY 10174

**STEWART, ELLEN D.,** theater producer; Former fashion designer; founder, dir. La MaMa Exptl. Theatre Club, NYC, 1961—. Vis. prof. Inst. Drama, Republic of Korea. Prodr. innovative theatre, most recently Antigone, a part of SEVEN: Seven Greek Plays in Repertory; dir., most recently Perseus, Great Jones Rep. Co.; active in internet theatre exch. Named Officer Ordre des Arts et Lettres, Republic France; named to Theatre Hall of Fame, 1993; recipient Margo Jones award, 1969, MacArthur Genius award, Les Kurbas award disting. svc. to art and culture, Ukraine, Order of Sacred Treasure Gold Rays with Rossette, Emperor Japan, 1994, Human Rights award, Philippines. Mem.: Seoul Internat. Theatre Inst. Office: La MaMa ETC 74A E 4th St New York NY 10003-8903 Office Phone: 212-254-6468. Business E-Mail: lamama@lamama.org.*

**STEWART, FRANK GRAHAM,** composer, clarinetist; b. La Junta, Colo., Dec. 12, 1920; s. Thomas Guy Stewart and Esther E. Higgins; m. Johanna L. Kluge, Apr. 28, 1950; 1 child, Terry Leigh Stewart Carroll. MusB in Composition and Clarinet, Eastman Sch. Music, Rochester, NY, 1942; MAT in Composition and Edn., Colo. State U., 1968; PhD in Composition and Theory, Mich. State U., 1971. Lifetime collg. credential in music (all grades) Calif. Clarinetist, arranger, composer US Army Field Band; Alice M. Ditson fellow in music composition Columbia U., NYC; composer, arranger, pianist San Francisco and LA; instr. Miss. State U. Faculty advisor Phi Mu Alpha; v.p., pres. Southea. Composers' League, 1977—80. Composer: Divertimento for 2 Flutes and Piano, 1977, Toccata Sonora for Flute, Trombone and Piano, 1979, (1 instrument with piano accompaniment) Sonata for Clarinet and Piano, 1939, 12 Etudes for Clarinet & Piano, 1944, Metamorph for Bassoon & Piano, 1972, Highlights for Piccolo, alternating with flute and Piano, 1984, Introduction & Scherzo for Oboe and Piano, 1984, Spacescape for Flute and Piano, 1984, Divertimento for Bass Trombone and Piano, 1997, (solo piano) Suite for Piano based on American Indian Songs, 1941, Sonata for Piano, 1946, Toccata, 1976, Piano Suite for Smaller Hands, 1983, Portrait: Early American, 1995, (vocal music) Three Epitaphs for Mixed Chorus, 1968, English As She Is Taught for Mixed Chorus & 4 Percussionists, 1969, The Phantom Train of Marshall Pass, for Narrator, 9 Woodwinds, 2 Percussionists, 1970, The First Joy of Marriage, for Mezzo-soprano voice and 2 Marimbists, 1970, To Let the Captive Go, an Opera in 3 Scenes, 1971, Mississippi: That Grand Old State of Mind, for Tenor and Piano, 1978, Tony and Nina: Christmas 1958, for Tenor and Piano, 1978, A Sunset, for Tenor, Flute, Flugelhorn & Piano, 1979, Trapped Lightnin', for Mezzo-soprano, Flute, Piano, 1981, From the 103d Psalm, for SATB and Piano, 1981. Named Nat. Arts Assoc., Sigma Alpha Iota, 1986; recipient prizes, Va. Coll. Band Dirs. Nat. Assn, Orpheus award, Phi Mu Alpha, award, Mannes Sch. Music, NYC. Mailing: PO Box 285 Johnson City TN 37605-0285 E-mail: fgstewart@brinet.com.

**STEWART, GEORGIANA LICCIONE,** writer; b. Mount Vernon, N.Y., May 18, 1943; d. Arthur Alfred and Grace Marie (Zuzzolo) Liccione; m. William Lawrence Stewart, July 18, 1975. BA, Columbia U., 1971; MA, Columbia Tchr.'s Coll., N.Y.C., 1973; MAT, Manhattanville Coll., 1973. Author, cons. Kimbo Ednl., Long Branch, NJ, 1970—; spl. edn. tchr. Bronxville (N.Y.) H.S., 1989—. Cons. NAEYC, SACUS, 1975-89, Pres.'s Coun. on Physical Fitness, 1979-81. Author: (69 children's musical activity records and books including) Adaptive Motor Learning, 1982, Bean Bag Activities, 1983, Preschool Aerobic Fun, 1989, Children of the World, 1991, ulticultural Rhythm Stick Fun, 1992, Toddlerific, 1993, World of Parachute Play, 1997, Children's Folk Dances, 1998, Moving with Mozart, 1999 (Early Childhood Dir.'s Choice award NAEYC), Nursery Rhyme Time, 2000, Cool Aerobics for Kids, 2001, Musical Scarves, 2002, Circle Time, 2004. Recipient Student Advocacy Overcoming the Odds award, 1997. Mem. AAHPERD, Nat. Assn. for Edn. of Young Children, So. Assn. for Children Under Six, Faculty Dance Educators Am., Assn. for Retarded Citizens, Columbia Club, Women's Nat. Rep. Club. Avocations: Heatsong music and art therapy program, organizing local benefit programs. Home: 81 Pondfield Rd # 328 Bronxville NY 10708-3818 Office: Kimbo Ednl PO Box 477 Long Branch NJ 07740-0477

**STEWART, GORDON CURRAN,** insurance association executive; b. Chgo., July 22, 1939; s. Henry Stewart and Evangeline (Williams) Bolton; m. Elizabeth Knorr, June 19, 1965 (div. 1968); m. Zanne Early, Dec. 20, 1995; 1 child, Katarina Guadalupe Hadley. BA, Oberlin Coll., 1960; MA, U. Chgo., 1962; student, U. Vienna, Austria, 1963; MFA, Yale U., 1967. Instr. Amherst Coll., Mass., 1967-68; dir. Bus. Comm. for Arts, NYC, 1969-71; exec. asst. Mayor of NYC, 1971-73; dir., writer NYC, LA, UK, 1973-78; dep. chief speechwriter President of US, Washington, 1978-81; instr. Bus. and Govt. Acad. forums, U.S. and fgn. countries, 1981-82; v.p. AMSE, NYC, 1982-89; exec. v.p. Ins. Info. Inst., NYC, 1989-91, pres., 1991—2006; ret. Cons. Am.

Bus. Conf., Washington, 1982-89, Internat. Commn. for Ctrl. Am., Washington, 1986-88, Coun. on Competitiveness, Washington, 1987-88, Def. Sci. Bd., Washington, 1988-89. Writer films: The Store, 1978, Joey, 1978, Gallery, 1978; dir. (play) The Elephant Man (1st US prodn.), 1977, Jesse, 1975, Cowboy Mouth, 1976, Sleep, 1977, (films) The Blazers, 1975; condr. Beggar's Opera, 1969, West Side Story, 1970. Dir. NY Urban Coalition, NYC, 1984-88; dir. policy Samuels for Gov., NY, 1974; speechwriter numerous dem. campaigns, 1974-81; mem. fin. coun. Dem. Nat. Com. 1984-88; mem. adv. coun. Dem. Leadership Coun., 1984-90. Woodrow Wilson fellow Woodrow Wilson Found., 1961. Mem. Writers Guild Am. (west), Judson Welliver Soc. of Chief Presdl. Speechwriters (sec.-treas.), Coun. Fgn. Rels., Century Assn., Phi Beta Kappa, Yale Club. Avocations: politics, music.

**STEWART, GREGORY WALLACE,** physician; b. Balt., July 8, 1961; s. Don Milton and Martha (Davis) S.; divorced; 1 child, Lauren Elizabeth; m. Bonnie Marie Johnson, June 8, 1991; children: Tess Marie, Shaid Michael. BS in Biology, Chemistry and Para-Med. Sports Therapy, Houston Baptist U., 1982; MD, U. Tex. Med. Br. Sch. of Medicine, 1986. Diplomate Am. Bd. Phys. Medicine and Rehab. Resident in phys. medicine and rehab. La. State U./Charity Hosp. in New Orleans, 1986-90; instr. and asst. residency Sect. Phys. Medicine and Rehab. La. State U. Sch. Medicine in New Orleans, 1990-92; clin. asst. prof. Dept. Orthop. Tulane U. Sch. Medicine, 1990-95; asst. prof. and residency program dir. Sect. of Phys. Medicine La. State U. Sch. Medicine in New Orleans, 1992-95; assoc. prof. orthopedics Tulane U. Sch. Medicine, 1995—, chief divsn. phys. medicine and rehab., 1995—, med. dir. Tulane Ctrs. for Phys. Medicine and Rehab., 1996—, co-dir. Tulane Inst. Sports Medicine, 1995—. Team physician New Orleans Night Arena Football Team, 1991-92, Tulane U., 1990—, Hahnville H.S., 1987—; physician Ballet Hysell, New Orleans; coord. sports medicine St. Charles and Plaquemines Parish Sch. Dists.; assoc. coord. sports medicine St. Bernard and Orleans Parish Sch. Dists.; mem. adv. coun. La. Sports Medicine and Safety; mem. U.S. Olympic Track and Field Trials Sports Medicine Staff, 1992; mem. sports medicine organizing com. NCAA Track and Field Championships, 1993. Contbr. numerous articles to med. jours. Mem., chmn. task force on disabling violence La. Adv. Coun. on Disability Prevention, 1990-93, mem. com. on prevention of secondary disabilties; med. cons. Weiss Rehab. Ctr.; chmn. divsn. of rehab. svcs. head injury tech. assistance com. State of La.; mem. adv. com. for phys. therapy asst. program Delgado C.C.; reviewer Medicine and Sci. in Sports and Exercise Jour. of Orthopaedic and Sports Phys. Therapy; abstract reviewer Nat. Head Injury Found.; grant reviewer Nat. Inst. Disability Rsch. and Rehab., prin. investigator, 1997-2001. Recipient Study of Personal Care Attendants for Indigent Quadriplegics grant Am. Assn. of Spinal Cord Injury Psychologists and Social Workers, 1991-93, Rehab. Long Term Tng. -Rehab. Medicine grant Rehab. Svcs. Adminstrn., 1993-95, La. Disability Prevention Program grant Sports Injury Surveillance in La., 1993-94. Fellow Am. Coll. Sports Medicine; mem. AMA, Am. Acad. Phys. Medicine and Rehab., Am. Congress Rehab. Medicine, Nat. Athletic Trainers Assn., S.E. Athletic Trainers Assn., La. State Med. Soc., La. Athletic Trainers Assn., Orleans Parish Med. Soc., La. Sports Medicine Soc. (edn. chmn. 1994-2002). Presbyterian. Avocations: gardening, genealogy. Home: 4905 Clearlake Dr Metairie LA 70006-1112 Office: Dept Orthopaedics SL32 1430 Tulane Ave New Orleans LA 70112-2699 E-mail: gstewart@tulane.edu.

**STEWART, HAROLD BROWN,** biochemist; b. Chatham, Ont., Can., Mar. 9, 1921; s. John Craig and Margaret Gertrude (Brown) S.; m. Audrey Pauline Blake, Oct. 14, 1950; 1 dau., Ann Margaret. MD, U. Toronto, 1944, PhD, 1950, Cambridge U., Eng., 1955. Prof. biochemistry U. Western Ont., London, 1956—; chmn. dept. biochemistry U. Western Ont., 1964-72, dean grad. studies, 1972-86, prof. emeritus, 1986—. Med. Research Council Can. vis. scientist dept. biochemistry U. Cambridge, Eng., 1971-72 Contbr. articles in biochemistry to sci. jours. Served with Royal Canadian Navy, 1945-46. Mem. Canadian, U.K. biochem. socs., Canadian Physiol. Soc., Am. Soc. Biochemistry and Molecular Biology, Coll. Physicians and Surgeons of Ont. Home: 118 Baseline Rd E London ON Canada N6C 2N8

**STEWART, JACK,** artist, educator, writer; b. Atlanta, Jan. 27, 1926; s. Jack Thomas and Lilly Ruth (Hemperley) Stewart; m. Margot S. Stewart (div.); 1 child, Brandon Burns; m. Regina Serniak, Dec. 10, 1976. BFA, Yale U., 1951; MA, NYU, 1975, PhD, 1989. Mem. faculty Columbia U. Grad. Sch. Art, N.Y.C., 1966—76; dept. chmn. art Cooper Union Sch. Art, N.Y.C., 1971—74; v.p., provost R.I. Sch. Design, Providence, 1976—77. Academician Nat. Acad., 1995. Exhibitions include George Binet Gallery, N.Y.C., 1950, Pa. Acad., Phila., 1953, Grippi and Waddell Gallery, N.Y.C., 1963—64, Collegeo Raffaello, Urbino, Italy, 1973, La Scuola di Teodora, Venice, 1976, Sheldon Swope Gallery, Terre Haute, Ind., 1978, Broome St. Gallery, N.Y.C., 1990, 1992, 1996, 2001, Nat. Acad. Mus., 1995—2003, Galeria Tonalli, Mexico City, 1997, Anita Shapolski Gallery, 1997, Silvermine Galleries, Conn., 1998, others, prin. works include mosiac murals Versaile Hotel, Miami Beach, Fla., Grace Line's SS Santa Paula, 1957, Facade of Aruba Carib Hotel, Netherlands Antilles, 1958, Pub. Sch. 28, N.Y.C., 1958, prin. works include stained glass Robin Internat. Cinarama, 1962, Cluett Shirt Group, Atlanta, 1990; editor: Modern Mosaic Techniques, 1967; contbr. articles to encys. and mags.; inventor laminated stained glass. Sgt. inf. U.S. Army, 1944—46, ETO. Mem.: Fine Arts Fedn. N.Y. (v.p. 2002, pres. 2003), Nat. Soc. Mural Painters (pres. 1996—2000), N.Y. Artists Equity Assn. (pres. 1987—96). Baptist. Home and Office: Stewart Studio 31 E 7th St New York NY 10003-8001

**STEWART, JACQUELIN MARIA CONNELLY,** psychology professor, consultant; b. Independence, Kans., Oct. 17, 1944; MS, Pittsburg (Kans.) State U., 1971; PhD, U. Kans., 1986, postdoctorate, 1988. Cert. school psychologist, Okla., Kans. Psychologist S.W. Mo. Mental Health, Nevada, 1973-77; school psychologist Tri County Spl. Edn., Independence, 1977-80, 88-92, coord. curriculum 1988-92; asst. prof. Pittsburg State U., Kans., 1980-83, rsch. assoc. U. Kans., Lawrence, 1985-88; instr. psychology Seminole (Okla.) State Coll., 1992—. Bus. cons. Stewart-Robbins Ins., Fredonia, Kans., 1988-92; psychol. cons. Connelly Psychol. Svcs., Pittsburg, 1980-85, Safe House, Inc., Pittsburg, 1980-85; ednl. cons. Seminole Pub. Schs., Okla., 1997-99. Co-author book chpt. Stimulus Properties of Drugs, 1978; contbr. articles to profl. jours. Mem. adv. bd. Arts Coun., Fredonia, 1970. Grantee Pub. Health Svc., 1986-87, Nat. Insts. Child Health and Human Devel., 1985-88, IBM Spl. Resources, 1992, Okla. Dept. Spl. Edn., 1992. Avocations: wax doll making, power point curriculum design, gardening. Office: Seminole State Coll Sci Dept Boren Blvd PO Box 351 Seminole OK 74818-0351 Office Phone: 405-382-9245.

**STEWART, JAMES B.,** journalist, writer; b. Quincy, Ill. BA in History, DePauw U., 1973; JD, Harvard U., 1976. Assoc. Cravath, Swaine & Moore LLP, 1976—79; exec. editor Am. Lawyer mag., 1979—83; sr. spl. writer Wall St. Jour., 1983—88, "Page One" editor, 1988-92; reporter The New Yorker mag., N.Y.C., 1993—; editor-at-large Smart Money mag. Bloomberg prof. bus. journalism Columbia U., NYC. Author: The Partners: Inside America's Most Powerful Law Firms, 1984, Wendell Phillips: Liberty's Hero, 1986, The Prosecutors: Inside the Offices of the Government's Most Powerful Lawyers, 1987, Den of Thieves, 1993, Blood Sport: The President and His Adversaries, 1996, Holy Warriors: The Abolitionists and American Slavery, 1997, Follow the Story: How to Write Successful Nonfiction, 1998, Blind Eye, 1999, Heart of a Soldier: The Story of Love, Heroism and September 11, 2002, Disney War: The Battle for the Magic Kingdom, 2005. Pulitzer prize for Explanatory Journalism, 1987, Gerald Loeb award, 1987, 1988, George Polk award, 1988, Edgar Allan Poe award Mystery Writers Am., 2000 Mem.: NY State Bar Assn. Office: The New Yorker 4 Times Square New York NY 10036 E-mail: jbs32@columbia.edu.*

**STEWART, JANE,** psychology professor; b. Ottawa, Ont., Can., Apr. 19, 1934; d. Daniel Wallace and Jessie Stewart; m. Dalbir Bindra, Aug. 5, 1959 (dec. 1981). BA with honours, Queen's U., Kingston, Ont., 1956; PhD, U. London, 1959; DSc (hon.), Queen's U., 1992. Sr. rsch. biologist Ayerst Labs., Montreal, Que., 1959-63; part-time instr. psychology Sir George, Montreal, 1962-63; assoc. prof. psychology Williams U., Montreal, 1963-69; prof.,

chmn. psychology SGW Univ. (now Concordia U.), Montreal, 1969-75; prof. psychology Concordia U., Montreal, 1975—. Dir. Ctr. for Studies in Behavioral Neurobiology, Concordia U., Montreal, 1990-97. Fellow: APA, AAAS, Can. Psychol. Assn., Royal Soc. Can.; mem.: NY Acad. Sci., Soc. for Neurosci. Office: Concordia Univ 7141 Sherbrooke St W Montreal PQ Canada H4B 1R6

**STEWART, JANE,** former Canadian government minister; b. Brantford, Ont., Can., Apr. 25, 1955; d. Robert Nixon; 2 sons. BS with honors, Trent U., 1978. Chair Nat. Liberal Caucus, 1994-96; Human Resources profl., to 1994; min. nat. revenue Govt. of Can., 1996-97, min. Indian Affairs and No. Devel., 1997-99, min. Human Resources devel., 1999—2003. Chair Econ. Union, 2002—. Liberal Party Can.

**STEWART, JOAN HINDE,** academic administrator; b. NYC, Aug. 11, 1944; d. Wade and Dorothy (Ronning) H.; m. Philip Robert Stewart, Jan. 31, 1970; children: Anna Faye, Justin. Université Laval Summer Sch., Quebec, 1963, Middlebury Coll. Summer Sch., 1964-65; BA summa cum laude, St. Joseph's Coll., 1965; student, Salzburg Summer Sch., Austria, 1966; MPhil, Yale U., 1969, PhD, 1970. Tchg. assoc. French Yale U., New Haven, 1967—69, acting instr. French, 1969—70; instr. French Wellseley Coll., 1970—71, asst. prof. French, 1971—72, NC State U., Raleigh, 1973—77, assoc. prof. French, 1977—81, prof. French, 1981—99, asst. head dept. fgn. langs. and lits., 1978—82, asst. dean rsch. and grad. programs, 1983—85, acting head dept. fgn. langs. and lits., 1984—85, head dept. fgn. langs. and lit., 1985—97; prof., dean liberal arts U. SC, 1999—2003; prof. French, pres. Hamilton Coll., Clinton, NY, 2003—. Author: The Novels of Mme Riccoboni, 1976, Colette, 1983, 1996, Gynographs: French Novels by Women of the Late Eighteenth Century, 1993; editor: Mme Riccoboni's Lettres de Mistriss Fanni Butlerd, 1979; co-editor: Isabelle de Charrière's Lettres de Mistriss Henley, 1993, Marie Riccoboni's Histoire d'Ernestine, 1998. Chmn. N.C. Humanities Coun., 1988-89. Fellow Camargo Found., Cassis, France, 1979, Nat. Humanities Ctr., 1982-83, (sr.) ctr. for humanities Wesleyan U., 1990; NEH summer seminar fellowship, Princeton U., 1980; NEH fellowship Coll. Tchrs. and Ind. Scholars, 1990-91, 1994-95; fellow Ctr. d'Etude du XVIII Siecle, U. Paul Valery, Montpellier, France, 1995, Liguria Study Ctr. for the Arts and Scis., Bogliasco, Italy, 1997, Beinecke Rare Book and Manuscript Libr., Yale U., 1997; stipend younger humanists NEH, 1973; travel grantee ACLS, 1983; travel to collections grantee NEH, 1984; vis. scholar European Humanities Rsch. Ctr., Oxford U., 1995. Mem. AAUP, MLA, Am. Assn. Tchrs. French. Address: Hamilton Coll Pres Office 198 College Hill Rd Clinton NY 13323 Office Phone: 315-859-4104. E-mail: jstewart@hamilton.edu.

**STEWART, JOANNE,** retired director; b. Vancouver, Wash., Mar. 10, 1944; d. Edward Charles and Claudine Marie Spencer; m. William Lemley Stewart, Sept. 2, 1966 (dec. June 1983); children: Amy Diane Stemple, Nicholas William. BS, Wash. State U., 1966, MA, 1973. Cert. tchr., Mont., Idaho, Wash., Calif. Tchr. foods Seaside High Sch., Monterey, Calif., 1966-67; tchr. home econs. Marysville (Wash.) High Sch., 1967-68, Palouse (Wash.) High Sch., 1968-73, Ennis (Mont.) High Sch., 1973-76, Genesee (Idaho) High Sch., 1976-77; instr. young family Missoula (Mont.) County High Sch., 1983-84; tchr. home econs. Woodman Sch., Lolo, Mont., 1985-86; travel cons. Travel Masters, Missoula, 1984-87; ticketing mgr. Blue Caboose Travel, Missoula, 1987-91; tchr. family and consumer scis. Victor (Mont.) High Sch., 1991-2001; dir. Victor 21st Century Learning Ctr., 2001—04; project dir. Reaching Out for Positive Edn. Success (ROPES) program After Sch. Learning Ctr. Co-pres. Lolo PTO, 1980-81; v.p. Lolo Cmty. Ctr., 1981, team of leaders, 2004—06; sec. Lolo Mosquito Control Bd., 1988—; mem. telecommunications com. Conrad Burns & Gov. Racicot; sec. state supt. edn. task force on vocat. edn., 1995-96; coord. Health Rocks!, Nat. 4-H Program, 2000-01 Recipient Wash. State U. Alumni Achievement award, 2005; Marysville Edn. Assn. scholar, 1962, Future Homemakers Am. scholar, 1962. Mem. AAUW (sec. 1986, program chmn. 1987), Forestry Triangle (pres. (hon.), Am. Family and Consumer Scis. Assn., Mont. Family and Consumer Scis. Assn. (bylaws chair 1994, pres. elect 1995-96, pres. 1996-97, Profl. of Yr. 1997), Mont. Vocat. Tchrs. Assn. (returning Rookie of Yr. 1992, Am. Federated Tchrs., Mont. Vocat. Family and Consumer Scis. Tchrs. (v.p. 1993-94, pres. 1994-95, Tchr. of Yr. 1998), Sassy, Intelligent Lolo Ladies in Excellent Shape (Queen team of Lolo Red Hat chpt. 2002-), Am. Cancer Soc. Relay for Life (team cpt. 2005-, chmn. of survivorship, 2006). Republican. Methodist. Avocation: swimming. Home: 1200 Lakeside Dr Lolo MT 59847-9705

**STEWART, JOHN HARGER,** music educator; b. Cleve., Mar. 31, 1940; s. Cecil Tooker and Marian (Harger) S.; m. Julia Wallace, Aug. 14, 1977; children: Barbara, Cecily Bronwen. BA, Yale U., 1962; MA, Brown U., 1972; cert., New Eng. Conservatory, 1965. With various operas including Santa Fe Opera, N.Y.C. Opera, Met. Opera, U.S. and Europe, 1965—; lectr. Mt. Holyoke Coll., South Hadley, Mass., 1988-90; dir. vocal activities Washington U., St. Louis, 1990—, dir. Friends of Music. Office: Dept Music Washington U Campus Box 1032 One Brookings Dr Saint Louis MO 63130-4899 Office Phone: 314-935-5597. Business E-Mail: jstewart@wustl.edu.

**STEWART, JOHN LINCOLN,** university administrator; b. Alton, Ill., Jan. 24, 1917; s. Frederick William and Hilda (Denovan) S.; m. Joan Elsdon Guthridge, Sept. 23 1939 (div. 1964); children: Leslie Cythera Stewart Chalmers, Ann Guthridge Stewart Nutt; m. Ruth Peabody Quinn, July 11, 1964; stepchildren: Geoffrey Cornelius Quinn, Andrew Dean Quinn. AB, Denison U., 1938, ArtsD (hon.), 1964; MA, Ohio State U., 1939, PhD, 1947. From tchg. asst. to instr. Ohio State U. Columbus, 1939-41; instr. UCLA, 1947-49; from asst. prof. to prof. English Dartmouth Coll., Hanover, N.H., 1949-64; prof. Lit. U. Calif., San Diego, 1964-87, provost John Muir Coll., 1965-87. Author: Exposition for Science and Technical Students, 1950, The Essay, 1952, John Crowe Ransom, 1962, The Burden of Time, 1965; (with others) Horizons Circled, 1974, Ernst Krenek, 1990; contbr. articles to profl. jours. Assoc. dir. Hopkins Ctr. for Arts, 1961-64; dir. Mandeville Ctr. for Arts, 1974-76; mem. Dartmouth Community Symphony Orch., 1949-58; trustee Kinhaven Music Sch., 1960-64, Fla. West Coast Symphony, 1958, Oakland Cmty. Orch., 1997-2002; bd. dirs. Theater and Arts Found. San Diego County, 1970; pres. La Jolla (Calif.) Friends Sch. Music, 1971-73, Friends of Music, U. Calif., San Diego. Served with Aus, 1942-45. Howard Found. fellow, 1953-54, Dartmouth Coll. fellow, 1962-63. Democrat. Avocation: performer with music ensembles. Home: 2361 E 29th St Oakland CA 94606-3511

**STEWART, JOHN MURRAY,** retired bank executive; b. Summit, NJ, Apr. 2, 1943; s. Robert John Stewart and Mary Catherine Grabhorn; m. Sandra Meyers Frazier, 1966 (div. 1997); children: Jennifer Bricar Crone, Catherine Dorothy Lochead; m. Rebecca Marie Mellen, July 10, 1998. BA, U. Va. Charlottesville, 1965; MBA, NYU, 1983. Trust officer, v.p. Bankers Trust Co., N.Y.C., 1965-82, Morgan Guaranty Trust Co., N.Y.C., 1982-83; mgr., pres., dir. Morgan Trust Co. Fla., Palm Beach, 1983-89; pres., dir. Bankers Trust Co. Fla., 1989-93; founder, pres. pvt. capital group SunTrust Bank, Orlando, Fla., 1993-96; pres., dir. Harris Trust/Bank of Montreal, West Palm Beach, 1996—2001; contbg. writer Cannon Fin. Inst., 2004—; sr. trust advisor Wachovia Bank, 2006—. Campaign chmn. Palm Beach Cmty. Chest, 1985, 1986; exec. com. Tampa Bay and Palm Beach County Local Initiatives Support Corp.; mem. planned giving coun. U. Va., 1997—, pres. alumni club, 1990—98; vestryman Bethesda By the Sea Ch., Palm Beach, 1986—89, 1992—94, treas., 1986—87, Cathedral Ch. of St. Luke, Orlando, 1996; bd. dirs. Orlando Opera Co., 1994—96, Palm Beach Opera Co., 1996—2001. Mem. Fla. Bankers Assn. (chmn. trust bus. devel. com. 1989, planning commn., chmn. trust legis. com. 1990), NY State Bankers Assn. (mem. trust bus. devel. com. 1978-82), NY Yacht Club (NYC), St. Petersburg Yacht Club, Isla del Sol Country Club (St. Petersburg), Monmouth Boat Club (Red Bank, NJ), SAR (pres. Palm Beach chpt. 1997-98). Home: 1049 Pinellas Bayway S Tierra Verde FL 33715 Office Phone: 407-649-5299. Personal E-mail: uva1965@msn.com.

**STEWART, JOHN TODD,** economist, consultant; AB, Stanford U., 1961; MA, Tufts U., 1962, MALD, 1970. With Am. Fgn. Svc., 1962-98; U.S. amb. to Republic of Moldova, 1995-98; dep. head U.S. diplomatic missions to Can., Costa Rica and Jamaica; dir. office maritime and land transport Dept. of State, Washington; dir. GATT affairs Pres.'s Spl. Rep. for Trade Negotiations; dep. dir. Inst. Internat. Econs., Washington, 1998—2002; diplomat-in-residence Am. U., 2003—04. Vis. fellow Inst. Internat. Econs., 2002—. Home and Office: PO Box 3200 Sun Valley ID 83353 Office Phone: 208-622-7343. E-mail: todd.stewart@stanfordalumni.org.

**STEWART, JOHN WRAY BLACK,** college dean; b. Coleraine, Northern Ireland, Jan. 16, 1936; s. John Wray and Margaret Reid (Black) S.; m. Felicity Ann Patricia Poole, Aug. 7, 1965; children: J.W. Matthew, Hannah Louise. BSc with honors, Queen's U., Belfast, Northern Ireland, 1958, BSA with honors, 1959, PhD, 1963, DSc, 1988. Registered profl. agrologist. Sci. officer chem. rsch. divsn. Ministry of Agr., Belfast, 1959-64; asst. prof. soil sci. dept. U. Sask., Saskatoon, Canada, 1966-71, assoc. prof., 1971-76, prof., 1976-81, dir. Sask. Inst. Pedology, 1981-89, dean Coll. Agr., 1989-99, prof. emeritus, 1999—, dean emeritus, 1999—, interim dir. Inter-Am. Inst. for Global Change Rsch., 2002, 2005. Tech. expert, cons. FAO/IAEA, U.N.D.P., Vienna, 1971, Vienna, 1974—75; mem. program com. Can. Global Change, 1985—98; sec.-gen. Sci. Com. on Problems of Environ., Paris, 1988—92, pres., 1992—95, editor-in-chief, 1999—2006; cons. UNESCO, Paris, 1990; trustee Internat. Inst. Tropical Agr., Nigeria, 1991—97; chair sci. adv. com. Inter-Am. Inst. for Global Change Rsch., 1994—2001. Contbr. articles to profl. publs., chapters to books. Fellow: Can. Soc. Soil Sci., Berlin Inst. Advanced Study, Am. Soc. Agronomy, Soil Sci. Soc. Am., Agrl. Inst. Can.; mem.: Internat. Soc. Soil Sci., Brit. Soc. Soil Sci. Avocations: golf, tennis. Personal E-mail: stew9250@telus.net.

**STEWART, JON (JONATHAN STEWART LEIBOWITZ),** comedian, actor; b. NYC, Nov. 28, 1962; m. Tracy McShane, 2000; children: Nathan Thomas, Maggie Rose. BS in Psychology, Coll. William and Mary, 1984. Actor: (TV films) Since You've been Gone, 1998; (films) Mixed Nuts, 1994, Wishful Thinking, 1997, Half Baked, 1998, The Faculty, 1998, Playing by Heart, 1998, Big Daddy, 1999, The Office Party, 2000, Jay and Silent Bob Strike Back, 2001, Death to Smoochy, 2002, (voice) Doogal, 2006; host: (TV series) Short Attention Span Theater, 1989; You Wrote It, You Watch It, 1992; The Daily Show, 1999— (Emmy award Outstanding Variety, Music or Comedy Series, 2004); (TV special) The Daily Show with Jon Stewart: Indecision 2000 (Emmy award, 2001, George F. Peabody award, 2001); The Daily Show with Jon Stewart: Indecision 2004 (George F. Peabody award, 2005); exec. prodr., writer: (TV series) The Daily Show, 1996—; writer, host The Jon Stewart Show, 1993; writer (TV series) The Sweet Life, 1989; author: (book) Naked Pictures of Famous People, 1998; co-author (with Ben Karlin and David Javerbaum): The Daily Show With Jon Stewart Presents America (The Book): A Citizen's Guide to Democracy Inaction, 2004 (Book of the Year, Publishers Weekly, 2004, Quills award for best humor book, best audio book, 2005, Thurber Prize for American Humor, 2005). Named one of Time Mag. 100 Most Influential People, 2005; recipient George F. Peabody award, 2005. Office: The Daily Show 604R W 52nd St New York NY 10019-5013*

**STEWART, JONATHAN TAYLOR,** psychiatrist, educator; b. Bethpage, N.Y., Mar. 15, 1956; s. Allen Theodore and Vivian (Dreiblatt) S.; m. Linda Sue Irvin, Oct. 27, 1984; children: Jacob Zachary, Aaron Joshua. BA with honors, Rollins Coll., 1976; MD, U. South Fla., 1979. Diplomate Am. Bd. Psychiatry and Neurology, Geriatric Psychiatry, Nat. Bd. Med. Examiners. Resident in psychiatry U. Fla. Coll. Medicine, Gainesville, 1979-83, assoc. prof. psychiatry, 1983-94; asst. chief psychiatry VA Med. Ctr., Gainesville, 1987-94; prof. psychiatry U So. Fla. Coll. Medicine, 1994—; chief geropsychiatry sect. Bay Pines (Fla.) VA Med. Ctr., 1994—. Contbr. articles to profl. jours., 1985—. Mem. Head Injury Adv. Coun. State of Fla., 1985-90. Fellow: Am. Geriatrics Soc., Am. Psychiat. Assn. (disting. fellow); mem.: Fla. Geriatrics Soc., Fla. Psychiat. Soc. Jewish. Avocations: cooking, bicycling, diving, travel, flying. Office: VA Med Ctr Psychiatry Service 116A Bay Pines FL 33744

**STEWART, JOSEPH D.,** career military officer, academic administrator; b. Balt., July 9, 1942; m. Kathleen Ellen Fitzpatrick; children: David, Kevin. Grad., U.S. Naval Acad., Annapolis, Md., 1964, Basic Sch., Quantico, Va., Supply Sch., Camp Lejeune, N.C.; MS in Ops. Rsch., U.S. Naval Postgrad. Sch., Monterey, Calif., 1970; grad., Command and Staff Coll., Quantico, 1980, U.S. Naval War Coll., Newport, R.I., 1984; MS in Mgmt., Salve Regina Coll. Commd. 2nd lt. USMC, 1964, advanced through grades to maj. gen., 1993; bn. supply officer, S-4 officer, platoon comdr. 1st Reconnaissance Bn.; supply officer 2nd Tank Bn., Camp Lejeune; bn. supply officer, co. comdr. 3rd Tank Bn., Okinawa, Japan; project officer Marine Corps Devel. Ctr., Quantico, Va.; asst. lt. col. monitor Hdqs. Marine Corps, Washington, 1973-76; instr. U.S. Naval Acad., 1976-79; supply support officer, comdg. officer 2nd Supply Bn. 2nd FSSG, Camp Lejeune, 1980-82; officer in charge SASSY Mgmt. Unit 3rd FSSG, Okinawa, 1982-83; sect. head, br. head with Materiel Mgmt. Ops. Br. Installations and Logistics Dept. Hdqs. Marine Corps, 1984-87; comdg. officer Def. Depot, Columbus, 1987-90; dir. logistics plans policies and strategic mobility divsn Installations and Logistics, U.S. Marine Corps Hdqs., 1990-91, asst. dep. chief of staff plans, 1991-93, dep. chief of staff, 1996—98; comdr. Marine Corps Logistics Bases, Albany, Ga., 1993-96; supt. U.S. Mcht. Marine Acad., Kings Point, NY, 1998—. Decorated Legion of Merit, Defense Superior Svc. Medal, Navy Commendation Medal, Combat Action Ribbon; recipient Sec. Transp.'s Gold Medal Office, U.S. Mcht. Marine Acad. Supt. 300 Steamboat Rd Kings Point NY 11024*

**STEWART, JOSEPH MELVIN,** manufacturing executive, former food products executive; b. Maringouin, La., Dec. 23, 1947; m. Clara St. Amant, June 18, 1967; children: Erick, Kendra. BS in Foods and Nutrition, So. U., Baton Rouge; postgrad., USDA Grad. Sch. Dir. food services, dir. child nutrition programs Washington Pub. Sch. System, 1971-80; dir. child nutrition div. U.S. food products Kellogg Co., Battle Creek, Mich., 1980-81, dir. corp. communications div. pub. affairs, 1981-85, v.p. pub. affairs, 1985—88, sr. v.p. corp. affairs, 1988—91; co-founder, CEO Stewart Industries, 1991—. Mem. adv. council food industry FEA, 1975. Mem. adv. council Coll. Agr. and Home Econs., So. U.; bd. govs. Pub. Affairs Council Am.; mem. nat. agrl. rsch. and extension users adv. bd. Dept. of Agr.; bd. dirs. Battle Creek Area Urban League; trustee W.K. Kellogg Found. Recipient Silver Plate award Foodservice Mfrs. Assn., 1974, Dale G. Griffin Healthcare Leadership award, 2005. Office: Stewart Industries 150 Mcquiston Dr Battle Creek MI 49015*

**STEWART, JOSEPH TURNER, JR.,** retired pharmaceutical executive; b. N.Y.C., Apr. 30, 1929; s. Joseph Turner and Edna (Pride) S.; m. Carol Graham, Aug. 7, 1954; children: Lisa D., Alison D. BS with honors, U.S. Mcht. Marine Acad., 1951; MBA, Harvard U., 1954. Systems analyst Warner Lambert Co., Morris Plains, NJ, 1954-56, budget dir. internat., 1956-60, asst. div. controller consumer products group, 1960-62, div. controller group, 1962-66; dir. adminstrn. and fin. Proprietary Drug div. Warner Lambert Co., 1966; dir. Lactona Products div. Warner Lambert Co., 1967; controller Beech-Nut subs. Squibb Corp., N.Y.C., 1968, v.p. fin., 1968-71, v.p. planning, corp. staff parent corp., 1971-79, v.p. fin. and planning parent co., 1979-82, sr. v.p. corporate affairs parent co., 1982-89; also bd. dirs.; cons. Johnson & Johnson, 1990-98. Bd. dirs. Gen. Am. Investment Corp. 1987-. Trustee Tax Found., 1985-89, US Mcht. Marine Acad. Found., 2004-; commr. N.J. State Commn. on Income and Expenditures, 1985-88; mem. adv. com. Grad. Sch. Indsl. Adminstrn., Carnegie Mellon U., 1986-91; trustee New Sch. for Social Rsch., 1990-98, U. Medicine and Dentistry of N.J. Found., 1989—; bd. dirs. Liposome Co., 1995-2000; vis. coun. Marine Biol. Lab., 1995—; bd. advisors U.S. Mcht. Marine Acad., 2002—; trustee alumni found., 2003— John Hay Whitney Opportunity fellow, 1952-54. Mem.: Harvard (N.Y.C.). Personal E-mail: kingpin497@aol.com.

**STEWART, JULIA A.**, food service executive; m. Jon Greenawalt (div.); 2 children. BA in Communications, San Diego State U., 1977. Regional mktg. dir. Carl's Jr. Restaurant, 1978—80; regional mktg. mgr. Burger King Corp., 1980—84; mktg. dir. Spoons Grill & Bar Stuart Anderson's Black Angus/Cattle Co. Restaurants, 1985, mktg. v.p., 1986—91; western region v.p. operations Taco Bell Yum! Brands, 1991, nat. v.p. franchise, license Taco Bell, 1997—98; pres. domestic div. Applebee's Internat., Inc., 1998—2001; pres, COO Internat. House Pancakes (IHOP), 2001—, CEO, 2002—, chmn. 2006—. Bd. dirs. Avery Denison, Town Hall, LA, Women's Franchise and Distbn. Forum; mem. Elliott Inst. Leadership Coun.; bd. visitors UCLA Anderson Sch. Mgmt.; trustee Calif. Sci. Ctr. Found. Named one of Top Fifty Women in foodservice, Nation's Restaurant. Mem.: Nat. Restaurant Assn. (pres. mktg. executives group), Calif. Restaurant Assn. (exec. bd. mem.), Women's Foodservice Forum (past pres., founding mem.). Avocations: cooking, skiing. Office: IHOP 450 N Brand Blvd Glendale CA 91203-1903*

**STEWART, J.W.**, energy executive, lawyer; b. Mar. 2, 1944; BSEE, Univ. Tex., Arlington, 1966; JD, Univ. Houston, 1973. V.p. legal, sec. Hughes Tool Co.; chmn., pres., CEO BJ Services, Houston, 1990—. Office: BJ Services 5500 N W Ctrl Dr Houston TX 77092 Mailing: BJ Services PO Box 4442 Houston TX 77210-4442

**STEWART, KENNETH L.**, lawyer; b. Nashville, Ark., Feb. 26, 1954; BSBA in Acctg., U. Ark., 1976; JD, Vanderbilt U., 1979. Bar: Tex. 1979. Ptnr.-in-charge, Dallas office and mem. corp. banking and bus. practice Fulbright & Jaworski, LLP, Dallas, 1979—. Editor: Vanderbilt Law Rev. Chmn. Dallas Bus. Hall of Fame, 2001, Jr. Achievement Dallas Inc., 2002—03. Mem. ABA, Dallas Bar Assn., State Bar Tex., Dallas Citizens Coun., Greater Dallas C. of C. (dir. 2005-06), Order of Coif. Office: Fulbright & Jaworski LLP 2200 Ross Ave Ste 2800 Dallas TX 75201-2784 Office Phone: 214-855-8000. Office Fax: 214-855-8200. Business E-Mail: kstewart@fulbright.com.

**STEWART, KENNETH SEAN**, music educator; b. Stuebenville, Ohio, Feb. 19, 1977; s. Charles Kenneth and Vicki Marie Stewart; m. Christy Ann Carson. MusB, Youngstown State U., 1999. Cert. tchr. Pa. Tchr. Shenango Area Sch. Dist., New Castle, Pa., 2002—. Mem.: Pa. Music Educators Assn. Office Phone: 724-658-5566.

**STEWART, KENT KALLAM**, analytical biochemistry educator; b. Omaha, Sept. 5, 1934; s. George Franklin and Grace S.; m. Margaret Reiber, June 10, 1956; children: Elizabeth, Cynthia, Richard, Robert. Student, U. Chgo., 1951-53; AB, U. Calif., Berkeley, 1956; PhD, Pa. State U., 1965. Guest investigator Rockefeller U., N.Y.C., 1965-67, research assoc., 1967-68, asst. prof., 1968-69; research chemist U.S. Dept. Agr., Beltsville, Md., 1970-75, lab. chief Nutrient Composition Lab., 1975-82; prof., head dept. food sci. and tech. Va. Poly. Inst. and State U., Blacksburg, 1982-85, prof. biochemistry, anaerobic microbiology, food sci./tech., 1985—96, prof. emeritus of biochemistry; adj. prof. dept. chemistry and biochemistry U. Tex., Austin, 1996—2004. Editor Jour. Food Composition and Analysis, 1987-97, also 3 books; contbr. articles to profl. jours., co-author book; patentee in field. Capt. USMCR, 1956-59. Fellow AAAS, Inst. Food Technologist. Home: 3900 Glengarry Dr Austin TX 78731-3812 Office Phone: 512-458-1072. E-mail: stewart.kent@gmail.com.

**STEWART, LEWIS MOORE**, finance educator; b. Columbus, Miss., Sept. 23, 1935; s. William Anderson and Mary Amanda (Moore) S.; m. Charlene Kimbro, June 1, 1957; children: Lewis Jr., Richard K. BS in Bus., Harding U., 1957; MBA, Tex. Tech U., 1960; postgrad., U. Ala., 1967-70. Instr., book store mgr. Lubbock (Tex.) Christian Coll., 1958-63; instr. fin. and econs. Tex. Tech U., Lubbock, 1963-66; asst. prof. econs. and fin. Miss. State Coll. for Women, Columbus, 1966-68; part-time instr. U. Ala., Tuscaloosa, 1968-70; asst. prof. fin. Ga. So. U., Statesboro, 1970-78, dir. Small Bus. Devel. Ctr., 1978-84, asst. prof., dir. external affairs New Coll. Bus., 1984—99, dir. alumni affairs, Coll. Bus. Adminstrn., 1996-98, ret., 1999. Exec. sec. bd. dirs. Ga. Christian Children's Home, Valdosta, 1980-88, bd. dirs. 1988—. Recipient Regional Econs. award Ford Found., 1961. Mem. Ea. Fin. Assn., Ga. So. Alumni Assn. (exec. sec. 1984-96), Delta Sigma Pi. Home: 211 Wildwood Dr Statesboro GA 30458-1678

**STEWART, LUCILLE MARIE**, retired special education coordinator, educator; b. Pitts., Feb. 24; d. William H. and Edna (Hoffman) S. BEd, Duquesne U.; MEd, U. Pitts.; postgrad., Columbia U., U. Calif., Calif. State U. Cert. elem. and secondary tchr., spl. edn. tchr., supr., adminstr. Tchr., group leader mentally retarded Ednl. Alliance, N.Y.C., 1950—53; instr. Lincoln (Ill.) State Sch., 1953; instr., program leader, sec. Edn. Alliance, N.Y.C., 1954-58; tchr. mentally retarded Ramapo Ctrl. Sch. Dist., Spring Valley, NY, 1958-60, tchr. seriously emotionally disturbed, 1960-64, supr. presch. program for educationally disadvantaged, 1965-67; program dir. Pomona (N.Y.) Camp for Retarded, summers 1960-63; tchr. mentally retarded Stockton Sch., San Diego, 1964-65; tchr. mentally retarded sch. Cathedral City Sch., 1967-78; program specialist spl. edn. Palm Springs (Calif.) Unified Sch. Dist., 1978-95, prin. elem. summer schs., 1971-72; tchr. elem. mentally retarded sch. Palm Springs (Calif.) Unified; prin.-tchr. Summer Extended Sch. for Spl. Students, summer 1979-99. Exec. com. U. Calif. Extension, area adv. com.; spl. edn. surrogate parent Palm Springs Unified Sch. Dist. Mem. NEA, AAUW, ASCD, Calif. Adminstrs. Spl. Edn. (desert cmty. mental health childrens com.), Coun. Exceptional Children (adminstrn. divsn., early childhood-learning handicap divsns.), Am. Assn. Childhood Edn., Autism Soc., Coachella Valley, Learning Disabilities Assn., Creative Desert, Desert Theater League, Alpha Kappa Alpha, Phi Delta Kappa, Delta Kappa Gamma.

**STEWART, MARGARET MCBRIDE**, biology professor, researcher; b. Guilford County, NC, Feb. 6, 1927; d. David Henry and Mary Ellen (Morrow) S.; m. Paul C. Lemon, June 1962 (div. 1968); m. George Edward Martin, Dec. 19, 1969. AB, U. N.C.-Greensboro, 1948; MA, U. N.C.-Chapel Hill, 1951; PhD, Cornell U., 1956; DSc (hon.), U. P.R., Mayaquez, 1996. Instr. biology Greensboro Evening Coll. U. N.C., Greensboro, 1950-51; instr. biology Catawba Coll., Salisbury, N.C., 1951-53; extension botanist Cornell U., Ithaca, N.Y., 1954-56; asst. prof. biology SUNY, Albany, 1956-59, assoc. prof., 1959-65, prof. vertebrate biology, 1965-97, disting. tchg. prof., 1977—, disting. tchg. prof. emerita, 1997; dir. Program in Biodiversity Conservation and Policy, 1997-2000. Faculty rsch. participant Oak Ridge Assoc. Univs., 1983. Author: (with A.H. Benton) Keys to the Vertebrates of the Northeastern States, 1964, Amphibians of Malawi, 1967; contbr. numerous articles and revs. to profl. jours. Bd. dirs. E.N. Huyck Nature Preserve, Rensselaerville, N.Y., 1976-86; bd. dirs. Ea. N.Y. chpt. Nature Conservancy, 1983-88, 90-96, 97-2004, N.Y. State chpt., 1987-90; mem. Albany Pine Bush Commn., 1993-2004. Recipient Citizen Laureate award SUNY Found., 1987, Oak Leaf Award Nature Conservancy, 1997; Am. Philos. Soc. rsch. grantee, 1975, 81, NSF grantee, 1978-80, Oak Ridge Assocs. Univs. grantee, 1983-97. Fellow Herpetologists' League (bd. dirs. 1978-80); mem. Soc. for Study of Amphibians and Reptiles (pres. 1979), Am. Soc. Ichthyologists and Herpetologists (bd. govs. 1975-80, 87-90, 96—, herpetology editor 1983-85, pres. 1996, historian 1999-2004, Johnson award 2005, Fitch award 2005), Ecol. Soc. Am., Assn. for Tropical Biologists, Soc. Study of Evolution, III World Congress of Herpetology (mem. exec. com. 1995-01), Sigma Xi, Sigma Delta Epsilon, Phi Beta Kappa (emeritus), Phi Kappa Phi. Democrat. Presbyterian. Avocations: photography, gardening, reading, travel. Office: SUNY Dept Biol Scis 1400 Washington Ave Albany NY 12222-1000

**STEWART, MARLENE METZGER**, financial planning practitioner, insurance agent; b. Portland, Oreg., Nov. 1, 1937; d. Eddie Charles and Helen M. (Grant) Metzger; m. Robert W. Stewart, Aug. 1, 1964 (dec. Jan. 1967); m. Melvin N. McBurney, Feb. 14, 1985. BA, U. Oreg., 1959; MA, U. Tex., El Paso, 1971. CLU, CFP. Exec. dir. Summer 72 Youth Com. Office of Mayor, Portland, 1972; registered rep. Mut. Life Ins. Co. N.Y., Portland, 1973-76; Prudential Life Ins. Co., Portland, 1976-77; ptnr. N.W. Fin. Planning, Portland, 1977-79; pres. Horizons Unltd. Fin. Planning, Portland, 1979-86;

prin. EMR Fin. Adv. Svcs., Inc., Portland, 1986-89; registered rep. KMS Fin. Svcs., Inc., Portland, 1979—; owner Stewart Fin. Group, 1991—. Mem.-at-large nat. bd. YMCA's, 1971-73; bd. dirs. Met. YMCA, Portland, 1971-75; bd. dirs. YWCA, Portland, 1989-92, treas., 1990-92, chmn. investment com.; chmn. planned giving com. Arthritis Found., 1984-86. Bill Bottler scholar Portland chpt. CLU and Chartered Fin. Cons., 1981. Mem. Fin. Planning Assn., Oreg. Soc. Inst. CFP's (treas. 1985-86, Internat. Assn. Fin. Planners (pres. Oreg. chpt. 1987-88), Nat. Assn. Ins. & Fin. Adv., Soc. of Fin. Svc. Profls. and Portland Chpt. (treas. Portland chpt. 1985-86), Fin. Planning Assn. (mem. nat. task force on career devel. 2002), Estate Planning Coun. Portland, Assocs. Good Samaritan (steering com., chmn. 1991-92), Rotary (past chmn. World Cmty. Svc. com. 1998-2000). Republican. Presbyterian. Avocations: swimming, travel, reading, gardening. Office: 5901 SW Macadam Ave Ste 135 Portland OR 97239 Office Phone: 503-224-2034. E-mail: stewfg@aol.com.

**STEWART, MARTHA KOSTYRA**, entrepreneur, lecturer, author; b. Jersey City, Aug. 3, 1941; d. Edward and Martha (Ruszkowski) Kostyra; m. Andy Stewart, July 1, 1961 (div. 1990); 1 child, Alexis Gilbert. BA European History and Archtl. History, Barnard Coll. Former model; former stockbroker N.Y.C.; former profl. caterer; mag. owner, editor-in-chief Martha Stewart Living, 1990—97; CEO Martha Stewart Living Omnimedia, 1997—2003, chief creative officer, 2003—04, chmn. 1997—2004, founding editl. dir., 2004—. Lifestyle cons. for K-Mart Corp., 1987; bd. dirs., NYSE, 2002-04. Host (TV show) Martha Stewart Living, 1993-2004, The Apprentice: Martha Stewart, 2005, (TV talk show) Martha 2005; Author: (with Elizabeth Hawes) Entertaining, 1982, Weddings, 1987; Martha Stewart Hors d'Oeurvres: The Creation and Presentation of Fabulous Finger Food, 1984, Martha Stewart's Pies and Tarts, 1985, Martha Stewart's Quick Cook Menus: Fifty-two Meals You Can Make in Under an Hour, 1988, The Wedding Planner, 1988, Martha Stewart's Gardening: Month by Month, 1991, Martha Stewart's New Old House: Restoration, Renovation, Decoration, 1992, Martha Stewart's Christmas, 1993, Martha Stewart's Menus for Entertaining, 1994, Holidays, 1994, Good Things: The Best of Martha Stewart Living, 1997, Four Seasons of Great Menus to Make Every Day, 1997, Hors D'Oeuvres Handbook, 1999, The Best of Martha Stewart Living: Weddings, 1999, The Barefoot Contessa Cookbook: Secrets from the East Hampton Specialty Food Store for Simple Food and Party Platters You Can Make at Home, 1999, (with Ina Garten) Favorite Comfort Food, 1999, The Martha Stewart Living Cookbook, 2000, Halloween: The Best of Martha Stewart Living, 2001, Classic Crafts and Recipes Inspired by the Songs of Christmas, 2002, Martha Stewart Living 2003 Recipes, 2002, Simple Home Solutions, 2004, The Martha Rules, 2005, Martha Stewart's Baking Handbook, 2005; appeared in semi-monthly cooking segment on Today Show; syndicated columnist, NY Times. Named one of World's 100 Most Influential People, Time Mag., 2005. Office: 10 Saugatuck Ave Westport CT 06880-5720 also: care Susan Magrino Agy 40 W 57th St Fl 31 New York NY 10019-4001*

**STEWART, MARY FRANCES**, English professor; d. William McKinley and Mary Frances Cunningham; m. Samuel Lee Stewart, Feb. 1, 1969; m. Roland Dennis Cantley, Jan. 23, 1960 (div. Apr. 11, 1967); children: William Preston, Duncan Laird. BA, Birmingham So. Coll., 1961; MA, U. Ala. Birmingham, 1977. Cert. class A Ala. prof. secondary edn. Ala. State Bd. of Edn., class B profl. secondary tchg. Ala. State Bd. of Edn., class B Ala. prof. secondary edn. Ala. State Bd. of Edn. Tchr. English Wapato Sr. HS, Wash., 1961—64, Rogers Area Vocat. Sch., Birmingham, 1969—70; tchr. English, drama, speech A.C. Davis Sr. HS, Yakima, Wash., 1964—66; instr. English Jefferson State CC, Birmingham, 1983—90, Lawson State CC, Birmingham, 1992—; realtor Realty South, Birmingham, 1991—2001. Mem. adv. bd. Birmingham News, 1985—86. Singer with Jean Golden Opera Workshop various operas, singer, actor with U. Ala. Town and Gown and Summerfest Thea Community Theater. Recipient Freshman Women's scholarship, Alpha Lambda Delta, scholarship in Romance langs., Phi Sigma Iota, B.B. Comer English medal, Andrew W. Mellon fellowship to Auburn U. Mem.: NEA, Ala. Ednl. Assn., Phi Beta Kappa (scholarship). Republican. United Methodist. Avocations: singing, reading, genealogy, biblical archaeology. Office: Lawson State C C 110 9th Ave SW Bessemer AL 35021 Office Phone: 205-426-7370. Office Fax: 205-424-5119. Business E-Mail: fstewart@lawsonstate.edu.

**STEWART, MELBOURNE GEORGE, JR.**, physicist, researcher; b. Detroit, Sept. 30, 1927; s. Melbourne George and Ottilie (Tuholke) S.; m. Charlotte L. Ford, Jan. 23, 1954; children: Jill K., John H., Kevin G. AB, U. Mich., 1949; MS, 1950; PhD, 1955. Research assoc. dept. physics AEC, Ames Lab., Iowa State U., 1955-56, asst. prof., 1956-62, assoc. prof., 1962-63; prof. Wayne State U., Detroit, 1963-94, prof. emeritus, 1994—, chmn. dept. physics, 1963-73, assoc. provost for faculty relations, 1973-86; hon. research fellow Univ. Coll., London, 1986-87,93. Editorial bd.: Wayne State U. Press, 1969-73. Served with AUS, 1946-47. Mem. Am. Phys. Soc., AAAS, Sigma Xi, Phi Beta Kappa. Home: 415 Bournemouth Rd Grosse Pointe Farms MI 48236-2817 Office: Dept Physics Wayne State U Detroit MI 48202

**STEWART, MICHAEL B.**, lawyer, mechanical and aerospace engineer; b. Royal Oak, Mich., Nov. 5, 1963; s. Colin M. and Jacqueline P. Stewart; children: Elizabeth and Caitlin. BSME, U. Mich. 1987, BA in English, 1987, MS in Aerospace Engring., 1988, JD, 1991. Assoc. Dykema Gossett PLLC, Bloomfield Hills, Mich., 1991-96; mnging. ptnr. Rader, Fishman & Grauer PLLC, Bloomfield Hills, 1996—. Contbr. articles to profl. jours. Named 40 Under 40 Honoree Crain's Detroit Bus., 1998. Mem. ABA, Intellectual Property Law Assn., Mich. Patent Law Assn., Mich. Bar Assn., Oakland County Bar Assn. (chmn. continuing legal edn. subcom. for IP com. 1998), Optimists (bd. dirs. 1993-97), Delta Theta Phi (dean., bd. govs., Detroit alumni senate). Avocations: bicycling, woodworking. Office: Rader Fishman & Grauer PLLC 39533 Woodward Ave Ste 140 Bloomfield Hills MI 48304-5098 E-mail: mbs@raderfishman.com

**STEWART, MICHAEL GLENN**, otolaryngologist, educator; b. Bowling Green, Ky., Sept. 17, 1962; s. Michael Joseph and Barbara (Weisser) S. B in Engring. summa cum laude, Vanderbilt U., 1984; MD, Johns Hopkins U., 1988; MPH, U. Tex., 1996; Gen. Surgery, Baylor Coll. Medicine, 1990, Otolaryngology, 1994. Diplomate Am. Bd. Otolaryngology. Asst. prof. Baylor Coll. Medicine, Houston, 1994-99, assoc. prof., 1999—2005, dir. residency edn. dept. otolaryngology, 1996—2005, asst. dean clin. affairs, 1998-2000, gen. dir. affil. med. svc., 1999—2005, assoc. dean clin. affairs, 2000—05; prof., chmn. Dept. Otorhinolaryngology Weill Cornell Med. Coll., NYC, 2005—; otorhinolaryngologist-in-chief NY Presbyn. Hosp., 2005—. Chief otolaryngology Ben Taub Gen. Hosp., 1994-2005; chmn. med. bd. Harris County Hosp. Dist., Houston, 1999-2000. Editor Rev. Head and Neck, 1994—; reviewer Archive Otolaryngology-Head and Neck, 1997—, Jour. Trauma, 1998—, Otolaryngology-Head and Neck Surgery, 1998—, Cancer, 2001—; assoc. editor, mem. editl. bd. Am. Jour. Rhinology, 2003—; mem. editl. bd. Archives of Otolaryngology-Head and Neck Surgery, 2005—. Recipient Outstanding Clin. Rsch. award Kelsey-Seybold Found., 1992, 93, Houston Disting. Surgeon award Assn. Perioperative Nurses, 2005. Fellow: ACS, Am. Rhinologic Soc., Am. Laryngol., Rhinol. and Otol. Soc., Am. Acad. Otolaryngology Head and Neck Surgery (Disting. Svc. award 2004). Office: Weill Cornell Medical Ctr 520 E 70th St ST 541 New York NY 10021

**STEWART, MICHAEL MCFADDEN**, speech professional; b. Eupora, Miss., Aug. 24, 1938; s. Judge Ernest and Billie Rivers (McFadden) S.; m. Barbara Ann Dickerson, June 2, 1962; children: Michael Jr., Mark Robert (dec. Dec. 1997). BS, La. State U., 1961. Cons. E.K. Williams & Co., Birmingham, Ala., 1964-66, br. mgr., 1966-68, Miami, Fla., 1968-69, Marcoin, Inc., Balt., 1969-73, dist. mgr. Falls Church, Va., 1973-74; v.p. Marcoin Western Ops., Inc., Houston, 1974-77; dir., v.p. Marcoin, Inc., Atlanta, 1977-85; pmr. Cherokee/G & S Assocs., Atlanta, 1985-88; pres. Stewart & Stewart, Inc., Dunwoody, Ga., 1988—; The Sales Power Resource Group, Inc., Atlanta, 1991-95. Cons., speaker AMA, N.Y.C., 1989—, Duffy-Vinet Inst., Langhorne, Pa., 1987-92, The Sullivan Group, Guilford, Conn., 1990-92; guest speaker SBA, Bell South Success Symposium Series, 1990-91. Author: How to Get Started with a Small Business Computer, 1984,

Quality Customer Service, 1990, Using Your Financial Statements to Boost Your Bottom Line Profits, 1990, Computerizing Your Business, 1991, The Magic of Customer Service, 1991, Bring Home the Bacon, 1992, Customer Service Excellence: How to Implement a Corporate-wide Program, 1992, Strategic Relationship Selling, 1992, Transition into Sales Management, 1992, Sales Managemcmt Call Reluctance Workshop, 1992, Negotiating with Style, 1992, Meeting Today's Competitive Challenges, 1992, Creative Management in Tough Economic Times, 1993, Relationship Empowered Technical Selling, 1993, Consultative Relationship Selling, 1993, Customer-Centered Sales Management Leadership, 1993, Customer Centered Selling, 1993, Being Different in a Niche Market, 1993, Moving, Shaking and Prospecting, 1993, 50/250 The Smart Way, 1993, Customer-Centered Relationship Selling, 1994, Working Successfully with Others, 1994, Fundamentals of Quality Customer Service, 1994, Sales Are The Life-Blood Service is the Heart Beat, 1994, Customer-Centered Value Selling, 1994, Customer-Centered Sales Management, 1994, Make the Number by Selling Value, 1995, Hiring Smart, 1995, Customer-Centered Sales Management, 1995, Live the Spirit, 1996, Sell Value, Not Price, 1996; contbg. author: Chicken Soup for the Soul at Work, 1996, Relationship Centered Value Selling, 1997, Professional Sales Skills, 1997, Sales Negotiation for Higher Profits, 1998; contbg. author: Reach for the Stars, 1998, Close More Sales!, 1999, Close More Sales With Premise, 2000, Developing A Productive Sales Orientation, 2000, Motivational Sales Management, 2000, Basic Sales Training Boot Camp, 2001, DNA of Sales Success: Hiring and Motivating Blue-Chip Sales Persons, 2002, Leading Explosive Growth-Encouraging Passionate Sales Performance, 2002, others; co-author: Embracing Change-Understanding and Managing Transitions in Life and Work, 2002, Target Your Time For Sales Success, 2005, The Dirty Dozen: 12 Killer Mistakes That Murder Sales, 2005, 24 Karat Sales Standards: Two Dozen Gold Nuggets to Help You Sell More New Business, 2005, Plan Every Call to Sell More New Business, 2006; contbr. articles to profl. jours. Fin. officer Atlanta Colts Youth Assn., 1979; vol. speaker Am. Cancer Soc., 1994—. Capt. U.S. Army, 1961-64. Recipient Silver award Carlson Learning Co., Mpls., 1990, numerous other awards. Mem. Ga. Speakers Assn. (past pres., past dir., Mem. of Yr. 1996), Nat. Spkrs. Assn. (cert. speaking profl.), Dunwoody Country Club, Dunwoody Gridiron Club (pres. 1981), Lambda Chi Alpha. Episcopalian. Avocation: golf. Home: 490 Tavern Cir Atlanta GA 30350-4455 Office Phone: 770-512-0022. Personal E-mail: mike@stewartsalesdynamics.com.

**STEWART, MICHAEL T.**, lawyer; b. Bristol, Pa., Apr. 18, 1959; s. Paige Daniel and Agnes Simeone Stewart; m. Linda Picini, Oct. 22, 1988; children: Emilie Catherine, Cristina Grace. AB, U. Chgo., 1981; JD, U. Pitts., 1985. Bar: N.J. 1985, Pa. 1985, N.Y. 1987. Law clk. Hon. Richard Newman, J.S.C., Newark, 1985—86; assoc. Budd Larner, Short Hills, NJ, 1986—90, Foyen & Peri, Short Hills, 1990—93; ptnr. Foyen & Ptnrs., Short Hills, 1993—2003; shareholder Klett Rooney Lieber & Schorling, Newark, 2003—06, Buchanan, Ingersoll & Rooney, P.C., Newark, 2006—. Author: (article) Corporate Criminal Liability, 2005, U.S. Export Regulations, 2006; exec. editor: U. Pitts. Sch. Law Jour. Law and Commerce. Mem. Am. Scandinavian Found., N.Y.C., 2000—; bd. dirs. Partnerships for People, Short Hills, 1995—2003, Am. Red Cross, Fairfield, NJ, 2003—, Norwegian Am. Chamber, N.Y.C., 2005—, Swedish Am. Chamber, Phila., 2005—. Mem.: ABA, N.J. Bar Assn. (legis. liaison internat. section). Avocations: golf, motorcyle touring. Office: Buchanan Ingersoll & Rooney PC 550 Broad St Ste 810 Newark NJ 07102 Business E-Mail: michael.stewart@bipc.com.

**STEWART, MILTON ROY**, lawyer; b. Clovis, N.Mex., Dec. 16, 1945; s. Virgil Maurice and E. Marie (Collins) S. BA, Ind. U., 1968, JD summa cum laude, 1971. Bar: Oreg. 1971, U.S. Ct. Appeals (9th cir.) 1971, U.S. Dist. Ct. (no. dist.) Oreg. 1971. Assoc. Davies, Biggs et al, Portland, Oreg., 1971-75; v.p., gen. counsel U.S. Datacorp, Portland, 1975-77; pvt. practice Portland, 1977-86; bus. devel. ptnr. Davis, Wright, Tremaine, Portland, 1987—. Bd. dir. Lex Mundi assn. internat. law firms. Past chmn., mem emeritus Oreg. chpt. Nat. Multisclerosis Soc., 1994—, immediate past mem.; bd. dirs. Nat. Multiple Sclerosis Soc.; emeritus bd. visitors Ind. U. Law Sch.; active Bd. Ind. U. Found. Capt. U.S. Army, 1968-78 State Farm Found. fellow, 1970, John H. Edwards fellow Ind. U. Found., 1971. Mem. Oreg. State Bar Assn., Wash. State Bar Assn., Multnomah Athletic Club, Astoria Golf and Country Club. Office: Davis Wright Tremaine 1300 SW 5th Ave Ste 2200 Portland OR 97201-5667 Business E-Mail: miltstewart@dwt.com.

**STEWART, MIRIAM KAY (MIMI STEWART)**, state legislator, educator; b. Sarasota, Fla., Jan. 27, 1947; d. Wilbur H. Stewart and Alice Miriam Beck; children: Boris Nathan Margolin, Hannah Beck Margolin. BA cum laude, Boston U., 1971; MS, Wheelock Coll., 1977. Spl. educator, 1977—2004; mem. N. Mex. Ho. of Reps., Albuquerque, 1994—. Democrat. Address: 313 Moon St NE Albuquerque NM 87123-1151 Office Phone: 505-880-8249 ext. 113. E-mail: mstewart@osogrande.com

**STEWART, MURRAY BAKER**, retired lawyer; b. Muskogee, Okla., May 16, 1931; s. Francis and Fannie Penelope (Murray) S.; m. Roseanna Furgason; children: Melinda, Jeffrey, Cheryl. BA, U. Okla., 1953, JD, 1955; postgrad., Georgetown U., 1958-59. Bar: Okla. 1955; CLU, ChFC. Judge adv. U.S. Army, 1955-59; ptnr. Stewart & Stewart, Tulsa and Muskogee, Okla., 1955, 62-72; asst. v.p. First Nat. Bank and Trust Co. of Tulsa 1959-62, 77-78; mem. Hutchins, Stewart, Stewart & Elmore, Tulsa, 1972-77; atty. cons. advanced underwriting Metlife Ins. Co., N.Y.C., 1978-94; assoc. Metlife Securities, Inc., SEC Registered Investment Advisors, 1984-94; of counsel Brumley & Bishop, Tulsa, 1997-99; ret., 1999. Cons. on Indian books; lectr. in field. Contbr. articles to profl. and hist. jours.; prodr. texts and videos on history, investment and bus. Fellow Life Mgmt. Inst.; mem. Okla. Bar Assn., Okla. Indian Bar Assn., Sons Confederate Vets. (judge advocate Army of Trans-Mississippi 1988-2005), Kans. divsn. 2002-05), Civil War Roundtable Tulsa. Office: PO Box 1000 Broken Arrow OK 74013-1000

**STEWART, PAMELA L.**, lawyer; b. Bogalusa, La., Mar. 13, 1953; d. James Adrian and Patricia Lynn (Wood) Lloyd; m. Steven Bernard Stewart, Aug. 31, 1974 (div. July 1980); 1 child, Christopher. BA, U. New Orleans, 1986; JD, U. Houston, 1990. Cert. debtor educator Coalition Consumer Bankruptcy Edn., lic. realtor Tex. Intern La. Supreme Ct., New Orleans, 1984, Councilman Bryan Wagner, New Orleans, 1984—85; legal asst. Clann, Bell & Murphy, Houston, 1988—89, Tejas Gas Corp., Houston, 1989—90; atty. Law Offices of Pamela L. Stewart, Houston, 1991—. Spkr. in field. Bd. dirs. Alliance for Good Govt., New Orleans, 1983-84, Attention Deficit Hyperactivity Disorder Assn. Tex., 1989-90; vol. Houston Vol. Lawyers Program, Houston, 1992—; bd. dirs. West Lane Place Civic Assn., sec., 2001-2003, v.p., 2003-06, block captain, 2002—; mem. com. Lawyers Against Waste, Habitat for Humanity; apptd. Harris County Appraisal Rev. Bd.; vice chair Tex. State Bar Bankruptcy Section Ch. 13 Survey Com. Innsbruck scholar, U. New Orleans, 1985. Fellow Inst. Politics, Houston Bar Found.; mem. ABA, Tax Freedom Inst., Nat. Assn. Consumer Bankruptcy Attys., Houston Bar Assn., Nat. Assn. of Chpt. 13 Trustees (assoc.), Katy Bar Assn. (3d v.p. 1997-98), Houston Assn. Debtors Attys. (pres. 1996-98), Upper Kirby Dist. Optimist Club (v.p. 2000-01, pres. 2001-02), Feng Shui Guild, Feng Shui Basics (pres.), Nat. Assn. Consumer Advs. Methodist. Avocations: music, cooking, swimming, politics. Office: 4265 San Felipe St Ste 1100 Houston TX 77027-2998 Home: 3326 Mid Ln Houston TX 77027 Office Phone: 713-622-3893. Personal E-mail: plsatty@swbell.net.

**STEWART, PATRICIA CARRY**, foundation administrator; b. Bklyn., May 19, 1928; d. William J. and Eleanor (Murphy) Carry; m. Charles Thorp Stewart, May 30, 1976. Student, U. Paris, 1948—49; BA, Cornell U., 1950. Fgn. corr. Irving Trust Co., N.Y.C., 1950-51; with Janeway Rsch. Co., N.Y.C., 1951-60, sec., treas., 1955-60; with Buckner & Co. and successor firms, N.Y.C., 1961-73, ptnr., 1962-70, v.p., treas., 1970-71, pres., treas., 1971-73; Knight, Carry, Bliss & Co., Inc., N.Y.C., 1971-73, G. Tsai & Co., Inc., 1973; v.p. Edna McConnell Clark Found. Inc., 1974-92. Dir. Cmty. Found. Palm Beach and Martin Counties, 1993-2001, chair, 1998, 2000; allied mem. N.Y. Stock Exch., 1962-73; past mem. nominating com. Am. Stock Exch., N.Y. Stock Exch., N.Y.C. Fin. Svcs. Corp.; dir. emeritus, past chmn. Investor

Responsibility Rsch. Ctr. Trustee emerita, vice chair Cornell U., mem. bd. life overseers Cornell Med. Coll.; mem. vis. com. Grad. Sch Bus., Harvard U., 1974-80; bd. dirs. NOW Legal Def. and Edn. Fund, 1984-92, Women in Founds./Corp. Philanthropy, 1980-86; v.p. fin. com. Women's Forum, 1982-90; vice chmn. CUNY, 1976-80; bd. dirs. United Way of Tri-State, 1977-81, Inst. for Edn. and Rsch. on Women and Work; voting mem. Blue Cross and Blue Shield Greater N.Y., 1975-82; trustee N.Y. State 4-H Found., 1970-76, Internt. Inst. Rural Reconstrn., 1974-79; mem. N.Y.C. panel White House Fellows, 1976-78; mem. bus. adv. coun. The Hosp. Chaplaincy. Recipient Elizabeth Cutter Morrow award YWCA, 1977, Catalyst award Women Dirs. in Corps., 1978, Trustee medal CUNY, 1983, Acomplishment award Wings Club N.Y. 1984, Women's Funding Coalition Innovators for Women$hare award, 1986, Banking Industry Achievement award Nat. Assn. Bank Women, 1987, Cert. Disting. Accomplishments Barnard Coll., 1989; named to YWCA Acad. Women Achievers. Mem. Fin. Women's Assn. N.Y., Country Club of Fla. (bd. dirs.), Univ. Club (N.Y.C.), Gullane Golf Club (Scotland), North Berwick Golf Club (Scotland), Dunbar Golf Club (Scotland), St. Andrews Club (Delray Beach, Fla.), Phi Beta Phi. Home and Office: 2613 N Ocean Blvd Delray Beach FL 33483-7367 also: Halfland Barns North Berwick EH395PW Scotland Personal E-mail: stewartpc@aol.com.

**STEWART, PATRICK,** actor; b. Mirfield, Eng., July 13, 1940; s. Alfred and Gladys (Barraclough) S.; m. Sheila Falconer, Mar. 3, 1966 (div. 1990); 2 children; m. Wendy Neuss, Aug. 25, 2000 (div. 2003). Trained, Bristol Old Vic Theatre Sch. Actor: (theatre) Treasure Island (U.K., debut), 1959, (U.S.) A Midsummer Night's Dream (Broadway debut), 1970, A Christmas Carol, 1991, 92, 94; (TV series) Star Trek: The Next Generation, 1987-94, Eleventh Hour, 2005-, (narrator) High Spirits with the Ghostman, 2005, (mini series) Fall of Eagles, 1974, I, Claudius, 1977, Tinker, Sailor, Soldier, Spy, 1979, Maybury, 1981, Smiley's People, 1982, Playing Shakespeare, 1983, When the Lion Roars, 1992, (voice) 500 Nations, 1995, Mysterious Island, 2005, (TV movies) The Gathering Storm, 1974, Anthony and Cleopatra, 1974 (Olivier award best supporting actor), North and South, 1975, The Madness, 1976, Hamlet, Prince of Denmark, 1980, Little Lord Fauntleroy, 1980, John Paul II, 1984, The Devil's Disciple, 1987, Death Train, 1993, In Search of Dr. Seuss, 1994, (also co-prodr.) The Canterville Ghost, 1996, Moby Dick, 1997, Safe House, 1998, (voice) Animal Farm, 1999, (also exec. prodr.) A Christmas Carol, 1999, (also exec. prodr.) King of Texas, 2002, The Lion in Winter, 2003; host on Saturday Night Live, 1994, (films) Hennessy, 1975, Hedda, 1975, Excalibur, 1981, The Plague Dogs (voice) 1982, Dune, 1984, Uindii, 1984, Lifeforce, 1985, Code Name: Emerald, 1985, Wild Geese II, 1985, The Doctor and the Devils, 1985, Lady Jane, 1986, L.A. Story, 1991, Robin Hood: Men in Tights, 1993, Gunmen, 1994, Star Trek: Generations, 1994, The Pagemaster, 1994 (voice), Jeffrey, 1995, Let It Me Be (aka Love Dance), 1995, Star Trek: First Contact, 1996, Conspiracy Theory, 1997, Safe House, 1997, Dad Savage, 1997, Master Minds, 1997, (voice) Prince of Egypt, 1998, X-Men, 2000, (voice) Jimmy Neutron: Boy Genius, 2001, Star Trek: Nemesis, 2002, X-Men 2, 2003, (voice) Back to Gaya, 2004, Steamboy, 2004, The Game of Their Lives, 2005, (voice) Chicken Little, 2005, X-Men: The Last Stand, 2006, assoc. prodr. Star Trek IX: Insurrection, 1998; assoc. artist with Royal Shakespeare Co., 1967—; recording: Prokofiev: Peter and the Wolf (Grammy award best spoken word album for children 1996). Office: Flying Freehold Productions 233 Wilshire Blvd Ste 600 Santa Monica CA 90401 also: William Morris Agy 151 El Camino Dr Beverly Hills CA 90212*

**STEWART, PAUL ARTHUR,** pharmaceutical company executive; b. Greensburg, Ind., Sept. 28, 1955; s. John Arthur and Alberta Jeannette (Densford) S.; m. Susan Rhodes, Dec. 20, 1975; children: John Rhodes, Daniel Robbins. BS, Purdue U., 1976; MBA, Harvard U., 1987. Grad. asst. Purdue U., West Lafayette, Ind., 1977; asst. treas. Stewart Seeds Inc., Greensburg, 1997-82, sec., treas., 1982-84; cons. The Boston Cons. Group Inc., Chgo., 1986; founder, owner PASCO Group, mgmt. and computer cons., aircraft leasing, 1979-87; mgr. bus. planning agrichems. Eli Lilly & Co., Indpls., 1987-88, dist. sales mgr. agrichems., 1989-90, tech. acquisition mgr. med. devices and diagnostics divsn., 1990-92; dir. mktg. info. and bus. devel. IVAC Corp. subs. Eli Lilly & Co., 1992-94, advisor corp. fin. and investment banking, 1994-96; mgr. global bus. devel. (animal health) Eli Lilly & Co., 1996—. Author: (nonfiction) A Harvard MBA's Advice to His Sons, 2005. Mem. Greensburg-Decatur County Bd. Airport Commrs., 1980-85, pres., 1980-81, 83; mem. Decatur County Data Processing Bd., 1982-85; deacon 2d Presbyn. Ch. Indpls., 1991-92, elder, 1996-99; bd. dirs. Friends of Nat. Inst. Nursing Rsch., NIH, 1995-98, Park Tudor Sch., Indpls., 1997-2003. Mem.: Indpls. Legal Aid Soc. (bd. dirs. 2004—), Harvard Bus. Sch. Alumni Assn. (bd. dirs. 1999—2003, v.p. 2001—03), Alpha Gamma Rho. Republican. Presbyterian. Office: Eli Lilly & Co Lilly Corp Ctr Indianapolis IN 46285-0001 Office Phone: 317-277-6120. Personal E-mail: pstewart@mba1987.hbs.edu.

**STEWART, PAUL JAMES, JR.,** history educator; b. Chgo., 1929; s. Paul James and Kathryn (Baird) S.; m. Josephine Smania, 1960; children: Heather, Thomas. BA, U. Ill., 1950, PhD, 1961; MA, Columbia U., 1956. Grad. asst. U. Ill., Urbana, 1955-59, vis. lectr.; 1967-68; asst. prof. U. Southwestern La., Lafayette, 1959-62, Lawrence U., Appleton, Wis., 1962-65, Wash. State U., Pullman, 1965-67; vis. asst. prof. U. Idaho, Moscow, 1966-67 summers; assoc. prof. U. Wis., Whitewater, 1968-70; vis. prof. U. New Haven, 1979; prof. history So. Conn. State U., New Haven, 1970-92, prof. emeritus, 1992—. Faculty staff NDEA Hist. Inst. (summers), 1966, 67; participant monthly seminar on 16th century Europe CUNY, 1977—78. Editor/translator: Vigil in Benicarlo, 1982, Portrait of an Unknown Man: Manuel Azaña and Modern Spain, 1995; mem. editl. bd. Republican Notes, Madrid, Spain, Jour. of the Ctr. for Republican Rsch. and Studies, 2002-; contbr. articles to profl. jours. and encys. Sr. warden Grace Episcopal Ch., Hamden, Conn., 1990; vestryman Grace Episc. Ch., Hamden, Conn., 1981-88; del. to Diocesan Convention, 1991-93; Cpl. arty. US Army, 1951-1953, Japan. Fulbright scholar, Spain, 1960-61. Mem. Am. Hist. Assn., Conn. Acad. Arts and Scis., Am. Acad. of Rsch. Historians of Medieval Spain, Soc. for Spanish and Portuguese Hist. Studies. Office: So Conn State Univ Dept History New Haven CT 06515

**STEWART, PAUL LEROY,** art educator, printmaker; b. Cleve., June 28, 1928; s. Leroy Hepburn and Zoa Irene Stewart; m. Eulalia Maria Kingma, June 15, 1958; children: Paul Heath, John Hepburn, James Hachet. Student, Cleve. Inst. Art, 1948—50; BA, Albion Coll., 1953; student, New Sch. Social Rsch., 1955; MA, U. Mich., 1959. Graphic designer Alastair Brown Assocs., N.Y., 1955—57; assoc. prof. Albion (Mich.) Coll., 1959—72; prof. U. Mich., Ann Arbor, 1973—98, ret., 1998. Included in: Smithsonian Institute Archives of American Art, 1973, New York Art Review, 3d edit., 1987, Artists in Michigan 1900-1976, 1989, Venue, 1996, The Best Printmaking, An International Collection, 1997; Represented in permanent collections The Met. Mus. Art, N.Y., The Nat. Gallery Art, Washington, D.C., The Bklyn. (N.Y.) Mus. Art, Libr. Congress, Washington, D.C., The Cleve. (Ohio) Mus. Art, Detroit (Mich.) Inst. Art, The Mpls. (Minn.) Inst. Art, Toledo (Can.) Mus. Art, Kharkov (USSR) Mus. Art, Balt. (Md.) Mus. Art, Taipei (Taiwan) Fine Arts Mus., Phila. (Pa.) Mus. Art, The Boston (Mass.) Mus. Art, Ga. Mus. Art, Athens, Ga., L.A. (Calif.) County Mus. Art, others. Cpl. USMC, 1946—48. Nominee Achievement award, Artists Soc. Internat., 1987; recipient Kurawsao-Pomorski Voivod Spl. prize, Internat. Print Triennial, 2000, Purchase prize, Internat. Print Exhbn., 1997, many others for art competitions; grantee, Great Lakes Colls. Assn., 1967—68, Mich. Coun. Arts, 1987—88. Avocations: building, photography, travel. Home: 4040 Danford Rd Ann Arbor MI 48105 Business E-Mail: pleroy@umich.edu.

**STEWART, PRISCILLA ANN MABIE,** art historian, educator; b. Iowa City, Iowa, Sept. 21, 1926; d. Edward Charles and Grace Frances (Chase) Mabie; m. Thomas Wilson Stewart, Aug. 28, 1949 (dec. Mar. 1996). BA, U. Iowa, 1948; MA, U. South Fla., 1971; EdS, Fla. Atlantic U., 1983. Coord. elem. art Manatee County, Fla., 1953-59; prof. art history, intercultural humanities, founder photography dept. Manatee C.C., Bradenton, Fla., 1959—. Organizer, dir. Pelican Perch Wild Bird Hosp., Bradenton, 1953-85; participant Women's Archives U. Iowa Librs. Apptd. charter mem. of adv. bd. to dean of Liberal Arts, U. Iowa, 1999—. Mem. AAUP, Pres.'s Club U. Iowa, Fla. Assn. C.C.s, Sarasota-Manatee Phi Beta Kappa Assn. (pres. 1984-86), Phi Beta Kappa, Alpha Xi Delta, Phi Kappa Phi. Episcopalian. Home: 2705 Riverview Blvd Bradenton FL 34205-4335 Office: Manatee Community Coll Dept Fine and Performing Arts 5840 26th St W Bradenton FL 34207-3522 Office Phone: 941-752-5548. Personal E-mail: stewarp@aol.com. Business E-Mail: stewarp@mccfl.edu.

**STEWART, RICHARD BURLESON,** law educator; b. Cleve., Feb. 12, 1940; s. Richard Siegfried and Ruth Dysert (Staten) Stewart; m. Alice Peck Fales, May 13, 1967 (div. June 1992); children: William, Paul, Elizabeth; m. Jane Laura Bloom, Sept. 20, 1992; children: Emily, Ian. AB, Yale U., 1961; MA (Rhodes scholar), Oxford U., Eng., 1963; LLB, Harvard U., 1966; D (hon.), Erasmus U., Rotterdam, 1993, U. Rome La Sapienza, 2005. Bar: DC 1968, U.S. Supreme Ct. 1971. Law clk. to Hon. Potter Stewart U.S. Supreme Ct., 1966-67; assoc. Covington & Burling, Washington, 1967-71; asst. prof. law Harvard U., 1971-75, prof.; 1975-82, Byrne prof. adminstrv. law, 1982-89, assoc. dean, 1984-86; asst. atty. gen. environment and natural resources div. Dept. Justice, Washington, 1989-91; prof. law NYU Law Sch., N.Y.C., 1992-94, Emily Kempin prof. law, 1994—2002, John Edward Sexton prof. law, 2002—, univ. prof., 2002—; of counsel Sidley & Austin, 1992—. Spl. counsel U.S. Senate Watergate Com., 1974; vis. prof. U. Calif., Berkeley Law Sch., 1979—80, U. Chgo. Law Sch., 1986—87, Georgetown U., 1991—92, Europen U. Inst., 1995; dir. Ctr. Environ. and Land Use Law, Health Effects Inst.; mem. adv. bd. Environ. Def. Author: (book) The Reformation of American Administrative Law (in Chinese), 2002; author: (with P. Menell) Environmental Law and Policy, 1994, author: (with S. Breyer, C. Sunstein and M. Spitzer) Administrative Law and Regulation, 1979, Administrative Law and Regulation, 5th edit., 2002; author: (with E. Rehbinder) Integration Through Law: Environmental Protection Policy, 1985, Integration Through Law: Environmental Protection Policy, paper edit., 1987; author: (with R. Revesz) Markets v. Environment?, 1995; author: (with R. Revesz and P. Sands) Environment, the Economy, and Sustainable Development, 2001; author: (with J. Wiener) Reconstructing Climate Policy, 2003; editor (with R. Revesz): (book) Analyzing Superfund: Economics, Science, and Law, 1995. Fellow: Am. Acad. Arts and Scis.; mem.: ABA, Am. Law Inst. Office: NYU Law Sch 40 Washington Sq S New York NY 10012-1099 E-mail: stewartr@juris.law.nyu.edu.

**STEWART, RICHARD DONALD,** internist, educator, writer; b. Lakeland, Fla., Dec. 26, 1926; s. LeRoy Hepburn and Zoa Irene (Hachet) S.; m. Mary Leeuw, June 14, 1952; children: R. Scot, Gregory D., Mary E. AB, U. Mich., 1951, MD, 1955, MPH, 1962; MA, U. Wis. Milw., 1979; PhD in English, U. Wis., Milw., 1997. Diplomate Am. Bd. Internal Medicine, Am. Bd. Med. Toxicology, Acad. Toxicol. Scis. Intern Saginaw (Mich.) Gen. Hosp., 1955-56; resident in internal medicine U. Mich. Med. Ctr., Ann Arbor, 1959-62; dir. med. rsch. sect. Dow Chem. Co., Midland, Mich., 1962-66; staff physician Midland Hosp., 1962-66; assoc. prof. preventive medicine Med. Coll. Wis., Milw., 1966-68, prof., chmn. dept. environ. medicine, 1968—78, prof. emergency med., 1989—91, adj. prof. dept. pharmacology and toxicology, 1978—. Cons. Children's Hosp. Wis., 1989-93, Internal Medicine St. Mary's Hosp., Racine, Wis., 1983-93; prof., dir. med. toxicology fellowship Dept. Emergency Medicine Milw. Regional Med. Ctr., 1989-91; sr. attending staff, 1967-90; staff Internal Medicine St. Luke's Hosp., Racine, 1983-93; med. dir. Poison Control Ctr. Southeastern Wis., 1989-93; corp. med. advisor S.C. Johnson & Son, Inc., Racine, 1971-78, corp. med. dir., 1978-89. Author: (med. biography) Leper Priest of Molokai, 2000. Mem. adv. med. staff Milw. Fire Dept., 1977—. Cadet USAF, 1945-46. Fellow ACP, Am. Coll. Occupl. Medicine, Am. Acad. Clin. Toxicology, Acad. Toxicological Scis.; mem. AMA, Soc. Toxicology, Wis. State Med. Soc., Racine Acad. Medicine, Rotary Internat., Phi Theta Kappa, Phi Kappa Phi, Sigma Tau Delta. Achievements include invention of medical devices including the hollow fiber artificial kidney and capillary artificial lung; being leader of team that performed first human dialyses with the Hollow Fiber Artificial Kidney, beginning Aug.4, 1967. This artificial kidney is universally used for long-term dialysis. Avocations: hiking, literature, creative writing. Home and Office: 5337 Wind Point Rd Racine WI 53402-2322 Office Phone: 262-639-6483.

**STEWART, RICHARD EDWIN,** insurance consulting company executive; b. Washington, Nov. 4, 1933; s. Irvin and Florence Elsie (Dezendorf) S.; m. Barbara Lewis Dickson, Oct. 29, 1993. BA, W.Va. U., 1955; BA (Rhodes scholar), Oxford U., Eng., 1957, MA, 1961; JD, Harvard, 1959. Bar: N.Y. 1960. Assoc. Royall, Koegel & Rogers, N.Y.C., 1960-63; asst. counsel to Gov. of N.Y., 1963-64, 1st asst. counsel, 1965-66; supr. ins. N.Y. State Ins. Dept., 1967-70; sr. v.p., gen. counsel First Nat. City Bank, N.Y.C., 1971-72; sr. v.p., dir. Chubb & Son Inc., N.Y.C., 1973-81; sr. v.p. Chubb Corp., N.Y.C., 1973-81, CFO, 1974-81; gov. N.Y. Ins. Exch., N.Y.C., 1979-81; chmn. Stewart Econs., Inc., N.Y.C., 1981-90, Chapel Hill, NC, 1990—2005, San Francisco, 2005—. Mem. adv. com. HUD, 1968-72; mem. Adminstrv. Conf. U.S., 1970-74; bd. dirs. Am. Arbitration Assn., 1970-80; mem. UN panel experts on Transnational Bank failure, 1991. Co-author: Automobile Insurance...For Whose Benefit?, 1970, Watergate: Implications for Responsible Government, 1974, Medical Malpractice, 1977, Managing Insurer Insolvency, 1988, Insurance Insolvency Guarantees, 1990, A Brief History of Underwriting Cycles, 1991, Niche Insurance Companies, 1997, Information Technology and Insurance Agent Licensing, 1998, The Loss of the Certainty Effect, 2002, Managing Insurer Insolvency, 2003, Arbitration and Insurance without the Common Law, 2004; author: Reason and Regulation, 1972, Insurance and Insurance Regulation, 1980. Trustee Coll. Ins., N.Y., 1970-78, Am. Coll. Life Underwriters, 1990-93; mem. Mayor's Com. on Taxi Regulation, 1979-82, ABA Com. to Improve Liability Ins. System, 1989; mem. panel experts on transnat. bank failure UN, 1991; mem. spl. panel U.S. Senate Com. on Presdl. Campaign Practice, 1974. Served with AUS, 1959. Mem. Nat. Acad. Pub. Adminstrn., Nat. Acad. Social Ins., Cosmos Club of Washington, Century Club of N.Y.C., Phi Beta Kappa Assn. Home and Office: One Embarcadero Ctr Ste 500 San Francisco CA 94111 Office Phone: 415-315-1771. Business E-Mail: res@stewarteconomics.com.

**STEWART, RITA JOAN,** academic administrator; b. Muncie, Ind., June 6, 1945; d. John Marion and Crystalee Masterson; children: Jon Lewis, Robert Forrest. BS, Ball State U., 1967, MA, 1974. Tchr. Blue River H.S., Mt. Summit, Ind., 1968-69, Sunnyside Elem. Sch., New Castle, Ind., 1967-68; copywriter, announcer Sta. WTIM, Taylorville, Ill., 1974-75; dir. Kitselman Conf. Ctr. Ball State U., Muncie, Ind., 1978-2000, dir. conf. and spl. events, 2000—. Contbr. articles to profl. jours. Precinct committeewoman Henry County Dem. Party, New Castle, Ind., 1969-70; precinct chmn. March of Dimes, New Castle, Ind., 1974-75; chmn. edn. com. West Viwe Sch. Coun., Muncie, 1987-88; sec., bd. dirs. PAL Club, Muncie, 1988-93; pres., bd. dirs. Altrusa Club Found., Muncie, 1997-98, v.p., 2001-01, pres., 2002. Mem.: AAUW (v.p. 1984—85), Ind. Conf. Dirs. Assn., Collegiate Conf. and Event Dirs. Internat. (dir. region 8 1999—2000, pres. elect 2006—, internat. bd. dirs., Mentor Yr. award 2004), Altrusa Club of Muncie (pres. 2002—03), Kappa Delta Pi (Disting. Svc. award 1995). Methodist. Office: Ball State U Confs and Spl Events Muncie IN 47306 Home: # 1-203 4501 N Wheeling Ave Muncie IN 47304-1277 Office Phone: 765-285-1396. Office Fax: 765-285-5457. Business E-Mail: conferences@bsu.edu.

**STEWART, ROD (RODERICK DAVID STEWART),** singer; b. North London, Eng., Jan. 10, 1945; m. Alana Collins, Apr. 6, 1979 (div. 1984); children: Kimberly, Sean; child with Kelly Emberg: Ruby Rachel; m. Rachel Hunter, Dec. 15, 1990; children: Renée, Liam; one child with Penny Lancaster. Singer with Jeff Beck Group, 1968-69, The Faces, 1969-75; albums include (with Jeff Beck Group) Truth, 1968, Beck-Ola, 1969; (with The Faces) The First Step, 1970, Long Player, 1971, A Nod Is As Good as a Wink...To a Blind Horse, 1971, Ooh La La, 1973, Coast to Coast/Overture & Beginners, 1973, Snakes and Ladders/The Best of Faces, 1976; (solo) An Old Raincoat Won't Ever Let You Down, 1969, Gasoline Alley, 1970, Every Picture Tells a Story, 1971, Never a Dull Moment, 1972, Sing It Again Rod, 1973, Smiler, 1974, Atlantic Crossing, 1975, The Best of Rod Stewart, 1976, The Best of Rod Stewart Vol. II, 1976, A Night on the Town, 1976, Foot Loose & Fancy Free, 1976, Blondes Have More Fun, 1978, Greatest Hits Vol. I, 1979, Foolish Behaviour, 1980, Tonight I'm Yours, 1981, Absolutely Live, 1981, Camouflage, 1984, (with Jeff Beck) Get Workin', 1985, Out of Order, 1988, Storyteller: The Complete Anthology 1964-1990, 1990, Downtown Train, 1990, Vagabond Heart, 1991, You Wear It Well, 1992, The Mercury Anthology, 1992, Once In A Blue Moon Vintage, 1993, Ridin High, The Rod Stewart Album, Unplugged...And Seated, 1993 (Grammy nomination, Best Pop Male Vocal for "Have I Told You Lately"), Spanner in the Works, 1995, Handbags and Gladrags, 1996, When We Were the New Boys, 1998, Human, 2001, It Had to Be You...The Great American Songbook, 2002, As Time Goes By...The Great American Songbook, Vol.:II, 2003, Stardust...The Great American Songbook, Vol.:III, 2004, Thanks for the Memory: The Great American Songbook, Vol. 4, 2005, Ain't That Loving You Baby, 2005, Gold, 2005; films include Rod Stewart - The Best of Rod Stewart, Rod Stewart and The Faces - The Final Concert, 1974, Rod Stewart and Faces, 1975, Rod Stewart Live at Los Angeles Forum, 1980, Rod Stewart-Tonight He's Yours, short and long versions, 1981, The Rod Stewart Concert Video, 1984, Rod Stewart -Storyteller 1984-91, 1991, Rod Stewart - Vagabond Heart; composer (films) Night at the Roxbury, 1998, Almost Famous, 2000, About Schmidt, 2002 and several others; performer Olympic Torch Concert Live, 2004 and several others. Named Rock Star of Year Rolling Stone mag., 1971; recipient British Rock and Pop Lifetime Achievement award, 1992; inducted into the Rock & Roll Hall of Fame, 1994. Office: Warner Bros Records 3300 Warner Blvd Burbank CA 91505-4694*

**STEWART, RUTH ANN,** public policy educator; b. Chgo., Apr. 4, 1942; d. Elmer Ashton and Ann (Mitchell) Stewart; m. David Levering Lewis, children: Allegra Stewart, Jason Lewis, Allison Lewis, Eric Lewis. Student, U. Chgo., 1960-61, Simmons Coll., 1963; BA, Wheaton Coll., Norton, Mass., 1963; MS, Columbia U., 1965; postgrad., Fisk U., 1970, Harvard U., 1976, postgrad., 1987. Mktg. mgr. Macmillan Co., N.Y.C., 1968-70; asst. chief Schomburg Ctr. Rsch. Black Culture, N.Y.C., 1970-80; assoc. dir. external svcs. N.Y. Pub. Libr., 1980-86; asst. Libr. Congress Nat. Programs, Washington, 1986-89; assoc. Dir. Resource Devel., Washington, 1989-95; sr. policy analyst arts, humanities & social legis. Congl. Rsch. Svc., Washington, 1989-97; rsch. prof. cultural policy Ctr. Urban Policy Rsch. Bloustein Sch. Planning and Pub. Policy, Rutgers U., New Brunswick, NJ, 1997—2003; clin. prof. Wagner Grad. Sch. Pub. Svc., NYU, N.Y.C., 2003—. Trustee, sec. Wheaton Coll., Norton, 1980—99; mem. libr. vis. com. Harvard U., 1975—88, MIT, 1986—90. Cons. editor: Jour. Arts Mgmt. Law and Soc., 1998—, founding co-editor: book series Public Life of the Arts, 1998—; bd. dirs. Nat. Pk. Found., Washington, 1978—84, Fund Folk Culture, Santa Fe, 1991—2003, Lab. Sch. Washington, 1992—94, Women's Fgn. Policy Group, 1999—2003, Bklyn. Bot. Garden, 2000—, Studio in Sch., 2000—, Cooper-Hewitt Nat. Design Mus., Smithsonian Instn., 2003—; mem. rsch. adv. coun. Ctr. Arts and Culture, Washington, 1997—2006; sch. com. Alvin Ailey Sch., 1998—. Fellow, NY State Coun. Arts. Mem.: Coun. Fgn. Rels., ArtTable (nat. bd. dirs. 2002—03), Friends of Edn., Mus. Modern Art. Office: NYU Wagner Sch 295 Lafayette St New York NY 10012 Office Phone: 212-998-7480.

**STEWART, S. JAY,** automotive executive; b. Pineville, W.Va., Sept. 18, 1938; s. Virgil Harvey and Lena Rivers (Repair) S.; m. Judith Ann Daniels, June 3, 1961; children: Julie Annette, Jennifer Amy, Steven Jay. BSChemE, U. Cin., 1960; MBA, W.Va. U., 1966. Various positions in engring., mfg., mktg. Monsanto Co., St. Louis, 1961-73; dir. mktg. Ventron Corp. subs. Thiokol, Inc., Beverly, Mass., 1973-77, gen. mgr., 1977-79; pres. Dynachem Corp. subs. Thiokol, Inc., Tustin, Calif., 1979-82; group v.p. Thiokol Corp., Newtown, Pa., 1982; group v.p. splty. chems. Morton Internat., Inc. (formerly Morton Thiokol, Inc.), Chgo., 1983-86; pres., chief oper. officer Morton Internat., Inc., Chgo., 1986-94, also bd. dirs., 1994—99, chmn. bd., CEO, 1994—99; chmn. Autolive, Inc., Stockholm, 2001—. Mem. Household Internat. Inc., Autoliv, Inc.; trustee Rush Presbyn.-St. Luke's Med. Ctr., Chgo., 1987—; Trustee Mus. Scis. and Industry; mem. exec. commn., Soc. Chem. Industry. Recipient Disting. Alumnus award U. Cin., 1984. Mem. Am. Chem. Soc., Am. Inst. Chem. Engrs., Chem. Mfrs. Assn. (bd. dirs. 1984-87, 94), Comml. Devel. Assn., Chem. Mktg. Assn. (bd. dirs. 1990), Comml. Club Chgo., The Chgo. Club, Econ. Club Chgo. Republican. Methodist. Office: Autolive Inc Klarabergsciadukten 70 Sec E Box 70381 SE 10724 Stockholm Sweden*

**STEWART, SANDRA KAY,** music educator; b. New Albany, Ind., Dec. 24, 1947; d. Dale F. and June V. (Martin) Byrne; m. William Lee Stewart, June 25, 1971. B Music Edn., Ind. U., 1969; MusM, Norfolk State U., 1992; D Mus. Arts, U. S.C., 1995. Cert. vocal music N.Y., Mo.; nat. cert., state cert. piano tchr. Vocal music tchr., choral dir. Ritenour Sch. Dist., St. Louis, 1969-75, Sch. Dist. # 54, Chgo., 1975-76, Waverly (N.Y.) Jr./Sr. H.S., 1977-78, Clarence (N.Y.) H.S., 1978-82; piano instr., show choir dir. Inst. Fine Arts, Reading, Pa., 1982-85; piano accompanist Berks Grand Opera Co., Reading, Pa., 1982-85, Va. Opera Co., Norfolk, 1986, U. S.C., Columbia, 1992-95, Jacksonville Masterworks Sr. Chorale, 1996-99, Bolles Sr. H.S., 1996-98, Pinewood Presbyn. Ch., 1996-98; piano and music theory instr. Acad. of Music, Virginia Beach, Va., 1986-91, 2002—03; piano instr., choral dir., vocal jazz dir., accompanist Jacksonville (Fla.) U., 1995—2000; chair vocal music dept. Douglas Anderson Sch. of Arts, 1998—2000; prof. music U. North Fla., Jacksonville, 2000—. Editor: Florida Music Teacher, 1999-2000; contbr. articles to profl. publs. Mem. Virginia Beach Pops Orch., 1989-91; founder, dir. North Fla. Piano Camp, 2000-2006. Recipient Fla. First Lady's Art Scholar award, 2000. Mem. AAUW (numerous offices 1975—), Am. Choral Dirs. Assn., Coll. Music Soc., Nat. Piano Found., Music Educators Nat. Conf., Nat. Guild Piano Tchrs., Music Tchrs. Nat. Assn., Delius Assn. Fla. (bd. dirs. 1997-99), Phi Kappa Lambda, Mu Phi Epsilon, Delta Kappa Gamma Soc. Internat., TRI-M Music Honor Soc. Office: 3764 Harpers Ferry Ln Jacksonville FL 32257-4544 Office: U North Fla 4567 St Johns Bluff Rd S Jacksonville FL 32224 Office Phone: 904-620-3854.

**STEWART, SHARON ROSE,** mathematics professor; b. Fillmore, NY, Dec. 16, 1946; d. Eldyn Benjamin and Elizabeth Ann Simons; m. Brian William Stewart, July 24, 1971; children: Sheila, David, Anna. BA, Houghton Coll., NY, 1968; MS in Edn., SUNY, Geneseo, 1971; A in Practical Theology, Christ Nations Inst., Dallas, 1978; cert. in libr. studies, Meml. U. of Nfld., St. John's, Can., 1992. Cert. tchr. N-9, tchr. math. 7-12 NY. Math. tchr. Corinth Ctrl. Sch., NY, 1968-69, Belmont Ctrl. Sch., NY, 1969—71, Lindsay Collegiate and Vocat. Inst., Ont., Canada, 1971—72; tchr. A. Garrigus Acad. and Collegiate Inst., St. Lunaire-Griquet, Nfld., 1973—74, 1982—83; libr. technician Ctrl. Nfld. Regional Coll., Grand Falls-Windsor, 1987—92, math. prof., 1992—96, Hazard Cmty. and Tech. Coll., Ky., 1997—. Bd. dirs. Evangel Pentecostal Assembly, Grand Falls-Windsor, 1996—97; adult tchr. Victory Assembly of God, Hazard, 1997—. Mem.: Ky. Math. Assn. of 2-Yr. Colls., Gideons Internat. Ladies Aux. Avocations: reading, travel, painting. Office: Hazard Cmty and Tech Coll 1 Community College Dr Hazard KY 41701 Office Phone: 606-487-3119. E-mail: sharon.stewart@kctcs.edu.

**STEWART, SHIRLEY ANNE,** elementary school educator; b. Bridgeville, Del., June 8, 1957; d. James Elliott and Pearline (Jacobs) Stewart. BS in Spl. Edn., U. Del., 1979, MEd in Curriculum and Instrn., 2001; MEd in Spl. Edn., Temple U., 1981; postgrad., Wilmington Coll., 2003—. Cert. tchr., Del. Spl. edn. tchr. Caesar Rodney Sch. Dist., Camden, Del., 1979, Indian River Sch. Dist., Frankford, Del., 1980—; tchr. Frankford Elem. Sch., 1980-91, Sussex Ctrl. Mid. Sch., Millsboro, Del., 1991-94; asst. prin. Woodbridge Elem. Sch., Greenwood, Del., 1994-96, Pleasantville Elem. Sch., New Castle, Del., 1996-98, McCullough Elem. Sch., New Castle, 1998—2001; prin. Martin L. King Jr. Elem. Sch., Wilmington, Del., 2001—03; asst. prin. George Read Mid. Sch., Newcastle, Del., 2003—04; prin. tchr. Wilmington Manor Elem., New Castle, Del., 2004—. Mem. Gov.'s Adv. Coun. for Exceptional Citizens, Dover, Del., 1986-91; mem. Coun. Exceptional Children, Dover, 1986—; mem. Statewide Multicultural Com., 1989-90; instr. Del. Tchr. Ctr., 1990; mem. mid. sch. adv. coun. State Del., 1990-91, adv. coun. on multicultural edn., 1991-92, Mid. Sch. Reading Com., 1992, Indian River Sch. Dist. Recruitment/Critical Shortage Com., 1992, instructional materials rev. com. 1993—; pres. Garden Cmty., Inc., 1999—. Mem. black recruitment com. U.

Del., 1987; mem. Minority Action Com., Dover, 1985-87, chmn. Martin L. King Jr. Writing Contest, 1987-88, mem. exec. bd., 1988-89, chmn. black history com., 1986-87, sec. local minority action com., 1985-88; mem. attendance com. Indian River Sch. Dist., 1987-88, recruitment & retention com., 1992, mid. sch. reading com., 1992, mem. materials rev. com., 1993—; chmn. Del. State Edn. Minority Action Com., 1989-90; mem. strategic planning com. Del. State Edn. Assn., 1989-90, issues for the 90's com., 1991; active Dept. Pub. Instrn. Multicultural Inst. Tng., 1989; mem. middle sch. com. State of Del., 1991; mem. Statewide Multicultural Adv. Com., 1991—; vol. Saturday Sch. Com., 1992-93; mem. New Directions Com., 1992-93, Del. Prin.'s Leadership Acad., 1995-96; mem. tech. task force Colonial Sch. Dist., 1998-99; pres. Garden Cmty. Inc., 1999-2000. Recipient Instrnl. Profl. Devel. award Minority Action Com., 1987, Del. Tchr. Ctr. Svc. award, 1989, Instrnl. Profl. Devel. award Del. State Edn. Assn., 1990, Outstanding Black Woman award Nat. Polit. Congress of Black Women, Inc., 1997, 21st Century award for Positive Sch. Leadership, 2003. Mem. NEA, NAACP, ASCD, Nat. Elem. Sch. Prins. Assn., Del. Assn. Sch. Adminstrs., Del. Elem. Sch. Prins. Assn., Del. State Edn. Assn. (chairperson minority action com. 1988-91, Instrnl. Profl. Devel. award 1991, Human and Civil Rights award 1992), Indian River Edn. Assn. (treas. 1989-91, chairperson minority action com. 1990-93), Adults and Children with Learning Disabilities. Democrat. Pentacostal/Apostolic. Avocations: reading, poetry. Home: 224 Becks Woods Dr Bear DE 19701-3831 Office Phone: 302-323-2901 ext. 1075. Business E-Mail: sstewart@colonial.k12.de.us.

**STEWART, SUE S.,** lawyer; b. Oct. 9, 1942; d. Fraizer McVale and Carolyn Eliabeth (Hunt) S.; m. Arthur L. Stern, III, July 31, 1965 (div.). m. children: Anne, Mark Alan; m. John A. Ciampa, Sept. 1, 1985 (div.); m. Stephen L. Raymond (dec.). BA, Wellesley Coll., 1964; postgrad., Harvard U. Law Sch., 1964-65; JD, Georgetown U., 1967. Bar: N.Y. 1968. Clk. to judges Juvenile Ct., Washington, 1967-68; mem. Nixon, Hargrave, Devans & Doyle (now Nixon Peabody LLP), Rochester, NY, 1968-74, ptnr., 1975—2001, mng. ptnr., 1998—2001, ret., 2001; v.p., gen. counsel U. Rochester, 2003—. Lectr. in field; trustee Found. of Monroe County (N.Y.) Bar, 1976-78; v.p. & Gen. Counsel Univ. Rochester, NY, 2003–. Author: Charitable Giving and Taxation. Sec., dir. United Cmty. Chest of Greater Rochester, 1973-87, 1992-; trustee, sec. Internat. Mus. Photography at George Eastman House, Rochester, 1974-97, 2000-03, Genesee Country Mus., Mumford, N.Y., 1976-2002; bd. dirs. Ctr. for Govtl. Rsch., 1990-97; trustee, chmn. United Neighborhood Ctr. of Greater Rochester Found., 1991-2003; trustee, chmn. exec. com. Nat. Ctr. Edn. and Economy, 1997-; dir. Canandaigua (N.H.) Nat. Bank, 2000-. Mem. ABA (chmn. task force on charitable giving, exempt orgns. com. tax sect. 1981-2003), N.Y. State Bar (exec. com. tax sect. 1974-76, chmn. com. exempt orgns 1975-76), Monroe County Bar Assn. (trustee 1974-75), BNA Portfolio, Pvt. Found. Distbns. (Athena award 2000, de Tocqueville award 2003). Office: Of Counsel 266 Wallis Hall PO Box 270040 Rochester NY 14627-0040 Office Phone: 585-273-2167.

**STEWART, SUSAN,** writer; b. 1952; BA, Dickinson Coll., 1973; MA, Johns Hopkins U., 1975; PhD, U. Pa., 1978. Assoc. prof. dept. English Temple U., Phila., 1978—81; assoc. prof., 1981—85, prof., 1986—87; Regan prof. English U. Pa., 1997—. Vis. scholar Getty Ctr. for the History of Art and the Humanities, Santa Monica, Calif., 1995. Author: Nonsense: Aspects of Intertextuality in Folklore and Literature, 1979, On Longing: Narratives of the Miniature, the Gigantic, the Souvenir, the Collection, 1984, Crimes of Writing: Problems in the Containment of Representation, 1991, poetry. Recipient Individual Writer's award, Lila Wallace-Reader's Digest Found., 1996; fellow, Nat. Endowment for the Arts, 1982, 1990, Pa. Coun. on the Arts, 1984, 1988, John Simon Guggenheim Meml. Found., 1987; MacArthur fellow, 1997. Office: Univ Pa Dept English 119 Bennett Hall 3340 Walnut St Philadelphia PA 19104-6273

**STEWART, THOMAS CLIFFORD,** investment company executive; b. Portland, Oreg., Oct. 25, 1950; s. Jack Fry Stewart and Naomi June Gedney Cuyler; m. Susan Elizabeth Sample; children: Andrew, Tommy, MacKenzie, Cortny. Student, U. Gothenborg, Sweden, 1971; BS, U. Oreg., 1974; MBA, UCLA, 1982. Exec. dir. Morgan Stanley & Co., N.Y.C., 1982—90; pres. Cort MacKenzie & Co., Portland, 1990—2003; dir. Acrymed, Lake Oswego, Oreg., 1995-96, Morley Fin. Svcs., Lake Oswego, Oreg., 1995-97; prin. Andew Thomas & Co. L.L.L., 2003—. dir. NCAA Leadership Adv. Bd., 2003—. Contbr. articles to profl. jours. Trustee U. Oreg. Found., 1994-2004; bd. dirs. Oreg. Air and Space Mus., 2001-05; chmn. U. Oreg. Pres.'s Assn. 1997-99; mem. exec. com. Lundquist Coll. of Bus., Univ. Oregon, 1998-2001, 03-05, bd. advisors Coll. Bus., U. Oreg., 1990—, mem. athletic dept. bd. advisors, 1998-2005; Oreg. State Commn. on Higher Bus. Edn., 1992-94; mem. leadership coun. U. Oreg., 1995-99; bd. dirs. Lake Oswego Sch. Found., 1996-2000; treas. adv. cabinet State of Oreg., 1993-94; adv. bd. Sec. of Navy Nat. Naval Res. Policy Bd., Washington, 1987-89; mem. edn. specification com. Eugene 4J, Oreg., 2001-04. Comdr. USN, 1974-80, USNR, 1980-91. Decorated Air medal, Navy Commendation for Valor; Baker scholar, 1981. Mem. Naval Res. Assn. (Jr. Officer of Yr. 1988), U.S. Navy League, ROA, Am. Legion, VFW, Beta Gamma Sigma, Beta Alpha Psi, Alpha Mu Alpha, Skull & Dagger.

**STEWART, TIMOTHY GLEN,** organist; b. Atlanta, Sept. 18, 1960; s. Glen A. Stewart and Carol Ann Hicks; m. Melodee Beth Adams, Sept. 6, 1986. BS in Chemistry, Ga. State U., Atlanta, Ga., 1982; MS in Metallurgy, Ga. Inst. of Tech., Atlanta, Ga., 1985; PhD in Ednl. Psychology, Ga. State U., Atlanta, Ga., 1992. Chemistry lab asst. DeKalb Coll., Decatur, Ga., 1978—79; organist/asst. choir dir. Tucker Christian Ch., Tucker, Ga., 1981—88; metallurgy lab instr. Ga. Tech, Atlanta, 1983—84; chemistry/math instr. DeKalb Coll., Decatur, Ga., 1986—88; organist Indian Creek Bapt. Ch., Stone Mountain, Ga., 1988—91; owner/operator Stewart Musical Svcs., Loganville, Ga., 1991—; dir. music ministries/organist Westminster Presbyn. Ch., Snellville, Ga., 1992—93; organist First Bapt. Ch., Avondale Estates, Ga., 1995—; v.p. Miller Pipe Organ Svcs., Inc., Buford, Ga., 1995—2002. Author: The Elemental Book of Facts, 1982; musician: (recordings) Christmas Music for Everyone, 1987, Music from Roswell United Methodist Church, 2002. Mem.: Planetary Soc., Am. Guild of Organists. Achievements include development of Advanced MIDI organ voice module. Avocations: genealogy, classic television, chemistry, extrabiblical studies, astronomy. Personal E-mail: tgstewart@earthlink.net.

**STEWART, TONY,** professional race car driver; b. Rushville, Ind., May 20, 1971; NASCAR Driver Joe Gibbs Racing Team. Recipient Hoosier Auto Racing Fans 1st-Yr. Driver award, 1989, USAC Sprint Rookie of Yr. award, 1991, Indpls. Speedrome midget series Rookie of Yr. award, 1991, ESPY award, Best Driver, 2006. Achievements include recognized as International Karting Foundation Grand National champion, 1983; recognized as World Karting Association National Champion, 1987; won his first USAC victory, Indpls., 1991; won first USAC national midget victory, Hut Hundred, Terre Haute, Ind., 1993; finished 5th in points, finished 2d Copper World Classic, Phoenix; won NASCAR Busch Series Grand National division debut, 1999; won Penzoil 400, 1999; won Checker Auto Parts/Dura-Lube 500, 1999; won Exide NASCAR 4000, 1999; won Winston Cup, 2002; won Brickyard 500, 2005; won Nextel Cup Championship, 2005; won his first Daytona 300, 2006. Office: c/o Joe Gibbs Racing 13415 Reese Blvd W Huntersville NC 28078-7933*

**STEWART, VERLINDSEY LAQUETTA,** accounting educator; b. Birmingham, Ala., Dec. 27, 1965; d. Nathan Jr. and Shirley Ruth Brown; m. Kelvin Lorenzo Stewart I, June 22, 1991 (div. Feb. 1999); 1 child, Kelvin Lorenzo II. BS in Acctg., Ala. A&M U., 1988, MS in Bus. Edn., 1995, AA Cert. in Bus., 1997; EdD in Higher Edn. Leadership, Nova Southeastern U., 2004. Cert. tchr. bus. 7-12 Ala. Jr. acct. Childress Acctg., Huntsville, Ala., 1990-93; acctg. clk. Appeal Beauty Salon, Huntsville, 1988-94; receptionist Coop. Ext., Normal, Ala., 1992-94; grad. asst. Ala. A&M U., Normal, 1995; student tchr. J.O. Johnson H.S., Huntsville, Ala., 1995; acctg. instr. J.F. Drake State Tech., Huntsville, 1996—. Cons. Jr. Achievement, Huntsville, 1995—96. Post-reviewer: (book) College Accounting 9th, 1999 (Honorarium

1999). Vol. Habitat for Humanity, Huntsville, 1995-97; vol. asst. leader Girl Scouts North Ala., Huntsville, 1995-96. Recipient Adminstrv. Acad. award Rust Coll., 1999, Emerging Leaders Sch. award Ala. Edn. Assn., 1994, Ala. Master Tchr. Seminar, 2001. Mem. Nat. Bus. Edn., Ea. Star Mitzpah Ctr., Phi Beta Lambda (adviser 1998—), Delta Sigma Theta. Democrat. Baptist. Avocations: aerobics, weights, reading, listening to jazz music. Office: JF Drake State Tech Coll 3421 Meridian St N Huntsville AL 35811-1544 Personal E-mail: vbdst28@aol.com.

**STEWART, VIRGINIA HAKEN,** elementary school educator; b. Germantown, Pa., Dec. 21, 1941; d. Barrett Godwin and Virginia (Bishop) Tawresey; m. John D. Stewart, Sept. 14, 1963 (div.); children: John Thomas, Susan Courtney. BA in English, Cedar Crest Coll., 1963; MA in Reading, Worcester State Coll., 1981. Credit mgr. Montgomery Ward, Portchester, N.Y., 1963-66; tchr. Dennis-Yarmouth Schs., South Yarmouth, Mass., 1976-79, Title I coord., 1979—. Mem. ASCD, Mass. ASCD, Nat. Coun. Tchrs. Math., Internat. Reading Assn., Barnstable County Reading Assn., Delta Kappa Gamma. Democrat. Avocations: crafts, tennis, swimming, restorations. Home: 230 Old Main St Bass River MA 02664-4524 Office: Station Avenue Elem South Yarmouth MA 02664 Office Phone: 508-398-7623. Business E-Mail: stewartv@dy-regional.k12.ma.us.

**STEWART, WARREN EARL,** chemical engineer, educator; b. Whitewater, Wis., July 3, 1924; s. Earl Austin and Avis (Walker) S.; m. Jean Durham Potter, May 24, 1947; children: Marilyn, David, Douglas, Carol, Margaret, Mary Jean. BS in Chem. Engring. U. Wis., 1945, MS in Chem. Engring. 1947; Sc.D. in Chem. Engring. Mass. Inst. Tech., 1951. Project chem. engr. Sinclair Research Labs., Harvey, Ill., 1950-56, cons., 1956-83; from asst. prof. to prof. chem. engring. dept. U. Wis., Madison, 1956—96, chmn. dept., 1973-78, McFarland-Bascom prof., 1983-96, prof. emeritus, 1997—; pres. Stewart & Assoc. Engring. Software, Inc., 1998—. Cons. Englehard Industries, Inc., Newark, 1956-58; instr. spl. courses transport phenomena Chemstrand Corp., Pensacola, Fla., 1962, Nat. U. La Plata, Argentina, 1962, Esso Rsch. & Engring. Co., 1963, 66, Phillips Petroleum Co., 1963, Am. Inst. Chem. Engrs., 1965, 68-69, Inst. Tec. Celaya (Mex.), 1983, U. Autonoma de Mex., 1985; Reilly lectr. Notre Dame U., 1993. Author: (with R.B. Bird and E.N. Lightfoot) Transport Phenomena, 1960, 2d edit., 2002, Special Topics in Transport Phenomena, 1965, (with R.B. Bird, E.N. Lightfoot and T.W. Chapman) Lectures in Transport Phenomena, 1969; editl. adv. Latin Am. Applied Rsch., Computers and Chem. Engring., 1977—. Recipient Benjamin Smith Reynolds teaching award, 1981, Byron Bird rsch. award, 1991. Fellow Am. Inst. Chem. Engrs. (Computing in Chem. Engring. award 1985); mem. NAE, Am. Chem. Soc. (Murphree award 1989), Am. Soc. for Engring. Edn. (Chem. Engring. Lectureship award 1983), Wis. Acad. Scis., Arts and Letters, Phi Beta Kappa, Sigma Xi, Alpha Chi Sigma (Rsch. award 1981), Phi Eta Sigma, Tau Beta Pi, Phi Lambda Upsilon, Phi Kappa Phi. Conglist. (deacon, moderator). Home: 734 Huron Hill Madison WI 53711-2955 Business E-Mail: stewart@wisc.engr.edu.

**STEWART, WILLIAM A.,** medical educator, neurosurgeon; b. Liberty Center, Ohio, Apr. 6, 1933; s. Cyrus Bryson Stewart, Ardis Marjory Hicks; m. Nancy Newell Travis, June 18, 1960; children: Katherine, Elizabeth, Janet, Sarah, Heather, Alexandra. AB, Miami U., Oxford, Ohio, 1954; MD, Ohio State U., 1958. Diplomate Am. Bd. Neurosurgery. Resident in gen. surgery/neurosurgery SUNY-Upstate Med. Univ., Syracuse, 1958—65; prof. clin. neurosurgery SUNY-Upstate Med. U. Inst. Med. Humanities; team dir. Project Hope, Ile Ife, Nigeria, 1974—75, Afgan Mujehadeen Field Hosps., 1986. Chmn. Profl. Med. Conduct N.Y. State Dept. Health, Albany, NY, 1989—91, adminstrn. rev. bd., 1992—98; reviewer Med. Soc. State of N.Y. Mannix awards. Lt. comdr. M.C. USNR, 1955—72, with M.C. USN, 1965—67, Vietnam. Fellow: ACS; mem.: AMA, Internat. Physician Assessment Coalition, Nat. Assn. Scholars, Congress of Neurologic Surgeons, Am. Assn. Neurologic Surgeons, Coalition for Physician Enhancement, Adam Smith Soc. Presbyterian. Avocations: gardening, coin collecting/numismatics. Home: 7595 Hunt Ln Fayetteville NY 13066 Business E-Mail: stewartw@upstate.edu.

**STEWART SIMPSON, DONNAMAY ANGELA,** interior designer; b. Mandeville, Jamaica, W.I., Dec. 31, 1965; d. Ermine Stewart and Mary Ester Stewart Bromfield; m. Everton Seymour Simpson (div.); 1 child, Dimitre Andre Simpson. Student, Miami Dade C.C., 1986. Sec. Jamaica Transformer Co., 1986—87; secretarial clk. Pat Thompson Constrn. Co., Jamaica, 1987—89; ops. mgr. Blaise Trust, Mandeville, Jamaica, 1989, Nat. Car Rental, Mandeville, Jamaica, 1989—90; sec., accounts clk. Simpsons Wholesale Co., Elizabeth, Jamaica, 1990—91; ops. mgr. Simpson Supermarket, Elizabeth, Jamaica, 1991—94, Wesley Plz., Mandeville, Jamaica, 1995-97; owner Angelique Enterprises, Miramar, Fla., 1997—; fgn. exch. teller Ft. Lauderdale Internat. Airport, 1999—2001. Songwriter: Hill Top Records, 2006, Amerecord. Interior decorator, stage performer Perfect Praise Sch. Dance, Fla., 2002; conf. spkr. Women's Empowerment Conf. Believers and Achievers Internat., 1998. Mem.: Reagan Ranch Found., Paralyzed Vets. Am., USO, U.S. Navy Meml., Internat. Poetry Soc. Avocations: dance, writing, design, motivational speaking. Home: 1980 SW 103d Terr Miramar FL 33025 Office: Angelique Enterprises 1980 SW 103d Terr Miramar FL 33025 Office Phone: 954-295-8694. E-mail: Dimitre01@aol.com.

**STEYER, THOMAS FAHR,** investment company executive; Grad., Yale U.; MBA, Stanford U., 1983. Mng. dir. Hellman & Friedman LLC, 1986—; sr. mng. mem. Farallon Capital Mgmt. LLC, 1986—; assoc. risk arbitrage dept. Goldman, Sachs & Co.; with mergers and acquisitions dept. Morgan Stanley & Co. Bd. dirs CapitalSource, Chevy Chase, Md. Office: Hellman & Friedman LLC One Maritime Plz 12th Fl San Francisco CA 94111

**STIBBE, AUSTIN JULE,** retired accountant; b. St. Paul, Mar. 29, 1930; s. Austin Julius and Agnes Dorothea (Delaney) S.; m. Mary Elizabeth King, May 29, 1952; children: Anne Marie, Craig Jule, David King, Karen Lee. BSB in Acctg., U. Minn., 1952. CPA, Minn., Wis. Tax acct. Ernst & Ernst, Mpls., 1955-60; corp. tax mgr. EcoLab, Inc., St. Paul, 1960-65; audit mgr. Coopers & Lybrand, Mpls., 1965-74; v.p. Wilkerson, Guthmann & Johnson, Ltd., St. Paul, 1974-93, of counsel, 1993—2006. Exec. officer Twin Cities Squadron, U.S. Naval Sea Cadet Corps, Mpls., 1974-80; bd. dirs., treas., mem. Twin Cities coun. Navy League, 1970—, pres., 1979-81, treas., 1975-79, 81-91; mem. adv. coun. to dept. acctg. U. Minn., Mpls., 1983-86; bd. dirs., chmn. audit com. St. Paul Area Coun. Chs., 1985-87; mem. adv. bd. Headwaters Soc., 1987-88; mem. fin. reporting com. United Way St. Paul Area, 1981-93, mem. audit com., 1991-93; dir. comm. staff Indianhead coun. Boy Scouts Am., 1962-65. Lt. USN, 1952-55. Mem. Minn. Soc. CPAs (life), U.S. Naval Inst. (life), Belle Taine Lake Assn. (dir. 1995-2001, treas. 1996-2001), Hubbard County COLA Print Com., 1995-98, Friends of Heritage, 1996—, Hubbard County Works of Improvement (steering com. 2001), VFW (life), Am. Legion. Presbyterian. Avocations: music, boating, history. Home: PO Box 41 Nevis MN 56467-0041 E-mail: austin30@msn.com.

**STIBER, JULIE ANNE,** social worker; b. Binghamton, N.Y., May 1, 1962; d. Max Linwood and Ruth Mary S. BA, Albertus Magnus, New Haven, Conn., 1984; MSW, So. Conn. State U., New Haven, Conn., 1991. LCSW Conn., 1993, DCSW Conn., 1996. Asst. dir. Coord. Coun. Children in Crisis, New Haven, 1996—99; clin. coord. social work Priority Care, New Haven, Bridgeport and Norwalk, Conn., 1999—2000; dir. social work svcs. New Eng. Home Care, Conn., 2000—; clin. cons. Dept. Children & Families, State of Conn. Mem.: Nat. Assn. Social Workers (children's com. 2001—), diplomate in clin. social work 1996). Democrat. Episcopalian. Avocations: running, painting, drawing, jewelry, cooking. Office: State of Conn Dept Children & Families 1 Long Wharf New Haven CT 06511

**STIBER, NEIL ALAN,** environmental scientist; BSE, Duke U., 1991; MS, PhD, Carnegie Mellon U., 1998. Staff engr. Woodward-Clyde Cons., Overland Park, Kans., 1992—94; rsch. and tchg. asst. Carnegie Mellon U., Pitts.,

1994—98; intern Pa. Dept. of Environ. Protection, Pitts., 1995; sr. assoc. engr. McLaren/Hart, Inc., Cleve., 1999—2000; project environ. scientist URS Corp., Farmington Hills, Mich., 2000—03; environ. scientist U.S. EPA, Washington, 2003—. Contbr. articles to profl. publs. Bd. dirs. Livnot U'lehibanot Alumni Bd., Jerusalem, 2004—05; mem., alt. team leader Chevra Kadisha of Greater Washington, Silver Spring, Md., 2003—05. Recipient Outstanding Civil Engring. Sr. award, ASCE, 1991; scholar, 1990; Summer Rsch. fellow, 1990, Walter P. Murphy fellow, Northwestern U. Sch. of Engring. and Applied Sci., 1991—92. Office: US EPA 1200 Pennsylvania Ave NW (8104-R) Washington DC 20460 Office Phone: 202-564-1573. E-mail: stiber.neil@epa.gov.

**STICE, DWAYNE LEE,** broadcasting company executive; b. Paducah, Ky., Aug. 10, 1956; s. Freeman D. and Dorris Olive (Lee) S.; m. Paducah Community Coll., 1976; BS, Murray State U., 1977; MS, Southern Ill. U., 1983. Lic. funeral dir., Ky. Dir. Johnson-Lambert Funeral Home, Calvert City, Ky., 1974-81; gen. mgr. Paducah Area Transit System, 1980-92; pres. Sta. WCCK-FM, Stice Comm., Inc., Calvert City, 1990—2001; human resources, programming WPSD-TV, Paducah, Ky., 2001—. Adj. bus. instr. Paducah Community Coll., 1979—, Lindsey Wilson Coll., Columbia, Ky., 1991; adj. reporter CBS Radio Network, 1997-2000. Contbr. articles to profl. jours. Bd. dirs. Calvert Area Mentoring Program; mem. Calvert Area Devel. Assn.; transp. com. Purchase Area Devel. Dist. Outstanding grantee Ky. Transp. Cabinet, 1985, 86. Mem. Ky. Pub. Transit Assn. (pres. 1988-91), Ky. Broadcasters Assn. (bd. dirs. 1997-2000), Marshall C. of C. (bd. dirs., vice chmn. govt. affairs 1998), Paducah C.C. Alumni Assn. (pres. 1983), Hon. Order Ky. Cols., Travelers Protective Assn. (pres. Paducah chpt. 1989-90), Lions, Masons (master Calvert City 1984), Shriners, Order Ea. Star, Phi Kappa Phi, Phi Theta Kappa. Methodist. Avocations: organist, travel, baseball, antique clocks, automobiles. Office: WPSD-TV 100 TV Ln Paducah KY 42003 E-mail: ky4202956@yahoo.com.

**STICH, ROBERTA LYNN,** not-for-profit fundraiser, social worker; b. N.Y.C., N.Y., May 23, 1948; d. Melvin Harold Stich and Shirley Pearl Kaplan-Stich. Student, U. Rochester, 1965—67; BA, Bklyn. Coll., 1970; MSW, Hunter Coll., 1972; postgrad. Stanford Law Sch., 1980—85. Lic. master social worker N.Y. Legal asst. Howard Deutsch Atty. at Law, N.Y.C., 1977—80, Donald Lindover Atty. at Law, N.Y.C., 1982; rsch. asst. sociology dept. Stanford (Calif.) U., 1986—87; rsch. asst. Merit Co., Jerusalem, 1989—91; fundraiser Nat. Symphony Orch. Assn., Washington, 1991—95, Nat. Rep. Senatorial Com., Washington, 1995—97, Nat. Capital Teleservices, LLC, Washington, 1997—. Telephone solicitor Nat. Children's Ctr. Value Village Project Inc., Adelphi, Md., 1992—. Mem. Smithsonian Instn., Washington, 1996—, Phillips Collection, 2005, U.S. Holocaust Mus., Washington, 2000—, Rep. Nat. Com., 2002—. Mem.: Nat. Trust Historic Preservation, Stanford Alumni Assn. (life). Republican. Jewish. Avocations: surfing the Internet, cassettes and videos, casino gambling, travel, fashion. Home: Apt 208 1255 New Hampshire Ave NW Washington DC 20036 Office: CAPTEL 300 5th St NE Washington DC 20002 Office Phone: 202-547-4614. E-mail: robersti@aol.com.

**STICH, STEPHEN PETER,** philosophy educator; b. NYC, May 9, 1943; s. Samuel Joseph and Sylvia Lucille (Siegel) S.; m. Judith Ann Gagnon, Dec. 20, 1971; children: Jonathan Andrew, Rebecca Elizabeth. BA summa cum laude with distinction, U. Pa., 1964; PhD, Princeton U., 1968. Teaching asst. Princeton U., 1965; asst. prof. U. Mich., 1968-73, assoc. prof., 1973-78, dir. grad. studies in philosophy, 1973-74, assoc. chmn. dept. philosophy, 1975-76; assoc. prof. U. Md., 1978-81, prof., 1981-86, dir. grad. studies in philosophy, 1982-83; prof. U. Calif., San Diego, 1986-89, dir. cognitive sci. program, 1988-89; prof. philosophy and cognitive sci. Rutgers U., New Brunswick, 1989—, acting chair dept. philosophy, 1992-93, dir. rsch. group on evolution and higher cognition, 1997—, bd. govrs. prof., 1998—. Prof. Linguistic inst., Linguistic Soc. Am., summer 1982; dir. Summer Seminar for Coll. Tchrs. NEH, 1983, 89; vis. sr. lectr. U. Sydney, 1984-85; vis. fellow Australian Nat. U., 1992; Jemison prof. humanities U. Ala., Birmingham, 1993; adj. prof. CUNY Grad. Ctr., 1994-97; Erskine fellow Canterbury U., Christchurch, New Zealand, 1996; cons. Pres. Commn. for Nat. Priorities in the Eighties, Pres. Commn. on Ethics in Medicine and Biomed. and Behavioral Rsch.; mem. selection com. Mellon Fellowships in the Humanities, 1983-84; mem. Fulbright Selection Com., 1981-83, chair, 1983; vis. fellow Australian Nat. U., Rsch. Sch. Social Scis., 1992; hon. prof. philosophy U. Sheffield, 2005-. Author: From Folk Psychology to Cognitive Science, 1983, The Fragmentation of Reason, 1990, Deconstructing the Mind, 1996, Mindreading, 2003; editor: Innate Ideas, 1975; (with others) The Recombinant DNA Debate, 1979, Philosophy and Connectionist Theory, 1991, Mental Representation, 1994; editor Evolution and Cognition Series; mem. editl. bd. Linguistics and Philosophy, 1984—, Mind and Language, 1985—; Cognitive Sci., 1990—, Minds and Machines, 1991—, Pragmatics and Cognition, 1991—, Philosophical Studies, 1992—, Philosophy of Sci., 1992—, Cognition, 1993—, Neural Network Modeling and Connectionism; mem. editl. adv. bd. Studies in Cognitive Sys.; contbr. articles to profl. jours., chpts. to books. Woodrow Wilson Nat. Fellowship Found. fellow, 1964-65, Woodrow Wilson dissertation fellow, 1967, Danforth grad. fellow, 1964-67, H.H. Ford fellow Princeton U., 1967, Coun. Philos. Studies Summer Inst. fellow, 1971, Am. Coun. Learned Socs. fellow, 1978-79, Rutgers U. competitive fellow, sch. liberal arts fellow U. Otago, Dunedin, New Zealand, 2001; recipient fellowships NEH, 1974, 83-84, 96, Ctr. for Advanced Study in Behavioral Scis., Stanford, Calif., 1983; Fulbright sr. rsch. scholar, Bristol (U.K.) U., 1978-79; grantee U.S.-Israel Ednl. Found., 1979, NRC and U.S. Nat. Com. for Internat. Union of History and Philosophy of Sci., Hannover, West Germany, 1979, NSF, 1981-82. Mem. Am. Philos. Assn., Soc. for Philosophy and Psychology (pres. 1982-83, exec. com. 1980-82, 83-84, chair program com. 1979-80), Philosophy of Sci. Assn., Brit. Soc. for Philosophy of Sci., Fulbright Alumni Assn. Office: Rutgers U Philosophy Dept Davison Hall Douglass Campus New Brunswick NJ 08901-2882 Office Phone: 732-932-9861 x131. E-mail: stich@ruccs.rutgers.edu.

**STICK, THOMAS HOWARD FITCHETT,** architect, construction litigation consultant; b. Balt., Feb. 28, 1938; s. Gordon M. F. and Anne Howard (Fitchett) S.; m. Rosalie Wade Reynolds, 1959 (div. 1982); children: H. Edward M., Alexander W., David F.; m. Joyce Yeargin Carr, 1982 (div. 1989); m. Alyce C. Cushing, 1989. BA in Psychology, Yale U., 1960; postgrad., Md. Inst., 1962, U. Pa. Grad. Sch. Arch., 1964. Registered arch., Pa., Md., Del., N.J., Va., Maine, N.Y., D.C., Mass., N.H., N.C., Vt., Tenn., Okla., Colo., Ind., Ga., Ill., Mich., Ky., Kans., Ohio, Peoples Republic of China; cert. recommendation Nat. Coun. Archtl. Registration Bds. Arch. Vincent G. Kling & Ptnrs., Phila., 1964-74, B.J. Hoffman & Assocs., Berwyn, Pa., 1974; ptnr. Grim & Stick, Ardmore, Pa., 1975-77; prin. Stick Assocs., Gladwyne, Pa., 1977-80; corp. arch. Gino's Inc., King of Prussia, Pa., 1980-81; mgr. constrn. adminstrn. Ballinger Co., Phila., 1981-83; sr. constrn. claims cons. MDC Sys. Corp., Phila., 1984-85; chief arch. Day & Zimmermann Inc., Phila., 1985—, discipline mgr., 1987—, corp. arch., 1995—; dir. Day & Zimmerman Internat. Corp., Phila., 2000—. V.p. F-S Found., 1986, also bd. mem. One-man show in photography Ea. Camera Gallery, 1972. Named Arch. of Best Food Plant of Yr., Food Engring. Mag., 1992. Mem. AIA, Pa. Soc. Archs., Bldg. Ofcls. and Code Adminstrs. Internat., Internat. Conf. Bldg. Ofcls., So. Bldg. Code Congress Internat., Constrn. Specifications Inst., Nat. Fire Protection Assn., Soc. War of 1812 (sec. 1977-82), Soc. of Cincinnati, Soc. Colonial Wars, SR, Descs. of Lords of the Md. Manors, Mil. Order of Loyal Legion of U.S., Huguenot Soc., Am. Clan Gregor Soc., St. Andrew's Soc. of Balt., St. George's Soc. of Balt., Merion Cricket Club (Haverford, Pa.), Yale Club, Sovereign Mil. of Temple of Jerusalem (comdr.), Sovereign Order of St. John of Jerusalem (Knight of Justice), Knights Malta, Zeta Psi. Home: 1501 Monticello Dr Gladwyne PA 19035-1206 Office: Day & Zimmerman Internat 240 Continental Dr Newark DE 19713-4328

**STICKEL, FREDERICK A.,** publishing executive; b. Weehawken, N.J., Nov. 18, 1921; s. Fred and Eva (Madigan) S.; m. Margaret A. Dunne, Dec. 4, 1943; children—Fred A., Patrick F., Daisy E., Geoffrey M., James E., Bridget A. Student, Georgetown U., 1939-42; BS, St. Peter's Coll., 1943. Advt.

salesperson Jersey Observer daily, Hoboken, N.J., 1945-51; retail advt. salesperson Jersey Jour., Jersey City, 1951-55, advt. dir., 1955-66, publisher, 1966-67; gen. mgr. Oregonian Pub. Co., Portland, Oreg., 1967-72, pres., 1972-86, publisher, 1975—. Bd. regents U. Portland; adv. bd. Portland State U., St. Vincent's Hosp.; bd. dirs Portland Rose Festival Assn., United Way Oreg.; chmn. Portland Citizens Crime Commn. Capt. USMC, 1942-45. Mem. Assn. for Portland Progress (dir.), Portland C. of C. (dir.), Oreg. Newspaper Pubs. Assn. (past pres.), Pacific N.W. Newspaper Assn. (past pres.), Newspaper Assn. Am., University Club, Multnomah Athletic Waverley Country Club, Arlington Club, Rotary. Office: Oregonian Pub Co 1320 SW Broadway Portland OR 97201-3499

**STICKLE, DAVID WALTER,** microbiologist; b. Boston, Apr. 18, 1933; s. Harold Edwards and Lucille Margaret (Magee) S.; m. Mary Elizabeth DeLong, July 29, 1972. BA in Chemistry, Biology, Tufts U., 1955; MS in Pharmacy and Health, Northeastern U., Boston, 1968; MPH, U. N.C., 1969, DrPH, 1971. Bacteriologist Mass. Dept. Pub. Health, Boston, 1959-63, supr. immunology unit, 1963-68; UNC/CDC lab. dir.'s program Ctrs. for Disease Control, Atlanta, 1968-71; chief, clin. lab. improvement program Divsn. Med. Labs./Minn. Dept. Health, Mpls., 1971-82, acting dir., 1977-78, asst. dir., 1978-88. Ex-officio mem. Minn. Soc. Clin. Pathologists Exec. Com., Mpls., 1977-78; mem. Proficiency Testing Com., Minn. Acad. Family Physicians, Mpls., 1977-83; adj. asst. prof. U. Minn., Mpls., 1977-88; assoc. prof. emeritus, U. Minn., 1988—. Editor: Med. Lab. Forum periodical, 1973-88. Proctor Nat. Registry of Microbiology, Mpls. Examinations for Minn., 1987-92; instr. Edina Community Edn. Programs, Minn., 1992. With U.S. Army, 1955-57. Lab. tng. grantee Ctr. for Disease Control, HEW, Atlanta, 1977-78, 1978-80, 1979 81. Mem. Am. Soc. Microbiology, Phi Sigma, Sigma Xi. Achievements include serologic tests for systemic candidiasis which were in use for many years by the Ctrs. for Disease Control, U.S. Dept. of Health and Human Svcs.

**STICKLE, DOUGLAS FRANKLIN,** biochemist; b. South Amboy, N.J., Mar. 16, 1958; BS in Chem. Engring., U. Tenn., Knoxville, 1980; MS in Chem. and Biochem. Engring., U. Pa., Phila., 1982; PhD in Biomed. Scis., U. Tex., Houston, 1989. Diplomate Am. Bd. of Clin. Chemistry, 1999. Assoc. prof., tech. dir. of clin. chemistry dept. pathology U. Nebr. Med. Ctr., Omaha, 1999—; dir. chem. terrorism preparedness lab. Nebr. Pub. Health Lab., Omaha, 2005—; chief immunochemistry dept. pathology Brooke Army Med. Ctr., San Antonio. Pres. Am. Bd. of Clin. Chemistry, 2005—06. Capt. U.S. Army, 1996—99. Fellow: Nat. Acad. of Clin. Biochemistry. Home: 4439 Pine St Omaha NE 68105 Office: Univ Nebr Med Ctr 983135 UNMC Omaha NE 68198-3135 Office Phone: 402-559-8785. Office Fax: 402-559-6018.

**STICKLER, GUNNAR BRYNOLF,** pediatrician; b. Peterskirchen, Germany, June 13, 1925; came to U.S., 1951, naturalized, 1958; s. Fritz and Astrid (Wennerberg) S.; m. Duci M. Kronenbitter, Aug. 30, 1956; children: Katarina Anna, George David. MD, U. Munich, Germany, 1949; PhD, U. Minn., Mpls., 1957. Diplomate Am. Bd. Pediatrics, ofcl. examiner and mem., 1965-95. Resident in clin. pathology Krankenhaus III Orden, Munich, 1950; resident in pathology U. Munich, 1950-51; intern Mountainside Hosp., Montclair, NJ, 1951-52; fellow in pediatrics Mayo Grad. Sch., Rochester, Minn., 1953-56; sr. cancer research scientist Roswell Park Meml. Inst., Buffalo, 1956-57; asst. to staff Mayo Clinic, Rochester, 1957-58, cons. in pediatrics, 1959-89, head sect. pediatrics, 1969-74; prof. pediatrics, chmn. dept. pediatrics Mayo Clinic and Mayo Med. Sch., 1974-80. Mem. test com. III Nat. Bd. Med. Examiners, 1973-75; vis. prof. at various univs and instns., including U. Dusseldorf (Germany) and U. Munich, 1971, Pahlavi U., Iran, 1975, Olga Hosp.: Stuttgart, Germany, 1978, Martin Luther King Hosp., Los Angeles, 1979, U. Man., 1981; mem. emeritus staff Mayo Clinic, 1989. Mem. editl. bd. Clin. Pediatrics, 1968-76, 79-97, European Jour. Pediatrics, 1976-84, Pediatrics, 1983-89; contbr. more than 290 articles to med. publs. Active parent support groups in field of cyclic vomiting syndrome; life pres. Stickler Syndrome support group, 1997—. Recipient Humanitarian award Chgo. region chpt. Nat. Found. Ileitis and Colitis, 1978, award for excellence of subject matter and presentation So. Minn. Med. Assn., 1978 Mem. Am. Acad. Pediatrics (Disting. Svc. award Minn. chpt. 1999), Soc. Pediatric Rsch., Am. Pediatric Soc., Nat. Coun. Reliable Health Info., Midwest Soc. Pediatric Rsch. (coun. 1967-69, pres. 1970-71, Founders award 1996), N.W. Pediatric Soc. (pres. 1973-74) Achievements include description of hereditary progressive arthropathymopathy in 1965, now called Stickler syndrome; and the treatment otitis media, hypophosphatemic rickets, renal disease; research in areas of parents' fears and the need of routine physical examinations in adolescents, and the excesses of alternative medicine. Office: Mayo Clinic Emeritus Ctr Rochester MN 55905

**STICKNEY, CAROL JEAN,** special education educator, consultant; b. Summit, N.J., Nov. 26, 1941; d. Donald Frank and Doris Elizabeth (Miller) Utess; m. Ronald Thomas Stickney, Dec. 14, 1963; children: Jennifer, James. BA in Elem. Edn., Trenton State Coll., 1963; MS in Spl. Edn. (fellow 1967-68), Newark State Coll., 1968. Cert. elem. tchr. N.J., tchr. mentally retarded N.J., tchr. handicapped N.J. Tchr. Hanover Twp. Schs., Whippany, NJ, 1963—65, spl. edn. tchr., 1965—67, Montgomery County Schs., Rockville, Md., 1968—71, Kittatinny Regional HS, Newton, NJ, 1987—2005. Mem. adv. bd. spl. edn. Sussex County CC, Newton, NJ, 1998—2001. Treas. Castlewood Civic Assn., Sparta, NJ, 1985—; bd. dirs Manna House, Newton, 2003—, Interfaith Hospitality Network, Newton, 2004—; missionary Haiti, Kenya; chmn. mission com. Branchville (N.J.) Presbyn. Ch., 2003—. Named Most Inspiring Tchr., Sussex County CC, 2003, Tchr. of the Yr., Wal-Mart, 2003; recipient Golden apple for Outstanding Tchr., Kittatinny Regional HS, 2000; scholar, Dept. Edn., 1959—63; Traineeship grantee, 1966. Mem.: NEA, N.J. Edn. Assn., Sussex County Edn. Assn. (Warren Cummings award for Excellence in Edn. 2001), Profl. Devel. Bd. Kittatinny Edn. Assn. (treas. 1996—2005). Avocations: reading, photography, travel, painting. Office: Ednl Consulting 58 Castlewood Trail Sparta NJ 07871

**STICKNEY, JESSICA,** former state legislator; b. Duluth, Minn., May 16, 1929; d. Ralph Emerson and Claudia Alice (Cox) Page; m. Edwin Levi Stickney, June 17, 1951; children: Claudia, Laura, Jeffrey. BA, Macalester Coll., St. Paul, Minn., 1951; PhD (hon), Rocky Mtn. Coll., Billings, Mont., 1986. Rep. State of Mont., 1989-92. Mem. Gov.'s Commn. on Post-Sec. Edn. Mont., 1973-75. Mem. Sch. Bd. Trustees, Miles City, Mont., 1968-74; mem., chmn. zoning bd., Miles City, 1975-89; mem. Govt. Study Commn., Miles City, 1974-76, United Ch. Christ Bd. Homeland Ministries 1975-81; chmn., conf. moderator United Ch. Christ Bd. Mont.-Northern Wyo. Conf., 1980-82; chmn. Town Meeting on the Arts, Mont., 1980; mem., chmn. Miles Community Coll. Bd., 1975-89, chmn. 1978-80. Mem. Mont. Arts Coun. (chmn. 1982-85), Western States Arts Found. (vice chmn. 1984), Nat. Assembly State Arts Agys. (bd. dirs. 1982-88), AAUW (pres. 1964-66). Democrat. Avocations: writing, sewing, painting, reading.

**STICKNEY, JOHN,** editor; BA, Williams Coll., 1968. With People mag., 1982, Money mag., 1983—88; mktg. comm. mgr. NY Times Syndication Sales Corp., 1997—2002, sr. editor, 2002—. Freelance writer; author: 2 books. Office: NY Times Syndication Sales Corp 14th Fl 122 E 42nd St New York NY 10168 Office Phone: 212-499-3341. Office Fax: 212-499-3382. E-mail: stick@nytimes.com.*

**STICKNEY, NANCY CARVER,** state legislator; b. Bethel, Maine, July 20, 1936; d. Irving L. and Ruth W. (Homsted) Carver; m. Wallace E. Stickney, 1957; children: Peter, Christopher J., Daniel C., Adam K. BS, U. NH, 1960. Mem. NH Ho. of Reps. (dist. 26), Concord, Maine, 1997—2000. Methodist. Home: PO Box 177 North Salem NH 03073-0177 Office: NH State Legis State House Concord NH 03301

**STICKNEY, ROBERT ROY,** fisheries educator; b. Minneapolis, July 2, 1941; s. Roy E. and Helen Doris (Nelson) S.; m. LuVerne C. (Whiteley), Dec. 29, 1961; children: Robert Roy, Marolan Margaret. BS, U. Nebr., 1967; MA, U. Mo., 1968; PhD, Fla. State U., 1971. cert. fisheries scientist Rsch. assoc.

Skidaway Inst. Oceanography, Savannah, Ga., 1971—73, asst. prof., 1973—75, Tex. A and M U., Coll. Sta., 1975—78, assoc. prof., 1978—83, prof., 1983—84; prof. zoology, dir. Fisheries Rsch. Lab., So. Ill. U., Carbondale, 1984—85; dir. Sch. of Fisheries U. Wash., Seattle, 1985—91, prof., 1985—96; dir. Sea Grant Coll. program Tex. A&M U., Coll. Sta., 1996—. Author: Principles of Warmwater Aquaculture, 1979, Estuarine Ecology of the Southeastern U.S. and Gulf of Mex., 1984; editor: Culture of Non Salmonid Freshwater Fishes, 1986, 1992, Flagship: A History of Fisheries at the U. of Washington, 1989; co-editor: Fisheries: Harvesting Life from Water, 1989, Culture of Salmonid Fishes, 1992, Fisheries: Harvesting Life from Water, 1995, Principles of Aquaculture, 1994, Fish Culture in the United States: A Hist. Survey, 1996, Responsible Marine Aquaculture, 2002, Aquaculture: An Introductory Text, 2005; editor: revs. in Fisheries Sci., Ency. of Aqua-culture, World Aquaculture mag.; contbr. articles to profl. jour. Served in USAF, 1959-63. Mem.: Sea Grant Assn. (pres. 2003—04). Office Phone: 979-845-3854. Personal E-mail: rrstickney@aol.com. E-mail: stickney@tamu.edu.

**STIDHAM, GREGORY L.,** pediatrician, educator; b. Lafayette, Ind., Feb. 9, 1951; s. John Walter Stidham and Marjorie Blanche Jansing; m. Pam Kinnin, Jan. 27, 2002; children: Christopher Vincent, Timothy Richard. BA, U. of Notre Dame, Ind., 1973; MD, Med. Coll. Ohio, 1976. Prof. of pediat. U. of Tenn., Memphis, 1988—, chief divsn. of critical care dept. pediats., 1980—. Home: 19 S Auburndale St Memphis TN 38104 Office: LeBonheur Children's Medical Center 50 N Dunlap St Memphis TN 38103 Office Phone: 901-572-3132. Office Fax: 901-572-5198. E-mail: gstidham@utmem.edu.

**STIEBER, TAMAR,** journalist; b. Bklyn., Sept. 15, 1955; d. Alfred and Florence (Spector) Stieber. Student, Rockland C.C., 1972—75, West London (Eng.) Coll., 1973—74; BA in Film cum laude, U. Calif., Berkeley, 1985, postgrad. in comparative lit., 1985—86; grad. Police Res. Acad. cum laude, Napa Valley Coll., 1988. Office mgr., confidential sec. AP, San Francisco, 1981—83; stringer Daily Californian, Berkeley, 1983—84; film rsch. tchg. asst. U. Calif., Berkeley, 1984—86; libr. and rsch. asst. Pacific Film Archive, Berkeley, 1984—86; intern San Francisco Examiner, 1984; reporter Sonoma (Calif.) Index-Tribune, 1987—88, Vallejo (Calif.) Times-Herald, 1988—89, Albuquerque Jour., 1989—94, freelancer, 1994—. Recipient Pulitzer Prize for specialized reporting, 1990, 1st pl. pub. svc. divsn., N.Mex. Press Assn., 1990, Pub. Svc. award, Albuquerque Press Club, 1990, 1st pl. newswriting, N.Mex. Press Assn., 1991, Hon. Mention, AP Mng. Editors, 1994. Mem.: AAUW, Phi Beta Kappa. Home: PO Box 9835 Santa Fe NM 87504-9835 E-mail: tstieber@isp.com.

**STIEBING, WILLIAM HENRY, JR.,** retired history professor; b. New Orleans, Dec. 21, 1940; s. William Henry and Eunice Sophie Stiebing; m. Ann Erma Thompson, Sept. 11, 1965; 1 child, Kimberly Ann Heston. BA, U. New Orleans, 1962; PhD, U. Pa., 1970. Instr. history U. New Orleans, 1967—70, asst. prof. history, 1970—73, assoc. prof. history, 1973—85, prof. history, 1985—2001, Seraphia D. Leyda tchg. prof. history, 2001—05. Staff mem. excavations Archaeological Expdn., U. Pa. Mus., Tell Es-Sa Idiyeh, Jordan, 1965; coord. European history U. New Orleans, 1974—83; pottery supr. excavations Archaeological Expdn., U. Pa. Mus., Sarafand, Lebanon, 1974. Author: (scholarly book) Ancient Astronauts, Cosmic Collisions and Other Popular Theories About Man's Past, 1984, Out of the Desert?: Archaeology and the Exodus/Conquest Narratives, 1989 (Named one of Choice Mag.'s Outstanding Acad. Books, 1990), Uncovering the Past: A History of Archaeology, 1993, Ancient Near Eastern History and Culture, 2003. Bd. dirs., v.p., pres., treas. Salem United Ch. of Christ, New Orleans, 1970—2004. Recipient Disting. Faculty award, La. State U. Alumni Fedn., 1985, Career award for Excellence in Rsch., U. New Orleans Alumni Assn., 2003; NDEA fellow, U. Pa., 1962—65. Mem.: Soc. Bibl. Lit., Archaeol. Inst. Am. (sec. New Orleans chpt. 1983—88), Am. Hist. Assn. Mem. United Church Of Christ. Avocation: travel. Personal E-mail: wstiebing@msn.com. E-mail: wstiebin@uno.edu.

**STIEF, LOUIS JOHN,** chemist; b. Pottsville, Pa., July 26, 1933; s. Louis Norman and Dorothy Elizabeth (Bassler) S.; m. Kathleen J. Talbot, Nov. 30, 1963 (div. 1980); children—Andrew, Lorraine. BA, La Salle Coll., 1955; PhD, Catholic U. Am., 1960. Nat. Acad. Scis.-NRC postdoctoral rsch. assoc. Nat. Bur. Standards, Washington, 1960-61; NATO postdoctoral fellow, ind. researcher chemistry dept. Sheffield (Eng.) U., 1961-63; sr. scientist, sr. chemist Melpar, Inc., Falls Church, Va., 1963-68; NAS-NRC sr. postdoctoral rsch. assoc. NASA/Goddard Space Flight Ctr., Greenbelt, Md., 1968-69, astrophysicist, 1969-76, head br. astrochemistry, 1976-90, sr. scientist, 1990—2004, emeritus scientist, 2004—. Adj. prof. chemistry Cath. U. Am. Research: numerous publs., especially in Jour. Chem. Physics and Jour. Phys. Chemistry. Recipient Alumni Achievement award Cath. U. Am., 1985; NASA fellow Queen Mary Coll., U. London, 1981-82 Fellow: Washington Acad. Sci.; mem.: Am. Astron. Soc. (divsn. planetary sci.), Am. Geophys. Union, Royal Soc. Chemistry, Am.Chem. Soc. (Hillebrand prize Chem. Soc. Washington 2002), Sigma Xi.

**STIEFEL, ETHAN,** dancer, performing company executive; b. Tyrone, Pa. s. Alan and Mima Stiefel. Studies with Mikhail Baryshnikov, Sch. Classical Ballet, 1987; student, Fordham U., 1995—. From mem. to prin. dancer NY City Ballet, 1989-95, prin. dancer, 1995-96, Am. Ballet Theatre, NYC, 1997—; artistic dir. Stiefel and Stars, 2002—, Stiefel and Students, 2004—, Ballet Pacifica, 2004—06; prin. dancer, artistic assoc. Kings of the Dance, 2006—. With Zurich Ballet, 1992-93; guest artist N.Y.C. Ballet, 1998-99, Atlanta Ballet, 1999, Royal Ballet, 1999—. Dancer prin. roles include Le Corsaire, Romeo & Julia, Giselle, Les Patineurs, Onegin, Swan Lake, Theme and Variations, Raymonda, Don Quixote, A Midsummer Night's Dream, La Bayadere, The Dream, The Four Temperaments, Apollo, Stars and Stripes, Harlequinade, Tarantella, Tchaikovsky Pas de Deux, Chaconne, Prodigal Son, La Fille Mal Gardee, The Nutcracker, Robbins' ballets Dances at a Gathering, West Side Story Suite, The Goldberg Variations, The Cage, Quiet City, Martins' ballets Fearful Symmetries, Ash, Tchaikovsky Pas de Quatre, The Sleeping Beauty, King of the Dance, others; appeared in PBS TV prodn. Le Corsaire, 1999, Born to be Wild, 2002, The Dream, 2004; artistic dir. Stiefel & Stars, 2001—; artistic dir Performance Project, 2004; guest artist Teatro Colon, 1999, Hamburg Ballet, 2000, Kirov Ballet, 2001, 04, Verona, Italy, 2003, Washington Opera, 2003, Budapest Opera, 2003, others; starring role: (film) Center Stage, 2000. Recipient Silver medal Prix de Lausanne, 1989, Statue award Princess Grace Found., 1999; emerging dance artist grantee Princess Grace Found. U.S.A., 1991-92 Office: care Peter S Diggins Assoc 133 W 71st St Ste 8-B New York NY 10023 Office Phone: 212-874-4534. Personal E-mail: festspiel@aol.com.

**STIEGEL, MICHAEL ALLEN,** lawyer; b. Greenfield, Mass., Sept. 15, 1946; s. Sid James and Ida Eleanor (Solomon) S.; m. Marsha Palmer, Sept. 10, 1983. BA, U. Ariz., 1968; JD cum laude, Loyola U., Chgo., 1971. Bar: Ill. 1971, U.S. Dist. Ct. Ill. 1971, U.S. Ct. Appeals (7th cir.) 1971, U.S. Ct. Appeals (1st cir.) 1975, U.S. Ct. Appeals (6th cir.) 1991, U.S. Supreme Ct. 1975, Wis. 1985, Fla. 1987. Law clk. to fed. judge William Lynch U.S. Dist. Ct. Ill., Chgo., 1971—72; mng. ptnr. Arnstein & Lehr, Chgo., 1985—98; ptnr. Michael Best and Friedrich, 1998—, co-chair trial dept., 1998—2003, elected mgmt. com., 2003—. Adj. prof. law Northwestern U.; faculty Nat. Inst. Trial Advocacy, La. State U. Trial Advocacy Program, 1995-2000. Contbr. articles to profl. jours. Mem. fin. com. Lynn Martin for Senate, Ill., 1989-90. Mem. ABA (pres., sects. on litig. and bus. law, vice chmn. trial evidence com. litig. sect. 1990-91, co-chmn. trial evidence com. 1991-95, lawyers conf. stds. an- dards for admissibility of technologically sophisticated evidence comm., co-chair nat. CLE programs 1999-97, coun. 1997-2000, mem. exec. coun. 2000—, budget officer 2000-02, revenue officer, 2002—, litig. sect. advisor, uniform laws commn., litig. sect. liaison, drafting com. on Model Punitive Damages Act, appointee to Nat. Conf. Attys. & CPA, 2005, atty.-client privilege task force liaison), Ill. Bar Assn., Fla. Bar Assn., Wis. Bar Assn., Chgo. Bar Assn. (chair large firm com. 2002-04), Econ. Club Chgo.

(membership com.). Avocations: sports, reading, horse racing syndications. Office: Michael Best Friedrich 70 W Madison St Ste 3500 Chicago IL 60602-4224 Office Phone: 312-836-5073. Business E-mail: mastiegel@michaelbest.com.

**STIEHM, E. RICHARD,** pediatrician, educator; b. Milw., Jan. 22, 1933; s. Reuben Harold and Marie Dueno S.; m. Judith Hicks, July 12, 1958; children: Jamie Elizabeth, Carrie Eleanor, Meredith Ellen. BS, U. Wis., 1954, MD, 1957. Diplomate Am. Bd. Pediat., Am. Bd. Allergy and Clin. Immunology (bd. dirs. 1977-83), Am. Bd. Diagnostic Lab. Immunology. Intern Phila. Gen. Hosp., 1957-58; fellow in physiol. chemistry U. Wis., 1959-61, asst. prof. pediat., 1965—68, assoc. prof., 1968—69; med. officer USNR, Johnsville, Pa., 1961-63; resident in pediat. Babies Hosp., NYC, 1963-65; fellow in pediat. immunology U. Calif., San Francisco, 1965-68; assoc. prof. UCLA, 1969—72, chief divsn. immunology, allergy and rheumatology, 1984—2003, prof., 1972—, assoc. dir. Ctr. for Interdisciplinary Rsch. in Immunologic Diseases, 1981-82, co-dir. Cystic Fibrosis Ctr., 1988—95, vice chair acad. affairs dept. pediat., 1989—99; vis. scientist metabolism br. Nat. Cancer Inst., Bethesda, Md., 1982-88. Vis. prof. Yale U., Mayo Clinic, U. Cin., Great Ormond St. Hosp., U.K., U. Wis.; bd. sci. dirs. Immune Deficiency Found., 1981—, Eczema Found., 1988—, Pediat. AIDS Found., 1989-99; task force on pediatric allergy NIH, 1977; mem. gen. clin. rsch. ctr. study sect. NIH, 1978-82, 84-88; adv. com. Hartford Fellowship, 1984-88; co-dir. LA Pediatric AIDS Consortium, 1988—. Editor: Immunologic Disorders in Infants and Children, 1972, 80, 89, 96, 2004; Am. editor: Pediatric Rsch., 1984-89; assoc. editor: Pediat. Update, 2003-; mem. editl. bd. Pediat., 1972-78, Pediat. in Rev., 1978-81, Jour. Allergy and Clin. Immunology, 1976-80, Jour. Clin. Immunology, 1985-89, Jour. Asthma Pediatric Allergy and Immunology, 1987-91, Am. Jour. Diseases of Children, 1987-97, Contemporary Pediat., 1991-96, Am. Jour. Clin. Nutrition, 1992-97; contbr. articles to profl. jours. Commr. HHS Commn. on Childhood Vaccines, 1988-90; mem. clin. rsch. adv. com. Nat. Found. March of Dimes, 1992-97, 2004-09. Recipient Career Devel. award Nat. Inst. Allergy and Infectious Diseases, 1967-69, E. Mead Johnson award for Pediat. Rsch., 1974, Alumni Citation award U. Wis. Med. Sch., 1988, Lifetime Achievement award Immune Deficiency Found., 1995, Med. Sci. award UCLA Med. Alumni, 1999, Disting. Alumni award Babies and Children's Hosp. Alumni Assn., N.Y., 1999; Markle scholar, 1967-72. Fellow AAAS; mem. Am. Assn. Immunologists, Western Soc. Pediat. Rsch. (coun. 1977-80, pres. 1983, Ross Rsch. award 1971), Soc. Pediat. Rsch., Am. Pediat. Soc., Am. Acad. Allergy, Asthma and Clin. Immunology, Am. Acad. Pediat. (infectious diseases com. 1971-77), Am. Soc. Clin. Investigation, Clin. Immunology Soc., Phi Beta Kappa, Alpha Omega Alpha. Office: UCLA Dept Peds Divsn Immunology 10833 Le Conte Ave Los Angeles CA 90095-3075 Office Phone: 310-825-6481. Business E-mail: estiehm@mednet.ucla.edu.

**STIEHM, JUDITH HICKS,** director, political scientist, educator; b. Madison, Wis., Oct. 9, 1935; d. Stratton Elson and Eleanor Spencer (Kilbourn) Hicks; m. E. Richard Stiehm, July 12, 1958; children: Jamie Elizabeth, Carrie Eleanor, Meredith Ellen. Student, Oberlin Coll., 1953; BA in E. Asian Studies, U. Wis., 1957; MA in Am. History, Temple U., 1961; PhD in Polit. Theory, Columbia U., 1969. Dir. resident hons. program U. So. Calif., LA, 1970-73, asst. prof., 1970-74, assoc. prof., 1974-83, dir. program for study of women and men in soc., 1975-81, prof. polit. sci., 1983, vice provost, 1984-87; provost Fla. Internat. U., Miami, 1987-91, prof. polit. sci., 1987—. Vis. prof. U. Wis., 1994, U.S. Army Peacekeeping Inst., U.S. Army War Coll., 1995-96, U.S. Army Strategic Studies Inst., U.S. Army War Coll., 1996, U. So. Calif., 2002-; lectr. U. Wis., Madison, 1966-69, UCLA, 1969-70; vis. lectr. San Francisco State U., 1965-66; affiliate NAS Project, 1981-82; cons. UN Div. for the Advancement of Women, Calif. Elected Women, Dept. HEW, AAUW, LWV L.A., UN Lessons Learned Unit, Dept. Peacekeeping Ops. Author: Nonviolent Power: Active and Passive Resistance in America, 1972, Bring Me Men and Women..., 1981, Arms and the Enlisted Woman, 1989, The U.S. Army War College: Military Education in a Democracy, 2002, Champions for Peace: Women Winners of the Nobel Peace Prize, 2006; editor: The Frontiers of Knowledge, 1976, Women and Men's Wars, 1983, Women's Views of the Political World of Men, 1984, It's Our Military, Too!, 1996, The U.S. Army War College: Military Education in a Democracy, 2002; mem. editorial bd. Western Polit. Quar., 1972-75, Signs, 1981-84, Women and Politics, 1986-88, 2000-. Mem. Calif. Postsecondary Edn. Commn., 1978, Calif. Adv. Coun. on Vocat. Edn., 1978-82, Def. Adv. Com. on Women in Svcs., 1979-82; bd. dirs. So. Calif. and Miami chpts. ACLU. Named Woman of Yr., Santa Monica YWCA, 1981, U. Wis. Disting Alumni, 2006; recipient Outstanding Civilian Svc. medal U.S. Army, 1996. Mem. Am. Polit. Sci. Assn. (exec. coun. 1989, sec. 2000), Western Polit. Sci. Assn. (pres. 1986), Women's Caucus Polit. Sci. (pres. 1996-97), Nat. Council for Research on Women (exec. council 1982), Council on Fgn. Relations, Phi Beta Kappa, Phi Kappa Phi (Victoria Schuck Book award 1990). Avocations: tennis, skiing, stained glass. Office: Fla Internat U Dept Polit Sci Tamiami Trl Miami FL 33199-0001 E-mail: stiehmj@fiu.edu.

**STIER, BYRON G.,** law educator; BA, U. Pa., Phila., 1989—93; JD, Harvard Law Sch., Cambridge, Mass., 1993—96; LLM, Temple U., Phila., 2003—05. Bar: NY. Assoc. Jones, Day, NYC, 1996—2001, Skadden, Arps, Slate, Meagher & Flom, LLP, NYC, 2001—03; Freedman fellow, law lectr. Temple U. Sch. Law, Phila., 2003—05; assoc. prof. law Southwestern U. Sch. Law, LA, 2005—. Sr. editor Harvard Jour. Law & Pub. Policy. Office: Southwestern Univ Sch Law 675 S Westmoreland Ave Los Angeles CA 90005 Office Fax: 213-738-6698. Business E-Mail: bstier@swlaw.edu.

**STIER, MARY P.,** publishing executive; b. Memphis, Nov. 9, 1956; m. Jeff Stier; 2 children. Grad. in comm., broadcasting, U. Iowa. With Gannett Co., 1982—; retail advt. mgr. Iowa City Press-Citizen, 1982—84, advt. dir. 1984 87, prod., pub., 1987—91, v.p. Cul. Region Newspaper Divsn., 1990—93; pres., pub. Rockford (Ill.) Register Star, 1991—2000; pres. Midwest Newspaper Group, 1993—2000; pres., pub. The Des Moines Register, 2000—; sr. group pres. Midwest Newspaper Group, 2000—. Bd. trustees Drake U. Mem.: The Greater Des Moines Partnership, Am. Press Inst., Iowa Newspaper Assn., Newspaper Assn. Am., Phi Beta Kappa. Office: Des Moines Register PO Box 957 Des Moines IA 50304-0957

**STIER, ROGER EDWIN,** chemist, researcher; b. Hackensack, NJ, Dec. 23, 1946; s. Edwin Richard and Irmtraut Margaret Stier; m. Nancy Louise Stier, Oct. 5, 1969; children: David Roger, Brian Roger, Kathlean Ann. BS magna cum laude, Fairleigh Dickinson U., 1968; PhD in Chemistry, Stafford U., 2003. Technician Burroughs Wellcome Co., Tuckahoe, NY, 1968-70; analytical chemist Schering, Union, NJ, 1970-73; rsch. assoc. Beecham Products Rsch., Parsippany, NJ, 1973-97; sr. chemist Noville, South Hackensack, NJ, 1997—, tech. dir., 2003—05; applied tech. mgr. oral care Firmenich, Princeton, NJ, 2005—. Cons. Proctor & Gamble, Cin., 1999—, Smith Klein Beecham, Parsippany, 1997—, Diamond Products, Tampa, Fla., 1997—. Author and inventor in field. Asst. scout master Boy Scouts Am., Eagle Scout, 1961, Clifton, N.J., 1957-64; minister New Apostolic Ch., Clifton, 1967—. Named Outstanding Citizen, B'nai B'rith, 1968. Mem. AAAS, Am. Chem. Soc., Soc. Cosmetic Chemists, Internat. Assn. Dental Rsch., Am. Assn. Pharmaceutical Scientists, Sigma Xi, Phi Zeta Kappa, Phi Omega Epsilon. Republican. Avocations: playing and teaching organ, reading, writing poems. Home: 265 Washington Ave Clifton NJ 07011 Office: Firmenich PO Box 5880 Princeton NJ 08543 Office Phone: 609-580-4362. Business E-Mail: roger.stier@firmenich.com.

**STIERLE, LINDA J.,** military officer; BSN magna cum laude, Incarnate Word Coll., 1978; grad., Air Command and Staff Coll., 1980; MSN with honors, U. Calif. San Francisco, 1983; grad., Air War Coll., 1986; grad. Interagy. Inst. Healthcare Execs., George Washington U., 1993; grad. CAP- STONE, Nat. Def. U., 1996. Commd. 2d. lt. USAF, 1970, advanced through grades to brigadier gen., 1995; staff nurse med. unit Wiesbaden (West Germany) USAF Med. Ctr., 1974-76, asst. charge nurse surg. unit, 1976; charge nurse female med. unit David Grant USAF Med. Ctr., Travis AFB, Calif., 1978-81, edn. coord. dept. nursing, 1981; divsn. chief, sr. mgmt. cons. mgmt. strategies/edn. dir. Leadership and Mgmt. Devel. Ctr., Maxwell AFB,

Ala., 1984-86; asst. chmn. dept. nursing David Grant USAF Med. Ctr., Travis AFB, 1986-88; chief nurse 48th Tactical Fighter Wing Hosp., RAF, Lakenheath, England, 1988-90; dep. chief divsn. nursing Wilford Hall USAF Med. Ctr., Lackland AFB, Tex., 1991-93; command nurse Office of Command Surgeon Air Mobility Command, Scott AFB, Ill., 1993-95; dir. nursing svds. Office of Air Force Surgeon Gen., Bolling AFB, DC, 1995, dir. Med. Readiness Doctrine and Planning and Nursing Svcs., 1995—99; CEO ANA, Washington, 2000—. Decorated Legion of Merit with oak leaf cluster, Meritorious Svc. medal with 3 oak leaf clusters, D.S.M. USAF. Mem. Am. Soc. Assn. Execs., Soc. Air Force Nurses, Am. Orgn. of Nurse Execs., Md. Nurses Assn., Sigma Theta Tau.

**STIERS, DAVID OGDEN,** actor, conductor; b. Peoria, Ill., Oct. 31, 1942; s. Kenneth Truman and Margaret Elizabeth (Ogden) S. Diploma drama div., Juilliard Sch., 1973. Actor, Actors Workshop, 1962, Calif. Shakespeare Festival, 1963-68, mem., The Committee, 1968-70, San Francisco (revue)/Broadway season City Center Acting Co., N.Y.C., 1974; Broadway appearances include Ulysses in Nighttown, 1974, The Magic Show, 1974-75; other stage appearances include King Lear, 1981; regular on TV series MASH 1977-83, Two Guys, a Girl, and a Pizza Place, 1998, Love & Money, 1999, Teacher's Pet (voice), 2000-02, The Dead Zone, 2002-, Lilo & Stitch: The Series (voice), 2003-; other TV appearances include Mary Tyler Moore Show, 1976, 77, Rhoda, 1977, Matlock, 1987, 88, 89, Alf, 1988, Wings, 1990, Dr. Quinn, Medicine Woman, 1997, Ally McBeal, 1998, The Practice, 1999, Bull, 2000, Arli$$, 2002, Touched by an Angel, 2003, Frasier, 2003; TV film appearances include Charlie's Angels, 1976, A Circle of Children, 1977, A Love Affair: The Eleanor and Lou Gehrig Story, 1978, Sergeant Matlovich Vs. the US Air Force, 1978, Breaking Up Is Hard To Do, 1979, Damien: The Leper Priest, 1980, The Day the Bubble Burst, 1982, Anatomy of an Illness, 1984, The First Olympics-Athens 1896, 1984, The Bad Seed, 1985, North and South, 1985, North and South Book II, 1986, Mrs. Delafield Wants to Marry, 1986, Perry Mason: Case of the Notorious Nun, 1986, Perry Mason: Case of the Shooting Star, 1986, The Kissing Place, 1990, How to Murder a Millionaire, 1990, American Eyes, 1991, The Last of His Tribe, 1992, Taking Liberty, 1993, Past Tense, 1994, To Face Her Past, 1996, Justice League of America, 1997, Murder, She Wrote: The Last Free Man, 2001, Black River, 2001, Cable Beach, 2004; film appearances include: Drive, He Said, 1972, Oh God!, 1977, The Cheap Detective, 1978, Magic, 1978, The Man With One Red Shoe, 1985, Creator, 1985, Better Off Dead, 1985, The Accidental Tourist, 1988, Another Woman, 1988, Doc Hollywood, 1991, Beauty and the Beast (voice), 1991, Iron Will, 1994, The Toolshed, 1994, Bad Company, 1995, Pocahontas (voice), 1995, Steal Big, Steal Little, 1995, Mighty Aphrodite, 1995, Everyone Says I Love You, 1996, The Hunchback of Notre Dame (voice), 1996, Meet Wally Sparks, 1997, Jungle 2 Jungle, 1997, Beauty and the Beast: The Enchanted Christmas (voice), 1997, Justice League of America, 1997, Belle's Magical World (voice), 1997, Reagan, 1998, Krippendorf's Tribe, 1998, Pocahontas: Journey to a New World (voice), 1998, MacArthur, 1999, Love & Money, 1999, The Stand-In, 1999, Tomcats, 2001, Atlantis: The Lost Empire (voice), 2001, The Majestic, 2001, The Assistant, 2001, Lilo & Stitch (voice), 2002, Stitch! The Movie (voice), 2003, Teacher's Pet (voice), 2004, Hoodwinked (voice), 2005; artistic assoc. The Acting Co., N.Y.C.; prin. guest condr. Yaquina Orch., 1989; now resident condr. Yaquina Chamber Orch.; guest condr. 70 orchs. including San Diego Symphony, Dallas Symphony Orch., Utah Symphony Orch., Chgo. Symphony Orch., Va. Symphony Orch., N.C. Symphony Philharm., Ft. Wayne Philharm., Calif. Symphony Orch., also orchs. in Honolulu, Portland, Maine, Grand Rapids, Mich., Peoria, Ill. Mem. NARAS, Conductors Guild, Am. Symphony Orch. League, Internat. Horn Soc., Magic Castle, Players Club. Office: Susan Smith and Assocs 121 N San Vicente Blvd Beverly Hills CA 90211-2303*

**STIFEL, FREDERICK BENTON,** minister, biochemist, nutritionist; b. St. Louis, Jan. 30, 1940; s. Carl Gottfried and Alma J. (Clark) Stifel; m. Gail Joane Stewart, Aug. 10, 1963; children: Tim, Faith, Seth, Elizabeth. BS, Iowa State U., 1962, PhD, 1967; MDiv., Melodyland Sch. Theol., Anaheim, Calif., 1979. Ordained to ministry Evang. Presbyn. Ch., 1981. Lab. supr., research chemist U.S. Army Med. Research and Nutrition Lab., Denver, 1968-74, Letterman Army Inst. Research, San Francisco, 1974-76; intern pastor Melodyland Christian Ctr., Anaheim, 1979-80; assoc. pastor Faith Presbyn. Ch., Aurora, Colo., 1980—; moderator bd. deacons, 1997—; pastor Outreach and Missions, 1999—. Chmn. care candidates com. Presbytery of West, Denver, 1985—88, Denver, 1991—94, Denver, 2003—; v.p. Love Inc. Metro Denver, 1987—90; regional coord. Nat. Assn. Single Adult Leaders, 1987—90, coord. Denver area, 1990—95; mem. Denver Seminary Commn., 1995—, mem. world outreach com., 1998—99; regional coord. Colo. Pregnancy Ctrs., Inc., 1992—94, Rocky Mountain Prayer Network, 1994—96, Christian Family Svcs., 1990—; bd. dirs. St. James Bible Coll., faculty, Ukraine; bd. dirs. Internat. Project Adv. Bd., Heart for the World, Inc. Contbr. articles to profl. jours. Young Life leader Hinkley HS, Aurora, 1968—74; vice chmn. Young Life com. Marin County, Calif., 1974—76; mem. parent adv. coun. IMPACT drug intervention team Rangeview HS, Aurora, 1985—89, mem. accountability com., 1989—96; mem. Friends of Arts, 1992—96; del. Iowa and Colo. State Rep. Conv., Denver, 1984, Colorado Springs, 2002. Capt. Med. Svc. Corps U.S. Army, 1967—70. Recipient Sci. Achievement award, U.S. Army Sci. Conf., 1968, 1970, Parents of the yr. award, Rangeview HS, 1992—93; Ralston Purina Rsch. fellow, 1962—63, Borden Agrl. scholar, 1962. Mem.: Am. Sci. Affiliation, Am. Soc. Clin. Nutrition, Am. Soc. Nutritional Scis., Evang. Theol. Soc., Sigma Xi, Kappa Sigma, Gamma Sigma Delta, Alpha Zeta, Phi Kappa Phi, Phi Eta Sigma. Avocations: reading, hiking, swimming, poetry, gardening. Home: 3492 S Blackhawk Way Aurora CO 80014-3909 Office: Faith Presbyn Ch 11373 E Alameda Ave Aurora CO 80012-1023 Office Phone: 303-364-7271. Business E-Mail: fstifel@faithpc.org.

**STIFF, ROBERT MARTIN,** newspaper editor; b. Detroit, Aug. 25, 1931; s. Martin L. and Gladys (Mathews) S.; m. Cindy Rose, Aug. 30, 1980; children: David Alan, Amy Anne, Kirsten Marie. BA in Radio and Journalism, Ohio State U., 1953. All-Am. sports editor Ohio State U., Daily Lantern, 1952—53; reporter, bur. chief, city editor Painesville Telegraph, Ohio, 1953-61; deskman, asst. city editor, sports editor, city editor, day editor, state editor, asst. mng. editor St. Petersburg Times, Fla., 1961-67; editor St. Petersburg Evening Ind., 1967-84; dir. St. Petersburg Times Pub. Co., 1969-84; exec. editor, v.p. Tallahassee Democrat, 1985-91; pres. Bob Stiff & Assocs., Tallahassee, 1991-95; exec. editor JMT Assocs., 1991—92, 1994—95; mng. editor About Fla., 1991-94; editor Lexington (NC) Dispatch, 1995—2006. Mem. Pulitzer Prize Jury, 1982-83; dir. devel. and pub. rels. Fla. Taxwatch Inc., 1992-94; bd. dirs. NC AP News Coun., 1995-2001, v.p., 1997-99, pres., 1999-2000; pres. Empty Stocking Fund, 1995-2006. Mem. Pulitzer Prize Jury, 1982—83; bd. dirs. NC AP News Coun., 1995—2001, v.p., 1997—99, pres., 1999—2000; bd. dirs. Cancer Svcs. Davidson County, 1996—2004, NC Open Govt. Coalition, 2004—06, U. NC, Chapel Hill, Sch. Journalism Found., 2004—06; pres. Capital Press Assn., 1998—2001; bd. dirs. NC Daily Newspaper Assn., 1995—2006, v.p., 1998—99, pres., 1999—2000. Mem.: Nat. Coun. Editl. Writers, NC Press Assn. (bd. dirs. 1999—2000, 2002—05), AP Mng. Editors Assn., Fla. Bar Found. (bd. dirs. 1990—92), Fla. Soc. Newspaper Editors (pres. 1975—76, dir. 1971—84, 1990—93), Am. Soc. Newspaper Editors Found. (bd. dirs., treas. 1986—90), Am. Soc. Newspaper Editors (dir. 1981—87), AP Assn. Fla. (pres. 1970—71), Lexington Kiwanis (bd. dirs. 1996—2000, 2003—06), Sigma Delta Chi (pres. West Coast chpt. 1970—71). Office Phone: 941-575-1074.

**STIFFLER, JACK JUSTIN,** electrical engineer; b. Mitchellville, Iowa, May 22, 1934; s. John Justin and Helen Irene (Roorda) S.; m. Ardis Ann Ackerman, Aug. 21, 1955; 1 child, Julia Alise; m. Sally Voris Burns, Apr. 22, 1989. AB magna cum laude in Physics, Harvard U., 1956; MS in E.E. Calif. Inst. Tech., 1957, PhD, 1962; postgrad., U. Paris, 1957-58. Engr. Hughes Aircraft Corp., Culver City, Calif., 1956-57; mem. tech. staff Jet Propulsion Lab., Pasadena, Calif., 1959-67; cons. scientist Raytheon Corp., Sudbury, Mass., 1967-81; co-founder, exec. v.p. Sequoia Systems, Inc., Marlborough, Mass., 1981—97; cons., 1997—. Lectr. Calif. Inst. Tech., U. So. Calif.,

UCLA, Northeastern U. Author: Theory of Synchronous Communications, 1971; contbr. chpts. to books, articles to profl. jours. Fellow: IEEE; mem.: Sigma Xi, Phi Beta Kappa. Office Phone: 508-353-5611. Personal E-mail: stiffler@capecod.net.

**STIFFLER, STUART ALDEN,** retired library director; b. St. Louis, Jan. 16, 1934; s. James Henry Stiffler and Marcella Eugenia Alden; m. Muriel Watkins (dissolved); children: Douglas, Christine. BA, Hiram Coll., 1955; MA, We. Res. U., 1956, MLS, 1957; postgrad., Ind. U., 1966; cert. in exec. mgmt., Miami U., 1976. Ref. asst. Enoch Pratt Free Libr., Balt., 1958—59; asst. to assoc. libr. Hiram (Ohio) Coll., 1960—67; dir. Shafer Libr., Findlay (Ohio) Coll., 1968—73; dir. libr. Behrend Coll., Pa. State U., Erie, 1974—77; dir. Cole Libr., Cornell Coll., Mt. Vernon, Iowa, 1978—83; dir. libr. Ky. Wesleyan Coll., Owensboro, Ky., 1983—85, Daymar Coll., Owensboro, 1986—97. Faculty Hiram Coll., 1965, honors program faculty, 1965—67; chair nominating com. Ohio Coll. Libr. Ctr., 1970, exec. com., 70; pres. Erie Area Libr. Consortium, Erie, Pa., 1974. Reviewer: Iowa History; contbr. articles to profl. jours. Mem. Friends of the Libr., Miram Coll., 1990, Friends of Libr., Juniata Coll., Huntington, Pa., 2003—; sponsor Children Internat., Kansas City, 1995—; exec. com. Boy Scout Am., Mt. Vernon, 1974—76; sponsor Big Brothers Big Sisters, Owensboro, 1994—96. Recipient Genealogist's Documentation award, Alden Kindred, Inc., 2002; scholar, We. Res. U., 1956. Mem.: ALA. Democrat. Unitarians. Avocations: numismatics, genealogy, history. Home: PO Box 522 401 4th St Huntingdon PA 16652-1423 Personal E-mail: stustiff@verizon.net.

**STIFF-ROBERTS, ADRIENNE D.,** electrical engineer, educator; d. Lee Vernon and Renee Flood Stiff; m. Francis L. Roberts, Jr., Aug. 11, 2001. BS in Physics, Spelman Coll., Atlanta, Ga., 1999; BSEE, Ga. Inst. Tech., Atlanta, Ga., 1999; MSEE, U. Mich., Ann Arbor, Mich., 2004, PhD in Applied Physics, 2004. Asst. prof. Dept. Elec. and Computer Engring. Duke U., Durham, NC, 2004—. Contbr. articles to profl. jours. Recipient Elec. and Computer Engring. Outstanding Sr. Scholar award, Ga. Inst. Tech., 1999, Excellence in Tech. Comm. commendation, 2005; fellow, David and Lucille Packard Found., 1999—2004, AT&T Labs., 1999—2004; grantee, NSF, 2006; scholar, NASA, 1994—99. Mem.: IEEE, Materials Rsch. Soc., Golden Key Honor Soc., Sigma Pi Sigma, Phi Beta Kappa. Office: Duke University Dept of ECE Box 90291 Durham NC 27708-0291 Office Phone: 919-660-5560. Office Fax: 919-660-5293. Business E-Mail: adrienne.stiffroberts@duke.edu.

**STIFTEN, EDWARD J.,** corporate financial executive; Corp. controller General Dynamics Corp.; exec. v.p., chief adminstrv. officer Clark Refining & Marketing, Inc.; v.p., CFO BJC HealthCare, 1998—2004; sr. v.p., CFO Express Scripts, Inc., Mo., 2004—. Office: Express Scripts Inc 13900 Riverport Dr Maryland Heights MO 63043 Office Phone: 314-702-7667. Office Fax: 314-702-7037.*

**STIGALL, PHYLLIS GRAHAM,** retired librarian; b. Ft. Wayne, Ind., Oct. 3, 1917; d. Edwin James and Mary Josephine (Palmer) Graham; m. Richard Patten Pooley, Apr. 4, 1943 (dec. Dec. 1950); 1 child, Samuel Graham Pooley; m. William Jasper Stigall Jr., Aug. 11, 1956 (dec. Sept. 2001). AA, Stephens Coll., 1937; AB, Northwestern U., 1939; MALS, U. Mich., 1952. Asst. counselor Stephens Coll., Columbia, Mo., 1939-42; asst. to dir. USO-YWCA Clubs, various locations, 1942-46; co-dir. U. Mich. Cmty. Ctr., Ann Arbor and Willow Run, 1946-47; libr., dean, instr. Lincoln (Ill.) Coll., 1952-66; mgr. publs. and librs. IBM Rsch. Ctr., Yorktown Heights, N.Y., 1966-88; ret. Author: Notes on 46 Women Writers, 1991, Journeys of the Brave, 1992, Ireland: Reader's Guide. Women, 1995; co-editor I Couldn't be Better, 2002. Mem. AAUW, LWV (chpt. bd. dirs., pres. 1947-66). Democrat. Episcopalian. Avocations: photography, research, biography, history, genealogy. Home: 2609 Doris Pl Honolulu HI 96822-1814

**STIGLER, STEPHEN MACK,** statistician, educator; b. Mpls., Aug. 10, 1941; s. George Joseph and Margaret (Mack) S.; m. Virginia Lee, June 27,1964; children: Andrew, Geoffrey, Margaret, Elizabeth. BA, Carleton Coll., 1963, DSc (hon.), 2005; PhD, U. Calif., Berkeley, 1967. Asst. prof. U. Wis., Madison, 1967-71, assoc. prof., 1971-75, prof., 1975-79, U. Chgo., 1979—, chmn. dept., 1986-92, 2005—, Ernest DeWitt Burton Disting. Svc. prof. Ill., 1992—. Trustee Ctr. for Advanced Study in the Behavioral Scis., Stanford, Calif., 1986-92, 93-99, 2000—, chmn., 1995-99, 2002-05. Author: The History of Statistics, 1986, Statistics on the Table, 1999; contbr. articles to jours. in field. Recipient Humboldt Found. rsch. award, 2005; Guggenheim Found. fellow, 1976-77; Ctr. for Advanced Study in Behavioral Scis. fellow, 1978-79. Fellow: AAAS, Royal Statis. Soc. (Fisher lectr. 1986), Am. Statis. Assn. (editor Jour. 1979—82), Inst. Math. Stats. (Neyman lectr. 1988, pres. 1993—94, LeCam lectr. 2006), Am. Acad. Arts and Scis. (mem. coun. 1995—99); mem.: Am. Philos. Soc., Brit. Soc. for History Sci., History of Sci. Soc., Bernoulli Soc., Statis. Soc. Can., Internat. Statis. Inst. (mem. coun. 1999—2001, pres. 2003—05), Quadrangle Club, Phi Beta Kappa, Sigma Xi. Office: U Chgo Dept Statistics 5734 S University Ave Chicago IL 60637-1514 Office Phone: 773-702-8328. Business E-Mail: stigler@galton.uchicago.edu.

**STIGLIANO, JOSE MARIA,** information technology executive, computer scientist; b. Buenos Aires, Dec. 9, 1953; s. Jose and Yvonne Suzanne (Engel) S.; m. Daniela Saida Farinelli, Dec. 14, 1988; children: Veronica Maria, Carolina Maria, Jose Nicolas. Cert. in electronics, L.A. Huergo Tech. Coll., 1973; cert. systems analysis, U. Del Salvador, 1975; BABA, Am. U., 1990; MS in Mgmt., Boston U., 1992; PhD in Mgmt., Clayton U., 1993; BS in Mgmt. Info. Systems, U. of State of N.Y., 1996; MSc in Computer Sci., Boston U., 1997. Programmer Ministry of Justice, Buenos Aires, 1973-76; analyst, programmer CTC Svc. Bur., Buenos Aires, 1976-77; systems analyst Aurora S.A., Buenos Aires, 1977-78; computer systems officer Internat. Fund Agrl. Devel. UN, Rome, 1981-88; info. tech.coord. Internat. Fund Agrl. Devel. of U.N., Rome, 1988–2005, dir. info. tech. divsn., 2006—. Lectr. U. Del Salvador, Buenos Aires, 1975-77; cons. in field. Contbg. author: Encyclopedia of Information Systems, 2002; inventor in field. Recipient IFAD Merit award, 1988, IFAD Svc. award, 1990. Mem. IEEE, IEEE Computer Soc., IEEE Comms. Soc., Engring. Mgmt. Soc., Software Engring. Tech. Coun., Soc. Internat. Devel. (life), Assn. Computing Machinery, Boston U. Gen. Alumni Assn., Argentine Soc. for Informatics and Ops. Rsch. Avocations: music, bass guitar. Office: Internat Fund Agrl Devel 107 Via Del Serafico 00142 Rome Italy Personal E-Mail: j.stigliano@computer.org. Business E-Mail: j.stigliano@ifad.org.

**STIGLITZ, JOSEPH EUGENE,** economics professor, former federal official; b. Gary, Ind., Feb. 9, 1943; s. Nathaniel David and Charlotte (Fishman) Stiglitz; m. Anya Schiffrin, Oct. 29, 2004; children from previous marriage: Siobhan, Michael, Edward, Julia. BA, Amherst Coll., Mass, 1964; DHL, Amherst Coll., 1974; PhD in Econs., MIT, 1966; MA (hon.), Yale U., 1970; D in Econs. (hon.), U. Leuven, 1994. Asst. prof. econs. MIT, 1966—67; asst. prof. Cowles Found., Yale U., New Haven, 1967—68, assoc. prof., 1968—70, prof. econs., 1970—74; vis. fellow St. Catherine's Coll., Oxford, England, 1973—74; Joan Kenney professorship Stanford U., 1974—76, prof. econs. & senior fellow, Hoover Inst., 1988—2001; Oskar Morgenstern dist. fellow Inst. Advanced Studies Math., Princeton, NJ, 1978—79; Drummond prof. polit. economy Oxford U., England, 1976—79; prof. econs. Princeton U., 1979—88; mem., Coun. Econ. Advisors Exec. Office of the Pres., Washington, 1993—97, chmn., 1995—97; sr. v.p., chief economist World Bank, Washington, 1995—2000; sr. fellow Brookings Inst., Washington, 2000; Stern visiting prof. Columbia U., 2000; prof. economics & fin. Columbia U. Grad. Sch. of Bus., Dept. of Econ. and Sch. of Internat. and Public Affairs, 2001—; prof. exec. MBA programs Columbia U.; chmn. Columbia U. Com. Global Thought. Tapp rsch. fellow Gonville and Caius Coll., Cambridge, England, 1966—70; vis. prof. dept. econs. U. Canterbury, Christchurch, New Zealand, 1967; sr. rsch. fellow social sci. divsn. Inst. for Devel. Studies U. Coll. Nairobi, 1969—71; cons. World Bank, State of Alaska, Seneca Indian Nation, Bell Comm. Rsch. Editor: Jour. Econ. Perspectives, 1986—93; Am. editor: Rev. of Econ. Studies, 1968—76, assoc. editor: Am. Econ. Rev. 1968—76, Energy Econs., Managerial and Decision Econs., mem. editl. bd.: World Bank Econ. Rev.; author: Whither Socialism?,

1996, Frontiers of Development Economics: The Future in Perspective, 2000, New Ideas About Old Age Security: Toward Sustainable Pension Systems in the 21st Century, 2001, Globalization and Its Discontents, 2002, The Rebel Within: Joseph Stiglitz and the World Bank, 2002, The Roaring Nineties, 2003; co-author (with C.E. Walsh): Principles of Macroeconomics, 2002, Economics, 2002; co-author: (with R. K. Sah) Peasants Versus City-Dwellers: Taxation and the Burden of Economic Development, 2002; co-author: (with B. Greenwald) Towards a New Paradigm in Monetary Economics, 2003; co-author: (with Andrew Charlton) Fair Trade For All: How Trade Can Promote Development (Initiative for Policy Dialogue Series), 2006. Recipient John Bates Clark award, Am. Econ. Assn., 1979, Internat. prize, Accademia Lincei, 1988, Union des Assurances de Paris prize, 1989, The Nobel Prize in Economic Sciences, 2001, Rechtenwald Prize, Germany, 1998; fellow, Guggenheim, 1969—70; scholar guest, The Brookings Inst., Washington. Fellow: Inst. for Policy Rsch. (sr. 1991—93), Brit. Acad. (corr.); mem.: NAS (fellow, 1988), Econometric Soc., Am. Acad. Arts and Scis.(fellow, 1983), Am. Econ. Assn. (exec. com. 1982—84, v.p. 1985). Office: Columbia U Uris Hall Rm 814 3022 Broadway New York NY 10027 E-mail: jes322@columbia.edu.*

**STIGWOOD, ROBERT COLIN,** film producer, television producer, radio producer, theater producer; b. Adelaide, Australia, Apr. 16, 1934; came to Eng., 1950; s. Gordon and Gwendolyn (Burrows) S. Student, Sacred Heart Coll., Adelaide. Worked as copywriter for advt. agy., Adelaide; opened talent agy. London, 1962; liquidated firm, 1965; became bus. mgr. for group Graham Bond Orgn.; became co-mng. dir. NEMS Enterprises, 1967; prin. Robert Stigwood Orgn., 1967; formed RSO Records, 1973; dir. Polygram, 1976; co-founder (with Rupert Murdoch) R&R Films, 1979. Founder Music for UNICEF. 1st ind. record producer in Eng. with release of single Johnny Remember Me; producer: films, including Jesus Christ Superstar, 1973, Bugsy Malone, Tommy, 1975, Survive, 1976, Saturday Night Fever, 1977, Grease I, 1978, Grease II, 1982, Moment By Moment, 1978, Sergeant Pepper's Lonely Hearts Club Band, The Fan, 1981, Times Square, 1980, Gallipoli, 1980, Staying Alive, 1983, Evita, 1996; stage musicals in Eng. and U.S., including, Hair, Oh! Calcutta, The Dirtiest Show in Town, Sweeney Todd, Pippin, Jesus Christ Superstar, Evita, Grease, Saturday Night Fever; TV producer in Eng. and U.S.: prodns. include The Entertainer (dramatic spl.); All in the Family (series), The Prime of Miss Jean Brodie (dramatic series). Bd. dirs. Police Athletic League, N.Y.C.; patron Australian Nat. Art Gallery. Recipient Tony award for best musical (Evita); named Internat. Producer of Yr. ABC Interstate Theatres, Inc., 1976, Knight of St. John of Jerusalem, Malta. 1985. Mem. Royal Bermuda Yacht Club. Clubs: Royal Bermuda Yacht. Avocations: yachting, tennis. Home: Barton Manor East Cowes Isle of Wight England

**STIKLESTAD, NICOLE LEIGH,** music educator; d. Rickie Lynn and Julene Marie Stiklestad. BA in Music Edn., U. Minn., 2002. Voice and piano tchr., Twin Cities, Minn., 2002—; vocal coach for mus. theater prodns. Burnsville H.S., Minn., 2002—. Mem.: Apple Valley Music Tchrs. Assn., Nat. Assn. Tchrs. of Singing. Avocations: piano, musical theater, concerts. E-mail: nicolestiklestad@yahoo.com.

**STILES, CHERYL,** writer, librarian, educator; b. Marietta, Ga., July 21, 1958; d. Ralph Stiles and Betty Joan Nelson. BA in Religion, Duke U., Durham, N.C., 1980; M in Libr. and Info. Mgmt., Emory U., Atlanta, 1983; diploma computer info. sys., N. Metro Tech. Coll., Acworth, GA, 1999; MA in Profl. Writing, Kennesaw State U., 2003; postgrad., Ga. State U., 2005—. Outreach svcs. libr. Moutrie (Ga.)-Colquitt County Regional Libr., 1983—84; audiovisual svcs. libr. Brunswick (Ga.)-Glynn Regional Libr., 1984—89; libr. II Cobb County Pub. Libr., Marietta, Ga., 1989—96; asst. libr. Floyd Coll., Rome, Ga., 1996—98; asst. libr., coord. libr. instrn. Kennesaw (Ga.) State U., 1998—. Reviewer Video Rating Guide Librs., San Diego, 1990—94, Audio-File, Maine, 1992—96; instr. continuing edn. Kennesaw State U., 1999—2002, conf. dir., 2002—03; adj. instr. Shorter Coll., Rome. Poetry editor: Kennesaw Rev., 2002—03; contbr. poems in jours. Grad. Leadership Cobb County, Marietta, 1995, Leadership Kennesaw State, Kennesaw, 1999; vol. libr., archivist Hambidge Ctr., Rabun Gap, Ga., 2003—04. Recipient Grad. Writing award for Poetry, Kennesaw State U., 2001, 2003; Artist's Residency fellow, Hambidge Ctr., 2003, Disting. scholar, Kennesaw State U., 2003. Mem.: MLA, ALA, Acad. Am. Poets, Associated Writing Programs, Sigma Tau Delta, Phi Kappa Phi. Avocations: arts & crafts, hiking, camping, travel, yoga. Office: Kennesaw State U 1000 Chastain Rd Kennesaw GA 30144 Office Phone: 770-423-6003. Business E-Mail: cstiles@kennesaw.edu.

**STILES, GARY LESTER,** cardiologist, molecular pharmacologist, educator; b. NYC, May 22, 1949; s. Robert L. and Vivian M. (Cano) S.; m. Alexis H. Stiles; children: Heather B., Wendy A. BS in Chemistry, St. Lawrence U., 1971; MD, Vanderbilt U., 1975. Diplomate Am. Bd. Internal Medicine, sub.-bd. Cardiovascular Medicine. Resident in internal medicine Vanderbilt U., Nashville, 1975-78; from fellow in cardiology to prof. Duke U., Durham, NC, 1978—90, prof. medicine, 1990—; CMO, v.p. Duke Health Sys., 1999—2004; exec. v.p. Wyeth Pharms., Collegeville, Pa., 2004—, chief med. officer, 2004—. Mem. sci. adv. coun. Alta. Heritage Found., Edmonton, Can., 1990-2006; mem. pharmacology study sect. NIH, Bethesda, Md., 1988-91. Mem. editl. bd. Jour. Biol. Chemistry, 1990-95, Molecular Pharmacology, 1991-99. Recipient Katz prize Am. Heart Assn., 1983, award Am. Fedn. Clin. Rsch., 1989; grantee Am. Heart Assn., 1987-90. Fellow Am. Coll. Cardiology (award 1993); mem. Internat. Churchill Soc., Assn. Am. Physicians, Am. Soc. Clin. Investigation. Republican. Achievements include patent in field. Office: D6106 Wyeth Pharms 500 Arcola Rd Collegeville PA 19426 Office Phone: 484-865-8700. Business E-Mail: stilesg@wyeth.com.

**STILES, JULIA,** actress; b. NYC, Mar. 28, 1981; d. John O'Hara and Judith Stiles. B in English, Columbia U., 2005. Actor: (TV films) Before Women Had Wings, 1997, The '60s, 1999; (films) I Love You, I Love You Not, 1996, The Devil's Own, 1997, Wicked, 1998, Wide Awake, 1998, 10 Things I Hate About You, 1999, Down to You, 2000, Hamlet, 2000, State and Main, 2000, Save the Last Dance, 2001 (Teens Choice Drama award, 2001), The Business of Strangers, 2001, O, 2001, The Bourne Identity, 2002, A Guy Thing, 2003, Carolina, 2003, Mona Lisa Smile, 2003, The Prince & Me, 2004, The Bourne Supremacy, 2004, Edmond, 2005, A Little Trip to Heaven, 2005, The Omen, 2006; TV guest appearances include Ghostwriter, 1992, Promised Land, 1996, Chicago Hope, 1994; actor: (plays) Fran's Bed, 2005. Volunteer Habitat for Humanity, Costa Rica, Amnesty Internat. Named one of 25 Hottest Stars under 25, Teen People mag., 2002; voted one of, People Mag.'s 50 Most Beautiful People, 2001. Democrat. Office: Clare Ryu c/o United Talent Agy 9560 Wilshire Blvd Beverly Hills CA 90212*

**STILES, KNUTE,** retired artist; b. Hudson, Wis., Sept. 14, 1923; s. Charles and Lorena Emma (Weldon) S. Grad., Calif. Sch. Fine Arts; student, St. Paul Sch Art, Black Mountain Coll, New Sch. Social Rsch. Reviewer, San Francisco corr. Artforum, San Francisco, 1963—71; tchr. painting and drawing San Francisco Art Inst., 1964—71; reviewer, feature writer KXKX-FM, San Francisco, Art in Am., N.Y.C., 1975—83; columnist art Calif. Voice, San Francisco, 1977-83; ret., 1983. One-man shows include 6 Gallery, San Francisco, 1955-56, Brata Gallery, N.Y.C., 1957-61, San Francisco Mus. Modern Arts, 1964, Staniford Gallery, San Francisco, 1969, Metart Gallery, Area Arts Gallery, Lucien Lebaudt Gallery; poet Poetry.com, MULE mag. With U.S. Army, 1943-46. Home: 5 Campbell St Bisbee AZ 85603

**STILES, MARY ANN,** lawyer, writer, lobbyist; b. Tampa, Fla., Nov. 16, 1944; d. Ralph A. and Bonnie (Smith) S.; m. Barry Smith. AA, Hills Community Coll., 1973; BS, Fla. State U., 1975; JD, Antioch Sch. Law, 1978. Bar: Fla. 1978. Legis. analyst Fla. Ho. of Reps., Tallahassee, 1973-74, 74-75; intern U.S. Senate, Washington, 1977; v.p., gen. counsel Associated Industries Fla., Tallahassee, 1978-81, gen. counsel, 1981-84, spl. counsel, 1986-97; assoc. Deschler, Reed & Crichfield, Boca Raton, Fla., 1980-81; founding ptnr. Stiles, Taylor, & Grace, P.A., Boca Raton, Tampa, Orlando, Jacksonville, Talahassee, and Miami, Fla., 1982—, shareholder, dir. Tampa; gen. counsel Associated Industries Ins. Co., Inc., 1996—, Associated Industries Fla., Inc.,

1997—, Associated Industries Ins. Svcs., Inc., 1997—. Shareholder, dir. Six Stars Devel. Co. of Fla., Inc. Platnum Bank; dr. Eclipse, Inc.; owner, pres. Styles by Stiles; shareholder, pres. 42nd St., The Bistro; mem. Workers' Compensation Task Force, 2000-01. Author: Workers' Compensation Law Handbook, 1980-94 edit. Bd. dirs., sec. Hillsborough C.C. Found., Tampa, 1985-87, 94-96; bd. dirs. Hillsborough Area Regional Transit Authority, Tampa, 1986-89, Boys and Girls Club of Tampa, 1986—; The Spring, 1992-93, What's My Chance, 1992-94; mem. Gov.'s Oversite Bd. on Workers' Compensation, 1990, Workers' Compensation Rules Com., Fla. Bar, 1990-95, 2000—, Workers' Compensation Exec. Counsel Fla. Bar, 1990-95, Jud. Nominating Commn. for Workers' Compensation Cts., 1990-93, trustee Hillsborough Cmty. Coll., 1994-99, vice-chair, 1995-96, chair, 1996-97; bd. dirs. Seminole Boosters, Inc., Tallahassee Fla. State U., 1996—. Mem. ABA, Fla. Bar Assn., Hillsborough County Bar Assn., Hillsborough Assn. Women Lawyers, Fla. Assn. Women Lawyers, Fla. Women's Alliance, Hillsborough County Seminole Boosters (past pres.), Tiger Bay Club (Tampa, past pres., sec.). Republican. Baptist. Avocations: boating, reading. Office: 315 S Plant Ave Tampa FL 33606-2325 also: 317 N Calhoun St Tallahassee FL 32301-7605 also: PO Box 310397 Miami FL 33231-0397 Address: PO Box 294349 Boca Raton FL 33429 also: PO Box 48190 Jacksonville FL 32247

**STILES, THOMAS BEVERIDGE, II,** retired investment company executive; b. Easton, Pa., Oct. 4, 1940; s. Ezra Martin and Vivien (de Fay) S.; m. Elaine Ann Patyk, July 2, 1966 (div. Oct. 1980); children— Thomas Beveridge III, Jonathan Ezra; m. Barbara Toll Alexander, Mar. 7, 1981. BA, Yale U., 1963; MBA, Harvard U., 1968. V.p: Laird, Inc., N.Y.C., 1968-73; sr. v.p., dir. Smith Barney Harris Upham and Co. Inc., N.Y.C., 1973-82; exec. v.p., dir. E.F. Hutton & Co. Inc., N.Y.C., 1982-87; chmn., CEO Shearson Lehman Advisors Asset Mgmt. Co., N.Y.C., 1988-90, 99—, Bernstein Macaulay, N.Y.C., 1988-90; CEO, chmn. Greenwich Street Advisors, N.Y.C., 1990-97; mng. dir. Smith, Barney, Inc., N.Y.C., 1993-99, retired, 1999—. Bd. dirs., pres. Cedar Lawn Cemetery, Paterson, N.J., 1973—. Bd. dirs. Sanford C. BErnstein Fund, 2003—. 1st lt. M.I., U.S. Army, 1963-66. Fellow Fin. Analysts Fedn.; mem. N.Y. Soc. Security Analysts, Spring Lake Bath and Tennis Club (N.J.), El Niguel Country Club (Calif.). Republican. Presbyterian. Avocations: political science, tennis, swimming. E-mail: tom.stiles@cox.net.

**STILES, VIRGINIA FORD,** data processing executive, poet; b. Memphis, June 3, 1961; d. Margaret Berry and John Edward Ford, adopted d. Mattie Virginia Martin; m. Allen Wesley Stiles, Aug. 9, 2003; children: Lakeisha Lashun Williams, Teresita Louise Cornelius. Lic. Tax Preparer, H&R Block Tax Sch., 1992. Data entry clk. H&R Block, LA, 1992—93; ms mgmt. specialist USN, Norfolk, Va., 1996. Tax examiner IRS, Memphis, 1987—88. Singer (author): (anthology) Memphis Miracle (Editor's Choice award, 2000); author: I Think (Best Poet, 2002). Recipient Veterans Integrity, Patrotism Recognition, Am. Legions, 2000, Pub. greeting cards, anthology, and CD, Internat. Libr. of Poetry, 2001. Mem.: Phi Theta Kappi Honor Soc. (hon.). Personal E-mail: virginiallen@aol.com.

**STILL, CHARLES HENRY, SR.,** lawyer; b. Lubbock, Tex., Sept. 22, 1942; s. Charles Alphonso and Henri Sue S.; m. Frances Eugenia Odell, Apr. 29, 1967; children: Charles Henry Jr., Kathryn Elizabeth. BBA in Acctg., Tex. Tech. U., 1965; JD with honors, U. Tex., 1968. Bar: Tex. 1968. Assoc. Fulbright & Jaworski, Houston, 1968-75, ptnr., 1975—, head corp. dept., 1984-99, mem. exec. com., 1992-99. Speaker numerous confs. and meetings; bd. dirs. Oyo Geospace Corp. Comment editor Tex. Law Rev., 1967-68. Bd. dirs. St. Luke's Episcopal Hosp., Houston, 1991—, Catalyst Found., Houston, 1992—; mem. vestry Christ Ch. Cathedral, Houston, 1981-84, sr. warden, 1983, chancellor, 1986-2002. Fellow Am. Bar Found., Tex. Bar Found., Houston Bar Found.; mem. ABA (bus. law sect. 1968—, corp. laws com. 1983-89, fed. regulation of securities com. 1976—, com. on legal opinions 1989—, law firms com. 1990—, chmn. 1998-2000, ethics 2000 task force 1999-2002, multiple disciplinary practice task force 1998—, profl. conduct com. 2002—), Am. Law Inst., State Bar Tex. (chmn. bus. law sect. 1984-85, mem. coun. 1982-86, chmn. securities law com. 1981-83, Forest Club, Petroleum Club, Order of Coif, Phi Delta Phi, Phi Kappa Phi, Gamma Phi Beta, Beta Alpha Psi, Phi Beta Theta, Phi Eta Sigma. Avocations: hunting, reading. Home: 3734 Locke Ln Houston TX 77027-4006 Office: Fulbright & Jaworski 1301 Mckinney St Ste 5100 Houston TX 77010-3095

**STILL, CHARLES NEAL,** retired neurologist, medical educator, consultant; b. Richmond, Va., Apr. 15, 1929; s. Charles Wright and Ruth (Kemp) S.; m. Dorothy Lee Varn, Dec. 27, 1958; children: Charles Herbert, Carl Nelson, Sara Alice. BS in Chemistry, Clemson U., 1949; MS in Biochemistry, Purdue U., 1951; MD, Med. U. S.C., 1959. Diplomate Am. Bd. Psychiatry and Neurology. Instr. chemistry Clemson (S.C.) U., 1951-52; rotating intern U. Chgo. Clinics, 1959-60; neurology fellow Sch. Medicine Johns Hopkins U., Balt., 1960-63; resident in neurology Johns Hopkins-Balt. City Hosp., 1960-63; NIH rsch. fellow Harvard U.-McLean Hosp., Belmont, Mass., 1963-65; chief neurology svcs. William S. Hall. Psychiat. Inst., Columbia, S.C., 1965-81, assoc. dir. gen. psychiatry and neurology, 1989-92; dir. C. M. Tucker Human Resources Ctr., Columbia 1981-88; clin. prof. neuropsychiatry USC Sch. Medicine, Columbia, S.C., 1981-88, prof. neuropsychiatry, 1989—2004, clin. prof. neuropsychiatry and behavioral sci. Sch. Medicine, 2004; ret., 2004. Instr. chemistry U.S. Mil. Acad., West Point, N.Y., 1953-55; assoc. clin. prof. neurology Med. U. S.C., Charleston, 1973-92; assoc. prof. neuropsychiatry U.S.C. Sch. Medicine, Columbia, 1976-78, prof. neuropsychiatry, 1978-81. Author: (with others) Handbook of Clinical Neurology, 1976, Neurologic Clinics, 1984, Movement Disorders, 1986; editor The Recorder Columbia Med. Soc., 1991-2003, editor emeritus, 2003—; mem. edit. bd. Jour. S.C. Med. Assn., 1980 2006, Jour. Applied Gerontology, 1983-88; contbr. articles to profl. jours. Chmn. grants rev. bd. S.C. Dept. Mental Health, Columbia, 1973-78; mem. exec. bd. Alzheimer's Assn. Columbia, 1985-93, pres. Mid-State chpt. Alzheimer's Assn., 1991-92; med. dir. Alzheimer's Disease Registry, Columbia, 1989-92, Alzheimer's Daycare Ctr., Columbia, 1989-92; mem. Gov.'s Adv. Coun. to Alzheimer's Disease and Related Disorders Resource Coordination Ctr., 1995-99. 1st lt. U.S. Army, 1952-55. Fellow: Am. Geriatrics Soc. (emeritus), Am. Acad. Neurology (emeritus), Gerontol. Soc. Am. (emeritus), Am. Inst. Chemists (life); mem.: AMA (life), Am. Chem. Soc. (emeritus). Baptist. Avocations: writing, photography. Home: 2 Culpepper Cir Columbia SC 29209-2234 Personal E-mail: cndstill@aol.com.

**STILL, DAVID BARNES,** bank executive, lawyer; b. Abington, Pa., June 2, 1949; s. Harold Ferguson and Virginia (Barnes) S.; m. Sheridan Shepherd, Nov. 1, 1984; 1 child, Meredith Susan Lynn; children by previous marriage: David Jr., Mark L. BA, St. Lawrence U., Canton, N.Y., 1971; MBA, U. Pa., 1972; JD, Temple U., 1987. Bar: Pa. 1989. V.p. Shawmut Nat. Bank, Boston, 1972-78; sr. v.p. Phila. Nat. Bank, 1978-84, CoreStates Fin. Corp., Phila., 1984—. Vice chmn., trustee Curtis Inst. Music, Phila., 1982—; trustee Mary Louis Curtis Bok Found., Phila., 1984—. Mem. Robert Morris Assocs., Pine Valley (N.J.) Golf Club, Merion Golf Club. Republican. Episcopalian. Office: CoreStates Fin Corp Broad & Chestnut Sts Philadelphia PA 19101

**STILL, HOMER I.,** information technology executive; Student in Bus. Mgmt. and Programming, Tulsa Jr. Coll.; AA in Liberal Arts, Okla. Mil. Acad.; BS in Indsl. and Managerial Psychology, Okla. State U., BA in History. Sr. EDP systems engr., computer security mgr. Am. Airlines, Inc., 1974—82; sr. cons. CAP Gemini Am. (Trans World Airlines (TWA)), 1982—87; advr. system engr., account mgr., bus. analyst, program/project mgmt. cons., worldwide bus. cons., sr. ptnr. IBM, 1987—93; chief operating and info. officer, exec. v.p. Genesis Industries, Inc., 1994—95; computer and operations cons., 1995—98; sr. mgr., program mgr. Sabre Inc., 1998—2001; security screener Dept. Homeland Security, 2002—03; sr. account mgr., program mgr., bus. analyst Capital One Auto Fin., 2003—04. Active reserve U.S. Army, 1967—70, intelligence officer, capt. U.S. Army, 1970—73, Vietnam, active reserve U.S. Army, 1974—79, 95th Infantry Divsn., Tulsa. Mem.: Phi Theta Kappa.

**STILLER, BEN,** actor, television producer; b. NYC, Nov. 30, 1965; s. Jerry Stiller and Anne Meara. m. Christine Taylor, May 13, 2000, children, Ella Olivia, Quinlin Dempsey. Student, UCLA. Actor: (theatre) The House of Blue Leaves, 1985, This Is How It Goes, 2005; (films) Hot Pursuit, 1987, Empire of the Sun, 1987, Fresh Horses, 1988, Next of Kin, 1988, That's Adequate, 1989, Elvis Stories, 1989, Stella, 1990, Highway to Hell, 1992, Reality Bites, 1994, Heavyweights, 1995, Happy Gilmore, 1996, Flirting With Disaster, 1996, Zero Effect, 1998, There's Something About Mary, 1998, Your Friends and Neighbors, 1998, Permanent Midnight, 1998, Nobody Knows Anything, 1998, The Suburbans, 1999, McClintock's Peach, 1999, Black and White, 1999, Mystery Men, 1999, The Independent, 2000, Keeping the Faith, 2000, Meet the Parents, 2000, The Royal Tannenbaums, 2001, Orange County, 2002, Duplex, 2003, Nobody Knows Anything, 2003, Along Came Polly, 2004, Envy, 2004, Meet the Fockers, 2004, Madagascar (voice), 2005, Danny Roane: First Time Director, 2006; actor, dir. (films) Reality Bites, 1994, The Cable Guy, 1996, Zoolander, 2001; actor, prodr. (films) Dodgeball: A True Underdog Story, 2004; actor, exec.prodr. (films) Starksy & Hutch, 2004; TV appearances include Kate McShane, 1975, Kate & Allie, 1986, Miami Vice, 1987, The Ben Stiller Show (also writer, dir.)(Emmy award for writing), 1992-93, Frasier, 1993, Duckman, 1995, Friends, 1997, Saturday Night Live, 1998, 2000, Freaks and Geeks, 2000, The Simpsons (voice), 2002, Undeclared, 2002, The King of Queens, 2002, Curb Your Enthusiasm, 2004, King of the Hill (voice), 2004, Arrested Development, 2004, 05; co-editor (with Marla Hamburg Kennedy) Looking at Los Angeles. Named one of 50 Most Powerful People in Hollywood, Premiere mag., 2005.*

**STILLER, JENNIFER ANNE,** lawyer; b. Washington, May 4, 1948; d. Ralph Sophian and Joy (Dancis) Stiller. AB in Econs. and History, U. Mich., 1970; JD, NYU, 1973. Bar: Pa. 1973, U.S. Dist. Ct. (mid. dist.) Pa. 1977, U.S. Supreme Ct. 1978, U.S. Dist. Ct. (ea. dist.) Pa. 1983, U.S. Ct. Appeals (3rd cir.) 1983, U.S.C. Ct. Appeals (D.C. cir.), 1996. Dep. atty. gen. Pa. Dept. Justice, Harrisburg, 1973-75, Pa. Dept. Health, Harrisburg, 1975-78; sr. staff atty. Am. Hosp. Assn., Chgo., 1978-80, mgr., dept. fed. law, 1980-81; gen. counsel Ill. Health Fin. Authority, 1981-82; sr. assoc. Berriman & Schwartz, King of Prussia, Pa., 1983-85, Wolf, Block, Schorr & Solis-Cohen, Phila., 1985-88, Montgomery, McCracken, Walker & Rhoads, LLP, Phila., 1988-90; ptnr. Montgomery, McCracken, Walker & Rhoads, Phila., 1990-2000, chair health law group, 1991-2000; sr. counsel Tenet Healthcare Corp., Phila., 2000-2001; pvt. practice Haverford, Pa., 2001—. Contbr. articles to profl. jours. Fellow Am. Health Lawyers Assn. (bd. dirs. 1997-2003, exec. com. 2002-03); mem. ABA (gov. com. Health Law Forum 1994-95), Pa. Soc. Healthcare Attys. (pres. 1995). Avocations: gardening, bicycling, hiking, music. Office: Law Office Jennifer A Stiller 625 Haydock Ln Haverford PA 19041-1207 Office Phone: 610-642-3366. Business E-mail: stiller@healthregs.com.

**STILLER, JERRY,** actor; b. NYC, June 8, 1927; s. William and Bella S.; m. Anne Meara, Sept. 14, 1953; children: Amy, Benjamin. BS in Speech and Drama, Syracuse U., 1950. Actor with nat. co. of Peter Pan, 1951, also at Henry St. Playhouse, 1941; Cherry Lane Theatre, N.Y.C., 1947, Billy Barnes Showboat, Chgo., 1950, Erie (Pa.) Playhouse, 1951, 52, Memphis Arena Theatre, 1952, Phoenix Theatre, 1954, 55, 56, Shakespeare Festival Theatre, Stratford, Conn., 1955, Compass Players, 1959, mem. Shakespeare Co. in Central Park, N.Y.C., 1957, 71, Two Gentlemen, 1971, Much Ado, 1988; Broadway appearances include The Golden Apple, 1954, The Ritz, 1975, Unexpected Guests, 1977, Hurlyburly, 1985, Three Men on a Horse, 1993, What's Wrong With This Picture?, 1994, The Three Sisters, 1997; film appearances include The Taking of Pelham 1-2-3, 1974, Airport '75, 1975, The Ritz, 1976, Those Lips, Those Eyes, 1979, Nadine, 1986, That's Adequate, 1986, Hairspray, 1986, Shoeshine (Acad. award nomination, short subject 1989), A Pair of Jokers, 1990, The Pickle, 1992, Stag, 1996, Camp Stories, 1996, The Deli, 1997, Die Story Von Monty Spinnerratz, 1997, The Fish in the Bathtub, 1998, The Independent, 2001, On the Line, 2001, Serving Sara, 2002, Zoolander, 2003; Off-Broadway appearances include Boubouroche, 1971, Passione, 1980, Prairie du Chien, 1985, After-Play, 1995-96; mem. comedy team, Anne Meara, 1961— Ed Sullivan Show 36 appearances; night club appearances include Compass Players, St. Louis, 1957, Happy Medium, Chgo., 1960, also Village Gate, Village Vanguard, Blue Angel, Bon Soir and Phase Two, N.Y.C., Mr. Kelly's, Chgo., Hungry I, San Francisco, The Establishment, London, The Sands, Flamingo, Las Vegas, Harrah's, Reno and Lake Tahoe, Trump Plaza, QE II; co-star: daily TV series Take Five with Stiller and Meara, 1977-78; actor TV series Joe and Sons, 1975, Tattinger's, 1987, The Detective, The Sunset Gang, PBS, 1991, Seize the Day, 1990, The Hollow Boy, American Playhouse, 1991, Seinfeld, 1993-98, Subway Stories, King of Queens, 1998—; commercials: Blue Nun, United Van Lines, Amalgamated Bank, Vermeer Liquor, Nike, AT&T, Glad Bags, Total Cereal; AOL, Video (co-host with Anne Meara): So You Want to be an Actor?; animation: Teachers Pet "Pretty Boy", 2000-02, Lion King III, 2003, Lion King 1Y2, 2004; author: Married to Laughter (Grammy nomination for audio), 2000. Recipient Disting. Alumnus award Syracuse U., 1973, Voice of Imagery award, 1975, Arents Pioneer Medal, 1979, 1st Biffy award Balt. Internat. Film Festival, Entertainment Father of Yr. award, 1977, Syracuse Walk of Stars, 1994, Syracuse U. award for Achievement in the Arts, Am. Comedy award for role in Seinfeld, 1998, Fourth Ann. Alan King award in Jewish humor (with Anne Meara), Am. Comedy award Seinfeld, 1998, Productive Aging award Jewish Coun. Aging, 2004, Thalia award (with Anne Meara) Humbert Coll., Toronto, 2004; nominated Emmy award for role in Seinfeld, 1997, Ellis Island Medal of Honor, 2000.

**STILLER, SHALE DAVID,** lawyer, educator; b. Rochester, NY, Feb. 23, 1933, s. Maurice Aaron and Dorothy (Sahtan) S.; m. Ellen M. Heller; children: Lewis B., Michael J., Kenneth R.; stepchildren: William Heller, Lawrence Heller. BA, Hamilton Coll., 1954; LLB, Yale U., 1957; MLA, Johns Hopkins U., 1977. Bar: Md. 1957. Ptnr. corp. and securities, tax, trusts and estates practices DLA Piper, Balt., 1992—. Lectr. U. Md. Law Sch., 1963—. Contbr. articles to profl. jours. Trustee Johns Hopkins U., Assn. Jewish Charities, Peabody Inst.; trustee, vice chmn. Johns Hopkins Hosp. and Sch. Medicine; pres. The Harry and Jeanette Weinberg Found., Leonard & Helen Stulman Found., Charles Crane Family Found.; bd. mem. Bright Star Found., Shelter Found., Hittman Family Found.; mem. adv. bd. Tax Mgmt., 1972-93; chmn. Jud. Nominating Commn., Balt., 1979-83; officer, bd. dirs. Park Sch., 1973-79, pres., 1982-86; pres. Jewish Family Agy., 1972-74. Mem. ABA, Am. Law Inst., Am. Coll. Tax Counsel, Am. Coll. Trust and Estate Counsel, Order of Coif. Democrat. Jewish. Office Phone: 410-654-6835. Office Fax: 410-654-4900. Business E-mail: sstiller@theweinbergfoundation.org.

**STILLINGS, DENNIS OTTO,** research association administrator, consultant; b. Valley City, N.D., Oct. 30, 1942; s. Harlow Cecil and Ruth Alice (Wolff) S. BA, U. Minn., 1965. Tchr. Henry (S.D.) Pub. Schs., 1965-66, Darby (Mont.) Pub. Schs., 1966-68; tech. rsch. libr., then mgr. hist. dept. Medtronic, Inc., Mpls., 1968-79; instr. humanities U. Minn., Mpls., 1970-72; founding dir., then curator Bakken Libr., Mpls., 1976-80; ind. antiquarian hist. cons. Mpls., 1979-81; sole proprietor Archaeus Project, Kamuela, Hawaii, 1981—2006; exec. dir. Five Mountain Med. Cmty., 1996-97, also bd. dirs., 1996—2006; ret., 2006. Ctr. for Sci. Anomalies Rsch., Ann Arbor, Mich., 1993—97; bd. mem. Kohala Ctr., 2001—06; bd. dirs. Dan Carlson Enterprises, Mpls. Columnist Med. Progress Through Technology, 1974-76; columnist Med. Instrumentation, 1973-76, guest editor, 1975; editor: Cyberphysiology: The Science of Self-Regulation, 1988, Cyberbiological Studies of the Imaginal Component in the UFO Contact Experience, 1989, The Theology of Electricity: On the Encounter and Explanation of Theology and Science in the 17th and 18th Centuries, 1990, Project 2010: On the Current Crisis in Health and Its Implications of the Hospital for the Future, 1992; founding editor: (jours.) Artifex, 1981-93, Archaeus, 1982-84, Healing Island. Fellow Am. Inst. Stress; mem. Soc. Sci. Exploration. Avocations: jungian psychology, golf, fishing, travel. Home and Office: 724 4th Ave NW Valley City ND 58072 E-mail: dstillings@archaeusproject.com

**STILLINGS, IRENE ELLA GRACE CORDINER,** retired foundation executive; b. Boston, Aug. 17, 1918; d. Matthew Wilson and Susan F. (Mason) Cordiner; m. Gordon A. Stillings, May 13, 1945; children: David Gordon, Susan Irene. Student, Radcliffe Coll., 1936-39; diploma, Burdett Coll., 1941. Sec., bookkeeper Boston Refrigerator Co., 1941-42; sec., tchr. Burdett Coll., 1942-44; sec., bookkeeper Gertrude Rittenburg, Boston, 1944-46. Town chmn. Heart Fund, Woodland, Maine, 1953-61; Brownie leader Girl Scouts U.S., 1954-58; pres. Woodland Woman's Club 1961-63; sec. PTA, 1961-62; chmn. Baileyville Superintending Sch. Com., 1962-64; chmn. women's activities Nat. Found., East Washington County, 1959-61; pres. Hosp. Aid, 1961-63; chmn. Newcomers Coll. group YWCA, 1965-66, chmn. theatre group, 1968-70, pres. Suburbanites, 1970-71; Stamford (Conn.) chmn. Expt. in Internat. Living, 1965-68; bd. dirs. YWCA of Stamford, 1969-78, chmn. antique show, 1960-77, chmn. devotion, 1970-92, ann. Antique Show benefit, 1970-77; pres. New Suburbanites, Stamford, 1994-95, ret. 1996. Mem. Mass. Hort. Soc., St. Luke's Guild (treas. 1954-63), Radcliffe Club, Stamford Woman's Club (treas. 1975-79, program com., co-chmn. Am. home dept. 1974, 75, pres. 1981-83, bd. dirs. 1981—, 2d v.p.v. fin. 1979-81, 83-85, 87-89, chmn. bldg. investment 1979-81, parliamentarian 1990—, pres., newcomers/suburbanites, 1994-95), Theta Alpha Chi. Episcopalian. Home: 277 W Hill Rd Stamford CT 06902-1708

**STILLITANO, JOSEPH MICHAEL,** music educator; b. Syracuse, NY, Nov. 30, 1977; s. William Nick Stillitano and Maureen Anne FitzPatrick; m. Heather Shannon Tryon, Nov. 9, 2003. MusB, Ithaca Coll., NY, 2000. Cert. tchr. NY, Mass. H.s. vocal music tchr. West Genesee Pub. Schs., Camillus, NY, 2001; vocal music tchr. Boston U., 2000—. H.s. and mid. sch. choral dir. Westborough (Mass.) Pub. Schs., 2001—. Mem.: Music Educators Nat. Conf. (Ctrl. Dist. h.s. choral chair 2004—05), Am. Choral Dirs. Assn. (h.s. repertoire and stds. chair 2003—05). Office: Westborough HS 90 W Main St Westborough MA 01581 Office Phone: 508-836-7720 ext 5192. Office Fax: 508-836-7723. E-mail: stillitj@westborough.k12.ma.us.

**STILLMAN, BRUCE,** molecular biologist; b. Melbourne, Australia, Oct. 16, 1953; came to U.S., 1979; s. Graham and Jessie (England) S.; m. Grace Begley, Mar. 21, 1981; children: Keith, Jessica. BSc with honors, U. Sydney, 1975; PhD, Australian Nat. U., 1979. Staff investigator Cold Spring Harbor Lab., NY, 1981-83; sr. staff investigator, 1984-85, sr. scientist, 1985-90, asst. dir., 1990-93, dir. cancer ctr., 1992—, dir., 1994—2003, pres., CEO, 2003—. Contbr. scientific papers to profl. publs. Apptd. to Order of Australia, 1999; Rita Allen Found. scholar, 1981-85; Cancer Rsch. fellow Damon Runyon-Walter Winchell, 1979-80, Alfred P. Sloane, Jr., GM Cancer Rsch. Found., 2004. Fellow Royal Soc. London; mem. AAAS, Am. Soc. Microbiology, Am. Soc. Biochem. and Molecular Biology, Am. Assn. Cancer Rsch., NAS. Office: Cold Spring Harbor Lab PO Box 100 Cold Spring Harbor NY 11724-0100*

**STILLMAN, CHARLES ALLEN,** lawyer; b. Bklyn., Sept. 8, 1937; s. Max and Anne (Parness) S.; m. Marilyn Norma Radezky, Aug. 30, 1959; children: Nina, Robert, Jay. BA, NYU, 1958, JD, 1962. Bar: NY 1962. Law clk. to Hon. Irving R. Kaufman, US Ct. Appeals (2d cir.), 1959-62; asst. US atty. So. Dist. NY, 1962-66; assoc. Phillips, Nizer, Benjamin, Krim & Ballon, 1966-68; assoc. Louis Bender, Esquire, 1968-69; ptnr. Botein Hays Sklar & Herzberg, NYC, 1969-72; practice, NYC, 1972-77; ptnr. Stillman & Friedman, NYC, 1977—; adj. assoc. prof. trial advocacy Fordham U., 1978-85; hearing officer for environ. protection hearings NY Conv. Ctr.; mem. spl. investigation Roosevelt Island Tramway Accident, 1981-82. Chmn. lawyers div. Am. Friends of Hebrew U.; mem. Lawyers Com. on the Crininal Justice Act, 1977-86, ABA, Fed. Bar, NYC Bar Assn., NY County Lawyers Assn., NY State Bar Assn., NY Coun. Def. Lawyers (dir., 1987-92); coun. mem. Am. Coll. Trial Lawyers, Internat. Acad. Trial Lawyers; trustee, NYC Sch. Constrn. Authority, 2000-03. Recipient: Torch of Learning award, Am. Friends of Hebrew U., lawyers divsn., 1984, Norman S. Ostrow award NY Coun. Def. Lawyers, 1992, Human Rels. award Anti-Defamation League, 1993, Louis Dembitz Brandeis Medal for Disting. Legal Svc., Brandeis U., 1997, Milton S. Gould award for Outstanding Advocacy, Office of Appellate Defender, 1999, Robert M. Morgenthau award Police Athletic League, 2003. Office: Stillman & Friedman PC 425 Park Ave New York NY 10022 E-mail: cstillman@stillmanfriedman.com

**STILLMAN, CORY,** professional hockey player; b. Peterborough, Ont., Can., Dec. 20, 1973; m. Mara Stillman; children: Riley, Madison, Chase. Left wing Calgary Flames, 1995—2001, St. Louis Blues, 2001—03, Tampa Bay Lightning, 2003—04, Carolina Hurricanes, 2005—. Achievements include being a member of Stanley Cup Champion Tampa Bay Lightning, 2004, Carolina Hurricanes, 2006. Office: Carolina Hurricanes RBC Ctr 1400 Edwards Mill Rd Raleigh NC 27607*

**STILLMAN, GREGORY N.,** lawyer; b. Portsmouth, Va., Apr. 29, 1948; BA, U. Richmond, 1970; JD, Washington & Lee U., 1974. Bar: Va. 1974. Mng. ptnr., litig, intellectual property, antitrust Hunton & Williams LLP, Norfolk, Va., and mem. exec. com. Contbr. The Va. Lawyer, 1980-86. Burls scholar. Fellow Am. Coll. Trial Lawyers (Va. State chmn., 1998-2000); mem. Va. Bar Assn., Fed. Bar Assn., Richmond Bar Assn., Va. Assn. Def. Attys., Norfolk-Portsmouth Bar Assn., Phi Delta Phi. Office: Hunton & Williams PO Box 3889 Crestar Bank Bldg 500 E Main St Ste 1000 Norfolk VA 23510-2204 Office Phone: 757-640-5314. Business E-Mail: gstillman@hunton.com.

**STILLMAN, JEANNE BETSOCK,** public health administrator, consultant; b. Bethlehem, Pa., Dec. 15, 1942; d. Paul Thomas and Juliana Habena Betsock; m. David George Stillman, 1965; children: J. Alexander, Gregory D., Juliana E. C. BA, Am. U., 1964; MSPH, U. N.C., 1971, postgrad., Columbia U. Sch. Pub. Health, 1979-81. Assoc. dir. Quaker Svc./AFSC, Lome, Togo, 1969-70; from instr. to lectr. health adminstrn. Sch. Pub. Health U. N.C., Chapel Hill, 1971-74, rsch. assoc. Population Ctr., 1971-74; staff assoc., Tunisia project mgr. The Population Coun., N.Y.C., 1982-83; dir. N.Y. office Inst. for Devel. Tng., N.Y.C., 1989-93; Nigeria project mgr. The Africa-Am. Inst., N.Y.C., 1993-96; prin. Strategies for Devel., Inc., Hastings-on-Hudson, NY, 1998—. Dep. dir. devel. The Children's Village, Dobbs Ferry, 2002; mem. adv. com. UN Population Fund, N.Y.C., 1998; cons. in field. Assoc. editor, contbr. International Encyclopedia of Population, 2 vols., 1982; editor: (tng. manuals) Training Course in Women's Health, 2nd edit., 11 vols., 1993; editor, writer: UNHCR Manual for Health Services in Afghan Refugee Camps, 1985; project dir.: (video) Population and People of Faith, 1991 (NY Internat. Film Festival Bronze medal 1992). Ch. coord. Habitat for Humanity, Hastings-on-Hudson, 1997—2000; vol. Internat. Microcredit Summit Meeting of Couns., NYC, 1998; bd. sec. Greater Westchester Youth Orch. Assn., Valhalla, NY, 1997-99; parent fund vol. Phillips Exeter Acad., 1998—; mem. Ch. Vestry, 2001-04; vol. Bus. Coun. of Westchester, 2002—; vol. emergency preparedness ARC, 2002-04; mem. adv. bd. youth symphony UN, 2006—. Mem. APHA, Assn. Devel. Officers (bd. dirs. 2003-06), UN Assn. USA (Westchester chpt., bd. dirs. 2006-, bd. dirs., sec. 2002—, Mid-Atlantic rep., mem. coun. of chpts. and divsns. steering com. 2005—, bd. dirs. So. N.Y. divsn. 2005-), Am. Freedom Assn. (hon. bd. dirs. 2003-). Democrat. Episcopalian. Avocations: reading, theater, music. Office: Strategies for Development Inc 166 Edgars Ln Hastings On Hudson NY 10706-1108 Office Phone: 914-478-3450. Office Fax: 914-478-7859. Business E-Mail: jbs@stratdev.com

**STILLMAN, NINA GIDDEN,** lawyer; b. N.Y.C., Apr. 3, 1948; d. Melvin and Joyce Audrey (Gidden) G. AB with distinction, Smith Coll., 1970; JD cum laude, Northwestern U., 1973. Bar: Ill. 1973, U.S. Dist. Ct. (no. dist.) Ill. 1973, U.S. Dist. Ct. (ea. dist.) Wis. 1979, U.S. Dist. Ct. (no. dist. trial bar) Ill. 1983, U.S. Ct. Appeals (7th cir.) 1974, U.S. Supreme Ct. 1981, U.S. Dist. Ct. (ctrl. dist.) Ill. 1994, U.S. Dist. Ct. (ea. dist.) Tex., 1996, U.S. Dist. Ct. (Colo.), 1999, U.S. Dist. Ct. (ND) 2002. Assoc. Vedder, Price, Kaufman & Kammholz, Chgo., 1973-79, ptnr., 1980—2004, Morgan, Lewis and Bockius, LLP, Chgo., 2004—. Adv. bd. occupational health and safety tng. program U. Mich., Ann Arbor, 1980-83; adj. faculty Inst. Human Resources and Indsl. Rels., Loyola U., Chgo., 1983-86, bd. advisors, 1986—. Author: (with others)

Women, Work, and Health: Challenge to Corporate Policy, 1979, Occupational Health Law: A Guide for Industry, 1981, Employment Discrimination, 1981, Personnel Management: Labor Relations, 1981, Occupational Safety and Health Law, 1988; contbr. author: Occupational Medicine: State of the Art Reviews, 1996; contbr. articles to profl. jours. Legal advisor, v.p. Planned Parenthood Assn. Chgo., 1979—81; sec. jr. governing bd. Chgo. Symphony Orch., 1983; trustee Merit Sch. Music, 2000—, vice chmn. bd. trustees, 2001—. Recipient Svc. award Northwestern U., 1994. Mem.: ABA (occupl. safety and health law com. 1978—), Human Resources Mgmt. Assn. Chgo. (bd. dirs. 1986—88, officer), Am. Inns of Ct. (v.p. Wigmore chpt. 1988—89), Chgo. Bar Assn. (chmn. labor and employment law com. 1986—87), Northwestern U. Sch. Law Alumni Assn. (pres. 1991—92), Univ. Club Chgo. (bd. dirs. 1988—2001, sec. 1999—2000, v.p. 2000—01), The Chgo. Com., Econ. Club Chgo., Lawyers Club, Smith Coll. Club Chgo. (pres. 1972). Avocations: travel, reading, the arts, collecting art. Office: Morgan Lewis and Bockius LLP 77 W Wacker Dr Ste 600 Chicago IL 60601 Office Phone: 312-324-1150. Business E-mail: nstillman@morganlewis.com.

**STILLS, STEPHEN,** musician, vocalist, composer; b. Dallas, Jan. 3, 1945; m. Kristen Stills; 2 children. Vocalist, guitarist Buffalo Springfield band, 1966-68, Crosby, Stills & Nash, 1968-69, 77, 82, Crosby, Stills, Nash, & Young, 1969-71, solo career, 1971—. Albums include Stephen Stills, 1970, Stephen Stills II, 1971, Stephen Stills, 1975, Illegal Stills, 1976, Thoroughfare Gap, 1978, Right by You, 1984, (with Buffalo Springfield) Buffalo Springfield, 1967, (with Buffalo Springfield) Buffalo Springfield Again, 1967, Last Time Around, 1969, (with Crosby, Stills, Nash, & Young) Deja Vu, 1970, Four Way Street, 1972, (with Crosby, Stills, Nash, Young) So Far, 1974, American Dream, 1989, (with Crosby, Stills, Nash) Crosby, stills and Nash, 1969, Crosby, Stills and Nash, 1977, Daylight Again, Live It Up, Replay (best of), After The Storm, 1994, (with Manassas) Manassasm 1972, Down The Roadm 1973; singles include (solo) Love the One You're With, 1971, Super Session, (with Buffalo Springfield) For What It's Worth, 1967, (with Crosby, Stills, Nash, & Young) Woodstock, Ohio, Teach Your Children, 1970, Stills Alone, 1991. Inducted into Rock and Roll Hall of Fame, 1997. Office: Vision Records 13385 W Dixie Hwy North Miami FL 33161-4134

**STILLWAGON, GARY BOULDIN,** radiation oncologist; b. Memphis, Dec. 30, 1951; s. Jack Wright and Ida Jean (Bouldin) S.; m. Leta Fern Miller, Jan. 20, 1979. BS in Physics, Ga. Inst. Tech., 1974, MS in Nuclear Engring., 1975, PhD, 1978; MD, U. Tenn., 1983. Diplomate Nat. Bd. Med. Examiners, Am. Bd. Radiology in Radiation Oncology; cert. FLEX, 1983. Med. physicist Meth. Hosp., Memphis, 1977, rsch. asst. Ga. Inst. Tech., Atlanta, 1975-78; radiation safety officer, physicist VA Med. Ctr., Memphis, 1978-80, cons. radiation safety, 1980-83; fellow in radiation oncology Johns Hopkins U. and Hosp., Balt., 1983-87; asst. prof. oncology and radiology Johns Hopkins U. Sch. Medicine, Balt., 1987—. Vis. rschr. radiobiology lab. U. Utah, 1978; com. mem., site visitor, radiation therapy oncology group, coop. group Nat. Cancer Inst., 1989—; cons. in field. Contbr. articles to profl. jours. Active Boy Scouts Am., Bapt. Ch. Sunday Sch. Dept. of Energy fellow, 1976-78, Clin. fellow Am. Cancer Soc., 1986-87. Fellow Am. Coll. Radiology; mem. AAAS, AMA, Health Physics Soc., Am. Assn. Physicists in Medicine, Am. Nuclear Soc., Am. Soc. Therapeutic Radiology and Oncology, Am. Soc. Clin. Oncology, Sigma Xi. Republican. Home: 655 River Chase Rd NW Atlanta GA 30328-3568 Office: 1000 Johnson Ferry Rd Atlanta GA 30342

**STILLWELL, ARLENE M.,** psychologist, educator; d. Frederick A. and Elizabeth R. Stillwell; m. John F. Tenbusch, June 5, 1993. BA, Baldwin Wallace Coll., Berea, Ohio; PhD, Case Western Res. U., Cleve., 1993. Asst. prof. of psychology SUNY, Potsdam, NY, 1993—99, assoc. prof. of psychology, 1999—. Recipient President's Award for Acad. Advising, SUNY Coll. at Potsdam, 2004. Mem.: Soc. for Personality and Social Psychology, APA, Omicron Delta Kappa, Phi Kappa Phi, Psi Chi (faculty advisor 1997—2006). Roman Catholic. Avocations: cross country skiing, hiking. Office: SUNY College at Potsdam 44 Pierrepont Ave Potsdam NY 13676 Office Phone: 315-267-4808. E-mail: stillwam@potsdam.edu.

**STILLWELL, R. NEWCOMB,** lawyer; b. Oct. 2, 1956; AB magna cum laude, Princeton Univ., 1979; JD cum laude, Harvard Univ., 1984. Bar: Mass. 1984. Assoc. Ropes & Gray, Boston, 1984—93, ptnr. corp. dept., 1993—, co-leader private equity practice group. Lectr. Harvard Law Sch. Former bd. dir. Hotchkiss Sch.; bd. dir. Volunteers of Am. of Mass. Office: Ropes & Gray 1 International Pl Boston MA 02110-2624 Office Phone: 617-951-7316. Office     Fax:     617-951-7050.     Business     E-Mail: newcomb.stillwell@ropesgray.com.

**STILLWELL, WALTER BROOKS, III,** lawyer; b. Whitehall, Wis., July 30, 1946; s. Walter Brooks Jr. and Selpha T. (Everson) S.; m. Carolyn E. Laws, Dec. 20, 1992; children: Walter, Haviland. BA cum laude, Wake Forest U., 1968; JD, U. Ga., 1971. Bar: Ga. 1971, U.S. Dist. Ct. (so. dist.) Ga. 1971, U.S. Ct. Appeals (D.C. cir.) 1976, U.S. Ct. Appeals (11th cir.) 1981, U.S. Dist. Ct. (no. dist. 1996) Ga., U.S. Supreme Ct., 1977. Assoc. Hunter, Maclean, Exley & Dunn, P.C., Savannah, Ga., 1971-74, ptnr., 1974—; dir. First Nat. Bank, 2002—. Trustee Savannah Tech. Coll. Found., 2002-; adv. dir. Century South Bank of Coastal Region, N.A., 1993-2001; v.p. and dir. W.E.T., Inc., 1991-96; adv. coun. Savannah (Ga.) Econ. Devel. Authority, 2004—. Alderman City of Savannah, 1974-92, mayor-pro-tem, 1990-92; chmn. Chatham County Bd. Elections, 1999-2002. Mem. State Bar of Ga. (real property sect., exec. com. 1986-93, chmn. 1992), Am. Coll. Real Estate Lawyers, Savannah Bar Assn. (pres. 1999-2000). Office: Hunter Maclean Exley & Dunn PC 200 E Saint Julian St Savannah GA 31401-2700

**STIMAC, JOHN ANTHONY,** small business owner, poet, cartoonist, inventor; b. Kansas City, Kans., Nov. 12, 1946; s. Max George and Lola Mae Stimac; m. Sherry Lynn Stimac, Apr. 30, 1965 (dec. Sept. 24, 2005); children: Mary Ann, John Anthony, Christopher John. Union painter Local 43, Leavenworth, Kans., 1973—79; owner Heritage Painting Co., Kansas City, Kans., 1979—85, J-Duncan's Painting Co., Kingsville, Mo., 1985—2001, John Stimac Painting Co., Kingsville, 2001—. Cartoons, Highlights for Children, 1983; contbr. poems to books and jours. With U.S. Army, 1963—65. Recipient Editors Choice awards, Internat. Libr. of Poetry, 2001—02. Mem.: Soc. of Poets (Lifetime Mem. award). Achievements include invention of inventive systems minor images. Avocations: guitar, instrumental music. Home and Office: 13 NW 1621 Rd Kingsville MO 64061 Office Phone: 816-682-5075.

**STIMMEL, BARRY,** cardiologist, educator, internist, dean; b. Bklyn., Oct. 8, 1939; s. Abraham and Mabel (Bovit) S.; m. Barbara Barovick, June 6, 1970; children: Alexander, Matthew. BS, Bklyn. Coll., 1960; MD, SUNY, Bklyn., 1964. Diplomate: Nat. Bd. Med. Examiners, Am. Bd. Internal Medicine. Resident Mt. Sinai Hosp., N.Y.C., 1964-65, 67-69; asst. dean admissions and student affairs Mt. Sinai Sch. Medicine, CUNY, 1970-71, assoc. dean, 1971-81, asst. prof. medicine, 1972-75, assoc. prof., 1975-83, prof. medicine and med. edn., 1984—, assoc. dean acad. affairs, 1975-81, assoc. attending physician, 1975-83, acting chmn. dept. med. edn., 1979-94, dean admissions, acad. affairs and student affairs, 1981-94, dean grad. med. edn., 1994—, attending physician, 1984—, Katherine and Clifford Goldsmith prof. medicine (cardiology), 1998—. Mem. com. planning, priorities and evaluation N.Y. Met. Regional Med. Program, 1971-73; adv. com. Nat. Ctr. Urban Problems CUNY, 1970-71; adv. com. methadone maintenance Office of Drug Abuse Svcs. State N.Y., 1976-79; sci. adv. bd. Nat. Coun. Drug Abuse, 1978-84, N.Y. State Bd. Profl. Med. Conduct, 1983-97; bd. dirs. Am. Soc. Addiction Medicine, N.Y. State Coun. on Grad. Med. Edn., Greater N.Y. Hosp. Assn. Task Force on Health Manpower. Author: Heroin Dependency: Medical Social and Economic Aspects, 1975, Cardiovascular Effects Mood Altering Drugs, 1979, Pain, Analgesia, Addiction, 1984, Ambulatory Care, 1983, The Facts about Drug Use, 1993, Drugs Abuse and Social Policy in America: The War That Must Be Won, 1996, Pain and Its Relief Without Addiction, 1997, Alcoholism, Drug Addiction and the Road to Recovery: Life on the Edge, 2002; editor Advances in Alcohol and Substance Abuse, 1980-91, Jour. Addictive Diseases, 1991—; assoc. editor Am. Jour. Drug and

Alcohol Abuse, 1979-85; contbr. chpts. to books, articles to profl. jours. With M.C. USNR, 1965—67. Mem. AAUP, Am. Assn. Physicians Assts. (adv. bd. 1972-73), Am. Assn. Higher Edn., Soc. Study of Addiction to Alcohol and Other Drugs, Assn. Med. Edn. and Rsch. Substance Abuse, Inst. Study of Drug Addiction, Am., N.Y. heart assns., Am., N.Y. State socs. internal medicine, Soc. Internal Medicine County of N.Y. (dir.), Am. Coll. Cardiology, Greater N.Y. Coalition on Drug Abuse, NYS Coun. on Grad. Medical Edn. N.Y. Acad. Medicine, Nat. Coun. Alcoholism, Rsch. Soc. on Alcoholism, Am. Ednl. Research Assn., Am. Fedn. Clin. Rsch., Am. Soc. Addiction Medicine. Office: Mt Sinai Sch Med 5 E 98th St Fl 3 New York NY 10029-6501 Office Phone: 212-241-6694. E-mail: barry.stimmel@mssm.edu.

**STIMPERT, MICHAEL ALAN,** agricultural products company executive; b. Madisonville, La., Aug. 21, 1944; s. Warren Eugene and Louisa (Beale) S.; m. Kim Kathleen Agee, Apr. 17, 1970 (div. 1985); 1 child, Kelly Kathleen; m. Helen Marie Evans, June 27, 1987; children: Katherine Helen, Michael Adam. Student, Washburn U., 1962-64, U. Copenhagen, 1964; BA, Western Res. U., 1967; MBA, Harvard U., 1974. Asst. to group v.p. Gold Kist Inc., Atlanta, 1974, mgr. internat. div., 1975-80, dir. spl. markets and staff services, 1980-81, group v.p., 1982-86; v.p. ops. and govt. affairs Golden Peanut Co., Atlanta, 1986-89, exec. v.p., 1989-95; sr. v.p. Gold Kist Inc., Atlanta, 1996—. Chmn. bd. dirs. Sunpower, Inc., Athens, Ohio, G.C. Properties, Atlanta, Luker Engring. Inc., Augusta, Ga., GKX Inc., Agana, Guam, Fundatropicos, Turrialba, Costa Rica; immediate past chmn. Global Health Action, Atlanta; chmn. Agra Trade Financing, Inc., Atlanta. Bd. dirs. Global Health Action, Tropics Found., Atlanta. Lt. (j.g.) USN, 1967-72, Vietnam. Mem. Assn. for Corp. Growth, Japan-Am. Soc. Ga., Harvard Bus. Sch. Club Atlanta, Cherokee Town and Country Club. Democrat. Roman Catholic. Office: Gold Kist Inc 244 Perimeter Center Pkwy NE Atlanta GA 30346-2397

**STIMPSON, CATHARINE ROSALIND,** literature educator, writer; b. Bellingham, Wash., June 4, 1936; d. Edward Keown and Catharine (Watts) Stimpson. AB, Bryn Mawr Coll., 1958; BA, MA, Cambridge U., Eng., 1960; PhD, Columbia U., 1967. Mem. faculty Barnard Coll., N.Y.C., 1963—80; prof. English, dean of grad. sch., vice provost grad. edn. Rutgers U., New Brunswick, NJ, 1980—92, univ. prof., 1991—; chmn. bd. scholars Ms. Mag., N.Y.C., 1981—92; dir. fellows program MacArthur Found., 1994—97; univ. prof., dean Grad. Sch. Arts and Sci. NYU, N.Y.C., 1998—. Author: Class Notes, 1979, Where the Meanings Are, 1988; editor: Signs: Jour. Women in Culture and Soc., 1974—81, Women in Culture and Society book series, 1981; contbr. Change Mag., 1992—93. Chmn. N.Y. Coun. Humanites, 1984—87, Nat. Coun. Rsch. on Women, 1984—89; trustee Bates Coll., 1990—; pres. Assn. Grad. Schs., 2000—01; bd. dir. Stephens Coll., Columbia, Mo., 1982—85, Legal Def. and Edn. Fund, 1991—96. Fellow, Woodrow Wilson Found., 1958, Nat. Humanities Inst., 1975—76; Fulbright fellow, 1958—60, Rockefeller Humanities fellow, 1983—84. Mem.: PBS (bd. dirs. 1994—2000), NOW, PEN, MLA (exec. coun., chmn. acad. freedom com., 1st v.p., pres. 1990). Democrat. Home: 29 Washington Sq W Apt 15C New York NY 10011-9199 Office: NYU 6 Washington Sq N New York NY 10003-6668 Office Phone: 212-998-8040. Business E-Mail: catharine.stimpson@nyu.edu.

**STIMPSON, SCOTT DAVID,** lawyer; b. Presque Isle, Maine, Apr. 16, 1964; s. Don Dillen and Rita Mary Stimpson; m. Lori Ann Hutchinson, Aug. 5, 1989; children: Don Robert, Tyler Gregory, Dillon Scott. BS in Mech. Engring. with distinction, U. Maine, 1986; JD, Wash. and Lee U., Lexington, Va., 1989. Registered: U.S. Patent and Trademark Office (patent attorney). Ptnr. Pennie & Edmonds LLP, N.Y.C., 1989—2003; atty. - ptnr. Morgan, Lewis & Bockius LLP, 2004—. Spkr. in field of intellectual property patent litigation. Contbr. articles to profl. jours. Recipient Maine Alumni mag. profile, A Patent for Success-N.Y.C. Atty., Scott D. Stimpson '86, a rising star in IP Law, 2003. Mem.: ATLA, ABA, N.Y. Intellectual Property Law Assn. Methodist. Avocations: Karate, baseball, golf. Home: 3051 Morehouse Hwy Fairfield CT 06824 Office: Morgan Lewis and Bockius LLP 101 Park Ave New York NY 10178 Office Phone: 212-309-6628. Business E-Mail: sstimpson@morganlewis.com.

**STINE, JOHN ANDREW,** communications engineer, researcher; b. Miami, Fla., Oct. 4, 1959; s. Carl William and Mary Biggers Stine; m. Martha Byrd Byrd, Apr. 13, 1985; children: Andrew Joseph, Harry James, Brian Edward, Mary Elizabeth, Bridget Anne, Christopher William. BS in Gen. Engring., U.S. Mil. Acad., West Point, N.Y., 1981; MSEE, U. Tex., Austin, 1990, MS in Mfg. Sys., 1990, PhD in Elec. Engring., 2001. Registered profl. engr., Va., 1992. Commd. 2d lt. U.S. Army, 1982, advanced through grades to maj., 1981, platoon leader A Co. 10th engr. bn. 3rd inf. div. Schweinfurt, Germany, 1982—83, exec. officer A Co. 10th engr. bn. 3rd inf. div., 1983—85, brigade engr. 2d brigade, 2d armored div. Ft. Hood, Tex., 1985—86, comdr. C Co. 17th engring. bn. 2d armored div., 1986—87, asst. divsn. engr. 2d armored div., 1987—88, operation rsch. sys. analyst test and experimentation command, 1993—96; constrm. mgr. Def. Spl. Weapons Agy. (now Def. Threat Reduction Agy.), Kirtland AFB, N.Mex., 1997—2001; asst. prof. elec. engring. U.S. Mil. Acad., West Point, NY, 1990—93; comm. engr. MITRE Corp., McLean, Va., 2001—04, prin. investigator in advanced tactical networking, 2004—. Contbr. articles to profl. jours. Decorated Army Commendation medal 3rd inf. divsn. U.S. Mil. Acad., Army Meritorious Svc. medal 2d armored divsn., Army Commendation medal U.S. Army Test and Experimentation Command, Army Meritorious Svc. medal, Def. Meritorious Svc. medal Def. Threat Reduction Agy.; recipient Best Dept. Rsch. award, U.S. Mil. Acad., 1993. Mem.: IEEE Comm. Soc. Roman Catholic. Achievements include patents pending for. Office: MITRE Corp 7515 Colshire Dr Mc Lean VA 22102 Office Phone: 703-983-6281. Office Fax: 703-983-1370. Personal E-mail: stine@ieee.org. Business E-mail: jstine@mitre.org.

**STINE, KATIE KRATZ,** state legislator; b. Dec. 6, 1956; BS, U. Cin.; JD, No. Ky. U. Atty.; mem. Ky. Ho. of Reps., Frankfort, 1995-98; senate pres. pro-tempore Ky. Senate, Frankfort, 1999—, mem. judiciary com. com. rules. Active Jr. League Cin., Episcopal Ch. Women, No. Ky. Right to Life; former vice chair Ft. Thomas Bd. Adjustments. Mem. DAR, Ky. Bar Assn., Ft. Thomas Garden Club. Republican. Office: Ky Senate 24th Dist 702 Capitol Ave Rm 204 Frankfort KY 40601-3448 Home: 21 Fairway Dr Southgate KY 41071-3023

**STINE, RICK D.,** editor; B in Journalism, English and Mathematics, U. of Richmond. Joined Dow Jones & Co., 1983, reporter Dow Jones Capital Markets Report, writer Dow Jones cable television dept.; news editor Dow Jones News Svc., 1989—95, asst. mng. editor, 1995—97, deputy mng. editor, 1997—99, mng. editor Jersey City, 1999—. Office: Dow Jones News Svc Harborside Fin Ctr 800 Plaza Two Jersey City NJ 07311-1199*

**STINE, ROBERT HOWARD,** retired pediatrician, allergist; b. Nov. 1, 1929; s. Harry Raymond and Mabel Eva (Newhard) S.; m. Lois Elaine Kihlgren, Oct. 22, 1960; children: Robert E., Karen E. Burnham, Jonathan N. BS in Biology, Moravian Coll., 1952. Diplomate in pediatrics and in pediatric allergy Am. Bd. Pediatrics, Bd. Allergy and Immunology. Intern St. Luke's Hosp., Bethlehem, Pa., 1960-61, resident in surgery, 1961-62; physician Jefferson Med. Coll., Phila., 1956-60; resident in pediatrics U. N.Y., Syracuse, 1962-64; resident in allergy Robert A. Cooke Inst. Allergy Roosevelt Hosp., N.Y.C., 1964-65; clin. instr. pediatrics U. Ill., Chgo., 1965-71; mem. courtesy staff Proctor Community Hosp., Peoria, Ill., 1966-77, mem. active staff, 1977—, chmn. dept. medicine, 1988—89; pres. elect. med. staff, 1990-91; pres. med. staff, 1991-92; mem. teaching staff St. Francis Hosp., Peoria, 1969—2002; clin. instr. pediatrics Rush-Presbyn. St. Luke's Hosp., Chgo., 1971—2002; ret. Vol. Heartland Cmty. Health Clinic, Peoria, Ill., 2002—04. Lt. (j.g.) USN, 1953—56. Fellow Am. Acad. Pediatrics (emeritus). Am. Acad. Allergy Asthma and Immunology, Am. Coll. Allergy and Asthma, Am. Assn. Cert. Allergists Am. Coll. Chest Physicians (emeritus); mem. Ill. Soc. Allergy and Clin. Immunology, Peoria Med. Soc. (pres.-elect 1993, pres. 1994), Christian Med. and Dental Soc. Home: 105 Hollands Grove Ln Washington IL 61571-9623

**STINE, R(OBERT) L(AWRENCE),** children's book author; b. Columbus, Ohio, Oct. 8, 1943; s. Lewis and Anne (Feinstein) S.; m. Jane Waldhorn, June 22, 1969. BA, Ohio State U., 1965. Assoc. editor Jr. Scholastic, N.Y.C., 1969-71; editor Search, N.Y.C., 1972-75, Barnas, N.Y.C., 1972-83, Maniac, N.Y.C., 1984-85. Author: The Time Raider, 1982, The Golden Sword of Dragonwalk, 1983, Horrors of the Haunted Musuem, 1984, Instant Millionaire, 1984, Through the Forest of Twisted Dreams, 1984, Indiana Jones and the Curse of Horror Island, 1984, Indiana Jones and the Giants of the Silver Tower, 1984, Indiana Jones and the Cult of the Mummy's Crypt, 1985, The Badlands of Hark, 1985, The Invaders of Hark, 1985, Demons of the Deep, 1985, Challenge of the Wolf Knight, 1985, Conquest of the Time Master, 1985, Cavern of the Phantoms, 1986, Operation: Deadly Decoy, 1986, Mystery of the Imposter, 1986, Blind Date, 1986, Twisted, 1986, The Baby-Sitter, 1989, Phone Calls, 1990, Curtains, 1991, Broken Date, 1991, Baby-Sitter II, 1991, Beach House, 1992, Dead Girlfriend, 1993, Halloween Night, 1993, Hitchhiker, 1993, Be Careful What You Wish For, 1993, Baby-Sitter III, 1993, Call Waiting, 1994, The Beast, 1994; (series) Fear Street, Fear Street Super Chiller, Fear Street Saga, Fear Street Cheerleaders, Ninety-Nine Fear Street: The House of Evil, Thrillers, Space Cadets, Goose Bumps; (as Jovial Bob Stine) The Absurdly Silly Encyclopaedia and Flyswater, 1978, How to Be Funny: An Extremely Silly Guidebook, 1978, The Complete Book of Nerds, 1979, The Dynamite Do-It-Yourself Pen Pal Kit, 1980, Dynamite's Funny Book of the Sad Facts of Life, 1980, Going out! Going Steady! Going Bananas!, 1980, The Pigs' Book of World Records, 1980, The Sick of Being Sick Book, 1980, Bananas Look at TV, 1981, The Beast Handbook, 1981, The Cool Kids' Guide to Summer Camp, 1981, Ghastly Gnomes, 1981, Don't Stand in the Soup, 1982, Bored with Being Bored!: How to Beat the Boredom Blahs, 1982, Blips! The First Book of Video Game Funnies, 1983, Everything You Need to Survive: Brothers and Sisters, 1983, Everything You Need to Survive: First Dates, 1983, Everything You Need to Survive: Homework, 1983, Everything You Need to Survive: Money Problems, 1983, Jovial Bob's Computer Joke Book, 1985, Miami Mice, 1986, One Hundred and One Silly Monster Jokes, 1986, The Doggons Dog Joke Book, 1986, Mostly Ghostly: Who Let the Ghosts Out?, 2004; (as Eric Affabee) G.I. Joe and the Everglades Swamp Terror, 1986, Attack of the King, 1986; (as Zachary Blue) The Petrova Twist, 1987, The Jet Fighter Trap, 1987.

**STINEHART, ROGER RAY,** lawyer; b. Toledo, Jan. 27, 1945; s. Forrest William and Nettie May (Twyman) S.; m. Martha Jean Goodnight, Sept. 19, 1970; children: Amanda Jean, Brian Scott. BS, Bowling Green State U., Ohio, 1968; JD, Ohio State U., 1972. Bar: Ohio 1972. Fin. analyst Gen. Electric, Detroit, 1968-69; assoc. Gingher & Christensen, Columbus, Ohio, 1972-76, ptnr., 1976-80; sr. v.p., gen. counsel, sec. G.D. Ritzy's, Inc., Columbus, 1983-85; ptnr. Jones, Day, Reavis & Pogue, Columbus, 1980-83, 85—. Adj. prof. law Capital U., Columbus, 1976-79; mem. adv. com. Ohio securities divsn. Dept. Commerce, Columbus, 1979—; fellow Columbus Bar Found., 1992—; adv. bd. The Entrepreneurship Inst., 1992-95. Contbr. Ohio State U. Coll. Law Jour., 1970-72. Gen. counsel, trustee Internat. Assn. Rsch. on Leukemia and Related Diseases, 1975—; v.p., trustee Hospice of Columbus, 1978-80; trustee Cen. Ohio chpt. Leukemia Soc. of Am., Columbus, 1983-93, v.p., 1985-87; trustee Ohio Cancer Rsch. Assocs., Columbus, 1983—, v.p., 1990—; dir. Rotary Internat., Columbus Chapter, 2004-, v.p., 2005-; chmn. Social Com., 2001-03, Internat. Com., 2003-04, Adopt-a-School Com., 2003-04, Dist. 6690, 2005-. With USMCR, 1963-68. Mem. ABA (bus. law com., franchise law com.), Ohio State Bar Assn. (corp. law com., franchise law com.), Columbus Bar Assn. (securities law com., chmn. 1981-83, bus. law com., franchise law com.), Sigma Tau Delta, Beta Gamma Sigma. Home: 2155 Waltham Rd Columbus OH 43221-4149 Office: Jones Day Reavis & Pogue 1900 Huntington Ctr Columbus OH 43215-6103

**STINEHART, WILLIAM, JR.,** retired lawyer; b. LA, Dec. 15, 1943; s. William Sr. and Martha T. S.; m. Patricia Kidney, June 22, 1968; children: Jacqueline Elaine, William III. BA with distinction, Stanford U., 1966; LLB, UCLA, 1969. Bar: Calif. 1970, US Dist. Ct. (cen. dist.) Calif. 1970. Assoc. Gibson, Dunn & Crutcher LLP, LA, 1969-76, ptnr. tax dept., 1977—; ret. 2005. Bd. dir. Tribune Co. Trustee Harvard Westlake Sch., N. Hollywood, 1983-89, SW Mus., 1986-89. Mem. LA County Bar Assn., Order of Coif, LA Country Club, Beach Club of Santa Monica, Calif., LA Tennis Club. Republican. Episcopalian. Office: Gibson Dunn & Crutcher LLP 2029 Century Pk E Los Angeles CA 90067-3026 Office Phone: 310-552-8557. Office Fax: 310-552-7027. Business E-Mail: wstinehart@gbsondunn.com.

**STINES, BETTY IRENE PARHAM,** artist; b. Stinesville, Ind., May 3, 1918; d. Claude Everett Parham and Helen Bryan Acuff Parham; m. Willard Russell Elliott, Oct. 11, 1936 (dec. Aug. 1969); children: Jerry Lee Elliott, Gillespie-Kathy Lyn Elliott Holtsclaw, Willard Keith Elliott; m. Edmond Glen Stines, Feb. 19, 1972. Grad. high sch., Bloomington, Ind. Organizer, mem. Hoosier Hills Art Guild, Bloomington, Ind., 1963—80; organizer Hoosier Hills Art Guild Ann. Student Art Exhibit, 1963—73; floral designer Unique Florist Shoppe, Ellettsville, Ind., 1963—69; hon. dir. Internat. Biog. Ctr., Cambridge, England. Oil and water color paintings, 1950—2001, exhibited in group shows at Ind. U., Manchester Coll., Swope Art Gallery, Terre Haute, Ind., Hoosier Hills Art Gallery, Bloomington, Ind., Owen County Art Gallery, Spencer, Ind., Represented in permanent collections, exhibited in group shows at Ind. State House Art Salon. Chmn., co-chair art exhibits Monroe County Festival, Ellettsville, Ind., 1950—60; Sunday sch. tchr. Gave Chalk Talks Bapt. Ch., 1950; leader Brownie Scouts, 1943—47. Recipient numerous First, Best in Show and Champion Exhibitor awards. Mem.: Ind. Women in Arts, Nat. Mus. Women in Arts. Baptist. Avocations: genealogy, antiques. Home: 7935 W Ratliff Rd Bloomington IN 47404-9685

**STINES, FRED, JR.,** publisher; b. Newton, Iowa, Mar. 16, 1925; s. Fred and Nella (Haun) S.; m. Dorothy G. McClanahan, Sept. 5, 1953 (dec.); children: Steven, Scott, Ann; m. Mary K. Devin, Sept. 12, 1989. B.C.S., U. Iowa, 1949. With Meredith Corp., Des Moines, 1949-90, sales promotion and mdse. mgr. 1955-63, advt. dir., 1963-66, pub., 1966-73, pub. dir. mag. div., 1973-76, v.p. gen. mgr. books and newspapers, 1976-83, sr. v.p., 1983-87, pres. book pub., 1986-90, corp. v.p. spl. projects, 1988-90; pres., prin. Concepts in Mktg., 1990—. Cert. instr. Dale Carnegie courses, 1958-63. Bd. dirs. Des Moines Ballet Assn., North Am. Outdoor Group, Mpls., 1992-95; bd. dirs., v.p. Jr. Achievement of Ctrl. Iowa. Served with AUS, 1946-49. Named Farm Marketing Man of Year, 1972 Mem. Future Farmers Am. Found. (nat. chmn. 1971), Rotary Internat., Des Moines Golf and Country Club, Phi Gamma Delta (sect. chief 1983, nat. bd. dirs. 1985-89), Alpha Kappa Psi, Alpha Delta Sigma. Clubs: Des Moines Golf and Country (dir., pres. 1981, pres. Ednl. Found.). Home: Concepts in Mktg 680 58th Pl West Des Moines IA 50266-6007

**STING, (GORDON MATTHEW SUMNER),** musician, songwriter, actor; b. Newcastle Upon Tyne, Eng., Oct. 2, 1951; s. Ernest Matthew and Audrey (Cowell) Sumner; m. Frances Eleanor Tomelty, May 1, 1976 (div. Mar. 1984); children: Joseph, Fuschia Katherine; m. Trudie Styler, Aug. 22, 1992; children: Brigette, Michael, Jake, Eliot, Paulina, Giacomo Luke. Grad., Warwick U., Coventry, Eng.; doctorate (hon.), Northumbria U., 1992; degree (hon.), Berklee Coll. Music, Boston, 1994. Schoolmaster, Newcastle Upon Tyne, Eng., 1975-77; songwriter, singer, bass player with rock group The Police, 1977-86; mng. dir. Kaliedescope Cameras, London, from 1982; singer, songwriter, 1986—. Albums (with The Police) Outlandos D'Amour, 1978, Reggatta De Blanc, 1979, Zenyatta Mondatta, 1980, Ghost in the Machine, 1981, Synchronicity, 1983, singles Every Breath You Take, 1986; appearance: (Broadway plays) Three Penny Opera, 1989; solo (albums) The Dream of the Blue Turtles, 1985, Bring On The Night, 1986, Nothing Like the Sun, 1987, The Soul Cages, 1991, Ten Summoner's Tales, 1993 (Grammy award, Best Long Form Music Video, 1994), Demolition Man, soundtrack, 1993, Mercury Falling, 1996, Brand New Day, 1999, Sacred Love, 2003 (Grammy award, Best Pop Collaboration With Vocals for song "Whenever I Say Your Name" with Mary J. Blige, 2003), appeared (films) Quadrophenia, 1979, The Secret Policeman's Other Ball, 1981, Brimstone and Treacle, 1982, Dune, The Bride, Plenty, 1985, Julia and Julia, 1987, Stormy Monday, 1988,

Resident Alien, 1990, The Grotesque, 1995, Lock, Stock and Two Smoking Barrels, 1998, voice artist (TV series) Captain Planet and the Planeteers, 1990—92, rec. soundtracks (films) Brimstone and Treacle, Party, Party, The Secret Policeman's Other Ball, 1982, The Emperor's New Groove, 2000. Recipient 15 Grammy awards with The Police and as solo artist, 13 BMI awards, 4 Brit awards, Downbeat mag. Readers' Poll Pop/Rock Musician of Yr. award, 1989, Downbeat mag. Readers' Poll Pop/Rock group award, 1989, Internat. Rock award for Video Legend, 1991, Star on the Hollywood Walk of Fame, 2000, Golden Globe award Kate and Leopold, 2001. Mem.: Rainforest Found. (co-founder), Amnesty Internat., Performing Rights Soc. also: Firstars 3520 Hayden Ave Culver City CA 90232-2413 also: A & M Records Inc 70 Universal City Plz Universal City CA 91608-1011 Office: KSM 826 Broadway Fl 4 New York NY 10003-4826

**STINGEL, RUDOLF,** artist; b. Merano, Italy, 1957; One-man shows include pittura austriae - Positionen aus Osterreich I/III, Galerie Elisabeth & Klaus Thoman, Innsbruck, 2000, Monochrome/Monochrome?, Florence Lynch Gallery, NYC, 2001, Stanze, Museo d'arte moderna e contemporanea, 2001, Collector's Choice, Neue Galerie Graz am Landesmuseum Joanneum, 2002, Penetration, Friedrich Petzel Gallery, NYC, 2002, Marianne Boesky Gallery, NYC, 2002, ReProdukton - Gruppenausstellung, Galerie Bernhard Knaus, Mannheim, 2002, International Landscape, Galerie Rodolphe Janssen, Brussels, 2002, Dreams and Conflicts: The Dictatorship of the Viewer, La Biennale di Venezia, Venice, 2003, Walk Ways, U. South Fla. Contemporary Art Mus., 2003, Invite - Silver Convention, Galerie Giti Nourbakhsch, Berlin, 2003, Ruina - Aesthetic of Destruction, Galeria Helga de Alvear, Madrid, 2004, Miradas y conceptos en la Coleccion Helga de Alvear, 2005, Home Depot, Museum fur Moderne Kunst, Frankfurt, 2004, Art Underfoot - Carpeting the Walker Entry, Walker Art Ctr., Mpls., 2004, Sadie Coles HQ, London, 2004, None of the Above, Si Swiss Inst., NYC, 2004, Singular Forms (Sometimes Repeated): Art from 1951 to the Present, Solomon R Museum, NY, 2004, Power, Corruption and Lies, Roth Horowitz, NYC, 2004, Museum fur Kunst, Frankfurt, 2004, Galleria Massimo de Carlo, Milan, 2004, EURAC tower, Bolzano, Italy, 2005, MART, Roverto, Italy, 2005, Hayward Gallery, London, 2005, Universal Experience: Art, Life, and the Tourist's Eye, Mus. Contemporary Art, 2005, The Red Thread, Howard House Contemporary, Seattle, 2005, exhibited in group shows at Examining Pictures, Mus. Contemporary Art Chgo., 1999, GOOD TIMING, Georg Kargl Fine Arts, Vienna, 2005, Whitney Biennial: Day for Night, Whitney Mus. Am. Art, NYC, 2006.*

**STINGER, FANCHON,** newscaster; d. Edward and Zelma Stinger; m. Tony Camilleri. BA in English and Commn., U. Mich., 1993. Reporter WJBK-TV, Detroit, 1997—, editor and co-anchor 5:30pm news, 2000—. Recipient 5 Emmy awards, NATAS, 1998—, Best Reporter award, AP-Mich., 2000, Insp. Gen.'s Integrity award, U.S. Dept. HHS, 2002. Office: WJBK-TV Fox 2 PO Box 2000 Southfield MI 48037-2000

**STINI, WILLIAM ARTHUR,** anthropologist, educator; b. Oshkosh, Wis., Oct. 9, 1930; s. Louis Alois and Clara (Larsen) S.; m. Mary Ruth Kalous, Feb. 11, 1950; children: Patricia Laraine, Paulette Ann, Suzanne Kay. BBA, U. Wis., 1960, MS, 1967, PhD, 1969. Planner cost acct. Kimberly-Clark Corp., Niagara Falls, NY, 1960-62; from asst. prof. to assoc. prof. Cornell U., Ithaca, NY, 1968-73; assoc. prof. U. Kans., Lawrence, 1973-76; prof. anthropology U. Ariz., Tucson, 1976—, prof. family and cmty. medicine, 1978—; panelist anthropology program NSF, 1976-78; cons. NIH, 1974—. Mem. Ariz. Cancer Ctr., 1995—; adj. prof. Nutritional Scis., 1997—; head dept. anthropology U. Ariz., 1980-89, prof. pub. health, 1998—; panelist NRC/NSF Grad. Fellowship Program, 1991-95. Author: Ecology and Human Adaptation, 1975, Nature, Culture and Human History - A Biocultural Introduction to Anthropology (with Davydd J. Greenwood), 1977, Physiological and Morphological Adaptation and Evolution, 1979 (with Frank E. Poirier and Kathy B. Wreden) In Search of Ourselves: An Introduction to Physical Anthropology, 1990, 5th edit., 1994; field editor phys. anthropology The Am. Anthropologist, 1980-83; editor-in-chief Am. Jour. Phys. Anthropology, 1983-89; assoc. editor Nutrition and Cancer, 1981-95; cons. editor Collegium Antropologicum, 1985—. Mem. Gov.'s Adv. Coun. on Aging, State of Ariz., 1980—83. Nat. Inst. Dental Rsch. tng. grantee, 1964-68; Clark Found. grantee Cornell U., 1973; Nat. Dairy Coun. grantee, 1985-88; Wenner-Gren Found. grantee, 1991—; fellow Linacre Coll., Oxford, 1985; vis. fellow U. London, 1991. Fellow AAAS (steering group sect. H 1987-91), Am. Anthrop. Assn., N.Y. Acad. Scis.; mem. Am. Assn. Phys. Anthropologists (exec. com. 1978-81, pres. 1989-91), Human Biology Assn. (exec. com. 1978-81), Soc. for Study Social Biology, Am. Soc. Nutritional Scis., Am. Soc. on Aging, Sigma Xi. Home: 6240 N Camino Miraval Tucson AZ 85718-3025 Business E-Mail: stini@u.arizona.edu.

**STINNETT, HESTER ANN,** artist, educator, art school administrator; b. Phila., June 29, 1956; s. Bernard J. and Hester E. (Durrett) S. BFA, Hartford Art Sch., 1978; MFA, Tyler Sch. Art, Phila., 1982. Lectr. U. of Arts, Phila., 1982-85, Bryn Mawr (Pa.) Coll., 1985-86; asst. prof. Tyler Sch. Art Temple U., Phila., 1986—; assoc. dean Tyler Sch. Art, Phila., 1992—. Vis. artist Pa. Acad. Fine Arts, Phila. 1984-85. Author: Water-Base Screenprinting, 1988; exhibited in group show Dolan/Maxwell Gallery, 1988; prodr. Electrical Matter, 1989-92; dir. Contemporary Viewpoints, 1987-89. Office: Office of the Dean Tyler Sch Arts Temple U 7725 Penrose Ave Elkins Park PA 19027 Office Phone: 215-782-2715. Fax: 215-782-2799. E-mail: hester.stinnett@temple.edu.

**STINNETT, J. DANIEL,** lawyer; b. 1945; BA, Vanderbilt U., 1967; JD, U. Mo., 1972. Bar Mo. 1972. Assoc. counsel Commerce Bank, Kans. City, Mo., 1975—78; v.p., dep. gen. counsel, asst. sec. Commerce Bancshares, Inc., Kans. City, Mo., 1978—95; sec. Commerce Bank 1978—95; sec. gen. counsel Commerce Bancshares, Inc., 1996—; sr. v.p. Commerce Bank, 1996—, gen. counsel.

**STINNETT, TERRANCE LLOYD,** lawyer; b. Oakland, Calif., July 22, 1940; s. Lloyd Monroe and Gertrude (Hyman) S. BS, Stanford U., 1962; JD magna cum laude, U. Santa Clara, 1969. Bar: Calif. 1970, U.S. Dist. Ct. (no. dist.) Calif. 1970, U.S. Dist. Ct. (ea. ctrl. and so. dists.) Calif. 1975, U.S. Ct. Appeals (9th cir.) 1970, U.S. Supreme Ct. 1975. Law clk. to judge Calif. Ct. Appeals, San Francisco, 1969-70; assoc. Hyman, Rhodes & Aylward, Fremont, Calif., 1970-71, Glicksberg, Kushner & Goldberg, San Francisco, 1972-77; mem. Goldberg, Stinnett Meyers & Davis, San Francisco, 1977—. Bd. dirs. Fremont Bancorp, Fremont Bank, vice-chmn. bd., 1998-2000. Mem. ABA, Calif. State Bar Assn., Bar Assn. San Francisco (chmn. bench bar liaison com. for U.S. Bankruptcy Ct., No. Dist. of Calif. 1997). Republican. Roman Catholic. Home: 131 Alamo Hills Ct Alamo CA 94507-2243 Office: Goldberg Stinnett Meyers & Davis 44 Montgomery St Ste 2900 San Francisco CA 94104-4803 Office Phone: 415-362-5045. E-mail: tstinnett@gsmdlaw.com.

**STINSMUEHLEN-AMEND, SUSAN,** artist; b. Balt., Nov. 5, 1948; d. William I. and Geraldine S. (Dodds) Hamilton; m. Richard E. Amend, Nov. 27, 1987; children: Jason Stinsmuehlen, Wyatt Amend. Student, Hood Coll., U. Tex. Designer, owner Renaissance Glass Co., Austin, 1973-87; artist, glass, paint and mixed media dba Impresa, Inc., L.A. and Ojai, Calif., 1987—. Mem. Art in Pub. Places Panel, Austin, 1986-87; cons. Nat. Endowment for the Arts, Washington, 1986, 87, Cmty. Redevel. Agy., L.A., 1990-92; artist trustee Am. Craft Coun., 1988-92; lectr., lead artist Hollywood Blvd. Streetscape Team, Hollywood, Calif., 1991-94; lead artist Canoga Park, Calif., Pedestrianscape and Madrid Theater Project, City of L.A., 1996-2000; mem. Arts Commn., Ojai, Calif., 2000—; mem. Hollywood Art and Design Adv. Panel, 1994-2003; head artist Canoga Pk., Calif., 1996-2000; guest lectr., artist Puchuck Glass Sch., 1980-92, 94-95, 97, 2005, R.I. Sch. Design, 1980, 2006, Mass. Coll. Art, 1980, Dallas Mus. Art, 1981, Japanese Glass Conf., 1985, Calif. Coll. Arts, Oakland, 1985, 89, Australian Glass Conf., 1987, Penland Sch. Craft, N.C., 1996; artist-in-residence Pilchuck Glass Sch., Wash., 2005; educator in field. One-woman shows include Mattingly Baker Gallery, Dallas, 1984, Kurland Summers Gallery, L.A., 1985, 88, 90, 92,

Traver Sutton Gallery, Seattle, 1986, Habatat Galleries, Detroit, 1991, The Nest Gallery, Ojai, Calif., 1997, The Glass Gallery, Bethesda, Md., 2000, Carnegie Mus. Art, Oxnard, Calif., 2004, Sandy Carson Gallery, Denver, 2005, D&A Fine Arts, L.A., 2005; exhibited in group shows at Whatcom Mus., Bellingham, Wash., 1992, 94, Finegood Art Gallery, West Hills, Calif., 1993-94, Miller Gallery, N.Y.C., 1994, The Wignall Mus., Chaffey Coll., Rancho Cucamonga, Calif., 1995, Traver Gallery, Seattle, 1995, Smithsonian Inst. Travelling Exhbn., 1999, Muckenthaler Cultural Arts Ctr., Calif., 1999, Loveland (Colo.) Mus. Gallery, 1998, 99, Fresno Art Mus., 1998, SOFA Chgo., 1998, Santa Cruz Mus. Art and History, 1999, Smithsonian Inst., 1998-2000, L.A. County Mus. Art, 1999, Orange County Mus. Art, 1999, L.A. Mcpl. Art Gallery, 2003, Reynolds Gallery, Richmond, Va., 2003, Nathan Larramendy Gallery, 2004, Ojai Valley Mus., 2003-05, San Francisco Mus. Craft & Design, 2005, L.A. Mcpl.Art Gallery, 2005, Beatrice Wood Ctr. Arts, 2005, others; represented in permanent collection Am. Airlines, Dallas, Renwick Gallery Nat. Mus. Art, Washington, The Jewish Mus., N.Y.C., The Corning (N.Y.) Mus. Glass, Detroit Inst. Arts, Leigh Yawkey Woodson Mus., Wausau, Wis., Oakland (Calif.) Mus., Wagga Wagga City Art Gallery, NSW, Australia, Nishida Mus., Toyoma, Japan, Pilchuck Glass Ctr., Stanwood, Wash., Mus. Art & Design, N.Y.C., L.A. (Calif.) County Mus. Art, Radisson Hotel, Austin, AT&T, Dallas, AT&T, N.Y.C., Marshall Fields Corp. Collection, Chgo., City of L.A., Mus. Am. Art/Smithsonian Instn., Carnegie Art Mus., Beatrice Wood Ctr. for Arts, Ojas Valley Cmty. Hosp., others plus numerous pvt. collections. Nat. Endowment for the Arts grantee, Washington, 1982, 88; Hauberg fellowship Pilchuck Glass Sch., 2001. Mem. Glass Art Soc. (hon. life; bd. dirs. 1982-86, pres. 1984-86), Mus. Contemporary Art (L.A.), L.A. County Mus. Avocations: gardening, swimming, walking, hiking, golf. E-mail: impresa@pobox.com.

**STINSON, ANDREA MARIA,** professional basketball player; b. Mooresville, N.C., Nov. 25, 1967; BA, N.C. State U., 1991. Guard Charlotte Sting 1997—. Named Kodak All-Am., 1990, 1991, MVP, ACC Tournament, ACC Player of Yr., 1991, lead scorer, Charlotte Sting, 1997—2001; named to All-ACC Tournament Team, Italian League All-Star Team, Ea. Conf. All-Star Team, 2001; recipient Gold medal, 1992 Jones Cup Team, Bronze medal, 1991 Pan Am. Team playing overseas for Thiene in Italy, 1996—97. Office: Charlotte Sting 100 Hive Dr Charlotte NC 28208-7707

**STINSON, KENNETH E.,** construction and mining company executive; b. Chgo, May 24, 1946; BS in Civil Engring., U. Notre Dame; MS in Civil Engring., Stanford U. Pres. Kiewit Constrn. Group Inc., Omaha, 1992-93, chmn., pres, 1993-96; pres. Peter Kiewit Sons' Inc., Omaha, 1997—2000, CEO, 1998—2004, chmn., 1997—; chmn. exec. com. Bd. dir. ConAgra Foods, Inc., Omaha, 1996—, Valmont Industries, Inc., Omaha, 1996—. Recipient Outstanding Projects and Leaders awards, ASCE, 2003. Office: Peter Kiewit Sons Inc 1000 Kiewit Plaza Omaha NE 68131 Office Phone: 402-342-2052. Office Fax: 402-271-2939.*

**STINSON, MARION DENNIS,** lawyer, land use planner, judge; b. Alton, Ill., Aug. 19, 1953; s. George Washington and Clara Alevia (Keene) S.; m. Shirley Joan Cartwright, Feb. 13, 1971; children: Casey René (dec.), Marion David. AA magna cum laude, Rogers State Coll., Claremore, Okla., 1992; BA summa cum laude, Northeastern State U., Tahlequah, Okla., 1997; JD, Oklahoma City U., 2002. Leadman Stresscon Inc., Tulsa, 1971-74; crane operator Gardner-Denver, Pryor, Okla., 1974-79; laborer Lone Star Industries, Pryor, 1979-88; owner, mgr. sml. bus. Pryor, 1988-90; concrete finisher United Bridge Constrn., Joplin, Mo., 1990-91; sec. Grand Gateway Econ. Devel. Assn., Vinita, Okla., 1991-93; coord. cmty. devel. Grand Gateway Econd. Devel. Assn., Vinita, Okla., 1993-94, dir. cmty. devel., 1994-95, dir. cmty./econ. devel. Big Cabin, Okla., 1995—2003, dep. exec. dir., 1999—2003. Bd. trustees Town of Salina, 1990-91; com. chmn. MESTA, Pryor, 1995-98; citizen's adv. com. chmn. Mayes County Commrs., Pryor, 1997-98; mem. oversight com. Multiple Local Govts., Delaware/Adair County, Okla., 1995-99; mem. Salina (Okla.) Bd. Edn., 1995-98, v.p., 1996-97, pres., 1997-98; precinct chmn. Dem. Party, Salina, 1996; chmn. bd. N.E. Okla. Little League, Salina, 1994-96; bd. dirs. Pryor Sr. Citizens, Inc., 1996, Cmty. Devel. Soc., 1995-2003; com. mem. Okla. Dept. Commerce, 1994-96, bd. govs., O.D. Mayor Found., 2003—. Recipient Acad. Achievement award Northeastern State U., 1997, scholarship Okla. Scholar Leadership Enhancement Program, 1996, Cert. of Achievement, Okla. Mcpl. League, 1995, 96, 97, 98. Mem. Okla. Floodplain Mgmt. Assn. (cert. floodplain mgr., sec. com. 1996-98), Am. Planners Assn., Salina Area C. of C. (bd. dirs. 1996), Phi Theta Kappa, Alpha Chi. Democrat. Baptist. Avocations: boating, golf, movies, football. Office: Stinson Law Firm PO Box 922 Pryor OK 74362 Office Phone: 918-825-3399. Personal E-mail: stinsonlawfirm@sbcglobal.net.

**STINSON, MARY FLORENCE,** retired nursing educator; b. Wheeling, W.Va., Feb. 11, 1931; d. Rolland Francis and Mary Angela (Voellinger) Kellogg; m. Charles Walter Stinson, Feb. 12, 1955; children: Kenneth Charles, Karen Marie Wiberg, Kathryn Anne Kartye. BSN, Coll. Mt. St. Joseph, 1953, postgrad., 1983; MEd, Xavier U., Cin., 1967; postgrad., U. Cin., 1981. Staff nurse contagious disease ward Cin. Gen. Hosp., 1953-54, asst. head nurse med. and polio wards, 1955, acting head nurse, clin. instr., 1955-56; instr. St. Francis Hosp. Sch. Practical Nursing, Cin., 1956-57; Good Samaritan Hosp. Sch. Nursing, Cin., 1957—66; instr. refresher courses for nurses Cin. Bd. Edn. and Ohio State Nurses Assn. Dist. 8, 1967-70; coord. sch. health office Coll. Mt. St. Joseph, Ohio, 1969-72, instr. dept. nursing, 1974-79, asst. prof., 1979-89; RN assessor pre-admission screening sys. providing options & resources today Coun. on Aging Southwestern Ohio, 1989-90, quality assurance coord. pre-admission screen sys. providing options & resources today program, 1990-93, quality assurance supr. pre-admission screen sys. providing options & resources today and elderly coord. Coun. on Aging Southwestern Ohio, 1995-2000; ret., 2000. Staff nurse St. Francis/St. George Hosp., Cin., 1988-89; vol. ombudsman Pro Srs. of S.W. Ohio, 2005—. Charter mem. Adoptive Parents Assn. St. Joseph Infant and Maternity Home, 1966—70; women's com. for performing arts series Coll. Mt. St. Joseph; chmn. by-law com. Coll. Mt. St. Joseph Nursing Honor Soc., 1996—98; active St. Antoninus Rosary Altar and Sch. Soc., 1973—84, St. Antoninus Athletic Club, com. chmn., 1969—70; bd. dirs. Coll. Mt. St. Joseph Alumni Assn., 1982—84, sec., 1968—69, v.p., 1969—70, pres., 1970—71, chmn. revision of constn., 1976—77; homecoming chmn. Coll. Mt. St. Joseph, 1970, co-chmn., 1977, co-chair com. to celebrate 75 years of nursing edn., 2001—02; mem. com. to plan 50th ann. of graduation Coll. Mt. St. Joseph Alumni Assn., 2003. Mem. River Squares Club (v.p. 1967), Sigma Theta Tau (charter Omicron Omicron chpt. 1998—), St. Antonious Adult Social Group (pres. 2005—). Democrat. Roman Catholic. Home: 5549 Cleander Dr Cincinnati OH 45238-4266 Personal E-mail: flostinson@current.net.

**STINSON, RICHARD FLOYD,** retired horticulturist, educator; b. Cleve., Feb. 4, 1921; s. Floyd Earl and Helen M. (Schiemann) S.; m. Lois D. Stinson; children: Leigh, Laurie, Glenn, Paul, Cathy. BS, Ohio State U., 1943, MS, 1947, PhD, 1952. Instr. floriculture SUNY, Alfred, 1947-48; asst. prof. floriculture U. Conn., Storrs, 1948-55; asst. prof. horticulture Mich. State U., East Lansing, 1955-59, assoc. prof. horticulture, 1959-67; assoc. prof. agrl. edn. and horticulture Pa. State U., University Park, 1967-73, prof., 1973-89, sr. faculty mem., 1979-89, prof. emeritus, 1990—. Cons. in field. Contbr. articles to profl. jours. Lt. (j.g.) USNR, 1943-46. Mem. N.Am. Assn. Colls. and Tchrs. Agr. (E.B. Knight Jour. award 1992), Sigma Xi, Alpha Tau Alpha, Gamma Sigma Delta, Phi Delta Kappa. Office: Pa State U 323 Agrl Adminstrn Bldg University Park PA 16802-2601 Office Phone: 814-863-3824. Business E-Mail: rfs5@psu.edu.

**STINSON, STANLEY THOMAS,** project manager; b. Dothan, Ala., Dec. 17, 1961; s. Leonis and Betty Lois (Harrison) S.; m. Sharin B. Clark, Aug. 25, 1984; children: Sarah Ashley, Amy Rebecca, Rachel Elizabeth, Thomas Clark. AS in Computer Sci., Enterprise State Jr. Coll. 1982; BSBA cum laude, Troy State U., 1984; MBA, Samford U., 1989. Fin. sys. engr. NCR Corp., Birmingham, Ala., 1984-87; sr. sys. specialist Systematics Inc.,

Birmingham, 1987-88, sys. engr., 1988-90, sr. sys. engr., 1990; cons. devel. analyst Systematics, Inc., Little Rock, 1990-92; sr. sys. engr. Systematics Fin. Svcs., Atlanta, 1992-93; sr. applications programmer/analyst Capital City Bank, Tallahassee, 1993-96; sys. cons. Consultec, Inc., Tallahassee, 1996-98; pvt. practice, 1998—2002; founder, pres. DP Answers Inc., 1999—2001; sr. sys. analyst Deutsche Fin. Svcs., St. Louis, 2002; sr. staff E-Trade Consumer Fin. Corp., 2003—05; sr. analyst IT applications GE Money, 2005—. Baptist. Avocations: golf, personal computer. Home and Office: 5998 Peachtree Dr Hillsboro MO 63050 Personal E-mail: banking_dp@earthlink.net.

**STIPE, MICHAEL,** musician, film producer; b. Decatur, Ga., Jan. 4, 1960; Student, U. Ga. Singer R.E.M., 1980—; owner C-OO. Albums (with R.E.M.) Chronic Town, 1982, Murmur, 1983 (Gold record, Rolling Stone Critics Poll Best Album of Yr., 1983), Reckoning, 1984 (Gold record, 1984), Fables of the Revolution, 1985 (Gold record, 1985), Life's Rich Pageant, 1986 (Gold record, 1986), Dead Letter Office, 1987 (Gold record, 1987), Document, 1987 (Platinum record, 1987), Eponymous, 1988 (Platinum record, 1988), Green, 1989 (Platinum record, 1989), Out of Time, 1991 (Platinum record, 1991, 7 Grammy nominations, 1992, Best Pop Vocals Grammy award for group, 1992), Automatic for the People, 1992 (Platinum record, 1992, 4 Grammy nominations, 1992), Monster, 1994, Songs That Are Live (4 song CD), 1995, New Adventures in Hi-Fi, 1996, Up, 1998, Reveal, 2001, In Time: The Best of R.E.M., 2003, guest artist for following groups 10,000 Maniacs, 1987, Indigo Girls, 1989, soundtrack Man on the Moon, 1999; prodr.: (films) Being John Malkovich, 1999, Saved!, 2004, (TV films) Olive, the Other Reindeer, 1999, Stranger Inside, 2001; exec. prodr.: (films) Velvet Goldmine, 1998, Spring Forward, 1999, Our Song, 2000, Thirteen Conversations About One Thing, 2001, Everyday People, 2004, Johnny Berlin, 2005. Named Rolling Stone Critics Poll Best New Group, 1983, Rolling Stone Group Artist of Yr., 1992, Rolling Stone Male Vocalist of Yr., 1992; recipient MTV Video Music Video of Yr. award, 1992, MTV Best Direction, Best Editing, Best Cinematography, and Breakthrough Video awards for "Everybody Hurts", 1994. Address: REM PO Box 8032 Athens GA 30603-8032

**STIPE, ROBERT EDWIN,** retired design educator; b. Easton, Pa., July 18, 1928; s. J. Norwood and Ethel M. Stipe; m. Josephine Davis Weedon, 1952; children: Daniel W., Frederick Norwood. AB in Econ., Duke U., 1950, LLB, 1953; MRP, U. N.C., 1959. Urban planning cons. City and Town Planning Assocs., Chapel Hill, NC, 1956-57; asst. dir. prof. pub. law and govt. U. N.C. Inst. Govt., Chapel Hill, NC, 1957-74; sr. Fulbright rsch. fellow London U., 1968-69; dir. Divsn. Archives and History N.C. Dept. Cultural Resources, Raleigh, NC, 1974-75; vis. prof. U. N.C., Chapel Hill, 1975-77; prof. design N.C. State U., Raleigh, 1976-89, emeritus prof. design, part time prof. design, 1989—2000. Lectr. Inst. Advanced Studies, Bratislava, Slovak Republic, 1992-96; bd. trustees U.S. com. Internat. Coun. on Monuments and Sites, Preservation Action, Nat. Coun. on Preservation Edn., Hist. Preservation Fund N.C., Alliance for Preservation Hist. Landscapes, Old Salem Inc., Stagville Ctr. for Preservation Tech.; emeritus trustee Nat. Trust for Hist. Preservation; mem. bd. adv. Nat. Alliance Preservation Commn. Author, editor articles and publs. in fields of historic preservation, landscape conservation, design, urban planning and planning law; contbr. chapters to books. Mem. Chapel Hill Design Review Bd.; trustee Chapel Hill Preservation Soc.; founder, trustee Chapel Hill HIstorical Soc. Fellow U.S. Com. Internat. Coun. on Monuments and Sites, 1986; recipient Disting. Svc. award Ruth Coltrane Cannon award, N.C. Soc. for Preservation of Antiquities, 1973, Sec. of Interior's Disting. Conservation Svc. award, 1978, Spl. award outstanding contbns. to landscape archicture Am. Soc. Landscape Archiects, N.C. chpt., 1985, Louise DuPont Crowninshield award for Superlative Lifetime Achievement in Historic Preservation, Nat. Trust for Historic Preservation, 1988, Dist. Svc. and Profl. Leadership award Nat. Coun. for Preservation Edn., 1989, Charles S. Murphy award, Duke U. Law Sch. Alumni Assn., 2003, Antoinette Downing Book award Soc. Archtl. Historians, 2005. Mem. Cosmos Club (Washington), Sigma Pi Kappa (First Disting. mem. 1994), Sigma Lambda Alpha (disting. mem. 1996), Phi Delta Phi. Home: 100 Pine Ln Chapel Hill NC 27514-4331

**STIPEK, DEBORAH JANE,** dean, education educator; BS in Psychology, U. Wash., 1972; PhD in Devel. Psychology, Yale U., 1977. Prof. Grad. Sch. Edn. UCLA, 1977—2000; co-dir. NIMH Tng. Program in Applied Human Devel.; dir. Corinne Seeds U. Elme. Sch., Urban Edn. Studies Ctr.; I. James Quillen dean, prof. edn. Stanford (Calif.) U. Grad. Sch. Edn., 2001—. Mem. bd. on children, youth and families NRC; dir. MacArthur Found. Network on Tchg. and Learning. Author: Motivation to Learn: From Theory to Practice, 2002; author: (with A. Bohart) Constructive and Destructive Behavior: Implications for Family, School, and Society, 2001; author: (with K. Seal) Motivated Minds: Raising Children to Love Learning, 2001. Congl. Sci. fellow, Soc. for Rsch. in Child Devel., Office Senator Bill Bradley, 1983—84. Office: Stanford Univ Sch Edn 485 Lasuen Mall Stanford CA 94305-3096

**STIPETIC, WERNER** See HERZOG, WERNER

**STIREWALT, JOHN NEWMAN,** coal company executive; b. Springfield, Ill., July 14, 1931; s. Newman Claude and Genevieve (Henton) S.; m. Joan Marie McCarthy, Dec. 26, 1957; children: Genevieve, Janice, James, Christopher. AB, U. Miami, 1953; grad. execs. program, Carnegie Mellun U., 1978. Salesman Kaiser Aluminum, Indpls., 1957-63; dist. sales mgr. Consol. Coal, Detroit, 1963-67, Cleve., 1967-73, gen. sales mgr. Detroit, 1973-76, asst. v.p., 1976-79; v.p. mktg. Youghiogheny and Ohio Coal Co., St. Clairsville, 1979-81; v.p. mktg. Crown Coal and Coke Co. Pitts., 1981-85, Arch Mineral, 1985-90; sr. v.p. Crown Coal & Coke Co., 1990—. Exec. reservist U.S. Dept. Interior emergency solid fuels adminstrn., 1971, U.S. Energy Dept., 1991-97. Chmn. coun. Cub Scouts, Highland, Mich., 1976; mem. Mich Energy Task Force, 1966; pres. bd. trustees Wheeling Country Day Sch., 1980-84; trustee Wheeling Symphony; bd. dirs. Teen Challenge for New Life Inc. Served with U.S. Army, 1954-56. Mem.: Vinyard Christian Fellowship, Symposiarchs, Wheeling Country Club, Sigma Chi. Home: 130 Spring Hill Ln Wheeling WV 26003-7746 Office: Crown Coal and Coke Co Pittsburgh PA 15220 Office Phone: 412-920-1908.

**STIRITZ, MARETTE MCCAULEY,** English language educator, consultant; b. Center Point, Ark., Dec. 9, 1931; d. Edrie Delos and Lucyle Virginia (Dautrieve) McCauley; m. Charles Wayne Jackson, July 1, 1950 (dec. June 1986); children: Charles, Retta, Shelia; m. John David Stiritz, Dec. 3, 1992. BSE, Ark. State U., 1962; MA, U. Ark., 1965, PhA, 1986. Tchr. elem. Plum Bayou (Ark.) Pub. Schs., 1950-52; tchr. Laura Connor H.S., Augusta, Ark., 1955-59, Swifton (Ark.) Elem. Sch., 1959-60, Swifton H.S., 1962-63; prof. English So. Ark. U., Magnolia, 1965-78, U. Cen. Ark., Conway, 1978—96; cons., 1996—. Cons. high schs., Conway, Morrilton, Vilonia, 1983—, Ark. Dept. Edn., Little Rock, 1982, 84; lectr. U. Chile, Santiago, 1989, Moscow Pedagogical U., 1991, 92, Academica Inst. Chileno-Norteamericano, Santiago, 1994; speaker 8th Bi-ann. Conf. Profs. Fgn. Langs., Chile, 1992, 9th Conf., Chile, 1994. Author: A Grammar for All Seasons, 1996, Using Language Effectively, 1996; editor: What the American Children Like to Read, 1995; contbr. articles to profl. jours.; book reviewer Ark. Elem. Coun., 1980—. Del. Faulkner County Dems., Conway, 1984; exec. sec., founder Columbia Tchrs. Eng.; Magnolia, 1974-78. Mem. Ark. Coun. Tchrs. English (pres. 1979-80, bd. dirs. 1989-93), Ark. Philol. Assn., Nat. Coun. Tchrs. English, Ark. Coll. Tchrs. English (pres. 1992-93), Conway Rotary Internat. Breakfast Club (charter), Conway Shakespeare Club (v.p. 2005-06, pres. 2006—), Alpha Chi (region II v.p. 1992-93. Democrat. Methodist. Home: 3414 Rhondas Ct Conway AR 72032-9168 Office Phone: 501-329-5048. Personal E-mail: JorMStiritz@conwaycorp.net.

**STIRITZ, WILLIAM P.,** food products executive; b. Jasper, Ark., July 1, 1934; s. Paul and Dorothy (Bradley) Stiritz; m. Susan Ekberg, Dec. 4, 1972; children: Bradley, Charlotte, Rebecca, Nicholas. BS, Northwestern U., 1959; MA, St. Louis U., 1968. Mem. mktg. mgmt. staff Pillsbury Co., Mpls., 1959—62; staff Gardner Advt. Co., St. Louis, 1963; with Ralston Purina Co., St. Louis, 1963—97, pres., CEO, chmn., 1981—97; chmn., CEO Agribrands Internat., St. Louis, 1997—2001; chmn. Ralcorp Holdings, St. Louis, Energizer Inc. Bd. dirs. Am. Freightways, Angelica Corp., Ball Corp., Boatmen's Bancshares, Inc., Gen. Am. Life Ins. Co., May Dept. Stores, S.C. Johnson & Son, Reins. Group Am., Vail Resorts; bd. dirs., chmn. Ralston Purina, Ralcorp.; chmn. Westgate Equity Group, LLC; bd. dirs. Fedennted Dept. Stores. Served USN, 1954—57. Business E-Mail: william.stiritz@purina.nestle.com.

**STIRLING, JAMES PAULMAN,** investment banker; b. Chgo., Mar. 30, 1941; s. Louis James and Beverly L. (Paulman) S.; m. Ellen Adair Foster, June 6, 1970; children— Elizabeth Ginevra, Diana Leslie, Alexandra Curtiss. AB, Princeton U., 1963; MBA, Stanford U., 1965. Chartered fin. analyst. Vice pres. corp. fin. Kidder, Peabody & Co. (now UBS), N.Y.C. and Chgo., 1965-71, 84-86, sr. v.p. corp. fin., 1987—; asst. to sec. U.S. Dept. Commerce, Washington, 1976-77. Chmn. bd. Northwestern Meml. Mgmt. Corp., Chgo., 1989—; trustee Northwestern Meml. Hosp., Chgo., 1985—. Pres. jr. bd. Chgo. Symphony, 1968—70; mem. exec. coun. Chgo. Metropolis 2020; trustee Chgo. Symphony, 1970—75, Tchrs. Acad. for Math. Sci., 1991—95. Mem. Investment Analysts Soc. (Chgo.), Bond Club of Chgo., Nat. Econ. Hon. Soc. Clubs: Chicago, Racquet (Chgo.); Onwentsia (Lake Forest, Ill.). Office: UBS Tower One N Wacker Dr Ste 2500 Chicago IL 60606-4302

**STIRPE, JOSH A.,** sales executive; b. Spokane, Wash., Apr. 24, 1973; BA in Mgmt., Ea. Wash. U., Cheney, Wash., 1996, MBA, 1999. Nat. acct. exec. Lucent / Avaya, Washington, 2000—03; dir. nat. sales Safeco, Liberty Lake, Wash., 2003—. Dir. CEA, Spokane, Wash., 2005—06. Home: 1923 E 54th Spokane WA 99223 Office Phone: 509-944-2161. Business E-Mail: jossti@safeco.com.

**STISKAL, JOSEPH ALEXANDER,** neonatologist; b. Elizabeth, NJ, June 13, 1962; s. Joseph and Matilda Stiskal; m. Helen D. Stiskal, June 18, 1988; 1 child, Alexander. BA, U. Pa., 1984; MD, Rutgers U., 1988. Cert. bd. cert. pediat., neonatology. Resident Georgetown U., Wash., 1988—91; fellow U. Toronto, Canada, 1991—94; neonatologist Main Line Neonatology, Bryn Mawr, Pa., 1994—99, Mid-Atlantic Neonatology, Morristown, NJ, 1999—. Reviewer articles to profl. jours., 1999—2003. Contbr. articles various profl. jours. Fellow: Am. Acad. Pediat. Democrat. Presbyterian. Achievements include publications and lectures on effects of maternal antidepressants on newborn babies. Avocation: long distance running. Home: 17 Harwich Rd Morristown NJ 07960 Office: Morristown Meml Hosp NICU 100 Madison Ave Morristown NJ 07962 Office Phone: 973-971-5488.

**STITES, SUSAN KAY,** writer, human resources specialist; b. Colorado Springs, Colo., Sept. 20, 1952; d. William Wallace and Betty Jane (Kosley) Stites; m. Gerald Frederick Simon, Aug. 14, 1988. BA, Wichita State U., 1974; MA, Northwestern U., 1979. Benefits authorizer Social Security Adminstrn., Chgo., 1974-77; trainer Chgo. Urban Skills Inst., 1977-79; human resources mgr. Montgomery Ward, Chgo., 1979-83; mgr. tng. Lands' End, Dodgeville, Wis., 1983-87; owner Mgmt. Allegories, Madison, 1987—. Author: Delegating for Results, 1992, Business Communications, 1992, Managing with a Quality Focus, 1994, Training Orientation for the Small Business, 1994, Powerful Performance Management, 1994, Safety Management Techniques, 1995, Teaching First Aid and CPR, 1995, Alive at 25, 1995, Strategic Thinking and Planning, 1995, Teaching Alice at 25, 1996, Fundamentals of Industrial Hygiene, 1996, Recruiting, Developing and Retaining Volunteers, 1996, Creating a Credit Union University: An Administrator's Guide, 1997, 2d. edit., 2001, Creating a Corporate University, 1997, Strategic Thinking for the Automotive Industry, 1997, Managing Sales and Service, 1997, Sales and Service Management in Credit Unions, 1997, Provide Training Without Straining Your budget, 1997, Car America Sales Training Manual, 1998, Introduction to Community Organizing, 1998, Car America Leader's Guide, 1998, Effective Loan Interviewing, 1999, Driven to Extremes, 2000, Safety Inspections, 2001, Job Safety Analysis, 2001, Incident Investigations, 2001, Ergonomics for the Small Business, 2003, Creating a Safety Culture: Strategies for Small Business, 2004, Preventing Slips, Trips and Falls, 2006, How May I Help You? Service with a Smile and a Story, 2006; editor: Backstay, 1999—2001. Vol. tutor Japanese students in English, Evanston, Ill., 1977—80; reader to the blind Chgo. Coun. for Blind, 1974—76. Named Outstanding Woman of the Yr., Wichita State U., 1974. Mem.: ASTD (v.p. membership 1986, chpt. pres. 1988, Region V awards chair 1992), Assn. Quality and Participation, Madison Area Quality Improvement Network, Soc. Applied Learning Tech., Mendota Yacht Club (treas. 1990—94), Rotary (vol. fundraiser). Avocations: sailing, windsurfing, gardening, cooking, travel. Office: Mgmt Allegories 3788 Highridge Rd Madison WI 53718-6206

**STITH, LAURA DENVIR,** state supreme court justice; b. St. Louis, Oct. 30, 1953; m. Donald George Scott; children: Lisa, Rebecca, Cynthia. BA magna cum laude, Tufts U., 1975; JD magna cum laude, Georgetown U., 1978. Law clk. to Hon. Robert E. Seiler, Mo. Supreme Ct., 1978—79; assoc. Shook, Hardy & Bacon, Kansas City, Mo., 1979—84, ptnr., 1984—94; judge. Mo. Ct. Appeals (we. dist.), 1994—2001; judge Mo. Supreme Ct., 2001—. Speaker Mo. New Judges Sch. Author: articles on appellate practice, products liability and civil procedure. Tutor, mentor Operation Breakthrough, St. Vincent's Sch.; founding dir. mem. Lawyers Encouraging Academic Performance. Mem. Assn. Women Lawyers of Greater Kansas City (speaker, past pres.), Mo. Bar Assn., Kansas City Metropolitan Bar Assn. Office: Supreme Ct Mo PO Box 150 Jefferson City MO 65102*

**STITH-CABRANES, KATE,** law educator; b. St. Louis, Mar. 16, 1951; d. Richard Taylor and Ann Carter (See) Stith; m. Jeffrey Leonard Pressman, Dec. 23, 1970 (dec. Mar. 1977); m. José Alberto Cabranes, Sept. 15, 1984; children: Alejo, Benjamin José; stepchildren: Jennifer, Amy. BA, Dartmouth Coll., 1973; MPP, J.F.K. Sch. of Govt., 1977; JD, Harvard U., 1977. Bar: D.C. 1979. Law clk. to Judge Carl McGowan US Ct. of Appeals, Washington, 1977-78; law clk. to Justice Byron White US Supreme Ct., Washington, 1978-79; staff economist Coun. of Econ. Advisers, Washington, 1979-80; spl. asst. Dept. of Justice, Washington, 1980-81, asst. U.S. atty. NYC, 1981-84; assoc. prof. Yale Law Sch., New Haven, 1985-90, prof. of law, 1990—97, Lafayette S. Foster prof. law, 1998—, dep. dean, 1999—2001, 2003—04; mem. adv com. Fed. Rules of Criminal Procedure, 1995—2001. Mem. Permanent Commn. on the Status of Women, State of Conn., Hartford, 1990-96. Author: (with José A. Cabranes) Fear of Judging: Sentencing Guidelines in the Federal Courts, 1998 (Cert. of Merit ABA); contbr. articles on criminal law and constl. law to profl. jours. Trustee Dartmouth Coll., Hanover, N.H., 1989-2000, Women's Campaign Sch., 1994—, Fed. Bar Found., 1998-2004. Mem. Am. Law Inst., Coun. Fgn. Rels., Conn. Bar Found. (bd. dirs. 1987—, chair 1999-2002). Office: Yale Law Sch PO Box 208215 New Haven CT 06520-8215 E-mail: kate.stith@yale.edu.

**STITLEY, JAMES WALTER, JR.,** food manufacturing executive; b. York, Pa., May 23, 1944; s. James Walter and Geraldine Salome (Horn) S.; m. Tresa Rose Adkins, 1996. BS in Chemistry, Millersville U., 1970. Med. technician York Hosp., 1962-66; rsch. biochemist Carter-Wallace, Inc., Cranbury, N.J., 1970-75; mgr. Ward Labs. divsn. Ward Foods, East Orange, N.J., 1975-77; mgr. tech. svcs. Pepperidge Farms, Inc., Norwalk, Conn., 1977-86; dir. tech. devel. Am. Inst. Baking, Manhattan, Kans., 1986-88; dir. baking and cereal sci. rsch. and biscuit product devel. internat. Campbell Soup Co., Camden, N.J., 1988-90; nat. dir. rsch. and tech. Domino's Pizza, Inc., 1990-91, divsn. v.p. consumer and product rsch., 1992—; pres., CEO TechnoVation Network, Inc., 1992—; dir. new product innovation Weider Nutrition Internat., Salt Lake City, 1999—. Cons. biochemistry and toxicology. Contbr. articles to profl.jours. Asst. scoutmaster Boy Scouts Am. Mem. AAAS, Am. Chem. Soc., Am. Mgmt. Assn., Am. Assn. Cereal Chemists, Am. Inst. Baking (ednl. adv. com. 1978—), Instrument Soc. Am. (assoc. dir.-food industry liaison), Am. Astron. Rsch. Group, York Astron. Soc. (v.p. 1960). Achievements include patents in field. Office: Schiff Nutrition Internat 2002 S 5070 W Salt Lake City UT 84104 Home: 5519 Philadelphian Ct West Jordan UT 84088-6232 E-mail: sitf2000@yahoo.com.

**STITT, DAVID TILLMAN,** judge; b. St. Louis, Apr. 9, 1943; s. David Leander and Jane Wilkinson (Dupuy) S.; m. Elizabeth Celia Santino, Apr. 30, 1981; children: Rachel Elizabeth Botkin, Samuel Thornton. AB, Davidson Coll., 1964; JD, U. Tex., 1969. Assoc. Galland, Kharasch, Calkins & Brown, Washington, 1969-71; asst. corp. counsel D.C., Washington, 1971-73, asst. U.S. atty., 1973-74; asst. county atty. Fairfax County, Va., 1975-80, county atty., 1980-91; ptnr. Venable, Baetjer & Howard, McLean, Va., 1991-95; judge Cir. Ct. Fairfax County, Va., 1995—. I.t. U.S. Army, 1964-66, Vietnam. Mem. Va. State Bar Coun. (exec. com. 1991-93), Local Govt. Attys. of Va. (pres. 1983-84, Disting. Svc. award 1991), Conf. of Local Bar Assn. (chmn. 1990-91), Fairfax Bar Assn. (pres. 1986-87). Presbyterian. Home: 6503 Smoot Dr Mc Lean VA 22101-4003 Office: Fairfax County Circuit Ct 4110 Chain Bridge Rd Fairfax VA 22030-4009 Office Phone: 703-246-2221.

**STITT, DOROTHY JEWETT,** journalist; b. Houston, Sept. 4, 1914; d. Harry Berkey and Gladys (Norfleet) Jewett; m. James Wilson Stitt, Feb. 14, 1939; children: James Harry (dec. 1999), Thomas Paul. AB, Rice U., 1937; MS, Columbia U., 1938. Reporter Houston Post, 1936-38, asst. city editor, 1938; editor of publs. Jewett Family of Am., 1971-94, editor emeritus, 1994—. Spl. asst. to pub. Jewett Genealogy Vols. III and IV, 1995-97; Jewett family Dir.-for-Life, 1995—; gen. chair Jewett Family Reunion, 1996; exec. com. Jewett 2000 Millennium Reunion. Author; editor: The 100th Anniversary Yearbook and History of the George Taylor Chapter, DAR, 1895-1995, 1994, Easton Red Cross Fiftieth Anniversary Booklet and History—Fifty Years of Service, 1967. Adv. bd. Easton Salvation Army, pub. chmn., 1956—, chmn. bd. dirs., 1964, bd. treas., 1981; bd. dirs., pub. chmn. Easton chpt. ARC, 1952-67, vol. Lehigh Valley chpt., 1995-96, 98; founding chmn., pres. Easton JC Wives, 1950-53; fin. com. Little Stone House Mus. Assn., 1974-76, 80, organizing bd. dirs. sec. and pub. chmn., 1974-91; bd. dirs. Easton United Comty. Chest/United Way, 1957-60, publicity chmn. for United Way 1st campaign, 1960; active Easton Civil Def. Comms., 1956-60; charter mem. bd. Montgomery County Pa. Girl Scouts USA, 1946-48, publicity chmn., initiator and editor county newsletter; den mother cub scouts Easton Boy Scouts Am., 1948-55; capt. renovation campaign area YWCA, 1956; mem. March Sch., Easton PTA, 1948-57, sec., 1952-54, v.p., 1954-56, bylaws chmn., 1953, Easton H.S., 1954-61, membership chmn., 1955-57, 59-60; bd. dirs. Easton Young Woman's Christian Assn., 1965-68, publicity chmn. Y-Teen com., 1953-68; sponsoring dir. Easton area H.S. Students weekly TV 30-minute news program, 1955-56; class agent 60th reunion Pulitzer Grad. Sch. Journalism Class of 1938 Columbia U., 1998 Recipient citation, United Way of Easton, 1960, cited for outstanding svcs., Easton chpt. ARC, 1967, cert. for outstanding svc. and support, 1997, Molly Pitcher Gold medal, SAR, 1980, plaques, Salvation Army, 1982, 1991, 2005, Vol. Svc. cert., 2005, plaques, Jewett Family of Am., 1993, citation for outstanding svc. in restoration and pub. of Little Stone Ho. Mus., Hist. and Geneal. Soc. Northampton County, 1993, cert. of recognition, State Senate of Pa., 2005. Mem. AAUW (treas. Easton br. 1950-52, newsletter initiator and editor 1951-60, rep. of br. to UN N.Y.C. conf. 1961-68, internat. rels. chair 1960-68; Pa. achievement award 2000), UDC (Jefferson Davis chpt./Houston), DAR (George Taylor chpt. regent 1974-80, 89-95, vice regent 1980-83, historian 1971-74, 95—, pub. chair 1969—, Pa. state chair vol. svcs. 1995-98, DAR chmn. Kressler Meml. Garden, Easton, 1999—), DAR, PEO (chpt. AF Houston), Easton Tavern House Soc., World Affairs Coun. Phila., Woman's Club of Easton (pres. 1961-64, bd. dirs. 1957—, pub. chair 1952-68, 70-82, 92-96, parliamentarian 1984-92, 2000—, spl. fin. chair 1969-78, legis. chair 1982-84, internat. affairs chair 1996-2000, history update chair 1997—, Outstanding Woman of Yr. 1992, Gold Medal of Honor 1992), Pa. Northeastern Dist. Regents Club (pres. 1980-83, treas. 1997—2003), Northampton Country Club (Niners' Golf chair 1957-91), Women's Golf Assn. (constn. and bylaws chair, publicity chmn. 1957-92, parliamentarian 1960-92), Libr. of Congress Assn. (founding nat. mem., charter assoc.). Republican. Episcopalian. Avocations: history, antiques, golf, swimming. Home: 110 Upper Shawnee Ave Easton PA 18042-1356

**STITT, FRANK,** food service executive; Chef Highlands Bar & Grill, Ala., 1982—, Chez FonFon. Named Culinary Legend and James Beard Best Chef of the Southeast, Am. Express, 2001. Office: Highlands Bar & Grill 2011 11th Ave Birmingham AL 35201 Office Phone: 205-939-1400.

**STITT, MARI LEIPPER,** poet; b. Salem, Ohio, May 1, 1923; d. Robert and Myrtle (Cost) Leipper; m. Rodney Dean Stitt, Apr. 22, 1944; children: Dana Lovelace, Rodney D. Jr. BA in Music, San Diego State U., 1946; MA in Human Rels., Calif. Western U., 1966. Dir. religious edn. Ctrl. Congl. Ch., 1941-50; tchr. sociology San Diego Evening Coll., 1966-84; writer poetry, 1984—. Home: The Academy Village 7761 S Vivaldi St Tucson AZ 85747-9632 Personal E-mail: marilstitt@cox.net. *Did we miss the point? Somehow the stories of the Garden of Eden, Cain and Abel, and the Tower of Babel seemed so simple—take only what you need, care for your brother, stay with your own kind. After all our pious ponderings, why don't we get it?.*

**STIVENDER, DONALD LEWIS,** mechanical engineering consultant; b. Chgo., May 8, 1932; s. Paul Macon and Grace (Larsen) S.; m. Margaret Ann Lourim, Apr. 14, 1956; children— Anne, Robert, Carole. BS in Engring, U.S. Coast Guard Acad., 1954; MS, U. Mich., 1959. Registered profl. engr., Mich. R & D engr. Rsch. Labs., GM Corp., Warren, Mich., 1959-92, sr. rsch. engr., 1968-92; owner, consulting engr. Stivender Engring. Assos., 1980—. Cons. engine, thermodynamics, emissions and systems engring. disciplines. Contbr. articles tech. jours. on diesel, gas turbine and spark ignition engine combustion, emission, constrn. and electronic control aspects. Engring. officer USCG, 1950-58. Fellow Soc. Automotive Engrs. (Arch T. Colwell award 1968, 69, 79, governing bd. 1971-73); mem. NAS (naval studies bd. 1990-92), ASME, NRC, Combustion Inst., Sigma Xi. Achievements include inventions of internal combustion engines and electronic control systems. Home: 1730 Hamilton Dr Bloomfield Hills MI 48302-0221 Office Phone: 248-334-7622. E-mail: stive@umich.edu.

**STOB, MARTIN,** retired physiology educator; b. Chgo., Feb. 20, 1926; s. Cornelius and Theodora (Sluis) S BS, Purdue U., 1949, MS, 1951, PhD, 1953. Mem. faculty Purdue U., Lafayette, Ind., 1953—, assoc. prof. animal scis., 1958-63, prof., 1963-92; ret., 1992. Contbr. articles to profl. jours. Patentee prodn. of fermentation estrogen Served with USN, 1944-46; ETO, PTO Name Best Tchr. Sch. Agr., 1970, Best Counselor Sch. Agr., 1977, Best Counselor Purdue U., 1977 Fellow AAAS Episcopalian. Home: 6218 W Rd 75 N West Lafayette IN 47906

**STOBAUGH, ROBERT BLAIR,** oil industry executive; b. McGehee, Ark., Oct. 15, 1927; s. Robert B. and Helen (Parris) S.; m. Beverly Ann Parker, Oct. 18, 1947 (dec. 1990); children: Blair, Susan, William (dec.), Clay; m. June Gray Milton, Dec. 7, 1991. BS in Chem. Engring., La. State U., 1947; DBA, Harvard Bus. Sch., 1968. Refinery engr. Exxon Corp., Baton Rouge and Venezuela, 1947-52; engring. mgr. Caltex Oil Co., N.Y., Bahrain, London, 1952-59; mgr. econ. evaluation Monsanto Co., Houston, 1959-65; lectr. Harvard Bus. Sch., Boston, 1967-70, assoc. prof., 1970-71, prof., 1972-83, Charles E. Wilson prof., 1984-96, Charles E. Wilson prof. emeritus, 1996—, chmn. doctoral programs 1984-89, dir. energy project, 1972-83, chmn. tech. and ops. mgmt. area, 1981-83. Bd. dirs. 11 cos.; adj. prof. mgmt. Rice U., 2002—. Co-author: Money in the Multinational Enterprise, 1973, Energy Future (best-seller list N.Y. Times and Time mag.), 1979, How To Build an Effective Small-Company Board, 1996; author: Nine Investments Abroad and Their Impact at Home, 1976, Innovation and Competition, 1988; co-editor: Technology Crossing Borders, 1984; contbr. articles to profl. jours. Mem. bd. advisors Inst. Estudios Superiores de la Empresa, Barcelona, Spain, 1973-80; co-chmn. The Dumbarton Oaks Symposium on Energy Efficiency, Washington, 1979; bd. dirs. Alliance to Save Energy, Washington, 1979-94; expert testimony Congress; adv. cabinet-level depts. White House and UN; trustee French Libr. and Cultural Ctr., Boston, 1995-2004 Named to Hall of Distinction, La. State U., 1987. Fellow Acad. Internat. Bus. (pres. 1979-80), Coun. on Fgn. Rels., Am. Econ. Assn., Nat. Assn. Corp. Dirs. (bd. dirs.

1996-2005, vice-chmn. blue rimmon commn.), Harvard Club (NY), Forest Club (Houston) Episcopalian. Office: Harvard Bus Sch Soldiers Field Rd Boston MA 02163-1317 E-mail: rstobaugh@hbs.edu.

**STOBB, MARY JEAN,** retired association administrator; b. Winnipeg, Man., Can., Oct. 16, 1934; came to U.S., 1955; d. Rudolph Edwin and Milla Elida (Corneliussen) Rasmussen; m. Gordon Wesley Stobb, June 14, 1958; children: Barbara Jean, David Gordon, William Eric. BS in Home Econs., U. Man., 1955. Cert. home economist. County home agt. U. Minn. at Stearns County, St. Cloud, 1955-58, U. Minn. at Mille Lacs County, Milaca, 1962-67; pvt. practice home economist Little Falls, Minn., 1967-71; interviewer Mid-Continent Surveys, Inc., Mpls., 1971-78, Rsch. Triangle Inst., Inc., Research Triangle Park, NC, 1976-78; dir. nutrition Region V Elderly Nutrition Program, Little Falls, Minn., 1978-80; dist. dir. Minn. unit Green Thumb, Inc., Wadena, Minn., 1980—89, mgr. field ops., 1989—95; field ops. coord. Green Thumb, Inc. (now Experience Works, Inc.), Minn., 1995—2003, ret., 2003. Key leader Riverwood Ramblers 4-H Club, Little Falls, 1968—70, 1971—79; county clothing leader Morrison County, Little Falls, 1974—75; chair adv. com. North Ctrl. Minn. Coun. on Aging, 2003—05; chair Ctrl. Minn. Coun. Aging, 2006—; commr. Little Falls Housing and Devel. Authority, 2005—; mem. adv. bd. Morrison County Interfaith Hospitality Network, 2004—06; pres. United Ch. Women's Assn., Little Falls, 1977—79; lay leader First United Ch., 2003—05, outreach chair, 1976—78, fin. chair, 1987—93, chair mission and ministry com., 1996—2002, mem. mission and ministry com., 2006—. Named 4-H Leader of Yr. Morrison County 4-H Leaders, 1974. Mem.: Minn. Home Econs. Assn. (dist. pres. 1969—71, chmn. home economists in homemaking 1972—73, by-laws chair 1977—78, del. 1981, 1982, dist. pres. 1986—87), Am. Assn. Family and Consumer Scientists (dist. pres. 1986—87), Internat. Fedn. Home Economists, Morrison Coast Interfailth Hospitality Network (host coord. 2005—), Mid-Sota Home Economists in Homemaking Club (Little Falls) (pres.). Methodist. Avocations: singing, gardening, walking. E-mail: maryjeans@charter.net.

**STOBBE, COLLEEN SUE,** elementary school educator, consultant; b. Modesto, Calif., July 9, 1947; d. Carroll Hipsher and Verdella Grace (Oberkamper) Keirn; m. Jeffrey Friedrich Stobbe, July 6, 1969; children: Finn Andrew, Scott Thomas. BA in Social Studies, San Jose State U., Calif., 1969, MA in Sch. Adminstrn., 2004; MA in Elem. Edn., U. San Francisco, 1975. Elem. tchr. Pajaro Valley Unified Sch. Dist., Watsonville, Calif., 1972—88, 1992—95, reading specialist, 1988—90; supr. student tchrs. U. Calif., Santa Cruz, 1990—92; advisor to new tchrs. Santa Cruz New Tchr. Project, Capitola, 1994—; program lead Santa Cruz/Silicon Valley New Tchrs. Project, Capitola, 2003—. Human resources com. Pajaro Valley Unified Sch. Dist., 1994—; outreach cons. New Tchr. Ctr., Santa Cruz, 2003—. Contbr. articles to profl. jours. Mem.: ASCD. Avocations: boating, camping, travel, reading. Office: Santa Cruz/Silicon Valley New Tchr Project 809H Bay Ave Capitola CA 95010 Office Phone: 831-477-5512. Fax: 831-479-1316. E-mail: cstobbe@santacruz.k12.ca.us.

**STOBER, WILLIAM JOHN, II,** economics professor; b. Boston, Mar. 24, 1933; s. Ralph William and Marjorie Cairncross (Duthie) S.; m. Jeannine Lynn Defries, Sept. 10, 1955. B.Sc., Washington and Lee U., 1955; MA, Duke U., 1957, PhD, 1965. Instr., then asst. prof. econs. N.C. State U., Raleigh, 1959-65; asst. prof., then assoc. prof. La. State U., 1965-69, acting head dept. econs., 1968-69; mem. faculty U. Ky., 1969—, prof. econs., 1974-97, chmn. dept., 1979-86, 90-95, dir. grad. studies, 1979-86, prof. emeritus, 1997—. Mem. Beta Gamma Sigma. Democrat. Home: 516 Mundys Lndg Versailles KY 40383-9468 E-mail: Stober@pop.uky.edu.

**STOBO, JOHN DAVID,** dean, educator, physician; b. Somerville, Mass., Sept. 1, 1941; BA, Dartmouth Coll., 1963; MD, SUNY, Buffalo, 1968. Intern Osler Med. Services, Johns Hopkins, Balt., 1968-69, asst. med. resident, 1969-70, chief med. resident, 1972-73; research assoc. NIH, Bethesda, 1970-72; asst. prof. Mayo Clinic and Research Found., Rochester, Minn., 1973-76; assoc. prof. Moffitt Hosp., San Francisco, 1976-82, prof., head section rheumatology, clin. immunology, 1982-85; William Osler prof. medicine, chmn. dept. medicine John Hopkins Hosp. and Univ., Balt., 1985-94, vice dean clin. sci., assoc. v.p. medicine, 1994—97; v.p. Johns Hopkins Health System, Balt., 1994—97; chmn., CEO Johns Hopkins Healthcare LLC, Balt.; pres. U. Tex. Med. Br., Galveston, 1997—. Mem. transp. and immunobiology com. NIAID, 1976—81; vice chmn. rsch. com. Arthritis Found., 1982—84, chmn. rsch. com., 1984—86, sr. investigator, 1974—77; mem. bd. sci. counselors Nat. Cancer Inst., 1982—; mem. sci. adv. bd. exec. com. Lupus Rsch. Inst.; mem. rsch. adv. bd. DuPont Co., 1987—94. Mem. editl. bd.: Jour. Immunology, 1981—86, Jour. Lab. and Clin. Investigation, 1977—82, Arthritis and Rheumatism, 1980—85, Jour. Reticuloendothelial Soc., 1982—84, Jour. Clin. Investigation, 1981—86, Jour. Clin. Immunology, 1982—87, Jour. Molecular and Cellular Immunology, 1984—86, Rheumatology Internat., 1984—86, Jour. Immunology, 1875—1987; contbr. numerous articles to profl. jours. Recipient Merck award, 1967, Maimonides Med. Soc. award, 1968. Fellow: ACP, Am. Clin. and Climatol. Assn.; mem.: AAAS, Assn. Profs. Medicine (sec.-treas. 1991—92, pres. 1994—95), Am. Soc. Clin. Investigation, Am. Fedn. Clin. Rsch., Assn. Am. Physicians, Am. Assn. Immunologists, Am. Rheumatism Assn. (sec., treas., 1st v.p. 1985—89), Am. Coll. Rheumatology (pres. 1989—90), Inst. Medicine, Md. Soc. Internal Medicine, Interurban Clin. Club, Balt. City Med. Soc., Alpha Omega Alpha. Office: U Texas Med Br Pres Office 301 University Blvd Galveston TX 77555-5302

**STOCK, ANN,** federal official; m. Stuart C. Stock; 1 child. Grad., Purdue U. Dep. press sec. to V.p. Walter F. Mondale, 1980, 84; regional dir. pub. rels. Bloomingdales Dept. Stores, 1982—86, v.p., 1986—89, v.p. pub. rels., 1989—93; dep. asst. to Pres. and Social Sec. The White House, Washington, 1993-97; v.p. institutional affairs The Kennedy Ctr., Washington, 1997—. Asst. sec. Kennedy Ctr. Bd. Trustees; bd. dirs. Young Concert Artists, Cultural Alliance Greater Washington, United Artists. Mem. Capital Children's Mus. (co-founder), The Women's Forum, N.Y. Fashion Group (former program chmn.), Washington Woman Roundtable (founder), "Race for the Cure" (co-founder). Office: Institutional Affairs The Kennedy Ctr Washington DC 20566-0001 Office Phone: 202-416-8703.

**STOCK, DAVID EARL,** mechanical engineering educator; b. Balt., Feb. 2, 1939; s. Walter E. and Minnie H. (Bauer) S.; m. Mary R. Wilford, Aug. 4, 1962; children: Joseph W., Katherine W. BS, Pa. State U., 1961; MS, U. Conn., 1965; PhD, Oreg. State U., 1972. Test engr. Pratt & Whitney Aircraft, East Hartford, Conn., 1961-65; vol. Peace Corps, Ghana, 1965-68; prof. Wash. State U., Pullman, 1972—, chair faculty senate, 1997-98. Contbr. articles to profl. jours. Fellow ASME (chair multiphase flow com. 1988-90, Freeman scholar 1994, chair exec. com. fluid engring. divsn., 2000-01). Office: Wash State U Sch Mech Materials Engr PO Box 642920 Pullman WA 99164-2920 Office Phone: 509-335-3223. Business E-Mail: stock@wsu.edu.

**STOCK, JAMES H.,** economics professor; b. Munich, Dec. 24, 1955; arrived in U.S., 1956; s. James H. and Barbara F. Stock; m. Anne E. Doyle; children: Christopher, Corey. BS, Yale U., 1978; MA, U. Calif., Berkeley, 1982, PhD, 1983. Asst. to assoc. prof. Harvard U., Cambridge, Mass., 1983—90, prof. polit. econ., 1991—2002, prof. econ., 2002—, U. Calif., Berkeley, 1990—91. Adv. panel Bus. Cycle Indicators, 1982—; cons. European Ctrl. Bank, 2000—; acad. adv. Fed. Res. Bank, Boston. Chair bd. editors: Rev. Econ. and Stats., 1992—2002; author: Introduction to Econometrics, 2003; contbr. articles to profl. jours. Grantee, Nat. Bur. Econ. Rsch., 1987—91, NSF, 2004; Sloan Rsch. fellow, 1988—90. Fellow: Am. Acad. Arts & Sciences; mem.: NSF (econ. panel mem.), Econometric Soc. Office: Harvard Univ M4 Littauer Ctr Cambridge MA 02138*

**STOCK, STEPHEN MICHAEL,** broadcast journalist; b. Colorado Springs, May 16, 1961; s. Ray Kesecker and Juanita Madeline (Keller) Stock; m. Lynn Victoria Peithman, July 20, 1985; 1 child, Michael Stephen Ray. BA, U.N.C., 1983. From engring. tech. to gen. assignment reporter WDBJ-TV, Roanoke,

Va., 1983-86; from investigative reporter to weekend anchor, producer WECT-TV, Wilmington, N.C., 1986-87; bur. chief Anderson, S.C. WYFF-TV, Greenville, S.C., 1987-91; investigative reporter-bur. chief Ocala, Fla. WESH-TV, Orlando, 1991—2005, chief investigative reporter, 2005—; standby SE corr. NBC NewsChannel, 1995—. Guest lecr. Marion County Sheriff's Office, Ocala, 1993—98, U. Fla. Press Club, Gainesville, 1993; participant Media Studies Initial Advanced Power Reporting Seminar The Poynter Inst., 1998, participant Getting Wired Seminar, 2001. Adv. bd. mem. Jack Eckerd Youth Camp E-Kel-Etu, Silver Springs, Fla., 1996—; founder Ocala/Marion County Town Mtg. on Violence, 1996; adv. bd. mem. Fla. Environthon, Ocala/Silver Springs, 1993; v.p., bd. dirs. Ocala Habitat for Humanity, 1996—99; elder First Presbyn. Ch., Ocala, 1996—99, Fort King Presbyn. Ch., Ocala, 2005—. Named TV Journalist of Yr., RTNDA of Carolinas, 1989; recipient TV Agrl. News Coverage award, S.C. Agr. Co., 1989, Fla. Media award, Fla. Emergency Mgmt. Assn., 1997, 5 Emmy awards, Alfred I. DuPont Columbia U. Silver Baton, 2004, George Foster Peabody award, 2004, Sigma Delta Chi award, 2003, 1st Pl. Individual Achievement award, AP, 2004, Best in Show-TV award, AP, 2005, Best Investigative Report award, 2005; Ethics fellow, Poynter Inst. Media Studies, 2004. Mem.: Ctrl. Fla. Press Club (Best Gen. News 1994, Merit Recognition for Spot News 1995, Best Spot News award 1996, Best Investigative Report award 1996, Merit Gen. News award 1996), Investigative Reporters and Editors Assn., Soc. Profl. Journalists (Finalist Non-deadline News 1999, 1st pl. TV Investigations Market 1-100 Green Eyeshade award 2000, Fla. Sunshine State award for best investigative reporting 2000, Sunshine State award Best Investigative 2006, RTNDA Communicator award of distinction, Green Eyeshade award 2006). Avocation: Avocations: wine collecting, photography, sports, gardening, carpentry. Office Phone: 352-208-2603. Business E-Mail: sstock@hearst.com.

**STOCK, STUART CHASE,** lawyer; b. St. Louis, July 19, 1946; s. Sheldon Harry and Muriel Cecil (Lovejoy) Stock; m. Judith Ann Stewart, July 18, 1970; 1 child, Frederick Chase. BS in Engring., with highest distinction, Purdue U., 1968; JD magna cum laude, Harvard U., 1971. Bar: Mo. 1971, Ind. 1973, DC 1974. Law clk. to Chief Judge Henry J. Friendly U.S. Ct. Appeals 2d cir., New York, 1971-72; law clk. to Justice Thurgood Marshall U.S. Supreme Ct., Washington, 1972-73; assoc. Covington & Burling, Washington, 1974-78, ptnr., 1978—, chmn. of firm, exec. com., chmn. mgmt. com. Lectr. law U. Va., Charlottesville, 1987—90. Mem.: Am. Law Inst. Office: Covington & Burling PO Box 7566 1201 Pennsylvania Ave NW Washington DC 20044 Office Phone: 202-662-5384. Office Fax: 202-662-6291. Business E-Mail: sstock@cov.com.

**STOCKAR, HELENA MARIE MAGDALENA,** artist; b. Bratislava, Czechoslovakia, Mar. 22, 1933; came to the U.S., 1968; d. Arnost J. and Helen R. (Strakova) Kubasek; m. Ivo J. Stockar, Oct. 31, 1959; children: David, Laura Bates. Diploma, Graficka Skola, Prague, 1952, Music Conservatory, 1954. Piano tchr. Music Sch., Prague, 1954-68; company pianist State Ballet/Breacrest Sch., R.I., 1968-74; piano tchr. Music Tchr. Assn., R.I. 1968-86. One-woman shows include Warwick (RI) Mus., 1986, Brown U., Providence, 1987, Westerly (RI) Art Gallery, 1987, Westerly Art Gallery/Morin-Miller, 1988—89, Galerie Horizon, Paris, 1989, Barnes & Noble, Warwick, 1999—2000, Bohemian Gallery, NYC, 1999, Nixie Gallery, Westerly, 2000, Happy White Gallery, Barrington, R.I., 2000, C.C. R.I., Lincoln, 2000, 2004, Pittenween Art Festival, Scotland, 2001, 2004, Pawtucket Congl. Ch., 2002, Bell St. Chapel, Providence, 2002, Courthouse Ctr. Arts, West Kingston, R.I., 2003, two-person shows, RI State Com. Nat. Mus. Women in the Arts, Triboro Studio, Providence, 1995, Bush Gallery, Bryce Studio, Providence, 2001, Monserat Gallery, Soho, 2002, Courthouse Ctr. for the Arts, West Kingston, R.I., 2002, De Blois Gallery, Newport, 2002, Stonington Vineyards Gallery, Conn., 2002, Teichman Gallery, Cape Cod, Mass., 2003, Gallery Z, Providence, 2003—04, one-man shows include McGrath Courthouse, Wakefield, RI, 2005, exhibited in group shows at World Congress Czechoslovak Soc. Art and Sci., Washington, 1988, Prague, 1992, Morin-Miller Internat., N.Y.C., 1989, Ariel Gallery, Soho, N.Y.C., 1989, Art Expo N.Y.C., 1989, New Eng. Internat. Art Expo, 1993, R.I. State Com. Nat. Mus. Women Arts, 1995, Providence Art Club, 1996—97, Sarah Doyle Galery, Brown U., Providence, 1997, Visions, Newport, 2001—02, Gallery Z, Providence, 2003—05, Krause Gallery, 2003, 2005, Breslin Fine Arts, Inc., Warwick, RI, 2003—05, Warwick Mus., 2003, Charmed Gallery, East Greenwich, RI, 2004—05, BFA Boston Internat. Fine Art Show, 2005, BFA Art Expo, N.Y.C., N.Y., 2005, BFA Contemporary Art Fair, Edinburgh, 2005, BFA Art Ireland, Dublin, 2005, Real Art Ways, Hartford, Conn., 2006, Ct. House Ctr. for the Arts, West Kingston, RI, 2006, Represented in permanent collections; featured on TV shows. Participant Art in Public Places: Convention Ctr., Providence, 1994. Recipient Second prize Nat. Competition of Children's Book Illustration, Prague, 1965. Mem.: Czechoslovak Soc. Art and Sci. Avocations: travel, gardening. Personal E-mail: istockar@aol.com.

**STOCKARD, JAMES ALFRED,** lawyer; b. Lake Dallas, Tex., Aug. 4, 1935; s. Clifford Raymond and Thelma Gladys (Gotcher) S.; m. Mary Sue Hogan, Aug. 17, 1956; children— Bruce Anthony, James Alfred, Paul Andrew. BA with honors, N. Tex. State U., Denton, 1956; LLB magna cum laude, So. Methodist U., 1959. Bar: Tex. 1959. Pvt. practice, Dallas, 1959-62; with Employers Casualty Co., Dallas, 1962-65; v.p. Southland Life Ins. Co., Dallas, 1965-77, sr. v.p., gen. counsel, dir., 1977-87; exec. v.p., gen. counsel, sec. Southland Fin. Corp., Dallas, 1978-87; dir. Tex. Life, Accident, Health and Hosp. Svc. Ins. Guaranty Assn., 1978-84, chmn. bd., 1980-84; ptnr. Butler & Binion, Dallas, 1987-2000; pvt. practice Dallas, 2000—; counsel Employers Gen. Ins. Group, Inc., 1994—. Bd. dirs. Ins. Systems Am., Atlanta; pres., bd. dirs. Dallas County Mcpl. Utility Dist 1, Irving, Tex.; gen. counsel, bd. dirs. Lone Star Life Ins. Co., 1988-99. Contbr. legal jours. Mem. exec. com., precinct chmn. Dallas County Dem. Com., 1971. Mem.: ABA, Tex. Bar Assn., Dallas Bar Assn., Assn. Life Ins. Counsel. Methodist. Home: 3607 Asbury St Dallas TX 75205-1848 Office: 7501 Inwood Rd Dallas TX 75209-4019 Personal E-mail: jastockard@sbcglobal.net.

**STOCKARD, SUSAN ANTONIA WILLIAMS** See CHANNING, STOCKARD

**STOCKBAUER, ROGER LEWIS,** physicist, researcher; b. Victoria, Tex., Feb. 3, 1944; s. Fred Ferdinand and Elizabeth (Nitschman) S.; m. Catherine Pauline Jones, June 10, 1972; children: Robbin Renee, Kathryn Elizabeth, Marc Daniel. BA, Rice U., 1966; MS, U. Chgo., 1968, PhD, 1973. Rsch. assoc. U. Chgo., 1972-73; rsch. physicist Nat. Inst. Stds. and Tech., Gaithersburg, Md., 1973-89; prof. physics La. State U., Baton Rouge, 1989—2005. Editor: High Tc Superconducting Thin Films, 1990; contbr. articles to profl. jours. Recipient Silver medal US Dept. Commerce, 1983; NRC fellow, 1973-75. Fellow Am. Phys. Soc.; Am. Vacuum Soc.; mem. AAAS, AAUP, Materials Rsch. Soc., Sigma Xi. Office Phone: 512-236-8326. Personal E-mail: rlstockbauer@mac.com.

**STOCKBURGER, JEAN DAWSON,** lawyer; b. Scottsboro, Ala., Feb. 4, 1936; d. Joseph Mathis Scott and Mary Frances (Alley) Dawson; m. John Calvin Stockburger, Mar. 23, 1963; children: John Scott, Mary Staci, Christopher Sean. Student, Gulf Park Coll., 1954-55; BA, Auburn U., 1958; M in Social Work, Tulane U., 1962; JD, U. Ark., Little Rock, 1979. Bar: Ark. 1979, U.S. Dist. Ct. (ea. dist.) Ark. 1980. Assoc. Mitchell, Williams, Selig, Gates & Woodyard and predecessor, Little Rock, 1979-85, ptnr., 1985-94, of counsel, 1994—. Bd. dirs., sec. Cen. Ark. Estate Counsel, Little Rock, 1984—85, 2d v.p., 1985—86, pres., 1987—88. Assoc. editor: U. Ark. Law Rev., 1978—79. Bd. dirs. Little Rock Cmty. Mental Health Ctr., 1994—, v.p., 1996—99, pres., 1999—2001; bd. dirs. Sr. Citizens Activities Today, Little Rock, 1983—88, treas., 1986—88; bd. dirs. Vol. Orgzn. for Ctrl. Ark. Legal Svcs., 1986—91, sec., 1987—88, chmn., 1989—91 H.I.R.E. Inc., 1994—2001. Mem. ABA, Ark. Bar Assn. (chmn. probate and trust law sect. 1986-88), Pulaski County Bar Assn. (bd. dirs. 1994-97), Ark. Bar Found.

---

Am. Coll. Trust and Estate Counsel. Democrat. Methodist. Office: Mitchell Williams Selig Gates & Woodyard 425 W Capitol Ave Ste 1800 Little Rock AR 72201-3525 Office Phone: 501-688-8818. E-mail: jstockburger@mwsgw.com.

**STOCKEBRAND, LARRY DEAN,** physical education educator, director; b. Iola, Kans., Dec. 25, 1956; s. Gerald D. Stockebrand and Carolyn Ann Orr; m. Janet Kay Brilke, Dec. 31, 1983; children: Eric, Steven, Paul. AA, Ft. Scott C.C., Ft. Scott, Kans., 1976; BSE, Emporia State U., Kans., 1979. Cert. phys. edn. tchr. Kans. K-8 phys. edn. tchr. Yates Ctr. Elem. Sch., Yates Center, Kans., 1980—. 1980—. Jump Rope for Heart coord., 1980—2006. Jr. h.s. track coach Yates Ctr. Jr. H.S., 1980—2006, jr. h.s. football vol. coach, 1980—87; basketball coach Yates Ctr. H.S., 1981—87. Mem.: NEA, Kans. Assn. Health, Phys. Edn., Recreation and Dance, Kans. Edn. Assn. Avocations: fishing, gardening, walking, hunting, fitness. Home: 1207 Nighthawk Rd Yates Center KS 66783 Office: Yates Center Elementary School Box 160 Yates Center KS 66783

**STOCKER, ARTHUR FREDERICK,** classics educator; b. Bethlehem, Pa., Jan. 24, 1914; s. Harry Emilius and Alice (Stratton) S.; m. Marian West, July 16, 1968. AB summa cum laude, Williams Coll., 1934; A.M., Harvard U., 1935, PhD, 1939. Instr. Greek Bates Coll., 1941—42; asst. prof. classics U. Va., 1946—52, assoc. prof. Va., 1952—60, prof. Va., 1960—84, prof. emeritus Va., 1984—, chmn. dept. Va., 1955-63, 68-78, assoc. dean Grad. Sch. Arts and Scis. Va., 1962—66; vis. asst. prof. classics U. Chgo., summer 1951. Editor: (with others) Servianorum in Vergilii Carmina Commentariorum Editio Harvardiana. Vol II, 1946, Vol. III, 1965, editor: Classical Outlook. Served with USAF, 1942-46; col. (ret.). Sheldon Traveling fellow, Harvard U., 1940—41. Mem. Va. Classical Assn. (pres. 1949-52), Mid. West and South Classical Assn. (pres. Sc. sect. 1960-62, pres. 1970-71), Nat. Huguenot Soc. (pres. gen. 1989-91), Am. Philol. Assn., Mediaeval Acad. Am., Poetry Soc. Va. (pres. 1966-69), Soc. Colonial Wars in the State of Va., Sons of the Revolution, S.A.R. (chpt. pres. 1972, 91), Huguenot Soc. Va. (pres. 1981-83), Raven Soc. (Raven award 1977), Phi Beta Kappa, Omicron Delta Kappa. Republican. Presbyterian (elder). Clubs: Masons, Red-Land (Charlottesville, Va.), Colonnade (Charlottesville, Va.), Farmington Country (Charlottesville, Va.), Commonwealth (Richmond, Va.), Williams (N.Y.C.), Army and Navy (Washington). Home: 250 Pantops Mountain Rd Charlottesville VA 22911-8682

**STOCKER, JOYCE ARLENE,** retired secondary school educator; b. West Wyoming, Pa., May 13, 1931; d. Donald Arthur and Elizabeth Mae (Gardner) Saunders; m. Robert Earl Stocker, Nov. 26, 1953; children: Desiree Lee Stocker Stackhouse, Rebecca Lois Stocker Genelow, Joyce Elizabeth Stocker Scrobola. Grad. cum laude, Coll. Misericordia, Dallas, 1953; Master's equivalency diploma, Pa. Dept. Edn., 1991. Cert. tchr., Pa. Tchr. music and lang. arts West Pittston (Pa.) Sch. Dist., 1953-60; tchr. music and choral Wyoming Area Sch. Dist., Exeter, Pa., 1970-78, tchr. English composition, 1978-93, chmn. lang. arts dept., 1982-90, dir. nat. history day activities, 1982-93. State cons. Nat. History Day, 1996—. Organist, choir dir. United Meth. Ch., Wyo., 1958—; dir. W. Wyo. Centennial Choir, 1998; mem. adminstrv. bd. West Wyo., 2000—; mem. worship com. United Meth. Ch. and Interch. Coun., Wyo. and West Wyo., chmn. worship com., dir. music, organist, mem. nominating com.; judge history day, Wyo., 1986—; chmn. centennial Wyo., 1988, organizer, dir. choirs various venues. Recipient Tchr. of Yr. award DAR, 1992-93, Wilkes U., 1990, citation Pa. Senator Musto, Pa. Rep. Mundy, Pres. Clinton, 1999, Medallion award Coll. Misericordia, 2003; named Outstanding Educator, Times Leader, 1993; honoree Wyo. United Meth. Ch. Choir, 1999. Mem. NEA, Pa. Edn. Assn., Wyo. Edn. Assn., N.E. Pa. Writing Coun., Nat. Coun. Tchrs. English, Women Educators Internat., Orgn. Am. History, Pa. Music Educators Assn., Music Educators Nat. Coun., Nat. Coun. Social Studies, Pa. Assn. Sch. Retirees (mem. vol. of yr. com., mem. exec. bd., mem. bd. region III, named Vol. of Yr. 1998), Pa. Sch. Employees Retirement Sys. (social svcs. com.), Pa. Retired Pub. Sch. Employees Assn. (Luzerne-Wyoming counties chpt.), Pa. Coun. Social Studies, Wyo. Monument Commemorative Assn., Delta Kappa Gamma (recording sec. 1991—, accompanist Pa. state chorus, 1999—, 2000—, pres. Alpha Rho chpt. 2002-04, chmn. nominating com., parliamentarian 2004-06), Phi Mu Gamma. Methodist. Avocations: reading, writing, sewing, hunting, fishing. Office: Wyoming Area Sch Dist 20 Memorial St Exeter PA 18643-2659

**STOCKER, MICHAEL AUBREY,** health insurance company executive; b. Mpls., 1942; Grad., U. Notre Dame; MD, Med. Coll. Wis., 1968; MPH, U. Mich., 1987. Intern Milw. County Gen. Hosp.; resident Mayo Clinic, U. Calif., San Joaquin Gen. Hosp.; assoc. chmn. dept. family practice Cook County Hosp., Chgo., 1975—80; med. dir. ANCHOR Rush Presbyn. St. Luke's Med Ctr., Chgo., 1980—85; exec. v.p., gen. mgr. NY area market US Healthcare, 1985—92; pres. CIGNA Health Plans, 1993—94; pres., CEO Empire Blue Cross and Blue Shield (subs. WellChoice Inc.), NYC, 1994—; CEO WellChoice Inc., NYC, 2002—05, pres., 2003—05; pres., CEO ea. region WellPoint Inc., Indpls., 2005—. Bd. dirs. Nat. Quality Forum, Am. Assn. Health Plans, Coun. Affordable Quality Healthcare, Sec.'s Coun. for Pub. Health Preparedness, HHS, 2002—. Bd. dirs. Arthur Ashe Inst. Served U.S. Army. Office: WellPoint Inc 120 Monument Circle Indianapolis IN 46204*

**STOCKHOLM, CHARLES M.,** diversified financial services company executive; BA, Stanford Univ.; Graduate Degree, American Graduate Sch. Internat. Mgmt. Sr. officer Citibank; chmn. Citibank Internat.; sr. exec. vice-pres. Crocker Nat. Bank; mng. dir. Trust Co. West; chmn. bd. dir. Matson Navigation Co., Inc., Alexander & Baldwin Inc. Trustee Am. Graduate Sch. Internat. Mgmt., Asian Art Mus., San Francisco. Office: Alexander & Baldwin 822 Bishop St Honolulu HI 96813-3924 Office Phone: 808-525-6611. Office Fax: 808-525-6652.

**STOCKMAN, DAVID ALAN,** investment banker; b. Ft. Hood, Tex., Nov. 10, 1946; s. Allen and Carol (Bartz) S. BA in Am. History cum laude, Mich. State U., East Lansing, 1968; postgrad., Harvard U. Div. Sch., 1968—70. Spl. asst. to Congressman John Anderson, 1970-72; exec. dir. Rep. Conf., Ho. of Reps., 1972-75; mem. 95th Congress from 4th Dist. Mich., Interstate and Fgn. Commerce Com., Adminstrn. Com.; chmn. Rep. Econ. Policy Task Force, 1977-81; dir. Office of Mgmt. and Budget, Washington, 1981-85; mng. dir. Salomon Bros., NYC, 1985-88; sr. mng. dir. The Blackstone Group, NYC, 1988-99; founder Heartland Indsl. Ptnrs., 1999—; CEO Collins & Aikman, 2003—05. Mem. Nat. Commn. on Air Quality, 1978. Author: The Triumph of Politics: Why the Reagan Revolution Failed, 1986. Fellow, Inst. Politics, 1974. Mem. Coun. on Fgn. Rels. Office: Heartland Indsl Ptnrs 55 Railroad Ave Greenwich CT 06830 Office Phone: 203-861-2622. Business E-Mail: david.stockman@heartlandpartners.com.

**STOCKMAN, JAMES ANTHONY, III,** pediatrician; b. Phila., 1943; MD, Jefferson Med. Coll., 1969. Diplomate Am. Bd. Pediat. Intern Childrens Hosp. Pa., 1969—70, resident in pediat., 1970—72; fellow in pediatric hematology/oncology SUNY, Syracuse, 1972—74; now clin. prof. Duke U.; also with U. N.C., Chapel Hill; pres. Am. Bd. Pediat., Chapel Hill. Office: Office of the Pres Am Bd Pediatrics 111 Silver Cedar Ct Chapel Hill NC 27514-1512

**STOCKMAN, JENNIFER BLEI,** political organization administrator; b. Phila., Dec. 5, 1954; d. William Harry and Florence (Sussberg) Blei; m. David A. Stockman, Nov. 10, 1983; children: Rachel, Victoria. BS, U. Md., 1976; MBA in Fin., George Washington U., 1983. Systems engr. IBM Corp., Washington, 1976-78, mktg. rep., 1978-81, staff mktg. mgr., 1981-83; dir. tech. trade Sears World Trade, Washington, 1983-84, v.p. tech. investment, 1984-85; founder Stockman & Associates Inc., Greenwich, Conn., 1985, past pres., CEO. Co-chair Rep. Majority for Choice (formerly Rep. Pro-Choice Coalition); bd. mem. WISH List. Pres. Solomon R. Guggenheim Mus., NYC, 2003—; phography com. MOMA; co-chair Bruce Mus. Council; nat. adv. bd.

---

Aspen Art Mus. Named Republican Woman of Year award, Conn. Women's Forum; recipient Heart of Greenwich, YMCA. Republican. Avocations: tennis, swimming, children. Office: Republican Majority For Choice 1660 L St NW Ste 609 Washington DC 20036-5676 Home: 1850 Henry Cowgill Rd Camden Wyoming DE 19934 Business E-Mail: jbstockman@aol.com.

**STOCKMEYER, NORMAN OTTO,** law educator, consultant; b. Detroit, May 24, 1938; s. Norman O. and Lillian R. (Hitchman) S.; m. Marcia E. Rudman, Oct. 1, 1966; children: Claire, Kathleen, Mary Frances. AB, Oberlin Coll., 1960; JD, U. Mich., 1963. Bar: Mich. 1963, U.S. Ct. Appeals (6th cir.) 1964, U.S. Supreme Ct. 1974. Legis. grad. fellow Mich. State U., 1963; legal counsel Senate Judiciary Com., Mich. Legislature, 1964; law clk. Mich. Ct. Appeals, 1965, commr., 1966-68, rsch. dir., 1969-76; assoc. prof. law Thomas M. Cooley Law Sch., 1977-78, prof., 1978—. Vis. prof. Harvard U. Law, 1986, Calif. Western Sch. Law, 1993; lectr. Mich. Judicial Inst., 1995. Editor Mich. Law of Damages, 1989; contbr. numerous articles to state and nat. legal jours. Named one of 88 Greats, Lansing State Jour., 1988. Fellow Am. Bar Found. (life); mem. ABA (chmn. Mich. membership 1972-73, ho. of dels. 1988-92, editl. bd. Compleat Lawyer 1990-99), Nat. Conf. Bar Founds. (trustee 1985-90, sec. 1988-89), Mich. State Bar Found. (pres. 1982-85, trustee 1971-92), State Bar Mich. (chmn. Young Lawyers sect. 1971-72, rep. assembly 1972-79, bd. commrs. 1985-93), Ingham County Bar Assn. (bd. dirs. 1981-85), Mich. Assn. Professions (bd. dirs. 1981-84, Profl. of Yr. 1988), Thomas M. Cooley Legal Authors Soc. (pres. 1982-83), Scribes (bd. dirs. 1994—, pres. 2005—), Delta Theta Phi (dean Christiancy Senate 1962, Outstanding Prof. 1984). Address: PO Box 13038 Lansing MI 48901-3038 Office Phone: 517-371-5140 x 2727. E-mail: stockmen@cooley.edu.

**STOCKS, DONNA BRANDENBURG,** school system administrator; b. Cin., Mar. 2, 1955; d. Donald and Norma Holbrook Brandenburg; children: Jonathan William children: Conrad Jason, Lesley Erin. BS, Georgetown Coll., Ky., 1977; BA, Fla. Atlantic U., 1980; MS, Nova Southeastern U., 2000. Cert. elem. tchr., early childhood edn. tchr., adminstr. Fla. Tchr. Port St. Lucie Elem. Sch., Fla., 1979—80, Palm City Elem. Sch., Fla., 1983—85, St. Michael's Ind. Sch., Stuart, Fla., 1985—2001, early childhood coord., 1994—2001, head of lower sch., 2001—. Mem.: ASCD (assoc.), Stuart Area Panhellenic (treas. 1990—96), Sigma Kappa Alumni Assn. (life). Home: Unit E 3624 SW Quail Meadow Tr Palm City FL 34990 Office: St Michael's Ind Sch 1300 E Tenth St Stuart FL 34996 Office Phone: 772-283-1222. Business E-Mail: dstocks@stmikesschool.org.

**STOCKS, RUNDELL KINGSLEY,** management, construction, education and general consultant; b. Kokstad, South Africa, Feb. 14, 1925; s. Gerald Restall and Edith Hannah (Duffy) S.; m. Janet Alma Parish, Mar. 23, 1949 (dec. 1964); 1 child, Virginia Anne Stocks Garde. Grad., Kingswood Coll., Grahamstown, South Africa, 1942. Chmn., mng. dir. Stocks Constrn., Port Alfred, South Africa, 1946-57; tech. clk. Vecor Ltd., Vanderbijlpark, South Africa, 1957-60; gen. mgr. F.A. Poole Group, Pretoria, South Africa, 1960-64; dir. gen. mgr. Stocks Group, Pretoria, South Africa, 1964-75; Pretoria dir. Eastern Province Bldg Soc., 1970-86; chmn. non exec. Habitech Group, Pretoria, 1975-85; chmn. Gem Valley Estates (Pty) Ltd., 1969—; external examiner U. Pretoria, 1970—2000. Mem. bldg. rsch. adv. com. Coun. for Sci. and Indsl. Rsch., 1972-88, nat. exec. com. Bldg. Industries Fedn. South Africa, exec. com. Master Builders Assn. of Pretoria, mgmt. com. Nat. Devel. Fund for British Industries, mem. South African affiliate Internat. Com. on Tall Bldgs. With South African Navy, 1943-46. Fellow Chartered Inst. Mgmt., Chartered Inst. Bldg. (hon., pres. 1977-78); mem. South African Inst. Mgmt. (hon. life), South African Inst. Pers. Mgmt. Christian Scientist. Home: Gem Valley Farm Pretoria Transvaal South Africa Office: 442 Clark St Waterkloof Pretoria Transvaal 0181 South Africa Office Phone: 012-460-7319.

**STOCKS, WILLIAM L.,** federal judge; Bar: N.C. Chief bankruptcy judge for mid. dist. N.C. U.S. Bankruptcy Ct., Greensboro, 1993—. Office: US Bankruptcy Ct 101 S Edgeworth St Greensboro NC 27401-2219 Office Phone: 336-333-5080.

**STOCKTON, DAVID A.,** lawyer; BA, Emory U., 1978; JD with honors, U. NC, Chapel Hill, 1982. Bar: Ga. 1982. Ptnr. Corp. Group Kilpatrick Stockton LLP, Atlanta. Mem.: ABA (mem. Fed. Regulation of Securities sub-com.), Atlanta Bar Assn., State Bar of Ga. (chmn. Bus. Law Sect.), Order of the Coif. Office: Kilpatrick Stockton LLP Ste 2800 1100 Peachtree St Atlanta GA 30309 Office Phone: 404-815-6500. Office Fax: 404-541-3402. E-mail: DStockton@KilpatrickStockton.com.

**STOCKTON, JOHN HOUSTON,** retired professional basketball player; b. Spokane, Wash., Mar. 26, 1962; m. Nada Stepovich, Aug. 16, 1986; 1 child, John Houston. Grad., Gonzaga U., 1984. With Utah Jazz, Salt Lake City, 1984—2003. Mem. U.S. Olympic Basketball Team, 1992. Named All-Star Co-Most Valuable Player, NBA, 1993; named one of 50 Greatest Players in NBA History, 1996; named to All-Star team, NBA, 1989—94, All-NBA 1st team, 1994. Achievements include being NBA Assists leader, 1987-92; sharing single-game playoff record for most assists, 24, 1988; leading NBA in most assists per game, 1988-93; leading NBA with highest steals per game avg., 1989, 92; being NBA Steals leader, 1989, 92; being holder of NBA single season rec. most assists, 1991.

**STOCKTON, SUSAN,** food products executive; Attended, U. Dayton, Mus. Sch., Peter Kump New York Sch. of Cooking. Owner landscape and floral design store, graphic design firm, Boston, catering co.; chef, food stylist Food Network, 1993, exec. chef, v p. Culinary Prodn. Goundling mom. Food Network Kitchens. Avocation: cooking. Office: Home of Food Network 75 9th Ave New York NY 10011*

**STOCKWELL, LINDA M.,** principal; b. Mpls., Oct. 8, 1948; d. Irving Gordon and Neomie Lillian Reishus; m. David Lewis Stockwell, Dec. 20, 1969 (div.); children: Joel David, Jaime Lynn O'Brien. BA in Elem. Edn., Augsburg Coll., 1970; MS in Curriculum and Supervision, No. Ill. U., 1985. Cert. elem. sch. tchr. 1-6, elem. sch. prin. Minn. Dept. Edn. Elem. sch. tchr. Bloomington Pub. Schs., Minn., 1970—72, Menominee Cath. Ctrl. Schs., Menominee, Mich., 1974—76, Valley View Pub. Schs., Romeoville, Ill., 1981—85, curriculum coord., 1985—88, assoc. prin., 1988—92; elem. sch. prin. Rochester Pub. Schs., Minn., 1992—. Com. mem. Gloria Dei Luth. Ch., Rochester, Minn., 1998—2005. Recipient Ofcl. Core Knowledge Sch., Core Knowledge Found., 2000-2005. Mem.: Rochester Elem. Sch. Prins. Assn. (pres., v.p., sec.), Nat. Assn. Elem. Sch. Prins., ASCD. Home: 605 29th St NW Rochester MN 55901 Office: Washington Elem School 1200 11th Ave NW Rochester MN 55901 Business E-Mail: listockwell@rochester.k12.mn.us.

**STOCKWELL, ROBERT PAUL,** linguist, educator; b. Oklahoma City, June 12, 1925; s. Benjamin P. and Anna (Cunningham) S.; m. Lucy Louisa Floyd, Aug. 29, 1946; 1 child, Paul Witten; m. Donka Minkova, Jan. 13, 2005. BA, U. Va., 1946, MA, 1949, PhD, 1952. Instr. English, Oklahoma City U., 1946-48; mem. linguistics staff Sch. Langs., Fgn. Service Inst., State Dept., 1952-56; mem. faculty UCLA, 1956-94, prof. English, 1962-66, prof. linguistics, 1966—94, chmn. dept., 1966-73, 80-84, prof. emeritus, 1994—. Mem. com. lang. programs Am. Coun. Learned Socs., 1965-69 Author: (with J.D. Bowen) Patterns of Spanish Pronunciation, 1960, Sounds of English and Spanish, 1965, (with J.D. Bowen, J.W. Martin) The Grammatical Structures of English and Spanish, 1965, The Major Syntactic Structures of English, 1973, (with P.M. Schachter, B.H. Partee) Foundations of Syntactic Theory, 1977, Workbook in Syntactic Theory and Analysis, 1977, (with Donka Minkova) English Words: History and Structure, 2001; also numerous articles.; editor: (with R.S.K. Macaulay) Linguistic Change and Generative Theory, 1972, (with Donka Minkova) Studies in the History of the English Language: A Millennial Perspective, 2003; assoc. editor: Lang., 1970-73, Festschrift: Rhetorica, Phonologica, Syntactica: A Festschrift for Robert P. Stockwell, 1988. Served with USNR, 1943-45. Am. Coun. Learned Socs.

fellow, 1963-64. Mem. Linguistic Soc. Am. (exec. com. 1965-68), Philol. Assn. Great Britain. Home: 1929 Manning Ave #301 Los Angeles CA 90025 Office: UCLA Linguistics Dept Los Angeles CA 90095 Business E-Mail: stockwel@ucla.edu.

**STOCKWELL, WILLIAM F.,** not-for-profit fundraiser, consultant; b. Belmont, Mass., Oct. 1, 1948; s. Fred F. and Marjorie (Werner) Stockwell; m. Sara Gray Stockwell, June 16, 1973; children: Quentin F., Carl W. BA, Rutgers U., 1971; MEd, Boston U., 1975. Dir. devel. Eaglebrook Sch., Deerfield, Mass., 1980-83, Hyde Sch., Bath, Maine, 1983-84, Western Regional Coun. on Alcoholism, Lewiston, Maine, 1992-94; dealer Target/1 Fundraiser, Auburn, Maine, 1985-95, 2006, Campagne Assn., Manchester, N.H., 1999—; cons. William F. Stockwell Fundraising and Nonprofit Mgmt. Cons., Waterford, Maine, 1984—. Dir. numerous workshops, presentations, retreats and studies including Arthur Griffin Ctr. for Photographic Art, Winchester, Mass., 1997, Shaw House, Bangor, Maine, 1998, Bear Mountain Learning Cmty., South Waterford, Maine, 1998, Cary Med. Ctr., Caribou, Maine, 1998, Deertrees Found., Ltd., Harrison, Maine, 1998, Calais Regional Hosp., 1998, Bridgton (Maine) Pub. Libr., 1998, Watershead Ctr. for Ceramic Arts, Nobleboro, Maine, 1999, Lincoln Home, Newcastle, Maine, 1999, Carriage and Driving Ctr., Skyline Farm, North Yarmouth, Maine, 1999, USM-Sr. Coll., Portland, Maine, 1999, Maine Bar Found., Augusta, 2000, Hyde Sch., Bath, Me., 2001, Eagle Hill Sch., Hardwick, 2001, among others. Trustee Western Maine Health, Norway, Maine, 1990—2005; dir., pres. Oxford Hills Assn. Devel. Corp., Norway, 1985-94; corporator Norway Savs. Bank, 1986—; Maine Health, 1999—2005; mem. annual fund steering com., parent vol. Eagle Hill Sch., 1999—2004. Mem. Maine Hosp. Assn. (healthcare governance coun. 1991—2004), Kiwanis (dir. Norway-Paris chpt. 1986-88). Republican. Avocations: semi-precious gems, gardening. Home: PO Box 84 264 Passaconaway Rd Waterford ME 04088-0084 Office: PO Box 84 Waterford ME 04088 E-mail: fndrsr@fndrsr.com.

**STODDARD, ALEXANDRA,** interior designer, educator, writer; b. Weston, Mass., Nov. 8, 1941; d. Robert Powell and Barbara Rutledge (Green) Johns; m. Brandon Stoddard (div.); children: Alexandra Brandon, Brooke Goodwin; m. Peter Megargee Brown, May 18, 1974. Diploma in design, N.Y. Sch. Interior Design, 1961. Designer McMillen, Inc., N.Y.C., 1963-77; pres., CEO Alexandra Stoddard Inc., N.Y.C., 1977—. Founder, pres. Design & Art Soc., Ltd., N.Y., 1987—. Author: Style for Living: How to Make Where You Live You, A Child's Place: How to Create a Living Environment for Your Child From Birth through Adolescence, Reflections on Beauty: Lectures and Notes on Interior Design, The Postcard as Art: Bring the Museum Home (Cert. of Merit award 1986), Living a Beautiful Life: 500 Ways to Add Elegance, Order, Beauty and Joy To Every Day of Your Life, 1997, Alexandra Stoddard's Living Beautifully Together, Alexandra Stoddard's Book of Color, Gift of a Letter, Daring to be Yourself, 1990, Creating a Beautiful Home, 1992, Grace Notes, Making Choices, Alexandra Stoddard's Tea Celebrations, The Art of the Possible, Mothers: A Celebration, Gracious Living in a New World, The Decoration of Houses, Open Your Eyes - 1000 Simple Ways to Bring Beauty into Your Home and Life Each Day, Feeling at Home - Defining Who You are and How You Want to Live, 1999, Choosing Happiness: Keys to a Joyful Life, 2002, Things I Want My Daughters to Know--A Small Book About the Big Issues in Life, 2004, Time Alive: Celebrate Your Life Every Day, 2005; contbg. editor Country Antiques and Collectibles, Decorating with Americana; back page columnist Design Times--The Art of Interiors; columnist McCall's mag.; contbr. articles to profl mags. and jours. Founding mem., chmn. spiritual direction com. Ch. of Heavenly Rest, 1975-77; former mem. bd. regents Cathedral St. John the Divine; dame Am. Soc. of Order of St. John Hosp. of Jerusalem. Recipient Burlington prize, 1975, award for design Greenwich Arts Coun., 1985, Interior Design award Brandeis U., 1986, cert. of spl. merit English Art Inst., Designer of Yr. award Kips Bay Boys and Girls Club, 1997, Disting. Womans' award Northwood U., 1999, Lit. Lion, 100th Anniversary prize 2000 Stonington (Conn.) Libr. Mem. English Speaking Union, New Eng. Soc. Republican. Episcopalian. Home: 1125 Park Ave New York NY 10128-1243 Office: Rev John Rathbone House 87 Water St Stonington CT 06378-1432 also: 1125 Park Ave Ste 6A New York NY 10128-1243 Office Phone: 212-289-5509.

**STODDARD, ALLAN LEE,** writer, musician; b. Perry, Okla., Sept. 1, 1944; s. Leland Luellan and Lena Ethel Stoddard; m. Katherin Ann Gilpen, Apr. 28, 1974; m. Diana Elizabeth Doyle, Apr. 21, 1973 (div. Sept. 1973). Musician The Intruders, Okla., 1959—67; lead guitar The Greenmen, 1965; band leader The Shirelles, 1967—71; prin., owner Cherokee Heart Pub. Co., Shawnee, Okla., 1967—. Musician The Drifters, 1966—67, The Olympics, 1966—67; band leader Mickey Hargitay, 1966—67, 1970, Wolfman Jack, 1966—67; prodr. for Mel Fender and Ashley Fender. Author: Single Pick, 1973 (featured Billboard mag., 1973), Lady You've Been On My Mind, 1973 (featured Billboard mag., 1973), Oklahoma Trade Tokens & Baggage Checks, 2003, Oklahoma Territory and Indian Territory Collectibles, 2003; appearances on (TV program) Danny's Day, Okla. City Channel 4, 1978, featured with Roy Clark, Dub Taylor, and Johnny Gimble (Roy Clark jam) Enid Quail Hunt, 1979; music video writer: Hit and Run Lover, 1990; contbr. articles to profl. jours. including Nat. Treasure Pubs. Vol. Alan Lee Christmas benefit party mentally handicapped children Enid State Sch., 1972; vol. Oklahoma Cystic Fibrosis Found., 2003; musician benefit fundraiser REST Homeless Shelter, Oklahoma City, 2000; mem. Nat. D-Day Mus., New Orleans, 2006; bd. dirs. Washington Irving Mus., Stillwater, Okla., 2000—. With Nat. Guard, 1961—67. Mem.: Philbrook Art Mus., Western Heritage Assn. Musician. Baptist. Avocations: metal detecting, treasure hunting, writing songs, collecting rare indian painting. Home: 1615 East Main Shawnee OK 74801 Office Phone: 405-878-0355.

**STODDARD, ANNE MAHER,** biostatistician, researcher, educator; b. Rochester, NY, Mar. 26, 1946; d. Robert Williamson and Mary Jane Gunter Maher; children: Joshua Forrest, Nathan Edward. AB, Hollins Coll., Roanoke, VA, 1964—68; MS, Harvard Sch. of Pub. Health, Boston, MA, 1971—73, ScD, 1973—78. Instr. in pub. health U. Mass., Amherst, 1977—78, asst. prof. pub. health, 1978—89, assoc. prof. pub. health, 1989—2003, assoc. prof. emerita, 2003—; sr. rsch. scientist New England Rsch. Inst., Watertown, Mass., 2003; dir. Ctr. for Statis. Analysis and Rsch., 2004—. Dir. UMASS/ Baystate Ctr. for Rsch. and Edn. in Women's Health, Amherst, Mass., 1997—2003; adj. lectr. Harvard Sch. of Pub. Health, Boston, 1997—; vis. scientist Dana Farber Cancer Inst., Boston, 2001—02. Fulbright Sr. Specialists grantee, 2004—05. Office: NERI 9 Galen St Watertown MA 02472 E-mail: astoddard@neriscience.com.

**STODDARD, ERIN,** actress, artist; d. Carl and Lynne Stoddard. BA, NYU, 1989—92. Actress: Evita, 1992—93; Cabaret, 1993—94; Joseph and the Amazing Technicolor Dreamcoat, 1996; Showboat, 1997—98; A Christmas Carol, 1994—95, 1999—2000; Beauty and the Beast, 2000—01; 42nd St, 2001—05; One Way Ticket to Hell, 2005—06; My One and Only, 2006; (films) That Old Song and Dance, 2004; (TV series) Common Space, 2005. Recipient White Sweater award, David Prouty H.S., 1989, Miss Dance of Conn., Dance Masters of Am., 1989; scholarship, Joffrey Ballet - NYC, 1983, Edward Villella - Cape Cod Conservatory, Overall scholarship, Dance Masters of Am., 1988. Mem.: Screen Actor's Guild, Actor's Fed. TV and Radio Assn., Actor's Equity Assn. Avocations: sculpting, writing, painting, tennis. Personal E-mail: erinstoddard@nyc.rr.com.

**STODDARD, PATRICK CLARE,** retired military systems consultant, computer engineer; b. June 13, 1941; s. Frank Eudaly and Mary Clarann (Burns) Stoddard; m. Anneliese Barg, Sept. 18, 1963; children: Patrick Frank, Conni Maryann. Student, Cleve. Inst. Electronics, 1967—68, U. Md., 1961—63. Enlisted USAF, 1959, radar technician, 1959—67, resigned, 1967; asst. engr. Univac divsn. Sperry Rand, Minn., 1967—68, field engr. Minn., 1968; sys. engr. Hydrospace Challenger Rsch., Inc., Md., 1968—73; sr. engr. Control Data Corp., Arlington, Va., 1973—74, prin. engr. computer scis., 1974—78, mil. sys. cons., 1978—2002; ret., 2002. Contbr. numerous studies in support of mil. sys. devel. Recipient Bill Norris Shark Club award, Control

Data Corp., 1978. Roman Catholic. Achievements include patents for electronic oil slick control. Home: 55 Mohegan Rd Groton CT 06340-5537 Personal E-mail: local538@mindspring.com.

**STODDARD, PETER HAWKINS,** education educator, consultant; b. Biloxi, Miss., June 10, 1949; s. Richard Williams Stoddard and Winifred Gertrude Hawkins; 1 child, Matthew Richard. BA, Hiram Coll., 1967—71; MSW, San Francisco State U., 1979—81; PhD, Case Western Res. U., 1981—83. Reporter Charlotte Observer, NC, 1971—73; transp. mgr. Jesica/Gunne Sax, Ltd., San Francisco, 1973—74; news editor Alameda Times Star, Calif., 1975—77; social worker San Francisco Welfare Dept., 1977—79; aid to the mayor City of San Francisco, 1979—81; prof. of social work Moorhead State U., Moorhead, Minn., 1983—84, U. of Tenn. Grad. Social Work Sch., Knoxville, 1984—88, Austin Peay State U., Clarksville, Tenn., 1988—. Dir. Ctr. for Social Rsch./ Coun. of Cmty. Services, Nashville, 1986—89; founder and exec. dir. Montgomery County Coun. of Cmty. Services, Clarksville, 1993—94; founder and dir. APSU Cmty. Outreach Partnership Ctr., Clarksville, 1992—96, Vol. Ctr. of Clarksville, Tenn., 1995—96; co-founder Family Guidance Ctr., Clarksville. Author: (book) An Atlas of Montgomery County, Tennessee; contbr. articles to profl. jours. Bd. mem. Nat. Assn. of Planning Councils, Dallas; governor's task force on social svc. block grants State of Tenn., 1996—97; task force mem. Governor's Task Force on Manpower Needs in Mental Health, Nashville, 1987—89, SF Mayor's Task Force on Housing Needs, San Francisco, 1980—81; sec. and bd. mem. Red River Improvement Corp., Clarksville, Tenn.; pres. Cmty. Services Orgn., Clarksville, Tenn., 1993—96, AAUP Austin Peay State U. Chpt., Clarksville, Tenn., 2000—03. Fellow NIMH fellowship, NIMH, 1981—82; grantee Austin Peay State U. Tower grant, Austin Peay State U., 1989. Mem.: Austin Peay State U. Faculty Senate (senator 1998—2002), Coun. on Social Work Edn. Accreditation Com. (licentiate; u. accreditation team insp. 1998—2003), AAUP (life; chpt. pres. 2000—03). Democrat-Npl. Unitarian Universalist. Office: Austin Peay State Univversity College St Clarksville TN 37040 Personal E-mail: stoddardp@apsu.edu.

**STODDARD, PHILIP HENDRICK,** foreign affairs analyst, consultant, writer; b. Iowa City, Apr. 30, 1929; s. George Dinsmore and Margaret (Trautwein) S.; m. Carol Cannon, Jan. 19, 1952 (div. 1959); children: Michele, Christopher, Eric; m. Doris Joyce Mills, Dec. 26, 1960; children: Leah, Evan. BA, U. Ill., 1950; MA, Princeton U., 1955, PhD, 1963. Asst. prof. SUNY New Paltz, 1956-60; analyst, 1963-80; with U.S. Dept. State, Washington, dep. asst. sec., 1980-83; exec. dir. Middle East Inst., Washington, 1983-87; cons. Nat. Intelligence Coun., Washington, 1988-90, dir., analytic group, 1990-94; ret., 1994; mem., dir. Ctrl. Intelligence's Sr. Rev. Panel, 1996-97. Author: Teskilat-i Mahsusa, 1993; editor: Change and the Muslim World, 1981; editor, co-translator: The Turkish Battle at Khaybar, 1997 (in English and Turkish); contbr. articles to profl. jours. State Dept. fellow Coun. Fgn. Rels., 1979-80. Sgt. USMC, 1951-53. Named Disting. Fed. Exec., U.S. Govt.; recipient Nat. Intelligence Disting. Svc. medal. Mem. Middle East Inst., Middle East Studies Assn., Turkish Studies Assn., Am. Fgn. Svc. Assn., Phi Beta Kappa, Sigma Chi. Home: 6000 Springfield Dr Bethesda MD 20816-1232 E-mail: dpstoddard@concast.net.

**STODDARD, ROBERT H.,** geography educator; b. Auburn, Nebr., Aug. 29, 1928; s. Hugh P. and Nainie L. (Robertson) S.; m. Sally E. Salisbury, Dec. 10, 1955; children: Martha, Andrew R., Hugh A. BA, Nebr. Wesleyan, Lincoln, 1950; MA, U. Nebr., 1960; PhD, U. Iowa, 1966. Instr. Nebr. Wesleyan, 1961-63, asst. prof., 1963-67, U. Nebr., Lincoln, 1967-71, assoc. prof., 1971-81, prof., 1981—2001. Vis. prof. Tribhuvan U., Kathmandu, Nepal, 1975-76, U. Colombo, Sri Lanka, 1986; inst. instr. Okla. State U., Stillwater, 1966; TV instr. Nebr. Ednl. TV Higher Edn., Lincoln, 1969; instr. Career Opportunity Program, Lincoln, 1973; dir. Geog. Edn. of Nebr., Lincoln, 1989-95. Author: Field Techniques, 1982; contbg. author: Human Geography, 2d edit., 1989; editor: Sacred Places, 1997. Mem. subcom. Lincoln-Lancaster Planning Com., 1974-78. Mem. Assn. Am. Geographers, Nat. Coun. for Geog. Edn. (Disting. Tchg. Achievement award 1992). Democrat. Unitarian Universalist. Office: U Nebr Geog Program Lincoln NE 68588-0368

**STODDARD, ROGER ELIOT,** scholar; b. Boston, Dec. 2, 1935; s. Merton Edgar and Helen (Bonney) S.; m. Helen Louise Heckel, May 24, 1958; children— Alison Louise, Christopher Paine AB, Brown U., 1957. Asst. curator Harris Coll. Am. Poetry and Plays, Brown U., Providence, 1961-63, curator, 1963-65; asst. to librarian Harvard U. Houghton Library, Cambridge, Mass., 1958-61, asst. librarian, 1965-69, assoc. librarian, 1969-85, sr. curator, 1995—2004; curator rare books Harvard Coll. Library, Cambridge, Mass., 1985—2004; lectr. English Harvard U., Cambridge, Mass., 1984-86, sr. lectr., 1986—2004, assoc., 2004—. Faculty mem. Columbia U. Rare Book Sch., N.Y.C., 1984-85; sec. Friends of Harvard Coll. Libr., Cambridge, Mass., 1983-98. Author: Catalogue of Books & Pamphlets Unrecorded in Wegelin's Early American Poetry, 1969, The Houghton Library 1942-82, 1982, Poet & Printer in Colonial & Federal America, 1983, The Parkman Dexter Howe Library, part 1: Early New England Books, 1983, Marks in Books, Illustrated and Explained, 1985 (N.E. Book Show award, 1986, Am. Libr. Assn. award, 1987), Put a Resolute Hart to a Steep Hill: William Gowans Antiquary and Bookseller, 1990; editor: A Glance at Private Libraries, 1991, Edmond Jabès in Bibliography, 1998, 2001, John Laurent, Maine Painter: An Annotated Register of Paintings, Prints and Drawings, 2000, Julien Offray de La Mettrie, 1709-1751: A Bibliographical Inventory, 2001, A Library-Keeper's Business: Essays, 2002, Abundant Bibliophiles: Hubbard Winslow Bryant on the Private Libraries of Portland 1863-1864, 2004; contbr. articles to profl. jours. Mem. Records and Archives Com., Concord, Mass., 1985-87; bd. dirs. Louisa May Alcott Meml. Assn., Concord, 1983—2004. Huntington Library fellow, San Marino, Calif., 1978, 2005; W.F. Milton fellow Harvard U. Med. Sch., Boston, 1978-80; D.W. Bryant fellow Harvard U., 1992. Mem. Bibliog. Soc. Am. (coun. mem. 1982-88), Bibliography of Am. Lit. (supervisory com. chmn. 1982-91, pres. 1996-2000), Am. Antiquarian Soc. (coun. mem. 1989-93), Assn. Internat. de Bibliophilie, Baxter Soc. Portland, Book Club Calif., Colonial Soc. Mass. (corr. sec. 1993-97), The Johnsonians, Bibliog. Soc. London (hon. sec. for Am. 1992—), Bibliog. Soc. Va., Grolier Club (N.Y.C.), Harvard Club (N.Y.C.), Club of Odd Vols. Boston (exec. com. 1985-87), Soc. of Printers Boston, Phi Beta Kappa. Home: 9 Birchwood Ln Lincoln MA 01773-4907 Office: Harvard Univ Barker Ctr 12 Quincy St Cambridge MA 02138-6502

**STODDARD, STEPHEN DAVIDSON,** ceramics engineer, retired state senator; b. Everett, Wash., Feb. 8, 1925; s. Albert and Mary Louise (Billings) S.; m. Joann Elizabeth Burt, June 18, 1949 (dec. Oct. 1993); children: Dorcas Ann, Stephanie Kay; m. Barbara L. Seitz, Feb. 18, 1995. Student, Tacoma Coll., Wash., 1944, Conn. Coll., New London, 1946; BS, U. Ill., Urbana, 1950. Asst. prodn. supr., asst. ceramic engr. Coors Porcelain Co., Golden, Colo., 1950-52; ceramics-powder metallurgy sect. leader Los Alamos (N.Mex.) Sci. Lab., U. Calif., 1952-82; pres., treas. Materials Tech. Assocs., Inc., 1978-94; cons. Ceramic Age Mag., 1958-60; Cons. Nuclear Applications for Ceramic Materials, 1958-60; Jury commr. Los Alamos County, 1969; justice of peace, 1956-62; mem. Los Alamos Sch. Adv. Council, 1966; mcpl. judge Los Alamos, 1976—77; chmn. Los Alamos Ordinance Rev. Com., 1958; Mem. Republican County and State Central Com., 1955—; county commr. Los Alamos, N.Mex., 1966-68; mem. Los Alamos County Planning Commn., 1962-63, N.Mex. Senate, 1980-92. Bd. dir. Los Alamos Econ. Devel. Corp., 1982-99, U. N.Mex. Los Alamos Found.; mem. Los Alamos Pub. Sch. Found., 2006-. Patentee in field. Vestryman Episcop. Ch., 1999—2002; bd. dirs. Sangre de Cristo coun. Girl Scouts U.S.A., 1965—71; N.Mex. chpt. Nature Conservancy, 1988—97, v.p., 1993—94, disting. trustee 2001; bd. dirs. Southwestern Assn. on Indian Affairs, Inc., 1987—91, chmn., 2000—02; chmn. bd. dirs. Los Alamos Vis. Nurses, 1995—2004; chmn. Gov.'s Commn. in Nat. and Cmty. Svc., 2001, Los Alamos County 50th Anniversary Com., 1998—99; trustee, vice chmn. Valles Caldera Nat. Preserve, 2000—02; chmn. Los Alamos Vis. Nurses, 2000—, Los Alamos 50th Anniversary Com., 1998—99; mem. Los Alamos Edn. Group, 1995—. With AUS, 1943—46. Decorated Bronze Star, Purple Heart, Combat Infantry Badge; recipient disting. alumni award U. Ill. Coll. Engring., 1986, Leopold

Conservation award N.Mex. Nature Conservancy, 1988, Cmty. Svc. award. Fellow Am. Inst. Chemists, Am. Ceramic Soc. (treas. 1972-74, pres. 1976-77, disting. life 1984); mem. Nat. Inst. Ceramic Engrs. (PACE award 1965, Greaves Walker award 1984), Am. Soc. Metals, N.Mex. Soc. Profl. Engrs. (Ingeniero Veterano de Neuvo Mejico award 1992), Los Alamos of C. (citizen of yr. award 1992), Living Treasure of Los Alamos, Masons, Shriners (pres. 1994-95), Elks (dist. dep. grand exalted ruler 1968-69), Los Alamos Golf Assn. (dir. 1964-66), Am. Legion (nat. legis. coun. 1992-94), Kiwanis (pres. 1964, lt. gov. 1968-69), Sigma Xi, Alpha Tau Omega. Episcopalian. Home: 4557 Trinity Dr Los Alamos NM 87544-1862 E-mail: sbstoddard@msn.com.

**STODDART, J. FRASER,** chemistry professor; b. Edinburgh, Scotland, May 24, 1942; BSc, Edinburgh U., Scotland, 1964; PhD, Edinburgh U., 1966, DSc, 1980. Postgrad. student U. Edinburgh, Scotland, 1964-66, Queen's U., Kingston, Ont., Canada, 1967-70; rsch. fellow U. Sheffield, England, 1970, lectr. in Chemistry, 1970-78; rschr. ICI Corp. Lab., Runcorn, England, 1978-81; reader in Chemistry U. Sheffield, England, 1981-90; prof. Org. Chem. U. Birmingham, England, 1990-97, head Sch. Chem., 1993-97; Winstein chair U. Calif., L.A., 1997—. Lectr. in supramolecular and macromolecular sci. Contbr. over 730 articles to profl. jours. Recipient Hope prize 1964, Carbohydrate Chemistry award 1978, RSC Perkin Divsn. Career award 1980, 81, 82, Internat. Izatt-Christensen award in macrocyclic chemistry, 1993, Chaire Bruylants award 1994, Arthur C. Cope Scholar award 1999, Nagoya Gold Medal award in organic chemistry, 2004; Leverhulme rsch. fellow, 1988-89. Fellow Royal Soc., German Acad. Natural Scis. Office: UCLA Dept Chem & Biochem 405 Hilgard Ave Los Angeles CA 90095-9000 Business E-Mail: stoddart@chem.ucla.edu.

**STODOLA, STEVEN JAMES,** science educator; b. Waterloo, Iowa, Nov. 11, 1949; s. Stanley John and Pauline Barbara Stodola; m. Deborah Lee Olsson, July 19, 1975; children: Joel Robert, Ryan Richard, Meegan Anne. BA, St. Mary's Coll., Winona, Minn., 1971; MA in Tech., Coll. St. Thomas, St. Paul, Minn., 1972. Lic. tchr. Maple Valley Cmty. Schs., St. Paul, 1971—73, Breck Acad., Mpls., 1973—75, Peace River (Can.) Sch. Dist., 1975—76; tchr. biology and chemistry Maple Valley Cmty. Schs., Mapleton, Iowa, 1976—. Adj. prof. Western Iowa Tech C.C., Sioux City, Iowa, 1986—. EMT Mapleton (Iowa) Area Ambulance Svc., 1976—88; mem. city coun. Mapleton (Iowa) City Coun., 1990—94. Mem.: NEA, Iowa State Edn. Assn. Democrat. Roman Catholic. Avocations: genealogy, pysanky. Home: 311 South 6th Street Mapleton IA 51034 Office: Maple Valley Community Schools 502 South 7th Street Mapleton IA 51034 Office Phone: 712-881-1317. Personal E-mail: stodola@longlines.com. Business E-Mail: sstodola@maple-valley.k12.ia.us.

**STODT, F. CHLOE,** piano educator; d. Leo Francis and Mary Ellen Stodt. BA in Music Edn. and Piano, St. Ambrose U., Davenport, Iowa, 1974; MMus in Piano Performance, U. Colo., 1976; MA in Theology and Liturgical Studies, U. Notre Dame, 1978; DMA in Piano Performance and Pedagogy, U. Iowa, 2003. Dir. music and liturgy St. Joseph's Parish, Stratford, Ontario, Canada, 1978—80, St. Patrick's Parish, Kansas City, Mo., 1980—84; asst. prof, then assoc. prof. music Black Hawk Coll., Moline, Ill., 1986—88; dir. cmty. music, instr. piano Augustana Coll., Rock Island, 1988—93; dir. music ministries South Pk. Presbyn. Ch., Rock Island, 1993—2005; instr. piano West Music Conservatory, Moline, Ill., 2005—. Recipient Music award, State Iowa, 1970—71; Italian Lang. scholar, U. Iowa, 1992, Piano Accompanying scholar, U. Colo., 1975, Presdl. scholar, St. Ambrose U., 1970—74. Mem.: Coll. Music Soc., Nat. Guild Piano Teachers, Am. Guild Organists (exec. bd. mem., sub-dean, newsletter editor 1984—2005), Pi Kappa Lambda. Independent. Avocations: swimming, bicycling, wildflowers, morel mushrooms. Office: 2201 7th Ave Moline IL 61265

**STOEBUCK, WILLIAM BREES,** law educator; b. Wichita, Mar. 18, 1929; s. William Douglas and Donice Beth (Brees) S.; m. Mary Virginia Fields, Dec. 24, 1951; children: Elizabeth, Catherine, Caroline. BA, Wichita State U., 1951; MA, Ind. U., 1953; JD, U. Wash., 1959; SJD, Harvard U., 1973. Bar: Wash. 1959, U.S. Supreme Ct. 1967. Pvt. practice, Seattle, 1959—64; asst. prof. law U. Denver, 1964—67; assoc. prof. U. Wash., Seattle, 1967—70, prof., 1970—95, Judson Falknor prof., 1995—99, prof. emeritus, 1999—; of counsel Karr, Tuttle, Campbell, Seattle, 1988—. Author: Washington Real Estate: Practice Law, 1995, 2d edit., 2004, Washington Real Estate: Transactions, 1995, 2d edit., 2004, Basic Property Law, 1989, Law of Property, 1984, 3d edit., 2000, Nontrespassory Takings, 1977, Contemporary Property, 1996, 2d edit., 2002; contbr. articles to profl. jours. Bd. dirs. Cascade Symphony Orch., 1978-83, Forest Park Libr., 1975-80. 1st lt. USAF, 1951-56. Mem. Pacific Real Estate Inst., Am. Coll. Real Estate Lawyers, Wash. State Bar Assn., Assn. Am. Law Schs., Order of Coif, Seattle Yacht Club. Home: 3515 NE 158th Pl Lk Forest Park WA 98155-6649 Office: Sch Law Univ Washington William H Gates Hall Seattle WA 98195-3020 Office Phone: 206-543-4917. Business E-Mail: stoebuck@u.washington.edu.

**STOECKER, DAVID THOMAS,** banker; b. St. Louis, June 8, 1939; s. John Garth and Marie (Zahler) S.; m. Ann E. Conrad, Aug. 18, 1962; children— Lisa Ann, Susan Jane. BS, Ind. U., 1963. Sr. v.p. comml. loans Mercantile Trust Co. N.Am., St. Louis, 1965-80; pres. Gravois-Merc. Bank, St. Louis, 1980-87; pres., chief exec. officer Bank of South County, St. Louis, 1987-95; chmn. bd., CEO Ctrl. West End Bank, St. Louis, 1996—. Served to 1st lt. AUS, 1963—65. Mem.: Robert Morris Assocs. (pres. St. Louis 1980), Sunset Country Club. Methodist. Office: 415 Debaliviere Saint Louis MO 63112

**STOEK, THOMAS,** management professional, sales professional; b. Friedberg, Germany, Dec. 2, 1964; s. Norbert Leo and Elke Astrid Stoek; 1 child, Robin. Degree in elect. engring., Darmstadt (Germany) U., 1992; IMD, Lausanne U. Cons. Interchip Unternehmensberatung, 1992-95; sr. cons. Softlab, Munich, 1995-96; sales mgr. Central Europe Seagate Software, Inc., Munich; mng. dir. and mem. European Bd. Guardian iT (formerly debis Systemhaus Guardian), London, 1997-2000; exec. v.p. sales & mktg. Cybernet, Inc., Munich, 2001—02; mng. dir. Ester GmbH Lyon & Maud, 2003—. Bd. dirs. Novento AG, Multicale AG. Contbr. articles to profl. jours. Active Bus. Angel Network Deutschland, Berlin, 2000—; chmn. McKinsey Social Projects. Served with German mil., 1984-85. Office: Cybernet IncEster GmbH 80868 Munich Germany Fax: 49 8152 981372. Office Phone: 49 89 700 007-10. E-mail: tstoek@t-online.de.

**STOELTING, CURTIS W.,** consumer products company executive; BS in Acctg., U. Ill. From v.p. fin. and ops. to CEO RC2 Corp., Bolingbrook, Ill., 1996—2003, CEO, 2003—; bd. dir. Office: Rc2 1111 W 22nd St Oak Brook IL 60523-1940

**STOELTJE, BEVERLY JUNE,** liberal studies educator; b. Rotan, Tex., Apr. 1, 1940; d. Roger Caswell and Laura Inez (Kennedy) Smith; children: Gretchen, Rachael; m. Richard Bauman, Nov. 26, 1977; children: Mark, Andrew. BA, U. Tex., 1961, MA, 1975, PhD, 1979. Asst. prof. English U. Tex., Austin, 1983-86; assoc. prof. anthropology, folklore/ethnomusicology Ind. U., Bloomington, 1986—, mem. Am. studies faculty, 1986—, mem. African studies faculty, 1989—. Cons. S.W. Ednl. Devel. Lab., Austin, 1976, Tex. Women's History Project, San Antonio, 1981; dir. Folk Arts Survey Tex., Austin, 1977, 78; dir. USIA linkage performance Ind. U. and U. Ghana, 1989-93; assoc. dir. Ind. Ctr. Global Change World Peace, 1994-95. Author: Children's Handclaps, 1979; editor: (with C.B. Cohen and R. Wilk) Beauty Queens on the Global Stage, 1996; editor (essay collection) Feminist Revision in Folklore Studies, 1988, Women, Language, and Law in Africa, 2002; contbr. articles to profl. jours. and chpts. in books. Fulbright rsch. fellow Ghana, 1989-90; grantee Tex. Commn. for Humanities, 1980; Weatherhead scholar Sch. Am. Rsch., 1997-98. Mem. African Studies Assn., Am. Folklore Soc. (exec. bd. 1981-84), Am. Anthropol. Assn., Law and Soc. Office: Dept Anthropology Student Bldg Ind U Bloomington IN 47405 Office Phone: 812-855-8014. Business E-Mail: stoeltje@indiana.edu.

**STOERI, WILLIAM R.,** lawyer; b. 1955; BA in History & Phil. summa cum laude, Kalamazoo Coll., 1978; student, Univ. Erlangen, Nurenberg, Germany, 1978—79; JD, Yale Univ., 1982. Bar: Minn. 1982. Law clerk, Hon. Diana E. Murphy US Dist. Ct., Minn. Dist., 1982—84; assoc. Dorsey & Whitney LLP, Mpls., 1984—89, ptnr., trial dept., 1990—, and co-chair, profl. malpractice group. Mem.: Phi Beta Kappa. Office: Dorsey & Whitney LLP Ste 1500 50 S Sixth St Minneapolis MN 55402-1498 Office Phone: 612-343-7942. Office Fax: 612-340-8800. Business E-mail: stoeri.bill@dorsey.com.

**STOESEN, ALEXANDER RUDOLPH,** retired history educator; b. Austin, Texas, Apr. 9, 1932; s. Andrew Robert William and Laura Tomine (Thompson) S.; m. Carol Annette Cronk, Aug. 22, 1959 (dec. Feb. 1999); children: Robert Andrew, William Darden, Carolyn Anne. BA, The Citadel, 1954; MA, U. Rochester, 1958; PhD, U. N.C., 1965. Tchr. Washington Sq. Reading Ctr., NYC, 1958-59; asst. prof. history Newberry Coll. SC, 1964-66; from asst. to prof. history Guilford Coll., Greensboro, NC, 1966-99, chmn. dept. history, 1972-77, 82-84, 90-91; Lilly fellow Duke U., Durham, NC, 1976-77. Mem. past chair NC Hwy. Hist. Marker Adv. Commn., Raleigh, 1986-91, 94-98, 2001—; v.p. So. Assn. Pre-Law Advisers, 1989-91, pres., 1991-93; mem. Pre-Law Advisers Nat. Coun., 1991-93, cons., 1993—. Author: Guilford College: On the Strength of 150 Years, 1987, Guilford County Since 1890, Part II of History of Guilford County, 1981, Guilford County: A Brief History, 1993; author: (with others) The North Carolina Experience, 1984, Encyclopedia of Southern History, 1979; contbr. articles to profl. jours. and reviews to newspapers. Mem. Greensboro Sit-Ins Twentieth Anniversary Com., 1979-80, 13th Anniversary Com., 1989-90, 40th Ann. Com., 1999-2000; chmn. bd. trustees Unitarian Ch. of Greensboro, 1979-81; trustee Greensboro Hist. Mus., 1997-99; vol. Habitat for Humanity, various countries, 2001 ; vol. Quaker workteam in Ramallah, Palestine, 1999, 2001. 1st lt. U.S. Army, 1955-57, capt. USAR, 1969. 1st lt. USAR, 1955—57, capt. USAR, 1969. Recipient Congl. Leadership award Thomas Jefferson dist. Unitarian-Universalist Assn., Excellence in Tchg. Award, Guilford Coll., 1995, Appreciation award Guilford County Bd. of Pub. Health, 2000, Christopher Crittenden award State NC, 1990, 2000; grantee NEH, 1975, 82. Mem. Am. Hist. Assn., Hist. Soc. NC (coun. 1988-90, sec. 1990-96, v.p. 1997-98, pres. 1998-99, Hugh T. Lefler undergrad. history award com. 1983, chmn. 1984), N.C. Lit. and Hist. Assn. (Mayflower Cup book prize com. 1987, 91), So. Hist. Assn., Orgn. Am. Historians (chmn. membership com., 1991-96), Assn. of Citadel Men (life). Democrat. Avocations: bicycling, bicentennial memorabilia collector, gardening, bird watching, whitewater rafting. Personal E-mail: astoesen1@bellsouth.net.

**STOESSINGER, JOHN GEORGE,** political science professor; b. Vienna, Oct. 14, 1927; came to U.S., 1947; s. Oscar and Irene Stoessinger; m. Carolyn Stoessinger, 1966 (div. 1985); children: Richard Victor, Anna. BA, Grinnell Coll., 1950, LLB (hon.), 1970; MA, Harvard U., 1952, PhD, 1954; LLB (hon.), Am. Coll. in Switzerland, Leysin, 1981. Prof. polit. scis. CUNY, N.Y.C., 1957-83; dir. polit. affairs divsn. UN, N.Y.C., 1967-74; disting. prof. internat. affairs Trinity U., San Antonio, 1983-2000; disting. prof. global diplomacy U. San Diego, 2000—. Teaching fellow Harvard U., Cambridge, Mass., 1952-54; asst. prof. polit. sci. Wellesley (Mass.) Coll., 1954-56; vis. prof. internat. affairs Columbia U., 1963-67, Princeton (N.J.) U., 1978. Author: The Might of Nations, 1962, 10th edit., 2000 (Bancroft prize 1963), Nations at Dawn, 1979, 6th edit., 1996, Henry Kissinger, 1979, Why Nations Go To War, 1983, 9th edit., 2004. Active UNA-USA, NY, 1960—. Mem. Coun. on Fgn. Rels. (book rev. editor Fgn. Affairs 1968-78). Jewish. Avocation: classical music. Office: U San Diego 5998 Alcala Park San Diego CA 92110 Home: 601 Neptune Ave Encinitas CA 92024 Office Phone: 760-632-8682. Personal E-mail: johngstoessinger@cox.net.

**STOFFEL, PAUL T.,** investment company executive; m. Gayle Stoffel. MBA, Harvard Bus. Sch. Various positions to bd. dirs. Comerica Corp.; chmn. Triple S Capital Corpn., Paul Stoffel Investments. Bd. dirs. Holly Corpn., Dallas, 2001—. Co-founder Gayle and Paul Stoffel Found.; bd. mem. Dallas Symphony Orch., Southwestern Med. Found., Zale Lipshy Hosp., St. Paul U. Hosp.; bd. dirs. Dallas Symphony Assn., Dallas Symphony Found. Named one of Top 200 Collectors, ARTnews mag., 2005—06. Mailing: 5949 Sherry Ln Ste 1465 Dallas TX 75225*

**STOFFERSON, TERRY LEE,** financial analyst; b. Omaha, Apr. 22, 1957; s. Dale Leslie and Alma Rose (Flores) S. BSBA, U. Nebr., Omaha, 1980; MBA, DBA, Calif. Coast U., Santa Ana, 1998. Auditor Alexander Grant & Co., CPA's, Omaha, 1979-81; budget mgr. Archbishop Bergan Mercy Hosp., Omaha, 1981-86; controller Lafayette (La.) Gen. Med. Ctr., 1986-87; chief fin. officer Opelousas (La.) Gen. Hosp., 1987-89; assoc. adminstr. fin. County of Fresno Valley (Calif.) Med. Ctr., 1989-94; v.p. fin. Trinity Med. Ctr., Minot, N.D., 1994-96; exec. v.p. St. Catherine Hosp., Garden City, Kans., 1996-2001; sr. v.p. Provena St. Joseph Hosp., Elgin, Ill., 2001—02; v.p. adminstr. La Rabida Children's Hosp., Chgo., 2003—05; CFO Twelve Oaks Med. Ctr., Houston, 2006—. Cons. in field. Mem. Healthcare Fin. Mgrs. Assn. (advanced), Nat. Assn. Accts. (contr.'s coun. 1988, 89), Am. Hosp. Assn., Am. Coll. Healthcare Execs Lodges: Optimist (pres. 1988). Republican. Presbyterian. Avocations: fishing, electronics, photography. Office Phone: 713-964-8780. E-mail: drterrbear@aol.com.

**STOFFLE, CARLA JOY,** university library dean; b. Pueblo, Colo., June 19, 1943; d. Samuel Bernard and Virginia Irene (Berry) Hayden; m. Richard William Stoffle, June 12, 1964; children: Brent William, Kami Ann. AA, So. Colo. State Coll., Pueblo, 1963; BA, U. Colo., 1965; MLS, U. Ky., 1969; postgrad., U. Wis., 1980. Head govt. publ. dept. John G. Crabbe Library, Eastern Ky. U., Richmond, 1969-72; from head pub. svcs. to asst. chancellor edn. svcs. U. Wis. Parkside Libr., Kenosha, 1972—85; dep. dir. U. Mich. Libr., Ann Arbor, 1986—91; prof. libr. sci. U. Ariz. Tucson 1991 , dean libr. and ctr. for creative photography, 1991—, acting dir. Sch. Info. Resources and Libr. Sci., 1999—2001. Adv. bd. Bowker Librs., NY, 1985—90; bd. dirs. Trejo Foster Found., 2000—; state adv. com. Ariz. State Dept. of Libr. Archives and Pub. Records, 2000—; adv. com. U. Mich. Sch. Libr. Sci., 1986—92, OCLC Rsch. Librs., 1995—2000. Co-author: Administration of Government Documents Collection, 1974, Materials and Method for History Research, 1979, Materials and Methods for Political Science Research, 1979; mem. editl. bd. The Collection Bldg., 1978—95, The Bottom Line, 1989—95, Internet and Higher Edn., 1998—99, The Univ. Ariz. Press, 1992—. Vol. Peace Corps, Barbados, West Indies, 1965—67. Named Outstanding Alumnus, Coll. Libr. and Info. Sci., U. Ky., 1989; recipient Pres.'s award, Ariz. Ednl. Media Assn., 1993, YWCA Tucson Outstanding Woman of 1992: A Woman on the Move award, 1992, Ariz. Libr. of Yr. award, 2000. Mem.: ALA (councilor 1983—93, exec. bd. dirs. 1985—93, treas. 1988—93, endowment trustee 1988—93, endowment campaign com. 1989—93, pres. adv. com. 1993—96, legis. com. 1994—96, nominations com. 1997, Lippincott award com. 1997, spectrum scholarship com. 1998—2002, endowment trustee 2001—, chair com. accreditation 2002—03, libr. and info. tech. svcs. adv. com. 1997-99, chair 1997-98, Miriam Dudley Bibliographic Instrn. Libr. of Yr. award 1991, Acad. Rsch. Libr. of Yr. 1992, Elizabeth Futas Catalyst for Change award 2002, Equality award 2003, Loleta Fyan award Jury 2003—04), Ctr. Rsch. Librs. (budget and fin. com. 1994—2001, exec. com., bd. dirs. 1998—, treas. 1999—2000, vice chair, bd. dirs. 2001—03, chair, bd. dirs. 2003), Ariz. State Libr. Assn., Assn. Coll. Rsch. Librs. (bd. dirs. 1978—84, mem. exec. com. 1981—84, pres. 1982—83, Planning Com. 1993—95, chair nat. conf. planning com. 1995—97), Assn. Rsch. Librs. (com. stats. and measurement 1994—2003, bd. dirs. 1997—2001, mem. steering com. Scholarly Pub. and Acad. Resource Coalition 1998—2001, mem. govt. documents digitization project work group 2004—, bd. dirs. info. policies com. 2004—). Office: U Arizona Main Libr 1510 E University Blvd Tucson AZ 85721-0055 Office Phone: 520-621-2101. E-mail: stofflec@u.library.arizona.edu.*

**STOHLER, CHRISTIAN S.,** dean, dental educator; DMD, U. Bern, Switzerland, 1972, DrMedDent, 1975. Cert. in oral surgery U. Bern, 1976, in prosthodontics U. Bern, 1979. Tchr. asst. prof. U. Mich., 1979—81; assoc. prof. prosthodontics U. Bern, 1981—83; vis. asst. prof. U. Mich. Sch.

Dentistry, 1983—84, assoc. prof., 1984—90, prof., 1990—95; rsch. scientist Ctr. for Human Growth and Devel., U. Mich., 1991—98; dir. rsch. U. Mich. Sch. Dentistry, 1994—97; chair dept. biologic and material sci. U. Mich., 1995—2003, William R. Mann prof., 1997—2002, Robert and Natalie Roberts prof., 2002—03; dean Balt. Coll. Dental Surgery. U. Md., 2003—. Mem. bd. scientific counselors Nat. Inst. Dental and Craniofacial Rsch., 2000—; past pres. IADR/AADR Neuroscience Group, Assn. of U. TMD/Orofacial Pain Groups. Assoc. editor: Journal of Orofacial Pain. Office: U Maryland Baltimore Coll Dental Surgery 666 W Baltimore St Baltimore MD 21201 Business E-mail: cstohler@dental.umaryland.edu.*

**STOHLMAN, BRUCE RICHARD,** secondary school educator; b. Lynwood, Calif., June 13, 1949; s. Robert Fischer Sr. and Carmen Margarita (Santiago) S.; m. Connie Suzanne Holmes, Sept. 14, 1991. BBA, U. Md., 1975; A in Space Communications Ops. Tech., Community Coll. of Air Force, Offutt AFB, Nebr., 1992. Chief master sgt. USAF, chief of tng. detachment 184 Europe Balikishir, Turkey, 1976-77; chief SAC tng. br. 308 Strategic Missile Wing Davis-Monthan AFB, Tucson, Ariz., 1977-80; command control tng. br. 36th Tactical Fighter Wing Bitburg (Germany) Air Base, 1980-82; supt. command control div. 406 Tactical Fighter Tng. Wing Zaragoza (Spain) Air Base, 1982-84; sr. non-commd. officer underground command ctr. Hdqs. SAC Offutt AFB, Omaha, 1984-85, supt. command control inspection Hdqs. SAC, 1985-89, chief space future concepts div. Hdqs. SAC, 1989-92; high sch. tchr. Bellevue (Nebr.) West High Sch., 1992—. Mem. Offense/Def. Integration Opportunities Working Group Def. Nuclear Agy., Alexandria, Va., 1989-92. Mem. PTA, Papillion, Nebr., 1987; scoutmaster Boy Scouts Am., 1960—. Decorated Meritorious Svc. medals; recipient Dist. Merit award, Boy Scouts Am., 2001, Silver Beaver award, 2003, James E. West award, 2006. Mem. Air Force Assn., USAF Chiefs Assn. (v.p. 1991-92), Nat. Tchrs. Orgn., Bellevue Ednl. Assn. Avocations: bible study, golf, tennis, playing bridge. Home: 205 Martin Dr Bellevue NE 68005-4795 Office: Bellevue West High Sch 1501 Thurston Ave Bellevue NE 68123-2499

**STOHR, DONALD J.,** federal judge; b. Sedalia, Mo., Mar. 9, 1934; s. Julius Leo and Margaret Elizabeth (McGaw) Stohr; m. Mary Ann Kuhlman, July 31, 1957; 5 children. BS, St. Louis U., 1956, JD, 1958. Bar: Mo. 1958, U.S. Dist. Ct. (ea. dist.) Mo. 1958, U.S. Ct. Appeals (8th cir.) 1966, U.S. Supreme Ct. 1969. Assoc. Hocker Goodwin & MacGreevy, St. Louis, 1958-63, 66-69; asst. counselor St. Louis County, 1963-65, counselor, 1965-66; U.S. atty. Ea. Dist. Mo., St. Louis, 1973-76; ptnr. Thompson & Mitchell, St. Louis, 1969-73, 76-92; judge U.S. Dist. Ct. (ea. dist.) Mo., St. Louis, 1992—. Mem. ABA, Mo. Bar Assn., Am. Judicature Soc., St. Louis Met. Bar Assn. Office: 111 S 10th St Rm 16 182 Saint Louis MO 63102

**STOHR, KATE (KATHERINE A. STOHR),** freelance journalist; b. Evanston, Ill., Oct. 24, 1976; d. Edward Albert and Marcia Gillan S. BA magna cum laude in Philos., NYU, 1995; MS in Journalism, Columbia U., 1998. Copywriter Austin Knight, NYC, 1993-95; assoc. prodr. Time Inc. New Media, NYC, 1995-97; producer J. Walter Thompson Specialized Comm., NYC, 1998—99; co-founder Architecture for Humanity, 1999—. Producer (documentary): Don's Dump on Us, 1998, Biography, Hist. Detectives, Escape From Death Row, Night Court, Teen Gambling; co-editor: Design Like You Give a Damn, 2006. Vol. Gen Art Film Festival, N.Y.C., 1998-99. Co-recipient WIRED Rave award-Architecture, 2006. Mem. Soc. Profl. Journalists. Office: Architecture for Humanity 23 1/2 N Tracy Ave Bozeman MT 59715-3556*

**STOIA, VIOREL G.,** life underwriter; b. Aberdeen, SD, Feb. 13, 1924; s. John and Seana (Biliboca) S.; m. Donna Marie Maurseth Stoia, Sept. 10, 1949; children: Marsha Jo, Nancy Kay, Gregory Allen, Thomas John, James Vincent. BBA, U. Minn., 1949; D in Pub. Svc. (hon.), No. State U., 2002. CLU, ChFC, Am. Coll. Sr. agt. Northwestern Mut. Life, Milw.; with Stoia Kusler and Assoc., Aberdeen, SD. Co-founder, chmn. bd. Student Loan Fin. Corp., 1978—2003; mng. ptnr. Aberdeen Real Estate Ptnrs., 1979—92; co-founder, mng. ptnr. Tel Serv, 1983—97; co-founder Northwest Regional Health and Fitness Ctr., 1999—. Co-founder, pres. Northeastern Mental Health Ctr., 1957-59, North Plains Hospice, 1980-84; sec. Edn. Asst. Corp., 1978-97; bd. dirs. SD Crippled Children's Hosp., Avera Health Sys., 1996-2003; trustee Aberdeen YMCA, 1969-73, St. Luke's Hosp., 1969-96; co-founder, trustee Northern State U. Found., 1972-99; co-founder Great Plains Edn. Found., 1999—, Aberdeen Downtown Assn., 1999, Blackstone Devel. Corp., 2000, N.E. Regional Health and Fitness Ctr., 1999—. USN, C.P.O., 1942-46. Named Outstanding Civic Leader of Am., 1967; recipient Jefferson award Nat. Inst. of Pub. Svc., Sioux Falls, 1980, George award Aberdeen C. of C., 1979, 94, Gov.'s award for excellence in econ. devel., 2000, Disting. Trustee award SD Assn. Healthcare Orgns., 2002. Mem. Aberdeen Devel. Corp. (pres. 1972-87), Aberdeen Jr. C. of C. (pres. 1956), S.D. Soc. CLU's (co-founder, pres. 1958-59), Nat. Assn. Life Underwriters, Aberdeen Dist. Life Underwriters (pres. 1953-54), S.D. Assn. Life Underwriters (pres. 1959-60), Million Dollar Round Table (life), Moccasin Creek Country Club (v.p. 1969-75). Republican. Roman Catholic. Avocations: jogging, hunting, reading. Home: 1022 N Main St Aberdeen SD 57401-2426 Office: Stoia Kusler & Assoc PO Box 98 304 1/2 S Main St Aberdeen SD 57401-4146 Office Phone: 605-225-3382. Personal E-mail: stoia@nvc.net.

**STOIBER, CARLTON RAY,** nuclear law consultant, freelance/self-employed cartoonist; b. Vallejo, Calif., July 5, 1942; s. Raymond F. and Grace Stoiber; m. Susanne Alexander, Sept. 10, 1966. BA summa cum laude, U. Colo., 1964, JD, 1969; LLM, U. London, 1975; diploma cum laude, Hague Acad. Internat. Law, 1975. Bar: Colo. 1969, DC 1970, US Supreme Ct. 1973. Atty. US Dept. Justice, Washington, 1969-71, dir. Office of Indian Rights, 1972-74; asst. gen. counsel US NRC, Washington, 1975-80, US Arms Control and Disarmament Agy., Washington, 1980-81; dir. Office Nuclear Export Control US Dept. State, Washington, 1981-85; dir. Office Nuclear Non-Proliferation Policy, 1988-91; dir. Office Nuclear Tech. and Safeguards, 1991-93; counselor US Mission to UN Agys., Vienna, 1985-88; dir. Internat. Programs USNRC, 1993-99; cons. Sci. Applications Internat. Corp., 1999—; cartoonist Issues in Sci. & Tech., 2000—. Rhodes scholar, 1964, Norlin award for disting. achievement U. Colo., 1994. Mem. Reform Club, Am. Soc. Internat. Law, Am. Assn. Editl. Cartoonists, Phi Beta Kappa. Avocations: mountain climbing, birding. Personal E-mail: crstoiber@earthlink.net.

**STOIBER, SUSANNE A.,** health science organization administrator; BA, MPA, U. Colo.; MS, London Sch. Econs. Principal analyst for health care fin. programs Congressional Budget Office; adminstr. of clinical research Nat. Inst. of Health; dir. divsn. soc. and econ. studies NRC US Dept. HHS, 1990-94, various sr. positions, 1994—98; exec. officer Inst. Medicine, 1998—. Contbr. articles to profl. jours. Recipient NIH Directors Award, 1985, Presidential Rank Award for lifetime achievement in Senior Exec. Service. Office: Inst Medicine 500 5th St NW Washington DC 20418-0007 Fax: 908-771-8618.

**STOICHEFF, BORIS PETER,** physicist, researcher; b. Bitol, Macedonia, June 1, 1924; s. Peter and Vasilka (Tonna) S.; m. Lillian Joan Ambridge, May 15, 1954; 1 child, Richard Peter. BSc, U. Toronto, 1947, MA, 1948, PhD, 1950, DSc (hon.), 1994, U. Skopje, Macedonia, 1981, York U., 1982, U. Windsor, 1989. McKee-Gilchrist postdoctoral fellow U. Toronto, Ont., Canada, 1950-51; postdoctoral fellow NRC Can., Canada, 1951-53, sr. rsch. officer, 1954-64; vis. scientist MIT, 1963-64; prof. physics U. Toronto, Canada, 1964-89, univ. prof., 1977-89, univ. prof. emeritus, 1989—, chmn. engring. sci., 1972-77, H.L. Welsh lectr., 1984; sr. fellow Massey Coll., 1979—; exec. dir. Laser and Lightwave Rsch. Ctr., Ont., Canada, 1988-91. Mem. NRC Can., 1977-83; govt. appointee to coun. Assn. Profl. Engr. Ont., 1985-91; vis. sci. Stanford U., 1978; Walter E. Kaskan lectr. SUNY, Binghamton, 1980; Elizabeth Laird Meml. lectr. U. Western Ont., 1985; UK/Can. Rutherford lectr., 1989; v.p. Internat. Union Pure and Applied Physics, 1994-96. Author: Gerhard Herzberg: An Illustrious Life in Science, 2002; contbr. articles to profl. jours. Decorated officer Order of Can., 1982; I.W. Killam scholar, 1977-79; Geoffrey Frew fellow Australian Acad. Sci., 1980. Fellow Royal Soc. Can. (co-fgn. sec. 1995-2000, Henry Marshall Tory

medal 1989), Royal Soc. London, Am. Phys. Soc., Optical Soc. Am. (pres. 1976, William F. Meggers award 1981, Frederic Ives medal 1983, Disting. Svc. award 2002), Indian Acad. Sci. (hon.), Macedonian Acad. Sci. and Arts (hon.), Am. Acad. Arts and Sci. (fgn. hon.); mem. Can. Assn. Physicists (pres. 1984, Gold medal 1974). Achievements include develop. of techniques for high resolution Raman spectroscopy of gases and determination of geometrical structures many molecules; use of lasers in spectroscopic investigations including Brillouin and Raman scattering and two photon absorption; observation of stimulated Raman absorption and stimulated Brillouin scattering resulting in generation of intense hypersonic waves in solids; use of Brillouin spectra to measure elastic constants of rare gas crystals; generation of tunable coherent VUV radiation for use in atomic and molecular spectroscopy. Home: 66 Collier St Apt 6B Toronto ON Canada M4W 1L9 Office: U Toronto Dept Physics Toronto ON Canada M5S 1A7 Office Phone: 416-978-2948. Business E-mail: bps@physics.utoronto.ca.

**STOJKOVIC, DEJAN B.,** physicist, educator; b. Vranje, Serbia-Montenegro, Feb. 4, 1971; arrived in US, 1997; s. Borivoje and Borka Stojkovic; m. Andrijana Stojkovic, May 5, 1998; children: Dejana, Natalia. BSc, U. Belgrade, 1994, MSc, 1997; PhD, Case Western Res. U., Cleve., 2001. Killam Meml. postdoctoral fellow U. Alta., Edmonton, Canada, 2001—03; Mich. Ctr. Theoretical Physics postdoctoral fellow U. Mich., Ann Arbor, 2003—05; asst. prof. Case Western Res. U., 2005—. Recipient Spl. award, City Coun., Vranje, 2002; fellow Serbian (Yugoslav) Ministry of Sci.; scholar Case Western Res. U., 1997—2001. Achievements include research in theoretical physics (cosmology, particle physics, gravity, field theory, extra dimensions, topological defects). Avocations: philosophy, swimming, travel. Office: Case Western Res U 10900 Euclid Ave Cleveland OH 44106-7079 Office Phone: 216-368-4070. Business E-Mail: dbs3@case.edu.

**STOJKOVIC, DUSAN,** lawyer; b. Zemun, Yugoslavia, Apr. 26, 1976; s. Sava and Dragica (Filip) Stojkovic. BA, Bernard M. Baruch Coll., 1997; JD, Harvard Law Sch., 2000. Bar: NY 2001. Assoc. LeBoeuf, Lamb, Greene & MacRae, L.L.P., NYC, 2000—05, Simmons & Simmons, London, 2005—. Mem. Sierra Club, NYC, 1995—2004. Belle Zeller scholar, CUNY, 1996. Achievements include fluently speaking four languages. Avocations: travel, writing on-line film reviews, rock concerts. Office: Simmons & Simmons CityPoint One Ropemaker St London EC2Y 9SS England Office Phone: 011-44-20-7825-4234. Office Fax: 011-44-20-7628-2070. Business E-Mail: dusan.stojkovic@simmons-simmons.com.

**STOKER, DANIEL J.,** academic administrator; s. Mary Phipps; m. Rebecca Wald Stoker, July 8, 2005. BA, SUNY, Potsdam, 1993; MS, Ind. State U., 1995. Program coord. for Greek and student orgns. Pittsburg (Kans.) State U., 1995—97, asst. dir. Overman Student Ctr. for Campus Activities, 1997—2003; dir. co-curricular programs U. of Indpls., 2003—06, exec. dir. for student svcs., 2006—. Exec. v.p. Assn. of Frat. Advisors, Indpls., 2002—04. Mem.: Assn. of Coll. Unions Internat., Coll. Student Educators Internat., Nat. Assn. of Student Pers. Adminstrs., Pi Kappa Alpha. Presbyterian. Office: U Indpls 1400 E Hanna Ave Indianapolis IN 46227 Office Phone: 317-788-3507. Office Fax: 317-788-3383. E-mail: dstoker@uindy.edu.

**STOKES, B. R.,** transportation executive, consultant; b. Anadarko, Okla., Feb. 20, 1924; s. Robert Allan and Ethel Nan (James) S.; m. Joan Pringle, Oct. 22, 1950; children: Timothy, Leigh, Lindsey, Celia. Student. U. Okla., 1941-44; BA, U. Calif., Berkeley, 1947. Reporter, writer Oakland (Calif.) Tribune, 1946-58; dir. info. San Francisco Bay Area Rapid Transit Dist., 1958-61, asst. gen. mgr., 1961-63, gen. mgr., 1963-74; exec. v.p. Am. Public Transit Assn., Washington, 1974-80; sr. v.p. internat. ATE Mgmt. and Service Co., Inc., 1980-95. Dir. gen. Saudi Arabian Public Transport Co., 1980-81 Served with USNR, 1942-46. Recipient Salzberg medal Syracuse U., 1975; inductee Am. Pub. Transit Assn. Transit Hall of Fame, 1996; Reid Found. fellow, 1954. Office: 1911 Fort Myer Dr Arlington VA 22209-1603

**STOKES, HENRY ARTHUR,** journalist; b. Jacksonville, Fla., Dec. 9, 1944; s. Henry Jasper and Waneta Marian (Lord) S.; m. Carolyn Elizabeth Morley, Aug. 6, 1966; children: Elizabeth, Virginia, Katherine. AA, St. Johns River Jr. Coll., Palatka, Fla., 1966; BS in Journalism with high honors, U. Fla., 1969. Reporter Daytona Beach (Fla.) News-Jour., 1966, Palatka (Fla.) Daily News, 1966-69, Fla. Times-Union, Jacksonville, 1969-71, night city editor, 1972; various editing positions Detroit News, 1972-88; asst. mng. editor Comml. Appeal, Memphis, 1988-92, mng. editor, 1992—2002, dir. adminstrn. and planning, 2003—. Mem. Memphis Literacy Coun., 1989-97, chmn., 1993, 94; bd. dirs. Friends Memphis/Shelby Co. Libr., 1991-2003, Found. for the Libr., 2003—; mem. pres. adv. coun. LeMoyne-Owen Coll., 1992-2000; bd. dirs. Memphis Downtown YMCA, 2001—. Recipient Emig award Coll. Journalism U. Fla., 1970. Mem. Soc. Profl. Journalists, Tenn. Press Assn. (bd. dirs. 2003-04, v.p. 2004—), The Egyptians, Rotary (bd. dirs. Memphis chpt. 2002-04). Episcopalian. Avocations: ornithology, fly fishing. Office: Comml Appeal 495 Union Ave Memphis TN 38103-3221 Office Phone: 901-529-2301. Business E-Mail: stokes@commercialappeal.com.

**STOKES, JAMES CHRISTOPHER,** lawyer; b. Orange, N.J., Mar. 19, 1944; s. James Christopher and Margaret Mary (Groome) S.; m. Eileen Marie Brosnan, Sept. 7, 1968; children: Erin Margaret, Michael Colin, Courtney Dorothy. AB, Holy Cross Coll., 1966; JD, Boston Coll., 1975. Bar: Hawaii 1975, U.S. Ct. Appeals (1st and 9th cirs.) 1976, Mass. 1977, U.S. Ct. Internat. Trade 1988. Officer USMC, 1966-72; assoc. Carlsmith, Carlsmith, Wichman & Case, Honolulu, 1975-76, Bingham, Dana & Gould (now Bingham McCutchen LLP), Boston, 1976-82, ptnr. London, 1980-84, Boston, 1982—. Contbr. articles to profl. jours. Active personnel bd. Town of Wellesley, Mass., 1984-89, chmn. bd. 1990-99, town moderator, 1992-97, trustee U.S.S. Constitution Mus. Capt. USMC, 1966-72, Vietnam. Mem. Hawaii Bar Assn., Mass. Bar Assn., Internat. Bar Assn., Boston Bar Assn., Harvard Club (Boston), Wellesley Club. Roman Catholic. Office: Bingham McCutchen LLP 150 Federal St Boston MA 02110-1713 Office Phone: 617-951-8222. Business E-Mail: james.stokes@bingham.com.

**STOKES, JAMES SEWELL,** environmental services administrator, not-for-profit developer; b. Englewood, NJ, Jan. 24, 1944; s. James Sewell III and Doris Mackey (Smith) S.; m. Esther Moger, Aug. 19, 1967; children: Jessica Neale, Elizabeth Sewell BA, Davidson (N.C.) Coll., 1966; LLB, Yale U., 1969. Bar: Ga. 1969. Asst. to gen. counsel Office Gen. Counsel of the Army, Washington, 1969-72; assoc. Alston, Miller & Gaines, Atlanta, 1972-77; Alston & Bird (previously Alston, Miller & Gaines), Atlanta, 1977—2005, chmn. environ. group, 1987—96, chmn. bus. devel. com., 1996—2005; mem. ptnr.'s com. Alston & Bird, Atlanta, 1995-98; chmn. mgmt. com., Atlanta, 1998; pres. Ga. Conservancy, Atlanta, 2005—. Mem. Ga.'s Environ. Adv. Coun., 1991-2004, chmn., 1997-99; chmn. Gov.'s Conf. on Pollution Prevention and the Environment, 1997; spkr. in field Contbr. articles to profl. jours. Mem. Metro Atlanta Chamber Clean Water Initiative, 2000, Ga. Future Forestry Commn., 2005, Atlanta Regional Commn. Environ. & Land Use Com., 2005; exec. com. Livable Cmtys. Coalition, 2005—; chmn. Metro Atlanta Chamber Water Com., 2002; mem. Trust for Public Land Ga. Bd., 1986-91; co-chmn. Spotlight on Ga. Artists V, 1986; mem. City of Atlanta Zoning Rev. Bd., 1978-85, chmn., 1984-85; bd. dirs. Brookwood Hills Civic Assn., 1975-77, pres., 1977; bd. dirs. Nexus Contemporary Arts Ctr., Atlanta, 1987-92, vice chmn. capital campaign, 1989, chmn. nominating com., 1988, chmn. fundraising com., 1987-88; bd. dirs. Butler St. YMCA N.W. br., 1973-75, Dynamo Swim Club, 1988-91, Arts Festival Atlanta, 1994-98; trustee Inst. Continuing Legal Edn., Athens, 1980-81, Trinity Sch., Atlanta, 1988, 1997-2003, Charles Loridans Found., 1994-2005; mem. session Trinity Presbyn. Ch., 1986-89, 1997-2000, clk. of session, 1987-89, chmn. cmty. concerns com., 1987-88, chmn. pers. com., 1989-90, 1999-2005, chmn. assoc. pastor search com., 1991-92, 2004-05; bd. dirs. Park Pride, 1992, Ga. C. of C., 1998-2005, Hambidge Ctr., 2000-2003, chmn. environ. com., 1987-92, environ. legal counsel, 1981-87; mem. spl. program Leadership Atlanta, 1979-80, Leadership Ga., 1985, Inst. Ga. Environ. Leadership, 2004. Capt. U.S. Army, 1969-72 Decorated D.S.M.; recipient Spl. award Atlanta chpt. AIA, 1988, Mayor Andrew Young, 1985; named one of 96 Most Influential

Atlantans, Atlanta Bus. Chronicle, 2005, One of 100 Most Influential Georgians, Ga. Trend Mag., 2006. Mem. ABA (natural resources sect.), State Bar Ga. (chmn. environ. law sect. 1979-82), Atlanta Bar Assn., City of Atlanta Hist. Preservation (policy steering com. 1989), Atlanta C. of C. (water resources task force 1982-87, solid waste task force 1989, air quality task force 1993-97, environ. affairs com. 1998—2005), Ga. Indsl. Developers Assn. (hazardous waste com. 1983-84), Phi Beta Kappa, Omicron Delta Kappa. Avocations: swimming, bird watching, community activities, travel. Office: Ga Conservancy Ste 200 817 W Peachtree St Atlanta GA 30308 Office Phone: 404-876-2900 ext. 200. Office Fax: 404-872-9229. Business E-Mail: jstokes@gaconservancy.org.

**STOKES, KALEDA MARYUM,** educational association administrator; b. Washington, Feb. 17, 1975; d. George O. and Katrina J. Stokes. BA, Fisk U., Nashville, Tenn., 1996. With Learning Ctr., Silver Springs, Md., 1996—2003; chief academic officer The Pneuma Acads., Washington, 2001—; cons. instrnl. design The Windwalker Corp., Tyson's Corner, Va., 2003; dir. Educate, Inc., Balt., 2004, dir. edn., 2004. Spkr. in field. Dir. fashion and dance ministry Thank God Im Blessed; trustee Options Pub. Charter Sch., Washington, 2000—01. Avocations: writing, singing, modeling.

**STOKES, KATHLEEN SARAH,** dermatologist, educator; b. Springfield, Mass., Oct. 18, 1954; d. John Francis and Margaret Cecelia (MacDonnell) Stokes; m. William Walter Greaves; children: Ian R., Spencer W., Malcolm W. BS, U. Utah, 1978, MS, 1980; MD, Med. Coll. Wis., 1987. Diplomate Am. Bd. Dermatology. Intern in internal medicine Med. Coll. Wis., Milw. 1987-88, resident in dermatology, 1988-90, chief resident, 1990-91, asst. clin. prof. dermatology, 1991—; pvt. practice, Milw., 1991—. Contbr. articles to med. jours., including Critical Care Medicine, Jour. Pediatric Dermatology. Named A Top Physician, Milw. mag., 1996, 2000, 04 Fellow Am. Acad. Dermatology, Milw. Acad. Medicine; mem. AMA, Wis. Dermatol. Soc. (sec.-treas. 2003-04, pres. 2005-06), Women's Dermatologic Soc., Tempo, Alpha Omega Alpha. Office: Affiliated Dermatologists 2300 N Mayfair Rd Milwaukee WI 53226-1505

**STOKES, LOUIS,** lawyer, former congressman; b. Cleve., Feb. 23, 1925; s. Charles and Louise (Stone) S.; m. Jeanette Francis, Aug. 21, 1960; children: Shelley, Louis C., Angela; Lorene. Student, Case We. Res. U., 1946—48; JD, Cleve. Marshall Law Sch., 1953; 26 hon. doctorate degrees, 1953—2001. Bar: Ohio 1953. Mem. 91st-105th Congresses from 11th (formerly 21st) Ohio dist., Washington, 1969—99; sr. counsel Squire, Sanders and Dempsey, Washington, 1999—. Former chmn. appropriations subcom. on VA, HUD and Ind. Agys.; Disting. vis. prof. Mandel Sch. Applied Social Scis. Case We. Res. U., 1999—. Served with AUS, 1943-46. Decorated Congl. DSM; recipient numerous awards for civic activities including Disting. Svc. award Cleve. br. NAACP; Certificate of Appreciation U.S. Commn. on Civil Rights. Mem. ABA, ACLU, Cuyahoga County Bar Assn., Cleve. Bar Assn., Urban League, Am. Legion, Masons, Kappa Alpha Psi. Democrat. Office: Squire Sanders & Dempsey Key Tower Bldg Cleveland OH 44114 Office Phone: 202-626-6697. Business E-Mail: lstokes@ssd.com.

**STOKES, MACK BOYD (MARION BOYD STOKES),** bishop; b. Won-san, Korea, Dec. 21, 1911; arrived in U.S., 1929; s. Marion Boyd and Florence Pauline (Davis) Stokes; m. Ada Rose Yow, June 19, 1942; children: Marion Boyd III, Arch Yow, Elsie Pauline. Student, Seoul Fgn. High Sch., Korea; AB, Asbury Coll., 1932; BD, Duke, 1935; postgrad., Boston U. Sch. Theol., 1935-37, Harvard, 1936-37; PhD, Boston U., 1940; LLD, Lambuth U., Jackson, Tenn., 1963; DD, Millsaps Coll., 1974. Resident fellow systematic theology Boston U., 1936-38, Bowne fellow in philosophy, 1938-39; ordained to ministry Meth. Ch., deacon, 1938, elder, 1940; vis. prof. philosophy and religion Ill. Wesleyan U., 1940-41; prof. Christian doctrine Candler Sch. Theology, Emory U., 1941-56, asso. dean, Parker prof. systematic theology, 1956-72, chmn. exec. com. div. of religion of grad. sch., 1956-72; acting dean Candler Sch. Theology, Emory U. (Candler Sch.), 1968-69; bishop-in-residence Peachtree Rd. United Meth. Ch. Atlanta, 1988—. Faculty mem. Inst. Theol. Studies Oxford U., 1958; del. Meth. Ecumenical Conf., 1947, 52, 61, 71, Holston, Gen. confs., S.E. Jurisdictional Conf., 1956, 60, 64, 68, 72; chmn. com. ministry Gen. Conf. Meth. Ch., 1960; nat. com. Nature Unity We Seek, 1956—; mem. gen. com. ecumenical affairs theol. study com. United Meth. Ch., 1968—72, com. on Cath.-Meth. rels., 1969—, bishop, 1972—. Author: (book) Major Methodist Beliefs, 1956, Major Methodist Beliefs, rev. 15th edit., 1990, The Evangelism of Jesus, 1960, The Epic of Revelation, 1961, Our Methodist Heritage, 1963, Crencas Fundamentals Dos Metodistas, 1964, Study Guide on the Teachings of Jesus, 1970, The Bible and Modern Doubt, 1970, Major United Methodist Beliefs, 1971, Major United Methodist Beliefs, Korean transl., 1977, Major United Methodist Beliefs, rev. with added study guide, 1998, The Holy Spirit and Christian Experience, 1975, The Holy Spirit and Christian Experience, Korean transl., 1985, Twelve Dialogues on John's Gospel, 1975, Jesus, The Master-Evangel, 1978, Can God See the Inside of an Apple?, 1979, Questions Asked by United Methodists, Philippine transl., 1980, The Bible in the Wesleyan Heritage, 1981, Respuestas A Preguntas Que Hacen Los Metodistas Unidos, 1983, The Holy Spirit in the Wesleyan Heritage, 1985, The Holy Spirit in the Wesleyan Heritage, Spanish transl., 1992, The Holy Spirit in the Wesleyan Heritage, Korean transl., 1992, Scriptural Holiness of the United Methodist Christian, 1988, Talking with God: A Guide of Prayer, 1989, Theology for Preaching, 1994, Questions and Answers about Life and Faith, 2000. Trustee Emory U., Millsaps Coll., Rust Coll., Wood Jr. Coll. Methodist. Home: PO Box 497 Waynesville NC 28786 *Faith in God and basic trust in people. Knowing the direction in which to go, and moving with divine assistance toward it with persistence, resourcefulness, imagination and patience.*

**STOKES, MELVIN KIRKLIN,** psychologist; b. Florence, SC, May 5, 1943; s. Roy Kirklin and Doris Proctor Stokes. BA in Psychology, Fairfield U., 1965; MA in Psychology, Temple U., 1967; PhD in Clin. Psychology, U. SC, 1978. Lic. psychologist Fla. Instr. psychology U. SC, Lancaster, 1970—73; clin. intern Devereux Found., Devon, Pa., 1973—74; dir., psychologist partial care dept. Comprehensive Mental Health Ctr., Savannah, Ga., 1974—76; dir. Counseling Ctr., asst. prof. psychology Eckerd Coll., St. Petersburg, Fla., 1977—80; dir. Knowledge Utilization, FMHI and Horthside CMHC, Tampa, Fla., 1980—83; pvt. practice clin. psychology St. Petersburg, 1980—. Tchg. assoc., intern rehab. counseling program U. South Fla., Tampa, 1978—80; bd. dirs. Christian Recovery Ctr., St. Petersburg, Westcare, AIDS and Substance Abuse Recovery Or4gn., St. Petersburg. Contbr. articles to profl. jours. Founder, pres. Bay Area Rights Coun., Tampa, 1981—82. Recipient Outstanding Psychologist award, Hillsboro County Mental Health Assn., Tampa, 1989, cert. of appreciation, People of Color AIDS Coalition, St. Petersburg, 1999, Svc. award, Christian Recovery Ctr., St. Petersburg, 1990. Mem.: APA. Democrat. Avocations: raising and breeding tropical birds, gardening, collecting old books. Home: 1250 10th St N Saint Petersburg FL 33705 Office: 4707 Central Ave Saint Petersburg FL 33713

**STOKES, PATRICK T.,** brewery company executive; b. Washington, 1942; married. BS, Boston Coll., 1964; MBA, Columbia U., 1966. Fin. analyst Shell Oil Co., 1966-67; v.p. materials acquisitions Anheuser-Busch Cos. Inc., St. Louis, 1979-81, v.p., group exec., 1981—; pres. Anheuser-Busch Co. St. Louis, 1990—; COO Campbell Taggart Inc. (subs. Anheuser-Busch Cos. Inc.), Dallas, 1986-90, CEO, 1990—; pres. Anheuser-Busch Inc.; chmn. Anheuser-Busch Internat.; CEO, sr. exec. v.p. Anheuser-Busch Co. Inc., 2000—02, pres, & CEO, 2002—. Served to 1st lt. U.S. Army, 1967-69. Office: Anheuser-Bush Co Inc 1 Busch Place Saint Louis MO 63118-1852*

**STOKES, PAUL MASON,** lawyer; b. Miami Beach, Fla., July 16, 1946; s. Walter Johnson and Juanita (Hemperley) S.; m. Carol Crocker, Sept. 12, 1970; children: Macon Lanford, Walter Ashley, Mary Juanita. BA, Duke U., 1968; JD, U. Chgo., 1971. Bar: Fla. 1971. Law clerk to hon. Milton Pollack U.S. Dist. Ct. (so. dist.) N.Y., 1971—72; assoc. Smathers and Thompson, Miami, Fla., 1972—77, ptnr., 1977—88, Kelley Drye & Warren L.L.P., Miami, 1988—99, Stokes McMillan Maracini & Autunez P.A., Miami,

1999—. Adj. prof. law U. Miami, Coral Gables, Fla., 1987-94, 2005-; pub. defender City of Miami Springs, Fla., 1974, City of Hialeah, Fla., 1974-75. Mem. Code Enforcement Bd. Miami Springs, 1990-92; regent Trinity Internat. U., Deerfield, Ill., 1989-98; mem. Permanent Jud. Commn., Presbytery of Tropical Fla., 1997-00; bd. dirs. Greater Miami Youth for Christ. Fellow Am. Coll. Trust and Estate Coun.; mem. Dade County Bar Assn. (probate and guardianship ct. com. 1988—, bd. dirs. 1989-92, 94-2000, 2004—05), Fla. Bar (cert. wills, trusts and estates), Am. Radio Relay League, Phi Beta Kappa, Order of Coif. Democrat. Presbyterian. Office: Stokes McMillan Marcini & Antunez PA One SE 3d Ave Ste 1750 Miami FL 33131 Office Phone: 305-379-4008. Business E-Mail: pstokes@smpalaw.com.

**STOKES, SUSAN,** political science professor; MA in Anthropology, Stanford U., 1985, MA in Polit. sci., 1986, PhD, 1988. Assoc. prof. polit. sci. U. Chgo. Contbr. articles to profl. jours.; author: Social Movements and the State in Peru, 1995, Neoliberalism by Surprise in Latin America; editor: Political Support for Market Reforms in New Democracies, 2001; co-editor: Democracy, Accountability, and Representation. Recipient Guggenheim fellowship, 2003.

**STOKEY, NANCY L.,** economist, educator; BA in Economics, U. Pa., 1972; PhD in Economics, Harvard U., 1978. Asst. prof. Kellogg Grad. Sch. Mgmt., Northwestern U., 1978—82, assoc. prof., 1982—83, prof., 1983—87, dept. chmn., 1987—89, Harold L. Stuart prof. managerial economics, 1988—90; vis. lectr. Harvard U., 1982; vis. prof. economics U. Minn., 1983, U. Chgo., 1983—84, prof. ecnomics, 1990—96, Frederick Henry Prince prof. economics, 1997—. Vis. scholar rsch. dept. Fed. Reserve Bank, Mpls., 2000—01. Author (with Robert E. Lucas, Jr. and Edward C. Prescott): Recursive Methods in Economic Dynamics, 1989. Fellow: Am. Econ. Assn. (v.p. 1996—97, nominating com. 1998, exec. com. 2000—02), Am. Acad. Arts and Scis., Econometric Soc. (coun. mem. 1996—98, 1999—2001); mem.: NAS. Office Phone: 773-702-0915. Office Fax: 773-702-8490. Business E-Mail: n-stikey@uchicago.edu.*

**STOKKE, DIANE REES,** lawyer; b. Kansas City, Mo., Jan. 29, 1951; d. William James and Marybeth (Smith) Rees; m. Larry Ernst Stokke, June 9, 1973; children: Michelle, Megan, Carly. AB magna cum laude, Gonzaga U., 1972; JD with high honors, U. Wash., 1976. Bar: Wash. 1976, U.S. Dist. Ct. (ea. dist.) Wash. 1976, U.S. Dist. Ct. (we. dist.) Wash. 1976, U.S. Ct. Appeals (9th cir.) 1980. Assoc. Preston, Thorgrimson, Ellis & Holman, Seattle, 1976-83; ptnr. Preston, Gates & Ellis LLP, Seattle, 1983—. Atty. Seattle Ctr. Found., 1977-83. Trustee Seattle Infant Devel. Ctr., 1984—86, Fremont Pub. Assn., 1994—2001, 2003—05. Gonzaga U. scholar, 1968. Mem. ABA, Wash. State Bar Assn. (spl. dist. counsel 1985-88), Seattle-King County Bar Assn., Wash. Women Lawyers, Order of Coif, Wash. Women Real Estate Lawyers, Am. Coll. of Mortgage Attys., Comml. Real Estate Women. Roman Catholic. Office: Preston Gates & Ellis LLP 925 Fourth Ave Ste 2900 Seattle WA 98104-1158 Office Phone: 206-623-7580. Business E-Mail: dianes@prestongates.com.

**STOKLOSA, GREGORY A.,** publishing executive; BS, U. Mich.; MA in Mgmt., Northwestern U. Various fin. positions Kraft Gen. Foods, Inc.; from asst. treas. global corp. fin. to exec. v.p., CFO RR Donnelley & Sons, Chgo., 1993—2000, exec. v.p., 2000—05, CFO, 2000—05; v.p., CFO Hollinger Internat. Inc., Chgo., 2005—. Office: Hollinger International Inc 350 N Orleans St Chicago IL 60654 Office Phone: 312-321-2299. Office Fax: 312-321-0629.*

**STOKOE, KENNETH H., II,** civil engineer, educator; BSCE, U. Mich., 1966, MSCE, 1967, PhD, 1972. Instr. Univ. Mich., 1971; asst. prof. Univ. Mass., 1972—73, Univ. Tex., Austin, 1973—78, assoc. prof., 1978—83, prof. civil engring., 1983—85, Brunswick Abernathy Regents prof., 1985—97, Cockrell Family Regents Chair, 1997—99, Jennie C. and Milton T. Graves chair in engring., 2000—. Contbr. articles to prof. jours. Mem.: Nat. Acad. Engring., Am. Soc. Civil Engineers, Am. Soc. Nondestructive Testing, Am. Soc. Testing & Materials, Earthquake Engring. Rsch. Inst., Internat. Soc. Soil Mech. & Geotechnical Engring., Seismological Soc. Am., Soc. Exploration Geophysicists, Transp. Rsch. Bd., Soc. Profl. Engineers. Office: U Tex at Austin Dept Archl and Environ Engring 1 Univeristy Sta C1792 Austin TX 78712-0280

**STOLAREVSKY, KATHRYN FELL,** music educator; b. Las Vegas, N.Mex. d. Herbert Elroy and Eunice Tamme Fell; m. Mihail Stolarevsky, June 14, 1946 (dec. Dec. 1974). BA, U. N.Mex., 1935; MusB, Conservatory Music, Cin., 1936, MusM, 1937; postgrad., Nat. Music Camp, Interlochen, Mich., 1937—38. Music dir. The Lotspeich Sch., Cin., 1936—45; music dir., piano tchr. The Ellis Sch., Pitts., 1945—79; music faculty piano Nat. Music Camp, Interlochen, 1946—48; music faculty U. Wis., Madison, 1948; faculty piano Chatham Coll. Music and Arts Day Camp, Pitts., 1956—74, dir., 1974—91; pvt. piano tchr. Pitts., 1991—. Adv. bd. Chatham Coll. Music and Arts Day Camp, Pitts., 1991—. Bd. mem. Concert Soc. Pitts., 1947—50; founder Stolarevsky Meml. Found., Pitts., 1976—. Recipient 1st prize piano competition, Piano Fedn. N.Mex., 1928. Democrat. Episcopalian. Avocations: concerts, theater, reading, exercise, cooking. Home: 5605 Darlington Rd Pittsburgh PA 15217

**STOLARIK, M. MARK,** history professor; b. St. Martin, Slovak Republic, Apr. 22, 1943; s. Imrich and Margita (Vavro) S.; m. Anne Helene Ivanco, June 15, 1968; children: Roman Andrej, Matthew Mark. BA, U. Ottawa, 1965, MA, 1967; PhD, U. Minn., 1974. Ast prof. history Cleve. State U., 1972-76; hist. rschr. Nat. Mus. of Man, Ottawa, Ont., Canada, 1977-78; pres. Balch Inst. for Ethnic Studies, Phila., 1979-91; prof. history, chair dept. Slovak history and culture U. Ottawa, 1992—. Cons. Harvard Ency. Ethnic Groups, Cambridge, Mass., 1976-80; advisor State Hist. Records Bd., Harrisburg, Pa., 1982-91; cons. Ency. Canada's Peoples, 1991—99. Author: film documentary Vianoce-Slovak Christmas, 1978 (2d prize 1979), Slovaks in Bethlehem, Pa., 1985, The Slovak Experience, 1870-1918, 1989. Mem. Pa. adv. com. to U.S. Commn. on Civil Rights, 1985-91. Lehigh U. fellow, 1976. Mem. 1st Cath. Slovak Union, Nat. Slovak Soc., Can. Slovak League (pres. 1994-99). Roman Catholic. Office Phone: 613-562-5800 x1286. Business E-Mail: stolarik@uottawa.ca.

**STOLBERG, MARY MARGARET,** historian; b. Denver, Colo., Sept. 8, 1956; d. David Fox and Anne Stewart (Brand) S.; m. Lynn Doyle, Jan. 18, 1986 (div. 2000). BA, U. Chgo., 1977; MA, U. Va., 1986, PhD, 1991. Reporter S.W. Times Record, Fort Smith, Ark., 1977-78, The Pitts. Press, 1978-84; lectr., asst. prof. Appalachian State U., Boone, N.C., 1990-93; ind. scholar Boone, N.C., 1993—. Author: Fighting Organized Crime, 1995, (Little Brown award 1995), Bridging the River of Hatred, 1998, Looking Beyond Race, 2000; also articles in Sat. Eve. Post, Jour. of Policy History. Democrat. Episcopalian. Home: PO Box 90 Vilas NC 28692-0090 Agent: David Hendin Lit Enterprises PO Box 990 Nyack NY 10960-0990

**STOLBERG, SHERYL GAY,** journalist; b. N.Y.C., Nov. 18, 1961; d. Irving and Marcia Dawn (Papier) S. BA, U. Va., 1983. Reporter Providence Jour. Bulletin, 1983-87, L.A. Times, 1987-97; sci. & med. corr. NY Times, Washington, 1997—2002, congl. corr., 2002—06, White House corr., 2006—. Recipient Unity award Lincoln U., 1987. Office: NY Times Wash Bur 7th Fl 1627 I St NW Washington DC 20006-4007*

**STOLL, GEORGE,** artist; b. Balt. 1954; Solo exhibitions include, Tupperware, A/B Gallery, LA, 1994, Newspaper & Plywood Drawings, Paper Towel Paintings, Fast Food Wrappers, TRI Gallery, LA, 1994, Sculpture, Morris Healy Gallery, NYC, 1995, New Sculpture, Paintings, and Drawings, 1997, Toilet Paper, Dan Bernier Gallery, Santa Monica, 1995, Snowflakes, 1996, 161 Tumblers 2 Ways, Daniel Weinberger Gallery, San Francisco, 1995, Windows, Bruxelles, Belgium, 1997, New Work, Thomas Healy Gallery,

NYC, 1998, Gallery Paule Anglim, San Francisco, 1999, George Stoll: thinking of christmas, Angles Gallery, Santa Monica, 2004—05. John Armstrong Chaloner Rome Prize Fellowship in Visual Arts, Am. Acad. in Rome, 2004—05.

**STOLL, HOWARD LESTER, JR.,** dermatologist; b. Buffalo, June 13, 1928; s. Howard L. and Margaret (Kahler) S.; m. Jacklyn Fay Straight, June, 1948; children— Shelley, Margaret, Amy, Howard III AB, Harvard U., 1948; MD, U. Pa., 1952. Diplomate Am. Bd. Dermatology. Intern E.J. Meyer Hosp., Buffalo, 1952, resident in dermatology, 1953-55; sr. cancer research surgeon Roswell Park Meml. Inst., Buffalo, 1955-59, assoc. cancer research dermatologist, 1959-67, chief, sect. dermatology, 1984-92; mem. courtesy staff Mercy Hosp., Buffalo, 1958-70; asst. in dermatology E.J. Meyer Meml. Hosp., Buffalo, 1962-72. Clin. assoc. prof. dermatology Sch. Medicine, SUNY-Buffalo, 1976-91, clin. prof., 1991—. Served to capt. U.S. Army, 1955-57 Mem. Am. Acad. Dermatology. Soc. Investigative Dermatology, Buffalo-Rochester Dermatologic Soc. Office: Roswell Park Meml Inst Elm & Carlto Sts 666 Elm St Buffalo NY 14263-0002

**STOLL, JOHN ROBERT,** lawyer, educator; b. Phila., Nov. 29, 1950; s. Wilhelm Friedrich and Marilyn Jane (Kremser) S.; m. Christine Larson, June 24, 1972; children: Andrew Michael, Michael Robert, Meredith Kirstin, Alison Courtney. BA magna cum laude, Haverford Coll., 1972; JD, Columbia U., 1975. Bar: Ind. 1975, U.S. Dist. Ct. (no. and so. dists.) Ind. 1975, U.S. Ct. Appeals (7th cir.) 1976, U.S. Dist. Ct. (no. dist.) Ill. 1980, (so. dist.) N.Y. 1993, Ill. 1981, N.Y. 1989. Atty. Barnes & Thornburg, South Bend, Ind., 1975-80, Mayer, Brown & Platt, Chgo., 1980—. Adj. prof. law Northwestern U., Chgo., 1985—, DePaul U., Chgo., 1987; lectr. in bus. St. Mary's Coll., Notre Dame, Ind., 1977-78. Contbr. articles to profl. jours. Mem. ABA, Ind. State Bar Assn., Am. Bankruptcy Inst., Phi Beta Kappa. Office: Mayer Brown & Platt 190 S La Salle St Ste 3100 Chicago IL 60603-3441

**STOLL, NEAL RICHARD,** lawyer; b. Phila., Nov. 7, 1948; s. Mervin Stoll and Goldie Louise (Serody) Stoll Wilf; m. Linda G. Seligman, May 25, 1972; children: Meredith Anne, Alexis Blythe. BA in History with distinction, Pa. State U., 1970; JD, Fordham U. 1973. Bar: N.Y. 1974, U.S. Dist. Ct. (ea. dist.) N.Y. 1974, U.S. Ct. Appeals (2d cir.) 1974, U.S. Ct. Appeals (11th cir.) 1982, U.S. Dist. Ct. (ea. dist.) Mich. 1983, U.S. Dist. Ct. (so. dist.) N.Y. 1974, U.S. Supreme Ct. 1986. Assoc. Skadden, Arps, Slate, Meagher & Flom, LLP, N.Y.C., 1973-81, mem., 1981—. Lectr. Practicing Law-Inst., N.Y.C. Author: (with others) Aquisitions Under the Hart Scott Rodino Antitrust Improvements Act, 1980; contbr. articles to profl. pubs. Mem. Assn. Bar City of N.Y. (mem. trade regulation com. 1983-85), ABA, N.Y. State Bar Assn. Democrat. Office: Skadden Arps Slate Four Times Sq New York NY 10036-6522 Office Phone: 212-735-3660. Business E-Mail: nstoll@skadden.com.

**STOLL, RICHARD GILES,** lawyer; b. Phila., Oct. 2, 1946; s. Richard Giles and Mary Margaret (Zeigler) S.; m. Susan Jane Nicewonger, June 15, 1968; children: Richard Giles III, Christian Hayes. BA magna cum laude, Westminster Coll., 1968; JD, Georgetown U., 1971. Bar: D.C. 1971, U.S. Dist. Ct. D.C. 1971, U.S. Ct. Appeals D.C. 1971, U.S. Ct. Appeals (4th cir.) 1977. Assoc. Arent, Fox, Kintner, Plotkin & Kahn, Washington, 1971-73; atty. Office of Gen. Counsel EPA, Washington, 1973-77, asst. gen. counsel, 1977-81; dep. gen. counsel Chem. Mfrs. Assn., Washington, 1981-84; ptnr. Freedman, Levy, Kroll & Simonds, Washington, 1984-2001, Foley & Lardner, Washington, 2001—. Instr. environ. law and policy U. Va., Charlottesville, 1981-90. Co-author: Handbook on Environmental Law, 1987, 88, 89, 91, Practical Guide to Environment Law, 1987; contbr. articles to profl. jours.; moderator, panelist legal ednl. TV broadcasts and tapes ABA and Am. Law Inst. Elder Georgetown Presbyn. Ch.; bd. dirs., mem. exec. com. Georgetown Ministry Ctr., 2004-06, pres. 2006—; bd. dirs. Westminster Ingleside Found., Washington, 2004—. Capt., USAR, 1968-76. Recipient Alumni Achievement award Westminster Coll., 1998. Mem. ABA (sect. environment, energy and resources, chmn. water quality com. 1982-83, hazardous waste com. 1983-85, coun. mem. 1985-88, sect. chmn. 1990-91, sect. adminstrv. law co-chmn. rulemaking com. 2004—, chmn. sponsorship com. 2004—, mem. coun. 2005—), Washington Golf and Country Club, Cosmos Club. Avocations: piano, golf, music composition. Office: Foley & Lardner 3000 K St NW Washington DC 20007 Business E-Mail: rstoll@foley.com.

**STOLL, SARAH MAY REICHERT,** elementary school educator; b. Torrington, Wyo., Nov. 8, 1967; d. Fred L. and Delores J. (See) Reichert. AA, Ea. Wyo. Coll., 1988; BA, U. Wyo., 1990; MA, Lesley U., 2005. Tutor math. and English Ea. Wyo. Coll., Torrington, 1987—88; assc. range mgmt. dept. U. Wyo., Laramie, 1989—90; tchr. 4th grade Arapahoe Sch. Fremont County Sch. Dist. #38, Wyo., 1991—2003, tchr. 3d grade Arapahoe Sch., 2003—04, kindergarten reading intervention specialist tchr., 2004—. Mem.: ASCD, NEA, Arapahoe Edn. Assn., Wyo. Edn. Assn., U. Wyo. Alumni Assn. E-mail: stoll@tribcsp.com.

**STOLL, WILHELM,** mathematics professor; b. Freiburg, Germany, Dec. 22, 1923; arrived in U.S., 1960; s. Heinrich and Doris (Eberle) S.; m. Marilyn Jane Kremser, June 11, 1955; children: Robert, Dieter, Elisabeth, Rebecca. PhD in Math, U. Tübingen, Fed. Republic Germany, 1953, habilitation, 1954. Asst. U. Tübingen, 1953-59, dozent, 1954-60, ausserplanmässiger prof., 1960; vis. lectr. U. Pa., 1954-55; temp. mem. Inst. Advanced Study, Princeton, 1957-59; prof. math. U. Notre Dame, 1960-88, Vincent J. Duncan and Annamarie Micus Duncan prof. math., 1988-94, prof. emeritus, 1994—, chmn. dept., 1966-68, co-dir. Ctr. for Applied Math., 1992. Vis. prof. Stanford U., 1968-69, Tulane U., 1973, U. Sci. and Tech., Hefei, Anhui, People's Republic of China, summer, 1986; adviser Clark Sch., South Bend, Ind., 1963-68; Japan Soc. Promotion Sci. fellow, vis. prof. Kyoto U., summer 1983. Publs. in field. Fellow: AAAS. Achievements include research in complex analysis several variables. Home: 2601 Covington Commons Dr #44-46 Fort Wayne IN 46804-7333

**STOLL, WILLIAM FREDERICK, JR.,** lawyer; b. Youngstown, Ohio, June 28, 1948; s. William Frederick and Elizabeth Jayne (Walsh) Stoll; m. Patricia Ann Musial, 1969 (div.); children: Eric Walsh, Todd William. BS in Fgn. Service, Georgetown U., 1969; JD, Case Western Res. U., 1973. Bar: Ohio 1973, U.S. Dist. Ct. (no. dist) Ohio 1974. Assoc. Roth & Stephens, Youngstown, Ohio, 1973—75; atty. Westinghouse Electric Corp., Pitts., 1975—77, counsel, 1977—78, chief counsel, 1978—82, asst. gen. counsel, 1982—84, assoc. gen. counsel, 1982—93, v.p., dep. gen. counsel, 1993—96; chief legal officer, exec. v.p. Borden, Inc., 1996—2003, Lennox Internat., 2004—. Mem. bd. dirs. AEP Industries, Inc. Mem. bd. of governors Georgetown U. Alumni Assn. Mem.: ABA. Office: Lennox Internat 2140 Lake Park Blvd Richardson TX 75080

**STOLL, WILLIAM HERMANN,** real estate company executive; b. Aug. 7, 1944; s. Gottfried Alois and Mary Elizabeth (Lochrie) Stoll; m. Elizabeth Anne Stoll, Aug. 5, 1967. BBA, U. Tex., Austin, 1970. Budget examiner Tex. Gov.'s Office, 1967—71; fin. grants administr. City Mgrs. Office, Austin, Tex., 1971—73; dir. program devel. Tex. Dept. Cmty. Affairs, Tex., 1973—78; gen. mgr. AIS Data Sys., Inc., Austin, 1978—81; pres. Submariner, Inc., Austin, 1981—86; sales mgr. Better Homes & Gardens, Austin, 1986—97; sales counselor Standard Pacific Homes, Austin, 1997—. Chmn. Southwest Nat. Bank, Austin, 1980—82; also bd. dirs.; chmn. Austin Bd. Realtors, Austin, 1987. Author (digest): Texas Water Plan, 1967. Chmn. North Austin Mental Health/Mental Retardation Com., 1975—76; rep. Goals for Austin Tomorrow, 1974—75; chmn. Allandale Neighborhood Assn., Austin, 1975—76; mem. LBJ Library Found.; mem. selection com. Austin Most Worthy Citizen award, 1993—94; mem. pledge com. Muscular Dystrophy Ann. Campaign, Williamson County, 1999—2001; mem. fin. com. KLRO-TV PBS sta., 1994—95; presiding judge Travis County Election Commn., Austin, 1976—79; fin. chmn. Travis County Dem. Party, 1977—78; vice chmn. Austin Planning and Zoning Commn., 1976—80. Mem.: Austin Soc. Pub. Adminstrn., Austin C. of

C., Exch. Park Toastmasters, U. Tex.-Austin Ex-students' Assn., Men's Polit Club Austin (co-founder), Young Men's Bus. Club, Kiwanis, Sigma Phi Epsilon (advisory dir. alumni assn. 1984—88). Home: 8704 Azalea Trl Austin TX 78759-7503

**STOLLAR, BERNARD DAVID,** biochemist, educator; b. Saskatoon, Sask., Can., Aug. 11, 1936; came to US, 1960. s. Percy and Rose (Direnfeld) S.; m. Carol A. Singer, Oct. 7, 1956; children: Lawrence, Michael, Suzanne. BA, U. Sask., Saskatoon, 1958, MD, 1959. Intern U. Sask. Hosp., 1959-60; postdoctoral fellow Brandeis U., Waltham, Mass., 1960-62; asst. prof. dept. pharmacology Tufts U. Schs. Medicine and Dental Medicine, Boston, 1964-67, asst. prof. dept. biochemistry, 1967-68, assoc. prof. biochemistry/pharmacology, 1968-74, prof., 1974—2005, prof. emeritus, 2005—, acting chmn. dept. biochemistry and pharmacology, 1984-86, chmn. dept. biochemistry, 1986-2001; interim dean Sackler Sch. Grad. Biomed Sci., Tufts U., 2002—04. Vis. prof. internat. course in immunology and immunochemistry Mexico City, 1971; sr. fellow Weizmann Inst. Sci., Rehovot, Israel, 1971-72; vis. prof. chemistry Wellesley Coll., Mass., 1976, U. Tromsö, Norway, 1981; Dozor vis. prof. Ben-Gurion U. Sch. Medicine, Beer Sheva, Israel, 1986; cons. USAF Office Sci. Rsch., 1966-69, Seragen, Inc., 1983-88, Cetus, 1982-85, Gene-Trak, 1986-89, Alkermes, Inc., 1989-94, Catalytic Antibodies, Inc., 1993-98; 3d ann. alumni lectr. U. Sask. Coll. Medicine, 1989; mem. allergy/transplantation rsch. com. NIH/NIAID, 1990-94; mem. sci. vis. com. Okla. Med. Rsch. Found., 1996-98; mem. panel Israel Cancer Rsch. Found., 1996-2000. Contbr. over 200 articles to profl. jours., chpts. to books; exec. editl. bd. Analytical Biochemistry, 1988—; editl. bd. Jour. Immunology, 1981-85, Molecular Immunology, 1980-95, Arthritis and Rheumatism, 1986-89, Jour. Immunological Methods, 1988—. Mem. adult edn. com. Temple Reyim, Newton, Mass., v.p., 2001-04, 1st v.p. 2004-05, pres. 2005-. Capt. USAF, 1962—64. Recipient (with Carol Stollar) 2d Century award Jewish Theol. Sem. and Temple Reyim, 1997; rsch. grantee NSF, NIH, 1964-2005; sr. fellow Weizmann Inst. Sci., 1971-72. Mem. AAAS, Am. Assn. Immunologists, Am. Soc. Biochemistry and Molecular Biology, Am. Coll. Rheumatology, Clin. Immunology Soc., NY Acad. Sci. Office: Tufts Univ Sch Medicine Dept Biochemistry 136 Harrison Ave Boston MA 02111-1800 Office Phone: 617-636-2948. Business E-Mail: david.stollar@tufts.edu.

**STOLLER, CLAUDE,** architect; b. N.Y.C., Dec. 2, 1921; s. Max and Esther (Zisblatt) S.; m. Anna Maria Oldenburg, June 5, 1946 (div. Oct. 1972); children: Jacob, Dorothea, Elizabeth; m. Rosemary Raymond Lax, Sept. 22, 1978. Student, Black Mountain Coll., N.C., 1942; M.Arch., Harvard U., 1949. Architect Architects Collaborative, Cambridge, Mass., after 1949, Shepley, Bulfinch, Richardson & Abbot, Boston, 1951; co-founder, partner firm Marquis & Stoller, San Francisco, 1956; pvt. practice architecture N.Y.C. and San Francisco, 1974-78; founder, partner Stoller/Partners, Berkeley, Calif., 1978, Stoller, Knoerr Archs., 1988-95. Mem. faculty Washington U., St. Louis, 1955-56, U. Calif., Berkeley, 1957-91, prof. arch., 1968-92, acting chmn. dept., 1965-66, chair grad. studies, 1984-91; mem. Berkeley Campus Design Rev. Bd., 1985-91, chmn., 1992-93; commr. Calif. Bd. Archtl. Examiners, 1980-90, mem. exam. com., 1985-88; mem. diocesan commn. arch. Episcopal Diocese Calif., 1961-98; vis. arch. Nat. Design Inst. Ahmedabad, India, 1963; planning commr. City of Mill Valley, 1961-66, Marin County Planning Commn., 1966-67; mem. pub. adv. panel archtl. svcs. GSA, 1969-71; citizens urban design adv. com. City of Oakland, Calif., 1968; vis. com. nat. archtl. accrediting bd. U. Minn. and U. Wis., Milw., 1971; coun. Harvard Grad. Sch. Design Assn., 1976-77; mem. design rev. com. The Sea Ranch, Calif., 1990-2002. Prin. works include St. Francis Sq. Coop. Apts., San Francisco, 1961, Pub. Housing for Elderly, San Francisco, 1974, Learning Resources Bldg, U. Calif., Santa Barbara, 1975, Menorah Park Housing for Elderly, San Francisco, 1979, San Jose State U. Student Housing Project, 1984, Delta Airlines Terminal, San Francisco Internat. Airport, 1988. Served with AUS, 1943-46. Recipient numerous awards including AIA Honor awards, 1963, 64, AIA Bay Region Honor award, 1974, Concrete Reinforced Steel Inst. award, 1976, AIA award, 1976, CADA Site I Solar Housing award Sacramento, Calif., 1980, State of Calif. Affordable Housing award, 1981, PG&E Sunthern award, 1981, San Francisco Housing Authority award, 1983, Orchid award City of Oakland, 1989, Citation for achievement and svc. U. Calif., Berkeley, 1991, Design award Berkeley Design Advocates. Fellow AIA. Home: 2816 Derby St Berkeley CA 94705-1325 Business E-Mail: stoller@berkeley.edu.

**STOLLER, JOHN R.,** lawyer; b. N.Y.C., Oct. 16, 1948; BA, Valparaiso U., 1970, JD, 1973. Bar: Minn. 1973, Colo. 1978, Mich. 1993. Editor-in-chief Calparaiso U. Law Rev., 1972—73; law clk. to Justice Walter F. Rogscheske Minn., 1973—74; assoc. HArstad & Rainbow, 1974—78; spl. asst. atty. gen. Minn. Dept. Transp., 1974—78; atty. The Mountain States Telephone and Telegraph Co., 1978—83; v.p., gen. counsel, sec. Beta West Properties, Inc., 1984—90; gen. counsel, sec. Pulte Homes, Inc., Bloomfield Hills, Mich., 1990—, sr. v.p., 1999-. Mem.: ABA, Am. Soc. Corp. Secs., Am. Corp. Counsel Assn., State Bar Mich., Denver Bar Assn., Colo. Bar Assn., Minn. Bar Assn. Office: Pulte Homes Inc 100 Bloomfield Hills Pky Ste 300 Bloomfield Hills MI 48304

**STOLLER, ROSE,** think-tank executive; With N.D. Dept. Human Svcs.; exec. dir. Mental Health Assn., ND, The Consensus Coun., Bismarck, ND, 2002—. Chairperson Bismarck Human Rels. Com.; vol. Mo. Slope United Way; grad. leadership program Bismarck C. of C. Recipient Mental Health Svcs. award, N.D. Psychiat. Soc., Welcome Back award, Eli Lilly Co. Office: The Consensus Coun Inc Ste 7 1003 E Interstate Ave Bismarck ND 58503-0500

**STOLLERMAN, GENE HOWARD,** internist, educator; b. N.Y.C., Dec. 6, 1920; s. Maurice William and Sarah Dorothy (Mezz) S.; m. Corynne Miller, Jan. 21, 1945 (dec. Mar. 1997); children: Lee Denise Stollerman Meyburg, Anne Barbara Stollerman DiZio, John Eliot; m. Vita Mark, Nov. 9, 1997. AB summa cum laude, Dartmouth Coll., 1941; MD, Columbia U., 1944. Diplomate Am. Bd. Internal Medicine. Clin. tng. Mt. Sinai Hosp., N.Y.C., 1944-46, chief med. resident, 1948; Dazian research fellow microbiology NYU Med. Sch., 1949-50, mem. dept. medicine, 1951-55; med. dir. Irvington House for Cardiac Children, 1951-55; prin. investigator Sackett Found. Research in Rheumatic Diseases, 1955-64; asst. prof. medicine Northwestern U., 1955-57, assoc. prof., 1957-61, prof. medicine, 1961-65; prof., chmn. dept. medicine U. Tenn., 1965-81, Goodman prof., 1977-81; physician-in-chief City of Memphis Hosps., 1965-81; prof. medicine Boston U. Sch. Medicine, 1981-95, prof. pub. health, 1991-95, prof. medicine and pub. health emeritus, 1996—. Chief staff gen. internal medicine Univ. Hosp., Boston U. Med. Ctr., 1983-86; Disting. physician VA Med. Ctr., Bedford, Mass., 1986-89; assoc. chief of staff Geriatrics and Extended Care, 1989-92; clin. dir. Bedford div. Geriatric Rsch., Ednl. and Clin. Ctr., 1989-92; dir. VA Health Svcs. Rsch. Field, 1990-93; chmn. research career program com. NIAMD-NIH, 1967-70; mem. commn. streptococcal and staphylococcal diseases U.S. Armed Forces Epidemiol. Bd., 1956-74; adv. bd. immunization practices Center for Disease Control, 1968-71; expert adv. panel cardiovascular disease WHO, 1966—; mem. Am. Bd. Internal Medicine, 1967-73, chmn. cert. exam. com., 1969-73, mem. exam. com., 1971-73; chmn. Panel on Bacterial Vaccines, FDA, 1973-80; mem. nat. adv. council Nat. Inst. Allergy and Infectious Diseases, NIH, 1978-82; mem. Dept. Health & Human Services nat. vaccine adv. com. Editor-in-chief Advances in Internal Medicine, 1968-93, Jour. Am. Geriatric Soc., 1984-88; co-editor Hosp. Practice, 1990—, editor, 1998—; contbr. chpts. to Braunwald's Textbook of Cardiology, Harrison's Textbook of Medicine, Cecil & Loeb Textbook of Medicine, others; contbr. articles to profl. jours. Served as capt. M.C., AUS, 1946-48. Recipient Bicentennial award in internal medicine Columbia U., 1967, Disting. Alumnus award Mt. Sinai Hosp., 1989, Thewlis award Am. Geriatric Soc., 1990, Mentor award Infectious Disease Soc. Am., 2004. Master ACP (bd. regents 1978, v.p. 1984, Bruce medal for preventive medicine 1985), Am. Coll. Rheumatology, Am. Heart Assn. (mem. exec. com., press. coun. on rheumatic fever and congenital disease 1965-67), Am. Fedn. Clin. Rsch., Am. Rheumatism Assn., Am. Soc. Clin. Investigation, Cen. Soc. Clin. Rsch. (v.p.

1973-74, pres. 1974-75), Assn. Profs. Medicine (pres. 1975-76), Am. Assn. Immunologists, Assn. Am. Physicians, Infectious Disease Soc. Am. (coun. 1968-70), Phi Beta Kappa, Alpha Omega Alpha. Personal e-mail: gstollerman@valley.net.

**STOLLEY, ALEXANDER,** advertising executive; b. Coethen Anhalt, Germany, May 12, 1922; arrived in US, 1923, naturalized, 1929; s. Mihail and Tatiana (Rainich) Stolarevsky; m. Patricia Martin, June 26, 1944 (dec. Aug. 1970); children: Christopher, Peter, Laura Stolley Smith, Annabel Stolley Hetzer, Megan Stolley Berry; m. Bette Scott Vogt, June 15, 1973. ME, U. Cin., 1948. With Cin. Milacron, Inc., 1941-50, dir. employee relations, 1948-50; with Northlich, Stolley, Inc., Cin., 1950-89, exec. v.p., 1959-67, pres., 1967-84; chmn. Northlich, Stolley, LaWarre, Inc. (formerly Northlich, Stolley, Inc.), Cin., 1984-89. Mem. exec. com. Cincinnatus Assn., 1968-73, sec., 1970-71, v.p., 1971-72, pres., 1972-73; mem. Cin. Council on World Affairs, 1969—; chmn. Contemporary Arts Center, Cin., 1966-67; mem. exec. com. Cin. Conv. and Visitors Bur., 1975, chmn. long range planning com., 1983; trustee Cin. Symphony Orch., 1969-75. Served to 1st lt. AUS, 1943-46. Mem. Bus., Profl. Advt. Assn., Greater Cin. C. of C. (exec. com. 1982-83) Clubs: Cin. Country, Literary, Gasparilla Beach, Lemon Bay Golf, Boca Bay Pass. Home: PO Box 1339 Boca Grande FL 33921-1339

**STOLLEY, PAUL DAVID,** medical educator, researcher; b. Pawling, NY, June 17, 1937; s. Herman and Rosalie (Chertock) Stolley; m. Jo Ann Goldenberg, June 13, 1959; children: Jonathan, Dorie, Anna. BA, Lafayette Coll., 1957; MD, Cornell U., 1962; MPH, Johns Hopkins U., 1968; MA (hon.), U. Pa., 1976. Diplomate Am. Coll. Preventive Medicine, Am. Coll. Epidemiology. Intern U. Wis. Med. Ctr., 1962—63, resident in medicine, 1963—64; med. officer USPHS, Washington, 1964—67; asst. prof. Johns Hopkins Sch. Pub. Health, Balt., 1968—71, assoc. prof., 1971—76; Herbert C. Rorer prof. medicine U. Pa. Sch. Medicine, Phila., 1976—91; prof. dept. epidemiology U. Md. Sch. Medicine, Balt., 1991—2002; staff epidemiologist Public Citizen Health Rsch. Group, 2002—04. Co-author: Foundations of Epidemiology, 3d edit., 1995, Epidemiology: Investigating Disease, 1995 (Am. Med. Writers Assn. award, 1996); contbg. author: Case-Control Studies, 1982, mem. editl. bd.: New Eng. Jour. Medicine, 1989—93, Millbank Quar., Health and Soc., 1986—, assoc. editor: Clin. Pharmacology and Therapeutics, 1987—93; contbr. articles to med. jours. Charter mem. Physicians for Social Responsibility, 1961—. Lt. comdr. USPHS, 1964—67. Fellow: ACP; mem.: Johns Hopkins Soc. Scholars, Internat. Epidemiol. Assn. (treas. 1982—84), Am. Epidemiol. Soc. (pres. 1994—), Soc. Epidemiol. Rsch. (pres. 1982—84), Inst. Medicine of NAS, Am. Coll. Epidemiology (pres. 1987—89). Office Phone: 410-706-3610. Personal E-mail: pstolley@aol.com.

**STOLLEY, RICHARD BROCKWAY,** journalist; b. Peoria, Ill., Oct. 3, 1928; s. George Brockway and Stella (Sherman) S.; m. Anne Elizabeth Shawber, Oct. 2, 1954 (div. 1981); children: Lisa Anne, Susan Hope, Melinda Ruth, Martha Brockway; m. Lïse Jane Hilboldt, 1997. BS in Journalism, Northwestern U., 1952, MS, 1953; LLD, Villa Maria Coll., 1976, Hartwick Coll., 2005. Sports editor Pekin (Ill.) Daily Times, 1944-46; reporter Chgo. Sun-Times, 1953; mem. staff weekly Life mag., 1953-73; bur. chief Los Angeles, 1961-64, Washington, 1964-68, sr. editor Europe, 1968-70, asst. mng. editor N.Y.C., 1971-73; mng. editor monthly Life mag., N.Y.C., 1982-86; founding mng. editor People mag., N.Y.C., 1974-82, Picture Week mag., N.Y.C., 1985-86; dir. spl. projects Time Inc., N.Y.C., 1987-89; editl. dir. Time Inc. Time Warner Inc., N.Y.C., 1989-93, sr. editl. adviser, 1993—. Author: Sinatra: An Intimate Portrait of a Very Good Year, 2002; introd. to Leigh A. Wiener, Marilyn: A Hollywood Farewell: The Death and Funeral of Marilyn Monroe, 1990 Introduction To Life: The Platinum Anniversary Collection, 2006; editor People Celebrates People: The Best of 20 Unforgettable Years, 1994, rev. edit., 1996, Life: Our Century in Pictures, 1999; Life: Century of Change, America in Pictures, 1900-2000, 2000, LIFE: World War 2, 2001; exec. prodr. (TV) Extra, 1995-96; editl. cons. Our American Century series Time-Life Books, 1998-99. Chmn. Twins Found.; Providence; bd. govs. Nat. Parkinson Found., Miami, Fla., Lensic Performing Arts Ctr., Santa Fe, N.Mex., 2005—. With USN, 1946-48. Recipient Alumni merit award Northwestern U., 1977, Alumni medal Northwestern U., 1994, Henry Johnson Fisher award for lifetime achievement in mag. pub., 1997, Mag. Profl. of Yr. award Assn. for Edn. in Journalism and Mass Comm., 2002; inducted into Am. Soc. Magazine Editors' Hall of Fame, 1996, Hall of Achievement Medill Sch. Journalism Northwestern U., 1997. Mem. Am. Soc. Mag. Editors (pres. 1982-84), Nat. Press Club, Overseas Press Club (pres. 2004-06), Century Assn., Kappa Tau Alpha, Sigma Delta Chi. Home: 1243 Canyon Rd Santa Fe NM 87501

**STOLOFF, CAROLYN,** artist, educator, poet; b. N.Y.C., Jan. 14, 1927; Student, U. Ill., 1944-46; pupil of, Xavier Gonzalez, Eric Isenburger, Hans Hofmann, Stanley Kunitz; BS in Painting, Columbia U., 1949. Tchr. painting and drawing Manhattanville Coll., Purchase, NY, 1957-74, chmn. art history and studio art, 1960-65, seminar in writing poetry, 1969-74; tchr. English and creative writing Baird House, 1973; vis. writer Stephens Coll., 1975; instr. Hamilton Coll., 1985. Vis. writer summer writers' workshop U. Rochester, NY, 1985. One-woman shows include Dubin Gallery, Phila., Manhattanville Coll. Gallery, 1957, 67, Arts and Crafts Gallery, Wellfleet, Mass., Open Studio, 1984, 87, Atlantic Gallery, 1985. Donnell Libr., Fine Pub. Libr., N.J., 1989, Pine Pub. Libr., Fairlawn, N.J., 1989, Tom Kendall Gallery, N.Y.C., 1990, others; exhibited in group shows at Whitney Mus., 1951, ACA Gallery, Audubon Artists, Pa. Acad. Fine Arts, Silvermine Guild, Nat. Assn. Women Artists, Krasner Gallery, City Ctr. Gallery, Laurel Gallery, Knickerbocker Artists, L.I. League of Painters and Sculptors, N.J. Soc. Painters and Sculptors, Nat. Exhbn. Contemporary Art U.S. in Los Angeles, Oakland Art Mus., Arthur Brown Gallery, Nat. Assn. Women Artists, 1986, Graphics Jury Audubon Artists, 1987, others. Author: Stepping Out, 1971; Dying to Survive, 1973; In the Red Meadow, 1973; Lighter-than-Night Verse, 1977; Swiftly Now, 1982; A Spool of blue, New and Selected Poems, 1983; You Came to Meet Someone Else, 1993, Greatest Hits, 2003, Reaching for Honey, 2004; contbr. poems to mags., anthologies. Tchr. Poets in Pub. Svc., 1989—90; vol. tutor Pub. Schs., 1995—96. Grantee MacDowell Colony, 1961, 62, 70, 76, Helene Wurlitzer Found., 1972, 73, 74, Ossabaw Island Project, 1976, R.I. Creative Arts Ctr., 1981; Michael Karolyi Meml. Found., 1983, Va. Ctr. Creative Arts, 1985, 1988, Millay Colony for the Arts, 1987, UCROSS Found., 1992; recipient Theodore Roethke award Poetry Northwest, 1967, Silver Ann. medal Audubon Artists, 1967, Achievement award Nat. Council on Arts, 1968, 1st prize for poetry Miscellany, 1972, Michael M. Engel Sr. Meml. award Audubon Artists, 1982, 3d place Concrete Poetry Competition, Gamut, 1983, Robert Philipps Meml. award for painting, 1990, Daler-Rowney award for oil painting, 1994, Art Students League award for oil, 1995, Grumbacher Gold medal for oils, 1998, Vi Gale award for poetry, 1999, Emily Lowe award for oil painting, 2000. Home: 24 W 8th St New York NY 10011-9019 Office: 32 Union Sq E Rm 911 New York NY 10003-3209 E-mail: cstoloff6@aol.com.

**STOLOV, WALTER CHARLES,** medicine physiatrist, educator; b. NYC, Jan. 6, 1928; s. Arthur and Rose F. (Gordon) S.; m. Anita Carvel Noodelman, Aug. 9, 1953; children: Nancy, Amy, Lynne. BS in Physics, CCNY, 1948; MA in Physics, U. Minn., 1951, MD, 1956. Diplomate Am. Bd. Phys. Med. and Rehab., Am. Bd. Electrodiagnostic Medicine. Physicist U.S. Naval Gun Factory, Nat. Bur. Stds., Washington, 1948-49; teaching and rsch. asst. U. Minn., Mpls., 1950-54; from instr. to assoc. prof. U. Wash., Seattle, 1960-70, prof., 1970-99, prof. emeritus, 1999—, also chmn., 1987-99, prof. emeritus, 1999—. Editl. bd. Archives Phys. Medicine and Rehab., 1967-78, Muscle and Nerve, 1983-89, 92-95; cons. Social Security Adminstrn., Seattle, 1975—; sec. Am. Bd. Electrodiagnostic Medicine, 1995—. Co-editor: Handbook of Severe Disability, 1981; contbr. articles to profl. jours. Surgeon USPHS, 1956-57. Recipient Townsend Harris medal CCNY, 1990. Fellow: AAAS, Am. Heart Assn.; mem.: Am. Spinal Cord Injry Assn., Am. Assn. Electrodiagnostic Medicine (pres. 1987—88, Lifetime Achievement award 2001), Assn. Acad. Physiatrists, Am. Congress Rehab. Medicine (Essay award

1959), Am. Acad. Phys. Medicine and Rehab. (Disting. Clinician award 1987). Avocations: dance, singing. Office: U Wash Box 356490 1959 NE Pacific St Seattle WA 98195-0001 Office Phone: 206-543-7065.

**STOLPER, EDWARD MANIN,** secondary school educator; b. Boston, Dec. 16, 1952; s. Saul James and Frances A. (Liberman) S.; m. Lauren Beth Adoff, June 3, 1973; children: Jennifer Ann, Daniel Aaron. AB, Harvard U., 1974, PhD, 1979; MPhil, U. Edinburgh, Scotland, 1976. Asst. prof. geology Calif. Inst. Tech., Pasadena, 1979-82, assoc. prof. geology, 1982-83, prof. geology, 1983-90, William E. Leonhard prof. geology, 1990—, chmn. divsn. geol. and planetary sci., 1994—2004, acting provost, 2004. Marshall scholar Marshall Aid Commemoration Commn., 1974-76; recipient Newcomb Cleve. prize AAAS, 1984, F.W. Clarke medal Geochemistry Soc., 1985, Arthur Holmes medal European Union Geosci., 1997; Geochemistry Soc. Geochem. Soc. and The European Assn. for Geochemistry, 1997. Fellow Meteoritical Soc. (Nininger Meteorite award 1976), Am. Geophys. Union (James B. Macelwane award 1986), Mineral Soc. Am., Am. Acad. Arts and Scis., Geol. Soc. Am. (Arthur L. Day medal 2004); mem. NAS, Sigma Xi. Office: Calif Inst Tech Div Geol Planetary Sci Pasadena CA 91125-0001

**STOLPER, PINCHAS ARYEH,** religious organization executive, rabbi; b. Bklyn., Oct. 22, 1931; s. David Bernard and Nettie (Rosch) S.; m. Elaine Liebman, Nov. 22, 1955; children: Akiva Psachia, Michal Hadassah Cohen, Malka Tova Kaweblum. BA, Bklyn. Coll., 1952; MA, New Sch. for Social Rsch., 1971. Rabbinical ordination Chaim Berlin-Gur Aryeh Rabbinical Acad., 1956; dir. L.I. Zionist Youth Commn., 1956-57; adminstrv. dean, adviser to English-speaking students Ponevez Yeshiva, Bnai Brak, Israel, 1957-59; also prin., instr. English and Talmud Nahalim Bnai Akiva H.S., 1959-77; nat. dir. youth div. Union Orthodox Jewish Congregations Am., Nat. Conf. Synagogue Youth, N.Y.C., 1959-76, founder NCSY, Torah Fund, Ben Zakai Honor Soc., 1959-76; editor Jewish Youth Monthly, 1967—; exec. v.p. Union Orthodox Jewish Congregations Am., 1976-94, sr. exec., 1994—. Adj. prof. Jewish studies Touro Coll., N.Y., 1975—; mem. publs., Israel, campus commns., staff mem. responsible for edn., Talmud Torah, day sch. commns. Union Orthodox Jewish Congregations Am., 1965—; del. White House Conf. on Children and Youth, 1961; cons. N. Am. Jewish Youth Conf., 1967—. Author: Tested Teen Age Activities, 1961, rev. edit., 1964, Day of Delight, 1961, Tefilah, Text and Source Book, 1963, Revelation What Happened on Sinai, 1966, Prayer, The Proven Path, 1967, The Road to Responsible Jewish Adulthood, 1967, Jewish Alternatives in Love, Dating and Marriage, 1985, The Sacred Trust, Love, Dating and Marriage, The Jewish View, 1996, Beyond Belief, Revelation for the Modern Jew, 1996, Living Beyond Time: The Mystery and Meaning of the Jewish Festivals, 2003, Purim in a New Light: Mystery, Grandeur and Depth, 2003, Chanukah in a New Light, 2005, Hidden Lights: Chanukah and the Jewish/Greek Conflict, 2005; contbr. numerous articles, plays, and revs. to Jewish publs.; columnist The Jewish Press, 1994. Nat. dir. Nat. Conf. Synagogue Youth, 1995-98; bd. dirs. Chaim Berlin Torah Schs.-Mesivta Rabbi Chaim Berlin-Rabbinical Acad., 1965—; pres. David Dov Found. Recipient Alumi Amudim award Mesivta Rabbi Chaim Berlin-Gur Aryeh Inst., 1967, award Assn. Orthodox Jewish Tchrs., 1975, citation Rabbinical Coun. Am., 1984, Jabotinsky medal, 1990, Alumnus of Yr. award Flatbush Yeshiva, 1989, Joseph K. Miller Achdut Yisrael award Shaalvim Yeshiva, 1993. Mem. Rabbinical Coun. Am. Jewish. Home: 603 Twin Oaks Dr Lakewood NJ 08701-7147 Office: Union Orthodox Jewish Cong of Am 11 Broadway New York NY 10004-1303 E-mail: PinchasStolper@aol.com.

**STOLPIN, WILLIAM ROGER,** printmaker; b. Flint, Mich., June 25, 1942; s. William and Dorothy Florence (Mitchell) S.; m. Kathleen Diane Poyner, Aug. 14, 1970; children: Krishna Ann, James Mitchell. BME, Kettering U., 1965; AA, Charles Stewart Mott C.C., Flint, 1978; postgrad., Ea. Mich. U., 1992. Jr. reliability engr. GM Corp., Flint, 1968—76, sr. reliability engr., 1976—80, supr. quality control, 1980—83, mgr. product assurance, 1983—89, asst. staff engr. Warren, Mich., 1990—93; printmaker, print pub. Flint, 1969—80; printmaker, print pub., co-founder DAS Print Co., Holly, Mich., 1980—; art faculty Flint Inst. Arts, Mich., 2000—. Faculty Flint Inst. of Arts, Flint, Mich., 2006—; resident artist Robert T. Longway Planetarium, Flint, 1975—. Printmaker: (lithograph) And the Santa Maria, 1969 (Smithsonian permanent collection 1973), (serigraph) One Giant Leap For Mankind, 1970 (Smithsonian permanent collection 1973), numerous pub. serigraphs, lithographs, intaglio prints and woodcuts, 1969—. Grant reviewer Greater Flint Arts Coun., 1989-90, 2000-02, v.p., 1973-74, programming and planning, 1988, mktg. and pub. rels., 1999—, bd. dirs., 1999—; pres. Buckham Fine Arts Project, Flint, 1993-94, bd. dirs., 1993-2000; bd. dirs. Whaley Hist. House, Flint, 1997-2000; adv. com. U. Mich. Flint Art Gallery, 1997-2000, Shiawassee Arts Coun., 1999-2000, Alma Coll., 1999-2001; accessions and collections com. Flint Inst. Arts, 2000—; grant reviewer Oakland County Office Arts, Culture and Film, 2002—. Recipient 1st in Graphics award Internat. Platform Assn., 1969, Koegler Meml. award Left Bank Gallery 1991, 1st in Overall Attitude, Mich. Renaissance Festival, 1998, 99, 1st prize all media award Left Bank Gallery, 1998, purchase prize Saginaw Art Mus., 1994, 98, hon. mention Ann Arbor Art Ctr., 2003, 04, 1st prize Flint (Mich.) Art Fair, 2004, Third prize 2006; Fed. Design and Art in Transp. grantee, 2002. Mem. AAAS, AIAA, Internat. Assn. for Astron. Arts, Am. Soc. for Quality, Nat. Stereoscopic Assn., Soc. Automotive Engrs., Soc. Am. Graphic Artists, Flint Artist's Market, Left Bank Gallery, Detroit Artist's Market, Assn. Sci. Fiction and Fantasy Artists, Mich. Assn. Printmakers, Am. Print Alliance, Am. Color Print Soc., Mid Am. Print Coun., Internat. Ctr. for the Print, Wood Engravers Network, Mich. Guild Artists and Artisans, Renaissance Artisans Guild. Avocations: directing community theater, participant in michigan renaissance festival, stereoscopic imaging. Studio: DAS Print Co 12201 Gage Rd Holly MI 48442-8339 Personal E-mail: bill@ntolpinod.com

**STOLTE, LARRY GENE,** marketing executive, retired computer and publishing company executive; b. Cedar Rapids, Iowa, Sept. 17, 1945; s. Ed August and Emma Wilhelmina (Tank) S.; m. Rebecca Jane Tappmeyer, June, 1970; children: Scott Edward, Ryan Gene. BBA with highest distinction, U. Iowa, 1971; MBA, Trinity U., 2000. CPA Ill., Mo., Minn., Mich., Wis., personal fin. specialist, Ill., Mo., Minn., Mich., Wis., cert. profl. econ. to mgmt., Nat. Bur. Profl. Mgmt. Cons. Tax and auditing acct. McGladrey Pullen & Co., Cedar Rapids, 1971—73; v.p., mng. mgr. TLS Co. (subs. CCH Computax Inc.), Cedar Rapids, 1973—92; re-engring. cons. CCH, Inc., Riverwoods, Ill., 1992—94; nat. mktg. McGladrey & Pullen, Cedar Rapids, 1994—97; sr. v.p., mng. dir. Web Site Dynamics & Stolte Enterprises, Cedar Rapids, 1997—2000; ptnr. NY Life Ins. Co. & NY Life Securities, Inc., Cedar Rapids, 2001—03; personal fin. advisor Thrivent Fin., 2004—. Sgt. USMC, 1964-67. Mem. AICPA, Nat. Assn. Computerized Tax Processors (pres.), Am. Mgmt. Assn., Am. Mktg. Assn., Inst. Mgmt. Accts. (cert.), Nat. Bur. Profl. Mgmt. Cons. (cert.), Sales and Mktg. Execs. Internat. (cert. mktg. exec., cert. sales exec.), Inst. Cert. Mgmt. Cons. (cert.). Methodist. Address: 3000-A Towne House Dr NE PO Box 0489 Cedar Rapids IA 52406-0489 Office Phone: 319-378-4697. Personal E-mail: larrystolte@hotmail.com.

**STOLTENBERG, DONALD HUGO,** artist, writer; b. Milw., Oct. 15, 1927; s. Hugo Adolph and Leora (Belitz) Stoltenberg. BS in Virtual Design, Ill. Inst. Tech., 1958. Instr. visual design Inst. Design, Chgo., 1952; instr. painting, print making DeCordova Sch., Lincoln, Mass., 1954—75; instr. printmaking, painting, drawing Cape Cod Conservatory Music and Art, Barnstable, Mass., 1970. Vis. critic RI Sch. Design, Providence, 1963. Author: The Artist and the Built Environment, 1980, Collagraph Printmaking, 1975. Fellow: Am. Soc. Maritime Artists; mem.: New Eng. Watercolor Soc., Am. Watercolor Soc. Home: 947 Satucket Rd Brewster MA 02631 E-mail: stollow@comcast.net.

**STOLTZ, ERIC,** actor; b. Whittier, Calif., Sept. 30, 1961; Studied with Peggy Fury, William Traylor, U. So. Calif. Actor: (stage prodns.) One Flew Over the Cuckoo's Nest, 1978, Hello, Dolly!, 1979, The Seagull, 1980, The Widow Claire, 1987, Our Town, 1988 (Tony award nomination Drama Desk nomination), The American Plan, 1990, Two Shakespearean Actors, 1992, Down the Road, 1993, The Importance of Being Earnest, 1996, Three Sisters, 1997, Arms and the Man, 1997, The Glass Menagerie, 1998, Light Up the

Sky, 2000, McReele, 2005; (feature films) Fast Times at Ridgemont High, 1981, Wild Life, 1983, Mask, 1984 (Golden Globe award nomination 1985), Lionheart, 1986, Some Kind of Wonderful, 1987, Sister, Sister, Haunted Summer, Code Name Emerald, 1988, Say Anything, 1989, Manifesto, 1989, The Fly II, 1989, Memphis Belle, 1990, Singles, 1991, The Waterdance, 1991, Naked in New York, 1993, Killing Zoe, 1993, God's Army (renamed The Prophesy), 1993, Pulp Fiction, 1994, Little Women, 1994, Rob Roy, 1995, Fluke, 1995, Kicking and Screaming, 1995, Grace of My Heart, 1995, Inside, 1996, Two Days in the Valley, 1996, Anaconda, 1996, Mr. Jealousy, 1997, Hi-Life, 1998, The House of Mirth, 1999, Havard Man, 2001, The Rules of Attraction, 2002, When Zachary Beaver Came to Town, 2003, The Butterfly Effect, 2004, Childstar, 2004, The Honeymooners, 2005; (TV movies) the Grass Is Greener, 1980, The Violation of Sarah McDavid, 1982, Thursday's Child, 1982, Paper Dolls, 1982, A Killer in the Family, 1983, Foreign Affairs, 1993, Roommates, 1994, Keys to Tulsa, 1997, Blackout Effect, 1997, The Passion of Ayn Rand, 1999, Our Guys, 1999, The Simean Line, 1999, The Harvard Man, 2000, The Last Dance, 2000, Things Behind the Sun, 2001, My Horrible Year!, 2001; (TV series) Chicago Hope, 1998-99, The Lot, 1999; (TV episodes) St. Elsewhere, 1983, Fallen Angels, 1994, (13 episodes) Mad About You, 1995, Partners, 1995, Homicide, 1997, Chicago Hope, 1998; actor, prodr. Bodies, at Rest and Motion, 1993, Sleep With Me, 1995, Mr. Jealousy, 1997, Highball, 1997; dir. (TV series) Once and Again, 1999-2002. Office: Creative Artists Agy care Jane Berliner 9830 Wilshire Blvd Beverly Hills CA 90212-1804*

**STOLTZFUS, EMILIE,** social policy analyst; b. Milford, Del., Aug. 5, 1964; d. Llewellyn Roy and Anna Elizabeth Stoltzfus; m. Eugene Stevanus, Aug. 6, 1994; children: Gabriel Llewellyn Stevanus, Elliott William Stevanus. BA in English & Comm., Goshen Coll., Ind., 1986; PhD in History, Claremont U., Calif., 1999. Mng. editor United Mine Workers Am., 1990—92; social legislation specialist Congl. Rsch. Svc., 2001—. Author: (monograph) Citizen, Mother Worker: Debating Public Responsibility for Child Care After the Second World War, 2003. Mem.: Orgn. Am. Historians, Am. Hist. Assn. Office: Congl Rsch Svc 101 Independence Ave SE Washington DC 20540-7440

**STOLTZMAN, RICHARD LESLIE,** clarinetist; b. Omaha, July 12, 1942; s. Leslie Harvey and Dorothy Marilyn (Spohn) S.; m. Lucy Jean Chapman, June 6, 1976; children: Peter John, Margaret Anne. MusB summa cum laude, Ohio State U., 1964; MusM magna cum laude, Yale U., 1967; postgrad., Columbia U. Tchrs. Coll., 1967-70. Mem. faculty Calif. Inst. Arts, 1970-75, New Eng. Conservatory, 1996. Western regional dir. Young Audiences, Inc., 1972-74, mem. nat. bd. Appeared in concerts throughout U.S., Europe, Japan, Hong Kong, Australia, 1976—; rec. artist, 1974—; debut LaScala, Milan, 1981, Carnegie Hall, N.Y.C., 1982; appeared in world premiere of Einar Englund concerto Helsinki Festival, 1991, Toru Takemitsu concerto (Fantasma/Cantos) Wales BBC, 1991, U.S. premiere of Lukas Foss concerto L.A. Philharm. Orch., 1991, Copland concert, 1993 (Emmy award for best performing arts video 1993), world premiere of Leonard Bernstein sonata for clarinet and orch. Pacific Music Festival, Sapporo, Japan, 1994, world premiere of Steven Hartke concerto PBS, 2001, world premiere of William Thomas McKinley concerto 9 Shades of Lament, Boston Civic Orch., 2001, of Einojuhani Rautavaara Concerto, Nat. Symphony, Carnegie Hall, 2002. Recipient Horatio Parker award Yale U., 1966, Avery Fisher prize, 1977, Martha Baird Rockefeller award, 1973, Grammy award, 1983, 95, Avery Fisher artist award, 1986, Disting. Alumnus award Ohio State U., 1990, Sanford medal Yale U., 2005. Home: 6 Lincolnshire Way Winchester MA 01890-3048 Office: 201 W 54th St Apt 4C New York NY 10019-5521 Office Phone: 212-581-5197. E-mail: stohome@comcast.net. *Be mindful of the breath. It gives life to the sound which sends music to the soul.*

**STOLWIJK, JAN ADRIANUS JOZEF,** physiologist, biophysicist; b. Amsterdam, Netherlands, Sept. 29, 1927; came to U.S., 1955, naturalized, 1962. s. Leonard and Cornelia Agnes (Van Der Bijl) S.; m. Deborah Rose, 1990. BS, Wageningen U., Netherlands, 1948, MS, 1951, PhD, 1955. Biophysicist John B. Pierce Found., New Haven, 1957-61; assoc. fellow John B. Pierce Found. Lab., 1961-64, fellow, 1964, assoc. dir., 1974-89; instr. dept. physiology Yale U. Sch. Medicine, New Haven, 1962-63, asst. prof., 1964-68, asst. prof. epidemiology, 1968-69, assoc. prof., 1969-75, prof., 1975-99, dir. grad. studies, dept. epidemiology and pub. health, 1992-99, chmn. dept. epidemiology and pub. health, 1982-89; rsch. fellow Harvard U., 1955-56. Cons. divsn. disease prevention Conn. Health Dept., 1977-99; cons. vehicle inspection program Dept. Motor Vehicles, 1979-83; mem. sci. adv. bd. EPA, 1985-93; mem. tech. adv. bd. Dept. Commerce, 1972-77. Mem. Am. Physiol. Soc., Biophys. Soc., Aerospace Med. Soc., Am. Pub. Health Assn., AAAS, Internat. Biometeorol. Soc., Soc. Occupl. and Environ. Health, Am. Conf. Govt. Indsl. Hygienists, ASHRAE, Conn. Acad. Sci. and Engring., Cosmos Club. Home: 4414 Harbour Town Dr Beltsville MD 20705-1081 E-mail: stolwijk@prodigy.net.

**STOLZ, BENJAMIN ARMOND,** foreign language educator; b. Lansing, Mich., Mar. 28, 1934; s. Armond John and Mabel May (Smith) S.; m. Mona Eleanor Seelig, June 16, 1962; children: Elizabeth Mona, John Benjamin. AB, U. Mich., Ann Arbor, 1955; certificat, U. Libre de Bruxelles, Belgium, 1956; A.M., Harvard U., 1957, PhD, 1965. Mem. faculty U. Mich., 1964-2001, prof. Slavic langs. and lits., 1972-2001, chmn. dept., 1971-85, 89-91; prof. emeritus, 2001—. Cons. in field. Editor: Papers in Slavic Philology, 1977, Studies in Macedonian Language, Literature, and Culture, 1995; co-editor: Oral Literature and the Formula, 1976, Cross Currents, 1982-85, Language and Literary Theory, 1984, Mich. Slavic Publs., 1990—; co-editor, translator: (Konstantin Mihailovic): Memoirs of a Janissary, 1975; contbr. articles to profl. pubs. Served to lt. (j.g.) USNR, 1957-60. Recipient Orion E. Scott award humanities U. Mich., 1954, Fulbright scholar, 1955-56; Fgn. Area fellow Yugoslavia, 1963-64; Fulbright-Hays rsch. fellow Eng. and Yugoslavia, 1970-71; grantee Am. Coun. Learned Socs., 1968-70, 73, Internat. Rsch. and Exchs. Bd., 1985, 87, Woodrow Wilson Ctr., 1992. Mem. Am. Assn. Advancement Slavic Studies, Am. Assn. Tchrs. Slavic and East European Langs., Huron Valley Tennis Club, Phi Beta Kappa, Phi Kappa Phi, Delta Upsilon. Democrat. Home: 3423 Riverbend Dr Ann Arbor MI 48105 Office: Univ Mich 3010 MLB Ann Arbor MI 48109*

**STOLZ, THEODORA,** psychologist; b. Athens, Greece, Jan. 13, 1958; d. Bernhard and Evelyn Stolz; children: Lynette, Constantine. BA in Psychology, Marymount Manhattan Coll., 1981; PhD, Hofstra U., 1991. Lic. psychologist N.Y., 1991, N.J., 1994. Pvt. practice, Staten Island and Bklyn., 1991—; assoc. psychologist, program mgr. Staten Island Devel. Disabilities Svcs, 1989—, bd. dirs., 1989—; contractual mil. psychologist Homeland Security, NJ, 2005—. Author: Cognitive Factors in Pathological Gambling, 1991., Hofstra U. fellow, 1989. Mem.: APA, Deborah Orgn. Avocations: dollhouse building, bicycling, needlepoint, music, meditation. Office: 68 Guyon Ave Staten Island NY 10306-2019

**STOLZBERG, MARK ELLIOTT,** psychologist; b. NYC, Apr. 30, 1944; s. Seymour and Ruth (Petesky) S.; m. Marilyn Goldberg, Mar. 18, 1972; children: Susan Beth, David Jonathan, Daniel Jason. BA, Hofstra U., 1966, PhD, 1986; MA in Exptl. Psychology, C.W. Post Coll., 1970; postgrad. in clin. psychology, SUNY, Albany, 1973. Diplomate in clin. psychology Am. Bd. Profl. Psychology. Intern in clin. psychology Maimonides Hosp., Bklyn., 1972-73; pres. Stolzberg Rsch., LLC, Stony Brook, NY, 1976—. Adj. lectr. Bklyn. Coll., 1973; faculty Coll. Optometry, SUNY, 1985-86; cons. clin. psychologist to numerous nursing homes, 1994—. Contbr. articles to profl. jours. Co-pres. North Shore SEPTA, 1999-2001. Grad. fellow C.W. Post Coll., 1968-70, SUNY, Albany, 1970-72, N.Y. State War Svc. scholar; recipient Disting. Achievement award for Rsch., N.Y. State Optometric Assn., 1983. Mem. Ind. Practitioners of Geropsychology (founder, past pres.), N.Y. State Psychol. Assn. (pres. divsn. on aging 2004), Aircraft Owners and Pilots Assn., Nat. Aeronautics Assn. Achievements include setting a U.S. transcontinental speed record for piston-engine aircraft. Home and Office: 3 Seabrook Ct Stony Brook NY 11790-3305 Personal E-mail: mstolzbe@optonline.net.

**STOMFAY-STITZ, ALINE MARIA,** education educator; b. Newark, N.J. d. Adolph and Irene (Badowska) Wegrocki; m. Emery Stomfay-Stitz (dec.); children: Peter, John, Robert. BA, Barnard Coll.; MA, Case We. Res. U.; EdD, No. Ill. U., 1984. Asst. prof. edn. St Scholastica, Duluth, Minn., 1984—85, St. Leo Coll., Fla., 1985—87, Nicholls State U., Thibodaux, La., 1989—91; assoc. prof. edn. Christopher Newport U., Newport News, Va., 1991—96. Vis. prof., assoc. prof. edn. U. No. Fla., Jacksonville, 1996-2003; assoc. editor Joun. Early Childhood Tchr. Edn. Author: Peace Education in America 1828-1990, 1993; author (book chpt.): Toward Education That is Multicultural, 1992, Multicultural Education for the 21st Century, 1993; contbr. articles to profl. jours. Mem.: Internat. Peace Rsch. Assn., Nat. Assn. for Early Childhood Tchr. Educators, Am. Ednl. Rsch. Assn. (SIG exec. coun.). Business E-Mail: astomfay@unf.edu.

**STONE, ALAN,** container company executive; b. Chgo., Feb. 5, 1928; s. Norman H. and Ida (Finkelstein) S.; m. Joanie B. Stone; children: Christie-Ann Stone Weiss, Joshua. BSE, U. Pa., 1951; cert. in Advanced Mgmt., U. Chgo., 1960. Trainee, salesman Stone Container Corp., Chgo., 1951-53, dir. mktg. service, 1954-64, gen. mgr., regional mgr., 1964-72, sr. v.p. adminstrn., gen. mgr. energy div., 1972—, also dir., sr. v.p. purchasing and transp.; pres. North La. and Gulf R.R./Ctrl. La. and Gulf R.R., 1985-92, Atlanta St. Andrews and Bay Line R.R., 1992-94, Abbeville-Grimes R.R., 1992-94, Apache R.R., 1992-94. Bd. dirs., exec. com. Stone Container Corp., 1960—; cons. Chgo. Mfg.; pres. No. La. Gulf Railroad, 1985, Ctrl. La. Gulf Railroad, 1985. Pres. Jewish Vocat. Svc., Chgo., 1975-77, bd. dirs., 2005—; v.p. Sinai Temple, Chgo., 1977-84; bd. dirs. Jewish Fedn. Chgo., 2005; vice-chmn. Roycemore Sch., Evanston, Ill., 1982-87; pres. Emergency Fund for Needy People, 1993-2003, chmn., 2003—; trustee Brewster Acad., Wolfeboro, N.H.; vol. exec. for overseas needs Citizen's Democracy Corps; vol. cons. Exec. Svc. Corps., 1992—, project mgr., 1997, bd. dirs., 2002—; bd. dirs. Gastrointestinal Rsch. Found., Intermodal Transp. Inst., U. Denver, 1997—; cancer adv. bd. Northwestern U. Mem. Standard Club, Tavern Club, Bryn Mawr Country Club, Tamarisk Country Club, Long Boat Key Club, Execs. Club Chgo., Beta Alpha Psi, Phi Eta Sigma, Zeta Beta Tau. Avocations: golf, sports, reading, travel, cultural activities. Office: Stone Container Corp 645 N Michigan Ave Ste 800 Chicago IL 60611-3775 Office Phone: 312-981-5016. Personal E-mail: alanstone3@aol.com.

**STONE, ALAN JAY,** retired academic administrator; b. Ft. Dodge, Iowa, Oct. 15, 1942; s. Hubert H. and Bernice A. (Tilton) S.; m. Jonieta J. Smith; 1 child, Kirsten K. Stone Morlock. BA, Morningside Coll., 1964; MA, U. Iowa, 1966; MTh, U. Chgo., 1968, DMin, 1970; PhD (hon.), Kyonggi U., Korea, 1985; LLD, Stillman Coll., 1991, Sogong U., Korea, 1992, Alma Coll., 2001; HD, Morningside Coll., 2001. Admissions counselor Morningside Coll., Sioux City, Iowa, 1964-66; dir. admissions, asso. prof. history George Williams Coll., Downers Grove, Ill., 1969-73; v.p. coll. relations Hood Coll., Frederick, Md., 1973-75; v.p. devel. and fin. affairs W.Va. Wesleyan Coll., Buckhannon, 1975-77; dir. devel. U. Maine, 1977-78; pres. Aurora (Ill.) U., 1978-88, Alma (Mich.) Coll., 1988-2000; pres., CEO Alzheimer's Assn., Chgo., 2001—02; ret., 2002. Home: 28897 N 94th Pl Scottsdale AZ 85262 Personal E-mail: stone5613@earthlink.net, thestones3@cox.net.

**STONE, ALAN JOHN,** manufacturing company executive, real estate company executive; b. Dansville, N.Y., Sept. 9, 1940; s. Guthrie Boyd and Doris Irene (Wolfanger) S.; m. Sandra Barber, Aug. 22, 1964; children: Teri, Timothy, Michael. BSME, Rochester Inst. Tech., 1963; MBA, U. Pitts., 1964. Engring. aide Xerox Corp., Webster, N.Y., 1963-67; gen. mgr. mech. component divsn. Stone Conveyor Co., Inc., Honeoye, N.Y., 1964-67, v.p. sales, 1968; co-founder, CEO Stone Constrn. Equipment Inc., Honeoye, 1969-86, also cons., bd. dirs., 1969—; founder, pres. Canandaigua Apts. Inc., NY, 1967—83; pres. Wildtrak, Inc. 1983—; founder, gen. prtnr. Stone Properties, 1986—2002; mng. mem. Stone Family Properties, LLC, 2002—. Dir., co-founder Baker Rental Svc., Inc., 1973-75; net. adv. bd. Chase Lincoln Bank, 1981-84; co-founder, dir. Royal Lines Ltd., 1989-91; v.p. Naples Biol. Rsch. Sta. Inc., 1996-98; bd. dirs. Canandaigua Nat. Bank & Trust Co., 1986-, chmn. 1994-2004; mem., City Mini Storage, LLC, 2001—; mng. mem., 2001-04. Patentee in field. Mem. Town of Richmond (N.Y.) Planning Bd., 1970-75, chmn., 1970-71; mem. Honeoye Ctrl. Sch. Bd. Edn., 1971-76, pres., 1974-75; com. chmn. pack 10 Boy Scouts Am., 1975-78; mem. Ontario County Overall Econ. Devel. Com., 1976-81; bd. dirs. F.F. Thompson Hosp., 1987-91; chmn. fin. com. United Meth. Ch., Allens Hill, 1995—2001; trustee Honeoye Pub. Libr., 1998-2003. Mem. Honeoye C. of C., Constrn. Industry Mfrs. Assn. (exec. mem. new bus. challenges coun. 1980-83), Honeoye Valley Assn. (dir. 1993-95), Griswold and Cast Iron Collectors Assn. (treas. 1994-96, chmn. fin. com. 1996-2002), Honeoye Area Hist. Soc. (bicentennial com. 1989), Grand Slam Club, Safari Internat., Found. N.Am. Wild Sheep. Methodist. Office Phone: 585-229-2700.

**STONE, ALEXANDER PAUL,** mathematics professor; b. West New York, N.J., June 28, 1928; s. Samuel Bradford and Violet Elizabeth (Schuessler) S.; m. Mary Ann Majeski, July 23, 1960; 1 child, Christopher Bradford. BSEE, Columbia U., 1952; MSEE, Newark Coll. Engring., 1956; PhD, U. Ill., 1965. Field engr. Western Elec./Bell Telephone Labs., Whippany, N.J., 1952-56; instr. in elec. engring. Manhattan Coll., Riverdale, N.Y., 1956-58; asst. prof. physics Dickinson Coll., Carlisle, Pa., 1958-60; asst. prof. math. U. Ill., Chgo., 1965-69, assoc. prof. math., 1969-70, U. N.Mex., Albuquerque, 1970-76, prof. math., 1976—, chmn. dept. math. and stats., 1991-97. Cons. Air Force Rsch. Lab., 1984—. Editor: Improperly Posed Boundary Value Problems, 1976; author: Transient Lens Synthesis, 1990; contbr. articles to profl. jours. With USN, 1946-48, 2d lt. U.S. Army, 1951-52. NSF grantee, 1966-70, AFOSR grantee, 1984-85, 95-96; Intergovtl. Personnel Act appt. Air Force Rsch. Lab., 1991-94, 97-99. Mem. Am. Math. Soc., Internat. Union of Radio Sci. (commn. E on electro-magnetic noise and interference). Avocations: tennis, golf, mountain climbing. Office: Univ NMex Dept Math And Stats Albuquerque NM 87131-1141 Office Phone: 505-277-5303. E-mail: astone@math.unm.edu.

**STONE, ALFRED DOUGLAS,** physicist, educator; b. New Haven, Conn., June 26, 1954; s. Alan A. and Sue Smart Stone; m. Mary Schwab, June 2, 1984; children: John Alan, William Schwab. BA in Social Studies summa cum laude, Harvard Coll., Cambridge, Mass., 1976; MA in Physics and Philosophy, Balliol Coll., Oxford, England, 1978; PhD in Theoretical Physics, MIT, Cambridge, Mass., 1983. Postdoctoral fellow IBM Rsch. Ctr., Yorktown Heights, NY, 1983-85; IBM postdoctoral fellow SUNY Stony Brook, NY, 1985—86; assoc. prof. Yale U., New Haven, 1986—90, prof. of applied physics and physics 1990—97, chmn. of applied physics, 1997—2003, Carl A. Morse prof. applied physics and physics, 2003—. Dir., divsn. of physical sci. Yale U., 2004—. Recipient William MacMillan award, U. Ill., 1987, Presdl. Young Investigator award, NSF, 1987—92, Outstanding Tech. Achievement award, IBM Corp., 1987; Alfred P. Sloan fellow, Alfred P. Sloan Found., 1990—91, Rhodes scholarship, Rhodes Trust, 1976—78. Fellow: Am. Phys. Soc. (life). Achievements include pioneer in new sub-field of solid state physics known as mesoscopic physics; wrote first published article using the term; patents for optical physics/lasers. Office: Applied Physics Yale U PO Box 208284 New Haven CT 06511 Office Phone: 203-432-4279.

**STONE, ANDREW GROVER,** lawyer; b. LA, Oct. 2, 1942; s. Frank B. and Meryl (Pickering) S.; 1 child, John Blair; m. Susan Anselmo, Feb. 14, 2003. BA, Yale U., 1965; JD, U. Mich., 1969. Bar: D.C. 1970, U.S. Dist. Ct. D.C. 1970, U.S. Ct. Appeals (D.C. cir.) 1972, Mass. 1981. Assoc. Rogers & Wells, Washington, 1969-71; atty. Bur. Competition, FTC, Washington, 1971-80; antitrust counsel Digital Equipment Corp., Maynard, Mass., 1980-83, mgr. N.E. law group, 1983-86, mgr. headquarters sales law group, 1986-88; asst. general counsel U.S. (acting), 1987, 88; corp counsel Washington, 1988-90; corp. counsel, pub. sect. mktg. Thinking Machines Corp., Cambridge, Mass., 1990-91, corp. counsel, 1992-95; pvt. practice on-site legal svcs. Marblehead, Mass., 1995—2006; v.p., gen. counsel Hologic Inc., Bedford, Mass., 2006—. Corp. mem. Tenacre Country Day Sch., Wellesley, Mass., 1981-88. Mem. ABA (bus. law sect.), Mass. Bar Assn. (internat. law steering com. 1993-94),

Boston Bar Assn. (membership com. 1998-2000, chair corp. counsel com. 1995-98, chair gen. counsel forum 1995—), Am. Arbitration Assn. (comml. arbitrator), New Eng. Corp. Counsel Assn.

**STONE, ANN ELIZABETH,** marketing agency executive, consultant, entrepreneur, volunteer; b. Bridgeport, Conn., Aug. 9, 1952; d. Jack Reginald and Edith Pauline (Christiansen) Wesche; m. Roger J. Stone, June 15, 1974 (div. Dec. 1990). BA in History and Comm., George Washington U., 1974; postgrad., Wharton Sch. Bus., Washington, 1975—76. Mktg. mgr. Human Events, Washington, 1974—76; v.p. polit. div. The Viguerie Co., Falls Church, Va., 1976—82; chmn. Capstone Lists, Alexandria, Va., 1983—; Unique Graphics, Alexandria, 1985—; vice chmn. George Washington Nat. Bank, Alexandria, 1988—; pres. Weintraub-Stone Direct, Inc., Woodland Hills, Calif., 1991—; pres. The Stone Group Inc. (formerly Ann E.W. Stone & Assocs.), Alexandria, 1982—. Bd. dirs. Action Products; spkr. in field. Co-host (TV show) The Alexandria Forum, TV appearances Larry King Live, Lehrer News Hour, Good Morning Am., Politically Incorrect, others; contbr. articles to profl. jours. Pres.'s exec. global adv. bd. European/Am. Women's Coun., 2003; internat. chair Empowered Women Internat. and Women Immigrant Network; arbiter Va. Bar Assn.; trustee apptd. by gov. Va. Hist. Preservation Found.; fin. dir. Alexandria Rep. Party, 1989—92; chmn. D.C. Young Reps., Washington, 1975—77; Republican candidate for mayor Alexandria, 1991; chmn., foundr Reps. for Choice, Alexandria, 1989—; bd. dirs. Campaigns and Elections Mag., Washington, 1987—, Am. Heart Assn., 1990—, chmn., 1993—94; bd. dirs. Nat. Womens History Mus., The Washington Ctr., Response mag., Influence mag. Named one of Women Who Changed Politics in Am., Campaigns and Elections mag., 1992. Mem. Direct Mktg. Assn. Washington (bd. dirs. 1974—), Renaissance Women (bd. dirs. 1985—), Alexandria C. of C. (bd. dirs. 1982), Alexandria Soc. for Preservation of Black Heritage, Animal Welfare League, Lions Club, Alexandria Seaport Fedn. (past bd. dirs.), Direct Mktg. Club (Washington). Lutheran. Avocations: reading, travel, historical renovation, rock collecting, music. Office: 205 S Whiting St 250 Alexandria VA 22304 Office Phone: 703-329-1982, 703-370-8282. Personal E-mail: tsgrp@aol.com.

**STONE, BETHANNE JULIA,** music educator; d. Theodore C. and Judith Claire Stone. BA, Loyola U. Chgo., 1995; MA, NYU, 2001; MEd, Columbia U., 2005. Registered Violin Istr. Suzuki Assn. Am. Asst. club. rels. coord. Coun. Jewish Elderly, Chgo., 1989—95; freelance performer and music instr. Chgo., 1995—2000; instr. music, music edn. NYU, N.Y.C., 2001—03; profl. chorister Chgo. Symphony Chorus, 2002—; dir. Stone Studios, N.Y.C., 2004—. Dir. Project Sing & Serve, Hoboken, NJ, 2004—05. Author (presenter): The Life and Work of Chicago Composer John Alden Carpenter. Presenter Thompson Symposium on Music Edn., Pa. State U., 2005; musician Archdiocese of Chgo., 1990—2000. Academic scholarship, Loyola U. Chgo., 1991-1995, Academci scholarship, NYU, 2000-2001, Elin J. Steene scholarship, Tchrs. Coll. Columbia U., 2001. Mem.: Am. Guild Musical Artists, Suzuki Assn. Am., Nat. Assn. Tchrs. of Singing, Music Tchrs. Nat. Assn., NY Singing Tchrs. Assn. (assoc.), The Lambs, Phi Beta Kappa. Achievements include research in understanding the dynamics of the voice studio. Avocations: hiking, travel. Home Fax: 201-792-0185. Personal E-mail: bethannestone@yahoo.com.

**STONE, CAROLINE FLEMING,** artist; b. N.Y.C., Mar. 26, 1936; d. Ralph Emerson and Elizabeth (Fleming) Stone; m. Oakleigh B. Thorne, June 1956 (div. 1969); children: Oakleigh, Henry; m. John Roderick Keating, July 2002. Student, Art Students' League, 1954-57, 71-72, Pratt Graphics, 1973-74. One-woman shows include Washington Art Assn., Conn., Ella Sharp Mus., Mich., 1980, San Diego Pub. Library, 1981, Trustman Gallery Simmons Coll., Boston, 1985, Mary Ryan Gallery, N.Y.C., 1989, Boston Pub. Libr., 1994, Messiah Coll., 1995; two-person shows include Mary Ryan Gallery, 1985, Katonah Gallery, N.Y., 1986, Davidson Gallery, Seattle, 1990, The Millbrook (N.Y.) Gallery, 1993; juried shows include Silvermine Nat. Printmaking, Conn., 1978, Print Club, Phila., 1981, Trenton State (Nat. Print Exhibn. Purchase award), 1982, Minot State Coll., N.D., 1985, Boston Printmakers (Jurors Commendation), 1986; group shows include Mus. N.Mex., 1984, De Cordova and Dana Mus., Nat. Acad. Art, N.Y.C., Boston Pub. Library, Mus. Contemporary Hispanic Art, N.Y.C., 1987, World Print Exhbn., San Francisco, Smith Coll. Gallery, Northampton, Mass., Mary Ryan Gallery, 1988, Virginia Lynch Gallery, R.I., 1989, 91, Accent on Paper, Lintas, N.Y., 1991, Women Printmaker's Nat. Touring Show, Boston Pub. Libr. 1991, The Tenth Anniversary Show Virginia Lynch Gallery, 1993; represented in permanent collections Art Inst. Chgo., Mid-West Mus. Am. Art, Ind., Mus. N.Mex., Nat. Mus. Am. Art, Boston Pub. Library, U. Chgo., U. Mich., The Portland Art Mus. Mem.: The Kitchen (bd. dirs.). Home and Office: C Stone Press 80 Wooster St New York NY 10012-4347

**STONE, CURTIS,** celebrity chef; b. 1976; Chef Savory Hotel, Melborne, Australia, The Grill Room, Café Royal, London; sous chef Mirabelle; head chef Quo Vadis, London, Restaurant 301. Host Dinner in a Box, UK Food, 2002, Surfing the Menu, ABC Australia, 2003, 2005, My Restaurant Rules, Network 7, Australia, 2004, Take Home Chef, TLC, 2006—; guest appearances Taste Today, Taste Network, Great Food Live, UK Food, Saturday Kitchen, BBC2, This Morning; author: Surfing the Menu, 2004, 2005; columnist Delicious Mag., Australia. Avocations: surfing, skiing.*

**STONE, DAVID M.,** former federal agency administrator, retired career military officer; m. Cynthia Faith Voth, 1987. Diploma, U.S. Naval Acad., 1974; MS in Nat. Security Affairs, U.S. Naval Postgrad. Sch., 1977, MA in Nat. Security/Strategic Studies, U.S. Naval War Coll., 1986; MS in Mgmt., Salve Regina Coll. Commd. ensign USN, 1974, advanced through ranks to rear adm., ret., 2002, various assignments to comdr. Middle East Force and Destroyer Squadron 50, 1994-96; chief of staff U.S. Sixth Fleet, 1996-98; comdr. NATO's Standing Naval Force Mediterranean, 1998-99; deputy director surface warfare USN, 99-00, Nimitz battlegroup comm., 2000-01; dir., environ. protection, safety & occupational health Office of the Chief of Naval Ops., Washington, 2001—02; fed. security dir. LA Internat. Airport, 2002—03; dep. chief of staff Transp. Security Adminstrn., US Dept. Homeland Security, 2003—04, acting adminstr., 2003—04; asst. sec. for Transp. Security Adminstrn. US Dept. Homeland Security, 2004—05. Decorated Legion of Merit (3 times), Def. Meritorious Svc. medal (2 times), Meritorious Svc. medal (3 times), Navy Commendation medal (3 times), Navy Achievement medal, others.

**STONE, DAVID PHILIP,** lawyer; b. NYC, Sept. 11, 1944; s. Robert and Laura Stone; m. Arlene R. Stone, June 11, 1966; children: Aaron J., Rachel E. AB, Columbia U., 1967; JD, Harvard U., 1970. Bar: N.Y. 1971. Assoc. Cahill, Gordon & Reindel, N.Y.C., 1970-74, Baer & McGoldrick, N.Y.C., 1974-76, Weil, Gotshal & Manges, L.L.P., N.Y.C., 1976-79, ptnr., 1979—2005. Office: Weil Gotshal & Manges LLP 767 5th Ave New York NY 10153-0119 Business E-Mail: david.stone@weil.com.

**STONE, DONALD DIAMOND,** investment and sales executive; b. Chgo., June 25, 1924; s. Frank J. and Mary N. (Miller) Diamondstone; m. Catherine Mauro, Dec. 20, 1970; 1 child, Jeffrey. Student, U. Ill., 1942-43; BS, DePaul U., 1949. Pres. Poster Bros., Inc., Chgo., 1950-71, Revere Leather Goods, Inc., Chgo., 1953-71; owner Don Stone Enterprises, Chgo., 1954—; v.p. Horton & Hubbard Mfg. Co. Inc. div. Brown Group, Nashua, N.H., 1969-71, Neevel Mfg. Co., Kansas City, Mo., 1969-71. Mem. adv. bd. San Diego Opera; founder Don Diego Meml. Scholarship Fund; mem. bd. overseers U. Calif., San Diego, chancellor's assoc.; mem. exec. bd. Chgo. Area council Boy Scouts of Am. Served with U.S. Army, 1943-46. Clubs: Bryn Mawr Country (Lincolnwood, Ill.) (dir.), Carlton, La Jolla Beach and Tennis, La Jolla Country, Del Mar Thoroughbred. Home: 1001 Genter St Apt 5C La Jolla CA 92037

**STONE, DONALD RAYMOND,** lawyer; b. Madison, Wis., Mar. 6, 1938; s. Donald Meredith and June Dorothy (Graffenberger) S.; m. Dorothy Tetzlaff, June 23, 1962; children: Randall, Brian. BS in Physics, U. Wis., 1960, JD,

1963. Bar: Minn. 1963, D.C. 1987, U.S. Supreme Ct. 1987. Patent atty. Honeywell, Inc., Mpls., 1963-66; patent atty. firm Burd, MacEachron, Braddock, Bartz & Schwartz, Mpls., 1966-68; with Medtronic, Inc., Mpls., 1968-87, v.p., then sr. v.p. product assurance and regulation, 1973-77, sr. v.p., sec., gen. counsel, 1977-80, sr. v.p., 1980-85, v.p., 1985-87; ptnr., mem. Burditt, Bowles & Radzius, Chartered, Washington, 1987-90; ptnr. McKenna & Cuneo, L.L.P., Washington, 1990-2001, Kirkpatrick & Lockhart LLP, Washington, 2001—03, of counsel, 2003; ret., 2003. Condr. seminars, 1974—. Contbr. articles to profl. jours. Bd. dirs., 1st v.p. East Side Neighborhood Services, Inc., Mpls., 1976-80; bd. dirs. Guthrie Theater Found., 1979-85; mem. allocations com. United Way Mpls., 1979-86, chmn. allocations com., 1985, bd. dirs. 1985-86; mem. Citizens League of Twin Cities, 1965-86. Mem. ABA, D.C. Bar Assn., Fed. Bar Assn., Hennepin County Bar Assn., Am. Soc. Quality, Am. Intellectual Property Law Assn., Advanced Med. Tech. Assn. (past chmn. legal and regulatory sect., std. sect., 1975-87), Nat. Elec. Mfrs. Assn. (past chmn. med. electronics sect., 1970-76), Minn. State Bar Assn., Minn. Intellectual Property Law Assn. (past sec.), Minn. Corp. Counsel Assn., Order of Coif, Phi Delta Phi, Kappa Sigma. Episcopalian.

**STONE, EDWARD C.,** physicist, researcher; b. Knoxville, Iowa, Jan. 23, 1936; s. Edward Carroll and Ferne Elizabeth (Baber) Stone; m. Alice Trabue Wickliffe, Aug. 4, 1962; children: Susan, Janet. AA, Burlington Jr. Coll., 1956; MS, U. Chgo., 1959, PhD, 1964, DSc (hon.), 1992, Washington U., St. Louis, 1992, Harvard U., 1992, U. So. Calif., 1998. From rsch. fellow in physics to prof. Calif. Inst. Tech., Pasadena, Calif., 1964—94, Voyager project scientist, 1972—, chmn. divsn. physics, math. and astron., 1983—88, v.p. 1988—2001, dir. jet propulsion lab., 1991—2001, David Morrisroe prof. physics, 1994—, mem. Draper Lab., 2001, vice provost for spl. projects, 2004—. Cons. Office of Space Sci., NASA, 1969—85, adv. com. outer planets, 1972—73; high energy astrophysics mgmt. oper. working group NASA, 1976—84, cosmic ray program working group, 1980—82, outer plantets working group, 1981—82, solar sys. exploration com., 1981—82, U. rels. study group, 1983; exec. com. Com. on Space Rsch. Interdisciplinary Sci. Comm., 1982—86; com. on space astronomy and astrophysics Space Sci. Bd., 1979—82, steering group study on maj. directions for space sci., 1984—85; mem. Space Sci. Bd., NRC, 1982—85; commnr. on phys. sci., math. and resources NRC, 1986—89; adv. com. vis. sr. scientist program NASA/Jet Propulsion Labs., 1986—90; com. on space policy NAS/NAE, 1988—89; chmn., chief sci. advisor The Astronomers, KCET, 1989—91; chmn. adv. panel NAS/WQED TV program "Sail on, Voyager!", 1989—90; v.p. COSPAR Bur., 2001—. Mem. editl. bd. Space Sci. Instrumentation, 1975—81, Space Sci. Rev., 1982—85, Astrophysics and Space Sci., 1982—, Sci. mag. Bd. dir. W.M. Keck Found., 1994—. Named an asteroid Edward C. Stone in his honor, 1996; named to Hall of Fame, Aviation Week and Space Tech., 1997, Hall of Honor, Burlington Comm., 1999; recipient medal for exceptional sci. achievement, NASA, 1980, Am. Edn. award, 1981, Disting. Svc. medal, 1981, 1998, 2001, Dryden award, 1983, Disting. Pub. Svc. medal, 1985, Outstanding Leadership medal, 1986, 1995, Achievement award, Soc. for Tech. Comm., 1984, Space Achievement award, AIAA, 1986, Oppenheimer Mem. Lecture Aviation Week and Space Tech. Aerospace Laureate, 1989, Sci. Man of Yr. award, ARCS Found., 1991, Nat. Medal of Sci., 1991, Golden Plate award, Am. Acad. Achievement, 1992, COSPAR award, 1992, LeRoy Randle Grumman medal, 1992, Disting. Pub. Svc. award, Aviation/Space Writers Assn., 1993, Internat. von Karman Wings award, 1996, Space Flight Award, Am. Astron. Soc., 1997, Alumni award, S.E. C.C., Burlington, Iowa, 1997, CEO of Yr. award, ARC, 1998, Allan D. Emil Meml. award, Internat. Astronautical Fedn., 1999, Carl Sagan award, Am. Astronautical Soc. and Planetary Soc., 1999, Prof. Achievement award, Alumni, U. Chgo., 2002, Nat. Award for Op., Assn. for Unmanned Sys., Nat. Medal of Sci., Pres. Bush; fellow Sloan Found., 1971—73. Fellow: AAAS (award 1993), AIAA (assoc.; Calif. coun. sci. and tech. 1996—2001, Space Sci. award 1984, von Karman lectureship in astronautics 1999), Internat. Astron. Union, Am. Geophys. Union, Am. Phys. Soc. (exec. com. 1974—76, chmn. cosmic physics divsn. 1979—80); mem.: NAS, Sci. Edit. Bd., Comm. of Phys. Sci., Math., and Applications, NRC, Am. Philos. Soc., Calif. Assn. Rsch. in Astronomy (bd. dirs., vice-chmn. 1986—88, vice-chmn. 1986—2003, bd. dirs., vice-chmn. 1991—94, chmn. bd. dirs. 1994—97, bd. dirs., vice-chmn. 1997—2000, chmn. bd. dirs. 2000—03), Royal Aero. Soc., Nat. Space Club (bd. govs., Sci. award 1990), Astron. Soc. Pacific, Am. Philos. Soc. (Magellanic award 1992), Am. Astron. Soc. (divsn. planetary sci. com. 1981—84, Space Flight award 1997). Internat. Acad. Astronautics (trustee 1989—2001, v.p. 2001—). Office: Calif Inst Tech Space Radiation Lab M/C 220-47 Pasadena CA 91125 Office Phone: 626-395-8321. Business E-Mail: ecs@srl.caltech.edu.

**STONE, EDWARD HARRIS, II,** landscape architect; b. Lanesboro, Pa., Aug. 28, 1933; s. Frank Addison and Beth Lee (Brennan) S.; m. Diane Gertrude Berg, June 11, 1955; children: Randel Harris, Deborah Dee. BS, SUNY, 1955. Landscape architect Harmon, O'Donnell & Henninger, Denver, 1955-56, U.S. Forest Service, Colo., 1958-61; regional landscape architect Alaska, 1961-64; regional landscape architect, Colo., 1964—65; chief landscape architect U.S. Forest Service, U.S. Dept. Agr., Washington, 1966-79, asst. dir. for recreation, 1979-85; ret., 1985; with C-3 Co., Bowie, Md., 1986—. With U.S. Army, 1956—58. Recipient Arthur S. Flemming award for outstanding fed. govt. service U.S. Jr. C. of C., 1969 Fellow Am. Soc. Landscape Architects (pres. 1975-76); mem. Sigma Lambda Alpha (hon.) Home and Office: 13200 Forest Dr Bowie MD 20715-4390

**STONE, EDWARD HERMAN,** lawyer; b. July 20, 1939; s. Sidney and Ruth Stone; m. Penni G. Gray (dec. 1990); children: Andrew, Matthew; m. Elaine Ornitz, Dec. 22, 1995. DS in Acctg., U. Ill., 1961, JD, John Marshall Law Sch., 1967. Bar: Ill. 1967, Calif. 1970, cert.: Calif. (specialist probate, estate planning, and trust law). With IRS, 1963—71; assoc. Eilers, Baranger, Myers & Smith, 1971—72; pvt. practice Newport Beach, Calif., 1972—88, Santa Ana, Calif., 1988—89; mem. Davis, Samuelson, Goldberg & Blakely (formerly Cohen, Stokke & Davis), Santa Ana, 1984—88; ptnr. Edward H. Stone A Law Corp., Irvine, Calif., 1990—. Instr. income and estate taxes Western States U. Sch. Law, 1971—72; mem. joint adv. com. CEB, Calif.; temporary judge Orange County Superior Ct.; moderator, spkr. Calif. Trust and Probate Litig. CEB, 1999; mediator IRS ADR tax cases in appeals, 2000—; moderator, spkr. postmortem trust adminstrn. CEB, Calif., 2004; moderator, spkr. Calif. Trust and Probate Litig. CEB, 2000—02, 2004—05. Contbr. articles to profl. jours. Pres. Jewish Family Svcs. Orange County, 1975; v.p., bd. dirs. Jewish Fedn. Orange County, 1985—88; bd. dirs. Heritage Points Orange County, 1992—95, Eastbluff Homeowners Cmty. Assn., Newport Beach, 1980—82, pres., 1981—82. Mem.: Orange County Bar Assn. (vice-chmn. estate planning probate and trust law sect. 1976—77, chmn. sect. 1977—78, instr. Probate Clinic 1980, chairperson ADR com. 1996, spkr. in substantive law, dir. 1977—82, past chmn. profl. edn. coun., chmn.del. real property and probate sect., chmn. del. real property and probate sect. state bar conv. 1992—), Phi Alpha Delta (pres. alumni chpt. 1975—77). Office Phone: 949-833-7705.

**STONE, EDWARD LUKE,** investor, realtor; b. Englewood, N.J., Jan. 18, 1937; s. James and Anna (Druskin) S.; m. Cassandra Reeve, Mar. 15, 1969. BA, Yale U., 1958; postgrad., Cambridge U., Eng., 1959; MBA, Harvard U., 1966. Dir. fin. planning Yale U., New Haven, 1966-69; pres. HDC, Inc., Boston, 1970-77; ptnr. Dane, Falb, Stone, Boston, 1977-81; exec. dir. White House Preservation Fund, Washington, 1981-90; trustee Newport Art Mus., 1991-94; mem. Stone and Cranwell, Newport, R.I., 1995-99; pres. Hogan and Stone, Newport, 1996-99; broker Benchmark Assocs., Middletown, RI, 1999—2001; chmn. Edward L. Stone Realty llc, Newport, 2002—. Cons. Booz Allen Hamilton, Bethesda, Md., 1987-88. Trustee Mus. of Women in the Arts, Washington, 1988-96; v.p. Newport Sym., 1988-95, The Washington Home, 1988-95, Touro Synagogue Friends, 1996—, Royal Arts Found., 2006—; gov. Newport Health Care Corp., 1997—; co-chmn. The Isaac Bell House, 1995—. Mem. Newport Reading Rm., Spouting Rock Beach Assn., Somerset Club, Elizabethan Club, Phi Beta Kappa. Avocation: early 19th century american decorative arts. Home: 519 Bellevue Ave Newport RI 02840 Office Phone: 401-849-9262. E-mail: estone3137@aol.com.

**STONE, ELIZABETH CECILIA,** anthropology educator; b. Oxford, Eng., Feb. 4, 1949; d. Lawrence and Jeanne Cecilia (Fawtier) S.; m. Paul Edmund Zimansky, Nov. 5, 1976. BA, U. Pa., 1971; MA, Harvard U., 1973; PhD, U. Chgo., 1979. Lectr. anthropology SUNY, Stony Brook, 1977-78, asst. prof., 1978-85, assoc. prof., 1985-95, prof., 1995—2002. Participated archaeol. in Eng., Iran, Iraq, Afghanistan; dir. archaeol. projects Ain Dara, Syria, Tell Abu Duwari, Iraq, Ayanis Survey, Turkey. Author: Nippur Neighborhoods, 1987; co-author: (monograph) Old Babylonian Contracts from Nippur 1, 1976, Adoption in Old Babylonian Nippur and the Archive of Mannum-meshulissur, 1991, The Iron Age Settlement at Ain Dara, Syria, 1999, The Anatomy of a Masopotamian City: Survey and Soundings of Mashkan-Shapin, 2004; co-editor: The Cradle of Civilization Recent Archaeology in Iraq-Biblical Archaeologist, 1992, Velles Paraules: Ancient Near Eastern Studies in Honor of Miguel Civil on the Occasion of His 65th Birthday, 1991; mem. editl. bd. Bull. Am. Schs. Oriental Rsch., 1993-95, 99—; contbr. articles to profl. jours. Assoc. trustee Am. Schs. of Oriental Rsch., 1983-90. Recipient P.E. MacAllister Field Archaeology award Am. Sch. Oriental Rsch., 2002, SUNY Rsch. Recognition award, 2003, Am. Schs. of Oriental Rsch. Spl. Recognition award, 2004; named Woman of the Yr. in Sci., Three Village Cmty., 2004; Fulbright fellow, 1986-87; rsch. grantee Ford Found., 1974, Nat. Geog. Soc., 1983, 84, 88, 90, 97-99, 2002, 03, Am. Schs. of Oriental Rsch., 1987, 88, NSF, 1989-95, 2000—, NEH, 1989-93, Andrew Mellon Found., 2003, USAID, 2003-4. Office: SUNY Dept Anthropology Stony Brook NY 11794-0001 Office Phone: 631-632-7627. Business E-Mail: estone@notes.cc.sunysb.edu.

**STONE, F. L. PETER,** lawyer; b. Wilmington, Del., Feb. 24, 1935; s. Linton and Lorinda (Hamlin) S.; m. Therese Louise Hannon, Apr. 7, 1969; 1 child, Lisa Judith. AB, Dartmouth Coll., 1957; LLB, Harvard U., 1960. Bar: Del. Supreme Ct. 1960, U.S. Ct. Appeals (3d cir.) 1964, U.S. Supreme Ct. 1965, U.S. Ct. Appeals (fed. cir.) 1983. Assoc. Connolly, Bove & Lodge, Wilmington, 1960-64; dep. atty. gen. State of Del., Wilmington, 1965-66; atty. Del. Gen. Assembly, Dover, 1967-68; counsel Gov. Del., Dover, 1969; U.S. atty. Dist. of Del., Wilmington, 1969-72; ptnr. Connolly, Bove, Lodge, & Hutz, Wilmington, 1972-97; counsel Trzuskowski, Kipp, Kelleher & Pearce, Wilmington, 1997—98, 2001—02; dep. atty. gen., counsel to ins. dept. State of Del., 1998-2001; dep. commr. Del. Ins. Dept., 2002—05. Mem. Del. Agy. to Reduce Crime, 1969-72, Del. Organized Crime Commn., 1970-72, State Drug Abuse Coun., 1990-93, State Judicial Nominating Commn., 1991-93, State Coun. Corrections, 1992-99; co-founder, adj. prof. criminal justice progra, West Chester (Pa.) U., 1975-79; chmn. Gov.'s Harness Racing Investigation Com., 1977, Del. Jai Alai Commn., 1977-78, Del. Govs. Corrections Task Force, 1986-88. Contbr. articles to profl. jours. Chmn. UN Day, Del., 1989; mem. Del. Gov.'s Task Force on Prison Security, 1994—95; trustee Leukemia Soc. Am., N.Y.C., 1972—74, Marywood Coll., Scranton, Pa., 1974—79, Ursuline Acad., Wilmington, 1974—80; bd. dirs. Boys and Girls Club Del., 1997—, Seamen's Ctr., Port of Wilmington, 2001—; Rep. candidate for atty. gen. Del., 1990; mem. Rep. exec. com. Wilmington region, 1991—2000; chmn. re-election campaign Del. Ins. Commr., 1996. Mem. Port of Wilmington Maritime Soc. (bd. dirs., chair 1998-2000), Wilmington Country Club, Rehoboth Beach Country Club, Lincoln Club Del. (pres. 1994), Wilmington Rotary (bd. dirs. 1995-97), Nat. Assn. Former U.S. Attys. (bd. dirs. 1995-98). Roman Catholic. Avocations: hiking, tennis, golf, music, mountain climbing. Office: F L Peter Stone Atty Law PO Box 325 Mendenhall PA 19357 Office Phone: 302-571-1782. Business E-Mail: flps@tkkp.com. *My major accomplishment has been establishing and maintaining a close relationship with my family, first and foremost, regardless of what activities and accomplishments were pursued in my professional, political and community life.*

**STONE, FLORENCE SMITH,** film producer, consultant; b. Balt., June 15, 1938; d. Howard Chandler and Mary (Burnam) Smith; m. Roger David Stone; 1 child, Leslie Burnam. BA, Vassar Coll., 1960; cert. Inst. Arts Adminstrn., Harvard U., 1978. Asst. to v.p. for pub. rels. Transam. Corp., San Francisco, 1962—64; newsletter editor U.S. Embassy, Rio de Janeiro, 1964—66; coord. cmty. rels. Am. Mus. Natural History, N.Y.C., 1970—79, coord. spl. progrm, 1977—84; dir. Washington Office Earthwatch, 1985—90; ind. cons. to mus. and ednl. orgns. Washington, 1990—; artistic dir., founder Environ. Film Festival, Washington, 1993—. Co-chmn. Margaret Mead Film Festival, 1977-84. Trustee The Textile Mus., Washington, 1994—, Laura Boulton Found., N.Y.C., 1980-99, Mus. of the Hudson Highlands, Cornwall-on-Hudson, N.Y., 1974-96; mem. adv. com. Margaret Mead Film Festival, N.Y.C., 1992—; active Trees for Georgetown Com., Washington, 1996—. Mem.: Textile Soc., Women in Film and Video, Ind. Film and Video Assn., Internat. Documentary Assn., Am. Assn. Mus., Cosmos Club, Cosmopolitan Club, Georgetown Garden Club. Democrat. Avocations: textiles, films, trees, performing arts, outdoor activities. Office: Environ Film Festival 1228 1/2 31st St NW Washington DC 20007-3402 Office Phone: 202-342-2564. Business E-Mail: flostonc@igc.org.

**STONE, FRED MICHAEL,** lawyer; b. Bklyn., Jan. 20, 1943; s. Nathan and Rose (Silverman) Stone; m. Bonnie B. Dobkin, Aug. 14, 1965; children: Jonathan, Jennifer. AB cum laude, Bklyn. Coll., 1964; JD, Harvard U., 1967; LLM, NYU, 1971. Bar: N.Y. 1968. Assoc. Cadwalader, Wickersham & Taft, N.Y.C., 1967-69; asst. gen. counsel Standard & Poor's/Intercapital, Inc., N.Y.C., 1969-71; v.p. gen. counsel Mocatta Funds, 1971-73, Mocatta Metals Corp., N.Y.C., 1973-76; sr. v.p., gen. counsel Am. Stock Exch., Inc., N.Y.C., 1976-86; exec. v.p., gen. counsel Jamie Securities Co., Caronan Ptnrs., N.Y.C., 1986-88; sr. v.p., gen. counsel, sec. M.D. Sass Assocs., Inc., N.Y.C., 1989-2000; chmn. exec. com. Amex Commodities Exch., 1980-81; dir. Am. Gold Coin Exch., Inc., 1981-85; exec. v.p., dir. Revere Copper and Brass, Inc., 1986-88; dir. Ea. Electric Motor Co., Inc., 1987-88; mng. dir. Chase & M.D. Sass Ptnrs., 1998-2000; sr. mng. dir. Millennium Ptnrs., L.P., N.Y.C., 2000—. Ofcl. advisor drafting com. to Revise Uniform Securities Act Nat. Conf. Uniform State Law Commrs., 1981—85; sec., treas. steering com. Taxaple Mcpl. Bondholders Protective Com., 1990—95; lectr. in field. Mem. Manalapan (N.J.) Twp. Zoning Bd. Adjustment, 1975—86, 2000—03, chmn., 2001—02; mem. N.J. regional adv. com. Anti-Defamation League of B'nai B'rith, 1991—; vice chmn. Manalapan Dem. Com., 1988—96; Dem. candidate Manalapan Twp. Com., 1989, 1993. Mem.: ABA (task force pvt. investment entities 1994—), Nat. Futures Assn. (mem. nominating com. 1986—88), Nat. Assn. Securities Dealers (arbitrator 1986—), Assn. Bar City of N.Y. (mem. chorus), Harvard U. Law Sch. Assn. Democrat. Jewish. Home: 15 Kingsley Dr Manalapan NJ 07726-3134 Personal E-mail: fstone@mlp.com.

**STONE, GEOFFREY RICHARD,** lawyer, educator; b. Nov. 20, 1946; s. Robert R. and Shirley (Weliky) S.; m. Nancy Spector, Oct. 8, 1977; children: Julie, Mollie. BS, U. Pa., 1968; JD, U. Chgo., 1971. Bar: N.Y. 1972. Law clk. to Hon. J.S. Kelly Wright U.S. Ct. Appeals (D.C. cir.), 1971-72; law clk. to Hon. William J. Brennan Jr. U.S. Supreme Ct., 1972-73; asst. prof. U. Chgo. 1973-77, assoc. prof., 1977-79, prof., 1979-84, Harry Kalven Jr. disting. svc. prof., 1984—, then Lee. Harry Kalven Jr., 1987-93, provost, 1994—2002, Harry Kalven, Jr. Disting. Svc. Prof. Law, 2002—. Author: Constitutional Law 1986, 5th edit., 2005, The Bill of Rights in the Modern State, 1992, The First Amendment, 1999, Eternally Vigilent: Free Speech in the Modern Era, 2001, Perilous Times: Free Speech in Wartime, 2004 (25th Annual Robert F. Kennedy Book award, 2005); editor The Supreme Ct. Rev., 1991—; contbr. articles to profl. jours. Recipient Robert F. Kennedy Book award, Los Angeles Times Book prize for Best Book of Yr. in History. Fellow AAAS; mem. Chgo. Coun. Lawyers (bd. govs. 1976-77), Am. Law Inst. Assn. Am. Law Schs. (exec. com. 1990-93), Order of Coif. Office: U Chgo 1111 E 60th St Chicago IL 60637-5418 Business E-mail: gstone@uchicago.edu.

**STONE, GEORGE CLIFFORD,** education educator, researcher; b. Harrisburg, Ill., Sept. 17, 1938; s. Clifford Lavender and Melba Rose Stone; m. Helen Ruth Gluesenkamp, Aug. 20, 1961; children: Scott Mitchell, Jeffrey Clifford, Gregory George, Kelly Kristin Stone-Ault, Brett Alan. BA, So. Ill. U., 1964, MA, 1965, PhD, 1973; postgrad., Ball State U., 1965—66. Nat. tchg. fellow in social sci. Paducah (Ky.) Jr. Coll., 1967—68; instr. in edn., interim asst. dean Coll. Liberal Arts and Scis. So. Ill. U., Carbondale, 1968—71; prof. of history, philosophy and edn. Sterling (Kans.) Coll., 1971—90; Rountree Caldwell Bryan disting. prof. edn. Lyon Coll., Batesville, Ark., 1990—99; dean Sch. Edn. Buena Vista U., Storm Lake, Iowa, 1999—2001; prof. of edn., chmn, divsn. edn. U. of Ozarks, Clarksville, Ark., 2001—. Mem. Santa Fe (N.Mex.) Trail nat. adv. coun. U.S. Pk. Svc., 1988—92; cons. NEH, Washington, 1992—99. Contbr. articles to profl. publs. Grant evaluator Kans. Arts and Humanities Commn., Topeka, 1987—90; mem. Spring Conf. in Edn., 1991—99; chmn. Lyons Pub. Libr., 1979—90; chmn. seminar on archaeology and history of Coronado and the Quivirian Indians in Rice County Rice County Mus., Lyons, 1985. Recipient McCreery award for Excellence in Tchg., Sterling Coll., 1979, 1985; Wye fellow, Aspen Inst. of Queenstown, Md., 1991, Dewey scholar, Ctr. Dewey Studies, So. Ill. U., 1974—. Fellow: Philosophy of Edn. Soc.; mem.: Soc. Professors Edn., Soc. Philosophy and History of Edn. (pres. 2003—05), Trail of Tears Assn., John Dewey Soc., Quarter Century Wireless Assn., Inc. (50th Anniversary Award, Disting. Mem. for Fifty Years of Svc. 15 June 2004), U.S. Army Mil. Affiliate Radio Sys., Kiwanis (pres. Clarksville chpt. 2003—05, Outstanding Sec. Kans. dist. 1985, Kiwanian of Yr. Clarksville chpt. 2003—04, 2004—05), Phi Delta Kappa (pres. 1996—97), Pi Gamma Mu, Phi Kappa Phi, Kappa Delta Pi. Democrat. Methodist. Avocations: reading, travel, boating, amateur radio, music. Home: 205 Bayview Cir Knoxville AR 72845 Office: U of the Ozarks 415 North College Ave Clarksville AR 72830 Office Phone: 479-979-1410. Office Fax: 479-979-1328. Personal E-mail: gstone@starband.net. E-mail: gstone@ozarks.edu.

**STONE, GLENDA LEE,** librarian, genealogist; b. Cleburne, Tex., July 27, 1948; d. Herbert Roy Johnson and Ida Corene Roe; m. Ray Stone, Oct. 28, 1969; MLS, Tex. Woman's U., 1986. Clk. typist Dick Smith Libr. Tarleton State U., Stephenville, Tex., 1970—72, libr. asst., 1972—88, libr., 1988—91, libr. III, 1991—2002, libr. IV, head cataloging dept., 1991—. Presenter on local history, genealogy, Stephenville area. Co-author: Thomas Getzendaner of Maryland and South Carolina. Developer Cross Timbers Hist. Images Project. Recipient Cert. for support of today's youth, Stephenville H.S. History Honor Soc., 1999; grantee Cross Timbers Hist. Images digitization project, Tex. Coun. for the Humanities, 2002—03, Ralph and Dossie Rogers Collection digitization project, Tex. State Libr. Tex Treasures, 2002—03. Mem.: Tex. Libr. Assn., ALA, Erath County Geneal. Soc. (exec. officer, ex-officio advisor 2003—04). Methodist. Avocations: local history, genealogy, arts and crafts, travel.

**STONE, GREGORY PAUL,** lawyer; b. Ventura, Calif., July 21, 1952; BS, Calif. Inst. Tech., 1974, MS; JD, Yale U., 1977. Bar: Calif. 1977. Law clk. to Hon. William Matthew Byrne, Jr. US Dist. Ct. (ctrl. dist.) Calif., 1977—78; ptnr. Munger, Tolles & Olson LLP 1978—. Bd. dirs. Constitutional Rights Found., Pasadena Playhouse. Named one of Top 10 Trial Lawyers in Am., Nat. Law Jour., 2006; recipient Jack E. Froelich Meml. award, Donald S. Clark award, John F. Casky Prize for trial advocacy. Mem.: ABA, State Bar Calif., LA County Bar Assn. Office: Munger Tolles & Olson LLP 355 S Grand Ave 35th Fl Los Angeles CA 90071 Office Phone: 213-683-9255. Office Fax: 213-683-5155. E-mail: Gregory.Stone@mto.com.*

**STONE, HAROLD B.,** artist, educator; b. Ft. Worth, Sept. 26, 1951; s. Harold Ben and Joy Walker Stone; m. Ann Nelson, Mar. 6, 1976; 1 child, Stephen Thomas. BS, Tex. A&M U., 1972; MA, MFA, U. Tulsa, Okla., 1981. Instr. drawing and design Dunwoody Coll. of Tech., Mpls., 1988—2005; dir. Mpls. Drawing Workshop, 1996—. Fine art instr. Tulsa Jr. Coll., 1981—84; instr. art and art history Century C.C., Mahtomedi, Minn., 1988—95. Author: Exploring Life Drawing, 2006. Office: Mpls Drawing Workshop 250 3rd Ave N # 328 Minneapolis MN 55403 Office Phone: 612-267-3550.

**STONE, HAZEL ANNE DECKER,** artist; b. Salt Lake City, Oct. 30, 1934; d. Carl Marcellus and Hazel Sheets (Van Cott) Decker; m. William Samuel Stone, July 20, 1956; children: Cynthia Anne Stone Barkanic, Lisa Marie. BS, RN, U. Utah, 1956; postgrad. in art and humanities, Ariz. State U., 1979-81; studied with various artists, Ariz., N.Mex., 1985—. Nurse out-patient dept. Salt Lake County Hosp., 1956-57; instr. med.-surg. nursing U. Utah Coll. Nursing, 1957-59; watercolor fine artist. One-woman shows include Sun Cities Museum of Art, Sun City, Ariz., 1997, Downtown Deli, Phoenix, 1999, Galerie van Friend, Scottsdale, Ariz., 2003—04, two person exhbns., Church of the Beatitudes, Phoenix, 1994—95, 2003, Gallery Nineteen, 1996, three person exhbns., Gammage Meml. Auditorium, Ariz. State U., 2002, Casa Grande Art Mus., 2002, exhibited in group shows at Ariz. Artists Guild, 1986, 1988—90, 1992—97, 2005, Tucson Mus. of Art, 1988, Ariz. Watercolor Assn., 1989 (Merchant award), 1991, 1993—95 (Award of Merit, 1998), 1997—99, 2001—04 (Award of Merit, 2005), Vistas, 1989, 1991, 1993, Contemporary Watercolorists of Ariz., 1994—2004 (award of Excellence, Merit award, Merchant award, Award of Excellence, 2004), Foothills Art Ctr., Golden, Colo., 1994, Q Artists, 1995—96, 1998, 2000—02, Bareiss Gallery, Taos, N.Mex., 1995, Stables Gallery, Taos, 1996, Van Vechten-Lineberry Taos Art Mus., 1997, Chandler Ctr. for Arts, Ariz., 1997, 2000, Wenatchee Valley Coll., Wash., 1997, 1999—2000, West Valley Art Mus., Surprise, Ariz., 1999, Sangre de Cristo Arts Ctr., Pueblo, Colo., 1999, Tubac Ctr. of the Arts, Ariz., 1999, 2003, Sun Cities Art Mus., 1994, Farmington Mus., Gateway Pk N.Mex., 1999, Watercolor Gallery, Pitts., 1999—2000, Woodmere Art Gallery, Phila., 2000, Crary Art Gallery, Warren, Pa., 2000, Colo. Springs Fine Arts Ctr., 2001, Bellevue Art Mus., Wash., 2001, U. Miami, Oxford, Ohio, 2001, Showcase Gallery, San Diego, 2001 (Merchant award), 2005, Acad. of Art Gallery, Calif., 2002, Minnetrista Cultural Ctr., Muncie, Ind., 2002, Noyes Mus. of Art, Oceanville, NJ, 2002, Albuquerque Art Mus., 2002, City of Brea Gallery, Calif., 2002, Fine Arts Ctr., Colo. Springs, 2003, Western Colo. Ctr. for Arts, Grand Junction, 2003, Beverly Arts Ctr., Chgo., 2003 (Merit award), Mill Atelier Gallery, Santa Fe, 2003, Cynon Valley Mus., Aberdare, Wales, 2004 (ISEA USA Wales medalion, 2003, 2004), John Stobart's Three Rivers Gallery, Pitts., 2003, AIS, Seattle, 2004, Plains Art Mus., Fargo, ND, 2004, Springfield Art Mus., Mo., 2004, Lee County Alliance of Arts, Ft. Myers, Fla., 2004 (Medallion, 2004), Wichta Art Mus., Kans., 2004, Wichita Art Mus., 2005, So. Alleghenies Mus. Art, Loretto, Pa., 2005, Showcase Gallery, San Diego, 2005, Shemer Art Ctr. and Mus., 2005, Chandler Ctr. for the Arts, 2005, Mountain Shadow Gallery, Tucson, 2005, Internat. Soc. Expl. Artists, Cardiff, Wales, 2005, So. Alleghenies Mus. Art, Loretto, Pa., 2005, Wichta Art Mus., Kans., 2005, galleries, Vision Gallery, Chandler, Ariz., 1997— (2d Place award, Chandler Ostrich Festival Fine Arts Print Contest, 1998), The Park Gallery, Litchfield Park, Ariz., 2003—04, Gallerie van Friend, Scottsdale, Ariz., 2003—04, mag., The Artist's Mag. exhibitions include Lee County Alliance of the Arts, Fort Meyers, Fla., 2004 (Medallion, 2004), Berman Mus. Art, Collegeville, Pa., 2005—06, Kirsten Gallery, Seattle, 2005, Showcase Gallery, San Diego, 2005, So. Alleghenies Mus. Art, Loretto, Pa., 2005; contbr. Docent Phoenix Art Mus., 1979-80, master docent, 1989-96; mem. Ariz. Women's Caucus Art, 1988-91. Mem.: Transparent Watercolor Soc. Am., Waterworks, Q Artists, Contemporary Watercolorists Ariz. (gen. chmn. 2002—04, exhbns. chmn. 2004—, signature), Ariz. Watercolor Assn. (assoc. 1985—88, juried 1988—, bd. mem. 1994—2001, Coatimundi Honor Soc. 1995, Nat. Watercolor Exhbn. co-chair 1999, Royal Scorpion 2000, Nat. Watercolor Exhbn. chair 2000, signature), Ariz. Artists Guild (juried 1986—), Watercolor West (juried), Watercolor Art Soc. - Houston, Taos Nat. Soc. Watercolorists (signature), Phila. Water Color Soc. (signature), Pa. Watercolor Soc. (signature), N.W. Watercolor Soc. (signature), Mo. Watercolor Soc., Internat. Soc. Exptl. Artists (signature), Calif. Watercolor Assn., San Diego Watercolor Soc. (assoc.), Nat. Watercolor Soc. (assoc.), La. Watercolor Soc. (assoc.), Am. Watercolor Soc. (assoc.). Home: 3621 E Pasadena Ave Phoenix AZ 85018-1511 Office Phone: 602-956-3783.

**STONE, HERBERT ALLEN,** management consultant; b. Washington, Sept. 14, 1934; s. Joseph and Marion (Solomon) S.; m. Marjorie Nelke Sterling, June 14, 1964; children: Joanna, Lisa. BSc, U. Mass., 1955, MSc, 1958; PhD, U. Calif., Davis, 1963. Specialist Exptl. Sta. U. Calif., Davis, 1961-62; food scientist SRI, Menlo Park, Calif., 1962-67, dir. food and plant sci., 1967-74; pres. Tragon Corp., Redwood City, Calif., 1974—; adj. prof. Fuzhou U., 2004—. Mem. adv. U. Mass. Food Sci., 1992—, Calif. Poly. U. Food Sci. and Nutrition, 1996—2001; chair leadership bd., food sci. dept. U. Calif., Davis, 2005—; vis. prof. So. Yangtze U., 2004—, Fuzhou U., 2004—. Author: Sensory Evaluation Practices, 2004; assoc. editor: Jour. Food Sci., 1977—80, 2000—, chair editl. bd.: World of Food Sci.; contbr. sci. and tech. articles to profl. jours. Fellow Inst. Food Sci. and Tech., Inst. Food Exec. Com. (pres. S.E. divsn. 1977-78, exec. com., pres. mktg. and mgmt. divsn.); mem. AAAS, Inst. Food Technologists (nat. exec. com. 1994-97, pres. 2004-05), Am. Soc. Enology, European Chemoreception Orgn., Ladera Oaks Club (Menlo Park, Calif.). Achievements include patents in field. Home: 990 San Mateo Dr Menlo Park CA 94025-5640 Office: Tragon Corp 365 Convention Way Redwood City CA 94063-1402 Business E-Mail: hstone@tragon.com.

**STONE, HOWARD S.,** retired baking industry executive, art collector; b. Mar. 1930; m. Donna Stone. Named one of Top 200 Collectors, ARTnews Mag., 2004. Avocation: collector of contemporary art. Home: 219 E Lake Shore Dr Chicago IL 60611

**STONE, JACQUELYN ELOIS,** lawyer; b. Williamsburg, Va., Jan. 7, 1958; d. William Thomas and Sara Elizabeth (Cumber) Stone. BA in Am. Govt., U.Va., 1980; JD, Harvard U., 1985. Bar: Va. 1985. Legis. asst. US Ho. of Reps., Washington, 1980-82; assoc. McGuire, Woods, Battle & Boothe, LLP (now McGuireWoods LLP), Richmond, Va., 1985—94, ptnr., 1994—, mem. bd. partners, firmwide hiring ptnr. & recruiting com. chair. Bd. mem. Arts Coun. of Richmond, past pres.; bd. mem. Jr. Achievement of Ctrl. Richmond, Richmond Eye & Ear Hosp., Richmond Renaissance, asst. sec.; exec. com. mem. Va. Performing Arts Found.; mem. local adv. com. Local Initiatives Support Corp.; bd. mem. Va. Commn. for the Arts. Recipient Outstanding Woman Award, YWCA, 2000. Mem.: ABA (mem. bus. law sect. 1985—), Am. Immigration Lawyers Assn., Old Dominion Bar Assn. (mem. exec. com. 1990—92), Va. Bar Assn. (exec. com. young lawyers sect. 1988—90, chmn. membership com. 1988—90), Va. State Bar. Baptist. Avocation: travel. Office: McGuireWoods LLP One James Ctr 901 E Cary St Richmond VA 23219-4030 Office Phone: 804-775-1046. Office Fax: 804-698-2183. Business E-Mail: jstone@mcguirewoods.com.

**STONE, JAMES HOWARD,** management consultant; b. Chgo., Mar. 4, 1939; s. Jerome H. and Evelyn Gertrude (Teitelbaum) S.; divorced; children: Margaret Elisa, Emily Anne, Phoebe Jane. AB cum laude, Harvard U., 1960; MBA, Harvard Bus. Sch., 1962. Cert. mgmt. cons., 1977. From staff analyst to exec. com. Stone Container Corp., Chgo., 1962—83, former exec. and audit coms., 1983—96; founder, owner, CEO, pres. Stone Mgmt. Corp., Chgo., 1969—; dir. privately-owned beverage mfr. Sheridan Beverage Co., Chgo., 1989—96; dir. privately-owned distributor and fabricator metals and metal products Fullerton Metals Co., Northbrook, Ill., 1993—98; pres. JEMP, Inc., Chgo., 2002—. Mem. strategic alliance Boston Cons. Group, 1990—; trustee, sec., exec. com. Roosevelt U., Chgo., 1983—, exec. com. edn. alliance, 1994—; co-chmn. commn. fgn. and domestic affairs Northwestern U., Evanston, Ill., 1981-85, bus. plan judge Kellogg Grad. Sch. Mgmt., 1994—; mem. vis. com. libr., lectr. U.Chgo., 1980—, The Chgo. Com., 1986—, Mid-Am. Com., Chgo., 1993-98; bd. overseers, lectr. IIT Stuart Sch. Bus., 1993—; bd. dirs. Cinema Chgo./Chgo. Film, Festival, Pilgrim Chamber Players, pres.; past pres., regional dir. Chgo. chpt. Inst. Mgmt. Cons.; past dir. Chgo. Roundtable Coun. Logistics Mgmt.; past pres., dir. Harvard Bus. Harvard Bus. Sch. Club Chgo. Contbr. articles in various trade jours. Mem. Chgo. Coun. Fgn. Rels., 1967, bd. dirs., 1974-78. Bd. dirs., mem. exec. com. NCCJ, Chgo., 1985, presiding co-chmn., 1990-97; trustee Hadley Sch. Blind, Winnetka, Ill., 1985-96, chmn. planning com., 1989-96, Hadley life trustee, 1996—; vice chmn. fin. com. North Shore Congregation Israel, 1995-98; bd. dirs. Suzuki-Orff Sch., 1997-03; pres. Pilgrim Chamber Players, 2002—; former presiding co-chair Chgo. region Nat. Conf. Christians and Jews; sec., trustee, mem. exec. com. Roosevelt U.; mem. Chgo. Alliance Com.; life trustee Hadley Sch. for the Blind; vis. com. libr., patron U. Chgo.; with Northwestern U. Asher Sch. Psychiatry, Med. Sch.; bd. overseers Ill. Inst. Tech. Stuart Sch. Bus.; pres.'s cir., former dir. Chgo. Coun. Fgn. Rels.; advisor DCFS; mem. JVS Duman Loan Com.; dir. Blue Gargoyle, Little City Found.; past vice chmn. fin. com. North Shore Congregation Israel. Recipient Spirit of Life award, 2003. Mem. Coun. Logistics Mgmt. (dir. Roundtable-Chgo. 1990-94, lectr. Northwestern U. Ill. Inst. Tech.), The Exec. Club Chgo., Econs. Club Chgo., Harvard Club Chgo. (dir. 1995—), Harvard Bus. Sch. Club Chgo. (dir. 1992—, pres. 1997-99), Traffic Club Chgo., Std. Club. Northmoor Country Club, Mid-Day Club, The Casino Club, MidAm. Club, Arts Club, Juvenile Protective Assn. (trustee 1999—, dir.), The East Bank Club, Little City Found. Avocations: family-centered activities, reading, golf, travel. Office Phone: 312-236-0800.

**STONE, JAMES ROBERT,** surgeon; b. Greeley, Colo., Jan. 8, 1948; s. Anthony Joseph and Dolores Concetta (Pietrafeso) S.; m. Kaye Janet Friedman, May 16, 1970; children: Jeffrey, Marisa. BA, U. Colo., 1970; MD, U. Guadalajara, Mex., 1976; MBA, Madison U., 2002. Diplomate Am. Bd. Surgery, Am. Bd. Surg. Critical Care, Am. Bd. Forensic Medicine. Intern Med. Gen. Hosp., Balt., 1978-79; resident in surgery St. Joseph Hosp., Denver, 1979-83; pvt. practice Grand Junction, Colo., 1983-87; staff surgeon, dir. critical care Va. Med. Ctr., Grand Junction, 1987-88; dir. trauma surgery and critical care, chief surgery St. Francis Hosp., Colorado Springs, Colo., 1988-91; pvt. practice Kodiak, Alaska, 1991-92; with Summit Surg. Assocs., 1992-96; asst. dir. trauma Tristate Trauma System, Erie, Pa., 1996-99; med. dir. LifeStar Aeromed, Erie, Pa., 1997-99; dir. trauma, sr. assoc. physician, med. dir. emergency svcs. ISJ Mayo Health, 1999—2001; also dir. trauma/EMS med. dir., sr. assoc.; gen., thoracic and vascular surgery Caylor-Nickel Clinic, Bluffton, Ind., 2001—02, Emergency Medicine of Ind., Ft. Wayne, Ind., 2002—04; CEO Guymon Surg. Cons., Okla., 2004—. Asst. clin. prof. surgery U. Colo. Health Sci. Ctr., Denver, 1984-96; pres. Stone Aire Cons., Grand Junction, 1988—; owner, operator Jjnka Ranch and Stuno Ranch, Flourissant, Colo.; spl. advisor CAP, wing med. officer, 1992-96; advisor med. com. unit, 1990-92; advisor Colo. Ground Team Search and Rescue, 1994-96; cons. Am. Med. Forensic Specialists, Berkeley, Ca., 2002-; Guymon surgical cons., 2004—. Contbr. articles to profl. jours.; inventor in field. Bd. dirs. Mesa County Cancer Soc., 1988-89, Colo. Trauma Inst., 1988-91; chmn. Guymon Pioneer Days Rodeo. Colo. Speaks out on Health grantee, 1988; recipient Bronze medal of Valor Civil Air Patrol. Fellow Denver Acad. Surgery, Southwestern Surg. Congress, Am. Coll. Chest Physicians, Am. Coll. Surgeons (trauma com. Colo. chpt.), Am. Coll. Critical Care; mem. Am. Coll. Physician Execs., Soc. Critical Care (task force 1988—), Assn. Air Med. Physicians. Roman Catholic. Avocations: horse breeding, hunting, fishing. Office Phone: 580-338-6666. Business E-Mail: jrstone@ptsi.net.

**STONE, JEREMY JUDAH,** professional society administrator; b. N.Y.C., Nov. 23, 1935; s. I.F. and Esther (Roisman) S.; m. Betty Jane Yannet, June 16, 1957. BS magna cum laude, Swarthmore Coll., 1957, LL.D. (hon.), 1985; PhD, Stanford U., 1960. Research mathematician Stanford Research Inst., 1960-62; mem. profl. staff Hudson Inst., Croton-on-Hudson, 1962-64; research assoc., arms control and disarmament Harvard Ctr. Internat. Affairs, 1964-66; asst. prof. math., lectr. polit. sci. Pomona Coll., Claremont, Calif., 1966-68; pres. Fedn. Am. Scientists, Washington, 1970-2000, Catalytic Diplomacy, 1999—. Author: Containing the Arms Race; Some Concrete Proposals, 1966, Strategic Persuasion, 1967, "Every Man Should Try." Adventures of a Public Interest Activist, 1999. Recipient award for pub. svc. Forum on Physics and Soc., Am. Phys. Soc., 1979, Fedn. of Am. Scientists Pub. Svc. award, 1994; Social Sci. Rsch. Coun. fellow in econs. Stanford U.,

1968-69, Coun. Fgn. Rels. internat. affairs fellow, 1969-70. Mem. Coun. Fgn. Rels., Internat. Inst. Strategic Studies, Phi Beta Kappa. Home and Office: 5615 Warwick Pl Bethesda MD 20815-5503 E-mail: Jstone@catalyticdiplomacy.org.

**STONE, JOHN TIMOTHY, JR.,** writer; b. Denver, July 13, 1933; s. John Timothy and Marie Elizabeth (Briggs) S.; m. Judith Bosworth Stone, June 22, 1955; children: John Timothy III, George Williams. Student, Amherst Coll., 1951—52, U. Mex., 1952; BA, postgrad., U. Miami, 1955, U. Colo., 1959—60. Sales mgr. Atlas Tag, Chgo., 1955-57; br. mgr. Household Fin. Corp., Chgo., 1958-62; pres. Janeff Credit Corp., Madison, Wis., 1962-72, Recreation Internat., Mpls., 1972-74, Continental Royal Svcs., N.Y.C., 1973-74; dir. devel. The Heartlands Group/Tryon Mint, Toronto, Ont., Can., 1987-89; spl. cons. Creative Resources Internat., Madison, 1988-90, Pubs. Adv. Group, 1990—; spl. cons. art and antiques Treasure Hunt Assocs., 1994—. Bd. dirs. Madison Credit Bur., Wis. Lenders' Exch. Author: Made, 1973, Going for Broke, 1976, The Minnesota Connection, 1978, Debby Boone So Far, 1980, (with John Dallas McPherson) He Calls Himself "An Ordinary Man", 1981, Satiacum, The Chief Who's Winning Back the West, 1981, Runaways, 1983, (with Robert E. Gard) Where the Green Bird Flies, 1984, The Insiders Guide to Buying Art, 1993, Anyone's Treasure Hunt, 1995; syndicated columnist The Great American Treasure Hunt, 1983-87. Served with CIC, U.S. Army, 1957-59. Mem. Minarani Club, African First Shotters Club, Sigma Alpha Epsilon. Presbyterian.

**STONE, JOSS (JOSCELYN EVE STOKER),** singer; b. Dover, Eng., Apr. 11, 1987; d. Wendy. Winning contestant Jr. Star for a Night, BBC TV talent show, 2002; former back-up singer for Britney Spears. Spokeswoman The Gap, 2005. Singer: (albums) Soul Session, 2003, Mind Body & Soul, 2004 (Capital Award, London's favourite UK album, 2005), Alfie soundtrack, 2004, Spoiled, 2005. Recipient Brit Award best British female solo artist, 2005, Brit Award best British urban act, 2005, Grammy Nomination best new artist, 2005, Grammy Nomination best female pop vocal performance, 2005, Grammy Nomination best pop vocal performance, 2005.

**STONE, KAREN,** opera company director; b. Horsforth, Yorkshire, England, 1952; Degree, Royal Academy of Music, 1970—73, Conservatorio di Musica "Santa Celilia", 1973—76. Asst. dir. Freiburg Opera, 1982—85; dir. English Nat. Opera, 1985—86; prod. and dir. various organizations including Maggio Musicale Fiorentino (Italy), Brighton Festival (Eng.), Royal Opera House (Covent Garden), Teatro Lirico di Parma (Italy), Glyndebourne Festival Opera (Eng.), et al, 1986—94; dep. dir. Cologne Opera, Germany, 1995; gen. mgr. Theaters of Graz, Austria, 2000—03; gen. dir. Dallas Opera, 2003—. Office: Dallas Opera Campbell Centre I 8350 N Central Expy Ste 210 Dallas TX 75206*

**STONE, LAWRENCE D.,** software company executive; BS in Math., Antioch Coll., 1964; MS in Math., Purdue U., 1966, PhD in Math., 1967. With Daniel H. Wagner Assocs., 1967—85; v.p. Metron, Inc., Reston, Va., 1986—89, sr. v.p., COO, 1990—2003, CEO, 2004—. Author: Theory of Optimal Search (Ops. Rsch. Soc. Lanchester prize), 1975, Bayesian Multiple Target Tracking, 1999. Mem. NAE. Office: Metron Inc 11911 Freedom Dr Ste 800 Reston VA 20190-5602 Fax: 703-787-3518. Office Phone: 703-787-8700. E-mail: stone@metsci.com.

**STONE, LAWRENCE MAURICE,** lawyer, educator; b. Malden, Mass., Mar. 25, 1931; s. Abraham Jacob and Pauline (Bernstein) S.; m. Anna Jane Clark, June 15, 1963; children: Abraham Dean, Ethan Goldthwaite, Katharine Elisheva. AB magna cum laude, Harvard U., 1953, JD magna cum laude, 1956. Bar: Mass. 1956, Calif. 1958. Rsch. asst. Am. Law Inst., Cambridge, Mass., 1956-57; assoc. Irell and Manella, L.A., 1957-61, ptnr., 1963, 79-96, of counsel, 1997—; internat. tax coordinator U.S. Treasury Dept., Washington, 1961-62, vis. legis. counsel, 1964-66; prof. law U. Calif., Berkeley, 1966-78. Vis. prof. law Yale U., New Haven, 1969, Hebrew U. Jerusalem, 1973-74, U. So. Calif., L.A., 1984; mem. adv. group to commr. IRS, Washington, 1973-74; mem. President's Adv. Commn. on Tax Ct. Appointments, Washington, 1976-80; tax advisory bd. Little Brown Co., 1994-96. Author: (with Doernberg) Federal Income Taxation of Corporations and Partnerships, (with Klein, Bankman and Bittker) Federal Income Taxation; bd. editors Harvard Law Rev., 1955-56. Fellow Am. Coll. Tax Counsel; mem. ABA, Am. Law Inst., Internat. Fiscal Inst., Am. Arbitration Assn., L.A. County Bar Assn. (recipient Dana Latham award 1995), Phi Beta Kappa. Office: Irell & Manella 1800 Avenue Of The Stars Los Angeles CA 90067-4276 Office Phone: 310-203-7525.

**STONE, LAWRENCE MYNATT,** publishing executive; b. Balt., June 24, 1945; s. David G. and Clara Ruth (Coxey) S.; m. Lois V. Smith, June 10, 1967; children: Bradley Michael, Geoffrey David. BA, U. Iowa, 1968. Prof. Northeastern Bible Coll., Essex Fells, NJ, 1968-69; missionary Africa Evangelical Fellowship, Ndola, Zambia, 1969-71; asst. to production mgr. Am. Bible Soc., N.Y.C., 1971-72; book club mgr. Iversen-Norman Assocs., N.Y.C., 1972-75; editl. v.p. Thomas Nelson Pubs., Nashville, 1976-85; pres. Rutledge Hill Press, Nashville, 1985-99, pub., 1999—2004, pub. emeritus, 2005—. Book and libr. adv. com. U.S. Info. Agency, Washington, 1984-88; editor in field; ghost writer. Office: Rutledge Hill Press PO Box 141000 Nashville TN 37214-1000 Personal E-mail: larryrhp@aol.com. Business E-Mail: lstone@rutledgehillpress.com.

**STONE, LINDA,** former computer company executive, consultant, speaker, writer; Grad., Evergreen State Coll.; M. in Edn., Cognitive Psychology, and Librarianship, U. of Washington. Primary sch. teacher; sch. librarian Seattle; systems analyst, market devel. mgr., software evangelist and asst. for special projects for CEO John Sculley Apple Computer, 1986—93; joined as dir. special projects under Nathan Myhrvold Microsoft Corp., 1993, co-founder, dir. Virtual Worlds Group / Social Computing Group, v.p. corp. and industry initiatives, 2000—02; cons., 2002—. Adj. faculty NYU Tisch Sch. Arts, 1998—99; speaker, expert online social life and virtual communities. Contbr. NY Times, Newsweek, Wired, The Economist, The Boston Globe and hundreds of blogs. Nat. bd. World Wildlife Fund, Philanthropic Collaborative for Integrative Medicine; advisory bd. Rochester Inst. Tech. Lab Social Computing; advisor hidden brain drain task force Center for Work-Life Policy. Named Outstanding Regional Volunteer of the Year, F.I.R.S.T, 2002; named one of 100 leaders of the digital revolution, Upside mag., 1996. Achievements include coined the term continuous partial attention to describe the way people work and live with information and communication overload.*

**STONE, MARC J.,** lawyer; b. N.Y.C., Dec. 21, 1960; m. Amy Wheeler Solt, Mar. 23, 2002; children: Alexandra Paige, Justin Alexander, Dylan Mackenzie, Jackson Taylor. AB, Brown U., 1982; JD, U. Calif., Berkeley, 1985. Bar: N.Y., Fla. Assoc., corp. dept. Rubin Baum Levin Constant & Friedman, N.Y.C., 1985-87, Rubin Baum Levin Constant Friedman & Bilzin, Miami, Fla., 1987-92, ptnr., 1993-97; v.p., gen. counsel, sec. TradeStation Group, Inc., Plantation, Fla., 1997—. Mem.: AMEX, ABA, NYSE, N.Y. State Bar Assn. E-mail: mstone@tradestation.com.

**STONE, MARVIN JULES,** hematologist, oncologist, educator; b. Columbus, Ohio, Aug. 3, 1937; s. Roy J. and Lillian (Bedwink) S.; m. Jill Feinstein, June 29, 1958; children: Nancy Lillian, Robert Howard. Student, Ohio State U., 1955-58; SM in Pathology, U. Chgo., 1962, MD with honors, 1963. Diplomate Am. Bd. Internal Medicine, (Hematology, Med. Oncology). Intern ward med. svc. Barnes Hosp., St. Louis, 1963-64, asst. resident, 1964-65; clin. assoc. arthritis and rheumatism br. Nat. Inst. Arthritis and Metabolic Diseases, NIH, Bethesda, Md., 1965-68; resident in medicine, ACP scholar Parkland Meml. Hosp., Dallas, 1968-69; fellow in hematology-oncology, dept. internal medicine U. Tex. Southwestern Med. Sch., Dallas, 1969-70, instr. dept. internal medicine, 1970-71, asst. prof., 1971-73, assoc. prof., 1974-76, clin. prof., 1976—, chmn. bioethics com., 1979-81; mem. faculty and steering com. immunology grad. program, Grad. Sch. Biomed. Scis., U.

Tex. Health Sci. Ctr., Dallas, 1975, adj. mem., 1976—. Dir. Charles A. Sammons Cancer Ctr., chief oncology, dir. immunology, co-dir. divsn. hematology-oncology, attending physician Baylor U. Med. Ctr., Dallas, 1976—; v.p. med. staff Parkland Meml. Hosp., Dallas, 1982. Contbr. chpts. to books, articles to profl. jours. Chmn. com. patient-aid Greater Dallas/Ft. Worth chpt. Leukemia Soc. Am., 1971-76, chmn. med. adv. com., 1978-80, bd. dirs., 1971-80; mem. v.p. Dallas unit Am. Cancer Soc., 1977-78, pres., 1978—; mem. adv. bd. Baylor U. Med. Ctr. Found., Marvin J. Stone Libr., Baylor Inst. Immunology Rsch., 1999. With USPHS, 1965-68. Recipient Wings of Eagles award, Baylor Health Care Sys., 2001, Disting. Svc. award, U. Chgo., 2002, Lifetime Achievement award, Internat. Soc. Study of Waldenstrom's Macroglobulinemia, 2004. Master ACP (gov. No. Tex. 1993-97, laureate Tex. chpt. 2000); fellow Royal Soc. Medicine (London); mem. AMA, Am. Assn. Immunologists, Am. Soc. Hematology, Internat. Soc. Hematology, Coun. Thrombosis, Am. Heart Assn. (established investigator 1970-75), Am. Soc. Clin. Oncology (edn. com. 2002-05, career devel. com. 2002-05), Am. Osler Soc. (bd. govs. 1997-2000, 2005—, v.p. 2001-03, pres. 2003-04), Am. Assn. for Cancer Rsch., So. Soc. Clin. Investigation, Tex. Med. Assn., Dallas County Med. Soc., Clin. Immunology Soc., Phi Beta Kappa, Sigma Xi, Alpha Omega Alpha. Office: Baylor U Med Ctr Charles A Sammons Cancer Ctr 3500 Gaston Ave Dallas TX 75246-2096 Business E-Mail: marvins@baylorhealth.edu.

**STONE, MARY ANN,** literature and language educator; b. Freelandville, Ind., Jan. 30, 1934; d. Ralph D. and Leona Green; m. Paul R. Stone, Dec. 27, 1953; children: Sunny, Karen, Kerry, Kevin. BS, Ind. State U., 1964, MS, 1983. Lang. arts tchr. Ganada HS, Ganada, Ariz., 1983—2002. Pres. Ganada Edn. Assn., Ganada, Ariz., chmn. lang. arts; faculty coun. Ganada HS. Chmn. bd. dirs. Ganada Presbyn. Avocations: reading, gardening, needlecrafts. Home: 586 Bay N Ct Franklin IN 46131 E-mail: magreenstone@earthlink.net.

**STONE, MARY SAINZ,** elementary school educator; b. St. Louis; m. James E. Stone; children: Elizabeth Sainz, Katherine Sainz, Joseph Sainz. BS, U. of Mo., St. Louis, 1972; MA, Maryville U., St. Louis, 1991. Cert. tchr. Mo. Social studies dept. coord. Francis Howell Mid. Sch., St. Charles, Mo., 1998—. Recipient Excellence In Tchg. award, Emerson Electric Co., Tchr. of the Yr. award, Francis Howell Mid. Sch., 2005-2006. Office: Francis Howell Mid Sch 825 O'Fallon R Saint Charles MO 63304 Office Phone: 636-851-4933. Business E-Mail: mary_stone@fhsd.k12.mo.us.

**STONE, MATT,** animator; b. Houston, May 26, 1971; s. Gerald and Sheila Stone. Student, U. Colo. Creator, writer, dir., prodr., actor (films) The Spirit of Christmas (also titled Jesus vs. Frosty), 1992; creator, writer, dir., prodr., actor: (films) The Spirit of Christmas (also titled Jesus vs. Santa), 1995 (Los Angeles Film Critics award for Best Animation, 1997); creator, writer, dir., exec. prodr., actor (TV series) South Park, 1997—, also voices of characters Kyle Broslofski, Kenny McCormick, Terrance Henry Stoot, Pip Pirrup, Leopold "Butters" Stotch, Saddam Hussein, Stuart McCormick, Jesus Christ, others (CableACE award for Animated Programming Special or Series, 1997); composer, prodr., actor: (film) Orgazmo, 1997; composer, actor BASEketball, 1998; writer, actor, prodr., composer South Park: Bigger, Longer, and Uncut, 1999 (MTV Movie award Best Musical Performance, 1999, Los Angeles Film Critic Assn. award for Best Music, 1999, New York Film Critics Circle award for Best Animated Film, 1999); writer, prodr.: TV series That's My Bush, 2001; actor: (films) Bowling for Columbine, 2002; actor, writer, prodr.: Team America: World Police, 2004; exec. prodr., singer: Chef Aid: The South Park Album, South Park: Bigger, Longer & Uncut, Mr. Hankey's Christmas Classics, Timmy and the Lords of the Underworld.

**STONE, MERRILL BRENT,** lawyer; b. Jersey City, N.J., Aug. 16, 1951; s. Leonard and Clare (Orlean) S.; m. Geri Ellen Satkin, Nov. 24, 1976; children: Jacqueline Blair, Erica Lauren. AB summa cum laude, Rutgers U., 1973; JD, Columbia U., 1976. Bar: N.J. 1976, N.Y. 1977, Fla. 1981, U.S. Dist. Ct. N.J. 1976, U.S. Dist. Ct. (so. dist.) N.Y. 1977, U.S. Dist. Ct. (so. dist.) Fla. 1983. Assoc. Kelley Drye & Warren, N.Y., 1976-84, resident Miami, 1983-85, ptnr. N.Y.C., 1985—, mng. ptnr., 1992—2003. Editor: (comments section) Columbia Human Rights Law Rev., N.Y.C., 1975-76. Trustee Greater Miami C. of C., 1984-85. Named Harlan Fiske Stone Scholar, Columbia Law Sch., N.Y.C., 1975-76. Mem. ABA (bus. bankruptcy com. sect. on bus. law, banking law com.), Am. Soc. Corp. Secs., Fla. Bar Assn., Club 101, Phi Beta Kappa, Pi Sigma Alpha. Office: Kelley Drye & Warren LLP 101 Park Ave New York NY 10178-0002 Business E-Mail: mstone@kelleydrye.com.

**STONE, MICHAEL HOWARD,** psychiatry educator; b. Syracuse, N.Y., Oct. 27, 1933; s. Moses Howard and Corinne (Gittleman) S.; m. Clarice Joan Kestenbaum, (div. 1979); children: David, John; m. Beth Janine Eichstaedt. BA, Cornell U., 1954, MD, 1958. Diplomate Am. Bd. Psychiatry and Neurology. Residency in psychiatry Columbia Coll. of Physicians & Surgeons, N.Y.C., 1963-66; asst. prof. psychiatry Columbia Coll. Physicians and Surgeons, N.Y.C., 1973-77; assoc. prof. Cornell Med. Coll., N.Y.C., 1977-80; prof. psychiatry U. Conn., Farmington, 1980-84; clin. dir. U. Conn. Dept. Psychiatry, Farmington, 1980-84; prof. clin. psychiatry Mt. Sinai Sch. Medicine, N.Y.C., 1984-85, Cornell Med. Coll., N.Y.C., 1985-88, Columbia Coll. Physicians and Surgeons, N.Y.C., 1988—; dir. research Middletown (N.Y.) Psychiat. Ctr. Visiting prof. psychiatry Albert Einstein Med. Ctr., N.Y.C., 1987—; lectr. in field, 1987-; prof. clin. psychiatry Columbia Coll. Physicians and Surgeons. Author: The Borderline Syndromes, 1980, The Fate of Borderline Patients, 1990; editor: Borderline Disorders, 1981, Treating Schizophrenic Patients, 1983, Essential Papers on Borderline, 1985, Personality Disorders: Treatable and Untreatable, 2006; contbr. over 200 articles to profl. jours. Recipient Hematology Fellowship NIH, 1961-63. Fellow Am. Psychiat. Assn.; mem. Am. Pschopathol. Assn., Am. Coll. Psychiatrists. Republican. Jewish. Avocations: piano, collecting rare books, languages. Home and Office: 225 Central Park W New York NY 10024-6027 Office Phone: 212-758-2000. Personal E-mail: mhstonemd@yahoo.com.

**STONE, OLIVER,** film director, film producer, scriptwriter; b. NYC, Sept. 15, 1946; s. Louis and Jacqueline (Goddet) S.; m. Najwa Sarkis May 22, 1971 (div. 1977); m. Elizabeth Stone June 6, 1981 (div. 1993); 2 children. Student, Yale U., 1965; BFA, NYU Film Sch., 1971. Tchr., Cholon, Vietnam, 1965-66; wiper U.S. Mcht. Marine, 1966; taxi driver NYC, 1971. Screenwriter: Midnight Express, 1978 (Acad. award for screenplay, Writers Guild Am. for screenplay), Evita, 1996; screenwriter, dir.: Seizure, 1974 The Hand, 1981, (with John Milius) Conan, the Barbarian, 1982 (writer), Scarface, 1983, (writer with Michael Cimino) Year of the Dragon, 1985, (writer with David Lee Henry) 8 Million Ways to Die, 1986; dir., writer (with Richard Boyle) Salvador, 1986, Platoon, 1986 (Acad. award for best dir., Dirs. Guild award, British Acad. award),(documentary) Looking for Fidel, 2004; co-writer, dir.: Wall Street, 1987, Talk Radio, 1988, The Doors, 1991, Any Given Sunday, 1999; screenwriter, prodr., dir.: Born on the Fourth of July, 1989 (Acad. award for best dir. 1990), Heaven & Earth, 1993, Comandante, 2003, Looking for Fidel, 2004, Alexander, 2004, World Trade Center, 2006; co-writer, prodr., dir.: JFK, 1991, Natural Born Killers, 1994, Nixon, 1995 (Acad. award nominee for best screenplay with Stephen J. Rivele and Christopher Wilkinson 1996); prodr.: Love, Death, 1972, Sugar Cookies, 1973, Reversal of Fortune, 1991, South Central, 1992, Zebrahead, 1992, The Joy Luck Club, 1993, The New Age, 1994, The People vs. Larry Flynt, 1996, Savior, 1998, The Corruptor, 1999, (TV mini-series) Wild Palms, 1993; exec. prodr. The Iron Mze, 1991, Freeway, 1996, Killer: A Journal of Murder, 1996, Indictment: The McMartin Trial, 1995 (Emmy award), Cold Around the Heart, 1997, The Last Days of Kennedy and King, 1998, The Day Reagan was Shot, 2003; dir. only (short film) Last Year in Viet Nam, 1971, Mad Man of Martinique, 1979, U-Turn, 1992, Persona Non Grata, 2003; film appearances include The Battle of Lover's Return, 1971, The Hand, 1981, Platoon, 1986, Wall Street, 1987, Born on the Fourth of July, 1989, The Doors, 1991, Nixon (voice only), 1995, Any Given Sunday, 1999. Served with U.S. Army, 1967-68. Decorated Purple Heart with oak leaf cluster, Bronze Star; Lifetime

Achievement award, Stockholm Internat. Film Festival, 2004. Mem. Writers Guild Am., Dirs. Guild Am., Acad. Motion Picture Arts and Scis. Office: 1207 4th St PH 1 Santa Monica CA 90401-1340*

**STONE, PAMELA ANN,** accountant; b. Flint, Mich., Jan. 10, 1954; d. Leslie Elwood and Aloha Augusta (Wegener) S. AS in Acctg., Baker Bus. U., 1980; BS in Acctg., Detroit Coll. Bus., 1981; AS in Computer Programming, Baker Jr. Coll., 1983; MS in Profl. Accountancy, Walsh Coll., 1986; MS in Info. Sys. Mgmt., Ferris State U., 1996; PhD in Counseling, Universal Life Ch., 2003. Acct., bus. mgr. Drury Bros. Inc., Durand, Mich., 1982-85; instr. Pontiac (Mich.) Bus. Inst., 1985-86; software tng. mgr. Gateway, 1999—2001; founder, pres. Bright Futures Bus. Sch., Flint, 2001—. Pvt. practice, Flint, 1985—; instr. Baker Coll., Flint, 1986-99, Detroit Coll. Bus., Flint; vocat. edn. tchr. Shiawassee Intermediate Sch. Dist. Avocations: piano, organ, tennis, bowling, needlepoint. Office: Bright Futures Bus Sch PO BOx 7906 3717 Van Slyke Rd Ste 1 Flint MI 48507 Office Phone: 810-341-9533. Personal E-mail: brightfutures@aol.com.

**STONE, PATRICIA A.,** special education services professional, consultant; d. Henry and Rita Belair; m. James Henry Stone, Oct. 27, 1984; children: Cassandra L., Allison M., Brian J. BS, Fitchburg State Coll., Mass., 1984; MEd, Lesley Coll., Cambridge, Mass., 1989; cert. in advanced grad. study in ednl. leadership, Rivier Coll., Nashua, NH, 2006. Cert. elem. edn. N.H., Mass., spl. edn N.H., Mass., assessment specialist N.H., spl. edn. adminstrn. N.H. Tchr. spl. edn. Sch. Adminstrv. Unit 28 Windham Sch. Dist., NH, 1985—99, Sch. Adminstrv. Unit 57 Salem Sch. Dist., 1999—2001, assessment specialist, 2001—04, asst. dir. student svcs., 2004—, dir. student svcs., 2006—. Chmn. bd. Windham Coop. Kindergarten, NH, 1996—97; adj. instr. U. N.H., Durham, 2004—; exec. bd. United Way Success by 6, Salem, 2004—. Mem.: ASCD, N.H. Assn. Spl. Edn. Adminstrs., N.H. Assn. Sch. Psychologists, Coun. Exceptional Children, Assn. Specialization Intellectual Functioning, Alpha Delta Kappa. Avocations: reading, crafts. Home: 11 Brookdale Rd Salem NH 03079-1902 Office: SAU 57 Salem Sch Dist 38 Geremonty Dr Salem NH 03079

**STONE, PAUL ALAN,** biologist, educator; b. Henderson, Ky., Nov. 21, 1960; s. Charles Ronnie Stone and Patricia Deanne Thomas; m. Marie Elizabeth Babb, Jan. 3, 2005; children: Megan Ann, Zachary Spider. BS, U. Fla., Gainesville, 1987; MS, Auburn U., Ala., 1990; PhD, U. N.Mex, Albuquerque, 1995. Prof. biology U. Ctrl. Okla., Edmond, 1995—. Contbr. articles to profl. jours. Office: U Ctrl Okla Biology Dept 100 N University Dr Edmond OK 73034 Office Phone: 405-974-5791. Business E-Mail: pstone@ucok.edu.

**STONE, RICHARD JAMES,** lawyer; b. Apr. 30, 1945; s. Milton M. and Ruth Jean (Manaster) S.; m. Lee Lawrence, Sept. 1, 1979; children: Robert Allyn, Katherine Jenney, Grant Lawrence. BA in Econs., U. Chgo., 1967; JD, UCLA, 1970. Bar: Calif. 1971, Oreg. 1994, D.C., 2000, Wash. State, 2004. Assoc. O'Melveny & Myers, L.A., 1971-77; dep. asst. gen. counsel U.S. Dept. Def., Washington, 1978-79; asst. to sec. U.S. Dept. Energy, Washington, 1979-80; counsel Sidley & Austin, L.A., 1981, ptnr., 1982-88; ptnr., head litig. dept. Milbank, Tweed, Hadley & McCloy, L.A., 1988-94; mng. ptnr. Zelle & Larson, LLP, L.A., 1994-97; counsel Ball Janik LLP, Portland, Oreg., 1998—. Gen. counsel and staff dir. Study of L.A. Civil Disturbance for Bd. Police Commrs., 1992; adj. prof. law Lewis and Clark Northwestern Sch. Law, 1998-99; lawyer rep. 9th Cir. Jud. Conf., 1998-99; mem. legal ethics com. Oreg. State Bar, 2002-03, com. on spl. rules, 2002-03. Editor-in-chief: UCLA Law Rev., 1970. Mem. Pub. Sector Task Force, Calif., State Senate Select Com. on Long Range Policy Planning, 1985-86, U.S. del. Micronesian Polit. Status Negotiations, 1978-79; mem. U.S. Mil. Acad. at West Point, Oreg. Field Force, 2003—; mem. adv. panel Coun. Energy Resource Tribes, 1981-85; mem. vestry St. Aidan's Episcopal Ch., 1990-93, 97-98, sr. warden, 1998; dir. Legal Aid Found. L.A., 1991-99, officer, 1994-98, pres., 1997-98; dir. Portland City United Soccer Club, 1999-2000; classic coach, 2002-04. Recipient Amos Alonzo Stagg medal and Howell Murray Alumni medal U. Chgo., 1967; honoree Nat. Conf. Black Mayors, 1980; recipient spl. citation for outstanding performance Sec. Dept. Energy, 1981. Fellow Am. Bar Found.; mem. ABA, Fed. Bar Assn., Calif. Bar Assn. (trustee 1986-88), D.C. Bar Assn., Wash. Bar Assn., L.A. County Bar Assn. (trustee 1986-88), D.C. Bar Assn., Wash. Bus. Trial Lawyers, Multnomah County Bar Assn., Phi Gamma Delta. Home: 3675 NW Gordon St Portland OR 97210-1285 Office: Ball Janik LLP 101 SW Main St Portland OR 97204-3228 Office Phone: 503-228-2525. Business E-Mail: rstone@bjllp.com.

**STONE, ROBERT G., JR.,** water transportation executive; BA Class of 1945, Harvard Univ., 1947. Chmn. & pres. States Marine Lines; chmn. Kirby Corp., 1983—95, chmn. emeritus & dir., 1995—. Bd. dir. Chubb Corp., Core Industries Inc., Corning Inc., NovaCare Inc., Pittston Co., Russell Reynolds Assoc., Tandem Computers Inc., Tejas Gas Corp.; mem. bd. adv. Arcadia Partners; lead investor Industrial Capital Group, Intersouth Partners, Morgan Holland Venture Partners, Mayfield Fund. Fellow Harvard Corp., 1975—95, sr. fellow, 1995—2002. With U.S. Army, 1943—45. Fellow: Am. Acad. Arts & Sci.; mem.: N.Y. Yacht Club (commodore), Augusta Nat. Golf Club. Achievements include world record in 2000 meter heavyweight crew, captain, 1947. Office: Kirby Corporation Suite 1000 55 Waugh Dr PO Box 1745 Houston TX 77251-1745

**STONE, ROGER DAVID,** environmentalist; b. N.Y.C., Aug. 4, 1934; s. Patrick William and Kathleen Mary Stone; married; 1 child. BA in English, Yale U., 1955. Asst. to pub. Time Mag., 1959-61, corr., news bur. chief San Francisco, Rio, Paris, 1961-68; asst. to pres. Time Inc., N.Y.C., 1968-70; v.p. Inter-Am. Rels., N.Y.C., 1975-82; v.p. World Wildlife Fund, 1982-86, sr. fellow, 1986-90; vis. fellow, cons. on environ. issues Coun. on Fgn. Rels., 1990-92; vice chmn. ECO Inc., Washington, 1992-96; pres. Sustainable Devel. Inst., Washington, 1993—. Vis. lectr. Yale Ctr. Internat. and Area Studies, 1994-95; mem. external adv. bd. Yale Inst. Biospheric Studies. Author: Dreams of Amazonia, 1985, The Voyage of the Sanderling, 1990, Wildlands and Human Needs, 1991, The Nature of Development: Reports from the Rural Tropics on the Quest for Sustainable Economic Growth, 1992, Fair Tide: Sailing Toward Long Island's Future, 1996, Tropical Forests and the Human Spirit = Journeys to the Brink of Hope, 2001; contbr. chpts. to books; contbr. articles to Time, Life, Life en Espanol, Fgn. Affairs, N.Y. Times, Internat. Herald Tribune, Christian Sci. Monitor, Harvard Bus. Rev., USA Today Mag., Cruising World, Conservation Found. Letter, numerous others. Bd. dirs. Astrolabe, Inc., Cintas Found.; v.p. Armand G. Erpf Fund, Sotterley Found.; sec. St. Mary's River Watershed Assn.; former bd. dirs. U. Andes Found.; former bd. dirs. and exec. com. World Wildlife Fund-U.S., Ctr. for Inter-Am. Rels., Ams. Found., Accion Internat., Arts Internat., others. Lt. (j.g.) USN, 1956-59. Mem.: Century Assn. Democrat. Episcopalian. Avocation: sailing. Home: 1527 30th St Nw # B-32 Washington DC 20007 Fax: 202-337-9639. Office Phone: 202-338-1017. E-mail: susdev@igc.org.

**STONE, SANDRA,** writer, artist; b. Portland, Oreg., Apr. 4, 1934; Visual arts cons. to individual collectors; editor Breitenbush Books, Portland, 1977-81; artist cons. Green Tiger Press, 1985. Exhibited in group shows at Portland Art Mus., 1975-80, 95, White Bird Gallery, Cannon Beach, Oreg., 1980, White Bird Gallery, 1981, N.W. Artist's Workshop, 1981, Contemporary Crafts Gallery, Portland, 1983, Am. Inst. Architects Gallery, 1994, Ricciardi Gallery, Astoria, Oreg., 1994, Orlo Found., 1994, Marylhurst Coll., Portland, 1994, Am. Inst. Architects Gallery, Portland, 1994, Spokane Ctrl. Libr. Art Gallery, 1994, Broders Books, 1995, Old City Hall, Gresham, Oreg., 1996; commd. works by Oreg. State Archives Bldg., Salem, 1991-92, Tacoma Firehouse, 1993, Spokane Ctrl. Libr., 1993-95, Portland CC Libr., 1994-96, Midland Regional Libr., Portland, 1994-96, U.S. Fed. Courthouse, Portland, 1995-97, Riverfront Park, Salem, Oreg., 1996-97; author: (poems) Cocktails with Brueghel in the Museum Cafe, 1996, also essays for art catalogues. Active Young Audiences Bd., Portland Art Mus., N.W. Artist's Workshop, Portland Ctr. for Visual Arts, Contemporary Crafts Gallery, Oreg. Sch. Arts and Crafts,

others. Artist's fellow Va. Ctr. for Creative Arts, 1986, Oreg. Lit. Arts, 1992; recipient Purchase award U. West Fla., 1995. Mem. N.W. Dramatist's Guild, Soc. Children's Book Writers and Illustrators, Acad. Am. Poets (assoc.).

**STONE, SHARON,** actress; b. Meadville, Pa., Mar. 10, 1958; d. Joe and Dorothy S; m. George Englund Jr. (div.); m. Michael Greenburg, Aug. 18, 1984 (div. Jan. 20, 1987); m. Phil Bronstein, Feb. 14, 1998 (div. Jan. 29, 2004); 3 adopted sons, Roan Joseph, Laird Vonne, Quinn. Diploma in Creative Writing and Fine Arts, Edinboro State U. Model Eileen Ford Modeling Agy.; owner Chaos prodn. co. Actress (films) Stardust Memories, 1980, Deadly Blessing, 1981, Irreconcilable Differences, 1984, King Solomon's Mines, 1985, Allan Quatermain and the Lost City of Gold, 1986, Cold Steel, 1987, Police Academy 4: Citizens on Patrol, 1987, Action Jackson, 1988, Above the Law, 1988, Beyond the Stars, 1989 (Personal Choice award), Total Recall, 1990, Year of the Gun, 1991, Diary of a Hitman, 1991, He Said/She Said, 1991, Scissors, 1991, Basic Instinct, 1991, Where Sleeping Dogs Lie, 1992, Last Action Hero, 1993, Sliver, 1993, Intersection, 1994, The Specialist, 1994, (also co-prodr.) The Quick and the Dead, 1995 (also co-prodr.), Casino, 1995 (Golden Globe award for best actress in film 1996, Acad. award nominee for best actress 1996), Diabolique, 1996, Last Dance, 1996, Sphere, 1998, The Mighty, 1998 (Golden Global nominee), Antz, 1998 (voice), Gloria, 1999, The Muse, 1999, Simpatico, 1999, Beautiful Joe, 2000, Picking Up the Pieces, 2000, Cold Creek Manor, 2003, Cold Creek Manor, 2003, Catwoman, 2004, Jiminy Glick in La La Wood, 2004, Broken Flowers, 2005, Alpha Dog, 2006, Basic Instinct 2, 2006; TV appearances include Not Just Another Affair, 1982, Bay City Blues, 1983, Calendar Girl Murders, 1984, The Vegas Strip Wars, 1984, War and Remembrance, 1988, Tears in the Rain, 1988, (guest) The Larry Sanders Show, 1994, Big Guns Talk: The Story of the Western (tv spl.), 1997; narrator: Harlow: The Blond Bombshell, 1993, If These Walls Could Talk 2, 2000, Harold and the Purple Crayon, 2001, Cold Creek Manor, 2003, A Different Loyalty, 2004. Office: Care Guy McElwaine PO Box 7304 North Hollywood CA 91603-7304*

**STONE, STUART LEE MORRISON,** librarian, language educator; b. St. Louis, June 4, 1949; s. Norwood Lee Stone and Antoinette Aubouchon Engle. BS in Edn., The U. Mo., 1971; M of Libr. and Info. Sci., The Cath. U. Am., 1979, postgrad., 1980—82. Cert. secondary edn. U. Mo., 1971, English as a fgn. lang. tchr. The Cambridge Sch., Ltd., London, 1982. Quadri-lingual rsch. asst. The Inter-Am. Def. Coll. / OAS, Washington, 1972—75; tchr. French, Spanish, & history The Wash. Ethical Soc. H.S., 1975—77; sr. staff asst. The U.S. Ho. Subcom. Postal Pers. and Modernization, 1980—82; tchr. English and Am. history The Am. Lang. Inst., Lisbon, Portugal, 1982—86; asst. libr. IMF, Washington, 1986—87; sr. cataloger, Portuguese-French-Spanish-Gaelic Libr. Congress, 1987—2002, recommending officer Scots-Gaelic, 1997—, sr. acquisitions specialist Europe and L.Am., 2000—, founder, coord. Scots Gaelic Lang. Table, 2004—. Instr. beginning Scots-Gaelic Am. Gaelic Soc., Alexandria, Va., 1999—; mem. planning com. US Nat. Mod., 2006—. Translator (seminar instr. / U. Sao Paulo): (international library online networking) Training Manual / MARC Name Authorities; author: (ednl. discussion kit) Inauguration: An American Beginning (Presdl. Inaugural Com. award, 1981). Ward rep. bldgs. and grounds com. Fairlington Villages, Arlington, Va., 2003—. With U.S. Army, 1972—75. Decorated Joint Svc. Commendation medal Sec. Def. Pentagon. Fellow: Soc. Antiquaries Scotland; mem.: Libr. Congress (profl. assoc.), Am. Gaelic Soc. (newsletter editor asst. 1997—2000, Gaelic instr. 1997—), Am. Legion. Home: 3079 S Buchanan St C-2 Arlington VA 22206 Business E-Mail: ssto@loc.gov.

**STONE, SUSAN A.,** lawyer; b. 1961; BA summa cum laude, Yale U., 1983; JD cum laude, Harvard U., 1987. Bar: Calif. 1987, U.S. Dist. Ct. (no. dist.) Calif. 1987, U.S. Ct. Appeals (9th cir.) 1987, U.S. Dist. Ct. (ctrl. dist.) Calif. 1988, Ill. 1990, U.S. Dist. Ct. (no. dist.) Ill. 1990, U.S. Ct. Appeals (7th cir.) 1990. Asst. U.S. atty. U.S. Dept. Justice, LA; law clk. to Judge William J. Orrick, U.S. Dist. Ct. for No. Dist. Calif.; ptnr. Sidley & Austin (until 2001 merger), Chgo.; ptnr. litig. Sidley Austin Brown & Wood, Chgo., 2001—, and co-chair practice devel. com. Named one of Top Young Litigators Under 40, Ill. Legal Times, One of 40 Attorneys Under 40, Chgo. Lawyer. Mem. ABA, Ill. Bar Assn., Calif. State Bar, Phi Beta Kappa. Office: Sidley Austin Brown & Wood LLP Bank One Plz 10 S Dearborn St Chicago IL 60603 Fax: 312-853-7036. Office Phone: 312-853-2177. E-mail: sstone@sidley.com.

**STONE, THERESA M.,** communications executive; b. Boston, 1944; Grad., Wellesley Coll.; grad. studies Cornell U.; MS, Sloan Sch. Mgmt., Mass. Inst. Tech., 1976. With Chubb Corp., 1990—97; pres. CEO Chubb Life Ins. Co. Am., 1994—97; with Morgan Stanley & Co., 1976—90; pres. Jefferson Pilot Comm., Greensboro, NC, 1997, exec. v.p., CFO, 1997—. Mem.: Burlington Industries Bd., Fed. Res. Bd., Richmond Br., MIT Corp., Greensboro United Way 1999 Campaign (pacesetters chair), Greensboro O of C. Office: Jefferson Pilot Corp PO Box 21008 Greensboro NC 27420

**STONE, VAN COURTRIGHT,** not-for-profit developer; b. Deland, Fla., June 22, 1946; s. Wilfred Arthur and Catherine Louise Stone; m. Nancy M. Stone, July 19, 1969 (div. 1989); 1 child, Edana A. Stone Neundorf; m. Lisa L. Stone, Dec. 22, 1990; children: Melisa A., Wesley Alan. BA, Wichita State U., 1968; JD, Washburn U., 1974. Exec. v.p., officer S.W. State Bank, Topeka, Kans., 1974-81; pres. Nat. Bank of Andover, Kans., 1985-87; corp. atty. various corps., 1987-91; COO Gerber Bus. Devel. Corp., Petaluma, Calif., 1991-94; exec. dir. Lions of Ill. Found., Sycamore, 1995—. Bd. dirs. Ill. Sch. for the Visually Impaired, Jacksonville, Ill. Eye Fund, Chgo., mng. dir. Lions of Ill. Endowment Fund, 1995—; pres., N.Am. Conf. of Lions Founds., 2000—. Author: (newsletter) Lions Share, 1995—; contbr. articles to profl. journs. Capt. U.S. Army, 1968-71. Decorated 3 Bronze Stars; recipient Presl. medal of honor Ill. Coll. of Optimetry, 1999, Meritorious Svc. award Deicke Ctr., 1999; Lions of Ill. Found. fellow laureate, 2002. Mem. VFW, No. Aurora Lions Club, Lions Club Internat. (Melvin Jones fellow), Andover C. of C. (pres. 1986), Phi Sigma Rho, Tau Kappa Alpha, Phi Alpha Delta. Republican. Methodist. Avocations: golf, running, bridge, writing, bowling. Office: Lions Ill Found 2814 Dekalb Ave Sycamore IL 60178-3117 Office Phone: 815-756-5633 227.

**STONE, WILLIAM DAVID,** secondary school educator, consultant; b. San Mateo, Calif., July 6, 1948; s. Frederick Hamilton and Jeanne Evelyn Stone; children: Vernon Donald, Frederick Hamilton, William Ruben Lumas, Micah Merritt. BA, St. Louis U., 1970. Educator East St Louis Sch. Dist. 189, East St Louis, Ill., 1970—2006. Chmn. lang. arts dept. M. L. King Jr. H.S., East St Louis, Ill., 1971—75, chmn. social studies dept., 1977—80; scholastic team leader Younge Mid. Sch., 2000—06. Leader Boy Scouts Am., East St. Louis, 1972—76. Mem.: Am. Fedn. Tchrs. (assoc.). Avocations: woodworking, travel, camping, hiking, chess, billiards. Home: 10 Lakewood Dr Belleville IL 62223-3119 Office Phone: 618-646-3760. Personal E-mail: dyhams@sbcglobal.net.

**STONE, WILLIAM EDWARD,** academic administrator, consultant; b. Peoria, Ill., Aug. 13, 1945; s. Dean Proctor and Katherine (Jamison) S.; m. Deborah Ann Duncan; children: Jennifer, Allison, Molly. AB, Stanford U., 1967, MBA, 1969. Asst. dean Stanford U., 1969—71, asst. to pres., 1971—77; exec. dir. Stanford Alumni Assn., 1977—90, pres., CEO, 1990—98; pres., dir. Stanford Alumni Assn. divsn. Stanford U., 1998—2001, Stanford Sierra Programs LLC, South Lake Tahoe, Calif., 1998—2001, Alpine Chalet, Inc., Alpine Meadows, Calif., 1987—2001; pres.-emeritus Stanford Alumni Assn. Stanford U., 2001—, cons. in ednl. advancement, 2001—; prin. eAdvancement Consortium, 2001—. Dir. Coun. Alumni Assn. Execs., 1989-93, v.p., 1990-91, pres., 1991-92; trustee Coun. for Advancement and Support of Edn., 1988-91; bd. dirs. Univ. ProNet, Inc., chmn., 1990-92, sec. 1996-00. Bd. dirs. North County YMCA, 1975-76; bd. dirs., chmn. nominating com. faculty club Stanford U., 1979-81; trustee Watkins Discretionary Fund, 1979-82; mem. cmty. adv. bd. Resource Ctr. Women; dir. Stanford Hist. Soc., 2002—, v.p., 2003-06, pres., 2006—. Recipient K.M. Cuthbertson award Stanford U., 1987, Tribute award Coun. for Advancement

and Support of Edn., 1991, Steuben Apple award, 2002. Mem.: Stanford Assoc., Stanford Faculty Club. Home: 1061 Cathcart Way Stanford CA 94305-1048 Office Phone: 650-494-6959. Business E-Mail: stone@eadvancement.org.

**STONECIPHER, DAVID A.,** insurance company executive; b. 1941; m. Nancy Berend; 4 children. Degree, Vanderbilt U., 1962; M Agrl. Sci., Ga. State U., 1967. With Life Ins. Co. Ga., Atlanta, 1967-92, sr. v.p., actuary Atlanta, 1978—84, exec. v.p., 1984—89, pres., COO, 1989—91, CEO, 1991—92, Southland Life Ins. Co, Atlanta, 1991—92; CEO elect Jefferson-Pilot Corp., Greensboro, NC, 1992; pres., CEO Jefferson Pilot Corp., Greensboro, NC, 1993—2004, Jefferson-Pilot Life Ins. Co., 1993—2004; chmn. Jefferson-Pilot Corp., Greensboro, NC, 1998—2004, non-exec. chmn., 2005—06. Bd. dir. Bassett Furniture Industries, Inc., McKenney's Corp., Internat. Home Furnishings Ctr., Inc., Fin. Services Roundtable, Lincoln Nat. Corp., Phila., 2006—. Bd. dirs. McCallie Sch. Served U.S. Army, 1962—64. Fellow, Soc. of Actuaries, 1970. Mem.: Am. Acad. Actuaries, Soc. Actuaries, Am. Coun. Life Insurers (past chmn.). Office: Lincoln Nat Corp Ctr Sq W Tower Ste 3900 1500 Market St Philadelphia PA 19102-2112*

**STONEHILL, ERIC,** lawyer; b. Rochester, N.Y., Feb. 27, 1950; BA with distinction, Northwestern U., 1970; JD, Cornell U., 1973, MBA, 1981, cert. hosp. and health svc. adminstrn., 1981. Bar: N.Y. 1974, D.C. 1981, U.S. Dist. Ct. (we. dist.) N.Y. 1974, U.S. Dist. Ct. (no. dist.) N.Y. 1976. Assoc. Harris Beach PLLC, Rochester, 1973—81, ptnr., 1982—. Adj. instr. Rochester Inst. Tech., 1990-92. Contbr. articles to profl. jours. Bd. dirs. Rochester Eye and Human Parts Bank, 1983-91, 92-2001, pres., 1987-90. Mem. Am. Health Lawyers Assn., N.Y. State Bar Assn. (mem. health law sect.), D.C. Bar Assn., Monroe County Bar Assn., Sloan Alumni Assn., Phi Beta Kappa. Office: Harris Beach PLLC 99 Garnsey Rd Pittsford NY 14534 Office Phone: 585-419-8641.

**STONEHILL, LLOYD HERSCHEL,** gas industry executive, mechanical engineer; b. South Bend, Ind., May 20, 1927; s. Charles Myers and Bertha M. (Reed) S.; m. Jean Carole Herzer, Dec. 30, 1961; children: Mark, Bill, John, Rob. BSME, Purdue U., 1949. Registered profl. engr., La. Chief engr. Rothschild Boiler & Tank Works, Shreveport, La., 1949-54; chmn. bd. dirs. Frankfort (Ind.) Bottle Gas, Inc., 1956—. Patentee in field. Founding pres. Clinton County Hosp. Authority, Frankfort, 1974; membership chmn. Clinton County Hosp. Found., Frankfort, 1982-83, 89. With U.S. Army, 1954-56. Recipient Heroism award Elks Lodge, Frankfort, 1959. Mem. Nat. Propane Gas Assn. (mktg. awards 1986, 87), Am. Legion, Purdue Alumni Assn. (Clinton County Chpt. mem. pres.' coun.), Hudson Inst., Rotary (sec. 1963-65, Paul Harris fellow), Lambda Chi Alpha (sec. 1946-47). Republican. Mem. Christian Ch. Avocations: collecting old violins, sailing, reading. Home: 1258 Forest Dr Frankfort IN 46041-3230 Office: Frankfort Bottle Gas Inc 1555 McKinley Ave Frankfort IN 46041-1805

**STONEMAN, MARK L.,** lawyer; b. Cleveland, Jan. 11, 1971; s. Dean L. and Diana G. Stoneman; m. Jill L. Stoneman, June 24, 2000; children: William J., Nathaniel D. BS in Bus. Adminstrn., U. Mo., Columbia, 1993, JD, 1996; master degree in Accountancy, U. Mo., St. Louis, 2002. Lic.: Mo. 1996, Ill. 1997. Assoc. Armstrong Teasdale LLP, St. Louis, 1996—2004, ptnr., 2004—. Contbr. chapters to books. Tchg. vol. Jr. Achievement, St. Louis, 2004; bd. mem. Metro Theater Co., St. Louis, 2001—04. Recipient Order of the Coif, U. Mo., 1996, Fred L. Howard award for Excellence in Appellate Advocacy, 1996, Pacioli award, 2002; scholar Lynn and Peggy Ewing Scholar, U. Mo. Law Sch. Found., 1994-95, Curator's Scholar, U. Mo., 1994-95, Mary Fiser Meml. Scholar, 1994-95, Law Rev. Fellows Scholar, 1995-96. Mem.: Phi Kappa Phi, U. Mo. Law Rev. Office: Armstrong Teasdale LLP One Metropolitan Sq Ste 2600 Saint Louis MO 63102 Office Phone: 314-621-5070. Office Fax: 314-621-5065. Business E-Mail: mstoneman@armstrongteasdale.com.

**STONER, GARY DAVID,** cancer researcher; b. Bozeman, Mont., Oct. 25, 1942; married; 2 children. BS, Mont. State U., 1964; MS, U. Mich., 1968, PhD in Microbiol., 1970. Asst. rsch. scientist U. Calif., San Diego, 1970-72, assoc. rsch. scientist, 1972-75; cancer expert Nat. Cancer Inst., 1976-79; assoc. prof. pathology Med. Coll. Ohio, 1979-83; prof. pathology, 1983-92; prof. internal medicine and pathology Ohio State U., Columbus, 1992, assoc. dir. Ctr. for Molecular and Environ. Health, 1993—2003, assoc. dir. basic rsch. Comp Cancer Ctr, 1994—, prof., chmn. divsn. environ. health scis. Sch. Pub. Health, 1995—2003; prof. internal medicine, dir. program Ohio State U. Comprehensive Cancer Ctr., Columbus. Cons. Nat. Heart Lung & Blood Inst., 1974—, EPA, 1979—, Nat. Cancer Inst., 1979—, Nat. Toxicol. Program, 1981—; mem. study sect. NIH, 1980-92, 2003—, Am. Cancer Soc., Ohio, 1982—, Am. Cancer Soc., 1995-2002. Grantee Nat. Cancer Inst., EPA, U.S. Army R & D Command. Fellow AAAS; mem. Soc. Toxicology, Am. Assn. Cancer Rsch., Am. Assn. Pathologists, Internat. Soc. Cancer Chrmopre. Achievements include research in carcinogenesis in human and animal model respiratory and esophagal tissues, carcinogen metabolism, mutagenesis, in vitro transformation of epithelial cells, chemoprevention. Office: Ohio State U Divsn Hematology/Oncology Dept Internal 1148 CRH 300 W 10th Ave Columbus OH 43210-1240 Office Phone: 614-293-3268. Business E-Mail: stoner.21@osu.edu.

**STONER, JAMES LLOYD,** retired foundation administrator, clergyman; b. Point Marion, Pa., Apr. 23, 1920; s. Martin Clark and Bess (Hare) S.; m. Janice Faller Evans, Aug. 28, 1943; children: Thomas Clark, James Douglas and Geoffrey Lloyd (twins). BS, Bethany Coll., 1941, DD (hon.), 1958; BD, MA, Yale U., 1944. Ordained to ministry Christian Ch., 1943; minister in Hamden, Conn. 1947-44, asst. dir. univ. rec. U. Tex. YMCA, 1944-45; dir. Student Christian Fellowship, Bowling Green State U., 1945-47, Univ. Christian Mission, Fed. Council Ch. and Nat. Council Chs. 1947-56; minister North Christian Ch., Columbus, Ind., 1956-66; asst. gen. sec. for exec. operations Nat. Council Chs., 1966-72; sr. minister Central Christian Ch., Austin, Tex., 1972-80; dep. exec. dir. Found. for Christian Living, Pawling, N.Y., 1980-83, exec. dir., 1983-87. Chmn. com. recommendations Internat. Conv. Christian Chs., 1962-65; bd. mgrs. United Christian Missionary Soc., 1956-63; mem. adv. bd. Am. Bible Soc., 1966-72; life mem. coun. Christian Unity, Christian Ch.; a founder, 1st pres. ISIK Award, Ridgewood, N.J., 1966-72; mem. Austin Coun. Chs., pres., 1973-75; rep. Tex. Conf. Chs., 1976-80; mem. goals com. Austin Tomorrow; mem. adv. bd. 1st Comml. Bank of Lakeway, Austin, Tex., 1990-95. Author: Down-to-Earth Meditations That Give You a Lift, 2000; contbr. articles to profl. publs. A founder, bd. dirs. Fellowship Christian Athletes, Kansas City, Mo., 1956-68; trustee Tougaloo (Miss.) Coll., 1968-74; trustee emeritus Lakeway Ch.; v.p., mem. exec. com. Ecumenical Ctr. Continuing Edn., Yale, 1966-72; mem. exec. com. Boy Scouts Am., Austin, 1980, Dutchess County council, 1981-82; bd. mgrs. New Milford Hosp., 1983-88; bd. dirs. Holiday Hills YMCA, 1983-87; com. mem. Town of Pawling 200th Anniversary, 1985-88, Lakeway Ecumenical Ch.; co-founder Holy Week Palm Observance, Lakeway, Tex. Mem. Pawling C. of C. (exec. com. 1984-87), Fellowship of Christian Athletes (nat. adv. bd. 1994—), Masons (32 degree), Pawling Rotary Club (pres. 1983-84, dist. gov.-elect 1991-92, dist. gov. 1992-93, Paul Harris fellow), Shriners, Austin Rotary Club (spl. lifetime mem.), Lake Travis/Lakeway Rotary Club (hon.), Alpha Psi Omega, Beta Theta Pi. Home: Summit 1034 Liberty Pk Dr 323 Austin TX 78746 *Fill every day with rainbow colors, and punctuate life with a positive outlook... Even the Cross of Christ is a positive sign.*

**STONER, JOHN RICHARD,** federal agency administrator; b. Ypsilanti, Mich., May 11, 1958; s. Richard P. and Marjorie G. Stoner; m. Diane Leslie Snow. BA in Govt., Lawrence U., 1981, B in Music Edn., 1981; MS in Mgmt., U. Md., 2004, MBA, 2005. Staff asst. Senator Robert Kasten Jr., Washington, 1981-82; staff assoc. Wis. Office Fed.-State Rels., Washington, 1982-83; intergovtl. rels. officer U.S. Dept. Transp., Washington, 1983-86, congl. rels. officer, 1989-91; dir. Office of Program and Policy Support, Rsch. and Spl. Programs Adminstrn., Dept. Transp., Washington, 1991-93; exec. dir. Republican Nat. Lawyers Assn., 1993-97; rep. Primerica Fin. Svcs., 1993-97, mortgage banker, 1998—; state govt. rels. mgr. Am. Trucking Assn., Inc.,

Alexandria, Va., 1986-88; researcher George Bush for Pres. Com., 1988; staff asst. Office of Pres.-Elect, Washington, 1988-89; state dir. The Century Coun., Washington, 2000—03. Admissions contact Washington area Lawrence U., 1986-87; football team mgr. Montgomery County Recreation League. Recipient Eagle Scout award Boy Scouts Am., 1972; Mortar Bd. scholar, 1980; Senate Rep. Policy Com. Legis. fellow, 1993-96. Republican. Mem. Ch. of Christ, Scientist. Avocations: water-skiing, organ. Home: 10409 Brunswick Ave Silver Spring MD 20902-4845 Office: The Century Coun 1310 G St NW Washington DC 20005-3000

**STONER, LEONARD D.**, automotive parts company executive; b. Galion, Ohio, Feb. 19, 1950; s. Kenneth M. and Delores I. (Fix) S.; m. Katharine I. Wiese, Feb. 14, 1980; children: Elisha, Cameron, Aaron. AS in Electronics Engring. Tech., Bell Howell U., 1974-76; student, U. Nebr., 1976-80; BS of Bus. Adminstrn. in Tech. Svcs., Bellevue U., 1995. Maintenance stores Keeper Control Data Corp., Omaha, 1978-85; prodn. control mgr. Douglas and Lamason, Richmond, Mich., 1986-87; ops. mgr. Johnson Controls, Lapeer, Mich., 1987-89; project mgr. Dohrman Machine Prodn. Inc., Omaha, 1990-92; mgr. prodn. and inventory control Stuart Entertainment, Inc., Council Bluffs, Iowa, 1995-96; materials control mgr. Sears Mfg., Davenport, Iowa, 1996-98; prodn. control mgr. Nishikawa Standard Co., Topeka, 1998-2000; materials mgr. RoMech, Red Oak, Iowa, 2001—02; self employed, 2002—. Assoc. cons. Internat. Purchasing Svc., Dearborn. With USAF, 1970-77. Mem. Am. Prodn. & Inventory Control Soc., Am. Radio Relay League. Avocations: amateur radio, camping, boating, woodworking, car repair. Office: RoMech 2700 N Broadway Red Oak IA 51566 Home: 14884 320th St Treynor IA 51575 E-mail: LeonardStoner@msn.com; lamboy51503@stratomail.com

**STONER, LOIS CAROLE**, biology educator; b. Gardner, Mass., Dec. 25, 1949; d. Olavi Adolph and Dorothy Beatrice Oja; m. Thomas T. Stoner, Aug. 25, 1973. BS in Edn., Indiana U. Pa., 1971; MS in Edn., Pa. State U., State College, 1979. Instrnl. level II tchg. cert. Tchr. Chestnut Ridge Sch. Dist., New Paris, Pa., 1971—. Jr., sr. class advisor Chestnut Ridge HS, New Paris, 1973—89; conservation educator Pa. Fedn. Sportsmen's Club, 1992; key club advisor Kiwanis, Bedford, Pa., 2003—06. Envirothon advisor Bedford County Conservation Dist., 1975—2005; pres. Summer Women's Bowling, Bedford, 1996—2006. Named Conservation Educator of the Yr., Bedford County Conservation Dist., 2005; recipient Examplary Programs, Shippensburg U. Pa., 1993. Mem.: Chestnut Ridge Edn. Assn. (bldg. rep. 2004—05), Nat. Wild Turkey Fedn. (mem. banquet com. 1996—2006), Everett Sportmen's Club, Delta Kappa Gamma (com. chair, newsletter editor 1992—2006). Avocations: golf, bowling, photography, hunting. Office: Chestnut Ridge HS 2588 Quaker Valley Rd New Paris PA 15554

**STONESIFER, PATTY (PATRICIA Q. STONESIFER)**, foundation administrator; b. Indpls., 1956; m. Michael Kinsley; 2 children from previous marriage. BA, Ind. U., 1982. Editor-in-chief Que Corp., Indpls.; sr. mgr. Microsoft Press, 1988-89; gen. mgr. Microsoft Can., 1989-90; gen. mgr., then v.p. product support svcs. consumer divsn. Microsoft Corp., Redmond, Wash., 1990-93, sr. v.p. consumer divsn., 1993—96; chairwoman, pres. Gates Learning Found., 1997—99; co-chair, pres., CEO Bill & Melinda Gates Found., Seattle, 2000—. Mem. US delegation to UN Gen. Assembly Spl. Session on AIDS; mem., bd. dirs. Viacom Inc., 2000—; The Seattle Found., Amazon.com. Mem. bd. regents Smithsonian Inst. Named one of 25 Most Influential People in Am., Time mag., 1996. Fellow: Am. Acad. Arts & Sci. (founding bd. mem.). Office: Bill & Melinda Gates Found PO Box 23350 Seattle WA 98102*

**STONG, ROGER ALAN**, lawyer; b. Chgo., May 2, 1962; s. Robert Evert and Therese (Countess Raczynski) Stong; m. Phyllis Ann Hoffman, Apr. 9, 1994; 1 child, Heather Nicole Ross. BA, U. Va., 1983; JD, Ind. U., 1985; MBA, U. Okla., 1986. Bar: Okla. 1986, U.S. Dist. Ct. (we dist. Okla.) 1991. Assoc. Crowe & Dunlevy, Oklahoma City, 1986—93, dir., shareholder, 1993—. Asst. sec. Okla. Lawyers for Children, Oklahoma City, 1998—. Fellow: Okla. Bar Found.; mem.: ABA, Oklahoma County Bar Assn., Okla. Bar Assn. (chairperson Bus. and Corp. Law sect. 2002—03), U. Va. Alumni Assn., U. Okla. Alumni Assn., Ind. U. Alumni Assn., Okla. Hist. Soc. Republican. Roman Cath. Home: 2205 NW 56th St Oklahoma City OK 73112 Office: Crowe & Dunlevy 20 N Broadway Oklahoma City OK 73102 Office Phone: 405-235-7700. Office Fax: 405-272-5255. Business E-Mail: stongr@crowedunlevy.com.

**ST-ONGE, DENIS ALDERIC**, geologist, research scientist, educator; b. Ste-Agathe, Man., Can., May 11, 1929; s. Adolphe and Jeanne M. (Ritchot) St-Onge; m. Jeanne Marie Behaegel, Jan. 7, 1955; children: Marc R, Nicole J M. BA, Coll. St-Boniface, 1951; Lic. Sci., U. Louvain, Belgium, 1957, DSc, 1962; DSc (hon.), U. Man., 1990. Research scientist Geol. Survey, Ottawa, Ont., Canada, 1958-68, sect. head, 1982-85; chief sub. div. Quaternary Geology, 1985-87, dir. terrain scis. div., 1987-91, sci. advisor Polar Continental Shelf Project, 1991-97; prof. geography U. Ottawa, 1968-82, chmn. geography, 1974-77, vice dean grad. studies, 1977-80, prof. emeritus, 1998—, bd. govs., 2000—; scientist emeritus Geol. Survey Can., 1997—. Chmn. bd. dirs. Fluxnet Can., 2002—, Arctic Net, 2003—04. Author: (book) Geomorphologie Ellef-Ringnes Island, 1965, Quaternary Geology, Inman River Region, N.W.T. Canada, 1995; contbr. articles to profl jours. Pres Ont Francophone PTA, 1967—69. Decorated Officer Order of Can; recipient medal, Queen Elizabeth II, 1979, Commemorative medal, Govt. of Can., 1992, Medal of Honor, Univ Liege, Belgium, 1980, medal, A Cailleux, 1991, Can 125, 1992, Royal Scottish Geog. Soc, 1994, Golden Jubilee medal, Queen Elizabeth II, 2002. Fellow: Explorers Club (internat. fellow 2005), Arctic Inst. N.Am., Geol. Assn. Can. (pres. 1984—85, J. W. Ambrose medal 2001), Royal Can. Geog. Soc. (bd. dirs. 1980—2001, pres. 1992—98, chmn. Partnership Group Sci. Engrs. 1999—2001, Camsell medal 2005, 75th Ann. medallion 2005); mem.: Can. Geosci. Coun. (pres. 1996—97), Assn. Quebecoise pour l'etude du Quaternaire (hon.), Can. Quaternary Assn., Internat. Union Quaternary Rsch. (hon.), Can. Assn. Geographers (pres. 1979—80, Award Svc. to Profession 2000). Avocations: swimming, skiing, photography. Office: Geolog Survey of Canada 601 Booth St Ottawa ON Canada K1A 0E8 Home: 1188 Agincourt Rd Ottawa ON Canada K2C 2H9 Office Phone: 613-947-1652. Business E-Mail: dstonge@nrcan.gc.ca.

**STONNINGTON, HENRY HERBERT**, physician, educator, medical association administrator; b. Vienna, Feb. 12, 1927; arrived in U.S.; 1969; m. Constance Mary Leigh Hammersly. MB, BS, Melbourne U., Victoria, Australia, 1950; MS, U. Minn., 1972. Diplomate Am. Bd. Phys. Medicine and Rehab., 1973. Pvt. practice, Sydney, N.S.W., Australia, 1955-65; clin. tchr. U. N.S.W., Sydney, 1965-69; resident in Phys. Medicine and Rehab. Mayo Clinic, Rochester, Minn., 1969-72, asst. prof. 1972-83; assoc. prof. Mayo Med. Sch., Rochester, 1975-83; chmn. dept rehab. medicine Med. Coll. Va., Va. Commonwealth U., Richmond, 1983-88, prof. rehab. medicine, 1983-89, dir. rsch. tng. ctr., 1988-89; v.p. med. svcs. Sheltering Arms Hosp., Richmond, 1985-92; prof. and chmn. dept. phys. medicine and rehab. U. Mo., Columbia, 1992-94; med. dir. Meml. Rehab. Ctr., Savannah, Ga., 1994-97; clin. prof. rehab. medicine Emory U., Atlanta, 1997—2000; clin. prof. medicine sect. phys. medicine and rehab. La. State U., 2001—. Med. dir. rehab. svcs. Meml. Hosp., Gulfport, Miss., 1998—; clin. prof. phys. med. and rehab. La. State U. Med. Sch., 2001—. Editor: Brain Injury, 1987—2001, Pediatric Rehabilitation, 1997—2000; contbr. articles to profl. jours. Recipient award Rsch. Tng. Ctr. Model Systems, Nat. Inst. Disability and Rehab. Rsch., Washington, 1987, 88, Disting. Clinician award Am. Acad. Phys. Medicine and Rehab., 2002. Fellow Australian Coll. Rehab. Medicine, Australasian Faculty Rehab. Medicine, Royal Coll. Physicians Edinburgh (Scotland), Am. Acad. Phys. Medicine and Rehab. (named Disting. Physician 2002), Am. Coun. Rehab. Medicine, Am. Assn. Acad. Physiatrists; mem. Internat. Brain Injury Assn. (v.p. for sci. affairs 1998—, bd. govs., Founder's award 2004). Personal E-mail: hencon2731@bellsouth.net.

**STOOKEY, NOEL PAUL**, folksinger, composer; b. Balt., Dec. 30, 1937; s. George William and Dorothea (St. Aubrey) S.; m. Mary Elizabeth Bannard, Sept. 4, 1963; children: Elizabeth Drake, Katherine Darby, Anna St. Aubrey. Student, Mich. State U., 1955-58; HHD (hon.), Husson Coll., 1978. Prodn. mgr. Cormac Chem. Corp., N.Y.C., 1959-60; artist in residence Northfield Mount Hermon Sch., 1999. Released album of songs Birds of Paradise, 1954; sang professionally, master ceremonies events, Mich. State U., 1955-58; profl. singer, Greenwich Village, N.Y.C., 1960-61; mem. folksinging group, Peter, Paul and Mary, 1961—; solo rec. artist for Warner Bros., 1971-74; producer folk albums for Scepter Records, Verve/Folkway Records; founder, Neworld Media, rec. studio Neworld Records, 1977-81; rec. artist: Paul And, 1971, One Night Stand, 1972, Real to Reel, 1976, Something New and Fresh, 1978, Band and Bodyworks, 1979, Wait'll You Hear This, 1982, There is Love, 1985, State of the Heart, 1985, In Love Beyond Our Lives, 1990; host Maine Pub. TV broadcasting series "E-Maine", 1997. Mem. AFTRA, Screen Actors Guild, ASCAP, Delta Upsilon. Clubs: St. Botolph's (Boston). Personal E-mail: stook@celestat.com. Business E-mail: neworld@celestat.com.

**STOOPLER, MARK BENJAMIN**, physician; b. N.Y.C., Sept. 29, 1950; s. Alex and Blanche Sylvia (Kappel) S.; m. Lynn Sara Fruchter, Jan. 10, 1982; children: David Andrew, Emily Rachel, Jesse Bryan. BS, Tulane U., 1971; MD, Cornell U., 1975. Diplomate Am. Bd. Internal Medicine, Am. Bd. Oncology. Intern and resident in internal medicine North Shore U. Hosp., Manhasset, N.Y., 1975-78, Meml. Sloan-Kettering Cancer Ctr., N.Y.C., 1975-78, asst. chief resident in medicine, 1978, fellow in med. oncology, 1978-80; asst. attending physician Presbyn. Hosp., N.Y.C., 1980-93, assoc. attending physician, 1993—; asst. clin. prof. medicine Columbia U. Coll. of Physicians and Surgeons, N.Y.C., 1980-93; assoc. clin. prof. medicine, 1993—. Contbr. articles to profl. jours. Recipient U. scholar Tulane U., 1970-71; named one of America's Top Doctors, A Castle Connolly Guide, 2003, 2004, 2005. Fellow ACP; mem. Am. Soc. of Clin. Oncology, Am. Fedn. for Clin. Research, Internat. Assn. for the Study of Lung Cancer, Phi Beta Kappa. Office: Columbia-Presbyn Med Ctr 161 Fort Washington Ave New York NY 10032-3713 Office Phone: 212-305-8230.

**STOOPS, BOB**, college football coach; b. Youngstown, Ohio, Sept. 16, 1960; BS, Univ. Iowa, 1983. Grad. asst. coach Univ. Iowa, 1983—84, vol. coach, 1985—87; asst. coach Kent State, 1988; defensive backs coach Kans. State, 1989—90, co-defensive coord., 1991—95; def. coord., asst. head coach Univ. Fla., 1996—98; head football coach Univ. Okla., 1998—. Recipient Nat. Coach Yr., Am. Heart Assn., 2000, 2000, Football News, 2000, Walter Camp awards, 2000, 2003, Big 12 Coach Yr., 2000, 2003. Office: OU Football 180 W Brooks St Norman OK 73019*

**STOPFORD, PHILIP**, lawyer; LLB with honors, Brunel U., 1977; LLM, U. Va., 1978. Bar: DC 1980, NY 1981. Solicitor: England and Wales 1993. Ptnr. White & Case, London. Contbr. articles to profl. jours. Office: White & Chase 5 Old Broad St London EC2N 1DW England Office Phone: 44-20-7532-2300. Office Fax: 44-20-7532-1001. E-mail: pstopford@whitecase.com.

**STOPLER, TRACY**, dietician, educator; b. Bronx, NY, July 7, 1964; BS, SUNY, Oneonta, 1986; MS, NYU, NYC, 1989. Nutrition rsch. Office of Dr. Victor Herbert/Bronx VA Med. Ctr., 1987—99; clin. dietician surgery and psychiatry Bronx VA Med. Ctr., 1989—90; clin. dietician, program dir. Great Neck (NY) Cardiovascular Ctr., 1990—93; pres. Nutrition ETC, Inc., Plainview, NY, 1991—. Adj. prof. Adelphi U., Garden City, NY, 1996—; nutrition cons. Rockland County (NY) Dept. Health, 2005—06; spkr. in field. Author: Nutrition ETC for the Millennium, 1999; editor: Total Nutrition, 1995. Fundraiser Elizabeth Glazer Pediat. AIDS. Mem.: Am. Coll. Sports Medicine, Am. Dietetic Assn. Avocation: marathons.

**STOPNIK, SCOTT H.**, lawyer; BBA, U. Miami, 1992; JD, NY Law Sch., 1995. Bar: NY 1996, US Dist. Ct. Ea. Dist. NY, US Dist. Ct. So. Dist. NY. Ptnr. Wilson, Elser, Moskowitz, Edelman & Dicker LLP, NYC. Mem.: Assn. of the Bar of the City of NY. Office: Wilson Elser Moskowitz Edelman & Dicker LLP 150 E 42nd St 23rd Fl New York NY 10017-5639 Office Phone: 212-490-3000 ext. 2747. Office Fax: 212-490-3038. Business E-Mail: stopniks@wemed.com.

**STOPPARD, TOM (TOMAS STRAUSSLER)**, playwright; b. Zlin, Czechoslovakia, July 3, 1937; arrived in Eng., 1946; s. Eugene and Martha Stoppard Straussler, Kenneth Stoppard (Stepfather); m. Jose Ingle, 1965 (div., 1972), 2 sons; m. Miriam Moore-Robinson, 1972 (div. 1992), 2 sons MLitt (hon.), U. Bristol, Eng., 1979, Brunel U., 1979, U. Sussex, 1980. Journalist Western Daily Press, Bristol, Eng., 1954-58, Evening World, Bristol, 1958-60; free-lance reporter, 1960-63. Bd. dir. Royal Nat. Theatre, London, 1989—. Author: (plays) The Gamblers, 1965, Rosencrantz and Guildenstern Are Dead, 1966 (Plays and Players Best Play award 1967, Best Play Tony award 1968), Enter a Free Man, 1968, The Real Inspector Hound, 1968, Albert's Bridge, 1969 (Prix Italia 1968), If You're Glad I'll Be Frank, 1966, After Magritte, 1970, Dogg's Our Pet, 1971, Jumpers, 1972 (Evening Standard Best Play award 1972, Plays and Players Best Play award 1972), Travesties, 1974 (Evening Standard Best Play award, Best Play Tony award 1976), Dirty Linen and New-Found-Land, 1976, Every Good Boy Deserves Favor, 1974, Night and Day, 1978 (Evening Standard Best Play award 1978), Dogg's Hamlet, Cahoot's Macbeth, 1979, The Real Thing, 1982 (Evening Standard Best Play award 1982, Best Play Tony award 1984), Best Fgn. Play Tony award 1984), Hapgood, 1988, Artist Descending a Staircase, 1988, Arcadia, 1993 (Evening Standard Best Play award 1993, Oliver award 1994), Indian Ink, 1995, Invention of Love, 1997 (Evening Standard Best Play award 1997); (play adaptations) Tango by Slawomir Mrozek, 1966, The House of Bernarda Alba by Federico Garcia Lorca, 1973, Undiscovered Country (based on Das Weite Land by Arthur Schnitzler), 1979, On the Razzle (based on Einen Jux will er sich machen by Johann Nestroy), 1981, Rough Crossing (based on The Play's the Thing by Ferenc Molnar), 1984, Dalliance (based on Liebelei by Arthur Schnitzler), 1986; (radio plays) The Dissolution of Dominic Boot, 1964, M is for Moon Among Other Things, 1964, If You're Glad I'll Be Frank, 1966, Albert's Bridge, 1967, Where Are They Now?, 1970, Artist Descending a Staircase, 1972, The Dog It Was That Died, 1982, In the Native State, 1991, also episodes of radio serials The Dales, 1964, A Student's Diary, 1965; (screenplays) The Romantic Englishwoman, 1975, Despair, 1978, The Human Factor, 1980, (with Terry Gilliam and Charles McKeown) Brazil, 1985 (Best Screenplay Acad. award nominee 1985, Best Screenplay L.A. Critics Circle award 1985), Empire of the Sun, 1987, The Russia House, 1990; (author, dir.) Rosencrantz and Guildenstern Are Dead, 1990 (Grand prize Venice Film Festival 1990), Billy Bathgate, 1991, (with Marc Norman) Shakespeare in Love, 1998 (Golden Globe award and Oscar for best screenplay); (teleplays) A Walk on the Water, 1963, A Separate Peace, 1966, Teeth, 1967, Another Moon Called Earth, 1967, Neutral Ground, 1968, The Engagement (based on his radio play The Dissolution of Dominic Boot), 1970, One Pair of Eyes, 1972, (with Clive Exton) Boundaries, 1975, Three Men in a Boat, 1975, Professional Foul, 1977, Squaring the Circle: Poland 1980-81, 1985; (translator) Largo Desolato by Vaclav Havel, 1987; (novel) Lord Malquist and Mr. Moon, 1966; contbr. short stories to Introduction 2, 1964. In 1977, a visit to Russia raised concerns for human rights issues; concerns are manifested in work and involvement with orgns. such as Amnesty Internat., Com. Against Psychiatric Abuse, and Index on Censorship. Decorated knight comdr. Order Brit. Empire; Ford Found. grantee, 1964; recipient John Whiting award Arts Coun. Great Britain, 1967, Evening Standard Most Promising Playwright Drama award, 1972, Shakespeare prize Hamburg, Germany, 1979. Fellow: Royal Soc. Literature. Office: Peters Fraser Dunlop Drury Ho 34-43 Russell St London WC2B 5HA England

**STORANDT, MARTHA**, psychologist; b. Little Rock, June 2, 1938; d. Farris and Floy (Montgomery) Mobbs; m. Duane Storandt, Dec. 15, 1962; 1 child, Eric AB, Washington U., St. Louis, 1960, PhD, 1966. Lic. psychologist, Mo. Staff psychologist VA, Jefferson Barracks, Mo., 1967-68; asst. prof. to prof. Washington U., St. Louis, 1968—. Mem. nat. adv. council on aging Nat. Inst. on Aging, 1984-87; editor-in-chief Jour. Gerontology, 1981-86 Author:

Counseling and Therapy with Older Adults, 1983; co-author: Memory, Related Functions and Age, 1974; co-editor: The Clinical Psychology of Aging, 1978, The Adult Years: Continuity and Change, 1989, Neuropsychological Assessment of Dementia and Depression in Older Adults: A Clinician's Guide, 1994. Recipient Disting. Service award Mo. Assn. Homes for the Aging, 1984. Fellow APA (pres. divsn. 20 1979-80, council rep. 1983-84, 86-88, Disting. Sci. Contbn. award divsn. adult devel. and aging 1988, Master Mentor award divsn. adult devel. and aging 2000, Disting. Contbns. to Clin. Geropsychology divsn. clin. psychology 2002), Gerontol. Soc. Am. Office: Washington U Dept Psychology Saint Louis MO 63130

**STORB, URSULA BEATE**, molecular genetics and cell biology educator; b. Stuttgart, Germany; came to U.S., 1966; d. Walter M. Stemmer and Marianne M. (Kämmerer) Nowara. MD, U. Freiburg, Germany, 1960. Asst. prof. dept. microbiology U. Wash., Seattle, 1971-75, assoc. prof., 1975-81, prof., 1981-86, head. div. immunology, 1980-86; prof. molecular genetics and cell biology U. Chgo., 1986—. Mem. editl. bd. Immunity, Current Opinion in Immunology, Internat. Immunology, Immunol. Revs.; contbr. articles to sci. jours. Grantee NIH, NSF, Am. Cancer Soc., 1973—. Fellow Am. Acad. Arts and Scis.; mem. AAAS, Assn. Women in Sci., Am. Assn. Immunologists. Office: U Chgo 920 E 58th St Chicago IL 60637-5415 E-mail: stor@midway.uchicago.edu

**STORCH, ARTHUR**, theater director; b. Bklyn., June 29, 1925; s. Sam and Bessie (Goldner) S.; children: Max Darrow, Alexander English, Bess Martin. BA, New Sch. Social Research, 1949. Actor in Broadway prodns. End as a Man, 1953, Time Limit, 1955, Girls of Summer, 1956, Look Homeward, Angel, 1957, Night Circus, 1958, The Long Dream, 1960, The Best Man, 1961; motion pictures The Strange One, 1956, Girls of the Night, 1959, The Exorcist, 1974; dir. off-Broadway Two by Saroyan, 1961, Three by Three, 1962, Talking to You (London debut), 1962, The Typists and the Tiger, 1963, The Owl and the Pussycat, 1964, The Impossible Years, 1965, The Local Stigmatic, 1970, Under the Weather, 1965, Golden Rainbow, 1967, The Chinese and Dr. Fish, 1969, Promenade All, 1970, 42 Seconds from Broadway, 1973, Tribute, 1978, Twice Around the Park, 1982, Clarence, 1986; Of Mice and Men, 1988; dir. nat. tour The King and I, 1989; dir. Syracuse Stage Waiting for Lefty, Noon, Of Mice and Men, 1974, 75, La Ronde, The Butterfingers Angel. Mornings at Seven, Dynamo, 1975-76, A Quality of Mercy, The Seagull, 1976-77, 1976-77, Love Letters on Blue Paper, End of the Beginning, 1977-78, Loved, 1978, Naked, 1979, The Comedy of Errors, 1980, The Impromptu of Outremont, 1982, The Double Bass, 1984, Arms and the Man, Handy Dandy, Cyrano de Bergerac, Romeo and Juliet, 1986, Of Mice and Men, N.Y.C., 1987, Fugue, 1988, Seven By Beckett, 1988, Look Homeward Angel, Wait Unitl Dark, Dangerous Corner, 1990, A Walk in the Woods, 1989, Finding Donis Ann, 1990, Androcles and the Lion, 1991; Lend Me a Tenor, 1992; Awake and Sing, 1993; dir., actor Love Letters, 1992. Founder, producing artistic dir. Syracuse Stage; chmn. drama dept. Syracuse U., 1974-92, Arthur Storch Theatre, 1992. Home: 400 W 43d St Apt 21H New York NY 10036

**STORCH, DAVID**, manufacturing executive; Degree, Ithaca Coll., NY, 1975. Pres. AAR Aircraft Turbine Ctr.; pres., COO AAR Corp., Wood Dale, Ill., 1989—; CEO, 1996—. Bd. dirs. AAR Corp., Whittman-Hart Inc., Prentice Women's Hosp. Bd. trustees Ithaca (N.Y.) Coll., 2000—. Mem.: Young Pres. Org. Internat., Econ. Club Chgo. Office: AAR Corp 1100 North Wood Dale Rd Wood Dale IL 60191

**STORCH, GERALD L.**, retail executive; BA cum laude, Harvard U., 1978, MBA with hons., 1981, JD magna cum laude, 1982. Ptnr. McKinsey & Co., Boston, 1982—93; sr. v.p. strategic planning Dayton Hudson Corp., Mpls., 1993—98; pres. fin. services & new bus. Target Corp., Mpls., 1999—2001, vice chmn., 2001—05; CEO Toys R Us Inc., Wayne, NJ, 2006—. Office: Toys R Us Inc 1 Geoffrey Way Wayne NJ 07470*

**STORER, MARYRUTH**, law librarian; b. Portland, Oreg., 1953; d. Joseph and Carol Storer; m. David Bailey, 1981; children: Sarah, Allison. BA in History, Portland State U., 1974; JD, U. Oreg., 1977; M in Law Librarianship, U. Wash., 1978. Bar: Oreg. 1978. Assoc. law libr. U. Tenn., Knoxville, 1978-79; law libr. O'Melveny & Myers, L.A., 1979-88; dir. Orange County Pub. Law Libr., Santa Ana, Calif., 1988—. Mem. Am. Assn. Law Libris. (exec. bd. 1999-2002), So. Calif. Assn. Law Libris. (pres. 1986-87), Coun. Calif. County Law Libris. (sec./treas. 1990-94, pres. 1994-96), Arroyo Sero Libr. Network (chair 2000-03). Democrat. Episcopalian. Office: Orange County Public Law Library 515 N Flower St Santa Ana CA 92703-2304 Office Phone: 714-834-3002.

**STOREY, BRIT ALLAN**, historian; b. Boulder, Colo., Dec. 10, 1941; s. Harold Albert and Gladys Roberta (Althouse) S.; m. Carol DeArman, Dec. 19, 1970; 1 child, Christine Roberta. AB, Adams State Coll., Alamosa, Colo., 1963; MA, U. Ky., 1965, PhD, 1968. Instr. history Auburn (Ala.) U., 1967-68, asst. prof., 1968-70; dep. state historian State Hist. Soc. Colo., Denver, 1970-71, acting state historian, 1971-72, rsch. historian, 1972-74; hist. preservation specialist Adv. Coun. on Hist. Preservation, Lakewood, Colo., 1974-88; sr. historian Bur. Reclamation, Lakewood, 1988—. Contbr. articles to profl. publs. Mem. Fed. Preservation Forum (pres. 1990-91), Nat. Coun. Pub. History (sec. 1987, pres.-elect 1990-91, pres. 1991-92), Orgn. Am. Historians (com. 1983-86, 1985-86), Victorian Soc. Am. (bd. dirs. 1977-79), Western History Assn. (chmn. com. 1982-86), Colo.-Wyo. Assn. Mus. (sec. 1974-76, pres. 1976-77), Cosmos Club (Washington). Avocation: birding. Home: 7264 W Otero Ave Littleton CO 80128-5639 Office: Bur Reclamation Denver Fed Ctr D 5300 Bldg 67 Denver CO 80225-0007

**STOREY, CHARLES PORTER**, lawyer; b. Austin, Tex., Dec. 4, 1922; s. Robert Gerald and Frances Hazel (Porter) S.; m. Helen Hanks Stephens, Oct. 14, 1950; children: Charles Porter, Harry Stephens, Frederick Schatz. BA, U. Tex., 1947, LLB, 1948; LLM, So. Methodist U., 1952. Bar: Tex. 1948. Pvt. practice law, Dallas, 1948—; sr. counsel Carrington Coleman Sloman & Blumenthal, LLP. Pres. Dallas Day Nursery Assn., 1958, Greater Dallas Coun. Chs., 1970-71; internat. Com. YMCA, 1969-71; nat. bd. dirs. U.S. YMCA, 1964-75; pres. Children's Devel. Ctr., Dallas, 1959; trustee Baylor Coll. Dentistry, 1981-90, Hillcrest Found., 1994—; trustee emeritus Southwestern Legal Found., chmn. 1980-90; dir. Zale Lipshy U. Med. Ctr., 1999—. 1st lt., pilot USAAF, 1943-45, ETO. Decorated Air medal. Master emeritus Dallas Inn of Ct. (pres. 1991-93); fellow Am. Coll. Trial Lawyers, Am. Bar Found., Tex. Bar Found.; mem. ABA, Tex. Bar Assn. (bd. dir. 1976-79), Dallas Bar Assn. (pres. 1975), Philos. Soc. Tex., Dallas Country Club, Crescent Club, Phi Delta Phi, Phi Delta Theta. Mem. Christian Ch. (Disciples Of Christ). Home: 5855 Farquhar Ln Dallas TX 75209 Office: 200 Crescent Ct Ste 1500 Dallas TX 75201-7839 Fax: 214-758-3753. Office Phone: 214-855-3052. E-mail: cstorey@ccsb.com.

**STOREY, GREGORY DEAN**, publisher, editor; b. Denver, Sept. 16, 1950; s. Harold Robert and Grace Marcella (Wright) S.; m. Charlene Komar, May 28, 1983. Student, U.S. Mcht. Marine Acad., 1968-70; BA with honors, U. Conn., 1973; MS in Journalism, So. Ill. U., 1984. Reporter, editor Norwich (Conn.) Bull., 1973-76; press dir. Vt. Pres. Ford Com., Burlington, 1976; reporter Naples (Fla.) Star, 1977; freelance writer, copy editor Ill., 1978-79; maritime reporter Jour. Commerce, N.Y.C., 1980-82, editl. writer, 1982-84, editor west coast San Francisco, 1984-86; dir. pub. rels., corp. sec. N.Y. Shipping Assn., N.Y.C., 1986-95, v.p. corp. rels., 1995—; ed. dir. Jour. of Commerce, N.Y.C.; columns editor Daily Deal, 2000—. Contbr. articles to profl. jours. Mem. Soc. of the Silurians, Phi Kappa Phi, Kappa Tau Alpha. Avocations: maritime and NYC history, Irish culture.

**STOREY, J. BENTON,** horticulturist, educator; BS in Horticulture, Tex. A&M U., 1949, MS, 1952; PhD in Botanical Sci. and Plant Physiology, U. Calif., LA, Calif., 1957. Prof. Tex. A & M Univ., College Station, 1950—. Editor: The Pecan Quar., 1967—81. Recipient Outstanding Grad. Educator award, 1992. Office: Texas A&M University Dept Horticultural Scis College Station TX 77843-0001

**STOREY, JAMES MOORFIELD,** lawyer; b. Boston, Apr. 12, 1931; s. Charles Moorfield and Susan Jameson (Sweetser) S.; m. Adair Miller, Aug. 28, 1954 (div. 1973); children: Barbara Sessums Storey McGrath, Mary Sweetser Storey Meley, Susan Adair Storey Frank, Eliza Allison Tebo Storey Anderson, Alice Leovy Storey Wille; m. Isabelle Helene Boeschenstein, May 17, 1973. AB, Harvard U., 1953, LL.B., 1956. Bar: Mass. 1956. Atty. SEC, Washington, 1956-57, legal asst. to chmn., 1957-59; assoc. Gaston, Snow, Motley & Holt, Boston, 1959-62; ptnr. Gaston, Snow, Motley & Holt (name changed to Gaston Snow & Ely Bartlett), Boston, 1962-87, Dechert Price & Rhoads, Boston, 1987-94, ret., 1994, profl. trustee, corp. dir., 1994—. Trustee Mt. Auburn Cemetery, Cambridge, Mass., 1980-. Co-author: Mutual Fund Law Handbook, 1998, The Uneasy Chaperone, 2000. Mem. ABA, Boston Bar Assn., Tavern Club Boston (pres. 1985-87), Century Assn. of N.Y. Unitarian Universalist. Home: 89A Mt Vernon St Boston MA 02108-1330 Office: 5 Boylston Pl Boston MA 02116 Office Phone: 617-728-0429. Personal E-mail: jandistorey@worldnet.att.net.

**STOREY, KENNETH BRUCE,** biology professor; b. Taber, Alta., Can., Oct. 23, 1949; s. Arthur George and Madeleine Una (Mawhinney) S.; m. Janet Margaret Collicutt, June 6, 1975; children: Jennifer, Kathryn. BSc with honors, U. Calgary, Alta., 1971; PhD, U, B.C., Vancouver, Can., 1974. Asst. prof. Duke U., Durham, NC, 1975-79; assoc. prof. Carleton U., Ottawa, Ont., Canada, 1979-85, prof., 1985—. - Can. Rsch. chair, 2001—. Chmn. rsch. molecular physiology, Canada; adj. prof. in botany and zoology Stellenbosch U., South Africa; lectr. in field. Editor Cell and Molecular Responses to Stress; mem. editl. bd. Jour. Comparative Physiology, 1995—; contbr. over 500 articles to profl. jours. Recipient E.W.R. Steacie award Nat. Sci. and Engring. Rsch. Coun. Can., 1984-86, Killam Sr. Rsch. fellow, 1993-95. Fellow AAAS, Royal Soc. Can.; mem. Can. Biochem. Soc. (Ayerst award 1989), Can. Soc. Zoology, Soc. Cryobiology. Avocations: movies, music, renaissance art. Office: Carleton U Dept Biology 1125 Colonel By Drive Ottawa ON Canada K1S 5B6 E-mail: kenneth_storey@carleton.ca.

**STOREY, NORMAN C.,** lawyer; b. Miami, Fla., Oct. 11, 1943; BA cum laude, Loyola-Marymount U., L.A., 1965; JD, U. Ariz., 1968. Bar: Ariz. 1968. Law clk. to Hon. James A. Walsh U.S. Dist. Ct. Ariz.; ptnr. Squire, Sanders & Dempsey, L.L.P., Phoenix. Mens art coun. Phoenix Art Mus.; fin. coun. Diocese Phoenix Cath. Ch. Mem.: State Bar Ariz. Office: 40 N Central Ave Ste 2700 Phoenix AZ 85004-4498 Business E-Mail: nstorey@ssd.com.

**STOREY, PAMELA T.,** elementary school educator; b. Fayetteville, Tenn., Jan. 12, 1960; d. Rex Carter and Patricia Henson Talley; m. Michael Neal Storey, June 6, 1981; children: Ryan, Brent, Tyler. BA, Mid. Tenn. State U., Murfreesboro, 1981, MA in Curriculum/Instrn., 1987. Spl. edn. tchr. Highland Pk. Elem., Columbia, Tenn., 1982—98, tchr., 1998—. Mem. adv. bd. Jr. Cotillion, Columbia, 1997—2001; Sunday sch. tchr. 1st Presbyn. Ch., Columbia. Named Tchr. of the Yr., Highland Pk. Elem. Sch., 1993, 2003. Mem.: NEA, Maury County Edn. Assn. (sec. 1996—98). Avocations: travel, decorating, music. Home: 3218 Carrington Ln Columbia TN 38401 Office: Highland Pk Elem 1606 Highland Ave Columbia TN 38401

**STOREY, ROBERT DAVIS,** lawyer; b. Tuskegee, Ala., Mar. 28, 1936; s. Dewitt Herald and Katie Pearl (Johnson) S.; m. Juanita Kendrick Cohen, May 9, 1959; children: Charles Kendrick, Christopher Robert Ransom, Rebecca Kate. AB, Harvard U., 1958; JD, Case Western Res. U., 1964; LHD, Tri-State U., 2000. Bar: Ohio, 1964. Atty. East Ohio Gas Co., Cleve., 1964-66; asst. dir. Legal Aid Soc., Cleve., 1966-67; assoc. Burke, Haber & Berick, Cleve., 1967-70, ptnr., 1971-93, Thompson, Hine & Flory, L.L.P., Cleve., 1994—. Bd. dirs. Procter & Gamble Co., Cin., May Dept. Stores Co., St. Louis, Verizon Comm., N.Y.C. Trustee Kresge Found., George Gund Found., Case Western Res. U., Spelman Coll., Univ. Sch., Great Lakes Sci. Ctr., Phillips Exeter Acad., 1968-83; trustee Cleve. State U., 1971-80, chmn., 1979-80; bd. overseers Harvard U., 1978-84. Capt. USMC, 1958-61. Recipient Charles Flint Kellog award Assn. Episcopal Colls., 1984; named Chief Marshal, 25th Reunion, Harvard Class of 1958, 1983. Mem. Soc. Benchers, Union Club. Episcopalian. Home: 1803 Asturias St Saint Augustine FL 32080-4074 Office: Thompson Hine & Flory LLP 3900 Key Ctr 127 Public Sq Cleveland OH 44114-1216 E-mail: RDStorey@thompsonhine.com.*

**STOREY, SUSAN,** investment banker; b. Dublin; 1 child. Student, U. Coll. Dublin, York U., Toronto, Can. Fgn. exch. trader CIBC Wood Gundy, 1982—87, v.p., 1987—88, with bank derivatives group London, 1988—90, derivatives mgr. Toronto, 1990—96, head global derivatives trading, 1996—98, mng. dir., head global trading Debt Capital Markets, 1998—. Former chair Can. Com. for Professionalism; past pres. Forex Can.; voting mem. Fed. Res. Bank, N.Y. Fgn. Exch. Com.; ex-officio mem. Can. Fgn. Exch. Com. Bank Can. Chair CIBC Wood Gundy Children's Miracle Found.; vice chair Children's Aid Found.; bd. mem. Ireland Fund. Named one of 25 Most Powerful Women in Banking, U.S. Banker, 2003. Office: BCE Place 161 Bay St PO Box 500 Toronto ON Canada M5J 2S8

**STORIE, ERIC DUANE,** science administrator; b. Lenoir, NC, May 20, 1954; s. Clarence Lee and Daisy Puett Storie; m. Jean Ward Bumbarger; children: Kathryn Elizabeth, Erin Christine. MS in Biology, U. NC, Charlotte, 1983. Dir. environ. tech. Roanoke-Chowan C.C., Ahoskie, NC, 1997—2003; dir. biotech. Coll. of The Albemarle, Elizabeth City, NC, 2003—. Mem. com. on anti-bioterrorism curricula NC Dept. of C.C.s, Raleigh, 2002—03. Mem. Am. Inst. Biol. Scis., Human Anatomy and Physiology Soc. Avocations: hiking, bicycling. Office: Coll of The Albemarle 1208 N Road St Elizabeth City NC 27909 Office Phone: 252-335-0821 ext 2202. Office Fax: 252-335-2011. E-mail: estorie@albemarle.edu.

**STORIN, MATTHEW VICTOR,** academic administrator, educator, retired editor; b. Springfield, Mass., Dec. 24, 1942; s. Harry Francis and Blanche Marie S.; m. Keiko Takita, Aug. 1, 1975; 1 child, Kenyatta; children by previous marriage: Karen, Aimee, Sean. BA, U. Notre Dame, 1964. Reporter Springfield Daily News, 1964-65, Griffin-Larrabee News Bur., Washington, 1965-69; Washington corr., city editor, Asian corr., nat. editor, asst. mng. editor, dep. mng. editor Boston Globe, 1969-85; dep. mng. editor U.S. News & World Report, Washington, 1985-86; editor, sr. v.p. Chgo. Sun-Times, 1986-87; editor The Maine Times, Topsham, 1988-89; mng. editor N.Y. Daily News, 1989-91, exec. editor, 1991-92, Boston Globe, 1992-93, editor, 1993—2001; assoc. v.p., prof. Am. studies U. Notre Dame, 2002—. Recipient Disting. Polit. Reporting award Am. Assn. Polit. Sci., 1969, Yankee Quill award New Eng. Chpt. Sigma Delta Chi, 1997. Home: 1333 Oliver Cir South Bend IN 46614-7218 Office Phone: 574-631-8696. E-mail: mstorin@nd.edu.

**STORING, PAUL EDWARD,** retired foreign service officer; b. Ames, Iowa, Oct. 24, 1929; s. James Alvin and Edith Nora (Ryg) S.; children: Mimi Storing Harlan, Felice Storing Kite. Student, U Oslo, Norway, 1950-51; BA, Allegheny Coll., 1952; MA with honors, Colgate U., 1956; postgrad., U. Wis.-Madison, 1955-59. Fgn. service officer Dept. State, Washington, Mex. and Scandinavia, 1960-80; spl. asst. U.S. Sect. Internat. Boundary and Water Commn. U.S. And Mex., Washington, 1980-99; ret. Contbr. articles to profl. jours. Served to cpl. U.S. Army, 1953-55 Fellow U. Wis., 1957-58; Fulbright fellow U. Oslo, 1959-60 Mem. Am. Fgn. Svc. Assn., Fulbright Assn., Phi Beta Kappa, Delta Tau Delta (pres. Alpha chpt. 1949-50). Baptist. Avocations: music, photography, travel. Home: 9006 Opera Alley Manassas VA 20110 E-mail: storingpe@netscape.net.

**STORK, CHRISTINE MARY,** toxicologist, pharmacist; d. Alfred John and Diane Theresa Stork; m. Joe Medicis, July 1, 1995; children: Zachary Joseph Medicis, Julia Christine Medicis, Emily Teresa Medicis. BS in Pharmacy, Albany U., NY, 1991; DSc in Pharmacy, St. John's U., 1993. Diplomate Am. Bd. Applied Toxicology, 1996; lic. pharmacist N.Y., 1991. Clin. dir. Upstate Poison Ctr. Upstate Med. U., Syracuse, NY, 1995—. Assoc. prof. Dept. Emergency Medicine, Syracuse, NY. Contbr. articles to profl. jours. Mem.: Am. Acad. Clin. Toxicology (bd. dirs. 2000—03). Office: Upstate NY Poison Center 750 East Adams Street Syracuse NY 13210 Office Phone: 315-464-7078.

**STORK, DONALD ARTHUR,** advertising executive; b. Walsh, Ill., June 17, 1939; s. Arthur William and Katherine Frances (Young) S.; m. Joanna Gentry, June 9, 1962; 1 child, Brian Wesley. BS, So. Ill. U., 1961; postgrad., St. Louis U., 1968—69. With Naegele Outdoor Advt., Mpls. and St. Louis, 1961—63; acct. exec. Richard C. Lynch Advg., 1963—64; media exec. Gardner Advt. Co., 1964—69; v.p. mktg. Advanswers Media/Programming, 1975—79; pres. Advanswers Bur., Wells/BDDP, N.Y.C., 1979—98; pres. Advanswers unit Omnicom, St. Louis, 1998—2002, pres. PHD unit, 2002—04, chmn., 2004; ret., 2004. Bd. dirs. Trailblazers, Inc.; corp. devel. St. Louis Art Mus., 1999—2005; dir. Audit Stds. Media Mgmt., Inc., 2005—. Pres. Signal Hill Sch. Assn. Parents Tchrs. Capt. Mo. Air N.G., 1961-67. Recipient Journalism Alumnus of Yr. award So. Ill. U., Alumni Achievement award. Mem. St. Louis Advtsg. Club, Mensa, Mo. Athletic Club, St. Clair Country Club (bd. dirs. 2001), Alpha Delta Sigma (Aid to Advtg. Edn. award). Home: 27 Symonds Dr Belleville IL 62223-1905 Office: Media Mgmt Inc 14755 N Outer Forty Dr Chesterfield MO 63017 Office Phone: 636-812-0042 x 214. Personal E-mail: dastork@sbcglobal.com.

**STORK, GILBERT,** chemistry professor; b. Brussels, Dec. 31, 1921; s. Jacques and Simone (Weil) Stork; m. Winifred Stewart, June 9, 1944 (dec. May 1992); children: Diana, Linda, Janet, Philip. BS, U. Fla., 1942; PhD, U. Wis., 1945; DSc (hon.), Lawrence Coll., 1961, U. Paris, 1979, U. Rochester, 1982, Emory U., 1988, Columbia U., 1993, U. Wis., 1997. Sr. rsch. chemist Lakeside Labs., 1945—46; instr. chemistry Harvard U., 1946—48, asst. prof., 1948—53; assoc. prof. Columbia U., N.Y.C., 1953—55, prof., 1955—67, Eugene Higgins prof., 1967—92, prof. emeritus, 1992—, chmn. dept., 1973—76. Lectr. and cons. in field; chmn. Gordon Steroid Conf., 1958—59. Recipient Baekeland medal, 1961, Harrison Howe award, 1962, Edward Curtis Franklin Meml. award, Stanford, 1966, Gold medal, Synthetic Chems. Mfrs. Assn., 1971, Nebr. award, 1973, Roussel prize in steroid chemistry, 1978, Edgar Fahs Smith award, 1982, Nat. Medal of Sci., 1982, Linus Pauling award, 1983, Tetrahedron prize, 1985, Remsen award, 1986, Cliff S. Hamilton award, 1986, Mony Ferst award, Sigma Xi, 1987, George Kenner award, 1992, Robert Robinson award, 1992, Chem. Pioneer award, Am. Inst. Chemists, 1992, Welch Found. award in chemistry, 1993, Allan R. Day award, 1994, Wolf prize in chemistry, Wolf Found., Israel, 1996, Phila. Chemists Club award, 1998, Barton Gold medal, U.K., 2002, Ryoji Noyori award, Soc. Synthetic Organic Chemistry Japan, 2003, Eminent Scientists award, Japanese Soc. for the Promotion Sci., 2005; fellow, Guggenheim, 1959. Fellow: NAS (award in chem. sci. 1982), Am. Philos. Soc., Am. Acad. Arts and Scis., Royal Soc., French Acad. Scis., Royal Soc. Chemistry (Barton Gold medal 2002); mem.: Am. Chem. Soc. (chmn. organic chemistry divsn. 1967, award in pure chemistry 1957, award for creative work in synthetic organic chemistry 1967, Nichols medal 1980, Arthur C. Cope award 1980, Willard Gibbs medal 1982, Roger Adams award in organic chemistry 1991, Herbert C. Brown award in organic chemistry 2005), Chem. Soc. Japan (hon.), Pharm. Soc. Japan (hon.), Chemists Club (hon.). Home: 188 Chestnut St Englewood Cliffs NJ 07632-1908 Office: Columbia U Dept Chemistry Chandler Hall New York NY 10027 Office Phone: 212-854-2178. Business E-Mail: gjs8@columbia.edu.

**STORM, HANNAH,** newscaster; b. Oak Pk., Ill., June 13, 1962; B in Polit. Sci. and Comm., U. of Notre Dame, 1983. Sports anchor, reporter KTXH-TV, Houston; Home Sports Entertainment; KNCN-FM Radio, Corpus Christi, Tex., WNDU-TV, South Bend, Ind., 1982—88; sports reporter, anchor WPQC-TV, Charlotte, NC, 1988—89; anchor CNN Sports Tonight, 1989—92; anchor, reporter NBC Sports, 1993—2002; anchor The Early Show, 2002—. Host NBC coverage of the NBA, 1997—2002, NBC coverage of Major League Baseball, 1996—2002, NBC coverage of Major League Baseball World Series, 1995, 97, 99. Author: (sports guide for parents) Go Girl!, 2002. Recipient Gracie Allen award, Am. Women in Radio and TV.

**STORM, J. RENI,** nurse, consultant; d. Edmund Francis and M. Helen (Saltzmann) Corrado; m. John A. Storm, Feb. 14, 1970 (div. Sept. 1990); 1 child, Kierston L Storm-Dubois. AAS in Nursing cum laude, Dutchess C.C., Poughkeepsie, NY, 1978; BS in Health Care Studies, SUNY, New Paltz, 1987; workshop, Scottsdale Sch. for Artists, 2001; MA in Legal and Ethical Studies, U. Balt., 2003. RN NY. Cmty. mental health nurse Dutchess County Dept. Mental Hygiene, Millbrook, NY, 1980—84; nurse Vassar Bros. Hosp., Poughkeepsie, NY, 1984—87; health svc. cons. Empire Blue Cross & Blue Shield, NYC, Albany, Poughkeepsie, 1987—92; cons. nurse III St. Vincent Hosp., Santa Fe, 1992—. Cmty. edn., mental health players NY State Psychiat. Ctr., Poughkeepsie, 1984—86; pvt. practice consulting legal nurse, Santa Fe, 2003—; surveyor trainee Accreditation Assn. for Ambulatory Health Care, Inc. Contbg. editor: (novel) Seas Raging, White Horse Flying; contbg. costume designer The Jungle Book, N.Mex. Ballet, creator (coloring book); exhibitions include 1st Nat. Bank Santa Fe, Limner Gallery, NYC, Santa Fe Soc. Artists, Kiva Gallery; actor: (debut) Inherit the Wind, Agatha Christie's Spider Web (Critical acclaim reviews, 1990); polit. cartoon strip, Udn. Mem. Santa Fe Coun. on Internat. Rels., N.Mex., 2002—03; mem., educator Cmty. Mental Health Players, Poughkeepsie, NY, 1984—86; tutor for cmty. immigrants Literacy Vols., Santa Fe, 2001—02; mem. founding group Santa Fe Living Wage Network, 2003—; rehab. group leader for stroke patients Santa Fe Care Nursing Home, 1999—2000; pres., bd. dirs. Mid Hudson Kennel Club, 1986—88; sponsor World Vision, Rhinebeck, NY, 1989—99; nursing, health care advisor KSK Buddhist Ctr., Santa Fe, 2001—03; AKC judges edn. coord. Mastiff Club Am., Rhinebeck, NY, 1986—88; pres. Dutchess County SPCA, Poughkeepsie, NY, 1986—88; v.p. Santa Fe Soc. Artists, 1997—98. Recipient Cmty. Svc. award for Devel. Contbn., Dutchess County SPCA Bd. Dirs., 1988; scholar, Union Plus, 2002. Mem.: Legal Nurse Consultants (Puget Sound chpt.), Am. Assn. Legal Nurse Cons. Achievements include development of long range plan for community project/Dutchess County SPCA. Avocations: world travel and cultures, cartooning, painting, writing, public speaking. Office Phone: 360-894-0549. Office Fax: 360-894-0549.

**STORM, JANET S.,** psychiatric social worker; b. Indpls. d. Charles R. and Evelyn M. (Seitz) Howard; children: Beth A., Mary J. BSW with high distinction, Ind. U., 1982, MSW, 1984. Cert. ACSW; lic. clin. social worker; lic. marriage and family therapist; cert. diplomate in psychotherapy. Pvt. indsl. social work therapist Supportive Systems Inc., Indpls.; med. social worker Wishard Meml. Hosp., Indpls.; social work cons. State of Ind., Indpls.; psychiat. sr. mental health clinician Community Hosp., Indpls.; pscyhiat. social worker Adult and Child Mental Health Ctr., Indpls.; psychiat. social worker St. Francis Counseing Ctr.; pvt. practice Indpls. Mem. NASW, Sigma Pi Alpha. Home: PO Box 47461 Indianapolis IN 46247-0461 E-mail: sto340@aol.com.

**STORM, SUZANNE,** state representative; b. Spokane, Wash., July 17, 1941; 1 child, Carmen. BA, William Jewell Coll., 1963; MS, U. Kans., 1984. Tchr. pub. schs., 1964—78; tchr. Shawnee Mission, Kans., 1978—; mem. Kans. Ho. of Reps., 1996—. Mem.: Shawnee Mission Edn. Found., Mainstream Coalition, Kans. Nat. Edn. Assn. (bd. dirs.). NEA (pres. 1992—96). Democrat. Baptist. Office: 272-W State Capitol 300 SW 10th Ave Topeka KS 66612 Address: 8145 Mackey Overland Park KS 66204-3121 Business E-Mail: sstorm@sbcglobal.net.

**STÖRMER, HORST LUDWIG,** physicist; b. Frankfurt-Main, Fed. Republic Germany, Apr. 6, 1949; arrived in U.S., 1977; s. Karl-Ludwig and Marie (Ihrig) S.; m. Dominique A. Parchet, 1982. Studied Physics, JW Goethe Univ.; PhD, U. Stuttgart, 1977. From tech. staff to dir. phys. rsch. lab. AT&T Bell Labs., Murray Hill, NJ, 1977—97; prof. physics and applied physics Columbia U., NYC, 1998—. Adj. physics dir. Lucent Tech., 1997—. Decorated Officier de la Legion d'Honneur France, Grosses Verdienstkreuz Mit Stern Germany; recipient Otto Klung prize, 1985, Benjamin Franklin medal in physics, 1998, Nobel prize in Physics, 1998, N.Y.C. Mayor's award for excellence in sci. and tech., 2000; fellow Bell Labs., 1983. Fellow: NAS, Am. Acad. Arts and Scis., Am. Phys. Soc. (Buckley prize 1984). Office: Columbia U Dept Physics 538 W 120th St New York NY 10027-6601 also: Lucent Technologies 700 Mountain Ave New Providence NJ 07974-1208*

**STORMER, JOHN ANTHONY,** retired minister, writer, publisher; b. Altoona, Pa., Feb. 9, 1928; s. Regis Walter and Mary Ann (Forr) S.; m. Elizabeth Ruth Lewis, July 2, 1951; 1 child, Holly. BS in Journalism, San Jose (Calif.) State U., 1954; DLitt (hon.), Manahath Sch. Theology, Hollidaysburg, Pa., 1965; LittD (hon.), Shelton Coll., 1976. Ordained to ministry Bapt. Ch., 1968. Pastor Heritage Bapt. Ch., Florissant, Mo., 1968-86; supt. Faith Christian Acad., Florissant, 1968—99; owner Liberty Bell Press, Florissant, 1963—. Bd. dirs. Internat. Coun. Christian Chs., 1965-87; dir. I Chronicles 12:32 Ministry, Florissant, 1985—; leader bible studies for legislators, Jefferson City, Mo., 1977—. Author: None Dare Call It Treason, 1964, The Death of a Nation, 1968, Growing of God's Way, 1984, NDCIT—25 Years Later, 1990, None Dare Call It Education, 1999, Betrayed by the Bench, 2005. Mem. rep. state com., state chmn. Mo. Young Reps., 1962-64, state del. Rep. Nat. Conv., San Francisco, 1964; tchr. legis. bible studies Mo. State Capital, Jefferson City, Mo., 1977—. With USAF, 1950-53. Mem. Coun. for Nat. Policy, Am. legion, Rotary Internat. Office: PO Box 32 Florissant MO 63033 Office Phone: 314-838-1477. *Through the resurrected life of the Lord Jesus Christ, individuals who have received Him have everything they need to be and do all that God the Father calls them to.*

**STORMES, JOHN MAX,** systems analyst; b. Manila, Oct. 7, 1927; s. Max Clifford and Janet (Heldring) S.; m. Takako Sanae, July 29, 1955; children: Janet Kazuko Stormes-Pepper, Alan Osamu. BS, San Diego State U., 1950; BA, U. So. Calif., 1957, MA, 1967. Cert. secondary and community coll. tchr., sr. profl. human resources. Editing supr. Lockheed Propulsion Co., Redlands, Calif., 1957-61; proposals supr. Rockwell Internat., Downey, Calif., 1961-62; publs. dir. Arthur D. Little, Inc., Santa Monica, Calif., 1962-63; publs. coord. Rockwell Internat., Downey, 1963-68; project dir. Gen. Behavioral Systems, Inc., Torrance, Calif., 1969-73; tng. and comm. cons. Media Rsch. Assocs., Santa Cruz, Calif., 1973—; instrl. design supr. So. Calif. Gas Co., L.A., 1985-2001; adj. assoc. prof. Alliant U., Alhambra, Calif., 2001—02. Lectr. Calif. State U., Northridge, 1991-2003; tng. cons. Nat. Ednl. Media, Chatsworth, Calif., 1966-81, comm. cons. Mission Rsch. Calif., Long Beach, 1974-. Co-author: TV Communications Systems For Business and Industry, 1970; contbg. author: ASTD's In Action series of casebooks, 1996-99. Curriculum adv. bd. communications dept. Calif. State U., Fullerton, 1964-78. Sgt. U.S. Army, 1953-55, Japan. Mem. Soc. Tech. Communication (sr. mem., 2nd v.p. Orange County chpt. 1962-63), Internat. Soc. Performance and Instruction (v.p. L.A. chpt. 1989, pres. 1990). Democrat. Episcopal. Avocations: photography, sailing. Home and Office: 136 Alamo Ave Santa Cruz CA 95060 Personal E-mail: jmstormes@comcast.net.

**STORMONT, RICHARD MANSFIELD,** hotel executive; b. Chgo., Apr. 4, 1936; s. Daniel Lytle and E. Mildred (Milligan) S.; m. Virginia Louellen Walters, Nov. 21, 1959; children: Stacy Lee Freeman, Richard Mansfield, John Frederick. BS, Cornell U., 1958. Cert. hosp. adminstrn.; cert. hosps. industry profl. Food cost analyst, sales rep. Edgewater Beach Hotel, Chgo., 1957-58; asst. sales mgr. Marriott Hotels, Inc., Washington, 1962-64, dir. sales Atlanta, 1964-68, resident mgr., 1969-71; gen. mgr. Marriott Hotel, Dallas, 1971-73, Phila., 1973-74, Atlanta, 1974-79; pres. Hardin Mgmt. Co., 1979-80; v.p. Marriott Franchise div. Marriott Corp., Washington, 1980-83, v.p. ops. Courtyard by Marriott, 1981-83; pres. The Stormont Cos. Inc., 1984—2004; chmn. Stormont Trice Corp., 1993-2000, Stormont Noble Devel. LLC, 2004—06; pres. The Stormont Cos., LLC, 2004—. Pres. Atlanta Conv. and Visitors Burs., 1975-76, vice chmn. bd., 1976-77, chmn., 1998-99, chmn. bd. exec. com., 1998-2000; trustee Young Harris Coll.; bd. dirs. Better Bus. Bur.; exec. com. Ctrl. Atlanta Progress, 1979-80; exec. coun. Boy Scouts Am.; bd. dirs., chmn. tourism divsn. Ga. Dept. Industry, Trade and Tourism, 1999-2001; trustee Lenbrook Square Found., Inc., 2003—05, vice chmn., 2005-06; chmn. bd. dirs. Atlanta St. Patricks Day Found., 2005-06. Recipient Disting. Salesman of Yr. award Marriott, 1967, Obi T. Brewer award for Decade of Outstanding Svc., 1979, Atlanta Hospitality Hall of Fame award, 2006. Mem. Sales and Mktg. Execs. (exec. v.p. 1969-70, pres. Atlanta 1970-71), Am. Hotel-Motel Assn. (exec. com., bd. dirs. 1993-95, Most Valuable Vol. Ga. 1999), Ga. Hospitality and Travel Assn. (founder 1975, bd. dir., pres. 1989-90, chmn. bd. 1991-92, Hotelier of Yr. award 1977, Hall of Fame 2001), Ga. Bus. and Industry Assn. (bd. dirs.), Atlanta Hotel Assn. (pres. 1976), So. Innkeepers Assn., Atlanta C. of C. (v.p. 1978-79), Gwinnett C. of C. (bd. dirs.), Cornell Soc. Hotelmen (pres. Ga. chpt. 1976, regional v.p. 1989-91), Cornell U. Hotel Soc. (SE Hotelier of Yr.), Rotary Club of Atlanta (chmn. program com. 1998, bd. dirs. 1999-2002, chmn. membership com., 2003, alt. sec. 2004-05, bd. dirs. 2005—, Paul Harris fellow Rotary Internat., 2003, pres.-elect). Home and Office: 2980 Nancy Creek Rd NW Atlanta GA 30327-2000 Office Phone: 404-355-4038. E-mail: dstormont@bellsouth.net.

**STORMS, CLIFFORD BEEKMAN,** lawyer; b. Mount Vernon, NY, July 18, 1932; s. Harold Beekman and Gene (Pertak) S.; m. Barbara H. Grave, 1955 (div. 1975); m. Valeria N. Parker, July 12, 1975; children: Catherine Fitamis Fischer, Clifford Beekman. BA magna cum laude, Amherst Coll., 1954; LLB, Yale U., 1957. Bar: N.Y. 1957. Assoc. Breed, Abbott & Morgan, NYC, 1957—64; with CPC Internat., Inc., Englewood Cliffs, NJ, 1964—97, v.p. legal affairs, 1975-78, v.p., gen. counsel, 1975—88, sr. v.p., gen. counsel, 1988—97, atty. alternate dispute resolution, corp. dir., 1997—; bd. dirs. Corn Products Internat. Inc., 1997—2005; pvt. practice Greenwich, Conn., 1997—. Bd. dirs. Atlantic Legal Found., Indian Harbor Yacht Club; mem. Conn. Alternate Dispute Resolution panel Ctr. Pub. Resources. Trustee emeritus Food and Drug Law Inst. Mem. ABA (com. of corp. gen. counsel), Am. Arbitration Assn. (panel arbitrators large complex case program), Assn. Gen. Counsel (pres. 1992-94), Assn. Bar City NY (sec., com. on law depts. 1979-81), Phi Beta Kappa. Home: 19 Burying Hill Rd Greenwich CT 06831-2604 Office: Ste 100 Two Sound View Dr Greenwich CT 06830 Office Phone: 203-622-4995. Personal E-mail: cbstorms@aol.com.

**STORPER, DAVID H.,** bank executive; b. N.Y.C., Aug. 27, 1965; s. Stanley Arnold and Vivian Cecile (Schwartz) S. BS in Applied Math., Columbia U., 1987, MBA in Acctg./Fin., 1989. Corp. banking officer Wells Fargo Bank, N.Y.C., L.A.'s. rsch. analyst Libra Investments, Credit Suisse First Boston Corp.; mng. dir. WL Ross LLC, N.Y.C.; mng. dir., 2000—. mem. Tau Beta Pi. Office: WL Ross & Co LLC Manhattan Tower 101 E 52nd St New York NY 10022

**STORR, ROBERT,** curator, art educator, painter; b. Portland, Maine, Dec. 28, 1949; s. Richard J. and Virginia V. Storr; m. Rosamund Helen Morley, Sept. 1, 1979; children: Katharine, Susannah. BA, Swarthmore Coll., 1972; postgrad., Sch. Art Inst. of Chgo., 1975-78; MFA, Skowhegan (Maine) Sch. Painting and Sculpture, 1978. Assoc. dean N.Y. Studio Sch., NYC, 1987-88; asst. prof. Tyler Sch. Art, Phila., 1989; Avery prof. Bard Coll., Annandale On Hudson, NY, 1990-91; sr. curator painting and sculpture Mus. Modern Art, NYC, 1991—2002; Rosalie Solow prof. of modern art NYU Inst. of Fine Arts, NYC, 2002—06; dean Sch. Art Yale Univ., New Haven, 2006—. Vis. artist Cooper Union, NYC, 1988-89; vis. artist, critic R.I. Sch. Design, Providence, 1988; lectr. art mus., univs. and art schs. in U.S. and abroad; coordinating curator at Moma, 1995. Author: Philip Guston, 1986; co-author: Chuck Close, 1987, (with Lawrence Hudson) Susan Rothenberg 15 Years a Survey, 1990, (with Kirk Varnedoe) From Bauhaus to Pop: Masterworks Given By Phillip Johnson, 1996; also exhbn. catalogues; contbg. editor Art in Am.;

mem. editorial bd. Art Jour.; contbr. articles to profl. jours.; exhibitions include Inst. Contemporary Art Phila., 1991, Moma, 1991, 93, 94, 95, 96. Penny McCall Found. grantee, 1988, Peter Norton Family Found. grantee, 1990. Mem. Internat. Assn. Art Critics. Office: Yale Univ Sch Art Holcombe T Green Jr Hall 1156 Chapel St New Haven CT 06511-8921*

**STORRER, WILLIAM ALLIN,** theater educator, consultant; b. Highland Park, Mich., Mar. 22, 1936; s. Fredrick Ray and Margaret Ann (Pitts) S.; m. Carol A. Tuthill, Nov. 6, 1964 (div. June 1969); 1 child, Kirsten; m. Patricia Alice Whalley Dec. 30, 1976. Student, Albion Coll., 1954-56; AB in Engring. Scis., Harvard U., 1959; MFA in Theatre Arts, Boston U., 1962; PhD in Comparative Arts, Ohio U., 1968. Electronics engr. Raytheon Co., Wayland, Mass., 1958-60; tech. dir. small stage Boston Arts Festival, 1961, 62; dir. dramatics Melrose (Mass.) H.S., 1962-63; dir. playhouse and repertory theatre, instr. drama-speech Hofstra U., 1963-66, instr. opera, 1965; asst. prof. theatre, dir. univ. theatre, U. Toledo, 1968-69; assoc. prof. radio and t.v., dir. Southampton Coll., L.I. U., 1969-73; asst. cinema studies and still photography Ithaca (N.Y.) Coll., 1973-76; assoc. prof. media arts U. S.C., Columbia, 1976-82; pres. MINDaLIVE Creative Mind Enhancement, Newark, 1980—. Assoc. prof. theater and speech World Campus Afloat, Chapman Coll., 1972; edn. media specialist Newark Bd. Edn., 1990-94, Linden Bd. Edn., 1994-95, Harrison Bd. Edn., 1995-96, Rosa Parks Fine and Performing Arts H.S., Paterson, N.J., 1996-2004, dir. Storrer/Storre/Storer Family Inst., adj. prof. U. Tex., 2004—. Author: The Architecture of Frank Lloyd Wright, 1974, 3d edit. 2002, The Frank Lloyd Wright Companion, 1993, 2 edit., 2006; contbr. articles to popular mags. and profl. jours. Grantee Graham Found. for Advanced Studies in Fine Arts, 1987, 94. Home: Frankfort MI 49635-1121 Office: PO Box 1121 Frankfort MI 49635 Office Phone: 231-352-9343.

**STORRS, ELEANOR EMERETT,** science administrator, consultant; b. Cheshire, Conn., May 3, 1926; d. Benjamin Porter and Alta Hyde (Moss) S.; m. Harry Phineas Burchfield, Jr., Nov. 29, 1963; children: Sarah Storrs, Benjamin Hyde. BS with distinction in Botany, U. Conn., 1948; MS in Biology, NYU, 1958; PhD in Chemistry, U. Tex., 1967. Asst. biochemist Boyce Thompson Inst. for Plant Rsch., Yonkers, NY, 1948-62; rsch. scientist Clayton Found. Biochem. Inst., U. Tex., Austin, 1962-65; biochemist Pesticides Rsch. Lab., USPHS, Perrine, Fla., 1965-67; dir. dept. biochemistry Gulf South Rsch. Inst., New Iberia, La., 1967-77; adj. prof. chemistry U. Southwestern La., Lafayette, 1974-77; rsch. prof. biology Fla. Inst. Tech., Melbourne, 1977-94, cons. on leprosy-armadillo programs, 1975-94, mem. Faculty Senate, 1979-84, prof. emeritus, 1994—. Cons. in rehab. and prevention deformities leprosy Pan Am. Health Orgn., WHO, Venezuela, Argentina, Brazil, Mex., 1972-90; dep. v.p. Coll. Hansenology in Endemic Countries, 1980-85 Author: (with H.P. Burchfield) Biochemical Applications of Gas Chromatography, 1962, (with Burchfield, D.E. Johnson) Guide to the Analysis of Pesticide Residues, 2 vols, 1965; also articles, book chpts. Grantee NIH, 1968-88, CDC, 1969-73, WHO, 1973-93, Leprosy Program, 1978-93, German Leprosy Relief Assn., 1973-78, Nat. Coun. Episc. Ch., 1975-77, Brit. Leprosy Relief Assn., 1981-88; recipient plaque La. Health Dept., 1972, Disting. Alumni award U. Conn., 1975, Gold award Am. Coll. Pathologists and Am. Soc. Clin. Pathologists, 1974, Gerard B. Lambert award for spl. recognition, 1975. Fellow AAAS; mem. AAUW, Internat. Leprosy Assn., Am. Recorder Soc., Early Music Assn., Sigma Xi. Episcopalian (vestryman). Clubs: Appalachian (Boston); Green Mountain (Bear Mountain, N.Y.). Achievements include pioneering devel. leprosy in exptl. animal (armadillo) reproduction. Home: 72 Riverview Ter Melbourne FL 32903-4640 *Children display interests early in their lives, and in my life, this early interest - in animals, and the beauty of nature - is one which I have never lost, but one which seems to become more important now with the passing of years. Parents can help mold a child, but should mold the child in the child's interests as my parents did, not in a mold designed by them.*

**STORTZ, THOMAS C.,** lawyer, communications executive; b. Apr. 11, 1951; m. Diane Stortz; children: Tara Lynne, Troy. BBA, U. Iowa; JD, Creighton U. Bar: Nebr. 1976. Atty. Peter Kiewit Sons', Inc., 1981—91, v.p., gen. counsel, 1991—98, Kiewit Constrn. Group, Inc., 1991—98; sr. v.p., gen. counsel, sec. Level 3 Comm., Inc., 1998—2000, group v.p., gen. counsel, sec., 2000—04, exec. v.p., chief legal officer, sec., 2004—. Office: Level 3 Comm Inc 1025 Eldorado Blvd Broomfield CO 80021

**STORY, BERNARD J,** academic administrator; b. Bethlehem, Pa., Feb. 1, 1958; s. Bernard J. and Eleanor Story; m. Margaret A. Bartos, July 23, 1958; children: Mary Katherine, Michael, Allison. BA, Moravian Coll., 1980. Secondary Instructional Commonwealth of Pa., 1980. Dean of admissions and fin. aid Moravian Coll., Bethlehem, Pa., 1987—97, v.p. for enrollment, 1997—. Cons. The Coll. Bd., NYC, 1990—. Pres. Boys and Girls Club, Bethlehem, Pa., 1985—2006. Recipient William Harris award of Excellence, The Coll. Bd., 2004. Mem.: Coll. Bd. (chair, mid. states regional coun. 2000—03), Pa. Assn. of Coll. Admission Counseling, Nat. Assn. of Coll. Admission Counseling. Avocations: travel, golf, writing. Office: Moravian Coll 1200 Main St Bethlehem PA 18018 Office Phone: 610-861-1320.

**STORY, JOAN H.,** lawyer; b. Parsons, Kans., Feb. 7, 1944; AB, Occidental Coll., 1965; MA, UCLA, 1968; JD, U. Calif., Davis 1977. Bar: Calif. 1977. Ptnr., mem. exec. com. Sheppard, Mullin, Richter & Hampton LLP, San Francisco. Co-chair Calif. adv. bd. Trust for Pub. Land. Volume editor U. Calif. at Davis Law Rev., 1976-77. Mem. alumni bd. govs. Occidental Coll., 1982-85. Mem.: Practicing Law Inst. (real estate law adv. com.), Am. Coll. Real Estate Lawyers, Bar Assn. San Francisco, State Bar Calif. (mem. real property law sect.), U. Calif. Davis Law Sch. Alumni Assn. (bd. dirs.), Lambda Alpha. Office: Sheppard, Mullin, Richter & Hampton LLP 17 Fl Four Embarcadero Ctr San Francisco CA 94111 Office Phone: 415-774-3211. Office Fax: 415-434-3947. E-mail: jstory@sheppardmullin.com.

**STORY, JULIE ANN,** language educator; b. Muncy, Pa., Aug. 6, 1959; d. Phillip Mason Story and Mary Lee Peters. BA in English, Lock Haven U., 1982; MA in English, Ind. U. Pa., 1984. Assoc. dir. undergraduate writing ctr., lectr. English Pa. State U., U. Pk., 1987—2003; English instr. Juniata Coll., Huntingdon, Pa., 1987—89; dir. writing ctr., writing specialist Lock Haven U., Pa., 1998, 2003—. Internship coord. writing ctr. Pa. State U., University Park; cons. in field; faculty advisor Dangling Modifier. Mem. Pa. State Commn. for Women, University Park. Grantee, Ctr. Excellence Learning and Tchg., 2001. Mem.: NOW, Nat. Coun. Tchrs. English, Conf. Coll. Composition Comm., Ctrl. Pa. Writing Ctrs. Assn. (bd. dirs.), Nat. Conf. Peer Tutoring in Writing (adv. bd.), Mid-Atlantic Writing Ctrs. Assn. (bd. dirs.), Internat. Writing Ctrs. Assn., Phi Kappa Phi, Sigma Tau Delta. Democrat. Avocations: gardening, walking, photography, reading, movies. Home: 33 Julia Dr Lock Haven PA 17745 Office: Lock Haven Univ Pa 19 Russell Hall Lock Haven PA 17745 Business E-Mail: jstory@lhup.edu.

**STORY, TIMOTHY KEVIN (TIM STORY),** film director; b. LA, Mar. 13, 1970; married; 1 child. Grad., U. So. Calif. Dir.: (films) One of Us Tripped, 1997, Barbershop, 2002, Taxi, 2004, Fantastic Four, 2005; dir., co-editor, writer (films) The Firing Squad, 1999, writer Urban Menace, 1999; prodr., dir.: (TV series) Standoff, 2006; The 12th Man, 2006.*

**STOSS, FREDERICK WARREN,** librarian, educator; b. Gloversville, NY, Aug. 12, 1950; s. Dayton Robert and Katherine Gretchen (Ruzicka) Stoss; m. Dorothy Katherine Holderle, Aug. 24, 1974; 1 child, Kaeti Elizabeth. BA in Biology, Hartwick Coll., 1972; MS in Zoology, SUNY, Brockport, 1974; MLS, Syracuse U., 1982. Tech. rsch. assoc. U. Rochester Med. Ctr., NY, 1974—78; rsch. assoc. Syracuse Rsch. Corp., 1978—82; libr. dir. Ctr. for Environ. Info., Rochester, 1982—90; rsch. assoc. U. Tenn., Knoxville, 1990—96; scis. libr. U. Buffalo, 1996—. Lab. instr. U. Rochester, 1975—78; adj. lectr. Syracuse U., 1983—85; vis. lectr. U. Buffalo, 1997—2002; mem. editl. adv. bd. Environment Abstracts, 1988—, Electronic Green Jour., 1990—, Counterpoise, 1999—2005. Assoc. editor: Information Resources in Toxicology, 2001. Pres. Seth Green chpt. Trout Unlimited, Rochester,

1989—90; mem. spkrs. bur. Susquahanna River Basin Commn., 2005—; mem. panel on environment Rochester Dem. and Chronicle Readers, 2005—. Mem.: ALA (chair task force on the environment 1995—99, coord. social responsibilities round table 1999—2002, OLOS adv. com. 2003—06, STS/ACRL cont. edn. subcom. co-chair 2005—, publ. com. 2005—, team trainer Librs. Build Sustainable Cmtys. Team), N.Y. State Outdoor Edn. Assn., Spl. Librs. Assn. (chair environ. info. divsn. 1988, pres. So. Appalachian chpt. 1994—95, Outstanding Divsn. Mem. award, Environ. Resource Mgmt. divsn., Environment and Resource Mgmt. Divsn. 1994), Nat. Sci. Tchrs. Assn., N.Y. Libr. Assn., SUNY Libr. Assn., Sierra Club (chair environ. edn. com. 2001—06), Sigma Xi (Outstanding Grad. Rsch. award 1974). Democrat. Lutheran. Avocations: fly fishing, nature photography. Office: Univ Buffalo Sci Eng Libr 228-B Capen Hall Buffalo NY 14260 Office Phone: 716-645-2947 ext. 224. Business E-Mail: fstoss@buffalo.edu.

**STOSSEL, JOHN,** news analyst; BA in Psychology, Princeton U., 1969. Prodr., reporter Sta. KGW-TV, Portland, Oreg.; consumer editor WCBS-TV, N.Y.C., Good Morning Am.; consumer corr. 20/20, 1981—, ABC news corr. Weekly consumer reporter ABC Radio Info. Network, Author: Shopping Smart: The Only Consumer Guide You'll Ever Need, 1980, Give Me a Break, 2004, Myths, Lies and Downright Stupidity: Get Out the Shovel--Why Everything You Know Is Wrong, 2006. Recipient 19 Emmy awards, 5 awards for Excellence in Consumer Reporting Nat. Press Club, award Nat. Environment Devel. Assn., award Retirement Rshc. Found., George Polk award Outstanding Local Radio and Television Reporting. Office: 20/20 147 Columbus Ave Fl 8 New York NY 10023-5900*

**STOSSEL, SCOTT HANFORD,** editor, writer; b. Boston, Aug. 7, 1969; s. Thomas Peter and Anne (Hanford) Stossel; m. Susanna Joy Pueschel, July 1, 2000. BA, Harvard Coll., 1991. Spl. projects editor Atlantic Monthly, Boston, 1992-93, staff editor, 1993-96, editl. dir. new media, 1994-96; assoc. editor The Am. Prospect, Cambridge, Mass., 1996-97, exec. editor, 1997—2002; sr. editor The Atlantic Monthly, Boston, 2002, mng. editor Washington, 2006—. Contbr. columns in newspapers; contbr. The New Yorker, The New Republic; author: (biography) Sarge: The Life and Times of Sargent Shriver, 2004. Mem. Harvard Club Boston, Belmont Hill Club. Episcopalian. Avocations: tennis, squash, soccer, basketball. Office: The Atlantic Monthly The Watergate 600 New Hampshire Ave NW Washington DC 20037*

**STOSSEL, THOMAS PETER,** medical educator, researcher, director; b. Chgo., Sept. 10, 1941; m. Kerry Maguire, 1997. AB, Princeton U., 1963; MD, Harvard U., 1967; MD (hon.), U. Linkoping, Sweden, 1989, U. Geneva, 2004. Diplomate Am. Bd. Internal Medicine. Ho. staff medicine Mass. Gen. Hosp., Boston, 1967-69, chief hematology-oncology, 1976-90; staff assoc. NIH, Bethesda, Md., 1967-71; fellow to sr. assoc. Med. Ctr. Children's Hosp., Boston, 1971-76; prof. medicine Harvard Med. Sch., Boston, 1982—; chief divsn. exptl. medicine Brigham Women's Hosp., Boston, 1991—, co-dir. hematology divsn., 1991—. Sci. bd. Biogen Corp., 1987—2002, Dyax Corp., 1996—2002; clin. rsch. prof. Am. Cancer Soc., 1987—; bd. dirs. Zymequest, Inc. Author (with B. Babior): (book) 2d edit., 1984, Hematology, A Pathophysiological Approach, 1994; editor (with R. Handin and S. Lux): Blood, Principles & Practice of Hematology, 1995, 2d edit., 2003; contbr. articles to profl. jours. Bd. dirs. Am. Coun. Sci. and Health, 2006—. Lt. comdr. USPHS, 1969—71. Mem.: NAS, Am. Acad. Arts and Scis., Assn. Am. Physicians, Am. Soc. Cell Biology, Am. Soc. Hematology (pres. 1997, Damashek prize 1983, Thomas prize 1993), Am. Soc. Clin. Investigation (pres. 1987), Am. Fedn. Clin. Rsch., Inst. Medicine. Achievements include patents in field. Office: Brigham & Womens Hosp Karp 625 1 Blackfan Cir Boston MA 02115 Office Phone: 617-355-9001. Business E-Mail: tstossel@rics.bwh.harvard.edu.

**STOTLAR, DOUGLAS W.,** transportation executive; b. Newbury, Ohio; BS, Ohio State Univ. Freight ops. supr. through regional mgr. Con-Way Transp. Svcs., Ann Arbor, Mich., 1985—96, v.p., gen mgr. Con-Way NOW, 1996—99, exec. v.p. ops., 1999—2002, exec. v.p., COO, 2002—04, pres., CEO, 2004—05, CNF Inc., Palo Alto, Calif., 2005—. V.p., mem. exec. com. Am. Trucking Assn.; bd. dir. Am. Transp. Rsch. Inst. Office: Cnf Inc 2855 Campus Dr Ste 300 San Mateo CA 94403-2512*

**STOTLER, ALICEMARIE HUBER,** federal judge; b. Alhambra, Calif., May 29, 1942; d. James R. and Loretta M. Huber; m. James Allen Stotler, Sept. 11, 1971. BA, U. So. Calif., 1964, JD, 1967. Bar: Calif. 1967, U.S. Dist. Ct. (no. dist.) Calif. 1967, U.S. Dist. Ct. (ctrl. dist.) Calif. 1973, U.S. Supreme Ct. 1976; cert. criminal law specialist. Dep. Orange County Dist. Attys. Office, 1967-73; mem. Stotler & Stotler, Santa Ana, Calif., 1973-76, 83-84; judge Orange County Mcpl. Ct., 1976-78, Orange County Superior Ct., 1978-83, U.S. Dist. Ct. (ctrl. dist.) Calif., L.A., 1984—. Assoc. dean Calif. Trial Judges Coll., 1982; lectr., panelist, numerous orgns.; standing com. on rules of practice and procedure U.S. Jud. Conf., 1991-98, chair, 1993-98; chair 9th cir. Pub. Info. and Cmty. Outreach, 2000-04; mem. exec. com. 9th Cir. Jud. Conf., 1989-93, Fed. State Jud. Coun., 1989-98, jury com., 1990-92, planning com. for Nat. Conf. on Fed.-State Jud. Relationships, Orlando, 1991-92, planning com. for We. Regional Conf. on State-Fed. Jud. Relationships, Stevens, Wash., 1992-93; chair dist. ct. symposium and jury utilization Ctrl. Dist. Calif., 1985, chair atty. liaison, 1989-90, chair U.S. Constn. Bicentennial com., 1986-91, chair magistrate judge com., 1992-93; mem. State Adv. Group on Juvenile Justice and Delinquency Prevention, 1983-84, Bd. Legal Specializations Criminal Law Adv. Commn., 1983-84, victim/witness adv. com. Office Criminal Justice Planning, 1980-83, U. So. Calif. Bd. Councilors, 1993-2001; active team in rcsp. Leukemia Soc. Am., 1993, 95, 97, 2000; legion lex bd. dirs. U. So. Calif. Sch. Law Support Group, 1981-83. Winner Hale Moot Ct. Competition, State of Calif., 1967; named Judge of Yr., Orange County Trial Lawyers Assn., 1978, Most Outstanding Judge Orange County Bus. Litig. Sect., 1990. Mem. ABA (jud. adminstrn. divsn. and litig. sect. 1984—, nat. conf. fed. trial judges com. on legis. affairs 1990-91), Am. Law Inst., Am. Judicature Soc., Fed. Judges Assn. (bd. dirs. 1989-92), Nat. Assn. Women Judges, U.S. Supreme Ct. Hist. Soc., Ninth Cir. Dist. Judges Assn., Calif. Supreme Ct. Hist. Soc., Orange County Bar Assn. (mem. numerous coms., Franklin G. West award 1984), Calif. Judges Assn. (mem. com. on jud. coll. 1978-80, com. on civil law and procedure 1980-82, Dean's coll. curriculum commn. 1981), Calif. Judges Found. Office: Ronald Reagan Fed Bldg & Courthouse 411 W 4th St Santa Ana CA 92701-4500 Office Phone: 714-338-4730.

**STOTLER, EDITH ANN,** retired grain company executive; b. Champaign, Ill., Oct. 11, 1946; d. Kenneth Wagner and Mary (Odebrecht) S. Student, Mary Baldwin Coll., 1964-66; BA, U. Ill., 1968. Asst. v.p. Harris Trust and Savs. Bank, Chgo., 1969-83; mgr. Can. Imperial Bank of Commerce, Chgo., 1983, sr. mgr., 1983-85, asst. gen. mgr. group head, 1985-88, v.p., dir. utilities, 1988-90; ptnr. Stotler Grain Co., Champaign, Ill., 1990—2002; pres. Homer Grain Co., Champaign, 1990-2000; pres., bd. dirs. S&I Grain Co., 1990-2000, SEMCO Energy Inc., 1987—2004. Bd. dirs., audit com., fin. com. SEMCO Energy Inc.; compensation com. Strategic Capital Bancorp, Inc., 2002—03. Past pres. liberal arts and scis. constituent bd., mem. pres.'s coun. U. Ill.; trustee, mem. fin. com. Countryside Sch., 1997—2000; dean's bus. coun. and exec. com. U. Ill. Bus. Coll., 1998—2005; bd. dirs. Champaign County YMCA, 2000—03; bd. dirs., treas. bd., chair investment and fin. coms. Champaign Pub. Libr. Found.; past mem. investment com., bd. trustees 4th Presbyn. Ch.; bd. dirs Spurlock Mus., Urbana. Mem.: U. Ill. Found., Art Club (past pres., v.p.), Krannert Art Mus. Coun., Champaign Country Club (chair house com.), U. Ill. Found., Book Club. Avocations: needlepoint, reading, tennis, golf, cooking. Home: 1010 W Clark Champaign IL 61821

**STOTT, BRIAN,** software company executive, consultant; b. Eccles, Eng., Aug. 5, 1941; came to U.S., 1983; s. Harold and Mary (Stephens) S.; m. Patricia Ann Farrar, Dec. 3, 1983. BSc, Manchester U., 1962, MSc, 1963, PhD, 1971. Asst. prof. Mid. East Tech. U., Ankara, Turkey, 1965—68; lectr. Inst. Sci. and Tech., U. Manchester, England, 1968—74; assoc. prof. U. Waterloo, Ont., Canada, 1974—76; cons. Electric Energy Rsch. Ctr. Brazil, Rio de Janeiro, 1976—83; prof. Ariz. State U., Tempe, 1983—84; chmn.

Power Computer Applications Corp., Mesa, Ariz., 1984—2000; pres. Stott Inc. Cons. in field. Contbr. numerous articles to rsch. publs. Fellow IEEE (Millennium medal); mem. NAE. Home and Office: 10222E Southwind Lane #1004 Scottsdale AZ 85262 Business E-Mail: brianstott@ieee.org.

**STOTT, DON S.,** precious metals products executive; b. Washington, Feb. 17, 1934; s. Marion McClelland Stott and Mabelle Louise (Maidem) Vanice; m. Dorothy Greene, June 21, 1962 (div.); children: David Michael, Melissa Ann; m. Bonnie Jean Peltomen, Dec. 4, 2002. Owner DS Theatres, DC and Phila., 1956—67; Bijou Iced Creme Parlours, Phila., 1967—71; hotel owner Wyman, Alma House and Grand Imperial Hotels, Silverton, Colo., 1971—94; pres. Colo. Gold, Montrose, 1977—. Author: Where the Mountains Meet the Sky, Three Feet to Silverton, Trails Among the Columbines, Consequences, numerous newspaper columns. Past pres. Montrose Hist. Soc., Valley Symphony, Kiwanis Club, Early Words Toastmasters, Am. Theatre Organ Soc., Silverton C. of C.; bd. dirs. Ariz. Opera. Republican. Avocations: trains, antiques, architecture. E-mail: gold@gwe.net.

**STOTT, GRADY BERNELL,** lawyer; b. Bailey, N.C., Sept. 19, 1921; s. William Willard and Zettie Harriett (Bissette) S.; m. Mays Beal, May 9, 1952; children: Sue J., Caroline Beal. AB, Duke U., 1947, JD, 1952. Bar: N.C. 1952. Dist. atty. 27th Jud. Dist., Gastonia, NC, 1957-62; partner firm Stott, Hollowell, Palmer & Windham, Gastonia, 1960—. Served with USMC, 1943-48. Fellow Am. Bar Found., Am. Coll. Trial Lawyers; mem. N.C. State Bar (pres. 1978-79), Am. Bar Assn. (del. 1980), N.C. Bar Assn., Assn. Ins. Attys. Clubs: Masons. Democrat. Methodist. Office: 401 E Franklin Blvd Gastonia NC 28054-7152 Office Phone: 704-846-3425. Personal E-mail: gbs@shpw.com.

**STOTT, PETER WALTER,** investment company executive; b. Spokane, Wash., May 26, 1944; s. Walter Joseph and Rellalee (Gray) S.; m. Julie L. Neupert, Oct. 12, 1996; 1 child, Preston. Student, Portland State U., 1962-63, 65-68, U. Americas, Mexico City, 1964-65. Founder, bd. chmn. emeritus Market Transport Ltd., Portland, Oreg., 1969—2006; pres. Columbia Investments, Ltd., Portland, 2005—; vice chmn., prin. ScanlanKemperBard Cos., Portland, 2005—. Pres., CEO, prin. Crown Pacific, 1988-2004; bd. dirs. Con-Way Inc. Mem. pres.'s adv. bd. for athletics Portland State U., mem. cabinet Building Our Future campaign; trustee Portland Art Mus.; founding bd. dirs. Crater Lake Nat. Park Trust. With USAR, 1966-72. Mem. Nat. Football Found. and Hall of Fame, Oreg. Sports Hall of Fame (lifetime), Stop Oreg. Litter and Vandalism (founders' circle), Arlington Club, Mazamas Club, Multnomah Athletic Club, Portland Golf Club, The Racquet Club, Univ. Club, Waverly Country Club, Valley Club. Republican. Roman Catholic. Office: Columbia Investments Ltd Ste 2600 1211 SW Fifth Ave Portland OR 97204 Business E-Mail: peter.stott@cipdx.com.

**STOTTER, HARRY SHELTON,** banker, lawyer; b. N.Y.C., Aug. 28, 1928; s. Jack and Adele Stotter; m. Marilyn H. Knight, Nov. 7, 1954; children: Jeffrey Craig, Cheryl dee. Student, L.I. U., 1948-49; JD, St. John's U., 1952; postgrad., NYU Law Sch., 1956-57. Bar: N.Y. 1952, N.J. 1974, U.S. Supreme Ct. 1983. Pvt. practice in, N.Y.C., 1952-53, 54-56; atty. U.S. Dept. Def., 1953; with trust div. Bank of N.Y., 1956-63; exec. v.p., sr. mgmt. com. Summit Bank (now Bank of Am.), NJ, 1963-84; exec. v.p. Chase Manhattan Bank, N.Y.C., 1984-94; dir., vice chmn. Chase Manhattan Trust Co. Fla., Palm Beach, Fla., 1984-87; pvt. trust and estates law practice NJ, 1974-2000; former mem. probate com. N.J. Supreme Ct. Jud. Conf. Mem. N.Y.C. and Bergen County estate planning couns.; former pres. Bergen County coun. Girl Scouts Am.; bd. dirs., pres., chief exec. officer Bergen County United Way; treas. 2d Century Fund, Hackensack Hosp.; bd. dirs. Holy Name Hosp., Teaneck, N.J. With USN, World War II; brig. gen. Army N.G. Mem. ABA (co-chmn. nat. conf. lawyers and corp. trustees 1991-93), Am. Bankers Assn. (chmn. trust counsel com. 1991-93), N.Y. Bar Assn., N.J. Bar Assn., N.Y. County Lawyers Assn., Bergen County Bar Assn. (former trustee, former chmn. probate and estate planning coms.), Fed. Bar Assn., N.Y. Militia Assn., Nat. Guard Assn. U.S.

**STOTTER, LAWRENCE HENRY,** lawyer; b. Cleve., Sept. 24, 1929; s. Oscar and Bertha (Lieb) S.; m. Ruth Rapoport, June 30, 1957; children: Daniel, Jennifer, Steven. BBA, Ohio State U., 1956, LLB, 1958, JD, 1967. Bar: Calif. 1960, U.S. Supreme Ct. 1973, U.S. Tax Ct. 1976. Pvt. practice, San Francisco, 1963—; ptnr. Stotter and Coats, San Francisco, 1981-97; sole practitioner, 1997—; mem. faculty Nat. Judicial Coll.; mem. Calif. Family Law Adv. Commn., 1979-80. Editor in chief: Am. Bar Family Advocate mag, 1977-82; TV appearances on Phil Donahue Show, Good Morning America. Pres. Tamalpais Conservation Club, Marin County, Calif.; U.S. State Dept. del. Hague Conf. Pvt. Internat. Law, 1979-80; legal adv. White House Conf. on Families, 1980—. Served with AUS, 1950-53. Mem. ABA (past chmn. family law sect.), Am. Acad. Matrimonial Lawyers (past nat. v.p.), Calif. State Bar (past chmn. family law sect.), San Francisco Bar Assn. (past chmn. family law sect.), Calif. Trial Lawyers Assn. (past chmn. family law sect.) Home and Office: 2244 Vistazo St E Belvedere Tiburon CA 94920-1970 Office Phone: 415-435-3568. Personal E-Mail: lhstotter@aol.com.

**STOTTLEMYER, DAVID LEE,** federal official; b. Waynesboro, Pa., June 1, 1935; s. Omar Samuel and Miriam (Noll) S.; m. Jane Ann Hembree, Aug. 26, 1961; children: Todd Andrew, Kristen Elizabeth, Kathryn Ann. AB, Miami U., Oxford, Ohio, 1959; M. Pub. and Internat. Affairs (NDEA fellow), U. Pitts., 1964, also postgrad. Program and budget analyst Exec. Office of Pres., Office of Mgmt. and Budget, Washington, 1964-69; sr. mgmt. officer UN, N.Y.C., 1969-70; adviser internat. orgn. affairs U.S. Mission to UN, N.Y.C., 1971-72; counsellor internat. orgn. affairs, 1973-75, counsellor UN resources mgmt., 1976-77; also mem. U.S. del. 26th-31st gen. assemblies, mem. UN Com. on Contbns., 1971; mem. UN Adv. Com. on Adminstrv. and Budgetary Questions, 1973-77; dir. policy mgmt. staff Bur. Internat. Orgn. Affairs, U.S. Dept. State, Washington, 1977-80, exec. asst. to sec. of state for internat. orgn. affairs, 1980; mem. staff office of Vice-Pres., Washington, 1981-83; dir. adminstrv. mgmt. service UN, N.Y.C., 1984-85; exec. asst., dir. Office of Under-Sec.-Gen. for Adminstrn. and Mgmt., UN, N.Y.C., 1986-87; pvt. practice as cons., 1987-90; dir. industry rels. NASA, Washington, 1990-91, dir. office nat. svc., 1992-93; retired, 1993; cons. pvt. practice, 1993—. Served with AUS, 1953-56. Recipient Superior Honor award State Dept., 1975 Mem. Am. Pub. Serv. Assn. Home and Office: 5920 Sherborn Ln Springfield VA 22152-1035 Office Phone: 703-644-7348. E-mail: dave.stot@verizon.net.

**STOTTLEMYER, TODD A.,** business association executive; BA, Coll. William and Mary; JD cum laude, Georgetown U., 1991. Corp. v.p. BDM Internat. Inc.; exec. v.p., CFO, chief adminstrv. officer BTG Inc.; mng. dir. McGuireWoods Capital Group; pres. McGuireWoods Cons.; CEO Apogen Technologies; pres., CEO Nat. Fedn. Ind. Bus., Washington, 2006—. Mem. Profl. Svcs. Coun.; vice chmn. bd. dirs. No. Va. Tech. Coun. Bd. dirs. Fairfax County C. of C., Am. Red Cross of Nat. Capital Region, INOVA Health System Foundation. Mem.: Phi Beta Kappa. Home: Nat Fedn Ind Bus 1201 F St NW Ste 200 Washington DC 20004*

**STOTTS, DENNIS MARTIN,** lawyer; b. St. Louis, Dec. 15, 1950; s. Donald Alvin Stotts and Rose Mary Marshall; m. Gail Pamela Tolsma, Nov. 10, 1979; children: Jessica, Darren. BS Chemistry, Eckerd Coll., St. Petersburg, Fla., 1972; MS Pub. Health, Environ. Scis. and Engring., U. N.C., Chapel Hill, 1976; JD cum laude, Stetson U. Coll. Law, Gulfport, Fla., 1983. Bar: Fla. 1984, U.S. Dist. Ct. (so. dist.) Fla. 1987. Environ. permitting specialist Fla. Dept. Environ. Regulations, Ft. Lauderdale, 1974—75, head enforcement sect. West Palm Beach, 1975—81; assoc. environ. law Peeples Earl & Blank, Miami, Fla., 1984—86; ptnr. Earl Blank Kavanaugh & Stotts, Miami, 1986—2003, Katz Barron Squitero Faust, Miami, 2003—. Lectr. Fla. Bar, 1987—, Fla. C. of C., 1987—. Govt. appointee adv. com. Fla. Recycling Markets, 1993—99; mem. master plan adv. com. City of Hollywood, Fla., 2001. Named Top Lawyer, South Fla. Legal Guide, 2005, 2006; recipient Recognition award, Legal Environ. Assistance Found., 1997, Outstanding

Adv. award, Stetson U. Coll. Law, 1982. Mem.: ABA, Fla. Acad. Profl. Mediators, Fla. Bar Assn. (exec. coun.Environ. and Land Use Law sect. 1990—96, chair Environ. and Land Use Law sect. 1996—97, Stephens/Register Meml. award 1993), Lambda Alpha. Office: Katz Barron Squitero Faust 2699 S Bayshore Dr 7th Fl Miami FL 33133

**STOTTS, TERRY,** professional basketball coach; b. Cedar Falls, Iowa, Nov. 25, 1957; s. Frank and Jayne (Phelps) Stotts; m. Jan Stotts. BS in zoology, U. Okla., 1983, MBA, 1988. Second round draft choice Houston Rockets, NBA, 1980; player Montana Golden Nuggets, CBA, Spain, France; head coach Albany Patoons, 1990—91; asst. Fort Wayne Fury, 1991—92; advance scout Seattle SuperSonics, 1992—93, asst. coach, 1994; coach Western Conf. NBA All-Star Game, 1994, 1996, 1998; asst. coach Milw. Bucks, NBA, 1998—2002, head coach, 2005—; asst. coach Atlanta Hawks, 2002, head coach, 2002—04. Office: Milwaukee Bucks 1001 N Fourth St Milwaukee WI 53203*

**STOTZKY, GUENTHER,** microbiologist, educator; b. Leipzig, Germany, May 24, 1931; arrived in US, 1939; s. Moritz Stotzky and Erna (Angres) Kester; m. Kayla Baker, Mar. 17, 1958; children: Jay, Martha, Deborah. BS, Calif. Poly. State U., 1952; MS, Ohio State U., 1954, PhD, 1956. Spl. sci. employee Argonne Nat. Lab. USAEC, Lemont, Ill., 1955; rsch. assoc. dept. botany U. Mich., Ann Arbor, 1956-58; head soil microbiology Ctrl. Rsch. Labs. United Fruit Co., Norwood, Mass., 1958-63; chmn., microbiologist Kitchawan Rsch. Labs. Bklyn. Botanic Garden, Ossining, NY, 1963-68; assoc. prof. dept. biology NYU, 1967-70, prof. dept. biology, 1970—, chmn. dept. biology, 1970-77. Editor: Soil Biochemistry, 1990-2000; series editor Marcel Dekker, Inc., 1986-92; contbr. over 280 articles to profl. jours., chpts. to books. With USCG, 1957. Recipient Selman A. Waksman Hon. Lecture award Theobald Smith Soc., 1989, Honored Alumnus of Yr. award Calif. Poly. State U., 1992, fellowship Japanese Soc. for Promotion of Sci., 1996; named Disting. Vis. Scientist, U.S. EPA, 1986-89. Fellow AAAS, Am. Soc. Agronomy, Soil Sci. Soc. Am.; mem. Am. Acad. Microbiology, Am. Soc. Microbiology (Fisher Co. award for applied and environ. microbiology 1990, Excellence in Tchg. award N.Y.C. for 1994). Jewish. Avocations: gardening, reading, music. Office: NYU Dept Biology 1009 Silver Ctr New York NY 10003 Office Phone: 212-998-8268. Business E-Mail: gs5@nyu.edu.

**STOUCK, JERRY,** lawyer; b. Washington, Mar. 24, 1955; s. Alex and Eileen Marion (Tepper) S.; m. Mindy A. Buren, Feb. 18, 1984; children: Danielle, David, Rachel. BA magna cum laude, Wesleyan U., 1977; JD, NYU, 1980. Bar: U.S. Dist. Ct. D.C. 1981, U.S. Ct. Fed. Claims 1981, D.C. Ct. Appeals, 1981, Md. Ct. Appeals 1983, U.S. Ct. Appeals (4th cir.) 1983, U.S. Dist. Ct. Md. 1985, U.S. Ct. Appeals (fed. cir.) 1992, U.S. Supreme Ct. 1993, U.S. Ct. Appeals (D.C. cir.) 1997. Law clk. to hon. Pettine U.S. Dist. Ct. R.I, 1980-81; assoc. McKenna, Conner & Cuneo, Washington, 1981-83; Shulman, Rogers, Gandel, Rockville, Md., 1984-87; Spriggs & Hollingsworth, Washington, 1983-84, 87-89, ptnr., 1989—2005; shareholder Greenberg Traurig, LLP, Washington, 2005—. Mem. Phi Beta Kappa. Office: Greenberg Traurig LLP 800 Connecticut Ave NW Washington DC 20006 Office Phone: 202-331-3173. Business E-Mail: stouckj@gtlaw.com.

**STOUDEMIRE, AMARE CARSARES,** professional basketball player; b. Lake Wales, Fla., Nov. 16, 1982; Player Phoenix Suns, 2002—. Mem. US Olympic Basketball Team, Athens, Greece, 2004. Named NBA Rookie of the Year, 2003, MVP, Rookie Challenge, 2004; named to NBA All-Rookie Team, 2003. Achievements include The only high school student selected in the 2002 NBA Draft. Office: c/o Phoenix Suns 201 E Jefferson St Phoenix AZ 85004*

**STOUDENMIRE, MYUNGSOOK SONG,** music educator; b. Seoul, Republic of Korea, Jan. 27, 1962; arrived in US, 1988; d. Byungchul Song and Jungja Cha; m. John David Stoudenmire, II, June 29, 1991; 1 child, Esther Song. MusB in Piano Performance, Sungshin Women's U., 1984, MusM in Piano Performance, 1986; MM in Piano Performance, Columbia Coll., 1990; D of Musical Art, U. SC, 1997. Instr. Trident Tech. Coll., Charleston, SC, 1997, Sch. Art-Charleston County, Charleston, SC, 1998—99, Trident Tech. Coll., 2000—; adj. prof. Clarleston So. U., 2000—, Columbia Internat. U., SC, 2000—03. Dist. chair SC Music Tchrs. Adminstrn., Charleston, 2003—. Mem.: SC Music Educators, Nat. Piano Guild, SC Piano Festival.

**STOUDT, HOWARD WEBSTER,** biological anthropologist, consultant; b. Pitts., May 13, 1925; s. Howard Webster and Harriet Catharine (Powers) S.; m. Jean Gorey Henderson, Feb. 14, 1953; children: Katharine Webster, Roberta Henderson. AB, Harvard Coll., 1949; MA, U. Pa., 1953, PhD, 1959; SM in Hygiene, Harvard U., 1963. Rsch. asst. Harvard Sch. Pub. Health, Boston, 1952-55; rsch. specialist Air U., U.S. Air Force, Montgomery, Ala., 1955-57; rsch. assoc. Harvard Sch. Pub. Health, Boston, 1957-66, asst. prof., 1966-73; prof. community medicine Mich. State U., East Lansing, 1973-88, chmn. dept., 1973-78, prof. emeritus, 1988—; cons. Stoudt Assocs., Bath, Maine, 1988—. Cons. U.S. Army, USAF, NASA, USPHS, VA, NRC, NAS, pvt. industry, 1952—. Author: Physical Anthropology of Ceylon, 1961; co-author: Human Body in Equipment Design, 1971; contbr. over 40 articles to profl. jours. Sgt. U.S. Army, 1943-46, Europe. Harrison fellow U. Pa., Phila., 1951-52, USPHS fellow, Boston, 1961-62. Fellow Human Biology Coun.; mem. AAAS, Am. Assn. Phys. Anthropologists, Human Factors and Ergonomics Soc. Democrat. Home and Office: 4 Schooner Ridge Rd Ste 4 Bath ME 04530-1662 Office Phone: 207-442-9714. Personal E-mail: hjstoudt@verizon.net.

**STOUFFER, NANCY KATHLEEN,** publishing company executive; b. Hershey, Pa., Feb. 14, 1951; d. William Lawrence Sweeny O'Brian and Edna Luttrell m. David Ira Thornton, July 19, 1980; children: Jennifer Belle, Vance David. Pres. André Pub. Co., Inc., Camp Hill, Pa., 1985-88; pres., chmn. B.C.I., Camp Hill, Pa., 1988-90; v.p. R&D E.S.P. Inc., N.Y.C., 1989-90; v.p. corp. planning Nu-Tek Labs., Hershey, Pa.; exec. rschr. Assocs. in Law and Corp. Devel., Camp Hill, 1995—; owner RealMuggles.com and RealMuggles LLC. Exec. rschr Com. on Advanced Studies in Learning Disabilities Med. and Profl., SPECTRA. Author: Your Basic Guide to Creative Survival, 1991; contbr. articles on dyslexia and learning disabilities to popular mags.; author children's books; developer of Reading Genie, EZ read program, Real MUGGLES, LLC, RealMUGGLES.com Republican. Address: 1619 S York St Mechanicsburg PA 17055 Personal E-Mail: alcdch@aol.com. Business E-Mail: chiefmuggle@realmuggles.com.

**STOUGHTON, W. VICKERY,** healthcare executive; b. Peoria, Ill., Mar. 1, 1946; s. Warner Vickery and Mary Olive (McNamara) S.; m. Anne Stoughton; children: Zachary Benjamin, Samantha. BS, St. Louis U., 1968; MBA, U. Chgo., 1973. Asst. dir. Boston Hosp. for Women, 1973-74, Peter Bent Brigham Hosp., Boston, 1975-77, dir., 1978-80; pres. The Toronto Hosp., Ont., Can.; asst. prof. U. Toronto, 1982-90, assoc. prof., 1991; vice chancellor health affairs, chief exec. officer Duke U. Hosp., Durham, N.C., 1991-92; pres. Smithkline Beecham Clin. Labs., Collegeville, Pa., 1992-95, Smithkline Beecham Diagnostic Systems, King of Prussia, Pa., 1996; chmn., CEO Careside, Culver City, Calif., 1996—; dir. Biomira, 1988—. Bd. dirs. Sun Life Assurance Co. Bd. dirs. Toronto Symphony, 1983-86, Toronto United Way. Served to capt. AUS, 1969-72. Fellow Am. Coll. Hosp. Adminstrs. Home: 8820 Lookout Mountain Ave Los Angeles CA 90046-1820

**STOUT, ANGELA KAY,** music educator; b. Tucson, Feb. 13, 1984; d. Alan and Vivian Greynolds; m. Matthew Paul Stout. MusB, U. Ariz., 2006—. Pvt. clarinet tchr., Tucson, 2001—; condr., coord. U. Ariz. Mid. Sch. Outreach Band, Tucson, 2004—. Robert C. Byrd scholar, U.S. Dept. Edn., 2002, Nat. Merit scholar, 2002. Mem.: Collegiate Music Educators Nat. Conf. Avocations: clarinet, tap dance, Spanish, German, travel.

**STOUT, DONALD EVERETT,** real estate developer, environmental services administrator; b. Dayton, Ohio; s. Thorne Franklin and Lovella Marie (Sweeney) m. Gloria B. McCormick; children: Holly Sue, Scott Kenneth.

BS, Miami U.; postgrad., Appraisal Inst. Lic. real estate broker, Ohio, U.S. V.I.; cert. gen. appraiser, Ohio. Pres. various real estate groups. Developer 1st transp. ctr. for trucking Ohio; pres. Falls Estates, Wright Gate Tech. Ctr., Edglo Land Recycle, Donald E. Stout, Inc.; developer, instr. real estate courses. Contbr. articles to profl. jours. With U.S. Army and USN. Named Outstanding Real Estate Salesmen State, Ohio Bd. Realtors. Mem. Nat. Assn. Real Estate Bds., Appraisal Inst. (sr. real estate analyst, sr. residential appraiser), Soc. Indsl. Office Realtors, Dayton Area Bd. Realtors (co-founder, 1st pres. salesman divsn.), U.S. Naval Res. Officers Assn., Raymond M. Hughes Soc., Exhausted Roosters, Masons (32d degree), Shriner, Phi Delta Theta. Office: 1344 Woodman Dr Dayton OH 45432-3442 Personal E-Mail: stoutde@sbcglobal.net.

**STOUT, ELVA CAROLYN FRASER,** elementary school educator; b. Independence, Mo., Oct. 20; d. Gertrude Alleen Warnke, Charles Allen Fraser; m. Forrest Eugene Stout; children: Sherri Jones, Karrie Henricks, F. Evan, Eric. BS, Appalachian State U., 1972; MEd, Augusta State U., 1978; postgrad., U.S.C., 1984—88. T-6 profl. tchg. cert. Tchr. T. A. Dugger Jr. High, Elizabethton, Tenn., 1972—74, A. C. Griggs, Augusta, Ga., 1974—75, Bel Air Elem., Evans, Ga., 1975—88, Lakeside Mid. Sch., Evans, 1988—92, Riverside Mid. Sch., Evans, 1992—2003; astronomy, earth scis. cons., 2003—. Field tester Am. Geol. Inst., 1999; evaluator Scope poster, 2000; reviewer, evaluator Astronomy Edn. Rev., 2002. Adult Sunday sch. tchr. First Bapt. Ch., Augusta, 1975—. Named Outstanding Sci. Tchr., Sigma Xi, 1994, AASTRA Tchr., Am. Astron. Soc., 1996, 1997, Rsch. Based Sci. Edn. Tchr., Nat. Optical Astronomy Observatories, 1999, Best Tchr. in Sci. and Math. 1991, Best Tchr. in Sci. and Tech., 1993—94; recipient Internat. Educator of the Yr., Internat. Biog. Centre/Cambridge, England, 2004. Mem.: Profl. Assn. Ga. Educators (membership coord. sch. 1980—91), Ga.'s Sci. Tchrs.' Assn., Nat. Earth Sci. Tchrs. Assn. (presenter), Nat. Assn. Geoscience Tchrs. (Ga.'s Outstanding Earth Sci. Tchr. 1996), Phi Delta Kappa (assoc.), Alpha Delta Kappa (assoc.; dist. chaplain 1980—82). Baptist. Avocations: fossil "hunter", amateur astronomer, painting, travel. Home: 4800 Woodbridge Pl Evans GA 30809 Personal E-Mail: TeacherES@aol.com.

**STOUT, JOHN WILSON,** academic administrator; b. Reading, Pa., Oct. 3, 1942; s. John Wellington and Helen Mary (Rothermel) S.; m. Jayne Frances Atherton, Mar. 25, 1965 (div. Dec. 1976); 1 child John R.; m. Helen Jean Hosty, July 30, 1977; 1 child, Katie Irene. BA, Dickinson Coll., 1964; MA, Northeastern U., 1966; MPA, Nova Southeastern U., 1980. Instr. R.I. Coll. Providence, 1971; mem. faculty U. Without Walls, Providence, 1972-74; asst. to pres. Roger Williams U., Bristol, RI, 1974-75, dir. Open Disnv., 1974-90, dean Sch. Social Sci., 1990-93, dean Cont. Sch. Edn., 1990—, dean Cont. Sch. Edn. Univ. Coll., 1994—, dean Open Coll., 2000—, dean Sch. Continuing Studies, 2004—. Sr. lectr. Northeastern U., Boston, 1967—; cons. head start, model cities, Providence and Pawtucket, 1971-74; rsch. coordinator Urban Observ. R.I., 1970-75. Mem. budget panel United Way Southwestern New Eng., Providence, 1972; mem. comm. Planning Project Post Secondary Edn., Providence, 1975. Recipient Achievement cert. Northeastern U., 1982, 92, 97, Army Comdr.'s award for pub. svc., 2000, Disting. Tchg. award Roger Williams Alumni Assn., 1974, Svc. award N.J. N.G., 1998, 2001. Mem. ASPA (pres. 1979-80), NEA, Am. Dem. Action, Coun. Adult and Exptl. Learning. Democrat. Mem. Ch. of Christ. Home: 3 Nathaniel Rd Barrington RI 02806-3825 Office: Roger Williams U 150 Washington St Providence RI 02903 Office Phone: 401-254-3530. E-mail: jstout@rwu.edu.

**STOUT, LEON JAMES,** archivist, librarian; b. Long Branch, N.J., Oct. 10, 1947; s. Leon E. Stout and Verna May Porter; m. Dolores Anne Altmyer, Aug. 22, 1969; children: David James, Christine Anne Smith. BA, Pa. State U., 1969, MA, 1972; MLS, U. of Pitts., 1974. Archivist Pa. State U. Librs., University Park, 1974—2002, head, pub. svcs. and outreach spl. collections, 2002—. Cons. in field. Author: (reference book) Pennsylvania State University in International Dictionary of Library Histories; contbr. articles to profl. jours. Mem. U.S. Nat. Hist. Pubs. and Records Commn., Washington, 2002—, Pa. State Hist. Records Adv. Bd., Harrisburg, 1989—; apptd. rep. State Coll. Borough Hist. Resources Commn., State College, Pa., 1992—. Recipient Award for Outstanding Contbns. to Librs., Pa. State U. Librs., 1991, Fellows' Posner prize for Outstanding Articles in the Am. Archivist, Soc. of Am. Archivists, 1995; fellow Andrew K. Mellon Rsch. fellow in archives, Bentley Hist. Libr., U. of Mich., 1987; grantee Archival Rsch. grantee, U.S. Nat. Hist. Pubs. and Records Commn., 1991—93, Archives and Records Mgmt. grantee, Pa. Hist. and Mus. Commn., 1985—86. Fellow: Soc. of Am. Archivists (pres. 2001—02); mem.: Midwestern Archives Conf., Mid-Atlantic Regional Archives Conf. (chair 1989—91). Roman Catholic. Avocations: travel, golf, genealogy, photography. Office: Pennsylvania State University 104 Paterno Library University Park PA 16802 Office Phone: 814-863-3381. E-mail: lys2@psu.edu.

**STOUT, MARY WEBB,** dean; b. Richmond, Va., Dec. 24, 1947; d. Frank Edmond Webb and Edith Diiguid (Harris) Webb Steger; m. Teddy Alvin Stout, July 8, 1972. BA, Mary Washington Coll., 1970; MEd, U. Va., Charlottesville, 1972; Edn. Specialist, Coll. William and Mary, 1991, EdD, 1995; cert. in Multimedia Devel., George Mason U., 2003. Cert. Red Cross water safety instr. Tchr. Harrisonburg City Sch., Va., 1970-71, Buckingham County Sch., Va., 1972-73; guidance counselor So. European Task Force US Army, Vicenza, Italy, 1973-78, edn. specialist Quartermaster Sch. Ft. Lee, Va., 1978-80, edn. specialist Tng. Support Ctr. Ft. Eustis, Va., 1980-82; edn. specialist Hdqs. Tng., Doctrine Command, Ft. Monroe, Va., 1982-83; edn. svc. specialist Combined Arms Ctr., Ft. Leavenworth, Kans., 1983-88; instrnl. systems specialist Hdqs. TRADOC, Ft. Monroe, 1988-98; supervisory edn. svc. specialist Hdqs. US Army Pers. Command, Alexandria, Va., 1998-2000; edn. program specialist OSD Office of Chancellor Edn. and Profl. Devel., Arlington, Va., 2000—03, online faculty U. Phoenix, 2002—; edn. program specialist OSD Civilian Pers. Mgmt. Svcs., Arlington, 2003—05; acad. dean, dep. dir. U.S. Marine Corps War Coll., Quantico, Va., 2005—. Mem. devel. bd. Sch. Edn. Coll. William and Mary, 2002—. Legis. affairs rep. Running Man Homeowners Assn., Yorktown, Va., 1996—98; treas. Massanetta Springs Alumni Assn., Harrisonburg, Va., 1988—2002, membership chmn., 1998—2002, pres., 2002—04, reunion com., 2004—06. Recipient Alumni award Massanetta Springs Alumni Assn., 1996. Mem.: ASTD, U.S. Distance Learning Assn., Assn. for Instnl. Rsch., Assn. Study Higher Edn., Mary Washington Coll. Alumni Assn., U. Va. Alumni Assn., Coll. William and Mary Alumni Assn., Kappa Delta Pi. Presbyterian. Avocation: running. Home: 6006 River Dr Mason Neck VA 22079-4127 Office: Marine War Coll Marine Corps Univ 2076 South St Quantico VA 22134 Office Phone: 703-432-4542. Personal E-mail: mstout8895@aol.com.

**STOUT, PATRICIA A.,** communications educator; b. St. Louis, Jan. 21, 1950; BA in Anthropology, U. Ariz., 1979; postgrad., U. Minn., 1979-81; PhD in Comm., U. Ill., 1985. Asst. mgr. alumni publ. U. Mont., Missoula, 1978-79; acct. mgmt. Judge Advt., Pub. Rels., Helena, Mont., 1979; tchg. asst., Sch. Journalism & Mass Comm. U. Minn., Mpls., 1979-80; project asst. Minn. Cmty. Prevention Program, 1980-81; vis. lectr. dept. advt. U. Ill., Urbana, 1981-84; asst. prof. dept. advt. U. Tex., Austin, 1984-90, assoc. prof. dept. advt., 1990—, assoc. dean acad. affairs Coll. Comm., 1996—; vis. rsch. prof. Ctrs. for Disease Control and Prevention, Atlanta, 1993-94; vis. assoc. prof. dept. mktg. and internat. bus. U. Auckland, New Zealand, 1994; chmn. 5 doctoral coms., numerous masters theses, profl. reports U. Tex., Austin, mem., reader numerous others; dir. grad. studies dept. advt. U. Tex., Austin, Fall 1990, Summer 1993; ad hoc reviewer Jour. Advt., Jour. Consumer Rsch., Jour. Pub. Policy & Mktg., Journalism Quar., Critical Studies in Mass Comm., Jour. Bus. Rsch. Author: (with John D. Leckenby and Nugent Wedding) Advertising Management, (with Michael Solomon and Kim Rotzoll) The Advertising Around Us: A Consumer Perspective on Marketing Communications; editor procs. of 1990 Am. Acad. of Advt. Conf.; contbr. tech. papers, procs., articles to profl. jours. Recipient in field. Recipient Internat. cartoon caption contest first place award Olympia Beer Distbrs., Missoula, Mont., 1978-79, Jour. Advt. best article award Am. Acad. Advt., 1993, vis. rsch. prof. intergovernmental pers. act award Nat. AIDS Edn. and Info. Program, Ctrs. for Disease Control and Prevention, Atlanta, 1993-94; Pub. Health Svc. Tng.

fellow Lab. Physiological Hygiene, U. Minn., 1980-81, Houston Harte Centennial Comm. fellow U. Tex., Austin, 1987-88, Am. Acad. Advt. Industry fellow Advt. Rsch. Found, N.Y., 1993-94; dissertation rsch. grantee U. Ill., 1984-85, summer rsch. grantee U. Tex., Austin, 1984-85, direct support grantee U. Tex., 1985-86, 86-87, rsch. grantee Am. Acad. Advt., 1985-86, U. Rsch. Inst. spl. rsch. grantee U. Tex., 1988-89, 95-96, Columbia U. Tech. Studies Seminar grantee Freedom Forum Media Studies Ctr., 1992-93, immunization of Tex. children co-investigator grantee Tex. Dept. Health, 1995-96, an exploratory study on appropriate internet content and use standards for children co-investigator grantee Hogg Found. for Mental Health, 1996-97. Mem. Internat. Comm. Assn. (ad hoc reviewer), Am. Acad. Advt. (treas. 1989, v.p. 1990, pres. elect 1991, pres. 1992, past pres. 1993, publs. com. 1997—, ad hoc reviewer), Assn. Consumer Rsch. (ad hoc reviewer), Assn. Edn. in Journalism and Mass Comm., Soc. Consumer Psychology, Phi Kappa Phi, Kappa Tau Alpha, Alpha Delta Sigma. Avocations: photography, hiking. Home: 5508 Great Divide Dr Austin TX 78738-6123 Office: Univ Tex Dept Advt CMA 7142 Austin TX 78712

**STOUTENBURG, JANE SUE WILLIAMSON,** nurse practitioner, fund raiser, actress; b. Davenport, Iowa, Mar. 10, 1949; d. George Baker and Hazel Elaine (Kline) W.; m. Noel Wayne Stoutenburg, Aug. 25, 1979 (div. July 1996); 1 child, Karen Elaine. AS with honors, Black Hawk Jr. Coll., East Moline, Ill., 1970; BA, BS, Augustana Coll., 1973, 75; Cert. in Fire Sci. with honors, Harper Coll., Palatine, Ill., 1982; AS in Nursing with high honors, Elgin Community Coll., 1987. EMT; cert. paramedic; cert. tchr. Rsch. technologist Rush-Presbyn. St. Luke's Med. Ctr., Chgo., 1974-75; acct. supr., pvt. investigator Per Mar Security Sys., Davenport, Iowa, 1975-77; pre-trial release investigator 7th Jud. Ct. Dist., Davenport, Iowa, 1976-77; pharm. rep. Bristol Labs., Syracuse, N.Y., 1977-80; dir. safety tng. Zee Med., Irvine, Calif., 1981-83; tng. specialist ARC, Chgo., 1983-86, Lake County Fire Rescue, Barrington, Ill., 1981—; nurse practitioner Boy Scouts of Am., St. Charles, Ill., 1990—; nurse trainer Buehler YMCA, Palatine, Ill., 1990-94. Emergency med. svc. coord. Robbins (Ill.) Fire Dept., 1985—; bd. dirs. Barrington Area Devel. Coun., 1981-90; EMS coord. Lake Counte Fire Rescue, 1980—, owner, Snail's Pace Gifts, Barrington, IL, 1997—, pres. Karyn Etcetera Inc., 1997—. Author: Academy of Science, 1967, (poetry), 1970, actress: ER, 1997—, First Edition, 1998—, Backdraft, A Normal Life, Relic, My Best Friends Wedding. Troop leader Girl Scouts, Barrington, 1990-95; book fair chmn. Lines Sch. PTO, Barrington, 1991-94; camp nurse Boy Scouts Am., Camp Big Timber, Ill., YMCA Camp Duncan, Fox Lake, Ill.; pageant judge Miss Am. System, 1995—.bd. dirs. Elgin C.C., 1998—, NW Suburb Chgo. Vol. Bur., 1998—. Recipient Ill. EMT of the Yr. award, 1989-90, Disting. Svc. award ARC, 1989, Disting. Svc. key Alpha Phi Omega, 1989, Key, Phi Theta Kappa, 1989, Vol. of the Yr. award Chgo. Vol. Bur., 1993, J.C. Penney Golden Flame award, 1993. Mem. Am. Soc. Safety Engrs., Am. Trauma Soc., Am. Acad. Sci., Internat. Soc. Fire Sci. Instrs., Prehosp. Care Providers of Ill., Alpha Phi Omega (mem. bd. dirs. 1995—, publicity com.), P.E.O. Sisterhood. Episcopalian. Avocations: poetry, camping, firefighting, girl scouts, dixieland jazz.

**STOVAL, LINDA,** political party official; b. Kans. m. Toby Stoval. Worked on staff campaigns Gov. Dean, Senator Kerry, former Dem. Gov. Mike Sullivan, and others; local to presdl. activist, organizer, strategist, owner Gravitas Coaching Internat., Wyo.; chairperson Wyo. Dem. Party, 2001—03; polit. leadership coach, 2005—. Former chair Make-A-Wish, Wyo.; former vice chair Habitat for Humanity, Wyo.; former chair Wyoming (Americorps). Mailing: Gravitas Coaching Internat 737 Kirk Ave Casper WY 82601-3324 Office Phone: 877-734-8624. Business E-Mail: linda@gravitascoaching.com.

**STOVALL, APRIL LEANNE,** music educator; b. Aurora, Ill., Apr. 19, 1968; d. Vernon Albert and Bobette Lee Shoger; m. James Brian Stovall, Nov. 24, 1990. MusM Edn., Bob Jones U., S.C., 1990. Cert. Svc. Playing Am. Guild of Organists, 1999. Pvt. piano tchr., bus. owner Artistry by Apr. Studios, North Aurora, Ill., 1990—; accompanist St. Charles Singers, Ill., 1999—2002; assoc. organist Baker Meml. United Meth. Ch., St. Charles, Ill., 1999—; music faculty Waubonsee C.C., Sugar Grove, Ill., 1999—; dir. music, choirmaster, organist St. Charles Episcopal Ch., Ill., 2002—. Local bd. mem., fox valley chpt. Am. Guild of Organists, Batavia, Ill., 2001—; nat. steering com. mem. Chgo. AGO Nat. Conv., 2001—; accompanist Elgin Choral Union, Ill., 2003—. Musician: (musical recording) Live at Cambridge U., Eng. Tour, 2000, Lenten Artists Series, Baker United Meth. Ch. Accompanist, world tours St. Charles Singers, Ill., 2000; dir. children's chorus St. Charles Episcopal Ch., Ill., 2002. Recipient Superior Rating, Nat. Piano Guild, 1990. Mem.: Ill. State Music Tchrs. Assn. (life; music educator 1990), DAR. Conservative. Avocations: travel, art, reading, skiing, mountain biking. Home: 209 April Ln North Aurora IL 60542-1205 Office: St Charles Episcopal Ch 994 N Fifth Ave Saint Charles IL 60174 Personal E-mail: jimapril1124@sbcglobal.net. E-mail: stcharles@anet.com.

**STOVALL, BETH ROOP,** music educator; b. Owensboro, Ky, Aug. 24, 1962; d. Joe Franklin Roop and Sara Jane Brackett; m. James Philip Stovall (div.); children: Sara C., Leslie A., James Philip IV. B in Music Edn., Ky. Wesleyan Coll., 1984; MusM in Vocal Performance, U. NC, Greensboro, 1987. Cert. Kindermusik Instructor. Music dir. Shepherd of the Hill Luth. Ch., Sylva, NC, 1990—96; early music educator Kindermusik of the Smokies, Sylva, 1990—96, Montessori Sch., Sylva, 1990—96; music dir. Blakemore United Meth. Ch., Nashville, 1995—96; tchr. Children's House Montessori, Nashville, 1995—96; music dir. Settle Meml. U. MC, Owensboro, Ky., 1997—; vocal instr. Ky. Wesleyan Coll., Owensboro, 1997—. Music cons. Rose Curtain Players, Owensboro, 2003—; tchr. Pvt. Studio, Owensboro, 1997—. Performer (soloist) Owensboro Symphony Orch., 1998—. Recipient Cmty. Svc. award, Ky. Wesleyan Coll., 2003, 2004. Mem.: Am. Choral Dir. Assn., Ky. Music Educators, Delta Omicron. Democrat. United Meth. Home: 1200 Cary Ct Owensboro KY 42301 Office: Settle Meml UMC 202 E 4th St Owensboro KY 42303

**STOVALL, CARLA JO,** former state attorney general; b. Hardner, Kans., Mar. 18, 1957; d. Carl E. and Juanita Joe (Ford) Stovall. BA, Pittsburg State U., Kans., 1979; JD, U. Kans., 1982, MPA, 1993. Bar: Kans. 1982, U.S. Dist. Ct. Kans. 1982. Pvt. practice, Pitts., 1982—85; atty. Crawford County, Pitts., 1984—88; gov. Kans. Parole Bd., Topeka, 1988—94; atty. gen. State of Kans., Topeka, 1995—2002. Lectr. law Pittsburg State U., 1982—84. Mem. bd. govs. U. Kans. Sch. Law; Nat. Ctr. Missing and Exploited Children; Am. Legacy Found.; Nat. Crime Prevention Coun.; Coun. State Govts.; mem. bd. govs. Kans. Children's Cabinet; pres. NAAG, 2001—02, chmn. exec. com. midwest region, sexually violent predator com., 1995—96; Bd. dirs., sec. Pittsburg Family YMCA, 1983—88. Named Outstanding Atty. Gen., Nat. Assn. Attys. Gen., 2001, Topeka Fraternal Order of Police's Amb. to Law Enforcement; recipient Champion award, Campaign Tobacco Free Kids, 2002, Adam Walsh Children's Fund Rainbow award, Nat. Ctr. Missing and Exploited Children, 2001, Kelley-Wyman award, Nat. Assn. Attys. Gen., 2001, Person of the Yr., Kans. Peace Officer Assn.'s Law Enforcement, Morton Baud Allied Profl. award, Nat. Orgn. Victim Assistance, Father Ken Children award, Nat. Parents Murdered Children, Disting. Svc. to Kans. Children award, Kans. Children's Svc. League, Woman of Achievement award, Miss Kans. Pageant. Mem.: NAAG (pres. 2001—02), AAUW (bd. dirs. 1983—87), ABA, Bus. and Profl. Women Assn. (Young Careerist award 1984), Nat. Coll. Dist. Attys. Assn., Kans. County and Dist. Attys. Assn., Crawford County Bar Assn. (sec. 1984—85, v.p. 1985—86, pres. 1986—87), Kans. Bar Assn., Kans. Assn. Commerce and Industry (Leadership Kans. award 1983), Pittsburg Area C.C. (bd. dirs. 1983—85, Leadership Pitts. award 1984), Pittsburg State U. Alumni Assn. (bd. dirs. 1983—88). Republican. Methodist. Avocations: travel, photography, tennis. Home: 138 S Blue Bells Ct Garden Plain KS 67050-9225

**STOVALL, FRANCES MIDDAGH,** journalist, preservationist; b. Lawrenceville, Ill., Dec. 7, 1921; d. John Judy and Rebecca (Fowler) Middagh; m. Jack N. Stovall, Aug. 16, 1941 (dec. 2004); children: Richard Middagh Stovall, Frances Judy S. Upchurch, John Fowler Stovall, Susan

Calvert G. Carter. Student, McMurry Coll., 1938-41. Woman's Page editor Odessa (Tex.) News Times, 1937-40; reporter Abilene (Tex.) Reporter News, 1938-41. Author: Clear Springs and Limestone Ledges, A History of San Marcos and Hays County, 1986; editor: San Marcos Bicentennial Cookbook, 1976, Cottage Kitchen Cookbook, 1983, Cottage Kitchen, Second Helping, 1986, Twenty Years In Cottage Kitchen, 1996, Historical Markers in Hays County, 2005-06; columnist San Marcos Daily Record, 1988-2005. Founder Heritage Assn. San Marcos, 1975, bd. dirs., 1975-2006, hon. life mem., 1989—; chmn. City of San Marcos Bicentennial Commn., 1972-76, Hays County Hist. Commn., 1987-2006; initiator Main St. in San Marcos, 1989; founder Preservation Assocs., Inc., 1986, Friends of Hays County Hist. Commn., 1990-95. Named Woman of Yr. Beta Sigma Phi, San Marcos, 1976, 96, Vol. of Yr., Rotary Club San Marcos, 1995; recipient Tex. award for hist. preservation Tex. Hist. Commn., Austin, 1990, John Ben Shepperd Leadership award Tex. Hist. Commn., Austin, 1991, Lifetime Achievement award Tex. Hist. Commn., Austin, 1993; Preservation award named in her honor, 1999, The Frances Stovall Collection within the San Marcos City libr. dedicated in her honor, 2001. Mem. DAR, Nat. Trust for Hist. Preservation, Tex. Hist. Found., Tex. State Hist. Assn., Spring Lake Garden Club, Magna Charta Dames. Avocation: history. Home: 20 Timbercrest St San Marcos TX 78666-3018

**STOVALL, JERRY (COLEMAN STOVALL),** insurance company executive; b. Houston, July 31, 1936; s. Clifford Coleman and Maxine (Lands) S.; m. Elsie Hostetter, June 20, 1959; 1 child, Brent Allen. BBA, U. Houston, 1968. Adminstr. home office Am. Gen. Life, Houston, 1955-63, agt., agy. mgr., 1963-66, agy. mgr., regional dir. agys., regional v.p., 1969-74; sr. brokerage cons. Conn. Gen. Life, Houston, 1966-69; sr. v.p., dir. mktg. Capitol Life Inst. Co., Denver, 1974-78; v.p., dir. mktg. Integon Life Ins. Corp., Winston-Salem, N.C., 1978-81; pres. Life of Mid-Am. Ins. Co., Topeka, 1981-85, Victory Life Ins. Co., Topeka, 1981-85, chmn., pres., chief exec. officer, 1981-87; pres., retired chief exec officer Integon Life Ins. Co., Winston-Salem, N.C., 1987-91; pres. Lamar Life Ins. Co., 1992-95, ret., 1995; pres., CEO Am. Pub. Holding Inc., 1996-2000, ret., 2000. Bd. dirs., vice-chmn., Ga. Internat. Life; vice-chmn. Mktg. One Inc. Bd. dirs. Jr. Achievement Miss., Inc.; bd. trustees Miss. Bapt. Found. With U.S. Army, 1955-57. Mem. Nat. Assn. Life Cos., Nat. Assn. Life Underwriters, Am. Soc. CLUs (Gold Key soc.), Am. Coun. Life Ins., Exec. Round Table (chmn. 1995), The Country Club of Jackson. Home: 1406 Mossycup Ln Livingston TX 77351-3074

**STOVALL, LOU,** printmaker; b. Athens, Ga., Jan. 1, 1937; Attended, RI Sch. Design; BFA, Howard U. Founder & dir. Workshop Inc., 1968—. Ind. Day invitation, White House (at Nancy Reagan's request), 1982, Am. Beauty Rose print, DC Area Host Com. Dem. Nat. Conv. (at Mayor Marion Barry's request), 1988, Breathing Hope print, Howard U. pres. inauguration, exhibitions include Art Lou Stovall, Strathmore Hall, 2004, Art Silkscreen Printmaking, Howard U. Gallery, 2001. Named Washingtonian Yr., 1979; recipient Bd. Dir.'s Award, Source Theatre Co., Washington DC, 1988, Mayor's Art Award Excellence Artistic Design, Washington DC, 1985; Workshop Grants, Nat. Endowment Arts, 1972, 1973, 1974, Individual Artist Fellowship Grant, 1972, Stern Family Grant Fund, 1968—74. Mem.: DC Commn. Arts & Humanities. Office: Workshop Inc 3145 Newark St NW Washington DC 20008 Office Phone: 202-966-4202. Office Fax: 202-362-0116. E-mail: lou@loustovall.com.

**STOVALL-BROOKS, PATRICIA,** elementary school educator, writer; b. Gillett, Ark., Mar. 8, 1951; d. Ambrose Poke and Addie Britton Stovall; 1 child, Sheldon Leon Brooks. BS in Edn. cum laude, Ark. Bapt. Coll., 1972; MS, Nat. Louis U., 1982. Cert. tchr. Ill., 1981. Tchr. Chgo. Pub. Schs., 1973—. Cons. U.S. Dept. Edn., Washington, 2002. Author: Except The Lord Builds The House/Relationships. Rec. sec. Women Empowered For Change, Chgo., 1999—2003; choir mem. mass choir and gospel choir Chancel Choir/Du Page A.M.E.Ch., Lisle, Ill.; active mem. Women's Missionary Soc., Lisle, 2002—03. Recipient Disting. Svc. award, Greater Instnl. A.M.E. Ch., 1999, Dedicated Svc. award, Greater Instl. Guild, 2002. Avocations: singing, cooking, writing. Office: Chicago Public Schs 125 S Clark St Chicago IL 60605 Office Phone: 630-886-8711. Personal E-mail: pbstovall@aol.com.

**STOVER, CARL FREDERICK,** foundation executive; b. Pasadena, Calif., Sept. 29, 1930; s. Carl Joseph and Margarete (Müller) S.; m. Catherine Swanson, Sept. 3, 1954; children: Matthew Joseph, Mary Margaret Stover Marker, Claire Ellen Stover Herrell; m. Jacqueline Kast, Sept. 7, 1973. BA magna cum laude, Stanford U., 1951, MA, 1954. Instr. polit. sci. Stanford U., 1953-55; fiscal mgmt. officer Office Sec. Dept. Agr., 1955-57; assoc. dir. conf. program pub. affairs Brookings Instn., 1957-59, sr. staff govtl. studies, 1960; fellow Center Study Democratic Instns., Santa Barbara, Calif., 1960-62; asst. to chmn. bd. editors Ency. Brit., 1960-62; sr. polit. scientist Stanford Research Inst., 1962-64; dir. pub. affairs fellowship program Stanford U., 1962-64; pres. Nat. Inst. Pub. Affairs, Washington, 1964-70, Nat. Com. U.S.-China Relations, 1971-72; pres., dir. Federalism Seventy-Six, Washington, 1972-74; dir. cultural resources devel. Nat. Endowment Arts, 1974-78; pres., dir. Cultural Resources, Inc., Washington, 1978-85; bd. dirs. H.E.A.R. Found., 1976-86, treas., 1976-80, pres., 1980-86. Bd. dirs. Ctr. for World Lit., pres., 1987-90, chmn., 1990-92; pvt. profl. cons., 1970—; scholar-in-residence Nat. Acad. Pub. Adminstrn., 1980-82; cons. in field. Author: The Government of Science, 1962, The Technological Order, 1963; Founding editor: Jour. Law and Edn., 1971-73; pub. Delos mag., 1987-92. Treas. Nat. Com. U.S.-China Rels., 1966-71, 82-87, 89-94, bd. dirs., 1966-74, 79-98, dir. emeritus, 1998—; bd. dirs. Council Com. Lit. Mags., 1966-68, H.E.A.R. Found., 1976-86, treas., 1976-80; trustee Inst. of Nations, 1972-76, Nat. Inst. Pub. Affairs, 1967-71, Kinesis Ltd., 1972-78; vol. Nat. Exec. Svc. Corps, 1984-89; mem. Fellowship of Reconciliation Fellow AAAS, Phi Beta Kappa (hon. lectr. 1972-87); mem. Am. Soc. Pub. Adminstrn., Nat. Acad. Pub. Adminstrn. (hon.), Internat. Devel. Jordan Soc. (dir. 1982-84), Nat. Acad. Pub. Adminstrn. (hon.), Internat. Soc. Panetics (pres. 1991-95, chmn. 1995-98, chmn. emeritus 1999—, bd. govs. 1991—, founding mem. 1991—). Democrat. Presbyterian. Home and Office: 4109 Metzerott Rd College Park MD 20740-2082 E-mail: carlfstover@aol.com.

**STOVER, DIANE ELIZABETH,** internist; d. Harry Stourr and Yolanda Marie Caproni; m. Anthony John Pepe, June 7, 1970; 1 child, Dana. BS magna cum laude, St. John's U., Queens, N.Y., 1966; MD, The Albert Einstein Coll. Medicine, Bronx, N.Y., 1970. Diplomate Am. Bd. Internal Medicine, 1975, in pulmonary disease Am. Bd. Internal Medicine, 1978, lic. physician N.Y., 1970. Intern Harlem Hosp., N.Y.C., 1970—72; sr. resident Hosp. Cornell U., N.Y.C., 1974—75; fellow pulmonology Albert Einstein, Bronx, 1975—77; from asst. attending physician to attending physician Meml. Hosp. Cancer and Allied Diseases, N.Y.C., 1977—91, attending physician, 1991—, chief Pulmonary Svc. Dept. Medicine, 1987—. Instr. Weill Cornell Med. Coll. Cornell U., N.Y.C., 1977—; lectr. in field. Contbr. over 40 articles to profl. jours. Maj. U.S. Army, 1972—74. Named one of Best Doctors in N.Y., New Yorker Mag., 1992, Best Doctors in N.Am., Woodward White Inc., 1992, 1994; recipient Physician's Recognition award, 83, Paul Sherlock Tchg. award, 1985, 2000; grantee, Ancell Clin. Studies Fund, 1983. Fellow: Am. Coll. Chest Physicians (mem. membership com. 1991—93, chmn. coun. govs. 1992—97, gov. N.Y.C. chpt. 1992—97, chmn. task force 1996—2002, chmn. nat. coalition 1998—2002, numerous other coms.); mem.: Am. Soc. Program Dirs., Assn. Subspecialty Profs., N.Y. State Lung Assn. (mem. respiratory svcs. com. 1989—89), N.Y.State Thoracic Soc. (sec. 1995—96, treas. 1995—96, v.p. 1996—97, pres. 1998—99), Am. Thoracic Soc. Roman Cath. Office: Meml Sloan Kettering Cancer Hosp 1275 York Ave H819 New York NY 10021

**STOVER, ELLEN L.,** health scientist, psychologist; b. Bklyn., Nov. 21, 1950; d. Ralph and Charlotte (Tulchin) Simon; m. Alan B. Stover, June 3, 1973; children: Elena Randall Simon, Randall Alan Simon. Andrew Simon. BA with honors, U. Wis., 1972; PhD, Catholic U., 1978. Cons. NIMH, Rockville, Md., 1972-74, exec. sec. drug abuse rsch. review com., 1974-76, spl. asst. to assoc. dir. extramural programs Rockville, Md., 1976-77, chief, small grants program, 1977-79, asst., acting & chief rsch. resources br.,

1980-85, dep. dir., div. basic scis., 1985-88, dir. office AIDS, 1988-97, dir. divsn. mental disorders, behavioral rsch. and AIDS, 1997—; dir. Ctr. Mental Health Rsch. on AIDS. Dir. divsn. AIDS, health, behavior NIMH. Recipient Superior Svc. award USPHS, 1987, 92, 93, Dir.'s award NIH, 1996, Presdl. Rank award, 2001. Mem. APA, Am. Psychol. Soc. Avocations: gardening, dance. Office: NIMH 6001 Executive Blvd Rm 6217 Bethesda MD 20892-0001 Office Phone: 301-443-9700. Business E-Mail: estover@nih.gov.

**STOVER, JOHN FORD,** railroad historian, educator; b. Manhattan, Kans., May 16, 1912; s. John William and Maud (Ford) S.; m. Marjorie Ellen Filley, Aug. 21, 1937; children: John Clyde, Robert Vernon (dec.), Charry Ellen Stover. AB, U. Nebr., 1934, MA, 1937; PhD, U. Wis. 1951. Instr. social studies Arcadia H.S., Nebr., 1936—37; instr. history and govt. Bergen Jr. Coll., NJ, 1937—41; grad. asst. history U. Wis., 1941—42, 1946—47, fellow, 1946; from instr. to assoc. prof. Purdue U., West Lafayette, Ind., 1947—59, prof. history, 1959—78, prof. emeritus, 1978—. Chmn. Pres.'s adv. coun. on retirement Purdue U., 1980-81. Author: The Railroads of the South, 1865-1900, 1955, American Railroads, 1961, rev. edit., 1997, A History of American Railroads, 1967, Turnpikes, Canals and Steamboats, 1969, The Life and Decline of the American Railroad, 1970, Transportation in American History, 1970, History of Illinois Central Railroad, 1975, Iron Road To The West, 1978, Sixty-Five Years of Kiwanis in Indiana, 1981, History of the Baltimore & Ohio Railroad, 1987, Seventy-Five Years of Kiwanis and Indiana, 1990, The Routledge Historical Atlas of the American Railroads, 1999; contbr. chpts. to books, articles to profl. jours. Chmn. edn. com., exec. com. Ind. Sesquicentennial Commn., 1962-67; hon. mem. Indiana Rev. Revolution Bicentennial commn., 1972-82; adv. coun. Centennial History of Ind. Gen. Assembly, 1979-83; pres. Lafayette Kiwanis Found., 1977-78, 2d lt. to capt. USAAF, 1942-46; Res., 1946-53, ret., 1953. XL grantee Purdue Rsch. Found., 1957, 1959; fellow Coll.-Bus. Exch. Program I.C.R.R., 1962, George F. Hixson fellow, 1996; named Sagamore of Wabash Gov. Ind., 1978; recipient Alumni Achievement award U. Nebr., 1985. Fellow Soc. Am. Historians; mem. AAUP, Ind. Acad. Social Scis., We. History Assn., Bus. History Conf. (trustee 1973-76), Am. Hist. Assn., So. Ind. Hist. Assn. (com. on libr. 1975-91), Nebr. Hist. Assn., Tippecanoe County Hist. Assn. (pres. 1972-74), Lexington Group (R.R. historians), Ind. History Tchrs. Assn. (pres. 1958-59), Orgn. Am. Historians, Newcomen Soc. N.Am., Rlwy. and Locomotive Hist. Soc. (editl. adv. bd. for R.R. History jour., 1970-94, Sr. Achievement R.R. History award 1983), Soc. Ind. Pioneers, Civil War Round Table of Nebr., Nat. Rlwy. Hist. Soc., Phi Beta Kappa (hon.), Phi Alpha Theta, Delta Sigma Rho. Clubs: Fortnightly, Lincoln Open Forum. Lodges: Kiwanis (local pres. 1973-74, disting. lt. gov. 1978-79, historian hist. dist. 1980-81, 83-90. 91-92). Republican. Congregationalist. Avocations: golf, model railroading, stamps. Home: Apt 318 Grand Lodge 4400 S 80th St Lincoln NE 68516

**STOVER, KENNETH ALAN,** sales executive; b. Lynn, Mass., Aug. 27, 1952; s. Homer Nelson and Elizabeth Ann (Dryer) Stover. AB, Boston U., Mass., 1978. Chemist Stohler Isotope Chemicals, Waltham, Mass., 1979—85, Strem Chemicals Inc., Newburyport, Mass., 1985—96; cons. sales assoc. Sears, Roebuck & Co., Peabody, Mass., 1998—2004. Mem.: North Shore Computer Soc.

**STOVER, LEON (EUGENE STOVER),** retired anthropology professor, critic, writer; b. Lewistown, Pa., Apr. 9, 1929; s. George Franklin and Helen Elizabeth (Haines) S.; m. Takeko Kawai, Oct. 12, 1956. BA, Western Md. Coll., 1950, LittD (hon.), 1980; MA, Columbia U., 1952, PhD, 1962. Instr. Am. Museum Natural History, N.Y.C., 1955-57; asst. prof. Hobart and William Smith Colls., Geneva, NY, 1957-63; vis. asst. prof. Tokyo U., 1963-65; assoc. prof. Ill. Inst. Tech., Chgo., 1966-74, prof. anthropology, 1974-94, prof. emeritus, 1995—. Founder, 1st chmn. John W. Campbell Meml. Award, 1972; guest lectr. Brit. Film Inst., 1986; humanities cons. Champaign (Ill.) Pub. Library H.G. Wells Traveling Exhbn., 1986. Author: La Science Fiction Americaine, 1972, The Cultural Ecology of Chinese Civilization, 1974, China: An Anthropological Perspective, 1976, The Shaving of Karl Marx, 1982, The Prophetic Soul: A Reading of H.G. Wells's "Things to Come", 1987, Robert A. Heinlein for Twayne's United State Authors Series, 1987, Harry Harrison for Twayne's United States Authors Series, 1990, The Annotated H.G. Wells: The Time Machine, 1996, The Annotated H.G. Wells: The Island of Docotor Moreau, 1996, The Annotated H.G. Wells: The Invisible Man, 1998, The Annotated H.G. Wells: The First Men in the Moon, 1998, The Annotated H.G. Wells: When the Sleeper Wakes, 2000, The Annotated H.G. Wells: The War of the Worlds, 2001, The Annotated H.G. Wells: The Sea Lady, 2001, Science Fiction from Wells to Heinlein, 2002, The Annotated H.G. Wells: Man Who Could Work Miracles, 2002, Stonehenge City: A Reconstruction, 2003, Imperial China and the State Cult of Confucius, 2004, Things to Come, The Annotated H.G. Wells, 2006; sr. author: Stonehenge: The Indo-European Heritage, 1979; co-author: Stonehenge: Where Atlantis Died, 1983; sr. editor: Apeman, Spaceman, 1968; co-editor: Above the Human Landscape, 1972; sci. editor: Amazing, Stories, 1967-69; cons. editor: Contemporary Authors, 1987. Recipient Chris award for best ednl. film, 1974; recipient Cine award Internat. Council Non-Theatrical Events, 1973; named Disting Faculty Lectr. Sigma Xi, 1978; honored with Stover Day Western Md. Coll., 1981 Mem. H.G. Wells Soc., Sci. Fiction Writers Am. Home: 3100 S Michigan Ave Apt 602 Chicago IL 60616-3825

**STOVER, MILES RONALD,** management consultant; b. Glendale, Calif., Dec. 23, 1948; s. Robert Miles and Alberta Mae (Walker) S.; m. Cynthia McNeil, Jan. 25, 1975; children: Christopher, Matthew. BS, U. So. Calif., 1974; MBA, Pepperdine U., 1979; PhD, Kennedy Western U., 2005. Cert. fraud examiner; cert. turnaround profl.; cert. profl. cons.; cert. mgmt. cons.; cert. confidentiality officer; cert. insolvency advisor. V.p., gen. mgr., CFO Johnson Controls Inc., L.A., 1974-82; gen. mgr. MG Products Inc., San Diego, 1982-84; exec. v.p., gen. mgr. ICU Med. Inc., Mission Viejo, 1984-86; v.p., COO B.P. John Inc.. Santa Ana, Calif., 1986-88; gen. mgr. MG Products Inc., San Diego, 1988-90; pres. Lucks Co., Kent, Wash., 1991-96, also bd. dirs.; prin. Crossroads LLC, 1998—2002; pres. Turnaround, Inc., 1996—98, 2002—. Cons. Turnaround Mgmt. Assn., Tacoma, 1990. With USN, 1967-71. Decorated Gallantry Cross USN; recipient award for Productivity U.S. Senate, 1978. Mem. Inst. Mgmt. Cons., Turnaround Mgmt. Assn., Am. Bankruptcy Inst., Nat. Assn. Corp. Dirs., Assn. Cert. Fraud Examiners, Assn. Insolvency and Restructuring Advisors, Inst. Mgmt. Accts., Mensa. Republican. Methodist. Home: 3415 A St NW Gig Harbor WA 98335-7843 Office Phone: 253-857-6730. Business E-Mail: mstover@turnaround-inc.com.

**STOVER, RICHARD L.,** investor; b. Uniontown, Pa., Oct. 11, 1942; s. Louis John and Sarah Virginia Stover; m. Dorothea Gerber Stover, June 19, 1965; children: Kristin Stover Matheny, Douglas Richard. BSBA, The Pa. State U., 1965. Sr. v.p. Mellon Fin. Corp., Pitts., 1969—89; exec. v.p. Bank of New Eng. Corp., Boston, 1989—91; exec. v.p. and chief credit officer Equimark Corp., Pittsburgh, Pa., 1991—93; mng. dir. GE Capital Corp., Stamford, Conn., 1993—94; founder and prin. Stover & Assocs., Wexford, Pa., 1994—96; founder and mng. dir. ARC Capital, Pittsburgh, Pa., 1995—96; pres. First Western Bancorp, Inc., New Castle, Pa., 1996—99; mng. prin. Birchmere Capital, Wexford, Pa., 2000—. Dir. SAFAS Corp., Clifton, NJ, 1995—; Bliley Technologies, Inc., Erie, Pa., 1999—; Ductmate Industries, Inc., Charleroi, Pa., 2004—. Bd. dirs. Inst. for Transfusion Medicine, Pitts., 1978; chmn. bd. suprs. Marshall Twp., Wexford, Pa., 1995—2001; chmn., fin. com. WQED Multimedia, Pitts., 2002. Lt. USN, 1965—69. Mem.: Bonita Bay Club, Treeesdales Golf and Country Club, The Duquesne Club. Avocations: golf, travel, exercise, history. Office: Birchmere Capital 500 Stonewood Dr Ste 220 Wexford PA 15090 Office Phone: 724-940-2300. Office Fax: 724-940-2383. E-mail: rstover@birchmere.net.

**STOVER, WILBUR G., JR.,** manufacturing executive; BSBA, Wash. State U., 1975. Audit mgr. Cooper & Lybrand; with Micron, 1989, dir. subs. sales; v.p. fin., CFO, Micron Semiconductor, 1992; v.p. fin., CFO Micron Tech., Inc., Boise, Idaho, 1994—. Office: Micron Tech Inc PO Box 6 8000 S Federal Way Boise ID 83707-0006

**STOWE, ALEXIS MARIANI,** accountant, consultant; b. Binghamton, N.Y., May 3, 1950; d. Albert Joseph and Gilda Ann (DiNardo) Mariani; m. Dennis James Stowe, June 3, 1972 (dec. Nov. 1988); children: Cort Andrew, Derek Anthony, Jilda Ann. Student, Le Moyne Coll., 1968-70; BS in Acctg., SUNY, Buffalo, 1972; MS in Acctg., SUNY, Albany, 1974; MS in Taxation, Southeastern U., 1980. CPA, N.Y., Va., cert. fraud examiner; cert. govt. fin. mgr., cert. info. sys. auditor. In-charge acct. Ernst & Young, CPA's, Buffalo, 1973-74; sr. corp. acct. Moog, Inc., East Aurora, N.Y., 1974-76; auditor U.S. Gen. Acctg. Office, Washington, 1976-78, 79-80; tax law specialist IRS, Washington, 1978-79; pvt. practice CPA Woodbridge, Va., 1980-87; v.p., contr. M.T. Hall, Ltd., Woodbridge, 1987-91; audit mgr. U.S. Dept. Health and Human Svcs., Washington, 1991-93; oversight mgr. Resolution Trust Corp., Washington, 1993-94; v.p., prin. Gardiner, Kamya, CPA's, Washington, 1994-97; v.p., ptnr. Leon Snead & Co., PC, Rockville, Md., 1998—2002; v.p., prin. Gardiner, Kamya, CPAs, Washington, 2002—05; dir. profl. svcs. Mgmt. Concepts., Washington, 2005; dir. Washington fed. practice Price Waterhouse Coopers, Washington, 2005—, 2005—. Trustee pension plan M.T. Hall, Ltd., Woodbridge, 1987—90; team leader CFO task force Pres.'s Coun. on Integrity and Efficiency, Washington, 1991—93; instr. Inspector Gen. Auditor Tng. Inst., Ft. Belvoir, Va., 1992—2000; mem. task force on grants Govtl. Acctg. Stds. Bd., Norwalk, Conn., 1992—96; mem. faculty Assn. Cert. Fraud Examiners, 1995—. Contbr. articles to profl. jours. N.Y. Regents scholar, 1968-72. Mem.: AICPA, Inst. Internal Auditors, Info. Sys. Audit Control Assn., Assn. Cert. Fraud Examiners, Assn. Govt. Accts. (vice chair publs. 1994—98, Author's award 1991), Va. Soc. CPAs, Cath. Daus. of Am., Beta Gamma Sigma, Chi Omega. Roman Catholic. Home: 1320 N Veitch St #819 Arlington VA 22201 Office: 1800 Tysons Blvd Mc Lean VA 22102 Office Phone: 703-918-1049. Business E-Mail: alexis.m.stowe@us.pwc.com.

**STOWE, CHARLES ROBINSON BEECHER,** management consultant, educator, lawyer; b. Seattle, July 18, 1949; s. David and Edith Beecher (Andrade) Stowe; m. Laura Everett, Mar. 9, 1985. BA, Vanderbilt U., 1971; MBA, U. Tex., Dallas, 1975; JD, U. Houston, 1982; PhD, U. Warsaw, Poland, 1998. Bar: Tex. 1982, US Dist. Ct. (so. dist.), Tex. 1984, US Tax Ct. 1984. Acct. exec. Engleman Co., Dallas, 1974-75; dir. Productive Capital Assoc., 1975-81; instr. Richland Coll., Dallas, 1976; acct. Arthur Andersen and Co., 1976-78; pres. Stowe and Co., 1978—; prof. dept. gen. bus., fin. Coll. Bus. Adminstrn., Sam Houston State U., 1982—, dir. office internat. programs, 1997-2001. BD dir., office internat. programs Sam Houston State U., Tex., adminstrv. intern asst. to pres., 1985; cons. in field. Editor: Houston Journal International Law, 1981—82; co-editor: Knowledge Cafe for Intellect Product and Intellectual Entrepreneurship, 2001, Knowledge Cafe for Intellectual Entrepreneurship, Intellectual Product, Intellectual Capital, 2001; author: Bankruptcy I Micro-Mash Inc., 1989, 3d edit., 2005, The Implications of Foreign Financial Institutions on Poland's Emerging Entrepreneurial Economy, 1999; co-author: CPA; contbr. articles to profl. jour. Team chief, US Mil. liaison, Rep., 1994; founder Young Am.'s Found., 1969—; trustee Stowe-Day Found., 1979—80; vol. faculty State Bar Tex., Profl. Devel. Program, 1988—; vol., mediator Dispute Resolution Ctr., Montgomery County; mediator so. dist. US Dist. Ct., Tex., 1993; pub. affairs officer George C. Marshall European Ctr. Security Studies, 1997; vestry St. Stephen's Episcopal Ch., Huntsville, Tex., 2002—05. Capt. Res. USNR, 1971—74. Decorated Navy Achievement medal, Gold Star Navy, US, Def. Meritorious Svc. medal (oak leaf cluster), Navy Meritorious Svc. award, Legion of Merit; recipient Freedoms Found. award; fellow Summer fellow Tex. Coordinating Bd., 1988, Prince-Babson Fellow Entrepreneurship Symposium, 1991. Mem.: Res. Officers Assn., Naval Res. Assn., Tex. Assn. Realtors, Pub. Rels. Soc. Am., Assn. Computer Educators Tex. (bd. dirs. 2000—03, editor 2002—05), Tex. State Bar Coll. (bd. dirs. 2001—05), Walker County Bar Assn. (pres. 1987—88), State Bar Tex. (vol. faculty profl. devel. program 1988—90, vice chmn. profl. efficiency and econ. rsch. com. 1993, chmn. law office mgmt. com. 1993—94), Am. Arbitration Assn., ABA, US Navy League, Dallas Vanderbilt Club (pres. 1977—78). Office: PO Box 537 Huntsville TX 77342-0537

**STOWE, ROBERT LEE, III,** textile company executive; b. Charlotte, N.C., July 3, 1954; s. Robert Lee Jr. and Ruth Link (Harding) S.; m. Christine Ruth Edwards, Jan. 15, 1983; children: Christine Ruth, Lillian Rhyne. BA, Davidson (N.C.) Coll., 1976. Dir. mgmt. trainee R.L. Stowe Mills, Inc., Belmont, N.C., 1976-77, v.p., 1977-79, exec. v.p., 1979-84, chmn. bd., 1984—. Sec., treas. Lakeview Farms, Inc.; pres. Robrt Lee Stowe Jr. Found., Belmont, 1978—; bd. mgrs. Wachovia Bank of N.C., Gaston County; mem.-mgr. McAdams & Stowe, LLC; bd. dirs. John Locke Found. Trustee Belmont Abbey Coll., 1987-90, Mint Mus. Art, Charlotte, 1989-92, Crossnore (N.C.) Sch., 1987-98, Sci. Museums, Charlotte, 1989-91, Gaston Day Sch., 1994-97, Gaston County C. of C., 1992-95, Mis. of New South; trustee Daniel Jonathan Stowe Conservancy, 1990, pres., 1996-2000, vice-chmn., 2000; deacon, elder local Presbyn. Ch.; bd. dirs. Downtown Belmont, Inc., Gaston County Edn. Found., Gaston County YMCA, John Locke Found., 2005—; trustee Presbyn. Hosp. Found., Charlotte, N.C. Named one of Outstanding Young Men Am., 1979. Mem. Am. Textile Mfrs. Inst. (bd. dirs. 1989-92), Newcomen Soc. U.S., N.C. Textile Found. (bd. dirs. 1986—), Net. Club N.Y., Charlotte Country Club, Gaston Country Club. Republican. Avocations: golf, boating, church activities. Home: 135 N Main St PO Box 232 Belmont NC 28012-0232 Office: RL Stowe Mills Inc 100 N Main St Belmont NC 28012-3104 Office Phone: 704-825-5314. Business E-Mail: rlstowe3@rlstowe.com.

**STOWELL, CHRISTOPHER R.,** artistic director, choreographer, retired dancer; b. NYC, June 8, 1966; s. Kent and Francia (Russell) S. Student, Pacific N.W. Ballet Sch., 1979-84, Sch. Am. Ballet, 1984-85. Entered corps de ballet San Francisco Ballet, 1986, promoted to soloist, 1987, prin., 1990—2001; freelance choreographer for ballet and opera cos., 2001—; ballet master Balanchine Trust, 2001—; artistic dir. Oreg. Ballet Theater. Guest artist Ballet Met, Ohio, Pacific N.W. Ballet, Seattle, and with Jean Charles Gil, Marseilles, France, Asami Maki Ballet, Tokyo. Created leading roles in Handel-A Celebration, Con Brio, The Sleeping Beauty, New Sleep, Connotations, Pulcinella, Meistens Mozart; other roles include Calcium Light Night, Rubies, The Sons of Horus, The Four Temperaments, Hearts, Tarantella, Flower Festival, La Fille Mal Garde, Haffner Symphony, Forgotten Land, The End, Agon, In the Middle Somewhat Elevated, Le Quattro Stagioni, Swan Lake, Job, Company B, Tchaikousky Pas de Deux, Maelstrom, Mercutio in Romeo and Juliet, The Dance House, Stars and Stripes, Ballo Della Regina, Drink to me only With Thine Eyes, Pacific; performed in Reykjavik Arts Festival, Iceland, 1990, San Francisco Ballet at the Paris Opera Garnier, 1994, Bolshoi Theatre, Moscow, 1998; artistic dir. Oreg. Ballet Theatre, Portland, 2003—. Avocations: cooking, reading, camping. Office: 818 SE 6th Ave Portland OR 97214*

**STOWELL, KENT,** ballet director; b. Rexburg, Idaho, Aug. 8, 1939; s. Harold Bowman and Maxine (Hudson) S.; m. Francia Marie Russell, Nov. 19, 1965; children: Christopher, Darren, Ethan. Student, San Francisco Ballet Sch., Sch. Am. Ballet, LHD (hon.) Seattle U., 2003, PhD (hon.) 2004; Lead dancer San Francisco Ballet, 1957-62, NYC Ballet, 1962-68; ballet dir., ballet master Frankfurt (Fed. Republic Germany) Opera Ballet, 1973-77; artistic dir. Pacific NW Ballet, Seattle, 1977—; prof. dance Ind. U., Bloomington, 1969-70; bd. dirs. Sch. of Am. Ballet, Dance/USA, Washington, 1986—. Choreographer: Silver Lining, Cinderella, Carmina Burana, Coppelia, Time & Ebb, Faurè Requiem, Hail to the Conquering Hero, Firebird, Over the Waves, Nutcracker, The Tragedy of Romeo and Juliet, Delicate Balance, Swan Lake, Time and Ebb, Through Interior Worlds, Quaternary, Orpheus. Bd. dirs. Sch. of Am. Ballet, NYC, 1981—; mem. Goodwill Games Arts Com., Seattle, 1987—; chmn. dance panel NEA, 1981-85. Grantee NEA, 1980, 85, fellow NEA, 1979. Recipient Arts Service award King County Arts Commn., 1985, Outstanding Contbn. to Pacific NW Ballet State of Was., 1987, Best Dance Co. award The Weekly Newspaper, Seattle, 1987, Gov. Arts award, 1988, Dance Mag. award, 1996, Lifetime Achievement award U. Utah, 2004,

Lifetime Achievement in Arts award ArtsFund, 2004, award Seattle (Wash.) Ctr., 2004, Entrepreneur of Yr. award Ernst and Young, 2004, Mayor's Art award, 2004. Office: Pacific NW Ballet 301 Mercer St Seattle WA 98109-4600*

**STOWELL, ROBERT EUGENE,** pathologist, retired educator; b. Cashmere, Wash., Dec. 25, 1914; s. Eugene Francis and Mary (Wilson) S.; m. Eva Mae (Chambers), Dec. 1, 1945; children: Susan Jane, Robert Eugene Jr. Attended, Whitman Coll., 1932-33; BA, Stanford Univ., 1936, MD, 1941; PhD, Washington Univ., 1944. Fellow in cytology Wash. U. Sch. Medicine, St. Louis, 1940-42; rsch. fellow Barnard Free Skin and Cancer Hosp., St. Louis, 1940-42; rsch. assoc., 1942-48; asst. resident in pathology Barnes, McMillan, St. Louis Children's Hosps., St. Louis, 1942-43, resident in pathology, 1943-44, asst. pathologist, 1944-48; instr. in pathology Washington U. Sch. Medicine, St. Louis, 1943-45, asst. prof., assoc. prof., 1948; advanced med. fellow Inst. for Cell Rsch., Stockholm, 1946-47; chmn. dept. oncology U. Kans. Med. Ctr., Kansas City, Kans., 1948-51, prof. pathology and oncology, dir. cancer rsch., 1948-59, chmn., 1951-59; sci. dir. Armed Forces Inst. Pathology, Washington, 1959-67; chmn. dept. pathology Sch. of Medicine U. Calif., Davis, 1967-69, asst. dean Sch. Medicine, 1967-72, prof. pathology Sch. Medicine, 1967-82, prof. emeritus, 1982—; dir. div. pathology Sacramento Med. Ctr., 1967-69. Vis. prof. U. Md. Sch. Medicine, Balt. 1960-67; acting dir. Nat. Ctr. for Primate Biology, U. Calif., Davis, 1968-69, dir., 1969-71; cons. U.S. Atomic Energy commn., Los Alamos, N.Mex., 1949-54; NIH, 1949-74; Cancer Control Div. USPHS, 1949-59, others; mem. adv. med. bd. Leonard Wood Meml. found., Washington, 1965-67; numerous univs.; prin. investigator, chmn. Expert Panel on Authentication Review of Selected Materials Submitted to the FDA Relative to Application of Searle Lab. to Market Aspartame, 1977-78; Assessment of the Practical Risk to Human Health from Nitrilotriacetic Acid in Household Laundry Products, 1984-85. Contbr. 121 articles, 34 abstracts to jour. in field; editor 35 biomed. books, monographs and conf. reports, 1941-88; mem. editorial bd. Cancer Rsch., 1949-59, Lab. Investigation, 1952-71, editor, 1967-71. Recipient Meritorious Svc. Award, Dept. Army, 1963; Exceptional Civilian Svc. Award, Dept. Army, 1965; Disting. Svc. Award U. Calif., 1988, Robert E. Stowell ann. Med. Student Award Outstanding Excellence in Pathology, 1981—; Robert E. Stowell ann. lectureship established U. Calif. Sch. Medicine, 1991 and Am. Registry of Pathology, Washington, 1991; endowed Robert E. Stowell professorship, 2002-. Mem. AMA; Am. Registry of Pathology (bd. dir. 1976-83, exec. com. 1976-82, v.p. 1976-78, pres. 1978-79, Disting. Svc. Award 1995), Am. Assn. Cancer Rsch., Am. Assn. Pathologists (Gold-headed Cane Award 1990), Am. Assn. Pathologists and Bacteriologists (councilor 1965-72, v.p. 1969-70, pres. 1970-71), Am. Soc. Clin. Pathologists; Am. Soc. Exptl. Pathology (councilor 1962-66, v.p. 1963-64, pres. 1964-65); Calif. Med. Soc.; Calif. Soc. Pathologists; Binford-Dammin Soc. Infectious Disease Pathologists; Coll. Am. Pathologists; Histochem. Soc.; Internat. Acad. Pathology (councilor 1954-61, pres.-elect 1958-59, pres. 1995-60); Disting. Svc. Award 1970; Diamond Jubilee Award 1981; Stowell-Orbison Award established 1982—); Soc. Cryobiology (bd. gov. 1968-71); Soc. Exptl. Biology and Medicine; U.S. and Can. Acad. Pathology; Yolo County Med. Soc.; Assn. Mil. Surgeons U.S. (sustaining membership award 1965), Univ. Associated for Rsch. and Edn. in Path. (bd. dir. 1975-90, sec.-treas. 1978-82, hon. dir. 1990-2002); Sigma Xi; Alpha Omega Alpha. Home: 44752 N El Macero Dr El Macero CA 95618-1090

**STOWERS, CARLTON EUGENE,** writer; b. Brownwood, Tex., Apr. 14, 1942; s. Ira Milton and Fay Eloise (Stephenson) S.; m. Patricia Ann Folks, Mar. 2, 1981; children: Anson, Ashley. Student, U. Tex., Austin, 1961-63. Sportswriter Abilene (Tex.) Reporter News, 1963-64; sports editor Roswell (N.Mex.) Daily Record, 1964-65; sportswriter Lubbock (Tex.) Avalanche Jour., 1965-67; sports editor Amarillo (Tex.) Globe News, 1967-72; reporter, columnist Dallas Morning News, 1972-81; freelance writer Cedar Hill, Tex., 1981—. Editor Dallas Cowboys Weekly, 1985-89. Author: The Randy Matson Story, 1971, Spirit, 1973; author: (with E.B. Hughes) Doc, 1976; author: (with Trent Jones) Where the Rainbows Wait, 1978; author: (with Wilbur Evans) Champions, 1978; author: The Overcomers, 1978; author: (with Roy Rogers and Dale Evans) Happy Trails, 1979; author: pub. softcover as Terlingua Teacher, 1982, 2005, The Unsinkable Titanic Thompson, 1982, 1988, Journey to Triumph, 1988; author: (with Steve Perkins and Greg Aiello) Dallas Cowboys Bluebook III, 1982; author: Partners in Blue: The 100-Year History of the Dallas Police Department, 1983, with Greg Aiello: Dallas Cowboys Bluebook IV, 1983;; author: (with Billy Olson) Reaching Higher, 1984; author: The Dallas Cowboys: The First 25 Years, 1984, The Cowboy Chronicles, 1984; author: (ghosted for Pam Lontos) Don't Tell Me It's Impossible Until I've Already Done It, 1988; author: Careless Whispers, 1986 (Edgar Allan Poe award Mystery Writers Am., Oppie award S.W. Booksellers Assn.), The Cotton Bowl: The First 50 Years, 1986; author: (with Jarret Bell) Dallas Cowboys Bluebook IX, 1988; author: (with Wiliam C. Dear) Please...Don't Kill Me: The True Story of the Milo Murder, 1989 (Literary Guild selection); author: (with Larry Wansley) The FBI Undercover: The True Story of Special Agent 'Mandrake', 1989; author: Innocence Lost, 1990, A Hero Named George, 1991, Hard Lessons, 1994, Open Secrets, 1994, Sins of the Son, 1995; author: (with Marcus Allen) Marcus, 1997; author: To the Last Breath, 1998 (Edgar Allan Poe award Mystery Writers Am.); author: (with Rev. Carroll Pickett) Within These Walls, 2002 (Violet Crown award, 2002, PEN S.W. Book award finalist, 2002); author: Scream at the Sky, 2003, Death in a Texas Desert, 2003, Where Dreams Die Hard, 2005. Recipient Katie awards Dallas Press Club, 1985-2004, Stephen Philben awards Dallas Bar Assn., 1987-92, other journalism awards. Home: 1015 Randy Rd Cedar Hill TX 75104-3035 Office Phone: 972-291-4831 E-mail: antowers1@comcast.net.

**STOWERS, JAMES EVANS, JR.,** investment company executive; b. Kansas City, Mo., Jan. 10, 1924; s. James Evans Sr. and Laura (Smith) S.; m. Virginia Ann Glasscock, Feb. 4, 1954; children: Pamela, Kathleen, James Evans III, Linda. AB, U. Mo., 1946, BS in Medicine, 1947. Chmn. bd. Am. Century Investment Mgmt. Inc., Am. Century Cos., Inc.; Am. Century Group of Mutual Funds, Kansas City, 1958—. Author: Why Waste Your Money on Life Insurance, 1967, Principles of Financial Consulting, 1971, Yes, You Can...achieve financial independence, 1992. Co-founder, chmn. Stowers Inst. for Med. Rsch., Kansas City, 1995—. Capt. USAAF, 1943-45; with USAFR, 1945-57. Mem. Kansas City Co. U.S. Capital Svc Club Republican Chmn. Am Century Svcs 4500 Main St Kansas City MO 64111-1816*

**STOWERS, MARK DAVID,** chemicals executive; b. Houston, Feb. 9, 1957; s. Charles Henry Stowers, Jr. and Eleanor Ann (Schurz) Fowler; m. Sarah Kent Upham, Sept. 2, 1984; children: Rosemary Diane, Samuel Huntington, Elizabeth Ann. BS in Biology, Appalachian State U., Boone, N.C., 1977; MS in Microbiology, N.C. State U., 1980, PhD in Microbiology, 1982. Postdoctoral assoc. Cornell U., Ithaca, NY, 1982-83; sr. project leader NPI, Inc., Salt Lake City, 1983-86; head, biol. scis. rsch. Eastman Kodak Co., Rochester, NY, 1986-89; bus. dir. Monsanto Co., St. Louis, 1989-95, v.p. ops. Naples, Fla., 1996—97; v.p. mktg. Seminic Inc., Oxnard, Calif., 1996—98, v.p. bus. devel., 1998—2000; pres., CEO MBI Internat., Lansing, Mich., 2000—, Draths Corp. Bd. dirs. BioPlastics Inc., Natura, Inc., MBI Internat. Bd. dirs. Pierce Coll. Found., 2000—01. Rsch. grantee NSF, 1984, AID, 1985, Dept. Energy, 2001—, EPA, 2001-03, USDA, 2002—; named Disting. Alumnus, Coll. Agr. and Life Scis. N.C. State U., 2003. Mem. AAAS, Am. Soc. for Microbiology, Soc. for Indsl. Microbiology, Assn. Univ. Tech. Mgrs., Coun. of Logistic Mgmt., Am. Mgmt. Assn., Inst. Food Technologists, Comml. Devel. Assn., Produce Mktg. Assn., United Fresh Fruit and Vegetable Assn. (sci. and tech. com.), Fla. Fruit and Vegetable Assn. (bd. dirs.). Conservative. Methodist. Achievements include patents for use of a protease in the extraction of Chlamydial, Gonococcal and Herpes Antigens. Avocations: golf, cross country skiing, basketball, fly fishing. Home: 480 Juneberry Ln Okemos MI 48864-4126 Office: MBI Internat 3900 Collins Rd Lansing MI 48910 Office Phone: 517-336-4612. Personal E-mail: mdstowers@yahoo.com

**STOWMAN, DAVID L.,** lawyer; b. Rothsay, Minn., 1943; m. Judy Stowman; 4 children. BA, Moorehead State Univ.; JD, Univ. N.D. Co-founder NW Minn. Legal Services. Capt. USMC, 1965—69, Vietnam (1968-69). Named one of Minn. Top 25 Lawyers, Law & Politics mag., 2001. Mem.: ABA, Minn. State Bar Assn. (pres.-elect 2003, pres. 2004). Achievements include completing the Boston Marathon. Avocations: running, water-skiing. Office: Stowman Law Office PO Box 845 Detroit Lakes MN 56502-0845 also: Stowman Law Office 1100 W Lake Dr Detroit Lakes MN 56501 Office Phone: 218-847-5644.

**STOYTCHEVA, LILIA STEFANOVA,** concert pianist, educator; b. Sofia, Bulgaria, July 13, 1962; arrived in US, 1995; d. Stefan Sotirov Stoytchev and Liliana Georgieva Sarafova. Studied with Liuba Entcheva, Bulgarian State Conservatory, M in Piano summa cum laude, 1987; M of Music summa cum laude, Winthrop U., 1997; MusD in Piano Performance, U. Iowa, 2005. Instr. piano Bulgarian State Conservatory, Sofia, 1988—92; asst. prof. piano Sofia's U. "Kliment Ohridski", 1988—90; prof. piano State Conservatory, Czech Republic, 1992—95; asst. prof. Ctrl. State U. Wilberforce, Ohio, 2003—06; assoc. prof. North Greenville U., Tigerville, SC, 2006—. Composer: 1300 Anniversary Bulgaria, 1981; musician (solo pianist): Symphony Orch. of the Bulgarian State Conservatory, 1987, Symphony Orchestra of Biel/Bienne, 1992, The Jihoceske Chamber Orchestra of South Bohemia, 1992, Academic Symphony Orch. U. Iowa; musician: (pianist) Hancher Auditorium, 2002, Harper Hall, 2001, 2002, Clapp Hall, 2001, 2002, Rudolf Steiner House and St. Cyprianus Ch. Eng., 2001, Concert Hall at the Conservatory of Stravanger, 2002, Salle Munch at Ecole Normal de Musique, 2002. Recipient award, Nat. Composition Competition, Bulgaria, 1981, Internat. Piano Competition, Italy, 1988, John Simms award, 1998, 1999, 2001, award, Maia Quartet Competition, 2001; fellow Internat. Piano Master Classes with Norma Fisher, London, UK, 2001, Internat. Piano Master Classes with Nelson Delle-Vigne, John Perry, Phillippe Entremont and Einar Nokleberg, Paris, 2002; grantee, George Soros Found. Open Soc., Sofia, 1992; scholar Internat. Piano Master Classes with Rudolf Buchbinder and Victor Merzhanov, Switzerland, 1992, 1993, Walter Hautzig Piano Master Classes, S.C., 1995, 1996, U. Iowa, 2001, Internat. Piano Workshop, Stavanger, Norway, 2002. Mem.: Studio of the Young Musician, Coll. Music Soc., Phi Kappa Phi. Avocations: travel, fine arts, languages. Personal E-mail: lstoytch@hotmail.com.

**STRAATSMA, BRADLEY RALPH,** ophthalmologist, educator; b. Grand Rapids, Mich., Dec. 29, 1927; s. Clarence Ralph and Lucretia Marie (Nicholson) S.; m. Ruth Campbell, June 16, 1951; children: Cary Ewing, Derek, Greer. Student, U. Mich., 1947; MD cum laude, Yale U., 1951; DSc (hon.), Columbia U., 1984; JD cum laude, U. West LA, 2002. Diplomate Am. Bd. Ophthalmology (vice chmn. 1979, chmn. 1980). Intern New Haven Hosp., Yale U., 1951-52; resident in ophthalmology Columbia U., N.Y.C., 1955-58; spl. clin. trainee Nat. Inst. Neurol. Diseases and Blindness, Bethesda, Md., 1958-59; assoc. prof. surgery/ophthalmology UCLA Sch. Medicine, 1959-63, chief div. ophthalmology, dept. surgery, 1959-68, prof. surgery/ophthalmology, 1963-68, prof. ophthalmology, 1968—2001, dir. Jules Stein Eye Inst., 1964-94, chmn. dept. ophthalmology, 1968-94, prof. emeritus, 2001—; ophthalmologist-in-chief UCLA Med. Ctr., 1968-94. Lectr. numerous univs. and profl. socs. 1971—; cons. to surgeon gen. USPHS, mem. Vision Research Tng. Com., Nat. Inst. Neurol. Diseases and Blindness, NIH, 1959-63, mem. neurol. and sensory disease program project com., 1964-68; chmn. Vision Research Program Planning Com., Nat. Adv. Eye Council, Nat. Eye Inst., NIH, 1973-75, 75-77, 85-89; mem. med. adv. bd. Internat. Eye Found., 1970-79; mem. adv. com. on basic clin. research Nat. Soc. to Prevent Blindness, 1971-87; mem. med. adv. com. Fight for Sight, 1960-83; bd. dirs. So. Calif. Soc. to Prevent Blindness, 1967-77, Ophthalmic Pub. Co., 1975-93, v.p. 1990-93, Pan-Am. Ophthalmol. Found., 1985-95; chmn. sci. adv. bd. Ctr. for Partially Sighted, 1984-87; mem. nat. adv. panel Found. for Eye Research, Inc., 1984-94; mem. com. Palestra Oftalmologica Panamericana, 1976-81; coord. com. Nat. Eye Health Edn. Program, 1989; mem. sci. adv. bd. Rsch. to Prevent Blindness, Inc., 1993—2003. Editor-in-chief Am. Jour. Ophthalmology, 1993-2002; mem. editorial bd. UCLA Forum in Med. Scis., 1974-82, Am. Jour. Ophthalmology, 1974-91, Am. Intra-Ocular Implant Soc. Jour., 1978-79, EYE-SAT Satellite-Relayed Profl. Edn. in Ophthalmology, 1982-86; mng. editor von Graefe's Archive for Clin. and Exptl. Ophthalmology, 1976-88; contbr. over 500 articles to med. jours. Trustee John Thomas Dye Sch., Los Angeles, 1967-72. Lt. USNR, 1952-54. Recipient William Warren Hoppin award N.Y. Acad. Medicine, 1956, Univ. Service award UCLA Alumni Assn., 1982, Miguel Aleman Found. medal, 1992, Benjamin Boyd Humanitarian award Pan Am. Assn. Ophthalmology, 1991, Lucian Howe medal, Am. Ophthalmological Soc., 1992, Internat. Gold Medal award 3rd Singapore Nat. Eye Ctr. Internat. Meeting and 11th Internat. Meeting on Cataract, Implant, Microsurgery and Refractive Keratoplasty, 1998, award of merit in retinal rsch. Retina Rsch. Found., 2002, Jose Rizal gold medal Asia-Pacific Acad. Ophthalmology, 2003, Gold medal Barraquer Inst., 2005. Fellow Royal Australian Coll. Ophthalmologists (hon.); mem. Academia Ophthalmologica Internationales (pres. 1998-2002), Am. Acad. Ophthalmology (bd. councillors 1981, Life Achievement award 1999), Found. of Am. Acad. Ophthalmology (trustee 1989, chmn. bd. trustees 1989-92), Am. Acad. Ophthalmology and Otolaryngology (pres. 1977), Am. Soc. Cataract and Refractive Surgery, AMA (asst. sec. ophthalmology sect. 1962-63, sec. 1963-66, chmn. 1966-67, coun. 1970-74), Am. Ophthalmol. Soc. (coun. 1985-90, v.p. 1992, pres. 1993), Assn. Rsch. in Vision and Ophthalmology (Mildred Weisenfeld award 1991), Assn. U. Profs. of Ophthalmology (trustee 1969-75, pres.-elect 1973-74, pres. 1974-75), Assn. VA Ophthalmologists, Calif. Med. Assn. (mem. ophthalmology adv. panel 1972-94, chmn. 1974-79, sci. bd. 1973-79, ho. of dels. 1974, 77, 79), Chilean Soc. Ophthalmology (hon.), Columbian Soc. Ophthalmology (hon.), Glaucoma Soc. Internat. Congress of Ophthalmology (hon.), Heed Ophthalmic Found. (chmn., bd. dirs., 1990-98), Hellenic Ophthalmol. Soc. (hon.), Internat. Coun. Ophthalmology (bd. dirs. 1993-, Internat. Duke-Elder medal 2006), LA County Med. Assn., LA Soc. Ophthalmology, Pan-Am. Assn. Ophthalmology (coun. 1972—, pres. elect 1985-87, pres. 1987-89), Peruvian Soc. Ophthalmology (hon.), Retina Soc., Barraquer Inst. Ophthalmology (pres. 1996-05), Academia Ophthalmol. Internat. (pres. 1998-02), Internat. Coun. Ophthalmology (pres. found. 2002-, Jules Francois medal 2002, Philip M. Corboy award 2005, Internat. Duke-Elder medal 2006), The Jules Stein Club. Presbyterian. Avocations: music, scuba diving. Home: 3031 Elvido Dr Los Angeles CA 90049-1107 Office: UCLA 100 Stein Plz Los Angeles CA 90095-7065 Office Phone: 310-825-5051. Business E-Mail: straatsma@jsei.ucla.edu.

**STRACHAN, LINDA AVERY,** federal agency administrator; BA, Greensboro Coll. Spl. asst. to asst. administr., Offices Pesticides & Toxic Substances EPA; spl. asst. to asst. sec, Bur. Oceans, Internat. Environ. & Scientific Affairs US Dept. State, Washington; dir. congl. affairs Monsanto Co.; asst. sec. for congl. rels. USDA, Washington, 2006—. Office: USDA 1400 Independence Ave SW Washington DC 20250

**STRACHER, DOROTHY ALTMAN,** education educator, consultant; b. N.Y.C., May 11, 1934; d. Joseph and Gussie (Newman) Altman; m. Alfred Stracher, July 4, 1954; children: Cameron Altman, Adam Reed, Erica Terri. BA, Bklyn. Coll., 1955; MA, Columbia U., 1957; postgrad., U. Copenhagen, 1958-59; acad. vis., Oxford (Eng.) U., 1973-74; PhD, Hofstra U. 1979. Cert. English and social sci. tchr. N.Y. Coord. secondary reading Ctrl. Moriches (N.Y.) Sch. Dist., 1974-78; coord. reading East Williston (N.Y.) Sch. Dist., 1978-79; specialist reading and writing SUNY, Old Westbury, 1979-81; adj. prof. dept. reading Hofstra U., Hempstead, NY, 1979-82; asst. prof. edn. L.I. U., Bklyn., 1982-83, Coll. New Rochelle, 1983-85; sr. learning diagnostic specialist child devel. div. L.I. Jewish Hosp., Bklyn., 1985-86; prof. Dowling Coll., Oakdale, NY, 1986—, acad. chair Sch. Edn., 1991-93, coord. elem. edn. dept., 2000-01; acad. chair Sch. Edn., 2001-05. Cons. Johnson & Johnson, Inc., Princeton, NJ, 1982—; Sanford (Fla.) Sch. Dist., 1983, Lawrence (N.Y.) Sch. Dist., 1984, Sch. Dist. 7, N.Y.C., 1984—; vis. prof. U. East London, 1994. Author (with others): First the Fundamentals, 1980, What Do You Call a Well-Behaved Martian?, A Manual for Thinkers' Parents, 1981, Integrating Assessment, 1982; editor: Differentiated Curricula, 1986, A Literature Based Integrated Curriculum: Grades Pre-K, 1989, Successful Strategies for Learning Disabled College Students: Reading, Writing and Reasoning, 1991, 3d edit., 2005; co-author: Commitment to Excellence, 2002; contbr. articles to profl. jours. Bd. dirs. Roslyn (N.Y.) Sch. Dist., 1975—84, v.p., 1980—82, pres., 1982—84; mem. adv. bd. Children's Sch. Sci., Wood Hole, Mass., 1976—82. Recipient Academic Excellence award, Dowling Coll., 2005. Mem.: NOW, LWV (bd. dirs. 1961—70), Nat. Assoc. Gifted Edn., Internat. Reading Assn., Orton Soc., Coun. Exceptional Children, Kappa Delta Pi. Avocations: reading, writing, travel. Home: 47 The Oaks Roslyn NY 11576-1704 Office Phone: 631-244-3306. Personal E-mail: dastracher@cs.com. Business E-Mail: strached@dowling.edu.

**STRACHER, GLENN BLAIR,** geology educator, research scientist; b. Albany, N.Y., Mar. 31, 1949; s. Bernard and Lillian (Sussman) S.; m. Janet Lynn Stracher. BS in Geol. Sci., U. Wash., 1980; MS in Geology, U. Nebr., 1986, PhD in Geology, 1989. Grad. tchg. asst. U. Nebr., Lincoln, 1984-89; asst. prof. geology Bloomsburg U. Pa., 1992; prof. geology East Ga. Coll., Swainsboro, 1992— vis. assoc. prof. Ga. Inst. Tech., Atlanta, 1996—; convener AAAS, 2003. Author: (with Donald L. Johnson) Thermodynamic Loop Applications in Materials Systems, Vol. I, 1995, Vol. II, 1995, Introduction to Thermodynamics for Materials Science-Application of Thermodynamic Loop Analysis, 1998; editor Jour. Math. Geology, 1998—, Internat. Jour. Coal Geology, 2004; contbr. numerous articles to profl. jours. Tutor for Ga. Sci. Olympiad, Swainsboro Middle Sch., 1992—; Coll. for Kids instr. East Ga. Coll., Swainsboro, 1992—, tchr. continuing edn. geology courses, 1994—. Grantee Geol. Soc. Am., 1986, 87, U. Nebr., Schramm and Meyer Scholastic Fellowships, 1986-87, Univ. Sys. of Ga., 1994, 97-2006, others; Lady Davis postdoc. fellow Inst. Earth Scis., Hebrew U. Jerusalem, 1989-90. Mem. Am. Geophys. Union, Geol. Soc. Am. (convener wild coal fires symposia 2004), Sigma Xi, Sigma Gamma Epsilon (pres. chpt.). Jewish. Avocations: rock and mineral collecting, hiking, model railroading, classic car restoration. Office: East Ga Coll Divsn Sci and Math 131 College Cir Swainsboro GA 30401-3643 Office Phone: 478-289-2073. Business E-Mail: stracher@ega.edu.

**STRACK, HAROLD ARTHUR,** retired electronics executive, military officer, financial consultant, writer; b. San Francisco, Mar. 29, 1923; s. Harold Arthur and Catheryn Jenny (Johnsen) S.; m. Margaret Madeline Decker, July 31, 1945; children: Carolyn, Curtis, Tamara (dec.). Student, San Francisco Coll., 1941, Sacramento Coll., 1947, Sacramento State Coll., 1948. U. Md., 1962, Indsl. Coll. Armed Forces, 1963. Commd. 2d lt. USAAF, 1943; advanced through grades to brig. gen. USAF, 1970; comdr. 1st Radar Bomb Scoring Group Carswell AFB, Ft. Worth, 1956-59; vice comdr. 90th Strategic Missile Wing SAC Warren AFB, Cheyenne, Wyo., 1964; chief, strategic nuclear br., spl. studies group Joint Chiefs of Staff, 1965-67, dep. asst. to chmn. JCS for strategic arms negotiations, 1968; comdr. 90th Strategic Missile Wing SAC Warren AFB, Cheyenne, 1969-71; chief Studies, Analysis and Gaming Agy. Joint Chiefs Staff, Washington, 1972-74, ret., 1974; v.p., mgr. MX Peacekeeper Program v.p. strategic planning Northrop Electronics Divsn., Hawthorne, Calif., 1974-88; ret., 1988. 1st clarinetist, Cheyenne Symphony Orch., 1969-71. Mem. Cheyenne Frontier Days Com., 1970-71. Decorated D.S.M., Legion of Merit, D.F.C., Air medal, Purple Heart, Presdl. citation, Army, Air Force and Joint Svc. Commendation medals. Mem. Inst. Nav., Am. Def. Preparedness Assn., Air Force Assn., Aerospace Edn. Found., Am. Fedn. Musicians, Orde Pour le Merite, Cheyenne Frontier Days "Heels". Home: 707 James Ln Incline Village NV 89451-9612 *The precepts which have guided me recognize the dignity of the individual and human rights. I believe that living by the Golden Rule contributes to the quality of life by making us better and more useful citizens while favorably influencing others. Integrity, ideals, and high standards reinforce one's own character. While taking pride in accomplishment, show gratitude for opportunity and humility for success. Lead by example and always do your best. Service to humanity and country is the highest calling, and the satisfaction of a job well done, approbation, respect and true friendship are one's greatest rewards.*

**STRACK, STEPHEN NAYLOR,** psychologist; b. Rome, NY, Nov. 13, 1955; s. Ralph and Grace (Naylor) S.; m. Leni Ferrero. BA, U. Calif., Berkeley, 1978; PhD, U. Miami, Fla., 1983. Psychologist L.A. County Dept. Mental Health, 1984-85; staff psychologist VA Outpatient Clinic, L.A., 1985—, dir. tng., 1992-97. Clin. assoc. U. So. Calif., L.A., 1986-95; adj. prof. Calif. Sch. Profl. Psychology, L.A., 1989—; clin. prof. Fuller Grad. Sch. Psychology, Pasadena, Calif., 1986—. Author (test): Personality Adjective Check List, 1987; co-author: Differentiating Normal and Abnormal Personality, 1994, 2d edit., 2006, Death and the Quest for Meaning, 1997, Essentials of Million Inventories Assessment, 1999, 2d edit., 2002, Handbook of Personology and Psychopathology, Pioneers of Personality Science, 2005, Millon Coll. Counseling Inventory, 2006; cons. editor Jour. Personality Disorders, 1992—, Omega, 1997—, Jour. Personality Assessment, 1999—. U.S. Dept. VA grantee, 1986-93, 96-2000. Fellow APA, Soc. for Personality Assessment; mem. Internat. Soc. for the Study of Personality Disorders, Calif. Psychol. Assn., Soc. for Interpersonal Theory and Rsch., Soc. for Rsch. in Psychopathology, Western Psychol. Assn., Sigma Xi. Office: VA Outpatient Clinic 351 E Temple St Los Angeles CA 90012-3328 Personal E-mail: snstrack@aol.com.

**STRADER, JAMES DAVID,** lawyer; b. Pitts., June 30, 1940; s. James Lowell and Tyra Fredrika (Bjorn) S.; m. Ann Wallace, Feb. 8, 1964; children: James Jacob, Robert Benjamin. BA, Mich. State U., 1962; JD, U. Pitts., 1965. Bar: Pa. 1966, US Dist. Ct. (we. dist.) Pa. 1966, US Dist. Ct. (ea. dist.) Pa. 1973, US Dist. Ct. (mid. dist.) Pa. 1985, US Ct. Appeals (4th and 5th cirs.) 1977, US Ct. Appeals (3d and 11th cirs.) 1981, US Supreme Ct. 1982, W.Va. 1996, Assoc. Peacock, Keller & Yohe, Washington, 1967 6ft. atty. UB Dist.1 Corp., Pitts., 1968-77, gen. atty. worker's compensation, 1977-84; assoc. Caroselli, Spagnolli & Beachler, Pitts., 1984-87; ptnr. Dickie, McCamey & Chilcote, Pitts., 1987—. Bd. trustees Mt. Lebanon Pub. Libr., 2002—, pres., 2004—05; del. Dem. Mid-Yr. Conv., 1974; mem. Dem. Nat. Platform Com., 1976; commr. Mt. Lebanon, Pa., 1974—78. Capt. U.S. Army, 1965—67. Mem. ABA (sr. vice-chmn. worker's compensation com. 1978-94), Pa. Bar Assn. (chmn. worker's compensation law sect. 1994-95), Pa. Bar Inst. (bd. dirs. 2001-), State Bar W.Va., Allegheny County Bar Assn., Valley Brook Country Club. Democrat. Presbyterian. Office: Dickie McCamey & Chilcote 2 PPG Pl Ste 400 Pittsburgh PA 15222-5491 Office Phone: 412-392-5419. Business E-Mail: jstrader@dmclaw.com.

**STRADLEY, WILLIAM JACKSON,** lawyer; b. Houston, Oct. 27, 1939; s. Samuel and Mary Stradley; m. Emmalee H. Stradley, Apr. 16, 1960; children: Lisa D., William M. BS, U. Houston, 1964, JD, 1967. Bar: Tex. 1967, U.S. Dist. Ct. (so. dist.) Tex. 1967, U.S. Ct. Appeals (5th cir.) 1967, U.S. Supreme Ct. 1970, cert.: (civil trial law), Tex. Bd. Legal Specialization (personal injury trial law). Of counsel Mithoff Law Firm; mem. faculty trial advocacy course Law Sch. U. Houston, 1982. Pres. Police Adv. Com., 1981—84, sec., 1980—81; bd. dirs. Houston Coun. Human Rels., 1982—84; mem. adminstrv. bd. St. Luke's United Meth. Ch.; co-chair fed. judiciary appts. com. State Bar Tex., 1991, mem. cont. legal edn. com., 1991, adminstrn. justice com., spl. com. professionalism. Named Texas Super Lawyers, 2005; named one of, 2003, 2004; recipient Pub. Svc. award, Houston Police Dept., 1984, Texas Super Lawyers, 2006. Mem.: Assn. Trial Lawyers Am., Tex. Trial Lawyers Assn. (dir. emeritus, chmn. ethics com., by-laws com.), Houston Bar Assn. (chmn. tort and compensation sect. 1980—81, chmn. cont. legal edn. com., com. on professionalism), Houston Trial Lawyers Assn. (bd. dirs. 1980—82, v.p. 1983—84, pres. 1985—86), Am. Bd. Trial Advocates (pres., treas. 1980—82, v.p. Houston 1983—84). Houston Bar Found. (charter), The Houstonians Club, Houston Club. Home: 64 E Broad Oaks Dr Houston TX 77056-1226 Office: 3450 One Allen Ctr Houston TX 77002 Office Phone: 713-654-1122.

**STRAFER, G. RICHARD,** lawyer; b. Evanston, Ill., Jan. 19, 1951; s. BA, U. Wis.-Madison, 1976; JD, Northeastern U., 1980; LLM, Georgetown U., 1983. Bar: DC, U.S. Dist. Ct., DC, U.S. Ct. Appeals, DC Cir. 1980, Fla. 1984. Appellate law fellow Appellate Litig. Clin. Prog. Georgetown U. Law Ctr.,

1981—83; pvt. practice G. Richard Strafer, PA. Contbr. articles to law jours. Mem.: ABA. Office: 2400 S Dixie Highway Ste 200 Miami FL 33133 Office Phone: 305-857-9090. E-mail: straferpa@aol.com.

**STRAHAN, MICHAEL ANTHONY,** professional football player; b. Houston, Nov. 21, 1971; s. Gene and Louise Strahan; m. Wanda Hutchins, 1992 (div. 1996); children: Tanita, Michael Jr.; m. Jean Strahan, July 18, 1999 (div. July 20, 2006); children: Isabella, Sophia. Grad, Tex. State U., 1992. Defensive end N.Y. Giants, 1993—. Co-chair Meet the Giants Fundraisers. Named First Team All-American, 1992, NFL Defensive Player of the Yr., 2001; named to NFL Pro-Bowl, 1997—99, 2001—03, 2005. Achievements include set NFL single season sack record (22.5), 2001. Office: Giants Stadium East Rutherford NJ 07073*

**STRAHILEVITZ, MEIR,** inventor, researcher, psychiatry educator; b. Beirut, July 13, 1935; s. Jacob and Chana Strahilevitz; m. Aharona Nattiv, 1958; children: Michal, Lior. MD, Hadassah Hebrew U. Med. Sch., 1963. Diplomate Am. Bd. Psychiatry and Neurology, Royal Coll. Physicians and Surgeons Can. Asst. prof. Washington U. Med. Sch., St. Louis, 1971-74; assoc. prof. So. Ill. U., Springfield, 1974-77, U. Chgo., 1977, U. Tex. Med. Br., Galveston, 1978-81; chmn. dept. psychiatry Kaplan Hosp., Rehovot, Israel, 1987-88; clin. assoc. prof. U. Wash., Seattle, 1981-88; prof. U. Tex. Med. Sch., Houston, 1988-92. Contbr. articles to profl. jours. Fellow Am. Psychiat. Assn., Royal Coll. Physicians and Surgeons Can. Achievements include discovery of protective effects of nitric oxide on psychiatric patients; invention of the use of antibodies to receptors and their fragments as drugs of immunoadsorption treatment of hyperlipidemia, cancer, autoimmune disease, atherosclerosis and coronary artery disease; patents for immunological and affinity adsorption methods; specific adsorption devices with automatic regeneration of adsorbent utilized in automated fluid purification and analytical and preparatory applications; treatment methods for psychoactive drug dependence; immunological methods for treating psychoactive drug intoxication; methods of improved targeting of drugs and visualization ligands, particularly in the treatment and diagnosis of cancer; immunoassay methods for psychoactive drugs; devices for removing species from the blood circulatory system. Office: PO Box 25008 Seattle WA 98165-1908 Personal E-mail: mstrahilevitz@pol.net.

**STRAHLMAN, RICHARD SCOTT,** pediatrician; s. Richard and Carol Ann Strahlman; m. Teresa Flores, May 11, 1996; children: John Wesley, Stephanie Leigh, Matthew Scott, Michael Allen. MD, Johns Hopkins U., Balt., 1978. Diplomate Am. Bd. Pediats. Instr. in pediats. Johns Hopkins U. Sch. of Medicine, Balt., 1995—; chief of pediats. Patuxent Med. Group, Columbia, Md., 1997—2004; pediatrician Columbia Med. Practice, Md., 2004—. Cons. in field, Columbia, 1995—. Author: (chpts. in med. textbooks) Primary Pediatric Care. Named Top Doc, Balt. Mag., 2002. Fellow: Am. Acad. Pediats. Office: Columbia Med Practice 5500 Knoll N Dr Columbia MD 21045 Office Phone: 410-964-6300. Office Fax: 410-964-6227.

**STRAHM, SAMUEL EDWARD,** veterinarian; b. Fairview, Kans., Feb. 9, 1936; s. Silas Tobias and Martha Mary (Beyer) S.; m. Barbara Jean Wenger, June 1, 1958; children: Gregory Lee, Bryan Scott, Andrea Marie Enloe. BS, DVM, Kansas State U., 1959. Owner Osage Animal Clinic Inc., Pawhuska, Okla., 1959—, pres., 1985—. Bd. dirs. 1st Nat. Bank, Pawhuska, Okla.; cons. Profl. Exam Svc., 1990-2000; adv. bd. USDA Users, 1991-95; adv. com. Pew Nat. Health Profession Vet. Medicine, 1991; state adv. coun. Okla. Coop. Extension Svcs., 2000—, chmn.-elect, 2000-01, chmn., 2001-06. Bd. dirs. Okla. Sch. Bd. Assn., 1977-98, 2d v.p., 1993, 1st v.p., 1994, pres., 1996; active Okla. All-State Sch. Bd. Assn., 1993, Pawhuska Sch. Bd., 1974-98, 2001—, pres., 1991-98, 2003—; active Pawhuska Planning Commn., 1965-70, Okla. State U. Centennial Commn., Stillwater, 1986-91; bd. dirs. Nat. Sch. Bd. Assn., 1996-98, exec. com., 1997-99, western reg. chmn., 1996. Recipient Disting. Alumni award Coll. Vet. Medicine Kans. State U., 1994, Fairview HS, 2004, Outstanding Svc. award Nat. Sch. Bds. Assn., 1997, Disting. Svc. award Nat. Bd. Exam. Com., 2000, Friend of Yr. award Okla. Coop. Extension, 2002. Mem.: AVMA (pres. 1989—90, coun. govt. affair 1992—98, coun. edn. 2003—06, AVMA award 1986), Am. Vet. Med. Found. (chmn. 1995—98, treas. 2004—), Am. Assn. Theriogenealogy, Am. Assn. Bovine Practitioners (Practitioner of Yr. award 2005), Am. Vet. State Bds., Am. Assn. Vet. Specialty Bd. (rep. coun. on edn.), Am. Assn. Food Hygiene Vets. (bd. dirs. 2000—), Nat. Bd. Vet. Med. Examiners (Disting. Svc. award 2000), Okla. Vet. Med. Assn. (all offices 1959—, Veterinarian of Yr. 1990, Disting. Svc. award 1998), Kans. Vet. Med. Assn., Okla. Bd. Vet. Med. Examiners (pres.), Pawhuska C. of C. (pres. 1968), Toastmasters Club, Pawhuska Jaycees (all offices 1959—69). Republican. Baptist. Avocations: gardening, fishing, flying. Home: PO Box 1256 Pawhuska OK 74056-1256 Office: Osage Animal Clinic Inc PO Box 1209 Pawhuska OK 74056-1209

**STRAIGHT, ELSIE HOSKING,** retired librarian, sculptor; b. Moresby, Cumberland, Eng., 1914; arrived in U.S., 1923, naturalized, 1926; d. Thomas E. and Anne (Molyneaux) Hosking; 1 child, Elaine W. Sanders. AA, Art Inst. Pitts., 1940, NY Sch. Applied Design, 1941; BA, Roger Williams Coll., 1969; MLS, U. RI, 1974. Libr. St. Raphael Acad., Pawtucket, RI, 1960—68, Elmhurst Acad., Portsmouth, RI, 1968—74; libr. dir. Ringling Sch. Art and Design, Sarasota, Fla., 1974—81; ret.; cons. U. South Fla., Sarasota, 1981—. Manatee Art League, Bradenton, Fla., 1980—82, 1983, 1984, Plaza Art Show, Sarasota, 1983, Longboat Key Art Ctr., 1984, Represented in permanent collections Mus. of the Circus, Ringling Mus. Art; author: (novels) Between the Dark and the Daylight, 2001, Land of the Dead, 2002; contbr. articles to publs. Mem.: Manatee Writers Guild, Fla. West Coast Writers, Ringling Sch. Art Libr. Assn., Artcenter Manatee, Art Librarian's Soc. (dir. 1980). Avocation: writing. Home: 435 Edwards Dr Sarasota FL 34243-2038

**STRAIGHT, RICHARD COLEMAN,** photobiologist, natural philosopher; b. Rivesville, W.Va., Sept. 8, 1937; BA, U. Utah, 1961, PhD in Molecular Biology, 1967. Asst. dir. radiation biology summer inst. U. Utah, 1961-63; supervisory chemist med. svc. VA Hosp., 1965—; dir. VA Venom Rsch. Lab., 1975—; adminstrv. officer rsch. svc. VA Ctr., 1980—; dir. Dixon laser inst. U. Utah, Salt Lake City, 1985-90; pres. Western Inst. for Biomed. Rsch., Salt Lake City, 1990—2003. Dir. Utah Ctr. for Photo Medicine, Salt Lake City, 1993—; assoc. chief of staff for rsch. VA Salt Lake City Health Care Sys., 1997-2003; chmn. bd. dirs. VAMCU FEd. Credit Union, 1980-; cons. to NIH, NSF, Dept. Def., 1985-. Assoc. editor Lasers in Surgery and Medicine, 1990-95, Jour. Biomed. Optics, 1998—. Mem. Am. Chem. Soc., Am. Soc. Photobiology, Biophysics Soc., Am. Soc. for Laser Medicine and Surgery, Utah Life Sci. Industries Assn. (charter). Achievements include research in photodynamic action on biomonomers and biopolymers, tumor immunology, effect of antigens on mammary adenocarcinoma of C3H mice, biochemical changes in aging, venom toxicology, mechanism of action of photoactive drugs, optical imaging and spectroscopy. Office: Protherics-Utah Univ Utah PO Box 58603 Salt Lake City UT 84158 Office Phone: 801-913-4799. E-mail: rcsrcsrcs3@aol.com.

**STRAIN, HARRIET RICE,** retired secondary school educator; b. New London, Conn., Aug. 7, 1918; d. Charles Edward Rice and Harriet Burr Frink; m. James R. Strain, June 19, 1943 (dec.); 1 child, Carol Elizabeth. AB, Conn. Coll. for Women, New London; MA, U. Conn., Storrs; Profl. Cert., U. Conn. Social studies and English tchr. Hawley Sch., New Town, Conn., 1940—48; social sci. tchr. grades 7-12 Chester H.S., Conn., 1948—51; history and govt. tchr. Valley Regional H.S., Deep River, Conn., 1951—53, Old Saybrook H.S., Conn., 1953—89; ret., 1989. Pres. Valley Shore Animal Welfare League, Westbrook, Conn., 1998—; tchr. Literacy Vols., Westbrook. Mem.: NEA, Assn. Ret. Tchrs. Conn. (past pres., Middlesex County dir. and bd. mem. 1989—2005), Conn. Edn. Assn. Democrat. Avocations: travel, birding. Home: 306 Rt 81 Killingworth CT 06419

**STRAIN, JAMES ARTHUR,** lawyer; b. Alexandria, La., Oct. 11, 1944; s. William Joseph and Louise (Moore) S.; m. Cheryl Sue Williamson, Aug. 19, 1967; children: William Joseph, Gordon Richard, Elizabeth Parks. BS in

Econs., Ind. U., 1966, JD, 1969. Bar: Ind. 1969, U.S. Dist. Ct. (so. dist.) Ind. 1969, U.S. Ct. Appeals (7th cir.) 1972, U.S. Supreme Ct. 1975, U.S. Ct. Appeals (5th cir.) 1978. Instr. Law Sch. Ind. U., Indpls., 1969-70; law clk. to Hon. John S. Hastings 7th Cir. Ct. Appeals, Chgo., 1970-71; assoc. Cahill, Gordon & Reindel, N.Y.C., 1971-72; law clk. to Hon. William F. Rehnquist U.S. Supreme Ct., Washington, 1972-73; assoc. Barnes, Hickam, Pantzer & Boyd, Indpls., 1973-75; ptnr. Barnes, Hickam, Pantzer & Boyd (name changed to Barnes & Thornburg), 1976-96, Sommer Barnard, PC, Indpls., 1996—. Adj. asst. prof. law Ind. U. Sch. Law, 1986-92. Mem., bd. dirs. The Penrod Soc., Indpls., 1976—, Indpls. Symphonic Choir, 1988-91, Festival Music Soc., Indpls., 1990-96. Mem. 7th Cir. Bar Assn. (meetings chmn. Ind. chpt. 1979-88, portraits 1988-89, bd. govs. 1989—, 1st v.p. 1995, pres. 1996). Avocations: photography, music. Office: Sommer Barnard PC Ste 3500 One Indiana Sq Indianapolis IN 46204 Office Phone: 317-713-3500. Business E-mail: strain@sommerbarnard.com.

**STRAIN, JAMES ELLSWORTH,** pediatrician, educator, retired medical association administrator; b. Lincoln, Nebr., Apr. 23, 1923; s. Elmer Ellsworth and Tessa Elizabeth (Stevens) Strain; m. Ruby Lee Shepard; children: James A., John D., Janet M. Strain McKinney, Jeffrey Lee Phillips-Strain. AB, Phillips U., Enid, Okla., 1945; MD, U. Colo., Denver, 1947. Diplomate Am. Bd. Pediat. (examiner 1984-89, mem. 1989-93, emeritus mem. 1993—). Intern Mpls. Gen. Hosp., 1947—48; resident in pediat. Denver Children's Hosp., 1948—50, pres. med. staff, 1964, dir. genetic unit, 1982—86; pvt. practice specializing in pediat. Denver, 1950—86; exec. dir. Am. Acad. Pediat., Elk Grove Village, Ill., 1986—93, ret., 1993. Pres. med. bd. Colo. Gen. Hosp., 1969—70; clin. prof. pediat. U. Colo. Med. Ctr., 1969—86, 1993—, U. Chgo., 1987—93; mem. Colo. Med. Adv. Coun. for Title 19, 1968—75, chmn., 1968—71; mem. Task Force on Iowa Health Care Stds. Project, 1984—85; presenter numerous profl. confs. Editl. bd. Pediat. in Rev., reviewer Jour. Pediat.; contbr. articles to profl. publs. Mem. Colo. Commn. on Children and Youth, 1971—75; trustee Phillips U., 1974—. Capt. U.S. Army, 1953—55. Recipient Disting. Alumnus award, Phillips U., 1974, Florence Sabin award, U. Colo., 1984, Excellence in Pub. Svc. award, U.S. Surgeon Gen., 1988, Abraham Jacobi award, AMA and Am. Acad. Pediat., 1994, James E. Strain Child Advocacy award established in his name, Denver Children's Hosp., 1983. Fellow: Am. Acad. Pediat. (Clifford Grulee award 1985); mem.: AMA, APHA, Inst. Medicine NAS, Ambulatory Pediatric Assn., Can. Pediatric Soc., Denver Med. Soc., Colo. Med. Soc., Alpha Omega Alpha. Republican. Mem. Christian Ch. (Disciples Of Christ). Avocations: fishing, sports, reading. Personal E-mail: jstrain121@aol.com.

**STRAIN, MICHAEL L.,** music director, performing company executive; MusB, U. Cin., 1979, MusM in Choral Conducting, 1981. Dir. music Westwood First Presbyn. Ch., Cin., 1979—89; min. music Noroton Presbyn. Ch., Darien, Conn., 1989—99; dir. music and arts Clairmont Presbyn. Ch., Decatur, Ga., 1999—. Musician (dir.): (choral performance) Rutter Gloria. Mem.: Am. Guild Organists (bd. dirs. Fairfield West chpt. 1994—96, sub-dean 1996—98), Choristers Guild, Presbyn. Assn. Musicians, Am. Choral Dirs. Assn. Office: Clairmont Presbyterian Ch 1994 Clairmont Road Decatur GA 30033 Office Phone: 404-634-3355.

**STRAIT, GEORGE,** country music vocalist; b. Poteet, Tex., May 18, 1952; m. Norma Strait; 1 child, George Bubba Jr. Degree in Agr., S.W. Tex. State U. Singer Care Err Cooolsey, Tenn., 1983—. Albums include Blue Clear Sky (Country Music Assn. Album of Yr. 1996), Strait Out of the Box (boxed set), Easy Come, Easy Go, Right or Wrong, Strait from the Heart, Strait Country, Does Ft. Worth Ever Cross Your Mind, 1985 (Country Music Assn. Album of Yr. 1985), Pure Country, 1986, No. 7, Something Special, 1986, Ocean Front Property, 1987, If You Aint Lovin' (You Aint Livin'), 1988, Beyond the Blue Neon, 1989, Livin' It Up, 1990, Ten Strait Hits, 1991, Chill of An Early Fall, 1991, Greatest Hits Volume I, II, Lead On, 1994, Strait Out of the Box, 1995, Blue Clear Sky, 1996 (Country Music Assn. Album of Yr. 1996), Carrying Your Love With Me, 1997 (Country Music Assn. Album of Yr. 1997), One Step at a Time, 1998 (Country Music Assn. Album of Yr. 1998), Always Never the Same, 1999, Merry Christmas Wherever You Are, 1999, Latest Greatest Straitest Hits, 2000, George Strait, 2000, The Road Less Traveled, 2001, 20th Century Masters, 2002, Honkytonkville, 2003, 50 Number Ones, 2004, Somewhere Down in Texas, 2005, other platinum albums; #1 country hits include Fool Hearted Memory, 1982, Amarillo By Morning, 1983, You Look So Good in Love, 1984, The Chair, 1986, Baby Blue, 1989, Beyond the Blue Moon, 1989, Baby's Gotten Good At Goodbye, 1989, Love Without End, Amen, 1990, I've Come to Expect It From You, 1990, Chill of An Early Fall, 1991, If I Know Me, 1991, The Big One, 1995, Good News Bad News (Due with Lee Ann Womack), 2005 (Country Music Assn. Musical Event of Yr. 2005); (movie) Pure Country, 1992. Served with U.S. Army, until 1975. Recipient Entertainer of Yr. award Country Music Assn., 1989, 90, Entertainer of Yr. award Acad. Country Music, 1990; named Male Vocalist of Yr. Country Music Assn., 1985, 86, 96, Male Vocalist of Yr. Acad. Country Music, 1984, 85, 89, SRO Touring Artist of Yr., 1990, Top Country Vocalist Am. Music Awards, 1991, Entertainer of Yr. 1990, Country Music Assn., Tex Ritter Award for Pure Country, 1993, Voice of the Yr. ASCAP, 1995, Male Vocalist of Yr. 1997, Country Music Assn. Avocations: golf, skiing, fishing, hunting, Steer-roping.*

**STRAIT, VIOLA EDWINA WASHINGTON,** librarian; b. El Paso, Tex., Aug. 29, 1925; d. Leroy Wentworth and Viola Edwina (Wright) Washington; m. Freeman Adams, Mar. 6, 1943; 1 child, Norma Jean (Mrs. Louis Lee James); m. Clifford Moody, Jan. 8, 1950; 1 child, Viola Edwina III (Mrs. Paul M. Cunningham); m. Amos O. Strait, Dec. 9, 1972. Bus. cert., Tillotson Coll., 1946, BA, 1948; MS in Libr. Sci., U. So. Calif., 1954. Substitute tchr. El Paso Pub. Schs., 1948; sec. bookkeeper U.S.O.-YWCA, El Paso, 1948-50; libr. asst. Spl. Svcs. Libr., Ft. Bliss, Tex., 1950-53, libr., 1954-71; equal employment opportunity officer Ft. Bliss, 1971-72; dep. equal employment opportunity officer Long Beach (Calif.) Naval Shipyard, 1972-85; with Temp. Job Mart, Torrance, Calif., 1986-87; substitute tchr. Ysleta Ind. Sch. Dist., 1988-89; profl. libr. Eastwood Hts. Elem. Sch., 1989-90; sec. Shiloh Bapt. Ch., El Paso, 1991-92; br. mgr. El Paso Pub. Libr., 1992-96, retired, 1996. Host, prodr. (gospel music video with Viola Washington Strait), Time Warner TV, Cable Channel 15, 2003—04. Sec. Sunday sch. Bapt. Ch., 1956-66, 92-96, min. music, 1958-72, supr. young adult choir, 1966-72, pres. sr. choir, 1969-71; disc jockey Sta. KELP, El Paso, 1970-72; host radio show Sta. KTEP, U. Tex., El Paso, 1994-2004; hon. chmn. for ann. observance of Nat. Libr. Week, City of El Paso, 1970. Mem. ALA, Border Region Libr. Assn. (chmn. scholarship com. 1970), NAACP (sec. 1996), Alpha Kappa Alpha. Democrat. Baptist. Avocations: piano, reading. Personal E-mail: vstrait@aol.com.

**STRAJA, SORIN RADU,** chemical engineer, mathematician, computer programmer; b. Bucharest, Romania; s. Radu and Sonica Straja; m. Mihaela Cirstea, Mar. 26, 1982. MS, Poly. Inst., Bucharest, 1979, PhD, 1987. Chem. engr. Plastics Processing, Bucharest, 1979—81; rsch. and devel. cons. Chem. and Biochem. Energetics Inst., Bucharest, 1982—89; mem., vol. USDA, Washington, 1991—92; chemist U. Md., Balt., 1992—93; dir. occupl. health and safety dept. Temple U., Phila., 1993—95, asst. prof. stats., 1994—2001; v.p. Inst. Regulatory Sci., Columbia, Md., 1996—. Cons. Montgomery Investment Tech., Radnor, 1995—. Editor: Environmental International, 1993-99; contbg. editor: Technology, 1996—; contbr. numerous articles to profl. jours. Recipient Nicolae Teclu award Romanian Acad. Scis., 1983, Cert. Appreciation, USDA, 1992, Cert. Appreciation for Tchg., Temple U., 1999. Mem. AIChE, ACS. Avocations: history, geography. Home and Office: Inst Regulatory Sci 5406 Hildebrand ct Columbia MD 21044-1918 Office Phone: 410-997-6396. Business E-Mail: straja@nars.org.

**STRAKA, LASZLO RICHARD,** retired publishing consultant; b. Budapest, Hungary, June 22, 1934; came to U.S., 1950, naturalized, 1956; s. Richard J. and Elisabeth (Roeck) S.; m. Eva K. von Viczian, Jan. 20, 1962 (div. May 1981); children: Eva M., Monika E., Viktoria K. BA cum laude, NYU, 1959. Acct. Greatrex Ltd., N.Y.C., 1952-53; pres. Maxwell Macmillan Internat. Pub. Group, N.Y.C., 1991-92; with Pergamon Press, Inc., Elmsford, NY,

1954-90, v.p., 1964-68, exec. v.p., treas., 1968-74, pres., 1974-75, 80-88, chmn. bd., 1975-77, 88-90, vice chmn. bd., 1977-80, 88-89, also dir.; vice chmn. bd. Pergamon Books Ltd., Oxford, England, 1986-88; group v.p. Macmillan Inc., N.Y.C., 1989-91; pub. cons. Alta Loma, Calif., 1992—2005; ret., 2005. Treas. Brit. Book Centre, Inc., N.Y.C., 1956-67; pres. Pergamon Holding Corp., 1981-86; chmn. bd. Microforms Internat., Inc., 1971-87. D. dirs., sec. Szechenyi Istvan Soc., N.Y.C., 1967-80, 89-93. Mem. Phi Beta Kappa. Home: 6405 Caledon Pl Alta Loma CA 91737 Personal E-mail: nagyapul@yahoo.com.

**STRALEY, FORREST ALVIN CHIP,** theater educator, director, actor; b. Atlanta, July 16, 1958; s. Harrison Wilson Straley IV and Charlene Straley (Stepmother), JoAnn Straley; m. Betsy Lou Arnold, May 30, 1993; 1 child, Elizabeth Garnet. BA, Mary Wash. Coll., Fredericksburg, Va., 1980; MFA, Va. Commonwealth U., Richmond, 1993. Prof. ECPI Tech. Coll., Richmond, Va., 1998—2000; head theatre dept. Ariz. Western Coll., Yuma, 2000—. Com. mem. Dept. Arts and Recreation Performing Arts Com., Yuma, 2003—; cons. Planned Parenthood/Child Abuse Prevention Coun., Yuma, 2005—. Dir.: (stage prodn.) Arsenic and Old Lace, (touring musical theatre prodn.) Alice Through the Looking Glass; actor: (independent film) Altamont Now. Com. mem. Ariz. Commn. of the Arts, Phoenix, 2003—06. Mem.: Soc. Am. Fight Dirs. D-Liberal. Home: 1213 W 2nd St Yuma AZ 85364 Office: Arizona Western Coll 2020 S Ave 8E Yuma AZ 85365 Office Phone: 928-344-7592. Business E-mail: forrest.straley@azwestern.edu.

**STRAMPEL, WILLIAM DERKEY,** dean, medical educator; b. Saugatuck, Mich., Feb. 8, 1948; married; 3 children. BA, Hope Coll., 1970; DO, Chgo. Coll. Osteopathic Medicine, 1976. Intern Madigan Army Med. Ctr., Fort Lewis, Wash., 1976—77, resident in medicine, 1977—79; fellow in pulmonary disease Fitzsimons Army Med. Ctr., Aurora, 1980—82; staff internal medicine svc. and dir. intensive care 121 Evacuation Hosp., Seoul; pulmonary staff and dir. intensive care Fitzsimons Army Med. Ctr., Aurora, Colo.; divsn. surgeon First Infantry Divsn. Irwin Army Cmty. Hosp., Fort Riley, Kans., dep. comdr., dir. med. edn., Evans Army Cmty. Hosp., Fort Carson, Colo.; chief Quality Assurance Divsn., Dept. of Army, Office Surgeon Gen., 1991—94; dir. med. edn. Brooke Army Med. Ctr., 1994—96; comdr. Brooke Army Med. Ctr. and Great Plains Med. Command, 1996—97; dir. quality mgmt. Office Sec. Def.; chief med. officer Tricare Mgmt. Activity; spl. asst. for ops. and readiness to U.S. surgeon gen.; leader Mich. State U. Health Team; sr. assoc. dean Mich. State U., Coll. Osteo. Medicine, 1999—2002, prof. internal medicine, 2001—, acting dean, 2001—02, dean, 2002—. Served to col. U.S. Army. Office: A314 E Free Hall East Lansing MI 48824-1316*

**STRAND, CURT ROBERT,** hotel executive; b. Vienna, Nov. 13, 1920; naturalized Am. citizen, 1943; m. Fleur Lillian Emanuel, June 14, 1946; 1 child, Karen. BS, Cornell U., 1943. Supt. service Plaza, N.Y.C., 1947-49; asst. to v.p. Hilton Hotels Corp., 1949-53; v.p. Hilton Internat. Co., N.Y.C., 1953-64, exec. v.p., 1964-67, pres., chief exec. officer, 1967-86, chmn., 1986-87. Sr. v.p., dir. Trans World Air Lines, Inc.; lectr. Cornell U. Sch. Hotel Adminstrn., Ecole Superieure de Scis. Econs., Paris, NYU; sr. cons. Am. Express; mem. adv. panel com. Am. Hotel and Motel Assn.; dir. Sherry Netherland Corp.; mem. coun. Bd. Exec. Svc. Corps, Aspen. Mem. coun. Cornell U.; adv. bd. Aspen Found.; bd. govs. Snowmass Resort Assn., also pres.; fellow Aspen Inst. With Mil. Intelligence U.S. Army, 1943—46. Mem. Cornell Soc. Hotelmen (Hotelier of Yr. 1986), Aspen Exec. Svc. Corps (mem. bd., v.p.), Nat. Arts Club. Home: PO Box 6359 Snowmass Village CO 81615

**STRAND, MARGARET N.,** lawyer; b. White Plains, NY, Apr. 27, 1946; BA, U. Rochester, 1968; MA, U. RI, 1971; JD, Coll. William and Mary, 1976. Bar: Va. 1976, DC 1977, US Supreme Ct. Chief, environ. def. sect. environ. and natural resources divsn. U.S. Dept. Justice, Washington, 1984—91; ptnr. Oppenheimer Wolff & Donnelly, Washington, Venable LLP, Washington, 2001—. Lectr. George Washington U., 1993—2002; chair environ. law com. Transp. Rsch. Bd., Nat. Acad. Scis.; bd. dirs. Environ. Law Inst.; mem. editl. bd. Environ. Law Reporter, Nat. Wetlands News. Author: Wetlands Deskbook, 1997; contbr. chapters to books, articles to profl. jours. Named a Top Washington Lawyer, Washingtonian Mag., 2004, 2005. Mem.: ABA. Office: Venable LLP 575 7th St NW Washington DC 20004 Office Phone: 202-344-4699. Office Fax: 202-344-8300. Business E-Mail: mnstrand@venable.com.

**STRAND, MARK,** poet; b. Summerside, P.E.I., Can., Apr. 11, 1934; came to U.S., 1938. s. Robert Joseph and Sonia (Apter) S.; m. Antonia Ratensky, Sept. 14, 1961 (div. June 1973); 1 dau., Jessica; m. Julia Rumsey Garretson, Mar. 15, 1976; 1 son, Thomas Summerfield. BA, Antioch Coll., 1957; BFA, Yale, 1959; MA, U. Iowa, 1962. Instr. English U. Iowa, 1962-65; asst. prof. Mt. Holyoke Coll., 1967; assoc. prof. Bklyn. Coll., 1971-72; Bain-Swiggett lectr. Princeton, 1973; Hurst prof. poetry Brandeis U., 1974-75; prof. U. Utah, 1981-93; U.S. poet laureate Library of Congress, Washington, 1990-91; prof. Johns Hopkins U., 1994—97; Andrew MacLeish disting. svc. prof. U. Chgo., 1997—. Fulbright lectr. U. Brazil, Rio de Janeiro, 1965-66; adj. assoc. prof. Columbia U., 1969-72; lectr. U. Wash., 1968, 70, U. Va., 1977, Wesleyan U., 1979, Harvard U., 1980; vis. lectr. Yale, 1969-70, U. Va., 1976, Calif. State U., Fresno, 1977, U. Calif., Irvine, 1979. Author: Sleeping with One Eye Open, 1964, Reasons for Moving, 1968, Darker, 1970, The Story of Our Lives, 1973 (Edgar Allan Poe award Acad. Am. Poets 1974), The Sargeantville Notebook, 1974, The Monument, 1978, Elegy for My Father, 1978, The Late Hour, 1978, Selected Poems, 1980, The Planet of Lost Things, 1982, The Night Book, 1983, Mr. and Mrs. Baby and Other Stories, 1985, Rembrandt Takes a Walk, 1986, William Bailey, 1987, The Continuous Life, 1990, Dark Harbor, 1993, Hopper, 1994, Blizzard of One, 2000 (Pulitzer Prize), Man and Camel, 2006; Editor: The Contemporary American Poets, 1968, New Poetry of Mexico, 1970, 18 Poems from Quechua, 1971, The Owl's Insomnia, 1973, The Best American Poetry 1991, The Golden Ecco Anthology, 1994; co-author: 89 Clouds, 1999; co-editor: Another Republic: Seventeen European and South American Writers, 1976, The Art of the Real, 1983, Traveling in the Family, 1987; translator: Souvenir of the Ancient World, 1976. Recipient award Am. Acad. and Inst. Arts and Letters, 1975, Utah Gov.'s award in arts, 1992, Bobbitt Nat. prize for poetry, 1992, Bollingen prize for poetry Yale Univ. Libr., 1993; Fulbright scholar in Italy, 1960-61; Ingram Merrill Found. grantee, 1966; Nat. Endowment for Arts grantee, 1967-68, 78-79, 86-87; Rockefeller Found. grantee, 1968-69; Guggenheim fellow, 1975-76; Acad. Am. Poets fellow, 1979; MacArthur Found. fellow, 1987; Pulitzer Prize in Poetry, Blizzard of One, 1999. Fellow Acad. Am. Poets; mem. Am. Acad. and Inst. Arts and Letters.*

**STRAND, MELVIN LEROY,** English educator; b. Waseca, Minn., Mar. 15, 1936; s. Carl Morris and Dorothy Mae Reburn S. BS, Minn. State U., Mankato, 1961, MS in Edn., 1968; MS, Bemidji (Minn.) State U., 1972; EdD, U. S.D., 1976. Tchr. English Rockford (Ill.) Secondary Schs., 1960-61, Rochester (Minn.) Secondary Schs., 1961-63, Richfield (Minn.) Secondary Schs., 1963-82; asst. prof. English King Saud U., Abha, Saudi Arabia, 1982-92; prof. English Saudi Arabian Am. Oil Co., Dhahran, Saudi Arabia, 1994, Royal Saudi Navy, Dhahran, 1995-96, Ctrl. Tex. Coll., Killeene, 1996—. Author: The Basic Sentence, 1989, Sentence to Paragraph, 1990; subject of nat. Saudi Arabian telecast Guest of Kingdom, 1991; contbr. articles to jours. in field. Vol., instr. AARP 55-Alive; active Minnesotans for Responsible Recreation, Nat. Arbor Day Found., WASECA County DFL, Am. Refugee Com., Internat. Planned Parenthood Com., Stroke Assn., Disabled Am. Vets; com. mem. Dem. Congrl. Campaign; active Grace Luth. Ch. With USAF, 1955—59. Recipient, USAF Missile Badge, 1958. Mem. NEA, AARP, Minn. Edn. Assn., Nat. Coun. Tchrs. of English, Edn. Minn., Am. Vets, Vets for Common Sense, MSU Found., Minn. Young DFL, Minn. Sr. Fed., N.H. Arbor Day WASECA Arts Council, Alliance for Ret. Am., AARP, Sojourners, Am. Fedn. of Tchrs., Ret. Educators Assn. Minn., Edn. Minn., Sierra Club, World Wildlife Fund, Nature Conservancy, Nat. Parks Conservation Assn., Childreach Plan Internat., Pi Delta Epsilon. Democrat. Lutheran. Avocations: world travel, reading, writing, environmental concerns. Home: 13342 382nd Ave Waseca MN 56093 Personal E-mail: stranordic@lakes.com.

**STRAND, ROGER GORDON,** federal judge; b. Peekskill, NY, Apr. 28, 1934; s. Ernest Gordon Strand and Lisabeth Laurine (Phin) Steinmetz; m. Joan Williams, Nov. 25, 1961. AB, Hamilton Coll., 1955; LLB, Cornell U., 1961; grad., Nat. Coll. State Trial Judges, 1968. Bar: Ariz. 1961, U.S. Dist. Ct. Ariz. 1961, U.S. Supreme Ct. 1980. Assoc. Fennemore, Craig, Allen & McClennen, Phoenix, 1961-67; judge Ariz. Superior Ct., Phoenix, 1967-85, U.S. Dist. Ct. Ariz., Phoenix, 1985—2001, now sr. judge. Assoc. presiding judge Ariz. Superior Ct., 1971-85; lectr. Nat. Jud. Coll., Reno, 1978-87; mem. jud. conf. U.S. com. on info. tech., 1996-2002; mem. 9th Cir. Jud. Coun. Past pres. cen. Ariz. chpt. Arthritis Found. Lt. USN, 1955-61. Mem. ABA, Ariz. Bar Assn., Maricopa County Bar Assn., Nat. Conf. Fed. Trial Judges, Phi Delta Phi, Aircraft Owners and Pilots Assn. Lodges: Rotary. Avocations: computer applications, golf, fishing. Home: 5825 N 3rd Ave Phoenix AZ 85013-1537 Office: Sandra Day O'Connor US Courthouse SPC 57 401 W Washington Phoenix AZ 85003-2156 Office Phone: 602-322-7550. Business E-Mail: roger_strand@azd.uscourts.gov.

**STRANDBERG, MALCOM WOODROW PERSHING,** physicist; b. Box Elder, Mont., Mar. 9, 1919; s. Malcom and Ingeborg (Riestad) S.; m. Harriet Elisabeth Bennett, Aug. 2, 1947 (dec.); children— Josiah R.W., Susan Abby, Elisabeth G., Malcom B. S.B., Harvard Coll., 1941; PhD, M.I.T., 1948. Research asso. M.I.T., Cambridge, 1941-48, asst. prof. physics, 1948-53, asso. prof., 1953-60, prof., 1960-88, prof. emeritus, 1988—. Author: Microwave Spectroscopy, 1954; patentee in field. Fellow Am. Phys. Soc., Am. Acad. Arts and Scis., IEEE, AAAS; mem. Am. Assn. Physics Tchrs. Episcopalian. Home: 82 Larchwood Dr Cambridge MA 02138-4639 Office: Mass Inst Tech 26-351 Cambridge MA 02139 Office Phone: 617-253-2563. Business E-Mail: mwpstr@mit.edu.

**STRANDJORD, M. JEANNINE,** telecommunications industry executive; B in Acctg. and Bus. Adminstrn., U. Kans. CPA. V.p. fin. Macy's Midwest; with Kans. city Power & Light Co., Ernst and Whinney; v.p. fin. and distrbn. AmeriSource, Inc. (subs. Sprint), 1985—90, controller, 1986—90, sr. v.p., treas., 1990—98, sr. v.p. fin. global markets group, 1998—2003; sr. v.p. fin. svcs. Sprint Corp., 2003, sr. v.p., chief integration officer, 2003—. Bd. dirs. Am. Century Mutual Funds, DST Sys., Inc., Euronet Worldwide. Trustee Rockhurst U. Office: 6200 Spring Pkwy Overland Park KS 66251

**STRANG, RUTH HANCOCK,** pediatrician, educator, cardiologist, priest; b. Bridgeport, Conn., Mar. 11, 1923; d. Robert H.W. and Ruth (Hancock) Strang. BA, Wellesley Coll., 1944, postgrad., 1944—45; MD, N.Y. Med. Coll., 1949; MDiv, Seabury We. Theol. Sem., 1993. Diplomate Am. Bd. Pediat.; ordained deacon Episc. Ch., 1993, priest Episc. Ch., 1994. Intern Flower and Fifth Ave. Hosp., N.Y.C., 1949—50, resident in pediat., 1950—52; mem. faculty N.Y. Med. Coll., N.Y.C., 1952—57; fellow cardiology Babies Hosp., N.Y.C., 1956—57, Harriet Lane Cardiac Clinic, Johns Hopkins Hosp., Balt., 1957—59, Children's Hosp. Boston, 1959—62; mem. faculty U. Mich. Hosp., Ann Arbor, 1962—89; prof. pediat., 1970—89, prof. emeritus, 1989—; priest-in-charge St. Johns Episcopal Ch., Howell, Mich., 1994—. Dir. pediat. Wayne County Gen. Hosp., Westland, Mich, 1965-85; mem. staff U. Mich. Hosps., 1962-89; mem. med. adv. com. Wayne County chpt. Nat. Cystic Fibrosis Rsch. Found., 1966-80, chmn. med. adv. com. nat. found., Detroit, 1971-78; cons. cardiology Plymouth (Mich.) State Home and Tng. Ctr., 1970-81; diocesan coun. Diocese Mich., 2003-, mem. com. on nominations and elections Diocesan Conv., 2003, chmn. com., 2004. Author: Clinical Aspects of Operable Heart Disease, 1968; contbr. numerous articles to profl. jours. Mem. citizen's adv. coun. Juvenile Ct., Ann Arbor, 1968—76; mem. med. adv. bd. Ann Arbor Continuing Edn. Dept., 1968—77; v.p. Am. Heart Assn. Mich., 1989, pres., 1991; bd. dirs. Livingston Cmty. Hospice, 1995—99, Emrich Episcopal Conf. Ctr., 1998—; ctr. bd. Emrich Episcopal Retreat, 1998—, adv. bd., 1998—; mem. Diocesan Com. for World Relief, Detroit, 1970—72; trustee Episcopal Med. Chaplaincy, Ann Arbor, 1971—96; mem. bishop's com. St. Aidan's Episc. Ch., 1966—69, sec., 1966—88, vestry, 1973—76, 1978—80, 1984—86, 1990—91, sr. warden, 1975—76, 1978, 1986, 1990; del. Episc. Diocesan Conv., 1980, 1991; mem. Congl. Life Circle Episcopal Diocese Mich., 1995—2001, mem. loans and grants com., 1995—99, mem. com. on reference ann. diocesan conv., 1995-98, chmn., 1996; mem. Diocese Mich. Clergy Family Project, 1996—98; co-dean Huron Valley area coun. Diocese Mich., 1998—2000; bd. trustees Ecumenical Theol. Sem., 1996—, chair acad. affairs com., 2000—; mem. Congl. Devel. Commn., 2001—03; bd. dirs. Livingston County Cath. Social Svcs., 2004—; mem. diocesan coun. Episc. Diocese Mich., 2004—. Recipient Alumnae Life Achievement award, Baldwin Sch., 2005. Mem. AMA, Am. Acad. Pediat., Am. Coll. Cardiology, Mich. Med. Soc., Washtenaw County Med. Soc., N.Y. Acad. Medicine, Am. Heart Assn., Women's Rsch. Club (membership sec. 1966-67), Ambulatory Pediat. Assn., Am. Assn. Child Care in Hosps., Am. Assn. Med. Colls., Assn. Faculties of Pediat. Nurse Assn./Practitioners Programs (pres. 1978-81, exec. com. 1981-84), Episc. Clergy Assn. Mich., Northside Assn. Ministries (pres. 1975, 76, 79-80), Soc. Companions of Holy Cross. Home: 4500 E Huron River Dr Ann Arbor MI 48105-9335

**STRANG, WILLIAM GILBERT,** mathematician, educator; b. Chgo., Nov. 27, 1934; s. William Dollin and Mary Catherine (Finlay) S.; m. Jillian Mary Shannon, July 26, 1958; children— David, John, Robert. SB, MIT, 1955; BA (Rhodes scholar), Oxford U., Eng., 1957; PhD (NSF fellow), UCLA, 1959. Asst. prof. mathematics MIT, 1959-63, assoc. prof., 1963-66, prof., 1966—. Pres. Wellesley-Cambridge Press; hon. prof. Xian Jiaotong U., People's Republic of China, 1980. Author: An Analysis of the Finite Element Method, 1973, Linear Algebra and Its Applications, 1976, Introduction to Applied Mathematics, 1986, Calculus, 1990, Introduction to Linear Algebra, 1993, Wavelets and Filter Banks, 1996, Linear Algebra, Geodesy, and GPS, 1997, Recipient Chauvenet prize Math. Assn. Am., 1977; Sloan fellow, 1966-67, Hon. fellow Balliol Coll., Oxford, 1999; Fairchild scholar, 1981. Mem. Soc. Indsl. and Applied Math. (pres. 1999-2000). Home: 7 Southgate Rd Wellesley MA 02482-6606 Office: MIT Math Dept Rm 2-240 Cambridge MA 02139 Office Phone: 617-253-4383. Business E-Mail: gs@math.mit.edu.

**STRANGE, DONALD ERNEST,** healthcare company executive; b. Ann Arbor, Mich., Aug. 13, 1944; s. Carl Britton and Donna Ernestine (Tenney) Strange; m. Lyn Marie Purdy, Aug. 3, 1968 (div. Mar. 2001); children: Laurel Lyn, Chadwick Donald. BA, Mich. State U., 1966, MBA, 1968. Asst. dir. Holland (Mich.) City Hosp., 1968-72, assoc. dir., 1972-74; exec. dir. Bascom Palmer Eye Inst./Anne Bates Leach Eye Hosp., U. Miami, Fla., 1974-77; v.p. strategic planning and rsch. Hosp. Corp. Am., Nashville, 1977-80, group v.p. Boston, 1980-82, regional v.p., 1982-87; chmn., chief exec. officer HCA Healthcare Can., Toronto, 1985-87; exec. v.p. Avon Products, Inc., N.Y., 1987-89; chmn. Sigecom, Ltd., Greenwich, Conn., 1989-94, U.S. HomeCare Corp., 1990-91; exec. v.p., COO, dir. EPIC Healthcare Group, Dallas, 1991-93; chmn, CEO TransCare Corp., Dallas, 1993-95; chmn, CEO First New Eng. Dental Ctrs., Inc., Boston, 1996-98; pres., CEO Behavioral Healthcare Ptnrs., Inc., Quincy, Mass., 2000; sr. v.p. Bon Secours Health Sys. Inc., Mariottsville, Md., 2001—06, COO, 2006—. Dir. Altoona (Pa.) Regional Health Sys., 2004—, Bon Secours Cottage Health Sys., Grosse Pointe, Mich., 2002—. Trustee Boston Ballet, 1998—2001, chmn. bd. overseers, 1999—2001. Mem. Harvard Club (Boston), Nat. Arts Club (N.Y.). Episcopalian. Office: Bon Secours Health Sys Inc 1505 Marriottsville Rd Marriottsville MD 21104-1399 Office Phone: 410-442-5511. Business E-Mail: don_strange@bshsi.com.

**STRANGE, HENRY HAZEN,** judge; b. Oleary, P.E.I., Can., July 26, 1939; s. Henry Hazen and Marion Yvonne (Copp) S.; m. Heather Susan Carson, July 30, 1966; children: Elizabeth Marion, Jennifer Jody. BBA, U. N.B., Fredericton, 1961, BA, 1963, B in Civil Laws, 1964. Pvt. practice barrister, solicitor, N.B., 1964-66; sgt. asst. to dir. of pub. rels. Centennial Commn., Ottawa, Ont., Canada, 1966-67; crown prosecutor Dept. Justice, Fredericton, N.B., 1967-71, dir. pub. prosecutions N.B., 1971-81; judge Provincial Ct., N.B., 1981—, chief judge N.B., 1987-97. Chmn. Can. Coun. Chief Judges, 1995. Apptd. as Queen's Counsel, N.B., 1977. Avocations: salmon fishing, sports.

Home: 664 Woodstock Rd Fredericton NB Canada E3B 5N7 Office: Provincial Ct PO Box 6000 Fredericton NB Canada E3B 5H1 Office Phone: 506-453-2120. E-mail: hazen.strange@gnb.ca.

**STRANGE, J. LELAND,** computer company executive; b. Dallas, May 15, 1941; s. James Alton and Ola (Johnson) S.; m. Jane Hendrix Strange, Aug. 28, 1965; children— Mark, Cary, Ryan. BS Indsl. Mgmt., Ga. Tech. U., 1965, MBA, Ga. State U., 1968. Gen. mgr. Colonial Film & Equipment Co., Atlanta, 1967-69; pres. Cheese Villa Stores, Inc., 1969-74, Quadram Corp., 1981-83, Intelligent Systems Corp., 1983— (all Atlanta); prof. mktg. Mercer U., 1976-83; bd. dirs. Healthdyne Corp., Atlanta, Intelligent Systems Corp., Wave Air Corp, IQ Software Corp. Republican. Baptist. Office: Intelligent Systems Corp 4355 Shackleford Rd Norcross GA 30093-2948

**STRANGHOENER, LARRY W.,** manufacturing executive; BS, St. Olaf Coll., Northfield, Minn.; MBA, Northwestern U. CFA. Investment analyst Dain Bosworth, Mpls.; with Honeywell, Inc., 1983—99; dir. investor rels., dir. mktg./internat. sales Honeywell Centra, Germany, dir. corp. fin. planning/bus. analysis, asst. treas., 1992—93; v.p. fin. Honeywell Indsl. Automation and Control, Phoenix, 1993—96; v.p. bus. devel. Honeywell, Inc., Mpls., 1996—97, v.p., CFO, 1997-99; exec. v.p., CFO Techies.com, Edina, Minn., 2000—01; CFO Lutheran Brotherhood, 2001—02, Thrivent Financial for Lutherans (formerly Lutheran Brotherhood), Mpls., 2002—.

**STRANO, MICHAEL,** chemical engineer; BS, Polytechnic U., Bklyn., 1997; PhD, U. Del., 2002. Asst. prof. dept. chem. & biomolecular engring. U. Ill., Urbana-Champaign. Contbr. articles to profl. jours. Named one of Top 100 Young Innovators, MIT Tech. Review, 2004; recipient DuPont Young Investigator award, 2004. Office: Dept Chem & Biomolecular Engring 118 RAL MC-712 Box C-3 600 S Matthews Ave Urbana IL 61801

**STRANTZ, NANCY JEAN,** law educator, consultant; b. Calgary, Alta., Can., 1958; 1 child. LLB, U. Alta., 1981; JD, South Tex. Coll. Law, Houston, 1990; BA in Social Scis., U. N.D., Grand Forks, 1997. Bar: Alta. 1982. Articling lawyer Carma Developers Ltd., Calgary, 1981-82; barrister and solicitor Stewart & Stewart, Barristers and Solicitors, Calgary, 1982-83; rsch. asst., author Can. Inst. Resources Law, U. Calgary, 1984-85; corp. counsel Chevron Can. Resources, 1985-90, Gulf Can. Resources, 1991-94, 98; asst. prof. U. N.D. Sch. Law, Grand Forks, 1994-97. Land and legal cons. N.J. Strantz Cons., Calgary, 1991-94; adj. faculty U. Calgary, Mt. Royal Coll., So. Alta Inst. Tech., Calgary, 1991-94. Co-author: A Reference Guide to Hardrock Mining in Canada; contbr. articles to profl. jours. Trustee Rocky Mountain Mineral Law Found., 1994-97. Pvt. Can. Dept. Nat. Def., Naval Res., 1975. Recipient award and grants. Mem. Law Soc. Alta. Avocation: swimming.

**STRAS, PENNY LYNN,** director; b. Fergus Falls, Minn., Sept. 13, 1951; d. Orville James and Mildred Georgia Stras; m. Wade Elson Olson, Dec. 19, 1974 (div. Sept. 1977); 1 child, J. D. Olson. AA, Yankton Coll., 1981. BA, 1982, U. Mont., 1991, MPA, 1993. From adminstrv. asst. to case mgr. Vietnam Vets. Childrens Asst. Program, Missoula, Mont., 1989—92; advocacy specialist Mont. Advocacy Program, Helena, 1992—93; child devel. specialist Comprehensive Devel. Ctr., Missoula, 1993—95; pvt. practice acct. Libby, Mont., 1995—99; asst. dir. Missoula Head Start, 1999—2000; bus. office coord. Ashby (Minn.) Care Ctr., 2001; dir. Grand Portage (Minn.) Head Start, Grand Portage, 2001—03, SEMCAC Head Start, Rushford, Minn., 2003—. Grant writer Dept. HHS, 1989—93. Vol. Spl. Olympics, Yankton, SD, 1981—82, Missoula, Mont., 1991—93. Grantee Fed. grant, Dept. Health & Human Svcs., 2001. Avocations: refinishing furniture, latch hook rugs. Office: SEMCAC Head Start 204 S Elm Rushford MN 55971 Home: 102 2nd St Glendive MT 59330-3506 E-mail: nvrtool8@yahoo.com.

**STRASBAUGH, JOAN TIMMIS,** publishing executive; BS in Dance, U. Wis., 1975. Mktg. mgr. A-R Editions, Madison, Wis., 1994; book divsn. mgr. Zino Press, Madison, Wis., 1996; adminstr. U. Wis. Ctr. for Humanities, Madison, 2000—02; pub. Jones Books, Madison, Wis., 2002—. Author: (book) Acorn Guide to Milwaukee, 1995; choreographer (modern dance) You Call This Dance? Dance in the Plain Style, Jazz Dinner; coord. (Humanities Festival) Jane Austen in the 21st Century. Mem.: Jane Austen Soc. of N.Am. Office: Jones Books 309 N Hillside Ter Madison WI 53705 Office Phone: 608-236-9259. Office Fax: 608-236-0225. Business E-Mail: info@jonesbooks.com.

**STRASBAUGH, WAYNE RALPH,** lawyer; b. Lancaster, Pa., July 20, 1948; s. Wayne Veily and Jane Irene (Marzolf) S.; m. Carol Lynne Taylor, June 8, 1974; children: Susan, Wayne T., Elizabeth. AB, Bowdoin Coll., 1970; AM, Harvard U., 1971, PhD, 1976, JD, 1979. Bar: Ohio 1979, Pa. 1983, U.S. Tax Ct. 1980, U.S. Ct. Fed. Claims 1980, U.S. Ct. Appeals (fed. cir.) 1982, U.S. Dist. Ct. (no. dist.) Ohio 1979, U.S. Dist. Ct. (ea. dist.) Pa. 1983. Assoc. Jones Day Reavis & Pogue, Cleve., 1979-82, Morgan Lewis & Bockius, Phila., 1982-84, Ballard Spahr Andrews & Ingersoll, LLP, Phila., 1984-88, ptnr., 1988—, chmn. tax group, 2001—. Mem. ABA (tax sect., chmn. com. 1992-94), Am. Coll. Tax Counsel (regent 2003—), Phila. Bar Assn. (tax sect., chmn. fed. tax com. 1992, coun. mem. 1995, sec.-treas. 1996, vice-chmn. 1997-98, chmn. 1999-2000). Episcopalian. Office: Ballard Spahr Andrews & Ingersoll LLP 1735 Market St Ste 5100 Philadelphia PA 19103-7599 E-mail: strasbaugh@ballardspahr.com.

**STRASBURGER, VICTOR C.,** pediatrician; b. Balt., Oct. 7, 1949; s. Arthur Charles and Marjorie (Cohen) S.; m. Alison Reeve, Aug. 18, 1984; children: Max, Katya. BA summa cum laude, Yale U., 1971; MD, Harvard U., 1975. Intern Children's Hosp. U. Wash., Seattle, 1975-76; residency, 1976-77; Boston Children's Hosp., 1977-78; dir. adolescent medicine Bridgeport (Conn.) Hosp., 1979-86; vis. lectr. St. Mary's Hosp. Med. Sch., London, 1986-87; chief div. adolescent medicine sch. medicine U. N.Mex., Albuquerque, 1987—, prof. pediats., 1997—. Cons. Nat. PTA, Washington and Chgo., 1978-86. Author: Rounding Third and Heading Home, 1974, Adolescent Medicine: A Practical Guide, 1991, 2d edit., 1998, Getting Your Kids to Say No in the '90's When You Said Yes in the '60's, 1993, (with B. Wilson) Children, Adolescents, and the Media, 2002, (with R. Brown, P. Braverman, C. Holland, P. Rogers and S. Coupey) Care of the Adolescent: A Handbook for Primary Care, 2006; editor: Basic Adolescent Gynecology, 1990; editor-in-chief Adolescent Medicine: State of the Art Revs., 1989—. Recipient Adele Hofmann award, 2000. Fellow Am. Acad. Pediatrics (Holyroyd-Sherry award 2000), Soc. for Adolescent Medicine; mem. Phi Beta Kappa. Office: U NM Sch Medicine Dept Pediatrics MSC10 5590 1 Univ New Mexico Albuquerque NM 87131-0001 Office Phone: 505-272-0338. E-mail: vstrasburger@salud.unm.edu.

**STRASFOGEL, IAN,** stage director, playwright; b. NYC, Apr. 5, 1940; s. Ignace and Alma (Lubin) S.; m. Judith Hirsch Norell, Feb. 15, 1973; children: Daniella Elizabeth, Gabrielle Sarah. BA, Harvard U., 1961. Administr. asst. N.Y.C. Opera Co., 1962-64, stage dir., 1964—; tchr. music Julliard Sch. Music, N.Y.C., 1965-66, Augusta (Ga.) Coll., 1967-68; founder, previous artistic dir. Augusta Opera Co., from 1967; chmn. dept. opera New Eng. Conservatory, Boston, 1968-72; prof. music U. Mich., Ann Arbor, 1980; freelance opera dir., playwright Rosenstone & Wander Agency, N.Y.C., 1982—. Stage dir. Balt. Civic Opera, Kansas City Lyric Theatre, Netherlands Opera Co., 1973—, N.Y.C. Opera, San Francisco Opera, Stuttgart Opera, Alte Oper Frankfurt, Edinburgh Festival, Aix-en-Provence Festival, Aspen Music Festival; dir. music theatre project Tanglewood Festival, Lenox, Mass., 1971-73; gen. dir. Opera Soc. Washington, 1972-75; artistic cons. Phila. Lyric Opera, 1973; dir. New Opera Theatre, Bklyn. Acad. Music, 1976-79. Author: Il Musico (music by Larry Grossman), 1990-91 The Caregiver (play), 1999, Jewish Ensemble Theatre, Detroit; editor: Ba-Ta-Clan, 1970. Served with AUS, 1966-68. Henry Russell Shaw travelling fellow, 1961-62; Ford Found. internship in performing arts, 1962-64; grantee: Internat. Inst. Edn., 1965, Berrillon Kerr Found., 1997 (for The Caregiver). Mem. Phi Beta Kappa. Home: 915 W End Ave New York NY 10025-3535

**STRASSBURGER, JOHN ROBERT,** academic administrator; b. Sheboygan, Wis., Apr. 6, 1942; s. J. Robert and Elizabeth (Mathewson) S.; m. Gertrude Hunter Mackie, Aug. 24, 1968; children: Sarah Electa, Gertrude Hunter. BA, Bates, 1964; Honours degree, Cambridge (Eng.) U., 1966; PhD, Princeton U., 1976. Faculty Hiram (Ohio) Coll., 1970-82; program officer NEH, Washington, 1982-84; prof. history, exec. v.p., dean Coll., Knox Coll., Galesburg, Ill., 1984-94; pres. Ursinus Coll., Collegeville, Pa., 1995—; CEO Philip & Muriel Berman Mus. Art at Ursinus Coll., Collegeville, Pa. Mem. commn. govt. rels. Am. Coun. Edn., 1997—. Contbr. articles to profl. jours. Bd. trustees Perkiomen Sch., 1997—. Mem. Am. Conf. Acad. Deans (chair 1990-91), Sunday Breakfast Club (Phila.). Office: Ursinus Coll Office of Pres PO Box 1000 Collegeville PA 19426-1000

**STRASSER, GABOR,** management consultant; b. Budapest, Hungary, May 22, 1929; s. Rezso and Theresa (Seiler) S.; m. Linda Casselman Pemble, Aug. 16, 1958 (div. 1976); children: Claire Margaret, Andrew John; m. Joka Verhoeff, Feb. 2, 1978; children: Steven Verhoeff, Tessa Christina. BCE, City Coll. N.Y., 1954; MS, U. Buffalo, 1959; PMD, Harvard, 1968; MDiv, Va. Theol. Sem., 1992. Research engr. Bell Aircraft Co., Buffalo, 1956-61; project leader Boeing Airplane Co., Seattle, 1961-62; dept. head Mitre Corp., Bedford, Mass., Washington, 1962-68; v.p. Urban Inst., Washington, 1968-69; tech. asst. to pres.'s sci. adviser White House, 1969-71, exec. sec. pres.'s sci. and tech. policy panel, 1970-71; dir. planning Battelle Meml. Inst., Columbus, Ohio, 1971-73; pres. Strasser Assocs., Inc., Washington, 1973-92. Author, editor: Science and Technology Policies-Yesterday, Today, Tomorrow, 1973; Contbr. articles to profl. jours. and theol. lit. Served to 1st lt., C.E. USAR. Recipient 1st nat. award Gravity Research Found., 1952

**STRASSER, RICHARD JOSEPH, JR.,** federal agency administrator; b. NYC, July 15, 1947; s. Richard Joseph Sr. and Lillian Mary (Murray) Strasser; m. Christine Therese Avery, Oct. 18, 1969; children: Richard, Mary Patricia, Therese, Clare, Moira, Christine. BA in Govt., Seton Hall U., 1969; M. in Pub. Adminstrn., Am. U., 1983. Mgmt. intern US Postal Svc., Washington, 1969-71, acting postmaster Walnut Creek, Calif., 1972, mgr. mktg. Washington, 1973-80, dir. office of policy, 1981-86, asst. postmaster gen. planning, 1987-90, sr. asst. postmaster gen. mktg. and customer svc., exec. v.p., CFO, 2000—. Mem. Corp. Planning 100, N.Y.C., 1986—; Conf. Bd. Coun. on Svcs. Mktg., 1991—. Soccer coach, Arlington, 1982-85, 88—. Roman Catholic. Office: US Postal Svc 475 Lenfant Plz SW Rm 5021 Washington DC 20260-0004*

**STRASSER, ROBERT,** architectural firm executive; Grad., City U. Joined Swanke, Hayden, Connell Archs., N.Y.C., 1989, prin., CFO, 1993—, ptnr., 1998—. Mem.: AIA (CFO large firm roundtable), Fin. Execs. Internat. (pres. N.Y. chpt.). Office: SHCA 295 Lafayette St New York NY 10012

**STRASSLER, MARC A.,** corporate lawyer; b. 1948; m. Meryl Strassler. BA, Bklyn. Coll., CUNY; JD, George Washington U. Bar: 1973. Joined Pathmark Stores Inc., Carteret, NJ, 1974, v.p., gen. counsel, sec., sr. v.p., gen. counsel, sec., 1998—. Office: Pathmark Stores Inc 200 Milik St Carteret NJ 07008

**STRASSNER, HOWARD TAFT, JR.,** obstetrician, educator; b. Tulsa, Okla., Dec. 2, 1948; BA in Biochemistry, U. Chgo., 1970, MD, 1974. Diplomate Am. Bd. Ob-gyn. Intern Columbia Presbyn. Med. Ctr., N.Y.C., 1974, resident ob-gyn., 1974—78; fellow maternal fetal medicine L.A. County-U. So. Calif. Med. Ctr., 1978—80; physician, dir. sect. maternal fetal medicine Rush U. Med. Ctr., Chgo., 1980—, co-dir. Rush Perinatal Ctr. John M. Simpson prof., chmn. Rush U. Med. Ctr., Chgo. Office: Rush Med Ctr 1653 W Congress Pkwy Chicago IL 60612 Office Phone: 312-997-2229. Business E-Mail: howard.t.strassner@rush.edu.

**STRATAS, TERESA (ANASTASIA STRATAKI),** soprano; b. Toronto, Ont., Can., May 26, 1938; Studied with Irene Jessner, 1956-59; grad., U. Toronto, 1959; LLD (hon.), McMaster U., 1986, U. Toronto, 1994; degree (hon.), Juilliard Sch. Music, 1995, Eastman Sch. Music, 1998, U. Rochester, 1998. Winner Met. Opera auditions, 1959; major roles in opera houses throughout world include: Mimi in La Bohème; Tatiana in Eugene Onegin; Susanna in The Marriage of Figaro; Nedda in Pagliacci; Marenka in The Bartered Bride; Three Heroines in Il Trittico; Violetta in La Traviata; title role in Rusalka; Jennie in Mahagonny; created title role in completed version of Lulu (Alban Berg), Paris Grand Opera, 1979; film appearances Kaiser von Atlantis, Seven Deadly Sins; Zefirelli's La Traviata, Salome, Lulu, Paganini, Zarewitsch, Eugene Oregin; Broadway debut in Rags, 1986; creator the role of Marie Antoinette Ghosts of Versailles world premiere Met. Opera, 1992; sang both female leading roles Il Tabarro, Pagliacci double bill opening Met. Opera, 1994, numerous recs. including Richard Strauss' Salomé, Songs of Kurt Weill. Decorated Order of Can.; recipient 3 Grammy awards, Emmy award, Drama Desk award, 1986, 3 Grammy nominations, Tony nomination, 1986, Tiffany award, 1994, Highest Paedeia award, 1996, Gemini award, 1997; named Performer of Yr., Can. Music Council, 1979. Home: 6150 Blackjack Ct N Punta Gorda FL 33982-9606

**STRATHAIRN, DAVID,** actor; b. San Francisco, Calif., Jan. 26, 1949; m. Logan Goodman; 2 children. Attended, Williams Coll., Ringling Bros. Clown Coll. Numerous stage appearances including: I'm Not Rappaport, Salonika, A Lie of the Mind, The Birthday Party, Danton's Death, Mountain Language, L'Atelier, A Moon for the Misbegotten, Temptation; Actor (films) Return of the Secaucus Seven, 1980, Lovesick, 1983, Silkwood, 1983, The Brother From Another Planet, 1984, Iceman, 1984, Enormous Changes at the Last Minute, 1985, When Nature Calls, 1985, At Close Range, 1986, Matewan, 1987, Eight Men Out, 1988, Stars and Bars, 1988, Dominick and Eugene, 1988, Call Me, 1988, The Feud, 1989, Memphis Belle, 1990, City of Hope, 1991, Big Girls Don't Cry...They Get Even, 1992, Bob Roberts, 1992, Shadows and Fog, 1992, A League of Their Own, 1992, Sneakers, 1992, Passion Fish, 1992, April One, 1993, Lost in Yonkers, 1993, The Firm, 1993, A Dangerous Woman, 1993, The River Wild, 1994, Dolores Claiborne, 1995, Losing Isaiah, 1995, Home for the Holidays, 1995, Mother Night, 1996, Beyond the Call, 1996, Song of Hiawatha, 1997, The Climb, 1997, Bad Manners, 1997, L.A. Confidential, 1997, With Friends Like These..., 1998, Simon Birch, 1998, Meschugge, 1998, A Small Miracle, 1998, A Midsummer Night's Dream, 1999, A Map of the World, 1999, Limbo, 1999, Harrison's Flowers, 2000, A Good Baby, 2000, The Victim, 2001, Ball in the House, 2001, Speakeasy, 2002, Blue Car, 2002, The Root, 2003, Twisted, 2004, Heavens Fall, 2005, Missing in America, 2005, Good Night, and Good Luck (Coppa Volpi award for Best Actor, Venice Film Festival), 2005, The Notorious Bettie Page, 2005, Steel Toes, 2006, The Shovel, 2006; (TV movies) Broken Vows, 1985, The Feud, 1989, Wiseguy, 1990, Heat Wave, 1990, Judgment, 1990, Without Warning: The James Brady Story, 1991, Lethal Innocence, 1991, O Pioneers!, 1992, The American Clock, 1993, Beyond the Call, 1996, In the Gloaming, 1997, Evidence of Blood, 1998, Freedom Song, 2000, The Miracle Worker, 2000, Lathe of Heaven, 2002, Master Spy: The Robert Hanssen Story, 2002, Paradise, 2004; (TV series) Another World, 1987, The Days and Nights of Molly Dodd, 1988-90, Big Apple, 2001; (TV appearances) Miami Vice, 1985, Spense: For Hire, 1987, The Equalizer, 1988, Day One, 1989, Wiseguy, 1990, Big Apple, 2001, The Sopranos, 2004*

**STRATHERN, JEFFREY N.,** medical researcher; PhD, U. Oreg., 1977. Sr. staff mem. Yeast Genetics Lab. Cold Spring Harbor Lab.; joined ABL-Basic Rsch. Program Nat. Cancer Inst., Frederick, 1984, joined Divsn. Basic Sciences (now Ctr. Cancer Rsch.), 1999; now chief Gene Regulation and Chromosome Biology Lab. Ctr. Cancer Rsch., Nat. Cancer Inst., Frederick, also head Genome Recombination and Regulation Sect. Office: Gene Regulation and Chromosome Biology Lab Nat Cancer Inst at Frederick PO Box B Bldg 539 Rm 152 Frederick MD 21701-1201 Office Phone: 301-846-1274. Office Fax: 301-846-6911. E-mail: strather@mail.ncifcrf.gov.

**STRATIGOS, WILLIAM NARGE,** computer company executive; b. Huntington, N.Y., Mar. 14, 1946; s. Narge G. and Portia R. (Kleros) Stratigos; m. Deborah Feller, Jan. 4, 1981; children: Stephanie, Elena. BA in Biology cum laude, NYU, 1972, DDS, 1977. Lic. dentist N.Y. Mgr. div. Med. Ctr. NYU, N.Y.C., 1966-74; mng. ptnr., dentist Stratigos et al, N.Y.C., 1978-88; pres. Sigma Imaging Sys. Inc., N.Y.C., 1988-95; also bd. dirs. Sigma Imaging Sys., Inc., N.Y.C., NY; v.p. Wang Software, N.Y., Inc., N.Y.C., 1995-97, Eastman Software, Inc., N.Y.C., 1997; v.p., bd. dirs. R2K, Inc., N.Y.C., 1997—; pres. Comfidex Corp., N.Y.C., 1998—. Bd. dirs. Animal Med. Ctr. Author: (book) Hot Spot, 1993. Fellow: NYU Acad. Oral Rehab.; mem.: First Dist. Dental Soc., Dental Soc. State of N.Y., Assn. Image & Info. Mgmt. Internat. (bd. dirs., treas. exec. com., chmn. accreditation com.), Omicron Kappa Upsilon. Greek Orthodox. Achievements include patents in field. Avocations: writing, chess, bowling. Office: R2K Inc 83 Maiden Ln New York NY 10038 Personal E-mail: wstratigos@aol.com.

**STRATMAN, DEBORAH,** filmmaker, film and video educator; Attended, U. Ill., 1985—86; BFA, Sch. of the Art Inst. of Chgo., 1986—90; MFA, Calif. Inst. of the Arts, 1992—95. Asst. instr. Cmty. Film Workshop, Chgo., 1988; contact printer Allied Film & Video, Chgo., 1989; tech. programmer, visiting artists; program Sch. Art Inst. Chgo., Chgo., 1989—90; staff audio visual dept. Mich. & Adams, 1990—91; projectionist, The Film Ctr. Art Inst. Chgo., 1990—92; co-op & tech. dir. Chgo. Filmmakers, 1991—92; 35 mm projectionist Cal Arts, Valencia, Calif., 1992—95; dir./prodr. Ind. Film/ Video Prodn. Pythagoras Productions, 1995—2002; visiting instr. -live action film/video Calif. Inst. Arts, Valencia, 2002; adj. asst. prof.-dept. film, video & new media Sch. Art Inst., Chgo., 1998—2003; adj. asst. prof.-art & architecture dept. U. Ill., Chgo., 2003—. Prodr.: (films) My Alchemy, 1990, Upon a Time, 1991, A Letter, 1992, Possibilities, Dilemmas, 1992, the train from l.a. to l.a., 1992, In Flight: Day No. 2,128, 1993, Palimpsest, 1993, Waking, 1994, Iolanthe, 1995, On the Various Nature of Things, 1995 (Ann Arbor Film Festival, 1996), From Hetty to Nancy, 1997 (Athens Internat. Film/Video Festival: best experimental, 1998), The BLVD, 1999 (Athens Internat. Film/Video Festival: best documentary, 2000), Untied, 2001, In Order Not to Be Here, 2002 (THAW Film/Video Festival: best of festival, 2002, Chgo. Underground Film Festival: best experimental, 2002, Film Festival: Gecko Award, 2002, Media City Film Festival: hon. mention, 2003, Ann Arbor Film Festival: best experimental & best narrative integrity, 2003), Meet Adiljan, 2003. Bd. dirs. Experimental Film Coalition, 1989—92, Chgo. Filmmakers, 2000—01. John Simon Guggenheim Meml. Found., 2003, prodn./post-prodn. grant, Daniel Film Inst. Workshop, 1995—96, Fulbright Grant, Iceland, 1995—96, Baltic-Nordic Fund, Denmark, 1996, finalist stipend, Studio Film & Tape, Roy W. Dean Film Grant, 1998, Chinese Adventure Capital Grant, Durfee Found., 2000, Pub. Art Grant, Gunk Found., 2000, Cmty. Arts Assistance Grants, 1999, 2000, 2001, Wendover Residency, Ctr. Land Use Interpretation, 2001, audio post prodn. residency, Experimental Sound Studio, 2001, Ill. Arts Coun. Spl. Assistance Grant, 1995, 1997, 2002, post prodn. residency, Wexner Ctr. Arts, 1998, 1999, 2001, 2002, Cal Arts Deans Coun. Grant, 2002, Artist's Fellowship-Media Arts, Ill. Arts Coun., 2000, 2002, Guggenheim Fellowship, 2003. Mailing: Pythagoras Productions PO Box 6167 Chicago IL 60680*

**STRATON, JOHN CHARLES, JR.,** investment banker; b. Warwick, N.Y., Apr. 18, 1932; s. John Charles and Helen (Sanford) S.; m. Sally M. Strawhand (div. Mar. 1970); children: John Charles III, Sara; m. Marion S. Holder, Feb. 18, 1974 (div. Mar. 1997); 1 child, Ashley Holder Straton; m. Donna S. DeCoursey, June 24, 1998. BA, U. Va., 1954. With Jas. H. Oliphant and Co., N.Y.C., 1956—; gen. ptnr., 1962—, 1st v.p., 1972-75; v.p. Spencer Trask & Co., Inc., N.Y.C., 1975-77, Hornblower, Weeks, Noyes & Trask, N.Y.C., 1977-78, Loeb Rhoades, Hornblower & Co., 1978-79, Shearson Loeb Rhoades, 1979-81; v.p., fin. cons. Shearson Lehman Bros., N.Y.C., 1981-93; sr. v.p. Smith Barney, N.Y.C., 1993—, Saloman Smith Barney, N.Y.C., 1997—, Smith Barney, N.Y.C., 2004—. Assessor Village of Tuxedo Park, N.Y., 1963-70. Vestryman St. Mary's, Tuxedo, N.Y. Served to maj. AUS, 1954-56; ret. Mem. U. Va. Alumni Assn. N.Y. (pres., treas. 1973-90), Mil. Order Fgn. Wars (comdr. 1981-86, treas. 1986—), Pilgrims of U.S. Am. Legion, Tuxedo Park Club, Sigma Phi Epsilon. Home: 2 Ledge Rd Tuxedo Park NY 10987 Office: 450 Lexington Ave New York NY 10017

**STRATOS, KIMARIE ROSE,** lawyer, sports association executive; b. Miami, Fla., Aug. 24, 1960; d. Jack Sloshower and Charmaine (McDougal) S. BS with high honors, U. Fla., 1981, JD with honors, 1984. Bar: Fla. 1985, U.S. Dist. Ct. (so. and mid. dist.) Fla. 1987. Ptnr. Shutts & Bowen, Miami, 1984—85, 1986—96; chair sports law dept., law clk. to judge U.S. Dist. Ct. for So. Dist. Fla., Miami, 1985-86; prin. Kimarie R. Stratos, PA, 1996—; gen. counsel Miami Children's Hosp. Bd. dirs. Fla. Sports Found., 1992—, vice chmn., 1995, chmn., 1996—; mem. Miami's 1999 Super Bowl Com. Co-author, asst. editor: Facility Development and the Sports Authority, Law of Professional and Amateur Sports; asst. editor: Clark Boardmen, 1990; contbr. articles to profl. jours. Inducted into U. Fla. Hall of Fame. Mem. ABA, Fla. Bar (bd. govs. young lawyers sect. 1987-93, exec. coun. entertainment, arts and sports law sect. 1988—), Fla. Assn. Women Lawyers, Sports Lawyers Assn. (nat. v.p. 1988-90, 93—, bd. dirs. 1990—), Phi Delta Phi, Fla. Blue Key. Avocations: running, travel. Office: Miami Children's Hosp 3100 SW 62nd Ave Miami FL 33155-3009 E-mail: kimarie.stratos@mch.net.

**STRATT, RICHARD MARK,** chemistry researcher, educator; b. Phila., Feb. 21, 1954; s. Stanford Lloyd and Florence Clair (Sussman) S. SB in Chemistry, MIT, 1975; PhD, U. Calif., Berkeley, 1979. Postdoctoral rsch. assoc. U. Ill., Champaign, 1979-80; NSF postdoctoral rsch. assoc., 1980; asst. prof. chemistry Brown U., Providence, 1981-85, assoc. prof., 1986-88, prof., 1988—, dept. chair, 1996—99, Harrison S. Kravis prof., 1999—2000, Newport Rogers prof. chemistry, 2004—. Mem. editl. bd. Jour. Chem. Physics, 2002-04, Molecular Physics, 2003—; mem. adv. bd. Jour. Phys. Chemistry, 1999—; contbr. articles to profl. jours. Alfred P. Sloan fellow, 1985-89; Fulbright scholar Oxford U., 1991-92. Fellow Am. Phys. Soc.; mem. Am. Chem. Soc. (chmn.-elect theoretical chem. subdivsn. 1997-98, chair 1998-99, program chair phys. chem. divsn. 2000-01, chair 2001-02), Sigma Xi, Phi Lambda Upsilon. Office: Brown U Dept Chemistry Providence RI 02912-0001 Office Phone: 401-863-3418. Business E-mail: Richard_Stratt@brown.edu.

**STRATTON, EVELYN LUNDBERG,** state supreme court justice; b. Bangkok, Feb. 25, 1953; came to U.S., 1971 (parents Am. citizens); d. Elmer John and Corrine Sylvia (Henricksen) Sahlberg; children: Luke Andrew, Tyler John; m. Jack A. Lundberg. Student, LeTourneau Coll., Longview, Tex., 1971-74; AA, U. Fla., 1973; BA, U. Akron, 1976; JD, Ohio State U., 1978. Bar: Ohio 1979, U.S. Dist. Ct. (so. dist.) Ohio 1979, U.S. Ct. Appeals (6th cir.) 1983. Assoc. Hamilton, Kramer, Myers & Cheek, Columbus, 1979-85; ptnr. Wesp, Osterkamp & Stratton, 1985-88; judge Franklin County Ct. Common Pleas, 1989-96; justice Ohio Supreme Ct., 1996—. Vis. prof. Nat. Jud. Coll., 1997—; spkr. legal seminars. Contbr. articles to profl. jours. Trustee Ohio affiliate Nat. Soc. to Prevent Blindness, 1989—, bd. dirs., trustee Columbus Coun. World Affairs, 1990-99, chmn. bd. dirs., 1999—; bd. dirs., trustee Dave Thomas Adoption Found., 1996—, ArChSafe Found., 1997—; mem. women's bd. Zephyrus League Cen. Ohio Lung Assn., 1989—; mem. Alliance Women Cmty. Corrections, 1993—. Recipient Gold Key award LeTourneau Coll., Gainesville, Fla., 1974, Svc. commendation Ohio Ho. of Reps., 1984, Scholar of Life award St. Joseph's Orphanage, 1998. Mem. ABA, ATLA, Columbus Bar Assn. (bd. govs. 1984-88, 90—; lectr.), Ohio Bar Assn. (jud. adminstrv. and legal reform com., coun. dels. 1992-96, Ohio Cmty. Corrections Orgn. (trustee 1995—), Columbus Bar Found. (trustee 1986-91, officer, sec. 1986-87, v.p. 1987-88), Am. Inns of Ct., Women Lawyers Franklin County, Phi Alpha Delta (pres. 1982-83). Office: Ohio Supreme Ct 65 S Front St Columbus OH 43215*

**STRATTON, GREGORY ALEXANDER,** application developer, director, mayor; b. Glendale, Calif., July 31, 1946; s. William Jaspar and Rita Phyllis (Smith) S.; m. Yolanda Margot Soler, 1967 (div. 1974); 1 child, Tiffany Schwarzer; m. Edith Carter, Sept. 27, 1975; stepchildren: Paul Henkell,

D'Lorah Henkell Wismar. Student, Harvey Mudd Coll., 1964-65; BS in Physics, UCLA, 1968; MBA, Calif. Luth. U., 1977. Elec. engr. Naval Ship Weapon System Engring. Sta., Port Hueneme, Calif., 1968-73; sr. staff mem. Univac, Valencia, Calif., 1973-74; v.p. Digital Applications, Camarillo, Calif., 1974-75; cons. Grumman Aerospace, Point Mugu, Calif., 1975-76; F-14 software mgr. Pacific Missle Test Ctr., Pt. Mugu, Calif., 1976-84; software mgr. Teledyne Systems, Northridge, Calif., 1984-92, dir. engring. software dept., 1992-93; dep. dir. software engring. Teledyne Electronic Systems, Northridge, Calif., 1993-94; software mgr. Litton Guidance and Controls, Woodland Hills, Calif., 1995-2001, Northrop/Grumman Nav. Sys., Woodland Hills, Calif., 2001—. Mem. strategic planning Simi Valley Hosp. Mem. City Coun., City of Simi Valley, Calif., 1979-86, mayor, 1986-98; mem. Rep. County Cen. Com., Ventura County, 2000-04; mem. Rep. State Cen. Com., Calif., 1990—; bd. dirs. Simi Valley Hosp., 1987-2001; pres. Simi Valley Cultural Arts Found., 1999-2005; trustee Simi Valley Unified Sch. Dist, 2002—. Mem. Rotary (Paul Harris award Simi Sunrise chpt. 1989), Jaycees (pres. Simi Valley chpt. 1974-75, nat. bd. dirs. 1975-76, v.p. Calif. state 1976-77). Republican. Lutheran. Office: Northrop Grumman Navigation Sys 5500 Canoga Ave Woodland Hills CA 91367-6698 Office Phone: 818-715-2371. Personal E-mail: gastratton@sbcglobal.net. Business E-mail: greg.stratton@ngc.com.

**STRATTON, JACK,** artist, art educator, curator, conservator; b. Hickory, N.C., Dec. 17, 1953; d. John Albert and Peggy Ann (Mason) Stratton; m. Sara Jane Mann, Apr. 22, 1997; m. Clara Ann Palmer Kelly (div.). BFA in Painting, U. N.C., Greensboro, 1977. Bookbinder Jackson Libr. U. N.C., Greensboro, 1982—92; preparator Weatherspoon Art Mus., Greensboro, NC, 1992—. Instr. art Art Alliance, Greensboro, NC, 2004—; freelance exhibition cons.; artist. One-man shows include Founders Hall, Guilford Coll., Greensboro, N.C., 1981, EUC Gallery, Greensboro, 1994, U. N.C. Wilmington, 2004, exhibitions include N.C. Mus. Art, Raleigh, 1987, Matress group, Atlanta, 1988, exhibited in group shows at 360 Broadway Gallery, N.Y.C., 1995, exhibitions include Green Hill Ctr. for N.C. Art, Greensboro, 2005, Represented in permanent collections High Point (N.C.) Arts Coun. Avocations: guitar, scuba diving. Office: Weatherspoon Art Mus Spring Garden at Tate St Greensboro NC 27412 Home: 1507 Fairmont St Greensboro NC 27403 Office Phone: 336-256-1446.

**STRATTON, JOHN ALFRED,** electrical engineer, educator; b. Rochester, N.Y., Sept. 12, 1941; s. Burton Elbridge and Alice Adele (Howie) Stratton; m. Lois Averett; children: Thomas C., Linda S. Palmer, Ann-Marie Gianossa. AAS, Rochester Inst. Technology, 1962, BS, 1964; MSEE, Rensselaer Poly. Inst., Troy, N.Y., 1966. Profl. engr. Sys. planning engr. N.Y. State Elec. & Gas, Binghamton, 1966—69; assoc. prof. Alfred State Coll., NY, 1969—71; from prof. elec. engring. tech. to chair dept., assoc. dean Rochester Inst. Tech., 1971—99, chair mfg. & mech. engring. technology, pckg. sci., 1999—2003, prof. elec./mech. engring., 2003—. Cons. in field. Pres. Classis of Rochester Reformed Ch. in am. Mem. IEEE, Inst. Power Engring. Soc., Am. Soc. Engring. Edn. (chair elect zone 1). Avocation: riding trains. Home: 43 Queensway Rd Rochester NY 14623-4627 Office: Rochester Inst Technology 78 Lomb Memorial Dr Rochester NY 14623-5604 Office Phone: 716-475-2017. Business E-mail: jasite@rit.edu.

**STRATTON, MARGARET ANNE,** minister; b. Concordia, Kans., Oct. 10, 1948; d. Charles Edward and Marie Teresa Mary; m. Mick Stratton, June 9, 1973; children: James, Grace. BS Home Econs., Kans. State U., 1973; M Theology, Caribbean Comty. Ministerial Acad., Orlando, Fla., 1994; MDiv, So. Meth. U., 2000. Ordained elder United Meth. Ch., 2003. Pastor United Meth. Diamond Hill Parish and Mission, Ft. Worth, 2000—06, Robinson Dr. United Meth. Ch., Waco, Tex., 2006—. Chmn. Task Force on Hunger, Ctrl. Tex. Conf.; mem. Hispanic com.; mem. Confessing Movement United Meth. Ch.; clergy leadership initiative Tex. Meth. Found.; bd. dirs. Johnson Hill Children's Program, Eutaw, Ala., 1993—95. Recipient grants in field. Mem.: Confession Movement, Battalion of Deborah, Lifewatch, Nat. Assn. United Meth. Evangelists. Avocation: wood sculpting and carving. Office: 2801 Robinson Dr Waco TX 76706 Office Phone: 254-662-3155. Business E-mail: margaretstratton@sbcglobal.net.

**STRATTON, MARIANN,** retired military nursing executive; b. Houston, Apr. 6, 1945; d. Max Millard and Beatrice Agnes (Roemer) S.; m. Lawrence Mallory Stickney, nov. 15, 1977 (dec.). BSN, BA in English, Sacred Heart Dominican Coll., 1966; MA in Mgmt., Webster Coll., 1977; MSN, U. Va., 1981. Cert. adult nurse practitioner. Ensign USN, 1966, advanced through grades to rear adm., 1991; patient care coord. Naval Regional Med. Ctr., Charleston, SC, 1981-83; nurse corps plans officer Naval Med. Command, Washington, 1983-86; dir. nursing svcs. U.S. Naval Hosp., Naples, Italy, 1986-89, Naval Hosp., San Diego, 1989-91; chief pers. mgmt. Bur. Medicine & Surgery, Washington, 1991-94; dir. USN Nurse Corps, Washington, 1991-94; ret. USN, 1994. Decorated Disting. Svc. medal, Meritorious Svc. medal with two stars, Naval Achievement medal, Navy Commendation medal. Mem. Interagy. Inst. Fed. Health Care Execs., Am. Volksporting Assn., Tex. Wanders, D'Vine Women, Garden Vols. of South Tex., U. Va. Raven Soc., Fiber Artists San Antonio.

**STRATTON, MICHAEL RUDOLF,** medical educator, researcher; b. June 22, 1957; BA in Physiol.Sci., Brasenose Coll., Oxford, Eng., 1979; MB BS, Guys Hosp., London, 1982; PhD, Inst. Cancer Rsch., London, 1989. House surgeon Guy's Hosp., London, 1982—83; house physician Beckenham Hosp., 1982—83; Ellen Russell Smith rsch. fellow Inst. Psychiatry, 1983; sr. house officer in pathology Westminster Hosp., 1984; registrar in histopathology Royal Postgrad. Med. Sch., Hammersmith Hosp., 1984—86; MRC tng. fellow Inst. Cancer Rsch., Inst. Psychiatry, 1986—89; sr. registrar dept. neuropathology Inst. Psychiatry, 1989—91; team leader in molecular carcinogenesis Inst. Cancer Rsch., Sutton, 1991—, joint head ICR Cancer Gene Cloning Lab., 1996—2000, prof. cancer genetics, sect. chmn., 1997—; head cancer genome project Sanger Inst., 2000—. Hon. cons. Royal Marsden Hosp., Sutton, 1992—; mem. joint rsch. com. Royal Marsden Hosp. Trust; bd. mgmt. Wellcome Trust Sanger Inst.; mem. Cambridge Addenbrookes Local Rsch. Ethics Com. Recipient Lennox K Black award for excellence in medicine, Thomas Jefferson U., Phila., 2002, Tom Connors award lecture, Brit. Assn. Cancer Rsch., 2001, Kettle Meml. Lecture, Assn. Clin. Pathologists, 1998; grantee, CRC, 1992, 1995, 1996, 1998, 1999, Wellcome Trust, 1999—2000, 2002, Kadoorie Found., 2005, many others. Fellow: Acad. Med. Scis.; mem.: Royal Coll. Pathologists. Achievements include patents for breast cancer susceptibility gene; patents pending for familial cylindromatosis tumour suppressor gene; application of mutations in BRAF for diagnostics and therapeutics in relation to human cancer; application of mutations in ERBB2 for diagnostics and therapeutics in relation to human cancer; application of mutations in other genes mutated in lung cancer for diagnostics and therapeutics. Office: Wellcome Trust Sanger Inst Wellcome Trust Genome Campus Hinxton Cambridge CB10 1SA England Address: Haddow Labs Inst Cancer Rsch 15 Cotswold Rd Sutton Surrey SM2 5NG England

**STRATTON, ROBERT,** retired electronics executive; b. Vienna, Aug. 14, 1928; came to U.S., 1959, naturalized, 1966; s. Kenneth Kurt and Eugenie (Schwatzer) S.; m. Elfriede Karlberger, Jan. 11, 1980; children: David Alexander, Valerie Pam. B.Sc. in Physics, Manchester U., 1949, PhD in Theoretical Physics, 1952. Rsch. physicist Met. Vickers Elec. Co. Manchester, Eng., 1952-59; with Tex. Instruments, Inc., Dallas, 1959-94, dir. physics rsch. lab., 1963-71, assoc. dir. cen. rsch. labs., 1971-72, dir. semiconductor R & D, 1972-75, dir. cen. rsch. labs., 1975-77, asst. v.p., dir. cen. rsch. labs., 1977-82, v.p. corp. staff, dir. cen. rsch. labs., 1982-94; dir. Indsl. Outreach Elec. Materials Sci. Tech. Ctr., dir. Engring. and Tech. Inst., U. Tex., Austin, 1994-96. Contbr. articles to profl. jours. Bd. dirs. Indsl. Rsch. Inst., 1993-88, Coun. on Superconductivity for Am. Competitiveness, 1987-90; adv. bd. dirs. Tex. Ctr. for Superconductivity, 1989-2000. Fellow IEEE, Inst. Physics (U.K.), Am. Phys. Soc.; mem. NAE. Personal E-mail: rstratton@comcast.net.

**STRATTON, WALTER LOVE,** lawyer; b. Greenwich, Conn., Sept. 21, 1926; s. John McKee and June (Love) Stratton; m. DeAnna Weinheimer, Oct. 1, 1994; children from previous marriage: John, Michael, Peter(dec.), Lucinda. Student, Williams Coll., 1943; AB, Yale U., 1948; LLB, Harvard U., 1951. Bar: N.Y. 1952. Assoc. Casey, Lane & Mittendorf, N.Y.C., 1951-53, Donovan, Leisure, Newton & Irvine, N.Y.C., 1956-63, ptnr., 1963-84, Gibson, Dunn & Crutcher, 1984-93, Andrews Kurth, N.Y.C., 1993-95; of counsel Andrews Kurth, N.Y.C., 1996—. Asst. U.S. atty. U.S. Dist. Ct. (so. dist.) N.Y., N.Y.C., 1953—56; lectr. Practising Law Inst. With USNR, 1945—46. Fellow: Am. Coll. Trial Lawyers; mem.: ABA, N.Y. State Bar Assn., Fed. Bar Coun., Greenwich Riding and Trails Assn., Colo. Arlberg Club, Indian Harbor Yacht Club. Home: 434 Round Hill Rd Greenwich CT 06831-2639 Office: Andrews Kurth 450 Lexington Ave 15th Fl New York NY 10017-3911 Office Phone: 212-850-2821. Business E-mail: walterstratton@akllp.com.

**STRATTON-CROOKE, THOMAS EDWARD,** financial consultant; b. NYC, June 28, 1933; s. Harold and Jeanne (Stifft) children: Karen, John Ryland; m. Suzanne Williams, Oct. 21, 1989 Student, Hunter Coll., 1951-52; BS in Marine Engring. and Transp., U.S. Maritime Acad., 1952-56; student, Washington U., St. Louis, 1961; MBA in Internat. Mktg., Banking and Fin., NYU, 1967. Commd. ensign USN, 1956, advanced through grades to lt., 1957; with Goodyear Internat. Corp., Akron, Ohio, 1960-63, Esso Internat., N.Y.C., 1958-60; dir. market info. and devel. Hotel Corp. Am., Boston, 1964-68; with Continental Grain Co., N.Y.C., 1968-72; dir. charter contracts Conoco, Stamford, Conn., 1973-75; cons. A. T. Kearney, Cleve., 1976-81; investment banker E. F. Hutton, Cleve., 1981-83, AG Edwards and Sons, Inc., Cleve., 1983-89; sr. fin. advisor, registered investment advisor, asst. v.p.; sr. fin. cons. Merrill Lynch, Cleve., 1989—. Chmn. Indsl. Devel. Resch. Coun., Atlanta, 1970, Indsl. Devel. Resch. Coun., Snow Mass, Colo., 1971; lectr. bus. U. R.I., Kingston, 1968-70, tchr. Bus. Coll. Internat., 1986-89 Contbr. articles to profl. jours. Mem. Findley Lake (N.Y.) Hist. Soc.; mem. Nat. Task Force Reps. for Pres. Reagan, Cleve., 1982—Officer (ret.) USN. Mem. Naval Res. Officers Assn., Naval Res. Assn., Great Lakes Hist. Soc., Soc. Naval Architects/Engrs., Findley Lake N.Y. Area C. of C., Navy League, Civil War Roundtable, NYU Alumni Assn., U.S. Coast Guard Club (Cleve.), Univ. Club, Circumnavigators Club (life), Internat. Shipmasters Assn., Propeller Club, Army Club, Navy Club, French Creek Hist. Soc., Town Club (Jamestown, N.Y.), Masons (32d degree), Naval Masonic Lodge, Shriners, Cleve. City Club, Kings Point Alumni Assn., Civil War Round Table, U.S. Mcht. Marine Acad., English Speaking Union (chpt. bd. dirs.), York & Scottish Rites Avocations: sailing, skiing, birdwatching, gardening, sports car and motorcycle enthusiast. Office: Merrill Lynch One Cleveland Ctr 1375 E 9th St Cleveland OH 44114-1798 Office Phone: 216-363-6717. Personal E-mail: tommyes@aol.com.

**STRAUB, CHESTER JOHN,** federal judge; b. Bklyn., May 12, 1937; s. Chester and Ann (Majewski) Straub; children: Chester, Michael, Christopher, Robert. AB, St. Peter's Coll., 1958; JD, U. Va., 1961. Bar: N.Y. 1962, U.S. Dist. Ct. (so. and ea. dists.) N.Y. 1963, U.S. Ct. Appeals (2d cir.) 1967, U.S. Supreme Ct. 1978. Assoc. Willkie Farr & Gallagher, N.Y.C., 1963—71, ptnr., 1971—99; mem. N.Y. State Assembly, 1967—72, N.Y. State Senate, 1973—75, Dem. Nat. Com., 1976—80; judge U.S. Ct. Appeals (2d cir.), 1998—. Past mediator U.S. Dist. Ct. (so. dist.) N.Y.; neutral evaluator U.S. Dist. Ct. (ea. dist.) N.Y.; chmn. jud. screening com. State of N.Y., 1988—94, first dept. jud. screening com., 1983—94, Senator Moynihan's jud. selection com., 1976—98. Trustee Lenox Hill Hosp.; Cardinal's com. laity Cath. Charities, N.Y. With U.S. Army, 1961—63. Mem.: ABA, Assn. of Bar of City of N.Y.C., N.Y. State Bar Assn., Kosciuszko Found. Office: US Ct Appeals 2530 US Courthouse 500 Pearl St New York NY 10007*

**STRAUB, GREGORY S.,** priest; b. Irvington, NJ; Degree, Dickinson Coll., 1970; MDiv, Phila. Div. Sch., 1973; DMin, Drew U., 1990. Ordained deacon, 1973, priest, 1974; deacon intern St. Thomas Ch., Lancaster, Pa., priest asst. to rector, interim rector; rector Emmanuel Ch., Chestertown, Md., 1976—2005; exec. officer Gen. Conv., NYC, 2005—. Dep. Gen. Conv. triennial meeting, 1985, 97, 2000, 03, asst. sec. for voting, 03. Mem.: Nat. Episcopal Historians and Archivists Orgn., Episcopal Hist. Soc. Episc. Office: DFMS Gen Conv Office 815 2nd Ave 4th Fl New York NY 10017

**STRAUB, PETER FRANCIS,** novelist; b. Milw., Mar. 2, 1943; s. Gordon Anthony and Elvena (Nilsestuen) S.; m. Susan Bitker, Aug. 27, 1966; children: Benjamin Bitker, Emma Sydney Valli. BA, U. Wis., 1965; MA, Columbia U., 1966. English tchr. Univ. Sch., Milw., 1966-68. Bd. dirs. U. Wis: Author: Marriages, 1973, Julia, 1975, If You Could See Me Now, 1977, Ghost Story, 1979, Shadowland, 1980, Floating Dragon, 1983, Leeson Park and Belsize Square, 1984, Wild Animals, 1984, Blue Rose, 1985, Koko, 1988, Mystery, 1989, Houses Without Doors, 1990, Mrs. God, 1991, The Throat, 1993, The Hellfire Club, 1994, Mr. X, 1999, Pork Pie Hat, 1999, Magic Terror, 2000, Lost Boy Lost Girl, 2003, In the Night Room, 2004; (with Stephen King) The Talisman, 1984, Black House, 2001; editor: Peter Straub's Ghosts, 1995. Conjunctions #39, 2002, Library of America H.P. Lovecraft Tales, 2005. Bd. dirs. Fence, Conjunctions, Am. Poetry Rev., Poets & Writers. Recipient Brit. Fantasy award, August Derleth award, 1983, World Fantasy awards World Fantasy Conv., 1989, 93, World Horror Assn. awards, 1993, 98, 99, 2000, 03, 04, Grand Master award World Horror Conv., 1997, award Internat. Horror Guild, 1999, 2003, Lifetime Achievement award HWA, 2006; sponsor Peter Straub Disting. Lectureship on Popular Culture, U. Wis. Mem. PEN, Horror Writers Assn. Avocations: jazz, opera, classical music. Personal E-mail: pstraub@nyc.rr.com.

**STRAUB, PETER THORNTON,** lawyer; b. St. Louis, Mar. 27, 1939; s. Ralph H. and Mary Louise (Thornton) S.; m. Wendy B. Cubbage, Dec. 29, 1964; children: Karl Thornton, Philip Hamilton, Ellen Elizabeth. AB, Washington and Lee U., 1961, LLB, 1964. Bar: Mo. 1964, Va. 1968, U.S. Dist. Ct. (ea. dist.) Mo. 1967, U.S. Circuit Ct. Appeals (8th cir.) 1969, U.S. Supreme Ct. 1970. U.S. Circuit Ct. Appeals (D.C. cir.) 1971, Ct. Mil. Appeals 1970, U.S. Tax Ct. 1971, U.S. Bankruptcy Ct. 1991. Assoc. Evans & Dixon, St. Louis, 1966-68; asst. pub. defender St. Louis County, St. Louis, 1968-69; asst. U.S. Atty. St. Louis, 1969-71; trial atty. internal security div. Dept. Justice, Washington, 1971-72, atty.-adviser office of dep. atty. gen., 1972-73, dir. office criminal justice, spl. asst. to atty. gen., 1974; minority counsel com. on judiciary U.S. Ho. of Reps., Washington, 1973-74; gen. counsel SSS, Washington, 1974-76; pvt. practice Law Offices of Peter T. Straub, Alexandria, Va., 1976—. Pres., gov. bd. Alexandria Cmty. Mental Health Ctr., 1982—95; mem. No. Va. Estate Planning Coun., 1981—; mem. pres.'s coun. Trinity Coll., Washington, 1980—87; mem. adv. bd. Am. Heart Assn., Alexandria, 1991—92, Salvation Army, Alexandria, 1991—, v.p., 1994—96, chmn., 1997—99, Alexandria Cmty. Shelter Adv. Bd., 1995—97; Va. escheat atty. City of Alexandria, 1994—2002; dist. chmn. Boy Scouts Am., 1998—2001; mem. adv. bd. Hospice No. Va., 2000—; bd. dirs. Friends of the Washington and Old Dominion Trail, 2002—, Parc East Condominium, 1990—, sec., 1992—; bd. dirs. Sigma Nu Ednl. Found., Inc., 2000—; charter mem. bd. dirs. Alexandria Country Day Sch., 1983—90. With U.S. Army, 1964—66, capt. USAR, 1966—72. Recipient certificate of award Dept. Justice, 1970, certificate of appreciation Law Enforcement Assistance Administn. Dept. Justice, 1974, Silver Beaver award Boy Scouts Am., Washington, 1987, Collins award Alexandria Coun. Persons with Disabilities, 1993, Cmty. Svc. award Am. Indian Alliance, 1995. Mem.: FBA, ABA, Nat. Acad. Elder Law Attys., Va. Trial Lawyers Assn., Alexandria Bar Assn., Mo. Bar Assn., Bar Assn. Met. St. Louis, Va. State Bar Assn., Optimists (bd. dirs., pres. Alexandria chpt. 1984, lt. gov. Nat. Capitol Va. Dist. 1987—89, treas. 1999—2001), Nat. Eagle Scout Assn., Nat. Lawyers Club, Sigma Nu. Republican. Congregationalist. Avocations: scouting, reading, bicycling. Office: 1225 Martha Custis Dr # 103 Alexandria VA 22302-2040 Office Phone: 703-820-3600. Office Fax: 703-820-8602. Business E-mail: pstraub@straublawoffices.com.

**STRAUCH, EDWARD HUGO,** writer, retired literature and language professor; b. Chgo., June 18, 1925; s. Moritz Franz and Ida (Pfeffer) Strauch; m. Patricia A. D'Andrea (div.); 1 child, Jason Edward; m. Arlene M. Russie, 1954 (div. 1959); children: Julia, Lydia. Diplôme Supérieur, Sorbonne U., Paris, 1950; BA in English and French, Calif. State U., LA, 1958, MA in English and Edn., 1961; PhD in Comparative Lit., Ind. U., Bloomington, 1969. Cert. instr. Calif. Dir. humanities program Nasson Coll., Caen, France, 1966—70; assoc. prof. English U. Guam, Mangilao, 1971—75; vis. prof. English Pahlavi U., Shiraz, Iran, 1975—76; writer multimedia English Free U., Teheran, 1976—77; prof. English Mohammed V U., Rabat, Morocco, 1977—78; head English dept. U. Maiduguri, Nigeria, 1979—86; assoc. prof. English U. Guam, Mangilao, 1987—95; ret., 1995. Author: How Nature Taught Man to Know, Imagine and Reason, 1995, Beyond Literary Theory: Literature as a Search for the Meaning of Human Destiny, 2001, The Creative Conscience as Human Destiny, 2004; contbr. articles to profl. jours. Ensign USN, 1943—46. Mem.: MLA. Avocations: art, writing, music. Home: U Guam PO Box 5256 Mangilao GU 96923

**STRAUCH, JOHN L.,** lawyer; b. Pitts., Apr. 16, 1939; s. Paul L. and Delilah M. (Madison) S.; m. Gail Lorraine Kohn, Dec. 5, 1991; children: Paul L., John M., Lisa E. BA summa cum laude, U. Pitts., 1960; JD magna cum laude, NYU Sch. Law, 1963. Law clk. to Judge Sterry Waterman US Ct. Appeals (2d cir.), St. Johnsbury, Vt., 1963-64; assoc. Jones, Day, Reavis & Pogue, Cleve., 1964-70, ptnr., litig. group, 1970—, chair, litig. group, 1993—2004. Mem. Statutory Com. on Selecting Bankruptcy Judges, Cleve., 1985-88; mem. lawyers com. Nat. Ctr. for State Cts. Editor-in-chief: NYU Law Rev., 1962-63; contbr. chpt. to book. Pres., trustee Cleve. Task Force on Violent Crimes, 1985-88; trustee Legal Aid Soc., Cleve., 1978, Cleve. Greater Growth Assn., 1985-86, Citizens Mental Health Assembly, 1989-90, lawyers com. Nat. Ctr. for State Cts., 1989—. Fellow Am. Coll. Trial Lawyers (life); mem. ABA, Ohio Bar Assn., Cleve. Bar Assn. (trustee 1980-83, pres. 1985-86), Fed. Bar Assn. (trustee Cleve. chpt. 1978-79, v.p. Cleve. chpt. 1979-80), Sixth Fed. Jud. Conf. (life), Ohio Eighth Jud. Conf. (life), Order of Coif, Inns of Ct., Oakmont Country Club, The Country Club, Kiawah Island Club, Phi Beta Kappa. Office: Jones Day North Point 901 Lakeside Ave Cleveland OH 44114-1190

**STRAUCHON-VERNER, KIMBERLY,** lawyer; b. Troy, N.Y., Jan. 14, 1968; d. William V. and Joanne M. Strauchon; m. Arthur Scott Verner, Sept. 27, 1998; children: Liam Scott Verner, Luca Jane Verner. Mem. Bethlehem Bus. Builders, Albany, NY, 2004—, Network Empowering Women, Albany, 2006—. Pres. bd. dirs. Capital Dist. Ctr. for Independence, Albany, 2004—; bd. dirs., 2001—; amb. So. Sarasota County C. of C., Clifton Park, NY, 2005—; soccer coach Bethelehem Soccer Club, Delmar, NY, 2006.

**STRAUGHAN, WILLIAM THOMAS,** engineering educator, structural engineering consultant; b. Shreveport, La., Aug. 2, 1936; s. William Eugene and Sara Chloetilde (Harrell) S.; m. Rubie Ann Barnes, Aug. 20, 1957; children: Donna Ann, Sara Arlene, Eugene Thomas. BS, MIT, 1959; MS, U. Tex., 1986; PhD, Tex. Tech. U., 1990. Registered profl. engr., Fla., Ill., Iowa, La., Tex., Wash. Project engr. Gen. Dynamics Corp., Chgo., 1959—60; chief project, design engr. Gen. Foods Corp., Kankakee, Ill., 1960—64; mgr. plant engring. Std. Brands Inc., Clinton, Iowa, 1964—66; regional mgr. Air Products & Chems., Inc., Creighton, Pa., 1966—68; gen. mgr. Skyline Corp., Harrisburg, NC, 1968—70; cons. Charlotte, NC, 1970—72; dir. engring. and Fla. ops. Zimmer Homes Corp., Pompano Beach, 1972—73; v.p. engring. and mfg. Nobility Homes, Inc., Ocala, Fla., 1973—78, Moduline Internat., Inc., Lacey, Wash., 1978—85; rsch. engr. U. Tex., Austin, 1985—86; lectr., rschr. Tex. Tech. U., Lubbock, 1987—90; assoc. prof. U. New Orleans, 1990—92; asst. prof. dept. civil engring. La. Tech. U., Ruston, 1992—98. Tchr. 30 different courses, 1987—; adj. prof. Coll. Engring., La. Tech. U., 2001-05, vis. prof., 2005-; cons. in field, Dubach, La., 1992—; condr. workshops in field; apptd. spokesman Mfrd. Housing Industry before U.S. Congress. Contbr. articles to numerous profl. jours. Vol. engring. svcs. Lubbock Fire Safety House, 1990; judge sci. fair Ben Franklin H.S., New Orleans, 1990. Recipient T.L. James Svc. award La. Tech. U., 1994; grantee Urban Waste Mgmt. and Rsch. Ctr. New Orleans, 1991, Shell Devel. Co., 1993, La. Edn. Quality Support Fund, Insituform Techs., Inc., Trenchless Tech. Ctr., PABCO, Inc., InLiner USA, Inc., 1995, others; numerous grants in field. Mem. ASME (life), ASCE (Student chpt. Tchr. of Yr. award 1995, 98), Nat. Coun. Structural Engrs. Assns., Structural Engrs. Assn. La., Phi Kappa Phi, Sigma Xi, Chi Epsilon. Avocations: flying, skiing, motorcycling, camping, reading. Home: 199 Sellers Rd Dubach LA 71235-3218 Personal E-mail: drtomstraughan@msn.com.

**STRAUMANIS, JOHN JANIS, JR.,** psychiatrist, educator; b. Riga, Latvia, Apr. 22, 1935; arrived in U.S., 1950; s. Janis and Ella (Fredrichson) S.; m. Carol A. Sharar, Aug. 8, 1959; children: John, Susan. BA, U. Iowa, 1957, MD, 1960, MS, 1964. Intern Georgetown U. Hosp., Washington, 1960-61; resident U. Iowa, Iowa City, 1961-64; asst. prof. Temple U., Phila., 1966-71, assoc. prof., 1971-77, prof., 1977-85; prof. psychiatry La. State U., Shreveport, 1985-92; prof. psychiatry, dir. rsch. Tulane U. Med. Sch., New Orleans, 1992—. Cons. Camden County Hosp., Blackwood, NJ, 1967—85, VA Hosp., Shreveport, 1985—92, New Orleans, 1992—. Contbr. articles to profl. jours. Lt. comdr. USN, 1964—65. Recipient Rsch. Career Devel. award, NIMH, 1966. Fellow Am. Psychiat. Assn.; mem. Am. Psychopathol. Assn., Soc. Biol. Psychiatry, Phi Eta Sigma, Phi Beta Kappa, Alpha Omega Alpha. Avocations: travel, music, photography. Office: Tulane U Med Ctr Dept Psychiatry & Neurology 1430 Tulane Ave New Orleans LA 70112-2699 Office Phone: 504-988-7530.

**STRAUME, TORE,** biophysicist, researcher; s. Oddvard Jorik and Ella Dorothea Straume; m. Andrea Bernice Haines, Mar. 1, 1968; children: Shawn Tor, Erik Jorik, Lisa Andrea. BS, U. Wash., Seattle, 1973, MS, 1976, PhD, U. Calif., Davis, 1982. Radiation biophysicist Lawrence Livermore Nat. Lab., Livermore, Calif., 1975—97; rsch. prof. U. Utah, Salt Lake City, 1997—2004; chief scientist Ames Rsch. Ctr., Life Scis. Divsn. NASA, Moffett Field, Calif., 2004—; pres., founder GenMetrix, LLC, Salt Lake City, 2000—04. Contbr. over 150 articles to profl. jours. Recipient Spl. Achievement award, U.S. Dept. Energy, 2006; fellow, USPHS, 1973—75. Achievements include reconstructing the radiation doses received by Hiroshima survivors; the measurement of radioiodine from Chernobyl; the development of chromosome painting; neutron and tritium radiation health effects studies; biotechnology development; 6 patents in field. Office: NASA Ames Research Center Life Sciences Division Moffett Field CA 94035 Office Phone: 650-604-3943. Business E-Mail: tstraume@mail.arc.nasa.gov.

**STRAUS, DAVID A.,** architectural firm executive; b. Medford, Oreg., 1943; m. Sherry Straus; 2 children. BArch, U. Oreg., 1967. Registered architect, Oreg. Founding ptnr. Skelton, Straus & Seibert, Medford, 1989—. Mem Oreg Transp Comn, Rogue Valley Area Comn Transp. Past pres Medford Arts Comn, Arts Coun Southern Oreg; coach Rogue Valley Soccer Asn; leader Boy Scouts Am; bd dirs, past pres Schneider Mus Art SOSC; bd dirs Medford YMCA, Rogue Valley Art Asn. Lt USNR, Vietnam. Mem.: AIA (pres. so. Oreg. chpt.), Archit Found Oreg (past bd. dirs.), Medford/Jackson County CofC (past bd. dirs., Mem of the Yr 2000), Univ Oreg Alumni Asn, Oreg Club Southern Oreg (past pres.), Univ Club Medford (past pres.), Rotary. Office: Skelton Straus & Seibert Arch 26 Hawthorne St Medford OR 97504-7114 Office Phone: 541-779-4363. Business E-Mail: dstraus@sssarchitects.com.

**STRAUS, KATHLEEN NAGLER,** academic administrator, educator; b. NYC, Dec. 3, 1923; d. Maurice and Mildred (Kohn) Nagler; m. Everet M. Straus, May 29, 1948 (dec. Nov. 1967); children: Peter R., Barbara L. BA in Econs., Hunter Coll., 1944; postgrad., Columbia U., 1944—45, Am. U., 1946—47, Wayne State U., 1976—78. Various positions, 1944—50, 1966; dep. dir. Model Neighborhood Agy., City of Detroit, 1968—70; dir. social svcs. Southeastern Mich. Coun. Govts., Detroit, 1970—74; staff coord. Edn. Task Force, Detroit, 1974—75; exec. dir. People and Responsible Orgns. for Detroit, 1975—76; staff dir. edn. com. Mich. Senate, Lansing, 1976—79; assoc. exec. dir. Mich. Assn. Sch. Bds., Lansing, 1979—86; dir. cmty. rels.

and devel. Ctr. for Creative Studies, Detroit, 1986—87, pres., 1987—91; mem. Mich. Bd. Edn., 1992—, pres., 2003. Mem. Mich. Bd. for Pub. Jr. and C.C.s, Lansing, 1980-92, v.p., 1989, pres., 1991; cons. Met. Columbus (Ohio) Schs. Com., 1975-76; mem. steering com. Mich. Edn. Seminars, 1979-86; mem. Adv. Com. on Higher Edn. Needs in S.W. Mich., 1971-72, Ad Hoc Com. on Equal Access to Higher Edn., 1970-71, Citizens Action Com. on Sch. Fin. Contbr. articles to profl. jours. Active numerous civic orgns.; vice chmn. downtown br. Met. Detroit YWCA, 1970-74; bd. dirs. Citizens for Better Care, Inc., 1973-78; mem. edn. com. New Detroit, Inc., 1972—; trustee Detroit Sci. Ctr., Inc., 1975—; founder, pres. Mich. Tax Info. Coun., 1982—; v.p. bd. dirs. Univ. Cultural Ctr. Assn., 1986-91; trustee Comprehensive Health Planning Coun. Southeastern Mich., 1977-78; mem. Wayne County Art and History Commn., 1988; co-chmn. Nat. Arts Program, 1987-88; bd. dirs. North Ctrl. Regional Edn. Libr.; bd. dirs. North Ctrl. Regional Edn. Lab. Recipient Amity citation, Detroit, 1966, Disting. Cmty. Svc. award Am. Jewish Com., 1988, Common Coun., Detroit, 1976, resolution Mich. Ho. of Reps., 1986, Mich. Senate, 1988, Educator of Yr. Wayne State U., 1999, Disting. Warrior award Detroit Urban League, 2000; named to Mich. Edn. Hall of Fame, 1997; inducted into Mich. Women's Hall of Fame, 2000, Lifetime Achievement award Anti Defamation League, 2004, Multi Cultural Edn. award Nat. Conf. Cmty. and Justice, 2004. Mem.: LWV (pres. Detroit 1961—63), Alpha Chi Alpha. Democrat. Avocations: travel, theater, concerts. Home: 7431 Deep Run 210 Bloomfield Hills MI 48301 Office: State Bd Edn PO Box 30008 Lansing MI 48909-7508 Office Phone: 517-373-3900. Business E-Mail: strausk@michigan.gov.

**STRAUS, LEON STEPHAN,** physicist; b. Takoma Park, Md., May 29, 1943; s. Sidney and Ruth Straus; m. Cheryl Sarran Straus, Apr. 4, 1970; children: Jonathan, Jennifer. BS in Physics, Antioch Coll., Yellow Springs, Ohio, 1965; M Physics, Georgetown U., 1970, PhD in Physics, 1971. Mem. rsch. staff Ctr. Naval Analyses, Alexandria, Va., 1973-75, field rep. CTF 69 Naples, Italy, 1975-77, project mgr. Alexandria, 1977-79, field rep. CTF 69 and CTF 66/67 Naples, Italy, 1979-82, assoc. dep. dir. Alexandria, 1982-85, field rep. CTF 72 Kamiseya, Japan, 1985-87, program mgr. Alexandria, 1987-90, field rep. COMSIXTHFLT Gaeta, Italy, 1990-92, project mgr. Alexandria, 1992-95, tech. dir. spl. projects, 1995-97, dep. dir. info. ops. warfare team, 1997-2000; pvt. contractor, 2001—. Asst. AEC, Germantown, Md., 1968-71. Contbr. articles to profl. jours. Vol. Jewish lay leader USN, Naples, 1975-77, 79-82. Recipient Fellowship Georgetown U., Washington, 1965-68. Mem. Acoustical Soc. Am., Navy Submarine League. Jewish. Achievements include planning, evaluating and documenting tests/exercises and conducting studies associated with U.S. Navy and joint strategy, tactics, force planning, communication and technology. Office Phone: 954-298-2513. Personal E-mail: strausconsult@aol.com.

**STRAUS, MARC JOSHUA,** internist, poet; b. NYC, 1943; married; 2 children. AB, Franklin and Marshall Coll., 1964; MD, SUNY, Bklyn., 1968. Straight med. intern Kings County Hosp., Bklyn., 1968-69; staff assoc. Nat. Cancer Inst., NIH, Bethesda, Md., 1969-71; sr. cancer rsch. internist, head Cell Kinetics Lab. Barnes Hosp., St. Louis, 1972—74, resident in medicine, 1971-72, fellow in hematology, 1974; chief sect. med. oncology Univ. Hosp., Boston, 1974-78; assoc. prof. medicine Boston U. Sch. Medicine, 1974-78; prof. medicine NY Med. Coll., Valhalla, 1978—, chief divsn. neoplastic diseases, 1978-82; pvt. practice, White Plains, NY, 1982—. Rsch. pathologist Mallory Inst. Pathology, Boston, 1974-78; chief oncology Westchester County Med. Ctr., 1978-82; staff physician St. Agnes Hosp., White Plains, St. Joseph's Hosp., Yonkers, Hudson Valley Hosp., Peekskill, NY, Putnam Hosp., Carmel, NY; co-founder (with Livia Straus) Hudson Valley Center for Contemporary Art, Peekskill, NY, 2002-. Recipient Robert Penn Warren award lectr. Yale U. Med. Sch., 1998; Yaddo fellow in poetry, 1993. Fellow ACP, Am. Coll. Physician Execs.; mem. Am. Assn. for Cancer Rsch., Am. Soc. Clin. Oncology. Office: 707 Westchester Ave Ste 110 White Plains NY 10604-3155 also: Hudson Valley Ctr for Contemporary Art 1701 Main St PO Box 209 Peekskill NY 10566 Office Phone: 914-788-7166. Business E-Mail: mstraus@mdx-med.com, info@hvcca.com.

**STRAUS, MATTHEW,** wine director; b. 1973; Studied European Cuisine, Pacific Inst. Culinary Arts, Vancouver, 2005. Worked at The Tuscan Grill, Boston, The Harvest, Boston, The Federalist, Boston, Campanile, LA, L'Orangerie, LA, Sona, LA; wine dir. Grace, LA, Wilshire, LA; owner Heirloom. Named one of LA's Rising Stars, StarChefs.com, 2006. Office: Wilshire 2454 Wilshire Blvd Santa Monica CA 90403 Office Phone: 310-586-1707.*

**STRAUS, OSCAR S., II,** foundation executive; b. NYC, Nov. 6, 1914; s. Roger Williams and Gladys (Guggenheim) S.; m. Marion Miller Straus, 1941 (div. 1982); 1 child, Oscar S. III; m. Joan Sutton, 1982. AB, Princeton U., 1936; postgrad., U. Dijon, summer 1936, Sch. Bus. Adminstrn. Harvard U., 1938. Pvt. sec. Internat. Labor Office, Geneva, 1937-38; U.S. fgn. svc. officer, 1940-42; divisional asst. Dept. State, 1942-43, 44-45; treas., dir., v.p., chmn. fin. com. Am. Smelting & Refining Co., 1945-59; ptnr. Guggenheim Bros., 1959-83; pres., dir. Guggenheim Exploration Co., Inc., 1963-73; gen. ptnr. Straus Minerals, 1973-88; chmn., bd. dirs. Daniel and Florence Guggenheim Found., N.Y.C. Chmn., bd. dirs. Fred L. Lavanburg Found. Trustee emeritus Am. Mus. Natural History, Mystic Seaport, Conn.; hon. chmn. Rensselaerville (N.Y.) Inst.; trustee Congregation Emanu-El. Mem.: Coun. Fgn. Rels., Knickerbocker Club, Doubles Club, Megantic Fish and Game Club, Cruising Club Am. Jewish. Home: 40 S Howells Point Rd Bellport NY 11713 Office: 950 3rd Ave New York NY 10022

**STRAUS, ROBERT,** behavioral sciences educator; b. New Haven, Jan. 9, 1923; s. Samuel Hirsh and Alma (Fleischner) Straus; m. Ruth Elizabeth Dawson, Sept. 8, 1945; children: Robert James, Carol Martin, Margaret Dawson, John William. BA, Yale U., 1943, MA, 1945, PhD, 1947. Asst. prof. Yale U., 1948—51, rsch. assoc. applied physiology, 1951—53; acting dir. Conn. Child Study and Treatment Home, New Haven, 1952—53; prof. med. preventive medicine SUNY Upstate Med. Ctr., 1953—56; prof. med. sociology U. Ky., Lexington, 1956—59, prof. med. dept. behavioral sci. Coll. Medicine, also chmn. dept., 1959—87; dir. for sci. devel. Med. Rsch. Inst. San Francisco, 1991—93. Vis. fellow Yale U., 1968—69; vis. prof. U. Calif., Berkeley, 1978, 86; sec. Com. Med. Sociology, 1955—57; chmn. Coop. Com. Study Alcoholism, 1961—63, Nat. Adv. Com. on Alcoholism, 1966—69; mem. Nat. Adv. Coun. on Alcohol Abuse and Alcoholism, 1984—87; trustee Med. Rsch. Inst. San Francisco, 1988—93; mem. Calif. Pacific Med. Ctr. Rsch. Coun., 1993. Author: Medical Care for Seamen, 1950; author: (with S.D. Bacon) Drinking in College, 1953; author: Alcohol and Society, 1973, Escape From Custody, 1974, A Medical School is Born, 1996; co-editor: Medicine and Society, 1963; mem. editl. bd.: Jour. Studies on Alcohol, 1950—2000. Pres. Bluegrass R.R. Mus., 1980. Mem.: Inst. Medicine NAS, Acad. Behavioral Medicine Rsch., Am. Pub. Health Assn. (lifetime achievement award sect. on alcohol, tobacco and other drugs 1993), Assn. Behavioral Scis. and Med. Edn. (pres. 1974), Am. Sociol. Assn. (chmn. med. sociology sect. 1967—68, Leo G. Reeder award Disting. Contbn. Med. Sociology 1998), Sigma Xi, Phi Beta Kappa. Home: 656 Raintree Rd Lexington KY 40502-2874 Personal E-mail: randrstraus@insightbb.com. Business E-Mail: rstraus@uky.edu.

**STRAUS, STEPHEN EZRA,** federal agency administrator, biomedical researcher; b. NYC, Nov. 23, 1946; s. Samuel Lieb and Dora Beatrice (Drattel) S.; m. Barbara Ellen Portnoy, June 24, 1973; children: Kate, Julie, Benjamin. BS, MIT, 1968; MD, Columbia U., 1972. Diplomate in internal medicine and infectious diseases Am. Bd. Internal Medicine. Intern and resident in internal medicine Washington U., St. Louis, 1972-73, 75-76; sr. investigator Nat. Inst. Allergy and Infectious Diseases, Bethesda, Md., 1979—, chief Lab. Clin. Investigation, 1991—2003; dir. Nat. Ctr. Complementary and Alternative Medicine, NIH, Bethesda, Md., 1999—. Contbr. over 400 articles to profl. jours. Med. dir. USPHS, 1973-75, 79-2000. Recipient 5 medals USPHS, 1983, 87, 90, 98, 2000. Mem. Assn. Am. Physicians, Am. Soc. for Clin. Investigation, Infectious Diseases Soc. Am. Achievements include research and fundamental discovery on treatment and pathogenesis of human viral infections and immunological disorders. Office: Dept Health & Human Svcs/Nat Ctr Complementary and Alternative Medicine 31 Center Drive Bethesda MD 20892-0001

**STRAUSBAUGH, CARL ALAN,** plant pathologist; s. Carl Dennis and Mary Katie Strausbaugh; m. Cynthia Strausbaugh, June 0, 1989; 1 child, Ben Lee. PhD, Wash. State U., Pullman, 1988. Rsch. plant pathologist USDA-ARS, Kimberly, Idaho, 2004—. Office: USDA-ARS 3793 North 3600 East Kimberly ID 83341 Office Phone: 208-423-6594. Office Fax: 208-423-6555. Business E-Mail: carls@nwisrl.ars.usda.gov.

**STRAUSBERG, ROBERT L.,** federal agency administrator; Head, sequencing tech. br. Nat. Ctr. for Human Genome Rsch., NIH, 1994—96; dir., office of cancer genomics Nat. Cancer Inst., NIH, 1999—; v.p., rsch. The Inst. for Genomic Rsch., 2003—04; v.p. human genomic medicine J. Craig Venter Institute, Rockville, Md., 2004—. Office: J Craig Venter Institute 9704 Medical Ctr Dr Rockville MD 20850

**STRAUSER, ROBERT WAYNE,** lawyer; b. Little Rock, Aug. 28, 1943; s. Christopher Columbus and Opal (Orr) S.; m. Atha Maxine Tubbs, June 26, 1971 (div. 1991); children: Robert Benjamin, Ann Kathleen; m. Terri D. Seales, Oct. 17, 1998. BA, Davidson Coll., N.C., 1965; postgrad., Vanderbilt U., Nashville, 1965-66; LLB, U. Tex., 1968. Bar: Tex. 1968, U.S. Ct. Mil. Appeals 1971. Staff atty. Tex. Legis. Coun., Austin, 1969-71; counsel Jud. Com., Tex. Ho. of Reps., Austin, 1971-73; chief counsel Jud. Com., Tex. Constl. Conv., Austin, 1974; exec. v.p. and legis. counsel Tex. Assn. Taxpayers, Austin, 1974-85; assoc. Baker Botts, LLP, Austin, 1985-87, ptnr., 1988—. Assoc. editor Tex. Internat. Law Jour., 1968. Mem. Tex. Ho. Speakers Econ. Devel. Com., Austin, 1986-87; assoc. dir. McDonald Obs. Bd. Visitors, 1988—; bd. dirs. Tex. Assn. Bus. and C. of C., 2000-2002; mem. Dean's Roundtable, U. Tex. Law Sch.; bd. dirs. Austin Symphony Orch. Soc., 1985—, v.p., 1993-94, nominating com., 1998-2002. Capt. USNR, ret. Named Rising Star of Tex., Tex. Bus. Mag., 1983. Fellow Tex. Bar Found.; mem. State Bar of Tex. (tax sect.), Austin Bar Assn., Austin Bar Found., Headliners Club (Austin). Office: Baker & Botts 1600 San Jacinto Blvd Austin TX 78701 Office Phone: 512-322-2535. E-mail: robert.strauser@bakerbotts.com.

**STRAUSER, SUSAN PARKYN,** performing arts educator, singer; d. Harold Mann and Helen Ruth (Knapp) Parkyn; m. George John Strauser; 1 child, Andrew. BS in Music Edn., West Chester U., Pa., 1964; MEd in Music, West Chester U., 1967; postgrad., Ind. U., 1976—80. Profl. singer, 1959—; prof. voice William Paterson U., Wayne, NJ, 1974—75; artistic dir. Vocal Arts Studio, Wallkill, NY, 1985—; voice seminar dir. Delaware Valley Opera, Narrowsburg, NY, 1985—86; prof. voice SUNY, Orange/Middletown, 1990—2004, voice program dir. Ulster/Stone Ridge, 2000—. Seminar presenter in field; artistic dir. Empire Artists of N.Y., Wallkill, 1992—; appeared with N.J. Symphony Orch., Hudson Valley Philharmonic Orch., West Chester Symphony, Ind. U. Philharm. and Opera Theatre; guest artist West Islip Symphony Orch. of L.I.; performances with opera and musical theatre cos. as well as in concert, oratorio and recital presentations include numerous leading roles; numerous appearances for cable TV Lunch N Listen series, Heroines-Women of the Musical Stage. Contbr. articles to profl. jours. Bd. dirs. Delaware Valley Opera, 1986. Recipient U.S. Congl. Citation in the Benjamin Gilman Congress, 1995, Theodore Presser Found. award, Westchester U., 1962, N.J. Opera Festival winner, Nat. Arion award. Avocation: genealogy. Home and Office: PO Box 412 37 DuBois St Wallkill NY 12589 Office Phone: 845-895-3959. Personal E-mail: parkyn@frontiernet.net.

**STRAUSS, ALBRECHT BENNO,** retired language educator, editor; b. Berlin, May 17, 1921; came to U.S., 1940; s. Bruno and Bertha (Badt) S.; m. Nancy Grace Barron, July 30, 1978; 1 child, Rebecca Ilse; stepchildren: Carolyn, Kathryn Ba, Oberlin Coll., 1942; MA, Tulane U., 1948; PhD, Harvard U., 1956. Instr. English Brandeis U., 1951-52; teaching fellow gen. edn. Harvard U., 1952-55; instr. English Yale U., 1955-59; asst. prof. English U. Okla., Norman, 1959-60, U. N.C., Chapel Hill, 1960-64, assoc. prof., 1964-70, prof., 1970-91, prof. emeritus, 1991—; lectr. Duke Inst. for Learning in Retirement, 1993—2005. Editor Studies in Philology, 1974-80; sec. editorial com. Yale Edit. of Works of Samuel Johnson, 1975—; mem. editorial com. Ga. edit. works of Tobias Smollett, 1973-95; contbr. articles to lit. publs. Served with U.S. Army, 1942-46 Recipient Tanner Teaching award U. N.C., 1966; Fulbright fellow, Germany, 1983-84 Mem. MLA, South Atlantic MLA, Am. Soc. Eighteenth-Century Studies (pres. Southeastern group 1980-81), Johnsonians Republican. Jewish. Home: 396 Lakeshore Ln Chapel Hill NC 27514-1728 Personal E-mail: strausshaus@mindspring.com.

**STRAUSS, CAROLYN,** broadcast executive; b. NYC, July 13, 1963; BA, Harvard U., 1985. Temp Documentaries Dept. HBO, 1986, asst. original programming, 1986—89, mgr. original programming, 1989—90, dir. original programming, 1990—94, v.p. original programming, 1994—99, sr. v.p. original programming, 1999—2002, exec. v.p. original programming, 2002—04, pres. entertainment, 2004—. Mailing: HBO Entertainment 1100 Avenue of Americas New York NY 10036*

**STRAUSS, DAVID A.,** law educator; b. 1952; AB summa cum laude, Harvard U., 1973, JD magna cum laude, 1978; BPhil in Politics, Magdalen Coll., Oxford U., 1975. Bar: DC 1980, US Supreme Ct. Law clk. to Hon. Irving L. Goldberg US Ct. Appeals 5th Cir., 1978—79; atty.-advisor Office Legal Counsel US Dept. Justice, 1979—81; asst. to Solicitor Gen. of US, 1981—85; asst. prof. law U. Chgo. Law Sch., 1985—89, prof., 1989—92, Harry N. Wyatt prof. law, 1992—; vis. prof. law Georgetown U. Law Ctr., 1989—90; editor The Supreme Ct. Rev. U. Chgo. Law Sch., 1989—; spl. counsel Com. on Judiciary US Senate, 1990. Mem. bd. trustees U. Chgo. Lab. Schools, 1999—, chmn., 2003—. Fellow: Am. Acad. Arts & Sciences. Office: U Chgo Law Sch 1111 E 60th St Chicago IL 60637 Office Phone: 773-702-9601. E-mail: d-strauss@uchicago.edu.

**STRAUSS, DEBORAH,** foundation administrator; AB, MA, U. Chgo. Cert. Fund Raising Exec. Dir. devel. pub. rels. Chgo. Child Care Soc.; exec. dir. IT Resource Ctr., Chgo., 1985—. Mem. mgmt. team Nat. Strategy for Nonprofit Tech.; chair Tech. Resource Consortium; bd. mem. Alliance for Nonprofit Mgmt., Donors Forum of Chgo.; mem. Mayor's Coun. of Tech. Advisors, co-chair Bridging the Digital Divide Com. Mem.: Assn. of Fundraising Profs. (mem. Chgo. Chap. Bd., Benjamin Franklin Award 1998). Office: IT Resource Ctr Ste 1005 29 E Madison St Chicago IL 60602-4529 Office Phone: 312-372-4872. Office Fax: 312-372-7962. E-mail: dstrauss@itresourcecenter.org.*

**STRAUSS, DIANE CAROL WHEELER,** librarian, educator, writer; b. Milw., Feb. 14, 1943; d. Charles Clifton and Olga (Bondeli) Wheeler; m. Robert P. Strauss, Nov. 26, 1969 (div. 1973). BS, U. Wis., Milw., 1966; MS in Libr. Sci., U. Wis., 1967. Young adult libr. Enoch Pratt Free Libr., Balt., 1967-68; materials analyst U. Wis., Madison, 1968-69; legis. libr. Dept. Labor Libr., Washington, 1970-72; social scis. libr. U. N.C., Chapel Hill, 1972-75, head bus. adminstrn./social scis. reference dept., 1975-92, assoc. univ. libr., 1992—, interim head collections, 2005—. Author: Handbook of Business Information, 1988; also articles. Mem. ALA (Gale Rsch. award 1990), Spl. Librs. Assn. (pres. N.C. chpt. 1980-81), N.C. Online Users Group (pres. 1978), Beta Phi Mu (pres. Epsilon chpt. 1991-93). Office: U NC Davis Libr CB #3900 Chapel Hill NC 27514-8890 Office Phone: 919-962-1301. Business E-Mail: dstrauss@email.unc.edu.

**STRAUSS, DIANE JAYNE,** retired elementary and secondary school educator, small business owner; b. Crawfordsville, Ind., July 6, 1940; d. Harold and Madge Virginia Wright. BS, Purdue U., 1964; MS, Butler U., 1971, postgrad., 1974—. Ind. Vocat. Tech. Coll., 1983—. Ind.-Purdue U., 1980—. With Am. United Life Ins. Co., Indpls., 1959-64; tchr. St. Matthews Elem. Sch., Indpls., 1962-63, Decatur Twp. Sch. System, Indpls., 1964-71;

reading coord. Benton County Sch. System, Fowler, Ind., 1971-73; tchr. Ctr. Grove High Sch., Greenwood, Ind., 1978-79; coord. title 1 dept. corrections curriculum projects Ind. U.-Purdue U., Indpls., 1980-82; tchr. Indpls. Pub. Schs., 1986—2005, instrl. coach, 2002—06; Title I reading tchr. grades 6-8 John Marshall Middle Sch., 2004—05, Cripus Attucks Mid. Sch., 2005—06; ret., 2006. Owner, co-dir. Bus. Personal Devel. Ctr., Indpls., 1971-86, Strauss Learning Ctr., Indpls., 1971-90, Strauss Enterprises, 1991—. Pres. Decatur Twp. Tchrs. Assn., Indpls., 1970, enld. lobbist, 1964-97. Mem.: Mem. ASCD, NEA, Ind. State Tchrs. Assn., Indpls. Assn. (life), Phi Delta Kappan. Home and Office: 7370 Lions Head Dr A Indianapolis IN 46260-3460

**STRAUSS, HARLEE SUE,** environmentalist, consultant; b. New Brunswick, NJ, June 19, 1950; d. Robert Lemuel and Helene (Marcus) S. BA, Smith Coll., 1972; PhD, U. Wis., 1979. Postdoctoral fellow dept. biology MIT, Cambridge, 1979-81; congrl. sci. fellow U.S. House of Reps., Washington, 1981-83; spl. asst. Am. Chem. Soc., Washington, 1983-84; spl. cons. Environ. Corp., Washington, 1984-85; rsch. assoc. Ctr. for Tech., Policy and Indsl. Devel. MIT, Cambridge, 1985-86, rsch. affiliate, 1986-92; sr. assoc. Gradient Corp., Cambridge, 1986-88; pres. H. Strauss Assocs., Inc., Natick, Mass., 1988—. Exec. dir. Silent Spring Inst., 1994-95; adj. assoc. prof. Sch. Pub. Health, Boston U., 1990-94; lectr. Sch. Medicine, Tufts U., Boston, 1988-95; mem. steering com. Boston Risk Assessment Group, 1986-95. Co-editor, author Risk Assessment in Genetic Engineering, 1991; author: Biotechnology Regulations, 1986, book chpts. in field. Active Instl. Biosafety Com., Army Rsch. Lab., Natick, 1989—94, Army Sci. Bd., 1994—2001. Mem. AAAS, Am. Chem. Soc., Assn. for Women in Sci. (chmn. com. New England chpt. 1986-88, co-chmn. legis. com 1985-93), Biophys. Soc. (chmn. com. 1983-84, Congl. Sci. fellow 1981-83), Soc. for Risk Analysis (pres. New England chpt. 1991-92, pres.-elect 1995-2000). Jewish. Avocations: travel, hiking. Office: H Strauss Assocs Inc 21 Bay State Rd Natick MA 01760-2942 Office Phone: 508-651-8784. Personal E-Mail: hstrauss@aol.com. Business E-Mail: h.strauss@rcn.com.

**STRAUSS, HERBERT LEOPOLD,** chemistry professor; b. Aachen, Germany, Mar. 26, 1936; came to U.S., 1940, naturalized, 1946; s. Charles and Joan (Goldschmidt) S.; m. Carolyn North Cooper, Apr. 24, 1960; children: Michael Abram, Rebecca Anne, Ethan Edward. AB, Columbia U., 1957, MA, 1958, PhD, 1960; postgrad, Oxford U., 1960-61. Mem. faculty U. Calif., Berkeley, 1961—, prof. chemistry 1973—2003, prof. grad. divsn., 2003—, vice chmn. dept. chemistry 1975-81, 92-95, asst. dean Coll. Chemistry, 1986-92, assoc. dean, 1995—. Vis. prof. Indian Inst. Tech., Kanpur, 1968-69, Fudan U., Shanghai, 1982, U. Tokyo, 1982, U. Paris du Nord, 1987; mem. IUPAC Commn. I.1, 1994—. Author: Quantum Mechanics, 1968; assoc. editor Ann. Rev. Phys. Chemistry, 1976-85, editor, 1985-2000. Recipient Bomen-Michaelson award Coblentz Soc., 1994, Ellis Lippincott award Optical Soc. Am., 1994, The Berkeley Citation, 2003; Alfred P. Sloan fellow, 1966-70. Fellow Am. Phys. Soc., AAAS; mem. Am. Chem. Soc., Sigma Xi, Phi Beta Kappa, Phi Lambda Upsilon. Achievements include research in elucidation of vibrational spectra associated with large amplitude molecular motion in gases, liquids and solids. Home: 2447 Prince St Berkeley CA 94705-2021 Office: U Calif Dept Chemistry Berkeley CA 94720-1420 Office Phone: 510-642-7114. Business E-Mail: hls@cchem.berkeley.edu.

**STRAUSS, JEROME FRANK, III,** reproductive endocrinologist, educator; b. Chgo., May 2, 1947; s. Jerome Frank (Jr.) and Josephine (Newberger) Strauss; m. Catherine Blumlein, June 20, 1970; children: Jordan L., Elizabeth J. BA, Brown U., 1969; MD, U. Pa., 1974, PhD, 1975. Asst. prof. U. Pa. Sch. Medicine, Phila., 1976—83, assoc. prof., 1983—85, prof., 1985—, assoc. chair, 1987—, assoc. dean, 1990—98; Luigi Mastroianni jr. prof. and founding dir. Ctr. Rsch. on Women's Health and Reproduction, Phila., 1990—94; prof. Inst. Medicine NAS, 1994—; dean, exec. v.p. med. affairs, prof. ob-gyn. Va. Commonwealth U. Sch. Medicine, Richmon, 2005—. Biochem. endocrinology study sect. NIH, 1983—87, Nat. Adv. Child Health and Human Devel. Coun., 2002—; chmn. population rsch. com. Nat. Inst. Child Health and Human Devel., 1989—92; chair Reproductive Scientist of the Ams. Network, 1995—; dir. Ctr. Excellence in Women's Health, 1996—2002; co-chair Indo-U.S. Joint Working Group on Reproductive Sci. and Contraceptive Tech., 1999—; bd. dirs. Burroughs Wellcome Fund, 2003—; bd. trustees Berlex Found., 2005—. Editor: Lipoprotein and Cholesterol Metabolism in Sterodogenic Tissues, 1985, Current Topics in Membrane Research, 1987, Uterine and Embryonic Factors in Early Pregnancy, 1991, New Achievements in Research of Ovarian Function, 1995, Cell Death in Reproductive Physiology, 1997, Molecular Biology in Reproductive Medicine, 1999, Ovarian Function Research: Present and Future, 1999, Reproductive Medicine Molecular, Cellular and Genetic Fundamentals, 2002, New Frontiers in Contraceptive Research, 2004, Yen and Jaffe's Reproductive Endocrinology, 2004, Steroids jour., 1993—; assoc. editor Ency. of Reproduction, 1998—, assoc. editor, mem. editl. bd. Jour. Lipid Rsch., 1982—90, corr. editor Jour. Steroid Biochem. and Molecular Biology, 1990—99, mem. editl. bd. Endocrinology, 1986—90, 1997—2000, Biology of Reprodn., 1986—90, 1999—2003, Jour. of Women's Health, 1991—, Jour. Soc. Gynecologic Investigation, 1993—, Placenta, 1995—98, Trends in Endocrinology and Metabolism, 1999—, Reference in Gynecologie Obstetrique, 1999—, Seminars in Reproductive Endocrinology, 2000—, Jour. Endocrinology, 2000—, Human Reproduction Update, 2001—05, Science, 2004—. Recipient Transatlantic medal, Brit. Endocrine Soc., 1998, Disting. Grad. award, U. Pa., 2005, NAS Inst. Medicine, 2005. Fellow: Internat. Acad. Human Reproduction; mem.: Perinatal Rsch. Soc., Am. Soc. for Reproductive Medicine, Soc. for Study of Reproduction (bd. dirs. 1989—91, Rsch. award 1992), Endocrine Soc., Soc. Gynecologic Investigation (pres. 2003, Pres.'s Achievement award 1990, Disting. Scientist award 2006), Am. Physiol. Soc., Am. Assn. Pathologists. Home: 2808 Monument Ave Unit 3 Richmond VA 23221 Office: Va Commonwealth U Dean's Office Sch Medicine 1101 E Marshall St Rm 1-070 Richmond VA 23298 Business E-Mail: jfstrauss@vcu.edu.

**STRAUSS, JOHN STEINERT,** dermatologist, educator; b. New Haven, July 15, 1926; s. Maurice Jacob and Carolyn Mina (Ullman) Strauss; m. Susan Thalheimer, Aug. 19, 1950; children: Joan Sue, Mary Lynn. BS, Yale U., 1946, MD, 1950. Intern U. Chgo., 1950-51; resident dermatology U. Pa., Phila., 1951-52, 54-55, fellow dermatology, 1955-57, instr., 1956-57; mem. faculty Boston U. Med. Sch., 1958-78, prof., 1966-78; head dept. dermatology U. Iowa, Iowa City, 1978-98, prof. dermatology, 1978-00, prof. emeritus, 2000—. Mem. editl. bd.: Archives of Dermatology, 1970—79, Jour. Am. Acad. Dermatology, 1979—89, Jour. Investigative Dermatology, 1977—82; contbr. articles to profl. jours. With USNR, 1952—54. Fellow James H. Brown Jr., 1947—48, USPHS, 1955—57; grantee. Fellow: Am. Acad. Dermatology (pres.); mem.: Internat. Com. Dermatology (pres. 1992—97), Internat. League Dermatol. Socs. (pres. 1992—97), 18th World Congress Dermatology (pres.), Am. Bd. Med. Spltys. (exec. com. 2001—04), Coun. Med. Splty. Socs. (pres.), Am. Fedn. Clin. Rsch., Ctrl. Soc. Clin. Rsch., Assn. Am. Physicians, Am. Dermatol. Assn. (sec., pres.), Am. Bd. Dermatology (bd. dirs., assoc. exec. dir., exec. cons.), Dermatology Found. (pres.), Soc. Investigative Dermatology (sec.-treas., pres.). Achievements include research in sebaceous glands and pathogenesis of acne. Office: U Iowa Hosp & Clinics Dept Dermatology 200 Hawkins Dr # BT2045-1 Iowa City IA 52242-1009 Office Phone: 319-356-7546.

**STRAUSS, JON CALVERT,** retired academic administrator; b. Chgo., Jan. 17, 1940; s. Charles E. and Alice C. (Woods) S.; m. Joan Helen Bailey, Sept. 19, 1959 (div. 1985); children: Susan, Stephanie; m. Jean Anne Sacconaghi, June 14, 1985; children: Kristoffer, Jonathon. BSEE, U. Wis., 1959; MS in Physics, U. Pitts., 1962; PhD in E.E., Carnegie Inst. Tech., 1965; LLD (hon.), U. Mass., 1996. Assoc. prof. computer sci., elec. engring. Carnegie Mellon U., Pitts., 1966-70; dir. computer ctr., prof. computer sci. Tech. U. Norway, Trondheim, Norway, 1970; vis. assoc. prof. elec. engring. U. Mich., Ann Arbor, 1971; assoc. prof. computer sci. Washington U., St. Louis, 1971-74, dir. computing facilities, 1971-73; dir. computing activities U. Pa., Phila., 1974-76, faculty master Stouffer Coll. House, 1978-80, prof. computer, info. scis., prof. decision sci. Wharton Sch., 1974-81, exec. dir. Univ. Budget,

1975-78, v.p. for budget, fin., 1978-81; prof. elec. engring. U. So. Calif., Los Angeles, 1981-85, sr. v.p. adminstrn., 1981-85; pres. Worcester Poly. Inst., Mass., 1985-94; v.p., chief fin. officer Howard Hughes Med. Inst., Chevy Chase, Md., 1994-97; pres. Harvey Mudd Coll., Claremont, Calif., 1997—2006. Cons. Electronics Assocs., Inc., 1965, IBM Corp., 1960-64, Westinghouse Elec. Corp., 1959-60; bd. dirs. Transamerica Income Fund, Variable Ins. Fund, United Educators Ins., mem. NSF Nat. Sci. Bd., 2004-. Contbr. articles on computer systems and university mgmt. to profl. jours.; co-holder patent. Bd. dirs. Presbyn.-U. Pa. Med. Ctr., Phila., 1980-81, U. So. Calif. Kenneth Norris Jr. Cancer Hosp., L.A., 1981-85, Med. Ctr. of Ctrl. Mass., 1986-94, Worcester Acad., 1986-91, Mass. Biotech. Rsch. Inst., 1985-94. Mem. New. Eng. Assn. Schs. and Colls., Inc., Commn. on Instns. of Higher Edn., Nat. Collegiate Athletic Assn. (pres.'s commn 1990-94). Avocations: hiking, running, swimming. Office: Harvey Mudd Coll Kingston Hall Rm 201 301 E 12th St Claremont CA 91711-5980 Office Fax: 909-321-8360. Business E-Mail: jon_strauss@hmc.edu.*

**STRAUSS, PAUL,** shadow senator; b. NYC; m. Kathy Strauss; 1 child, Abigail. BA, Am. U.; JD, Wash. Coll. Law. Various locally elected govt. positions including at-large mem. of Dem. State Com. and chmn. of Dem. Party Statehood Com., Washington; chmn. to commr. Advisory Neighborhood Commn., 1986—96; U.S. senator Washington, 1996—97; shadow senator, 1997—2006. Legis. asst. council's com. on consumer and regulatory affairs, Washington; union organizer Hotel and Restaurant Employee's Local 25. Pres. NW Youth Alliance, Inc.; atty. mem., panel chmn. Bd. Real Property Assessment and Appeals, Washington. Mem.: Internat. Assn. Assessment Officers, African-Am. Coalition (hon. chmn.). Democrat.*

**STRAUSS, PETER L(ESTER),** law educator; b. NYC, Feb. 26, 1940; s. Simon D. and Elaine Ruth (Mandle) S.; m. Joanna Burnstine, Oct. 1, 1964; children: Benjamin, Bethany. AB magna cum laude, Harvard U., 1961; LLB magna cum laude, Yale U., 1964. Bar: DC 1965, US Supreme Ct. 1968. Law clk. US Ct. Appeals DC Cir., 1964-65, US Supreme Ct., 1965-66; lectr. Halle Selassie U. Sch. Law, Addis Ababa, Ethiopia, 1966-68; asst. to solicitor gen. Dept. Justice, Washington, 1968-71; assoc. prof. law Columbia U., 1971-74, prof., 1974—, Betts prof., 1985—, vice-dean, 1996, 2001—02. Gen. counsel Nuclear Regulatory Commn., 1975-77, Adminstrv. Conf. U.S., 1984-95; Byrne vis. prof. Sch. Law Harvard U., Cambridge, Mass., 1994; bd. dirs. Ctr. for Computer Assisted Legal Instrn., 2002—. Mem. adv. bd. Lexis Electronic Author's Press, 1995-99; editor: SSRN Administrative Law Abstracts, 1997-2006; author: (with Abba Paulos translator) Fetha Negast: The Law of the Kings, 1968; (with others) Administrative Law Cases and Comments, 2003, Administrative Justice in the United States, 2002, Legal Methods: Understanding and Using Cases and Statutes, 2005, Administrative Law Stories, 2005, Legislation: Understanding and Choosing State Fees, 2006; contbr. articles to profl. jours. Recipient John Marshall prize Dept. Justice, 1970, Disting. Svc. award Nuclear Regulatory Commn., 1977. Mem. ABA (chair sect. administrv. law and regulatory practice 1992-93, Disting. Scholarship award 1988), Am. Law Inst. Office: Columbia U Law Sch 435 W 116th St New York NY 10027-7201 Office Phone: 212-854-2370. Business E-Mail: strauss@law.columbia.edu.

**STRAUSS, ROBERT PHILIP,** economics professor; b. Cleve., May 11, 1944; s. Harry and Carrie S.; m. Celeste G. Meade, Jan. 11, 1980; children: Sarah Elizabeth, David Anthony, Elena Nicole. AB in Econs., U. Mich., 1966; MA, U. Wis., 1968, PhD in Econs., 1970. Fellow Inst. Research on Poverty, 1968-69; asst. prof. econs. U. N.C., Chapel Hill, 1969-73, assoc. prof., 1973-79; econ. policy fellow Brookings Instn., Washington, 1971-72; economist U.S. Congress Joint Com. Taxation, 1975-78; prof. econs. and pub. policy Carnegie-Mellon U., Pitts., 1979—, assoc. dean Sch. Urban and Pub. Affairs, 1981-83, dir. Ctr. for Pub. Fin. Mgmt., 1984-91; dir. research Pa. Tax Commn., 1979-81. Vis. prof. econs. and pub. policy U. Rochester, 1992-94. Mem. Pa. Local Tax Reform Commn., 1987; sec. faculty Carnegie-Mellon U., 1991-92. Recipient Exceptional Service award U.S. Treasury, 1972, Disting. Service award Pitts. Tax Execs. Inst., 1987, Georgescu Roegen award, 1998, Steven B. Gold award Pub. Policy and Mgmt. Nat. Tax Adminstrs., Fedn. Tax Adminstrs., 2005; named to Alumni Hall of Fame, Cleveland Heights H.S., 2004; grantee NSF, U.S. Dept. Labor, U.S. Treasury, HUD, Social Security Adminstrn.; William C. Lincoln fellow, 2005-06. Mem. Am. Econ. Assn., Econometric Soc., Nat. Tax Assn., Pub. Choice Soc., Assn. for Pub. Policy and Mgmt., Am. Soc. for Pub. Adminstrn., Nat. Tax Assn. (bd. dirs. 1995-98). Clubs: Cosmos. Home: 2307 Country Pl Export PA 15632-9059 Office: 5000 Forbes Ave Pittsburgh PA 15213-3890 Office Phone: 412-268-4798. E-mail: rpstrauss@att.net.

**STRAUSS, ROBERT SCHWARZ,** lawyer, retired ambassador; b. Lockhart, Tex., Oct. 19, 1918; s. Charles H. and Edith V. (Schwarz) S.; m. Helen Jacobs, 1941; children: Robert A., Richard C., Susan. LL.B., U. Tex., 1941. Bar: Tex. 1941, DD 1971. Spl. agt. FBI, 1941-45; founding ptnr. Akin Gump Strauss Hauer & Feld LLP, Dallas, 1945-77, 81—, now sr. exec. ptnr. Washington and Dallas; and chmn. AG Global Solutions (joint venture between Akin Gump and First Internat. Resources, Inc.); treas. Dem. Nat. Com., 1970-72, chmn., 1973—76; chmn. election campaigns for Pres. Carter, 1976, 1980; spl. rep. for trade negotiations with rank of amb. Pres., 1977-79; Pres.'s personal rep. for Mid. East negotiations, 1979-81; US amb. to Russia, 1991—92. Bd. dirs. Archer-Daniels-Midland Co., Decatur, Ill., Gulf Stream Corp., Savannah, Ga., Gen. Instruments, NYC; lectr. in field. Contbr. articles to profl. jours. Co-chmn. Nat. Econ. Commn., 1988—. Recipient Presdl. medal of freedom, 1981; Lifetime Achievement award The Am. Lawyer, 2004. Mem. ABA, Dallas Bar Assn., DC Bar Assn. Home: Akin Gump Strauss Hauer & Feld LLP 1333 New Hampshire Ave NW Washington DC 20036-1564 also: 1700 Pacific Ave Ste 4100 Dallas TX 75201-4675 Office Phone: 202-887-4000, 214-969-2800. Office Fax: 202-887-4288, 214-969-4343.

**STRAUSS, SIMON WOLF,** chemist, materials scientist; b. Bedzin, Keltz, Poland, Apr. 15, 1920; arrived in U.S., 1929; s. Israel Calvin and Anna (Hops) S.; m. Mary Jo Boehm, Dec. 27, 1957; children: Jack Calvin, Ruth Ann. BS in Chemistry, Poly. Inst. Bklyn., 1944, MS in Chemistry, 1947, PhD in Chemistry, 1950. Rsch. chemist Nat. Bur. Stds., Washington, 1951-55; from phys. chemist to head chem. metallurgy sect. Naval Rsch. Lab., Washington, 1955-63; sr. staff scientist Air Force Systems Command, Washington, 1963-80; ind. tech. cons. Washington, 1980—. Mem. bd. civil svc. examiners for sci. and tech. pers. U.S. Naval Dist. of Washington, 1959-63; mem. air force panel expert tech. reviewers patents for secrecy considerations Office Air Force Judge Adv. Gen., Washington, 1965-80; co-chair com. on career planning and appraisal of sci. and engrs. Air Force Sys. Command, Washington, 1966-67; air force mem. in-house com. mgmt. rev. tech. info. program, Dept. Def., 1967; chair rsch. steering com. Air Force Dir. of Sci. Tech., Washington, 1976-80; mem., chair editl. adv. com. Washington Acad. Jour., 1983-87, chair com. on scholarly activities, 1984-88. Author: Advanced Composites: An Historical Perspective, Retiring Presidential Lecture, 1987; prin. compiler 75 Years of Scientific Thought, 1987; mem. bd. reviewers Jour. Chem. Engring. Data, 1965-66; contbr. articles to profl. jours. Judge Internat. Sci. Engring. Fair, 1970, 72, 73; nat. evaluator space shuttle student involvement program NSTA, NASA, Washington, 1984, 85. With U.S. Army, 1944-45. Recipient Air Force Exceptional Civilian Svc. medal, 1980, first Disting. Career in Sci. award Wash. Acad. Sci., 1988, Disting. Svc. award, 1990. Fellow AAAS, Wash. Acad. Scis. (first Disting. Scien-in-Residence 1984-89, pres.-elect 1985-86, pres. 1986-87, life mem. fund trustee 1988—), Am. Inst. Chemists; mem. Math. Assn., Am. Air Force Assn., Cosmos Club, Air Force Materials Lab. (hon. life), Sigma Pi Sigma, Phi Lambda Upsilon, Sigma Xi. Achievements include 3 patents for electrodeposition of Cadmium on high strength steel; research and development of advanced composites technology; the development of equations for the estimation of surface tensions, viscosities and densities of liquid metals as a function of temperature. Home: 4506 Cedell Pl Temple Hills MD 20748-3805 *Living a life not just for oneself contributes not only to the elevation of humankind, but also to the ennoblement and enrichment of one's own life.*

**STRAUSS, STANLEY ROBERT,** lawyer; b. NYC, June 3, 1915; s. Maurice M. and Blanche Anna (Danciger) S.; m. Margaret Inglis Forbes, Mar. 13, 1944 (div. 1950); m. Helen Anne Cummings, Dec. 31, 1975 (dec. 1980). BA cum laude, Williams Coll., 1936; LLB, Columbia U., 1940. Bar: N.Y. 1941, D.C. 1964, U.S. Ct. Appeals (1st cir.) 1977, U.S. Ct. Appeals (3d cir.) 1986, U.S. Ct. Appeals (4th cir.) 1974, U.S. Ct. Appeals (5th cir.) 1970, U.S. Ct. Appeals (6th cir.) 1977, U.S. Ct. Appeals (8th cirs.) 1975, U.S. Supreme Ct. 1965. Assoc. Howard Henig, N.Y.C., 1940-41; atty. NLRB, Washington, 1946-52, supervising atty., 1953-59, chief counsel, 1959-63; assoc. Vedder, Price, Kaufman & Kammholz, Washington, 1963-65, ptnr., 1965-90; of counsel Ogletree, Deakins, Nash, Smoak & Stewart, Washington, 1990—. Co-author: Practice and Procedure Before the National Labor Relations Board, 3d edit., 1980, 4th edit., 1987, 5th edit., 1996. Officer U.S. Army, 1941—45, PTO. Decorated Bronze Star; Horn scholar, Columbia U. Law Sch., 1937—40. Mem. ABA, Fed. Bar Assn., D.C. Bar Assn., Kenwood Country Club. Avocations: golf, tennis. Home: 4956 Sentinel Dr Bethesda MD 20816-3594 Office: Ogletree Deakins Nash 2400 N St NW Fl 5 Washington DC 20037-1154 Office Phone: 202-887-0855. E-mail: stanleystrauss@odense.com.

**STRAUSS, ULRICH PAUL,** chemist, educator; b. Frankfurt, Germany, Jan. 10, 1920; s. Richard and Marianne (Seligmann) S.; m. Esther Lipetz, June 20, 1943 (dec. Sept. 1949); children— Dorothy, David; m. Elaine Greenbaum, Nov. 23, 1950; children— Elizabeth, Evelyn. AB, Columbia U., 1941; PhD, Cornell U., 1944. Sterling fellow Yale U., 1946-48; faculty Rutgers U., New Brunswick, NJ, 1948—, prof. phys. chemistry, 1960-90, prof. emeritus, 1990—; also dir. Sch. Chemistry, 1965-71, chmn. dept. chemistry, 1974-80. Prof. emeritus Rutgers U., 1990—. Mem. editorial bd. Macromolecules, 1990-93; contbr. articles to profl. jours. Recipient Sci. achievement award Johnson Wax Co., 1986; NSF sr. fellow Nat. Center Sci. Research, Strasbourg, France, 1961-62; Guggenheim fellow U. Oxford, Eng., 1971-72. Fellow N.Y. Acad. Scis.; mem. Am. Chem. Soc. (chmn. phys. chemistry group N.J. sect. 1956, councillor 1961-72, honored by 1-day symposium at nat. meeting N.Y.C. 1986, Excellence in Edn. award N.J. sect. 1994). Home: 227 Lawrence Ave Highland Park NJ 08904-1837 Office: Rutgers U Dept Chemistry New Brunswick NJ 08903 Business E-Mail: strauss@rci.rutgers.edu.

**STRAUSSLER, TOMAS See STOPPARD, TOM**

**STRAUTINS, VILNIS,** music educator, retired performing company executive; b. Lubana, Madona, Latvia, Dec. 28, 1939; s. Fricis Strautins and Emma (Bundzis) Strautina; m. Dzidra Markevica, Dec. 31, 1964; children: Ineta, Peteris. MA, Latvian Music, Riga, 1965. Prin. flutist Latvian Nat. Symphony Orch., Riga, 1961-89, mng. dir., 1989-97; prof. flute Latvian Music Acad., Riga, 1971—. Mem.: Latvian Correspondence Chess Fedn. (pres. 2001—). Lutheran. Avocation: correspondence chess. Office: Latvian Music Acad Kr Barona 1 LV-1050 Riga Latvia E-mail: vstrautins@apollo.lv.

**STRAVINSKA, SARAH,** dance educator; b. Pitts., Nov. 12, 1940; d. Robert Edwin Williams and Alice Elizabeth Markey Hildeboldt; m. George Lawrence Denton, May 10, 1959 (div. 1973); children: Kathryn, Michael, Laura, David. BFA in Dance, Fla. State U., 1977, MFA in Dance, 1979; Cert. in Ballet, Vaganova Inst., Leningrad, Russia, 1990; Cert., Raoul Gelabert Kinesiology Ins, N.Y.C., 1980. Dancer Ballet Russe, N.Y.C., 1957-58; dance choreographer Dutchess County Ballet, Beacon, NY, 1966-65; instr. Brevard C.C., Cocoa, Fla., 1969-73; chair dept. dance Randolph/Macon Woman's Coll., Lynchburg, Va., 1979-84; asst. prof. dance U. So. Miss., Hattiesburg, 1984-86; prof. and coord. dance U. La., Lafayette, 1986—. Dir. State of La. Danse Project, Lafayette, 1991-94. Choreographer original dance works: Mama! Stop the Bombs, 1989, The Yellow Wallpaper, 1990, Spring Night, 1998, Serrano!, 2002, Feather, Stone and Light, 2003, The Littlest Angel, 2005; reconstructor of classical ballets: Les Sylphides, 1991, Giselle, 1992, Swan Lake, 1993, Raymonda, Pas de Quatre, 1994. Dir. concerns for children La Danse with Acadiana Arts Coun., Lafayette, 1987-93; mem. Arts in Edn. Program, Lafayette, 1987—, coord. The Othello Project, 2003-04. Grantee Mellon Found., 1982. Mem. Am. Coll. Dance Festival Assn. (bd. dirs., festival coord. 1989-91), Dance History Scholars, CORPS de Ballet Internat. (founder), Phi Kappa Phi. Episcopalian. Avocations: writing, music, reading, biking. Office: Univ of La PO Box 43690 Lafayette LA 70504-3690 Personal E-mail: dancepro@m.efriends.net.

**STRAW, CAROLE ELLEN,** history professor; b. Hollywood, Calif., Apr. 8, 1948; d. Rex Ellis Straw and Marie Louise Olson; m. Frederick John McGinness, July 26, 1980. PhD, U. Calif., Berkeley, 1979. Harper fellow U. of Chgo., 1979—80; asst. to full prof. Mt. Holyoke Coll., South Hadley, Mass., 1980—. Cons. Hist. Rsch. Assocs., South Hadley, 1990—. Author: (book) Gregory the Great: Perfection in Imperfection (Medieval Acad. of Am., John Nicholas Brown Prize for first book of outstanding quality, 1992), Gregory the Great (Authors of the Middle Ages 12); co-editor (with Richard Lim): The Past Before Us: The New Historiographies of Late Antiquity. Fellow, Am. Coun. of Learned Socs., 1991, NEH, 1990—91. Mem.: Medival Acad. of Am., N.Am. Patristics Soc., Am. Hist. Assn. Home: 29 Silver St South Hadley MA 01075-1615 Office: Mount Holyoke Coll Dept History South Hadley MA 01075-1616 Office Phone: 413-538-2377.

**STRAW, LEE,** music educator, actor; b. Lima, Ohio, July 2, 1954; s. Wayne L. and Julia Wood Straw; m. Laurie Anne Stevens, Aug. 18, 2001; 1 child, Julia Straun. MusB, Ohio State U., 1977; MusM, Eastman Sch. Music, 1982, D of Mus. Arts, 1987. Voice performer's cert. Eastman Sch. Music, 1982, opera performer's cert. Eastman Sch. Music, 1987. Assoc. prof. voice No. Ill. U., DeKalb, 1982—93; tchr. voice San Francisco, 1993—. Voice area coord. No. Ill. U., DeKalb, 1985—93. Performer: (mus. theatre) The Phantom of the Opera, 1993—99, John Muir in Mountain Days, 2000—05, (opera) S.F. Opera Chorus, 2002—04. Mem.: Nat. Assn. Tchrs. of Singing, Am. Guild of Mus. Artists, Actors Equity Assn. Office: Lee Straw Voice Studio 965 Mission St Ste 115 San Francisco CA 94103

**STRAWDERMAN, WILLIAM E.,** statistics educator; b. Westerly, R.I., Apr. 25, 1941; s. Robert Lee and Alida Browning (Dow) S.; m. Susan Linda Grube; July 20, 1985; children: Robert Lee, William Edward, Heather Lynne. BS, U. R.I., 1963; MS, Cornell U., 1965, Rutgers U., 1967, PhD, 1969. Mem. tech. staff Bell Tel. Labs., Holmdel, NJ, 1965-67; vis. asst. prof. Stanford (Calif.) U., 1969-70; instr. Rutgers U., New Brunswick, NJ, 1967-69, prof. stats., 1970—. Contbr. more than 140 articles to profl. jours. Fellow: Inst. Math. Stats., Am. Statis. Assn. Office: Rutgers U Statistics Dept Hill Ctr-Busch Campus New Brunswick NJ 08903 Office Phone: 732-445-2697. Business E-Mail: straw@stat.rutgers.edu.

**STRAWHECKER, PAUL JOSEPH,** fundraising consultant; b. Oct. 31, 1947; s. John Leslie and Leone Francis (Kalamaja) Strawhecker; m. Margaret Ellen Baumann, Aug. 31, 1974; children: Risa Nicole, Ryan John. Student, St. Joseph's Sem., 1963-67, Blessed John Neumann Coll., 1968-68; BA, Creighton U., 1970, postgrad. Law Sch., 1971-73; MPA, U. Nebr., 1980. Advanced cert. fundraising exec. Assn. Fundraising Profls. Rsch. associate mayor's office City of Omaha, 1970, spl. asst. to mayor, 1971, mgr. spl. programs, 1972-73; dir. spl. resources Father Flanagan's Boys Home, Boys Town, Nebr., 1974-81; v.p. for devel. Luth. Hosps. and Homes Soc. Am., Fargo, N.D., 1982-86; asst. administr. Sacred Heart Gen. Hosp., Eugene, Oreg., 1986-87; v.p. Northwood U., Midland, Mich., 1987-94; pres. Paul J. Strawhecker, Inc., Omaha, 1995—. Adj. prof. U. Nebr., Omaha, 1995—; treas. Credit Union, 1975; clk., treas. liaison officer Village of Boys Town, 1974-81; writer Am. Soc. Planning Ofcls.; past owner The Wooden Spoon Ltd., Omaha; exec. com. Assn. Philanthropic Counsel. Author: Fund Raising, 1997, Capital Campaigns, 1998, Resource Development, 1999. Chmn. Met. Area Planning Agy. Coun. Ofcls. Goals Com. for Human Svcs., 1976; mem. Omaha/Douglas County Criminal Justice Commn., 1977-80; mem. adv. com. Douglas County Office on ChildrenYouth, Midland County Cmty. Corrections, 1991-92; bd. dirs. "Say Yes" to Youth, 1990-92; chmn. urban affairs com. Met. Area

Planning Agy. Mem. Assn. Fundraising Profls. (cert., pres. ND area chpt., bd. dirs. 1994-95, pres. Mich. chpt. bd. dirs. 1987-90, pres. Nebr. chpt. bd. dirs. 1997-99, vice chair nat. bd. 1991, nat. found. bd. 2000—, bd. mem. chair elect 2005, Internat. Found.), Nat. Assn. Hosp. Devel. (spkr. 1983), Internat. City Mgmt. Assn. (spkr. 1971), Multi Hosp. Devel. Assn. (pres. 1986), Leadership Midland (alimni and steering com. 1990-92), Phi Kappa Psi. Roman Catholic. Home: 3424 N 129th Cir Omaha NE 68164-4240 Office: Paul J Strawhecker Inc 4913 Dodge St Omaha NE 68132-2917 Office Phone: 402-556-5785. Business E-Mail: paul@pjstraw.com.

**STRAWN, MELVIN NICHOLAS,** artist, educator; b. Boise, Aug. 5, 1929; s. Milton Rozell and Irma Belle Strawn; m. Bernice Iva Strawn, June 14, 1951; children: Clare Lynn, Daniel Paul, Stanley Milton, Benjamin Joseph, Angela Mary, Thomas Melvin. BFA, Calif. Coll. Arts and Crafts, 1955, MFA, 1956. Art instr. Midwestern U., Wichita Falls, Tex., 1956—57, Mich. State U., East Lansing, 1957—59; asst./assoc. prof. Antioch Coll., Yellow Springs, Ohio, 1959—69; prof., dir. U. Denver, 1969—85; prof., chair art dept. Western Mich. U., Kalamazoo, 1985—88; prof. emeritus U. Denver, 1985—. Juror Colo. Watercolor Soc., Denver. Major retrospective exhbn., Denver Ctrl. Libr., 2006. Vol., designer Steam Plant Cmty. Ctr., Salida, Colo., 1990—2000. Pvt. U.S. Army, 1951—53. Avocations: fly fishing, photography, cross country skiing, hiking. Home: 8905 Hwy 285 Salida CO 81201 Office Phone: 719-539-2637. Personal E-mail: mels@chaffee.net.

**STRAWSER, JERRY R.,** dean; BBA in acctg., Tex. A&M U., 1983, MS in acctg., 1984, PhD in acctg., 1985. CPA Tex., 1985. Asst. prof. La. State U., 1985—90, Arthur Andersen & Co. rsch. fellow, 1989—90; assoc. prof. Conn. Bauer Coll Bus. U Houston, 1990—97, assoc. dean academic and rsch. programs, 1995—99, prof. and Arthur Anderson & Co. alumni prof. acctg. and taxation, 1997—2001, interim dean, 1999—2001; dean Mays Bus. Sch., Tex. A&M U., 2001—, Devel. Coun. chair bus., 2001—, Leland/Weinke chair acctg., 2001—. Mem. editl. bd. Issues in Acctg. Edn., 1998—. Co-author: (books) Auditing Theory and Practice, 1985—2001, Managerial Accounting, 1990—2000, Auditing & Assurance Services, 2004. Recipient Outstanding Tchg. award, Alpha Kappa Psi, 1985, George W. Fair award for tchg. excellence, 1986, Melcher award for rsch. excellence, 1992, 1995, Master Tchg. award, NationsBank, 1994, Disting. Faculty award, Exec. MBA Alumni Assn., 2000; Arthur Andersen rsch. fellowship, 1989, Melcher tchg. fellow, 1991, Melcher svc. fellow, 1993. Mem.: Am. Assn. Acctg., Assn. to Advance Collegiate Schools of Bus. Office: Tex A&M U Mays Bus Sch 4113 TAMU College Station TX 77843-4113 Office Phone: 979-845-4711. Office Fax: 979-845-6639. Business E-Mail: jstrawser@tamu.edu.*

**STRAYER, BARRY LEE,** retired judge; b. Moose Jaw, Sask., Can., Aug. 13, 1932; s. Carl John and Nina Naomi Strayer; m. Eleanor Lorraine Staton, July 2, 1955; children: Alison Lee, Jonathan Mark, Colin James. BA, U. Sask., Can., 1953, LLB, 1955; BCL, Oxford U., Eng., 1957; SJD, Harvard U., 1966. Bar: Sask., 1959. Crown solicitor Gov. Sask., Regina, 1959-62; prof. law U. Sask., 1962-68; dir. constitutional rev. Gov. Can., Ottawa, 1968-72, dir. constitutional law, 1972-74, asst. dep. minister justice, 1974-83; judge trial divsn. Fed. Ct. Can., Ottawa, 1983-94; jud. mem. Competition Tribunal Can., Ottawa, 1986-93; judge Fed. Ct. Appeal of Can., 1994—2004; chief justice Ct. Martial Appeal Ct. of Can., 1994—2004. Sessional lectr. U. Ottawa, 1973-78; constitutional advisor Rep. Seychelles, 1979; adviser Hongkong Govt. Bill of Rights, 1989. Author: Judicial Review of Legislation, 1968, Canadian Constitution and the Courts, 1983, 3d edit., 1988; contbr. articles to profl. jours. Mem.: Larrimac Golf Club, Rideau Club. Home: 504 Queen Elizabeth Dr Ottawa ON Canada K1S 3N4

**STRAZZERI, JAMES C.,** orthopedist, surgeon, health facility administrator; b. Albany, NY, July 16, 1954; s. James Frank and Fern Elaine Strazzeri; m. Dawn Kinns, Mar. 20, 1983; children: Michael Glenn, Craig James, Kyle Christopher, Mark Anthony. MD, Albany Med. Coll., 1980. Diplomate Am. Bd. Orthop. Surgery. Pvt. practice orthop. surgeon. Mission Hills, Calif., 1985—; chief surgery Holy Cross Med. Ctr., Mission Hills, 1987—88, chief orthop. surgery, 1989—99; med. dir., pres. Holy Cross Surgery Ctr., Mission Hills, 1992—2005. Orthop. trauma med. dir. Providence Holy Cross Med. Ctr., Mission Hills, 2005—; asst. prof. U. Calif., Irvine, 1985—. Named Best Orthop. Surgeon, Nation's Best Doctors Publ., 2004—06. Home: 11550 Indian Hills Rd #351 Mission Hills CA 91345 Office: 11550 Indian Hills Rd #351 Mission Hills CA 91345 Office Phone: 818-368-8291. Office Fax: 818-898-0866.

**STREAMAS, JOHN,** ethnic and American studies professor; s. Edward Streamas and Hideko Kato; m. Valerie Boydo, Oct. 31, 1996. AB, Miami U., Oxford, Ohio, 1977; MA, Syracuse U., NY, 1981; PhD, Bowling Green State U., Ohio, 2001. Grad. tchg. asst. Syracuse U., NY, 1979—80, Miami U., Oxford, Ohio, 1981—85, rsch. asst., 1978—83; instr. Franklin U., 1985—94; grad. asst. Bowling Green State U., Bowling Green, 1996—98; asst. prof. Wash. State U., Pullman, 2001—. Proofreader Ross Lab., Columbus, Ohio, 1987—2001; tchr. langs. Berlitz Sch. Langs., Ft. Thomas, Ky., 1981. Author short stories, poems, (plays) The Serving Class. Mem.: Am. Studies Assn. (minority scholars com. 2005—), Western Lit. Assn., Japanese Am. Nat. Mus., Nat. Japanese Am. Hist. Soc., Multi-Ethnic Lit. US. Assn. Asian Am. Studies, Internat. Soc. Study Time, Am. Studies Assn. (Wise Susman prize 2000), MLA, AAUP. Office: Wash State U PO Box 644010 Wilson Hall 112A Pullman WA 99164-4010 Office Phone: 509-335-4791. E-mail: streamas@wsu.edu.

**STREAR, JOSEPH D.,** public relations executive; b. N.Y.C., Nov. 5, 1933; s. Morris and Betty (Birenbaum) S. BA, CCNY, 1955. Pres. AC&R Pub. Relations, Inc., N.Y.C., 1972-82; mng. ptnr. Kanan, Corbin, Schupak & Aronow, Inc. N.Y.C., 1982-84; pres. David & Mlufoth, Inc., N.Y.C., 1984-91; prin. Joseph Strear Pub. Rels., N.Y.C., 1992—. 1st lt. U.S. Army, 1955-57. Mem. Pub. Rels. Soc. Am. Avocation: sports. Office: 408 W 57th St New York NY 10019-3053

**STREATOR, EDWARD,** retired diplomat, management consultant; b. N.Y.C., Dec. 12, 1930; s. Edward James and Ella (Stout) S.; m. Priscilla Craig Kenney, Feb. 16, 1957; children: Edward James, III, Elinor Craig Garcia-Garcia, Abigail Merrill Squance. AB, Princeton U., 1952. Commd. fgn. service officer Dept. State, 1956; assigned ICA, 1956-58; 3d sec. embassy Addis Ababa, Ethiopia, 1958-60; 2d sec. embassy Lome Togo, 1960-62; intelligence research specialist Office Research and Analysis for Africe, Dept. State, Washington, 1962-63; staff asst. to sec. state, 1964-66, chief polit.-mil. affairs unit, 1966-67; dep. dir. polit.-mil. affairs, 1967-68; dep. dir. polit. affairs U.S. Mission to NATO, 1968-69; dep. dir. Office NATO and Atlantic Polit.-Mil. Affairs, Dept. State, 1969-73; dir. office, 1973-75; dep. U.S. permanent rep. to NATO, dep. chief U.S Mission to NATO, 1975-77; minister, dep. chief of mission Am. embassy, London, 1977-84; ambassador, U.S. rep. OECD Paris, 1984-87. Bd. dirs. South Bank, 1991-99; chmn. New Atlantic Initiative, 1996—. U.S. dels. NATO and OECD Ministerial Meetings, 1964, 66, 69-75, 85-87; mem. 10th SEATO Coun. Min. Meeting, 1965; 2d spl. Inter-Am. Conf., 1965, Conf. Security and Coop., Europe, 1973; mem. Coun., Royal United Svcs. Inst., 1987-92, vice patron, 1991—; exec. com. The Pilgrims, U.K., 1988—, Internat. Inst. Strategic Studies, 1988-99; coun. mem. Royal United Svcs. Inst. Def. Studies, 1988-1992; gov. Ditchley Found., 1988—, English Speaking Union, 1988-94; mem. Am. C. of C., U.K., 1988-94; chmn. European Coun. Am. C. of C., 1992-94; bd. dirs. Brit-Am. Arts Assn., 1987-99; dir. Brit. Mus. Natural History Internat. Found.; devel. com. Nat. Gallery, U.K., 1993-99; adv. bd. Inst. U.S. Studies-U. London, 1993-99; mem. coun. Oxford Inst. Am. Studies, 1989-2001; adv. com. Fulbright Commn., 1995-2001; pres., trustee Northcoate Parkinson Fund, 2004—. Recipient Presdl. Meritorious Svc. award, 1986, Wilbur Carr award Dept. of State, 1987, Benjamin Franklin medal Royal Soc. Arts, 1992. Mem. Knickerbocker Club (N.Y.), Pilgrims (N.Y.), Met. Club (Washington), Beefsteak Club, Garrick Club, White's Club (London), Mill Reef Club (Antigua), Century Assn. Episcopalian. Mailing: 535 Park Ave New York NY 10021 Office Phone: 212-486-6688. Personal E-mail: estreator@nyc.rr.com.

**STREB, ELIZABETH A.,** choreographer, dancer; b. Rochester, NY, Feb. 23, 1950; d. Leonard and Carolyn (Gale) S. BS in Modern Dance, SUNY, Brockport, 1972. Dean's special scholar, Draper program NYU; artistic dir. Streb/Ringside Co., NYC, 1978—, Streb Lab for Action Mechanics, Brooklyn, 2003—. Choreographer (dance): Airlines, Airwaves, Fall Line, Freeflight, Pole Vaults, Amphibian, 1985, Mass, 1991, Ringside, 1994, Up, 1996, Lookup, 1993, Bounce, 1995, Fly, 1997, All/Wall, 1998, Action Heroes, 2001-02, PopAction, 2004-05, SLAM show, 2005. Recipient Bessie award, 1989, Brandeis award, Brandeis U., 1991, Bessie award, 1999, Nat. Dance Residency Program award, Pew Charitable Trust, Nat. Dance Program award, New England Found. for Arts; fellow Guggenheim Found., 1989, Nat. Endowment for the Arts, 1990-93, MacArthur Fellowship, 1997. Office: Streb Lab for Action Mechanics 51 N 1st St Brooklyn NY 11211

**STREB, PAUL GERARD,** arbitrator; b. Balt., Dec. 8, 1945; s. Edwin and Marie (W.) S.; m. Mary Ament, Nov. 16, 1973. AB in Philosophy, Mount St. Mary's Coll., 1967; JD, U. Balt., 1973. Bar: Md. 1973, U.S. Ct. Appeals (Fed. cir.) 1986. Adminstrv. judge U.S. Civil Svc. Commn. and U.S. Merit Systems Protection Bd., Washington, 1973-83; atty. U.S. Merit Systems Protection Bd., Washington, 1983-90, dep. dir. regional ops., 1990-91; adminstrv. law judge U.S. Dept. HUD, Washington, 1991-94; chief adminstrv. law judge U.S. Merit Systems Protection Bd., Washington, 1994-2001; bd. dirs. fgn. svc. grievance bd. U.S. Dept. State, Washington, 2001—03. Sec. Fed. Administrative Law Judges Conf., 1993-94; arbitrator Fed. Mediation and Conciliation Svc., 2002-. Vol. atty. for Homeless Persons Representation Project, Balt., 1990-91. Lt. U.S. Army, 1967-70, Vietnam. Decorated Purple Heart, U.S. Army; recipient Chmn.'s Legal Excellence award Merit Systems Protection Bd., 1987. Avocations: running, swimming, biking, travel, the arts.

**STRECKER, DAVID EUGENE,** lawyer; b. Carthage, Mo., Nov. 29, 1950; s. Eugene Albert and Erma Freida (Wood) S.; m. Katherine Ann Pugh; children: Charles David, Carrie Christina. BA, Westminster Coll., 1972; JD, Cornell U., 1975, M in Indsl. Labor Rels., 1976. Bar: N.Y. 1976, Okla. 1981, U.S. Dist. Ct. (no. dist.) N.Y. 1976, U.S. Dist. Ct. (ea. dist.) Okla. 1984, U.S. Dist. Ct. (we. dist.) Okla. 2000, U.S. Dist. Ct. (we and ea. dists.) Ark. 2000, U.S. Ct. Appeals (no. dist.) Okla. 1981, U.S. Ct. Appeals (10th cir.) 1982, U.S. Ct. Appeals (6th cir.) 1990, U.S. Supreme Ct. 1991. Assoc. Conner & Winters, Tulsa, 1980-85, ptnr., 1985-91, Shipley, Inhofe & Strecker, Tulsa, 1991-95, Strecker & Assocs. P.C., Tulsa, 1995—. Instr. paralegal program Tulsa Jr. Coll., 1985—, mem. adv. com., 1986-91; mem. Cornell Secondary Schs. Com., Tulsa, 1985—; adj. instr. labor rels. Okla. State U., 1995—; master Am. Inns of Ct. Bd. dirs., v.p. Tulsa Sr. Svcs., 1988-91; mem. pers. com. Philbrook Art Mus. Capt. JAGC, U.S. Army, 1976-80. Mem. ABA, Okla. Bar Assn. (chmn. labor sect. 1990-91), Tulsa County Bar Assn. (continuing legal edn. com. 1981—), Soc. for Human Resource Mgmt., Tulsa Area Human Resources Assn. (gen. counsel 1989-2000, v.p. 1994-98, bd. dirs. family and children's svcs. 2000—04), Kappa Alpha. Democrat. Episcopalian. Avocations: jogging, golf. Home: 5112 E 107th St Tulsa OK 74137-7238 Office: Midcontinent Tower 401 S Boston Ste 2150 Tulsa OK 74103-4009 Office Phone: 918-582-1716. E-mail: destreck@juno.com, david.strecker@streckerlaborlaw.com.

**STRECKER, JUDY ELLEN,** music educator; d. Robert Joseph and Tressie Eulala Gibson; m. Jerome John Strecker, Dec. 28, 1990. MusB, Incarnate Word U., 1965; MA, Eastman Sch. Music, 1971; D of Musical Arts, U. Colo., 1979. Chair music dept. Incarnate Word Coll., San Antonio, 1971—76; dir. music St. Alphonsus Ch., Greenwell Springs, La., 1985—87; chair music dept. St. Mary of Plains Coll., Dodge City, Kans., 1987—90, Frank Phillips Coll., Borger, Tex., 1992—. V.p. faculty assoc. Frank Phillips Coll., 1996—98; adjudicator Nat. Guild Piano Tchrs., 1990—; organist 1st Meth. Ch., Pampa, 1992—94. Musician: (albums) Afternoon of Jazz, 1998, Recorder Music. Regional dir. Tex. Jr. Colls. Choral Festival, San Antonio, 1997—98; organist various chs., Borger, 1992—. Recipient NISOD Excellence award, U. Tex., Austin, 1998; fellow, Eastman Sch. Music, Rochester, N.Y., 1976—79. Mem.: Am. Coll. Musicians (piano judge 1990—), Tex. Assn. Music Schs., Tex. Music Educators Assn. Home: Box 835 Fritch TX 79036 Office: Frank Phillips Coll 1301 W Roosevelt Borger TX 79008 Personal E-mail: judystrecker@aol.com.

**STREEB, GORDON LEE,** diplomat, economist; b. Windsor, Colo., Dec. 24, 1935; s. Gerhard O. and Amelia (Martin) S.; m. Alice Junette Thomas, Aug. 11, 1962; children: Kurt, Kent, Kerry-Lynn. BSBA, BSChemE, U. Colo., 1959; PhD in Econs., U. Minn., 1978. Fgn. service officer U.S. Dept. State, Berlin, 1963-65; vice consul Am. Consulate, Guadalajara, Mex., 1965-67; instr. econs. U. Minn., 1968; examiner Bd. Examiners, 1972-73; internat. economist for trade policy Bur. Econ. and Bus. Affairs, Washington, 1973-77; econ. counselor U.S. mission European Office of the UN and other internat. orgns., Geneva, 1977-80; exec. asst. to undersec. of state on econ. affairs Washington, 1980-81; dep. asst. sec. state for econ. and social affairs Bur. Internat. Orgn. Affairs, Washington, 1981-84; dep. chief mission Am. Embassy, New Delhi, 1984-88; sr. inspector Dept. State, Washington, 1988-90; amb. to Zambia Am. Embassy, Lusaka, 1990-93; diplomat-in-residence The Carter Ctr., Atlanta, 1994-95, assoc. exec. dir. peace program, 1995—2004; vis. prof. Emory U., Atlanta, 2004—. Bd. dirs. Coun. on Fgn. Rels., Friendship Force Internat.; mem. adv. bd. Engrs. Without Borders-USA. Home: 2680 Churchwell Ln Tucker GA 30084-2402 Business E-Mail: gstreeb@emory.edu.

**STREEM, JAMES KENNETH,** musician, educator; b. Cleve., Jan. 15, 1934; s. Irving Earl and Geraldine W. Streem; m. Prudence Vitale, July 4, 1968 (dec. June 29, 2000). BS, Juilliard, 1956, MS, 1959. Mem. piano faculty Cleve. Music Sch. Settlement, 1960—68; prof. piano Fla. State U., Tallahassee, 1968—; concert debut Carnegie Hall, N.Y.C., NY, 1966. Trio in field Composer: (film score) Double Stop, 1967; author: 125 Pianists on the Legend of Vladimir Horowitz, 1996; performer: Steinway concert series, Kosciusko Found., Alice Tully Hall, numerous recitals throughout U.S.; soloist: with symphony orch. Trustee Temple Israel, Tallahassee, 1975—82, 1987—93. With U.S. Army, 1958—63. Home: 2604 Stonegate Dr Tallahassee FL 32308 E-mail: jks1115@aol.com.

**STREEP, MERYL (MARY LOUISE STREEP),** actress; b. Summit, N.J., June 22, 1949; d. Harry, Jr. and Mary W. Streep; m. Donald J. Grummer, Sept. 15, 1978; children: Henry, Mary Willa, Grace, Louisa. BA, Vassar Coll., 1971; MFA, Yale U., 1975, DFA (hon.), 1983, Dartmouth Coll. 1981. Co-founder Mothers & Others for a Livable Planet. Appeared with: Green Mountain Guild; actress: (Broadway plays) Trelawny of the Wells, 1975; (plays) 27 Wagons Full of Cotton (Theatre World award); A Memory of Two Mondays; Henry V; Secret Service; The Taming of the Shrew; Measure for Measure; The Cherry Orchard; Happy End; Wonderland; Taken in Marriage; Alice in Concert (Obie award, 1981); Mother Courage, 2006; (films) Julia, 1977; The Deer Hunter, 1978 (Best Supporting Actress award nat. Soc. film Critics, Acad. award nomination, 1978); Manhattan, 1979; The Seduction of Joe Tynan, 1979; Kramer vs. Kramer, 1979 (N.Y. Film Critics' award, Los Angeles Film Critics' award, both for best actress, Golden Globe award, Acad. award for best supporting actress, 1980); The French Lieutenant's Woman, 1981 (Los Angeles Film Critics award for best actress, Brit. Acad. award, Golden Globe award for best actress, Acad. award nomination, 1982); Sophie's Choice, 1982 (Acad. award for best actress, Los Angeles Film Critics award for best actress, Golden Globe award for best actress, 1983); Still of the Night, 1982; Silkwood, 1983 (Acad. award nomination); Falling in Love, 1984; Plenty, 1985; Out of Africa, 1985 (Los Angeles Film Critics award for best actress, Golden Globe award, 1985); Heartburn, 1986; Ironweed, 1987 (Acad. award nomination); A Cry in the Dark, 1988 (named Best Actress N.Y. Film Critics' Circle, Best Actress Cannes Film Festival, 1989, Acad. award nomination); She-Devil, 1989; Postcards From the Edge, 1990; Defending Your Life, 1991; Death Becomes Her, 1992; The House of Spirits, 1993; The River Wild, 1994; The Bridges of Madison County, 1995 (Acad. award nominee for best actress, 1996); Before and After, 1996; Marvin's Room, 1996; Dancing at Lugnasa, 1998; One True Thing, 1998; Music of the Heart, 1999 (Acad. award nominee for best actress); The Hours,

2002; Adaptation, 2002 (Southeastern Film Critics Assn. award for best supporting actress, 2002, Chgo. Film Critics Assn. award for best supporting actress, 2003, Golden Globe for best supporting actress, 2003); The Manchurian Candidate, 2004; Lemony Snicket's A Series of Unfortunate Events, 2004; Prime, 2005; A Prairie Home Companion, 2006; The Devil Wears Prada, 2006; (voice only) Rabbit Ears: The Tale of Peter Rabbit, 1987; Rabbit Ears: The Tale of Jeremy Fisher, 1987; The Tailor of Gloucester, 1988; Rabbit Ears: The Fisherman and His Wife, 1989; Chrysanthemum, 1999; Artificial Intelligence: AI, 2001; The Ant Bully, 2006; actress: (TV films) Secret Service, 1977; The Deadliest Season, 1977; Uncommon Women and Others, 1979; Alice at the Palace, 1982; actress, exec. prodr. First Do No Harm, 1997; narrator The Velveteen Rabbit, 1984 (Emmy award Best Children's Rec.); A Vanishing Wilderness, 1990; actress: (TV miniseries) Holocaust, 1978 (Emmy award for Outstanding Lead Actress in a Mini-series, 1978); Angels in America, 2003 (Screen Actors Guild Award for best actress, Golden Globe for best actress, Emmy award Outstanding Lead Actress in a Mini-series or a movie, 2004). Named Officer, French Ordre des Arts et des Lettres, 2000; named one of 100 Most Influential People, Time Mag., 2006; recipient Mademoiselle award, 1976, Woman of Yr. award, B'nai Brith, 1979, Hasty Pudding Soc., Harvard U., 1980, Best Supporting Actress award, Nat. Bd. of Rev., 1979, Best Actress award, 1982, Star of Yr. award, Nat. Assn. Theater Owners, 1983, People's Choice award, 1983, 85, 86, 87, 1990, Women in Film Crystal award, 1998, Gotham award for Lifetime Achievement, 1999, Bette Davis Lifetime Achievement award, 1999, Lifetime Achievement award, Am. Film Inst., 2004, most nominated actor ever for an Academy Award. Office: Creative Artists Agy 9830 Wilshire Blvd Beverly Hills CA 90212 1825*

**STREET, DAVID HARGETT,** investment company executive; b. Oklahoma City, Dec. 4, 1943; s. Bob Allen and Elizabeth Anne (Hargett) S.; m. Betty Ann Nichols, Oct. 1, 1966; children: Elizabeth Ann, Randall Hargett, Jeffrey David. BA in English, U. Okla., 1965; MBA in Fin., U. Pa., 1970. Vice pres. SEI Corp., 1970; v.p., prin. Street & Street, Inc., N.Y.C., 1970-74; v.p., mgr. San Francisco regional office First Nat. Bank Chicago, 1974-78; sr. v.p., CFO, treas. Bangor Punta Corp., Greenwich, Conn., 1978-84; v.p., treas. Penn Cen. Corp., Greenwich, 1984-86, v.p. fin., 1986-87, v.p. fin. Cin., 1987-92; exec. v.p. Gen. Cable Corp., Highland Heights, Ky., 1992-94, also bd. dirs.; pres., CEO Street Capital Group, Duluth, Ga., 1994—. Mem. adv. bd. Mfrs. Hanover Trust Co., 1982-88. 1st lt. M.I. U.S. Army, 1966—67. Mem. St. Ives Country Club. Republican. Presbyterian.

**STREET, DEBORRA LYNN,** fine arts director; b. Ft. Payne, Ala., Feb. 25, 1953; d. John M. and Mary (Adams) Long. B in Music Edn., Troy State U., 1976, MEd, 1982, EdS, 1994; student, Birmingham U. Sch. Law. Tchr. music S. Hall Jr. High Sch., Oakwood, Ga., 1976-77, Slocomb (Ala.), 1977-79, U.S. Collegiate Wind Bands European (summer) Tours, 1978-88, Judson Coll., Marion, Ala., 1980—, Marion Mil. Inst., 1980—, Marion Acad., 1987-88. Band camp instr. 22 U.S. Univs., 1968—; band judge U.S. music festivals, 1977—; asst. conductor U.S. Collegiate Wind Bands European Tours, 1979; sponsor Drama Soc., Marion, 1985—. Prodr.(over 30 musicals and plays):. Sunday sch. tchr. United Meth. Ch., Marion, 1987-88; chmn. Marion Mil. Inst. Fine Arts Coun., 1989-90; mem. steering com. Citizens for a Better Community, Marion, 1990-91; conductor Community Instrumental Ensemble, Marion, 1990—. Mem. Nat. Band Assn., Music Educators Nat. Conf., Women Band Dirs. Nat. Assn. (Indsl. chmn. 1988), DAR, Perry County Hist. Soc., Am. Legion Aux. (Americanism award 1971), Delta Kappa Gamma, Perry County Arts and Humanities Council, AAUW, Tau Beta Sigma, Kappa Kappa Psi, Delta Gamma. Avocations: music, drama, swimming. Home: 803 Washington St Marion AL 36756-3027 Office: Marion Mil Inst Washington St Marion AL 36756-1822

**STREET, HUSTON,** professional baseball player; b. Austin, Tex., Aug. 2, 1983; s. James, Janie. Attended, Tex. Univ., 2002—03. Relief pitcher Oakland Athletics, 2004—. Named Ctrl. Tex. Coll. Pitcher Yr, 2003, USA Baseball Athlete Yr., 2003; recipient Rookie of the Yr., Major League Baseball Am. League, 2005. Achievements include first-team NCAA All-American, 2003; two-time first-tem All-Big 12, 2002-2003. Office: Oakland Athletics 7000 Colliseum Way Oakland CA 94621*

**STREET, JEANNE,** psychologist; b. Lexington, Va., Oct. 1, 1952; d. Marion Scott and Wilma Mae Street; m. Clif Dopson, Nov. 23, 1979; 1 child, Lorna Street Dopson stepchildren: Jennifer Ellen Rennix, Steven Eric Dopson. BA, U. Fla., 1973, MA, 1975, PhD, 1978. Lic. Psychologist U.S. State Bd. Profl. Examiners. Staff psychologist Chapel Hill Mental Health Ctr., NC; pvt. practice Shreveport, La. Assoc. prof. La. State U. Health Scis. Ctr., Shreveport; consulting psychologist Brentwood Hosp., Shreveport, DeSoto Parish Office Children's Svcs., Mansfield, La. Mem. Highland Restoration Assn., Shreveport, 1982—, Highland Area Partnership, Shreveport, 1990—; bd. mem. Noel Children's Learning Ctr., Shreveport, 2005. Recipient Best Tchr. 2003, La. State U. Health Scis. Ctr., Shreveport. Mem.: APA, Soc. Personality Assessment, Southeastern Psychol. Assn., Phi Beta Kappa. Office: 610 Herndon Ave Shreveport LA 71101 Office Phone: 318-424-3867.

**STREET, JOHN CHARLES,** linguistics educator; b. Chgo., Apr. 3, 1930; s. Charles Larrabee and Mary Louise (Rouse) S.; m. Eve Elizabeth Baker, June 4, 1975. BA, Yale, 1951, MA, 1952, PhD, 1955. Asst. prof. English Mich. State U., 1957-59; asst. prof. linguistics and Mongolian langs. Columbia, 1959-62; vis. asst. prof. linguistics U. Wash., 1962-63; assoc. prof. linguistics U. Wis., Madison, 1963-65, prof. linguistics, 1965-92, prof. emeritus Madison, 1992—. Author: The Language of the Secret History of the Mongols, 1957, Khalkha Structure, 1963, The Journal of Oliver Rouse, 1983, An Ellis Family of Devon and Newfoundland, 1994, A Genealogy of the Rouses of Devon, 2002. Research asso. Am. Council Learned Socs., 1959-62. Served with AUS, 1955-57.

**STREET, JOHN F.,** mayor; b. Norristown, Pa., Oct. 15, 1943; m. Naomi Street; children: Sharif, Rasida, Lateef, Akeem. BA in English, Oakwood Coll., 1966; JD, Temple U., 1975. Pvt. law practice, 1975—80; city councilman City of Phila., 1979-98, pres., 1992-98, past chmn. licenses and inspections, appropriations coms., chmn. Whole, Rules & Fiscal Stability, Intergovt. coop. com., 1992—; mem. Phila. Gas Commn., 1984-89, chmn., 1992—; mayor City of Phila., 2000—. Named one of 100 Most Influential Black Americans, Ebony mag., 2006. Avocations: running, bicycling. Office: City Hall Rm 215 Philadelphia PA 19107*

**STREET, PAUL SHIPLEY,** lawyer; b. Klamath Falls, Oreg., Mar. 4, 1948; s. Leon Rex and Mary Rebecca (Shipley) S.; children: Adam, Blake. BA, Coll. Idaho, 1970; JD, U. Wash., 1973. Bar: Idaho 1973, U.S. Dist. Ct. Idaho 1973, Idaho Supreme Ct. 1973. Law clerk Idaho Supreme Ct., Boise, 1973-74; pres., mng. ptnr. Moffatt, Thomas, Barrett, Rock & Fields, Boise, 1974—99; sr. v.p., gen. counsel, corp. sec. Bldg. Materials Holding Co., San Francisco, 1999—, chief adminstrv. officer, 2001—. Sec. BMC West Corp., Boise, 1987—. Co-author: Idaho Law Review, 1991, Digest of Environmental Law of Real Property, 1991. Pres. Coll. Idaho Alumni Assn., Caldwell, 1986—, Am. Diabetes Assn., 1984—; bd. dirs. First United Meth. Ch., Boise, 1985—; chairperson United Way of Ada County, Boise, 1982-83. Mem. ABA (sec. mem. patent, trademark and copyright law; litigation, econs. law practice), Am. Soc. Med. Assn. Coun. Law and Medicine, Am. Arbitration Assn., Idaho State Bar (chmn. corp. and securities law sect. 1992-93), Boise Bar Assn., Boise Ins. Adjusters Assn., Real Estate Lawyers Assn., Boise Area C. of C. (vice chmn. 1991—). Avocation: bird hunting. Office: Bldg Materials Holding Corp Four Embarcadero Ctr Ste 3250 San Francisco CA 94111 Office Phone: 415-627-9100. Office Fax: 415-627-9119.

**STREET, PICABO,** Olympic athlete; b. Triumph, Idaho, Apr. 3, 1971; Downhill skier U.S. Ski Team, 1994—. Autobiography Picabo: Nothing to Hide. Named World Cup Downhill Women's Champion, 1995, 1996; recipient Silver medal Women's Downhill Alpine Skiing, Olympic Games,

Lillehammer, 1994, Bronze and Gold medals, World Championships, 1996, Gold medals (3) Women's Super Giant Slalom Alpine Skiing, Nagano, Japan, 1998, medal, Winter Olympics. Office Phone: 208-578-9880.

**STREET, ROBERT LYNNWOOD,** civil, mechanical and environmental engineer; b. Honolulu, Dec. 18, 1934; s. Evelyn Mansel and Dorothy Heather (Brook) S.; m. Norma Jeanette Ensminger, Feb. 6, 1959; children: Brian Clarke (dec.), Deborah Lynne, Kimberley Anne. Student, USN ROTC Program, 1952-57; MS, Stanford U., 1957, PhD (NSF grad. fellow 1960-62), 1963. Mem. faculty Sch. Engring. Stanford U., 1962—2005, prof. civil engring., assoc. chmn. dept. Sch. Engring., 1970-72, chmn. dept. Sch. Engring., 1972-80, 94-95, prof. fluid mechanics and applied math. Sch. Engring., 1972—2004, founding dir. environ. fluid mechanics lab. Sch. Engring., 1985-91, assoc. dean rsch. Sch. Engring., 1971-83, vice provost acad. computing and info. sys., 1983-85, vice provost, dean rsch. and acad. info. sys., 1985-87, v.p. for info. resources, 1987-90, acting provost, 1987, v.p. librs. and info. resources, 1990-92, vice provost, dean of librs. and info. resources, 1992—94, William Alden and Martha Campbell prof. Sch. Engring., 1997—2004, prof. emeritus fluid mechanics, applied math, 2005. Vis. prof. U. Liverpool, Eng., 1970-71, Ctr. for Water Rsch., U. Western Australia, 1985; vis. prof. mech. engring. James Cook U. Australia, 1995; trustee Univ. Corp. Atmospheric Rsch., 1983-94, chmn. sci. programs evaluation com., 1984; fellow N.E. Asia-U.S. Forum on Internat. Policy at Stanford U., 1985-89; named to Beverly Hills HS Hall of Fame, 2005. Fellow: AAAS; mem.: NAE, ASME (R.T. Knapp award 1986), ASCE (chmn. publs. com. hydraulics divsn. 1978—80, Walter Huber prize 1972, Hilgard Hydraulic Engring. prize 2002, Rouse Hydraulic Engring. award 2005), Am. Meteorol. Soc., Oceanographic Soc., Am. Geophys. Union, Sigma Xi, Phi Beta Kappa, Tau Beta Pi. Office: Stanford U Environ Fluid Mechs Lab Dept Civil/Environ Engring Stanford CA 94305-4020 Office Phone: 650-723-4969. Business E-Mail: street@stanford.edu.

**STREET, SUSAN LEE,** elementary school educator; b. Kansas City, Kans., Aug. 4, 1955; d. Charley E. Taylor and Betty Lee Milum; m. Thomas D. Street, Dec. 20, 1980; children: Amanda Lee, Jordan Thomas. BS in Elem. Edn., Ark. Tech. U., 1977. Tchr. kindergarten Jasper (Ark.) Elem.; tchr. elem. Woodland Heights Sch., Harrison, Ark. Tchr. Bible Sch. Home: RR 6 Box 60K Harrison AR 72601-8808

**STREET, TERRI M.,** artist, educator; b. Bklyn., Dec. 11, 1929; d. William George Nappenbach and Marie Virginia Caron; m. Norman Street, Oct. 11, 1962 (dec. Sept. 1979); children: Lesa, David. Student, Chinourd Art Sch., 1948, Art Students League, 1950—53, Am. Art Sch., 1953—54, NYU Inst. Fine Art, 1953—54, Nat. Acad. Design, 1953—58, Vrijy Acad., 1956. Cert. tchr. Calif. Instr. Traphagen Sch. Design, NY, 1959, Conejo Valley Adult Sch., Thousand Oaks, Calif., 1980—93; art dir. Dwight Sch. for Girls, NJ, 1960—62, Carden Conejo Sch., Calif., 1976—93; exhibit specialist Smithsonian, Wash., 1962—63; founder, dir. Burke Sch. Art, Va., 1968—70; art cons. for occupl. therapists Pediatric Rehabilitation, Poland, Slovakia, Hungary, 1988—90; founder, dir. Hawthorne Studio, Portland, Oreg., 1993—. Instr. St. Francis Svcs., Portland, 2000—. Exhibitions include Knickerbocker Art Guild, 1955, Allied Artists Nat. Acad. Design, NY, 1956, Smithsonian Art Inst., Wash., DC, 1964, Gallery 33, Portland, Oreg., 1997—98, Hawthorne Studio; illustrator: Problem Solving in Occupational Therapy; numerous pvt. collections. Cons. park and recreation Children's Art Festival, Calif.; charter mem. Nat. Women's Mus.; coun. mem. St. Francis Ch., Portland. Fogg Mus. of Haravard U. scholar, 1954, Louis Comfort Tiffany fellow, 1956. Mem.: Allied Artists, Oriental Art Soc., Oreg. Soc. Artists, Keizer Art Assn., Watercolor Soc. Oreg., Nat. Watercolor Soc. (assoc.), Northwest Watercolor Soc. (assoc.), Art Students League (life). Home and Office: Hawthorne Studio 3436 SE Madison Portland OR 97214 E-mail: tstreetart@msn.com.

**STREET, WILLIAM MAY,** beverage company executive; b. Louisville, 1938; Grad., Princeton U., 1960; MBA, Harvard U., 1963. V.p. Brown-Forman Corp., Louisville, 1969, dir., mem. exec. com., 1971, sr. v.p., 1977, vice chmn., 1983, pres., 2000; pres., COO Brown-Forman Beverage Co. Divsn., Louisville, 1986-94; pres., CEO Brown-Forman Beverages Worldwide Divsn., 1994—; pres. Brown-Forman Corp., 2001—03; ret., 2003. Dir. Papa John's Internat. Chmn. Ky. Horse Racing Authority. Office: Brown-Forman Beverages Worldwide 850 Dixie Hwy Louisville KY 40210-1038

**STREETEN, BARBARA WIARD,** ophthalmologist, medical educator; b. Candia, N.H., Mar. 3, 1925; d. Robert Campbell Wiard and Gertrude Sarah Matheson; m. David Henry Palmer Streeten, Aug. 2, 1952; children: Robert Duncan, Elizabeth Anne, John Palmer. AB magna cum laude, Tufts U., 1945, MD cum laude, 1950. Diplomate Am. Bd. Ophthalmology. Jr. resident in gen. pathology Mallory Inst., Boston City Hosp., 1951-52; fellow in ophthalmic pathology Mass. Eye and Ear Infirmary, Boston, 1952-53; resident in ophthalmology Wayne County Gen. Hosp., Eloise, Mich., 1953-56; from jr. to sr. clin. instr. ophthalmology U. Mich. Med. Sch., Ann Arbor, 1956-60; from asst. prof. to prof. ophthalmology SUNY Health Sci. Ctr. (now called SUNY Upstate Med. U.), Syracuse, 1964—, dir. eye pathology lab., 1966—; from asst. prof. to prof. pathology SUNY Health Sci. Ctr., Syracuse, 1968—. Contbr. more than 120 articles to profl. jours., chapters to books. Mem. vision study sect. Nat. Eye Inst., NIH, Bethesda, Md., 1977-80, mem. bd. sci. counselors, 1982-86; mem. editl. bd., mem. editl. adv. com. Ophthalmology jour., 1982-94; gen. editor Investigative Ophthalmology and Visual Sci., 1979-82, mem. editl. bd., 1987-92. Grantee Nat. Eye Inst., NIH, 1975—2002. Mem. Am. Assn. Ophthalmic Pathologists (charter, past pres., bd. dirs., Zimmerman medal 1997), Am. Acad. Ophthalmology (honor award 1990), Verhoeff Ophthalmic Pathology Soc. (past pres.), Assn. for Rsch. in Vision and Ophthalmology (past sect. chmn.), Internat. Soc. Ophthalmic Pathology (co-v.p. N.Am. 1990-92), Phi Beta Kappa, Alpha Omega Alpha. Episcopalian. Achievements include establishment of elastic system nature of the suspensory ligament of the ocular lens; ultrastructural and immunopathologic contributions to diseases of the ocular connective tissue matrix, particularly those related to cataract and glaucoma. Home: 334 Berkeley Dr Syracuse NY 13210-3000 Office: SUNY Upstate Med Univ WH Rm 2107 766 Irving Ave Syracuse NY 13210-1602

**STREETER, JOHN WILLIS,** information systems manager; b. Topeka, Sept. 3, 1947; s. Jack and Edith Bernice (Vowels) S.; m. Nancy Ann Buck, June 15, 1968 (div. 1985); children: Sarah Beth, Timothy Paine; m. Linda Lea Wenrich Weisbender, Sept. 13, 1986; stepchildren: Michael Leon Weisbender II, Debra Ann Weisbender, Dawn Marie Weisbender. BS in Computer Sci., Kans. State U., 1973, MBA in Mgmt., 1974; postgrad., Harvard U., 1992. Computer programmer U.S.M.C., 1965-70, Kans. State U. Manhattan, 1970-74; cons., mgr., prin. Am. Mgmt. Systems, Inc., Arlington, Va., 1974-83; systems planning analyst Fed. Nat. Mortgage Assn., Washington, 1983-85; assoc. dir. computing and telecomm. Kans. State U. Manhattan, 1985-91, dir. info. systems, 1991—. Mem. State of Kans. Info. Tech. Adv. Bd., 1997-98. Author: Streeter Genealogy, 1985. Staff sgt. USMC, 1965-70. Recipient Navy Achievement medal in data processing Sec. Navy, 1971. Mem. SR, KC, Am. Inst. Cert. Computer Profls., Educause, Inc. (Kans. State U. voting mem. rep. 1987—), Streeter Family Assn. (bd. dirs. 1988—, v.p. 1990-95), Am. Legion. Republican. Roman Catholic. Avocations: genealogy, history, book collecting. Home: 6765 Salzer Rd Wamego KS 66547-9636 Office: Kans State U Info Sys 2323 Anderson Ave Ste 215 Manhattan KS 66502-2912 Office Phone: 785-532-4758. Business E-Mail: jws@ksu.edu.

**STREETER, ROBERT DAVENPORT,** electrical engineer, consultant; b. Springfield, Mass., Sept. 17, 1941; s. William Allen Streeter and Muriel Ethel Davenport; m. Carole Janet Riley, Mar. 21, 1970 (dec. Nov. 2004); children:

John Riley, Susan Streeter Billian; m. Donna Jean Preston, Feb. 18, 2006. B in Elec. Engring., Ohio State U., 1964; MSEE, Purdue U., 1968. Registered profl. engr., Ind. Engr. WBNS Radio-TV, Columbus, Ohio, 1961—64, Ohio State U. Rsch. Found., Columbus, 1962—64, The Magnavox Co., Fort Wayne, Ind., 1965—82; pres. A M Stereo, Inc., Fort Wayne, 1982—; engring. fellow Raytheon, Fort Wayne, 1985—. Contbr. articles to profl. jours. Mem.: IEEE, Eta Kappa Nu (life). Achievements include invention of AM stereo, microelectromechanical systems. Avocations: private pilot, amateur radio, bicycling. Home: 6111 Eagle Creek Dr Fort Wayne IN 46814-3213 Office: Raytheon 1010 Production Rd Fort Wayne IN 46808 Personal E-mail: r.streeter@ieee.org

**STREETER, STEPHANIE ANNE,** printing company executive; b. Boston, Sept. 19, 1957; d. Andrew Geoffrey Galef and Suzanne Jane (Cohen) Sidy; m. Edward Stanley Streeter, Feb. 22, 1980. BA in Polit. Sci., Stanford U., 1979. Mgr. market analysis Xerox Small Bus. System, Sunnyvale, Calif., 1980-81; regional sales mgr. Xerox Office Products Divsn., Sunnyvale, Calif., 1981-83; product mgr. Decision Data Computer Corp., Horsham, Pa., 1983-85; sr. product mgr. Avery Dennison Corp., Covina, Calif., 1985-88, bus. mgr. indexes, 1988-89, bus. mgr. computer supplies, 1989-90, dir. mktg., computer products, 1990-91, v.p. gen. mgr. label divsn. Diamond Bar, Calif., 1991-93, v.p., gen. mgr., Avery Dennison Brands, 1993—96, worldwide group v.p., 1996—2000; COO idealab!, Pasadena, Calif., 2000; pres., COO Banta Corp., Menasha, Wis., 2001—02, dir., 2001—, pres., CEO, 2002—04, chmn., pres., CEO, 2004—. Bd. dirs. Wis. Mfrs. and Commerce. Fellow Internat. Women's Forum. Democrat. Avocations: bicycling, skiing. Office: Banta Corp 225 Main St Menasha WI 54952*

**STREETMAN, BEN GARLAND,** electrical engineering educator; b. Cooper, Tex., June 24, 1939; s. Richard E. and Bennie (Morrow) S.; m. Lenora Ann Music, Sept. 9, 1961; children: Paul, Scott. BS in Elec. Sci., 1961, MS, 1963, PhD, 1966. Fellow Oak Ridge Nat. Lab., 1964-66; asst. prof. elec. engring. U. Ill., 1966-70, assoc. prof., 1970-74, prof., 1974-82; rsch. prof. Coordinated Sci. Lab., 1970-82; prof. elec. engring. U. Tex., Austin, 1982—, dir. Microelectronics Rsch. Ctr., 1984—96, Dula D. Cockrell Centennial chair engring., 1989—, dean Coll. Engring., 1996—. Bd. dirs. Nat. Instruments, Zix Corp. Author: Solid State Electronic Devices 6th edit., 2005. Recipient Frederick Emmons Terman award Am. Soc. Engring. Edn., 1981, AT&T Found. award, 1987; named Disting. Alumnus, U. Tex. at Austin, 1998, Aldert Vander Ziel award, 2005. Fellow IEEE (life, Edn. medal 1989, Aldert van der Ziel award 2005), Electrochem. Soc.; mem. NAE, Am. Acad. Arts and Scis., Tau Beta Pi, Eta Kappa Nu, Sigma Xi. Office: U Tex at Austin Dean of Engring 1 University Sta C2100 Austin TX 78712-0284

**STREETMAN, JOHN WILLIAM, III,** museum director; b. Marion, N.C., Jan. 19, 1941; s. John William, Jr. and Emily Elaine (Carver) S.; children: Katherine Drake, Leah Farrior, Burgin Eaves. BA in English and Theatre History, Western Carolina U., 1963; cert. in Shakespeare studies, Lincoln Coll., Oxford (Eng.) U., 1963. Founding dir. Jewett Creative Arts Ctr., Berwick Acad., South Berwick, Maine, 1964-70; exec. dir. Polk Mus. Art, Lakeland, Fla., 1970-75; dir. Mus. Arts and Sci., Evansville, Ind., 1975—; chmn. mus. adv. panel Ind. Arts Commn., 1977-78. Mem. Am. Assn. Museums, Assn. Ind. Museums (bd. dirs.) Episcopalian. Office: Evansville Mus Arts History and Sci 411 SE Riverside Dr Evansville IN 47713-1037

**STREFF, WILLIAM ALBERT, JR.,** lawyer; b. Chgo., Aug. 12, 1949; s. William Albert Streff Sr. and Margaret (McKeough) Streff Fisher; m. Kathleen Myslinski, Sept. 29, 1984; children: Amanda, William III, Kimberly. BS, Northwestern U., 1971, JD cum laude, 1974. Bar: Ill. 1974, U.S. Dist. Ct. (no. dist.) Ill. 1974, U.S. Dist. Ct. (no. dist.) N.Y. 1987, U.S. Dist. Ct. (no. dist.) Calif. 1988, U.S. Ct. Appeals (7th cir.) 1980, U.S. Ct. Appeals (9th cir.) 1988, U.S. Ct. Customs and Patent Appeals, 1978, U.S. Ct. Appeals (3rd cir.), 1992, U.S. Ct. Internat. Trade, 1996, Supreme Ct. State Ill. Legal writing instr. Law Sch. Northwestern U., Chgo., 1973—74; assoc. Kirkland & Ellis LLP, Chgo., 1974—80, ptnr., 1980—. Lectr. Ill. Inst. Continuing Legal Edn., 1984; adj. prof. Northwestern U. Law Sch., 1992-94, 97-2000, Chgo. Kent-IIT Law Sch., 1998, John Marshall Law Sch., 2000-03. Contbr. articles to profl. jours. Mem. adv. bd. Ill. Inst. Tech./Chgo.-Kent, 1983-86; trustee Northwestern U., Evanston, 1984-86, mem. vis. com. Law Sch., Chgo., 1988-94. Mem. ABA. Office: Kirkland & Ellis LLP 200 E Randolph Dr Chicago IL 60601-6636 Office Phone: 312-861-2126. Office Fax: 312-861-2200. Business E-Mail: wstreff@kirkland.com.

**STREHLKE, CARL BRANDON,** art historian, curator; b. Newton, Mass., July 15, 1955; s. Richard Brandon and Rose Maria (Ravera Barocco) S. BA, Columbia U., 1978, MA, 1979, M in Philosophy, 1981, PhD, 1985. Researcher Bkyln. Mus., 1979-82; asst. curator Phila. Mus. Art, 1984—. Vis. assoc. prof. of art history, Johns Hopkins U., 1990—. Collaborator The Burlington Mag., London. Office: John G Johnson Coll Phila Mus Art Philadelphia PA 19101

**STREICHER, JAMES FRANKLIN,** retired lawyer; b. Ashtabula, Ohio, Dec. 6, 1940; s. Carl Jacob and Helen Marie (Dugan) S.; m. Sandra JoAnn Jennings, May 22, 1940; children: Cheryl Ann, Gregory Scott, Kerry Marie. BA, Ohio State U., 1962; JD, Case Western Res. U., 1966. Bar: Ohio 1966, U.S. Dist. Ct. (no. dist.) Ohio 1966. Assoc. Calfee, Halter & Griswold, Cleve., 1966—2005; ret., 2005. Bd. dirs. Provider Gateway, Inc., Sensir Technologies, Stamford, Conn., Mid Am. Consulting; mem. Divsn. Securities Adv. Bd., State of Ohio; lectr. Case Western Res. U., Cleve. State U.; mem. pvt. sector com. John Carroll U. Former trustee Achievement Ctr. for Children, Western Res. Hist. Soc., Make-A-Wish Found. Endowment. Mem. ABA, Fed. Bar Assn., Ohio State Bar Assn., Assn. for Corp. Growth, Ohio Venture Assn., No. Ohio Venture Assn. (trustee), Greater Cleve. Bar Assn. (founding chmn. corp., banking, bus. law sect.), Ohio State U. Alumni Assn., Case Western Res. U. Alumni Assn., Newcomen Soc., Bluecoats Club (Cleve.), Mayfield Country (bd. dirs. 1985-89), Union Club, The Pepper Pike Club, The Tavern Club, Beta Theta Pi, Phi Delta Phi. Roman Catholic. Republican. Office Phone: 216-408-3919. Office Fax: 216-241-0816. Business E-Mail: jstreicher@comcast.net.

**STREIFF, ARLYNE BASTUNAS,** business owner, educator; b. Sacramento, Calif., Nov. 04; d. Peter James and Isabel (Gemnas) Bastunas; children: Peter Joshua, Joshua Gus. BS, U. Nev., 1965; postgrad., U. Calif., Davis, 1965-68, Calif. State U., Chico, 1968, 71. Cert. elem. tchr., Calif., Nev., cert. in English-specially designed lang. acad. instrn. devel. in English. Tchr. reading, lang. and kindergarten Enterprise Elem. Sch. Dist., Redding, Calif., 1965-98, tchr. kindergarten, 1988-98; owner, pres. Arlyne's Svcs., Redding, Calif., 1990—. Author: Niko and His Friends, 1989, Niko The Black Rottweiler, 1995, Color-Talk-Spell. Mem. Rep. Women, Five County Labor Coun., Redding, 1974-93, Calif. Labor Fedn., 1974-93, AFL-CIO, 1974-97. Named Tchr. of Yr., Enterprise Sch. Dist., 1969. Mem. AAUW, Am. Fedn. Tchrs., Calif. Tchrs. Assn. (bargaining spokesperson 1968-72, exec. bd. dirs.), United Tchrs. Enterprise (pres. 1979-80, chmn. lang. com.), Calif. Reading Assn., Enterprise Fedn. Tchrs. (pres. 1974, pres.-elect 1995-97), Calif. State Fedn. Tchrs. (v.p. 1974-75, exec. bd. 1995-97), Redding C. of C., Women of Moose, Elks. Avocations: home interior design, real estate, construction, creative writing, educational advancement. Office: Arlynes Svcs 1468 Benton Dr Redding CA 96003-3116

**STREISAND, BARBRA JOAN,** singer, actress, film director; b. Bklyn., Apr. 24, 1942; d. Emanuel and Diana (Rosen) S.; m. Elliott Gould, Mar. 1963 (div.); 1 son, Jason Emanuel; m. James Brolin, July 1, 1998. Grad. high sch. Bklyn.; student, Yeshiva of Bklyn.; Doctorate of Arts and Humanities (hon.), Brandeis U., 1995. NY theatre debut Another Evening with Harry Stoones, 1961; appeared in Broadway musicals I Can Get It for You Wholesale, 1962, Funny Girl, 1964-65; motion pictures include Funny Girl, 1968, Hello Dolly, 1969, On a Clear Day You Can See Forever, 1970, The Owl and the Pussy Cat, 1970, What's Up Doc?, 1972, Up the Sandbox, 1972, The Way We Were, 1973, For Pete's Sake, 1974, Funny Lady, 1975, The Main Event, 1979, All

Night Long, 1981, Nuts, 1987, Meet the Fockers, 2004; actor, prodr. (film): A Star is Born, 1976; prodr., dir., actor: Yentl, 1983, The Prince of Tides, 1991, The Mirror Has Two Faces, 1996 (ASCAP Award for score, 1996); exec. prodr.: (TV movie) Serving in Silence: The Margarethe Cammermeyer Story, 1995; TV spls. include My Name is Barbra, 1965 (5 Emmy awards), Color Me Barbra, 1966, Barbra Streisand: The Concert, 1995 (Cable ACE award for best performance and for best direction, Two Emmy awards), Barbra Streisand: Timeless, 2001 (Emmy award); rec. artist on Columbia Records; Gold record albums include People, 1965, My Name is Barbra, 1965, Color Me Barbra, 1966, Barbra Streisad: A Happening in Central Park, 1968, Barbra Streisand: One Voice, Stoney End, 1971, Barbra Joan Streisand, 1972, The Way We Were, 1974, A Star is Born, 1976, Superman, 1977, The Stars Salute Israel at 30, 1978, Wet, 1979, (with Barry Gibb) Guilty, 1980, Emotion, 1984, The Broadway Album, 1986, Til I Loved You, 1989; other albums include: A Collection: Greatest Hits, 1989, Just for the Record, 1991, Back to Broadway, 1993, Concert at the Forum, 1993, The Concert Recorded Live at Madison Square Garden, 1994, The Concert Highlights, 1995, Higher Ground, 1997, A Love Like Ours, 1999, Christmas Memories, 2001, The Essential Barbara Streisand, 2002, The Movie Album, 2003, Guilty Pleasures, 2005, Guilty Too, 2005, Nur das Beste, 2006. Recipient Emmy award, CBS-TV spl. (My Name Is Barbra), 1964, Acad. award as best actress (Funny Girl), 1968, Golden Globe award (Funny Girl), 1969, co-recipient Acad. award for best song (Evergreen), 1976, Georgie award AGVA 1977, Grammy awards for best female pop vocalist, 1963, 64, 65, 77, 86, for best song writer (with Paul Williams), 1977, 2 Grammy nominations for Back to Broadway, 1994; Nat. Acad. of Recording Arts & Sciences Lifetime Achievement Award, 1994, Cecil B. Demille Lifetime Achievement Award, 2000, Life Achievement award, Am. Film Inst., 2001, Liberty & Justice Award, Rainbow/PUSH Coalition, 2001, Humanitarian award, Human Rights Campaign, 2004. Office: Barbra Streisand c/o Martin Erlichman Assoc Inc 5670 Wilshire Blvd Ste 2400 Los Angeles CA 90036 also: Nigro Karlin Segal 10100 Santa Monica Blvd Ste 1300 Los Angeles CA 90067

**STREIT, MICHAEL J.,** state supreme court justice; b. Sheldon, Iowa, Apr. 14, 1950; married; 1 child. BA, U. Iowa, 1972; grad., U. San Diego Sch. Law, 1975. Cert.: (U.S. Ct. Appeals) 1996. Atty. priv. practice, 1975—83; asst. atty. Lucas County, 1975—79, atty., 1979—83; judge Iowa Dist. Ct., Fifth Judicial Dist., 1983—96, Iowa Ct. of Appeals, 1996—2001; justice Iowa Supreme Ct., 2001—. Mem. Iowa Supreme Ct. Education Advisory Com., Iowa Supreme Ct. Judicial Technology Com., Judges Assn. Education Com. Mem.: Iowa State Bar Assn., Blackstone Inn of Ct., Iowa Jud. Inst. Office: Iowa Supreme Ct Jud Branch Bldg 1111 E Ct Ave Des Moines IA 50319*

**STREITWIESER, ANDREW, JR.,** chemistry professor; b. Buffalo, June 23, 1927; s. Andrew and Sophie Streitwieser; m. Mary Ann Good, Aug. 19, 1950 (dec. May 1965); children: David Roy, Susan Ann; m. Suzanne Cope Beier, July 29, 1967 (dec. Apr. 2006). AB, Columbia U., 1949, MA, 1950, PhD, 1952; postgrad. (AEC fellow), MIT, 1951-52. Faculty U. Calif, Berkeley, 1952-92, prof. chemistry, 1963-92, prof. emeritus, 1993—. Cons. to industry, 1957—. Author: Molecular Orbital Theory for Organic Chemists, 1961, Solvolytic Displacement Reactions, 1962, (with J.I. Brauman) Supplemental Tables of Molecular Orbital Calculations, 1965, (with C.A. Coulson) Dictionary of Pi Electron Calculations, 1965, (with P.H. Owens) Orbital and Electron Density Diagrams, 1973, (with C.H. Heathcock and E.M. Kosower) Introduction to Organic Chemistry, 4th edit., 1992, A Lifetime of Synergy with Theory and Experiment, 1996; also numerous articles; co-editor: Progress in Physical Organic Chemistry, 11 vols., 1963-74. Recipient Humboldt Found. Sr. Scientist award, 1976, Humboldt medal, 1979, Berkeley citation, 1993. Fellow AAAS; mem. NAS, Am. Chem. Soc. (Calif. sect. award 1964, award in Petroleum Chemistry 1967, Norris award in phys. organic chemistry 1982, Cope scholar award 1989), Am. Acad. Arts and Scis., Bavarian Acad. Scis. (corr.), Phi Beta Kappa, Sigma Xi. Achievements include research in organic reaction mechanisms; application molecular orbital theory to organic chemistry; chemical structures on carbon acidities; f-element organometallic chemistry. Office: U Calif Dept Chemistry Berkeley CA 94720-1460 Office Phone: 510-642-2204. Business E-Mail: astreit@berkeley.edu.

**STREKOWSKI, LUCJAN,** chemistry professor; came to U.S., 1981; s. Antoni and Janina S.; m. Alewtina Smirnova, Oct. 14, 1967; children: Rafal, Anna. BS in Polymer Chemistry with distinction, Mendeleev Inst. Chemistry, Moscow, 1967; PhD in Organic Chemistry, Polish Acad. Scis., 1972; DSc in Chemistry, Adam Mickiewicz U., Poznan, Poland, 1976. Instr. organic chemistry Adam Mickiewicz U., Poznan, 1971-72, asst. prof. dept. chemistry, 1972-78, assoc. prof. dept. chemistry, 1978-81; rsch. assoc. dept. chemistry U. Fla., Gainesville, 1981-84; asst. prof. dept. chemistry Ga. State U., Atlanta, 1984-89, assoc. prof. dept. chemistry, 1989-96, prof. dept. chem., 1996—. Vis. prof. U. Fla., Gainesville, 1979-80, 81, Australian Nat. U., 1980, U. Kans., Lawrence, 1972-73. Editor: Pyridine-Metal Complexes, Vol. 14, Part 6, 1985; N.Am. editor Heterocyclic Comms., mem. editl. bd. Arkivoc; contbr. more than 250 articles to profl. jours.; patentee in field. Recipient award, Polish Ministry Sci., 1997, Polish Chem. Soc., 1973, Polish Acad. Scis., 1972, Ga. State U., 1993; grantee Am. Chem. Soc.-Petroleum Rsch. Fund, 1985—2006, Solvay Pharms., 1992—93, Nat. Diagnostics, 1991—93, NIAID/NIMH, 1988—89, Rohm and Hass Co., 1988, Am. Cancer Soc., 1987—89, Rsch. Corp., 1985—94, Milheim Found. Cancer Rsch., 1985—86, DuPont Co., 1996—2000, Small Bus. Innovation Rsch. Program, 2000—02, FBI, 2002—, Coley Pharms., 2003—04, Ga. Rsch. Alliance, 2004—05. Mem. Am. Chem. Soc., Internat. Soc. Heterocyclic Chemistry, Internat. Acad. Scis. of Nature and Soc. (mem. presidium). Avocation: classical music. Office: Ga State Univ Dept Chemistry Atlanta GA 30303 Office Phone: 404-651-0999. Business E-Mail: lucjan@gsu.edu.

**STRENA, ROBERT VICTOR,** lab administrator, director; b. Seattle, June 28, 1929; s. Robert Lafayette Peel and Mary Oliva (Holmes) S.; m. Rita Mae Brodovsky, Aug. 1957; children: Robert Victor, Adrienne Amelia. AB, Stanford U., 1952. Survey mathematician Hazen Engring., San Jose, Calif., 1952-53; field engr. Menlo Sanitary Dist., Menlo Park, Calif., 1954-55; ind. fin. reporter Los Altos, Calif., 1953-59; asst. dir. Hansen Labs. Stanford U., 1959-93, asst. dir. emeritus Ginzton Lab., 1993—. Ind. fin. cons., Los Altos, 1965—; mem. restoration adv. bd., Moffett Fed. Airfield, 1994-2003. Active Edn. System Politics, Los Altos, 1965-80, local Boy Scouts Am., 1968-80, Maj. USAR, 1948-70. Mem. AAAS, Mus. Soc., Big X (Los Altos), Cherry Chase Golf Club. Republican. Avocations: golf, sailing. Home: 735 Raymundo Ave Los Altos CA 94024-3139 Office: Stanford U Ginzton Lab Stanford CA 94305 Office Phone: 650-960-1776. Business E-Mail: strena@stanford.edu.

**STRENG, WILLIAM PAUL,** lawyer, educator; b. Sterling, Ill., Oct. 17, 1937; s. William D. and Helen Marie (Conklen) S.; children: Sarah, John. BA, Wartburg Coll., 1959; JD, Northwestern U., 1962. Bar: Iowa 1962, Ill. 1962, Ohio 1964, Tex. 1975. Law clk. to U.S. circuit judge Lester L. Cecil, Cin., 1963-64; assoc. firm Taft, Stettinius & Hollister, Cin., 1964-70; atty.-advisor Office Sec. Tax Policy, Office Tax Legis. Counsel, Dept. Treasury, Washington, 1970-71; dep. gen. counsel Export-Import Bank U.S., Washington, 1971-73; prof. law Sch. Law, So. Methodist U., Dallas, 1973-80; vis. prof. Coll. Law Ohio State U., Columbus, 1977; ptnr. firm Bracewell & Patterson, Houston, 1980-85; Vinson & Elkins prof. of law U. Houston Law Ctr, 1985—. Vis. prof. Rice U., NYU Law Sch., 1990, U. Tex. Sch. Law, 2002, Yokohama (Japan) Nat. U., 2005; disting. vis. prof. U. Hong Kong Law Faculty, 1992; Fulbright prof. U. Stockholm Law Faculty, 1993; vis. fellow law faculty Victoria U., Wellington, New Zealand, 1996; vis. law lectr. U. Leiden, The Netherlands, 1997, The Netherlands, 98, The Netherlands, 2000; cons. Bracewell & Patterson (now Bracewell & Giuliani), 1985—; lectr. various confs. Am. Law Inst., World Trade Inst., Practicing Law Inst. Internat. Fiscal Assn., ABA, Tex. State Bar. Author: International Business Transactions-Tax and Legal Handbook, 1978, Estate Planning, 1991, 2006, International Business Planning: Law and Taxation, 6 vols., 1982, 2005, Tax Planning for Retirement, 2001, revised edit., 2005, Doing Business in China, 1990, 1996, Federal Income Taxation of Corporations and Shareholders--

Forms, 1995—2005, 2005, Choice of Entity, 1994, 1999, U.S. International Estate Planning, 1996, revised, 2006. Served with USMC, 1962. Lutheran. Home: 1903 Dunstan Rd Houston TX 77005-1619 Office: U Houston Law Ctr Houston TX 77204-6060 Office Phone: 713-743-2148. Business E-Mail: wstreng@uh.edu.

**STRETCH, JOHN JOSEPH,** social worker, educator, management consultant; b. St. Louis, Feb. 24, 1935; s. John Joseph and Theresa Carmelita (Fleming) S.; children: Paul, Leonmarie, Sylvan, Adrienne, Sharonalice; m. Barbara Ann Stewart, Mar. 16, 1985; children: Margaret, Thomas. AB, Maryknoll Coll., Glen Ellyn, Ill., 1957; MSW, Washington U., St. Louis, 1961; PhD, Tulane U., 1967; MBA, St. Louis U., 1980. LCSW 1985. Instr. Tulane U., 1962—68, asst. prof., 1968; assoc. prof. social work St. Louis U., 1968—71, prof., 1972—, asst. dean Sch. Social Service, 1976-87, dir. doctoral studies, 1976-94, dir. MSW. program, 1985-86, bd. dirs., exec. com. Ctr. for Social Justice, 1987—, instnl. rev. bd. Sch. Social Svc., 1987—92; dir. rsch. Social Welfare Planning Coun. Met. New Orleans, 1962—68. Cons. to United Way Met. St. Louis, Cath. Charities of Archdiocese of St. Louis, Cath. Svcs. for Children and Youth, Full Achievement, Mo. Province of S.J., Cath. Commn. on Housing, Cath. Family Svcs., Youth Emergency Svcs., Mo. State Dept. Social Svcs., U. Mo. Extension Svc., St. Joseph's Home for Boys, Marian Hall Ctr. for Adolescent Girls, Boys Town-Girls Town of Mo., A World of Difference, Anti Defamation League of B'nai Brith, Prog. Youth Ctr., Foster Care Coalition of Greater St. Louis, Rankin-Jordan Children's Rehab. Hosp., 1999-2000, Ill. St. Claire County Sch. Sys.'s Old Man River Project, 2002—2005; expert witness on homeless U.S. House Select Com. on Families, Children and Youth, 1987; resource spl. task force on homeless Office of Sec. U.S. Dept. HUD, 1989, survey design cons. U.S. Office of The Insp. Gen., 1990; methodology expert on homelessness U.S. Census Bur., 1989; expert homeless policy GAO hearings, 1992; chair Mo. Assn. for Social Welfare Low Income Housing, 1982—; chmn. St. Louis Low Income Housing Preservation Com., 1985; mem. Comprehensive Housing Affordabiltiy Strategies (CHAS) Mo. Statewide Planning Group, Mo. Housing Devel. CHAS citizen's com., State of Mo. Affordable House Task Force, Mo. Housing Devel. Corp., 1998-2002, Mo. Inst. Psychiatry, 1995, University City Sch. Dist., 1990; mgmt. cons. People's Issues Task Force Agrl. div. Monsanto Chem. Inc., 1992, regional office NCCJ, 1990-92; vis. prof. Nat. Cath. U. Am. Sch. Social Svcs., 1991, 92, U. Bristol, Eng., 1992, U. Calif. Sch. Pub. Health, Berkeley, 1990; cons. Mo. Speaker of the Ho. statewide legis. task force, 1990-92, Russian Am. Summer U., 2000; statewide grant project reviewer emergency shelter grant program Mo. Dept. Social Svcs., 1989—, chair, 2000—; homeless svcs. grant reviewer City of St. Louis, 1996-97. Mem editl. bd. Social Work, 1968-74, Health Progress, 1988—01, Social Work Administration, 2003—; manuscript referee Jour. Social Svc. Rsch., 1977-99; mgmt. and evaluation content referee Wadsworth Press, Human Svcs. Press, Allyn and Bacon Press, Haworth Press; editor, contbr. chpts. to books, articles to profl. jours. Bd. dirs. Beyond Housing, Inc. 1985—, pres., 1993-95, St. Louis U. Ctr. for Social Justice, 1990—, Housing Comes First, 1995-99, Adequate Housing for Missourians, 2002—, Neighborhood Housing Svcs., 2004—2005, Nat. Coalition for Homeless, 2004—; mem. Mo. Assn. Social Welfare, 1980—, DuBourg Soc. of St. Louis U., 1989; mem. Salvation Army Family Haven, 1987, 2000—, mem. adv. bd., 1988-92; bd. dirs., exec. com. Cmty. Asset Mgmt. Co. chmn. United Way of Greater St. Louis venture grant com., 1988-91, vice chmn. day care allocation com., 1985-95, mem. process and rev. com., 1991-93, inter-orgnl. priorities com., 1991-93; mem. leadership coun. Success By Six, 1990—2004; organizer Mo. State Nat. Coalition for the Homeless, 1989; appointee instl. representation nat. Jesuits social concern group St. Louis U., 1993—; mem. exec. and support tng. group, St. Louis U., 1987-92; mem. instnl. rev. bd., 1979-99. NIMH Career Leadership Devel. fellow, 1965-67, Fed. Ednl. grantee Ill. Sch. Sys., 2002; recipient Scholar of Yr. award Sch. Social Svc., St. Louis U., 1987; named Vol. of Yr. Ecumenical Housing Prodn. Corp., 1990; Presdl. scholar Sch. Social Svc., 1992, Fulbright Sr. scholar, 2004—. Mem. AAUP (St. Louis U. chpt. exec. com. 1990—2003, pres. 1994—2003), ACLU (chair compensation benefits com. St. Louis faculty senate 2004-2005), Acad. Cert. Social Workers (charter mem.), Nat. Assn. Social Workers, Mo. Assn. for Social Welfare (bd. dirs., Outstanding State-Wide Mem. of Yr. 1987, nominee Elaine Aber Humanitarian award 2005), Coun. on Social Work Edn., Common Cause, Amnesty Internat., Nat. Consumer's Coun. on vital and health stats.), U.S. Census Bur. (subcom. on health stats. for minorities and other spl. populations of U.S. Dem.). Democrat. Roman Catholic. Home: 9100 Litzsinger Rd Saint Louis MO 63144-2214 Office: 3550 Lindell Blvd Saint Louis MO 63103-1021 Office Phone: 314-977-2715. Business E-Mail: stretchj@slu.edu. *My entire professional life has been in the field of social work. My personal and professional values are derived from a dual commitment to empower the uniqueness of individuals and to enhance the development of caring communities. These goals have organized and directed my professional practice, teaching and writing. I believe that the profession of social work has a unique and singular mission in society. That mission is to advocate for and consciously bring about the social development of all people.*

**STREVEY, TRACY ELMER, JR.,** army officer, surgeon, health facility administrator; b. Shorewood, Wis., Apr. 24, 1933; s. Tracy Elmer and Margaret (Rees) S.; m. Victoria Crowley (div.); children: Virginia Ann, Tracy Elmer III, Andrew Victor; m. Elizabeth Sommers; children: Stephanie Jean, James Sommers. Student, Pomona Coll., 1951-54; MD, U. So. Calif., 1958; student, Armed Forces Staff Coll., 1970-71, U.S. Army War Coll., 1977-78. Diplomate Am. Bd. Surgery, Am. Bd. Thoracic Surgery. Intern Los Angeles County Gen. Hosp., 1958-59; commd. officer U.S. Army, 1959, advanced through grades to maj. gen., 1983; resident in gen. surgery Letterman Gen. Hosp., San Francisco, 1962-66; resident in thoracic and cardiovascular surgery Walter Reed Gen. Hosp., Washington, 1968-70; commdg. officer 757 Med. Detachment OA, Ludwigsburg, Germany, 1959-61; ward officer orthopaedic svc. 75th Sta. Hosp., Stuttgart, Fed. Republic Germany, 1961-62; chief profl. svc., chief surgery 85th Evacuation Hosp., Qui Nhon, Vietnam, 1967; commdg. officer 3d Surg. Hosp., Dong Tam, Vietnam, 1967-68; asst. chief thoracic and cardiovascular surgery service Fitzsimons Army Med Ctr., Denver, 1971-73, chief thoracic and cardiovascular surgery service, 1973-75; asst. dir. med. activities and dir. Profl. Edn. Gorgas Hosp., Panama Canal Zone, 1975-77; chief dept. surgery Walter Reed Army Med. Ctr., Washington, 1978-81; commdr. Brooke Army Med. Ctr., Ft. Sam Houston, Tex., 1981-83, Tripler Army Med. Ctr., Hawaii, 1983-86, U.S. Army Health Svcs. Command, San Antonio, 1986-88; ret. U.S. Army, 1988; CEO Nassau County Med. Ctr., 1988-93; pres., CEO N.Y. Hosp Med. Ctr. Queens, N.Y.C., 1993-94; v.p. N.Y. Hosp. Care Network, N.Y.C., 1994-95; v.p. for med. affairs Sisters of Mercy Health Sys., St. Louis, 1995-99; prin. Strevey Cons. Assocs., LLC, 1999—2003. Asst. clin. prof. surgery U. Colo. Med. Ctr., Denver, 1973-75; prof. surgery Uniformed Services U. Health Scis., Bethesda, 1978-2003, vice chmn. dept. surgery, 1978-81 Contbr. articles to profl. jours. Mem. reg. bd. Am. Heart Assn. Decorated D.S.M., Legion of Merit with 2 oak leaf clusters, Meritorious Service medal with 2 oak leaf clusters, Purple Heart, Army Commendation Medal for Valor, Vietnam Cross of Gallantry with Palm; recipient Outstanding Service award U. So. Calif. Alumni Assn., 1983 Fellow ACS, Am. Coll. Chest Physicians, Am. Coll. Cardiology, Am. Coll. Physician Execs. (disting.); mem. Assn. Mil. Surgeons U.S., Soc. Thoracic Surgeons, Western Thoracic Surg. Assn., Am. Assn. Thoracic Surgery, Masons. Avocations: ham radio, scuba diving, golf, computers. Home and Office: 1509 Woodgate Dr Saint Louis MO 63131-4724 Personal E-mail: tstrevey@aol.com.

**STREVIG, JANICE LEE,** music educator; b. Baltimore, Md., Oct. 19, 1957; BS, Towson U., Towson, Maryland, 1975—79; postgrad., U. Iowa, 1980—90, Temple U., 1980—90, Bucknell U., 1980—90, Towson U., 1980—90, Peabody Conservatory, 1980—90. Tchr. Balt. County Pub. Schools, Baltimore, Md., 1980—. Freelance pit musician, Md., 1980—; performer Sentimental Journey Big Band, Balt., 1980—; pvt. clarinet tchr., Balt., 1979—95. Girls fastpitch softball coach Lansdowne (Md.) H.S. Jayvee, 1989—97; soloist Catonsville (Md.) United Meth. Ch., 1998—, dir. vocal ensemble, 2000—. Mem. Md. Music Educators Assn. (chm. exhibits 1987—,

bd. dirs. 1987—), Music Educators Nat. Conf. (25 Yr. Svc. award 2004), Kappa Delta Pi (v.p. 1978—79). United Methodist. Avocations: playing women's baseball, crossword puzzles, reading. Office Phone: 410-887-0854. Personal E-mail: jbrahms@comcast.net.

**STRIANESE, MICHAEL T.,** corporate financial executive; CPA. With Ernst & Young; dir. spl. projects Loral Skynet, 1991—96; v.p. & contr., C31 & systems integration ctr. Lockheed Martin, 1996—97; v.p. fin., contr. L-3 Communications, NYC, 1997—2000, sr. v.p. fin., 2000—05, sr. v.p., CFO, 2005—; interim CEO L-3 Commnucations, NYC, 2006—. Office: L-3 Communications 600 Third Ave New York NY 10016*

**STRICK, JEREMY,** curator; BA in History of Art with highest honors, U. Calif., Santa Cruz, 1977; postgrad., Harvard U. Asst. curator 20th Century art Nat. Gallery Art, Washington, 1986-89, assoc. curator 20th Century art, 1989-93, acting dept. dept. 20th Century art, 1992-93, curator Nat. Sculpture Garden project, 1989-93; curator modern art St. Louis Art Mus., 1993-96; Frances and Thomas Dittmer curator 20th Century painting and sculpture Art Inst. Chgo., 1996-99; dir. Mus. Contemporary Art, L.A., 1999—. Curator N.Y. Interpreted: Joseph Stella and Alfred Stieglitz, Nat. Gallery Art, 1987, Milton Avery, 1990, Mark Rothko: The Spirit Myth, 1990-95, asst. curator A Century of Modern Sculpture: The Patsy and Raymond Nasher Collection, 1987, co-curator Twentieth-Century Art: Selections for the Tenth Anniversary of the East Building, 1987; curator Brice Marden: A Painting, Drawings, Prints, St. Louis Art Mus., 1993, Currents 58: Susan Crile—The Fires of War, 1994, Louise Bourgeois: The Personages 1946-1954, 1995, Currents 60: Jerald Ioans, 1994, Masterworks from Stuttgart: The Romantic Age in German Art, 1995, Currents 66: Michael Byron, 1996, Currents 67: Leonardo Drew, 1996; curator The Sublime Is Now: The Early Work of Barnett Newman, Walker Art Ctr., Mpls., Pace Gallery, N.Y.C., 1994; curator In the Light of Italy: Corot and Early Open-Air Painting, Nat. Gallery Art, Bklyn. Mus., St. Louis Art Mus., 1996; lectr., symposia participant and organizer, 1981—; juror Showhegan awards, 1995. Contbg. author: Works by Antoine-Louis Barye in the Collection of the Fogg Art Museum, Vol. IV, 1982; contbr. articles to exhbn. catalogs, newspapers, mags., ency. Instnl. fellow Samuel H. Kress Found., Paris, 1983-85, fellow Mrs. Giles Whiting Found., 1985-86. Office: Mus Contemporary Art Dept 20th Century Painting 250 S Grand Ave Los Angeles CA 90012-3021 Home: 261 N Bundy Dr Los Angeles CA 90049-2825 E-mail: jstrick@moca.org.

**STRICK, PETER LEONARD,** psychiatrist, neurologist, educator; PhD in Neuroanatomy, U. Penn. Rschr. NIH, 1972—76; prof. neurosurgery & physiology Syracuse U., 1976—89; prof. dept. psychiatry & neurobiology U. Pittsburgh, 2000—; co-dir. Ctr. for Neural Basis of Cognition, Caregie Mellon U., 2004—. Fellow: Am. Acad. Arts & Sciences; mem.: Soc. for Neuroscience (former treasurer). Office: U Pittsburgh W1640 Biomedical Science Tower 200 Lothrop St Pittsburgh PA 15261 also: Carnegie Mellon U Ctr Neural Basis of Cognition 4400 Fifth Ave Pittsburgh PA 15213

**STRICKHOLM, JEAN,** retired elementary school educator, musician; b. Madison, Wis., Oct. 27, 1933; d. Hulsey and Eloise May (Boeker) Cason; m. Harry Jean Cason Strickholm, June 30, 1956; children: Karen, Sally Tayeb, Douglas, Glenn. Student, Red Fox Music Camp, Marlboro, Mass., 1952—54; BS, U. Rochester, Rochester, N.Y., 1955; MS, Queens Coll., Flushing, N.Y., 1959. Cert. tchr. N.Y. Dept. Edn., 1955; elem. edn. K-12 N.J. Dept. Edn., 1969, tchr. social studies K-12 N.J. Dept. Edn., 1973. Tchr. Gt. Neck Pub. Schs., Gt. Neck, NY, 1955—58, Tenefly Pub. Schs., NJ, 1969—70, Englewood Pub. Schs., NJ, 1970—98, ret., 1998. Co-dir., mgr., fund raiser, performer All Seasons Chamber Players, Demarest, NJ, 1981—. Chmn. Bergen County Equal Opportunities Study Com., Hackensack, NJ, 1969—70; active Civil Rights Movement Bergen County, 1961—70. Recipient award, Bergen County Fair Housing Coun., 1961—70. Mem.: Chamber Music Am. (assoc.). Democrat. Avocations: swimming, gardening, reading. Office Phone: 201-768-1331.

**STRICKLAND, ANITA MAURINE,** retired business educator, librarian; b. Groom, Tex., Sept. 24, 1923; d. Oliver Austin and Thelma May (Slay) Pool; m. LeRoy Graham Mashburn, Aug. 12, 1945 (dec. Mar. 1977); 1 child, Ronald Gene; m. Reid Strickland, May 27, 1978. BBA, West Tex. State U., 1962, MEd, 1965; postgrad. in library sci., Tex. Women's U., 1970. Cert. tchr., Tex.; cert. librarian. Employment interviewer Douglas Aircraft Co., Oklahoma City, 1942-45; cashier, bookkeeper Southwestern Pub. Services, Groom and Panhandle, Tex., 1950-58; acct. Gen. Motors Outlet, Groom, 1958-62; tchr. bus., lang. arts Groom Pub. Schs., 1962-68; bus. tchr., librarian Amarillo (Tex.) Pub. Schs., 1968-81. Vol. Amarillo Symphony, 1980—, Amarillo Rep. Com., 1981—, Lone Star Ballet, 1981-92; docent Amarillo Mus. Art, 1987—, sec. 1982-90, 93-94, treas., 1987-91; sec. Amarillo Art Alliance, 1989-90. Mem. AAUW (legis. com. 1986-88, sec. 1989-90, bd. dirs. 1989-91), Amarillo C. of C. (vol. women's divsn. 1981-86), Amarillo Christian Women's Club (asst. prayer advisor 1989-90, treas. 1995-96). Baptist. Avocations: piano, reading, swimming, tennis. Home: 6513 Roxton Dr Amarillo TX 79109-5120

**STRICKLAND, ANTHONY,** state representative; b. Fort Ord, Calif., Feb. 17, 1970; m. Audra Strickland. Student, Cochise C.C., Ariz.; BA in Polit. Sci., Whittier Coll. Calif. Mem. Calif. Assembly, 1998—. Mem. adv. bd. Food Share; founding pres. So. Calif. Taxpayers' Alliance; hon. bd. dirs. Doris Tate Crime Victims' Bur.; bd. dirs.Go N Strong Basketball Camp; hon. bd. dirs. Moorpark Boys & Girls Club; bd. dirs. Ventura County United Way. Republican Office: PO Box 942849 Rm 4098 Sacramento CA 94249 Address: 2659 Townsgate Rd Westlake Village CA 91361

**STRICKLAND, ARVARH EUNICE,** history professor; b. Hattiesburg, Miss., July 6, 1930; s. Eunice and Clotiel (Marshall) S.; m. Willie Pearl Elmore, June 17, 1951; children: Duane Arvarh, Bruce Elmore. BA, Tougaloo Coll., 1951; MA, U. Ill., 1953, PhD, 1962. Tchr. Hattiesburg Schs., 1951-52; instr. Tuskegee Inst., 1955-56; prin. supr. Madison County Schs., Canton, Miss., 1956-59; asst. prof. history Chgo. State U., 1962-65, assoc. prof. history, 1965-68, prof. 1968-69, U. Mo., Columbia, 1969-96, prof. emeritus, 1996—, chmn. dept. history, 1980-83, interim dir. black studies program, 1994-96, sr. faculty assoc., Office of V.P. acad. affairs, 1987-88, assoc. v.p. acad. affairs, 1989-91. Author: History of the Chicago Urban League, 1966, reprint, 2001, (with Reich and Biller) Building the United States, 1971, (with Reich) The Black American Experience to 1877, 1974, The Black American Experience since 1877, 1974; editor: Working with Carter G. Woodson, (with Lorenzo J. Greene) The Father of Black History: A Diary, 1930-33, 1989, Selling Black History for Carter G. Woodson: A Diary, 1930-33, 1996, (with Robert E. Weems) The African American Experience: A Historiographical and Bibliographical Guide, 2000. Commr. Planning and Zoning, Columbia, Mo., 1977-80, Boone County Home Rule Charter, 1982, Mo. Peace Officers Standards and Tng. Commn., 1988-89; co-chmn. Mayors Com. to Commemorate Contbns. of Black Columbians, Columbia, 1981; mem. exec. subcom. Mayor's Ad Hoc Election '82 Com., 1982; bd. dirs. Harry S. Truman Library Inst., 1987-96, U. of Mo.-Columbia Health Sys., 2003—. Recipient Disting. Svc. award Ill. Hist. Soc., 1957, Byler Disting. Prof. award U. Mo., 1994, St. Louis Am.'s Educator of Yr. award, 1994, Disting. Faculty award U. Mo.-Columbia Alumni Assn., 1995, Tougaloo Coll. Alumni Hall of Fame, 1995, Alumni Achievement U. Ill. Coll. Liberal Arts and Scis., 1997, Disting. Svc. award State Hist. Soc. Mo., 1997. Mem. Orgn. Am. Historians, Am. Hist. Assn., Assn. Study Afro-Am. Life and History (Carter Godwin Woodson Scholars medallion 1999), So. Hist. Assn., State Hist. Soc. Mo. (Disting. Svc. award 1997), Boone County Hist. Soc. 1998-2002, 2d v.p. 1999, 1st v.p. 2000-02), Kiwanis, Alpha Phi Alpha, Phi Alpha Theta (internat. v.p. 1991-93, pres. 1994-95, chair adv. bd. 1996-97, Disting. Svc. award 1997, Columbia Values Diversity award, 2005). Democrat. Methodist. Home: 4100 Defoe Dr Columbia MO 65203-0252 Office: U Mo Dept History 101 Read Hall Columbia MO 65211-7500 E-mail: stricklanda@missouri.edu.

**STRICKLAND, BONNIE RUTH,** psychologist, educator; b. Louisville, Nov. 24, 1936; d. Roy E. and Billie P. (Whitferd) S. BS, Ala. Coll., 1958; MS, Ohio State U., 1960, PhD (USPHS fellow), 1962. Diplomate: clin. psychology Am. Bd. Examiners in Profl. Psychology. From asst. to asso. prof. psychology Emory U., Atlanta, 1962—73, dean of women, 1964—67; prof. psychology U. Mass., Amherst, 1973—2003, prof. emeritus, 2003—, chmn. dept. psychology, 1976—77, 1978—82, assoc. to chancellor, 1983—84. Mem. adv. coun. NIMH, 1984-87; Sigma Xi nat. lectr., 1991-93. Adv. editor numerous psychology jours., acad. pub. houses; contbg. author texts personality theory.; contbr. of numerous articles on social personality and clin. psychology to profl. jours.; contbg. author of two citation classics. Recipient Outstanding Faculty award Emory U., 1968-69; Chancellor's medal disting. service U. Mass., 1983. Fellow APA (pres. divsn. clin. psychology 1983, pres. divsn. gen. psychology 2005, chmn. bd. profl. affairs 1980-83, chmn. policy and planning bd. 1985, pres. 1987, bd. dirs. 1986-87, Outstanding Leadership award 1992, Disting. Contbns. and Psychology in the Pub. Interest award 1999, Presdl. Citation 2001), Am. Psychol. Soc. (founder 1988, bd. dirs. 1989-93), New Eng. Psychol. Assn. (Disting. Contbns. award 2002), Am. Assn. Applied and Preventive Psychology (founder 1990, bd. dirs. 1990-94, pres. 1992-94), Acad. Clin. Psychology (chmn. 1982-83). Home: 558 Federal St Belchertown MA 01007-9754 Office: U Mass Dept Psychology Amherst MA 01003-7710

**STRICKLAND, DELPHENE COVERSTON,** judge; b. Ponca City, Okla. d. Harry Ethelbert and Mary Louise (Reed) Coverston; m. Thomas Whitney Strickland, Aug. 31, 1946; children: Mary Herrington, Thomas Whitney. BA, John B. Stetson U., 1944; JD, U. Fla., 1945; postgrad., Fla. State U., 1965, 70, Nat. Jud. Coll., Reno, 1979-84. Bar: Fla. 1945, US Dist. Ct. (so. dist.) Fla. 1946, US Dist. Ct. (no. dist.) Fla. 1966, US Dist. Ct. (no. dist.) Tex. 1979, US Dist. Ct. Hawaii 1980, US Supreme Ct. 1980, US Ct. Appeals (11th cir.) 1983. Assoc. Rogers & Morris, Ft. Lauderdale, Fla., 1945-46, Clayton, Arnow, Johnson & Duncan, Gainesville, Fla., 1946-51; pvt. practice Delphene Strickland Law Offices, Gainesville, 1951-59; legal rsch. asst. Fla. Supreme Ct., Tallahassee, 1960-68, exec. asst., 1968-70, mem. legis. ref. com., 1970—72; gen. counsel Fla. Dept. Transp., 1972; adminstrv. law judge Tallahassee; ret., 1982; part time gen. practice DC Strickland, 2002—. Adj. prof. U. Fla., Gainesville, Fla. State U., Tallahassee; Fla. del. to 1983 11th Cir. Jud. Conf.; mem. Fla. Bd. Bar Examiners, 1970-; sr. mem. 1980-; sr. mem. Fla. Traffic Ct., 1970—; mem. efficiency com. Fla. Supreme Ct., 1984—; organizer, charter mem. Leon Safety Coun. Contbr. articles to law jours. Sunday sch. tchr. St. Paul United Meth. Ch., Tallahassee, 1970-2002. Mem. ABA (chmn. nat. conf. adminstrv. law jduges 1983-84, exec. coun. 1985—), Fla. Govt. Bar Assn. (past pres., Earnie Webb award 1988), Fla. Assn. Women Lawyers (past pres.), Tallahassee Women Lawyers Assn. (past pres., founder,), Nat. Assn. Women Lawyers (Fla. del., charter mem.), Nat. Assn. Women Judges (charter mem.), Am. Arbitration Assn., AAUW (past pres. Gainesville), Supreme Ct. Hist. Soc., Fla. Supreme Ct. Hist. Soc. (organizer, charter, trustee), Fla. Govt. Bar Assn. (organizer, charter, past pres.), Tallahassee Bar Assn., North Fla. Legal Svcs., DAR (state del. Tallahassee, 99th nat. congress Washington 1989—), Capital City Country Club, Am. Camellia Soc., Tallahassee Camellia Soc., Am. Rose Soc., Tallahassee Rose Soc., Thomasville Camellia Soc, Thomasville Rose Soc., Apalachee Audubon Soc., Saint Andrew Soc. (organizer, charter mem.), Zonta, Phi Alpha Delta. Home: 2802 Sterling Dr Tallahassee FL 32312-3030 Office Phone: 850-385-1976.

**STRICKLAND, DOROTHY,** education educator; BS, Newark State Coll.; MA, PhD, NYU. Elem. sch. tchr. N.J. pub. sch. sys., reading cons., learning disabilities specialist; prof. edn. Rutgers U., New Brunswick, NJ, 1985—, Samuel DeWitt Proctor Prof. Edn., 2002—. Active in numerous organ. and nat. adv. bds. Author: Language Literacy and the Child, Process Reading and Writing: A Literature Based Approach, The Administration and Supervision of Reading Programs, Educating Black Children: America's Challenge, Family Storybook Reading, Listen Children: An Anthology of Black Literature, Families: An Anthology of Poetry for Young Children, Teaching Phonics Today, 1998, Beginning Reading and Writing, 2000, Supporting Struggling Readers and Writers, 2002, Preparing Our Teachers, 2002, Language Arts: Learning and Teaching, 2003, Learning About Print in Preschool Settings, 2004. Inducted into the Reading Hall of Fame, pres., 1997-98. Mem. Nat. Coun. Tchrs. English (Rewey Belle Inglis award for Outstanding Woman in English Education Annual Conv., rsch. award, Outstanding Educator in Lang. Arts award 1998), Internat. Reading Assn. (past pres., Outstanding Tchr. Educator of reading award). Home: 131 Coccio Dr West Orange NJ 07052-4121 Office: Rutgers U Dept Edn Grad Sch Edn New Brunswick NJ 08903

**STRICKLAND, HUGH ALFRED,** lawyer; b. Rockford, Ill., May 3, 1931; s. Hugh and Marie (Elmer) S.; m. Donna E. McDonald, Aug. 11, 1956; children: Amy Alice, Karen Ann. AB, Knox Coll., 1953; JD, Chgo. Kent Coll. Law, 1959. Bar: Ill. 1960. Partner firm McDonald, Strickland & Clough, Carrollton, Ill., 1961—; asst. atty. gen. Ill., 1960-67; spl. asst. gen. Ill., 1967-69; pres. McDonald Title Co. Mem. Greene County Welfare Svcs. Com., 1963—, Ill. Heart Assn., 1961-65; trustee Thomas H. Boyd Meml. Hosp., 1972-95; pres. Long Lake Assn. Vilas County, Inc., 2002—. With AUS, 1953-55. Recipient award for meritorious service Am. Heart Assn., 1964 Fellow Ill. Bar Found. (charter); mem. ABA, Ill. Bar Assn., Greene County Bar Assn. (past pres.), Southwestern Bar Assn. (past pres.), Ill. Def. Counsel, Am. Judicature Soc., Def. Rsch. Inst., Elks Club, Westlake Country Club (v.p. 1968-70, dir.), Big Sand Lake Country Club, Phi Delta Theta, Phi Delta Phi. Methodist. Home: 827 7th St Carrollton IL 62016-1421 Office: 524 N Main St PO Box 71 Carrollton IL 62016-1027 Office Phone: 217-942-3115. Personal E-Mail: mcdslawyers@aol.com. Business E-Mail: has3@irtc.net

**STRICKLAND, JULIA B.,** lawyer; b. San Francisco, Aug. 21, 1954; Student, Dartmouth Coll.; BA with honors, Univ. Calif., San Diego, 1975; JD, UCLA, 1978. Bar: Calif. 1978. Summer intern Stroock & Stroock & Lavan LLP, LA, 1977, ptnr., chair, fin. svcs. litig. practice, mem., operating exec. com., 1996—. Chair, consumer fin. svcs. litig. program Practising Law Inst., 1997—. Bd. of editors Banking Law Jour., editorial bd. Wall St. Lawyer, frequent lectr., writer in field. Named a Super Lawyer, LA Mag.; named one of Top 50 Women Litigators, LA Daily Jour., 2004. Mem.: Mortgage Bankers Assn., Assn. Bus. Trial Lawyers (bd. dir.). Office: Stroock & Stroock & Lavan LLP 2029 Century Pk E Los Angeles CA 90067-3086 Office Phone: 310-556-5806. Office Fax: 310-556-5959. Business E-Mail: jstrickland@stroock.com.

**STRICKLAND, LEE STEPHEN,** educator, consultant; b. Birmingham, Ala., Jan. 4, 1950; s. Warren Candler and Mary Stone Strickland; m. Karen L. Lucas, June 20, 1994. BS, U. Ctrl. Fla., 1970; M in Computer Sci., U. Va., 1971; JD, U. Fla., 1974. Bar: D.C. 1975, Va. 1981. Atty. CIA, Washington, 1975—2003, cons., 2004—. Vis. prof. U. Md., College Park, 2000—. Recipient Intelligence Commendation medal, Dir. Ctrl. Intelligence, 1999. Mem.: ACLU, IEEE, ALA, Soc. Competitive Intelligence Profls., Am. Soc. for Info. Sci. and Tech. Achievements include research in information policy balancing civil liberties and government powers; restructuring national intelligence functions; design of quality methodologies in IT gravitational efforts. Office: Univ Maryland 4105 Hornbake Library South Wing College Park MD 20742 Office Phone: 301-405-1741. Personal E-mail: lee.s.strickland@gmail.com. Business E-Mail: lstrickl@deans.umd.edu.

**STRICKLAND, MARSHALL HAYWARD,** bishop; b. Rome, Ga., Oct. 8, 1933; s. Albert A. Strickland and Elzie Greer Strickland Morton; 1 child, Marshall H. II. BA, Livingstone Coll., 1951; PhD, St. Mary's Sem. Balt.; MDiv, Hood Theol. Sem., 1955, DD (hon.), Allen U. Pastor Patten Meml. AME Zion Ch., Chattanooga, David Stan AME Zion Ch., Lancaster, SC, Hood Meml. AME Zion Ch., Bristol, Tenn., Big Zion AME Ch., Mobile, Ala., Pa. Ave. AME Zion Ch., Balt.; bishop Mid Atlantic I dist. AME Zion Ch., Balt.; sec.; bishop AMEZ, Balt., 1992—. Bd. bishops AME Zion Ch., chmn. commn. judiciary, chmn. Am. Bible Soc., 1st vice chair brotherhood pension svc., 1st vice chair Christian edn., 2d vice chair bicentennial commn., trustee

Livingstone Coll.; past mem. Ala. Consultation Ch. Union; guest pastor Gen. Conf. AME Ch., St. Paul Cathedral, others; spkr. in field; guest on various radio and TV stas. Author: William E. Fine: Kennedy-The Dreamer, Church and State: Not Separate, Our Heritage is Our Religion, The Black Church: Black America's Salvation, The Black Church: Solving Black America's Crisis, Health Care: Preaching Prevention from the Pulpit, Rebuilding Our Cities in Partnership with the Black Church: A Master Plan; contbr. articles to profl. jours. Former chmn. bd. dirs. Mobile Community Action Authority; past mem. Commn. Organic Union; founder Sterling Outreach Ctr., Balt. Recipient Humanitarian award, Zion Outreach Svcs. Associated Black Charities, Econ. Devel. award, HUB, Flood Relief Support award, Jamaican Assn. Md. Mem.: NAACP (past pres. Bristol chpt., Recognition awards Bristol and Balt. chpts.). Office: 2000 Cedar Circle Dr Baltimore MD 21228-3743

**STRICKLAND, ROBERT LOUIS,** retired retail executive; b. Florence, SC, Mar. 3, 1931; s. Franz M. and Hazel (Eaddy) S.; m. Elizabeth Ann Miller, Feb. 2, 1952; children: Cynthia Anne, Robert Edson. AB, U. N.C., 1952; MBA with distinction, Harvard U., 1957. Bd. dirs. Lowe's Cos., Inc., North Wilkesboro, NC, 1961—2000, sr. v.p., 1970—76, exec. v.p., 1976—78, chmn. bd., 1979—98, chmn. exec. com., 1988—98, mem. office of pres., 1970—78, chmn. emeritus, 1999; founder Sterling Advt., Ltd., 1966. V.p.; mem. adminstrv. com. Lowe's Profit-Sharing Trust, 1961-87, chmn. ops. com., 1972-78; mgmt. com. Lowe's ESOP Plan, 1978-97; bd. dirs. Lowe's Cos., Wilkesboro, NC, T.Rowe Price Assocs., Balt., 1991-2001, Hannaford Bros. Co., Portland, Maine, Krispy Kreme Corp., Winston-Salem, NC, Wholesale Club, Indpls., Summit Comms., Atlanta; vice chair, bd. dirs. Revelstroke Co., Calgary, Can.; panelist investor rels. field, 1972-99; spkr., panelist employee stock ownership, 1978-2000; spkr. on investor rels., London, Edinburgh, Glasgow, Paris, Zurich, Frankfurt, Milan, Vienna, Singapore, Tokyo. Author: Lowe's Cybernetwork, 1969, Lowe's Living Legend, 1970, Ten Years of Growth, 1971, The Growth Continues, 1972, 73, 74, Lowe's Scoreboard, 1978; contbr. articles to profl. jours. Mem. NC Ho. of Reps., 1962-64, Rep. Senatorial Inner Circle, 1980-95; exec. com. NC Rep. Com., 1963-73; trustee U. NC, Chapel Hill, 1987-95, chmn. bd., 1991-93; dir., dep. chmn. Fed. Res. Bank of Richmond, 1996-98; com. on bus. laws and the economy NC, 1994-97; dir. US Coun. Better Bus. Burs., 1981-85; bd. dirs., v.p. Nat. Home Improvement Coun., 1972-76; bd. dirs. NC Sch. Arts Found., 1975-79, NC Bd. Natural and Econ. Resources, 1975-76, bd. dirs. govt. affairs com. Home Ctr. Inst., co-chmn. Home Ctr. to Israel Del., 1984; trustee, sec. bd. Wilkes CC, 1964-73; chmn., pres. bd. dirs. Do-It-Yourself Rsch. Inst., 1981-89; pres. Hardware Home Improvement Coun. City of Hope Nat. Med. Ctr., LA, 1987-89. With USN, 1952-55, lt. Res. 1955-62. Named Wilkes County NC Young Man of Yr., Wilkes JC, 1962; recipient Bronze Oscar of Industry award Fin. World, 1969-74, 76-79, Silver Oscar of Industry award, 1970, 72-74, 76-79, Gold Oscar of Industry award as best of all industry, 1972, 87, Excellence award in corp. reporting Fin. Analysts Fedn., 1970, 72, 74, 81-82, cert. of Distinction Brand Names Found., 1970, Retailer of Yr. award, 1971, 73, Disting. Mcht. award, 1972, Spirit of Life award City of Hope, 1983, Free Enterprise Legend award Students Free Enterprise, 1994; named to Home Ctr. Hall of Fame, 1985. Mem. Nat. Assn. Over-Counter Cos. (bd. advisers 1973-77), Newcomen Soc., Employee Stock Ownership Assn. (pres. 1983-85, chmn. 1985-87), James Madison Club, Federalist Soc., Forsyth Country Club, Piedmont City Club, Roaring Gap Club (NC), Ponte Vedra Inn and Club (Fla.), Harvard Club (NY), Scabbard and Blade, Phi Beta Kappa, Pi Kappa Alpha. Home: 226 N Stratford Rd Winston Salem NC 27104-3132 also: 721 5th Ave Apt GH New York NY 10022 Office: 2000 W 1st St Winston Salem NC 27104-4225 Home: 67 Ponte Vedra Blvd Ponte Vedra Beach FL 32082 Personal E-mail: lowchair@aol.com.

**STRICKLAND, SIDNEY,** neurobiologist; educator; b. 1946; m. Carol Colclough Strickland, 1968. BS, Rhodes Coll., Memphis, Tenn., 1968; PhD, Univ. Mich. Lead prof., dir., genetics program SUNY, Stony Brook; and assoc. dir. Stony Brook Inst. of Cell and Developmental Biology; now v.p., ednl. affairs, dean grad. and post-grad. studies and rsch. prof. Rockefeller Univ., NYC. Avocation: performs with Southern Blots musical ensemble of scientists. Office: Neurobiology and Genetics lab Rockefeller Univ 1230 York Ave New York NY 10021 Office Phone: 212-327-8705 Lab. Business E-Mail: strickland@rockefeller.edu.

**STRICKLAND, SYLVIA RAYE,** social worker; b. Grand Prarie, Tex., Feb. 21, 1945; d. Nathaniel and Flora Evelyn Strickland; m. Julian B. Angel, Oct. 6, 1973 (div. Apr. 1983); 1 child, Sarah Renee Angel. BSW, U. So. Colo., Pueblo, 1986; MSW, N.Mex. Highlands U., Las Vegas, N.Mex., 1987. Lic. psychotherapist 1998, cert. grief recovery specialist Grief Recovery Inst., 2005. Social worker Highland Park Nursing Home, Pueblo, 1988; social worker III El Paso County Social Svcs., Colorado Springs, Colo., 1988—89; resident svcs. coord. Villa Santa Maria, Colorado Springs, Colo., 1990—91; ballot initative circulator, 1992; social worker Medalion Health Ctr., Colorado Springs, 1993—; coord. activities Medalion Health Ctr. and Personal Care Unit, 1993—96. Vol. Hospice of Comforter, 1994—96; active St. Paul's Cath. Ch.; sec. Social Work Action Team, U. So. Colo., 1984—85. Mem.: Satellite S.W. Avocations: choir, water colors, attending concerts, quilting. Home: PO Box 38123 Colorado Springs CO 80937-8123 Office Phone: 719-381-4967.

**STRICKLAND, TED,** congressman, clergyman, psychology educator, psychologist; b. Lucasville, Ohio, Aug. 4, 1941; m. Frances Smith. BA in Hist., Asbury Coll., Wilmore, Ky., 1963; MDiv, Asbury Theol. Seminary, Wilmore, Ky., 1967; PhD in Counseling Psych., U. Ky., Lexington, 1980. Min.; dir. social svcs. Ky. Meth. Home; consulting psychologist So. Ohio Correctional Facility, 1985—92, 1994—96; asst. prof. Shawnee State U., Portsmouth, Ohio, 1988—92, 1994—96; mem. US Congress from 6th Ohio dist., 1993—95, 1997—, mem. energy and commerce com., mem. vets. affairs com., ranking minority mem. oversight and investigations subcommittee. Dem. nominee for Governor, Ohio, 2006. Co-recipient Outstanding Psychologist award, Nat. Alliance Mentally Ill, 2004. Mem.: Ohio Psychol. Assn., APA. Democrat. Methodist. Office: US Ho Reps 336 Cannon Ho Office Bldg Washington DC 20515-3506 Office Phone: 202-225-5705.*

**STRICKLAND, WILLIAM JESSE,** lawyer; b. Newport News, Va., Mar. 21, 1942; BSBA, U. Richmond, 1964, JD, 1969. Bar: Va. 1969, US Dist. Ct. Ea. Dist. Va., US Dist. Ct. We. Dist. Va., US Ct. Appeals 4th Cir., US Ct. Claims, US Tax Ct. Mem McGuire Woods LLP, Richmond, Va., 1969—, firm mng. ptnr., 1996—. Bd. dirs. Cableform Inc., Zion Crossroads, Va., Eimeldingen Corp., Indpls, World Affairs Coun., Greater Richmond. Mem. exec. com. Va. Found. for Rsch. & Econ. Edn., Inc., bd. dirs. U. Richmond Law Sch. Found.; mem. coun. Va. Inst. Marine Sci.; founder Marine Corps Heritage Found.; bd. dirs. World Affairs Coun. Greater Richmond. Capt. USMC, 1964—67. Mem. ABA (com. on tax exempt fin.), Va. Bar Assn., Richmond Bar Assn., Nat. Assn. Bond Lawyers, Va. Govt. Fin. Officers Assn., Va. Local Govt. Attorneys Assn. Baker & Bond Club. Office: McGuire Woods LLP One James Ctr 901 E Cary St Richmond VA 23219-4030 Office Phone: 804-775-4350. Office Fax: 804-698-2185. Business E-Mail: wstrickland@mcguirewoods.com.

**STRICKLER, DENNIS JOHNSON,** research scientist; b. New Haven, June 27, 1949; s. Thomas David and Mildred Martin Strickler; m. Candice Shelton, Aug. 7, 1971; children: Sarah Elizabeth, Thomas Martin. BA in Math., Berea Coll., 1971; MA in Math., U. Ky., 1973. Rsch. staff Oak Ridge (Tenn.) Nat. Lab., 1974—2005; ret., 2005. Pres. Oak Ridge City Tennis League, 1979. Tennis Assn., 1985, 1988, 2004, 2005. Mem.: US Tennis Assn. Achievements include collaborating on development spherical torus magnetic fusion energy confinement concept; development of a computational method for designing complex magnetic coils for compact stellarator magnetic fusion energy confinement devices. Avocation: tennis. Home: 395 Mississippi Ave Oak Ridge TN 37830 Business E-Mail: stricklerdj@comcast.net.

**STRICKLER, IVAN K.,** dairy farmer; b. Carlyle, Kans., Oct. 23, 1921; s. Elmer E. and Edna Louise (James) S.; m. Madge Lee Marshall, Aug. 7, 1949; children— Steven Mark, Thomas Scott, Douglas Lee. BS, Kans. State U., 1947. Owner, mgr. dairy farm, Iola, Kans., 1947—; tchr. farm mg. to vets. World War II, 1947-54; judge 1st and 2d Nat. Holstein Show, Brazil, 1969-70, Internat. Holstein Show, Buenos Aires, 1972, Nat. Holstein Show, Ecuador, 1978, 10th Nat. Holstein Show, Brazil, 1980, Holstein Show, Australia, Mex. and Argentina, 1981, Lang Lang, 1984, Adelaide (Australia) Royal Show, 1987; pres Mid-America Dairymen, Inc., Springfield, Mo., 1981—. Appointed chmn. Nat. Dairy Bd., 1985-90; dairy leader 4-H Club, 1962-75; dir. Iola State Bank; rep. U.S. Internat. Dairy Symposium, 1994, Belo Horinzote, Brazil. Author: Wholly Cow We Did It, 1996 (Centennia Honor roll 1997). Trustee Allen County Community Jr. Coll.; mem. agr. edn. and rsch. com. Kans. State U. (recipient Medallion-highest honor, 2000), U.S. Agrl. Trade and Devel. Mission, Algeria and Tunisia, 1989. With USN, 1942-46, PTO. Recipient Silver award Holstein Friesian Assn. Brazil, 1969, Top Dairy Farm Efficiency award Ford Found., 1971, Master Farmer award Kans. State U. and Kans. Assn. Commerce and Industry, 1972, Gold award Holstein Friesian Assn. Argentina, 1972, Richard Lynng award Nat. Dairy Bd., 1990, award of merit Gamma Sigma Delta, 1987, Alumni medallion Kans. State U., 1999; named Man of Yr. World Dairy Exposition, 1978; portrait in Dairy Hall of Fame Kans. State U., 1974; Guest of Hon. Nat. Dairy Shrine, 1985; selected First Dairy Leader of Yr., 1996; inductee Kans. Co-op Hall of Fame, 1999. Mem. Mid Am. Dairymen (sec. corporate bd. 1971-81, pres. 1981-95), Holstein Friesian Assn. Am. (nat. dir. 1964-72), Dairy Shrine (nat. dir. 1971-81), United Dairy Industry Assn. (dir. 1971-79), Nat. Holstein Assn. Am. (pres. 1979-80), Alpha Gamma Rho (highest honor 1989, Hall of Fame 1998). Mem. Christian Ch. (elder, bd. dirs.). Club: Nat. Dairy Shrine (pres. 1978). Home: PO Box 365 Iola KS 66749-0365 Office: Mid America Dairymen Inc 1641 N Dakota Rd Iola KS 66749

**STRICKLER, JEFFREY HAROLD,** pediatrician; b. Mpls., Oct. 14, 1943; s. Jacob Harold and Helen Cecelia (Mitchell) S.; m. Karen Anne Stewart, June l8, l966; children: Hans Stewart, Liesl Ann. BA, Carleton Coll., l965; MD, U. Minn., l969. Diplomate Am. Bd. Pediatrics. Resident in pediatrics Stanford U., Calif., 1969-73; pvt. practice Helena, Mont., 1975—2005; chief staff Shodair Children's Hosp., Helena, 1984-88. Dir. maternal-child health Lewis and Clark County, Helena, 1978-88; chief of staff St. Peters Hosp., Helena, 1994-96; bd.chmn. Helena Health Alliance, 1996-99; founding mem., bd. dirs. Caring Found. Mont., 1992-2005. Mem. Mont. Gov.'s Task Force on Child Abuse, 1978-79; mem. steering com. Region VIII Child Abuse Prevention, Denver, l979-82; bd. dirs. Helena Dist. 1 Sch. Bd., 1982-88, vice chmn., 1985-87. Maj. M.C., USAF, l973-75. Fellow: Am. Acad. Pediatrics (vice chmn. Mont. chpt. 1981—84, chmn. 1984—87, mem. nat. nominating com. 1987—90, chmn. 1989—90, coun. on govt. affairs 1990—96, future of pediatric edn. II 1996—2000, Wyeth award 1987); mem.: Am. Bd. Pediatrics (PMCP-G practice performance com. 2001—), Rotary (youth exch. chmn. dist. 539 1984—88, pres. Helena 1988—89, polio plus chair dist. 5390 1996—, asst. gov. dist. 5390 2002—04, dist. gov. elect 2005—). Avocations: skiing, hiking. Home: PO Box 161815 2125 Yellowtail Rd Big Sky MT 59716-1815 Personal E-mail: j.strickler@3rivers.net.

**STRICKLER, MATTHEW M.,** lawyer; b. Bryn Mawr, Pa., June 27, 1940; s. Charles S and Mary Webster (Cornman) S.; m. Margaret Renshaw, Sept. 3, 1966; children: Matthew David, Andrew Kellogg, Timothy Webster, Edward Charles. AB, Haverford Coll., 1962; JD, Harvard U., 1965. Bar: Pa. 1965, U.S. Supreme Ct. 1975. Assoc. Ballard, Spahr, Andrews & Ingersoll, Phila., 1965-74, ptnr., 1974—2002, sr. counsel, 2003—; dir. legal affairs Sch. Medicine Temple U., Phila., 2003—. Adj. prof. Temple U. Sch. Law, Phila., 1993—. Editor: Representing Health Care Facilities, 1981. Bd. dirs. Phila. chpt. Girl Scouts Am., 1978-96, v.p., 1984-90, 94-96; bd. dirs. Kardon Inst. Arts, 2000—, treas., 2003-05, chmn., 2005—. Mem. ABA, Pa. Bar Assn., Phila Bar Assn., Am. Acad. Healthcare Attys., Am. Health Lawyers Assn., Nat. Assn. Coll. and Univ. Attys., Union League Phila., Pocono Lake Preserve, Meridian Bridge Club. Office: Temple U Sch Medicine 3420 N Broad St Rm 107 Philadelphia PA 19140 Office Phone: 215-707-6766. Business E-Mail: mstrick@temple.edu.

**STRICKON, HARVEY ALAN,** lawyer; b. Bklyn., Nov. 9, 1947; s. Milton and Norma (Goodhartz) S.; m. Linda Carol Meltzer, July 2, 1972; children: Joshua Andrew, Meredith Cindy, Erica Stacey. BBA, CCNY, 1968; JD, NYU, 1971. Bar: N.Y. 1972, U.S. Dist. Ct. (so. and ea. dists.) N.Y. 1973, U.S. Ct. Appeals (2d cir.) 1973, U.S. Supreme Ct. 1975, U.S. Dist. Ct. (no. dist.) N.Y. 1980, U.S. Dist. Ct. (we. dist.) N.Y. 1981, U.S. Dist. Ct. Ariz. 1991, U.S. Dist. Ct. Conn., 1996. Law clk. U.S. Dist. Ct. (ea. dist.) N.Y., Bklyn., 1971-73; assoc. Moses & Singer, N.Y.C., 1973-80; from assoc. to ptnr. Kaye, Scholer, Fierman, Hays & Handler, N.Y.C., 1980-91; from ptnr. to counsel Paul, Hastings, Janofsky & Walker LLP, N.Y.C., 1991—. Mem. complaint mediation panel, departmental disciplinary com. appellate div., 1st dept. Supreme Ct. State N.Y.; mem. mediation panel U.S. Dist. Ct. (ea. dist.) N.Y.; mem. mediation register U.S. Bankruptcy Ct. (so. and ea. dists.) N.Y. Co-author: Enforcing Judgments and Collecting Debts in New York, 1996. Mem. Nassau County Rep. Com., Great Neck, N.Y., 1982—; chmn. bd. dirs. Flushing Community Vol. Ambulance Corps. Inc., N.Y., 1981-86, vice chmn., 1987-92. Mem. ABA, N.Y. State Bar Assn., Assn. Bar City N.Y. (chmn. complaint mediation panel com. on profl. discipline), Am. Judicature Soc., Assn. Comml. Fin. Attys., N.Y. Law Inst., Bankruptcy Lawyers Bar Assn., (bd. govs. 1987-89, corr. sec. 1989—), Am. Bankruptcy Inst. Republican. Jewish. Home: 11 West Brook Rd Great Neck NY 11024-1219 Office: Paul Hastings Janofsky & Walker LLP 75 E 55th St New York NY 10022-3205 Office Phone: 212-318-6380. E-mail: harveystrickon@paulhastings.com, hastrick@optonline.net.

**STRIDER, MARJORIE VIRGINIA,** artist, educator; b. Guthrie, Okla. d. Clifford R. and Marjorie E. (Schley) S. BFA, Kansas City Art Inst., 1962. Faculty Sch. Visual Arts, N.Y.C., 1970-2001; artist-in-residence City U. Grad. Ctr. Mall, N.Y.C., 1976, Fabric Workshop, Phila., 1978, Grassi Palace, Venice, Italy, 1978. One-woman shows include Pace Gallery, N.Y.C., 1963-64, Nancy Hoffman Gallery, N.Y.C., 1973-74, Weather Spoon Mus., U.N.C., Chapel Hill, 1974, City U. Grad. Center Mall, 1976, Clocktower, N.Y.C., 1976, Sculpture Center, N.Y.C., 1983, Steinbaum Gallery, N.Y.C., 1983, 84, Andre Zarre Gallery, 1993, 95, Outdoor Installation, N.Y.C., 1997, Selby Gallery, Ringling Sch. of Art, Sarasota, Fla., 1998, Neuberger Mus., Purchase, N.Y., 1999; exhibited in group shows at Sculpture Center, N.Y.C., 1981, Drawing Biennale, Lisbon, Portugal, 1981, Newark Mus., 1984, William Rockhill Nelson Mus., Kansas City, 1985, Danforth Mus., Framingham, Mass., 1987, Delahoyd Gallery, N.Y.C., 1992; represented in permanent collections Guggenheim Mus., N.Y.C., U. Colo., Boulder, Albright-Knox Mus., Buffalo, Des Moines Art Center, Storm King (N.Y.) Art Center, Larry Aldrich Mus., Ridgefield, Conn., City U. Grad. Center, N.Y.C., Hirschhorn Mus. and Sculpture Garden, Washington, Santa Fe (N. Mex.) Mus. of Art, also pvt. collections. Grantee Nat. Endowment for Arts, 1973, 80, Longview Found., 1974, Pollock-Krasner Found., 1990, Florsheim Art Fund, 1998, 2000; Va. Ctr. for Creative Arts fellow, 1974, 92, Millay Colony for Arts fellow, 1992, Yaddo Colony, 1996-97 Office Phone: 845-246-1301. Business E-Mail: m_strider@hvc.rr.com.

**STRIDIRON, IVER ALLISON,** former attorney general; b. St. Thomas, V.I., May 29, 1945; m. Priscilla Blyden; 4 children. BA Lincoln U., 1969; JD, Howard U. Sch. of Law, 1974. Atty. U.S. Nuclear Regulatory Commn., U.S. Commn. on Civil Rights, Washington, 1974—77; pvt. practice St. Thomas, V.I., 1977—99; mem. V.I. Legis., 1981—83, 1985—89, pres., 1987—88; atty. gen. V.I., 1999—2004. Democrat.

**STRIEBY, B. LORRAINE,** artist; b. Morgantown, W.Va., Dec. 5, 1938; d. Charles Willis Ayer and Margaret Ann Ferko; m. Michael Strieby (dec.); children: Vicki Parzyk, Lisa Maginot, Lori Constantine, Ann; m. Stanley Veerin Gunn, Nov. 22, 2003. BA in Bus. Edn., Calif. State U., Northridge, 1976, secondary tchg. credential, 1977. Tchr. L.A. Unified Sch. Dist., 1978—81. Pres. Women Painters West, L.A., 1995—97. Exhibitions include

Art Concepts Gallery, Tacoma, 1997, Black Sheep Gallery, Hardwarden Castle, Wales, 1999, Westminster Gallery, London, 1999, S.E. La. U. Gallery, Hammond, 2000, Segreto Gallery, Santa Fe, 2002, Barlow Gallery, New Orleans, 2004, Mus. Making Music, Carlsbad, Calif., 2004, Williamson Art Gallery and Mus., Liverpool, Eng., 2004, Sotto South Gallery, Savannah, Ga., 2004—06, Barrie Holt Gallery, New Orleans, 2006, Charlevoix Street Gallery, Albuquerque, 2006, Adobe Ranch Gallery, Chatsworth, Calif. Various positions Rep. Women West Valley, L.A., 1990—99. Recipient Golden Products award, Nat. Acrylic Painters Assn. Home: PO Box 4928 Chatsworth CA 91311 Office Phone: 818-261-3968. E-mail: adobeart818@earthlink.net.

**STRIEFEL, KAREN JOYCE,** music educator; b. Maddock, N.D., Feb. 19, 1951; d. William Peter and Betty Christine (Stark) Zeien; m. Randy Rene Striefel, Mar. 2, 1973; 1 child, Sarah Joy. BS, Mayville State Coll., N.D., 1973. Choir tchr. Velva Pub. Sch., ND, 1974—76; music tchr. Butte Pub. Sch., ND, 1976—81, Goodrich Pub. Sch., ND, 1981—82, 1992—2004, Anamoose Pub. Sch., ND, 1988—92; music educator Fessenden-Bowdon Sch., ND, 2004—. Choir dir. St. Martin Lutheran Ch., Anamoose, ND, 1986—88. Named Educator of Yr., Farm Bur. Sheridan County, 2001. Mem.: NEA, Am. Choral Dirs. Assn., Music Educator's Nat. Conf.

**STRIEFSKY, LINDA A(NN),** lawyer; b. Carbondale, Pa., Apr. 27, 1952; d. Leo James and Antoinette Marie (Carachilo) S.; m. James Richard Carlson, Nov. 3, 1984; children: David Carlson, Paul Carlson, Daniel Carlson. BA summa cum laude, Marywood Coll., 1974; JD, Georgetown U., 1977. Bar: Ohio 1977. Assoc. Thompson Hine LLP (formerly Thompson, Hine & Flory), Cleve., 1977-85, ptnr., 1985—. Loaned exec. United Way N.E. Ohio, Cleve., 1978; trustee ideastream, Mus. Theater Edn. Programming. Mem. ABA (real estate fin. com. 1980-87, vice chmn. leader liability com. 1993-97, mem. non-traditional real estate fin. com. 1987—, chair securitization and spl. financing techniques com. 2006-), Am. Bar Found., Am. Coll. Real Estate Lawyers (bd. govs. 1994-98, 06-, treas. 1999), Internat. Coun. Shopping Ctrs., Nat. Assn. Office and Indsl. Parks, Urban Land Inst. (chmn. Cleve. dist. coun. 1996-2000), Cleve. Real Estate Women, Ohio Bar Assn. (bd. govs. real property sect. 1985-97), Greater Cleve. Bar Assn. (chmn. bar applicants com. 1983-84, exec. coun. young lawyers sect. 1982-85, chmn. 1984-85, mem. exec. coun. real property sect. 1980-84, Merit Svc. award 1983, 85), Pi Gamma Mu. Democrat. Roman Catholic. Home: 2222 Delamere Dr Cleveland OH 44106-3204 Office: Thompson Hine LLP 3900 Key Ctr 127 Public Square Cleveland OH 44114-1216 Office Phone: 216-566-5733. Business E-Mail: linda.striefsky@thompsonhine.com.

**STRIER, KAREN BARBARA,** anthropologist, educator; b. Summit, N.J., May 22, 1959; d. Murray Paul and Arlene Strier. BA, Swarthmore Coll., 1980; MA, Harvard U., 1981, PhD, 1986. Lectr. anthropology Harvard U., Cambridge, Mass., 1986—87; asst. prof. Beloit Coll., Wis., 1987—89, U. Wis., Madison, 1989—92, assoc. prof., 1992—95, prof., 1995—, dept. chair, 1994—96. Panel mem. U.S. Dept. Edn., Washington, 1989—92. Author: (book) Faces in the Forest, 1999, Primate Behavioral Ecology, 2d edit., 2003; co-author: Planning, Purposing, and Presenting Science Effectively; mem. editl. bd.: Internat. Jour. Primatology, 1990—, Primates, 1991—, Yearbook of Phys. Anthropology, 1990—. Recipient Presdl. Young Investigator award, NSF, 1989—94, NAS, 2005. Fellow: AAAS (coun. del. anthropology sect. 1998—2000), Am. Anthropol. Assn. (chair elect anthropology sect. 2005); mem.: NAS, Animal Behavior Soc., Internat. Primatological Soc., Am. Assn. Phys. Anthropologists. Office: U Wis Dept Anthropology 5403 Social Sci Bldg 1180 Observatory Dr Madison WI 53706-1320 Office Phone: 608-262-0302. E-mail: kbstrier@wisc.edu.

**STRIGL, DENNIS F.,** telecommunications industry executive; BBA, Canisius Coll.; MBA, Dickinson U. With NY Tel. Co., 1968, AT&T; v.p. product mgmt. network svcs. Bell Atlantic, 1989—91; pres., CEO Bell Atlantic Mobile and Bell Atlantic Global Wireless, 1991—97, Bell Atlantic Global Wireless, 1997—2000, Verizon Wireless Joint Venture, 2000—; exec. v.p. Verizon Comm., Inc., Bedminster, NJ, 2000—. Office: Verizon Wireless 180 Washington Valley Rd Bedminster NJ 07921

**STRIKER, CECIL LEOPOLD,** archaeologist, educator; b. Cin., July 15, 1932; s. Cecil and Delia (Workum) S.; m. Ute Stephan, Apr. 27, 1968. BA, Oberlin Coll., 1956; MA, NYU, 1960, PhD, 1968; MA (hon.), U. Pa., 1972. From instr. to asst. prof. Vassar Coll., 1962-68; assoc. prof. U. Pa., Phila., 1968-78, prof. history art, 1978—2006, chmn. dept. history of art, 1980-87, prof. emeritus, 2006—; field archaeologist Dumbarton Oaks Center for Byzantine Studies, 1966-80, fellow, 1972-73. Adj. prof. Sabanci U., 1999—; dir. survey and excavation, Myrelaion, Istanbul, 1965-66; co-dir. Kalenderhane Archaeol. Project, Istanbul, 1966-78, Aegean Dendrochronology Project, 1977-88; gen. archaeol. coun. Istanbul Metro and Bosphorus Tunnel Project, 1985-87; dir. Archtl. Dendrochronology Project, 1988—; cons. Integrated Study of Hagia Sophia Structure, 1991-95. Mem. editorial bd. Architectura: Zeitschrift für Geschichte der Architektur, 1986—. Adv. bd. Ctr. for Advanced Study in the Visual Arts, 1986-88, Samuel H. Kress Found. Art History Fellowship Program, 1986-87. With U.S. Army, 1954-57. Fulbright grant in Germany, 1960-62, NEH grant, 1985-86; art historian in residence Am. Acad. in Rome, 1973. Mem. Archaeol. Inst. Am., Coll. Art Assn., Am. Rsch. Inst. in Turkey (fellow 1965-66, pres. 1978-84, hon. dir. 2002), Coun. Am. Overseas Rsch. Ctr. (chmn. 1980-84), Soc. Archtl. Historians, Turkish Studies Assn., U.S. Nat. Com. for Byzantine Studies, Koldewey Gesellschaft, German Archaeol. Inst. (corr.). Office Phone: 215-573-9702. Business E-Mail: cstriker@sas.upenn.edu.

**STRIMBU, VICTOR, JR.,** lawyer; b. New Phila., Ohio, Nov. 25, 1932; s. Victor and Veda (Stancu) S.; m. Kathryn May Schrote, Apr. 9, 1955 (dec. 1995); children: Victor Paul, Michael, Julie, Sue; m. Marjorie Bichsel, Oct. 23, 1999. BA, Heidelberg Coll., 1954; postgrad., Western Res. U., 1956-57; JD, COlumbia U., 1960. Bar: Ohio 1960, U.S. Supreme Ct. 1972. With Baker & Hostetler LLP, Cleve., 1960—, ptnr., 1970—. Bd. dirs. North Coast Health Ministry; mem. Bay Village (Ohio) Bd. Edn., 1976-84, pres., 1978-82; mem. Bay Village Planning Commn., 1967-69; life mem. Ohio PTA; mem. Greater Cleve. Growth Assn.; trustee New Cleve. Campaign, 1987-94—, North Coast Health Ministry, 1989-2001, Heidelberg Coll., 1996—; mem. indsl. rels. adv. com. Cleve. State U., 1979—, chmn., 1982,1999, vice chmn., 1998. With AUS, 1955-56. Mem. ABA, Ohio Bar Assn., Greater Cleve. Bar Assn., Ohio Newspaper Assn. (minority affairs com. 1987-90), Ct. of Nisi Prius Club. Republican. Presbyterian. Office: Baker & Hostetler LLP 3200 National City Ctr 1900 E 9th St Ste 3200 Cleveland OH 44114-3485 Office Phone: 216-621-0200.

**STRINER, HERBERT EDWARD,** economics professor; b. Jersey City, Aug. 16, 1922; s. Harry and Pearl (Strynar) S.; m. Erma Steinert, Dec. 9, 1943 (div. 1970); children: Richard Alan, Deborah Jane; m. Iona V. Meredith. AB, Rutgers U., 1947, MA, 1948; PhD (Maxwell fellow 1949-50), Syracuse U., 1951. Asst. prof. Syracuse U., 1951; economist Interior Dept., 1951-54; program dir. NSF, 1954-55, Nat. Planning Assn., 1955-57; sr. analyst Operations Research Office, Johns Hopkins, 1957-59; program dir. Brookings Inst., 1959-61, Stanford Research Inst., 1961-62; program devel. dir. Upjohn Inst., Washington, 1962-69; dean Coll. Continuing Edn. Am. U., Washington, 1969-72, dean Coll. Bus., 1974-81, prof. econs. and mgmt., 1981-89; cons. Los Alamos Nat. Lab., 1970-71; chief planning and policy NIH, 1972-73; pres. U. Research Corp., 1973-74; assoc. faculty mem. Johns Hopkins U., 1997. Chmn. bd. dirs. NetTalon Corp. Inc., 2002—04. Author: Toward a Fundamental Program for the Training, Employment and Economic Equality of the American Indian, 1968, Continuing Education as a National Capital Investment, 1972, Regaining The Lead: Policies for Economic Growth, 1984; co-author: Local Impact of Foreign Trade, 1960, Civil Rights, Employment and the Social Status of American Negros, 1966; Contbr. profl. jours. Mem. rev. panel Pres.'s Cabinet Com. Juv. Delinquency, 1961-63, D.C. Youth Employment Com., 1963, Pres.'s Task Force Am. Indians, 1967, White House

Conf. Aging, 1971; bd. dirs. Opportunities Industrialization Ctr., NAACP, Washington. Officer inf. U.S. Army, 1943-46. Decorated Breast Order of Yun Hui with Ribbon, World War II Govt. China. Home: 3158 Gracefield Rd # 416 Silver Spring MD 20904

**STRINGEL, GUSTAVO,** pediatric surgeon; b. Mier, Mex., Sept. 29, 1945; s. Gustavo Sr. and Magdalena (Toledo) S.; m. Lina Guertin, Dec. 29, 1978; children: Mariana, Virginia, Patricia, Alexander. MD, U. Mex., 1969. Intern Hispana Benevolent Soc., Mexico City, 1969; rotating intern Hosp. Espanol de Mex., Mexico City, 1971; resident in pediatrics Hosp. Infantil de Mex., Mexico City, 1971-72; rotating intern St. Michael's Hosp., Toronto, 1972-73; resident in gen. surgery Gallie Course, U. Toronto, 1973-77; resident in pediatric surgery Hosp. for Sick Children, 1977-79; asst. prof. surgery U. Ottawa, Can., 1979-85; assoc. prof. surgery U. Tex., Dallas, 1985-92, SUNY, Stony Brook, 1992-94; prof. surgery N.Y. Med. Coll., Valhalla, 1994—. Surgeon in chief The Maria Fareri Children's Hosp. Fellow ACS, Am. Acad. Pediatrics, Royal Coll. Physicians and Surgeons of Can., Am. Coll. of Physician Executives; mem. AMA, Am. Pediatric Surg. Assn., Can. Assn. Pediatric Surgeons, Larchmont Yacht Club. Roman Catholic. Home: 21 Addison St Larchmont NY 10538-2744 Office: Westchester Co Med Ctr Valhalla NY 10595

**STRINGER, C. VIVIAN,** college basketball coach; b. Edenborn, Pa. m. William D. Stringer (dec.); children: David, Janine, Justin. Grad., Slippery Rock State Coll. Head coach Cheyney State Coll., 1971—83, U. Iowa, 1983—95, Rutgers U., 1995—. Head coach US Select Team tour China, 1980, World U. Games, Kobe, Japan, 1985, World Championship Zone Qualification Tournament, San Paulo, Brazil, 1989, US Pan-American Games, Havana, Cuba, 1991. Finalist Naismith Nat. Coach of Year award, 2000, 2001, 2003; named to Women's Basketball Hall of Fame, 2001; recipient Phila. Sportswriters' Coach of Year, 1980, Phila. Sportswriters' Coach of Year, 1981, NCAA, Wade Trophy Women's Nat. Coach of Year, 1982, Converse Women's Nat. Coach of Year, 1988, Naismith award, Converse, Sports Illustrated, USA Today, Los Angeles Times and Black Coaches Assn. Women's Coach of the Year, 1993. Mem. Amateur Basketball Assn. U.S. (bd. dirs.). Achievements include 1st person (male or female) to lead 3 different schools to the NCAA final four; recorded 750th career win, 2006.*

**STRINGER, GRETCHEN ENGSTROM,** consulting volunteer administrator; b. Pitts., Feb. 25, 1925; d. Birger and Gertrude Anne' (Schuchman) Engstrom; m. Loren F. Stringer, Oct. 3, 1953 (dec. Sept. 1992); children: Lizbeth, Pamela, William E., Frederick E. BA, Oberlin Coll., 1946; Cert. in Teaching, U. Pitts., 1951, SUNY, Buffalo, 1964, M, 1996. Cert. vol. adminstr. Owner, founder, pres. Vol. Cons., Clarence, NY, 1979—; owner, founder, officer Non Profit Mgmt. Ctr., Buffalo, 1995-2000. Founding pres. bd. dirs. Ctrl. Referral Svc. Author: The Board Manual Workbook, 1980, rev., 2004, The Instructors Guide, 1982, A Magical Formula, 1980; co-author: Non Profit Management Education, 1998; contbr. articles to profl. jours. Exec. dir. Vol. Action Ctr., United Way Buffalo and Erie County, 1988-81; founding vice chair Erie County Commn. on Status of Women, 1989-2000; pres. Girl Scout Coun. of Buffalo and Erie County, 1980-84; chair, gen. mgr. cadette encampment; bd. dirs. Clarence Ctrl. Sch. Dist., 1976-86; chair, gen. mgr. Buffalo and Erie County Bicentennial Parade, 1976, Erie County Ski Swap; bd. dirs. Longview Protestant Home for Children Bd., Millard Fillmore Jr. Bd., Prevention is Primary, N.Y. Bd. State Foster Care Youth Ind. Project, others; Cmty. Hero Torch Bearer Summer Olympics, 1996; del. White House Conf. on Small Bus., 1995; vol. steering com. Martin House Restoration Corp., 1988—. Recipient Pinny Wilson Vol. award Buffalo and Erie County, 1981, Continuing Svc. award Mass. Mutual, 1987, Girl Scouts Thanks Badge, 1983, Susan Reid Greene Russell award Jr. League of Buffalo, 1994, Assoc. of Yr. award Am. Bus. Women, 1997, Women Bus. Advocate of Yr. Small Bus. Adminstrn., 1998, Prime Time award Council Care, 1999, Woman of Achievement award AAUW, Buffalo chpt., 2001, Woman of Achievement award Every Woman Opportunity Ctr., 2004. Mem. Nat. Assn. Women Bus. Owners (bd. pres. Buffalo chpt. 1998-2000), N.Y. Assn. Vol. Ctrs. (founding exec. bd.), Vol. Adminsntrs. Western N.Y. (founding pres. 1980), Buffalo Ambassadors of C. of C. (bd. dirs.), Women's Pavilion Pan Am. Centennial 2001 (founder, pres. bd. dirs. 1999-2001), Jr. League Buffalo, Inc. (sustainer v.p. 1998-2000), Assn. Vol. Adminstrn. (chair, gen. mgr. nat. conf. 1986, nat. trainer, re-cert. chair, subcom. vol. adminstrn. higher edn.). Office: Vol Cons 9015 Cliffside Dr Clarence NY 14031-1460 Office Phone: 716-633-8264. E-mail: gestringer@adelphia.net.

**STRINGER, SIR HOWARD,** electronics company executive, retired media executive; b. Cardiff, Wales, Feb. 19, 1942; arrived in U.S., 1965, naturalized, 1985; s. Harry and Marjorie Mary (Pook) Stringer; m. Jennifer Kinmond Patterson, July 29, 1978; children: David Ridley, Harriot Kinmond. BA, MA in Modern History, Oxford U., Eng.; doctorate, PhD, London Inst., 2003, U. Glanorgan, 2005. Prodr., dir. CBS News, NYC, 1973—76, pres., 1986—88; exec. prodr. CBS Reports, 1976—81, CBS Evening News with Dan Rather, 1981—84; exec. v.p., 1984—86; pres. CBS Broadcast Group, 1988—95; chmn., CEO Tele-TV, 1995—97, Sony Canada, 1997—; chmn. Sony Electronics, 1998—; chmn., CEO Sony Corp. Am. 1998—; pres. Sony Broadband Entertainment, 2000—; dir. Sony Corp., 1999—, vice chmn., 2003—, COO, entertainment bus. group, 2005—, chmn., CEO, rep. corp. exec. officer, 2005—; corp. head Sony Group in the Americas, chmn., exec. officer. Bd. dirs. Sony Corp., 1999—, Sony Europe, Sony BMG Music Entertainment; chmn. Sony Canada; bd. dirs. Intercontinental Hotel Group; spkr. Consumer Electronics Show, Las Vegas, 2006. Chmn. Bd. trustees Am. Film Inst.; bd. dirs. Am. Theatre Wing, NY Presbyn. Hosp., Am. Friends of the British Mus., Corp. Leadership Com. Lincoln Ctr. for the Performing Arts, InterContinental Hotel Group; bd. trustee Miss TV and Radio; trustee Teach for Am. Sgt. U.S. Army, 1965—67, Vietnam. Decorated knight bachelor Eng.; US Army Commendation medal for meritorious achievement for svc. in Vietnam; named a Living Legend of NY, 2005; named hon. fellow Merton Coll., Oxford, 2000, hon. fellow Welsh Coll. Music and Drama, 2001; named one of World's 100 Most Influential People, Time Mag., 2005; named to Broadcasting and Cable Hall of Fame, 1996, Royal TV Soc. Welsh Hall of Fame, Wales, 1999; recipient Emmy award, NATAS, 1973, 2 Emmy awards, 1979, 1981, 4 Emmy awards, 1983, Columbia Dupont award, Columbia Journalism Sch., 1979, 1981, Overseas Press Club awards, 1974, 1979, 1982, IRTS Found. award, 1994, First Amendment Leadership award, Radio and TV News Dirs. Found., 1996, Steven J. Ross Humanitarian award, UJA-Federation NY, 1999, Pub. Svc. award, Phoenix House, 2002, Britannia award for contbns. to worldwide entertainment, BAFTA, 2003, Gold medal, St. George Soc., 2004, highest award, Ctr. for Communications, 2000, award, Literary Partners, NY Hall of Sci. Mem.: Coun. on Fgn. Rels. Presbyterian. Office: Sony Corp of Am 550 Madison Ave 33rd Fl New York NY 10022-3211 also: Sony Corp 7-35 Kitashinagawa 6-chrome Shinagawa-ku Tokyo 141-0001 Japan Business E-Mail: howard_stringer@sonyusa.com

**STRINGER, JOHN,** retired materials scientist; b. Liverpool, Eng., July 14, 1934; came to U.S., 1977, naturalized, 1996; s. Gerald Hitchen and Isobel (Taylor) S.; m. Audrey Lancaster, Feb. 4, 1957; children: Helen Caroline, Rebecca Elizabeth. BS in Engring., U. Liverpool, 1955, PhD, 1958, D in Engring., 1974. Chartered engr., U.K. Lectr. Univ. Liverpool, England, 1957-63, prof. materials sci., 1966-77; fellow Battelle Columbus (Ohio) Labs., 1963-66; sr. project mgr. Electric Power Rsch. Inst., Palo Alto, Calif., 1977-81, sr. program mgr., 1981-87, dir. tech. support, 1987-91, dir. applied rsch., 1991-95, tech. exec. fellow, 1995-96, exec. tech. fellow, 1997—2004; ret. Chmn. Sci. and Tech. Edn., Merseyside, Liverpool, 1971-74; press. Corrosion and Protection Assn., London, 1972; mem. Nat. Material Adv. Bd., 1992-95, basic energy scis. adv. com., U.S. Dept. Energy, 1992-98, chmn., 1996-98. Mem. editl. bd.: Oxidation of Metals Jour., 1971—; author: An Introduction to the Electron Theory of Solids, 1967; editor: (book) High Temperature Corrosion of Advanced Materials, 1989, Chlorine in Coal, 1991, Applied Chaos, 1992; contbr. over 350 articles to profl. jours. Recipient U.R. Evans award Inst. Corrosion, U.K., 1993, Campbell Meml. Lectr. of ASM

Internat., 1995. Fellow AAAS, NACE Internat. (Willis Rodney Whitney award 2004), AIME, Inst. Energy, Royal Soc. Arts, Instn. Corrosion (hon.), ASM Internat. Personal E-mail: jstringer@izambard.com, johnstringer@comcast.net.

**STRINGER, L. E. (DEAN STRINGER),** retired lawyer; b. Sayre, Okla., June 22, 1936; s. Rex Herman and Bessie (Morris) S.; m. Carol Ann Woodson, Aug. 31, 1963; children: Craig Woodson, Laura DeAnn. BA, Okla. State U., 1958; LLB, Harvard U., 1961. Bar: Okla. 1961, US Ct. Appeals (10th cir.) 1962, US Dist. Ct. (we. dist.) 1963, US Supreme Ct. 1972. Assoc. Crowe, Boxley, et al (now Crowe & Dunlevy), Oklahoma City, 1961—68, mem., dir., 1968—2000, chmn. bd., 1999—2000. Pres. Crowe & Dunlevy, P.C., 1979-81, chmn. litigation dept., 1987-2000, ret. 2000; bd. dirs. Okla. Inst. for Child Advocacy, 2003—, v.p., 2004, pres.-elect, 2005, pres. 2006. Pres. Okla. State U. Alumni Assn., 1972-73; bd. regents Okla. State U. and A&M Colls., Stillwater, 1986-94, vice-chmn., 1989-90, chmn., 1990-91; chmn. Okla. State U. Found., Stillwater, 1982-85; pres. Friends of the Libr., Okla. State U., 2000—; bd. dirs. Okla. Heritage Assn., 1995-2000; pres. adv. com. Okla. State U./OKC, 1998—, chmn., 2000—; mem. regents edn. adv. com. Okla. State Regents for Higher Edn., 1995-2001; trustee Youth Svcs. Oklahoma County, Inc., 2001—, vice chmn. 2002-04, chmn. 2004—. Maj. Okla. N.G., 1961-71. Recipient Disting. Alumnus award Okla. State U., 1979, Neil E. Bogan Professionalism award, Okla. Bar Assn., 2005; inducted Hall of Fame Okla. State U. Alumni Assn, 1998. Fellow Am. Bar Found. (adv. rsch. com. 1996-2000); mem. Okla. Bar Assn. Democrat. Methodist. Home: 325 NW 17th St Oklahoma City OK 73103-3424

**STRINGER, SCOTT M.,** city manager, former state legislator; b. NYC, Apr. 29, 1960; BA, John Jay Coll. Mem. NY State Assembly, Dist. 67, Albany, NY, 1992—2005, mem. Edn., Higher Edn., Housing, and Judiciary coms.; borough pres. Manhattan, NY, 2006—. Dist. coord. NY State Assemblyman Jerrold Nadler. Mem.: NAACP, Nat. Women's Polit. Caucus, West Side Crime Prevention Program, NYC Americans for Dem. Action, Manhattan New Dem. Coalition. Office: Office Manhattan Borough Pres 1 Centre St 19th Fl New York NY 10007*

**STRINGER, WILLIAM JEREMY,** university official; b. Oakland, Calif., Nov. 8, 1944; s. William Duane and Mildred May (Andrus) S.; m. Susan Lee Hildebrand; children: Shannon Lee, Kelly Erin, Courtney Elizabeth. BA in English, So. Meth. U., Dallas, 1966; MA in English, U. Wis., 1968, PhD in Ednl. Adminstrn., 1973. Dir. men's housing Southwestern U., Georgetown, Tex., 1968-69; asst. dir. housing U. Wis., Madison, 1969-73; dir. residential life, assoc. dean student life, adj. prof. Pacific Luth., Tacoma, 1973-78; dir. residential life U. So. Calif., 1978-79, asst. v.p., 1979-84, asst. prof. higher and post-secondary edn., 1980-84; v.p. student life Seattle U., 1984-89, v.p. student devel., 1989-92, assoc. provost, 1989-95, assoc. prof. edn., 1990—, chair ednl. leadership, 1994—97, chair strategic planning, 1997—2000, chair profl. studies, 2001—. Author: How to Survive as a Single Student, 1972, The Role of the Assistant in Higher Education, 1973. Bd. dirs. N.W. Area Luth. Social Svcs. of Wash. and Idaho, pres.-elect, 1989, pres., 1990-91; bd. dirs. Seattle Coalition Ednl. Equity; chair parents' coun. Pacific Luth. U., 2006-. Recipient John Hubbard Leadership award, 1984; Danforth Found. grantee, 1976-77. Mem. AAUP, Nat. Assn. Student Pers. Adminstrs. (bd. dirs. region V 1985-97, mem. editl. bd. Jour. 1995-2001, Disting. Svc. to Profession award 2000, faculty fellow 2002-, chair 2005-), Am. Coll. Pers. Assn., Phi Eta Sigma, Sigma Tau Delta, Phi Alpha Theta, Lambda Chi Alpha Lutheran. Home: 4553 169th Ave SE Bellevue WA 98006-6505 Office: Seattle U Dept Edn Seattle WA 98122 E-mail: stringer@seattleu.edu.

**STRINGFELLOW, CATHERINE VERONIQUE,** computer scientist, educator; b. France, June 4, 1962; d. Oron Ray and Marie-Odile Stringfellow. BS in math. and Computer Sci., Cameron U., 1984; MS in Computer Info. Sys., Ohio State U., 1986; PhD in Computer Sci., Colo. State U., 2000; BA in Art, N.Mex. Highlands U., 2002. From asst. to assoc. prof. N.Mex. Highlands U., Las Vegas, 1991—2002; from assoc. to full prof. Midwestern State U., Wichita Falls, Tex., 2002—. Contbr. articles to profl. jours. Vol. Meals on Wheels, Wichita Falls, Tex., 2003—04, Habitat for Humanity, Wichita Falls, Tex., 2004; chair Math., Sci. and U Girls Conf., Wichita Falls, Tex., 2004—05. Mem.: Consortium for Computing Scis. in Colls., Assn. Computing Machinery, IEEE Computer Soc. Avocations: painting, reading, baking, collecting postcards. Office: Midwestern State Univ 3410 Taft Blvd Wichita Falls TX 76308

**STRINGFELLOW, GERALD B.,** engineering educator; b. Salt Lake City, Apr. 26, 1942; s. Paul Bennion and Jean (Barton) S.; m. Barbara Farr, June 9, 1962; children: Anne, Heather, Michael. BS, U. Utah, 1964; PhD, Stanford U., 1968. Staff scientist Hewlett Packard Labs., Palo Alto, Calif., 1967-70, group mgr., 1970-80; disting. prof. elec. engring., materials sci. U. Utah, Salt Lake City, 1980—, chmn., 1994-98, adj. prof. physics, 1988—, dean Coll. Engring., 1998—2003. Cons. Tex. Instruments, Dallas, 1995-97, AT&T-Bell Labs., Holmdel, N.J., 1986-90, Brit. Telecom.; London, 1989-92; editor-in-chief Phase Diagrams for Ceramics, Vol. IX. Author: Organometallic Vapor Phase Epitaxy, 1989, 2d edit., 1999; editor: Metal Organic Vapor Phase Epitaxy, 1986, 2004, American Crystal Growth, 1987, Alloy Semiconductor Physics and Electronics, 1989, Phase Equilibria Diagrams-Semiconductors and Chalcogenides, 1991, High Brightness LEDs, 1997; prin. editor Jour. Crystal Growth, 1998-2003; letters editor Jour. Electronic Materials, 1992-99; contbr. over 360 articles to profl. jours. Recipient U.S. Sr. Scientist award Alexander von Humboldt Soc., Bonn, Germany, 1979, Gov.'s Sci. Tech. medal State of Utah, 1997, John Bardeen award TMS, 2003; guest fellow Royal Soc., London, 1990. Fellow IEEE, Japan Soc. Promotion of Sci ; mem. Am. Phys. Soc., Electronic Materials Com. (pres. 1985-87), Nat. Acad. Engring. Achievements include pioneering development of organometallic vapor phase epitaxy, development of theories of thermodynamic properties of alloy semiconductors; discovery of phenomenon of compositional latching in alloy semiconductor layers grown by epitaxial techniques. Office: U Utah Dept ECE 3280 MEB Salt Lake City UT 84112-1109 Business E-Mail: stringfellow@coe.utah.edu.

**STRINGFELLOW, JULIA,** archivist; d. Nancy and Charles Cardona (Stepfather). MusB, Ouachita U., 2000; Master of Libr. and Info. Sci., MA in History, U. Wis.-Milw., 2002. Archives intern divsn. archives and spl. collections U. Wis.-Milw., 2001—02; archivist SE Ashian archive, spl. collections and archives dept. U. Calif., Irvine, 2003—05; archivist and reference libr. Lawrence U., Seeley G. Mudd Libr., Appleton, Wis., 2005—. Sec. student chpt. Soc. Am. Archivists, U. Wis.-Milw., 2002; mentor Soc. Am. Archivists Mentoring Program, Appleton, Wis., 2003—; local arrangements com. mem. Soc. Calif. Archivists, Irvine, 2004; mem. diversity team U. Calif., Irvine Librs., 2003—05, mem. Bridging the Gap program, 2003—05. Contbr. presented at profl. conf.; co-curator (exhibit) A SEAA of Memories: Documenting the Southeast Asian American Experience. Recipient Beth Mason scholarship, Am. Assn. Univ. Women, North Shore br., 2001. Mem.: Midwest Archives Conf., Soc. Calif. Archivists, Soc. Am. Archivists. Avocations: travel, writing, reading. Home: 111 E Water St #103 Appleton WI 54911 Office: Lawrence Univ Seeley Mudd Libr 113 S Lawe St Appleton WI 54911 Office Phone: 920-832-6753. Business E-Mail: julia.stringfellow@lawrence.edu.

**STRINGFIELD, SHERRY,** actress; b. Colorado Springs, Colo., June 24, 1967; m. Larry Joseph, 1998; 1 child. BFA, SUNY, Purchase, 1989. Theater appearances include Goose and Tom Tom, Hurly Burly, Devil's Disciple, A Dream Play, Hotel Baltimore, The Kitchen, Tom Jones; appeared in (TV series) Guiding Light, 1989-92, NYPD Blue, 1993, ER, 1994-96, 2001-(Emmy nominee Outstanding Lead Actress in a Drama Series, 1995), Going Home, 2000; (films) Burnzy's Last Call, 1995, 54, 1998, Borderline, 1998, Autumn in New York, 2000, Viva Las Nowhere, 2001; (TV movies) Border Line, 1999, Going Home, 2000; (TV appearances) Touched by an Angel, 1999, Third Watch, 2002.

**STRINGHAM, LUTHER WINTERS,** retired economist, retired health facility administrator; b. Colorado Springs, Colo., Dec. 14, 1915; s. Luther Wilson and Fern (Van Duyn) S.; m. Margret Ann Pringle, Dec. 1, 1942 (dec. May 1998); 1 child, Susan Jean; m. Kathryn Cochran Baehr, June 19, 1999. BA summa cum laude, U. Colo., 1938, MA in Econs., 1939; Rockefeller fellow pub. adminstrn., U. Minn., 1939-40, Nat. Inst. Pub. Affairs, 1940-41. Economist Dept. Commerce, also OPA, 1941-43; intelligence officer Def. Dept., 1946-55; program analysis officer Office of the Sec. HEW, 1956-63, chmn. sec.'s com. mental retardation, 1961-63; exec. dir. Nat. Assn. for Retarded Children, 1963-68; intergovtl. relations officer HEW, 1968-77; planning dir. Central Va. Health Systems Agcy., 1977-83. Dir. TV series Healthy Virginians, 1981-83. Mem. Pres.'s Com. Employment Handicapped, 1963-68; pres. Music for People, Inc., 1971-74; lectr. CUNY, 1971-76; mem. nat. coun. Boy Scouts Am., 1963-83; co-founder Older Virginians for Action, 1983-84; bd. dirs. Capital Area Agy. Aging, 1984-87; Midlothian Dist. rep. Keep Chesterfield Clean Corp. Capt. AUS, 1943-46; lt. col. USAFR, 1946-56. Mem. Greater Richmond C. of C. (mem. quality coun. 1993-94), Va. Hist. Soc., Phi Beta Kappa, Pi Gamma Mu, Delta Sigma Rho. Home: 2500 Durhamshire Pl Cheltenham Midlothian VA 23113 E-mail: lstringham2005@comcast.net.

**STRINGHAM, PHYLLIS JOAN,** retired music educator; b. Grand Rapids, Mich., Jan. 30, 1931; d. Wilhelmina Johanna and Harry Newton Stringham. MusB, Calvin Coll., Grand Rapids, Mich., 1952; MusM, U. Mich., Ann Arbor, Mich., 1955. Organist Chatham (Va.) Hall Girls Sch., 1955—59; prof. of music Carroll Coll., Waukesha, Wis., 1959—2001. Owner and mgr. Phylllis Stringham Concert Mgmt., Waukesha, Wis., 1964—. Musician concert organist. Mem.: Am. Guild of Organists. Avocation: reading. Home: 1101 Belmont Dr Waukesha WI 53186 Office: Phyllis Stringham concert Mgt 1101 Belmont Dr Waukesha WI 53186 Office Phone: 262-542-7197. Business E-Mail: pstringh@cc.edu.

**STRINGILE, MARIE ELIZABETH,** educational administrator; b. Bayonne, N.J., May 13, 1954; d. Orlando Salvatore and Amelia Mary (Prisco) S. BA in edn., Jersey State Coll., 1976; MA in adminstrn., St. Peter's Coll., 1988; PhD in Edn. Adminstrn., 1976. Cert. elem. tchr., prin./supr., sch. adminstr., N.J. Tchr. St. James Sch., Newark, N.J., 1976-79; remedial math tchr. Ind. Child Study Teams, Jersey City, N.J., 1979-88, assoc. dir., 1988-90, adminstr., 1990—97, dir. ednl. programs, rsch. and evaluation mgr., 1997—2000; edn. program devel. specialist N.J. Dept. Edn., 2000—. Data documentation monitor Ind. Child Study Teams, Jersey City, 1990—, testing and curriculum specialist, 1990—, staff inservices, 1990—, data collection on all eligible remedial students, 1990—; cons. Devel. Remedial Math. Curriculum, 1993, resource room, 1985-88. Bd. dirs. O.L. Assumption Sch. Bd., 1991-93. Mem. ASCD, Sisters of St. Joseph of Peace (assoc.), Nat. Coun. Tchrs. Math., Internat. Reading Assn., Disabled Vets. Am., Medic Alert Found., Handyman Club Am., Black Seal Boiler Operator, Phi Delta Kappa. Avocations: carpentry, gardening, reading, mechanics, educational research. Home: 133 W 25th St Bayonne NJ 07002-1715 Office: NJ State Dept Edn Program Improvement 240 S Harrison St South Orange NJ

**STRIPLING, KAYE,** school system administrator; BS in Health and Phys. Edn., Tex. Woman's U., 1962; EdM in Spl. Edn., U. Houston, 1967, ED in Curriculum and Instrn., 1985. Tchr. spl. edn. Houston Ind. Sch. Dist., 1964—75, prin. elem. and mid. schs., 1975—87, supt. Adminstrv. Dist. XIV, 1987—90, asst. supt. staff devel., 1990—94, supt. S.W. Adminstrv. Dist., 1995—2001, acting supt. schs., 2001, supt. schs., 2001—. Named Disting. Alumna, Tex. Woman's U., 2002. Office: Houston Ind Sch Dist 3830 Richmond Ave Houston TX 77027

**STRITCH, ELAINE,** singer, actress; b. Detroit, Feb. 2, 1925; d. George Joseph and Mildred (Jobe) S.; m. John M. Bay, Feb. 2, 1973 (dec. 1973). Student drama workshop, New Sch. for Social Research; studies in singing with Burt Knapp, Drama Workshop, from 1948. Appeared in Broadway prodns. Loco, 1946, Three Indelicate Ladies, 1947, Yes M'Lord, 1949, Pal Joey, 1962, On Your Toes, Bus Stop, 1955, Sail Away, 1961, Who's Afraid of Virginia Woolf?, 1962, 65, Wonderful Town, 1967, Private Lives, 1968, Company, 1970, also London prodn., 1972, At Home at the Carlyle, 2005, 2006; appeared in Follies in Concert, N.Y.C., 1982; (films) The Scarlet Hour, 1956, Three Violent People, 1956, A Farewell to Arms, 1957, The Perfect Furlough, 1958, Who Killed Teddy Bear?, 1965, Pigeons, 1971, The Spiral Staircase, 1975, Providence, 1977, September, 1988, Cocoon II: The Return, 1988, Cadillac Man, 1990, Out to Sea, 1997, Screwed, 2000, Small Time Crooks, 2000; numerous television appearances, including (series) My Sister Eileen, 1960-61, The Trials of O'Brien, 1965-66, (British) Two's Company, 1975-76, The Ellen Burstyn Show, 1987, Stranded, 1986; (TV movie) Chance of a Lifetime, 1991; (TV miniseries) An Inconvenient Woman, 1991, Elaine Stritch: At Liberty, 2002 (Emmy award Outstanding Individual Performance in a Variety or Music Program, 2004, Drama Desk award, outstanding solo performance, Drama Desk award, outstanding book of a musical); author: Am I Blue?: Living With Diabetes and, Dammit, Having Fun, 1984. Recipient Nightlife award, outstanding cabaret female vocalist in a major engagement, 2006.

**STRITTMATTER, PETER ALBERT,** astronomer, educator; b. London, Eng., Sept. 12, 1939; came to U.S. 1970. s. Albert and Rosa S.; m. Janet Hubbard Parkhurst, Mar. 18, 1967; children— Catherine D., Robert P. BA, Cambridge U., Eng., 1961, MA, 1963, PhD, 1967. Staff scientist Inst. for Astronomy, Cambridge Eng. 1967-70; staff scientist dept. physics U Calif.-San Diego, La Jolla, 1970-71; assoc. prof. dept. astronomy U. Ariz., Tucson, 1971-74, prof. dept. astronomy, 1974—; Regent's prof., 1994—. Dir. Steward Observatory, Tucson, 1975—; mem. staff Max Planck Inst. Radio-astronomy, Bonn, W. Germany, 1981— Contbr. articles to profl. jours. Recipient Sr. award Humboldt Found., 1979-80, Karl Schwarzschild medal, 1998. Fellow Royal Astron. Soc.; mem. Am. Astron. Soc., Astronomische Gesellschaft. Office: U Ariz Steward Obs Tucson AZ 85721-0001

**STRNAD, JEFF (JAMES FRANK STRNAD II),** law educator; b. Aug. 23, 1952; AB in Physics, magna cum laude, Harvard Coll., 1975; JD, Yale U., 1979, PhD in Economics, 1982. Bar: Calif. 1980. Asst. prof. law U. So. Calif. 1981—83, assoc. prof., 1983—86, prof., 1986—89, John B. Milliken prof. taxation, 1989—97; asst. prof. law and economics Calif. Inst. Tech., 1984—86, assoc. prof., 1986—92, prof., 1992—97; prof. law Stanford Law Sch., 1997—2003, Charles A. Beardsley prof. law, 2003—, Helen L. Crocker faculty scholar, 1997—2003. Vis. prof. law Yale U., 1987—88. Office: Stanford Law Sch Crown Quadrangle 559 Nathan Abbott Way Stanford CA 94305-8610 Office Phone: 650-723-9674. Business E-Mail: jstrnad@stanford.edu.

**STROBEL, PAMELA B.,** energy executive; b. Chgo., Sept. 9, 1952; BS highest honors, U. Ill., 1974, JD cum laude, 1977. Bar: Ill. 1977, U.S. Dist. (ctrl. and no. dists.) Ill. 1977, U.S. Ct. Appeals (7th cir.) 1981, U.S. Claims Ct. 1983, U.S. Ct. Appeals (fed. cir.) 1985. Ptnr. Sidley & Austin, Chgo., 1988-93; exec. v.p. gen. counsel Commonwealth Edison Co., Chgo., 1993—2000; exec. v.p. gen. counsel Commonwealth Edison Co., Chgo., 1993—2000; exec. v.p. Exelon Corp., Chgo., 2000—, exec. v.p., chief adminstrv. officer, 2003—; pres. Exelon Energy Delivery Co., Chgo., 2000—, vice-chair, 2000—01, CEO, vice-chair, 2001—02, chmn., CEO, 2002—03. Mem. Kappa Tau Alpha (staff 1975-77). Office: Exelon Corp PO Box 805398 Chicago IL 60680-5398

**STROBEL, RUSS M.,** gas industry executive, lawyer; b. N.Y.C., May 2, 1952; BA, Northwestern U., 1974; JD magna cum laude, U. Ill., 1977. Bar: Ill. 1977. Ptnr. Jenner & Block, Chgo., Friedman & Koven; sr. v.p., gen. counsel, & sec. Nicor Inc., Naperville, Ill., 2000—02; pres. Nicor Gas, Naperville, Ill., 2002—, CEO, 2003—, chmn., 2005—; exec. v.p. Nicor Inc., Naperville, Ill., 2002, pres., 2002—, chmn., CEO, 2005—. Dir., mem. exec.

com. Am. Gas Assn. Bd. dir. USO Ill.; mem. adv. com. Gene Siskel Film Ctr., Art Inst. Chgo. Mem.: Econ. Club Chgo., Comml. Club Chgo. (mem. civic com.), Order of the Coif. Office: Nicor Inc 1844 Ferry Rd Naperville IL 60563-9600*

**STROBELL, DAN F.,** bank executive, writer; b. Whittier, Calif., Dec. 16, 1951; s. Joseph B. Strobel and Maxine G. Tuttle; m. Cindy L. Boggs, May 5, 1998; m. Michele C. Cooper, Feb. 21, 1975 (dec. Feb. 3, 1992); children: Amanda C. Bird, Tim J., Scott F., Ken D., Kevin C. BA, Brigham Young U., Provo, Utah, 1975. V.p. US Bank, St. George, Utah, 1992—2000; chief adminstr. officer SunFirst Bank, St. George, Utah, 2000—. Author: (religious) Justice & Mercy. Pres. La Casita Found., St. George, Utah, 1998—2004. Mem.: Rotary (pres. 1990—91, Rotarian of the Yr. 1984, 2000). Lds. Avocations: travel, international service projects. Office: SunFirst Bank 146 E St George Blvd Saint George UT 84770

**STROBER, FRANCINE LEE,** librarian, archivist; d. Stanley A and Maryanne K Strober. MS in Libr. Info. Sci., L.I. U., Brookville, N.Y., 2004. Lic. pub. libr. N.Y., 2004. Program coord. Am. Movie Classics Networks, Bethpage, NY, 1998—99; libr. (trainee) Hewlett-Woodmere Pub. Libr., Hewlett, NY, 2001—03; archivist (trainee) Am. Express Corp. Archives, New York, NY, 2002—03; libr. (trainee) Rockville Centre Pub. Libr., Rockville Centre, NY, 2003—04; archives rschr. NBC Universal, N.Y.C, NY, 2004—05; libr. N.Y.C (N.Y.) Pub. Libr., 2005—. Mem.: Spl. Libr. Assn.

**STROBER, MYRA HOFFENBERG,** education educator, consultant; b. NYC, Mar. 28, 1941; d. Julius William Hoffenberg and Regina Scharer; m. Samuel Strober, June 23, 1963 (div. Dec. 1983); children: Jason M., Elizabeth A.; m. Jay M. Jackman, Oct. 21, 1990. BS in Indsl. Rels., Cornell U., 1962; MA in Econs., Tufts U., 1965; PhD in Econs., MIT, 1969. Lectr., asst. prof. dept. econs. U. Md., College Park, 1967-70; lectr. U. Calif., Berkeley, 1970-72; asst. prof. grad. sch. bus. Stanford (Calif.) U., 1972-86, assoc. prof. sch. edn., 1979-90, prof. edn., 1990—, assoc. dean acad. affairs, 1993-95, interim dean, 1994; program officer in higher edn. Atlantic Philanthropic Svcs., Ithaca, N.Y., 1998-2000. Organizer Stanford Bus. Conf. Women Mgmt., 1974; founding dir. ctr. rsch. women Stanford U., 1974-76, 79-84, dir. edn. policy inst., 1984-86, dean alumni coll., 1992, mem. policy and planning bd., 1992-93, chair program edn. adminstrn. and policy analysis, 1991-93, chair provost's com. recruitment and retention women faculty, 1992-93, chair faculty senate com. on coms., 1992-93; mem. adv. bd. State of Calif. Office Econ. Policy Planning and Rsch., 1978-80; mem. Coll. Bd. Com. Develop Advanced Placement Exam. Econs., 1987-88; faculty advisor Rutgers Women's Leadership Program, 1991-93. Author: (with others) Industrial Relations, 1972, 1990, Sex, Discrimination and the Division of Labor, 1975, Changing Roles of Men and Women, 1976, Women in the Labor Market, 1979, Educational Policy and Management: Sex Differentials, 1981, Women in the Workplace, 1982, Sex Segregation in the Workplace: Trends, Explanations, Remedies, 1984, The New Palgrave: A Dictionary of Economic Theory and Doctrine, 1987, Computer Chips and Paper Clips: Technology and Women's Employment, Vol. II, 1987, Gender in the Workplace, 1987, Challenge to Human Capital Theory: Implications for the HR Manager, American Economic Review, 1995, Rethinking Economics Through a Feminist Lens, Feminist Economics, 1995, Making and Correcting Errors in Economic Analyses: An Examination of Videotapes, (with Agnes M.K. Chan) the Road Winds Uphill All the Way: Gender, Work, and Family in the U.S. and Japan, 1999, (with Jay M. Jackman) Fear of Feedback, 2003, Children As a Public Good, 2004, Can Harvard Ever Play a Positive Role for Women in Higher Education?, 2005; editor (with Francine E. Gordon) Bringing Women Into Management, 1975, (with others) Women and Poverty, 1986, Industrial Relations, 1990, Challenges to Human Capitol Theory: Implications for HR Managers, 1995, (with Sanford M. Dornbusch) Feminism, Children and the New Families, 1988, Rethinking Economics Through a Feminist Lens, 1995, (with Agnes M.K. Chan) The Road Winds Uphill All The Way: Gender, Work and Family in the U.S. and Japan, 1999, (with Jay M. Jackman) Fear of Feedback, 2003, Application of Mainstream Economics Constructs to Education: A Feminist Analysis, 2003, Children as a Public Good, 2004, Feminist Economics: Implications for Education, 2005, Can Harvard Ever Play a Positive Role for Women in Higher Education, 2005; mem. bd. editors Signs: Jour. Women Culture and Soc., 1975-89, assoc. editor, 1980-85; mem. bd. editors Sage Ann. Rev. Women and Work, 1984—; mem. editorial adv. bd. U.S.-Japan Women's Jour., 1991—; assoc. editor Jour. Econ. Edn., 1991—; contbr. chpt. to book, articles to profl. jours. Mem. rsch. adv. task force YWCA, 1989—; chair exec. bd. Stanford Hillel, 1990-92; bd. dirs. Resource Ctr. Women, Palo Alto, Calif., 1983-84; pres. bd. dirs. Kaider Found., Mountain View, Calif., 1990-96; bd. trustees Mills Coll., 2004—. Fellow Stanford U., 1975-77, Schiff House Resident fellow, 85-87. Mem.: NOW (bd. dirs. legal def. and edn. fund 1993—98), Ctr. Gender Equality (bd. dirs. 2000—), Internat. Assn. Feminist Econs. (assoc. editor Feminist Econs. 1994—, pres. 1997), Indsl. Rels. Rsch. Assn., Am. Ednl. Rsch. Assn., Am. Econ. Assn. (mem. com. status of women in profession 1972—75). Office: Stanford U School Edn Stanford CA 94305 Office Phone: 650-723-0387. Business E-Mail: myra.strober@stanford.edu.

**STROBER, SAMUEL,** immunologist, educator; b. NYC, May 8, 1940; s. Julius and Lee (Lander) S.; m. Linda Carol Higgins, July 6, 1991; children: William, Jesse; children from a previous marriage: Jason, Elizabeth. AB in Liberal Arts, Columbia U., 1961; MD magna cum laude, Harvard U., 1966. Intern Mass. Gen. Hosp., Boston, 1966-67; resident in internal medicine Stanford U. Hosp., Calif., 1970-71; rsch. fellow Peter Bent Brigham Hosp., Boston, 1962-63, 65-66, Oxford U., England, 1963-64; rsch. assoc. Lab. Cell Biology Nat. Cancer Inst. NIH, Bethesda, Md., 1967-70; instr. medicine Stanford U., 1971-72, asst. prof., 1972-78, assoc. prof. medicine, 1978-82, prof. medicine, 1982—, Diane Goldstone Meml. lectr., 1978-97, John Furman Merrill Meml. lectr., chief div. immunology & rheumatology, 1978-97. Investigator Howard Hughes Med. Inst., Miami, Fla., 1976-81; chmn., bd. dirs. La Jolla Inst. for Allergy and Immunology; founder Dendreon, Inc. Assoc. editor: Jour. Immunology, 1981-84, Transplantation, 1981-85, 99—, Internat. Jour. Immunotherapy, 1985—, Transplant Immunology, 1992—, Biol. Bone Marrow Transplantation, 1999—; contbr. articles to profl. jours. Served with USPHS, 1967-70. Recipient Leon Reznick Meml. Rsch. prize, Harvard U., 1966. Mem. Am. Assn. Immunology, Am. Soc. Clin. Investigation, Am. Coll. Rheumatology, Transplantation Soc. (councilor 1986-89), Am. Soc. Tranplantation Physicians, Western Soc. Medicine, Am. Assn. Physicians, Clin. Immunology Soc. (mem. 1996), Alpha Omega. Office: Stanford U Sch Medicine 300 Pasteur Dr Palo Alto CA 94304-2203

**STROBLE-THOMPSON, COLETTE MARY HOULE,** construction executive; b. Manchester, N.H., Aug. 10, 1947; d. George Albert and Mary Agnes (Sala) Houle; children: B.J., Danielle, Aiden; m. Dennis W. Thompson. Student, CAP Regional Staff Coll. Tex., 1985, 86. Lic. real estate agt., stucco/plasterer. Switchboard operator Leavitt's Dept. Store, Manchester, NH, 1965-66, with credit office, 1966-67, merchandiser, advertiser, 1966-69; advt. marketer Ariz. wide K-Mart, Mesa; owner, mgr. Colette's Boutique, Mesa, 1980-82; co-founder, CEO, pres. Stroble Plastering, Gilbert, Ariz., 1977—. Cons. area wide constrn. firms, Phoenix, 1979—; contractor plastering and stucco, Phoenix, 1987-90; realtor personal real estate property, Phoenix, 1988-90. Author, editor Wing Tips, 1985-86; co-inventor, electronic locator transmitter. Maj., squadron leader, fin. officer, personnel officer CAP, Mesa, 1990; active Dept. Disabled/Disadvantaged, Phoenix, 2000. Recipient Humanitarian award Dept. Econ. Security, Mesa, 1989, Letters of Appreciation, Leper Colony, Mexico, 1989. Mem. Nat. Assn. Search and Rescue (life), World Wing Kung Fu Assn., Rosicrucian Order Amorc (dep. master, master). Avocations: collector of masks & fetishes of all cultures, fishing, travel, real estate, boating. Office: Stroble Plastering 1440 S Clearview Ave Ste 104 Mesa AZ 85209-3381

**STROCK, CARL A.,** career military officer; b. GA; BCE, Va. Military Inst.; MCE, Miss. State U. Registered profl. engr., Mo. Commd. 2d. lt. U.S. Army, 1972, advanced through grades to lt. gen., 2004; various assignments Columbus AFB, 1980—83; with 307 Engr. Battalion, 82nd Airborne, Ft.

Bragg, NC, 1983—86; sr. tactics instr. British Royal Sch. Military Engring.; cols. assignment officer, personnel staff officer Office of Dep. Chief Staff for Personnel Hqs. Dept. Army, 1991—94; comdr. engr. brigade 24th Infantry Divsn., Ft. Stewart, Ga., 1994—96; chief of staff US Army Engr. Training Ctr., Ft. Leonard Wood, Mo., 1996—97; comdr., divsn. engr. Pacific Ocean Divsn. US Army CE, Ft. Shafter, Hawaii, 1997—99; comdr. Northwestern Divsn. US Army CE, Portland, Oreg., 1999—2001, dir. military programs Washington, 2001—03, dir. civil works, 2003—04, chief of engineers, commdg. gen. Washington, 2004—06; dep. dir. ops. Coalition Provisional Authority, Iraq, 2003. Decorated Legion of Merit with one oak leaf cluster, Bronze Star with one oak leaf cluster, Meritorious Svc. medal with two oak leaf clusters, Southwest Asia Svc. medal with three battle stars.

**STROCK, JAMES MARTIN,** communications executive, writer, entrepreneur; b. Austin, Tex., Aug. 19, 1956; s. James Martin Strock Sr. and Augusta (Tenney) Cumby. AB, Harvard U., 1977, JD, 1981; postgrad, New Coll. Oxford U., 1981—82. Bar: Colo. 1983. Tchg. asst. Harvard U., 1980—81; spl. cons. to majority leader U.S. Senate, Washington, 1982—83; spl. asst. to adminstr. EPA, Washington, 1983—85, asst. adminstr. for enforcement, 1989—91; spl. counsel U.S. Senate Com. on Environment and Pub. Works, Washington, 1985—86; assoc. Davis, Graham & Stubbs, Denver, 1986—88; acting dir., gen. counsel U.S. Office Pers. Mgmt., Washington, 1988—89; sec. for environ. protection State of Calif., Sacramento, 1991—97; prin. James Strock & Co., Scottsdale, Ariz., 1997—; sr. fellow, exec. edn. R.H. Smith Sch. bus. U. Md., 2003—. Adj. prof. U. So. Calif., 1996-97; mem. Intergovtl. Policy Adv. Com., rep. U.S. Trade, 1991-97; mem. Calif. State Pers. Bd., 1998; guest prof. U. Konstanz, 1998; bd. dir. Raoul Wallenberg com. of the U.S.; mem. Calif. State Personnel Bd., 1997-99; spkr. in field Author: Reagan on Leadership, 1998, Theodore Roosevelt on Leadership, 2001; contbr. articles to profl. jours. Capt. JAGC USAR, 1987—96. Recipient Ross Essay award ABA, 1985, Environ. Leadership award Calif. Environ. Bus. Coun., 1994, Fed. Republic Germany Friendship award, 1996; Environ. Soc. India fellow, 1997, commendation Calif. Dist. Attys. Assn., 1997 Mem. Coun. Fgn. Rels., Pacific Coun. on Internat. Policy, Nat. Spkrs. Assn., Authors' Guild, Phi Beta Kappa. Republican. Office: Ste B-111-601 15029 N Thompson Peak Pky Scottsdale AZ 85260 Business E-Mail: jms@jamesstrock.com.

**STROCK, MARCUS,** lawyer; b. Boston, Jan. 4, 1941; s. Moses and Bernice S.; m. Geniel Gwin, Apr. 18, 1970; children: Alden, Justin, Owen. AB, Harvard U., 1965, MA in Teaching, 1967; JD, NYU, 1971. Bar: N.Y. 1972, U.S. Ct. Appeals (1st cir.) 1972, U.S. Tax Ct. 1984. Law clk. to Hon. Edward M. McEntee U.S. Ct. Appeals, Providence, 1971-72; assoc. Debevoise & Plimpton, N.Y.C., 1972-81, ptnr., 1982—. Mem. ABA, N.Y. State Bar Assn., Assn. of Bar of City of N.Y. Home: 234 W 101st St New York NY 10025-4905 Office: Debevoise & Plimpton 919 3rd Ave Fl 47 New York NY 10022-3902 Office phone: 212-909-6861.

**STROCK, ROBERT S.,** retired education educator; b. Sewickley, Pa., Oct. 19, 1921; s. Paul Blazier and Jessie Serene Strock. BS, Geneva Coll., 1947; EdM, Shippensburg U., 1964; postgrad., Colo. State U., 1965, U. Tenn., 1966, U. Miami, 1968, Ind. U., 1969. Cert. tchr. Dept. Pub. Instrn., Pa., Nat. Coun. Bus. Schs. Acctg. tchr. Duffs Iron City Coll., Pitts., 1947—50; stock control clk. H.H. Robertson Co., Inc., Ambridge, Pa., 1950—57; tchr. Baden (Pa.)-Economy Sch. Dist., 1957—67; asst. prof. Slippery Rock (Pa.) U., 1967—72; assoc. prof. Indiana U. Pa., 1972—99, prof. emeritus, 2002—. Dir. homecoming parades Ind. U. Pa., 1974—98, Geneva Coll., 2000, 05, 06. Mem. bd. elections Beaver (Pa.) County Election Bur., 1982—84; councilman Ind. Boro Coun., 1991—94; mem. 27th Air Transport Group. Staff sgt. USAF, 1943—45. Recipient Outstanding Prof. award, Student Pa. State Edn. Assn., 1992, Patriotic Achievement award, Mil. Order of the World Wars Chpt. 200, 1993, Pres. medal of distinction, Indiana U. Pa., 1998. Mem.: Friends of Nat. Parks Gettysburg, Nat. Trust Hist. Preservation, Beaver Heritage Soc. (bd. trustees), Beaver County Geneal. Soc., CWPT History Channel Club (life), Am. Legion, Alpha Phi Omega, Delta Pi Epsilon (treas. Beta Alpha chpt. 1973—76), Theta Xi (past advisor Beta Lambda chpt. 1972—75). Republican. Methodist. Avocations: genealogy, travel, collecting miniature bottles, collecting postcards. Home: 222 Fourth St Beaver PA 15009

**STROCK, WILLIAM C.,** lawyer; b. Cleve., Sept. 22, 1942; s. Harry Kenneth and Mabel T. (Moseley) S.; m. Anne B. Turner, June 26, 1965; children: William Matthew, Anne Elizabeth. BA, So. Meth. U., 1964, JD, 1967. Bar: Tex. 1967, admitted to practice: US Supreme Ct., US Ct. Appeals (5th Cir.), US Ct. Appeals (8th Cir.), US Ct. Appeals (11th Cir.), US Dist. Ct. (No. Dist.) Tex., US Dist. Ct. (So. Dist.) Tex., US Dist. Ct. (Ea. Dist.) Tex., US Dist. Ct. (We. Dist.) Tex., US Dist. Ct. (Dist. Colo.), Supreme Ct. Tex. Labor rels. atty. Gen. Dynamics Co., Ft. Worth, 1967-70; ptnr. Seay, Gwinn, Crawford, Mebus & Blakeney, Dallas, 1970-82; ptnr., labor and employment law Haynes & Boone LLP, Dallas, 1982—. Mem. adj. faculty So. Meth. U., 1983—90, mem. adj. faculty employment law & labor law, 1990. Contbg. editor Developing Law Law, 2nd edit., 1983; editor: Employment Law Handbook, 1989; assoc. editor Jour. of Air Law and Commerce, 1966—67. Named a Tex. Super Lawyer, Tex. Monthly Mag., 2003, 2004; named one of Best Lawyers in Dallas, D Magazine, 2001, 2003. Fellow: Coll. of Labor & Employment Lawyers; mem.: Labor Law Tex. Bd. of Legal Specialization (adv. com.), Tex. Assn. Bus. (chmn. employment law subcom. 1988), Tex. Bar Found., ABA (labor and employment law sect.). Republican. Presbyterian. Office: Haynes and Boone LLP 901 Main St Ste 3100 Dallas TX 75202-3789 Office Phone: 214-651-5623. Office Fax: 214-200-0655. Business E-Mail: bill.strock@haynesboone.com.

**STRODE, JOSEPH ARLIN,** lawyer; b. DeWitt, Ark., Mar. 5, 1946; s. Thomas Joseph and Nora (Richardson) S.; m. Carolyn Taylor, Feb. 9, 1969; children: Tanya Briana, William Joseph. BSEE with honors, U. Ark., 1969, JD, So. Meth. U., 1972. Bar: Ark. 1972. Design engr. Tex. Instruments Inc., Dallas, 1969-70; patent agent Tex. Instruments, Dallas, 1970—72; assoc. Bridges, Young, Matthews, Drake, Pine Bluff, Ark., 1972-74, ptnr., 1975—. Chmn. Pine Bluff Airport Commn., 1993; bd. dirs. United Way Jefferson County, Pine Bluff, 1975-77, campaign chmn., 1983, pres., 1986, exec. com., 1983-87; bd. dirs. Leadership Pine Bluff, 1983-85. Mem. Ark. Bar Assn., Jefferson County Bar Assn. (pres. 1995), Pine Bluff C. of C. (dir. 1981, 84, 94, 97), Ark. Wildlife Fed. (dir. 1979-81), Jefferson County Wildlife Assn. (dir. 1973-80, pres. 1976-77), Kiwanis (lt. gov. Mo.-Ark. divsn. 1983-84, chmn. lt. govs. 1983-84), Order of Coif, Tau Beta Pi, Eta Kappa Nu. Home: 7600 Jay Lynn Ln Pine Bluff AR 71603-9387 Office: 315 E 8th Ave Pine Bluff AR 71601-5005 Office Phone: 870-534-5532. Business E-Mail: joestrode@bridgesplc.com.

**STRODE, WILLIAM HALL, III,** photojournalist; b. Louisville, Aug. 6, 1937; s. William Hall and Margaret (Diehl) S.; m. Elizabeth Ann Wheeler, Nov. 26, 1960 (div. 1973); children: Alissa Michelle, Erin Hall; m. Hope Powel Alexander, Nov. 12, 1977 (div. 1997); children: Hope Ives, Charlotte Alexander. BS, Western Ky. U., 1959. News photographer Courier Jour. and Louisville Times, 1960-64, asst. dir. photography, 1968-75; photographer Courier Jour. mag., 1964-77; formed William Strode Assocs., photog. and pub. co., Louisville, 1978—, Harmony House pubs., 1984—. Author 24 books; exhbns. include Fine Arts III, 1961, Profile in Poverty, Smithsonian Instn., 1966, Documerica, in Corcoran Gallery, Washington, 1972, 73, Picture of the Year Travelling Exhibits; one man show includes Speed Mus. Active local Boy Scouts Am., Eagle Scout; founder Nat. Press Photographers Found., 1975. Served with AUS, 1959. Recipient Headliners best photojournalism award, 1965; award for excellence for best mag. photog. reporting Overseas Press Club, 1967; co-recipient Pulitzer Prize for pub. service Courier Jour., 1967, for feature photography, 1976; Art Dirs. Gold medal, 1980, World Press Photog. Arts and Scis. award, 1985 Mem. Nat. Press Photographers Assn. Soc. Profl. Journalists, Masons (32 deg.), Scottish Rite, Knights Templar, Sovereign

Colonial Wars, Sigma Chi (Significant Sig award, 2005), Kappa Alpha Mu. Methodist. Home and Office: 1008 Kent Rd Goshen KY 40026-9768 Office Phone: 502-228-4446. Personal E-mail: harmonyhousepub@bellsouth.net.

**STROEVE, PIETER,** chemical engineering researcher, educator; b. Velp, Gelderland, The Netherlands, Sept. 15, 1945; arrived in US, 1959; s. Antonie and Frederika Wilhelmina Stroeve; m. Diane Barrett; children: Dale, Maryke, Yoly, Jodie. Student, Contra Costa Coll., 1962-65; BSChemE, U. Calif., Berkeley, 1967; MSChemE, MIT, 1969, ScD, 1973. Sr. scientist Weizmann Inst. Sci., Rehovot, Israel, 1973—74; asst. prof. U. Nijmegen, The Netherlands, 1974-77; postdoctoral rschr. Weizmann Inst. Sci., 1977; from asst. to assoc. prof. SUNY, Buffalo, 1977-81; assoc. prof. U. Calif., Davis, 1981-83, prof. dept. chem. engring. and material sci., 1983—. Cons. Los Alamos (N.Mex.) Nat. Lab., 1983—86, Ames Nat. Lab., 1995—97, Procter and Gamble Co., 2003; vis. prof. Max-Planck Inst., Mainz, Germany, 1996; Frontis prof. nanotech. Wageningen U., Netherlands, 2003—04; co-dir. NSF Ctr. on Polymer Interfaces and Macromolecular Assemblies; co-founder ATA Co., Nanotech. Co. Solar Cells, QlNanoSys. Author, editor (books): Integrated Circuits, 1985, Biomedical Engineering, 1983; editor: Transport with Chemical Reaction, 1981, Molecular Engineering of Ultrathin Polymeric Films, 1987, Macromolecular Assemblies in Polymeric Systems, 1992; author: (book) Polymer-Layered Silicate and Silica Nanocomposites, 2005; contbr. over 190 articles to profl. jours. Recipient Tchg. award, U. Calif., Davis, 1984, 1990, 1991, 1995, 2006, 2d Pl. award Big Bang bus. plan competition, 2005; grantee NSF, 1985, 1987—89, 1994—2002; P.J. Flory fellow, IBM Almaden Rsch. Ctr., 1988—89. Mem. Am. Inst. Chem. Engrs., Am. Chem. Soc. Office: U Calif Davis Dept Chem Engring and Material Sci Davis CA 95616 Office Phone: 530-752-0400, 530-752-8778. Business E-Mail: pstroeve@ucdavis.edu.

**STROGER, JOHN H., JR.,** county official; BS, Xavier U.; JD, DePaul Law Sch. Pres. Forest Preserve Dist. of Cook County, Chgo.; spl. atty. to gen. atty.; atty.; commr. Cook County; pres. Cook County Bd. Commr., Chgo., 1994—. Named one of 100 Most Influential Black Americans, Ebony mag., 2006. Achievements include had the John H. Stroger, Jr. Hosp. of Cook County named after him. Office: Cook County Bd Commr 118 N Clark St Rm 537 Chicago IL 60602*

**STROH, RAYMOND EUGENE,** retired personnel executive; b. Bloomington, Ill., Aug. 13, 1942; s. Harry William and Felcie Cleo (Weaver) S.; m. Peggy Jane Whitacre, June 12, 1966 (dec. Jan. 2002); children: Rebecca Jane, David Ray. BA, So. Ill. U., 1966, U. Ill., 1977. Pers. technician Ill. Dept. Mental Health, Springfield, Ill., 1966-67; pers. officer Andrew McFarland Mental Health Ctr., Springfield, 1967-68, Manteno (Ill.) State Hosp., 1968-69; chief pers. officer Ill. Dept. Law Enforcement, Springfield, 1969-75, Ill. Dept. Revenue, Springfield, 1975-81, Ill. Dept. Mental Health, Springfield, 1981-82; pers. exec. Ill. Dept. Cen. Mgmt. Svcs., Springfield, 1982-2001; ret. State govt. chmn. U.S. Savs. Bond Campaign, Springfield, 1978-82. Bd. dirs. Consumer Credit Counseling Svc., Springfield, 1988-94, sec., 1994; coun. exec. bd. Boy Scouts Am., Springfield, 1987—, v.p., 1987-99, dist. commr., 1979-86, unit commr., 1970-79; bd. dirs. State Employees Credit Union, 1984-85. Recipient Patriotic Svc. awards U.S. Treasury Dept., 1979-82, Silver Beaver award Boy Scouts Am., 1987, Dist. award of merit, 1981, Area Pres. awards, 1985, 86, Scouters Key award, 1976, Order of the Arrow Vigil Honor, 1998, James E. West Fellowship award, 1998. Mem. NRA, U. Ill. Alumni Assn., So. Ill. U. Alumni Assn., Exptl. Aircraft Assn., Aircraft Owners and Pilots Assn., Cessna Owner Orgn., Ponce De Leon Inlet Lighthouse Assn., Nat. Geog. Soc., Cornell U. Lab. of Ornithology, Ill. Audubon Soc., Abraham Lincoln Gun Club, Appalachian Trail Conf., Union County (Tenn.) Hist. Soc., Wabash R.R. Hist. Soc., Am. Rose Soc., Theta Delta Chi. Republican. Lutheran. Avocations: aviation, hunting, fishing, model railroading, gardening. Home: 2111 Warwick Dr Springfield IL 62704-4147

**STROHECKER, LEON HARRY, JR.,** orthodontist; b. Schuylkill Haven, Pa., Aug. 14, 1932; s. Leon Harry and Anna (Fabian) S.; m. Juanita Mary Puyoou, Apr. 13, 1957; children: Sandra Lee Strohecker Beckett, Leon Harry III. Student, U. Pa., 1950-53, DDS, 1957, orthodontic cert., 1960. Bd. cert. Am. Bd. Orthodontics. Pres., pvt. practice, Lansdale, Pa., 1961—; dir. Face Head & Neck Pain and Trauma Ctr., Lansdale, 1987. Bd. dirs. Artman Home Retirement Ctr., Ambler; treas., bd. dirs. Valley Ctr. Mental Health Clinic, Lansdale, 1984—2002; guest lectr. in field. Pres. Lansdale Rotary Club, 1967-68; coun. mem. Trinity Luth. Ch., Lansdale, 1977-85, chmn. fin. com., 1980-85. Lt. (j.g.) USN, 1957-59. Named Internat. Health Profl. of Yr., Internat. Biographical Ctr., 2003; recipient Spoke award, Jr. C. of C., 1963, Spark Plug award, 1963, Widsom award of Honor, Best Orthodontist vote, 2 Lansdale area newspapers, One Thousand Great Ams. award, Internat. Biographical Ctr., 2001, 2002. Mem. ADA, Internat. Acad. Head, Neck and Facial Pain, Internat. Coll. Cranio-Mandibular Orthopedics, Am. Acad. Pain Mgmt. (diplomate), Am. Assn. for Functional Orthodontics, Am. Profl. Practice Assn., Am. Soc. Dentistry for Children, Am. Acad. Oral Medicine, Am. Assn. Orthodontists, Am. Assn. Stomatologists, Am. Acad. Oral Medicine, Middle Atlantic Orthodontic Soc., Pa. Orthod ontic Soc., Phila. Orthodontic Soc., Pa. Dental Assn., Second Dist. Dental Assn., Montgomery-Bucks Dental Soc., Alpha Omega, Omicron Kappa Epsilon. Avocations: tennis, travel, bridge, water sports. Home: 1512 Cedar Hill Rd Ambler PA 19002-1406 Office: 456 E Hancock St Lansdale PA 19446-3803 Office Phone: 215-855-7717. Personal E-mail: lstrohecker@hotmail.com.

**STROHM, BRUCE C.,** lawyer, real estate company executive; b. 1955; BS, U. Ill.; JD, Northwestern U. Ptnr. Rosenberg & Liebentritt, PC, Chgo.; exec. v.p., gen. counsel, sec. Equity Residential, Chgo., 1995—. Office: Equity Residential 2 N Riverside Plaza Chicago IL 60606

**STROHM, DAVID,** venture capitalist; BA, Dartmouth Coll.; MBA, Harvard Bus. Sch. Gen. ptnr. Greylock Partners, Waltham, Mass., 1980—83, gen. ptnr., opened Palo Alto office, 1983—. Bd. dirs. Legato Systems, Inc., 1988—2003, AccelChip, AtHoc, Successfactors, CoWare, Decru, Double-Click, EMC Corp., Internet Security Systems, Mobile Automation, Wily Technol. Office: Greylock Ptnrs 2929 Campus Dr Ste 400 San Mateo CA 94403 Office Phone: 650-493-5525. Office Fax: 650-493-5575. Business E-Mail: dstrohm@greylock.com.

**STROHMENGER, THOMAS C,** lawyer; BA, Fordham U.; JD, St. John's U. Sch. of Law; M, NYU. Bar: Conn., Fla., NY. Counsel Am. Ins. Assn.; with Aetna, 1978—; v.p. and chief compliance officer Aetna Inc., 2001—. Office: Aetna Inc 151 Farmington Ave Hartford CT 06156

**STROHMEYER, JOHN,** writer, retired editor; b. Cascade, Wis., June 26, 1924; s. Louis A. and Anna Rose (Saladunas) S.; m. Nancy Jordan, Aug. 20, 1949 (dec. 2000); children: Mark, John, Sarah; m. Sylvia Ciernick Broady, Oct. 25, 2003. Student, Moravian Coll., 1941—43; AB, Muhlenberg Coll., 1947; MA in Journalism, Columbia U., 1948; LHD (hon.), Lehigh U., 1983. With Nazareth Item, Pa., 1940—41; night reporter Bethlehem Globe-Times, Pa., 1941—43, 1945—47; investigative reporter Providence Jour.-Bull., 1949—56; editor Bethlehem Globe-Times, 1956—64, v.p., 1961—84, dir., 1963—84. African-Am. journalism tchr. in Nairobi, Freetown, 1964; Atwood prof. journalism U. Alaska, Anchorage, 1987-88, writer-in-residence, 1989—; Clendinen Prof., U. S. Fla., 2001. Author: Crisis in Bethlehem: Big Steel's Struggle to Survive, 1986, Extreme Conditions: Big Oil and The Transformation of Alaska, 1993, Historic Anchorage, 2001. Lt. (j.g.) USNR, 1943-45. Pulitzer Traveling fellow, 1948; Nieman fellow, 1952-53; recipient Comenius award Moravian Coll., 1971; Pulitzer prize for editl. writing, 1972; Alicia Patterson Found. fellow, 1984, 85. Mem. Am. Soc. Newspaper Editors, Pa. Soc. Newspaper Editors (pres. 1964-66), Anchorage Racquet Club. Home: 6633 Lunar Dr Anchorage AK 99504-4550 E-mail: jstroh@gci.net.

**STROJNIK, TADEJ,** neurosurgeon, researcher; b. Ljubljana, Slovenia, July 11, 1963; s. Franc and Marija (Petrič) S.; m. Irena Šurca, June 6, 1987; children: Tom, Maša. MD, U. Ljubljana, 1989, MSc, 1994, PhD, 1998.

Physician Health Ctr., Ptuj, Slovenia, 1989-90; resident in neurosurgery Univ. Clinic Neurosurgery, Ljubljana, 1995—96, Tchg. Hosp., Maribor, Slovenia, 1990-95, neurosurgeon, 1996—; asst. prof. U. Ljubljana, 2002—. Aitken Clin. Rsch. fellow, 1998-99. Mem. Med. Chamber Slovenia, Slovene Med. Soc., Slovenian Neurosurg. Soc. (sec. 1997-2001), European Assn. Neurosurgeons, Ctrl. European Neurosurg. Soc. (bd. dirs.). Roman Catholic. Avocations: photography, fishing, reading. Office: Tchg Hosp Dept Neurosurgery Ljubljanska 5 2000 Maribor Slovenia Business E-Mail: t.strojnik@siol.net.

**STROJUY, JOAN E.,** writer; d. Julius and Florence Rose Strojuy; children: Gerald Jeffrey Thomas, Pamela Lynn Ferraro, Jill Patricia Miller. BS, U. Md., 1973. Reporter McGraw-Hill Info. Sys., San Francisco, 1980—81, Reno Gazette Jour., Battle Moutain, Nev., 1981—83; reporter, stringer Porterville Recorder & AP, Porterville, Calif., 1983—84; mng. editor Battle Mountain Bugle, Battle Mountain, Nev., 1981—83; stringer UPI, Battle Moutain, Nev., 1981—83; polit. action adminstr. Citizens Action League & ACORN, San Francisco, 1984—88, L.A., 1984—88, Sacramento, 1984—88, San Diego, 1984—88; writer various locations, Calif., 1988—95, NY, 1988—95, self-employed, DC, 1998—99, fiction writer, 2001—; newspaper reader Burrelles Press Svc., Wash., 1995—98; editl. asst., reader Marcourt, San Antonio, 1999—2001. Author: (novels) Mapmaker, 2004. Vol. Plattsburg Nursing Home, NY, 1995, Mead Start, Plattsburg, NY, 1995; bd. dirs. Bexar County Rep. Women, San Antonio, 2002—. Avocations: hiking, photography, fishing, gardening. Home: 2400 Oakhill Rd # 1008 San Antonio TX 78238 Personal E-mail: jestroj@sbcglobal.net.

**STROKE, HINKO HENRY,** physicist, researcher; b. Zagreb, Croatia, June 16, 1927; came to U.S., 1943, naturalized, 1949; s. Elias and Edith (Mechner) S.; m. Norma Richlick, Jan. 14, 1956; children: Ilana Lucy, Marija Tamar. BEE, N.Y. Inst. Tech., 1949; MS, MIT, 1952, PhD, 1955. From rsch. asst. to rsch. assoc. Princeton (N.J.) U., 1954-57; rsch. staff lab. electronics, lectr. dept. physics MIT, 1957-63; assoc. prof. physics NYU, N.Y.C., 1963-68, prof., 1968—. Dept. chmn. NYU, 1988-91; prof. associé. U. Paris, 1969-70, École Normale Supérieure, 1976; vis. scientist Max Planck Inst. für Quantenoptik, Garching, U. Munich, 1977-78, 81-82, 93; cons. Atomic Instrument Co., MIT Sci. Translation Svc., Tech. Rsch. Group, Cambridge Air Force Rsch. Ctr., Am. Optical Corp., ITT Fed. Labs., NASA, others; mem. com. on line spectra of elements NAS-NRC, 1976-82; sci. assoc. CERN, Geneva, 1983—. Contbg. author: Nuclear Physics, 1963, Atomic Physics, 1969, Hyperfine Interactions in Excited Nuclei, 1971, Francis Bitter: Selected Papers, 1969, Atomic Physics 3, 1973, Nuclear Moments and Nuclear Structure, 1973, A Perspective of Physics, Vol. 1, 1977, Atomic Physics 8, 1983, Lasers in Atomic, Molecular, and Nuclear Physics, 1989—, Symposium on Probing Luminous and Dark Matter, 2000; editor: Comments on Atomic, Molecular and Optical Physics, The Physical Review-The First Hundred Years, Benjamin Bederson: Works, Comments and Legacies, Advances in Atomic, Molecular and Optical Physics, Vol. 51. Mem. Chorus Pro Musica, 1951—54, 1957—63, Münchener Bach-Chor, Munich, 1977—82, 1992; Choeur pro Arte Lausanne, 1983—; mem. Collegiate Chorale, NY, 1964—94, Dessoff Choirs, 1994—, Westchester Oratorio Soc., 2001—. Recipient Sr. U.S. Scientist award Alexander von Humboldt Found., 1977; NATO sr. fellow in sci., 1975 Fellow Am. Phys. Soc. (publs. oversight com. 1991-93), Optical Soc. Am., AAAS; mem. IEEE (life), European Phys. Soc., Soc. Française de Physique, Sigma Xi, Tau Beta Pi, Omicron Delta Kappa. Office: NYU Dept Physics 4 Washington Pl New York NY 10003-6621 Office Phone: 212-998-7679. Business E-Mail: henry.stroke@nyu.edu.

**STROM, BRIAN LESLIE,** internist, educator; b. NYC, Dec. 8, 1949; s. Martin and Edith (Singer) S.; m. Elaine Marilyn Moskowitz, June 4, 1978; children: Shayna Lee, Jordan Blair. BS, Yale U., 1971; MD, Johns Hopkins U., 1975; MPH, U. Calif., Berkeley, 1980. Diplomate Am. Bd. Internal Medicine, Am. Bd. Epidemiology. Intern in medicine U. Calif., San Francisco, 1975-76, resident in medicine, 1976-78, research fellow in clinical pharmacology, 1978-80; from asst. prof. to assoc. prof. medicine and pharmacology U. Pa., 1980-93, prof. medicine, 1993—, prof. biostatistics & epidemiology, 1995—. Adj. asst. prof. clin. pharmacy Phila. Coll. of Pharmacy and Sci., 1981-90, adj. assoc. prof., 1990-93, adj. prof., 1993—; mem. U. Pa. Cancer Ctr., 1981—; attending staff Hosp. U. Pa., 1980—, co-dir Clin. Epidemiology Unit, 1980-91, dir., 1991-2001; dir. Clin. Pharmacology Cons. Svc., 1981-82; dir. Ctr. for Clin. Epidemiology and Biostats., 1993—, chair dept. biostats. and epidemiology, 1995—; lectr. in field; George S. prod. pub. health and preventive medicine, 2002—; cons. CDC, 1981, Coun. for Internat. Orgn. of Med. Scis., Geneva, Switzerland, 1981-83, Office of Tech. Assessment, Congress of U.S., 1980-81, Aging Rev. Com., Nat. Inst. Aging, 1982, Ministry of Pub. Health, State of Kuwait, 1982, Royal Tropical Inst. Amsterdam, 1983, others. Editl. cons. Johns Hopkins U. Press, J.B. Lippincott; referee Annals of Internal Medicine, Archives of Internal Medicine, Clin. Pharmacology and Therapeutics, Digestive Diseases and Sci., Internat. Jour. Cardiology, Internat. Jour. Epidemiology, Jour. AMA, Jour. Gen. Internal Medicine, Med. Care, Primary Care Tech., Sci.; editor Pharmaepidemiology and Drug Safety; mem. editl. bd. 7 jours.; contbr. numerous articles to profl. jours. Nat. Acad. Scis. grantee, Rockefeller Found. grantee, NIH grantee, many others. Fellow ACP, Am. Coll. Epidemiology, Am. Epidemiology Soc.; mem. Am. Fedn. Med. Rsch., Am. Pub. Health Assn., Am. Soc. Clin. Pharmacology and Therapeutics, Am. Soc. Clin. Investigation, Am. Assn. Physicians, Internat. Soc. Pharmacoepidemiology, Internat. Epidemiol. Assn., Soc. for Epidemiologic Rsch., Soc. Gen. Internal Medicine, Inst. Medicine, Inst. Medicine. Democrat. Jewish. Avocations: hiking, bicycling, camping, skiing. Home: 332 Hidden River Rd Narberth PA 19072-1111 Office Phone: 215-898-2368. Business E-Mail: bstrom@cceb.med.upenn.edu.

**STROM, DEBRA ELAINE,** social studies educator; b. Marshall, Minn., Dec. 15, 1953; d. Norman James and Virginia Margaret Evans; m. Roger Lloyd Buoni, June 29, 1974. BS, Dakota State U., Madison, 1977; MA, U. S.D., Vermillion, 1982. Bus. instr. Sinte Gleska U., Mission, SD, 1977—83; social studies and health tchr. Huron Pub. Schs., SD, 1983—. State examiner S.D. Gen. Ednl. Devel., Sioux Falls, 2004—. Named Outstanding Educator of Am., 1987. Mem.: S.D. Edn. Assn., S.D. Bus. and Office Edn. (sec. 1983—85, pres. 1985—87). Avocation: travel. Office: Huron Pub Schs/Huron HS PO Box 949 801 18th SW Huron SD 57350

**STROM, DORIS MARIE,** music educator; b. Chgo., June 28, 1933; m. Edward R. McLaughlin. BA, U. Sioux Falls, 1953; MA, U. S.D., 1969. Tchr. music, English Sioux Falls, Philip Sch. Dist., Baltic Sch. Dist., Canton Sch. Dist., SD, 1955—73; ins. agt., exec. Prudential Ins. Co., Aberdeen, Rapid City, 1974—86; ednl. svcs. mgr., promotion mgr. Rapid City Jour., SC, 1986—92. Adj. teacher. Nat. Am. U., Rapid City, 1980—89, 1999—, S.D. State U., Brookings, 1988—92; choir dir. 1st Congl. Ch., 1999—. Author: In the Village, 1996; co-author: Reflections, 1994. Avocations: gardening, cooking, reading.

**STROM, KRISTINA CHASE,** writer, consultant; b. Schenectady, NY, Dec. 28, 1948; d. Raymond Olaf and Lois Moulton Strom; children: Kia Strom Kuresman, Kamala Strom Kuresman, Kimberly Strom Kuresman, Kara Strom Kuresman. PhD, Universal Life Sem. Lic. Insurance OH; Ordained Clergy OH. Asst. buyer, buyer Hess's Dept. Store, Allentown, Pa., 1968—69; educator Xavier U., New Orleans, 1970; columnist Denver Free Press, 1972; co-founder, owner New World Ctr. Bookshop and Foodshop, 1973—74; tchr. Beth Adam Religious Sch., Cin., 1981—88, art dir., 1987—89, prin., 1988—89; editor Beth Adam Newsletter, Cin., 1982—86; designer Del Favero Enterprises, Cin., 1984—90; store mgr. B. Dalton Books, Cin., 1990—91; systems operator TriStateOnline Greater Cin. Consortium Colls. and Univs., 1999, adminstr., 1999; pvt. practice Glendale, Ohio, 1968—; freelance artist, 1970—; design and bus. cons., 1985—. Columnist, staff writer Silent Messages, Cin., 1996—99; moderator Wells List, 1995—; owner, mgr. CelestialPerspectives.com, Cin., 1999—. Exhibitions include Mich. State U., 2003—04, Represented in permanent collections Millennium Challenge; author: Denim and Lace, An historical mystery of first love, timeless love, numerous poems; co-editor, contbr. From Eulogy to Joy, A

Heartfelt Anthology, Feathered Star, 2003, Monkey Wrench New Quilts from an Old Favorite, 2004, Seven Sisters New Quilts from an Old Favorite, 2005; contbr. articles to profl. jours. Pres. Kindervelt #17 Cin. Children's Hosp. Aux., 1983—85. Mem.: Smithsonian Nat. Mus. Am. Indian, Nat. Ctr. for Preservation of Medicinal Herbs, The Nature Conservancy, Nat. Audubon Soc., Am. Quilter's Soc., Sierra Club, Twilight Club Ctr. Evolutionary Ethics. Avocations: gardening, genealogy, book collecting, anthropology, archaeology. Home: 171 West Sharon Road Glendale OH 45246-4334 Personal E-mail: kristinastrom@celestialperspectives.com.

**STROM, LYLE ELMER,** judge; b. Omaha, Nebr., Jan. 6, 1925; s. Elmer T. and Eda (Hanisch) Strom; m. Regina Ann Kelly, July 31, 1950 (dec.); children: Mary Bess, Susan Frances(dec.), Amy Claire, Cassie A., David Kelly, Margaret Mary, Bryan Thomas. Student, U. Nebr., 1946-47; AB, Creighton U., 1950, JD cum laude, 1953. Bar: Nebr. 1953. Assoc. Fitzgerald, Brown, Leahy, Strom, Schorr & Barmettler and predecessor firm, Omaha, 1953-60, ptnr., 1960-63, gen. trial ptnr., 1963-85; judge U.S. Dist. Ct. Nebr., Omaha, 1985-87, chief judge, 1987-94, sr. judge, 1995—. Adj. prof. law Creighton U., 1959-95, clinical prof., 1996—; mem. com. pattern jury instrns. and practice and proc. Nebr. Supreme Ct., 1965-91; spl. legal counsel Omaha Charter Rev. Commn., 1973; chair gender fairness task force U.S. Ct. Appeals (8th cir.), 1993-97. Exec. com. Covered Wagon Coun. Boy Scouts Am., 1953—57, bd. trustees, exec. com. Mid-Am. Coun., 1988—; chmn. bd. trustees Marian H.S., 1969—71; mem. pres. coun. Creighton U., 1990—95. With U.S. Maritime Svc., 1943—46. Fellow Am. Coll. Trial Lawyers, Internat. Acad. Trial Lawyers; mem. Nebr. Bar Assn. (ho. of dels. 1978-81, exec. coun. 1981-87, pres. 1989-90), Nebr. Bar Found. (bd. trustees 1998    ), Omaha Bar Assn. (pres. 1980-81), Am. Judicature Soc., Midwestern Assn. Amateur Athletic Union (pres. 1976-78), Rotary (pres. 1993-94), Alpha Sigma Nu (pres. alumni chpt. 1970-71). Republican. Roman Catholic. Office: US Dist Ct Roman Hruska Courthouse 111 S 18th Plz Ste 3190 Omaha NE 68102

**STROM, MILTON GARY,** lawyer; b. Rochester, NY, Dec. 5, 1942; s. Harold and Dolly (Isaacson) S.; m. Barbara A. Simon, Jan. 18, 1975; children: Carolyn, Michael, Jonathan. BS in Econ., U. Pa., 1964; JD, Cornell U., 1967. Bar: N.Y. 1968, U.S. Dist. Ct. (W. dist.) N.Y. 1968, U.S. Ct. Claims 1969, U.S. Ct. Mil. Appeals 1969, U.S. Ct. Appeals (D.C. cir.) 1970, U.S. Supreme Ct. 1972, U.S. Dist. Ct. (so. dist.) N.Y. 1975. Atty. SEC, Washington, 1968-71; assoc. Skadden, Arps, Slate, Meagher & Flom, N.Y.C., 1971-76, ptnr., 1977—2004, of counsel, 2004—. Served with USCGR, 1967-73. Mem. ABA, N.Y. State Bar Assn. (corp. law sect.), Assn. of Bar of City of N.Y., Internat. Bar Assn., Beach Point Club. Republican. Jewish. Avocations: tennis, skiing, golf. Office: Skadden Arps Slate Meagher & Flom 4 Times Sq Fl 42 New York NY 10036-6522 E-mail: mstrom@skadden.com.

**STROMAN, SUSAN,** choreographer, theater director; b. Wilmington, Del., Oct. 17, 1954; d. Charles and Frances Stroman; m. Mike Ockrent, 1996 (dec. Dec. 2, 1999); stepchildren: Ben, Natasha. Grad., U. Del. Choreographer Flora Roberts Inc. Dancer Chgo., 1977—78, Whoopee!, 1979, Richard III, 1980, Peter Pan, 1983, choreographer (off-Broadway) Broadway Babylon, 1984, Sayonara, 1987, Flora, the Red Menace, 1987, Shenandoah, 1988, Slasher, 1988, Rhythm Ranch, 1989, The Roar of the Greaspaint-The Smell of the Crowd, 1990, Gypsy, 1991, And the World Goes 'Round, 1991 (Outer Critics' Cir. award for choreography, 1991), A Christmas Carol, 1994, (Broadway plays) Crazy for You, 1992 (Tony award for best choreography, 1992, Drama Desk award for choreography, 1992, Outer Critics' Cir. award, 1992, Laurence Olivier award for choreography, 1993), Picnic, 1994, Show Boat, 1994 (Tony award for best choreography, 1995, Astaire award Theatre Devel. Fund, 1995), Big, 1996 (Tony nomination for best choreography, 1996), Oklahoma, 2002 (Laurence Olivier Award for choreography, 2002, Tony nomination for best choreography, 2002), (Operas) Don Giovanni, 1989, A Little Night Music, 1990, 100 in the Shade, 1992, (spl.) Liza Minnelli: Stepping Out at Radio City Music Hall, 1991 (Emmy nomination for choreography, 1993), (films) The Producers, 2005; choreographer, conceiver (Broadway plays) Steel Pier, 1997 (Tony nomination for best choreography, 1997), dir., choreographer The Music Man, 2000 (Tony nomination for best choreography, 2000, Tony nomination for best dir., 2000), The Producers, 2001 (Tony award for best choreography, 2001, Tony award for best dir., 2001, Drama Desk Award for best dir. musical, 2001, Touring Broadway award, best direction, League Am. Theatres and Producers, 2005), The Frogs, 2004, dir., choreographer, conceiver Contact, 2000 (Tony award for best choreography, 2000, Lucille Lortel Award for outstanding direction, 2000, Tony nomination for best dir., 2000), Thou Shalt Not, 2001, Double Feature, 2004, co-conceiver Trading Places, Equity Libr. Theatre Informals, 1983, dir., co-conceiver (off-Broadway) Living Color, 1986, co-conceiver, choreographer (TV spl.) Sondheim-A Celebration at Carnegie Hall, 1992, asst. dir., asst. choreographer (Broadway plays) Musical Chairs, 1980; dir.(TV spl.): An Evening With the Boston Pops-A Tribute to Leonard Bernstein, 1989. Recipient Disting. Achievement in Musical Theatre Award, Drama League, 2001, Elan award, 2005. Address: Flora Roberts Agy Penhouse A 157 W 57th St New York NY 10019-2210*

**STROMBERG, CLIFFORD DOUGLAS,** lawyer; b. NYC, June 1, 1949; s. George M. and Greta (Netzow) Stromberg; m. Ava S. Feiner, June 25, 1972; children: Kimberly, Eric. BA summa cum laude, Yale U., 1971; JD, Harvard U., 1974. Bar: NY 1975, DC 1979, US Dist. Ct. (so. and ea. dists.) NY 1975, US Ct. Appeals (DC cir.) 1975, US Ct. Appeals (2nd cir.) 1975, US Supreme Ct. 1980. Law clk. to judge U.S. Dist. Ct. (ea. dist.) N.Y., 1974-75; assoc. Arnold & Porter, Washington, 1975-78, 80-83; dep. exec. sec. HHS, Washington, 1978-80; cons. FTC, Washington, 1980; ptnr. Dorsey & Whitney, Washington, 1983-84; Hogan & Hartson, Washington, 1984—. Adj. asst. prof. emergency medicine George Washington U. Sch. Medicine, 1991-97. Co-author: Mental Health and Law: A System in Transition, 1975, Alternatives to the Hospital: Ambulatory Surgery Centers and Emergicenters, 1984, Entrepreneurial Health Care: How to Structure Successful New Ventures, 1985, The Psychologist's Legal Handbook, 1988, Access to Hospital Information: Problems and Strategies: 4 Frontiers of Health Services Management 3-33, 1987, Healthcare Provider Networks: Antitrust Issues and Practical Considerations in Devels. in Antitrust Law, 1990, Healthcare Credentialing: Implications for Academic Medical Centers, 1991; mem. editl. bd. Harvard Law Rev., 1972-73; editor in chief Healthspan: The Report of Health Business and Law, 1984-87; cons. editor: Managed Care Law Strategist, 1999-2002; contbr. articles to profl. jours. Bd. dirs. Nat. Children's Eye Care Found., Washington, 1985-87. Teaching fellow in govt. Harvard U., 1973-74. Fellow Am. Bar Found.; mem. ABA (chair working group health care reform 1993-96, state membership chmn. 1984, bd. dirs. forum com. health law 1987-90, adv. com. govt. affairs 1993-98, governing bd., individual rights and responsibilities sect., exec. coun., 1980-90, sec. 1984-87, chair-elect 1987-88, chair 1988-89, legal aid and indigent defendants com. 1982-87), Am. Health Lawyers Assn., Nat. Assn. Coll. and Univ. Attys., Phi Beta Kappa. Office: Hogan & Hartson 555 13th St NW Washington DC 20004-1161 Office Phone: 202-637-5699. Business E-Mail: cdstromberg@hhlaw.com.

**STROMBERG, GREGORY,** printing ink company executive; b. Milw., Feb. 10, 1948; s. Clifford Norman and Margaret Betty (Hoover) S.; m. Gail Elizabeth Steinbach, Aug. 22, 1970; children: Christopher, Brian, Ellen. BS, Marquette U., 1970; MBA, Jones Internat. U., 2006. Office product salesman Continental Can Co., Milw., 1970-78; sales rep. Sun Chem. Co., Milw., 1978-82; v.p. gen. mgr. Acme Printing Ink Co., Milw., 1982—; exec. v.p. Can. ops. Acme Printing Ink Can. Ltd., 1985—, pres., 1990—, v.p. sales/mktg. metal divsn., 2000—. Bd. dirs. Can. Ops. Acme Inks of Can., pres. Toobee Internat., Inc., Milw., 1981—; v.p., dir. mktg. and advertising sales INX Internat. Ink Co., 1991—. Author: Toobee Air Force Flight Training Manual, 1983. Advisor Milw. Jr. Achievement, 1974; sponsor Muscular Dystrophy, 1983; asst. mem. com. toys for Tots, Children's Hosp., Milw., 1983; active United Meth. Men. Mem. Internat. Metal Decorators Assn., Am. Mgmt. Assn. Internat., Am. Soc. Quality Control, Nat. Metal Decorators

Assn., Nat. Assn. Printers and Lithographers, Nat. Assn. Printing Equipment and Suppliers, Exec. Agenda of Wis Home: N69w23448 Donna Dr Sussex WI 53089-3245 Office Phone: 414-438-4384. E-mail: mitze@execpc.com.

**STROMBERG, JEAN WILBUR GLEASON,** lawyer; b. St. Louis, Oct. 31, 1943; d. Ray Lyman and Martha (Bugbee) W.; m. Gerald Kermit Gleason, Aug. 28, 1966 (div. 1987); children: C. Blake, Peter Wilbur; m. Kurt Stromberg, Jan. 3, 1993; 1 child, Kristoffer Stromberg. BA, Wellesley Coll., 1965; LLB cum laude, Harvard U., 1968. Bar: Calif. 1969, D.C. 1978. Assoc. Brobeck, Phleger & Harrison, San Francisco, 1969-72; spl. counsel to dir. div. corp. fin. SEC, Washington, 1972-76, assoc. dir. div. investment mgmt., 1976-78; of counsel Fulbright & Jaworski, Washington, 1978-80, ptnr., 1980-96; dir. fin. instns. and market issues GAO, Washington, 1996-97; cons. Washington, 1997—. Mem. adv. panel on legal issues GAO, 1992—96; mem. NASD select com. on NASDAQ, 1994—96; trustee AARP Intestment Program and AARP Scudder Mut. Funds, 1997—2000; bd. dirs. Scudder Mut. Funds., Svc. Source, Inc., Mut. Fund Dirs. Forum. Dir. William and Flora Hewlett Found., 2000—; overseer Wellesley Ctrs. Women, 2003-. Mem. ABA (chmn. subcom. on securities and banks, corp. laws com., bus. sect. 1982-93), D.C. Bar Assn. (chmn. steering com. bus. sect. 1982-84), FBA (chair exec. coun., securities com. 1993-95), Am. Bar Retirement Assn. (bd. dirs. 1986-90, 94-96), Phi Beta Kappa. Home and Office: 3816 Military Rd NW Washington DC 20015-2704*

**STROMBERG, PATRICIA ROBERTS,** retired school librarian; b. Cin., Apr. 23, 1932; d. Richard Bickmore and Ruth Hessler Roberts; children: Mark Alan Stromberg, Ruth Ann Stromberg Batson, BS in Edn, U. Cin., Ohio, 1954; postgrad., Our Lady of the Lake Coll., San Antonio, 1973-75; MA in Edn., U. Colo., Denver, 1979. Tchr. Cin. Pub. Schs., 1954-56, 1970-71, Mt. Healthy (Ohio) Pub. Schs., 1972-73; library media specialist Jefferson County Pub. Schs., Golden, Colo., 1976—97; ret. Mem. basic list com., Jefferson County Schs., 1976-77, Pleasant View Sch., 76-90, Peiffer Sch., 1990-97; computer cons. JEFFCO Schs., 1983-88; co-chair gifted and telented com. Pleasant View Sch., Golden, Colo., 1987-90; pres. JEFFCO Ednl. Media Specialists, 1990-92. Ruling elder on session Green Mt. Presbyn. Ch., 1982-84, 88-91, 2001-03, 06—, chair worship and fellowship/evangelism coms., 1988, 89, 2003-05, ch. mission com., 2006—; mem. social justice and peacemaking commn. Presbytery of Denver, 1989-92; mem. ministry evaluation, 1992 Cmty. Green Mt. Presbyn. Ch. Title IV-C Drama grantee Pleasant View Sch., 1981-84, Jeff Found. Venture grantee, 1985, CCIRA Star grantee, 1996. Mem. AAUW, Nat. Assn. Advancement and Perpetuation of Storytelling, Spellbinders, Jefferson County Internat. Reading Assn. (sec. 1978-79, area membership rep. 1991-95), Jefferson County Ret. Sch. Employees Assn. (vol. Colo. Coun. (chair Books for Kids com. 1998—) Internat. Reading Assn. (workshop presenter), Jefferson County Spellbinders Assn., Phi Delta Kappa. Republican. Avocations: internat. study children's lit., travel, storytelling, gardening, photography. Home: 12834 W Iliff Ave Lakewood CO 80228-4334 Office Phone: 303-988-3563. Personal E-mail: pstrawberry32@aol.com.

**STROMBERG, ROSS ERNEST,** lawyer; b. Arcata, Calif., May 5, 1940; s. Noah Anders and Anne Laura (Noyes) S.; m. Toni Nicholas, Dec. 16, 1961; m. Margaret Telonicher, Oct. 3, 1965; children: Kristin, Matthew, Gretchen, Erik. BS, Humboldt State U., 1962; JD, U. Calif., Berkeley, 1965. Bar: Calif. 1966, U.S. Dist. Ct. (no. dist.) Calif. 1966, U.S. Ct. Appeals (9th cir.) 1966. Assoc. Hanson Bridgett, San Francisco, 1965-70, ptnr., 1970-85, Epstein Becker Stromberg & Green, San Francisco, 1985-90, Jones Day, San Francisco, 1990—. Past chmn. Jones Day's Healthcare Specialized Industry Practice; pres. Stromberg Vineyards, Healdsburg, Calif., 2002—. Author: Economic Joint Venturing, 1985, Acquisition and Enhancement of Physician Practices, 1988. Pres. Am. Acad. Hosp. Attys. of Am. Host. Assn., Chgo., 1978; bd. dirs. Sutter Med. Ctr., Santa Rosa, 2001—, chair, 2003—; pres. East Bay AHEC, Oakland, Calif., 1984—87; bd. dirs. Am. Cancer Soc., Oakland, 1984—95, Wildflowers Inst., San Francisco, 1984—; chair Pediat. Dental Initiative of the North Coast, Healdsburg, Calif., 2004. Mem.: Am. Health Lawyers Assn. Democrat. Office: Jones Day 26th Fl 555 Calif St San Francisco CA 94104 Office Phone: 415-875-5724. Business E-Mail: restromberg@jonesday.com.

**STROMBOM, DAVID GLEN,** designer; b. Pullman, Wash., Apr. 18, 1951; s. Donald A. and Dona S.; m. Cathy J. (Powers), June 17, 1972; 1 child, Paul Davis. Student, Whitman Coll., 1968—70; BS in Architecture, Wash. State U., 1973; MArch, Harvard U., 1977. Registered arch., Wash. Vol. U.S. Peace Corps, Marrakech, Morocco, 1973-75; designer Seattle, 1982-87; prin. The Strombom Architects, Seattle, 1982-91; dir. David Roberts Bowman, Ltd., 1991—; assoc. Internat. Devel. Bus. Cons., Washington, 1996—, Islamabad, Pakistan, 1996, Port au Prince, Haiti, 1997-99, Bali, Indonesia, 1999, Chiang Mai, Thailand, 1999, Venice, Italy, 2002. Fulbright scholar Ahmedabad, India, 1977-78; vis. prof. Ahmedabad Sch. Architecture; designer Ctr. Devel. Studies and Activities, Pune, India. Office Phone: 206-283-1023. Business E-Mail: cpstrombom@aol.com.

**STROME, STEPHEN,** distribution company executive; b. Lynn, Mass., June 20, 1945; s. David and Rose (Cantor) S.; m. Phyllis Ruth Fields, Jan. 14, 1967; children: Michael, Rochelle. BA, Hillsdale Coll., 1967; MBA, Wayne State U., 1968. Trainee KMart Corp., Detroit, 1968-69, mgr. work measurement Troy, Mich., 1970-73; mgr. tng., edn. Fruehauf Corp., Detroit, 1974-76, regional mgr. labor relations, 1978; dir. ops. Handleman Co., Clawson, Mich., 1978-80, account exec., 1980-82, v.p. computer software div. Troy, 1983-85, pres. computer software/video div., 1986-87, exec. v.p., 1987-89, exec. v.p., chief oper. officer, 1989-90, pres., CEO, 1991-2001, chmn., CEO, 2001—. Home: 4597 Kiftsgate Bnd Bloomfield Hills MI 48302-2331 Office: Handleman Co 500 Kirts Blvd Troy MI 48084-4142

**STROMINGER, JACK LEONARD,** biochemist; b. NYC, Aug. 7, 1925; AB, Harvard U., 1944; MD, Yale U., 1948; DSc (hon.), Trinity Coll., Dublin, 1975, Washington U., 1988. From asst. prof. to prof. pharmacology sch. med. Washington U., St. Louis, 1955-61, prof. pharmacology and microbiology, 1961-64; prof. pharmacology and chem. microbiology med. sch. U. Wis., Madison, 1964-68; prof. biochemistry Harvard U., 1968-83, chmn. dept. biochemistry and molecular biology, 1970-73, Higgins prof. biochemistry, 1983—; head tumor virol. divsn. Dana-Farber Cancer Inst., Boston, 1977—. Recipient John J. Abel award, 1960, Paul-Lewis Lab award, 1962, Rose Payne award Am. Soc. Histocompat. & Immunogen., 1986, Hoechst-Roussel award, 1990, Pasteur medal, 1990, Albert Lasker Award for Basic Med. Rsch., 1995; named Passano Found. laureate, 1993. Mem. NAS (mem. study medicine, Microbiology award 1968, Selman Waxman award 1968), AAAS, Am. Soc. Biol. Chemists, Am. Soc. Pharmacology & Exptl. Therapeutics, Am. Assn. Immunologists, Am. Soc. Microbiologists, Am. Chem. Soc., Am. Acad. Arts & Sci., European Molecular Biol. Orgn., Sigma Xi. Address: Harvard U Dept Molecular & Cell Bio 7 Divinity Ave Cambridge MA 02138-2019 Office: Dana Farber Cancer Inst Dept Biochem 44 Binney St Boston MA 02115-6084 Office Phone: 617-495-2733, 617-632-3083. E-mail: jlstrom@fas.harvard.edu.*

**STROMMEN, LINDA SUE,** music educator, musician; b. Oconomowoc, Wis., July 6, 1957; d. Dean R. and Eleanor M. Strommen. Student, Northwestern U., 1974—76; MusB, MusM, Cleve. Inst. Music, 1978. Instr. Preparatory Dept. Cleve. (Ohio) Inst. Music, 1977—79; artist in residence U. Wis., Milw., 1979—80; instr. U. Hawaii, Honolulu, 1981; asst. prof. Wichita (Kans.) State U., 1981—90; adj. instr. Yale U., 1990—91; mem. faculty The Mannes Coll. Music, 1990—97, The Juilliard Sch., 1993—; em. faculty SUNY, Purchase, 1993—94; prin. oboe The Am. Sinfonietta, 1994—; prof. music La. State U., 1997—2002; second oboe The Brandenburg Ensemble, 1997—; prof. oboe Ind. U., Indpls., 2002—; prin. oboe People (Ind.) Chamber Orch., 2002—. Mem. adv. com. N.Y. String Orch. Seminar, N.Y. Musician: (albums) Sejong Plays Ewazen, 2002. Recipient Paul Harris award, Rotary Internat., 2004. Mem.: Pi Kappa Lambda. Avocations: reading, swimming. Office: Indiana Univ Sch Music 1201 E Third St Bloomington IN 47401

**STROMQUIST, KENNETH JAMES, JR.,** pilot, retired military officer; m. Edna Dyrud; children: Virginia, Paul. BBA, U. Minn., 1968; grad., USMC Weapons, Tactics Instrn., 1969, Air Command Staff Coll., 1979, Air War Coll., 1993. Commd. 2d lt. USAF, 1968, forward air controller Bien Hoa AFB, Vietnam, 1969-70; pilot instr. T-41, T-33 USAF Acad. Aerospace Defense Command, Peterson AFB, Colo., 1970-73; pilot, flight comdr., unit plans officer, officer in charge of alert forces Duluth (Minn.) Air Nat. Guard, 1973-90; comdr. detachment 1, 148 Fighter Wing USAF, Tyndall AFB, Fla., 1990-93; advisor Air Nat. Guard NORAD/USSPACECOM, Peterson AFN, Colo.; air comdr. 148 fighter wing Duluth Air Nat. Guard Base, 1995-98, wing comdr. 148 fighter wing, 1997-98; vice comdr. First Air Force USAF, Tyndall AFB, Fla., 1998-99, ret.; pilot Frontier Airlines, Denver. Past Minn. State pres. Nat. Guard Assn. U.S. Decorated Legion of Merit, Disting. Flying Cross, Purple Heart, Air medal, Meritorious Svc. medal.

**STRONACH, BELINDA,** former retail executive; b. Newmarket, Ont., Can., May 2, 1966; d. Frank Stronach; m. Donald Walker, 1990 (div. 1995); children: Nikki 2 children; m. Johann Olov Koss, 2000 (div. 2003). Student, York U., Toronto; JD (hon.), McMaster U. With Magna Internat. Inc., Aurora, Ont., Canada, 1985—2004, CEO, 2001—04, pres., 2002—04. Mem., bd. dirs. Magna Internat. Inc., 1988—2004, U.S. Chamber of Commerce; mem., Dean's Coun. J.F.K. Sch. Govt., Harvard U.; mem., Dean's Advisory Coun. Joseph L. Rotman Sch. Mgmt., U. Toronto; ran for leadership of Can. Conservative Party, 2004; mem. Parliament for Newmarket-Aurora, Ont.; internat. trade critic Official Opposition, Canada; mem. standing com. on fgn. affairs and internat. trade Ho. Commons; founding mem. Can. Automotive Partnership Coun.; mem. Ont. Task Force on Productivity, Competitiveness and Econ. Progress; dir. Yves Landy Found. Named Most Powerful Business-woman in Can., Nat. Post, 2001, Global Leader of Tomorrow, World Econ. Forum, 2001, #2 World's Most Powerful Women in Bus., Fortune mag., 2002; named one of World's 100 Most Influential People, Time Mag., 2004.

**STRONACH, CAREY ELLIOTT,** physicist, researcher; b. Boston, Aug. 8, 1940; s. Ralph Howard and Frances Burns (Maynard) S.; m. Joan Alice Louise Venner, Aug. 20, 1966; children: John Maynard, Howard Stanley. BS, U. Richmond, Va., 1961; MS, U. Va., Charlottesville, 1963; PhD, Coll. William and Mary, 1976. Instr. physics Va. State U., Petersburg, 1965-66, asst. prof., 1966—76, assoc. prof., 1976—80, prof., 1980—2006, prof. emeritus, 2006—. Dir. Muon Spin Rotation Rsch. Program, 1977-2006, Superconducting Materials Rsch. Program, 1988-97, Nanostructured Materials Rsch. Program, 1997-2001, Galactic Cosmic Radiation Rsch. Program, 1993-97, U.S.-France Joint Muon Spin Rotation Rsch. Program, 1985-91, Magnetic Materials Lab. Devel. Program, 1999-2001; radiation safety officer; mem. Solid State Physics Rsch. Inst., 1983-87; founding dir. Ctr. Interactive Micromagnetics, 2001-06; vis. assoc. prof. U. Alta, 1978-79; guest scientist Brookhaven Nat. Lab.; organizing com. Internat. Symposium on the Electronic Structure and Properties of Hydrogen in Metals, 1982, Internat. Symposium on the Physics and Chemistry of Small Clusters, 1986, From Clusters to Crystals, 1991, Sci. and Tech. Atomically Engineered Materials, 1995, Internat. Symposium on Cluster and Nanostructure Interfaces, 1999, Internat. Symposium Clusters and Nano-Assemblies: From Physical to Life Sciences, 2003; sci. adv. com. European Workshop Spectroscopy of Subatomic Species in Non-Metallic Solids, 1985, govs. com. on Superconducting Supercollider, 1987; TV physics lectr., 1991-94; adv. com. Internat. Conf. Muon Spin Rotation, 1996-2005, chmn., 1999-2002; assoc. Va. Inst. Pub. Policy, 2004-; cons. Marco Polo Project AAAS, 2002—. Contbr. numerous articles to publs. in field; playwright; editor of sci. textbooks for several pub. cos. Mem. internat. adv. com. on acad. freedom Bar Ilan U., Israel, 2005—; pres. Petersburg area chpt. Va. Coun. Human Rels., 1965—67; active Petersburg Commn. Cmty. Rels. Affairs, 1974—77; long-range transp. adv. com. City of Petersburg, 1994—98; steering com. Gilmore for Gov., 1997; active Dramatists Guild; sec. adv. coun. bds. and commns. Commonwealth Coun., 1998—2002; active Richmond Playwrights Forum, 1999—, Virginians for Warner, 2001; reviewer of rsch. proposals Nat. Sci. Found.; corr. sec. Petersburg Dem. Com., 1974—77, active, 1972—85, vice chmn., 1981—85. Fellow duPont Corp., 1961-63, NSF, 1971-72, NASA, 1976; recipient Patrick Henry award Va. Gov. James C. Gilmore III, 2001. Mem.: AAUP (chpt. pres. 1968—70), AAAS, Air Force Assn., Internat. Soc. on Muon Spectroscopy (founding mem.), WWII Meml. Soc. (charter), Sci. Netlinks Adv. Bd., N.Y. Acad. Scis., Planetary Soc., High Speed Rail/Maglev Assn. (govt. rels. com. 1992—97, Maglev task force 1994—97), Va. Assn. Scholars (bd. govs. 1999—, pres. 2004—), Southeastern Univs. Rsch. Assn. (site sel. com. 1980—81, materials sci. com. 1983—86, trustee 1983—98, sci. and tech. com. 1986—88, rules com. 1988—92, edn. com. 1992—94, new projects com. 1994—95, Jefferson Lab. com. 1995—98), Va. Acad. Sci. (sec. astronomy, math. and physics sect 1983—84, chmn. 1984—85), Nat. Assn. Scholars, Am. Assn. Physics Tchrs., Am. Phys. Soc., Tri-univ. Meson Facility Users Group, Coun. Secular Humanism (assoc.), Richmond Area Free Thinkers, Pi Mu Epsilon, Sigma Pi Sigma, Sigma Xi (chpt. sec. 1977—78, chpt. pres. 1980—84, 1987—88), Phi Beta Kappa. Achievements include co-devel. of low-energy muon beam line at the AGS of Brookhaven Nat. Lab.; rsch. in pion-nucleus interactions, heavy-ion reactions, muon spin rotation studies of high-temperature superconductors and related materials, fullerenes, heavy-fermion materials, ferromagnetic metals, metal hydrides, fatigue in metals and other materials; participation in the establishment of the Southeastern Universities Research Association and the Thomas Jefferson Nat. Accelerator Facility; discovery of formation of muonium and muonated radicals in Buckminsterfullerene; discovery of simultaneous high-temp. superconductivity and magnetic ordering in strontium yttrium ruthenate. Home: 2241 Buckner St Petersburg VA 23805-2207 Office Phone: 804-732-8993. Personal E-mail: cestronach@adelphia.net.

**STRONE, MICHAEL JONATHAN,** real estate consultant, lawyer; b. NYC, Feb. 26, 1953; s. Bernard William and Judith Semel (Sogg) S.; m. Andrea Nan Acker, Jan. 27, 1979; children: Noah Gregory, Joshua Samuel. BA cum laude, Colby Coll., 1974; JD, Fordham Law Sch., 1978. Bar: N.J. 1978, N.Y. 1979, Conn. 1988, U.S. Ct. Appeals (2d and 3d cirs.) 1979, U.S. Dist. Ct. (so. and ea. dists.) N.Y. 1979, U.S. Dist. Ct. N.J. 1979. Assoc. Ratheim Hoffman et al, N.Y.C., 1978-80, Botein Hays et al, N.Y.C., 1980-84; v.p., assoc. gen. counsel, asst. sec. GE Investment Corp., Stamford, Conn., 1984-2000; v.p., gen. counsel real estate GE Asset Mgmt., Inc., 2000—02, sr. cons., 2002—; CEO Oracle Investment Advisors, LLC, 2002—, Oracle Fin., LLC, 2004—. Cons. First Am. Title Ins. Co., 2002—05, Title Assoc., 2004—; bd. dirs. Internat. Netsuke Soc., Holm & Drath, 2005—, spl. counsel, 2005—. Contbr. articles to profl. jours. in field; columnist: Jour. Internat. Netsuke Soc., 2002—. Bd. dirs. NY chpt. Juvenile Diabetes Found., NYC, 1981-89, vice chmn., 1981-88; mem. fin. com. Juvenile Diabetes Found. Internat., 1981-86; asst. prin. bassist Westchester Symphony Orch., Scarsdale, NY, 1982-2000, pres., 1982-87, chmn. bd., 1982-90, exec. mng. dir., 1990-93; vice chmn. ann. dinner NCCJ, 1987; bd. dirs. Parkinson's Disease Found., 1989-96, chmn. merger com., 1991-96; bd. dirs. Parkinson's Action Network, 1994-98; founding mem. trustee Congregation Sulam Yaakov, 2005—; trustee Jewish Cmty. Ctr. of Harrison, 1996-2003, mem. ritual com., 1996-2004, chmn., 2000-03, chmn. alt. svcs. com., lay cantor, 1997-2005; founding mem., cantor Congregation Sulam Yaakor, 2005—; chmn. county United Way Campaign, 1999, bd. dirs., gen. coun. Harrison Little League, 2001—; coach, 1989-, bd. dirs., v.p., gen. counsel Mariners Hockey, Inc., 2003-04, v.p. adminstrn., 2004-05, exec. mng. dir., 2005—; mem. zoning bd. appeals, Village of Harrison, 2003—; mem. bd. dirs. NY Gilbert & Sullivan Players, 2006-, mem. exec. com., 2006, chmn. Spl. Task Force, 2006; chmn. Strategic Task Force, 2006—; coach Little League, 1989-2005, Babe Ruth League, 2006-, WBA, 2006-, Jr. Little League, 2006-. Recipient Gerald I. Phillippe Dist. Cmty. Svc. award, Juvenile Diabetes Found., 1994, Lifetime Achievement award, 2003. Mem. ABA (chmn. pension plan investments 1988-91, chmn. asset mgmt. 1992-94, 95-97, significant legis. issues 1985-92, chmn. subcom. on joint ventures 1988-90), Am. Coll. Real Estate Lawyers (com. professional-ism 1994—, vice chmn. 1999-2000), Am. Polit. Items Collectors, The Corp. Bar Assn., Nat. Assn. Real Estate Investment Mgrs. (sr. legal officers adv. com. 1993-2003, ann. forum chair 1997), Colby Coll. Alumni Coun. (nominating com. 1994-97), Fordham Law Alumni Assn., The Internat.

Netsuke Soc. Republican. Jewish. Avocations: Japanese art, politial memorabilia, antiquarian books, coaching. Home: 10 Genesee Trail Harrison NY 10528-1802 Office: PO Box 6 Harrison NY 10528-0006 Office Phone: 914-899-9000. Personal E-mail: michael@strone.org. Business E-Mail: mstrone@oracleinvest.com.

**STRONG, ANNSLEY CHAPMAN,** interior designer, volunteer; b. Paterson, N.J., July 18, 1947; d. Donald John and Margaret Brawley Chapman; m. George Gordon Strong, Jr., Nov. 30, 1974; children: George Gordon III, Courtney Chapman Strong Thomas, Meredith Annsley, Alexis Palmer. BA, Wheaton Coll., Norton, Mass., 1969. Cert. N.Y. Sch. Design, 1969, Interior Designers Guild, 1975. V.p. Environs, La Canada, Calif., 1984—. Treas., commr. AYSO Region 13, Pasadena, Calif., 1993—97; co-founder La Canada Sports Coalition, 1996; mem. pres.'s commn. Wheaton Coll., Norton, Mass., 1998—2004; bd. chair Hathaway Sycamores, Pasadena, Calif., 2006—; bd. sec. Verdugo Hills Hosp., Glendale, 2002—05; bd. chmn. Verdugo Hills Hosp. Found., 2002—05. Recipient 20th Century award, Pasadena YMCA, 1990, Bill Carroll Lifetime Achievement award, Am. Youth Soccer Orgn., 2000. Republican. Avocations: painting, piano, bridge, skiing, golf. Office Phone: 818-957-0086.

**STRONG, BRENDA,** actress; b. Brightwood, Oreg., Mar. 25, 1960; BA, Ariz. State U. Actor(guest appearances): (TV series) St. Elsewhere, 1985, MacGyver, 1986, Cheers, 1986, Dallas, 1987, Hotel, 1987, Star Trek: The Next Generation, 1988, Matlock, 1989, Father Dowling Mysteries, 1990, Anything But Love, 1991, Twin Peaks, 1991, Blosson, 1991, 1992, Murphy Brown, 1991, 1996, Scorch, 1992, Sibs, 1992, Herman's Head, 1992, 1993, Picket Fences, 1993, The John Larroquette Show, 1996, Party of Five, 1996, 3rd Rock from the Sun, 1996, Seinfeld, 1996, 1997, Any Day Now, 1999, Sports Night, 1999, 2000, Get Real, 2000, Michael Richards Show, 2000, Ally McBeal, 2001, CSI: Crime Scene Investigation, 2001, Gilmore Girls, 2001, Dawson's Creek, 2001, 7th Heaven, 2001, 2002, The Court, 2002, Malcolm in the Middle, 2002, Nip/Tuck, 2003, Everwood, 2002, 2003, 2004, 2005, Desperate Housewives, 2004— (Screen Actors Guild Award for outstanding performance by an ensemble in a comedy series, 2005, 2006,: (TV films) Kenny Rogers as the Gambler, Part III: The Legend Continues, 1987, Spaceballs, 1987, People Like Us, 1990, Island City, 1994, Going to the Mat, 2004; (films) Malice, 1993, My Life, 1993, The Craft, 1996, Get a Job, 1998, Black Dog, 1998, Undercurrent, 1999, The Deep End of the Ocean, 1999, Terror Tract, 2000, Teddy Bears' Picnic, 2002, Red Dragon, 2002, Missing Brendan, 2003, The Work and the Glory, 2004, The Work and the Glory: American Zion, 2005. Bd. dirs. Montana Shakespeare Co., Helena. Office: Desperate Housewives Touchtone Television 100 Universal City Plaza Bldg 2128 Ste G Universal City CA 91608*

**STRONG, GARY EUGENE,** librarian; b. Moscow, Idaho, June 26, 1944; s. Authur Dwight and Cleora Anna (Nirk) S.; m. Carolyn Jean Roetker, Mar. 14, 1970; children: Christopher Eric, Jennifer Rebecca. BS in Edn., U. Idaho, 1966; AMLS, U. Mich., 1967. Adminstrv. and reference asst. U. Idaho, 1963-66; extension libr. Latah County Free Libr., Moscow, 1966; head librarian Markeley Residence Libr. U. Mich., 1966-67; library dir. Lake Oswego Pub. Libr., Oreg., 1967-73, Everett Public Libr., Wash., 1973-76; asso. dir. services Wash. State Libr., Olympia, 1976-79, dep. state librarian, 1979-80; state librarian Calif. State Libr., Sacramento, 1980-94; dir. Queens Borough Pub. Libr., Jamaica, NY, 1994—2003; dir. emeritus Calif. State Library Found., 1994—2003; univ. libr. UCLA, 2003—. Adj. prof. Queens Coll. Grad. Sch. of Libr. and Info. Scis., 2000-03; chief exec. Calif. Libr. Svcs. Bd., 1980-94; founder, bd. dirs. Calif. State Libr. Found., 1982-94, Calif. Literary Campaign, 1984-94, Calif. Rsch. Bur., 1992; bd. dirs. No. Regional Libr. Bd., 1983-94, Queens Libr. Found., 1994-2003; mem. adv. bd. Ctr. for Book in Libr. of Congress, 1983-86; mem. nat. adv. com. Libr. of Congress, 1987-89; chmn. adv. bd. Calif. Libr. Constrn. and Renovation Bond Act Bd., 1989-94; vis. lectr. Marylhurst Coll., Oreg., 1968, Oreg. Divsn. Continuing Edn., 1972, San Jose State U. Sch. Libr. Svc., 1990; mem. N.Y. State Adv. Coun. Librs., 1996-97; mem. chancellor's task frrce ednl. tech. and librs. CUNY, 1996-97; convenor Archons of the Colophan, 1997-98; regents adv. coun. librs. N.Y. State, 1999-2003; lectr. and cons. in field. Host, producer: cable TV Signatures Program, 1974-76, nationwide videoconfs. on illiteracy, censorship, 1985; author: On Reading-in the Year of the Reader, 1987, U.S. Patriot's Act: Protecting Patron's Rights, 2002; editor Calif. State Library Found. Bull., 1982-94 (H.W. Wilson Periodical award 1988), Western Americana in the Calif. State Library, 1986, On Reading-In the Year of the Reader, 1987, Chinatown Photographer: Louis J. Stellman, 1989, Local History Genealogical Resources, 1990, Literate America Emerging, 1991; curator Queens Libr. Gallery, 1998; contbr. articles to profl. jours.; editor, designer and pub. of various books. Bd. dirs., v.p. Pacific N.W. Bibliog. Ctr., 1977-80; bd. dirs. Thurston Mason County Mental Health Ctr., 1977-80, pres., 1979-80; bd. dirs. Coop. Library Agy. for Sys. and Svcs., 1980-94, vice chmn., 1981-84; bd. dirs. Sr. Svcs. Snohomish County, 1973-76, HISPANEX (Calif. Spanish lang. database), 1983-86; bd. govs. Snohomish County Hist. Assn., 1974-76; mem. psychiat. task force St. Peters Hosp., Olympia, 1979-80; co-founder Calif. Ctr. for the Book, bd. dirs., 1987-94; mem. adv. bd. Calif. State PTA, 1981-86, Gov.'s Tech. Conf., 1993-94; mem. adv. com. Sch. Libr. Sci., UCLA, 1991-94, Sch. Libr. and Info. Studies, U. Calif., Berkeley, 1991-94, Libr. Sch. Queens Coll., 1996-2003, libr. sch. St. John's U., 1996-98; mem. Oreg. Coun. Pub. Broadcasting, 1969-73, Calif. Adult Edn. Steering Com., 1988-94, N.Y. State Adv. Coun. on Libr., 1996-97; chmn. collaborative coun. Calif. State Literacy Resource Ctr., 1993-94; bd. dirs. Queens coun. Boy Scouts Am., 1994-2003; v.p. 100 Yr. Assn. N.Y., 1996-2003; mem. Chancellor's Task Force on Ednl. Tech. and Librs., CUNY, 1996-97; participant N.Y. Pub. Libr. Conf. of World Libr. Leaders, 1996; trustee Flushing Cemetery Assn., 1998-2003; mem. com. on intellectual property rights and the engring. info. infrastructure Nat. Rsch. Coun., 1998-2000; chair organizing com. China-U.S. Libr. Conf., 2001, 05; mem. info. tech. planning bd. UCLA, 2003—, mem. privacy and data protection adv. bd., 2004—, mem. accreditation steering com. Western Assn. Schs. and Colls., 2004—. Oreg. Libr. scholar, 1966; recipient Disting. Alumnus award U. Mich., 1984, Disting. Svc. award Calif. Library Inc., 1985, Spl. Achievement award Literacy Action, 1988, Assn. Specialized and Coop. Libr. Agys. Exceptional Achievement award 1992, Gov.'s award of Achievement Govt. Tech. Conf., 1994, Advancement of Literacy award Pub. Libr. Assn., 1994, John Cotton Dana award Libr. Adminstrn. and Mgmt. Assn., 1994, Chartie Robinson award PLA, 2002; named Libr. of Yr. Calif. Assn. Libr. Trustees and Commrs., 1994, Disting. Svc. award Chinese Am. Libr. Assn., 1996, 21st Century Libr. award Syracuse U., 2002, Bus. Person of Yr., Queens C. of C., 2002. Mem.: The Digital Dilemma, Assn. of Coll. and Rsch. Libraries, Assn. Specialized and Coop. Libr. Agys., Western Coun. State Libr. (pres. 1989—91), Chief Officers of State Libr. Agys. (pres. 1984—86), Calif. Libr. Assn. (govt. rels.com. 1980—94), Pacific N.W. Libr. Assn. (hon. life mem., pres. 1978—79), Oreg. Libr. Assn. (hon. life mem., pres. 1970—71), Assn. of Rsch. Libraries, Libr. Adminstrn. and Mgmt. Assn. (bd. dis. 1980—88, pres. 1984—85), Am. Printing History Assn., ALA (legis. com. 1980—82, commn. on freedom and equality of access to info. 1983—86, legis. com. 1995—97, chair intellectual property subcom. 1995—98, chmn. conf. librs. Beijing 1996, rep. Internat. Fedn. of Libr. Assn. nat. organizing com. 1996—2001, intellectual property com. 1998—2001, Fedn. of Libr. Assn. UN rep. 2001—03, IFLA governing bd. 2004—, chair U.S. planning com. for chair U.S. libr. coop. conf. 2001, Humphrey award for Internat. Librarianship 2003), METRO (bd. dirs. 1994—2003, treas. 1996—99, 1st v.p. 1999—2001), Everett Area C. of C. (bd. dirs. 1974—76), Queens County C. of C. (bd. dirs. 1996—2003, named Bus. Person of Yr. 2002), Jamaica Devel. Corp., Zamorano Club, The Typophiles, Guild of Book Workers, Grolier Club, The Book Collectors Club of L.A., Roxburghe Club, Sacramento Book Collectors Club, Book Club of Calif. Office: UCLA Libr Box 951575 Los Angeles CA 90095-1575 Business E-Mail: gstrong@library.ucla.edu.*

**STRONG, GEORGE GORDON, JR.,** lawyer, management consultant; b. Toledo, Apr. 19, 1947; s. George Gordon and Jean Boyd (McDougall) S.; m. Annsley Palmer Chapman, Nov. 30, 1974; children: George III, Courtney,

Meredith, Alexis Phillips. BA, Yale U., 1969; MBA, Harvard U., 1971; JD, U. San Diego, 1974. Bar: Calif. 1974, U.S. Dist. Ct. (cen. dist.) Calif. 1974; CPA, Calif., Hawaii, cert. mgmt. cons. Contr. Vitredent Corp., Beverly Hills, Calif., 1974-76; sr. mgr. Price Waterhouse, L.A., 1976-82, ptnr., 1987—2001, mng. ptnr. west region dispute analysis and corp. recovery, 1993—99, mem. policy bd., bd. dirs., 1995-98, mem. combination bd., 1997-98; bd. ptnrs., prin. Pricewaterhouse Coopers LLP, L.A., 1998-2001, mem. global oversight bd., 1998—2001; exec. v.p., COO Internat. Customs Service, Long Beach, Calif., 1982-84; CFO Uniform Software Systems, Santa Monica, Calif., 1984-85; exec. v.p., COO Cipherlink Corp., 1986; pres. Woodleigh Lane, Inc., Flintridge, Calif., 1985-87; mng. dir., gen. counsel Cornerstone Rsch., 2002—. Chmn. bd. dirs. L.A. SPCA. Mem. ABA, AICPA, Calif. State Bar, Calif. Soc. CPAs, Andover Abbott Alumni So. Calif. (bd. dirs., treas.), Inst. Mgmt. Cons., Harvard Bus. Sch. Alumni Assn. (bd. dirs. 1996-99), Harvard Bus. Sch. Assn. So. Calif. (chmn. bd. trustees scholarship fund 1992—, pres. 1988-89, dir. 1996-99, 2001-03, 06—), Harvard Club NY, Harvard Club Boston, Yale Club NY, Lincoln Club, Calif. Club, Olympic Club, Jonathan Club, Annandale Golf Club, Coral Beach and Tennis Club, Mid Ocean Golf Club, Royal Bermuda Yacht Club, Valley Hunt Club, Tuckers Point Golf Club (Bermuda), Park Meadows Country Club. Republican. Presbyterian. Avocations: golf, tennis, bridge. Home: 5455 Castle Knoll Rd La Canada Flintridge CA 91011-1319 Office: 515 S Flower St #2900 Los Angeles CA 90071-2300 Office Phone: 213-553-2600. Personal E-mail: gstrong@cornerstone.com.

**STRONG, GEORGE HOTHAM,** private investor, consultant; b. Johnstown, Pa., July 15, 1926; s. George Hite and Mary Elizabeth (Hotham) S.; m. Mary Louise Lyon, Sept. 19, 1953; children: Cynthia Strong Hibbard, Dexter, Sarah Strong Bornstein. AB magna cum laude, Allegheny Coll, 1949; MBA, Harvard U., 1951. V.p. Smith Barney & Co., NYC & Boston, 1951-67, Norlin Corp., NYC, 1967-73, Am. Medicorp, Bala-Cynwyd, Pa., 1974-78; cons. A.D. Little, Cambridge, Mass., 1973-74; sr. v.p., dir. Universal Health Svcs., King of Prussia, Pa., 1978-84; pvt. practice investor NYC, 1985—. Served on 16 pub. and pvt. corp. bds. Served to sgt. U.S. Army, 1944—46, Italy. Mem. Harvard Club (NYC), Union League Club (Phila.), Seabright (NJ) Lawn Tennis Club, Seabright Beach Club, Rumson (NJ) Country Club, Phi Beta Kappa. Republican. Episcopalian. Home: 946 Navesink River Rd Rumson NJ 07760-2330

**STRONG, HENRY,** foundation executive; b. Rochester, NY, Oct. 6, 1923; s. L. Corrin and Alice (Trowbridge) S.; m. Malan Swing, June 30, 1951; children: Sigrid Anne, Barbara Kirk, Dana Elizabeth, Henry Lockwood. AB, Williams Coll., 1949; LHD, Mt. Vernon Coll., 1999. Joined Fgn. Service, 1950; with State Dept., 1950-51; vice consul The Hague, 1951-54, Washington, 1954-55; 2d sec. US Embassy, Copenhagen, 1955-58, State Dept., 1958-62, Djakarta, Indonesia, 1962-64; resigned, 1968; chmn. bd., pres. Hattie M. Strong Found., 1968—. Mem. D.C. Commn. Arts, 1968-75; mem. DC Bd. Higher Edn., 1973-76; vice chmn. bd. trustees J.F. Kennedy Ctr. for Performing Arts, 1975-90, hon. trustee, 1991—; bd. dir. Nat. Symphony Orch., Pomfret Sch., 1967-1990, M.M. Post Found. DC, Community Found. of Greater Washington, 1974-91, Mt. Vernon Coll., 1969-88, 91-98, Nat. Capital chpt. ARC, 1994—. Lt. (j.g.) USNR, 1943-46. Mem.: Chevy Chase; Metropolitan (Washington); Gibson Island (Md.). Republican. Episcopalian. Home: 5039 Overlook Rd NW Washington DC 20016-1911 Office: Hattie M Strong Found 1620 I St NW Ste 700 Washington DC 20006-4005

**STRONG, JOHN DAVID,** insurance company executive; b. Cortland, N.Y., Apr. 12, 1936; s. Harold A. and Helen H. Strong; m. Carolyn Dimmick, Oct. 26, 1957; children: John David, Suzanne. BS, Syracuse U., 1957; postgrad., Columbia U., 1980. With Kemper Group, 1957-90, Kemper Corp., 1990-96, Empire sales divsn. mgr., 1972-74, CEO, 1988-93, chmn. bd., 1989-93; vice chmn. Millikin Assocs., 1993-96, chmn., 1996; exec. v.p., dir. Facilitators, Inc., 1995-98. Mem. adv. coun. Sch. Bus., Millikin U., 1975-79, 84—; bd. dirs. United Way of Decatur and Macon County, Ill., 1976-83, campaign chmn., 1978-79, pres. bd. dirs., 1979-81; pres. United Way of Ill., 1981-83; bd. dirs. DMH Commn. Svcs. Corp., 1985-97, chmn., 1988-90; bd. dirs. Decatur-Macon County Econ. Devel. Found., 1983-88, DMH Health Systems, 1987-94, Richland C.C. Found., 1987-90, Symphony Orch. Guild of Decatur, 1992-96, DMH Found., 1988-97; bd. dirs. Ill. Ednl. Devel. Found., 1983-90, pres., 1986-87; bd. dirs. Decatur Meml. Hosp., 1985-94, vice chmn., 1988, chmn., 1990-92; bd. dirs. Ctrl. Ill. Health Assocs., Inc., 1994, vice chmn., 1994-96; mem. steering com. Decatur Advantage, 1981-93, pres., 1988-93. Capt. USAR, 1958-69. Mem. Metro Decatur C. of C. (bd. dirs. 1977-80, chmn. 1983-84), Decatur Club (bd. dirs. 19080-83, pres. 1983), Country Club of Decatur (bd. dirs. 1993-99, pres. bd. 1995-97), Alpha Kappa Psi. Personal E-mail: jack@strongs.net.

**STRONG, JOHN OLIVER,** plastic surgeon, educator; b. Montclair, NJ, Feb. 1, 1930; s. George Joseph and Olivia (LeBrun) S.; m. Helen Louise Vrooman, July 19, 1958 (dec. Mar. 1973); m. Deborah Sperberg, May 20, 1978; children: John Jr., Jean LeB., Andrew D. BS, Yale U., 1952; MD, U. Pa., 1957. Cert. vol. paleontologist Calif. Practice medicine specializing in plastic and reconstructive surgery, Santa Ana, Calif., 1964-97; asst. clin. prof. plastic and reconstructive surgery U. Calif., Irvine, 1970—. Chief of staff Western Med. Ctr., Santa Ana, 1996-97, interim chmn. bd., 1996-97, bd. dirs.; bd. dirs. United Western Med. Ctrs., Healthcare Found. Orange County, chmn.; vol. Anza Borrego Desert State Pk., steering com., 1998-2003. Vol. Anza -Borrego Desert State Pk. Fellow ACS; mem. Calif. Med. Assn. (chmn. sci. adv. panel 1983-89), Calif. Soc. Plastic Surgeons (pres. 1991-92). Republican. Office: PO Box 94 Borrego Springs CA 92004-0094 Address: 511 Seaward Rd Corona Del Mar CA 92625-2600 Personal E-mail: jostrong1@sbcglobal.net, jhnos@netscape.net.

**STRONG, JOHN SCOTT,** finance educator; b. Phila., Aug. 28, 1956; s. John S. and Thelma J. (Willard) S. BS, Washington & Lee U., 1978; M of Pub. Policy, Harvard U., 1981, PhD in Bus. Econs., 1986. Rsch. fellow Harvard U., Cambridge, Mass., 1983-85, 89-90, 93, vis. asst. prof. econs., 1989-90; prof. fin. Coll. William and Mary, Williamsburg, Va., 1985—. Cons. on econs. and fin. Republic of Indonesia, 1987-89, MITI, Japan, 1988-89, European Bank for Reconstruction and Devel., 1993-95, Govt. of Bolivia, 1994, Govt. of Russia, 1996, Govts. of Brazil, Argentina and Uruguay, 1997, Govt. of Peru, 1998, World Bank, 1997—, Inter-Am. Devel. Bank, 2002—, U.S. Dept. Transp., 1999-02. Author: Why Airplanes Crash: Aviation Safety in a Changing World, 1992, Moving to Market: Restructuring Transport in the Former Soviet Union, 1996; co-author 2 books on airline deregulation; contbr. articles to profl. jours. Fulbright scholar, 1978-79; grad. fellow NSF, 1979-82.

**STRONG, JOHN WILLIAM,** lawyer, educator; b. Iowa City, Aug. 18, 1935; s. Frank Ransom and Gertrude Elizabeth (Way) S.; m. Margaret Waite Cleary, June 16, 1962; children— Frank Ransom, Benjamin Waite. BA, Yale U., 1957; JD, U. Ill., 1962; postgrad. U. N.C., 1966-67. Bar: Ill. 1963, Oreg. 1976. Assoc. firm LeForgee, Samuels, Miller, Schroeder & Jackson, Decatur, Ill., 1963-64; asst. prof. law U. Kans., 1964-66; assoc. prof. Duke U., 1966-69; prof. U. Oreg., 1969-75; legal counsel Oreg. Task Force on Med. Malpractice, 1976; prof. U. Nebr., 1977-84, dean, 1977-82, vice chancellor for acad. affairs, 1981-84; Rosenstiel Disting. prof. law U. Ariz., 1984-98, prof. emeritus, 1998—. Nat. sec.-treas. Order of the Coif, 1992-98; cons. Nat. Judicial Coll. Author: (with others) Handbook on Evidence, 5th edit., 1999. Served with U.S. Army, 1957-59. Mem. Ill. Bar Assn., Oreg. Bar Assn., ABA, Am. Law Inst., Phi Delta Phi. Independent. Congregationalist. Office: U Ariz Coll Law Tucson AZ 85721-0001 Home: PO Box 8063 Black Butte Ranch OR 97759 Business E-Mail: strong@law.arizona.edu.

**STRONG, JUDITH ANN,** chemist, educator; b. June 19, 1941; d. Philip Furnald and Hilda Bernice (Hubbard) S. BS cum laude, SUNY, Albany, 1963; MA, Brandeis U., 1966, PhD, 1970. Asst. prof. chemistry Moorhead State U. Minn., 1969—73, assoc. prof., 1973—81, prof., 1981—, chmn. chemistry dept., 1984—86, dean social and natural scis., 1986—97, assoc. v.p. acad. affairs, 1997—. Recipient Gov.'s Acts of Kindness Vol. award, 1997; fellow, NSF, 1965—67. Mem.: Minn. Acad. Sci., Assn. Women in Sci., Am. Chem. Soc., Soroptimist Internat. (gov. North Ctrl. region 2002—04, program coun.

2004—), Sigma Xi. Home: 1209 12th St S Moorhead MN 56560-3707 Office: Minn State U Moorhead Academic Affairs Moorhead MN 56563-0001 Office Phone: 218-477-2075. Business E-Mail: strong@mnstate.edu.

**STRONG, LOUISE CONNALLY,** geneticist; b. San Antonio, Apr. 23, 1944; d. Ben Clarkson and Sarah Nell (Allen) Connally; m. Beeman Ewell Strong III, Jan. 10, 1970; children: Beeman Connally, Larkin Louise. BA, U. Tex., 1966; MD, U. Tex. Med. Br., Galveston, 1970. Diplomate Tex. State Bd. Med. Examiners. Faculty Grad. Sch. Biomed. Scis. U. Tex. Health Sci. Ctr., Houston, 1972—, rsch. assoc. Med. Genetics Ctr., 1972-73; asst. prof. pediatrics and biology, asst. geneticist U. Tex. M.D. Anderson Cancer Ctr., 1976-79, assoc. prof. exptl. pediatrics, assoc. geneticist, 1979—, Sue and Radcliffe Killam prof., 1981—. Part-time asst. prof. U. Tex. Health Sci. Ctr., 1973-78; vis. prof. pediatrics, U. Tex. Med. Sch., U. Tex. Health Sci. Ctr., 1988-95; nat. adv. bd. Dept. Health and Human Svcs., Nat. Cancer Inst., NIH, Bethesda, Md., 1984—; bd. scientific counselors Div. Cancer Etiology, Nat. Cancer Inst., 1981-84; mem. search com. for dep. dir. Div. Extramural Activities, Nat. Cancer Inst., speaker in field, others. Contbr. articles to profl. jours., books and abstracts. Named Warren E. Wheeler Vis. Prof., Children's Hosp., Columbus, Ohio, 1989; recipient Marjorie W. Margolin Award for Outstanding Achievement in Retina Rsch., Retina Rsch. Found., Houston, 1987, Outstanding Achievement in Field of Oncology, State Pres.'s BPW award Tex. Fedn. Bus. and Profl. Women's Clubs, 1984, several scholarships; grantee NIH, 1984-92, John S. Dunn Rsch. Found., 1989-91, Retina Rsch. Found., 1982-90, Joe and Jessie Crump Fund Med. Rsch., 1982-83, Kelsey-Leary Found., others. Mem. AAAS, Am. Assn. Cancer Rsch. AMA, Am. Med. Women's Assn., Am. Men and Women in Sci., Am. Soc. Human Genetics, Am. Soc. Preventive Oncology, Environ. Health Inst., Tex. Genetics Soc., Phil. Soc. Tex., GM Adv. Council, Cancer Rsch. Found. Avocation: tennis. Office: 1515 Holcombe Blvd HMB Box #209 Houston TX 77030

**STRONG, SUSAN CLANCEY,** writer, communications executive, editor; b. Cin., Nov. 10, 1939; d. William Power and Elizabeth (Browne) Clancey; m. Oliver Swigert, 1957 (div. 1972); children: Silvia, David Mack; m. Richard Devon Strong, 1977. BA, Northwestern U., 1965; MA, U. Calif., Berkeley, 1972, PhD, 1979. Tchr. Helen Bush Parkside Sch., Seattle, 1965-66, Taipei (Taiwan) Lang. Inst., 1967-68; acting instr. U. Calif., Berkeley, 1972-78, teaching fellow, 1979, lectr., 1979-84, St. Mary's Coll., Moraga, Calif., 1982-85; pvt. practice Orinda, Calif., 1985-90, 97—; sr. rsch. assoc. Ctr. for Econ. Conversion, 1990-96. Mem. Contra Costa County Conflict Resolution Panels, Calif., 1987-90; affiliate Support Ctr./CTD, San Francisco, 1987-90; del. UN Conf. on Econ. Conversion, Moscow, 1990; co-founder "The Who's Counting?" Project, 1996; founder The Metaphor Project, 1997. Author: The GDP Myth: How It Harms Our Quality of Life, and What Communities are Doing About It, 1995; editor Deficit Delirium, 1993, Shaping A New Conversion Agenda, 1995; author poetry; columnist, book reviewer, film reviewer. Mem. Bay Area Global Tomorrow Com., 1986; co-founder Peace Economy Working Group, 1988; co-founder Peace Economy Campaign, 1988; mem. Peace Action Nat. Strategy Com., 1989-95, co-chair strategy com., 1992-93; conf. co-chmn. Nat. Sane/Freeze Congress, 1989-90, rep. nat. bd. advisors Nat. Peace Action, Washington, 1989-95; mem. bd. advisors Peace and Environ. Project, San Francisco, 1986-88; chmn. No. Calif. Sane Freeze, San Francisco, 1985-89; co-convenor The Natural Step Open Space Com. Conf., San Francisco, 1997. Mem. Phi Beta Kappa. Democrat. Episcopalian. Avocations: music, gardening. Mailing: PO Box 892 Orinda CA 94563-2124 Office Phone: 925-254-7198. Office Fax: 925-254-3304. Business E-Mail: sstrong@metaphorproject.org.

**STRONG, VIRGINIA WILKERSON,** freelance writer, former special education educator; b. Vernal, Utah, Mar. 19, 1935; d. Arbon C. and Mildred (Wyman) Wilkerson; m. David Smith, Oct. 6, 1950 (div. Jan. 1960); children: Anna Smith Blyton, Dorothy Smith Wolf, Wendell Lee Smith, Ava Smith Eatman, Karen Smith Ritter; m. Lawrence D. Strong, June 1961 (div. May 1973); children: Lawrence D. Jr., Jeffrey A. BA, U. Miss., 1970, MEd, 1972; PhD, Ohio U., 1985; postgrad., UCLA. Cert. elem. edn. tchr., spl. edn. K-12 tchr., ednl. adminstrn., cert screenwriter, UCLA, 1995. Rsch. asst. U. Miss., University, 1968-70, Utah State U., Logan, 1974-78; tchr. spl. edn. various schs., nr. Oxford, Miss., 1969-74; instr. spl. edn., project coord., rsch. asst. Ohio U., Athens, 1978-82; supr. spl. edn. Meigs County Bd. Edn., Pomeroy, Ohio, 1982-84; tchr. spl. edn., dept. chmn. L.A. Unified Sch. Dist., 1986-93, co-facilitator alcohol drug abuse, 1990-93; freelance writer, owner, mgr. Fenix Devel., Culver City, Calif., 1990—. Early childhood adv. Utah Bd. Edn., Salt Lake City, 1976, evaluator edn. programs, Salt Lake City and Logan, 1976-77; acting dir. cons. North Miss. Retardation Ctr., Oxford, 1993-94; curriculum developer Meigs County, 1982-84; dir. gifted edn. workshop Ohio U., 1980. Author: The Role of the Special Education Supervisor, 1985, (screenplays) To See the Elephant, Dark Encounters; contbr. articles to newspapers. Elector Dem. Party, Logan, 1976; religious instr. LDS Ch., various locations, 1953-97. U.S. Dept. Edn. grantee Utah State U., 1976. Mem. ASCD, Kappa Delta Pi, Phi Delta Kappa. Avocations: genealogy, gemology, photography, history buff, travel. Business E-Mail: fenix711@sbcglobal.net.

**STRONG-CUEVAS, ELIZABETH,** sculptor; b. St. Germain en Laye, France, Jan. 22, 1929; Am. citizen; d. George and Margaret (Strong) de Cuevas; 1 child, Deborah Carmichael. BA, Vassar Coll., Poughkeepsie, N.Y., 1952. Instr. Arts Students' League, NYC; student John Hovannes. One-woman shows include Lee Ault Gallery, NYC, 1977-78, Tower Gallery, Southampton, NY, 1980, Iolas-Jackson Gallery, NYC, 1983, 85, Guild Hall Mus., East Hampton, NY, 1985, Benton Gallery, Southampton, NY, 1987, Kerr Gallery, NYC, 1988, Grounds for Sculpture, Hamilton, NJ, 1999, Island Weiss Gallery, NYC, 2004-05, Vassar Coll., Poughkeepsie, NY, 2006; group shows include Guild Hall, East Hampton, 1980, 84, 98, Art Students League of NY, 1982, Bruce Mus., Greenwich, Conn., 1984, 93, Tower Gallery, NYC, 1984, Kouros Gallery, Ridgefield, Conn., 1985, Andre Zarre Gallery, NYC, 1985, Susan Blanchard Gallery, NYC, 1986, Ruth Vered Gallery, East Hampton, 1986-88, Benton Gallery, Southampton, 1987, 1990, Benson Gallery, Bridgehampton, NY, 1989, 99, Koln Art Fair, Germany, 1989, 1991, Feingarten Galleries, NYC, 1990, Marisa del Re Biennale III, 1993, IV, 1994, Parrish Mus., Southampton, 1994, Grounds for Sculpture, Hamilton, NJ, 1994-96, Shidoni, Tessuque, N.Mex., 1995-98, Barnard-Biderman Fine Art, Southampton, 1997, The Tolman Collection, Singapore, 1997-98, Earl McGrath Gallery, 1998, Bulgari, NY, 2000, Grounds for Sculpture, Hamilton, 2000, 02, Russian Am. Cultural Ctr., 2001, Clark Fine Art, Southampton, 2001, 2003, The Ross Sch., East Hampton, 2003, Island Weiss Gallery, NYU, 2004-05, Kouros Gallery, NYC, 2003, UBS Bank Gallery, 2005, Ann Novton Sculpture Gardens, West Palm Beach, Fla., 2006; represented in pvt. collections at Bruce Mus., Greenwich, Grounds for Sculpture, Hamilton, NJ Guild Hall Mus., Heckscher Mus., Huntington, NY, East Hampton Garden, East Hampton, 1982, Park Ave. Ter., NY, 1997. Recipient First prize, Guild Hall, NY, 1985. Mem. Vassar Club (NY). Avocation: yoga. Personal E-mail: strongworks@sc-sculpture.com.

**STRONGIN, JONATHAN DAVID,** physician; b. Kingston, N.Y., June 19, 1951; s. Jack and Thelma (Kaufman) S.; m. Ellen Wells Seely, June 11, 1983; children: Jessica, Matthew. BA, Columbia Coll., 1973; PhD, MD, Columbia U., 1982. Diplomate Am. Bd. Internal Medicine, Am. Bd. Pulmonary Disease, Am. Bd. Critical Care Medicine. Intern, resident Cambridge (Mass.) Hosp., 1982-84; med. resident Beth Israel Hosp., Boston, 1984-85; pulmonary fellow Mass. Gen. Hosp., Boston, 1985-97; physician Pulmonary Assocs. of Greater Boston, 1994—96. Pres. med. staff Whidden Meml. Hosp., Everett, Mass., 1995-97; trustee Melrose Wakefield Health Care Corp., 1996-98; med. dir. respiratory care, pres. med. staff Cambridge Health Alliance. Fulbright scholar, 1976-77. Fellow Am. Coll. Physicians, Am. Coll. Chest Physicians. Avocation: running.

**STRONG-TIDMAN, VIRGINIA ADELE,** marketing professional; b. July 26, 1947; d. Alan Ballentine and Virginia Leona (Harris) Strong; m. John Fletcher Tidman, Sept. 23, 1978. BS, Albright Coll., Reading, Pa., 1969; postgrad., U. Pitts., 1970-73, U. Louisville, 1975-76. Exec. trainee Pomeroy's

divsn. Allied Stores, Reading, 1969-70; mktg. rsch. analyst Heinz U.S.A., Pitts., 1970-74; new products mktg. mgr. Ky. Fried Chicken, Louisville, 1974-76; dir. Pitts. office M/A/R/C, 1976-79; assoc. rsch. dir. Henderson Advt., Inc., Greenville, SC, 1979-81; sr. v.p., dir. rsch. Bozell, Jacobs, Kenyon & Eckhardt, Inc., Dallas, 1981-86, sr. v.p., dir. rsch. and strategic planning Atlanta, 1986-88; sr. v.p., dir. mktg. svcs. Bozell, Inc., Atlanta, 1988-91; sr. v.p., mng. ptnr. Henderson Adv., Inc., 1991-95; prin. Ender-Ptnr., Inc., 1995-96; v.p. mktg. Booth Rsch. Svcs., Inc., 1996-98; COO Moore & Symons, Inc., 1998—. Cons. mktg. rsch. Greenville Zool. Soc., 1981; adj. prof. So. Meth. U., 1984-85. Mem. Am. Mktg. Assn. (Effie award N.Y. chpt. 1982). Republican. Episcopalian. Home: 146 Northshores Dr Seneca SC 29672

**STROOCK, DANIEL WYLER,** mathematician, educator; b. NYC, Mar. 20, 1940; s. Alan Maxwell and Katherine (Wyler) S.; m. Lucy Barber, Nov. 21, 1962; children: Benjamin, Abraham. AB, Harvard Coll., 1962; PhD, Rockefeller U., 1966. Vis. mem. Courant Inst., N.Y. U., 1966-69, asst. prof., 1969-72; assoc. prof. math. U. Colo., Boulder, 1972-75, prof., 1975-84, chmn. dept. math, 1979-81; Simons prof. math. MIT, 1984—. Adj. prof. U. Colo., Beijing Normal U. Author: (with S.R.S. Vanadhan) Multidimensional Diffusion Processes, 1979, (with J.D. Deutschel) Large Deviations, 1989, Probability Theory, An Analytic View, 1993, An Introduction to the Analysis of Paths on a Rieman Manfold, 1999, Markov Processes from K. Ito's Perspective, 2003; editor Math. Zeitschrift, 1992-2000, Ill. Jour. Math., 1976-82, Transactions of Am. Math. Soc., 1974-80, Annals of Probability, 1988-93, Advances in Math., 1995—, Jour. Functional Analysis, 1994—; contbr. articles on probability theory to profl. jours. Guggenheim fellow, 1978-79 Mem. Am. Acad. Arts and Scis., Nat. Acad. Scis., Polish Acad. Arts & Scis. (fgn. mem.). Democrat. Jewish. Home: 55 Frost St Cambridge MA 02140-2247 Office: MIT Dept Math Cambridge MA 02139

**STROOCK, MARK EDWIN, II,** public relations company executive; b. NYC, Nov. 6, 1922; s. Irving Sylvan and Blanche (Loeb) S.; m. Hanna Marks Eiseman, June 24, 1945 (dec. May 2003); children— Mark E., Carolyn E. BA, Bard Coll., 1947. Reporter The New York Journal of Commerce, 1947-50; writer Barrons, N.Y.C., 1950-51; mng. editor Fairchild Publ., N.Y.C., 1952-53; bus. editor World Mag., N.Y.C., 1953-54; contbg. editor Time Mag., N.Y.C., 1954-56; with Young & Rubicam Inc., N.Y.C., 1956-87, sr. v.p., dir. corp. rels., cons., 1987—. Bd. trustees N.Y. Urban League, 1971-78, Alvin Ailey Dance Theatre, N.Y.C., 1977-84, Friends of the Theatre Mus. City N.Y., 1977-85, Arts Horizons, N.Y.C., 1998—; vice-chmn. Covenant House, N.Y.C., 1978-90; exec. com., mktg. and communications com., assoc. nat. commr. Anti-Defamation League, 1992—. With U.S. Army, 1943-46. Democrat. Jewish. Home: 50 Park Ave Apt 11B New York NY 10016-3075 Office: Young & Rubicam Inc 285 Madison Ave New York NY 10017-6486

**STROOCK, THOMAS FRANK,** oil and gas company executive; b. NYC, Oct. 10, 1925; s. Samuel and Dorothy (Frank) S.; m. Marta Freyre de Andrade, June 19, 1949; children: Margaret, Sandra, Elizabeth, Anne. BA in Econs., Yale U., 1948; LLB (hon.), U. Wyo., 1995; PhD (hon.), Universidad del Valle, Guatemala, 2001. Landman Stanolind Oil & Gas Co., Tulsa, 1948-52; pres. Stroock Leasing Corp., Casper, Wyo., 1952-89, Alpha Exploration, Inc., 1980-89; ptnr. Stroock, Rogers & Dymond, Casper 1960-82; dir. First Wyo. Bank, Casper, 1967-89; mem. Wyo. Senate, 1969-89, chmn. appropriations com., 1983-89, co-chmn. joint appropriations com., 1983-89, mem. mgmt. and audit com., pres., 1988-89; mem. steering com. Edn. Commn. of States; amb. to Guatemala Govt. of U.S., 1989-93; pres. Alpha Devel. Corp., 1992—; prof. pub. diplomacy U. Wyo., Laramie, 1993—; chmn. internat. adv. bd., 2001—. Dir. Wyo. Med. Ctr., 1996-2004. Rep. precinct committeeman, 1960-68; pres. Natrona County Sch. Bd., 1966, 69; pres. Wyo. State Sch. Bds. Assn., 1965-66; chmn. Casper Cmty. Recreation, 1955-60; chmn. Natrona County United Fund, 1963-64; chmn. Wyo. State Rep. Com., 1975-78, exec. com. 1954-60; del. Rep. Nat. Conv., 1956-76, 92; regional coord. campaign George Bush for pres., 1979-80, 87-88; chmn. Western States Rep. Chmn. Assn., 1977-78; chmn. Wyo. Higher Edn. Commn., 1969-71; mem. Nat. Petroleum Coun., 1972-77; chmn. trustees Sierra Madre Found. for Geol. Rsch., New Haven; chmn. Wyo. Nat. Gas Pipline Authority, 1987-88; bd. dirs. Ucross Found., Denver; mem. Nat. Pub. Lands Adv. Coun., 1981-85; chmn. Wyo. Health Reform Commn., 1993-95; trustee Nature Conservancy, 1993-2005; chmn. Universidad del Valle Found., Guatemala City, 1995-2000, trustee, 2000-2005; chmn. Wyo. Health Access Task Force, 2003-2004. Sgt. USMC, 1943-46. Mem. Rocky Mountain Oil and Gas Assn., Petroleum Assn. Wyo., Kiwanis, Casper Country Club, Casper Petroleum Club, Yale Club N.Y. Republican. Unitarian Universalist. Home and Office: PO Box 2875 Casper WY 82602-2875 Office Phone: 307-234-8925.

**STROPKI, JOHN M., JR.,** electric power industry executive; BS indsl. engring., Purdue Univ.; MBA, Ind. Univ. Sales trainee Lincoln Electric Holdings, 1972, dist. mgr., nat. sales mgr., 1992—94, exec. vice-pres., 1996, dir., 1998—, COO, 2003—04, CEO, 2003—, pres., chmn., 2004—. Mem. Am. Lung Assn.; Juvenile Diabetes Research Found.; mem. bd. Greater Cleveland Growth Assn., Great Lakes Sci. Ctr. Mem.: Nat. Electrical Manufacturers Assn. (mem. bd. gov.), Gas & Welding Distbr. Assn., Manufacturers Alliance/MAPI (pres. coun.), Am. Welding Soc. (exec. bd.). Office: Lincoln Electric Holdings 22801 St Clair Ave Cleveland OH 44117 Office Phone: 216-481-8100. Office Fax: 216-486-1751.*

**STROSCIO, MICHAEL ANTHONY,** physicist, researcher; b. Winston-Salem, NC, June 1, 1949; s. Anthony and Norma Lee (Sidbury) S.; m. Mitra Dutta; children: Elizabeth de Clara, Charles Marshall Sidbury, Gautam Dutta. BS, U. N.C., 1970; MPhil in Physics, Yale U., 1972, PhD in Physics, 1974. Physicist Los Alamos Sci. Lab., N.Mex., 1975-78; sr. staff mem. Johns Hopkins U. Applied Physics Lab., Laurel, Md., 1978-80; prof. mgr. for electromagnetic research Air Force Office of Sci. Research, Washington, 1980-83; spl. assst. to research dir. Office of Under Sec. Def., Washington, 1982-83; policy analyst White House Office of Sci. and Tech. Policy, Washington, 1983-85; prof. dir. for microelectrons, prin. scientist U.S. Army Research Office, Research Triangle Park, NC, 1985—2001; adj. prof. depts. physics and elec. and computer engring. N.C. State U., Raleigh, 1985—; Richard and Loan Hill prof. depts. bioengring. elec. and computer engring., physics U. Ill., Chgo., 2001—, dir. grad. studies, 2002—04. Adj. prof. depts. elec. engring. and physics Duke U., Durham, 1986-2005, dept. physics U. Ill. Chgo., 2002—; vis. prof. dept. elec. engring. U. Va., Charlottesville, 1990-95, U. Md., College Park, 1996-97; mem. compl. coun. Duke U. Chapel, 1989-91; lectr. UCLA, 1987, U. Mich., 1988; cons. U.S. Dept. Energy, Washington, 1985-90; vice-chmn. White House Panel on Sci. Comm., Washington, 1983-84; chmn. Dept. Def. Rsch. Instrumentation Com., Washington, 1982; assoc. mem. Adv. Group on Electron Devices, 1985-91, liaison Nat. Laser Users Facility, Rochester, N.Y., 1984; liaison Panel on Sci. Comm. and Nat. Security, NAS, 1982, Panel on Materials for High-Density Electron Packaging, 1987-90; U.S. Army liaison to JASON, 1992-2001; mem. U.S. Govt. coord. com. on Semicond. Rsch. Corp., 1992-2001; reviewer Irish Sci. Found. Author: Positronium: A Review of the Theory, 1975, Onslow Families, 1977, Quantum Heterostructures: Microelectronics and Optoelectronics, 1999, Phonons in Nanostructures, 2001, Biological Nanostructures and Applications of Nanostructures in Biology, 2004; editor: Quantum-Based Electronic Devices and Systems, 1998, Advanced Semiconductor Lasers and Applications to Optoelectronics, 2000, Advanced Semiconductor Heterostructures, 2003; reviewer: Army Rsch. Office, US Dept. Energy, NSF, Office of Naval Rsch., Dept. Commerce and the Natural Scis., Engring. Rsch. Coun. Can., 1981—, Irish Sci. Found. 2003, referee jours., —; contbr. articles to profl. jours. Capt. USAF, 1974-75. Grantee Los Alamos Sci. Lab., 1977, Air Force Office Sci. Rsch., 2002—, Army Rsch. Office, 2003—, Def. Advanced Rsch. Projects Agy., 2002—, NSF, SRC, 2004-06. Fellow AAAS, APS, IEEE (exec. com. for plasma sci. 1983—, Harry Diamond Meml. award 1998), Yale Sci. and Engring. Assn. (exec. bd. dirs. 1983—), Army Rsch. Lab.; mem. Nat. Geneal. Soc., DHS, DTRA, Phi Beta Kappa. Achievements include patents in

field. Home: 2045 Central Ave Wilmette IL 60091-2383 Office: U Ill Dept Elec and Computer Engring MC154 851 S Morgan St Chicago IL 60607 Office Phone: 312-413-5968. Business E-Mail: stroscio@uic.edu, m.stroscio@gte.net.

**STROSS, JEOFFREY KNIGHT,** internist, educator; b. Detroit, May 2, 1941; s. Julius Knight and Molly Ellen S.; m. Ellen Nora Schwartz; children: Wendy, Jonathan. BS in Pharmacy, U. Mich., 1962, MD, 1967. Diplomate Am. Bd. Internal Medicine. Intern Univ. Mich. Hosp., Ann Arbor, 1967-68, resident in internal medicine, 1971-73; instr. internal medicine U. Mich., Ann Arbor, 1973-74, asst. prof., 1974-79, assoc. prof., 1979-87, prof., 1987—. Contbr. numerous articles to med. jours. Served to maj. USAF, 1969-71. Nat. Heart, Lung and Blood Inst. grantee, 1975—. Fellow ACP; mem. Soc. for Gen. Internal Medicine (regional chmn. 1984-86). Jewish. Home: 824 Asa Gray Dr Ann Arbor MI 48105-2853 Office: U Mich Med Sch 3119 Taubman Ann Arbor MI 48109-0376 E-mail: jstross@umich.edu.

**STROSS, RANDALL E.,** business history professor, columnist; BA, Macalester Coll.; PhD in History, Stanford Univ. Prof. bus. history San Jose State Univ. Digital Domain columnist New York Times; columnist U.S. News & World Report; vis. scholar History Dept. & Prog. in History and Philosophy of Sci. and Tech., Stanford Univ. Author: eBoys: The First Inside Account of Venture Capitalists at Work, Steve Jobs and the NeXT Big Thing, The Microsoft Way, Technology & Society in Twentieth-Century America; contbr. articles to Wall Street Journal, The New Republic, Fortune. Rsch. fellowship, Nat. Endowment for the Humanities Mailing: New York Times 229 W 43d St New York NY 10036 Office Phone: 212-556-7395.*

**STROSSEN, NADINE,** legal association administrator, law educator; b. Jersey City, Aug. 18, 1950; d. Woodrow John and Sylvia (Simicich) S.; m. Eli Michael Noam, Apr. 25, 1980. AB, Harvard U., 1972, JD magna cum laude, 1975; LHD (hon.), U. Vt., 1992; LHD, U. R.I., 1992; JD (hon.), San Joaquin Coll. Law, 1996; LHD (hon.), Rpcky Mountain Coll., 1996, Mass. Sch. Law, 2000. Jud. clk. Minn. Supreme Ct., St. Paul, 1975-76; assoc. Lindquist & Vennum, Mpls., 1976-78, Sullivan & Cromwell, N.Y.C., 1978-83; prof. clin. law, supervising atty. Civil Rights Clinic, Sch. Law, NYU, 1984-88; prof. law N.Y. Law Sch., N.Y.C., 1988—; adj. prof. Columbia U., 1990—; pres. ACLU, N.Y.C., 1991—. Editor Harvard Law Rev., 1975; contbr. book chpts., articles to profl. jours.; author: In Defense of Pornography: Free Speech and the Fight for Women's Rights, 1995. Mem. Coun. Fgn. Rels., 1994—. Recipient Outstanding Young Person award Jaycees Internat., 1986; named one of Ten Outstanding Young Amers., U.S. Jaycees, 1986; adj. fellow Yale U. Calhoun Coll., 1997-. Mem. ACLU, Nat. Coalition Against Censorship (bd. dirs. 1988—), Human Rights Watch (exec. com. 1989-91), Harvard Club (N.Y.C.). Avocations: travel, skiing, singing. Office: NY Law Sch 57 Worth St New York NY 10013-2960 also: ACLU 125 Broad St 18th Fl New York NY 10004 E-mail: nstrossen@aclu.org.

**STROTE, JOEL RICHARD,** lawyer; b. NYC, Apr. 19, 1939; s. Jack and Fortuna (Benezra) S.; children: Jared, Noah, Sebastian; m. Elisa Ballestas, Dec. 14, 1991. BA, U. Mich., 1960; JD, Northwestern U., 1963. Bar: N.Y. 1964, D.C. 1965, Calif. 1967, U.S. Dist. Ct. (cen. dist.) Calif. 1967, U.S. Supreme Ct. 1971, Nev., 2003. Assoc. Damman, Blank, Hirsh & Heming, N.Y.C., 1964-65, ICC, Washington, 1965-66, Capitol Records, Hollywood, Calif., 1966-67; ptnr. Strote & Whitehouse, Beverly Hills, Calif., 1967-89; of counsel Selvin, Weiner & Ruben, Beverly Hills, Calif., 1989-94; ptnr. with Cohen, Strote & Young, 1992-94; sole practice law, 1994—. Judge pro tem L.A. County Mcpl. Ct., 1973—; probation monitor Calif. State Bar Ct., L.A., 1985—; pres. Liberace Found., Las Vegas, Nev., 1987-2005; bd. chmn. Tuesday's Child, L.A., 1989-91. Mem. Thousand Oaks Arts Commn., 1997-99. Cpl. USMC, 1963-64. Mem. Calif. State Bar Assn., L.A. County Bar Assn., L.A. Copyright Soc., Beverly Hills Bar Assn., Assn. Internat. Entertainment Lawyers, Internat. Fedn. of Festival Orgns. Democrat. Jewish. Avocations: swimming, bicycling, hiking, opera, travel. Office: Joel R Strote 2801 Townsgate Rd # 222 Westlake Village CA 91361-3003 Office Phone: 818-707-1923. Personal E-mail: joelstrote@verizon.net.

**STROTHER, ALLEN,** biochemical pharmacologist, researcher; b. Nolan County, Tex., Feb. 20, 1928; s. Henry Allen and Minnie Etta (Taylor) S.; m. Julia Ann Gutch, Feb. 7, 1957; children: Wesley Allen, Lori Ann. BS, Tex. Tech U., 1955; MS, U. Calif., 1957; PhD, Tex. A&M U., 1963. Rsch. asst. Tex. A&M, Coll. Sta., 1959-63; rsch. biochemist FDA, Washington, 1963-65; asst. prof. pharmacology Loma Linda (Calif.) U., 1965-70, assoc. prof., 1970-75, prof., 1975-95, retired, vol. faculty, 1995—, prof. emeritus Physiology and Pharmacology, 1997—. Cons. WHO, Geneva, 1982-86. Contbr. numerous articles to profl. jours.; chpt. to WHO Bull. Pilot CAP/USAF Search and Rescue San Bernardino, Calif., 1967-95; pilot examiner CAP Air Force Aux., Norton AFB, 1970-86. Named Investigator of Yr. Walter E. McPherson Soc., Loma Linda U., 1984, Basic Sci. Fellow of Yr., 1986, Outstanding Faculty Rschr. of Yr. award, 1997. Mem. Am. Soc. Pharmacology and Exptl. Therapeutics, Am. Chem. Soc., Xzenobiotic Soc. Avocations: flying, golf. Home: 74448 Nevada Cir E Palm Desert CA 92260-2269 Office: Loma Linda U Sch Medicine Dept Physiology and Pharmacology Loma Linda CA 92354

**STROTHER, JAMES M.,** lawyer; b. 1951; BA, JD, Univ. Minn. Pvt. practice, Mpls.; asst. gen. counsel Norwest Corp. (now Wells Fargo Home Mortgage), 1986—98; gen. counsel Wells Fargo Home Mortgage, 1998—2001; dep. gen. counsel Wells Fargo & Co., San Francisco, 2001—03, exec. v.p., gen. counsel, 2004—. Office: Wells Fargo & Co 633 Folsom St San Francisco CA 94107

**STROTHMAN, JAMES EDWARD,** editor-in-chief; b. Pitts., Mar. 27, 1939; s. Edward Charles and Harriet Hope (Jones) S.; m. Eleanor Shawfield Jacobs, Sept. 9, 1961; children— Joseph, Jill, Stuart. BA in Journalism, Pa. State U., 1961. Asst. city editor, city hall reporter Williamsport Pat, 1961-64; with Miami Herald, Fla., 1964-67; aerospace writer AP, Cape Kennedy, Fla., 1967-69; reporter Los Angeles bur. Electronic News, 1969-71, sr. editor computer news sect., 1971-73, mng. editor, 1973; sr. info. rep. corp. hdqrs., then program adminstr. data processing divsn. hdqrs. IBM Corp., 1973-77, mgr. ea. area comm. data processing divsn., 1977-79, field comm. mgr. data processing divsn., 1979-81, mgr. comm. rsch. divsn., 1981; free-lance writer and cons. Strothman Assocs., 1981-82; editor-in-chief MIS Week, N.Y.C., 1982-88; free-lance writer, cons., 1988-89; editor-in-chief Computer Pictures, Chappaqua, NY, 1989-94; news editor InTech Mag. and ISA On Line Instrument Soc. Am. (ISA), Research Triangle Park, NC, 1994-2000. Online editor, eCommerce Bus. Mag., 2000-01; assoc. editor InTech Mag., 2001-02; freelance writer, mktg. comm. cons., 2003—. Episc.

**STROTHMAN, WENDY JO,** literary agent; b. Pitts., July 29, 1950; d. Walter Richard and Mary Ann (Hodtum) S.; m. Mark Kavanaugh Metzger, Nov. 25, 1978; children: Andrew Richard, Margaret Ann. Student, U. Chgo., 1979-80; AB, Brown U., 1972. Copywriter, mktg. U. Chgo. Press, 1973-76, editor, 1977-80, gen. editor, 1980-83, asst. dir., 1983; dir. Beacon Press, Boston, 1983-95; v.p., pub. adult, trade and reference Houghton-Mifflin, Boston, 1995-96, exec. v.p. trade and reference divsn., 1996—2002, lit. agent, 2003—. Trustee Brown U., 1990-96, Deerfield Acad., 2003—. Edtl. adv. bd. Scholarly Pub., 1993-94; bd. editors Brown Alumni Monthly, 1983-89; chmn., 1986-89. Bd. dirs. Editorial Project for Edn., trustee, 1987-91, treas., 1988-90. Fellow Brown U., 1997—. Mem. Renaissance Soc. (bd. dirs. 1980-83), Assn. Am. Pubs. (Freedom to Read com.), Pubs. Lunch Club (N.Y.C.), PEN New Eng. (adv. bd.), Examiner Club, NacRe Reins. Soc. (bd. dirs.). Office: The Strothman Agy LLC One Faneuil Hall Marketplace Third Fl Boston MA 02109

**STROUCKEN, ALBERT P. L.,** chemical company executive; Exec. v.p. industrial chemicals divsn. Bayer Corp., 1992—97; gen. mgr. inorganic chemicals divsn. Bayer AG, 1997—98; pres., CEO H.B. Fuller Co., St. Paul,

1998—, chmn., 1999—. Bd. dir. Baxter Internat., Owens Illinois. Bd. dir. Twin Cities United Way; chmn. Minn. Bus. for Early Learning. Office: HB Fuller Co PO Box 64683 1200 Willow Lake Blvd Saint Paul MN 55164-0683

**STROUD, JAMES STANLEY,** retired lawyer; b. Wimbledon, N.D., Jan. 26, 1915; s. Herbert Montgomery and Amanda Getchell (Longfellow) S.; m. Marjorie Marsh Hovey, Sept. 11, 1940; children: Jay Stanley, Steven Hovey. AB, Jamestown Coll., 1936; JD, U. Chgo., 1939. Bar: Ill. 1939, U.S. Supreme Ct. 1945, D.C. 1972. Counsel Ill. Mepl. Code Commn., Chgo., 1939-40; bill drafter Ill. Legis. Ref. Bur., Springfield, 1941; from assoc. to ptnr. Mayer, Brown Row & Maw LLP, Chgo., 1941-71, ptnr.-in-charge Washington, 1972-80, ret., 1982. Bd. dirs. Chgo. Community Renewal Found., 1962-70; mem. adminstrv. bd. Nat. United Meth. Ch., Washington, 1982-84; coord. Extended Family Program, 1981-82. Capt. AUS, 1943-46. Home: Cottage 304 3300 Darby Rd Haverford PA 19041-1063

**STROUD, JOHN FRED, JR.,** judge; b. Hope, Ark., Oct. 3, 1931; s. John Fred and Clarine (Steel) S.; m. Marietta Kimball, June 1, 1958; children: John Fred III, Ann Kimball, Tracy Steel. Student, Hendrix Coll., 1949-51; BA, U. Ark., 1959, LLB, 1960. Bar: Ark. 1959, Tex. 1988, U.S. Supreme Ct. 1963, cert.: Ark. (mediator). Ptnr. Stroud & McClerkin, 1959-62; city atty. City of Texarkana (Ark.), 1961; legis. asst. to U.S. Senator John L. McClellan, 1962-63; ptnr. Smith, Stroud, McClerkin, Dunn & Nutter, 1963-79, 81-95; assoc. justice Ark. Supreme Ct., Little Rock, 1980; judge Ark. Ct. Appeals, Little Rock, 1996—2001, chief judge, 2001—04. Chmn. Texarkana Airport Authority, 1966-67, Texarkana United Way Campaign, 1988; pres. Caddo area coun. Boy Scouts Am., 1971-73; former trustee Ark. Nature Conservancy; former bd. dirs. Ark. Cmty. Found.; former pres. Red River Valley Assn.; former commr. Red River Compact Commn.; past vice chmn. Ark. Water Code Study Commn.; chmn. bd., chmn. coun. ministries Meth. Ch. Lt. col. USAR, 1951-56, Res. ret. Recipient award of exceptional accomplishment Ark. State C. of C., 1972, 86, Silver Beaver and Disting. Eagle awards Boy Scouts Am.; named Outstanding Young Man of Texarkana, 1966, One of Five Outstanding Young Men of Ark., 1967, Outstanding Alumnus of U. Ark. Law Sch., 1980. Fellow Am. Bar Found.; mem. ABA, Ark. Bar Assn. (chmn. exec. coun. 1979-80, pres. 1987-88, C.E. Ransick award of excellence 1990-91, Presdl. award of excellence and Charles L. Carpenter Meml. award 1997-98), Four States Area Estate Planning Coun. (past chmn.), State Bar Tex., Miller County Bar Assn. (past pres.), Texarkana Bar Assn. (pres. 1982-83), Ark. Bar Found. (chmn. 1974-75, chmn. trust com. 2003-06), Am. Coll. Trust and Estate Counsel (chmn. Ark. chpt. 1986-91), S.W. Ark. Bar Assn., N.E. Tex. Bar Assn., Assn. Atty.-Mediators, Texarkana C. of C. (pres. 1969, C.E. Palmer award 1979), U. Ark. Law Alumni Soc. (bd. dirs.), Texarkana Country Club (pres. 1990-92), Rotary (pres. Texarkana 1965-66). Avocations: tennis, golf, hunting, fishing. Office: Box 8030 Ste 6 State Line Pl Texarkana AR 71854 Office Phone: 870-772-0718. Personal E-mail: jstroudadr@yahoo.com.

**STROUD, PATRICIA TYSON,** writer; b. Phila., Dec. 22, 1932; d. George Peterson and Jane (Chapman) Huber; m. Noel J. Tyson, Sept. 8, 1956 (dec. July 1982); children: John Tyson II, Peter H. Tyson, Lisa Tyson Ennis; m. Morris Wistar Stroud III, Mar. 11, 1989 (dec. Apr. 1990); m. Alexander McCurdy III, Nov. 16, 1991. AB, Smith Coll., Northampton, Mass., 1955. Writer, pub. rels. releases First Pa. Bank, Phila., 1968-69; editor, Frontiers Acad. Natural Scis., Phila., 1979-82; writer pvt. practice, Phila., 1982—. Author: Thomas Say: New World Naturalist, 1992, The Emperor of Nature: Charles Lucien Bonaparte and His World, 2000, The Man Who Had Been King: The American Exile of Napoleon's Brother Joseph, 2005; contbr. articles to profl. jours. Pres. bd. dirs. Ga. Farm Found., 1990—; bd. dirs. Hist. Bartram's Garden, 1992—98, U. Pa. Press, 1999—2003. Avocations: reading, gardening, piano.

**STROUD, ROBERT ARLEN,** medical equipment company executive; b. Lake Charles, Ill., Nov. 26, 1937; s. Grover Cleveland Stroud and Dolly Lucille (Mericle) S.; m. Mary Erin Coge, Oct. 1, 1965; children: Shannon Dene Stroud Dowden, Robert Arlen II. BS, La. State U., 1962. Sales rep. Chemetron Corp. Nat. Cylinder Gas, Inc., New Orleans, 1962-64; SE regional mgr. Orthopedic Equipment Corp., New Orleans, 1964; dist. mgr. Ohio Med. Products, Inc. Airco, New Orleans, 1964-75; v.p. sales and mktg. Med. Equipment Co. Inc., New Orleans, 1975-76, pres., CEO, 1976—. Pres., CEO Clin. Svcs. Inc., New Orleans, 1983-99. Contbr. papers to profl. jours. Chmn. bd. dirs. New Eng. Presch. Acad., Windsor Locks, Conn., 1992-99; chmn. bd. civil svc. bd. City of Slidell, La., 1977-97; state bd. adv. coun. La. Dept. Edn., Baton Rouge, 1977-82; adv. bd., small bus. coun. La. Assn. Bus. and Industry, Baton Rouge, 1985-96. Mem. Internat. Camellia Soc. (bd. dirs. 2000—), Am. Camellia Soc. (bd. dirs. 1989-99, dir.-at-large 1991-96, v.p. 1997-99, endowment bd. 1993-99, pres. 2002—), Gulf Coast Camellia Soc. (pres., v.p., treas. 1985-99, Dedication award 1996), Camellia Club (pres., v.p. 1999-99, Dedication award 1996). Republican. Avocation: camellia hobbyist. Home: 2 Oak Grove Way Slidell LA 70458-5328 E-mail: bobcamelia@aol.com.

**STROUP, DARRYL RAY,** systems engineer; b. Denver, Colo., Aug. 5, 1953; s. Norman Glen and Darlene Edna (Porath) Stroup; m. Mary Meta Vensel, Dec. 9, 1972; children: Jared Norman, Caryn Meta Hill (Stroup), Jared Norman, Caryn Meta Hill (Stroup), Elizabeth Marie. BSEE cum laude, U. Utah, 1977; MSEE, Air Force Inst. Tech., Dayton, Ohio, 1981. System Flight Test Engineer, U. S. Naval Test Pilot Sch., Md., 1987; Program Management Def. Sys. Mgmt. Coll., Va., 1991. Chief FB-111 AMP avionics test engr. USAF, McClellan AFB, Calif., 1985—86, chief B-2 offensive avionics test engr. Edwards AFB, Calif., 1986—89; chief advanced sys. br. Asst. Sec. of Air Force (Acquisition), Pentagon, DC, 1989—90; lead F-15 program element Fighter Divsn., Asst. Sec. of Air Force (Acquisition), Pentagon, 1990—92; mgr. avionics, nav., and precision targeting sys. Adroit Sys. Inc, Alexandria, Va., 1992—96; lead sys. integration engr. USN, Patuxent River, Md., 2003—. Contbr. articles to jours. Rsch. asst. Program in Occupl. Therapy Wash. Sch. of Medicine, St Louis, Mo., 1999—99; rsch. design engr. Ctrl. Inst. for the Deaf, St Louis, Mo., 2000; vol. Luth. Family Assn. and Luth. Hour Ministries, St Louis, 1999—2003. Maj. USAF, 1972—92. Decorated Meritorious Svc. medal USAF, Air Force Commendation medal.: mem.: Swedish Colonial Soc. Lutheran - Missouri Synod. Office: USN 453 Bldg 2272 Rm 351 Patuxent River MD 20670 Office Phone: 301-757-6760. Office Fax: 301-757-6459. E-mail: darryl.stroup@navy.mil.

**STROUP, KALA MAYS,** former education commissioner, educational alliance administrator; BA in Speech and Drama, U. Kans., 1959, MS in Psychology, 1964, PhD in Speech Comm. and Human Rels., 1974; EdD (hon.), Mo. Western State Coll., 1996; LHD (hon.), Harris-Stowe State Coll., 2000. V.p. acad. affairs Emporia (Kans.) State U., 1978-83; pres. Murray State U., Ky., 1983-90, S.E. Mo. State U., Cape Girardeau, 1990-95, Am. Humanics, Kansas City, Mo., 2002—; commr. higher edn., mem. gov.'s cabinet State of Mo., Jefferson City, 1995—2002. Pres. Mo. Coun. on Pub. Higher Edn.; mem. pres.'s commn. NCAA; cons. Edn. Commn. of States Task Force on State Policy and Ind. Higher Edn.; adv. bd. NSF Directorate for Sci. Edn. Evaluation; adv. coun. Dept. Health, Edn. and Welfare, chair edn. com.; citizen's adv. coun. on state of Women U. S. Dept. Labor, 1974-76. Mem. nat. exec. bd. Boy Scouts Am., nat. exploring com., former chair profl. devel. com., mem. profl. devel. com., exploring com., Young Am. awards com., 1986-87, north ctrl. region strategic planning com., bd. trustees, nat. mus. chair; mem. Gov.'s Coun. on Workforce Quality, State of Mo.; bd. dirs. Midwestern Higher Edn. Commn.; chair ACE Leadership Commn.; mem. bd. visitors Air U.; v.p. Missourians for Higher Edn.; bd. dirs. St. Francis Med. Ctr. Found., 1990-95, Cape Girardeau C. of C., 1990-95, U. Kans. Alumni Assn.; pres. Forum on Excellence, Carnegie Found.; adv. bd. World Trade Ctr., St. Louis, Svc. Mems. Opty. Colls., 1997—; mem. Mo. Higher Edn. Loan Authority, 1995—, depts. econ. devel. & agrl. Mo. Global Partnership, 1995—, Mo. Tng. & Employment Coun., 1995-2002, Concordia U. Sys. Advancement Cabinet, State Higher Edn. Exec. Officers, 1995—, mem. com. workforce edn. and tng., 1996; bd. dirs. Heartland's Alliance Minority Participation, 1995-2002; chair, mem. workforce devel. com. NPEC coun. U.S. Office of Edn., 1997—; bd. dirs. Midwestern Higher Edn.

Distributed Learning Workshop, 1998-2002, Dept. Natural Resources Minority Scholarship Adv. Bd.; chair Show Me Results sub-cabinet Educated Missourians; mem. Pub. Policy Initiative Stakeholder Com., 1999—; mem. Coun. Higher Edn. transfer and pub. interest com.; mem. access/diversity com. State Higher Edn. Exec. Officers; trustee, mem. adv. coun. Assn. Governing Bds. of Univs. and Colls. Ctr. for Pub. Edn., 2000—. ACE fellow; recipient Alumni Honor Citation award U. Kans., Award Distinction Profl. Black Men's Club, S.E. Mo., 1990, Dist. Svc. to Edn. award Harris-Stowe State Coll., 1996; named to U. Kans. Womans Hall of Fame, Ohio Valley Conf. Hall of Fame, 1997. Mem. Am. Assn. State Colls. and Univs. (past bd. dirs., mem. Pres.'s Commn. on Tchr. Edn., Task Force on Labor Force Issues and Implications for the Curriculum), Mortar Board, Phi Beta Kappa, Omicron Delta Kappa, Phi Kappa Phi, Rotary (found. Ednl. awards com.). Office: Am Humanics 4601 Madison Ave Kansas City MO 64112 Office Phone: 816-561-6415.

**STROUP, RICHARD L.,** lawyer; b. Shelby, Ohio, May 17, 1948; BSME, Ohio Northern U., 1970; JD, U. Va., 1976. Bar: Va. 1976, DC 1977, lic.: US Ct. Appeals (Fed. Cir.) 1982, registered: US Patent & Trademark Office. Law clk. to Hon. Francis C. Brown Trial Divsn., US Ct. of Claims, 1976—77; patent examiner US Patent & Trademark Office; ptnr. Finnegan, Henderson, Farabow, Garrett & Dunner LLP, Washington, leader, Litig. Sect. Mem.: Internat. Trademark Assn., Am. Intellectual Property Law Assn., ABA, Va. Bar Assn., Bar Assn. DC, DC Bar Assn., Phi Kappa Phi, Tau Beta Pi. Office: Finnegan Henderson Farabow Garrett & Dunner LLP 901 New York Ave NW Washington DC 20001-3315 Office Phone: 202-408-4000. Office Fax: 202-408-4400. Business E-mail: richard.stroup@finnegan.com

**STROUP, RICHARD LYNDELL,** economist, educator, writer; b. Sunnyside, Wash., Jan. 3, 1943; s. Edgar Ivan and Inez Louise (Kellett) S.; m. Sandra Lee Price, Sept. 13, 1962 (div. Sept. 1981); children— Michael, Craig; m. Jane Bartlett Steidemann Shaw, Jan. 1, 1985; 1 child, David. Student, MIT, 1961-62; BA, MA, U. Wash., 1966, PhD in Econs., 1970. Asst. prof. econs. Mont. State U., Bozeman, 1969-74, assoc. prof. econs., 1974-78; dir. Office Policy Analysis, Dept. Interior, 1982-84; prof. econs. Mont. State U., 1978—, dept. head, 2003—. Vis. assoc. prof. Fla. State U., Tallahassee, 1977-78; sr. fellow Property and Environ. Rsch. Ctr., Bozeman, 1980-. Author: Economics, 2003; co-author: Natural Resources, 1983, Economics: Private and Public Choice, 11th edit., 2005, Basic Economics, 1993, What Everyone Should Know About Economics and Prosperity, 1993, Common Sense Economics, 2005; editor: Cutting Green Tape, 2000; also articles, 1972—; mem. editorial bd. Regulation, 1993—. Adj. scholar Cato Inst., 1993—. Mem. Am. Econ. Assn., Western Econ. Assn., So. Econ. Assn., Mont Pelerin Soc., Phila. Soc., Assn. Pvt. Enterprise Edn. (Hayeck Endowed chair econs. 2005). Episcopalian. Home: 9 W Arnold St Bozeman MT 59715-6127 Office: PERC 2048 Analysis Dr Ste A Bozeman MT 59718-6829 Business E-Mail: rstroup@montana.edu.

**STROUP, RODGER EMERSON,** historian; b. St. Louis, Oct. 4, 1946; s. Robert Melvin and Mary Claire Stroup; m. Martha Porter Smith, Dec. 22, 1968; 1 child, Mary Page. BA, Wofford Coll., 1968; MA, U. S.C., 1972, PhD, 1980. Dir./curator Hist. Columbia (S.C.) Found., 1974—79; curator history S.C. State Mus., Columbia, 1979—86, chief curator, 1986—89; dir. collections and interpretation, 1989—97; dir. and state hist. preservation officer S.C. Dept. Archives and History, Columbia, 1997—. Pres. S.C. Hist. Assn., Columbia, 1988—89, S.C. Fedn. Museums, Columbia, 1991—93; trustee Nat. History Day, College Park, Md., 1990—; coun. mem. Drayton Hall Site Coun., Charleston, SC, 1997—. Curator (history exhbns.) South Carolina History Exhibits. Pres. Hist. Columbia Found., Columbia, 1992—93; chair Richland County Hist. Preservation Commn., Columbia, 1994—95; vestry mem., jr. warden, treas. St. John's Episcopal Ch., Columbia, 1986—2005; pres. Shandon Neighborhood Coun., Columbia, 1985—86. First lt. U.S. Army, 1968—70, South Korea. Named Preservationist of the Yr., Hist. Columbia Found., 2002—03; recipient Profl. Svc. award, S.C. Fedn. Museums, 1992, David Phillips Disting. award, Men of St. John's Episcopal Ch., 1994. Mem.: Am. Assn. for State and Local History (coun. mem. 2004—), Loblolly Soc. (pres. 2004—05). Episcopalian. Avocations: genealogy, railroad history, reading, civic volunteer. Office: SC Dept Archives & History 8301 Parklane Rd Columbia SC 29223-4905 Office Phone: 803-896-6187. Office Fax: 803-896-6186. Business E-Mail: stroup@scdah.state.sc.us.

**STROUP, SALLY,** federal agency administrator; b. Harrisburg, Pa. Grad., Ind. U. Pa., Loyola U. From staff atty. to sr. v.p. legal svcs. and chief counsel Pa. Higher Edn. Agy.; mem. profl. staff com. on edn. and the workforce US Ho. of Reps., 1993—2001; dir. industry and govt. affairs Apollo Group Inc./U. Phoenix; asst. sec. postsecondary edn. US Dept. Edn., Washington, 2001—. Office: US Dept Edn Office Postsecondary Edn 1990 K St NW Rm 7115 Washington DC 20006 Office Phone: 202-502-7750, 202-502-7714. Office Fax: 202-502-7875.

**STROUSE, DEBRA J.,** director; b. Mt. Vernon, Ohio, May 15, 1955; d. Ralph Bernard and Ann Helen Ferry; m. Roy Edward Strouse, Sept. 9, 1979; children: Joshua C., Jenna C. BA in Edn., Mt. Vernon Nazarene U., Ohio, 1979; MA in Ednl. Adminstrn., Ohio State U., Columbus, 1982. Nat. bd. cert. tchr. NBPT, 1999, cert. Praxis assessor 2002, prin. edn. adminstr. 2005, OPE facilitator 2005. Social studies tchr. Mt. Vernon City Schs., 1979—2004, lang. arts tchr., 2004—19, achievement coord. grades 6-12, 2006—. Bd. mem. student tchr./tchr. program Mt. Vernon Nazarene U., 2000—; Praxis assessor Ohio Dept. Edn., Columbus, 2002—, SIRI workshop presenter, 2005—; COTC prof. comp I, II Ctrl. Ohio Tech. Coll., Mt. Vernon, 2006—. Mem.: Mt. Vernon Adminstrs. Assn., Middle Sch. Assn., Mental Health Assn. Avocations: bicycling, running, walking, golf. Home: 201 E Gambier St Mount Vernon OH 43050 Office: Mt Vernon City Schs 298 Martinsburg Rd Mount Vernon OH 43050

**STROUSE, JEAN,** writer; b. L.A., Sept. 10, 1945; d. Carl David and Louise (Friedberg) S. BA, Radcliffe Coll., 1967. Editl. asst. N.Y. Rev. of Books, 1967-69; freelance writer N.Y.C., 1969-72; editor Pantheon Books, N.Y.C., 1972-75; freelance writer N.Y.C., 1975-79, 1983-2003; book critic Newsweek Mag., N.Y.C., 1979-83; dir. Cullman Ctr. for Scholars and Writers N.Y. Pub. Libr., N.Y.C., 2003—. Selection com. J.S. Guggenheim Found., N.Y.C., 1995-97, trustee, 1987-94, 2001—04, fellow, 1977, 86; exec. coun. Authors Guild; Ferris prof. journalism Princeton U., 1998; John J. Rhodes chair in Am. instns. and pub. policy Barrett Honors Coll., Ariz. State U., 2003. Author: Alice James, A Biography, 1980, Morgan American Financier, 1999; editor: Women & Analysis: Dialogues on Psychoanalytic Views of Femininity, 1974. Recipient Bancroft prize, Columbia U., 1981; fellow, NEH, 1976, 1992, John D. and Catherine T. MacArthur Found., 2002—. Mem. Am. Acad. Arts & Sci.; mem. Soc. Am. Historians (pres. 2001-02), Am Philos Soc, The Century Assn., Phi Beta Kappa (vis. scholar 1996-97).

**STROUSS, CARLETON O.,** lawyer; BA, Bucknell Univ., 1974; JD, Pa. State Univ., 1977. Bar: Pa. 1977. Atty. Pa. Dept. Transp., 1980—85; chief counsel Pa. Turnpike Commn., 1985—87; adminstrv. ptnr. & mem. mgmt. com. Kirkpatrick & Lockhart Nicholson Graham LLP, Harrisburg, Pa. Trustee emeritus Wilson Coll.; mem. Transp. Rsch. Bd. Com. Contract Law. Master: James S. Bowman Am. Inn of Ct.; mem.: ABA (Forum on Constrn. Industry), Pa. Bar Assn. (chmn. Civil Litigation sect. 1991—93, chmn. Constrn. Litigation Com. 1986—90). Office: Kirkpatrick & Lockhart Nicholson Graham LLP Payne Shoemaker Bldg 240 N Third St Harrisburg PA 17101-1507 Office Phone: 717-231-4503. Office Fax: 717-231-4501. Business E-Mail: cstrouss@klng.com.

**STROUTH, BARON HOWARD STEVEN,** geologist, mining engineer; b. Frankfurt, Germany, Sept. 28, 1919; arrived in U.S. 1941; s. Baron Karl Siegfried and Ida (Morck) von Strauss; m. Penelope Ann Creamer-Osteen, Nov. 3, 1951. BSc, U. Sorbonne, 1939; PhD in Engring., Bretton Woods U., 1965; PhD in Engring. (hon.), Rochedale U., Can., 1970. Asst. mgr. Drexel Bros. Ltd., NYC, 1941—43; pres. Std. Mining, NYC, 1951-58, Stanleigh

Uranium Mine, Toronto, Can., 1954-61; mng. dir. Norsul Oil and Mining Quito, Ecuador, 1961-71; dir., officer Mining and Oil Cos., various locations; founder, operator Stanleigh Uranium and Norsul Oil. Sr. trustee Weingueter Baron K. S. von Strauss, Erben Trust, Vaduz, 1954—. Translator: author Rilke The Cornet, 1960, A Window to the Morrow, 1963, A Sonata for Frankfurt, 1967, Cities of the Break of Dawn, 1988, Beauty is Forever, 1996. Maj. USAR, 1943-69, ret. Recipient Conspicuous Svc. Cross, Gov. Dewey, 1947, French, Czech, Cambodian decorations. Fellow Explorers Club; mem. Can. Inst. Mining Engrs. (life), Am. Inst. Mining Engrs. (sr.; Legion of Honor), St. James Club (London), Ontario Club Toronto. Achievements include patents for mining and oil processes. Avocations: collector, antique books, precolombian art, antique maps.

**STROYAN, SUSAN ELIZABETH,** librarian, administrator; b. Lincoln, Ill., Mar. 16, 1950; d. Charles William and Mary Jane (Gayle) Anderson; m. Richard Lee Stroyan, Aug. 7, 1971 (div.); children: Kathryn, Emily, Peter, David Alikah; m. Carl Richard Bennett, May 16, 1992. BS, Ill. State U., 1972; MLS, U. Ill., 1973, PhD, 1986. Head adult svcs. Bloomington (Ill.) Pub. Libr., 1974-78; instr. Ill. State U., Normal, 1977-82; dir. health scis. libr. BroMenn Regional Healthcare, Bloomington, 1981-88; asst. exec. dir. Ill. Valley Libr. System, Pekin, 1988-92; libr. Ill. Wesleyan U., Bloomington, 1992—. Cons. healthcare librs., 1979—. Author: (chpt.) Sources of Medical Evidence, 1997; author (booklet) Library Facility Planning, 1993; bd. dirs. Highsmith Press Editl. Bd., 1992-99. Mem. McLean County Arts Coun., Bloomington, 1976-78; v.p. Alumni Assn., Ill. State U., Normal, 1977-82. Recipient grants Japan Found., 1993, netILLINOIS, 1993, James Kemper Found., 1993, Ill. State Librr., 1994. Mem. ALA (councilor 1994-98), Ill. Librr. Assn. (v.p. 1994-95, pres. 1995-96), Libr. Adminstrn. and Mgmt. Assn. (pres. 1991-92), Med. Librr. Assn., Med. Librr. Assn. of Health Info. Profls. (cert., disting. mem.), Ill. Librr. Computer Sys. Orgn. Consortia (pres. 2003-2005), Beta Phi Mu (elected bd. dirs. 1999-2005). Lutheran. Avocation: beading. Office: Ill Wesleyan Univ PO Box 2899 Bloomington IL 61702-2899 Home: 1515 Sweetbriar Dr Bloomington IL 61701-8326 E-mail: sstroyan@titan.iwu.edu.

**STROYD, ARTHUR HEISTER, JR.,** lawyer; b. Pitts., Sept. 5, 1945; 1 child, Elizabeth. AB, Kenyon Coll., 1967; JD, U. Pitts., 1972. Bar: Pa. 1972, U.S. Dist. Ct. (we. dist.) Pa. 1972, U.S. Ct. Appeals (3d cir.) 1972. Law clk. to judge U.S. Ct. Appeals (3d cir.), Phila., 1972—75; with Reed, Smith, LLP, Pitts., 1975—, mng. ptnr., Allegheny Region, 1997—2001. Mem. Nat. Adv. Coun. on Child Nutrition, U.S. Dept. Agriculture, 1984-85. Mem. Mt. Lebanon Zoning Hearing Bd., 1978-81; pres. bd. dirs. Mt. Lebanon Sch. dist., 1981-87; solicitor Allegheny County Rep. Com., 1988-95; pres. bd. dirs. Ctr. for Theatre Arts, Pitts., 1984-93; grad. Leadership Pitts., 1991-92; chair bd. dirs. Mt. Lebanon Hosp. Authority, 1990-91; bd. dirs. Neighborhood Legal Svcs. Assn., 1989-91, U. Pitts. Cancer Inst., 1993—, Leadership Pitts. Inc., 2006—; mem. alumni coun. Kenyon Coll., 1996-00; bd. dirs. Edn. Policy and Issues Ctr., 2000-03. Lt. USNR, 1969-71. Fellow Am. Coll. Trial Lawyers; mem. ABA, Pa. Bar Assn. (commn. for justice initiatives in Pa. 2004—), Allegheny County Bar Assn. (past pres., bd. govs., past chair civil litig. sect., past chmn. judiciary com.), Acad. Trial Lawyers (pres., bd. govs.), mem. Pa. Supreme Ct. Civil Procedural Rules Com., Duquesne Club, Pitts. Golf Club, Hist. Soc. We. Pa. (bd. dirs. 2000—). Episcopalian. Avocations: skiing, motorcycling, golf. Office: Reed Smith LLP 435 6th Ave Pittsburgh PA 15219-1886 Office Phone: 412-288-3110. Business E-Mail: astroyd@reedsmith.com.

**STRUBBE, THOMAS R.,** insurance industry executive; b. Ft. Wayne, Ind., Mar. 30, 1940; s. Rudolph C. and Maverne E. (Wagoner) S.; children: Tracy Lynn, Patrick Thomas, Christina Lee. BS, Ind. U., 1962; JD, Tulane U., 1965. Bar: Ind. 1965, Ill. 1969. Atty. Lincoln Nat. Life Ins. Co., Ft. Wayne, Ind., 1965-66, asst. counsel, 1967-68; with Washington Nat. Corp., Evanston, Ill., 1968-90, counsel, 1968-73, gen. counsel, 1973-79, corp. sec., 1974-84, v.p., 1975-79, sr. v.p., 1979-83, exec. v.p., 1983-84, pres., 1984-90, also bd. dirs., mem. exec. com.; pres., CEO Osborn Labs. Inc., Olathe, Kans., 1990-98, Guarantee Res. Life Ins. Co., Chgo., 1998-99, also bd. dirs., ret., 2000. V.p., bd. dirs., exec. com. Chgo. chpt. Epilepsy Found. Am., 1975—79; trustee Glencoe (Ill.) Union Ch., 1984—87; Stephen min. Trinity Luth. Ch., Kans., 2003—; bd. dirs. Assn. Retarded Citizens Ill., 1985—89, Northlight Theater, 1984—89. Lt. USNR, 1965—71. Lincoln Found. grantee, 1964. Mem. ABA, Assn. Life Ins. Counsel, Nat. Investor Rels. Inst., Am. Soc. Corp. Secs., Home Office Life Underwriters Assn., Ind. Bar Assn., Ill. Bar Assn., Skokie Country Club (Ill.), Shadow Glen Golf Club (Kans.), Hallbrook Country Club (Kans.), Hideaway Beach Club (Fla.), Rotary, Lambda Chi Alpha, Delta Sigma Pi. Home (Summer): 9210 Oak Valley Dr De Soto KS 66018-7994 Home (Winter): 6000 Royal Marco Way Unit 350 Marco Island FL 34145 Personal E-mail: thomstrubbe@yahoo.com.

**STRUBEL, ELLA DOYLE,** advertising executive, public relations executive; b. Chgo., Mar. 14, 1940; d. George Floyd and Myrtle (McKnight) D.; m. Richard Craig G'sell, Apr. 26, 1969 (div. 1973); m. Richard Perry Strubel, Oct. 23, 1976; stepchildren: Douglas Arthur, Craig Tollerton. BA magna cum laude, U. Memphis, 1962; MA, U. Ill., 1963. Staff asst. Corinthian Broadcasting Co., N.Y.C., 1963-65; dir. advt. and pub. rels. WANE-TV, Ft. Wayne, Ind., 1965-66; asst. dir. advt. WBBM-TV, Chgo., 1966-67, mgr. sales promotion, 1967-69, v.p. advt. sales promotion and info. svcs., 1969-70; dir. pub. rels. Waltham Watch Co., Chgo., 1973-74; mgr. advt. promotion and pub. rels. WMAQ-TV, Chgo., 1974-76; v.p. corp. rels. Kraft, Inc., Glenview, Ill., 1985-87; sr. v.p. corp. affairs Leo Burnett Co., Inc., Chgo., 1987-92, exec. v.p., 1992-98; mng. dir. EllaQuent Designs, 2002—. Pres. women's bd. Rehab. Inst. Chgo., 1982—84; chair Chgo. Network, 1994—95, Rehab. Inst. Chgo., 1998—2001; vice chair Chgo. Pub. Libr. Found.; bd. dirs. Rehab. Inst. Chgo. Named Outstanding Woman in Comms. in Chgo., YWCA, 1995, one of 100 Most Influential Women in Chgo., Crain's Chgo. Bus., 1996, Who's Who in Chgo. Bus. 2002. Mem. Casino Club, Econ. Club (bd. dirs.). Democrat. Presbyterian. Home and Office: 55 W Goethe St Chicago IL 60610-7406 Office Phone: 312-255-0235. Business E-Mail: estrubel@aol.com.

**STRUBEL, RICHARD PERRY,** Internet company executive; b. Evanston, Ill., Aug. 10, 1939; s. Arthur Raymond and Martha (Smith) S.; m. Linda Jane Freeman, Aug. 25, 1961 (div. 1974); children: Douglas Arthur, Craig Tollerton; m. Ella Doyle G'sell, Oct. 23, 1976. BA, Williams Coll., 1962; MBA, Harvard U., 1964. Assoc. Fry Cons., Chgo., 1964-66, mng. prin., 1966-68; with N.W. Industries, Inc., Chgo., 1968-83, v.p. corp. devel., 1969-73, group v.p., 1973-79, exec. v.p., 1979-83, pres., 1983; chmn. bd., pres. Buckingham Corp., N.Y.C., 1972-73; pres., chief exec. officer Microdot Inc., Chgo., 1973-83; mng. dir. Tandem Ptnrs. Inc., Chgo., 1990-99; with UNext Inc., Deerfield, Ill., 1999, pres., COO, 1999—2004, vice chmn., dir., 2004—. Trustee Mut. Funds of The No. Trust Co., Chgo., and various mutual funds of Goldman Sachs Asset Mgmt., N.Y.C.; bd. dirs Gildan Activewear, Inc., Montreal, Que., Can. Trustee U. Chgo.; mem. visiting com. Divinity Sch., U. Chgo.; mem. adv. bd. Martin Marty Ctr. Mem. Casino Club, Chicago Club, Comml. Club, Racquet Club of Chicago, Commonwealth Club, Econ. Club. Presbyterian. Office: UNext Inc Ste 455 111 N Canal St Chicago IL 60606

**STRUBLE, DAN,** academic administrator; m. Karen Brown Struble; children: Amanda, Benjamin. BS with merit, U.S. Naval Acad., 1983; MA in Comparative Politics, U. So. Calif., 1989, PhD in Am. Politics, 1993. Asst. prof. pub. adminstrn. Navy ROTC Dept. U. So. Calif., 1987—9; from asst. to assoc. to acting dir. Major and Planned Giving Office Occidental Coll., L.A., 1999-; prin. gifts U.S. Naval Acad., 1995—2004; pres. Montreat (N.C.) Coll. Active Christ Our Anchor Presbyn. Ch. Commdr. USNR. Office: Montreat Coll PO Box 1267 Montreat NC 28757

**STRUBLE, JAMES CURTIS,** ambassador; b. Visalia, Calif., Oct. 29, 1953; s. Arthur James and Ezella Ruby (Meek) S.; m. Susan Mary Briggs, Dec. 9, 1976; children: Peter James, Dale. BA in Slavic Lang. & Lit., U. Calif., Berkeley, 1975, BA in History, 1975. Vice consul Am. Consulate Gen., Monterrey, Mex., 1977-79; consul Am. Embassy USSR, Moscow, 1981-83;

first sec. Am. Embassy Spain, Madrid, 1983-86; consul gen. Am. Embassy Honduras, Tegucigalpa, 1986-88; program assoc. Hoover Institution, Stanford, Calif., 1988—89; gen. consul Am. Embassy Thailand, Bangkok, 1994—96; dep. chief of mission Am. Embassy Ecuador, Quito, 1996—99; dir., office of Brazilian and So. cone affairs U.S. Dept. State, Washington, 1999—2001, dep. asst. sec., bureau of western hemisphere affairs, 2001—02, prin. dep. asst. sec., 2002, acting asst. sec., 2002—03, U.S. amb. to Peru Lima, 2003—. Mem. Am. Fgn. Svc. Assn. Avocations: coin collecting/numismatics, history. Office: Am Embassy APO Lima AA 34031-5000 Peru

**STRUCK, NORMA JOHANSEN,** artist; b. West Englewood, NJ, Feb. 17, 1929; d. Hans Christian and Amanda (Solberg) Johansen; m. H. Walter Struck, Aug. 21, 1955; children: Steven, Laurie. Student, N.Y. Phoenix Sch. Design, 1946-50, Art Students' League, N.Y.C., 1976-77. Staff artist Norcross, inc., N.Y.C., 1950-60, free-lance artist, 1967-75; artist portraits, prints Scafa-Tornabene, Nyack, NY, 1976—; artist portraits, paintings U.S.N., U.S. Coast Guard, Washington, 1976—. Com. ed. mem. Navy Art Coop. Liaison, N.Y.C., 1976-80, Coast Guard Art Program, N.Y.C., 1980—, Navy Hist. Mus., Washington. One-woman shows include Valley Cottage Gallery, NY, Bergen Co. Playhouse, Oradell, NJ, NY Yacht Club, 2003, Nabisco Co., Fairlawn, NJ, 1987; exhibited in group shows Navy Hist. Mus., Washington, 1976, Navy Combat Art Gallery, Washington, World Trade Ctr., 1979, USCG, New Eng. Air Mus., Windsor Locks, Conn., 1984, Fed. Hall, NYC, 1986, 93-97, Salmagundi Club, NYC, Officers Club, Governor's Island, Hudson Valley Show, White Plains, NY, Intrepid Mus., NYC, Alexander Hamilton U.S. Custom House, Newington-Cropsey Mus., NY, Bergen County Mus. Art & Sci., NJ; represented in permanent collections U.S. Pentagon, Washington, Henie-Onstad Mus., Oslo, World Figure Skating Hall of Fame and Mus., Colorado Springs, Alexander Hamilton Custom House, NYC, Nat. Arts Club, NYC. Recipient Louis E. Seley award, Navy Art Program, 1979; Grumbacher award, Catherine Lorillard Wolfe, Nat. Arts Club, N.Y.C., 1978; George Gray award Coast Guard Art Program, Governors Island, N.Y., 1983, 89. Fellow Am. Artists Profl. League (pres.'s award 1979); mem. Portrait Soc. Am., Art Students League (life), Hudson Valley Assn. (bd. dirs. 1985-88, M. Dole award 1980), Soc. Illustrators, Salmagundi Club, Nat. Arts Club, Inc., Mus. of Women in the Arts (charter). Avocations: antiques, gourmet cooking. Home: 910 Midland Rd Oradell NJ 07649-1904 E-mail: njstruck99@cs.com.

**STRUCK, PETER T.,** classicist, educator; AB, U. Mich., 1987; MA, U. Chgo., 1991, PhD, 1997. Lectr. dept. comparative lit. U. Chgo. 1996; sr. lectr. dept. classics Ohio State U., 1997—98; asst. prof. and co-dir. program in classical langs. and lit. U. Mo., Kansas City, 1998—99; asst. prof. dept. classical studies U. Pa., Phila., 1999—2005, assoc. prof. classical studies, 2005—. Rschr. and reporter U.S. News & World Report, 1988—89; copy editor The New Republic, 1987—88; editl. asst. Critical Inquiry, 1992—94; mng. editor book series History, 1997—98; mem. rev. com. comparative lit. U. Chgo., Chgo., 1994, preceptor MA program in Humanities, 1996—97, instr. dept. classics summer intensive Greek program, 1996; mem. undergraduate com. U. Mo., Kansas City, 1998—99; freshman advisor U. Pa., Phila., 1999—; interim faculty fellow Hamilton Coll. Ho. U. Penn., 1999—2000; faculty fellow Stouffer Coll. Ho. U. Penn., 2000—; discussion leader Penn Reading Project, 2000; mem. writing com. U. Pa., 2001—02, mem. Mellon postdoctoral tchg. fellowship rev. com., 2001. Contbr. chapters to books, articles to profl. jours.; author: Birth of the Symbol, 2004. Vol. Latin tutor H.S. students, Chgo, 1992—94. Fellow, U. Chgo., 1989—94; grantee, 1994, 1995, 1996, Distributed Learning Venture Fund, U. Pa., 2000, 2001, Andrew Mellon/ACLS Jr. Faculty fellow, 2002—03; Whiting fellow, 1995—96, Robert F. and Margaret S. Goheen fellow, Nat. Humanities Ctr., 2002—03. Mem.: Soc. of Biblical Lit., Am. Acad. of Religions, Am. Philological Assn. Office: U Pa 201 Logan Hall 249 S 36th St Philadelphia PA 19104

**STRUDLER, ROBERT JACOB,** real estate development executive; b. N.Y.C., Sept. 22, 1942; m. Ruth Honigman, Aug. 29, 1965; children: Seth, Keith, Craig. BS in Indsl. and Labor Relations, Cornell U., 1964; LLB, Columbia U., 1967. Bar: N.Y. 1967, Fla. 1973. Assoc. firms in, N.Y.C., 1967-71; v.p., chmn. operating com. U.S. Home Corp., Clearwater, Fla., 1972-76, v.p. legal affairs, 1976-77, v.p. ops., 1977-79; sr. v.p. ops. Houston, 1979-81, sr. v.p. acquisitions, 1981-84, pres., chief operating officer, 1984-86, CEO, 1986-2000; vice-chmn. Lennar Corp., Miami, Fla., 2000—04, COO, 2000—04, chmn., 2004—. Pres., trustee Sch. for Young Children; mem. pres.' adv. coun. U. St. Thomas. Co-recipient Builder of Yr. award Profl. Builder Mag., 1994, Bronze award Wall Street, 1995, Hearthstone Builder Lifetime Pub. Svc. award, 2003, Legend of Residential Mktg. award Nat. Sales and Mktg. Coun., 2004; elected to Nat. Housing Hall of Fame, 2000. Mem. ABA, N.Y. State Bar Assn., Fla. Bar Assn., Cornell Real Estate Coun., Nat. Assn. Homebuilders (chmn. high prodn. coun. 1991-93). Office: Lennar Corp 10707 Clay Rd Houston TX 77044*

**STRUELENS, MICHEL MAURICE JOSEPH GEORGES,** political science professor, consultant; b. Brussels, Mar. 10, 1928; m. Godelieve De Wilde, Aug. 2, 1949; children: Alain, Patricia, Brigitte, Bernard, Jean Paul (dec.). BA, Coll. St. Pierre, Brussels, 1944; MA, Antwerp U., Belgium, 1949; PhD, Am. U., Washington, 1968. Insp. econ. affairs Congo Govt., Leopoldville, 1954-50, chief insp. econ. affairs, 1954-55, dep. commr. transp., 1955-57; dir. Info. and Public Relations Office for Congo, Brussels, 1957-58, Congo Tourism Pavillion, Internat. World's Fair, Brussels, 1958-59; dir. gen. Belgian Congo and Ruanda Urundi Tourist Office, Congo, 1959; chmn. African Commn. Internat. Union Ofcl. Travel Orgns., Geneva, 1959-60; ofcl. Katanga rep. in U.S., 1960-63; dir. gen. Internat. Inst. for African Affairs in Can., 1963-64; spl. asst. to prime minister Democratic Republic Congo, fgn. affairs minister, adviser to Congo UN del., adviser Congo embassy Washington, N.Y.C., 1961-66; dir. Eurafrica Consultants on Fgn. Affairs, Washington, 1966—; prof. polit. sci., French, internat. bus. Am. U., 1968-93; prof. emeritus, 1993; dir. Ctr. Rsch and Documentation on European Community Am. U., 1971—, chmn. faculty rels. com., 1986-87, chmn. grad. studies com., 1989-90; dir. E.C. Inst. in Europe, 1978-93; U. Antwerp Exchange Program, 1979-83. Dir. EPSCI/ESSEC (France) Exchange Program, 1980-84, chmn. internat. bus. dept., 1980-84; dir. exchange program Bus. Sch. of Poly., U. Madrid, 1981-84; investment adviser, 1977—; adminstr. French Parish., 1974-75. Ctr. Studies on Internat. Relations, 1987-96, Econs. and Bus., La Rochelle, France, 1987-96; exec. v.p. Eglise St. Louis Corp., French-Speaking Union, Washington, 1974-75; mgr. by agreement with European Communities, European Documentation Ctr. (CERDEC), accessing by satellite EC Data Banks, 1985— and providing through WCL Libr. of Am. U., On Line Pub. Access Cataloging, 1991—. Author: (with Inforcongo) Congo Belge et Ruanda-Urundi, 1958; monograph Le Canada à l'Heure de l'Afrique, 1964; The United Nations in the Congo - or ONUC and International Politics, 1976. Recipient Internat. Union Ofcl. Travel Orgns. Poster award Brussels, 1958, Etoile de Service en Argent King of Belgium, 1956; chevalier de l'Ordre Royal du Lion, 1957; Faculty award for outstanding contbn. to acad. program devel. Coll. Bus. Adminstrn., Am. U., 1979; Faculty award for outstanding teaching, 1980, 82, 84; Faculty award for outstanding service to Am. U., 1981 Mem. Golden Key, Phi Sigma Alpha. Clubs: Cosmos (Washington); Bukavu Royal Sports (founder 1950, pres. 1951-54, hon. pres. 1957) (Congo). Lodges: Rotary. Home: 1374 Woodside Dr Mc Lean VA 22102-1536 Office: Am U 4400 Mass Ave NW Washington DC 20016-8071 "Ad Augusta per Angusta". Using Latin, French writer Victor Hugo said it all! Nothing comes easy and "success," a very personal perception indeed, requires a great deal of luck, perseverance and hard work. True success, though, is directly related to the pursuit of happiness, which in turn is a state of mind. If and when I reach eternity, I'll then be able to tell how successful I was during my passage on earth.

**STRUKOFF, RUDOLF STEPHEN,** retired music educator; b. Rostov, Don, Russia, July 18, 1935; came to U.S., 1957; s. Stephen and Olga (Flemming) S.; m. Donna Lee Hill, May 31, 1959; children: Rudolf Stephen, Jr., Robbin Stanley, Regan Stuart. B Music Edn., Andrews U., 1960; MusM, Mich. State U., 1964, PhD in Music, 1970. Instr. music Mich. State U., East Lansing,

1963-65; asst. prof. Ind. State U., Terre Haute, 1966-69; assoc. prof. Andrews U., Berrien Springs, Mich., 1969-76; prof. music Gov's. State U., Univ. Park, Ill., 1977-97. Chorus master Ill. Philharm. Chorus, Park Forest, Ill., 1982-84; music dir. Univ. Cmty. Chorale, Univ. Park, Ill., 1978-96, Chamber Orch., Univ. Park, 1978-96. Composer: The Greatest of These, 1970, Childhood Sketches, 1973; singer (opera) Attila by Verdi, 1979; condr. Christmas Oratorio by Saint-Saens, 1986, Stabat Mater by Rossini, 1988, German Requiem by Brahms, 1989, Requiem by Mozart, 1990, Mass in C by Beethoven, 1991, Mass in E Flat by Schubert, 1992, Requiem in C Minor by Cherubini, 1993, Cathedral Series, Joliet, Ill., Mass in B Flat by Haydn, St. Liborius, Steger, Ill., 1994, Symphony #2 (Hymn of Praise), Temple Anshe Sholom, 1994, Olympia Fields, Ill., Requiem by Mozart, St. Liborius, Steger, Ill., 1995, Messiah by Handel, Ctr. for Performing Arts, University Park, Ill., 1995, Concert Overture and Requiem by Cherubini, 1996; rec. artist (CD) How Great Thou Art, 2003, My Native Land, 2003. Lectr. Lyric Opera, Chgo., 1979-89, Libr. Lectr. Series, Park Forest, 1982, Career Days, Chgo., 1982-97, Symposium on Soviet Russia, Univ. Park, 1985, Ill. Philharmonic Workshop Series, 1991-96. Mem. ASCAP, Chgo. Singing Tchrs. Guild (pres. 1984-86, 91-93, bd. dirs. 1986-96), Am. Choral Dirs. Assn., Nat. Assn. Tchrs. Singing, Nat. Assn. Schs. Music, Pi Kappa Lambda. Avocations: antiques, golf, reading.

**STRULL, GENE,** technology consultant, retired manufacturing executive; b. Chgo., May 15, 1929; s. Albert and Helen (Wolf) S.; m. Joyce Landsbaum, July 6, 1952; children: David Jay, Brian Lee. BSEE, Purdue U., 1951; MS, Northwestern U., 1952, PhD in Elec. Engring., 1954. With Westinghouse Electric Corp., Pitts., later Balt., 1954-93, supervisory engr., adv. cngr., mgr. solid state tech.-aerospace, 1958-68, mgr. sci. and tech. systems devel. div., mgr. advanced tech. labs., 1968-78, dep. gen. mgr. systems devel. div., 1979-81, gen. mgr. advanced tech. div., 1981-93, exec. dir. tech., 1987-93. Cons. Army Sci. Bd., 1979-83, NRC-NAS, 1980-82, Def. Sci. Bd., 1981-83, NSF, 1992—; cons. NASA, 1967-87, com. chmn., 1976-78; adv. com. panel USNR, 1989. Contbg. author: Integrated Electronic Systems, 1970, Integrated Circuit Technology, 1967; contbr. articles to profl. jours.; patentee in field. Gene Strull Tech. Ctr. at Westinghouse Electric Corp. Advanced Tech. Labs. named in his honor, Balt.; named Outstanding Elec. Engr. award Purdue U., 1994. Fellow IEEE (life, Govt. Industry Svc. award 1987, Frederik Philips award 1991); mem. Md. Acad. Scis. (chmn. 1978-80). Home: One Gristmill Ct # 606 Baltimore MD 21208

**STRUM, BRIAN J.,** real estate company officer; b. Bklyn., Nov. 27, 1939; s. Max J. and Beatrix (Galitzky) S.; m. Mickey Weiss, Nov. 19, 1966; children: Ira, Howard, Beth. BA, Bklyn. Coll., 1960; LLB, NYU, 1963. Bar: N.Y. 1964, N.J. 1969; CLU; counselor of real estate. Atty. Gilbert, Segall and Young, N.Y.C., 1963-65; assoc. res. atty. Prudential Ins. Co. Am., N.Y.C., 1965-67, various positions, law dept., 1967-75, v.p. real estate investments, 1975-86; chmn. Prudential Property Co., Newark, 1986—94; CEO Prudential Realty Group, Newark, 1992-94; Silverstein chair of real estate devel. NYU, 1995-98. Pres., trustee Prudential Realty Trust, 1985-94; mem. adv. bd. Chgo. Title & Trust Co., N.Y.C., 1982-96. Editor: Financing Real Estate in the Inflationary Eighties, 1981; contbr. articles to profl. jours. With USAR, 1963-69. Recipient Disting. Cmty. Svc. award Brandeis U., 1983, Urban Leadership award NYU, 1990, Good Scout award N.Y.C. coun. Boy Scouts Am., 1991, Nat. Achievement awrd D.A.R.E. Am., 1993. Fellow Anglo Am. Real Property Inst. (charter); mem. ABA (chmn. real property, probate and trust law sects. 1984-85), N.Y. State Bar Assn. (chmn. real property sect. 1975-76), Urban Land Inst. (coun. mem.), Am. Coll. Real Estate Lawyers (charter). Home: 435 Pine Ln Haworth NJ 07641-1308 Office Phone: 201-384-1400. Personal E-mail: mstrum77@aol.com.

**STRUM, JAY GERSON,** lawyer; b. N.Y.C., July 6, 1938; s. John and Dorothy (Chaikind) S.; m. Patricia Ann Burtis, Jan. 25, 1969; children: Daniel, Jennifer. BA in polit. sci. magna cum laude, CCNY, 1959; LLB, Harvard U., 1962. Bar: N.Y. 1963, U.S. Dist. Ct. (so. and ea. dists.) N.Y. 1963, U.S. Ct. Appeals (2d cir.) 1965, U.S. Supreme Ct. 1979. Ptnr. SEC, NYC, 1963-65, Coon, Dubow, Kleinberg & Strum, 1965-67; assoc. Kaye, Scholer, Fierman, Hays & Handler, 1967-70; ptnr. Kaye, Scholer LLP, 1971—. Mem. ABA, Assn. of Bar of City of N.Y., Harvard Club (N.Y.C.), Phi Beta Kappa. Clubs: Harvard (N.Y.C.). Office: Kaye Scholer Fierman Hays & Handler LLP 425 Park Ave New York NY 10022-3506

**STRUM, PHILIPPA,** political science professor, researcher; b. N.Y.C., Dec. 14, 1938; d. Joseph B. and Ida P. Strum; 1 child, David Strum Weiss. BA, Brandeis U., 1959; MEd, Harvard U., 1960; PhD, New Sch. for Social Rsch., 1964. From instr. to assoc. prof. Rutgers U., Newark, 1964-72; vis. prof. Barnard Coll., N.Y.C., 1978-79; vis. scholar NYU, N.Y.C., 1982-83; prof. polit. sci. CUNY, N.Y.C., 1972-99, prof. polit. sci. emeritus, 1999—; dir. U.S. Studies Woodrow Wilson Internat. Ctr. for Scholars, 2001—. Vis. prof. constl. law Wayne State U., 2000—01; sr. Fulbright lectr. Bosphorus U., Istanbul, 1995. Author: The Supreme Court and "Political Questions", 1974, Brandeis: Justice for the People, 1984, 1984, Brandeis: Beyond Progressivism, 1993, Privacy: The Debate in the U.S. Since 1945, 1998, When the Nazis Came to Skokie, 1999, Women in the Barracks, 2002. Bd. dirs. ACLU, N.Y.C., 1979—; pres. Am.-Israeli Civil Liberties Coalition, N.Y.C., 1981-91. Guggenheim Found. rsch. fellow, 1986-87, ACLS rsch. fellow, 1980-81; Fulbright Exch. Program tchg. fellow, Istanbul, 1995; Woodrow Wilson Internat. Ctr. for Scholars rsch. fellow, 1997-98. Avocations: travel, music. Office: Wilson Center 1300 Pennsylvania Ave NW Washington DC 20004-3027 Office Phone: 202-691-4129 Business E-Mail: philippa.strum@wilsoncenter.org.

**STRUNCK, JUERGEN,** printmaker; b. Germany, 1943; naturalized; Student, Univ. Munich, Germany, 1964—65, student, 1966—76, Wichita State Univ., Kans., 1965—66; MA, MFA, Univ. Dallas, Irving, Tex., 1970. Faculty Cistercian Prep. Sch., Irving, Tex., 1967—68; prof. printmaking Univ. Dallas, Irving, Tex., 1968—; faculty So. Meth. Univ., Dallas, 1973, 1975—76; summer faculty Univ. Wash., Seattle, 1976. One-man shows include Martha Gault Art Gallery, Slippery Rock Univ., Pa., 1990, Slocumb Galleries, Ea. Tenn. State Univ., 1993, Warehouse Living Arts Ctr., Corsicana, Tex., 1993, Dutch Phillips & Co. Fine Art, Fort Worth, Tex., 1994, Univ. Art Gallery, Baylor Univ., Waco, Tex., 1994, Univ. Tex., Tyler, 1995, Museu Nacional de Bellas Artes, Rio de Janeiro, Brazil, 1995, Spring Creek Gallery, Collin County CC, Plano, Tex., 1996, exhibited in group shows at 10th Norwegian Internat. Print Triennale, Fredrikstad, Norway, 1992, So. Graphics Coun., Univ. Tenn., Knoxville, 1992, Nat. Inst. Coll. of Art, Balt., 1993, Nat. Ctr. for Fine Arts of Egypt, Giza, 1993, 1st Internat. Print Triennale Colour in Graphic Art, Dist. Mus., Old Town Hall, Torun, Poland, 1994, San Angelo Mus. Fine Arts, Tex., 1994, 170th Annual Exhbn., NAD, NYC, 1995, La Societe Internat. des Beaux-Arts, Trammell Crow Ctr., Dallas, 1996, ArtCentre of Plano, Tex., 2003, others, Represented in permanent collections Libr. of Congress, others; workshop presenter, lectr., panelist, juror. Mem: NAD (academician 1994—). Office: Art Dept Univ Dallas 1845 E Northgate Dr Irving TX 75062 Office Phone: 972-721-5000.

**STRUNK, ROBERT CHARLES,** physician; b. Evanston, Ill., May 29, 1942; s. Norman Wesley and Marion Mildred (Ree) S.; m. Juanita; children: Christopher Robert, Alix Elizabeth. BA in Chemistry, Northwestern U., 1964, MS in Biochemistry, 1968, MD, 1968. Lic. MD, Ariz., Colo., Mass., Mo. Resident in pediatrics Cin. Children's Hosp., 1968-70; pediatrician Newport (R.I.) Naval Hosp., 1970-72; rsch. fellow in pediatrics Harvard Med. Sch., Boston, 1972-74; asst. prof. pediatrics U. Ariz. Health Sci. Ctr., Tucson, 1974-78; dir. clin. svcs. Nat. Jewish Ctr. for Immunology and Respiratory Med., Denver, 1978-87; sabbatical leave Boston Children's Hosp., 1984-85; dir. divsn. allergy and pulmonary medicine Children's Hosp., St. Louis, 1987-98; pediatrician Barnes and Allied Hosp., St. Louis, 1987—; prof. pediatrics Washington U. Sch. Medicine, St. Louis, 1987—, Strominger prof.,

2002—. Recipient Allergic Disease Acad. award Nat. Inst. Allergy and Infectious Disease of NIH. Mem. Am. Acad. Allergy and Immunology, Am. Thoracic Soc. Office: Washington U Sch Med Dept Pediatrics 1 Childrens Pl Saint Louis MO 63110-1002

**STRUPP, HANS HERMANN,** psychologist, educator; b. Frankfurt am Main, Germany, Aug. 25, 1921; came to U.S., 1939, naturalized, 1945; s. Josef and Anna (Metzger) S.; m. Lottie Metzger, Aug. 19, 1951; children: Karen, Barbara, John. AB with distinction, George Washington U., 1945, AM, 1947, PhD, 1954; MD (hon.), U. Ulm, Fed. Republic of Germany, 1986. Diplomate in clin. psychology Am. Bd. Profl. Psychology; lic. clin. psychologist, Tenn. Research psychologist Human Factors Ops. Research Labs., Dept. Air Force, Washington, 1949-54; supervisory research psychologist, personnel research br. Adj. Gen.'s Office, Dept. of Army, Washington, 1954-55; dir. psychotherapy research project Sch. Medicine, George Washington U., Washington, 1955-57; dir. psychol. services, dept. psychiatry U. N.C. Sch. Medicine, Chapel Hill, 1957-64, assoc. prof. psychology, 1957-62, prof., 1962-66; prof. dept. psychology Vanderbilt U., Nashville, 1966-76, dir. clin. tng., dept. psychology, 1967-76, disting. prof., 1976-94, Harvie Branscomb disting. prof., 1985-86; disting. prof. emeritus, 1994—. Mem. editorial adv. bd. Psychotherapy: Theory, Research and Practice, 1963-97, Jour. Cons. and Clin. Psychology, 1964—, Jour. Nervous and Mental Disease, 1965—, Jour. Am. Acad. Psychoanalysis, 1972—, Jour. Contemporary Psychology, 1972-86, Psychiatry Research, 1979-86, Jour. Profl. Psychology, 1976-89; founding editor Psychotherapy Rsch., 1990-95; others; contbr. chpts. to books, articles and revs. to profl. jours. Recipient Helen Sargent meml. prize Menninger Found., 1963; Alumni Achievement award George Washington U., 1972; Disting. Profl. Achievement award Am. Bd. Profl. Psychology, 1976, Disting. Profl. Contbns. to Knowledge award Am. Psychol. Assn., 1987; others Fellow Am. Psychol. Assn. (mem. exec. council 1964, exec. bd. 1969-72, council of reps. 1970-73, chmn. com. on fellows div. psychotherapy 1970-74, pres. div. clin. psychology 1974-75, recipient Disting. Profl. Psychologist award 1973, Disting. Scientist award 1979), Tenn. Psychol. Assn., AAAS; mem. Eastern Psychol. Assn., Southeastern Psychol. Assn., Am. Psychopathol. Assn., Am. Psychoanalytic Assn. (hon.), Soc. for Psychotherapy Research (pres. 1972-73, Career Contbr. award 1986), Psychologists Interested in Advancement of Psychoanalysis, Phi Beta Kappa, Sigma Xi. Mailing: 6666 Brookmont Terr #408 Nashville TN 37205 Personal E-mail: hansstrupp@comcast.net. As a refugee from Nazi Germany, I remain deeply grateful for the opportunities my adopted country has provided me.

**STRUTHERS, MARGO S.,** lawyer; BA, Carleton Coll., 1972; JD cum laude, U. Minn., 1976. Atty., shareholder Moss & Barnett, P.A. and predecessor firms, Mpls., 1976-93; ptnr. Oppenheimer Wolff & Donnelly, LLP, Mpls., 1993—. Mem. Am. Health Lawyers Assn., Minn. State Bar Assn (bus. law sect., former chair nonprofit com., former chair and former mem. governing coun. health law sect.). Office: Oppenheimer Wolff & Donnelly LLP Plaza VII 45 S 7th St Ste 3300 Minneapolis MN 55402-1614 Office Phone: 612-607-7427, 612-607-7000. Business E-Mail: mstruthers@oppenheimer.com.

**STRUTZ, WILLIAM A.,** lawyer; b. Bismarck, N.D., May 13, 1934; s. Alvin C. and Ina Vee (Minor) S.; m. Marilyn Seagly, Aug. 31, 1957; children: Heidi Jane Mitchell, Colin Christopher, Nathaniel Paul. Student, Drake U., 1952-53; BA, North Ctrl. Coll., 1956; postgrad., Washington and Lee U., 1956-57; JD, U. N.D., 1959. Bar: N.D. 1959, U.S. Dist. Ct. N.D. 1959, U.S. Ct. Appeals (8th cir.) 1961. Atty., pres. Fleck, Mather & Strutz, Ltd., Bismarck, ND, 1959—. Mem. grievance com. N.D. Supreme Ct., Bismarck, 1974-77, chmn. supreme ct. svcs. com., 1979—. Bd. dirs. Vets. Meml. Pub. Libr., Bismarck, Shiloh Christian Sch., Bismarck, 1979—; pres. student body North Ctrl. Coll., 1956. Recipient Herbert Harley award Am. Judicature Soc., 1991. Mem. ABA, Am. Bd. Trial Advs. (adv.), Lions Club. Methodist. Avocations: reading, rare book collecting, music, sports. Home: 1238 W Highland Acres Rd Bismarck ND 58501-1259 Office: Fleck Mather Strutz Ltd 400 E Broadway Ave Bismarck ND 58501-4038

**STRUVE, GUY MILLER,** lawyer; b. Wilmington, Del., Jan. 5, 1943; s. William Scott and Elizabeth Bliss (Miller) S.; m. Marcia Mayo Hill, Sept. 20, 1986; children: Andrew Hardenbrook, Catherine Tolstoy, Frank Leroy Hill, Guy Miller, Beverly Marcia Wise Hill (dec.), Elena Wise Struve-Hill. AB summa cum laude, Yale U., 1963; LLB magna cum laude, Harvard U., 1966. Bar: NY 1967, DC 1986, US Dist. Ct. (so. dist.) NY 1970, US Dist. Ct. (ea. dist.) NY 1973, US Dist. Ct. (no. dist.) Calif. 1979, US Dist. Ct. DC 1987, US Dist. Ct. (we. dist.) NY 1991, US Dist. Ct. (no. dist.) NY 2000, US Ct. Appeals (2d cir.) 1969, US Ct. Appeals (DC cir.) 1973, US Ct. Appeals (8th cir.) 1976, US Ct. Appeals (9th cir.) 1979, US Supreme Ct. 1971. Law clk. Hon. J. Edward Lumbard, Chief Judge United States Ct. Appeals for 2d Circuit, 1966-67; assoc. Davis Polk & Wardwell, NYC, 1967-72, ptnr., 1973—, Ind. Counsel's Office, 1987-94. Mem. ABA, NY State Bar Assn., Assn. Bar City NY (chmn. com. antitrust and trade regulation, 1983-86, chmn. com. fed. cts. 1998-2001), Am. Law Inst, Civil War Preservation Trust (trustee), Juvenile Diabetes Rsch. Found. (lay rev. com.). Home: 116 E 63rd St New York NY 10021-7325 Office: Davis Polk & Wardwell 450 Lexington Ave Fl 30 New York NY 10017-3982 Office Phone: 212-450-4192. Business E-Mail: struve@dpw.com.

**STRUYK, PIETER M.,** music educator; b. Arlington, Va., June 9, 1970; s. Raymond Jay Struyk; m. Ali Kathleen Primus, July 29, 2000. B of Music Performance, U. Mich., 1992; studied with Michael Udow, Salvatore Rabbio, Albert Merz, Gerald Cleaver. Faculty Clark U., Worcester, Worcester Poly. INst., Coll. Holy Cross, Anna Marin Coll., Concord Acad.; percussion specialist Northborough Pub. Schs., Mass., 2001—; Artist endorser Sabian Cymbals, 1997; percussion coll. Coll. Holy Cross, Worcester, 2001—; adj. prof. percussion Worcester Polytechnic Inst., 2001—, Anna Maria Coll., Paxton, Mass., 2001—. Contbr. articles to mags.; musician: (recs. with Big Dave and the Ultrasonics) Love and Money, 1993, No Sweat Live!, 1996, Big Dave and the Ultrasonics, 1999; percussionist Coll. Holy Cross, Worcester, 2000—, Worcester Chorus Orch., 2001—, New Bedford Symphony Orch., Mass., 2001—, Chorus N. Shore, Danvers, Mass., 2002—, Foothills Theatre, Worcester, Mass., , appearances include (TV series) Much Music Lunch TV, 1995, (radio) House of Blues Radio Show, L.A., 1999. Mem.: Boston Musicians Assn., Am. Fedn. Musicians, Percussive Arts Soc. Democrat. Avocations: martial arts, ballroom dancing. Home: 19 Brookfield Cir Framingham MA 01701-4036

**STRUYK, ROBERT JOHN,** lawyer; b. Sanborn, Iowa, May 17, 1932; s. Arie Peter and Adriana (VerHoef) S.; m. Barbara Damon, Sept. 7, 1963; children: Arie Franklin, Damon Nicholas, Elizabeth Snow. BA, Hope Coll., 1954; MA, Columbia U., 1957; LLB, U. Minn., 1961. Bar: Minn., U.S. Dist. Ct. Minn. Secondary tchr. Indianola (Iowa) Pub. Schs., 1957-58; assoc., then ptnr. Dorsey & Whitney, Mpls., 1961—. Mem.: Mpls., Minikahda Club. Episcopalian. Office: Dorsey & Whitney 50 S 6th St Ste 2200 Minneapolis MN 55402-1498

**STRYER, LUBERT,** biochemist, educator; b. Tientsin, China, Mar. 2, 1938; BS with honors, U. Chgo., 1957; MD magna cum laude, Harvard U., 1961; DS (hon.), U. Chgo., 1992. Helen Hay Whitney fellow Harvard U., also Med. Research Council Lab., 1961-63; from asst. prof. to assoc. prof. biochemistry Stanford U., 1963-69; prof. molecular biophysics and biochemistry Yale U., 1969-76; Winzer prof. neurobiology Stanford U. Sch. Medicine, 1976—2004, chmn. dept. structural biology, 1976-79, prof. emeritus, 2004—; chmn. sci. adv. bd. Affymetrix, Inc., 1993—; chmn., chief sci. officer Senomyx, Inc., La Jolla, Calif., 1999-2001, chmn. sci. adv. bd., 2001—. Cons. NIH, NRC; pres. sci. dir. Affymax Rsch. Inst., Palo Alto, Calif., 1990. Mem. sci. adv. bd. Jane Coffin Childs Fund, 1982-90, Rsch. to Prevent Blindness, 1984-93; Pew Scholars Profs. in Biomed. Scis.; chmn. sci. adv. bd. Affymetrix, Inc., 1993—. Mem. editorial bd.: Jour. Molecular Biology, 1968-72, Jour. Cell Biology, 1981-84; assoc. editor: Annual Revs. Biophysics and Bioengineering, 1970-76. Trustee Helen Hay Whitney Found., 1997—2001, McKnight Endowment for the Neurosis., 1999—. Recipient Am. Chem. Soc. award in biol.

chemistry Eli Lilly & Co., 1970, Alcon award in vision Alcon Rsch. Inst., 1992, Molecular Bioanalytics award German Soc. Biochemistry and Molecular Biology, 2002. Fellow AAAS (Newcomb Cleveland prize 1992), Am. Acad. Arts and Scis.; mem. NAS, Am. Chem. Soc., Am. Soc. Biol. Chemists, Biophys. Soc., Phi Beta Kappa. Office: Stanford Sch Medicine Fairchild Ctr D221 Stanford CA 94305-5125

**STRYKER, DAVID MICHAEL**, lawyer; b. Bloomington, Ind., Nov. 5, 1958; m. Josie Bizzari; children: Joshua, Joseph, Hannah, Samuel. BA in English lit., Ind. U., 1980, JD magna cum laude, 1983. Bar: Ill. 1984, NY 1990. Clk. to Hon. Robert H. Bork US Ct. Appeals, DC Cir., 1984; ptnr. Kirkland & Ellis, 1984—94; sr. litig. counsel Siemens Corp., NYC, 1994—98, assoc. gen. counsel, 1998—2004, corp. compliance officer; sr. v.p., gen. counsel BASF Corp., Florham Park, NJ, 2004—. Exec. editor Ind. Law Jour., 1982—83. Mem.: Order of Coif. Avocations: running, camping, fishing. Office: BASF Corp 100 Campus Dr Florham Park NJ 07932 Office Phone: 973-245-6000.*

**STRYKER, JAMES WILLIAM**, retired automotive executive, former military officer; b. Grand Rapids, Mich., Apr. 20, 1940; s. John Alvin and Marian (Anderson) S.; m. Eleanor Marie Finger, Sept. 26, 1964; children: James William II, Marian Marie Jenkins, Kathryn Alison Greenbauer. BS, U.S. Mil. Acad., 1963; student, Def. Lang. Inst., 1968—69; MA, U. Mich., 1972; postgrad., U.S. Army Command and Gen. Staff Coll., 1978. Commd. 2d lt. U.S. Army, 1963, battery exec. officer 6th/20th field arty. Ft. Carson, Colo., 1964-65, advisor JUSMAG Vietnam, 1965—66, battery comdr. 4th/3d field arty. Ft. Hood, Tex., 1967-68, advisor TMAG Thailand, 1969—70; S-3 ops. officer 1st/7th F.A., Ft. Riley, Kans., 1972-73; asst. prof. history U.S. Mil. Acad., West Point, NY, 1973-77; chief nuc. ops. Cen. Army Group NATO, Heidelberg, Germany, 1978-81; dir., project mgr. tank-automotive command U.S. Army, Warren, Mich., 1981-86, ret., 1986; program mgr. military vehicles operation GMC Truck, Pontiac, Mich., 1987-95; cross brand portfolio mgr. Pontiac-GMC Divsn. GM Corp., Detroit, 1996-98, asst. brand mgr. product full size and mid size vans, 1999-2001, asst. brand mgr. product alternative fuels and mobility, 2001—02, product mgr. alternative fuels and mobility, 2002—04; ret., 2004. Author: (with others) Encyclopedia of Southern History, 1977; co-author: Early American Wars, 1978. Torch bearer Olympic Winter Games, Salt Lake City, 2002. Decorated Legion of Merit, Bronze Star medal, Def. Meritorious Svc. medal, Meritorious Svc. medal with oakleaf cluster, Army Commendation medal with oakleaf cluster, U.S. Army/Vietnamese Cross of Gallantry with palm and gold star; Olympic torchbearer Winter Olympics, 2002. Mem.: NRA (endowment), Nat. Def. Indsl. Assn. (dir. Detroit chpt. 1991—97, 2d v.p. 1995, 1st v.p. 1995—96, pres. 1996—97, adv. 1997—2000), Trout Unltd., Ruffed Grouse Soc. (banquet com. Detroit 1998—2003), Assn. U.S. Army (dir. Detroit chpt. 1990—95), Ducks Unltd., Pheasants Forever, Nodrog Setter Club Mich., Gordon Setter Club Am. Avocations: hunting, skeet shooting, trout fishing, field training english and gordon setters. Home: 168 First St Romeo MI 48065-5000

**STRYKER, STEVEN CHARLES**, retired lawyer; b. Omaha, Oct. 26, 1944; s. James M. and Jean G. (Grannis) S.; m. Bryna Dee Litwin, Oct. 20, 1972; children: Ryan; Kevin, Gerrit, Courtney. BS, U. Iowa, 1967, JD with distinction, 1969; postgrad. studies, Northwestern U. Grad. Sch. Bus, 1969-70, DePaul U., 1971. Bar: Iowa 1969, Tex. 1986; CPA Ill., Iowa. Sr. tax acct. Arthur Young & Co., Chgo., 1969-72; fed. tax mgr. Massey Ferguson, Des Moines, 1972-74; fed., state tax mgr. FMC Corp., Chgo., 1974-78; gen. tax atty. Shell Oil Co., Houston, 1978-81, asst. gen. tax counsel, 1981-83, gen. mgr., 1983-86, v.p., gen. tax counsel, 1986—2000, ret., 2000; pvt. practice, 2000—. Mem. ABA, AICPA, Tex. Bar Assn., Tax Execs. Inst., Am. Petroleum Inst. Home: 2120 Kipling Apt 404 Houston TX 77098

**STRYKER, TERENCE WAYNE**, secondary school educator; b. Daytona Beach, Fla., Nov. 21, 1956; s. Judson Phillip and Irene Lillian Stryker; m. Lynn Lyda. B in Music Edn., Fla. State U., 1980; M in M in Music Edn., Trinity Coll., 2001. Cert. network engr.; music tchr. grades K-12 Fla. Choral dir. Port St. Joe (Fla.) H.S., Port St. Joe, 1985—89; band dir. Wewahitchka (Fla.) H.S., 1989—. Named All USA Tchr. Team, USA Today, 1999, Tchr. of Yr., Gulf County Schs., 2000. Mem.: Fla. League Arts Tchrs., Fla. League Tchrs., Music Educator's Nat. Conf., Fla. Music Educator's Assn., Fla. Bandmaster's Assn. Baptist. Avocations: coin collecting/numismatics, auto restoration, woodworking, technology. Home: 4801 Sunset Dr Panama City FL 32404 Office: Wewahitchka HS One Gator Circle Wewahitchka FL 32465 Personal E-mail: stryker_t@firn.edu. Business E-Mail: tstryker@wewahigh.com

**STRYSICK, MICHAEL OTTO**, ecologist, physicist, microbiologist, researcher; b. Sheboygan, Wis., Jan. 13, 1931; s. Michael Sr. and Agnes (Czaja) S.; m. Carol Ann Greiner, June 25, 1955 (dec. July 1992); children: Peter Michael, Mary Susan. Terrestrial ecologist, rschr., Sheboygan, Wis., 1954—. Cons. Master Gardner program U. Wis. Ext. Svcs., Sheboygan Falls, Wis., 1988—; rschr. Neem Oil Margosan-O, 1992. Cubmaster to commr. Boy Scouts Am.; treas. Cath. Com. Scouting, Sheboygan, 1970-97. With U.S. Army, 1950-54, Korea. Recipient St. George medal Boy Scouts Am., 1984. Mem. AAAS, Korean War Vets. Assoc., VFW, Am. Legion. Achievements include Neem Oil development in the 1980s and field studies; Hanta Virus verification in Ams. as med. problem, 1990—; researcher in Myology 2000, a post-genome 30 protein complex of the nucleus of human cells; cell protein atom chemistry in female cumulus cell; Krebs/Calvincycle phenomena citric TNF alpha beta gamma omega role of un P on Ca polarity to transfat and uric acid lactic acidosis in human diabetes; symbiotic GUT thermobacteria excess citric acid as source of H3 and of NH3 and to NO and excess uric acid and E. coli or salmonella muntation, or UVB radiation induced cancers; including all life forms cycle of reproduction avoidance of overpopulation and evolutionary adaptation; and use of woodchip mulch, adverse effects in anerobic conditions in 1970-80. Home and Office: 1002 N 16th St Sheboygan WI 53081-3825 E-mail: gardnersenvy@bytehead.com.

**STUART, ALICE MELISSA**, lawyer; b. NYC, Apr. 7, 1957; d. John Marberger and Marjorie Louise (Browne) S. BA, Ohio State U., 1977; JD, U. Chgo., 1980; LLM, NYU, 1982. Bar: NY 1981, Ohio 1982, Fla. 1994, U.S. Dist. Ct. (so. dist.) Ohio, 1983, U.S. Dist. Ct. (so. and ea. dists.) NY 1985. Assoc. Schwartz, Shapiro, Kelm & Warren, Columbus, Ohio, 1982-84, Paul, Weiss, Rifkind, Wharton & Garrison, NYC, 1984-85, Kassel, Neuwirth & Geiger, NYC, 1985-86, Phillips, Nizer, Benjamin, Krim & Ballon, NYC, 1987—92; pvt. practice NYC, 1992—98; atty. LeBoeuf, Lamb, Greene & MacRae, NYC, 1998—. Adj. prof. Su. Coll., Orlando, Fla., 1997-98. Surrogate Speakers' Bur. Reagan-Bush Campaign, NYC, 1984; mem. Lawyers for Bush-Quayle Campaign, NYC, 1988; bd. dirs. Mayflower Soc. in State of NY, 1998-, counsellor, 2002-. Mem. ABA, NY State Bar Assn., Women's Nat. Rep. Club (bd. dirs. 2004-), Winston Churchill Meml. Libr. Soc., Jr. League, Soc. Mayflower Descs. in State of NY (bd. dirs. 1999-, counselor 2002-), Women's Nat. Rep. Club (bd. dirs. 2004-), Phi Beta Kappa, Phi Kappa Phi, Alpha Lambda Delta. Republican. Office: LeBoeuf Lamb Greene & MacRae 125 W 55th St New York NY 10019-5369 Office Phone: 212-424-8669. Business E-Mail: astuart@llgm.com

**STUART, CAROLE**, publishing executive; b. N.Y.C., Feb. 22, 1941; d. Frank and Sally (Stern) Rose; m. Lyle Stuart, Feb. 4, 1982; 1 child, Jennifer Susan Livingston. Student, Bklyn. Coll. Pub. Lyle Stuart, Inc., Secaucus, NJ; assoc. pub. Carol Pub. Group, N.Y.C.; pub. Barricade Books, N.Y.C. Author: Why Was I Adopted?, To Turn You On, 39 Sex Fantasies for Women; author: (with Claire Ciliotta) Why Am I Going to the Hospital?; author: I'll Never Be Fat Again, How To Lose 5 Pounds Fast, The Thank You Book. Mem.: Authors Guild, Women's Media Group, Wine and Food Soc. N.Y. Home: 1530 Palisade Ave Apt 6L Fort Lee NJ 07024-5402 Office: Barricade Books Ste 308A 185 Bridge Plz N Fort Lee NJ 02024

**STUART, CHARLES EDWARD**, electrical engineer, oceanographer; b. Durham, NC, Feb. 9, 1942; s. Charles Edward and Wilma Kelly Stuart; m. Margaret Ann Robinson, Jan. 9, 1982; children: Marjorie Kelly, Heather Alison. BSEE, Duke U., 1963. Engr. Westinghouse Electric Corp., Balt., 1963-65; sr. engr. Booz Allen Hamilton, Chevy Chase, Md., 1966-68; rsch. dir. B-K Dynamics Inc., Huntsville, Ala., 1969-78; oceanographer Office of Naval Rsch., Arlington, Va., 1979-84; dir. Maritime System Office Advanced Rsch. Projects Agy., Arlington, 1985-98; with def. programs U.S. Dept. Energy, Washington, 1998-99; pres. Competitive Enterprise Solutions, LLC, Arlington, 2000—. Contbr. articles to profl. jours. Recipient Am. Def. Preparedness Assn. Bushnell award career contbns. undersea warfare, 1996. Mem. IEEE (sr., ad. com. 1991-93), Assn. Unmanned Vehicle Systems (trustee 1989-93). Methodist. Achievements include rsch. in antisubmarine warfare, cybersecurity and unmanned undersea vehicle technology. Office: Competitive Enterprise Solutions LLC PO Box 567 Slidell LA 70458 Business E-Mail: cstuart@cesllc.com.

**STUART, CYNTHIA MORGAN**, retired academic administrator; b. Harrisburg, Pa, June 29, 1949; d. Paul William and Bernice Leona (Boyer) M.; m. David Edward Stuart, June 14, 1971. Student, Elizabethtown (Pa.) Coll., 1967-69; BA, U. N.Mex., 1971, MPA, 1982, ABD in Ednl. Leadership, 2003. Admissions counselor U. N.Mex., Albuquerque, 1974-77, asst. dir. admissions, 1977-80, assoc. dir. admissions, 1980-83, dir. admissions, 1983—2005, Univ. articulation officer, 1989—2005, dir. student outreach svc., 1991-95, enrollment mgmt. team mem., 1998—2005; ret., 2005. Mem. N.Mex. Coordinating Coun. Secondary Sch. and Coll., 1983-92; chair Coun. for Common Concerns, Albuquerque, 1987-95; mem. N.Mex. Articulation Com., Santa Fe, 1983-95; mem. adv. bd. Albuquerque Tech. Vocat. Inst., 1991—. Compiler, editor Statewide Statistical Profile Report, N.Mex. HS, 1983-90; cover photographer Prehistoric New Mexico, 2d edit., 1994, Glimpses of the Ancient Southwest, 1995. Coord. United Way, Albuquerque, 1980-81; elected del. N.Mex. Dem. Conv., 1982; mem. issues and advocacy com. Albuquerque Bus. Edn. Compact, 1991-93; mem. Am. Indian Edn. Initiative, Albuquerque, 1992—; Coll. Bd. del., 1991—. Recipient sys. devel. grant Commn. on Higher Edn., Santa Fe, 1995. Mem. Am. Assn. Collegiate Registrars and Admissions Officers (reporting officer of transfer credit N.Mex. 1979—), Rocky Mountain Assn. Collegiate Registrars and Admissions Officers (v.p. 1979-81, pres. 1983-84), N.Mex. Assn. Collegiate Registrars and Admissions Officers (sec.-treas. 1978-82, pres. 1991-92, Outstanding Svc. award 1990), N.Mex. Am. Coll. Testing Coun. (chair 1996-97, state rep. 1997—2005, trustee Am. Coll. Testing 1999-2002, del. to Coll. Bd. 1991—2005). Democrat. Avocations: photography, travel, drawing, music. Home: 423 Tulane Dr SE Albuquerque NM 87106-1417 E-mail: cstuart@unm.edu.

**STUART, DABNEY**, poet, language educator; b. Richmond, Va., Nov. 4, 1937; s. Walker Dabney Jr. and Martha (vonSchilling) S.; m. Sandra Westcott, Jan. 20, 1983; children: Martha, Nathan vonSchilling, Darren Wynne AB, Davidson Coll., 1960; AM, Harvard U., 1962. Instr. Coll. William and Mary, Williamsburg, Va., 1961-65; prof. English Washington and Lee U., Lexington, Va., 1965—2002, S. Blount Mason Jr. prof. English, 1991—2002. Vis. prof. Middlebury (Vt.) Coll., 1968-69, Ohio U., Athens, 1975, U. Va., Charlottesville, 1981-83. Author: The Diving Bell, 1966, A Particular Place, 1969, The Other Hand, 1974, Friends of Yours, Friends of Mine, 1974, Round and Round, 1976, Nabokov: The Dimensions of Parody, 1978, Rockbridge Poems, 1981, Common Ground, 1982, Don't Look Back, 1987, Narcissus Dreaming, 1990, Sweet Lucy Wine, 1992, Light Years: New and Selected Poems, 1994, Second Sight: Poems for Paintings by Carroll Cloar, 1996, Long Gone, 1996, The Way to Cobbs Creek, 1997, Settlers, 1999, Strains of the Old Man, 1999, No Visible Means of Support, 2001, The Man Who Loves Cezanne, 2003, Family Preserve, 2005. Recipient Dylan Thomas prize Poetry Soc. Am., 1965, Gov.'s award State of Va., 1979; NEA lit. fellow, 1975, 82, Guggenheim fellow, 1987-88, Individual Artist fellow Va. Commn. for Arts, 1995, resident fellow Rockefeller Study and Conf. Ctr., Bellagio, Italy, 2000. Avocations: food, travel, painting. Home: 30 Edmondson Ave Lexington VA 24450-1904

**STUART, DAVID EDWARD**, anthropologist, writer, educator; b. Calhoun County, Ala., Jan. 9, 1945; s. Edward George and Avis Elsie (Densmore) S.; m. Cynthia K. Morgan, June 14, 1971 BA, W.Va. Wesleyan Coll., 1967; MA Anthropology, U. N.Mex., 1970, PhD, 1972, postdoctoral, 1975—76; LHD (hon.), W.Va Wesleyan Coll., 2001. Rsch. assoc. Andean Ctr., Quito, Ecuador, 1970; instr. continuing edn. anthropology U. N.Mex., 1971—72; asst. prof. Eckerd Coll., St. Petersburg, Fla., 1972—74; rsch. archeologist Office Contract Archeology U. N.Mex., 1974, rsch. coord., 1974—77, asst. prof. anthropology, 1975—77, assoc. prof. anthropology, 1984—99, prof. anthropology, 1999—, asst. v.p. acad. affairs 1987—95, assoc. v.p. acad. affairs 1995—99, assoc. provost, 1999—2004, prof. anthropology, 2001—. Cons. archeologist right-of-way divsn. Pub. Svc. Co. N.Mex., Albuquerque, 1977-78; cons. anthropologist Bur. Indian Affairs, Albuquerque, 1978, Historic Preservation Bur. N.Mex., Santa Fe, 1978-81, Nat. Park Svcs., 1980, Albuquerque Mus., 1981; sr. rsch. assoc. Quivira Rsch. Ctr., Albuquerque, 1984-86; pres., bd. dirs. Rio Grande Heritage Found., Albuquerque and Las Cruces, 1985-87; advisor Human Sys. Rsch., Inc., Tularosa, N.Mex., 1978-80, sr. rsch. assoc., 1981-83; advisor Albuquerque Commn. on Hist. Preservation, 1984-86. Co-author: Archeological Survey: 4 Corners to Ambrosia, N.Mex., 1976, A Proposed Project Design for the timber Management Archeological Surveys, 1978, Ethnoarcheological Investigations of Shepherding in the Pueblo of Laguna, 1983; author: Prehistoric New Mexico, 1981, 3d edit., 1989, Glimpses of the Ancient Southwest, 1985, The Magic of Bandelier National Monument, 1989, Power and Efficiency in Eastern Anasazi Architecture, 1994, Anasazi America, 2000, The Guaymas Chronicles, 2003, The Zone of Tolerence, 2005, The Ecuador Effect, 2006; columnist New Mexico's Heritage, 1983-87; editor: Archeological Reports, No. 1, 1975, No. 2, 1982. Trustee Hibben Trust, 2005—. Grantee Eckerd Coll., 1973, Historic Preservation Bur., 1978-80; recipient Essayist award N.Mex. Humanities Coun., 1986 Mem. Am. Anthrop. Assn., N.Mex. Archeol. Coun., Albuquerque Archeol. Soc. (pres. 1986-88), Descs. Signers Declaration Independence, Sigma Xi, Phi Kappa Phi Office: U NMex Dane Smith Hall Rm 217 Albuquerque NM 87131-0001 Office Phone: 505-265-5459. Business E-Mail: dstuart@unm.edu. *Personal philosophy: In academics, as in life, reliability, integrity, and compassion are far more precious than mere intellectual brilliance.*

**STUART, DONALD BRUCE**, lawyer; b. New Zealand, Dec. 26, 1964; arrived in US, 1976; s. Bruce and Doreen Stuart; m. Katherine Stuart, May 9, 1992; children: Colin, Michael, Lauren. BS, Bradley U., 1987; JD, Mich. State U., 1995; LLM in Taxation, U. Fla., 1997. Bar: Mich. 1995, Tenn. 1998. Atty. Michael R. Kluck & Assocs., Okemos, 1995—96, Waller Lansden Dortch & Davis, PLLC, Nashville, 1997—. Editor: (law rev.) Thomas M. Cooley Law Rev., Fla. Tax Rev.; contbr. articles to profl.jours. Recipient Am. Jurisprudence award, Lawyers Coop. Pub., 1992. Mem.: ABA, Nashville Bar Assn., Am. Health Lawyers Assn., Tenn. Bar Assn., Mich. Bar Assn., Cool Springs C. of C. Office: Waller Lansden Dortch & Davis LLP 511 Union St Ste 2700 Nashville TN 37219 Office Phone: 615-850-8845. Office Fax: 615-244-6804. E-mail: dstuart@wallerlaw.com

**STUART, FRANCES DEADERICK**, retired music educator; b. Ft. Worth, Tex., Nov. 8, 1911; d. Claude Taylor Deaderick and Nina Clara Staiti; m. John James Stuart (dec.); children: John James Jr., Betty Lynne. MusB, postgrad., So. Meth. U.; cert. tchr., NY Sch. Music Arts. Cert. tchr. piano/music. Tchr. piano theory and pedagogy, Dallas. Judge Nat. Guild Piano Tchrs.; pres. emeritus Van Katwije Piano Club; patron chmn. Mu Phi Epsilon. Chmn. Sunday concert series J. Erik Jonsson Found., Dallas. Avocations: dance, interior decorating. Home: 3725 Maplewood Ave Dallas TX 75205

**STUART, FRANK ADELL**, county official; b. Tahoka, Tex., Dec. 18, 1928; s. John Franklin and Mary Elizabeth (Reed) S.; m. Mary Louise Wheat Crelia, Feb. 2, 1962; children: Rita, Donna, Franklin, Burce, Susan, Mary, Chris. BBA, Tex. Tech U., 1979. Asst. cashier Am. State Bank, Lubbock, Tex., 1949-52, Citizen Nat. Bank, Lubbock, 1953-59; acct. in pvt. practice

Lubbock, 1960-63; asst. mgr. Gibson Discount Ctr., Lubbock, 1964-77; tax. assessor and collector Lubbock County, Lubbock, 1979-94, ret., 1994. Served to col. Tex. State Guard, 1988-98. Mem. Tax Assessor-Collectors Assn. Tex., Lubbock C. of C., Masons, YorkRite, Scottish Rite, Shriners, Yellow House Lodge, Daylight Lodge. Baptist. Home: 2704 57th St Lubbock TX 79413-5605 E-mail: stuart2704@aol.com.

**STUART, GERARD WILLIAM, JR.**, investment company executive, alderman, city official; b. Yuba City, Calif., July 28, 1939; s. Gerard William and Geneva Bernice (Stuke) S.; m. Lenore Frances Lorona, 1981. Student, Yuba Jr. Coll., 1957-59, Chico State Coll., 1959-60; AB, U. Calif., Davis, 1962; MLS, U. Calif., Berkeley, 1963. Rare book libr. Cornell U., 1964-68; bibliographer scholarly collections Huntington Libr., San Marino, Calif., 1968-73, head acquisitions libr., 1973-75; sec.-treas., dir. Ravenstree Corp., 1969-80, pres, chmn. bd., 1980—, William Penn Ltd., 1981—. Councilman City of Yuma, 1992-96, deputy mayor, 1995; bd. dirs Ariz. Humanities Coun., 1993-99, Yuma Libr. Found., 1997, chmn., 1997-98, 99-2001, 05—. Lilly fellow Ind. U., 1964-63. Mem. Bibliog. Soc. Am., Rolls-Royce Owners Club, Grolier Club (N.Y.C.), Zamorano Club (L.A.), Phi Beta Kappa, Alpha Gamma Sigma, Phi Kappa Phi.

**STUART, GLEN R(AYMOND)**, lawyer; b. Kimpese, Congo, Mar. 4, 1959; came to U.S., 1960; s. Charles H. and Jeannette B. (Spinney) S.; m. Susan K. Sharpless, May 26, 1984; children: Jennifer Jacqueline, David Charles, Andrew William. BA, Franklin and Marshall Coll., 1981; JD, U. Va., 1984. Bar: Pa. 1984, U.S. Dist. Ct. (ea. dist.) Pa. 1984, U.S. Dist. Ct. (mid. dist.) Pa. 1986, U.S. Ct. Appeals (3rd cir.) 1988, U.S. Supreme Ct. 1997. Hiring ptnr. Morgan, Lewis & Bockius, LLP, Phila., 1984—. Mem. ABA, Pa. Bar Assn., Phila. Bar Assn., Order of Coif. Democrat. Baptist. Avocations: soccer, golf, softball, tennis. Home: 21 Harvey Ln Malvern PA 19355-2907 Office: Morgan Lewis & Bockius LLP 1701 Market St Philadelphia PA 19103-2903 Office Fax: 215-963-5001. Business E-Mail: gstuart@morganlewis.com.

**STUART, JACQUELYN L.**, state supreme court justice; b. Atmore, Ala., Sept. 23, 1955; m. George Stuart; children: Tucker, Shepard, Kelly. BA in Sociology and Edn., Auburn U., 1977; JD, U. Ala., 1980. Asst. atty. gen. State of Ala.; exec. asst. to commr. and spl. asst. atty. gen. Ala. Dept. Corrections; asst. dist. atty. Baldwin County; dist. judge, 1989—97; judge Ala. Cir. Ct., 1997—2001; justice Ala. Supreme Ct., 2001—. Faculty advisor Nat. Judicial Coll., Reno; former pres. Ala. Council of Juvenile & Family Ct. Judges; pres. Blue Ridge Inst. for Juvenile & Family Ct. Judges, 2002. Former pres. Heritage Junior Women's Club, Bay Minette Kiwanis Club, Jubilee Woman's Club; bd. mem. Ala. Federation of Women's Clubs. Republican. Office: Ala Supreme Ct 300 Dexter Ave Rm 3-215 Montgomery AL 36104-3741 Office Phone: 334-242-4584. Business E-Mail: lstuart@appellate.state.al.us.

**STUART, JEFFREY L.**, mathematics professor, consultant; m. Susan Stuart. BA in Math. & Physics, Pomona Coll., Claremont, Calif., 1980; MS in Math., PhD in Math., U. Wis., Madison, 1986. Vis. asst. prof. math. No. Ill. U., DeKalb, 1986—87; prof. math. U. So. Miss., Hattiesburg, 1987—2001, Pacific Luth. U., Tacoma, 2001—. Recipient K.T. Tang Faculty Excellence in Rsch. award, Pacific Luth. U., 2004—05, Faculty Excellence in Tchg. award, U. So. Mississippi, 2000, Disting. Tchg. award, Miss.-La. Sect. Math. Assn. Am., 2000. Mem.: Soc. Indsl. and Applied Math., Math. Assn. Am., Am. Statis. Assn. (v.p. Miss. chpt. 2000—01), Internat. Linear Algebra Soc. (sec.-treas. 2000—), Phi Beta Kappa. Office: Math Dept Pacific Lutheran Univ Tacoma WA 98447 Office Phone: 253-535-7403. Business E-Mail: jeffrey.stuart@plu.edu.

**STUART, JILL**, apparel designer; m. Ron Curtis, 1986; children: Morgan, Chloe, Sophie. Student, RI Sch. of Design. Sold jewelry and handbag designs Bloomingdales, NYC; founded accessory line Jill Stuart, NYC, founded women's wear line, 1993—, launched intimate apparel, eyewear, denim and footwear lines, 2000—. Office: Jill Stuart Offices 550 7th Ave New York NY 10018 Office Phone: 212-921-2600.*

**STUART, JOSEPH MARTIN**, art museum administrator; b. Seminole, Okla., Nov. 9, 1932; s. Arch William and Lillian (Lindsey) S.; BFA in Art, U. N.Mex., 1959, MA in Art, 1962; m. Signe Margaret Nelson, June 18, 1960; 1 dau., Lise Nelson Stuart. Dir., Roswell (N.Mex.) Museum and Art Center, 1960-62; curator U. Oreg. Mus. Art, 1962-63; dir. Boise (Idaho) Gallery Art, 1964-68, Salt Lake (City) Art Ctr., 1968-71, S.D. Art Mus., Brookings, 1971-93; prof. art S.D. State U., 1971-93; represented in permanent collections: Civic Fine Arts Ctr., Sioux Falls, S.D., Coll. Idaho, Eureka Coll., Salt Lake Art Ctr., Sioux City (Iowa) Art Ctr., U. N.Mex. Art Mus., West Tex. State U. With USN, 1951-55. Mem. Phi Kappa Phi. Unitarian. Author: Index of South Dakota Artists, 1974; Art of South Dakota, 1974, Harvey Dunn: Son of the Middle border, 1984, Art for a New Century, 1989; The Legacy of South Dakota Art, 1990; author numerous exhbn. catalogs. Office Phone: 505-466-6625.

**STUART, KIEL**, writer; b. NYC, Nov. 20, 1951; m. Howard Austerlitz, June 20, 1978. Student, SUNY, New Paltz, 1992—93, SUNY, Stony Brook, 1993—95. Freelance writer, L.I., NY, 1976—; exec. dir. Writers Alliance, Stonybrook, NY, 1982—85; editor Sci. Fiction Writers of America's Forum Mag., Wharton, NJ, 1985—88, Poetry Bone Mag., Lake Grove, NY, 1999—2001. Cons. O-C-G, Farmingdale, N.Y., 1986-87, Marine Sci. Rsch. Ctr., Stony Brook, 1986-87, Steinetics, St. James, N.Y., 1985. Author: (chapbook) Shivery River, 2001, Multitasking, 2003, From Parts Unknown, 1991, Shivery River, 2001, Math Tasking, 2003; editor: Keystrokes, 1992, Island Women, 1984. Mem. Authors Guild, Sci. Fiction Writers Am. Avocations: anime, Japanese language. E-mail: poetrybone@yahoo.com

**STUART, LORI AMES**, public relations executive; b. Hempstead, N.Y., Oct. 23, 1957; d. Henry Aschner and Janet (Hackel) Goldman; m. John Robert Ames, Jan. 30, 1982 (div. July 1990); 1 child, Robert Walter Ames; m. Robert John Stuart, July 27, 1991. BA, Hofstra U., 1979. Publicist Jane Wesman Pub. Rels., N.Y.C., 1980-84, v.p., 1991—; publicist, publicity mgr. William Morrow & Co., N.Y.C., 1984-89, publicity dir., 1989-90. Lectr., mentor NYU, 1994—. Jewish. Avocations: fishing, travel, reading, writing. Office: Jane Wesman Public Rels 322 8th Ave Ste 1702 New York NY 10001-6766

**STUART, MARIE JEAN**, physician, hematologist, researcher; b. Bangalore, India, Sept. 11, 1943; came to U.S., 1967; d. Norman and Dorothy (Dias) S. BS, MB, Madras (India) U. Asst. prof. pediatrics SUNY Health Sci. Ctr., Syracuse, 1972-76, assoc. prof., 1976-81, prof. pediatrics, 1981-87; prof. chief hematology and oncology div. St. Christophers Hosp. for Children and Temple U., Phila., 1987-97; prof. thrombosis rsch. Temple U., 1987-97; dir. NIH Comprehensive Sickle Cell Ctr. Thomas Jefferson U., Phila., 1998—. Mem. nat. child health com. Nat. Inst. Child Health and Human Devel., Bethesda, Md., 1982-86; mem. nat. heart, lung and blood rsch. tng. com., NIH, Bethesda, 1990—2000; mem. NIH Sickle Cell Disease Adv. Coun., 2000-04; mem. NIH Erythrocyte and Leucocyte Biology Study Sect., 2003—. Mem. editl. bd. Biology of the Neonate, 2000—; contbr. chpts. to books, articles to profl. jours. Docent Phila. Mus. Art, 2005. Recipient Rsch. award Temple U., 1997. Mem. Am. Fedn. Clin. Research. Am. Pediatric Soc., Soc. for Pediatric Research. Avocations: music, art. Home: 227 S 6th St Apt 1 NW Philadelphia PA 19106 Office Phone: 215-955-9820. Business E-Mail: marie.stuart@jefferson.edu.

**STUART, MICHELLE RAE**, artist; b. Borrego Springs, Calif., Feb. 10, 1940; d. Charles Cameron and Ramona (Hagenauer) S. Painter, sculptor, printmaker. Represented in numerous permanent collections including The Coll. of Wooster, Ohio, The Bklyn. Mus., Cin. Art Mus., Mus. Contemporary Art, Chgo., Mus. Modern Art, N.Y.C., Phila. Mus. Art, and others; exhibited in group shows at Denver Art Mus., New Orleans Art Mus., Pa. Acad. Art, Balt. Art Mus. and others; one-woman shows include Rose Art Mus., Brandeis U., Waltham, Mass., 1988, Galerie Ueda-Ginza, Tokyo, 1987, The Parrish Art Mus, NY, The Mus. of Contemporary Art, Los Angeles, Whitney

Mus. of Am. Art, N.Y.C. and others. Recipient numerous grants including Artist-In-Residence, Art Gallery of Western Australia and Curtin U. of Tech., Perth, 1989, N.Y. Found. for the Arts Artists' Fellowship, 1987, Finnish Art Assn. Fellowship, Helsinki, Finland, 1985, Nat. Endowment Arts grants, 1974, 77, 80, 89, John Simon Guggenheim Found. Fellowship, N.Y. State Creative Artists Pub. Svc. Grant, 1975, Ford Found. Tamarind Inst. Grant, Artist-In-Residence Program, Albuquerque, 1974, MacDowell Fellowship, Am. Acad. in Rome fellowship, Academician of the Nat. Acad. fellowship Avocation: photography. Gallery: Diane Villani Gallery 285 Lafayette St New York NY 10012-3225 also: B R Kornblatt Gallery 406 7th St NW Washington DC 20004-2217 E-mail: michellestuart38@aol.com.

**STUART, NANCY GIOVINAZZO,** secondary school educator; b. L.A., Aug. 8, 1931; d. Joseph and Carmelita Mary (Frontino) Giovinazzo; m. Jay William Stuart, Jr., July 28, 1951; children: Tani Lynn Stuart Robertson, Joel Vanni; 1 foster child, Hilary Davis. AA, UCLA, 1952, BS, 1954, MS, 1967. Tchr. Washington High Sch., L.A. Unified Sch. Dist., 1954-60, tchr. Gardena High Sch., 1960-63, tchr. Carson High Sch., 1963-91, chair dept. health, master tchr., 1970—91, retired, 1991, preferred substitute tchr., 1992—; mentor Calif. Acad. Math. and Sci. at Calif. State U., Dominguez Hills, 1993—2000. Drill team-pep units sponsor, 1968-81; founder Bird Seed Baby Parenting Experience, Carson H.S., 1970-91, sponsor peer counseling tng. program, 1984-91; workshop leader in field. Author: Death and Dying: A Teaching Guide and Workbook for Health Education, 1989, For Phsical Edn. and Dance, 1956, Adaptive Physical Edn., 1958, For Health Edn. CPR, 1976, 1980. Tchr. rep. L.A. Unified Sch. Dist. on City of L.A. Drug Commn., 1968-69. Grantee State of Calif., 1985. Mem. Calif. Assn. for Health, Phys. Edn., Recreation and Dance (Health Edn. Tchr. of Yr. 1988), AAUW, Calif. Ret. Tchrs. Assn., Delta Kappa Gamma, Alpha Delta Kappa. Home: 17502 Valmeyer Ave Gardena CA 90248-3356 Office: Carson High Sch 22328 Main St Carson CA 90745-4599 Personal E-mail: ngs54@earthlink.net.

**STUART, NANCY RUBIN (NANCY ZIMMAN STETSON),** journalist, writer, television producer; b. Boston, Nov. 25, 1944; d. Stuart Wendell and Ethel (Rabinovitz) Zimman; m. William W. Stetson, Apr. 28, 2001; children: Elisabeth, Jessica. BA, Tufts U., 1966; MA in Teaching, Brown U., 1967; PhD (hon.), Mt. Vernon Coll., 1995. Playwright, dir. Equity Library Theatre, Roundabout, Joseph Jefferson and St. Clement's theaters, N.Y.C., 1971-74; freelance reporter Westchester-Gannett newspapers and mags., 1975-77, N.Y. Times, N.Y.C., 1977—. Faculty affiliate Bush Ctr. in Child Devel., Yale U., New Haven, 1981-86; mem. Westchester County Women's Adv. Bd., chair, 1988; bd. dirs. Women Writing Women's Lives Seminar; mem. faculty SUNY, Purchase, 1994-95, Fordham U., N.Y.C., 1996-99. Author: The New Suburban Women, Beyond Myth and Motherhood, 1982, The Mother Mirror: How a Generation of Women is Changing Motherhood in America, 1984, Isabella of Castile: The First Renaissance Queen, 1991, American Empress: The Life and Times of Marjorie Merriweather Post, 1995, Club Dance: The Show, The Steps, The Spirit of Country, 1998, The Reluctant Spiritualist: The Life at Maggie Fox, 2005; writer, assoc. prodr.: TV series America's Castles for A&E Network, 1996—99 (Telly award, 1999, Telly award '3, 2001, Writing Communicator award, 1999), The Gold Coast for The Grand Tour A & E TV, 1997, writer prodr., prodr.: TV series Restore America, 1999; writer prodr., prodr. (TV series) Restore America, 2001 (3 Telly awards); writer/assoc. prodr.: TV series Eccentrics, 1999 (Crystal award, Telly award), The N.Y. Times, 1977—; writer prodr. Baltimore Sun, American History Magazine; contbg. editor: Parents mag., 1987—91.; McCalls, Savvy, Travel & Leisure, Ladies Home Jour., 1980—92; theater critic: Stamford Advocate, 1994—96; co-prodr.: Recipient Washington Irving award Westchester Libr. Assn., 1993, Telly award finalist, 2001; Am. Antiquarian Soc. fellow, 2005; Time, Inc.-Bread Loaf Writers' Colony scholar, 1979. Fellow MacDowell Colony; mem. Author's Guild, Am. Soc. Journalists and Authors (Author of Yr. award 1992, hon. mention gen. nonfiction 2006), PEN, Nat. Arts Club. Avocations: skiing, sailing, ballet, classical music, dance.

**STUART, ROBERT,** container manufacturing executive; b. Oak Park, Ill., Aug. 3, 1921; s. Robert S. and Marie (Vavra) Stuart; m. Lillian C. Kondelik, Dec. 5, 1962 (dec. May 1978); m. Lila Winterhoff Peters, May 21, 1982. BS, U. Ill., 1943; LLD, U. Ill., Chgo. 1982. Sec.-treas., gen. mgr. Warren Metal Decorating Co., 1947-49; asst. to gen. mgr. Cans, Inc., 1950-52; asst. to v.p., then v.p. Nat. Can Corp., Chgo., 1953-59, exec. v.p., 1959-63, pres., 1963-69, chief exec., 1966-69, chmn. bd., chief exec. officer, 1969-73, chmn. bd., 1973-83, chmn. fin. com., 1983, mem. corp. devel. com., until 1986, chmn. emeritus, 1986—. Past pres., bd. dirs. Corp. Responsibility Group of Greater Chgo. Past pres., bd. dirs. Chgo. Crime Commn.; past dir. Nat. Crime Prevention Coun.; founding chmn. Nat. Minority Supplier Devel. Coun., 1972-73, Lloyd Morey Scholarship Fund: Freedoms Found. at Valley Forge, past trustee; past mem. adv. bd. Salvation Army, Broader Urban Involvement and Leadership Devel.; chmn. emeritus World Federalist Assn.; past bd. dirs., past moderator Millard Congl. Ch.; trustee, past pres. Ctrl. Ch. Chgo.; chmn. emeritus Assn. to Unite the Democracies. Capt. AUS, 1943-46. Mem. Chgo. Club, Comml. Club, Yacht Club, Little Ship Club (London), Mason (32 degree, Red Cross of Constantine), Rotary (past pres. Chgo. club, past dist. gov.), Alpha Kappa Lambda (past nat. pres.). Lutheran. Home and Office: 233 SW 43d Ter Cape Coral FL 33914

**STUART, ROBERT ALLAN, JR.,** lawyer; b. Sept. 8, 1948; s. Robert Allan and Elizabeth (Pexton) Stuart; m. Kirsten Christianson, June 16, 1973 (div. Mar. 1975); children: Elizabeth Corinne, Christopher Todd; m. Margaret Anne Griffith, Apr. 2, 1977. BA, Bowdoin Coll., 1970, JD, U. Ill., 1973. Bar: Ill. 1973, U.S. Dist. Ct. (so. dist.) Ill. 1973, U.S. Supreme Ct. 1980, U.S. Tax Ct. 1981. Assoc. Brown Hay & Stephens, Springfield, Ill., 1973—78, ptnr., 1979—. Pres. Sangamon County Hist. Soc., 1983; exec. bd. Abraham Lincoln coun. Boy Scouts Am., 1986, pres. Abraham Lincoln coun., 1991—92; bd. dir. Goodwill Industries, Springfield, Ill., 1983—92; chmn. spl. gifts capital fund drive YMCA, Springfield, 1986, bd. dirs. capital fund drive, 1989—92; chmn. fund raising Sangamon County unit Am. Heart Assn., 1984; chmn. United Way Found. Sangamon County, 1999—2000, United Way Campaign, 1996, sec.; bd. dir. Nat. Recreation Found.; bd. trustees Ill. State Mus. Soc. Meml. Med. Ctr. Found., 2001—04; chmn. Springfield C. of C., 2003—; trustee 1st Presbyn. Ch., Springfield, 1987—90, elder. Recipient Silver Beaver award, Boy Scouts Am. Fellow: Am. Bar Found., Am. Coll. Trust Estate Coun.; mem.: Abraham Lincoln Assn. (treas.), Chgo. Bar Assn., St. Louis Bar Assn. Sangamon Valley Estate Planning Council (bd. dirs. 1982—83), Ill. Bar Assn. (estate planning coun. 1981—87, chmn. 1986—87), ABA, Shriners, Masons (33d degree), Rotary (dist. gov. 1985—86, zone inst. chmn. 1987, 1997, dir. 2005—, citation Meritorious Svc. 2005—), Nat. Eagle Scout Assn. (chmn. Abraham Lincoln coun. 1984, Disting. Eagle award). Home: 610 Williams Blvd Springfield IL 62704-2802 Office: PO Box 2459 205 S 5th St Ste 700 Springfield IL 62705 Business E-Mail: rstuart@bhslaw.com.

**STUART, ROBERT KENNETH,** internist, hematologist, oncologist, educator; b. Baton Rouge, July 6, 1948; s. Walter Bynum and Rita Bess (Kleinpeter) m. Gail Elaine Wiscarz, June 12, 1971 (div. Dec. 1988); children: R. Morgan, Elaine C.; m. F. Charlene Gates, Nov. 2, 1991. BS, Georgetown U., 1970; MD, Johns Hopkins U., Balt., 1974. Diplomate Am. Bd. Internal Medicine. Resident in medicine Johns Hopkins Hosp., Balt., 1974-76, oncology fellow Oncology Ctr., 1976-78; rsch. fellow Sloan-Kettering Inst., N.Y.C., 1978-79; asst. prof. Johns Hopkins U., Balt., 1979-84, assoc. prof., 1984-85; prof. medicine Med. U. S.C., Charleston, 1985—; assoc. dir. Hollings Cancer Ctr., Charleston, 1993-97; chmn. dept. oncology King Faisal Specialist Hosp and Rsch. Ctr., Riyadh, Saudi Arabia, 1997-2001; prof. medicine Med.U. S.C., Charleston, 2001—. Bd. dirs. Aplastic Anemia Found., Balt., 1982-93, med. adv. bd., 1993-98; mem. nat. team Tour of Hope, 2004. Democrat. Roman Catholic. Office: Medical Univ of South Carolina 171 Ashley Ave Charleston SC 29425-0100 E-mail: stuartrk@musc.edu.

**STUART, SHERRY BLANCHARD,** artist; b. Newport, Ark., Feb. 19, 1941; d. Walter Thomas Blanchard and Eathel Gladys Faulkner; m. Michael John Scholl, 1963 (div. 1970); 1 child, Aaron John Scholl; m. Roy Otto Stuart, Oct. 5, 1973; 1 child, Ross. BFA, Mpls. Coll. Art and Design, 1964. Designer logos. Exhibited in group shows at Bennington Ctr. for the Arts, 1999, Ariz. Hist. Mus./Joan Cawley Gallery, 1998, Merrill Johnson Gallery, Denver, 2001, Desert Caballeros Western Mus., 2001, Hilligoss Galleries, Chgo., 2002, Nita Stewart Haley Libr. and History Ctr./Elieb Biek Art Mus., 2002, Am. Artists Profl. League, N.Y.C., 2002, Nichols Fine Art Gallery, Taos, N.Mex., 2003, Ky. Horse Park, Lexington, 2003, Breckenridge Fine Arts Ctr., 2003, Harness Tracks of Am. 26th Ann. Art Show and Auction, Lexington, 2003, Stewart Gallery, 2004, Phoenix Civic Ctr. Plaza, 2004, Phippen Mus., 2004, Howard/Mandville Gallery, Kirkland, Wash., 2004, El Presidio Gallery, Tucson, 2005, Norby Gallery, Cave Creek, Ariz., 2004, Mus. of the S.W., 2004, one-woman shows include Gold Nugget Art Gallery, Wickenburg, Ariz., 2003, exhibited in group shows at numerous other group shows, juried and invitational. Recipient People's Choice award, Am. Acad. Women Artists, 1999, 2d Ann. Western ARt Classic, Mpls., 1985, 1st place and Best of Show, Minnetonka Ctr. Arts, 1979, Award of Excellence, Chinese Artists Assn. N.Am., 2003, numerous other 1st and 2d place awards various exhbns., juried shows. Mem.: Western Artists of Am., Am. Plains Artists (signature mem.), Oil Painters of Am. (signature mem.), Am. Acad. Women Artists (signature mem.), Creative Women of Pinnacle Peak (founding mem.). Republican. Avocations: antiques, photography, cooking, golf, horseback riding. Business E-Mail: whoswho@sherryblanchardstuart.com.

**STUART, SPENCER RAYMOND,** management consultant; b. Balt., Sept. 25, 1922; s. William Moore Stuart and Helen Lenore Raymond; m. Eugenia Presler Birdsall, Sept. 24, 1949; children: Spencer Raymond Stuart Jr., Cooper B., Eugenia Anne. BS, Haverford Coll., 1947. Mgr. mktg. and advt. Martin Senour Paint Co., Chgo., 1947—52; cons. Booz Allen and Hamilton, Chgo., 1952—55; prin. Heidrick and Struggles, Chgo., 1955; founder, CEO Spencer Stuart, Exec. Search Consultants, Chgo., 1956—74, founder, chmn. N.Y.C., 1974—, Dean Witter Coun. of Mgmt. Advisors, N.Y.C., 1990—92; mgmt. cons., corp. dir. Palm City, Fla., 1974—2001. Dir., chmn. compensation and mgmt. succession com., chmn. corp. governance com. Enhance Fin. Svcs. Group, N.Y.C., 1986—2001; dir., chmn. audit com., mem. compensation stock option and mgmt. succession com. UST, Inc., Greenwich, Conn., L.P., N.Y.C., 1997; dir., mem. exec. com., chmn. compensation and mgmt. succession com. Western Airlines, L.A., 1984—87; dir., chmn. compensation and corp. strategy coms. Allegheny Internat., Pitts., 1984—89; panelist Am. Mgmt. Assn., Presidents Assn., N.Y.C., 1960—72; exec. compensation Blue Ribbon com. Nat. Assn. Corp. Dirs., Washington, 1974—97; past dir. Assn. Exec. Recruiting Consultants, N.Y.C.; dir. Mass. Co./Keystone Custodian Funds, Boston, 1982—97. Contbr. articles to newspapers and profl. jours. Reception com. Econ. Club. Chgo., 1956—65; chmn. exploring divsn. Boy Scouts Am., Stamford, Conn., 1974—86, founder, chmn. corp. adv. bd. Fairfield County, Conn., 1975—86; trustee, pres. Silvermine Guild of Artists, New Canaan, Conn., 1972—79; trustee Green Mountain Coll., Poultney, Vt., 1980—84; chmn. fundraising dinner com., athlete of decade program Am. Cancer Soc., N.Y.C., 1977—82; panelist Aspen (Colo.) Inst. Humanistic Studies, 1948—58; mem. Conf. Christians and Jews, Conn., 1960—68. 1st lt. AUS, 1943—46, ETO. Decorated Bronze Star, Purple Heart; recipient Wm. H. Spurgen III award for disting. svc., Nat. Exploring Coun., Boy Scouts Am., 1978, Profl. Leadership award, Newcomen Soc. Am., 1981, Heidrick award, Assn. Exec. Search Consultants, 1995. Mem.: Hassayampa Golf Club, The Sky Club, Eldorado Country Club, Univ. Club N.Y.C. Avocations: golf, exercise, writing, computers, art.

**STUART, WALTER BYNUM, III,** retired banker; b. Baton Rouge, Oct. 5, 1922; s. Walter Bynum and Rosa (Gauthreaux) S.; m. Rita Kleinpeter, May 20, 1944; children: Walter Bynum IV, Robert, Douglas, Ronald, Scott. BS, La. State U., 1943. Adminstrv. mgr. Kaiser Aluminum & Chem. Corp., 1946-63; v.p. First Nat. Bank Commerce, New Orleans, 1963-65, sr. v.p., 1965, exec. v.p., 1965-73; vice chmn. bd., dir. 1st Nat. Bank Commerce, New Orleans, 1973-75, exec. v.p. 1st Commerce Corp., New Orleans, 1972-73, pres., 1973-75, vice-chmn. bd., 1975-78, dir., 1973-78; pres. Am. Bank & Trust Co., Lafayette, La., 1978-86, cons., ret., 1986. Assoc. dir., mem. faculty Sch. Banking La. State U., 1973-75, dir., 1975-78; mem. Faculty Assemblies for Bank Dirs. Campaign group chmn. industry com., mem. United Fund for Greater New Orleans Area, 1974; mem. research com. Pub. Affairs Research Council La., 1973-76, v.p., trustee, 1973-76; bd. dirs. Bur. Govtl. Research, 1973-77, Council Better La., 1975—; pres. New Orleans Indsl. Devel. Bd., 1973-75. Served to lt. (j.g.) USNR, 1943-46. Mem. C. of C. of Greater New Orleans Area (v.p. 1973-75, bd. dirs.), Am. Bankers Assn., La. Bankers Assn. (pres. 1977), Am. Mgmt. Assn., Kappa Alpha, Delta Sigma Pi, Beta Gamma Sigma. Democrat. Roman Catholic. Home: 10100 Hillview Dr Apt 2109 Pensacola FL 32514-5481 Recognizing that life is the experiencing of reality, and that reality is simply a continual series of problems, I long ago decided that I would treat a problem as an opportunity. Every incident of difficulty has always invited my intense interest as a challenge, and my thoughts have been immediately marshalled for positive effort. My life has been most rewarding because I believe that "a problem is an opportunity!".

**STUART, WALTER BYNUM, IV,** lawyer; b. Grosse Tete, La., Nov. 23, 1946; s. Walter Bynum III and Rita (Kleinpeter) S.; m. Lettice Lee Binnings, May 18, 1968; children: Courtney Lyon, Walter Burke V. Student, Fordham U., 1964—65; BA, Tulane U., 1968, JD, 1973. Bar: La. 1973, N.Y 1980, U.S. Dist. Ct. (ea. and we. dists.) La. 1974, U.S. Tax Ct. 1974, U.S. Supreme Ct. 1981, U.S. Dist. Ct. (so. dist.) Colo. 1987, U.S. Dist. Ct. (so. dist.) Tex. 1989. Ptnr. Stone, Pigman, Walther, Wittman and Hutchinson, New Orleans, 1971—73; Jager Huntvr Levine Seeman and Stuart, New Orleans, 1978—81, Gordon, Arata, McCollam and Stuart, New Orleans, 1981—88, Vinson & Elkins LLP, Houston, 1988—, adminstrv. ptnr. N.Y.C., 2003—. Instr. Tulane U. Law Sch., 1978-82; mem. faculty Banking Sch. of the South; bd. dirs. Inst. Politics; mem. adv. bd. City Atty.'s Office, New Orleans, 1978-79. Bd. dirs. gen. counsel Houston Grand Opera, 1992-2003. Mem. ABA, La. Bar Assn., Tex. Assn. Bank Counsel (pres. 1994-95), La. Bankers Assn. (chmn. bank counsel com.). Office: Vinson & Elkins 666 Fifth Ave 26th Fl New York NY 10103-0040 also: First City Tower 1001 Fannin St, Ste 2300 Houston TX 77002-6760 Office Phone: 212-237-0020, 212-237-0007. E-mail: wstuart@velaw.com.

**STUART, WILLIAM CORWIN,** judge; b. Knoxville, Iowa, Apr. 28, 1920; s. George Corwin and Edith (Abram) S.; m. Mary Elgin Cleaver, Oct. 20, 1946; children: William Corwin II, Robert Cullen, Melanie Rae, Valerie Jo. BA, State U. Iowa, 1941, JD, 1942. Bar: Iowa 1942. Pvt. practice, Chariton, 1946-62; city atty., 1947-49; mem. Iowa Senate from Lucas-Wayne Counties, 1951-61; justice Supreme Ct. Iowa, 1962-71; judge U.S. Dist. Ct., So. Dist. of Iowa, Des Moines, 1971-86, sr. judge, 1986—. With USNR, 1943-45. Recipient Outstanding Svc. award Iowa Acad. Trial lawyer, 1987, Iowa Trial Lawyers Assn., 1988, Spl. award Iowa State Bar Assn., 1987, Disting. Alumni, U. Iowa Coll. Law, 1987. Mem. ABA, Iowa Bar Assn., Am. Legion, All For Iowa, Order of Coif, Omicron Delta Kappa, Phi Kappa Psi, Phi Delta Phi. Clubs: Mason (Shriner). Presbyterian. Home: PO Box 130 Chariton IA 50049-0130

**STUBBART, DAVID JAMES,** elementary school educator; b. Framingham, Mass., Sept. 26, 1977; s. John Crawford and Fern Elizabeth Stubbart; m. Laura Michelle Opdenbrouw, July20, 2006. BS in Edn., Framingham State Coll., 1999, EdM, 2003; postgrad., Boston Coll., 2006—. Cert. elem. edn. grades 1-6 Mass., 2000, reading tchr. grades K-12 Mass., 2004. Educator grade 1 Town of Natick, Mass., 1999—99; educator-grade 1 Town of Westborough, Westborough, Mass., 2000—03; educator-grade 3 Town of Southborough, Mass., 2003—. Unit leader YMCA, Hopkinton, Mass., 1999—2000. Coord. Boy Scouts Am. Ashland, Mass., 1995—95. Mem.: Alpha Upsilon Alpha (assoc.). Office: Town of Southborough 28 Cordaville Rd Southborough MA 01772 Office Phone: 508-229-1250. Personal E-mail: davidstubbart@yahoo.com

**STUBBE, JOANNE,** chemistry professor; BA in Chemistry, U. Pa., 1968; PhD in Organic Chemistry, U. Berkeley, 1971. Asst. prof. dept. chemistry Williams Coll., 1972—77; asst. prof. dept. pharmacology Yale U. Sch. Medicine, 1977—80; asst. prof. biochemistry U. Wisconsin-Madison, 1980—83, assoc. prof., 1983—85, prof., 1985—87; Ellen Swallow Richards Prof. Chemistry MIT, 1987, prof. biology, 1990, John C. Sheehan Prof. Chem., 1992, Ciba-Geigy Professor of Chemistry, 1996, Novartis prof. chemistry and biology Cambridge. Recipient NIH Career Development Award, 1983—88, Arthur C. Cope scholar award, Am. Chemistry Soc., 1993; NIH pre doctoral fellowship, 1969—71, NIH postdoctoral fellowship, 1975—77. Mem.: Am. Academy of Arts & Sciences, NAS, Am. Philosophical Society. Office: MIT Dept Chemistry 77 Massachusetts Ave Dept Cambridge MA 02139-4307

**STUBBE, RAY WILLIAM,** minister, writer; b. Milw., Aug. 15, 1938; s. Clarence Arnold and Ruby Otillie (Mueller) Stubbe. *Grandfather, Julius F. Mueller, emigrated in 1889 from Germany at age 4. Though he lost both his parents, and was schooled only through 8th grade, he eventually worked his way up to become a superintendent in a cast iron foundry. In later years, his innovative techniques drew inquiries from numerous foreign foundry men and, upon retirement, he traveled to Sao Paulo, Brazil where he successfully modernized a foundry. His boundless energy and value on education was the reason that he flew bi-planes in the 1920's, built a reflecting telescope in the 1930's, sang in a civic male chorus, and travelled by car to every state including Canada and Mexico.* BA, St. Olaf Coll., 1960; MDiv, Northwestern Luth. Theol. Sem., 1965; postgrad., U. Chgo. 1967. Ordained to ministry Evang. Luth. Ch. Am., 1965. Mission devel. bd. Am. missions Luth Ch. in Am., Oak Creek, Wis., 1965-66; organizer, pastor All Saints Luth Ch., Oak Creek, 1966-67; enlisted USN, 1955; commd. ensign USNR, 1963, advanced through grades to lt., comdr. chaplain corps, 1971; augmented to USN, 1971; chaplain, 1967-85; ret. USN, 1985. Interviews on national televised programs. Author: Inside Force Recon, 1989, Khe Sanh Chaplain, 1970, Paddles, Parachutes, Patrols, 1979, Aarugha, 1989, Valley of Decision, 1991, The Final Formation, 1995, Khe Sanh and the Mongol Prince, 2002, Battalion of Kings, 2005, B5-T8 in 48 QXD: The Secret Official History of the North Vietnamese Army of the Siege at Khe Sanh, Vietnam, Spring, 1968, 2006, numerous poems; editor: Khe Sanh Veteran/Red Clay, 1996—98; contbr. articles to profl. jours. Founder, pres. emeritus Khe Sanh Vets., Inc., 1988—; spkr. numerous vet. assemblies; chaplain Wis. Vietnam Vets., Milw., 1984—, 3d Marine Divsn. Assn., 1988. Decorated Bronze Star with combat V; recipient Legion of Honor award, Chapel Four Chaplains. Mem.: DAV (life), VFW (life), Wis. Acad. Scis., Arts and Letters (life), Spl. Ops. Assn. (life), 3d Marine Divsn. Assn. (life), Spl. Forces Assn. (life), Force Reconnaissance Assn. (life), Soc. Bibl. Lit., Vietnam Vets. Am. (life), Wis. Vietnam Vets. (life), Mil. Officers Assn. Am. (life), Marine Corps Hist. Found. (life), Pi Kappa Delta. Lutheran. Avocation: boxing. Home: 8766 Parkview Ct Wauwatosa WI 53226-2729 Office: Redeemer Luth Church 631 N 19th St Milwaukee WI 53233-2152 Office Phone: 414-771-9987. *The most powerful Words of God have always been communicated to me by the occasional people encountered in life's pathways. These are the quiet ones whose very being reflect possibilities of being the image of God we all are; living Words of God who make us know we are free, forgiven, loved, blessed with value and future; heroes, who at great risk and pain to themselves, transform negatives into positives; great, good people who empty themselves into servants and incarnate love into all human conditions. When the vision they offer becomes life's task of who to become, all of life becomes a gift of everdeepening wells which nourish everything living with the deep underground stream, which is God.*

**STUBBEN, DOLUS JANE (D. J. STUBBEN),** advertising executive; b. Clovis, N.Mex., Sept. 12, 1951; d. Joseph P. Harmon and Maurine Yvonne (Simmons) McDonald; m. Ronald Patrick Day, Apr. 11, 1970 (div.); m. John David Stubben, Sept. 23, 1999 (div.); 1 child, Patricia Joan. Student, West Tex. State U., 1969—70. Instr. Amarillo Coll., Tex., 1971—73; advt. cons. Amarillo, 1976—78; advt. mgr. Montgomery Ward, Amarillo, 1978—80; owner, mgr. Welcome Pardner!, Amarillo, 1981—. Arbitrator Better Bus. Bur., Amarillo, 1978-79; musician Furr's Cafeteria, 1978-80; piano bar musician, comedienne Quigley's Restaurant, Eugene, Oreg., 1980-81, Jolly's Comedy Club, Amarillo, 1986-88, Sheraton Towers Amarillo, 1988-89 Author: #555 Death Row, 1981 (Nat. Press Women 2d pl. award 1982), Dog Pause..., 1981 (Nat. Press Women 2d pl. award 1982, Hon. Mention award 1987), It's a Secret, I Can't Tell You, 1984, poems; songwriter Media chmn. Am. Cancer Soc., Amarillo, 1978-79; media dir. Bralley's 4th July Picnic, Amarillo, 1977-78; media rels. com. St. Jude's Hosp. Tex. Com., Amarillo, 1983; publicity chmn. Miss Amarillo Area, 1993—; nominating com. Tex. plains Girl Scouts U.S.A., 1999; bd. dirs. Panhandle Ind. Living Ctr., High Plains Food Bank; active Panhandle Film Commn., 1999—Top 10 Women award Am. Mktg., 1996; recipient Entrepreneur award Center City BPW, 1999, Achievement of Decade award, 1999, Hall of Fame award Tex. Panhandle Broadcasters, 2003, Oxygen Network Winner, 2004, Vol. of Yr. award Amarillo C. of C., 2005; NBC4 award Pardners 4 Paws, 2006 Mem.: Tex. Panhandle Broadcasters Assn. (treas. 1998—99), Tex. Press Women (v.p. 1982, state treas. 1986, membership chmn. 1986, First Pl. (2) awards 1988), INFORMS, Sigma Xi, Sigma Tau, Tau Beta Pi, Lions Club (chmn. pub. rels. com. 1990—, Rookie of Yr. Downtown 1989—90, Lions Fellow award 1999). Office: Welcome Pardner PO Box 30926 Amarillo TX 79120-0926 Office Phone: 806-356-1555. E-mail: stubben@amaonline.com.

**STUBBERUD, ALLEN ROGER,** electrical engineering educator; b. Glendive, Mont., Aug. 14, 1934; s. Oscar Adolph and Alice Marie (LeBlanc) S.; m. May B. Tragus, Nov. 19, 1961; children: Peter A., Stephen C. BS in Elec. Engring., U. Idaho, 1956, MS in Engring., UCLA, 1958, PhD, 1962. From asst. prof. to assoc. prof. engring. UCLA, 1962-69; prof., then prof. emeritus, elec. engring. U. Calif., Irvine, 1969—, assoc. dean engring.. 1972-78, dean engring., 1978-83, chair elec. and computer engring., 1993-98, interim dean engring., 1994-96; chief scientist U.S. Air Force, 1983-85. Dir. Elec. Communications and Systems Engring. divsn. NSF, 1987-88. Author: Analysis and Synthesis of Linear Time Variable Systems, 1964, (with others) Feedback and Control Systems, 2d edit., 1990, (with others) Digital Control System Design, 2d edit., 1994; contbr. articles to profl. jours. Recipient Exceptional Civilian Svc. medal USAF, 1985, 90, Meritorious Civilian Svc. medal, 1996. Fellow IEEE (Centennial medal 1984, Millennium medal 2000), AIAA, AAAS, NYAS; mem. INFORMS, Sigma Xi, Sigma Tau, Tau Beta Pi, Eta Kappa Nu. Office: Univ Calif Elec Engring Dept zotcode 2625 Irvine CA 92697-2625 E-mail: arstubbe@uci.edu.

**STUBBLEFIELD, JOHN K., JR.,** food products executive; m. Sharon Stubblefield; 2 children. BBA in Acctg., U. Houston, 1970. V.p. administr. Langazorta Internat., 1976-84; controller Sysco Corp., Houston, 1984-86, v.p. fin., Denver, 1986-92, v.p., controller, sr. v.p. finance, Houston, 1993—99, CFO, 1994—, sr. v.p. fin. & admin., 1999—2003, exec. v.p. fin. and adminstrn., 2003—, also bd. dirs., 2003. Office: Sysco Corp 1390 Enclave Pkwy Houston TX 77077-2099*

**STUBBS, DONALD CLARK,** retired secondary school educator; b. Providence, Mar. 6, 1935; s. Edward J. and Margaret Eleanor (Clark) S.; m. Lorraine Alice Thivierge, Apr. 3, 1969 (dec. Jan. 1986); 1 child, Derek C.; m. Sarah E. Andrews, Apr. 23, 1999. AB, Cath. U. Am., Washington, 1959, MS, 1966; postgrad., St. John's U., N.Y.C., 1960. Tchr. Bishop Loughlin Meml. High Sch., Bklyn., 1959-61, Bishop Bradley High Sch., Manchester, NH, 1961-66; tchr., sci. dept. chair LaSalle Mil. Acad., Oakdale, NY, 1966-69, Ponaganset Regional High Sch., Glocester, RI, 1969-2000; ret. 2000. Home: 35 Shove St Woonsocket RI 02895-5741 E-mail: naddad@aol.com.

**STUBBS, GERALD,** biochemist, educator; b. Hobart, Australia, May 9, 1947; came to the US, 1976; m. Rebecca Lynn Harris; children: Andrew, Tamsin, Anneliese, Rachel. BSc, Australian Nat. U., 1968; DPhil, Oxford U., 1972. Sci. asst. Max Planck Inst., Heidelberg, Germany, 1973-76; rsch. assoc. Brandeis U., Waltham, Mass., 1976-83; asst. prof. Vanderbilt U., Nashville,

1983-87, assoc. prof., 1987-90, prof., 1990—. Contbr. articles to profl. jour. Achievements include determination of molecular structure of tobacco mosaic virus. Office Phone: 615-322-2018. Business E-mail: gerald.stubbs@vanderbilt.edu.

**STUBBS, KATRINA CHILDS,** management consultant, educator; b. Atlanta, Feb. 10, 1964; d. Theodore Roosevelt Childs and Jacqueline Louise (Clark) Childs-Taylor; children: Kayla Laranza, Kiara Danielle. BS in Chemistry, Dillard U., 1985; MBA, Albany State U., 1991. Cert. profl. tutor Nat. Tutoring Assn., 2004. Med. specialist U.S. Army Res., Chamblee, Ga., 1981-87; technologist/chemist Miller Brewing Co., Albany, Ga., 1987-93; bus. cons. UGA Bus. Outreach Svc., Albany, 1993—; prin., owner Elite Profl. & Tutoring Svcs., Inc., 1999—. Minority student dir. UGA Bus. Outreach Svc., Albany, 1994-95; grant cons. Union Mission Outreacy Ctr., 2000—; math. instr. Darton Coll., 2004—. Mem. NAFE. Democrat. Baptist. Avocations: working with youths, aerobics, listening to gospel, reading. Personal E-mail: katrina.stubbs@att.net.

**STUBBS, KENDON LEE,** retired librarian; b. Washington, Apr. 6, 1938; s. Donald Harrison and Rosalee Adelia (Brown) S.; m. Patricia Townsend, June 3, 1961; children: Christopher, Peter, Timothy. BA, St. John's Coll., Annapolis, Md., 1960; MA, U. Va., 1964; MS, Columbia U., 1965. Sr. asst. in manuscripts U. Va. Libr., Charlottesville, 1965, reference libr., 1966-76, acting acquisitions libr., 1967-68, assoc. univ. libr., 1976-87, assoc. univ. libr. for pub. svcs., 1987-92, acting univ. libr., 1993, assoc. univ. libr., 1994-98, dep. univ. libr., 1998—2003, ret., 2003. Cons. US Dept. Edn., Washington, 1982—84. Author: Quantitative Criteria for Academic Research Libraries, 1984; editor: Cumulated Assn. Research Libraries Statistics, 1981, Rsch. Libr. Statistics, 1990, ARL Statistics, 1992-95, Japanese Text Initiative on World Wide Web, 1995—; contbr. articles on library stats., rsch. to profl. publs., Internet. Mem. Assn. of Rsch. Librs. (mem. stats. com., vis. program officer 1995-97), Bibliog. Soc. U. Va. (pres. 1975-78, v.p. 1978-99).

**STUBBS, SUSAN CONKLIN,** retired statistician; b. Washington, July 26, 1935; d. Maxwell Robertson and Marcia (Nye) Conklin; m. LeRoy Carter Hostetter, May 20, 1975 (div. 1988); m. Joel Richard Stubbs, Sept. 20, 1992. BA, Pa. State U., 1957. Economist Bur. of Census, Suitland, Md., 1973—74, Bur. of Labor Stats., Washington, 1974—79, supervisory economist, 1979—84; statistician IRS, Washington, 1984—95, chief rschr. stats. of income divsn., 1989—92, coord. for indsl. classification, 1994—95; ret., 1995. Cons. joint com. on taxation U.S. Congress, 1992-94; OPM legis. fellow, 1988. Contbr. articles to profl. jours.; editor govtl. statis. publs. Leader, del., bd. dirs., v.p., chmn. nominating com. Nation's Capital coun. Girl Scouts U.S., 1968—; sec.-treas. Middlesex Beach Assn., Bethany, Del., 1991—94; jobs. editor Caucus for Women in Stats., Washington, 1992—95; mentor Mentors Inc., Washington, 1992—94; treas. Smith Point Sea Rescue, 1997—2004; docent Reedville Fisherman's Mus., 1997—, chmn. Christmas house tour, 2000—02, mem. steering com. Christmas house tour, 2002—03, fin. chmn., Christmas on Cockrell's Creek, 2002, treas., 2003, chmn. fin., 2003, chmn. planning giving com.; active Boy Scouts Am. Campaign for Family Values; tutor and mentor People Helping People; mem. Tax Economist Forum, 1990—97; mentor Northumberland Mid. Sch. in Tobacco grant program; treas. Region II, Episc. Diocese of Va., 1999—2005; bd. dirs. Rice's Hotel/Hughlett's Tavern Found., 1998—2000, Rappahannock CC Found., treas., 2003—05. Mem.: Northumberland Assn. for Progressive Stewardship (edn. com. 1997—), St. Stephen's Episcopal Ch. ECW (v.p. 2002, treas. 2003—04, del. to coun. 2005—06, mem. com. on resolutions 2006), Bus. and Profl. Women Essex County and No. Neck (sec. 1999—2001), Va. Federated Women's Clubs (pres. Northumberland County chpt. 1996—98, pres Ea. area Lee dist. 1998—2000), Rivers Bend Assn. (bd. dirs. 1996—98, chair fin. com. 1998—2001, v.p. bd. dirs. 2001—, chair bylaws com., chair long range planning com., chair fin. com. 2003—). Avocations: sailing, swimming, gardening, reading. Home: 776 Riverview Dr Heathsville VA 22473-4011 Personal E-mail: stubbs@crosslink.net.

**STUBBS, THOMAS HUBERT,** public relations executive; b. Americus, Ga., Aug. 16, 1944; s. Hubert F. and Elizabeth (Askew) S.; m. Mary Louise Quarles, Mar. 19, 1965; children: Thomas C., Chad P. BS, Auburn U., 1966. CPA, Ala., Ga., Miss. Sr. acct. Peat, Marwick, Mitchell and Co., Birmingham, Ala., 1966-72; supr. L. Paul Kassauf and Co., CPA's, Birmingham, 1972-73; staff mem. Snow, Stewart and Bradford, Birmingham, 1973-75; v.p. Cen. Computer Svcs., Inc., Birmingham, 1975-79; Cen. Bancshares of the South, Birmingham, 1979-81; ptnr. Bradford and Co., CPA's, Gulf Shore, Ala., 1981-82; v.p., trust officer Deposit Guaranty Nat. Bank, Jackson, Miss., 1983; treas. Data Supplies, Inc., Norcross, Ga., 1983-88, Stevens Graphics, Inc., Atlanta, 1988-89, v.p., 1989-90, pres. bus. products div., 1990-93, v.p., CFO, 1994—2002; fin. cons. LPL Fin. Svcs., Buford, Ga., 2002—; CFO The WOW Factory, Atlanta, 2003—04; v.p. fin. Data Supplies, Inc., Duluth, Ga., 2004—, treas., 2004—. Served with USNG, 1966-72. Mem. Am. Inst. CPA's, Ala. Soc. CPA's, Ga. Soc. CPA's, Miss. Soc. CPA's. Republican. Presbyterian. Avocations: tennis, jogging, golf. Home: 2875 Towne Village Dr Duluth GA 30097-7616 Office: 11300 Laksfield Dr Duluth GA 30189 Office Phone: 770-476-4455. Business E-mail: mlq3020@becgrowth.net, tstubbs@datasuppliesinc.com.

**STUBBS, TIMOTHY JOHN,** physicist; b. Salisbury, Eng., Dec. 18, 1975; s. Sally Ann and David John Stubbs; m. Charlotte Sarah Atkinson, Oct. 27, 2004; 1 child, Ethan Alexander. MSc, Imperial Coll., London, 1998, PhD in Space Physics, 2002. Rsch. asst. Imperial Coll., London, 2000—02; NRC rsch. assoc. NAS/GSFC, Washington, 2002—05; asst. rsch. scientist U. Md., Baltimore County, 2005—. Mem. lunar airborne dust toxicity adv. group NASA-USRA, Washington, 2005—, NRC rsch. assoc., 2002—05. Fellow: Royal Astron. Soc.; mem.: Am. Inst. Physics, Inst. of Physics (assoc.), Am. Geophys. Union. Achievements include development of dynamic dust fountain model for charged dust in the lunar exosphere. Office: NASA Goddard Space Flight Ctr Mail Code 6123 Greenbelt MD 20771 Office Phone: 301-286-1524. E-mail: timothy.j.stubbs.1@gsfc.nasa.gov.

**STUBBS, WILL, JR.,** pharmaceutical company manager; b. Birmingham, Ala., Feb. 26, 1955; s. Will, Sr. and Elizabeth S.; 1 child, Will III. BS in Mgmt. and Econs. cum laude, Fisk U., 1977. Sys. engr. Procter & Gamble, Jackson, Tenn., 1977-78; prodn. team mgr., 1978-80; large parenterals labeling/packaging supr. Abbott Labs., Rocky Mount, N.C., 1980-81, large parenterals terminal sterile filling supr., 1981-85, aseptic sterilization supr., 1985-88, small parenterals terminal sterile fill supr., 1988-90, aseptic filling supr., 1990-93, sr. prodn. supr., 1993-95, pharm. prodn. mgr., 1995-2001, terminal sterile filling prodn. mgr., 2001—02, small volume parenterals labeling/packaging prodn. mgr., 2002—04, pharm. prodn. mgr., 2004; labeling and packaging prodn. mgr. Hospira Inc., Rocky Mount, 2004—. Contbr. poetry to Fisk Herald. Mem. econ. growth task force Rocky Mount City Coun., 1992-94; bd. dirs. Nash Edgecombe Econ. Devel. Inc., Rocky Mount, 1994-99, vice-chmn. bd. dirs., 1998, chmn., 1999; mem. Adult Basic Edn. Bd., 1980-84; pres. Rocky Mount Pan Hellenic Coun., 1991-93. Named to Outstanding Young Men of Am., Jaycees, 1983, 5th Dist. Scholar of the Yr., Omega Psi Phi, 1977; recipient internship Mobil Oil Corp. Mem. Omega Psi Phi (Vice-Basileus grad. chap. 1989-91). Democrat. Baptist. Avocations: community service, travel, music, swimming, jogging. Home: 1028 Niblick Dr Rocky Mount NC 27804-9655 Office: 4285 N Wesleyan Blvd Rocky Mount NC 27804-8612 Office Phone: 252-977-5961. Business E-mail: will.stubbsjr@hospira.com.

**STUBER, CHARLES WILLIAM,** retired genetics educator, researcher; b. St. Michael, Nebr, Sept. 19, 1931; s. Harvey John and Minnie Augusta (Wilks) S.; m. Marilyn Martha Cook, May 28, 1953; 1 child, Charles William Jr. BS, U. Nebr., 1952, MS, 1961; PhD, N.C. State U., 1965. Vet., agrl. instr. Broken Bow HS, 1956-59; rsch. asst. U. Nebr., Lincoln, 1959-61; rsch. geneticist Agrl. Rsch. Svc., USDA, Raleigh, NC, 1962-75, supervisory rsrch. geneticist, rsch. leader, 1975-98, collaborator, 1998—; prof. genetics & crop sci. NC State U., Raleigh, 1975-98, prof. emeritus, 1998—. Assoc. editor Crop Sci. Jour., 1979-82, tech. editor, 1984-86, editor, 1987-89; contbr. over

200 articles to profl. jour., chpt. to books. Chmn. coun. on ministries and numerous offices Highland United Meth. Ch., Raleigh. Lt. USN, 1952-56. Named Outstanding Sci. of Yr., USDA-ARS, 1989; recipient Genetics and Plant Breeding award Nat. Coun. Comml. Plant Breeders, 1995, Award of Merit, U. Nebr. Alumni Assn., 1997; inductee USDA-Agrl. Rsch. Svc. Sci. Hall of Fame, 1999; Vol. 45 of MAYDICA dedicated to Charles W. Stuber, 2000. Fellow: Crop Sci. Soc. Am. (editor-in-chief 1987—91, pres. 1992—93, Crop Sci. Rsch. award 1995, DeKalb Genetics Crop Sci. Disting. Career award 1999), Fellow Am. Soc. Agronomy (pres. 2002); mem.: Am. Genetic Assn. (sec. 1984—86), Genetics Soc. Am., Phi Kappa Phi, Sigma Xi. Avocations: windsurfing, water-skiing. Home: 1800 Manuel St Raleigh NC 27612-5510 Office: USDA-ARS NC State U Dept Genetics PO Box 7614 Raleigh NC 27695-7614 Personal E-mail: cstuber2@aol.com.

**STUBER, SCOTT,** film company executive; Past mktg. dept. Universal Pictures; exec. Donner/Schuler-Donner Prodns.; v.p. prodn. Universal Pictures, Universal City, Calif., 1997—2000, exec. v.p. prodn., 2000—01, co-pres. prodn., 2001—03, vice chmn., worldwide prodn., 2003—05, prodr., 2006—. Assoc. prodr.: (films) Volcano, 1997; prodr.: The Break-Up, 2006, You, Me and Dupree, 2006; exec. prodr.: (films) Accepted, 2006. Office: Universal Pictures 100 Universal City Plaza Universal City CA 91608*

**STÜBGEN, JOERG-PATRICK,** neurologist; b. Tripoli, Libya, Sept. 7, 1959; s. Fritz Hans Georg and Marie-Louise Hildegard Stübgen; m. Dana Annenberg; 1 child, Charlotte. MD, U. Pretoria, South Africa, 1983. Diplomate Am. Bd. Psychiatry and Neurology. Intern Grey's Hosp., Pietermaritzburg, South Africa; neurology resident U. Pretoria, South Africa, 1984—89, neuromuscular fellow, asst. prof. dept. neurology, 1990—91, assoc. prof., 1991—92; asst. prof. Cornell U. N.Y.C., 1995—99, assoc. prof. dept. neurology, 2000—. Contbr. over 30 articles to profl. jours., chapters to books. Named one of Best Doctors in Am., 2003—04, America's Top Physicians, Consumer's Rsch. Coun. Am., 2005, Top Doctors N.Y. Metro Area, Castle Connelly Med. Ltd., 2006. Fellow: Am. Assn. Electro-Diagnostic Medicine, Royal Coll. Physicians and Surgeons Can., Coll. Physicians South Africa; mem.: AMA, Med. Soc. State N.Y., N.Y. Med. Soc., Am. Acad. Neurology. Lutheran. Avocations: road running, travel. Office: Cornell Univ Med College 525 E 68th St New York NY 10021 Office Phone: 212-746-2334. Business E-mail: pstuebge@med.cornell.edu.

**STUCK, ROGER DEAN,** electrical engineering educator; b. Ventura, Calif., Nov. 6, 1924; s. William Henry and Marian Grace (Ready) S.; m. Opal Christine Phillips, July 25, 1948; children: Dean, Phyllis, Sandra. BSEE, Calif. Inst. Tech.; 1947; MSEE, N.C. State U., 1957. Elec. engr. Warren Wilson Coll., Swannanoa, NC, 1947—, instr. elec. engring. physics, 1948-69, dean students, 1969-72, instr. physics, elec. engr., 1972-86. Author: (charts) The Periodic Table of Physical Concepts, 1977, The Periodic Table of Physical Concepts with Economic Concepts, 1980; (book) The Periodic Table of Physical Concepts Book of Definitions, 1987. Lt. (j.g.) USNR, 1942-46. Mem. Sigma Xi. Republican. Presbyterian. Achievements include an elliptical response for the creative theory and the identification of gravitational inductance, capacitance and splendor (MVVV) and energy-spread (hc) as a fundamental initial concept of physical creation relating mass and charge which is fundamental to any Grand Unification Theory; the statement of a quantized conservation law for energy-spread to establish an internal and external structure for neutrons, protons, electrons and neutrinos. Home: 65 Green Forest Rd Swannanoa NC 28778-2246

**STUCKERT, CAROLINE MORRIS,** retired non-profit executive, anthropologist; b. Phila., Apr. 7, 1940; d. Howard Morris Stuckert and Henrietta Scott Gay, Thomas Seward Gay (Stepfather); m. David Charles Toomey, Aug. 17, 1963 (div. Sept. 1973); children: Charles Scott Toomey, Christopher Melcher Toomey. BA, Bryn Mawr Coll., 1962; MA, U. Pa., 1976, PhD, 1985. Cert. instr. horseback riding. Instr. Coll. Gen. Studies U. Pa., Phila., 1977—79; instr. Muhlenberg Coll., Allentown, Pa., 1978; registrar Mus. Archaeology and Anthropology U. Pa., Phila., 1980—83; dir. Buten Mus. Wedgwood, Merion, Pa., 1983—84; pres. MACC Assocs., Inc., Havertown, Pa., 1986—96; site adminstr. Pa. Hist. and Mus. Commn., Harrisburg, 1996—2001; exec. dir. Hist. Yellow Springs, Inc., Chester Springs, Pa., 2001—02, Nat. Assn. Watch and Clock Collectors, Inc., Columbia, Pa., 2003—06. Grants reviewer mus. programs Pa. Hist. and Mus. Commn., Harrisburg, 2002—03; grants peer reviewer NSF, Washington, 1983, Inst. Mus. and Libr. Svcs., Washington, 1999—2001, Washington, 2006; pres. Lancaster (Pa.) County Mus. Coun., 1996—98; mem. heritage tourism adv. bd. Lancaster County Planning Commn., 1996—98; mem. adv. bd. Pa. Dutch Conf. and Visitors Bur., Lancaster, 1996—98; bd. dirs., chair interpretation com. Brandywine Battlefield Preservation Task Force, Chadds Ford, Pa., 1999—2001. Author: Cataloging From Scratch: A Manual for Cataloging Undocumented Collections in Small Museums, 1991; editor: (spl. jour. issue) The Museologist, 1989; contbr. articles to profl. jours. Choir mem. Ch. of Redeemer, Bryn Mawr, 1985—2005; founding mem. Sylvan Opera Festival, Wynnewood, Pa., 1994—96; chair internat. com. Concordville-Chadds Ford (Pa.) Rotary Club, 2000—01. Grantee, NSF, 1976; post doctoral fellow, Dept. Anthropology, U. Pa., 1985—87. Mem.: Mid-Atlantic Assn. Mus., Am. Assn. Mus., Pa. Fedn. Mus. and Hist. Orgns., Lancaster Rotary Club. Republican. Episcopalian. Achievements include research in physical anthropology of Romano-British Winchester, England; archaeological fieldwork in Ireland (1973), England (1974-77); West Saxon skeletal sample from Blacknall Field, England, funded by English Heritage. Avocations: singing, reading. Office: NAWCC Inc 514 Poplar St Columbia PA 17512-2130 Office Phone: 717-684-8261 209.

**STUCKEY, ELLEN MAE,** music educator; d. Charles Franklin and Mary Dolores Helsingborg; m. Joseph Bruce Stuckey, Jr., June 9, 1979; children: Laura L., Aaron N. BS in Music Edn., West Chester U., 1977; MEd in Music Edn., Pa. State U., 1981. Cert. music tchr. Pa. Dept. Edn. Music tchr. K-5 Everett (Pa.) Area Sch. Dist., 1977—82; pvt. music tchr. Martinsburg, 1982—; tchr. jr./sr. high vocal/gen. music Hollidaysburg (Pa.) Area Sch. Dist., 1988—89; music tchr. K-5 No. Bedford County Sch. Dist., Loysburg, Pa., 1990—, now music tchr. K-5. Dir. adult choir 1st Bapt. Ch. Altoona, Pa., 1977—87; Martinsburg Grace Brethren Ch., 1989—2006. Composer, lyricist: songs Hail to You, O Northern Bedford, 1995; contbr. to profl. mags.; composer 3 songs, co-author: mus. drama The Ark of Faith, 2003. Founder Aaron N. Stuckey Meml. Found.; dir. luminary svc. Am. Cancer Soc., Martinsburg, 2002, 2003; mistress of ceremonies Little Miss pageant Roaring Spring (Pa.) Lions Club, 1996, 1997, 1998. Mem.: Pa. State Educator's Assn., Nat. Guild Piano Tchrs., Am. Choral Dirs. Assn., Pa. Music Educators Assn. Republican. Grace Brethren. Avocations: spending time with family, gardening, photography, songwriting. Office: No Bedford County Sch Dist 217 NBC Dr Loysburg PA 16659 Office Phone: 814-766-2221 x 343. Business E-mail: estuckey@nbcsd.k12.pa.us.

**STUCKEY, JAMES P.,** real estate developer; b. Bklyn., Feb. 15, 1954; s. John McRae and Ethel Lilian Stuckey; m. Deborah Marie Stuckey, Apr. 6, 1974; children: Nicole Marie, James P. Jr., Danielle Antionette. BS in Psychology, St. John's U., 1975, MA, 1977, St. Joseph Seminary and Coll., 2002. Various Office Econ. Devel., 1977-80, N.Y.C. Pub. Devel. Corp., 1980-86; pres., CEO NYC Pub. Devel. Corp., 1986-89; mng. dir. Gronich & Co., Inc., 1990-93; exec. v.p., dir. comml. and residential devel. Forest City Ratner Cos., Bklyn., 1994—; pres. Atlantic Yards devel. group, 2006—. Lectr. Columbia U., Yale U., St. John's U., NYU, John Jay Coll., Pratt Inst. Mem. Westside Task Force N., N.Y.C.-Mcpl. Water Fin. Authority, Ctr. Family Life, Nat. Trust Historic Preservation, Art Commn. N.Y.C.; vice chmn. Cmty. Bd. 2, S.I.; chmn. Ctr. Against Domestic Violence Recipient Henry Hart Rice Award for Most Ingenious Deal of the Yr., NYC Real Estate Bd., 1992. Mem. Nat. Assn. Corp. Real Estate Execs., Urban Land Inst., Coun. Urban Econ. Devel., Inst. Urban Design (mem. regional adv. coun.), Am. Assn. Individual Investors. Avocations: music, bicycling, racquetball, golf. Office: Forest City Ratner Corp 1 Metrotech Ctr N Brooklyn NY 11201-3831 E-mail: jstuckey@fcrs.com.*

**STUCKI, MARGARET ELIZABETH,** art gallery director, writer, painter; b. West New York, N.J., Jan. 9, 1928; d. William Eugene and Elise (Hohl) Stucki. BA in Philosophy, Barnard Coll., 1949; MA in Fine Art, Columbia U., 1959; postgrad., Art Students League N.Y.C., 1949-51; ABD, NYU, 1961; PhD, Freedom U., Orlando, Fla., 1975. Prof. art Hartwick (N.Y.) Coll., 1962-72; dir. Stucki-Linstead Art Gallery and Mus., Pocatello, Idaho, 1994—. Founded A.D. 2000+ Christian Greeting Cards, 1999. One-woman shows include Wichita Art Assn., Kans., 1967, Swiss Ctr., N.Y.C., 1975, Capitol Bldg., Augusta, Maine, 1978, U.S. Senate, Washington, 1987, Idaho TV 8, 1998, Idaho State U. Women's Art Show, 2000, exhibitions include Treasure Valley Juried Exhbn., Boise State U., 1998, prin. works include oil painting The Crucifixion, Temple Bapt. Ch., Tallahassee, portraits; author: The Revolutionary Mission of Modern Art or Crud and Other Essays on Art, 1973, War on Light: The Destruction of the Image of God in Man Through Modern Art, 1975, Eco-Elegia: Elegies in Ecology, 1981, Gullible's Travels: An Educational Tax Exempt Trip Around the World in a Hot Air Balloon, 1987, October: A Thoreaunal, 2002, Margaret Stucki: A Pictorial Autobiography of the Swiss-American Artist (1928—), 2004, Croak: USSR-USA Top Secret Weather Control Tesla-Tech, 2005. Pub. spkr. Rorschach Soc. Projective Techniques, London, 1968, 3d Internat. Congress Social Psychiatry, Zagreb, Yugoslavia, 1970, Women for Constl. Gov., Washington, 1975, nat. convs., Boston, 1977, West Palm Beach, Fla., 1988, Rotary Club, Farmington, Maine, 1979. Recipient 4 awards for photography, 1951, 1961, 1997, 1999, Poetry prize, Swiss Civic Cultural Soc., 1983; grantee, Rsch. Coun., Finger Lakes, N.Y., 1967. Office: Stucki-Linstead Mus & Art Gallery 1050 E Center St Pocatello ID 83201-5201 Office Phone: 208-234-0478.

**STUCKY, SCOTT WALLACE,** lawyer; b. Hutchinson, Kans., Jan. 11, 1948; s. Joe Edward and Emma Clara (Graber) S.; m. Jean Elsie Seibert, Aug. 18, 1973; children: Mary-Clare, Joseph. BA summa cum laude, Wichita State U., 1970; JD, Harvard U., 1973; MA, Trinity U., 1980; LLM with high honors, George Washington U., 1983; postgrad., Nat. War Coll., 1993. Bar: Kans. 1973, U.S. Dist. Ct. Kans. 1973, U.S. Ct. Appeals (10th cir.) 1973, U.S. Ct. Mil. Appeals 1974, U.S. Supreme Ct. 1976, D.C. 1979, U.S. Ct. Appeals (D.C. cir.) 1979. Assoc. Ginsburg, Feldman & Bress, Washington, 1978-82; chief docketing and svc. br. Nuclear Regulatory Commn., Washington, 1982-83; legis. counsel U.S. Air Force USAF, Washington, 1983-96, gen. counsel sen. com. on armed svcs., 1996—2001, 2003—, prin. minority counsel, 2001—03. Lectr. bus. law Maria Regina Coll., Syracuse, N.Y., 1977; congrl. fellow Office Senator John Warner, 1986; res. judge adv. USAF Res., Washington, 1982-2003; col. Appellate Mil. Judge, USAF Ct. Criminal Appeals, 1991-95, 97-98, 2001-03; sr. reservist USAF Judiciary, 1995-97, Air Res. Pers. Ctr., 1998-99, Air Force Legal Svcs. Agy., 1999-2001. Contbr. articles to profl. jours. Capt. USAF, 1973-78. Decorated Legion of Merit, Air Force Meritorious Svc. medal with two oak leaf cluster. Mem. Fed. Bar Assn., Judge Advs. Assn. (bd. dirs. 1984-88), Res. Officers Assn., Wichita State U. Alumni Assn. (pres. chpt. 1981-86, nat. bd. dirs. 1986-92), Adoption Svc. Info. Agy. (bd. dirs. 1998-2002, 2004—), Army and Navy Club (Washington), Mil. Order of Loyal Legion U.S. (state comdr. and recorder 1984-92, nat. treas. 1987-89, nat. vice comdr. 1989-93, nat. comdr.-in-chief 1993-95), Sons of Union Vets Civil War (chpt. vice-comdr 1986-88), Phi Delta Phi, Phi Alpha Theta, Phi Kappa Phi, Omicron Delta Kappa, Sigma Phi Epsilon. Republican. Episcopalian. Home: 11004 Homeplace Ln Potomac MD 20854-1406 Office: Sen Armed Svcs Com 228 Senate Office Bldg Washington DC 20510-0001 Office Phone: 202-224-8629.

**STUCKY, STEVEN (EDWARD),** composer, conductor; b. Hutchinson, Kans., Nov. 7, 1949; s. Victor Eugene and Louise Doris (Trautwein) Stucky; m. Melissa Jane Whitehead, Aug. 22, 1970; children: Maura Catharine, Matthew Steven. MusB, Baylor U., 1971; MFA, Cornell U., 1973, DMA, 1978. Vis. asst. prof. Lawrence U., Appleton, Wis., 1978-80; prof. Cornell U., Ithaca, NY, 1980—, chmn. dept. music, 1992-97; vis. prof. Eastman Sch. of Music, 2001—02; Ernest Bloch vis. prof. U. Calif., Berkeley, 2003. Composer-in-residence L.A. Philharm. Orch., 1988—, Am. Acad. Rome, 2006. Author: Lutoslawski and His Music, 1981 (Deems Taylor award ASCAP 1982); composer: Sappho Fragments, 1982, Voyages, 1984, Boston Fancies, 1985, Dreamwaltzes, 1986, Concerto for orch., 1987, Son et Lumière, 1988, Angelus, 1990, Impromptus, 1991, Four Poems of A.R. Ammons, 1992, Ancora, 1994, Double Flute Co., 1994, Fanfares and Arias, 1994, Pinturas de Tamayo, 1995, Music for Saxophones and Strings, 1996, Cradle Songs, 1997, Concerto Mediterraneo, 1998, Ad Parnassum, 1998, American Muse, 1999, Nell'ombra, nella luce, 2000, Etudes, 2000, Partita-Pastorale, after J.S.B., 2000, Concerto for Percussion and Wind Orchestra, 2001, Skylarks, 2001, Colburn Variations, 2002, Whispers, 2002, Album Leaves, 2002, Spirit Voices, 2003, Jeu de timbres, 2003, Second Concerto for Orchestra, 2003 (Pulitzer Prize for music, 2005), To Whom I Said Farewell, 2003, Sonate en forme de préludes, 2004, Piano Quartet, 2005, Three New Motets, 2005; received commn. from Nat. Endowment for Arts, 1982, Koussevitzky Found., 1991, Meet the Composer, 1995, 2004. Bd. advisors Barlow Endowment, 1993-97; bd. dirs. MacDowell Colony, 1993-95, Kousservitzky Found., 2006—. Fellow Guggenheim Found., Nat. Endowment for the Arts, Bogliasco Found., Goddard Lieberson fellow Am. Acad. Arts and Letters. Fellow: Am. Acad. Arts & Scis. Office: c/o Philip Wilder 21C Media Group 162 56th St Ste 201 New York NY 10019 Office Phone: 212-245-2110 ext. 205. Personal E-mail: stevenstucky@mac.com.

**STUDDARD, RUBEN (CHRISTOPHER RUBEN STUDDARD),** singer; b. Birmingham, Ala., July 14, 1978; s. Kevin Studdard Sr. and Emily Studdard. Graduated, Ala. A&M U., 2000. Singer, and soul band Just a Few Cats; singer, gospel group God's Gift. Backup singer: American Idol: The Search for a Superstar, 2002; singer, 2003 (named American Idol, 2003), (single) Flying Without Wings, 2003, (albums) Soulful, 2003, I Need an Angel, 2004, The Return, 2006; singer: (with various artists) American Idol Season 2: All Time, 2003; cameo Scooby Doo 2: Monsters Unleashed, 2004; nominee commentator: I Wanna Thank My Mama: The BET Awards 2004 Nomination Special; performer: American Idol Tour, 9th Annual Walk of Fame Honoring Aretha Franklin, 2003, Fromage, 2003, American Idol Christmas, 2003, 3rd Annual BET Awards, 2003, Good Morning America, 2004; guest appearances Oprah Winfrey Show, 2003, 2004, Making the Video, Ruben Studdard: Flying Without Wings, 2003, American Juniors, 2003, Sharon Osbourne Show, 2003, Late Show with David Letterman, 2004, The Ellen DeGeneres Show, 2004, Mad TV, 2004, One on One, 2004, Jimmy Kimmel Live, 2004. Nominee Grammy award for best male vocal R&B performance. He was nicknamed the 'Velvet Teddy Bear' by the legendary soulful diva Gladys Knight. During the competition he acknowledged his home town of Birmingham, Alabama by wearing a t-shirt adorned with the city area code "205." The state declared March 11 'Ruben Studdard Day.' Office: J Records 745 5th Ave New York NY 10151 Office Phone: 646-840-5600.

**STUDEBAKER, JOHN MILTON,** utilities engineer, consultant, educator; b. Springfield, Ohio, Mar. 31, 1935; s. Frank Milton and Monaruth (Beatty) S.; m. Virginia Ann Van Pelt, Mar. 12, 1960; 1 child, Jacqueline Ann Allcorn. BS in Law, LaSalle U., Chgo., 1969; MS and PhD in Indsl. Engring., Columbia Pacific U., San Rafael, Calif., 1984. Cert. plant engr. Am. Inst. Plant Engrs., profl. cons. Acad. Profl. Cons. & Advisors. Indsl engr. Internat. Harvest Co., 1957-60, supr. indsl. engring., 1960-66, gen. supr. body assembly, 1967-68, mgr. indsl. engring., 1968-70; mgr. manufacturing engring. Lamb Electric Co., 1970—76, Cascade Corp., 1976—88; engring. mgr. Bundy Tubing Corp., Winchester and Cynthia, Ky., 1988—98; chmn. The Studebaker Group, Inc., Alexandria, Va., 1998—; pres. Studebaker Energy Cons., LLC, 1998—. Instr. numerous univs. including Boston U., Clemson U., Cornell U., Harvard U., Duquesne U., U. Ala., U. Ill., U. Wis., Ga. State U., James Madison U., Tex. Tech. U., U. Calif., Calif. State U., Columbia U., Fairleigh Dickinson U., San Francisco State U.; instr. Am. Mgmt. Assn., Rochester Inst. Tech., Ctr. for Profl. Advancement. Author: Slashing Utility Costs Handbook, Natural Gas Purchasing Handbook, Electricity Retail Wheeling Handbook, Electricity Purchasing Handbook, Utility Negotiation

Handbook, ESCO Handbook. Mem. NSPE, Am. Inst. Facility Engrs. (cert.), Assn. Energy Engrs. (instr.). Republican. Home and Office: PO Box 708 Winchester KY 40392-0708 Office Phone: 859-744-1018. Business E-Mail: jstudebaker@studebakerenergy.net.

**STUDEMAN, BILL (WILLIAM OLIVER STUDEMAN),** aerospace transportation executive, former federal agency administrator, retired naval officer; b. Brownsville, Tex., Jan. 16, 1940; s. Oliver Jennings and Gail (McDavitt) S.; m. Gloria Diane Jeans, Sept. 12, 1964; children: Kimberly, Michael, Kate. BA, U. of S. Sewanee, 1962; student, Def. Intelligence Sch., 1966-67; M in Internat. Affairs, George Washington U., 1973; postgrad., Naval War Coll., 1973, Nat. War Coll., 1981; DSc in Strategic Intelligence (hon.), Def. Intelligence Coll., 1987. Commd. ensign USN, 1963, advanced through grades to admiral, 1992; ret. 1995; analyst Naval Intelligence Support Ctr., Washington, 1974-75; exec. asst. Office Naval Intelligence, Washington, 1975-76; officer in charge FOSIC Norfolk, CINLANTFLT, Norfolk, Va., 1976-78; asst. chief of staff COMSIXTHFLEET, Gaeta, Italy, 1978-80; exec. asst. Office of VCNO, Washington, 1981-82; comdg. officer Navy Operational Intel Command, Washington, 1982-84; dir. long range planning USN, Washington, 1984-85; dir. Naval Intelligence, Washington, 1985-88, Nat. Security Agy., MD, 1988-92; dep. dir. CIA, Washington, 1991-95; sr. v.p., dep. gen. mgr. for intelligence & info. superiority, Northrop Grumann Mission Systems Northrop Grumman Corp. (formerly TRW), Reston, Va., 1996—. Mem. Commn. on Intelligence Capabilities of the US Regarding Weapons of Mass Destruction, 2004. Decorated Legion of Merit with two gold stars, Naval and Intelligence D.S.M.; recipient President's Nat. Security medal. Mem. Armed Forces Comm. and Electronics Assn., Nat. Mil. Intelligence Assn., Naval Intelligence Profls., Assn. Former Intelligence Officers, Episcopalian. Avocations: sailing, rebuilding cars. Office: Northrop Grumman Mission Systems 12011 Sunset Hills Rd Reston VA 20190

**STUDER, LOUIS,** priest, religious organization administrator; b. Algona, Iowa, Oct. 24, 1949; s. Paul Otto and Marcella Bertha (West) Studer. BA in Sociology, Lewis U., 1971; MDiv in Theology, Weston Coll. Sch. Theology, 1975; MS in Edn. Adminstrn. and Supervision, So. Ill. U., 1979; PhD in Philosophy of Edn., St. Louis U., 1984. Ordained priest Roman Cath. Ch., 1976. Assoc. pastor St. Patrick's Parish, McCook, Nebr., 1976—77; prin. St. Henry's Seminary, Belleville, Ill., 1977—84; dir. campus ministry U. Minn., Duluth, Minn., 1984—86; dir. Pre-Novitiate Program, Omaha, 1986—89, St. Louis, 1989—91; vocation dir. Oblate House Theology, Chgo., 1991—96; sabbatical program Jerusalem, Israel, Cambridge, Mass., 1996—97; dir. Shrine of Our Lady of the Snows & Missionary Assn. of Mary Immaculate, Belleville, 1997—. Provincial coun. mem. Oblates of Mary Immaculate, St. Paul, 1990—99. Author: (book) The High School Seminary in U.S. Today, 1984. Bd. dirs. Bethany Place, Belleville, 1998—. Home: 442 S De Mazenod Dr Belleville IL 62223 Office: Nat Shrine of Our Lady of the Snows 442 S DeMazenod Dr Belleville IL 62223

**STUDER, PATRICIA S.,** psychologist; b. Ft. Scott, Kans., Sept. 3, 1942; d. Herb E. Studer and Mary Edith (McElroy) Cook; children: Mary Paige, Catherine Ann. BS, Cen. Mo. State U., Warrensburg, 1964; MS, Pittsburg (Kans.) State U., 1975; PsyD, U. Minn., 1999. Lic. psychologist N.Y., Mo.; cert. elem. tchr. Mo. Supervisory tchr. Cen. Mo. State U., 1966; tchr. Consolidated Sch. Dist. 1, Hickman Mills, Mo., 1964-68; clin. psychologist Nevada (Mo.) State Hosp., 1977-80, chief unit psychologist, 1980-83; dir. psychology dept., staff psychologist Raphael Ctr. Hosp., Nevada, 1982-83; exec. dir., psychologist Nevada Counseling Ctr., 1983-91; adj. med. staff Nevada Regional Med. Ctr., 1983-99; exec. dir. Ctr. for Human Devel., Nevada, Mo., 1992-95. Practicum supr. Pittsburg State U., 1980-95; clin. supr. Cmty. Counseling Cons., Cinton, Mo., 1987-88; cons. psychologist Barton County Meml. Hosp., 1993-95, Heartland Hosp., Nevada, 1995, South Oaks Hosp., L.I., 1999-2000, Clin. PsychAssocs., N.Y., 2000—; mem. Com. for Drug Free Schs., Nevada, 1988-95, cons. psychologist, 1988-90; cons. psychotherapist Nevada Child Abuse Coun., 1981-82; pvt. practice, Long Island, N.Y., 2001. Mem. The Nelson-Adkins Mus. Art; mem. Mo. Regional Adv. Coun. on Alcohol and Drug Abuse, 1985-94, v.p., 1988, 92; bd. dirs. Mental Health Adv. Bd., 1993-95, Sch. Health Adv. Com., 1994-95. Mem. APA (assoc.)., Mo. Psychol. Assn., Soroptimist Internat. of Nevada (pres. 1992-93), Rotary Internat., Nevada Vernon County C. of C. Avocations: gardening, interior decorating, environmental issues. Home: 6 Mt Morris Park West New York NY 10027

**STUDER, WILLIAM ALLEN,** security consultant, retired military officer; b. Chgo., July 27, 1939; s. William Gotlieb and Annette Elizabeth (Bruzek) S.; m. Donna Barnes Bray, Dec. 26, 1961; children: Scott, Shannon. BS in Indsl. Mgmt., Ga. Inst. Tech., 1961; MS in Guidance and Counseling, Troy State U., 1975, MS in Mgmt., 1978; student, Air War Coll., Maxwell AFB, Ala., 1980-81. Commd. 2d lt. USAF, 1961, advanced through grades to maj. gen., 1989; legis. liaison U.S. Senate, Washington, 1981-83; dir. fighter ops./tng. USAF Hdqrs. Europe, Ramstein AB, Fed. Republic Germany, 1983-84; vice comdr. 10th Tactical Reconnaissance Wing RAF USAF, Alconbury, Eng., 1984-85, comdr. 10th Tactical Reconnaissance Wing RAF, 1985-86, cmdr. 81st Tactical Fighter Wing RAF Bentwaters, Eng., 1986-87, comdr. 316th Air Div/Kaiserslautern Ramstein AB, Fed. Republic Germany, 1987-88, vice comdr. 12th Air Force/U.S. So. Command Bergstrom AFB, Tex., 1988-90, comdr. 13th Air Force Clark AFB, The Philippines, 1990-91; dir. ops. CENTCOM/J-3, MacDill AFB, Fla., 1992-94; ret. USAF, 1994; dir. pub. safety dept. Hillsborough County, Tampa, Fla., 1994—2005, emergency preparedness cons., 2005—; pres. Studer & Assoc., Tampa. Decorated D.S.M., Legion of Merit with oak leaf cluster, DFC with three oak leaf clusters, Bronze Star, Air medal with 35 oak leaf clusters; Legion of Honor, Bronze Cross medal (The Philippines). Mem. Daedalians, Quiet Birdmen, Rotary. Avocations: golf, reading. Home: 5309 Bayshore Blvd Tampa FL 33611 Office: Studer & Assoc Tampa FL 33611 Personal E-mail: studerdm@verizon.net.

**STUDER, WILLIAM JOSEPH,** library director; b. Whiting, Ind., Oct. 1, 1936; s. Victor E. and Sarah G. (Hammersley) S.; m. Rosemary Lippie, Aug. 31, 1957; children: Joshua E., Rachel Marie. BA, Ind. U., 1958, MA, 1960, PhD (Univ. fellow), 1968. Grad. asst. divsn. libr. sci. Ind. U., 1959-60, reference asst., 1960-61; spl. intern Libr. of Congress, 1961-62, reference libr., sr. bibliographer, 1962-65; dir. regional campus libr. Ind. U., Bloomington, 1968-73, assoc. dean univ. librs., 1973-77; dir. librs. Ohio State U., Columbus, 1977-2000, prof. emeritus libr. sci., 2000—, coord. univ. oral history program, 2001—. Mem. Libr. Svcs. and Constrn. Act Adv. Com. of Ind., 1971-76; mem. Adv. Coun. on Fed. Libr. Programs in Ohio, 1977-85, chmn., 1980-81; adv. coun. Libr. Svcs. and Tech. Act, 1997-99; mem. ARL Office Mgmt. Studies Adv. Com., 1977-81, ARL Task Force on Nat. Libr. Network Devel., 1978-83, bd. dirs., 1981-84, chmn., 1981-83, com. on preservation, 1985-88, vice-chmn., 1989-90, chmn., 1992-93, task force on scholarly comm., 1983-87, com. stats. and measurement, 1993-99, chmn., 1997-98; network adv. com. Libr. Congress, 1981-88; libr. study com. Ohio Bd. Regents, 1986-87; mem. steering com. Ohio Libr. and Info. Network (OhioLINK), 1987-90; vice-chmn. Ctr. Rsch. Librs., 1993-94, chmn., 1994-95, sec., chmn. membership com., 1990-93; adv. coun. OhioLink Libr., 1992-2000, chmn., 1991-92, policy adv. coun., governing bd., 1991-92. Contbr. articles to profl. jours. Trustee Online Computer Libr. Ctr. Inc., 1977-78; del. Online Computer Libr. Ctr. Users Coun., 1983-91; rsch. librs. adv. com. Online Computer Libr. Ctr., 1989-95, vice-chmn., chmn.-elect, 1993-94, chmn., 1994-95; bd. dirs. Ohio Network of Librs. Ohionet, 1977-87, chmn., 1980-82, 86-87, treas., 1983-86; mem. Columbia U. Sch. Libr. Svc. Conservation Programs, vis. com., 1987-90; nat. adv. coun. to preserve. on preservation and access, 1989-92; treas. Monroe County (Ind.) Mental Health Assn., 1968-76; budget rev. com. United Way, 1975-77; bd. dirs. Mental Health Assn. Recipient citation for participation MARC Insts., 1968-69, Disting. Alumni award Ind. U., 1978, OhioLINK Founders award, 2002. Mem. ALA, Ohio Libr. Assn. (bd. dirs. 1980-83), Assn. Coll. and Rsch. Librs. (bd. dirs. 1977-81, com. on activities model for 1990, 1981-82, chmn. libr. sch. curriculum task force 1988-89), Ohio State U. Retirees Assn. (pres.-elect 2004-05, pres. 2005-06), Acad. Libr. Assn. Ohio, Torch Club (pres. 1993-94),

Phi Kappa Phi (pub. rels. officer 1982-83, sec. 1983-85), Phi Eta Sigma, Alpha Epsilon Delta., Beta Phi Mu. Home: 724 Olde Settler Pl Columbus OH 43214-2924 Office: Ohio State U William Oxley Thompson Meml Libr 1858 Neil Ave Columbus OH 43210-1286 Office Phone: 614-688-0204. Business E-Mail: studer.2@osu.edu.

**STUDEVANT, LAURA,** medical association administrator; Pres. Nat. Environ. Health Assn., Denver; regional health mgr. Amtrak, Chgo. Address: Regional Pub Health Mgr Amtrak 210 S Canal Chicago IL 60606 Office: National Environ Health Assn 720 S Colorado Blvd Ste 970S Denver CO 80246-1925

**STUDIN, JAN,** publishing executive; From acct. mgr. to v.p. Woman's Day, 1982—95, v.p., advt. dir., 1995—96; v.p., pub. Woman's Day Hachette Filipacchi Mags., Inc., NYC, 1996—2002; v.p., pub. Parents Mag., 2002—06, Better Homes & Gardens Mag., 2006—. Office: Better Homes & Gardens 125 Park Ave New York NY 10017 Office Phone: 212-557-6600.*

**STUDLEY, JAMIENNE SHAYNE,** lawyer, educator; b. NYC, Apr. 30, 1951; d. Jack Hill and Joy (Cosor) Studley; m. Gary J. Smith, July 14, 1984. BA magna cum laude, Barnard Coll., 1972; JD, Harvard U., 1975. Bar: DC 1975, U.S. Dist. Ct. DC 1978. Assoc. Bergson, Borkland, Margolis & Adler, Washington, 1976—80; spl. asst., sec. U.S. HHS, 1980—81; assoc. Weil, Gotshal & Manges, Washington, 1981—83; assoc. dean law sch. Yale U., New Haven, 1983—87; lectr. law, 1984—87; exec. dir. Nat. Assn. for Law Placement, Washington, 1987—90; syndicated columnist Am. Lawyer Media, 1990—91; exec. dir. Calif. Abortion Rights Action League, 1992—93; dep. gen. counsel U.S. Dept. Edn., 1993—99, acting gen. counsel, 1997—99; pres. Skidmore Coll., Saratoga Springs, NY, 1999—2003; scholar-in-residence Carnegie Found. for the Advancement of Tchg., Palo Alto, Calif., 2003—04; pres. Pub. Advocates, Inc., 2004—. Vis. scholar adj. faculty U. Calif., Berkeley Law Sch., 1992; bd. dirs. Assn. Am. Colls. & U., 2001—, treas., 2006—; bd. dirs. Adirondack Trust Co., 1999—2003; vis. com. Harvard Law Sch., 1999—2005; vice chair for program The Annapolis Group, 2001—03; chair legis. com. Commn. on Ind. Colls. and Univs. N.Y. State, 2002—03. Pres. Conn. Women's Ednl. and Legal Fund, Hartford, 1986—87; co-founder Washington Area Women's Found., 1997; founding bd. dirs. Wood Art Collectors; mem. Jacob Javits fellowship bd. U.S. Dept. Edn., 2000—03; mem. policy com. Campus Compact, 2002—; co-chmn. Calif. Coalition for Civil Rights, 2005—; bd. dirs. The Urban Sch., San Francisco, 2004—; San Francisco Mus. Craft and Design, 2004—, Am. Craft Coun., 2005—. Mem.: ABA (commn. on women in the profession 1991—94, chair editl. bd. Perspectives 1991—99, chair coord. com. legal edn. 1996—97, com. on loan repayment and forgiveness 2001—03), Nat. Adv. Coun., First Book, Nat. Assn. for Ind. Colls. and Univs. (accountability com. 1999—2002), DC Bar Assn., Barnard in Washington (pres. 1977—78), Assn. Alumnae Barnard Coll. (bd. dirs. 1978—81), Phi Beta Kappa. Office: 131 Steuart St 300 San Francisco CA 94105-1241 Office Phone: 415-431-7430.

**STUDNESS, CHARLES MICHAEL,** economist; b. Mpls., Nov. 2, 1935; s. Leo C. and Alma (Mehus) S.; m. Harriet Leah Katz, Oct. 27, 1968; children: Erica, Lisa, Roy. BA, U. Minn., 1957, MA, 1958; PhD in Econs., Columbia U., 1963. Lectr. CCNY, 1961-64, U. Minn., Mpls., 1964-65; economist Fed. Res. Bank N.Y., N.Y.C., 1965-67, N.Y. Stock Exchange, N.Y.C., 1967-68, Eastern Airlines, N.Y.C., 1968-70, Baker Weeks, N.Y.C., 1970-76, E.F. Hutton, N.Y.C., 1976-79; pres. Studness Rsch., Manhasset, NY, 1979—; lectr. Baruch Coll., N.Y.C., 1968-74. Contbg. editor Public Utilities Fortnightly, 1990—. Columnist, Pub. Utilities Fortnightly, 1979—. Personal E-mail: studness@optonline.net.

**STUDWELL, WILLIAM EMMETT,** librarian, writer; b. Stamford, Conn., Mar. 18, 1936; s. Alfred Theodore and Mary Alice (Baker) S.; m. Ann Marie Stroia, Aug. 28, 1965 (dec. 2003); 1 child, Laura Ann. BA, U. Conn., 1958, MA, 1959; MLS, Cath. U. Am., 1967. Tech. abstracter Libr. Congress, Washington, 1963-66, asst. editor decimal classification office, 1966-68; head libr. Kirtland C.C., Roscommon, Mich., 1968-70; head/prin. cataloger No. Ill. U., DeKalb, 1970-2000; freelance writer, editor, 2001—. Mem. U.S. Adv. Com. to Chemistry Sects., Universal Decimal Classification, 1968-72; chmn. adv. group Libr. Rsch. Ctr., Urbana, Ill., 1982-84. Author: Chaikovskii, Delibes, Stravinskii, 1977, Christmas Carols, 1985, Adolphe Adam and Leo Delibes, 1987, Ballet Plot Index, 1987 (named One of Outstanding Acad. Books by Choice Mag. 1988-89), Cataloging Books, 1989, Library of Congress Subject Headings, 1990, Opera Plot Index, 1990, Christmas Card Songbook, 1991, Subject Access to Films and Videos, 1992, Popular Song Reader, 1994, Christmas Carol Reader, 1995, National and Religious Song Reader, 1996, Americana Song Reader, 1997, Minor Ballet Composers, 1997, State Songs of the United States, 1997 (acad. best seller), Publishing Glad Tidings, 1998, College Fight Songs, 1998, Barbershops, Bullets, and Ballads, 1999, Circus Songs, 1999, The End of the Year, 1999, The Classic Rock and Roll Reader, 1999, They Also Wrote, 2000, The Big Band Reader, 2000, The Clandestine Classical Music Reader, 2000, Forward! Forward! Is the Word, 2000, College Fight Songs II, 2001, Lest We Forget, 2001, A Fable, A Fantasy, and a Farewell, 2002, The French Violin School, 2002, Suzannah's Redemption, or The Devil Gets His Due, 2003, The Man Who Invented God and Other Fantastic Tales, 2004, Ten Terrible Tales, 2005, College Fight Songs III, 2005, The Christmas Carol in the New Millennium, 2006, An Easy Guide to Christmas Carols, 2006; asst. editor Western Assn. of Map Librs. Info. Bull., 1989-94; editor Music Reference Svcs. Quarterly, 1991-99, Resources in Music History Book Series, 1999—; text editor (Christmas music) The Millennia Collection, 2000—; contbg. editor Technicalities, 1996-2004; contbr. about 400 articles to profl. jours.; over 720 radio, TV and print media appearances. U.S. expert on Christmas Carols; internat. recognized expert on Am. Coll. fight songs; internat. leader to devel. standardization code for use, congress subject headings; leading internat. proponent multinat., multicultural and multilingual subject access sys. Named most productive author among librs. in U.S., Coll. and Rsch. Librs. Mag., 1983-87, 93-97, Outstanding Alumnus, Sch. Libr. and Info. Sci., Cath. U. Am., 2002. Mem. Ill. Assn. Coll. and Rsch. Librs. (exec. bd. 1980-85, newsletter editor 1980-85, lifetime achievement award 1992), Ill. Libr. Assn., Librs. for Social Responsibility (editor newsletter 1986-87, bd. dirs. 1986-94). Home: 3332 S Forrester St Bloomington IN 47401-7115

**STUDZINSKI, JOHN JOSEPH PAUL,** investment banking executive; b. Mass., Mar. 19, 1956; arrived in Eng., 1984; s. Alfred and Jennie S. AB, Bowdoin Coll., 1978; MBA, U. Chgo., 1980. Investment banker Morgan Stanley & Co. Ltd., N.Y.C., 1980; head, corp. fin. Morgan Stanley Internat. Inc., London, 1989—92, head, mergers & acquisitions European bus., 1992—97, head, investment banking Europe, 1997—2001, dep. chmn. 2001—03; co-chief exec. corp. investment banking, and markets (CIBM) HSBC Holdings, 2003—. Chmn. Bus. Action on Homelessness, London, 1999—; founder Passage Day Centre, London, 2000—; trustee Tate Gallery, 1998—; life trustee Sir John Soane Mus., 1999—; trustee Human Rights Watch, N.Y.C., 1999—, Bowdoin Coll. Named to Knight of the Order of St. Gregory, Pope John Paul II, 2001; recipient Prince of Wales Ambassador's award, 2000, dist. alumnus U. Chgo., 2002. Avocations: performing arts, hiking, outdoor survival. Office: HSBC Holdings 8 Canada Sq London E14 5HQ England

**STUEBING, EDWARD WILLIS,** research scientist; b. Cin., Sept. 9, 1942; s. Edward Norman and Ruth Marcella (Glass) S.; m. Mary Ann Brown (div. 1980); children: Barbara Jean, Jennifer Jane. BS with high honors, U. Cin., 1965; PhD, Johns Hopkins U., Balt., 1970. Rsch. scientist U.S. Army Frankford Arsenal, Phila., 1971—77; U.S. Army, Edgewood R&D Ctr., Aberdeen Proving Ground, Md., 1977—; joint svcs. bus. area mgr. CB Def. Supporting Sci. and Tech., 1994—2003, chief scientist for physical scis., 1999—2001, team leader aerosol sci., 1992—. Adj. prof. Drexel U., Phila., 1973-1976; invited lectr. nat. and internat. scientific meetings. Contbr. articles to profl. jours. Dir. Civic Assn., Kingsville, Md., 1989-92; pres. Gunpowder Valley Conservancy, Md., 1990-94, treas., 1995—; elder Presbyn. Ch., Franklinville, Md., 1993—. Capt. U.S. Army, 1970-71. Recipient Army R&D

Achievement award, 1974, 85, medal for Meritorious Civilian Svc., 1984, The Outstanding Fed. Profl. of 1984 award Fed. Exec. Bd., 1984, William H. Walker award, 1989. Mem. Am. Assn. for Aerosol Rsch. (chmn. nat. meeting 1983, dir. 1998—2001), Am. Chem. Soc., Am. Phys. Soc., Phi Beta Kappa, Sigma Xi. Avocations: trombone, sailing. Home: PO Box 233 Gunpowder MD 21010-0233 Office: Attn AMSRD ECB RT TA Bldg E5951 5183 Blackhawk Rd Aberdeen Proving Ground MD 21010-5424

**STUEBNER, ERWIN AUGUST, JR.,** internist; b. Phila., Oct. 9, 1944; s. Erwin August and Frances Badge (Quinn) S.; m. Jane Sigrid Christensen, Sept. 21, 1968; children: Eric Jay, Andrew Todd, Scott August. AB, Dartmouth Coll., 1966; MD, Northwestern U., Chgo., 1970. Diplomate Am. Bd. Internal Medicine. Intern, resident U. Mich., Ann Arbor, 1970-74; physician Williamstown (Mass.) Med. Assocs., 1976—; chmn. dept. medicine North Adams (Mass.) Regional Hosp., 1991—2003, 2005—. Corporator North Adams Regional Hosp., 1992-; bd. dirs. Med. Profl. Mut. Ins. Co., Boston, 1995-. Fundraising chmn. Campaign for New Athletic Field, Williamstown, Mass., 1995-96. Maj. U.S. Army, 1974-76; trustee No. Berkshire Health Sys., 2002—. Mem. ACP, Am. Heart Assn. (exec. com. 1978-94), Mass. Med. Soc. (trustee 1988-94, 2000—06, alt. trustee 1994-2000, 06—), Berkshire Dist. Med. Soc. (pres. 1984-86, exec. com. 1982-). Avocations: hiking, tennis, travel, classical music. Office: Williamstown Med Assn 197 Adams Rd Williamstown MA 01267-2930

**STUEBNER, JAMES CLOYD,** real estate developer, contractor; b. Phila., Dec. 15, 1931; s. Erwin A. and Frances (Quinn) Stuebner; children: Kathleen, Stephen, James, Susan, Elizabeth. BA, Dartmouth Coll., 1953. Sales engr. Rohm & Haas Co., Phila., 1956-69; pres. Structural Plastics Corp., Mpls., 1961-69; pres., gen. ptnr. Stuebner Properties, Mpls., 1969—; pres. Northland Inn and Exec. Conf. Ctr., 1988—; CEO Five Star Realty and Devel. Co., Mpls., 1992—; Boone 94 Properties (Sleep Inn Hotel), 1998. Mem. Minn. Conv. Ctr. Commn., St. Paul, 1988; commr. Minn. Econ. Devel. Commn., St. Paul, 1985; bd. dirs. Bach Soc. of Minn., Mpls., 1986—, Minn. Orchestral Assn., Mpls., 1988-91. Sgt. U.S. Army, 1953-55. Mem. Nat. Assn. Office and Indsl. Parks (bd. dirs. Minn. chpt. 1976-85, 81-90, pres. 1978-80, 92-93, nat. pres. 1983-84, v.p. 1981-81, Developer of Yr. award 1987, Minn. Bus. Person of Yr. award 1990, vice chmn. indsl. devel. forum 1996, chmn. 1997). Avocations: sailing, running, singing. Office: Stuebner Properties 7000 Northland Dr N Minneapolis MN 55428-1502 Office Phone: 763-535-5093. Business E-Mail: jstuebner@qwest.net.

**STUEHRENBERG, PAUL FREDERICK,** librarian; b. Breckenridge, Minn., Mar. 14, 1947; s. Henry Ernest Frederick and Marian Violet (Sandberg) S.; m. Suzanne Elaine Draper, June 14, 1969 (div. Apr. 1982); m. Carole Lee DeVore, Aug. 1, 1983. BA, Concordia Sr. Coll., 1968; MDiv, Concordia Sem., 1972; STM, Christ Sem., 1974; MA, U. Minn., 1978, PhD, 1988. Asst. libr. U. Minn., Mpls., 1974-82; monographs libr. Yale Divinity Libr., New Haven, 1982-91, div. libr., 1991—; adj. assoc. prof. in theol. lit. Yale Divinity Sch., New Haven, 1993—. Asst. pastor Christ Meml. Luth. Ch., Plymouth, Minn., 1974-82; adj. pastor Bethesda Luth. Ch., New Haven, 1984—; sec. Luth. Student Found., Mpls., 1978-81. Contbr. articles to profl. jours. Sec. North Haven (Conn.) Libr. Bd., 1989-2003. Mem. Am. Theol. Libr. Assn. (pres. 2004-05), Soc. Bibl. Lit., Am. Acad. Religion, North Haven Meml. Libr. Assn. Home: 280 Bayard Ave North Haven CT 06473-4307 Office: Yale U Div Sch Libr 409 Prospect St New Haven CT 06511-2167 E-mail: paul.stuehrenberg@yale.edu.

**STUHAN, RICHARD GEORGE,** lawyer; b. Braddock, Pa., July 1, 1951; s. George and Pauline Madeline (Pavlocik) S.; m. Mary Ann Cipriano, Aug. 23, 1975; children: Brendan George, Sara Katherine, Brian Christopher, Caitlin Emily. BA summa cum laude, Duquesne U., 1973; JD, U. Va., 1976. Bar: Va. 1976, D.C. 1977, U.S. Ct. Appeals (D.C. cir.) 1977, U.S. Ct. Appeals (4th cir.) 1977, U.S. Claims Ct. 1979, U.S. Supreme Ct. 1980, U.S. Ct. Appeals (3d cir.) 1981, U.S. Ct. Appeals (11th cir.) 1982, U.S. Dist. Ct. (no. dist.) Ohio 1985, Ohio 1986. Assoc. Arnold & Porter, Washington, 1976-84; of counsel Jones Day, Cleve., 1984-86, ptnr., 1987—. Pres. Womankind Maternal and Prenatal Care; chmn. devel. com. Doan Brook Watershed Partnership. Mem. Va. Law Review, 1974-76. Recipient Gold Medal for Gen. Excellence, Duquesne U., 1973; named Ohio Super Lawyer, Law and Politics Media, Inc. Mem. Cleve. Bar Assn. (chmn. jury svc. com.), Internat. Assn. Def. Counsel, Order of Coif. Democrat. Roman Catholic. Avocations: tennis, swimming, basketball, home repair. Home: 2865 Falmouth Rd Shaker Heights OH 44122-2838 Office: Jones Day 901 Lakeside Ave Cleveland OH 44114-1190 Office Phone: 216-586-7148. Business E-Mail: rgstuhan@jonesday.com.

**STUHL, OSKAR PAUL,** scientific and regulatory consultant; b. Dec. 23, 1949; s. Johannes Alexander and Johanna Wilhelmine (Hoelling) S. S. Dipl. Chem., U. Duesseldorf, 1976, Dr.rer.nat., 1978. Tutor Inst. Organische Chemie U. Duesseldorf, 1975-76, sci. assoc., 1976-79; mgr. product devel. Drugofa GmbH, Cologne, Fed. Republic of Germany, 1980; mgr. sci. rels. RJRN, Cologne, 1981-88, mgr. sci. svcs., 1989-94; co-founder, co-owner WRKM Internat., 1996—. Cons. in field, 1995—. Mem. editl. bd. Beitraege zur Tabakforschung Internat., 1986-96; contbr. articles to profl. jours.; patentee in field. Mem. Duesseldorf Mus. Verein, Verein der Freunde des Hetjens-Museums, Verein de Freunde des Stadtmuseums Duesseldorf, Met. Mus. Art, N.Y.C., Friends Royal Acad. Arts, London, Friends of Tate Gallery, London, Art Soc. of Rheinlande and Westfalen, Gesellschaft der Freunde der Kunstammlung NRW, Gesellschaft der Freunde und Foerderer der Univ. Duesseldorf, Zuercher Kunstgesellschaft, Freundeskreis Theatermuseum, Duesseldorf, Foerderverein NRW-Stiftung, Forum fuer Film, Duesseldorf, Freunde und Foerder der Akademie fuer Kommunikations Design, Duesseldorf, Deutsch-Japanische-Gesellschaft. Mem. AAAS, Gesellschaft Deutscher Chemiker, Gesellschaft Deutscher Naturforscher und Aerzte, Max-Planck-Gesellschaft, Deutsche Gesellschaft fuer Arbeits hygiene, Am. Chem. Soc. (including various chmns.), Chem. Soc. Japan, N.Y. Acad. Scis., Royal Soc. Chemistry, Am. Pharm. Assn., Acad. Pharm. Rsch. and Sci., Internat. Union Pure and Applied Chemistry, Am. Soc. Pharmacognosy, Fedn. Internat. Pharmaceutic, Christlich Demokratische Union, Vereinigung AC Club Duesseldorf, PCL Club (London), KDStV Burgundia-Leipzig Club, Golf Club Velbert. CDU-Mittelstands und Wirtschaftsvereinigung. Roman Catholic. Office: PO Box 140544 D-40075 Düsseldorf Germany

**STUHLINGER, ERNST,** physicist; b. Niederrimbach, Germany, Dec. 19, 1913; came to U.S., 1946, naturalized, 1955. s. Ernst and Pauline (Werner) S.; m. Irmgard Lotze, Aug. 1, 1950; children: Susanne, Tilman, Hans Christoph. PhD, U. Tuebingen, Germany, 1936; PhD (hon.), Tech. U., Berlin. Asst. prof. Technische Hochschule, Berlin, Germany, 1936-41; guidance and control equipment rocket Devel. Center, Peenemuende, Germany, 1943-45; with Guided Missile Devel. Office, Ft. Bliss, Tex., 1946-50; physicist Ordnance Missile Labs., Huntsville, Ala., 1950-56, Army Ballistic Missile Agy., 1956-60; dir. Space Scis. Lab., George C. Marshall Space Flight Center, NASA, Huntsville, Ala., 1960-68; assoc. dir. for sci. George C. Marshall Space Flight Center, NASA, 1968-76; sr. research scientist, adj. prof. U. Ala. at Huntsville, 1976-84; sr. research assoc. Teledyne Brown Engring. Corp., Huntsville, 1984-88; cons. aerospace cos. Vis. scientist Tech. U. Munich, W. Germany, 1978, Max Planck Inst. Nuclear Physics, Heidelberg, 1983-85; cons. Teledyne-Brown Engring., 1984-90. Author: Ion Propulsion for Space Flight, 1964; co-author: Skylab, A Guidebook, 1973, Project Viking, 1974, Aufbruch in Den Weltraum, 1992, Wernher von Braun, Crusader for Space, 1994. Served with German Army, 1941-43, Russian Campaign. Recipient Humboldt prize Tech. U. Munich, 1978, Rainer Bauer award Ala.-Germany Partnership, 2002; induction Ala. Aviation Hall of Fame, 2001. Fellow Am. Astronautical Soc., mem. Von Braun Astron. Soc. (dir.), German Physikalische Ges., Hermann Oberth Assn. (hon.), Internat. Foerderkreis fuer Raumfahrt (hon. pres. 2004—). Rsch. cosmic rays, nuclear physics, electric space propulsion, manned missions to Mars. Home: 3106 Rowe Dr SE Huntsville AL 35801-6151

**STUHLMILLER, DAVID FE,** emergency physician; m. Christine M. Watters; 1 child, Sarah Christine. MD, Temple U. Sch. Medicine, Phila., 1998. Diplomate Am. Bd. Emergency Medicine, 2002. Attending physician and sr. instr. MetroHealth Med. Ctr., Case Western Res. U., Cleve., 2001—04; attending physician and asst. emergency med. dir. Emergency Med. Assocs. of Westchester Med. Ctr., Valhalla, NY, 2005—; med. dir., lifenet of N.Y. Air Methods, Valhalla, 2005—. Fellow: Am. Coll. Emergency Physicians (councillor 2006, bd. mem.); mem.: Soc. Academic Emergency Medicine, Nat. Assn. EMS Physicians (asst. chair, air med. transport com. 2004—06), Air Med. Physician Assn. Achievements include research in EMS and medical helicopter transport. Office: Westchester Med Ctr Maria Fareri Children's Hosp Rm 1250 Valhalla NY 10595 Office Phone: 914-493-7656. Office Fax: 914-493-8298. Business E-Mail: stuhlmillerd@wcmc.com.

**STUHR, ELAINE RUTH,** state legislator; b. Polk County, Nebr., June 19, 1936; m. Boyd E. Stuhr, 1956; children: Cynthia (Stuhr) Zluticky, Teresa (Stuhr) Robbins, Boyd E., Jr. BS, U. Nebr. Tchr. jr. and sr. vocat. h.s. Nebr. schs.; senator Nebr. Unicameral, Lincoln, 1994—; chmn. Nebr. retirement sys. com.; vice chair natural resources com.; commr. edn. com. of states; farmer Bradshaw, Nebr. Former asst. instr. U. Nebr., Lincoln; participant farmer to farmer assignment to Russia with Winrock, Internat., 1993, to Lithuania with Vol. Overseas Coop. Asistance, 1993; former pres. Agrl. Womens Leadership Network; former mem. bd. dirs. Feed Grains Coun., Nebr. Corn Bd. Past pres., bd. dirs. Found. for Agrl. Edn. and Devel.; former mem. exec. com. and bd. dirs. Agrl. Coun. Am.; nat. pres. Women Involved in Farm Econs., state pres.; mem. adv. com. Nebr. Extension Sv.; bd. dirs. Heartland Ctr. for Leadership Devel.; past chmn. Nebr. Agrl. Leadership Coun. Republican. Office: Nebr State Capitol Dist # 24 Lincoln NE 68509 Office Phone: 402-471-2756. E-mail: estuhr@unicam.state.ne.us.

**STUKEL, JAMES JOSEPH,** academic administrator, mechanical engineer, educator; b. Joliet, Ill., Mar. 30, 1937; s. Philip and Julia (Mattivi) S.; m. Mary Joan Helpling, Nov. 27, 1958; children: Catherine, James, David, Paul. BS in Mech. Engring. Purdue U., 1959; MS, U. Ill., Urbana-Champaign, 1963, PhD, 1968. Research engr. W.Va. Pulp and Paper Co., Covington, Va., 1959-61; mem. faculty U. Ill., Urbana-Champaign, 1968—, prof. mech. engring., 1975—, dir. Office Coal Research and Utilization, 1974-76, dir. Office Energy Research, 1976-81, dir. pub. policy program Coll. Engring., 1981-84, assoc. dean Coll. Engring. and dir. Expt. Sta., 1984-85; dean Grad. Coll., vice chancellor for research U. Ill. at Chgo., 1985-86, exec. vice chancellor, vice chancellor academic affairs, 1986-91, interim chancellor, 1990-91, chancellor, 1991-95, pres., 1995—. V.p. Chgo. Tech. Park Corp., 1985-88, pres., 1990-91; exec. sec. midwest Consortium Air Pollution, 1972-73, chmn. bd. dirs., 1973-75; mem. adv. bd. regional studies program Argonne (Ill.) Nat. Lab., 1975-76; adv. com. Energy Resources Commn., 1976; chmn. panel on dispersed electric generating techs. Office Tech. Assessment, U.S. Congress, 1980-81; chmn. rev. adv. bd. tech. rev. dist. heating and combined heat and power systems Internat. Energy Agy, OECD, Paris, 1982-83; cons. in field. Contbr. articles to profl. jours. Pres. parish council Holy Cross Roman Cath. Ch., Urbana, 1967-68. Mem. ASCE (State-of-the-Art of Civil Engring. award 1975), ASME, AAAS, Sigma Xi, Phi Kappa Phi, Pi Tau Sigma. Home: 2650 N Lakeview Ave Apt 1610 Chicago IL 60614-1819 Office: 364 Henry Adm Bldg M/C 346 Urbana IL 61801

**STULA, NANCY,** museum director, curator; b. Hartford, Conn., Oct. 10, 1961; d. George and Wanda Stula. BA summa cum laude, U. Hartford, Conn., 1985; PhD in Art History, Columbia U., N.Y., 1997. Dep. dir. Lyman Allyn Art Mus., New London, Conn., 2003—, chief curator, 2003—. Trustee Hartford Art Sch., West Hartford, Conn., 2005—. Mem.: Am. Assn. Mus., Coll. Art Assn. Office: Lyman Allyn Art Mus 76 Lyme St Old Lyme CT 06371

**STULBERG, SAMUEL DAVID,** surgeon, physician; b. Lansing, Mich., Jan. 14, 1943; s. Julius and Esther (Leiberman) Stulberg; m. Jann Dragovich, Aug. 17, 1996; children: Lisa Michele, Debra Beth, Mark Jeffrey. BA cum laude, Harvard Coll., Cambridge, Mass., 1961—65; MD, U. Mich. Med. Sch., Ann Arbor, 1965—69; D Honoris Causa (hon.), U. Mediterrean, Marseilles, France, 1997. Orthop. surg. resident Harvard U., Cambridge, Mass., 1970—75; founder and dir., joint reconstruction and implant svc. Northwestern Meml. Hosp., Chgo., 1986—; prof., clin. orthop. surgery Northwestern U., Feinberg Sch. Medicine, Chgo., 1994—. Author: (book) Arthritis of the Hip & Knee; contbr. chapters to books, articles to profl. jours. Bd. dirs. Rehab. Inst. Chgo., 1996—2005; bd. mem. ACLU, Chgo., 1986—2005. Recipient Elven J. Berkheiser Prize, Inst. Medicine Chgo., M.E. Muller award, Helsinki, 2005; fellow, Orthopaedic Rsch. and Edn. Found. Fellow: Am. Acad. Orthop. Surgeons (life); mem.: Internat. Soc. for Computer Assisted Orthop. Surgery (pres. 2003—04), Internat. Soc. for Tech. in Arthroplasty, Internat. Soc. Arthroscopy, Knee Surgery and Orthop. Sports Medicine, Knee Soc. N.Am., Hip Soc. N.Am., Am. Assn. Hip and Knee Surgeons, Am. Orthop. Assn. Liberal. Jewish. Achievements include being a leader in the development of the field of computer-assisted orthopedic surgery; being a leader in the development of concepts, techniques and instruments for minimally invasive orthopedic surgery; design of multiple joint replacement systems, including: The Columbus Computer Assisted Knee System, The Continuum Knee System, The MicroLoc Knee System; patents for a computer-assisted surgical system; methods and instruments for performing radial impaction grafting for revision total hip surgery; invention of surgical systems for carrying out robotic and computer assisted surgery. Avocations: travel, running, photography, boating. Office: Northwestern Orthop Inst 680 N Lake Shore Dr #1028 Chicago IL 60611 Office Phone: 312-664-6848. Office Fax: 312-475-5624. E-mail: jointsurg@northwestern.edu.

**STULL, DONALD DAVID,** anthropologist, educator; b. Sebree, Ky., June 25, 1946; s. Emerson Bosse and Marjorie Dunville Stull; m. Laura Kriegstrom Poracsky, Mar. 25, 1947; m. Paula Jean Jensen (div.); children: Todd Weldon, Erin Kirsten McAnulty. BA, U. Ky., Lexington, 1968; MA, U. Colo., Boulder, 1970, PhD, 1973; MPH, U. Calif., Berkeley, 1975. Assoc. dir. nat. clearinghouse on child neglect and abuse, children's divsn. Am. Humane Assn., Denver, 1973—74; prof. anthropology U. Kans., Lawrence, 1975—, chair, dept., 1994—2001. Author: (book) Slaughterhouse Blues: The Meat and Poultry Industry in North America, Doing Team Ethnography: Warnings and Advice, Kiikaapoa: The Kansas Kickapoo; editor: Any Way You Cut It: Meat Processing and Small-Town America, Collaborative Research and Social Change: Applied Anthropology in Action, Culture and Agriculture Jour., Human Organization Jour.; prodr.: (ethnographic films) Neshnabek: The People; Return to Sovereignty: Self-Determination and the Kansas Kickapoo; Another Wind Is Moving: The Off-Reservation Indian Boarding School; contbr. articles to profl. jours. Recipient Louise Byrd Grad. Educator award, U. Kans., 1998, Hon. Citizen, Garden City, Kans., 2001, Irvin Youngberg award for Rsch. Achievement in Applied Sci., Kans. Endowment Assn., 2002, Wally and Marie Steeples Faculty award for Outstanding Svc. to People of Kans., U. Kans., 2004. Fellow: High Plains Soc. Applied Anthropology (Omer C. Stewart Meml. Award 1995), Am. Anthrop. Assn., Soc. Applied Anthropology (pres. 2005—06); mem.: Nat. Assn. Practice of Anthropology, Phi Kappa Phi. Achievements include being one of the first to conduct modern social science research on the consequences of the meat and poultry industry for workers and communities in the United States. Avocation: novice trick roper. Office: Univ Kans 1415 Jayhawk Blvd 622 Fraser Hall Lawrence KS 66045 Office Phone: 785-864-2641. Office Fax: 785-864-5224. E-mail: stull@ku.edu.

**STULL, DONALD LEROY,** architect; b. Springfield, Ohio, May 16, 1937; s. Robert Stull and Ruth Branson; m. Patricia Ann Ryder, Dec. 29, 1959 (div. Dec. 1985); children: Cydney Lynn, Robert Branson, Gia Virginia. BArch, Ohio State U., 1961; MArch, Harvard U., 1962. Registered arch. Calif., Conn., Fla., Ky., Maine, Md., Mass., Mo., N.H., N.J., N.Y., Pa., R.I., Tenn., Va., D.C., Wash. Pres. Stull Assocs., Inc., Boston, 1966-83; Stull and Lee, Inc., Boston, 1983—. Nat. Loeb fellowship com. Harvard Grad. Sch. Design, Cambridge, 1969-80; mem. adv. bd. Boston Archtl. Ctr., 1972-80

Mus. Nat. Ctr. of Afro-Am. Artists, Boston, 1978—, Ohio State U. Sch. Architecture, 1980—; design prof. Harvard Grad. Sch. Design, 1974-81; mem. vis. design studio, Rice U., Houston, spring 1993; mem. vis. com. Yale Sch. Art and Architecture, New Haven, 1972-76, William Henry Bishop chair Yale Sch. Architecture, 1975; mem. nat. presdl. design award jury Nat. Endowment for Arts, 1984, 88; bd. overseers The Inst. of Contemporary Art, Boston, 1996-98. Trustee Shaw U., 1973-75, Boston Found. for Architecture 1992—; mem. design adv. panel, Balt., 1976-80; Mass Art Commn., Boston, 1978-80; commr. Boston Art Commn., 1980-92; mem. Design Adv. Group, Cambridge, 1980-90, 94—; commr. Boston Civic Design Commn. 1987—; adv. com. Suffolk Sch. Bus. Mgmt., 1989-95; bd. dirs Hist. Boston, 1990-98, Mus. of Afro-Am. History, Boston, 1979—; trustee Mass. Coll. Art, 1995-2000, 03-. Recipient Presdl. Design award Nat. Endowment for Arts, 1988; named one of Outstanding Young Men of Boston, 1969, Outstanding Young Men in Am., 1970, Centennial Yr. Outstanding Alumnus Ohio State U., 1970. Fellow AIA (nat. design com. 1972-84); mem. Boston Soc. Archs. (bd. dirs. 1969, 1999-2001, AIA Regional Design award 1975, 80-89, Honor award 1997), Nat. Coun. Archtl. Registration Bds., Mass. Soc. Archs. (bd. trustees 1995). Office: Stull and Lee Inc 38 Chauncy St Ste 1100 Boston MA 02111-2301 Office Phone: 617-426-0406. E-mail: dstull@stullandlee.com

**STULL, ELIZABETH CROSBY,** retired education educator; d. Francis Anthony Crosby and Anna Rose Lucas; m. Lorren Lamar Stull, July 31, 1975. BS in Edn., SUNY, Brockport, 1959, MS in Edn., 1967; PhD in Edn., Ohio State U., 1975. Cert. supr. NY, prin. Ohio. Elem. tchr. Greece (NY) Ctrl. Sch., 1959—70, Pittsford (NY) Ctrl. Sch., 1970—72; asst. prof. Ohio State U., Marion, 1975—76, adj. prof., 1994—99; asst. prof. Ohio Wesleyan U., Delaware, 1978—80; assoc. prof. Otterbein Coll., Westerville, 1986—94. Edn. writer Prentice-Hall/Pearson, Englewood Cliffs, NJ, 1980—2002; cons. Columbus (Ohio) Pub. Schs., 1999; cons., writer Publs. Internat., 2000. Author: Kindergarten Teachers Survival Guide, 1997, Let's Read, 2000, Global Discovery Activities, 2004, 10 activity books; contbr. articles to profl. jours. Mem. Columbus Mus. Art, 2000—, ARC, Columbus, 2000—, High Rd. Gallery, Worthington, Ohio, 2004—. Mem.: Worthington Area Art League, Internat. Reading Assn., Ohio State U. Alumni Assn., Delta Kappa Gamma (scholar 1974), Phi Delta Kappa. Avocations: fine arts, travel, reading, theater. Home: 6658 Schreiner St W Columbus OH 43085

**STULL, GARY EVAN,** secondary school educator, writer; b. Waynesboro, Pa., Aug. 4, 1947; s. Mark McKean and Evelyn Rebecca Stull; m. April Lee Walker, Mar. 21, 1970; 1 child, Andrew Evan. BS, Ohio State U., 1969, MA, 1984, postgrad., 1986. Tchr. Mohawk Jr.-Sr. H.S. Columbus City Schs., Ohio, 1970—71, tchr. Ridgeview Jr. H.S., 1971—79, tchr. Ridgeview Mid. Sch., 1980—. Named Educator of Yr., PTA, 1985, 1995. Mem.: NEA, Ohio Edn. Assn., Columbus Edn. Assn. Presbyterian. Avocations: writing, travel, photography, carpentry, reading. Office: Ridgeview Mid Sch 4241 Rudy Rd Columbus OH 43214 Office Phone: 614-365-5506. E-mail: gstull@columbus.rr.com.

**STULL, KENNETH LEE,** social studies educator; b. Columbia, Mo., Feb. 16, 1962; s. Thurman Louis Stull and Nancy Louise Grabe; m. Susan Jean Hopkins, July 28, 1987; children: Joseph Cecil, Jacob Samuel, Caleb Michael, Rebecca Jean. BSc, NE Mo. State, Kirksville, 1987; MEd, City U., Bellevue, Wash., 1992; MA, Truman State U., Kirksville, Mo., 1998. Tchr. Rock Bridge H.S., Columbia, 1988—90, Everett H.S., Wash., 1990—92, Chillicothe H.S., Mo., 1994—. Coach football, wrestling, track Rock Bridge H.S., Columbia, 1988—90, Everett H.S., 1990—92, Chillicothe H.S., 1994—. Scout master troop 122 Boy Scouts Am., Chillicothe, 2005—06; served mission LDS Ch., Philippines, 1981—82. Mem.: Nat. Coun. Social Studies. Republican. Lds Ch. Office: Boy Scouts Am Scout Master Old 190 Chillicothe MO 64601

**STULTING, ANDRIES ANDRIESSEN,** ophthalmologist; b. Cape Town, South Africa, Aug. 29, 1948; s. Andries Andriessen and Magdalena (Van Huyssteen) S.; m. Leanné Fouché, Dec. 15, 1973; children: Lizette, Liesl. MB ChB, U. Pretoria, 1973, MMed in Ophthalmology, 1981. Intern S.A. Def. Force, Pretoria, 1974; sr. houseman H.F. Verwoerd and Kalafong Hosps., Pretoria, 1975-76, med. officer, 1976, sr. med. officer, 1976-77, sr. med. officer, registrar dept. ophthalmology, 1977-81, sr. specialist, 1982; head dept. ophthalmology U. of the Free State, 1982—. V.p. Colls. of Medicine of South Africa, 1990—. Chmn. Bloemfontein Children's choir, 1992-97; chmn. Free State Govern Sch. Bodies, 1993-97; vice chmn. South African Schs. Governing Bodies, 1993-97; chmn. Ctrl. H.S., 1992-97. Recipient Bloemfonteiner of Yr., Publicity Com. of Bloemfontein, 1996. Fellow ACS, Am. Acad. of Ophthalmology; mem. Ophthalmol. Soc. of South Africa (pres. 1989-91, 97-99), Health Professions Coun. of South Africa, South African Med. Assn. (past vice chmn., past pres. free state br.). Dutch Reformed Ch. Avocations: reading, writing, light classical music, sport photography. Home: 50 Gascony Crescent Bloemfontein 9301 South Africa Office: Dept Ophthalmology PO Box 339 Bloemfontein South Africa Office Phone: 0027514052151. Personal E-mail: aaseyedoc@lantic.net. Business E-Mail: stultinga@fshealth.gov.za.

**STULTS, WALTER BLACK,** management consultant, trade association administrator; b. Hightstown, N.J., Oct. 25, 1921; s. C. Stanley and Nettie M. (Black) S.; m. Ann D. Haynes, June 28, 1947 (dec. 2002); children: Andrew Haynes, Thomas Stanley; m. Jean Morris Curtin, 2003. BA, Williams Coll., 1943; MA (Woodrow Wilson fellow), Princeton U., 1949. Teaching asst. Princeton (N.J.) U., 1946-49; legis. asst. to U.S. Senator Robert Hendrickson, Washington, 1949-50; staff dir. U.S. Senate Small Bus. Com., Washington, 1950-61; pres. Nat. Assn. Small Bus. Investment Cos., Washington, 1961-86; prin. W.B. Stults, Cons., Chapel Hill, NC, 1979-99. Dir. Pardee & Curtin Lumber Co., Pardee Resources Co., Phila.; chmn. Coun. Small and Ind. Bus. Assns., 1976-81. Pres. Carol Woods Residents Assn.; dir. Carol Woods Retirement Comty., 1995-97, 2001—. With USAAF, 1943-46. Mem. Am. Soc. Assn. Execs., The Exchequer Club, Masons. Congregationalist.

**STULTZ, CILLA HOLMES,** psychologist; d. Jeffrey Lynn and Cynthia Anne Holmes; m. Jay Allen Stultz, July 12, 1998. BA in Psychology, U. Tex.-San Antonio, 1994, MS in Psychology, 1997; MA in Sch. Psychology, Trinity U., 1999. Nat. cert. sch. psychologist Md., cert. tchr. Tex., 1999, lic. specialist in sch. psychology, psychol. assoc. Lic. specialist sch. psychology Judson Ind. Sch. Dist., San Antonio, 1999—2003, Northside Ind. Sch. Dist., San Antonio, 2003—. Examiner Tex. RioGrande Legal Aid, San Antonio, 2005—. Contbr. articles to profl. jours.; presenter posters. Mem. Deerfield Homeowners' Assn., San Antonio, 2002—. Grantee Grad. Student Small Grant Program, U. Tex.-San Antonio, 1996; Pauline W. and Samuel W. Cochran fellow, 1996—97. Mem.: Tex. Coun. Adminstrs. of Spl. Edn. (assoc.). Episcopalian. Avocations: travel, scuba diving. Office Phone: 210-397-3526.

**STULTZ, JACK C.,** career military officer; m. Lauralyn Brown; 4 children. BA, Davidson Coll., 1974; grad., Command Gen. Staff Coll., Army War Coll. Advanced through grades to Lt. Gen. U.S. Army, 1974—; platoon leader, exec. officer, comdr. Co. B. 20th engr. battalion, 1974—79; various positions including brigade asst. ops. officer, battalion personnel officer, comdr., divsn. asst. ops. officer, 108th divsn. U.S. Army Reserve, 1979—87; with 32d Transp. Group, 1987—91, group exec. officer, 1991—95, comdr., 1998—99, 257th Transp. Battalion, Gainsville, Fla., 1995—98; dep. comdg. gen. 143rd Transp. Command (TRANSCOM), 1999—2002, comdr. Orlando, 2002—04; dir. movements, distbn., transp. combined forces land land component command, Kuwait, 2003—04; dep. comdg. gen. U.S. Army Reserve Command, 2005—06; chief U.S. Army Reserve, 2006—; comdg. gen. U.S. Army Reserve Command, 2006—; ops. mgr. Proctor and Gamble, Orlando, Fla. Decorated Def. Superior Svc. Medal, Legion of Merit, Bronze Star with oak leaf cluster, Meritorious Svc. Medal with three oak leaf clusters, Army Commendation Medal with four oak leaf clusters, Army Achievement Medal. Office: US Army Reserve 1401 Deshler St SW Fort Mcpherson GA 30330-2000*

**STULTZ, NEWELL MAYNARD,** retired political science professor; b. Boston, June 13, 1933; s. Irving Washburn and Marjorie May (MacEachern) S.; m. Elizabeth Petronella Olckers, Apr. 6, 1958; children: Elliot Andries, Amy Elizabeth. AB, Dartmouth Coll., 1955; MA, Boston U., 1960, PhD, 1965; MA hon., Brown U., 1968. Fulbright exchange scholar U. Pretoria, South Africa, 1955-56; asst. prof. Northwestern U., Evanston, Ill., 1964-65; asst. prof. to prof. polit. sci. Brown U., Providence, 1965—2003, assoc. grad. dean, 1970-74, assoc. dean of faculty, 1993-98, assoc. provost, 1998-2000; ret., 2003. Vis. fellow Yale U.-South African Research Program, 1977; vis. prof. U. South Africa, Pretoria, 1980; James Gathings lectr. Bucknell U., Lewisburg, Pa., 1980 Author: Afrikaner Politics in South Africa, 1974, Who Goes to Parliament?, 1975, Transkei's Half Loaf, 1979, (bibliography) South Africa, 1989, 2d edit., 1993; co-author: South Africa's Transkei, 1967; co-editor: Governing in Black Africa, 1970, 2d edit., 1986 V.p. World Affairs Council R.I., 1983. Served as lt. (j.g.) USN, 1956-59. Fulbright fellow, 1955-56; NDEA grantee, 1959-62; Ford Found. fellow, 1962-64; Rockefeller Found. fellow, 1976-77 Unitarian Universalist. Home: 371 New Meadow Rd Barrington RI 02806-3729 Office: Brown U Dept Polit Sci PO Box 1844 Providence RI 02912-1844 Office Phone: 401-863-1567. Business E-Mail: newell_stultz@brown.edu.

**STUMBO, GREGORY D.,** state attorney general; b. Huntington, W.Va., Aug. 14, 1951; s. Harold James and Pluma Jean (Martin) S.; m. Mary Karen Henderson, Aug. 18, 1973; children: Brooks, Elizabeth Morgan, Kassidy Ream. B Gen.Sci., U. Ky., Lexington, 1973; JD, U. Louisville, 1975. Asst. county atty. Floyd County, Prestonsburg, Ky., 1976-78; trial commr. to dist. ct. Adminstrv. Office of Cts., State Ky., Prestonsburg, 1978-79; mem. Ky. Ho. of Reps., Frankfort, 1980—2003, majority fl. leader, 1985—2003; atty. gen. State of Ky., 2003—. Bd. dirs. First Guaranty Nat. Bank, Martin, Ky. Mem. Gov.'s Task Force on Coal Transp., Frankfort, 1983, Ky. Lottery Commn., Frankfort, 1988, Ky. Task Force on Edn. Reform, 1989—. Recipient Disting. Svc. award Ky. Cir. Judges Assn., 1980, Cert. of Appreciation, Western Ky. U., Bowling Green, 1982, Disting. Aumni award, U. Louisville, 1985. Mem. ABA, Ky. Bar Assn. Democrat. Baptist. Avocations: hunting, fishing, golf. Address: 108 Ridgewood Dr Prestonsburg KY 41653 Office: Office of the Attorney General State Capitol Suite 118 700 Capitol Ave Frankfort KY 40601 Office Phone: 502-696-5300.*

**STUMMER, HELEN M.,** photographer; b. Newark, Jan. 8, 1936; d. George and Regina Stummer; m. Douglas W. Tatton, June 10, 1984; children: Patricia Stuart, Nicholas Greulich, Jeanine Palotas. BA in Studio Art/Psychology, Kean U., 1977; MA in Visual Sociology, Vt. Coll./Norwich U., 1987. Cert. tchr. N.J. Ind. photographer social documentaries, 1972—; tchr. sociology and art St. Anthony H.S., Jersey City, 1982—84; tchr. photography Scotch Plains (N.J.) /Fanwood H.S., 1984—88; asst. prof. photography Kean U., Union, NJ, 1988—91. Lectr. County Coll. Morris, 1972—; leader photography workshops N.J. Ctr. for Visual Arts, Summit, NJ, 1988—2001. Author: No Easy Walk, Newark, 1980-1993, 1994, Out of Darkness, 1999, Out of Darkness, translated and pub. in France, 2004; Represented in permanent collections Libr. of Congress, N.J. Hist. Soc., N.Y. Hist. Soc., Bklyn. Mus., Mus. of City of N.Y., Newark Mus., Jersey City Mus., numerous pvt. collections. Recipient Nat. Gracie Allen award, Am. Women in Media; fellow, N.J. State Coun. on Arts, 1995, 2000, Geraldine Dodge Found., 1992. Home: 171 High St Metuchen NJ 08840

**STUMP, DAVID JAMES,** philosopher, educator; b. Santa Monica, Calif., Mar. 21, 1955; s. John and Sarah Stump. BA, U. Calif., Berkeley, 1977; MA, Northwestern U., Ill., 1984, PhD, 1988. Assoc. prof., philosophy U. San Francisco, 1992—. Editor: Disunity of Science. Postdoctoral fellowship, NSF, 1989-1990. Mem.: The Internat. Soc. History of Philosophy of Sci. (steering com. 2003—06). Office: U San Francisco 2130 Fulton St San Francisco CA 94118 Office Phone: 415-422-6153.

**STUMP, EARL SPENCER,** psychologist; b. Parkersburg, W.Va., Dec. 12, 1943; s. Amos Earl Stump and Harriet Gertrude (White) Stiff; m. Ann Chadwick, Sept. 30, 1967 (div. 1985); 1 child, Andrea Renee; m. Joan Irene Croft, Sept. 28, 1985; m. Suzan Woodland, March 19, 2005. BA, Ohio State U., 1966; MS in Corrections, Xavier U., 1971; PhD, Ohio U., 2000. Lic. psychologist, Ohio; profl. clin. counselor; cert. rehab. counselor. Psychiat. aide Harding Hosp., Worthington, Ohio, 1965-67; psychology trainee Athens (Ohio) State Hosp., 1966-67; psychologist Ohio Dept. Rehab. and Correction, Columbus, 1967-97; supr. psychology and clin. dir. Chillicothe (Ohio) Correctional Inst., 1977-97. Pvt. practice psychology Columbus Mental Health Clinic, Columbus, 1976-77; instr. psychology Hocking Tech. Coll., Chillicothe, 1973-78; adj. prof. Ohio U., Athens, 2002; psychologist Scioto Point Valley Mental Health Ctr., Chillicothe. Mem.: APA, Ohio Psychol. Assn. Home: 15 N May Ave Athens OH 45701-1817 Office Phone: 740-593-6420. Personal E-mail: estump@eurekanet.com.

**STUMP, JOHN SUTTON,** retired lawyer; b. Clarksburg, W.Va., Aug. 7, 1929; s. John Sutton and Helen (Mannix) S.; m. Elaine Claire Scammahorn, Sept. 14, 1968; children— John Sutton IV, James Felix. Student, Washington and Lee U., 1946-47, LL.B., 1957; BS in Commerce, U. N.C., 1951. Bar: W.Va. 1957, Va. 1957, D.C. 1983. Assoc. Jackson, Kelly, Holt & O'Farrell, Charleston, W.Va., 1957-58, Boothe, Dudley, Koontz & Boothe, Alexandria, Va., 1958-61, Boothe, Dudley, Koontz & Blankinghip, Fairfax and Alexandria, Va., 1962-63; ptnr. Boothe, Dudley, Koontz, Blankinghip & Stump, Fairfax and Alexandria, 1963-71, Boothe, Prichard & Dudley, 1971-87, McGuire, Woods, Battle & Boothe LLP, 1987-99. Served to lt. comdr. USNR, 1951-54, 61-62. Fellow Am. Coll. Trial Lawyers; mem. Am. Law Inst. Home: 8329 Weller Ave Mc Lean VA 22102-1717 Office: 1750 Tysons Blvd Mc Lean VA 22102-4208

**STUMP, M. PAMELA,** sculptor; b. Detroit, July 8, 1928; d. Clarence Homer S. and Gladys Greening Bogue; m. David Everet Walsh, Aug. 1950 (div. 1975); children: Kimberly Klaerr, Sara Greening Walsh Munro, John Klaerr II; m. Richard Taylor White, March, 1989. B of Design, U. Mich., 1950, M of Design, 1951. Educator Ann Arbor (Mich.) Adult Edn., 1950-51, Saginaw (Mich.) Mus. Schs., 1963-68, Birmingham (Mich.) Bloomfield Art Assn., 1969, Washtenaw C.C., Ypsilanti, Mich., 1968-69, Cranbrook Ednl. Cmty., Bloomfield Hills, Mich., 1969-90. Group and one-woman shows include Cranbrook Kingswood, Bloomfield Hills, 1969-90, Mich. Women's Hist. Ctr. & Hall of Fame, Lansing, 1994, 2005, Swann Gallery, Detroit, 1997; exhibited in group shows at Cranbrook Kingswood, 1950, 70, 87, City Art Mus., St. Louis, 1951, Terry Art Inst., Miami, Fla., 1951, Temple Israel, Detroit, 1951, 58, Ceceile Gallery, N.Y.C. (3rd prize), 1956, Pa. Acad. Fine Arts, Phila., 1958, Horace H. Rackham Sch. Grad. Studies, Detroit, 1960, Detroit Artists Market, 1961, R and R Robinson Gallery, Naples, Fla., 1962, Rubiner Gallery, West Bloomfield, Mich., 1963, Mich. Fine Arts Competition (Juror's award), 1983, 87, Slusser Gallery, U. Mich., 1989, Outdoor Sculpture II, III, Southfield, Mich., 1990, 91, N.Y. Acad. Scis., N.Y.C., 1991, Oakland U., 1991-92, Urban Park, Detroit, 1991, 92, Arc Gallery, Chgo., 1992, 1 Heritage Place, Southgate, Mich., 1993, Art Ctr., Sarasota, Fla., 2000, Downriver Coun. for the Arts, Taylor, Mich., 2002, Outside the Lines, Grosse Ile, Mich., 2003, (Artist award) Wayne County Coun. for the Arts, 2004, Keep Mich. Beautiful award), Nat. Assn. Women Artists, N.Y.C., 2005 (Cleo Hartwig award for sculpture); prin. works include courtyard sculpture Kingswood Sch., steel sculpture Sister City, Tokushima, Japan, 10 bronze sculptures for Cranbrook Schs., Bloomfield Hills, Civic Ctr., Saginaw, bronze fountain at Presbyn. Ch., Grosse Ile, Mich. bronze sculpture of history of U. of Mich. Women, Ann Arbor, Mich. Bell Telephone Co., Saginaw, bronze sculpture at Providence Hosp., Southfield, meml. for poet T. Roethke Saginaw Valley State U., bronze sculpture at First Presbyn. Ch., Pompano Beach, Fla., Rochester Hills Libr., Saginaw Mus., Western Mich. U., Kalamazoo, numerous others. Mem. Emily's List, Planned Parenthood. Recipient Artist award, Coun. for the Arts, 2004. Mem. ACLU, NOW, LWV, Nat. Assn. Women Artists (Cleo Hartwig award, 2005), Nat. Mus. Women in Arts (charter), Detroit Artist Market, Detroit Inst. Arts Founders Soc., Internat. Sculptors. Avocations: reading, writing. Home: 19629 Parke Ln Grosse Ile MI 48138-1024 E-Mail: lcolntu@gatecom.com.

**STUMP, PATRICK MARTIN,** musician; b. Glenview, Ill., Apr. 27, 1984; Lead singer, guitarist Fall Out Boy, 2001—. Musician: (albums) Fall Out Boy's Evening Out With Your Girlfriend, 2002, Take This to Your Grave, 2003, From Under the Cork Tree, 2005, (songs) Sugar, We're Going Down, 2003 (MTV2 award, MTV Video Music Awards, 2005), Dance, Dance, 2005 (Choice Music Single award, Choice Rock Track award, Teen Choice Awards, 2006, Viewer's Choice award, MTV Video Music Awards, 2006); actor: (films) Bedussey, 2005. Recipient Choice Music Rock Group award, Teen Choice Awards, 2006. Office: Fall Out Boy Inc Box 219 1187 Wilmette Ave Wilmette IL 60091*

**STUMP, RICHARD CARL,** environmental services administrator, consultant; b. Reading, Pa., Aug. 14, 1952; s. Richard Carl Stump; m. Brenda Lee Roughton, Jan. 11, 1974; children: Richard, Nathan, Jonathan Grad. high sch., Muhlenberg, Pa. Cert. radon testing specialist. Pres. Suburban Water Testing Labs., Temple, Pa., 1978—; Suburban Property Inspections, Inc., Temple, Pa., 1996—. Cons. to various news media and pubs. of books and mags. on drinking water issues; expert witness. Mem. Am. Water Works Assn., Am. Assn. Radon Scientists and Technologists, Pa. Assn. Accreditation Environ. Labs., Am. Chem. Soc., Aircraft Owners and Pilots Assn. Avocations: amateur radio, aviation, private pilot. Office: Suburban Water Testing Labs 4600 Kutztown Rd Temple PA 19560-1548

**STUMPE, WARREN ROBERT,** county official, retired engineering executive; b. Bronx, N.Y., July 15, 1925; s. William A. and Emma J. (Mann) S.; children: Jeffrey, Kathy, William. BS, U.S. Mil. Acad., 1945; MS, Cornell U., 1949; MS in Indsl. Engring, N.Y. U., 1965; grad., Command and Gen. Staff Coll., 1972, Army War Coll., 1976; PhD (hon.), Milw. Sch. Engring, 1987 Registered profl. engr., N.Y., Fla., Wis. Commd. 2d lt., C.E. U.S. Army, 1945, advanced through grades to capt., 1954; with (65th Engr. Bn.), 1945-48; asst. prof. mechanics U.S. Mil. Acad., 1951-54; resigned, 1954; from capt. to col. Res., 1958-79; dep. gen. mgr., gen. engring. div. AMF, Stamford, Conn., 1954-63; exec. v.p. Dortech, Inc., Stamford, 1963-69; dir. systems mgmt. group Mathews Conveyor div. REX, Darien, Conn., 1969-71; dir. research and devel. Rexnord, Inc., Milw., 1971-73, v.p. corp. research and tech., from 1973, v.p. bus. devel. sector, 1981-83, v.p., chief tech. officer, 1983-86; pres. Rexnord Techs., Milw., 1986-87; v.p. Radian Corp., Milw., 1987—90; civilian aide to sec. army for State of Wis., 1981-85; alderman City of Mequon, 1994—97, pres. coun., 1996—97, county supr., 1998—. Mem. adv. bd. technology transfer program U. Wis.-Whitewater. Contbr. articles to profl. jours. Founder, pres. No. Little League, Stamford, 1965-69; pres. Turn of River Jr. High Sh. PTA, 1967-68; vice chmn. for Wis. Dept. Def., Nat. Com. Employer Support Guard and Res.; bd. regents Milw. Sch. Engring.; mem. liaison coun. Coll. Engring., U. Wis., also mem. indsl. adv. coun.; mem. adv. coun. Marquette U.; mem. Wis. Gov.'s Task Force on Energy, Coun. Great Lakes Govs.' Regional Econ. Devel. Commn., 1987-88; bd. dirs. MRA-Inst. Mgmt., Inc. Mem. Am. Water Pollution Control Fedn., Indsl. Rsch. Inst. (pres., dir.), Wis. Assn. Rsch. Mgrs. (founder), West Point Soc. Wis., Tau Beta Pi, Phi Kappa Phi. Clubs: Wis., Ozaukee Country. Office Phone: 262-241-9560. Personal E-mail: warrenstumpe@aol.com.

**STUMPF, DAVID ALLEN,** pediatric neurologist; b. LA, May 8, 1945; s. Herman A. and Dorothy F. (Davis) S.; children: Jennifer F., Kaitrin E.; m. Elizabeth Dusenbery, Feb. 2, 1989; children: Todd Coleman, Shilo Walker. BA, Lewis and Clark Coll., 1966; MD cum laude, U. Colo., 1972, PhD, 1972. Diplomate Am. Bd. Pediat., Am. Bd. Psychiatry and Neurology, lic. MD State of Ill. Pediatric intern Strong Meml. Hosp., Rochester, NY, 1972-73, resident, 1973-74; resident in neurology Harvard Med. Sch., Boston, 1974-77; dir. pediatric neurology U. Colo. Health Sci. Ctr., Denver, 1977-85; chief neurology Children's Meml. Hosp., Chgo., 1985-89; chmn. neurology, Benjamin and Virginia T. Boshes prof. Northwestern U., 1989-98, prof. neurology and pediatrics, 1999—2001; pres. and CEO Oyxis, LLC, 1999—2001; med. dir. United Healthcare, Chgo., 2005—. Mem. sci. adv. com. Muscular Dystrophy Assn., 1981-87; bd. dirs. Northwestern Meml. Corp., Chgo. Mem. editl. bd. Neurology, 1982-87; contbr. articles to sci. jours. Recipient Lewis and Clark Coll. Disting. Alumni award, 1991; NIH grantee, 1979-84; Muscular Dystrophy Assn. grantee, 1977-89; March of Dimes grantee, 1983-85. Fellow Am. Acad. Neurology (treas. 2005-07); mem. Child Neurology Soc. (counsellor 1982-84, pres. 1985-87), Am. Neurol. Assn., Am. Pediatric Soc., Soc. Pediatric Rsch., Internat. Child Neurology Assn. (sec. 2002-04). Presbyterian. Home: 540 Judson Ave Evanston IL 60202-3084 Office Phone: 312-424-6905. E-mail: david@stumpf.org.

**STUMPF, HEINRICH JOSEF,** psychometrician, research consultant; b. Cologne, Germany, Dec. 10, 1951; came to U.S., 1991; s. Friedrich Hubert and Johanna Luise (Bauer) Stumpf; m. Doris Elisabeth Hoffmann, May 10, 1990. Diploma in Psychology, U. Bonn, Germany, 1975, PhD, 1978. Sci. employee German Nat. Scholarship Found., Bonn, Germany, 1978-91; sr. rsch. assoc. Ctr. for Talented Youth, Johns Hopkins U., Balt., 1991-95; rsch. cons. Ctr. for Talented Youth Johns Hopkins U., Balt., 1996—. Contbr. to German Encyclopedia of Psychology. Mem. German Psychol. Assn., Am. Psychol. Assn., N.Y. Acad. Scis. Achievements include: sr. author of the Cube Perspective Test of Spatial Ability, 1983, the German Personality Research Form, 1985 and the Spatial Test Battery of the Ctr. for Talented Youth; contbr. to German Ency. Psychology; contbr. about 50 scientific publications. Personal E-mail: stumpfhj@aol.com.

**STUMPF, JOHN G.,** bank executive; b. Minn. B of Acctg., St. Cloud U.; M in Fin., U. Minn. Sr. v.p., chief credit officer Norwest Bank, Minn., 1982—89; exec. v.p. Southwestern Banking, 1988; regional pres. Norwest Bank, Colo., 1990—94, head Tex., 1994—98; head southwestern banking group Wells Fargo & Co., San Francisco, 1998—2000, exec. v.p. w. banking group, 2000—02, group exec. v.p. cmty. banking, 2002—05, pres., COO, 2005—. Bd. chmn. Visa U.S.A. Bd. dir. San Francisco Zool. Soc., Bay Area chpt. Jr. Achievement; treas. Bay Area Council. Office: Wells Fargo & Co 420 Montgomery St San Francisco CA 94163*

**STUMPF, MARK HOWARD,** lawyer; b. Chgo., Jan. 25, 1947; s. Samuel Enoch and Jean (Goodman) S.; m. Elizabeth Bruce, Nov. 18, 1972; children: Nicholas, Anna, Lawrence, Gillian. AB, Harvard U., 1969, JD, 1972. Bar: N.Y. 1973, D.C. 1977, U.S. Dist. Ct. (so. and ea. dists.) N.Y. 1973. Assoc. Paul, Weiss, Rifkind, Wharton & Garrison, N.Y.C., 1972-76, Arnold & Porter LLP, Washington, 1976—80, ptnr., 1981—92, sr. ptnr., 1993—. Bd. dirs. Martha's Table, Inc., Washington. Co-author: Shark Repellents and Golden Parachutes; author: (with others) Latin American Sovereign Debt Management, 1990. Decorated Order of Generalísimo Francisco de Miranda, 1st Class (Republic of Venezuela) 1991. Mem. ABA, Harvard Club N.Y.C. Democrat. Episcopalian. Home: 3820 Jocelyn St NW Washington DC 20015-1920 Office: Arnold & Porter LLP 555 12th St NW Washington DC 20004-1206 E-mail: mark_stumpf@aporter.com.

**STUMPF, PAUL KARL,** biochemistry professor emeritus; b. NYC, Feb. 23, 1919; s. Karl and Annette (Schreyer) S.; m. Ruth Rodenbeck, June 1947; children: Ann Carol, Kathryn Lee, Margaret Ruth, David Karl, Richard Frederic. AB, Harvard Coll., 1941; PhD, Columbia U., 1945. Instr. pub. health U. Mich., Ann Arbor, 1946-48; faculty U. Calif., Berkeley, 1948-58, prof., 1956-58, Davis, 1958-84, prof. emeritus, 1984—. Chief scientist Competitive Rsch. Grants Office USDA, Washington, 1988-91; cons. Palm Oil Rsch. Inst., Kuala Lumpur, Malaysia, 1982-92; mem. sci. adv. bd. Calgene, Inc., Davis, 1990-93; mem. sci. adv. panel Md. Biotech. Inst., 1990-92; Inaugural lectr. Tan Sri Dato'Seri B. Bek-Nielsen Found., Kuala Lumpur, 1996. Co-author: Outlines of Enzyme Chemistry, 1955, Outlines of Biochemistry, 5th edit., 1987; co-editor-in-chief Biochemistry of Plants, 1980; exec. editor Archives of Biochemistry/Biophysics, 1965-88; contbr. over 250 articles to profl. jours. Planning commn. City of Davis, 1966-68; bd. dirs. Internat. House, Davis, 2002—. Guggenheim fellow, 1962, 69; recipient Lipid Chemistry award Am. Oil Chemists Soc., 1974, Sr. Scientist award Alexander von Humboldt Found., 1976, Superior Svc. Group award USDA, 1992, Award of Excellence, Calif. Aggie Alumni Found., 1996. Fellow AAAS; mem. NAS, Royal Danish

Acad. Scis., Am. Soc. Plant Physiologists (pres. 1979-80, chmn. bd. trustees 1986-90, Stephen Hales award 1974, Charles Reid Barnes Life Membership award 1992), Internat. Ho. Davis (mem. bd. dirs. 2002-2005). Avocation: golf. Home: 764 Elmwood Dr Davis CA 95616-3517 Office: U Calif Molecular & Cellular Biology Davis CA 95616 Business E-Mail: pkstumpf@ucdavis.edu.

**STUMPF, WALTER ERICH,** cell biology and pharmacology professor, researcher; b. Oelsnitz, Sachsen, Germany, Jan. 10, 1927; arrived in U.S., 1963; m. Ursula Emily Schwinge, May 20, 1961; children: Andrea, Martin, Carolin, Silva. MD summa cum laude, Humboldt U., Berlin, 1952; PhD in Pharmacology, U. Chgo., 1967; D of Human Biology (hon.), U. Ulm, Germany, 1987. Resident in neurology and psychiatry Humboldt U., Berlin, 1954-57, U. Marburg, Germany, 1957-61, resident in radiobiology, 1961-62; rsch. assoc. U. Chgo., 1963-67, asst. prof., 1967-70; assoc. prof. U. N.C. Chapel Hill, 1970-73, prof., 1973-95, mem. labs. for reproductive biology and neurobiology program, mem. Cancer Rsch. Ctr., Carolina Population Ctr., mem. curriculum in toxicology. Vis. psychiatrist Maudsley Hosp., London, 1959; vis. prof. Max-Planck Inst. for Cell Biology, Wilhelmshaven, Germany, 1975, U. Ulm, 1981, U. Sao Paulo, Brazil, 2000-02; rsch. advisor Chugai Pharm. Co., Ltd., Tokyo, 1992-95; lectr. U. São Paulo, 1997, 2000, Ain Shams U., Cairo, 1998; cons. Harris Mfg. Co., North Billerica, Mass., Rsch. Triangle Inst., Chemistry and Life Scis. Divsn., Rsch. Triangle Park, N.C., Merck Sharp and Dome, Westpoint, Pa., Glaxo Wellcome, Rsch. Triangle Park; exec. com. NRC, Inst. of Lab. Animal Resources, NAS, 1979-81, coun. Inst. of Lab. Animal Res., 1978-81, com. Soc. for Exptl. Biology and Medicine, 1987-92, founder Internat. Inst. Drug Distbn. Cytopharmacology and Cytoxicology, Chapel Hill, 1995. Editor: Autoradiography of Diffusible Substances, 1969, Anatomical Neuroendocrinology, 1975, Autoradiography and Correlative Imaging, 1995; author: Drug Localization in Tissues and Cells, 2003; mem. editl. bd. Neuroendocrinology Letters, 1979-87, Exptl. Aging Rsch., 1975-85, Jour. Histochemistry and Cytochemistry, 1982-90, Cell and Tissue Rsch., 1982-88, Molecular and Cellular Neurosci., 1989-94, Biomed. Rsch., 1991-94, Histochemistry, 1992-96; contbr. articles to profl. jours. Recipient Humboldt Found. award, 1989. Mem. AAAS, Am. Assn. Anatomists, N.Y. Acad. Scis., Soc. for Exptl. Biology and Medicine, Soc. for Neurosci., Endocrine Soc., Internat. Brain Rsch. Orgn., Am. Soc. Zoologists, Histochem. Soc. (coun. 1977-81), Histochem. Gesellschaft (Feulgen lectureship 1982), Internat. Soc. Study Xenobiotics (charter), Internat. Inst. Drug Distbn. Cytopharmacology and Cytotoxicology (founder). Home: U NC Sch Medicine 2612 Damascus Church Rd Chapel Hill NC 27516-8043 Office: Internat Inst Drug Distribution Cytopharmacology & Cytotoxicology Chapel Hill NC 27516 Office Phone: 919-942-8646. Business E-Mail: stumpfwe@email.unc.edu.

**STUMPFF, ROBERT THOMAS,** retired academic administrator; b. Lewistown, Pa., June 25, 1945; s. Harry Clarence and Marjorie Louise (Bossinger) Stumpff; m. Sylvia Simmons, Apr. 22, 1972; children: Robert Dale, Cherie Lynn Stumpff Zimmer. BS, U. Md., 1968; cert. U. Ky., 1978. Asst. dir. athletics U. Md., College Park, 1968-69, asst. dir. Md. student union, 1969-72, assoc. dir. Md. student union, 1973-80, acting dir. Md. student union, 1974-75, bus. mgr. athletics, 1980-81, asst. athletic dir., 1982-88, asst. dir. gen. svcs., facilities mgmt., 1988—2005; dir. pub. works City of College Park. Cons. U.S. Naval Acad. Athletic Assn., Annapolis, Md., 1984; dir. pub. works City of Coll. Park, Md., 2005—. Author, editor: Maryland Wrestling, 1964—65, 1968—69, asst. editor: Maryland Basketball, 1964—65, 1968—69, Maryland Football Guide, 1966—69. Asst. min. St. Paul's Luth. Ch., Fulton, Md., 1996—; mem. ch. coun. Abiding Savior Luth. Ch., Columbia, Md., 1986—87; mem. Luth. campus ministry bd. U. Md., 1995—. Mem.: Nat. Recycling Coalition, Md. Recyclcers Coalition (bd. dirs. 1997—, chair 2003—), Md.-Del. Solid Waste Assn., Nat. Solid Wastes Mgmt. Assn., Solid Waste Assn. N.Am. (bd. dirs. Mid-Atlantic chpt. 1992—94, cert. mcpl. solid waste mgr.), Am. Pub. Works Assn., U. Md. M Club Found. (life; bd. dirs. 1970—, past pres.), U. Md. Alumni Assn. (life), U. Md. Terrapin Club, Omicron Delta Kappa (Sigma chpt. faculty sec.-treas. 1972—76, faculty adviser 1976—91, faculty coord. 1991—2005). Avocations: reading, sightseeing. Home: 8206 Bubbling Spring Laurel MD 20723-1079 Office Phone: 301-474-4194. Business E-Mail: rstumpff@collegepark.md.gov.

**STUNKARD, ALBERT JAMES,** psychiatrist, educator; b. NYC, Feb. 7, 1922; s. Horace Wesley and Frances (Klank) Stunkard. BS, Yale U., 1943; MD, Columbia U., 1945; MD (hon.), U. Edinburgh, 1992. Intern in medicine Mass. Gen. Hosp., Boston, 1945—46; resident physician psychiatry Johns Hopkins Hosp., 1948—51; rsch. fellow psychiatry, 1951—52; 1rsch. fellow medicine Columbia U. Svc., Goldwater Meml. Hosp., N.Y.C., 1952—53; Commonwealth rsch. fellow, then asst. prof. medicine Cornell U. Med. Coll., 1953—57; mem. faculty U. Pa., 1957—73, 1976—, prof. psychiatry, 1962—73, 1976—, Kenneth Appel prof. psychiatry, 1968—73, chmn. dept., 1962—73; prof. psychiatry Med. Sch., Stanford U., 1973—76. Contbr. 450 articles on psychol., physiol., sociol., therapeutic and genetic aspects of obesity to profl. jours. Capt. M.C. AUS, 1946—48. Recipient Disting. Svc. award, Am. Psychiat. Assn., 1994, Goldberger award, AMA, 1990, Willendorf award, Internat. Assn. Study of Obesity, 1998, Sarnot award mental health, NAS Inst. Medicine, 2004, Disting. Achievement medal medicine, Columbia U. Coll. Physicians and Surgeons, 2005; fellow, Ctr. Advanced Study in Behavioral Scis., 1971—72. Mem.: Soc. Behavioral Medicine (past pres.), Assn. Rsch. Nervous and Mental Diseases (past pres.), Am. Psychosomatic Soc. (past pres.), Acad. Behavioral Medicine Rsch. (past pres.), Am. Assn. Chmn. Depts. Psychiatry (past pres.), Inst. Medicine of NAS. Achievements include contributions to the behavioral, pharmacological, community and surgical treatment of obesity and to understanding of sociological, physiological, psychological and genetic aspects of the disorder; contributions also to nosology and treatment of the eating disorders. Office: U Pa Sch Medicine Dept Psychiatry 3535 Market St 3rd Flr Philadelphia PA 19104-2641 Office Phone: 215-898-7314. Business E-Mail: stunkard@mail.med.upenn.edu.

**STUNTEBECK, CLINTON A.,** lawyer; b. Hibbing, Minn., May 25, 1938; s. Robert F. and S. Mary Stuntebeck; m. Mary Joan Carmody; children: Robin, M. Alison, Susan, John, William. BA US Psychology, U. Minn., 1960; LLB, U. Maine, 1968. Bar: Pa. 1969, U.S. Dist. Ct. (ea. dist.) Pa. 1969. Ptnr. emeritus, chmn. corp. fin. and securities, mem. exec. com. Schnader, Harrison, Segal & Lewis, Phila. Bd. dirs. HMG Courtland Properties, Cimento Tupi Shipping, Markel Corp., Greater Phila. First Partnership for Econ. Devel.; lectr. corp. and securities law. Contbr. articles to profl. jours. Pres. Radnor (Pa.) Twp. Bd. Commn., 1981—83, 1992—2001; founder, bd. dirs. Radnor Enhancement Cmty. Trust; bd. visitors U. Maine Sch. Law; trustee Cabrini Coll.; bd. dirs. Am. Heart Assn., Ctr. for Responsible Leadership and Governance, Villanova U. Capt. USAF, 1960—68. Mem. ABA, Am. Law Inst., Pa. Bar Assn., Phila. Bar Assn., Securities Industry Assn. (law and compliance com.), Nat. Assn. Corp. Dirs., U. Maine Law Alumni Assn. (pres. 1974-76), Federalist Soc., AF Assn., Mil. Order Fgn. Wars US, Union League Phila., Phila. Country Club, Sunday Breakfast Club, Corinthian Yacht Club. Avocations: sailing, skiing, golf. Office: Schnader Harrison Segal 1600 Market St Ste 3600 Philadelphia PA 19103-7287 Office Phone: 215-751-2034. E-mail: cstuntebeck@schnader.com.

**STUNTZ, JEAN ALLISON,** history professor; b. Orange, Tex., Apr. 8, 1957; d. Homer Clyde and Billie Williams Stuntz. JD, Baylor Law Sch., 1980; PhD, U. No. Tex., 2000. History prof. West Tex. A&M U., Canyon, Tex., 2001—. Author: (historical monograph) Hers, His, and Theirs: Community Property Law in Spain and Early Texas. Office: West Texas A&M Univ 2402 N 3rd Canyon TX 79016 Office Phone: 806-651-2404. Business E-Mail: jstuntz@mail.wtamu.edu.

**STUNTZ, WILLIAM JOHN,** law educator; b. Hyattsville, Md., July 3, 1958; s. John Walter and Marian Johnson Stuntz; m. Ruth Anne Councill, Aug. 2, 1980; children: Sarah Ruth, Samuel David, Andrew William. AB in History and English, Coll. of William and Mary, 1980; JD, U.Va., 1984. Law clk. to Hon. Louis H. Pollak, Phila., 1984-85; law clk. to Assoc. Justice Lewis H. Powell Jr. US Supreme Ct., Washington, 1985-86; asst. prof. law U. Va.,

Charlottesville, 1986-90, prof., 1990-96, E. James Kelly rsch. prof., 1991—94, Horace W. Goldsmith rsch. prof., 1995—2000, class of 1962 prof. law, 1996—2000; prof. law Harvard Law Sch., Cambridge, Mass., 2000—. Vis. prof. law Yale U., New Haven, Conn., 1996-97, Harvard U., 1998. Co-author: Constitutional Criminal Procedure, 1995, Comprehensive Criminal Procedure, 2001; contbr. articles to profl. journals. Bd. dirs. Ctr. for Christian Study, Charlottesville, 1993-97. Presbyterian. Office: Harvard Law Sch 1563 Massachusetts Ave Cambridge MA 02138 Office Phone: 617-496-0555. Office Fax: 617-496-4865. Business E-Mail: stuntz@law.harvard.edu.

**STUNZ, JOHN HENRY, JR.,** retired physician, consultant; b. Freeland, Pa., May 20, 1921; s. John Henry and Anna Amelia (Gross) Stunz; m. Geraldine Kutz, July 2, 1944 (dec. Oct. 10, 2003); children: Beverly A. Stunz Boyd, Geri Stunz Konstantin. BA, U. Pa., 1943, MD, 1946. Diplomate Am. Bd. Occupl. Medicine. Intern U.S. Naval Hosp., Saint Albans, NY, 1946-47; pvt. practice Freeland, 1949-50; plant physician Harrison Radiator div. Gen. Motors Corp., Lockport, NY, 1950-52, med. dir., 1952-78, Cadillac Motor Car div. Gen. Motors Corp., Detroit, 1978-86; occupational medicine cons. Preferred Med. Assocs., Southfield, Mich., 1987-98, ret., 1998. Pres. Niagara County (N.Y.) Bd. Health, 1966; acting commr. health Niagara County, 1972-73. Lt. (j.g.) M.C., USNR, 1946-49. Fellow Am. Coll. Occupl. and Environ. Medicine; mem. Mich. State Med. Soc., Oakland County Med. Soc. (environ. health com. 1988), Mich. Occupl. and Environ. Med. Assn. (bd. dirs. 1985-88), Detroit Occupl. Physicians Assn. Republican. Presbyterian. Avocations: stamp collecting/philately, boating, golf. Home: 735 Ardmoor Dr Bloomfield Hills MI 48301-2417

**STUPAK, BART T.,** congressman, lawyer; b. Milw., Feb. 29, 1952; m. Laurie Ann Olsen; children: Ken, Bart Jr. (dec.). AA in Criminal Justice, Northwestern Mich. C.C., Traverse City, 1972; BS in Criminal Justice, Saginaw Valley State Coll., 1977; JD, Thomas M. Cooley Law Sch., 1981. Patrolman Escanaba City Police Dept., 1972-73; state trooper Mich. Dept. State Police, 1973-84; instr. State Police Tng. Acad., 1980-82; atty., 1981-84, Hansley, Neiman, Peterson, Beauchamp, Stupak, Bergman P.C., 1984-85; ptnr. Stupak, Bergman, Stupak P.C., 1985-88; mem. Mich. Ho. of Reps., 1989-90; prin. Bart T. Stupak P.C., 1991—; mem. US Congress from 1st Mich. dist., 1993—. Mem. commerce subcom., ranking dem. on oversights and investigation, telecom. and Internet, environment and hazardous materials, commerce trade, consumer protection. Nat. committeeman Boy Scouts Am., coach Menominee Youth Baseball Assn., Little League; active Wildlife Unltd., Menominee Woods and Streams Assn., Menominee County Hist. Soc.; adv. com. Bay Pines Juv. Detection Ctr.; bd. dir. Cmty. Action Agy. Recipient Fed. Legislator of Yr. award, Mich. Credit Union League, Great Lakes legis. of Yr. award, Great Lakes Maritime Task Force, 2003. Mem. Nat. Rifle Assn., Sons of the Am. Legion, Knights of Columbus, Elks Club, State Employees Retirees Assn., fin. com. Holy Spirit Catholic Ch. Democrat. Roman Catholic. Office: US Congress 2352 Rayburn House Office Bldg Washington DC 20515-2201 also: Iron County Courthouse Ste 2 3 Sixth St Crystal Falls MI 49920-1438 Office Phone: 202-225-4735, 906-875-3751. Office Fax: 202-225-4744, 906-875-3889. E-mail: stupak@mail.house.gov.*

**STUPAK, MARY JO,** psychotherapist, educator; d. Carl Elmer Cross and Georgianna Viola Jones; children: John Jr., Joseph, Michael, Steven, Carol, Curt. BS (hon.), U. Wis., 1973, MS in Cmty. Counseling, 1985. Lic. profl. counselor State of Wis. Intermediate tchr. Cathedral Sch., Superior, Wis., 1972—73; family resource coord. Head Start, Superior, 1974—76; tchr. Douglas County Citizens, Superior, 1977—82, Rape and Incest Victim Orgn., Superior, 1983—85; psychotherapy Human Resource Ctr., Superior, 1985—95; latch key lead tchr. Cathedral Sch., Superior, 2000—. Cons. Head Start, Superior, 1982—83. Contbr. articles to profl. jours. Pres. St. Williams Altar Soc., Foxboro, Wis., 1952—; organist St. Williams Ch., Foxboro, Wis., 1952—. Democrat. Roman Catholic. Avocations: painting, folk art, music, reading.

**STUPPARD-BYARS, DORIS J.,** minister; b. El Dorado, Ark., Feb. 19, 1941; d. Jimmy D. and Mozella Massey; m. Mark Byars, July 31, 2004; m. Emanuel Stuppard, Aug. 1, 1986 (div. Sept. 1, 1995); m. Van J. Whaley, Mar. 1962 (div. June 1983); children: Stephanie A. Whaley-Jones, Ralph S. Whaley, Tiffany L. Whaley-LeConte. BA in Family Life Ed & Ministry, Spring Arbor U., Spring Arbor, Mich., 1997; BS in Psychology, Detroit Inst. of Tech., Detroit, Mich., 1991. Mn Dept. of Pub. Health, Mich., 1994; cert. Tchg. Fla. State Bd. of Edn., Fla., 1985, Child Care Adminstrn. Dade County C.C., Fla., 1987. Girl scouts leader Girl Scouts Of Am., Detroit, 1966—68; exec. dir. & founder Multi-Racial Family Study & Del. Ctr., Ypsilanti, Mich., 1979—; pres. of cloverlawn block club Cloverlawn Block Club, Detroit, 1970—71; leader Adult Deliverance Study, Detroit, 1976—78; alternative sch. tchr. Ace Sch., Detroit, 1976—78; outreach min. Old Path Temple COGIC, Detroit, 1977—83; pres. of chalmers block club Chalmers Block Club, Detroit, 1978—79; evangelist (min.) Trinity Deliverance Ch., Detroit, 1979—; asst. pastor Outer Dr. United Meth. Ch., Detroit, 1995—97; leader Children's Refuge Ho. (MRFDC), Brightmoor Cmty., Mich., 1993—95. Cons. Noble Med. Sch., Detroit, 2000—01; youth group counselor Go Lightly Elem. & Jr. High, Detroit, 1998—99; learning for life instr. Boy Scouts Of Am., Detroit, 1997—97. Author: (religous novel) The Unction it Takes to Function, (religous instruction) Hey Churchmember! Put Your Money Where Your Mouth Is!; singer (soprano): (concert) 2nd Annual Women's Conf. of Institutional Bapt. Ch. 100 Woman Concert; speaker 2nd Annual Women's Conf. of Inst. Bapt. Ch. Candidate for city coun. Detroit City Coun., Detroit, 2001—01; candidate state rep. State of Mich., Detroit, 2002—02; candidate charter commr. City of Detroit, Detroit, 1980—80. Recipient Cert. of Appreciation, Wayne County Sherrif Dept.: Exec. Dir. Robert Ficano, 2003, Cert. of Appreciation for Children's Feeding Program, City Of Detroit 1979 Mayor Word Of Deliverance (assoc., evangelist 2004—05); mem.: Hartford Meml. Bapt. Ch. (min. 1993—2000), Leadership To Go (corr.; exec. dir. 2004—05). Independent. Achievements include Outstanding Young Woman of the Yr. DIT: 1977; Outstanding Young Woman of Am.: 1978. Avocation: traveling evangelist. Home: 51360 Mich Ave Apt 2 Belleville MI 48111-5002 Office: Multi-Racial Family Study & Devel 2430 E Mich Ave Ste D Ypsilanti MI 48198 Office Phone: 734-483-0557. Personal E-mail: messengerd7@aol.com.

**STUPPLES, KAREN,** professional golfer; b. Dover, Eng., June 24, 1973; Attended, Fla. State U. Winner Women's British Open, 2004, Welch's/Fry's Championships, 2004. Second-team All-Am. Fla. State U., 1995; represented England Curtis Cup, 1996, 98. Avocations: cooking, movies, football. Office: c/o LPGA 100 International Dr Daytona Beach FL 32124-1092

**STURDEVANT, KATHERINE SCOTT,** historian, educator; b. San Francisco, Feb. 13, 1955; d. James Alexander and Barbara Harper Scott; m. Rick Willard Sturdevant, Aug. 31, 1984. BA in History, San Francisco State U., 1977, MA in History, 1981; postgrad., U. Calif., Santa Barbara, 1984. Rev. editor The Pub. Historian, Santa Barbara, 1981—84; tchg. asst. U. Calif., 1982—84; hist. editor State Hist. Soc. Iowa, Iowa City, 1984—85; chair social scis. Pikes Peak C.C., Colorado Springs, 1991—97, faculty history, 1992—, chair history, 2002—. Adj. faculty 4 colls., Colorado Springs, 1986—92; speaker in field. Author: Bringing Your Family History to Life Through Social History, 2000, Organizing Your Heirloom Documents, 2002; rev. editor: Jour. Southwest, 1987—97. Mem. Pikes Peak Local History Consortium, 2002—; Hist. Preservation Bd., 1986—88, Friends Pioneer Mem.: Colo. Edn. Assn. Recipient Nat. Inst. Staff & Orgnl. Devel. Excellence award. Mem.: Colo. Edn. Assn. (bd. dirs. 1999—2005, Tchg. Excellence award 2004). Avocations: collecting old movies, birdwatching, singing. Office: Pikes Peak CC 11195 Hwy 83 Colorado Springs CO 80921 E-mail: katherine.sturdevant@ppcc.edu.

**STURDIVANT, JAMES M.,** lawyer; b. Tulsa, Sept. 14, 1937; s. Ben S. and Elizabeth (Carlock) S.; m. Carol A. Baker, 1961 (div. Feb. 1975); children: Anne Carol, Catherine Abby; m. Barbara Dorn, Feb. 4, 1978; children: David Andrew, John Michael. BBA, U. Okla., 1959, JD, 1964. Bar: Okla. 1964, U.S. Tax Ct. 1964, U.S. Ct. Claims 1964, U.S. Dist. Ct., no. we. & so. dist. Okla.

1964, U.S. Ct. Appeals, 10th circuit 1971, U.S. Supreme Ct. 1975. Lawyer Gable & Gotwals, Inc., Tulsa, 1964—. Trustee River Parks Authority, Tulsa County, Okla., 1989-97; Okla. Jud. Nomin. Commn. 1981-87, chmn. 1985-87; Ctr. Am. & Internat. Law, trustee 1997-, rsch fellow 2000-; bd. dir. Tulsa Area United Way 2003- (exec. comm. 2003-, Alexis de Tocqueville Soc. chmn. 2004); bd. visitors Univ. Okla. Coll. Arts & Sci. 1997-, Coll. Law 2002-. Officer infantry USMC, 1959—61. Mem. ABA (house del. 1992-04, bd. gov. 2004-); Am. Coll. Trial Lawyers (fellow, state chmn. 2000-02), Okla. Bar Assn. (v.p., bd. gov. 1976, chmn. profl. responsibility commn. 1978, chmn. adminstrn. justice comm.1994-97, mem. tort reform task force, 2004), Okla. Bar Found. (trustee 1988—); Tulsa County Bar Assn.(Dist. Svc. award, 1992, Outstanding Young Lawyer, 1968). Life Fellow, Am. Bar Found; Okla. Bar Found; Am. Inns of Ct. (founding master, Hudson-Hall-Wheaton chptr.). Republican. Methodist. Office: Gable & Gotwals 1100 ONEOK Plz 100 W 5th St Tulsa OK 74103-4217 Office Phone: 918-595-4800. Business E-Mail: jsturdivant@gablelaw.com.

**STURGILL, JAMES AARON,** museum administrator; b. Cincinnati, Ohio, June 9, 1978; s. James and Rosemarie Sturgill; m. Erin Rosella Meekhof, May 26, 2001. AS, Hocking Coll., 1999; BA, Grand Valley State U., 2002; MA, Ea. Ill. U., 2004. Dir. Athens (Ohio) County Hist. Soc. and Mus., 2003—04; mgr. edn. and external relation Mahoning Valley Hist. Soc., Youngstown, Ohio, 2005—. Contbr. exhibition. Vol. Bush-Cheney 2004 Campaign, Athens, 2004; coord. county campaign Lanzinger for Justice, Athens, 2004; vice chmn. ctrl. com. Athens (Ohio) County Rep. Party, 2003—04. Mem.: Hist. Adminstrn. Program Assn. (v.p. 2005—), Assn. Midwest Mus., Honorary Order Ky. Cols. Republican. Lutheran. Avocations: poetry, reenacting. Office: Mahoning Valley Historical Society 648 Wick Avenue Youngstown OH 44502 Office Phone: 330-743-2589.

**STURGULEWSKI, ARLISS,** state legislator, director; b. Blaine, Wash., Sept. 27, 1927; BA, U. Wash.; LLD (hon.), U. Alaska, Anchorage, 1993. Mem. Assembly Municipality of Anchorage; interim exec. dir. Alaska Sci. and Tech. Found., 1995. Vice chmn. New Capital Site Planning Commn., mem. Capital Site Selection Com.; chmn. Greater Anchorage Area Planning and Zoning Commn.; mem. Alaska State Senate, 1978-93; Rep. nominee Office Gov. Alaska, 1986, 90. Home: 2957 Sheldon Jackson St Anchorage AK 99508-4469 Office: 3201 C St Ste 405 Anchorage AK 99503-3967 Business E-Mail: a.sturgulewski@swallingcpas.com.

**STURKEN, CRAIG C.,** retail executive; Sr. v.p. Big Star Food Stores, 1989—90; chmn. Can. ops. Spartan Stores Inc., 1990—93, group v.p. Mich. ops., then pres. A&P Mich., 1993—97, chmn., CEO midwest region, 1997—2000, pres., CEO atlantic region, 2000—03, chmn., pres., CEO 2003—. Office: Spartan Stores 850 76th St SW Grand Rapids MI 49518

**STURLEY, MICHAEL F.,** law educator; b. Syracuse, N.Y., Feb. 14, 1955; s. Richard Avern and Helen Elizabeth (Fisher) S.; m. Michele Y. Deitch, July 2, 1989; children: Jennifer Diane, Elizabeth Claire. BA, Yale U., 1977, JD, l981; MA in Jurisprudence, Oxford U., 1980, MA, 1985. Bar: N.Y. 1984, U.S. Dist. Ct. (so. and ea. dists.) N.Y. 1984, U.S. Supreme Court 1987. Law clk. to Judge Amalya L. Kearse, U.S. Ct. Appeals for 2d Cir., N.Y.C., 1981-82; law clk. to Justice Lewis F. Powell, Jr. U.S. Supreme Ct., Washington, 1982-83; assoc. Sullivan & Cromwell, N.Y.C., 1983-84; asst. prof. law U. Tex. Law Sch., Austin, 1984-88, prof., 1988—. Vis. prof. Queen Mary and Westfield Coll., U. London, 1990, advisor Restatement (3d) of Property (servitudes), 1989-2000. Author: (with David W. Robertson and Steven F. Friedell) Admiralty and Maritime Law in the United States, 2001; compiler, editor: The Legislative History of the Carriage of Goods by Sea Act and the Travaux Préparatoires of The Hague Rules, 3 vols., 1990; mem. editl. bd. Jour. Maritime Law and Commerce, 1989—, book rev. editor, 1993—; contbg. author: Benedict on Admiralty, 1990—; contbr. articles to legal jours. Mem. Am. Law Inst., Maritime Law Assn. (proctor), Comité Maritime Internat. (titulary) Office: U Tex Sch Law 727 E Dean Keeton St Austin TX 78705-3224 Office Phone: 512-232-1350.

**STURM, SUSAN P.,** law educator; BA, Brown U., 1976; JD, Yale U., 1979. Law clk. to Hon. Charles E. Stewart US Dist. Ct. (So. Dist.) NY; faculty mem. U. Pa., 1986—99, Columbia Law Sch., NYC, 2000—, George M. Jaffin Prof. of Law and Social Responsibility. Mem. Presdl. Adv. Commn. on Diversity Initiatives. Co-author: Whose Qualified? The Future of Affirmative Action, 2001; author: Equality and the Forms of Justice, 2003, Law's Role in Addressing Complex Discrimination, 2005. Office: Columbia Law Sch Rm 617 435 W 116th St New York NY 10027 Office Phone: 212-854-0062. Office Fax: 212-854-7946. E-mail: ssturm@law.columbia.edu.

**STURM, WILLIAM CHARLES,** lawyer; b. Milw., Aug. 4, 1941; s. Charles William and Helen Ann (Niesen) S.; m. Kay F. Sturm, June 10, 1967; children: Patricia, Elizabeth, Katherine, William, Susan. BS in Bus. Adminstrn., Marquette U., 1963; JD, 1966. Bar: Wis. 1966, U.S. Dist. Ct. (ea. dist.) Wis. 1966, U.S. Supreme Ct. 1980. Sole practice, Milw., 1966—77; ptnr. Rausch, Hamell, Ehrle & Sturm, S.C., Milw., 1977—81, Rausch, Hamell, Ehrle, Sturm & Blom, Milw., 1981-83, Rausch, Hamell, Ehrle & Sturm, 1983-95, Rausch, Hamell, Sturm & Israel S.C., 1995-98, Rausch, Sturm, Israel & Hornik, S.C., 1999—. asst. prof. Marquette U., 1982-91; lectr. U. Wis., Milw., 1991-97, sr. lectr. 1997-2002. Contbr. articles to profl. jours. Mem. adv. bd. Pallotine Order, 1985—; bd. dirs. Pius XI H.S., 2002-2004. Recipient Editors award Wis. Med. Credit Assn., 1980, Recipient Outstanding Alumni Pius XI H.S., 2002. Mem. ABA, Wis. Bar Assn., Comml. Law League Am. (exec. coun. midwestern dist. 1981-83, 86-88, chmn. state membership com. 1981-88, nat. nominating coun. 1984-86, 1988-89, 2004-05, sec., 2d v.p midwestern dist. 1989-90, 1st v.p. midwestern dist. 1990-91, chmn. 1991-92, nat. bd. govs. 1997-2000, pres. elect 2000-01, pres. 2001-02), Acad. Legal Studies in Bus., Midwest Bus. Law Assn. (sec. 1988-89, v.p. 1989-90, pres. 1990-91), Healthcare Fin. Mgmt. Assn., Beta Alpha Psi (faculty v.p. Psi chpt. 1985-88, Eta Theta chpt. 1992-99), Midwest Bus. and Health Assn. (v.p. procs. 1987-88, v.p. program 1988-89, pres. 1989-90), Westmoor Country Club (Milw.); Kiwanis (pres. 1979, lt. gov. div. 5, 1980). Office: 2448 South 102nd St Milwaukee WI 53227 Office Phone: 414-328-1400. E-mail: wsturm@wiscollect.com.

**STURMAN, DEBORAH MUSCHA,** lawyer, columnist; d. Herman Getzie and Gladys Freiman Sturman; 1 child, Rachel Zipporah. Prix D'Excellence, Royal Brussels Conservatory of Music, Belgium, 1992; JD, UCLA, 1995. Bar: Calif. 1995, D.C. 2000, NY 2001. Of counsel Milberg Weiss Bershad Hynes & Lerach LLP, N.Y.C., 1995—2001, Milberg, Weiss, Bershad, & Schulman, 2001—06, Law Office of Deborah Sturman, 2006—. Legal columnist Mgr. Magazin, Hamburg, Germany, 2003—. Musician (French horn soloist): Telemann Concerti Mozart Chamber Music; musician: (French horn sect. leader) Royal Philharmonic Belgium; musician: West German Broadcasting Orch.; dir.(prodr.): (radio and TV) Lieder und Schwenke aus der Klosterschenke, Aus dem Leben eines Taugenichts. Mem. Calif. Holocaust Era Ins. Oversight Com., Sacramento, 2000—. Democrat. Jewish. Avocations: music, writing. Office: Sturman LLP 112 Madison Ave New York NY 10016 Office Phone: 843-216-9000. Business E-Mail: sturman@sturman.ch.

**STURMAN, GEORGE,** poet; b. N.Y., Oct. 19, 1914; s. Benny and Anna Sturman; m. Mary Kruse, Oct. 18, 1953 (dec. June 27, 1993). Student, C.C. N.Y. Adminstr. officer U.S. Gen. Svc. Adminstrn., Washington, 1935—78. Editl. adv. Truth Seeker; pub. rels. Rancho Bernardo Sun, Poway, Calif. Author: (poetry) A Sonnet to Pavarotti; contbr. articles to profl. jour.; prof. listener (Royal Caribbean cruise line). Vol. Marriott's Remington Ret. Facility, San Diego. Home: Recipient Vol. of the Yr., Marriotts Remington Ret. facility., 2002. Home: 11098 Picaza Pl San Diego CA 92127

**STURMAN, GLORIDA J.,** lawyer; b. Cortez, Colo., June 26, 1957; BS cum laude, Ariz. State U., 1979, JD, 1982. Bar: Ariz. 1982, Nev. 1983. Atty. Edwards, Hale, Sturman, Atkin & Cushing, Ltd., Las Vegas. Mem.: ABA, So.

Nev. Assn. Women Attys. (pres. 1988—89), Clark County Bar Assn. (pres. 1994), State Bar Nev. (pres. 2002—03, bd. govs.), State Bar Ariz. Office: Edwards Hale Sturman et al 415 S Sixth St Ste 300 Las Vegas NV 89101-6937

**STURNER, LYNDA,** performing company executive; b. Buffalo, July 1, 1941; d. Samuel S. and Rachel Louise Sturner; m. Jerome S. Traum, Sept. 23, 2001 (dec.); children: Daniel Matthew Traum, Edward Hart Traum stepchildren: David A. Traum, Norman D. Traum. BFA, Boston U., 1963. Actress Broadway Oliver, N.Y.C., 1964—66; artistic dir. Playwrights Forum Inc., N.Y.C., 1982—88; co-prodr. The Juniper Tree, N.Y.C., 1982; prodr. Triangle Prodns., N.Y.C., 1981—87; artistic dir. Provincetown (Mass.) Repertory Theatre, 2004—. Bd. dirs., v.p. Music Theatre Group, N.Y.C., 1981—2001; tchr. Boston U., 1983—96; playwright Woman's Project Lab., 1989—97; bd. dirs. Castle Hill Truro Ctr. for the Arts, 1980—99, Provincetown Theatre Co., 1999—2003; artistic dir. Provincetown Repertory Theatre, 2004—05. Author: (plays) Look What You Made Me Do, 2000 (Audience Choice award, 2001), Art Brute, 2001, (on-line work) TheatreMania.com, 1999—2002; co-author: (plays) Sextet, 2001; author The Death of Huey Newton. Mem.: League of Profl. Theatre Women, Screen Actors Guild, Actors Equity Assn. Democrat. Jewish. Office: Provincetown Repertory Theatre 238 Commercial St Provincetown MA 02657 E-mail: lynda_sturner@yahoo.com.

**STURR, JAMES WILLIAM, JR.,** bandleader, recording industry executive, clarinetist, saxophonist, small business owner; b. Springfield, Mass., Sept. 25, 1952; s. James William Sr. and Margaret Lillian (Gallagher) S. AA, Valley Forge Mil. Acad., 1964; BA, U. Scranton, 1966. Pres., bus. owner Starr Record Co., 1969—; pres. United Polka Artists; owner Jimmy Sturr Travel Agy. Composer: Men Don't Leave; album I'm Sturr Crazy (Album of Yr.); song A Little Bit of Poland (Song of Yr.); albums include Live at Gilly's, 1991, When It's Polka Time at Your House, 1991, A Jimmy Sturr Christmas, 1992, Sturr It Up, 1992, Polka Christmas, 1993, Polka Saturday Night, 1994, Polka Your Troubles Away, 1994, Attitude in Polkas, 1994, I Love to Polka, 1995, Saturday Night Polka, 1995, Polka! All Night Long, 1996, Living On Polka Time, 1997, Polka Favorites, 1997, Pure Polka, 1997, Dance With Me, 1998, Life's A Polka, 1998, Polkapalooza, 1999, Jimmy Sturr Polka, 2000, Touched By a Polka, 2000, Gone Polka, 2001, Top of the World, 2002, Let's Polka 'Round, 2003, Rock 'N Polka, 2004, Shake, Rattle and Polka!, 2005 and others; has featured a number of high profile guest on albums such as, Willie Nelson, Jo-El Sonnier, Flaco Jimenez, Bill Anderson, Oak Ridge Boys, Brenda Lee, Arlo Guthrie, Mel Tillis, Rhonda Vincent, Béta Fleck and Boots Randolph; appeared at the Grand Old Opry, Carnegie Hall, NY, Lincoln Ctr., NYC, Avery Fisher Hall, NYC, Palace of Culture, Warsaw, Poland, The Nashville Network, Mohegan Sun Casino, Uncasville, Conn., Tropicana and Taj Mahal, Atlantic City, NJ, Patowatomi Casino, Milwaukee, Wis., Soaring Eagle, Mt. Pleasant, Mich., The President's Casino, Biloxi, Miss., Mountaineer Race Track and Gaming Resort, Chester, West Va., Stardust Hotel and Casino, Las Vegas; host, nationally syndicated TV show; guest appearances on CNN, ABC, NBC, FOX News, and Saturday Night Live, (TV commercials) Budweiser, Pontiac, Mrs. T's Pierogies (Nat. spokesperson for Mrs. T's Pierogies); owner of music publishing co.; owner, host syndicated radio show, Polka Session, 1964-. Anchorman Cerebral Palsy telethons, Am. Cancer Soc. telethons, active numerous others. Recipient 15 Grammy awards (including Best Polka Album), 5 Gold Album awards, (with orchestra) Commendation of Excellence, Broadcast Music Inc. (the only one ever awarded in the polka field); named #1 Polka Band in the country, Man of Yr., Valley Forge Military Acad.; inducted into Polka Hall of Fame. Mem. Elks. Achievements include receiving more consecutive Grammy nominations then anyone in history of musical awards; honored with a Star of Fame in the walkway of Main Street in small hometown of Florida, NY. Also on display signs at each entrance of the small town, Hometown of Polka King Jimmy Sturr.

**STURROCK, PETER ANDREW,** space science and astrophysics educator; b. South Stifford, Essex, Eng., Mar. 20, 1924; came to U.S., 1955; s. Albert Edward and Mabel Minnie Sturrock; m. Marilyn Fern Stenson, June 29, 1963; children: Deirdre, Colin; 1 child from previous marriage, Myra. BA, Cambridge (Eng.) U., 1945, MA, 1948, PhD, 1951. Scientist Telecomms. Rsch. Establishment, Malvern, England, 1943-46, Nat. Bur. Standards, Washington, 1949-50, Ecole Normale Superieure, Paris, 1950-51, Atomic Energy Rsch. Establishment, Harwell, 1951-53; fellow St. John's Coll., Cambridge U., 1952-55; rsch. assoc. Stanford (Calif.) U., 1955-61, prof. dept. applied physics, 1961-98, dir. Inst. for Plasma Rsch., 1964—74, 1980—83; dep. dir. Ctr. for Space Sci. and Astrophysics, 1983-92, dir., 1992-98. Author: Static and Dynamic Electron Optics, 1955, Plasma Physics, 1993, The UFO Enigma, 1999; editor: Plasma Astrophysics, 1967, Solar Flares, 1980, Physics of the Sun, vols. I, II, III, 1986. Recipient Gravity prize Gravity Found., 1967, Hale prize Am. Astron. Soc., 1986, Henryk Arctowski medal NAS, 1990, Space Sci. award AIAA, 1992; European Ctr. for Nuclear Rsch. fellow, 1957-58. Fellow AAAS, Royal Astron. Soc., Am. Phys. Soc.; mem. Internat. Astron. Union, Internat. Acad. Astronautics, Soc. Sci. Exploration (pres. 1982-2001, Dinnsdale prize 2006). Office: Stanford U Dept Physics Varian Bldg Rm 302 Stanford CA 94305

**STURTEVANT, BRERETON,** retired lawyer, retired federal official; b. Washington, Nov. 24, 1921; d. Charles Lyon and Grace (Brereton) S. BA, Wellesley Coll., 1942; JD, Temple U., 1949; postgrad., U. Del., 1969-71. Bar: D.C. 1949, Del. 1950. Research chemist E.I. duPont DeNemours & Co., 1942-50; law clk. Del. Supreme Ct., 1950; gen. practice law Wilmington, Del., 1950-57; partner Connolly, Bove & Lodge, Wilmington, 1957-71; examiner-in-chief U.S. Patent and Trademark Office Bd. Appeals, Washington, 1971-88. Adj. prof. law Georgetown U., 1974-79. Trustee Holton-Arms Sch., Bethesda, Md., 1977-96, chmn. or mem. all coms., trustee emerita, 1997—. Mem. ABA, Exec. Women in Govt. (charter mem., chmn. 1978-79) Clubs: Wellesley College, Washington-Wellesley (pres. 1982-84). Episcopalian. Achievements include first woman law clerk, Delaware Supreme Court; first woman patent examiner-in-chief. Home: 1227 Morningside Ln Alexandria VA 22308-1042

**STURTEVANT, PETER MANN, JR.,** television news executive; b. Northampton, Mass., Feb. 27, 1943; s. Peter Mann and Katharine Bryan (Hobson) S.; m. Anne Elizabeth Fitzpatrick, July 12, 1969 (div. Dec. 1984); 1 child, Amanda Hadden; m. Toni E. Siegel, Apr. 14, 1985; 1 child, Gillian Lee. BA in Polit. Sci., Wilmington Coll., 1965; MA in Journalism, U. Iowa, 1967. Assoc. prodr. CBS News, Washington, 1967-71, bur. chief Viet Nam Saigon, 1971-73, nat. news editor N.Y.C., 1974-80, asst. v.p. spl. events, 1981-83, producer 60 Minutes, 1984-85; exec. bus. news editor CNN, N.Y.C., 1985-86; prodr. Today's Bus. Buena Vista TV, N.Y.C., 1987; dir. news coverage CNBC, Fort Lee, NJ, 1988-90, v.p., mng. editor Ft. Lee, NJ, 1991-94; sr. v.p. Internat. Bus. News NBC, 1994-98; disaster relief, instr. Am. Red Cross, 1999—. Trustee Wilmington Coll., 2000—. Named Disting. Alumnus, Wilmington Coll., 1975, 97; named to Journalism Hall of Fame, U. Iowa Grad. Sch. Journalism, 1988; named to Wilmington Coll. Sports Hall of Fame, 1997. Mem. Nat. Acad. Cable Programming (nominated ACE award 1992, 93, 94), Soc. Profl. Journalists, Deadline Club N.Y., The Asia Soc., Overseas Press Club (bd. dirs.). Episcopalian. Avocations: racquet sports, landscaping, travel, stamp collecting/philately, parenting. Home: 90 Riverside Dr # 8D New York NY 10024-5306

**STURTS, DONNA JEAN,** music educator; b. Shelby, Ohio, Feb. 11, 1940; d. Charles Gilbert Burky and Martha Mabel Schwert; m. Delmar Dean Sturts, Apr. 8, 1961; children: Erica Lynn, Erin Elizabeth, Blair Alan. Cert. music tchr. Am. Coll. Musicians, 2002. Bank teller Citizens Bank, Shelby, Ohio, 1958—64; choir dir. Ctrl. Meth. Ch., Mansfield, Ohio, 1982—2000; piano tchr. Sturts Studio of Music, Mansfield, 1974—; vocal soloist various area churches, Mansfield, 1962—. Mem. Mansfield Symphony Chorus, 2004—. Gold cup chmn. Fedn. of Music Clubs, Dist. IV, Ohio, 1999—. Recipient Service award, Centra United Meth. Ch., 1986, 1996, State Gold Cup Chairmanship award, Ohio Fedn. Music Clubs, 2004. Mem.: Am. Coll. Musicians, Ohio Music Teachers Assn. (25 Yr. award 2002), Ohio Music

Teachers Assn., Music Teachers Nat. Assn. (ribbon festival chmn., Richland County 1997—), Nat. Fedn. Music Clubs, Mansfield Music Study Club. Avocations: painting, woodworking, needlecrafts, travel. Home: 92 Stewart Ave Mansfield OH 44906

**STURTZ, DONALD LEE,** surgeon, educator, military officer; b. Coshocton, Ohio, Apr. 18, 1933; s. Walter Raymond and Helene Josephine (Kubic) S.; m. Alice Marie McGuire, June 11, 1955; children: Jimalee, Janel. BS, U.S. Naval Acad., 1955; MD, U. Pa., 1965; diploma med. care catastrophe, Soc. Apothecaries London, 1996. Diplomate Am. Bd. Surgery. Surg. resident USN, Phila., 1965-70, ship's surgeon, 1970-71; staff surgeon Bethesda Naval Hosp., USN, 1971-80; chief of surgery San Diego Naval Hosp., USN, 1980-84; exec. officer Oakland (Calif.) Naval Hosp., USN, 1984-85; prof. clin. surgery USN, Bethesda, Md., 1985-87; commd. Naval Med. Command, 1987-88, Atlantic fleet surgeon, Supreme Allied Command surgeon Norfolk, Va., 1989-91; prof. surgery USUHS, Bethesda, Md., 1991—. Contbr. articles to profl. jours. Recipient B.D. Larrey award for Surgical Excellence, Surgical Dept. USUHS, Bethesda, 1988, Exceptional Svc. medal, Uniformed Svcs. U., 1998. Fellow ACS (gov. 1985-88); mem. Am. Assn. for Surgery of Trauma, Assn. Mil. Surgeons, USN Inst. Republican. Presbyterian. Avocations: travel, gardening, antiques, music, reading. Office: USUHS Dept Surgery 4301 Jones Bridge Rd Bethesda MD 20814-4799 Office Phone: 301-295-3155. E-mail: sturtz@aol.com.

**STUTTS, JAMES F.,** lawyer; b. Dec. 1944; BA in English, U. Va., 1967; MBA, U. Pa., 1970; JD, U. Richmond 1977. Bar: Va. 1977, Pa. 1992. V.p. corp. fin. Wheat, First Securities; ptnr. McSweeney Stutts & Burtch, Richmond, Va.; assoc. McGuire Woods Battle & Boothe LLP, Richmond, Va., 1985—87, ptnr., 1987—97; v.p., gen. counsel Dominion Resources Inc., Richmond, Va., 1997—. Office: Dominion Resources Inc 120 Tredegar St Richmond VA 23219

**STUTZ, PEARL HEWLETT,** retired photojournalist; b. Rochester, N.Y., Apr. 28, 1927; d. Herbert Henry Hewlett and Carolyn Amanda Brockmann; m. Peter Swan Stutz, May 23, 1953 (dec. July 1988); children: Eric Edward, Carolyn Edith Stutz Kourofsky. BA in Journalism, Ohio State U., 1949; MLS, SUNY, Geneseo, 1971. Cert. profl. libr. and media specialist, N.Y. Reporter Pampa (Tex.) Daily News, 1949, Great Falls (Mont.) Tribune, 1950; staff photographer Democrat and Chronicle, Rochester, 1950-56; libr. dir. Irondequoit Pub. Libr., Rochester, 1976-91; ret., 1991. Libr. cons. Cancer Action, Inc., Rochester, 1992-01. Named Disting. Communicator, Women in Comms., 1996. Achievements include first woman press photographer for large-city newspaper.

**STUTZMAN, DONNA J.,** minister; b. Lemoyne, Ohio, Apr. 29, 1936; d. David O. Kaser and Opal M. Stockwell; m. Darrell A. Stutzman, June 7, 1958 (dec. Sept. 1993); children: Denzel, Devon, Dawn, Dara, Desmond. BS in Child and Family Cmty. Svc., Bowling Green State U., Ohio, 1987; MA in Christian Psychology, Cornerstone U., Lake Charles, La., 1992. Ordained minister Nat. Conservative Christian Ch., 1999; lic. social worker Ohio. Pvt. piano tchr., Wauseon, Ohio, 1958—; case mgr. Fulton County Maumee Valley Guidance Ctr., Defiance, Ohio, 1987—89; assoc. pastor First Ch. of God, Wauseon, 1989—91; mental health profl. Fulton County Health Ctr., Wauseon, 1991—99; social worker, music coord. Fulton Manor Nursing Home, Wauseon, 1998—; hospice chaplain Cmty. Health Profls., Archbold, Ohio, 1999—; pastor Hope Christian Fellowship, Wauseon, 1991—. Spirituality group facilitator Fulton County Health Ctr. Psychiat. Unit, 2003—. Vol. coord. Habitat for Humanity, 2003. Mem.: AAUW, Am. Acad. Bereavement, Am. Assn. Christian Counselors, Nat. Christian Counselors Assn., Phi Upsilon Omicron. Avocations: reading, music. Home: 701 Burr Rd Unit 5 Wauseon OH 43567 E-mail: djstutzman@aol.com.

**STUTZMAN, L. LEE,** pastor; b. Clinton, Okla., June 13, 1953; s. Clamens L. Stutzman and Viola Darlene (Waters) Bonn; m. Connie R. Stutzman, June 3, 1972; children: Elizabeth, Jonathan, Rebecca. BA in Theology, Vision Christian U., MS in Theol. Studies, D in Ministry. With traveling ministry, 1972-78; founder Liberty Temple, Lima, Ohio, 1978-88, Christ Cathedral, 1988—; with nat. traveling ministry; apostle Liberty Network of Chs., Dayton, Ohio, 1986—. Author: From the Ground Up, 1987; producer (TV show) Foundation for Faith, 1985—; motivational spkr., Sci. of Empowered Living Forum. Author: From the Ground Up, 1987, Order Out of Chaos, 1995, Spiritual Gifts, 1992, Invisible Lines of Supply, 2002; prodr. (TV show) Life Without Limit, 1985—. Republican. Office: Christ Cathedral 51 Best St Dayton OH 45405 *The greatest key to Godly success: you've got to start where you're at to get where you're going.*

**STUTZMAN, SANDRA LOUISE,** advanced nurse practitioner; b. Ashland, Pa., Nov. 10, 1953; d. Mary (Tersavige) S. Diploma, Sacred Heart Hosp. Sch., Norristown, Pa., 1979; LPN, Pottstown Meml. Med. Ctr.; diploma, St. Joseph Sch. Nursing, Reading, Pa., 1983; BS, Pa. State U., Reading, 1991; MS, U. South Fla., 1994. Advanced RN practitioner. Staff nurse Pottstown Meml. Med. Ctr., 1983—91; advanced RN practitioner Infectious Disease Ctr., Tampa (Fla.) Gen. Hosp., 1995—98; advanced RN practitioner EverCare, Tampa, Fla., 1998-99, Sergio H. Vallejo, M.D., Lakeland, Fla., 1999—2002, Advent Christian Village, Dowling Park, Fla., 2002—. Mem. Am. Acad. Nurse Practitioners, Fla. Nurses Assn., Sigma Theta Tau.

**STUTZMAN, THOMAS CHASE, SR.,** lawyer; b. Portland, Oreg., Aug. 1, 1950; s. Leon H. and Mary L. (Chase) S.; m. Wendy Jeanne Craig, June 5, 1976; children: Sarah Anne, Thomas Chase Jr. BA with high honors, U. Calif. Santa Barbara, 1972; JD cum laude, Santa Clara U., 1975. Bar: Calif. 1976; cert. family law specialist. Pvt. practice, San Jose, Calif. 1976—79; pres., sec., CFO Thomas Chase Stutzman, PC, San Jose, 1979—. Instr. San Jose State U., 1977—78. Bd. dirs. Santa Cruz Campfire, 1978-80, Happy Hollow Park, 1978-80, 83-86, Pacific Neighbors, pres., 1991-92. Mem. Calif. Bar Assn., Santa Clara County Bar Assn. (chmn. environ. law com. 1976-78, exec. com. family law), Assn. Cert. Law Specialists, San Jose Jaycees (Dir. of Yr. 1976-77), Lions (dir. 1979-81, 2d v.p. 1982-83, 1st v.p. 1983-84, pres. 1984-85), Scottish Rite, Masons, Phi Beta Kappa. Congregationalist. Office: 1625 The Alameda Ste 626 San Jose CA 95126-2207 Business E-Mail: stutzman@tomstutzman.com

**STUZIN, JAMES M.,** plastic surgeon; b. Miami, Fla., June 1, 1952; BA, U. Fla., Gainesville, 1974, MD, 1978. Cert. in gen. surgery 1985, in plastic surgery 1989. Intern, gen. surgery U. Wash. Hosps., Seattle, 1978—79, resident, gen. surgery, 1979—83; fellow, plastic surgery NYU Hosps., N.Y.C., 1984—86; craniofacial fellow U. Miami Hosps., Fla., 1986, UCLA Sch. Medicine, 1987, asst. clin. prof., plastic surgery 1987; clin. instr., dept. plastic surgery U. Miami Sch. Medicine, Fla., 1989—95, clin. asst. prof., plastic surgery, 1995—. Mem. editl. bd. Annals of Plastic Surgery, 1993—. Mem.: Am. Soc. for Aesthetic Plastic Surgery (treas.), Alpha Omega Alpha, Phi Beta Kappa.

**STWALLEY, WILLIAM CALVIN,** physics professor, chemistry professor; BS, Calif. Inst. Tech., 1964; PhD, Harvard U., 1968. Asst. prof. U. Iowa, Iowa City, 1968-72, assoc. prof., 1972-75, prof. chemistry, 1975-93, prof. dept. physics and astronomy, 1977-93, dir. Iowa Laser Facility, 1979-93, dir. Ctr. for Laser Sci. and Engring., 1987-89, George Glockler prof. physical scis., 1988-93; program dir. NSF, Washington, 1975-76 (leave of absence); prof. and head dept. physics, prof. chemistry U. Conn., Storrs, 1993—, bd. trustees disting. prof., 2002—. Program chmn. Internat. Laser Sci. Conf., 1985, co-chmn., 1986, chmn., 1987; lectr. Chinese Acad. Scis., 1986. Editor books in field; contbr. numerous articles to profl. publs. Recipient Conn. medal of sci., 2005—; Japan Soc. for Promotion of Sci. fellow, 1982; Sloan fellow, 1970-72; numerous grants in field, 1970—. Fellow AAAS, Am. Phys. Soc. (sec.-treas. divsn. chem. physics 1984-92, vice chair/chair Topical Group on Laser Sci. 1989-92, vice chair/chair divsn. atomic, molecular and optical physics 2005-), Optical Soc. Am. (William F. Meggers award 1998), Conn.

Acad. Sci. and Engring., Conn. Acad. Arts and Scis.; mem. Am. Chem. Soc. Office: U Conn Unit 3046 Dept Physics Storrs Mansfield CT 06269-3046 Office Phone: 860-486-4924. Business E-Mail: w.stwalley@uconn.edu.

**STYCOS, MARIA NOWAKOWSKA,** adult education educator; b. Lwow, Poland, June 4, 1937; arrived in U.S., 1964; d. Marian Zygmunt Nowakowski and Julia Demska Nowakowska; m. Joseph Mayone Stycos; 1 child, Marek. BA, King's Coll. U. London, London, 1958; MA, Cornell U., 1967, PhD, 1977. Part time asst. prof. Ithaca Coll., NY, 1975—81; dir. Handwerker Art Gallery, Ithaca, NY, 1981—82; asst. prof. State U. of N.Y., Cortland, NY, 1982—86; sr. lectr. Cornell U., Ithaca, NY, 1986—. Cons. Cornell U., Costa Rica, 1986; faculty adv. com. Johnson Mus. Art, Cornell U. Co-author (with E. Sanchez-Blake): Voces Hispanas Siglo XXI Entrevistas con autores en DVD, 2005; contbr. chapters to books, articles to profl. jours. including Asociacion Internat. de Letras y Cultura Femenina Hispanica, Revista/Rev, Interamericana P.R., Dictionary of the Lit. of the Iberian Peninsula, others. Planning bd. mem. Village of Lansing, NY, 2002—. Mem.: MLA, Congreso Internat. Sobre Lit. Centroamericana, Assn. Internat. Hispanistas. Avocations: music, art, gardening, travel, poetry. Office: Romance Studies Cornell Univ Ithaca NY 14853 Business E-Mail: mns2@cornell.edu.

**STYER, DENISE MARIE,** psychologist; d. Kenneth James and Mary Ellen Styer; 1 child, James Kenneth Marketti. BA, U. Wisc., 1990; MA, Alfred Adler Inst. Minn., 1995; PsyD, Adler Sch. Profl. Psychology, 2001. Lic. Profl. Counselor Ill., 2001. Therapist, intake coord. SAFE Alternatives, Naperville, Ill., 2000—01; clin. coord. Self Injury Recovery Svcs. Alexian Bros. Behavioral Hosp., Hoffman Estates, Ill., 2001—. Mem.: APA (prevention rschr. adv. bd. 2005). Office Phone: 708-638-8235 Personal E-mail: d.denisestyer@aol.com.

**STYER, JOANNE LOUISE,** retired dietician; b. Melin, Oreg., Nov. 23, 1931; d. Raymond Louis Hosford and Gladys Lorraine Loomis; m. Lawrence Henry Styer, Aug. 20, 1955. BS in Foods and Nutrition and Instnl. Mgmt., U. Wis., Stout, 1954; postgrad., George Washington U., U. Md., U.S. Internat. U. Lic. reg. dietitian. Intern St. Mary's Hosp., Rochester, Minn., 1955; chief therapeutic dietitian Glen Dale Hosp., Washington, 1956; chief dietitian George Washington U. Med. Ctr., Washington, 1956—68; asst. dir. food svc. Montgomery County (Md.) Pub. Schs., 1968—69, dir. food svc., 1969—92; dietetic cons. Carriage Hill Nursing Home; cons. N.Y.C. Homeless Food Svc., Montgomery County Pub. Schs., USDA Commodity Processing, N.Y.C. Prison Food Svc. Evaluation; mem. adv. bd. D.C. Dairy Coun.; mem. industry adv. bd. Nat. Frozen Food Assn. Mem. editl. review panel Sch. Food Svc. Rsch. Review. Past chmn. nutrition com. D.C. Heart Assn.; nutrition com. Am. Heart Assn.; food chmn. Montgomery County Disaster Com.; nutrition com. Montgomery County Heart Assn.; expert task force USDA, Am. Cancer Soc. Named Disting. Alumni, U. Wis., Stout, 1989. Mem.: Md. Sch. Bus. Ofcls. (sect. chmn. food svc.), Md. Sch. Food Svc. Assn. (past pres.), D.C. Dietetic Assn. (past pres.), Md. Dietetic Assn., Am. Dietetic Assn. (chmn. dietetic practice group for sch. food svc.). Home: 11342 Kings Valley Dr Damascus MD 20872 Personal E-mail: lcapthook1@aol.com.

**STYMIEST, BARBARA,** stock exchange executive; MBA, Richard Ivey Sch. Bus. Audit ptnr., Fin. Svcs. Group Ernst & Young, 1978—87; exec. v.p., CFO Nesbitt Burns Corp., Ltd., Canada, 1992—99; chair, bd. govs. Toronto Stock Exch. (now TSX Group Inc.), 1997—99, CEO, 1999—, also. bd. dirs.; COO Royal Bank Can. Mem. ICAO Task Force, 1996; gov. Can. Investor Protection Fund, 1996; chair Joint Industry Coord. Com., 1995—97; alt. gov. Can. Securities Inst., 1995, gov. 1997—; mem. task force on std. setting CICA, 1996—98. Mem. ofcl. Bd. Forest Hills United Ch., 1984; bd. mem. Rehab. Inst. Toronto, 1996, Hincks Dellcrest Children's Ctr., 1990—97, chair, bd. dirs., 1993—96. Named one of 50 Most Powerful Women, Fortune Mag., 2005; grantee Inst. Charted Accts. Ont. Fellow: Inst. Chartered Accts. Ont. Office: Royal Bank Canada 200 Bay St M5J 2J5 Toronto ON Canada*

**STYNE, DENNIS MICHAEL,** physician, educator; b. Chgo., July 31, 1947; s. Irving and Bernice S.; m. Donna Petre, Sept. 5, 1971; children: Rachel, Jonathan, Juliana, Aaron. BS, Northwestern U., 1969, MD, 1971. Diplomate Am. Bd. Pediat. Intern in pediatrics U. Calif., San Diego, 1971-72, resident in pediatrics, 1972-73, Yale U., New Haven, 1973-74; fellow in pediatric endocrinology U. Calif., San Francisco, 1974-77, asst. prof. pediatrics, 1977-83, assoc. prof. Davis, 1983-90, prof., 1990—, chair pediatrics, 1989-97; prof., sect. chief and Rumsey chair of pediatric endocrinology U. Calif. Davis Med. Ctr., Sacramento, 1997—. Author numerous book chpts., contbr. articles to profl. jours. Mem. Endocrine Soc., Soc. Pediat. Rsch., Am. Pediat. Soc., Am. Acad. Pediat., Lawson Wilkins Soc. for Pediat. Endocrinology, Western Assn. of Physicians. Avocations: sailing, music. Office: UC Davis Med Ctr Dept Pediat 2516 Stockton Blvd Fl 3 Sacramento CA 95817-2208

**STYNES, STANLEY KENNETH,** retired chemical engineer, educator; b. Detroit, Jan. 18, 1932; s. Stanley Kenneth and Bessie Myrtle (Casey) S.; m. Marcia Ann Meyers, Aug. 27, 1955; children: Peter Casey, Pamela Kay, Suzanne Elizabeth. BS, Wayne State U., 1955, MS, 1958; PhD, Purdue U., 1963. Lab. asst. U. Chgo., 1951; instr. Purdue U., 1960-63; asst. prof. chem. engring. Wayne State U., Detroit, 1963-64, assoc. prof., 1964-71, prof., 1971-92, dean engring., 1972-85, prof. emeritus, 1992—. Dir. Energy Conversion Devices, Inc., Rochester Hills, Mich., 1978—2005, MacMedia, Holland, Mich.; cons. Schwayder Chem. Metallurgy Co., 1965, chemistry dept. Wayne State U., 1965—66, Claude B. Schneible Co., Holly, Mich., 1968. Contbr. engring. articles to profl. jours. Mem. coun. on environ. strategy S.E. Mich. Coun. Govts., 1976—81; sec.-treas. Mich. Ednl. Rsch. Info. Triad; trustee Sci. Ctr. Met. Detroit, 1980—92; mem. ops. com. MACTV, 2000; sec. Friends of Herrick Dist. Libr., 2003; bd. dirs. Program for Minorities in S.E. Mich., Sci. and Engring. Fair of Met. Detroit, pres. 1983; bd. dirs. Midwt. Program for Minorities in Engring., Friends of Herrick Dist. Libr.; treas. bd. dirs. Mac Media, 2002—; bd. dirs. Hope Acad. Sr. Profls., 2004. Ford Found. fellow, 1959-63; DuPont fellow, 1962-63; Wayne State U. faculty research fellow, 1964-65 Fellow: AIChE (past chmn. Detroit sect.), Mich. Soc. Profl. Engrs. (pres. 1987—88), Engring. Soc. Detroit (past bd. dirs.); mem.: Adult Learning Inst. (bd. dirs. 1994—99), Engring. Sci. Devel. Found. (pres. 1992—94), Am. Chem. Soc., Hope Acad. Sr. Profls. (bd. dirs. 2004—), Phi Lambda Upsilon, Omicron Delta Kappa, Tau Beta Pi, Sigma Xi. Presbyterian. Home: 145 Columbia #609 Holland MI 49423-2980 Personal E-mail: stynes@macatawa.org.

**STYRON, ROSE,** human rights activist, poet, journalist; b. Balt., Apr. 4, 1928; d. Benjamin Bernei and Selma (Kann) Burgunder; m. William Styron, May 4, 1953; children: Susanna, Polly, Thomas, Alexandra. BA, Wellesley Coll., 1950; MA, Johns Hopkins U., 1952; LHD (hon.), Briarcliff Coll., 1976, SUNY, Purchase, 1991, Trinity Coll., 2000. Bd. dirs Amnesty Internat., USA, N.Y.C., 1973-83, chair nat. adv. coun., 1984-94. Author: (poems) From Summer to Summer, 1965, Thieves' Afternoon, 1973. By Vineyard Light, 1995; co-author, translator: Modern Russian Poetry, 1972; contbr. editorials, profiles, articles, book revs. and poetry to maj. newspapers and mags. Chair, judge Robert F. Kennedy Meml. Human Rights Award, 1983—; mem. adv. bd. Reebok Found. for Human Rights, 1987—; mem. exec. bd. Human Rights Watch, N.Y.C., 1975-94; bd. dirs. Acad. of Am. Poets, 1995—, Equality Now, 1993—; chmn. adv. coun. Roxbury (Conn.) Libr., 1990-92; bd. dirs. N.Y. Found. for Arts, N.Y.C., 1986-94, Lawyers Com. for Human Rights, N.Y.C., 1981—, Rainforest Found., 1989-95, Assn. to Benefit Children, 1993—, Folger Shakespeare Libr., 1994-00; bd. overseers NYU Faculty of Arts and Scis., 1994—. Mem. P.E.N. (chair freedom-to-write com. 1983-89, bd. dirs. 1983-93), Coun. Fgn. Rels., Vineyard Haven Yacht Club. Democrat. Home: 12 Rucum Rd Roxbury CT 06783-1906

**STYRON, WILLIAM,** writer; b. Newport News, Va., June 11, 1925; s. William Clark and Pauline Margaret (Abraham) S.; m. Rose Burgunder, May 4, 1953; children: Susanna Margaret, Paola Clark, Thomas, Claire Alexandra. Student, Christchurch Sch., Davidson Coll.; Litt.D., Davidson Coll., 1986; AB, Duke U., 1947, Litt.D., 1968. Fellow Am. Acad. Arts and Letters at Am.

Acad. in Rome, 1953; fellow Silliman Coll., Yale, 1964-99. Jury pres. Cannes Film Festival, 1983. Author: novels Lie Down in Darkness, 1951, The Long March, 1953, Set This House on Fire, 1960, The Confessions of Nat Turner, 1967 (Pulitzer prize 1968, Howells medal Am. Acad. Arts and Letters 1970), Sophie's Choice, 1979 (Am. Book award 1980), In the Clap Shack (play), 1972, This Quiet Dust, 1982, Darkness Visible, 1990, A Tidewater Morning, 1993; also articles, essays, revs.; editor: Best Stories from the Paris Rev., 1959; adv. editor: Paris Rev., 1953—; mem. editorial bd. The Am. Scholar, 1970-76. Decorated Commander de l'Ordre des Arts et des Lettres, Commandeur Legion d'Honneur (France); recipient Duke U. Disting. Alumni award, 1984, Conn. Arts award, 1984, Prix Mondial del Duca, 1985, Elmer Holmes Bobst award for fiction, 1989, Edward MacDowell medal for excellence in the arts, 1988, Nat. Mag. award, 1990, Nat. medal of Arts, 1993, Medal of Honor, Nat. Arts Club, 1995, Common Wealth award, 1995, F. Scott Fitzgerald award, 1996. Mem. Am. Acad. Arts and Scis., Am. Acad. Arts and Letters, Soc. Am. Historians, Signet Soc., Harvard, Académie Goncourt, Phi Beta Kappa. Democrat.

**STYSLINGER, LEE JOSEPH, JR.,** manufacturing executive; b. Birmingham, Ala., June 28, 1933; s. Lee Joseph and Margaret Mary (McFarl) S.; m. Catherine Patricia Smith, Apr. 30, 1960; children: Lee Joseph III, Jon Cecil, Mark Joseph. Student, U. Ala., 1952. Pres., chief exec. officer Altec, Inc. and predecessors, truck equipment mfrs., Birmingham, 1956-89, chief exec. officer, chmn. bd., 1989-92, chmn., 1992—. Bd. dirs. Jemison Investment Co., Birmingham, Ala., Electronic Healthcare Systems. Mem. Country Club Birmingham, Mountain Brook Club, Shoal Creek Club, Willow Point Golf and Country Club, Jupiter Island Club (Hobe Sound, Fla.), Seminole Golf Club (Juno Beach, Fla.), Lyford Cay Country Club (Bahamas), Rotary, NY Yacht Club (N.Y.C.). Roman Catholic. Home: 3260 E Briarcliff Rd Birmingham AL 35223-1305 Office: 210 Inverness Center Dr Birmingham AL 35242-4834

**SU, KENDALL LING-CHIAO,** engineering educator; b. Fujian, China, July 10, 1926; came to U.S., 1948; s. Ru-chen and Sui-hsiong (Wang) S.; m. Jennifer Gee-tsone Chang, Sept. 10, 1960; children: Adrienne, Jonathan. BEE, Xiamen U., Peoples Republic China, 1947; MEE, Ga. Inst. Tech, 1949; PhD, Ga. Inst. Tech., 1954. Jr. engr. Taiwan Power Co., Taipei, Republic China, 1947-48; asst. prof. Ga. Inst. Tech., Atlanta, 1954-59, assoc. prof., 1959-65, prof., 1965-70; Regents prof., 1970-94, Regents' prof. emeritus, 1994—. Mem. tech. staff Bell Labs., Murray Hill, N.J., 1957. Author: Active Network Synthesis, 1965, Time-Domain Synthesis of Linear Networks, 1969, Fundamentals of Circuits, Electronics, and Signal Analysis, 1978, Handbook of Tables for Elliptic-Function Filters, 1990, Fundamentals of Circuit Analysis, 1993, Analog Filters, 1996. Fellow IEEE (life); mem. Sigma Xi (pres. Ga. Inst. Tech. chpt. 1968-69, 72-73, Faculty Rsch. award 1957), Phi Kappa Phi, Eta Kappa Nu. Methodist. Office: Ga Inst Tech Sch Elec & Comp Engring Atlanta GA 30332-0250 Business E-Mail: ksu@ece.gatech.edu.

**SU, SUNYU,** physicist; b. Jinjiang, Fujian, China, Apr. 8, 1955; s. Guangjun Su and Linfeng Wang; m. Rong Luo, Dec. 29, 1986; children: Charles, Robin. MSc, U. of NB, 1986; PhD, U. of Toronto, 1991. Postdoctal fellow U. of Toronto, 1991—93; rsch. assoc. NRC Can., Winnipeg, 1993—96; MRI scientist Toshiba Am. MRI, Inc., South San Francisco, 1996—2000; mgr., open MRI coils GE Med. Systems, USA Instruments, Inc., Aurora, Ohio, 2000—03; open segment program mgr. GE Med. Sys.-USA Instruments, Inc., 2003—06; program mgr. GE Healthcare Coils, Aurora, Ohio, 2006—. Cons. Toshiba Am. MRI, Inc., South San Francisco, 2000—02. Reviewer: Internat. Soc. Magnetic Resonance in Medicine Ann. Meeting Procs. Abstracts; contbr. articles to profl. jours. Recipient CEO award, GE Healthcare Coils, 2006, Mgmt. award, GE Healthcare Coils, 2006. Mem.: Internat. Soc. of Magnetic Resonance in Medicine. Achievements include development of solenoidal array concept for magnetic resonance imaging; patents for sandwiched solenoidal array coil; flexible, region-selectable inherently de-coupled sand-wiched solenoidal array coil; uneven counter-rotational coil; double counter-rotational coil; quadrature detection coil for interventional MRI; open structure breast coil and support arrangement for interventional MRI; patents pending in field. Office: GE Healthcare Coils 1515 Danner Dr Aurora OH 44202 Office Phone: 330-995-8586. Business E-Mail: sunyu.su@med.ge.com.

**SU, XIAOGANG,** statistician, educator; b. Oct. 8, 1974; BS in Math., Beijing Normal U.; MS in Stats., U. Calif., Davis, 1998, PhD in Stats., 2001. Risk analysis Household Credit Svcs., Salinas, Calif., 2001; asst. prof. U. Ctrl. Fla. Dept of Stats. & Actuarial Sci., Fla., 2001—. Recipient Julius Blum Meml. award for Outstanding Grad. Students, Dept of Stats., U. Calif. Davis, 1998; grantee In-House Rsch. grant, U. Ctrl. Fla. Office of Rsch., 2005, Multivariate Survival CART with Application to Dental Prognosis, NIH, 2005—, WDW Mktg. Strategic Devel., Walt Disney World, 2004—05. Mem.: Am. Statis. Assoc. Office: Dept of Stats & Actuarial Sci University of Central Florida Orlando FL 32816 Office Phone: 407-823-2940. Business E-Mail: xsu@pegasus.cc.ucf.edu.

**SU, ZHENDONG,** computer scientist, educator; BA in Math., U. Tex., Austin, 1992—95, BS in Computer Sci., 1992—95; MS in Computer Sci., U. Calif., Berkeley, 1995—97, PhD in Computer Sci., 1995—2002. Rsch. fellow NASA Ames Rsch. Ctr., Moffett Field, Calif., 2002—02; asst. prof., computer sci. U. Calif., Davis, 2002—. Spkr. in field. Contbr. papers to profl. jours. and pubs. Recipient Dean's Honored Grad. of Yr. in Computer Sci., U. Tex., Austin, Coll. Natural Sciences, 1995, CAREER award, NSF, 2006; grantee Presdl. scholarship, U. Tex., Austin, 1994—95, Regents fellowship, U. Calif., Berkeley, 1995—96. Mem.: IEEE. Achievements include development of techniques to improve software security and reliability. Office: Univ Calif 2063 Kemper Hall Davis CA 95616 Office Phone: 530 751 5376

**SUAREZ, LUIS EDGARDO,** civil engineering educator; b. Jujuy, Argentina, May 14, 1957; came to U.S., 1983; s. Luciano and Maria Mercedes (Colche) S.; m. Rosana Martinez-Cruzado, Dec. 30, 1994. MS in Engring. Mechanics, Va. Poly Inst., 1984, PhD in Engring. Mechanics, 1986. Jr. engr. Atomic Energy Commn. Argentina, Cordoba, 1981; instr. part-time dept. of structures U. Cordoba, 1981-82, asst. prof. grad. programs, 1987-89; rsch. asst. engring. sci. and mechanics Va. Poly. Inst., Blacksburg, 1983-86, asst. prof. engr. sci. and mechanics dept., 1986-87; asst. prof. gen. engring. dept. U. P.R., Mayaguez, 1989-91, assoc. prof. gen. engring. dept., 1991-96, prof. civil engring., 1996—. Proposal reviewer U.S. Army Rsch. Office, Mayaguez, 1991, NSF, Washington, 1994-95; paper reviewer Jour. Vibration and Acoustics, Jour. Engring. for Industry, Jour. Engring. Structures, Jour. Engring. Mechanics, Jour. Vibration and Control, Mayaguez, AIAA Jour., Jour. of Sound and Vibration, Jour. Nonlinear Dynamics; panelist to select scholarships Battelle, Mayaguez, 1991-92; chmn. 5th Pan Am. Congress of Applied Math., 1997. Co-author: Multinational Seismic Design Codes, Handbook, 1992, A Visual Introduction to SAP 2000, 2002; mem. editl. bds. Jour. Engineering Structures, Vibration and Control Mechanics; co-editor Jour. Revista Internacional de Desastres Naturales, Accidentes e Infraestructura Civil; contbr. articles to profl. jours. Cunningham fellow Va. Poly. Inst., 1986, Disting. prof., dept. gen. engring., 1994, Disting. prof. civil engring., 1996, 99; grantee U.S. Army Rsch. Office, 1990, Nat. Ctr. for Earthquake Engring. Rsch., 1992-96, Langley Rsch. Ctr. NASA, 1999, FEMA, 2001-03, U.S. Army Corps. Engrs., 2003-05, U.S. Geol. Survey, 2003-04. Mem. ASCE, ASME, AIAA, Internat. Coll. Bldgs. Offcls., Soc. Exptl. Mechanics, Earthquake Engring. Rsch. Inst., The Vibration Inst., Am. Soc. Engring. Edn., Am. Acad. Mechanics, Sigma Xi (Rsch. award Va. Tech. chpt. 1987). Roman Catholic. Achievements include development of methods for seismic analysis of mechanical equipment that are used in industry, several methods for dynamic analysis of large structural systems. Office: Univ Puerto Rico Civil Engring Dept PO Box 9041 Mayaguez PR 00681-9041 Office Phone: 787-832-4040 ext. 3669. E-mail: lsuarez@uprm.edu.

**SUAREZ, MARIA C.,** health care plan company executive; BA in math/computer sci., Queens Coll., CUNY; MBA in quantitative analysis/computer info. systems, St. John's U. Applications developer Coo-

pers & Lybrand; tech. lead managed care project North Shore U. Hosp.; dir. internet/intranet Empire BlueCross BlueShield, privacy officer, now asst. v.p. security assurance. Named one of Premier 100 IT Leaders, Computerworld, 2005. Office: Empire BlueCross BlueShield 15 Metro Tech Pl Brooklyn NY 11201 Office Phone: 212-476-1000, 718-312-5006. Office Fax: 212-476-1281. Business E-Mail: maria.suarez@empireblue.com.

**SUAREZ, SALLY ANN TEVIS,** health facility administrator, nurse, consultant; b. Jersey City, Jan. 23, 1944; d. Paul John and Gertrude Marie (Clancey) Tevis; 1 child, Maria E. Diploma, St. Mary Hosp. Sch. Nursing, 1965; BA in Health Edn. and Nursing, Jersey City State Coll., 1966, MA in Health Sci., 1977. Staff nurse St. Mary Hosp., Hoboken, N.J., 1965, Bayonne (N.J.) Hosp., 1966, Jersey City Med. Ctr., 1965-66; adminstr. Hoboken Med. Arts Family Health Ctr., 1969-75; adj. faculty Jersey City State Coll., 1976-77; adminstrv. supr. St. Mary Hosp., Hoboken, 1977-80; dir. North Hudson Commn. Action Corp. Clinic, West New York, N.J., 1979-88; nursing clin. dir. St. Mary Hosp., Hoboken, 1988-89; corp. dir. nursing Francisan Health System N.J., 1989-92; dir. maternal child health svcs. St. James Hosp., Newark, 1992-93, dir. Family Care Ctr., Cathedral Healthcare Sys., 1993-97, dir. nursing, 1996, 1996; cons. quality improvement preventive health Rutherford, NJ, 1996—; QI coord. United Health Care, 1998; v.p. Med. Resource Network, 1998—2000; coord. case mgmt. U. Medicine and Dentistry N.J. Univ. Hosp., 2006—. Instr. nursing St. Mary Hosp. Sch. Nursing; cons. Creative Concepts in Counseling, Rutherford, N.J., 1979-82, Com. for Cytogenetics, Newark, 1986-88; cons. in health svcs., 1996—; v.p. Med. Resource Network 1998-2003; case mgr. workers' compensation, critical care MCR, 2000-2003; case mgr. workers' compensation Corvel Corp., 2003-2004; health ctr. coord. North Hudson Cmty. Action Corp. Health Ctr., 2004-2006; case mgr. and coord UMDNJ, 2006—. Active Hudson County ARC, 1984-88, United Way, 1984-94; mem. Hudson County Perinatal Consortium Bd., 1987-92, Gateway Consortium, 1993-96; mem. adv. bd. Health Start, 1995-97, N.J. Assn. Women Bus. Owners, 1996-98; bd. dirs. Passaic Head Start; mem. adv. bd. Harrison Care Inst., 2005—. Mem. U.S. Assn. Women Bus. Owners, Am. Cancer Soc., N.J. Family Planning Forum (exec. com. 1980-86), Family Planning Assn. N.J. (exec. com. 1986-88). Democrat. Roman Catholic. Avocation: alternative healing. Home: 113 Wilson Ave Rutherford NJ 07070-2726 Personal E-mail: nursesrch@aol.com, nursescch@netzero.net.

**SUAREZ-MURIAS, MARGUERITE C.,** retired language educator, retired literature educator; b. Havana, Cuba, Mar. 23, 1921; arrived in U.S., 1935, naturalized, 1959; d. Eduardo R. and Marguerite (Vendel) Suarez-Murias. AB, Bryn Mawr Coll., 1942; MA, Columbia U., 1953, PhD, 1957. Lectr. in Spanish Columbia U., 1954-56; pub. rels. officer med. divsn. Johns Hopkins U., 1957-58; asst. prof. Spanish and French Sweet Briar Coll., 1958-59; asst. prof. Hood Coll., 1960-61; lectr. Cath. U., 1960-63, asst. prof., summers 1960-62, assoc. prof., summers 1964-66; asst. prof. dept. langs. and linguistics Am. U., 1961-63, assoc. prof., 1963-66; prof. dept. classical and modern langs. Marquette U., Milw., 1966-68; prof. Spanish and Portuguese U. Wis., Milw., 1968—83, chmn., 1972-75; ret., 1983. Guest Milw. prof. U. South Africa, Pretoria, 1980. Author: (book) La Novela Romántica en Hispanoamérica, 1963, Antología Estilística de la Prosa Moderna Española, 1968, Essays on Hispanic Literature/Ensayos de Literatura Hispana, 1982; editor: Gironella's Los Cipreses Creen en Dios, 1969; contbr. articles to profl. jours.; Mem.: Nat. Trust Historic Preservation. Roman Catholic. Achievements include designing, building and landscaping two homes. Home: 1315 Cold Bottom Rd Sparks MD 21152-9518

**SUAREZ-OROZCO, CAROLA ELISABETH,** psychology professor; b. Switzerland, Mar. 16, 1957; arrived in U.S., 1962; d. Rene Guy Jacqnat-Francillan and Carola Marietta Peters; m. Marcelo Mario Suarez-Orozco, Jan. 15, 1977; 1 child, Lucas. BA in Devel. Studies, U. Calif., Berkeley, 1978; MA in Clin. Psychology, John F. Kennedy U., 1980; PhD in Clin. Psychology, Calif. Sch. Profl. Psychology, 1993. Vis. scholar Harvard U., Grad. Sch. Edn., 1994—95, lectr., 1997—2002, mng. dir. immigrant projects, 1997—2002; exec. dir. David Rockefeller Ctr. for Latin Am. Studies Harvard U., 2002—03; sr. rsch. assoc. Harvard U., Grad. Sch. Edn., 2003—04; assoc. prof. N.Y. U., Steinhardt, 2004—05, prof., 2005—, chair applied psychology, 2005—. Author (M. Suarez-Orozco): Transformations: Immigration, Family Life & Achievement Motivation Among Latino Adolescents, 1995 (Best Book award Soc. Rsch. on Adolescents, 1996); co-author (M. Suarez-Orozco and D. Qin-Hillard): Interdisciplinary Perspectives on the New Immigration, 6 vols., 2001; author: (M. Suarez-Orozco): Children of Immigration, 2001; author: (I. Todorova) Understanding the Social World of Immigrant Youth, 2003; author: (M. Suarez-Orozco and D. Qin-Hillard) Immigration: An Interdisciplinary Reader, 2005; contbr. chapters to books, to profl. jours. Mem.: Am. Psychol. Assn., Soc. Rsch. Adolescence, Am. Ednl. Rschrs. Assn. Achievements include research in intersection of cultural and psychological factors in adaptation of immigrant and ethnic minority youth. Avocations: reading, gardening, travel. Office: NY Univ Applied Psychology 239 Greene St 4th Flr New York NY 10003

**SUBAK-SHARPE, GERALD EMIL,** electrical engineer, educator; b. Vienna, June 15, 1925; came to U.S., 1959, naturalized, 1967; s. Robert and Nelly (Brull) S.; m. Genell Jackson, Nov. 23, 1963; children: David, Sarah and Hope (twins). BS with 1st class honors, Univ. Coll., London, 1951; PhD, U. London, 1965; ScD, Columbia U., 1969. Rsch. engr. Brit. Telecommunications Rsch., Taplow, England, 1951-58; mem. tech. staff Bell Labs., Murray Hill, NJ, 1959-64, cons., 1977-78; assoc. prof. elec. engring. Manhattan Coll., Bronx, NY, 1966-68; prof. elec. engring. CCNY, N.Y.C., 1968—; v.p. G.S. Sharpe Communications Inc., 1981—. Author: (with A.B. Glaser) Integrated Circuit Engineering, 1978; contbr. articles on network structure and with bonor theory to profl. jours. Served as lt. Royal Warwickshire Regt., 1944-47. Recipient Prof. of Yr. award Eta Kappa Nu/CCNY, 1985-86. Fellow Instn. Elec. Engrs. (London); mem. IEEE (sr.), N.Y. Acad. Scis., Nat. Trust for Historic Preservation Home: 606 W 116th St Apt 71 New York NY 10027-7024 Office: CCNY Dept Elec Engring Convent Ave New York NY 10027 also: Knollcroft East Chatham NY 12060

**SUBER, DIANNE BOARDLEY,** educational administrator; b. Tallahassee, May 22, 1949; d. John Wilkerson and Barbara Ann (Baker) Boardley; BS with honors, Hampton Inst., 1971; ME., U. Ill., 1973; postgrad. Hampton U.; MEd, Old Dominion U., doctoral studies Va. Poly. Insst. and State U.; children: Nichole Reshan, Raegan Latrese; m. Robert B. Suber. Elem. tchr. Greensboro (N.C.) Public Schs., 1971-72; tchr. Newport News (Va.) Public Schs., 1973-77, asst. prin., 1977-79, 80-82, acting prin., 1979-80; elem. prin. Williamsburg, Va., 1982-85; prin. Newport (Va.) News, 1986-89, 91—, program devel. specialist, 1989-91; owner/prin. DBS and Assocs.; adj. instr. Hampton U. grad. sch. edn., 1986—; owner Child Care Resources Inc.; guest lectr. Coll. William and Mary, Williamsburg; owner human resources devel. cons. DBS & Assoc. Mem. Coalition for Good Govt. Mem. Nat. Assn. Elem. Sch. Prins., Nat. Assn. Edn. Young Children, Assn. Supervision and Curriculum Devel., Nat. Alliance Black Sch. Educators, Hampton Crusade for Votes League, Black Child Inst.; represent nat. conf. Am. Assn. Sch. Adminstrs. State Dept. Edn., Va. and N.C. Mem. Am. Assn. Sch. Adminstrs. Democrat. Roman Catholic.

**SUBER, ROBERT L., SR.,** toxicologist, researcher; m. Christine Bonar, Aug. 12, 1972; children: R. Lee Jr., Alison M. BS, U. of Fla., Gainesville, 1971; MS, U. of Fla., Gainesville, Florida, 1975, PhD, 1979. Diplomate Am. Bd. Toxicology, Am. Bd. Forensic Medicine. Asst. prof. of pathology U. of Ark. for Med. Scis., Little Rock, 1979—84, adj. asst. prof. of toxicology, 1982—84; toxicologist and chief, clin. pathology Nat. Ctr. for Toxicological Rsch., FDA, Jefferson, Ark., 1979—84; dir. sci. affairs RJR-Nabisco, Winston Salem, NC, 1984—92, v.p., product integrity and regulatory affairs, 1992—2002; advisor DarPharma, Chapel Hill, NC, 2001—02, Office of Tech. Transfer, U. Fla., Gainesville, 2002—. Assoc. editor Jour. of Pharm. Scis., N.Y.C., 1979—84; aerosols and tech. options com. UN Environ. Policy Com., N.Y.C., 1991—2001, methyl bromide options com., 1992—96; food additives com. Flavor and Extract Mfr.'s Assn., Washington, 1984—86, govt. rels.

com., 1984—86, internat. regulatory affairs com., 1985—92; exec. com., toxicology and safety evaluation com. Inst. of Food Tech., Washington, 1988—91; safety issues task force Grocery Mfrs. Am., Washington, 1985—91; rsch. program rev. com. USDA, Washington, 1990—2003; sci. com. Methyl Bromide Task Force, GMA, Washington, 1990—96; sci. adv. bd., sensory rsch. inst. Fla. State U., Tallahassee, 1999—2002. Fellow: Acad. Toxicological Scis.; mem.: Soc. of Regulatory Affairs Profls., Am. Assn. for Pharm. Scis., Soc. of Toxicology. Home: 3510 Stancliff Rd Clemmons NC 27012 Personal E-mail: robertsuber@aol.com.

**SUBER, ROBIN HALL,** former medical and surgical nurse; b. Bethlehem, Pa., Mar. 14, 1952; d. Arthur Albert and Sarah Virginia (Smith) Hall; m. David A. Suber, July 28, 1979; 1 child, Benjamin A. BSN, Ohio State U., 1974. RN, Ariz., Ohio. Formerly staff nurse Desert Samaritan Hosp., Mesa, Ariz. Lt. USN, 1974-80. Mem. ANA, Sigma Theta Tau.

**SUBIN, ELI HAROLD,** lawyer; b. Phila., June 25, 1935; s. Benjamin and Freda (Kalen) S.; m. Suzon Bette Rosenbluth, Oct. 21, 1962; children: Andrea Beth Craig, Ben William. BA, U. Pa., 1957; LLB, U. Miami, Coral Gables, Fla., 1961. Bar: Fla., 1961, U.S. Dist. Ct. (mid. dist.) Fla., 1961, U.S. Supreme Ct., 1964, U.S. Ct. Appeals (5th, 11th cirs.), 1966. Trial atty. antitrust divsn. U.S. Dept. Justice, Phila., 1962-63; rsch. aide Dist. Ct. Appeal (1st dist.) Fla., Tallahassee, 1963-64; atty. Roth Segal & Levine, Orlando, Fla., 1964-72, Subin Shams, et. al. P.A., Orlando, 1972-96; city atty. City of Orlando, 1980-82; atty. Maguire, Voorhis & Wells, P.A., Orlando, 1997-98, Holland & Knight LLP, Orlando, 1998—. Referee Supreme Ct. Fla., Tallahassee, 1975; mem. Fla. Bd. Bar Examiners, 1982-87, chmn., 1986-87. Mem. exec. com. Seminole County Dems., Sanford, Fla., 1970-74; mem. jud. nominating com. 9th cir. Fla., 1976-79; dir. Fla. Bar Found., Orlando, 1992-00. 1st lt. USAR, 1957-64. Mem. Am. Law Inst., Am. Bd. Trial Advs. (assoc.), Orange County Bar Assn. (dir. 1968-71). Jewish. Office: Holland & Knight LLP PO Box 1526 Orlando FL 32802-1526 E-mail: esubin@hklaw.com.

**SUBKOFF, TARA,** actress, apparel designer; b. 1973; Designer, co-founder Imitation of Christ clothing line, 2000—. Collaborator Easy Spirit shoe line, 2005. Actor: (films) When the Bough Breaks, 1993, Freeway, 1996, True Crime, 1996, Black Circle Boys, 1997, All Over Me, 1997, Lover Girl, 1997, As Good as It Gets, 1997, The Last Days of Disco, 1998, Mascara, 1999, The Cell, 2000, Looking for Jimmy, 2002, Undermind, 2003, The Notorious Bettie Page, 2005. Office: Designers Mgmt Agy c/o Marc Beckman 446 Broadway 4th Fl New York NY 10013*

**SUBLER, EDWARD PIERRE,** advertising executive; b. Shelby, Ohio, Mar. 24, 1927; s. Leo John and Dorotha (Armstrong) S.; m. Alice Ellen Carpenter, Sept. 8, 1956; children: Leo, Scott, Dorotha. BA, Denison U., Granville, Ohio, 1950; grad. advanced mgmt. course, Emory U., Atlanta. Mgr. product advt. Westinghouse Electric Co., Mansfield, Ohio, 1950—65; mgr. advt. and sales promotion Bell & Howell Co., Chgo., 1965-69; v.p. mdsg. Westinghouse Consumer Products Co., 1969-76; sr. v.p. Ketchum Advt., Pitts., 1976-92, ret., 1992; v.p. Pacific Garden Co., Millheim, Pa., 1988—2005, pres., bd. dir. Trustee BCB Anglers, Baie Jeanne Assn., Tanglewood Assn. Served with USN, 1945-46. Mem. Am. Mktg. Assn., Am. Assn. Advt. Agencies (regional chmn.), Catawba Island Club, Bus./Profl. Adv. Assn. (Pitts. Advt. Exec. of Yr. 1988), U.S. Power Squadron, Baie Jeanne Assn. (bd. dir.). Home: 2465 Circleville Rd Unit 122 State College PA 16803-3390 E-mail: esubler@yahoo.com.

**SUBLETT, ROGER H.,** academic administrator; b. Ark. m. Cynthia Sublett; 3 children. BS, MA, U. Ark.; PhD in Am. History, Tulane U. Assoc. v.p. academic affairs U. Evansville, Ind., dean Coll. of Grad. and Continuing Studies Ind., dir. spl. programs Coll. of Alternative Programs Ind.; dir. Kellogg Nat. Fellowship/Leadership Program W. K. Kellogg Found., 1991—2001, program dir. Higher Edn. and Leadership, 1991—2001; faculty mem. Union Inst. & Univ., Cin., 2001—; interim v.p. for nat. undergraduate programs, provost, COO, acting pres., pres., 2003—. Co-author: Leading from the Heart. Bd. trustees Ctr. for Ethical Leadership, Seattle, OmniMed, Boston. Named Leadership Scholar, James MacGregor Burns Acad. of Leadership, U. Md.; recipient Spirit of Leadership Award, Kellogg Fellows Leadership Alliance, 2005. Fellow: James MacGregor Burns Acad. Leadership; mem.: Coalition for Adult Edn. Orgns. (pres. 1989—90), Assn. for Continuing Higher Edn. (life; v.p. 1984—89, Outstanding Svc. Award), Ctr. for Ethical Leadership (sr. scholar). Office: Union Inst & Univ Nat Hdqs 440 E McMillan St Cincinnati OH 45206-1925

**SUBOLESKI, STANLEY C.,** federal agency administrator, mining engineer; BS, Pa. State U., 1963, PhD in Mining Engring., 1978; MS, Va. Tech. U., 1968. Mining engr. North American Coal Corp., 1963—65; gen. supt. Underground Mines, Ctrl. Div. Consolidation Coal Co., 1969—74; v.p. Mining Div. Continental Ill. Nat. Bank, 1977—81; v.p. mining devel, treas. A.T. Massey Coal Co., 1981—88, v.p. ops. strategy, pres. United Coal Co., v.p. Norfolk Southern Ops., 1993—97; cons. mining engr., 2000—01; exec. v.p., interim COO Massey Energy Co., 2001—03; commr. Fed. Mine Safety and Health Review Commn., Washington, 2003—. Instr. Va. Tech. U., 1963—65, prof., head Dept. Mining Engring., 1998—2000; instr. Pa. State U., 1974—77, Centennial professor mining engring., chmn. Mining Engring. Sect., 1988—93. Mem.: NAE, Soc. Mining, Metallurgy and Exploration (mem. exec. com. Coal and Energy Div.). Office: Fed Mine Safety and Health Review Commn 601 New Jersey Ave NW, Ste 9500 Washington DC 20001 Office Phone: 202-434-9921.*

**SUBOTNICK, ALI,** curator, writer; Receptionist Artforum; with editl. office Art News; host radio program WPS1.org; co-founder The Wrong Gallery, NYC. Vis. critic sch. of arts Columbia U.; spkr. in field. Curator MFA Thesis Exhibition, Columbia U. Sch. of Arts, 2004, 4th Berlin Biennial, 2006; editor: Parkett mag.; co-editor: Charley mag.; contbr. articles to profl. jours. Office: c/o Columbia Univ Sch of Arts 2960 Broadway New York NY 10027-6902*

**SUBPRASOM, KITTI,** civil engineer; b. Phetchabun, Thailand, Feb. 8, 1974; s. Chuan and Vanich Subprasom. B in civil engring., King Mongkut's U. of Tech. Thonburi, 1993—97; MS in civil and environ. engring., Utah State U., 1998—2000. Civil engr. Dept. of Hwy., Bangkok, Thailand, 1997—98; spl. lectr. King Mongkut's U. of Tech. Thonburi, Bangkok, Thailand, 1997—98; rsch. assoc. Utah State U., Dept. of Civil and Environ. Engring., 1999—2000, PhD candidate, 2000—. Contbr. articles to profl. jours. Royal Thai Govt. scholarship, Royal Thai Govt., 1998, 2000. Master: Thai Student Assn.; mem.: Inst. for Ops. Rsch. and Mgmt. Sci. (corr.), Inst. of Transp. Engineers Student Chapters (assoc.). Office: Utah State U Dept Civil and Environ Engring Logan UT 84322-4110 E-mail: sls9r@cc.usu.edu.

**SUBRAMANIAM, SHIVAN SIVASWAMY,** insurance company executive; b. Madras, India, Feb. 15, 1949; came to U.S., 1970; s. Kodaganullor Sivaswamy and Seethalakshmi S. B.E. in Mech. Engring. with honors, Birla Inst. Tech., Pilani, India, 1970; MS in Ops. Research, Poly. Inst. Bklyn., 1972; S.M. in Mgmt., MIT, 1978. Indsl. engr. Midland Container Corp., Ridgewood, N.J., 1971-74; mgmt. sci. analyst Allendale Ins. Co., Johnston, RI, 1974-76, sr. mgmt. sci. analyst 1976-77, sr. fin. staff officer, 1978-80, v.p., treas., 1980-83, sr. v.p. fin., chief fin. officer, 1983-91, exec. v.p., 1991-92, pres., 1992-93, CEO, 1993-95, chmn., pres., CEO, 1995—99; pres., CEO FM Global, Johnston, RI, 1999—2002, chmn., pres., CEO, 2002—. Mem. Fin. Execs. Inst. (membership chmn. 1982-84, Providence chpt. pres. 1985-86), Nat. Assn. Corp. Treas. Office: FM Global 1301 Atwood Ave Johnston RI 02919*

**SUBRAMANIAN, GUHAN,** law educator; b. 1970; BA in Economics, Harvard U., 1992, JD, MBA, Harvard U., 1998. Bar: NY 1999. Assoc. McKinsey & Co., 1998—99; lectr. Harvard Bus. Sch., 1999—2001; Joseph Flom asst. prof. law and bus. Harvard Law Sch., Cambridge, Mass.,

2002—04, Joseph Flom prof. law and bus., 2004—. Office: Harvard Law Sch 1563 Massachusetts Ave Cambridge MA 02138 Office Phone: 617-495-9784. Office Fax: 617-496-5156. Business E-mail: subraman@law.harvard.edu.

**SUBRAMANIAN, MANI N.,** chemistry professor; b. Madras, India, Oct. 2, 1950; arrived in U.S., 1972; s. Narayanan and Alamelu; children: Nathan, Jeffrey, Rachel. BS, MS, U. Madras; PhD, U. Akron, Ohio, 1975. Mem. faculty Solano Coll., Calif., 2002—, Coll. Marin, Kentfield, Calif., 2002—; prof. chemistry Dominican U., San Rafael, Calif., 2002—. Project mgr. Biorad, Calif.; scientist Zeneca, Calif. Scholar, Fulbright Found., 1972. Mem.: Am. Chem. Soc. Republican. Achievements include patents in field. Home: 130 Hollyhock Hercules CA 94547

**SUBRAMANIAN, MAS,** research scientist; PhD, Indian Inst. Tech., Madras, 1982. Rsch. fellow DuPont Ctrl. R&D, Wilmington, Del., 1985—. Contbr. over 230 papers to profl. jours. and pubs. Recipient Charles Pedersen medal, DuPont, 2004. Mem.: Materials Rsch. Soc. (assoc.). Achievements include discoveries in the area of materials science/chemistry; 41 patents held. Office: DuPont Central R&D Exptl Sta E328/219 Wilmington DE 19880-0328 Office Phone: 302-695-2966. Business E-mail: mas.subramanian@usa.dupont.com.

**SUCATO, ROBERT ALAN,** filmmaker, director; b. San Francisco, Aug. 17, 1966; s. Edward and Cheryl Anne Sucato; m. Tracy Lynn Hohs, Oct. 18, 1997; children: Emma Alise, Noah Robert. B, U. Advancing Tech., Tempe, Ariz., 2000—03. CEO Monsoon Films, Phoenix, 1999—2005. Exec. dir. Phoenix Film Project, 2003—05. Dir.: (films) The Journey Home, Real Gone Cat. E-4 USN, 1987—91, San Diego. Office: Monsoon Films 429 W Jackson Phoenix AZ 85003 Business E-mail: rob@monsoonfilms.com.

**SUCHER, DOROTHY,** writer, psychotherapist; b. Bklyn., May 18, 1933; d. Henry Glassman and Shirley Hankin Bryant; m. Joseph Sucher, Aug. 10, 1952; children: Gabriel, Michael, Anatol, Anne. BA, Bklyn. Coll., 1954; postgrad., Columbia U., 1954-55; M Mental Health, Johns Hopkins U., 1975. Lic. cert. social worker, Md. Assoc. editor Greenbelt (Md.) News Rev., 1959—70, 1993—2004; psychotherapist Group Health Assn., Washington, 1975-80; pvt. practice psychotherapy, Greenbelt, 1978-85; tchr. creative writing Writer's Ctr., Bethesda, Md., 1988-92, Prince George's C.C., 2005—06; writer, 1988—. Author: Dead Men Don't Give Seminars, 1988, Dead Men Don't Marry, 1989, The Invisible Garden, 1999. Mem. Greenbelt Arts Adv. bd., 1990-97; active founding Greenbelt Hist. Mus., 1985-86; coord. state and local consciousness raising NOW, Greenbelt, 1977-80. Mem.: Sisters in Crime, Greenbelt Writers' Group (founder, planning coord. 1995—2003). Avocations: gardening, painting. Address: 3116 Gracefield Rd Apt 421 VP Silver Spring MD 20904 Personal E-mail: dorothysucher@netscape.net.

**SUCHOMEL, MARK,** publishing executive; With Contemporary Books, Chgo.; sales mgr. Chgo. Rev. Press (acquired by IPG), Chgo., 1986—87; with Independent Pub. Group, Chgo., 1987—, v.p. sales, mktg., pres., 1998—. Exec. coun. The Quills. Named One of 11 for the Millennium-those who will help shape publ. in 21st century, Publishers Weekly. Office: IPG 814 N Franklin St Chicago IL 60610 Office Phone: 312-337-0747. Office Fax: 312-337-0747.

**SUCKIEL, ELLEN KAPPY,** philosophy educator; b. June 15, 1943; d. Jack and Lilyan Kappy; m. Joseph Suckiel, June 22, 1973 AB, Douglass Coll., 1965; MA in Philosophy, U. Wis., 1969, PhD in Philosophy, 1972. Lectr. philosophy U. Wis., Madison, 1969-71; asst. prof. philosophy Fla. State U., Tallahassee, 1972-73, U. Calif., Santa Cruz, 1973-80, assoc. prof., 1980-95, prof., 1995—; provost Kresge Coll., 1983-89, provost Stevenson Coll., 2004—. Author: The Pragmatic Philosophy of William James, 1982, Heaven's Champion: William James's Philosophy of Religion, 1996, also articles, book introductions and chpts. Mem. Am. Philos. Assn., Soc. for Advancement Am. Philosophy Office: UCSC Stevenson Coll Provost's Office 101 McLaughlin Dr Santa Cruz CA 95064 Office Phone: 831-459-2328. Business E-Mail: suckiel@ucsc.edu.

**SUD, PAMELA RANI,** pulmonary and critical care physician, consultant; b. Knoxville, Tenn., Mar. 19, 1968; d. Mohinder N. and Leela B. Sud. BA in Zoology, U. Tenn., 1986, BS in Biology & Biomedical Engring., 1986; MD, St. George's U. Sch. Med., 1993. Diplomate Am. Bd. Internal Medicine, cert. in pulmonary and critical care. Med. resident U. Tenn. Ctr. Health Scis., Memphis, 1993—96; fellow U. N. Mex., Albuquerque, 1996, La. State U. Health Sci. Ctr., Shreveport, 1997—2000; pvt. practice Knoxville, 2001—03; physician Sloan-Kettering Meml. Hosp., NYC, 1997, Overton-Brooks VA Med. Ctr., Shreveport, 2003—04, Signal Mountain Imaging, Chattanooga, 2005—. Bd. dirs. Signal Mountain Imaging, Chattanooga. Vol. Am. Found. AIDS Rsch., NYC, 1992. Named Outstanding Sr. Resident, U. Tenn. Ctr. Health Scis., 1994; recipient Merita Humanities Social Svc. award, Webb Sch., 1978; fellow, LSU Health Sci. Ctr., 2000. Mem.: AMA, ACP, Am. Coll. Chest Physicians. Avocations: art, music, languages, travel.

**SUDAK, HOWARD STANLEY,** psychiatrist, educator; b. Cleve., Nov. 13, 1932; s. Sol and Leona (Simms) S.; m. Diane M. Ressler, Dec. 25, 1955 (dec.); children: Ellen, Nancy, Janet, David; m. Donna M. Miller, Mar. 25, 1995. AB in Chemistry magna cum laude, Case Western Res., 1954, MD, 1958. Diplomate Am. Bd. Psychiatry and Neurology (sr. examiner 1991—). Intern in medicine Univ. Hosps. Cleve., 1958-59, resident in psychiatry, 1959-62; clin. assoc. NIMH, Bethesda, Md., 1962-64; chief psychiatry Cleve. VA Med. Ctr., 1964-84; asst. prof. psychiatry Case Western Res. U., Cleve., 1964-74, assoc. prof., 1974-82, prof., 1982—, vice dean Med. Sch., 1985-92; chmn. dept. psychiatry The Pa. Hosp., Phila., 1992-2001; psychiatrist-in-chief Inst. of Pa. Hosp., Phila., 1992-96; clin. prof. psychiatry U. Pa. Sch. Medicine, 1993-94, 97—; prof. psychiatry, vice chmn. psychiatry/human behavior Thomas Jefferson U., Phila., 1994-96; project supr. AFSF Evidence-Based Suicide Prevention Programs, 2003—. Mem. profl. adv. coun. Youth Suicide Nat. Ctr., Washington, 1986—; com. mem. Ctrs. for Disease Control, Atlanta, 1990-91. Editor: Suicide in the Young, 1984, Clinical Psychiatry, 1985; cons. editor Suicide and Life Threatening Behavior, 1988—; contbr. numerous articles to profl. jours., chpt. to books. Dir. Inst. for Urban Health, Cleve., 1990-92. Grantee NIMH, 1972-73, 83-86. Fellow Am. Psychiat. Assn., Am. Coll. Psychiatrists, Am. Coll. Psychoanalysts; mem. Am. Assn. Suicidology (trustee 1988-90), Am. Suicide Found. (trustee 1987—, pres. 1989-91), Phi Beta Kappa, Alpha Omega Alpha. Avocations: biking, sailing, reading, skiing, jazz and classical music. Home: 321 S Lawrence Ct Philadelphia PA 19106-4220 Office: John Ross House 401 S Second St Ste 402 Philadelphia PA 19147-1612 Office Phone: 215-238-0409. Business E-Mail: hsudak@afsp.org.

**SUDANOWICZ, ELAINE MARIE,** government executive; d. John Anthony and Helen Mary Sudanowicz. Student, Fontbonne Acad., Milton, Mass., 1974; BA, Boston State Coll., 1978; MPA, Suffolk U., Boston, 1986; grad. Exec. Leadership Devel. Program, Dept. of Def., 1993. Cert. level 2 contractor, level 3 in program mgmt., Mass. Pub. rels. office mgr. MacDonald & Evans Inc. Litho., Dorchester, 1974-78; rsch. asst. Nat. Commn. Neighborhoods, Washington, 1978; polit. cons. various nat., state and local polit. campaigns, 1974-86; telephonist supr., cons. ARC, Boston, 1980-81; adminstrv. asst. Suffolk County Courthouse Commn., Boston, 1981-82; exec. asst. sheriff Suffolk County Sheriff's Office, 1982-86; presdl. mgmt. fellow ESD/PK Air Force Systems Command, Hanscom AFB, Mass., 1986-89, advanced copper CAP Andrews AFB, Md., 1989-90; contract negotiator Hdqrs., Electronic Systems divsn. Joint STARS Program, Hanscom AFB, Mass., 1990-92; program mgr. Hdqrs., Electronic Sys. Ctr., EN-1, Hanscom AFB, 1992-95; asst. program dir. bus. acquisition re-engring. Elec. Sys. Ctr., Hanscom AFB, 1994-95; dep. commr. for transp. City of Boston, 1995—2006; inter-agy. coord. Mayor's Office Homeland Security Emergency Mgmt., 2006—; Mayor's interagency liaison Boston Emergency Mgmt. Agy., 1995—; guest spkr. Armed Forces Comm. and Elecs. Assn., 2000-; guest lectr. Suffolk U., Sawyer Sch. Mgmt., 2001-; panelist Neighborhood Issues

Forum, 2002. Author: Constitutional Vignette, Separation of Powers and Contracting in the Bureaucrat, 1987; contbr. PMInformer, 1989—; also articles; apt. cons Theatre Arts-Play 1988—. Vol., cons. City & State Pub. Agys.-Pub. Sector, Boston; literacy vol., 1988-89; task force Transp. Rsch. Bd. on Critical Transp. Infrastructure Security, 1999—. Recipient Spl. Achievement award U.S. Dept. Transp., 1989, Outstanding Alumnus award Suffolk U., 1990 Mem. Am. Soc. Pub. Adminstrn. (coun. mem. 1996—, mem. exec. bd. emergency and crisis mgmt. sect. 1999—), Nat. Contract Mgmt. Assn. (bd. dirs. 1996—, photographer No. Va. chpt. 1989-90, cert. profl. contracts mgr., nat. chair program mgmt. spl. topics com.), Presdl. Mgmt. Alumni Group (nat. bd. dirs. 1989-90, N.E. field bd. dirs. 1990—, Outstanding Alumnus award 1990), Trustees of Reservations Mass., Dept. Def. Sr. Profl. Women's Assn., Boston Network for Women in Govt. and Politics, Pi Alpha Alpha (pres. Suffolk U. chpt.). Democrat. Roman Catholic. Avocations: art, cross country and downhill skiing, hiking, outdoors, gardening.

**SUDARSKY, JERRY M.,** industrialist; b. Russia, June 12, 1918; s. Selig and Sara (Ars) S.; m. Mildred Axelrod, Aug. 31, 1947; children: Deborah, Donna (dec.). Student, U. Iowa, 1936—39; BS in Chem. Engrging., Poly. U. Bklyn., 1942; DSc (hon.), Poly. U. N.Y., 1976; PhD Hebrew U. Jerusalem (hon.), 2002. Founder, CEO Bioferm Corp., Wasco, Calif., 1946-66; cons. to Govt. of Israel, 1966—72; founder, chmn. Israel Chems., Ltd., Tel Aviv, 1967-72; chmn. I.C. Internat. Cons., Tel Aviv 1971-73; vice chmn., bd. dirs. Daylin, Inc., L.A., 1972-76; pres., chmn. J.M.S. Assocs., L.A., 1976—; vice chmn. bd. dirs. Jacobs Engring. Group Inc., Pasadena, Calif., 1982-94; chmn., CEO Health Sci. Prop. Holding Corp., Pasadena, 1997—. Mem. Alexandria Real Estate Equities Inc., Pasadena, 1997—. Mem. sci. adv. bd. Calif. Tech. Ventures, Pasadena, 2000—. Patentee in field of indsl. microbiology. Bd. govs. Hebrew U., Jerusalem; trustee Polytechnic U. N.Y., 1976—; bd. dirs. Mgmt. Edn. Assn., UCLA, 1990-99. Served with USNR, 1943-46. Mem. AAAS, Am. Chem. Soc., Brentwood Country Club, Sigma Xi. Office Phone: 310-556-1077.

**SUDBRACK, ELI (ASSUME VIVID ASTRO FOCUS),** artist; b. Rio de Janeiro, 1968; B, Pontificia Universidade Catolica, Rio de Janeiro, 1992; degree, Internat. Ctr. Photography, NY, 1999. Walking on Thin Ice, peres projects, LA, 2002, canopy, Skate Ctr., Ctrl. Pk., NYC, 2004, avaf8 (floorscape), 2004, exhibited in group shows at GNS: Global Navigation Sys., Palais de Tokyo, Paris, 2003, K48 Teenage Rebel: The Bedroom Show, galerie du jour, 2003, Popstraction, Deitch Projects, NY, 2003, Whitney Biennial Am. Art, Whitney Mus. Am. Art, 2004, Videodrome: 27 Internat. Artists, Santa Barbara Contemporary Arts Forum, Calif., 2005, one-man shows include, Galeria Triângulo, São Paulo, Brazil, 2004, Midway Contemporary Gallery, Saint Paul, Mich., 2003, Resodiversion, Paris, 2003. Mailing: c/o Santa Barbara Cmtemporary Arts Forum 653 Paseo Nuevo Santa Barbara CA 93101

**SUDBRINK, JANE MARIE,** sales and marketing executive; b. Sandusky, Ohio, Jan. 14, 1942; niece of Arthur and Lydia Sudbrink. BS, Bowling Green State U., 1964; postgrad., Kinderspital-Zurich, Switzerland, 1965. Field rep. Random House and Alfred A. Knopf Inc., Mpls., 1969-73, Ann Arbor, Mich., 1973, regional mgr. Midwest and Can., 1974-79, Can. rep., mgr., 1980-81; psychology and ednl. psychology adminstrv. editor Charles E. Merrill Pub. Co. div. Bell & Howell Corp., Columbus, Ohio, 1982-84; sales and mktg. mgr. trade products Wilson Learning Corp., Eden Prairie, Minn., 1984-85; fin. cons. Merrill Lynch Pierce Fenner & Smith, Edina, Minn., 1986-88; sr. editor Gorsuch Scarisbrick Pubs., Scottsdale, Ariz., 1988-89; regional mgr. Worth Publs., Inc. - von Holtzbrinck Pub. Grp., N.Y.C., 1989-97; mktg. assoc. Harcourt Brace Coll. Pubs., Northbrook, Ill., 1997-98, cons. Mid-Atlantic Redion, Midwest, Manitoba, Can., 1998—; mktg. assoc. W.W. Norton & Co., Northbrook, Ill., 1998—. Lutheran. Home and Office: 3801 Mission Hills Rd Northbrook IL 60062-5729 Business E-Mail: jsudbrink@wwnorton.com.

**SUDBURY, DAVID MARSHALL,** lawyer; b. Blytheville, Ark., Oct. 31, 1945; s. John Graham and Avis Wheatley (Miller) S.; m. Holly Jane Ritger, Dec. 27, 1967; children: Erin Elizabeth, Gregory Marshall. BA, So. Meth. U., 1967, JD, 1970. Bar: Tex. 1970, Okla. 1971, U.S. Dist. Ct. (we. dist.) Okla. 1971, U.S. Dist. Ct. (so. dist.) Tex. 1974, U.S. Dist. Ct. (no. dist.) Tex. 1976, U.S. Ct. Appeals (5th cir.) 1979, U.S. Supreme Ct. 1981. Asst. sec., atty. Wilson & Co. Inc., Oklahoma City, 1970-74; ptnr. Nelson and Harding, Houston, 1974-76; v.p., gen. counsel, sec. Comml. Metals Co., Dallas, 1976—. Bd. dirs. Dallas Repertory Theatre, 1982-85; bd. dirs. The 500 Inc., Dallas, 1978-82, pres., 1980-81. Mem. ABA, Tex. Bar Assn., Dallas Bar Assn. (bd. dirs. corp. counsel sect. 1987-93, chmn. 1992-93), Houston Bar Assn., Okla. Bar Assn., Am. Soc. Corp. Secs. (dir. 1984-86, pres., officer Dallas regional group 1978-81). Office: Comml Metals Co 6565 N MacArthur Blvd #800 Irving TX 75039-2461

**SUDBURY, JOHN DEAN,** religious organization administrator; b. Natchitoches, La., July 29, 1925; s. Herbert J. and Mary Flora S.; m. Jean Elizabeth Jung, July 18, 1947; children: John Byron, James Vernon (dec.), Linda Gail. BS, U. Tex., Austin, 1943, MA, 1947, PhD, 1949; DDiv (hon.), Okla. Christian U., 2003. Registered profl. engr., Okla. With Conoco Inc., various locations, 1949-83, asst. to v.p. tech. N.Y.C., 1970-72, v.p. coal research Conoco Coal Devel. Co. subs. Pitts., 1972-83; pres. Ea. European Mission and Bible Found., Houston, 1983-98, pres. emeritus, 1999—. Author: Oil Well Corrosion, 1956; contbr. articles to profl. jours.; patentee in energy field. Mem. Ponca City (Okla.) Sch. Bd., 1965-67; trustee Okla. Christian U., 1968—; bd. dirs. Am. Christmas Village, 2003—. Served with USN, 1943-45. Recipient Frank Newman Speller award Nat. Assn. Corrosion Engrs., 1967 Mem. Am. Chem. Soc., N.Y. Acad. Scis., AAAS, Sigma Xi. Republican. Mem. Ch. of Christ. Home and Office: 25485 Princeton Ln Oklahoma City OK Office Phone: 405-475-2162. Home Fax: 281-440-1955. Personal E-mail: jejs@evi.net.

**SUDDABY, GLENN T.,** prosecutor, lawyer; b. 1956; BA, SUNY, 1980; JD, Syracuse U., 1985. Bar: N.Y. 1986, Mass. 1986, Fed. Dist Ct. 1986. Asst. dist. atty. Onondaga County Dist. Atty.'s Office, 1986—89; assoc. Menter, Rudin & Trivelpiece, Syracuse, NY, 1989—92; chief asst. dist. atty. Onondaga County Dist. Atty.'s Office, 1992; 1st chief asst. dist. atty. Onandaga County Dist. Atty.'s Office, 1999—2002; US atty. (no. dist.) NY US Dept. Justice, 2002—. Office: PO Box 7198 100 S Clinton St Syracuse NY 13261 Office Phone: 315-448-0672.*

**SUDERS, JOAN MARY,** elementary school educator; b. Phila., Apr. 20, 1948; d. John Joseph and Stephany Rita Povilaitis; m. Daniel Charles Suders, Aug. 2, 1975; children: Daniel John, Stephany Rebecca. BS, Gwynedd-Mercy Coll., 1970; MEd, Shippensburg U., 1998. Cert. reading specialist Pa., reading recovery specialist Shippensburg U. Tchr. Cumberland Valley Sch. Dist., Mechanicsburg, Pa., 1970—. Tchr. religious edn. St Katharine Drexel Ch., Mechanicsburg, 1994—2006; min. of eucharist St Katherine Drexel Parish, Mechanicsburg, 1996—2006. Mem.: Beta Sigma Phi (officer Laureate Epsilon chpt.). Office Phone: 717-766-0217. Business E-Mail: jsuders@cvschools.org.

**SUDHIVORASETH, NIPHON,** pediatrician, immunologist, allergist; b. Bangkok, 1940; MD, Chulalongkorn Hosp. U., Bangkok, 1966. Diplomate Am. Bd. Pediatrics, Am. Bd. Allergy and Immunology. Intern Ch. Home Hosp., Balt., 1967-68; resident in pediatrics St. Lukes Hosp., N.Y.C., 1968-69, Beth Israel Hosp., N.Y.C., 1969-70; fellow in allergy Metro Hosp., N.Y. Med. Coll., N.Y.C., 1970-72; staff Marshall Meml. Hosp., Tex., 1978—; pvt. practice. Mem. AMA, Am. Acad. Allergy, Asthma, and Immunology, Am. Acad. Pediats., Am. Coll. Allergy and Immunology. Office: PO Box 2087 705 S Grove St Marshall TX 75670-5220

**SUDHOF, THOMAS CHRISTIAN,** molecular genetics educator; b. Göttingen, Germany, Dec. 22, 1955; Degree in medicine, RWTH, Aachen, Germany, 1977; MD, Georgia Augusta U., Göttingen, Germany, 1982. Postdoctoral fellow Max-Planck-Inst. Biophysikalische Chemie, Göttingen,

1982-83; postdoctoral fellow dept. molecular genetics U. Tex. Southwestern Med. Ctr., Dallas, 1983-85, asst. prof. dept. molecular genetics, 1987-89; asst. investigator U. Tex. Southwestern Med. Ctr., Howard Hughes Med. Inst., Dallas, 1986-89, assoc. prof. dept. molecular genetics, 1989-91, prof. dept. molecular genetics, 1991—, Gill disting. chair neurosci. rsch., 1995—, dir. center for neurosci., 1998—. Loyd B. Sands disting. chair in neurosci.; mem. molecular, cellular and devel. neurobiology rev. com. NIMH, 1995—. Mem. editl. bd. Jour. Biol. Chemistry and of Neuron; contbr. numerous articles to profl. publs. Recipient W. Alden Spencer award Columbia U., 1993, Wilhelm Feldberg award, 1994, Molecular Biology award NAS, 1997, MetLife award for Alzheimers Rsch. MetLife Found., 2004, Freedom to Discover Achievement award for Neuro-Science, Bristol-Myers Squibb, 2004. Office: UT Southwestern Med Ctr 5323 Harry Hines Blvd Dallas TX 75390-9111

**SUDMEYER, ALICE JEAN,** art gallery owner; b. Goldbeach, Oreg., Feb. 17, 1946; d. Harold Leo Enz Sr. and Zoa Jane (Mercer) Enz; m. Larry Gene Orrell, Jan. 11, 1970 (div. July 1974); children: Aaron Jay, Zoa Jean Easterling; m. Larry Everett Sudmeyer, Apr. 28, 1978. A Fine Arts and Letters, Mt. Hood C.C., 1977. Adminstr. dir. Art's OK!, San Diego, 1987—93; with Margaret Harwell Art Mus., Poplar Bluff, Mo., 1999—; owner, operator, artist Alice Jean Sudmeyer Artworks Gallery and Studio, Fredericktown, 2000—. With USAR, 1970—2006, ret. USAR, 2006. Decorated Liberation of Kuwait medal, Army Commendation medal, Southwest Asia medal. Mem.: DAV (life), VFW (life), Am. Legion (life). Avocations: gardening, yoga, music. Home and Office: 715 South Wood Ave Fredericktown MO 63645 Personal E-mail: jean4me@charter.net.

**SUE, ALAN KWAI KEONG,** dentist; b. Honolulu, Apr. 26, 1946; s. Henry Tin Yee and Chiyoko (Ohata) S.; m. Ginger Kazue Fukushima, Mar. 19, 1972, 1 child, Dawn Marie. BS in Chemistry with honors, U. Hawaii, 1968; BS, DDS, U. Calif., San Francisco, 1972. Film editor, photographer Sta. KHVH-TV ABC, Honolulu, 1964-71; staff dentist Strong-Carter Dental Clinic, Honolulu, 1972-73; dentist Waianae Dental Clinic, Honolulu, 1972-73; pvt. practice Pearl City, Hawaii, 1973—; chief exec. officer Dental Image Specialists, Pearl City, 1975—; dental dir. Hawaii Dental Health Plan, Honolulu, 1987—; dental cons. Calif. Dental Health Plan, Tustin, 1987—; Pacific Group Med. Assn., The Queen's Health Care Plan, Honolulu, 1993—. Dental cons. Pacific Group Med. Assn., 1994—; cons. Hawaii Mgmt. Alliance Assn., 1996—; bd. dirs. Kula Bay Tropical Clothing Co., Hawaiian Ind. Dental Alliance; mem. exec. bd. St. Francis Hosp., Honolulu, 1976-78, chief dept. dentistry, 1976-78; mem. expert med. panel Am. Internat. Claim Svc., 1995—. Mem. adv. bd. Health Svcs. for Sr. Citizens, 1976—; mem. West Honolulu Sub-Area Health Planning Coun., 1981-84; mem. dental task force Hawaii Statewide Health Coordinating Coun., 1980, mem. plan devel. com., 1981-84; vol. oral cancer screening program Am. Cancer Soc.; v.p. Pearl City Shopping Ctr. Merchants Assn., 1975-84, 92-93, pres., 1994—. Regents' scholar U. Calif., San Francisco, 1968-72. Fellow Pierre Fauchard Acad., Acad. Gen. Dentistry; mem. ADA, Acad. Implants and Transplants, Am. Acad. Implant Dentistry, Hawaii Dental Assn. (trustee 1978-80), Honolulu County Dental Soc. (pres. 1982), Am. Acad. and Bd. Head, Facial, Neck Pain and TMJ Orthopedics, Intertel, Internat. Platform Assn., Mensa, Porsche Club, Pantera Owners Club, Mercedes Benz Club. Democrat. Avocations: cars, tennis, photography, gardening. Office: Dental Image Specialists 850 Kam Hwy Ste 116 Pearl City HI 96782-2691 Office Phone: 808-455-4191. E-mail: oraldr928@tennis.com.

**SUE, MICHAEL ALVIN,** allergist; b. LA, Apr. 15, 1956; MD, U. Chgo., 1980. Diplomate Am. Bd. Internal Medicine, Am. Bd. Allergy and Immunology. Intern, resident and fellow West Los Angeles VA Med. Ctr., L.A., 1980-86; allergist Kaiser Permanent, Panorama City, Calif., 1986—. Fellow Am. Coll. Allergy, Asthma, and Immunology; mem. Am. Acad. Allergy, Asthma, and Immunology. Office: Kaiser Permanente 13652 Cantara St Panorama City CA 91402-5497

**SUEDFELD, PETER,** psychologist, educator; b. Budapest, Hungary, Aug. 30, 1935; emigrated to US, 1948, naturalized, 1952; s. Leslie John and Jolan (Eichenbaum) Field; m. Gabrielle Debra Guterman, June 11, 1961 (div. 1980); children: Michael Thomas, Joanne Ruth, David Lee; m. Phyllis Jean Johnson, Oct. 19, 1991. Student, U. Philippines, 1956-57; BA, Queens Coll., 1960; MA, Princeton U., 1962, PhD, 1963. Rsch. assoc. Princeton U.; lectr. Trenton State Coll., 1963-64; vis. asst. prof. psychology U. Ill., 1964-65; asst. prof. psychology Univ. Coll. Rutgers U., 1965-67, assoc. prof., 1967-71, prof., 1971-72, chmn. dept., 1967-72; prof. psychology U. B.C., Vancouver, 1972-2001, head dept., 1972-84, dean faculty grad. studies, 1984-90, disting. scholar-in-residence, P. Wall Inst. Adv. Studies, 2000, dean and prof. emeritus, 2001—. Chmn. Can. Antarctic Rsch. Program, 1994—98; Disting. vis. scholar Ohio State U., 2000—03; affiliated prof. U. Haifa, 2005—; cons., lectr. in field. Author: Restricted Environmental Stimulation: Research and Clinical Applications, 1980; editor: Attitude Change: The Competing Views, 1971, Personality Theory and Information Processing, 1971, The Behavioral Basis of Design, 1976, Psychology and Torture, 1990, Restricted Environmental Stimulation: Theoretical and Empirical Developments in Flotation REST, 1990, Psychology and Social Policy, 1991, Light from the Ashes, 2001; editor Jour. Applied Social Psychology, 1975-82; assoc. editor Environment and Behavior, 1992—; contbr. articles to profl. jours. Served with US Army, 1955-58. Recipient Antarctica svc. medal, NSF, US Navy, 1994, Zachor award, Parliament of Can., 2000; grantee, NIMH, 1970—72, Can. Coun., 1973—2006, Nat. Rsch. Coun. Can., 1973—90, NIH, 1980—84, Can. Space Agy., 2003—. Fellow Royal Soc. Can., Can. Psychol. Assn. (pres. 1998-99, Donald O. Hebb award 2001), APA, Am. Psychol. Soc., Acad. Behavioral Medicine Resch., Soc. Behavioral Medicine, N.Y. Acad. Sci.; mem. Internat. Soc. Polit. Psychol. (v.p. 1999-2001, Harold D. Lasswell award 2001, Roberta Sigel award 2005), Internat. Acad. Astronautics (corr.), Soc. Exptl. Social Psychology, Phi Beta Kappa, Sigma Xi. Office: U BC Dept Psychology Vancouver BC Canada V6T 1Z4 Office Phone: 604-822-5713. Business E-mail: psuedfeld@psych.ubc.ca.

**SUEDMEYER, WILLIAM KIRK,** veterinarian; b. St. Louis, Mar. 13, 1961; s. Robert and Mary Margaret Suedmeyer; m. Joyce Ellen Nelson, June 23, 1983; children: Jennifer, Jonathan, Austin, Taylor. BS in zoology, E.M.T., Northeast Mo. State U., 1983; DVM, UMC Coll. Vet. Medicine, 1987. Diplomate bd. cert. Am. Coll. Zoo. Medicine. Staff vet. Potawtomi Zoo, South Bend, Ind., 1989—92; staff vet. to sr. staff vet. to dir. animal health Kansas City Zoo, 1992—. Contbr. articles various profl. jours.; editor (assoc.): Jour. of Zoo and Wildlife Medicine, 2003—. Bd. dirs. Ind. Wildlife Rehab. Ctr., South Bend, Ind., 1990—92; chmn. Kansas City Zoo Sci. Study Com., 1994—. Recipient Pub. Employee Recognition award, Fed. Govt., Kansas City, 2001, CVM Phi Zeta Judge, UMC Coll. Vet. Medicine, 2003. Avocations: fishing, falconry, artistry. Office: Kans City Zoo 6700 Zoo Dr Kansas City MO 64132 Office Phone: 816-513-4669. E-mail: wksahc@juno.com.

**SUEHR, CINDY L.,** social studies educator, language educator; b. Decatur, Ill., Jan. 27, 1964; d. David L. and Jane U. Boyd; m. Jeff S. Suehr, June 28, 1986; children: Rose, Alexis, Ashley. BA, Olivet Coll., Mich., 1988; Master's, Mich. State U., East Lansing. Tchr. grade 5 Perry Mid. Sch., Mich.; tchr. grades 2-5 Haslett Elem. Sch., Mich Achievements include State Champion-Record Holder, swimming, 1979. Avocations: reading, travel, sports. Office: Perry Pub Schs 2775 W Britton Rd Perry MI 48872 Business E-Mail: suehrc@perry.k12.mi.us.

**SUELTZ, PATRICIA C.,** computer company executive; BA in Polit. Sci., Occidental Coll. With Installation and Repair Divsn. Pacific Telephone and Telegraph Co.; from various tech. positions to gen. mgr. Java Software IBM Corp., 1979—98, gen. mgr. Java Software, 1998—99; exec. v.p. gen. mgr. Software Sys. Group Sun Microsystems Inc., 1999—2002, exec. v.p. Enterprise Svcs. Group, 2002—04; pres. mktg., tech. and sys. Salesforce.com Inc., San Francisco, 2004—, exec. v.p., 2004—. Bd. dirs. Delphi Automotive Sys., Amgen Inc. Named one of 50 Most Powerful Women in Bus., Fortune Mag., 2000; fellow, Rockefeller Found.

**SUEN, CHING YEE,** computer scientist, educator, researcher; b. Chung Shan, Kwang Tung, China, Oct. 14, 1942; s. Stephen and Sin (Kan) S; m. Sheung Ling Chan, May 12, 1970; children: Karwa, Karnon. BSc in Engring., U. Hong Kong, 1966, MSc in Engring., 1968; MASc., U. B.C., 1970, PhD, 1972. Asst. prof. computer sci. Concordia U., Montreal, Can., 1972-76, assoc. prof., 1976-79, prof., 1979—, chmn., 1980-84, dir. Centre for Pattern Recognition and Machine Intelligence, 1988—, assoc. dean faculty engring. and computer sci., 1993-97, disting. chair artificial intelligence and pattern recognition, 2001—. Vis. scientist Rsch. Lab. of Electronics, MIT, Cambridge, 1975, 76, 78-79; invited prof. Ecole Polytechnique Fédérale de Lausanne, Switzerland, 1979, Institut de Recherche d'Informatique et d'Automatique, Rocquencourt, France, 1976, 78, 79, founder, Vision Interface, 1986; founder, co-chmn. Internat. Conf. on Document Analysis and Recognition, St.-Malo, France, 1991, Tsukuba Sci. City, Japan, 1993, chmn., Montreal, Can., 1995; founder, chmn. Internat. Workshop on Frontiers in Handwriting Recognition (hon. chair, 2002), gen. chair Internat. Conf. on Pattern Recognition, Quebec City, Canada, 2002; organizer numerous confs. Author: Computational Analysis of Mandarin, 1979, Computational Studies of the Most Frequent Chinese Words and Sounds, 1986, (with Z.C. Li, T.D. Bui, Y.Y. Tang) Computer Transformation of Digital Images and Patterns, 1989; editor: (with R. De Mori) Computer Analysis and Perception Vol. 1, Visual Signals, 1982, Computer Analysis and Perception Vol. 2, Auditory Signals, 1982, (with R. De Mori) New Systems and Architectures for Automatic Speech Recognition and Synthesis, 1985, (with R. Plamondon and M.L. Simner) Computer Recognition and Human Production of Handwriting, 1989, Frontiers in Handwriting Recognition, 1990, Operating Expert System Applications in Canada, 1992, (with P.S.P. Wang) Thinning Methodologies for Pattern Recognition, 1994; assoc. editor Signal Processing, 1979—, Pattern Recognition Letters, 1982—, Pattern Recognition, 1993—, IEEE Transactions on Pattern Analysis and Machine Intelligence, 1986-89, Internat. Jour. Pattern Recognition and Artificial Intelligence, 1986—, Pattern Analysis and Applications, 1998—, Internat. Jour. on Document Analysis and Applications, 1998—; founder, editor-in-chief Computer Processing of Chinese and Oriental Langs., 1982-93; adviser IEEE Transactions on Pattern Analysis and Machine Intelligence, 1989-92; author more than 300 publs.; patentee in field. Recipient award Fedn. Chinese Can. Profls., 1988; rsch. fellow Concordia U., 1998; Swire scholar U. Hong Kong, 1967, ITAC/NSERC award Info. Tech. Assn. Can. and Natural Scis. and Engring. Rsch. Coun. Can., 1992, Internat. Assn. Pattern Recognition and Internat. Conf. Document Analysis and Recognition award, 2005. Fellow IEEE (advisor Computer Soc.), Royal Soc. Can., Internat. Assn. for Pattern Recognition; mem. (life) Chinese Lang. Computer Soc. (v.p. 1987-90, pres. 1990-93, award 1988), Can. Image Processing and Pattern Recognition Soc. (pres. 1984-90, award 1997). Office: Concordia Univ Dept Computer Sci 1455 Maisonneuve W Ste VE-3-189 Montreal PQ Canada H3G 1M8 Office Phone: 514-848-2424 x3006.

**SUENRAM, ANDY,** lawyer; b. Lakeport, Calif., May 24, 1961; BA in Econs., U. Calif., Santa Cruz, 1985; JD, U. Mont., 1988. Bar: Mont. 1988, U.S. Dist. Ct. Mont. 1988. Atty. Erb & Suenram, Dillon. Mem.: ABA (econs. of law practice, natural resources law sects.), State Bar Mont. (exec. com. 1997—, pres.-elect 2001—02, pres. 2003). Beaverhead County C. of C. (dir. 1990—91). Office: Erb and Suenram PO Box 1366 134 E Reeder St Dillon MT 59725-1366

**SUER, MARVIN DAVID,** architectural consultant; b. Phila., Apr. 4, 1923; m. Gertrude Litvin, 1947; children: Marsha Suer Clark, Sharon, Deborah Suer Berman. BArch, U. Pa., 1950. Registered architect, Pa. Ptnr. Suer & Livingston, 1961-62, Suer, Livingston & Demas, 1962-69; dir. tech. prodn. Eshbach, Pullinger, Stevens & Bruder, Phila., 1969-74; assoc. Ballinger, Phila., 1974-79, Bartley Long Mirenda, Phila., 1979-85, S.T. Hudson Internat., Phila., 1986-95; archtl. cons., 1996—. Archtl. works include State Hosp. for Crippled Children addition, 1964, Huey Elem. Sch., Phila., 1964, Dist. No. 4 Health Ctr., Phila., 1967, Stephen Smith Towers, 1969, Foxchase Br. Libr., 1969. Chmn. bd. trustees Phila. Found. for Architecture, 1980-81. With C.E., AUS, 1943-46. Fellow AIA (pres. Phila. chpt. 1968, 125th Yr. citation 1982); mem. Tau Sigma Delta. Home: 305 Overlook Ave Willow Grove PA 19090-2806

**SUESS, JAMES FRANCIS,** retired clinical psychologist; b. Evanston, Ill., Aug. 8, 1950; s. James Francis and Rae Love (Miller) S.; m. Linda Grace Powell, July 31, 1976; 1 child, Misty Lynne. BS, U. So. Miss., 1974, MS, 1978, PhD, 1982. Lic. psychologist, NY, Ala.; diplomate Am. Bd. Profl. Psychology, Am. Bd. Med. Psychotherapists, Profl. Assn. Custody Evaluators, Am. Coll. Forensic Examiners, Am. Bd. Forensic Medicine. Assoc. psychologist State of Miss., Ellisville, 1978-80; clin. psychologist SUNY Med. Sch./Erie County Med. Ctr., Buffalo, 1982-84, supervising clin. psychologist, 1984-87, assoc. dir., 1987—2005; prof. dept. psychology Clinic South Ala., 2001—05; prof. emeritus SUNY, 2005—. Dir. practica SUNY Med. Sch., 1982-90, faculty counsel, 1988—; cons. Buffalo Dept. Social Svcs., 1985—; mem. spkrs. bur. Erie Alliance for Mentally Ill, 1986—; vis. prof. U. Guadalajara Sch. Medicine, 1985—; clin. dir. Stickney Adolescent Ctr. Mobile MHC, 1993-97; clin. dir. Physicans' Psychiat. Clinic, 1997—; CEO Stillwood Clin. Group, 1998—; adj. prof. dept. psychology U. South Ala., 2000—; clin. dir. Adm. Mc Collough Inst. of Rejuvenology. Author: Annotated Bibliography of Sex Roles, 1972, Personality Disorder and Self Psychology, 1991, (textbook) Enduring My Journey Throug Life: The Borderline Personality Disorders, 2005; contbr. chpts. to books, numerous articles to refereed jours. including Perceptual and Motor Skills, Jour. Clin. and Consulting Psychology, Am. Annals of Deaf, Assessment of Children, Threats in Schools. Mem. small bus. adv. coun. Nat. Congl. Com., 2005—. With USAR, 1969-76. Fellow Am. Orthopsychiat. Assn (diplomate), Sov. Personality Assessment; mem. APA, Ala. Llc. Psychol. (pres.), Mobile Assn. Psychol. (pres.). Home: 507 Evergreen Rd Mobile AL 36608-3845 Office: The Stillwood Clin Grp 717 Executive Park Dr Ste B Mobile AL 36606-2843 Office Fax: 251-342-8599. E-mail: drjfsuess@comcast.net.

**SUESS, JAMES FRANCIS,** retired psychiatry educator; b. Rock Island, Ill., Nov. 27, 1919; s. Joseph John and Elizabeth Ida (Dalton) S.; m. Rae Love Miller, Mar. 24, 1946; children: Rae Anne, James Francis, John Randall. B Med. Sci., Northwestern U., 1950, MD, 1952; postgrad., Coll. Physicians and Surgeons, Columbia U. and N.Y. Psychiat. Inst., 1958. Diplomate Am. Bd. Psychiatry and Neurology (examiner various times). Intern USPHS Hosp., New Orleans, 1952-53; resident in psychiatry Warren (Pa.) State Hosp., 1953-56, clin. dir., 1956-62; asst. prof. psychiatry U. Miss. Med. Sch., Jackson, 1962-65, assoc. prof., 1965-69, prof., 1969-82; prof. emeritus, 1982—; chmn. dept., 1967-69, 73-75; asst. dean, 1978-82. Assoc. chief staff for educ. VA Med. Ctr., Jackson, 1978-82; vis. prof. Inst. Psychiatry, London, 1977, 83; ref. editl. bd. Am. Jour. Psychiatry, Washington; invited cons. to 5 Soviet republics, USSR, 1979; invited cons. in psychiatry, China, 1979. Contbr. articles to med. jours., including Am. Jour. Psychiatry, Jour. Med. Edn., chpts. to books. Capt. U.S. Army, 1941-45. Fellow Am. Psychiat. Assn., So. Psychiat. Assn. (edn. com. 1973-77), Miss. Psychiat. Assn. (pres. 1968-69); mem. Am. Assn. Dirs. Psychiat. Tng. (a founder, exec. bd. 1969-71). Avocations: piano, organ, golf, duplicate bridge. Home: 1415 Radcliffe St Jackson MS 39211-4824 E-mail: jamespsychman@cs.com.

**SUFFIELD, JUDITH KREUTZ,** secondary school educator; b. Fargo, ND, Aug. 31, 1944; d. Palmer L. and Opal L. (Rood) Kreutz; m. Martin J. Suffield, June 11, 1966; children: Kristine, Peter. BA in English Edn., U. Ill., 1962; MS in Secondary Edn., Ind. U., Indpls., 1987. Tchr. Byrns L. Darden Elem. Sch., New Providence, Tenn., 1966-67, George Mason Jr.-Sr. HS, Falls Ch., Va., 1967-69, Edgewood Jr. HS, Highland Park, Ill., 1969-71; supr. student teaching Edgewood Coll., Columbia, Mo., 1975; tchr. English dept. Western HS, Russiaville, Ind., 1982—, chair, 1999—. Mem. adj. faculty Ind. U., Kokomo, 1987—, Bloomington, 2003—. Recipient Outstanding Faculty mem. award, Western H.S., Russiaville, Ind., 1993, Tchg. Excellence Recognition award, Ind. U., Kokomo, 1998, 2000, Claude Rich award for Excellence in Tchg., 2004; fellow Lilly Creativity fellow, Lilly Found., 1992.

Mem. NEA, Western Edn. Assn., Kappa Kappa Kappa, Chi Omega. Avocations: reading, quilting. Office: Western High Sch 600 W CR 250 S Russiaville IN 46979-9802 Office Phone: 765-883-5541. Business E-Mail: jsuffiel@western.k12.in.us.

**SUFFOLK, RANDALL,** museum director, curator; BA, Conn. Coll.; MA in higher edn. adminstrn., Columbia U.; MA in art hist., Bryn Mawr Coll. Assoc. W. Graham Arader III Galleries, Phila., NYC; cons. Arts Corp., Ltd., Phila.; curator The Hyde Collection, Glen Falls, NY, 1995—98, dep. dir. 1998—99, acting dir., 1999—2000, dir., 2000—. Mem. strategic planning com. Univ. Art Mus., SUNY, Albany; review panel mem. for Spl. Opportunity Stipend Grants NY State Coun. on Arts. Bd. dirs. Adirondack/Lake George Regional Tourism Bd., The Feeder Canal Alliance. Office: The Hyde Collection 161 Warren St Glens Falls NY 12801 E-mail: suffolk@hydecollection.org.

**SUFLAS, STEVEN WILLIAM,** lawyer; b. Camden, NJ, Oct. 7, 1951; s. William V. and Dorothy (Stafre) S.; m. Rochelle B. Volin, Apr. 15, 1978; children: Rebecca, Whitney. BA, Davidson Coll., 1973; JD with honors, U. N.C., 1976. Bar: N.J. 1976, Pa. 1978, U.S. Dist. Ct. N.J., U.S. Ct. Appeals (3d cir.). Field atty. NLRB, Phila., 1976-80; assoc. Archer & Greiner P.C., Haddonfield, NJ, 1980-86, ptnr., 1986—2002, Ballard, Spahr, Andrews & Ingersoll LLP, Voorhees, NJ, 2002—. Fellow Coll. of Labor and Employment Lawyers; mem. ABA, Pa. Bar Assn., Phila. Bar Assn., NJ Bar Assn. (exec. com. labor and employment law sect. 1985—, chmn. 1999-2001), Order of Coif, Omicron Delta Kappa. Office: Ballard Spahr Andrews & Ingersoll Plaza 1000 Ste 500 Main St Voorhees NJ 08043-4636 Office Phone: 856-761-3466. Business E-Mail: suflas@ballardspahr.com.

**SUGAHARA, BYRON MASAHIKO,** transportation executive; b. Jan. 22, 1940; s. Kay and Yone (Kuwahara) Sugahara; m. Nancy Shaw Hall, June 5, 1977; children: Christopher, Abigail, Alexandra. BA, Harvard Coll., 1962. From v.p. to pres. St. Geo. Am. Lines, Roseland, NJ, 1985—. Bd. dirs. Peck Sch., Morristown, NJ, 1993—95. 1st lt. U.S. Army, 1963—65. Mem.: Am. Bur. Shipping. Tokyo Club, Henryville Conservation Club. Avocations: fly fishing, golf. Office: Great American Lines 5 Becker Farm Rd Ste 4 Roseland NJ 07068-1779 Home: 533 Indian Harbor Rd Vero Beach FL 32963

**SUGAR, JOSEPH ROBERT,** music educator, conductor, musician; b. Worcester, Mass., Dec. 14, 1928; s. Elias George and Emily Angeline (David) S.; m. Clara Anne Steele, Dec. 26, 1955; children: Thomas Elias, Robert Albert. AA, Bergen Jr. Coll., Teaneck, N.J., 1948; BA, L.I. U., 1950; MA, Columbia U., 1955; profl. diploma, 1956. Brass instr. L.I. U., N.Y., 1949; asst. in bands. Ind. U., Bloomington, Ind., 1950; dir. Instrumental Music, Matawan, N.J., 1954-56; band dir. Upsala Coll., East Orange, N.J., 1956-57; band. dir., instr. music Bethpage (N.Y.) Elem. Sch., 1957-66; instr. baton twirling Bethpage High Sch., 1957-67; band. dir. Hewlett-Woodmere (N.Y.) Jr. High Sch., 1966-78; asst. band dir., instr. baton twirling Hewlett High Sch., 1967-69, band dir., 1983-84, dir. jazz ensemble, 1983-89; band dir. Dowling Coll., Oakdale, N.Y., 1977-79; dist. dir. music Hewlett-Woodmere Pub. Schs., 1978-89; advisor to music chmn. for courses music edn. C.W. Post Coll. L.I. U., Greenvale, N.Y., 1990—; prof., 1990—; dir. music edn., 1990-2001. Summer band sch. co-dir Manasquan, N.J., 1955-64; creative music cultural workshop, Bethpage, 1959-62; youth choir dir. Levittown (N.Y.) Presbyn. Ch., 1966; dir. N.Y. Jazz Ensemble, Hempstead, 1976; dir. Kismet Shrine Temple Band, 1997—; clinician numerous music festivals, 1970—; choral dir., instrumentalist, Air Force Band of Rockies, US Air Force Acad. Band, 504th Air Force Band, Colorado Springs. Performer Indpls. Symphony Orch., 1950, Joe Sugar and the Big Band, 1980—; accompanist numerous entertainers including Vic Damone, Diahann Carroll, Al martino, Jerry Vale, Georgia Gibbs, Toni Arden, Johnny Ray, Eddie Fisher, Cab Calloway, Marilyn Michaels, Frankie Lane, Henny Youngman, Anna Maria Alberghetti, Patti Page, Bobby Rydel, Buddy Grecco, Billy Eckstine, Julius La Rose, The Four Aces, Don Cornell, Connie Francis; rec. artist with Audio-Fidelity, 20th Century Fox, Paramount, MGM, 1958-61; author: Presidents march, 1982, Twirling Tips in 3 Volumes, 1963, Where Are We Headed in Music Education?, 1960; composer, condr. (album) Ten Nights in a Harem, 1963. Mem. Boy Scouts Am. With USAF, 1950-52. Grantee Ford Found., 1962; recipient Merit award Music Belongs, 1972, 1st pl. award East Nat. Music Festival, 1977, Appreciation of Outstanding Leadership award Black Music Caucus, 1982, Cert. of Merit award N.Y. State Senate, 1982, citation Town of Hempstead, 1982, Disting. Svc. award, Hewlett-Woodmere Pub. Schs., 1989; named Man of Yr. Wantagh C. of C., 1979; named to Tchr. Hall of Fame, Hewlett-Woodmere Pub. Schs., 1990. Mem. Music Educators Nat. Conf. (life, pres. Eastern divsn. 1985-87), N.Y. State Administrs. Music Edn. (pres. 1987—), N.Y. State Sch. Music Assn.(pres. 1980-82, Disting. Svc. award 1989), Nassau Music Educators (pres. 1970, Pres. award 1970, Svc. awards 1973, 87), Nat. Assn. Jazz Educators, Internat. Trumpet Guild, N.Y. State Coun. Music Adminstrs., DAV (life), Wantagh Friends of Libr., Am. Legion (past commander, award 1978), Jones Beach Power Squadron (sr.), Kiwanis (past pres. award 1979), Masons, Wantagh Dads and Booster (pst pres.), Wantagh Spiked Shoe (past pres. award 1979), Phi Delta Kappa, Phi Mu Alpha (life), Kappa Kappa Psi, Phi Mu Alpha, Tri M. Republican. Home: 1594 Milburn Ct Wantagh NY 11793-3330 Office: LI U CW POst Coll Music Dept 720 Northern Blvd Brookville NY 11548-1319 Personal E-mail: jsugar@liv.edu.

**SUGAR, RONALD D.,** aerospace executive; BSEE summa cum laude, UCLA, 1968, MS, 1969, PhD, 1971. Dir. advanced R & D programs TRW Inc., Cleve., 1981-83, chief engr., dep. program mgr. Milstar Satellite payload program, 1983-87, v.p., gen. mgr. space comms. divsn., 1987-92, v.p. strategic bus. devel. space and def. sector, 1992-94, exec. v.p., CFO, 1994-96, exec. gen. mgr. automotive electronics group 1996-98, exec. v.p. opt. program 1998-99, pres., COO space and info. sys. sector, 1999-2000; pres., COO Litton Industries, Inc., Woodland Hills, Calif., 2000—01, Northrop Grumman Corp., LA, 2001—03, pres., CEO, chmn., 2003—. Mem. Nat. Security Telecom. Adv. Com.; bd. dirs. Chevron Corp. Nat. trustee Boys & Girls Clubs of Am.; dir. LA Philharmonic Assn.; trustee U. So. Calif. Fellow: Royal Aeronautical Soc., Am. Inst. of Aeronautics and Astronautics; mem.: NAE, Aerospace Industries Assn. (vice chmn.), Assn. of US Army. Office: Northrop Grumman Corp 1840 Century Park E Los Angeles CA 90067-2199*

**SUGARMAN, ALAN WILLIAM,** educational consultant; b. Boston, Sept. 26, 1924; s. Henry and Dorothy (Adams) S.; m. Alice Mulhall, 1974; children: Michael, Susan, Ellen, William, Jane, James. BS, Boston U., 1948; MA, Columbia U., 1949, EdD, 1967; postgrad., SUNY, Albany, 1954-56. Entrance examiner Boston U., 1947-48; tchr. Public Schs. Hudson, NY, 1950-54, prin. jr. high sch., 1954-56, prin. sr. high sch., 1956-61; prin. Spring Valley (N.Y.) Sr. High Sch., 1961-67; dir. secondary edn. Ramapo Central Sch. Dist. No. 2, Spring Valley, 1967-69, asst. supt. instrn., 1969-73; prin. Ramapo Sr. High Sch., Spring Valley, 1969; supt. schs. Connetquot Central Sch. Dist. Islip, Bohemia, NY, 1973-80, Ft. Lee (N.J.) Sch. Dist., 1980—2000; nat. spkr., cons., 2000—. Adj. prof. N.Y. U., N.Y., 1967, prof. Río Piedras, Hofstra U., 1967—; prof. Fordham U., N.Y.C., 1969 Athletic dir. East River Day Camp, N.Y.C., summer 1949; group worker St. John's Guild, summer 1950; asst. dir. Tenn. Work Camp, Unitarian Service Com., summer 1951; dir. spl. activities Hudson Youth Bur., Hudson, N.Y., summer 1952; exec. dir. Jewish Community Center, Hudson, 1953-56; chmn. vis. coms. Middle States Commm. Colls. and Secondary Schs., 1958-76; chmn. county leadership tng. com., mem. Rockland County exec. council Boy Scouts Am., 1956; bd. dirs. Bergen County Red Cross; corr. sec. Rockland County Negro Scholarship Fund, Inc.; pres. Spring Valley Youth Activities Com., 1956-58; bd. dirs., past campaign co-chmn. Greater Hudson Community Chest; bd. dirs., 2d v.p. Hudson Youth Recreation Center, 1958-61; bd. dirs. Rockland County br. Am. Cancer Soc., 1958-61, Columbia Meml. Hosp., 1959-61; chmn. Town of Islip Health Usage Com., 1973-80. bd. dirs. Am. Heart Assn. NJ affiliate, 1993—. Served with AUS, 1944-46, ETO. Recipient Disting. Svc. award Hudson Jr. C. of C., 1960, Ft. Lee Citizen of Yr. award VFW, Bergen County Citizen of Yr. award VFW, 1989, N.J. State Elks Alcohol and Drug Prevention award, 1989, St. Michael's award, 1992, PBA Silver Life Card award, 1993, EIA award Greek Orthodox Archdiocese, 1993; named Adminstr. of Yr., Fordham U., 1990, B'nai Brith Man of Yr., 1995. Mem. Nat. Honor Soc. Secondary Schs. (hon.), Nat. PTA (hon. life), Am. Assn. Sch. Adminstrs., Assn. Supervision and Curriculum Devel., Nat. Sch. Public Relations Assn., Assn. Sch. Bus. Ofcls., Nat. Soc. Study Edn., DAV, VFW, Jewish War Vets., Rotary (bd. dirs.), Phi Delta Kappa (Adminstr. of Yr. award 1990), Kappa Delta Pi, Pi Gamma Mu. Office: 400 Fairview Ave Fort Lee NJ 07024 Home: 494 Country Club Dr Egg Harbor City NJ 08215-5132 E-mail: amwsintac@msn.com.

**SUGARMAN, GEORGE,** artist; b. N.Y.C., May 11, 1912; s. Herman and Rachel S. BA, CCNY, 1935. Adj. prof. art Hue Hunter Coll., 1961-68, also Yale U., Princeton U. One-man shows Widdifield Gallery, N.Y.C., 1958, Radich Gallery, N.Y.C., 1961, 64, 65, 66, Phila. Art Alliance, 1965, Dayton's Gallery 12, Mpls., 1966, Galerie Schmela, Dusseldorf, Germany, 1967, Galerie Ziegler, Zurich, Switzerland, 1967, 70, Kaiser Wilhelm Mus., Krefeld, Germany, 1969, Stadtsches Mus., Leverkusen, 1969, Kunsthalle, Basel, Switzerland, 1970, Haus Am Waldsee Mus., Berlin, 1970, Stedelijk Mus., Amsterdam, 1970, Gallery 118, Mpls., 1971, Zabriskie Gallery, N.Y.C., 1974, Dag Hammarskjold Plaza Sculpture Garden, N.Y.C., 1974, Robet Miller Gallery, N.Y.C., 1977, 78, Galerie Liatowitsch, Basel, 1979, Rudolf Zwirner Gallery, Cologne, W. Ger., 1981, Joslyn Art Mus (retrospective), Omaha, 1981-82, Fuller-Goldeen Gallery, San Francisco, 1984, Robert Miller Gallery, N.Y.C., 1985, Whitney Mus. Am. Art, N.Y.C., 1985, Contemporary Sculpture Ctr., Tokyo, 1993; group shows include, São Paulo (Brazil) Biennale, 1963, Whitney Mus. Am. Art, 1966, Los Angeles County Mus. Art, 1967, Internat. Pavilion, Biennale, Venice, Italy, 1968, Mus. Modern Art, N.Y.C., 1969, Whitney Mus., 1976, Washburn Gallery, NYC, 2006; represented in permanent collections, Walker Art Center, Mpls., Kunstmuseum, Zurich, Mus. Modern Art, Whitney Mus. Am. Art, Art Inst. Chgo., Met. Mus., N.Y.C.; sculpture commns., World Trade Center, Brussels, Albert M. Greenfield Sch., Phila., Empire State Mall, Albany, N.Y., Fed. Ct. Bldg., Balt., Akron (Ohio) Public Library, Lincoln Nat. Life Found., Ft. Wayne, Ind., Internat. Airport, Miami, Fla., Detroit Gen. Hosp., Wills Eye Hosp., Phila., Summer-Best Sta., Buffalo, Southland Life Bldg., Dallas, Columbia Plaza, Cin., Allegheny Landing, Pitts., Joslyn Sculpture Garden, Omaha, Bellevue Park, Wichita Falls, Tex., VA Hosp., Martinsburg, W.Va., Columbia Plaza, Cin., Storm King Art Ctr., Mountainville, N.Y., Mercantile Bank, San Antonio, GTE, Irving, Tex., NCNB Pla., Tampa, Fla., Koll Ctr. Irvine, North Irvine, Calif., The Pavillions at Buckland Hills, Manchester, Conn., Crystal Tower, Kobe, Japan, Mitsui Marine Co., Chiba, Japan, Cultural Ctr., Miyazaki, Kyushu, Japan, Suderman Sq., Jakarta, Indonesia. With USN, 1941—45. Recipient 2d prize Pitts. Internat., 1961-62; Am. Acad. and Inst. Arts and Letters award; Longview Found. grantee, 1961, 62, 63; Ford Found. grantee, 1965; Nat. Found. Arts grantee, 1966, special award Sculpture Triennale Osaka, Japan, 1992. Home: 230 Park Ave Rm 545 New York NY 10169-0599*

**SUGARMAN, IRWIN J.,** lawyer; b. Dayton, Ohio, June 17, 1943; s. Nathan and Esther (Goldstein) S.; 1 child, Alexander David Sugarman. BA, Rutgers U., New Brunswick, N.J., 1965; JD, Rutgers U., Newark, 1968. Bar: N.Y. 1968. Law clk. to Judge Edmund Palmieri U.S. Dist. Ct. for So. Dist. N.Y., N.Y.C., 1968-69; assoc. Debevoise Plimpton Lyons & Gates, N.Y.C., 1969-79; ptnr. Schulte Roth & Zabel, N.Y.C., 1979—. Bd. dirs. Santa Fe Opera, 1989-94. Office: Schulte Roth & Zabel 919 3rd Ave Fl 23 New York NY 10022-4774 E-mail: irwin.sugarman@srz.com.

**SUGARMAN, MICHAEL,** physician, rheumatologist; b. Galveston, Tex., May 26, 1945; s. Harold and Amelia Sugarman; m. Hilda Roberta Krug, Aug. 26, 1967; children: Jason, Steven. BS, U. Calif., Berkeley, 1966; MD, U. Calif., San Francisco, 1970. Diplomate Am. Coll. Physicians, Am. Coll. Rheumatology. Rheumatologist Fullerton (Calif.) Internal Medicine Ctr., Fullerton, Calif., 1976-94. Pres. St. Jude Heritage Med. Group, 1996—. Bd. trustees St. Jude Hosp. Fellow Am. Coll. Rheumatology, Orange County Rheumatism Soc.; mem. AMA, Orange County Med. Assn. Office: St Jude Heritage Med Group 433 W Bastanchury Rd Fullerton CA 92835-3404

**SUGARMAN, MYRON GEORGE,** lawyer; b. San Francisco, Nov. 7, 1942; s. Irving Carden and Jane Hortense (Weingarten) S.; m. Cheryl Ann Struble, June 8, 1968 (div. 1993); children: Andrew, Amy, Adam; m. Cynthia Wilson Woods, Apr. 16, 1994. BS, U. Calif., Berkeley, 1964, JD, 1967. Assoc Cooley Godward LLP, San Francisco, 1972-77, ptnr., 1977—. Trustee found. U. Calif., Berkeley. Served to capt. U.S. Army, 1968-71. Fellow Am. Coll. Trust and Estate Counsel, Am. Coll. Tax Counsel, Am. Bar Found.; mem. U. Calif. Alumni Assn. (bd. dirs. 1985-88), U. Calf. Berkeley Found. (bd. trustees), San Francisco Tax Club (pres. 1990), San Francisco Grid Club, Order of Coif, Phi Beta Kappa, Beta Gamma Sigma. Avocations: skiing, tennis. Office: Cooley Godward LLP 101 California St 5th Fl San Francisco CA 94111 Office Phone: 415-693-2040. Personal E-mail: msugarman@cooley.com.

**SUGARMAN, PAUL RONALD,** lawyer, educator, academic administrator; b. Boston, Dec. 14, 1931; m. Susan J. Sugarman; children: Amy J., Ellen L. AA, Boston U., 1951; JD cum laude (Law Week award 1954, assoc. editor law rev. 1952-54), 1954; LLD (hon.), Suffolk U., 1989. Bar: Mass. 1954, U.S. Supreme Ct. 1965. Ptnr. Sugarman & Sugarman, Boston, 1967-90, 94—; prof. law, dean Suffolk U. Law Sch., Boston, 1990-94. Mem. Atty. Gen. Mass. Hwy. Law Study Commn., 1965, Mass. Gov.'s Select Com. on Jud. Needs, 1976; bd. bar overseers Supreme Jud. Ct., 1984-88, chmn., 1985-88; advocate Am. Bd. Trial Advocates; spl. master, commr. Boston Mcpl. Ct. Report Supreme Jud. Ct. of Mass., 1990. Trustee Mass. Bar Found., 1980-81; bd. visitors Boston U. Sch. Law, 2005—. Served as officer AUS, 1955-58. Recipient Courageous Adv. award, Mass. Acad. Trial Attys., 1984, William O. Douglas First Amendment Freedom award, Anti-Defamation League, 1986, Silver Shingle award for svc. to legal profession Boston U. Sch. Law, 1989, Jurisprudence award Am. Orgn. for Rehab. through Tng. Fedn., 1991, Civil Justice award Am. Bd. trial Adv., 1993. Fellow: Internat. Soc. Barristers, Mass. Bar Found., Am. Coll. Trial Lawyers, Am. Bar Found.; mem.: ATLA (gov. 1966—68, pres. Mass. chpt. 1968—70), ABA, Boston U. Sch. Law Alumni Assn. (pres. 1979—80), Boston Bar Assn., Mass. Bar Assn. (pres. 1976—77, chmn. com. on recall of ret. judges 1982—86, chmn. Jud. Adminstrn. Sect. Coun., chmn. 2000—01, Task Force on Jud. Conduct Commn., Gold Medal award 1991). Office: Sugarman and Sugarman PC One Beacon St Boston MA 02108 Business E-mail: psugarman@sugarman.com.

**SUGERMAN, ABRAHAM ARTHUR,** psychiatrist, educator; b. Dublin, Jan. 20, 1929; came to U.S., 1958, naturalized, 1963; s. Hyman and Anne (Goldstone) S.; m. Ruth Nerissa Alexander, June 5, 1960; children: Jeremy, Michael, Adam, Rebecca. BA, Trinity Coll., 1950, MB, BChir, BA in Obstetrics, 1952; DSc, SUNY Bklyn., 1962. Diplomate Am. Bd. Psychiatry and Neurology. House officer Meath Hosp., Dublin, 1952—53, St. Nicholas Hosp., London, 1953—54; sr. house physician Brook Gen. Hosp., London, 1954; registrar in psychiatry Kingsway Hosp. Derby and Kings Coll. Med. Sch., Newcastle, England, 1955—58; clin. psychiatrist Trenton Psychiat. Hosp., NJ, 1958—59; rsch. fellow Downstate Med. Ctr., Bklyn., 1959—61; chief investigative psychiatry sect. N.J. Bur. Rsch., Princeton, 1961—73; cons. psychiatry, 1964—80; cons. rsch., assoc. psychiatrist Carrier Clinic, Belle Mead, NJ, 1968—72, 1978—90, dir. outpatient svcs., 1972—74, 1977—78, med. dir., 1974—77; dir. rsch. Carrier Found., Belle Mead, 1972—79; med. dir. addiction recovery svcs. Cmty. Mental Health Ctr. U. Medicine and Dentistry of N.J., Piscataway, 1990—93; cons. psychiatry Med. Ctr., Princeton, 1972—2001, assoc. in psychiatry, 2001—03, attending, 2003—, sr. attending, 2005—; clin. assoc. prof. psychiatry Rutgers Med. Sch. (now Robert Wood Johnson Med. Sch.), New Brunswick, NJ, 1972—78, clin. prof., 1978—. Vis. prof. Rutgers Ctr. for Alcohol Studies, 1977-83, Hahnemann Med. Coll., Phila., 1978-93; contbg. faculty Grad. Sch. Applied and Profl. Psychology, Rutgers U., 1974-78. Editor: (with Ralph E. Tarter) Alcoholism: Interdisciplinary Approaches to an Enduring Problem, 1976, Expanding Dimensions of Consciousness, 1978; contbr. articles to profl. jours. Bd. dirs. N.J. Mental Health R & D Fund, Princeton, 1968-74; v.p. Jewish Family Svc., Trenton, 1972-78; 1st v.p. Trenton Hebrew Acad., 1972-75. Fellow Am. Psychiat. Assn. (disting. life), Am. Coll. Neuropsychop-

harmacology, Am. Coll. Clin. Pharmacology, Am. Coll. Psychiatrists, Royal Coll. Psychiatrists; mem. AMA, Soc. Biol. Psychiatry, Assn. Rsch. Nervous and Mental Diseases. Office: 256 Bunn Dr Princeton NJ 08540-2859 Office Phone: 609-924-6711.

**SUGG, ROBERT PERKINS,** retired judge; b. Eupora, Miss., Feb. 21, 1916; s. Amos Watson and Virgie Christian (Cooper) S.; m. Elizabeth Lorraine Carroll, June 23, 1940; children: Robert Perkins, Charles William, John David. Student, Wood Jr. Coll., 1933—34, Miss. State U., 1935—37, Jackson Sch. Law, 1939—40; MS, First Bapt. Sem. Europa. Bar: Miss. Practice law, 1940; chancery judge, 1951—71; assoc. justice Miss. Supreme Ct., 1971—83; county pros. atty. Webster County, Miss., 1949—50; spl. chancery judge Hinds, Scott and Jasper counties, Miss., 1989; sr. judge, 1990—2000. Mem. adv. coun. Nat. Ctr. for State Cts., 1973-79. Bd. govs. Miss. Jud. Coll., 1973-80; literacy missions assoc. Home Mission Bd. of So. Bapt. Conv., 1983—; tchr. internat. class First Bapt., Ch., Jackson, Miss., 1980-2004, tchr. adult Bible class, 1973-2002, mem. fin. com. 1995-98, vision com. 1996-97, legal com. 1998-2001, missions com., 1997-2001. Named Outstanding Citizen, Eupora Jr. C. of C., 1970, Alumnus of Year, Wood Jr. Coll., 1973; recipient Svc. to Humanity award Miss. Coll., 1976, Literacy Missions Svc. award Home Mission Bd. of So. Bapt. Conv., 1995. Mem. Miss. State Bar, CAP (Miss. Wing, squadron comdr. 1974-76), Am. Legion (post comdr. 1950) Democrat. Baptist (chmn. bd. deacons 1964). Home: 1067 Meadow Heights Dr Jackson MS 39206-6021 Personal E-mail: judgesugg@jam.rr.com.

**SUGGS, KENNETH,** lawyer; b. Greenville, S.C., Sept. 24, 1946; BA Economics, Clemson Univ., 1964; JD cum laude, Univ. of S.C. Bar: S.C. Bar 1975, Fourth Cir. Ct. of Appeals, Eleventh Cir. Ct. of Appeals, U.S. Supreme Ct. Found.; ptnr. Suggs & Kelly, PC, Janet, Jenner, & Suggs. Pres. S.C. Trial Lawyers Assoc, 1981; bd. gov. Assoc. of Am. Trial Lawyers (ATLA); founding fellow So. Trial Lawyers Assoc.; pres. Richmond County Bar Assoc., 1999; bd. gov. Assoc. of Am. Trial Lawyers (ATLA), 1989—2000, parliamentarian 2000—01, treas., 2001—02, sec., 2002—03, v.p., 2003—04, pres. elect, 2004—. Communications technician USN, 1968—72. Recipient S.C. Trial Lawyers Assoc. Pres. Award, 1988, S.C. Trial Lawyers Public Citizen Award, 2002; fellow Am. Coll. of Trial Lawyers, Clemson Univ. Alumni, 2000. Office: Janet, Jenner & Suggs Woodholme Center 1829 Reisterstown Rd Suite 320 Baltimore MD 21208

**SUGGS, LEO H.,** transportation executive; Sr. v.p. Yellow Freight System Inc.; CEO Preston; chmn., CEO Overnite (a UPS co.), Richmond, Va., 1996—. Mem.: Am. Trucking Assn. (treas.). Office: Overnite 1000 Semmes Ave Richmond VA 23224

**SUGIHARA, KENZI,** publishing executive; b. Kearny, NJ, Oct. 4, 1940; s. Kyuichi and Shinobuko (Yamaguchi) S.; m. Roslyn Forbes, Dec. 1966; children: Kenichi, Takeo, Akira, Fumio; m. Nancy Elizabeth Kirsh, June 8, 1981; 1 child, Toshiro. BA, NYU, 1963. Supr. McGraw Hill, Inc., N.Y.C., 1965-67; assoc. dir. coll. product dept. Harcourt Brace Jovanovich Inc., N.Y.C., 1978-82, dir. electronic pub., 1982-83; v.p., pub. Bantam Electronic Pub. div., pub. Bantam Reference Books, Bantam Profl. Books, Bantam Doubleday Dell, N.Y.C., 1983-93; v.p., pub. Random House Reference & Electronic Pub. (Random House Inc.), N.Y.C., 1993-95; pres. Sugihara and Rose, N.Y.C., 1995—; pres., pub. ToExcel divsn. Kaleidoscope Software Corp., N.Y.C., 1998—2001; pub. Iuniverse; CEO, pres. SelectBooks, Inc., N.Y.C., 2001—. Democrat. Presbyterian. Home: 585 West End Ave Apt 15D New York NY 10024-1715 Office: SelectBooks One Union Sq West Ste 909 New York NY 10003 Office Phone: 212-206-1997. Business E-Mail: kenzi@selectbooks.com.

**SUGIKI, SHIGEMI,** ophthalmologist, educator; b. Wailuku, Hawaii, May 12, 1936; s. Sentaro and Kameno (Matoba) Sugiki; m. Bernice T. Murakami, Dec. 29, 1958; children: Kevin S., Boyd R. AB, Washington U., St. Louis, 1957, MD, 1961. Intern St. Luke's Hosp., St. Louis, 1961-62; resident in ophthalmology Washington U., 1962-65; chmn. dept. ophthalmology Straub Clinic, Honolulu, 1965-70, Queens Med. Ctr., Honolulu, 1970-73, 80-83, 88-90, 93-2000; clin. prof. ophthalmology Sch. Medicine U. Hawaii, 1997. Maj. M.C., AUS, 1968-70. Decorated Hawaiian N.G. Commendation medal, 1968. Fellow ACS; mem. AMA, Hawaii Med. Assn., Honolulu County Med. Soc., Am. Acad. Ophthalmology, Contact Lens Assn. Ophthalmologists, Pacific Coast Oto-Ophthal. Soc., Pan-Pacific Surg. Assn., Am. Soc. Cataract and Refractive Surgery, Am. Glaucoma Soc., Internat. Assn. Ocular Surgeons, Am. Soc. Contemporary Ophthalmology, Washington U. Eye Alumni Assn., Hawaii Ophthal. Soc., Rsch. To Prevent Blindness. Home: 2398 Aina Lani Pl Honolulu HI 96822-2024 Office: 1380 Lusitana St Ste 714 Honolulu HI 96813-2443 Personal E-mail: vision2damax@yahoo.com.

**SUGINTAS, NORA MARIA,** healthcare executive; b. Evergreen Park, Ill., Mar. 12, 1956; d. George and Mary (Navickas) S. BS in Biol. Scis. with highest distinction, U. Ill., Chgo., 1978; DVM, U. Ill., 1982. Lic. veterinarian Ill. Profl. hosp. specialist Abbott Labs., Detroit, 1983—87; anesthesia and critical care patient monitoring equipment acct. exec. Shiley, Inc., Detroit, 1987—91; anesthesia and critical care monitoring equipment sales exec. and cons. Ohmeda, Detroit, 1991—94; regional mgr. Criticare Systems, Detroit, 1994—95, nat. acct. dir., 1995—96; dir. corp. accounts Isolyser Health Care, 1996—98; cons. healthcare industry, 1998—2000; v.p. HealthCare Partnerships Healthgrades, Inc., Detroit, 2001—. Journalist The Lithuanian World-Wide Daily Newspaper, 1975; author: The Production of S-Adenosylmethionine by Saccharomyces cerevisiae and Candida utilis. Troop leader Girl Scouts Lithuanian, Chgo., 1972-77, camp dir., 1977; mem. Mirage Mid. Eastern Dance Ensemble. Recipient Louis Pasteur award for Acad. Excellence in the Biol. Scis. and Ind. Rsch. U. Ill., 1978. Mem. Internat. Platform Assn., Chelsea Park Assn. (bd. dirs., treas.), Mich. Orchid Soc., Econ. Club Detroit, Kirk Garden Guild, Phi Beta Kappa. Republican. Avocations: hiking, nature preservation, photography, dance, international politics.

**SUGIYAMA, KAZUNORI,** music producer; b. Tokyo, Aug. 18, 1950; came to U.S., 1976; s. Hiroshi and Michiko (Maeda) S.; m. Emi Fukui, Aug. 11, 1981. BS, Waseda U., 1974, postgrad., 1974-75; MA, Boston U., 1977. Jr. adminstrv. officer Japanese Mission to UN, N.Y.C., 1978-88; rep. N.Y. Toshiba EMI Records, Jazz Div., Tokyo, 1990-93; rep. U.S., exec. producer DIW/Avant Records, Tokyo, 1991—; exec. producer Tzadik Records, N.Y.C., 1995—; mem. adv. bd. The New Grove Dictionary of Jazz, 1997—2004. Corr. Jazz Life, Tokyo, 1980-88; columnist OCS News, N.Y.C., 1982-90; columnist Asahi Newspaper, 1998-99. Rec. engr. (album) Bud and Bird/Gil Evans, 1988 (Grammy); prodr. V/Ralph Peterson, 1990 (Jazz Album of Yr.); co-prodr. The Nurturer/Geri Allen, 1991 (2d pl. Jazz Album of Yr.), Big Band & Quartet/David Murray, 1992 (Best Prodn. Jazz Album of Yr.), Picasso/David Murray, 1993 (3d pl. Jazz Album of Yr.); translator Autobiography of Miles Davis, 1989. Mem. NARAS, USTA. Avocations: tennis, travel. Office: 93 Mercer St Apt 3W New York NY 10012-4452 E-mail: info@tzadik.com.

**SUGIYAMA, TORU TOM,** automotive executive; b. Hiratsuka, Japan, Aug. 15, 1956; s. Tadatsugu and Hatsue S. MBA, Calif. State U., 1994, MS in Acctg., 1997; MS in Engring., Oakland U., 1997, PhD in Engring., 2003. CPA Ill., 2005. Mgr. Denny's Japan Co., Ltd., Tokyo, 1979—80; indsl. engr. NHK Spring Co., Ltd., Yokohama, Japan, 1980—82; acct. mgr. NHK Spring Co., Ltd., Yokohama, 1983—89; mgr. NHK Internat. Corp., Southfield, Mich., 1992—96, corp. sec., treas., 1996—2001; treas. Gen. Seating Can., 2001—05; bd. dirs. Gen. Seating Am., 2001—03; pres., CEO NHK Internat. Corp., Wixom, Mich., 2001—03. Lectr. Oakland U., Rochester, Mich., 1998—. Avocations: golf, tennis, swimming. Office: NHK Internat Corp 50706 Varsity Ct Wixom MI 48393

**SUGLIA, JOSEPH VINCENT,** writer, educator; s. Theresa Joyce and Robert Louis Suglia. BA, Binghamton U., 1994; PhD, Northwestern U., 2002. Lectr. English, DePaul U., Chgo., 2000—; Roosevelt U., Chgo., 2002—; lectr.

English St. Augustine, Chgo., 2004—, Columbia Coll., Chgo., 2005—. Author: (novels) Years of Rage, 2005, Watch Out, 2006, (literary criticism) Hölderlin and Blanchot on Self-Sacrifice, 2004. Personal E-mail: josephsuglia@yahoo.com.

**SUGRUE, DENNIS PATRICK,** psychologist; b. Detroit, Oct. 28, 1949; s. Francis Michael and Diane (Reckinger) S.; m. Bernadette Tomasik, June 11, 1976; children: Dennis Patrick II, Sean Michael Francis. BA magna cum laude, Sacred Heart Sem., 1971; MA, U. Detroit, 1976; MS, Ea. Mich. U., 1976; PhD, U. Windsor, Ont., Can., 1981. Sr. staff psychologist Henry Ford Hosp., Detroit, 1979-85; clin. instr. psychiatry Med. Sch. U. Mich., 1985-92; founder, dir. Henry Ford Ctr. Human Sexuality, Farmington Hills, Mich., 1986-95; asst. clin. prof. psychiatry Med. Sch. U. Mich., Ann Arbor, 1992-93; regional clin. dir. dept. psychiatry Henry Ford Hosp., West Bloomfield, Mich., 1993-95; assoc. divsn. head outpatient psychiatry Henry Ford Health Sys., Detroit, 1995-98; pvt. practice Bloomfield Hills, Mich., 1998—. Asst. adj. prof. psychiatry Coll. Human Medicine Mich. State U., 1991; lectr. on human sexuality; cons. U. Mich. Comprehensive Gender Svcs. Program, 1994—; clin. assoc. prof. psychiatry Med. Sch. U. Mich., Ann Arbor, 1999—. Co-author: Sex Matters for Women, 2002; contbr. chpts. in books, articles to profl. jours. Den leader Farmington Hills Boy Scouts Am., 1988-91; coach South Farmington Little League Baseball, Farmington Hills, 1990-96. Mem. Harry Benjamin Internat. Gender Dysphoria Assn., Internat. Coun. Psychologists (chair counseling and psychotherapy), Soc. Sci. Study Sex, Am. Assn. Sex Educators, Counselors and Therapists (Mich. chair, profl. edn. chair, bd. dirs., cert. sex therapist, diplomate in sex therapy, pres.), Phi Kappa Phi. Roman Catholic. Avocations: golf, bridge, tae kwon do (1st degree black belt). Office: Affil Psychologists Mich 74 W Long Lake Ste 104 Bloomfield Hills MI 48304-2770 Office Phone: 248-888-8390. E-mail: dsugrue@umich.edu.

**SUGRUE, THOMAS J.,** history professor, social sciences educator; b. Detroit, July 24, 1962; s. Thomas J. and Sharon R. Sugrue; m. Dana L. Barron, May 30, 1993; children: Anna Linn Barron, John Michael Barron. BA in History summa cum laude, Columbia U., 1984; BA in History with honors, Cambridge Univ., 1986; AM in History, Harvard U., 1987; MA in History, Cambridge U., 1989; PhD in History, Harvard U., 1992. Lectr. history U. Pa., Phila., 1991—92, asst. prof. history, 1992—97, assoc. prof. history, 1997—98, assoc. prof. history and sociology, 1998—2000, Bicentennial Class of 1940 prof. history and sociology, 2000—04, Kahn prof. history and sociology, 2004—. Rsch. fellow Brookings Instn., Washington, 1990—91; vis. assoc. prof. NYU, NYC, 1998; trustee and vice chair of bd. Hist. Soc. Pa., Phila., 2000—; dir. Urban History Assn., Cin., 2000—02; vis. prof. Ecole des Hautes Etudes en Sciences Sociales, Paris, 2002. Author: The Origins of the Urban Crisis (Bancroft Prize in History 1998, Taft Prize in Labor History 1997, President's Book Award SSHA, 1996, Urban History Assn. Best Book Award 1997); editor: (book series) Politics and Culture in Modern America; editor, author (collection of essays) W.E.B. DuBois, Race, and the City. Founding mem. Scholars, Artists, and Writers for Social Justice, NYC, 1996—98; vice chair and chmn. Phila. Hist. Commn., Phila., 2001—; bd. mem. Bread and Roses Cmty. Fund, 2004—. Recipient Phi Beta Kappa, Columbia U., 1983, Sidney Hillman Found. award. for Nat. Teach-In with the Labor Movement., 1997, Disting. Lectr., Orgn. of Am. Historians, 2002—, John Simon Guggenheim fellowship, 2005; fellow, Alphonse Fletcher Sr. Found., 2005; grantee program in non-profits, univs., cmtys., schs., Kellogg Found. through U. Pa.Ctr. Cmty. Partnerships, 1998—2001, grant for Cand. (co-PI), Nat. Endowment Humanities, 1994-96; scholar, Harry S. Truman Found., 1982-84, 1986-88, Josephine De Kármán Found. fellow, 1989-90, Com. for Rsch. on the Urban Underclass, Dissertation grant and fellow, Social Sci. Rsch. Coun., 1990-91, Am. Coun. of Learned Societies fellow, ACLS, 1995-96. Mem.: Inst. for Advanced Study, Social Sci. History Assn. (program com. chair 1997—98), Am. Studies Assn., Am. Sociol. Assn., Urban History Assn. (bd. mem., prize com. mem., program com. mem. 2000—04), Orgn. of Am. Historians (program com. 2001—03). Avocations: architecture, travel, gardening. Home: 129 Carpenter Ln Philadelphia PA 19119 Office: U Pa 208 College Hall Philadelphia PA 19104 Office Phone: 215-898-0293. Personal E-mail: tsugrue@sas.upenn.edu.

**SUH, BYUNGSE,** medical educator; b. Ansung, Korea, Mar. 6, 1941; came to U.S., 1964; s. Sang Keun and Chong Sang (Lee) S.; m. Youngjoo Lee, Dec. 21, 1974; children: Jason, Jessica, Janice. BS, Chungang U., Seoul, Korea, 1962; MA, U. Kans., 1967, PhD, 1969; MD, U. Miami, 1973. Diplomate Am. Bd. Internal Medicine; diplomate Am. Bd. Infectious Diseases. Asst. prof. medicine Temple U. Sch. Medicine, Phila., 1978-83, assoc. prof. medicine, 1983-90, prof. medicine, 1990—. Contbr. articles to profl. jours. Fellow Infectious Diseases Soc. Am., Am. Coll. Physicians, Coll. Physicians Phila., Am. Coll. Clin. Pharmacology; mem. Am. Soc. Microbiology, Alpha Omega Alpha. Office: Temple U Sch Medicine Sect Infectious Diseases Broad and Ontario Sts Philadelphia PA 19140 Office Phone: 215-707-3807. Business E-Mail: bingsuh@temple.edu.

**SUH, DAE-SOOK,** political science professor; b. Hoeryong, Korea, Nov. 22, 1931; came to U.S., 1952; s. Chang-Hee and Chong-Hee (Paek) S.; m. Yun-Ok Paek, Oct. 29, 1960; children: Maurice, Kevin. BA, Tex. Christian U., 1956; MA, Ind. U., 1958; PhD, Columbia U., 1964. Asst. prof. U. Houston, 1965-67, assoc. prof., 1967-72; prof. polit. sci., dir. Ctr. for Korean Studies, U. Hawaii, Honolulu, 1972-95, Korea Found. prof. policy studies, 1994-99; George L. Paik prof. Yonsei U., 1999; prof. polit. sci. U. Hawaii, Manoa, Hawaii, 1972—. Vis. prof. polit. sci. UCLA, 2005. Author: The Korean Communist Movement, 1967, Documents of Korean Communism, 1970, Korean Communism, 1980, Kim Il Sung, 1988, Kim Il Sung and Kim Jong Il, 1996. Mem. Conv. Ctr. Authority, Honolulu, 1989-94. Grantee Social Sci. Rsch. Coun.-Am. Coun. Learned Socs., 1963, East-/West Ctr., Columbia U., 1971, The Woodraw Wilson Internat. Ctr. for Scholars, 1985, Fulbright, 1988. Mem. Am. Polit. Sci. Assn. (life), Assn. for Asian Studies. Avocations: tennis, golf. Office: U Hawaii Manoa Dept Political Sci 2424 Maile Way Honolulu HI 96822-2223 Home: 5150 Via EL Molino Thousand Oaks CA 91320-6996 E-mail: daesook@adelphia.net.

**SUH, JUNG SOOK KY,** personnel consultant; d. Keum Joon and Jung Ja Suh. BA, Calif. State U., Fullerton, 1996; MS in Orgnl. Psychology, Alliant Internat. U., Alhambra, Calif., 2001, PhD, 2005; postgrad., Oxford U., Eng., 2000. V.p. Packy B., Inc., Bellflower, Calif., 1995—2001; cons. Optimal Mgmt. Consulting, Long Beach, Calif., 2001—. Adj. faculty Long Beach City Coll., 2002—, Mt. San Antonio Coll., Walnut, 2005—. Mem.: NEA, Calif. Tchrs. Assn. Office: Mt San Antonio Coll 1943 Campus Ave B133 Upland CA 91786 Office Phone: 909-921-1714.

**SUH, MARY,** editor; Nat. editor Ms; editor Newsday; op-ed editor NY Times, Week in Review editor. Contbr. Minerva: Quar. Report on Women & the Military. Office: NY Times 229 W 43rd St New York NY 10036 Office Phone: 212-556-1748. Office Fax: 212-556-3738.*

**SUH, NAM PYO,** mechanical engineering educator; b. Seoul, Apr. 22, 1936; arrived in U.S., 1954, naturalized, 1963; s. Doo Soo and Joon Joo (Lee) S.; m. Young Ja Surh; children: Mary M., Helen H., Grace J., Caroline Y. SB, MIT, 1959, SM, 1961; PhD, Carnegie-Mellon U., 1964; D of Engring. (hon.), Worcester Poly. Inst., 1986; LHD (hon.), U. Mass., Lowell, 1988; D of Tech. (hon.), Royal Inst. Tech., Sweden, 2000. Devel. engr. Guild Plastics Inc., Cambridge, Mass., 1958-60; sr. rsch. engr. project mgr. USM Corp., Beverly, Mass., 1961-65; asst. prof. U. SC, Columbia, 1965-68, assoc. prof., 1968-69; assoc. prof. mech. engring. MIT, Cambridge, 1970-75, prof., 1975—, Ralph E. and Eloise F. Cross prof., 1989—, dir. Lab. Mfg. and Productivity, 1977-84, dir. industry polymer processing program, 1973-84, dir. Mfg. Inst. (now Park Ctr. for Complex Sys.), 1989—2006, Cross prof., dept. head mech. engring., 1991-2001; presdl. appointee asst. dir. for engring. NSF, Washington, 1984-88; pres. Korea Advanced Inst. Sci. and Tech., 2006—. Bd. dirs. Axiomatic Design Software, Inc., Boston, Tribotek, Inc., Burlington, Mass., Parker Vision, Inc., Jacksonville, Fla., Therma Wave, Inc., Fremont, Calif., Integrated Device Tech., Inc., San Jose, Calif.; former cons. Lawrence

Livermore Nat. Lab.; advisor Korea Elec. Power Rsch. Inst.; former mem. sci. and tech. rev. bd. Nat. Engring. Lab., mem. NRC rev. panel, 1986—90; mem. vis. com. (statutory) Nat. Inst. Stds. and Tech., 1990—94; mem. tech. adv. com. Alcan Aluminum Corp., 1989—90; editor advanced mfg. series Oxford U. Press; hon. prof. Univ. Hong Kong, 2003—; disting. vis. prof. Korea Advanced Inst. of Sci. and Tech., 2002—; cons. prof. Shangai Jiatong U., 2005. Author (with A.P.L. Turner): Mechanical Behavior of Solids, 1975; author: The Principles of Design, 1990; author: (with others) Manufacturing Engineering, 1990; author: Axiomatic Design: Advances and Applications, 2001, Complexity: Theory and Applications, 2005; co-author: Axiomatic Design and Fabrication of Composite Structures, 2006; editor (with N. Saka): Fundamentals of Tribology, 1980; editor: (with N. Sung) Science and Technology of Polymer Procs., 1979; editor: The Delamination Theory of Wear, 1977; editor: (with B.M. Kramer) University/Industry Cooperation, 1982; former co-editor-in-chief Robotics and Computer Aided Manufacturing, contbr. over 280 articles to profl. jours. Former chmn. bd. Korean-Am. Soc. New Eng., 1979. Named Fed. Engr. of Yr., NSF/NSPE, 1987; recipient Best Paper award, Soc. Plastics Engrs., 1981, Citation Classic, Inst. for Sci. Info., 1981, Disting. Svcs. award, NSF, 1988, Mainstream Am. award, 1991, scholarly award, Korea Broadcasting Svc., 1994, The Mensforth Internat. Gold Medal, U.K. Instn. Elec. Engrs., 2000, The Hills Millennium Internat. award, U.K. Instn. Engr. Designers, 2001, Gold medal of Honor, Acad. Transdisciplinary Learning and Advanced Studies, 2006, Gen. Nicolau award, CIRP, 2006; USM Corp. fellow, 1962—63. Fellow: ASME (Gustus L. Larson Meml. award 1976, Blackall award 1982, W.T. Ennor Mfg. Tech. award 1993, Best Tribology Paper award 1993, Ho.-Am. prize for Engring. Ho.-Am. com. 1997), Soc. Mfg. Engrs. (F.W. Taylor Rsch. award 1986); mem.: AAAS, Korean Acad. Sci. and Engring., Royal Swedish Acad. Engring. Sci. (fgn.), Internat. Acad. Produn. Engring., Am. Soc. Engrng. Edn. (Centennial medal 1993, Gen. Nicolau award 2006), Phi Kappa Phi, Pi Tau Sigma, Sigma Xi. Achievements include holder 50 U.S. patents. Office: MIT Rm 35-237 Dept Mech Engring Cambridge MA 02139 Office Phone: 617-253-2225.

**SUH, WONSUK WARREN,** radiation oncologist; s. Chai-Pill and Myung-Hi Suh; m. Jeewon Park, Nov. 22, 2000; children: Ryan Joonwon, Sidney Chaewon. BA, Cornell U., 1991; MD, U. Chgo., 1996; MPH, Harvard U., 1996. Diplomate Am. Bd. Internal Medicine. Resident internal medicine Mayo Clinic, Rochester, Minn., 1996—99; from radiation oncology resident to chief resident U. Mich., Ann Arbor, 2000—04; radiation oncologist, internist Brigham & Women's Hosp., Boston, 2004—. Contbr. articles to profl. jours. Named Eminent Scientist Yr., Internat. Rsch. Prom Coun., 2006; recipient H. Hughes award, 1990. Mem.: Mayo Clinic Plummer Soc., Am. Soc. Clin. Oncology (health svcs. outcome rsch. com. 2002—, Merit award 2003). Office: Brigham & Women's Hosp Dana Farber Cancer Inst 75 Francis St Boston MA 02115 Office Phone: 617-732-7936.

**SUH, YONGSOOK VICTORIA,** plastic surgeon; b. Iri-City, Chunbuk, Republic of Korea, Apr. 24, 1963; arrived in U.S., 1973; d. Dong Suk and Okye Suh; m. James Lee, Apr. 17, 1999. B in Neurosci. and English Lit., Amherst Coll., 1986; MD, N.Y. Med. Coll., 1990. Diplomate Am. Bd. Plastic Surgeons. Gen. surgery resident N.Y. Med. Coll., Valhalla, 1990; plastic surgery resident Ohio State U., Columbus, 1998; assoc plastic surgeon New Image Plastic Surgery, Reston, Va., 1998—2000; pres. Victoria Plastic Surgery Ctr., Fairfax, Va., 2000—. Mem. med. adv. bd. Divsn. Motor Vehicles, Va., 2003—; presenter in field. Contbr. chapters to books, articles to profl. jours. Active Korean Am. Family Counseling Ctr., Vienna, Va., 1998—2002, Fairfax County Skin Deep Tattoo Removal, Arlington, Va., 1999—. Recipient First Pl. Clin. Rsch., Columbus Surg. Soc., 1998, Best Pediat. Paper award, Plastic and Reconstructive Surgery, 1998. Mem.: No. Va. Surg. Soc., Nat. Capital Soc. Plastic Surgeons, Korean Am. Med. Assn., Am. Soc. Plastic Surgeons. Avocations: ballet, model train collecting, knitting, running. Office: Victoria Plastic Surgery Ctr 8503 Arlington Blvd #130 Fairfax VA 22031 Office Phone: 703-846-0097. E-mail: vus846@aol.com.

**SUHLER, JOHN STUART,** investor; b. Des Moines, May 10, 1943; s. Lester F. and Irene (Holmberg) S.; m. Charlotte Kay Thompson, Dec. 30, 1966; children: Ashley Thompson, Courtney Ruth, Brooke Thompson. BS, U. Kans., 1965. Co-owner Eldon (Mass.)-Hinsdale News, 1965-66; promotion writer Look mag., Des Moines, 1965-66; cons. Benson, Stagg & Assos., NYC, 1966-68; salesman Metromail div. Metromedia, NYC, 1968-69; circulation dir. Psychology Today, CRM div. Boise Cascade, Del Mar, Calif., 1969-70, assoc. pub., 1970-71, pub., 1971-73; v.p., pub. Psychology Today Pub. Group, 1973-74, Ziff Davis Pub. Co.; pres. CBS Publs., Consumer Pub. div. CBS Inc., NYC, 1974-79, CBS/Pub. Group, v.p. CBS Inc., 1979-81, Veronis, Suhler and Assocs. Inc. (now Veronis Suhler Stevenson), 1981—; gen. ptnr. VS&A Communications Ptnrs., L.P., 1987—. Pub. Univ. Daily Kansan, 1964-65; bd. dirs. Access Intelligence. Trustee William Allen White Found. Mem. Mag. Pubs. Assn. (former dir.), Nat. Assn. Broadcasters, Assn. Bus. Pubs., Direct Mktg. Assn., Assn. Am. Pubs. (former dir.), Info. Industry Assn., Wee Burn Club, Edgartown (Mass.) Yacht Club, Vineyard (Mass.) Golf Club, Long Boat Key (Fla.) Club, Sigma Chi. Office: Veronis Suhler Stevenson 350 Park Ave New York NY 10022

**SUHR, PAUL AUGUSTINE,** lawyer; b. Sonwunri, Chonbuk, Korea, Jan. 20, 1940; arrived in US, 1966; s. Chong-ju and Oksuk (Pang) So; m. Angeline M. Kang Suhr; 1 child, Christopher. BA, Campbell Coll., Buies Creek, N.C., 1968; MA, U.N.C., Greensboro, 1970; MS, U. N.C., Chapel Hill, 1975; JD, N.C. Cen. U., 1988. Bar: N.C. 1989, U.S. Dist. Ct. (ea. and mid. dist.) N.C. 1989, U.S. Ct. Appeals D.C. 1990, U.S. Ct. Appeals (4th cir.) 1992. Bibliographer N.C. Div. of State Libr., Raleigh, 1975-78; dir. Pender County Pub. Libr., Burgaw, NC, 1978-80; libr. Tob. Lit. Svc., U. Raleigh, 1980-85; pvt. practice law Law Offices of Paul A. Suhr, PLLC, Raleigh and Fayetteville, NC, 1989—. Author short stories and novelettes various lit. mags., jours and to Meru. Human Resources and Human Rels. Adv. Commn., City of Raleigh, 1990-95, chmn., 1994-95. N.C. Humanities Com. grantee, 1979-80; recipient Presdl. award President of Korea, 1992. Mem. ABA, ATLA, Am. Immigration Lawyers Assn., NC Bar Assn., NC Trial Lawyers Assn., Wake County Bar Assn. (bd. dirs. 1996-97, 2003—), DC Bar Assn. Democrat. Roman Catholic. Avocations: gardening, fishing, writing. Office: 1110 Navaho Dr Ste 502 Raleigh NC 27609-7322 Office Phone: 919-876-4707. Personal E-mail: paulsuhr@aol.com.

**SUHRHEINRICH, RICHARD FRED,** federal judge; b. Lincoln City, Ind., 1936; BS, Wayne State U., 1960; JD cum laude, Detroit Coll. Law, 1963; LLM (hon.), U. Va., 1990, Detroit Coll. Law, 1992. Bar: Mich. Law clerk Stringari, Fritz & Fiott, 1963; assoc. Moll, Desenberg, Purdy, Glover & Bayer, 1963—67; asst. prosecutor Macomb County, 1967; ptnr. Rogensues, Richard & Suhrheinrich, 1967; assoc. Moll, Desenberg, Purdy, Glover & Bayer, 1967—68; ptnr. Kitch, Suhrheinrich, Saurbier & Drutchas, 1968—84; assoc. prof. of law Detroit Coll. of law, 1975—85; judge U.S. Dist. Ct. (ea. dist.) Mich., Detroit, 1984—90, U.S. Ct. Appeals (6th Cir.), Lansing, 1990—2001, sr. judge, 2001—. Law prof. Thomas M Cooley Law Sch., 2003—; mem. State of Mich. Atty. Discipline Bd., Atty. Grievance Commn. Bd. trustees Brighton Hosp. Mem.: Ingham County Bar Assn., State Bar Mich., Mich. State Univ.-Detroit (bd. trustees 1985—2003, pres. 1999—2001). Office: US Ct Appeals 6th Cir USPO & Fed Bldg 315 W Allegan St Rm 241 Lansing MI 48933-1514*

**SUHRSTEDT, BARBARA LYNN,** concert pianist, voice educator; b. Massillon, Ohio, Dec. 6, 1945; d. Donald Charles and Elizabeth Ann Fetrow; m. Gerhardt John Suhrstedt, Oct. 25, 1969 (dec. Dec. 29, 2005). MusB, Oberlin Conservatory Music, Ohio, 1967; MusM, Boston U., 1970. Instr. piano South Shore Conservatory of Music, Hingham, Mass., 1971—84; pvt. piano studio Newton, Watertown and Somerville, Mass., 1975—90; concert pianist, 1980—2005; soprano Ch. of the Adent, Boston, 1980—90; pvt. voice studio Newton, Watertown and Somerville, 1982—. Artist, clinician state convs. Music Tchrs. Nat. Assn., 1989—2002; mem. internat. jury 3d Igor Stravinsky Competition for Young Pianists Stravinsky Sch. Music and Art, Lamonosov, Russia, 2002; participant St. Petersburg (Russia) Arts Festival, 2002. Musician: (CDs) A Four-Hand Feast, 1989, Dances for Duettists, 1998,

Peterhof's Grand Palace, Rimsky-Korsakov Conservatory, 1998—2001. Bd. dirs. FLAME Russian sister-city orgn., Framingham, Mass., 1999—. Mem.: Nat. Assn. Tchrs. of Singing. Episcopalian. Avocation: reading. Home: 112 Central St # 4 Somerville MA 02143-1200 E-mail: suhrfet@compuserve.com.

**SUI, ANNA,** fashion designer; b. Dearborn Heights, Mich., 1955; d. Paul and Grace S. Grad., Parsons Sch. Design. Founder, designer Anna Sui, 1988—. Opened outlet SoHo dist., 1992, NYC, Anna Sui Boutiques, Osaka, Tokyo, 1997; designer Sui Anna Sui, 1995-, Anna Sui cosmetic line, fragrance line, 1999, skincare line, 2000. First runway show, 1991. Recipient Perry Ellis award new fashion talent Coun. Fashion Designers Am., 1992. Address: Anna Sui Corp 275 W 39th St Fl 9 New York NY 10018-3107*

**SUINN, RICHARD MICHAEL,** psychologist; b. Honolulu, May 8, 1933; s. Maurice and Edith (Wong) S.; m. Grace D. Toy, July 26, 1958; children: Susan, Randall, Staci, Bradley. Student, U. Hawaii, 1951-53; BA summa cum laude, Ohio State U., 1955; MA in Clin. Psychology, Stanford U., 1957, PhD in Clin. Psychology, 1959; Doctorate (hon.), Calif. Sch. Profl. Psychology, 1999. Lic. psychologist, Colo.; diplomate Am. Bd. Profl. Psychology. Counselor Stanford (Calif.) U., 1958-59, rsch. assoc. Med. Sch., 1964-66; asst. prof. psychology Whitman Coll., Walla Walla, Wash., 1959-64; assoc. prof. U. Hawaii, Honolulu, 1966-68; prof. Colo. State U., Ft. Collins, 1968-99, head dept. psychology, 1972-93, emeritus prof., 2000—. Cons. in field; psychologist U.S. Ski Teams, 1976, Olympic Games, U.S. Women's Track and Field, 1980 Olympic Games, U.S. Ski Jumping Team, 1988, U.S. Shooting Team, 1994; mem. sports psychology adv. com. U.S. Olympic Com., 1983-89; reviewer NIMH, 1977-80, 94-98. Author: The Predictive Validity of Projective Measures, 1969, Fundamentals of Behavior Pathology, 1970, The Innovative Psychological Therapies, 1975, The Innovative Medical-Psychiatric Therapies, 1976, Psychology in Sport: Methods and Applications, 1980, Fundamentals of Abnormal Psychology, 1984, 88, Seven Steps to Peak Performance, 1986, Anxiety Management Training, 1990; editorial bd.: Jour. Cons. and Clin. Psychology, 1973-86, Jour. Counseling Psychology, 1974-91, Behavior Therapy, 1977-80, Behavior Modification, 1977-78, Jour. Behavioral Medicine, 1978-83, Behavior Counseling Quar., 1979-83, Jour. Sports Psychology, 1980-91, Clin. Psychology: Science and Practice, 1994-97, Professional Psychology, 1994-97; author: tests Math. Anxiety Rating Scale, Suinn Test Anxiety Behavior Scale, Suinn-Lew Asian Self-identity Acculturation Scale. Mem. City Council, Ft. Collins, 1975-79, mayor, 1978-79; mem. Gov.'s Mental Health Adv. Council, 1983, Colo. Bd. Psychologist Examiners, 1983-86. Recipient cert. merit U.S. Ski Team, 1976, APA Career Contbr. to Edn. award, 1995, Lifetime Contbn. to Ethnic Minority Issues award, 2004, Raymond D. Fowler award, 2005; NIMH grantee, 1963-64; Office Edn. grantee, 1970-71. Fellow APA (chmn. bd. ethnic minority affairs 1982-83, chmn. edn. and tng. bd. 1986-87, policy and planning bd. 1987-89, publs. bd. 1993-97, bd. dirs. 1990-93, pres.-elect 1998, pres. 1999, chmn. membership com. 2005, chmn. presdl. task force on enhancing diversity, 2005), Behavior Therapy and Rsch. Soc. (charter); mem. Am. Psychol. Found. (trustee 2000-04), Assn. for Advancement Psychology (trustee 1983-86), Assn. for Advancement Behavior Therapy (sec.-treas. 1986-89, pres. 1992-93), Asian Am. Psychol. Assn. (bd. dirs. 1983-88), Am. Bd. Behavior Therapy (bd. dirs. 1987-2000), Phi Beta Kappa, Sigma Xi. Home: 808 Cheyenne Dr Fort Collins CO 80525-1560 Office: Colo State U Dept Psychology Fort Collins CO 80523-0001 Office Phone: 970-491-1351. Business E-Mail: suinn@lamar.colostate.edu.

**SUISSA, DAVID,** advertising executive; Exec. creative dir., chmn. bd. Suissa Miller Advt. (merged with Dailey & Assoc.), LA; co-vice chmn. Dailey & Assoc., LA, 2004. Publ.: OLAM Mag. Office: Dailey and Associates 8687 Melrose Ave West Hollywood CA 90069

**SUIT, HERMAN DAY,** radiation oncologist, medical educator; b. Houston, Feb. 8, 1929; BA, U. Houston, 1948; MD, Baylor U., 1952; PhD, Oxford (Eng.) U., 1956. Cert. Radiation Oncology (England), 1956, Radiation Oncology, 1957. Intern Jefferson David Hosp., Houston, 1952-53, resident in radiation oncology, 1953-54; postdoctoral tng., radiation oncology Oxford United Hosp., England, 1957, Nat. Cancer Inst., 1959; house surgeon registrar Churchill Hosp., Oxford, 1954, rsch. asst. radiobiol. lab., 1954-56, registrar in radiotherapy, 1956-57; sr. asst. surgeon radiation br. Nat. Cancer Inst., 1957-59; asst. radiotherapist U. Tex. M.D. Anderson Hosp. and Tumor Inst., Houston, 1959-63, assoc. radiotherapist, 1963-68, radiotherapist, 1968-71, chief sect. exptl. radiotherapy, 1962-70; Andres Soriano Disting. prof. radiation oncology Harvard Med. Sch., 1970—; head dept. radiation oncology Mass. Gen. Hosp., Boston, 1970—2000, radiologist, oncologist. Mem. staff NASA Manned Spacecraft Ctr., 1969-71; annual oration in radiation oncology, Radiological Soc. of N.Am., 1997. Named a Disting. Alumnus, U. Houston, 2005; named Disting. Alumni Assn. award, Baylor College of Medicine, 1978, Janeway Lectr., Am. Radium Soc., 1987; recipient Charles F. Kettering prize, GM Cancer Rsch. Found., 1997, Gray medal, Internat. Comm. on Radiation Units and Measurments, Inc., 2001. Mem. AAAS (subcom. radiation biology), AMA, Am. Coll. Radiology, Am. Soc. Therapeutic Radiology and Oncology (pres. 1980-81, recipient Gold medal, 1990), Am. Assn. Cancer Rsch. Office: Mass Gen Hosp Cancer Ctr Dept Radiation Therapy 55 Fruit St Boston MA 02114 Office Phone: 617-724-1155. Office Fax: 617-726-4805.*

**SUITOR, DORCAS P.,** elementary school educator; b. Albany, Vt., Aug. 5, 1944; d. Abner Joseph and Eulalee Dorothy Poutry; m. David Douglas Suitor, Dec. 24, 1966; children: Daphne Joan Morris, Dorothea Joy Alter. BS in Edn., Johnson State Coll., 1966. Tchr. 2d grade C.P. Smith Sch., Burlington, Vt., 1966—67, Swanton Elem. Sch., 1967—71; tchr. title I Sheldon Elem. Sch., 1973—75 St Anne's Elem. Sch., Swanton 1974—75, tchr 1st grade Swanton Elem. Sch., 1975—94, tchr. k-1, 1994—99, tchr. 1st grade, 1999—. Mem. adv. bd. Project Scope, Swanton, 2002—; mem. local stds. bd. Franklin Northwest Dist., 1999—; mem. tech. task force Swanton Elem. Sch., 1999—; presenter in field. Mentor new tchr. FNW Supervisory Union, Swanton, 2003—; supr. student tchrs. U. Vt. and Johnson State Coll. Swanton Elem. Sch., 2001—04; trustee Meml. United Meth. Ch., Swanton, 2005—, Swanton Town Libr., 2005—. Mem.: Franklin Northwest NEA (30 Yrs. Svc. to Children award 1999), Vt. Coun. Reading. Democrat. United Methodist. Avocations: reading, cooking, making educational games, gardening. Home: 17 Dunning St Swanton VT 05488 Office: Swanton Elem Sch 113 Grand Ave Swanton VT 05488 Personal E-mail: davdor1@aol.com.

**SUITS, BERNARD HERBERT,** philosophy educator; b. Detroit, Nov. 25, 1925; s. Herbert Arthur and Helen Dorothy (Carlin) S.; m. Nancy Ruth Berr, July 3, 1952; children— Mark, Constance; m. Cheryl Ann Ballantyne, June 14, 1996. BA, U. Chgo., 1944, MA, 1950, PhD, U. Ill., 1958. Investigator venereal disease USPHS, 1950-51; personnel officer Detroit Civil Service Commn., 1952-54; instr. philosophy U. Ill., Urbana, 1958-59; asst. prof. Purdue U., 1959-66; assoc. prof. U. Waterloo, Ont., 1966-72, prof. philosophy, chmn. dept., 1971-74, asso. dean arts for grad. affairs, 1981-84. Vis. prof. U. Lethbridge, Alta., Can., 1980, U. Bristol, Eng., 1980, disting. prof. emeritus U. Waterloo, 1995. Author: The Grasshopper: Games, Life, and Utopia, 1978, paper, 1990, 2d edit., 2005; contbr. to profl. jours. and books; featured guest on seven-week TV Ontario series The Academy of Moral Philosophy, 1982. Served with USNR, 1944-46. Recipient Disting. Tchg. award U. Waterloo, 1983. Mem.: Philosthic Soc. Study of Sport (pres. 1973). Office: U Waterloo Dept Philosophy Waterloo ON Canada E-mail: bernard.suits@sympatico.ca.

**SUITS, JANICE CRYE,** elementary school educator; b. Cleveland, Tenn, Mar. 21, 1947; d. Luther Leall and Mary Rosealthe (Lacy) Crye; children: Karen Lacy Rector, Stephanie Lynne. BA, Tenn. Wesleyan U., 1969; MEd, U. Tenn., 1979; postgrad., Trevecca Coll., 1990-91. Cert. elem. tchr., Tenn., Ga. Tchr. McMinn County Bd. of Edn., Athens, Tenn., 1969-70; tchr. remedial reading Bradley County, Cleveland, 1970-72, 75-76, tchr. 6th grade, 1973, 76—, tchr. 4th grade, 1973—; SS tchr. Wesley Meml. Ch., Cleve., 1988—93, prin., 1993—2000; tchr. Cohutta (Ga.) Elem., 2000—05. Active Easter Seals, Cleve., 1970-94; Sunday sch. tchr. Wesley Meml. Ch., Cleve., 1988-91;

neighborhood commn. March of Dimes, Cleve., 1972-02; mem. Nat. Multiple Sclerosis Soc., Cleve., 1972-98. Named Disting. Tchr. of Br., Bradley County, 1989, Tchr. of Yr., 1991, Disting. Bradley County Adminstr. of Yr., 1996, Bradley County Edn. Assn.,Teacher of the Yr. at Cohutta Elem., 2001-02. Mem. NEA, Tenn. Edn. Assn., Internat. Reading Assn., Bradley County Edn. Assn., Red Clay Reading Coun., Alpha Delta Kappa, Beta Sigma Phi. Methodist. Avocations: walking, reading, sweepstakes, rafting. Home: 2703 Parkwood Trail Cleveland TN 37312-3627 Office Phone: 706-694-8812. Business E-Mail: janice_suits@whitfield.k12.ga.us. E-mail: sui46@aol.com.

**SUJANSKY, EVA BORSKA,** pediatrician, geneticist, educator; b. Bratislava, Slovak Republic, Feb. 14, 1936; d. Stefan and Terezia (Kaiserova) Borsky; m. Eduard Sujansky, Apr. 2, 1960 (dec. Sept. 1979); children: Paul, Walter. MD, Comenius U., Bratislava, Czechoslovakia, 1959. Diplomate Am. Bd. Pediats., Am. Bd. Med. Genetics. Resident in pediats. U. Iowa, Iowa City, 1969-71; fellow in human genetics Mt. Sinai Sch. Medicine, N.Y.C., 1971-73; clin. geneticist Beth Israel Hosp., N.Y.C., 1973-74; dir. clin. genetics Sch. Medicine, U. Colo., Denver, 1974-90, assoc. prof. pediats., 1981—, assoc. prof. biochemistry, biophysics and genetics, 1981—98; co-dir. divsn. genetic svcs. The Children's Hosp., U. Colo., Denver, 1990—2000. Contbr. articles to profl. jours. Fellow Am. Acad. Pediats., Am. Soc. Human Genetics, Am. Coll. Med. Genetics (founding fellow). Avocations: fine arts, reading, travel. Office: U Colo Med Ctr/TCH 1056 E 19th Ave Denver CO 80218-1007 Office Phone: 303-861-6395. Business E-Mail: sujansky.eva@tchden.org.

**SUKAPDJO, WILMA IRENE,** language educator; b. Indpls., Nov 8, 1936; d. Wilson Homer and Della Irene Warren; m. Humam Sukapdjo, Apr. 12, 1960; children: Tina, Stephen, Amye. AB, Butler U., 1958, MS, 1967. Tchr. French U. Wis., Madison, Gadjah Mada U., Jakarta, Indonesia, Plainfield H.S., Ind., Columbus Jr. H.S., Ben Davis H.S., Indpls.; tchr. langs. Iupui Continuing Edn., Wilhum Acad., Carmel, Oasis, Indpls. Vol. guide Eiteljorg Indian Mus., 1999—2006. Mem.: Colonial Williamsburg Found., Indpls. (Ind.) Mus. Art, Tomodachi Japan-Am. Club (pres.), Phi Kappa Phi. Republican. Presbyterian. Avocation: travel. Office: Wilhum Acad Foreign Lang 622 S Range Line Rd Ste I Carmel IN 46032-2152 Office Phone: 317-843-2874.

**SUKHATME, JAI,** research scientist; s. Suhas and Shobha Sukhatme. BTech, Indian Inst. of Tech., Bombay, 1995; MS, U. of Calif., Davis, 1998; PhD, U. of Chgo., 2003. Postdoctoral fellow Nat. Ctr. for Atmospheric Rsch., Boulder, Colo., 2003—05; rsch. assoc. U. of Wis., Madison, 2006—. Contbr. scientific papers to profl. jours. Recipient rsch. and tchg. scholarship, U. of Calif. - Davis, 1996—98, U. of Chgo., 1998—2003, postdoctoral fellowship, Nat. Ctr. for Atmospheric Rsch., 2003—05. Mem.: Am. Geophys. Union. Achievements include research in Passive Scalar Decay in Smooth Flows. Office Phone: 608-263-3603.

**SUKO, LONNY RAY,** judge; b. Spokane, Wash., Oct. 12, 1943; s. Ray R. and Leila B. (Snyder) Suko; m. Marcia A. Michaelson, Aug. 26, 1967; children: Jolynn R., David M. BA, Wash. State U., 1965; JD, U. Idaho, 1968. Bar: Wash. 1968, U.S. Dist. Ct. (ea. dist.), Wash. 1969, U.S. Dist. Ct. (we. dist.), Wash. 1978, U.S. Ct. Appeals (9th cir.) 1978. Law clk. U.S. Dist. Ct. Ea. Dist., Wash., 1968—69; assoc. Lyon, Beaulaurier & Aaron, Yakima, Wash., 1969—72; ptnr. Lyon, Beaulaurier, Weigand, Suko & Gustafson, Yakima, Wash., 1972—91, Lyon, Weigand, Suko & Gustafson, Yakima, Wash., 1991—95; U.S. magistrate judge Yakima, Wash., 1971—91, 1995—2003; judge U.S. Dist. Ct., 2003—. Mem.: Phi Kappa Phi, Phi Beta Kappa. Office: PO Box 2726 Yakima WA 98907-2726

**SUKOPP, KARL MARTIN,** sculptor, painter, graphic artist; b. Mannersdorf, Austria, Nov. 4, 1928; s. Karl and Magdalena (Rossner) S.; m. Margaretha Anna Meidl, Feb. 21, 1953; children: Krl, peter, paul, Margaretha, Barbara, Do-Hee Kim. Student graphic arts and design, Vienna, 1946-50; diploma in sculpture, Acad. Applied Arts, Vienna, 1959; MA, Acad. Applied Arts, 1984. Free-lance artist, Schwechat, Austria, 1953-74, 79—. Artistic collaborator workshops of Pub. theatre Union, Vienna, 1974-79. One man shows include Gallery ZB, Austria, 1966, Galeria Galeria de Arte, Naharro, Zaragoza, 1971, The Austria-Days, Kiev, 1974, Salzburger Kunstverein, 1980; group shows include The New Hagenbund, Warsaw, 1968, La Chaux de Fonds, 1969, House of Artists, vienna, 1973, Salzburg, 1977, Vienna, 1983, Paris, 1983, Schwechat Anniv. Exposition, 1988, Gladbeck, 1992, Schwechat Anniv. Exposition, 1998, Europe '99, Neustadt; represented in permanent collections including State Govt. Lower Austria, Fed. Ministry of Edn., Bldg. Soc. Vienna, nat. and internat. assns.; prin. works include Vietcong/resistance (Biennale Rzezby with Metalu Warzawa 1968), 1964, 3 sculptures in bronze (House of Arts prize 1973), 1969, 70, 73, dep. chmn. of the new hagenbund, Vienna, 1957, others. Recipient prize Union f Arts, 1967, Vienna Festival, 1983, Chapel of St. Laurentius' Home, 1984, 85, badge of honour in gold, 1998, ring of honour Schwechat, 1998, badge of honour in gold, 1998. Mem. House of Arts Salzburg, Union of Artists of Austria, Union of Artists. Soc. Social Dem. Party. Roman Catholic.

**SUKUMAR, SREENIVAS RANGAN,** operations research specialist, electrical engineer, computer engineer; s. Chellappa and Malathi Sukumar. Bachelor in Engring., U. Madras, Chennai, 2002; MS, U. Tenn., Knoxville, 2004. Rsch. asst. Imaging, Robotics and Intelligent Sys. Lab., Knoxville, 2002—. Author: (paper) Jour. of Electronic Imaging; editor: Electronics and Communication Engineering Department Mag. Mem.: Omicron Delta Kappa, Phi Kappa Phi. Achievements include research in System integration for robotic inspection of hazardous environments; Automatic 3D mapping for multi-sensor surveillance in unstructured dynamic environments; 3D imaging system for airport runway/ pavement inspection; Laser-based 3D imaging for reverse engineering of as-built automotive components; 3D imaging for inspection, surveillance and modeling for simulations; Quantifying 3D perceptual surface shape complexity.

**SUL, YI CHUL,** neurologist; b. Seoul, Korea, May 5, 1947; came to U.S., 1976; s. Tae Woon Sul and Jung Sook Suh; m. Kyu Won, Nov. 21, 1976; children: Caroline, Douglas, Joseph. MD, Yonsei U., Seoul, 1972. Bd. cert. in neurology Am. Bd. Psychiatry and Neurology, subspecialty clin. neurophysiology. Clin. instr. Vanderbilt U., Nashville, 1981-82; v.p. Lakeside Neurology, PC, Grosse Pointe Woods, Mich., 1985—; asst. clin. prof. Mich. State U., Lansing, 1995—; chief neurology sect. St. John Northeast Cmty. Hosp., Detroit, 2002—03; mem. neurosci. adv. group St. John Health Sys., Mich., 2004—. Adj. clin. asst. prof. U. Osteo. Medicine and Health Sci., 1998-99; clin. asst. prof. Coll. Osteo. Medicine U. Health Sci., 2000-; med. mission, Thailand, 1994, China, 1997; mem. neurosci. adv. group St. John Health Sys., 2004—. Chairperson adminstrv. bd. Korean United Meth. Ch., Detroit, 1997-98, chairperson bd. trustees, 2001; pres. Lakeside Neurology, 2005-; sec. Christian Assn. for Med. Mission, Detroit, 1991-95. Capt. Korean Army, 1972-75, Korea. Grantee Muscular Dystrophy Assn., 1981-82. Fellow Am. Assn. Electrodiagnostic Medicine; mem. AMA, Am. Acad. Neurology, Am. Clin. Neurophysiology Soc., Mich. State Med. Soc., Christian Assn. for Med. Mission (pres. 1999-2001). Home: 20720 Green Ct Grosse Pointe Woods MI 48236-1459 Office: Lakeside Neurology PC 20867 Mack Ave Ste 6 Grosse Pointe Woods MI 48236-1356 Office Phone: 313-882-2922. Personal E-mail: yisul21@comcast.net.

**SULAK, PATRICIA JANE,** gynecologist, educator; b. Hillsboro, Tex., Nov. 6, 1952; m. Jeffrey Alan Waxman, Dec. 6, 1980; children: David Bartholomew Waxman, Gabriel Waxman. B in pharmacy, U. Houston, 1975; MD, U. Tex. Health Sci. Ctr., San Antonio, 1980. Cert. MD Tex. State Bd. Medicine, 1980, Am. Bd. Obstetrics and Gynecology; Pharmacist Tex., 1975. Intern Bexar County Tchg. Hosp., 1980—81; obstetrics/gynecology preceptorship DeWill Army Hosp., Ft. Belvior, 1981—82; resident obstetrics/gynecology Walter Reed Army Med. Ctr., Washington, 1982—85; physician. maj. Darnall Army Cmty. Hosp., Ft Hood, Tex., 1985—; obstetrician, gynecologist Scott and White Hosp., Tex. A&M U., Temple, Tex., 1987—; prof. Tex. A&M Coll. Medicine, Temple, Tex., 1987—. Dir. Scott and White Dept. of Ob/gyn, Temple, Tex., 1995—; founder, dir. Scott and

White Sex Edn. Program, Temple, Tex., 1996—2004. Author: Worth The Wait (Hero For Children), Tex. State Bd. Edn., 1999, Am. Coll. Obstetricians and Gynecologists Dist. VII Presdl. award for Cmty. Svc., 2004); contbr. articles to profl. jours. Maj. U.S. Army, 1981—87, Walter Reed Army Med. Ctr. and Darnall Army Com. Hosp. Recipient Hero for Children award for establishing a sex edn. curriculum in Ctrl. Tex., Tex. State Bd. Edn., 1999. Fellow: Am. Coll. Obstetricians and Gynecologists; mem.: Am. Bd. Obstetricians and Gynecologists (assoc. examiner), Alpha Omega Alpha. Achievements include research in redesign of oral contraceptives to eliminate monthly menstruation. Office: Scott and White Hosp Tex A&M U Sys 2401 S 31st St Temple TX 76508 Office Phone: 254-724-4034. Business E-Mail: psulak@swmail.sw.org.*

SULBARAN, TULIO, education educator, researcher; PhD, Ga. Inst. Tech., Atlanta. Faculty The U. So. Miss., Hattiesburg, 2002—. Office: The Univ So Miss 118 College Dr # 5138 Hattiesburg MS 39406 Office Phone: 601-266-6419. Office Fax: 601-266-5717.

SULC, JEAN LUENA (JEAN L. MESTRES), lobbyist, consultant; b. Worcester, Mass., Mar. 17, 1939; d. Emilio Beija and Julia Luena; m. Lee Gwynne Mestres, Oct. 9, 1965 (div. Dec. 1973); m. Lawrence Bradley Sulc, Nov. 4, 1983. BS in Psychology, Tufts U., 1961; M in Urban and Regional Planning, U. Colo., 1976. Lic. real estate, Va.; lic. pvt. pilot. Mem. staff U.S. fgn. svc. Dept. State, Washington, 1962-65; intern Adams County Planning Dept., Brighton, Colo., 1974-75; cons. office policy analysis City and County of Denver, 1976; program dir. Coun. Internat. Urban Liaison, Washington, 1976-79; asst., dir. internat. Cities Svc. Oil & Gas Corp., Washington, 1980-81; govt. affairs rep. Cities Svc., OXY USA Inc., Washington, 1982-89; mgr. fed. rels. OXY USA Inc., Washington, 1990-95; pres. EdgeSystem.XXI, Washington, 1996—. Chmn. govt. affairs com. L.P. Gas Clean Fuel Coalition, Irvine, Calif., 1990-92. Author, editor: (newsletter) Dayton Climate Project, 1979-80; contbr. articles to newsletters. Vol. Reagan/Bush and Bush/Quayle Presdl. Campaigns and Inaugural Coms., Washington, 1984-89; pres. Hale Found., Nathan Hale Inst., Washington, 1984-85; mem. nat. panel consumer arbitrators Better Bus. Burs., Va., 1991—. Recipient Presdl. citation Nat. Propane Gas Assn., 1992; Minority Intern grantee Denver Regional Coun. Govts., 1974-76. Mem. ASTD, ABA (assoc., arbitration sect.), Am. League Lobbyists (bd. dirs. 1994-97, 2nd v.p. 1996-97, emeritus 1999—), Assn. Image Cons. Internat. (ea. regional adv. 1998—), Greater Beaufort C. of C., Psi Chi. Episcopalian. Avocations: skiing, sports shooting.

SULDS, JONATHAN L., lawyer; b. NYC, Feb. 6, 1950; s. Irvin D. adn Vivienne (Sheinberg) S.; m. Katharine Cooper, June 24, 1978; children: Amy, Benjamin, Michael. BA, MA, Colgate U., 1971; JD, Harvard U., 1974. Ptnr., co-chmn. mgmt. com. Gibson Dunn and Crutcher, NYC, 1984—98; now ptnr., labor and employment practice group Akin Gump Strauss Hauer & Feld LLP, NYC, 1998—. Lectr. Cornell U. Sch. Indsl. and Labor Rels., Ithaca, NY, 1985—. Author: New York Employment Law, 1998, New York Employment Discrimination Handbook, 2001; contbr. numerous articles profl. journals. Office: Akin Gump Strauss Hauer & Feld LLP 590 Madison Ave New York NY 10022-2524 Office Phone: 212-872-1042. Office Fax: 212-872-1002. Business E-Mail: jsulds@akingump.com.

SULENTIC, ROBERT E., real estate company executive; Various positions Trammell Crow Co., Dallas, 1984—94, pres. Trammell Crow NE, Inc., 1995—98, exec. v.p., nat. dir. devel. and investment, 1997—98, exec. v.p., CFO, 1998—2000, pres., CEO, 2000—, chmn., 2002—. Office: Trammell Crow Co Trammell Crow Ctr 2001 Ross Ave Dallas TX 75201

SULG, MADIS, manufacturing executive, entrepreneur; b. Tallinn, Estonia, May 25, 1943; came to U.S., 1950; s. Hand Eduard and Erika (Turk) S.; m. Mary Diane Detellis, Dec. 30, 1967; children: Danielle Marie, Michaella Erika. SB in Engring. Mgmt., MIT, 1965, SM in Mgmt., 1967. Cons. Barss, Reitzel & Assocs., Cambridge, Mass., 1970—71; mgr. planning and research Converse Rubber Co., Wilmington, Mass., 1971—75; dir. bus. planning and devel. AMF, Inc., Stamford, Conn., 1975—79; sr. v.p. planning and devel. Bandag, Inc., Muscatine, Iowa, 1978—88; pres. Prime Investments, 1988—, Muscatine Natural Resources Corp., 1981—88; chmn., CEO Sieg Auto Parts, Davenport, Iowa, 1989—93; COO Hammer's Plastic Recycling, Iowa Falls, Iowa, 1994, PURethane, Inc., West Branch, Iowa, 1994—98; COO, Bytec, Inc., Clinton Township, Mich., 1999—2001; prin. M&D Mgmt. Assocs., 1989—; mng. mem. Maddi's Gallery, LLC, 2001—. With U.S. Army, 1968-70. Presbyterian. Avocations: bridge, jogging, swimming. Home: 11238 Home Place Lane Charlotte NC 28227 Office Phone: 704-907-1289. Personal E-mail: madissulg@aol.com.

SULICH, VASSILI, artistic director; b. Island of Brac, Yugoslavia, Dec. 29, 1929; came to U.S., 1964; s. Thomas and Vjekoslava (Orlandini) Sulic. From co. mem. to Dancer Etoile various dancing cos., Paris, 1952-64; prin. dancer Broadway prodn. Follies Bergere, N.Y.C., 1964, prin. dancer, ballet master Las Vegas prodn., 1964-72; ind. choreographer Europe and U.S., 1964—; founder, artistic dir. Nev. Dance Theatre, Las Vegas, 1972-97, cons., advisor, 1997-98. Choreographer: Suite Lyrique, Oedipe roi, Idomeneo with Luciano Pavarotti; creator, choreographer numerous dance works including Mantodea, Walls in the Horizon, Cinderella; prin. dancer: La Dryade, L'Echelle, Combat, Cyrano de Bergerac, Lovers of Teruel; performer (TV show) Geraldine starring Geraldine Chaplin. Named Outstanding Individual Artist Gov. of Nev., 1981, Disting. Nevadan U. Nev. Bd. Regents, 1987. Office: Nev Theater Ballet 1555 E Flamingo Rd Las Vegas NV 89119-5258

SULIGA, JOSEPH, small business owner; N.J. state assemblyman Dist. 20, 1994—2002; NJ state senator Dist 22, 2002—03; owner Kool Scoop Italian Ices, Linden, NJ. Office: Kool Scoop Italian Ices 19 W 11th St Linden NJ 07036

SULIMIRSKI, WITOLD STANISLAW, banker; b. Lwow, Poland, May 18, 1933; came to U.S., 1957; s. Tadeusz and Olga (Lepkowska) S.; m. Teresa Maria Boniecka, Dec. 28, 1957; children: Elizabeth Blakeslee Lannelger, Adam, Edward BA with honors, Cambridge U., 1953, MA, 1957. With Irving Trust Co., N.Y.C., 1957-89, exec. v.p., 1986-89; pres. Servus Assocs., Inc., N.Y.C., 1989-95; chmn. exec. com. Intercap Investments, Inc., N.Y.C., 1989—2000. Chmn. Am. Bank in Poland, Warsaw, 1989-91, LBS Bank NY, 1990-2002; exec. dir. Am. Investment Initiative in Poland, Warsaw, 1992-94; bd. dirs. Bank Pekao S.A., Warsaw, Big Bank Gdanski SA, Warsaw, Bicentennial Publ's, N.Y.C. Dir. Polish Inst. Arts and Scis., Inc., N.Y.C., 1976-97; vice-chmn. Kosciuszko Found., Inc., N.Y.C., 1983-97, chmn. 1997—; chmn. Polish Assistance Inc., N.Y.C., 1984-92; bd. dirs. Middle East Policy Coun., Washington, 1984-98, Nat. U.S.-Arab C. of C., Washington, 1987-93. Mem. Bronxville Field Club, Knights of Malta. Roman Catholic. Office: The Kosciuszko Found 15 East 65th St New York NY 10021 Office Phone: 212-734-2130.

SULKIN, HOWARD ALLEN, academic administrator; b. Detroit, Aug. 19, 1941; s. Lewis and Vivian P. (Mandel) S.; m. Constance Annette Adler, Aug. 4, 1963; children— Seth R., Randall K. PhB, Wayne State U., 1963; MBA, U. Chgo., 1965, PhD, 1969; LHD (hon.), De Paul U., 1990. Dir. program rsch., indsl. rels. ctr. U. Chgo., 1964-72; dean Sch. for New Learning, De Paul U., Chgo., 1972-77; v.p. De Paul U., Chgo., 1977-84; pres. Spertus Inst. Jewish Studies, Chgo., 1984—. St. Paul's vis. prof. Rikkyo U., Tokyo, 1970—; cons., evaluator North Ctrl. Assn., Chgo., 1975—. Contbr. articles to profl. jours. Sec.-treas. Grant Park Cultural and Ednl. Cmty., Chgo., 1984—; bd. dirs. Chgo. Sinai Congregation, 1972—, pres., 1980-83; bd. dirs. S.E. Chgo. Commn., 1980—, United Way, 1984—; Crusade of Mercy United Way, 1990—, Grant Park Conservancy, Exec. Svc. Corps., Legacy Charter Sch.; bd. dirs., chmn. Parliament of World's Religions, 1989—. Mem.: Tavern, The Standard. Office: Spertus Inst of Jewish Studies 618 S Michigan Ave Chicago IL 60605-1901

SULLEBARGER, JOHN THOMPSON, internist, educator, cardiologist; b. Plainfield, N.J., May 2, 1957; s. Franklyn Jackson and Joanne Abbott (Aspinall) S.; m. Lorrie Jeanne Miller, June 14, 1980; children: Jeffrey Franklyn, Melissa Jeanne. Student, U. Mainz, 1977; AB, Dartmouth Coll., 1979; MD, Johns Hopkins U., 1983. Intern U. Rochester, NY, 1983-84, resident in medicine, 1984-86, fellow in cardiology, 1986-89; from sr. instr. to asst. prof., 1989-92; asst. prof. U. South Fla., Tampa, 1992-96, assoc. prof., 1997-99; dir. CCU Tampa Gen. Hosp., 1997—; clin. assoc. prof. U. South Fla., Tampa, 2004—. Dir. Cardiac Catheterization Lab. James Haley VA Hosp., Tampa, 1992—99; dir. interventional cardiology U. South Fla., 1994—99; attending physician Strong Meml. Hosp., Rochester, 1989—92; pres. Fla. Cardiovascular Inst., 2004—. Author: (with others) book chapters; contbr. articles to profl. jours. Chmn. Bd. Christian Svc., 1st Bapt. Ch., Rochester, 1991-92. Fellow ACP, 1992, Am. Coll. of Cardiology, 1991, Counc. on Clin. Cardiology of Am. Heart Assn., 1991, N.Y. Cardiological Soc., 1992. Fellow ACP, Soc. Cardiac Angiography and Interventions, Am. Coll. Cardiology (chmn. Fla. chpt.). Mem. Am. Heart Assn. (fellow coun. on clin. cardiology), Tampa Internat. Heart Found. (founder 2004-). Avocation: music. Office: 509 S Armenia Ste 200 Tampa FL 33609 Office Phone: 813-353-1515.

SULLENBERGER, ARA BROOCKS, mathematics professor; b. Amarillo, Tex., Jan. 3, 1933; d. Carl Clarence and Ara Frances (Broocks) Cox; m. Hal Joseph Sullenberger, Nov. 2, 1952; children: Hal Joseph Jr., Ara Broocks Sullenberger Switzer. Student, Randolph-Macon Woman's Coll., 1951—52, So. Meth. U., 1952, U. Tex., Arlington, 1953, Amarillo Coll., 1953—54; BA in Math., Tex. Tech. U., 1955, MA, 1958; postgrad., Tex. Christian U., 1963—67, U. N. Tex., 1969—80, Tarrant County Coll., 1972—83. Cert. tchr., Tex. Math. tchr. Tom S. Lubbock H.S., Tex., 1955—56; instr. math. Tex. Tech U., Lubbock, 1956—63; tchg. fellow math. Tex. Christian U., Ft. Worth, 1963—64; chmn. dept. math. Ft. Worth Country Day Sch., 1964—67; instr. math. Tarrant County Coll.-South, Ft. Worth, 1967—70, asst. prof. math., 1970—74, assoc. prof. math., 1974—95; prof. emeritus, 1995—; ret., 1995. Adj. prof. math. Tex. Christian U., 1996; cons. Project Change, Ft. Worth, 1967-68; math. scis. advisor Coll. Bd., Princeton, N.J., 1979-83; math. book reviewer Prentice-Hall, McGraw Hill, D.C. Heath, Prindle, Weber & Schmidt, MacMillan, Harcourt, Brace Jovanovich, West, Worth, Saunders, Wadsworth. Contbr. articles to profl. jours.; author book supplement to Intermediate Algebra, 1990. Active Jr. League, Ft. Worth, 1954—73, sustaining mem., 1973—; editor newsletter Crestwood Assn., Ft. Worth, 1984, 1986, 1991, membership sec., 1985, 1990—91, 1995, 1999, pres., 1988—89, 1998—99, crime patrol capt., 1993, 2000—01, v.p., 1993, treas., 1987, 1996, 2003, sec., 1997—98, crime patrol sec., 1999, crime patrol sec.-treas., 2001—05, fin. chmn., 2004—06, fin. com. chair, 2004—05, 2006—. Recipient award for excellence in teaching Gen. Dynamics, 1968. Mem. Math. Assn. Am. (life), Nat. Coun. Tchrs. Math. (life), Am. Math. Assn. Two-Yr. Colls. (life), Tex. Math. Assn. Two-Yr. Colls. (charter, v.p. 1997-99), Tex. Jr. Coll. Tchrs. Assn., Ft. Worth League Neighborhood Assn. (v.p. 1999-2000, del. 2004-05), Pi Beta Phi. Republican. Episcopalian. Avocations: reading, walking, writing. Home: 600 Eastwood Ave Fort Worth TX 76107-1020 Personal E-mail: halandara@aol.com.

SULLENDER, JOY SHARON, retired elementary school educator; b. Bloomington, Ind., Apr. 9, 1932; d. Fred Laymond and Edith (Parrish) Medaris. BS, Ind. U., 1959, MS, 1965; postgrad., Ind. U./Purdue U., Indpls., 1991. Cert. tchr. elem. edn. 1-8. Tchr. Monroe Sch., Salem, Ind., 1952-55, Pekin (Ind.) Sch., 1955-61, Highland Park (Ill.) Sch., 1961-62, George Julian Sch. #57, Indpls., 1962—2000; ret., 2000. Mem. prin.'s adv. coun. Indpls. Pub. Schs., 1985-95, supts. adv. coun., 1982-90; state mentor student tchrs., 1969—. Author col.: Let's Be Informed, 1993-95. Class sponsor Best Friends, Indpls., 1990—; vol. Toys for Foster Children, Indpls., 1991—; workshop presenter Alpha Epsilon State, Anderson, South Bend, 1994, 95. NSF grantee 1971. Mem. PTA (tchr. rep. 1993-95), Ind. Sch. Women's Club (v.p. 1989-91, pres. 1992-94), Woman's Dept. Club (v.p. 2002—), Delta Kappa Gamma (pres. 1978-80, state comm. 1989—, state corr. sec. 1997-99). Office: George Julian School 5435 E Washington St Indianapolis IN 46219-6411 Home: 1310 N Bazil Ave Indianapolis IN 46219-4244

SULLINS, KEN, mathematics, science and computer science educator; BA in Math., Oakland U., Rochester, Mich., 1970; MAT in Math., Oakland U., 1975. Tchr. 8th grade math. East Hills Jr. High, Bloomfield Hills, Mich., 1972; tchr. 7th grade math. and sci. Imlay City (Mich.) Jr. High, 1972—73; tchr. math. Croswell (Mich.)-Lexington HS, 1973—76; tchr. Carsonville (Mich.)-Port Sanilac Jr.-Sr. HS, 1976—81; tchr. pre-calculus St. Clair C.C., Port Huron, Mich., 1977—81; tchr. Chelsea (Mich.) HS, 1981—99; tchr. math. Ripley (Tenn.) HS, 1998—99; press operator JAC Products, Saline, Mich., 2000; text layout technician Sheridan Books, Inc., Ann Arbor, Mich., 2000—01; instr. Mansfield (Pa.) U., 2001—; adj. instr. math., sci., computer tech. Empire State Coll., Corning, NY, 2004—. Presenter in field. Contbr. articles to profl. jours. Mailing: RR 2 Box 74 Tioga PA 16946 Office Phone: 607-962-1421. Business E-Mail: kenneth.sullins@esc.edu.

SULLIVAN, ALFRED DEWITT, academic administrator; b. New Orleans, Feb. 2, 1942; s. Dewitt Walter and Natalie (Alford) Sullivan; m. Marilyn Janie Hewitt, Sept. 1, 1962 (div. May 1989); children: Alan, Sean; m. Dorothy Madeleine Hess, Apr. 1993. BS, La. State U., 1964, MS, 1966; PhD, U. Ga., 1969. Asst. prof. Va. Poly. Inst. and State U., Blacksburg, 1969—73; assoc. prof., then prof. Miss. State U., Starkville, 1973—88; dir. Sch. Forest Resources Pa. State U., University Park, 1988—93; dean coll. natural resources U. Minn., St. Paul, 1993—2002, vice provost Mpls., 2002—. Assoc. Danforth Found., 1981. Contbr. articles to profl. jours. Fellow, Am. Coun. Edn., 1987—88, NDEA fellow, U. Ga., 1966—69. Mem.: Soc. Am. Foresters. Office: U Minn 234 Morrill Hall 100 Church St SE Minneapolis MN 55455 E-mail: alsull@umn.edu.

SULLIVAN, ALISON ELIZABETH, pediatrician, child psychiatrist; b. Bronx, N.Y., May 17, 1976; d. Shirley Anne and Colm Sullivan. BA, Coll. of the Holy Cross, Mass., 1998; MD, Columbia U., N.Y., 2002. Resident in pediat., adult psychiatry and child psychiatry Mt. Sinai Hosp., N.Y.C., 2002—. Home: 215 East 95th St Apt 7G New York New York NY 10128 Personal E-mail: alison.sullivan@mssm.edu.

SULLIVAN, ANDREW M., online journalist, editor, news blogger; b. Aug. 1963; BA, Magdalen Coll., Oxford; MPA, Harvard John F. Kennedy Sch. Govt., 1986, PhD, 1990. Editl. writer intern The Daily Telegraph, London, Centre For Policy Studies; intern The New Republic, 1986, assoc. editor, dep. editor, 1990, acting editor, 1991, editor, 1991—96, currently sr. editor; taught moral and polit. theory in govt. dept. Harvard John F. Kennedy Sch. Govt., 1987; freelancer Wall Street Journal, Washington Post, Daily Telegraph, Esquire and NY Mag., Telegraph, 1990; started monthly column Esquire, 1990; columnist Time Mag., 2000—; blogger, editor andrewsullivan.com, 2000—; blog writer time.blogs.com/daily-dish, 2006—. Testified before Congress on the Defense of Marriage Act in 1996; spkr. in field at many universities and colleges. Author: (essay) The Politics of Homosexuality, 1993, What's So Bad About Hate, 1999, Virtually Normal: An Argument About Homosexuality, 1995, Love Undetectable: Notes on Friendship, Sex, and Survival, 1998, The Conservative Soul: How We Lost It, How to Get It Back (Hardcover), 2006, (reader) Same-Sex Marriage: Pro and Con, (cover stories) When Plagues End, NY Times, 1996, The Scolds, NY Times, 1998, Why Are Men So Different (provoked a cover story in Time and documentary on the Discovery Channel), 2000; contbg. writer, columnist NY Time Mag., regular contbr. NY Times Book Review, weekly columnist Sunday Times of London, contbg. columnist The Advocate, LA, Calif., contbg. editor NY Sun, regular guest Real Time with Bill Maher, Chris Matthews Show, guest appearances Nightline, Face the Nation, Meet the Press, Crossfire, Hardball, The O'Reilly Factor, Larry King Show, Reliable Sources, Hannity and Colmes, and many others. Named Editor of Yr., Adweek Mag., 1996; Harkness Fellowship, Harvard John F. Kennedy Sch. Govt., 1984. Office: The New Republic 1331 H St NW Ste 700 Washington DC 20005 Address: Sunday Times of London One Pennington St London E9 81ST England also:

The Advocate 6922 Hollywood Blvd Ste 1000 Los Angeles CA 90028 also: NY Sun 105 Chambers St New York NY 10007 Office: Time & Life Bldg Rockefeller Ctr 1271 Avenue of the Americas New York NY 10020-1393 Office Phone: 202-508-4444, 800-788-7197, 323-871-1225, 212-406-2000, 212-522-1212. Office Fax: 202-628-9383, 323-467-6805, 212-522-0003. E-mail: andrewmsullivan@aol.com, andrew@andrewsullivan.com.*

SULLIVAN, AUSTIN PADRAIC, JR., retired diversified food company executive; b. Washington, June 26, 1940; s. Austin P. and Janet Lay (Patterson) Sullivan; m. Judith Ann Raab, June 1, 1968 (dec. Oct. 1995); children: Austin P. III, Amanda, Alexander; m. Marie Elise de Golian, Aug. 1, 1997; stepchildren: Lauren Gibbons, Georgia Gibbons, Samuel Gibbons. BA cum laude, Princeton U., 1964. Spl. asst. to dep. dir. N.J. Office Econ. Opportunity, Trenton, NJ, 1956—66; prof. staff mem. Com. on Edn. and Labor, U.S. Ho. of Rep., Washington, 1967—71, legis. dir., 1971—76; dir. govt. relations Gen. Mills, Inc., Mpls., 1976—78, v.p., corp. dir. govt. rels., 1978—79, v.p. pub. affairs, 1979—93, v.p. corp. commn. and pub. affairs, 1993—94, sr. v.p. corp. rels., 1994—2005; ret., 2005. Lectr. fed. labor market policies Harvard U., Mass., 1972—76, Boston U., 1972—76. Mem. Nat. Commn. on Employment and Tng., 1979—81, U.S. Sec. Agr. Adv. Com. on Agrl. Biotech., 2000—03; chmn. Governor's Coun. on Employment and Tng., 1976—82; bd. dir., exec. com. Urban Coalition Mpls., 1978—80, Guthrie Theatre, Mpls., 1978—84, Minn. Citizens for the Arts, 1980—83; co chmn. Governor's Commn. on Dislocated Workers, Minn., 1988—89; chmn. Pub. Affairs Coun., 1993—94; bd. dir. Minn. C. of C., 1993—99; trustee Minn. Pub. Radio, 1999—; bd. advisors Dem. Leadership Coun., 1986—. Served in USMC, 1957—59. Recipient Eleanor Roosevelt Fellow in Interracial Rels., 1964—65. Mem.: Grocery Mfr. Assn. (govt. affairs coun. 1991—2004, chmn. biotech. task force 1999—2004), Coun. of Pub. Affairs Exec. (chmn. 1989—90), Medica (bd. dir. 2001—), Greater Mpls. C. of C. (exec. com. 1980—86, 1990—93, bd. dir.), Mpls. Club (bd. governor's 2001—). Home: 17830 County Rd 6 Minneapolis MN 55447-2905 Office: Ste 252 700 Twelve Oaks Center Dr Wayzata MN 55391

SULLIVAN, BARRY, lawyer; b. Newburyport, Mass., Jan. 11, 1949; s. George Arnold and Dorothy Bennett (Furbush) S.; m. Winnifred Mary Fallers, June 14, 1975; children: George Arnold, Lloyd Ashton. AB cum laude, Middlebury Coll., 1970; JD, U. Chgo., 1974. Bar: Mass. 1975, Ill. 1975, Va. 1995, U.S. Dist. Ct. (no. dist.) Ill. 1976, U.S. Ct. Appeals (7th cir.) 1976, U.S. Ct. Appeals (10th cir.) 1977, U.S. Supreme Ct. 1978, U.S. Ct. Appeals (11th cir.) 1986, U.S. Ct. Appeals (5th and 9th cirs.) 1987, U.S. Ct. Appeals (fed. cir.) 1993, U.S. Ct. Appeals (DC cir.) 1994, U.S. Ct. Appeals (4th cir.) 1997, U.S. Ct. Appeals (2d and 3d cirs.) 2002, U.S. Ct. Appeals (6th and 8th cirs.) 2004. Law clk. to judge John Minor Wisdom U.S. Ct. Appeals (5th cir.), New Orleans, 1974-75; assoc. Jenner & Block, Chgo., 1975-80; asst. to solicitor gen. of U.S. U.S. Dept. of Justice, Washington, 1980-81; ptnr. Jenner & Block, Chgo., 1981-94, 2001—; prof. law Washington and Lee U., Lexington, Va., 1994-2001, dean, 1994-99, v.p., 1998-99; Fulbright prof. U. Warsaw, Poland, 2000—01; lectr. in law U. Chgo., 2001—02; spl. asst. state's atty. Cook County, Ill., 2002—03. Vis. fellow Queen Mary and Westfield Coll., U. London, 2001; spl. asst. atty. gen. State of Ill., 1989—90; lectr. in law Loyola U., Chgo., 1978—79; adj. prof. law Northwestern U., Chgo., 1990—92, 1993—94, vis. prof., 1992—93; vis. prof. Ctr. for Am. law studies U. Warsaw, 2002—03, 2005; sr. lectr. Irving B. Harris Grad. Sch. Pub. Policy, U. Chgo., 2005—; Jessica Swift Meml. lectr. constl. law Middlebury Coll., 1991; Rufus Monroe and Sophie Payne lectr. U. Mo., Columbia, 2003; Charles L. Ihlenfeld lectr. pub. policy and ethics W.Va. U., 2005. Assoc. editor U. Chgo. Law Rev., 1973-74; mem. editl. bd. Dublin U. Law Jour., 2004-; contbr. articles to profl. jours. Mem. nat. adv. bd. Ctr. for Religion, The Professions, and The Pub., U. Mo., Columbia, 2003—; trustee Cath. Theol. Union at Chgo., 1993—2003, trustee emeritus, 2003—; mem. vis. com. Irving B. Harris Grad. Sch. Public Policy Studies U. Chgo., 2001—, U. Chgo. Divinity Sch., 1987—2001; mem. adv. panel Fulbright Sr. Specialist Program, 2001—04; mem. adv. bd. Internat. Human Rights Inst. DePaul U., 2003—; trustee U. Chgo. Court Theatre, 2003—05; mem. bd. visitors So. Ill. U. Sch. Law, 2006—. Fellow, Woodrow Wilson Found., 1970; scholar, Yeats Soc. scholar, 1968; Nat. Honor scholar, Univ. Chgo., 1970—74. Fellow: Am. Bar Found., Phi Beta Kappa; mem.: Internat. Bar Assn., ABA (chmn. coord. com. on AIDS 1988—94, standing com. on amicus curiae briefs 1990—97, coun. sect. individual rights and responsibilities 1993—98, sect. legal edn. com. on law sch. adminstrn. 1994—98, chair sect. legal edn. com. on professionalism 1999—2000, co-chair sect. individual rights/responsibilities com. amicus briefs 2002—04, sect. legal edn. stds. rev. com. 2002—05, co-chair sect. individual rights/responsibilities com. bill rights 2002—, standing com. amicus curiae briefs 2004—, coun. sect. legal edn. 2006—), Internat. Bar Assn., Lawyers Club Chgo., Supreme Ct. Hist Soc. (Ill. membership chair 2002—03), Ill. State Bar Assn., Appellate Lawyers Assn., Am. Law Inst., Bar Assn. 7th Fed. Cir. (vice chmn. advminstrv. justice com. 1985—86), Va. State Bar (chair sect. on legal edn. 1997—99). Democrat. Roman Catholic. Home: 5555 S Everett Apt A1-2 Chicago IL 60637 Office: Jenner & Block One IBM Plz Chicago IL 60611 E-mail: bsullivan@jenner.com.

SULLIVAN, BERNARD JAMES, accountant; b. Chgo., June 25, 1927; s. Bernard Hugh and Therese Sarah (Condon) S.; m. Joan Lois Costello, June 9, 1951; children: Therese Lynn Scanlan, Bernard J., Geralyn M. Snyder. BSc, Loyola U., Chgo., 1950. CPA, Ill. Staff Bansley and Kiener, Chgo., 1950-66, ptnr., 1966-82, mng. ptnr., 1982—. Bd. dirs. Associated Acctg. Firms, Internat.; exec. com. Moore Stephens and Co., U.S.A., 1984—. Arbitrator Nat. Assn. Security Dealers. Served with USN, 1945-46. Mem. Am. Inst. CPA's, Ill. Soc. CPA's, Govt. Fin. Officer Assn., Internat. Found. Employee Benefit Plans, Delta Sigma Pi. Clubs: Beverly Country (Chgo.), Metropolitan (Chgo.). Lodges: Elks, K.C. Avocations: golf, sports, travel. Home: 9636 S Kolmar Ave Oak Lawn IL 60453-3214 Office: Bansley & Kiener 8745 W Higgins Rd Ste 200 Chicago IL 60631-2704 Office Phone: 312-263-2700. Business E-Mail: bsullivan@bk-cpa.com.

SULLIVAN, BETTYE YARBOROUGH, foundation administrator; d. John Marion and Elise Barnette Yarborough; children: Elizabeth Sullivan Turello, Margaret Sullivan Harvey. BA, U. Miss., 1963. Exec. dir. Wilson Rsch. Found. Meth. Rehab. Ctr., Jackson, Miss., 1993—. Named one of Top 12 of Mississippi's Leading Bus. Women, Miss. Bus. Jour., 2001; recipient Governor's Disting. Svc. award, Gov. of Miss., 1984, Mar. of Dimes Tribute, Woman of Achievement, Mar. of Dimes, 1986, Athena award, Jackson Area Alumnae Panhellenic Assn., 1994, Salute to Vol. award, Goodwill Industries, 1987. Mem.: Miss. Arts Festival (exec. bd. of dirs. 1976—77), Miss. Symphony Orch. Bd. of Govs. (exec. com. 1974—75), Miss. Rep. Women (pres. 1990—91), Rsch. Club (pres. 1991—92), Goodwill Industries of Miss. (pres. 1982—83), Goodwill Industries Internat. (pres. - volunteers 1985—87), Jackson Symphony League (pres. 1973—74), Chi Omega (Outstanding Alumna of Miss. 1986). Baptist. Avocations: reading, music, travel. Home: 1437 Sheffield Dr Jackson MS 39211 Office: Wilson Rsch Found 1350 East Woodrow Wilson Drive Jackson MS 39216 Office Phone: 601-364-3598.

SULLIVAN, BILLY, artist; b. NYC, 1946; Ed., Sch. Visual Arts, NY, 1968. One-man shows include Fischbach Gallery, NY, 1986, 1989, 1990, 1990, 1992, 1997, Rebecca Ibel Gallery, 1994, 1994, 1998, 2000, 2001, Photographs, New Mus. Contemporary Art, NY, 2002, New York, Nicole Klagsbrun, NY, 2003, North Fork/South Fork: EastEnd Art Now, Parrish Art Mus., South Hampton, 2004, Galleria Francesca Kaufmann, Milan, Italy, 2005, exhibited in group shows at Face Value: American Portraits, Parrish Art Mus., 1995, Summer 1996, Rebecca Ibel Gallery, 1996, Reflection, 2001, Summertime, 2002, Ten Years in Columbus: Part 3, 2003, Fabulous, 2005, Sex/Industry, Stefan Stux Gallery, NY, 1997, Summer, Lennon, Weinberg, Inc., NY, 1998, Couples, Cheim & Read Gallery, NY, 2000, Whitney Biennial: Day for Night, Whitney Mus. Am. Art, NY, 2006. Mailing: c/o Rebecca Ibel Gallery 1055 North High St Columbus OH 43201*

SULLIVAN, BRENDAN PAUL, state official, consultant, communications educator; b. Boston, Apr. 20, 1949; s. Francis Joseph and Margaret Rita (McDonough) S.; m. Debra Marie Fitzgerald, Feb. 11, 1988; children: Erin,

Patrick. BS, Boston State Coll., 1970; MA in Comms., Fairfield U., 1976; MBA, Boston Coll., 1995. Tchr. Boston Pub. Schs., 1970-81; mgr. adminstrn. Mass. State Lottery, Braintree, 1981-91; asst. clk.-magistrate Commonwealth of Mass. Superior Ct., Brockton, 1993—. Adj. prof. Massasoit C.C., Brockton, 1996—, mem. mediation adv. bd., 1999—; adj. prof. Regis Coll., Weston, Mass. Mem. Plymouth County Dem. League, Abington, Mass., 2000—. Mem.: Furnace Brook Golf Club (gov. 1976—). Democrat. Roman Catholic. Avocations: golf, fishing, coaching baseball. Home: 220 Plymouth Ave Quincy MA 02169 Office: 72 Belmont St Brockton MA 02301-5248 Office Phone: 508-583-8250 377. E-mail: brensullivan@comcast.net.

**SULLIVAN, BRENDAN V., JR.,** lawyer; b. Providence, Mar. 11, 1942; AB, Georgetown U., 1964, JD, 1967. Bar: R.I. 1967, D.C. 1970, U.S. Dist. Ct. D.C. 1970, U.S. Ct. Appeals (D.C. cir.) 1970, U.S. Supreme Ct. 1972, U.S. Dist. Ct. Md. 1974, U.S. Ct. Appeals (4th cir.) 1981, U.S. Ct. Appeals (3d cir.) 1979, U.S. Ct. Appeals (6th cir.) 1991, U.S. Ct. Appeals (9th cir.) 1996, U.S. Ct. Fed. Claims 1998, U.S. Ct. Appeals (fed. cir.) 2003. Mem. Williams & Connolly LLP, Washington. Lectr. Practicing Law Inst., 1981—, Md. Inst. for Continuing Profl. Edn. of Lawyers, Inc., 1979—, D.C. Criminal Practice Inst., 1975-81. Author: Grand Jury Proceedings, 1981, Techniques for Dealing with Pending Criminal Charges or Criminal Investigations, 1983, White Collar Criminal Practice Grand Jury, 1985. Named one of 75 Best Lawyers In Washington, Washingtonian survey mag., 2002. Fellow Am. Coll. Trial Lawyers; mem. ABA, R.I. Bar Assn., D.C. Bar. Office: Williams & Connolly 725 12th St NW Washington DC 20005-5901 Office Phone: 202-434-5800.

**SULLIVAN, BRIANNE MAY,** history educator, educational program director; b. Springfield, Mass., June 4, 1980; d. Michael Joseph Sullivan and Donna Marie Brunton. BA in History, Framingham (Mass.) State Coll., 2002; MA in History, U. Mass., Boston, 2006. Summershops tchr. Old Sturbridge (Mass.) Village, 2001; dir., adminstr. Coll. Academy/Coll. Gate, Stoughton, Mass., 2002—; history tchr. Marlborough (Mass.) HS, 2002—; tchrs. asst. U. Mass., Boston, 2004—05. Faculty advisor SADD, Marlborough, 2005—. Mem.: Am. Hist. Soc. Home: 15 Spring St Apt 3 Natick MA 01760 E-mail: breezy6480@aol.com.

**SULLIVAN, CHARLES,** dean, educator, author; b. Boston, May 27, 1933; s. Charles Thomas and Marion Veronica (Donahue) S.; divorced; children: Charles Fulford, John Driscoll, Catherine Page. BA in English, Swarthmore Coll., 1955; MA, NYU, 1968, PhD in Social Psychology, 1973; MPA, Pa. State U., 1978. Predoctoral fellow NYU, 1964-68; postdoctoral fellow Ednl. Testing Svc., Princeton, NJ, 1973-74; asst. prof. psychology Ursinus Coll., Collegeville, Pa., 1973-78; mgmt. cons., 1978-86; adj. prof. Pa. State U., Radnor, Pa., 1978-80; prof., head dept. pub. adminstrn., dir. student svcs. Southeastern U., Washington, 1986-89; asst. dean Grad. Sch. Arts and Scis. Georgetown U., Washington, 1989-92, assoc. dean Grad. Sch. Arts and Scis., 1992-97, professorial lectr., dept. psychology, 1994-95; exec. dir. Doylestown Found., Doylestown, Pa., 1958-73; assoc. dean, prof. Coll. Profl. Studies U. San Francisco, 1997-98. Adj. prof. social and behavioral scis. U. Md., 1984-96; lectr., spkr. on lit. and art Cooper-Hewitt Mus., N.Y.C., Nat. Soc. Arts and Letters, Washington, Martin Luther King Jr. Libr., Washington, Met. Mus. Art, N.Y.C., Smithsonian Instn., Washington, Children's Book Fair, N.Y.C., Nat. Mus. Women in Arts, Lombardi Cancer Rsch. Ctr., Georgetown U., Arts Club of Washington, Phillips Collection, Corcoran Gallery of Art, U. San Francisco Multicultural Lit. Program, Nat. Mus. Am. History, New Coll. of Calif., others. Author: Alphabet Animals, 1991, The Lover in Winter, 1991, Numbers at Play, 1992, Circus, 1992, Cowboys, 1993, A Woman of A Certain Age, 1994, Out of Love, 1996, American Folk, 1998, In a Certain Place, 1999, The Lovers' Companion, 2002; editor: America in Poetry, 1988, 2d edit., 1992, 3d edit., 1996, Imaginary Gardens, 1989, Ireland in Poetry, 1990, Children of Promise, 1991, 2d edit., 2001, Loving, 1992, American Beauties, 1993, Here Is My Kingdom, 1994, Fathers and Children, 1995, Imaginary Animals, 1996, Dancing in the Wind, 2002. Trustee Folger Poetry Bd., 1988-92; Nat. Soc. Arts and Letters, 1992-94, 2002-04, Am. Acad. Liberal Edn., 1995—, San Francisco Art Inst., 2000-05, Pacific Ctr. for Photog. Arts, 2003—; pres. Am. Found. Arts, 1995—; collectors com. Nat. Gallery Art, Washington, 1998-2006; mem. Dir.'s Cir., San Francisco Mus. Modern Art, 1998-2006. Recipient Best Books for Young Adults award, Young Adult Libr. Svcs. Assn., 1992, 1998, Best Books for Teens award, N.Y. Pub. Libr., 1992, 1993. Mem.: The Family Club, Cosmos Club. Personal E-mail: artsfound@earthlink.net.

**SULLIVAN, CHARLES, JR.,** retired lawyer; b. Beaumont, Tex., Oct. 20, 1943; BS, Lamar U., 1967; JD, U. Houston, 1973. Bar: Tex. 1973. Mem. Fulbright & Jaworski LLP, Houston, retired ptnr. Mem. ABA, State Bar Tex., Houston Bar Assn. Office: Fulbright & Jaworski LLP 1301 Mckinney St Ste 5100 Houston TX 77010-3031 E-mail: csullivan@fulbright.com.

**SULLIVAN, CHRISTOPHER,** restaurant executive; Founder, pres. Outback Steakhouse, Tampa, Fla., 1987—, chmn., CEO, 1991—. Founding stockholder, dir., v.p. Sunstate Restaurant Corp, Chili's Grill and Bar Restaurants in Fla. and Ga., 1983-87; former exec. v.p. S&A Restaurant Corp. (then subs. of Pillsbury). Office: Outback Steakhouse 2202 Westshore Blvd Tampa FL 33607

**SULLIVAN, CHRISTOPHER DAVID,** real estate broker, real estate attorney; b. N.Y.C., Oct. 6, 1966; m. Anne Marie Houlihan, Sept. 3, 1966. JD, U. of the Pacific, 1997. Bar: Nev. 2002, Utah 1998. Mng. ptnr. Sullivan/Brown The Law Firm, Las Vegas, Nev., 2004—; broker, owner Chris Sullivan Realty, Las Vegas, 2005—. Mem. Urban Land Inst., Las Vegas, 2004—. Bd. dirs. Project Sunshine, Las Vegas, 2003—06. Mem.: Clark County Bar Assn., State Bar of Utah (assoc.), State Bar of Nev. (assoc.). Office: Sullivan-Brown 332 S Jones Blvd Las Vegas NV 89107 Office Phone: 702-471-0112, 702-547-0115, Office Fax: 702 367 0116. E-mail: thisisyourleader@yahoo.com.

**SULLIVAN, CONNIE CASTLEBERRY,** artist; b. Cin., Jan. 8, 1934; d. John Porter and Constance (Alf) Castleberry; m. John J. Sullivan, June 6, 1959; children: Deirdre Kelly, Margaret Graham. BA, Manhattanville Coll., 1957. Spl. lectr. Cin. Contemporary Art Ctr., 1984, Toledo Friends of Photography, 1991, U. Ky. Art Mus., 1993, Dennison U. Sch. Art, 1993, El Instituto de Estudios Norte Americanos, Barcelona, 1994, Ctr. for Photography, Bombay, India, 1997, Miami U. Art Mus., Oxford, Ohio, 1998, Alice and Harris K. Weston Gallery, Aronoff Ctr. for the Arts, Cin., 2000, Columbus Mus. Art, Ohio, 2001, Mus. Fine Arts St. Petersburg, Fla., 2002. One-woman shows include Contemporary Art Ctr. Cleve., 1982, Cin. Contemporary Arts Ctr., 1983, Fogg Art Mus., Cambridge, Mass., 1983, 90, Neikrug Gallery, N.Y.C., 1984, Camden Arts Ctr., London, 1987, Evanston Art Ctr., Chgo., 1987, Silver Image Gallery Ohio State U., Columbus, 1988, Jean-Pierre Lambert Galerie, Paris, 1988, 96, David Winton Bell Gallery, Brown U., Providence, 1989, Toni Burckhead Gallery, Cin., 1989, Rochester Inst. Tech., 1991, Fotomus. im Münchner Stadtmus., Munich, 1992, U. Ky. Art Mus., Lexington, 1993, internat. Photography Hall, Kirkpatrick Mus. complex, Oklahoma City, 1993, Institut d'Estudios Fotografics de Catalunya, Barcelona, Spain, 1994, Cheekwood Art Mus., Nashville, 1994, Museo Damy di Fotografia Contemporanea, Brescia, Italy, 1995, Photography Gallery U. Notre Dame, Ind., 1995, Louisville Visual Art Assoc., Watertower, Louisville, KY, 1995, Jean-Pierre Lambert Galerie, 1996, Museo Damy, Milan, 1997, Ctr. for Photography, Bombay, India, 1997, Miami U. Art Mus., Oxford, Ohio, 1998, Aronoff Ctr. for the Arts, Cin., 2000, Vine St. Studios, Houston, 2000, Columbus Mus. Art, 2001, Visual Studies Worshop Gall. Rochester, NY, 2000, NuNatte Duo Centre Photography, OP Photo Gall., Hong Kong, 2000, FotoFest, 2000; exhibited in numerous group shows including Robert Klein Gallery, Boston, 1981, Cin. Art Mus., 1981, 84, 85, 93, Witkin Gallery, N.Y.C., 1984, Milw. Art Mus., 1986, Dayton (Ohio) Art Inst., 1987, J.B. Speed Art Mus., Louisville, 1988, Trisolini Gallery Ohio U., 1989, Ohio U., Athens, 1989, Centre Nat. Photographie, Paris, 1989, Cleve. Ctr. for Contemporary Art, 1991, Tampa Mus. Art, 1991, 93, Images Gallery 1991, Dayton Art Inst./Mus. Contemporary Art Wright State U., Dayton, 1992, Bowling Green State U. Sch Art, 1992, Carnegie Arts Ctr., Covington, Ky., 1993,

POLK Mus. Art, Lakeland, Fla., 1993, Tampa (Fla.) Mus. Art, 1993, Adams Landing Fine Art Ctr., Cin., 1995, Checkwood Mus. Art, Nashville, 1995, Photo Forum Gallery, 1995, 96, Jean-Pierre Galerie, 1996, Soros Ctr. Contemporary Art, Kiev, Ukraine, 1996, Dom Khudozhnikiv, Kharkiv, Ukraine, 1996, Wolf Photographic Galleries, Cin., 1996, Columbus Mus. Art, 1996, Mus. fine Arts, St. Petersburg, Fla., 1997, Louisville Visual Art Assn., Water Tower, 1997, Mus. Damy di Fotografia Contemporanea, Brescia, Italy, 1998, Kharkiv Mcpl. Art Gallery, Kharkiv, Ukraine, 1999, Jean-Pierre Lambert Gallery, Paris, 1999, Huntington (W.Va.) Mus. Art, 2000, Centre Socio-Cultural Galerie Pierre Tal Coat, Hunnebont, France, 2000; represented in numerous permanent collections Tampa Mus. of Art, Münchner Stadt Mus., Munich, Germany, Museo Damy, Brescia, Italy, Ctr. Creative Photography, Tucson, Detroit Inst. Arts, Biblioteque National, Paris, Internat. Photography Hall of Fame and Mus., Kirkpatrick Ctr. Mus. Complex, Okla. City, Nelson Gallery-Atkins Mus., Kansas City, Ctr. for Photography, Bombay, Milw. Art Mus., Mus. Photography Arts, San Diego, Musee Nat. D'Art Modern, Cin. Art Mus., High Mus., Atlanta, Mus. Fine Arts, St. Petersburg, Fla., Centre Georges Pompidou, Paris, Denver Art Mus., Boston Mus. Fine Arts, Stanford U. Mus. Art, Palo Alto, Indpls. Art Mus., New Orleans Mus. Art, Fogg Mus., Cambridge, Mass., numerous others; also pvt. collections; author: Petroglyphs of the Heart, Photographs by Connie Sullivan, 1983; work represented in numerous publs. Trustee Images Ctr. for Fine Photography, Cin., 1986-94. Named Hyde Park Living Person of Yr., 1996; recipient Juried Show, Toledo Friends Photography, 1986, Best of show, 1988, Images Gallery, 1986, Pres.'s Coun. for Arts award, Manhattanville Coll., 1991, Treasure of the Month award, Mus. Fine Arts St. Petersburg, Fla., 1995; fellow Arts Midwest fellow, NEA, 1989—90; grantee Aid to Individual Artists grantee, Summerfair, 1987, travel grantee, Ohio Arts Coun., 1995, 1997, 2000, Artist Projects, 1999, 2000. Mem. McDowell Soc. Avocations: travel, reading, gardening, music. Home: 1950 Mount Vernon Dr Fort Wright KY 41011 Fax: 513-871-6931.

**SULLIVAN, DANIEL F.,** academic administrator, sociologist, educator; b. Jan. 19, 1944; m. Ann H. Sullivan; 3 children. BS in Math., St. Lawrence U., 1965; PhD in Sociology, Columbia U., 1971. Ctrl. office supr. N.Y. Tel. Co., Syracuse, 1966—67; rsch. assoc. Barnard Coll., 1969—73, instr. sociology, 1970—71; asst. prof. sociology, sr. rsch. assoc. Cornell U., 1974—76; asst. prof. sociology Carleton Coll., 1971—79, assoc. prof. sociology, 1979—86, dean acad. devel. and planning, 1979—81, v.p. for planning and devel., 1981—86, sec. of the coll., 1981—86; pres. Allegheny Coll., Meadville, Pa., 1986—96, prof. sociology, 1986—96; pres. St. Lawrence U., Canton, NY, 1996—, prof. sociology, 1996—. Mem. adv. com. NSF Divsn. Undergrad. Edn., 1991—; chair bd. trustees St. Lawrence Aquarium and Ecol. Ctr., 1998—; bd. dirs. N.Y. Commn. for Ind. Colls. and Univs., mem. exec. com., 2003; trustee Commn. on Ind. Colls. and Univs., 2002—. Co-author: Research on Human Subjects: Problems and Processes of Social Control in Bio-Medical Experimentation, 1973, Applying Market Research in College Admissions, 1983, What Works: Building Natural Science Communities, 1991. Mem.: Western Pa. Hist. Soc. (trustee 1994—), Am. Assn. Colls. and Univs. (bd. dirs. 2003—). Office: St Lawrence Univ 23 Romoda Dr Canton NY 13617

**SULLIVAN, DANIEL J.,** artistic director; b. Wray, Colo., June 11, 1940; s. John Martin and Mary Catherine (Hutton) Sullivan; children: Megan, John, Rachel M. BA, San Francisco State U. Actor Actor's Workshop, San Francisco, 1963—65; actor, dir. Lincoln Ctr. Repertory Theatre, NYC, 1965—73; resident dir. Seattle Repertory Theatre, 1979—81, artistic dir., 1981—97. Actor: (plays) Tiger at the Gates, 1968, Camino Real, 1970, The Good Woman of Setzuan, 1970, The Playboy of the Western World, 1971, Enemies, 1972, The Merchant of Venice, 1973, A Streetcar Named Desire, 1973; asst. dir. (plays) Hair, 1968; dir.: (plays) I'm Not Rappaport, 1985, 2002, The Heidi Chronicles, 1989, Conversations With My Father, 1992, The Sisters Rosensweig, 1993, An American Daughter, 1997, A Moon for the Misbegotten, 2000, Proof, 2000 (Tony award best direction), Major Barbara, 2001, Morning's at Seven, 2002, Short Talks on the Universe, 2002, A Retreat from Moscow, 2003, Sight Unseen, 2004, Brooklyn Boy, 2005, Julius Caesar, 2005, After the Night and the Music, 2005, Rabbit Hole, 2006, Stuff Happens, 2006 (OBIE award Village Voice, 1966). Recipient Drama Desk award, NY Theatre Critics award, 1972. Mem.: Nat. Endowments for Arts. Democrat. Office: Seattle Rep Theatre PO Box 900923 Seattle WA 98109-9723*

**SULLIVAN, DANIEL JOSEPH,** theater critic; b. Worcester, Mass., Oct. 22, 1935; s. John Daniel and Irene Ann (Flagg) S.; m. Helen Faith Scheid, 1965; children: Margaret Ann, Benjamin, Kathleen. AB, Holy Cross Coll., 1957; postgrad., U. Minn., 1957-59, U. So. Calif., 1964-65, Stanford U., 1978-79. Reporter Worcester Telegram, Mass., 1957, Red Wing Republican Eagle, Minn., 1959, St. Paul Pioneer Press, 1959-61; music and theater critic Mpls. Tribune, 1961—64; comedy writer Dudley Riggs' Brave New Workshop, 1961-64; arts reporter/theater reviewer N.Y. Times, 1965-68; theater critic L.A. Times, 1969-90. Dramaturg Eugene O'Neill Theatre Ctr., Waterford, Conn., 1972-73, 93-98; instr. O'Neill Critics Inst., Waterford, 1977-92, assoc. dir., 1993-98, dir., 1999—; adj. prof. U. Minn., Mpls., 1990—; juror theater panel Nat. Endowment for Arts, 1983; juror Pulitzer Prize for Drama, 1985, 89, 92; pres. L.A. Drama Critics Circle, 1970-71, Ctr. for Arts Criticism, St. Paul, 1992-95. Mem. Am. Theater Critics Assn. (founding). Office Phone: 612-522-9053. Personal E-mail: sulli98@yahoo.com.

**SULLIVAN, DANIEL JOSEPH,** biology professor, priest; b. N.Y.C., Apr. 22, 1928; s. Daniel Joseph and Margaret Mary Sullivan. BS in Biology, Fordham U., NY, 1950, MS in Biology, 1958; PhD in Entomology, U. Calif., Berkeley, 1969. Prof. biology, entomology dept. biol. scis. Fordham U. 1969—. Vis. scientist Centro Internacional Agricultura, Cali, Colombia, 1988—89, Internat. Agr. Icrisat, Hyderabad, India, 1999—2000; vis. scholar U. Calif., Berkeley, 2003, Berkeley, 05. Co-author (hyperparasitism) Annual Rev. of Entomology, 1999; author: Encyclopedia of Insects, 2003, Encyclopedia of Entomology, 2004. Named to Hall of Fame, ROTC; Fulbright rsch. fellowship, U.S. Govt., Nigeria, 1984-85. Mem.: N.Y. Entomological Soc. (former pres.), Soc. Sigma Xi (former pres. Fordham chpt.), Entomological Soc. Am. Roman Catholic. Office: Fordham Univ Biology Dept 441 E Fordham Rd Bronx NY 10458 Business E-Mail: sullivan@fordham.edu.

**SULLIVAN, DANIEL S.,** federal agency administrator; married; 3 children. B in Economics magna cum laude, Harvard U.; JD, MS in Fgn. Svc. cum laude, Georgetown U. Law clk. to Hon. Andrew Kleinfeld US Ct. Appeals (9th cir.); law clk. to Chief Justice Warren Matthews Alaska Supreme Ct.; atty. Perkins Coie, LLP; dir., acting sr. dir. Internat. Econ. Directorate The White House, Washington; asst. sec. for econ. and bus. affairs US Dept. State, Washington, 2006—. With USMC, strategic advisor, spl. asst. to comdr. U.S. Ctrl. Command (CENTCOM) USMC, 2005—06. Decorated Def. Meritorious Svc. Medal; named one of 10 Outstanding Young Americans, U.S. Jr. C. of C.; recipient Outstanding Svc. award, Nat. Security Coun. Office: US Dept State Bur Econ and Bus Affairs 2201 C St NW Washington DC 20520*

**SULLIVAN, DENNIS C.,** lawyer; b. San Francisco, 1946; AB, U. Calif., Berkeley, 1968, JD, 1972. Bar: Calif. 1972. Counsel Pacific Gas & Elec. 1972—76; assoc. Wilson Sonsini Goodrich & Rosati, 1976—78; founding ptnr. Mosher Pooley & Sullivan, 1978—88; ptnr. Graham & James, Palo Alto, Calif., 1988—93, Gray Cary Ware & Freidenrich, 1993—2004; ptnr., co-chmn. Capital Markets practice group DLA Piper Rudnick Gray Cary, Ea. Palo Alto, Calif., 2005—. Office: DLA Piper Rudnick Gray Cary 2000 University Ave Palo Alto CA 94303 Office Phone: 650-833-2243. Office Fax: 650-833-2001. Business E-Mail: dennis.sullivan@dlapiper.com.

**SULLIVAN, DENNIS JAMES, JR.,** retired hospitality and music executive; b. Jersey City, Feb. 23, 1932; s. Dennis James and Mary Theresa (Coyle) S.; m. Constance Rosemary Shields, Jan. 31, 1953; children: Denise Sullivan Morrison, Mary Agnes Sullivan Wilderotter, Colleen Sullivan Bastkowski, Andrea Sullivan Doelling. AB, St. Peters Coll., 1953; postgrad., U. Md., 1955; MBA, U. Pa., 1973. Various line and staff positions N.J. Bell, 1955-61, N.Y. Telephone Co., 1961-64, 67-68, AT&T, N.Y.C., 1964—67, 1968—72, dir. mktg., 1972-74, asst. v.p., 1974-76; v.p. mktg. Ohio Bell Telephone Co.,

Cleve., 1976-78; v.p. consumer info. services AT&T-Am. Bell, Parsippany, N.J., 1978-83; exec. v.p. Cin. Bell Telephone Co., 1983-84, pres., 1984-87, also bd. dirs.; exec. v.p., chief fin. officer Cin. Bell Inc., 1987-93; exec. counselor Dan Pinger Pub. Rels., 1993-2000; pres., CEO Gaylord Entertainment, Nashville, 2000—02. Bd. dirs. Fifth Third Bancorp & Bank, Anthem Ins. Co., The Future Now, Intefrated Techs. Inc., Kalthoff Internat. Author: Videotex, IEE Nat. Conf., 1981. Bd. dirs. Boy Scouts, Cin. Bell Inc., 1993-97; gen. chmn. United Way, 1990—. Lt. (j.g.) USN, 1953-55, ret. comdr. USNR, 1976. Mem. Fin. Exec. Inst., Commonwealth Club, Cin. Country Club, Queen City Club, Legatus. Roman Catholic. E-mail: dennisj37@marcocable.com.

**SULLIVAN, DENNIS P.,** mathematics professor; b. Port Huron, Mich., 1941; PhD, Princeton U., 1965; doctorate (hon.), Ecole Normale Superieure de Lyon, France, 2002. Albert Einstein chair in Sci., grad. ctr. CUNY; disting. prof. math. SUNY, Stony Brook. Invited spkr. Internat. Congress of Math., 1970, 86. Recipient Elie Cartan prize, French Acad. Sciences, 1981, King Faisal Internat. prize of Math., 1994, Nat. Medal Science in Math., 2004. Mem.: Am. Math. Soc. (Veblen prize 1971, Leroy P. Steele prize for Lifetime Achievement 2006), NAS. Office: Graduate Ctr CUNY 365 Fifth Ave New York NY 10016-4309

**SULLIVAN, DIANE P.,** lawyer; b. Elizabeth, NJ; BA cum laude, Fairfield U., 1984; JD, U. Pa., 1987. Bar: NJ 1987, U.S. Dist. Ct. (NJ Dist.) 1987, U.S. Dist. Ct. (So. and ea. dist. NY) 2003. Ptnr. mass torts and product liability group Dechert LLP, Princeton, NJ, 2001—. Bd. trustees Trial Attys. NJ, 2000—04; mem. policy com. Dechert LLP; lectr. in field. Named one of Top 40 Litigators Under 40, Nat. Law Jour., 2002, Top 10 Lawyers in the Country, Lawyers Weekly USA, 2005. Mem.: ABA, Internat. Assn. Def. Counsel (mem. trial acad. faculty 2002), Def. Rsch. Inst., NJ State Bar Assn. Office: Dechert LLP Princeton Pike Corp Ctr PO Box 5218 Princeton NJ 08543-5218 Office Phone: 609-620-3232. Office Fax: 609-620-3259. E-mail: diane.sullivan@dechert.com.

**SULLIVAN, DOROTHY RONA,** state official; b. Jan. 7, 1941; d. Lewis Robert and Dorothy (Hopkins) Sullivan. BA, Boston U., 1963; MEd, State Coll. Boston, 1966; CAGS, Boston U., 1972; postgrad., Northeastern U., 1970—71, Boston Coll., 1974—78, U. Mass., 1980. Rsch. asst. Boston Lying-In Hosp., 1963—64; employment counselor Mass. Divsn. Employment Security, Boston, 1964—66, sr. employment counselor, 1966—67, prin. employment counselor, 1967—70, employment office mgr., 1970—75, supr., 1975—78, chief rsch. dept., 1978—88, dir. def. employment analysis, 1985—87; chief rsch. dept. Mass. Divsn. Employment and Tng., 1989—98, 1998—2002. Supr. cmty. counselor interns and rehab. adminstrn. interns Northeastern U. Grad. Sch. Edn., 1968—74; supr. pub. adminstrn. interns Suffolk U., 1976; supr. econ. interns Boston U., 1979, Regis Coll., 1984, U. Mass.-Boston, 1998; presenter in field. Author: Boston Employment Service Guide, 1969, Careers and Training in the Allied Health Field, 1989, Higher Skills, Higher Wages and Higher Achievement, 1997, Career Families and Career Paths, 1997, Massachusetts Cities and Towns, 1978—82, Outplacement Program, 1993, Presentation and Performance Portfolio, 1998; editor: Mass. Trends, 1978—82; mem. editl. bd. Memos to the Gov., Mgmt. Advice from the Commonwealth's Experts in Pub. Adminstrn., 2003; contbr. articles to profl. jours.; exhibitions include Brookline Arts Ctr., Brookline Pub. Libr., Chatham Creative Arts Ctr. Recorder Gov.'s Conf. on Rehab., 1970; mem. Gov.'s Commn. Employment of Handicapped, 1972—78, Pres.'s Com. Employment of Handicapped, 1975—78; exec. bd. Greater Boston coun. Camp Fire Girls, 1971—73; R.S.V.P. adv. bd. Boston Commn. Affairs of the Elderly, 1977—78; mem. adv. com. equal employment opportunity practices Dept. Pers. Adminstrn., 1984—85; mem. adv. group Mass. Occupl. Info. Coordinating Com., 1991—98; mem. adv. bd. Mass. Ctr. Civic Edn., 2001—; bd. dirs. Doric Dames, Mass. State Ho., 2004—; 2nd v.p. Doric Docents, 2006; bd. dirs. Ethas (Boston Sr. Svcs. Agy.), 2004—. Recipient Recognition award, Nat. Occupl. Info. Coordinating Com., 1994, Exceptional Achievement award, U.S. Sec. Labor, 2003, Pres. Vol. Svc. award, 2004. Mem.: APGA (nat. recorder conf. 1968), ASPA, AACD, ACA (recorder), Am. Bus. Women's Assn. (del. nat. conv. 1980, 1983, pres. Boston chpt. 1982, Woman of Yr.. Boston chpt. 1983), Am. Econ. Assn., Am. Acad. Polit. and Social Sci., Am. Fedn. State, County and Mcpl. Employees (exec. bd. local 164 1972—73, 1974—76), Nat. Rehab. Assn. (Mass. sec. 1971—72, exec. bd. 1972—74, v.p. 1974—75, pres. 1976—77), Nat. Career Devel. Assn., Am. Soc. Pub. Adminstrn. (life; region I-II liaison, sect. women in pub. adminstrn. 1988—90, Mass. chpt. coun., officer, treas. 1997, sec. 1998, v.p. 1998—, pres.-elect 1999, pres. 2000, nat. coun. campaign for internat. rels.), Charitable Irish Soc., Rockport Art Assn. (patron), Boston Ctr. for Internat. Visitors, Chatham Swim Club. Home: 33 Morey Rd Roslindale MA 02131-1037 also: Eldredge Sq Chatham MA 02633

**SULLIVAN, E. THOMAS,** law educator; b. Amboy, Ill., Dec. 4, 1948; s. Edward McDonald and Mary Lorraine (Murphy) S.; m. Susan A. Sullivan, Oct. 2, 1971. BA, Drake U., 1970; JD, Ind. U., Indpls., 1973. Bar: Ind. 1973, Fla. 1974, D.C. 1975, Mo. 1980. Law clk. to Judge Joe Eaton, U.S. Dist. Ct. for So. Dist. Fla., Miami, 1973-75; trial atty. U.S. Dept. Justice, Washington, 1975-77; sr. assoc. Donovan, Leisure, Newton & Irvine, Washington, 1977-79; prof. law U. Mo., Columbia, 1979-84; assoc. dean, prof. Washington U., St. Louis, 1984-89; dean U. Ariz. Coll. Law, Tucson, 1989-95; William S. Pattee prof. law, dean U. Minn. Law Sch., Mpls., 1995—2002, Irving Younger prof. law, 2002—, sr. vice-pres., provost, 2004—. Fellow Am. Bar Found.; mem. Am. Law Inst., Am. Econ. Assn. Office: U Minn Law Sch Walter F Mondale Hall Office 381 229 19th Ave S Minneapolis MN 55455 Home: 182 Bank St Se Minneapolis MN 55414-1042

**SULLIVAN, EDMUND BERTRAM,** writer; b. Salem, Mass., Jan. 28, 1928; s. Michael Lawrence and Eleanor Bertram Sullivan; m. Marie Dianne Sullivan, Aug. 28, 1954 (dec.); children: Geoffrey, David, Maura, Mark. BS in History, Mass. State Coll., 1953, MEd, Boston Coll., 1954; EdD, Boston U., 1968. Prin. New Hampton Pub. Schs., NH, 1954—56; critic tchr., instr. North Adam State Coll., North Adams, Mass., 1956—58; critic secondary schs. Newton, Mass., 1958—62; dean faculty Mass. State C.C., Greenfield, 1963—68; prof. edn. found. U. Hartford, West Hartford, Conn., 1968—85, mus. dir., cur., 1985—93, prof. emeritus, 1993—. Dir. U.S. Peace Corps, East Africa and Zaire, 1973—74; cons. NEH, Detroit, 1989; vis. lectr., scholar U. San Diego, 1996. Author: Collecting Political Americana, 1980, Hellbent for the White House, 1989, Campaigning with James M. Curley, 2000; co-author: Images of American Radicalism, 1999. Vice chmn. Conn. State Libr. Bd., Hartford, 1991—2003; mem. Suffield Libr. Bd., 1972—2003, Conn. State Mus. Adv. Bd., Hartford, 1991—; founding dir. Mus. of Am. Polit. Life U. Hartford, 2005—; tour dir. Bicentennial Tour of U.K., 1976. With USN, 1945—46, with USMC, 1950—52. Named Disting. Alumnus, Mass. State Coll., 1998; NEH grantee 1983—85, Inst. for Mus. Svc. grantee, 1988—89. Fellow: John Dewey Soc.; mem.: Nat. Assn. Atomic Vets., New Eng. Hist. Assn., Am. Assn. Mus. Democrat. Avocations: hiking, Irish American studies. Home: 70 Valley View Dr Suffield CT 06078

**SULLIVAN, EDWARD DELANO,** lawyer, investor; s. Joseph Daniel and Eugenia Rose Sullivan; m. Elizabeth Wilhelmina Frank, June 26, 1954; children: Elizabeth Sullivan Rolfe, Kathleen Sullivan Fleming, Maureen Sullivan Fengler, Caroline Sullivan Piper, Alice Sullivan Tucker, April Sullivan Fitzgerald, Virginia Elaine. BS in Bus. Adminstrn., U. Conn., Storrs, 1954; JD, U. Okla. Coll. Law, Norman, 1958; grad. Judge Advocate Course Res., U. Va., Charlottesville, 1965; grad. Nat. Sec. Seminar, Indsl. Coll. of Armed Forces, 1974; grad. Sr. Staff Judge Advocate course, Air U., 1976; grad., U.S. Air Force War Coll., 1978. Bar: Okla. 1958, Conn. 1960, U.S. Supreme Ct. 1967, Fla. 1979; cert. in mgmt. devel. Fla. Atlantic U., 1977, pub. purchasing officer Nat. Inst. Govtl. Purchasing, Inc., comml. pilot with seaplane rating FAA. Pvt. practice, Bridgeport, Conn., 1960—, Fort Lauderdale, Fla., 1979—. Dir. Nat. Inst. Govtl. Purchasing, 1965—68 Col. JAG USAF, 1954—84. Decorated Commendation medal with Oak Leaf Cluster USAF, Humanitarian medal, Meritorious Svc. medal, Legion of Merit medal;

named Hon. Lt. Col. Aide-de-Camp, Ala. State Militia, 1976, Hon. Mayor, City of San Antonio, 1996; recipient Committment to Corporate Spirit plaque, Warren Robins AFB, GA, 1984, Boston Bar Assn. award, 1971. Mem.: SAR (chpt. pres. 1990—91, Fla. state pres. 1998—99, nat. trustee 1999—2000, pres. coun. of state pres.'s 1999—2000), ABA (sr.), Ga. Govtl. Purchasing Assn. (hon.), Freedon Found. (life), Air Force Assn., Pilgrim John Howland Soc., Delano Kindred (com. mem.), Gen. Soc. of Mayflower Descendants (asst. gen. 1996—99, dep. gov. gen. 1999—2002, counsellor gen. 2003—05, gov. gen 2005—), Res. Officers Assn. U.S. (life), Nat. Gavel Soc. (life), Mil. Officers Assn. (life), Mayflower Soc. State of Fla. (gov. John Alden Colony (Ft. Lauderdale chpt.) 1988—90, state dep. gov. 1990—93, state gov. 1993—96, Fla. counsellor 2003—05), Hugenot Soc. Fla. (pres. (Louis Du Bois chpt.), Alden Kindred, Phi Alpha Delta. Address: 2837 NE 27th St Fort Lauderdale FL 33306-1912

**SULLIVAN, EDWARD JOSEPH,** lawyer; b. Bklyn., Apr. 24, 1945; s. Edward Joseph and Bridget (Duffy) S.; m. Patte Hancock, Aug. 7, 1982; children: Amy Brase, Molly Elsasser, Mary Christine. BA, St. John's U., 1966; JD, Willamette U., 1969; MA, cert. Urban Studies, Portland State U., 1973; LLM, Univ. Coll., London, 1978; diploma in law, Univ. Coll., Oxford, 1984; MA, U. Durham, 1999. Bar: Oreg. 1969, D.C. 1978, Wash. 2001, U.S. Dist. Ct. Oreg. 1970, U.S. Ct. Appeals (9th cir.) 1970, U.S. Supreme Ct. 1972. Counsel Washington County, Hillsboro, Oreg., 1969-75; legal counsel Gov. of Oreg., Salem, 1975-77; ptnr. O'Donnell, Sullivan & Ramis, Portland, Oreg., 1978-84, Sullivan, Josselson, Roberts, Johnson & Kloos, Portland, Salem and Eugene, Oreg., 1984-86; Mitchell, Lang & Smith, Portland, 1986-90; Preston Gates & Ellis, Portland, 1990—2003; owner Garvey Schubert Barer, Portland, Oreg., 2003—. Bd. dirs., pres. Oreg. Law Inst. Contbr. numerous articles to profl. jours. Chmn. Capitol Planning Commn., Salem, 1975-77, 78-81. Mem. ABA (local govt. sect., com. on planning and zoning, adminstrv. law sect.) Oreg. State Bar Assn., (J.C. State Bar Assn., Wash. State Bar Assn., Am. Judicature Soc., Am. Polit. Sci. Assn. Democrat. Roman Catholic. Office: Garvey Schubert Barer 121 SW Morrison Ste 1100 Portland OR 97204-3141 Office Phone: 503-228-3939. Business E-Mail: esullivan@gsblaw.com.

**SULLIVAN, EMMET G.,** judge; b. Washington, June 4, 1947; s. Emmet A. and Eileen G. Sullivan; m. Nan Sullivan; children, Emmet, Erik. BA in Polit. Sci., Howard U., 1968, JD, 1971. Law clk. to Hon. James A. Washington, Jr. Superior Ct. D.C.; from assoc. to ptnr. Houston and Gardner, 1973-80; ptnr. Houston, Sullivan & Gardner, 1980-84; judge Superior Ct. D.C., 1984-92, U.S. Dist. Ct., 1992—94, U.S. Ct. Appeals, D.C. cir., 1994—. Commr. D.C. Judicial Nominating Commn. Mem. bd. bd. & exec. com. Council for Ct. Excellence, Washington; mem. Com. on Criminal Law & chmn. legis. subcommittee Judicial Conf. U.S.; mem. bd. bd. dir. Frederick Abramson Memorial Found., DC. Reginald Heber Smith fellow; recipient Thurgood Marshall Award of Excellence. Office: US Courthouse Rm 2327 333 Constitution Ave NW Washington DC 20001-2822

**SULLIVAN, EUGENE JOHN JOSEPH,** manufacturing executive, director; b. NYC, Nov. 28, 1920; s. Cornelius and Margaret (Smith) S.; m. Gloria Roesch, aug. 25, 1943; children: Eugene John Joseph, Edward J., Robert C., Elizabeth Ann Hansler. BS, St. John's U., 1942, D in Commerce, 1973; MBA, NYU, 1948. With chem. divsn. Borden, Inc., N.Y.C., 1946—; beginning as salesman, successively asst. sales, 1957-58, exec. v.p., 1958-64; pres. Borden Chem. Co. divsn. Borden, Inc.; v.p. Borden, Inc., 1964-67, exec. v.p., 1967-73, pres., COO, 1973-79, chmn., pres., CEO, 1979-86; prof. St. John's U., 1987—2003. Bd. dirs. W.R. Grace & Co.; chmn. bd. dirs. Hamilton Fund; trustee Atlantic Mut. Ins. Co. Trustee, vice chmn., past sec. St. John's U., chmn. bd. dirs., 1999—; trustee N.Y. Med. Coll., Cath. Health Assn., Cath. Charities U.S.A., 1999—; chmn. Commn. on Cath. Health Care. Served as lt. USNR, 1942-46; lt. Res. Mem. Coun. Fgn. Rels., Knights of Malta, Knights of Holy Sepulchre, Knights of St. Gregory. Univ. Club, Plandome Country Club. Personal E-mail: gene5978@aol.com.

**SULLIVAN, EUGENE RAYMOND,** judge; b. St. Louis, Aug. 2, 1941; s. Raymond Vincent and Rosemary (Kiely) S.; m. Lis Urup Johansen, June 18, 1966; children— Kim, Eugene II. BS, U.S. Mil. Acad., 1964; JD, Georgetown U., 1971; HDL (hon.), New Eng. Sch. Law, 2001. Bar: Mo. 1972, D.C. 1972. Law clk. to Hon. M.C. Matthes U.S. Ct. Appeals (8th cir.), St. Louis, 1971—72; assoc. Patton Boggs & Blow, Washington, 1972—74; asst. spl. counsel The White House, Washington, 1974; trial counsel U.S. Dept. of Justice, Washington, 1974—82; dep. gen. counsel U.S. Air Force, Washington, 1982—84; gen. counsel Nat. Reconnaissance Office, 1982—86; gov. of Wake Island, 1984—86; judge U.S. Ct. Appeals Armed Forces, Washington, 1986—90, 1995—2002, chief judge, 1990—95, sr. judge, 2002—; cofounder, prin. Gavel Consulting Group, 2003—; adj. prof. IMPAC U., Punta Gorda, Fla. Mem. Fed. Commn. To Study Honor Code at West Point, 1989-90. Author: (book) The Majority Rules, 2005. Trustee U.S. Mil. Acad., 1989—; mem. U.S. Army Ranger Trng. Brigade, 2006. With US Army, 1964-69. Decorated Bronze Star, Air medal, airborne badge, ranger badge, others; Castle award, West Point Soc., 2001. Republican. Roman Catholic. Office: Phone: 202-390-5959. Business E-Mail: esullivan@gavelconsultinggroup.com. E-mail: judgesullivan@west-point.org.

**SULLIVAN, FRANK, JR.,** state supreme court justice; b. Mar. 21, 1950; s. Frank E. and Colette (Cleary) S.; m. Cheryl Gibson, June 14, 1972; children: Denis M., Douglas S., Thomas R. AB cum laude, Dartmouth Coll., 1972; JD magna cum laude, Ind. U., 1982; LLM, U. Va., 2001. Bar: Ind. 1982. Mem. staff Office of U.S. Rep. John Brademas, 1974-79, dir. staff, 1975-78; with Barnes & Thornburg, Indpls., 1982-89; budget dir. State of Ind., 1989-92; exec. asst. Office of Gov. Evan Bayh, 1993; assoc. justice Ind. Supreme Ct., 1993—. Chair Ind. Supreme Ct. Judicial Technology & Automation Com. Mem. ABA (jud. divsn. liaison to commn. on racial & ethnic diversity, co-chair jud. clerkship program), Ind. State Bar Assn., Indpls. Bar Assn. Home: 5854 Lawton Loop West Dr Indianapolis IN 46216-2009 Office: Ind Supreme Ct State House Rm 321 Indianapolis IN 46204-2728 Office Phone: 317-232-2548.

**SULLIVAN, FRANK C.,** manufacturing executive; BA, U. N.C., 1983. Various comml. lending corp. fin. 1st Union Nat. Bank and Harris Bank, 1983-87; regional sales mgr. AGR Co. RPM Group, Inc., 1987-89, dir. corp. devel., 1989-91, v.p., 1991-93, CFO, 1993-98, exec. v.p., 1998-99, pres., 1999—, CEO, 2002—. Bd. dir. Timken Co. Bd. mem. Greater Cleveland Chpt., Am. Red Cross, Cleveland Rock & Roll Hall of Fame & Mus. Morehead scholar, 1983. Mem.: Cuyahoga County Bluecoats. Office: RPM International PO Box 777 2628 Pearl Rd Medina OH 44256 Office Phone: 330-273-5090.

**SULLIVAN, G. CRAIG,** household products executive; b. 1940; BS, Boston Coll., 1964. With Procter & Gamble Co., 1964-69, Am. Express Co., 1969-70; regional sales mgr. Clorox Co., Oakland, Calif., 1971-76, v.p. mktg., 1976-78, mgr. food svc. sales devel., mgr. bus. devel., 1978-79, gen. mgr. food svc. products divsn., 1979-81, v.p. food svc. products divsn., 1981, v.p. household products, 1981-89, group v.p. household products, 1989-92, chmn. bd., pres., CEO, 1992-99, chmn. bd., CEO, 1999—2003; ret., 2003.

**SULLIVAN, GEORGE EDWARD,** writer; b. Lowell, Mass. Aug. 11, 1927; s. Timothy Joseph and Cecilia Mary (Shea) S.; m. Muriel Agnes Moran, May 24, 1952; 1 son, Timothy. BS, Fordham U., 1952. Pub. relations mgr. Popular Library, N.Y.C., 1952-55; pub. relations dir. AMF, N.Y.C., 1955-63. Adj. prof. Fordham U. Author: Mathew Brady, His Life and Photographs, 1994(named a Notable Children's Trade Book in Field of Social Studies, Nat. Coun. Social Studies and Children's Book Coun., Teenage Book of Yr. NY Pub. Libr., Recommended Children's Book for Reading and Sharing, 1994, Recommended as a Book of Gt. Interest, GA, Books for Boys, 1998), Slave Ship, The Story of the Henrietta Marie, 1994 (named Best Book of 1994 Selection, Parents Mag., Best Children's Book of Yr. Selection, Children's Book Com., Bank St. Coll. Edn.), The Day Women Got the Vote, 1994, Pitchers: Twenty

Seven of Baseball's Greatest, 1994(named Teenage Book of Yr., NY Pub. Libr., A Recommended Book for Reluctant Young Adult Reader, ALA), Black Artists in Photography, 1995, Women War Spies, 1996, Alamo, 1996, Black Artists as Photographers, 1840-1940, 1996(named Teenage Book of Yr., NY Pub. Libr., A Best Children's Book of Yr. Selection, Children's Book Com., Bank St. Coll. Edn.), Glovemen: Twenty-Seven of Baseball's Greatest, 1996(named a Teenage Book of Yr., NY Pub. Libr., A Recommended Book for Reluctant Young Adult Reader, ALA), Not Guilty: Six Times When Justice Failed, 1996, To the Bottom of the Sea, 1998, Burnin' Rubber: Behind the Scenes in Stock Car Racing, 1998, One Hundred Years in Photographs, 1999, Picturing Lincoln: Famous Photographs that Popularized the President, 1999(Selected as a Notable Social Studies Trade Book, Children's Book Coun., named a Best Children's Book of Yr. Selection, Children's Book Com., Bank St. Coll. Edn.), Portraits of War, Civil War Photographers and Their Work, 2000, One Hundred Years in Photographs, 2000, The Civil War at Sea, 2001 (Selected as a Notable Social Studies Trade Book, Children's Book Coun., named a Teenage Book of Yr., NY Pub. Libr.), In Their Own Words: Lewis & Clark, 2001, In Their Own Words: Harriet Tubman, 2001, In Their Own Words: Helen Keller, 2001 (named a Best Children's Book of Yr. Selection, Children's Book Com., Bank St. Coll. Edn.), Power Football, 2001, In Their Own Words: The Wright Brothers, 2002 (Selected by US Agy. for Internat. Devel. to Promote Reading in North Africa, reprinted in Arabic), In Their Own Words: Abraham Lincoln, 2002 (Named a Best Children's Book of Yr. Selection, Children's Book Com., Bank St. Coll. Edn.), Mr. President: A Book of U.S. Presidents, 2004, The Civil War Photographs of Mathew Brady, 2004, Journalists at Risk: Reporting America's Wars, 2005, Built to Last, 2005, Berenice Abbott, Photographer: An Independent Vision, 2006. Served with USN, 1945-48. Mem. PEN, Authors Guild, Soc. Children's Book Writers & Illustrators. Roman Catholic. Personal E-mail: gjsbooks@rcn.com.

**SULLIVAN, GEORGE MURRAY,** transportation executive, consultant, retired mayor; b. Portland, Oreg., Mar. 31, 1922; s. Harvey Patrick and Viola (Murray) S.; m. Margaret Eagan, Dec. 30, 1947; children: Timothy M., Harvey P. (dec. July 1996), Daniel A., Kevin Shane, Colleen Marie, George Murray, Michael J., Shannon Margaret, Casey Eagan. Student pub. schs.; D.P.A. (hon.), U. Alaska, 1981. Line driver Alaska Freight Lines, Inc., Valdez-Fairbanks, 1942-44; U.S. dep. marshal Alaska Dist., Nenana, 1946-52; mgr. Alaska Freight Lines, 1952-56; Alaska gen. mgr. Consol. Freightways Corp. of Del., Anchorage, 1956-67; mayor of Anchorage, 1967-82; exec. mgr. Alaska Bus. Council, 1968; sr. cons. to pres. Western Air Lines Inc., 1982-87; former legis. liaison for Gov. of Alaska; now cons. Past mem. Nat. Adv. Com. on Oceans and Atmosphere, Joint Fed.-State Land Use Planning Commn.; past chmn. 4-state region 10 adv. com. OEO; mem. Fairbanks City Council, 1955-59, Anchorage City Council, 1965-67, Greater Anchorage Borough Assembly, 1965-67, Alaska Ho. of Reps., 1964-65. Trustee U. Alaska Found.; chmn. Anchorage Conv. and Visitors Bur.; bd. dirs. Western council Boy Scouts Am., 1958-59. Served with U.S. Army, 1944-46. Mem. Nat. Def. Transp. Assn. (life mem., pres. 1962-63), Nat. League Cities (dir.), Pioneers of Alaska, Alaska Mcpl. League (past pres.), Anchorage C. of C. (exec. com. 1963-65, treas. 1965-66, dir.), Alaska Carriers Assn. (exec. com.), Alaska Transp. Conf. (chmn.), U.S. Conf. Mayors (exec. com.), VFW (comdr. Alaska 1952) Clubs: Elks. Home and Office: George M Sullivan Co 1345 W 12th Ave Anchorage AK 99501-4252 Office Phone: 907-272-2918. *America is truly the land of opportunity, and I feel that the success with which God has blessed my life attests to this fact. I have been blessed four times. Not only was I born in America, but I have lived my life in Alaska. My other two blessings are my wonderful and supportive wife and our eight healthy children.*

**SULLIVAN, GLENN D.,** music educator; b. Ridgewood, NJ, Mar. 1, 1975; s. Gerald W. and Beverly Sullivan. MusB Music Mgmt., William Paterson U., 1998. Music instr. Partesi Music Svcs., Inc., South Plainfield, NJ, 1993—. Pvt. music instr., Wayne, NJ, 1991—. Asst. dir. N.J. Diocesan Honors Band, 1998—; asst. music dir. Pentecostal Lighthouse Ch., Paterson, NJ, 1990—98, Midvale Gospel Ch., Wanaque, NJ, 2000—02, 2004—. Mem.: Music Educators Nat. Conf. Avocations: computers, music. Home: 31 Emerson Pl Wayne NJ 07470 E-mail: gds3175@optonline.net.

**SULLIVAN, GORDON R.,** retired career officer; b. Boston, Sept. 25, 1937; s. Russsell Edgar and Penuel Edith (Gordon) S.; m. Miriam Gay Loftus, June 20, 1965; children: John, Mark, Elizabeth. BA in History, Norwich U., 1959, D Mil. Sci. (hon.), 1991; MA in Polit. Sci., U. N.H., 1974. Commd. 2d lt. U.S. Army, 1959, advanced through grades to gen., 1990; student Armor Officer Basic Course U.S. Army Armor Sch., Ft. Knox, Ky., 1959-60; platoon leader Co. B, 1st Medium Tank Bn., 66th Armor, 2d Armored Div., Ft. Hood, Tex., 1960; student Armor Communication Class U.S. Army Armor Sch., Ft. Knox, 1960; communications officer 1st Medium Tank Bn., 66th Armor, 2d Armored Div., Ft. Hood, 1960-61; comdr. Co. A, 1st Medium tank Bn., 66th Armor, 2d Armored Div., Ft. Hood, 1961; bn. communications officer 3d Medium Tank Bn. (Patton), 40th Armor, U.S. Army Pacific, Republic of Korea, 1961-62; platoon leader Co. A 3d Medium Tank Bn., 40th Armor, U.S. Army Pacific, Korea, 1962; asst. civil guard/self def. corps advisor 21st Inf. Div., Mil. Assistance Adv. Group, Vietnam, 1962-63; adminstrv. officer, later exec. asst. Office of Asst. Chief of Staff, J2 Div., Mil. Assistance Command, Vietnam, 1963-64; student Armor Officer Advanced Course U.S. Army Armor Sch., Ft. Knox, 1964-65; S-4 (Logistics) 3d Bn., 32d Armor, 3d Armored Div., U.S. Army Europe, 1965-66; comdr. Co.A, 3d Bn., 32d Armor, 3d Armored Div., U.S. Army Europe, 1966; assignment officer, later staff officer Combat Arms Sect., Mil. Pers. Div., Office of Dep. Chief of Staff for Pers., U.S. Army Europe, 1966-68; student U.S. Army Command Gen. Staff Coll., Ft. Leavenworth, Kans., 1968-69; pers. svcs. officer Plans and Ops Div., G-1, Hdqrs., I Field Force, Vietnam, 1969-70; pers. mgmt. officer Pers. Actions Sect., Armor Br., Office of Pers. Ops., Washington, 1970-73; student Internat. Rels. U. N.H., Durham, 1973-74; comdr. 4th Bn., 73d Armor, 1st Inf. Div. (Forward), U.S. Army Europe, 1975-76; chief of staff 1st Inf. Div. (Forward), U.S. Army Europe, 1976-77; student U.S. Army War Coll., Carlisle Barracks, Pa., 1977-78; asst. chief of staff G-3 (Ops.)/Dir. Plans and Tng., 1st Inf. Div. and Fort Riley, Kans., 1978-79, G-3 (Ops.), VII Corps, U.S. Army Europe, 1980-81; comdr. 1st Brigade, 3d Armored Div., U.S. Army Europe, 1981-83; chief of staff 3d Armored Div., U.S. Army Europe, 1983; asst. comdt. U.S. Army Armor Sch., Ft. Knox, 1983-85; dep. chief of Staff for support Cen. Army Group, Europe, 1985-87; dep. comdt. U.S. Army Command and Gen. Staff Coll., Ft. Leavenworth, 1987-88; comdg. gen. 1st Inf. Div. (Mechanized), Ft. Riley, 1988-89; dep. chief of staff for ops. and plans U.S. Army/Army Sr. Mem., Mil. Staff Com., UN, Washington, 1989-90; vice chief of staff Office of the Chief of Staff, U.S. Army, Washington, 1990-91; chief of staff U.S. Army, Washington, 1991-95. Editor: Portrait of an Army, 1991. Decorated D.S.M., Def. Superior Svc. medal, Legion of Merit, Bronze Star, Purple Heart, Meritorius Svc. medal with oak leaf cluster, Joint Svc. Commendation medal, Army Commendation medal with oak leaf cluster, Army Achievement medal, Combat Infantryman badge. Mem. Assn. of U.S. Army, Armor Assn. Office: Assn of the US Army 2425 Wilson Blvd Arlington VA 22201

**SULLIVAN, JAMES EDWARD,** poet; b. Cohasset, Mass., July 11, 1928; s. James J. Jr. and E. Louise (Hyland) S.; m. Frances Elizabeth Lynch, Aug. 11, 1963 (dec. Oct. 1976); children: Julia Marietta, John Franklin Joseph. AB, Boston Coll., 1948, MA, 1950. Dir. Woods Meml. Libr., Barre, Mass., 1967-94; ptnr. Crisis and Climax, 1989—. Lectr. in history, Boston Coll., 1962-63. Author: American Town: Barre, Mass., 1774-1974, 1974, In Order of Appearance: 400 Poems, 1988, numerous poems, plays; weekly contbr. original poetry Barre (Mass.) Gazette, 1981—. Selectman, Town of Barre, 1986-92, bd. chmn. 1988-92. Sgt. US Army, 1950-52. Mem.: Am. Legion (past comdr. Barre Post 2). Democrat. Roman Catholic. Home: PO Box 451 Barre MA 01005-0451

**SULLIVAN, JAMES F.,** physicist, researcher; b. Cin., Mar. 7, 1943; s. James E. and Alma L. (Lienesch) S.; m. Sylvia J. Kasselmann, Aug. 16, 1969; 1 child, Robert L. BS, Xavier U., 1965, MS, 1969. Instr. physics Brebeuf Prep. Sch., Indpls., 1965-67, OMI Coll. Applied Sci., U. Cin., 1968-71, asst. prof.

physics, 1971-77, assoc. prof. physics, 1977-88, prof. physics, 1988—; dept. head math., physics, computing tech. U. Cin. OMI Coll. of Applied Sci., 2002. Summer faculty researcher Solar Energy Rsch. Inst., Golden, Colo., 1980; mem. high sch. evaluation team N. Ctrl. Assn., Cin., 1983-85; vis. prof. Arcada Polytechnic Inst., Finland, 2002; rep. U. Cin. Grad. Ceremony, Delta Acad. Mansoura, Egypt, 2004. Author: Technical Physics, 1988; Co-author: Laboratory Manual for General Physics, 1973, 83, 90, 92, Physics for Technology Laboratory Manual, 1995, 97. Organizer of events St. Xavier H.S. Alumni, Cin., 1983—; vol. examiner Am. Radio Relay League for U.S. Fed. Comm. Commn., Newington, Conn., 1984—; judge physics category Ohio State Sci. Fair, Delaware, Ohio, 1986—; chief negotiator faculty and librs. U. Cin., 1995. Received John B. Hart award (disting. svc. to Southern Ohio sect. of Am. Assn. of Physics Tchrs.), 2001; named Faculty Mem. of Yr., Gamma Alpha chpt. Tau Alpha Phi, 1983. Fellow Ohio Acad. Sci.; mem. AAUP (v.p. U. Cin. chpt. 1994-96), Am. Assn. Physics Tchrs. (founder, past pres., assoc. sec. So. Ohio sect. 1993—, com. on instrnl. media 1994-98, chief organizer and presenter Fundamentals of Radio workshop Toronto 1985, Columbus, Ohio 1986, Bozeman, Mont. 1987, Orono, Maine 1992, Boise, Idaho 1993, South Bend, Ind. 1994, College Park, Md. 1996, Denver, 1997, com. on metric measurements, 2000-03), Ohio Valley Amateur Radio Assn. (pres. 1997—), Am. Soc. Engring. Edn. Achievements include supervising successful attempt of OMI Coll. Applied Sci. contact of shuttle Challenger during STS-51F mission, 1985. Office: Univ Cin 2220 Victory Pkwy Cincinnati OH 45206-2822

**SULLIVAN, JAMES GERALD,** small business owner; b. Bad Axe, Mich., Sept. 13, 1935; s. John Thomas and Frances Eugena (O'Henley) Sullivan; m. Florence Marie Tack, Sept. 12, 1959; children: Kevin Michael, Kathleen Marie. Student, U. Detroit 1957—58, Highland Park Coll., 1959—60. Owner Jerry's Barber Shop, Kinde, Bad Axe, Mich., 1963-66, 79—; purchasing agt. Thumb Elec. Coop., Ubly, Mich., 1966-79, Walbro Corp., Cass City, Mich., 1979-80; sales rep. Thumb Blanket, Bad Axe, Mich., 1980-81, Sta. WLEW, Bad Axe, 1981-82; regional mgr. Pri Am. Fin. Svcs., Bad Axe, 1985—; treas. Colfax Twp., Bad Axe, 1979-90; rural letter carrier U.S. Postal Svc., Bad Axe, 1982-98, ret., 1998. Loss clk., Toplis & Harding Wagner & Gliddon, Detroit, 1959-61; inventory control clk., Carrick Products Co., Royal Oak, Mich., 1957-59; Eucahristic minister. Pres. Huron County Twp. Assn., Mich., 1988—90; leader Boy Scouts Am., Bad Axe, 1975—77; lector Ushers Club, Sacred Heart Ch., Eucharistic min. With U.S. Army, 1954—56. Mem. Huron County Rural Letter Carriers Assn. (pres. 1988-2003), Armed Forces Vets. Club of the Nat. Rural Letter Carriers Assn. (Mich. divsn., state sec. 1999—), Am. Legion, 4-H Club (pres. 1948-50), Lions (pres. 1979-80, 2006-07), Cmty. Club (pres. 1976-77), KC (mem. coun. #1546), Tip of the Thumb Dance Club (pres. 2005). Republican. Roman Catholic. Avocations: gardening, golf, swimming, fishing. Home: 122 W Richardson Rd Bad Axe MI 48413-9108

**SULLIVAN, JAMES KIRK,** management consultant; b. Greenwood, SC, Aug. 25, 1935; s. Daniel Jones and Addie (Brown) S.; m. Elizabeth Miller, June 18, 1960; children: Hal N., Kim J. BS in Chemistry, Clemson U., 1957, MS, 1964; PhD, 1966; postgrad. program for sr. execs., MIT, 1975; DSc (hon.), U. Idaho, 1990. Prodn. supr. FMC Corp., South Charleston, W.Va., 1957-62, tech. supt. Pocatello, Idaho, 1966-69, mktg. mgr. N.Y.C., 1969-70; v.p. govtl. and environ. affairs Boise (Idaho) Cascade Corp., 1970-98; exec. com., chmn. trust and investment com., dist. bd. dirs. Key Bank of Idaho, 1983—2006; sr. ptnr. Veritas Advisors, LLP, 1999—2006. Bd. dirs., chmn. audit com. Key Trust Co. of the West; chmn. adv. bd. U. Idaho Coll. Engring., 1966-70, 80-87, centennial campaign, 1987-89, rsch. found., 1980-82; mem. Accreditation Bd. Engring. and Tech., Inc., 1994-99; bd. dirs. Pub. Employees Retirement Sys. of Idaho, St. Al's Regional Med. Ctr.; bd. trustees, chmn. bldg. com.; chmn Idaho State Rep. Party; mem. Rep. Nat. Com. Contbr. articles to profl. jours.; patentee in field. Mem. Coll. of Forest and Recreation Resources com. Clemson U., Idaho Found. for Pvt. Enterprise and Econ. Edn., Idaho Rsch. Found., Inc., Idaho Task Force on Higher Edn.; bd. dirs. Idaho Found. for Excellence in Higher Edn., Exptl. Program to Stimulate Competitive Rsch. NSF, N.W. Nazarene Coll., 1988-90, Boise Philharm., 1996-99, mem. Len B. Jordan Pub Affairs Symposium; trustee Idaho Children's Emergency Fund, 1984-90; trustee Bishop Kelly H.S., 1987-89; chmn. adv. bd. U. Idaho Coll. Engring., Am. Forest and Paper Assn., Govtl. Affairs Com., Environ. Com., Options Adv. Group, Idaho State Rep. Com.; bd. dirs. Boise Master Chorale, 1995-98; pres. Ore-Ida coun. Boy Scouts Am., St. Al's Found.; trustee St. Al's Med Ctr. 1st lt. U.S. Army, 1958-59. Recipient Presdl. Citation U. Idaho, 1990, Disting. Eagle award Boy Scouts Am., 2005, Good Shepard award Presbyn. Ch., 2005. Mem. AIChE, Am. Chem. Soc., Bus. Week Found. (chmn. Bus. Week 1980), Am. Forest and Paper Assn. (environ. and health coun., product and tech. com., solid waste task force), Bus. Roundtable (environ. com.), Idaho Assn. Commerce and Industry (past chmn. bd. dirs.), C. of C. of U.S. (pub. affairs com.). Republican. Home: 5206 Sorrento Cir Boise ID 83704-2347 Office Phone: 208-863-2851. Personal E-mail: j.kirksullivan@att.net.

**SULLIVAN, JAMES LEO,** organization executive; b. Somerville, Mass., Dec. 11, 1925; s. James Christopher and Anna Agnes (Kilmartin) S.; m. Anne Dorothy Hevner, Jan. 20, 1951; children: Maura, Mark, Lianne, Christopher. BS in History and Govt. cum laude, Boston Coll., 1950, MEd in Adminstrn. and Fin., 1958; DCS (hon.), Suffolk U., 1990. Asst. town mgr., Arlington, Mass., 1957-62; town mgr. Watertown, Conn., 1962-65; chief adminstrv. officer Town of Milton, Mass., 1965-68; city mgr. Cambridge, Mass., 1968-70, 74-81, Lowell, Mass., 1970-74; sr. rsch. asst. MIT, Cambridge, 1970-71; pres. Greater Boston C. of C., 1981-91, H.M.S. Mktg., Boston, 1991—. Chmn. Mass. Gov.'s Local Govt. Adv. Com., 1978; del. to Orgn. Econ. and Coop. Devel., Paris, 1979; chmn. New Eng.-Can. Bus. Coun., 1983; pres. Careers for Later Years, 1983; bd. dirs. Input-Output Computer Svcs., Imugen Inc., Mass. Bus. Devel. Corp., New Eng. Cert. Devel. Corp. Trustee Emerson Coll., 1984-88, mem. fin. and investment com., 1985-88; bd. dirs. Bunker Hill C.C. Coll. Found., 1988—; mem. Adv. Com. on Reorgn. of Mass. Ct. Sys., 1991—, chmn. budget subcom. 1991—; bd. overseers Univ. Hosp. Boston. With USN, 1943-46. Mem. Mass. League of Cities and Towns (pres. 1978), Mass. Mayors Assn., Internat. City Mgmt. Assn., Nat. League Cities, Am. C. of C. Execs. (bd. dirs. 1988—), World Trade Club (bd. govs. 1986—). E-mail: jls1225@aol.com.

**SULLIVAN, JAMES M.,** federal agency administrator; Attended, Bunker Hill Coll., Northeastern U. Firefighter, EMT, Arlington, Mass., 1976—80; with U.S. Marshals Svc., 1980—, dep. U.S. marshal, acting. U.S. marshal So. Dist. Calif.; dep. dir. U.S. Nat. Ctrl. Bur. INTERPOL, 2000—03, dir., 2003—. Sgt. USMC, Vietnam. Office: US Dept Justice INTERPOL US Nat Ctrl Bur Washington DC 20530 E-mail: james.sullivan@usdoj.gov.

**SULLIVAN, JENNIFER CASE,** research scientist; b. Watertown, N.Y., Feb. 2, 1974; d. Roger and Jane Slater Case; m. Gregory Sullivan, Oct. 9, 1999; children: Margaret Elizabeth, Kelly Louise. PhD, Albany Med. Coll., 2000. Postdoctoral fellow Med. Coll. of Ga., Augusta, 2000—03, asst. rsch. scientist, 2003—. Contbr. articles to profl. jours. Sponsor Am. Heart Assn., 2002—06. Recipient Rsch. Recognition award, Am. Physiol. Soc., 2003; grantee, NIH; H. Victor Moore Rsch. grant, MCG Children's Med. Ctr., 2003, Postdoctoral Fellowship in Physiol. Genomics, Am. Physiol. Soc., 2001-2003, Advanced Predoctoral Fellowship in Pharmacology and Toxicology, Pharma Found., 1999-2000. Mem.: Nat. Kidney Found., Am. Heart Assn., Am. Physiol. Soc. Office: Med Coll of Ga 1459 Laney Walker Blvd Augusta GA 30912 Office Phone: 706-721-6164. Business E-Mail: jsullivan@mail.mcg.edu.

**SULLIVAN, JERRY STEPHEN,** electronics executive; b. Havre, Mont., July 17, 1945; s. Patrick Joseph and Evangeline (O'Neil) S.; m. Sharon Lee Horton, June 17, 1967; children: Garrett, Mindy, Darren. BS, U. Colo., 1967, MS, 1969, PhD, 1970; advanced mgmt. program, Harvard U. Bus. Sch., 1986. Tech. mgr. N.V. Philips Co., Eindhoven, Netherlands, 1971-75; group dir. N.Am. Philips Corp., Briarcliff Manor, NY, 1975-80; dir. Tektronix, Beaverton, Oreg., 1981-83, div. gen. mgr. 1983-85, corp. dir., 1985-88; v.p.

Microelectronics & Computer Tech. Corp., Austin, Tex., 1988-92; pres. CEO, Design Techs. Inc., Austin, 1992—. Chmn. bd. MBA Techs., Inc., Phoenix; bd. dirs. Sherpa Corp., San Jose, Calif., Ontos, Inc. Boston, MBA Tech. Inc., Phoenix; mem. adv. bd. Ctr. Integrated Sys., Stanford U., Palo Alto, Calif., 1982—. Mem. adv. com. Coll. Engring., U. Tex., Austin, 1989—, bd. dirs. Edn. Found., 1990—. Mem. IEEE, Am. Phys. Soc., Assn. Computing Machinery, Am. Mgmt. Assn., Nat. Assn. Corp. Dirs. Avocations: scuba diving, golf, chess, sailing. Office: Design Techs Inc 107 Ranch Rd 620 S Austin TX 78734-3942

**SULLIVAN, JIM,** artist; b. Providence, Apr. 1, 1939; s. James Henry, Jr. and Frances Winifred (Welch) S.; m. Marie-Louise Paulson. BFA, R.I. Sch. Design, 1961; postgrad., Stanford U., 1962-63. Prof. emeritus art Bard Coll., Annandale-on-Hudson, NY, 1966-95, prof. emeritus, 1995—. One-man shows Paley and Lowe Gallery, N.Y.C., 1971, 73, Henri Gallery, Washington, 1974, Fischback Gallery, N.Y.C., 1974, Willard Gallery, N.Y.C., 1978, Nancy Hoffman Gallery, N.Y.C., 1983, 92, 84, 86, 88, 2004, Foker Skulima Gallery, Berlin, Germany, Anne Jaffe Gallery Bay Harbor Islands, Fla. 1990; exhibited in group shows including, Whitney Mus., Mus. Modern Art, Columbus Gallery Fine Arts, Worcester Art Mus., Corcoran Gallery Art, Washington; pub. collections including Met. Mus., Whitney Mus., Albany State Mus., Wadsworth Atheneum, Philip Morris INc., Owens Corning Coll., Amerada Hess, Carie Secrist Gallery, 2006. Juror Fulbright Fellowship Program, 1996, 1999; bd. dirs. Schoharie Land Trust. Recipient Hinda and Richard Rosenthal award, Am. Acad. Arts and Letters, 1973; grantee Stanford U., 1962—63, R.I. Sch. Design European Honors program, Rome, 1960—61, Nat. Endowment for Arts, 1982; Fulbright fellow, 1961—62, Guggenheim fellow, 1972—73. Address: Box 219 Rum Hill Rd Jefferson NY 12093 also: 59 Wooster St New York NY 10012

**SULLIVAN, JOHN,** news correspondent; Corr. Trenton Bur. NY Times. Office: NY Times Trenton Bur PO Box 021 Trenton NJ 08625-0021 also: NJ State House 125 W State St Trenton NJ 08625-0021 Office Phone: 609-292-5173 ext. 3. E-mail: jsullivan@nytimes.com.*

**SULLIVAN, JOHN A.,** congressman; b. Tulsa, Okla., Jan. 1, 1965; s. Daniel and Mag Sullivan; m. Judith Marie Beck; children: Tommy, Meredith, Sydney, Daniel. BA, Northeastern State U., Tahlequah, Okla., 1992. Real estate broker; mem. Okla. State Ho. Reps., 1995—2002, US Congress from 1st Okla. dist., 2002—, mem. energy and commerce com., asst. majority whip. Republican. Office: US Ho Reps 114 Cannon Ho Office Bldg Washington DC 20515-3601 Office Phone: 202-225-2211.*

**SULLIVAN, JOHN CORNELIUS, JR.,** lawyer; b. Erie, Pa., Oct. 23, 1927; s. John Cornelius and Catherine J. S.; m. Helen E. Kennedy, Feb. 3, 1951; children: John III, Timi Ann, Michael, Elizabeth. BA in Econs., Allegheny Coll., 1953; LLB, Dickinson Sch. Law, 1959. Bar: Pa. 1960, U.S. Supreme Ct. 1976. Sales rep. IBM Corp., 1953-56; mem. firm Nissley, Clecker & Fearen, Harrisburg, Pa., 1959-63; of counsel Nauman, Smith, Shissler & Hall, Harrisburg, 1964—. asst. city solicitor City of Harrisburg, 1964-68, city solicitor, 1968-70; gen. counsel Harrisburg Redevel. Authority, 1964-68, Harrisburg Mcpl. Authority, 1964-87; solicitor Silver-Spring Twp., 1970-81; dir. accounts and fin. City of Harrisburg, 1963; mem. Pa. House of Reps., 1963-64. Assoc. editor Dickinson Law Rev., 1958-59; editor Dauphin County Reporter, 1961-63. Chmn. bd. dirs. Harrisburg Pub. Library, 1965-73; bd. dirs., sec. Harrisburg Hosp.; bd. dirs. Harrisburg Hosp. Found., 1975-89. Mem. Pa. Bar Assn., Dauphin County Bar Assn. (past. dir.), The Pa. Soc. (N.Y.C.), Phi Gamma Delta. Home: 107 Sample Bridge Rd Mechanicsburg PA 17050-1940 Office: 200 N 3rd St Fl D18 Harrisburg PA 17101-1518

**SULLIVAN, JOHN DAVID,** business association executive; b. Bisbee, Ariz., Jan. 13, 1948; s. Lloyd John and Marjorie Jane (Kingsbury) S.; m. Patricia Mary Mathis, 1999. BA, U. Pitts., 1969, MA, 1972, PhD, 1983. Rschr. Inst. for Econ. Rsch., L.A., 1974-75; mem. rsch. staff Pres. Ford Com., Washington, 1976; dir. bus. edn. U.S.C. of C., Washington, 1977-82; asst. dir. The Democracy Program, Washington, 1982-83; program coord. Ctr. for Internat. Pvt. Enterprise, Washington, 1984-89; dir. Washington office Internat. Ctr. for Econ. Growth, 1989-91; exec. dir. Ctr. for Internat. Pvt. Enterprise, Washington, 1991—. Trustee Internat. Devel. Conf., Washington, 1988—. Contbr. articles to jours. in field; mem. editl. bd. Econ. Reform Today, 1991—. Speechwriter, vol. Reagan-Bush campaign, Washington, 1980, 84. Mem. Internat. Studies Assn. Republican. Roman Catholic. Avocations: photography, cooking. Office: Ctr for Internat Pvt Enterprise 1615 H St NW Washington DC 20062-0001

**SULLIVAN, JOHN DOMINIC,** theater producer, writer; b. La Crosse, Wis., Oct. 6, 1963; s. Arthur John and Eleanor Elizabeth (Skemp) Sullivan. BFA, U. Wis., Superior, 1986. Asst. dir. Duluth Playhouse, Minn., 1985; freelance arts cons. La Crosse, Wis., 1993—; play prodr. Great River Steamboat Co., La Crosse, Wis., 1996—97; stage mgr. La Crosse Cmty. Theatre, Wis., 1997; mng. dir. Fairbanks Shakespeare Theatre, Alaska, 1997. Author: (plays) Murder on the Mississippi, 1996, The Cabaret Killer, 1997. Social concerns com. mem. St. Joseph Cathedral, La Crosse, Wis., 1995—. Democrat. Roman Catholic.

**SULLIVAN, JOHN F., III,** lawyer; BBA with highest honors, Univ. Okla., 1984; JD with honors, Univ. Houston, 1987. Bar: Tex. 1987, US Dist. Ct. (so., ea., no., and we. dists.) Tex., US Ct. Appeals (5th cir.), bar: U.S. Supreme Ct. Joined Fulbright & Jaworski LLP, 1987—, now ptnr. and chair, hiring com. Houston. Assoc. editor Houston Law Rev. Trustee Oncology Svcs. Found. Fellow: Tex. Bar Found., Houston Bar Found.; mem.: ABA, Tex. Assn. Civil Trial and Appellate Specialists, State Bar of Tex., Houston Bar Assn., Tex. Assn. Def. Counsel, Order of Coif. Beta Gamma Sigma. Office: Fulbright & Jaworski LLP Ste 5100 1301 McKinney Houston TX 77010-3095 Office Phone: 713-651-5637. Office Fax: 713-651-5246. Business E-Mail: jsullivan@fulbright.com.

**SULLIVAN, JOHN J.,** lawyer; BA, Brown U.; JD, Columbia U. Law clk. to Justice David H. Souter U.S. Supreme Ct.; counselor to asst. atty. gen. office of legal counsel U.S. Dept. Justice; ptnr. Mayer, Brown, Rowe & Maw, LLP, 1993—2004; legal counsel, dep. gen. counsel US Dept. Def., Washington, 2004—05; gen. counsel US Dept. Commerce, Washington, 2005—. Office: US Dept Commerce Herbert Clark Hoover Bldg 14th St and Constitution Ave NW Rm 5870 Washington DC 20230 Office Phone: 202-482-4772. Office Fax: 202-482-0042.

**SULLIVAN, JOHN W.,** lawyer; b. NYC, Oct. 30, 1947; BA, SUNY, Stony Brook, 1968; JD, NYU, 1973. Bar: NY 1974, US Dist. Ct. No., So., Ea. & We. Districts NY. Ptnr. Wilson, Elser, Moskowitz, Edelman & Dicker LLP, NYC. Mem.: ABA, NY County Lawyer's Assn., Assn. of the Bar of the City of NY, NY State Bar Assn. Office: Wilson Elser Moskowitz Edelman & Dicker LLP 150 E 42nd St 23rd Fl New York NY 10017-5639 Office Phone: 212-490-3000 ext. 2454. Office Fax: 212-490-3038. Business E-Mail: sullivanj@wemed.com.

**SULLIVAN, JOSEPH PETER,** risk and insurance management consultant; b. Boston, Sept. 8, 1939; s. Joseph Francis and Mary Anna S.; m. Rachael Anne Cullen, Dec. 22, 1974; children: Philip, Sandra, Susan, Frederick. B Gen. Studies, U. Nebr., 1968; MA, U. No. Colo., 1973, Cen. Mich. U. 1976. Sr. acct. exec. Arkwright Ins., Greenwich, Conn., 1977-83; v.p. Frenkel & Co., N.Y.C., 1983-84; sr. account exec. Republic Hogg Robinson, N.Y.C., 1984-85; v.p. Alexander & Alexander, N.Y.C., 1985-92, Hugh Wood Inc., N.Y.C., 1992-93, Crawford-THG, N.Y.C., 1993-98; sr. v.p. Frontline Ins. Mgrs., Tampa, Fla., 1998—. Assoc. Miller-Heiman Internat., 1986-92; instr. Dale Carnegie and Assocs., 1980-87; ajd. prof. ins. The Coll. of Ins., N.Y.C., 1991-98. Mem. membership com. Red Cross, Rep. Club; bd. advisors The Salvation Army. With U.S. Army, 1956—77, with ETO, Korea and Vietnam. Decorated Bronze Star. Mem. Assn. Former Intelligence Officers (life), Ret. Officers Assn. (bd. dirs. Knickerbocker chpt.), Soc. CPCU's, Am. Soc. CLU's, Nat.

Assn. Health Underwriters, Profl. Liability Underwriting Soc., N.Y. Soc. Security Analysts, Soc. Competitive Intelligence Profls., Toastmasters, N.Y. Athletic Club, Rotary, Masons, Shriners. Republican. Roman Catholic. Avocations: american history, photography, collecting old photographic prints and antique photographic equipment. Home and Office: 15920 Dawson Ridge Dr Tampa FL 33647-1324 Office Phone: 813-903-8073. Personal E-mail: sully15920@earthlink.net.

**SULLIVAN, KATHLEEN ANN,** secondary school educator; b. Palmerton, Pa., Feb. 15, 1946; d. Henry Aloysius and Elizabeth Rose (Pennell) S. AAS, Harriman (N.Y.) Coll., 1966; student. Columbia U., N.Y.C., 1966-69; BS, St. Peter's Coll., Jersey City, 1971. Cert. English educator, N.J. Tchr. 6th grade Immaculate Conception, Bronx, N.Y., 1965-67, tchr. 7th grade, 1967-68; tchr. 8th grade St. Fortunata, Bklyn., 1968-69; tchr. 7th grade St. Augustine, Union City, N.J., 1969-71, tchr. 8th grade, 1971—, vice prin., 1971—. Mem. adv. bd. St. Augustine CYO, Union City, N.J., 1971—, Coll. St. Elizabeth, Morristown, N.J., 1986-92; trustee Weehawken (N.J.) Libr. Bd., 1976-2000. Mem. Natl. Cath. Edn. Assn., Nat. Coun. Tchrs. Math., Assn. Tchrs. Math. N.J. Home: 1400 70th St Apt 1 North Bergen NJ 07047 Office: St Augustine School 3920 New York Ave Union City NJ 07087-4887

**SULLIVAN, KATHLEEN MARIE,** lawyer, educator, former dean; BA, Cornell U., 1976, Oxford (Eng.) U., 1978; JD, Harvard U., 1981. Law clk. Hon. James L. Oakes U.S. Ct. Appeals (2d cir.), 1981-82; pvt. practice, 1982-84; asst. prof. Harvard U., Cambridge, Mass., 1984-89, prof., 1989-93, Stanford U. Law Sch., Calif., 1993—, Robert E. Paradise fellow, 1995-96, Stanley Morrison prof., 1996—, dean, Richard E. Lang prof. law, 1999—2004; of counsel Quinn Emanuel Urquhart Oliver & Hedges LLP, Redwood Shores, Calif., 2005—. Vis. prov. U. So. Calif. Law Ctr., 1991, Stanford U., 1992; lectr., commentator on constnl. law. Co-editor: (with Gerald Gunther) Constitutional Law, 15th edit., 2004. Named one of 100 Most Influential Lawyers Nat. Law Jour., 2000; recipient Albert M. Sacks-Paul A. Freund award for Teaching Excellence, Harvard, 1992, John Bingham Hurlbut award for excellence in tchg. Stanford U., 1996. Fellow Am. Acad. Arts and Scis, Am. Philosophical Soc.; bd. trustees, The Century Found. Office: Quinn Emanuel Urquhart Oliver & Hedges LLP 555 Twin Dolphin Dr Ste 560 Redwood City CA 94065 also: Stanford U Law Sch Crown Quadrangle 559 Nathan Abbott Way Stanford CA 94305-8610 Office Phone: 650-801-5000. Business E-Mail: sullivan@law.stanford.edu.

**SULLIVAN, KATHRYN D.,** geologist, former astronaut, former science association executive; b. Paterson, N.J., Oct. 3, 1951; d. Donald P. and Barbara K. Sullivan (dec.). BS in Earth Scis., U. Calif., Santa Cruz, 1973; PhD in Geology, Dalhousie U., Halifax, N.S., Can., 1978; Dr. (hon.), Halhousie, Halifax, N.S., Can., 1985, SUNY, Utica, 1990, Stevens Inst., 1992, Ohio Dominican U., 1998, Kent State U., 2002; Doctorate (hon.), St. Bonaventure U., 2005. Astronaut NASA, 1979—93, mission specialist flight STS-41G, 1984, mission specialist flight STS-31, 1990, payload comdr. flight STS-45, 1992; chief scientist NOAA, Washington, 1993—96; pres., CEO Ctr. Sci. and Industry, Columbus, Ohio, 1996—2005, sci. advisor. Adj. prof. Rice U., Houston, 1985-92, geology, Ohio State U., Columbus, Ohio; mem. Nat. Commn. on Space, 1985-86; mem. exec. panel Chief of Naval Ops., 1988-96; chair, Ohio Aerospace and Defense Adv. Coun., 2003; mem. Nat. Sci. Bd., 2005—; served on Pews Oceans Commn.; advisor, Nat. Geographic, Smithsonian Inst., Pub. TV; bd. dirs. Am. Electric Power. Oceanography officer, Capt. USNR; private pilot. Recipient Space Flight medal NASA, 1984, 90, 92, Exceptional Svc. medal, 1988, 91, Nat. Air and Space Mus. trophy Smithsonian Instn., 1985, Outstanding Leadership medal, 1992, AAS Space Flight Achievement award, 1991, AAS Prather Eva award, 1992, Lone Sailor award, US Navy Meml. Found., 1997, Juliette award for Nat. Women of Distinction, Girl Scouts U.S.A., 2002, Aviation Week & Space Tech. Aerospace Legend award, 2005; named one of Ten Outstanding Young People of the World award, Jaycees Internat., 1987, Ten Outstanding Young Americans award, US Jaycees, 1987; inductee Ohio Veteran's Hall of Fame, 2001, Ohio Women's Hall of Fame, 2002, Astronaut Hall of Fame, 2004. Fellow AAAS; mem. AIAA (Haley Space Flight award, 1991, Legends Aerospace Laureate 2005), Geol. Soc. Am., Am. Geophys. Union, Soc. Women Geographers, Nat. Sci. Bd. (Public Svc. award, 2003), Explorers Club, Woods Hole Oceanographic Institution, Assn. Space Explorers. First Am. woman to walk in space.

**SULLIVAN, KATHRYN MEARA,** telecommunications industry executive; b. Schenectady, NY, Sept. 20, 1942; d. Vincent Thomas and Agnes (Pendergast) Meara; m. Paul William Sullivan; children: Mary Margaret, Paul Hammond, Patricia Eileen. BS in Physics, Bucknell U., 1964; MBA, Fairleigh Dickinson U., 1981. Software developer GE Corp., Phila., 1964-65; account exec. Honeywell Corp., Phila., 1975-77; regional sales mgr. Nicolet Instrument Corp., Northvale, NJ, 1977-81; mktg. mgr. AT&T, Basking Ridge, NJ, 1981-83, bus. devel. mgr. Berkeley Heights, NJ, 1983-86; pres. AT&T-Pixel Machines, Somerset, NJ, 1986-90; dir. sales ops. and support AT&T Computer Sys., Morristown, NJ, 1990-91, dir. sales transition Parsippany, NJ, 1991-92; dir. info. svcs. AT&T Bus. Commn. Svcs., Parsippany, 1992-93; dir. bus. applications and info. svcs. AT&T, Bedminster, NJ, 1993-95, dir. cross market product mgmt., 1995-96, dir. bus. transformation team, 1997-98, v.p. bus. markets and alliance mgmt. Europe, Mid. East, Africa, 1998—2000. Chairperson career options for women com. YWCA, Plainfield, NJ, 1989-91; bd. dirs. Marco Island Civic Assn., 2003—, treas., 2004, 05; bd. dirs. Marco Island Police Found., 2004—; Citizens for a Better Marco, 2004-05; Marco Island Found. for the Arts, 2005—. Recipient Anthony Gervino award Fairleigh Dickinson U., 1989, Pinnacle award, 1991. Mem. Nat. Computer Graphics Assn. (assoc. mem., com. bd. dirs. 1989—). Avocations: reading, travel. Personal E-mail: pandksullivan@yahoo.com.

**SULLIVAN, KENNETH WAYNE,** engineer; b. N.Y.C., Apr. 15, 1957; s. William A. and Helen J. Sullivan; m. Christina A. Eastwood, Sept. 10, 1983 (div. Apr. 1997); children: Daniel, Sarah. AAS, SUNY, Farmingdale, 1978, BS, 2003. Draftsman, jr. designer Cosentini Assoc., N.Y.C., NY, 1981—84; sr. designer Syska & Hennessy Engrs., N.Y.C., NY, 1984—88; project engr. Sikorski Engring. Assn., Jericho, NY, 1990—93, Lehr Assocs., N.Y.C., 1993—99, Sear Brown, Melville, NY, 1999—2003; project mgr. Estee Lauder Co., 2003—05; project engr. AKF Engrs., N.Y.C., 2005—. Recipient award, Am. Sch. and Univ. Archtl. Portfolio, 1997. Mem.: ASHRAE, Prevect Mgmt. Inst., Nat. Trust Hist. Preservation, Delta Mu Delta. Roman Catholic. Avocations: reading, history, music, running. Home: 21 Ferney St Hicksville NY 11801-5147 Office: AKF Engrs 1501 Broadway New York NY 10036 E-mail: sullk11801@yahoo.com

**SULLIVAN, KEVIN B.,** lieutenant governor, former state legislator; b. Hartford, Conn., Aug. 20, 1949; s. John (dec.) and Gwendolyn Price (Bancroft) S.; m. Carolyn Thornberry, 1985. AB, Trinity Coll., 1971; JD, U. Conn., 1982. Polit. cons. in pvt. practice, West Hartford, Conn., 1973-74; adminstrv. clk. com. Conn. Ho. of Reps., Hartford, 1974-76; legis. asst. State Commr. Edn., 1976-81; atty. Byrn Slater Sandler Shulman & Rouse, Hartford, 1981—; councilman Town of West Hartford, 1981-86, mayor, 1983-85, dep. mayor, 1985-86; mem. from Dist. 5 Conn. Senate, Hartford, 1986—2004, Pro Tempore, 1997—2004; lt. gov. State of Conn., 2004—. Chmn. edn. com., mem. internship and transp. coms., dep. minority leader Conn. State Senate. Mem. ABA, Hartford Bar Assn., Greater Hartford Jaycees (Man of Yr. 1983), Pi Gamma Mu. Founded State Capitol Vietnam Veterens Meml. Democrat. Office: Office Lt Governor Rm 304 State Capitol Hartford CT 06106 Office Phone: 860-524-7384. Office Fax: 860-524-7304. E-mail: ltgovernor.sullivan@ct.gov.*

**SULLIVAN, KEVIN F.,** federal official; b. Chgo., 1958; m. Jo Anne Y. Sullivan; 4 children. BS, Purdue U., 1980; MS in Mass Comm., Iona. With Dallas Mavericks; v.p. sports comm. NBC, 2000—04; sr. v.p. comm. and media rels. NBC Universal, 2004—05; asst. sec. for comm. & outreach US Dept. Edn., Washington, 2005; asst. to Pres. for comm. The White House, Washington, 2006—. Office: The White House 1600 Pennsylvania Ave Washington DC 20500 Office Phone: 202-401-0768.*

**SULLIVAN, LAURA PATRICIA,** lawyer, insurance company executive; b. Des Moines, Oct. 16, 1947; d. William and Patricia S. BA, Cornell Coll., Iowa, 1971; JD, Drake U., 1972. Bar: Iowa 1972. Various positions Ins. Dept. Iowa, Des Moines, 1972-75; various legal positions State Farm Mut. Auto Ins. Co., Bloomington, Ill., 1975-81, sec. and counsel, 1981-88, v.p., counsel and sec., 1988—; v.p., sec., dir. State Farm Cos. Found., 1985—; sec. State Farm Lloyd's, Inc., 1987—; v.p., counsel and sec. State Farm Fire and Casualty Co., 1988—, State Farm Gen. Ins. Co., 1988—, also bd. dirs.; v.p. counsel, sec., dir. State Farm Life and Accident Assurance Co.; v.p. counsel, sec. State Farm Annuity and Life Assurance Co., State Farm Life Ins. Co.; dir. State Farm Indemnity Co., Bloomington, Ill., 1995—; sec., dir. State Farm Fla. Ins. Co., 1998—. Bd. dirs. Ins. Inst. for Hwy. Safety, Nat. Conf. Ins. Guaranty Funds, chmn., 1995-97. Trustee John M. Scott Indsl. Sch. Trust, Bloomington, 1983-86, Cornell Coll., 1999—; bd. dirs. Scott Ctr., 1983-86, Bloomington-Normal Symphony, 1980-85, YWCA of McLean County, 1993-95; chmn. Ins. Inst. for Hwy. Safety, 1987-88. Mem. ABA, Iowa State Bar Assn., Am. Corp. Counsel Assn., Am. Soc. Corp. Secs. Office: State Farm Mut Automobile Ins Co 1 State Farm Plz Bloomington IL 61710-0001

**SULLIVAN, LAWRENCE MATTHEW,** lawyer; b. Wilmington, Del., Sept. 5, 1937; BA Philosophy, Kings's Coll., 1959; LLB, Cath. U. Am., 1964. Bar: US Supreme Ct./Del. 1965, US Dist. Ct./Del. 1966. Pvt. practice, 1965; asst. county atty. New Castle County, 1966—67, register of wills, 1966—70; pub. defender State of Del., 1970; instr. bus. and real estate law Wilmington Coll., 1969—78, Del Tech. and Cmty. Coll., 1978—80, Del. State Coll., 1980—82, Brandywine Coll.; vice chmn. and mem. various com., Criminal Justice Coun., Del. Co-author: Del. Fundamentals of Real Estate, 1980. Named Del. Outstanding Young Rep. of Yr., Del., 1965, Wilmington's Young Man of Yr., Wilmington Del., 1966, one of Outstanding Young Men of Am., 1968. Mem.: New Castle County Officials Assn. (pres. 1968—70), Del Trial Lawyers Assn., Del. Bar Assn., Trial Lawyers Am., Am. Arbitration Assn., ABA, Sentencing Accountability Commn., Gov. Crime Reduction Task Force, Del. Agy. to Reduce Crime, Del Supreme Ct. Commn. on Del. Ct. 2000, Del Supreme Ct. Planning and Long Range Ct. Planning Com., Phi Alpha Delta. Office: Lawrence M Sullivan Pub Defender Del 1010 Concord Ave # 201 Wilmington DE 19802-3367

**SULLIVAN, MARCIA WAITE,** lawyer; b. Chgo., Nov. 30, 1950; d. Robert Macke and Jacqueline (Northrop) S.; m. Steven Donald Jansen, Dec. 20, 1975; children: Eric Spurlock, Laura Macke, Brian Northrop. BA, DePauw U., 1972; JD, Ind. U., 1975. Assoc. Arnstein, Gluck, Weitzenfeld & Minow, Chgo., 1975-76; ptnr. Greenberger and Kaufmann, Chgo., 1976-86, Katten Muchin Rosenman LLP, Chgo., 1986—. Adj. prof. Kent Coll. Law, Ill. Inst. Tech., Chgo., 1991—94; pres. Chgo. Real Estate Exec. Women, 2000—01. Mem. editl. adv. bd. Real Estate Chgo., 2001—02. Mem. NNCREW Found. Grant Making Com, 2003—04. Mem.: ABA, Chgo. Bar Assn. Avocations: bicycling, cross country skiing, gardening, camping. Office: Katten Muchin Rosenman LLP 525 W Monroe St Chicago IL 60661-3693 Office Phone: 312-902-5538. Business E-Mail: marcia.sullivan@kattenlaw.com

**SULLIVAN, MARGARET M.,** editor; d. John and Elaine (Saab) Sullivan; m. Charles "Bud" Anzalone; children: Alex, Grace. BA in English, Georgetown U., 1979; MS with distinction, Medill Sch. Journalism, Northwestern U., 1980. Clk. Washington bur. Gannett News Svc., 1977—80; Buffalo-area stringer N.Y. Times, 1984—89; reporter, news-feature reporter, columnist Buffalo News, 1980—87, asst. city editor, 1987—89, asst. mng. editor, 1989—98, mng. editor, 1998—99, editor, 1999—. Instr. journalism SUNY, Buffalo, 1991—93. Named One of Buffalo's Outstanding Young Bus. Leaders, Bus. 1st newspaper, 1992; named to Medill Sch. Journalism Hall of Achievement, 2003; recipient Award for Internat. Understanding, Rotary Found., 1987, Young Leadership award, YMCA, 1987. Mem.: Kappa Tau Alpha. Office: Buffalo News The News Plaza Buffalo NY 14203

**SULLIVAN, MARGARET WOLAN,** research psychologist, educator; b. Elizabeth, NJ, Sept. 24, 1952; d. Julian and Bertha (Szpiech) Wolan; m. Dennis J. Sullivan, June 20, 1976; children: Heather Jean, Meredith Clare. BA magna cum laude, Kean Coll., 1974; MS, Rutgers U., 1976, PhD, 1979. Mem. rsch. staff Ednl. Testing Svc., Princeton, 1978-82; asst. prof. pediatrics and child devel. U. Medicine and Dentistry N.J. Robert Wood Johnson Med. Sch., Piscataway, N.J., 1982-90, assoc. prof., 1990—99, prof., 1999—; dir. infant learning and emotion project Inst. for Study Inst. for Study of Child Devel., Piscataway, N.J., 1983—. Presenter in field. Mem. editl. bd. Infants and Young Children; contbr. articles to profl. jours. Trustee Friends of Wallace House and Old Dutch Parsonage/N.J. State Hist. Site; mcpl. rep. Co. Somerset Cultural and Heritage Commn., Somerville Bd. Health, 2002-06. Grantee Nat. Inst. Child Health and Devel., 1983-85, 87-90, Robert Wood Johnson Found., 1986-90, NSF, 1991-94, Harry Frank Guggenheim Found., 1991-94, NIMH, 1996-99, 1999—, NIH, 1997-99; recipient Eleanor Roosevelt award Somerset County Fedn. Dem. Women, 2001. Mem. AAUW, APA (divsn. 37), Am. Psychol. Soc., Soc. for Rsch. in Child Devel., Interant. Soc. for Inf. Rsch., Polish Am. Geneol. Assn. Roman Catholic. Avocations: gardening, reading. Office: UMDNJ-RWJ Med Sch 97 Paterson St New Brunswick NJ 08901-2160 Business E-Mail: sullivan@umdnj.edu.

**SULLIVAN, MARISSA M.,** elementary school educator; b. Butte, Mont., Nov. 04; d. Walter A. and Gerry T. Sullivan BA in Biology and Sociology, Gonzaga U., 1984, MA, 1993. Cert. tchr., Wash. 3d grade tchr. Ea. Hoffsetter Sch., Colville, Wash., 1986-87; tchr. grade 2-3 Bemiss, Spokane, 1987-88; kindergarten tchr. Adam Sch., Spokane, Wash., 1988-89; 4th grade tchr. Arlington Elem. Sch., Spokane, 1989-90, 3d grade tchr., 1990-92, 2d grade tchr., 1992-94, Whitman Elem. Sch., Spokane, 1994—97; kindergarten tchr. Brown e li Sch., Spokane, 1997—; dept. chair, 2000—05. Mem. Dist. 81 Assessment Com. Spokane, 1992-93, Report Card Rev. Com., Spokane, 1993-94; spkr. N.W. Math. Conf., Victoria, B.C., 1994, Seattle, 1993; mem. site coun. PTO, 2002-03, dept. chmn., prin. selection com., 2002-03. Site coun. rep. Roosevelt Parent Tchr. Orgn. Mem. Nat. Tchrs. Math. Avocations: rubber stamp art, travel.

**SULLIVAN, MARK J.,** federal agency administrator; b. Arlington, Mass. m. Laurie Bell; 3 children. BA, St. Anselm Coll. Spl. agent office inspector gen. HUD, 1978—83; spl. agent U.S. Secret Svc., U.S. Dept. Homeland Security, Detroit, 1983—90, spl. agent fraud divsn. Washington, 1990—, spl. agent presdl. protection divsn., 1991—96, asst. spl. agent in charge office protective ops., 1996—97, resident agent in charge Columbus, Ohio, 1997—98, spl. agent in charge conterfeit divsn., 1998—99, asst. spl. agent in charge presdl. protective divsn., 1999—2000, dep. asst. dir. office protective ops. fed. sr. exec. svc., 2000—02, dep. spl. agent in charge vice presdl. protective divsn., 2002—03, dep. asst. dir. office human resources and training, asst. dir. office protective ops., 2003—06, dep. dir., 2006—, dir., 2006—. Recipient Disting. Presdl. Rank award, 2005. Office: US Secret Svc Personnel Divisn 245 Murray Dr Bldg 410 Washington DC 20223*

**SULLIVAN, MARTIN J.,** insurance company executive; With fin. dept. Am. Internat. Underwriters Ltd., 1971—83, property mgr., 1983—88, London office mgr., regional mktg. mgr. for U.K. and Ireland, 1988—89, asst. mng. dir., 1989—91, CEO, 1991—93, pres.; UK/Ireland div., 1993—95, pres., 1997—98; sr. v.p. Am. Internat. Group, Inc., 1995—98, exec. v.p. N.Y.C., 1998—2002, co-COO, 2002—05, vice chmn., 2002—05, pres., CEO, 2005—. Office: Am Internat Group Inc 70 Pine St New York NY 10270*

**SULLIVAN, MARY ANN,** artist; b. Columbus, Ohio, June 17, 1952; d. Thomas Joseph and Mary Jane (neeHouck) Sullivan; 1 child, Benjamin James. BFA in Illustration, Columbus Coll. Art and Design, 1974. Designer, illustrator Gibson Greeting Cards, Cin., 1974—78; freelance commel. artist Artwear, Albuquerque, 1984—90; exhibiting fine artist Fine Arts Ctr. En Taos, Taos, N.Mex., 1984—86, Spangler Cummings Gallery, Columbus, 1984—88, El Taller Gallery, Taos, N.Mex., 1984—94, Roberta Kuhn Gallery, Columbus, 1988—92, various galleries, 1992—. Songs of the Earth, 1976, one-woman shows include El Taller Gallery, N. Mex., 1988, 1990, Wilmington Coll., 2001, exhibited in group shows at Ohio State Fair, 1974—2001, Spangler Cummings Gallery, Ohio, Roberta Kuhn Gallery, Grand Ctrl. Galleries, N.Y.C., 1985, Society of Illustrators, NYC, others. Mem.: Ohio Art League. Avocations: books, interior decorating.

**SULLIVAN, MARY ANNE,** lawyer, government agency administrator; BA in Philosophy summa cum laude, Fordham U., 1973; JD, Yale U., 1976. Law clk. to Hon. Walter K. Stapleton U.S. Dist. Ct., Wilmington, Del., 1976-77; assoc. Hogan & Hartson, Washington, 1977-84, ptnr., 1985-94; dep. gen. counsel Environ. and Civilian and Def. Nuclear Programs, U.S. Dept. Energy, Washington, 1994-98; gen. counsel U.S. Dept. Energy, Washington, 1998—. Instr. Lawyers Com. for Civil Rights; spkr. in field. Contbr. articles to profl. jours. Active Dem. Party, 1982—; sr. domestic issues advisr Geraldine Ferraro in Mondale Campaign; with debate prep. team Senator Bentsen in Dukakis Campaign; counsel to Clinton Campaign and Clinton/Gore Transition Team, 1992. Office: US Dept Energy Gen Counsel Rm 6A-245 1000 Independence Ave SW Washington DC 20585-0001 Fax: 202-586-1499.

**SULLIVAN, MARY BROSNAHAN,** advocate, social services administrator; m. John Sullivan, Apr. 21, 2001. Degree in Comm., Notre Dame U., 1983. With Universal Studios; press aide 1988 Dem. Presdl. Campaign; joined Coalition for the Homeless, N.Y.C., 1989, exec. dir., 1990—. Recipient Dr. Thomas A. Dooley award, Notre Dame U., 2002. Office: Coalition for the Homeless 129 Fulton St New York NY 10038

**SULLIVAN, MARY E.,** retired secondary educator, past state legislator; b. June 29, 1932; m. Charles M. Sullivan; children: Charles M. Jr., Ethel M., Mary E., Kathleen M., Mark C., Ursula M. AB, Regis Coll., 1954; MA, Boston Coll., 1955. Asst. prof. stats. Bentley Coll., Waltham, Mass., 1966-72; asst. prof., registrar Husson Coll., 1973-79; mem. staff Maine Dept. Manpower Affairs Rsch., 1980-81; math. tchr. John Bapst Meml. H.S., 1981-97; also mem. Maine Ho. of Reps., 1992-94. City councilor City of Bangor, Maine, 1985—, mayor, 1988-89. Mem. Maine Munic Assn. (past pres.). Democrat. Home: 143 Bright St Waltham MA 02453-6584

**SULLIVAN, MARY ROSE,** retired English language educator; b. Boston, May 13, 1931; d. John Joseph and Elinor May (Crotty) Sullivan BA, Emmanuel Coll., Boston, 1952; MA, Cath. U. Am., 1957; PhD, Boston U., 1964. Tchr. Woburn Pub. Schs., Mass., 1957-60; faculty Emmanuel Coll., Boston, 1960-66; prof. English U. Colo., Denver, 1966-96; ret., 1996. Book reviewing staff San Diego Mag., 1980—90. Author: Browning's Voices in the Ring and the Book, 1969; co-editor: (3 vols.) letters of E.B. Browning to M.R. Mitford, 1836-54, 1983, Women of Letters: Selected Letters of E.B. Browning to M.R. Mitford, 1987, Crime Classics, 1990, Elizabeth Barrett Browning: Selected Poetry and Prose, 1993; editl. bd. English Lang. Notes, 1970-96. Served to capt. USNR, 1952—83. Am. Coun. Learned Socs. fellow, 1973. Mem. MLA, Boston Browning Soc., Mystery Writers of Am.

**SULLIVAN, MICHAEL,** writer, retired mathematics professor; b. Chgo., Jan. 8, 1942; s. Michael and Catherine Sullivan; m. Mary Rita Doody (dec.); children: Kathleen, Michael III, Dan, Colleen. BS, DePaul U., Chgo., 1962; MS, Ill. Inst. Tech., Chgo., 1963, PhD, 1967. Prof. math. Chgo. State U., 1965—97; prof. emeritus, 1997—. Dir. Scott-Jones Inc., Half Moon Bay, Calif., 1987—2006; com. Authors Coalition of Am., 2001—. Author: 15 textbooks. Chmn. Oak Lawn Youth Commn., Ill., 1979—85; pres. St. German Sch. Bd., Oak Lawn, 1985—88, St. German Holy Name Soc., Oak Lawn, 1984. Mem.: Text and Acad. Authors Assn. (pres. 2001—04). Avocations: tennis, chess, gardening, travel. Home: 9529 S Tripp Ave Oak Lawn IL 60453

**SULLIVAN, MICHAEL EVAN,** investment company executive; b. Phila., Dec. 30, 1940; s. Albert and Ruth (Liebert) S. BS, N.Mex. State U., 1966, MA, 1967; BS, U. Tex., 1969; MBA, U. Houston, 1974; MS, U. So. Calif., 1976, MPA, 1977; BS in Acctg., U. La Verne, 1981; PhD in Adminstrn., U. So. Calif., 1983. Sr. adminstrv. and tech. analyst Houston Lighting & Power Co., 1969—74; electronics engr. U.S. Govt., Point Mugu, Calif., 1974—77; mem. tech. staff Hughes Aircraft Co., El Segundo, Calif., 1977—78; staff program adminstr. Ventura divsn. Northrop Corp., Newbury Park, Calif., 1978—79; divsn. head engring. Navastrogru, Point Mugu, 1978—82; br. head, divsn. head spl. programs head operational sys. Pacific Missile Test Ctr., Calif., 1983—90, head tech. devel. office, head capability devel., 1993—98; regional coord. far west, exec. com., exec. bd. Fed. Lab. Consortium, 1999—. CNO, dir. rsch., devel. and acquisiiton The Pentagon, Washington, 1987-88, dir. rsch. devel. test and evaluation and tech., 1990-93; pres., chmn. bd. Diversified Mgmt. Sys., Inc., Camarillo, Calif., 1978—. Author: The Management of Research, Developoment, Test and Evaluation Organizations; Organization Behavior Characteristics of Supervisors-Public versus Private Sectors; Self-Actualization in RDT & E Organizations: Self-Actualization in a Health Care Agency; others. V.p., bd. dirs. Ventura County Master Chorale and Opera Assn.; bd. dirs. So. Calif. Assn. of Pub. Adminstrn. (also mem. fin. com., programs com., student aid com., exec. bd., exec. com. fed. lab. consortium). Served with U.S. Army, 1958-62. Ednl. Rsch. Info. Clearing House fellow, 1965-67, Ednl. Rsch. Tng. Program fellow N.Mex. State U., 1967. Mem. IEEE, Am. Math. Soc., Math. Assn. Am., Am. Statis. Assn., IEEE Engring. Mgmt. Soc., Am. Soc. Pub. Adminstrn., So. Calif. Assn. Pub. Adminstrn. (bd. dirs., various coms.), Assn. Fedn. Tech. Transfer Execs., Fed. Mgrs. Assn., Am. Assn. Individual Investors, Mcpl. Mgmt. Assts. So. Calif., Acad. Polit. Sci., Internat. Soc. for the Sys. Scis., Assn. MBA Execs., Tech. Transfer Assn., Internat. Fedn. for Sys. Rsch., Phi Kappa Phi, Pi Gama Mu. Home: PO Box 273 Port Hueneme CA 93044-0273 Office: PO Box 447 Camarillo CA 93011-0447 Personal E-mail: mikedmsinc@aol.com.

**SULLIVAN, MICHAEL J.,** prosecutor; b. Oct. 3, 1954; m. Terry Sullivan, 1975; children: Joseph, Kelly, Allyson, James. Grad., Boston Coll., 1979; JD, Suffolk U., 1983. Assoc. Bolles and Pritchard, 1983—90; ptnr. McGovern and Sullivan, 1990—95; mem. Mass. Ho. Reps. (dist. 7), 1991—95; dist. atty. Plymouth County, Mass., 1995—2001; US atty. Us Dept. Justice, Boston, 2001—. Office: US Attys Office John Joseph Moakley Courthouse 1 Courthouse Way Boston MA 02210*

**SULLIVAN, MICHAEL J.,** labor union administrator; b. Indpls., 1945; Sheet metal worker Brad Snodgrass Sheet Metal Inc., R.M. Cotton Inc. Nyland Sheet Metal Inc.; bus. rep. Sheet Metal Workers' Internat. Assn., 1973, 1976, bus. mgr. and fin. sec./treas., Local 20, 1979—94, gen. exec. coun., 1983—94, gen. sec./treas., 1994—99, pres., 1999—. Pres. Ind. Bldg. and Constrn. Trades Coun.; v.p. State AFL-CIO; mem. Ind. Workers Compensation Comm.; chmn. Labor Inst. Tng.; pres. Sheet Metal Workers' Internat. Assn.'s Mich.-Ind. Coun.; bd. dir. Nat. Coordinating Com. for Multiemployer Plan, ULLICO, Washington, Am. Cmty. Partnerships. Mem. Hoosier Alliance Against Drugs. Office: Sheet Metal Workers' Internat Assn 1750 New York Ave NW Washington DC 20006*

**SULLIVAN, MICHAEL JOHN,** lawyer, former ambassador; b. Omaha, Sept. 22, 1939; s. Joseph Byrne and Margaret (Hamilton) S.; m. Jane Metzler, Sept. 2, 1961; children: Michelle, Patrick, Theresa. BS in Petroleum Engring., U. Wyo., 1961, JD, 1964. Bar: Wyo. 1964, U.S. Ct. Appeals (10th cir.) 1968, U.S. Supreme Ct. 1980. Assoc. Brown, Drew, Apostolos, Barton & Massey, Casper, Wyo., 1964-67; ptnr. Brown, Drew, Apostolos, Massey & Sullivan, Casper, 1967-86, 95-98; gov. State of Wyo., Cheyenne, 1987—95; amb. to Ireland Dublin, 1998-2001; spl. counsel Rothgerber, Johnson & Lyons, LLP, Casper, Wyo., 2001—. Trustee St Joseph's Children's Home, Torrington, Wyo., 1986-87; bd. dirs. Natrona County Meml. Hosp., Casper, 1976-86. Mem. ABA, ATLA, Wyo. Bar Assn., Wyo. Trial Lawyers Assn., Rotary (pres. Casper club). Democrat. Roman Catholic. Avocations: fly fishing, golf, tennis, jogging. Office: Casper Bus Ctr 123 W 1st St Ste 200 Casper WY 82601 Home: 1124 S Durbin St Casper WY 82601-4328 E-mail: msullivan@rothgerber.com.

**SULLIVAN, MICHAEL JOSEPH,** lawyer; b. Dunkirk, N.Y., Mar. 19, 1960; s. Thomas C. and Claudia Sullivan; divorced. BA, U. Dayton, 1981; JD, Syracuse Coll., 1983. Bar: N.Y. 1985, U.S. Dist. Ct. (we. dist.) N.Y. 1990, U.S. Ct. Appeals (3d cir.) 1991. Dep. county atty. County of Chautauqua, Mayville, N.Y., 1985-92; pvt. practice Fredonia, N.Y., 1985—. Chmn. Salvation Army Adv. Bd., Dunkirk, N.Y., 1992-97, sec., 1997—; treas. Chautauqua County Rep. com., 1994-2001; trustee Village of Fredonia, 1986-90, 95-99; mem. Coll. Coun., SUNY Fredonia, 1997—. Republican. Roman Catholic. Office: 7 E Main St PO Box 182 Fredonia NY 14063-0182 Office Phone: 716-673-9595. Business E-Mail: mjsullivan@netsync.net.

**SULLIVAN, MIKE,** former professional hockey coach; m. Kate Sullivan; children: Kaitlin, Kiley, Matthew. Degree, Boston U., 1990. Center San Jose Sharks, 1991—94, Calgary Flames, 1994—97, Boston Bruins, 1997—98, Phoenix Coyotes, 1998—2002; head coach Providence Bruins, 2002—03; asst. coach Boston Bruins, 2003, head coach, 2003—06. Asst. coach USA Hockey Team, Olympic Games, Torino, Italy, 2006.

**SULLIVAN, MITZI,** accountant; b. Chattanooga, Feb. 6, 1948; d. James Warren and Maysell Lucille Sullivan; m. Hassan Zayed, Sept. 27, 1975 (div. Oct. 1983); 1 child, Janine Amira Zayed. BA Liberal Arts, U. Tenn., 1971; MS Mgmt., Fla. Internat U., 1977. French and English tchr. Hamilton County Dept. Edn., Chattanooga, 1971—75; social worker Divsn. Retardation, Miami, 1975—78; employment specialist City of Wichita, Kans., 1985—98, accountant Kans., 1998—; owner Internat. Dairy Queen, Kingman, Kans., 1998—2000. Bd. dirs., 1st v.p. City of Wichita Deferred Compensation Bd., 1998—. Mem.: Wichita Irish Assn. (membership chmn. 1989—92), Wichita Hispanic Assn. (v.p. 1988—90). Buddhist. Avocations: writing, gardening, quilting, cooking, reading. Home: 942 S Longfellow St Wichita KS 67207-2737 Office: City Wichita Career Devel Office 444 E Wiliam Wichita KS 67202 Personal E-mail: mitzigsullivan@hotmail.com.

**SULLIVAN, MORTIMER ALLEN, JR.,** lawyer; b. Buffalo, Sept. 19, 1930; s. Mortimer Allen Sr. and Gertrude (Hinkley) S.; m. Maryanne Calella, Nov. 20, 1965; children: Mark Allen, Michael John. BA, U. Buffalo, 1954. Bar: N.Y. 1964, U.S. Dist. Ct. (we. dist.) N.Y. 1966, U.S. Dist. Ct. (no. dist.) N.Y. 1967, U.S. Supreme Ct. 1970. Counsel liability claims Interstate Motor Freight System, Grand Rapids, Mich., 1964-82. V.p. J.P.M. Sullivan, Inc., Elmira, N.Y., 1959-67; govt. appeal agt. U.S. Selective Service System, 1967-71; dep. sci. staff Erie County (N.Y.) Sheriff's Office, 1971—, lt., 1986—. Inventor (with others) in field; creator, dir. video depiction JudiVision, 1969; composer High Flight, 1983. Chmn. com. on Constn. and Canons Episcopal Diocese of Western N.Y., 1975-96; bd. dirs. Erie County Law Enforcement Found., Inc., 1987—; bd. dirs. Orchard Park (N.Y.) Symphony Orch., 1975-97, v.p., 1977-79, 91-94. With USAF, 1954-57; spl. agt. Air Force Office of Spl. Investigations, 1972-87, col. res. ret. Decorated Legion of Merit. Mem. Erie County Bar Assn. (chmn. law and tech. com., 1970-81), Transp. Lawyers Assn., Kappa Alpha Soc., Wanakah (N.Y.) Country Club. Republican. Avocation: aviation. Home: 19 Knob Hill Rd Orchard Park NY 14127-3917 Office: 88 S Davis St PO Box 1003 Orchard Park NY 14127-8003 Office Phone: 716-667-7800. Personal E-mail: masulaw@aol.com.

**SULLIVAN, NANCY ELIZABETH,** pediatric neuropsychologist; b. San Francisco, Jan. 21, 1950; d. Arthur James and Evelyn Lavelle Sullivan; m. Hal C. McMillen, Aug. 31, 2001; 1 child, Elizabeth Sullivan Thornton-Jackson. PhD, Pacific Grad. Sch. of Psychology, Palo Alto, Calif., 1996. Lic. psychologist Calif. Staff neuropsychologist Children's Health Coun., Palo Alto, Calif., 1996—; pvt. practice Menlo Park, Calif., 1996—. Mem.: APA. Green Party. Roman Catholic. Avocations: cooking, wine, tennis, yoga. Office: PO Box 338 Menlo Park CA 94026 Office 650-245-8685. Personal E-mail: nesphd@aol.com.

**SULLIVAN, NEIL MAXWELL,** oil and gas company executive; b. May 25, 1942; s. Thomas James and Jane Mason (Ginn) S.; m. Holly Abolt; children: Margaret Blair, Mason Pedrick. BS, Dickinson Coll., 1970; MS, Tulane U., 1994; postgrad., U. S.C., 1992. Exploration geologist Bass Enterprises, Midland, Tex., 1976—77; dist. geologist Am. Trading and Prodn. Co., Midland, 1977—78; divsn. geologist Anadarko Prodn. Co., Midland, 1978—79, chief geologist, 1979—80, v.p exploration, regional mgr. Houston, 1980—82; mgr. exploration ops. Valero Producing Co., San Antonio, 1982—85, v.p. exploration New Orleans, 1985—87; pres. Bluebonnet Petroleum Co., New Orleans, Eastover, 1987—97; v.p. exploration Forcenergy, Inc., Houston, 1997—98; pres. GAPCO Energy, Houston, 1998—2001; COO Tex. Keystone, Inc., Pitts., 2002—; v.p. exploration and prodn. Gulf Keystone Petroleum, Ltd., 2002—. Mem. Dept. adv. bd. Interior Outer Continental Shelf Com., 1985-87 Editor: Petroleum Exploration in Thrust Belts and Their Adjacent Forelands, 1976, Ancient Carbonate Reservoirs and Their Modern Analogs, 1977, Guadalupian Delaware Mountain Group of West Texas and Southeast New Mexico, 1979, Deep Water Sands in the Gulf Coast Region, 1988, Offshore Louisiana Geology: An Onshore Exploration Model, 1988, Risk: Evaluation and Management, 1989, Volga-Ural Basin Analysis, 1993, Northern Marginal Zone of the Pricaspian Basin, 1996. Bd. dirs. Permian Basin Grad. Ctr, Midland, 1979; com. chmn. Mus. of S.W., Midland, 1978. Served with USAF, 1964-68. Mem. Geol. Soc. Am., Am. Assn. Petroleum Geologists (cert. petroleum geologist), Houston Geol. Soc., New Orleans Geol. Soc. (chmn. continuing edn. com. 1987-89), South Tex. Geol. Soc. (chmn. nominating com. 1985), Soc. Econ. Paleontologists and Mineralogists (pres. Permian Basin sect. 1979), Elks. Home: 3894 Ash Dr Allison Park PA 15101-3103 Office Phone: 412-352-7799. E-mail: nsullivan525@yahoo.com.

**SULLIVAN, NICHOLAS G.,** science educator; b. Phila., Dec. 20, 1927; s. Edward James and Florence (Delaney) S. BS, Cath. U. Am., l950; MSc, U. Pitts., 1954; PhD, U. Notre Dame, l96l. Asst. prof. U. Notre Dame (Ind.), 1961-63; asst. prof., assoc. prof., prof. La Salle Coll., Phila., 1963-78, asst. to pres., 1972-74; prof. sci. Manhattan Coll., Riverdale, NY, 1979—. Vis. prof. U. Alaska, Anchorage, l961, U. NSW, Sydney, Australia, 1963; chmn. U.S. Deep Caving Team. Author: Speleology, the Study of Caves, 1962; contbr. over 200 articles on speleology to profl. jours. Trustee Gwynedd (Pa.) Mercy Coll., 1963-75, Nat. Speleological Found., Washington, 1978-84, Charles Lindbergh Found., 1989—. Fellow Nat. Speleological Soc. (hon. life, trustee 1955-79, pres. l957-63), Royal Geog. Soc., AAAS, N.Y. Acad. Scis., Explorers Club (pres. 1989-92, trustee 1968—, Explorer's medal Phila. chpt. 1978, Sweeney medal 1979); mem. Sydney Speleological Soc. (hon. life), South African Speleological Soc. (hon. life), Rittenhouse Club, Bankstown Sports Club (Sydney). Avocation: speleology.

**SULLIVAN, PATRICIA,** journalist; b. Joliet, Ill., Feb. 2, 1955; d. William L. and Elizabeth J. (Reed) S. BA, Marquette U., 1977. Reporter Herald-News, Joliet, 1977-78, Ft. Lauderdale (Fla.) Sun-Sentinel, 1979-84; reporter, editor Missoulian, Missoula, Mont., 1985-95; freelancer Sullivan Freelance, Missoula, 1995-96; online editor Mercury Ctr., San Jose, Calif., 1996—. John S. Knight Fellow, Stanford U., 1992-93.

**SULLIVAN, PATRICIA A.,** academic administrator; b. S.I. m. Charles Sullivan. AB cum laude, St. John's U., 1961; MS in Biology, NYU, 1964, PhD in Biology, 1967. Tchg. fellow, NIH pre-doctoral fellow NYU; post-doctoral fellow in cell biology Upstate Med. Ctr., Syracuse, NY; vis. fellow Cornell U., 1976; tchr. Wells Coll., NY; dir. biology honors program Tex. Woman's U., 1979-81; dean Salem Coll., Winston-Salem, 1981-87; v.p. acad. affairs Tex. Woman's U., 1987-94, interim pres., 1993-94; chancellor U. N.C. Greensboro, 1995—. Pres. Assn. Tex. Colls. and Univs. Acad. Affairs Officers, Assn. So. Colls. for Women, N.N.C. Assn. Chief Acad. Officers; active numerous coms. Tex. Higher Edn. Coordinating Bd.; lectr. in field. Contbr. articles to profl. jours. Office: U NC at Greensboro Office of Chancellor PO Box 26170 Greensboro NC 27402-6170

**SULLIVAN, PATRICIA W. (TERRY SULLIVAN),** real estate trainer; b. Hempstead, N.Y., July 25, 1936; d. Gilbert Hudson and Vera (Morgan) Wehmann; m. Richard J. Sullivan, June 8, 1957 (div. Apr. 1982); children: Katherine, Gillian Stewart, Adam W. BS, Skidmore Coll., 1958; MS, Syracuse U., 1965. Mgr. Purtell & Wigdale, Inc., Cedarburg, Wis., Merrill Lynch Real Estate, Cedarburg; office mgr. Coldwell Banker Real Estate, Cedarburg; sales mgr. Coldwell Banker Residential Brokerage, Mequon, WI; owner, trainer, cons. Terry Sullivan Tng. and Seminars, Belgium, Wis., 1991—; sales mgr. Coldwell Banker, Mequon, Wis. Contbr. articles to profl. jours. Named Wis. Cert. Real Estate Brokerage Mgr. of Yr., 1990. Mem.: Wis. Cert. Residential Brokers (cert., pres. 1988), Wis. Cert. Residential Specialists (cert., pres. 1982, Cert. Residential Specialist of Yr. 1993), Wis. Realtors Assn. (v.p. 1982—83, bd. dirs. 1983—86, GRI 1975, Instr. of Yr. 1988, Disting. Svc. award 1992), Realtors Nat. Mktg. Inst. (dir. RS coun. 1983—86, CRS 1978, CRB 1981), Oazukee Bd. Realtors (pres. 1979, bd. dirs. 1977—79, Realtor of Yr. 1979), Women's Coun. Realtors (pres. Milw. chpt. 1982, bd. dirs. 1983—90, PMN 2005, WCR of Yr. 1983), Nat. Women's Coun. Realtors (pres. 1990), Nat. Assn. Realtors (bd. dirs. 1989—90, Omega Tau Rho award 1983, Outstanding Educator of Yr. award for medium states 1989). Address: Terry Sullivan Tng & Seminars 5342 Sandy Beach Ln Belgium WI 53004-9731 E-mail: rlterry@hotmail.com.

**SULLIVAN, PATRICK ALLEN,** strategic management educator; b. Peoria, Ill., Oct. 31, 1932; s. Francis Richard and Carmela Marie (Smith) S.; m. Gwendolyn Jo Herndon, Aug. 25, 1958; children: Richard John, Sharon Louise Little, Patrick Michael, Cecelia Anne, Catherine Marie Markee. BCE, Marquette U., 1955; MBA, San Diego State U., 1975; DBA, U.S. Internat. U., San Diego, 1988. Engr. USMC, 29 Palms, Calif., 1958-63, USN, San Diego, 1963-67, mgmt. analyst, 1967-88; asst. prof. strategic mgmt. U.S. Internat. U., San Diego, 1988-89, assoc. prof. strategic mgmt., 1989-94, prof. strategic mgmr., 1994—2000, prof. emeritus, 2000—. Ptnr. Sullivan and Assocs. Mgmt. Cons., San Diego, 1988-2005; pres. Ansoft Inst., 2001-2006. Pres. St. Pius Ch. Parish Coun., Chula Vista, Calif., 1984. 1st lt. USMC, 1955-58. Mem. ASCE (life), Japan Strategic Mgmt. Soc. (dir.), K.C., Chi Epsilon, Tau Beta Pi, Sigma Iota Epsilon, Beta Gamma Sigma. Republican. Roman Catholic. Home: 98 E Emerson St Chula Vista CA 91911-3545 Personal E-mail: patsullivan2@cox.net.

**SULLIVAN, PATRICK GILES,** education educator, researcher; b. Louisville, Ky. s. Al and Mary Giles Sullivan; m. Diana Kay Erickson; children: Kyle Patrick, Erin Marie. PhD, U. Ky., Lexington, 1996—2000. Asst. prof. U. Ky., 2002—06, assoc. prof., 2006—. Ceo Nano-Mite Technologies LLC, Lexington, 2004—. Recipient Outstanding Student Presentation, Nat. Neurotrauma Soc., 1998, Wethington Excellence in Rsch. award, U. Ky. Coll. Medicine, 2004, 2005, 2006; grantee R01, NIH, 2004—, 2004—, R21, 2004—06. Mem.: Soc. Neuroscience, Am. Epilepsy Soc., Nat. Neurotrauma Soc. Achievements include research in mitochondrial targeted therapeutics for neuroprotection. Office: Univ Ky 375 BBSRB 741 S Limestone Lexington KY 40536-0509 Office Phone: 859-323-4684. Office Fax: 859-257-5737. Business E-Mail: patsullivan@uky.edu.

**SULLIVAN, PATRICK JAMES,** lawyer; b. Orange, Calif., Sept. 17, 1943; s. Leo Charles Sullivan and Virginia (Wohosky) Souza; m. Pamela Pressler, Aug. 17, 1974; children: Shannon, Erin. BA, U. So. Calif., 1965; JD, Loyola U., Los Angeles, 1974. Bar: (Calif.) 1974, U.S. Ct. Appeals (9th cir.) 1978, (U.S. Supreme Ct) 1979, U.S. Ct. Appeals (3d cir.) 1983, U.S. Tax Ct. 1986, U.S. Ct. Appeals (2d and 8th cirs.) 1989. Trial atty. U.S. Dept. Justice, Washington, 1974—75; ptnr. Sullivan, Jones & Archer, San Diego and San Francisco, 1975—83, Hewitt, Sullivan & Marshall, San Diego, 1983—87, King & Ballow, 1987—90, The Sullivan Law Firm, San Diego, 1990—. Arbitrator San Diego Superior Ct., 1979—83; lectr. U. Calif. Securities Regulations Inst., 1985; chmn. Am. Law Inst. Anti-Trust Conf., 1988, 91; mem. faculty Hastings Ctr. for Trial and Appellate Advocacy, 1989—92, Calif. Continuing Edn. of Bar, 1989—. Served to 1st lt. U.S. Army, Vietnam. Decorated Bronze Star. Fellow: Am. Bar Found. (life); mem.: ABA (litigation and anti-trust sects., ho. dels.), Am. Bd. of Trial Advocates, Nat. Inst. Trial Adv. (faculty 1986—), Am. Judiciary Soc., Am. Law Inst., Am. Inn Ct. (master 1992—2002), Rotary (Newhall, Calif.). Republican. Roman Catholic. Home: 335 Whitewood Pl Encinitas CA 92024-3137 Office: 810 Mission Ave Ste 300 Oceanside CA 92054

**SULLIVAN, PAUL E.,** lawyer, oil industry executive; BA in acctg., U. Maine, Bangor; LLD, Boston Coll. Law Sch. Legal asst. tax dept. Exxon Corp., N.Y.C., 1969; tax counsel Esso Inter-Am., Coral Gables, Fla.; mgr. tax dept. Exxon Co. Internat., 1977; sr. tax counsel tax planning Exploration and Prodn. Divsn.Exxon Corp., N.Y.C., 1976; mgr. tax planning Exploration and Prodn. Divsn. Exxon Corp., N.Y.C., 1979; gen. tax counsel Exxon Chem. Co., Darien, Conn., 1981, Exxon Co. U.S.A., 1989—94; v.p. and gen. tax counsel Exxon Corp., 1994—. Vice chmn. tax policy com. Am. Petroleum Inst. Mem.: ABA, Tax Execs. Inst., N.Y. State Bar Assn. Mailing: ExxonMobil Corp 5959 Las Colinas Blvd Irving TX 75039-2298

**SULLIVAN, PAUL F.,** career officer; b. Wellesley, Mass. m. Ann Sullivan; children: Shane, Morgan. BS with distinction, U.S. Naval Acad., 1970; MS in Ocean Engring., MIT, 1975; postgrad., Nuclear Power Sch. Commd. ensign USN, 1970, advanced through grades to rear adm.; supply officer USS Caiman; various engring. assignments USS Dace; engr. officer USS George C. Marshall; exce. officer USS Richard B. Russell; commdr. USS Birmingham, Pearl Harbor, Hawaii, USS Flask, Bangor, Wash.; mem. tactical analysis group COMSUBDEVRON 12; dep. commdr. tng. & ops. COMSUBDERVON 17; dep. dir. current ops. Ops. Directorate Joint Staff, Washington; commdr. Submarine Group 9, Silverdale, Wash., now rear admiral. Decorated Def. Superior Svc. Medal, Legion Merit award, 2 Meritorious Svc. Medals, 3 Navy Commendation Medals, 3 Navy Achievement Medals.

**SULLIVAN, PEGGY,** librarian, consultant; b. Kansas City, Mo., Aug. 12, 1929; d. Michael C. and Ella (O'Donnell) Sullivan. AB, Clarke Coll., 1950; MS in Libr. Sci., Cath. U. Am., 1953; PhD, U. Chgo., 1972. Children's pub. libr., Mo., Md., Va., 1952-61; sch. libr. specialist Montgomery County (Md.) Pub. Schs., 1961-63; dir. Jr. Coll. Libr. Info. Ctr., 1968-69; asst. prof. U. Pitts., 1971-73; dir. Office for Libr. Pers. Resources, ALA, Chgo., 1973-74; dean of students, assoc. prof. Grad. Libr. Sch., U. Chgo., 1974-77; asst. commr. for ext. svcs. Chgo. Pub. Libr., 1977-81; dean Coll. Profl. Studies, No. Ill. U., DeKalb, 1981-90; dir. univ. librs. No. Ill. U., 1990-92; exec. dir. ALA, 1992-94; assoc. Tuft & Assocs., 1995-98; dean Grad. Sch. Libr. and Info. Sci. Rosary Coll., 1995-97. Instr. grad. libr. edn. programs, 1958-73, UNESCO cons. on sch. librs., Australia, 1970; trustee Clarke Coll., 1969-72; sr. ptnr. Able Cons., 1987-92; cons. in field. Author: The O'Donnells, 1956, Many Names for Eileen, 1969, Problems in School Media Management, 1971, Carl H. Milam and the American Library Association, 1976, Opportunities in Library and Information Science, 1977, Realization: The Final Report of the Knapp School Libraries Project, 1968; co-author: Public Libraries: Smart Practices in Personnel, 1982. Mem.: ALA (dir. Knapp Sch. libr. project 1963—68), Ill. Libr. Assn., Cath. Libr. Assn., Caxton Club, Chgo. Lit. Club. Roman Catholic. Home and Office: 2800 N Lake Shore Dr Apt 816 Chicago IL 60657-6266 Office Phone: 773-549-5361. Business E-Mail: pslibcon@alumni.uchicago.edu. *Opportunities to use my abilities in a variety of public services have enriched my life, as I hope the results have enriched and empowered others.*

**SULLIVAN, ROBERT EDWARD,** lawyer; b. San Francisco, May 18, 1936; s. Edward C. S. and Mary Jane (Sullivan). m. Maureen Lois Miles, June 14, 1958 (dec. 1972); children: Teresa Ann, Andrew Edward, Edward Braddock; m. Lynn Bryant, Aug. 28, 2002. BS, U. San Francisco, 1958; LLB, U. Calif-Berkeley, 1961. Bar: Calif. 1962. Assoc. Pillsbury, Madison & Sutro, San Francisco, 1963-70, ptnr., 1971—2000, Pillsbury Winthrop LLP, San Francisco, 2001—05, Pillsbury Winthrop Shaw Pittman LLP, San Francisco, 2005—. Lectr. bus. law Calif. Continuing Edn. Bar and Practicing Law Inst.; v.p., treas., dir. MPC Ins., Ltd., 1986-93. Contbr. articles to profl. jours. Bd. dirs., exec. com. mem., sec. San Francisco Opera Assn., 1993—. 1st lt. U.S.

Army, 1961-63. Mem. ABA, State Bar Calif. (com. corps. 1979-82, chmn. 1981-82, mem. exec. com. bus. law sect. 1982-85, vice chmn. 1983-84, chmn. 1984-85, advisor 1985-86, mem. partnership com. 1990-92, chmn. ltd. liability co. drafting com. 1992-93), San Francisco Bar Assn., Bankers Club San Francisco (bd. dirs., sec.). Democrat. Roman Catholic. Office: Pillsbury Winthrop Shaw Pittman LLP 50 Fremont St San Francisco CA 94105-2228

**SULLIVAN, ROBERT EMMET, JR.,** lawyer; b. Detroit, Oct. 2, 1955; s. Robert Emmett Sr. and Gloria Marie (Lamb) S. BA in Polit. Sci. and Sociology, Wayne State U., 1977; M in Urban Planning, U. Mich., 1979; JD, U. Detroit, 1983; postgrad., Oxford (Eng.) U., 1981. Bar: Mich. 1984, U.S. Dist. Ct. (we. dist.) Mich. 1984, U.S. Dist. Ct. (ea. dist.) Mich. 1984, U.S. Ct. Appeals (6th cir.) 1984, U.S. Ct. Appeal (D.C. cir.) 1984, U.S. Tax Ct. 1984, D.C. 1985, U.S. Supreme Ct. 1987. Planning commr. City of Detroit, 1982-85; shareholder Sullivan, Ward, Asher & Patton, P.C., Detroit, 1984-; mem., bd. dirs. Internat. Inst. Metro. Detroit. Contbr. articles to profl. jours. Active St. Scholastica Parish Ch., North Rosedale Park Civic Assn., Detroit Hist. Soc. Moffitt scholar, 1982, 83. Mem. AIA, Detroit Bar Assn., Am. Planning Assn., Am. Inst. Cert. Planners. Roman Catholic. Home: 7464 Wilshire West Bloomfield MI 48322-2875 Office: Sullivan Ward Asher & Patton PC 25800 Northwestern Hwy Southfield MI 48075-1000 Office Phone: 248-746-2738. Business E-Mail: rsullivanjr@swappc.com.

**SULLIVAN, ROBERT EMMETT,** pediatric dentist, educator; b. Sioux City, Iowa, May 28, 1932; s. Joseph A. and Daisy B. (Stanieforth) S.; m. Mary Ann Haerer, Sept. 22, 1961. BA, Morningside Coll., 1954; DDS, U. Nebr., 1961, MSD, 1963. Diplomate Am. Bd. Pediat. Dentistry. Prof., chair pediat. dentistry U. Nebr. Coll. Dentistry, Lincoln, 1963-, prof. pedIats. U. Nebr. Coll. Medicine, Omaha, 1969-. Contbr. articles to profl. jours. With U.S. Army. Fellow Am. Acad. Pediat. Dentistry, Am. Coll. Dentists, Internat. Coll. Dentistry; mem. ADA, VFW, Am. Soc. Dentistry for Children, N.E. Nebr. Dental Assn., Lincoln Dist. Dental Assn. Democrat. Avocation: music. Home: 2530 Ridge Rd Lincoln NE 68512-2418

**SULLIVAN, ROBERT JOHN,** lawyer; b. Butte, Mont., Feb. 22, 1954; s. James David and Margorie (Ostoj) S.; m. Mary R. White, Feb. 18, 1984; children: Brian Robert, Patrick Leland. BA, U. Mont., 1976, JD, 1980; attended, Nat. Inst. Trial Advocacy, 1985. Bar: Mont. 1980, U.S. Dist. Ct. Mont. 1980, U.S. Ct. Appeals (9th cir.) 1980. Dep. county atty. Missoula (Mont.) County Atty.'s Office, 1980-85; assoc. Boone Karlberg P.C., Missoula, 1985—87, ptnr., 1987—. Mem. ABA, Western Mont. Bar Assn. (treas. 1989, v.p. 1990, pres. 1990-91), Mont. State Bar Assn. (trustee, mem. character and fitness com., 1991-, chmn. 2001-02, pres.-elect 2002-03, pres. 2003-04, past pres. 2004-05). Avocations: biking, skiing, outdoors. Office: Boone Karlberg PC 201 W Main St Ste 300 PO Box 9199 Missoula MT 59807-9199

**SULLIVAN, ROBERT S.,** college dean; BA in Math., Boston Coll., 1966; PhD in Ops. Mgmt., Pa. State U., 1968; MBA in Prodn. Mgmt., Cornell U., 2003. Various U. Tex., Austin, 1968—91; dean graduate sch. Indsl. Adminstrn. Carnegie Mellon U., Pitts., 1991-95; dir. IC2 inst. U. Tex., Austin, 1995-97; dean Kenan-Flagler U. N.C., Chapel Hill, 1998—2003; dean Rady Sch. Mgmt. U. Calif., San Diego, 2003—. Peace Corps. vol. Addis Ababa U., 1968-70. Office: U Calif Rady Sch Mgmt 9500 Gilman Dr La Jolla CA 92093-0093 Office Phone: 858-822-0830. Business E-Mail: rss@ucsd.edu.

**SULLIVAN, ROY MICHAEL,** aerospace engineer, researcher; b. Pitts., Pa., July 30, 1960; s. Jeremiah Bonaventure and Majorie Lorain Sullivan; m. Traci Ann Fabian; Dec. 31, 1988; children: Bonny Skye Palsa, Kyle Michael, Clare Eyles, Conor Fallon, Emma Doran. BS, The Pa. State U., U. Park, Pa., 1982; MS, The Va. U., Charlottesville, Va., 1984; PhD, The Pa. State U., U. Park, Pa., 1990. Registered profl. engr., Va., 1983. Aerospace engr. Marshall Space Flight Ctr. NASA, Huntsville, Ala., 1985—98, sr. rsch. engr. Glenn Rsch. Ctr. Cleve., 1998—. Adj. faculty The U. Ala., Huntsville, Ala., 1991—98. Achievements include development of coupled numerical solution methods for predicting the thermo-structural response of thermally-decomposing polymer composite materials; a novel numerical analysis method for predicting the oxidation behavior in carbon fiber-reinforced silicon carbide composite structures. Office Phone: 216-433-3249.

**SULLIVAN, SHAUN STUART,** lawyer; b. Albany, NY, Dec. 25, 1940; s. Charles Patrick and Dorothy Beatrice (Stuart) S.; m. Bonnie Sullivan; children: Sara Stuart, Jennifer Landon. AB with honors, Fairfield U., 1962; LLB, Fordham U., 1966. Bar: N.Y., Conn., U.S. Dist. Ct. (so. dist.) N.Y., U.S. Dist. Ct. Conn., U.S. Ct. Appeals (2d cir.), U.S. Supreme Ct. Assoc. Cahill, Gordon, N.Y., 1966-69, Wiggin & Dana, New Haven, 1969—. Fellow Am. Coll. Trial Lawyers (chair ADR comm., chair state of Conn. 1997-99, Best Lawyers 1987-2005), Internat. Acad. Trial Lawyers (chmn. state of Conn. 2004—); mem. Internat. Bar Assn. (chair litig. sect. bus. law 1999-2001), Am. Bar Found., Conn. Bar Found. Home: 40 Cliff St New Haven CT 06511-1344 Office Phone: 203-498-4400. Business E-Mail: ssullivan@wiggin.com

**SULLIVAN, STEVEN R.,** lawyer; b. St. Louis, Aug. 1960; BBA summa cum laude, U. Mo. St. Louis, 1981; JD with distinction, U. Mo. Kans. City Sch. Law, 1994. pub. acct. 1982. Atty. Arthur Andersen & Co., Kohn, Shands, Elbert, Gianoulakis & Giljum, 1989-95, Union Electric Co. (now Ameren EU), 1987—95; assoc. gen. counsel Anheuser-Busch Co., 1995—98; v.p. regulatory policy, gen. counsel, sec. Ameren EU, 1998—2003; sr. v.p. regulatory affairs, gen. counsel, sec. Ameren Corp., St. Louis, 2003—. Mem.: Mo. Bar Assn., Bar Assn. Met. St. Louis, Mo. Soc. Cert. Pub. Accts., Am. Soc. Corp. Sec., Edison Electric Inst. Office: Ameren Corp Legal Dept 1 Ameren Plz Saint Louis MO 63103 Home: 1895 Casa Dr Arnold MO 63010 1277 Office Phone: 314 031 3333. Office Fax: 314-554-3801.

**SULLIVAN, STUART FRANCIS,** anesthesiologist, educator; b. Buffalo, July 15, 1928; s. Charles S. and Kathryn (Duggan) S.; m. Dorothy Elizabeth Faytol, Apr. 18, 1959; children: John, Irene, Paul, Kathryn B., Canisius Coll., 1950; MD, SUNY, Syracuse, 1955. Diplomate Am. Bd. Anesthesiology. Intern Ohio State U. Hosp., Columbus, 1955—56; resident Columbia Presbyn. Med. Ctr., 1958—60; fellow Columbia-Bellevue Hosp. Ctr., N.Y.C. 1960—61; instr. anesthesiology Columbia U. Coll. Physicians and Surgeons, N.Y.C., 1961—62, assoc., 1962—64, asst. prof., 1964—69, assoc. prof., 1969—73; prof. dept. anesthesiology UCLA, 1973—91, vice chair anesthesiology, 1974—77, exec. vice chair, 1977—90, acting chmn., 1983—84, 1987—88, 1990—91, prof. emeritus 1991—. Capt. M.C., USAR, 1956-58. Fellow NIH, 1960-61; recipient research career devel. award NIH, 1966-69. Mem. Assn. Univ. Anesthetists, Am. Physiol. Soc., Am. Soc. Anesthesiologists. Home: 101 Foxtail Dr Santa Monica CA 90402-2047 Office: UCLA Sch Medicine Dept Anesthesiology Los Angeles CA 90095-0001

**SULLIVAN, TERESA ANN,** law and sociology educator, academic administrator; b. Kewanee, Ill., July 9, 1949; d. Gordon Hager and Mary Elizabeth (Finnegan) S.; m. H. Douglas Laycock, June 14, 1971; children: Joseph Peter, John Patrick. BA, Mich. State U., 1970; MA, U. Chgo., 1972, PhD, 1975. Asst. prof. sociology U. Tex., Austin, 1975-76, assoc. prof. sociology, 1981-87, dir. women's studies, 1985-87, prof. sociology, 1987—, prof. law, 1988—, assoc. dean grad. sch., 1989-90, 1992-95, chair dept. sociology, 1990-92, vice provost, 1994-95, v.p., grad. dean, 1995—2002; asst. prof. sociology U. Chgo., 1977-81; exec. vice-chancellor acad. affairs U. Tex. Sys., 2002—06; provost, exec. v.p. academic affairs U. Mich., Ann Arbor, 2006—. Pres. Southwestern Sociol. Assn., 1988-89; mem. faculty adv. bd. Hogg Found. Mental Health, 1989-92; mem. sociology panel NSF, 1983-85. Author: Marginal Workers Marginal Jobs, 1978; co-author: As We Forgive Our Debtors, 1989 (Silver Gavel 1990), Social Organization of Work, 1990, 2d edit. 1995; co-author: The Fragile Middle Class, 2000; contbr. articles and chpts. to profl. jours. Bd. dirs. Calvert Found., Chgo., 1978, CARA, Inc., Washington, 1985; mem. U.S. Census Bur. Adv. Com., 1989-95, chmn., 1991-92; mem. sociology panel NSF, 1983-85; trustee St. Michael's Acad., 1996-2001. Leadership Tex. 1994. Fellow AAAS (liaison to Population Assn.

Am. 1989-91, chair sect. K 1996), Sociol. Rsch. Assn., Am. Sociol. Assn. (sec. 1995—, editor Rose Monograph Series 1988-92), Philos. Soc. Tex., Soc. Study of Social Problems (chair fin. com. 1986-87), Population Assn. Am. (bd. dirs. 1989-91, chair fin. com. 1990-91), Assn. Grad. Schs. (pres. 2001-2002). Roman Catholic. Avocation: reading. Office: 503 Thompson St Ann Arbor MI 48109-1340 Home: 2197 Gray Fox Ct Ann Arbor MI 48103 Office Phone: 734-764-9292. Business E-Mail: tsull@umich.edu.

**SULLIVAN, THOMAS CHRISTOPHER,** coatings company executive; b. Cleve., July 8, 1937; s. Frank Charles and Margaret Mary (Wilhelmy) S.; m. Sandra Simmons, Mar. 12, 1960; children: Frank, Sean, Tommy, Danny, Kathleen, Julie. BS, Miami U., Oxford, Ohio, 1959. Div. sales mgr. Republic Powdered Metals, Cleve., 1961-65, exec. v.p., 1965-70; chmn. bd., CEO RPM, Internat., Medina, Ohio, 1971—2002, chmn. bd., 2003—. Bd. dirs. Agil Ysys Co., Cleve., Cleve. Clinic Found., Kaydon Corp., Ann Arbor, Mich. Trustee emeritus Culver (Ind.) Ednl. Found.; former trustee Cleve. Tomorrow; bd. advisors Urban Cmty. Sch., Cleve., Malachi House, Cleve.; trustee City Year Cleve.; trustee Cath. Diocese of Cleve. Found. Lt. (j.g.) USNR, 1959-60. Mem.: Nat. Assn. Securities Dealers (bd. govs. 1986—88, long-range strategic planning com.), Nat. Paint and Coatings Assn. (past chmn. bd., CEO, mem. exec. com.). Roman Catholic. Office: RPM Internat 2628 Pearl Rd Medina OH 44256-7623 Business E-Mail: tsullivan@rpminc.com.

**SULLIVAN, THOMAS PATRICK,** lawyer; b. Evanston, Ill., Mar. 23, 1930; s. Clarence M. and Pauline (DeHaye) Sullivan; m. Anne Landau; children from previous marriage: Margaret Mary, Timothy Joseph, Elizabeth Ann. Student, Loras Coll., 1947—49; LLB cum laude, Loyola U., Chgo., 1952; LLD (hon.), U. Notre Dame, 2006. Bar: Ill. 1952, Calif. 1982, N.Mex 1997. Assoc. Jenner & Block, Chgo., 1954—62, ptnr., 1963—77, 1981—; U.S. atty. No. Dist. Ill., Chgo., 1977—81. Co-chair Ill. Gov.'s Commn. Capital Punishment, 2000—02; chair Capital Punishment Reform Study Com., 2005—. Contbr. articles to profl. jours. With U.S. Army, 1952—54. Decorated Bronze Star; named laureate, Acad. Ill. Lawyers, Person of Yr., Chgo. Lawyer Mag., 2004; recipient medal of excellence, Loyola U. Law Sch., 1965, Damen award, 2004, award, Ill. Pub. Defender Assn., 1972, Justice John Paul Stevens award, 2000, Ctr. on Wrongful Convictions award, Northwestern U., 2003, Albert E. Jenner, Jr. Pro Bono award, 2003, Lifetime Achievement award, Legal Assistance Found. Chgo., 2005. Fellow: Am. Coll. Trial Lawyers; mem.: ABA (John Minor Wisdom Pub. Svc. and Professionalism award 2003), Chgo. Coun. Lawyers, Am. Judicature Soc. (Justice award 2004), Am. Law Inst., Nat. Bar Assn., Fed. 7th Cir. Bar Assn., Ill. Bar Assn. Office: Jenner & Block 1 Ibm Plz Fl 4100 Chicago IL 60611-5697 Office Phone: 312-923-2928. E-mail: tsullivan@jenner.com.

**SULLIVAN, THOMAS PATRICK,** academic administrator; b. Detroit, July 8, 1947; s. Walter James and Helen Rose (Polosky) S.; m. Barbara Jean Fournier, Aug. 9, 1968; children: Colleen, Brendan. BA in English, U. Dayton, 1969; M. Edn. and Adminstrn., Kent State U., 1971; postgrad., U. Mich., 1988. Tchr. Resurection Elem. Sch., Dayton, Ohio, 1968-69; administr. residence hall Kent (Ohio) State U., 1969-71; program mgr. residence hall Ea. Mich. U., Ypsilanti, 1971-73, adminstrv. assoc., 1973-76, dir. housing, 1976-83; assoc. provost Wayne County Community Coll., Belleville, Mich., 1983-84, dir. budget and mgmt. devel. Detroit, 1984-85, sr. v.p. acad. affairs, acting provost, 1985-86, acting exec. dean Belleville, 1986-88, dir. budget and mgmt. devel. Detroit, 1988-89; pres. Cleary Univ., Ypsilanti, 1989—. Part-time instr. English and math. Schoolcraft Coll., Livonia, Mich., 1980-90. Home: 9835 Whisperwood Ln Brighton MI 48116-8859 Office: Cleary Univ 3601 Plymouth Rd Ann Arbor MI 48105-2659

**SULLIVAN, TIMOTHY,** lawyer; b. Detroit, May 16, 1948; s. Paul Gilmary and Virginia (Rosier) S.; m. Marsha Rosenberg Sullivan, June 19, 1971; children: Eileen A., Hugh V. BA Journalism, U. Mich., 1970; JD, Georgetown U., 1975. Bar: 1975, D.C. 1976. Contract negotiator CIA, Washington, 1973-75; assoc. Fried, Frank, Harris, Shriver & Kampelman, Washington, 1975-78; ptnr. Capell, Howard, Knabe & Cobbs P.A., Washington, 1978-83, Dykema Gossett, Washington, 1983-95, Adduci, Mastriani & Schaumberg, LLP, 1995—2001. Lectr. in field. Narrator (audio cassette) How to Negotiate Government Contracts, 1986. Citizen mem. Alexandria Commn. Persons with Disabilities, Va., 1992-99, vice-chmn. 1997-98, 98-99. Sgt. U.S. Army, 1970-73. Mem. ABA, Nat. Contract Mgmt. Assn., U. Club Washington (bd. govs. 2003-2004, sec. 2003-05, v.p. 2005-06, pres. 2006—), Congl. Country Club (v.p. 1998-99, bd. govs. 1995-2000, pres. 1999-2000). Roman Catholic. Avocations: reading, sports. Office: Thompson Coburn LLP 1909 K St NW 6th Fl Washington DC 20006-1167

**SULLIVAN, TIMOTHY JACKSON,** lawyer, educator, retired academic administrator; b. Ravenna, Ohio, Apr. 15, 1944; s. Ernest Tulio and Margaret Elizabeth (Caris) Sullivan; m. Anne Doubet Klare, Jan. 21, 1973. AB, Coll. William and Mary, 1966; JD, Harvard U., 1969; LLD (hon.), U. Aberdeen, Scotland, 1993, Old Dominion U., 2005. Asst. prof. law Coll. William and Mary, Williamsburg, Va., 1972—75, assoc. prof., 1975—78, prof., 1978—85, Bryan prof. law, dean, 1985—92, pres., 1992—2005, pres. emeritus, 2005—; exec. asst. for policy Office of Gov. Charles S. Robb, Richmond, Va., 1982—85; atty. Freeman, Drapers' Co., London, 1992. Vis. prof. law U. Va., Charlottesville, 1981; exec. dir. Gov.'s Commn. on Va.'s Future, Richmond, 1982—84; vice-chmn. Gov.'s Commn. on Fed. Spending, Richmond, 1986; mem. Gov.'s Fellows Selection Com., 1985—90, Gov.'s Commn. on Sexual Assault and Substance Abuse on the Coll. Campus (chmn. enforcement subcom.), 1991—92; counsel Commn. on Future of Va.'s Ind. Sys. 1997–89, chair VA Rhodes Scholarship Commn., 1998—2005; mem. Livery Drapers Co., 2003; chair appeals panel Internat. Commn. Holocaust Era Ins. Claims, 2002—. Mem. Va. State Bd. Edn., Richmond, 1987—92; chair Gov.'s Task Force on Intercollegiate Athletics, 1992—93; pres. The Mariner's Mus., Newport News, Va., 2006—. Decorated Bronze Star; named Outstanding Virginian, Va. 4-H Found., 1999. Fellow: Va. Bar Fedn., Am. Bar Fedn.; mem.: ABA, Va. Bar Assn., Va. State Bar, Am. Arbitration Assn. (bd. dirs. 2000—03), Cosmos Club, Univ. Club (N.Y.C., Washington), Bull and Bear Club, Omicron Delta Kappa, Phi Beta Kappa. Democrat. Avocations: wine, swimming, reading, golf. Office: Coll William and Mary Office of Pres Emeritus PO Box 8795 Williamsburg VA 23187-8795 Office Phone: 752-221-1256. E-mail: tjsull@wm.edu.

**SULLIVAN, TIMOTHY PATRICK,** telecommunications company executive; b. Springfield, Ill., Mar. 4, 1942; s. Jeremiah Joseph and Genevieve Anastasia (Stapleton) S.; m. Kathleen Veronica Logue, May 4, 1974; children: Timothy Patrick Jr., Michael Sean, Shannon Kathleen, Jennifer Hillary, Thomas Brennan. BSEE, U. Notre Dame, 1964; postgrad., Syracuse U., 1966-67. Tech. mgr. IBM Corp., Poughkeepsie, NY, 1964—68, Hursley, England, 1968—69, middle mgr. Poughkeepsie, San Jose, 1969—77, sr. mgr. Research Triangle Park, NC, 1977—81, corp. com. Armonk, NY, 1981—83, product mgr. Research Triangle Park, NC, 1983—85; v.p., officer No. Telecom, Richardson, Tex., 1985—92; pres., CEO Connectware, Inc., 1993—97; CEO Com World, Inc., 1997—98; pres. Optical Networking SBU, Lucent Techs., Richardson, Tex., 1998—2000; pres. optical networking group Lucent Techs.; Holmdel, NJ, 2001—03; pres., CEO Cebatech Inc., 2004—. Bd. dirs. com. Corp. for Open Systems, McLean, Va., 1992; bd. dirs. AXONLINK; mem. adv. bd. Monmouth U., Corrigent Sys., Reactive Nanotech., Arcana Networks, Carrius Techs.; mem. exec. adv. coun. Nat. Comms. Forum, Chgo., 1989-90; chmn. bd. Osinet Corp., 1991. Inventor storage subsystems in field, 1969-71; author: Captain, 1974; contbr. articles to profl. jours. Adv. bd. Dallas Mus. of Art, 1988-92; mem. North Tex. Commn., Dallas, 1988-91. Republican. Roman Catholic. Avocations: creative writing, chess, golf. Home: 170 Red Hill Rd Middletown NJ 07748 Office: Cebatech Inc 444 Route 35 Eatontown NJ 07724-2200 Office Phone: 908-601-2244. Personal E-mail: tpskvs@ix.netcom.com. Business E-Mail: sullivan@cebatech.com.

**SULLIVAN, TRUDY F.,** apparel executive; Buyer Jordan Marsh; mgmt. positions with The Avenue, Decelle, T. Deane, Filene's; pres. J. Crew Group Inc., 1997—2001; group pres. Liz Claiborne casual & Liz Claiborne woman Liz Claiborne Inc., NYC, 2001—02, exec. v.p., 2002—06, pres., 2006—. Office: Liz Claiborne Inc 1441 Broadway New York NY 10018*

**SULLIVAN, WILLIAM BEAUMONT,** lawyer; b. Kansas City, Mo., May 12, 1945; s. Raymond Sidney and Georgia Belle (Sykes) S.; m. Donna Ray Daniel, Nov. 25, 1966; 1 child, Georgia Marie. BA magna cum laude in Economics, U. Va., 1967; JD cum laude, Harvard U., 1970. Bar: DC 1970, NC, 1990, US Ct. Appeals DC, 3rd, 4th, 6th, and 11th Circuits, various dist. and bankruptcy courts. Assoc. Arent, Fox, Kintner, Plotkin & Kahn, Washington, 1970-77, ptnr., 1978-90, head bankruptcy dept., 1982-90; mem. Womble, Carlyle, Sandridge & Rice PLLC, Winston-Salem, NC, 1990—, bankruptcy and creditors' rights practice group leader. Fellow Am. Bar Found., Am. Coll. Bankruptcy; mem. ABA, NC Bar Assn., Am. Bankruptcy Inst., Am. Arbitration Assn., Harvard U. Law Sch. Assn., Walker Chandler Inn of Ct. Avocations: word puzzles, music, golf. Office: Womble Carlyle Sandridge & Rice PLLC PO Box 84 Winston Salem NC 27102 Office Phone: 336-721-3506. Office Fax: 336-733-8365. Business E-Mail: wsullivan@wcsr.com.

**SULLIVAN, WILLIAM FRANCIS,** lawyer; b. San Francisco, May 6, 1952; s. Francis Michael and Jane Frances (Walsh) S.; children: Matthew, Meghan, Kathleen; m. Kait Sullivan. AB, U. Calif., Berkeley, 1974; JD, UCLA, 1977. Bar: Calif. 1977, U.S. Dist. Ct. (no. dist.) Calif 1977, U.S. Ct. Appeals (9th cir.) 1977, U.S. Dist. Ct. (ea. dist.) Calif. 1978, U.S. Ct. Appeals (5th cir.) 1979, U.S. Ct. Appeals (fed. cir.) 1985, U.S. Dist. Ct. (so. dist.) Calif. 1986, U.S. Dist. Ct. (cen. dist.) Calif. 1990, U.S. Supreme Ct. 1986. Assoc. Chickering & Gregory, San Francisco and Washington, 1977-81, Brobeck, Phleger & Harrison, San Diego and San Francisco, 1981-84, ptnr., 1984—2002, mng. ptnr. San Diego, 1992-96, 2001—03, securities litig. group leader, 2002—, firmwide mng. ptnr., 1996-98; ptnr. Paul Hastings Janofsky & Walker LLP, San Diego, 2003—, chair nat. securities litig. practice group, mem. litig. steering com., 2003—, mng. ptnr., 2005. Panelist Calif. Continuing Edn. Bar; instr. Fed. Practice Program, U.S. No. Dist., chair litig. sect., 1992, U.S. Dist. Ct. (no. dist.) Calif., 1980; instr. Coll. of Advocacy, Hastings Law Sch.; adv. bd. AMICUS Info. Svcs. Mem. ABA, Assn. Bus. Trial Lawyers (bd. govs. San Diego chpt. 1993-95), Calif. Bar Assn. (litig. sect.), San Francisco Bar Assn., San Diego Bar Assn., Barristers Club San Francisco (bd. dirs. 1984-86, pres. 1985), Calif. Young Lawyers Assn. (bd. dirs. 1986-89, sec. 1987-99, 1st v.p. 1988-89). Democrat. Roman Catholic. Office Phone: 858-720-2500. Business E-Mail: williamsullivan@paulhastings.com

**SULLIVAN, WILLIAM J.,** state supreme court justice; b. Waterbury, Conn., Mar. 12, 1939; Student, St. Thomas Sem., 1958-59; BA in Polit. Sci., Providence Coll., 1962; B in Civil Law, Coll. William and Mary, 1965, JD, 1970. Priv. practice, Waterbury, 1967—78; civil service commr. State of Conn., 1974—75; corp. counsel City of Waterbury, 1976—78; judge Conn. Superior Ct., 1978-97, Conn. Appellate Ct., 1997-99; assoc. justice Conn. Supreme Ct., 1999-2001, chief justice, 2001—06, sr. justice, 2006—. Captain U.S. Army, 1965-66. Decorated 2 Bronze Stars for meritorious svc. US Army, Air Medal. Office: Conn Supreme Ct Supreme Ct Bldg 231 Capitol Ave Hartford CT 06106-1548 Office Phone: 860-757-2116.

**SULLIVAN, WILLIAM JOHN,** osteopath; b. Pittsburg, Kans., Nov. 5, 1963; s. William Leroy and Joan Elizabeth (Prete) S; div.; 1 child, Lauren Marie. BS in Biology, Pittsburg State U., 1986; DO, U. Health Scis., Kansas City, Mo., 1990. Diplomate Nat. Bd. Osteo. Med. Examiners, Am. Bd. Internal Medicine, Am. Assn. Med. Rev. Officers. Intern Riverside Hosp., Wichita, Kans., 1990-91; resident Deaconess Hosp., St. Louis, 1991-94; pvt. practice Med. Cons. of Pitts., LLC, Kans., 1994—; active staff Mt. Carmel Med. Ctr., 1994—, med. dir. occupl. health, med. dir. employee health, 1995—2002, med. dir. cardiomyopathy clinic, 1997—, chief medicine, 1998—, chief-of-staff-elect, 1999—, pres. med. staff, 2001—. Mem. adv. bd. dirs. Cmty. Nat. Bank, Pittsburg; med. staff sec. Mt. Carmel Med. Ctr., Pittsburg, 1999; clin. instr. Pittsburg State U. Sch. Nursing; participating physician Pittsburg Free Clinic; clin. adv. Pittsburg State U. Pre-Med Club; mem. health occupations adv. bd. Unified Sch. Dist. #250; physician Congl. Health Ministries. Mem. exec. bd. dirs. Pitts. Family YMCA, pres.-elect, 2003, pres., 2004—, chief internal medicine, 1995—; bd. dirs. Pitts. State U. Alumni Assn., nat. 2d v.p., 2003-04. Lt. col. Kans. Army N.G., 1988—. Fellow ACP; mem. VFW, Kans. Med. Soc., Am. Assn. Med. Rev. Officers, N.G. Assn. U.S., KC, Crawford County Med. Soc. (pres. 2000), Am. Legion, Sigma Chi (life loyal Sig program). Republican. Roman Catholic. Avocations: music, golf, stamp collecting/philately. Office: Med Consultants Pitts LLC 1015 Mt Carmel Pl Pittsburg KS 66762 Home: 1502 Woodland Terr Pittsburg KS 66762 Office Phone: 620-231-8849.

**SULLIVAN, WILLIAM LITSEY,** lawyer; b. Harrodsburg, Ky., Nov. 1, 1921; s. Charles Blount and Anne Litsey Sullivan; m. Elizabeth Dorsey Sullivan, Apr. 21, 1951; children: John Charles, William L. Jr. BA, Centre Coll. Ky., Danville, 1943; LLB, U. Ky., Lexington, 1948; degree in Humanities (hon.), Henderson C.C., Ky., 2004. Founder and ptnr. Dorsey and Sullivan, Henderson, Ky., 1956—95; ptnr. Sullivan and Sullivan, 1995—99; of counsel Stoll Keenan Ogden PLLC, 1999—. Mem. Ky. State Senate, Frankfort, Ky., 1953—58, 1966—82; commr. aeronautics State of Ky., Frankfort, Ky., 1959—60; acting judge Ky. Supreme Ct., 1978; chmn. Ky. State Lottery, Louisville, 1988—89; mem. Ky. Racing Commn. 1990—99. Chmn. Coll. Found., Inc., Henderson, Ky., 1980—. 1st lt. USAAF, 1943—45. Named winner, Internat. Formula One Air Race, France, 1976, Outstanding Alumnus, Centre Coll., 1976, Disting. Citizen, City of Henderson, Ky., 2004; named to Ky. Aviation Hall of Fame, Ky. Aviation Mus., 2004. Mem.: ABA, Ky. Bar Assn. Democrat. Presbyterian. Avocations: hunting, fishing, golf, flying. Office: Stoll Keenan Ogden PLLC 201 C N Main Henderson KY 42420 Office Phone: 270-831-1900.

**SULLIVAN, WILLIAM P.,** electronics executive; b. Yakima, Wash.; 1949; BS, U. Calif.-Davis. With Hewlett-Packard Co., 1976—99, various positions, 1976—95, gen. mgr. Optical Comm. Divsn., 1995—97, gen. mgr. Comm. Semiconductor Solutions Divsn., 1997—98, gen. mgr., v.p. Components Group (now Semiconductor Products Group), 1998—99; senior v.p., gen. mgr. SPG Agilent Technologies Inc. (spin-off from HP Co.), 1999—2002; exec. v.p., COO Agilent Technologies Inc., 2002—05, pres., CEO, 2005—. Bd. dir. Children's Discovery Mus., San Jose, Calif., Lumileds, URS Corp., 2006—. Office: Agilent Technologies Inc 395 Page Mill Rd Palo Alto CA 94306*

**SULLIVAN STEMBERG, MAUREEN,** interior designer; b. Brookline, Mass., July 8, 1951; d. Loretta McDermott and Herbert Michael Sullivan; m. Thomas George Stemberg, Mar. 11, 1975 (div. Sept. 9, 1989). AA in polit. sci., Newton Jr. Coll., 1969—71; degree in art history, Boston Coll., 1972—73; Fine Arts Program, Mus. of Fine Arts Sch., 1973—75; Architecture and Design, Boston Ctr. of Architecture, 1982—85. ASID, MA, 1987. CEO, interior designer Interiors of Wellesley, Inc., Wellesley, Mass., 1977—80; CEO, head designer Maureen Sullivan Stemberg Interiors, Boston-Palm Beach, 1980—98; design and fashion editor Palm Beach Illus., Palm Beach, Fla., 1990—95; CEO BabySuites.Com, Boston, 2003—04; chief creative officer Connoisseur Pub., Inc., Boston, 2004—. Chmn. and co-chairman, ann. flower show Mass. Hort. Soc., Boston, 1990—94. Designer Mahaney Baseball Club House, U. Maine (Top 5 Design winner for Baseball Complex Devel., 1994), Various Hotel Interiors (Top 20 Hotel Designers for Holiday Inns Inc., 1991), Trump Plaza, other Club Colette, Palm Beach, Fla.; contbr. articles to mag. Fund raiser Barcelona Summer Olympics, Mass., Spain, 1990—92, Am. Cup, Boston, 1993—95; trustee Boston Opera Co., 1977—81. Mem.: United Way of Mass. Bay, Nat. Trust for Hist. Preservation, Dana Farber Cancer Inst. Pediat. (hon.; dir. 1996—97), Nat. Museum of

Women in the Arts (hon.; coun. mem. 1991—93), Am. Soc. of Interior Designers (assoc.). Home: 118 Huntington Ave Ste 1403 Boston MA 02116 Office Phone: 617-266-5664. E-mail: maureen@connoiseurpublishing.com, intdesignmss@aol.com.

SULLIVAN-SZUTS, BETTY ANNE, academic administrator, educator; b. Phila., Dec. 23, 1939; d. Rowland Thomas and Elizabeth Catherine Moriarty; m. Robert Lloyd Sullivan, Sept. 21, 1957 (div.); children: Lisa Anne Sullivan, Brent Rowland Sullivan, Jamie Alexandra Sullivan; m. Ivan Ramon Szuts, May 6, 1995. BS in Home Econs. Edn., Douglass Coll., 1975; EdM in Supervision and Adminstrn., Rutgers U., 1978, EdD in Adult and Continuing Ednl. Adminstrn., 1989. Cert. sch. adminstr. N.J., prin./supr. N.J., tchr. home econs. N.J. Tchr. home econs. Freehold Regional H.S. Dist., NJ, 1975—80; state supr. home econs. edn. N.J. State Dept. Edn., Trenton 1980—81; dir. and tchr. in-svc. Rutgers U., New Brunswick, NJ, 1981—89; vice prin. Monmouth County Vo-Tech H.S. Dist., Middletown, NJ, 1990—91; dir. Suffolk County Respite Care Program, Patchogue, NY, 1991—94; dir. gerontology program and instr. aging courses Union County Coll., Cranford, NJ, 1994—96; supr. student tchrs. Georgian Ct. Coll., Lakewood, NJ, 1994—96; vis. prof. dept. sociology Wheaton Coll., Norton, Mass., 1996—97; dir. model Tex. safe home program N.W. Assistance Ministries, Houston, 2000—02; grant coord. N. Harris Coll., 2002—03; seminar leader Spirited Elder and Assocs. Adj. prof. profl. studies grad. program LI U., Southampton, NY, 1991—94; rschr. Aging Tex. Well Coalition, 2002—; seminar leader Spirited Elder and Assocs., 2004—; presenter in field. Author: Spiritual Elders: Women of Worth in the Third Millennium, 1999. Chair edn. Harris County Area Agy. Aging, tng. com.; chair adv. bd. Acad. Lifelong Learning, North Harris Coll.; mem. Acts 16:5 task force Presbytery New Covenant, Houston; ruling elder North Woods Presbyn. Ch., 2006—. Recipient Cmty. Svc. award, North Harris Coll., 2003; grantee The Aging Tex. Well Grant, 2002—03. Mem.: Phi Delta Kappa, Kappa Delta Pi, Omicron Nu. Avocations: tennis, ballroom dancing, writing, playing the organ. Home and Office: Spirited Elder and Assocs 14311 Champions Dr Houston TX 77069 Office Phone: 281-895-0321. Personal E-mail: bettyanne.ivan@sbcglobal.net.

SULLOWAY, FRANK JONES, social sciences educator, historian; b. Concord, NH, Feb. 2, 1947; s. Alvah Woodbury and Alison (Green) Sulloway; 1 child, Ryan. AB summa cum laude, Harvard U., 1969, AM in History Sci., 1971, PhD in History Sci., 1978. Jr. fellow Harvard U. Soc. Fellows, 1974-77; mem. Sch. Social Sci. Inst. Advanced Study, Princeton, NJ, 1977-78; rsch. fellow Miller Inst. Basic Rsch. Sci. U. Calif., Berkeley, 1978-80, vis. Miller rsch. prof., 1999—2000, vis. prof., 2000—; rsch. fellow MIT, Cambridge, 1980-81, vis. scholar, 1989-98; postdoctoral fellow Harvard U., Cambridge, 1981-82, vis. scholar, 1984-89; rsch. fellow U. Calif., London, 1982-84; Vernon prof. biography Dartmouth Coll., Hanover, NH, 1986. Author: (book) Freud, Biologist of the Mind, 1979 (Pfizer award History Sci. Soc., 1980), Born to Rebel, 1996; contbr. articles to profl. jours. Recipient Randi award, Skeptics Soc., 1997, Golden Plate award, Am. Acad. Achievement, 1997; fellow, NEH, 1980—81, NSF, 1981—82, John Simon Guggenheim Meml. Found., 1982—83, MacArthur Found., 1984—89, Dibner Inst., MIT, 1993—94, Ctr. Advanced Study Behavioral Scis., Stanford, Calif., 1998—99. Fellow: AAAS (mem. electorate nominating com. sect. L 1988—91, 1994—97), Linnean Soc. London; mem.: History Sci. Soc. (mem. fin. com. 1987—92, mem. com. devel. 1988—92), Human Behavior and Evolution Soc., Am. Psychol. Soc. Home: 1709 Shattuck Ave Apt 205 Berkeley CA 94709-1753 Office: U Calif Dept Psychology IPSR 4125 Tolman Hall Berkeley CA 94720-1603 Office Phone: 510-642-7139. Business E-Mail: sulloway@berkeley.edu.

SULTAN, ALTOON, artist; b. Bklyn., Sept. 29, 1948; BFA, Bklyn. Coll., 1969, MFA in Painting, 1971; student, Skowhegan Art Sch., Maine, 1970. Vis. critic Univ. Pa., Phila., 1985—88; resident faculty Skowhegan Sch. Painting & Sculpture, Maine, 1988; asst. prof. San Jose State Univ., Calif., 1991—94; vis. prof. Dartmouth Coll., NH, 1998—2001; founder Mount Ara Designs, Groton, Vt. Author: The Luminous Brush: Painting with Egg Tempera, 1999; one-woman shows include First St. Gallery, NYC, 1971, 1973, 1975, Univ. SD, Vermillion, 1975, Marlborough Gallery, NYC, 1977, 1979, 1982, 1984, 1985, 1988, 1990, 1993, 1995, 1998, Marlborough Fine Art Graphics, London, 1987, Galleria Marieschi, Monza, Italy, 1999, Tibor de Nagy Gallery, NYC, 2001, exhibited in group shows at Suffolk Mus., Stony Brook, NY, 1971, Allan Frumkin Gallery, NYC, 1975, Davis & Long Gallery, 1977, Thorpe Intermedia Gallery, Sparkill, NY, 1980, Downtown Br., Whitney Mus., NYC, 1982, Mus. Fine Arts, Boston, 1982, One Penn Plaza, NYC, 1985, Veranneman Found., Belgium, 1986, David Adamson Gallery, Washington, 1988, Flint Inst. of Arts, Mich., 1991, Am. Acad. and Inst. of Arts & Letters, NYC, 1992, Sleeth Gallery, W. Va. Wesleyan Coll., 1996, numerous others. Recipient Prix Duc de Valverde d'Ayala Valva, Fondation Monaco, 1999, Acad. award in art for egg tempera painting, Am. Acad. Arts and Letters, 1999; grantee Nat. Endowment for Arts, 1983, 1989. Mem.: NAD (academician 1995—). Studio: PO Box 2 Groton VT 05046 Office: Tibor de Nagy Gallery 724 Fifth Ave New York NY 10019

SULTAN, MARK R., plastic surgeon; BS, Brandeis U.; MD, Columbia U. Coll. Physicians and Surgeons, 1982. Diplomate rgery, Am. Bd. Plastic Surgery. Resident in gen. surgery Columbia-Presbyn. Med. Ctr., N.Y.C., 1983—87, resident in plastic surgery, 1987—88, 1989—90; fellow in head and neck surgery/microvascular reconstrn. Emory U. Affiliated Hosps., Atlanta, 1988—89; attending physician dept. plastic surgery St. Luke's Roosevelt, N.Y. Eye and Ear Infirmary, N.Y.C., 1990—; chief divsn. plastic and reconstructive surgery Beth Israel Hosp.; pvt. practice plastic surgery N.Y.C. Assoc. prof. clin. surgery Columbia U. Coll. Physicians and Surgeons, N.Y.C. Mem.: Am. Soc. Reconstructive Microsurgery, Am. Soc. Plastic and Reconstructive Surgeons, Am. Soc. Aesthetic Plastic Surgery. Office: 1100 Park Ave New York NY 10128*

SULTAN, WAFA, psychiatrist; b. Baniyas, Syria, 1958; arrived in US, 1989, naturalized; m. David Sultan; 3 children. MD, Aleppo Univ. Syria. Lic. CA. Named one of 100 Most Influential People in World, Time Mag., 2006. Outspoken critic of violence in Muslim world saying violence destroys Islam. Home: Los Angeles CA*

SULTANOV, NAMIG, 2D BARONET, musician, music educator; b. Baku, Azerbaijan, June 9, 1948; arrived in USA, 2002; s. Abdulhamid Sultanov and Kubra Sultanova; m. Sevil Agalarova Sultanova, July 10, 1970; children: Nigyar Sultanova, Narmina Sultanova. MusB piano, MusM piano, State Conservatory of Music, Moscow, Russia, 1965—70, Mus D piano, 1970—73. Faculty mem., assoc. prof. piano dept. Azerbaijan State Conservatory of Music, Baku, Azerbaijan, 1971—91; vis. assoc. prof. Faculty of Music and Performing Arts, Bilkent Univ., Ankara, Turkey, 1991—2002, chmn. piano dept., 1991—2002, vice dean, 1991—2002; faculty mem., piano The Gorin Sch. of Music, Mountain View, Calif., 2002—. Named Hon. Title of State Artist, Pres. of Azerbaijan/ Baku, Azerbaijan, 1991; recipient Diploma for Student's Achievements, Third Internat. Young Pianists Compet. in Memory of v. Horowitz, 1999. Mem.: Juri mem. of Nat. and Internat. Piano Competitions, Music Tchr. Nat. Assoc. Achievements include conduct internat. master classes; Numerous students won prizes in Nat. and Internat. Piano competitions. Home: 362 LaStrada Dr #21 San Jose CA 95123 E-mail: namiksultan@yahoo.com.

SULTZBAUGH, JOHN STEPHAN, historian, educator; b. Harrisburg, Pa., July 25, 1950; s. John Leroy Sultzbaugh and Kathryn Mikhailovna Sass; m. Gayle Rene Reitenbach, May 3, 1980; children: Elisabeth Yvonne, Andrew John. B.Humanities summa cum laude, Pa. State U.-Harrisburg, 1972, MA, 1975; PhD, Greenwich U., Norfolk Island, Australia, 1999. Cert. tchr. Pa. Hydrologist USGS, Harrisburg, Pa., 1973—74; hydrologic technologist Susquehana River Basin Commn., Mechanicsburg, Pa., 1974—75; tchr. history, govt. Upper Dauphin Area Sch. Dist., Lykens, Pa., 1975—. Adj. journalist and photographer Upper Dauphin Sentinel, Millersburg, Pa., 1978—88; Daily News, Lebanon, Pa., 1981—83; Sunday Pa., Lebanon, 1982, Pa. Mag., Harrisburg, 1990; mem. Nat. Jr. Honor Soc. Bd./Upper Dauphin

Area Sch. Dist., 2002—03; coord. student assistance program Upper Dauphin Sch. Dist., 1991—98; cons. reader Pa. History Textbook Commn., Harrisburg, 2003. Contbr. poetry in jours. Recipient Editors award, Poetry.com, 2004. Mem.: Nat. Edn. Assns., Am. Soc. Authors and Pubs., Intersoc. Color Coun. Republican. Eastern Orthodox. Achievements include patents for variable pitch fluid impeller; research in blending colored music for instructional and theraupeutic applications; entry in Guinness Book of World Records. Avocations: aquatics, classical music, photography, philosophy. Home: 261 Romberger Ln Elizabethville PA 17023 Office: Upper Dauphin Area Sch Dist 2668 State Rt 209 Lykens PA 17048 Office Phone: 717-580-6719.

SULYK, STEPHEN, retired archbishop; b. Balnycia, Western Ukraine, Oct. 2, 1924; s. Michael and Mary (Denys) Sulyk. Student, Ukrainian Cath. Sem. of Holy Spirit, Fed. Republic Germany, 1945—48, St. Josaphat's Sem., 1948—52; Licentia in Sacred Theology, Cath. U. Am., 1952. Ordained priest Ukrainian Cath. Ch., 1952. Assoc. pastor, Omaha, 1952; assoc. pastor Bklyn., 1953, Minersville, Pa., 1954, Youngstown, Ohio, 1955; pastor Ch. Sts. Peter and Paul, Phoenixville, Pa., 1955, St. Michael's Ch., Frackville, Pa., 1957—61, Assumption of Blessed Virgin Mary Ch., Perth Amboy, NJ, 1962—81; sec. Archeparchy Chancery, 1956—57; adminstr. St. Nicholas, Phila., 1961; archbishop Met. of Ukraine-Rite Catholics of Archeparchy, Phila., 1981—2000; ret., 2000. Vice-chmn. Priests Senate, 1977—78, chmn.; pres. Ascension Manor, Inc.; archbishop Ukranian Rite Caths. Archeparchy Phila., Met. Ukranian-Rite Caths. U.S.A.; chmn. ad-hoc inter-rite com. Nat. Cath. Conf. Bishops/U.S. Cath. Conf., 1991. Mem.: Presidium of Synod of Ukranian Cath. Bishops (treas.), Coll. Bishops of Roman Cath. Ch., Providence Assn. Am. (Supreme Protector). Office: Archdiocese of Phila 827 N Franklin St Philadelphia PA 19123-2004

SULYOK, PAUL DAVID, music educator, composer; b. St. Johnsbury, Vt., July 14, 1958; s. Kalman Laszlo and Catherine Hagerman Sulyok. MusB in Music Edn., Westminster Choir Coll., 1981. Cert. Music Comprehensive 2100 N.J., 1981. Dir. activities Childrens' Fresh Air Home, North Wildwood, NJ, 1976—86; vocal, choral, drama tchr. East Windsor (N.J.) Schs., 1983—91, Upper Freehold Schools, Allentown, NJ, 1991—; childrens' theater dir. Green Apple Theater, Hightstown, NJ, 1993; music dir. On With The Show Bravo Cable Network, N.Y.C., 2001. Guild mem., entertainer Boheme Opera N.J., Trenton, 1993; musical dir., accompanist Off Broad St. Theater, Hopewell, 1995. Composer (and author): (musical play) Audition, 1993; composer: (author) (musical plays) Luigi's, 1995; composer: (and author) many children's musicals. Hospice vol. Hyacinth Orgn., New Brunswick, 1988—91; sch. bd. mem. Ewing Presbyn. Nursery Sch., 1998—2000; mem. choir, pianist Ewing Presbyn. Ch., 1995. Mem.: NEA, Ctrl. N.J. Orff-Schulwerk Assn., Music Educators Nat. Conf., Boheme Opera N.J. Guild (adv. bd./fundraising 1993). Democrat. Presbyterian. Avocations: piano, composing, travel, theater. Home: 27 Chippin Ct Robbinsville NJ 08691 Office: Upper Freehold Regional Schools 27 High St Allentown NJ 08501 Personal E-mail: sulyokpaul@aol.com.

SULZBERGER, ARTHUR OCHS, newspaper executive; b. N.Y.C., N.Y., Feb. 5, 1926; s. Arthur Hays and Iphigene (Ochs) Sulzberger; m. Barbara Grant, July 2, 1948 (div. 1956); children: Arthur Ochs, Karen Alden; m. Carol Fox, Dec. 19, 1956 (dec. Aug. 1995); 1 adopted child, Cathy 1 child, Cynthia Fox; m. Allison Stacey Cowles, Mar. 9, 1996. BA, Columbia, 1951; LL.D., Dartmouth, 1964, Bard Coll., 1967; L.H.D., Montclair State Coll., 1972, Tufts U.; LLD (hon.), U. Scranton; L.H.D., Columbia U., 1992. With N.Y. Times, N.Y.C., 1951—, asst. treas. 1958—63, pres., 1963—79, pub., 1963—92, chmn., CEO, 1963—97, chmn. emeritus, 1997—, also bd. dirs. Dir. Times Printing Co., Chattanooga. Trustee emeritus Columbia U.; trustee Met. Mus. Art, chmn. bd. trustees, 1987—. Capt. USMCR, WWII, Korea. Mem.: SAR, Met. Club (Washington), Explorers Club, Overseas Press Club. Office: NY Times Co 229 W 43rd St New York NY 10036-3959

SULZBERGER, ARTHUR OCHS, JR., newspaper publisher; b. Mt. Kisco, NY, Sept. 22, 1951; s. Arthur Ochs Sulzberger and Barbara Winslow Grant; m. Gail Gregg, May 24, 1975; children: Arthur Gregg, Ann Alden. BA, Tufts U., 1974; grad. Prog. for Mgmt. Dev., Harvard U. Bus. Sch., 1985. Reporter The Raleigh (N.C.) Times, 1974—76; corr. AP, London, 1976—78; Washington corr. NY Times, 1978—81, city hall reporter, 1981, asst. metro editor, 1981—82, group mgr. advt. dept., 1983—84, sr. analyst corp. planning, 1985, prodn. coordinator, 1985—87, asst. pub., 1987—88, dep. pub., 1988—92, pub., 1992—; chmn. bd. dirs. NY Times Co., 1997—. Chmn. NY Outward Bound Ctr., 2002—. Office: The NY Times 229 W 43rd St New York NY 10036-3959*

SUMANTH, DAVID JONNAKOTY, industrial engineer, educator; b. Machilipatnam, India, Jan. 28, 1946; arrived in U.S., 1972; s. John Devraj and Nancy (David) Jonnakoty; m. Chaya J. Victor, June 26, 1974; children: John J., Paul J. BE, Osmania U., India, 1967, ME, 1969; MS in Indsl. Engring., Ill. Inst. Tech., 1974, PhD in Indsl. Engring., 1979. Tchg./rsch. asst. Ill. Inst. Tech., Chgo., 1973-78, instr., 1979; asst. prof. indsl. engring. U. Miami, Coral Gables, Fla., 1979-83, founding dir. productivity research group, 1979—, dir. grad. studies, 1980-83, assoc. prof. indsl. engring., 1983-88, Coll. Engring. coordinator MBA/MSIE, 1984-93, prof. indsl. engring., 1987—. Chmn. confs. Author: Productivity Engineering and Management, 1984, internat. student edit., 1985, Spanish edit., 1990, Indian edit., 1990, coll. custom series edit., 1994, also instrs. manual, (script) Total Productivity Management, 1985; editor: Productivity Management Frontiers-I, 1987, II, 1989, Productivity and Quality Management Frontiers III, 1991, IV, 1993, V, 1995, VI, 1997, VII, 1998, X, 2004; author: Total Productivity Management, 1998. Recipient over 65 honors, awards and recognitions including YMCA Edn. Gold medal, 1969, Freedoms Found., 1987;, Alexander Orr award of Tchg. Excellence, U. Miami, 2000; fellow U. Miami Eaton Honors Coll., 1986, fellow World Acad. Productivity Sci., 1989; gov.'s appointee as sr. judge Fla. Sterling award, 1992-93, judge, 1993-98. Mem. Am. Inst. Indsl. Engrs. (sr. mem., pres. Miami chpt. 1982-83, bd. dirs. 1983-84, nat. asst. dir. productivity mgmt. 1984—, chairperson rsch. com. 1987, Outstanding Indsl. Engr. of Yr. Miami chpt. 1983, 84); Productivity Ctr. (trustee 1985-89), Internat. Soc. for Productivity and Quality Rsch. (founder 1993, founding pres. 1993-95, chmn. 1995-97, pres. 2004—., Distinguished Prof. Univ. Francise Marroguin, 2006). Republican. Baptist. Avocations: reading, writing, people. Office: U Miami Productivity Rsch Group Coral Gables FL 33124 Office Phone: 305-284-2366. Business E-Mail: dsumanth@miami.edu.

SUMBLIN, ANNE STONE, lawyer; b. Bay Minette, Ala., Nov. 14, 1960; d. Norborne Clarke and Patricia (Bartlett) Stone; m. Martin Anthony Sumblin, Nov. 16, 1996. BS in Acctg., U. Ala., 1983, JD, 1987. Bar: Ala. 1987. Law clk. to Hon. Sam C. Pointer, Jr., U.S. Dist. Ct. for No. Dist. Ala., 1987-88; Ptnr. Walston, Wells, Anderson & Bains, L.L.P., Birmingham, Ala., 1995—. Bd. dirs. U. Ala. Sch. of Law Found., 1997—; chmn. bd. bar examiners Ala. State Bar. Mem. Ala. State Bar Assn. Office: Walston Wells & Birchall LLP PO Box 345 Kinston AL 36453-0345

SUMERIX, KENDALL J., science educator; b. Lachine, Mich., Aug. 12, 1964; s. Kenneth and Joan Sumerix; m. Melony Sumerix; children: Clarissa, Andrew. BS in Biochemistry, Mich. State U., East Lansing, 1988, MS, 1991. Instr. sci. Alpena Cmty. Coll., Mich., 1991—. Named Tchr. of Yr., Alpena Cmty. Coll., 1999, 2004. Office: Alpena Cmty Coll 666 Johnson St Alpena MI 49707-1495 Home: 2650 Calcut Rd Lachine MI 49753 Office Phone: 989-358-7347.

SUMIDA, GERALD AQUINAS, lawyer; b. Hilo, Hawaii, June 19, 1944; s. Sadamy and Kimiyo (Miyahara) S. AB summa cum laude, Princeton U., 1966; JD, Yale U., 1969. Bar: Hawaii 1970, U.S. Dist. Ct. Hawaii 1970, U.S. Ct. Appeals (9th cir.) 1970, U.S. Supreme Ct. 1981. Rsch. assoc. Ctr. Internat. Studies, Princeton U., 1969; assoc. Carlsmith, Ball, Honolulu, 1970-76, ptnr., 1976-99; gen. counsel Asian Devel. Bank, 1999—. Mem. cameras in courtroom evaluation com. Hawaii Supreme Ct., 1984-86. Co-author: (with

others) Legal, Instutional and Financial Aspects of An Inter-Island Electrical Transmission Cable, 1984, Alternative Approaches to the Legal, Instutional and Financial Aspects of Developing an Inter-Island, Electrical Transmission Cable System, 1986; editor Hawaii Bar News, 1972-73; contbr. chpts. to books. Mem. sci. and statis. com. Western Pacific Fishery Mgmt. Coun., 1979-99; mem. study group on law of armed conflict and the law of the sea Comdr. in Chief Pacific, USN, 1979-82; chmn. Pacific and Asian Affairs Coun. Hawaii, 1991, pres., 1982-91, bd. govs., 1976-96; bd. govs. ARC, 1994-2000, mem. exec. com., 1996-2000, chmn. human resources com., 1996-2000, chmn. Hawaii chpt., 1983-99, bd. dirs., 1983-99, vice chmn., 1990; chmn. Hawaii C. of C., 1997-98, bd. dirs., 1990-99; vice chmn. Honolulu Com. Fgn. Rels., 1983—; pres., dir., founding mem. Hawaii Ocean Law Assn., 1978—; mem. Hawaii Adv. Group for Law of Sea Inst., 1977-85; pres. Hawaii Inst. Continuing Legal Edn., 1979-83, dir., 1976-87; pres., founding mem. Hawaii Coun. Legal Edn. Youth, 1980-83, dir., 1983-88; chmn. Hawaii Commn. Yr. 2000, 1976-79; mem. Honolulu Cmty. Media Coun., 1976-99, exec. com., 1976-84, Legal coun., 1979-83; bd. dirs. Hawaii Imin Centennial Corp., 1983-90, Hawaii Pub. Radio, 1983-88, Legal Aid Soc. Hawaii, 1984; founding gov., exec. v.p., chmn. rules and procedures Ctr. Internat. Comml. Dispute Resolution, 1987—; exec. com. Pacific Aerospace Mus., 1991—; exec. com. Pacific Islands Assn., 1988—; exec. com. Asia-Pacific Ctr. Res. Internat. Bus. Disputes, 1991-95; mem. Coun. Asia-Pacific Dispute Rsch. Ctrs., 1991-95; bd. dirs. U.S.C. of C., 1998—; mem. Pacific Basin Econ. Coun., 1993—; mem. mgmt. com. PBEC-U.S. Nat. Com., 1994-99. Recipient cert. of appreciation Gov. of Hawaii, 1979, resolutions of appreciation Hawaii Senate and Ho. of Reps., 1979; grantee Japan Found., 1979. Mem. ABA, Hawaii Bar Assn. (pres. young lawyers sect. 1974, v.p. 1984), Japan-Hawaii Lawyers Assn., Am. Soc. Internat. Law, Internat. Bar Assn., Am. Judicature Soc., Inter-Pacific Bar Assn., Internat. Law Assn., Plaza Club (Honolulu), Colonial Club (Princeton). Democrat. also: Gen Coun Asian Devel Bank PO Box 789 0980 Manila Philippines E-mail: gsumida@adb.org.

SUMIDA, GREGORY ZIO, artist, photographer, musician, astronomer; b. L.A. One-man shows include Palm Springs Desert Mus., 1973, Desert S.W. Art Gallery, 1974, Pioneer Mus. and Haggin Art Gallery, 1975, Potlatch Art Gallery, 1976, Maxwell Galleries, San Francisco, 1977, Smith Gallery, N.Y.C., Troy's Gallery, Ariz., 1984, 1986, 1986, Zantman Galleries, Palm Desert, Calif., 1990, Legacy Gallery, 1991, 2002, exhibited in group shows, Scottsdale, 2000, Artist Focus Show Legacy Gallery, 2000—01, Eitejorg Mus., 2002, Visions of the West, 2003—06, Legacy of Am. West, 2003, 2005, Weatherburn Gallery, 2003, Mountain Oyster's Club Art Show, 2003—06, Contemporary Western Art Show, 2003—05, Sylvan Gallery's Miniature Show, 2003, 2005—06, Trees Pl. Small Works Holiday Exhbn., 2003—06, Big Horn Galleries Summer Roundup, 2004—06, Tex. Art Gallery Auction, 2004—06, Phippen Mus. Miniature Masterpieces Art Show, 2005, 2006, Settlers West Show, 2005—06, Nat. Exhibits Found. Mus. Show, Lubbock, Tex., 2005, Trees Pl. Gallery, 2006, numerous others; contbr. artwork to mags. and jours. including Cowboys and Indian Mag., Jour. Pharm. Med., Art Talk, and Southwest Art. Mem.: Oil Painters Am., Soc. Am. Impressionism. Office: PO Box 9210 Stockton CA 95208-1210 Personal E-mail: ziogregory@hotmail.com.

SUMIYOSHI, TOMIKI, psychiatrist, researcher; b. Tokyo, Dec. 18, 1964; s. Hiroshi and Fusako (Naganuma) S.; m. Sawako Suemasa, Apr. 4, 1993. MB, MD, Kanazawa (Japan) U., 1989, PhD, 1993. Med. diplomate. Resident Fukui Prefectural Psychiat. Hosp., Japan, 1990; ward adminstr., dir. neurochemistry rsch. Kanazawa U. Hosp., Japan, 1991—93; rsch. assoc. dept. psychiatry Case Western Res. U., Cleve., 1993-95; asst. prof. dept. psychiatry, dir. psychopharmacology rsch. Saitama Med. Sch., Japan, 1995—96; asst. prof. dept. neuropsychiatry, dir. neurochemistry rsch. Toyama Med. and Pharm. U., Japan, 1996—2000; assoc. prof. dept. neuropsychiatry U. Toyama Sch. Medicine, 2000—; apptd. psychiatrist Health and Welfare Ministry Japan, 1996—. Vis. prof. dept. psychiatry Vanderbilt U., Nashville, 2000—02; rsch. bd. adv. Am. Biog. Inst., Inc., 2005—; cons. in field. Author: Clinical Perspective of the New Antipsychotic Drugs, 2001, Relapse in Schizophrenia, 2002; contbr. articles to profl. jours. Rep. athlete The Nat. Athletic Meeting, Hachinohe, Japan, 1993. Recipient Psychiat Rsch. award, Saburo Matsubara Meml. Fund, Kanazawa, Japan, 1993, Young Investigator award, Nat. Alliance for Rsch. on Schizophrenia and Depression, Chgo., 1995, NY, 2001, Meml. Travel award, Am. Coll. Neuropsychopharmacology, 2001; fellow Rsch. fellow, Min. Edn. and Sci., Japan, 2000—02; scholar, Rotary, 1994—95. Mem. Soc. Neurosci., NY Acad. Scis., World Fedn. Socs. Biol. Psychiatry, Coll. Internat. Neuropsychopharmacologicum, Schizophrenia Internat. Rsch. Soc., Japanese Soc. Psychiatry and Neurology, Japanese Soc. Biol. Psychiatry (prize 1994), Japanese Soc. Neuropsychopharmacology, Japanese Soc. Clin. Neuropsychopharmacology, Japanese Soc. for Brain Scis., Japanese Soc. Clin. Neurophysiology, Japan Soc. Psychiat. Diagnosis, Japanese Soc. Prevention in Psychiat. Disorders, Japanese Soc. Schizophrenia Rsch. Avocations: foreign languages, classical music, figure skating, foreign travel. Home: 144-14-B2 Nishiaraya Toyama 939-8251 Japan Business E-Mail: sumiyo@med.u-toyama.ac.jp.

SUMLIN, MARGARET BROWN, special education educator; b. Ann Arbor, Mich., Nov. 2, 1950; d. Willis Radcliff and Eulalie (Draughon) Brown. BS, U. Ala., 1972; MA, U. South Ala., 1976. Cert. spl. edn. tchr., Ala. Spl. edn. tchr. Morningside Elem. Sch., Tuscaloosa, Ala., 1972-73; spl. edn. tchr., community coord. A.P. Brewer Developmental Ctr., Mobile, Ala., 1973-75; spl. edn. tchr. Crichton Elem. Sch., Mobile, 1975-77, Scarborough Mid. Sch., Mobile, 1977-82, Cornerstone Group Home, Mobile, 1982; spl. edn. tchr., edn. coord. Brookwood Recovery Ctr., Mobile, 1984-90, Wilmer Hall Children's Home, Mobile, 1991, art therapy tchr., 1991—92; spl. edn. coord., tchr. The Murray Sch. at Wilmer Hall, Mobile, 1992—2002, prin., spl. edn. coord., 2003—. Ednl. cons. Parkside Recovery Ctr., Mobile, 1989-90; art therapy coord. Wilmer Hall Children's Home, 1991—; founder, organizer Friends of Wilmer Hall, 1992—. Author: (program model) Classroom Structure for Emotionally Disturbed Students, 1984. Bd. dirs. Women of Ch., St. Paul Ch., Mobile, 1991—, Mobile Pub. Libr., 1992—; vol. fundraiser Am. Cancer Soc., 1992; vol. tutor Project Hope Group Home, 1974, Rotary Rehab. Ctr., 1976; vol. coord. Vol. Mobile, 1982, Mobile County Sch. System, 1984; bd. dirs. Cornerstone Group Home (pres. 1985-86); vol. Mobile Pre-Sch. for the Deaf, 1979, Rotary Rehab. Ctr. In-Patient Svcs., 1977. Named a Point of Light by Pres. George Bush, 1991. Mem. Jr. League of Mobile (vol. fundraiser 1990-91). Episcopalian. Avocations: reading, hand sewing, beach activities. Office: Wilmer Hall Childrens Home Old Shell Rd Mobile AL 36608

SUMLIN, PEGGY MCDONALD, elementary school educator; d. James Edward and Peggy Joyce McDonald; m. James H. Sumlin, Jan. 12, 1973; children: Robert, Matthew, Lorena. AA, Pensacola Jr. Coll., 1973; BA in Sociology, U. West Fla., 1975; MAT in Edn., Olivet Nazarene U., 1992. Cert. tchr. Ill., SC, nat. bd. cert. mid. childhood generalist tchr. Presch. tchr., asst. dir. 1st Bapt. Childcare, Loxley, Ala., 1986—89, dir., prin., 1989—90; dir. Childcare, Loxley, 1989—90; tchr. asst. Odell (Ill.) Elem., 1990—91, kindergarten tchr., 1992—93; acad. coach Waccamaw Elem., 2002—06, elem. tchr. Pawleys Island, SC, 1996—2006. Home: 6424 Pleasant Hill Dr Hemingway SC 29554 Personal E-mail: psumlin@hotmail.com. E-mail: psumlin@we.gcsd.k12.sc.us.

SUMMAR, SHARON KAY, elementary school educator; b. Decatur, Ill, Jan. 27, 1948; d. Robert Dean and Leola (Warren) S. BS in Edn., Ill. State U., 1970, MS in Math., 1988. Tchr., computer coord. Green Valley Grade Sch., Ill., 1970-91; tchr. Midwest Cent. Primary Sch., 1991—2004; ret., 2004. Tchr. asst. U. Ill., Urbana, 1986. Mem. Nat. Coun. Tchr. Math., Ill. Coun. Tchr. Math. Avocations: computer programming, stamp collecting/philately, reading. E-mail: ssummar@ntslink.net.

SUMME, GREGORY LOUIS, health products executive; b. Ft. Mitchell, Ky., Nov. 25, 1956; s. James Augustine and Mary Elizabeth (McQueen) S.; m. Susan Louise Stevie, Aug. 1, 1981; children: Heather, Erin. BSEE, U. Ky.,

1978; MS, U. Cin., 1980; MBA with distinction, U. Pa., 1983. Design engr. Mostek Corp., Dallas, 1980-81; mktg. specialist Gen. Electric Plastics Europe, The Netherlands, 1982; ptnr. McKinsey & Co. Inc., Atlanta and Hong Kong, 1983—92; gen. mgr., comml. motors GE, 1992—93; pres. automotive products group, aerospace engines, gen. aviation avionics Allied Signal Inc., 1993—98; pres., COO PerkinElmer, Inc., Wellesley, Mass., 1998—99, pres., pres., CEO, 1999—. Contbr. articles to profl. jours. Alex Proudfoot fellow Wharton Sch., U. Pa., 1981-83; named to Univ. Ky. Coll. Engring. Hall of Distinction. Mem. IEEE, Eta Kappa Nu. Roman Catholic. Avocations: running, squash, golf. Office: PerkinElmer Inc 45 William St Wellesley MA 02481*

**SUMMER, DONNA (LA DONNA ADRIAN GAINES),** singer, songwriter, actress; b. Boston, Dec. 31, 1948; d. Andrew and Mary Gaines; m. Helmut Sommer (div.); 1 child, Mimi; m. Bruce Sudano; children: Brooklyn, Amanda. Has sold over 20 million records. Singer, 1967—; actress: (German stage prodn.) Hair, 1967-75, (Vienna Folk Opera prodns.) Porgy and Bess, (German prodns.) The Me Nobody Knows, (cable TV spl.) Donna Summer Special, 1980; recorded albums including The Wanderer, Star Collection, Love To Love You Baby, Love Trilogy, Four Seasons of Love, I Remember Yesterday, The Deep, Shut Out, Once Upon A Time, Bad Girls, On The Radio, Walk Away, She Works Hard For The Money, Cats Without Claws, All Systems Go, 1988, Another Place and Time, 1989, Mistaken Identity, 1991, Endless Summer, 1994, Christmas Spirit, 1994, I'm a Rainbow, 1996, Live & More Encore, 1999; subject My Life VH1 Concert, 1999; recorded theme song for Hunchback of Notre Dame, Disney; forerunner of disco style. Named Best Rhythm and Blues Female Vocalist, Nat. Acad. Rec. Arts and Scis., 1978, Best Female Rock Vocalist, 1979, Favorite Female Pop Vocalist, Am. Music Awards, 1979, Favorite Female Vocalist of Soul Music, 1979, Soul Artist of Yr., Rolling Stone mag., 1979; recipient Best Favorite Pop Single award, 1979, Best-selling Black Music Album for Female Artist award Nat. Assn. Record Merchandizers, 1979, Ampex Golden Reel award for album On the Radio, 1979, Best-selling Album for Female Artist, 1980, Ampex Golden Reel award for single On the Radio, 1980, Ampex Golden Reel award for album Bad Girls, Best of Las Vegas Jimmy award for best rock performance, 1980, Grammy award for best inspirational performance, 1984. Office: 2401 Main St Santa Monica CA 90405-3515

**SUMMER, EMILY EUGENIA,** artist, art educator; d. Charles Edgar and Emily Eugenia Summer. BS, Miss. U. for Women, 1945; LHD (hon.), Miss. U. for Women, 2005; MA, Columbia U., 1948. Supr. art Clarksdale (Miss.) City Schs., 1948—49; adj. prof. art Miss. U. for Women, Columbus, 1949—58, assoc. prof. art, 1958—78, prof. art, 1978—80, asst. dean Sch. Arts and Scis., 1980—82, head divsn. fine and performing arts, 1982—85, prof. emerita art, 1985—. One-woman shows include Ricks Meml. CArnegie Libr., Yazoo City, Miss., 1962, First Nat. Bank, Jackson, Miss., 1974, Mcpl. Libr., Amory, Miss., 1975, Miss. State U., Starkville, 1978, Rosenzweig Arts Ctr., Columbus, 2001, Fine Arts Gallery, Miss. U. for Women, 02, exhibitions include Hunter Gallery, 1963, Birmingham Mus. Art, 1968, Nat. Arts Club, 1980, numerous others, exhibited in group shows at Itawamba Jr. Coll. Gallery, Fulton, Miss., 1986, Hinds C.C. Gallery, Raymond, Miss., 1987, Shelton State C.C. Gallery, Tuscallosa, Ala., 1988, Miss. U. for Women, 1970—86, Miss. Mus. Art, Jackson, 2002, Miss. Gov.'s Mansion, 2001, Represented in permanent collections Miss. Mus. Art, Miss. U. for Women, also numerous pvt. and corp. collections. Bd. govs. artist registry Brooks Meml. Art Mus., Memphis, 1971—72; Miss. rep. bd. dirs. Southeastern Coll. Art Assn., 1964—71; rschr., trainer Nat. Mus. Am. Art, Washington, 1992—93; mem. Columbus/Lowndes County United Way, 1997—. Recipient Alumni Achievement award, Miss. U. for Women, 1986, Honored Artist, Nat. Mus. Women Artists, 2001, Lowndes County Alumni Svc. award, Plymouth Bluff Ctr., Columbus, 2003, Medal of Excellence, Miss. U. for Women, 2003, numerous others; Eugenia Summer Art Gallery named in her honor, Miss. U. for Women, 2002, Danforth assoc., 1977—83, rsch. grantee, Miss. U. for Women, 1976, 1978, 1979. Mem.: Miss. Mus. Art Rembrandt Soc., Nat. Audubon Soc., Lauren Rogers Mus. Art, Nat. Mus. Women in Arts (honored artist 2002), Coll. Art Assn. Am. (life), Nature Conservancy, John Muir Soc., Sierra Club, Garden Clubs Miss. (life), Kappa Pi, Phi Kappa Phi. Democrat. Roman Catholic. Home: 915 5th Ave S Columbus MS 39701

**SUMMER, EVAN D.,** artist, art educator; BS in Chem., SUNY, Cortland, 1970; BFA, SUNY, Buffalo, 1973; MFA in Printmaking, Yale Univ., 1975. Artist-in-residence Univ. Pa., Phila., 1978—88; instr. Tyler Sch. of Art, Elkins Park, Pa., 1979, Pratt Graphics Ctr., NYC, 1983, Kutztown Univ., Pa., 1984—85, asst. prof. Pa., 1987—91, assoc. prof. Pa., 1991—. Exhibited in group shows at Chongqing and Tianjin Arts Coll., Tianzin, People's Republic of China, 1986, Pa. Acad. Fine Arts, 1987, Bklyn Mus., 1989, Hewlett Gallery, Carnegie-Mellon Univ., Pitts., 1991, Internat. Print Triennale and Intergrafia, Krakow, Poland, Katowice, Poland, 1991, 1st Egyptian Internat. Print Tirennale, 1993, Represented in permanent collections Nat. Gallery Art, Washington, Corcoran Gallery Art, Bklyn. Mus., Taipei City Mus. Fine Arts, NAD, NYC, others. Recipient Berthe von Moschzisker prize, 1982, Juror's award, Pacific States Nat. Biennial Print Exhbn., Univ. Hawaii, 1992, Silver medal, 10th Norwegian Internat Print Triennial, Fredrikstad, Norway, 1992, Leo Meissner prize, NAD, 1999. Mem.: Boston Printmakers, Internat. print Triennial Soc., NAD (academician 1994—). Studio: Sharadin Art Studio 2AG Kutztown University Kutztown PA 19530 Office Phone: 610-683-4535. Business E-Mail: summer@kutztown.edu.

**SUMMER, ROBERT E.,** automotive executive, educator; b. Salem, Ohio, Apr. 28, 1944; s. Raymond Evertt Summer and Jane T Hulit; m. Linda F Gilreath, Mar. 5, 1966; 1 child, Sheila Ruth Lawlus. BSOE, WAYLAND, Lubbock, 1984—89 Ase Master Certified NIASE 1996 Iuo Seminolo H.S., Seminole, Tex., 1986—. Past pres. LION'S, Seminole, Tex., 1976—2005. Recipient Lion Of The Yr., Seminole Lion's, 1985—86. Mem.: ACTE, Tex. Automotive Instructors Assn. (pres. 1997—2000), Tex. Indsl. Vocat. Assn. (pres. 1995—96). Avocations: hunting, fishing, travel. Home: Rt 4 Box137 Seminole TX 79360 Office: Seminole HS 2100 Nw Ave D Seminole TX 79360 Office Phone: 432-758-5873. E-Mail: bsummer@seminole.k12.tx.us.

**SUMMER, THOMAS S.,** food products executive; BA in Econ., Harvard U., 1980; MBA, U. Chgo., 1982. CPA. Several positions, corp. fin. and internat. treasury PepsiCo, Inc., 1987—91; v.p., treas. Cardinal Health, Inc., 1991—97; sr. v.p. Constellation Brands, Inc., Fairport, NY, 1997—2000, exec. v.p., 2000—. Office: Constellation Brands Inc 370 Woodcliff Dr Ste 300 Fairport NY 14450-4238

**SUMMERFIELD, GALE,** director, educator; children: Tai Hsiao, Thomas Hsiao. PhD, U. Mich., 1987. Assoc. prof. Monterey (Calif.) Inst. Internat. Studies, 1987—98, U. Ill., Champaign, Ill., 1998—, dir. WGGP, 1998—. Author: Women and Gender Equity in Development Theory and Practice, Women's Rights to House and Land: China, Laos, Vietnam; contbr. articles to profl. jours. Bd. dirs. Nat. Coun. Rsch. on Women, N.Y., 2004—05; trustee Assn. Social Econs., 2002—05. Office: University of Illinois at Urbana 910 South Fifth St Champaign IL 61820 Office Phone: 217-333-1977. Office Fax: 217-333-6270. Business E-Mail: summrfld@uiuc.edu.

**SUMMERFIELD, JOHN ROBERT,** textile curator; b. St. Paul, Feb. 21, 1917; s. Isaac and Irene (Longini) S.; m. Anne Benson, July 14, 1945. SB in Mech. Engring., MIT, 1938. MBA, U. Calif., Berkeley, 1947, PhD in Econs., 1954. Asst. prof. Sloan Sch. Mgmt., MIT, 1952-54; br. chief CIA, Washington, 1954-56; project leader The Rand Corp., Santa Monica, Calif., 1956—62; corp. economist Douglas Aircraft Co., Santa Monica, Calif., 1962—66; v.p. econ. planning Western Airlines, L.A., 1966-70; staff v.p. econ. planning Pan Am. Airways, N.Y., 1970-71; pres. Summerfield Assocs., Pacific Palisades, Calif., 1972-92; vis. curator Fowler Mus. Cultural History, UCLA, 1993—. Co-curator exhbns. of antique Minangkabau ceremonial textiles from West Sumatra, Textile Mus., Washington, 1990-91, Santa Barbara (Calif.) Mus. Art,

1991, Bellevue (Wash.) Art Mus., 1992, Utah Mus. Fine Art, 1992, Fowler Mus. of Cultural History, UCLA, 1999, Iris and B. Gerald Cantor Gallery, Coll. Holy Cross, 2003. Served to lt. USNR, 1942-45. E-mail: summrfld@arts.ucla.edu.

**SUMMERFIELD, JUDITH PEARL,** dean, English language educator; b. McKeesport, Pa., Sept. 26, 1941; d. Martin and Bessie Judkovitz Pearl; m. Philip Michael Anderson, Jan. 3, 1995; m. Geoffrey Summerfield, Dec. 31, 1983 (dec.); m. Ross Fishman, June 9, 1962 (div. Jan. 1, 1983); children: Sharon Brady, Lauren Azuolay. BA, U. Pitts., 1963, MA, 1966; PhD, NYU, 1987. Tchr. English and social studies Schenley H.S., Pitts., 1963—64; instr., rsch. asst., grad. tchg. asst. U. Pitts., Pitts., 1964—68; instr. Bronx Cmty. Coll., CUNY, 1969—72; from lectr. to full prof. Queens Coll., CUNY, Flushing, NY, 1972—2005; dir. freshman yr. initiative Queens Coll., Flushing, 1992—99, acting dean of arts and humanities, 1999, dean undergrad. studies, 2000—03; univ. dean undergraduate edn. CUNY, N.Y.C., 2003—, doctoral faculty, urban edn., grad. sch., 2005—; leader Carnegie Acad. for Scholarship of Tchg. and Learning Leadership Program, 2006—. Prin. investigator funded projects Fund for the Improvement of Postsecondary Edn., Washington, 1993—2000. Author: (book) Negotiations, Readings, Texts and Contexts (MLA Mina Shaughnessy prize, 1987), Frames of Mind, Responding to Prose, Random House Guide to Writing. Named N.Y. Prof. of Yr., Carnegie Found. for Advancement of Tchg., 1998; recipient Theodore M. Hesburgh Cert. of Excellence Award for Faculty Devel. to Enhance Undergrad. Learning for Freshman Yr., Tchr.'s Ins. Annuity Assn. - Coll. Retirement Equities Fund, 1996, Queens Coll. Presdl. Rsch. award, Queens Coll., 1996, Multicultural Curriculum Work in English grant, Ford Found., 1992. Mem.: MLA, Nat. Coun. Tchrs. English. Achievements include development of award-winning programs for urban students. Home: 405 Weaver St Larchmont NY 10538 Office: CUNY 535 East 80th St New York NY 10021 Office Phone: 212-794-5367. E-mail: judith.summerfield@mail.cuny.edu.

**SUMMERFORD, BEN LONG,** retired artist, educator; b. Montgomery, Ala., Feb. 3, 1924; s. Ben Long and Ollie Jo (Gilchrist) S.; m. Christene Morris, Jan. 30, 1951 (dec.); children: Jeffrey (dec.), Rebecca, James. Student, Birmingham-Southern Coll., 1942-43; BA, Am. U., 1948, MA, 1954; student, Ecole des Beaux Arts., Paris., 1949-50. Staff art dept. Am. U., 1950-88, chmn. dept., 1957-66, 70-86, prof., 1960-88; prof. emeritus, 1988—; artist in residence Dartmouth Coll., 1993. One-man shows include, Balt. Mus. Art, Goucher Coll., Franz Bader Gallery, Washington, Jefferson Place Gallery, Washington, Phillips Collection, Washington, Washington County Mus. Fine Arts, Hagerstown, Md.; represented in permanent collection, Watkins Gallery, Phillips Gallery Art, Corcoran Gallery Art, all Washington, 50 yr RetoSelective exhibitions Wah. County Mus. of Fine Arts, Md, 2004, numerous group shows of paintings. Served to ensign USNR, 1943-46. Fulbright fellow, France, 1949-50; J. Paul Getty scholar, Phillips Collection, 1990-91. Home: 257 Ashley Dr Shepherdstown WV 25443

**SUMMERHILL, RONALD RAYMOND,** psychotherapist, psychologist; s. Walter Edward Summerhill and Vernon Joenell Goldsmith; m. Wanda Jean Owens, Dec. 31, 1979 (div. Jan. 24, 1994); children: Valorie Lenee Summerhill Mullins, Ronald Raymond II. BA in Bus. Mgmt., St. Mary's Coll. of Calif., Moraga, Calif., 1985; MS in Adminstrn., Ctrl. Mich. U., Mt. Pleasant, Mich., 1992; M in Human Rels., U. Okla., Norman, Okla., 1993; D of Psychology, Argosy U., Phoenix, 2004. Lic. Master Social Worker Iowa, 1996; cert. Sch. Psychologist Ariz., 2001, Nat. Counselor NBCC, 1996, lic. Profl. Counselor Nebr., 1996, Mental Health Practitioner Nebr., 1996. Capt., navigator USAF, Omaha, 1986—92; social worker Nebr. HHS, Omaha, 1994—96; exec. dir. Tiller Therapeutic Svcs., Inc., Bellevue, Nebr., 1996—99; psychologist assoc. Ariz. Dept. of Juvenile Corrections, Phoenix, 1999—2000; clin. supr. ValueOptions, Phoenix, 2000—00; psychology assoc. Ariz. Dept. of Health, Phoenix, 2000—01; sch. psychologist Cave Creek Unified Sch. Dist., Cave Creek, Ariz., 2001—03, Scottsdale Unified Sch. Dist., Scottsdale, Ariz., 2004—. Internship neuropsychology Kingsbrook Jewish Med. Ctr., Bklyn., 2003—04. Capt. USAF, 1986—92, Omaha, Nebr. Decorated Achievement Medal USAF, Accommodation Medal. Mem.: APA, ACA, NASP. R-Consevative. Protestant. Avocations: travel, musician, outdoorsman. Office: Scottsdale Unified Sch Dist #48 6720 E Continental Scottsdale AZ 85257-3226 Office Phone: 480-484-5828. Office Fax: 480-484-5801. Business E-Mail: rsummerhill@susd.org.

**SUMMERLIN, DEBORAH LYNN,** theater technician, video technician; b. Tyler, Tex., Sept. 10, 1951; d. George Ethridge Summerlin and Janey Elizabeth Nantz. BS in Elem. Edn., East Tex. State U., Commerce, 1974. Cert. Theatre and Speech East Tex. State U., 1997. Kindergarten and 1st grade tchr. Highland Pk. Elem. Sch., San Antonio, 1974—76; sci., theatre and social studies tchr. Connell Mid. Sch., San Antonio, 1976—80; theatre and speech tchr. Spring Oaks Jr. HS, Houston, 1980—91; theatre/video technician Northbrook Mid. Sch., Houston, 1991—. Voice/musical theatre dir. Ft. Bend Music Ctr., Stafford, Tex., 2004—. Dir.: (musical) Godspell; soloist Moscow Chamber Orchestra, St. Petersburg, Russia. Vol. Houston Zoo, 2003—06. Mem.: NEA, Tex. State Tchrs. Assn., Tex. Edn. Theatre Assn. (bd. dirs. k-12, Tchr. of Yr. 1995), Spring Br. Edn. Assn. (pres., bd. dirs. 1980—2006), Nat. Wildlife Def., Whale Adoption Project, Nat. Wildlife Fund, World Wildlife Fund. Methodist. Avocations: travel, singing, birdwatching. Home: 16538 Tranquil Dr Sugar Land TX 77478 Office: Northbrook Middle Sch 3030 Rosefield Houston TX 77080 Office Phone: 713-329-6510.

**SUMMERLIN, GLENN WOOD,** retired advertising executive; b. Dallas, Ga. Apr. 1, 1934; m. Anne Valley, Oct 16, 1971, 1 child, Wudd Hampton ;children from previous marriage: Glenn Wood III, Edward Lee. Student, Ga. Inst. Tech., 1951-52; BBA, Ga. State U., 1956, MBA, 1967. Prodn. mgr. Fred Worrill Advt., Atlanta, 1956-65; v.p. sales Grizzard, Atlanta, 1965-74, pres., 1974-94, vice chmn., 1994-99; retired, 1999. Vice chmn. Polaris dist. Boy Scouts Am., 1967, Ga. State U. Found., 1974; chmn. distributive edn. adv. com. DeKalb Coll., 1974—76; bd. founders Geo. M. Sparks Scholarship Fund; bd. dirs. Atlanta Humane Soc., 1971—, treas., 1973, 1981—82, 1984—86, asst. treas. for capital devel., 1987—99, 2005—, chmn., 2000—02, investment com., 1996—; mem. steering com. to honor Hank Aaron, 1982; lay rep. animal care com. Emory U., 1984—85; mem. adv. bd. Families in Action, 1985—86; bd. dirs. Travelers Aid Metro, Atlanta, 1989—90; mem. adv. bd. Emmaus House, 2000—03; chmn.'s coun., mem. mktg. adv. com. Crow Canyon Archaeol. Ctr., 1993—95. Recipient C.S. Bolen award Soc. Coun. Indsl. Editors, 1967; named Outstanding Young Man in DeKalb County, DeKalb Jaycees, 1967, Alumnus of Yr., Ga. State U., 1973; recipient Direct Mail Spokesman award Direct Mktg. Assn., 1973. Mem. Nat. Soc. Fund Raising Execs. (bd. dirs. Ga. chpt. 1984, cert. 1983-99), Ga. Assn. Bus. Communicators (pres. 1966-67), Ga. State Alumni Assn. (pres. 1971-72, dir. 1966-78), Sales and Mktg. Execs. Atlanta (dir. 1969-71), Ga. Bus. and Industry Assn. (bd. govs. 1975-76), Ga. Arms Collectors Assn. (dir. 1974-76, Pres.'s award 1973), Southeastern Antique Arms Collectors (charter, bd. dirs. 1978—, v.p. 1999—), Assn. Am. Sword Collectors (charter), Mid-Am. Antique Arms Soc. (charter) Mensa, Soc. Animal Welfare Adminstrs. (Disting Svc. award 2000), Travelers Aid of Atlanta (bd. dirs. 1989-90), Omicron Delta Kappa. Home: 1133 Ragley Hall Rd NE Atlanta GA 30319-2511

**SUMMERLIN, WILLIAM TALLEY,** allergist, immunologist, dermatologist; b. Anderson, S.C., 1938; MD, Emory U., 1964. Diplomate Am. Bd. Allergy and Immunology, Am. Bd. Dermatology, Am. Bd. Dermatopathology. Intern U. Tex. Med. Br., 1964-65; resident in dermatopathology Stanford, Palo Alto, 1967-70; resident in immunology U. Minn., Mpls., 1971-73, fellow in immunology, 1971-73; staff mem. St. Mary's Hosp., Rogers, Ark.; pvt. practice Regional Dermatology and Allergy Ctr., Rogers, Ark. Mem. AMA, Am. Acad. Dermatology, Am. Coll. Allergy and Immunology, Am. Acad. of Cosmetic Surgery, Am. Soc. for Mohs Surgery, Am. Subspecialty Bd. of Dermatopathology.

**SUMMERS, ANITA ARROW,** finance educator; b. NYC, Sept. 9, 1925; d. Harry I. and Lillian (Greenberg) Arrow; m. Robert Summers, Mar. 29, 1953; children: Lawrence H., Richard F., John S. BA, Hunter Coll., 1945, DHL (hon.), 1995; MA, U. Chgo., 1947. Sr. econ. analyst Standard Oil Co. N.J., N.Y.C., 1947-54; asst. in econs. Yale U., New Haven, 1956-59; lectr. dept. econs. Swarthmore (Pa.) Coll., 1965-71; sr. economist Fed. Res. Bank Phila., 1971-75, research officer, 1975-79; adj. prof. pub. policy U. Pa., Phila., 1979-82, prof. pub. policy and mgmt., 1982—, dept. chair, 1983-88, univ. ombudsman, 2001—03, co-dir Wharton Urban Decentralization Project, 1987-97, dir. rsch. Wharton Real Estate Ctr., 2003—, sr. scholar Nat. Ctr. on the Edn. Quality of the Workforce, 1991—95. Expert witness schs. fin. Md., Mass., Va., 1980-85, Md., Va., 1996, Calif., 2003, bd. dirs. William Penn Found., Phila., 1993-98; chair bd. dirs. Mathematica Policy Rsch., Inc., Princeton, N.J., 1993—. Author: Economic Report on the Philadelphia Metropolitan Area, 1985, Economic Development within the Philadelphia Metropolitan Area, 1986, Local Fiscal Issues in the Philadelphia Metropolitan Area, 1987; editor: Urban Change in the United States and Western Europe, 1992, 99; contbr. articles to profl. jours. Chair econ. subcom. Pa. Three Mile Island Commn., Harrisburg, 1979; pres. Lower Merion (Pa.) LWV, 1963-65; mem. Mayor's Econ. Roundtable, Phila., 1984-88; mem. rsch. policy coun., 1992-94, Com. for Econ. Devel. Rockefeller Found. resident scholar, Bellagio, Italy, 1986. Mem. Am. Econ. Assn., Assn. for Pub. Policy and Mgmt. (policy coun. 1986), Phi Beta Kappa. Avocations: needlepoint, cooking. Home: 1400 Waverly Rd V-11 Gladwyne PA 19035-1271 Office: U Pa Wharton Sch Dept Pub Policy and Mgmt Philadelphia PA 19104 Office Phone: 215-898-4076. Business E-Mail: summers@wharton.upenn.edu.

**SUMMERS, BERTIE JEAN,** secondary school educator; b. Waco, Tex., Feb. 12, 1946; d. Frank Gulizia and Martha Jane (Chenault) Byrd; m. Thomas Sydney Summers; children: Shannon Adele Vowell, Samantha Ann Parson, Sasha Alise Best. BA, U. Tex.-Permian Basin, Odessa, 1984, MA, 1991. Cert. secondary tchr. Tex. Tchr. Bradley Mid. Sch., San Antonio, 1987—98, Whitewright HS, Tex., 1998—. Chmn. UIL-one-act, 2001; mem. site-based com. Whitewright Sch. Dist., 2004—06, mem. prin. selection com., 2006. Founder, gen. dir. Whitewright Players Cmty. Theatre, 1999—; tchr., chmn. com., mem. adv. coun., ann. conf. del. First United Meth. Ch., Whitewright, 2000—. Named Tchr. of Yr., Bradley HS PTA, 1984, Best Actress-Drama, San Antonio Alamo Arts Coun., 1995, 1997. Mem.: Tex. Classroom Tchrs. Assn. (Tchr. of Yr. 1999). Republican. Methodist. Avocations: community theater, painting, poetry, writing, reading. Home: PO Box 965 Whitewright TX 75491 Office: Whitewright HS PO Box 888 Whitewright TX 75491

**SUMMERS, CAROL,** artist; b. Kingston, NY, Dec. 26, 1925; s. Ivan Franklin and Theresa (Jones) S.; m. Elaine Smithers, Oct. 2, 1954 (div. Aug. 1967); 1 son, Kyle; m. Joan Ward Toth, May 6, 1974 (dec.1998). BA, Bard Coll., 1951, DFA (hon.), 1974. Tchr. Hunter Coll., Sch. Visual Arts, Haystack Mountain Sch. Crafts, Bklyn. Mus. Art Sch., Pratt Graphic Art Ctr., Chelterham Twp. Art Ctr., Valley Stream Community Art Ctr., U. Pa., Columbia Coll., U. Calif., Santa Cruz, San Francisco Art Inst., U. Utah, Logan, Art Study Abroad, Paris, Casa de Espiritus Alegres Marfil, Mex., USIS workshop tour, India, 1974, 79; folk art and textiles tour leader to Rajasthan, India, 1995-05. Represented in permanent collections at, Mus. Modern Art, Bklyn. Mus., N.Y. Pub. Libr., Libr. of Congress, Nat. Gallery, Victoria and Albert Mus., London, Bibliotheque Nationale, Paris, Kunstmuseum, Basil, Lugano (Switzerland) Art Mus. Grenchen (Switzerland) Art Mus., Malmo (Sweden) Mus., Los Angeles County Mus., Phila. Mus., Balt. Mus., Seattle Mus., Boston Mus., Art Inst. Chgo., Am. embassies in Russia, Can., India, Thailand, Fed. Republic Germany and Eng.; traveling exhibit, Mus. Modern Art, 1964-66; retrospective exhbn. Brooklyn Mus., 1977, Nassau County Mus. Art, 1990, Belles Artes, San Miguel de Allende, Mex., 1992, Miami U. Art Mus., Oxford, Ohio, 1995, Egon Schiele Centrum Český Krumlov, Czech Republic, 1997-98; 50-yr. retrospective at Mus. Art and History, Santa Cruz, 1999, Woodstock (N.Y.) Artists Assn., 1999, San Francisco Mus. Modern Art Rental Gallery, 2000; author: A Treasury of Indian Folk Textiles, 2002, Another Treasury of Indian Folk Textiles, 2006. Served with USMCR, 1944-48, PTO. Named Artist of Yr., Santa Cruz County Arts Commn., 2001; recipient Outstanding Printmaker award, Mid Am. Print Coun., 2004; fellow, Louis Comfort Tiffany Found., 1955, 1960, John Simon Guggenheim Found., 1959, Fulbright, Italy, 1961; study grantee, Italian govt., 1954—55, rsch. grantee, Coun. Internat. Exch. Scholars, India, 1993—94. Mem. NAD (academician, 1994-). Calif. Soc. Printmakers. Office Phone: 831-423-0181. Personal E-Mail: carol@casaspirit.com

**SUMMERS, CATHLEEN,** film producer; b. Chgo. d. Paul and Elizabeth Summers; m. Patrick Crowley. BA, U. So. Calif., 1973. Film editor, comml. producer, dir.'s asst. Roman Polanski, Rome, 1972; story editor Albert S. Ruddy Prodns. Paramount Pictures, L.A., 1973-74; exec. v.p. sr. v.p. producer Martin Ransohoff Prodns. Columbia Pictures, 1976; sr. v.p. Tri-Star Pictures, Century City, Calif., 1984-87; motion picture producer Cathleen Summers Prodns., L.A., 1989—; ptnr. ESN, Film Prodn. Resource Co.; cons., ptnr. Estudio Network. Motion picture producer, ptnr. Summers-Kouf Prodns., Burbank, 1986-87; motion picture producer Cathleen Summers Prodns., L.A., 1987, Summers-Quaid Prodns., Century City, Culver City, Calif., 1988—. Producer: (motion picture) Stakeout, 1987, DOA, 1991, Vital Signs, 1990, Mystery Date, 1991, Dogfight, 1991, The Sandlot, 1993, Stakeout II, 1993; exec. prodr. Derivations, Who New/The Real Deal, 2003. Co-founder Diane Thomas Scholarship, UCLA, 1988—; bd. dirs. L.A. chpt. Nat. Parkinsons Found.; founding bd. dirs. U.S. Comedy Arts Festival, Aspen, Colo. Mem. Am. Film Inst. (pres. 3d Decade Coun. 1995, 96, 97). Personal E-mail: july4bu@charter.net.

**SUMMERS, CLYDE WILSON,** law educator; b. Grass Range, Mont., Nov. 21, 1918; s. Carl Douglas and Anna Lois (Yontz) S.; m. Evelyn Marie Wahlgren, Aug. 30, 1947; children: Mark, Erica, Craig, Lisa. BS, U. Ill., 1939, JD, 1942, LLD, 1998; LLM, Columbia U., 1946, JSD, 1952; LL.D., U. Leuven, Belgium, 1967, U. Stockholm, 1978, U. Ill., 1998. Bar: N.Y. 1951. Mem. law faculty U. Toledo, 1942-49, U. Buffalo, 1949-56; prof. law Yale U., New Haven, Conn., 1956-66, Garver prof. law, 1966-75; Jefferson B. Fordham prof. law U. Pa., 1975-90, prof. emeritus, 1990—. Hearing examiner Conn. Commn. on Civil Rights, 1963-71 Co-author: Labor Cases and Material, 1968, 1982, Rights of Union Members, 1979, Legal Protection for the Individual Employee, 1989, 1996, 2002; co-editor: Labor Relations and the Law, 1953, Employment Relations and the Law, 1959, Comparative Labor Law Jour., 1984—97. Chmn. Gov.'s Com. on Improper Union Mgmt. Practices N.Y. State, 1957-58; chmn. Conn. Adv. Council on Unemployment Ins. and Employment Service, 1960-72; mem. Conn. Labor Relations Bd., 1966-70, Conn. Bd. Mediation and Arbitration, 1964-72. Guggenheim fellow, 1955-56; Ford fellow, 1963-64; German-Marshall fellow, 1977-78; NEH fellow, 1977-78, Fullbright fellow, 1984-85. Mem. Nat. Acad. Arbitrators, Internat. Soc. Labor and Social Legislation (pres.). Congregationalist. Office: U Pa Sch Law 3400 Chestnut St Philadelphia PA 19104-6204 Home: 608 W Phil Ellena St Apt 1a Philadelphia PA 19119-3525 Office Phone: 215-898-6867. Business E-Mail: csummers@law.upenn.edu.

**SUMMERS, DAVID PATRICK,** chemist, astrobiologist; s. Ernest and Virginia Joy Summers. BS signum laudis, SUNY, Albany, 1975; PhD, MIT, Cambridge, Mass., 1984. Electrochemist SRI Internat., Menlo Park, Calif., 1984—89; Nat. Rsch. Coun. sr. fellow NASA Ames Rsch. Ctr., Mountain View, Calif., 1990—92; prin. investigator SETI Inst., Mountain View, 1993—. Recipient Undergrad. Award in Analytical Chemistry, Am. Chem. Soc., 1978. Mem.: Sigma Xi, Phi Beta Kappa. Achievements include patents in field; invention of. Office: SETI Inst NASA Ames Rsch Ctr Mail Stop 239-4 Mountain View CA 94035-1000 Office Phone: 650-604-6206. Office Fax: 650-604-1088. E-Mail: dsummers@mail.arc.nasa.gov.

**SUMMERS, DAVID STEWART,** neurologist, consultant; b. Canton, Ohio, Feb. 16, 1932; s. William Edward and Stewart (Jordan) Summers; m. Ada Ernestine Cumber, Nov. 30, 1957; children: David Stewart II, Timothy C. BS, Va. State U., 1954; MD, U. Va., 1959. Diplomate Am. Acad. Pain Mgmt.

Resident in neurology SUNY, Syracuse, 1960—63; asst. prof. neurology U. Rochester, NY, 1968—72; asst. prof. U. Utah Coll. Medicine, Salt Lake City, 1972—76; staff neurologist St. Vincent Health Ctr., Erie, Pa., 1976—91, Meadville Med. Ctr., Pa., 1991—93; neurologist Warren State Hosp., Pa., 1993—2000; investor, 2000—. Cons. Reflex Sympathetic Dystrophy Assn., Erie, 1988—97; mem. adv. coun. HHS, Washington, 1974—77. Contbg. author The Black Humanist Experience, 2003; contbr. articles to profl. jours. Supporter City Mission, Erie, 1991—, Planetary Soc., 2005—, Am. United Separation Ch. and State, NOW, ACLU, Am. Humanist Assn., People for the Am. Way, Ctr. Reproductive Law and Policy, Planned Parenthood, The Freedom from Religion Found., others; advisor to gov. Coun. Black Affairs, Salt Lake City, 1975; mem. Human Rights Campaign, Population Connection. Capt. M.C. USAR, 1964—67, Landstuhl, Germany. Grantee, Nat. Med. Fellowships, 1956—59; A. A. Rockefeller scholar, Williamsburg, Va., 1951—54. Mem.: AAAS, NAACP, Nat. Ctr. for Sci. Edn., The Planetary Soc., Nat. Soc. Scabbard & Blade, NY Acad. Scis., Menninger Soc., Am. Epilepsy Soc., Nat. Med. Assn., Am. Acad. Neurology, U. Va. Alumni Assn., Am. Legion (life). Democrat. Avocations: reading, hiking, walking.

SUMMERS, GERALD HOWARD (JERRY SUMMERS), lawyer; b. Chattanooga, May 28, 1941; s. Homer Howard and Millie (Dean) S. BA in Bus. Adminstrn. with honors, Auburn U., U. of South, 1963; LLB, U. Tenn. 1966. Bar: Tenn. 1966, U.S. Ct. Appeals (6th cir.) 1970, U.S. Supreme Ct. 1972. Asst. dist. atty. City of Chattanooga, 1966-69; sole practice, Chattanooga; ptnr. Summers & Wyatt; mem. Tenn. Law Revision Commn. 1976; city judge City of Soddy-Daisy (Tenn.), 1976-83; mem. Tenn. Supreme Ct. Com. on Jud. Planning, 1976, Commn. on Advt., 1978; mem. bd. advisors paralegal program Cleveland State Community Coll., 1975-76; mem. faculty polit. sci. U. Tenn., 1982; mem. Law Enforcment Commn. Hamilton County; bd. dirs. Project First Offender; mem. br. adv. bd. United Bank Chattanooga; mem. Speedy Trial Planning Commn. for Eastern Dist. Tenn. 1977-78; mem. Commn. on Criminal Rules, Tenn. Supreme Ct., 1982-83; lectr. in field. Named Young Man of Yr., Chattanooga Jaycees, 1973, 76-77, Outstanding Young Man Am., U.S. Jaycees, 1974; U. Tenn. univ. scholar, 1963-64. Fellow Tenn. Bar Found., Am. Bd. Trial Advocates (founding mem., pres. Tenn. chpt. 1986-87), Internat. Soc. Barristers, Am. Bd. Criminal Lawyers; mem. ABA, NACDL (gov. 1975-76), Tenn. Bar Assn. (chmn. criminal justice sect. 1976), Assn. Trial Lawyers Am. (chmn. young lawyers sect. 1975, bd. govs. 1985-87), Tenn. Trial Lawyers Assn. (v.p. 1972-73, pres. 1977-78), Tenn. Assn. Criminal Def. Lawyers (pres. 1975-76), Chattanooga Bar Assn. (mem. bd. govs. 1978, sec. 1981, pres.-elect 1982, pres. 1983-84), Chattanooga Trial Lawyers Assn. (pres. 1972-73), Central High Alumni Assn. (pres. 1971-73), Phi Gamma Delta (v.p. chpt. 1962-63). Club: Civitan (Chattanooga). Author: Law Office Management Manual, 1974. Office: Summers & Wyatt PC 500 Lindsay St Chattanooga TN 37403-3496 Office Phone: 423-266-2385. Office Fax: 423-266-5211. E-mail: jsummers@summersandwyatt.com.

SUMMERS, LAWRENCE HENRY, former academic administrator, former secretary of the treasury; b. New Haven, Nov. 30, 1954; s. Robert Summers and Anita A. (Summers); m. Victoria Joanne Perry, 1984 (div.); children: Pam, Ruth, Harry; m. Elisa New, Dec. 11, 2005. BS, MIT, 1975; PhD, Harvard U. 1982. Mem. faculty MIT, 1979-82; domestic policy economist, Coun. Econ. Advisors The White House, 1982-83; v.p. devel. economics, chief economist World Bank, 1991-93; prof. economics Harvard U., Cambridge, Mass., 1983-93, Nathaniel Ropes prof. polit. economy, 1987—91, pres., 2001—06; under sec. for internat. affairs US Dept. Treasury, Washington, 1993-95, dep. sec., 1995-99, sec., 1999-2001; Arthur Okun Disting. Fellow in Econ., Globalization, and Governance Brookings Instn., Washington, 2001. Author Understanding Unemployment, 1990; co-author Reform in Eastern Europe, 1991; editor series Tax Policy and the Economy; contbr. numerous articles to profl. jours. Recipient Alan Waterman Award NSF, 1987, John Bates Clark Medal, 1993, Disting. Achievement Award Boys' & Girls' Club Greater Washington, 2000, Patriot Award Concord Coalition, 2000, Stephen P. Guggan Award Int. Internat. Edn., 2000; named one of 100 Most Influential People of 2005, Time mag. Fellow NAS, Econometric Soc., Am. Acad. Arts and Scis., Brookhaven Sci. Assocs. (bd. dirs.), Nat. Acad. Sci. Office: Kennedy Sch Govt Littauer 244 79 John F Kennedy St Cambridge MA 02138*

SUMMERS, LORRAINE DEY SCHAEFFER, retired librarian; b. Phila., Dec. 14, 1946; d. Joseph William and Hilda Lorraine (Ritchey) Dey; m. F. William Summers, Jan. 28, 1984. BA, Fla. State U., 1968, MS, 1969. Ext. dir. Santa Fe Regional Libr., Gainesville, 1969-71; pub. libr. cons. State Libr. of Fla., Tallahassee, 1971-78, asst. state libr., 1978-84; dir. adminstrv. svcs. Nat. Assn. for Campus Activities, Columbia, SC, 1984-85; asst. state libr. State Libr. of Fla., Tallahassee, 1985—2001, ret., 2001—. Bd. dirs., sec. Southeastern Libr. Network, Inc.; cons. in field. Contbr. articles to profl. jours. Del. Pres.'s Com. on Mental Retardation Regional Forum, Atlanta, 1975; del. Fla. Gov.'s Conf. on Libr. and Info. Svcs., 1978, 90. Mem. ALA (orgn. com. 1979-83, coun. 1982-84, 93-97, resolutions com. 1983-85, mem. legislation com. 1993-95, nominating com. 1996, awards com. 1998-99, Spectrum awards jury 1999-2000), Assn. Specialized and Coop. Libr. Agys. (dir. 1976-82, chmn. planning and orgn. com. 1976-80, chmn. nominating com. 1980-81, chmn. by laws com. 1985-86, exec. bd. state libr. agy. sect. 1983-86, pres. 1987-88, chmn. stds. rev. com. 1990-92), Southeastern Libr. Assn. (exec. bd. 1976-80, v.p., pres.-elect 1994-96, pres. 1996-98, past pres. 1998-2000, nominating com. 2000-02), Fla. Libr. Assn. (sec. 1978-79, dir. 1976-80, nominating com. 1995-96), Zonta (dir. 1992-95, sec. 1999-2001). Democrat. Methodist. Personal E-mail: lorsummers@worldnet.att.net.

SUMMERS, MARC, TV host, TV personality; b. Indpls., 1951; m. Alice Summers; 2 children. Comedian, LA; magician, comedian Magic Castle; studio page CBS, LA; guest announcer Joker's Wild, 1973. Nat. spokesperson Obsessive Compulsive Found. Performer (audience warm-ups): (TV series) Soap, Alice, Star Search; host, programming cons., prodr. (TV series) Double Dare, Nickelodeon, 1986—94, host What Would You Do?, host, creator, exec. prodr. Pick Your Brain, host Home Show, ABC, Our Home, Lifetime, Biggers and Summers, Great Day Am., PAX-TV, Unwrapped, Food Network, Trivia Unwrapped, appearances on The Next Food Network Star, Oprah, The Today Show, Dateline, The Howard Stern Show, The Tonight Show, Politically Incorrect, featured in People mag., USA Today; author: Everything In It's Place, 1999.*

SUMMERS, MICHAEL EDWARD, music educator; b. Hubbard, Ohio, Nov. 26, 1966; s. George E. and Lydia P. Summers; m. Debra K. Bachani, July 9, 1994; children: Andrew M., Leslie A. B Music Edn., Youngstown State U., 1995; MA, Nova Southeastern U., 2003. Cert. tchr. Ohio. Assoc. dir. bands Hubbard Schs., 1990—94; dir music Western Res. Local Schs., Boardman, Ohio, 1994—98; dir. instrumental music Liberty Local Schools, Liberty Twp., Ohio, 1998—, chmn. music dept., 2002—. Pvt. trumpet instr., Ohio, 1996—. Composer: (young band composer) W.S. Samba Guy. Dir. student instrumental music Good Hope Luth. Ch., Boardman, Ohio, 2002—05. Mem.: Liberty Assn. Sch. Employees, Music Educators Nat. Conf., Ohio Music Edn. Assn. (dist. chmn. jr. high/mid. sch. band contest 2002—, local chmn. solo and ensemble festival 2003—), Tri M Music Honors Soc (advisor local chpt. 2003—). Lutheran. Avocations: devotional reading, music, golf. Office: Liberty HS 1 Leopard Way Youngstown OH 44505 Office Phone: 330-759-1637 163. E-mail: michael.summers@neomin.org.

SUMMERS, PAUL G., state attorney general; b. Somerville, Tenn., Mar. 28, 1950; BS, Miss. State U.; JD, U. Tenn. Dist. atty. gen. 25th Jud. Dist., Somerville, Tenn., 1982—90; judge Ct. of Criminal Appeals, Nashville, 1990—99; atty. gen. State of Tenn., Nashville, 1999—. Adj. prof. law U Memphis; former adj. faculty Cumberland U.; pres. elect Tenn. Dist. Atty's Gen. Conf.; mem. Ct. Criminal Appeals, 1990—99; lectr. in field. Former mem. Tenn. Sentencing Commn.; col. Tenn. Army N.G. With USAF. Mem.: Tenn. Dist. Attys. Gen. Conf. (pres.), Tenn. Bar Assn. (former gov.). Democrat. Avocations: racquetball, rollerblading, Karate (black belt), martial arts. Office: Office of Atty General 500 Charlotte Ave Nashville TN 37243*

SUMMERS, ROBERT, economics professor; b. Gary, Ind., June 20, 1922; s. Frank and Ella (Lipton) Samuelson; m. Anita Arrow, Mar. 29, 1953; children: Lawrence Henry, Richard Fredric, John Steven. BS, U. Chgo., 1943; PhD, Stanford, 1956; postgrad. (Social Sci. Research Council fellow), King's Coll., U. Cambridge, Eng., 1951-52. Instr. Stanford, 1949-50; mem. faculty Yale, 1952-59, asst. prof., 1956-59; staff mem. Cowles Found., 1955-59; economist RAND Corp., Santa Monica, Calif., 1959-60, cons., 1960-80. Mem. faculty U. Pa. Wharton Sch., 1959—, prof., 1967—, chmn. grad. group in econs., 1967-70, 73-76 Author: (with Lawrence R. Klein) The Wharton Index of Capacity Utilization, 1966, (with others) Strategies for Research and Development, 1967, (with others) A System of International Comparisons of Gross Product and Purchasing Power, 1975, (with others) International Comparisons of Real Product and Purchasing Power, 1978, (with others) World Product and Income, 1982; contbr. articles to profl. jours. Served with AUS, 1944-46. Ford Found. faculty rsch. fellow London Sch. Econs., 1966-67; NSF grantee 1957-59, 63-66, 80-82, 86-90, 92-94, 95-97, 97-2000, 00—03; resident scholar Rockefeller Found. Study Ctr., 1986. Fellow: AAAS, Am. Econ. Soc. (disting.), Econometric Soc. Home: 1400 Waverly Rd V-11 Gladwyne PA 19035-1271 Office: U Pa Dept Econ Philadelphia PA 19104-6297 Office Phone: 215-898-7717, 215-898-7624. Business E-Mail: rsummers@econ.upenn.edu.

SUMMERS, ROBERT SAMUEL, lawyer, author, educator; b. Halfway, Oreg., Sept. 19, 1933; s. Orson William and Estella Bell (Robertson) S.; m. Dorothy Millicent Kopp, June 14, 1955; children: Brent, William, Thomas, Elizabeth, Robert. BS in Polit. Sci., U. Oreg., 1955; postgrad. (Fulbright scholar), U. Southampton, Eng., 1955-56; LLB, Harvard U., 1959; postgrad. rsch., Oxford U., 1964-65, 74-75, 81-82, 88-89; LLD (hon.), U. Helsinki, Finland, 1990, U. Göttingen, Germany, 1994. Bar: Oreg. 1959, NY 1974. Asso. King, Miller, Anderson, Nash and Yerke, Portland, Oreg., 1959-60; asst. prof. law U. Oreg., 1960-63, asso. prof., 1964-68; vis. asso. prof. law Stanford U., 1964-65; prof. U. Oreg., 1968-69, Cornell U., 1969-76, McRoberts rsch. prof. law, 1976—. Summer vis. prof. Ind. U., 1969, U. Mich., 1974, U. Warwick, Eng., 1975, Australia Nat. U., U. Sydney, Australia, 1977; vis. Fulbright prof. U. Vienna, Austria, 1985; Goodhart vis. prof. Cambridge U., Eng., 1991-92; H. Hurst Eminent vis. scholar U. Fla., 1995; rsch. fellow Merton Coll., oxford U., 1981-82, Exeter Coll., Oxford U., 1988-89; cons. Cornell Law Project in publ. schs., N.Y., 1969-74, Law in Am. Soc. project Chgo. Bd. Edn., 1968-69; instr. Nat. Acad. Jud. Edn., 1976—; mem. faculty Salzburg Seminar in Am. Studies, 1990; ofcl. advisor Drafting commn. on New Civil Code for Russian Fedn., 1994-96. Author: Law, Its Nature, Functions and Limits, 1986; (with Hubbard and Campbell) Justice and Order Through Law, 1973; (with Bozzone and Campbell) The American Legal System, 1973; (with Speidel and White) Teaching Materials on Commercial Transactions, 1987, Collective Bargaining and Public Benefit Conferral-A Jurisprudential Critique, 1976, The Uniform Commercial Code, 1988, 4th edit., 1995; (with White) Het Pramatisch Instrumentalisme, 1981, Instrumentalism and American Legal Theory, 1982, Lon L. Fuller-Life and Work, 1984; (with Atiyah) Form and Substance in Anglo-American Law, 1987; (with Hillman) Contract and Related Obligation, 1987; (with MacCormick and others) Interpreting Statutes-A Comparative Study, 1991, Nature of Law and Legal Reasoning, 1993; contbr. book revs. and articles to profl. jours.; editor: Essays in Legal Philosophy, vol. 1, 1968, vol. 2, 1971. Social Sci. Research Council fellow, 1964-65 Mem. Am. Law Inst., Assn. Am. Law Schs. (chmn. sect. jurisprudence 1972-73), Am. Soc. Polit. and Legal Philosophy (v.p. 1976-78), Internat. Acad. Comp. Law, Internat. Assn. of Legal and Social Philosophy Am. Soc. (pres. 1989-91), Austrian Acad. of Scis., Phi Beta Kappa. Republican. Congregationalist. Office: Cornell U S Law Myron Taylor Hall Ithaca NY 14853

SUMMERS, STANLEY EUGENE, mechanical engineer; b. Sterling, Colo. s. Matthew Marion and Hazel J. (Snider) S.; m. Dorothy E. Hanneman, June 15, 1944 (div. Oct. 1977); children: Daniel E., Shirley A.; m. Jaclyn A. Marquart, Oct. 15, 1977; children: Stephanie Ann, Jeffrey E. BSME, UCLA, 1964. Mech. engr. Interstate Engring., El Segundo, Calif., 1947-59, Ametek Calmec, L.A., 1959-90, Ketema A&E, El Cajon, Calif., 1990—. Recipient Douglas Aircraft VIP award, 1968, NASA Achievement award, 1971, MacDonnell Douglas Pres.'s award, 1991, Spirit of Excellence award, 1992 NASF Snoopy award, 2004. Mem.: ASME. Republican. Avocations: woodworking, R.C. models. Home: 2576 Katherine Ct El Cajon CA 92020-2062 Office: Ketema A&E 790 Greenfield Dr El Cajon CA 92021-3101 E-mail: ssumm2@cox.net.

SUMMERS, SUZANNE FRANCES HEMENWAY, elementary school educator; b. Battle Creek, Mich., June 23, 1950; d. Robert Walter and Irene (Hodges) Hemenway; m. Jacob George Summers, June 23, 1973; children: Braxton, Jennifer, Dondra. BS in Home Econs., E. Carolina U., 1972; MEd, Campbell U., 1997. Lic. elem. tchr., N.C.; cert. tchr. Nat. Bd. Profl. Tchg. Standards, Va., 2005. Substitute tchr. Wake County Pub. Schs., Raleigh, N.C., 1973-74; presch. tchr. Greenwood Forest Bapt. Kindergarten, Cary, N.C., 1978-80; substitute tchr. Wake County Pub. Schs., Raleigh, 1980-96, tchr. elem., 1996—; tchr. Cary Elem. Sch. 2d team chair Cary Elem. Sch., rep. sch. improvement 2d and 3d grades; chmn. 2d grade sci. steering com. Wake County Pub. Schs., mem. sci. leadership com. Mem. NEA, N.C. Assn. Educators, Kappa Delta Pi, Phi Kappa Phi, Phi Upsilon Omicron. Republican. Baptist. Avocations: cooking, decorating homes. Home: 239 E Cornwall Rd Cary NC 27511-3907 Office Phone: 919-460-3455. Business E-Mail: ssummers@wcpss.net.

SUMMERS, THOMAS CAREY, lawyer; b. Frederick, Md., Feb. 9, 1956; s. Harold Thomas and Doris Jean (Culler) S.; m. Robin Ann Stalnaker, May 12, 1990; children: Kristin, Heather, Lindsay. BA, Dickinson Coll., 1978; JD, U. Balt., 1981. Bar: Md. 1981, U.S. Dist. Ct. Md. 1981, D.C. 1986. Assoc. Ellin & Baker, Balt., 1979-89, Peter G. Angelos, Balt., Md., 1989—. Adj. prof. law U. Balt. Sch. of Law. Mem. ABA, Md. State Bar Assn., Md. Trial Lawyers Assn. Democrat. Lutheran. Avocation: golf. Office: Law Offices of P G Angelos One Charles Ctr Baltimore MD 21201 Office Phone: 410-649-2000. Business E-Mail: tsummers@lawpga.com.

SUMMERS, WILLIAM B., JR., brokerage house executive; b. 1950; With McDonald & Co. Investments Inc., Cleve., 1971—; pres., CEO and chmn. McDonald & Co. Securities, Cleve., 1983—; chmn. McDonald Investments Inc., Cleve., 1995—; exec. v.p. KeyCorp, 1998—2000; chmn. Key Capital Partners, 1998—2000. Office: McDonald Investment Inc 800 Superior Ave E Cleveland OH 44114-2601

SUMMERS, WILLIAM COFIELD, science educator; b. Janesville, Wis., Apr. 17, 1939; s. Crosby Hungerford and Rebecca Delores (Cofield) S.; m. Wilma Jean Poos, July 24, 1965; 1 child, Emily Alexandra. BS, U. Wis., 1961, MS, 1963, Phd, MD, 1967; MA, Yale U., 1977. Post-doctoral fellow MIT, Cambridge, Mass., 1967-68; asst. prof. Yale U., New Haven, 1968-70, assoc. prof., 1970-77, prof., 1977—. Cons. NIH, Bethesda, Md., 1976—. Editor Nucleic Acids Research Jour., 1977-79, Gene jour., 1984-91; contbr. articles to profl. jours. Joanna Fuller Fund, New Haven, 1973-88, Searle Scholars Program, Chgo., 1980-84; trustee Leukemia Soc. Am., N.Y.C., 1981-85, Yale-China Assn., New Haven, 1982-88, 94-98. Mem. Am. Soc. for Microbiology, History Sci. Soc., Am. Assn. History of Medicine. Office: Yale U Box 208114 New Haven CT 06520-8114 E-mail: william.summers@yale.edu.

SUMMERS, WILLIAM KOOPMANS, psychiatrist, internist, researcher; b. Jefferson City, Mo., Apr. 14, 1944; s. Joseph S. and Amy Lydia (Koopmans) Summers; m. Angela Forbes McGonigle, Oct. 2, 1972 (div. Apr. 1985). Student, Westminster Coll., Fulton, Mo., 1962-64; BS, U. Mo., 1966; MD, Washington U., St. Louis, 1971. Internal medicine intern Barnes Hosp-Washington U., St. Louis, 1971—72; resident in internal medicine Jewish Hosp., St. Louis, 1972—73; resident in psychiatry Washington U. Sch. Medicine, St. Louis, 1973—76; asst. prof. U. Pitts., 1976—78, U. So. Calif., L.A., 1978—82; asst. clin. prof. UCLA, 1982—88; rschr. Arcadia, Calif., 1988—92, Albuquerque, 1992—; pres., CEO Alzheimers Corp., Albuquerque, 1999—. Mem.: ACP, AMA, Am. Fedn. Clin. Rsch. Soc.

Neurosci., N.Y. Acad. Scis., Am. Psychiat. Assn. Episcopalian. Achievements include holder of 8 patents in neuropharmacology and neuroceuticals. Avocation: gardening. Office: Alzheimers Corp 6000 Uptown NE Ste 308 Albuquerque NM 87110

SUMMERS, WILLIAM LAWRENCE, lawyer; b. Ravenna, Ohio, Mar. 6, 1942; s. Samuel Long and Harriet Cordellia (Jones) S.; m. Barbara A. Herbert; children: Melinda Ann, Shannon Lea, Heather Colleen, Kelly Lynn, Michael Patrick, Kevin James. BA in Polit. Sci. and Sociology, Kent State U., 1965; postgrad., U. Miami, 1966; JD, Cleve. State U., 1969. Bar: Ohio 1969, Ky. 1988, U.S. Dist. Ct. (no. dist.) Okla. 1971, U.S. Ct. Appeals (6th cir.) 1973, U.S. Ct. Appeals (3d and 5th cirs.) 1979, U.S. Ct. Appeals (8th and 5th cirs.) 1981, U.S. Ct. Appeals (7th cir.) 1982, U.S. Ct. Appeals (9th and 10th cirs.) 1983, U.S. Ct. Appeals (11th cir.), 1984, U.S. Supreme Ct., 1973, U.S. Tax Ct. 1973, U.S. Dist. Ct. (so. dist.) Ala. 1988, U.S. Dist. Ct. (so. dist.) Ohio 1985, U.S. Dist. Ct. (ea. and we. dists.) Ky. 1988. Ptnr. Summers & Vargas Co. LPA, Cleve. and Lexington, Ky., 1969—. Cons. on death penalty State Pub. Defender, Santa Fe, 1980-83; lectr. in field. Named one of Ten Outstanding Young Men of Cleve., Cleve. Jaycees, 1972, Five Outstanding Young Men of Ohio, Ohio Jaycees, 1972. Fellow Am. Acad. Trial Lawyers (Roscoe Pound award 1971); mem. ABA (criminal justice sect.), Ohio State Bar Assn. (ho. of dels. 1973-75, 2002-2004), Cuyahoga County Bar Assn. (trustee 1972-76, treas. 1976-79, pres. 1982-83, other coms.), Cuyahoga County Bar Assn., Cuyahoga County Criminal Ct. Bar Assn. (pres. 1977-79), Fed. Bar Assn., Portage County Bar Assn., Ohio Assn. Criminal Def. Lawyers (bd. dirs. 1988—), Ky. Assn. Criminal Def. Lawyer (bd. dirs. 1987-2000), Bar Assn. Greater Cleve., Nat. Assn. Criminal Def. Lawyers (trustee 1977-88, chmn. various coms. Pres.'s award 1981, 1986, 90, Robert C. Heeney award 1982), Am. Judicature Soc., Thoroughbred Club Am., Delta Theta Phi, Canterbury Golf Club, Elks. Roman Catholic. Avocation: thoroughbred horse breeding. Home: 17549 Merry Oaks Trl Chagrin Falls OH 44023-5643 Office: 55 Public Square Ste 2000 Cleveland OH 44113 Office Phone: 216-591-0727. Personal E-Mail: wlslawyer@aol.com.

SUMMERTREE, KATONAH See WINDSOR, PATRICIA

SUMMERVILLE, RICHARD M., mathematician, academic administrator; BS in Math., Clarion State Coll., Pa., 1959; AM in Math., Washington U., St. Louis, 1965; PhD in Math., Syracuse U., 1969. Provost Christopher Newport U. Office: Christopher Newport U Office of the Provost 1 University Pl Newport News VA 23606-2998 E-mail: rsummer@cnu.edu.

SUMMIT, STUART A., lawyer; b. Canton, Ohio, Apr. 18, 1936; s. William A. and Dorothy Jean (Cohen) S.; children: Joshua, Ian. BS, Ohio State U., 1957, JD summa cum laude, 1959. Bar: Ohio 1960, NY 1961, U.S. Dist. Ct. (so. dist.) NY 1965, U.S. Dist. Ct. (ea. dist.) NY 1965, U.S. Ct. Appeals (2d cir.) 1966, U.S. Supreme Ct. 1973, U.S. Ct. Appeals (5th cir.) 1975, DC 1978. Law clk. to judge Appellate Div., Supreme Ct. NY, 1962-63; assoc. Mudge, Stern, Baldwin & Todd, and successors, NYC, 1960-66; prtnr. Miller & Summitt, NYC, 1967-76, Summit Rovins & Feldesman and predecessor firm, NYC, 1976-93, Phillips Nizer Benjamin Krim & Ballon, NYC, 1993—; counsel N.Y. State Commn. Jud. Nomination, 1978—; exec. sec. Mayor's Com. on Judiciary, NYC, 1966-77. Sr. editor: Federal Litigation Guide, New York and Connecticut, 1998; contbr. articles to profl. jours. Alumni adv. coun. Ohio State U., chmn. 1982-85; nat. coun. Ohio State U. Law Coll. Mem. Ohio State U. Law Alumni Assn. (pres. 1978-79, trustee 2006—), adv. coun. Fashion Inst. Tech., 1993-96; trustee Boys & Girls Club Am., 1980-91, NYC Bar Assn., NY State Bar Assn., ABA, Fed. Bar Coun., Am. Judicature Soc., Fed. Bar Found. (trustee). Home: 240 Centre St Apt 6M New York NY 10013-3215 also: 15 Lakeview Ct Southampton NY 11968-2311 Office: 666 5th Ave New York NY 10103-0001 Office Phone: 212-841-0715. Business E-Mail: ssummit@phillipsnizer.com

SUMMITT, PATRICIA HEAD, college basketball coach; b. Henrietta, Tenn., June 14, 1952; d. Richard and Hazel Head; m. R.B. Summitt; 1 child, Ross Tyler. BS in Phys. Edn., U. Tenn., Martin, 1974; MS in Phys. Edn., U. Tenn., Knoxville, 1975. Basketball player U. Tenn., Martin, 1970—74; head women's basketball coach Knoxville, 1974—. Head coach 1st U.S. Jr. Nat. team, 1977 (2 gold medals in internat. play), U.S. Nat. team William R. Jones Cup Games, 1979, World Championships, 1979, Pan Am. Games, 1979 (2 gold medals, 1 silver medal); asst. coach U.S. Women's Olympic Basketball team, 1980-84, head coach, 1984 (gold medal); assoc. athletics dir., U. Tenn.; past v.p. USA BASKETBALL; past Olympic rep. adv. com. to USA BASKETBALL; bd. trustees Basketball Hall of Fame; bd. dirs. Women's Basketball Hall of Fame. Active Big Bros./Big Sisters; Active spokesperson United Way, Race for the Cure, Juvenile Diabetes; hon. chair Tenn. Easter Seal Soc., 1985, 87, 88, 89; Tenn. chair Am. Heart Assn., 1994. Named Naismith Coach of Yr., 1987, 1989, 1994, 1997, Naismith Coach of Century, 2000, WBCA/Converse Coach of Yr., 1983—95; named one of Women of Yr., Women in Sports and Events, 1999; named to Women's Sports Foundation Hall of Fame, 1990, Nat. Assn. for Sport and Phys. Edn., 1996, Women's Basketball Hall of Fame, 1999, Basketball Hall of Fame, 2000; recipient silver medal, Olympic Games, 1976, gold medal, Pan Am. Games, 1975, silver medal, U.S. World Univ. Games, 1973, Wooden Award, 1997, ARETE Award for Courage in Sports, 1999. Mem. Chi Omega. Achievements include coach U. Tenn. women's basketball NCAA Championship teams, 1987, 89, 91, 96, 97, 98; coach U. Tenn. women's basketball SEC Championship teams, 1980, 85, 90, 93, 94, 95, 98, 99, 2000, 01, 02, 03; became the all-time winningest coach in NCAA basketball history, March 21, 2005; first female coach ever to win 300 games, 2006.*

SUMNER, DANIEL ALAN, economist, educator; b. Fairfield, Calif., Dec. 5, 1950; BS in Agrl. Mgmt., Calif. State Poly. U., 1971; MA in Econs., Mich. State U., 1973, U. Chgo., 1977, PhD, 1978. Post-doctoral fellow, labor and population group, econ. dept., Rand Corp., Santa Monica, Calif., 1977-78; asst. prof. N.C. State U., Raleigh, 1978-83, assoc. prof., 1983-87, prof., 1987-92; resident fellow Resources for the Future, Washington, 1986-87; sr. economist Pres.'s Council of Econ. Advisers, 1987-88; dep. asst. sec. for econs. USDA, 1990-91, asst. sec. for econs., 1992-93; Frank H. Buck Jr. prof. dept. agrl. econs. U. Calif., Davis, 1993—. Dir. U. Calif. Agrl. Issues Ctr., 1997—; chair Internat. Agrl. Trade Rsch. Consortium, 1997-99. Author and editor books and monographs; contbr. chpts. to books, articles in profl. jours. Named Alumnus of Yr., Calif. State Poly. U., 1991; recipient Quality of Rsch. Contbn. award Am. Agrl. Econ. Assn., 1996, Policy Contbrn., 1995, fellow, 1999. Mem. Am. Econ. Assn., Econometric Soc., Am. Agrl. Econs. Assn., Internat. Assn. Agrl. Economists. Office: U Calif Davis Dept Agrl Econ Davis CA 95616 Office Phone: 530-752-1668. Business E-Mail: dasumner@ucdavis.edu.

SUMNER, DAVID GEORGE, association executive; b. Norwich, Conn., Apr. 22, 1949; s. Raymond W. and Ruth M. (Crooks) S.; m. Linda Ann Churma, June 27, 1980; 1 child, Deryn Anne. BA in Polit. Sci., Mich. State U., 1970; MBA, U. Conn., 1979. Corr. Travelers Ins. Co., Hartford, Conn., 1971-72; asst. sec. Am. Radio Relay League, Newington, Conn., 1972-76, asst. gen. mgr., 1976-82, gen. mgr., 1982-85, exec. v.p., 1985—. Bd. dirs. Windham Regional Planning Agy., Willimantic, Conn., 1991-98; mem. Coventry Dem. Town Com., 1995—; mem. spectrum planning and policy adv. com. U.S. Dept. Commerce, 1994—; sec. Internat. Amateur Radio Union, 1982-89, 99—; mem. Coventry Zoning Bd. Appeals, 1997—, chmn., 1999—. Recipient Calcutta Key, Radio Soc. Gt. Britain, 1989, Region I award Internat. Amateur Radio Union, 1989; Radio Club Am. fellow, 1991. Mem. Newington C. of C. (bd. dirs. 1988-90). Democrat. Congregationalist. Avocation: amateur radio. Office: Am Radio Relay League 225 Main St Newington CT 06111-1400

SUMNER, DAVID SPURGEON, surgeon, educator; b. Asheboro, N.C., Feb. 20, 1933; s. George Herbert and Velna Elizabeth (Welborn) S.; m. Martha Eileen Sypher, July 25, 1959; children: David Vance, Mary Elizabeth, John Franklin. BA, U. N.C., 1954; MD, Johns Hopkins U., 1958. Diplomate

Am. Bd. Surgery; cert. spl. qualification gen. vascular surgery. Intern Johns Hopkins Hosp., Balt., 1958-59, resident in gen. surgery, 1960-61, U. Wash. Sch. Medicine, Seattle, 1961-66; clin. investigator in vascular surgery VA Hosp., Seattle, 1967, 70-73; asst. prof. surgery U. Wash. Sch. Medicine, Seattle, 1970-72, assoc. prof. surgery, 1972-75; prof. surgery, chief sect. peripheral vascular surgery So. Ill. U. Sch. Medicine., Springfield, 1975-84, Disting. prof. surgery, chief sect. peripheral vascular surgery, 1984-98, disting. prof. emeritus, 1998. Staff surgeon Seattle VA Hosp., 1973-75, Univ. Hosp., Seattle, 1973-75, St. John's Hosp., Springfield, 1975-98, Meml. Med. Ctr., Springfield, 1975-98; mem. VA Merit Review Bd. Surgery, 1975-78; mem. vascular surgery rsch. award com. The Liebig Found., 1990-95, chmn., 1994; bd. dirs. Am. Venous Forum Found., 1993-95; vis. prof. Cook County Hosp., Chgo., 1971, Washington U., St. Louis, 1976, U. Tex., San Antonio, 1978, Wayne State U., Detroit, 1978, U. Ind., Indpls., 1979, Ea. Va. Med. Sch., Norfolk, 1979, Case-Western Res. U., Cleve., 1980, U. Chgo., 1981, U. Manitoba, Winnipeg, Can., 1983, others; dist. lectr. Yale U., 1982; guest examiner Am. Bd. Surgery, St. Louis, 1982, assoc. examiner, 1989; lectr. in field. Author: (with D.E. Strandness Jr.) Ultrasonic Techniques in Angiology, 1975, Hemodynamics for Surgeons, 1975; (with R.B. Rutherford, V. Bernhard, F. Maddison, W.S. Moore, M.O. Perry) Vascular Surgery, 1977; (with F.B. Hershey, R.W. Barnes) Noninvasive Diagnosis of Vascular Disease, 1984; (with R.B. Rutherford, G. Johnson Jr., R.F. Kempczinski, W.S. Moore, M.O. Perry, G.W. Smith) Vascular Surgery, 3d edit., 1989; (with A.N. Nicolaides) Investigation of Patients With Deep Vein Thrombosis and Chronic Venous Insufficiency, 1991; (with R.B. Rutherford, G. Johnson, K.W. Johnston, R.F. Kempczinski, W.C. Krupski, W.S. Moore, M.O. Perry, A.J. Comerota, R.H. Dean, P. Gloviczki, K.H. Johansen, T.S. Riles, L.M. Taylor Jr.) Vascular Surgery, 4th edit., 1995; (with K.A. Myers, A.N. Nicolaides Lower Limb Ischaemia, 1997; author 150 chpts. to books; mem. editl. bd. Vascular Diagnosis and Therapy, 1980-84, Jour. Soc. Non-Invasive Vascular Tech., 1987—, Jour. Vascular Surgery, 1987-97; series editor Introduction to Vascular Tech., 1990—; mem. exec. editl. com. Phlebology, 1987-91, mem. internat. editl. adv. bd., 1991-2000; mem. editl. com. Internat. Angiology, 1992—; contbr. over 150 articles to profl. jours. Lt. col. U.S. Army, 1967-70. Fellow in surg. rsch. Johns Hopkins U. Sch. Medicine, 1959-60, Am. Cancer Soc., Inc. fellow, 1965-66; Appleton-Century Crofts scholar, 1956, Mosby scholar, 1958. Fellow Am. Coll. Surgeons (Wash. chpt. 1971-75, Ill. chpt. counselor 1981-83), Cyprus Vascular Soc. (hon.); mem. AMA, Soc. Univ. Surgeons, Soc. Vascular Surgery (constn. and by-laws com. 1983, Wiley Fellowship com. 1990), Internat. Soc. Cardiovascular Surgery (N.Am. chpt. program com. 1985-88), Am. Surg. Assn., Am. Heart Assn. (stroke coun., cardiovascular surgery coun. 1978), Soc. Noninvasive Vascular Tech. (hon.), Vascular Surgery Biology Club, Am. Venous Forum (organizing com. 1987, founding mem. 1988, chmn. membership com. 1988-91, treas. 1992-95, pres. elect 1998, pres. 1999-2000), Cardiovascular Sys. Dynamics Soc., Internat. Soc. Surgery, Vascular Soc. So. Africa (hon.), North Pacific Surg. Assn., Ctrl. Surg. Assn., Midwestern Vascular Surg. Soc. (counselor 1977-79, pres.-elect 1980-81, pres. 1981-82), So. Assn. for Vascular Surgery, Ill. Heart Assn., Ill. Med. Soc., Ill. Surg. Soc., Chgo. Surg. Soc., Seattle Surg. Soc., Sangamon County Med. Soc., Henry N. Harkins Surg. Soc., Harbinger Soc., Phi Eta Sigma, Phi Beta Kappa, Sigma Xi, Alpha Omega Alpha. Presbyterian. Achievements include research in surgical hemodynamics and noninvasive methods for diagnosing peripheral vascular disease. Home: 2324 W Lake Shore Dr Springfield IL 62712-9521 E-mail: dsumner1@aol.com.

**SUMNER, GORDON, JR.,** retired military officer; b. Albuquerque, July 23, 1924; s. Gordon and Esstella (Berry) S.; m. Frances Fernandes, May, 1991; children: Ward T., Holly Rose. AS, N.Mex. Mil. Inst., 1943; BA, La. State U., 1955; MA, U. Md., 1963. Commd. 2d. lt. U.S. Army, 1944, advanced through grades to lt. gen., 1975, ret., 1978; founder, chmn. Cypress Internat., 1978-96; chmn. La Mancha Co., Inc., 1981-89, Sumner Assoc. Coos. U.S. Depts. State and Def; ambassador at large for Latin Am.; spl. advisor U.S. Dept. State; nat. security advisor Pres.' Bi-Partisan Commn. Cen. Am.; cons. Los Alamos Nat. Lab. Contbr. articles to profl. jours. Decorated D.S.M., Silver Star, Legion of Merit with three oak leaf clusters, D.F.C., Air medal with 13 oak leaf clusters, Bronze Star, Army Commendation medal with oak leaf cluster, Purple Heart. Mem. Phi Kappa Phi, Pi Sigma Alpha. Office: La Mancha Co 100 Cienega St Ste D Santa Fe NM 87501-2003 Office Phone: 505-984-8041.

**SUMNER, GORDON MATTHEW See STING**

**SUMNER, STEPHEN C.,** academic administrator; m. Pamela Sumner. Prof. U. Tulsa, dir. div. fine & performing arts, 1994—2001; provost New World Sch. Art, Miami, 2001—03; pres. Rocky Mountain Coll. Art & Design, Colo. Office: Office of President Rocky Mountain Coll Art & Design 1600 Pierce St Denver CO 80214 Office Phone: 303-753-6046. E-mail: ssumner@rmcad.edu.

**SUMPTER, WAYNE,** military officer, physician; b. Tampa, Fla., Nov. 6, 1961; BS in Biology, USAF Acad., 1983; MD, MPH, Uniformed Svcs. U. of Health Scis., 1987. Diplomate Am. Bd. Family Practice, 2004, in aerospace medicine Am. Bd. Preventive Medicine, 2000, in occupl. medicine Am. Bd. Preventive Medicine, 2001. Commd. lt. USAF, advanced through grades to col., flight comdr. 12th Aeromedical-Dental Squadron Randolph AFB, Tex., 2000—02, squadron comdr. 319th Aeromedical-Dental Squadron Grand Forks AFB, ND, 2002—04, chief aerospace medicine 55th Med. Group Offutt AFB, Nebr., 2004—. Decorated Bronze Star USAF. Mem.: Assn. Mil. Surgeons U.S., Soc. USAF Flight Surgeons, Aerospace Med. Assn., Am. Acad. Family Physicians, USAF Acad. Assn. Grads. (life). Office: 55th Medical Group 2501 Capehart Rd Offutt Afb NE 68113 Office Phone: 402-294-9027. Business E-Mail: wayne.sumpter@offutt.af.mil.

**SUMWALT, ROBERT LLEWELLYN III,** commissioner, pilot; b. Columbia, S.C., June 30, 1956; s. Robert Llewellyn Jr. and Joyce (Mills) S.; m. Anne Macdonald, Dec. 22, 1978; 1 child, Kaylyn Mackenzie. BS, U. S.C., 1979. Flight engr., first officer Piedmont Airlines, Winston-Salem, N.C., 1981-83, chief flight engr., 1983, capt., airline instr. Charlotte, NC, 1984-89; capt. U.S. Airways, Charlotte, 1989—2005; mgr. aviation SCANA Corp., 2005—06; mem. Nat. Transp. Safety Bd. (NTSB), Washington, 2006—, vice chmn., 2006—. Chmn. Richland County Airport Commn., Columbia, S.C., 1987-89; pres. Aviatrends, Inc., Columbia, 1992—; aviation safety rsch. cons. NASA Aviation Safety Reporting Sys.; mem., Air Line Pilots Assn. Accident Investigation Bd., 2002-04, US Airways Flight Ops. Quality Assurance, 2002-04; instr. Aviation Safety & Security Program, U. So. Calif., 2003- Author: Terminal Checklist, 1991; editl. adv. bd. Profl. Pilot Mag., Alexandria, Va., 1986—; contbr. articles to profl. jours. Recipient Laura Taber Barbour award, Flight Safety Found., 2003, Air Safety award, Air Line Pilots Assn., 2004. Mem. Airline Pilots Assn. (chmn. human hactors and ergonomics com.). Presbyterian. Achievements include research on aviation safety and aircraft accident investigation. Office: Nat Transp Safety Bd (NTSB) 490 L Enfant Plz SW Washington DC 20594*

**SUN, ALBERT YUNG-KWANG,** pharmacologist, educator; b. Amoy, Fukien, Peoples Republic of China, Oct. 13, 1932; came to U.S., 1959, naturalized, 1972; s. Pehcheng and SuiHo Kuo Wu; m. Grace Yen-Chi Cheung Sun, May 9, 1964; 1 child, Aggie Yee-Chun. BS in Agrl. Chemistry, Nat. Taiwan U., Taipei, 1957; PhD in Biochemistry, Oreg. State U., 1967. Postdoctoral rsch. assoc. Case-Western Res. U., Cleve., 1967-68; sr. rsch. scientist Cleve. Psychiat. Inst., 1968-74; project dir. Ohio Mental Health Rsch. Ctr., Cleve., 1972-74, rsch. prof./assoc. prof. biochemistry, 1974—91, prof. pharmacology, 1991—2003, prof. med. pharmacology and physiology, 2003—. Mem. adv. panel NSF, Washington, 1984-85. Editor: Neural Membranes, 1983, Molecular Mechanism of Alcohol, 1989. Advisor Chinese Christian Fellowship Group, Columbia, 1974—. Grantee Nat. Inst. Alcohol Abuse and Alcoholism, 1974-78, 82-98, Nat. Inst. Neurol. Communicable Disease and Stroke, 1975-79, Nat. Cancer Inst., 1979-83, NIEHS, 2000-05, Nat. Inst. Aging, 2001-. Mem. Rsch. Soc. Alcoholism, Am. Soc. Neurochemistry, Am. Soc. Neurosci., Am. Soc. Biochemistry and Molecular Biology, Am. Chem. Soc. Current work: Structure-functional relationship of neural membranes using biochemical and biophysical approaches, study on the

biochem.mechanism of aging and Alzheimer's Disease in the brain. Subspecialies: Biochemistry (medicine); Neurochemistry. Home: 2908 Shoreside Dr Columbia MO 65203-0941 Office Phone: 573-882-1565. Business E-Mail: suna@missouri.edu.

**SUN, BOMIN,** environmental scientist; s. Shanbei Sun and Wanqing Xie. PhD, U. Mass., Amherst, 2001. Postdoc investigator WHOI, Falmouth, Mass., 2000—01; rsch. scientist STG/NCDC/NESDIS, NOAA, Asheville, NC, 2002—. Achievements include research in cloud cover change, air-sea heat flux and USCRN normals product. Home: 20 Sweetbriar Asheville NC 28803

**SUN, CHENGHUA,** composer, music educator; b. Shao Xing, Zejiang, China, Sept. 17, 1942; arrived in U.S., 1991; s. Zhiliang Sun and Fuzhen Cai; m. Ai-Yue Ding, Jan. 17, 1968; children: Tian, Sun. Bachelors Degree in Violin Performance, Conservatory of Music, Shanghai, 1966. Group leader composition Song and Dance Theatre, Hunan, China, 1974—84; dir. song and dance group Opera & Dance Theatre, Jiangsu, China, 1986—91; founding dir. Chinese Youth Orch., Dallas, 1995—99; dir. Chinese Lucky-Star Choir, Dallas, 1995—. Advisor Little Red Flower Arts Group, Nanjing, China, 1987, Greatland Choral Soc., Dallas, 1995—2000, 2005; soloist Chinese Erhu Philharm. Symphony Orch., Irving, Tex., 1996, Voice of Change Inc., Dallas, 1998; soloist Dallas Chamber Orch., 2004—05. Composer: (songs) Album of Best Songs of China Since 1949, 1980 (1st prize), violin concerto. Named Life-time Art Dir., Opera and Dance Theatre, Jiangsu, 1991; recipient Grand prize for dance music, Nat. Edn. Dept., Beijing, 1989. Mem.: Am. String Tchr.'s Assn., Chinese Muiscians Assn., Music Tchrs. Nat. Assn., Assn. Chinese Profls. (advisor 2000), Dallas Chinese Artist Assn. (dir. 1999—2003), Chinese Music Soc. Dallas (founding dir. 1994—, prodr. first Dallas Chinese Music Festival 2004). Avocations: sports, games. Personal E-mail: sunding@juno.com. E-mail: sunding421217@yahoo.com.

**SUN, DONGLIAN,** meteorologist; d. Detian Sun and XianZhi Shiao; m. XiaoBiao Fan, May 1, 1990; 1 child, Jean Fan. BS in Synoptic Dynamics, Nanjing Inst. Meteorology, China, 1986; MS in Numerical Model and Simulation, Chinese Acad. Meteorol. Scis., Beijing, 1989, U. Md., College Park, 1998, PhD in Satellite Remote Sensing, 2003. Sr. scientist Raytheon ITSS Inc, Lanham, Md., 1998—2000; sr. software engr. Titan/AverStar, Vienna, Va., 2000—01; rsch. scientist, severe weather ctr. lead George Mason U., Fairfax, Va., 2001—. Achievements include development of new algorithms for improving atmospheric water vapor, surface temperature and emissivity retrieval from current and future satellite measurements; the study of coastal upwelling, hurricanes, and earthquakes by combining numerical model simulations with satellite remote sensing. Home: 21700 Seneca Ayr Dr Boyds MD 22830 Office: George Mason Univ Rsch Bldg 1 Room #252 MS:5C3 4400 University Dr Fairfax VA 22030 Office Phone: 703-993-4736. Home Fax: 703-993-1980; Office Fax: 703-943-1980. Personal E-mail: dsun@gmu.edu. Business E-Mail: sun@atmos.umd.edu.

**SUN, EDWARD CHIH-YU,** surgeon, orthopedist; s. Raymond and Susan Sun; m. Jacqueline T. Koo. MD, Harvard U., 1996; BA, Stanford U., Calif., 2001. Diplomate Nat. Bd. Med. Examiners, 1996. Resident orthopaedics Med. Ctr. U. Calif., L.A., 1996—2001; fellow pediatric orthopaedics Childrens' Hosp., Boston, 2002—03; fellow spine surgery Twin Citiies Spine Ctr., Mpls., 2003—04; staff surgeon SpineCare Med. Group, Daly City, Calif., 2004—. Fellow, NIH, 1995. Fellow: Scoliosis Rsch. Soc., Am. Acad. Orthopaedic Surgeons; mem.: North Am. Spine Soc. Achievements include research in clinical outcome following spinal procedures. Avocation: travel. Office: SpineCare Medical Group 1850 Sullivan Ave Suite 200 Daly City CA 94015 Office Phone: 650-985-7540. Office Fax: 650-985-7506.

**SUN, JUNPING,** computer science professor; BE in Computer Sci., SE U., Nanjing, China, 1982; MS, Wayne State U., Detroit, 1987; PhD, Wayne State U., 1992. Asst. and assoc. prof. Nova Southeastern U., Ft. Lauderdale, Fla., 1992—2002, prof., 2002—. Assoc. editor Jour. Engring. Letter, Hong Kong, 2005—, Internat. Jour. Computers and Their Applications, Cary, NC, 2005—. Mem.: IEEE (sr.), Assn. Computing Machinery (assoc.), Upsilon Pi Epsilon. Office: Nova Southeastern U 3301 College Ave Fort Lauderdale FL 33314 Office Phone: 954-262-2082. Office Fax: 954-262-3915.

**SUN, KELI,** electrical engineer, researcher; PhD in Fluid Mechanics, Peking U., Beijing, 1994—97; MS in Electromagnetics, Dartmouth Coll., Hanover, N.H., 1999—2001. Lectr. Tsinghua U., Beijing, 1997—99; rsch. assoc. Dartmouth Coll., Hanover, NH, 2001—. Reviewer IEEE Trans. on Geosciences and Remote Sensing, 2004—. Achievements include discovery of the fluid dynamic mechanism of thrombus formation in an artificial thrombus machine and studied the effect of magnetic field; research in the interaction of particles in the process of electrophoresis and created an empirical formulation for estimating electrophoresis speed; development of an algorithm for studying the Electromagnetic Induction (EMI) sensing of metallic objects, especially for the cases where field penetration is samll but not negligible; fast algorithms for estimating electromagnetic response of underground objects and applied them on Unexploded Ordnance detection and discrimination; inverse algorithms for inferring target information from measurement data, and applied them on unexploded ordnance detection and discrimination. E-mail: skl03755@yahoo.com.

**SUN, LI,** statistician; b. Changchun, Jilin, China, Aug. 5, 1957; s. Enhou Sun and Chongxin Li; m. Nancy Xiaoning Ha, Feb. 21, 1982; children: Rosy, George. BSc, U. Jilin, Changchun, Jilin, China, 1982; MSc, Acad. Sci. China, 1984; PhD, U. Toronto, 1992. Rsch. fellow U. B.C. Cancer Agcy., Vancouver, 1992—2000; sr. statis. engr. Ericsson Inc, Berkeley, Calif., 2001 01; sr. statistician Edmunds.com Inc., Santa Monica, Calif., 2002—. Contbr. articles to profl. jours., chapters to books. Fellow, Natural Sci. and Engring. Rsch. Coun. Can., 1992—94; Connaught scholar, U. Toronto, 1989—92. Mem.: Am. Stats. Assn. Office: Edmunds.com Inc Ste 250 2401 Colorado Ave Santa Monica CA 90404 Office Phone: 310-309-4982. E-mail: lsun@edmunds.com.

**SUN, NORA CHI-JUN,** pathologist; b. Shanghai, June 16, 1937; came to U.S., 1966; d. K.F. and S.W. Sun; m. David T. Sung; children: Thomas C.K. Lee, Anthony D. Sung. MD, Shanghai 2d Med. Coll., 1960; MS in Pathology, U. Minn., 1973. Demonstrator U. Hong Kong, 1964-66; rsch. biologist A.H. Robins Co., Richmond, Va., 1966-67; resident Med. Coll. Va., 1967—68; clin. teaching asst. Boston U. Sch. Medicine, 1968-70; resident Mallaory Inst. Pathology, 1968—70; fellow Mayo Clinic and Grad. Sch., 1970—73; asst. prof. pathology U. So. Calif., L.A., 1973-76; staff pathologist John Wesley Hosp., L.A., 1973-76; asst. prof. UCLA Sch. Medicine, L.A., 1976-82; staff pathologist, head hematopathology Harbor-UCLA Med. Ctr., Torrance, Calif., 1976—2002; assoc. prof. UCLA Sch. Medicine, L.A., 1982-88, prof. pathology, 1988—2002, prof. emeritus, 2002—. Recipient Women Achievement award Delta Kappa Gamma, Rochester, Minn., 1972, Disting. Svc. award Am. Soc. Clin. Pathologists, 1996. Mem. Internat. Assn. Chinese Pathologists (pres.-elect 1991-93, pres. 1993-95), Harbor-UCLA Med. Ctr. Faculty Soc. (pres.-elect 1990-91, pres. 1991-92). Office: Harbor UCLA Med Ctr 1000 W Carson St Torrance CA 90502-2004 Business E-Mail: ncjsun@ucla.edu.

**SUN, QIANG,** scientist, educator; arrived in US, 2002, permanent resident, 2006; s. Li Xian Sun and Si Ying Hou; m. Qian Wang, July 4, 1987; 1 child, Tony. BS in Physics Edn., Southwest U., Chongging, China, 1984, MS in Theoretical Physics, 1987; PhD in Condensed Matter Physics, Nanjing U., China, 1996. Asst. prof. Tohoku U., Sendai, Japan, 1997—2003; rsch. asst. prof. Va. Commonwealth U., Richmond, 2003—. Contbr. articles to profl. jours. Recipient Outstanding Rsch. award, Japan Inst. of Metals Rsch., 2000. Mem.: Japan Soc. Nano Sci. and Tech., Am. Materials Rsch. Soc., Am. Chem. Soc., Am. Physical Soc. Achievements include research in nanostructures applied to spin electronics, catalysis, biomedicine, environmental science, and hydrogen storage. Office: Va Commonwealth Univ W Main St 1020 Richmond VA 23284-2000 Office Phone: 804-828-7079. Office Fax: 804-828-7073. Business E-Mail: qsun@vcu.edu.

**SUN, RENSHENG,** electrical engineer, educator; s. Shouzhi Sun and Jingrong Xu; m. Wei Zhang, July 19, 2001. BSEE, Tsinghua U., Beijing, 1999; MSEE, Villanova U., Pa., 2002; PhD, Mich. State U., East Lansing, 2005. Vis. asst. prof. Dept. Elec. and Computer Engring. Mich. State U., 2005; sr. application engr. EM Software & Sys. Inc., Hampton, Va., 2006—. Mem.: IEEE, Phi Beta Delta, Tau Beta Pi, Eta Kappa Nu. Avocations: travel, music, jogging. Office: EM Software & Sys Inc 144 Research Dr Hampton VA 23666

**SUN, ROBERT ZU JEI,** manufacturing company executive, inventor, educator; b. Shanghai, July 5, 1948; s. David C.H. and Evelyn (Lee) S.; m. Nan Jennifer Ronis, Sept. 20, 1986; children: Matthew Nyland, Michael Elias. BS in Elec. Engring., U. Pa., 1970. Sr. project engr. Drexelbrook Engring. Co., Horsham, Pa., 1970—78; pres., chmn. bd. Suntex Internat., Inc., Easton, 1981—. Inventor 24 Math Game, Mhing Card Game; author First In Math. online program; 5 patents in field. Pres. Coalition of Religious and Civic Orgns., Easton, 1979-81; mem. transition team Pa. Gov.-elect Tom Ridge, 1994; apptd. by Gov. Ridge to Pa. State Bd. Edn., 1995, Team Pa. Amb. Coun., 1999; mem. fin. comm. Moravian Acad., 2001, trustee, 2004; planning commr. City of Easton, 2005; mem. Eisenhower Commn., 2006. Recipient 2 Excellence awards for Mhing pkg. Nat. Paperbox and Pkg. Assn., 1984-85. Office: 3311 Fox Hill Rd Easton PA 18045 Office Phone: 610-253-5255.

**SUN, WEI,** electrical engineer; b. Jilin, China, Sept. 15, 1969; arrived in US 1997; m. Xueqin Wu, July 15, 1997; 1 child, Olivia Qing. BEE, Xidian U., China, 1992; MS, Chinese Acad. Telecom. Tech., 1995; PhD, Stevens Inst. Tech., 2001. Mem. tech. staff Bell Labs Lucent Technologies, Holmdel, NJ, 2001—02; post-doctoral rsch. fellow Villanova U., Pa., 2002—04; asst. prof. Temple U., Phila., 2004—05; sr. comm. engr. Magnolia Broadband Inc., Bedminster, NJ, 2005—. Author: Signal Processing for Mobile Communications Handbook, 2004; contbr. scientific papers to profl. jours. Mem.: IEEE, Eta Kappa Nu. Home: 104 Bluebird Dr Hillsborough NJ 08844 Personal E-mail: wsun@ieee.org.

**SUN, YUEFENG,** research scientist, educator; b. Liangshan, Shandong, China, Apr. 5, 1962; s. Xueqian Sun and Shuyuan She; m. Lilai Yan; 1 child, Yusha Yan Sun. BS, Petroleum U. China, Donying, Shandong, 1981; MS, Columbia U., NYC, 1988, PhD, 1994. Geophysicist China Nat. Petroleum Corp., Urumqi, Xinjiang, 1982—87; grad. tchg. fellow Columbia U., NYC, 1988—94; postdoctoral fellow Lamont Doherty Earth Obs., Columbia U., Palisades, 1995—97, Doherty rsch. scientist, 1998—2005; assoc. prof. The Petroleum Inst., Abu Dhabi, 2006—. Mem.: Soc. Exploration Geophysicists (assoc.), Am. Math. Soc. (assoc.), Am. Phys. Soc. (assoc.), Am. Geophys. Union (assoc.). Achievements include invention of work on relating permeability to wave velocity implemented and referred to as the Sun model by Shell Oil Co., which improves world hydrocarbon reserves and production; research in theory invention; patents for method of estimation of gas hydrates; systems and methods of detecting living organisms in rocks. Home: 49 Bluefield Ave Harrington Park NJ 07640 Office: The Petroleum Inst Geosci PO Box 2533 Abu Dhabi United Arab Emirates Office Phone: 971-2-5085334. Office Fax: 971 2 5085200. Personal E-mail: yfsun3@yahoo.com. Business E-Mail: ysun@pi.ac.ae.

**SUN, ZUO,** mechanical engineer, researcher; b. Shenyang, Liaoning, China, July 3, 1970; arrived in U.S., 1996; s. Dianfu Sun and Shuxiang Liu; m. Xinxin Zhou. PhD in Theoretical and Applied Mechanics, Northwestern U., 2001; MS, BS, Tsinghua U. Sr. mech. engr. Corning (N.Y.) Inc., 2001—02; rsch. scientist Va. Tech, Blacksburg, 2002—03; mech. engr. GE Global Rsch. Ctr., Schenectady, NY, 2003—. Cons. Hewlett-Packard Comp., Portland, Oreg., 2001—02, State Nuc. Safety Bur. in China, Beijing, 1993—95. Contbr. articles to profl. jours. Recipient First Class award, Tsinghua U., Beijing, 1989; Grad. fellow, 1994, Grad. scholar, Northwestern U., 1997—2003. Mem.: ASME, AIAA (corr.), Sigma Xi (hon.). Achievements include development of new models to predict long term behavior and life of composite materials; tools to characterize micro/nano scale systems; physics-based modeling of commercial aircraft engines; design of Micro-electro-mechanical Systems; investigation of adhesion science. Home: 6 Hollandale Ln Apt C Clifton Park NY 12065 Office Phone: 518-387-5578. Personal E-mail: zuosun@yahoo.com.

**SUNAMI, JOHN SOICHI,** designer; b. N.Y.C., June 10, 1949; s. Soichi and Suyeko (Matsushima) S.; m. Marialyce Norman, Apr. 14, 1983; children: Christopher Andrew-Soichi, Jennifer Kiyoko. BA, CCNY, 1969. Cert. Gemological Inst. Am. Vol. Peace Corps, Jamaica, W.I., 1969-71; jeweler N.Y.C. and Columbus, Ohio, 1971-82; dir. mktg. Knight's Inn/Cardinal Industries, Columbus, 1982; founder, exec. designer Nimbus, Columbus, 1983—. Designer/sculptor pub. artwork IntroCenter, 1990; designer logo identities for various cos.; exhibited paintings and sculpture; author poems and essays. Bd. dirs. William H. Thomas Gallery, Columbus, 1992-93; v.p., bd. dirs. South Side Settlement House, Columbus, 1982-93; mem. cultural diversity outreach com. United Way of Franklin County, 1993-01. Recipient 1st prize Macworld Gallery/Macworld Mag., 1985. Mem.: Ctrl. Ohio Machine Knitters. Avocations: music, travel. Home: 408 Fairwood Ave Columbus OH 43205-2244 Office: Nimbus 413 Fairwood Ave Columbus OH 43205-2202 Office Phone: 614-253-0453. Office Fax: 614-253-0257. Personal E-mail: design@nimbus-art.com.

**SUNDARAM, MURALI M.,** manufacturing engineer, researcher; M in Tech., Indian Inst. Tech.-Madras, Chennai, 1997—98; PhD, Nanyang Technol. U., Singapore, 2004. US. scientist, engr. Indian Space Rsch. Orgn., Trivandrum, 1993—2002; postdoctoral rsch. assoc. U. Nebr., Lincoln, 2005—. Scholar Rsch. Schlorship, Nanyang Technol. U., Singapore 2002-2005. Office: Univ Nebr 175 Nebraska Hall Lincoln NE 68588-0518 Office Phone: 402-472-6239. Office Fax: 402-472-1384. Personal E-mail: dr.murali.us@gmail.com. Business E-Mail: murali@unlnotes.unl.edu.

**SUNDARARAJAN, ARUN,** economist, educator; b. Epping, England, June 14, 1971; s. Mahadeva and Kalyani Sundararajan; m. Swati Sharma. BS in Tech., Indian Inst. Tech., 1993; PhD, U. Rochester, 1998. Prof. NYU, N.Y., 1998—. Co-founder Aftermind Inc.; organizer summer workshop NYU. Author (associate editor): Management Science, Information Systems Research. Recipient Best Overall Rsch. Paper award, Internat. Conf. Info. Sys., 2004, Best Paper Editor's Choice award, U.S. Assn. Small Bus. and Entrepreneurship, 2006. Mem.: Am. Econ. Assn. Office: New York University 44 West 4th Street KMC 8-93 New York NY 10012 Office Phone: 212-998-0833. Business E-Mail: arun@stern.nyu.edu.

**SUNDBERG, CARL-ERIK WILHELM,** telecommunications executive, researcher; b. Karlskrona, Sweden, July 7, 1943; came to U.S., 1984; s. Erik Wilhelm and Martha Maria (Snaar) S. MEE, U. Lund, Sweden, 1966, PhD, 1975. Tchr., rsch. asst., lectr. U. Lund, 1966-75, rsch. prof. (docent), 1977-84; rsch. fellow European Space Agy., Nordwijk, The Netherlands, 1975-76; disting. mem. tech. staff AT&T Bell Labs., Murray Hill, NJ, 1984-96, Lucent Technologies, Bell Labs., 1997-2000; with media signal processing rsch. dept. Agere Sys., 2000—01, iBiquity Digital, Warren, NJ, 2002—03; prin., owner SundComm, Chatham, NJ, 2003—. Cons. L.M. Ericsson, Gothenburg, Sweden, 1975-76, Bell Labs., Crawford Hill, NJ, 1981-82; instr. Carl Cranz Gesellschaft, Oberpfaffenhofen, Fed. Republic Germany, 1990-93; vis. prof. Korea U., Seoul, 2003-04 Co-author: Digital Phase Modulation, 1986, Source-Matched Mobile Communications, 1995; contbr. articles to profl. jours.; patentee in field. Served in Swedish Navy, 1968. Fellow IEEE (Best Paper award 1986, guest editor Jour. on Selected Areas in Comm. 1988-89, 2005—, 2 papers named among 50 most influential 2002), IEE Marconi Premium (Best Paper award 1989); mem. Swedish Union Radio-Scientifique Internat Lutheran. Avocations: travel, history, photography. Home and Office: SundComm 25 Hickory Pl Apt A11 Chatham NJ 07928-1465 Business E-Mail: cews@ieee.org.

**SUNDBERG, GORDON NEIL,** retired mathematics and computer sciences instructor; b. Linn Grove, Iowa, Aug. 24, 1935; s. Nels George and Edna Josephine (Johnson) Sundberg; m. Marjorie Mae Mindemann, Aug. 9, 1959; children: Brenda Marie, Keith Nathan. BS, Iowa State U., 1957; MS, U. No. Iowa, 1965. Cert. tchr. Iowa. Math. and sci. tchr. LaPorte City (Iowa) HS, 1957—58, math. tchr., 1960—64; instr. NSF, Cedar Falls, Iowa, 1965; math. tchr. Geneseo HS, Buckingham, Iowa, 1965—66, Iowa Ctrl. C.C., Ft. Dodge, 1966—79. Served with U.S. Army, 1958—60. Mem.: Masons, Phi Delta Kappa, Acacia. Congregationalist. Avocations: woodworking, reading, volunteering, tutoring. Home: 902 SW 1 Eagle Grove IA 50533

**SUNDBERG, MARSHALL DAVID,** biology professor; b. Apr. 18, 1949; m. Sara Jane Brooks, Aug. 1, 1977; children: Marshall Isaac, Adam, Emma. BA in Biology, Carleton Coll., 1971; MA in Botany, U. Minn., 1973, PhD in Botany, 1978. Lab. technician Carleton Coll., Minn., 1973-74; teaching asst. U. Minn., Mpls., 1974-76, rsch. asst., 1976-77; adj. asst. prof. Biology U. Wis., Eau Claire, 1978-85, mem. faculty summer sci. inst., 1982-85; instr. La. State U., Baton Rouge, 1985-88, asst. prof. Biology, 1988-91, coord. dept. Biology, 1988-93, assoc. prof. Biology, 1991-97; prof., chair dept. biol. scis. Emporia State U., 1997—. Author: General Botany Laboratory Workbook, 5th revision, 1984, General Botany 1001 Laboratory Manual, 1986, General Botany 1002 Laboratory Manual, 1987, Biology 1002 Correspondence Study Guide, 1987, Boty 1202: General Botany Laboratory Manual, 1988, Biol 1208: Biology for Science Majors Laboratory Manual, 1988, 2d edit., 1989, Instructor's Manual for J. Mauseth, Introductory Botany, 1991; contbr. articles to profl. jours. Brand fellow U. Minn., 1976-77, Faculty Grants scholar U. Wis., 1984-85. Fellow Linnaean Soc. London; mem. NSTA, AAAS, Am. Inst. Biol. Scis. (coun. mem. at large 1992-95, edn. com. 1994-95, 98-2002), Nat. Sci. Tchrs. Assn., Assn. Biology Lab. Edn., Soc. Am. (chmn. tchg. sect. 1985-86, workshop com. tchg. sect. 1983-84, slide exch./lab. exch. tchg. sect. 1980-89, edn. com. 1991, 92, editor Plant Sci. Bull. 2000—, Charles H. Bessey award 1992, Centennial award 2006), Internat. Soc. Plant Morphologists, Nat. Assn. Biology Tchrs. (Outstanding 4-Yr. Coll. Tchr. award 1997, 2003), Soc. Econ. Botany, The Nature Conservancy, Sigma Xi (chpt. sec. 1982-84, 93-95, 2000-02, v.p. 1984-85, 96-97, pres. 1996, 99, 2005). Home: 1912 Briarcliff Ln Emporia KS 66801-5404 Office: Emporia State U Dept Biol Scis 1200 Commercial St Emporia KS 66801-5087

**SUNDBERG, RICHARD JAY,** chemistry professor; b. Sioux Rapids, Iowa, Jan. 6, 1938; BS, U. Iowa, 1959; PhD, U. Minn., 1962. Faculty dept. chemistry U. Va., Charlottesville, 1964-74, prof., 1974—. Author (with F. A. Carey) Advanced Organic Chemistry, 4th edit., 2000. Served to 1st lt. U.S. Army, 1962-64 Mem. Am. Chem. Soc. Lutheran. Office: U Va Dept Chemistry Box 400319 Charlottesville VA 22904-4319 Office Phone: 434-924-3233.

**SUNDBERG, RUTH DOROTHY,** hematologist, educator; b. Chgo., July 29, 1915; d. Carl William and Ruth (Chalbeck) S.; m. Robert H. Reiff, Dec. 24, 1941 (div. 1945). Student, U. Chgo., 1932-34; BS, U. Minn., 1937, MA, 1939, PhD, 1943, MD, 1953. Diplomate: Am. Bd. Pathology. Instr., asst. prof. anatomy U. Minn., 1939-53, assoc. prof., 1953-60, prof., 1960-63, prof. of lab. medicine and anatomy, 1963-73, prof. lab. medicine, pathology and anatomy, 1973-84, emeritus prof., 1984—; hematologist, dir. Hematology Labs., 1945-74, hematologist, co. dir., 1974-84. Editorial bd.: Soc. Exptl. Biology and Medicine, until 1975; mem. editorial bd.: Blood, 1960-67; assoc. editor, 1967-69. Recipient Lucretia Wilder award for research in anatomy, 1939 Mem.: Sigma Xi. Home (Summer): 322 Bishopsbridge Dr Cincinnati OH 45255-3947 Home (Winter): 12558 Shanandoah Ct Marco Island FL 34145-5023

**SUNDBORG, STEPHEN V.,** academic administrator; s. George and Mary Sundborg. PhD, Pontifical Gregorian Univ., Rome, 1982. Ordained Jesuit, 1974. Tchr. religion and Latin Gonzaga Prep. Sch., Spokane, Wash., Jesuit High, Portland, Oreg.; tchr. theology Seattle U.; rector Seattle U. Jewish Cmty., 1986-90; provincial Oreg. Province, 1990-97; pres. Seattle U., 1997—. Office: Admin Bldg 109 900 Broadway Seattle WA 98122-4340

**SUNDE, DOUGLAS,** plastic surgeon; b. Evanston, Ill., May 18, 1960; s. Edward Albert and Marilyn S.; m. Linda Neff, 1989; children: Samuel, Joseph. AB, Stanford U., 1982; MD, U. Calif., San Francisco, 1986. Diplomate Am. Bd. Plastic Surgery. Resident in plastic surgery Stanford (Calif.) U., 1986-92, clin. instr., 1992; fellow in aesthetic surgery Manhattan Eye Ear and Throat Hosp., N.Y.C., 1990; fellow in hand, microsurgery Davies Med. Ctr., San Francisco, 1993; pvt. practice Monterey, Calif., 1994—. Clin. asst. prof. Stanford Med. Ctr., 1998—. Contbr. articles to profl. jours. Named Nat. Merit scholar 1977. Fellow ACS; mem. Am. Bd. Plastic Surgery, Am. Soc. Plastic Reconstructive Surgery, Calif. Soc. Plastic Surgery, Alpha Omega Alpha. Office Phone: 831-372-0200.

**SUNDEL, ALFRED,** retired medical writer; s. Charles and Helen (Salzman) Sundel; 1 child, David. BA in Humanities, NYU, 1954. Editor, writer McGraw-Hill Pub. Co., N.Y.C., 1956—57, Franklin Watts Pub. Co., N.Y.C., 1958—59, Classics Illustrated Pub. Co., N.Y.C., 1960—76; sr. writer MD Pub., N.Y.C., 1966—68, Mc Adams Advertising Agency, N.Y.C., 1969—70, J. Walter Thompson Ad Agency, N.Y.C., 1970—71; copy chief, dept. head Wesson and Warhaftiq Ad Agency, N.Y.C., 1971—78; ret., 1978. Creative dir., v.p. Carrafiello Diehl Ad Agency, Irvington, NY, 1989—2005; pres. Al Sundel & Assoc., Hartsdale, NY, 1981—2005. Author: The Aztecs and the Mayas, 1967, Columbus, 2002. Donor Ben Gurion U., Beersheba, Israel, 2000—05, Hebrew U., Jerusalem, 2000—05, Boystown Jerusalem, Jerusalem, 1998—2005. Pvt. 1st class US Air Corps, 1946—47. Decorated Commendation for Rescue US Air Force; recipient 2 month residence award, Yaddo Writers Colony, 1956, Honor Roll award for Best Am. Short Stories, Houghton Mifflin Pub. Co., 1953. Avocations: swimming, literature, films. Home: 400 High Point Dr Hartsdale NY 10530

**SUNDEL, MARTIN,** management consultant, psychologist, educator; b. Bronx, NY, Sept. 22, 1940; s. Louis and Pauline (Brotman) S.; m. Sandra Stone, Aug. 22, 1971; children: Adam Daniel, Jenny Rebecca, Ariel Pauline. BA cum laude, St. Mary's, 1961; MSW., Our Lady of the Lake Univ., 1963; MA, PhD, U. Mich., 1968. Social group work supr. Valley Cities Jewish Cmty. Ctr., Van Nuys, Calif., 1963-65; asst. prof. U. Mich. Sch. Social Work, Ann Arbor, 1968-71; postdoctoral fellow Harvard U. Lab. Community Psychiatry, Boston, 1971-72; dir. rsch. and evaluation River Region Mental Health-Mental Retardation Bd., Louisville, 1972-77; adj. prof. Kent. Sch. Social Work-U Louisville, 1972-77, assoc. in psychology, 1975-77; sr. research assoc. The Urban Inst., Washington, 1977-80; pvt. practice psychology Dallas, 1980-95; Dulak Disting. prof. U. Tex., Arlington, 1980-89, prof., 1980-95, Fla. Internat. U., Miami, Fla., 1995-2000; faculty assoc. S.E. Fla. Ctr. on Aging, 1996-2000; pres. Sundel Cons. Group, 2000—. Mental health cons. UN High Commn. for Refugees in Cyprus, 1993-95; profl. adv. coun. Dallas Geriatric Rsch. Inst., 1980-89; long-range planning com. Dallas Jewish Coalition for the Homeless, 1986-95; coordinating com. Arlington Human Svcs. Project, 1981-90; Mayor's Forum on Human Svc. Needs Assessment, Ft. Worth, 1983-86; vis. prof. U. So. Calif. Sch. Social Work, spring 1985; sr. consortium rsch. fellow, Dept. Def., 1996-99. Author: (with Sandra Stone Sundel) Behavior Change in the Human Services, 1975, 5th edit., 2005; Be Assertive, 1980; co-author: Women at Midlife, 2002; co-editor: Assessing Health and Human Service Needs, 1983, Individual Change Through Small Groups, 2d edit., 1985, Midlife Myths, 1989; mem. editl. bds. and cons. to profl. jours. Named Nat. Table Tennis Champion, U1600 Round Robin Age Group of 40 Yrs. and Older, 2005. Fellow Prescribing Psychologists Register (diplomate), Internat. Coun. Prescribing Psychology (diplomate in psychopharmacology); mem. Behavior Therapy and Rsch. Soc. (charter clin. fellow). Home: 3804 Barbados Ave Hollywood FL 33026-4659 E-mail: sundelm@bellsouth.net.

**SUNDELL, RANDY,** music educator; b. Chgo., June 17, 1969; s. Robert and Martha Sundell. BA in Math., Northwestern U., 1992, MusB in Edn., 1992, M in Music Edn., 1996. Band dir. Oak Grove Sch. Dist. #68, Green Oaks, Ill., 1992—96; assoc. dir. bands Libertyville (Ill.) H.S., 1996—2000; dir. bands Vernon Hills (Ill.) H.S., 2000—. Named Chgo. Outstanding Music Educator, Quinlan & Fabish Music Co., 2004. Mem.: Ill. Music Educators Assn. (dist. jazz rep. 2003—04), Music Educators Nat. Conf. Office: Vernon Hills HS 145 N Lakeview Pky Vernon Hills IL 60061 Office Phone: 847-932-2162.

**SUNDERMAN, DUANE NEUMAN,** chemist, research and development company executive; b. Wadsworth, Ohio, July 14, 1928; s. Richard Benjamin and Carolyn (Neuman) S.; m. Joan Catherine Hoffman, Jan. 31, 1953; children: David, Christine, Richard. BA, U. Mich., 1949, MS, 1954, PhD in Chemistry, 1956. Researcher Battelle Meml. Inst., Columbus, Ohio, 1956-59, mgr., 1959-69, assoc. dir., 1969-79, dir. internat. programs, 1979-84; sr. v.p. Midwest Rsch. Inst., Kansas City, Mo., 1984-90, exec. v.p., 1990-94, Golden, Colo., 1990-94. Dir. Nat. Renewable Energy Lab., Golden, Colo., 1990-94, dir. emeritus, 1994—. Contbr. numerous articles to profl. jours. Bd. dirs. Mid-Ohio chpt. ARC, 1982-83, U. Kansas City, 1985-90, Mo. Corp. for Sci. and Tech., Jefferson City, 1986-90, Colo. Energy Sci. Ctr., 2000-04. With USNR, 1949—59. Mem. Am. Chem. Soc. Republican. Presbyterian. Avocation: computers. E-mail: dsunderm@columbus.rr.com.

**SUNDERMEYER, MICHAEL S.,** lawyer; b. Kansas City, Mo., Feb. 8, 1951; s. Edgar W. and Ruth (Shobe) S.; m. Susan Talarico; children: Kim Marie, Mark Shobe. BA, U. Kans., 1973; JD, U. Va., 1976. Bar: D.C., Md., Va., U.S. Dist. Ct. D.C., U.S. Dist. Ct. Md., U.S. Dist. Ct. (ea. dist.) Va., U.S. Dist. Ct. (no. dist.) Okla., U.S. Ct. Appeals (D.C. cir.), U.S. Ct. Appeals (2d, 3d, 4th, 5th, 6th, 9th and 11th cirs.). Law clk. to Hon. John Minor Wisdom U.S. Ct. Appeals (5th cir.), New Orleans, 1976-77; law clk. to Hon. Harry A. Blackmun U.S. Supreme Ct., Washington, 1977-78; assoc. Williams & Connolly, Washington, 1978-84, ptnr., 1985—. Editor-in-chief Va. Law Rev., 1975-76. Mem. ABA. Office: Williams & Connolly LLP 725 12th St NW Washington DC 20005-5901 Office Phone: 202-434-5000. E-mail: msundermeyer@wc.com.

**SUNDGREN, DONALD E.,** construction executive; BS, La. State U. V.p. exec. dir. Dillingham Constrn., Holdings, Inc., Pleasanton, Calif., 1996-97; pres., CEO Dillingham Construction Corp., Pleasanton, Calif., 1997—. Office: Dillingham Construction Holdings PO Box 1268 Placerville CA 95667-1268

**SUNDHEIM, GEORGE (DUF),** lawyer, political organization worker; b. Chgo., Dec. 11, 1952; m. Cheryl Sundheim; children: Jordan, Eric. BA with hons., Stanford U., 1975; JD, Northwestern U., 1980. Bar: Calif. 1981, U.S. Dist. Ct. Calif. 1981. Of counsel Doty Sundheim & Gilmore, Palo Alto, Calif.; chmn. Calif. Rep. Party, Burbank, Calif., 2003—. Guest spkr. Peninsula This Week. Fellow, State Farm. Mem.: Santa Clara Bar Assn., State Bar Calif. (trustee 1992, Wiley W. Manuel award), Palo Alto Area Bar Assn. (pres. 1992), Calif. State Bar (Pro Bono award), Bay Area Rep. Lincoln Club (pres.). Office: Doty Sundheim & Gilmore 260 Sheridan Ave Ste 200 Palo Alto CA 94306 Mailing: California Republican Party Chmn 1903 W Magnolia Blvd Burbank CA 91506

**SUNDHEIM, NANCY STRAUS,** lawyer; b. Phila., June 25, 1951; B in History, U. Pa., 1973; JD, Harvard U., 1978. With Arnold & Porter, Washington, Ropes & Gray, Boston, Dechert Price & Rhoads, Phila.; chief acquisitions counsel Unisys Corp., Blue Bell, Pa., 1987, dep. counsel, head corp. law group, 1990, corp. v.p., corp. sec., 1999, mem. exec. com., 1999—; sr. v., gen. counsel, 2001. Office: Unisys Corp Unisys Way Blue Bell PA 19424 Office Phone: 215-986-4011. Office Fax: 215-986-2312.

**SUNDICK, SHERRY SMALL,** author, journalist, poet; b. Washington, July 17, 1946; d. Charles Haskell and Ruth (Behrend) Small; B.A., Am. U., 1970; m. Gary Norman Sundick, Aug. 3, 1969; children— Amy Beth, Suzanne Faye. Columnist, Today Newspapers, Rockville, Md., 1973-75; journalist The Jour. Newspapers, Chevy Chase, Md., 1975—, The Potomac Almanac, 1976-80. Recipient N.Am. Mentor Mag. Ann. Mentor Poetry award, 1973. Mem. Nat. League Am. Pen Women, Writers Center, World Poetry Soc. Jewish. Author: Celebration, 1977; (with Ruth Small) Potpourri, 1978; contbr. articles to various mags. and jours. including Md. Mag., No. Va. Mag. Design, Maine Life, Feelings, Smile, The Pen Women, Haiku Headlines, others. Address: 11809 Hunting Ridge Ct Potomac MD 20854-2152

**SUNDIN, MATS JOHAN,** professional hockey player; b. Sollentuna, Sweden, Feb. 13, 1971; Selected 1st round NHL entry draft Que. Nordiques, 1989, right wing, 1990—94, Toronto Maple Leafs, 1994—. Played in Europe NHL Lockout, 1994—95; mem. Swedish League All-Star Team, 1990—91, 1991—92; player NHL All-Star Game, 1996—2004. Achievements include being a member of gold medal winning Swedish Hockey Team, Torino Olympics, Italy, 2006. Office: Toronto Maple Leafs Air Canada Ctr 40 Bay St Ste 300 Toronto ON Canada M5J 2X2*

**SUNDLOF, STEPHEN FREDERICK,** veterinary administrator; DVM, U. Ill., 1980, PhD in Toxicology, 1980. Diplomate Am. Bd. Vet. Toxicology. From instr. to prof. U. Fla. Coll. Vet. Medicine, 1980-94; dir. Ctr. for Vet. Medicine FDA, Washington, 1994—. Chmn. WHO/FAO Codex Alimentarius Com.; presenter in field. Contbr. articles to profl. jours. Recipient Presidential Rank Award, 2000. Mem. Am. Acad. Vet. Pharmacology and Therapeutics (past pres.). Office: Ctr Vet Medicine Office Dir 7500 Standish Pl Rockville MD 20855-2764 Fax: 301-827-4401.*

**SUNDLUN, BRUCE,** former governor; b. Providence, Jan. 19, 1920; s. Walter I. and Jan Z. (Colitz) Sundlun; m. Susan Garvin Dittelman, Jan. 1, 2000; children: Tracy, Stuart, Peter, Kara; stepchildren: Heather Conover, Max Dittelman. BA, Williams Coll., 1942; LLB, Harvard U., 1949; grad., Air Command and Staff Sch., 1948; DSBA (hon.), Bryant Coll., 1980; DBA (hon.), Roger Williams Coll., 1980; LLD (hon.), Johnson and Wales U., 1993, Williams Coll., 1993, U. RI, 1998; DHL (hon.), New Eng. Inst. Tech., 2005. Bar: RI and DC 1949. Asst. U.S. atty., Washington, 1949-51; spl. asst. to U.S. atty. gen., Washington, 1951-54; ptnr. Amram, Hahn & Sundlun, Sundlun, Tirana & Scher, Washington, 1958—76; v.p., gen. counsel, dir. Outlet Co., Providence, 1960-76, Outlet Comms. Inc.; pres., CEO Outlet Co., Providence, 1976-84, chmn. bd., CEO, 1984-88. Pres. Exec. Jet Aviation, Inc., Columbus, Ohio, 1970—76; apptd. by Pres. Kennedy incorporator, bd. dirs. Comm. Satellite Corp., 1962—92; bd. dirs. Worthington Industries, Nat. Bank of Washington, Miriam Hosp. Mem. adv. group Nat. Aviation Goals, 1961; chmn. Inaugural Medal Com., Washington, 1961, 65; vice chmn. Inaugural Parade Com., 1961; appointed by Pres. Carter, bd. visitors USAF Acad., 1978-80; mem. RI Capital Center Commn., 1980, RI Legis. Pay Commn., 1980; vice chmn. Providence Rev. Com., 1981, chmn., 1982-85; mem. Providence Sch. Bd., 1985-90; mem. Providence Housing Authority, 1987, chmn. 1987-90; elected del. Dem. Nat. Conv. 1964, 68, 80, 88, 92, RI Constl. Conv., 1985; Dem. candidate for gov. RI, 1986, 88, 90, 92; gov. RI, 1990-92, 1992-95; mem. exec. com. Dem. Gov. Assn., 1990-94; vice chmn. CONEG, 1992-94, chmn., 1994, chmn., vice chmn. Com. on Economy Nat. Gov. Assn., 1992-94, chmn. NE Gov. Assn., 1994; pres. Washington Internat. Horse Show, 1970-75, trustee, 1975-90; pres. Providence Performing Arts Ctr., 1978-90; bd. dirs. Touro Synagogue, Newport, RI, 1979—, Miriam Hosp., 1985-90; bd. dirs. Temple Beth El, Providence, 1979-84, v.p. 1984-88, pres., 1988-91; bd. dirs. Trinity Repertory Theater, 1980-90, chmn., 1984-90; trustee RI Philharm. Orch., 1981-90; trustee Providence Preservation Soc. 1981-90, v.p., 1987-90; trustee Newport Art Mus., 1985, pres., 1987-91; founding chmn., pres. Providence Found., 1985-86; pres. RI C. of C. Fedn., 1981-84, bd. dirs., 1977-81; pres. Greater Providence C. of C., 1978-81, bd. dirs. 1976-85; bd. dirs. New Eng. Coun., 1978, vice chmn., 1980-81, chmn., 1981-83; trustee Bryant Coll., 1989-98; gov.-in-residence U. RI, 1995—; dir. Providence Facilities Mgmt. Corp., 1998—; appointed by Pres. Clinton dir. Nat. Security Edn. Bd., 2000-05; dir. Sargent Rehab. Ctr., 1995—, Ft. Adams

Found., 2000—. Lt. USAAF, 1941-45; Capt. USAFR, ret., 1980. Decorated D.F.C., Air medal with oak leaf cluster, Purple Heart; chevalier Legion d'Honneur (France); Prime Minister's medal (Israel). Mem.: Aurora Assn., Spouting Rock Beach Assn., Dunes Club, Hope Club, Clambake Club, Delta Upsilon. Democrat. Office: U RI Carlotti Bldg 175 Lower College Rd Kingston RI 02881 Home: 280 Seaside Dr Jamestown RI 02835-3031 Office Phone: 401-874-4000. Business E-mail: sundlun@uri.edu.

**SUNDQUIST, ALEXANDRA (ALIX SUNDQUIST),** diplomat, consultant; BA in Govt. cum laude, Smith Coll.; MA in Econ., N.Y.U. Entered fgn. svc. U.S. Dept. State, 1979; with Chase Manhattan Bank, N.Y.C., Chemical Bank, 1970—79; comml. attache U.S. Embassy, Jeddah, Saudi Arabia, 1980—82, 1st sec. (energy attache) Paris, 1982—86, consul gen. Bordeaux, 1991—94, counselor econ. affairs Rabat, Morocco, 1995—98; economist Bur. Econ. and Bus. Affairs Dept. State, Washington, 1986—90, chief spl. trade activities divsn., 1998—99; ret., 1999; ind. fgn. affairs advisor, 1999—. Cons. U.S. Dept. State, Washington, 1999; chargé a'Affaires, Valletta, Malta; trade policy advisor Bill Bradley Pres. Campaign. Mem.: Am. Fgn. Svc. Assn., U.S. Assn. Energy Econ., Middle East Inst., Diplomatic and Consular Officers, Retired, Inc. (gov., trustee Bacon Ho. Found.). Address: 3016 N Florida St Arlington VA 22207-1808

**SUNDQUIST, DON,** retired governor, retired congressman, sales executive; b. Moline, Ill., Mar. 15, 1936; s. Kenneth M. and Louise (Rohren) S.; m. Martha Swanson, Oct. 3, 1959; children: Tania, Andrea, Donald Kenneth. BA, Augustana Coll., 1957. Div. mgr. Josten's, Inc., 1961-72; exec. v.p. Graphic Sales of Am., Memphis, 1972, pres., 1973-82; mem. 98th-103rd Congresses from 7th Tenn. dist., Washington, 1983-94; gov. State of Tenn., Nashville, 1995—2003. Vice chmn. bd. Bank of Germantown, Tenn. Past mem. White House Commn. Presdl. Scholars; past chmn. Jobs for High Sch. Grads. of Memphis; chmn. Congl. Steering Com. George Bush for Pres., 1988, 92; nat. campaign mgr. Howard Baker for Pres., 1979; dir. com. ops., alt. del. Republican Nat. Conv., 1980; chmn. Shelby County Rep. Party, 1975-77; alt. del. Rep. Nat. Conv., 1976; exec. com. Rep. Nat. Com., 1971-73; nat. chmn. Young Rep. Nat. Fedn., 1971-73; sec. Bedford County Election Commn., 1968-70; chmn. Tenn. Young Rep. Fedn., 1969-70; dir. Mid-South Coliseum, Am. Council Young Polit. Leaders, 1972-74, U.S. Youth Council, 1972-75; bd. govs. Charles Edison Meml. Youth Fund; nat. adv. bd. Distributive Edn. Clubs Am.; mem. U.S. del. study tour, People's Republic of China, 1978, study tour, USSR, 1975. Served with USN, 1957-59. Mem. Kiwanis. Republican. Lutheran. Mailing: PO Box 28 Townsend TN 37882

**SUNDQUIST, JAMES LLOYD,** retired political scientist; b. West Point, Utah, Oct. 16, 1915; s. Frank Victor and Freda (Carlson) S.; m. Beth Ritchie, Dec. 25, 1937 (dec. 1982); children: Erik L., Mark L., James K.; m. Geraldine Coote, Dec. 3, 1983. Student, Weber Coll., 1932-34, HHD (hon.), 1990; student, Northwestern U., 1934-35; BS, U. Utah, 1939; MS in Pub. Adminstrn, Syracuse U., 1941; DDS (hon.), Carthage Coll., 1987. Reporter Salt Lake Tribune, 1935-39; adminstrv. analyst U.S. Bur. Budget, 1941-47, 49-51; reports and statistics officer Office Def. Moblzn., 1951-53; dir. mgmt. control European Command, U.S. Army, Berlin, 1947-49; asst. to chmn. Democratic Nat. Com., 1953-54; asst. sec. to gov. NY, 1955-56; asst. to U.S. Senator Clark, 1957-62; dep. under sec. agr., 1963-65; sr. fellow Brookings Instn., 1965-85, emeritus, 1985—, dir. govtl. studies, 1976-78; adj. prof. Smith Coll., 1975-78. Sec. platform com. Dem. Nat. Conv., 1960, 68 Author: Politics and Policy: The Eisenhower, Kennedy and Johnson Years, 1968, Making Federalism Work, 1969 (Louis Brownlow award for best pub. adminstrn. book), Dynamics of the Party System, 1973, 2d edit., 1983, Dispersing Population: What America Can Learn form Europe, 1975, The Decline and Resurgence of Congress, 1981 (Hardeman prize for best book on Congress), Constitutional Reform and Effective Government, 1986, 2d edit., 1992, Deseret Boy: Memories of a Utah Childhood, 2003; editor: Internat. Rev. Adminstrv. Scis., 1980—89, Beyond Gridlock?, 1993, Back to Gridlock?, 1995. Mem. Gov.'s Commn. on Va.'s Future, 1983-84 Recipient Exceptional Civilian Svc. award War Dept., 1945, Lifetime Achievement award Maxwell Sch. (Syracuse U.) Alumni Assn., 1994; sr. Rsch. fellow U. Glasgow, Scotland, 1972-73. Mem. Nat. Acad. Pub. Adminstrn., Am. Soc. Pub. Adminstrn., Am. Polit. Sci. Assn. (treas. 1980, Charles E. Merriam award 1985, Eldersveld award 1994), Am. Acad. Arts and Scis. Home: 900 N Taylor St Unit 2117 Arlington VA 22203 Office Phone: 703-294-4226.

**SUNDSTROM, AILEEN LOIS,** speech educator; b. Detroit, Mar. 2, 1925; d. Raymond and Gertrude B. (Meyer) Richard; m. Arthur E. Sundstrom, July 10, 1954. BA, Wayne State U., 1946 MA, 1947, PhD, 1964, postgrad., 1977. Tchr. speech, radio Highland Park (Mich.) High, 1947-48; English tchr. Denby High, 1948-49, Barbour Jr. High, 1949-50, Jefferson Jr. High, 1950-52, Denby High, 1952-53, Northwestern High, 1953-56, Cass Tech. High, 1957-65; asst. prof. Mercy Coll., Detroit, 1965-67; instr. performing arts dept. Henry Ford C.C., Dearborn, Mich., 1967—. Dept. spokesperson Henry Ford C.C., 1980-82, chair, 1982-88; speaker in field; text book reviewer; dir., evaluator Interpretative Reading Festival Workshops; chair various coms. Henry Ford C.C.; participant NEH, summer 1994; spl. lectr. performance communication, Oakland U., 1999-2005; forensic evaluator I.E. events, 2000-05; sponsor performance sect. Meeting of Minds, 2003, 04, 05. Contbr. articles to profl. jours. Recipient Ford Found. scholarship, 1961-62. Mem. Assn. Speech Communication, Am. Forensic Assn., Am. Assn. Univ. Women Ednl. Found., Academically Gifted and Talented, Excellence in Interpretative Reading, Mich. Assn. of Speech Communication (pres. 1985-86, presenter, chair confs. 1967—, Disting. Svc. award for festivals 1992, 93), Mich. Intercollegiate Speech League (bd. dirs. Oral Interpretation Festival/Workshops 1977—, pres. 1993-94), Speech Comm. Assn. (presenter, chair conf. programs 1967-2002), Ctrl. States Speech Assn. (presenter, chair conf. programs 1978-2001, participant NEH summer seminar 1994), Mich. High Sch. Forensic Assn., Beta Sigma Phi, Alpha Beta Pi.

**SUNDSTROM, HAROLD WALTER,** public relations executive; b. Chgo., Jan. 26, 1929; s. Elmer A. and Rosalind Lillian (Busse) S.; m. Mary Olin, Oct. 1, 1955; children: Geoffrey Lee, Lori Lynn, Deborah Barron. AA, Wright Jr. Coll., 1949; BA, Mich. State U., 1952, MA, 1954. Fgn. svc. info. officer USIA, Tokyo, Jakarta, Seoul, 1955-61; sr. pub. rels. assoc. Eli Lilly and Co., Indpls., 1962-66; v.p., dir. pub. rels. Eisenhower People to People Program, Kansas City, Mo., and Copenhagen, 1966-68; govt. and pub. affairs rep. North Ctrl. States Automobile Mfrs. Assn., Kansas City, 1968-69; speechwriter, pub. rels. cons. Commdr.-in-Chief U.S. Pacific Forces, Aiea, 1969-75; pres. No. Ariz. Comm., Inc., Flagstaff, 1975-79; asst. sec., dir. pub. affairs U.S. Internat. Trade Commn., Washington, 1977-87; v.p. pub. affairs and publs. Export-Import Bank U.S., Washington, 1987-89; pres. Halamar, Inc., Manassas, Va. and Easley, SC, 1983—, Silver Springs, Fla., 1983-98. Mem. Pres.'s Consumer Affairs Couns., 1977-89; freelance writer and poet. Author: The American West, 1956, Indonesia: Its People and Politics, 1957, Garuda, Introducing Indonesia, 1962, Faces of Asia: Korea, 1965, The Northern Arizona Scene, 1976, American Collie Champions, Vol. I, 1979, Vol. II, 1980, Vol. III, 1987, Collies - A Complete Pet Owners Manual, 1994, 2d edit., 2005; editor, pub. Hawaiian Dog Rev., The Alaska Cir., The Arizona Cir., Internat. Lhasa Apso Rev., Sandwich Isles Dog Gazette, 1972-76, Collie Cues, 1983-86, Travel Writer, Honolulu Sun Press, 1972-76. Active Civil War Preservation Trust, Colonial Williamsburg, Nat. Trust for Hist. Preservation, Hist. Mount Vernon, Va. With U.S. Army, 1947-48, 52-53. Recipient People to People Disting. Svc. award, 1967, George Washington Honor medal Freedom Found., 1968, Silver Beaver award Boy Scouts Am., 1975. Fellow Japan Soc. N.Y., Pub. Rels. Soc. Am. (past pres. Hawaii chpt., Silver Anvil award 1973); mem. Dog Writers Assn. Am. (pres. 1984-92, Disting. Svc. award 1993), Dog Writers Ednl. Trust (vice chmn., chmn. 1999-2005), Collie Club Am. (pres. 1984-86), Collie Club Am. Found. (life, pres. 1990-92), Am. Kennel Club (del. 1986—), Pi Sigma Alpha, Phi Kappa Sigma. Republican. Avocations: pure-bred dog breeding and showing, travel, photography, conservation, preservation of historic properties. Home and Office: 1 Wadsworth Ct Greer SC 29651

**SUNG, KYU-TAIK,** social worker, educator, gerontologist, researcher; b. South Kyungsang, Republic of Korea, Sept. 9, 1930; arrived in U.S., 1967; s. Jang Hwan Sung and Kyu Soon Nam; children: Choon-ho, Jin-ho, Yoon-ho, Vera. BA, Seoul Nat. U., 1956, MA, 1961; MSW, U. Mich., 1972, PhD, 1974. Prof. U. Wis. Sch. Social Work, Madison, 1975—78; prof. dept. social work Yonsei U., Seoul, Republic of Korea, 1978—96; prof. Mich. State U. Sch. Social Work, East Lansing, Mich., 1996—98; Frances Wu endowed chair prof. U. So. Calif. Sch. Social Work, 2004—; vis. prof. U. Mich. Sch. Social Work, Ann Arbor, 2004—. Dir., founder Ctr. for Social Welfare Rsch. Yonsei U., 1982—96; exec. dir., founder Elder Respect, Inc., 2002—; sr. rschr. Korean Inst. Gerontology; presenter/spkr. in field. Author: Social Welfare Administration, 1993, Filial Piety in Modern Times: A New Look at Intergenerational Relationship, 1995, Filial Piety in Modern Times: Changing Expressions in Modern Times, 1996, Filial Piety in Modern Times: Timely Adaptation and Practicing Patterns, 2000, Filial Piety in Modern Times: Care and Respect for the Elderly, 2005, Care and Respect for the Elderly: Filial Piety in Modern Times in East Asia, 2005; contbr. articles to profl. jours. With U.S. Army, 1950—53. Mem.; Korean Acad. Social Welfare (past pres.), Korean Gerontol. Soc. (past pres.). Recipient Achievements include identified components of filial piety (East Asian value of care and respect for the elderly) based on empirical data and introduced them in US profl. jours. Avocations: collecting Buddhist paintings, visiting museums. Home: 1812 Longshore Dr Ann Arbor MI 48105 Office: Univ Mich Sch Social Work 1080 S University Ann Arbor MI 48109-1106 Office Phone: 734-936-8645.

**SUNGAILA, MARY-CHRISTINE (M.C. SUNGAILA),** lawyer; BA in Polit. sci., Stanford U., 1988; JD, UCLA, 1991. Bar: Calif., Ctrl. Dist. Calif., U.S. Ct. Appeals (9th cir.) 1991, U.S. Supreme Ct 1995 Extern The Honorable Dorothy W. Nelson, U.S. Ct. Appeals (9th cir.), 1990; law clk. The Honorable Alicemarie H. Stotler, U.S. Dist. Ct., Ctrl. Dist. Calif., 1991—92, The Honorable Ferdinand F. Fernandez, U.S. Ct. Appeals (9th cir.), 1993—94; litigation assoc. Irell & Manella LLP, Newport Beach, Calif., 1994—97; assoc. Horvitz & Levy LLP, Encino, Calif., 1997—2002, ptnr., 2003—. Spkr., panelist, lectr. various legal speaking engagements. Founding editor: The Newsletter of the Woman Advocate Com. of the ABA, 1996—97; contbg. editor: Jurist: Books-on-Law, 2000—01; author: articles in numerous legal publs. and jours. Mem. Gender Equity Com. Orange County Bar Assn., 1996—2000; bd. dirs. Opera Pacific, 1996—2006; bd. govs. Women Lawyers Assn. L.A., 2000—. Office: Horvitz & Levy 15760 Ventura Blvd 18th Fl Encino CA 91436 Office Phone: 818-995-0800. Office Fax: 818-995-3157. Business E-Mail: msungaila@horvitzlevy.com.

**SUNI, ELLEN Y.,** dean, law educator; BA magna cum laude, CCNY; JD magna cum laude, Boston U. Law clerk to Chief Justice Mass. Supreme Judicial Ct., dep. legal asst. to Justices; dir. legal writing prog. Boston U. Sch. Law, asst. dean, lectr.; faculty mem. U. No.-Kansas City Sch. Law, 1986—, interim assoc. dean, interim dean, prof. law, 2004—, Marvin Lewis Rich Faculty Scholar. Fed. prosecutor U.S. Atty. Office, 1987—88; mem. Eighth Cir. Criminal Jury Instrns. Sub-com.; bd. mem. Pub. Interest Litigation Clinic, Police Law Inst. Contbr. articles to law jours. Legal dir. Kansas City Youth Ct.; pres. Midwestern Innocence Project. Recipient Legal Leader of Yr. Award, 2004. Office: U Mo-Kansas City Sch Law 5100 Rockhill Rd Kansas City MO 64110 Office Phone: 816-235-2372. E-mail: sunie@umkc.edu.

**SUNIA, AITOFELE TOESE F.,** lieutenant governor; b. Mar. 26, 1943; JD, U. of San Francisco. Various gov. positions including asst. atty. gen., temp. dist. ct. judge Ter. of Am. Samoa, territorial treas., 1997—2003, lt. gov., 2003—. Democrat. Office: Office Lt Governor Territory American Samoa Pago Pago AS 96799 Office Phone: 684-633-4116. Office Fax: 684-633-2269.*

**SUNIA, MUAGUTUTIA FITI,** former attorney general; Asst. atty. gen. Am. Samoa Govt., Pago Pago, 1997—2001, acting atty. gen., 2001—02, atty. gen., 2002—05.

**SUNLEY, EMIL MCKEE,** economist; b. Morgantown, W.Va., July 30, 1942; s. Emil McKee and Nelle Berniece (Traer) S.; m. Judith Evelyn Steere, Dec. 23, 1966; children: Rachel Anne, Gillian Traer, Neil Steere. BA, Amherst Coll., 1964; MA, U. Mich., 1965, PhD, 1968. Economist office tax analysis Dept. Treasury, Washington, 1968-73, assoc. dir. office tax analysis, 1973-75, dep. asst. sec. for tax policy, 1977-81; sr. fellow Brookings Instn., Washington, 1975-77; dir. tax analysis Deloitte & Touche, Washington, 1981-92; asst. dir. fiscal affairs dept. Internat. Monetary Fund, 1992—. Mem. editl. bd. Nat. Tax Jour., 1992-95. Mem. Commn. on RR Retirement Reform, 1987-90. Mem. Am. Econ. Assn., Nat. Tax Assn. (pres. 1995-96), Tax Analysts (bd. dirs. 1982-93). Episcopalian. Office: Internat Monetary Fund Fiscal Affairs Dept Washington DC 20431-0001 Business E-Mail: esunley@imf.org.

**SUNSHINE, PHILIP,** pediatrician; b. 1930; MD, U. Colo., 1955. Bd. cert. neonatal-perinatal medicine Am. Bd. Pediat. Resident Stanford Hosp. and Clinics, 1957, 1961, fellow, 1963; co-dir. MCCPOP Stanford U. Sch. Medicine, Palo Alto, Calif.; staff mem. Lucile Packard Childrens Hosp. Recipient Virgina Apgar award, Am. Acad. Pediat., 2001. Avocations: tennis, bicycling. Office: Stanford Univ Sch Medicine MC 5731 750 Welch Rd #315 Palo Alto CA 94304-1510 Office Phone: 650-723-5711. E-mail: psunshine@stanford.edu.

**SUNSHINE, STEVEN H.,** lawyer; AB, UCLA, 1973, JD, 1976. Bar: Calif. 1976. Ptnr., mem. exec. com. Bryan Cave LLP, Irvine, Calif. Office: Bryan Cave LLP 2020 Main St, Ste 600 Irvine CA 92614 Office Phone: 949-223-7200. E-mail: shsunshine@bryancave.com.

**SUNSTEIN, BRUCE DAVID,** lawyer; b. Phila., May 27, 1944; s. David E. and Phylis (Eisenberg) S.; 1 child, Aaron E. BS, MIT, 1965; MA, Ind. U., 1969; JD, U. Calif., Berkeley, 1973. Bar: Calif. 1973, U.S. Dist. Ct. (no. dist.) Calif. 1973, U.S. Ct. Appeals (9th cir.) 1973, U.S. Patent and Trademark Office 1974, Mass. 1977, U.S. Tax Ct. 1977, U.S. Supreme Ct. 1977, U.S. Ct. Appeals (1st cir.) 1978, U.S. Ct. Appeals (fed. cir.) 1982. Assoc. Cooper, White & Cooper, San Francisco, 1973-77; ptnr. Bromberg & Sunstein LLP, predecessor firms, Boston, 1977—. Contbr. articles to profl. jours.; author: Investor Relations Meets Intellectual Property, 2003. Named one of top Boston lawyers, Boston Mag., 2002. Mem.: Boston Patent Law Assn., Boston Bar Assn., Mass. Bar Assn., Licensing Execs. Soc., Am. Intellectual Property Lawyers Assn., IEEE, ABA. Office: Bromberg & Sunstein LLP 125 Summer St Ste 1100 Boston MA 02110-1618 Office Phone: 617-443-9292. Office Fax: 617-443-0004. Business E-Mail: bsunstein@bromsun.com.

**SUNSTEIN, CASS ROBERT,** law educator; b. Salem, Mass., Sept. 21, 1954; AB, Harvard U., 1975, JD, 1978. Law clk. to Hon. Benjamin Kaplan Supreme Jud. Ct. of Mass., 1978—79; law clk. to Hon. Thurgood Marshall US Supreme Ct., Washington, 1979-80; atty.-advisor, Office of Legal Counsel US Dept. Justice, Washington, 1980-81; asst. prof. U. Chgo. Law Sch., 1981—83, U. Chgo. Law Sch. & U. Chgo. dept. polit. sci., 1983—85, prof. law, 1985—88, Karl N. Llewellyn Prof. Jurisprudence, 1988—93, Karl N. Llewellyn Disting. Svc. Prof. Jurisprudence, 1993—. Assoc. editor Ethics, 1986—88; bd. editors Studies Am. Polit. Devel., 1989—, Constitutional Polit. Econ., 1991, Jour. Polit. Philosophy, 1991—; contbg. editor The Am. Prospect, 1989, The New Republic, 1999—; vis. prof. Columbia Law Sch., NYC, 1986, Harvard Law Sch., Cambridge, Mass., 1987, 2005; co-dir. Ctr. Constitutionalism Ea. Europe U. Chgo., 1990—97; mem. Presdl. Adv. Com. Pub. Svc. Obligations of Digital TV, 1997—98; cons. project on social norms IRS, 1999—. Author: (book) After the Rights Revolution: Reconceiving the Regulatory State, 1990, Democracy and the Problem of Free Speech, 1993 (Goldsmith Book Award, 1994), The Partial Constitution, 1993, Legal Reasoning and Political Conflict, 1996, Free Markets and Social Justice, 1997, One Case At A Time: Judicial Minimalism on the Supreme Court, 1999, Designing Democracy: What Constitutions Do, 2001, Republic.com, 2001, Free Markets and Social Justice, 2002, Risk and Reason, 2002, The Cost-Benefit State, 2002, Why Societies Need Dissent, 2003, The Second Bill of Rights: Franklin Delano Roosevelt's Constitutional Vision and Why We Need It More Than Ever, 2004, The Laws of Fear: Beyond the Precautionary Principle, 2005, Radicals in Robes: Why Extreme Right-Wing Courts Are Wrong for America, 2005; co-author: Administrative Law and Regulatory Policy, 1999, The Cost of Rights, 1999, Constitutional Law, 2001, Punitive Damages: How Juries Decide, 2002; editor: Feminism and Political Theory, 1990, Behavioral Law and Economics, 2000; co-editor: The Bill of Rights and the Modern State, 1992, Clones and Clones: Facts and Fantasies About Human Cloning, 1998, The Vote: Bush, Gore & the Supreme Court, 2001, Animal Rights: Current Controversies and New Directions, 2004. Mem.: ABA (vice chmn. Sect. Govtl. Orgn. & Separation Powers 1986—87, coun. Sect. Adminstr. Law 1987—88, vice-chmn. Jud. Rev. Com. 1991—, co-chair Com. Regulatory Policy 2001—, Cert. Merit Award 1991), Am. Acad. Arts and Sci., Am. Law Inst., Inst. Medicine Com., World Wildlife Fund. Office: Sch Law U Chgo 1111 E 60th St Chicago IL 60637-2776 E-mail: csunstei@midway.uchicago.edu.

**SUNTRA, CHARLES RATAPOL,** surgeon, educator; b. Detroit, Dec. 4, 1968; s. Sathien and Malee Suntra. BA summa cum laude, St. Louis U., 1991, MD cum laude, 1995. Diplomate Am. Bd. Otolaryngology, bd. eligible Am. Bd. Facial Plastic and Reconstructive Surgery. Intern gen. surgery Boston U. Sch. Medicine/Boston Med. Ctr., 1995—96; resident otolaryngology-head and neck surgery Boston U. Sch. Medicine, 1996—2000; chief resident Boston Med. Ctr./Boston U., 1999—2000; fellow facial plastic and reconstructive surgery Park Ctrl. Inst./Forest Park Hosp., St. Louis, 2000—01; med. staff Forest Pk. Hosp., St. Louis, 2000—01, Sutter Gould Med. Found., Modesto, Calif., 2001—, Doctors Med. Ctr., Modesto, 2001; asst. clin. prof. Sch. Medicine U. Calif., Davis. Presenter in field. Contbr. articles to profl. jours. Fellow: ACS, Am. Bd. Otolaryngology; mem.: Thai Physicians Assn. Am., Am. Rhinologic Soc., Am. Acad. Facial Plastic and Reconstructive Surgery, Am. Acad. Otolaryngology-Head and Neck Surgery, Phi Eta Sigma, Alpha Epsilon Delta, Beta Beta Beta, Alpha Sigma Nu, Phi Beta Kappa, Alpha Omega Alpha. Office: Gould Med Group 600 Coffee Rd Modesto CA 95355 Office Phone: 209-550-4770. Business E-Mail: suntrac@sutterhealth.org. E-mail: csuntra@email.com.

**SUNUNU, JOHN EDWARD,** senator; b. Boston, Sept. 10, 1964; s. John H. Sununu; m. Kitty (Halloran) Sununu; 3 children BS in Mech. Engring., Mass. Inst. Tech., 1986, MS in Mech. Engring., 1987; MBA with honors, Harvard Grad. Sch. Bus., 1991. Design engr. Remec, Inc., 1987-90; mgr. ops. specialist Pittiglio, Rabin, Todd & McGrath, 1990-92; chief fin. officer, dir. ops. Teletrol Sys. Inc., Manchester, NH, 1992—96; cons. JHS Assocs., Ltd.; mem. US Congress from 1st NH dist., 1997—2003; US senator from NH, 2003—. Com. banking, housing and urban reform US Senate, com. commerce, sci., and transp., com. fgn. relations, joint econ. com. Active NH C. of C., NH Bus. and Industry Assn., NH High Tech Coun. Recipient Friend of the Taxpayer award, Americans for Tax Reform, Guardian of Small Bus. award, Nat. Fedn. Independent Bus., Spirit Enterprise award, US C. of C. Mem.: NH Bus. and Industry Assn. Republican. Office: US Senate 111 Russell Senate Bldg Washington DC 20510 also: District Office Ste 3 1589 Elm St Manchester NH 03101 Office Phone: 202-224-2841, 603-647-7500. Office Fax: 202-228-4131, 603-647-9352.*

**SUNWOLF,** law educator, writer; b. Denver, July 4, 1946; d. Frederick Lorraine and Ruth Johanningsmeier Hotes. BA summa cum laude, Calif. State U., 1971; JD, U. Denver, 1976; MA, U. Calif., Santa Barbara, 1997, PhD, 1998. Tng. dir. Colo. Pub. Defender's Office, Denver, 1978—93; assoc. prof. Santa Clara U. Sch. Law, 1998—; faculty Nat. Criminal Def. Coll., Macon, Ga., 1990—2006, Bryan R. Shechmeister Death Penalty Coll., Santa Clara U. Coll. Law, 1998—2006. Lectr. Calif. Pub. Defenders Assn., Sacramento, 1995—; mem. editl. bd. Jour. Applied Comm. Rsch., DC, 1998—, Comm. Studies, Ephrata, Pa., 2002—06, Small Group Rsch., Thousand Oaks, Calif., 2004—; lectr. Fla. Bar Assn., Miami, Fla., 2005—, Nev. Bar Assn., Dallas, 2005, State Bar of Ariz., Phoenix, 2005, NC Acad. Trial Lawyers, Sunset Beach, NC, 2006—, SC State Bar Assn., Charleston, SC, 2006—; pro bono faculty Nat. Criminal Defense Coll., Bryan Shechmeister Death Penalty Coll. Author: (books) Practical Jury Dynamics, 2004, Jury Thinking, 2005, Juror Competency Jury Compassion, 2006, (DVD) Jury Talk; special issue editor Jour. Storytelling, Self, Soc., 2005. Recipient Order St. Ives, U. Denver, Coll., 1976, Edwin R. Schoell award for excellence in tchg., Comm. Dept., U. Calif., 1995, Dennis S. Gouran Rsch. award, Nat. Comm. Assn., 2000, Most Outstanding Scholarly Article award, 2005, Career Dedication award for pro bono work, Am. Soc. Trial Cons., 2005. Mem.: ATLA, ABA, Soc. Children's Book Writers & Illustrators, Internat. Assn. Relationship Rsch., Nat. Comm. Assn. (chair applied comm. divsn. 2001—01, Most Outstanding Scholarly Article 2000, Most Outstanding Scholarly Article award 2005), Nat. Storytelling Network, Nat. Assn. Criminal Def. Lawyers (lectr., featured spkr. 1991—2006), Am. Soc. Trial Cons. Achievements include publication of a new theory of communication; translating research from scientific research into practical tools for trial attorneys. Avocations: storytelling, knitting, gardening, reading, dance. Office: Santa Clara Univ 500 El Camino Real Santa Clara CA 95053 Business E-Mail: sunwolf@scu.edu.

**SUP, STUART ALLEN See ALLEN, STUART**

**SUPANICH, BARBARA ANN,** physician; b. Detroit, Sept. 24, 1952; d. Donald George and Mildred Mary (Stanovich) Supanich. BS in Chemistry, Mercy Coll. Detroit, 1974; MD, Mich. State U., 1980. Diplomate Am. Bd. Family Practice, lic. physician Mich., Fla.; joined Sisters of Mercy, 1973. Resident in family practice Creighton U. Affiliated Hosps., Omaha, 1900—03, pvt. practice Eaton Rapids, Mich., 1983—86, Houghton Lake, Mich., 1986—92; fellow in clin. ethics Ctr. Ethics Mich. State U., East Lansing, 1992—93, asst. prof. family practice, 1993—97, assoc. prof., 1998, assoc. chair clin. svcs., dept. family practice, 1995—99, assoc. residency dir. family practice residency Munson, 1999—; fellow palliative medicine & hospice care Mayo Clinic, Jacksonville, Fla., 2005. Cons. Mich. Dept. Cmty. Health, Lansing, 1996—99. Contbr. chapters to books, articles to profl. jours. Fellow: Am. Acad. Family Physicians (bd. dirs., regional dir. 2000—04, 2d v.p. 2004—05); mem.: Am. Med. Women's Assn., Mich. Acad. Family Physicians. Roman Catholic. Avocations: swimming, bicycling, mystery and science fiction novels. Home: Apt 1602 9803 Creekfront Rd Jacksonville FL 32256 Office: Mayo Clinic Dept Family Medicine 4500 San Pablo Rd Jacksonville FL 32224 Office Phone: 904-953-6722. Personal E-mail: bsupanich@comcast.net.

**SUPANVANIJ, JANIKAN,** finance educator; b. Bangkok, Aug. 6, 1971; arrived in U.S., 1993; d. Vitaya and Sopha Supanvanij. BBA, Thammasat U., Bangkok, 1993; MFN in Fin., St. Louis U., 1995, MBA in Fin. and Econs., 1997, PhD in Fin., 2003. Cert. tchg. skills. Internat. banking facility fgn. exch. dealer The Thai Mil. Bank, Ltd., Bangkok, 1993; instr. St. Louis U., 1997—2003; asst. prof. St. Cloud State U., Minn., 2003—06, assoc. prof., 2006—. Contbr. articles to profl. jours. Recipient Rsch. Collaboration award, St. Cloud State U., 2000—05, Disting. Rsch. award, 2000—05, Tchg. Excellence award, 2004—05. Mem.: St. Louis U. Grad. Student Assn. (webmaster 1997—2002, GSA rsch. symposium program co-chair 2001—02, pres. 2002—03), Beta Gamma Sigma, Alpha Epsilon Lambda. Office: St Cloud State U 720 4th Ave S Saint Cloud MN 56301

**SUPERNEAU, DUANE WILLIAM,** geneticist, physician; b. Ogden, Utah, Dec. 31, 1950; s. Richard Edwin and Mary Ellen Superneau; children: Adam, Ashley, Allison. BA, Carroll Coll., 1973; MD, U. Wash., 1977. Diplomate Am. Bd. Pediat., Am. Bd. Med. Genetics. Asst. prof. dept. med. genetics U. So. Ala., Mobile, 1982-87, assoc. prof. dept. med. genetics, 1987-91; chief sect. med. genetics Ochsner Clinic, New Orleans, 1991—2005; dir. Genetic Svcs. La., Baton Rouge, 2005—. Clin. assoc. prof. La. State U., New Orleans, 1992—. Bd. dirs. The ARC Greater New Orleans, 1991—, pres. 1994-96; bd. dirs. ARC of La., 1994—, pres., 1999-2001; bd. dirs. Jefferson Parish Human Svcs. Authority, Jefferson Parish, La., 1992-99. Roman Catholic. Office: Genetic Svcs of La 5412 Dijon Dr Baton Rouge LA 70808 Office Phone: 225-766-4088. Business E-Mail: duane.superneau@womans.org.

**SUPINO, PHYLLIS GAIL,** medical researcher, educator; m. Rene Patrick Supino, June 7, 1980; children: Lisa Michelle, Christopher Davies. BS in Biol. Scis., CCNY, 1964; EdD in Sci. Edn., Rutgers U., 1976. Instr. psychology, rsch. assoc. in cognitive psychology Princeton U., 1975—77; dir. rsch. and evaluation The Ednl. Improvement Ctr. divsn. NJ. State Dept. Edn., West Orange, 1977—79; adj. instr. environ. cmty. medicine, adj. instr. family medicine Robert Wood Johnson Med. Sch./U. Medicine and Dentistry NJ, Piscataway, 1979—90; asst. prof. pub. health in medicine, dir. data mgmt. Cornell U. Med. Coll., N.Y.C., 1995—99; rsch. assoc. prof. emergency medicine, rsch. assoc. prof. med. edn., dir. rsch. in emergency medicine Mt. Sinai Sch. Medicine, N.Y.C., 1996—99; assoc. rsch. prof. pub. health in medicine, dir. data mgmt., epidemiology and ednl. programs Weill Med. Coll. of Cornell U., N.Y.C., NY, 1999—. Mem. editl. bd.: Vol. Morocco VI US Peace Corps, Washington. Recipient Phi Delta Kappa award, Rutgers U., 1976, The Howard Gilman award, The Howard Gilman Found., 1995, Best Mentor of the Yr. award, Mt. Sinai Sch. Medicine, 1998, Best Nat. Sci. Abstract award, Am. Soc. Nuc. Cardiology and Internat. Affiliates, 2001; grantee Pilot Rsch. award, Weill Med. Coll. of Cornell U. Fellow: NY Acad. Medicine (mem. evidence based medicine working group); mem.: Heart Valve Soc. Am., Am. Soc. Nuc. Cardiology, Am. Heart Assn., Am. Statis. Assn. (editl. bd.), Am. Fedn. for Med. Rsch., Kappa Delta Pi (life). Achievements include development of first comprehensive approved course on clinical research methodology for physicians at Weill Medical College and Mount Sinai School of Medicine; Research mentor to more than 50 residents, fellows and junior faculty in medicine. Avocations: theater, vocal music. Office: Weill Medical College/Cornell University 525 E 68th Street; F467 New York NY 10021 Office Phone: 212-746-2118. Business E-Mail: phs2002@med.cornell.edu.

**SUPLEE, DENNIS RAYMOND,** lawyer; b. Phila., Jan. 20, 1943; s. Raymond C. and Miriam C. (Morris) S.; m. Patricia H. Hickey; children: David A., Christopher D., Richard C. BS, St. Joseph's U., 1964; LLB, U. Pa., 1967. Bar: Pa. 1967. Assoc. Schnader, Harrison, Segal & Lewis, Phila., 1967-74, ptnr. litig. practice, 1975—, mem. exec. com., 1986-89, 91-92, chmn. exec. com., 1992—98. Mem. Sec. Navy's Adv. Bd. on Edn. and Tng., Washington, 1985-86. Author: (with others) The Deposition Handbook, 4th edit., 2002, Expert Witness: Law and Practice, 1993; contbr. articles to profl. jours. Mem. adv. com. Dorland Global Health Communications, 2003-; trustee St. Joseph's U., Phila., 2004-; mem. bd. gov. Mercy Fitzgerald Hosp., 2005-. Equal Justice award, Cmty. Legal Svcs., 2003. Fellow Am. Coll. Trial Lawyers (Pa. state chmn. 1998-2000, regent for NJ & Del. 2001-). Internat. Acad. Trial Lawyers (dir. 2000-); mem. Pa. Bar Assn. (ho. of dels. 1988-89), Phila. Assn. Def. Counsel (pres. 1994-95), U. Pa. Law Sch. Am. Inn of Ct. (master), Union League. Democrat. Roman Catholic. Avocations: tennis, badminton. Office: Schnader Harrison Segal & Lewis Ste 3600 1600 Market St Philadelphia PA 19103-7286 Home: 40 S Roberts Rd Bryn Mawr PA 19010-2622 Office Phone: 215-751-2068. Office Fax: 215-751-2205. Business E-Mail: dsuplee@schnader.com.

**SUPPES, CHRISTINE JOHNSON,** publishing executive; b. L.A., Mar. 3, 1953; d. Robert and Jane Johnson; m. Patrick Suppes; children: Alexandra Christine, Michael Patrick. Copygirl/editl. asst. San Francisco Examiner, 1972—73; pres. Gravure At Home, Stanford, Calif., 1997—2001; pub., editor-in-chief www.Fashionlines.com, Stanford, Calif., 1999—; chief designer Jewels by Christine, 2002—. Advt. cons. Clarum Corp., Palo Alto, Calif., 1997—, Gravure Corp., Dallas, 1997—2000; chief designer www.jewelsbyChristine.com, Stanford, Calif., 2003—; Am. rep. Of Silk, of Gold and Silver Assn., France. Author: Amanda Prescott, 1984, Clinic, 1985; contbr. revs. to San Francisco Chronicle, articles to SF Moda. Organizer, Teacher's Fund Bing School, Stanford, 1995—2001; mem. Peninsula Chpt. NARAL, Palo Alto, 1997—2000; supporter ARC, Palo Alto, 2001. Recipient Angel of Fashion com. award, N.Y.C., 1999—. Mem.: French Heritage Soc. No. Calif. (bd. dirs. 2005), Fashion Group Internat., Camera Nazionale della Moda Italiana, Federation Francaise de la Couture. Office: Fashionlines 678 Mirada Ave Stanford CA 94305 Business E-Mail: suppes@fashionlines.com.

**SUPPES, PATRICK,** statistician, philosopher, psychologist, educator; b. Tulsa, Mar. 17, 1922; s. George Biddle and Ann (Costello) Suppes; m. Joan Farmer, Apr. 16, 1946 (div. 1970); children: Patricia, Deborah, John Biddle; m. Joan Sieber, Mar. 29, 1970 (div. 1973); m. Christine Johnson, May 26, 1979; children: Alexandra Christine, Michael Patrick. BS, U. Chgo., 1943; PhD (Wendell T. Bush fellow), Columbia U., 1950; LLD, U. Nijmegen, Netherlands, 1979; Dr. honoris causa (hon.), U. Rene Descartes, Paris, 1982, U. Regensburg, Germany, 1999, U. Bologna, Italy, 1999. Instr., Stanford U., 1950—52, asst. prof., 1952—55, assoc. prof., 1955—59, prof. philosophy, statistics, psychology and edn., 1959—92, prof. emeritus. Founder, CEO Computer Curriculum Corp., 1967—90. Author: Introduction to Logic, 1957, Axiomatic Set Theory, 1960, Sets and Numbers, books 1-6, 1966, Studies in the Methodology and Foundations of Science, 1969, A Probabilistic Theory of Causality, 1970, Logique du Probable, 1981, Probabilistic Metaphysics, 1984, Estudios de Filosofia y Metodología de la Ciencia, 1988, Language for Humans and Robots, 1991, Models and Methods in the Philosophy of Science, 1993, Representation and Invariance of Scientific Structures, 2002; author: (with Davidson and Siegel) Decision Making, 1957; author: (with Richard C. Atkinson) Markov Learning Models for Multiperson Interactions, 1960; author: (with Shirley Hill) First Course in Mathematical Logic, 1964; author: (with Edward J. Crothers) Experiments on Second-Language Learning, 1967; author: (with Max Jerman and Dow Brian) Computer-assisted Instruction, 1968, ..., Stanford Arithmetic Program, 1968, author: (with D. Krantz, R.D. Luce and A. Tversky) Foundations of Measurement, Vol. 1, 1971, Vol. 2, 1989, Vol. 3, 1990; author: (with M. Morningstar) Computer-Assisted Instruction at Stanford, 1966-68, 1972; author: (with B. Searle and J. Friend) The Radio Mathematics Project: Nicaragua, 1974-75, 1976; author: (with Colleen Crangle) Language and Learning for Robots, 1994; author: (with Mario Zanotti) Foundations of Probability with Applications, 1996. Served to capt. USAAF, 1942-46. Recipient Nicholas Murray Butler Silver medal, Columbia U., 1965, Disting. Sci. Contbr. award, APA, 1972, Tchrs. Coll. medal for disting. svc., 1978, Nat. medal Sci., NSF, 1990, Henry Chauncey award for disting. svc., Ednl. Testing Svc., 2003, Lakatos Book Award prize, London Sch. Econs., 2003, Lauener Prize in Philosophy, Lauener Found., 2004; fellow, Ctr. for Advanced Study Behavioral Scis., 1955—56, NSF, 1957—58. Fellow: APA, AAAS, Assn. Computing Machinery, Am. Acad. Arts and Scis.; mem.: NAS, Chilean Acad. Scis., European Acad. Scis. and Arts, Norwegian Acad. Sci. and Letters (fgn.), Russian Acad. Edn. (fgn.), Am. Edn. Rsch. Assn. (pres. 1973—74), Internat. Union History and Philosophy of Sci. (pres. divsn. logic, methodology and philosophy of sci. 1975—79), Finnish Acad. Sci. and Letters, Internat. Inst. Philosophy, Croatian Acad. Scis. (corr.), Brazilian Acad. Philosophy (corr.), Nat. Acad. Edn. (pres. 1973—77), Acad. Internat. de Philosophie des Scis. (titular), Am. Math. Soc., Assn. Symbolic Logic, Am. Philos. Soc., Am. Philos. Assn., Math. Assn. Am., Sigma Xi. Office Phone: 650-725-6030. E-mail: psuppes@stanford.edu.

**SUPRUN, HARRY ZVI,** pathologist; b. San Antonio, Aug. 19, 1924; arrived in Israel, 1934; s. Joseph Jacob and Bertha Batya (Payes) S.; m. Hedva Storch-Chassidi, Mar. 26, 1950; children: Ilana Sarah, Leora Oli. BA in Medicine, Am. U. Beirut, 1948; MD, cert. med. studies, U. Lausanne, Switzerland, 1952. Rotating intern Beilinson Med. Ctr., Petah Tikvah, Israel, 1953-54; gen. practice, Affuleh, Israel, 1954-55; resident in pathology Ctrl. Emek Hosp. and Med. Ctr., Affuleh, 1955-58; resident and chief resident in anatomic pathology Tel Aviv U.-Mcpl. Tchg. Med. Ctrs., 1958-62, specialist in anatomic pathology, assoc. attending, 1961; tng. in cytopathology, rsch. fellow Sloan-Kettering Inst., N.Y.C., 1962-63; instr., asst. pathologist Ohio State U. Med. Coll., Columbus, 1963-64; instr. Tel Aviv U. Med. Sch. Tchg. Hosps., 1964-65; clin. instr., founder dept. pathology and cytology Regional Med. Ctr. West Galilee, Nahariyya, Israel, 1965-91; lectr. gynecologic, gastrointestinal, fine needle aspiration cytology and urol. cytopathology Tel Aviv U.

Postgrad. Med. Sch., 1987-92; lectr. anatomic pathology, U.S. students Tel Aviv U., 1990-92. Lectr. normal histology Technion Med. Sch., Haifa, Israel, 1977-82; mem. Internat. Bd. Cytopathology, 1986-92; head orgn. com. Israel Soc. Cytology, 1971; fellow Internat. Acad. Cytology, 1971-73. Nat. editor Acta Cytologica, 1971-93, mem. European rev. bd., 1982-93; assoc. editor The Cervix and Lower Female Genital Tract, 1987-90, mem. editl. bd., 1989-91; mem. N.Am. rev. bd. Acta Cytol, 1997—; contbr. more than 100 articles to profl. publs. Rsch. fellow Israel Cancer Rsch. Fund, 1979-82. Fellow Internat. Acad. Cytology (continuing edn. and quality assurance com. 1992—), Israel Soc. Cervical Pathology and Colposcopy (pres. 1986). Achievements include correlative study on incidence of pulmonary cancer and other lung diseases associated with squamous metaplasia of bronchial epithelium.

**SUPUT, RAY RADOSLAV,** librarian; b. Columbus, Ohio, May 13, 1922; s. Elias and Darinka (Balac) S.; m. Mary Grace Hansen, May 23, 1953 (dec. Nov. 1980); children: David Ray, Dorothy Mary; m. Milana Preradov, July 12, 1986. BA, Ohio State U., 1950; MSL.S., Case Western Res. U., 1951, PhD, 1972; MA, U. Chgo., 1955. Librarian Northwestern U., Evanston, Ill., 1951-52; reference and circulation librarian Law Library, U. Chgo., 1952-54, cataloger, 1954-57; asso. librarian Garrett-Evang. Theol. Sem., Evanston, 1957-58, head librarian, 1958-64; asst. dir. libraries and adj. lectr. dept. Slavic and E. European langs. Sch. Library Sci. Case Western Res. U., Cleve., 1964-67, acting dir. libraries, 1967-68; adj. instr. Case Western Res. U. (Sch. Library Sci.), 1965-69; librarian Case Western Res. U. (Freiberger Library), 1968-69; dir. univ. library, head dept. and prof. library sci. Ball State U., Muncie, Ind., 1969-78, univ. librarian, head dept. and prof. library service, 1978-81, prof. library service, also adj. prof. library sci., 1981-82, chmn. dept. library and info. sci., prof. library sci., 1982-87, prof. library sci., info. sci. emeritus, 1987—. Contbr. articles to profl. jours. Nat. Endowment for Humanities and Council on Library Resources Inc. grantee. Mem.: AAUP, ALA, Ohio Hist. Soc., Serb Nat. Fedn., Am. Theol. Libr. Assn., African Violet Soc. Am. Eastern Orthodox. E-mail: suputi@sbcglobal.net.

**SURABIAN, CAROL ANNE,** language educator, consultant; b. Fresno, Calif., Aug. 1, 1948; d. Harvey Graham and Jeannette Agnes Corbett; m. Ronald Dave Surabian; children: Jennifer Carol, Shelley Rebecca Vizcarra, David Christopher. BA, Calif. State U., Fresno, 1971; M, Fresno Pacific U., 2001. Tchr. Washington Intermediate Sch., Dinuba, Calif., 1984—. Organist Sts. Sahag-Mesrob Armenian Ch., Reedley, Calif., 1982—2006. Mem.: Calif. Assn. Tchrs. English (pres. Tulare County coun. 1997—2006). Avocations: reading, needlecrafts, travel. Home: 589 E Sycamore Reedley Ca 93654 Office: Washington Intermediate Sch 1150 N Hayes Dinuba CA 93618 Office Phone: 559-595-7252. Personal E-mail: csurab132@yahoo.com. Business E-mail: csurabia@dinuba.k12.ca.us.

**SURACE, THERESA,** special education educator; b. Rochester, NY, Sept. 14, 1958; d. Richard R. Goeltz and Ellen C. Lipani; m. Rick Surace, May 1, 1999; children: Christie Leathersich, Michele Cope. BS, St. John Fisher Coll., 2003; AAS, Monroe Cmty. Coll., 2001. Special Education Teacher State of NY Edn. Dept., 2004, Elementary School Teacher, including Pre-Kindergarten and Kindergarten State of NY Edn. Dept., 2004. Client svc. rep. IBM, Rochester, NY, 1989—99; spl. edn. tchr. Rochester City Sch. Dist., 2004—. V.p. Chpt. of the Coun. for Exceptional Children, Rochester, 2002—04. Recipient Outstanding Adult Student, Rochester Area Colleges Continuing Edn., 2003. Mem.: Coun. for Exceptional Children (assoc.). Office: Monroe High Sch 164 Alexander St Rochester NY 14607 Office Phone: 585-232-1530. E-mail: theresa.surace@rcsdk12.org.

**SURACI, CHARLES XAVIER, JR.,** retired federal agency administrator, air transportation executive, consultant; b. Washington, Feb. 10, 1933; s. Charles Xavier and June Celcia (Hunter) Suraci; m. Florence Patricia De Mino, May 23, 1970. Cadet, Penn Mil. Coll. (now Widener U.), 1951—55; grad., Nat. Acad. Broadcasting Sch., Washington, 1959; student, Columbia Union Coll., 1962-63, 72, Catholic U., 1969; grad. extension course, CAP Staff Coll., 1974; BA, Calif. Christian Coll., 1977, HHD (hon.), 1977; grad., USAF Inspectors Gen. Sch., Eglin AFB, Fla., 1982; also grad. numerous other govt. schs. and courses. Served with USAF, 1953-57; enlisted CAP, 1957, commd. 1st lt., 1961; advanced through ranks to Col. CAP USAF Aux, 1974, co-founder Wheaton-Silver Spring Cadet Squadron; comdr. Nat. Capital Wing, 1973-76; dep. chief of staff cadet activities Middle East region, 1977-79, dir. cadet tng., 1979-82, insp. gen., 1982—. With Henry Diamond Lab. U.S. Army, Adelphi, Md., 1963—, materials publs. asst. Harry Diamond Lab., 1963—68, later asst. to motor transp. officer, now supply specialist, logistics sect.; bd. dirs. Centro Tepeyac Crisis Pregnancy Ctr., Silver Springs, Md. Mem. youth com. YMCA, Silver Spring, 1962—69, mem. bd. mgmt., 1967—; bd. dirs. Am. Youth Com.; mem. Commn. on Children and Youth Bd., Montgomery County, Md., Montgomery County Juvenile Ct. Com., 1978—86; co-chmn. Right to Life com. KC-Rosensteel Coun.; bd. dirs. Pregnancy Aid Ctr., College Park, Md.; choir mem. Blessed Sacrament Cath. Ch., Washington. Nominee Pres.'s Vol. Action award, Pres. of U.S., 1988, 1991; named Air Man of Month, USAF, 1956, Grand Marshall Meml. Day Parade, Rockville, Md., 1971, Man of Yr. State of Md., Air Force Assn., 1993; recipient Leader and Svc. award, YMCA Silver Spring, 1968, 1969, CAP Meritorious Svc. award, Dept. Def., 1969, 1977, Cert. of Commendation, Pres. Richard Nixon, 1970, CAP Exceptional Svc. award, Congressman Lester Wolff of N.Y., 1972, award, Montgomery County C. of C., 1973, Commendation, Gov. of Tenn., 1975, Letter of Commendation, Washington Mayor Walter Washington, 1977, Outstanding Patriotic Civilian Svc. award, Dept. Def., 1977, Md. Vol. Cmty. honor award, Montgomery County, 1981, Vol. Activist award, 1984, George Washington honor medal, Valley Forge Freedom Found., 1995, Patrick Henry medal for Patriotic Achievement, Mil. Order of World Wars, 1995, Honor, Md. Ho. Dels., 1974, D.C. Govt., 1977, numerous AF and CAP ribbons and medals, Dept. of Army Spl. Act or Svc. award, Dept. of Army Superior Performance award, 1987, Cmty. Svc. award, Wheaton-Kensington News, Bethesda Chevy Chase Current, Montgomery County Press Assn., 1990, Outstanding Support Aviation Career Day Tuskegee Airmen and Commdg. Gen. of D.C., Air Nat. Guard, 1992, Spl. award for tng. over 1000 youth cadets in CAP in 31 yrs., State of Md., 1986, Plaque Name Displayed at U.S. Army-Harry Diamond Lab., Pro-Life award, KC-Rosensteel Coun., 1992, 1999—2002, Frank G. Brewer Meml. Aerospace award-CAP Mid. East Region HQ, 1984, 1991, 1992, CAP-USAF Aux. Meritorious Svc. award, Mid. East Region HQ, 1993, Cert. Appreciation Aerospace Edn. of Md., Air Force Assn., 1993—95, Exceptional Svc. award, USAF Aux., 1994—95, Sr. Officer of Yr. Mid East Region, USAF Aux.-CAP, 1998, Colonel Robinson Lifetime Leadership award, Nat. Capital Wing, 2001, Leadership award, Cen. East Region Air Force Assn., 2001, numerous others. Mem.: Md. Pvt. Industry Coun. (bd. dirs. Opportunity Skyway program), Md. Press. Assn. Montgomery County, Nat. Officers Assn., Mil. Order of World Wars (jr. vice comdr. Bethesda chpt. 1996—, Outstanding staff officer of the yr. 2005), Tuskegee Airmen Inc., Fed. Ret. Employees Assn., Army Aviation Assn., Navy League, Nat. Aerospace Assn., Air Force Assn. (v.p. aerospace edn. Thomas W. Anthony chpt. 1996—, pres. Thomas W. Anthony chpt. 1998—, bd. dirs., nat. liaison officer to Civil Air Patrol-Aux. USAF 2004, Medal of Merit 1990, Exceptional Svc. award 1991, Disting. Svc. as Inspector Gen. 1991, Exceptional Svc. award 1994, Commd. Officer of Yr. 1995, Spl. Cert. Appreciation 1996, Mem. Distinction award Thomas W. Anthony chpt. 2000—02, Cen. East Region Chpt. Pres. of Yr. 2004, Thomas W. Anthony chptr. pres. of the Yr. 2005), Alumni Assn. Widener U., Andrews AFB Officers Club, KC (chmn. Pro-Life Father Rosensteel coun., Outstanding Leadership Pro-Life activities 1990—91), Outstanding Svc. award 1993—94, Honored Guest of Yr. 1996—97, Outstanding Cmty. award 2003, 2004, Achievement award of the Yr. 2005), Chester Lodge. Democrat. Achievements include 2 plaques in his name displayed at Columbia Union Coll., Takoma Park, Md., Widener U. (formerly Pa. Mil. Coll.), Chester. Home: Rock Creek Hills 9817 La Duke Dr Kensington MD 20895-3156 Office: USAF Aux CAP Mid East Region Hdqrs Office of Insp Gen 9817 La Duke Dr Kensington MD 20895-3156 Office Phone: 301-585-0081.

**SURBER, DAVID FRANCIS,** public relations executive, consultant, television producer, journalist; b. Covington, Ky. s. Elbert and Dorothy Kathryn (Mills) Surber. BA in Physics, Thomas More Coll., 1960; LLD (hon.), London Inst. Applied Rsch., 1973. Owner P.R. Co., pub. affairs counseling, Covington, 1960—. Judge Brit. Airways Tourism Tomorrow awards, London, 2000—. Spl. corr.: Am. newspapers to Vatican II, 1965; prodr.: (TV series) Make Peace with Nature, Sta. WKRC-TV, 1973—, Strip Mining: Two Views, 1972, Energy: Where Will It Come From, How Much Will It Cost, 1975, Atomic Power for Ohio, 1976, A Conversation with the Vice President, 1976, The Bad Water, 1977, The Trans-Alaska Pipeline: A Closeup Report, 1977, Acid Rain: A World View, 1986—89, Energy Independence in the U.K., 1992, Unhappy Prospects: Acid Rain & Global Climate Change, 1995, The Kyoto Summit: Was It Global and Will It Work, 1997—98. Apptd. by Sec. of Energy to Nat. Coal Coun., 1992, 1994, 1996, 1998, 2000, 2002, 2004, chmn. comm. com., 1999—; mem. Bd. Zoning Appeals, Covington, 1964—84, chmn., 1971—84, Covington Environ. Commn., 1971—72, Commn. Strip Mining, 1967—82; pub. interest adv. com. Ohio River Valley Water Sanitation Commn., 1976—82; water quality adv. com. Ohio-Ky.-Ind. Regional Coun. Govts., 1975—82; environ. adv. coun. City of Cin, 1981—84; rehab. com. Cmty. Chest Greater Cin., 1972—78, mem. agy. admissions com., 1972—78, mem. priorities com., 1972—78; pres. bd. dirs. Cathedral Found., 1968—70; trustee Montessori Learning Ctr., 1973—75, Bklyn. Spanish Youth Choir; founding mem. Mayor's Task Force on the Environment, Cin., 1972—73; mem. Ky. Nature Preserves Commn., 1976—79; Dem. candidate for U.S. Ho. Reps., 1972. Recipient Cmty. Svc. award, Thomas More Coll., 1975. Mem.: ACLU, AFTRA, Nat. Inst. Urban Wildlife (bd. dirs. 1987—96), Tri-State Air Com. (chmn. 1973—74), Mousquetaires d'Armagnac, Izaak Walton League (pres. Ky. 1973—98, bd. dirs. Ky., nat. bd. dirs.). Office: PO Box 15555 Covington KY 41015-0555 Office Phone: 859-491-5000. E-mail: surber@surber.com.

**SURDAM, ROBERT MCCLELLAN,** retired banker; b. Albany, N.Y., Oct. 28, 1917; s. Burke and LeMoyne (McClellan) S.; m. Mary Caroline Buhl, July 8, 1946; children— Peter Buhl, Robert McClellan, Mary Caroline. BA cum laude, Williams Coll., 1939. With Nat. Bank Detroit, 1947-88, exec. v.p., 1964-66, pres., 1966-72, chmn. bd., 1972-82, also bd. dirs., 1966-88. Served to lt. comdr. USNR, 1941-46. Recipient, Navy and Marine Corps. medal. Mem. Detroit Club, Country Club of Detroit, Yondotega Club, Jupiter Island Club (Hobe Sound, Fla.), Jupiter Hills Club (Tequesta, Fla.), Little Traverse Yacht Club (Harbor Springs, Mich.), Rolling Rock Club (Ligonier, Pa.), Hobe Sound Yacht Club, Little Harbor Club (Harbor Springs, Mich.). Home: 396 Provencal Rd Grosse Pointe Farms MI 48236-2959

**SURERUS, DOROTHEA KAE,** elementary school educator; b. Brocket, ND, May 22, 1938; d. Stanley Gustave and Alma (Kalliokoski) Berg; married, June 3, 1961 (div., Jan. 1979); children: Kristene, Kelly, Kory. BS, Mayville State U., 1961. Tchr. third grade Beulah (ND) Pub. Sch., 1958-59; tchr. fourth grade Cavalier (ND) Pub. Sch., 1959-60; tchr. second and fourth grade Neche (ND) Pub. Sch., 1962; tchr. basic skills Moorhead (Minn.) Pub. Sch., 1969-70; tchr. elem. edn. Cooperstown (ND) Pub. Sch., 1970—99; tutor Griggs County (ND) Ctrl. Pub. Sch., 1999—2006. Mem. NEA, N.D. Edn. Assn., Cooperstown Edn. Assn. (pres. 7 yrs.). Home: PO Box 624 1417 Roberts Ave NE Cooperstown ND 58425-0624 Office: Cooperstown HS Cooperstown ND 58425

**SURESH, SUBRA,** materials engineer, educator; B. Technol., Indian Inst. Technol., 1977; MS, Iowa State U., 1979; ScD, MIT, 1981. Asst. prof. engring. Brown U., 1983; R. P. Simmons Endowed Professorship MIT, 1993, head Dept. Materials Sci. and Engring., 2000—, Ford Prof. of Engring., 2002—. Clark B. Millikan Endowed Chair for visiting professorship Calif. Inst. Tech., Pasadena, 1999—2000. Author: Fatigue of Materials, 2nd ed., 1998; co-author (with A. Mortenson): Fundamentals of Functionally Graded Materials, Institute of Materials, 1998; co-author: (with L.B. Freund) Thin Film Materials: Stress, Surface Evolution and Failure, 2003; contbr. articles to profl. jours. Named one of The Most "Highly Cited Researchers" in the World in the broad area of Materials Science, Inst. for Scientific Info., 2002; recipient Outstanding Scientific Accomplishment award, U.S. Dept. of Energy, 1982, Robert Lansing Hardy Gold medal, The Metallurgical Society of AIME, 1983, Champion H. Matthewson Gold medal, 1985, Presidential Young Investigator award, NSF, 1985—90, Ford Found. Rsch. award, 1985—87, Allied Signal Found. Rsch. award, 1989, Allied Signal Found. Merit award, 1990, Disting. Alumnus award, Indian Inst. of Technol., 1997. Fellow: TMS (Disting. Scientist/Engineer award 2001), ASME, ASM Internat., Am. Acad. Arts and Sciences, Am. Ceramic Society (Ross Coffin Purdy award 1992); mem.: US Nat. Acad. Engring., NAE, Materials Rsch. Society of India (hon.). Achievements include patents in field. Office: MIT Room 8-303 77 Massachusetts Ave Cambridge MA 02139

**SURFACE, JAMES LOUIS, SR.,** trust officer, lawyer; b. Roanoke, Va., May 20, 1941; s. Thomas James and Elizabeth (Abbott) S.; m. Judith Marcia Woodford, Aug. 11, 1962; children: Susanna Elizabeth, James Louis Jr. BA cum laude, Washington & Lee U., 1963, JD cum laude, 1965. Bar: W.Va. Assoc. Spilman, Thomas, Battle & Klostermeyer, Charleston, W.Va., 1965-71; trust officer Kanawha Valley Bank, N.A., Charleston, 1971-77; v.p., trust counsel Liberty Nat. Bank & Trust Co., Louisville, 1977-84; v.p., trust officer United Va. Bank, Richmond, 1984-85; v.p., sr. trust officer First Citizens Nat. Bank, Dyersburg, Tenn., 1985-93; sr. v.p., sr. trust officer SunTrust Bank East Tenn., Johnson City, 1993—2003; retired, 2003. Mem. administr. bd. First United Meth. Ch., Dyersburg, 1988-90, pres., bd. dirs. Cmty. Concert Assn. Dyersburg, 1988-93; treas., bd. dirs. Louisville-Jefferson County Youth Orch., Louisville, 1980-84; pres., bd. dirs. W.Va. Opera Theater, Inc., Charleston, 1972-77; elder First Presbyn. Ch., Johnson City, 1998-2000; bd. dirs. Tipton-Haynes Hist. Site, 2001-06. Mem. ABA (chmn. subcom. on duties and responsibilities of successor trustee real property, probate and trust sect., Charleston 1974-75), W.Va. Bar Assn., Tenn. Bankers Assn. (treas. trust divsn. Nashville chpt. 1988-89, sec. 1989-90, v.p. 1990-91, pres. 1991-92), W.Va. Bankers Assn. (chmn. trust divsn. Charleston chpt. 1974-75), Rotary (bd. dirs. Dyersburg chpt. 1987-88), East Tenn. State U. Friends of Music (bd. dirs. 1994-99, 2000—). Democrat. Avocations: tennis, racquetball, photography, reading.

**SURGENOR, TIMOTHY R.,** neurotechnology company executive; BA in Biochemistry, Williams Coll., 1981; MBA, Harvard Bus. Sch., 1987. Various positions in ops. Integrated Genetics; exec. v.p., CFO Biosurface Technology, Inc.; pres.. Genzyme Tissue Repair Genzyme Corp., Cambridge, Mass., 1994—99; exec. v.p. Haemonetics Corp., Braintree, Mass., 1999—2003, mem. investor team; pres., CEO, dir. Cyberkinetics Neurotechnology Systems, Inc., Foxborough, Mass., 2003—. Office: Cyberkinetics Neurotechnology Systems Inc 100 Foxborough Ste 240 Foxboro MA 02035 Office Phone: 508-549-9981. Office Fax: 508-549-9985.

**SURGUCHOV, ANDREI P.,** biochemist, ophthalmologist, researcher; m. Irina G. Surgucheva; 1 child, Alexei A. Surguchev. DS, PhD, Moscow State U. Head lab. molecular biology Cardiology Rsch. Ctr., Moscow, 1986—91; asst. prof. Baylor Coll. Medicine, Houston, 1992—95; sr. rschr. U. Utah, Salt Lake City, 1995—98; assoc. prof. Wash. U. St. Louis, 1998—2001; assoc. prof., rsch. biologist VA Med. Ctr. and Kans. U. Med. Ctr., Kansas City, Mo., 2001—. Grantee, Alzheimer's Disease Rsch. Ctr., 1999, Reevs Found., 1999, NIH, 2001—04, VA Ctrl. Office, 2005. Mem.: Am. Acad. Neurology, Soc. Neurosci., Assn. Rsch. Vision and Ophthalmology. Office: VA Med Ctr 4801 Linwood Blvd Kansas City MO 64128 Office Phone: 816-861-4700 57078. Business E-Mail: asurguchov@kumc.edu.

**SURH, GERALD,** history professor; b. Tucson, Feb. 24, 1939; s. Young Oak Kim (Stepfather); Nora Chung Kim; m. Nelia Berko, Jan. 4, 1984; 1 child, Alexander Berko. PhD, U. Calif., Berkeley, 1967. Acting asst. prof. dept. history & ethnic studies UCLA, 1976—79; vis. asst. prof. dept. history Reed Coll., Portland, Oreg., 1981—82; assist. prof. dept. history NC State U., Raleigh, 1982—88, assoc. prof. dept. history, 1988— Editor (with robert e. weinberg): (collection of articles) Labor, Thought, and Society in Russia and

the Soviet Union; author: (book) 1905 in St. Petersburg: Labor, Society, and Revolution, (pub. 1989). Co-chair U.S. Green Party, 2003—04. Fellow Rsch. fellow, NEH, 1990—91. Mem.: Am. Assn. Advancement Slavic Studies, So. Conf. Slavic Studies (life; pres. 1996—97), Carolina Godiva Track Club. Green Party. Avocation: running. Office: North Carolina State University Department of History Box 8108 Raleigh NC 27695-8108 Office Phone: 919-513-2219. Office Fax: 919-515-3886. E-mail: surh@ncsu.edu.

**SURI, JASJIT S.,** research scientist; BS in Computer Engring., Regional Engring. Coll., Bhopal, India, 1988; MS, U. Ill., Chgo., 1991; PhD in Elec. Engring., U. Wash., 1997. Lectr. dept. electronic and computer engring. Regional Engring. Coll., Bhopal, 1988-89; rsch. asst. biomed. visualization dept. U. Ill., Chgo., 1989-90; rsch. programmer image sci. group IBM Palo Alto (Calif.) Sci. Ctr., summer 1990-91; rsch. assoc. U. Wash., Seattle, 1992-97; rsch. software engr. radiation treatment planning group Siemens Med. Sys., Calif., 1991-92; rsch. scientist Gammex Inc., Middleton, Wis., 1997, Sch. Medicine, U. Wis., Madison, 1997; rsch. scientist software devel. TSI, N.Y., 1997; rsch. staff scientist image guided surgery dept. Image Processing and Computer Graphics Picker Internat., Cleve., 1999—. With Bharat Heavy Elec. Ltd., Bhopal, 1986, Larson & Tubro Ltd., Bombay, India, 1987, Nat. Info. Tech. Ltd., Bhopal, 1987; presenter in field; mem. Mayo Clinic Procs., Rochester, Minn.; rev. com. Internat. Conf. in Pattern Analysis and Applications, Plymouth, Eng., 1998. Author: (with others) Model Based Segmentation, 2d. rev. edit., 2000; mem. editl. bd. Radiology, Jour. Computer Assisted Tomography, Internat. Jour. Pattern Analysis and Applications, Internat. Conf. Pattern Analysis and Applications; contbr. over 150 articles. to profl. jours.; patentee in field. Scholar Regional Engring. Coll., 1985-88 Mem. IEEE, Assn. Computing Machinery, Artificial Intelligence, Optical Engring. Soc. Am., Engring. in Medicine and Biology Soc. (mem. editl. bd.), Am. Assn. Artificial Int., USENIX-Tcl/Tk. Office: Case Western Res U Biomed Engring Dept Cleveland OH Office Phone: 720-936-6362. Personal E-mail: suri0256@msn.com.

**SURJI, KEMAL M.,** health facility administrator, consultant; PhD in Health Adminstrn., Kennedy Western U., Cheyenne, Wyo., 2005. Registered respiratory therapist NBRC/TN, 1993. Respiratory therapist HCA Summit Med. Ctr., Hermitage, Tenn., 1993—2002; pres. EMS Med. Staffing Svcs., Inc, Centerville, Tenn., 2002—. Respiratory care cons. EMS Med. Svcs., Centerville, 2002—; patient educator on pulmonary diseases. Achievements include Patient Education of Pulmonary Disease. Office: EMS Med Staffing Svcs Inc PO Box 249 Dickson TN 37056 Office Phone: 615-477-3421. Home Fax: 615-446-7152; Office Fax: 615-446-7152. Business E-Mail: kemal.surji@emsstaffing.com.

**SURKIN, ELLIOT MARK,** lawyer; b. Phila., Apr. 22, 1942; s. Hersh M. and Minnie (Shore) S.; m. Carol E. Foley, May 26, 1973; 1 child, Jennifer Dykema. AB, Princeton U., 1964; LLB, Harvard U., 1967. Bar: Mass. 1967. Assoc. Hill & Barlow, P.C., Boston, 1967-73, mem., 1973—2003, chmn. mgmt. com., 1988-92, chmn. real estate dept., 1996-2001; mng. ptnr. Boston DLA Piper Rudnick Gray Cary, 2003—. Lectr. law Harvard U., 1975-96, MIT, Ctr. for Real Estate, 1996—. Chmn. bd. Boston Ctr. Arts, 1972-81, dir., mem. exec. com., 1981-83; trustee, mem. exec. com. Wang Ctr. for Performing Arts, Boston, 1980—, mem. fin. com., 1995—2005, vice chmn. bd., 1997—2005; mem. New Eng. com. Legal Def. Fund NAACP, 1976-93; chmn. bd. Trustees of Reservations, 1997-2003, bd. dir., 2003—, chmn. Chappaquiddick local com. 1986-97, trustee 1985—, mem. standing com. 1994-2003, mem. exec. com. 1996-2003; dir. Sheriff's Meadow Found., 1994-97. Mem. ABA, Am. Law Inst., Am. Coll. Real Estate Lawyers, Mass. Bar Assn., Boston Bar Assn., St. Botolph Club, Harvard Club of Boston, Edgartown Yacht Club, Country Club of Brookline, Mass., Kiawah Island Club. Office: DLA Piper Rudnick Gray Cary 33 Arch St 26th Fl Boston MA 02110-1447 Office Phone: 617-406-6030. Office Fax: 617-406-6130. Business E-Mail: elliot.surkin@dlapiper.com.

**SURLES, CAROL D.,** academic administrator; b. Pensacola, Fla., Oct. 7, 1946; d. Elza Allen and Versy Lee Smith; divorced; children: Lisa Surles, Philip Surles. BA, Fisk U., 1968; MA, Chapman Coll., 1971; PhD, U. Mich., 1978. Personnel rep. U. Mich., Ann Arbor, 1973-78, vice-chancellor-adminstrn. Flint, 1987-89; exec. asst. to pres., assoc. v.p. for human resources U. Ctrl. Fla., Orlando, 1978-87; v.p. acad. affairs Jackson State U., Miss., 1989-92; v.p. adminstrn. and bus. Calif. State U. Hayward, 1992-94; pres. Tex. Woman's U., Denton, 1994-99, Ea. Ill. U., Charleston, 1999—. Trustee Pub. Broadcasting Ch. 24, Orlando, 1985-87; bd. dirs. First State Bank, Denton, Tex., Tex.-N.Mex. Power Co., TNP-Enterprise. Recipient Outstanding Scholar's award Delta Tau Kappa, 1983. Mem. AAUW, Am. Assn. Colls. and Univs., Golden Key Honor Soc., Mortar Bd. Soc., Dallas Citizens' Coun., Dallas Women's Found., Coun. of Pres. (Austin, Tex.), Phi Kappa Phi, Alpha Kappa Alpha. Methodist. Avocation: piano. Office: Ea Ill U 600 Lincoln Ave Charleston IL 61920-3011

**SURLES, RICHARD HURLBUT, JR.,** retired law librarian; b. Norfolk, Va., Mar. 28, 1943; s. Richard H. and Elda Florine (Belvin) S.; m. Judith Louise Coffin, May 29, 1964; children— Stephanie Anne, Richard H. BA, Tex. A&M U., 1963; JD, U.Houston, 1967; M.L.L., U.Wash., 1969. Bar: Colo. 1971. Asst. to law librarian U. Houston, 1966-68; asst. to law librarian King county Law Library, Seattle, 1968-69; dir. of law library, prof. law U. Denver, 1969-71, U. Tenn., Knoxville, 1971-76, U. Oreg., Eugene, 1976-81, U. Ill., Champaign, 1981—98; ret., 1998. Author: Legal Periodical Management Data, 1977 Mem. Am. Assn. Law Libraries Republican. Personal E-mail: Beretta@KTC.com.

**SURMA, JOHN P., JR.,** metal products executive; b. Pitts., 1954; BS Acctg., Pa. State Univ., 1976. CPA. Acct. Price Waterhouse, 1976—81, mgr., 1981—85, sr. mgr., 1985—87, ptnr., 1987—97; sr. v.p. Marathon Oil Co., 1997—99; pres. Speedway SuperAmerica LLC, 1998—2000; sr. v.p. Marathon Ashland Petroleum LLC, 2000, pres., 2001; asst to chmn. USX Corp., 2001; vice chmn., CFO US Steel Corp., 2002—03, pres., COO, 2003—04, pres., CEO, 2004—. Exec. staff asst. to vice chmn. Fed Reserve Bd. Pres. Exec. Exchange Prog., 1983; bd. dirs. Mellon Fin. Corp., 2004—, Calgon Carbon Corp., 2000—, Nat. Assn. Mfr.; dir. & mem. exec. com. Internat. Iron & Steel Inst.; mem. Pa. Bus. Roundtable. Dir. & mem. exec. com. Allegheny Conf. Cmty. Devel.; mem. bd. vis. Univ. Pitts. Katz Graduate Sch. Bus., Pa. State Univ. Smeal Coll. Bus. Mem.: Am. Inst. CPAs, Pitts. Celebrity Hockey Team. Office: US Steel Corp 600 Grant St Pittsburgh PA 15219-2800*

**SURMAN, OWEN STANLEY,** psychiatrist; b. Boston, Apr. 21, 1943; s. Aaron Harry and Edith Anne (Silver) S.; m. Lezlie Anne Humber, July 19, 1969 (dec. Nov. 5, 1994); children: Craig Bruce Hackett, Kathleen Bridget Lezlie; m. Amy Johnson, Oct. 1, 2000. BSc with honors, McGill U., 1964, MD, CM, 1968. Diplomate Am. Bd. Psychiatry and Neurology. Intern Balt. City Hosp., 1968—69; clin. fellow in medicine Johns Hopkins U., Balt., 1968—69; resident in psychiatry Mass. Gen. Hosp., Boston, 1969—72; clin. fellow in psychiatry Harvard Med. Sch., Boston, 1969—72; clin. asst. in psychiatry Mass. Gen. Hosp., Boston, 1975—76, asst. in psychiatry, 1977—80, asst. psychiatrist, 1980—86, assoc. psychiatrist, 1986—89; psychiatrist, 1990—; instr. psychiatry Harvard U. Med. Sch., Boston, 1975—80, asst. prof., 1980—90, assoc. prof., 1990—. Psychiat. cons. Boston Ctr. Heart Transplant, 1988-94; mem. ethics com. Mass. Ctr. Organ Transplantation, 1988—; mem. subcom. Human Studies, Mass. Gen. Hosp., 1982—, acting chmn., 1996-97; vis. co-vice-chmn., 1999-2001, cons. transplant unit, 1975—, vice-chmn. xenotransplant adv. com., 1997-98, living related partial liver donor oversight com., 2000—; mem. Inst. for Study of Smoking Behavior and Policy, John F. Kennedy Sch. Govt., 1982-89; vis. prof. Tokyo U., 2001; mem. N.Y. State Com. on Quality Improvement in Living Liver Donation, 2002—. Contbr. articles and letters to profl. jours., chpts. to books, After Eden: A Love Story, 2005. Bd. dirs. Unitarian-Universalist Area Ch., Sherborn, Mass., 1983-86, 93-96; advancement officer troop 1 Boy Scouts Am., Sherborn, 1983-91. Lt. comdr. M.C., USNR, 1972-75. Grantee Milton Fund, 1969-70, Upjohn Corp., 1982-84, Burroughs Wellcome Co., 1984-85, Eli Lily Corp., 1989, 90-92. Fellow Am. Psychiat. Assn. (Disting.), Am. Acad.

Psychosomatic Medicine (ethics com., awards com. 1994-97); mem. AAAS, Mass. Med. Soc., N.Y. Acad. Scis., Mass. ACLU, Libr. of Boston Athenaeum, Ford Hall Forum, New Eng. Poetry Club, Boston Authors Club. Avocation: creative writing. Office: Mass Gen Hosp Wang ACC 815 15 Parkman St Boston MA 02114 Office Phone: 617-724-0846. Business E-Mail: osurman@partners.org.

**SURMATIS, JOSEPH D.,** retired chemist; b. Dickson City, Pa., Mar. 22, 1913; s. George and Constance (Mickulski) Surmatis; m. Geraldine Duff, Feb. 12, 1945; 1 child, Anthony. BS, Penn. State U., 1936, MS, 1937, PhD, 1942. Instr. chemistry Penn. State U., State Coll., Pa., 1940—42; cons., tech. G.J. Esslen, Inc., Boston, 1942—44; sr. tech. fellow Hoffman-La Roche, Nutley, NJ, 1945—78; ret., 1978. Chmn. Internat. Symposium Carotinoid Chemistry, New Mex. State U., 1969, Internat. Symposium Cartenoid Chemistry, Cluj, Romania, 1972. Contbr. scientific papers over 20; referee (Jour. of Organic Chemistry), 1978. Fellow: Am. Assn. Advancement of Sci., Am. Inst. of Chemists; mem.: NY Acad. of Sci. Achievements include patents in field of indsl. synthesis including vitamins E, A, biotin, myxin and beta-carotene (over 100). Home: 4 Sunset Rd West Caldwell NJ 07006

**SURO-BREDIE, CARMEN CECILIA,** federal official; b. Washington, Aug. 19, 1947; d. Guillermo Antonio and Piedad (Castillo) Suro; m. Joseph W.B. Bredie, Oct. 26, 1974; children: Nicholas Alexander, Christopher Anthony. BA, Manhattanville Coll., 1969; MA, Johns Hopkins U., 1972; MBA, Harvard U., 1981. Dep. asst. U.S. Trade Rep. for Investment and the Uruguay Round, Washington, 1989-92, asst. for environment and intellectual property, 1992-93, asst. for L.Am., Africa and the Caribbean, 1993-95; sr. policy advisor Bur. Interam. Affairs Dept. State, Washington, 1995-96; sr. policy advisor and exec. sec. U.S. Trade Rep., Washington, 1996-00, asst. U.S. trade rep. for policy coord., 2000—. Contbr. articles to profl. publs. Coach No. Ireland Women's Coalition. Named one of Elite Women, Hispanic Bus. mag., 2005; recipient Nat. Cuban Am. Women's Assn. award, 1992. Roman Catholic. Avocations: antiques, gourmet cooking. Office: Exec Office of the Pres US Trade Rep 600 17th St NW Washington DC 20850 Office Phone: 202-395-9541. Business E-Mail: csuro-bredie@ustr.eop.gov.

**SUROVELL, EDWARD DAVID,** real estate company executive; b. Washington, Mar. 20, 1940; s. Samuel and Florence Deborah (Starfield) S.; m. Barbara Ann Bartelmes, Apr. 26, 1958 (div. Jan. 1974); children: David Alexander, Claire Katherine; m. Natalie A. Sallade, June 3, 1999. BA, Columbia U., 1962; postgrad., U. Mich., 1968-71. Lic. real estate broker, Mich. Copy editor Harcourt, Brace & World, Inc., N.Y.C., 1963-65; editor Princeton (N.J.) U. Press, 1965-67, Scott, Foresman Co., Glenview, Ill., 1967-68, U. Mich., Ann Arbor, 1968-72; real estate agt. Fletcher & Klein, Inc., Ann Arbor, 1973-75; sales mgr. Charles Reinhart Co., Ann Arbor, 1975-82; pres. Edward Surovell Realtors Ann Arbor, 1982—. Dir. United Bank and Trust, Washtenaw, 2001—. Mem. Ann Arbor City Planning Commn., 1988-91, 95-98, Downtown Devel. Authority, Ann Arbor, 1991-95; trustee Ann Arbor Dist. Libr., 1996—, pres., 2004—06; trustee Libr. Mich. Found., 2005-; bd. dirs. Mich. Shakespeare Festival, 1999—, Jackson Symphony Orch., 2000—, Chamber Music Am., 2004—; mem. Mich. Bd. Profl. Cmty. Planners, 1988-92. Mem. Nat. Assn. Realtors, Hist. Soc. Mich. (trustee 1992—, v.p. 1996-97), Ann Arbor Area Bd. Realtors (v.p. 1984, pres. 1985, Realtor of Yr. 1990), Univ. Mus. Soc. (bd. dirs. 1992-98, trustee Mich. Ctr. for the Book 1998-2002), Mich. Hist. Commn. (bd. mem. 2005-). Avocations: book collecting, arts philanthropy. Home: 1000 Forest Rd Ann Arbor MI 48105-1047 Office: Edward Surovell Realtors 1884 W Stadium Blvd Ann Arbor MI 48103-4504 Business E-Mail: esurovell@surovell.com.

**SUROWIEC, ANDREW JULIUS,** biophysicist, researcher; b. Lwów, Poland, Apr. 13, 1940; arrived in US, 1986; s. Jan Jakub and Maria (Knobloch) S.; m. Irene Regina Baranowski, Apr. 27, 1977; 1 child, Caroline Maria. Engr., Tech. U., Gliwice, Poland, 1962, MS, 1964; PhD, Silesian U., Katowice, Poland, 1972. Cert. elec. engring. Asst. prof. Silesien Sch. Medicine, Katowice, 1964-82; postdoctoral fellow Ctr. d'Etude L'Energie Nucleaire, Mol, Belgium, 1973-74; disting. vis. scientist U. Ottawa, Ont., Canada, 1983-87; asst. prof. Bowman U. Sch. Medicine, Winston-Salem, NC, 1987-88, U. So. Calif., L.A., 1988-93; sr. physicist Centennial Med. Ctr., Nashville, 1993—. Peer reviewer: Cancer, Internat. Jour. Am. Cancer Soc., 1993; contbr. articles to Physics in Medicine and Biology, Bioelectromagnetics, IEEE Transactions Biomed., Internat. Jour. Hyperthermia, Biopolymers, Jour. Chem. Soc. Faraday Transactions. Grantee Nat. Sci. and Engring. Rsch. Coun., 1985. Fellow Radiation Rsch. Soc.; mem. Internat. Clin. Hyperthermia Soc., N.Y. Acad. Scis. Achievements include patent for recording system for rotating viscometer; finding of simulated materials for electromagnetic studies and cancer treatment; findings of dielectric spectroscopy of normal and cancer tissues; finding of dielectric and hydrodynamic properties of DNA. Home: 8209 Londonberry Rd Nashville TN 37221-4640 Office: Centennial Med Ctr Radiation Therapy 2300 Patterson St Nashville TN 37203-1528 Office Phone: 615-342-4850. Personal E-mail: andsur@aol.com.

**SURPLUS, ROBERT WILBUR,** retired music educator; b. Scranton, Pa., Sept. 1, 1923; s. Willard K. and Olive T. (Wrightson) S.; m. Jean Craig, June 25, 1976; children: Amy, Melanie. BS, Susquehanna U., 1945; MA, Columbia U., 1947, EdD, 1968. Music tchr., Mineola, N.Y., 1945-46, Butler, N.J., 1946-47; music supr. Red Lion, Pa., 1947-56; assoc. prof. Shippensburg (Pa.) State U., 1956-58; music tchr. Fox Lane Sch., Bedford, N.Y., 1958-59; instr. Columbia U., N.Y.C., 1959-61; asst. prof. U. Minn., Mpls., 1961-65; prof. music Ea. Ky. U., Richmond, 1965-94; ret., 1994. Rsch. chmn., So. Div., Music Educators Nat. Conf., 1974-80, rsch. coun. mem., 1974-80; cons. Nat. Assn. Jr. Colls., 1973-75. Author: Follow the Leader, 1962, The Alphabet of Music, 1963, The Beat of the Drum, 1963, The Story of Musical Organizations, 1963; editor: A Guidebook for State Music Education Associations, 1985, Beyond the Classroom Informing Cultural, 1987; contbr. articles to profl. jours. Mem.: Ky. Alliance for Arts Edn. (pres. 1974—82, adv. bd.), Ky. Music Educators Assn. (bd. dirs., pres. 1971—73, Disting. Svc. award 1983, Citation for Svc. 2004), Music Educators Nat. Conf. (pres. so. divsn. 1982—84).

**SURPRIS, JOSEPH W.,** research scientist; BA in biol. sciences, Hunter Coll., 1994—99. Howard Hughes student fellow Hunter Coll. Gene Ctr., NYC, 1996—2000; rsch. asst. Rockefeller U., NYC, 1998; assoc. rsch. scientist Burke Med. Rsch. Inst., Inc, White Plains, NY, 2001—. Student mentor Liberty Partnership Program, NYC, 1999; intern Cmty. Food Resource Ctr., Inc., NYC Health Rsch. Tng. Program, NYC, 1998; vol. Meml. Sloan-Kettering Cancer Ctr., NYC, 1997—98; musical dir./ch. bd. mem. Eben-Ezer Fresh Seventh-day Adventist Ch., Bklyn, NY, 2001; vol. Project Health Care, Bellevue Hosp. Ctr., NYC, 1998—98. Howard Hughes Med. Inst. Scholar award, Howard Hughes Med. Inst., 1997—99. Mem.: NY Acad. of Sciences, AAAS, Sigma Xi, The Sci. Rsch. Soc. (assoc.), Golden Key Nat. Honor Soc. (life), Alpha Phi Omega Nat. Svc. Frat. (pub. rels. 1998—99). Seventh-Day Adventist. Achievements include research in the effects of EMF on cancer. Office: Burke Med Rsch Inst Inc 785 Mamaroneck Ave White Plains NY 10605 E-mail: jsurpris@burke.org.

**SURPRISE, JUANEE,** chiropractor, nutrition consultant; b. Gary, Ind., Apr. 28, 1944; d. Glenn Mark and Willia Ross (Vasser) Surprise; m. Peter E. Coakley, Feb. 12, 1966 (div. Jan. 1976); children: Thaddeus, Mariah, Darius; m. Robert T.Howell, Feb. 24, 1984. RN, Phila. Gen. Hosp. Sch. Nursing, 1965; D of Chiropractic summa cum laude, Life Chiropractic Coll., Marietta, Ga., 1981. Diplomate Nat. Bd. Chiropractic Examiners, Am. Acad. Pain Mgmt., Am. Acad. Integrated Medicine, Internat. Acad. Clin. Nutrition; bd. cert. naturopathic med. doctor; cert. clin. nutritionist, acupuncturist, Thompson technique, Nimmo receptor tonus technique. Staff nurse Children's Hosp., Balt., 1966-67; charge nurse Melrose-Wakefield Hosp., Mass., 1967-68; hosp. adminstr. Animal Hosp. of Wakefield, Mass., 1967-79; chiropractor Chiropractic Clinic of Greenville, NC, 1982-84, Family Med.-Chiropractic Clinic, Denton, Tex., 1984—; dean Sch. Nutrition Quantum-Veritis Internat. Univ. Sys., 2003—; dir. Ctr. Clin. Sci., Parker Coll. Chiropractic, Dallas, 1996-97, dir. diplomate and certification programs, 1997-2000. Mem. postgrad. faculty Northwestern U. Health Scis. Mem., chmn. Cmty. Planning Commn., North Reading, Mass., 1976-79; chmn. bldg. com. Immaculate Conception Ch., Denton, 1987-90, parish coun., 1990-92; v.p. Property Owners Assn., 2000-02. Fellow Am. Acad. Integrated Medicine; mem. Am. Assn. Pain Mgmt., Am. Chiropractic Assn., Am. Chiropractic Bd. on Nutrition (past pres.), Tex. Chiropractic Assn. (past chair), Pi Tau Delta. Republican. Roman Catholic. Avocation: health education. Office: Family Med and Chiropractic Clinic 1100 Dallas Dr Denton TX 76205-5121 Office Phone: 940-566-0000. Personal E-mail: doctormomdc@hotmail.com. Business E-Mail: info@familymedandchiro.com.

**SURRIDGE, STEPHEN ZEHRING,** lawyer, writer; b. N.Y.C., Dec. 12, 1940; s. Robert George and Florence Elizabeth (Zehring) S.; m. Helen Frances McKenna, Mar. 15, 1969; children: Christopher S., Jonathan R., Matthew W., Martha H. BA magna cum laude, Yale U., 1962; MBA (with distinction), JD, U. Mich., 1969. Bar: Wis. 1969, Mich. 1969. Assoc. Quarles & Brady, Milw., 1969-76, ptnr., 1977-89; freelance writer, tchr., 1990—. Author: (monograph) Seven Thunders of Revelation, 1985, Revelation Revisited, 1995, Fatima's 'Third Secret' is Future Warning, 2004. 1st lt. U.S. Army, 1963-65. Mem. Phi Beta Kappa. Mem. Christian Ch. Home: 4480 N Ardmore Ave Milwaukee WI 53211-1418

**SURWIT, RICHARD SAMUEL,** psychology professor; b. Bklyn., Oct. 7, 1946; s. David and Ethel S.; m. Sandra E. Cummings, May 23, 1982; children: Daniel Alan, Sarah Jeanne. AB, Earlham Coll., 1968; PhD, McGill U., Montreal, Que., Can., 1972; postgrad., Harvard U., Boston. Postdoctoral fellow Harvard Med. Sch., 1972-74, instr., 1974-76, asst. prof., 1976-77; assoc. prof. psychiatry Duke U. Med. Ctr., Durham, NC, 1977-83, prof., 1980, 83—, vice chmn., 1993—; chief divsn. med. psychology Duke U., 1997, prof. psychology, 1991—; chmn. bd. dir. ZyCare Inc. (formerly Healthware Corp.), Chapel Hill, 1983—. Author: Fear: Learning to Cope, 1978, Behavioral Approaches to Cardiovascular Diseases, 1982, The Mind-Body Diabetes Revolution, 2004. Recipient rsch. devel. award NIMH, 1980, rsch. scientist award NIMH, 1993. Fellow APA, Soc. Behavioral Medicine (pres. 1994), Acad. Behavioral Medicine Rsch. Achievements include co-discovery in 1997, of UCP2, a novel gene related and diabetes and immunity; co-developer of the Diacare-diabetes disease management system, Coag-Care anticoagulation management system. Home: 3804 Sweeten Creek Rd Chapel Hill NC 27514-9706 Office: Duke U Med Ctr PO Box 3842 Durham NC 27702-3842 Business E-Mail: richard.surwit@duke.edu.

**SURYANARAYANAN, RAJ GOPALAN,** pharmacist, researcher, consultant, educator; b. Cuddalore, Tamil Nadu, India, Apr. 19, 1955; came to U.S., 1985; s. Natesan and Pushpa (Subramanian) Rajagopalan; m. Shanti Venkateswaran, Nov. 24, 1985; children: Priya Mallika Sury, Meera Sindu Sury. B in Pharmacy, Banaras Hindu U., Varanasi, India, 1976, M in Pharmacy, 1978; MS, U. BC, Vancouver, Can., 1981, PhD, 1985. Mgmt. trainee Indian Drugs and Pharms. Ltd., Rishikesh, India, 1978; supr. Roche Products, Bombay, India, 1979; tchg. asst. U. B.C., Vancouver, Can., 1979, 82-83; asst. prof. pharmaceutics U. Minn., Mpls., 1985-92, assoc. prof., 1992-99, prof., 1999—, dir. grad. studies, 1994-98. Cons. numerous pharm. cos. in U.S., 1987—. Contbr. articles to profl. jours; patentee quantitative analysis of intact tablets. Recipient numerous grants for rsch., U.S., 1985—. Mem. Am. Assn. Pharm. Scientists, Am. Assn. Colls. Pharmacy. Hindu. Avocation: sports. Office: U Minn Coll Pharmacy 308 Harvard St SE Minneapolis MN 55455-0353 Home: 2025 Autumn Pl Saint Paul MN 55113-5417 Office Phone: 612-624-9626. E-mail: surya001@umn.edu.

**SUSAC, JOHN OBREN,** neurologist, consultant; b. Powhatan Point, Ohio, Feb. 27, 1940; s. John William and Eunice Marie Susac; Glenn Howard Morris (Stepfather); m. Lois Ann Green, Sept. 5, 1959; children: Holly Beth Tabernilla, Heather Megan, John Arthur, Jeremy Lawton. MD, Ohio State, Columbus, 1965. Lic. Ohio, 1965. Neurologist Neurology, Neurosurgery, Winter Haven, Fla., 1978—. Assoc. prof. Uniformed Svcs. Health Scis., Washington, 1973—78; cons. neuroophthalmologist U.S. Dept. Army. Lt col. U.S. Army, 1965—70. Fellow: Am. Acad. Neurology. Achievements include discovery of Susac's syndrome. Avocations: travel, hiking. Home: 300 W Lake Otis Dr SE Winter Haven FL 33880 Office: Neurology Neurosurgery 50 2d St Winter Haven FL 33880 Office Phone: 863-293-2107. Home Fax: 863-294-9314; Office Fax: 863-294-9314. Business E-Mail: jsusac@neurohaven.com.

**SUSCHITZKY, PETER,** cinematographer; Cinematographer The Skouras Agy., 1987—. Cinematographer: (films) It Happened Here, 1962, Privilege, 1967, A Midsummer Night's Dream, 1968, Charlie Bubbles, 1968, Leo the Last, 1970, Melody/Swalk, 1971, The Pied Piper, 1972, Henry VIII and His Six Wives, 1972, That'll Be the Day, 1974, All Creatures Great and Small, 1975, Lisztomania, 1975, The Rocky Horror Picture Show, 1976, Valentino, 1977, The Empire Strikes Back, 1980, Krull, 1983, Falling in Love, 1984, Dead Ringers, 1988, Where the Heart Is, 1990, Naked Lunch, 1992, The Public Eye, 1992, The Vanishing, 1993, M. Butterfly, 1993, Immortal Beloved, 1994, Crash, 1996, Mars Attacks!, 1996, eXistenZ, 1998, The Man in the Iron Mask, 1998, The Empire Strikes Back - Spl. Edition, 1999, Star Wars Trilogy- Spl. Edition, 1999, The Red Planet, 1999, Spider, 2005, A History of Violence, 2005, Shopgirl, 2005, le concile de pierre, 2005. Office: The Skouras Agency 1149 3rd St #3 Santa Monica CA 90403

**SUSCOVICH, DAVID J.,** neuropsychologist, marriage and family therapist; b. Mt. Pleasant, Pa., Sept. 20, 1952; s. Joseph Anthony and Helen G. Suscovich; m. Edith P. Suscovich, May 23, 1980 (div. Sept. 15, 2001); children: Joseph Alfred, John David, Mark Andrew. BS/BA in Psychology and Sociology, U. Pitts., 1973, postgrad.; FRM, MA in Marriage and Family Therapy, U. Conn, 1977; PsyD in Clin. Psychology, Antioch New Eng., 1997. Cert. marriage family therapist Conn.; diplomate Am. Coll. Forensic Examiners, Nat. Bd. Addiction Examiners; lic. marriage and family therapist Am. Assn. Marriage and Family Therapists, Conn.; Psychiat. clinician psychiatry dept. Waterby (Conn.) Hosp., 1974—80; pvt. practice individual and marriage and family therapy Naugatuck, Conn., 1987—. Clin. cons. Waterby Youth Svcs., Inc., 1988—, Salvation Army Youth Shelter, Waterby, 1995—, Conn. Dept. children and Families, 2001—03; clin. neuropsychology examiner Conn. Resource Group, LLC, Waterby, 1988—, Conn. Edn. Svcs., Middletown, 2001—; mental health cons. Danby (Conn.) Head Start, Conn., 1994—97; adj. faculty So. Conn. State U., New Haven, 1992—, Yale U. Sch. Medicine, New Haven, 2002—; full adj. prof., adj. Ctrl. Conn. State U., New Britain, Conn., 1994—; presenter in field; co-facilitater G.R.A.S.P. parent advocacy and support group. Weeblos Cub Scout leader Boy Scouts Am. Pack 110, Naugatuck, 1989—98; troop com. mem. Boy Scouts Am. Troop 109, Naugatuck, 1997—. Mem.: Electroencephalography and Clin. Neurosci. Soc., Conn. Assn. Marriage and Family Therapy (chair state election com. 2002—), Phi Kappa Phi. Democrat. Roman Catholic. Achievements include research in negative neurophysiological effects of stress on children and teens delaying development of executive brain functions; neurofeed back training for brain disorders. Avocations: camping, canoeing, fishing, woodworking, music. Home: 23 May St Naugatuck CT 06770 Office: 16 Orchard St Naugatuck CT 06770 Office Phone: 203-729-2565. Personal E-mail: dr_suscovich@msn.com.

**SUSKIND, DENNIS A.,** investment banker; b. Staten Island, N.Y., Dec. 13, 1942; s. Morris and Ida (Levine) S.; m. Cynthia Ann Leverenz, Sept. 14, 1968; children— Brian, John Paul, Pamela Claire, Audrey Elizabeth. Student, Pace Coll., N.Y.C. Vice pres. J. Aron & Co., N.Y.C., 1962-81; ptnr. Goldman Sachs & Co., N.Y.C., 1981—; Intl. ptnr., 1990—. Bd. dirs. Merc. Exchange, 1972-80, Gold Inst., Washington, 1980-90; bd. dirs. Commodity Exchange, Inc., N.Y.C., 1980-87, 1st vice chmn., 1989-91; lectr. Fin. Times Conf., 1983, 84, 86-90. Bd. dirs. East End chpt. Nature Conservancy, Arthur Ashe Inst. for Urban Health, pres.; trustee Collegiate Sch., N.Y.C., Marymount Sch., N.Y.C.; councilman Southampton, NY. Recipient Pillar of NY award, NY State Preservation League, 2005. Mem. AIME, Silver Inst., Futures Industry Assn. (Hall of Fame 2005), Southampton Golf Club, Atlantic Golf Club (Bridgehampton, N.Y.). Home: 73 Wo0ster St New York NY 10012

**SUSKIND, RONALD STEVEN,** journalist, writer; b. Kingston, NY, Nov. 20, 1959; s. Walter Burton and Shirley Lila (Berman) Suskind; m. Cornelia Kennedy, May 4, 1986; children: Walter Kennedy, Harry Owen. BA in Govt. and Fgn. Affairs, U. Va., 1981; MS in Journalism, Columbia U., 1983. No. Va. field coord. Charles Robb for Gov., Alexandria, Va., 1981; campaign mgr. John Downey for U.S. Senate, New Haven, 1982; news asst., interim reporter The New York Times, 1983—85; city/state reporter The St. Petersburg Times, Fla., 1985—86; sr. editor Boston Bus. Mag., 1987—88, editor, 1988—90; staff reporter The Wall St. Jour., Boston, 1990—93, sr. nat. affairs writer Washington, 1993—2000, project reporter; contr. NY Times Mag., Esquire Mag. Instr. advanced journalism Harvard U., Cambridge, Mass., 1987—93; commentator Sta. WBUR, Boston, 1989—93. Author: (non-fiction) A Hope in the Unseen: An American Odyssey from the Inner City to the Ivy League, 1998, The Price of Loyalty: George W. Bush, the White House, and the Education of Paul O'Neill, 2004 (Investigative Reporter's and Editor's Book of Yr. award, 2004), The One Percent Doctrine: Deep Inside America's Pursuit of Its Enemies Since 9/11, 2006. Recipient Pulitzer Prize for feature writing, 1995, Benjamin Fine award, Nat. Assn. Secondary Sch. Prins., 1995, Nat. Writing award, Ball State U., 1995, Bus. Book of Yr. award, Forbes Mag., 2004. Office: c/o The Harry Walker Agency Inc 21st Fl 355 Lexington Ave New York NY 10017 Business E-Mail: ronsuskind@ronsuskind.com.

**SUSKIND, SIGMUND RICHARD,** microbiology educator; b. N.Y.C., June 19, 1926; s. Seymour and Nina Phillips S.; m. Ann Parker, July 1, 1951; children: Richard, Mark, Steven. AB, NYU, 1948; PhD, Yale U., 1954. Research asst. biology div. Oak Ridge Nat. Lab., 1948-50; USPHS fellow NYU Med. Sch., N.Y.C., 1954-56; mem. faculty Johns Hopkins U., Balt., 1956—, prof. biology, 1965-96, univ. prof., 1983-96, prof. emeritus, 1996—, Univ. ombudsman, 1988-91, dean grad. and undergrad. studies, 1971-78, dean Sch. Arts and Scis., 1978-83. Head molecular biology sect. NSF, 1970-71; cons. NIH, 1966-70, Coun. Grad. Schs., Mid States Assn. Colls. and Secondary Schs., 1973—, NSF, 1986; vis. scientist Weizmann Inst. of Sci., Israel, 1985; trustee Balt. Hebrew U., 1985-93; mem. adv. bd. La. Geriatric Ctr., 1990—. Author: (with P.E. Hartman) Gene Action, 1964, 69, (with P.E. Hartman and T. Wright) Principles of Genetics Laboratory Manual, 1965; editor: (with P.E. Hartman) Foundations of Modern Genetics series, 1964, 69; mem. sci. editorial bd. Johns Hopkins U. Press, 1973-76, 88-91. With USNR, 1944—46. NIH grantee, 1957-76 Fellow AAAS; mem. Am. Soc. Microbiology, Genetics Soc. Am., Am. Soc. Immunology, Am. Soc. Biol. Chemistry and Molecular Biology, Coun. Grad Schs., Assn. Grad. Schs., Northeastern Assn. Grad. Schs. (exec. com. 1975-76, pres. 1977-78). Avocation: research in microbial biochemical genetics and immunogenetics. Office: Johns Hopkins U Dept Biology and McCollum-Pratt Inst 34th and Charles Sts Baltimore MD 21218 Business E-Mail: sigr@dmv.com.

**SUSLICK, KENNETH SANDERS,** chemistry professor; b. Chgo., Sept. 16, 1952; s. Alvin and Edith Suslick. BS with honors, Calif. Inst. Tech., 1974; PhD, Stanford U., 1978. Rsch. and tchg. asst. Stanford (Calif.) U., 1974-78; chemist Lawrence Livermore (Calif.) Lab., 1974-75; asst. prof. U. Ill., Urbana, 1978-84, assoc. prof., 1984-88, prof. chemistry, 1988—; prof. Beckman Inst. for Advanced Sci. and Tech., Urbana, 1989-92; prof. materials sci. and engring. U. Ill., Urbana, 1993—, William H. and Janet Lycan prof. chemistry, 1997—2004, Marvin T. Schmidt prof. chemistry, 2004—; founder ChemSensing, Inc., 2001—. Vis. fellow Balliol Coll., Inorganic Chemistry Lab., Oxford (Eng.) U., 1986; cons. in field. Editor: High Energy Processes in Organometallic Chemistry, 1987, Ultrasound: Its Chemical, Physical and Biological Effects, 1988, Comprehensive Supramolecular Chemistry, vol. 5, 1996; co-editor: Sonochemistry and Sonoluminescence, 1999; editl. bd. Ultrasonics, 1992-96, Ultrasonic Sonochemistry, 1996—, Accounts of Chemical Research, 2005—, Jour. Am. Chem. Soc., 2006-; patentee isotope separation by photochromatography, sonochemistry, protein microspheres, drug delivery, blood substitutes, sensors, smell-seeing, artificial olfaction; contbr. articles to profl. jours. Fellow DuPont Found., 1979-80, Sloan Found., 1985-87; A.C. Sr. Cope scholar, 2004; recipient Rsch. Career Devel. award NIH, 1985-90, NSF Spl. Creativity award 1992-94, Material Rsch. Soc. medal, 1994. Fellow AAAS, Am. Acoustical Soc. Royal Soc. Arts, Mfrs. and Commerce (Silver medal 1974); mem. Am. Chem. Soc. (chmn. sect. 1987-89, Nobel Laureate Signature award 1994, Sr. Cope Scholar award 2004). Avocations: sculpting, music. Office: U Ill Dept Chemistry 600 S Mathews Ave Urbana IL 61801-3602 Business E-Mail: ksuslick@uiuc.edu.

**SUSMAN, MILLARD,** geneticist, educator; b. St. Louis, Sept. 1, 1934; s. Albert and Patsy Ruth S.; m. Barbara Beth Fretwell, Aug. 18, 1957; children: Michael K., David L. AB, Washington U., St. Louis, 1956; PhD, Calif. Inst. Tech., 1962. With microbial genetics research unit Hammersmith Hosp., London, 1961-62; asst. prof. genetics U. Wis., Madison, 1962-66, assoc. prof., 1966-72, prof., 1972—2002, prof. emeritus, 2002—, chmn. lab. genetics, 1971-75, 77-86, assoc. dean med. sch., 1986-95, acting dean Sch. Allied Health Professions, 1988-90, vice dean med. sch., 1994-95, spl. advisor to the dean med. sch., 1995; dir. Ctr. for Biology Edn., Madison, 1996—2002. Phage course instr., Cold Spring Harbor, N.Y., 1965; v.p. scis., Wis. Acad. Scis., Arts and Letters, 2000—. Co-author: Life on Earth, 2d edit., 1978, Human Chromosomes: Structure, Behavior, Effects, 3d edit., 1992; contbr. articles to sci. jours. Mem Genetics Soc. Am., AAAS, Sigma Xi, Phi Beta Kappa, Phi Eta Sigma, Omicron Delta Kapp. Home: 2707 Colgate Rd Madison WI 53705-2234 Office: 2432 Genetics/Biotech Ctr Bldg Madison WI 53706 Office Phone: 608-263-5075. E-mail: msusman@wisc.edu.

**SUSMAN, MORTON LEE,** lawyer; b. Aug. 6, 1934; m. Nina Meyers, May 1, 1958; 1 child, Mark Lee. BBA, So. Meth. U., 1956, JD, 1958. Bar: Tex. 1958, U.S. Dist. Ct. (so. dist.) Tex. 1961, U.S. Ct. Appeals (5th cir.) 1961, U.S. Supreme Ct. 1961, U.S. Ct. Appeals (11th cir.) 1981, DC 1988, U.S Ct. Appeals (DC cir.) 1980, N.Y. 1990, Colo. 1996. Asst. U.S. atty., Houston, 1961-64; 1st asst. U.S. atty., 1965-66; U.S. atty., 1966-69; ptnr. Weil, Gotshal & Manges and predecessor firm Susman & Kessler, Houston, 1969-97; ret., 1998. Lt. USNR, 1958—61. Fellow: Am. Coll. Trial Lawyers, Tex. Bar Found.; mem.: FBA (dir., Younger Fed. Lawyer award 1968), ABA, Tex. Bar Assn. Democrat.

**SUSMAN, STEPHEN DAILY,** lawyer; b. Houston, Jan. 20, 1941; m. Ellen Spencer, 1999; children: Stacy, Harry. BA magna cum laude, Yale U., 1962; LL.B. with highest honors, U. Tex., 1965. Bar: US Supreme Ct. 1970, Tex. 1965, DC 1999, NY 2000, Colo. 2002. Law clk. to Hon. John R. Brown US Ct. Appeals (5th cir.), New Orleans, 1965-66; law clk. to Justice Hugo L. Black USSupreme Ct., Washington, 1966-67; ptnr. Fulbright & Jaworski LLP, Houston, 1966-75; spl. counsel to atty. gen. Mandell & Wright, PC, Houston, 1975-80; founding ptnr. Susman Godfrey LLP, Houston, 1980—. Vis. prof. law U. Tex., Austin, 1975; chmn. adv. com. on discovery Tex. Supreme Ct. Contbr. articles to profl. jours. Bd. dirs. Contemporary Arts Mus., 1988-94, 1998-2004, Yale Art Gallery, 1998—, Yale Devel. Fund, Southwest Legal Found., Inns of Ct., Houston Grand Opera, 1998—, Phoenix House, 1998-2001, Lawyers Com. for Civil Rights, 1997-, Human Rights First, 1998—, ADL, 1999-; mem. U.S. Holocaust Meml. Coun., 2000-2002 (devel. comm.), Million Dollar Advocates Forum, (life), 2000—, others. Recipient ADL Jurisprudence award, 1995, Disting. Counselor award, State Bar Tex., 2005; named one of Top 10 Trial Lawyers in Am., Nat. Law Jour., yearly since 1998. Mem. ABA (antitrust sect., mem. coun. litigation sect., chmn. task force on fast track litigation), Houston Bar Assn., Dallas Bar Assn., DC Bar Assn., NY Bar Assn., Colo. Bar, State Bar Tex., Am. Law Inst., Assn. Trial Lawyers Am., Am. Bar Trial Advocates, Houston Bar Assn., Southwestern Legal Found. Rsch. Fellows, Yale Club (Houston, NYC), Houston Trial Lawyers Assn. (dir.), Tex. Assn. Civil Trial and Appellate Specialists (former pres., dir.), Order of the Coif, Finrs, Phi Delta Phi. Avocations: skiing, hiking. Office: Susman Godfrey LLP Ste 5100 1000 Louisiana St Houston TX 77002-5096 Business E-Mail: ssusman@susmangodfrey.com.

**SUSSBERG, MILTON JOEL,** marketing professional; b. New Rochelle, N.Y., Oct. 5, 1949; s. Darwin Ralph and Carol G Sussberg; m. Linda Aland, June 27, 1971; children: Matthew H, Jordan A. BBA with distinction, U. Wis., Madison, 1971; MBA, Columbia U., 1973. Car. mktg. & sales Pearl-Wick

Corp., Long Island City, N.Y., 1973-76; v.p. M. Ware Assocs., N.Y.C., 1976-79, Meteor/SKelly, Inc., Stamford, Conn., 1979-84; pres. Robot-Coupe Internat., Norwalk, Conn., 1984-86; CEO, founder Sussberg & Co., Inc., White Plains, N.Y., 1986—; owner Savannah (Ga.) Sand Gnats Baseball Club, 1991—2005. Adj. prof. mktg. Fordham U., Bronx, NY, 1996—99. Mem.: Trump Nat. Golf Club, Phi Kappa Phi. Avocations: golf, skiing. Office: Sussberg & Co Inc Ste 308W 701 Westchester Ave White Plains NY 10604

**SUSSE, SANDRA SLONE**, lawyer; b. Medford, Mass., June 1, 1943; d. James Robert and Georgie Coffin (Bradshaw) Slone; m. Peter Susse, May 10, 1969 (div. May 1993); 1 child, Toby. BA, U. Mass., 1981; JD, Vt. Law Sch., 1986. Bar: Mass. 1986, U.S. Dist. Ct. Mass. 1988, U.S. Ct. Appeals (1st cir.) 1995. Staff atty. Western Mass. Legal Svcs., Springfield, 1986—. Mem. ABA, Hampden County Bar Assn. Avocations: hiking, german literature, films, skating. Address: Western Mass Legal Serv 127 State St Fl 4 Springfield MA 01103-1905 Office Phone: 413-781-7826 ext. 124. Business E-Mail: ssusse@wmls.org.

**SUSSKIND, LAWRENCE ELLIOTT**, urban planner, educator, mediator; b. NYC, Jan. 12, 1947; s. David J. and Marjorie H. (Friedman) S.; m. Miriam Mason, June 8, 1968 (div. Dec. 1982); m. Leslie Webster Tuttle, Dec. 12, 1982; children: Noah Gates, Lily Webster. AB in Sociology, Columbia U., 1968; M.C.P., MIT, 1970, PhD in Urban Planning, 1973. Asst. prof. urban and environ. planning MIT, Cambridge, 1971-74, assoc. prof., 1974-82, prof., 1982-95, Ford prof., 1995—, head dept., 1978-82, dir. MIT-Harvard Pub. Disputes Program, 1980—; exec. dir. program on negotiation Harvard Law Sch., 1984-87, visiting prof. law, 2001—. Founder Consensus Bldg. Inst., 1993— Author: Paternalism, Conflict and Co-Production, 1983, Proposition 1 1/2; Its Impact on Massachusetts, 1983, Resolving Environmental Regulatory Disputes, 1983, Breaking the Impasse, 1987, Environmental Diplomacy, 1994, Reinventing Congress for the 21st Century, 1995, Dealing With an Angry Public, 1996, Consensus Building Handbook, 1999, Negotiating on Behalf of Others, 1999, Negotiating Environmental Agreements, 1999, Better Environmental Policy Studies, 2001, Transboundary Environmental Negotiation, 2002, Breaking Roberts's Rules, 2006; sr. editor, founder Environ. Impact Assessment Rev., 1980-96; mem. editl. bd. Negotiation Jour., 1984—. Recipient Disting. Planning Educator award, Assn. Collegiate Sch. Planning, 2005. Mem. Am. Inst. Cert. Planners, Assn. for Conflict Resolution. Jewish. Home: 32 Jericho Hill Rd Southborough MA 01772-1007 Office: MIT 9-332 Cambridge MA 02139 Office Phone: 617-492-1414. Business E-Mail: susskind@mit.edu.

**SUSSKIND, LEONARD**, physicist, educator; BS, CCNY, 1962; PhD, Cornell U., 1965. NSF postdoc. fellow Cornell U., Ithaca, NY, 1965-66; from asst. to prof. Physics Belfer Grad. Sch. Sci. Yeshiva U., NYC, 1966-79; Felix Bloch prof. Physics Stanford U., Stanford, Calif., 1979—. Visiting prof. Physics U. Tel Aviv 1971-72. Co-author (with James Lindesay): An Introduction To Black Holes, Information And The String Theory Revolution, 2004; author: The Cosmic Landscape: String Theory and the Illusion of Intelligent Design, 2005. Recipient Pregel award 1975, J.J. Sakurai prize 1997; Loeb lectr. Harvard U. 1976. Mem. AAAS, Nat. Acad. Sci. Achievements include being credited as the father of String Theory; co-inventor, Holographic Principle. Office: Dept Physics Varian Bldg Rm 108 Stanford Univ Stanford CA 94305-4060*

**SUSSKIND, TERESA GABRIEL**, publishing executive; came to U.S., 1945; d. Aaron and Betty (Fox) Gabriel; m. Charles Susskind, May 1, 1945; children: Pamela Pettler, Peter Gabriel, Amanda. Student, U. London, 1938-40. Profl. libr. Calif. Inst. Tech., Pasadena, 1946-48, Yale U., New Haven, 1948-51, Stanford (Calif.) U., 1951-52, SRI Internat., Menlo Park, Calif., 1953; founder, pres. San Francisco Press, Inc., 1959—. Active in cultural affairs; bd. govs. San Francisco Symphony, 1986-89. With Women's Royal Naval Svc., 1943-45. With Women's Royal Naval Svc., 1943—45. Mem. Town and Gown Club (Berkeley, Calif.; pres. 1984-85). Office: 660 Spruce St Berkeley CA 94707-1730

**SUSSMAN, ALEXANDER RALPH**, lawyer; b. Bronx, NY, Sept. 24, 1946; s. Herman R. and Claire (Blumenson) S.; m. Edna Rubin, Mar. 24, 1973; children: Jason, Carl, Matthew, Eric. AB cum laude, Princeton U., 1968; JD, Yale U., 1972. Bar: N.Y. 1973, U.S. Dist. Ct. (so. and ea. dists) N.Y. 1974, U.S. Ct. Appeals (1st, 2d, 3d, 5th, 6th, 8th, 10th, and 11th cirs.) 1983, U.S. Supreme Ct. Law clk. to Hon. Constance Baker Motley U.S. Dist. Ct., N.Y.C., 1972-73; assoc. Cravath, Swaine & Moore, N.Y.C., 1974-76, Fried, Frank, Harris, Shriver & Jacobson, N.Y.C., 1977-79, ptnr., 1979—. Author: (with A. Fleischer, Jr.) Responses to Takeover Bids, 2004, Takeover Defense, 2 vols., 2004; editor Yale Law Jour., 1971-72. Bd. dirs. N.Y. Lawyers for Pub. Interest, 1983—; bd. dirs., mem. exec. com. Legal Aid Soc., 1987-93. Fulbright scholar U. Bordeaux, 1969. Mem. ABA, Am. Law Inst., N.Y. State Bar Assn., Assn. of Bar of City of N.Y. (fed. cts. com. 1984-87, jud. com. 1987-90, chmn. legal assistance com. 1988-91, Marden lectr. com. 1991-94, chmn. mergers and acquisitions com. 1995-99). Home: 20 Oak Ln Scarsdale NY 10583-1627 Office: Fried Frank Harris Shriver & Jacobson 1 New York Plz Fl 25 New York NY 10004-1980 E-Mail: Alex.Sussman@ffhsj.com.

**SUSSMAN, BARRY**, writer, demographer, editor; b. N.Y.C., July 10, 1934; s. Samuel and Esther (Rosen) S.; m. Peggy Earhart, Jan. 20, 1962; children: Seena, Shari. BA, Bklyn. Coll., 1956. Reporter Herald Courier, Bristol, Va., 1960-62, mng. editor, 1962-65; editor Washington Post, 1965-69, city editor, 1970-73, spl. Watergate editor, 1972-74, pollster, pub. opinion analyst, 1975-87; co-founder, co-dir. Washington Post-ABC News poll, 1981-87; columnist Washington Post Nat. Weekly, 1983-87; mng. editor nat. affairs UPI, Washington, 1987; ind. pub. opinion analyst and pollster, 1988—. Adv. bd. Innovation news media cons. group, 1994—; editor Watchdog Project of the Nieman Found. for Journalism at Harvard U., 2003—. Author: The Great Coverup: Nixon and the Scandal of Watergate, 1974, What Americans Really Think, 1988, (with Lowell P. Weicker, Jr.) Maverick, 1995; editor: (with J.A. Giner) Innovations in Newspapers: The 1999 Global Report, 1999, The 2000 Global Report, 2000, The 2001 Global Report, 2001, 02, 03, 04. Recipient Drew Pearson award for Nat. Reporting, 1972, 1st Prize award Washington Newspaper Guild, 1973, Editor of Yr. award Washington Newspaper Guild, 1973. Mem. Am. Assn. for Pub. Opinion Rsch. (exec. coun. 1985-87), Am. Soc. Newspaper Editors. Jewish. Avocation: chess. Personal E-Mail: bsussman@his.com. Business E-Mail: bsussman@niemanwatchdog.org.

**SUSSMAN, DEBORAH EVELYN**, interior designer, small business owner; b. NYC, May 26, 1931; d. Irving and Ruth (Golomb) S.; m. Paul Prejza, June 28, 1972. Student, Bard Coll., 1948-50, DHL (hon.), 1998; student, Inst. Design, Chgo., 1950-53, Black Mountain Coll., 1950, Hochschule für Gestaltung Ulm, Germany, 1957-58. Art dir. Office of Charles and Ray Eames, Venice, Calif., 1953-57, 61-67; graphic designer Galeries Lafayette, Paris, 1959-60; prin. Deborah Sussman and Co., Santa Monica, Calif., 1968-80; founder, pres. Sussman-Prejza and Co., Inc., Santa Monica, Calif., 1980-90, Culver City, Calif., 1990—. Spkr., lectr. UCLA Sch. Arch., Archtl. League N.Y.C., Smithsonian Inst., Stanford Conf. on Design, Am. Inst. Graphic Arts Nat. Conf. at MIT, Design Mgmt. Inst. Conf., Mass.; spl. guest Internat. Design Conf., Aspen, Colo.; Fulbright lectr., India, 1976; spkr. NEA Adv. Coun., 1985, Internat. Coun. Shopping Ctrs., 1986, USIA Design in Am. seminar, Budapest, Hungary, 1988. One-woman shows include Visual Arts Mus. Sch. Visual Arts, N.Y.C., 1995; participant exhbn., Moscow, 1989, Walker Art Ctr., Mpls., 1989; mem. editl. adv. bd. Arts and Arch. Mag., 1981-85, Calif. Mag.; Arch. Calif. Fulbright grantee Hochschule für Gestaltung Ulm, 1957-58; recipient award AIA Nat. Inst. Honors, 1985, 88, Am. Inst. Graphic Arts, Calif. Coun. AIA, Comms. Arts Soc., LA County Bd. Suprs., Vesta award Women's Bldg. LA, Golden Arrow award Soc. Environ. Graphic Designers, 2006. Fellow Soc. Environ. Graphic Design; mem. AIA (hon., Medal for XXIII Olympiad 2004), Am. Inst. Graphic Arts (bd. dirs. 1982-85, founder LA chpt., chmn. 1983-84, Legacy medal 2004), Am. Ctr. Design (hon.), LA Art Dirs. Club (bd. dirs., award), Alliance Graphique Internat., Archs., Designers, and Planners Social Responsibility, Calif. Women in Environ. Design (adv. d.), Trusteeship (affiliate Internat. Women's

Forum, chmn.'s cir. Town Hall). Democrat. Jewish. Avocation: photography. Office: Sussman/Prejza & Co Inc 3525 Eastham Dr Culver City CA 90232 E-mail: dsussman@sussmanprejza.com.

**SUSSMAN, GERALD**, publishing company executive; b. Balt., Feb. 21, 1934; s. Hyman Jacob and Sylvia (Applebaum) S.; m. Arla Ilene Ellison, Aug. 25, 1963; children: Daniel Leonard and Louis. BA, U. Md., 1956. Co-founder, prin. Investors Service of Md., Balt., 1956-60; cabl. traveller Oxford U. Press, Inc., N.Y.C., 1961-62, coll. sales mgr., 1962-69, gen. sales mgr., 1970-73, v.p., dir. mktg., 1974-79, sr. v.p., dir. mktg., 1979-83, sr. v.p., dir. adminstrn. and planning, 1983—97; project mgr. Guide to the Sandia Mountains. V.p. Friends of Sandai Mountains. Mem. Assn. Am. Pubs. (chmn. mktg. com.), Assn. Am. Univ. Presses (chmn. mktg. com. 1980-81), Pubs. Advt. Club, Phi Alpha Theta. Home: 10424 City Lights Dr NE Albuquerque NM 87111-7536 Office: Oxford U Press Inc 198 Madison Ave Fl 9 New York NY 10016-4341 Personal E-mail: agsuss@comcast.net.

**SUSSMAN, HOWARD SIVIN**, lawyer; b. NYC, Feb. 12, 1938; s. Joseph and Dora (Sivin) S. AB cum laude, Princeton U., 1958; LLB, Columbia U., 1962. Bar: N.Y. 1964, U.S. Dist. Ct. (so. and ea. dists.) N.Y. 1967, U.S. Ct. Appeals (2d cir.) 1967, U.S. Tax Ct. 1969, U.S. Dist. Ct. (no. dist.) N.Y. 1970, U.S. Supreme Ct. 1970, U.S. Ct. Appeals (5th cir.) 1982. Assoc. Chadbourne, Parke, Whiteside & Wolff, N.Y.C., 1963-71; asst. U.S. atty. So. Dist. N.Y., 1971-77; assoc. prof. law U. Houston, 1977-82; of counsel Wood, Lucksinger & Epstein, Houston, 1982-83; pvt. practice, N.Y.C., 1983-94; ptnr. Sussman Sollis Ebin Tweedy & Wood, LLP, N.Y.C., 1995—. Instr. continuing legal edn. U. Houston, Nat. Inst. for Trial Advocacy; 1985-89, Stockholm, 2003-. Editor Columbia U. Law Rev., 1960-62; contbr. articles to profl. jours. Harlan Fiske Stone scholar, 1959-61, Edvard Cassels Stiftelse vis. scholar, Stockholm, 1962-63; travelling fellow Parker Sch. Fgn. and Comparative Law Columbia U., 1962-63. Mem. assn. Bar City N.Y (com. adminstrv. law 1974-76, profl. conf. 1979, com. fed. legis. 1984-87, com. criminal law 1987-90, com. lectr. and continuing edn. 1990-93, com. fgn. and comparative law 1993-96, arbitration com. 2002-2003), Fed. Bar Coun., Swedish Am. C. of C. (dir. N.Y. chpt. 1996—). Clubs: Princeton N.Y. Office: 212-688-7373. Business E-Mail: howard.sussman@ssetw.com.

**SUSSMAN, JANET I.**, social sciences educator; b. N.Y.C., Sept. 24, 1952; d. Joseph I. and Selma H. Sussman. BA, Douglas Coll., 1974. Pub. Harcourt Brace, N.Y.C., 1974—76, Van Nostrand Reinhold, 1975—77, Sky & Telescope Mag., Cambridge, Mass., 1977—80, Wholistic Edn. & Svcs., Inc., Charlotte, NC, 1984—90, No. Star Dimensions, Charlotte, 1986—; pub., cons. Time Portal Pubs., Fairfield, Iowa, 1993—. Author: Timeshift: The Experience of Dimensional Change, 1996; musician: (CD) Bridges, 2002; author: The Reality of Time, 2005. E-mail: timeport@lisco.com.

**SUSSMAN, JEFFREY BRUCE**, public relations and marketing executive; b. NYC, Mar. 15, 1943; m. Suzy Hirschland-Prudden, 1964 (div. 1981); 1 child, Robert; m. Barbara Ramsay, 1984. BA in English, NYU, 1969. Pres. Suzy Prudden Studios, N.Y.C., 1975—81; v.p. Zachary and Front, N.Y.C., 1981—88; pres. Jeffrey Sussman, Inc., N.Y.C., 1988—, Sweet Silver Prodns., 2005—. Instr. mktg. The New Sch. U., N.Y.C. Author: Creative Fitness for Baby and Child, 1972, Suzy Prudden's Family Fitness Book, 1975, Fit for Life, 1977, See How They Run, 1978, Suzy Prudden's Spot Reducing Program, 1979, Suzy Prudden's Pregnancy and Back-To-Shape Exercise Program, 1980, I Can Exercise Anywhere, 1981, How to Sleep Without Drugs, 1986, Power Promoting: How to Market Your Business to the Top!, 1997; book rev. editor The Manhattan Tribune, 1969-75; contbr. book revs. to N.Y. Times Book Rev., 1974; bi-monthly columnist Weight Watchers Mag., 1977-79; monthly columnist Fortune Small Business, 2000—; contbr. articles to profl. jours. including Bottom Line Bus., Independent Bus., Small Bus. Report, N.Y. Real Estate Jour., East Hampton Star, M World mag. Press sec. N.Y.C. Coun.-Henry Stern, 1981; pvt. sec. to Nobel prize winning author Isaac Bashevis Singer. Avocations: photography, writing, music, painting, drawing. Home and Office: 249 E 48th St New York NY 10017-1526 Office Phone: 212-421-4475. Personal E-mail: marketingpro@aol.com.

**SUSSMAN, JOSEPH**, engineering educator, researcher; BCE, City Coll. NY; MSCE, U. N.H.; PhD, Mass. Inst. Tech. Dir. ctr. transp. and logistics Mass. Inst. Tech., Cambridge, Mass., 1986—91, JR East prof. civil and environ. engring. and engring. systems. Author: (book) Introduction to Transportation Systems, 2000. Named in honor Joseph M. Sussman Leadership award, Intelligent Trasp. Systems, 2002; recipient award, Coun. Univ. Transp. Ctrs., 2003, Roy W. Crum award, Transp. Rsch. Bd., 2001. Achievements include development of new methodology for regional strategic transportation planning, ReS/SITE (Regional Strategies for the Sustainable Intermodal Transportation Enterprise); Complex, Large-Scale, Integrated, Open Systems (CLIOS) process; worked extensively on intelligent transportation systems in the U.S., Bangkok, Western Europe and Japan. Office: Mass Inst Tech 77 Massachusetts Ave Bldg 1-163 Cambridge MA 02139-4307 Office Phone: 317-253-4430. Business E-mail: sussman@mit.edu.

**SUSSMAN, LAUREEN GLICKLIN**, elementary school educator; b. NYC, Mar. 21, 1953; d. Harry and Ruth (Goldstein) G.; m. Alan Neil Sussman, May 30, 1977; children: David Efrem, Adam Jacob, Daniel Joshua. BA in English, Bklyn. Coll., 1974; MS, MSc, Hofstra U., 1998. Cert. tchr. nursery-6, spl. edn. tchr. all grades. Sec. McCann-Erickson, Inc., N.Y.C., 1974-75; adminstrv. asst., tour operator EasTours divsn. Fgn. Tours, N.Y.C., 1975-78; adminstrv. asst. Alan N. Sussman, CPA, Woodmere, NY, 1978-96; kindergarten tchr. Hebrew Acad. Long Beach (N.Y.), 1996-97; jr. HS tchr. Torah Acad. Girls, Far Rockaway, NY, 1997—. Participant Instrumental Enrichment/IRI Skylight, N.Y., 1995, 98, Dynamic Assessment project Touro Coll., N.Y.C., 1996; CSE parent rep., adv. Lawrence (N.Y.) Pub. Schs., 1992-97; trainer Life Tech., Cedarhurst, N.Y., 2004—05. Contbr. articles to profl. jours. Mem. Spl. Edn. PTA Lawrence Schs., 1986-2003, Sisterhood Congregation Bais Tefilah, 1990-2003; mem. Sisterhood East Meadow Jewish Ctr., chair social action, Israel affairs, 1979-81; mem. adv. bd. Kulanu of the South Shore of Nassau County, 2000—; mem. Sisterhood Kehillah Aish Kodesh, Emunah of Am. Mem.: AMIT Women (Masada chpt.), OTSAR (founder Nassau County chpt. 1987—; nat. bd. dirs., pres. Nassau chpt. 1987—2002). Democrat. Avocations: Israeli and simcha dancing, walking, reading, needlepoint. Office: Torah Acad Girls 444 Beach 6 St Far Rockaway NY 11691 Personal E-mail: lauglick@aol.com.

**SUSSMAN, LEONARD RICHARD**, foundation executive; b. NYC, Nov. 26, 1920; s. Jacob and Carrie (Marks) S.; m. Frances Rukeyser, May 9, 1942 (div. 1958); m. Marianne Rita Gutmann, May 28, 1958; children: Lynne, David William, Mark Jacob. AB, NYU, 1940; MS in Journalism, Columbia U., 1941. Copy editor N.Y. Morning Telegraph, news editor radio sta. WQXR, 1941; cable editor San Juan (P.R.) World Jour., also corr. Business Week mag., 1941-42; editor fgn. broadcast intelligence svc. FCC, 1942; press sec. to Gov. of P.R., 1942-43; dir. info. in N.Y. for Govt. of P.R., 1946-49; regional dir., then nat. exec. dir. Am. Coun. Judaism, 1949-66; cons. pub. affairs cons. Nationwide Ins. Cos. (and indsl. subs.), 1955-57; mem. editorial com. Coun. Liberal Chs., 1956-59; exec. dir. Freedom House, 1967-88, 96, sr. scholar in internat. communications, 1988—; evaluator Fulbright Program Bd. Fgn. Scholarships, 1990-92; exec. dir. Willkie Meml., 1970-88. Adj. prof. journalism and mass comm. NYU, N.Y.C., 1990-99; adj. prof. Sch. for Internat. and Pub. Affairs, Columbia U., 2000-01; organizer, dir. Freedom House/Books USA, 1968-85; editor Freedom at Issue, bimonthly, 1970-81; mem. U.S. Dels. to Conf. World Communicaiton Yr./83, 1982-83; organizer acad. confs.; participant Internat. Coun. on Press Freedom, Venice, Italy, 1976, 77, Cairo, 1978, Talloires, 1981, 83, San Jose, Costa Rica, Johannnesburg, and Santiago Chile, 1987, others; panel competition in space Congl. Office Tech. Assessment, 1982-83. Author: American Press-Under Siege?, 1973, Mass News Media and The Third World Challenge, 1977, Glossary for International Communications: Warning of a Bloodless Dialect, 1983, Spanish version, 1987, Power, The Press and the Technology of Freedom: The Coming of Age of ISDN, 1990, The Culture of Freedom: The Small World of Fulbright Scholars, 1992, Good News Bad News, 1994, Can A Free Press Be

Responsible? To Whom?, 1995, The Press: Pressed and Oppressed, 1995, The Journalist as Pariah: Press Freedom, 1996, The Global Airscape, 1996, Democracy, Yes; Press Freedom, Maybe, 1997, Press Law Epidemic: Press Freedom, 1997, Global Warning: Press Controls Fuel the Asian Debacle, 1998, The News of the Century, 1999, Censor Dot Gov: The Internet and Press Freedom, 2000, Press Freedom in Our Genes, A Human Need, 2001, How Free? The Web and the Press, 2001, Democracy's Advocate: The Story of Freedom House, 2002, The Press at War: Marksman and Target, 2002, repub. in Freedom and Responsibility Yearbook, 2001-2002, A Global Survey of Media Independence, 2003, A Passion for Freedom: My Encounters with Extraordinary People, 2004, Historic Aspects of Freedom of the Press and New World Information and Communication in the Encyclopedia of International Media and Communications, 2003, The Unesco Withdrawal Syndrome: Shoot The UN in Americans for UNESCO, 2005; editor: Three Years at the East-West Divide, 1983, Today's American: How Free?, 1986; contbr. sects. to books, articles to profl. jours. and newspapers; project dir.: Big Story-How the American Press and Television Reported and Interpreted the Crisis of Tet-1968 in Vietnam and Washington, 1977; editor: textbook series, also quar. mag. Issues, 1953-66; mem. editl. bd. Polit. Comm. and Persuasion. Trustee Internat. Coun. on Future of Univ., 1973-84; bd. dirs. World Press Freedom Com., 1977—; chmn. Friends of Survey Mag. Charitable Trust, London, 1978-92; mem. U.S. Nat. Commn. for UNESCO, 1979-85, vice chmn., 1983-85; mem. U.S. dels. to internat. conf. on space, African Aid, UNESCO, London Info. Forum; mem. Internat. Freedom of Expression Exch., 1995-2003, mem. coun., 1997-99. 2001-2002. Decorated Legion of Merit; recipient Ann. First Amendment award N.Y. br. Soc. Profl. Journalists, 1988. Mem. Internat. Inst. Comm., Internat. Press Inst., Internat. Assn. Mass Comm. Rsch., Century Club. Home: 215 E 73d St New York NY 10021-3653 Office: 120 Wall St Fl 26 New York NY 10005-3904 Business E-Mail: sussman@freedomhouse.org.

**SUSSMAN, MONICA HILTON**, lawyer; b. NYC, Apr. 2, 1952; BA cum laude, Syracuse U., 1973; JD, Hofstra U., 1977. Bar: Va. 1977, DC 1978. Legis. coun. NY State Gov's. Office, Washington, 1977-79; spl. asst. to under sec. US Dept. HUD, Washington, 1979-80; br. chief office State Agy. and Bond Fin. programs, 1980-82, office gen. counsel, 1982-83, also bd. dirs., 1988-95, v.p., 1989-93, treas. Nat. Housing Conf., 1990-93, pres. Nat. Housing Conf., 1997—2000, also programs and regulations dep. gen. counsel; ptnr. McDermott, Will & Emery, Washington, Peabody & Brown, Washington, 1996-99, Nixon Peabody LLP, Washington, 1999—. Mem.: ABA, Mortgage Bankers Assn., Nat Leased Housing Assn., Va. State Bar, DC Bar Assn. Office: Nixon Peabody LLP 401 9th St NW Ste 900 Washington DC 20004 Office Fax: 202-585-8080. E-mail: msussman@nixonpeabody.com.

**SUSSMANE, JEFFREY BRETT**, pediatrician; BS in Chemistry, U. Miami, 1977; MD, St. Georges U., 1982; MBA, U. Miami, 2000. Pediat. residency Miami (Fla.) Children's Hosp.; pediat. critical care fellowship Children's Hosp., Pittsburgh, Pa.; pediat. pulmonary fellowship Hahnemann, Pa.; pediat. intensivist Miami (Fla.) Children's Hosp., 1988—, dir. ECLS (Extracorporel Life Support), 1988—. Mem. med. bd. Miami Childrens Hosp.; mem. Miami Childrens Hosp.-PHO. Bd. dirs. Deering Bay Estates, Miami. Grantee, Miami Childrens Hosp. Found., 1995, 1999, 2002. Fellow: SCCM (diplomate), ACCP (diplomate), AAP (diplomate 2000—02); mem.: Fla. Assn. Pediat. CCM (Critical Care Medicine) (pres. 1997—2002). Office: Divsn Critical Care Medicine Miami Childrens Hosp Miami FL 33155

**SUSSNA, EDWARD**, economist, educator; b. Phila., Nov. 26, 1926; s. Louis and Manya (Prytzycka) Sussna; m. Sylvia Fishman, Mar. 8, 1953; children: Audrey Francine, Ellen Sondra. BA, Bklyn. Coll., 1950; MA, U. Ill., 1952, PhD, 1954. Instr. U. Ill., 1952-54; asst. prof. Lehigh U., 1956-57; prof. bus. adminstrn. and econs. U. Pitts., 1957—; dir. ctr. for exec. edn. Grad. Sch. Bus., acad. dir. mgmt. program for execs. Center for Econ. Edn., Grad. Sch. Bus., acad. dir. mgmt. program in Hong Kong and Peoples Republic China, spring 1989, 95; inaugural prof. MBA program Bratislava Sch. Econs., Slovakia, 1996. Vis. Fulbright prof. U. Tehran, Iran, adviser, 1972—73; cons. Bur. Budget, HEW, Dept. Transp., UN Indsl. Devel. Orgn., Bell Tel. Co., Alcoa, Westinghouse Corp., NSF, Pitts. Nat. Bank, Japanese Regional Bankers Assn., others; vis. prof. UCLA, 1970, Ecole Superieure des Scis. Economiques et Commerciales, Paris, 1976—77, U. E. Asia, Hong Kong, Macau, 1986; vis. scholar Internat. Inst. Mgmt., Berlin, 1982. Contbr. articles to profl. jours. With U.S. Mcht. Marine, 1944—47, with U.S. Army, 1954—56. Ford Found. Fellowship Vis. prof., Harvard, 1960—61, Ford Found. Fellowship Guest scholar, Brookings Instn., 1962—63. Mem.: Strategic Mgmt. Inst., Am. Fin. Assn., Am. Econ. Assn., Omicron Delta, Beta Gamma Sigma. Home: 1538 S Negley Ave Pittsburgh PA 15217-1420 Personal E-mail: sussna@katz.pitt.edu.

**SUSTAR, T. DAVID**, religious organization administrator; Pres. East Coast Bible Coll., Ch. of God, Charlotte, NC, 1996-99; evangelism and home missions dir. Western N.C. Ch. of God, Charlotte, 1999—2002; sr. pastor Easley Ch. God, Easley, SC, 2004—. Pentecostal. Home: 100 Muirfield Dr Easley SC 29642-2414 Office: PO Box 443 Easley SC 29641 Office Phone: 864-859-1631. Personal E-mail: tdsustar@bellsouth.net.

**SUTARDJA, SEHAT**, information technology executive; b. China; m. Weili Dai; 2 children. BSEE, U. Calif., Berkeley, MS in Elec. Engring. and Computer Sci., PhD in Elec. Engring. and Computer Sci., U. Calif., Berkeley. Mgr., prin. project engr. 8X8, Inc., 1989—95; co-founder Marvell Semiconductor Inc., chmn., pres., CEO, 1995—. Named one of 400 Richest Ams., Forbes mag., 2006. Office: Marvell Semiconductor Inc 5488 Marvell Ln Santa Clara CA 95054*

**SUTCLIFFE, RICK (RICHARD LEE SUTCLIFFE)**, professional baseball player; b. Independence, Mo., June 21, 1956; m. Robin Ross. Profl. baseball player Los Angeles Dodgers, 1976-81, Cleve. Indians, 1982-84, Chgo. Cubs, 1984—91, Balt. Orioles, 1992—93, St. Louis Cardinals, 1994; sportscaster, and baseball analyst ESPN, 2000—. Mem. Am. League All-Star Team, 1983, Nat. League All-Star Team, 1989; recipient Cy Young award Nat. League, 1984. Office: ESPN ESPN Plz 935 Middle St Bristol CT 06010*

**SUTCLIFFE, TAMI**, web page designer; m. David Sutcliffe, 1993. BA in English, Tex. Woman's U., 1997, M in Libr. and Info. Scis., 1998; M in Art History, Calif. State U., Dominguez Hills, 2004. Cert. county libr. grade I Tex. State Libr. and Archives Commn., 1999. Instrnl. designer U. North Tex., Denton, 2004—; bibliographic instrn. specialist Collin County C.C., McKinney, Tex.; knowledge mgmt. analyst Verizon - Strategy, Planning and Metrics, Irving, Tex.; rschr./tech. writer Alcatel, Plano, Tex.; libr. dir. S.W. area KPMG, Dallas; web page designer Tex. Woman's U., Denton. Presenter in field. Office: Univ North Texas Information Sciences Building Room 205 Denton TX 76203-1068 Office Phone: 877-ASK-SLIS. Office Fax: 940-565-3101. Personal E-mail: tami.sutcliffe@gmail.com. Business E-Mail: tsutcliffe@lis.admin.unt.edu.

**SUTER, ROBERT EDUARD**, emergency physician, educator; b. Decatur, Ill., Aug. 29, 1961; s. Robert Koester and Erika Ilse Suter; children: Robert E Jr., Joseph E, Jennifer E. B. Washington U., 1982; M in Healthcare Adminstrn., Des Moines U., 1989, D of Osteopathy, 1988. Diplomate Am. Bd. Emergency Medicine. Chmn. emergency svcs. Eisenhower Army Med. Ctr., Ft. Stewart, Ga., 1993—95, Providence Hosp. and Med. Ctrs., Detroit, 1995—97; regional med. dir. Questeore Med. Svcs., Dallas, 1997—2001; chmn. emergency dept. Spring Br. Med. Ctr., Houston, 2001. Pres. Tex. Emergency Physicians; prof. Med. Coll. Ga.; bd. dirs. Am. Coll. Emergency Physicians. Bd. dirs. Nat. Emergency Medicine, Washington, 2003—05; bd. dirs. alumni assn. Des Moines U. Coll. Osteo. Medicine, Des Moines U., 1978—. Recipient Founders award, Continuing Edn. Coord. Bd. for EMS, 2004, Wackerle Founders award, Emergency Medicine Residents Assn., 1998, Alumnus of the Yr., Des Moines U., 2005. Fellow: Am. Coll. Osteopathic Emergency

Physicians, Am. Coll. Emergency Physicians (pres. bd. dirs. 2001—); mem.: Soc. for Academic Emergency Medicine. Cath. Mailing: P O Box 670785 Dallas TX 75367 Home: 5926 St Marks Cir Dallas TX 75230

**SUTER, TRACY A.,** finance educator; s. Jerry E. and Darlene C. (Weir) Suter; m. Kristen J. Lundquist; children: Camille H., Emma G. BBA, Wichita State U., Kans., 1989; MBA, U. Ark., Fayetteville, 1992, PhD, 1997. Asst. prof. mktg. U. So. Miss., Hattiesburg, 1998—2001, Okla. State U., Tulsa, 2001—. Dir. mktg. behavioral lab. Okla. State U., Stillwater, 2001—. Recipient President's Outstanding Faculty award, Okla. State U., Tulsa, 2005. Mem.: Am. Mktg. Assn. (dir. at large 2006), Soc. for Mktg. Advances (v.p., mem. services 2004—05). Office Phone: 918-594-8394.

**SUTERA, SALVATORE PHILIP,** mechanical engineer, educator; b. Balt., Jan. 12, 1933; s. Philip and Ann (D'Amico) S.; m. Celia Ann Fielden, June 21, 1958; children: Marie-Anne, Annette Nicole, Michelle Cecile. BS in Mech. Engring, Johns Hopkins, 1954; postgrad., U. Paris, 1955-56; MS, Calif. Inst. Tech., 1955; PhD, Cal. Inst. Tech., 1960; MA (hon.), Brown U., 1965. Asst. prof. mech. engring. Brown U., Providence, 1960-65, asso. prof., 1965-68, exec. officer div. engring., 1966-68; prof. dept. mech. engring. Washington U., St. Louis, 1968-97, chmn. dept., 1968-82, 86-97, Spencer T. Olin prof. engring. and applied sci., 1997—2003, prof. biomed. engring., 1997—2003, sr. prof., 2003—. Vis. prof. U. Paris VI, 1973. Assoc. editor: Jour. Biomech. Engring., 1993-97; mem. editorial bd. Circulation Rsch., 1975-82. Pres. St. Louis-Lyon Sister Cities, Inc., 2000—. Fulbright fellow Paris, 1955; recipient Nat. Marconi Sci. award UNICO, 1999. Fellow ASME, Am. Inst. of Med and Biol. Engring. (founding); mem. Biomed. Engring. Soc. (bd. dirs. 1997-2000), Internat. Soc. Biorheology, N.Am. Soc. Biorheology (pres.-elect 1986-89, pres. 1989-90), Am. Soc. Artificial Internal Organs, Am. Soc. Engring. Edn., AAAS (Lindbergh award St. Louis sect. 1988), AIAA, European Acad. Sci., Tau Beta Pi, Pi Tau Sigma. Republican. Roman Catholic. Achievements include research in fluid mechanics, heat transfer, blood flow, rheology of suspensions. Home: 830 S Meramec Ave Saint Louis MO 63105-2539 Business E-Mail: sps@wustl.edu.

**SUTHERLAND, ALAN ROY,** business educator; b. NYC, Jan. 15, 1944; s. Arthur Abbott and Margaret Louise (Schweitzer) S. BFA, Pratt Inst., Bklyn., 1964; MPA, NYU, 1969, PhD, 1984. Personnel dir. Manhattan Psychiat. Ctr., N.Y.C., 1966-72; dep. dir. Rockland Children's Psychiat. Ctr., Orangeburg, NY, 1972-74, L.I. Devel. Ctr., Melville, NY, 1974-78, dir., 1978-80; program dir. Vols. Am., N.Y.C., 1983-86; sr. staff officer Nat. Acad. Scis., Washington, 1986-88; dep. dir. U.S. Interagy. Coun. on Homeless, Washington, 1988-89; exec. dir. Travelers Aid Internat., Washington, 1989-91; AIDS Ctr. of Queens County, Rego Park, NY, 1992-96; chair dept. mgmt. studies Southeastern U., Washington, 1998-99. Prof. U. Md., College Park, 1998—. Editor: Homelessness, Health and Human Service Needs. Recipient citation N.Y.C. Coun., 1986, Stanley J. Drazak Excellence in Tchg. award U. Md., 2004. Mem. ASPA, World Futurist Soc. Lutheran. Avocation: weightlifting. Home: 1301 Delaware Ave SW #N-806 Washington DC 20024 Office: Univ of Maryland 3501 University Blvd E Adelphi MD 20783-7998

**SUTHERLAND, ANDREW C.,** actor, educator; b. Sacramento, Calif., July 3, 1965; MFA in Acting, So. Meth. U., Dallas, Tex., 1996. Cert. stage combat tchr. Dueling Arts Internat., 2006. Prof. U. So. Miss., Hattiesburg, 2000—03, Calif. State U., Turlock, 2003—. Shakespeare Festival founder and dir. Calif. State U., Turlock, 2005—. Actor: (various stage prodns.). Mem.: SAG, Equity, Aftra. Home: 4414 Bellevue Dr Turlock CA 95382 Office: Calif State Univ 801 W Monte Vista Ave Turlock CA 95382 Office Phone: 209-667-3455. Personal E-mail: asutherland@csustan.edu.

**SUTHERLAND, BETSY MIDDLETON,** biologist; m. John C. Sutherland, Aug. 28, 1965. BS, Emory U., 1964, MS, 1965; PhD, U. Tenn., 1967. Postdoctoral fellow Walter Reed Army Med. Ctr., Washington, 1967—69, U. Calif., Berkeley, 1969—72, asst. prof. Irvine, 1972—75, assoc. prof., 1975—77; sr. scientist Brookhaven Nat. Lab., Upton, NY, 1977—, head biology dept., radiobiology support group. Named to Alumni Hall of Fame, U. Tenn., Knoxville; recipient Outstanding Svc. to Sci. award, Suffolk County, NY, E. O. Lawrence award, U.S. Dept. Energy, 1985, Rsch. Career Devel. award, NIH; grad. fellow, Emory U., 1964—65, Oak Ridge Associated Universities, 1965—67. Achievements include patents in field. Office: Brookhaven Nat Lab Bldg 463 Biology 50 Bell Ave Upton NY 11973-5000 Office Phone: 631-344-3380.

**SUTHERLAND, DANIEL ELLYSON,** historian; b. Detroit, Mar. 5, 1946; s. Daniel E. Sutherland and Dorothy Nell Parrish; 1 child, Christopher M. BS, Wayne State U., Detroit, 1968, MA, 1973; PhD, Wayne State U., Detroit. Prof. history McNeese State U., Lake Charles, La., 1977—89, U. Ark., Fayetteville, 1989—. Bankhead lectr. U. Ala., 2003; Douglas Southall Freeman prof. U. Richmond, 2004; vis. fellow Wolfson Coll., U. Cambridge, 2005—06. Author: Confederate Carpetbaggers, 1988, Seasons of War, 1995, Guerrillas, Unionists and Violence on Confederate Home Front, 1999; contbr. articles to profl. jours. With USNR, 1968—70. Recipient Disting. Achievement award, U. Ark. Alumni Assn., 1999; rsch. grantee, NEH, 1978, 1988, 2000, Mellon Found., 1995. Mem.: Hist. Soc., Coll. Art Assn., So. Hist. Assn. Avocations: opera, gardening, hockey. Home: 1048 E Glenn Ln Fayetteville AR 72703 Office: Dept History Univ Ark Fayetteville AR 72701

**SUTHERLAND, DANIEL W.,** lawyer; b. 1961; BS, U. Louisville; JD, U. Va. Bar: 1985. Atty. office civil rights U.S. Dept. Edn., Washington, 1987—89; atty. civil rights divsn. U.S. Dept. Justice, Washington, 1989—2003; officer civil rights and civil liberties U.S. Dept. Homeland Security, Washington, 2003—. First exec. dir. Brown v. Bd. Edn. 50th Anniversary Comm. Co-author: (book) Religion In the Workplace, 1998. Office: US Dept Homeland Security 3801 Nebraska Ave Washington DC 20528

**SUTHERLAND, DEBORAH ALICE,** music educator; b. Des Moines, Aug. 6, 1951; d. Max Allen Sutherland and Dorothy Mathilda Kinne; m. Michael Charles Hulfactor, June 15, 1991. BMus Edn., Valparaiso U., 1973; postgrad., Drake U., 1976—79; MA Edn., Stanford U., 1985. Tchr. music Argos Cmty. Schs., Ind., 1973—74; various clerical Drake U., Des Moines, 1976—79; asst. libr., mgr. office, dir. student svcs., fin. administr. Stanford U., Calif., 1979—96; dir. music Bethany Luth. Ch., Menlo Park, Calif., 1994—. Instr. voice Drake U., Des Moines, 1976—79; soloist mezzo- soprano First United Meth. Ch., Des Moines, 1976—79; dir. choir and handbell choir various churches, Palo Alto, Calif., 1979—94. Named Outstanding Staff Mem., Stanford U. Sch. Edn., 1985; recipient Good Citizenship award, DAR Des Moines, 1969.

**SUTHERLAND, DONALD,** actor; b. St. John, N.B., Can., July 17, 1935; m. Lois Hardwick, 1959 (div. 1966); m.Shirley Douglas, 1966. (div. 1970); children: Kiefer, Rachel; m. Francine Racette, 1972; children: Roeg, Rossif, Angus. Grad., U. Toronto, 1958. Actor: London Acad. Music and Dramatic Art, Perth Repertory Theatre, Scotland, also Nottingham, Chesterfield, Bronley, Sheffield, (plays) The Spoon River Anthology, The Male Animal, The Tempest, August for People (London debut), On a Clear Day You Can See Canterbury, The Shewing Up a Balance Posnet, Enigma Variations, 2000, Ten Unknowns, 2001 (films) The World Ten Times Over, 1963, The Castle of the Living Dead, 1964, Dr. Terror's House of Horrors, 1965, Fanatic, 1965, The Bedford Incident, 1965, Promise Her Anything, 1966, The Dirty Dozen, 1967, Billion Dollar Brain, 1967, Oedipus the King, 1967, Sebastian, 1968, Interlude, 1968, Joanna, 1968, The Split, 1968, Start the Revolution Without Me, 1970, The Act of the Heart, 1970, M*A*S*H, 1970, Kelly's Heroes, 1970, Alex in Wonderland, 1970, Little Murders, 1971, Klute, 1971, Johnny Got His Gun, 1971, Lady Ice, 1973, Steelyard Blues, 1973, Don't Look Now, 1973, Alien Thunder, 1974, S*P*Y*S, 1974, The Day of the Locust, 1975, End of the Game, 1975, Fellini's Casanova, 1976, 1900, 1976, The Eagle Has Landed, 1976, The Kentucky Fried Chicken Movie, 1977, The Disappearance, 1977, Blood Relatives, 1978, Animal House, 1978, Invasion of the

Body Snatchers, 1978, The Great Train Robbery, 1979, Murder by Decree, 1979, Bear Island, 1979, A Man, A Woman and a Bank, 1979, North China Commune (voice), 1980, Nothing Personal, 1980, Ordinary People, 1980, Eye of the Needle, 1981, Gas, 1981, The Disappearance, Blood Relative, Threshold, 1981, Max Dugan Returns, 1983, Crackers, 1984, Heaven Help Us, 1985, Revolution, 1985, The Wolf at the Door, 1986, The Trouble with Spies, 1987, The Rosary Murders, 1987, Apprentice to Murder, 1988, Lock Up, 1989, Lost Angels, 1989, A Dry White Season, 1989, Bethune: The Making of a Hero, 1990, Buster's Bedroom, 1991, Backdraft, 1991, JFK, 1991, Eminent Domain, 1991, Cerro Torre: Schrei aus Stein, 1991, Buffy the Vampire Slayer, 1992, The Setting Sun, 1992, Shadow of the Wolf, 1992, The Railway Station Man, 1992, Younger and Younger, 1993, Six Degrees of Separation, 1993, The Shadow Catcher (voice), 1993, Red Hot, 1993, Benefit of the Doubt, 1993, Punch, 1994, The Puppet Masters, 1994, Disclosure, 1994, Outbreak, 1995, Bethune: The Making of a Hero, 1990, FTA, A Time to Kill, 1996, Hollow Point, 1996, The Shadow Conspiracy, 1997, The Assignment, 1997, Fallen, 1997, Without Limits, 1998, Free Money, 1998, Toscano, 1999, CSS Hunley, 1999, Virus, 1999, Instinct, 1999, Panic, 2000, Space Cowboys, 2000, The Art of War, 2000, Threads of Hope(voice), 2000, Final Fantasy: The Spirit Within(voice), 2001, Da wan, 2001, Five Moons Plaza, 2003, The Italian Job, 2003, Baltic Storm, 2003, Cold Mountain, 2003, Aurora Borealis, 2005, Fierce People, 2005, Pride & Prejudice, 2005, Lord of War, 2005, An American Haunting, 2006; (TV movies) Terry-Thomas, 1963, Marching to the Sea, Hamlet at Elsinore, 1964, The Death of Bessie Smith, 1965, The American Civil War, 1965, The Sunshine Patriot, 1968, Bethune, 1977, The Saint, The Avengers, Gideon's Way, The Champions, The Winter of Our Discontent, 1984, Ordeal By Innocence, 1984, Quicksand: No Escape, 1992, The Lifeforce Experiment, 1994, Oldest Living Confederate Widow Tells All, 1994, Citizen X, 1995 (Emmy award), Natural Enemy, 1997, Behind the Mask, 1999, The Hunley, 1999, The Big Heist, 2001, Uprising, 2001, Path to War, 2002, Salem's Lot, 2004, Frankenstein, 2004; (TV mini series) A Farewell to Arms, 1966; (TV series) Commander in Chief, 2005-06; guest appearance Suspense, 1963, Gideon's Way, 1966, The Saint, 1965, 1966, Man in a Suitcase, 1967, 1968, The Name of the Game, 1969, (voice) The Simpsons, 1996 and others; narrator The Poky Little Puppy's First Christmas, 1992; exec. prodr. Steelyard Blues, 1973. Decorated officer dans l'Ordre des Artes et des Lettres (France); officer Order of Can. Office: c/o Creative Artists Agy Katherine Olin 9830 Wilshire Blvd Beverly Hills CA 90212-1804*

**SUTHERLAND, DONALD WOOD,** cardiologist; b. Kansas City, Mo., July 29, 1932; s. Donald Redeker and Mary Frances (Wood) S.; m. Margaret Sutherland, Sept. 11, 1954 (div. 1994); children: Kathleen Massar, Ellen Baltus, Richard, Ann, Julia McMurchie; m. Roslyn Ruggiero Elms, Mar. 31, 1995. BA, Amherst Coll., 1953; MD, Harvard U., 1957. Intern, resident Mass. Gen. Hosp., Boston, 1957-60; fellow in cardiology U. Oreg., Portland, 1961-63; pvt. practice Portland, 1963—. Assoc. clin. prof. medicine Oreg. Health Sci. U., Portland, 1967—; chief of staff St. Vincent Hosp. and Med. Ctr., Portland, 1971-72. Contbr. articles to profl. jours. Fellow Am. Heart Assn., Am. Coll. Cardiology (pres. Oreg. chpt. 1972); mem. Multnomah Athletic Club, North Pacific Soc. Internal Medicine (pres. 1985), Pacific Interurban Clin. Club (pres. 2000). Avocations: flying, scuba diving. Home: 4405 SW Council Crest Dr Portland OR 97239 Office: Columbia Cardiology Assocs 9427 Barnes Rd Ste 498 Portland OR 97225-6629 Personal E-mail: dwscardio@comcast.net.

**SUTHERLAND, IVAN E.,** computer scientist; b. Hastings, Nebr., May 16, 1938; children: Juliet, Dean. BSEE, Carnegie Inst. Tech., 1959; MSEE, Calif. Inst. Tech., 1960; PhD in Elec. Engring., MIT, 1963; MA (hon.), Harvard U., 1966. Elec. engr., 1st lt. Nat. Security Agy., 1963; dir. office info. processing techniques Advance Rsch. Projects Agy., 1964-66; prof. elec. engring. Harvard U., 1966-68, U. Utah, Salt Lake City, 1968—73; co-founder Evans & Sutherland, 1968; rschr. Rand Corp., 1975; chmn. dept. computer sci. Calif. Inst. Tech., 1976—80; established, v.p. Tech. dir. Sutherland, Sproull, and Assocs., 1980; fellow, v.p. Sun Microsystems Lab., Menlo Park, Calif., 1990—. Honored guest spkr., elec. engring. computer sci. dept. U. Calif. Berkeley, 2006; spkr. in field. Contbr. articles to profl. publs. Recipient Smithsonian Price Waterhouse Info. Tech. Leadership award for Lifetime Achievement, Fellow award, Computer History Mus., 2005; co-recipient, R&D 100 award, 2004. Fellow Assn. Computing Machinery (A.M. Turing award 1988); mem. NAE (First Zworkin award 1972), NAS, IEEE (John von Neumann medal 1998). Achievements include pioneer in computer graphics; inventor of computer program, known as Sketchpad, and head-mounted three-dimensional display, an integral part of many virtual reality systems; several patents in field. Office: Sun Microsystems Lab 16 Network Cir umpk16-161 Menlo Park CA 94025

**SUTHERLAND, JOHN CAMPBELL,** pathologist, educator; b. Tamingfu, Hopei, People's Republic of China, Oct. 28, 1921; came to US, 1926; s. Francis Campbell and Ann Findlay (Bowman) S.; m. Eunice Lucille Kindschi, June 16, 1950; 1 child, John Mark. AB, N.W. Nazarene Coll., 1941; MD, Med. Coll. Wis., 1946. Intern Milw. Hosp., 1946-47; resident in pathology St. Francis Hosp., Wichita, Kans., 1950-52, Barnes Hosp., St. Louis, 1952-54, Stanford Med. Ctr., Calif., 1967-68; gen. practitioner Mangum Clinic, Nampa, Idaho, 1949-50; gen. med. officer Raleigh Fitkin Meml. Hosp., Manzini, Swaziland, 1955-56, Ethel Lucas Meml. Hosp., Acornhoek, South Africa, 1956-61, 62-67; acting head biology dept. N.W. Nazarene Coll., Nampa, 1961-62; head rsch. pathology dept. Balt. Cancer Rsch. Ctr., 1968-74; asst. prof. dept. pathology U. Md., Balt., 1974-76, assoc. prof., 1976-84; mem. grad. faculty, 1982-84; vis. assoc. prof. dept. surgery U. Ariz., Tucson, 1984 96; dep. med. examiner Midland County, Ariz., 1996 2000. Co-author: Guinea Pig Doctors, 1984, Behind the Silence, 1999; contbr. articles to sci. jours. Capt. USAF, 1947-49. Mem. Alumni Assn. of N.W. Nazarene Coll. (Profl. Achievement award 1984), Toastmasters, Gideons. Republican. Mem. Wesleyan Ch. Avocations: reading, bird watching, speaking. Address: PO Box 737 Atkinson NE 68713-0737 Home: 408 W Central Atkinson NE 68713-0737 E-mail: johsut@elkhorn.net.

**SUTHERLAND, KIEFER,** actor; b. London, Eng., Dec. 21, 1966; s. Donald and Shirley Douglas S.; m. Camelia Kath, Sept. 12, 1987 (div.1990); 1 child, Sarah Jude; m. Kelly Winn, June 29, 1996 (div.) Appearances include (theater) debut in Throne of Straw, 1977, (films) Max Dugan Returns, 1983, The Bay Boy, 1984 (Genie award nominee 1984), At Close Range, 1986, Crazy Moon, 1986, Stand By Me, 1986, The Lost Boys, 1987, The Killing Time, 1987, Promised Land, 1987, 1969, Bright Lights, Big City, 1988, Young Guns, 1988, Renegades, 1989, Chicago Joe and the Showgirl, 1990, Flashback, 1990, Flatliners, 1990, The Nutcracker Prince (voice), 1990, Young Guns II, 1990, Article 99, 1991, Twin Peaks: Fire Walk With Me, 1992, A Few Good Men, 1992, The Vanishing, 1993; The Three Musketeers, 1993, The Cowboy Way, 1994, Eye for an Eye, 1995, A Time to Kill, 1996, The Last Days of Frankie the Fly, 1996, Freeway, 1996, Truth or Consequences N.M, 1997, Dark City, 1997, Sweetheart of the Song Tra Bong, 1998, Ground Control, 1998, (voice) Dinosaur, 1998, The Breakup, 1998, Dark City, 1998, Woman Wanted, 1999, The Red Dove, 1999, Hearts and Bones, 1999, Beat, 2000, Picking Up the Pieces, 2000, Ring of Fire, 2000, The Royal Way, 2000, The Right Temptation, 2000, To End All Wars, 2001, Paradise Found, 2001, Desert Saints, 2002, Dead Heat, 2002, Behind the Red Door, 2002, Phone Booth, 2002, Taking Lives, 2004, Jiminy Glick in La La Wood, 2004, (voice) The Wild, 2006, The Sentinel, 2006; (TV movies) Trapped in Silence, 1986, Brotherhood of Justice, 1986, Last Light, 1993; (TV series) 24, 2001-(Best Performance by Actor in TV Series Drama Golden Globe award 2002, Best Performance by Actor in a Drama Series Golden Satellite award 2002, nominee Outstanding Lead Actor in Drama Series Emmy award 2002, Screen Actors Guild Award for best actor in a drama series, 2004, Screen Actors Guild Award for Outstanding Performance by a Male Actor in a Drama Series, 2006, Emmy Award for Outstanding Lead Actor in a Drama Series, 2006). Office: William Morris Agency attn: Steve Dontanville 151 El Camino Dr Beverly Hills CA 90212*

**SUTHERLAND, L(EWIS) FREDERICK,** food products executive; b. Charleston, W.Va., Jan. 1, 1952; s. Lewis Frederick and Dorothy Louise (Droddy) S.; m. Barbara Hall Hoover, Aug. 24, 1974; children— Matthew, Mark BS, Duke U.; MBA, U. Pitts. V.p Chase Mahattan Bank, N.Y.C.; asst. treas. Aramark Corp., Phila., 1980-83, treas., 1983-85, v.p., treas. 1985-87, v.p. corp. fin. and devel., 1987-91, sr. v.p., 1991-93, exec. v.p. and pres. Uniform Svcs. sector, 1993-96, exec. v.p., CFO, 1997—. Trustee WHYY, Phila.; bd. dirs. Consol. Edison. Trustee People's Light and Theatre Co. Named Treas. of Yr., Cash Flow mag., 1987. Office: Aramark Corp 1101 Market St Ste 45 Philadelphia PA 19107

**SUTHERLAND, MARION IDA,** music educator; b. Merrill, Wisc. d. Edwin August and Erna Martha Hackbarth; m. Robert D. Sutherland, Sept. 22, 1962. B in Music Edn., St. Louis Inst. of Music, 1954; M in Music, Eastman, 1956. Cert. music educator 1974. Music edn. St. Louis Inst. Music, Clayton, Mo., 1956—58; acting vocal music dir. Carleton Coll., Northfield, Minn., 1959—60; choral music dir. Concordia Coll., River Forest, Ill., 1960—61, Chippewa Falls Med. Sch., Wis., 1975—81; music educator St. Therese Sch., Rothschild, Wis., 1981—85, St. Paul's Sch., Bloomer, Wis., 1988—93; piano and voice educator Wausau Conservatory Music, Wis., 1982—2003; ret. Mem. libr. bd. St. Louis Inst. of Music, Clayton, 1956—58; cert. music adj. Wis. Music Festivals, 1982—2000, master music adj., 2000—. Author: (booklet) Life of P. Tschaikovsky, 1963. Full Yr. scholarship, Eastman, 1955—56. Mem.: Nat. Assn. of Tchrs. of Singing, Kiwanis Club (pianist 1948—50), Rotary Club (pianist 1945—50, Internat. Found. fellowship for European study 1958—59), Sigma Alpha Iota (life). Lutheran. Avocations: reading, walking, swimming, needlecrafts. Home: N3822 Hanke Rd Bryant WI 54418

**SUTHERLAND, PETER EDWARD,** electrical engineer; AS in Elec. Engring. Tech., U. Maine, 1979, BSEE with honors and highest distinction, 1983; MScE, U. N.B., Fredericton, Can., 1986; PhD Electric Power Engring., Reusselaer Polytechnic Inst., 2003. Registered profl. engr., Maine, N.Y., Pa.; radiotelephone lic. FCC. Test engr. Accutest Corp., Chelmsford, Mass., 1979-80, 82, design engr., 1983-84; planning engr. Maine Pub. Svc. Co., Presque Isle, 1983; grad. tchg. and rsch. asst. U. N.B., 1984-86; power sys. engr. GE Co., Schenectady, 1987-89, 93, lead tng. specialist, 1989-92, sr. engr., 1994—2001, Super Power Inc., Schenectady, 2001—03; cons. engr. EPRI Solutions, Inc., Schenectady, 2003—04; lead cons. G-E Energy, 2004—. Contbr. articles to profl. jours. Mem. IEEE (sr., chpt. chair Brown Book working group, chpt. co-chair Gray Book working group, power sys. protection com., London chartered engr.), IEE (London), Tau Beta Pi, Eta Kappa Nu, Phi Kappa Phi. Achievements include patents pending for; patents for power system instrumentation. Office: GE Energy 180 Rotterdam Indsl Pk Schenectady NY 12306 E-mail: peter.sutherland@ieee.org.

**SUTHERLAND, ROGER COLLIN,** civil engineer, consultant; b. Denver, Colo., Apr. 29, 1950; s. Ian Reid and Irene Frances Sutherland; m. Jill Kathleen Fries, Apr. 7, 1955; children: Colin James, Kyle Robert. BCE, Univ. Md., Coll. Pk., Md., 1972, MCE, 1975. Cert. profl. engr., Oreg., 1983. Engr. in tng. J.E. Griener Corp., Balt., 1972—73; water resources specialist Harza Engring., Chgo., 1975—77; water resources engr. CH2M Hill, Portland, Oreg., 1977—84; pvt. cons. self employed, Aloha, Oreg., 1984—86; dir. water resources engring. OTAK, Inc., Lake Oswego, Oreg., 1986—93; v.p. Kurahashi and Assoc. Inc., Tigard, Oreg., 1993—98; pres. owner Pacific Water Resources, Beaverton, Oreg., 1998—. Co-editor Stormwater Treatment N.W. Newsletter, Seattle, 1996—; lectr. & tnr. in field. Contbr. articles pub. to over 30 profl. jour. Mem.: Assn. of State Floodplain Mgrs., Water Environ. Fedn., Am. Pub. Works. Assn., Am. Water Resources Assn., Chi Epsilon. Democrat. Avocations: white-water rafting, golf, horse racing. Office Phone: 503-671-9709.

**SUTHERLAND, VANNA RAE,** psychiatrist; BS in Biology, Tulane U., 1992, MD, 1996. Resident in psychiatry U. Calif., San Francisco, 1996—2000; adult psychiatrist City and County of San Francisco, 2000—03; adult psychiatrist student health ctr. Hastings Coll. Law, San Francisco, 2000—06; pvt. practice San Francisco, 2000—05, San Mateo, Calif., 2005—. Mem.: No. Calif. Psychiat. Soc., Am. Psychiat. Assn. Office: 205 E Third Ave Ste 207 San Mateo CA 94401 Office Phone: 650-375-8077.

**SUTHERLAND, WILLIAM OWEN SHEPPARD,** retired language educator, consultant; b. Wilmington, NC, Jan. 19, 1921; s. William Owen Sheppard and Mary Owen (Green) S.; m. Madeline Ethel Cooley, Sept. 12, 1947; children: Madeline, William, John, Thomas. AB in English with honors, U. N.C., 1942, MA, 1947, PhD, 1950. Instr. English. U. N.C., Chapel Hill, 1950-51, Northwestern U., Evanston, Ill., 1951-54; asst. prof. U. Tex., Austin, 1954-58, assoc. prof., 1958-65, prof., 1965-98, Robert A.-Thomas H. Law Centennial prof. humanities emeritus, 1998—, chmn. dept., 1983-90, faculty humanist rep. Deans of Humanities of S.W. Conf., 1980; cons. Ednl. Testing Svc. and Coll. Bd., Princeton, NJ, 1965-72, NEH, Washington, 1971—; prof. emeritus U. Tex., 1998 yet, 1998. Author: Art of the Satirist, 1965; co-editor: The Reader, 1960, Six Contemporary Novels, 1961, An Index to 18th Century Periodicals, 1800, 1956. Served to capt. C.E. U.S. Army, 1942-45. Recipient Scarborough Excellence in Tchg. award U. Tex. Austin, 1959, Liberal Arts Pro Bene Meritis award, 1996, Pres. Assocs. Tchg. award, 1982; NEH grantee, 1978-79. Mem. MLA, South Central MLA (exec. com. 1967-69), AAUP (state v.p. 1970-71), Nat. Council Tchrs. English (dir. 1974-78) Democrat. Episcopalian. Home: 3610 Highland View Dr Austin TX 78731-4033 Office: U Tex Dept English Austin TX 78712 Business E-Mail: woss@mail.utexas.edu.

**SUTHERS, JOHN WILLIAM,** state attorney general, former prosecutor; b. Denver, Oct. 18, 1951; s. William Dupont and Marguerite A. (Ryan) S.; m. Janet Gill, May 21, 1976; children: Alison, Catherine. BA in Govt. magna cum laude, U. Notre Dame, 1974; JD, U. Colo., 1977. Bar: Colo. 1977, U.S. Dist. Ct. Colo. 1977, U.S. Ct. Appeals (10th cir.) 1979, U.S. Supreme Ct. 2003. Dep. dist. atty. 4th jud. dist. State of Colo., Colorado Springs, 1977-79, chief dep. dist. atty. 4th jud. dist., 1979-81, dist. atty. 4th jud. dist., 1989—97; assoc. Sparks, Dix, Enoch, Colorado Springs, 1981-82; ptnr. Sparks, Dix, Enoch, Suthers & Winslow, Colorado Springs, 1982-89; sr. counsel Sparks, Dix, Colorado Springs, 1997—99; exec. dir. Colo. Dept. Corrections, 1999—2001; US atty. dist. Colo. US Dept. Justice, 2001—05; atty. gen State of Colo., Denver, 2005—. Mem. adv. bd. Sec. of State, Denver, 1983—89; Colo. commr. Uniform State Laws, 1993—97. Author: Fraud and Deceit, 1982, How to Liquidate a Lemon, 1983. Pres., chmn. bd. dirs. Cmty. Corrections of Pikes Peak Region Inc., 1984—87; bd. dirs. Crimestoppers, Inc., Colorado Springs, 1985—88; mem. exec. com. Colo. Dist. Atty.'s Coun. 1992—97, pres., 1994—95, treas., 1993; El Paso County Rep. Ctrl. com. Colorado Springs, 1985—2001; Colo. State Rep. Ctrl. com., 1989—2001. Zimmerman Found. scholar, 1970-74. Mem. Colo. Bar Assn. (com. chmn.), El Paso County Bar Assn. (pres. 1990-91), Notre Dame Colorado Springs (pres. 1983-84). Republican. Roman Catholic. Avocations: baseball cards, golf. Office: Colo Dept Law 1525 Sherman St 5th Fl Denver CO 80203 Office Phone: 303-866-3557. Business E-Mail: john.suthers@state.co.us.

**SUTIN, ALAN N.,** lawyer; b. New Haven, Apr. 29, 1958; BA, Emory Univ., Atlanta, 1979; JD, Univ. Ga., 1984. Bar: Ga. 1984, NY 1985, US Ct. Appeals (DC cir.), US Dist. Ct. (so., ea. districts) NY. Shareholder, chair nat. tech. media, telecom. practice Greenberg Traurig LLP, NYC. Articles editor Ga. Journ. Internat. and Comparative Law; contbr. articles to profl. journals. Mem.: ABA, State Bar of Ga., NY State Bar Assn., Assn. Bar of NYC, Computer Law Assn. Office: Greenberg Traurig LLP MetLife Bldg 200 Park Ave New York NY 10166 Office Phone: 212-801-9286. Office Fax: 212-801-6400. Business E-Mail: sutina@gtlaw.com.

**SUTIN, NORMAN,** chemist, researcher; b. Ceres, Sept. 16, 1928; arrived in US, 1956, naturalized; s. Louis and Clara (Goldberg) S.; m. Bonita Sakowski, June 29, 1958; children: Lewis Anthony, Cara Ruth. B.Sc., U. Cape Town, S. Africa, 1948, M.Sc., 1950; PhD, Cambridge U., Eng., 1953. Research fellow

Durham U. (Eng.), 1954-55; research assoc. Brookhaven Nat. Lab., Upton, NY, 1956-57, assoc. chemist, 1958-61, chemist, 1961-66, sr. chemist, 1966—2001, dept. chmn., 1988-95; affiliate Rockefeller U., N.Y.C., 1958-62; vis. fellow Weizmann Inst., Rehovoth, Israel, 1965; vis. prof. SUNY-Stony Brook, 1968, Columbia U., N.Y.C., 1968-69, Tel Aviv U., Israel, 1973-74, U. Calif.-Irvine, 1977, U. Tex. Austin, 1979; disting. prof. Rutgers U., 1999—2001; ret., 2001. Editor: Comments on Inorganic Chemistry Jour., 1980-87; mem. editorial bd. Jour. Am. Chem. Soc., 1985-89, Inorganic Chem., 1986-89, Jour. Phys. Chem., 1987-92; contbr. articles to profl. jours. Mem. NAS, Am. Acad. Arts and Scis., Am. Chem. Soc. (recipient award for disting. svc. in advancement of inorganic chemistry 1983). Office: Brookhaven Nat Lab Dept Chemistry Upton NY 11973 Business E-Mail: sutin@bnl.gov.

**SUTMAN, FRANCIS XAVIER,** university dean; b. Newark, Dec. 20, 1927; s. Joseph L. and Ella (Joyce) S.; m. Mabel Ranagan, Apr. 1, 1956; children: Frank J., Catherine J., Elizabeth A. AB, Montclair State U., 1949, MA, 1952; EdD, Columbia U., 1956. Tchr. pub. secondary schs., NJ, 1949-55; instr. chemistry Upsala Coll., 1953-55; asst. prof. Wm. Paterson Coll., 1957-58; chmn., assoc. prof. natural scis. Inter-Am. U. P.R., 1957-58; prof. gen. edn., chmn. SUNY, Buffalo, 1958-62; prof. sci. edn., chmn. dept. secondary edn. dir. Merit Bilingual Center Temple U., Phila., 1962—98; dean Coll. Edn. Fairleigh Dickinson U., 1982-88. Tech. rsch. staff Exxon Engring. & Rsch. Lab., Linden, N.J., 1955; vis. lectr. Rutgers U.; cons. India AID Project; vis. prof., scientist Hebrew U., Israel; sr. scholar Temple U., 1988-2004, Morgan State U., 1999-2002, Richard Stockton Coll. N.J., 2004—; vis. sci. educator, program dir. edn. and human resources NSF, 1989-93; exec. dir. curriculum devel. coun., Rowan U., N.J.; sr. scholar U. Miami, 1995-2000; del. OAS Coun. Sci. Edn. and Culture, 1971; co-dir. Environ. Edn. Conf. Environ. Protection Svc., Jerusalem, 1975; cons. fed., state, local schs. dists.; dir. sci. tech. project Huazhong U., China, 1980-87; co-dir. chem. edn. conf. Tianjin Normal U., 1984. Author: Concepts in Chemistry, 1962, 2d edit., 1968, What Kind of Environment Will Our Children Have?, 1971, Chemistry in Today's Environment (U.S. and Israel), 1977, Educating Personnel for Bilingual Settings: Today and Beyond, 1979, Learning English Through Science, 1986, Improving Learning in Science and Basic Skills Among Diverse Student Populations, 1995, We Need a Better Understanding of Inquiry in Instruction, Harvard Edn. Letter, 2000, Practicing Student Inquiry/Discovery in Teaching Science: A Guidebook for Science and other Educators, 2006. Active Haddonfield (N.J.) Bd. Edn., 1976-79; v.p. alumni bd. Montclair State U., 1982-88; mem. chem. and tech. bd. Burlington County Coll., 1994—. Recipient Air Force Assn. award, 1968, N.J. Gov.'s Albert Einstein Edn. award, 1987, award Hispanic Congress of Pa., 1980, Alumni Citation Montclair State U., 1988. Fellow AAAS; mem. NSTA, Am. Chem. Soc., Am. Assn. Colls. Tchr. Edn. (chief instnl. rep. 1968-87), Nat. Assn. Rsch. Sci. Tchg. (pres.), N.J. Gov.'s Acad., Coun. Sci. Soc. Presidents, Sigma Xi, Phi Delta Kappa (pres. chpt. 2000-02). Home: 311 W Royal Ave Linwood NJ 08221-1458 Personal E-mail: fmsutman@msn.com. *Professional success comes when one accepts the paradoxes of human activity and accepts conflict and criticism, and gives of one's self for a worthy cause.*

**SUTNICK, ALTON IVAN,** medical educator, consultant, dean, internist, researcher; b. Trenton, NJ, July 6, 1928; s. Michael and Rose (Horwitz) S.; m. Mona Reidenberg, Aug. 17, 1958; children: Amy Sutnick Plotch, Gary Benjamin Sutnick. AB, U. Pa., 1950, MD, 1954; student in Biomed. Math., Drexel U., 1961—62; student in Biometrics, Temple U., 1969—70. Diplomate Am. Bd. Internal Medicine. Rotating intern Hosp. U. Pa., 1954—55, resident in anesthesiology, 1955—56, resident in medicine, 1956, USPHS postdoctoral research fellow, 1956—57; asst. instr. anesthesiology, then asst. instr. medicine U. Pa. Sch. Medicine, 1955—57; resident in medicine Wishard Meml. Hosp., Indpls., 1957—58, chief resident in medicine, 1960—61; resident instr. medicine Ind. U. Sch. Medicine, Indpls., 1957—58; USPHS postdoctoral research fellow Temple U. Hosp., 1961—63; instr., then assoc. in medicine Temple U. Sch. Medicine, 1962—65; mem. faculty U. Pa. Sch. Medicine, 1965—75, assoc. prof. medicine, 1971—75; clin. asst. physician Pa. Hosp., 1966—71; research physician, then assoc. dir. Inst. Cancer Research (now Fox Chase Cancer Ctr.), Phila., 1965—75; vis. prof. medicine Med. Coll. Pa., Phila., 1971—74; prof. medicine Drexel U. Coll. Medicine (formerly Med. Coll. Pa.), 1975—; dean Med. Coll. Pa., 1975—89, sr. v.p., 1976—89; v.p. Ednl. Commn. Fgn. Med. Grads, 1989—95; dir. internat. med. edn. Carelift Internat., 1997—2005. Dir. clin. devel. Am. Oncologic Hosp., Phila., 1973-75; attending physician Phila. VA Hosp., 1967-89, Allegheny U. Hosps., 1971-95; cons. in field; mem. U.S. nat. com. Internat. Union Against Cancer, 1969-72; mem. Nat. Conf. Cancer Prevention and Detection, 1973, Nat. Cancer Control Planning Conf., 1973; vice chmn. Gov. Pa. Task Force Cancer Control, 1974-76, chmn. com. cancer detection, 1974-76; mem. health rsch. adv. bd. Commonwealth of Pa., 1976-78; mem. diagnostic rsch. adv. group Nat. Cancer Inst., 1974-78; chmn. coord. com., comprehensive cancer ctr. program Fox Chase Cancer Ctr., U. Pa. Cancer Ctr., 1975; cons. WHO, Govt. of India, 1979, Govt. of Indonesia, 1980, entire S.E. Asia region, 1981, U. Zimbabwe, 1989, Minister of Health of Poland, 1992, Israel Sci. Coun., 1992, U. Autonoma de Guadalajara, Mex., 1993, Generalitat de Catalunya, Spain, 1993, Ministry of Health Russian Fedn., 1993; mem. Inst. de Pos-Graduacao Medica Carlos Chagas, 1993, Fondazione Smith Kline, Italy, 1995, Assn. Med. Schs. Europe, 1995-99, U. Jordan, 1995, U.S.-China Ednl. Inst., 1996, Georgian Postgrad. Med. Found., 1996, Instituto Universitario de Ciencias Biomedicas, Argentina, 1996, faculty of medicine U. Saarland, Germany, 1996, Ctr. for Med. Edn., Ben Gurion U., Israel, 1996-, Hungarian Nat. Health Ins. Fund, 1996, Carelift Internat., 1997, Intercoll., Cyprus, 1997, Open Soc. Inst., 1997-99, Aieti Med. Sch., Republic of Georgia, 1997-2001, Tartu U., Estonia, 1998-99, WHO European Office, 1998, Vilnius U. and Kaunas Med. U., Lithuania, 1998-99, U. Zagreb, Croatia, 1998-99, Larnaca Hosp., Cyprus, 1998, Netherlands and Russian med. schs., Temple U., others; faculty of medicine Moldova State Med. and Pharm. U., 1997-, vis. prof., 2002, prof. assoc., 2003-; rep. for internat. med. and health scis. MCP Hahnemann U. of the Health Scis., 1996-99; adv. com. Open Soc. Inst. Muskie Fellowship Program, 1997, working group on implementation of presdl. policy on internat. edn., 2000, selection comm. Internat. Consortium for the Advancement of Med. Edn., 2001-05; mem. adv. com. internat. health program Temple U., 2005—. Author numerous articles in field.; asst. editor: Annals Internal Medicine, 1972-75; mem. editl. bd. other med. jours. Bd. dirs. Israel Cancer Rsch. Fund, 1975—95, Am. Assocs. for Democracy in Georgia, 2000—; nat. bd. dirs. Am. Assocs. Ben Gurion U., 1991—; bd. Internat. Med. Scholar Program, 1988—89, Sight Savers Internat., 1988—91; adv. commn. Internat. Participation Phila. '76, 1973—76; bd. dirs. Phila. Coun. Internat. Visitors, 1972—77; nat. bd. dirs. Phila. divsn. Am. Assocs. Ben Gurion U., 1986—; assoc. chair, 1993—95, 2000—. Capt. M.C. U.S. Army, 1958—60. Recipient Torch of Learning award Am. Friends of Hebrew U., 1981, medal Ben Gurion U. of Negev, Israel, 1985, medal U. Cath. de Lille, France, 1987, medal U. Belgrade, Yugoslavia, 1988, Founder's award and medal Med. Coll. Pa., 1989, St. Thomas Aquinas award Santo Tomas U. Med. Alumni Assn., The Philippines, 1989, medal Kiev Med. Inst., Ukraine, 1991, Benjamin Albagli medal Inst. de Pos-Graduacao Medica Carlos Chagas, Brazil, 1993, shield Coll. Physicians and Surgeons, Pakistan, 1993, medal Ukrainian State Med. U., 1994, medal Universidad de Cantabria, Spain, 1999, medal Hadassah-Hebrew U. Dental Sch., 1999, Negev award Am. Assocs., Ben Gurion U., 2000. Fellow ACP (internat. adv. network), Coll. Physicians Phila. (censor 1977-86, councillor 1977-86); mem. AMA (Arnold and Marie Schwartz award in medicine, 1976, Dr. William Beaumont award), AAAS, Am. Fedn. Clin. Rsch. (pres. Temple U. chpt. 1964-65), Am. Assn. Cancer Rsch., Am. Soc. Clin. Oncology, Am. Dermatoglyphics Assn., Assn. Am. Cancer Insts., Assn. Am. Med. Colls., Northeast Consortium on Med. Edn. (treas. 1983-89, chmn. 1986-87), Council of Deans of Pvt. Free-Standing Med. Schs. (co-founder, nat. chmn. 1983-85), Pa. Council Deans (chmn. 1987-89), Am. Cancer Soc. (vice chmn. service com. Phila. div. 1974-76, bd. dirs. 1974-80, chmn. awards com. 1976), Am. Lung Assn., Am. Heart Assn., NAFSA-Assn. Internat. Educators, Am. Med. Assn., Phila. Coop. Cancer Assn., N.Y. Acad. Scis., Pa. Heart Assn., Heart Assn. Southeastern Pa., Pa. Med. Soc., Phila. County Med. Soc. (chmn. com. internat. med. affairs 1964-72), Pa. Lung Assn., Phila. Assn. for Clin. Trials (bd. dirs. 1980-81), Health Systems Agy. Southeastern Pa. (gov.

---

bd., exec. com. 1983-87, sec. 1985-87), Am. Assn. Ben Gurion U. (bd. dirs. 1986—), Soc. des Medecins Militaires Français, Assn. Med. Edn. in Europe, Soc. Española de Educacion Medica, Internat. Med. Sch. Affiliates Consortium (co-founder, vice chmn. 1985-87), Phi Beta Kappa, Sigma Xi, Alpha Omega Alpha (councillor 1963-65) Achievements include discovery of association of hepatitis B surface antigen with hepatitis; performed 1st studies of pulmonary surfactant in adult human lung disease; developed cancer screening system based on risk status; pioneer in describing non-A non-B hepatitis C, pioneer in showing relationship of body iron stores to cancer susceptibility and life expectancy; organized first symposium on problems of foreign medical graduates; coined word "ergasteric" for lab.-contracted disease; responsible for advances in assessment of clinical competence; demonstrated validity of clinical competence assessment using standardized patients; demonstrated reliability of clinical competence assessment across six different languages and cultures. Personal E-mail: alton@sutnick.com.

**SUTRO, EDMUND J.,** secondary school educator, consultant; b. L.A., Aug. 4, 1946; s. Paul and Ethelwyn (Ziegler) S. AA, L.A. Valley Coll., Van Nuys, 1966; AB, U. So. Calif., L.A., 1969, MSc, 1971; PhD, Stanford U., 1979. Cert. tchr. Calif. Tchr. Pasadena (Calif.) H.S., 1969-92, Arcadia (Calif.) H.S., 1992—. Commr. Calif. Commn. on Tchg. Credentials, Sacramento, 1992-95; mem. adv. bd. Occidental Coll., L.A., 1990—, L.A. Times, 1971-72; reviewer Dept. Edn., Washington; guest lectr. U. So. Calif., Calif. State Coll., L.A., Calif. Inst. Tech., Stanford U.; spkr. Pasadena Star News; acad. cons., L.A.; manuscript reviewer Social Edn. Contbr. articles to profl. jours. Co-chair Calif. chpt. Bush-Quayle '92, 1992; trustee Flintridge Prep. Sch., La Canada, Calif., 1992—, Pilgrim Sch., L.A., 1990—; bd. dirs. L.A. Bach. Festival, Pasadena Chamber Orch.; prodn. chair, bd. dirs., mem. adv. bd. Hollywood Bowl Easter Sunrise Svc.; vol. Head Start, Bell Gardens/Montebello; vol. fundraiser Sta. KCET Channel 28, L.A.; charter mem. Greater L.A. Zoo Assn. Mem. ASCD, Ednl. Excellence Network, Nat. Coun. for the Social Studies, Calif. Coun. for the Social Studies, Phi Delta Kappa, Tau Kappa Epsilon (pres., past pledge trainer). Republican.

**SUTTELL, PAUL ALLYN,** state supreme court justice; b. Providence, Jan. 10, 1949; s. Allyn Kingsley and Pauline Louise (Stickney) S.; m. Mary Wood Cissel, May 24, 1980; children: William Theodore Stickney, Grace Wood. BA, Northwestern U., 1971; JD, Suffolk U., 1976. Assoc. Beals & DiFiore, Providence, 1977-90; legal counsel RI Home Minority Leader, 1979-82; mem. RI Ho. of Reps., Providence, 1983—90; assoc. justice RI Family Ct., Providence, 1990—2003; justice RI Supreme Ct., 2003—. Mem. Little Compton (R.I.) Rep. Town Commn., 1981-90; del. R.I. Rep. State Com., 1981-90, Rep. Nat. Conv., 1988; bd. dirs. Friends of Sakonnet Lighthouse; bd. dirs. Little Compton Hist. Soc., chmn., 1999—; mem. bd. deacons Little Compton Congregational Ch., 1995-99, chair, 1997-99. Mem. Sakonnet Preservation Assn., R.I. Agrl. Lands Preservation Com. Office: RI Supreme Ct Frank Licht Judicial Complex 250 Benefit St Providence RI 02903 E-mail: psuttell@counts.state.ri.us.*

**SUTTENFIELD, DIANA,** artist; b. Washington, Nov. 20, 1944; BFA, Md. Inst. Coll. Art, 1972. Co-founder German St. Gallery, Shepherdstown, W.Va., 1973-76, Boarman Arts Ctr., Martinsburg, W.Va., 1982-92. Author: Shepherdstown Sketchbook, 1976, Martinsburg Sketchbook, 1978, Harpers Ferry—Pen and Ink Drawings, 1979, The C and O Canal-An Illustrated History, 1981, Elegy for Barns, 2002; exhbns. include Aqueous Open '83, Balt. Watercolor Soc.(award), 1987 Johns Hopkins U., Pastel Soc. Am. fall exhbn., (award 1991, 93), Nat. Arts Club N.Y.C., Shades of Pastel Md. Pastel Soc., (award 1991, 93), Washington County Mus. of Fine Art, 1984, Art in Embassies 1999-2005, U.S. Dept. State, 2005; affiliated galleries include Mary Bell Galleries, Chgo., Callen McJunkin Gallery, Charleston, W.Va., AIIA, Sheperdstown, W.Va Founder; pres. Friends of the Shepherdstown River Front, 2002—05; bd. mem., co-founder River Front Frmty. Art Ctr., 2006. Named Woman of the Yr. in Art, W.Va. Women's Commn., 1985; recipient Artist of the Yr., Women's Garden Coun. Club, 1985. Home: PO Box 832 Shepherdstown WV 25443-0832 Personal E-mail: sutenfield@aol.com.

**SUTTER, BRUCE (HOWARD SUTTER),** retired professional baseball player; b. Lancaster, Pa., Jan. 8, 1953; m. Jaymie Sutter; children: Joshua, Chad, Ben. Baseball player Chgo. Cubs, 1976-80; baseball player St. Louis Cardinals, 1981-85, Altanta Braves, 1985—88. Mem. Nat. League All-Star Team, 1978-81, 84. Recipient Cy Young award Nat. League, 1979; named Nat. League Fireman of Year Sporting News, 1979, 81, 82, 84; inducted to MLB Hall of Fame, 2006. Office: c/o Baseball Hall of Fame 25 Main St Cooperstown NY 13326*

**SUTTER, DARRYL JOHN,** professional sports team executive, former professional hockey coach; b. Viking, Alta., Can., Aug. 19, 1958; m. Wanda Sutter; children: Brett, Christopher, Jessie. Player Chgo. Blackhawks, 1980-86, asst. coach, 1987-88, assoc. coach, 1991-92, head coach, 1992-95, cons., 1995-97; head coach San Jose Sharks, 1997—2002, Calgary Flames, 2002—06, gen. mgr., 2003—. Named to Alberta Sports Hall of Fame, 2000; recipient Dudley Red Garrett Meml. Trophy, 1980, Commrs. Trophy, 1990. Office: Calgary Flames PO Box 1540 Stn M Calgary AB Canada T2P 3B9*

**SUTTER, ELEANOR BLY,** retired diplomat; b. NYC, Oct. 21, 1945; d. Samuel M. and Sylvia Gertrude Bly; children: Deborah Nelson, Willis. BA, Swarthmore Coll., 1966; MA, Am. U., 1978; diploma in strategic studies, U.S. Army War Coll., 1997. Instr. English Thammasat U., Bangkok and Udornthani Tchr. Tng. Coll., 1967-71, Lomonosov State U., Moscow, 1973-74; rschr. Kennan Inst. for Advanced Russian Studies, 1977-79; fgn. svc. officer Office Soviet Internal Affairs Dept. of State, 1979-80, fgn. svc. officer Office of Strategic Nuc. Policy, 1986-88, fgn. svc. officer Office of Soviet Union Affairs, 1988-90, office dir. Washington, 1997-99, sr. inspector Office Inspector Gen., 1999-2001, dir. Office of Proliferation Threat Reduction, 2001—02; fgn. svc. officer U.S. Embassy, Kinshasa, 1980-82, London, 1982-85, Moscow, 1990-92, charge d'affaires ad interim Bratislava, 1993, dep. prin. officer, 1993-95, dep. chief of mission, 1995-96. Exec. dir., exec. sec., advisor U.S. Del. to Nuclear and Space Talks, Geneva, 1987-91; teaching fellow Russian lit. The Am. U., 1976-77; escort interpreter and translator Dept. of State, 1976. Co-author: Final Report of the Kennan Institute's Soviet Research Institutes Project, 1981. Founder Camp Wocsom, Moscow, 1974. Mem. Am. Fgn. Svc. Assn. Avocations: music, folk dance.

**SUTTER, JANE ELIZABETH,** conservationist, science educator; b. St. Louis, Nov. 27, 1939; d. Richard A. and Elizabeth Henby Sutter. AB in Sociology and English, Vassar Coll., 1961; MA in Health Facilities Mgmt., Webster Coll., St. Louis, 1979. Healthcare analyst, Chgo. and St. Louis, 1966-83; asst. dir. radio, TV and motion picture dept. AMA, Chgo., 1966-67; staff coord.; rsch. assoc. Chgo. water quality study and environ. health study Inst. of Medicine of Chgo., 1967-69; dir. environ. health planning Comprehensive Health Planning, Inc., Chgo., 1969-73; planning assoc., spl. asst. to med. dir. Sutter Clinic, Inc., St. Louis, 1975-84; vol. activist, educator; founder, dir. for conservation and gardening for birds Wild Birds for the 21st Century (a non-profit ednl. svc.), 1994—; ednl. writer www.wildbirds.org. Author: City Approved Medical Emergency Plan of Operation O'Hare International and Midway Airports, 1971. Chmn. Opera Theatre of St. Louis Newsletter, Recitative, Vol. 1, No. 1, 1980, Vol. 1, No. 2, 1980; co-founder, com. mem. 1st Internat. Alewife Festival of Chgo., Chgo. Yacht Club, summer 1968; appointee Gov.'s Com. for Pure Air and Water, Chgo., 1968; spl. advocate N.Am. Migratory Birds particularly hummingbirds; mem. Ladue Chapel. Mem. Nat. Garden Clubs, Inc. (regis. Federated Garden Clubs of Mo., Inc., Clayton Garden Assn., Mo. Bot. Garden, St. Louis Artists' Guild (mem. artists' sect. 1992-95, portraitist), Mo. Bird Conservation Initiative, Neotropical Bird Club (UK), Univ. Club St. Louis, Vassar Club St. Louis, Bradenton C. of C. Avocations: gardening, writing. Home: 7376 Pershing Blvd Saint Louis MO 63130-4206

---

**SUTTER, JOSEPH F.,** aeronautical engineer, consultant, retired air transportation executive; b. Seattle, Mar. 21, 1921; m. Nancy Ann French, June 14, 1943. BA, U. Wash., 1943; Doctorate, Nova Gorcia Poly. Inst., 2004. Various engring. positions Boeing Comml. Airplane Co., Seattle, 1946—65, dir. engring. for Boeing 747, 1965—71, v.p., gen. mgr. 747 div., 1971—74, v.p. program ops., 1974—76, v.p. ops. and product devel., 1976—81, exec. v.p., 1981—86, cons., 1986—87, 1987—. Chmn. aerospace safety adv. panel NASA, 1986; mem. Challenger Accident Commn., 1986. Served to lt. j.g. USN, 1943—45. Named Joseph F. Sutter professorship established in his honor, U. Wash., Boeing Co., 1992; named to. Interant. Air Cargo Assn. Hall of Fame, Gallery of Legends, Pacific Asian Travel Assn., 2005; recipient Master Design award, Product Engring. mag., 1965, Franklin W. Kolk Air Transp. Progress award, Soc. Aero. Aerospace Coun., 1980, Elmer A. Sperry award, 1980, Nuts & Bolts award, Transport Assn., 1983, Nat. Medal Tech., U.S. Pres. Reagan, 1985, Sir Kingsford Smith award, Royal Aero. Soc. in Sydney, 1980, Wright Bros. Meml. Trophy, 1986, Alumnus Summa Laude Dignatus award, U. Wash., 2001. Fellow: AIAA (Daniel Guggenheim award 1990), Royal Aero Soc. (hon.); mem.: Internat. Fedn. Airworthiness (pres. 1989), Slovenian Acad. Engring. (hon.). Office: Boeing Co PO Box 3707 Seattle WA 98124-2207

**SUTTER, LAURENCE BRENER,** lawyer; b. NYC, Feb. 5, 1944; s. Meyer and Beatrice Sutter; m. Betty A. Satterwhite, June 9, 1979. AB, Columbia Coll., 1965; JD, N.Y.U., 1976. Bar: N.Y. 1977, U.S. Dist. Ct. (so. and ea. dists.) N.Y. 1977. Assoc. Shea & Gould, N.Y.C., 1976-80, Meyer, Suozzi, English & Klein P.C., Mineola, NY, 1980-82; assoc. counsel publs. Gen. Media Comm., Inc., N.Y.C., 1982-96, sr. v.p., gen. counsel, sec., 1997—2004; sr. counsel Penthouse Media Group Inc., 2004—. With N.Y. Army N.G., 1966-72. Mem. Assn. of Bar of City of N.Y. (mem. com. on civil rights 1986-89, mem. com. on comm. and media law 1989-92, mem. com. on copyright and lit. property 1994-97), First Amendment Lawyers Assn., Nat. Arts Club, Orient (N.Y.) Yacht Club (dir. 1997-2000, sec. 2000-2001). Democrat. Jewish. Avocations: music, sailing.

**SUTTER, LAWRENCE A.,** lawyer, educator; b. Barberton, Ohio, Oct. 24, 1963; BA, Glenville State Coll., 1986; JD, U. Akron, 1989. Bar: Ohio 1989, U.S. Dist. Ct. (no. dist) Ohio 1991, U.S. Ct. Appeals (6th cir.) Tenn. 2001. Mng. ptnr. Sutter, O'Connell, Mannion & Farchione, Franklin, Tenn. Prof. U. Akron, 2001—. dir. Trial Advocacy Sch. Law. Named one of Top Ten Trial Lawyers, The Nat. Law Jour., 2002. Mem.: ABA, Ohio State Bar Assn., Cuyahoga County Bar Assn., Cleve. (Ohio) Bar Assn., Akron (Ohio) Bar Assn., Anthony D. Celebrezze Inn Ct. Office: Sutter OConnell Mannion & Farchione 217 Second Ave South Franklin TN 37064-2622

**SUTTER, WILLIAM PAUL,** lawyer; b. Chgo., Jan. 15, 1924; s. Harry Blair and Elsie (Paul) S.; m. Helen Yvonne Stebbins, Nov. 13, 1954; children: William Paul, Helen Blair Sutter. AB, Yale U., 1947; JD, U. Mich., 1950. Bar: Ill. 1950, Fla. 1977, U.S. Supreme Ct. 1981. Assoc. Hopkins & Sutter (and predecessors), Chgo., 1950-57, ptnr., 1957-89, of counsel, 1989—2001. Mem. Ill. Supreme Ct. Atty. Registration Commn., 1975-81 Contbr. articles on estate planning and taxation to profl. jours. Chmn. Winnetka Caucus Com., 1966-67; pres., trustee Lucille P. Markey Charitable Trust, 1983-98; precinct capt. New Trier Twp. (Ill.) Rep. party, 1960-68; asst. area chmn. New Trier Rep. Orgn., 1968-72; trustee Gads Hill Center, pres., 1962-70, chmn., 1971-80; trustee Northwestern Meml. Hosp., 1983-98, life trustee, 1998—; bd. dirs. Chgo. Hort. Soc., 1982-2005, life dir., 2005—; mem. dean's coun. Sch. Medicine, Yale U., 1991-97; bd. visitors Waisman Ctr., U. Wis., 1996-2002; corr. sec. Yale U. Class of 1945, 1990—. Served to 1st lt. AUS, 1943-46 Fellow Am. Bar Found., Am. Coll. Trust and Estate Counsel (bd. regents 1977-83, exec. com. 1981-83); mem. ABA (ho. dels. 1972-81, chmn. com. on income estates and trusts, taxation sect. 1973-75), Ill. Bar Assn. (bd. govs. 1964-75, pres. 1973-74), Chgo. Bar Assn. (chmn. probate practice com. 1963-64), Am. Law Inst., Internat. Acad. Estate and Trust Law, Am. Judicature Soc., Ill. LAWPAC (pres. 1977-83), Order of Coif, Phi Beta Kappa, Phi Delta Phi, Chi Psi, Mid-Day Club, Indian Hill Club, Gulf Stream Golf Club, Country Club Fla., Ocean Club (Fla.) (bd. govs. 1993-99, sec. 1993-97, pres. 1997-99), Lawyers Club Chgo. Episcopalian. Home: 2 Par Club Cir Village Of Golf FL 33436 Personal E-mail: WPSutter@aol.com.

**SUTTERBY, LARRY QUENTIN,** internist; b. North Kansas City, Mo., Sept. 11, 1950; s. John Albert and Wilma Elizabeth (Henry) Sutterby; m. Luciana Risos Magpuri, July 5, 1980; children: Leah Lourdes, Liza Bernadette. BA in Chemistry, William Jewell Coll., 1972; MD, U. Mo., Kans. City, 1976. Resident in internal medicine Mt. Sinai Hosp., Chgo., 1976-79; physician Mojave Desert Health Svc., Barstow, Calif., 1979-86; pvt. practice Barstow, 1986-2001; med. cons. State of Calif., L.A., 2001—. Med dir Mojave Valley Hospice, 1983—2001, VNA Hospice, Barstow, 1994—2001, Optioncare Home Health Servs, 1995—2001. Recipient Loving Care Award, Vis Nurse Assn Inland Counties, 1988. Democrat. Roman Catholic. Avocation: astronomy. Office: 311 S Spring St Ste 900 Los Angeles CA 90013

**SUTTIE, JOHN WESTON,** biochemist; b. La Crosse, Wis., Aug. 25, 1934; married; 2 children. BS, U. Wis., 1957, MS, 1958, PhD, 1960. Fellow biochemist Nat. Inst. Med. Rsch, England, 1960-61; asst. prof. to assoc. prof. biochemistry U. Wis., Madison, 1961-69, prof., 1969—2001, chair nutrition sci., 1988-97, Katherine Berns Van Donk Steenbock prof. nutrition, 2000, prof. emeritus, 2002—. Mem. Bd. on Agriculture & Natural Resources, 1996—2001. Assoc. editor Jour Nutrition, 1991-97; editor Jour. Nutrition, 1997—2003. Recipient Disting. Achievement in Nutrition Rsch., Bristol-Myers Squibb/Mead Johnson, 2002. Fellow Am. Heart Assn. Coun. Nutrition, Physical Activity and Metabolism, Am. Soc. for Nutrition Scis. (Osborne and Mendel award 1980, Mead Johns award 1974, Conrad Elvehjem award, 2004); mem. NAS, Am. Soc. Expl. Biology and Medicine, Am. Soc. Biochemistry and Molecular Biology, Am. Soc. Clin. Nutrition, Internat. Soc. Thrombosis and Hemostasis (Hemostasis Career award 1989). Business E-Mail: suttie@biochem.wisc.edu.

**SUTTON, ALBERT PHILIP,** urologist; s. Jack Sutton and Pauline Aaron; m. Beverly G. Kolodney, Oct. 22, 1949; children: Elizabet Sutton Thompson children: Ira J., Jodi J. Gershel. BA cum laude, U. Buffalo, 1944; MD, 1949. Attending urologist LI Jewish Med. Ctr., Queens, NY, 1955—96, chief urology, 1977—81, cons., 1981—96. Mem.: Am. Urology Assn. (pres. NY sect. 1989—90), Alpha Omega Alpha, Phi beta Kappa. Achievements include research in technique of ureteral transplant. Avocations: gardening, golf.

**SUTTON, BEVERLY JEWELL,** psychiatrist; b. Rockford, Mich., May 27, 1932; d. Beryl Dewey and Cora Belle (Potes) Jewell; m. Harry Eldon Sutton, July 7, 1962; children: Susan, Caroline. MD, U. Mich., 1957. Diplomate Am. Bd. Pediat., Am. Bd. Psychiatry and Neurology. Rotating intern St. Joseph Mercy Hosp., Ann Arbor, Mich., 1958; resident in child psychiatry Hawthorne Ctr., Northville, Mich., 1958-62; resident in pediat. U. Hosp./U. Mich. Med. Ctr., Ann Arbor, 1959-61; resident in psychiatry Austin (Tex.) State Hosp., 1962-64, dir. children's svc., 1964-89, dir. psychiat. residency program, 1989—, dir. tng. and rsch., 1993-98. Cons. in field. Contbr. articles to profl. jours. Active numerous civic orgns. Recipient Outstanding Achievement award, YWCA, 1989, Jackson Day award, Tex. Soc. Child and Adolescent Psychiatry, 1989, Showcase award, Tex. Dept. Mental Health/Mental Retardation, 1990. Fellow Am. Acad. Child and Adolescent Psychiatry (life), Am. Psychiat. Soc., Am. Pediatric Assn.; mem. Tex. Soc. Child and Adolescent Psychiatry (pres. 1979-80), Tex. Soc. Psychiat. Physicians (Disting. Svc. award 1990), AMA, Tex. Med. Assn., Am. Genetics Soc. Office: Seton Shoal Creek Hosp 3501 Mills Ave Austin TX 78731 Business E-Mail: bsutton@seton.org.

**SUTTON, CARL,** finance educator; m. Andrea Celmer, May 24, 1969. AS Bus. Adminstrn., Wilkes Barre Bus. Coll., 1968; BBA, Coll. Misericordia, Dallas, Pa., 1982; MS Edn., Wilkes U., 1999. Bus. educator Canton Area Sch. Dist., Pa., 1983—. Adj. prof. Lackawana Coll., Scranton, Pa., 1995—2005.

Past treas. Canton Area Nursing Assn., 1986—89. Mem.: Masons (assoc.). Republican. Avocations: antique cars and trucks, toy trains. Home: 21 S Minnequa Ave Canton PA 17724 Personal E-mail: sutts@epix.net.

**SUTTON, CECILIA (CECE SUTTON),** bank executive; b. Charlotte, NC; B in Psychology, U. SC; MBA, Winthrop U. Branch manager First Union Corp., Raleigh and Cary, NC, consumer credit sales mgr. Charlotte, NC, 1984—86, consumer banking mgr. Greenville, SC, 1986—89, consumer bank training dir. Charlotte, NC, 1988—89, area exec. Rock Hill, SC, 1989—92, head SC Gen. Banking Group Greenville, SC, 1992—93, area exec. Rock Hill, SC, 1993—95, consumer banking exec, SC, exec. v.p. SC, 2001; exec. v.p., head retail Wachovia Corp. (merged with First Union Corp), Charlotte, 2001—. Office: Wachovia Corp 301 S Coll St Charlotte NC 28288-0018

**SUTTON, DOLORES,** actress, writer; b. N.Y.C. BA in Philosophy, NYU. Appeared in broadway plays including Man With the Golden Arm, 1956, Career, 1958, Machinal, 1960, Rhinoceros, Liliom, She Stoops to Conquer, Hedda Gabler, Anna Karenina, Eccentricities of a Nightingale, Brecht on Brecht, Young Gifted and Black, Luv, The Friends, The Web and the Rock, The Seagull, Saturday, Sunday, Monday, The Little Foxes, What's Wrong With This Picture, The Cocktail Hour, My Fair Lady (Broadway revival), 1994, My Fair Lady (nat. tour), 1993-94; films include The Trouble With Angels, Where Angels Go, Trouble Follows, Crossing Delancey, Crimes and Misdeameanors, Tales of the Darkside; TV appearances include Studio One, Hallmark Hall of Fame Prodn. An Wilderness, Theatre Guild of the Air: Danger, Suspense, Gunsmoke, Valiant Lady, General Hospital, From These Roots, As the World Turns, Edge of Night, F Scott Fitzgerald in Hollywood, Patty Hearst Story, All in the Family, Bob Newhart Show, All My Children, others, (TV writer) Lady Somebody, 1999, The Secret Storm, Loving; playwright: Down at the Old Bull and Bush, The Web and the Rock, Born Yesterday, 1995, A Perfect Ganesh, 1995, Detail of a Larger Work, 1995, The Front Page, 1996, The Exact Center of the Universe, 1997, A Drop in the Bucket, 1997, Spring Storm (newly discovered Tennessee Williams play), 1997, Signs and Wonders, 1998, It Gives Me Great Pleasure, 2000, Company Comin', 2005; prodns. Free Ascent, 2001, Burial Society, 2001, The Find, 2002. Mem. Actors Studio, League of Profl. Theatre Women (bd. dirs.), Ensemble Studio Theatre (bd. dirs.).

**SUTTON, FRANCIS XAVIER,** social services administrator, consultant; b. Oneida, Pa., July 7, 1917; s. Frank James and Rose Marie (Burns) S.; m. Ruth Jacqueline Young, Aug. 24, 1948 (dec. July 2002); children: Peter, Sean, Philip, Elizabeth. BS, Temple U., 1938; MA, Princeton U., 1940, Harvard U., 1941, PhD, 1950; DLitt (hon.), Aga Khan U., Karachi, 2003. Jr. fellow, Soc. Fellows Harvard U., Cambridge, Mass., 1946-49, asst. prof., lectr., 1949-54; program officer, overseas rep. Ford Found., N.Y.C., 1954-67, dep. v.p., acting v.p., 1968-83; cons. Ford Found. and Harvard U., 1983-85; acting pres. Social Sci. Rsch. Coun., N.Y.C., 1985-86, also bd. dirs., chmn., 1985-92; cons. Rockefeller Found, U.S. Agy. for Internat. Devel. and World Bank, N.Y.C. and Washington, 1987-92; acting dir. Rockefeller Study and Conf. Ctr., Bellagio, Italy, 1990-92; cons. Aga Khan U., 1992—. Author: The American Business Creed, 1956; editor: A World to Make/Development in Perspective, 1989; contbr. articles to profl. jours. and chpts. to books. Pres. Am. Found. for Intellectual Coop. with Europe, N.Y.C., 1987-93; mem. bd. fgn. scholarships Dept. State, Washington, 1961-63; bd. dirs. Nat. Ctr. on Adult Literacy, U. Pa., Phila., 1990-97; mem. adv. bd. Ctr. on Philanthropy, City Univ., N.Y.C., 1988—. Capt. U.S. Army Air Corps, 1941-45. Fellow AAAS; mem. Council on Fgn. Relations, Assn. for Asian Studies (Disting. Service award 1984). Clubs: Century Assn. (N.Y.C.). Democrat. Avocation: piano playing. Home: 80 Bellair Dr Dobbs Ferry NY 10522-3504 E-mail: fxsutton@aol.com.

**SUTTON, GREGORY PAUL,** obstetrician, gynecologist; b. Tokyo, Dec. 12, 1948; (parents Am. citizens); s. Vernon S. and Vonna Lou (Streeter) S.; m. Judith Craigie Holt, June 26, 1977; children: Anne Craigie, James Streeter. BS in Chemistry with honors, Ind. U., 1970; MD, U. Mich., 1976. Diplomate Am. Bd. of Ob/Gyn. Prof. gynecol. oncology Ind. U. Sch. Medicine, Indpls., 1986-97; Mary Fendrich Hulman prof. Gynecologic Oncology Ind. U. Sch. Med., Indpls., 1997-2000; mem. staff St. Vincent Hosp. and Health Svcs., 2000—01. Cancer Clin. fellow Am. Cancer Soc., Phila., 1981-83; recipient Career Devel. award Am. Cancer Soc., 1986-89. Fellow: Am. Coll. Obstetrics and Gynecology (chair Ind. sect. 2000—03); mem.: ACS (com. on cancer, Ind. state liaison), Hoosier Oncology Group, Soc. of Gynecologic Oncologists, Bayard Carter Soc., Ind. State Med. Soc., Marion County Med. Soc., Gynecologic Oncology Group (cert. Spl. Competence in Gynecologic Oncology 1985). Avocations: swimming, bicycling, woodworking, sailing, crossword puzzles. Office: 8301 Harcourt Rd Ste 202 Indianapolis IN 46260-1453 E-mail: gsutton@stvincent.org.

**SUTTON, HAL EVAN,** professional golfer; b. Shreveport, La., Apr. 28, 1958; s. Howard Everett and Mary Alice (Rogers) S.; m. Ashley; children: Samantha, Sara, Sadie. BS in Sci., Centenary Coll. Professional golfer, 1981—. Named Player of Yr., Profl. Golf Assn., 1983; winner Disney Classic, 1982, Profl. Golf Assn. Championship, 1983, Tournament Player's Championship, 1983, 2000, Memphis Classic, 1985, Phoenix Open, 1986, Meml. Tournament, 1986, Ryder Cup Team, 1987; B.C. Open, 1995; Westin Texas Open, 1998; The Tour Championship, 1998, Bell Canadian Open, 1999, Greater Greensboro Chrysler Classic, 2000. Office: Sutton Enterprises 212 Texas St Ste 117 Shreveport LA 71101-3287 Home: 909 Trabue St Shreveport LA 71106-1114

**SUTTON, HARRY ELDON,** geneticist, educator; b. Cameron, Tex., Mar. 5, 1927; s. Grant Edwin and Myrtle Dovie (Fowler) S.; m. Beverly Earlene Jewell, July 7, 1962; children: Susan Elaine, Caroline Virginia. BS in Chemistry, U. Tex., Austin, 1948, MA, 1949; PhD in Biochemistry, U. Tex., 1953. Biologist U. Mich., 1952-56, instr., 1956-57, asst. prof. human genetics, 1957-60; assoc. prof. zoology U. Tex., Austin, 1960-64, prof., 1964-99, chmn. dept. zoology, 1970-73, assoc. dean Grad. Sch., 1967-70, 73-75, v.p. for research, 1975-79, Ashbel Smith prof. emeritus molecular genetics and microbiology, 2000—. Mem. adv. council Nat. Inst. Environ. Health Scis., 1968-72, council sci. advs., 1972-76; mem. various coms. Nat. Acad. Scis.-NRC; cons. in field; bd. dirs. Associated Univs. for Research in Astronomy, 1975-79, Argonne Univs. Assn., 1975-79, Univ. Corp. for Atmospheric Research, 1975-79, Associated Western Univs., 1978-79 Author: Genes, Enzymes, and Inherited Disease, 1961, An Introduction to Human Genetics, 1988, Genetics: A Human Concern, 1985; editor: First Macy Conference on Genetics, 1960, Mutagenic Effects of Environmental Contaminants, 1972, Am. Jour. Human Genetics, 1964-69. Trustee S.W. Tex. Corp. Public Broadcasting, 1977-80, sec., 1979-80; bd. dirs. Ballet Austin, 1978-84, 98-2004; mem. Austin Arts Commn., 1991-95. Served with U.S. Army, 1945-46. Mem. AAAS, Am. Soc. Human Genetics (dir. 1961-69, pres. 1979), Genetics Soc. Am., Am. Soc. Biochem. and Molecular Biology, Am. Chem. Soc., Tex. Genetics Soc. (pres. 1979), Am. Genetic Assn., Headliners Club (Austin), Town and Gown Club. Achievements include research and publications in human genetics. Home: 1103 Gaston Ave Austin TX 78703-2507 Office: Univ Tex Sect Molecular Genetics & Microbiology Austin TX 78712 Business E-mail: eldon.sutton@mail.utexas.edu.

**SUTTON, JEFFREY PAUL,** physician, scientist; b. NYC, July 6, 1958; MD, U. Toronto, Ontario, Can., 1982; MSc in med. sci., 1985; PhD in physics, 1988. Intern U. Toronto, 1982-83, fellow in med. sci., 1983-84; fellow Can. Psychiat. Research Found., 1984-85; research fellow Med. Research Coun. of Can., 1985-88; clin. fellow in psychiatry Harvard Med. Sch., Boston, 1988-91; vis. scientist in brain and cognitive scis. MIT, Cambridge, 1988-95, rsch. affiliate in brain and cognitive scis., 1995—; instr. psychiatry Harvard Med. Sch., Boston, 1991-93, asst. prof., 1993—; dir. neural sys. group Mass. Gen. Hosp., 1995—2001; dir. Nat. Space Biomed. Rsch. Inst., 2001—. Recipient NIH Rsch. Career Scientist award, 1994—. Mem. AMA, Am. Phys. Soc., Am. Psychiat. Assn., Soc. for Neurosci. Office: Nat Space Biomed Rsch Inst One Baylor Plaza NA-425 Houston TX 77030*

**SUTTON, JEFFREY S.,** federal judge; b. Dhahran, Saudi Arabia, 1960; BA, Williams Coll., 1983; LLB, Ohio State Univ., 1990. Clk. Second Circuit Ct. for Judge Thomas Meskill, 1990—91, Supreme Ct. for Justice Scalia and ret. Justice Powell, 1991—92; assoc. Jones, Day, Reavis & Pogue, Columbus, Ohio, 1992—95; adj. law prof. Ohio State Univ., Ohio, 1994—; Solicitor Ohio State, Ohio, 1995—98; ptnr. Jones, Day, Reavis & Pogue, Columbus, Ohio, 1998—2003; judge US Ct. Appeals, (6th cir.), Cin., 2003—. Office: Office Clerk US Ct Appeals 6th Cir 532 Potter Stewart US Cthse 100 E 5th St Cincinnati OH 45202-3988*

**SUTTON, JOHN EWING,** lawyer; b. San Angelo, Tex., Oct. 7, 1950; s. John F. Jr. and Nancy (Ewing) S.; 1 son, Joshua Ewing; 1 stepson, Michael Brandon Ducote. BBA, U. Tex., 1973, JD, 1976. CPA Tex.; bar: Tex. 1976, U.S. Tax Ct. 1977, U.S. Ct. Claims 1977, U.S. Ct. Appeals (5th cir.) 1978, U.S. Dist. Ct. (we. dist.) Tex. 1979, U.S. Supreme Ct. 1980. Tax specialist Peat, Marwick, Mitchell & Co., CPAs, Dallas, 1976-77; ptnr. Shannon, Porter, Johnson, Sutton and Greendyke Attys. at Law, San Angelo, 1977-87; judge 119th Dist. Ct. of Tex., 1987-99; pvt. practice Law Offices of John E. Sutton, 1999—. Treas. Good Shepherd Episcopal Ch., San Angelo, 1979-81; co-chmn. profl. divsn. United Way, San Angelo, 1980-82; trustee Angelo State U. Found., 1987-99, pres. 1988-91, 95-97, v.p. 1992-94, 98-99, sec.-treas., 1991-92. Fellow Tex. Bar Found. (life); mem. ABA, Tex. Bar Assn., Tex. Criminal Def. Lawyers Assn., Tom Green County Bar Assn. (sec.-chmn. young lawyers 1977-78), AICPAs, Tex. Soc. CPAs (bd. dirs. 1980-87, pres. San Angelo chpt. 1980-81, mem. state exec. com. 1981-82, 86-87, state sec. 1986-87, chmn. profl. ethics com. 1985-86, Young CPA of Yr. 1984-85), Concho Valley Estate Planning Coun. (v.p. 1979-80, also dlr.). Office: Law Office of John E Sutton 117 S Irving St San Angelo TX 76903-6419

**SUTTON, JOHN F., JR.,** lawyer, educator, dean; b. Alpine, Tex., Jan. 26, 1918; s. John F. and Pauline Irene (Elam) S.; m. Nancy Ewing, June 1, 1940; children: Joan Sutton Parr, John Ewing. JD, U. Tex., 1941. Bar: Tex. 1941, U.S. Dist. Ct. (we. dist.) Tex. 1947, U.S. Ct. Appeals (5th cir.) 1951, U.S. Supreme Ct. 1960. Assoc. Brooks, Napier, Brown & Matthews, San Antonio, 1941; spl. agt. FBI, Washington, 1942—45; assoc. Matthews, Nowlin, Macfarlane & Barrett, San Antonio, 1945—48; ptnr. Kerr, Gayer & Sutton, San Angelo, Tex., 1948—50, Sutton, Steib & Barr, San Angelo, 1951—57; prof. U. Tex.-Austin, 1957—65, William Stamps Farish prof., 1965—84, A.W. Walker centennial chair, 1984—88, emeritus, 1988—, dean Sch. Law, 1979—84. Editor: (with Wellborn) Materials on Evidence, 8th edit., 1996, (with Dzienkowski) Cases and Materials on Professional Responsibility of Lawyers, 1989, (with Schuwerk) Guideline to the Texas Disciplinary Rules of Professional Conduct, 1990, (with Dzienkowski) Cases and Materials on Professional Conduct, 2d edit., 2002; contbr. articles to profl. jours. Served to 1st lt. JAGC USAR, 1948—51. Fellow Am. Bar Found. (life), Tex. Bar Found. (life); mem. ABA (com. on ethics 1970-76), State Bar Tex. (com. on rules of profl. conduct, com. adminstrn. rules of evidence), Philos. Soc. Tex., Order of Coif, U. Tex. Club, Phi Delta Phi, North Austin Rotary (pres. 1969). Presbyterian. Home: 3830 Sunset Dr San Angelo TX 76904-5956 Office: U Tex Sch Law 727 E Dean Keeton St Austin TX 78705-3224 Business E-Mail: jsutton@mail.law.utexas.edu.

**SUTTON, JOHN PAUL,** lawyer; b. Youngstown, Ohio, July 24, 1934; m. Jane Williamson, Aug. 20, 1958; children: Julia, Susan, Elizabeth. BA, U. Va., 1956; JD, George Washington U., 1963. Bar: Calif. 1965. Patent examiner U.S. Patent Office, Washington, 1956, 59-62; law clk. U.S. Ct. Customs and Patent Appeals, Washington, 1962-64; assoc. Flehr, Hohbach, Test, Albritton & Herbert, San Francisco, 1964-68; ptnr. Limbach, Limbach & Sutton, San Francisco, 1969-91; spl. counsel Heller, Ehrman, White & McAuliffe, San Francisco, 1992-95; of counsel Medlin & Carroll, San Francisco, 1995, Bryan, Hinshaw & Barnet, San Francisco, 1996-99; sole practice San Francisco, 2000—. Adj. instr. Practicing Law Inst., 1968-69; continuing edn. program Calif. State Bar, 1972, 75, U. Calif. Law Sch., Berkeley, 1975, 84. Contbr. articles to legal jours. Served with USNR, 1956-59. Mem.: Am. Chem. Soc., Fedn. Internat. des Conseils en Propriete Indal. (pres. U.S. sect. 2003—), State Bar Calif. (exec. com. patent sect. 1975—77), San Francisco Patent Law Assn. (pres. 1976), Calif. Patent Law Assn. (pres. 1975). Democrat. Episcopalian. Home and Office: 2421 Pierce St San Francisco CA 94115-1131 Office Phone: 415-929-7408. Personal E-mail: JohnPSutton@earthlink.net.

**SUTTON, JOHNNY KEANE,** prosecutor, lawyer; b. June 1960; B in Internat. Bus., U. Tex., 1983, JD, 1987. Criminal trial prosecutor Harris County Dist. Atty. Office; asst. dist. atty. Harris County Dist. Atty.'s Office, 1987—95; criminal justice policy dir. to Gov. State of Tex., 1995—2000; assoc. dep. atty. gen. US Dept. Justice, Washington, 2001; policy coord. Bush-Cheney Transition Team, US Dept. Justice; US atty. (we. dist.) Tex. US Dept. Justice, 2001—. Avocation: baseball (played for the Longhorns, starting lef-fielder on 1983 Nat. Championship team). Office: US Attys Office 601 NW Loop 410 Ste 600 San Antonio TX 78216*

**SUTTON, JONATHAN MARK,** lawyer; b. Flint, Mich., Nov. 21, 1959; s. James Owen and Rachel Bernice (Pederson) S. Bachelor's Degree, Ctrl. Mich. U., 1982; JD, U. Tulsa, 1992. Bar: Okla. 1992, U.S. Dist. Ct. (ea., we. and no. dists.) Okla. 1994, U.S. Ct. Appeals (10th cir.) 1994, U.S. Supreme Ct. 1997. Corp. counsel United Parcel Svc., Atlanta, 1993. Guardian for disabled vets. VA, Tulsa, 1996—. Mem. ATLA, Okla. Bar Assn. Avocations: skiing, scuba diving, hunting, motorcycles, adventure racing. Office: 4401 S Harvard Ave Tulsa OK 74135-2638 Fax: (918) 747-8884

**SUTTON, JULIA,** musicologist, dance historian; b. Toronto, July 20, 1928; d. Samuel L. and Anne R. (Rubin) Sumberg. AB summa cum laude, Cornell U., 1949; MA, Colo. Coll., 1952; PhD, U. Rochester, 1962. Instr. music history New Sch. for Social Rsch., 1962-63; instr. music Queens Coll., CUNY, 1963-66; instr. music history and musicology New Eng. Conservatory Music, 1967—90, instr. and prof. musicology, 1967—90, chmn. dept. music history and musicology, 1971-90, chmn. faculty senate, 1971-73, prof. emerita, 1992. Vis. assoc. prof. George Peabody Coll. for Tchrs., 1966-67; instr. NYU, summers 1963, 64; pvt. tchr. piano, 1949-65; lectr., rsch. dir. in musicology, music as related to the dance; presenter numerous workshops and summer insts. on Renaissance dance. Dance dir. N.Y. Pro Musica prodn. An Entertainment for Elizabeth, Caramoor, N.Y., Saratoga, N.Y., U. Ariz., Stanford U., UCLA, 1969, ann. nationwide tours, 1970-1973; dance dir. Descent of Rhythm and Harmony, Colorado Springs, Colo., 1970, Renaissance Revisited, Phila., 1972, An Evening of Renaissance Music and Dance, York U., Toronto, 1974; author: Jean Baptiste Besard's Novus Partus 1617, 1962; editor: Thoinot Arbeau: Orchesography 1588, 1967; translator, editor: Fabritio Caroso: Nobiltà di dame 1600, 1986, reprinted 1995; producer, co-dir. (tng. video) Il Ballarino, 1991; contbr. numerous articles to profl. jours. and Internat. Ency. of Dance, The New Grove Dictionary of Music and Musicians 1st and 2d edit., Die Musik in Geschichte und Gegenwart, 1st edit. Mem. Am. Musicological Soc., Soc. of Dance History Scholars, Phi Beta Kappa. Office Phone: 781-893-0856. E-mail: julia-sutton@rcn.com.

**SUTTON, KAREN E.,** museum director; b. New Brunswick, N.J., Aug. 26, 1952; d. Alfred Michael and Carmen (Collado) Sutton; children: Sloane, Brooke, Devon, Megan, Christopher. BA, Hofstra U., 1974; postgrad., NYU, 1987—89. Asst. to dir. Mus. Am. Folk Art, N.Y.C., 1975-76, acting dir., 1976-77, bd. dirs., exec. com. officer, 1980-88, gallery dir., 1989-92, dir. ops., 1992-94, dep. dir. planning and administra, 1994-95; v.p. Sotheby's, N.Y.C., 1995-96, sr. v.p. adminstrn., 1996-2001, sr. v.p. worldwide mktg., 2001—. Bd. dirs. Family Dynamics, N.Y.C., 1976-80. Mem.: NY Women in Real Estate, Cosmopolitan Club (younger members Phila.). Democrat. Episcopalian. Office: Sotheby's 1334 York Ave New York NY 10021-4806 Home: 132 E 72 St New York NY 10021 Office Phone: 212-606-7410. E-mail: karen.sutton@sothebys.com.

**SUTTON, LYNN SORENSEN,** librarian; b. Detroit, July 31, 1953; d. Leonard Arthur Edward and Dorothy Ann (Steele) Sorensen. AB, U. Mich., 1975, MLS, 1976. Dir. Med. Libr. South Chgo. Cmty. Hosp., 1976-77; corp. dirs. librs. Detroit-Macomb Hosp. Corp., Detroit, 1977-86; dir. librs. Harper Hosp., Detroit, 1987-88; dir. Sci. and Engring. Libr. Wayne State U., Detroit, 1989-95, dir. undergrad. libr., 1996—2004; dir. Z Smith Reynolds Libr. Wake Forest U., Winston-Salem, NC, 2004—. Cons. Catherine McAuley Health Sys., Ann Arbor, Mich., 1993. Contbr. articles to profl. jours. Mem. ALA, Assn. Coll. and Rsch. Librs. (budget and fin. com. 1995—), Mich. Health Scis. Librs. Assn. (pres. 1987-88), Met. Detroit Med. Libr. Group (pres. 1983-84), Phi Beta Kappa, Beta Phi Mu. Office: Z Smith Reynolds Libr Wake Forest U Box 7777 Reynolda Station Winston Salem NC 27109 Office Phone: 336-758-5090. Business E-Mail: suttonls@wfu.edu.*

**SUTTON, MARK B.,** diversified financial services company executive; b. Oct. 19, 1954; BSBA finance, U. Ark., 1978. With Merrill Lynch & Co., 1978—80; joined Rotan Mosely, 1980, PaineWebber Inc., 1983, office mgr. Houston, 1985—86, divsn. mgr., Rotan divsn., 1986—88; with Mitchell Hutchins Asset Mgmt., 1988—91; COO, mng. dir., investment svcs. div. Kidder, Peabody & Co., 1992—94, CEO investment svcs. divsn., CEO brokerage unit, 1994; exec. v.p. PaineWebber Inc., 1995—98, pres. pvt. client group, 1998—2000; head U.S. pvt. client group UBS Fin. Svcs., N.Y.C., 2001—02; pres., COO UBS Wealth Mgmt. USA, N.Y.C., 2002—04, CEO, 2004—. Named hon. initiate, Betta Gamma Sigma, Sam H. Walton Coll. of Bus., U. Ark., 2003. Office: UBS Fin Svcs 1285 Avenue of the Americas New York NY 10019-6028

**SUTTON, NANCY THURMOND,** music educator; d. A. L. Thurmond and Rosetta Irene (Posey) Thurmond-Hale; m. Geoffrey Coe Sutton, June 25, 1977 (div. 1999); 1 child, Brittany Bradford. BMus, U. Memphis, 1969, MusM, 1979; cert., Royal Sch. Ch. Music, Croydon, Eng., 1994; D of Musical Arts, U. Calif., L.A., 2000. Organist, Church St. Paul's Episcopal Ch., Memphis, 1965—68; organist, dir. music St. George's Episcopal Ch., Germantown, Tenn., 1968—97; dir. choral activities U. N.C., Charlotte, NC, 2000—. Dir. St. George's Festival of Music, Germantown, 1982—97; music instr. U. Memphis 1975—76; faculty Sewanee Music Conf., 1995; tchr., mentor Memphis City Schs., 1969—73. Conductor Andrew Lloyd Webber's Requiem, 1986, Arvo Part's Miserere, 1990, Lalo Schifren's Cantos Aztecas, American Premier, 1992, pub. Sun Splendor, 2000. Organist, choirmaster St. Christopher's Cath. Ch., Dickson, Tenn., 2003—05; dir. choral workshops Roman Cath. Dioceses, Tenn., Ky.; organist, dir. music Church of the Most Holy Trinity, Augusta, Ga., 2005—., Musician Artist Trust Fund grantee, 1980—97. Mem.: Orch. League, Assn. Anglican Musicinas (conv. chair 1982), Am. Guild Organists (dean 1980—81). Episcopalian. Avocations: horseback riding, walking, reading, water-skiing, skiing. E-mail: nants@knology.net.

**SUTTON, NEAL S.,** lawyer; b. Grand Forks, ND, Sept. 9, 1945; BA, U. Houston, 1969, JD, 1972. Bar: Tex. 1972, US Ct. Appeals 5th Cir. 1972. Atty. pvt. practice; gen. counsel, sec. Cameron Iron Works (acquired by Cooper Industries Inc. in 1989), Houston, 1977—89; assoc. gen. counsel Cooper Industries Inc., Houston, 1989—91; v.p., gen. counsel Smith Internat. Inc., Houston, 1991—92, v.p. adminstrn., gen. counsel, sec., 1992—94, sr. v.p. adminstrn., gen. counsel, sec., 1994—. Adj. assoc. prof. adminstrv. sci. Jones Grad. Sch. Adminstrn., Rice U., 1989—93; gulf coast dist. dir. Petroleum Equipment Suppliers Assn. Bd. dirs. Harris County Edn. Found., 1997—. Mem.: Am. Corp. Counsel Assn. (dir. Houston chpt. 1984—87, pres. Houston chpt. 1985—86, mem. nat. bd. 1993—96), State Bar Tex., Houston Bar Assn. (dir. corp. counsel sect. 1991—93), ABA. Office: Smith Internat Inc 411 N Sam Houston Pkwy Ste 600 Houston TX 77060

**SUTTON, PETER U.,** military officer; BSCE, USAF Acad., 1972; MSCE, U. Ill., 1973; grad., Squadron Officer Sch., 1976, Air Command and Staff Coll., 1986, Air War Coll., 1988, Indsl. Coll. of Armed Forces, 1991. Commd. 2d lt. USAF, 1972, advanced through grades to brigadier gen., 1998; spl. asst. air staff tng. program, Dep. Chief of Staff Ops., Plans and Readiness, Hdqs. USAF, The Pentagon, Washington, 1979-80; asst. prof. aerospace studies Air Force Res. Officer Tng. Corps Detachment 105, U. Colo., Boulder, 1980-83; RF-4C flight comdr. 91st Tactical Reconnaissance Squadron, Bergstrom AFB, Tex., 1983-84; aide to comdr. 12th Air Force, Bergstrom AFB, 1984-85; T-38 ops. officer 25th Flying Tng. Squadron, comdr. 8th Flying Tng. Squadron, Vance AFB, Okla., 1986-88; dep. chief intelligence, electronic combat, test/tng. divsn. Directorate Programs & Eval., Hdqs. USAF, The Pentagon, Washington, 1988-90; exec. officer to dep. comdr. in chief UN Command, Yongsan AFB, South Korea, 1991-92; chief Yongsan relocation divsn. J-5, U.S. Forces Korea, Yongsan AFB, 1992-93; comdr. 71st Support Group, Vance AFB, 1993-95; vice comdr. 47th Flying Tng. Wing, Laughlin AFB, Tex., 1995-96; comdr. 11th Wing, Bolling AFB, 1996-98, Air Force Recruiting Svc., Randolph AFB, Tex., 1998-2000, comdr. 12th Flying Tng. Wing, 2000—. Decorated Def. Superior Svc. medal, Legion of Merit, Meritorious Svc. medal with 6 oak leaf clusters.

**SUTTON, ROBERT EDWARD,** investment company executive; b. Burlington, Vt., July 3, 1943; s. Rollin Robert and Blanche Margaret (Deforge) S.; m. Julie Robin Levine, Feb. 1, 1975; children: Katherine Vanessa, David Robert. BA in Econs., St. Michaels Coll., 1962-66. V.p. Competic, Inc., Beverly Hills, Calif., 1967-70; brokerage cons. Conn. Gen. Life Ins. Co., Denver, 1970-74; pres. The Core Corp., Denver, 1975-80; mng. dir. Willshire Investments & Holding Co. Denver, 1981-91; pres., chmn Gen Capital Inc Denver, 1991-93, pres, CEO WR Capital Advisors, Inc., Denver, 1994—; prin., owner Sutton Motorsports, 2002—; co-owner MBZ Motorsports, 2005—. Dir. NAt. Assn. Indep. Contr., Denver. 1991—, Nat. Endowment Trust, Denver, 1990—, Tri Corp, Denver, 1980-89, Nat. Acceptance Corp. L.A., 1991—. Nat. Investment Holdings, L.A., 1990—; chmn. Centrix Findmiol, LLC, 1998—, EIF, Inc., 1998—, Centrix Fin., LLC Mem. Nat. Rep. Eagles, Washington, 1986-90, Inner Circle, Washington, 1985-90, Denver Ctr. Performing Arts, 1976-86; bd. trustees St. Michaels Coll., Burlington, Vt.; bd. dirs St. John's Hospice, Make-a-Wish Found Mem. Am. Cancer League, Glenmoor Country Club. Home: 4949 South Fairfax St Littleton CO 80121

**SUTTON, ROBERT JAMES,** social studies educator, special education educator; b. Frankfort, Germany, Mar. 23, 1956; arrived in U.S., 1956; s. James Estus and Mary Elizabeth Sutton; m. Kathy Standley Sutton, Dec. 23, 1989; 1 child, Joshua James. BS in Secondary Edn., U. So. Miss., Hattiesburg, 1990, EdM, 1995. History and spl. edn. educator Oak Grove H.S., Hattiesburg, Miss., 1990—. Named to George Washington Tchr. Inst., Ladies of Mt. Vernon, 2004; recipient Master Tchr. award, Oak Grove H.S., 2002, Teach Vietnam award, Vietnam Veterans, 2005. Achievements include development of greenhouse project for students with severe learning disabilities; horticulture and landscaping job skills program. Avocations: historical wargaming, reading. Office: Oak Grove HS 5198 Old Hwy 11 Hattiesburg MS 39402-6222 Office Phone: 601-264-9058. Fax: 601-264-0160. Personal E-mail: rjsutton56@comcast.net.

**SUTTON, RONNIE NEAL,** state legislator, lawyer; b. Pembroke, N.C., June 17, 1941; s. Willie French and Vergie Mae (Oxendine) S.; m. Genny Chavis, June 19, 1967; children: Ronette, Fonda Lynn. BA, U. West Fla., 1970; MS, Naval War Coll., 1977; MA, Ctrl. Mich. U., 1979; JD, U. N.C., 1985. Commd. ensign USN, 1958, advanced through grades to comdr., ret., 1982; atty. Sutton Law Office, Pembroke, 1985-97; rep. N.C. Ho. of Reps., Raleigh, 1993—. Bd. dirs. Lumber River Legal Svcs., Pembroke, N.C. Cancer Inst., Lumberton. Chmn. Robeson County Dem. Party, Lumberton, 1991-92. Mem. Pembroke Kiwanis Club (pres. 1991-92, Kiwanian of Yr. 1992). Democrat. Home: 2940 Philadelphus Rd Pembroke NC 28372-8308 Office: NC Ho of Reps Jones St Raleigh NC 27601 Office Phone: 910-521-4797. E-mail: rons@ncleg.net.

**SUTTON, THOMAS C.,** insurance company executive; b. Atlanta, June 2, 1942; m. Marilyn Sutton; children: Stephen, Paul, Matthew, Meagan. BS in Math. and Physics, U. Toronto, 1965; postgrad., Harvard U., 1982. With Pacific Mut. Life Ins. Co., Newport Beach, Calif., 1966-69, successively asst. actuary, assoc. actuary, asst. v.p., 2d v.p., v.p. individual ins., 1969-80, successively v.p. individual fin., sr. v.p. corp. devel., exec. v.p. individual ins., 1980-87, pres. 1987—90, bd. dir. 1987—; chmn., CEO Pacific Life Corp., Newport Beach, Calif., 1990—. Bd. dir. Irvine Co. Edison Internat.; dir & past chmn. Am. Council Life Insurers, Assn. Calif. Life & Health Ins. Cos., Health Ins. Assn. Am. Trustee South Coast Repertory 1984-94, pres. 1992-94; bd. dir. Orange County Perf. Arts Ctr. 1995-98, Calif. C. of C.; chmn. Pub. Policy Inst. Calif. Fellow Soc. of Actuaries (mem. numerous coms.); mem. Am. Acad. Actuaries (com. on dividend prins. and practices, 1978), Pacific States Actuarial Club, L.A. Actuarial Club (sec. 1974-75, pres. 1978-79). Office: Pacific Mut Life Ins Co 700 Newport Center Dr Newport Beach CA 92660-6307*

**SUTTON, WILLIAM BLAYLOCK,** pastor; b. Little Rock, Aug. 10, 1942; s. Richard Otto and Bettye (Blaylock) S.; m. Martha Davis, Apr. 19, 1968; children: Blake, Bryan, Stephen. BBA, Baylor U., 1964; BD, Southwestern Bapt. Theol. Sem., Ft. Worth, 1967; ThM, Internat. Theol. Sem., Orlando, Fla., 1982, DD, 1984. Ordained to ministry So. Bapt. Conv., 1965. Pastor North Hopkins Bapt. Ch., Sulphur Springs, Tex., 1965-67, 1st Bapt. Ch. Pine Hills, Orlando, 1969-77, Windsor Park Bapt. Ch., Ft. Smith, Ark., 1977-86; assoc. pastor Dauphin Way Bapt. Ch., Mobile, Ala., 1968-69; pastor 1st Bapt. Ch., McAllen, Tex., 1986—. V.p. Fla. Bapt. Pastors Conf., Orlando, 1973, So. Bapt. Conv. Tex., 2003—04; pres. Ark. Bapt. Pastors Conf., Ft. Smith, 1983; trustee fgn. mission bd. So. Bapt. Conv., Richmond, Va., 1990—. Bd. visitors Criswell Coll., Dallas, 1991. Office: 1st Bapt Ch 1200 Beech Ave Mcallen TX 78501-4687

**SUTTON-CREECH, DONNA LYNN,** gifted and talented educator; b. Arcadia, La., Dec. 14, 1963; d. Jerry Lamar and Betty Muse Sutton; m. Stephen Orel Creech, July 9, 2005. BA, La. Tech. U., 1984, MA, 1985, EdD in curriculum and instruction, 2002. Compensatory edn. tchr. Bienville Parish Sch. Sys., Arcadia, La., 1985—90; parttime computer instr. Northwest La. Tech. Coll., Minden, La., 2002—04; gifted program tchr. Bienville Parish Sch. Sys., Arcadia, 1990—. Computer workshop presenter Bienville Parish La. Libr., Arcadia, La., 2003. Publr. genealogy column, Bienville Democrat. Participant Tech Rome 1987, La. Tech. U. Named Tchr. of Yr., Ringgold Elem. Sch., 1995; recipient Daughters of Am. Revolution Outstanding Jr. Mem. award, Dorcheat-Bistineau, 1997; La. Heritage Edn. grant, La. Divsn. Archaeology and Hist., 2003. Mem.: DAR (Dorcheat-Bistineau chpt. officer, regist & historian, chpt. chair, Dorcheat-Bistineau chpt. scholarship com., Good Citizens award), Phi Delta Kappa, Krewe of Gemini, Colonial Dames Seventeenth Century (state jr. mem. chair 2001—04, Martha Randolph chpt. v.p. 2002—04, state pages chair), Nat. Soc. Magna Carta Dames and Barons, USA Order of Crown of Charlemagne. Republican. Baptist. Avocations: genealogy, reading, travel, painting.

**SUVARI, MENA,** actress; b. Newport, RI, Feb. 9, 1979; d. Ando and Candance Suvari; m. Robert Brinkmann, Mar. 4, 2000. Actor: (TV films) Atomic Train, 1999; (TV series) Six Feet Under, 2004—; (films) Nowhere, 1997, Snide and Prejudice, 1997, Kiss the Girls, 1997, Slums of Beverly Hills, 1998, The Rage: Carrie 2, 1999, American Pie, 1999, American Beauty, 1999, American Virgin, 2000, Loser, 2000, Sugar & Spice, 2001, American Pie 2, 2001, The Musketeer, 2001, Sonny, 2002, Spun, 2002, Trauma, 2004, Beauty Shop, 2005, Domino, 2005, Rumor Has It..., 2005. Office: c/o Gersh Agy 232 N Canon Dr Beverly Hills CA 90210*

**SUWYN, MARK A.,** building products executive; b. Denver, Aug. 8, 1942; BS in Chemistry, Hope Coll., Holland, Mich., 1964; PhD in Inorganic Chemistry, Wash. State U., 1967. From R&D to gen. mgmt. positions DuPont Co., 1967-91, sr. v.p. imaging and med. products, 1989-92; exec. v.p. Internat. Paper, Purchase, N.Y., 1992-95; CEO Louisianna Pacific Corp., Portland, 1995—. Office: Louisiana Pacific 805 SW Broadway Ste 740 Portland OR 97205-3344

**SUYCOTT, MARK LELAND,** program manager, retired military officer; b. Riverside, Calif., Oct. 3, 1956; s. Morgan L. Suycott and Dixie L. (Drury) Bobbitt; m. Lisa Lyn Brammer, Oct. 1, 1983. BSCE, U. Mo., 1979; MS in Aero. Engring., Naval Postgrad. Sch., Monterey, Calif., 1987; test flight officer, U.S. Naval Test Pilot Sch., Patuxent River, Md., 1987; student, Def. Sys. Mgmt. Coll., Ft. Belvoir, Va., 1994. Commd. ensign USN, 1979, advanced through grades to comdr., 1995; aviation armament divsn. officer Fighter Squadron 33, Virginia Beach, Va., 1981-84; flight test project officer Pacific Missile Test Ctr., Point Mugu, Calif., 1987-89; air ops. officer Comdr. U.S. 7th Fleet, Yokosuka/Manama, Japan/Bahrain, 1989-91; ops./maintenance officer Fighter Squadron 11, San Diego, 1992-93; dep. asst. program mgr. Naval Air Sys. Command, Arlington, Va., 1994-97; prof. Def. System Mgmt. Coll., Fort Belvoir, Va., 1997-99; sr. sys. engr. SAIC Space and Def. Group, San Diego, 2000-01, prin. sys. engr. and program mgr., 2001—03, sr. project mgr., program mgr., 2004—. Asst. dist. commr. Boy Scouts Am.; chaplain Al Bahr Shrine, 2006. Decorated Def. Meritorious Svc. medal, Meritorious Svc. medal (2), Navy Commendation medal (2), Navy Achievement medal; named Outstanding Grad., U.S. Naval Test Pilot Sch.; recipient Woodbadge, Distng. Comm'r. and Commr.'s Key awards, Boy Scouts Am. Mem.: VFW, AIAA (sr.), Inst. Navigation, Naval Aviation Found., Nat. Eagle Scout Assn. (life), Masons (life), Tailhook Assn., Scottish Rite (32d degree), Am. Legion, Shriners (life), Chi Epsilon, Tau Beta Pi, Omicron Delta Kappa, Alpha Phi Omega (life). Avocations: bicycling, sailing, skiing. Address: SAIC 10260 Campus Point Dr MS c2 San Diego CA 92121-1522

**SUYDAM, JOHN J.,** lawyer; b. NYC, 1960; BA, SUNY, Albany, 1982; JD, NYU, 1985. Bar: NY 1986. Chmn. O'Sullivan LLP, NY; head O'Melveny & Myers LLP, NY, mem. policy com., co-chair merger and acquisitions/private equity practice group. Mem.: ABA. Office: O'Melveny & Myers LLP Times Square Tower 7 Times Square New York NY 10036 Office Phone: 212-408-2471. Office Fax: 212-326-2061.

**SUYENAGA, ELSIE SAKAE,** retired elementary school educator; b. Honolulu, Dec. 19; d. Shigeharu Shimizu-Jinbo and Misao Jinbo; m. James Saburo Suyenaga; 1 child, Matthew Masao. BA, Pasadena Coll., 1963; postgrad., U. Hawaii, 1963—81. Sec. Nuuanu Bapt. Ch., 1954—62; tchr. Ewa Beach (Hawaii) Elem. Sch., 1964—89. Exch. tchr. Laurel Elem. Sch. LA Sch. Dist., 1968—69; advisor student coun. Laurel Elem. Sch. Sec. Palisades Cmty. Assn., 1977; treas. Neighborhood Bd., Pearl City, 1982; legis. chmn., treas. Pearl City Cmty. Assn., 1984—85; treas. local chpt. PTA; active polit. campaigns. Recipient Student Coun. Advisor award, Ewa Beach Elem. Sch., 1978, Dist. award, PTA, 1976, Merit Cert., Pearl City Cmty. Assn., 1977, Recognition award, Ewa Beach Kiwanis, 1986; Fed. grant, 1963. Mem.: DAV, Am. Mus. Natural History, Hawaii Edn. Assn. (bd. trustees 1986—), Leeward Tchrs. Assn. (treas., polit. sect. chmn. 1986), Hawaii State Tchrs. Assn. (dir. 1981—83, sec. fin. com. 1981, vice-chmn. 1982, Merit Cert. 1969), Alpha Delta Kappa (treas. Lambda chpt. 1980—81). Democrat. Baptist. Home: 6354 San Diego Ave Riverside CA 92506 E-mail: suyenaga@charter.net.

**SUZIEDELIS, VYTAUTAS A.,** retired engineering corporation executive; b. Kaunas, Lithuania, June 22, 1930; s. Simas and Antanina. BS, Northeastern U., 1954; MS, N.Y. U., 1955. With Stone & Webster Engring. Corp., Boston, 1956-90, chief power engr., 1972-74, v.p., 1974-76, sr. v.p., 1976-79, exec. v.p., 1979-87, dir., 1975-87, cons., 1987-90; pres. Vasair Corp., Brockton, Mass., 1977-91; ret., 1991. Mem. ASME, Aircraft Owners and Pilots Assn.; Pi Tau Sigma (hon.). Republican. Roman Catholic. Home: 6849 Grenadier Blvd Ph 5 Naples FL 34108-7223 Personal E-mail: vasuziedelis@cs.com.

**SUZUKI, AKIRA,** physics professor; b. Tokyo, Apr. 14, 1949; s. Masatsugu and Takako (Tanbo) S.; m. Keiko Sawamura, Sept. 13, 1992. BSc, Sci. U. Tokyo, 1973; PhD, U. Reading, Eng., 1982. Rsch. assoc. Purdue U., West Lafayette, Ind., 1982-85; chief scientist Canon Rsch. Ctr., Atsugi, Japan, 1986-93; assoc. prof. Sci. U. Tokyo, 1993-98, prof. physics, 1998—, chmn., 2002—; prof. Inst. Pure and Applied Physics Tokyo U. Sci., 1998—. Contbr. articles to profl. jours. Mem. IEEE, Am. Phys. Soc., NY Acad. Scis. Avocations: tennis, golf, music. Office: Sci U Tokyo Ctr Solid State Physics 1-3 Kagurazaka Tokyo 162 Japan

**SUZUKI, BOB H.,** retired academic administrator; b. Jan. 1936; MS mech. engring., Univ. Calif. Berkeley. Formerly v.p. acad. affairs Calif. State Univ., Northridge; pres. Calif. State Poly. Univ., Pomona, 1991—2003; ret., 2003. Recipient Human Rights award Leadership Asian and Pacific Island Affairs, NEA, 1976. Home: 3012 W Ross Ave Alhambra CA 91803

**SUZUKI, HIDETARO,** violinist; b. Tokyo, June 1, 1937; arrived in U.S., 1956; s. Hidezo and Humi (Sakai) S.; m. Zeyda Ruga, May 16, 1962; children: Kenneth Hideo, Nantel Hiroshi, Elina Humi. Diploma, Toho Sch. Music, Tokyo, 1956, Curtis Inst. Music, 1963. Prof. violin Conservatory Province Que., Canada, 1963-79, Laval U., Quebec, Canada, 1971-77, Butler U., Indpls., 1979—. Concertmaster Que. Symphony Orch., 1963-78, Indpls. Symphony Orch., 1978-2005; performed as concert violinist Can., U.S., Ea. and Western Europe, Cuba, Japan, S.E. Asia, India, USSR 1951-; guest condr. orchs. in numerous concerts, broadcasts, 1968—; mem. jury Mont. Internat. Competition, 1979, Internat. Violin Competition, 1979, Internat. Violin Competition of Indpls., 1982, 86, 90, 94; artistic dir. Suzuki and Friends chamber music series, 1980—; rec. artist (CDs, violin and piano) Dialogue, Dialogue II, Pas de deux.

**SUZUKI, HOWARD KAZURO,** retired anatomist, educator; b. Ketchikan, Alaska, Apr. 3, 1927; s. Goerge K. and Tsuya S.; m. Tetsuko Fujita, Sept. 12, 1952; children: Georganne, Joan, James, Stanley. BS, Marquette U., 1949, MS, 1951; PhD, Tulane U., 1955. Instr. anatomy Yale U. Sch. Medicine, 1955-58; asst. prof. anatomy U. Ark. Med. Center, Little Rock, 1958-62, assoc. prof., 1962-67, prof., 1967-70; prof. anatomy, asso. dean health related professions U. Fla., Gainesville, 1970-71; prof. anatomy U. Fla. (Coll. Medicine), 1970-71; dean U. Fla. (Coll. Health Related Professions), 1971-79; prof. anatomy U. Fla. (Coll. Medicine and Health Related Professions), 1979-90, ret., 1990. Cons. NIH, VA, NASA; vis. research prof. U. Utah Sch. Medicine, 1962 Contbr. articles to profl. jours. Bd. dirs. Civitan Regional Blood Bank, 1977—; regional v.p. Fla. Retarded Citizens Assn., 1974-76; mem. Fla. Adv. Council on Vocat. Edn., 1978-86, chmn., 1981; active United Way. Fellow AAAS; mem. Soc. Exptl. Biol. Medicine, Am Assn. Anatomists, Am. Soc. Allied Health Professions, Am. Soc. Marine Artists, Sigma Xi. Episcopalian. Home: 4331 NW 20th Pl Gainesville FL 32605-3436 E-mail: hksuzuki@aol.com.

**SUZUKI, ICHIRO,** professional baseball player; b. Kasugai, Japan, Oct. 22, 1973; Player Orix Blue Waves, Japan, 1992—2001; right field Seattle Mariners, 2001—. Named a mem. of the All-Tourney Team, World Baseball Classic, 2006; named Am. League Rookie of the Year, 2001, Am. League MVP, 2001; named to Am. League All-Star Team, 2001—06; recipient Matsutaro Shoriki prize, 1994, Pacific League MVP, 1994, Matsutaro Shoriki prize, 1995, Pacific League MVP, 1995, 1996, Gold Glove Awards (seven), Nippon Professional Baseball League, 7 Best Nine Team (Japan) titles, Am. League Gold Glove Award, 2001—05. Achievements include being the second player in history to win rookie and MVP award in the same season; being second player in MLB history to lead league in batting average and stolen bases in a season, 2001; being first player in MLB history to have over 200 hits in each of his first four years; holding MLB record for singles in a season (225), 2004; holding MLB record for hits in a single season (262), 2004; leading American League in Batting Avg. (.371), 2004; helping his national team Japan win the first ever World Baseball Classic 2006. Office: Seattle Mariners PO Box 4100 Seattle WA 98104*

**SUZUKI, JON BYRON,** medical educator, periodontist, microbiologist; s. George K. and Ruby Suzuki. BA in Biology, Ill. Wesleyan U., 1968; PhD in Microbiology magna cum laude, Ill. Inst. Tech., 1971; DDS magna cum laude, Loyola U., 1978. Lic. lab. dir. Hawaii Dept. Health. Med. technologist Ill. Masonic Hosp. and Med. Ctr., Chgo., 1966—67; instr. lab. in histology and parasitology Ill. Wesleyan U., Bloomington, 1967—68; med. technologist Augustana Hosp., Chgo., 1968—69; rsch. assoc., instr. microbiology Ill. Inst. Tech., Chgo., 1968—71; clin. rsch. assoc. U. Chgo. Hosps., 1970—71; clin. microbiologist St. Luke's Hosp., Columbia Coll., Physicians and Surgeons, N.Y.C., 1971—73; assoc. med. dir. Paramed Tng. and Registry, Vancouver, BC, Canada, 1973—74; dir. clin. labs. Registry of Hawaii, 1973—74; chmn. clin. labs. edn. Kapiolany C.C., U. Hawaii, Honolulu, 1974; lectr. periodontics, oral pathology Loyola U. Med. Ctr., Maywood, Ill., 1974—90; lectr. stomatology Northwestern U. Dental Sch., Chgo., 1982—90; NIH rsch. fellow depts. pathology and periodontics Ctr. for Rsch. in Oral Biology, U. Wash., Seattle, 1978—80; prof. dept. periodontics and microbiology U. Md. Coll. Dental Surgery, Balt., 1980—90; attending faculty divsns. dentistry and oral and maxillofacial surgery Johns Hopkins Med. Inst., Balt., 1985—96; practice specializing in periodontics Balt. and Pitts.; prof., dean Sch. Dental Medicine U. Pitts., 1989—2000, prof., dir. periodontics residency program, 2002—04. Cons. Dentsply Internat., York, Pa., U.S. Army, Walter Reed Med. Ctr., Washington, U.S. Army, Ft. Gordon, Ga., USN, Nat. Naval Med. Command, Bethesda, The NutraSweet Col., Chgo., FDA, Rockville, Md., 1995—, Phillips Oral Health Care, Snoqualmie, Wash.; oral biology/medicine study sect. NIH, Bethesda, 1985-90; nat. adv. dental rsch. coun. NIH/NIDCR, Bethesda, 1994-98; vis. scientist Moscow State U., USSR, 1972, NASA, Houston, 1976-92; lectr. Internat. Congress allergology, Tokyo, 1973. Author: Clinical Laboratory Methods for the Medical Assistant, 1974; mem. editl. bd. Jour. Clinical Dentistry, Jour. Practical Hygiene, Jour. Acad. Gen. Dentistry; contbr. articles on rsch. in microbiology, immunology and dentistry to profl. jours. Instr. water safety ARC, Honolulu, 1973—90. Recipient Pres.'s medallion Loyola U., Chgo., 1977; named Alumnus of Yr., Ill. Wesleyan U., 1977, Loyola U., Chgo., 1997. Fellow Acad. Dentistry Internat., Am. Coll. Dentists, Internat. Coll. Dentists, Am. Coll. Stomatologic Surgeons; mem. ADA (chair coun. sci. affairs 1998), AAUP, Am. Acad. Periodontology (diplomate), Am. Dental Edn. Assn., Am. Inst. Biol. Scis., Internat. Soc. Biophysics, Internat. Soc. Endocrinologists, Ill. Acad. Sci., Am. Internat. Assn. Dental Rsch. (pres. Md. chpt.), Am. Coll. Microbiology (diplomate, examiner), Am. Soc. Clin. Pathology (specialist microbiology), N.Y. Acad. Scis., Sigma Xi, Omicron Kappa Upsilon (past nat. pres., exec. sec. 1989—, treas. 2006—), Beta Beta Beta. Office: Temple Univ Dentistry Office of the Dean 3223 N Broad St Philadelphia PA 19140 E-mail: jsuzuki@temple.edu.

**SUZUKI, JUNICHI,** computer scientist; s. Hanichiro and Nobuko Suzuki; m. Kumiko Nakano, Feb. 11, 2001. PhD in Computer Sci., Keio U., Yokohama, Japan, 2001. Tech. analyst, dir. Soken Planning Co., Ltd., Tokyo, 1992—96; tech. dir. Object Mgmt. Group Japan, 1996—2001; co-founder, chief tech. officer Tech Atlas Comm., Inc., Austin, Tex., 1997—98; lectr. dept. econs. Keio U., Yokohama, Japan, 2000—01; adv. bd. Synergy Rsch. Corp., Tokyo, 2001—02; adv. bd. mem. Software Engring. Ctr., Osaka Gas Info. Sys. Rsch. Inst. Co., Ltd., 2001—; chief scientist Object Mgmt. Group Japan Inc., 2003—; adv. bd., 2003—03; asst. prof. U. Mass., Boston, 2004—. Mem. std. com. Internat. Std. Orgn., 2004—; specification co-leader Object Mgmt. Group, Super Distributed Objects Domain SIG, 2000—04. Author: (technical book) Software Patterns Revisited, LiveWire Primer: Building Programmable Internet Servers; contbr. chapters to books. Fellow, U. Calif., Irvine, 2001—04. Mem.: IEEE, ACM. Achievements include research in Technical Standard Specification, Platform Independent Model (PIM) and Platform Specific Model (PSM) for Super Distributed Objects. Office: U Mass 100 Morrissey Blvd Boston MA 02125 Office Phone: 617-287-6264.

**SUZUKI, KUNIHIKO,** biomedical educator, researcher; b. Tokyo, Feb. 5, 1932; arrived in U.S., 1960; s. Nobuo and Teiko (Suzuki) Suzuki; m. Kinuko Ikeda, Dec. 20, 1960; 1 child, Jun. BA in History and Philosophy of Sci., Tokyo U., 1955, MD, 1959; MA (hon.), U. Pa., 1971. Diplomate Nat. Bd. Med. Licensure Japan. Rotating intern USAF Hosp. Tachikawa, Tokyo, 1959-60; asst. resident in neurology Bronx (N.Y.) Mcpl. Hosp. Ctr.-Albert Einstein Coll. Medicine, 1960-61, resident in neurology, 1961-62, clin. fellow in neurology, 1962-64; instr. in neurology Albert Einstein Coll. Medicine, Bronx, 1964, asst. prof., 1965-68; assoc. prof. U. Pa. Sch. Medicine, Phila., 1969-71, prof. neurology and pediatrics, 1971-72; prof. neurology Albert Einstein Coll. Medicine, 1972-86, prof. neurosci., 1974-86; prof. neurology and psychiatry, faculty curriculum in neurobiology U. N.C. Sch. Medicine, Chapel Hill, 1986—2002, prof. emeritus neurology and psychiatry, 2002—; dir. UNC Neurosci. Ctr., Chapel Hill, 1986-99, dir. emeritus, 1999—; prof. Future Sci. and Tech. Joint Rsch. Ctr. Tokai U., Japan, 2003—, dir. Inst. Glycotechnology, 2003—. Staff dept. neuropsychiatry Tokyo U. Faculty Medicine, 1960, U. Pa. Inst. Neurol. Scis., 1969—72; attending physician Bronx Mcpl. Hosp. Ctr., 1976—86, Hosp. Albert Einstein Coll. Medicine, 1977—86; vis. prof. fellowship Japan Soc. for Promotion Sci., 1980, Yamada Sci. Found.; mem. neurology B study sect. NIH, 1971—75, guest scientist, 1984—85, program com. mental retardation and devel. disabilities, 1989—92; mem. basic neurosci. task force Nat. Inst. Neurol. and Communicative Disorders and Stroke, 1978, adv. panel directions and opportunities for future rsch., 83; bd. sci. counselors NIH, 1980—84; mem. adv. com. on fellowships Nat. Multiple Sclerosis Soc., 1974—77; jury St. Vincent Internat. award for Med. Sci., 1979; mem. adv. com. Eunice Kennedy Shriver Ctr., Waltham, Mass., 1974—84; mem. U.S. Nat. Com. for Internat. Brain Rsch. Orgn., 1985—89. Editor: Ganglioside Structure and Function, 1984; editor: (chief) Jour. Neurochemistry, 1977—82; dep. chief editor Jour. Neurochemistry, 1975—77, mem. editl. bd. Jour. Neuropathology and Exptl. Neurology, 1981—83, Neurosci., 1975—, Molecular Chem. Neuropathology, 1983—, Neurochem. Rsch., 1985—89, Metabolic Brain Disease, 1985—87, Molecular Brain Rsch., 1985—, Jour. Molecular Neurosci., 1987—, Devel. Neurosci., 1987—, Jour. Neurosci. Rsch., 1993—97; contbr. Mem. Nat. Adv. Commn. on Multiple Sclerosis, 1973—74; mem. med. adv. bd. United Leukodystrophy Found., 1982—86, 1997—, Nat. Tay-Sachs and Allied Diseases Assn. 1971—2001, Canavan Found., 1992—. Recipient A. Weil award, Am. Assn. Neuropathologists, 1970, Saul R. Korey Lecturship, 1993, M. Moore award, 1975, Jacob K. Javits Neurosci. Investigator award, NIH, 1985, 1992, Humboldt Sr. Rsch. award, Humboldt Found., 1990, Eminent Scientist award, Inst. Phys. Chem. Rsch., Japan, 1995, Japan Acad. prize, 2002. Mem.: AAAS, Japan Soc. Inherited Metabolic Disease (hon.), Am. Soc. Human Genetics, Internat. Brain Rsch. Orgn., Japanese Neurochem. Soc., Japanese Med. Soc. Am. (Disting. Scientist award 1985), Am. Acad. Neurology, Am. Soc. Biochemistry and Molecular Biology, Soc. for Neurosci., Internat. Soc. for Neurochemistry (coun. 1987—89, treas. 1989—93, pres. 1993—95), Am. Soc. for Neurochemistry (pres. 1985—87, coun. 1973—77, 1987—91, Basic Neurochemistry Lectureship 1995), Inst. Medicine NAS. Avocations: piano, photography, birdwatching, skiing. E-mail: kuni.suzuki@attglobal.net.

**SUZUKI, NOBUTAKA,** chemistry professor; b. Nishio, Aichi, Japan, Nov. 8, 1942; s. Kihachiro and Masayo (Miwa) S.; m. Fumiko Sato, Mar. 21, 1971; children: Mina, Kumi. B of Chemistry, Nagoya U., Japan, 1966, D of Chemistry, 1972. Asst. prof. dept. chemistry Mie U., Tsu, Japan, 1971-88, assoc. prof., 1988; sr. rschr. Biophoton project JRDC, Sendai, Japan, 1988-90; assoc. prof. Shimonoseki (Japan) Nat. U. Fisheries, 1990-92, prof., 1993—2002, Hiroshima U., Japan, 2002—06, dean dept. biol. functional chemistry, 2004—05; chief Internat. Tech. Exch. Soc. Rsch. Inst., Nagoya, Japan, 2006—. Postdoctoral staff Johns Hopkins U., Balt., 1977-79; vis. prof. Asian Sch. Internat. Tech. Exch. Soc. Rsch. Inst., Brunswick, Ohio, 2000—. Author: Natural Products Chemistry, 1975, 2d rev. edit., 1983, Bioluminescence and Chemiluminescence, Current Status, 1991, Oxygen Radicals, 1992, Chemistry of Functional Dyes, Vol. 2, 1993, Bioluminescence and Chemiluminescence, Status Report, 1993, Bioluminescence and Chemiluminescence: Fundamentals and Applied Aspects, 1994, Maillard Reactions in Chemicals, Food, and Health, 1994, Food Factors: Chemistry and Cancer Prevention, 1997, Bioluminescence and Chemiluminescence, Molecular Reporting and Photons, 1997, Food Factors for Cancer Prevention, 1997, The Maillard Reaction in Foods and Medicine, 1998, Recent Research Developments in Agricultural and Biological Chemistry, Vol. 2, 1998, Advances in Shrimp Biotechnology, 1998, Dictionary of Biochemistry, 3d edit., 1998, Bioluminescence and Chemiluminescence: Perspectives for the 21st Century, 1999, Recent Development of Food Factors for the Aging Prevention, 1999, Agricultural and Biological Chemistry, Vol. 3, 1999, Future in Fisheries Science, 1999, Food Sciences, 2001, Bioluminescence and Chemiluminescence, 2000, 01, Bioluminescence and Chemiluminescence, Progress and Current Applications, 2002, Research Advances in Food Science, 2002, Trends in Comparative Biochemistry and Physiology, 2002, Near Infrared Spectroscopy, 2002, Trends in Comparative Biochemistry & Physiology, Vol.9, 2002; editor: (The Roles of Oxygen in Chemistry and Biochemistry, 1988, (book/tape) Scientific English in Fisheries, 1992, English for Science and Technological Experiments, 1994, English for Pharmacy and Medical Science, 1995, English for International Conference, 1995, Oxidative Degradation and Antioxidative Activities of Food Constituents, 2002, Life-style Related Diseases and Food Functions, 2003, Amazing Power of Marine Foods, 2003, Biological Sciences in Foods, 2004, Current Topics in Food Science & Technology, 2005; mem. editl. bd. ITE Letters on Batteries, New Techs. and Medicine, 2000—, award com. chmn., 2000—. Recipient Rsch. award Internat. Battery Material Assn., 1997, Spl. award Internat. Tech. Exch. Soc.-Internat. Battery Material Assn., 1998, Kozawa award, 2003, Yeager-Kozawa award, 2004; grantee Naito Meml. Found., 1977, Tokai Sci. Rsch. Found., 1986, Agrl. Biol. Chemistry Japan, 1990, Kiei-Kai Sci. Rsch. Found., 1991-96, Skylark Rsch. Found., 1992, The Sci. and Tech. Agy., Japan, 1994-96, Internat. Tech. Exch. K-Found., 1996-97, Internat. Battery Material Assn., 1998—, Nakatani Electronic Measuring Tech. Assn. Japan, 1998-99, Daikin Rsch. Inst., Japan, 2002-03; grant-in-aid Sci. and Tech. Agy. of Japan, 1998—, Rsch. Devel. Corp. Japan, 1998, Small Bus. Promotion Corp., Japan, 2000, grantee Daikin Rsch. Inst., Japan, 2000-2004, Taki Chem. Co., 2004—, Catalysts of Chems. Ind. Co., 2005-2006, Nishimura Co. Japan, 2005—, Yokota Md., 2005—. Mem. Am. Soc. for Photobiology, Agrl. Biol. Soc. Japan, Chem. Soc. Japan, Internat. Tech. Exch. Soc. (award 1995, bd. dirs. 1995—, v.p. 2000—, grantee 1998—). Office: Grad Sch Biosphere Sci Hiroshima Univ Hagashi Hiroshima 739-8528 Japan Business E-Mail: suzukin@hiroshima-u.ac.jp.

**SUZUKI, TSUNEO,** molecular immunologist; b. Nagoya, Aichi, Japan, Nov. 23, 1931; s. Morichika and Toshiko (Kita) S.; widowed; children: Riichiro, Aijiro, Yozo. BS, U. Tokyo, 1953, MD, 1957; PhD, U. Hokkaido, 1967. Asst. prof. U. Kans. Med. Ctr., Kansas City, 1970-79, assoc. prof., 1979-83, prof., 1983—2003, prof. emeritus, 2003—, interim chair, 1994-98. Mem. NIH Study Sect., Washington, 1983-87. Contbr. articles to profl. jours. Fellow U. Wis., 1963-66, 69-70, U. Lausanne, Switzerland, 1966-67, U Toronto, 1967-69; recipient Travel award Fulbright Found., 1962, Sr. Investigator award U. Kans. Med. Ctr., 1990. Mem. Am. Assn. Immunologists, Am. Soc. Biological Chemists (Travel award 1988). Home: 3620 W 73rd St Prairie Village KS 66208-2903 Office: U Kans Med Ctr/Dept Microbiology 3901 Rainbow Blvd Rm 3001 Orr Major Kansas City KS 66160-0001 E-mail: tsuzuki@kumc.edu.

**SUZUKI, YASUHIKO,** retired law educator; b. Mishima, Japan, Sept. 6, 1936; arrived in U.S., 68; s. Heijo and Hiro Suzuki; m. Kyoko Teraizumi Suzuki, May 14, 1961; children: Iori, Anri, Claude. LLB, Chuo U., Tokyo, 1960; LLM, Georgetown U., 1972. V.p. Nissan Motor Corp., Gardena, Calif., 1968—85; chmn. bd. dirs. Pacific Trade & Investment Corp., Washington, 1985—90; prof. U. Va., Charlottesville, 1991—93, Showa Joshi U. Tokyo, 1994—96, George Mason U., Fairfax, Va., 1996—2003. Vice chmn. Automobile Importers Am., Washington, 1975—85; lectr. in field. Author: Washington Lobby, 1990, The American Nation, 1999, The Constitution of the United States - The Evolving Constitution, 2000, Is the Second Amendment Anachronism? - The Right to Keep and Bear Arms, 2003. Bd. dirs. Japanese C. of C., N.Y.C., 1978—85, Washington, 1979—85. Named to Automotive Hall of Fame, 1984; recipient cert. of recognition for outstanding contbns. and efforts, Humane Soc. of Washington, DC, 1980, Youth for Understanding, 1981. Mem.: Internat. Law Inst. Japan, Acad. Polit. Sci. Home: 31242 Avenida Terramar San Juan Capistrano CA 92675

**SVAHN, JOHN ALFRED,** federal agency administrator; b. New London, Conn., May 13, 1943; s. Albert Russell and Esther Marilu (Caffero) S.; m. Jill Weber, July 12, 1977; children: Kirsten Marie, John Alfred III. BA in Polit. Sci, U. Wash., 1966; postgrad., U. Pacific, 1970-73, Georgetown U., 1973-74. Spl. asst. to dir. Calif. Dept. Public Works, 1968-70; chief dep. dir. Calif. Dept. Social Welfare, 1971-73, dir., 1973; acting commr. Community Services Adminstrn., HEW, Washington, 1973-74; commr. Assistance Payments Adminstrn., 1973-76; dep. adminstr. Social and Rehab. Service, 1974-75; adminstr. Social and Rehab. Svcs., 1975-76; mgr. Haskins and Sells, 1976-79; pres. John A. Svahn, Inc., Annapolis, Md., 1979-81; U.S. commr. social security Balt., 1981-83; undersec. HHS, Washington, 1983-84; asst. to Pres. for policy devel. Washington, 1984-86; chmn. Maximus Inc., Washington, 1988-92; U.S. commr. Commn. for Study of Alternatives for Panama Canal, 1987-92; exec. v.p. The Wexler Group, Washington, 1995—; chmn. Captial Assocs., Inc., 1994—; bd. dirs. Logisticare, Inc., 2000—, EpicEdge, Inc., 2001—. Mem. Nat. Devel. Disability Adv. Council, 1975-76, Pres.'s Transition Team, 1980-81, Calif. Health Care Commn., 1972, pub. affairs com. United Way Am., 1987—; chmn. Govs. Commn. on Corrections Health Care, Md., 1990—; assoc. mem. Calif. Republican State Cen. Com., 1970-72; bd. dirs. Nat. Aquarium, Balt.; bd. dirs. Health Care Svcs. NAS Inst. Medicine, 1987-92; bd. dirs. Logisticare, Inc., 2001-; bd. dirs. Epic Edge, Inc., 2001-04; mem. Gov.'s Privatization Coun., 1992—. Served to lt. USAF, 1966-68. Named Outstanding Young Man in HEW, 1974; recipient Sec.'s citation, 1975. Adminstr.'s spl. citation, 1975 Mem. Annapolis Yacht Club, Sailing Club of the Chesapeake, Kent Island Yacht Club, Phi Delta Phi, Zeta Psi. Republican. Office: 4790 Caughlin Pkwy 317 Reno NV 89509 Personal E-mail: jackswahn@aol.com.

**SVALYA, PHILLIP GORDON,** lawyer; b. Ferndale, Mich., June 28, 1943; s. John Michael and Anne Marie Svalya; children: Daniel Gordon, Karina Renee. BS, U.S. Naval Acad., Annapolis, Md., 1966; JD, U. Santa Clara, Calif., 1973. Bar: Calif. 1974, U.S. Dist. Ct. (no. dist.) Calif. 1974. Pvt. practice, Sunnyvale, Mountain View, Calif., 1974-81, Cupertino, Calif., 1981—. Officer, bd. dirs. Albanian Health Fund, Phillis Found. Lt. USN, 1966-70, capt. USN SEAL ret., 1970-91. Mem. Calif. Bar Assn., Santa Clara County Bar Assn., Sunnyvale/Cupertino Bar Assn., Underwater Demolition Team-SEAL Assn., Million Dollar Advocates Forum. Republican. Avocations: hiking, gardening. Office: Phillip G Svalya Inc 10455 Torre Ave Cupertino CA 95014-3203 Office Phone: 408-252-5211.

**SVAMBERA, BEATRICE ALICE,** secondary school educator; b. El Paso, Tex., July 28, 1942; d. Jose Jesus Ramirez and Angelina Manilla; m. Milan Joe Svambera, Feb. 14, 1973; children: Kelli Anne, Mark Anthony. BA, U. Tex., El Paso, 1964. Speech and drama tchr. Austin H.S., El Paso, 1964—68, Jefferson H.S., El Paso, 1968—74; ESL tchr. Rusk Elem., El Paso, 1975—78, Burle Sch., 1978—79; world history tchr. Baker Jr. High, LaPorte, Tex., 1985—87; Tex. and Am. history tchr. LaPorte Jr. High, 1987—. Curator Tex. and Am. History Mus., LaPorte, 1997—; presenter in field. Sec. of edn. Tejano Preservation Assn., Houston, 1988—91. Named Am. History Tchr. of the Yr., DAR, 2002; recipient Leon Jaworsky Edn. award, State Bar Tex., 2001, Spirit of Anne Frank Educator award, Anne Frank Ctr., 2002, Robert Goldman award for Tchg. Excellence in Holocaust Edn., Jewish Found., 2002. Mem.: NEA, Tex. Coun. for the Social Studies, Tex. State Tchrs. Assn., Sons of Rep. Tex., Daus. of Rep. Tex., Tejano Preservation Assn., U. Tex. El Paso Alumni Assn., Bay Area Heritage Soc., Bay Area Vets. Assn. Home: 3207 Lazy Pine La Porte TX 77571

**SVENDSBYE, LLOYD AUGUST,** academic administrator, theologian, educator; b. Hamlet, N.D., May 26, 1930; s. Anders A. and Gudrun J. (Birkelo) S.; m. Annelotte Frieda Erika Moertelmeyer, Dec. 20, 1958. BA, Concordia Coll., Moorhead, Minn., 1951, DD (hon.), 1983; BTh, Luther Theol.Sem., 1954; postgrad. U. Erlangen, Germany, 1954-55, Columbia U., 1959-60; ThD, Union Theol. Sem., 1966; LLD (hon.), Gettysburg Coll., 1977; LHD (hon.), Kilian C.C., 1992. Ordained to ministry, 1955; asst. pastor Our Saviours Luth. Ch., Mpls., 1955-56; adminstrv. asst. to dir. 3d Assembly Luth. World Fedn., 1956-57; asst. prof. religion Concordia Coll., 1957-59; asst. pastor Trinity Lutheran Ch., Bklyn., 1959-61; chmn. dept. religion Concordia Coll., 1962-66; editor in chief Augsburg Publ. House, Mpls., 1966-71; v.p., dean St. Olaf Coll., 1971-74; pres., prof. ch. history Luther Theol. Sem., St. Paul, 1974-82; pres. Northwestern Luth. Theol. Sem., 1976-82, Luther Northwestern Theol. Sem., 1982-87, prof. ch. history, 1982-87; pres. Augustana Coll., Sioux Falls, SD, 1987-92. V.p. Am. Luth. Ch., 1981-87; Mem. Am. Luth. Ch.-Luth. Ch. Am. coop. com., 1974-78; Luth. World Fedn. Com. on Info. Services, 1971-76; mem. Com. on Luth. Unity, 1978-82, Commn. To Form a New Luth. Ch., 1982-86. Chmn. senate dist. 49A, Dem. Farm Labor Com., 1970-71; bd. dirs. Luth. Brotherhood, 1970-95, Luth. Gen. and Health Care Sys., Park Ridge, Ill., 1981-87; trustee Luth. Deaconess Hosp., Mpls., 1970-71, Fairview-Southdale Hosp., 1975-87, Fairview Cmty. Hosps., 1979-87. Recipient Alumni Achievement award Concordia Coll., 1974 Mem. Phi Beta Kappa. Home: 2500 Quentin Ct Minneapolis MN 55416-1900 E-mail: annelloy@aol.com.

**SVENDSEN, ALF,** artist, art educator; b. Bklyn., Mar. 24, 1930; s. Alf and Anna Thordina (Fjeldberg) S. BFA cum laude, Syracuse U., 1955; MFA summa cum laude, U. Notre Dame, 1965. Asst. sculptor Ivan Mestrovic, Notre Dame, Ind., 1955-56; sculptor Hall of African Man Am. Mus. Natural History, N.Y.C., 1966-68; tchr. art Mt. Anthony H.S., Bennington, Vt., 1969-71; prof. Delaware County C.C., Media, Pa., 1971-89. Exhibited work at New Sch. Social Rsch., N.Y.C., 1958, N.Y. Six Gallery, 1962, Berkshire (Mass.) Mus., 1970, Gallery 14 Sculptors, N.Y.C., 1974, Dartmouth (N.H.) Coll., 1978, Deshong Mus., Chester, Pa., 1981, Art Sutton Que., 1998, Mary Bryan Gallery, Jeffersonville, Vt., 1999. With USN, 1948-52. Home: 465 Daigle Dr Enosburg Falls VT 05450-5088 E-mail: alfsvenden@earthlink.net.

**SVENGALIS, KENDALL FRAYNE,** law librarian, educator, publishing executive; b. Gary, Ind., May 16, 1947; s. Frank Anthony and Alvida Linnea (Matheus) S.; children: Hillary Linnea, Andrew Kendall; m. Ellen Christine Haffling, June 16, 2001. BA, Purdue U., 1970, MA, 1973; MLS, U. R.I., 1975. Reference librarian Roger Williams Coll., Bristol, RI, 1975, Providence (R.I.) Coll., 1975-77; asst. law librarian R.I. State Law Library, Providence, 1976-82, state law librarian, 1982—2002. Adj. prof. libr. and info. studies U. R.I., 1987—; pres. RI Law Press, 1996—. Author: The Legal Information Buyer's Guide and Reference Manual, 1996 (Best Legal Reference Book of 1996), 10th edit., 2006, Gary, Indiana: A Centennial Celebration, 2006; editor: The Criv Sheet, 1988—94; contbr. articles to profl. jours. Chmn. jud. branch United Way Com. R.I., 1980; pres. Verdandi Male Chorus, 2000—. Recipient AALL Joseph L. Andrews Bibliographical awd. Mem. Am. Assn Law Librs. (state, ct. and county libr. spl. interest sect., Connie E. Bolden Significant Publ. award 1993, 99, bd. dirs. 1986-88, 96-99), Law Librs. New Eng. (treas. 1983-85, 1985-86, pres. 1986-87), Com. on Rels. with Info. Vendors (editor 1988-94), New Eng. Law Libr. Consortium (v.p. 1990-92, pres. 1992-94), Jussi Bjorling Soc. (v.p.), R.I. Swedish Heritage Assn. (v.p.) Republican. Lutheran. Home: 204 Wyassup Rd North Stonington CT 06359 Personal E-mail: ksven@comcast.net, rilawpress@comcast.net.

**SVENSON, CHARLES OSCAR,** investment banker; b. Worcester, Mass., June 28, 1939; s. Sven Oscar and Edahjane (Castner) S.; m. Sara Ellen Simpson, Nov. 15, 1968; children: Alicia Lindall, Tait Oscar. AB, Hamilton Coll., 1961; LL.B., Harvard U., 1964; LL.M., Bklyn. Law Sch., 1965. Bar: N.Y. 1965, U.S. Dist. Ct. (so. dist.) N.Y. 1965, U.S. Ct. Appeals (2d. cir.) 1965. Atty. Dewey, Ballantine, Bushby, Palmer & Wood, NYC, 1964-68; v.p. Goldman Sachs & Co., NYC, 1968-75; sr. v.p. Donaldson, Lufkin & Jenrette, NYC, 1975-89, mng. dir., 1989-2000; sr. mng. dir. Brock Capital Group LLC, NYC, 2002—. Trustee Kirkland Coll., Clinton, N.Y., 1976-78; trustee Hamilton Coll., Clinton, 1979-83, 90—. Mem. ABA, N.Y. State Bar Assn., Assn. of Bar of City of N.Y. Clubs: Tuxedo (Tuxedo Park, N.Y.); Harvard

(N.Y.C.). Home: 1185 Park Ave New York NY 10128-1308 Office: Brock Capital Group LLC 295 Madison Ave 46th FL New York NY 10017 Office Phone: 212-209-3000. Business E-mail: csvenson@brockcapital.com.

**SVENSSON, ROBERT CHARLES WILHELM,** physicist, researcher; b. Göteborg, Sweden, Sept. 11, 1947; s. Carl-Eric George and Lilly Maria S. BS in Physics, Göteborgs U., 1983, MS in Physics, 1991, PhD in Environ. Scis. with specialization in Phys. Chemistry, 1994. Lectr. Merchant Marine Acad., Göteborg, 1983—; physicist Applied Scis., Inc., Cedarville, Ohio, 1991-92; electronic design engr. Göteborg, 1982—; instr. Merchant Marine Acad., Göteborg, 1982-93; asst. prof. Chalmers U. Technology, Göteborg, 1994-96, assoc. prof., 1996—. Organizer Conf. TEC '93, Chalmers U. of Tech., 1993; guest speaker workshop, U. Eindhoven, Holland, 1993; cons. physicist Applied Scis., Cedarville, 1991-92, Space Exploration Assoc., 1993; specialist Thermionic Energy Conversion Conf.; presenter MIT, 1999; invited TEC specialist US Nat. Rsch. Coun. 2000; invited spkr., Russia, 2003; vis. rsch. prof. W. Va. U., Morgantown, 2004, 2005. Contbr. articles to profl. jours; patentee in field. Mem. ASME, Soc. Automotive Engrs. Lutheran. Avocations: artistic photography, electronics design, power sports. Home: Dörravägen 1 Landvetter S-43893 Sweden Office: Chalmers U Tech S-40272 Göteborg Sweden Office Phone: 46-31-772-5728, 304-692-3046. Personal E-mail: drlomo@yahoo.com. Business E-mail: term@chalmpos.se.

**SVENSSON, SVEN EILIF,** civil engineer, consultant; b. Copenhagen, Dec. 15, 1945; s. Palle and Agnes Svensson; m. Dorte Merete Ahlbom, Aug. 10, 1968; children: Trine, Rikke, Jakob. MSc, Tech. U. Denmark, 1970, PhD, 1973; postgrad., Univ. Coll., London. Civil engring. Ramboel & Hannemann, Copenhagen, 1974-85, dir., 1985-90, ES Cons. Ltd., Copenhagen, 1990—. Cons. Great Belt Link Brige, Copenhagen, 1990—, Oresund Link Bridge, Copenhagen, 1993—; vis. prof. U. Coll., London, 1997—. Contbr. articles to profl. jours. Mem. ASCE, Nat. Acad. of Tech. Scis. Denmark. Avocations: music, tennis. Home: Bistrupvej 92B Birkeroed 3460 Denmark Office: ES-Consult DTU Scion Dr Neergaards Vej 15 DK 2970 Horsholm Denmark E-mail: eilif@es-consult.dk.

**SVERDLOVE, ZOLITA,** artist, painter, printmaker; b. NYC, Feb. 21, 1936; d. Harry and Leah (Rothman) S.; m. Donald Rapp, May 30, 1956; children: Melissa Rapp, Erica Rapp. Cert., Cooper Union Coll., N.Y.C., 1956, BFA, 1977. Chmn. fine arts com. U. Tex., Dallas, 1972-73, exhibits dir., 1973-74. Prints reproduced in Mondus Artium, 1976; one-woman shows include U. Tex., 1973-74, Dallas Mus. Fine Arts (1st prize), 1975, Purdue U. (1st prize) 1970, Marymount Coll., 1969, Toledo Mus. 1976, Maturango Mus., Ridgecrest, Calif., 2001, U. Judaism, 2001, Tirago Gallery, Pasadena, Calif, 2005; exhibited in group shows at Tirage Gallery, Pasadena, Calif.; 2005 NEA grantee, 1973-74. Mem. L.A. Printmaking Soc. (bd. dirs. 1981-83, chmn. new mems. 1983), Graphic Arts Coun., LA County Mus., Phila. Print Club Home and Office: 1445 Indiana Ave South Pasadena CA 91030-4109 Office Phone: 323-254-3389. E-mail: zsverdlove@earthlink.net.

**SVETLOVA, MARINA,** ballerina, retired choreographer; b. Paris, May 3, 1922; arrived in U.S., 1940; d. Max and Tamara (Andreieff) Hartman. Studied with Vera Trefilova, Paris, 1930-36, studied with L. Egorova and M. Kschessinska, 1936-39; studied with A. Vilzak, N.Y.C., 1940-57; D (hon.), Fedn. Francaise de Danse, 1988. Ballet dir. So. Vt. Art Ctr., 1959-64; dir. Svetlova Dance Ctr., Dorset, Vt., 1965-95; prof. ballet dept. Ind. U., Bloomington, 1969-92, prof. emeritus, 1992—, chmn. dept., 1969-78. Choreographer Dallas Civic Opera, 1964—67, (ballets) Ft. Worth Opera, 1967—83, San Antonio Opera, 1983, Seattle Opera, Houston Opera, Kansas City Performing Arts Found., The Fairy Queen, 1966, L'Histoire du Soldat, 1968, ballerina Ballet Russe de Monte Carlo, 1939—41, guest ballerina Ballet Theatre, 1942, London's Festival Ballet, Teatro dell Opera, Rome, Nat. Opera Stockholm, Suomi Opera, Helsinki, Finland, Het Nederland Ballet, Holland, Cork Irish Ballet, Paris Opera Comique, London Palladium, Teatro Colon, Buenos Aires, others, prima ballerina Met. Opera, 1943—50, N.Y.C. Opera, 1950—52; performer: (ballets) Graduation Ball; contbr. articles to profl. jours. Mem.: Nat. Soc. Arts and Letters (nat. dance chmn.), Conf. Ballet in Higher Edn., Am. Guild Mus. Artists (bd. dirs.). Office: 2100 E Maxwell Ln Bloomington IN 47401-6119

**SVEZIA, VERA TISHEFF,** concert pianist; b. Alliance, Ohio; d. Thomas and Anna (Tarpov) Tisheff; m. Rudolph Svezia; children: Alexander, Alexandra. Studied with Rosina Lhevinne, Julliard Sch. Music; MusB, Mich. State U.; MusM, Eastman Sch. Music; studied with Bruce Simonds, Yale U. Creator Verex Entertainment; active as classical pianist, vocal coach, vocalist music prodr. Concert performances with leading orchs. in U.S. and Europe; solo concerts, U.S. and European cities. McDowell Music Colony scholar; recipient Martha Baird Rockefeller award Internat. Platform Assn. award U.S. Congl. Adv. Bd. citation, various other awards. Mem. AAUW, Phi Omega Phi, Delta Omicron. Home: 130 E Hamilton Ave Englewood NJ 07631-3016

**SVIOKLA, JOHN JULIUS,** technology consultant; b. Brockton, Mass., July 3, 1957; s. Sylvester Charles and Katherine Bravendar (McCraig) S.; m. Eileen Marie Harvey, Aug. 12, 1987; children: John, Michael, Patrick. BA, Harvard U., 1979, MBA, 1983, D of Bus. Adminstrn., 1986. Banker Mark Twain Bank Inc., St. Louis, 1986; asst. prof. to assoc. prof. Harvard Bus. Sch., Boston, 1986—98; v.p. DiamondCluster Internat., Chgo., 1998—2001, vice chmn., 2000—. Dir. Cosmo, Inc., Braintree, Mass., Dir. Expert Systems, Cambridge, Mass. Dir. Found. Faces of Children-At-Children's Hosp., Boston 1987 Recipient Detur prize Harvard U., 1979 IBM fellow Harvard U., 1982. Mem. Am. Assn. Artificial Intelligence. Inst. Mgmt. Sci. Clubs: Harvard Faculty (Cambridge); Harvard (Boston). Avocations: drawing, bicycling. Office: DiamondCluster Internat Inc 875 North Michigan Ave Ste 3000 Chicago IL 60611

**SVOBODA, JANICE JUNE,** nurse; d. Alfred A. and Jessie (Boor) Hinke; m. Glenn R. Svoboda, July 20, 1957; children: Melora, Kevin, Craig. Diploma, Luther Hosp., 1954; cert., U. Wis., 1955; student, U. Wis., Madison, 1955—57; BS in Health Edn. cum laude, U. Wis., Milw., 1980; student, Alverno Coll., 1991-92. Pub. health nurse Ozaukee County, Wis., 1979, 86; asst. instr. nursing Milw. Area Tech. Coll., 1979-83; instr. seminar Cardinal Stritch Coll., Milw., 1985-87; nutritional counselor Nutri-Sys., Grafton, Wis., 1987-90. Instr. seminar Milw. Area Tech. Coll., 1983, 90, coping with stress course, 1985-86, assertiveness training course, 1985, health seminars Alverno Coll., Milw., 1991-95, designed and implemented alternative health and healing seminar, Alverno Coll., 1994-97; pvt. practice holistic nurse cons., nutrition and herbal therapy, 1997—; lectr. pub. on nutrition and anti aging. Mem. Am. Holistic Nurses Assn. (charter cert. and recert.), Ctr. for Sci. in the Pub. Interest. Office Phone: 262-372-1242.

**SVOBODA, JOANNE DZITKO,** artist, educator; b. Dec. 24, 1948; d. John Richard and Joanna Frances (Rygiel) Dzitko; m. Peter W. Svoboda, Sept. 3, 1972; children: Kimberly Anne, Lauren Anne. Student, Parsons Sch. Design, 1966, Kean Coll., 1970; BA, Jersey City State Coll., 1970, MA, 1975; postgrad., Tchrs. Coll., Columbia U., 1972, Chubb Inst., 1983-84. Art tchr. Jersey City, 1966-70, Henry Snyder H.S., Jersey City, 1970-80; tng. specialist Johnson & Johnson Baby Products, Skillman, N.J., 1984-89; owner, curriculum revision cons. Jersey City Bd. Edn., 1976; mem. Washington Twp. Shade Tree Commn., 1979-81, chmn., 1981; mem. Washington Twp. Hist. Heritage Commn., 1981-85; active encouraging establishment of hist. zone Long Valley, landmarks, Jersey City and Washington Twp. Grantee N.J. State Dept. Edn., 1973; recipient awards N.J. Fedn. Jr. Woman's Clubs: black and white photography, 1979, crafts, 1979, 1st pl. color photography, 1980, free form,

1981. Mem. Am. H.S. Assn. (asst. exec. dir. 1997-99, 2000-), Inst. Raritan Valley CC. (2000-). Office: PO Box 1216 Marshalls Creek PA 18335 Office Phone: 570-223-9600. E-mail: joan@joansvoboda.com.

**SVOBODA, MARY BETH,** health physicist, environmental science educator; d. Arthur Earl and Rosemary Irene S. Grad. with honors, III Corps Nuclear, Biol. and Chem. Warfare Sch., 1986; BS, U. Ariz., Tucson, AZ, 1993. Radiation safety officer Oakland U., Rochester, Mich., 1998—2001; health physicist Wayne State U., Detroit, 2001—. Adj. faculty environ. health sci. Wayne State U., Detroit, 2001—. Sgt. U.S. Army, 1984—87. Mem.: Am. Acad. of Health Physics (assoc.), Phi Theta Kappa, Golden Key. Home: PO Box 25941 Yuma AZ 85367 Office: Wayne State U 5425 Woodward Ave Ste 300 Detroit MI 48202 Office Phone: 313-577-0019. E-mail: aj8368@wayne.edu.

**SVOBODA, PATRICIA HELEN,** art historian; b. Washington, Dec. 22, 1950; d. Ladislav Maurice and Marie Martina (Vojta) S. BFA in Graphic Design, U. Wash., 1974, BA in Art History, 1974, MA in Art History, 1980. Graphic artist freelance, Seattle, Washington, 1971—86; art history rschr. for exhbns. Collaboration of Seattle Art Mus. & U. Wash., Seattle, 1977—78; graphic artist U. Rsch. Tech. Edn. Ctr., Rockville, Md., 1984; graphic artist, adminstrv. asst. U.S. Dept. Commerce Office Pubs. Svc., Washington, 1984—88; lectr. art history Phillips Collection, Washington, 1987—; coord. rsch. Smithsonian Instn. Nat. Portrait Gallery, Washington, 1988—; lectr. art history Georgetown U., Washington, 1989—97. Rep. Art Svcs. Internat., Alexandria, Va., 1990-92; contbr. Inst. for Classical Studies, Prague, Czech Republic, 1993-94, Inst. for the Classical Tradition, Boston U., 1995, Mus. of Decorative Arts, Prague, Czech Republic, 1996. Author: Zoe Dusanne, 1980; interviewer for Northwest Traditions, 1978; prin. work includes Seattle YMCA mural Olympic Race, 1982; contbr. articles to profl. jours. Keyworker Combined Fed. Campaign, Washington, 1985-88; participant Internat. Partnerships among Mus. Programs Am. Assn. Mus., 2003-05. Recipient Nat. Pks. Sec. Purchase Prize award Soc. Illustrators, 1974, Cert. of Performance award Smithsonian Instn., 1989-2006. Mem. Am. Assn. Mus., Internat. Coun. Mus., Coll. Art Assn., Czechoslovak Soc. Arts & Scis., Internat. Soc. for Classical Tradition, U. Wash. Alumni Assn. Avocations: literature, history, langs., music, photography. Office: Smithsonian Instn Nat Portrait Gallery Victor Bldg-Ste 8300 PO Box 37012 Washington DC 20013-7012 Business E-Mail: svobodap@si.edu.

**SVOBODA, ROBERT RAY,** music educator; b. Seward, Nebr., May 13, 1957; s. Edward Vladislav and Rosella Fay (Holman) Svoboda; m. Sarah Elizabeth Farmer, July 20, 2002; children: Christopher, Christopher, Tiffany, Miranda, Rachel. BFA in fine arts, Peru State Coll., 1980; attended, NW Mo. State U., U. Nebr., Wichita State. Cert. vocal, instrumental tchg. K-12 Mo., Physical Edn. K-12 Mo. Music tchr. Fairfax Schs., Fairfax, Mo., 1980—91; instrumental, vocal tchr. Mound City (Mo.) Schs., 1991—95; instrumental tchr., head football coach Nodaway Holt Schs., Graham, Mo., 1995—. Working musician various bands, 1970—; instr. Mo. Hunter Edn. Project, Mo., 1985—; product quality officer B&B Inc., Graham, Mo., 2002—. Leader Fellowship of Christian Athletes, Fairfax, Mo., 1982—90, Boy Scouts, Mound City, 1991—92. Mem.: Mo. Football Coaches Assn., Cmty. Tchrs. Assn. (pres. 1997—99), Mo. State Tchrs. Assn., Mo. Music Educators Assn., Music Educators Nat. Conf. Avocations: raising horses, powerlifting. Home: 33171 Fortune Rd Graham MO 64455 Office: Nadaway Holt Schs 318 S Taylor Graham MO 64455 Office Phone: 660-939-2135. Office Fax: 660-939-2200. E-mail: bandball@hotmail.com.

**SWACKER, FRANK WARREN,** lawyer; b. N.Y.C., May 18, 1922; m. Irene Maloney Michael; children: Carolyn, Frances, Michele, Ruth. BA, Union Coll., Schnectady, 1947; JD, U. Va., 1949; LLM in Internat. Law, NYU, 1961. Bar: Va. 1948, N.Y. 1950, Ohio 1962, Wis. 1969, D.C. 1977, Fla. 1991, U.S. Ct. Internat. Trade 1978, U.S. Supreme Ct. 1952. Pvt. practice, N.Y.C., 1949—54, 1964—68, Washington, 1977—84, Clearwater, Fla., 1984—89, St. Petersburg, Fla., 1994—; atty. Caltex Petroleum Corp., N.Y.C., 1955—60, Marathon Oil Co., Ohio, 1961—63; counsel Shearman & Sterling, N.Y.C., 1964—67; internat. counsel Allis-Chalmers Corp., Milw., 1968—78; sr. mem. Swacker & Assocs., P.C., Springfield, Va., 1980—84, chmn., pres. firm, sr. mem. Largo, Fla., 1989—93; vice chmn. Lasergate Sys., Inc., 1995—99. Spl. asst. dep. atty. gen. State of N.Y., 1950; govtl. adviser U.S., P.I., Algeria; lectr. Ohio No. U., 1962, N.Y. World Trade Inst., 1976; adj. prof. Stetson U. Coll. Law, St. Petersburg, Fla., 1996-2000, LLM internat. adv. coun., 1997—. Author: Business International Guide for Going Global, 1999, Boardroom Conspiracies, 2005; co-author: World Trade Without Barriers: World Trade Organization and Dispute Resolution, vol. 2, 1996; co-editor, contbr.: Bus. and Legal Aspects of Latin Am. Trade and Investment, 1977, Reference Manual on Doing Business with Latin America, 1979; contbr. articles to profl. jours. Mem. internat. bus. adv. bd. U. So. Fla., 1993-94. Lt. (j.g.) USN, 1943-46, WWII. Mem. ABA (lectr. 1978, internat. commission com. 1991—), Nat. Law Inst., Am. Arbitration Assn. (roster of neutrals, 1960-2005), Nat. Arbitration Forum (arbitration panel), World Intellectual Property Orgn. (arbitration panel), CPR Internat. Inst. for Conflict Prevention and Resolution (internst. and Fla. arbitration panels 2005—) Office Phone: 727-394-0265. E-mail: frankswacker@aol.com.

**SWAGER, CLEO MARIE,** secondary school educator; b. Columbus, Ind., Feb. 21, 1951; d. Louis Cleo and Mable Marie Swager. BS in Edn., St. Francis Coll., Ft. Wayne, Ind., 1974, MS in Edn., 1982. Tchr. Paulding (Ohio) Exempted Village Sch., 1975—2005. Camp dir. Girl Scouts Lumberlost, 1976—78, 1980—82, Luth. Outdoor Ministries, Indpls., 2006. Life mem., leader Girl Scouts; reading camp dir. Luth. Outdoor Ministries. Mem.: Beta Sigma Phi.

**SWAGER, TIMOTHY MANNING,** chemistry educator; b. Sheridan, Mont., July 1, 1961; married; two children. BS in Chemistry with highest honors, Mont. State U., 1983; PhD in Chemistry, Calif. Inst. Tech., 1988. Postdoctoral fellow MIT, Cambridge, Mass., 1988-90; asst. prof. chemistry U. Pa., 1990-96, prof. chemistry, 1996, MIT, Cambridge, 1996—, John D. MacArthur prof., Chem. Dept. head. Cons. EPA, 1993-95, Hannoch Weisman, Counselors at Law, 1996-97, Wolf, Greenfield & Sacks P.C., 1999—; mem Internat. Adv. Com. for Metallomesogens, 1994—; co-organizer Materials Chemistry Workshops, 1995-97; mem. sci. adv. bd. E-ink, Cambridge, 1999—, Polaroid Corp., 1999—, Nomadics, Inc., Stillwater, Okla., 1999—; lectr. and presenter in field. Mem. editl. adv. bd. Chemistry of Materials, 1997—, Accounts Chem. Rsch., 1998—, Jour. Polymer Sci., 1999—, Jour. Am. Chem. Soc., 2000; contbr. numerous articles to profl. jours. Recipient Merck Index Undergrad. Chemistry award, 1983, DuPont Young Faculty award, 1993-96, Phila. Sect. award Am. Chem. Soc., 1996, Union Carbide Innovation Recognition award, 1997, 98, Homeland Security award, Christopher Columbus Fellowship Found., 2003, 2005; named Young Investigator NSF, 1992-97, Young Investigator, Office Naval Rsch., 1992-95; Camille Dreyfus Tchr. scholar, 1995-97, Arthur C. Cope scholar Am. Chem. Soc., 2000; IBM grad. fellow, 1984-87, Advanced Techs. Grad. fellow Aerojet Gen., GM, TRW, 1988, Alfred P. Sloan rsch. fellow, 1994-96. Mem. Internat. Liquid Crystal Soc.; fellow Am. Acad. Arts & Sciences Achievements include patents for Ring-Opening Polymerization of 3,4-Dimethylene Cyclobutene Derivatives, Synthesis of Polyacetylene from High Energy Polymer Formed by Ring-Opening Metathesis Polymerization, Calixarene-based Transition Metal Complexes and Photonic Devices Comprising the Same, Derivatized Polythiophenes and Devices Comprising Same, Electroluminescence in Light Emitting Polymers Featuring Deaggregated Polymers, Conducting Polymer Hybrid Materials and Sensors, Stable Chemically Sensitive Fluorescent Polymer Films; research on polymer science, liquid crystals, synthetic conductors, chemical, molecular recognition, molecular electronics. Office: MIT Room 18-597 77 Massachusetts Ave Cambridge MA 02139-4307 Fax: 617-253-7929. E-mail: tswager@mit.edu.*

**SWAILES, WILLIAM E.,** counseling administrator; b. Balt., July 28, 1945; m. Heidi Robin Raudleht, May 19, 1968. Stockbroker Foster & Marshall, Bellevue, Wash., 1978—81; investment mgr. Advanced Personal Finances,

Medina, Wash., 1982—; chmn. EWR, Inc., Bellevue, 2002—. Author: (book) Money in your Life, 1986. Chgo. area chmn. Ill. Coll. Rep. Fedn., 1968—69; hon. chmn. for Wash. state NRCC Bus. Adv. Coun., 2004; founder, min. Leyden Tolerants Ch., 1973—. With U.S. Army, 1964—67, Germany and Vietnam. Recipient Ronald Reagan Rep. Gold Medal, Nat. Rep. Congl. Com., 2004, Wash. State Businessman of Yr., 2005; Monmouth Honor scholarship, Monmouth Coll., 1963. Mem.: Am. Assn. Retired Persons (past pres. Bellevue chpt.).

SWAIM, C. HALL, lawyer; b. Delta, Colo., Dec. 31, 1939; s. H. Albert and Janet S.; m. Patricia Fahey, Oct. 9, 1976. Grad. Geophys. Engr., Colo. Sch. Mines, 1961; JD, NYU, 1964. Asst. counsel Tex. Instruments Inc., Dallas, 1964-71; assoc. Hale and Dorr LLP, Boston, 1971-74, ptnr., 1974—. Served to capt. U.S. Army, 1965-67, Vietnam. Mem. ABA, Mass. Bar Assn., Boston Bar Assn., Comml. Law League Am. Office: Wilmer Hale 60 State St Boston MA 02109-1816 Office Phone: 617-526-6716. Personal E-mail: hall.swaim@wilmerhale.com.

SWAIM, MARK WENDELL, physician, molecular biologist, gastroenterologist, photographer; b. Winston-Salem, N.C., Dec. 4, 1960; s. Donnie Lee and Bernice Earline (Brown) S. BA summa cum laude, U. N.C., 1983; MD, Duke U., 1990, PhD with honors, 1990. Diplomate Am. Bd. Internal Medicine, Am. Bd. Gastroenterology and Hepatology. Resident dept. medicine Duke U. Med. Ctr., Durham, NC, 1990-93, fellow gastroenterology, 1993-97, clin. med. instr., 1994-2000, fellow in advanced hepatology and endoscopy, 1997-98, attending physician, 1998-2000, Durham VA Med. Ctr., 1998-2000; asst. prof. medicine Gastrointestinal Ctr., U. Tex.-M.D. Anderson Cancer Ctr., Houston, 2000—02; dir., prin. investigator, med. dir. Regional Rsch. Inst., Jackson, Tenn., 2002—; founder Southeastern Liver Inst., Jackson, 2002—. Assoc. dept. medicine Duke U., 1998-2000; instr. clin. medicine Duke U. Sch. Medicine, 1994-2000, mem. admissions com.; instr. U. Tenn. Sch. Medicine, 2004—; asst. prof. medicine Gastrointestinal Ctr., U. Tex. M.D. Anderson Cancer Ctr., Houston; vis. med. resident Nat. Taiwan U., Taipei, 1991, 92; vis. physician Saratov (Russia) Med. U., 1995; faculty senator U. Tex. M.D. Anderson Cancer Ctr., 2000-02; book rev. panelist The Pharos of Alpha Omega Alpha; cons. physician Al-Jazeira Hosp., Abu Dhabi, United Arab Emirates; mem. med. adv. bd. Axium Pharms., Inc.; cons. Inttermune Pharms. Contbr. articles to profl. jours., Ency. Brit. Great Ideas Today, 1996; photography pub. in Am. Photo. Recipient Brody award for history of medicine, 1998, Davison award for tchg. excellence, 2000; NIH Med. Sci. Tng. Program fellow, 1983-90, numerous acad. scholarships and grants. Fellow: ACP (winner assocs. competition 1994); mem.: European Assn. for Study of Liver, Houston Acad. Medicine, Tex. Med. Assn., Am. Liver Found. (bd. dirs. Tex. chpt.), Engel Soc., Am. Coll. Forensic Examiners, Reticuloendothelial Soc., Am. Assn. for Study Liver Diseases, Am. Soc. for Gastrointestinal Endoscopy, Am. Coll. Gastroenterology, Sigma Pi Sigma, Phi Lambda Upsilon, Sigma Xi, Phi Beta Kappa, Alpha Omega Alpha (pres. Duke chpt. 1989). Avocations: photography, chamber music, writing, travel. Home: 61 Valley Oak Loop Jackson TN 38305 Office: 45 Physicians Dr Jackson TN 38303 Office Phone: 731-664-2200. Personal E-mail: markswaim@msn.com.

SWAIM, MICHAEL E., lawyer, former mayor; BA, UCLA, 1967, MA, 1968, JD, 1971. Lawyer Simon, McKinsey & Miller, 1971-78; pvt. practice, 1978—; mayor City of Salem, Oreg., 1997—2003. Office: Law Office 270 Cottage St NE Salem OR 97301 E-mail: mswain@open.org.

SWAIMAN, KENNETH FRED, pediatric neurologist, educator; b. St. Paul, Nov. 19, 1931; s. Lester J. and Shirley (Ryan) S.; m. Phyllis Kammerman Sher, Oct. 1985; children: Lisa, Jerrold, Barbara, Dana. BA magna cum laude, U. Minn., 1952, BS, 1953, MD, 1955; postgrad., 1956-58. Diplomate Am. Bd. Psychiatry and Neurology, Am. Bd. Pediatrics, Am. Bd. Psychiatry and Neurology with Spl. Competence in Child Neurology. Intern Mpls. Gen. Hosp., 1955-56; resident in pediatrics, fellow in pediatrics to chief resident U. Minn. Hosp., 1956-58, spl. fellow in pediatric neurology, 1960-63, dir. pediatric neurology tng. program, 1968-94, various to interim head dept. neurology, 1994-96; chief pediatrics U.S. Army Hosp., Ft. McPherson, Ga., 1958-60; asst. prof. pediatrics, neurology U. Minn. Med. Sch., Mpls., 1963-66, prof., dir. pediatric neurology, 1996-96, mem. internship adv. coun. exec. faculty, 1966-70, interim head dept. neurology, 1994-96; postgrad. fellow pediatric neurology Nat. Inst. Neurologic Diseases and Blindness, 1960-63, assoc. prof., 1966-69. Cons. pediatric neurology Hennepin County Gen. Hosp., 1963—, Mpls., St. Paul Ramsey Hosp., St. Paul Children's Hosp., Mpls. Children's Hosp.; vis. prof. numerous univs. including Loyola U., 1982, U. N.Mex., 1982, U. Ind. Med. Sch., 1983, U. Kyushu, Shiga, Nagoya, Tokyo, 1985, Driscoll Children's Hosp., Corpus Christi, Tex., 1986, Inst. Nacional de Pediatria, Mexico City, 1986, U. de Concepion, Chile, 1989, Beijing U. Med. Sch., 1989, Xian Med. U., China, 1989, Children's Hosp. of Mich., Detroit, 1990, Hong Kong Child Neurology Soc., 1995, Tartu, Estonia, 1997, Krem, Austria, 1997, Santiago, Chile, 1997, Kaunas, Lithuania, 1998, ICNA Ednl. Seminar, Tartu, 1998, Montevideo, Uruguay, 1999, others; lectr. in field; guest worker NIH, NICHD, Bethesda, Md., 1978-79, 79-81. Author: (with Francis S. Wright) Neuromuscular Diseases in Infancy and Childhood, 1969, Pediatric Neuromuscular Diseases, 1979, (with Stephen Ashwal) Pediatric Neurology Case Studies, 1978, 2d edit., 1984, Pediatric Neurology: Principles and Practice, 1989, 4th edit., 2006; editor: (with John A. Anderson) Phenylketonuria and Allied Metabolic Diseases, 1966, (with Francis S. Wright) Practice Pediatric Neurology, 1975, 2d edit., 1982; mem. editorial bd.: Annals of Neurology, 1977-83, Neurology Update, 1977-82, Pediatric Update, 1977-85, Brain and Devel. (Jour. Japanese Soc. Child Neurology), 1980—, Neuropediatrics (Stuttgart), 1982-92; editor-in-chief: Pediatric Neurology, 1984—; contbr. articles to sci. jours. Chmn. Minn. Gov.'s Bd. for Handicapped, Exceptional and Gifted Children, 1972-76; mem. human devel. study sect. NIH, 1976-79, guest worker, 1978-81. Served to capt. M.C. U.S. Army, 1958-60. Fellow Am. Acad. Pediatrics, Am. Acad. Neurology (rep. to nat. coun. Nat. Soc. Med. Rsch., A.B. Baker Neurol. Edn. Lifetime Achievement award 2005); mem. Soc. Pediatric Rsch., Ctrl. Soc. Clin. Rsch., Ctrl. Soc. Neurol. Rsch., Internat. Soc. Neurochemistry, Am. Neurol. Assn., Minn. Neurol. Soc., AAAS, Midwest Pediatric Soc., Am. Soc. Neurochemistry, Child Neurology Soc. (1st pres. 1972-73, Hower award 1981, Founder's award 1996, chmn. internat. affairs com., 1991-96, mem. long range planning com. 1991-97, chmn. fin. com. 1995—), Internat. Assn. Child Neurologists (exec. com. 1975-79, chmn. global edn. com. 1996-99), Profs. of Child Neurology (1st pres. 1978-80, mem. nominating com. 1986-92), Japanese Child Neurology Soc. (Segawa award 1986, mem. nominating com. 1986-92, chair internat. affairs com. 1991—, mem. long range planning com. 1991-98), Soc. de Psiquiatria y Neurologia de la Infancia y Adolescencia, Internat. Child Neurology Assn. (chair internat. edn. com. 1996-99), Lithuanian Child Neurology Soc. (hon., pres. 2000—), Child Neurology Found. (pres. 2000-03), Phi Beta Kappa, Sigma Xi. Office: U Minn Med Sch Dept Pediatric Neurology 1821 University Ave W Saint Paul MN 55104-2801 also: UMHC Box 486 420 Delaware St SE Minneapolis MN 55455-0374 E-mail: pncomm@uswet.net, cnfc@childneurologyfoundation.org.

SWAIN, CLIFFORD H., lawyer; b. Phila., 1941; married. BA, Yale Univ., 1963; LLB, Univ. Pa., 1968. Bar: Pa. 1968. With Drinker Biddle & Reath LLP, 1993—, ptnr., real estate practice group, former adminstrv. chair, former mng. ptnr. Office: Drinker Biddle & Reath LLP One Logan Sq 18th & Cherry Sts Philadelphia PA 19103-6996 Office Phone: 215-988-2796. Office Fax: 215-988-2757. Business E-mail: clifford.swain@dbr.com.

SWAIN, DAVID O., manufacturing executive; b. Lizton, Ind., July 30, 1942; B of Aeronautical Engring., Purdue U., D (hon.), Rose-Hulman Inst. Tech. Engr. Gemini project McDonnell Douglas, 1954—72, engr. tactical missile programs, tomahawk and harpoon/standoff land attack missile, 1972—87; v.p., gen. mgr. strategic bus. devel. McDonnell Douglas Astronautics Co., 1987—91; sr. v.p., c-17 program mgr. McDonnell Douglas Aerospace, 1981—94; v.p. gen. mgr. advances sys. and tech. Phantom Works McDonnell Douglas, 1994—97; v.p. engring. The Boeing Co., 1997—99; pres. Boeing Phamtom Works, 1999—2001; exec. v.p. The Boeing Co., 2002—, chief

operating officer integrated defense systems, 2003—. Chmn. NASA Aerospace Tech. Adv. Com. Bd. dirs. Nat. Action Coun. Minorities in Engring., Chgo.'s Mus. Sci. and Industry. Recipient Disting. Engring. ALumnus award, Purdue U., 1993, Outstanding Aerospace Engr. award, 1999. Fellow: AIAA, Royal Aeronautical Soc.; mem.: Soc. Automotive Engrs. Office: The Boeing Co PO Box 516 Saint Louis MO 63166

SWAIN, DONALD CHRISTIE, retired academic administrator, historian, educator; b. Des Moines, Oct. 14, 1931; s. G. Christie and Irene L. (Alsop) S.; m. Lavinia Kathryn Lesh, Mar. 5, 1955; children: Alan Christie, Cynthia Catherine. BA, U. Dubuque, 1953; MA in History, U. Calif., Berkeley, 1958, PhD, 1961; D (hon.), U. Louisville, 1995, Bellarmine Coll., 1995. Asst. rsch. historian U. Calif., Berkeley, 1961-63, mem. faculty Davis, 1963-81, prof. history, 1970-81, acad. asst. to chancellor, 1967-68, asst. vice chancellor acad. affairs, 1971, vice chancellor acad. affairs, 1972-75; acad. v.p. U. Calif. System, Berkeley, 1975-81; pres. U. Louisville, 1981-95, pres. emeritus, 1995—, prof. history, 1981-95; ret., 1995. Author: Federal Conservation Policy, 1921-33, 1963, Wilderness Defender: Horace M. Albright and Conservation, 1970; co-editor: The Politics of American Science 1939 to the Present, 1965. Recipient William B. Hellestine award Wis. State Hist. Soc., 1967, Disting. Tchg. award U. Calif., Davis, 1972, Wilson Wyatt award U. Louisville Alumni Assn., 1995; named Louisvillian of Yr., 1995. Democrat. Presbyterian. Office: U Louisville Alumni Ctr Louisville KY 40292-0001 E-mail: dcsandlls@aol.com.

SWAIN, JAMES EDWARD, psychiatrist, researcher; b. Scarboroughj, Ont., Can., Nov. 4, 1966; s. John Kenneth and Virginia Swain. BS, U. Toronto, Ontario, Canada, 1988, MS, 1990, PhD, 1994, MD, 1997. Asst. prof. child psychiatry Yale U., New Haven, 2005—. Mentor Yale U., 2003—. Recipient Summer Undergraduate Life Sci. award, U. Toronto, 1988, Upjohn Can. award, U. Toronto, Depts. Physiology and Pharmacology, 1992, Dr. Francesco Lamensa award, U. Toronto, Faculty Medicine, 1993, Samuel Castrilli Rsch. award, 1994—97, Crocker Found. award, 1994, Clin. Excellence Tchg. award, Ottawa Gen. Hosp., 1998, Outstanding Resident award, NIMH, 2001, Travel award, Ann. Wis. Symposia Emotion, 2002—05, Rsch. award, Inst. Rsch. Unlimited Love, 2002—04, ACNP Travel award, Am. Coll. Neuropsychopharmacology, NIMH, 2003; fellow, U. Toronto, 1985—87, U. Toronto, Massey Coll., 1988, U. Toronto, U. Arts and Scis., 1989, U. Toronto, Dept. Physiology, 1993, U. Toronto, Dept. Pharmacology, 1994, Yale U., 2002—05, Internat. Soc. Magnetic Resonance Medicine, 2003, Internat. Acad. Child and Adolescent Psychiatry and Allied Profls., 2004; scholar, Ont., 1984, U. Toronto Med. Alumni Assn., 1995. Mem.: AMA, Am. Acad. Child and Adolescent Psychiatry (assoc.), Orgn. Human Brain Mapping (assoc.), Can. Acad. Child and Adolescent Psychiatry (assoc.), Cognitive Neurosci. Soc. (assoc.), Soc. Biol. Psychiatry (assoc.), Internat. Soc. Magnetic Resonance Medicine (assoc.), Conn. Psychiat. Assn. (assoc.), NY Acad. Scis. (assoc.). Avocations: travel, movies, squash, history. Office: Yale University 230 South Frontage Rd New Haven CT 06520 Office Phone: 203-785-6973. Office Fax: 203-785-7611. Business E-Mail: james.swain@yale.edu.

SWAIN, JUDITH LEA, cardiologist, educator; b. Long Beach, Calif., Sept. 24, 1948; m. Edward W. Holmes. BS in Chemistry with deptl. honors, UCLA, 1970; MD, U. Calif., San Diego, 1974. Diplomate Am. Bd. Internal Medicine, cardiovasc. disease; lic. physician Calif., Pa., N.C. Intern in medicine Duke U. Med. Ctr., 1974-75, resident in medicine, 1975-76, fellow in cardiology, 1976-80, assoc. in medicine, 1979-81, from asst. prof. medicine to assoc. prof. medicine, 1981-91, asst. prof. physiology, 1981-88, assoc. prof. microbiology & immunology, 1988-91, Herbert C. Rorer prof. med. scis., prof. genetics, 1991-92, mem. molecular biology grad. group, 1991-92, chief cardiovasc. divsn., 1991-92; chair dept. medicine Stanford (Calif.) U., 1996—; dir. Coll. Integrated Life Scis. U. Calif., San Diego, 2004—. Vis. asst. prof. dept. genetics Harvard Med. Sch., Boston, 1985-86; mem. search com. for dir. Ctr. for Aging, Duke U. Med. Ctr., 1991—, mem. exec. com. deptl. awards selection, 1992—, chmn. combined degree dir. search com., 1993, mem. clin. rsch. ctr. adv. com., 1993-94, mem. grad. student admissions com., 1993, mem. search com. for chief cardiovasc. surgery, 1992, dept. medicine intern selection com., 1992—; mem. instnl. rev. com. Pa. Muscle Inst., 1993; cardiology adv. com. Nat. Heart, Lung, & Blood Inst., 1989-93; dir. USA-Russia Cardiovasc. Rsch. Program, 1992—; mem. NIH Task Force on Heart Failure, 1992-93, dirs. standing com. on clin. rsch. NIH, 1995—; cons. Netherlands Rsch. Initiative in Molecular Cardiology, 1993; external adv. com. Ctr. for Prevention of Cardiovasc. Disease, Harvard Sch. Pub. Health, 1993—; adv. coun. NHLBI, 1995—, Friends of NHLBI com., 1996—, lectr. in field. Exec. editor: Trends in Cardiovascular Medicine, 1990-93; mem. editl. bd. Circulation Rsch., 1991—, Circulation, 1991—, Jour. Clin. Investigation, 1992—; cons. editor: Circulation, 1993—; contbr. articles to med. jours. Mem. exec. com. Coun. on Basic Sci., Am. Heart Assn., 1986-93, chmn. Katz Prize Award Com., 1989-92, rsch. rev. com., 1990-93, fellowship rsch. com., 1992—, program com., 1992—, mem. Levine Young Investigator Awards Com., Coun. on Clin. Cardiology, 1994—, mem. Basic Sci. Coun.; bd. dirs. Southeastern Pa. Heart Assn., 1992—. Recipient Bristol-Myers Squibb Cardiovasc. Achievement award, 1992, also numerous rsch. grants. Fellow Am. Coll. Cardiology (internat. edn. com. 1994—, chair cardiovasc. rsch. com. 1996—), Coll. Physicians of Phila.; mem. Assn. Univ. Cardiologists, Assn. Am. Physicians, Assn. Prof. of Cardiology, Am. Soc. Cell Biology, Am. Fedn. Clin. Rsch., Am. Soc. Clin. Investigation (pres.-elect 1994—, councilor 1991—), Internat. Soc. Heart Rsch. (councilor 1988—), Interurban Clin. Club, Clin. and Climitol. Soc., John Morgan Soc. Office: U Calif Sch Medicine 410 Pepper Canyon Hall 9500 Gilman Dr La Jolla CA 92093-0602 Office Phone: 858-534-7658. E-mail: jlswain@ucsd.edu.

SWAIN, LAURA TAYLOR, federal judge; b. Bklyn., 1958; d. Justus E. and Madeline V. (Allgood) Taylor; m. Andrew J. Swain, 1991. AB, Harvard U., 1979, JD, 1982. Bar: Mass. 1982, N.Y. 1983, U.S. Dist. Ct. (so. and ea. dists.) N.Y. 1983. Law clk to chief judge U.S. Dist. Ct. (so. dist.) N.Y., 1982-83; assoc. Debevoise & Plimpton, N.Y.C., 1983-95, counsel, 1995-96; U.S. bankruptcy judge U.S. Bankruptcy Ct., Bklyn., 1996-2000; judge U.S. Dist. Ct. (So. Dist.), NY, 2000—. Mem. N.Y. State Bd. Law Examiners, Albany, 1986-96; mem. multistate bar exam. com. Nat. Conf. Bar Examiners, 1987-99, mem. testing, R&D devel. com., 1990-94, mem. long range planning com., 1994-96; cons. N.Y. Profl. Edn. Project, 1995-96; adv. com. for fules of banruptcy procedures Judicial Conf. U.S., 2002-. Co-contbr. articles on employee benefits, employee stock ownership plans, acctg. and bankruptcy to profl. publs.; contbg. author: New York Insurance Law, 1991. Trustee Diocese of N.Y. (Episcopal), 1991-92; mem. Dessoff Choirs, N.Y.C., 1984-92; bd. dirs. Episcopal Charities, Inc., 1996-2003, Coalition Consumer Bankruptcy Debtor Edn., 1996—. Mem. ABA, Assn. of Bar of City of N.Y., Met. Black Bar Assn., N.Y. State Bar Assn., Nat. Conf. Bankruptcy Judges, Nat. Assn. Women Judges, Fed. Judges Assn. (bd. dirs. 2005-). Episcopalian. Avocation: music. Office: US Courthouse 40 Centre St Rm 1205 New York NY 10007

SWAIN, MARY ANN PRICE, university official; b. Chardon, Ohio, Apr. 20, 1941; d. David and Mary A. Price; m. Donald B. Swain, June 27, 1964; children: Judy, Brenda. BA in Psychology, DePauw U., 1963; MA in Psychology, U. Mich., 1964, PhD in Psychology, 1969. Dir. Sch. Nursing Doctoral Program U. Mich., Ann Arbor, 1975—76, chmn. dept. nursing rsch., 1977—82, assoc. v.p. acad. affairs 1983—93, interim co-dir. pers., 1986—88, interim dir. affirmative action, 1988—89, interim v.p. student svcs., 1990—92; provost and v.p. acad. affairs SUNY, Binghamton, 1993—. Evaluation site visotor U. Balt. Sch. Law, 1996—97, Tes. Wesleyan U., 1998—99, U. Va. Sch. Nursing, Charlottesville, 1994—95; chmn. coun. acad. affairs Nat. Assn. State Univs. and Land Grant Colls., 1998—99. Co-author (with H. Erickson and E. Tomlim): Modeling and Role-modeling: A Theory and Paradigm for Nursing, 1983. Chmn. campaign United Way Broome COunty, Binghamton, 1998—99; pres. bd. dirs. Vis. Nurses Assn. Huron Valley, Ann Arbor, 1989—92. Fellow Woodrow Wilson fellow, 1963. Mem.: Am. Psychol. Soc., Am. Assn. Higher Edn., Am. Soc. Quality Control, Sigma

Theta Tau, Phi Beta Kappa, Golden Key Hon. Soc. Office: SUNY at Binghamton Provost Office PO Box 6000 Binghamton NY 13902-6000 Office Phone: 607-777-2141. E-mail: mswain@binghamton.edu.

SWAIN, MARY MADGALENE DICKERSON, pediatrics nurse; b. Talladega, Ala., May 4, 1954; d. Quincy Jackson and Dorothy Arizona Dickerson; m. Michael Swain, May 3, 1986; children: Cassandran Averitte, Victor Dickerson, Tumika Shears. AAS, Gadsden State C.C., 1996; LPN, N.F. Nunnelley Tech. Coll., 1985. Lic. clin. skills observer Ala.; cert. minister of health Ala., 2005. LPN, acting unit mgr., unit coord. Northport Health Svcs., Lineville, Ala., 1987—95; case mgr. Dixie Nursing Svc., Batesville, Miss., 1995—97; DON Ball Healthcare Svc., Roanoke, Ala., 1997—2000; RN postpartum Coosa Valley Bapt. Med. ctr., Sylacauga, Ala., 2000—02; dir. parish nurse svcs. Christ Deliverance Christian Ctr., Talladega, 2001—, RN supr. Talladega Healthcare Ctr., 2002—03; staff parish nurse Sylacauga Alliance for Family Enhancement, 2002—03; Author: He Has Always Been There, 2003. Avocations: writing, reading, learning. Home: 709 Glenwood Rd Talladega AL 35160-2954 Office: A Remnant's Place 121 N Court Sq Talladega AL 35160

SWAIN, ROBERT, artist; b. Austin, Tex., Dec. 7, 1940; s. Robert O. and Beth (Brower) S.; m. Annette Carol Leibel, Oct. 4, 1969. BA, Am.U., 1964. Prof. fine arts Hunter Coll.; vis. artist to various schs., univs., including Bklyn. Mus. Art Sch., 1975, 77, 78; dept. architecture Harvard U. Grad. Sch. Design, 1977 One-man shows, Thenan Gallery, N.Y.C., 1965, Fischbach Gallery, N.Y.C., 1968-69, Everson Art Museum, N.Y.C., 1974, Susan Galdwell Gallery, N.Y.C., 1974, 75, 78, Tex. Gallery, Houston, 1975, Columbus (Ohio) Gallery Fine Arts, 1976, Nina Freundenhein Gallery, Buffalo, 1978, group shows include, Mus. Modern Art, N.Y.C., 1968, Grand Palais, Paris, 1968, Kunsthaus, Zurich, Switzerland, 1969, Tate Gallery, London, 1969, Corcoran Gallery Art, Washington, 1969, Whitney Mus. Am. Art, N.Y.C., 1971, Albright-Knox Gallery, Buffalo, 1971, Mus. Modern Art Internat. Circulating Exhbn.-Latin Am., 1974-75; represented in permanent collections, Corcoran Gallery Art, Walker Art Center, Mpls., Va. Mus. Fine Arts, Richmond, Everson Art Mus., Columbus Gallery Fine Arts, Detroit Inst. Art, Albright-Knox Mus., works include archtl. installations, Am. Republic Ins. Co., Des Moines, 1969, N.K. Winston Corp., N.Y.C., 1969, Schering Labs., Bloomfield, N.J., 1970, Skidmore, Owings and Merrill, N.Y.C., 1970, Kahn & Mallis Assocs., N.Y.C., 1972, Harris Bank, Chgo., 1977, Powell/Kleinschmidt Chgo., 1977, Travenol Labs., Deerfield, Ill., 1977, Skidmore, Owings and Merrill, Chgo., 1977. John Simon Guggenheim Meml. Found. fellow, 1969; Nat Endowment for Arts grantee, 1976 Home and Office: 57 Leonard St Fl 4 New York NY 10013-2919

SWAIN, SUSAN MARIE, communications executive; b. Phila., Dec. 23, 1954; d. Samuel B. Swain and Marie Paget. BA in Comms. magna cum laude, U. Scranton, Pa., 1976, Doctorate (hon.), 2000. Reporter Sta. WDAU-TV, Scranton, 1975-76; pub. rels. staff Up With People, Inc., Tucson, 1976—78; supr. Raytheon Service Co., Cambridge, Mass., 1978-80; research assoc. Nat. Counsel Assocs., Washington, 1980-82; producer C-SPAN Cable Network, Washington, 1982-83, dir. pub. relations, 1983-87, v.p. corp. communications, mem. exec. mgmt. com., 1987-89, sr. v.p., 1989—95, exec. v.p., co-chief oper. officer, 1995—; also creator & host "American Writers", C-SPAN. Officer The Nat. Cable Satellite Corp.; bd. mem. C-SPAN Ednl. Found.; bd. mem., dir. Talbot's Inc. Moderator (TV program) C-SPAN Viewer Call-In, 1982—; editl. mgr. Booknotes, 1997, Booknotes: Life Stories, 1999, Booknotes: Stories from History, 2001, Booknotes: On American Character, 2004. Trustee U. Scranton, 1992—2000. Recipient Alumni award U. Scranton, 1976, Disting. Achievement award, 1991. Mem. Cable Telecom. Adminstrn. and Mktg., Mus. TV and Radio, Cable TV Pub. Affairs Assn. (bd. dirs. 1986-90, sec. 1988-89), Washington Cable Club, Alpha Sigma Nu. Roman Catholic. Avocations: sailing, biking. Office: C-SPAN 400 N Capitol St NW Ste 650 Washington DC 20001-1550 E-mail: sswain@c-span.org.

SWAINSON, JOHN, software company executive; b. Canada; 3 children. BS in Engring., U. British Columbia. Joined as systems engr. IBM, Vancouver, Canada, 1978, various mgmt. positions in mktg. and services and mfg. and devel., mgr. market devel. and support, IBM Canada Software Solutions Lab. Toronto, Canada, 1991—93, dir. application devel. mktg., software solutions div., 1993—94, v.p., application devel. solutions and dir., IBM Canada Software Solutions Lab. Toronto, Canada, 1994, gen. mgr. applications and integration middleware, 1997—2004, v.p. sales software div., 2004; pres. Computer Associates Internat. Inc., Islandia, NY, 2004—, CEO-elect, 2004—05; CEO Computer Associates Internat. Inc. (now named CA, Inc.), Islandia, NY, 2005—, also bd. dir. Mem. IBM Worldwide Mgmt. Coun., IBM Strategy Team, IBM Sr. Leadership Team; bd. gov. IBM Acad. Technology. Office: Computer Associates Internat Inc (CA Inc) One Computer Associates Plz Islandia NY 11749*

SWAISGOOD, HAROLD EVERETT, biochemist, educator; b. Ashland, Ohio, Jan. 19, 1936; s. Ray Weaver and Jennie (Morr) S.; m. Janet Cromwell, Sept. 15, 1956; children: Mark Harold, Ronald Ray. BS, Ohio State U., 1958, PhD in Chemistry (NIH fellow), Mich. State U., 1963. Rsch. assoc. Mich. State U., 1963-63; rsch. assoc. NIH, 1963—64; asst. prof. food sci. and biochemistry N.C. State U., 1964-67, assoc. prof., 1967-72, prof., 1972-84, William Neal Reynolds prof., 1984—2001, prof. emeritus William Neal Reynolds, 2001—, Alumni Disting. Grad. Rsch. prof., 1997. Vis. prof. U. Lund, Sweden, 1974, chmn. biotech. program, 1986-92; bd. mem. Coun. Agrl. Sci. and Tech., 2004—. Editor for Ams., Comments on Agr. and Food Chemistry; assoc. editor Jour. Food Biochemistry, 1983-2000; mem. editl. bd. Jour. Dairy Sci. 1975-85, Jour. Food Sci. 1978-83; regional editor Nahrung-Food, 1995-2002; contbr. articles, chpts. to profl. publs. USPHS fellow, 1963-64. Fellow Am. Chem. Soc. (agriculture food chem. divsn., award advancement of application of agrl. and food chemistry sponsored by IFF 1994), Am. Dairy Sci. Assn. (pres. 1999-2000, dairy rsch. found. award, 1985, Borden award 1987); mem. AAAS, Am. Inst. Nutrition, Am. Soc. Biochemists and Molecular Biologists, Inst. Food Technologists, Coun. Agrl. Sci. and Tech. (bd. dir.), Sigma Xi, Phi Kappa Phi, Gamma Sigma Delta. Democrat. Methodist. Achievements include research in protein structure, interactions, and functionality; characteristics and applications of immobilized enzymes; patents in field. Office: NC State U Dept Food Sci Raleigh NC 27695-7624 Business E-mail: harold_swaisgood@ncsu.edu.

SWALIN, RICHARD ARTHUR, scientist, company executive; b. Mpls., Mar. 18, 1929; s. Arthur and Mae (Hurley) S.; m. Helen Marguerite Van Wagenen, June 28, 1952; children: Karen, Kent, Kristin. BS with distinction, U. Minn., 1951, PhD, 1953. Rsch. assoc. GE, 1954-56; mem. faculty U. Minn., Mpls., 1956-77, prof., head Sch. Mineral and Metall Engring., 1962-68, assoc. dean Inst. Tech., 1968-71, dean Inst. Tech., 1971-77; acting dir. Space Sci. Center, 1965; v.p. tech. Eltra Corp., N.Y.C., 1977-80; v.p. R & D Allied-Signal Corp., Morristown, N.J., 1980-84; dean Coll. Engring. and Mines U. Ariz., Tucson, 1984-87, prof., 1984-94; pres. Ariz. Tech. Devel. Corp., Tucson, 1987; prof. emeritus U. Ariz., Tucson, 1995—. Guest scientist Max Planck Inst. für Phys. Chemie, Göttingen, Fed. Republic Germany, 1963, Lawrence Radiation Lab., Livermore, Calif., 1967; cons. to govt. and industry; bd. dirs. emeritus Medtronic Corp., BMC Industries; corp. adv. bd. AMP Inc., 1990-93. Author: Thermodynamics of Solids, 2d edit, 1972; Contbr. articles to profl. jours. Dir. div. indsl. coup. U. Ariz. Found., 1985-86; trustee Midwest Research Inst., 1975-78, Sci. Mus. Minn., 1973-77, Nat. Tech. U., 1983-90. Recipient Disting. Teaching award Inst. Tech., U. Minn., 1967, Leadership award U. Minn. Alumni, 1993; NATO sr. fellow in sci., 1971. Mem. Sigma Xi, Tau Beta Pi, Phi Delta Theta, Gamma Alpha. Home: 5143 E Calle Brillante Tucson AZ 85718-1823 Personal E-mail: rswalin@yahoo.com.

SWALLOW, KATHLEEN CLINEDINST, chemistry professor; b. Balt., Jan. 21, 1948; d. Clinton Richard and Virginia Catherine (Martin) Clinedinst; m. Stephen Thaxter Swallow, June 20, 1970; children: Lindsey Ellen, Clinton Peloubet. BS, U. Richmond, 1970; PhD, MIT, 1978; Dr. Honoris Causa, U. West, Timisoara, Romania, 2006. Asst. prof. Wellesley Coll., Mass.,

1977—82, 1989—90; pres. Interstate Labs., Newburyport, Mass., 1980—82; mgr. Analytical Labs MODAR, Inc., Natick, Mass., 1982—85; sr. assoc. Gradient Corp., Cambridge, Mass., 1986—89; from assoc. prof. to prof. Merrimack Coll., North Andover, Mass., 1990—97, prof., 1997—, dean sci. and engring. dept., 1998—2003. Chair dept. chemistry Merrimack Coll., North Andover, 1995—97, 2005—; vis. scientist, prof. MIT, 1996—, Fulbright sr. specialist in environ. sci., Mass., 2004—; cons. MODAR, Inc., 1985—92. Contbg. author: Ground Water Quality and Analysis at Hazardous Waste Sites, 1992; patentee supercritical water oxidation. Moderator, Town of West Newbury, 1985—; chmn. governing bd. First Religious Soc. of Newburyport, 1984, 2002. Disting. Alumna Westhampton Coll. Class of 1970, Richmond, Va., 1995 Mem. Am. Chem. Soc. (chmn. Norris com. northea. sect. 1996), Sigma Xi, Gamma Sigma Epsilon, Phi Beta Kappa Unitarian Universalist. Home: 131 River Rd West Newbury MA 01985-1103 Office: Merrimack Coll 315 Turnpike St North Andover MA 01845-5806 Business E-Mail: kathleen.swallow@merrimack.edu.

**SWALM, THOMAS STERLING,** aerospace transportation executive, retired military officer; b. San Diego, Sept. 28, 1931; s. Calvin D. and Margaret A. (Rynning) S.; m. Charlene La Vern Garner, June 26, 1954; children: Edward Steven, Lori Ann. BS, U. Oreg., 1954; MS in Pub. Adminstrn., George Washington U., 1964; grad., Air Command and Staff Coll., 1964, Nat. War Coll., 1974. Commd. USAF, 1954, advanced through grades to maj. gen., 1982, instr. fighter-interceptor weapons sch. Tyndall AFB, Fla., 1956, pilot 434th Fighter-Day Squadron George AFB, Calif., 1957-58, engring. test pilot and flight examiner 50th Tactical Fighter Wing, 10th Tactical Fighter Squadron Toul-Rosieres AFB, France, and Hahn AFB, Fed. Republic Germany, 1958-61, hdqrs. 12th Waco, Tex., 1961-64, instr. pilot, flight examiner 4453d Combat Crew Tng, Wing Davis-Monthan AFB, Ariz., 1965-66, flight comdr. 12th Tactical Fighter Wing Cam Ranh Bay AFB, Republic Vietnam, 1966-67; comdr. air-to-air flight, instr. and chief R&D/OT&E sect. Fighter Weapons Sch., Nellis AFB, Nev., 1967-70; comdr., leader Thunderbirds USAF, 1970-73, chief fighter attack directorate Kirtland AFB, N.Mex., 1974-75, dep. dir. test and evaluation, 1975-76, from vice comdr. to comdr. 8th Tactical Fighter Wing Kunsan AFB, Republic of Korea, 1976-78, comdr. 3d Tactical Fighter Wing Clark AFB, Philippines, 1978-79, comdr. 57th Fighter Weapons Wing, comdt. fighter weapons sch. Nellis AFB, Nev., 1979-80, comdr. 833d air div. Holloman AFB, N.Mex., 1980-81, comdr. tactical air warfare ctr. Eglin AFB, Fla., 1981-86, ret., 1986; pres. T. Swalm and Assocs., Ft. Walton Beach, Fla., 1986-91; v.p. Melbourne Systems Div. Grumman Corp., 1991-95; pres. T. Swalm and Assocs., Melbourne, Fla., 1995—. V.p. Applications Group Internat., Inc., Atlanta, 1986—89; bd. dirs. Nat. Correlation Working Group. Mem. editorial bd. Jour. Electronic Def., 1983-86; contbr. articles to profl. jours. Hon. chmn. Heart Assn., Las Vegas, Nev., 1972; exec. dir. Boy Scouts Am., Las Vegas and Alamagordo, N.Mex., 1970-81; chmn. AFA Scholarship Found., 1989-91; active Fla. Govs. Coun. for TQM, 1992-94; bd. dirs. Jr. Achievement, Ctrl. Fla., 1992-94; mem. USAF scientific adv. bd., 1994-98. Decorated D.S.M., Legion of Merit with two oak leaf clusters, DFC, Air medal with 14 oak leaf clusters, Vietnam Service medal with three service stars, Republic Vietnam Campaign medal; recipient R.V. Jones Trophy Electronic Security Command, 1984, Exceptional Civilian Svc. award USAF, 1999. Mem. Air Force Assn. (exec. advisor, Jerome Waterman award 1985, Jimmy Doolittle fellow 1986), Thunderbirds Pilots Assn., Old Mission Beach Athletic Club (founder), Assn. Old Crows (editl. bd. R.V. Jones trophy 1984), Order of Daedalians (flight capt.), Melbourne C of C. (trustee 1993-95), Sigma Nu. Republican. Presbyterian. Avocations: golf, tennis, sailing.

**SWAMIDOSS, STEPHENSON,** pathologist, health facility administrator; b. Tanjore, Tamil Nadu, India, Apr. 11, 1946; Came to U.S., 1973; s. Asirwatham and Alice Flora; m. Premila M.K., Jan. 15, 1973; children: Cynthia, Philip. Asst. pathologist Holy Spirit Hosp., Camp Hill, Pa., 1978-82, assoc. pathologist, 1983-96, med. dir. lab. medicine, 1997—; clin. asst. prof. pathology Penn State U. Hershey Med. Ctr., Hershey, Pa., 1995—. Organizer, dir. implementation of thin prep PAP test Holy Spirit Hosp., 1997. Fellow: Internat. Acad. Cytologists, Am. Soc. Clin. Pathologists, Coll. Am. Pathologists; mem.: AMA, Nat. Soc. for Histotechnology, Dauphin County Med. Soc., Pa. Assn. Pathologists, Pa. Med. Soc., Am. Soc. Cytology, Am. Soc. Cytopathologists. Lutheran. Avocations: photography, gardening. Home: 13 Northwatch Ln Mechanicsburg PA 17050-1775 Office: Holy Spirit Hosp-Lab 503 N 21st St Camp Hill PA 17011-2204 Office Phone: 717-763-2209. E-mail: stepswam@msn.com.

**SWAMIKANNU, XAVIER,** environmental engineer, state official; b. Penang, Malaysia, Aug. 1, 1958; s. Swamikannu Savarimuthu and Rosary Swamikannu; m. Laveeza Bhatti, Apr. 21, 1959; 1 child, Romin Swamikannu Savri. PhD in Environ. Sci. & Engring., U. Calif., L.A., 1994. Environ. engr. Calif. EPA - Water Quality Control Bd., LA, 1989—99, chief, coastal storm water program, 1999—2003, spl. asst., storm water pollution control, 2003—04, chief storm water permitting, 2005—. Tech. adv. on storm water pollution USEPA Office of Water, Washington, 1989—; expert panelist Nat. Water Rsch. Inst., Pomona, Calif., 1997—97. Lector St. Anastasia Cath. Ch., LA, 1999—2004. Named Disting. scholar, U. Calif., 1993. Mem.: ASCE, Water Environment Fedn., Internat. Water Assn., Am. Water Works Assn. Roman Catholic. Achievements include development of water quality design stds. for Calif; So. Calif. storm water monitoring; Santa Monica Bay restoration policy; storm water pollution control. Avocation: travel. Home: 7732 Stewart Ave Los Angeles CA 90045 Office: Calif EPA - Water Quality Control Bd 320 W 4th St Los Angeles CA 90013 Office Phone: 213-620-2094. Home Fax: 310-242-9222; Office Fax: 213-576-6625. Business E-Mail: xswamikannu@waterboards.ca.gov.

**SWAMINATHAN, SETHURAMAN,** pediatrician, cardiologist; b. Chennai, India, 1967; MBBS, U. Madras, India, 1990; MD in Pediat., U. Calicut, India, 1993. Diplomate Am. Bd. Pediat. (sub-bd. cardiology), Indian Bd. Pediat. Asst. prof. clin. pediat. Miller Sch. Medicine, U. Miami, 2001—. Mem.: Am. Soc. Echocardiography. Achievements include research in tissue Doppler echocardiography in children. Office: U Miami Miller Sch Medicine 1611 NW 12 Ave Rm 5043 Miami FL 33156 Office Phone: 305-585-6683. Office Fax: 305-324-6012.

**SWAN, ANNALYN,** writer; b. Biloxi, Miss. d. Ethelynn Swan; m. Mark Whitney Stevens, June 12, 1977; children: Emmelyn Swan, Julia Philippa. Former writer Time mag.; former music critic & sr. arts editor Newsweek; has also written for The New Republic, The Atlantic Monthly, NY Times Mag. Co-author (with Mark Stevens): de Kooning: An American Master, 2004 (Nat. Book Critics Circle Award for biography/autobiography, 2005, Pulitzer Prize for biography, 2005).

**SWAN, GEORGE STEVEN,** law educator; b. St. Louis; s. Raymond Albert and Lorene Catherine (Kennedy) Swan. BA, Ohio State U., 1970; JD, U. Notre Dame, 1974; LLM, U. Toronto, 1976, SJD, 1983. Bar: Ohio 1974, U.S. Dist. Ct. (so. dist.) Ohio 1975, U.S. Supreme Ct. 1987, U.S. Ct. Appeals (6th and 11th cirs.) 1993, U.S. Ct. Appeals (10th cir.) 1994, DC 1997, Ga. 1997, Fla. 1997, U.S. Dist. Ct. (no. dist.) Ga. 1997, Minn. 1998, La. 1999, Mass. 1999; CLU, ChFC, CFP. Asst. atty. gen. State of Ohio, Columbus, 1974-75; jud. clk. Supreme Ct. Ohio, Columbus, 1976-78; asst. prof. Del. Law Sch., Wilmington, 1980-83, assoc. prof., 1983-84; prof. law St. Thomas U. Law Sch., Miami, Fla., 1984-88; jud. clk. U.S. Ct. Appeals (7th cir.), Chgo., 1988-89; assoc. prof. N.C. Agrl. & Tech. State U., Greensboro, 1989—. Vis. prof. John Marshall Law Sch., Atlanta, 1996—97, Atlanta, 2000—01. Contbr. articles to profl. jours. Mem.: Am. Polit. Sci. Assn., Fin. Planning Assn., Soc. Fin. Svc. Profls., La. State Bar Assn., Nebr. State Bar Assn., Mass. Bar Assn., Fla. Bar, State Bar Ga., DC Bar, Ohio State Bar Assn., Phi Kappa Phi. Office: Merrick Hall 1601 E Market St Greensboro NC 27411 Office Phone: 336-334-7656 ext 7022. Business E-Mail: swan@ncat.edu.

**SWAN, KENNETH CARL,** surgeon; b. Kansas City, Mo., Jan. 1, 1912; s. Carl E. and Blanche (Peters) S.; m. Virginia Grone, Feb. 5, 1938; children: Steven Carl, Kenneth, Susan. AB, U. Oreg., 1933, MD, 1936. Diplomate: Am.

Bd. Ophthalmology (chmn. 1960-61). Intern U. Wis., 1936-37; resident in ophthalmology State U. Iowa, 1937-40; practice medicine specializing in ophthalmology Portland, Oreg., 1945—; staff Good Samaritan Hosp.; asst. prof. ophthalmology State U. Iowa, Iowa City, 1941-44; assoc. prof. U. Oreg. Med. Sch., Portland, 1944-45, prof. and head dept. ophthalmology, 1945-78, prof. emeritus, 2004—. Chmn. sensory diseases study sect. NIH; mem. adv. council Nat. Eye Inst.; also adv. council Nat. Inst. Neurol. Diseases and Blindness. Contbr. articles on ophthalmic subjects to med. publs. Recipient Proctor Rsch. medal, 1953, Disting. Svc. award U. Oreg., 1963, Meritorious Achievement award U. Oreg. Med. Sch., 1968, Howe Ophthalmology medal, 1977, Aubrey Watzek Pioneer award Lewis and Clark Coll., 1979, Disting. Alumnus award Oreg. Health Scis. U. Alumni Assn., 1988, Disting. Svc. award, 1988, Mentor award Oreg. Health Scis. Found., 1996; named Oreg. Scientist of Yr. Oreg. Mus. Sci. and Industry, 1959. Mem. Assn. Research in Ophthalmology, Am. Acad. Ophthalmology (v.p. 1978, historian), Soc. Exptl. Biology and Medicine, AAAS, AMA, Am. Ophthal. Soc. (Howe medal for distinguished service 1977), Oreg. Med. Soc., Sigma Xi, Sigma Chi (Significant Sig award 1977) Home: 4645 SW Fairview Blvd Portland OR 97221-2624 Office: Oreg Health Scis U Ophthalmology Dept Portland OR 97239-4197

**SWAN, MICHAEL K.,** lawyer; b. Kilgore, Tex. BBA, Tex. A&M, 1964; LLB, Univ. Tex., 1967. Bar: Tex. 1967, US Supreme Ct. 1971, US Dist. Ct. (so., no., we., ea. districts) Tex., cert.: Civil Trial Law, Tex. Bd. Legal Specialization. Assoc. Reynolds White Allen & Cook, 1971—75, mng. ptnr., 1981—88; ptnr., gen. litig. Andrews & Kurth, 1988—92; now ptnr.-in-charge Houston, head litig. practice and mem. mgmt. com. Akin Gump Strauss Hauer & Feld LLP, Houston, 1992—. Mem. JAGC U.S. Army, 1967—71. Fellow: Houston Bar Found., Tex. Bar Found.; mem.: ABA, Am. Bd. Trial Advocates, State Bar of Tex. (dir. 1982—85), Houston Bar Assn., Phi Alpha Delta. Office: Akin Gump Strauss Hauer & Feld LLP 44th fl 1111 Louisiana St Houston TX 77002-5200 Office Phone: 713-220-5862. Office Fax: 713-236-0822. Business E-Mail: mswan@akingump.com.

**SWAN, PEER ALDEN,** public utility executive; b. Beverly, Mass., 1944; s. E.M. and Stella Swan; m. Nancy Carol Mosier, Jan. 24, 1969; children: Michael, Ashley. AA, Orange Coast Coll., Costa Mesa, Calif., 1966; BA, Calif. State U., Fullerton, 1973. Fin. analyst Brunswick, Costa Mesa, 1974-76; asst. treas. Pacific Sci. Co., Newport Beach, Calif., 1977-84, treas., 1984-98. Dir. SC Bancorp, Downey, Calif., 1992-97, Met. Water Dist. of So. Calif., 1999-2002. Dir. Irvine (Calif.) Ranch Water Dist., 1979—, Orange County Sanitation Dist., Fountain Valley, Calif., 1985—2001, So. Calif. Water Com., Irvine, 1984—92, Nat. Water Rsch. Inst., Fountain Valley, 1991—2001. Capt. U.S. Army, 1966—71, Vietnam. Avocations: sailing, hiking. Home: 7 Terraza Dr Newport Coast CA 92657-1510 Business E-Mail: pswan@ix.netcom.com.

**SWAN, PHILIP GEORGE,** librarian, educator, director, artist; b. Camp Springs, Md., Feb. 7, 1969; s. Philip George and Diana Morse Swan; m. Jennifer Marguerite Hubert, Sept. 27, 2001. BA, U. Mich., 1991; MA, Coll. William and Mary, 1994; MS in Info., U. Mich., 1996. Libra, asst. mgr. Queensborough Pub. Libr., Jamaica, NY, 1997—99; head libr., assoc. prof. Hunter Coll., NYC, 2000—. Chesebrough Pond's Nat. Arts Competition, 1987, juried exhibition, The Haven (Second Pl. Nationally, 1987), Dansforth Gallery, 2000, Longbeach Island Found. Arts, 2002; author: (peer reviewed article) Collection Building (Emerald Publishing's 2003 Highly Commended Award, 2002); contbr. articles to profl. jours. Scholar, Coll. William and Colonial Williamsburg Found., 1993—94. Mem.: ALA, Libr. Assn. CUNY (co-chair 2002—04, co-chair electronic info. svcs. com. 2002—04), Assn. Coll. and Rsch. Libr. (coll. libr. sect. comm. 2001—04). Office: Hunter Coll 129 E 79th St 2nd Flr New York NY 10021

**SWAN, ROBERT H.,** information technology executive; BS in mgmt., SUNY, Buffalo; MBA, SUNY, Binghamton. Fin. positions Gen. Electric, 1985—99; CFO GE Transportation Systems, 1994—97; v.p. fin. GE Med. Systems, 1997—98; v.p.fin., CFO GE Lighting, 1998—99, Webvan Group, 1999—2001, COO, 2000—01, CEO, 2001; CFO, exec. v.p. TRW Inc., 2001—02; exec. v.p., CFO EDS, Plano, Tex., 2003—06; sr. v.p. fin., CFO eBay Inc., San Jose, Calif., 2006—. Office: eBay Inc 2145 Hamilton Ave San Jose CA 95125 Office Phone: 972-604-6000. Office Fax: 972-605-6033.*

**SWAN, SUSAN LINDA,** history professor; b. Everett, Wash., May 31, 1943; d. Joseph William Franckevitch and Doris Aline (Doolittle) Berry; m. Victor LaMarr Swan, June 19, 1965 (div. Apr. 1994); 1 child, Kerrigan Aline. BA in History, U. Wash., 1965, BA in English, 1965; MA in History, Western Wash. U., 1969; PhD in History, Wash. State U., 1976. Employment interviewer Wash. State Employment Security, Tacoma, 1971-72; asst. prof. history Wash. State U., Pullman, 1977-82, student affairs officer III, 1984-94, assoc. prof. gen. edn. program, 1994—; rsch. assoc. Nat. Coord. Spl. Hist. Projects, Mex., 1991-92. Student affairs com. Wash. State U., chair acad. advising and reinstatement subcom., mus. adv. subcom.; chpt. advisor Alpha Phi Omega, 1995—99; advisor Sikh Student Assn., 2002—04. Co-author: Breve Historia de las Sequias en Mexico, 1995; adaptation editor: Study Guide for the Heritage of World Civilizations, vol. I, 2001, vol. II, 2002; contbg. editor: Reading About the World, I, II, 3d edit., 1999; contbr. articles to profl. jours Vol. Pullman Meml. Hosp. Aux., 1983—92; group leader Sacajawea coun. Camp Fire, Pullman, 1984—90. Recipient Faculty award, Wash. State U. Multicultural Student Svcs., 2002. Mem.: AAAS, Assn. Faculty Women (treas. 1998—99), Am. Mus. Women in the Arts, N.Y. Acad. Scis., Seattle Art Mus., Phi Kappa Phi, Phi Alpha Theta (pres. 1974—75). Avocations: watercolors, gardening. Home: PO Box 1284 Pullman WA 99163-1284 Office: Wash State Univ Dept History Pullman WA 99164-4030

**SWAN, WILLIAM,** actor; b. Buffalo, Feb. 6, 1932; s. Earl B. and Irene (Hall) S. Student, Geller Workshop, L.A. Appeared in films including Lady in a Cage, Hotel, The Parallax View, Bombers B-52; over 200 TV guest appearances include Streets of San Francisco, Quincy, Perry Mason, Felony Squad, Twilight Zone, Have Gun Will Travel, Cannon, Barnaby Jones; appeared in off-Broadway plays including Anne of a Thousand Days, Night Fishing in Beverly Hills, The Locked-In Syndrome; appeared in regional theatre prodns. of A Delicate Balance, The Rehearsal, The Cocktail Hour, California Suite, The Middle Ages, Stained Glass, What the Butler Saw, The Price, Golf with Alan Shepard, Moby-Dick-Rehearsed, Medea and Electra, The Miracle Worker, All the Way Home, The Night of the Iguana, 2006, and others; actor: (TV) Walter Hines on All My Children, 1982-2000, Dr Ralph Jennings on The Young and the Restless, Rex Whitmore on As The World Turns. Trustee Berkshire Theatre Festival, Stockbridge, Mass., 1984-2001. Sgt. U.S. Army, 1948-49, ETO. Mem. Acad. TV, Arts and Scis., The Players, The Yale Club. Democrat. Avocation: tennis. Home: 141 E 55th St Apt 12B New York NY 10022-4034 also: Barberry Close Monterey MA 01245

**SWANAGAN, JEFFERY S.,** aquarium administrator; BS, Ohio State U.; MS in Tech. and Sci. Policy, Ga. Inst. Tech. With Columbus Zoo; dir. edn. to dep. zoo dir. Zoo Atlanta, 1987—98; exec. dir. Fla. Aquarium, Tampa, 1998—2002, Ga. Aquarium, 2003—. Bd. dirs. Atlanta Convention & Visitors Bur., Leadership Atlanta. Mem.: Am. Zoo and Aquarium Assn. Office: Ga Aquarium 225 Baker St Atlanta GA 30313 Office Phone: 404-581-4000.*

**SWANER, LYNN E,** education educator; d. Norris S and Susan L Gaynor; m. Damon K Swaner, Aug. 10, 1996; 1 child, Ashley E. EdD, Columbia U., 2003. Nat. cert. counselor. Asst. prof. C.W. Post Campus of L.I. U., Brookville, NY, 2005—. Cross-site evaluator, mem. planning bd. Bringing Theory to Practice Project, Am. Assn. Colls. and Univs., Washington, 2004—. Sec. South Yaphank Cmty. Assn., Yaphank, NY, 2004—05. Recipient Binghamton U. award for the Humanities, 1996. Mem.: Phi Beta Kappa. Achievements include commissioned literature review on mental health, engaged learning, and civic development published by Am. Assn. Colls. and Univs. Office: CW Post Campus of LI U Dept of Counseling 720 Northern Blvd Brookville NY 11548 Office Phone: 516-299-2815.

**SWANER, PAULA MARGETTS,** clinical psychologist; b. Salt Lake City, Nov. 23, 1927; d. Sumner Gray and Pauline (Moyle) Margetts; m. Leland Scowcroft, May 22, 1951; children: Leland S., Jr., Sumner Margetts, Paula June Swaner-Sargetakis. BA in Eng. Lit., U. Utah, 1949, MA in Eng. Lit., 1972, MS in Ednl. Psychol., 1978, PhD in Clin. Psychology, 1986; postgrad., Washington Sch. Psychiatry, 1991, Mill Valley Calif. Acad., 1990; MA, in Mythological Studies, Pacifica Grad. Inst., 2003. Lic. clin. psychologist, Utah. Psychotherapist Granite Mental Health Ctr., Salt Lake City, 1978-80; intern Mental Health Unit, Juvenile Ct., Salt Lake City, 1984-87; pvt. practice Salt Lake City, 1986—. CEO Evergreen Coalition, 1993—2002; faculty Internat. Psycotherophay Inst., Chevy Chase, Md., 1996—; dir., Salt Lake City, 1996, founder, 2000, Infant Observation Teleconferencing Satellite Program, 2000; established master tchrs. svcs. IPI Videoconf. Supervision and Clin. Application Program, 2001. Chair Swaner Nature Preserve Found., 1993-2002; established Rock Mountain Psychol. Ctr. for Therapy and Tng., Salt Lake City, 2003. Mem.: APA, Utah Psychol. Assn. (mem. task force 2002—06). Democrat. Avocations: hiking, cross country skiing, swimming.

**SWANGO, COLLEEN JILL,** science educator; b. Izmir, Turkey, Sept. 8, 1956; d. Charles Irvan Swango and Altamae Silva. BS in Edn., Ind. U., 1978; MS in Edn., Ind. U.-Purdue, 1984. Lic. tchr. Ind. Tchr. Share's Inc., Shelbyville, Ind., 1978—85, supervising tchr., 1979—85; sci. tchr. Brownsburg (Ind.) Jr. High, 1986—, chair sci. dept., 1993—. Co-prodr.: Help! I'm Teaching Middle School Science, 2003. Mem.: Nat. Sci. Tchrs. Assn., Hoosier Assn. Sci. Tchrs., Brownsburg Classroom Tchrs. Assn. (past pres., rep.). Independent. Avocations: music, reading, theater, travel. Home: 104 Sterling Dr Pittsboro IN 46167

**SWANK, HILARY ANN,** actress; b. Lincoln, Nebr., July 30, 1974; m. Chad Lowe, Sept. 28, 1997 (separated 2006). Actor: Buffy the Vampire Slayer, 1992, The Next Karate Kid, 1994, Sometimes They Come Back...Again, 1996, Kounterfeit, 1996, The Way We Are, 1997, Heartwood, 1998, Boys Don't Cry, 1999 (Golden Globe for Best Actress, 2000, Academy award for Best Actress, 2000), Affair of the Necklace, 2000, The Gift, 2000, The Affair of the Necklace, 2001, Insomnia, 2002, The Core, 2003, Million Dollar Baby, 2004 (best actress, Boston Film Critics Award, 2004, Golden Globe award for best actress, 2005, Screen Actors Guild award, for outstanding performance by female actor in leading role, 2005, Acad. award for Best Actress, 2005), The Black Dahlia, 2006; (TV movies) Cries Unheard: The Donna Yaklich Story, 1994, Terror in the Family, 1996, Dying to Belong, 1997, The Sleepwalker Killing, 1997, Iron Jawed Angels, 2004; (TV series) Evening Shade, 1991-92, Camp Wilder, 1992, Beverly Hills, 90210, 1997-98, Leaving L.A., 1997; actor, exec. prodr. (films) 11:14, 2003; (TV appearances) Growing Pains, 1985, Harry and the Hendersons, 1991. Named one of Time Mag. 100 Most Influential People, 2005; recipient Little Screen/Big Star award, TV Land, 2006. Avocations: sky diving, river rafting, skiing, swimming. Office: William Morris Agy 151 S El Camino Dr Beverly Hills CA 90212*

**SWANK, WILLIAM GEORGE,** historian, writer; b. Chgo., June 17, 1940; s. William George and Estelle Jensen Swank; m. Jeri Lynne Bessie; children: William Corey, Eric William, Karen Estelle. BS, San Diego State Coll., 1962. Supervising probation officer County of San Diego, 1963—94; historian, lectr., writer San Diego, 1994—. Baseball historian San Diego Hall of Champions, 1988—, San Diego Hist. Soc., 1994—; chmn. Gavy Cravath Hall of Fame Com., Johnny Ritchey Commemorative Task Force, 2003—. Author: The Lane Field Padres, 2 vols., 1997, Echoes from Lane Field, 1999, Gold Leather Helmets/Black Hightop Shoes, 2003, Baseball in San Diego: From the Plaza to Petco, 2 vols., 2004, Bob Chandler's Tales From the San Diego Padres, 2006; editor: Whitey Wietelmann Box Score Collection, 1969—, (newsletter) Echoes from Lane Field, 1995—. Coach youth soccer, baseball, basketball, San Diego, 1975—93; judge Greater San Diego Science and Engring. Fair, San Diego, 1992—; Santa Claus, Christmas on the Prado, Balboa Park, San Diego, 2002—; House of David Baseball Team, 2003. Mem.: Soc. for Am. Baseball Rsch. (dead ball era com. 1998—). Avocations: scale model of Lane Field, baseball scrapbooks. Home: 3474 Via Beltran San Diego CA 92117-5729

**SWANKIN, DAVID ARNOLD,** lawyer, consumer products company executive; b. Boston, Jan. 18, 1934; s. Max and Anne (Rotefsky) S.; m. Jeanne Phyllis Herrick; 1 dau., Sheryl. AB, Brandeis U., 1954; JD, U. Wis., 1957; JD, George Washington U., 1962. Mgmt. intern U.S. Dept. Labor, Washington, 1957-60, spl. asst. to asst. sec. labor, 1961-63, dep. asst. sec. labor, 1967; dir. Bur. Labor Standards, 1967-68; exec. sec. Pres.'s Consumer Adv. Council, Washington, 1964; exec. dir. Pres's Com. on Consumer Interests, Washington, 1965-66; Washington rep. Consumer's Union, 1969-71; exec. dir. Consumer Interests Found., 1971-73; sr. partner Swankin & Turner, 1973—. Pres. Citizen Advocacy Ctr. 1994—; cons. U.S. Dept. Labor; pres. Citizen Advocacy Ctr., 1994—. Mem. president's coun. Brandeis U., 1968-69; mem. PEW Health Profls. Commn., 1997-98. Served with AUS., 1954-56. Recipient Jump award U.S. Govt., 1969 Home: 2305 N Van Buren Ct Arlington VA 22205 Office: 1400 16th St NW Washington DC 20036-2217 Business E-Mail: davidswankin@cacenter.org

**SWANN, BRIAN,** writer, humanities educator; b. Wallsend, Northumberland, Eng., Aug. 13, 1940; came to U.S., 1963, naturalized, 1980; s. Stanley Frank and Lilyan Mary (Booth) S.; m. Roberta Metz. BA, Cambridge U., Eng., 1962, MA, 1965; PhD, Princeton U., 1970. Instr. Princeton U., 1964-65, lectr., 1968-70, asst. prof., 1970-72; instr. Rutgers U., 1965-66; asst. prof. humanities Cooper Union for Advancement Sci. and Art, N.Y.C., 1972-75, assoc. prof., 1975-80, prof., 1980—, acting dean, 1990-91. Dir. Bennington Writing Workshops, 1988-91. Author: The Middle of the Journey 1982, A Basket Full of White Eggs, 1988, Song of the Sky: Versions of Native American Song-Poems, 1993, The House With No Door, 1998, Wearing the Morning Star: Native American Song-Poems, 1996, Autumn Road, 2005, Snow House, 2005, other books, translations; editor: Smoothing The Ground: Essays of Native American Oral Literature, 1983; (with Arnold Krupat) Recovering the Word, 1987, I Tell You Now: Autobiographical Essays by Native American Writers, 1987, Coming to Light: Contemporary Translations of the Native American Literatures, 1992, (with Krupat) Here First: Autobiographical Essays by Contemporary Native American Writers, 2000, Voices from Four Directions: Contemporary Translations of the Native Literatures of North America, 2003; editor The Smithsonian Series of Essays on Native American Literatures, 1990-98, Algonquian Spirit: Contemporary Translations of the Algonquian Literatures of North America, 2005. NEA fellow, 1981; Creative Arts in Pub. Service grantee, 1982. Office: Cooper Union Adv Sci & Art Faculty Humanities & Social Sci Cooper Sq New York NY 10003

**SWANN, CHARENA RAI,** psychotherapist, social worker; b. Chamersburg, Pa., June 18, 1962; d. Nathaniel McNabb and Brenda Keepler; m. Lynn Swann, June 23, 1991; children: Shafer, Braxton. BA Social Work, Calif. U. Pa., Calif., Pa., 1984; MA Social Work, U. Pitts., 1985, PhD, 2002. Psychiatric soc. worker Western Psychiatric Inst. & Clinic, Pitts., 1994—; psychotherapist Sewickley Valley Hosp., Pitts., 1995—. Adv. bd. Summerbridge Pitts., 1999—2002; bd. mem. Children's Mus., 1998—. Fundraiser, mentor Girls Hope Pitts., 1998—2002. Mem.: Am. Psychol. Soc., Link, Jack and Jill of Am. Baptist. Avocations: reading, exercise.

**SWANN, LYNN CURTIS,** sportscaster, former professional football player; b. Alcoa, Tenn., Mar. 7, 1952; s. Willie and Mildred (McGarity) Swann; m. Charena Swann; 2 children. BA, U. So. Calif., 1974. Wide receiver Pitts. Steelers, 1974-83; commentator ABC Sports, 1976—; founder, pres. Swann, Inc. Bd. dirs. H.J. Heinz Co., Wyndham Internat. Inc.; chairman President's Coun. Phys. Fitness and Sports, 2002. Entertainment and media apppearances as dancer with Twyla Tharp and Peter Martines Omnibus TV Spl., 1980, guest star Night of 100 Stars I, 1982, 100 Stars II, 1985; host and narrator Britten's Young Person's Guide to Orchestra, Wheeling Symphony Orch., 1982; host of 13 part edn. spl. Arts Alive, PBS, 1984; major character in episodes Paper Chase, 1984, Hotel, 1984, Love American Style, 1985; other appearances on various TV shows including 20/20, Good Morning America, Merv

Griffin, Hollywood Squares, others; intermittent host daily talk show Pittsburgh 2Day, 1985 Spokesman for Big Bros./Big Sisters Assn.; trustee Pitts. Ballet Theatre, creator youth scholarship program; bd. dirs. Scott Newman Juvenile Drug and Alcohol Prevention Found.; bd. dirs. U. So. Calif. Sch. Journalism Alumni Assn. Named All Pro, 1976 77, 78, Most Valuable Player in Super Bowl X, 1976, Pitts. Multiple Sclerosis Athlete of Yr., 1980, NFL Man of Yr., 1981; holder 4 Super Bowl records, 2d in 2 categories; mem. Pitts. Steelers All-Time Team, 50th Anniv.; named to NFL Hall of Fame Team of Decade/1970's, AP, UPI, Kodak All Am. Teams, Pop Warner Hall of Fame; recipient Image award NAACP, 1979, Ebonics Soc. award, Outstanding Alumni award U. So. Calif., 1984, Oleg Cassini Competitors Fashion award, 1985. Mem. Screen Actors Guild, AFTRA. Office: Swann Inc 506 Hegner Way #2 Sewickley PA 15143-1552

**SWANN, NAT HENDERSON, JR.,** physician; b. Danville, Va, Nov. 2, 1927; s. Nat Henderson, Sr. and Mary Stokes S.; m. Sarah Hayes, Aug. 7, 1952; children: Nat H. III, Wayland Hayes. AB in Chemistry, U. N.C., Chapel HIll, 1950, MD, 1954. Fellow Royal Soc. Medicine/London. Resident in internal medicine Med. Coll. Va., 1954-56, Boston VA Hosp., 1956-57, Cleve. VA (Crile) Hosp., 1957-58; specialist internal medicine Chattanooga 1958—. Med. dir. Chattem, Inc., Chattanooga, 1960—; cons. rheumatic heart clin. Children's Hosp., Chattanooga, 1959-63; chief of staff Downtown Gen. Hosp., Chattanooga, 1986-90. Contbr. articles to profl. jours. Dir. Physician's Giving, United Way, Chattanooga, 1980; mem. Chattanooga Met. Coun., 1961; bd. spkr. Air Pollution Control Bd., Chattanooga, 1962; bd. dirs. The Salvation Army. With U.S. Army Med. Corps, 1946-47. Recipient Disting. Achievement award Am. Heart Assn. Fellow: Internat. Coll. Angiology, Royal Soc. Medicine, Am. Coll. Angiology, Am. Coll. Chest Physicians (assoc.); mem.: ACP, AMA, Am. Coll. Cardiology, Athenians Club (Chattanooga), Torch Club (Chattanooga), Mountain City Club (bd. dir.), Rotary (bd. dir.). Avocations: short story and novel writer, golf, tennis. Home: 412 Brady Point Rd Signal Mountain TN 37377-2206 E-mail: natswann@mindspring.com.

**SWANN, RICHARD ROCKWELL,** lawyer, banker; b. Orlando, Fla., May 7, 1940; s. Pervie P. and Maesther (Mears) Swann; m. Doris Orr (dec. Oct. 1983); children: Dorothy Orr, Christian Mears, Campbell Thornal, Doris Reed. AB, Duke U., 1961, JD, 1963. Bar: Fla. 1963. Mem. Swann & Haddock, Orlando, 1963—90, Swann & Hadley, 1990—. Chmn. bd. First Fidelity Savs. & Loan, Orlando. Am. Pioneer Savs. Bank, Orlando, Am. Pioneer, Inc., Orlando; dir. Overseas Pvt. Investment Corp., Washington, 1977—82; bd. govs. Overseas Investment Reins, 1978—82. Mem.: ABA, Fla. Bar Assn., Orange County Bar Assn. Democrat. Office Phone: 497-647-2777. E-mail: rswann@swann.hadley.com.

**SWANSBURG, RUSSELL CHESTER,** nursing educator, consultant, health facility administrator; b. Cambridge, Mass., Aug. 6, 1928; s. William W. and Mary A. (Pierce) S.; m. Laurel Clark, Sept. 1951; children: Philip Wayne, Michael Gary, Richard Jeffrey. Diploma, N.S. Hosp. Sch. Nursing, 1950; BSN, Western Res. U., 1952; MA in Nursing Edn., Columbia U., 1961; PhD, U. Miss., 1984. CNAA. Asst. administr. U. of S. Ala. Med. Ctr., Mobile; v.p. U. South Ala., Mobile; prof. Auburn U., Montgomery, Ala., Med. Coll. of Ga., Augusta; instr. Univ. of the Incarnate Word, San Antonio, 1986—. Mil. cons. USAF Surgeon Gen., 1972; sr. med. svc. cons., 1973-76; nurse cons. VA Med. Ctr., Tuskegee, Ala., 1987-88; mem. editl. adv. bd. Nursing Adminstrn. Manual. Author: Team Nursing: A Programmed Learning Experience, 1968, Inservice Education, 1968, The Measurement of Vital Signs, 1970, The Team Plan, 1971, Management of Patient Care Services, 1976, Strategic Career Planning and Development, 1984, The Nurse Manager's Guide to Financial Management, 1988, Management and Leadership for Nurse Managers, 1990 (Book of Yr. Selection, Am. Jour. Nursing 1990), 3d edit., 2002 (Book of Yr. Selection, Am. Jour. Nursing 2002), 4th edit., 2006, Introductory Management and Leadership for Clinical Nurses, 1993, 2d edit., 1999 (Book of the Yr. Selection, Am. Jour. Nursing 1999), Staff Development: A Component of Human Resource Development, 1994, Budgeting and Financial Management for Nurse Managers, 1997, (audiovisual course) Nurses & Patients: An Introduction to Nursing Management, 1980; contbr. articles to profl. publs Bd. dir. Air Force Village Found., Alzheimer's Care and Rsch. Found. Col. USAF, 1956-76. Decorated Air Medal with oak leaf clusters, Legion of Merit; recipient award for outstanding work in hosp. adminstrn. Ala. State Nurses' Assn., 1985, Outstanding Nursing Svc. Adminstrn. award, 1981, Outstanding Nurse Rschr. 1984, Disting. Svc. award Air Force Village Found., 1999, Disting. Alumnus award Frances Payne Bolton Sch. Nursing Case Western Res. U., 2006. Fellow AONE, Ala. Orgn. Nurse Execs. (past state pres.); mem. Coun. Grad. Edn. Adminstrn. in Nursing (sec.), Ala. Acad. Sci., Sigma Xi, Phi Kappa Phi, Sigma Theta Tau. Home and Office: 4917 Ravenswood Dr Apt 1711 San Antonio TX 78227-4356 Office Phone: 210-673-9475. Personal E-mail: lswansburg@sprintmail.com.

**SWANSEN, SAMUEL THEODORE,** lawyer; b. Milw., June 6, 1937; s. Theodore Lawrence and Clarinda Dingwall (Crittenden) S.; m. Donna Rae Elizabeth Maloney, June 27, 1959; children: Jessica Swansen Bonelli, Theodor Andrew, Christopher Currie. AB, Dartmouth Coll., 1959; JD, U. Wis., 1962. Bar: Wis. 1962, Pa. 1964, U.S. Supreme Ct. 1969, accredited estate planner: Nat. Assn. Estate Planners & Couns. 1995. Law clk. to presiding justice Wis. Supreme Ct., Madison, 1962-63; assoc. Dechert, Price & Rhoads, Phila., 1963-68, 70-73, ptnr., 1973-93; asst. dist. atty. City of Phila. Dist. Atty.'s Office, 1968-70, chief frauds div., 1969; pvt. practice Phila., 1963—93, Blue Bell Pa., 1994—. Adj. prof. Law Temple U., Phila., 1970-80; lectr. Pa. Bar Inst., Nat. Bus. Inst., Ctr. Profl. Edn., 1985—. Editor, author U. Wis. Law Rev., 1960-62. Corp. mem. Anna T. Jeanes Found., Fox Chase, Phila, 1985—93, Associated Svcs. for the Blind, Phila, 1974—91, Bach Festival of Phila., 1989—, pres., 1993—97, 2003—06; founding dir. Global Bach Cmty., 2000—, pres., 2001—2003—06; violinist North Penn Symphony Orch., 1973—, trombonist, 1973—; mem. Nat. Network of Estate Planning Attys., 1993—; mem. wealth counsel Nat. Acad. Elder Law Attys., 1993—; bd. dirs. Friends Rehab. Program, Inc., Phila., 1966—73, 1985—94, Franklin Found., Phila., 1969—; v.p., sec., bd. dirs. Foulkeways at Gwynedd, 1979—97, pres., 1986—97; chmn. bd. dirs. Friends Life Care at Home, Inc., 1990—, bd. dirs., 1990—; Friends Retirement Concepts, Inc., Gwynedd, sec. bd. dirs., 1985—96; hon. bd. dirs. Friends Neighborhood Guild; pres. Greater Phila. Fedn. Settlements, 1970—72; dir., sec. Energy Islands Internat., Inc., 1963—; pres. emeritus Foulkeways at Gwynedd, 1997; mem. Gwynedd Monthly Meeting of Friends, 1974—. Fellow Esperti Peterson Inst. Wealth Strategies Planning, 1996—. Mem. ABA, Pa. Bar Assn., Phila. Bar Assn., Dartmouth Club Phila., Delta Upsilon, Phi Delta Phi. Republican. Mem. Soc. Of Friends. Home: 221 Morris Rd Ambler PA 19002-5202 Office: 660 Sentry Pky Ste 200 Blue Bell PA 19422-2317 Office Phone: 610-834-9810. Personal E-mail: sam@samswansen.com.

**SWANSEY, MICAH KASSIO,** psychologist; b. Joseph and Annie Swansey; m. Sherri Shannon, June 28, 1998; children: Meyoh Korchez children: Micah Kassio Jr., Ryenne Shaw. D of Clin. Psychology, Adler Sch. Profl. Psychology, 2001. Lic. clin. psychologist Ill. Dept. Profl. Regulation, 2005, clin. profl. counselor IL Dept Profl. Regulation, 1998; cert. addictions counselor Iodappca, 2001. CEO Cons. Profls. Inc., Calumet, City, Ill., 2000—. Mem.: Kappa Alpha Psi. Office: Cons Profls Inc 593 Burnham Ave Calumet City IL 60409 Office Phone: 708-832-1002. Home Fax: 708-832-1099; Office Fax: 708-832-1099. Personal E-mail: mswansey@aol.com.

**SWANSON (MCNUTT), BEVERLEY KAY,** special education educator; b. Oranjestad, Aruba, May 29, 1974; d. Maxine Sims and Beverly Daniel McNutt; m. Donald John Swanson, Sept. 27, 1997; 1 child, Katie Elizabeth Swanson. BA in Edn., Mercer U., 1996; MEd in Interrelated Spl. Edn., Kennesaw State U., 2000. Cert. Learning disabilities tchr. Ga. Profl. Stds., 1996, interrelated spl. edn. tchr. Ga. Profl. Stds., 2000, preschool handicapped endorsement Ga. Profl. Stds., 2001. Spl. edn. tchr. Cobb County Schs.-Awtrey Mid. Sch., Kennesaw, Ga., 1997—98; interrelated spl. edn. resource tchr. Cobb County Pub. Schs.-Lewis Elem., Kennesaw, Ga., 1998—2001; spl. needs preschool tchr. Cobb County Pub. Schs.- Rocky Mt. Elem., Kennesaw,

Ga., 2001—. Spl. instr., evaluator Babies Can't Wait, Marietta, Ga., 1998—2005; Ga. Pines parent advisor Ga. Dept. of Edn., Atlanta, 2001—05. Sibling moderator Assn. for Retarted Citizens, 2001—06; sibling advisor Ga. Sensory Assistance Project, Atlanta, 2003—06; mem. Christ Episcopal Ch., Kennesaw, Ga., 1998—2006. Recipient Tchr. of the Yr. award, Ga. Sensory Assistance Project, 2004. Office Phone: 770-591-5050.

**SWANSON, CARL D.,** music educator, singer; B in Music Edn., U. R.I., 1978; EdM, Suffolk U., 1988. Tchr. Duxbury (Mass.) Pub. Schs., 1983—; voice prof. Northeastern U., Boston, 2001—. Under Providence Gay Men's Chorus, 1995—98. Editor: Jour. Singing; contbr. articles to profl. jours. Mem.: Nat. Assn. Tchrs. Singing (gov. New Eng. region 2002—06, R.I. dist. gov. 2000—06, v.p. discretionary funds and field activities 2006—). Office Phone: 781-934-7630.

**SWANSON, DAVID CARL,** engineering educator, researcher; s. Arthur Smith and Violet Jean Swanson; m. Nadine Marie Sharp, Oct. 17, 1987; children: Drew Alexander, Anya Elise, Erik Arthur, Ava Irene. BEE, U. Del., Newark, Del., 1981; MS Acoustics, Pa. State U., Univ. Pk., Pa., 1984; PhD Acoustics, Pa. State U., 1986. EIT NCEE Del., 1981, cert. Bd. Cert. Noise Control, Inst. of Noise Control Engrs., 1994. Sr. scientist Textron Def. Sys., Wilmington, Mass., 1986—89; sr. rsch. assoc. The Applied Rsch. Lab., State College, Pa., 1989—. Author: (textbook) Signal Processing for Intelligent Sensor Systems. Fellow: Acoustical Soc. Am. (life); mem.: IEEE, Inst. Noise Control Engrs. R-Consevative. Achievements include patents for Sys. and method for detection, localizing, or classifying a distrubance using a waveguide sensing sys. USP6371210. Avocations: guitar, woodworking, home and car renovation, beer brewing, football. Office: Pa State U 121 ARL West PO Box 30 State College PA 16804 Office Phone: 814-865-2448.

**SWANSON, DAVID P.,** lawyer; b. 1955; BA, St. Cloud State Univ., 1978; JD, Vanderbilt Univ., 1981. Bar: Ill. 1981, Minn. 1983. Ptnr., co-chair, project devel., fin. group Dorsey & Whitney LLP, Mpls., and chair, agribus., coop. law. Dir. North Country Devel. Fund, Ralph K. Morris Found., John Brandt Meml. Found. Recipient Honored Cooperator award, Nat. Coop. Bus. Assn. Mem.: Nat. Soc. of Accountants for Cooperatives, Legal Services Coop., Nat. Coop. Bus. Assn. Office: Dorsey & Whitney LLP Ste 1500 50 S Sixth St Minneapolis MN 55402-1498 Office Phone: 612-343-8275. Office Fax: 612-340-7800. Business E-mail: swanson.dave@dorsey.com.

**SWANSON, DIANE L.,** business management and economics educator, researcher; b. Manhattan, Kans., Oct. 6, 1950; d. Harold Albin Swanson and Betty Jo Lusby; m. Michael Dale Scott, Aug. 5, 1970 (dec. July 19, 1975); 1 child, Christopher William Scott. BS Mgmt. and Fin., Avila U., Kansas City, Mo., 1980; MA Econs., U. Mo., Kansas City, 1982; PhD Bus. Adminstrn., U. Pitts., 1996. Instr. econs., interim dir. Inst. Mgmt. Old Dominion U., Norfolk, Va., 1984—86; asst. prof. fin. Hampton U., Va., 1987—88; asst. prof. bus. econs. U. Pitts., 1988—89; assoc. prof. mgmt. Robert Morris Coll., Pitts., 1989—97, Kans. State U., Manhattan, 1997—; instr. corp. continuing ethics edn. acctg., 2005—. Mem. Pres.'s Commn. on Women Kans. State U., Manhattan, 2000—01, mentor Developing Scholars Program for Minority Students, 2000—01; instr. exec. edn. program Dartmouth Coll., 2005—; von Waaden prof. bus. adminstrn., founder and chair Bus. Ethics Edn. Initiative Kans. State U., 2002—; instr. continuing edn. in acctg. ethics, Kans. 2005—06; presenter in field; spkr. in field. Book rev. editor, consulting editor: Internat. Jour. Orgnl. Analysis, 1994—2005, mem. editl. bd.: Ethics in Film, 2005—06, Organizational Analysis, Research in Management, Education and Development Books Series, 2005, mem. editl. team spl. issues: Acad. Mgmt. Rev., 2005, mem. editl. bd.: Oxford Handbook of Corporate Social Responsibility, 2006—, Media Source, 2002—; contbg. editor: Managing Ego Energy, 1994; spl. issue editor: Jour. Individual Employment Rights, 2002—03, assoc. editor: Business Ethics and Society Encyclopedia, 2004—; assoc. editor website Acad. Mgmt. Profl. Devel., 2005; assoc. editor: Acad. Mgmt. Profl. Devel. in Ethics, 2005, reviewer: Acad. Textbooks, 1998—2005; contbr. chapters to books, articles to profl. jours. Co-founder Nat. Campaign to Improve Bus. Ethics Edn., 2002—; bd. dirs. Women's Intercultural Network, San Francisco, 1994—2002, People's Coop., Manhattan, 1998—2000, All Acad. Task Force on Mentoring, 2002—04. Recipient nat. award for tchg. excellence, Bell and Howell, 1982, award for entrepreneurial leadership, Advances in Mgmt. Conf., 1996, Best Article on Bus. and Soc. award, Internat. Assn. for Bus. and Soc. and Calif. Mgmt. Rev., 1999, Outstanding Bus. Ethics Educator award, 2004, Japha Hon. for rsch. on exec. compensation, U. Colo., 2004; grantee, Beard Ctr. for Ethics, Duquesne U., 2000, Australian Grad. Sch. Mgmt., 2000—01;. David Berg Family Found. in Bus. Ethics fellow, 1994, Weatherford fellow, Oreg. State U., 2004. Mem.: Nat. Acad. Mgmt. (governing bd. Social Issues in Mgmt. 1998—, chair nat. ethics curriculum devel. com. 2003—05), Beta Gamma Sigma. Democrat. Avocations: yoga, meditation, travel, gardening, cat rescue. Office: Kans State U 101 Calvin Hall Manhattan KS 66506 Office Phone: 785-532-4352. Business E-mail: swanson@ksu.edu.

**SWANSON, DON RICHARD,** university dean; b. L.A., Oct. 10, 1924; s. Harry Windfield and Grace Clara (Sandstrom) S.; m. Patricia Elizabeth Klick, Aug. 22, 1976; children— Douglas Alan, Richard Brian, Judith Ann. BS, Calif. Inst. Tech., 1945; MA, Rice U., 1947; PhD, U. Calif., Berkeley, 1952. Physicist U. Calif. Radiation Lab., Berkeley, 1947-52, Hughes Research and devel. Labs., Culver City, Calif., 1952-55; research scientist TRW, Inc., Canoga Park, Calif., 1955-63; prof. Grad. Library Sch., U. Chgo., 1963-92, dean, 1963-72, 77-79, 86-90, prof. bio-sci. coll. divsn. and divsn. humanities, 1992-96, prof. emeritus, 1996—. Mem. Sci. Info. Council, NSF, 1960-65; mem. toxicology info. panel Pres.'s Sci. Advisory Com., 1964-66; mem. library vis. com. Mass. Inst. Tech., 1966-71; mem. com. on sci. and tech. communication Nat. Acad. Scis., 1966-69 Editor: The Intellectual Founds. of Library Education, 1965, The Role of Libraries in the Growth of Knowledge, 1980; co-editor: Operations Research: Implications for Libraries, 1972, Management Education: Implications for Libraries and Library Schools, 1974; mem. editorial bd.: Library Quarterly, 1963-93; contbr.: chpt. to Ency. Brit., 1968—; sci. articles to profl. jours. Trustee Nat. Opinion Research Center, 1964-73; Research fellow Chgo. Inst. for Psychoanalysis, 1972-76. Served with USNR, 1943-46. Recipient Award of Merit Am. Soc. for Info. Sci. and Tech., 2000. Mem.: Am. Soc. for Info. Sci. Home: 5468 S Ingleside Ave Chicago IL 60615-5062 Office: U Chgo Humanities 1010 E 59th St Chicago IL 60637-1512 Business E-mail: d-swanson@uchicago.edu.

**SWANSON, DONALD ALAN,** geologist; b. Tacoma, July 25, 1938; s. Leonard Walter and Edith Christine (Bowers) S.; m. Barbara Joan White, May 25, 1974. BS in Geology, Wash. State U., 1960; PhD in Geology, Johns Hopkins U., 1964. Geologist U.S. Geol. Survey, Menlo Park, Calif., 1965—68, 1971—80, Hawaii National Park, 1968—71; sr. geologist Cascades Volcano Obs. Vancouver, Wash., 1980—90, rsch. scientist-in-charge, 1986—89, sr. geologist Seattle, 1990—96; assoc. dir. Volcano Systems Ctr. U. Wash., 1993—96; scientist-in-charge Hawaiian Volcano Obs., 1997—2004. Affiliate prof. U. Wash., 1992—; adj. prof. U. Hawaii, 2002--; cons. U.S. Dept. Energy, Richland, Wash., 1979-83; volcanologist New Zealand Geol. Survey, Taupo, 1984; advisor Colombian Volcano Obs., Manizales, 1986. Assoc. editor Jour. Volcanology and Geothermal Rsch., 1976—, Jour. Geophys. Rsch., 1992-94; editor Bull. of Volcanology, 1985-90, exec. editor 1995-99; contbr. numerous articles to profl. jours. Recipient Superior Svc. award U.S. Geol. Survey, 1980, Meritorious Svc. award U.S. Dept. Interior, 1985, Disting. Svc. award, U.S. Dept. Interior, 2005; postdoctoral fellow NATO, 1964-65. Fellow Geol. Soc. Am., Am. Geophys. Union, AAAS; mem. Sigma Xi. Avocation: hiking. Home: 417 Linaka St Hilo HI 96720-5927 Office: US Geol Survey Hawaiian Volcano Obs PO Box 51 Hawaii National Park HI 96718-0051 Office Phone: 808-967-8863. Business E-mail: donswan@usgs.gov.

**SWANSON, DONALD FREDERICK,** retired food company executive; b. Mpls., Aug. 6, 1927; s. Clayton A. and Irma (Baiocchi) S.; m. Virginia Clare Hannah, Dec. 17, 1948; children— Donald Frederick, Cynthia Hannah, Janet Clare Webster. BA, U. Minn., 1948. With Gen. Mills, Inc., 1949-85, div. v.p.,

dir. marketing flour, dessert and baking mixes, 1964-65, v.p., gen. mgr. grocery products div., 1965-68, v.p., corporate adminstrn. officer consumer foods group, fashion div., transp. and purchasing depts., advt. and marketing services, 1969, exec. v.p. craft, game and toy group, fashion group, direct marketing group, travel group, dir., 1968-76, sr. exec. v.p. consumer non-foods, 1976-85, chief financial officer, 1977-79, sr. exec. v.p. restaurants and consumer non-foods, 1980-81, vice chmn. restaurants and consumer non-foods, 1981-85. Ret. chmn. bd. Soo Line Corp. Served with AUS, 1946-47. Mem. Mpls. Club, Wayzata Country Club, Royal Poinciana Golf Club, Phi Kappa Psi. Home: 2171 Gulf Shore Blvd N Apt 504 Naples FL 34102-4685 Office: 641 Lake St E Wayzata MN 55391-1760

**SWANSON, DOUGLAS E.,** oil industry executive; BA, Cornell Univ. CPA. Exec. v.p. Cliffs Drilling Co., 1978—92, chmn., CEO, 1992—99; pres., CEO Oil States Internat., Houston, 2000—. Bd. dir. Boots & Coots Internat. Well Control, Flint Energy Services Ltd. Office: Oil States Internat 3 Allen Ctr Ste 4620 333 Clay St Houston TX 77002*

**SWANSON, ERIK CHRISTIAN,** museum director; b. Breckenridge, Colo., June 17, 1940; s. Glen Leonard and Eveitte Leona (Snell) S.; m. Elizabeth Jane Thompson, Aug. 22, 1976; children: Johannah Elizabeth, Nils Christian. Student, Royal U., Lund, Sweden, 1960-64; BA in History, German Lang., tchg. cert., U. No. Colo. Curator South Pk. City Mus., Fairplay, Colo., 1974-89; dir. Alma (Colo.) Fire House Mus., 1976-82; exec. dir. Cripple Creek (Colo.) Dist. Mus., 1988—. Chief of police Alma, Colo., 1977-80. With U.S. Army, 1966-68. Mem. Odd Fellows (past grand South Park Lodge # 10, Fairplay, Colo.), Swedish Order of VASA (Lodge #178), Masons (sr. warden Cripple Creek chpt. 1995), Elks. Republican. Home: PO Box 27 Alma CO 80420-0027 Office Phone: 719-689-9540.

**SWANSON, JACQUELINE V.,** academic administrator, educator, women's health nurse practitioner; b. Houston, Feb. 12, 1944; d. Ivan Jack and Edith Wilson; m. James Swanson, Aug. 21, 1965; children: Jim, Charlotte, Robert, Guy, Danny. BS, Tex. Woman's U., 1967, MS, 1974; PhD, U. North Tex., Denton, 1989. Cert. clin. nurse specialist, in maternal-newborn health, women's health nurse practitioner Planned Parenthood of Rocky Mountains, sexual assault nurse examiner. Various clin. nursing positions, Tex. and Kans., Tex., 1967-73; supr. obstet. and nursery Harris County Hosp. Dist., Houston, 1970-73; instr. Prairie View (Tex.) A&M U., 1973-75; asst. prof. Tex. Woman's U., Denton, 1975-85; labor and delivery nurse Tarrant County Hosp. Dist., Ft. Worth, 1987-89; assoc. prof., chmn. dept. nursing Ft. Hays State U., Hays, Kans., 1989-94; dir. BS nursing program Lamar U., Beaumont, Tex., 1994-95; prof. nursing, 1998-2000; assoc. prof. nursing Tarleton State U., 2000—03, women's health nurse practioner Student Health Clinic, 2003—04; clin. instr. Tex. Christian U., 2005; dean Sch. Nursing Bacone Coll., 2005—. Contbr. articles to profl. jours.; presenter U.S. and internat. Mem. Denton Area War on Drugs. Mem. AAUP, ANA, Nat. Assn. Nurse Practioners Women's Health, Assn. Women's Health, Obstetric and Neonatal Nurses, Kans. State Nurses Assn., Tex. Nurses Assn., Tex. Nurse Practioner's Assn., Mont. Nurses Assn., Internat. Coun. on Women's Health Issues, Internat. Soc. for Univ. Nurses, Sigma Theta Tau. Home: 416 N 16th Muskogee OK 74401

**SWANSON, JANET M.,** retired secondary school educator; b. Abilene, Tex., June 6, 1941; d. Edwin E. and Marjorie (Munger) Middleton; div.; children: Kristen, Eric. BA, Tex. Christian U., 1963; MA, So. Meth. U., 1965; student, Hollins Coll., Roanoke, Va., 1959-61. Cert. secondary tchr., Tex. Tchr. Richardson (Tex.) H.S., 1964-67, Park Acad., Dallas, 1985-88; grant writer Elsie Robertson Lancaster H.S., Lancaster, Tex., 1995-96, 10th grade English tchr., 1988—2004, chmn. English dept. 1998—2004; ret., 2004. Vol. student conservatory So. Meth. U., 1980-87, bd. dirs. Cross Plains Pub. Libr.; vol. Project Pride, Cross Plains, Big Bros. Big Sisters, 2004-05. Recipient Jack Harvey Exemplary Tchr. award Weatherford Coll., 1998. Mem.: AAUW, Abilene Ret. Tchrs. Assn., Abilene Writers Guild, Cross Plains Pub. Libr. Bd., Callahan Cty. Hist. Commission. Avocations: old books, ranching, treasure hunting, crafts, Texas history. Home: 16301 Private Rd 4595 Cross Plains TX 76443-4419 Personal E-mail: jswan1941@aol.com.

**SWANSON, KURT,** small business owner, artist; b. Denver, Colo., July 9, 1957; s. Weldon Arthur Swanson and Eileen Reiquam; m. Lisa R. Schwartz, Aug. 31, 1986; 1 child, Oliver. BA, Coll. Idaho, Caldwell, 1981; MFA, Mass. Coll. Art, Boston, 1983. Pres. Pinkwater Glass Inc., Carmel, NY, 1983—. Art blass, furniture, lighting, sculpture. Recipient award for Ltd. Prodn. Design, Urban Glass, NY, 1998; fellow, NY Found. Arts, 1990.

**SWANSON, LYNNETTE SUE,** special olympics coordinator, special education educator; d. Carl Robert and Betty Jane Krambier; m. David John Swanson, June 2, 1984. BS cum laude, Brenau U., 2004. Cert. spl. edn. Ga., 2005. Spl. edn. paraprofl. Gwinnett County Pub. Schs., Lawrenceville, Ga., 1994—2000, coord. spl. olympics, 2000—. Coach Ga. women's volleyball team Spl. Olympics USA, Dublin, 2003. Mem.: Nat. Rlwy. Hist. Soc., Kappa Delta Pi, Phi Theta Kappa. Avocations: volunteer coaching, travel, crafts. Home: 4875 Five Forks Trickum Rd Lilburn GA 30047 Office: Gwinnett County Spl Olympics 950 McElvaney Ln Lawrenceville GA 30044 Office Phone: 678-985-3592. E-mail: lynnette_swanson@gwinnett.k12.ga.us.

**SWANSON, PATRICIA KLICK,** retired academic administrator, retired foundation administrator; b. St. Louis, May 8, 1940; d. Emil Louis and Patricia (McNair) Klick; 1 child, Ivan Clatanoff. BS in Edn., U. Mo., 1962; postgrad., Cornell U., 1963; MLS, Simmons Coll., 1967. Reference librarian Simmons Coll., Boston, 1967-68, U. Chgo., 1970-79, sr. lectr. Grad. Library Sch., 1974-83, 86-88, head reference service, 1979-83, asst. dir. for sci. libraries, 1983-93, acting asst. dir. for tech. svcs., 1987-88, assoc. provost, 1993-98; program officer MacArthur Found., 1999—2005; ret., 2005. Project dir. Office Mgmt. Svcs., Assn. Rsch. Librs., 1982-83; speaker in field; cons. on libr. mgmt., planning and space. Author: Great is the Gift that Bringeth Knowledge: Highlights from the History of the John Crerar Library, 1989; contbr. articles to profl. jours. Program officer MacArthur Found., 1999—2001.

**SWANSON, PEGGY EUBANKS,** finance educator; b. Ivanhoe, Tex., Dec. 29, 1936; d. Leslie Samuel and Mary Lee (Reid) Eubanks; m. B. Marc Sommers, Nov. 10, 1993. BBA, U. North Tex., 1957, M. Bus. Edn., 1965; MA in Econs., So. Meth. U., 1967, PhD in Econs., 1978. Instr. El Centro Coll., Dallas, 1967-69, 71-78, bus. div. chmn., 1969-71; asst. prof. econs. U. Tex., Arlington, 1978-79, asst. prof. fin., 1979-84, assoc. prof., 1984-86, chmn. dept. fin. and real estate, 1986-88, prof. fin., 1987—, interim dean Coll. Bus. Adminstrn., 1999—2000, John and Judy Goolsby disting. prof., 2004—. Expert witness various law firms, primarily Tex. and Calif., 1978—; cons. Internat. Edn. Program, 1992-99; curriculum cons. U. Monterrey, Mexico, 1995, New Saudi Arabia U., 1999. Contbr. articles to acad. profl. jours. Vol. Am. Cancer Soc., Dallas, Arlington, 1981—, Meals on Wheels, Arlington, 1989—; mem. adv. bd. Ryan/Reilly Ctr. for Urban Land Utilization, Arlington, 1986-88. Mem. Fin. Exec. Inst. (chmn. acad. rels. 1987-88), Internat. Bus. Steering Com. (chmn. 1989-91), Am. Fin. Assn., Am. Econ. Assn., Fin. Mgmt. Assn. (hon. faculty mem. Nat. Honor Soc. 1985-86, program com. 1998-99), Southwestern Fin. Assn. (program com. 1987-88, 96), Midwest Fin. Assn. (program com. 1997-98, 98-99), Acad. of Internat. Bus. (program com. 1992-95), Acad. Disting. Tchrs., Phi Beta Delta (membership com. 1987-89). Republican. Episcopalian. Avocations: tennis, gardening. Home: 4921 Bridgewater Dr Arlington TX 76017-2729 Office: U Tex at Arlington PO Box 19449 Arlington TX 76019-0001 Office Phone: 817-272-3841. Business E-mail: swanson@uta.edu.

**SWANSON, RICHARD EVERETT,** physics professor, dean; b. Biloxi, Miss., Dec. 15, 1948; s. Dustin Herbert and Dorothy Mae Swanson; m. Leigh Ross Ross, June 5, 1970; children: Serena Bree, Shane Richard, Kyle Ross. B, USAF Acad., Colorado Springs, Colo., 1970; M, Ohio State U., Columbus,

1971; PhD, U. N.Mex, Los Alamos, 1981. Commd. 2d lt. USAF, 1966, advanced through grades to lt. col.; weapons devel. Air Force Armament Lab., Eglin AFB, Fla., 1971—73; explosives rsch. Los Alamos Nat. Lab. 1973—75; physics instr. U.S. Mil. Acad., West Point, NY, 1976—77; laser rsch. Air Force Weapons Lab., Albuquerque, 1977—79; guest scientist Los Alamos Nat. Lab., 1979—81; physics prof. USAF Acad., Colorado Springs, 1981—88. C.c. rep. N.C. Transfer Adv. Com., Raleigh, NC, 2003—. Co-author (videodisc) Skylab Physics, Physics of Flight. Sec. United Way of Moore County, Pinehurst, NC, 2000—04; bd. dirs. Sandhills Food Bank, Southern Pines, NC, 2004—06. Decorated Joint Meritorious Svc. medal U.S. European Command; grantee, N.C. C.C. Sys., 1993—95. Mem.: Am. Assn. Physics Tchrs. (assoc.), Phi Kappa Phi, Pi Mu Epsilon. Mem. Lds Ch. Avocations: handball, horseback riding. Home: PO Box 2258 Southern Pines NC 28388 Office: Sandhills Cmty Coll 3395 Airport Rd Pinehurst NC 28374 Office Phone: 910-695-3715. Business E-Mail: swanson@sandhills.edu.

**SWANSON, RICHARD OSCAR,** history educator, department chairman; s. Richard Eric Swanson and Lynda Rose Crowley; m. Christine Anna Leahy, Aug. 10, 2002; children: Kathleen Rose, Theodore Richard. BA in History, Coll. of Holy Cross, Worcester, Mass., 1992; MA Tchg. in History, Bridgewater State Coll., Mass., 2003. Tchr. Inner-City Tchg. Corps., Chgo., 1992—93, asst. dir., 1993—95; tchr. Silver Lake Regional HS, Kingston, Mass., 1995—2002; tchr., head social studies dept. Duxbury (Mass.) HS, 2002—. Office: Duxbury HS 130 S George St Duxbury MA 02332

**SWANSON, RICHARD WILLIAM,** retired statistician; b. July 26, 1934; s. Richard () and Erma Marie (Herman) Swanson; m. Laura Yoko Arai, Dec. 30, 1970. BS, Iowa State U., 1958, MS, 1964, Ops. analyst Stanford Rsch. Inst., Monterey, Calif., 1958—62; statistician ARINC Rsch. Corp., Washington, 1964—65; sr. scientist Booz-Allen Applied Rsch., Vietnam, 1965—67, L.A. 1967—68; sr. ops. analyst Control Data Corp., Honolulu, 1968—70; mgmt. cons. Honolulu, 1970—73; exec. v.p. SEQUEL Corp., Honolulu, 1973—75; bus. cons. Hawaii Dept. Planning and Econ. Devel., Honolulu, 1975—77; tax rsch. and planning offider Dept. Taxation, 1977—82; ops. rsch. analyst U.S. Govt., 1982—89, shipyard statistician, 1989—97; ret., 1997. Mem.: Hawaiian Acad. Sci., Sigma Xi. Home: 583 Kamoku St Apt 3505 Honolulu HI 96826-5241 Personal E-Mail: hnlrichardswanson@msn.com.

**SWANSON, ROBERT DRAPER,** college president; b. Sioux City, Iowa, Aug. 6, 1915; s. Alfred and Tida Ruth (Draper) S.; m. Roberta B. Clements, May 5, 1941 (dec. Oct. 1975); children: Sara Louise, Mark Robert; m. Dorothy B. Howe, Aug. 4, 1979. AB, Park Coll., 1937; student, U. Iowa, 1937; B.D., McCormick Theol. Sem., 1941; D.D., James Millikin U., 1950; L.H.D., Tusculum Coll., 1966, Olivet Coll., 1971, Central Mich. U., 1979, Alma Coll., 1981; LL.D., Hillsdale Coll., 1968, Hope Coll. 1981. Dir. athletics, phys. edn. Park Coll., 1937-38; ordained to ministry Presbyn. Ch., 1941; pastor Second Presbyn. Ch., Tulsa, 1941-45; dean of students McCormick Sem., 1946-47, v.p., prof. preaching, 1948-56; pres. Alma Coll. 1956-80, pres. emeritus, 1980—. Dir. Gen. Telephone Co. Mich. Served as lt. (j.g.), Chaplain's Corps USNR, 1945-46. Recipient Disting. Alumni award, Pk. Coll., 1971, Disting. Alumnus award, McCormick Theol. Sem., 1981, Higher Edn. Honors award, Presbyn. Ch., 2002. Mem. Phi Beta Kappa. Clubs: Rotary (Alma). Home: 1267 Masonic Ct Alma MI 48801-1167 Business E-Mail: swanson@alma.edu.

**SWANSON, ROBERT LAWRENCE,** oceanographer, academic program administrator; b. Balt., Oct. 11, 1938; s. Lawrence Wilbur and Hazel Ruth Swanson; m. Dana Lamont, Sept. 12, 1963; children: Lawrence Daniel, Michael Nathan BSCE, Lehigh U., 1960; MS Oceanography, Oreg. State U., 1965, PhD Oceanography, 1971. Cert. hydrographer. Commd. ensign U.S. Coast and Geodetic Survey (now NOAA), 1960, advanced through grades to capt., 1978; ops. offider U.S. Pathfinder, 1965; comdg. officer U.S. Mariner, 1966; chief oceanog. divsn. Nat. Ocean Survey, NOAA, Rockville, Md., 1969—72; mgr. Marine Ecosys. Analysis, N.Y. Bight project, Stony Brook, 1973—78; dir. Office Marine Pollution Assessment NOAA, Rockville, 1978—83, rsch. assoc. Sea Grant Stony Brook, 1983—84; comdg. officer U.S. Rschr., Miami, Fla., 1984—86; chief internat. activities group NOAA, Rockville, 1986, exec. dir. Office Oceanic and Atmospheric Rsch., 1986—87; dir. Waste Reduction and Mgmt. Inst. SUNY, Stony Brook, 1987—, assoc. dean Marine Scis. Rsch. Ctr., 2003—. Adj. prof. Marine Scis. Rsch. Ctr., SUNY, Stony Brook, 1976—; mem. Suffolk County Coun. Environ. Quality, 1988—, vice chair, 1996—2006, chair, 2006—; mem. N.Y. State Oversight Com. Brookhaven Nat. Lab., 1996—2000; mem. Coastal Mgmt. Commn. Villages Head-of-the-Harbor and Nissequogue, 1994—2002; chmn. Coastal Mgmt. Commn. Villages Head Harbor and Nissequogue, 1995—97, 1999—2001; trustee Three Village Hist. Soc., 1994—2002; co-chair L.I. Environ. Econ. Roundtable, 1995—2000; adv. bd. Evan L. Lit Meml. Fund, 1998—; trustee Village of Head of the Harbor, 2002—, deputy, 2003—, cons. in field. Co-author, co-editor: Oxygen Depletion and Associated Benthic Mortalities in N.Y. Bight, 1979; co-editor: Floatable Wastes and the Region's Beaches; mem. editl. bd. N.Y. Bight Monograph Series, 1973-81, Chemistry and Ecology, 1995-2003; co-author Images of America, Stony Brook, 2003; co-pub. Waste Mgmt. Rsch. Report, 1988-95; mem. adv. bd. L.I. Hist. Jour., 1995-2003, mem. editl. bd., 2004- Recipient Karo award Am. Soc. Mil. Engrs., 1972; Silver medal Dept. Commerce, 1973; Program and Adminstrn. Mgmt. award NOAA, 1975, Unit citation, 1987; sr. exec. fellow John F. Kennedy Sch. Govt., Harvard U., 1983, Spl. Achievement award, 1987, NOAA Corps. Commendations, 1987; named Man of Yr. for environment Three Village Times, 1998 Mem. N.Y. Acad. Scis., ASCE (clem. hydrography and oceanography com. 1972-74), AAAS, Am. Geophys. Union, Marine Tech. Soc. (chmn. marine pollution com. 1982-92), Cosmos Club, Sigma Xi (pres. SUNY Stony Brook chpt. 1998—) Presbyterian. Home: 46 Harbor Hill Rd Saint James NY 11780-1217 Office: SUNY Waste Reduction And Mgmt Inn Stony Brook NY 11790 5000 Business E-Mail: lswanson@notes.cc.sunysb.edu.

**SWANSON, ROBERT LEE,** lawyer; b. Fond du Lac, Wis., July 15, 1942; s. Walfred S. and Edna F. (Kamp) S.; m. Mary Ruth Francis, Aug. 19, 1967; children: Leigh Alexandra, Mitchell Pearson. BS, U. Wis., 1964; JD, Valparaiso U., 1970; LLM, Boston U., 1979. Bar: Wis. 1970, U.S. Dist. Ct. (ea. dist.) Wis. 1970, U.S. Dist. Ct. (we. dist.) Wis. 1974, U.S. Dist. Ct. (we. dist.) Okla. 2002, U.S. Tax Ct. 1981, U.S. Dist. Ct. (cen.) Ill. 1988, Okla. 1999, U.S. Ct. Appeals (7th cir.) 1999. Atty. Kasdorf, Dahl, Lewis & Swietlik, Milw., 1970-73; atty., ptnr. Wartman, Wartman & Swanson, Ashland, Wis., 1973-80; city atty. City of Ashland, Wis., 1976-80; atty., ptnr. DeMark, Kolbe & Brodek, Racine, Wis., 1980-95; ptnr. Hartig, Bjelajac, Swanson & Koenen, Racine, 1995-99, Okla. Indigent Def. Sys., Lincoln County, 2000—02; pvt. practice Robert Lee Swanson Law Office, 2000—. Lectr. civil rights and discrimination laws, 1980—; lectr.bus. law Cardinal Strich U., 1996—99; lectr. bus. law U. Wis.-Parkside, 1997—99; adj. prof. civil procedure Northeastern State U., Broken Arrow, Okla., 2005—; participating atty. Alliance Def. Fund, 2000—; legal columnist Burlington Std. Press, 1991—95, Wis. Restaurant Assn. Mag., 1986. Bd. dirs. North Ctrl. Regional Airport, Chandler, 2003—; chmn. Ashland County Rep. Party, 1976—79; v.p., bd. dirs. Menell. Med. Ctr., Ashland, 1975—80; bd. trustees Kendrick Mcpl. Authority, Okla., 2001—; vice comdr. USCG Aux. Bayfield (Wis.) Flotilla, 1975—81; vol. atty. ACLU Wis., 1975—90. 1st lt. U.S. Army, 1964—66. Named one of Outstanding Young Men of Am. Jaycees, 1978; recipient Disting. Achievement in Art and Sci. of Advocacy award Internat. Acad. Trial Lawyers, 1970. Mem. Okla. Criminal Def. Lawyers Assn., Racine County Bar Assn. (bd. dirs. 1986-89), Wis. Acad. Trial Lawyers, Def. Rsch. Inst., AM Hockey Assn. U.S. (coach, referee 1983-90), Am. Legion, Okla. Limousin Assn. (parliamentarian, treas. 2004, bd. dirs. 2005-). Avocations: softball, volleyball, hockey. Home: RR 1 Box 478 Stroud OK 74079-9723 Office: 109 1/2 W 9th St Chandler OK 74834 Office Phone: 405-258-4850. Personal E-Mail: rswanson.atty@sbcglobal.net.

**SWANSON, ROY ARTHUR,** classicist, educator; b. St. Paul, Apr. 7, 1925; s. Roy Benjamin and Gertrude (Larson) S.; m. Vivian May Vitous, Mar. 30, 1946; children: Lynn Marie (Mrs. Gerald A. Snider), Robin Lillian, Robert

Roy (dec.), Dyack Tyler, Dana Miriam (Mrs. Jon Butts). BA, U. Minn., 1948, BS, 1949, MA, 1951; PhD, U. Ill., 1954. Prin. Maplewood Elementary Sch., St. Paul, 1949-51; instr. U. Ill., 1952-53, Ind. U., 1954-57; asst. prof. U. Minn., Mpls., 1957-61, assoc. prof., 1961-64, acting chmn. classics, 1963-64, prof. classics, chmn. comparative lit., 1964-65; prof. English Macalester Coll., St. Paul, 1965-67, coord. humanities program, 1966-67; prof. comparative lit. and classics U. Wis.-Milw., 1967—, prof. English, 1990-96, prof. emeritus, 2003—, chmn. classics dept., 1967-70, 86-89, chmn. comparative lit., 1970-73, 76-83, coord. Scandinavian studies program, 1982-96. Cons. St. Paul Tchrs. Sr. High Sch. English, 1964 Author: Odi et Amo: The Complete Poetry of Catullus, 1959, Heart of Reason: Introductory Essays in Modern-World Humanities, 1963, Pindar's Odes, 1974, Greek and Latin Word Elements, 1981, The Love Songs of the Carmina Burana, 1987, Pär Lagerkvist: Five Early Works, 1989; editor Minn. Rev., 1963-67; Classical Jour., 1966-72; contbr. articles to profl. jours. With AUS, 1944-46. Decorated Bronze Star; recipient Disting. Teaching award U. Minn., 1962, Disting. Teaching award U. Wis.-Milw., 1974, 91, 99. Home: 11618 N Bobolink Ln Mequon WI 53092-2804 Office: U Wis French/Italian/Comp Lit PO Box 413 Milwaukee WI 53201-0413 Personal E-Mail: rexroy333@aol.com. Business E-Mail: rexcy@uwm.edu.

**SWANSON, STEPHEN OLNEY,** minister, retired English educator; b. Mpls., Aug. 31, 1932; s. Carl R. and Dorothy Olney Swanson; m. Judith Seleen Swanson, June 10, 1956; children: Scott, Shelley, Noel, Kim, Brian. BA, St. Olaf Coll., 1954; grad. in theology, Luther Theol. Sem., St. Paul, 1958, BD, 1960; MA, U. Oreg., 1964, ArtsD, 1970. Ordained to ministry Evang. Luth. Ch. Am. 1958, Instr. theology Augustana Coll., Sioux Falls, SD, 1957; instr. writing U. Oreg., Eugene, 1964—66; asst. prof. English and writing Tex. Luth. Coll., Seguin, 1966—70; assoc. prof. English and writing Camrose (Alta.) Univ. Coll., 1970—73; prof. writing St. Olaf Coll., Northfield, Minn., 1976—99. Parish pastor Luth. congregations, Minn., 1958-61, Oreg., 1962-65, Sask., 1973-74; interim pastor 40 congregations, Minn., Iowa, Wis., Alta., Sask., 1956—; dir. creative writing Tex. Luth. Coll., 1966-70, Camrose Univ. Coll., 1970-73; coach wrestling, football, volleyball, hockey, Tex., Can., Minn.; co-owner Nine-Ten Press, Northfield, 1997—; adj. Waldorf Coll., Forest City, Iowa, 2004—. Author 26 books for adults, teens and children, including Is There Life After High Sch., 1991, The Earthkeeper Mystery Series, 4 vols., 1994, Moving Out on Your Own, 1995, The First Fall: Ytterboe Hall, 1946, 1997; playwright 6 plays; contbr. articles to jours.; columnist Now and Then, 1998-99; metal sculpture exhbns. include Luth. Brotherhood Corp. Gallery, Mpls., 1992, 94, 98, Waldorf Coll., Forest City, Iowa, 1999, Luther Coll., Decorah, Iowa, 2002, Art Ctr. of St. Peter, Minn., 2003, Thrivent Fin. Corp. Gallery, Mpls., 2003, St. Olaf Coll. Northfield, Minn., 2003, Am. Swedish Inst., Mpls., Minn., 2004, Edge Gallery, Big Fork, Minn., 2005 Mem. Northfield Human Rights Commn., 2006—. Recipient award Minn. Arts Bd., 1987, Blandin Found., Grand Rapids, Minn., 1988-89; fellow NDEA, Washington, 1968-69. Mem.: Blue Key (hon.), Am. Swedish Inst. Avocations: metal sculpture, fishing, Volvo repair. Home: 910 St Olaf Ave Northfield MN 55057

**SWANSON, VICTORIA CLARE HELDMAN,** lawyer; b. Aug. 28, 1949; d. Paul F. and Anne F. (Thomas) Schmitz; m. Louis M. Heldman, Sept. 21, 1971 (div. 1973); m. John Askins, Feb. 28, 1975 (div. 1977); m. Thomas C. Swanson, Feb. 13, 1988 (div. 2004). BA in journalism with distinction, Ohio State U., 1972; JD, U. Detroit, 1975. Bar: Mich. 1975, Colo. 1984, U.S. Dist. Ct. (ea. and we. dists.) Mich. 1975, U.S. Ct. Appeals (6th cir.) 1977, U.S. Ct. Appeals (3d cir.) 1980, U.S. Supreme Ct. 1983, U.S. Ct. Appeals (10th cir.) 1984, U.S. Ct. Appeals (5th cir.) 1989, cert.: NBTA (civil trial advocate) 1994. Assoc. Lopatin, Miller, Bindes & Freedman, Detroit, 1973—76; ptnr. Schaden, Swanson & Lampert, Detroit, 1977—90, Sears, Anderson & Swanson, P.C., Colorado Springs, Colo., 1991—96, Sears & Swanson, Colorado Springs, 1997—. Adj. prof. U. Detroit Sch. Law, 1982. Author (chpt.): (non-fiction) Anatomy of a Personal Injury Lawsuit, 1992; author, editor: handbook Colorado Auto Litigators Handbook, 1995, Colorado Courtroom Handbook, 1998, author, editor: 2nd edit., 2006, Colorado Evidence Handbook, 1995; co-author (with Richard F. Schaden): (non-fiction) Product Design Liability, 1982; co-author (with others) Women Trial Lawyers: How They Succeed in Practice and in the Courtroom, 1986. Mem.: Mich. Trial Lawyers Assn., Colo. Trial Lawyers Assn. (past pres.), Kripke Lifetime Achievement award 2005), Assn. Trial Lawyers Am., Colo. Bar Assn., Mich. Bar Assn. Office: Sears & Swanson 2 N Cascade Ave Colorado Springs CO 80903-1631 Office Phone: 719-471-1984. Business E-Mail: victoria@searsandswanson.com.

**SWANSON, WALLACE MARTIN,** lawyer; b. Fergus Falls, Minn., Aug. 22, 1941; s. Marvin Walter and Mary Louise (Lindsey) S.; children: Kristen Lindsey, Eric Munger. BA with honors, U. Minn., 1962; LL.B. with honors, So. Methodist U., 1965. Bar: Tex. 1965. Assoc. Coke & Coke, Dallas, 1965-70; ptnr. Johnson & Swanson, Dallas, 1970-88; prin. Wallace M. Swanson, P.C., Ennis, Tex., 1988—; chmn., CEO Ace Cash Express Inc., Irving, Tex., 1987-88, State St. Capital Corp., 1990—. Served with USNR, 1960-65. Mem. Tex. Bar Found., State Bar Tex. (securities com. 1972-86, chmn. 1978-80, coun. bus. law sect. 1980-86), Crescent Club. Methodist. Address: 6234 FM 879 Ennis TX 75119 Office Phone: 214-520-7000. Personal E-Mail: wallaceswanson@yahoo.com.

**SWANSON, WILLIAM FREDIN, III,** manufacturing executive; b. Pitts., Mar. 6, 1960; s. William Fredin Jr. and Marjorie Beatrice (Davis) S.; m. Jane Anne Crosby, June 30, 1990; children: Elisabeth Anne, William Fredin IV. BSME, U. Va., 1982; M in Mgmt., Northwestern U., 1985. Asst. to v.p. mfg. Bridgestone/Firestone, Inc., Akron, Ohio, 1985-87, project mgr. Decatur, Ill., 1987-89 operating mgr, 1989-92; plant mgr Am Roller Co, Wälkerton, Ind., 1992-95, mfg. mgr. Union Grove, Wis., 1995—2002; pres. Diamond Holding Corp., Marietta, Ga., 2002—. Mem. alumni admissions orgn. Kellogg Grad. Sch. Mgmt., Northwestern U., Evanston, Ill., 1986-97, CEO roundtable Cobb County, 2002—; chmn. long range planning com. Antioch (Ill.) United Meth. Ch., 1997-98, adminstrv. coun., 2000-02, lay leader, 2001-02; coach youth soccer YMCA, 2003-2004, t-ball, 2004, basketball, 2004-2005. Mem.: Kiwanis. Avocations: golf, spectator sports, reading. Home: 1701 Kenbrook Ct Acworth GA 30101 Office: Diamond Holding Corp 150 Marr Ave Marietta GA 30060 Office Phone: 770-795-8556. Personal E-mail: wfswansoniii@bellsouth.net. Business E-Mail: bills@diamondroller.com.

**SWANSON, WILLIAM HENRY,** equipment manufacturing company executive; b. Bakersfield, Calif., Feb. 9, 1949; s. William H. and Rosemary O. (Pavicich) Swanson; m. Cheryl K. Allen, Dec. 21, 1968. BSIE, Calif. Poly. State U., 1972; MBA, Golden Gate U., 1977; JD (hon.), Pepperdine U., 2002. Assoc. engr. Raytheon Co., 1972—74; project engr., 1974—75, mfg. program mgr., 1977—80, test engring. mgr., 1977—80, mgr. mfg. group, 1980—81; mfg. mgr. Equipment div. Waltham, Mass., 1981—83; plant mgr., Missile Systems div. Andover, Mass., 1984—90; asst. gen. mgr., Missile Systems div., 1989—90; sr. v.p., gen. mgr., Missile Systems div., 1990—95; exec. v.p. Raytheon Co., 1995—2002; gen. mgr. Electronic Systems div., 1995—97; chmn., CEO Raytheon Systems Co., 1997—99; pres., Electronic Systems div., 1999—2002; pres. Raytheon Co., 2002—03, pres., CEO, 2003—, chmn., 2004—. Mem. President's Nat. Security Telecommunications Adv. Com. Exec. com. Bus.-Higher Edn. Forum; mem. Sec. Air Force Adv. Bd.; bd. advs. CIA Officers Meml. Found.; bd. dir. Medal Honor Found., Rose Fitzgerald Kennedy Greenway Conservancy; mem. Calif. Poly. State U. President's Cabinet, Pepperdine U. Bd. Regents. Named Outstanding Indsl. Engring. Grad., Calif. Poly. State U., 1972, Outstanding Indsl. Engring. Alumni, 1981; recipient Captains Industry Award, Inst. Indsl. Engr., Semper Fidelis Award, USMC Scholarship Found., 2002, Laurel Award, Aviation Week & Space Tech., 2003. Fellow: Royal Aero. Soc. (UK), Am. Inst. Aeronautics & Astronautics, Tau Beta Pi; mem.: Aerospace Industries Assn., Nat. Def. Indsl. Assn., Air Force Assn., Navy League (Rear Adm. John J. Bergen Leadership Medal for Industry), Assn. US Army, Blue Key, Alpha Pi Mu. Republican. Roman Catholic. Office: Raytheon Co 870 Winter St Waltham MA 02451*

**SWANSTROM, THOMAS EVAN,** economist; b. Green Bay, Wis., May 17, 1939; s. Alfred Enoch and Elizabeth Nan (Thomas) S.; m. Nancy Anne Roche; children: Amy, Scott. Student, U. Notre Dame, 1957-59; BA, U. Wis., 1962, MA, 1963; postgrad., Am. U., 1963-66. Economist, U.S. Bur. Labor Statistics, Washington, 1963-66. Dir. rsch/ Population Ref. Bur., Washington, 1966-68; economist Sears, Roebuck & Co., Chgo., 1968-70, market analyst, 1970-72, mgr. catalog rsch., 1972-75, asst. mgr. econ. rsch., 1974-80, chief economist, 1980-90; pres. Consumer Econs., Chgo., 1991—; mem. bus. rsch. adv. coun. Bur. Labor Stats. Contbr. articles to industry pubs. Mem. Conf. Bus. Economists, The Caxton Club. Personal E-mail: tevanswan@aol.com.

**SWANTON, SUSAN IRENE,** retired library director; b. Rochester, N.Y., Nov. 29, 1941; d. Walter Frederick and Irene Wray S.; m. Wayne Holman, Apr. 12, 1969 (div. June 1973); 1 child, Michael; ptnr. James Donald Lathrop; children: Kathryn, Kristin. AB, Harvard U., 1963; MLS, Columbia U., 1965. Libr. dir. Warsaw (N.Y.) Pub. Libr., 1963-64, Gates Pub. Libr., Rochester, NY, 1965—2003; ret., 2003. Pres. Drug and Alcohol Coun., Rochester, 1985-91, mem. adv. coun., 1992-94; bd. dirs., co-chair info. svcs. Rochester Freenet, 1995—; sec. Gates Hist. Preservation Commn., 2000-03, Friends of Rochester Pub. Libr., 2004—; chmn. Gates Dem. Com., 2004—; v.p., sec. Friends of Gates Pub. Libr., 2004—; newsletter editor Empire (N.Y.) Friends Roundtable, 2004—. Mem. Gates Hist. Soc. (bd. dirs., pres. 1998—2002, v.p. 2002—03), Gates-Chili C. of C. (pres. 1982, sec. 1990-94, 2004—, bd. dirs. 2003, Citizen Yr. 1994), Harvard Club of Rochester (mem. adv. bd.). Home: 284 Gatewood Ave Rochester NY 14624-1622 E-mail: sswanton@ggw.org.

**SWARD, ANDREA JEANNE,** information and computer scientist, musician; b. Hackensack, NJ, June 25, 1951; d. George Frederick and Carol Jeanne (Snoad) Lankow; m. Jeffrey Edwin Sward, June 7, 1975. Student, U. Minn., Duluth, 1969-72; BA in Psychology, Calif. State U., Fullerton, 1973, MS in Info. Sci., 1974, MS in Edn., 1976; cert. Bus. Intelligence and Data Warehousing, U. Calif. Irvine, 2003. Librarian, prof. Calif. State U., Fullerton, 1972—97; violist Anaheim Cultural Arts Ctr. Orch., Calif., 1978-80, Anaheim Civic Light Opera, 1978-80, Calif. European Tour Orch., Fullerton, 1978-79, Fullerton Cmty. Orch., Fullerton, 1978—86; computer programmer, analyst Hughes Aircraft, Fullerton, 1980-81, Smith-Kline/Beckman, Fullerton, 1981-83, ConAgra/Hunt-Wesson, Irvine, 1983—2004; librarian Downey City Library, Calif., 1985, Orange Pub. Library, Calif., 1985—90, Huntington Beach Library, Calif., 1985—; analyst New Century Mortgage, Irvine, Calif., 2004—. Editor Vis À Vis; An Interdisciplinary Journal, 1972-74. Contbr. articles to profl. jours. Mem., contbr. Newport Harbor Art Mus., Newport Beach, Calif., 1975—, Los Angeles County Mus. of Art, 1975—; ACLU, 1976—; Cousteau Soc., 1978—; Audubon Soc., 1985—; Amigos de Bolsa Chica, 1985—; Spl. Olympics, 1987—; wildlife rehabilitator Wetlands and Wildlife Care Ctr., Orange County, 1999—; Fridley (Minn.) Edn. Assn. scholar, 1969, Spl. Edn. Assn. scholar, 1972; Edwin Carr fellow, 1976; Ptnrs. in Excellence grantee, 1979. Mem. ALA. Assn. for Computing Machinery, Calif. Library Assn., Calif. Reading Assn., Reading Educators Guild, Penguini Poets and Philosophers Guild of Placentia (co-founder). Democrat. Avocations: sports, reading, dance, theater, art. Home: PO Box 7019 Huntington Beach CA 92615-7019 E-mail: ajsward@yahoo.com.

**SWARLIS, LINDA,** library and information scientist; d. Clarence Leroy and Helen Louise Jacobs; children: Amber, Andrew. BS in Edn., Clarion U., Pa., 1979; MLS, U. Pitts., Pa., 1984. Libr. dir. Winchester Thurston Sch., Pittsburgh, Pa., 1984—88, Sewickley Acad., Sewickley, Pa., 1988—95; head libr. Lincoln H.S., Gahanna, Ohio, 1995—97; dir. of info. services and libr. Columbus Sch. for Girls, Columbus, Ohio, 1997—. Pres. Pitts. Area Ind. Schools Assn., Pa., 1993—95. Recipient Outstanding Svc. award, Gahanna Kiwanis Club for Key Club Leadership, 1995—97; Distance Ind. scholarship, U. North Tex., 2004—. Office: Columbus Sch for Girls 56 S Columbia Ave Columbus OH 43209 Office Phone: 614-252-0781 129. Office Fax: 614-252-0571. E-mail: lswarlis@columbusschoolforgirls.org.

**SWARTOUT, HANK B.,** oil and gas industry executive; b. Apr. 6, 1951; m. Carol Swartout; 4 children. Student in Petroleum Engring. Technol., Southern Alberta Inst.of Technol., 1972; BS with honours in Petroleum Engring., U. Wyo., 1976. Prodn. engr. Amerada Hess, ND, 1977; v.p. constuction Nabors Drilling, 1978; rig design and construction Dreco; mgr. Bawden Western Oceanic Offshore; pres. Cypress Drilling (acquired Precision Drilling), 1985; chmn., pres., CEO Precision Drilling Corp., Calgary, AB, Canada, 1987—. Recipient Disting. Alumnus, Southern Alberta Inst. of Technol., 1999, Pinnacle award, Fraser Milner Casgrain LLP, 2003. Office: Precision Drilling Corp 4200 150-6th Ave SW T2P 3Y7 Calgary AB Canada

**SWARTOUT, TORIN SHERWIN ROBERTS,** logistics executive, transportation consultant; b. Brockport, N.Y., Mar. 14, 1952; s. Sherwin George and Eileen May (Tavenner) S.; m. Anne Elizabeth Washington, July 21, 1978; children: Jesse, Jason, Katherine Lynne, Joseph. BA in Philosophy, Antioch Coll., 1972; cert. custom house broker, World Trade Inst., 1978, cert. of chartering, 1979. Lic. customhouse brokers. European sales mgr. Antioch Bookplate Co., Yellow Springs, Ohio, 1971; pres. Alternative Living, Inc., Brockport, NY, 1972-76; import mgr. Spies Shipping Corp., N.Y.C., 1976-77; equipment control mgr. Hansen and Tidemann, N.Y.C., 1977-78; intermodal ops. mgr. Star Shipping of N.Y., Inc., N.Y.C., 1979-81; mgr. container svcs., 1981-85; dist. mgr. midwest Star Shipping, Inc., Des Plaines, Ill., 1985-86, 87-89; v.p. sales Tokyo, 1986-87, trade mgr. U.S. gulf Stamford, Conn., 1989-91; gen. traffic mgr. Atlantic Trades, 1991-96; pres. Viking Homes, Hempstead, NY, 1981-85. Bd. dirs. Alternative Living, Inc., Brockport, 1977-91, Viking Homes, Ridgefield, Conn.; custom house broker T. Swartout CHB, Chgo., 1978—; cons. TransNat. Shipping Corp., N.Y.C., 1981-88; owners' rep. Spliethoff's, 1996—; mng. dir. Ocean Transport Svcs., Ridgefield, Conn., 1996—. Vice pres. N.W. Civic Assn., Hempstead, 1983, Georgetown Manor Homeowners Assn., Arlington Heights, 1987; cubmaster pack 74 Cub Scouts, Ridgefield, Conn. Mem. Midwest Fgn. Commerce Club, Ocean Freight Agts. Assn., Norwegian-Am. C. of C., Japanese C. of C. (affiliate), Holland Soc., Sons of Norway (v.p. 1981-82, 90-91, pres. 1983-84), Conn. Maritime Assn., Internat. Forest Products Transport Assn., Railway Industrial Clearance Assn., Project Mgmt. Inst. Congregationalist. Avocations: hiking, farming, travel, coaching, norwegian language. Office: Ocean Transport Svcs 68 Great Hill Rd Ridgefield CT 06877-2629 E-mail: otsusa@aol.com.

**SWARTOUT, WILLIAM R.,** education educator, director; s. Charles W. and June Swartout; m. Janet P. Swartout; children: Robin, David. BS in Math. Scis., Stanford U., Palo Alto, Calif., 1970—74; MS in Elec. Engring. & Computer Sci., MIT, Cambridge, Mass., 1973—77, PhD in Computer Sci., 1977—81. Dir., intelligent sys. divsn. U. So. Calif. Info. Scis. Inst., Marina del Rey, 1999—; dir. of tech. U. So. Calif. Inst. for Creative Technologies, Marina del Rey, 1999—. Mem. Air Force Sci. Adv. Bd., Washington, 2004—, Bd. Army Sci. and Tech., Washington, Joint Forces Command Transformation Adv. Group, 2004. Fellow: Am. Assn. Artificial Intelligence (mem. bd. councilors 1992—); mem.: Assn. Computing Machinery (chair Spl. Interest Group on Artificial Intelligence 1985—87). Office: Univ So Calif Inst Creative Technologies 13274 Fiji Way Marina Del Rey CA 90292 Office Phone: 310-574-5705.

**SWARTZ, B(ENJAMIN) K(INSELL), JR.,** archaeologist, educator; b. LA. June 23, 1931; s. Benjamin Kinsell and Maxine Marietta (Pearce) S.; m. Cyrilla Casillas, Oct. 23, 1966; children: Benjamin Kinsell III, Frank Casillas. AA summa cum laude, L.A. City Coll., 1952; BA, UCLA, 1954, MA, 1958; PhD, U. Ariz., Tucson, 1964. Curator Klamath County Mus., Oreg., 1959-61, rsch. assoc., 1961-62; asst. prof. anthropology Ball State U., Muncie, Ind., 1964-68, assoc. prof., 1968-72, prof., 1972-2001, prof. emeritus, 2001—. Vis. sr. lectr. U. Ghana, 1970-71; exch. prof. U. Yaounde, Cameroon, 1984-85; field rschr. N.Am. and West Africa; mem. exec. bd., Am. Com. to Advance the Study of Petroglyphs and Pictographs and its rep. to Internat. Fedn. Rock Art Orgns.; mem. overseas ed. bd. Rock Art Rsch.; mem. adv. bd. Am. Com. for Preservation of Archaeol. Collections. Contbr. revs. and articles to profl. jours.; author books, monographs in field, including: West African

Culture Dynamics, 1980, Indiana's Prehistoric Past, 1981, Rock Art and Posterity, 1991, Procs. of 1st Internat. South African Rock Art Assn. Conf., 1991. Klamath County chmn. Oreg. Statehood Centennial, 1959. With USN, 1954-56. Fellow AAAS, Ind. Acad. Sci.; mem. Current Anthropology (assoc.), Soc. Am. Archaeology, Internat. Com. Rock Art, Sigma Xi, Lambda Alpha (nat. coun., exec. sec.). Home: 805 W Charles St Muncie IN 47305-2235 Personal E-mail: 01bkswartz@bsu.edu.

SWARTZ, CHARLES ROBERT, lawyer; b. Norfolk, Va., Jan. 28, 1944; BA, U. Va., 1965; JD, U. Ga., 1968. Bar: Va. 1968. Ptnr. McGuireWoods LLP, Richmond, Va., 1969—. Fellow Am. Coll. Real Estate Lawyers. Office: McGuireWoods LLP 1 James Ctr 901 E Cary St Richmond VA 23219-4057 E-mail: cswartz@mcguirewoods.com.

SWARTZ, DONALD PERCY, physician; b. Preston, Ont., Can., Sept. 12, 1921; s. Simon Wingham and Lydia Ethel Swartz; m. Norma Mae Woolner, June 24, 1944 (dec. May 1980); children: Ian Donald, Rhonda Swartz Peterson; m. Isabelle Liz Dales, Apr. 21, 1984. BA, U. Western Ont., 1951, MD cum laude, 1951, MSc cum laude, 1953. Intern Victoria Hosp., London, Ont., 1951-52; asst. resident Westminster Hosp., London, 1953-54; resident Johns Hopkins U., Balt., 1954-58; asst. prof. ob-gyn. U. Western Ont., London, 1958-62; prof. Columbia U., N.Y.C., 1962-72; dir. ob-gyn. Harlem Hosp.; prof. dept. ob-gyn. Albany (N.Y.) Med. Coll., 1972-99, prof. emeritus, 2000—, chmn., 1972-79, chief sect. gen. gynecology, 1982-88, head. div. gen. gynecology, 1988—99, acting chmn., 1992. Vis. prof. dept. Ob-Gyn. U. Rochester, N.Y., 1981 Assoc. editor: Advances in Planned Parenthood. Vice pres., pres. Assn. Planned Parenthood Physicians, 1972-74. Served with RCAF, 1942-45. NRC Can. fellow, 1952-53; Am. Cancer Soc. fellow, 1956-57; Markle scholar, 1958-63 Fellow ACOG, Royal Coll. Surgeons Can.; Am. Gynecologic Soc., Am. Gyn-Ob Soc., Am. Fertility Soc., Royal Soc. Health, Soc. Gynecologic Surgeons. Home: 24 Devon Rd Delmar NY 12054-3534 Office: Albany Med Coll 47 New Scotland Ave Albany NY 12208-3412 E-mail: swartzd@mail.amc.edu. *It has been a privilege and a challenge to participate in the forefront of the revolutionary changes in the health care of women during the past five decades. Acceptance, initiation and implementation of positive change have been guidelines for gratifying action.*

SWARTZ, EUGENE ROBERT, JR., music educator, minister; b. Cleve., Mar. 19, 1957; s. Eugene Robert and Sarah Jane Swartz; m. Vicki Ann Masters, July 31, 1959; children: Sarah Frances Bourque, Amanda Leah Dickens. AAS in Engring. Tech., Dabney Lancaster C.C., Clifton Forge, Va., 1977; BS in Music Edn., U. Tenn., Knoxville, 1987, MS in Music Edn., 1989. Cert. music edn. Md. State Dept. Edn., 2005. Worship pastor Friendship Bapt. Ch., Sykesville, Md., 1999—2003; dept. chair, dir. choral activities Owings Mills H.S., 2003—. Music dir. Wash. Bible Coll., Lanham, Md., 1994—97. Bd. mem. Adult Literacy Bd., New Roads, La., 1990—92. Hamilton Conducting scholar, U. Tenn., 1986—87. Mem.: Md. Music Educators Assn. (state choral festival dir. 1998—99), Nat. Educators Assn., Am. Choral Dirs. Assn., Music Educators Nat. Conf. Conservative. Baptist. Avocation: car and truck shows. Home: 665 Tanglewood Dr Eldersburg MD 21784 Office: Owings Mills High Sch 124 Toll Gate Rd Owings Mills MD 21117 Office Phone: 410-887-1700. Personal E-mail: jeeps4jesus@aol.com. E-mail: eswartz@bcps.org.

SWARTZ, JACK, retired chamber of commerce executive; b. Nov. 24, 1932; s. John Ralph and Fern (Cave) S.; m. Nadine Ann Langlois, Aug. 4, 1956; children: Dana, Shawn, Tim, Jay. AA, Dodge City C.C., 1953; student, St. Mary of Plains Coll., 1953-55, 58; BBA, Washburn U., 1973, BA in Econs., 1974. V.p. D.C. Terminal Elevator Co., Dodge City, Kans., 1957-65; exec. v.p. Kans. Jaycees, Hutchinson, 1965-68, Kans. C. of C. and Industry, Topeka, 1968-82; pres. Nebr. C. of C. and Industry, Lincoln, 1982—2000, ret., 2000. Past chmn., bd. regents U.S. C. of C. Inst. U. Colo. With U.S. Army, 1955-57, USAR, 1961. Named Outstanding Local Pres. in State, Kans. Jaycees, 1961, Outstanding Young Man of Yr., Dodge City Jaycees, 1961, Outstanding State V.P., U.S. Jaycees, 1962, Outstanding Nat. Dir., 1963; named to Nebr. Bus. Hall of Fame, 2000, Sublette H.S. Wall of Honor, 2002. Mem. Am. Soc. Assn. Execs. (cert.), Am. C. of C. Execs. (bd. dirs., cert.), Nebr. C.of C. Execs. (sec.-treas.), Nebr. Soc. Assn. Execs. (past pres.), Nebr. Fedn. Bus. Assns. (pres. 1986-88), Nebr. Thoroughbred Breeders Assn. (past bd. dirs.), Washburn U. Alum. (past bd. dirs.). Am. Legion, Rotary. Republican. Roman Catholic. Home: 625 W Gibraltar Ln Phoenix AZ 85023-5243

SWARTZ, JAMES EDWARD, chemistry professor, educator, dean; b. Washington, June 12, 1951; s. Donald M. and Geneva R. (Henderson) S.; m. Louanne L. Curtis, June 6, 1980 (dec. 1986); m. Cynthea Mosier, Apr. 1, 1988. BS in Chemistry, Stanislaus State Coll., Turlock, Calif., 1973; PhD in Chemistry, U. Calif., Santa Cruz, 1978. Intern U. Calif., Santa Cruz, 1978; rsch. fellow Calif. Inst. Tech., Pasadena, 1978-80; asst. prof. Grinnell (Iowa) Coll., 1980-86, assoc. prof. chemistry, 1986-93, prof., 1993—, v.p. acad. affairs, dean, 1998—. Vis. prof. U. Minn., Mpls., 1986—87; mem. adv. coun. Iowa Energy Ctr.; cons.-evaluator Commn. Higher Edn., N. Cent. Assn., 1995—; bd. dirs. Am. Conf. Acad. Deans, 2000—; mem. exec. com. Associated Colls. of the Midwest, 2004—. Contbr. articles to profl. jours. Grantee Petroelum Rsch. Fund, 1981-83, Rsch. Corp., 1981-83, 84-86, 86-88, NSF, 1982-84, 90-93, 91-94. Mem. Am. Chem. Soc., Iowa Acad. Scis., Am. Wind Energy Assn. Home: 1233 Summer St Grinnell IA 50112-1547 Office: Grinnell Coll Office of Dean Grinnell IA 50112-1690 Office Phone: 641-269-3100. Business E-mail: swartz@grinnell.edu.

SWARTZ, JAMES R., chemical engineer, educator; B in Chem. Engring., S.D. Sch. Mines and Tech.; DSci, MIT, 1978. Rsch. scientist Eli Lilly & Co., Indpls., Genentech, Inc., San Francisco, 1981—2003, dir. dept. fermentation rsch. and process devel.; prof. chem. engring. Stanford U., Palo Alto, Calif., 2003—. Mem. NAE, Am. Chem. Soc. Office: Dept Chem Engring Stanford U Keck 185 381 North South Mall Stanford CA 94305-5025 E-mail: swartz@chemeng.stanford.edu.

SWARTZ, JEFFREY B., apparel executive; MBA, Amos Tuck Sch. Dartmouth Coll. Exec. vice-pres. Timberland Co., 1990—91, COO, 1991—98, pres., CEO, 1998—. Office: Timberland 200 Domain Dr Stratham NH 03885*

SWARTZ, JON DAVID, psychologist, educator; b. Houston, Dec. 28, 1934; s. Orville Elmo and Nina June (Baker) S.; m. Carol Joseph Hampton, Oct. 20, 1966; children: Eric Jason McFarland, Sally Katherine Baker, Edward Joseph Bryson. BA, U. Tex., Austin, 1956, MA, 1961, PhD, 1969, postgrad., 1973-74. Rsch. and tng. asst. dept. psychology U. Tex., 1956-62, asst. prof. dept. ednl. psychology, 1969-72; assoc. prof. psychology, chmn. U. Tex.-Permian Basin, 1974-78, chmn. anthropology and sociology, 1975-78, field dir., 1962-65; asst. dir. Austin Longitudinal Rsch. project, 1965-69, co-dir., 1969-74; research scientist Hogg Found. for Mental Health, 1972-74; prof. edn. and psychology Southwestern U., Georgetown, Tex., 1978-90, vis. prof. psychology, 1991, dir. testing and guidance, 1978-81, holder Brown vis. chair, 1978-82, assoc. dean for librs. and learning resources, 1981-90; coord., adminstrv. head Killeen office Cen. Counties Ctr. for MHMR Svcs., Temple, Tex., 1990-91; chief psychol. svcs. Temple, Tex., 1991-99; pvt. practice Temple, 2000—. Lectr. Nat. U., Mexico, 1962, U. Ctrl. Tex., 1994, Temple Coll., 1994. Author: (with W.H. Holtzman) Inkblot Perception and Personality, 1961, (with C.C. Cleland) Mental Retardation: Approaches to Institutional Change, 1969, Administrative Issues in Institutions for the Mentally Retarded, 1972, Exceptionalities Through the Lifespan: An Introduction, 1982, Multihandicapped Mentally Retarded, 1973, (with W.H. Holtzman, R. Diaz-Guerrero) Personality Development in Two Cultures, 1975; editor: (with C.C. Cleland, L.W. Talkington) Profoundly Mentally Retarded, 1976, (with R.K. Eyman, C.C. Cleland) Research with the Profoundly Retarded, 1978, Holtzman Inkblot Technique: An Annotated Bibliography (supplement), 1988, (with R.C. Reinehr, W.H. Holtzman) Holtzman Inkblot Technique: An Annotated Bibliography 1956-1982, 1983, (with R.C. Reinehr) Handbook of Old-Time Radio, 1993, Holtzman Inkblot Technique: Research Guide and

Bibliography, 1999, Southwestern University Bibliographic Series, 1986-1990; contbr.: Handbook of Texas, 1996; editl. assoc. Current Anthropology, 1971-77; assoc. editor: Am. Corrective Therapy Jour., 1971-81, Exceptional Children, 1982-84; mem. editl. bd. Tex. Psychologist, 1979-83, Phi Kappa Phi Jour./Nat. Forum, 1976-80; editl. cons. Mental Retardation, 1972-77; rev. editor Jour. Biol. Psychology, 1972-80, Revista Interamericana de Psicologia, 1983-89; reviewer Sci. Books, Films, 1978—; cons. editor Jour. Personality Assessment, 1981-90; spl. features editor: Scientifiction: The First Fandom Report, 2002—; rev. editor The National Fantasy Fan, 2003—; frequent contbr. Paperback Parade, 2004—; contbr. over 500 articles to profl. jours. Mem. Mayor's Drug Abuse Panel, Odessa, Tex., 1975-78; chmn. adv. bd. Human Potentials Ctr., Permian Basin Cmty. Ctrs. for Mental Health and Mental Retardation, Odessa and Midland, Tex., 1975-78; bd. govs. Mood-Heritage Mus., 1984-90. U.S. Office Edn. fellow, 1964-66, U. Tex. fellow, 1973-74; recipient Franklin Gilliam prize Humanities Rsch. Ctr. U. Tex., 1965, Spencer Rsch. award Nat. Acad. Edn., 1972, Faculty Fellowship award Southwestern U., 1981 Fellow AAAS, Am. Psychol. Soc., Soc. Personality Assessment (life); mem. Western Rsch. Conf. on Mental Retardation, Am. Acad. Mental Retardation, Southwestern Psychol. Assn., Bell County Psychol. Assn., Sigma Xi, Psi Chi, Mu Alpha Nu, Delta Tau Kappa, Phi Kappa Phi, Phi Delta Kappa. Personal E-mail: jon_swartz@hotmail.com. *All my life I have had teachers, in school and out, who challenged me to do more than I thought I was capable of doing. Any success I have achieved, I owe to them and their efforts in my behalf.*

SWARTZ, JULIANNE, artist; b. Phoenix, Apr. 29, 1967; BA in Photography and Creative Writing, U. Ariz., 1989; postgrad., Skowhegan Sch. for Painting and Sculpture, 1999; MFA, Bard Coll., 2002. One-woman shows include currents1: Julianne Swartz, Colby Coll. Mus. Art, Waterville, Maine, 2004, Speculative Mechanics *persistant optimism, Josee Bienvenu Gallery, NY, 2004, Partial Excavation (in pink), Angles Gallery, Santa Monica, Calif., 2005, Elevator Music 4, Frances Young Tang Mus., Skidmore Coll., Saratoga Springs, NY, 2005, exhibited in group shows at Shadow House, Ricco/Maresca Gallery, NY, 2000, Luminous, Bellevue Art Mus., Seattle, 2000, Pop Mechanics, Susquehanna Art Mus., Harrisburg, Pa., 2000, Interval: New Art for New Space, Sculpture Ctr., NY, 2001, Landing - the Bubble (with Piot Brehmer), 123 Watts, NY, 2001, Bklyn.!, Inst. Contemporary Art, Palm Beach. Fla., 2001, Periphera, Murray Guy Gallery, NY, 2002, Garden Details, Imported and Compressed, Schroeder Romero, NY, 2002, Line Drawing, Artist Space Project Rm., NY, 2003, Plastic Gardens, Cristinerose I Josee Bienvenu Gallery, NY, 2003, Breaking Away, P.S. 1 Inst. Contemporary Art, Queens, NY, 2003, Counter Culture, New Mus. Contemporary Art, NYC, 2004, Biennial, Whitney Mus. Am. Art, NY, 2004, Press Play, Green on Red Gallery, Dublin, Ireland, 2005, Sixteen:One, Santa Monica, 2005. Artist in Residence grant NY Found. Arts, 1997, Spl. Editions grant, Lower East Side Printshop, 1998, Artist in Marketplace, Bronx Mus. Arts, 1999, Richard Kelly Found. grant, 1999, Cite Internationale des Arts, Paris, 2000, grant, P.S. 1 Mus., Nat. and Internat. Studio Program, 2002, Pub. Art Fund, NY, 2002, Art Omi Internat. Artists Colony, Ghent, NY, 2003. Mailing: c/o Josee Bienvenu Gallery 529 W 20th St New York NY 10011 E-mail: info@joseebienvenu.com.

SWARTZ, MICHAEL D., statistical geneticist; b. Boston, Jan. 24, 1974; s. Robert J. and Adele M. Swartz. BA, BS, Trinity U., San Antonio, 1997; MA, Rice U., Houston, 2002, PhD, 2004. Pre-doctoral fellow dept. epidemiology M.D. Anderson Cancer Ctr., U. Tex., Houston, 1999—2004, post-doctoral fellow, 2004—; rsch. asst. prof. statis. dept. Tex. A&M U., College Station, 2004—06. Contbr. articles to profl. jours. Vol. Kairos Found., Houston, 1989. Recipient Chairman's award for svc. to dept. stats., Rice U. Dept. Chair, 2002; fellow Tng. fellowship in cancer prevention, Nat. Cancer Inst., M.D. Anderson Cancer Ctr., 2006, Nat. Cancer Inst. & Dept. Stats., Tex. A&M U., 2004—; Keck fellowship in computational biology, Keck Ctr., Rice U., 1998—2000, Tng. fellowship in cancer prevention, Nat. Cancer Inst., M.D. Anderson Cancer Ctr., 2000—04. Mem.: Am. Stats. Assn., Internat. Genetic Epidemiology Soc., Phi Beta Kappa. Achievements include development of a new method for gene mapping. Avocation: swing dancing. Office: U Tex MD Anderson Cancer Ctr Dept Epidemiology Unit PO Box 301439 Houston TX 77230 Business E-mail: mswartz@alumni.rice.edu.

SWARTZ, MICHAEL FREDERICK, physician assistant; b. Nyskauna, N.Y., Sept. 2, 1979; s. Kurt and Julie Swartz. BS, D'Youville Coll., Buffalo N.Y., 2001. Physician's asst. SUNY Upstate Med. U., Syracuse, 2001—. Contbr. articles to profl. jours. Recipient Du Couet Musarra scholar, D'Youville Coll., 2001, Good Citizenship award, Am. Legion, 1996. Mem.: Lambda Sigma (life; treas. 1998—98). Democrat-Npl. Episcopal. Achievements include research in Prevention of muscle damage during a heart attack. Office: SUNY Upstate Medical University 750 E Adams St Syracuse NY 13210 Office Phone: 315-464-6255.

SWARTZ, MORTON NORMAN, medical educator; b. Boston, Nov. 11, 1923; s. Jacob H. and Janet (Heller) Swartz; m. Cesia Rosenberg, Sept. 18, 1956; children: Mark David, Caroline Joan. BA, Harvard Coll., 1945; MD, Harvard U., 1947; MD (hon.), U. Geneva, Switzerland, 1988. Diplomate Am. Bd. Internal Medicine. Med. intern and resident Mass. Gen. Hosp., Boston, 1947—50, chief resident in medicine, 1953—54, chief infectious disease unit, 1956—90, chief James Jackson Firm, med. svcs., 1990—; USPHS postdoctoral rsch. fellow Johns Hopkins U., McCollum-Pratt Inst. Enzymology, Balt., 1954—56; assoc. prof. medicine Harvard Med. Sch., Boston, 1967—73, prof., 1973—. Vis. assoc. prof. biochemistry Stanford Med. Sch., Palo Alto, Calif., 1969—70; chmn. Nat. Inst. Child Health and Devel., 1995—97, bd. sci. counselors. Co-author: Osteomyelitis, 1971; editor: Current Clinical Topics in Infectious Diseases, 1980—2002; assoc. editor: New Eng. Jour. Medicine, 1981—2002; contbr. articles to profl. jours. 1st lt. U.S. Army, 1950—52. Mem.: ACP (Disting. Tchr. award 1989), Inst. Medicine, Infectious Diseases Soc. Am. (Bristol award 1984, Feldman award 1989, Soc. Citation award 2003), Assn. Am. Physicians, Am. Soc. for Clin. Investigation, Am. Soc. Biochemistry and Molecular Biology. Jewish. Avocations: biology, birdwatching, cosmology. Home: 54 Shaw Rd Chestnut Hill MA 02467-3122 Office: Mass Gen Hosp Dept Medicine Bulfinch Bldg #127 Boston MA 02114-2696 Office Phone: 617-726-7865. Business E-mail: mswartz@partners.org.

SWARTZ, RENEE BECKER, civic volunteer; b. Newark, Feb. 25, 1935; d. Sidney David and Adeline (Kleinberg) Becker; m. Harry Mason Swartz, Mar. 8, 1931; children: Stephen, Addi-Lyn, Sidney. Student, Rutgers U., 1950-52, Bryn Mawr Coll., 1952-53; BA, Barnard Coll.-Columbia U., 1955. Planning com. N.J. White Ho. Conf. on Librs. and Info. Sci., 1975-79, del. selection com., mem. programs com., 1978-79; chair del. White Ho. Conf., 1979; re-elected permanent N.J. rep. Nat. Commn. Follow-up Activities White Ho. Conf., 1991, chairperson nat. awards com., 1984-86, chair fundraising com., 1989-90; chmn. N.J. Del. White Ho. Conf. of Librs. and Info. Svcs., 1991—. Pres. Friends of Monmouth County Libr. Assn., 1964-68; founding mem. N.J. Citizens for Better Librs., 1982; chair bldg. com. Dorothy L. Spiwak Meml. Libr., Rumson, N.J., 1971-73, trustee, 1971—; active N.J. Libr. Devel. Com., 1973-84; chair, bd. trustees Grad. Sch. of Comm., Info. and Libr. Studies, Rutgers U., 1980—, chair, 1983—; gov. appointee N.J. State Libr. Adv. Coun., 1975, chair, 1986—, Monmouth County Libr. Commn., 1965—, chair, 1976—; past trustee Barnard Coll., pres. Alumnae Assn., 1981-84, trustee, 1981-85; founder NJ Ctr. in the Book, 2001—, chair, state coord.; presdl. appointee Nat. Inst. Mus. and Libr. Svcs., 2004— Recipient Hanna G. Solomon award Greater Red Bank sect. Nat. Coun. Jewish Women, 1979, Pres. medal Barnard Coll.-Columbia U., 1984, Columbia U. medal, 1985, Woman or Achievement award Monmouth County Adv. Com., 1991; named Nat. Trustee of Yr. ALA, 1991. Mem. Nat. Citizens Com. for Pub. Libraries (steering com. 1980-84), Am. Library Trustee Assn. (pres. com. 1983, nat. intellectual freedom com. 1984—), N.J. Library Assn. (centennial com. 1986-89, chairperson N.J. Ednl. Inst. com. 1987-88, N.J. Trustee of Yr. 1980, 99), N.J. Library Trustee Assn. (exec. com. 1976-81, regional rep. 1983-86), Assn. N.J. Library Commrs. (pres. 1973-75), Capitol Hill Club, Lotus Club

N.Y., Ocean Club NJ, Cosmos Club Avocations: tennis, sailing, walking. Home: 136 Rumson Rd Rumson NJ 07760-1238 Office Phone: 732-431-7235. Business E-mail: rswartz@co.monmouth.nj.us.

SWARTZ, ROSLYN HOLT, real estate company executive; b. L.A., Dec. 9, 1940; d. Abe Jack and Helen (Canter) Holt; m. Allan Joel Swartz, June 2, 1963. AA, Santa Monica (Calif.) Coll., 1970; BA summa cum laude, UCLA, 1975; MA, Pepperdine U., 1976. Cert. CC instr., student-pers. worker Calif. Mgr. pub. rels. Leader Holdings, Inc., L.A., 1968-75, pres., 1991—, sec., treas. North Hollywood, Calif., 1975-81, pres., 1981-91; CEO Beverly Stanley Investments, L.A., 1979—. Pres. Leader Properties, Inc., Leader Fairfax, Inc., Leader 358, Inc., Leader 359, Inc., Leader Ventura, Inc., 1996—; condr. Oral History Elderly Jewish Cmty. Venice, Calif. Los Angeles County Planning Dept. Libr., 1974. Founder Pres.'s Cir. L.A. County Mus. Art, UCLA Affiliates Sch. of Medicine Scholarship Com., 2004—06; past trustee Odyssey Theatre Ensemble; mem. coun. Libr. Found.; supporting founding mem. Kirk Douglas Theatre; founder Disney Hall; hon. chmn. bus. adv. coun. Nat. Rep. Congl. Com.; bd. dirs. House Ear Inst.; hon. bd. dirs. West L.A. Symphony. Mem.: NAFE, ARCS Found., Inc. (Achiev. rewards for coll. scientists), KCET Womens Coun., Comml. Real Estate Women, Am. Pharm. Assn., First Century Soc. at UCLA, Royce Ctr. Cir., UCLA Las Donas (exec. bd.), Friends of Robinson Gardens, Town Hall (life), UCLA Alumni Assn. (life), Santa Monica Coll. Alumni Assn. (life), Nat. Mus. Women in Arts (So. Calif. coun.), Friends of Fox, UCLA Chancellor's Assocs. (mem. leadership coun. W. L.A. chpt.), Women's Guild Cedars-Sinai Med. Ctr., Fashion Cir. Costume Coun. of LACMA, UCLA Prytanean Alumnae Assn., Ctr. Dance Assn. (charter), Women and Philanthropy at UCLA (cir. level.), The Blue Ribbon Club, Club 100, Westwood Women's Bruins Club, Order Eastern Star, Phrateres Internat., Phi Beta Kappa (Bicentennial fellow), Pi Lambda Theta, Pi Gamma Mu, Phi Delta Kappa, Alpha Kappa Delta, Alpha Gamma Sigma, Phi Alpha Theta. Avocation: horticulture. Office: PO Box 241866 Los Angeles CA 90024-9666

SWARTZ, STEVEN R., publishing executive; Grad., Harvard Coll. Report The Wall St. Jour., Phila., 1984-86, N.Y.C., 1986-89, page one editor, 1989-91; editor SmartMoney mag., N.Y.C., 1991-95, pres., CEO, editor-in-chief, 1995—; CEO, editor-in-chief Hearst Newspapers, 1995—2000, exec. v.p., 2001—. Bd. dirs. Dow Jones Profit Sharing Plan; dir. Settlement Housing Fund, N.Y.C. Mem. investment com. Whitney Mus. Am. Art.

SWARTZ, THOMAS R., economist, educator; b. Phila., Aug. 31, 1937; s. Henry Jr. and Elizabeth (Thomas) S.; m. Jeanne Marie Jourdan, Aug. 12, 1961; children: Mary Butler, Karen Miller, Jennifer, Anne, Rebecca. BA, LaSalle U., 1960; MA, Ohio U., 1962; PhD, Ind. U., 1965. Asst. prof. U. Notre Dame, Ind., 1965-70, assoc. dept. chair Ind., 1968-70, assoc. prof. Ind., 1970-78, acting dir. grad. studies Ind., 1977-78, prof. econs. Ind., 1978—85, dir. program econ. policy Ind., 1982-85; resident dir. U. Notre Dame London Program, 1990-91, U. Notre Dame Austraulia Program, Fremantle, 1996. Vis. prof. U. Notre Dame London Program 1982, 85, 90-91, 2001—; fellow Inst. for Ednl. Initiatives, 1997-2005; dir. London Summer Program, 2001—; found. bd. Mich. Coll., 2004—; fiscal cons. Ind. Commn. State Tax, Indpls., 1965-68, spl. tax cons., 1971-81, City of South Bend, Ind., 1972-75; cons. in field. Co-editor: The Supply Side, 1983, Changing Face of Fiscal Federalism, 1990, Urban Finance Under Siege, 1993, Taking Sides, 11th edit., 2004, America's Working Poor, 1995; contbr. articles to profl. jours. Bd. dirs. Forever Learning Inst., South Bend, Ind., 1988-93; mem. steering com. Mayor's Housing Forum, South Bend, 1989-95; chair Com. Svcs. Block Grant, South Bend, 1985-90, Econ. Devel. Task Force, South Bend, 1985; Rsch. fellow Nat. Ctr. Urban Ethnic Affairs, 1979-85, Found. Bd. S.W. Mich. Coll. Bd., 2004-, v.p., 2005-. Rsch. fellow Nat. Ctr. Urban Ethnic Affairs, 1979-85, Found. Bd. S.W. Mich. Coll. Bd., 2004-, v.p., 2005-; recipient Danforth Assoc. award Danforth Found., 1972-86, Tchg. award Kan Nazajian Found., 1974, Tchg. awards Notre Dame; Rsch. grantee Mellon Found., 1998-2003. Fellow Inst. Ednl. Initiatives. Democrat. Roman Catholic. Avocations: racquetball, golf. Office: U Notre Dame Dept Econs and Policy Studies 414 Decio Hall Notre Dame IN 46556-5644 Office Phone: 574-631-7737. Business E-mail: swartz1@nd.edu.

SWARTZBAUGH, MARC L., lawyer; b. Urbana, Ohio, Jan. 3, 1937; s. Merrill L. and Lillian K. (Hill) S.; m. Marjory Anne Emhardt, Aug. 16, 1958 (deceased May 20, 2000); children: Marc Charles, Kathleen Marie, Laura Kay. BA magna cum laude, Wittenberg Coll., 1958; LLB magna cum laude, U. Pa., 1961. Bar: Ohio 1961, U.S. Dist. Ct. (no. dist.) Ohio 1962, U.S. Claims Ct. 1991, U.S. Ct. Appeals (6th cir.) 1970, U.S. Ct. Appeals (3d cir.) 1985, U.S. Ct. Appeals (Fed. cir.) 1995, U.S. Supreme Ct. 1973. Law clk. to judge U.S. Ct. Appeals (3d cir.), Phila., 1961-62; assoc. Jones, Day, Reavis & Pogue, Cleve., 1962-69, ptnr., 1970-98; ret., 1998; cons., 1998—. Note editor U. Pa. Law Rev., 1960-61; co-author: Ohio Legal Ethics, 2001, Ohio Legal Ethics under the New Rules, 2006. Co-chmn. Suburban Citizens for Open Housing, Shaker Heights, Ohio, 1966; v.p. Lomond Assn., Shaker Heights, 1965-68; trustee The Dance Ctr., Cleve., 1980-83; amb. People to People Internat., 1986; chmn. legal divsn. Cleve. campaign United Negro Coll. Fund, 1989-96; tutor Cleve. Reads, 2003; endower of Marjory and Marc L. Swartzbaugh chair, Cleve. Orch., 2004. Mem. ABA (litigation sect., sr. lawyers divsn.), Fed. Bar Assn., Ohio Bar Assn., Cleve. Bar Assn., Rowfant Club, Order of Coif, Beta Theta Pi. Democrat. Avocations: poetry, painting, music, photography, rare book collecting. Office: Jones Day N Point 901 Lakeside Ave E Cleveland OH 44114-1190

SWARTZENTRUBER, DON MICHAEL, artist, educator; b. Seaford, Del., Aug. 23, 1966; s. John Mark and Marjorie Swartzentruber; m. Christine Damer, Nov. 19, 1994; children: Drake, Keller. BS in Edn., Grace Coll., 1993; MFA, Norwich U., 2000. Cert. tchr. Ind., 1993. Freelance artist, Winona Lake, Ind., 1983—; dir. art WMDT-TV47, Salisbury, Mass., 1988—89; computer animator, illustrator Noteworthy Graphics, Mansfield, Ohio, 1988—89; visual art instr. Warsaw (Ind.) H.S., 1993—. Adj. prof. Ind. U., Purdue, 2001—02, Grace Coll., Winona Lake, 2002—. Exhibitions include Totem Triptychs, 2000. Grantee, Ind. Arts Commn., 2001, 2003. Avocation: art. Home: PO Box 262 Winona Lake IN 46590

SWARTZLANDER, EARL EUGENE, JR., engineering educator, former electronics company executive; b. San Antonio, Feb. 1, 1945; s. Earl Eugene and Jane (Nicholas) S.; m. Joan Vickery, Aug. 9, 1968. BSEE, Purdue U., 1967; MSEE, U. Colo., 1969; PhD, U. So. Calif., 1972. Registered profl. engr., Ala., Calif., Colo., Tex. Devel. engr. Ball Bros. Rsch. Corp., Boulder, Colo., 1967-69; Hughes fellow, mem. tech. staff Hughes Aircraft Co., Culver City, Calif., 1969-73; mem. rsch. staff Tech. Svc. Co., Santa Monica, Calif., 1973-74; chief engr. Geophys. Systems Corp., Pasadena, Calif., 1974-75; staff engr. to sr. staff engr., 1975-79, project mgr., 1979-84, lab. mgr., 1985-87; dir. ind. R&D TRW Inc., Redondo Beach, Calif., 1987-90; Schlumberger Centennial prof. engring. dept. elec. and computer engring. U. Tex., Austin, 1990—; mem. tech. adv. bd. Arithmatica. Gen. chmn. Internat. Conf. Wafer Scale Integration, 1989, Internat. Conf. Application Specific Array Processors, 1990, 94, 11th Internat. Conf. on Computer Arithmetic, 1992, 31st Ann. Asilomar Conf. on Signals, Sys., and Computers 1997, others; chmn. 3d Internat. Conf. Parallel and Distributed Sys., Taiwan, 1993, 12th Internat. Conf. on Application-Specific Systems, Architectures and Processors, 2000; mem. tech. adv. bd. ECIT, Queen's U., Belfast, 2005—. Author: VLSI Signal Processing Systems, 1986; editor: Computer Design Development, 1976, Systolic Signal Processing Systems, 1987, Wafer Scale Integration, 1989, Computer Arithmetic Vol. 1 and 2, 1990, Application Specific Processors, 1996; editor-in-chief Jour. of VLSI Signal Processing, 1989-95, IEEE Transactions on Computers, 1991-94, IEEE Transactions on Signal Processing, 1995; editor: IEEE Transactions on Computers, 1982-86, IEEE Transactions on Parallel and Distributed Systems, 1989-90; hardware area editor ACM Computing Revs., 1985—; assoc. editor: IEEE Jour. Solid-State Circuits, 1984-88; contbr. more than 300 articles to profl. jours. and tech. conf. procs. Bd. dirs. Casiano Estates Homeowners Assn., Bel Air, Calif., 1976-80, pres., 1978-80; bd. dirs. Benedict Hills Estates Homeowners Assn., Beverly Hills, Calif., 1984-2006, pres., 1990-95. Recipient Disting. Engring.

Alumnus award Purdue U., 1989, U. Colo., 1997, Outstanding Elec. Engr. award Purdue U., 1992, knight Imperial Russian Order St. John of Jerusalem (Knights of Malta), 1993. Fellow: IEEE (hist. com. 1996—2004, fellows com. 2000—03, 3d Millennium medal 2000); mem.: IEEE Solid-State Cirs. Coun. (sec. 1992—93, treas. 1994—97), IEEE Signal Proc. Soc. (bd. govs. 1992—94), IEEE Computer Soc. (bd. govs. 1987—91, Golden Core award 1996), Omicron Delta Kappa, Sigma Tau, Eta Kappa Nu. Office: U Tex Austin Dept Elec Computer Engring Austin TX 78712 Office Phone: 310-702-5756.

**SWARZ, JEFFREY ROBERT,** investment banker, biotechnologist, neuroscientist; b. Nov. 9, 1949; s. Irvin Brad and Blanche S. (Marcus) S.; m. Kathy Helen Kafer, June 20, 1976. BS with hons., U. Calif., Irvine, 1971; PhD, U. Rochester, 1976. Postdoctoral fellow in neurovirology Johns Hopkins U. Sch. Medicine, Balt., 1976-79; staff fellow infectious diseases NIH, Bethesda, Md., 1979-80; dir. biotech. group Teknekron Rsch. Inc., McLean, Va., 1980-81; pres. AgroBiotics, Inc., Balt., 1981-82; from sr. scientist to dir. mktg. and sales Pall Corp., Glen Cove, N.Y., 1982-85, dir. mktg. and sales, 1985-86; biotech./healthcare analyst Goldman Sachs & Co., Glen Cove, N.Y., 1986-92; dir. CS First Boston, N.Y.C., 1992-99; ptnr. Partner-Eagle Ptnrs., N.Y.C., 1999—; prodr. Shadow Prodns.; mng. dir. Life Sci. Group, 2001—. Cons. U.S. Senate Subcom. on Sci., Tech. and Space, 1979-80; prodr. Shadow Prodns., 1998—. Author: (with others) Genetic Engineering: Issues and Trends, 1982; contbr. articles to profl. jours. Recipient Rsch. award Bank of Am., 1970-71, Nat. Rsch. Svc. award 1976-79; NIH fellow 1975-76. Mem.: N.Y. Acad. Sci., N.Y. Athletic Club, U. Club. Democrat. Jewish. Office: Life Sci Group 1 Sound Shore Dr Greenwich CT 06830-5449 Office Phone: 203-422-6500. E-mail: jswarz@investinlife.com.

**SWATOS, WILLIAM HENRY, JR.,** priest, sociologist; b. Paterson, N.J., Sept. 25, 1946; s. William H. Sr. and Lucille (MacNab) S.; children (by previous marriage): Giles S., Eric B.; m. Joanne Longstreet, Oct. 29, 2002. AB, Transylvania U., 1966; MDiv summa cum laude, Episc. Theol. Sem., Lexington, Ky., 1969; MA, U. Ky., 1969, PhD, 1973. Ordained to ministry Episcopal Ch., 1969. Mem. sociology faculty King Coll., Bristol, Tenn., 1973-80; vicar St. Mark's Episc. Ch., Silvis, Ill., 1980-94; mem. sociology faculty No. Ill. U., 1984-88; chair dept. edn. Diocese of Quincy, 1988-90, 93-96. Mem. faculty Black Hawk and Scott C.C., Moline, Ill., Bettendorf, Iowa, 1988-96; adj. faculty Augustana Coll., Rock Island, Ill., 2005—. Editor: Time, Place and Circumstance, 1990, Religious Politics in Global and Comparative Perspective, 1989, Religious Sociology, 1987; editor Sociol. Analysis/Sociology of Religion, 1989-94; editor-in-chief Encyclopedia of Religion and Society, 1998; mng. editor Interdisciplinary Jour. Rsch. on Religion, 2004—; contbr. articles to profl. jours. Recipient Templeton prize in humility theology, 1996; full grantee World Soc. Found., Zurich, Switzerland, 1987, grantee NEH, 1974, 79, 85, 89, rsch. grantee Soc. for the Sci. Study of Religion, 1984-85, 91-92; Inst. Studies Religion sr. fellow Baylor U., 2004—; named Disting. Alumnus Dept. of Sociology, U. Ky., Lexington, 1990. Fellow Soc. Sci. Study of Religion (program chair 2004); mem. Assn. for the Sociology of Religion (editor 1989-94, book rev. editor 1986-88, exec. coun. 1984-86, exec. officer 1996—, gen. editor Religion and the Social Order Series 2004—), Religious Rsch. Assn. (sec. 1990-91, bd. dirs. 1986-89, exec. officer 1994—). Home and Office: 618 SW 2nd Ave Galva IL 61434-1912 E-mail: bill4329@hotmail.com.

**SWATT, STEPHEN BENTON,** communications executive, consultant; b. LA, June 26, 1944; s. Maurice I. and Lucille E. (Sternberger) S.; m. Susan Ruth Edelstein, Sept. 7, 1968; 1 child, Jeffrey Michael. BSBA, U. Calif., 1966, M in Journalism, 1967. Writer San Francisco Examiner, 1967; reporter United Press Internat., L.A., 1968-69; producer news Sta. KCRA-TV, Sacramento, 1969-70, reporter news, 1970-79, chief polit. and capitol corres., 1979-92; mng. ptnr. NCG Porter Novelli, Sacramento, 1992—2003, sr. counselor, 2003—. Adj. prof., guest lectr. Calif. State U., Sacramento. Contbr. articles to profl. jours. With USCG, 1966. Recipient No. Calif. Emmy NATAS, 1976-77, Pub. Svc. award Calif. State Bar, 1977, Exceptional Achievement Coun. advancement and Support of Edn., 1976, Nat. Health Journalism award Am. Chiropractic Assn., 1978. Mem. Soc. Profl. Journalists (8 awards), Capitol Corres. Assn., U. Calif. Alumni Assn., Sacramento Press Club. Avocations: hiking, jogging, fishing. Office: Porter Novelli 1215 K St # 2100 Sacramento CA 95814 Office Phone: 916-443-3354. Business E-Mail: steve.swatt@porternovelli.com.

**SWAYZE, CHARLES J., JR.,** lawyer; b. Greenwood, Miss., May 14, 1944; BBA, Univ. Miss., 1966, JD, 1969; LLM, George Washington Univ., 1973. Prosecuting atty. City of Greenwood, Miss., 1974—75, Leflore County, 1976—2000; mem. Whittington, Brock & Swayze PA, Greenwood, Miss. Pres. So. Conf. of Bar Pres. Capt. JAGC U.S. Army, 1969—73. Fellow: Miss. Bar Found.; Am. Bar Found.; mem.: ABA, Miss. Bar Assn. (pres. 2004), Phi Delta Phi. Office: Whittington Brock & Swayze PA 308 Fulton St PO Box 931 Greenwood MS 38930

**SWAYZE, PATRICK,** actor, dancer; b. Houston, Aug. 18, 1952; s. Patsy Swayze. Student, Harkness Sch., Joffrey Ballet Sch. Dancer (Broadway) Goodtime Charley, Grease; film appearances include (debut) Skatetown, U.S.A., 1979, The Outsiders, 1983, Uncommon Valor, 1983, Red Dawn, 1984, Grandview U.S.A., 1984, Youngblood, 1986, Dirty Dancing, 1987, Steel Dawn, 1987, Tiger Warsaw, 1988, Road House, 1989, Next of Kin, 1989, Ghost, 1989, Point Break, 1991, City of Joy, 1992, Father Hood, 1993, Tall Tale, 1994, To Wong Foo, Thanks for Everything, Julie Newmar, 1995, Three Wishes, 1995, Letters From a Killer, 1997, Vanished, 1998, Black Dog, 1998, Letters from a Killer, 1998, Without a Word, 1999, The Winddriver, 2000, Wakin' Up In Reno, 2000, Forever Lulu, 2000, Green Dragon, 2001, Donnie Darko, 2001, Waking Up in Reno, 2002, One Last Dance, 2003, 11:14, 2003, Dirty Dancing: Havana Nights, 2004; (tv series) Hollywood Squares, 1998; (TV movies) King Solomon's Mines, 2004; (off-Broadway) Guys and Dolls, 2006. Recipient Golden Apple award. Office: William Morris 151 S El Camino Dr Beverly Hills CA 90212-2775*

**SWAZEY, JUDITH POUND,** academic administrator, science educator; b. Bronxville, N.Y., Apr. 21, 1939; d. Robert Earl and Louise Titus (Hanson) Pound; m. Peter Woodman Swazey, Nov. 28, 1964; children: Elizabeth, Peter. AB, Wellesley Coll., 1961; PhD, Harvard U., 1966. Rsch. assoc Harvard U., 1966-71, lectr., 1969-71, rsch. fellow, 1971-72; cons. com. brain scis. NRC, 1971-73; staff scientist neuroscis. rsch. program MIT, Cambridge, 1973-74; assoc. prof. dept. socio-med. scis. and cmty. medicine Boston U., 1974-77, prof., 1977-80, adj. prof. Schs. Medicine and Pub. Health, 1980—; exec. dir. Medicine in the Pub. Interest, Inc., Boston and Washington, 1979-82, 89-93; pres. Coll. of the Atlantic, Bar Harbor, Maine, 1982-84, Acadia Inst., Bar Harbor, 1984-2001, founding pres., sr. scholar, 2001—. Mem. Army Sci. Bd., 1987-92. Author: Reflexes and Motor Integration, the Development of Sherrington's Integrative Action Concept, 1969, (with others) Human Aspects of Biomedical Innovation, 1971, (with R.C. Fox) The Courage to Fail, a Social View of Organ Transplants and Hemodialysis, 1975, rev. edit., 1978, 02 (hon. mention Am. Med. Writers Assn., C. Wright Mills award Am. Sociol. Assn.), Chlorpromazine in Psychiatry, a Study of Therapeutic Innovation, 1974, (with K. Reeds) Today's Medicine, Tomorrow's Science, Essays on Paths of Discovery in the Biomedical Sciences, 1978; editor: (with C. Wong) Dilemmas of Dying, Policies and Procedures for Decisions Not to Treat, 1981, (with F. Worden and G. Adelman) The Neurosciences: Paths of Discovery, 1975, (with R.C. Fox) Spare Parts, Organ Replacement in American Society, 1992, Japanese transl., 1999, (with C. Messikomer and A. Glicksman) Society and Medicine. Essays in Honor of Renée Fox, 2002; assoc. editor IRB: A Jour. of Human Subjects Rsch., 1979-00; mem. editl. bd. Sci. and Engring. Ethics, 1994—; contbr. articles to profl. jours. Mem. Maine Dept. Human Svcs. Bioethics Adv. Com. (chair 1991-94); mem. Commn. on Rsch. Integrity, 1994-95; bd. dirs. Maine Bioethics Network, 1994-99. Wellesley Coll. scholar, 1961; Wellesley Coll. Alumnae fellow Harvard U., 1966, NIH predoctoral fellow, 1966, Radcliffe Coll. Coll. grad. fellow, 1966. Fellow AAAS (sci. freedom and responsibility com. 1986-89, nominations com. 2003-2004), Inst. Medicine of NAS (mem. health scis. policy bd.

1986-89), Grad. Record Exam. (bd. dirs. 1987-91), Phi Beta Kappa, Sigma Xi (mem. ethics com. 2004-). Office: PO Box 243 Bar Harbor ME 04609-0243 Business E-Mail: jswazey@verizon.net.

**SWEARER, WILLIAM BROOKS,** lawyer; b. Hays, Kans. Grad., Princeton U., 1951; law degree, U. Kans., 1955. Bar: Kans. 1955. Pvt. practice, Hutchinson, Kans., 1955—; ptnr., now counsel Martindell, Swearer & Shaffer, LLP, Hutchinson, 1955—. Mem. Kans. Bd. Discipline for Attys., 1979-92, chmn., 1987-92; mem. Kans. Commn. on Jud. Qualifications, 2003-. With U.S. Army, 1952-53, Korea. Mem. ABA (ho. of dels. 1995-2000), Am. Bar Found. (state chair 1998-2002), Kans. Bar Assn. (pres. 1992-93, various offices, mem. coms.), Kans. Assn. Sch. Attys. (pres. 1989-90), Reno County Bar Assn. Office: PO Box 1907 Hutchinson KS 67504-1907 Office Phone: 620-662-3331. Business E-Mail: wbs@martindell-law.com.

**SWECKER, CHRIS (CHRISTOPHE E. SWECKER),** protective services official, former federal agency administrator; b. El Ferrol, Spain, July 14, 1956; married; 3 children. BS, Appalachian State U., 1978; JD, Wake Forest U., 1981. Bar: Va., NC, U.S. Ct. Appeals (4th cir.), U.S. Supreme Ct. Asst. dist. atty. (1st dist.) State of NC, 1981—82; various positions FBI, 1981—87, supr., acting asst. spl. agent in charge Miami, 1987—94, asst. spl. agent in charge Houston, 1994—98, insp., 1998—99, spl. agent in charge Charlotte, NC, 1999—2004, asst. dir. Criminal Investigative Divsn. Washington, 2004—06, acting exec. asst. dir. for law enforcement services, 2006; head corp. security Bank of Am. Corp., Charlotte, NC, 2006—. Office: Bank of Am Corp 100 N Tryon St Bank of Am Corp Ctr Charlotte NC 28255*

**SWEE, DAVID ETHAN,** physician; b. NYC, Sept. 3, 1947; s. Eugene and Joan (Shalit) S.; m. Karen Virginia Hermanson, Dec. 30, 1971; children: Kendra Olivia, Julia Elizabeth. BA, Grinnell Coll., 1969; MD, Dalhousie U., 1975. Diplomate Am. Bd. Family Practice. Dir. premed. programs dept. family medicine U. Medicine and Dentistry NJ-Robert Wood Johnson Med. Sch., Piscataway, NJ, 1977-85, dir. fellowship program, 1985-87, med. dir. family practice ctr., vice chair dept. New Brunswick, 1987-91, prof., chmn. dept. family medicine, 1991—2005, acting sr. assoc. dean. edn., 2005—. Chief dept. family medicine Robert Wood Johnson U. Hosp., New Brunswick, 1991-05; site surveyor Accreditation Coun. Continuing Med. Edn., Chgo., 1993—, site surveyor, liaison com. on med. edn., 2001—, accreditation rev. com., 2005—. Editor, main author: Teaching Family Medicine in Medical School: A Companion to Predoctoral Education in Family Medicine, 1991. Grantee Prudential Ins. Co., 1987-89, US Dept. HHS, 1984-87, 91-04, 93-96, 96-99, 99-02, 02-05; Bishop fellow Am. Coun. Edn., 2002-03. Fellow Am. Acad. Family Physicians; mem. Soc. Tchrs. Family Medicine (bd. dirs. 1985-89, group on predocotoral edn. 1984—, group on faculty devel. 1985—). Avocations: music (piano), writing. Home: 259 Lawrence Ave Highland Park NJ 08904-1837 Office: 675 Hoes Ln Rm R102 Piscataway NJ 08854 Business E-Mail: swee@umdnj.edu.

**SWEED, PHYLLIS,** publishing executive; b. NYC, Dec. 6, 1931; d. Paul and Frances (Spitzer) S.; m. Leonard Bogdanoff (dec. Oct. 1975); children: Patricia Romano (dec. June 1994), James Alan. BA, NYU, 1950. Asst. buyer Nat. Bellas Hess, N.Y.C., 1950; assoc. editor Fox-Shulman Pub., N.Y.C., 1951-57; significant products and components editor Product Engring. mag. McGraw-Hill Pub., N.Y.C., 1957—61; mng. editor Haire Pub., N.Y.C., 1962-66; editor Gifts & Decorative Accessories Mag., 1966-78; sr. v.p. Geyer-McAllister Pub., N.Y.C., 1978-98, editor-in-chief, co-pub., 1978—98; dir. editl. devel. Gifts & Decorative Accessories, N.Y.C., 1998-99; prin. P.S. Comms. & Mktg., 1999—; editor-in-chief, pub. Gift Executive, 1999—. Bd. dirs. Frances Hook Scholarship Fund, 1989-96. Recipient Editl. Excellence award Indsl. Mktg., 1964, Nat. Assn. Ltd. Edit. Dealers award, 1993, 96, MagWeek Excellence award, 1992, Dallas Mktg. Ctr. award, 1980, 82. Mem. Nat. Assn. Ltd. Edit. Dealers (assoc.), Internat. Furnishings and Design Assn. Avocations: gardening, collecting antique Belleek. Office: 505 La-Guardia Pl Ste 17D New York NY 10012-2004 Personal E-mail: psweed505@aol.com.

**SWEEM, BILLY DON,** archbishop; b. Bartlesville, Okla., Aug. 7, 1942; s. Verl D. and Viola J. (Benner) Sweem; m. Roberta Marie Hawthorn, Dec. 26, 1990; children: Mark A., Kevin L., Chad D. Dipl., Internat. Bible Inst. & Sem., Portsmouth, Fla.; ThD magna cum laude, Bethel Full Gospel Sem., Okla. Ordained to ministry Gospel Mins. and Chs. Internat., 1991, Ind. Assemblies Fellowship, 1991. Evangelist Lighthouse Temple, Colorado Springs, Colo., 1977-80, Tulsa, 1980-85; youth pastor Echoes of Faith, Las Vegas, Nev., 1985-89; exec. dir. Billy Sweem Gospel Ministries, Tulsa, 1990—. Evangelist United Meth. Coop. Ministries, Tulsa, 1990—. Missionary India, Pakistan and Philippines. Special interest in church planting and mission works with orphans and troubled teens world-wide. Home: Internat Independent Assemblies Inc Global Faith Outreach Ministries PO Box 2171 Bartlesville OK 74005-2171 Office Phone: 918-337-6104. Personal E-Mail: sayaprayer7@yahoo.com.

**SWEENEY, ANNE M.,** cable television company executive; b. Nov. 4, 1957; m. Philip Miller; children: Rosemary, Christopher. BA, Coll. of New Rochelle, N.Y., 1979; EdM, Harvard U., 1980. With Nickelodeon/Nick at Nite, 1981-93, sr. v.p. program enterprises; chmn., CEO Fx Networks, NYC, 1993-96; exec. v.p. Disney/ABC Cable Networks, pres. Disney Channel Walt Disney Co., 1996—98, pres. Disney/ABC Cable Networks, Disney Channel, 1998—2000, pres. ABC Cable Networks Group, Disney Channel Worldwide, 2000—04, co-chair Media Networks divsn., pres. Disney/ ABC TV, 2004—. Bd. dirs. Mus. Radio & TV; hon. chair Cable Positive. Bd. trustees Coll. of New Rochelle, Harvard U. Found., hon. chair Cable Positive; bd. dirs. Walter Kaitz Found, Spl. Olympics Internat. Named one of 50 Most Powerful Women in Bus., Fortune mag., World's 100 Most Powerful Women, Forbes mag., 100 Most Powerful Women in Entertainment, Hollywood Reporter, 2004, 2005, 100 Most Powerful Women, Forbes mag., 2005—06, 50 Women to Watch, Wall St. Journal, 2005; named to Hall of Achievement, Am. Advt. Fedn., 1996; recipient Lucy award, Women in Film, 2002, Chair Award, Caucus for TV Prodrs., Writers, and Dirs., 2003, President's award, Cable TV Pub. Affairs Assn., 2004. Mem. Nat. Acad. Cable Programming (bd. dirs.), Women in Cable NY (founding mem.), Women in Cable (Exec. of Yr. 1994, Woman of Yr. 1997, Advocate Leader award So. Calif. Chpt. 1998). Office: The Walt Disney Co 500 S Buena Vista St Burbank CA 91521

**SWEENEY, CLAYTON ANTHONY,** business executive; b. Pitts., Oct. 20, 1931; s. Denis Regis and Grace Frances (Roche) S.; m. Sally Dimond, Oct. 4, 1958; children: Sharon, Lorrie, Maureen, Clayton Anthony, Tara, Megan. BS, Duquesne U., 1957, LLB, 1962. Bar: Pa. 1962, U.S. Supreme Ct. 1968. Supr. transp. claims H.J. Heinz Co., Pitts., 1955-57; mgr. market research Murray Corp. Am., Pitts., 1957-62; ptnr. Buchanan, Ingersoll, Rodewald, Kyle and Buerger, Pitts., 1962-78; sr. v.p. Allegheny Ludlum Industries, Inc., Pitts., 1978-81; exec. v.p., chief administrv. officer Allegheny Internat., Inc., Pitts., 1981-84, vice chmn., 1984-85; ptnr., mng. dir. Dickie, McCamey & Chilcote, Pitts., 1986-98, also bd. dirs.; pres. Sweeney Metz Fox McGrann & Schermer, 1998-2000; with Schnader Harrison Segal & Lewis, LLP, Pitts., 2000—. Bd. dirs. Wilkinson Sword Group Ltd., U.K., Landmark Savs. and Loan Assn., Liquid Air N.Am., Halbouty Energy Co., Koppers Holding Corp., Koppers Industries, Inc., Schaefer Mfg., Inc., Schaefer Marine, Inc., Schaefer Equipment, Inc.; adj. prof. Duquesne U. Sch. Law; lectr. Pa. Bar Inst.; mem. procedural rules com. Supreme Ct. Pa. Named Disting. Alumnus Sch. Law Duquesne U., 1997. Bd. dirs. Met. Pitts. Pub. Broadcasting, Inc., Diocesan Sch. Bd., Roman Cath. Diocese Pitts., Toner Inst., Christian Assocs. of Southwestern Pa., Wesley Inst., Inc., Jr. Achievement S.W. Pa., YMCA Western Pa.; chmn. Seton Hill Coll.; mem. St. Thomas More Sch. Bd., Bethel Park, Pa.; chmn. St. Francis Med. Ctr., St. Francis Health System; chmn. bd. DePaul Inst. With U.S. Army, 1953-55. Named one of 100 Most Disting. Living Alumni, Duquesne U. Century Club, 1978. Mem. Acad. Trial Lawyers Allegheny County, ABA, Pa. Bar Assn., St. Thomas

More Soc. Home: 232 Thornberry Cir Pittsburgh PA 15234-1025 Office: Schnader Harrison Segal & Lewis LLP Ste 2700 Fifth Ave Pl 120 Fifth Ave Pittsburgh PA 15222-3010 Office Phone: 412-577-5225. Business E-Mail: csweeney@schnader.com.

**SWEENEY, DAVID BRIAN,** lawyer; b. Seattle, June 23, 1941; s. Hubert Lee and Ann Louise (Harmon) S.; m. Janice Kay Goins, June 18, 1983; children: Stuart, Jennifer, Ann, Katharine. BA Magna cum laude, Yale U., 1963; LLB, Harvard U., 1967. Bar: Wash. 1968, U.S. Dist. Ct. (we. dist.) Wash. 1968, U.S. Ct. Appeals (9th cir.) 1968. Assoc. Roberts, Shefelman, Lawrence, Gay and Moch, Seattle, 1968-75; ptnr. Roberts, Shefelman, Lawrence, Gay & Moch (then Robert & Shefelman, then Foster, Pepper & Shefelman), 1976—2002; of counsel Smith & Zuccarini, P.S., Bellevue, Wash., 2002—. Mem. Seattle-King County Bar Assn., Wash. State Bar Assn., ABA, Estate Planning Coun. Seattle, College Club, Harbor Club. Home: 17506 SE 46th St Bellevue WA 98006-6527 Office: Smith & Zuccarini PS 2155 112th Ave NE Bellevue WA 98004 Office Phone: 425-990-1586. Business E-Mail: d.sweeney@smithzuccarini.com.

**SWEENEY, DEIDRE ANN,** lawyer; b. Hackensack, NJ, Mar. 17, 1953; AB cum laude, Mt. Holyoke Coll., 1975; JD, Fordham U., 1978. Assoc. Curtis, Mallet-Prevost, Colt & Mosle, N.Y.C., 1978—84, Eaton & Van Winkle, N.Y.C., 1984—86; ptnr. Jacobs, Persinger & Parker, N.Y.C., 1986—2002; of counsel McCanliss and Early, LLP, N.Y.C., 2002—. Hi-five scholarship com. CUNY, 2000—. Mem. Assn. of Bar of City of N.Y. (uniform state laws com. 1982-85).

**SWEENEY, DON PATRICK,** music coordinator, conductor; b. N.Y.C., Jan. 8, 1952; s. John James and Eileen Bernadett (Gillen) S.; m. Catherine Mary Burkhimer, Sept. 19, 1981; 1 child, Jennifer William. Grad. high sch., Fresh Meadows, N.Y. Music coord. Carson/Tonight Prodn., Burbank, Calif., 1976-92; music supr. Jay Leno Tonight Show, 1992-95; ind. prodr. TV spls. and commls., 1995—; bandleader SRO Orchestra, Canoga Park, Calif., 1980—. Featured drummer Earl Rose Trio, concerts thoughout Can., U.S.; with symphonies Corpus Christi, Tex., Asheville, N.C., Pacific Symphony, Calif.

**SWEENEY, GERALD BINGHAM,** lawyer; b. Waterbury, Conn., July 4, 1946; s. James W. and Aletha E. (Bingham) S.; m. Carolyn S. Chin, Sept. 18, 1976; 1 child, Patricia M. Chin-Sweeney. BS in Engring., Rensselaer Poly. Inst., 1968; JD, Columbia U., 1971. Bar: NY 1972, NJ 1976, Calif. 1986, Ill. 1998. With Owen and Turchin, NYC, 1971—74; atty. Avon Products, Inc., NYC, 1974-76; sr. counsel Revlon, Inc., NYC, 1976-81, regulatory counsel, 1981-83, v.p. divsn. counsel, 1983-87; v.p. gen. counsel Barnes-Hind, Inc., Sunnyvale, Calif., 1987-88, Coburn Optical Industries, Inc., Tulsa, 1987-88; prin. Sweeney & Assocs., Parsippany, NJ, 1988-92; mng. mem. Sweeney Law, Montclair, NJ, 1992—; dirs., treas. Crane Bldg. Assn., Inc., 2004—06; dir., pres. C.S. Properties, Inc. (real estate), 1995—; dir. Addition Tech., Inc. (med. devices), 2001—; dir., voting mem. Tech. Dirs., LLC (angel investing), 1998—; gen. counsel Wesley Jessen Visioncare Inc., 1998—2000, Large Scale Biology Corp., 2005. Exec. v.p. NJ Common Cause, Trenton, 1983; trustee Hosp. Ctr., Orange, NJ, 1986-95. Mem. ABA, NY Bar Assn., NJ Bar Assn., Calif. Bar Assn., Ill. Bar Assn. Home: 24 Oak Bend Llewellyn Pk West Orange NJ 07052 Office Phone: 973-509-1800.

**SWEENEY, JACK,** publishing executive; b. Jersey City; m. Ellie Sweeney; children: Jake, Jessica. BA in English, King's Coll., Wilkes-Barre, Pa. With adv. dept. Washington Post, 1968—74; adv. dir. Trenton Times, 1974—78, Boston Herald, 1978—80, Houston Chronicle, 1980—83, dir. sales and mktg., 1983—86, v.p. sales and mktg., 1986—91, v.p., gen. mgr, 1991, assoc. pub., 1998—2000, pres., 1998—, pub., 2000—. Exec. com., bd. trustees United Way Tex. Gulf Coast; exec. com., bd. dirs. Greater Houston Partnership; chmn. Be A Super Host Com. Super Bowl 2004, Houston. Mem.: Tex. Daily Newspaper Assn. (Pat Taggart Meml. Award 2000), Newspaper Assn. Am. Office: Houston Chronicle 801 Texas Ave Houston TX 77002*

**SWEENEY, JAMES RAYMOND,** retired lawyer; b. Chgo., Feb. 19, 1928; s. John Francis and Mae J. (McDonald) S.; m. Rhoda W. Davis, May 15, 1987; children from previous marriage: Margaret Elizabeth, John Francis, Thomas Edward. BS, U. Notre Dame, 1950; JD, Northwestern U., 1956. Bar: Ill. 1956. With Schroeder, Hofgren, Brady & Wegner, Chgo., 1956-61; ptnr. Hofgren, Wegner, Allen, Stellman & McCord, Chgo., 1962-71, Coffee, Wetzel, Sweeney, Chgo., 1971-72, Coffee & Sweeney, 1972-76, Mason, Kolehmainen, Rathburn & Wyss, Chgo., 1976-82, Mann, McWilliams, 1983-86, Mann McWilliams Zummer and Sweeney, 1986—89, Lee, Mann, Smith, McWilliams & Sweeney, 1989-91, Lee, Mann, Smith, McWilliams, Sweeney & Ohlson, 1991—2002; dir. ctr. intellectual property law John Marshall Law Sch., 1988—2003; ptnr. Barnes & Thornburg, 2003—04, ret., 2004. Commr. for disbarment matters Ill. Supreme Ct., 1963-73; mem. hearing div. Atty. Registration and Discipline Commn., 1974-77, chmn commn. 1983-90; chmn. Ctr. for Intellectual Property Law adv. bd. John Marshall Law Sch., 1997-2002. Bd. dirs., sec. Highland Park (Ill.) Hosp., 1972-79. Served as 1t. (j.g.) USN, 1950-53; 1t. comdr. Res. ret. Mem. ABA (coun. patent, trademark and copyright sect., sec. 1978-82), Ill. State Bar (assembly 1990-96), Chgo. Bar Assn. (sec. 1977-79), Bar Assn. 7th Cir., Intellectual Property Law Assn. Chgo., Patent Law Assn. Chgo. (pres. 1974), The Law Club, Skokie (Ill.) Country Club, Union League Club. Home: 505 N Lake Shore Dr Chicago IL 60611-3427 Business E-Mail: jrsweeney@btlaw.com.

**SWEENEY, JOHN E.,** congressman; b. Troy, NY, Aug. 9, 1955; m. Gayle Ford; 3 children. AA in Liberal Arts, Hudson Valley CC, 1978; BA in Polit. Sci. and Criminal Justice, Russell Sage Coll., 1981, JD, Western New Eng. Sch. Law, 1991. Bar: NY 1991. Dir. Rensselaer County Stop-DWI prog., Troy; ptnr. Cholakis, Sweeney and Wollowitz, Troy, 1991—95; exec. dir., chief counsel NY State Rep. Party, 1992—94; commr. labor State of NY, Albany, 1995-97, dep. chief of staff to Gov. George Pataki, 1997—98; mem. US Congress from 20th NY dist., 1999—, mem. Rep. steering com., mem. appropriations com., vice chmn. transp., treasury and housing and urban devel. appropriations subcommittee. Recipient President's award, Mental Health Assn. NY State, Inc., 2002, Friend of Farm Bur. award, NY Farm Bur., 2004, Guardian award, Partnership for Drug-Free Am., 2004. Republican. Roman Catholic. Office: Us Ho Reps 416 Cannon Ho Office Bldg Washington DC 20515-3220 Office Phone: 202-225-5614.*

**SWEENEY, JOHN FRANCIS,** lawyer; b. Washington, Nov. 26, 1946; s. Albert Eugene and Mildred (Mattimore) S.; m. Noreen Castelli, Aug. 9, 1969; children: Matthew John, Laura Marie. BS in Math., Carnegie-Mellon U., 1968; JD, Georgetown U., 1973. Bar: NY 1974, U.S. Supreme Ct. 1980, U.S. Ct. Appeals (fed. cir.) 1982, U.S. Ct. Appeals (2d cir.) 1975, U.S. Ct. Appeals (3d cir.) 1981, U.S. Dist. Ct. (So. dist.) NY 1975, U.S. Dist. Ct. (Ea. dist.) N.Y. 1984. Mathematician U.S. Army Strategy and Tactics Analysis Group, Bethesda, Md., 1968-70; computer analyst U.S. Army Computer Sys. Support and Evaln Command, Arlington, Va., 1970-73; assoc. Morgan & Finnegan and predecessor firm Morgan Finnegan Pine Foley & Lee, N.Y.C., 1973-81, ptnr., 1981—, mem. exec. com., 1983—. Author: (poems) Rhymes, 1984. Mem. ABA, Assn. of Bar of City of N.Y. (mem. patent com. 1983—), NY Patent, Trademark and Copyright Law Assn., Head of the Bay Club (Huntington Bay, N.Y.), New York Intellectual Property Law Assn. (pres. 2000-2001). Democrat. Roman Catholic. Home: Tulipwood Lloyd Ln Lloyd Harbor NY 11743 Office: Morgan & Finnegan 3 World Fin Ctr New York NY 10281-2101 Office Phone: 212-415-8525. Office Fax: 212-415-8701. E-mail: jfsweeney@morganfinnegan.com.

**SWEENEY, JOHN JOSEPH,** labor union administrator; b. Bronx, NY, Feb. 5, 1934; m. Maureen Sweeney; children: John, Patricia. Degree in Econs., Iona Coll. Rsch. asst. Internat. Ladies' Garment Workers; v.p., chair exec. coun. com. on health care Am. Fedn. Labor and Indsl. Orgns.; contract dir., NYC Local 32B Svc. Employees Internat. Union, 1960, pres., 1980; v.p. AFL-CIO, 1980—95, pres., 1995—. Author: America Needs A Raise:

Fighting for Economic Security and Social Justice, 1996; co-author: Solutions for the New Work Force, 1989; co-editor: Family & Work: Bridging the Gap, 1987. Mem.: Democratic Socialists of Am. Office: Am Fedn Labor & Indsl Orgns 815 16th St NW Washington DC 20006-4104*

**SWEENEY, LEO JOSEPH,** university administrator; b. Jan. 7, 1927; BA, U. Mo., Kansas City, 1951. Dir. admissions and registrar U. Mo., Kansas City, 1957-89, asst. vice chancellor, 1989-92, cons., 1992-99. Home: 9727 Aberdeen Dr Shawnee Mission KS 66206-2148 Office Phone: 816-236-1017. Business E-mail: sweeneyl@umbe.edu.

**SWEENEY, MARGARET MARY,** federal judge; b. 1955; BA in History, Coll. Notre Dame, Md., 1977; JD, Del. Law Sch., 1981. Bar: Supreme Ct. Pa., DC Ct. Appeals. Master Del. Family Ct., 1981—83; atty. Fedorko, Gilbert, & Lanctot, 1983—85; law clk. to Hon. Loren A. Smith US Ct. Fed. Claims, 1985—87; trial atty. gen. litigation sect., environ. and nat. resources divsn. US Dept. Justice, 1987—99, atty. adv. office intelligence policy and rev.; spl. master US Ct. Fed. Claims, 2003—05, judge, 2005—. Mem.: US Ct. Fed. Claims Bar Assn. (mem. bd. 1990—, pres. 1999). Office: US Ct Fed Claims 717 Madison Pl NW Washington DC 20005 Office Phone: 202-219-9657.*

**SWEENEY, NEAL JAMES,** lawyer; b. Paterson, NJ, Nov. 1, 1957; s. Bernard Thomas and Mary Agnes (Keneally) S.; m. Mary Elizabeth Finocchiaro, Oct. 27, 1984; children: Daniel Fulton, Clare Kenneally, Moira Ann. BA in History and Polit Sci., Rutgers U., 1979; JD, George Washington U., 1982. Bar: Ga. 1982, US Dist. Ct. (no. dist.) Ga. 1982, US Dist. Ct. (no. dist.) Tex. 1982, US Claims Ct. 1984, US Ct. Appeals (5th cir.) 1987. Assoc. Smith, Currie & Hancock, Atlanta, 1982-87, ptnr., 1988-98; ptnr. Construction and Pub. Contracts Practice Kilpatrick Stockton LLP, Atlanta, 1998—. Co-author: Construction Business Handbook, 1985, Holding Subcontractors to Their Bids, 1986, Subcontractor Default, 1987, The New AIA Design and Construction Documents, 1988, Proving and Pricing Claims, 1995, Fifty State Construction Lien and Bond Law, 2000, Who Pays For Defective Design?, 1997, Design-Build Contracting Claims, 1999, Design-Build Contracting Handbook, 2001; editor: Construction Subcontracting, 1991, Common Sense Construction Law, 1997, Aspen Construction Law Update, 1992—; notes editor G.W.U.J. Internat. Law and Econs., 1981-82. Mem. ABA (pub. contract law sect., forum com. on constrn. industry) Atlanta Bar Assn. (bd. mem. construct law sect.), Am. Arbitration Assn. (panel of arbitrators), Water Environment Fedn. (edit. adv. bd. 1994-97), Design Build Inst. of Am. (pres. SE chpt. 2006-). Roman Catholic. Home: 120 Forrest Lake Dr NW Atlanta GA 30327 Office: Kilpatrick Stockton LLP 1100 Peachtree St NE Ste 2800 Atlanta GA 30309-4530 Office Phone: 404-815-6616. Office Fax: 404-541-3408. Business E-mail: nsweeney@kilstock.com.

**SWEENEY, PAUL W., JR.,** lawyer; BA cum laude, Univ. So. Calif., 1972; JD, Columbia Univ., 1975. Bar: D.C. 1975, Calif. 1984. White House Fellow Chief of Staff Asst. to Pres. for Intergovernmental Affairs, Washington, 1979—81; adminstrv. ptnr. & mem. mgmt. com Kirkpatrick & Lockhart Nicholson Graham LLP, L.A. Contbr. articles to profl. jours. Bd. dir. Prevent Child Abuse Am., Hollywood Wilshire YMCA, Public Counsel. Mem.: Am. Law Inst. Office: Kirkpatrick & Lockhart Nicholson Graham LLP 7th Fl 10100 Santa Monica Blvd Los Angeles CA 90067-4003 Office Phone: 310-552-5055. Office Fax: 310-552-5001. Business E-mail: psweeney@klng.com.

**SWEENEY, RICHARD JAMES,** finance professor; b. San Diego, Jan. 13, 1944; s. John Joseph and Catherine Scott (Spahr) S.; m. Joan Long, June 19, 1965; children: Robin Scott, Erin Michaela. BA, UCLA, 1965; PhD, Princeton U., 1972. Acting assoc. prof. econs. UCLA, 1968-71; asst. prof. Tex. A&M U., College Station, 1971-73; dep. dir. office of internat. monetary research U.S. Dept. Treasury, Washington, 1973-77; Charles M. Stone prof. econs. and fin. Claremont (Calif.) McKenna Coll., 1977-89, chmn. dept. econs., 1987-89; Bolton Sullivan & Thomas A. Dean chair internat. fin. Georgetown U., Washington, 1989—. Vis. assoc. prof. econs. U. Va., Charlottesville, 1975; vis. prof. bus. adminstrn. Dartmouth Coll., Hanover, N.H., 1979; vis. prof. fin. Gothenburg (Sweden) Sch. Econs., 1991—. Author: A Macro Theory with Micro Foundations, 1974, Principles of Microeconomics, Macroeconomics, 1980, Wealth Effects and Monetary Theory, 1988, Profit-Making Speculation in Foreign Exchange Markets, 1992; author, editor: Capital Control in Emerging Market Economies, 1997, Exchange-Rate Policies for Emerging Market Economies, 1999; contbr. articles to profl. jours. Fellow Woodrow Wilson Found., 1965, NSF, 1966-68. Mem. Western Econ. Assn. (editor Econ. Inquiry jour. 1984-96), Am. Econ. Assn., Am. Fin. Assn., Western Fin. Assn., Phi Beta Kappa. Independent. Avocations: writing, weightlifting, walking, aerobics. Office: McDonough Sch Bus Georgetown U Washington DC 20057-0001 Office Phone: 202-687-3742. Business E-mail: sweeneyr@georgetown.edu.

**SWEENEY, ROBERT DAVID,** retired communications engineer; b. Nashville, Aug. 28, 1921; s. John Henry and A. Letty (Bateman) Sweeney; m. Mildred Kathleen Rose, July 14, 1941 (dec. Aug. 1973); children: Robert, Mary, Barbara; m. Marie Ruby Simmons, Dec. 14, 1974; children: Rick, Alan, Robbie. Comm. Engr., Capitol Radio Engring. Inst., Washington, 1942; Elec. Engr., U.S. Mil. Acad., West Point, N.Y., 1950. Commd. U.S. Army, 1951, advanced through grades to col., 1969; comm. and electronic instr. Norwich U., Norfield, Vt., 1948-50; asst. instr. U.S. Army Mil. Acad., West Point, 1950-51; bn. comdr., asst. divsn. signal officer 1st Armored Divsn., Ft. Hood, Tex., 1951-52; commdg. officer 59th Signal Support Co., 1952-53; radio engr. Japan Signal Bn., 1953-56; signal officer 61st Anti Aircraft Artillery Groups, Milw., 1956-60; officer in charge Down Island Comm. Systems, U.S. Comm. Detachment, Taiwan, 1960-61; comm.-electronics officer 28th N.Am. Air Defense Command, Hamilton AFB, Calif., 1961-64; chief Pacific field office U.S. Army Strategic Comm. Command, Okinawa, 1964-67; post signal officer The Infantry Ctr., Ft. Benning, Ga., 1967-68; dep. dir. Comm. Systems Engring. Mgmt. Agy., 1st Signal Brigade, Vietnam, 1968-69; dept. dir. comm.-electronics dept. U.S. Army Infantry Sch., Ft. Benning, 1969-73; congl. aide-dist. rep. Congressman 3rd Dist. Ga., Washington, 1974-83; ret. Counselor Boy Scouts Am., Ft. Riley, Kans., 1950—. Decorated Legion of Merit with oak leaf cross, Bronze Star with 3 oak leaf crosses, Air Medal, Purple Heart. Mem.: Armed Forces Comm.-Elec. Assn. (charter mem. 1968, Merit award), Assn. Elec. Engrs., Odd Fellows, Fraternal Order Eagles. Democrat. Baptist. Avocations: amateur radio, chess, football, baseball, tennis. Home: 4828 Allegheny Dr Columbus GA 31907-1734 Personal E-mail: sweeneyrd@hotmail.com.

**SWEENEY, SARINA MARIE,** psychologist, consultant; b. Chester, Pa., Nov. 20, 1978; d. William T. and Catherine M. Sweeney. BS, St. Joseph's U., Phila., 1997—2001; MA in Counseling Psychology, Immaculata U., 2004. Cert. sch. psychologist Pa., 2004. Therapeutic support staff Pvt., West Chester, Pa., 1999—2003; behavior specialist cons. Chester County Intermediate Unit, Downingtown, Pa., sch. psychologist, 2004—. Mem.: APA, Nat. Assn. Sch. Psychologists, Chi Sigma Iota. Office: Chester County Intermediate Unit 455 East Boot Rd Downingtown PA 19335 Office Phone: 484-237-5035.

**SWEENEY, SPENCER,** artist; BA, Pa. Acad. Fine Arts, Phila., 1993—97. Exhibitions include Free Coke, Greene Naftali Gallery, NYC, 1999, Legal Paper Work, Beyond Baroque, 2000, Paintings, Gavin Brown's Enterprise, 2002, Today's Man, John Connely, NY, 2003, Subway Series, Bronx Mus. Arts, NY, 2004, Modern Inst., Glasgow, Eng., 2005, Whitney Biennial: Day for Night, Whitney Mus. Am. Art, NY, 2006. Recipient Lewis S. Ware Meml. prize for exptl. work, Jimmy C. Leuders painting prize, Angelo Pinto Meml. prize exptl. work, Cuff/Sammack prize for abstract art; scholar Lucile Sorgenti scholar artistic excellence. Mailing: c/o Gavin Brown Enterprise 620 Greenwich St New York NY 10014*

**SWEENEY, THOMAS FREDERICK,** lawyer; b. Detroit, Feb. 10, 1943; s. Harold Eugene and Marion Genevieve (Lunz) S.; m. Susan Carol Horn, Dec. 27, 1968; children: Sarah Elizabeth, Neal Thomas. AB, U. Mich., 1965, JD, 1968. Bar: Mich. 1968, U.S. Dist. Ct. (ea. dist.) Mich, 1968, U.S. Tax Ct. 1979, U.S. Supreme Ct. 1985. Assoc. Fischer, Franklin, Ford, Simon & Hogg, Detroit, 1969—73, ptnr., 1974—85, Houghton, Potter, Sweeney & Brenner, Detroit, 1986—95; mem. Clark Hill, Birmingham, Mich., 1995—, mem. exec. com., 1999—2002. Spkr. Inst. CLE; guest lectr. U. Mich. Law Sch., 2001-03. Contbr. articles to legal jours. Mem. Birmingham (Mich.) Charter Rev. Commn., 1977; bd. dirs. Cmty. House Assn., 1990—98, pres., 1993—95; trustee Baldwin Pub. Library, Birmingham, 1981—, pres., 2001—03. Fellow Mich. State Bar Found.; mem. ABA, Oakland County Bar Assn. (chmn. taxation com. 1988-89), Forest Hills Swim Club (pres. 1985-87). Roman Catholic. Home: 1493 Buckingham Ave Birmingham MI 48009-5866 Office: Clark Hill 255 S Old Woodward Ave Ste 301 Birmingham MI 48009-6182 E-mail: tsweeney@clarkhill.com.

**SWEENEY, THOMAS JOSEPH, JR.,** lawyer; b. NYC, Oct. 29, 1923; s. Thomas Joseph and Johanna M. (Flynn) S.; m. Robin Virginia Thwaites, May 30, 1947; children: Thomas Joseph, III, Deidre Ann. BA, N.Y. U., 1947; JD, Columbia U., 1949. Bar: N.Y. 1949. Assoc. in law Columbia U. Law Sch. 1949-50; assoc. Cravath, Swaine & Moore, N.Y.C., 1950-62; with Morgan Guaranty Trust Co. N.Y., 1962-89, v.p., 1965-76, sr. v.p., tr. trust officer, 1976-89, chmn. instl. trust and investment com., 1989-99; ptnr. Decker, Hubbard, Welden & Sweeney, N.Y.C. Bd. dirs. W.R. Kenan Fund. Trustee Pinkerton Found., Jean and Louis Dreyfus Found. 2d lt. USAAF, 1943-45. Mem. N.Y. State Bar Assn. Democrat. Roman Catholic. Home: 525 Teaneck Rd Ridgefield Park NJ 07660-1100 Office: Decker Hubbard Welden & Sweeney 420 Lexington Ave New York NY 10170

**SWEENEY, TIMOTHY C.,** lawyer; b. Madison, Wis., Mar. 28, 1948; s. Raymond Patrick and Marian Elizabeth (Murphy) S.; m. Ann Elizabeth Jimieson, Aug. 30, 1969; children: Colleen, Patrick, Kathleen. BA in Econs., U. Notre Dame, 1970; JD, U. S.D., 1975. Bar: Wis. 1975, S.D. 1975, U.S. Dist. Ct. (we. dist.) Wis. 1975. Tchr., coach St. Francis (S.D.) Indian Sch., 1970-72; assoc. Walsh & Walsh, Madison, 1975-78; shareholder Walsh, Walsh, Sweeney & Whitney, S.C., Madison, 1978-86; ptnr. Foley & Lardner, Madison, 1986-94; pres. Sweeney & Sweeney, S.C., Madison, 1994—. Officer Wilderness Hotel & Resort, Inc., Wisconsin Dells, Wis., 1994. First chmn., trustee Edgewood H.S., Madison, 1985—; founding bd. dirs. Blessed Sacrament Athletic Assn., Madison, Dane County Sports Medicine Coun., Madison. Recipient svc. award Edgewood H.S., 1997. Mem. ABA, S.D. Bar Assn., Wis. Bar Assn., Dane County Bar Assn. (exec. com.). Avocations: golf, athletics, travel. Office: 440 Science Dr Madison WI 53711-1088 Fax: 608-238-8262.

**SWEENEY, STEPHEN JUDE,** academic administrator; b. N.Y.C., Sept. 15, 1943; s. Herbert Vincent and Isabel Mary (Dolan) S.; m. Barbara Mary Stasz, Aug. 7, 1976. BA in Spanish, Cath. U., 1966; MA in Theology, Manhattan Coll., 1971, MA in Counseling Psychology, 1976; PhD, NYU, 1991. Prin. Incarnation Elem. and Jr. High Sch., N.Y.C., 1969-73; dir. campus ministry Manhattan Coll., N.Y.C., 1973-76; asst. to provost Coll. of New Rochelle, N.Y., 1976-78, mem. edn. dept. N.Y., 1976—, exec. asst. to pres. N.Y., 1978-80, v.p. for planning N.Y., 1980-81, sr. v.p. N.Y., 1981-97, pres., 1997—. Bd. trustees exec. com., com. on fin. and adminstrn. Commn. Ind. Colls. and Univs.; bd. trustees, chmn. acad. affairs com., chmn., student affairs com. Coll. St. Elizabeth; bd. trustees strategic planning com., mem. com. LaSalle Acad., Network of Sacred Heart Schs.; membership com. Network of Sacred Heart Schs.; bd. dirs. Neylan Commn. Colls. and Univs., Cardinal McCloskey Svcs., Women's Coll. Coalition. Mem.: Soc. Friendly Sons St. Patrick (N.Y.C.), Soc. Friendly Sons of St. Patrick (Westchester), Sovereign Mil. Order of Malta (med. com.), Knights of the Holy Sepulchre. Roman Catholic. Office: The College of New Rochelle 29 Castle Pl New Rochelle NY 10805-2338

**SWEET, ALEC STONE,** law educator; BA, Western Washington U., 1982; MA, Johns Hopkins, 1984; PhD in Polit. Sci., U. Washington, 1990. Asst. prof. Middlebury Coll., 1990—91; U. Calif., Irvine, 1992—94, assoc. prof., 1994—97, prof., 1997—2002; Jean Monnet fellow Schuman Ctr., European U. Inst., Florence, Italy, 1996—97, 1998—99; Jean Monnet chair Inst. of Polit. Studies, Paris, 2001; official fellow, chair comparative govt. Nuffield Coll., Oxford, England, 1998—2004; Leitner prof. of law, politics, and internat. studies Yale U., New Haven, 2004—. Author: The Birth of Judicial Politics in France, 1992, Governing with Judges, 2000, The Judicial Construction of Europe, 2004; co-author: European Integration and Supranational Governance, 1998, The European Court and the National Courts, 1998, The Institutionalization of Europe, 2001, On Law, Politics, and Judicialization, 2002; contbr. articles to law jours. Office: Yale Law Sch PO Box 208215 New Haven CT 06520 E-mail: as657@pantheon.yale.edu.

**SWEET, DENNIS C., III,** lawyer; b. Jackson, Miss., 1955; married; 3 children. BS, Tougaloo Coll., 1977; JD, George Washington U. Nat. Law Ctr., 1980. Bar: DC 1981, Ala. 1984, US Supreme Ct. 1985, Miss. 1986. Former staff atty. Pub. Defender's Office, Washington; So. Poverty Law Ctr., Montgomery, Ala., 1984—86; del. Fifth Circuit Judicial Conf., 1987; mem. Miss. Ho. Reg., 1992—96; ptnr. Sweet & Freese, PLLC, Jackson, Miss., 2003—. Tchg. mem. Intro. Trial Advocacy, Harvard Law Sch., 1983—96. Named one of Am. Top Black Lawyers, Black Enterprise Mag., 2003. Mem.: Assn. Trial Lawyers Assn., Miss. Trial Lawyers Assn., DC Bar, Ala. State Bar, Miss. Bar (mem. bd. commrs. 1990—93), Hinds County Bar Assn., Magnolia County Bar Assn. Avocations: auto racing, fishing, horseback riding, basketball. Office: Sweet & Freese PLLC 200 S Lamar St Ste 410 N Tower Jackson MS 39207: PO Box 1178 Jackson MS 39215 Office Phone: 601-965-8700.

**SWEET, HARVEY,** set designer, lighting designer; b. Detroit, Oct. 27, 1943; s. Sam and Rose Sweet; m. Susan Perrett, Mar. 16, 1964 (div. Mar. 1975); children: Deborah Anne, Rebecca Lynn, Jason Aaron; m. Patricia Ravn, Sept. 9, 1978 (div. July 1987). BS, Ea. Mich. U., 1965; MS, U. Wis., 1967, PhD, 1974. Instr. U. N.D., Grand Forks, 1967-69; asst. prof. Boise (Idaho) State Coll., 1972-73; instr. U. Wis., Madison, 1973-74; prof. of theater arts U. No. Iowa, Cedar Falls, 1974-89; dir. lighting Landmark Entertainment Group, L.A. and Tokyo, 1989-91; cons. Advanced Tech., Tokyo, 1991; tech. writer Walt Disney Imagineering, Glendale, Calif., 1992; project mgr., sr. designer, sr. estimator, tech. writer Tru Roll, Inc., Glendale, Calif., 1993-99; project mgr. estimator tech. sales LVH Entertainment Sys., Oxnard, Calif., 1999—2002, mgr. theatrical rigging divsn., 2002—03, v.p. rigging systems, 2003—04, v.p. installation sys. and sales, 2004—05; v.p. sales L.A. Propoint, 2005—. Owner, operator Sweet Studios Theatrical Equipment, Cedar Falls, 1981-89; dir. theater tech. and design U. No. Iowa, 1974-87; mem. tech. stds. working group Entertainment Svcs and Tech. Assn., 2002-2004, mem. rigging cert. working group, 2002-2004, chair fire safety curtain task group, 2004—; mem.fire safety curtain stds. task group; chair El.22 Fire Safety Curtain Stds. Task Group, El.6-Powered Rigging Stds. Task Group. Author: Graphics for the Performing Arts, 1982, Handbook of Scenery, Properties and Lighting I and II, 1988, 2nd edit., 1995, The Complete Book of Drawing for the Theatre, 1995; scenic designer Summer Spl. Repretory Theatre, 1988, Timberlake Playhouse, 1988-89; lighting designer, scenic designer, tech. dir. various coll. theatrical prodns., 1964-89; themed lighting designer Sanrio Puroland, Tokyo, 1989, exec. dir. lighting, 1990. Mem. U.S. Inst. for Theatre Tech. (vice commr. 1979-81, commr. 1981-87, mem. graphic stds. bd. 1979-86, edn. commn. 1983-88, mem. publs. com. 1986-89, bd. dirs. 1989). Avocations: travel, cooking. Office: LA Propoint 9051 Sunland Blvd Sun Valley CA 91352 Office Phone: 818-767-6800, 818-767-6800.

**SWEET, JAMES M.,** lawyer; b. Mpls., Apr. 23, 1945; BA, Wheaton Coll., 1967; JD, Coll. William & Mary, 1973. Bar: Pa. 1973. Joined Drinker Biddle & Reath LLP, Phila., 1973, chmn., litig. dept., 1997—2000, chmn., CEO, mgmt. com., 2000—05, ptnr., insurance, pharm., medical device litig. practice areas. Founder, chmn. bd. Cornerstone Christian Acad. Officer USN. Fellow:

Salzburg Seminar, Austria. Office: Drinker Biddle & Reath One Logan Sq 18th & Cherry Sts Philadelphia PA 19103-6996 Office Phone: 215-988-2936. Office Fax: 215-988-2757. Business E-mail: james.sweet@dbr.com.

**SWEET, MARGARET ANN,** psychologist, educator; b. Lansing, Mich., Apr. 25, 1948; d. Roger Edward and Anna Goodsy Sweet. BA, Mich. State U., East Lansing, 1975, MA, 1983. Cert. psychoanalyst Mich. Psychoanalytic Coun., lic. profl. counselor, ltd. lic. psychologist. Therapist, cons. Comty. Mental Health, Lansing, 1984—92; therapist Family Mental Health, Lansing, 1992—94; pvt. practice clinician in psychotherapy, psychoanalysis East Lansing, 1995—; instr. psychology Lansing C.C., 1997—. Supporting mem. Internat. Ctr. for Study of Psychiatry and Psychology, N.Y.C., 2002—; invited participant Oxford Round Table, Oxford U., England, 2005; supr. undergrad. practicum in devel. psychology Lansing C.C., 1998—; guest lectr. Mich. State U., 2003—. Mem.: Mich. Psychoanalytic Coun. (cons. 2000, tng. analyst 2000—). Democrat. Avocations: backpacking, hiking, camping, gardening, nature conservation. Home: 812 W Mount Hope Ave Lansing MI 48901 Office: Lansing C C Social Sci PO Box 40010 Lansing MI 48901-7210

**SWEET, ROBERT WORKMAN,** federal judge; b. Yonkers, N.Y., Oct. 15, 1922; s. James Allen and Delia (Workman) S.; m. Adele Hall, May 12, 1973; children by previous marriage— Robert, Deborah, Ames, Eliza. BA, Yale U., 1944, LL.B., 1948. Bar: N.Y. 1949. Asso. firm Simpson, Thacher & Bartlett, 1948-53; asst. U.S. atty. So. Dist. N.Y., 1953-55; asso. firm Casey, Lane & Mittendorf, 1955-65, partner, 1957-65; counsel Interdepartmental Task Force on Youth and Juvenile Delinquency, 1958-78; dep. mayor City of N.Y., 1966-69; partner firm Skadden, Arps, Slate, Meagher & Flom, N.Y.C., 1970-77; mem. hearing office N.Y.C. Transit Authority, 1975-77; judge U.S. Dist. Ct. (So. Dist.) N.Y, 1978—, now sr. judge NY. Participant USIA Rule of Law Program in Albania, 1991; observer Albanian elections, 1992. Pres. Community Service Soc., 1961-78; trustee Sch. Mgmt. Urban Policy, 1970—; Taft Sch.; vestryman St. Georges Epis. Ch., 1958-63. Served to lt. (j.g.) USNR, 1943-46. Recipient Alumni citation of merit Taft Sch., 1985, various other awards, citations for service as dep't mayor N.Y.C. Mem. ABA, Assn. of Bar of City of N.Y., N.Y. Law Inst., N.Y. County Lawyers Assn., State Bar Assn., Am. Legion (comdr. Willard Straight Post) Clubs: Quaker Hill Country, Century Assn., Merchants, Indian Harbor Yacht, Mid City Rep. Office: US Courthouse 500 Pearl St Rm 1920 New York NY 10007-1316

**SWEET, VICTORIA,** medical educator, physician; BS in Math., Stanford U., 1971; MD, U. Calif., Irvine, 1977; PhD, U. Calif., San Francisco, 2003. Assoc. clin. prof. U. Calif., San Francisco, 1970—. Attending physician Laguna Honea Hosp., San Francisco, 1990—, San Francisco Gen. Hosp., San Francisco, 2005—. Author: Rooted in the Earth, Rooted in the Sky, 2006. Mem.: Am. Assn. History of Medicine. Office: Univ Calif 1947 Alameda De Las Pulgas Redwood City CA 94061-3211

**SWEETLAND, LORAINE FERN,** librarian, educator; b. Morristown Corners, Vt., Aug. 13, 1933; d. William Eric and Sibyl Bedina (Bailey) Bloomfield; m. Ronald David Sweetland, July 1, 1950; children: Kathy L. (dec.), Dale J. Bettis. BS in Elem. Edn., Columbia Union Coll., Takoma Pk., Md., 1968; MS in LS, Syracuse U., N.Y., 1973. Tchr. 1st and 2d grade Beltsville (Md.) Seventh-day Adventist Sch., 1960-67; asst. libr., cataloger Vt. Tech. Coll., Randolph Ctr., 1968-69; middle sch. libr. Barre (Vt.) City Schs., 1970-74; tchg. prin. Cen. Vt. Seventh-day Adventist Sch., Barre, 1974-76, Brooklawn Seventh-day Adventist Sch., Bridgeport, Conn., 1976-81; med. libr. Washington Adventist Hosp., Takoma Park, Md., 1981-85; dir. libr. svcs. Seventh-day Adventists World Hdqs., Silver Spring, Md., 1985-95. Med. libr. cons., Balt., 1983-95; pres. Oasis, 1993-94; tchr. Home Study Internat., Silver Spring, Md., 1995-98, IPS-Info. Problem Solvers, Crossville, Tenn., 1998-99. Book reviewer Libr. Jour., 1990-98. Trustee Randolph (Vt.) Pub. Library, 1970-71; sec. Nat. Area Hosp. Council, Washington, 1985; treas. Plateau Food Buying Club, 1999-2004. Mem. Laurel Rotary Club (bull. editor 1990-94). Republican. Avocations: gardening, computers.

**SWEETMAN, KIMBERLY BURKE,** librarian, consultant; b. Framingham, Mass., May 17, 1970; m. Peter Sweetman, May 14, 2003. BA in Film Studies, U. Mass., Amherst, 1992; MA, Emory U., Atlanta, Ga., 1994; MLS, Cath. U. Am., Washington, DC, 1995. Head Interlibrary Loan NYU Librs., NYC, 1998—2001, head Access Svcs. dept., 2001—. Cons. in field. Co-author: Access Services in ARL Libraries (SPEC Kit), 2005; author: Managing Student Assistants: A How to Do it Manual for Librarians, 2006. Mem.: ALA, Assn. Coll. and Rsch. Librs. (mem. rsch. com. 2004—). Office: Bobst Library 70 Washington Square South New York NY 10012 Office Phone: 212-998-2532.

**SWEETSER, SUSAN W.,** lawyer, advocate, retired state legislator; b. Dec. 13, 1958; d. Robert Joseph and Lucretia Rose (Donnelly) Williams. BA in Polit. Sci./Environ. Admin. with high honors, Johnson (Vt.) State Coll., 1982; JD magna cum laude, Vt. Law Sch., 1985; MBA, U. Pa., 2002. Bar: N.Y. 1986, Vt. 1986, U.S. Dist. Ct. Vt. 1989; CLU, ChFC, CFP. Confidential law clk. Appellate div. N.Y. Supreme Ct., Albany, 1985-86; assoc. Gravel & Shea, Burlington, Vt., 1986-90; atty. Nat. Life Ins. Co., Montpelier, Vt., 1990—2002; mem. Vt. State Senate, 1992-96; 2nd v.p. women's markets MassMutual Fin. Group, Springfield, Mass. Victims rights adv. Essex Junction, Vt., 1980—; adj. prof. bus. law St. Michael's Coll., Winooski, Vt., 1991—, Johnson State Coll., 1995-97; justice of peace Town of Essex, 1991-95; chair judiciary com., 1994-96; mem. Health and Welfare Com.; former mem. Appropriations Com.; mem. Housing and Conservation Trust Fund Study Com., Civil Rights Study Com., Adoption Law Reform Study Com. Author articles on victims rights. Trustee Vt. State Colls., Waterbury, 1979-81, Univ. Health Ctr., 1992-94, bd. dirs.; mem. ethics com. Fanny Allen Hosp., Winooski, Vt., 1989-92; v.p. Lyric Theatre, Burlington, 1989-95; mem. Vt. Rep. State Com., Montpelier, chmn. Rep. State Conv., 1988, 92, 96; founder, pres. Survivors of Crime, Inc. Recipient Achievement award Vt. Law Enforcement Coordinating Com., 1990, Vt. Ctr. for Prevention and Treatment of Sexual Abuse and The Safer Soc. Program, 1991, Nat. recognition for victims rights work The Giraffe Project, 1991, award Nat. Found. for Improvement of Justice, 1993; named 754th Point of Light by former Pres. George Bush, 1992, Am. Heroine Ladies Home Jour., 1991, Legislator of Yr. Nat. Rep. Legislators Assn., 1995, Working Mother Mag. Working Mother of Yr., 1998. Fellow AAUW, Life Mgmt. Inst.; mem. Vt. Bar Assn., N.Y. State Bar Assn., Internat. Assn. Fin. Planners (chmn. legis. affairs Greater Vt. chpt. 1988-91). Roman Catholic. Avocations: skiing, flower gardening, running, camping, horseback riding. Office: 15 Cindy Ln Essex Junction VT 05452-3307

**SWEEZY, CAROLINE,** mathematician, educator; d. Alan Richardson and Susan Shepherd Sweezy. BS, UCLA, 1980, MS, 1982, PhD, 1986. Instr. UCLA, 1986; asst. prof. N.Mex. State U., Las Cruces, 1986—96, assoc. prof., 1997—, chmn. undergrad. math. majors com., 1997—. Vis. rsch. assoc. U. Vt., Burlington, Vt., 2001. Mem.: Math. Assn. Am., Am. Math. Soc. Office: New Mexico State University Box 30001 3MB Las Cruces NM 88003

**SWEEZY, JOHN WILLIAM,** political party official; b. Indpls., Nov. 14, 1932; s. William Charles and Zuma Frances (McNew) S.; BS in Mech. Engring., Purdue U., 1956; MBA, Ind. U., 1958; student Butler U., 1953-54, U. Ga., 1954-55, Ind. Cen. Coll., 1959; m. Carole Suzanne Harman, July 14, 1956; children: John William, Bradley E. Design, test engr. Allison div. GM, Indpls., 1953-57; power sales engr. Indpls. Power & Light Co., 1958-69; dir. pub. works City of Indpls., 1970-72; chmn. Marion County Rep. Cen. Com., 1972—; bd. dirs. Lorco Engring., Indpls., Indpls. Industrial Products, Acme Screw & Mfg., Inc., Telnet, Inc., Landmarks Ltd., Innovative Investment Co. Bd. dirs. Indpls. Humane Soc.; chmn. 11th Dist. Rep. Com., 1970, 73—; chmn. Nat. Assn. Urban Rep. County Chmn.; alt. del. Rep. Nat. Conv., 1968, del., 1972, 76, 80, 84, 88, 92, 96, del., mem. credentials com., 1984, 88; mem. credentials com., 1980, spkr. presenter, 1996; mem. Rep. Nat. Com., 1984—, exec. com., 1984—; mem. Warren Schs. Citizens Screening Com., 1958-72; bd. dirs. Warren Devel. Com. With AUS, 1953-55. Mem. AMA, Mensa, Sigma Iota Epsilon. Home: 2089 S German Church Rd Indianapolis IN 46239-9620

**SWENDIMAN, ALAN ROBERT,** lawyer; b. Arlington, Va., Apr. 5, 1947; s. Robert Charles and Jessie (Birse) S.; m. Kathleen Shea, Oct. 8, 1977; children: Shelley Christine, Robert Alan. AB in Polit. Sci., U. N.C., 1969; JD, Georgetown U., 1973. Bar: Md. 1973, D.C. 1974, U.S. Dist. Ct. D.C. 1974, U.S. Dist. Ct. Md. 1974, U.S. Ct. Appeals (D.C. cir.) 1974, U.S. Ct. Appeals (4th cir.) 1974, U.S. Supreme Ct. 1980. Law clk. to chief judge US Dist. Ct. Md., 1973-74; ptnr. Jackson & Campbell, Washington, 1974—92, 1993—2005, mng. ptnr., 1989-90; gen. counsel Fed. Labor Rels. Authority, Washington, 1992-93, Gen. Services Adminstrn., Washington, 2005—. Edn. appeal bd. US Dept. Edn., 1982—90; gen. counsel Legal Svcs. Corp., Washington, 1983—84; adj. prof. George Mason Law Sch., 1988—91; mem. White House Presdl. Personnel, 1989. Gen. counsel Nat. Capital Cmty. Found.; past chmn. bd. Columbia Lighthouse for the Blind; bd. dirs. Jr. Achievement, Leadership Greater Washington, Providence Hosp. Found.; trustee Goodwill of Greater Washington. Mem. DC Bar Assn., Md. Bar Assn., Montgomery County Bar Assn., Jud. Conf. DC Cir., Greater Washington Bd. Trade, U. NC Alumni Assn., Barristers Club, Counsellors Club DC, Rotary, Phi Beta Kappa, Phi Eta Sigma. Office: Gen Svcs Adminstrn Office Gen Counsel 1800 F St NW Ste 4140 Washington DC 20405 Office Phone: 202-501-2200. Business E-Mail: alan.swendiman@gsa.gov.

**SWENSEN, CLIFFORD HENRIK, JR.,** psychologist, educator; b. Welch, W.Va., Nov. 25, 1926; s. Clifford Henrik and Cora Edith (Clovis) S.; m. Doris Ann Gaines, June 6, 1948; children— Betsy, Susan, Lisa, Timothy, Barbara BS, U. Pitts., 1949, MS, 1950, PhD, 1952. Diplomate Am. Bd. Profl. Psychology. Instr. U. Pitts., 1951-52; clin. psychologist VA, 1952-54; from asst. prof. to assoc. prof. U. Tenn., Knoxville, 1954-62; assoc. prof. psychology Purdue U., West Lafayette, Ind., 1962-65, prof., 1965—, dir. clin. tng., 1975-85; vice chair U. Senate, 1994-95. Vis. prof. U. Fla., 1968-69, U. Bergen, Norway, 1976-77, 83-84; cons. VA, 1981 White House Conf. on Aging, others; Am. Psychol. Assn.-NSF Disting. Sci. lectr., 1968-69; Fulbright-Hays lectr., Norway, 1976-77 Author: An Approach to Case Conceptualization, 1968; Introduction to Interpersonal Relations, 1973; contbr. chpts. to books, articles to profl. jours. Mem. Ind. Gov.'s Task Force Alzheimer's Disease and Related Senile Dementia, 1998—. Served with USN, 1944-46 Recipient Gordon A. Barrows Meml. award for disting. contributions to psychology, 1990; named to Hall of Fame, Brentwood Pa. H.S., 2001. Fellow APA (pres divsn. cons. psychology 1976-77, Presdl. citation 1999, Cert. achievement 2000), Am. Psychol. Soc., Soc. Personality Assessment, Am. Assn. Applied and Preventive Psychology, Acad. of Clin. Psychology; mem. Midwestern Psychol. Assn., Southeastern Psychol. Assn., Ind. Psychol. Assn., Gerontol. Soc., Sigma Xi, Psi Chi. Republican. Mem. Ch. of Christ Home: 1700 Lindberg Rd # 229 West Lafayette IN 47906 Office: Purdue U Dept Psychol Scis West Lafayette IN 47907 Office Phone: 765-494-6977. E-mail: cswensen@psych.purdue.edu.

**SWENSEN, COLE,** poet, educator; BA, MA, San Francisco State U.; PhD in Comparative Lit., U. Calif., Santa Cruz. Dir. creative writing prog. U. Denver; assoc. prof. U. Iowa Writers' Workshop. Author: It's Alive, She Says, New Math, 1988 (Nat. Poetry Series winner), Park, 1991, Numen, 1995, Noon, 1997 (New Am. Poetry Series Award), Try, 1999, Oh, 2000 (Iowa Poetry Prize), Such Rich Hour, 2001, Goest, 2004 (Nat. Book Award finalist, 2004); contbg. editor American Letters and Commentary, Shiny, translation editor How2. Office: Grad Prog Creative Writing U Iowa 102 Dey House Iowa City IA 52242-1408 Office Phone: 319-335-0416.

**SWENSEN, DAVID FREDERICK,** investment advisor; b. River Falls, Wis., Jan. 26, 1954; s. Richard David and Grace Marie (Hartman) Swensen; m. Susan Candler Foster, June 26, 1982 (div.); 3 children. BA, BS, U. Wis., 1975; MA, Yale U., 1976, M in Philosophy, 1978, PhD, 1980. Assoc. Salomon Bros., NYC, 1979-82; sr. v.p. Shearson Lehman, NYC, 1982-85; chief investment officer Yale U., New Haven, 1985—, adj. prof. investment strategy, lectr. ecess., 1985—. Bd. dirs. Endowment Advisors, Inc., Endowment Realty Investors Inc.; trustee Carnegie Inst. of Wash., 1991—; bd. mem., treas. Hopkins Sch. Com. of Trustees Inc., 1998—; mem. Yale New Haven Hosp. Investment Com., 2000—; com. mem. Courtauld Inst. Art Investment Com., 2002—; trustee Brookings Inst., 2004. Author: Pioneering Portfolio Management: An Unconventional Approach to Institutional Investment, 2000, Unconventional Success: A Fundamental Approach to Personal Investment, 2005. Fellow: Berkeley Coll.; mem.: Tchrs. Insurance and Annuity Assn. (trustee 2003—), Am. Fin. Assn., Am. Econ. Assn., Elizabethan Club (trustee 1991). Avocations: squash, tennis, skiing, bicycling. E-mail: swen@invsmtp.invest.yale.edu.

**SWENSON, ADA PEREZ,** artist; m. Roy Swenson, Oct. 30, 1994; children: Miguel Weissman, Wendy Robin Weissman. Student, Stony Brook U., 1965—66, Indian River C.C., 2002—05, Art Student League, 1951—54; studied with, Richard Cardoff, 1965—68, John Seerey Lester, 2004. One-woman shows include Bahia Redonda Resort and Marina, Venezuela, 1999, Port de Plaisance, St. Maarten, Netherlands, 1999, Harbor Village, Bonaire, Netherlands, 1999, Vero Beach Main Libr., Fla., 2002—06, Count Down Studio, N.Y.C., 2000—05, 2006, Everglades Nat. Park Mus., Homestead, Fla., 2005, exhibitions include Vero Beach Mus., Vero Beach Main Libr., 2001—04, 2005, Meghan Candler Gallery, Vero Beach, 2004, 2005, 2006, Arte Direct Galley, Naples, Fla., 2004—05, 2006, Everglades Nat. Park Visitors Ctr. Mus., 2005—06. Represented in permanent collections U. Fla. Rsch. Ctr., Ft. Pierce, S.C. State Park, Dillon, Littman Jewelers, Bonaire, Count Down Studio, Everglades Nat. Park; art coord. Indian River Main Libr., Vero Beach, 2006. Recipient Scholastic Art award Pratt II, 1948, awards, Art Duokun Mus., Ft. Pierce, 2002, Ctr. for the Arts, Vero Beach, 2002, Everglades Nat. Park, 2004. Mem.: Vero Beach Art Club, Nat. Acad. Profl. Plein Air Painters, Am. Impressionist Soc., Plein Air Painters of East Coast, Fla. Watercolor Soc. Home: 256 Marina Dr Fort Pierce FL 34949 Office Phone: 772-595-3158. Personal E-mail: apswenson@comcast.net.

**SWENSON, ERICK,** painter, artist; b. Phoenixville, Pa., 1972; BFA in Studio Art, Painting/Drawing, U. North Tex., 1999. Represented in permanent collections, Dallas Mus. Art, Modern Mus. Art, Fort Worth, Tex., one-man shows include Microwavable, Good/Bad Art Collective, Denton, Tex., 1996, Push to Prime, Diverse Works Art Space, Houston, 1996, Obviously a Movie, Angstrom Gallery, Dallas, 1998, Villa Stuck, Munich, Germany, 2002, UCLA Hammer Mus., 2003, James Cohan Gallery, NY, 2004, exhibited in group shows at el clumsio, Angstrom Gallery, Dallas, 1996, Mad, Good/Bad, and Dangerous to Know, Good/Bad Art Collective, Denton, Tex., 1996, Popo y Lupe, 1996, Isolation Chamber, 1996, Gay Art/Straight Play, 1997, One Person Show Featuring..., 1997, Strange Loops, 1997, Hallowmas, 1997, Wee Coma, 1997, Very Fake, but Real, Diverse Works Art Space, Houston, 1997, Welcome to Important Town, Conduit Gallery Annex, Dallas, 1998, Tex. Dialogues Parallels, Blue Star Art Gallery, San Antonio, 1998, Its a Peeece in Itself, Good/Bad Art Collective, Denton, Tex., 1998, Fire Sale 2000, Angstrom Gallery, Dallas, 1999, True Stories, Arlington Mus. Art, Tex., 1999, Natural Deceits, Fort Worth Mus. Modern Art, Tex., 2000, Out of the Ordinary: New Art From Tex., Contemporary Arts Mus., Houston, 2000, Swallow Swenson, Mus. Contemporary Art, Sydney, Australia, 2001, New Orleans Triennial, New Orleans Mus. Art, 2001, The Big Id, James Cohan Gallery, NY, 2001, Summer, 2002, Air, 2003, Erick Swenson & Ricky Swallow, Karen Lovegrove Gallery, LA, 2003, Summer Show, James Cohan Gallery, NY, 2004, Whitney Biennial, Whitney Mus. Am. Art, NY, 2004, Natural Histories: Realism Revisited, Scottsdale Mus. Contemporary Art, Ariz., 2004. Arch & Anne Giles Kimbrough Fund, Dallas Mus. Art, 1999. Mailing: c/o James Cohan Gallery 533 West 26th St New York NY 10001

**SWENSON, MARK GREGORY,** architect; b. Mpls., Nov. 29, 1949; s. Stanley S. and Linnea Marie (Anderson) S.; m. Marcy Gayle Stevenson, Apr. 6, 1974; 1 child, Gregory Peter. B in Environ. Design, U. Minn., 1971,

MArch, 1973. Registered architect, Minn., Colo., Ariz., Ohio, Fla., Ill., Iowa, La., Nev., Tex., N.J., Ga., S.D., Wis., Kans., Va. Project planner Ellerbe, Inc., Bloomington, Minn., 1972-78; prin., pres. BRW Architects, Inc., Mpls., 1978-96, also bd. dirs.; prin., pres., bd. dirs. Elness Swenson Graham Architects Inc., Mpls., 1996—. Lectr. architecture U. Minn., Mpls., 1974-82. Bd. edn. Minnehaha Acad., Mpls., 2000—04. Evans scholar, Western Golf Assn., 1968—71. Mem.: AIA (lectr. profl. devel. 1983—87, bd. dirs. Minn. chpt. 2001—, pres. Mpls. chpt. 2002, pres. elect Minn. chpt. 2005, pres. Minn. chpt. 2006), Urban Land Inst., Lambda Alpha. Home: 5501 Dever Dr Edina MN 55424-1641 Office: Elness Swenson Graham Architects Inc 500 Washington Ave S Minneapolis MN 55415-1130 Office Phone: 612-373-4625. E-mail: mark.swenson@esgarch.com.

**SWENSON, SHIRLEY RUTH,** retired elementary school educator; b. Provo, Utah, Dec. 22, 1935; d. Karl Warnick and Ruth Irene (Eldredge) S. BS, Brigham Young U., 1958, MEd, 1972. Cert. tchr. elem. edn., spl. edn., libr., Utah. Tchr. 2d grade Sevier Sch. Dist., Richfield, Utah, 1958-59, Jordan Sch. Dist., Sandy, Utah, 1959-61; tchr. 3d grade Alpine Sch. Dist., American Fork, Utah, 1963-71, resource tchr., 1971-97, team leader Barratt Elem., 1992-97; ret. Editor: Swen Swenson Descendants, 1955, Nebeker Family Book, 1979. Guide, Nauvoo (Ill.) Restoration, 1969-70; missionary LDS Ch., southern states, 1961-63. Mem. DAR, Mayflower Soc., Utah Ednl. Assn., Daus. Utah Pioneers (co. treas.) Avocations: genealogy, family history, needlecrafts.

**SWENSON, SUSIE DORIS A.,** music educator; d. Wade Francis and Dorothy Esther McDaniel; m. Richard Eric Swenson, July 24, 1976; children: Anna C. Tanner, David J. MusB, U. N.C., Greensboro, 1970; MA, Eastman Sch. Music, Rochester, N.Y., 1973; postgrad., New Eng. Conservatory Music, Boston, 1987—88. Nat. cert. tchr. music Music Tchrs. Nat. Assn. Grad. tchg. asst. Eastman Sch. Music, Rochester, 1971—72; instr. music R.I. Jr. Coll., Providence and Warwick, 1972—76, asst. prof. music Lincoln, 1976—88; chair music dept. C.C. of R.I., Providence, Warwick, Lincoln, and Newport, 1987—, assoc. prof. music Warwick, 1988—94, prof. music, 1994—. Co-min. music Evangelical Covenant Ch., Riverside, RI, 1981—87. Composer: (choral music) Blessed are They, 2004; composer, librettist: operetta Ring of Destiny, 2006. Bd. dirs., mem. The Providence Singers, Providence, 2003—06. Named Most Promising New Celtic Harpist, Scottish Highland Games, Grandfather Mountain, N.C., 2003. Mem.: R.I. Music Tchrs. Assn., Am. Choral Dirs. Assn. (chair 2-yr. coll. repertoire and stds. ea. divsn. 1997—2006), Pi Kappa Lambda, Mu Phi Epsilon. Avocations: travel, Celtic harp. Office: C C of RI 400 East Ave Warwick RI 02886

**SWENSSON, EARL SIMCOX,** architect; b. Nashville, July 28, 1930; s. Earl Ebenezer and Viola Lazelle (Simcox) Swensson; m. Suzanne Dickenson, June 6, 1953; children: Krista, Lin, Kurt. BS in Bldg. Design, Va. Poly. Inst. and State U., 1952, MArch, 1953, U. Ill., 1955. Registered 28 states. Founder, prin. Earl Swensson Assocs., Inc., Nashville, 1961—. Adj. prof. Va. Poly. Inst. and State U., Blacksburg, 1971—72, Auburn U., 1976—83; lectr. in field; apptd. chairholder Jennings and Rebecca Jones Chair of Excellence in Urban and Regional Planning, Mid. Tenn. State U., 1999. Contbr. articles to profl. jours.; author (with Richard L. Miller): (books) New Directions in Hospital and Healthcare Facility Design, 1995; author: (book) Hospital and Healthcare Facility Design 2d edit., 2002. Mem. arch. program adv. coun. Auburn U., 1990—94; bd. dirs. Metro Arts Commn., 1979—86; Middle Tenn. Health Systems (pres. 1972) AIA, 1973—78; Leadership Nashville Alumni Groups, 1984—; bd. advisors U. Tenn. Sch. Arch., 1982, chmn., 1985—88. Named Outstanding Nashvillian of Yr., Downtown Kiwanis Club, 1992, One of Top 100 Alumni of Greatest Distinction Throughout 128-yr. History, Va. Poly. Inst. and State U., 2001; recipient Jefferson award, Am. Inst. Pub. Svc. (Nashville chpt.), 1985. Fellow: AIA. Presbyterian. Achievements include patents for on systamodule for pharmacies. Office: Earl Swensson Assocs 2100 W End Ave Ste 1200 Nashville TN 37203-5239

**SWENSSON, EVELYN DICKENSON,** conductor, composer, librettist; b. Woodstock, Va., Sept. 18, 1928; d. Glenn Gilmer and Evelyn Christine (Ring) Dickenson; m. Sigurd Simcox Swensson, June 9, 1949; children: Lise, Karen, Erik, Jon. Cert. in piano, Ward-Belmont Coll., 1946; BA in Piano and Voice, Hollins Coll., 1949; MusM, West Chester U., 1972. Condr. Aldersgate Meth. Ch., Wilmington, Del., 1969—2002, Brandywiners Ltd., Kennett Sq., Pa., 1973—2004, Opera Del., Wilmington, 1974—, Bi-Centennial Chorus, Wilmington, 1976; guest condr. Del. Symphony Orch., Wilmington, 1977; condr. Ardensingers, Wilmington, 1978-80; condr. 200th Anniversary Meth. Ch. Am., Balt., 1984. V.p. Opera for Youth Inc.; dir. family opera theater Opera Del., Wilmington, 1974—. Condr.: inaugural concert for Gov. P.S. duPont IV, 1977, Sleeping Beauty (Respighi), 1977, The Zoo (Sullivan and Rowe), 1980, The Lion, the Witch and the Wardrobe (John McCabe), 1980, celebration of Swedes Landing, 1988, The Boy Who Grew Too Fast (Menotti), 1982, Charlotte's Web (Strouse), 1989, A Wrinkle in Time (Larsen), 1992, composer, condr.: The Enormous Egg, 1993, The Adventure of Beatrix Potter, 1994, The Jungle Book, 1995, Anne of Green Gables, 1996, The Homecoming, 1997, The Legend of Redwall Abbey, 1998, All Through the Night, 1999, The Trumpet of the Swan, 2000, The Mixed-Up Files of Mrs. Basil E. Frankweiler, 2002, Billy Lee's Washington, 2003, The Secret of NIMH, 2004, What Child is This?, 2005. Recipient W. W. Laird Music award, Opera Del., Wilmington, 1987, Internat. Reading Coun. Literacy award, 1989, Disting. Alumna award, West Chester U., 1989, 5 composition awards, Nat. League Am. Pen Women, 2000, Outstanding Svc. award, Nat. Opera Assn., 2004. Mem.: Am. Guild Organists (choir master). Home: 166 Heyburn Rd Chadds Ford PA 19317

**SWENTY, BRIAN JAY,** civil engineer, educator; m. Constance Fay Seiler, July 10, 1976; children: Matthew, Melissa, Michelle. BSCE, U. Mo., Rolla, 1976; PhD in Civil Engring., U. Mo., 1989: MSCE, U. Fla., Gainesville, 1977. Registered profl. engr., Calif., 1980, Fla., 1982, Mo., 1983, Ind., 1993, Ill., 1996. Sr. civil engr. Stottler, Stagg and Associates, Architects and Engineers, Cape Canaveral, Fla., 1981—83; dir. Mo. Dam and Reservoir Safety Program, Rolla, Mo., 1983—93; civil engring. prof. U. of Evansville, Evansville, Ind., 1993—. Cons. engr. Brian Swenty-Cons. Engr., Rolla, Mo., 1994—. Deacon, bd. of trustee chmn., sunday sch. supt., bldg. com. chair Calvary Assembly of God Ch., Rolla, Mo., 1983—2006. Capt. C.E. U.S. Army, 1977—81. Decorated Army Commendation Medal; recipient Dean's Outstanding Tchg. award, U. Evansville Coll. Engring. and Computer Sci., 1996, Alumni Outstanding Tchg. award, U. Evansville, 1998, Disting. Svc. award, Harlaxton Coll., Grantham, Eng., 2004. Mem.: Accreditation Bd. for Engring. and Tech. (civil engring. program evaluator 2001—06), Mo. Soc. of Profl. Engrs. (pres.-Rolla chpt., dir. 1989—91), Assn. of State Dam Safety Ofcls. (state rep. 1984—93, Midwest Region Award of Merit 1993, 1993), Am. Soc. for Engring. Edn., Soc. of Am. Mil. Engrs. (Outstanding Sr., ROTC 1976), ASCE, Chi Epsilon (Outstanding Tchg. award 1992, U. of Missouri-Rolla Outstanding Tchg. Award 1993). Avocations: running, bicycling. Office: University of Evansville 1800 Lincoln Ave Evansville IN 47722 Office Phone: 812-488-2661. Office Fax: 812-488-2780. Personal E-mail: cfswenty@rollanet.org. E-mail: bs3@evansville.edu.

**SWERDLOFF, RONALD S.,** medical educator, physician, researcher; b. Pomona, Calif., Feb. 18, 1938; s. Julius Lewis and Eva (Kelman) S.; m. Christina Wang; children: Jonathan Nicolai, Peter Loren, Paul Im, Michael Im. BS, U. Calif., 1959, MD, 1962. Diplomate Am. Bd. Internal Medicine, Am. Bd. Endocrinology. Intern U. Wash., Seattle, 1962-63, resident, 1963-64; rsch. assoc. NIH, Bethesda, Md., 1964-66; resident UCLA Sch. Medicine, 1966-67; rsch. fellow Harbor-UCLA Med. Ctr., Torrance, Calif., 1967-69, asst. prof., 1969-72, assoc. prof. divsn. Endocrinology, 1972-78, chief divsn. Endocrinology, 1973—, prof., 1978—, assoc. chair dept. medicine, 1997—; dir. UCLA Population Rsch. Ctr., Torrance, 1986-92, Mellon Found. Ctr. in Reproductive Medicine, 1997—. Dir. WHO Collaborating Ctr. Reproduction, Torrance, NIH Contraceptive Clin. Trials Ctr., 2005—, Torrance; cons. WHO Geneva, 1982-90, NIH, Bethesda, 1982—, UN Fertility Planning Assn., Geneva, 1983—, Am. Bd. Internal Medicine, Phila., 1989—; inaugural lectr. Australian Soc. Reproductive Biology, Perth, 1990; mem. tech. adv. com. Contraceptive R & D Agy. (CONRAD, AID), 1992—. Editor: 3 books;

contbr. chapters to books 100, articles 250 to profl. jours. Bd. dirs., vice chair Harbor-UCLA Rsch. and Edn. Inst; bd. dirs. Scaplanes Corp. Recipient Sherman Mellinkoff award, UCLA. Fellow: ACP; mem.: We. Soc. Clin. Rsch. (pres. 1983—84, Sherman Mellinkoff award UCLA, Mayo Soley award 2000), Endocrinology Soc., Pacific Coast Fertility (pres. 1984, Outstanding Rsch. award 1976, 1984, Wyeth award 1984, Squibb award), Am. Soc. Clin. Rsch. (pres. we. sect. 1972—73), Am. Assn. Physicians, Am. Soc. Andrology (pres. 1992—93, Serono award 1986, Disting. Andrologist award 2004). Office: Harbor UCLA Med Ctr Divsn Endocrinology 1000 W Carson St Torrance CA 90502-2004 Office Phone: 310-222-1867. Business E-Mail: swerdloff@labiomed.org

**SWERDLOW, AMY,** historian, educator, writer; b. N.Y.C., Jan. 20, 1923; d. Joseph and Esther (Rodner) Galstuck; m. Stanley H. Swerdlow, Nov. 27, 1949 (dec. Sept. 1991); children: Joan Swerdlow-Brandt, Ezra, Lisa, Thomas. BA, NYU, 1963; MA, Sarah Lawrence Coll., 1973; PhD, Rutgers U., 1984. Prof. emerita Sarah Lawrence Coll.; Bronxville, NY, 1981-95, dir. grad. studies in women's history, 1983-95, dir. women's studies program, 1983-95. Mem. adv. bd. Feminist Press, 1973-90. Editor: Memo, Women Strike for Peace, 1969—73; editor, co-author Families in Flux, 1980, (reprint), 1989; author: Women Strike for Peace, Traditional Motherhood and Radical Politics in the 1960s, 1993; editor: Feminist Perspective on Homework and Childcare, 1978; co-editor: Class, Race, and Sex: The Dynamics of Control, 1983, Rethinking Women's Peace Studies, 1995; co-author: The Readers Companion to U.S. Women's History (anon.), 1998, Notable American Women, 2004; contbr. book reviews to jours., essays to various pubs. Peace History Soc. non-govtl. rep. to UN, 1994—2005; panelist Bronx (N.Y.) Mus. History, 1995, Rutgers U. fellow, 1977-81, Woodrow Wilson Dissertation fellow, 1980. Mem. Berkshire Conf. in Women's History (program com.). Home: 33 Wheelock Walk East Hampton NY 11937-3937 Office Phone: 212-666-7227. Personal E-mail: amnerm@aol.com

**SWERDLOW, MARTIN ABRAHAM,** pathologist, educator; b. Chgo., July 7, 1923; s. Sol Hyman and Rose (Lasky) Swerdlow; m. Marion Levin, May 19, 1945; children: Steven Howard, Gary Bruce. Student, Herzl Jr. Coll., 1941—42; BS, U. Ill., 1945; MD, U. Ill., Chgo., 1947. Diplomate Am Bd Pathology. Intern Michael Reese Hosp. and Med. Center, Chgo., 1947-48, resident, 1948-50, 51-52, mem. staff, 1974—, chmn. dept. pathology, v.p. acad. affairs, 1974-90; pathologist Mennead Med Ctr, Kansas City, Mo., 1954—57. Asst prof, pathologist Univ Ill Col Med, Chicago, 1957—59, assoc prof, 1959—60, clin prof, 1960—64, prof, pathologist, 1966—72, assoc dean, prof pathology, 1970—72; prof pathology, chmn Univ Mo, Kansas City, 1972—74; prof pathology Univ Chicago, 1975—89, Geever prof, head pathology emeritus, 1991—; mem comt standards Chicago Health Sys Agency, 1976—. With MC U.S. Army, 1944—45. Recipient Alumnus of the Yr Award, Univ Ill Col Med, 1973, Instructorship Award, Univ Ill, 1960, 1965, 1968, 1971, 1972. Mem.: Inst. of Medicine, Am. Soc. Dermatopathology, Internat. Acad. Pathology, Coll. Am. Pathologists, Am. Soc. Clin. Pathologists, Chgo. Pathology Soc. (pres 1980—). Jewish. Office Phone: 847-831-2983. Business E-Mail: maswerdl@uic.edu. *My credo these years has been to care about patients, students, colleagues, employees, my institution and the many publics I serve. Honesty and thoroughness has been a basic life style, irrespective of the cost. With all, competence is a necessity and ongoing. Continuous responsibility for my education and learning is my way of living.*

**SWERLING, JACK BRUCE,** lawyer; b. N.Y.C., May 30, 1946; s. Benjamin Fidel and Jeanette (Fidler) S.; m. Erika Andrea Helfer, Jan. 17, 1970; children: Bryan, Stephanie. BA, Clemson U., 1968; JD, U. S.C., 1973. Bar: S.C. 1973, U.S. Dist. Ct. S.C. 1973, U.S. Ct. Appeals (4th cir.) 1974, U.S. Supreme Ct. 1978. Ptnr. Law Firm of Isadore Lourie, Columbia, SC, 1973-83, Swerling, Harpootlian & McCulloch, Columbia, 1983-92; pvt. practice Columbia, 1992—. Mem. Pre-Trial Intervention Adv. Com., 1980-82; mem. adv. com. Child Victim Ct. Notebook divsn. Pub. Safety Programs, 1987; mem. S.C. Bd. Law Examiners, 1987-92, S.C. Bd. Grievances and Discipline, 1994-97; adj. prof. U. S.C. Sch. Law, Columbia, 1986—; clin. prof. dept. Neuropsychiatry Sch. Medicine, 1988—; mem. S.C. Supreme Ct. com. on model criminal jury instructions, chmn. bule ribbon task force criminal docketing com. Author: South Carolina Criminal Trial Notebook, 1991; co-author: Criminal Trial Advocacy, 1998; contbr. articles to profl. jours. Co-pres. Jewish Cmty. Ctr., Columbia, 1977. Fellow Am. Coll. Trial Lawyers, Am. Acad. Appellate Lawyers, Am. Bd. Criminal Lawyers, S.C. Bar Found.; mem. ABA, ATLA, Am. Judicature Soc., Nat. Assn. Criminal Def. Lawyers, S.C. Trial Lawyers Assn. (chmn. criminal law sect. 1979-82), S.C. Bar Assn. (chmn. criminal law sect. 1985-86), Richland County Bar Assn. (chmn. criminal law sect. 1988-89). Democrat. Jewish. Avocation: shooting sporting clays. Office: 1720 Main St Ste 301 Columbia SC 29201-2850

**SWETLAND, DAVID WIGHTMAN,** real estate company executive, investment company executive; b. Cleve., Apr. 13, 1916; s. Fredrick L. and Pauline (Wightman) S.; m. Mary Ann Sears, May 15, 1943 (dec. Aug. 1969); children: David S., Ruth Swetland Eppig, Polly Swetland Jones; m. Jean Thomas, Sept. 23, 1971 (dec. Jan. 2005); stepchildren: Christine Anderson, Dane Anderson, Carol Juliano, Chace Anderson. AB, Williams Coll., 1938. Mgr. Swetland Co./Park Investment Co., Cleve., 1939-60; owner Park Investment Co., Cleve., 1960—2002, David W. Swetland Bldg. Co. Ltd., Cleve., 2002—. Life trustee Cleve. Mus. Natural History, Holden Arboretum, Vocat. Guidance Svcs., Cleve. Soc. for the Blind; trustee emeritus Western Res. Acad., Shaker Lakes Nature Ctr., Univ. Circle, Inc.; hon. trustee Cleve. Garden Ctr., Ohio chpt. Nature Conservancy. Capt. USAF, 1942-46. Mem. Cleve. Assn. Bldg. Owners and Mgrs. (life trustee), The Pepper Pike Club, Rowfant Club (Cleve.), Biscayne Bay Yacht Club, Wiscasset Yacht Club, Union Club, Home .1 0 Aubier Rd Ann Mit O15.15-0100 Office. David W Swetland Bldg Co Ltd 140 Public Sq Ste 907 Cleveland OH 44114-2213

**SWETLIK, WILLIAM PHILIP,** orthodontist; b. Manitowoc, Wis., Jan. 31, 1950; s. Leonard Alvin and Lillian Julia (Knipp) S.; m. Cheryl Jean Klein, June 30, 1973 (div.); children: Alison Elizabeth, Lindsey Ann, Adam William; m. Joyce M. Caris, Mar. 10, 1995. Student, Luther Coll., Decorah, Iowa, 1968-70; DDS, Marquette U., 1974; MS in Dentistry, St. Louis U., 1977. Diplomate Am. Bd. Orthodontics. Resident in gen. dentistry USPHS, Norfolk, Va., 1974-75; practice dentistry specializing in orthodontics Green Bay, Wis., 1977—. Instr. oral pathology NE Wis. Tech. Coll., Green Bay, 1979-86. Author: (with others) Orthodontic Headgear, 1977. Mem. Prevention Walking Club, Family Crisis Ctr. of Green Bay. Served as lt. USPHS, 1974-75. Fellow Coll. Diplomates Am. Bd. Orthodontics; mem. ADA, Am. Assn. Orthodontists, Wis. Dental Assn. (Continuing Edn. award 1986), Wis. Soc. Orthodontists, Orthodontic Edn. and Research Found., Brown Door Kewaunee Dental Soc. (program chmn. 1985-86, sec., treas. 1986-87, v.p. 1987-88, pres. 1988-89), Shawano County Dental Soc. (sec.-treas. 2005-06, pres. 2006—), St. Louis U. Orthodontic Alumni Assn. (pres. 1988-89), Acad. Gen. Dentistry, Violet Club of Am. Roman Catholic. Avocations: skiing, running, fitness training, raising violets, bicycling. Home: 2160 Greenleaf Rd De Pere WI 54115-8621 Office: 115 Alpine Ct Shawano WI 54166-2041 Office Phone: 715-526-2544. Personal E-mail: wswetlik@earthlink.net, jayecars@earthlink.net.

**SWETMAN, GLENN ROBERT,** literature and language professor, poet; b. May 20, 1936; s. Glenn Lyle and June (Read) S.; m. Margarita Ortiz, Feb. 8, 1964 (div. 1979); children: Margarita June, Glenn Lyle Maximilian, Glenda Louise. BS, U. So. Miss., 1957, MA, 1959; PhD, Tulane U., 1966. Instr. U. So. Miss., 1957-58; asst. prof., 1964-66; instr. Ark. State U., 1958-59, McNeese U., 1959-61; instr. English Univ. Coll. Tulane U., 1961-64, spl. asst. dept. elec. engring., 1961-64; assoc. prof. La. Inst. Tech., 1966-67; prof., head dept. langs. Nicholls State Coll., Thibodaux, La., 1967-69, head dept. English, 1969-71, prof., 1971-91; prof. emeritus William Carey Coll., Gulfport, Miss., 1991—. Writer in residence, prof. English William Carey Coll., Gulfport, 1991—; ptnr. Breeland Pl., Biloxi, 1960—; stringer, corr. Shreveport (La.) Times, 1966—; ptnr. Ormuba, Inc., 1975—; cons. tech. writing Union Carbide Corp., Am. Fedn. Tchrs. State v.p. Nat. Com. to Resist Attacks on

Tenure, 1974— . Book reviewer Jackson (Miss.) State Times, 1961; contbr. poetry to various publs. including Poet, Prairie Schooner, Trace, Ball State U. Forum, Film Quar., Poetry Australia, numerous others worldwide; author: (books of poems) Tunel de Amor, 1973, Deka #1, 1973, Deka #2, 1979, Shards, 1979, Concerning Carpenters, 1980, Son of Igor, 1982, Poems of the Fantastic, 1990; contbr. numerous articles to encys.; cons. editor (poetry) Paon Press, 1974— , Scott-Foresman, 1975; mem. editl. bd. Scholar and Educator, 1980— . Subdivsn. coord. Rep. Party, Hattiesburg, Miss., 1964. With AUS, 1957. Recipient Poetry awards KQUE Haiku contest, 1964, Coll. Arts contest, L.A., 1966, Black Ship Festival, Yoqosuka, Japan, 1967, Green World Brief Forms award Green World Poetry Editors, 1965. Mem. MLA, S. Cen. MLA, So. Literary Festival Assn. (v.p. 1975-76, 82-83, pres. 1984-85), Coll. Writers Soc. La. (pres. 1971-72, exec. dir. 1983— ), IEEE, Am. Assn. Engring. Edn., La. Poetry Soc. (pres. 1971-74, 86— ), Internat. Boswellian Inst., Nat. Fedn. State Poetry Socs. (2d v.p., nat. membership chmn. 1972-74, pres. 1976-77), Nat. Soc. Scholars and Educators (bd. dirs. 1982— , sec. exec. bd. 1986— , sec. bd. dirs. 1986— , sec. soc. 1989— , exec. edn. 2001-), Am. Fedn. Tchrs. (chpt. pres. 1973-78), Nat. Fedn. State Poetry Socs. (1st v.p. 1975-76, exec. bd. 1972-73), Phi Eta Sigma, Omicron Delta Kappa. Home: PO Box 146 Biloxi MS 39533-0146 Office: William Carey Coll 1856 Beach Dr Gulfport MS 39507-1508

**SWETNAM, MICHAEL S.,** think-tank executive; b. Espanola, N.Mex., Aug. 18, 1952; s. Fred R. and Grace M. (Thompson) S.; m. Karen T. Swetnam, June 15, 1971; children: Kelly M., Kevin M.; 1 foster child, Gerry Wild. BSEE, U. Okla., 1979. Program mgr. Nat. Security Agy., Ft. Meade, Md., 1980-83; R&D mgr. RAF Edzell, Scotland, 1983-86; dir. ctrl. intelligence staff CIA, Washington, 1986-90; mgr. strategic investments GTE Corp., Rockville, Md., 1990-92, dir. info. sys., 1992-94; co-founder Potomac Inst. for Policy Studies, Washington, 1994, chmn., 1994— ; v.p. Pacific-Sierra Rsch. Corp. Spl. cons. Pres.' Fgn. Intelligence Adv. Bd., Washington, 1990—92; mem. Tech. Adv. Group to US Senate Spl. Select Com. on Intelligence, Washington; bd. dirs. Space and Defense Sys. Inc., Gov. Bd. of Potomac Inst. of New Zealand, Dragon Hawk Entertainment Inc. Co-editor: Cyber Terrorism and Information Warfare: Threats and Responses, 1999; co-author: ETA: Profile of a Terrorist Group, 2001, Usama bin Laden's al-Qaida: Profile of a Terrorist Network, 2001; contbr. articles to profl. jours. Bd. dirs. Boy Scouts UK, Scotland, 1984-85; No. UK Scout Master, 1984-85; mem. Canyon (N.Mex.) Sch. Bd., 1970; pres. Pershinghill PTA, Ft. Meade, 1982-83, Cookroaches, Washington, 1992-95, Corp. Vol. Coun., Montgomery, Md., 1992-94; candidate from 5th dist. Md. for U.S. Ho. of Reps., Bowie, 1992; chmn. P.G. County Tax Referendum, Bowie, 1992. Comdr. USN, 1972-90. Recipient Presdl. Unit citation Naval Rsch. Lab., 1991. Mem.: Term Limits Referendum Com. (chmn. 1992—93), Armed Forces Comms. and Electronics Assn., Security Affair Soc. (mem. Ad. Bus. Roundtable (pres. 1993), Montgomery County Corp. Vol. Coun. (pres. 1993), Montgomery County Corp. Partnership for Managerial Excellence (pres. 1993), Old Crows. Republican. Roman Catholic. Achievements include invention of of glucose tape tester. Office: Potomac Inst for Policy Studies 901 N Stuart St, Ste 200 Arlington VA 22203 Office Phone: 703-525-0770. Office Fax: 703-525-0299.*

**SWETS, JOHN ARTHUR,** psychologist, researcher; b. Grand Rapids, Mich., June 19, 1928; s. John A. and Sara Henrietta (Heyns) Swets; m. Maxine Ruth Crawford, July 16, 1949; children: Stephen Arthur, Joel Brian. BA, U. Mich., 1950, MA, 1953, PhD, 1954. Instr. psychology U. Mich., Ann Arbor, 1954—56; asst. prof. psychology MIT, Cambridge, 1956—60, assoc. prof. psychology, 1960—63; v.p. Bolt Beranek & Newman Inc., 1964—69, sr. v.p., 1969—74, gen. mgr. rsch., devel. and cons., dir., 1971—74; chief scientist BBN Labs., 1975—98, chief scientist emeritus, 1998—; sr. rsch. assoc. dept. radiology Brigham and Women's Hosp., 1997—. Lectr. dept. clin. epidemiology Harvard Med. Sch., 1985—88, dept. health care policy, 1988—; mem. corp. Edn. Devel. Ctr., Newton, Mass., 1971—75; Regent's prof. U. Calif., 1969; advisor vision com., com. on hearing and bioacoustics NAS-NRC, 1960—96; mem. Commn. on Behavioral Social Scis. and Edn., NRC, 1988—92, vice chair, 1992—93, chmn., 1993—96; ex-officio mem. governing bd. NRC, 1994—96, mem. various coms., 1960—. Author: Signal Detection Theory and ROC Analysis in Psychology and Diagnostics, 1996; co-author (with D.M. Green): Signal Detection Theory and Psychophysics, 1966; co-author: (with R.M. Pickett) Evaluation of Diagnostic Systems: Methods From Signal Detection Theory, 1982; editor: Signal Detection and Recognition by Human Observers, 1964; editor: (with L.L. Elliott) Psychology and the Handicapped Child, 1974; editor: (with D. Druckman) Enhancing Human Performance, 1988; mem. editl. bd. Med. Decision Making, 1980—85, Psychol. Sci., 1989—94, 1999—2002, Psychol. Rev., 1995—97, Jour. Exptl. Psychology: Applied, 1995—97, Human Factors, 1997—2001; contbr. articles to profl. jours. Mem. bd. dirs. German-Am. Rsch. Coun. Found., 1999—2001; mem. corp. Winchester Hosp., Mass., 1981—84. Fellow rsch. rsch. fellow, Philips Labs., The Netherlands, 1958. Fellow: APA (Disting. Sci. Contbn. award 1990), AAAS (coun. 1986—89), Am. Psychol. Soc., Soc. Exptl. Psychologists (chmn. 1986, exec. com. 1986—89, Howard Crosby Warren medal 1985), Am. Acad. Arts and Scis., Acoustical Soc. Am. (exec. coun. 1968—71); mem.: NAS (chmn., Troland award com. 1991, chair psychology sect. 1998—2001, nominating com. 2001), Soc. Math. Psychology, Psychometric Soc., Psychonomic Soc., Tequesta Country Club, Sigma Alpha Epsilon, Sigma Xi. Congregationalist (Moderator). Home: 10411 SE Terrapin Pl 103-C Tequesta FL 33469-1827 E-mail: swets@bbn.com.

**SWETT, RICHARD NELSON (DICK SWETT),** diplomat, former congressman; b. Bryn Mawr, Pa., May 1, 1957; s. Philip Eugene Sr. and Ann (Parkhurst) S.; m. Yvonne Katrina Lantos, Aug. 29, 1980; children: Chelsea, Sebastian, Keaton, Chanteclaire, Kismet, Atticus, Sunday. BA in Architecture, Yale U., 1979. Lic. contractor, Calif.; lic. architect, Calif., N.H. Arch. Skidmore Owings & Merrill, San Francisco, 1979-82; pres. Bastion Group, Inc., San Mateo, Calif., 1982-87; project mgr. Grosvenor Properties, San Francisco, Calif. 1986-87; pres. Veritas Group Inc., Gilford, NH, 1987-90; mem. 101st-102d Congresses from 2nd dist. N.H., Washington, 1991—95; mem. pub. works and transp. com. U.S. Ho. of Reps., Washington, 1991-95; mem. sci., space, and tech. com., 1991-95, mem. select com. on aging, 1991-95; amb. to Denmark Am. Embassy, Copenhagen, 1998-2001; pres. Swett Assocs., Bow, NH, 2001—. State chmn. U.S. Olympic Com., 1992—98; founding mem. adv. bd. European Ctr. of Calif., 2001—; sr. counselor APCO Worldwide, 2001—; mem. U.S. Govt. Gen. Svcs. Adminstrn. Archtl. Peer Rev. Bd., 2000—; bd. dirs. AeroSat Corp., Amherst, NH, 2001—. Author: Leadership by Design: Creating an Architecture of Trust; contbg. author: A Nation Reconstructed. Bd. advisors Hans Christian Andersen Found., Denmark, 2001—, Architects for Humanity, N.Y.C., 2001—, Abildsø Fund, Oslo, 2002—, Project for Pub. Spaces, N.Y.C., 2003—. Presented 1st Comdr. Order of Danabrog, Queen Margrethe II of Denmark, 2001; named as one of Top Ten Outstanding Young Ams., U.S. Jr. C. of C., 1993. Fellow AIA, Design Futures Coun. (sr.); mem. Nat. Hist. Preservation Soc., Ind. Power Producers N.H. Assn., Yale Club N.H., Sierra Club, Winnipesaukee Yacht Club. Democrat. Avocations: athletics, piano, art, sailing. Office Phone: 603-774-1072. Business E-mail: rnswett@swettassociates.com. E-mail: info@swettassociates.com.

**SWETT, STEPHEN FREDERICK, JR.,** artist, educator; b. Englewood, N.J., Sept. 14, 1935; s. Stephen Frederick and Frances (Gulotta) S.; m. Annette Palazzolo, Nov. 18, 1961; children: Susan, Kimberly Ann, Stephen Laurence. BA, Montclair State Coll., 1959, MA, 1965; EdD in Ednl. Adminstrn., Rutgers U., 1976; grad., North Light Art Sch., 1995. Tchr. Long Branch (N.J.) Schs., 1961-62, Roselle Park (N.J.) H.S., 1962-73; rsch. asst. Rutgers U.; New Brunswick, NJ, 1973-74; instrnl. supr. Elmwood Park (N.J.) Schs., 1974-76, Morris Hills Regional Schs., Denville, NJ, 1976-77; asst. prin. Lawrence H.S., Lawrenceville, NJ, 1977-79; prin. Stafford Intermediate Sch., Manahawkin, NJ, 1979-94; recreation and art cons., 1994—. Participant NSF Inst. in physics, chemistry and math. Seton Hall U., 1964, Newark Coll. Engring., 1965, Stevens Inst. Tech., summers 1966-68; rschr. sch. fin. Exhibited in group shows at Sheldon Meml. Art Gallery, 1998, Period Gallery, Omaha, 1998, 99, Montserrat Gallery, N.Y.C., 2000, The Looking

Glass Art Gallery, Hawley, Pa., 2000, Annette Howell Turner Ctr. for the Arts, Valdosta, Ga., 2004, Schacknow Mus. Fine Arts, Plantation, Fla., 2005, 06. With AUS, 1959-61. Mem. Roselle Park Edn. Assn. (pres. 1971-73), Nat. Soc. Study Edn., Am. Assn. Physics Tchrs., Am. Inst. Physics, Am. Assn. Sch. Adminstrs., N.J. Assn. Sch. Adminstrs., Nat. Assn. Elem. and Mid. Sch. Adminstrs., N.J. Assn. Elem. and Mid. Sch. Adminstrs., Nat. Assn. Secondary Sch. Prins., Phi Delta Kappa (sec. Rutgers chpt. 1977-80, v.p. 1980-82, pres. 1983-84). Home: 306 Tenth Ave Belmar NJ 07719-2313

**SWIBEL, HOWARD JAY,** lawyer; b. Chgo., July 9, 1950; s. Charles Robert and Seena (Minkus) S.; m. Sheryl Siegel, June 19, 1973; children: Matthew, Brian, Justin, Alison. BA cum laude, Harvard U., 1972, JD cum laude, 1975. Bar: Ill. 1975, U.S. Dist. Ct. (no. dist.) Ill. 1975, U.S. Ct. Appeals (7th cir.) 1978. Ptnr. Kirkland & Ellis, Chgo., 1975-83, Arnstein & Lehr, Chgo., 1983—, exec. comm., 1983—2005. Mem. Nat. Conf. Commrs. on Uniform State Laws, Chgo., 1976— (pres.); vice chair Midwest Regional Bd. Anti-Defamation League; v.p. Holocaust Meml. Found. Ill., 2002— ; arbitrator, NASD Contbr. articles law jour. Mem. instl. rev. bd. Ill. Cancer Council, Chgo., 1986-90; pres. Cmty. Found. Jewish Ednl. Met. Chgo., 2000-02. Mem. ABA, Ill. Bar Assn., Chgo. Bar Assn., Harvard Club (bd. dirs. Chgo. 1975-85). Jewish. Avocations: investments, tennis, skiing, travel. Office: Arnstein & Lehr LLP 120 S Riverside Plz Ste 1200 Chicago IL 60606-3910 Office Phone: 312-876-7164. Business E-mail: hjswibel@arnstein.com.

**SWIBEL, STEVEN WARREN,** lawyer; b. Chgo., July 18, 1946; s. Morris Howard and Gloria Swibel; m. Leslie Swibel; children: Deborah, Laura. BS, MIT, 1968; JD, Harvard U., 1971. Bar: Ill. 1971, U.S. Dist. Ct. (no. dist.) Ill. 1971, U.S. Tax Ct. 1973, U.S. Ct. Appeals (7th cir.) 1981. Assoc. Sonnenschein Carlin Nath & Rosenthal, Chgo., 1971-78, ptnr., 1978-84, Rudnick & Wolfe, 1984-93, Schwartz, Cooper, Greenberger, Krauss Chartered, Chgo., 1993—. Adj. prof. taxation Ill. Inst. Tech. Kent Coll. Law, Chgo., 1989—2001; lectr. in field. Contbr. articles to profl. jours. Ednl. counselor MIT, 1979—; bd. dirs. MIT Alumni Fund, 1992—95, MIT Enterprise Forum, Chgo., 2002—, Kids in Danger, 1998—, Ragdale Found., 1987—2000, treas., 1987—92. Recipient Lobdell Disting. Svc. award, MIT Alumni Assn., 1989. Mem.: ABA (com. partnerships sect. taxation), Chgo. Bar Assn. (mem. exec. subcom. 1984—2004, chmn. subcom. real estate and partnerships 1986—87, vice-chmn. 1988—89, chmn. 1990, mem. fed. taxation com.), Ill. Bar Assn. (sec. 1980—87, dir. Chgo. chpt. 1980—91, pres. 1987—89, dir. Chgo. chpt. 1996—), Met. Club, Sigma Xi, Eta Kappa Nu, Tau Beta Pi. Office: Schwartz Cooper Greenberger & Krauss Chartered 180 N La Salle St Ste 2700 Chicago IL 60601-2757 Office Phone: 312-346-1300. Business E-Mail: sswibel@schwartzcooper.com.

**SWIBINSKI, EDWARD THOMAS,** internist, endocrinologist, educator; b. Jersey City, Jan. 26, 1950; s. Stanley Adolph and Celina Frances (Szymanski) S. BA, Rutgers U., 1972; MD, N.Y. Med. Coll., 1975. Diplomate Am. Bd. Internal Medicine, Am. Bd. Endocrinology and Metabolism. Resident in medicine N.Y. Med. Coll., N.Y.C., 1975-78; gen. internist Nat. Health Svcs. Corp., Camden, NJ, 1978-79; fellow in endocrinology Hosp. of U. Pa., Phila., 1979-80; fellow in endocrinology -R.W. Johnson Med. Sch. U. Medicine and Dentistry N.J., Piscataway, NJ, 1980-81, clin. prof. medicine R.W. Johnson Med. Sch.; divsn. chief endocrinology Our Lady of Lourdes Ctr. Mem. ACP, Phila. Endocrinology Soc. (v.p. 1993-94, bd. dirs. 1991-96, pres. 1994-95), Camden County Med. Soc., Phi Beta Kappa, Alpha Omega Alpha. Roman Catholic. Office: 1210 Brace Rd Cherry Hill NJ 08034-3213 Office Phone: 856-795-3597. Personal E-mail: marvoor@aol.com.

**SWIBOLD, GRETCHEN ANN,** librarian, writer; b. Holland, Mich., May 3, 1933; d. Jan B. and Margaret Ann (Raak) Vanderploeg; m. Richard Edward Swibold, Aug. 15, 1955; children: Katharine Margaret, Edward Jan. AB, Bryn Mawr Coll., 1955; postgrad., U. Ill., Urbana, 1958—59; MS, So. Conn. State Coll., 1970; postgrad., Cen. Conn. State Coll., 1973—82. Editl. asst. Our Wonderful World, Urbana, 1955—57; editor Spencer Press, Urbana, 1957—58; rsch. asst. U. Ill., Urbana, 1958—59; libr. Yale U. Polit. Sci. Rsch. Libr., New Haven, 1967—71, Canton (Conn.) Elem. Schs., 1971—97. Editor: Animals in Action, 1958, Rolling Wheels, 1959; contbr. articles to newspapers and profl. jours. Women's com. Yale U. Art Gallery, New Haven, 1967—71; active Canton Creative Arts Coun., 1980—97, v.p., 1987—88, treas., 1989—92; chmn., sec. Bd. Assessors, 1975—79; active Dem. Town Com., Canton, 1973—92, Charter Commn., Canton, 1983—84; bd. dirs. Creative Arts Workshop, New Haven, 1967—71. Mem.: LWV (bd. dirs. Canton chpt. 1992—, Conn. chpt. 1997—2000), ALA (com. on libr. svc. to children with spl. needs 1992—94), Bryn Mawr Coll. Alumni Assn. Democrat. Home: PO Box 306 North Canton CT 06059-0306 Personal E-mail: swibold@comcast.net.

**SWICK, TODD J.,** medical association administrator; b. N.Y.C., N.Y., Feb. 8, 1950; s. Adele Hantman; m. Marilyn L. Farkas, June 22, 2002; m. Lisa C. Bleiweiss, Apr. 14, 1973; children: Jennifer P., Blair J., Chad M. Ruoff. B, and MD, SUNY, Stony Brook N.Y., 1974. Med. dir. Houston Sleep Ctr., 1999—; sect. chief divsn. sleep medicine Meth. Neurol. Inst., Houston, 2006—. Fellow: Am. Acad. of Sleep Medicine, Am. Acad. of Neurology (life). Office: Houston Sleep Ctr Ste 525 7500 San Felipe Houston TX 77063 Office Phone: 713-465-9282. Office Fax: 713-465-9248. E-mail: tswick@houstonsleepcenter.com.

**SWICKLIK, MARY LOU MARQUARDT,** freelance/self-employed artist; b. Nyack, N.Y., Mar. 31, 1927; d. George C. and Gertrude Marquardt; m. Leonard J. Swicklik, Aug. 30, 1952; children: Catherine, Michael, Christine. BS, Mt. Mary Coll., Milw., 1948; AM, Columbia U., 1950; student, U. Pitts., 1950-53; BA, Empire State Coll., SUNY, Rochester, 1986. Prof. chemistry Monroe Community Coll., Rochester, N.Y., 1962-83; self-employed artist Rochester, N.Y., 1986—. Chmn. western sect. N.Y. State 2 Yr. Coll. Chemistry Tchrs. Assn., mid 1970's. Author: Answer Book to Accompany Chemistry Text, 1987; prin. works include collage Garden Play, painting Garden Lace; exhibited in one-woman shows at Link Gallery at City Hall, Rochester, 1994, AAUW Clubhouse, Rochester, 1994, My Sister's Gallery, 1996, 2003, Williams Gallery, Artists' Breakfast Group Bausch & Lomb Gallery, 1997, Rochester Art Club, 2002, Arena Group Dyer Art Ctr., 2003, Artist Breakfast Group. Pres. Assn. for Children with Learning Disabilties, Rochester, 1970-72; bd. dirs., exec. com. Finger Lakes Health Systems Agy., 1975-81. Recipient Citation award Health Assn., 1974. Mem. AAUW (pres. Rochester br. 1965), Arts for Greater Rochester (bd. dirs. 1987-92, artists com.), Meml. Art Gallery, Irondequoit Art Club (pres. 1986-88, Art Show awards 1980, 82-86, 88, 90, 94, 96-97, 1999-2006), Rochester Art Club, Arena Group.

**SWID, STEPHEN CLAAR,** communications executive, director; b. NYC, Oct. 26, 1940; s. David and Selma (Claar) S.; m. Nan Goldman, Mar. 1, 1963; children: Robin, Scott, Jill. BS, Ohio State U., 1962. Mgmt. trainee Alside Aluminum Co., Akron, Ohio, 1962-63; securities analyst Dreyfus Fund, NYC, 1963-66; sr. investment officer Oppenheimer Fund, NYC, 1966-67; gen. ptnr. City Associates, 1967-69, Swid Investors, NYC, 1970-78; co-chmn. bd. Gen. Felt Industries Inc., Saddle Brook, NJ, 1974-86, Knoll Internat., 1977-86; chmn. bd., CEO SBK Entertainment World Inc., NYC, 1986-89; chmn., CEO SCS Comm., NYC, 1989—, SESAC, 1992—. Trustee Solomon R. Guggenheim Mus., New Sch. U.; mem. vis. com. 20th century art Met. Mus. Art; past trustee Horace Mann Sch., NYC.; former exec. vp. bd. dirs. Lenox Sch. NY; dir. Mepl. Art Soc. Mem.: Coun. Fgn. Rels. Office: SESAC Inc 152 W 57th St New York NY 10019-3310

**SWIDARSKI, THOMAS W.,** manufacturing executive; B in Mktg., U. Dayton, Ohio; M in Bus. Mgmt., Cleve. State U. With various financial firms; mgr. PNC Bank; joined Diebold, Inc., Canton, Ohio, 1996—, sr. v.p., financial self-svc. group, pres., COO, 2005, pres., CEO, 2005—. Bd. dir. Diebold, Inc., Canton, Ohio, 2003—. Office: Diebold Inc 5995 Mayfair Rd PO Box 3077 Canton OH 44720-8077*

**SWIECICKI, MARTIN,** retired neurosurgeon; b. Camden, N.J., June 29, 1934; s. Martin E. and Annetta Swiecicki; m. Gloria J. Whelpley; children: Diane, Annette, Karen, Sheryl, Martin C. BA, Colgate U., 1956; MD, Hahnemann Med. Sch., 1960. Diplomate Am. Bd. Neurol. Surgery. Intern West Jersey Hosp., Camden, 1960—61; resident in neurol. surgery Jefferson U., Phila., 1961—65; mem. staff in neurol. surgery West Jersey Hosp., Camden, Berlin, NJ, 1967—2004, chief Neurol. Surgery, 1967—89; clin. assoc prof. Neurol. Surgery Hahnemann Med. Coll., Phila., 1977—2004; ret., 2004. Contbr. articles to profl. jours. Recipient N.J. Gov.'s award for Outstanding Svcs., 1970, 71, 72, 73, Award for Support and Svc. Boy Scouts Am., 1992. Fellow ACS; mem. AMA, Camden County Med. Soc. (v.p.1993, pres. 1995), West Jersey Med. Soc., N.J. State Med. Soc., N.J. Neurosurg. Soc.(sec.-treas. 978-79, pres. 1981, chmn. peer rev. com. 1983-89, mem. peer rev. com. 1977-2004), Camden County Med. Soc. (exec. com. 1977-2004, v.p. 1993, pres.- elect 1994, pres. 1995), Soc. Air Force Clin. Surgeons, Am. Assn. Neurol. Surgeons. Personal E-mail: mswiecicki@aol.com.

**SWIECICKI, PETER,** lawyer; b. Lancaster, Pa., June 29, 1954; s. Ignacy and Anna Pauline (Giebultowicz) S.; m. Susan Marie Reid. BS in Fgn. Svc., Georgetown U., 1976; MA, Columbia U., 1977; JD, U. Mich., 1982. Bar: Mich. 1982, U.S. Dist. Ct. (ea. dist.) Mich. 1982, U.S. Dist. Ct. (we. dist.) Mich. 1985, U.S. Ct. Appeals (6th cir.). Assoc. Dickinson, Wright, Moon, Van Dusen & Freeman, Detroit, 1982-87, ptnr. Detroit and Warsaw, Poland, 1988—96, Baker & McKenzie, Warsaw, 1996—2002, of counsel Chgo., 2002—. Advisor Ministers of Fin. and Fgn. Econ. Rels., Govt. of Poland, Warsaw, 1990-91; bd. dirs. Gen. Comml. Bank Lodz, Poland, 1991-95. Studium Pres. N.Am. Study Ctr. for Polish Affairs, Ann Arbor, Mich., 1987-90. Mem. ABA, Internat. Bar Assn., Mich. State Bar Assn., Detroit Bar Assn. Office: Baker & McKenzie 130 E Randolph Dr Chicago IL 60601

**SWIENTON, GREGORY T.,** transportation company executive; BBA in Mktg., Loyola U., Chgo., 1971; MBS in Bus. Admin., U. Chgo. Various sales and mktg. positions Ill. Bell and AT&T, Chgo., Mpls., 1971-82; former v.p., gen. mgr. DHL Airways, Inc., Chgo. and Houston; mng. dir. We. & Ea. Europe DHL Worldwide Express, Brussels, 1989-90, exec. dir. Europe and Africa, 1991—94; exec. v.p. Intermodal Bus.Unit Burlington No. Railroad, 1994—95; sr. v.p. Industrial Bus. Unit Burlington No. Santa Fe Corp., 1995—99; pres., COO Ryder System, Inc., Miami, 1999—2000, Chmn., CEO, 2000—. Mem. bd. dir. St. Thomas Univ. Bd. Trustees. Office: Ryder System Inc PO Box 20816 Miami FL 33102-0816*

**SWIER, JANET KAY,** secondary school educator; b. Sioux Falls, S.D., Oct. 9, 1972; d. Joseph and Donnabelle Schartz; m. Craig Eugene Swier, Aug. 10, 1996; children: Lincoln, Taya. BS, S.D. State U., 1994; MA, Augustana Coll., 2001. Sci. tchr. Wash. H.S., Sioux Falls, 1996—; sci. dept. chair. Office: Washington High School 501 N Sycamore Ave Sioux Falls SD 57110

**SWIERINGA, ROBERT JAY,** dean, accounting educator; BA in econs., Augustana Coll., 1964; MBA in acctg. and econs., U. Denver, 1965; PhD in acctg. and complex orgns., U. Ill., 1969. Asst. prof. acctg. Grad. Sch. Bus., Stanford U., Calif., 1968-74; assoc. prof. acctg. Johnson Grad. Sch. Mgmt., Cornell U., Ithaca, NY, 1974-81, prof. acctg., 1981-85, 1997—, Anne and Elmer Lindseth Dean, 1997—; mem. Fin. Acctg. Standards Bd., Norwalk, Conn., 1986—96; prof. in practice acctg. Yale Sch. Mgmt., 1996—97. Bd. dirs. GE, 2002—; adv. bd. mem. Columbia Bus. Sch. Ctr. for Excellence in Fin. Reporting and Security Analysis, 2003—; mem. editl. bd. Jour. Acctg. Rsch., 1975—97, Acctg. Horizons, 1996—. Co-author: (with R.T. Sprouse) Essentials of Financial Statement Analysis, 1972, (with R.H. Moncur) Some Effects of Participative Budgeting on Managerial Behavior, 1975; (with T.R. Dyckman) Cases in Financial Accounting, 1980, rev. 1981, 3rd edit. 1989; (with H. Bierman Jr.) Financial Accounting: An Introduction, 1987. Grantee Nat. Assn. Accts., 1970, Peat, Marwick, Mitchell & Co. Found., 1976; Recipient Justice Found. Award for Outstanding Teaching, Cornell U., 1976, PhD Alumni of Yr. Award, Accountancy Dept. U. Ill., 1988, Alumni Outstanding Achievement Award, Augustana Coll., 1989, Alumnus of Yr. Award, Sch. Accountancy U. Denver, 1994. Mem. Am. Acctg. Assn. (inducted into Northeast Regional Hall of Fame, 1996), Beta Gamma Sigma, Beta Alpha Psi, Assn. to Advance Collegiate Schs. of Bus. (peer review teams mem., 2001-), Grad. Mgmt. Admissions Coun. (bd. dirs., 2001-05, vice chair, 2002-03, chair, 2003-04). Office: Johnson Grad Sch of Management Cornell University 207 Sage Hall Ithaca NY 14853-6201 Office Phone: 607-255-6418. Office Fax: 607-255-5117. E-mail: rjs22@cornell.edu.

**SWIFT, CALVIN THOMAS,** electrical and computer engineering educator; b. Quantico, Va., Feb. 6, 1937; s. Thomas and Elsie (Hill) S.; m. Joanne Taylor, Sept. 5, 1959; children: Pamela, Janet. BS, MIT, 1959; MS, Va. Poly. Inst., 1965; PhD, William and Mary Coll., 1969. Research engr. N. Am. Aviation Co., Downey, Calif., 1959-62; aerospace technologist NASA, Hampton, Va., 1962-81; prof. elec. and computer engring. U. Mass., Amherst, 1981—2001, prof. emeritus, 2001—. Cons. engring., Amherst, 1981—; co-founder ProSensing (formerly Quadrant Engring., Inc.), Amherst, 1982 Editor: Transactions on Geoscience and Remote Sensing, 1980-84; assoc. editor: Jour. Oceanic Engring., 1980-84. F.L. Thompson fellow NASA, 1977; faculty fellow U. Mass., 1997. Fellow IEEE (life); mem. Internat. Union Radio Sci. (chmn. Commn. F 1988-91), Antennas and Propagation Soc. (adminstrv. com. 1974-77, 80-85), Geosci. and Remote Sensing Soc. (adminstrv. com. 1978-86, pres. 1985, Disting. Achievement award 1994). Office: U Mass Dept Elec & Computer Engring Amherst MA 01003 Personal E-mail: calswift@comcast.net.

**SWIFT, CHARLES,** career military officer, lawyer; married; Grad., US Navel Academy; JD, Seattle U. Sch. Law. Advanced through grades to lt. comdr. USN; atty. JAGC, USN, 1994—, defense counsel Mil. Com, 2003—. Office: Office of Chief Justice Counsel 1600 Defense Pentagon Washington DC 20301*

**SWIFT, DALE MATTHEW,** neurosurgeon; b. Lorain, Ohio, May 26, 1958; m. Denice Swift; 2 children. Degree, Coll. of Wooster, Ohio, 1980; MD, Case Western Res. U., 1984. Diplomate Am. Bd. Neurol. Surgery, Am. Bd. Pediat. Neurol. Surgery. Intern Columbia Presbyn. Hosp., N.Y.C., 1984—85, resident in neurol. surgery, 1985—91; fellow in pediat. neurol. surgery Children's Hosp. Pitts., 1991—92; neurosurgeon Neurosurgeons for Children, Dallas, 1992—. Attending neurosurgeon Children's Med. Ctr. Dallas, 1992—, Med. City Dallas Hosp., 1992—, Tex. Scottish Rite Hosp. for Children, 1992—; assoc. clin. prof. neurosurgery U. Tex. Southwestern Med. Sch., 1992—. Mem.: Alpha Omega Alpha, Phi Beta Kappa. Office: Children's Med Ctr-Neurosurgery 1935 Motor St Dallas TX 75235

**SWIFT, EDWARD FOSTER, III,** investment banker; b. Chgo., Nov. 1, 1923; s. Theodore Philip I and Elizabeth (Hoyt) S.; m. Joan McKelvy, July 2, 1947; children: Theodore Philip II, Edward McKelvy, Lockhart McKelvy, Elizabeth Hoyt; m. Carol Coffey Whipple, June 21, 1968. Grad., Hotchkiss Sch., 1941; BA, Yale U., 1945. With Esmark, Inc. (formerly Swift & Co.), 1947-75, asst. to v.p. charge meat packing plants, 1958, asst. v.p. 1958-59, v.p. for provisions, fgn., casings and storage, 1959-64, exec. v.p., 1964-75; vice-chmn. Chgo. Corp., 1975-79; vice chmn. Bacon, Whipple & Co., Chgo., 1980-84; mng. dir. A.G. Becker Paribas Inc., Chgo., 1984-85; with E.F. Hutton & Co., Chgo., 1985-87; mng. dir. Shearson Lehman Hutton Inc, Chgo., 1987-92. Bd. dirs. Santa Fe Pacific Pipelines, Inc. Chmn. So. Ind. chpt. United Negro Coll. Fund, 1956; trustee Northwestern U., Evanston, Ill.; bd. dirs. Northwestern Meml. Hosp., Chgo. Served to capt. U.S. Army, 1942-46. Mem. Chgo. Assn. Commerce and Industry (bd. dirs.), Scroll and Key, Chgo. Club, Racquet Club, Econ. Club, Valley Club, Comml. Club, Onwentsia Club, Old Elm ClubBirnam Wood Golf Club, Aurelian Honor Soc. Office: 70 W Madison St Ste 1400 Chicago IL 60602-4267

**SWIFT, FRANK MEADOR,** lawyer; b. NYC, Dec. 27, 1911; s. Frank Meador and Alberta (Rankin) S.; m. Harriet Elizabeth Simpson, May 30, 1944 (dec. Jan. 2003); children: Frank Meador (dec.), Thomas Lamar. Student,

Emory U., 1930-32; LL.B., U. Ga., 1935. Bar: Ga. 1935. Partner Swift, Currie, McGhee & Hiers, Atlanta, 1965-82, of counsel, 1982—. Served to comdr. USNR, 1942-46. Mem. Am., Ga. bar assns., Lawyers Club Atlanta, Clubs: Piedmont Driving. Republican. Presbyterian. Office: Swift Currie McGhee & Hiers 1355 Peachtree St NE Ste 300 Atlanta GA 30309-3238 Home: 12 Remegar Way Apt 220 Saint Simons Island GA 31522

**SWIFT, GREGORY,** physicist; b. Omaha, Nebr., July 7, 1952; BS in physics and math., U. Nebr., 1974; PhD in physics, U. Calif., Berkeley, 1980. Dir. postdoctoral fellow condensed matter and thermal physics group Los Alamos Nat. Lab., J. Robert Oppenheimer fellow condensed matter and thermal physics group, tech. staff mem. condensed matter and thermal physics group, lab. fellow condensed matter and thermal physics group. Author: Thermoacoustics: A Unifying Perspective for Some Engines and Refrigerators. Recipient Los Alamos Disting. Performance award, "Thermoacoustic natural-gas liquefier", 1996, R&D-100 award, "Acoustic Stirling Heat Enginge", R&D mag., 1999, World Oil's New Horizons Idea award, "Thermoacoustics for gas liquefaction", 2003, Ernest and Orlando Laurence award, US Dept Energy, 2004, Los Alamos Disting. Patent award, 2004, Los Alamos Disting. Licensing award, 2004. Fellow: Am. Physical Soc., Los Alamos Nat. Lab., Acoustical Soc. Am. (Silver Medal in Physical Acoustics 2000). Achievements include 24 patents. Office: Los Alamos Nat Lab PO Mail Stop K764 Los Alamos NM 87545

**SWIFT, JOHN FRANCIS,** retired health care advertising company executive; b. N.Y.C., June 15, 1935; s. John F. and Mary Veronica (Kehoe) S.; m. Eleanor H. Cunniff, Oct. 10, 1964; children— John Francis, Sharon Ann. BS in Bus. Adminstrn, Seton Hall U., 1960, postgrad., 1960-61. Mktg. research mgr. Lederle Labs. div. Cyanamid Internat., 1960-63; account exec. Robert A. Becker Advt. Agy., N.Y.C., 1963-66; mgr. new products Chesebrough Ponds Co., N.Y.C., 1966-68; v.p. Frohlich Intercon Co., N.Y.C., 1968-72; pres., CEO, Lavey/Wolff/Swift, Inc., N.Y.C., 1972-91, chmn., CEO, 1991-94; pres., CEO, BBDO Health & Med. Comms. Inc., 1977-91; chmn., CEO Health & Med. Comm. Inc., 1991-95, chmn. emeritus, 1995—, ret., 1995; vice-chmn. Lyons Lavey Nickel Swift, Inc., 1995—. Bd. govs. Cathedral Healthcare Systems, 1991-2004; chmn. emeritus Cathedral Healthcare Found., 1994-2004. Served with USN, 1955-57. Named to, Med. Advt. Hall of Fame, 2004. Mem. Pharm. Advt. Coun. (pres. 1979), Bio-Med. Mktg. Assn., Canoe Brook CC (Summit, N.J.), Manasquan River Golf Club, Skytop Club (Pa.), Royal Palm Yacht and Country Club, Boca Raton Resort and Club, N.Y. Athletic Club. Home: 12 Melrose Ln Green Village NJ 07935 also: 600 S Ocean Blvd Boca Raton FL 33432-6265 also: 76 Bay Point Harbour Point Pleasant NJ 08742-5509

**SWIFT, JONATHAN,** television personality, educator; b. Glasgow, Scotland, Apr. 26, 1932; arrived in U.S., 1948, naturalized, 1954; s. John Francis and Catherine Little (McGowan) S. MA, Wayne State U., 1957; postgrad., Ecole Normale Superieure, Paris, 1954-55; studied with Georges Jouatte, 1954-56; cert., Conservatoire Nat. de Musique, France, 1955; postgrad., U. Mich., 1959, Cambridge U., 1981; PhD, Mich. State U., 1983. On-camera tchr. French Sta. WTVS, Detroit, 1955-56, tchr. Am. lit., 1960-62; instr. French Wayne State U., Detroit, 1955-60; tchr. English, French and social studies Detroit Pub. Schs., 1957-64; tchr. English and history Glasgow Corp. Schs., 1967; tchr. English and French Livonia (Mich.) Pub. Schs., 1967; chmn. English dept. Stevenson H.S., Livonia, 1970-78, dir. Sch. Global Edn., 1978-98; dir. Ctr. Internat. Studies Madonna U., Mich., 1998—. Sr. lectr. Mich. State U. Debut in opera as Alfredo in La Traviata, 1961; host PBS TV and cmty. TV series Global Connections, Time Out for Opera, Dining Out With Jonathan Swift; leading tenor with Detroit Piccolo Opera Co., 1981-96, Detroit Grand Opera, 1965, Mich. Opera Co., 1961-64; concert soloist with major symphonies in U.S., Can., Europe, Australia, 1961-81; appeared as tenor soloist in various radio and TV programs, 1961-81; rec. artist with Scotia and Andis, U.K.; contbr. articles and poems to profl. and lit. jours. Mem. adv. bd. Am. Mid.-East Christian Congress, 2003—. Named Fulbright scholar, 1954—55; named to Hall of Fame, Mich. Model UN, 1999; recipient French Govt. medal, 1954, tribute, Mich. State Legislature, 1984, NEA Applegate-Dorros award, 1987, MEA Siddall Internat. award, 1987, Philo Farnsworth award, Alliance Cmty. Media, 1990, 1994, 1995, 1998, 1998, 1999, 2000, Hometown award, Nat. Fedn. Local Cable Programmers, 1994, 1999, 2001, Nat. TV award, Nat. Assn. Telecomm. Officers and Advs., 1995, Human Rels. award, Livonia, 1999, Multi-Cultural award, Birmingham, Mich., 2000, 2004. Mem.: decorated Chevalier de la Confrerie de la Chaine des Rotisseurs, Descs. Knights of Garter, Soc. Friends of St. George. Roman Catholic. also: 4200 Telegraph Rd # 489 Bloomfield Hills MI 48302-2038 Office Phone: 248-734-5669.

**SWIFT, MARY LOU,** art dealer, financial consultant; b. Syracuse, N.Y., July 25, 1942; d. Andrew G. Swift and E.R. Ensle. BA, Sarah Lawrence Coll., Bronxville, N.Y., 1964; postgrad., U. Pa., 1964-66, NYU Bus. Sch., 1967-69, N.Y. Inst. Finance, 1967-69. Registered stockbroker N.Y. Stock Exch. and Nat. Assn. Securities Dealers. Adminstrv. head of syndicate dept. Drexel Harriman Ripley, N.Y.C., 1966-71; product mgr. Fieldcrest Mills, N.Y.C., 1971-74; acct. supr. advtg. Rosenfeld Sirowitz Lawson, N.Y.C., 1974-76, BBDO, N.Y.C., 1976-78, Cavalieri, Kleier, Pearlman, N.Y.C., 1978-79; bus., mktg. cons. Mary Lou Swift & Co., N.Y.C., 1979-81; instnl. stockbroker Mabon Securities, N.Y.C., 1981-91; Gerard Klauer Mattison, N.Y.C., 1992-93; pvt. art dealer internat. modern and contemporary art Mary Lou Swift Fine Arts, N.Y.C., 1994—. Cons. Miller Tabak & Co., Inc., 1994—2006. Recipient Undergraduate Fellowship (2) Am. Mus. Nat. History, 1962, 63. Avocations: golf, travel, languages. Office: Mary Lou Swift Fine Arts 161 Breese Ln PO Box 1496 Southampton NY 11969

**SWIFT, MICHAEL RONALD,** internist, educator; b. NYC, Feb. 5, 1935; s. Herbert Allen and Estelle (Clafter) S.; m. Ronnie Elaine Gorman, Nov. 27, 1971; children— Melissa, Amy, Laura. BA, Swarthmore Coll., 1955; MA in Math., U. Calif.-Berkeley, 1958; MD, NYU Sch. Med., 1962. bd. cert. Am. Bd. Internal Medicine, 1969, Am. Bd. Med. Genetics, 1983. Intern med. Coll. Physicians and Surgeons, NY, 1962—63; asst. resident med. NYU Bellevue Hosp., 1963—64; Instr., then asst. prof. NYU Sch. Medicine, N.Y.C., 1966-70; asst. prof. med., 1970; assoc. prof., then prof. U. N.C., Chapel Hill, 1972-92, also chief genetics div.; prof. pediatrics, dir. Inst. for Genetic Analysis Diseases N.Y. Med. Coll., N.Y.C., 1992—2001, prof. med., pathology, 1998. Dir. Inst. Genetic Analysis Common Diseases, 1994—2001, Disease Insight Rsch. Found., 2004—; CEO Sci. dir. Life Testing LLC (now GenDex LLC), 2001—. Author: Malignant Neoplasms in the Families of Patients with Ataxia Telangiectasia, 1976, Breast Cancer and other Cancers in Ataxia-Telangiectasia Families, 1987, Incidence of Cancer in 161 Families affected by Ataxia-Telangiectasia, 1991, Molecular Genotyping shows that Ataxia Telangiectasia Heterozygotes are Predisposed to Breas Cancer, 1996. Mem. AAAS, Am. Soc. Human Genetics, Alpha Omega Alpha. Achievements include discovery of Mutations in the A-T gene predispose carriers in the general population to cancer, particularly female breast cancer. Avocations: hiking, fishing, travel, theater. Office: Disease Insight Rsch Found 410 Saw Mill River Rd Ardsley NY 10502 Business E-Mail: mikeswift@fcc.com.

**SWIFT, RICHARD J.,** engineering company executive; b. 1944; BS in Engring., U.S. Mil. Acad., 1966; MS in Engring., Purdue U., 1972; MBA, Fairleigh Dickinson U., 1972. With TVA, 1970—72, Union Carbide Corp., 1976—77; project mgr., process plants divsn Foster Wheeler Corp., Clinton, NJ, 1972—81; dir. comml. operations, process plants divsn, 1981—84, pres., COO, power systems group, 1987—89, CEO. group exec., power systems group, 1989—92, group exec., exec. v.p., energy equipment group, 1992, pres., COO Clinton, NJ, 1992—94, chmn., pres., CEO, 1994—2001; dir. contract ops. Foster Wheeler Corp. (Paris subsidiary), 1984—86; v.p. Foster Wheeler Internat. Corp., 1986—87. Bd. dir. PSE&G, 1994—, mem., audit com. and corp. governance; bd. dir. Ingersoll-Rand Ltd., 1995—, chmn., audit com, bd. dir. Hubbell, Inc., Kaman Corp.; chmn. Nuclear Com., Fin. Acctg. Standards Adv. Coun., 2002—. Past chmn. Nat. Foreign Trade Coun.; past mem. Bus. Roundtable, mem., trade and investment task force. Commd.

officer U.S. Army, 1966—70. Address: Fin Acctg Standards Bd 401 Merritt 7 PO Box 5116 Norwalk CT 06856-5116 Office Phone: 908-730-4000. Fax: 203-849-9714; Office Fax: 908-730-5315.

**SWIFT, ROBERT J.,** lawyer; b. Wilmington, Del., Jan. 17, 1948; BA, U. Del., 1972; JD, South Tex. Coll. Law, 1977. Bar: Tex. 1977. Assoc. Fulbright & Jaworski L.L.P., Houston, ptnr., 1985—, and co-head health law-litig. and adminstrn. dept. Mem. ABA, Am. Soc. Healthcare Risk Mgmt., State Bar Tex. (mem. health litigation/med. malpractice com.), Tex. Assn. Def. Counsel, Houston Bar Assn., Greater Houston Soc. Healthcare Risk Mgmt. Office: Fulbright & Jaworski LLP 1301 McKinney St Ste 5100 Houston TX 77010-3031 Office Phone: 713-651-5151. Office Fax: 713-651-5246. Business E-Mail: rswift@fulbright.com.

**SWIFT, RONNIE GORMAN,** psychiatrist, educator; b. N.Y.C., Sept. 13, 1948; d. Joseph Harry Gorman and Mollie Samuels; m. Michael Ronald Swift, Nov. 27, 1971; children: Melissa, Laura, Amy. BS, CCNY, 1969; MD, U. N.C., Chapel Hill, 1975. Lic. physician N.Y., N.C. Resident U. N.C., Chapel Hill, 1978; pvt. practice psychiatry Chapel Hill, 1979—92; psychiatrist, dir. divsn. psychiatry genetics N.Y. Med. Ctr., Valhalla, 1992—97; chief psychiatry Met. Hosp. Ctr., N.Y.C., 1998—, assoc. med. dirs., 1999—. Clin. assoc. prof. dept. psychiatry U. N.C., Chapel Hill, 1982—83, 1990—92, rsch. scientist Biol. Sci. Rsch. Ctr., 1988—92; dir. outpatient svcs., dept. psychiatry Westchester County Med. Ctr., NY, 1995—98; network chief psychiatry and behavioral health svcs. Generations+/No. Manhattan Health Network, Health and Hosps. Corp. Orgn., N.Y.C., 2001—; assoc. chmn. dept. psychiatry N.Y. Med. Coll., Valhalla, 2004—; med. dir. Open Gate Residential Ctr., Somer, NY, 1992—; chief psychiatry Westchester Inst. Human Devel., N.Y. Med. Coll. Orgn., Valhalla, 1999—2001; cons., spkr. in field; mem. CME adv. bd. Neurosci. Edn. Inst., Carlsbad, Calif., 2006—; psychiat. commentator various programs Fox 5 News; First Sidney E. Frank vis. prof. N.Y. Med. Coll., 2005. Contbr. articles to profl. jours. Fellow Falk fellow, Am. Psychiat. Assn., 1979. Mem.: Am. Psychiat. Assn., World Psychiat. Assn. (hon.), Alpha Omega Alpha. Avocations: cooking, reading, travel. Office: Metropolitan Hospital Center 1901 First Ave New York NY 10029

**SWIFT, STEPHEN CHRISTOPHER,** lawyer; b. NYC, Jan. 7, 1954; s. James Stephen and Rhoda Emma Jean (Howd) Swift. AA, Lansing CC, 1980; BA, Mich. State U., 1983; JD, Wayne State U., 1988. Bar: Mich. 1988, Hawaii 1989, U.S. Ct. Hawaii 1989, U.S. Ct. Fed. Claims 1990, U.S. Ct. Appeals (fed., DC and 9th cirs.) 1990, DC 1991, U.S. Supreme Ct. 1992, Va. 1995, U.S. Dist. Ct. (ea. and we. dists.) Va. 1995, U.S. Bankruptcy Ct. (ea. and we. dists.) Va. 1995, U.S. Ct. Appeals (4th cir.) 1995, U.S. Dist. Ct. DC 1997, U.S. Tax Ct. 1997, Md. 1998, U.S. Dist. Ct. Md. 1998, U.S. Ct. Internat. Trade 2000, U.S. Dist. Ct. (ea. dist.) Mich. 2002, registered: (patent atty.) 1994. Pvt. practice, Honolulu, 1989—94, Arlington, Va., 1995—2003, Alexandria, 2003—. Mem.: ABA, Am. Intellectual Property Law Assn., Fed. Cir. Bar Assn., Fed. Bar Assn. Office: Swift Law Office 1800 Diagonal Rd Ste 600 Alexandria VA 22314-2840 Office Phone: 703-418-0000. Business E-Mail: steve@swift.law.pro.

**SWIFT, STEPHEN JENSEN,** federal judge; b. Salt Lake City, Sept. 7, 1943; s. Edward A. and Maurine (Jensen) S.; m. Lorraine Burnell Facer, Aug. 4, 1972; children: Carter, Stephanie, Spencer, Meredith, Hunter. BS, Brigham Young U., 1967; JD, George Washington U., 1970. Trial atty. U.S. Dept. Justice, Washington, 1970-74; asst. U.S. atty. tax divsn. US Dept. Justice, San Francisco, 1974-77; v.p.; sr. tax counsel Bank Am. N.T. & S.A., San Francisco, 1977-83; judge US Tax Ct., Washington, 1983—88, 2000—, sr. judge, 1988—2000. Adj. prof. Golden Gate U., San Francisco, 1976-83, 2005—, U. Balt., 1987— Mem. ABA, Calif. Bar Assn., D.C. Bar Assn. Office: US Tax Ct 400 2nd St NW Washington DC 20217-0002

**SWIGER, ELINOR PORTER,** lawyer; b. Cleve., Aug. 1, 1927; d. Louie Charles and Mary Isabelle (Shank) Porter; m. Quentin Gilbert Swiger, Feb. 5, 1955; children: Andrew Porter, Calvin Gilbert, Charles Robinson. BA, Ohio State U., 1949, JD, 1951. Bar: Ohio 1951, Ill. 1979. Sr. assoc., now of counsel Robbins, Schwartz, Nicholas, Lifton & Taylor, Ltd., Chgo., 1979—. Author: (book) Mexico for Kids, 1971, Europe for Young Travelers, 1972, The Law and You, 1973 (Literary Guild award), Law in Everyday Life, 1977, Careers in the Legal Professions, 1978, Women Lawyers at Work, 1978. Mem. Glenview (Ill.) Fire and Police Commn., 1976—86; chmn. Glenview Zoning Bd. Appeals, 1987—97. Mem.: Chgo. Bar Assn. (chmn. legis. exec. com. 1990—92), Women Bar Assn. Ill., Ill. Coun. Sch. Attys. (past chmn.), Ohio State U. Coll. Law Alumni Coun., Soc. Midland Authors. Republican. Home: 1933 Burr Oak Dr Glenview IL 60025 Office: Robbins Schwartz Nicholas Lifton & Taylor 20 N Clark St Ste 900 Chicago IL 60602-4115

**SWIGER, ELIZABETH DAVIS,** chemist, educator; b. Morgantown, W Va., June 27, 1926; d. Hannibal Albert and Tyreeca Elizabeth (Stemple) Davis; m. William Eugene Swiger, June 2, 1948 (dec.); children: Susan Elizabeth Swiger Knotts-Case, Wayne William; m. James E. Coleman, Dec. 11, 2004. BS in Chemistry, W.Va. U., 1948, MS in Chemistry, 1952, PhD in Chemistry, 1964. Instr. math. Fairmont State Coll., 1948-49, instr. math. and phys. sci., 1956-57, instr. chemistry, 1957-60, from asst. prof. to assoc. prof., 1960-66, prof., 1966-92, chmn., divsn. sci., math, and health careers, 1991-92; NSF fellow rsch. W.Va. U., Morgantown, 1963-64, prof. emerita, 1992. Advisor Am. Chem. Soc. student affiliates, 1965-88. Author: Morton Family History, 1984-2004, Davis-Winters Family History, 1994—, Civil War Letters and Diary of Joshua Winters, 1991, 2d edit., 1996; contbr. articles to profl. jour. Chmn. Blacks Chapel Meml. Found., 1993—; rep. adv. coun. to Bd. Regents Fairmont State Coll., Charleston, W.Va., 1977—78, rep. instl. bd. advisors, 1990—92. NSF grantee, 1963; named Outstanding Prof. W.Va. Legislature, Charleston, 1990. Mem.: Am. Chem. Soc. (advisor student affiliates 1965—88, sec. chmn. North W.Va. 1975—83), W.Va. Acad. Sci. (life; pres. 1978—79, exec. com. mem. chmn. 1990—93), Nature Conservancy (bd. dir. W.Va. chpt. 1970—86, chmn. 1980—82), Prickett's Fort Meml. Found. (life; bd. dir. 1988—2000, chmn. elect 1990—92, chmn. 1992—96, bd. dir 2002—), Marion County Hist. Soc. (life), Fairmont Lions Club, Morning Gardeners Garden Club (pres. 1999—2003). Republican. Methodist. Avocations: local history, genealogy, gardening, computers, quilting. Home: 1599 Hillcrest Rd Fairmont WV 26554-4807 Home (Winter): 242 Laird Dr Freeport FL 32439

**SWIGER, L. A.,** agricultural studies educator; BS in Animal Husbandry, Ohio State U., 1954; MS, Iowa State U., 1957, PhD, 1960. Geneticist USDA, Lincoln, Neb., assoc. prof. animal sci., experiment sta. statistician, 1959—65; grad. chmn. Ohio State U. prof. animal sci. Va. Tech, Blacksburg, 1965—80, head dept. animal sci., 1980-86, assoc. dean rsch. Coll. Agrl. and Life Scis., 1986-92, interim dean, 1992-93, dean, 1993—. Recipient Rockefeller Prentice Meml. award Eta Sigma Delta, Nat. Soc., 1984. Office: Va Tech Coll Agrl and Life Sci Blacksburg VA 24061-0402 E-mail: swiger@vt.edu.

**SWIGERT, JAMES MACK,** lawyer; b. Carthage, Ill., Sept. 25, 1907; s. James Ross and Pearl (Mack) S.; m. Alice Francis Titcomb Harrower, July 7, 1931 (dec. 1990); children: Oliver, David Ladd, Sally Harper (Mrs. Hamilton). Student, Grinnell Coll., 1925-27; SB, Harvard U., 1930, LLB, 1935. Bar: Ill. 1935, Ohio 1937. With Campbell, Clithero & Fischer, Chgo., 1935-36, Taft, Stettinius & Hollister, Cin., 1936—, ptnr., 1948-79, sr. ptnr. and chmn. exec. com., 1979-85, of counsel, 1985—. Dir., mem. exec. com. Union Cen. Life Ins. Co., 1963-79; dir., chmn. audit com. Philips Industries, 1975-82. Author articles on labor rels. and labor law. Bd. dirs. Cin. Symphony Orch., 1976-78; trustee, chmn. exec. com. Cin. Music Scholarship Assn., 1987-92. Recipient Lifetime Achievement in Law award, Cin. Bar Fund, 2002, Great Living Cincinnatian award, 2004. Mem.: Harvard Law Club (past pres.), Recess Club (past pres.), Tennis Club (past pres.), Queen City Club, Queen City Optimists Club (past pres., psat bd. dirs.), Cin. Country Club (past v.p., dir.). Republican. Presbyterian. Home: 2121 Alpine Pl Cincinnati OH 45206-2690 Office: 425 Walnut St Ste 1800 Cincinnati OH 45202 Office Phone: 513-357-9300. Business E-Mail: swigert@taftlaw.com.

**SWIGGER, KEITH,** library and information scientist, educator; b. Hutchinson, Kans., Feb. 3, 1943; s. Paul Clarke and Loneta (Miller) S.; children: Jessica, Nathaniel; m. Cindy Johnson Potter, Nov. 29, 1997. BA, U. Chgo., 1965, MA, 1975, Ind. U., 1967; PhD, U. Iowa, 1973. Sketchwriter Marquis Who's Who, Chgo., 1963-67; teaching asst. Ind. U., Bloomington, 1967, U. Iowa, Iowa City, 1968-73, lectr., 1973-74, libr., 1976-77; asst. prof. East Tex. State U., Commerce, 1977-81; asst. prof. libr. scis. Tex. Woman's U., Denton, 1981-85, assoc. prof., 1985-89, prof., 1989—, dean Sch. Libr. Sci., 1991-92, dean Sch. Libr. and Info. Studies, 1992-2000, dir. Sch. Libr. and Info. Studies, 2001—02, dir. Ctr. for Consulting and Planning, 1997—, dean Coll. Profl. Edn., 2000—03, dir. Gear Up fed. grant program, 2002—03. Mem. adv. com. continuum libr. edn. We. Coun. State Libr., 2003—; cons. in field. Co-editor Jour. of Youth Svcs., 1997-2000; contbr. numerous articles to profl. jours. Bd. dirs. ACLU, Denton, 1990-92, Emily Fowler Pub. Libr., Denton, 1995-97, vice chair, 1997; mem. Tex. Edn. Tech. Coord. Coun., 2000-03; delegate Tex. Dem. Party state convention, 2004. Rsch. grantee OCLC, Inc., 1990-91, Career Tng. grantee U.S. Office Edn., 1990-98; postdoctoral fellow Coun. on Libr. Resources U. Chgo., 1974-75; recipient Svc. award Nat. Storytelling Assn., 1998. Mem. ACLU, Am. Studies Assn., ALA, Assn. Coll. and Univ. Librs. Office: Tex Womans U Sch Libr Info Studies PO Box 425438 Denton TX 76204-5438 E-mail: KeithSwigger@charter.net.

**SWIGGETT, HAROLD E. (HAL SWIGGETT),** writer, photographer; b. Moline, Kans., July 22, 1921; s. Otho Benjamin and Mildred (Spray) S.; m. Wilma Caroline Turner, Mar. 1, 1942; children: Gerald, Vernon. Grad. h.s. Ordained minister So. Bapt. Ch. Staff photographer San Antonio Express-News, 1947-67, head dept., 1955-67; free-lance writer/photographer San Antonio, 1947—; full-time, 1967—. Contbg. author books on game gunting, gun-oriented paperbacks; author: Hal Swiggett on North American Deer, 1980; sr. editor Harris Publs., Guns/Hunting; editor: Handguns 95; contbg. editor N.Am. Hunter. Minister So. Bapt. Ch. With USAAC, World War II. Recipient 10th ann. Outstanding Am. Handgunner award, 1982, Lifetime Cicero award, 1991, St. Gabriel Possenti medal, 1991; named to Am. Handgunner Hall of Fame, 1987, Anschutz/PSI Gun Writer of Yr., 1990, Handgun Hunter Hall of Fame, 1991. Mem. NRA (life), Wildlife Unltd. (pres. chpt. 1955-58), Outdoor Writers Assn. Am. (dir. 1969-72), Tex. Outdoor Writers Assn. (pres. 1967-68), Ducks Unltd., Tex. Rifle Assn. (life), Internat. Handgun Metallic Silhouette Assn. (life), Game Conservation Internat. Home: 539 Roslyn San Antonio TX 78204-2456

**SWIHART, JAMES W., JR.,** diplomat; b. Washington, July 25, 1946; s. James Wilbur and Ruth (Inge) S.; m. Ellen Jane Cendo Mar. 30, 1968; children: Jennifer Anne, Christopher John; m. Kimberly Ann Mack, May 12, 2001. BA, Columbia Coll., 1968. Vice consul Am. Embassy, Belize, Brit. Honduras, 1970-72, 2nd sec., polit. officer Belgrade, Yugoslavia, 1972-74; ops. officer ops. ctr. Dept. State, Washington, 1974-75, country officer for Italy and the Vatican, 1975-78, polit./mil. officer for U.S. Mission Berlin, 1978-82, officer C.S.C.E. Bur. European Affairs Washington, 1982-83, officer for Fed. Republic of Germany, 1983-84; consul gen., prin. officer U.S. Consulate Gen., Zagreb, Yugoslavia, 1984-1988; mem. sr. seminar Dept. State, Washington, 1988-89, dir. Bur. for Ea. European and Yugoslavia Affairs, 1989-1991; min. counselor, deputy chief of mission Am. Embassy, Vienna, Austria, 1991-94, Chargé d'Affaires ad interim, 1993, amb. to Lithuania Vilnius, 1994-97; sr. fellow Inst. for Strategic Studies/Nat. Def. U., Washington, 1997-99; polit. advisor US Space Command, Colorado Springs, Colo., 1999—. Avocations: piano, harpsichord, jogging, classical music. Office: US Space Command Peterson AFB 250 S Peterson Blvd Ste 116 Colorado Springs CO 80914-3285

**SWINAND, ANDREW,** advertising executive; b. 1968; BS economics, U. of Pa., 1990. Account supervisor BBDO, Los Angeles; brand mgr. Procter & Gamble Co., Cincinnati; gen. mgr. Starcom USA, San Francisco, 2000—02, Chicago, 2002—05, exec. v.p., 2005—. Reserve 3rd infantry div USAR, 1990—94. Named one of the best 40 under 40 in business, Crain's Chicago Business, 2005; scholar Reserve Officers' Training Corps, U.S. Army. Office: c/o Starcom 35 W Wacker Dr Chicago IL 60601*

**SWINBURN, CAROL DITZLER,** retired state and municipal agency administrator; b. Washington, July 9, 1945; d. John Nevin and Mildred Peterman Ditzler; m. Charles Swinburn, Dec. 16, 1972; children: Ann Elizabeth, Catherine Knowles. BA, Ursinus Coll., Collegeville, Pa., 1967. Founder, dir. The Healthy Gourmet, West Chester, Va., 1990—95; campaign exec. United Way, Alexandria, 1994—95; acting dir., counselor Women's Empowerment Program, Alexandria, 1995—97; dir., coord. Alexandria Criminal Justice Svcs., Va., 1997—2004; sr. staff Alexandria Criminal Justice Bd., 1997—2004. Author: (cookbook) Recipes from the Healthy Gourmet Cooking Classes. Shelter staff vol. Domestic Violence Program, Alexandria, 1995—97; shelter staff vol. teen runaway shelter This Way House, Alexandria, 1994—95; parent edn. chair PTO, Alexandria, 1986—90; fundraising chair Chadds Ford, Pa., 1986—90; bd. dirs. Delray Beach Condo Assn., 2006. Named Woman of Yr., Alexandria Commn. on Women, 1997. Mem.: NOW, Planned Parenthood, Emily's List, Boca Raton Resort & Club. Democrat. Avocations: travel, beachwalking, yoga.

**SWINBURN, CHARLES,** rail transportation executive; b. Bowness on Windermere, Cumbria, Eng., Apr. 11, 1947; came to U.S., 1949; s. Joseph and Myra (Sullivan) S.; m. Carol Ann Ditzler, Dec. 16, 1972; children: Ann Elizabeth, Catherine Knowles. BA in Psychology, Princeton U., 1963; MBA, Harvard U., 1971; JD, U. Pa., 1993. Industry analyst U.S. Dept. Transp., Washington, 1971-73, chief Industry Analysis Div., 1973-76, dep. asst. sec., 1979-83; assoc. adminstr. fed. assistance Fed. R.R. Adminstrn., Washington, 1976-79; v.p. PS Rollins Environ. Svcs. Inc., Wilmington, Del., 1983-90; atty. Morgan, Lewis & Bockius, Washington, 1993—2004; CEO RailAmerica, Inc., Boca Raton, Fla., 2004—. Capt. USMC, 1963-69; major USMCR, 1970-75. Decorated DFC (2), Air medal (35); recipient Presdl. Disting. Exec. award, 1980, Dept. Transp. Meritorious Achievement award, 1976, 78, 81 Office Phone: 561-226-1701. E-Mail: charles.swinburn@railamerica.com.

**SWINDELL, ARCHIE CALHOUN, JR.,** research biochemist, statistician; b. Sept. 26, 1936; s. Archie Calhoun and Louise Evelyn (Ellis) S.; m. Dolores Dyer Holland, Dec. 28, 1962; children: Randy Zidick, Matthew Earle. BS in Chemistry, So. Meth. U., 1958; M in Nutritional Sci., Cornell U., 1965, PhD in Biochemistry, 1968. NIH postdoctoral fellow Duke U. Med. Ctr., Durham, NC, 1968-70; rsch. sci. positions in biochemistry, pharmacology, stats. Pfizer, Inc., Groton, Conn., 1970-95; statis. cons., 1995—. Contbr. articles on cholesterol metabolism, hormone action, cell culture, actions of drugs, data analysis, stats. to profl. jours., 1968-2004; patentee several anti-atherosclerosis agts. Mem. Town Coun., Groton, 1991-95, Bd. of Edn., 1997—; bd. dir. LEARN, 2001—. With U.S. Army, 1958—61. Mem. AAAS, Am. Statis. Assn., Am. Heart Assn., Am. Assn. Artificial Intelligence, Sigma Xi, Conn. Botanical Soc., Math. Assn. Am. Avocations: nature photography, hiking, botany. Home and Office: 192 Monument St Groton CT 06340-3915 Office Phone: 860-449-8658. E-mail: swindellac@tvcconnect.net.

**SWINDELLS, SUSAN,** HIV specialist; b. Manchester, Eng., Apr. 11, 1954; came to US, 1979; d. Charles Hubert and Nanette May S.; m. Timothy A. Galbraith, Apr. 22, 1983; children: Emily, Charles. MB, BS, U. Coll., London, 1977. Med. house officer Univ. Coll. Hosp., London, 1977-78; surg. house officer Royal No. Hosp., London, 1978-79; resident family medicine U. Wash., Seattle, 1979-80; staff physician N.W. Emergency Physicians, Seattle, 1980-81; trainee gen. practitioner U. Manchester, England, 1981-82; resident psychiatry St. Bernard's Hosp., London, 1982-83; staff physician Cmty. Physicians, Inc., St. Louis, 1983-84; primary physician Southside Family Health Ctr. Columbus Health Dept., Ohio, 1985-91; clin. asst. prof. dept. medicine Ohio State U. Hosps., Columbus, 1988—91; preceptor dept. family medicine Grant Med. Ctr., Columbus, 1988—91; HIV clinic med. dir., asst. prof. medicine dept. internal medicine U. Nebr. Med. Ctr., Omaha, 1991—96, HIV clinic med. dir., assoc. prof., 1996—2000, co-dir. Ctr. Neurovirology and Neurodegenerative Disorders, 1998—, assoc. prof., 2000—02, Terry K.

Watanabe Disting. Chair HIV/AIDS Rsch. and Care, 2001—, prof., 2002—; prin. investigator AIDS Clin. Trial Grp. Subunit, 1992—; dir. Nebr. AIDS Edn. and Tng. Ctr., 1992—; asst. clin. prof. depts. med. microbiol. and medicine Creighton U. Sch. Medicine, Omaha, 1994—96. Cons. Columbus Health Dept., 1988—91, chair pharmacy rev. com., 1988—91; mem. AIDS tech. adv. com. Nebr. State Health Dept., 1991, chair drug utilization rev. com., 92, mem. care options subcommittee, 92, mem. health care workers and invasive procedures subcommittee, 92; mem. systemic mycoses pathogen study grp. AIDS Clin. Trials Grp., Rockville, Md., 1994—96. Contbr. articles to profl. jours., chapters to books; co-editor: Mountain-Plains Regional AIDS Edn. and Tng. Ctr., 5th edit., 1994. Vol. Columbus Free Clinic, Ohio, 1989-91; med. cons. AIDS Coalition for Empowerment, 1992; co-chair Nebr. Walk for AIDS; mem. adv. bd. Wellness Ctr., 1994; bd. dirs. Nebr. AIDS project 1996; mem. adv. com. Hospice House, 1997. Recipient Caregiver award, AIDS Interfaith Network Omaha, 1999. Mem.: Royal Coll. Gen. Practitioners, UK, Nebr. Med. Assn., Am. Acad. Family Practitioners, AMA, Internat. Soc. NeuroVirology (founding mem. 1998). Office: Dept Internal Medicine Sect Infectious Disease 985400 Nebr Med Ctr Omaha NE 68198-5400 E-mail: sswindells@unmc.edu.*

SWINDLE, RALPH WILSON, JR., research psychologist; b. Palo Alto, Calif., Nov. 17, 1951; s. Ralph Wilson and Jewel Marie Swindle; m. Renee Marie Pobuda, May 8, 1983; children: David Michael, Jeremy Christopher, Natalie Diane. BA Magna Cum Laude in social ecology, U. Calif., Irvine, 1973; PhD in clin. cmty psychology, Ind. U., 1983. Cert. Psychologist, Health Svcs. Provider Ind. Health Svcs. Profl. Bur., 1984. Psychol. intern Quinco Cons. Ctr., Columbus, Ind., 1977—78; program evaluator So. Ctrl. Cmty. Mental Health Ctr., Bloomington, Ind., 1978—87; rsch. psychologist VA Health Svcs. R&D, Stanford U., Palo Alto, Calif., 1987—94, VA Health Svcs. R&D, Ind. U., Indpls., 1994—99; mgr., outcomes rsch., us med. divsn. Eli Lilly & Co., Indpls., 1999—2005, sr. rsch. scientist, 2005—. Contbr. chapters to books, more than 50 articles to profl. jours. Recipient Nicolas Aeberhardt award, Outstanding Freshman. U. Calif., Irvine, 1969; fellow Clin. Traineeship in Alcoholism Rsch., NIAAA, 1975-1977; grantee NIMH Rsch. Grant (Heller & Swindle), NIMH, 1995-1998; Summer fellow in Evaluation Rsch., 1975, Pre-Doctoral Clin. Tng. fellowship, 1973-1975. Office: Outcomes Rsch USMD.DC 4113 Lilly Corp Ctr Indianapolis IN 46285 Office Fax: 317-276-8268. Personal E-mail: pobudaswindle@earthlink.net. Business E-mail: swindle@lilly.com.

SWING, WILLIAM LACY, ambassador; b. Lexington, N.C., Sept. 11, 1934; s. Baxter Dermot and Mary Frances (Barbee) S.; m. Yuen Fong Cheong; children: Brian Curtis, Gabrielle. AB, Catawba Coll., 1956, LLD (hon.), 1980; BD, Yale U., 1960; postgrad., Oxford U., Eng., U. Tuebingen, Germany, 1961, Hofstra U., LLD (hon.), 1994. Vice consul Am. Consulate, Port Elizabeth, Republic of South Africa, 1963-66; internat. economist Bur. Econ. Affairs US Dept. State, 1966-68; consul, chief consular sect. Am. Consulate Gen., Hamburg, Germany, 1968-72; internat. rels. officer, desk officer Fed. Republic Germany US Dept. State, Washington, 1972-74; dep. chief of mission, counselor Am. Embassy, Bangui, Ctrl. African Republic, 1974-76; fellow Ctr. for Internat. Affairs Harvard U., 1977-79; US amb. to People's Republic of Congo US Dept. State, 1979-81, US amb. to Republic of Liberia Monrovia, 1981-85, US amb. to South Africa, 1989-92, US amb. to Fed. Republic of Nigeria, 1992-93, US amb. to Haiti Port-au-Prince, 1993-98, US amb. to Dem. Republic of the Congo (formerly Zaire), Kinshasha, 1998—2001; spl. rep. of Sec-Gen. for Western Sahara UN, 2001—03, spl. rep. of Sec.-Gen. for Democratic Republic of Congo, 2003—. Dir. Fgn. Svc. Career Devel. and Assignments, 1985-87; sr. dep. asst. sec. state for pers., 1987-89. Co-editor: Education for Decision, 1963, U.S. African Policy and the Case of South Africe: Dilemas and Priorities, 1977, Haiti: In Physical Contact with History, 1995; chpt. chpts. to books. Bd. dirs. Outward Bound Found. South Africa. Recipient Meritorious Honor award USIA, 1971, Superior Honor award Dept. State, 1985, Presdl. Disting. Svc. award, 1985, Presdl. Meritorious Svc. award, 1987, 90, 94, Equal Employment Opportunity award Dept. State, 1988, Disting. Honor award, 1994, Valor award, 1995, Disting. Svc. award, 1996, Disting. Pub. Svc. award USCG, 1998, U.S. Presdl. Cert. of Commendation, 1998, Disting. Alumnus award, Yale U. Divinity Sch., 1995. Mem. Am. Acad. Diplomacy, Army and Navy Club. Yale Club (Washington and N.Y.C.), Harvard Club, Internat. Club, Lions. Mem. United Ch. of Christ. Home: 6002 Paradise Point Dr Miami FL 33157 Office: MONUC-HQ Kinshasa PO Box 4653 Grand Central Sta New York NY 10163-4653 Office Phone: 212-963-0103. E-mail: swing@un.org, swingwl@yahoo.com, ywswing@bellsouth.net.

SWINNEY, CAROL JOYCE, secondary school educator; Langs. tchr. Hugoton (Kans.) High Sch., 1972-98; dir. distance learning S.W. Plains Regional Svcs. Ctr., Kans., 1998—. Named Kans. Tchr. of Yr., Disney for Lang. Tchr. of Yr., 1993, Milken Nat. Educator, 1992. Office: PO Drawer 1010 Sublette KS 67877-1010

SWINNEY, HARRY LEONARD, physics professor; b. Opelousas, La., Apr. 10, 1939; s. Leonard Robert and Ethel Ruth (Bertheaud) S.; m. Gloria Luyas, Oct. 21, 1967 (dec. Oct. 1997); 1 child, Brent Luyas (dec.); m. Lizabeth Kelley, Aug. 12, 2000. BS in Physics, Rhodes Coll., 1961; PhD in Physics, Johns Hopkins U., 1968. Vis. asst. prof. Johns Hopkins U., 1970-71; asst. prof. physics NYU, 1971-73; assoc. prof. CCNY, 1973-77, prof., 1978; prof. physics U. Tex., Austin, 1978—, Trull Centennial prof., 1984-90, Sid Richardson Found. regents chair, 1990—, dir. Nonlinear Dynamics, 1985—. Morris Loeb lectr. Harvard U., 1982. Editor: Hydrodynamic Instabilities and the Transition to Turbulence, 1985; contbr. articles to profl. jours. Regents chair Sid Richardson Found., 1990—. Grantee NSF, Dept. Energy, NASA, Office Naval Rsch., Welch, others; Guggenheim fellow, 1982-83. Fellow AAAS, Am. Phys. Soc. (exec. bd. 1992-94, Fluid Dynamics prize 1996); mem. NAS, Am. Acad. Arts and Scis., Am. Assn. Physics Tchrs. Democrat. Methodist. Office: U Tex Dept Physics Ctr Nonlinear Dynamics Austin TX 78712 E-mail: Swinney@physics.utexas.edu.

SWINSON, SARA HOPE, writer; b. Denver, Sept. 10, 1964; d. Honey Constance Harriet Shulman and Thomas Stanley Swinson. BA in Bible and Religion, Montreat, NC, 1993; MA in Exegetical Theology, Covenant Theol. Sem., Mo., 1996. Social worker MERS, Goodwill Industries, St. Louis, 1998—2005; media coord. Zip for Senate, Jefferson County, Mo., 2005; with hosp. chaplaincy, clin. pastoral edn. St. Louis U. Hosp., 2005—06; vocat. evaluator, social worker Lakes Country Resource Ctrs., St. Louis, 2005—06; hosp. chaplain, resident in clin. pastoral edn. St. Luke's Hosp., St. Louis, 2006—. Columnist St. Louis Suburban Jours., 2004—05; staff writer Nighttimes.com, St. Louis, 2005—; freelance writer. Writer (humor columns, social critiques, revs.) Opinion Shaper's Columnist, archaeological (byzantine mosaic floor) Abila of the Decapolis; exhibit, Prophetic Self-Portrait. Staff writer New City Fellowship's Mainliner, St. Louis, 2001—. Mem.: St. Louis Writer's Guild, St. Mary's Hosp. Bioethics Com. (com. mem. representing patient's rights 2001—03), Ctr. for Culture and Bioethics. Independent. Avocations: travel, painting, acting, collecting globes and pens. Home: 10331 Oxford Hill Dr Apt 3 Saint Louis MO 63146 Personal E-mail: shswinson@yahoo.com.

SWINT-KRUSE, LISKIN, biochemist, educator; b. New Haven, Conn., Mar. 15, 1968; d. Richard Bennett and Susan Brown Swint; m. Joel Glen Kruse, Mar. 25, 1995; children: Kiel Bennett Kruse, Meredith Amber Kruse. BS in chem., Baylor U., 1990; PhD in biochem., U. of Iowa, 1995. Postdoctoral fellow Rice U., U. Houston, W. M. Keck Ctr. for Computational Biology, Houston, 1995—99, Rice U., Houston, 2000—02, sch. scientist, 2002—03; asst. prof. Dept. Biochem., Molecular Biology, U. Kans. Med. Ctr., Kansas City, Kans., 2004—. Recipient Postdoctoral Poster award, Sealy Ctr., UTMB Galveston, 2001. Mem.: AAAS, Am. Sci. Affiliation, Am. Chem. Soc. Christian. Avocations: reading, cooking. Office: BMB U Kans Med Ctr 3901 Rainbow Blvd MS 3030 Kansas City KS 66160 Office Phone: 913-588-0399. Personal E-mail: lswint-kruse@kumc.edu.

SWINTON, STEPHEN P., lawyer; b. Charles City, Iowa, Sept. 25, 1951; BS, Iowa State Univ., 1973; JD with honors, Drake Univ., 1982. Bar: Calif. 1982, US Dist. Ct. (so., no., ctrl. dist. Calif.), US Ct. Appeals (9th, Fed. cir.), US Patent & Trademark Office, US Supreme Ct. Process & mfg. engr. Proctor & Gamble; extern Judge Roy L. Stephenson, US Ct. Appeals, 8th cir.; ptnr., bus. litigation Cooley Godward LLP, San Diego, 1994—, chmn. Intellectual Property Litigation practice. Faculty mem. Nat. Inst. Trial Advocacy. Served surface line officer USN. Mem.: ABA, State Bar Calif., San Diego Bar Assn. Order of the Coif. Office: Cooley Godward LLP 4401 Eastgate Mall San Diego CA 92121-1909 Office Phone: 858-550-6028. Office Fax: 858-550-6420. Business E-mail: swintonsp@cooley.com.

SWIRNOFF, LOIS, artist, educator; b. Bklyn., May 9, 1931; d. Harold and Fannie (Goldstein) Swirnoff; m. Richard Boyce (dec.); 1 child, Dr. Joshua Avram Boyce; m. J. G. Charney (dec.). Cert. of graduation, Cooper Union Art Sch., N.Y.C., 1951; BFA, Yale U., 1953, MFA summa cum laude, 1956; studied with Josef Albers. Instr. art Wellesley (Mass.) Coll., 1954-58; from asst. prof. to prof. emerita UCLA, 1965—90, prof. emerita, 1990—; lectr. Harvard U., Cambridge, Mass., 1968-75; assoc. prof., chmn. art dept. Skidmore Coll., Saratoga Springs, N.Y., 1977-81; guest artist Cooper Union Art Sch., 1990-91, adj. prof., 1991—; Feltman chair Cooper Union, N.Y., 2000—02. Author: Dimensional Color, 1989, Van Nostrand Reinhold, 1992, The Color of Cities, 2000 (Hon. Mention Best Book on Arch. and Urban Studies, Assn. Am. Pubs.);: 2d edit., 2003, paperback edit., 1992; one-woman shows include Farnsworth Mus., 1958, Swetzoff Gallery, Boston, 1962, Inst. Internat. Edn., N.Y.C., 1978—79, NAS, Washington, 1982—83, The Woman's Bldg., L.A., Bradford Coll. Laura Knott Gallery, 1988, Wellesley Coll., Gallery BAI, N.Y.C., 1996, N.Y. Sch. of Interior Design, 2000—01, Parson's Sch. Design, 2005, exhibited in group shows at City Art Mus., St. Louis, 1951, Bklyn. Mus., 1951, Munson-Williams Proctor Inst., Unica, N.Y., 1956, Swetzoff Gallery, 1963—65, Inst. Contemporary Art, Boston, 1961, LaJolla (Calif.) Mus., 1968, L.A. County Mus., 1968, Represented in permanent collections Addison Gallery Am. Art at Andover, Wellesley Coll., Mary I. Bunting Inst., Radcliffe Coll, UCLA, Parsons Sch. Design, also pvt.collections. Fulbright fellow, Florence, Italy, 1951-52, Yale-Norfolk summer fellow, 1953, fellow Mary I. Bunting Inst., Radcliffe Coll., 1961-63, Yaddo fellow, 1985, 1987; Mellon faculty grantee Skidmore Coll., 1981, grantee Graham Found., 1988, 98, Internat. Interior Design Assn., 2004-05. Studio: 80 Monmouth St Brookline MA 02446-5607 Office Phone: 617-731-5071. Personal E-mail: lswirnoff@earthlink.net.

SWISHER, CHARLES FRANCIS, electrical engineer, consultant; b. Schenectady, NY, Mar. 8, 1934; s. Thomas Hyer and Frances Hannan Swisher. BSEE, U. Ill., 1956. Elec. engr. Dukane Corp., St. Charles, 1956—58; product mgr. Ampex Corp., Redwood City, Calif., 1958—65; v.p. Vega Electronics Corp., Cupertino, Calif., 1965—68; sr. cons. Jaffe Holden Acoustics, Inc., Norwalk, Conn., 1968—72; sound designer San Francisco Opera, 1974—79; v.p. Atlantic City Conv. Hall Organ Soc., Inc., Annapolis, Md., 1980—; exec. dir. The Am. Pipe Organ Mus., Lauderhill, Fla., 1994—. Pres. TBG Prodns., Lauderhill, 1971—. Artist, designer (outdoor symphonic sound sys) NY Philharm. Summer Parks Concerts; prodr.: (CD) The Auditorium Organ, John Balka Plays The Great Organ of St. Mary's Cathedral, San Francisco, (cassette recording) A Treasury of Hymns; dir., designer (music edn. and listening ctr.) The Sound Gallery, prodr., designer (opera and symphony audience expansion) Electronic Standing Rm. Chmn. Arts Commn., Springfield, Oreg., 1992—96. Fellow: Audio Engring. Soc. Achievements include discovery of technique to restore master audio tape recordings; first ever to record in a courtroom trial (1960); co-designer and operator of first PLAT (Pilot Landing Aid Television System), now installed on all US aircraft carriers (1961). Home: 3910 Inverrary Blvd B-608 Lauderhill FL 33319 Personal E-mail: cswisher@comcast.net.

SWISHER, STEPHEN G., thoracic surgeon; BA in Hist., Stanford U., 1982, BS in Biology, 1982; MD, U. Calif., 1986. Diplomate Nat. Bd. Med. Examiners, AM. Bd. Surgery, Am. Bd. Thoracic Surgery, lic. Tex. State Bd. Med. Examiners, Calif. State Bd. Med. Examiners. Intern U. Calif., Los Angeles Med. Ctr., 1986—87, resident, 1987—88, fellow surgical oncology, 1988—90, resident gen. surgery, 1990—93; clin. instr. gen. surgery U. Calif. Los Angeles Med. Ctr., 1993—94; registrar gen. surgery Nottingham, England, 1991; prof. surgery U. Tex., M.D. Anderson Cancer Ctr., fellow cardiothoracic surgery, 1994—96, jr. faculty assoc. to asst. prof. to assoc. prof. to prof., dept. throacic and cardiovascular surgery, 1995—; fellow cardiothoracic surgery St. Luke's Episc. Hosp., Tex. Heart Assn., 1994—96. Dir. esophageal cancer program, dept. thoracic and cardiovascular surgery U. Tex., M.D. Anderson Cancer Ctr., 2002—05, APN/PA dept. liaison, dept. thoracic and cardiovascular surgery, 2003—, dep. chair academic affairs, dept. thoracic and cardiovascular surgery, 2004—; reviewer various profl. jours.; speaker various nat. and internat. confs. Contbr. articles various profl. jours. and abstracts, chapters to books. Mem. ACS, 1982—86, 1996—98, assoc. fellow to fellow, 1996—2000; mem. mem. Med. Student Assn., 1982—86, Western Student Rsch. Med. Com., 1983—86, AMA, 1986—98. Nominee Clin. Scientist award in translational rsch., Burroughs Wellcome, 2000; named one of Best Doctors in Am., 2005; recipient Yale Book award, Menlo Sch., 1977, Fairclough award, Stanford U., 1982, Lange Publ. award, UCSD Med. Sch., 1986, Pres. award, Soc. Leukocyte Biology, 1989, Golden Scalpel Chief award, UCLA Med. Ctr. Resident, 1993; numerous rsch. grants. Mem.: Denton A. Cooley Cardiovascular Soc., Harris County Med. Soc., Tex. Med. Assn., Longmire Surgical Soc., Am. Assn. Thoracic Surgery, Am. Coll. Surgeons Oncology Group, Soc. U. Surgeons, Internat. Soc. Gastointestinal Cancer, Am. Soc. Gastrointestinal Oncology, Am. Radium Soc., Am. Assn. Cancer Rsch., So. Thoracic Surgical Assn., Soc. Thoracic Surgeons, Am. Bd. Thoracic Surgery, Internat. Soc. Diseases Esophagus, Am. Soc. Clin. Oncology, Internat. Assn. Study Lung Cancer, Soc. Surgical Oncology, Soc. Thoracic Radiology (hon.), Peruvian Soc. Med. Oncology (hon.), Gen. Thoracic Surgical Club, Phi Beta Kappa. Achievements include patents for induction of apoptotic or cytotoxic gene expression by adenoviral mediated gene codelivery; patents pending for methods of enhancing immune induction involving MDA7; proapoptotic adenoviral vectors and methods of use thereof; multigene vectors; compositions and methods involving MDA7 for the treatment of cancer. Office: Thoracic Cardiovascular Surgery 1515 Holcombe Blvd Unit 445 FC9 2044 Houston TX 77030 Home: 3423 Sunset Blvd Houston TX 77005

SWISTEL, DANIEL GEORGE, surgeon; b. Mar. 4, 1953; AB, Harvard Coll., 1975; MD, Rutgers U., 1979. Intern/resident gen. surgery St. Lukes/Roosevelt, 1979—84; resident in cardiovasc. surgery Albert Einstein/Montefiore Hosp. Med. Ctr., 1984—86; chief divsn. cardiothoracic surgery St. Luke/Roosevelt Hosp. Ctr., N.Y.C., 1998—, co-dir. hypertrophic cardiomypathy program. Assoc. prof. surgery Columbia U. Coll. Physicians and Surgeons, 1996—; co-dir. Hypertrophic Cardiopathy Program, 2000—; bd. dirs. Ukrainian Inst. Am., N.Y.C. Home: 25 E 86th St Apt 13D New York NY 10028-0553 Office Phone: 212-523-2705. E-mail: dwistel@chpnet.org.

SWITLO, JANICE GEORGINA ALICE E., barrister, solicitor, mediator, consultant; b. Vancouver, BC, Can., Jan. 10, 1959; d. Alexander Donald and Mary (Shutka) Switlo; married; 1 child. LLB, Osgoode Hall Toronto, 1986; B.Commerce, U. B.C., 1981. Mgmt. cons. Control Data Can. Ltd., Vancouver, 1981—83; articled student Ladner Downs, 1986—87; barrister, solicitor Aydin & Co., Vancouver, 1987—88; legal counsel Dept. Justice of Can., Vancouver, 1989—93; gen. counsel Westbank Indian Band, Westbank, BC, 1993—94; barrister, solicitor, cons. Switlo & Co. Peachland, BC, 1993-97; candidate fed. election Okanagan-Coquihaila, 1997; legal advisor Ministry Aboriginal Affairs Govt. N.W.T., 1999—2000. Mem. adv. coun. on multiculturalism, adv. coun. to Minister of Multiculturalism, B.C., 1996-98; presenter in field. Author: (book/screenplay) Sookinchute, 2001, (treatise) Trick or Treaty?, 1995, Apple Cede: First Nations Land Management Regime, 1999, In A Perfect World: Modern day colonialism in Canada, 2001, The River Forks Here: Canada's attempt to execute the 1969 White Paper and Indigenous Peoples, 2002, Ockham's Razor: Cutting Down a Worn Out Scarecrow, 2005, (book) Gustafsen Lake: Under Seige, 1997. Dir. B.C.

Parents in Crisis Soc., Vancouver, 1991—93, Orpheum Kids Club Soc., Vancouver, 1991, Vancouver Youth Theatre, 2001. Scholar, Univ. Mem. Internat. Bar Assn., Internat. Commn. Jurists (Can. sect.), Can. Counsel on Internat. Law, York U. Alumni Assn., U. B.C. Commerce Alumni Assn., Phi Delta Phi. Office: Switlo & Co 141-6200 McKay Ave Ste 955 Burnaby BC Canada V5H 4M9 Office Phone: 800-332-1191. E-mail: janice@switlo.com.

SWITZ, ROBERT E., telecommunications executive; BS in Mktg. and Econs., Quinnipiac Coll., 1969; MBA in Fin., U. Bridgeport, 1973. Sr. fin. mgmt. staff PepsiCo., AMF, Olin Corp.; v.p. European ops., ventures and fin. Burr-Brown Corp., Tucson, 1988-94; CFO ADC Telecom., 1994—2003, sr. v.p. to exec. v.p., 1997—2003, pres. broadband access & transport group, 2000—01, pres., CEO, 2003—. Bd. dirs. Hickory Tech. Corp., Mpls. Youth Trust. Office: ADC Telecommunications 13625 Technology Dr Eden Prairie MN 55344 E-mail: bob_switz@adc.com.*

SWITZER, CAROLYN JOAN, artist, educator; b. Petoskey, Mich., Apr. 20, 1931; d. Eugene Constant and Burnis Hazel (Lower) S. Student, Wayne State U., 1954-55, St. John's Coll., Santa Fe, N.Mex., 1993; BA, Mich. State U., 1953, MA, 1964. Cert. tchr. Mich. Art tchr. Ferndale Bd. of Edn., 1953-56, Birmingham Bd. of Edn., Mich., 1956-96; pvt. tchr. drawing and painting. Exhbns. include state and local shows, galleries and pvt. collections. Cons. Girl Scouts U.S., Birmingham, Petoskey, Mich.; mem. Crooked Tree Arts Coun., Petoskey; deacon, mem. choir First Presbyn. Ch. of Petoskey. Recipient recognition award for svc. to community, Birmingham Edn. Assn. Coun., 1967, Outstanding Sr. Woman Lantern Night MSU, 1953. Mem. AAUW (scholar, Mich. State U., 1962), Nat. Art Edn. Assn., Mich. Art Edn. Assn., Mich. Edn. Assn., Detroit Dist. Art, Nat. Mus. for Women in Arts, Mich. Coun. for Arts, Art Study Club of Petoskey, Zonta Internat., Crooked Tree Arts Ctr. Petoskey, PEO, Little Traverse Hist. Soc. Avocations: music/singing, reading, exercise class, walking, photography. Home: 805 Lindell Ave Petoskey MI 49770-3159

SWITZER, JO YOUNG, college president; b. Huntington, Ind., Mar. 4, 1948; d. John Frederick and Miriam Lucile (Kindy) Young; children: Sarah Kate Keller, John Christian Keller. BA, Manchester Coll., 1969; MA, U. Kans., 1977, PhD, 1980; postdoctoral, Ind. U., 1983, Harvard U., 1995. Asst. instr. U. Kans., Lawrence, 1977-79; asst. prof. Ind. U.-Purdue, Ft. Wayne, Ind., 1979-82; assoc. prof. Manchester Coll., North Manchester, Ind., 1982-87, Ind. U.-Purdue, Ft. Wayne, Ind., 1987-93; v.p., dean for acad. affairs and prof. comm. studies Manchester (Ind.) Coll., 1993—2004, pres., 2004—. Recipient E. C. Buehler award U. Kans., 1978; grantee NEH, 1983. Mem. Central States Comm. Assn. (Outstanding Young Educator award 1982), Coun. of Ind. Colls., Am. Coun. on Edn., Am. Assn. Colls. and Univs. Office: Manchester Coll Office of Pres 604 E College Ave North Manchester IN 46962-1276 Home: Tall Oaks 1408 East St North Manchester IN 46962 Office Phone: 260-982-5050. Office Fax: 260-982-5042. Business E-Mail: jyswitzer@manchester.edu.

SWITZER, JON REX, architect; b. Shelbyville, Ill., Aug. 22, 1937; s. John Woodrow and Ida Marie (Vadalabene) S.; m. Judith Ann Heinlein, July 7, 1962; 1 child, Jeffrey Eric. Student, U. Ill., 1955-58; BS, Millikin U., 1972; MA, U. Ill., Springfield, 1981. Registered architect Ill., Mo., Ohio, Colo.; registered interior designer, Ill. Arch. Warren & Van Praag, Inc., Decatur, Ill., 1970-72; prin. Decatur, 1972-81, Bloomington, Ill., 1981-83; arch. Hilfinger, Asbury, Cufaude, Abels, Bloomington, 1983-84; ptnr. Riddle/Switzer, Ltd., Bloomington, 1984-86; with bldg., design and constrn. divsn. State Farm Ins. Cos., Bloomington, 1986-89; arch. The Riddle Group, Bloomington, 1989-91; prin. J. Rex Switzer, Arch., Bloomington, 1991—. Elder Presbyn. Ch., 1996. With U.S. Army, 1958-61. Mem. AIA (pres. Bloomington chpt. 1983, Decatur chpt. 1976, v.p. Ill. chpt. 1986-87, sec. 1985, treas. 1984), Am. Archtl. Found., Chgo. Architecture Found., Nat. Trust Hist. Preservation, Frank Lloyd Found., Decatur C. of C. (merit citation 1974, merit award 1979), Am. Legion, Masons (32d degree). Republican. Presbyterian. Avocations: swimming, hunting, fishing, reading, drawing. Home: 9 Mary Ellen Way Bloomington IL 61701-2014 Office: 2412 E Washington St Ste 6A Bloomington IL 61704-1613

SWITZER, MAURICE HAROLD, journalist; b. Toronto, Ont., Can., Mar. 28, 1945; s. Harold Switzer and Ruby (Marsden) Hicks; m. Mary Helene Pavlik; children: Andrea Zimperi, Adin, Lisa Doracka. Student, Trent U., Peterborough, Ont., 1964-65. Journalist Belleville (Ont.) Intelligencer, Canada, 1965-67, sports editor, 1967-72, mng. editor, 1972-79, Oshawa (Ont.) Times, 1979-81; pub. Timmins (Ont.) Daily Press, 1981-86, Sudbury (Ont.) Star, 1986-92, Winnipeg (Man.) Free Press, 1992-94; owner Media Help Svcs., 1994—. Mem. faculty Aboriginal Media First Nations Tech. Inst., 1996—97; dir. comm. Assembly of First Nations, Ottawa, 1997—2000, Union Ont. Indians, North Bay, 2000—; mem. faculty Aboriginal Leadership and Mgmt. program Banff Ctr., 1998—; prof. comms. Huntington U., Sudbury, Ont., Canada, 2001—. Author: Bruno Cavallo a Conversation, 1991. Mem. elders coun. Mississaugas of Alderville First Nation. Office Phone: 705-497-4127. Personal E-Mail: swimau@anishinabek.ca.

SWITZER, ROBERT LEE, biochemistry professor; b. Clinton, Iowa, Aug. 26, 1940; s. Stephen and Elva Delila (Allison) S.; m. Bonnie George, June 13, 1965; children: Brian, Stephanie. BS, U. Ill., 1961; PhD, U. Calif., Berkeley, 1966. Research fellow Lab. Biochemistry, Nat. Heart Inst., Bethesda, Md., 1966-68; asst. prof. biochemistry U. Ill., Urbana, 1968—73, assoc. prof., 1973—78, prof. biochemistry and basic med. scis., 1978—2002, prof. emeritus, 2002—, dept. head, 1988—93. Mem. biochemistry study sect. NIH, 1985-89, chmn., 1987-89; guest prof. U. Copenhagen, 1995; mem. microbial physiology and genetics study sect., NIH, 1998-2000. Author: (with Liam F. Garrity) Experimental Biochemistry, 3rd rev. edit., 1999; mem. bd. editors Jour. Bacteriology, 1977-82, 1985—2002, Archives Biochemistry and Biophysics, 1977-98, Jour. Biol. Chemistry, 1980-85; contbr. articles to profl. jours. NSF predoctoral fellow, 1961-66; NIH postdoctoral fellow, 1966-68; Guggenheim fellow, 1975. Fellow Am. Acad. Microbiology; mem. Am. Soc. for Biochemistry and Molecular Biology, Am. Soc. Microbiology, Am. Chem. Soc., AAAS, Sigma Xi. Home: 404 W Michigan Ave Urbana IL 61801-4948 Office: U Ill Dept Biochemistry 600 S Mathews Ave Urbana IL 61801-3602 Office Phone: 217-333-3940. Business E-Mail: rswitzer@uiuc.edu.

SWOAP, DAVID BRUCE, government agency administrator, consultant, art director, state agency administrator; b. Kalamazoo, Mich., Aug. 12, 1937; s. Orlo Frederick and Aileen Esther (Hempy) S. BA in Govt. with honors, Denison U., 1959; MA in Govt., Claremont Grad. Sch., 1961; DSc (hon.), U. Osteo. Medicine and Health Scis., Des Moines, 1981. Asst. sec. Calif. State Pers. Bd., Sacramento, 1972-73; chief dep. dir., acting dir. Calif. State Dept. Social Welfare, 1973, dir., 1973-74, Calif. State Dept. Benefit Payments, 1974-75; sr. rsch. asso. Rep. Study Com., U.S. Ho. of Reps., Washington, 1975-76; profl. staff mem. U.S. Senate Com. on Fin., 1976-79; legis. dir. U.S. Senator William L. Armstrong, 1979-81; dep. sec. HHS, 1981-83; sec. health and welfare State of Calif., Sacramento, 1983-85; ptnr. Franchetti & Swoap, San Francisco, 1985-90; owner Mana Olana Farms, Hakalau, Hawaii, 1989—97; vice chmn. Sacramento Advs., 1991-98; owner The David Bruce Gallery, Carlsbad, Calif., 1995-97. Chmn. bd. Hope Unltd. for Children, Los Alamitos, Calif., 1991—96, mem. adv. bd., 1996—, chmn. adv. bd., 1996—2003. Elder Presbyn. Ch.; bd. dirs. Friends of SOS Children's Villages, 1989-91; bd. regents John F. Kennedy U., 1990-93; mem. Healthy Families Dorchester adv. bd., 2002-05, Md. State Bd. of Physicians, 2003-05. Rotary Club Found. fellow, 1961-62 Mem. Wycliffe Assocs., Phi Beta Kappa, Delta Upsilon. Republican.

SWOAP, THOMAS FRANK, JR., history educator; m. Rebecca R. Swoap; children: Victoria, Lindsey, Tamasin. BA in Polit. Sci., Emory and Henry Coll., Emory, Va. Tchr. history, Hanover County, Va., 1976—95, Bluestone Sr. H.S., Skipwith, Va., 1995—. Republican. Baptist. Avocations: reading, camping, farming, church activities.

**SWOFFORD, BETH,** agent; Motion picture agent Creative Artists Agency (CAA), Beverly Hills. Trustee Mus. of Contemporary Art, LA. Named one of Top 200 Collectors, ARTnews Mag., 2004. Avocation: Collector of Contemporary Art. Office: Creative Artists Agency 9830 Wilshire Blvd Beverly Hills CA 90212 E-mail: bswofford@caa.com.

**SWOFFORD, ROBERT LEE,** editor, journalist; b. Berryville, Ark., Aug. 22, 1949; s. Andrew Madison and Verna Mae (England) S.; m. Karen King, Jan. 24, 1969 (div. 1977); children: Teri, Toby; m. Sandra Dunn, 1978 (div. 1979); m. B. Joanna Rongren, Feb. 14, 1981 (div. 2001); 1 child, Tyler. AA, Coll. of the Sequoias, 1969; student, Calif. State U., 1969-71. Photographer, reporter, news editor The Advance-Register, Tulare, Calif., 1965-78; city editor The Record Searchlight, Redding, Calif., 1978-81; suburban editor, Neighbors editor The Sacramento Bee, 1981-86; assoc. metro. editor, cmty. editor The Orange County Register, Santa Ana, Calif., 1986-89; exec. news editor The Press Democrat, Santa Rosa, Calif., 1989-90, mng. editor, 1990—. Mem. Am. Soc. Newspaper Editors, Calif. Soc. Newspaper Editors (pres.). Office: The Press Democrat 427 Mendocino Ave Santa Rosa CA 95401-6385 Business E-Mail: bswofford@pressdemocrat.com.

**SWOGER, JAMES WESLEY,** magician; b. Wilkinsburg, Pa., Jan. 26, 1918; s. George Edmond and Iva Edna (Heacox) S.; m. Willie Williams, Jan. 8, 1944 (div. 1967); children: Melinda (dec.), James Michael, Andrina; m. Violet Elizabeth Pettit, Oct. 29, 1968. Owner House of Enchantment, Oceanside, Calif., 1937—. Owner, magician Museum of Magic, 1937, Magic Follies of Tomorrow, 1938-41; active numerous war bond drive shows, camp shows, ship entertainment and concert tours in Australia, New Guinea and the Philippines, 1943-46; starred in Magic on Showboat Rhododenron Season, 1965—, Mr. Roger's Neighborhood, Army Hour, 1943; lectr. Magic Castle, 1995; magician Pitts. Children's Theatre, 1941-43, Bascom Prodns., 1941-43, Austin Prodns., 1941-43; bd. dirs. Awesome Balloons, Inc. Magician for more than 80 yrs. Eagle Scout with 3 Palms BSA. Named Magician of Yr. 1960, 60 Yrs Svc. Magic, Internat. Magicians Ring 13 IBM, 1973, Faithful Yr. Svc. Magic, 42d Annual Magicfest, 1973, 60 Yr. Svc. Magic, 1983; named to Order of Arrow Boy Scouts Am.; recipient Internat. Brotherhood of Magician, 80 yrs. in Magic Conv., 2002. Mem.: Awesome Balloons (bd. dirs. 2000), Fellowship Christian Magicians, Acad. Magical Scis., Mystic 52 (pres.), Craftsmen Printers Guild, Internat. Brotherhood Magicians (pres., Order of Merlin Excalibur 1995, Presdl. citation 2001–02, 80 Yrs. in Magic plaque 2002, Order of Merlin Excelsior, 60 Yrs. of Continuous Svc. 2005), Soc. Am. Magicians (pres.). Republican. Avocations: inventing stage effects, model illusions. Home: 3542 Mira Pacific Dr Oceanside CA 92056-3932

**SWONGER, THOMAS K. H., JR.,** insurance company executive; s. Thomas K. H. and Mary Helen Swonger; m. Claudia Maria Arteaga, Feb. 6, 2004; children: Richard Thomas, Karli Elizabeth, Thomas K. H. III. BS in Bus. Mgmt., U. Phoenix, Orlando, Fla., 2001—04, MBA, 2004—05. Cert. in workers compensation WCCP, Fla., 1996. Mil. police US Army, Karlsruhe, Germany, 1987—92; police officier Daytona Beach Police Dept., Fla., 1992—93; claims examiner Exec. Risk Cons., Longwood, Fla., 1993—97; sr. claims examiner, claims supr. Gallagher Bassett Svcs., Orlando, Fla., 1997—2004; claims mgr. Sedgwick Claims Mgmt. Svcs., Lake Mary, Fla., 2004—. Youth instr. St. Isaac Joques, Orlando, 2003–05. Specialist U.S. Army, 1987—92, Germany. Decorated Good Conduct medal US Army, Drivers medal, Forgien Svc. medal, Combat citation. Mem.: WCCP (assoc.). Office: Sedgwick CMS 255 Primera Blvd Ste 400 Lake Mary FL 32746 Office Fax: 407-833-4111. Business E-Mail: tswonger@sedgwickcms.com

**SWOOPES, SHERYL DENISE,** professional basketball player; b. Brownfield, Tex., Mar. 25, 1971; d. Louise Swoopes; m. Eric Jackson, June 7, 1995 (div. 1999); 1 child, Jordan Eric Jackson. Student, South Plains Jr. Coll., Tex.; grad., Tex. Tech. U., 1993. Basketball player South Plains Jr. Coll., 1989—91, Tex. Tech U., 1991—93; profl. basketball player Houston Comets, WNBA, 1997—. Founder Sheryl Swoopes Found. for Youth. Named Nat. Player of Yr., USA Today, Sports Illustrated, others, 1993, Most Outstanding Player, NCAA Final Four, 1993, Most Valuable Player, WNBA, 2000, 2002, Defensive Player of Yr., 2000, 2002, 2003, Female Athlete of Yr., AP, 1993; named to First Team All-WNBA, 1998—2000, 2002, WNBA All-Star Team, 1999, 2000, 2002, 2003; recipient Coll. Performer of Yr. Award, ESPY award, 1994, Women's Pro Basketball Player of Yr. Award, 2001, Best WNBA Player, 2006. Achievements include mem., Texas Tech NCAA Championship Team, 1993; mem., US Women's Basketball Gold Medal Team, World Championships, 2002; mem., US Women's Basketball Gold Medal Team, Atlanta Olympics, 1996; mem., US Women's Basketball Gold Medal Team, Sydney Olympics, 2000; mem., US Women's Basketball Team, Athens Olympics, 2004; first woman to have a Nike shoe, the Air Swoopes, named after her. Office: Houston Comets 1510 Polk St Houston TX 77002-1099*

**SWOPE, DONALD DOWNEY,** retired banker; b. Martinsville, Ill., Feb. 26, 1926; s. Roy V. and Dorothy Irene (Downey) S.; m. Earla Long Markert, Aug. 16, 1960. BS, Ind. State U., 1950. With Ill. Savs. and Loan Commn., Springfield, Ill., 1950-77, chief dept. commr., 1971-77; exec. v.p. Bank for Savs. & Loan Assn., Chgo., 1977-81 pres., 1981-90. Bd. dirs. Country Fair White Elephant, Green Valley, Ariz., 1981—, treas., 1981-84. With USNR, 1944-63. Mem. VFW (life), Nat. Assn. State Savs. and Loan Suprs. (pres. 1972-73), Am. Legion (life), C. C. Green Valley, Kiwanis (pres. Crete, Ill. 1977-78, treas. Green Valley, Ariz. 1994, 95), Elks (treas.).

**SWOPE, JEFFREY PEYTON,** lawyer; b. Evanston, Ill., June 11, 1945; s. Oliver P. and Elspeth E. (Cahill) S.; m. Linda Lee, Aug. 26, 1967; children: Matthew, Gregory, Timothy. AB, Harvard U., 1967, JD, 1970. Bar: Mass. 1970, U.S. Dist. Ct. Mass. 1971, U.S. Ct. Appeals (1st cir.) 1973, U.S. Ct. Claims 1974, U.S. Supreme Ct. 1979. Assoc. Edwards Angell Palmer & Dodge, Boston, 1970-76, ptnr., 1977—. Treas. Social Law Libr., Boston, 1984-2003, pres., 2003-. Treas. Ella Lyman Cabot Trust, Holliston, Mass., 1979-. Home: 54 Hyde St Newton MA 02461-1206 Office: Edwards Angell Palmer & Dodge LLP 111 Huntington Ave Boston MA 02199-7613

**SWOPE, MEGAN ELIZABETH,** social studies educator; b. Princeton, NJ, Mar. 15, 1976; d. Thomas Eugene and Tozia Ann Engleman; m. Eric Allen Swope, Dec. 21, 2002; 1 child, Gavin William. BA, U. Rochester, 1998; MA, Gratz Coll., 2002. Cert. social studies tchr. Pa. Social studies tchr. Irondequoit (NY) HS, 1998—99, Pennsbury (Pa.) HS, 1999—. Mem.: Nat. Coun. Social Studies. Democrat. Lutheran. Avocation: home improvement. Home: 418 Washington Crossing Rd Newtown PA 18940-1615 Office: Pennsbury HS West 608 South Olds Blvd Fairless Hills PA 19030 Office Phone: 215-949-6780 72124. Personal E-mail: swope1221@verizon.net. Business E-Mail: mswope@pennsbury.k12.pa.us.

**SWOPE, WILLIAM CLARENCE,** computer scientist, researcher; b. Pasadena, Calif., Dec. 26, 1952; s. John and Joan Marie Ginter; m. Karen Marie Maschino, Dec. 27, 1984; children: Helen Claire Maschino, Alexander Phineas Maschino. AB Chemistry and Physics, Harvard U., Cambridge, Mass., 1975; PhD Chemistry, U. Calif., Berkeley, Calif., 1979. Sci. staff mem. IBM Palo Alto Sci. Ctr., Palo Alto, Calif., 1986—92; rsch. staff mem. IBM Almaden Rsch., San Jose, Calif., 1992—. Avocation: wine making. Office: IBM Almaden Rsch 650 Harry Rd San Jose CA 95120 Office Phone: 408-927-1706.

**SWORDS, WILLIAM EDWARD,** microbiologist, educator; b. Huntsville, Ala., Aug. 18, 1965; s. William Arthur and Mary Vandiver Swords; m. Tina Maria Reeves, July 6, 1996; children: Maria Kay, Molly Evelyn. BS, Auburn U., Ala., 1983—88; MS, Miss. State U., Starkville, 1988—90; PhD, U. Ala., Birmingham, 1990—96. Postdoctoral fellow Centers for Disease Control and Prevention, Atlanta, 1996—98, U. Iowa, Iowa City, 1998—2001; asst. prof., microbiology Wake Forest U. Health Sciences, Winston-Salem, NC, 2002—. Mem. Calvary Bapt. Ch., Winston-Salem, NC, 2002. Grantee ASM/NCID fellowship, Centers for Disease Control, 1996—97, K22 Transition award, NIAID, 2002—04, Rsch. grant, 2004—, NIDCHD, 2005—; NIH Postdoc-

toral Trainee, NIAID, 1999—2001. Mem.: Internat. Endotoxin Soc., Am. Soc. Microbiology. Baptist. Achievements include research in pathogenesis of chronic airway infections. Home: 3233 Paddington Ln Winston Salem NC 27106 Office: 5101A Gray Bldg Medical Center Blvd Winston Salem NC 27157 Office Phone: 336-713-5049.

**SWYERS, DONALD G.,** information scientist; b. Syracuse, N.Y., Mar. 30, 1958; s. William A. Swyers and Corinne Prall Neville; m. Nancy C. Bargesser, Jan. 2, 1993; 1 child, William Q. BS in Mgmt. Sci., SUNY, Geneseo, 1980; MBA in Corp. Investment, U. Hartford, 1991. Cert. computer profl. Inst. Cert. Computing. Database analyst Xerox, Webster, N.Y., 1980-87; computer automated sys. engring. tool cons. Aetna, Hartford, Conn., 1987-94; cons. Hartford, 1994-99; information engr. Citigroup-Travelers Life & Annuity, Hartford, 1999—. Home: 575 Bridge Rd Northampton MA 01062-1089 E-mail: dswyers@yahoo.com

**SWYGERT, HAYWOOD PATRICK,** academic administrator; b. Phila., Mar. 17, 1943; s. LeRoy and Gustina (Rogers) Huzzy; children: Haywood Patrick Jr., Michael Branson. AB in History, Howard U., 1965, JD cum laude, 1968. Bar: D.C. 1968, Pa. 1970, N.Y. 1970. Law clk. to chief judge U.S. Ct. Appeals (3d cir.), Phila., 1968—69; assoc. Debevoise, Plimpton, Lyons & Gates, N.Y.C., 1969—70; adminstrv. asst. to Congressman Charles B. Rangel NY, 1971—72; spl. asst. dist. atty. Phila., 1973; from asst. prof. to prof. law Temple U., 1972—90, v.p. adminstrn., 1982—88, exec. v.p., 1988—90; pres. SUNY, Albany, 1990—95, Howard U., Washington, 1995—. Bd. dirs. United Tech. Corp., Hartford Fin. Svcs. Group, Fannie Mae; adv. bd. Nat. Security Agency, 2002; chmn. HBCU Capital Fin., 2002—. Gov.'s rep. Southeastern Pa. Transp. Authority, 1987—90; bd. trustees Inst. Pub. Administrn., 1992—99; exec. com. Pub. Law Ctr., Phila., 1980—88; bd. dirs. NY State Coun. on Humanities, 1991—95; chmn. ednl. structure, policies and practices NY State Spl. Commn., 1993—95; co-chmn. joint task force grad. edn. Nat. Assn. State Univs. and Land Grant Colls./Am. Assn. State Coll. and Univs., 1993—95; chmn. capital financing program adv. bd. Historically Black Colls. and Univs., 2002—; mem. founding coun. Smithsonian Instn.'s Nat. Mus. of African Am. History and Culture, 2004; mem. DC Emancipation Commemoration Commn., 2004, Brown V Board Edn. Commemoration Commn., 2002, US Nat. Commn. UNESCO, 2004; chmn. award Congl. Black Caucus 34th Ann. Legis. Conf., 2004; bd. dirs. New Cmty. Devel. Corp., HUD, 1980—82, Nat. Pub. Radio, 1995—96. Recipient Bldg. Industry Assn. Achievement award, DC, Nat. Urban League award outstanding leadership in edn., 2005. Mem.: ABA, Victory Funds (trustee 1994—2002), Middle States Assn. Colls. and Schs. (commn. on higher edn. 1992—95). Office: Howard U Office of Pres 2400 6th St NW Ste 402 Washington DC 20059-0002 Office Phone: 202-806-2500.

**SYDNOR, DOUGLAS BRYAN,** architect, educator; b. Bremerton, Wash., Sept. 5, 1952; s. Reginald Gene and Dorothy Mae (Webb) S.; m. Sonia Poli Hechanova, Dec. 28, 1974; children: Ryan Douglas, Siena Marie, Elizabeth Anne. BArch, Ariz. State U., 1976; MArch, Harvard U., 1977. Registered arch., Ariz. Salesman Entz-White Lumber, Phoenix, 1969-71; constrn. laborere M.M. Sundt-Kitchell, Phoenix, summers 1971-73; draftsman Varney Sexton Sydnor, Phoenix, summers 1974-76; project designer, 1977-80; sr. assoc. Sydnor Archs., Phoenix, 1980-84; v.p., 1985-89; arch., sr. assoc. Lescher & Mahoney, Inc., Phoenix, 1989-93; pres. Douglas Sydnor Arch. & Assocs. Inc., Scottsdale, Ariz., 1993—. Faculty assoc. Ariz. State U., Tempe, 1980, vis. design critic, 1982—, vis. lectr., 1984—; mem. devel. rev. bd. City of Scottsdale, Ariz., 1988-91; mem. environ. awards com. City of Phoenix, 1992-95. Project designer St. Joseph Hosp. parking structure, 1981 (award excellence in concrete award Ariz. Rock Product Assn.), St. Joseph Hosp. expansion, 1981 (Ariz. Steel Field Erectors Assn. award), St. Luke's Health Ctr., 1983 (AIA Merit award), Baker Office Bldgs. (AIA Merit award 1984), Lazor Residence (Ariz. Home of Yr. hon. mention award 1989), Cummings Residence (Ariz. Home of Yr. Hon. award 1990, AIA Ariz. award for excellence, 1991, Helen C. Lincoln Learning Ctr. AIA Ariz. award for Excellence in Architecture 1991, AIA Ariz. Architects Medal award, Excellence in Design award Ariz. Masonry Guild, 1992, Citation Design award AIA Ariz. and the Prodrs. Coun. Imagination Cube 1994). Acitve Phoenix Art Mus., Scottsdale Cultural Coun., 1993-94; past bd. dirs. Mens Arts Coun., Samuel Gompers Meml. Rehab. Ctr., 1984-88; mem. adv. bd. Inst. Celebration Cultural Diversity, 1994—, Stagebrush Theater, Tempe 1994-96; chmn., bd. dirs. Ariz. Town Hall, 1996-1998, Friends Scottsdale Pub. Libr., 1998—; chmn. Historic Preservation Commn. City of Scottsdale, 1997-03. Recipient Am. Concrete Inst. award, 1996, Merit award Valley Forward Assn., 1997, Excellence in Masonry award Ariz. Masonry Guild, 1997, Gold Travel award ariz. Masonry Guild, 1998, S.W. Contractor Best of 1998 award, others. Mem. AIA (bd. dirs. 1980-81, 83, chmn. graphics com. 1980-81, programs com. 1981-82, publicity chmn. 1984, treas. 1987, pres. 1990, Western Mountain Region award, Citation award 1998), Ariz. Acad., Scottsdale C. of C. (bd. dirs. 1988-91), Scottsdale Leadership (bd. dirs. 1988-92, chmn. 1990-91, vice-chmn. adv. bd. Ctr. for Arts 1990-91), Kiwanis (past pres.). Republican. Methodist. Office: Douglas Sydnor Arch and Assocs 4434 N Civic Center Plz Ste 101 Scottsdale AZ 85251-3539 Office Phone: 480-423-1800.

**SYDOW, MICHAEL DAVID,** lawyer; b. Dec. 12, 1950; m. Kelli McDonald; children: Kristen, David, Wyatt. BA, Southwestern U., 1973; JD with honors, U. Tex., 1976. Bar: Tex. 1976, U.S. Ct. Claims 1977, U.S. Ct. Appeals (5th cir.) 1977, U.S. Dist. Ct. (so. dist.) Tex. 1977, U.S. Dist. Ct. (ea. dist.) Tex. 1979, U.S. Supreme Ct. 1980, U.S. Dist. Ct. (no. dist.) Tex. 1985, U.S. Dist. Ct. (we. dist.) Tex. 1986; cert. in civil trial law Tex. Bd. Legal Specialization. Trial atty. Office Gen. Counsel USN, Arlington, Va., 1976-77; mem. firm Eastham, Watson, Dale & Forney, Houston, 1977-84, Hagans & Sydow, LLP, Houston, 1985-90, Reynolds & Sydow LLP, Houston, 1993-94; pvt. practice, 1990-93, with Sydow & McDonald, LLP, 1995-97; shareholder Verner, Liipfert, Bernhard, McPherson & Hand, Houston, 1997—2002, Sydow, Kormack Carrigan & Eckerson, 2002—04, Sydow, McDonald, Kaiser & Ahmed, LLP, 2005—. Fellow Tex. Bar Found., Houston Bar Found.; mem. Houston Bar Assn. (chmn. jud. liaison com. 1988-90, Pres.'s award 1990), Maritime Law Assn. U.S. (mem. com. on gen. average 1977-88, practice and procedures com. 1988—), State Bar Tex., Phi Delta Phi. Address: Sydow McDonald Kaiser & Ahmed LLP 2000 Bering Dr Ste 700 Houston TX 77057 Home: 5773 Woodway Dr Houston TX 77057-1501 Office Phone: 713-355-4200. E-mail: msydow@smkalaw.com.

**SYED, ELIZABETH CHANCE,** health facility administrator, critical care nurse; b. Clermont, Fla., Oct. 18, 1958; d. Brooker Lawson and Beulah Catharine (Lord) Chance; m. Mohsin M. Syed, Dec. 30, 1993; children: Adam, Jibran. B in Gen. Studies, Howard Payne U., 1981; MA in Comm. without thesis, SW Bapt. Theol. Sem., 1985; ADN, Ea. N.Mex. U., 1988. Cert. CCRN, program nurse sr. options, med. office mgr. Critical care nurse Meml. Hosp. & Med. Ctr., Midland, Tex., 1990—94, Angelo Cmty. Med. Ctr., San Angelo, Tex., 1992; staff nurse ICU Med. Ctr. Hosp., Odessa, Tex., 1998; mental health nurse Glenwood Hosp., Midland, Tex., 1998—99; practice adminstr. Family Care Clinic and Med. Spa of Midland, 1999—. Instr. ACLS. Mem. Cmty. Chorale, Farmington, N.Mex., 1981, Roswell, N.Mex., 1989-90. Mem. AACN (rsch. assoc. Thunder Project 1991-92). Avocation: music. Office: Family Care Clinic 4506 Briarwood Ave Midland TX 79707-2642 Office Phone: 432-689-6818.

**SYED, IBRAHIM BIJLI,** medical educator, physicist; b. Bellary, India, Mar. 16, 1939; came to U.S., 1969, naturalized, 1975; s. Ahmed Bijli and Mumtaz Begum (Maniyar) S.; m. Sajida Shariff, Nov. 29, 1964; children: Mubin, Zafrin. BS with honors, Veerasaiva Coll., Bellary U., Mysore, 1959; MS with honors and distinction, Bangalore U., Mysore, 1962; diploma, U. Bombay, 1964; DSc, Johns Hopkins U., 1972; PhD (hon.), Malta, 1985. Cert. hazard control officer, 1980, internat. health care safety officer, 1980; diplomate Am. Bd. Radiology, Am. Bd. Health Physics. Lectr. physics Veerasaiva Coll., Bellary U., Mysore, 1962-63; med. physicist, radiation safety officer Victoria Hosp., India, 1964-67, Bowring and Lady Curz on Hosp. & Postgrad. Med. Rsch. Inst., Bangalore, India, 1964-67; cons. med. physicist, radiation

safety officer Ministry of Health, Govt. of Karnataka, India, 1964-67; Bangalore Nursing Home, India, 1964-67; med. physicist, radiation safety officer Baystate Med. Ctr., Springfield, Mass., 1973-79; assoc. prof. Springfield Tech. C.C.; also adj. prof. radiology Holyoke (Mass.) C.C., 1973-79; asst. clin. prof. nuclear medicine U. Conn. Sch. Medicine, Farmington, 1975-79; cons. med. physicist Mercy Hosp., Springfield, 1973-79, Wing Meml. Hosp., Palmer, Mass., 1973-79; med. physicist, radiation safety officer VAMC, Louisville, 1979—, exec. officer radiation safety com., 1979—; prof. medicine U. Louisville Sch. Medicine, 1979—; dir. nuclear med. scis., 1980—; mem. Instl. Review Bd. Veterans Admin. Medical Ctr., Louisville, 2000—. Guest lectr. religious studies program U. Louisville, 1979—; vis. prof. Bangalore U., 1987—88, Gulbarga U., India, 1987—88; vis. scientist Bhabha Atomic Rsch. Ctr., Bombay; invited spkr. Veerasaiva Coll., Bellary, India, 1996, Vijayanagar Coll., Hospet, 1996, Vajayanagar Inst. Med. Scis., Bellary, 1996, Deccan Coll. Med. Scis., Hyderabad, India, Bhabha Atomic Rsch. Ctr., Bombay, 1997, 15th Ann. Islamic Conf. New Eng., Islamic Coun. New Eng., 1999, Coun. for a Parliament of the World's Religions, Cape Town, South Africa, 1999, Garden City Coll. Bangalore, 2000, Veerasaiva Coll., Bellary, 2000, Islamic Rsch. Found.; Mumbai, India, 2001, Islamic Assn. of Essex, England, 2001, Assn. Muslim Social Scientists, Detroit, 2001, Darus Salam, Bangalore, India, 2005; invited faculty Assn. Muslim Social Scientists, Dallas, 2005; invited spkr. Islamic Orgn. Med. Scis., Cairo, 2002; PhD thesis examiner Allahabad U., 1996—; course dir. licensing for nuclear cardiologists U. Louisville, 1980—, mem. admissions com. nuclear medicine program, 1980—; guest relief examiner Am. Bd. Radiology, 1991, 2005; examiner in radiol physics, 1995, 97, 98, 2000; examiner in radiol. physics, 03, 05, 06; mem. panel of examiners Am. Bd. Health Physics; PhD thesis examiner U. Delhi, Internat. Inst. for Advanced Study, Clayton, Mo., 1985—, Allahabad (India) U., 1996—2005; faculty mem. Med. Physicists of India Ann. Meeting, 1987; IAEA tchr. expert in nuclear medicine on mission to People's Republic of Bangladesh, 86; to Guatemala, 94; founder, pres. Islamic Rsch. Found. Internat., Louisville, 1988—; convener Internat. Conf. on Islamic Renaissance: Action Plan for the 21st Century, Chgo., 1995; cons. Coun. Sci. and Indsl. Rsch., Govt. India, 0809—, Am. Coun. Sci. and Health, 1980—; cons. gastroenterology and urology divsn. FDA, HHS, 1988—, cons. radiopharm. divsn., 1989—; cons. Govt. India in nuclear medicine, diagnostic radiol. physics, therapeutic radiol. physics and radiation safety, 1992; cons. radiol. and med. nuc. physics Govt. India, Un Devel. Program, 1992; convenor Internat. Conf. on Islamic Renaissance, Chgo., 1995; guest spkr. Muslim Cmty. Ctr., Chgo. 1988; invited spkr. objective studies and Islamic voice, Bangalore, 96, Parliament of World Religions, Chgo., 1993, Cape Town, South Africa, 99, Cooper Mosque, Mississauga, Ont., Canada, 2002; invited faculty Assn. of Muslim Social Scientists, Dallas, 2005; invited spkr. Darus Salam, Bangalore, India, 2005. Author: Radiation Safety for Allied Health Professionals, Radiation Safety Manual, 1979, Intellectual Achievements of Muslims, 2002; contbg. editor Jour. of Islamic Food and Nutrition Coun. of Am., 1986—, health and sci. column Muslim Jour. 1989—; freelance writer Minaret Biweekly, N.Y.C., 1975—, Islamic Voice, India, 1988—, Al-Balaagh, Lenasia, South Africa, 1989—, AL'FURQAN Internat., Norcross, Ga., 1990, Message Internat., Jamaica, N.Y., 1990, Minaret Monthly Mag., L.A., 1995—, The Message, London, 1998—, The Minaret, Botswana, 1998—; editor: Science and Technology for the Developing World, 1988; mem. editl. bd. Jour. Islamic Med. Assn., 1981—; regular contbr. Pres.'s Page; manuscript reviewer for sci. and med. jours., 1973; assoc. editor AAlim, 1998—; contbr. more than 100 articles to sci. jours.; pub. internat. more than 300 articles on various topics of Islam in jours. and mags. Moderator fgn. policy workshop U.S. Dept. State, Louisville, 2000; spkr. Dayton Islamic Ctr., Dayton, 2000, Muslim Student Assn. U. Cin., 2000, Muslim Cmty. Ctr., Chgo., 2001; invited spkr. Muslim Assn. of Cleveland East, Cleve., 2002; bd. dir. Nur Islamic Sch., Louisville, 2003, Am. Muslim Assn. Louisville, 2003—; bd. dirs. Islamic Ctr. of Louisville, 1992—; founder, mgr., trustee Bijli Found. Charitable Trust, Bellary, India, 2005—. Recipient Disting. Cmty. Svc. award India Cmty. Found., 1982, Hind Rattan Jewel of India Title award Govt. India, 1994; WHO fellow, Govt. India scholar Bhabha Atomic Rsch. Ctr., Bombay, 1963-64; USPHS fellow Johns Hopkins U., 1969-72. Fellow Inst. Physics (U.K.), Am. Inst. Chemists, Royal Soc. Health, Am. Coll. Radiology, Internat. Acad. Med. Physics; mem. Am. Assn. Physicists in Medicine, Am. Coll. Nuclear Medicine, Health Physics Soc., Am. Acad. Health Physics, Soc. Nuclear Medicine (faculty mem. ann. meeting 1987, convenor internat. conf. 1995), Nat. Assn. Ams. of Asian Indian Descent (chmn. state pub. rels. com. 1982—), Islamic Med. Assn. N.Am. (life, faculty 1994, 96, 98), Internat. Inst. Islamic Medicine (faculty Orlando, Fla. 1996, 97, Birmingham, U.K. 1998), Islamic Soc. N.Am. (faculty Chgo. 1998), Islamic Soc. Balt. (founding mem.), Islamic Cultural Ctr.(sec. 1999-), Louisville, Islamic Assn. Maritime Provinces Can., Halifax, N.S. (asst. sec. 1967-69), Health Physics Soc. (chmn. med. health physics com. 1989—, affirmative action com. 1984—), Am. Assn. Physicists in Medicine (biol. effects com.), Assn. Muslim Scientists and Engrs. N.Am. (program chmn. ann. conf. 1987, treas. 1987-88, sec. 1988—), AAUP, Soc. Nuclear Medicine India (life, faculty mem. ann. meeting 1987, invited spkr. and faculty ann. meeting 1996), Assn. Med. Physicists India (life, invited spkr. and faculty ann. meeting Madras 1996), Med. and Biol. Physics (divsn. Can.) Assn. Physicists, Hosp. Physicists Assn., N.Y. Acad. Scis., Islamic Assn. Maritime Provinces of Can., Ky. Med. Assn., Jefferson County Med. Soc. (assoc.), Am. Physical Soc., Am. Muslim Assn. Louisville (bd. dirs. 2003—), Assn. Muslim Social Scientists, Sigma Xi Islamic. Home: 7102 W Shefford Ln Louisville KY 40242-4642 Office: 800 Zorn Ave Louisville KY 40206-1499 Office Phone: 502-287-6262. Business E-Mail: irfi@iname.com.

**SYKES, DIANE S.,** federal judge, former state supreme court justice; b. Milw., Dec. 23, 1957; 2 children. BA, Northwestern U., 1980; JD, Marquette U., 1984. Reporter Milw. Jour., law clk. to Hon. Terence T. Evans US Dist. Ct. (ea. dist.) WI, 1984—85; assoc. Whyte & Hirschboeck S.C., 1985—92; judge Milw. County Ct., 1992—99, Wis. Supreme Ct., Madison, 1999—2004, US Ct. Appeals (7th cir.), 2004—. Mem.: St. Thomas More Soc., Milw. Lawyers Chpt., Federalist Soc., Fairchild Inn, Am. Inns of Ct., Assn. for Women Lawyers, Seventh Cir. Bar Assn., Milw. Bar Assn., Wis. Bar Assn. Office: US Ct Appeals 7th Cir 371 US Court House 517 E Wisconsin Ave Milwaukee WI 53202 also: Dirksen Fed Bldg Rm 2742 219 S Dearborn St Chicago IL 60604 Office Phone: 414-727-6988.*

**SYKES, GRESHAM M'CREADY,** sociologist, educator, artist; b. Plainfield, NJ, May 26, 1922; s. M'Cready and Beatrice (Evans) S.; m. Carla Adelt, July 13, 1946. AB summa cum laude, Princeton U., 1950; PhD (Woodrow Wilson fellow 1950-51, Univ. fellow 1951-52), Northwestern U., 1953; MA (hon.), Dartmouth Coll., 1961. Instr. sociology Princeton U., 1952-54, asst. prof., bicentennial preceptor, 1954-58; assoc. prof. Northwestern U., Evanston, Ill., 1958-60; prof. sociology Dartmouth Coll., Hanover, NH, 1960-63, chmn. dept., 1961-63; exec. officer Am. Sociol. Assn., 1963-65; research prof. law and sociology, dir. adminstrn. of justice program U. Denver, 1965-72; chmn. dept. sociology U. Houston, 1973; prof. sociology U. Va., Charlottesville, 1974-88, chmn. dept., 1978-81, emeritus prof., 1988—. Chmn. Salzburg (Austria) Seminar in Am. Studies, summer 1965; working as artist, with frequent group and one-man exhbn., 1988—. Author: Crime and Society, rev. edit., 1967, The Society of Captives, 1958, Law and the Lawless, 1969, Social Problems in Am., 1971, Criminology, 1978, rev. edit., 1992, The Future of Crime, 1980; criminology editor Jour. Criminal Law, Criminology and Police Sci., 1959-64; assoc. editor Rev. Am. Sociol. Assn., 1960-62, Contemporary Sociology, 1977-80, Criminology, 1980-84; contbr. articles and revs. to Ency. Britannica, profl. jour. Served to capt., C.E. AUS, 1942-46, ETO. Recipient Edwin H. Sutherland award Am. Soc. Criminology, 1980. Home: 2197 Shepherds Ridge Road Charlottesville VA 22901

**SYKES, JOHN,** communications company executive; BS in Comm., Syracuse U. Staff CBS Records, 1977-80; mem. start-up team to v.p. programming MTV, 1980-86; agt. Creative Artists Agy., 1986-88; pres. Champion Entertainment, 1988—92; exec. v.p. talent acquisition and mktg. EMI Mus. Pub. Worldwide, 1992—94; pres. VH1, N.Y.C., 1994—2004; chmn., CEO Infinity Radio ops. Viacom Inc., 2004—05, with MTV Networks, 2005—. Bd. mem.

The Robin Hood Found., T.J. Martell Cancer Found., The City of Hope, Rock and Roll Hall of Fame; mem. adv. bd. Syracuse U. S.I. Newhouse Sch. Office: VH1 Viacom International 1515 Broadway Fl 20 New York NY 10036-8901

**SYKES, KATHRYN ROSEMARIE,** human resources specialist, consultant; d. William E. and Ruth A. Sykes. BSc, Fla. State U., 2002; MA, Appalachian State U., 2004. Jr. analyst Belle Enterprise & Tech., Inc., Harrisburg, Pa., 2004—05; human resources specialist Def. Logistics Agy., Harrisburg, Pa., 2004—05; human resouces specialist U.S. Army Corps. Engrs., N.Y., 2005—. Mem.: APA (assoc.), Soc. Human Resources Mgmt., Met. N.Y. Assn. Applied Psychology (assoc.), Chi Omega. Office Phone: 9177908126.

**SYKES, MELVIN JULIUS,** lawyer; b. Balt., Jan. 9, 1924; s. Philip Louis and Sara (Klein) S.; m. Judith Janet Konowitz, Sept. 24, 1950; children: David K., Rachel A. (dec.), Daniel E., Israel J. Grad., Balt. City Coll., 1940, Balt. Hebrew Coll., 1941; AB with honors, Johns Hopkins U., 1943; LLB magna cum laude, Harvard U., 1948. Bar: Md. 1949, U.S. Ct. Appeals (4th cir.) 1949, U.S. Dist. Ct. Md. 1950, U.S. Supreme Ct. 1955. Law clk. to Judge Morris A. Soper U.S. Ct. Appeals (4th cir.), 1948-49; pvt. practice Balt., 1949—. Draftsman Md. Dept. Legislative Reference, 1949—50; rsch. cons. Md. Commn. Adminstrv. Orgn., 1951—52; reporter Md. Commns. to Study Judiciary, 1953; Md. commns. to revise law relating to pub. svc. commn., 1953—55; mem. standing com. on rules of practice, procedure Md. Ct. Appeals, 1954—72, 1978—; mem. legis. coun. Commsn. on Revision Condemnation Laws, 1961—63; mem. Balt. Charter Revision Com., 1962—63; pres. Fund. Md. Bar Libr. Balt., 1962—63; mem. Md. Constl. Conv. Commn., 1966—67; cons. Gov. Md. Commn. to Revise Testamentary Laws, 1967—69; mem. Gov. Md. Commns. to study state aid to nonpub. edn., 1969—71, Md. Code Revision Commn., 1970—78. Co-author: West's Maryland Procedural Forms, 1964, Jewish Law (Mishpat Ivri), Cases and Materials, 1999; co-translator Elon, Jewish Law--History, Principles, Sources, 1994. Bd. dirs. Balt. Neighborhoods; mem. governing coun. Am. Assn. Jewish Edn., 1968—81; bd. dirs. Balt. Jewish Coun., 1970—72; bd. dirs. Balt. chpt. Am. Jewish Com.; bd. dirs. Inst. for Christian and Jewish Studies; former mem. and chmn. bd. trustees Balt. Hebrew U. With USAF, 1943—45. Fellow Am. Coll. Trial Lawyers, Am. Acad. of Appellate Lawyers, Am. Coll. Trust and Estate Counsel, Am. Bar Found.; mem. ABA, Am. Law Inst., Md. Bar Assn., Balt. City Bar Assn., Am. Jewish Congress, Balt. Zionist Dist., B'nai B'rith, Phi Beta Kappa Democrat. Home: 3811 Fords Ln Baltimore MD 21215-2804 Office: Ste 1701 120 E Baltimore St Baltimore MD 21202-6701 Office Phone: 410-727-3078. Business E-Mail: msykes@mjsykes.com.

**SYKES, PLUM,** writer; b. London, 1969; married. BA in Modern History, Oxford U. Fashion writer Vogue (British), 1993—97; contbg. editor Vogue (Am.), 1997—. Author: (novels) Bergdorf Blondes, 2004 (Publishers Weekly Bestseller lists), The Debutante Divorcee, 2006. Office: c/o Janklow & Nesbit 445 Park Ave New York NY 10022*

**SYKES, RICHARD NESBIT,** retired history professor, department chairman; b. Charlotte, N.C., Jan. 11, 1942; s. Richard Nesbitt and Sarah Elizabeth (Hovis) Sykes. AB in History and English summa cum laude, So. Wesleyan U., 1964; MA in Social Sci. and Reading Spec., Appalachian State U., 1965; PhD in History, Greenwich U., 2001. Cert. educator S.C., N.C. Instr. history and polit. sci. Gordon Coll., Barnesville, Ga., 1965—67; asst. prof. history and reading Gardner-Webb Coll., Boiling Springs, NC, 1967—69; instr. history and reading Ctrl. Piedmont C.C., Charlotte, 1969—70; coordinator secondary reading Chester County Schs., 1971—73; reading specialist Williamsburg County Schs., 1973—74; reading diagnostician Chesterfield County Schs., 1974—79; tchr., reading specialist Buford HS, Lancaster, SC, 1979—90; prof. history Aiken Tech. Coll., 1990—2005, dept. chair, 2001—05, ret., 2006. Nominee Gov.'s Disting. Prof. award, S.C. Comm. on Higher Edn., 2000; named Faculty Mem. of Yr., Aiken Tech. Coll., 1999; recipient medal, Nat. Inst. Staff and Orgnl. Devel., 2000. Mem.: S.C. State Employees Assn., S.C. Tech. Edn. Assn. (Educator of Yr. 1991—92, Nominee State Educator of Yr. 1991—92), Nat. Geog. Soc., Smithsonian Instn. Avocations: reading, walking, fishing. Home: 838 Osbon Dr Aiken SC 29801-4154

**SYKES, ROBIN ALEXIS,** plastic surgeon; b. McKeesport, Pa., May 17, 1954; d. Robert Thomas and Joyce Patrick Sykes; m. Thomas Richard Rowe, Aug. 12, 1989; children: Galen, Alexis. BA in Biology, Wells Coll., 1976; MD, Johns Hopkins U., 1980; postgrad., U. Miami, 1983, U. Kans., 1985. Diplomate Am. Bd. Med. Specialties. Pvt. practice, Jupiter, Fla., 1985—. Reporter Healthvision TV Sta. WPBF, 2001—02; spkr. in field. Mem.: Palm Beach County Plastic Surgeons, Am. Soc. for Laser and Medicine and Surgery, Am. Med. Womens Assn., Fla. Soc. Plastic Surgeons, Am. Soc. Plastic Surgeons, Fla. Med. Assn. Avocations: music, reading, travel, theater, movies. Office: Jupiter Plastic Surgery Ctr 2055 Military Tr Ste 305 Jupiter FL 33458 Office Phone: 561-746-9400. Personal E-mail: drrasplastic@aol.com.

**SYKES, WANDA,** comedienne, actress; b. Portsmouth, Va., Mar. 7, 1964; BS, Hampton U. Actor: (TV series) Best of Chris Rock, 1999, Larry David: Curb Your Enthusiasm, 1999, Crank Yankers, 2003—, Wanda Does It, 2004; (films) Tomorrow Night, 1998, Nutty Professor II: The Klumps, 2000, Down to Earth, 2001, Pootie Tang, 2001, Monster-in-Law, 2005, Clerks II, 2006, My Super Ex-Girlfriend, 2006, (voice) Over the Hedge, 2006, Barnyard: The Original Party Animals, 2006; actor, writer (TV series) The Chris Rock Show, 1997—2000 (Emmy award for outstanding writing, 1999), The Downer Channel, 2001, writer, creator, actor, prodr. Wanda at Large, 2003, writer The Keenen Ivory Wayans Show, 1997, guest appearances include The Drew Carey Show, Chappelle's Show; author: Yeah I Said It, 2004; appears on (TV series) Inside the NFL, 2002—. Recipient Am. Comedy award for Funniest Female Stand-Up Comic, 2001. Office: Creative Artists Agy 9830 Wilshire Blvd Beverly Hills CA 90212*

**SYKORA, PETR,** professional hockey player; b. Plzen, Czechoslovakia, Nov. 19, 1976; m. Reynata Sykora. Center Cleve. Lumberjacks, 1993—94, Detroit Vipers, 1994—95, Albany River Rats; right wing NJ Devils, 1995—2002, Anaheim Mighty Ducks, 2002—06, NY Rangers, 2006, Edmonton Oilers, 2006—. Mem. Czech Republic Nat. Hockey Team, World Cup of Hockey, 1996, 2004, Czech Republic Nat. Hockey Team, Olympic Games, Salt Lake City, 2002. Named to All-Rookie Team, NHL, 1996. Achievements include being a member of Stanley Cup Champion NJ Devils, 2000. Office: Edmonton Oilers Hockey Club 11230 - 110 St Edmonton AB T5G 3H7 Canada*

**SYLK, LEONARD ALLEN,** manufacturing executive, real estate developer; b. Phila., Feb. 25, 1941; s. Harry S. and Gertrude (Bardy) S.; m. Barbara Ann Lovenduski, Dec. 1, 1975; children: Tristan, Tyler, Galen. BS in Econs., U. Pa., 1963; MBA, Columbia U., 1965. Cert. comml. property builder. Founder, chmn. bd., CEO Shelter Systems Corp., Hainesport, NJ, 1965-99; ret.; prin. and CEO Property Mgmt. Svcs., Hainesport, 1996—. Vice pres. USA Bancshares, Inc., 1998-2000; chmn., bd. govs. Mid. East Forum; trustee Nat. Bldg. Sys. Coun., 1986—; presdl. advisor on housing trade with Soviet Union, 1990; bldg. industry advisor U.S. Dept. Commerce, 1997-99; mem. leadership coun. Franklin & Marshall Coll., 2006—. Contbr. articles to industry publs. Chmn. ann. awards dinner Jewish Nat. Fund, Phila., 1987, v.p.; bd. dir.; bd. dirs. Phila. Orch. Assn., 1990-98, emeritus, 1999—; bd. trustees Roman Catholic H.S., Phila., 2003—; bd. dir. Pa. Ballet, 1994-99, exec. com., 1996-99, vice-chmn., pres., 1998; bd. dir. Resources for Childrens' Health, 1993-96, Acad. Music, Phila. 1990-96, Rock Sch. of Pa. Ballet, 1995-98, Young Scholars Charter Sch., 2000—; bd. dir. Jewish Nat. Fund, 1987—, v.p., 2000—; trustee Hahnemann U. and Hosp., 1991-96; vice chmn., trustee St. Christopher's Hosp. Children, Phila., 1994-2002, chmn. St. Christophers Found. Children, 1999, v.p., bd. dir., 1999-2002; chmn. 1999, bd. dirs., vice chmn. St. Peter's Sch., Phila., 1995-03; trustee Allegheny U.

---

Hosps., 1999—; bd. trustees Compass Charter H.S., Phila., 2004; bd. mem. Hosp U. Pa. Cancer Ctr., 2004-; N.J. chmn. Builders Bush, 1988. Named Man. of Yr., 1988, Man of Yr., NJ C. of C., 2002, 2001; recipient Tree of Life award presented by R. Hon. Margaret Thatcher, 1995, Leadership award, Roman Cath. Sch. Sys., 2006. Mem. Nat. Assn. Homebuilders (com. chmn., nat. bd. dir. 1984—, mem. exec. com. 1990, 97, fundraising chmn. 1991, Man of Yr. in Industrialized Housing 1990), Wood Truss Coun. Am. (bd. dir. 1983—, pres. 1987, named to Hall of Fame 1990), Builders League South Jersey (v.p., bd. dir. 1984-94), N.J. Builders Assn. (bd. dir., com. chmn., exec. com. 1990-96), Merion Civic Assn. (bd. dir. 1999-2001), Le Club (N.Y.C.), Atlantic City Country Club, Vesper Club, Union League, Capitol Club (Washington), Masons. Republican. Home: 350 N Highland Ave Merion Station PA 19066-1708 Office: Property Mgmt Svcs PO Box 9 Hainesport NJ 08036-0009

**SYLK, ROBERT F.,** casino marketing executive; s. Harry Sylk; 1 child, Kelly Jo. Pres. Sylk Corp., Marina del Rey, Calif.; prin. Travel Agts. Internat., Marina del Rey; bldg. dir. La Quinta (Calif.) C. of C. Bd. dirs. NASDAQ Corp. Save the World Air. Founder Marina del Rey Food and Wine Festival; pres., founder Marina/Venice chpt. City of Hope; former del. L.A. Tourism and Trade Commn.; mem. adv. bd. Dept. Beaches and Harbors, Marina del Rey; commr. Cit of La Quinty Cmty. Svcs.; chief precinct officer, sr. inspector County Registrar's dist. 4; election ofcl. Riverside County; chief inspector Riverside County-La Quinta Elections; bd. dirs. La Quinta, USO of Greater L.A.; former sr. v.p., bd. dirs. Marina del Rey C. of C. With U.S. Army. Named City of Hope Man of Yr., 1997; recipient Tree of Life award, Jewish Nat. Fund. Mem.: La Quinta C. of C. (bd. dirs., exec. bd.), Cornerstone Club (past pres.). Office: 79675 Rancho Santa Margarita La Quinta CA 92253

**SYLVERN, CRAIG,** music educator; m. Robin Gale; 1 child, Isaac. MusB in Music Composition, Fla. State U., 1981, MusB in Music Edn., 1981, MusM in Performance, 1985; MusD in Music Composition, Ohio State U., 1996. Vis. asst. prof. Plattsburgh State U., NY, 1997—98; assoc. prof. Keene (N.H.) State Coll., 1998—. Mem.: Tech. Inst. Music Educators, N.Am. Saxophone Alliance, Assn. Tech. Music Instrn., Coll. Music Soc. Office Phone: 603-358-2185. Business E-Mail: csylvern@keene.edu.

**SYLVESTER, JOHN ANDREW,** social studies educator; b. Springfield, Mass., Dec. 20, 1935; s. Andrew Armour Sylvester and Stella Elizabeth Davies. AB cum laude, Harvard U., 1957; MA, U. Wis., 1959, PhD, 1967. Assoc. prof. history Okla. State U., Stillwater, 1970—95, asst. prof. history, 1966—70. Contbr. articles to profl. jours. Staff sgt. U.S. Army, 1958—62. Mem.: The Soc. for Historians of Am. Fgn. Rels., Orgn. of Am. Historians. Avocations: classical music, films, philately. Home: O4 Belden Ct Agawam MA 01001-3803

**SYLVESTER, ROBERT,** dean, musician; b. NYC; Dir. cultural affairs Western Wash. U., dean Sch. Fine & Performing Arts; pres. Portland State U., 1997—. Cofounder Chamber Music at Guggenheim Festival, N.Y.C., Cape & Island Festival, Cape Cod, Mass., Bellingham Festival Music. Avocation: cello. Office: Office of the Dean Sch Fine & Performing Arts Portland State U 349 Lincoln Hall Portland OR 97207-0751 Office Phone: 503-725-3105. E-mail: sylvester@pdx.edu.

**SYLVESTRE, JEAN GUY,** former national librarian; b. Sorel, Que., Can., May 17, 1918; s. Maxime Arthur and Yvonne Marie (Lapierre) S.; m. Francoise Poitevin, Feb. 27, 1943; children: Marie, Jean, Paul. BA, U. Ottawa, 1939, B.Ph., 1940, MA, 1942, D.L.S. (hon.), 1969, D.Litt. (hon.), 1970, LL.D. (hon.), 1974, 75, 82. Translator Dept. Can. Sec. of State, 1942-44; editor Wartime Info. Bd., 1944-45; asst. pvt. sec. to minister of justice, 1945-47; pvt. sec. to sec. of state for external affairs, 1947-48; pvt. sec. to prime minister, 1948-50; adminstrv. officer Dept. Resources and Devel., 1950-53; asst. librarian Library of Parliament, Ottawa, Ont., 1953-56, asso. parliamentary librarian, 1956-68, nat. librarian, 1968-83; pres., chmn. bd. Can. Inst. for Hist. Microprodns., 1983-86; chmn. Ottawa Valley Book Festival, 1988-92; hon. chmn., 1993—. Author: Louis Francoeur, journaliste, 1941, Situation de la poésie canadienne, 1941, Anthologie de la poésie canadienne-française, 1943, 58, 64, 66, 68, 74, Poètes catholiques de la France contemporaine, 1944, Sondages, 1945, Impressions de théâtre, 1950, Amours, délices et orgues, 1953, Panorama des lettres canadiennes-francaises, 1964, Canadian Writers, 1964, Literature in French Canada, 1967, A Century of Canadian Literature, 1967, The Future of the National Library of Canada, 1980, Guidelines for National Libraries, 1987 French, Spanish and Arabic edits., 1988; also articles in profl. jours., encys.; editor: A Canadian Errant (J.P. Manion), 1960; editor: Canadian Universities Today, 1961, Structures sociales du Canada francais, 1967. Chmn. Gov. Gen.'s Lit. Awards, 1960-62; organizer, chmn. World Poetry Conf., Expo 1967; chmn. Can. Council Com. on Aid-to-Publs., 1960-68; lectr. U. Ottawa Library Sch., 1954-71; v.p. Can. Library Week Council, 1965-67; Bd. dirs. Can. Writers Found., pres., 1960-61. Decorated comdr. Ordre International du Bien Public, officer Order of Can.; comdr. Order of Merit of Poland; recipient Centennial medal., Outstanding Pub. Service award, Internat. Fedn. Libr. Assn. medal. Fellow Royal Soc. Can. (hon. sec. 1959-62, pres. sect. 1 1963-64, hon. libr. 1969-91, pres. 1973-74); mem. Can. Libr. Assn. (life), Ont. Libr. Assn. (hon. life), Can. Assn. Info. Sci. (pres. 1971-72), Assn. Scis. et Techniques (life). Home: 2286 Bowman Rd Ottawa ON Canada K1H 6V6

**SYMANZIK, JUERGEN,** statistician, educator; m. Natascha Vukasinovic; 1 child, Alexandar. PhD, Iowa State U., Ames, Iowa, 1996. Assoc. prof. Utah State U., Logan, Utah, 1999—. Co-chmn. Interface Found. N.Am., Fairfax, Va., 2002—. Mem.: Am. Statis. Assn. (coun. sects. rep. 2002—06, rep., pres. Utah chpt. 2001—06, chmn. program 2002—06), Interface Found. of N.Am. (bd. of directors mem., 2003 co-chair 2002—). Office: Utah State University Department of Mathematics and Statistics Logan UT 84322-3900 Office Phone: 435-797-0696. Business E-Mail: symanzik@math.usu.edu.

**SYMCHOWICZ, SAMSON,** retired biochemist; b. Krakow, Poland, Mar. 20, 1923; came to U.S., 1954; s. Chiel and Esther M. S.; m. Sarah R. Nussbaum, May 24, 1953; children: Esther, Beatrice, Caren. Chem. engr., Poly. Inst. Prague, Czechoslovakia, 1950; MS in Chemistry, Bklyn. Poly. Inst., 1956; PhD in Biochemistry, Rutgers U., 1960. Asst. biochemist McGill U., Montreal, Que., Can., 1951-54, SUNY, 1954-56; research asst. Schering-Plough Corp., Bloomfield, N.J., 1956-73, assoc. dir. biol. rsch., 1973-80, dir. drug metabolism, 1980-92; ret. Editorial bd. Drug Metabolism and Disposition; contbr. over 90 sci. papers to profl. publs. Mem. Internat. Soc. Study of Xenobiotics, Am. Chem. Soc., N.Y. Acad. Sci., Soc. Pharmacology and Exptl. Therapeutics.

**SYME, DANIEL BAILEY,** rabbi, institution executive; b. Sharon, Pa., Feb. 6, 1946; s. Monte Robert and Sonia (Hendin) S.; m. Jill Susan Young; 1 child, Joshua. BA, U. Mich., Ann Arbor, 1967; BHL, MAHL, Hebrew Union Coll.-Jewish Inst. Religion, Cin., 1972; MEd, Columbia U., 1977, EdD, 1980. Ordained rabbi, 1972. Asst. dir. Nat. Fedn. Temple Youth, 1972-73; rabbi Stamford (Conn.) Fellowship for Jewish Learning, 1973-77; asst. nat. dir. edn. Union of Am. Hebrew Congregations, N.Y.C., 1973-77, 1977—; asst. dir. Commn. Jewish Edn. for Reform Movement, N.Y.C., 1973-77, 1977—, Union of Am. Hebrew Congregations TV Inst., N.Y.C., 1982-83, exec. asst. to pres., 1983-85, v.p., 1985-91, sr. v.p., 1991-96; sr. rabbi Temble Beth El, Bloomfield Hills, Mich., 1996—. Chmn. coalition for Alternatives in Jewish Edn., N.Y.C., 1978-80; mem. Nat. Assn. Temple Educators, 1972-91, Commn. on Teaching of Israel and Zionism, World Zionist Orgn., 1980-84; dir.-at-large Jewish Nat. Fund, Jewish Fedn. Met. Detroit, 2000—, internat. bd. Meml. Found. for Jewish Culture; nat. cabinet mem. Am. Zionist Movement, v.p. Am. Zionist Youth Movement; bd. dirs. United Israel Appeal, Ecumenical Inst. Author: 100 Essential Books for Jewish Readers, Finding God, My Body is Something Special, Prayer Is Reaching, I'm Growing, I Learn About God, Books Are Treasures, Jewish Home, What Happens After I Die?, Why I Am a Reform Jew, Drugs, Sex and Integrity, The Jewish Wedding Book, The Book of the Jewish Life; exec. prodr. T.V. programs A

---

Conversation with Menachem Begin, 1981, Choosing Judaism, 1981, To See the World Through Jewish Eyes, 1983, A Conversation with Yitzchak Navon, 1983, You Can Go Home Again, Jewish Youth and Cults, 1984; contbr. articles to religious publs. Mem. Rabbinic Adv. Coun., United Jewish Appeal, Nat. Religious Edn. Assn. (exec. bd.), Nat Coun. Jewish Edn. (exec. bd.), Econ. Club Detroit (bd. dirs.), Jewish Nat Fung (bd. dir.) Office: 7400 Telegraph Rd Bloomfield Hills MI 48301-3876

**SYMES, LAWRENCE RICHARD,** computer science educator, university dean; s. Oliver Lawrence and Maybell Melita Blanche Symes; m. Evelyn Jean Hewett, Apr. 3, 1964; children: Calvin Richard, Michelle Louise, Erin Kathleen. BA, U. Sask., Saskatoon, Can., 1963, postgrad. in math., 1964; MS, Purdue U., 1966, Phd, 1969. Asst. prof. Purdue U., West Lafayette, Ind., 1969-70; assoc. prof. computer sci. U. Regina, Sask., Canada, 1970-74, prof. Sask., 1974—, dir. computer ctr. Sask., 1970-75, head dept. computer sci. Sask., 1972-81, dean of sci. Sask., 1982-92, dean grad. studies, assoc. rsch. v.p. Sask., 1997-99, dir. info. svcs. Sask., 1999—. Dir. tng. Software Tech. Ctr., 1993-94; exec. dir. postsecondary svcs. br. Saskatchewan Edn. Tng. and Employment Govt. of Saskatchewan, 1994-95, exec. dir. multimedia learning, 1995-96; invited lectr. Xian Jiaotong U., 1983; invited lectr., Shandong Acad. Sci., China, 1987, guest prof.; vis. prof. Ednl. Inst. Jilin Province, Shandong U., Jinan, China; co-chair IT cluster Regina Regional Econ. Authority, 2002—. Contbr. articles to profl. jours. Bd. dirs. Hosp. Sys. Study Group, Saskatoon, 1978-94, chmn. bd., 1980-83; dir. SSTA Computer Svcs., Regina, 1972-89; mem. adv. coun. Can./Sask. Advanced Tech. Agreement, 1985-87; mem. Sask. Agrl. Rsch. Found. Bd., 1987-88; mem. steering com. IBM/Sask. Agreement, 1990-92; mem. adv. bd. Plant Biotech. Inst., NRC, Can. Fed. Govt. grantee, 1977-84. Mem. Assn. Computing Machinery, Can. Info. Processing (pres. 1979-80, accreditation com. 1988-94), IEEE Computer Soc., Sask. ADA Assn. (bd. dirs. 1990-93), Software Tech. Ctr. (bd. dirs. 1993-98), Regina Regional Econ. Authority (IT cluster co-chair). Office: U Regina Info Svcs 3737 Wascana Pkwy Regina SK Canada S4S 0A2

**SYMLAR, JESSE LEE,** finance executive; b. Cleve., Aug. 4, 1959; s. Jesse Lee and Willa Leeann S. BA in Pub. Adminstrn., Christopher Newport U., 1982; MBA in Tech. Mgmt., U. Md., 2001. Project mgr. VYCOR Corp., Washington, 1986-90; multimedia tng. Multimedia Tng. Inst., Washington, 1987-88; program analyst Det. Vets. Affairs, Washington, 1990; program mgmt. U.S. Dept. Agrl., Washington, 1990-93; program analyst Dept. Vets. Affairs, Washington, 1993-99; bus. process engr. Multimedia, Upper Marlboro, Md., 1998-2000; CEO Kyi Internat., Upper Marlboro, Md., 2000—. Author of poems. Mentor Each-One-Teach-One, Upper Marlboro, 1997-99. Sgt. USAF, 1975-79. Mem. Amherst Soc., Internat. Soc. Poets (disting.). Avocations: art, poetry, music, chess, sports, computers. Home: 3311 Old Largo Rd Upper Marlboro MD 20772-7811 E-mail: jsymlar@msn.com.

**SYMONDS, CRAIG,** historian, writer; b. Long Beach, Calif., Dec. 31, 1946; s. Lee and Virginia (Garrison) Symonds; m. Marylou Hayden, Jan. 17, 1969; 1 child, Jeffrey. BA, UCLA, 1967; MA, U. Fla., Gainesville, 1969, PhD, 1976. Prof. strategy U.S. Naval War Coll., Newport, RI, 1974—75; prof. history U.S. Naval Acad., Annapolis, Md., 1976—2005, prof. emeritus, 2006—; chief historian The Monitor Ctr. at The Mariners' Mus., 2005—. Prof. strategy Britania Royal Naval Coll., Dartmouth, England, 1994—95. Author: (Book) Navalists and Antinavalists, 1980, A Battlefield Atlas of the Civil War, 1983, A Battlefield Atlas of the American Revolution, 1986, Joseph E. Johnson: A Civil War Biography, 1992, Gettysburg (A Battlefield Atlas), 1992, The Naval Institute's Historical Atlas of the U.S. Navy, 1995, Stonewall of the West: Patrick Cleburne and the Civil War, 1997, Confederate Admiral: The Life and Wars of Franklin Buchanan, 1999, The American Heritage History of the Battle of Gettysburg, 2001, Decision at Sea: Five Naval Battles that Shaped American History, 2005; editor: Charleston Blockade, 1976, New Aspects of Naval History, 1980, Recollections of a Naval Officer, 1995, A Year on the Monitor and the Destruction of Fort Sumter, 1991. Home: 102 Hillmere Ct Annapolis MD 21401-3767 E-mail: macsymonds@aol.com.

**SYMONETTE, LYS,** foundation executive, musician, writer; b. Mainz, Germany, Dec. 21, 1920; came to U.S., 1936; d. Max Weinschenk and Gertrude (Metzger) Honheisser; m. Randolph Symonette, Sept. 1, 1949; 1 child, Victor. Student, Curtis Inst., Phila., 1937-39. Piano accompanist to internat. singers, 1940—. Musical asst. to Kurt Weill and L. Lenya, 1945-81; tchr. Curtis Inst., Phila., 1976—; musical exec., v.p. Kurt Weill Found., N.Y.C., 1981—. Translator operas from English to German and German to English, 1945—; co-editor Speak Low, Family Letters, 1996. Mem. Am. Fedn. Musicians, Alumni Assn. Curtis Inst. Music. Home: 160 W 73rd St New York NY 10023-3012 Office: Kurt Weill Found for Music 7 E 20th St New York NY 10003-1106

**SYMONS, EDWARD LEONARD, JR.,** lawyer, educator, investment advisor; b. Pitts., Dec. 21, 1941; s. Edward Leonard and Lillian Mae (Daniel) S.; m. Louise Quinn, July 18, 1970; children: Amy, Colin. BA, Cornell U., 1963; JD summa cum laude, U. Pitts., 1969. Assoc., ptnr. Reding, Blackstone, Rea & Sell, Pitts., 1969-72; asst. atty. gen., chief counsel Pa. Dept. Banking, Harrisburg, 1972-74; prof. law U. Pitts. Sch. Law, 1974-98; CEO Symons Capital Mgmt., Inc., 1983—. Tax cons., Wash., 1987, Del., 95; exec. v.p. investments Smithfield Trust Co., 1996—2000; mem. adv. coun. Conflict Resolution Ctr. Internat., 1994—2004; mem. bd. internat. scholars Ctr. for Comml. Law Studies, Queen Mary and Westfield Coll., U. London, 1993—2004. Co-author: Pennsylvania Professional Corporations, 1974, Banking Law Teaching Materials, 1984, 3d edit., 1991, Regulation of Financial Institutions, 1998; contbr. articles to profl. jours. Commr., Mt. Lebanon, Pa., 1976—80; chmn. St. Clair Hosp. Found., Pitts., 1996—; bd. dirs. Performing Arts for Children, Pitts., 1980—84, Mt. Lebanon Hosp. Authority, 1993—2004, St. Clair Hosp., 1995—. 1st. lt. arty., AUS, 1964—66. Mem.: Order Coif. Office: Symons Capital Mgmt Inc 250 Mount Lebanon Blvd Ste 301 Pittsburgh PA 15234-1248 Office Phone: 412-344-7690.

**SYMONS, ROBERT SPENCER,** electronics engineer; b. San Francisco, July 3, 1925; s. Spencer W. and Avesia (Atkins) S.; m. Alice Faye Smith, Dec. 21, 1960; children: Julia Ann, Robert Spencer Jr. BS, Stanford U., 1946, MS, 1948. Engr. Eitel-McCullough, Inc., San Bruno, Calif., 1947, Heinz & Kaufman, South San Francisco, 1948, Pacific Electronics Co., Los Gatos, Calif., 1949; sr. engring. mgr. Varian Assocs., Palo Alto, Calif., 1950-83; tech. dir. CTO Litton Sys., Inc., San Carlos, Calif., 1983—. Patentee in field. 1st lt. AUS, 1950-53. Recipient Charles B. Thornton award for Advanced Tech. Achievement, 1991, 99. Fellow IEEE (assoc. editor Transactions on Electron Devices jour. 1980-83); mem. Commonwealth of Calif. Club, Phi Beta Kappa, Tau Beta Pi. Home: 290 Surrey Pl Los Altos CA 94022-2180 Office: Litton Industries 960 Industrial Rd San Carlos CA 94070-4194

**SYMONS, VAN JAY,** humanities educator; b. Logan, Utah, June 5, 1945; s. Joseph Nathaniel Symons and Vivian Lavon Burrup; m. Ruth Alene Thomson; children: Amy Marie Ettore, Brandt Nathaniel, Cherilyn Andrea, Diana Christine, Karl Woodruff. AB, Brigham Young U., Provo, Utah, 1970; PhD, Brown U., Providence, R.I., 1974. Asst. prof. Whittier Coll., Calif., 1974—78; prof. Augustana Coll., Rock Island, Ill., 1978—. Dir. ASIANetwork Consultancy Adv. Program, Bloomington, Ill., 1998—99; program dir. ASIANetwork, Bloomington, 1999—2005; mem. editl. adv. bd. EastBridge Press, Norwalk, Conn., 2001—; sr. editl. adv. bd. Edn. About Asia, Ann Arbor, Mich., 2003—05; vis. prof. Brigham Young U., Provo, 1982—83; vis. Mansfield prof. of modern Asian affairs Maureen and Mike Mansfield Ctr., U. Mont., Missoula, 1990—91. Author: (book) Ch'ing Ginseng Management: Ch'ing Monopolies in Microcosm; co-author (with Sechin Jagchid): Peace, War, and Trade along the Great Wall: Nomadic Chinese Interaction through Two Millennia; co-editor: Asia in the Undergraduate Curriculum: A Case for Asian Studies in Liberal Arts Education. Vice-chair, chair ASIANetwork, Bloomington, 1995—99. Fellow, NEH, Summer Insts., 1978, 1980, 1994,

1995. Church Of Jesus Christ Of Latter-Day Saints. Home: 123 Fernwood Ave Davenport IA 52803 Office: Augustana Coll 639 - 38th St Rock Island IL 61201 Office Phone: 309-794-7413. Office Fax: 309-794-7702. Business E-Mail: vanjsymons@augustana.edu.

**SYNCLAIR, LARRY ROSS,** news correspondent, advocate; b. Fresno, Calif., June 27, 1960; s. Emily C. and Larry R. Griffith; m. S.E. Stinson, July 30, 1980 (div. Sept. 1981); m. S.V. Gavrilova, June 4, 1994 (div. Jan. 23, 2003); children: Jason, Larry Jr. AA, N. Idaho Coll., Coeur d'Alene, 1984; BA, Wash. State U., Pullman, 1986; MA, Calif. State U., Chico, 1990. Cert. grant writing Portland C.C., 2005. U. instr. Wash. State U., Pullman, Wash., 1986—86; ops. dir. KCHO-FM, Chico, Calif., 1987—90; assoc. prof. Calif. State U., Chico, 1991; radio prodr., announcer Radio Moscow, 1991—92; fgn. news corr. USA Radio Network, Moscow, 1991—94; news dir., morning show co-host Radio 7, Moscow, 1992—94; fgn. news corr. substitute NBC Radio News, Moscow, 1994; founder, pres. Synclair & Assoc., Moscow, 1994—98; state corr. Westwood One, Portland, Oreg., 2004—05; freelance writer, legal rschr. Portland, 1998—. Mem. Parental Abduction Prevention Work Group, Oreg. Commn. Children and Families), Salem, 2006; author Synclair-Cannon Child Abduction Prevention Act of 2003, Calif. family code sect. 3048. Recipient Spl. Recognition, Delta Kappa Gamma, 1990; KCPQ scholar, Kelly Broasdcasting, 1985, Athletic scholar, N. Idaho Coll., 1980.

**SYNEK, MIROSLAV,** physicist, chemist, world affairs consultant; b. Prague, Czech Republic, Sept. 18, 1930; came to U.S., 1958, naturalized, 1963; s. Frantisek and Anna (Kokrment) S.; children: Mary Rose, Thomas Robert. Cert., Indsl. Chemistry Tech. Sch., Prague, 1946-50; cert. in liberal arts, Prague, 1951; MS in Physics with distinction, Charles U., Prague, 1956; PhD in Physics, U. Chgo., 1963. Analytical chemist Indsl. Medicine Inst., Prague, 1950-51; rsch. physicist Acad. Scis., Prague, 1958; from asst. to assoc. prof. De Paul U., Chgo., 1962-67; prof. Tex. Christian U., Ft. Worth, 1967-71; lectr., rsch. U. Tex., Austin, 1971-75; tenured faculty U. Tex., San Antonio, 1975-95. Sci. advisor Tex. Edn. Agy., Austin, 1971-73, U. Tex., 1971-73; advisor Student Physics Soc., active numerous univ. coms. Contbr. numerous articles to sci. jours., abstracts to presentations. Campaigner United Way, San Antonio, 1975-95; judge Alamo Sci. Fairs and Tex. Acad. of Sci. Fairs, annually; grand award judge Internat. Sci. and Engring. Fairs, 1998, 99. Rsch. grantee Robert A. Welch Found., 1968-71, 76-83, 93-95. Fellow AAAS, Am. Phys. Soc. (life), Tex. Acad. Sci., Am. Inst. Chemists; mem. NEA, Tex. State Tchrs. Assn., AAUP, DAV Comdrs. Club, Am. Assn. Physics Tchrs., Am. Acad. Polit. Sci., Am. Mus. Natural History, Libr. Congress, Smithsonian Instn., Nat. Trust Hist. Preservation, N.Y. Acad. Scis., Am. Chem. Soc. (San Antonio edn. com. chmn.), Czechoslovak Nat. Coun. Am. (dist. sec. Chgo. 1961-63, chmn. 1967), Czechoslovak Soc. Arts and Scis. Am., Internat. Soc. Poets (disting. mem.), Sheriffs' Assn. Tex. (assoc.), San Antonio Astron. Assn., World Affairs Coun. San Antonio (diplomat mem.), Bexar County Czech Heritage Soc. of Tex., Sigma Xi (life), Sigma Pi Sigma (sustaining). Roman Catholic. Achievements include research in atomic structure calculations of laser-active lanthanides, analytical relativistic self-consistent field theory, approximate estimate of the extra-terrestrial intelligence probability, nuclear age requiring free elections, main dangers of our times, suggested priorities for human society. Home and Office: Independent Consultant PO Box 5937 San Antonio TX 78201-0937 Personal E-Mail: m.synek@juno.com.

**SYNNOTT, AIDAN JOHN,** lawyer; b. Cork, Ireland, July 1, 1964; arrived in U.S., 1987; s. Edward Christopher Synnott and Nora Mary Angela Walsh; m. Elizabeth Lauren Grayer, May 11, 2002; 1 child, Catherine Eve. B of Civil Law, Univ. Coll. Cork, 1985; LLM, U. Mich., 1989. Bar: Ireland 1987, N.Y. 1989, Barrister at Law: Hon. Soc. of King's Inns, Dublin 1987. With Paul, Weiss, Rifkind, Wharton & Garrison LLP, N.Y.C., 1988—2000, ptnr., 2000—. Assoc. editor: Antitrust Law Jour., 2000—. Named Alumnus of Yr. in Law, Univ. Coll. Cork, 2004. Fellow: ABA (leadership ptnr. antitrust sect. 2000—), Am. Bar Found.; mem.: N.Y. State Bar Assn. (chair com. on antitrust 1999—2002), Bar Assn. of City of N.Y. (mem. pro bono com. 2002—05). Home: 124 Hudson St New York NY 10013 Office: Paul Weiss Rifkind Wharton & Garrison LLP 1285 Avenue of the Americas New York NY 10019-6064

**SYNNOTT, MARCIA GRAHAM,** history professor; b. Camden, N.J., July 4, 1939; d. Thomas Whitney and Beatrice Adelaide (Colby) S.; m. Willard Edwin Sharp, June 16, 1979; children: Willard Sharp, Laurel Beth Sharp. AB, Radcliffe Coll., 1961; MA, Brown U., 1964; PhD, U. Mass., 1974. History tchr. MacDuffie Sch., Springfield, Mass., 1963-68; instr. U. S.C., Columbia, 1972-74, asst. prof., 1974-79, assoc. prof. history, 1979-97, dir. grad. studies history dept., 1990-92, prof. history, 1997—. Author: The Half-Opened Door, 1979; contbr. essays to books, articles to profl. jours. and to scholarly jours. Active university-wide cmty. svc. projects. Grantee, Am. Coun. Learned Socs., 1981; Fulbright scholar, 1988. Mem. Am. Hist. Assn., So. Hist. Assn., Orgn. Am. Historians (membership com. 1990-93), S.C. Hist. Assn. (pres. 1994-95), History of Edn. Soc. (mem. editl. bd. 1996, 97, 98, bd. dirs. 2000-02). Avocations: history, skiing, walking. Office: U SC Dept History Columbia SC 29208-0001 Office Phone: 803-777-2585. Business E-Mail: synnott@gwm.sc.edu.

**SYNNOTT, WILLIAM RAYMOND,** retired management consultant; b. Fall River, Mass., Dec. 29, 1929; s. William Joseph and Marie Aurore (Labrie) S.; m. Suzanne Pauline Moseley, Oct. 21, 1967; children— Dianne, Mark, Amy Grad. cert., Rutgers U., 1958; BS summa cum laude, Boston U., 1973; grad. advanced mgmt. program, Harvard Bus. Sch., 1973. Sr. v.p. Bank of Boston, 1967-87; sr. dir. The Yankee Group, Boston, 1987-88; dir. Nolan, Norton & Co., Lexington, Mass., 1988-91; pres. W.R. Synnott Assocs., Wellesley Hills, Mass., 1990-94; ret., 1994. Lectr., seminar leader on info. technology worldwide. Author: The Information Weapon, 1987; co-author: Information Resource Management, 1981. Served as sgt. U.S. Army, 1951-53, Korea. Avocations: skiing, tennis, golf. Home (Winter): 1630 Winding Oaks Way #101 Naples FL 34109 Home (Summer): 6 Iron Mountain Rd Jackson NH 03846 Personal E-Mail: wilsyn@aol.com.

**SYNOLAKIS, COSTAS E.,** engineering educator; b. Athens, Greece, Sept. 21, 1956; BS in Engring. and Applied Sci., Calif. Inst. Tech., 1978, MS in Civil Engring., 1979, PhD in Civil Engring., 1986. Asst. prof. civil and environ. engring. U. So. Calif., LA, 1985-91, assoc. prof. civil, environ. and aerospace engring., 1991-97, prof. civil, environ., mech. and aerospace engring., 1997—. Prime Minister's adv. sci. and tech., Greece, 1993; vis. prof. U. Calif., Berkeley, 1994. Contbr. articles to sci. jours., chapters to books; co-author: Long Wave Runup Models, 1997, Furious Earth: The Sci. of Earthquakes, Volcanoes and Tsunamis, 1999. Recipient Presdl. Young Investigator award, 1989—94; grantee Alexander Onassis Pub. Benefit Found. fellowship, 1981—83. Mem.: Internat. Assn. Hydraulic Rsch., NY Acad. Scis., Armenian Acad. Scis., Soc. Theoretical and Applied Mechanics, Assn. Asphalt Paving Technologists, Am. Geophys. Union, Am. Phys. Soc., AAUP, AAAS, ASCE, Chi Epsilon, Sigma Xi. Office: Dept Civil Engring U So Calif Los Angeles CA 90089-2531 E-mail: costas@usc.edu.*

**SYPHER, FRANCIS J.,** retired theology studies educator; s. Francis J. and Mildred A. Sypher; m. Marie-Claire Cournand, 1966 (div. 1969); 1 child, Eleanor H.; m. Eleanor C. Kramer, 1970 (div. 1983). AB, Columbia U., NYC, 1963, AM, 1964, PhD, 1968. Prof. Columbia U., 1965—68, U. NY, 1968—75; ret., 1975. Author: (biography) Frederick L. Hoffman; His Life and Works, Letitia Elizabeth Landon, (historical) Saint Agnes Chapel of the Parish of Trinity Church, New York Society of the Cincinnati; Biographies of Original Members and Other Continental Officers; editor: Minutes of Coroners Proceedings; City and County of New York, John Burnet, Coroner, 1748-1763; contbr. articles to jours. Rsch. grant, NY State Regents Fellowship, 1963-65, SUNY Rsch. Found., Mellon Found. Pub., Fullbright Sr. Lectureship Am. Lit. Mem.: Huguenot Soc. Am., St. Nicholas Soc. City NY (editor), NY State Soc. Cin., Cosmos Club.

**SYPHERS, JAMES EDGAR,** retired social worker; b. Exeter, NH, Feb. 21, 1933; s. Albion Lionel and Mary Pinkham (Gray) S.; m. Joyce Caswell, June 22, 1952 (div. Mar. 1969); m. Barbara Walters, Dec. 31, 1974; children: Gail N., Dale A., Paul N., Neal A., Dennis L. Walters, Marcia W. Turner. BA in Psychology, U. N.H., 1955; MSW, U. Pitts., 1965; BD, Oberlin Coll., 1968; PhD in Higher Edn., Walden U., 1978. Cmty. peace intern Am. Friends Svc. Com., NY, 1958—61, youth sec. Pitts., 1961—63; acting. coord., dir. cmty. affairs Hill House Assn., Pitts., 1965-69; instr., acting dir. human svcs. Lincoln U., Pa., 1969-75, assoc. prof., asst. dir. masters human svcs. program, 1977-79; asst. prof., dir. social work and human svcs. Widener U., Chester, Pa., 1975-76; assoc. prof., chair, field coord. dept. social work Saginaw Valley State U., University Center, Mich., 1980-87; asst. prof., field coord. dept. social work Western Carolina U., Cullowhee, NC, 1987-91; dir. social svc. Downingtown (Pa.) Indsl. and Agrl. Sch., 1991-92; asst. prof., acting chair dept. social work and gerontology California U. Pa., 1992—2002; ret., 2002. Evaluator gang control programs City of Phila. and Youth Svc. Inc., 1973-75; cons., evaluator Dauphin Commn. on Drugs and Alcohol, Harrisburg, Pa., 1978; sec. Saginaw County Mental Health/Mental Retardation Adv. Bd., 1982-86; cons. social work program Carlow Coll., Pitts., 1994-99. Author, co-editor: Community Action for Social Change, 1972; contbr. (booklet) The Community is Our Client, 1966. Mem. gen. com., devel. com. Friends Com. on Nat. Legislation, Washington, 1973-79. Recipient grad. fellowship NIMH, 1963-65, rsch. fellowship NIH, 1964, Human Svc. Program grant Social and Rehab. Svcs. of HEW, 1970-76. Mem. NASW (western N.C. unit sec. 1980—, Lifetime Achievement award Pa. 2002), NAACP (student chpt. v.p.), AAUP, Coun. on Social Work Edn. (del. 1980—), Mich. Assn. Baccalaureate Social Work Programs (pres. 1983-85), Pa. Assn. Undergrad. Social Work Edn. (pres. 1997), Phi Alpha. Democrat. Mem. Soc. Of Friends. Avocations: hiking, construction, travel, social justice activities, counseling. Mailing: 110 Martha Ave Hopwood PA 15445 Personal E-Mail: jsyphers33@verizon.net.

**SYPOLT, DIANE GILBERT,** retired judge; b. Rochester, N.Y., June 14, 1947; d. Myron Birne and Doris Isabell (Robie) Gilbert; m. Dwight Douglas Sypolt; children: Andrew, David Weinstein. BA, Smith Coll., Northampton, Mass., 1969; postgrad., Stanford U., 1977-78, Georgetown U., 1978; JD, Boston U., 1979. Bar: D.C. 1979, Mass. 1979. Law clk. to judge D.C. Ct. Appeals, Washington, 1979-80; assoc. Peabody, Lambert & Meyers, Washington, 1980-83; asst. gen. counsel Office of Mgmt. and Budget, Washington, 1983-86; dep. gen. counsel U.S. Dept. Edn., Washington, 1986-88, acting gen. counsel, 1988-89; legal counselor to V.P. of U.S., White House; counsel Pres.'s Competitiveness Coun., Washington, 1989-90; judge U.S. Ct. Fed. Claims, Washington, 1990—2005; ret., 2005. Bd. dirs. Democracy Devel. Inst. Recipient Young Lawyer's award Boston U. Law Sch., 1989. Mem. Fed. Am. Inn of Ct. (Master), Federalist Soc. Personal E-Mail: dgsypolt@yahoo.com.

**SYRDAHL, RICKELLE LYN,** biology professor; b. Encino, Calif., Sept. 1, 1964; d. Richard Preston and Marilyn Ann Johnson; m. Leif Frederick Syrdahl, July 14, 1990; 1 child, Kaelyn Ann. BA, U. Calif., Santa Barbara, 1986; MS, Calif. State U., Chico, 1993. Rsch. asst. Calif. State U., Chico, 1991—92, tchg. asst., 1992—93; instr. Vanguard Bound, Chico, 1993; rsch. asst. Jean Hubbell, Chico, 1993—94; lab mgr. Pepperdine U., Malibu, 1994—97; assoc. prof. Porterville (Calif.) Coll., 1997—. Adj. faculty Butte Coll., Oroville, Calif., 1994. Mem.: Nat. Science Biology Tchrs., Phi Kappa Phi. Avocations: camping, hiking, reading, photography. Office: Porterville Coll 100 E College Ave Porterville CA 93257 Office Phone: 559-791-2347. Business E-Mail: rsyrdahl@portervillecollege.edu.

**SYRON, DICK (RICHARD FRANCIS SYRON),** finance company executive, economist; b. Boston, Oct. 25, 1943; s. Dominick Richard and Elizabeth (McQuire) S.; m. Margaret Mary Garatoni, Oct. 21, 1972; children: Erin Elizabeth, Brendan Paul. BS in Econs.-Acctg. with high honors, Boston Coll., 1966; MA in Econs., Tufts U., 1969, PhD in Econs., 1971. Dep. dir. budget Commonwealth of Mass., 1973-74; v.p., economist Fed. Res. Bank of Boston, 1974-82, sr. v.p., econ. advisor, 1982-85; exec. asst. to sec. U.S. Dept. Treasury, Washington, 1979-80, dep. sec. for econ. policy, 1980-81; asst. to Chmn. Volcker Fed. Res. Sys., Washington, 1981-82; pres., CEO Fed. Home Loan Bank of Boston, 1986-88; pres., chief exec. officer Fed. Res. Bank of Boston, 1989-94; chmn. Am. Stock Exch., N.Y.C., 1994-99; chmn., CEO Thermo Electron, Waltham, Mass., 1999—2002, exec. chmn., 2002—03; chmn., CEO Fed. Home Loan Mortgage Corp. (Freddie Mac), McLean, Va., 2003—. Bd. trustees Boston Coll.; past chmn. Boston Pvt. Industry Coun.; bd. dirs. McKesson Corp., Nabors Industries. Author: Urban Fire Insurance, 1972; contbr. articles to profl. jours. Mem. Fed. Open Market Com., 1989—94. Teaching fellow Tufts U., 1966-69. Mem.: Comml. Club Boston, Boston Econ. Club, Clover Club Boston. Office: Freddie Mac 8200 Jones Branch Dr Mc Lean VA 22102-3110

**SYTSMA, FREDRIC A.,** lawyer; b. Grand Rapids, Mich., Jan. 12, 1944; BA, Mich. State U., 1964; JD, U. Mich., 1968. Bar: Mich. 1968. Mem. Varnum, Riddering, Schmidt & Howlett, Grand Rapids. Fellow Am. Coll. Trust and Estate Counsel; mem. ABA, State Bar Mich. (mem. coun. probate and estate planning sect. 1977—, chmn. 1986-87), Grand Rapids Bar Assn Office: Varnum Riddering Schmidt & Howlett PO Box 352 333 Bridge St NW Grand Rapids MI 49501-0352 Office Phone: 616-336-6000. Business E-Mail: fasytsma@varnumlaw.com.

**SYVERTSON, CLARENCE ALFRED,** management consultant, engineer; b. Mpls., Jan. 12, 1926; s. Alfred and Esther Louise (Goertemiller) S.; m. Helen Hammond Gonnella, May 4, 1953 (dec. May 1981); 1 child, Marguerite Louise.; m. JoAnn Mary Caruso, May 8, 1982; 1 stepchild, Lynn S. Sechrest. B. Aero. Engring., U. Minn., 1946, MS, 1948, DSc (hon.), 2004; postgrad., Stanford U., 1950. 57 engr. Ames and Mgmt. Program, Harvard U., 1977. Research scientist Ames Aero. Lab., NACA, Moffett Field, Calif., 1948-58; exec. dir. Joint Dept. Transp./NASA Civil Aviation Research and Devel. Policy Study, 1970-71; with Ames Research Center, NASA, Moffett Field, 1958-84, dep. dir., 1969-78, dir., 1978-84. Mem. adv. bd. Coll. Engring., U. Calif., Berkeley, 1980-85; cons. prof. Stanford U., 1985-88; hon. prof. Northwestern Poly. U., Xian, China, 1998. Served with U.S. Army, 1946-47. Recipient invention and contbn. award NASA, 1964, Exceptional Service medal, 1971, Disting. Service medal, 1984, Outstanding Achievement award U. Minn., 1982, Comdrs. award for civilian service U.S. Army, 1984 Fellow AIAA (Lawrence Sperry award 1957), Am. Astronautical Soc., Calif. Coun. Sci. and Tech.; mem. Nat. Acad. Engring. Home: 14666 Springer Ave Saratoga CA 95070-5748 Office Phone: 408-867-2663.

**SYVERUD, KENT DOUGLAS,** dean, law educator; b. Rochester, NY, Oct. 23, 1956; s. Warren Lukken and Janet (Thatcher) S.I; m. Ruth Chi-Fen Chen, May 22, 1982; children: Steven, Brian, David. BSFS, Georgetown U., 1977; JD, U. Mich., 1981, MA, 1983. Bar: D.C. 1982, Mich. 1993. Law clk. to Judge Oberdorfer U.S. Dist. Ct. D.C., Washington, 1983-84; law clk. Justice O'Connor Supreme Ct. U.S., Washington, 1984-85; assoc. Wilmer, Cutler & Pickering, Washington, 1985-97; exec. sec. Mich. Law Revision Commn., Lansing, 1993-95; prof. U. Mich. Law Sch., Ann Arbor, 1987-97; dean, Garner Anthony prof. Vanderbilt U. Law Sch., Nashville, 1997—2005; dean, Shepley prof. Wash. U. Law Sch., St. Louis, 2005—. Chair exec. com. Inst. CLE, Ann Arbor, 1995-97; chair, bd. trustees Law Sch. Admissions Coun., 2005-. Editor: Journal of Legal Education, 1988—90. Mem. Am. Law Inst., Law and Soc. Assn. Office Phone: 315-935-6420, 314-935-6420. Business E-Mail: syverud@wulaw.wustl.edu.

**SZABLYA, HELEN MARY,** writer, language educator; b. Budapest, Hungary, Sept. 6, 1934; came to U.S., 1963; d. Louis and Helen (Bartha) Kovacs; m. John Francis Szablya, June 12, 1951; children: Helen, Janos, Louis, Stephen, Alexandra, Rita, Dominique-Mary. Diploma in Sales, Mktg., U.B.C., 1962; BA in Fgn. Lange., Lit., Wash. State U., 1976. Freelance writer, translator, 1967—; columnist Cath. News, Trinidad, West Indies, 1980-91; adult educator TELOS Bellevue (Wash.) C.C., 1987-89; adult educator Pullman-Spokane (Wash.) C.C., 1976-80; faculty Christian Writers' Conf., Seattle, 1983-88, Pacific N.W. Writers' Conf., Seattle and Tacoma, 1987—92;

hon. consul for Wash., Oreg., Idaho Republic of Hungary, 1993—. Lectr. Washington Commn. for Humanities, 1987-89. Author (with others): Hungary Remembered, 1986 (Guardian of Liberty award, 1986, George Washington Honor medal, Freedoms Found. award, 1988); author: 56-os Cserkészcsapat, 1986; author: (with others) The Fall of the Red Star, 1996, Hungarian transl., 1999 (1st prize Wash. Press Assn., 1st prize Nat. Fedn. Press Women); pub., editor Hungary Internat. newsletter, 1990—93; columnist Hungarian Bus. Weekly, 1994—95; translator: Emlékezünk, 1986, Mind Twisters, 1987, A vörös csillag lehull, 1999. Recipient Nat. 1st place editl. Nat. Fedn. Press Women, 1987, Senator Tom Martin Meml. award Pacific N.W. Writers Conf., 1979, Pro Auxilio Cinum Hungarorum, Min. Fgn. Affairs, Republic of Hungary, 2003, Order of Merit, Republic of Hungary, 2005, Pro Communitate, City of Pecs, Hungary, 2006; grantee Hungarian Am. Assn. Wash., 1986, Wash. Com. for Humanities, 1986; named Cmty. Woman of Yr. Am. Bus. Women Assn., 1990. Mem. AAUW, Wash. Press Assn. (pres. 1987-88, 1st and 2nd place awards, several editl. and profile awards 1983, 87, 89, 90, 91, 92, 96, Communicator of Achievement award 1987, Nat. Fedn. Press Women (Affiliate Pres.' award 1988, bd. dirs. edn. fund N.W. quadrant, mem. 21st century planning com.), Authors Guild, Am. Translators Assn., Arpad Acad. (Gold medal 1987), Nat. Writers Club, Internat. PEN Club, Sigma Delta Chi (editl. award 1989). Avocations: children, reading, dance, swimming, travel. Home and Office: PO Box 578 Kirkland WA 98083-0578 Office Phone: 425-739-0631. Personal E-Mail: szablyahj@aol.com.

**SZABO, BARNA ALADAR,** engineering educator; b. Martonvasar, Hungary, Sept. 21, 1935; arrived in US, 1967, naturalized, 1974; s. Jozsef and Gizella (Ivanyi) S.; m. Magdalin Gerstmayer, July 23, 1960; children: Mark, Nicholas. BSc, U. Toronto, Ont., Can., 1962; MS, SUNY, Buffalo, 1966, PhD, 1968; D. honoris causa, U. of Miskolc, Hungary, 1998. Registered profl. engr., Mo. Mining engr. Internat. Nickel Co. Can., 1960-62; engr. Acres Cons. Services Ltd., Niagara Falls, Can., 1962-66; instr. SUNY, Buffalo, 1966-68; from mem. faculty to sr. prof. Washington U., St. Louis, 1968—2006, sr. prof. mech. engring., 2006—; chmn. Engring. Software R&D, Inc., St. Louis, 1989—. Author: (with Ivo Babuska) Finite Element Analysis, 1991; contbr. articles to profl. jours. Fellow, St. Louis Acad. Sci. Fellow U.S. Assn. Computational Mechanics (founding mem.); mem. ASME, Hungarian Acad. Sci. Home: 48 Crestwood Dr Clayton MO 63105-3033 Office: PO Box 1129 Saint Louis MO 63188-1129 Office Phone: 314-935-6352. Business E-Mail: szabo@wustl.edu.

**SZABO, DANIEL,** federal official; b. Budapest, Hungary, Mar. 23, 1933; came to U.S., 1950, naturalized, 1954; s. Alexander and Maria (Berger) S.; m. Corinne Holiber, July 3, 1955; children— Nancy Beth, Peter Stuart. BA, CCNY, 1957; MA, Johns Hopkins U., 1959. Internat. economist U.S. Tariff Commn., 1959-60; desk officer for Vietnam, Cambodia and Laos U.S. Dept. Commerce, 1960-63; spl. asst. to U.S. Senator Jacob K. Javits, 1963-69; dep. asst. sec. state for Inter-Am. Affairs, Washington, 1969-74; sr. adviser Inter-Am. Devel. Bank, Washington, 1974-95. Bd. dirs. Washington chpt., chmn. Md. legis. task force Am. Jewish Com.; Am. Jewish Com. advocate Md. Interfaith Legis. Com., 1999—. With U.S. Army, 1954—56. Home: 11600 Danville Dr North Bethesda MD 20852-3716 E-mail: ds3693@verizon.net. *In approaching life I want my work to represent a service to our society. I am attracted to new ideas and new ways of solving old problems.*

**SZABO, DENIS,** criminologist, educator; b. Budapest, Hungary, June 4, 1929; arrived in Can., 1958; s. Jenő and Catherine (Zsiga) Szabo; m. Sylvie Grotard; children: Catherine, Marianne. D in Social and Polit. Sci., U. Louvain, Belgium, 1956; diploma in Criminology, Sorbonne U., Paris, 1958; Doctorate (hon.), U. Sienna, Italy, 1983, U. Budapest, Hungary, 1985, U. Aix Marseille, 1992, Panteios U., 1996, U. Bucarest, 2004. Asst. in sociology U. Louvain, 1951—56; lectr. sociology Cath. Univ., Paris, Lyon, 1956—58; mem. rsch. group Ctr. Nat. de la Recherche Scientifique, Paris, 1954—58; asst. prof. to assoc. prof. U. Montreal, Canada, 1958—66, founder, dir. dept. criminology, 1960—70, prof., 1966—95; founder, dir. Internat. Ctr. Comparative Criminology, Canada, 1969—84; prof. emeritus U. Montreal, Canada, 1995—. Emeritus prof. law U. Ecuador, Quito, 1984. Author, editor: book Can. Criminal Justice Sys., 1977, Criminologie et Politique Criminelle, 1978, La Criminologie Empirique au PQ, 1985, Sci. et Crime, 1986, De L' Anthropologie a la Criminologie Comparee, 1993, La Criminologie: Ses Fondements et sa Fondation, 1998; author (with Marc LeBlanc): Le Traité de Criminologie Empirique, 1993, The Criminal Justice Sys., 2001. Decorated officer Order Can.; named Comdr., Nat. Order Merite Hungarian Republic, 1996; recipient Beccaria Award, German Soc. Criminology, 1970, Chevalier Des Arts et des Lettres, France, 1996. Fellow: Am. Soc. Criminology (exec. coun., Sutherland award 1968), Am. Sociol. Soc., Royal Soc. Can.; mem.: Acad. Sci. Morales et Politiques, Quebec Soc. Criminology (founder, 45 Yrs. Svc. award 2005), Can. Soc. Criminology (v.p. 1962—64), Hungarian Acad. Sci., Inst. France (corr.; corres. mem.), Basque Inst. of Criminology San Sebastian (hon.), Romanian Soc. Criminology (hon.; elected hon. mem. 2003), Medaille de l' Institut Basque de Criminology (hon.), Nat. Order Merit (comdr. Ivory Coast 1987), Internat. Assn. Sociology, Order Nat. du Que. (officer 1998—), Soc. de Criminology du Que. (sec.-gen. 1960—70), Soc. Criminology (v.p. 1962—64), Internat. Soc. Criminology (pres. 1978—85, hon. pres.). Roman Catholic. Avocations: swimming, gardening, travel. Home: 66 Carré Copp Georgeville PQ Canada J0B 1T0 Office: U Montreal Internat Ctr Com Criminology CP 6128 succursale Centre-ville Montreal PQ Canada H3C 3J7 Office Phone: 514-343-7065. Business E-Mail: denis.szabo@umontreal.ca.

**SZALKOWSKI, CHARLES C.,** lawyer; b. Amarillo, Tex., Apr. 14, 1948; s. Chester Casimer and Virginia Lee Szalkowski; m. Jane Howe, Dec. 28, 1971; children: Jennifer Lee, Stephen Claude. BA, BS in Acctg., Rice U., 1971; MBA, JD, Harvard U., 1975. Bar: Tex. 1975. Assoc. Baker Botts L.L.P., Houston, 1975-82, ptnr., 1983—. Speaker in field. Chmn. ann. fund campaign Rice U., Houston, 1991-93, chmn. Fund Coun., 1995-96; chmn. adminstrv. bd. St. Luke's United Meth. Ch., Houston, 1994, chmn. bd. trustees, 1997, 2003; chmn. DePelchin Children's Ctr., Houston, 2002-2004; bd. dirs. Meth. Children's Home, Waco, 1998-2001, 03—, MIT Enterprise Forum of Tex., Houston. Mem.: ABA (fed. regulation of securities com.), Assn. Corp. Growth, Tex. Bus. Law Found. (mem. exec. com. 1988—, chmn. 1998—2000, bd. dirs.), Harvard Law Sch. Assn. Tex. (pres. 1983—84), Houston Bar Assn. (corp. counsel sect. 1988—90, chmn.), State Bar Tex. (chmn. bus. law sect. 1991—92), Am. Law Inst., Assn. Rice U. Alumni (bd. dirs. 1999—2002). Office: Baker Botts LLP 1 Shell Plz 910 Louisiana St Ste 3000 Houston TX 77002-4991 Office Phone: 713-229-1480.

**SZALKOWSKI, DEBORAH,** music educator; b. Ithaca, N.Y., Nov. 25, 1956; d. Leslie Rudy and Mary Jane Worden; m. Mark James Szalkowski, July 21, 1990. MusB, Ithaca Coll., 1977; MEd, SUNY, Albany, 1982. Profl. tchg. cert. Fla.; N.Y. Tchr. vocal music Marathon (N.Y.) Ctrl. Schs., 1977—78; tchr. Voorheesville (N.Y. H.S., 1978—80, Troy (N.Y.) City Schs., 1980—85; choir dir. Guilderland (N.Y.) Ctrl. Schs., 1985—95; tchr. Pinellas County Schs., Tarpon Spring, Fla., 1995—96, choir dir. Largo, Fla., 1996—. Choral arranger: Mem.: Pinellas County Music Educators, Fla. Vocal Assn., Fla. Music Educators Assn. (1st Yr. Svc. award 2002), Music Educators Nat. Assn. Avocations: travel, boating. Home: 10111 Tarpon Dr Treasure Island FL 33706 Office: Pinellas Pk HS 6305 118th Ave N Largo FL 33773 Personal E-Mail: debchoir1@cs.com.

**SZALLER, JAMES FRANCIS,** lawyer; b. Cleve., Jan. 22, 1945; s. Frank Paul and Ellen Grace (O'Malley) S.; m. Roberta Mae Curtin, Oct. 23, 1967 (div. Aug. 1975); m. Charlene Nancy Smith, Apr. 28, 1984. AA, Cuyahoga C.C., Ohio, 1967; BA, Cleve. State U., 1970, JD cum laude, 1975. Bar: Ohio 1975, U.S. Dist. Ct. (no. dist.) Ohio 1975, U.S. Supreme Ct. 1982, U.S. Ct. Appeals (6th cir.) 1983, U.S. Ct. Appeals (4th cir.) 1986. Assoc. Metzenbaum, Gaines & Stern, Cleve., 1975—79; sr. ptnr. Brown & Szaller Co., L.P.A., Cleve., 1979—. Lectr. law Cleve. State U., 1977-81. Mem. editorial bd. Cleve. State U. Law Rev., 1973-75.; contbr. articles to profl. jours. Fellow Nat. Coll. Advocacy (co-chmn. Baycol Litigation Group, 2002—); mem.

Ohio State Bar Assn., Greater Cleve. Bar Assn., Cleve. Acad. Trial Lawyers, Ohio Acad. Trial Lawyers (trustee, 2002—, Disting. Svc. award 1996), Assn. Trial Lawyers Am., Democrat. Roman Catholic. Avocations: gourmet cooking, automobile racing. Office: Brown & Szaller Co LPA 14222 Madison Ave Cleveland OH 44107-4510 Office Phone: 216-228-7200. E-mail: szaller@lawandhelp.com.

**SZAMOSFALVI, JOZSEF,** corporate financial executive, consultant; arrived in US, 1994; s. Jozsef Szamosfalvi and Iren Hornyak. BS in Econs. and Internat. Politics, Brigham Young U., 2001. Chartered fin. analyst candidate level 2. V.p. Summit Ventures Internat. and Interlink Capital Strategies, Falls Church, Va., 2002—; mng. dir. New Europe Capital Mgmt., LLC, Va., 2003—; CAPPA FUND I, LLC, Falls Church, 2006—; intern divsn. programs coord. and evaluation Internat. Atomic Energy Agy., Vienna, 1998; rsch. asst. Brigham Young U., Provo, Utah, 1999—2001; CFO Rustico, Inc., Orem, Utah, 1999—2001; dir. of fin. Summit Ventures, LLC, Washington, 2003—. Vol. rep. Ch. of Jesus Christ of Latter-day Saints, Tirana, Albania, 1995—97. Mem.: NY Soc. Security Analysts, Nat. Assn. Bus. Econs. Conservative. Avocations: guitar, soccer, ballroom dancing. Office: Summit Ventures LLC 1101 30th St NW Washington DC 20007 Office Phone: 202-333-9055. Office Fax: 202-478-5111. Personal E-mail: jozsef@summit-ventures.com.

**SZÁRA, STEPHEN ISTVÁN,** pharmacologist, consultant; b. Budapest, Hungary, Mar. 21, 1923; arrived in U.S., 1957; s. János Szára and Mária Katona; m. Madeleine Gadányi, Sept. 5, 1959 (div. June 1980); 1 child, Christopher. D of Natural Scis., Petrus Pázmány U., Budapest, 1950; MD, Med. U. Budapest, 1951. Asst. prof. dept. biochemistry Med. U. Budapest, 1950—53; chief biochemistry lab. State Inst. for Nervous Disorders, Budapest, 1953—56; vis. scientist Clin. Sci. Lab. NIMH, Bethesda, Md., 1957—61, sect. chief Washington, 1961—71; br. chief NIDA NIH, Rockville, Md., 1971—90; sci. cons. Kensington, Md., 1990—. Assoc., clin. prof. psychiatry George Washington U., Washington, 1966—75; mem. adv. bd. Heffter Rsch. Inst., Santa Fe, 1993—. Co-author (with H. Weil-Malherbe): Biochemistry of Functional and Experimental Psychoses, 1971; co-editor (with M. Braude): The Pharmacology of Marihuana, 1976; co-editor: (with J.P Ludford) Benzodiazepines: A Review of Research Results, 1980; editor: Neurobiology of Behavioral Control of Drug Abuse, 1986; contbr. articles to profl. jours. Recipient Meritorious Achievement award, ADAMHA/PHS/DHHS, 1984, Kovats Freedom medal, Am. Hungarian Fedn., 2005. Fellow: Coll. Internat. Neuro-Psychopharmacologicum, Am. Coll. Neuro-Psychopharmacology; mem.: AAAS, Am. Soc. Pharmacol. Exptl. Therapy. Achievements include discovery of hallucinogenic effects of NN-Dimethyltryptamine in man. Avocations: sailing, computer programming. Home: 10901 Jolly Way Kensington MD 20895-1111 Personal E-mail: siszara@earthlink.net.

**SZARAWARSKI, CAROLLEE,** special education educator; b. Neptune, N.J., July 25, 1955; d. Charles Frank and Barbara Jean Moorefield; children: Charles Michael, Nicholas Bruno. BS, Coll. N.J., 1977; MAT, Marygrove Coll., 2005; supr. cert., Georgian Ct. U., 2006. Tchr. spl. edn. Princeton (N.J.) Sch. Exceptional children, 1977—78, Jr. #1, Trenton, NJ, 1978—81, Hightstown (N.J.) H.S., 1991—. Advisor, interact club Hightstown (N.J.) H.S., 1992—95, advisor student coun., 2003—. Leader Cub Scout Leader, Manalapan, NJ, 1987—93; supt. sunday sch. Presbyn. Ch., Tennant, NJ, 1988—90; pres. United Presbyn. Women, Tennant, NJ, 1991—94. Mem.: ASCD. Avocations: hiking, reading, writing, crafts. Home: 146 Freehold Rd Manalapan NJ 07726 Office: Hightstown High School 25 Leshin Lane Hightstown NJ 08520 Office Phone: 609-443-7835.

**SZAREK, STANISLAW JERZY,** mathematics professor; b. Ladek Zdroj, Poland, Nov. 13, 1953; arrived in US, 1988, naturalized, 1994; s. Mieczyslaw and Bronislawa (Brzezinska) S.; m. Malgorzata Chwascinska, June 22, 1980 (separated 1996, div. 2002); children: Martina, Natalia; 1 stepchild, Olga; m. Margaretmary Daley, May 15, 2004; 1 child, Emily; stepchildren: Blake, Devin. M in Math., Warsaw U., Poland, 1976; PhD in Math. Scis., Polish Acad. Scis., Warsaw, 1979. Rsch. asst. Math. Inst. Polish Acad. Scis., Warsaw, 1976-79, rsch. fellow, 1979-83; asst. prof. Case Western Res. U., Cleve., 1983-87, prof., 1987—, chair math. dept., 1994-96; prof. U. Paris, 1996—. Vis. positions U. Ill., Urbana; 1980, Ohio State U., Columbus, 1981, U. Tex., Austin, 1981-83, Inst. des Hautes Etudes Scientifiques, Bures-Sur-Yvette, France, 1986-89, U. Paris, 1990, 92, 95, Math. Scis. Rsch. Inst., Berkeley, Calif., 1996. Contbr. articles to profl. jours. Recipient Prize of Sci. Sect. Polish Acad. Scis., 1979; Rsch. grantee NSF, 1983—, U.S.-Israel Binat. Sci. Found., 1993-97, 2003—; Sloan fellow Alfred P. Sloan Found., 1988-89; invited spkr. Internat. Congress of Math. Madrid, 2006. Mem.: Am. Math. Soc. Avocations: skiing, sailing, diving, bridge, travel. Office: Case Western Res U Dept of Math Cleveland OH 44106 Office Phone: 216-368-2880. Business E-Mail: szarek@cwru.edu.

**SZAREK, WALTER ANTHONY,** chemist, educator; b. St. Catharines, Ont., Can., Apr. 19, 1938; s. Anthony and Sophia (Kania) S. BSc, McMaster U., 1960, MSc, 1962; PhD, Queen's U., 1964. Postdoctoral fellow in chemistry Ohio State U., Columbus, 1964-65; asst. prof. biochemistry Rutgers U., New Brunswick, N.J., 1965-67; asst. prof. chemistry Queen's U., Kingston, Ont., 1967-71, assoc. prof., 1971-76, prof., 1976—2003, emeritus prof., 2003—, dir. Carbohydrate Research Inst., 1976-85; founding mem., prin. investigator Neurochem, Inc., 1993—. Cons. to govt. and industry; mem. Premier's Coun. Tech. Fund. Mem. editl. adv. bd. Carbohydrate Rsch. jour., 1973-97, Jour. of Carbohydrate Chemistry, 1994-2001; contbr. articles to profl. jours. Recipient Tchg. Excellence award Queen's U. Arts and Sci. Undergrad. Soc., 1988-89, Tchg. Excellence in Chemistry award, 1993, 2000, 2002. Fellow Chem. Inst. Can.; mem. AAAS, Am. Chem. Soc. (chmn. divsn. carbohydrate chemistry 1982-83, councilor 2002—, Claude S. Hudson award in carbohydrate chemistry 1989, Melville L. Wolfrom award 1992), Inst. Theol. Encounter with Sci. and Tech., Royal Soc. Chemistry, N.Y. Acad. Scis., Soc. Glycobiology. Roman Catholic. Office: Dept Chemistry Queens Univ Kingston ON Canada K7L 3N6 Fax: 613-533-6532. Office Phone: 613-533-2643. Business E-Mail: szarekw@chem.queensu.ca.

**SZARKOWSKI, T(HADDEUS) JOHN,** museum administrator; b. Ashland, Wis., Dec. 18, 1925; s. Julius and Rose (Woychik); m. Jill Anson, Oct. 14, 1963; children: Nina, Natasha. BS, U. Wis., 1948; BS hon. degrees, Phila. Coll. Art, 1972; BS, Mpls. Coll. Art and Design, 1974. Photographer Walker Art Center, Mpls., 1948-51; instr. in photography U. Minn., 1950, Albright Art Sch., U. Buffalo, 1951-53; dir. dept. photography (emeritus) Mus. Modern Art, N.Y.C., 1962—. Author: The Idea of Louis Sullivan, 1956, The Face of Minn., 1958, The Photographer & the Am. Landscape, 1963, The Photographer's Eye, 1966, Walker Evans, 1971, Looking at Photographs, 1973, Mirrors & Windows: Am. Photography Since 1960, 1978, Irving Penn, 1984, Photography Until Now, 1990, Ansel Adams at 100, 1991, Atget, 2000, Photographs, 2005; co-author (with Alfred Stieglitz): Alfred Stieglitz at Lake George, 1995. With U.S. Army, 1945—46. Fellow John Simon Guggenheim Found., 1954, 1961. Mem.: Century Assn. Office: Museum Modern Art 11 W 53rd St New York NY 10019-5498

**SZASZ, THOMAS STEPHEN,** psychiatrist, educator, writer; b. Budapest, Hungary, Apr. 15, 1920; came to U.S., 1938, naturalized, 1944; s. Julius and Lily (Wellisch) S.; m. Rosine Loshkajian, Oct. 19, 1951 (div. 1970); children: Margot Szasz Peters, Susan Marie Szasz Palmer. AB, U. Cin., 1941, MD, 1944; DSc (hon.), Allegheny Coll., 1975, U. Francisco Marroquin, Guatemala, 1979; LHD (hon.), Towson U., 1999; D Sc(hon.), SUNY, 2001. Diplomate: Nat. Bd. Med. Examiners, Am. Bd. Psychiatry and Neurology. Intern 4th Med. Service Harvard, Boston City Hosp., 1944-45; asst. resident medicine Cin. Gen. Hosp., 1945-46, asst. clinician internal medicine div. out-patient dispensary, 1946; asst. resident psychiatry U. Chgo. Clinics, 1946-47; tng. research fellow Inst. Psychoanalysis, Chgo., 1947-48, rsch. asst., 1949-50, staff mem., 1951-56; practice medieine, specializing in psychiatry, psychoanalysis Chgo., 1949-54, Bethesda, Md., 1954-56, Syracuse, NY, 1956—; prof. psychiatry SUNY Health Sci. Ctr., Syracuse, 1956-90, prof. psychiatry emeritus, 1990—. Vis. prof. dept. psychiatry U. Wis., Madison, 1962, Marquette U. Sch. Medicine, Milw., 1968, U. N.Mex.,

1981; holder numerous lectureships, including C.P. Snow lectr. Ithaca Coll., 1970; E.S. Meyer Meml. lectr. U. Queensland Med. Sch.; Lambie-Dew orator Sydney U., 1977; Mem. nat. adv. com. bd. Tort and Med. Yearbook; cons. com. mental hygiene N.Y. State Bar Assn.; mem. research adv. panel Inst. Study Drug Addiction; adv. bd. Corp. Econ. Edn., 1977— Author: Pain and Pleasure, 1957, The Myth of Mental Illness, 1961, Law, Liberty and Psychiatry, 1963, Psychiatric Justice, 1965, The Ethics of Psychoanalysis, 1965, Ideology and Insanity, 1970, The Manufacture of Madness, 1970, The Second Sin, 1973, Ceremonial Chemistry, 1974, Heresies, 1976, Karl Kraus and the Soul-Doctors, 1976, Schizophrenia: The Sacred Symbol of Psychiatry, 1976, Psychiatric Slavery, 1977, The Theology of Medicine, 1977, The Myth of Psychotherapy, 1978, Sex by Prescription, 1980, The Therapeutic State, 1984, Insanity: The Idea and its Consequences, 1987, The Untamed Tongue: A Dissenting Dictionary, 1990, Our Right to Drugs: The Case for a Free Market, 1992, A Lexicon of Lunacy, 1993, Cruel Compassion, 1994, The Meaning of Mind, 1996, Fatal Freedom, 1999, Pharmacracy: Medicine and Politics in America, 2001, Liberation By Oppression: A Comparative Study of Slavery and Psychiatry, 2002, Words to the Wise: A Medical-Philosophical Dictionary, 2004, Faith in Freedom: Libertarian Principles and Psychiatric Practices, 2004, Szasz Under Fire: The Psychiatric Abolitionist Answers His Critics, 2004, My Madness Saved Me: The Madness and Mariage of Virginia Woolf, 2006; editor: The Age of Madness, 1973; cons. editor of psychiatry and psychology: Stedman's Medical Dictionary, 22d edit, 1973; contbg. editor: Reason, 1974—, Libertarian Rev., 1986—; mem. editl. bd. Psychoanalytic Rev, 1965—, Jour. Contemporary Psychotherapy, 1968—, Law and Human Behavior, 1977—, Jour. Libertarian Studies, 1977—, Children and Youth Services Rev, 1978—, Am. Jour. Forensic Psychiatry, 1980—, Free Inquiry, 1980—. Comdr. M.C., USNR, 1954-56. Recipient Stella Feiss Hofheimer award U. Cin., 1944, Holmes-Munsterberg award Internat. Acad. Forensic Psychology, 1969; Wisdom award honor, 1970; Acad. prize Institutum atque Academia Auctorum Internationalis, Andorra, 1972; Distinguished Service award Am. Inst. Pub. Service, 1974; Martin Buber award Midway Counseling Center, 1974, Thomas S. Szasz award Cir. Ind. Thought, 1990, Alfred R. Lindesmith award for achievement in field of scholarship and writing Drug Policy Found., 1991, Rollo May award APA, 1998; others; named Humanist of Year am. Humanist Assn., 1973; Hon. fellow Postgrad. Center for Mental Health, 1961, Mencken award, 1981, Humanist Laureate, 1984, Statue of Liberty-Ellis Island Found. Archives Roster, 1986, George Washington award Am. Hungarian Found., 2003. Fellow Am. Psychiat. Assn. (life), Am. Psychoanalytic Assn., Internat. Soc. Psychoanalytic Soc., Western N.Y. Psychoanalytic Soc. Home: 4739 Limberlost Ln Manlius NY 13104-1405 Office: 750 E Adams St Syracuse NY 13210-2306 Personal E-mail: tszasz@aol.com.

**SZAUTNER, CHRISTIAN ANDREAS,** lawyer; b. Bethlehem, Pa., Aug. 27, 1972; s. Johann and Kathleen Szautner; m. Michelle Janette Hain, Apr. 18, 1998; 1 child, Mikaela Maida. BA cum laude, Pa. State U., 1994; JD cum laude, U. Pa., 1997. Bar: Pa. 1998. Assoc. Ballard Spahr Andrews & Ingersoll, LLP, Phila., 1997—2005, ptnr., 2005—. Named A Pa. Rising Star Lawyer, Phila. (Pa.) Mag., 2005. Office: Ballard Spahr Andrews & Ingersoll LLP 1735 Market Street 51st Floor Philadelphia PA 19103 Office Phone: 215-864-8602. Business E-Mail: szautner@ballardspahr.com.

**SZCZERBIAK, WALLY,** professional basketball player; b. Mar. 5, 1977; Grad., U. Miami, Ohio, 1999. Basketball player Minn. Timberwolves, 1999—2006, Boston Celtics, 2006—. Named Mac Player Yr., 1999; named to Second Team All-Am., AP, 1999, All-Rookie Team, NBA, 1999—2000; recipient MVP Rookie Challenge, 2001. Office: Boston Celtics Fourth Fl 226 Causeway St Boston MA 02114-4714*

**SZCZUBLEWSKI, WENDY SUE,** small business owner, musician, freelance/self-employed writer; b. Dunkirk, NY; d. Bernard and Rosemary Dougherty; m. Michael Szczublewski, June 26, 1999; 1 child, Preston Thomas. BA in polit. sci. cum laude, SUNY Coll. at Fredonia, 1987—91. Project mgr. Vanstar Corp., Vienna, Va., 1996—97; proposal mgr. RS Info. Systems, Inc., McLean, Va., 1997—98; writer/editor Computer Assoc. Internat., Inc., Herndon, Va., 1999—2002; pres. and ceo WoBop Music, Columbia, Md., 2002—; owner Szuzublewski Music, Columbia, Md., 2005—. Mem.: Nat. Guild of Piano Teachers, Am. Coll. of Musicians, MENSA. Avocations: baking, gardening, reading, bicycling, hiking. Office Phone: 410-772-1097. Business E-Mail: wszczub@szczublewski.com.

**SZCZYRBA, IGOR NICHOLAS,** mathematical physicist, consultant; b. Prague, Czech Republic, May 20, 1946; s. Mikolaj and Rozalia Szczyrba; m. Halina Agnieszka Kocewiak; children: Rafal W, Anna P. MS, Warsaw U., 1969, PhD, 1973, Dr. Habilitatis, 1983. Tchg. and rsch. asst. Warsaw U., 1969—73, tenured prof., 1973—84; vis. prof. Warsaw Sch. Econs., 1973—77; rsch. fellow Inst. Theoretical Physics, Trieste, Italy, 1975; vis. prof. U. Heidelberg, Germany, 1977—81; asst. prof. U. No. Colo., Greeley, 1986—88, assoc. prof., 1988—90, full prof., 1990—. Linguistic cons. Internat. Lang. Engring., Boulder, Colo., 1988—99, LionBridge, Boulder, Colo., 2000—, Bowne Global Solutions, Montreal, Canada, 2003—; polit. scis. cons. U. No. Colo., Greeley, 1986—. Contbr. articles to profl. jours. Recipient Scholar of Yr. award, U. No. Colo., Coll. Arts and Scis., 1989, 2002—03. Mem.: Math. Assn. Am. Office: U No Colo Ross Hall Greeley CO 80639 Office Phone: 970-351-2011. Office Fax: 970-351-1225. E-mail: igor.szczyrba@unco.edu.

**SZE, MICHAEL MING-CHIH,** actuary, consultant; b. Shanghai, June 1, 1940; came to US, 1968; m. Elsie Sim-Yee Chin, Aug. 19, 1972; children: Benjamin, Samuel, Timothy. BS, Hong Kong, 1964; MS, Calif. State U., Hayward, 1969; PhD in Math., Ohio State U., 1975. CFA. Internat. pension and ins. cons., ptnr. Hewitt Assocs., Lincolnshire, Ill., 1975-96; pres., fin. planner Sze Assocs., Toronto, Canada, 1996—. Adj. prof. U. Mich., Ann Arbor, 1998—99; tech. panel adv. bd. Social Security Adminstrn., Washington, 1994—96, Washington, 1999; cons. in field. Mem. editl. bd. Jour. Actuarial Practice, 1996—; co-author: Carswell's Benefits Manual, 1999-2002. Fellow Soc. Actuaries (bd. govs. 1994-97), Can. Inst. Actuaries (com. on investment practice 1994-96); mem. Acad. Social Scis., NY Acad. Scis. Roman Catholic. Avocations: bridge, fitness workouts. Office: Sze Assocs 45 Francine Dr Willowdale ON Canada M2H 2G5 Office Phone: 416-756-2181. Business E-Mail: msze@szeassociates.com.

**SZE, SARAH,** sculptor; b. Boston, 1969; BA magna cum laude, Yale U., 1991; MFA, Sch. of Visual Arts N.Y., 1997. One-woman shows include, Mus. of Fine Arts, Boston, Inst. of Contemporary Art, London, The Found. Cartier, Paris, Walker Art Ctr., Mpls., 2002, The Whitney Mus. Am. Art, N.Y.C., 2003, Mus. of Contemporary Art, Chgo, Marianne Boesky Gallery, NY, 2000, 2005, exhibited in group shows, The Whitney Mus. of Am. Art, N.Y.C., The Carnegie Mus. of Art, Pitts., Mus. Modern Art, San Francisco, 48th Venice Biennial, The L.A. (Calif.) Mus. Contemporary Art, 1999. Recipient Paula Rhodes Meml. award, 1997, award, Louis Comfort Tiffany Found., 1999, Lotus Club Found. Prize, 2003; fellow John D. and Catherine T. MacArthur Found., 2003.*

**SZE, SING-HOI,** science educator, researcher; Asst. prof. Tex. A&M U., Coll. Sta., Tex., 2002—. Grantee Exact Computational Biology Algorithms with Small Parameters, NSF, 2003—06, Genetic and Functional Genomic Analysis of Early Events in Cotton Fiber Devel., 2004—.

**SZEFLER, STANLEY JAMES,** pediatrics and pharmacology educator; b. Buffalo, Aug. 24, 1948; s. Stanley and Bernice Laura (Platt) Szefler; m. Christine M. Drezek, Dec. 26, 1970; children: David, Paul. BS, SUNY, Buffalo, 1971, MD, 1975. Resident pediat. Children's Hosp. Buffalo, 1975—77; postdoctoral fellow in clin. pharmacology and allergy immunology SUNY, Buffalo, 1977—79, asst. prof. pediat. and pharmacology, 1979—82; assoc. prof. pediat. and pharmacology U. Colo., Denver, 1982—90, prof. pediat., pharmacology, 1990—. Dir. clin. pharmacology Children's Hosp., Buffalo, 1979—82, Nat. Jewish Ctr. for Immunology and

Respiratory Medicine, Denver, 1982—. Contbr. articles to profl. jours. Mem. steering com., Asthma Camp for Children Am. Lung Assn., Denver, 1987—96. Maj. USAR, 1979—88. Grantee NIH, 1980—84, 1990—, FDA, Denver, 1988—91. Fellow: Am. Acad. Pediat. (liaison mem. com. drugs), Am. Acad. Allergy, Asthma and Immunology (chmn. asthma, rhinitis and respiratory disease interest sect. 1995—97). Avocations: literature, history, reading. Office: Nat Jewish Med & Rsch Ctr Dept Pediat 1400 Jackson St Denver CO 80206-2761 Business E-Mail: szeflers@njc.org.

**SZEGO, CLARA MARIAN,** cell biologist, educator; b. Budapest, Hungary, Mar. 23, 1916; arrived in U.S., 1921, naturalized, 1927; d. Paul S. and Helen (Elek) S.; m. Sidney Roberts, Sept. 14, 1943. AB, Hunter Coll., 1937; MS, U. Minn., 1939, PhD, 1942. Instr. physiology U. Minn., 1942-43; Minn. Cancer Rsch. Found. fellow, 1943—44; rsch. assoc. OSRD, Nat. Bur. Stds., 1944-45, Worcester Found. Exptl. Biology, 1945-47; rsch. instr. physiol. chemistry Yale U. Sch. Medicine, 1947-48; mem. faculty UCLA, 1948—, prof. biology, 1960—. Contbr. articles to profl. jours., book chapters and revs. Garvan fellow U. Minn., 1939; Guggenheim fellow, 1956; named Woman of Year in Sci. Los Angeles Times, 1957-58; named to Hunter Coll. Hall of Fame, 1987. Fellow AAAS; mem. Am. Physiol. Soc., Am. Soc. Cell Biology, Endocrine Soc. (CIBA award 1953), Soc. for Endocrinology (Gt. Britain), Biochem. Soc. (Gt. Britain), Internat. Soc. Rsch. Reproduction, Phi Beta Kappa (pres. UCLA chpt. 1973-74), Sigma Xi (pres. UCLA chpt. 1976-77). Home: 1371 Marinette Rd Pacific Palisades CA 90272-2627 Office: U Calif Dept Molecular Cell & Devel Biology Los Angeles CA 90095-1606 Business E-Mail: cmszego@ucla.edu.

**SZEJNIUK, NATHAN M.,** disaster preparedness coordinator, health care preparedness consultant; s. Doris (Messenger) and Noach Szejniuk; m. Betty J. Payne, Jan. 26, 1946; children: Jennifer, Joseph. Degree in Pub. & Environ. Health, East Carolina U., Greenville, NC, 2001. Cert. environ. health technician Nat. Environ. Health Assn., 1988. Hosp. corpsman operational medicine US Navy, Norfolk, NC, 1976—96; risk mgmt/safety cons. Pvt. Consulting, Greenville, NC, 1998—2003; disaster mgmt. coord. U. NC Health Care Sys., Chapel Hill, 2003—. Cons./instr. FEMA, Anniston, Ala., 2004—. With Hosp. Emergency Incident Command Sys., Sacramento, 2005. Chief petty officer USN, 1976—96. Decorated Navy Achievement medal US Navy; named Disaster Vol. of Yr., ARC, 1999; recipient Dist. Award of Merit, Boy Scouts Am., 2000. Mem.: Epsilon Nu Eta. Avocations: chess, reading, hiking, camping, canoeing. Office: Univ NC 101 Manning Dr Chapel Hill NC 27514 Office Phone: 919-966-6429. Office Fax: 919-966-1973. Personal E-mail: nszejniuk@cox.net. Business E-Mail: nszejniu@unch.unc.edu.

**SZEKELY, ZOLTAN,** mathematics professor; b. Szekszard, Hungary, Nov. 26, 1958; s. Laszlo Szekely and Margit Lazar; m. Olga Csuka Szekely, July 6, 1991. MS in Math., JATE, Steged, Hungary, 1983, MA in Math. Edn., 1987; PhD in Math., U. SC, 1998, M of Engring., 2002. Asst. prof. JATE, Szegedy, Hungary, 1987—91, Gallaudet U., Washington, 1999—2004, assoc. prof., 2004—. Mem.: AAUP, Math. Assn. Am., Am. Math. Soc. Roman Catholic. Avocation: amateur chess. Home: Apt 22 3517 Toledo Ter Hyattsville MD 20782 Office: Gallaudet Univ 800 Florida Ave NE Washington DC 20002 Office Phone: 202-651-5315. Office Fax: 202-651-5828. Business E-Mail: zoltan.szekely@gallaudet.edu.

**SZELENYI, IVAN,** adult education educator; b. Budapest, Apr. 17, 1938; came to the U.S., 1981; s. Gusztav and Julianna (Csapo) S.; m. Valeria Vanilia Majoros; children: Szonja, Lilla, Balazs. PhD, Hungarian Acad. Scis., Budapest, 1973, DSc, 1990; doctorate (hon.), Budapest U. Econs., 1992; DLitt (hon.), Flinders U., 1997; dr. rer.pol. h.c. (hon.), Friedrich-Alexander U., 2003. Rsch. fellow Hungarian Acad. Scis., Budapest, 1963-75; found. prof. Flinders U., Adelaide, Australia, 1975-80; prof. U. Wis., Madison, 1981-86; disting. prof. CUNY Grad. Ctr., 1986-88; prof. UCLA, 1988-99; William Graham Sumner prof. sociology Yale U., New Haven, 1999—. Author: Urban Inequalities under State Socialism, 1983, Socialist Entrepreneurs, 1988 (C. Wright Mills award 1989); co-author: Intellectuals on the Road to Class Power, 1979, Making Capitalism without Capitalists, 1998, Theories of New Class, 2004. Mem. Hungarian Acad. Scis; fellow Am. Acad. Arts and Sci. Business E-Mail: ivan.szelenyi@yale.edu.

**SZEP, PAUL MICHAEL,** editorial cartoonist; b. Hamilton, Ont., Can., July 29, 1941; came to U.S., 1966; s. Paul Joseph and Helen (Langhorne) S.; m. Angela Diane Garton, Feb. 27, 1965 (div. 1976); children: Amy, Jason; m. Lyn Dunlop, June 3, 2003. A.O.C.A., Ont. Coll. Art, 1964; A.O.C.A. hon. degree, 1975, Framingham State Coll., 1975, Worcester State Coll., 1980, William Penn Coll., 1981. Sports cartoonist Hamilton Spectator, 1958-61; graphics designer Financial Post, Toronto, Ont., 1965-66; editorial cartoonist Boston Globe, 1966—2001. Vis. fellow Harvard U., 1981; lectr. various univs. Author: In Search of Sacred Cows, 1967, Keep Your Left Hand High, 1969, At This Point in Time, 1973, The Hader They Fall, 1975, Unvote for a New America, 1976, Them Demaned Pictures, 1977, Warts and All, 1979, To a Different Drummer, 1983, The Gang of Eight, 1985, The Next Szep Book, 1985, Often in Error, Never in Doubt, 1987, And Then Jack Said to Arnie, 1991, And Then Arnie Told Chi Chi and Then Chi Chi Said to Fuzzy, 1993, And Then Fuzzy Told Seve, 1996, Not Just Another Szep Book, 1997, And Then Seve Told Freddy, 1997, Then Freddy Told Tiger, 1998, And Then Tiger Told the Shark, Talking on Tour, 2001, And Then the Shark Told Justin, 2002; editl. cartoonist: Sta. WNEV-TV, creator comic strip: Mr. Zeep, 1999; contbr. Golf Digest, New Eng. Jour. Golf. Served with F.A. Royal Canadian Army, 1957-58. Recipient Pulitzer prize, 1974, 1977, award, Sigma Delta Chi, 1974, 1977, Toyl award, Boston Jaycees, 1976, Headliners award, 1977, Reuben award for best editl. cartoonist, Nat. Cartoonist Soc., 1979, Thomas Nast award, Internat. Cartoonist award, Best Sports Cartoonist award, Nat. Cartoonists Soc., 1988. Mem. Soc. Illustrators, Kittansett Club, Harvard Club, Weston Golf Club, Belleair Country Club.

**SZESCILA, ANDREW J.,** oil industry executive; BS, Miss. State U. From region engr. Baker Oil Tools to sr. v.p., COO Baker Hughes, Houston, 1973—98, sr. v.p. & COO, Oilfield Ops., 1998—. Office: Baker Hughes 3900 Essex Lane Houston TX 77027-5177

**SZETO, YVONNE,** architectural firm executive; b. Hong Kong, July 4, 1956; naturalized; BArch, U. Minn., 1977; MArch, Harvard U., 1979. Registered N.Y., cert. Nat. Coun. Archtl. Registration Bds. With I.M. Pei & Ptnrs., 1977—89, Pei Cobb Freed & Ptnrs., 1989—99; ptnr. Pei Cobb Freed & Ptnrs., N.Y.C., 1999—. Guest critic Yale U.; panel mem. Bilbao: The Transformation of the City Art Inst. Chgo.; jury Bus. Week/Archtl. Record Awards, 2000. Mem.: AIA (medal and Cert. of Merit 1977). Office: Pei Cobb Freed & Ptnrs LLP 88 Pine St New York NY 10005

**SZIGETI, JÁNOS,** physicist; b. Budapest, Hungary, Oct. 11, 1936; s. György and Zsuzsanna (Ziffer) S.; m. Boglárka Gulyás, Aug. 7, 1967; children: Andrea, Zsófia. Diploma, Roland Eötvös U., 1960; PhD, U. Leningrad, 1972. With Ctrl. Rsch. Inst. for Physics, 1960—91; sr. scientist Rsch. Inst. for Particle and Nuc. Physics 1991—96, sci. advisor, 1996—, head dept. laser spectroscopy, 1991—. Asst. scientific co-worker, 1960-66; scientific co-worker Acad. of Sci., 1966-72, sr. scientist, 1972-96, head dept. laser spectroscopy, 1993—, sci. advisor, 1996—; head of dept. Rsch. Inst. of Particles and Nuclear Physics, 1991—. Contbr. numerous articles to profl. jours. Mem. Roland Eötvös Phys. Soc., European Phys. Soc. Avocation: rowing on the danube. Home: Erzsebet u 27 app 40 1043 Budapest Hungary Office: Rsch Inst Particle & Nuc Physics PO Box 49 H-1525 Budapest Hungary Office Phone: 36-1-392-27-52. Business E-Mail: szigeti@rmki.kfki.hu.

**SZINI, ISTVAN JANOS,** electronics engineer; s. Istvan and Alice Vidal Szini; m. Luciana Rocha Silva, Feb. 20, 1988; children: Ferenc Janos, Lilla Katalin. Postgrad., U. SC, 2005—. Sr. engr. NEC of Brazil, Sao Paulo, 1989—98; prin. staff engr. Motorola Inc., Libertyville, Ill., 1998—. Mem.:

IEEE. Achievements include research in handsets internal and external antennas. Office: Motorola 600N US 45 Libertyville IL 60048 Office Phone: 847-523-8780. E-mail: istvan.szini@motorola.com.

**SZKODY, PAULA,** astronomy educator, researcher; b. Detroit, July 17, 1948; d. Julian and Pauline (Wolski) S.; m. Donald E. Brownlee, Mar. 19, 1976; children: Allison, Carson. BS in Astrophysics, Mich. State U., 1970; MS in Astronomy, U. Wash., 1972, PhD in Astronomy, 1975. Rsch. asst. Observatoire de Geneve, 1969, Kitt Peak Nat. Obs., 1970; rsch., teaching asst. U. Wash., Seattle, 1970-75, rsch. assoc., lectr., 1975-82, sr. rsch. assoc., 1982-83, rsch. assoc. prof., 1983-91, rsch. prof., 1991-93, prof., 1993—. Part-time mem. faculty Seattle U., 1974-75, 82, Bellevue Coll., 1975-77; vis. scientist Kitt Peak Nat. Obs., 1976; vis. instr. UCLA, 1977, adj. asst. prof., 1980, 81; vis. assoc. prof. U. Hawaii, 1978; vis. assoc. prof. Calif. Inst. Tech., 1978-79, 80, mem. XTE users com., 1996-99; mem. users com. Internat. Ultraviolet Explorer, 1983-85, 93-97; mem. A.J. Cannon adv. com. AAUW, 1986-91, chmn. 1988-90; mem. mgmt. ops. working group on Ultraviolet/Visual/Relativity, NASA, 1988-91; mem. rep. Assocs. U. Rsch. Astronomy, 2000—. Scientific editor ApJ, 2002—; contbr. numerous articles to profl. jours. Recipient Annie J. Cannon award, 1978. Fellow AAAS (mem. nominating com. 1990-93, chairperson 1993, mem.-at-large 1995-99); mem. Am. Assn. Variable Star Observers (coun. mem. 2004—), Am. Astron. Soc. (councilor 1996-99), Internat. Astron. Union; mem. commn. 42 organizing com. 1991—, v.p. 1997-00, pres. 2000—03), Astron. Soc. Pacific (bd. dirs. 1988-92), Phi Beta Kappa. Office: U Wash Dept Astronomy PO Box 351580 Seattle WA 98195-1580 Business E-Mail: szkody@astro.washington.edu.

**SZKUTAK, TOM,** corporate financial executive, married; 2 children. BS in Fin. magna cum laude, Boston U. From exec. v.p. fin. divsn. investments to CFO divsn. lighting GE, 1982—2002; sr. v.p., CFO Amazon.com, Seattle, 2002—. Office: Amazon.com 1200 12th Ave S Seattle WA 98144

**SZLAM, ALEKSANDER,** manufacturing executive; arrived in US, 1969; BEE, Ga. Tech., 1974, MEE, 1980. Designer, engr. Lockheed NCR; founder, chmn., CEO eshare Comm., Inc. (formerly Melita Internat., Inc.), Norcross, Ga.; chmn., CEO Szlam Enterprises, Inc. Co-author: Predictive Dialing, 1996. Named Entrepreneur of Yr. (Southern Region), Inc. mag., 1991, Pioneer in Industry, Call Ctr. mag., 1997. Achievements include more than 50 world patents; 150 more pending.*

**SZOKA, EDMUND CASIMIR CARDINAL,** archbishop; b. Grand Rapids, Mich., Sept. 14, 1927; s. Casimir and Mary (Wolgat) Szoka. BA, Sacred Heart Sem., 1950; JCB, Pontifical Lateran U., 1958, JCL, 1959. Ordained priest Roman Catholic Ch., 1954, elevated to cardinal 1988. Asst. pastor St. Francis Parish, Manistique, Mich., 1954—55; sec. to bishop Marquette, 1955—57, 1959—62; chaplain St. Mary's Hosp., Marquette, 1955—57; tribunal, defender of bond Marquette, 1960—71; asst. chancellor Diocese of Marquette, 1962—69, chancellor, 1970—71; pastor St. Pius X Ch., Ishpeming, Mich., 1962—63, St. Christopher Ch., Marquette, 1963—71; bishop Diocese of Gaylord, Mich., 1971—81; archbishop of Detroit, 1981—90. Sec.-treas. Mich. Cath. Conf., Lansing, 1972—77; mem. region VI Nat. Conf. Cath. Bishops, 1972—77; treas., adminstrv. bd. and adminstrv. com., budget and fin. com. Nat. Conf. Cath. Bishops/U.S. Cath. Conf., 1981—84; pres. Prefecture for Econ. Affairs of the Holy See, 1990—97, Pontifical Commn. Vatican City State, 1997—2006; mem. Secretariat of State 2d sect. Coun. for Rels. with States; pres. Governatorato Vatican City State, 2001—06. Trustee Nat. Shrine of the Immaculate Conception, Washington, 1981—90; chmn. bd. trustees Cath. Telecomm. Network Am., 1980—90; trustee, exec. com., chmn. com. for univ. rels. Cath. U. Am., 1981—90. Mem.: Congregation for Clergy, Congregation for Evangelization of Peoples, Congregation for Bishops, Congregation for Causes of Saints, Congregation for Insts. Consecrated Life and Socs. Apostolic Life. Roman Catholic. Address: Governatorato 00120 Vatican City Italy

**SZOKODY, ANIKO,** pianist, educator; b. Szeged, Hungary, Apr. 24, 1973; arrived in U.S., 1997; d. Fedor Sandor Szokody and Zsuzsanna Szlovak; m. Willis Dee Ottery III, Mar. 1, 2002; 1 child, Willis David. MusB, Zoltan Kodaly Spl. Musical Secondary Sch., Kecskemet, Hungary, 1991; Piano Performer Artist Degree, tchrs. diploma, Franz Liszt Acad. Music, Budapest, Hungary, 1997; MusM in Piano Performance, Ind. U., 2000; artist diploma (hon.), Conservatorio Beethoven, Buenos Aires, 1997. Assoc. instr. piano Ind. U., Bloomington, 1998—2000; instrumental accompanist, chamber music coach Chautauqua Instn., 1999—2002, head instrumental accompanist, chamber music coach, 2002—06. Guest instr. piano Conservatorio Beethoven, Buenos Aires, 1996—97; studio pianist for cellist Janos Starker Ind. U., Bloomington, 1998—2000; pvt. piano instr., Albany, NY, 2000—. Musician (pianist): (solo performances) Europe, North and South America. Grantee, Hungarian Nat. Cultural Found., 1996, Conservatorio Beethoven, 1996—97, for profl. career documentary, Hungarian Pub. TV, 2002; scholar, studio of Prof. Gyorgy Sebok, Ind. U., 1998—2000. Mem.: Am. Fed. Musicians, Capitol Chamber Artists, Adirondack Ensemble, N.Y. State Music Tchrs. Assn., Coll. Music Soc., Music Tchrs. Nat. Assn., Upper Hudson Musical Arts, Schenectady Musical Union, Albany Symphony Orch. Home: 819 Woodland Ave Schenectady NY 12309

**SZOLNOKI, JOHN FRANK,** special education educator, administrator; b. N.Y.C., Apr. 16, 1956; s. Jacob and Anna (Reinwald) S.; m. Kathleen Bascetta, Dec. 28, 2004; children: Melissa Beth, David Jacob, Elizabeth, Eric. BS, Manhattan Coll., 1978; MS, Coll New Rochelle, 1981; Med, Columbia U., 1983, EdD, 1988. Cert. tchr. spl. edn., sch. adminstr., supr., dist. adminstr., N.Y. Therapy aide Office Mental Health, N.Y. State Bronx Psychiat. Ctr., 1978; intn oei. fith-fith grades bch. Philip and James bch., Archdiocese of N.Y., 1978-79; program supr. occpl. edn. classes St. Mary's Habilitation Inst. Inst. Applied Human Dynamics, Bronx, 1979-83; sch. supr. Assn. for Help of Retarded Children Bronx Habilitation Ctr., N.Y.C., 1983-87; spl. educator Mt. Pleasant-Blythedale Union Free Sch. Dist., Valhalla, NY, 1987-88; spl. edn. educator Bd. Coop. Edni. Svcs. Westchester, White Plains, NY, 1988—, Dobbs Ferry (N.Y.) H.S., 1995-96, Harrison (N.Y.) H.S., 1996-97, Hommocks Mid. Sch., Larchmont, NY, 2002—05, West Lake H.S., Valhalla, 2005—. Adj. prof. Western Conn. State U., Danbury, 1988-89, St. Thomas Aquinas Coll., Sparkill, N.Y., 1990, 91, Coll. New Rochelle, N.Y., 2001-, CUNY Hunter, 1994-99; team leader Bd. Coop. Ednl. Svcs., So. Westchester, 1989-93, site coord. extended sch. yr. program Rye Lake campus, 1991-95; presenter in field; Ctr. Spl. Edn. and Tng. Resource Ctr., workshop presenter supts. day, 1995; mem. So. Westchester Bd. coop. Ednl. Svcs. Vol. firefighter, sec. hook & ladder Harrison (N.Y.) Fire Dept., 1993-95, lt., 1996-97 capt., 1998-99 (Firefighter of Yr. 1990); mem. exec. bd. Very Spl. Arts,White Plains, N.Y., 1990; parent rep. exec. bd. Harrison Children's Ctr., 1991-93, 95—; lector, tchr. catechism St. Gregory the Gt. Roman Cath. Ch., 1994-95, Secular Franciscan Order, Roman Cath. Ch., 2002—; sec. St. Francis Fraternity, N.Y., 2003—; EMT vol. Harrison Ambulance Corps, 1993-94; aux. police officer N.Y.C. Police Dept., 1975-77; mem. Ctrl. Westchester Vicariate Coun., Archdiocese of N.Y., 1998—99; mem. parish coun. St. Gregory the Great, 1998—99; panel mem. surrogate decision making com. N.Y. State Commn. on Quality Care for the Mentally Disabled, 1999—. Grantee: Readers Digest Found., Westchester Edn. Coalition, 1990, Innovation Network, Westchester, Rockland Impact II, Adaptor award, 1991, 92, 93, 94, 95, 97, 98, 2000 Mem. Am. Assn. on Mental Retardation (rsch. project norming examiner adaptive behavior scale 1991), Coun. for Exceptional Children (pres. Hunter Coll. chpt. 1997-2000, regional rep. to bd. 2000-03, treas. 1993-96, exec. bd. dirs. 1993-96, del. Nat. conv. 1998, co-chair N.Y. state conv. 1997, sec. 2002—, co-chmn. promotion/publicity subcom. local arrangements com. nat. annual conv. 2002, v.p. NY State Fedn. Chpts. Coun. Exceptional Children, 2003-04, pres.-elect, 2004-05, NY State CEC pres. 2005-), Kappa Delta Pi, Phi Delta Kappa. Avocation: marathon running. Office: Bd Coop Ednl Svcs So Westchester 1606 Old Orchard St White Plains NY 10604-1049 Home: 51 Holmes Ave Hartsdale NY 10530-1339 Office Phone: 914-948-7271. Personal E-mail: johnszolnoki@aol.com.

**SZOLOVITS, PETER,** computer scientist; BS, PhD, Calif. Inst. Tech. Prof. computer sci. & engring. MIT, Cambridge, Mass., 1974—, prof. health sciences & tech., head of Clin. Decision-Making Group, Computer Sci. & Artificial Intelligence Lab. (CSAIL). Contbr. articles, scientific papers. Fellow: Am. Coll. Med. Informatics, Am. Assn. Artificial Intelligence; mem.: Inst. Medicine. Office: MIT 32-254 EECS 77 Mass Ave Cambridge MA 02139-4307 Office Phone: 617-253-3476. E-mail: psz@mit.edu.*

**SZOSTAK, JACK WILLIAM,** molecular biologist, educator; b. London, Nov. 9, 1952; s. William J. and Viola (Munford) S.; m. Terri-Lynn McCormick, May 29, 1993. BS in Cell Biology, McGill U., Montreal, Can., 1972; PhD in Biochemistry, Cornell U., Ithaca, NY, 1977. Rsch. assoc. in biochemistry Cornell U., Ithaca, NY, 1977-79; asst. prof. dept. biol. chemistry Harvard Med. Sch./Sidney Farber Cancer Inst., Boston, 1979-83; assoc. prof. dept. biol. chemistry Harvard Med. Sch./Dana Farber Cancer Inst., Boston, 1983-84; assoc. prof. dept. genetics Harvard Med. Sch., Boston, 1984-87, prof., 1988—; assoc. molecular biologist, dept. molecular biology Mass. Gen. Hosp., Boston, 1984-87, molecular biologist, dept. molecular biology, 1988—, Alex Rich Disting. Investigator, dept. molecular biology, 2000—; investigator Howard Hughes Med. Inst., 1998—. Cons. Genetics Inst., 1980-87; mem. site visit team, NIH, 1982; mem. Presdl. Young Investigator Review Panel, 1984; mem. Nat. Sci. Found. Review Panel, 1985, NASA Exobiology Study Sect., 1997; NATO Advanced Study Course on RNA, Spetses, Greece, 1994; program dir., Genetics Cancer and Inherited Disease Tng. Grant, Harvard Med. Sch., 1986-92; mem. sci. adv. bd. Gilead Scis., Inc., 1990-98, Trans-Karyotic Therapies, Inc., 1990—, Cubist, Inc., 1993-97; ad hoc mem., NIH Molecular Biology Study Sect., 1992; mem. Subcommittee of Professors, Harvard Med. Sch., 1992-94 preliminary qualifying exam com., 1996-97, com. on postdoctoral fellow, 1997-98; mem. com. on sr. appointments, Mass. Gen. Hosp., 1992-97; co-chair, Nucleic Acids Gordon Conf., 1993, Keystone Symposium on RNA, 1996; Can. reallocation exercise external reviewer, NRC, 1998, mem. workshop on size limits of microorganisms, 1998, co-chair com. on the origin and evolution of life, 2003-; mem. partners com. on sr. appointments, 1997-; mem. bd. tutors, biochemical sciences, Harvard U., 2000-; mem. NIH Intramural Review Panel, 2001; invited lectr. Agouron Inst. Sponsored Geobiology Course, Catalina Island, 2002; vis. fellow, Brasenose Coll. and Astor Lectr., Oxford U., 2005; tchr. Introductory Lecture, RNA World Quarter Course, 2005. Contbr. articles to sci. jours. Recipient Louis Vuitton-Moet Hennesey 'Vinci of Excellence' award, 1996, Hans Sigrist prize U. Bern, Switzerland, 1997, Genetics Soc. Am. medal, 2000, Harrison Howe award, Am. Chemical Soc., Rochester sect., 2003; co-recipient Albert Lasker award for Basic Med. Rsch., Lasker Found., 2006 Fellow NY Acad. Scis.; mem. NAS (award in molecular biology 1994), Am. Acad. Arts & Sciences. Achievements include patents in field. Office: Howard Hughes Med Inst Mass Gen Hosp Dept Molecular Biology Boston MA 02114 also: CCIB 7215 Simches Research Ctr 185 Cambridge St Boston MA 02114 Address: Mass Gen Hosp 32 Fruit St Boston MA 02114 Business E-Mail: szostak@molbio.mgh.harvard.edu.*

**SZULIK, MATTHEW J.,** information technology executive; With Sapiens Internat., MapInfo Corp.; pres. Relativity Technologies, 1997—98; COO Red Hat, Inc., Raleigh, NC, 1998—99, CEO, 1999—, pres., 1999—, dir., 1999—, chmn., 2002—. Chmn. sci. and tech. bd. State NC Econ. Develop. Bd. Recipient 20/20 Vision award, CIO mag. Mem.: NC Electronics and Information Technologies Assn. (past chmn. and exec. dir.). Office: Red Hat Inc 1801 Varsity Dr Raleigh NC 27606-2072 Office Phone: 919-754-3700. Office Fax: 919-754-3701.*

**SZUMITA, PAUL MICHAEL,** pharmacist; b. Pawtucket, RI, May 18, 1975; s. Richard William and Sarah Ann Szumita. D in Pharmacy, Northeastern U., Boston, 1999. Diplomate Bd. Pharm. Specialties. Sr. pharmacist Brigham & Women's Hosp., Boston, 1999—2001, ICU clin. specialist, 2001—03, clin. pharmacy practice mgr., 2003—. Mem.: Am. Soc. Health Sys. Pharmacist. Achievements include research in high-dose corticotropin test to diagnose relative adrenal insufficiency in vasopressor-dependent septic shock; barriers to glucose control in the intensive care unit; vasopressin for vasopressor-dependent septic shock. Home: 111 Jersey St # 10 Boston MA 02215 Office: Brigham and Womens Hosp 75 Francis St Boston MA 02115 Office Phone: 617-732-7677.

**SZUWALSKI, ANDRE MICHAEL,** lawyer; b. Buffalo, Aug. 16, 1964; m. Angela Fontana. BS in Elec. Engring., U. Miss., 1987; JD cum laude, Tulane U., 1990. Bar: Tex. 1990, registered: US Patent & Trademark Office. Assoc. Jenkens & Gilchrist, P.C., Dallas, 1990—97, shareholder, 1997—, firm co-leader intellectual property practice group. Mem.: ABA, Am. Intellectual Property Law Assn., Dallas Assn. Young Lawyers, Dallas/Ft. Worth Patent Law Assn., Dallas Bar Assn., Tex. State Bar Assn. Office: Jenkens & Gilchrist PC Ste 3200 1445 Ross Ave Dallas TX 75202-2799 Office Phone: 214-855-4795. Office Fax: 214-855-4300. Business E-Mail: aszuwalski@jenkens.com.

**SZWALBENEST, BENEDYKT JAN,** lawyer; b. Poland, June 13, 1955; s. Sidney and Janina (Bleishtif) S.; m. Shelley Joy Leibel, Nov. 8, 1981. BBA, Temple U., 1978, JD, 1981. Law clk. Fed. Deposit Ins. Corp., Washington, 1980; law clk. to presiding justice U.S. Dist. Ct. (ea. dist.) Pa., Phila., 1980-81; staff atty., regulatory specialist Fidelcor, Inc. and Fidelity Bank, Phila., 1981-86; regulations specialist sr. regulatory staff Fed. Res. Bank of N.Y., N.Y.C., 1986-89; s.v.p. regulatory compliance, sec. Custodial Trust Co. subs. Bear Stearns, Princeton, 1990—2001, pres., CEO, dir., 2001—; mng. dir., prin. Bear Stearns & Co., Inc., 1998—. Author: Federal Bank Regulation, 1980. Mem. Commonwealth of Pa. Post-secondary Edn. Planning Commn., Harrisburg, 1977-79; trustee Pop Warners Little Scholars, Phila., 1981-86. Recipient E. Gerald Corrigan Pres.'s Award for Excellence, 1988. Mem.: ABA (nat. sec. treas. law student divsn, 1980—81 Silver Key award 1980, Gold Key award 1981), N.J. Bankers Assn. (legis. and compliance com. 1992—), Securities Industry Assn. (anti-money laundering com. 2001—), Temple U. Sch. Bus. Alumni assn. (sec. 1982—84, v.p. 1984—86, pres. 1986—88, bd. dirs. gen. alumni assn. 1986—88), Am. Bankers Assn. (cert. compliance specialist, lectr. 1984—), Am. Judicature Soc., Omicron Delta Epsilon. Avocations: baseball, tennis, skiing. Home: 1504 Brookfield Rd Yardley PA 19067-3930 Office: Custodial Trust Co 101 Carnegie Ctr Princeton NJ 08540-6231 Office Phone: 609-951-2313. E-mail: bswalbenest@bear.com.

**SZWARC, WLODZIMIERZ,** operations research professor; b. Kowel, Poland, Apr. 9, 1924; s. Maksym and Raja (Frenkel) S.; m. Maria Bass, Aug. 17, 1954 (div. Mar. 3, 1976); children: Michal, Ryszard; m. Rae Briker Lagen, Nov. 5, 1990. MS, U. Wroclaw, Poland, 1952, PhD in Math., 1960. Asst. prof. Tech. U., Wroclaw, 1952-60, adj. prof., 1960-67, assoc. prof., 1967-69; vis. prof. Carnegie-Mellon U., Pitts., 1970-71, U. Wis., Milw., 1971-72 prof. ops. rsch., 1972—97, prof. emeritus 1997—. Cons. Inst. Inner Trade, Warsaw, 1959-68, Budapest, 1963-64, Elec. Inst., Wroclaw, 1961-62, Transp. Inst., Warsaw and Wroclaw, 1967-69. Assoc. editor Naval Rsch. Logistics, 1977; contbr. over 93 rsch. papers to sci. jours. Mem. Ops. Rsch. Soc. Am., Inst. Mgmt. Sci. Achievements include research on transportation and linear programming problems, optimization techniques, production scheduling, discrete optimization techniques, application of mathematics to managerial problems and combinatorial methods. Office: U Wis-Milw PO Box 742 Milwaukee WI 53201-0742 Home: 650 San Antonio Rd unit 33 Palo Alto CA 94306 Office Phone: 414-229-3823. Personal E-mail: wlodek.1@comcast.net.

**SZYBALSKI, WACLAW,** geneticist, educator; b. Lwów, Poland, Sept. 9, 1921; arrived in U.S., 1950, naturalized, 1957; s. Stefan and Michalina (Rakowska) Szybalski; m. Elizabeth Hunter, Feb. 5, 1955; children: Barbara A. Szybalski Sandor, Stefan H. BSChemE, Politechnika Lwów, 1944; MSChemE, Politechnika Slaska, Gliwice, Poland, 1945; DSc, Inst. Tech., Gdansk, 1949, PhD (hon.), 2001, U. Marie Curie, Lublin, Poland, 1980, U. Gdansk, 1989, Med. Acad. Gdansk, 2000. Asst. prof. Inst. Tech., Gdansk, 1945—50; staff Cold Spring Harbor (N.Y.) Biol. Labs., 1951—55; asst. prof. Inst. Microbiology, Rutgers U., New Brunswick, NJ, 1955-60; prof. oncology McArdle Lab., U. Wis., Madison, 1960—. Mem. recombinant DNA adv. com. NIH, 1974—78; Wendel H. Griffith meml. lectr. St. Louis U., 1975; Raine vis. prof. U. Western Australia, Perth, 1997. Author: numerous papers, revs., abstracts and books in field; editor-in-chief: Gene, 1976—96, hon., founding editor-in-chief, 1996—; mem. editl. bd. other jours. Decorated Order of Merit Republic of Poland; recipient Karl A. Forster lectr. award, U. Mainz, 1970, A. Jurzykowski Found. award in biology, 1988, Hilldale award in biology, U. Wis., 1994, G. J. Mendel Gold medal for merit in biol. scis., Acad. Scis. Czech Republic, 1995, Cogene lectr. Internat. Union Biochemistry, Nairobi, 1987, Cairo, 1988, Harare, Zimbabwe, 1989;, chemistry bldg. at Inst. Tech. Gdansk named in his honor, 2004. Mem.: AAAS, Polish Inst. Arts and Scis. Am. (C. Funk Natural Sci. award 2003), Polish Acad. Scis., European Molecular Biology Orgns. (lectr. 1971, 1976), Am. Soc. Microbiologists (chmn. virology divsn. 1972—74, chmn. divsn. IV 1974—75), Genetic Soc. Am., Am. Soc. Biochemists, Polish Med. Alliance (hon.), Italian Soc. Exptl. Biology (hon.), Polish Soc. Microbiologists (hon.). Home: 1124 Merrill Springs Rd Madison WI 53705-1317 Office: U Wis McArdle Lab Madison WI 53706 E-mail: szybalski@oncology.wisc.edu. *The profession should also be the hobby and a constant source of enjoyment and satisfaction.*

**SZYDLOWSKI, JOSEPH EDWARD,** music librarian; b. Wyandotte, Mich., July 13, 1955; s. Joseph Victor and Hedwig Szydlowski. MusB, Ea. Mich. U., 1979; MusM, San Francisco State U., 1985; M in Info. and Libr. Studies, U. Mich., 1993. Libr. clk. U. Mich. Music Libr., Ann Arbor, 1991—93; libr., gen. reference Chgo. Pub. Libr., 1993—94, music libr., 1994—. Musician (classical guitarist) Spanish and Polish music concerts. Union trustee AFSCME, Chgo., 2001—02. Scholar Robert Guthrie Master Class, So. Meth. U., 1999. Mem.: Guitar Found. Am., Chgo. Classical Guitar Soc., Music Libr. Assn. (reviewer 2003—04). Roman Catholic. Avocations: politics, ecology, renaissance and baroque music, architecture, art. Office: Chicago Public Library - Main 400 S State St Chicago IL 60605 Office Phone: 312-747-4823. Office Fax: 312-747-4832. Business E-Mail: szydlows@chipublib.org.

**SZYDLOWSKI, RALPH,** retired metal products executive; b. Alpena, Mich., Nov. 14, 1942; s. Chester and Bridget (Romel) Sedloske; m. Geraldine Bryson, Oct. 8, 1971; children: Denise E., George S., Ruth A., Regina M. Assoc. in Indsl. Tech. summa cum laude, Baker Coll., Flint, Mich., 1991, B of Indsl. Mgmt. summa cum laude, 1994. With Flint Metal Ctr., Draw Die Tryout, 1972-96; die maker Flint Metal Ctr., 1996—2001, formability cons., 1995—2001; die engr. tech. staffing divsn. Trialon Corp., GM Metal Fabricating divsn., 2003—05; ret., 2005. Served with U.S. Army, 1962-69. Decorated Silver Star, Purple Heart. Mem. VFW, DAV, Am. Legion, Mil. Order of the Purple Heart, 26th Inf. Regt. Assn., Soc. 1st Inf. Divsn., Eagles. Roman Catholic. Avocations: woodworking, travel, books. E-mail: rsgs42@aol.com.

**SZYGENDA, RALPH J.,** automotive executive; b. McKeesport, Pa., Sept. 6, 1948; BS in Computer Sci., U. Mo., 1970; MEE, U. Tex., 1975; ED (hon.), U. Mo. With Tex. Instruments Inc., 1972—93; v.p., chief info. officer Bell Atlantic Corp., Arlington, Va., 1993—96, GM Corp., 1996—2000, group v.p., chief info. officer, 2000—. Bd. dir. Handleman Co. Mem.: GM Automotive Stratey Bd., U. Mo. Sch. Mgmt. Info. Sys. (chmn. advisory bd.), InformationWeek Mag. (editl. bd.), Rsch. Bd. Office: GM Corp 300 Renaissance Ctr PO Box 300 Detroit MI 48265-3000*

**SZYGENDA, STEPHEN A.,** electrical and computer engineering educator, researcher; b. McKeesport, Pa., Oct. 5, 1938; s. Stephen A. Sr. and Elizabeth B. (Zolczer) S.; m. Marie A. Deli, Apr. 2, 1960; children: Stephanie Burden, Diana Easton, Mark. BS, Fairleigh Dickinson U., 1965; MS, Northwestern U., 1967, PhD, 1968. Registered profl. engr., Tex. Engr. Comprehensive Design, NJ, 1959-62; mem. tech. staff Bell Tel. Labs., NJ, Ill., 1962-68; assoc. prof. elec. engring. and computer engring. U. Mo., Rolla, 1968-70; prof. elec. engring. and computer engring. So. Meth. U., Dallas, 1970-73, U. Tex., Austin, 1973-86, dir. Ctr. for Tech., 1986-89, Clint Murchison Sr. Chair of Free Enterprise prof., 1986-96, chmn. elec. and computer engring. dept., 1993-96; dean Sch. Engring. U. Ala., Birmingham, 1996-2000, So. Meth. U., Dallas, 2000—04, Cecil H. Green chair, 2004—. Pres. CCSS, Austin, 1972-81, Comsat Gen. Internat. Sys., Austin, 1981-83, SBI, Inc., Austin, 1985—; pres., CEO Rubicon Group, Austin, 1983-85; active Tex. Gov. Coun. for Sci. and Tech., 1984-87. Contbr. articles to profl. jours. Dir. Laguna Gloria Mus., Austin, 1981-83; pres. bd. Austin Ballet, 1983. With USN, 1956-59. Fellow IEEE (bd. dirs. 1973-75 Svc. awards 1977, 79, 83, 87, 96), IC2, Soc. for Design and Process Sci.; mem. Assn. Computing Machinery (Svc. award 1975, 79, 87, 88, Disting. lectr. 1991-95). Roman Catholic. Achievements include pioneering in CAD, simulation, fault tolerant computing, telecommunications, entrepreneurship, and software engineering. Home: 5227 Beckington Ln Dallas TX 75287 Office: Southern Methodist Univ Sch of Engring Dallas TX 75275 Office Phone: 214-768-3959. Personal E-mail: szygenda@msn.com.

**SZYMANCZYK, MICHAEL E.,** tobacco products executive; BS in Finance, Indiana U., 1972. Various sales and gen. mgmt. positions Procter & Gamble, 1971-87; v.p. sales Kraft Inc., Glenview, Ill., 1987-88, v.p retail ops., 1988; sr. v.p. Swift-Eckrich Inc., 1989; sr. v.p. sales Philip Morris USA (now divsn. of Altria Grp., Inc.), NYC, 1990-97, pres., CEO, 1997—, chmn., 2002—. Mem.: Indiana U. Kelley Sch. of Bus. Dean's Adv. Council (chmn.), bd. trustees Va. Found. for Independent Coll. Office: Philip Morris USA 120 Park Ave New York NY 10017-5592

**SZYMANSKI, BOLESLAW KAROL,** computer scientist, educator, entrepreneur; b. Paslek, Poland, Apr. 22, 1950; arrived in U.S., 1982; s. Kazlmierz and Aniela Marta (Langer) Szymanski; m. Emilia Haraf, Dec. 15, 1973; children: Petcr Rafal, Witold Andrew. M in Engring. Electronics, Warsaw Poly. Inst., Poland, 1973; PhD in Computer Sci., Nat. Acad. Scis., Warsaw, 1976. Asst. prof. Warsaw Poly. Inst., 1973-75; rschr. Inst. Technol. and Econ. Info., Warsaw, 1975-78; divsn. head Inst. STEI, Warsaw, 1979-82; postdoctoral fellow Aberdeen U., England, 1978; vis. asst. prof. U. Pa., Phila., 1982-85, assoc. prof. computer sci., 1985-89; prof. computer sci. CSCI, 1990—, acting chmn., 1993-94; assoc. dean info. tech. Rensselaer Poly. Inst., Troy, NY, 1997—2001, dir. Ctr. for Pervasive Computing and Networking, 2003—; founder/chmn. bd. dirs Premonitia, Inc., Boston, 2000; founder, pres., CEO Optimaret, Inc. Latham, NY, 2004. Chief sci. officer CCCC, Phila., 1984—87; cons. GE R & D Ctr., Schenectady, 1987—90, IBM Corp., Poughkeepsie, NY, 1992—96, Cardiomag, Inc., Schenectady, NY, 2001—. Internat. Med. Programs, Albany, 2003—; EPL parallel computer lang. expert witness U.S. Congress, Washington, 1997; expert UN Indsl. Devel. Office, Vienna, 1990—96. Author: Parallel Functional Languages and Compilers, 1993; editor-in-chief Sci. Computing IOS Press, Amsterdam, 2000—; editor: Languages, Compilers & RT Systems, 1996, Advances in Pervasive Computing and Networking, 2004. Recipient Wiley Disting. Faculty award, 2003, Tech. Innovation award, NASA, 1996, SuPaCup '93, German Computer Soc., Mannheim, 1993; Rsch. grantee, IBM, Lucent, CISCO, DARPA, ARO, NSF, ONR, 1966—. Fellow: IEEE; mem.: Assn. Computing Machinery (nat. lectr. 1987—88). Avocations: history, bridge. Home: 6 Hollow Rd Newtonville NY 12110-5100 Office: Rensselaer Poly Inst 110 8th St Troy NY 12180-3590 Office Phone: 518-276-2714. Personal E-mail: bkszym@yahoo.com. Business E-Mail: szymab@rpi.edu.

**SZYMANSKI, EDNA MORA,** dean; b. Caracas, Venezuela, Mar. 19, 1952; came to U.S., 1952; d. José Angel and Helen Adele (McHugh) Mora; m. Michael Bernard, Mar. 30, 1973. BS, Rensselaer Poly. Inst., 1972; MS, U. Scranton, 1974; PhD, U. Tex., 1988. Cert. rehab. counselor. Vocat. evaluator Mohawk Valley Workshop, Utica, N.Y. 1972-75; vocat. rehab. counselor N.Y. State Office Vocat. Rehab., Utica, 1975-80, sr. vocat. rehab. counselor, 1980-87; rsch. assoc. U. Tex., Austin, 1988-89; asst. prof. U. Wis., Madison, 1989-91, assoc. prof., 1991-93, assoc. dean sch. edn., 1993—99, dir. rehab. rsch. and tng. ctr., 1993-99, prof. rehab. psychology and spl. edn., 1997—99, chair dept. rehab. psychology and spl. edn., 1997-99, fellow tchg. acad., 1997; dean Coll. Edn. U. Md., College Park, 1999—2006; sr. v.p. acad. affairs, provost U. Maine, Orono, 2006—. Cons. Rsch. Assocs. Syracuse, N.Y.,

1988-90. Co-author various book chpts.; co-editor: Rehabilitation Counseling Basics and Beyond, 1992, 98, 2005; co-editor Work and Disability, 1996, 2003, Rehabilitation Counseling Bull., 1994-2000; contbr. articles to profl. jours. Mem. Pres.'s Com. on Employment of People with Disabilities, Washington, 1987-97. Recipient Rsch. award Am. Assn. Counselor Edn. and Supr., 1991. Mem. ACA (chair rsch. com. 1992-94, Rsch. awards 1990, 93, 95), Am. Rehab. Counseling Assn. (pres. 1985-86, rsch. award 1989, 94, Disting. Profl. award 1997, James F. Garrett award for disting. career in rehab. rsch. 1999), Coun. Rehab. Edn. (chair rsch. com. 1990-95, v.p. 1993-95, 97), Nat. Coun. Rehab. Edn. (chair rsch. com. 1992-99, Rehab. Rschr. of Yr. 1993, New Career in Rehab. Edn. award 1990). Office: U Maine Office of Provost 201 Alumni Hall Orono ME 04469 Personal E-mail: emsqy@aol.com.

**SZYMANSKI, PATRICK JOSEPH,** lawyer; b. Detroit, Jan. 18, 1949; s. Frank S. and Lillian F. (Mikula) S. Student, MIT, 1966-69; BA, Wayne State U., Detroit, 1973, JD, 1976. Bar: Mich. 1976, U.S. Ct. Appeals (D.C., 1st, 2d and 4th cirs.) 1977, U.S. Ct. Appeals (9th cir.) 1978, Calif. 1979, D.C. 1979, U.S. Dist. Ct. (no. dist.) Calif. 1979, U.S. Ct. Appeals (10th cir.) 1984, U.S. Supreme Ct. 1985, U.S. Dist. Ct. D.C. 1988, U.S. Dist. Ct. Md. 1988, U.S. Dist. Ct. Mich. (ea. dist.) 1991, U.S. Ct. Appeals (3d cir.) 1991. Appellate ct. br. NLRB, Washington, 1976-78, 83-88; assoc. Beeson, Tayer & Bodine, San Francisco, 1978-83, Baptiste & Wilder, P.C., Washington, 1988—2003. Mem. editorial bd. Wayne State U. Law Rev., 1975-76. Gen. counsel Internat. Brotherhood Teamsters, 1999—2006, Change to Win, 2006—. Democrat. Roman Catholic. Office Phone: 202-721-6035. Business E-Mail: patrick.szymanski@changetowin.org.

**SZYMCZAK, EDWARD JOSEPH,** mechanical engineer; b. Anderson, Tex., Sept. 28, 1938; s. Harold and Verna (Walkoviak) S.; m. Lorena Jane Sharp, Sept. 26, 1964; children: Denise, Lisa, Brian. Student, U. St. Thomas, 1958; BSME, Tex. A&M, 1961; MBA, U. Houston, 1970. Registered profl. engr., Tex. Engr. trainee to engring. mgr. Cameron Iron Works, Houston, 1961-90; dir. engring. Ea. hemisphere Cooper Oil Tool Div./Cooper Industries, London, 1990-91, dir. engring. Houston, 1991-95, Cameron div. Cooper Cameron Corp., Houston, 1995-97; mgr. design process tech. ABB Vetco Gray, Houston, 1998—2003; pvt. practice Spring, Tex., 2004—. Past chmn. indsl. adv. bd. U. La., Lafayette (formerly U. Southwestern La.), 1991—; trustee Tex. A&M U. Rsch. Found., College Station, 1994—; mech. engring. adv. bd. U. Tenn., Knoxville, 1996-2000; cons. in field. Patentee (8) on oil tool equipment. Bd. dir. Polish Home, Houston, 2004—. Mem. ASME, Tex. A&M Former Students Assn., Tex. A&M 12th Man Found., Tex. A&M Mech. Engring. Acad. Disting. Grads., Soc. Petroleum Engrs., Nat. Assn. Corrosion Engrs., Tau Beta Pi. Republican. Roman Catholic. Avocations: ranching, farming, design process technology, investing. Home and Office: 4002 Cypress Hill Dr Spring TX 77388-5717 Personal E-mail: szy_99@hotmail.com.

**SZYMONIAK, ELAINE EISFELDER,** retired state senator; b. Boscobel, Wis., May 24, 1920; d. Hugo Adolph and Pauline (Vig) Eisfelder; Casimir Donald Szymoniak, Dec. 7, 1943; children: Kathryn, Peter, John, Mary, Thomas. BS, U. Wis., 1941; MS, Iowa State U., 1977. Speech clinician Waukesha (Wis.) Pub. Sch., 1941-43, Rochester (N.Y.) Pub. Sch., 1943-44; rehab. aide U.S. Army, Chickasha, Okla., 1944-46; audiologist U. Wis., Madison, 1946-48; speech clinician Buffalo Pub. Sch., 1948-49, Sch. for Handicapped, Salina, Kans., 1951-52; speech pathologist, audiologist, counselor, resource mgr. Vocat. Rehab. State Iowa, Des Moines, 1956-85; mem. Iowa Senate, Des Moines, 1989—2000; ret., 2000. Bd. dir. On With Life, Terrace Hill Found. Adv. bd. Iowa State Inst. for Social and Behavioral Health; mem. Child Care Resource and Referral Cmty. Empowerment Bd., Greater Des Moines Coun. for Internat. Understanding, United Way, 1987—88, Urban Dreams, Iowa Maternal and Child Health com.; pres. Chrysalis Found., 1997; mem. City-County Study Commn.; Mem. Des Moines City coun., 1978—88; bd. dirs. Nat. League Cities, Washington, 1982—84, Civic Ctr., House of Mercy, Westminster House, Iowa Leadership Consortium, Iowa Comprehensive Health Assn. Named Woman of Achievement, YWCA, 1982, Visionary Woman, 1993, Young Women's Resource Ctr., 1989; named to Iowa Women's Hall of Fame, 1999; named Des Moines Woman of Influence, Bus. Record, 2000. Mem. Am. Speech Lang. and Hearing Assn., Iowa Speech Lang. and Hearing Assn. (pres. 1977-78), Nat. Coun. State Legislators (fed. state com. on health, adv. com. on child protection), Women's Polit. Caucus, Nexus (pres. 1981-82, mem. Supreme Ct. Select Com.), Wellmark Found. (adv. bd.), Des Moines (Iowa) Women's Club (bd. dir. 2003—), Prairie Club. Avocations: reading, travel, swimming, whitewater rafting. Home: 2909 Woodland Ave Apt 1011 Des Moines IA 50312-3877 Personal E-mail: ElaineSzy@aol.com.

**SZYSZKA, ROSWITA EVELYN,** artist; b. Chgo., Apr. 5, 1955; d. John and Regina (Rizinger) Schilli; m. Michael C. Szyszka, Jan. 29, 1977; children: David M., Eric S. AA, Am. Acad. Art, 1976. Illustrator The World Healing Book; artist: Looking Out, Looking In; featured Woodstock Colony of Arts Web Site (Top 100 artists of the 20th Century). Mem. Woodstock Artist Assn., The Woodstock Guild. Office Phone: 914-388-2967. E-mail: RoswitaSzyszka@hotmail.com.

**TAATI, POOPAK,** media director; d. Abdol Ali Taati and Mahin Dokht Farzan. PhD in Sociology, U. Tex., Austin, 1988. Asst. prof. of sociology Minn. State U., Moorhead, 1988—92; prof. sociology Georgetown U., Washington, 1995—96; prof. social scis. Montgomery Coll., Germantown, Md., 1999—2003; freelance journalist BBC, 2003—05; dir. Media for Thought, 2004—06. Vis. prof. anthropology & sociology Wittenberg U., Springfield, Ohio, 1987—88. Prodr.: (documentary film/video) When Authorities Turn Violent, (educational film/video) When Different is Beautiful. Treas. Ctr. Iranian Rsch. and Analysis, 1988—89; mem. tchg. com. Am. Sociol. Assn., 1997—98; mem. Iranian Professionals Assn., Washington, 1993—94, Iranian-American Cultural Assn., 1996—97. Recipient Tchg. and Svc. award, Montgomery Coll., 2002; fellow, NEH, 1991, 1997; grantee, MIT, Cambridge, 1990, U.S. Inst. Peace, 1996. Mem.: Gulf 2000. Independent. Spiritual Moslem. Avocations: participation in cultural activities, movies, travel, exercise, sauna.

**TABACHNICK, NORMAN DONALD,** psychiatrist, educator; b. Toronto, Ont., Can., Feb. 21, 1927; BS, U. Ill., 1947, MD, 1949; PhD in Psychoanalysis, So. Calif. Psychoanalytic Inst., 1977. Diplomate Am. Bd. Med. Examiners, Am. Bd. Psychiatry and Neurology. Intern Michael Reese Hosp., 1949-50; resident in psychiatry U.S. VA Hosp., Bedford, Mass., 1950-51, U.S. AFB, Biloxi, Miss., 1951-52, L.A. County Gen. Hosp., 1953-54; staff psychiatrist Sepulveda VA Hosp., 1976-78; pvt. practice L.A.; mem. staff Resthaven Sanitarium, U. So. Calif. Med. Ctr.; mem. staff Neuropsychiatric Hosp., Edgemont Hosp., Cedars-Sinai Med. Ctr.; mem. staff Neuropsychiatric Inst. UCLA; clin. prof. psychiatry U. So. Calif., L.A., 1970-75, UCLA, 1975—. Hon. mem. med. staff. Resthaven Cmty. Med. Health Ctr., 1973; guest lectr. Cedars-Sinai Med. Ctr., 1985; mem. adv. bd. divsn. psychoanalysis Nassau County Med. Ctr.; mem. faculty Calif. Sch. Profl. Psychology, L.A. Ctr. Group Psychotherapy, Grad. Ctr. Child Devel. and Psychotherapy; cons. L.A. County Coroner's Office, 1963-70, Bur. Vocat. Rehab., Jewish Family Svc., profl. adv. bd. Resthaven Sanitarium, Marianne Frostig Sch. Ednl. Therapy, W. Valley Ctr. Ednl. Therapy. Author: Accident or Suicide?, 1973; mem. edtl. bd. Jour. Acad. Psychoanalysis, book rev. editor, 1978; mem. edtl. bd. Internat. Jour. Psycho-analytic Psychotherapy, 1979-83; reviewer Am. Jour. Psychiatry, 1983—, Jour. Neuropsychiatry and Clin. Neuro Scis., 1988-90; contbr. articles to profl. jours.; cons. (film) Suicide Prevention: The Physician's Role, 1967, Highlights of the 1964 American Psychiatric Association; cons., participant The Thin Edge—Guilt., 1975; author book revs. Assoc. chief psychiatrist L.A. Suicide Prevention Ctr., 1968-76, prin. investigator; adv. com. Walter Briehl Human Rights Found., 1984; v.p., bd. dirs. Suicide Prevention Ctr., Inc.; bd. dirs. Inst. Suicide Prevention, L.A., 1996, chmn. funding a crisis line com., 1997; bd. dirs. We. divsn. Am. Found. Suicide Prevention, 1998, chair program com., 1999-2002. Recipient award for disting. creativity and leadership, Am. Found. for Suicide Prevention,

2003; rsch. grantee, Founds. Fund Rsch. Psychiatry, 1963, NIMH, 1970. Fellow Am. Psychiatric Assn. (life), Am. Acad. Psychoanalysis (pres. 1974, chmn. nominating com. 1975, trustee, chmn. com. on rsch., mem. editl. bd. The Acad., presdl. citation 1975); mem. Internat. Psychoanalytic Assn., Internat. Assn. Suicide Prevention, Am. Psychoanalytic Assn. (cert., mem. com. liason with AAAS 1977-80), Am. Assn. Suicidology, (founder, mem. editl. bd. Life-Threatening Behavior, cert. recognition 1996) Inst. Contemporary Psychoanalysis (founding mem., trustee 1990-93), So. Calif. Psychoanalytic Inst. (pres., tng. and supervising analyst, selection rsch. clin. assocs. com., dir. rsch. divsn. 1976-77, chief investigator 1976-88, chmn. com. rsch. award stds. 1979, pres.-elect 1980, 86, pres. 1981, 87-90, mem. tng. and supr. analyst, new ctr. for psychoanalysis), Am. Coll. Psychiatrists, Med. Rsch. Assn. So. Calif., So. Calif. Psychiat. Soc. (consultation and violence panel), L.A. County Med. Assn. Office: 505 N Bonhill Rd Los Angeles CA 90049-2325 Office Phone: 310-472-5044. Personal E-mail: ndtmd@aol.com.

**TABAK, LAWRENCE A.,** federal agency administrator, dentist; b. Bklyn., Dec. 15, 1951; BS in biology and chemistry, City Coll., CUNY, 1972; DDS, Columbia U., 1977; PhD in oral biology, SUNY, Buffalo, 1981. Certificate of Proficiency in Endodontics SUNY, Buffalo, 1985. Asst. prof. oral biology SUNY, Buffalo, 1980—81, asst. prof. endodontics and oral biology, 1981—85, assoc. prof., 1985—86; assoc. prof. dental rsch. and biochemistry Sch. Medicine and Dentistry, U. Rochester, 1986—92, prof., 1992—96, prof. dental rsch. and biochemistry and biophysics, 1996—97, prof. dentistry and biochemistry and biophysics, 1998—2000, chair dept. dental rsch., 1995—97, sr. assoc. dean for rsch., 1998—2000; dir. Nat. Inst. Dental and Craniofacial Rsch., NIH, 2000—; sr. investigator Nat. Inst. Diabetes and Digestive and Kidney Diseases, NIH, 2000—. Vis. scientist Nat. Inst. Dental Rsch., NIH, 1982—83. Named Alumnus of Yr., Sch. Dental and Oral Surgery, Columbia U., 1997. Fellow: AAAS; mem.: Inst. Medicine, Soc. Glycobiology, Am. Assn. for Dental Rsch., Internat. Assn. for Dental Rsch. (Disting. Scientist Award 1996). Office: Nat Inst Dental and Craniofacial Rsch Bldg 31 Rm 2C39 31 Center Dr MSC 2290 Bethesda MD 20892 Office Phone: 301-496-3571. Office Fax: 301-402-2185. E-mail: lawrence.tabak@nih.gov.*

**TABAKA, SANDRA LEE,** retired medical/surgical nurse; d. Elmer William and Elaine Verba Viehmann; m. John Lawrence Tabaka, Oct. 8, 1960 (div. Nov. 1985); children: James Lawrence, Anthony Michael, Theresa Lynn. ADN, St. Mary's Coll., O'Fallon, Mo., 1978; BSN, Webster U., 1993. RN Mo. Staff nurse St. Luke's Hosp., Chesterfield, Mo., 1978—82, assoc. head nurse, 1982—94, staff nurse, 1994—2004, ret., 2004. Founding mem. St. Charles Countians Against Hazardous Waste, 1982—84; bd. mem. Cedar Groves Townhomes Assn., St. Charles, 1999—2002. Mem.: Oncology Nursing Soc. (oncology cert. nurse). Home: 244 Cedar Grove Dr Saint Charles MO 63304

**TABATABAEE, VAHID,** architectural engineer, researcher; PhD, U. Md., College Pk., 1995—2003. Sr. architecture engr., co-founder Zagros Networks, Rockville, Md., 2001—03; rsch. assoc. U. Md., 2004—. Achievements include patents for method and apparatus for arbitration scheduling with a penalty for a switch fabric; method and apparatus for weighted arbitration scheduling separately at the input ports and the output ports of a switch fabric. Office: Dept Computer Sci Univ Md AV Williams Bldg College Park MD 20742 Office Phone: 301-405-3619.

**TABATABAI, JAY (MAGID),** travel company executive; b. Tehran, Calif., May 14, 1953; s. Ahmad and Robabeh Tabatabai; m. Zahra Bozorgzad, Jan. 28, 1954; children: Afshin Sean, Cyrus Sam. BS in Indsl. Engring.; M in Inds. and System Engring., U. So. Calif., 1978. Cert. in Application and Network Architecture Microsoft, 2004. Indsl. engr. Acme Lithonia Lighting, City of Industry, Calif., 1978—79; supr. indsl. engring. US and Mexico ops. Mattel Toys, City of Industry, 1979—82; application devel. mgr. Allied Signal Aerospace, Torrance, Calif., 1982—98; sr. project mgr. People Support, L.A., Calif., 1999—2002; chief tech. officer Altour Internat., LA, 2002—; dir. info. tech. Uniworld Cruises, Encino, Calif. Achievements include development of the enhancement of the Kosher sound system. Home: 26152 Kenrose Cir Calabasas CA 91302 Office: Altour International 12100 W Olympic Blvd Ste 300 Los Angeles CA 90064

**TABATABAI, M. ALI,** chemist, biochemist; b. Karbala, Iraq, Feb. 25, 1934; BS, U. Baghdad, 1958; MS, Okla. State U., 1960; PhD in Soil Chemistry, Iowa State U., 1965. Rsch. assoc. soil biochemistry Iowa State U., Ames, 1966-72, from asst. prof. to assoc. prof., 1972-78, prof. soil chemistry and biochemistry, 1978—. Cons. Electric Power Rsch. Inst., Palo Alto, 1978-83. Fellow AAAS, Am. Inst. Chemists, Am. Soc. Agronomy (Soil Sci. rsch. award 1992), Soil Sci. Soc. Am., Iowa Acad. Sci. (Disting. scientist, Disting. fellow); mem. Coun. Agrl. Sci. and Tech., Am. Chem. Soc., Am. Soc. Microbiology, Am. Soc. Agronomy, Soil Sci. Soc. Am., Assn. Univ. Profs. Iowa Acad. Sci., Gamma Sigma Delta (Alumni award of merit Iowa Beta chpt. 1993), Sigma Xi, Phi Kappa Phi. Achievements include research in soil enzymology and chemistry of sulfur, nitrogen and phosphorus in soils, nutrient cycling in the environment. Office: Iowa State U Sci & Tech Dept Agronomy Ames IA 50011-0001 E-mail: malit@iastate.edu.

**TABATZNIK, BERNARD,** retired cardiologist; b. Mir, Poland, Jan. 8, 1927; came to U.S., 1959, naturalized, 1966; s. Max and Fay (Ginsberg) T.; m. Marjorie Turner, Jan. 8, 1956; children: Darron Mark, Keith Donald, Ilana Wendy; m. Charline Edwards Harmon, Aug. 7, 1992. BSc, U. Witwatersrand, South Africa, 1945, MB, BChir, U. Witwatersrand, South Africa, 1949. Intern Baragwanath Hosp., Johannesburg, 1950-51, Hillingdon Hosp., Ashford Hosp., also rsch. unit Can. Red Cross Meml. Hosp., Taplow, England, 1951-54; med. registrar Ashford Hosp., 1954-56, Johannesburg Gen. Hosp., 1956-58; physician Baragwanath Hosp., 1958-59; fellow in medicine Sch. Medicine Johns Hopkins U., Balt., 1959-60, fellow in cardiology, 1960-61, asst. prof. medicine, 1966-97, ret., 1997; head cardiopulmonary divsn. Sinai Hosp., Balt., 1961-72, assoc. chief medicine, 1964-72; chief cardiology dept. North Charles Gen. Hosp., Balt., 1972; also dir. med. edn., dir. Postgrad. Inst., coord. ambulatory svcs.; mem. dir. Nurse Practitioner-Physician Asst. Program Ch. Hosp., Balt., 1987-90. Contbr. articles to profl. jours. Recipient Save-A-Heart Humanitarian award, 1977, Maimonides award, 1983, Shaarei Zion Humanitarian award, 1987. Fellow Royal Coll. Physicians (London); mem. South African Cardiac Soc., Am. Heart Assn., Md. Heart Assn. (chmn. health careers 1964-66), Laennec Cardiovasc. Sound Group. Home: HC 3 Box 180 Monterey VA 24465-9313 Personal E-mail: btabatznik@aol.com.

**TABAZADEH, AZADEH,** environmental scientist, researcher; b. Tehran, Iran, Feb. 17, 1965; came to U.S., 1982; d. Modjtaba and Fatema (Beigi) T.; m. Mark Z. Jacobson, Aug. 30, 1993; children: Dionna Shelly Jacobson, Daniel Forest Jacobson. BS in Chemistry, UCLA, 1988, MS in Chemistry, 1990, PhD, 1994. Rsch. tchg. asst. UCLA, 1989-94; postdoctoral NASA, Moffett Field, Calif., 1994-97, rsch. sci., 1997—. Lectr. in field. Contbr. articles to profl. jours. including Jour. Geophys. Rsch., Geophys. Rsch. Letters, Sci. NASA fellow, 1991-94, 94-97; recipient Presdl. Early Career award for Scientist and Engrs., 1998; named to Brilliant 10, Popular Science Mag., 2002. Mem. Am. Chem. Soc., Am. Geophysical Union (James B. Macelwane medal, 2001), Am. Assn. Aerosol Rsch., Air and Waste Mgmt. Assn., UCLA Chemist Assn. Achievements include discovery of narrow rings of cold air over the Earth's poles that help to form clouds which contribute to the destruction of the ozone layer. Fax: 650-604-3625. Business E-Mail: azadeh.tabazadeh-1@nasa.gov.

**TABB, VICKI CLARK,** mathematics professor; M, Delta State U., Cleveland, Miss., 1955. Mathamatics instr. Indianola Pub. Sch., 1999—99, Miss. Delta C.C., Moorhead, 1999—. Office: Miss Delta CC PO Box 668 Moorhead MS 38761 Office Phone: 662-246-6279. E-mail: vtabb@msdelta.edu.

**TABB, WALLER CROCKETT,** retired allergist, retired immunologist; b. Richmond, Va., 1935; MD, U. Va., 1959. Diplomate Am. Bd. Internal Medicine, Am. Bd. Allergy and Immunology. Intern U. Va. Hosp., Charlottesville, 1959-60, resident in internal medicine, 1964-66, fellow in allergy/immunology and pulmonary medicine, 1966-67; mem. staff Lakeland (Fla.) Regional Med. Ctr., 1967—; pvt. practice Watson Clinic, Lakeland, ret., 1997. Fellow ACP, Am. Acad. Allergy and Immunology, Am. Coll. Chest Physicians; mem. Alpha Omega Alpha. Address: PO Box 178 Ware Neck VA 23178-0178 Home: 6102 WAre Neck Rd Ware Neck VA 23178

**TABB, WINSTON,** librarian; b. Tulsa, Okla. BA magna cum laude, Okla. Baptist U., 1963; MA in Am. Lit., Harvard U., 1964; MLS, Simmons Coll., Boston, 1972. Various positions with Libr. of Congress, Washington, 1972—2002, asst. chief Gen. Reading Room, 1978—84, chief Copyright Info. & Reference Divsn., 1984—88, dir. Rsch. Svc., 1988—89, acting dep. libr., 1989—92, assoc. libr., 1992—2002; dean Univ. Libr. Johns Hopkins U., 2002—. Mem. Nat. Digital Libr. Fedn. Policy Com., Coun. Libr. & Info. Resources; mem. vis. com. Harvard Libr.; rsch. libr. adv. com. Online Computer Libr. Ctr. Past bd. mem. Soros Found. Served with U.S. Army, in Thailand. Recipient Melvil Dewey medal, ALA, 1998, Ainsworth Rand Spofford President's award, District of Columbia Libr. Assn., 2002. Mem.: ALA (Melvil Dewey Medal 1998), Internat. Fedn. of Libr. Assns. & Insts. (vice chmn. profl. bd., chmn. Nat. Libr. Sect., chmn. Coordinating Bd. Divsn. Rsch. Libr., chmn.IFLA Profl. Com. 2001—). Office: Milton S Eisenhower Libr Johns Hopkins Univ 3400 N Charles St Baltimore MD 21218 Office Phone: 410-516-8328. Office Fax: 410-516-5080. E-mail: wtabb@jhu.edu.

**TABBAL, NICOLAS G.,** plastic surgeon; b. Beirut, 1946; MD, Am. U., Beirut, 1972. Diplomate Am. Bd. Plastic Surgery, Am. Bd. Surgery. Intern Am. U. Med. Ctr., Beirut, 1971—72, resident in surgery, 1972—76; resident in plastic surgery Akron City Hosp., Ohio, 1977—79; fellow in gen. surgery Upstate Med. Ctr., Syracuse, NY, 1976—77; fellow in plastic reconstructive surgery NYU, 1979—80; pvt. practice plastic surgery N.Y.C., 1980—; attending plastic surgeon Manhattan EET Hosp. Clin. instr. plastic surgery NYU Med. Ctr. Office: 521 Park Ave New York NY 10021-1840 Office Phone: 212-644-5800. Business E-Mail: mail@tabbal.us.

**TABBARA, HADI,** director, researcher; PhD, Iowa State U., Ames, 2000. Rsch. assoc. USDA-ARS, Phoenix, 2001—02; lab. mgr. Ariz. State U., Tempe, 2005—. Recipient, USAID, 1973—76. Mem.: Am. Chem. Soc., Phi Lambda Upsilon. Office: BioDesign Institute- Arizona State U 1001 S McAllister Tempe AZ 85281 Office Phone: 480-727-0893. Home Fax: 480-727-0889; Office Fax: 480-727-0889. Business E-Mail: hadi.tabbara@asu.edu.

**TABBUT, LOREEN M.,** power industry executive; Dir. projects and applications services Calif. Ind. Sys. Operator (Cal ISO); v.p. info. services Calpine Corp., San Jose, Calif., 2001—. Named one of Premier 100 IT Leaders, Computerworld, 2005. Office: Calpine Corp 50 W San Fernando St San Jose CA 95113 Office Phone: 408-995-5115. Office Fax: 408-995-0505.*

**TABEA, EMILE VICTOR,** health facility administrator; b. Abidjan, Ivory Coast, June 6, 1959; s. Leon Kobe and Jeannette Saoua Tabea; m. Melanie Ayere Gbangninan; children: Joel Victor, Eunice Victoire. MS, U. Mass., 1992. Cert. human svcs. profl. Mass. Instr. French and ESL U. Mass., Lowell, 1984—90; coord. Tewksbury (Mass.) Hosp., 1989, discharge planner dept. pub. health, 1989. Deacon Bethel Internat. Ch., Everett, Mass., 2003—05. Recipient Performance Recognition award, Commonwealth of Mass., 2000. Mem.: Mass. Tchr. Assn. (assoc.). Mem. Independent Thinkers. Avocations: soccer, reading, travel. Home: 46 Barclay St Lowell MA 01851 Office: Tewksbury Hosp Dept Pub Health 365 East St Tewksbury MA 01876 Office Phone: 978-851-7321. Home Fax: 978-851-6743; Office Fax: 978-851-6743. Personal E-mail: emile_tabea@uml.edu. Business E-Mail: emile.tabea@state.ma.us.

**TABER, DAVID O.,** urological surgeon; b. Panama City, Panama, June 30, 1938; s. Alden Pugh and Virginia (Kresler) Taber; m. Rebecca M. (Smith); children: Sharon Taber Silverman, Jeffrey, Andrew, Richard; m. Rebecca M. Taber, Dec. 20, 1987. BA, Syracuse U., 1959; MD, George Washington U., 1963. Diplomate Am. Bd. Urology. Urologic surgeon in pvt. practice, El Paso, Tex., 1972—. Chief med. staff Columbia West Hosp., El Paso, 1975-76, chief of urology, 1998-99; chief of surgery Sierra Med. Ctr., El Paso, 1977-78, chief of urology, 1995-97; prof. urology Tex. Tech Sch. Medicine, El Paso, 1998—. Mem. state com. on prostate cancer Am. Cancer Soc., Austin, 1998-99, bd. dirs. El Paso unit, 1999; mem. Tex. Rangers Found., Waco, 1998-2005; judge Santa Fe Indian Market; med. exec. com. El Paso County; founder Am. Mus. Served to lt. U.S. Army, 1963-72. Lt. col. U.S. Army. Fellow ACS; mem. AMA, Urol. Soc. Internat. (adv.), Urostomy Assn. (adv.), Tex. Urol. Soc., Am. Urol. Assn., Tex. Med. Assn., Am. Fertility Soc., Am. Lithotripsy Soc., El Paso Med. Soc. (exec. com. 2004—m sec. 2006—), Mason (32 degree), Elmaida Shrine, Rotary, Alpha Epsilon Delta, Pi Sigma. Episcopalian. Avocations: photography, diving instructor. Office: 2201 N Stanton St El Paso TX 79902 Office Phone: 915-533-0800.

**TABER, GEOFFREY ALEXANDER,** quality assurance professional; s. Richard Allen Baldwin and Trudy Diane Drwenski; m. Michelle Renee Baker, Aug. 3, 2002; 1 child, Alexis Renee. BA in Psychology, U. Colo., Denver, 2001; MBA, U. Phoenix, Lonetree, Colo., 2004. Cert. six sigma black belt Tyco Internat., 2006. Quality assurance mgr. ADT Security Svcs. Inc., Aurora, Colo., 2001—03, bus. analyst, 2003—04, project mgr., 2004—04, six sigma black belt, 2004—. Mem.: Am. Soc. of Quality. Independent. Avocations: swimming, coaching, travel. Office Phone: 303-306-5524.

**TABER, KENNETH W.,** lawyer; b. Nov. 28, 1956; BS summa cum laude, Univ. Pa., 1977; JD, Yale Univ., 1980. Bar: NY 1981, US Dist. Ct. (so., ea. dist. NY) 1981. Ptnr. Pillsbury Winthrop Shaw Pittman, NYC, litigator employment, co-chmn. Product Liability Practice. Founder Interfaith Legal Outreach, Westchester County, NY. Office: Pillsbury Winthrop Shaw Pittman 1540 Broadway New York NY 10036 Office Phone: 212-858-1813. Office Fax: 212-858-8405. Business E-Mail: kenneth.taber@pillsburylaw.com.

**TABER, MARGARET RUTH,** retired engineering technology educator; b. St. Louis, Apr. 29, 1935; d. Wynn Orr and Margaret Ruth (Feldman) Gould Stevens; m. William James Taber, Sept. 6, 1958 B of Engring. Sci., Cleve. State U., 1958, BEE, 1958; MS in Engring., U. Akron, 1967; EdD, Nova Southeastern U., 1976; postgrad., Western Res. U., 1959-64. Registered profl. engr., Ohio; cert. engring. technologist. From engring. trainee to tng. dir. TOCCO divsn. Ohio Crankshaft Co., Cleve., 1954-64; from instr. elec.-electronic engring. tech. to prof. Cuyahoga CC, Cleve., 1964-79, chmn. engring. tech., 1977-79; assoc. prof. elec. engring. tech. Purdue U., West Lafayette, Ind., 1979-83, prof., 1983-2000, prof. emeritus, 2000—. Lectr. Cleve. State U., 1963-64; mem. acad. adv. bd. Cleve. Inst. Electronics, 1981—; cons. in field. Author: (with Frank P. Tedeschi) Solid State Electronics, 1976; (with Eugene M. Silgalis) Electric Circuit Analysis, 1980; (with Jerry L. Casebeer) Registers, 1980; (with Kenneth Rosenow) Arithmetic Logic Units, 1980, Timing and Control, 1980, Memory Units, 1980; 6809 Architecture and Operation, 1984, Programming I: Straight Line, 1984; contbr. articles to profl. jours. Bd. dirs. West Blvd. Christian Ch., deaconess, 1974-77, elder, 1977-79; deacon Federated Ch., 1981-84, 86-89, Stephen Leader, 1988—2002; mem. Cancer Support Group; vol. Lafayette Adult Resource Acad., 1992—; ednl. resource vol., vol. tchr. Sunburst Farm Rainbow Acres, Ariz., 1988—. Recipient Helen B. Schleman Gold Medallion award Purdue U., 1991, The Greater Lafayette Cmty. Survivorship award, 1994, Outstanding Alumni award U. Akron Coll. Engring., 1994, Disting. Alumni award, Cleve. State U., 2002; Margaret R. Taber Microcomputer Lab. named in her honor Purdue U., 1991; NSF grant, 1970-73, 78; Rainbow Acres Computer Lab named The Marge Taber Computer Lab., 2002. Fellow Soc. Women Engrs. (counselor Purdue chpt. 1983-94, Disting. Engring. Educator award 1987); mem. IEEE (life sr.), Am. Cancer Soc. (co-chair svc. and rehab com. 1992-94, vol. coord. CanSurmount 1993-98, chair Cmty. Connections, mem. Resource, Info. and Guidance CoreTeam, 1994-98, v.p. Tippecanoe bd. dirs. 1996-98, relay for life hon. chair 1999), Am. Bus. Women's Assn. (ednl. chmn. 1964-66), Am. Soc. Engring. Edn., Am. Tech. Edn. Assn., Tau Beta Pi (hon.), Phi Kappa Phi. Avocations: robotics; computers. Home: 3036 State Rd 26 W West Lafayette IN 47906-4743 Office: Purdue U Elec Engring Tech Dept Knoy Hall Tech West Lafayette IN 47907

**TABIN, CLIFFORD S.,** geneticist, educator; Prof. dept. genetics Harvard Med. Sch., Boston. Recipient award in molecular biology NAS, 1999. Office: Harvard Med Sch Warren Alpert Bldg 4th Fl 240 Longwood Ave Boston MA 02115

**TABIN, JULIUS,** lawyer, physicist; b. Chgo., Nov. 8, 1919; s. Sol and Lillian (Klingman) T.; m. Johanna Krout, Sept. 7, 1952; children: Clifford James, Geoffrey Craig. BS, U. Chgo., 1940, PhD in Physics, 1946; LLB, Harvard U., 1949. Bar: Calif., D.C. 1949, Ill. 1950. Jr. physicist metall. lab. U. Chgo., 1943-44; physicist Los Alamos Sci. Lab. (U. Calif.), N.Mex., 1944-45, Argonne Nat. Lab., AEC, Chgo., 1946; staff mem., group supr. Inst. Nuc. Studies, MIT, 1946-49; patent examiner U.S. Patent Office, Washington, 1949-50; assoc. firm Fitch, Even, Tabin & Flannery, Chgo., 1950-52; mem. firm Fich, Even, Tabin & Flannery, Chgo., 1952—. Lectr. U. Chgo., 1959. Mem. Am., D.C., Calif., Ill., Chgo. bar assns., Sigma Xi. Home: 162 Park Ave Glencoe IL 60022-1352 Office: 120 S La Salle St Chicago IL 60603-3403 Office Phone: 312-577-7000. E-mail: jtabin@fitcheven.com.

**TABLER, BRYAN G.,** lawyer; b. Louisville, Jan. 12, 1943; s. Norman Gardner and Sarah Marie (Grant) T.; m. Susan Y. Beidler, Dec. 28, 1968 (div. June 1987); children: Justin Elizabeth, Gillian Gardner; m. Karen Sue Strome, July 24, 1987. AB, Princeton U., 1969; JD, Yale U., 1972. Bar: Ind. 1972, U.S. Dist. Ct. (so. dist.) Ind. 1972, U.S. Dist. Ct. (no. dist.) Ind. 1976, U.S. Ct. Appeals (7th cir.) 1976, U.S. Supreme Ct. 1976. Assoc. Barnes & Thornburg, Indpls., 1972-79, ptnr., chmn. environ. law dept., 1979-94; v.p., gen. counsel, sec. IPALCO Enterprises, Inc., 1994—; sr. v.p., gen. coun., sec. Indpls. Power & Light Co., 1994—. Mem. exec. com. Environ. Quality Control, Inc., Indpls., 1985-97. Mem. Indpls. Mus. of Art, 1972—; bd. dirs. Indpls. Symphony Orch., 1995—. 1st lt. U.S. Army, 1964-68, Vietnam. Mem. ABA, Ind. Bar Assn., Bar Assn. of the 7th Cir., Indpls. Bar Assn. Avocation: golf. Home: 137 Willowgate Dr Indianapolis IN 46260-1471 Office: Indpls Power & Light Co One Monument PO Box 1595 Indianapolis IN 46206-1595

**TABLER, NORMAN GARDNER, JR.,** lawyer; b. Louisville, Oct. 15, 1944; s. Norman Gardner and Marie (Grant) T.; m. Dawn Carla Martin, May 6, 1989; 1 child, Rachel Ann Tabler. BA, Princeton U., 1966; MA, Yale U., 1968; JD, Columbia U., 1971. Bar: Ind. 1971, U.S. Dist. Ct. (so. dist.) Ind. 1971. Assoc. Baker & Daniels, Indpls., 1971-77, ptnr., 1978-96; sr. v.p. corp. affairs, gen. counsel, chief compliance officer, sec. Clarian Health Ptnrs., Inc., Indpls., 1996—. Adj. prof. Ind. U. Law Sch., Indpls., 1984-88; mem. adv. com. Ctr. for Law and Health, Ind. U., Indpls., 1987-91; mem. antitrust task force Ind. Dept. Health, 1993-94; lectr. Ind. U. Law Sch., 1992-96; chmn. bd. dirs. CH Assurance Ltd., 2002-, Clarian Health Risk Retention Group, Inc., 2004—, Emergency Medicine Group, Inc., 2004—. Bd. dirs. Ind. Repertory Theatre, Inc., Indpls., 1984-97, Indpls. Art Ctr., 1988-93, 2006—, chmn., 1989-92; bd. dirs. Indpls. 500 Festival, 1992-98, Brickyard 400 Festival, 1993-98, Found. of Indy Festivals, 1995-98, Indy Festivals, 1995-98; bd. dirs. Indpls. Pub. Broadcasting, 1992—, chmn., 1997-2001, 05-; mem. Ind. Sec. of State's Com. on Revision of Ind. Nonprofit Corp. Act, 1989-92, Ind. Ednl. Fin. Authority, 1989-93; mem. Ind. Recreational Devel. Commn., 1993—, vice chmn., 2002—; mem. Medicaid Task Force Ind. Commn. Health Policy, 1990-92, Ind. Commn. on CLE, 1999-2005; mem. nat. bd. lay reps. PBS, 1997-2003. Mem. ABA (health care com. sect. antitrust law, health law sect.), Ind. Bar Assn. (health law sect.), Indpls. Bar Assn. (health law sect.), Am. Health Lawyers Assn. (com. on antitrust, com. on fraud and abuse, self-referrals and false claims, in-house counsel com. and tchg. hosps., acad. med. ctrs. com.), Ind. Health and Hosp. Assn. (com. on hosp. governance 1999—), Ind. U. Parents Assn., Ind. U. Parents Ann. Fund (nat. chmn. 1995-98), U.S., Squash Racquets Assn., Princeton Alumni Assn. Ind. (pres. 1988-97), Indpls. Athletic Club (bd. dirs. 1994-2000), Skyline Club (bd. govs. 1992—), Princeton Club N.Y., Lawyers Club (Indpls.), Highland Golf & Country Club (Indpls.), Carmel Racquet Club (Ind.). Methodist. Avocations: reading biographies, squash, kayaking. Office: General Counsel & Sr VP Legal Dept Clarian Health Ptnrs Inc PO Box 1367 Indianapolis IN 46206-1367

**TABLER, SUSAN BEIDLER,** lawyer; b. Quakertown, Pa., Nov. 13, 1943; d. Henry Landis and Pauline Henrietta Beidler; m. Bryan Grant Tabler, Dec. 28, 1968 (div. July 1987); children: Justin Elizabeth, Gillian Gardner. BA, Wellesley Coll., 1965; JD summa cum laude, Ind. U., Indpls., 1975. Intern BBC, London, 1965-67; examiner Ednl. Testing Svc., Princeton, N.J., 1967-69; adminstrv. assoc. Long Wharf Theatre, New Haven, 1969-72; assoc. Ice Miller Donadio & Ryan, Indpls., 1975-81, ptnr., 1982—. Bd. dirs. Ind. Sports Corp., Indpls. Pres. bd. dirs. Julian Ctr., Indpls., 1975-80; bd. dirs. Cathedral Arts, Indpls., 1975-79. Fellow Ind. Bar Found.; mem. ABA (chmn. standing com. on Gavel awards 1985-88, labor law div. vice chair gen. practice sect. 1988-91), Ind. State Bar Assn., Indpls. Bar Assn., Ind. U. Alumni Assn. (bd. dirs. 1989—). Office: Ice Miller Donadio & Ryan 1 American Sq Indianapolis IN 46282-0020

**TABOADA, JAVIER GUSTAVO,** neurologist; b. Trujillo, Peru, Feb. 20, 1940; came to U.S. 1966; s. Manuel and Esperanza (Vega) T.; m. Martha Rivas-Plata, June 25, 1966; children: Lucia, Martha, Suzanne, Tina. BS, Nat. U. Trujillo, Peru, 1960, MD, 1966. Diplomate Am. Bd. Psychiatry, Am. Bd. Neurology. Neurology residency Georgetown U., Washington, 1968-72; capt. U.S. Army, 1969, advanced through grades to col., 2000; psychiatry residency N.Y. Hosp.-Cornell, White Plains, N.Y., 1972-75, chief geriatric unit; chief neurology svc. USPHS Hosp., S.I., N.Y., 1975-78; pvt. practice Assoc. Neurologists of N.J., PA, Trenton, 1978—, pres., 1990—; clin. asst. prof. SUNY Downstate, Bklyn., 1975-78; clin. asst. prof. neurology Hahneman U., Phila., 1980—; chief neurology svc. H. Fuld Med. Ctr., Trenton, N.J., 1994—. Fellow ACP, Am. Acad. Neurology, Royal Med. Soc.; mem. Mercer County Med. Soc. (exec. coun. 1990—, v.p. 1995-96, pres. 1997-98), KC Roman Catholic. Avocation: soccer. Personal E-mail: jtaboadamd@yahoo.com.

**TABOR, CURTIS HAROLD, JR.,** retired librarian, minister; b. Atlanta, July 3, 1936; s. Curtis Harold and Gerturde Olive (Casey) Tabor; m. Dorothy May Corbin, June 30, 1957 (dec. June 1996); m. Paulene C Pennington, July 12, 1997; children: Timothy M, John M. AA, Fla. Coll., Temple Terrace, 1957; BA, Harding Coll., 1960; MA, Butler U., 1969; MDiv, Bapt. Missionary Assn. Theol. Sem., Jacksonville, Tex., 1974; MLS, Tex. Woman's U., 1977. Min. Ch. of Christ, Bowling Green, Ky., 1960-61, Hamilton, Ont., Canada, 1961-64, Lindsay, 1964-67, Nacogdoches, Tex., 1967-75, Dallas, 1976-77, Columbus, Miss., 1977-79, Tampa, Fla., 1993-97, Maryville, Tenn., 1997—; reference libr. Blount County Pub. Libr., 1998—2006; ret., 2006. Tchr. Great Lakes Christian Coll., Beamville, Ont, Canada, 1961—64; Bible chair dir Stephen F Austin State U., Nacogdoches, Tex., 1967—75; participant archeological excavations, Tell Gezer, Israel, 1969, Tell Lachish, Israel, 80; profl. libr. sci. Fla. Coll., Temple Terrace, 1979—85, libr. dir., 1985—97; prin., owner Tabor Properties, Inc., 2005. Author (with others): (book) Resurrection, 1973, Biblical Authority, 1974, The Lord of Glory, 1980, Making A Difference: Florida College, the First Fifty Years, 1996. Cub master Boy Scouts Am. Nacogdoches, 1970—75; pres Nacogdoches Baseball Assn. 1974—75; vol driving instr 55 Alive AARP, 1998—2001. Recipient Scouters Key, Cub Scouts Am, 1975. Mem.: SAR, Tampa Bay Libr. Consortium (treas 1986—89), Beta Phi Mu, Eta Beta Rho. Republican. Mem. Ch. Of Christ. Avocations: amateur radio (KC4XS), locksmithing. Home: 1906 Raulston View Dr Maryville TN 37803-2868 Personal E-mail: haltabor@yahoo.com.

**TABORA, CAROLOS ALBERTO,** mathematician, educator; b. Jersey City, Dec. 22, 1969; s. Armando and Rudidia Tabora. BS in Mech. Engring., NJ Inst. Tech., 1993. Tchr. math. Acad. of Sacred Heart, Hoboken, NJ, 1996—. Office: Acad of Sacred Heart 713 Washington St Hoboken NJ 07030 Office Phone: 201-659-7139. E-mail: c2oA40T@aol.com.

**TABREZ, SHAMS S.M.,** gastroenterologist; b. Rawahindi, Pakistan, June 10, 1962; arrived in U.S., 1993; s. Sayeed S.M. Akhter and Sabira Khatoon; m. Salma Ali Tabrez, Aug. 5, 1993; children: Elsa, Mariam, Sana Shams. MB BS, Rawal Pindi Med. Coll., 1986. Diplomate Am. Bd. Internal Medicine. Emergency med. officer Dist. Hdqs. Hosp., Chakwal, Pakistan, 1986—87; lectr. pharmacology dept. Rawal Pindi Med. Coll., 1987—93; extern dept. pulmonary medicine VA Med. Ctr., 1995—96, resident in internal medicine NYU Med. Ctr., 1995—96, resident in internal medicine 1996—98; fellow in gastroenterology Yale U. Affiliated Hosp., Bridgeport, Conn., 1998—2001; attending physician gastroenterology and hepatology So. N.Mex. Med. Assn., Eastern N.Mex. Med. Ctr., Roswell, 2001—; cons. gastroenterologist So. N.Mex. Assocs., Roswell, 2001—. Contbr. articles to profl. jours., chapters to books. Recipient Physician award, AMA, 2001. Mem.: ACP, Am. Gastroent. Assn., Am. Coll. Gastroenterology. Avocations: literature review, travel. Home: 12 Berrendo Meadows Roswell NM 88201 Office: So NMex Med Assn 303 W Country Club Rd Roswell NM 88201

**TABRON, WENDY,** paper company executive; Pres. Document Enterprise Inc., Atlanta, 1997—.

**TACAL, JOSE VEGA, JR.,** retired public health official, veterinarian; b. Ilocos Sur, Philippines, Sept. 5, 1933; arrived in US, 1969; s. Jose Sr. and Cristina (Vega) T.; m. Lilia Caccam, 1959; children: Joyce, Jasmin, Jose III. DVM, U. Philippines, Quezon City, 1956; diploma, U. Toronto, 1964. Diplomate Am. Coll. Vet. Preventive Medicine; lic. vet., Calif. Provincial veterinarian Philippine Bur. Animal Industry, Manila, 1956-57; instr. vet. medicine U. Philippines, Quezon City, 1957-64, asst. prof., chmn. dept. vet. microbiology, pathology and pub. health, 1965-69; pub. health veterinarian San Bernardino (Calif.) County Dept. Pub. Health, 1970-83, sr. pub. health veterinarian, program mgr., sect. chief, 1984-2000. Zoonotic diseases lectr. Calif. State U., San Bernardino, 1984; lectr. U. Calif. Ext., Riverside, 1985; vis. prof. vet. pub. health U. Philippines at Los Banos, Laguna, 1988; participant 1st Internat. Conf. on Emerging Zoonoses, Jerusalem, 1996; presenter 4th Internat. Symposium on Ectoparasites of Pets, U. Calif., Riverside, 1997; presenter 8th Ann. Rabies in the Ams. Conf., Kingston, Ont., Can., 1997; rabies and ferret adv. group Calif. Dept. Health Svcs., 1998; presenter 48th Western Poultry Disease Conf., Vancouver, B.C., Can., 1999, 10th Rabies in Ams. Meeting, San Diego, 1999. Columnist LA Free Press, 1991, Pilipinas Times, 1993, Mabuhay Times, 1994-95; panelist Filipino-Ams. TV series The Many Faces of San Bernardino, California; contbr. more than 50 articles to profl. jours. Pres. Filipino Assn. of San Bernardino County, Highland, Calif., 1979; charter mem. Greater Inland Empire Filipino Assn., Highland, 1986—; del. First Filipino Media Conf. N.Am., LA, 1993; mem. San Bernardino County Africanized Honey Bee Task Force, 1993-2000; participant 1st Internat. Conf. on Emerging Zoonoses, Jerusalem, 1996; v.p. Friends of the Highland Libr., 2006. Recipient Donald T. Fraser Meml. medal, U. Toronto, 1964, cert. of merit, Philippine Vet. Med. Assn., 1965, cert. of appreciation, Calif. State Bd. Examiners in Vet. Medicine, 1979, 1984, cert. of recognition, Congressman George E. Brown Jr., 42d Congl. Dist. Calif., 1994, Assemblyman Joe Baca, 62d Assembly Dist., Calif. State Legis., 1994, Vet. Medicine/Journalism award, Greater Inland Empire Filipino Assn., 1999, cert. appreciation, San Bernardino County Libr., Highland Br., 2005, 2006; Colombo Plan Study fellow, Can./Philippine Govts., 1963—64, hon. fellow, Philippine Coll. Vet. Pub. Health, 2002. Mem.: ACLU, AVMA, AAAS, Highland Area Hist. Soc., Calif. Rare Fruit Growers (Inland Empire chpt.), Soc. for Advancement of Rsch., Western Poultry Disease Conf., Am. Vet. Med. History Soc., U. Philippines Alumni Assn. (life), Phi Sigma, Phi Kappa Phi. Office: PO Box 1023 Highland CA 92346-1023

**TACCONE, JORMA,** writer, director; b. Berkeley, Calif., Mar. 19, 1977; s. Tony. Grad., U. Calif. LA. Co-founder, mem. The Lonely Island, NYC, 2001—. Writer MTV Movie Awards, 2004, 2005, G-Phoria, 2004, Saturday Night Live, 2005—; actor(appearances): Saturday Night Live, 2005—06; guest appearances (TV Specials) 40 Most Awesomely Bad Dirrty Songs...Ever, 2004. Recipient WIRED Rave Award - TV, 2006. Office: United Talent Agency Inc 9560 Wilshire Blvd Ste 500 Beverly Hills CA 90212 Office Phone: 310-273-6700. Office Fax: 310-247-1111.*

**TACHA, ATHENA,** sculptor, artist, educator; b. Larissa, Greece, Apr. 23, 1936; arrived in U.S., 1963; MA, Nat. Acad. Fine Arts, Athens, Greece, 1959; MA in Art History, Oberlin Coll., 1961; PhD, U. Paris, 1963. Curator modern art Allen Art Mus., Oberlin, Ohio, 1963-73; prof. art Oberlin Coll., 1973-2000; adj. prof. art U. Md., College Park, 1999—. One-woman shows include Zabriskie Gallery, NY, 1979, 81, Max Hutchinson Gallery, NY, 1984, High Mus. Art, Atlanta, 1989, Franklin Furnace, NY, 1994, Beck Ctr., Cleve., 1998-99, Found. for Hellenic Culture, NY, 2001, Marsha Mateyka Gallery, Washington, 2004, Am. Univ. Mus., Washington, 2006, others; prin. pub. commns. include sculptures at Am. Airlines Ctr., Dallas., Strathmore Music Ctr., Bethesda, Md., City of Phila., Dept. Environ. Protection, Trenton, NJ, Case-Western Res. U., Cleve., Low Water Dam Riverfront Pk., Tulsa, Dept. of Transp., Hartford, Conn., Metrorail, Miami, Fla., Ecology Dept. U. Minn., St. Paul, Strathmore Music Ctr., Bethesda, Md., Am. Airlines Plz., Dallas, Metro Morgan Sta., Washington, Light Rail Sta., Newark, NY; collections include Hirshhorn Mus., Washington, Albright-Knox Art Gallery, Buffalo, Mus. Fine Arts, Houston, Nat. Coll. Fine Arts, Washington, Cleve. Mus. Art, Munson-Williams-Proctor Inst., Uttica, Nelson-Atkins Mus. Art, Kansas City, Allen Art Mus., Oberlin, Speed Art Mus., Louisville; author: (as A. T. Spear) Rodin Sculpture in the Cleveland Museum of Art, 1967, Brancusi's Birds, 1969; contbr. articles to profl. jours.; subject of book Cosmic Rhythms: Athena Tacha's Public Sculpture (E. McClelland), 1998, Dancing in the Landscape: The Sculpture of Athena Tacha, 2000. Recipient 1st prize May Show, Cleve. Mus. Art, 1968, 71, 79; NEA grantee, 1975; Bogliasco Found./Liguria Study Ctr. fellow, 2003; Bellagio Study Ctr. resident, 2007. Home: 3721 Huntington St NW Washington DC 20015-1817 E-mail: atacha@umd.edu.

**TACHA, DEANELL REECE,** federal judge; b. Goodland, Kans., Jan. 26, 1946; m. John Allen Tacha; children: John Reece, David Andrew, Sarah Nell, Leah Beth. BA, U. Kans., 1968; JD, U. Mich., 1971. Spl. asst. to U.S. Sec. of Labor, Washington, 1971—72; assoc. Hogan & Hartson, Washington, 1973, Thomas J. Pitner, Concordia, Kans., 1973—74; dir. Douglas County Legal Aid Clinic, Lawrence, Kans., 1974—77; assoc. prof. law U. Kans., Lawrence, 1974—77, prof., 1977—85, assoc. dean, 1977—79, assoc. vice chancellor, 1979—81, vice chancellor, 1981—85; judge U.S. Ct. Appeals (10th cir.), Denver, 1985—, chief judge, 2001—; mem. U.S. Sentencing Commn., 1994—98; nat. pres. mem. Am. Inns. of Ct., 2004—. Office: US Ct Appeals 643 Massachusetts St Ste 301 Lawrence KS 66044

**TACHER, ROBERT FREDERICK,** lawyer; b. Bklyn., Jan. 24, 1951; s. Abraham and Ilona Tacher; m. Nelly Bendrihem, 2005. BA, U. Miami, 1972, JD, 1977. Bar: Fla. 1977, U.S. Dist. Ct. (so. dist.) Fla. 1977, U.S. Ct. Appeals (5th cir.) 1978, Fed. Trial Bar 1986. Assoc. Law Office Arnold Levy, Miami, Fla., 1977-78, Law Office David Willing, Miami, 1978-80, Law Office Lawrence Friedman, Miami, 1980-82; sr. litigation atty. Nelson & Tacher, Miami, 1982-94; mng. atty. Law Office of Robert F. Tacher, Miami, 1994—, Law Office Robert F. Tacher, Ft. Lauderdale, 1996—. Mem. City of Lauderhill (Fla.) Planning and Zoning Bd., 1987-88. Mem. Fla. Bar Assn. (chmn. code and rules of evidence com. 2002-03). Office: 3230 W Commercial Blvd Fort Lauderdale FL 33309

**TACHNA, RUTH C.,** retired lawyer; b. NYC; d. Max and Rose (Rosenblatt) T.; m. Paul Bauman (dec.); children: Leslie Levy, Lionel Bauman. BA, Cornell U., 1935; LLB cum laude, Bklyn. Law Sch., 1937. Bar: N.Y. 1938, Calif. 1978, U.S. Dist. Ct. (so. dist.) N.Y. 1966, U.S. Ct. Appeals (2d cir.) 1966, U.S. Supreme Ct. 1956. Founding atty. Legal Aid, Westchester, N.Y., 1960-64; sr. ptnr., of counsel Tachna & Krassner, White Plains, NY, 1964—2001; ret. Prof. law Northrop U. Sch. Law, L.A., 1977-85; speech-writer for many office holders including Franklin D. Roosevelt. Group mng. editor Matthew Bender, N.Y.C., 1968-77; editor law rev. Bklyn. Law Sch. Staff atty., founder Legal Aid for Srs., Santa Monica, Calif., 1980-83. Mem. Calif. Bar Assn., L.A. County Bar Assn. Home: 5400 Eagles Point Cir Apt 106 Sarasota FL 34231-9154

**TACHNER, LEONARD,** lawyer; b. Bklyn., Jan. 18, 1944; BEE, CCNY, 1965; MSEE, Calif. State U., Long Beach, 1969; JD, Western State U., Fullerton, Calif., 1973. Bar: Calif. 1973, US Patent Office 1972. Supr. electronic counter measures sect. Ford Aerospace Corp., Newport Beach, Calif., 1969—73; patent atty. Reed L. Lawlor, LA, 1973—76, Rockwell Internat. Corp., Anaheim, Calif., 1976—78; ptnr. Fischer, Tachner & Strauss, Newport Beach, 1978—84; pvt. practice Irvine, Calif., 1984—. Instr. intellectual property Calif. State U., Long Beach, 1979—82; com. maintenance profl. competence Calif. State Bar, 1978—81. Mem. editl. bd. Western State U. Law Rev., 1972—73, columnist Interface Age mag., 1979—82, Bus.-to-Bus. mag., 1983—85. Mem.: Orange County Patent Law Assn., Calif. Bar Assn., Greater Irvine Indsl. League, Phi Kappa Phi. Office: 17961 Sky Park Cir Ste 38-E Irvine CA 92614 Office Phone: 949-752-8525. Personal E-mail: ltachner@aol.com.

**TACIROGLU, ERTUGRUL,** civil engineer, educator; PhD, U. Ill., Champaign-Urbana, 1998. Post-doctoral rsch. assoc. Ctr. for Simulation of Advanced Rockets, Urbana, 1998—2001; asst. prof. UCLA, 2001—. Contbr. articles to profl. jours. Recipient Career award, NSF, 2001—06. Mem.: ASCE (assoc.). Office: UCLA 5731E Boelter Hall Los Angeles CA 90095-1593 Office Phone: 310-267-4655. Office Fax: 310-206-2222.

**TACK, THERESA ROSE,** women's health nurse; b. Lunenburg, Vt., Nov. 10, 1940; d. Gustave L. and Blanche Rose Fournier; m. Dennis M. Tack, Sept. 2, 1961; children: Lynelle Scullard, Karyn Terry, LeAnn Gomez. Diploma, Cen. Maine Gen. Hosp., 1961. Cert. ACLS, neonatal resuscitation Am. Heart Assn. Staff nurse neurosurgery unit Hillcrest Med. Ctr., Tulsa, 1961-62; staff nurse cardiovascular unit Meth. Hosp., Houston, 1962-65; staff nurse St. John's Hosp., Red Wing, Minn., 1979-85, Wasatch County Hosp., Heber City, Utah, 1985-97. Columnist, Nurses Notes in Wasatch Wave, Heber City, Utah, 1990-97.

**TACKER, WILLIS ARNOLD, JR.,** medical educator, researcher; b. Tyler, Tex., May 24, 1942; s. Willis Arnold and Willie Mae (Massey) T.; m. Martha J. McClelland, Mar. 18, 1967; children: Sarah Mae, Betsy Jane, Katherine Ann. BS, Baylor U., 1964, MD, PhD, 1970. Lic. physician, Ind., Alaska, Tex. Intern Mayo Grad. Sch. Medicine Mayo Clinic, Rochester, Minn., 1970-71; pvt. practice Prudhoe Bay, Alaska, 1971; instr. dept. physiology Baylor Coll. Medicine, Houston, 1971-73, asst. prof. dept. physiology, 1973-74; clin. prof. family medicine Ind. U. Sch. Medicine, West Lafayette, Ind., 1981—; vis. asst. prof. Biomed. Engring. Ctr., Purdue U., West Lafayette, 1974-76, assoc. prof. Sch. Vet. Medicine, 1976-79; assoc. dir. William A. Hillenbrand Biomed. Engring. Ctr., Purdue U., West Lafayette, 1980-93, prof. Sch. Vet. Medicine, 1979—, acting dir., 1991-93; exec. dir. Hillenbrand Biomed. Engring. Ctr., 1993-95. Vis. rsch. fellow Sch. Aerospace Medicine, Brooks AFB, San Antonio, 1982; with Corp. Sci. and Tech., State of Ind., 1985-88; presenter, cons. in field. Author: Some Advice on Getting Grants, 1991; co-author: Electrical Defibrillation, 1980; author: (with others) Handbook of Engineering and Medicine and Biology, 1980, Implantable Sensors for Closed-Loop Prosthetic Systems, 1985, Encyclopedia of Medical Devices and Instrumentation, 1988, (with others) Defibrillation of the Heart, 1994; contbr. numerous articles to profl. jours. Chmn. bd. dirs. Assn. Advancemnt Med. Instrumentation Found., Arlington, Va., 1987-95. Mem. Am. Heart Assn. (bd. dirs. Ind. affiliate 1975-81, med. edn. com. 1975-81, pub. health edn. com. 1975-81, chmn. ad hoc com. CPR tng. for physicians 1976-77, rsch. review com. 1988-90), Am. Physiol. Soc., Ind. State Med. Assn., Tippecanoe County Med. Soc., Assn. Advancement Med. Instrumentation (chmn. various coms., bd. dirs. 1981-84, pres. 1985-86), Am. Men and Women Sci., Alpha Epsilon Delta, Beta Beta Beta, Soc. Sigma Xi. Achievements include research in biomedical engineering, cardiovascular physiology, medical education, emergency cardiovascular care, motor evoked potentials, skeletal muscle ventricle; patents for an apparatus and method for measurement and control of blood pressure, electrode system and method for implantable defibrillators, pressure mapping system with capacitive measuring pad. Office: Purdue U Basic Med Scis 625 Harrison St West Lafayette IN 47907-2006 E-mail: tacker@vet.purdue.edu.

**TACKETT, VITI LEE,** writer; d. Clarence James and America Jane (Mason) Hunt; m. Floyd Vernon Tackett, July 2, 1953; children: Floyd Randall, Terry Lynn, Lucinda Gail Tackett/Hines. Diploma, Inst. Children's Lit., West Redding, Conn. Author: (novel series) Roseanna, Belle's Restless Heart, Beyond the Tempest, Rainbow's End, Girl on the Run, Two Roads, Summer's Dream Betrayal. Office Phone: 870-572-7587. Personal E-mail: goviti@hotmail.com. E-mail: vititackett6@yahoo.com.

**TADDEI, LOIS ANNETTE MAGOWAN,** artist, interior designer; b. Phila., Sept. 17, 1935; d. Frank Rue Magowan and Grace Gloria (Valentino) Weinstein; m. Robert Matthew Taddei, May 21, 1960; 1 child, Robyn Grace Degree. Pleine Culi. Represented by Phila. Mus. of Art. Watercolor botanicals shown at Phila. Mus. Art; one-woman shows include Pa. Hort. Soc., Phila, La Grande Gallery, Moorestown, N.J., Camden County Libr.; group shows include Art at Armory, Phila, Great Galleries, New Hope, Pa., Hardcastle Gallery, Wilmington, Del., Hockessin, Del., Gallery I, Chadds Ford, Pa., Rhoads Gallery, Gwynedd Valley, Pa., Festival Arts, Cape May, N.J., Ocean City (N.J.) Arts Festival; designer Vassar Designers Showcase House, 1991-92, Haddonfield Design Showcase House, 1992, Barry Decorators Haddonfield & Cherry Hill, Interiors by Marilouise, West Chester, Pa., Rocco Marianni & Assoc. Interior Design, Haddonfield. Mem. Graphic Artist Guild, United Visual Artists, Burlington Country Art Guild. Avocations: gardening, needlepoint, ballet, museums.

**TADDESSE, SAMUEL,** economist, consultant; b. Addis Ababa, Shoa, Ethiopia, Oct. 16, 1944; came to U.S., 1968; s. Altaye and Askale (Yitabarek) T.; married Menbere Tshaey; children: Tsehay, Samson, David, Helen, Johannes. BSc, Haile Selassie 1st U., 1968; MBA, Fairleigh Dickinson U., 1970; PhD in Fin. and Applied Econs., U. Pa., 1975. Asst. prof. fin. and econs. Bernard Baruch Coll. CUNY, N.Y.C., 1973-77; sr. economist Fed. Res. Bank of N.Y., N.Y.C., 1977-80; dist. mgr. AT&T, Morristown, N.J., 1980-87; v.p. Debo Enterprises, Inc., Washington, 1987—2006; sr. rsch. scientist RTI Internat., Rsch. Triangle Pk., NC, 2006—. Sr. cons. Mgmt. Systems Internat., Washington, 1992—. Founder World Class Schs., Inc. Mem. Am. Bus. Assn. of Kenya, Internat. Soc. for African Devel., Soc. for Internat. Devel., Am. Econ. Assn., Washington Assn. Ethiopian Jews (pres.). Republican. Jewish. Avocation: camping. Home: 11104 Penderwood Ct Raleigh NC 27617-8573

**TADDIE, DANIEL LAWRENCE,** music educator; b. Cleve., Feb. 25, 1949; s. Lawrence John and Ritamarie Coletta (Bernard) T.; m. Ann Killebrew, Oct. 26, 1974; 1 child, Elena Louise DeZavala Taddie Cadle. B.A. summa cum laude, Marycrest Coll., 1971 (name changed to Teikyo Marycrest U.); M.A., U. Iowa, 1973, M.F.A., 1974, Ph.D., 1984. Adj. instr. mus. Luther Coll., Decorah, Iowa, 1974-77, Upper Iowa U., Fayette, 1975-77; instr. mus. Miss. County C. C., Blytheville, Ark., 1979-83; asst. prof. mus. Bethel Coll., McKenzie, Tenn., 1983-84, assoc. prof. music, 1988-90; Sheila Sutton Hunter prof. music, chair div. fine arts Maryville (Tenn.) Coll., 1990—. Choir dir. First Cumberland Presbyn. Ch., McKenzie, 1983-86; bd. dirs. Blytheville Very Little Theater, 1981-83, U. Tenn. Martin Arts Coun.,

1986-90, Miss. County Community Coll. Community concert Series, 1981-83. NEH fellow, 1986, 89, James Still fellow U. Ky., Lexington, 1994; recipient Rita Benton prize in musicology U. Iowa, 1985. Marycrest Coll. scholar, 1970-71, U. Iowa scholar, 1971-74; chorus master of Jackson (Tenn.) Symphony Chorus, 1989-90; hon. mem. Blytheville Orpheus Music Club, 1979-83. Mem. Coll. Mus. Soc., Am. Musicol. Soc. (v.p., program chair South Cen. chpt. 1991-92, pres., treas. 1992-93), Nat. Assn. Tchrs. of Singing, Am. Choral Dirs. Assn. (Tenn. repertoire/stds. chmn. cmty. choirs 1995-97, So. region chmn. 1996—), Nat. Assn. Schs. Music (sec. region 8 1996—), Sonneck Soc. Am Music, Tenn. Assn. Music Execs. in Colls. and Universities (pres. 1994-95), East Tenn. Vocal Assn. (coll. rep. and bd. dirs. 1996—). Democrat. Avocations: golf, swimming, reading, travel, photography. Office: Divsn Fine Arts Maryville Coll Maryville TN 37804-5907

**TADEPALLI, SRIKANTH**, mechanical engineer, researcher; s. Sitharamanjaneya Sastry and Syamala Tadepalli. BTech, Jawaharlal Nehru Technol. U., Hyderabad, 2001; MSE, U. Tex., 2003, postgrad., 2004—. In-plant trainee Indian Space Rsch. Orgn., Bangalore, 2000; project trainee Def. R&D Orgn., Hyderabad, 2001; tchg. asst. U. Tex., Austin, 2002—03, grad. rsch. asst., 2003—05; use condition devel. intern Intel Corp., Chandler, Ariz., 2005—. Recipient Excellence in Tchg. Fellowship award, H. Grady Rylander Longhorn Mech. Engring. Club, 2003; grantee NSF, 2003—. Mem.: ASME (assoc.), Soc. Mfg. Engrs. (assoc.). Achievements include research and development of the mathematical basis and the foundation principles for the systematic evolution of an innovative similitude method in empirical domain; work on the enhancement of the novel similarity process through the use of numerical procedures by incorporating the non-linearities of a mechanical system and the associated response parameters; work as part of a team in designing, developing and prototyping an assistive bowling device using mechanical design methodology tools. Avocations: reading, puzzles, chess. Office Phone: 512-471-5838. E-mail: tsrikanth@mail.utexas.edu.

**TADESSE, TSEGAYE**, climatologist, researcher; arrived in US, 1998; s. Tadesse Yifru and Tenagnework Merine; m. Betleham B Konjit, Dec. 19, 1998; children: Betselot (King) Tsegaye, Bemnet (Kate) Tsegaye. BSc in Physics, Addis Ababa U., Ethiopia, 1982; MSc, Internat. Space U., France, 1998; PhD, U. Nebraska-Lincoln, 2002—02. Meteorologist, team leader meteorol. comm. Nat. Meteorol. Svcs. Agy. Ethiopia, Addis Ababa, Ethiopia, 1984—97; rsch. assoc. Nat. Drought Mitigation Ctr., Lincoln, Nebr., 1998—; climatologist, asst. geoscientist, mem. faculty U. Nebr., Lincoln, 2006—. Contbr. articles to profl.jours. V.p Ethiopian Cmty. in Lincoln (Nebr.) Area, 2001—04. Mem.: Nat. Geog. Soc., Am. Meteorol. Soc. Achievements include research in modern drought monitoring tools. Home: 2201 Gunnison Dr Lincoln NE 68521 Office: National Drought Mitigation Center University of Nebraska Lincoln NE 68503 Office Phone: 402-472-3383. Personal E-mail: ttadesse2@unl.edu.

**TADROS, FAWZI M.**, educator; b. Mar. 12, 1934; came to U.S. 1967; BA in Library & Info. Scis., Cairo U., 1960; MA, U. Utah, 1972, Ind. U., 1973; MLS, U. Mich., Ann Arbor, 1974; PhD in Library & Info. Scis., Cairo U., 1979. Expert in libr. sci. Inspector Egyptian Nat. Libr., 1960-67; mem. faculty U. Utah, 1967-69, Ind. U., 1969-76; Arab area specialist Library of Congress, 1976—; mem., expert libr. sci. UNESCO, 1981-83. Cons. U. Libr. Saudi Arabia, Oman, Qatar, Bahrain, Kuwait, United Arab Emirates, Alexandria Libr. Com.; rep. UNESCO; vis. profl. Cairo U., U. Qatar, U. Bahrain, U. Oman; supr. World Global Gate Way between Libr. of Congress and Nat. Libr. Egypt. Pub. bibliography on the Holy Koran (among the best 60 Am. pub., 1994), others; contbr. articles to profl. jours. Mem. Congl. Del. State Qatar. Recipient Fulbright Sr. Awd., Univ. Qatar, 1990. Mem. AAUP, Middle East Studies Assn., Middle East Libr. Assn., Fulbright Assn. Achievements include first to exhibit in Qatar on the Holy Koran Manuscripts. Office Phone: 202-707-7311. Business E-mail: ftad@loc.gov.

**TADYCH, CHRISTOPHER ALLEN**, architectural firm executive, architectural engineer; s. Harry Allen and Mary Callaghan Tadych. BArch, U. Notre Dame, South Bend, Ind., 1988; MArch, U. Tex., Austin, 1993. Lic. Ohio Bd. Examiners Architects, 1994, Mich. Bd. Architects, 2001, Pa. State Architect's Lic. Bd., 2004, NC Bd. Architecture, 2000, Ga. State Bd. Architects & Interior Designers, 1999, Ind. Profl. Licensing Agy., 1999. Project mgr., project arch. Marr Knapp Crawfis Assocs., Inc, Mansfield, Ohio, 1995—97; assoc. ptnr., designer Richard Fleishman Architects Inc., Cleve., 1997—98; lead designer Richard L. Bowen & Assocs., Inc., 1998—99; pres. Christopher Architects LLC, 1999—; v.p. Chrysalis Environ. Devel. LLC, 2000—. Architect-of-record (design-build construction) Gurley Leep Volkswagen-Audi Dealership (Nat. Bldg. Yr., 2002). Commr. Hist. Preservation Commn., Mansfield, Ohio, 1995—97. Mem.: AIA (dir. networking 2002, dir. cmty. affairs 2005—06, chair govt. affairs com. 2005—06, chair renaissance com. 2005—06, regional dir. young architects forum com. 1997—2001), Notre Dame Club Mansfield (vice-president 1995—97). Roman Catholic. Avocations: travel, writing, drawing, painting. Office: Christopher @ Architects LLC 1433 West Bagley Road Suite 300 Berea OH 44017-2955 Office Phone: 440-239-9560. E-mail: christopher@architectsllc.cc.

**TAESCH, RICHARD EDMOND**, music educator; b. San Diego, Calif., Dec. 17, 1942; s. Edmond Thomas Taesch and Ann Marcella Simeone; m. Sandra Aiken, June 15, 1968 (div. Jan. 0, 1980). Cert. lit. Braille Libr. of Congress, 1988, music Braille Libr. of Congress, 1992; proofreader. Tchr. Adler Music Acad., Van Nuys, Calif., 1961—71; tchr. pvt. studio Van Nuys Music, 1971—94; tchr., chair dept. guitar So. Calif. Conservatory of Music, Sun Valley, 1976—; tchr., founder Braille music divsn., 1992—; tchr. L.A.City Coll., 1983—90. Br. pres. Music Tchrs. Assn. Calif, San Fernando East Valley, 1971—79; music specialist Calif. Transcribers and Educators of Visually Handicapped, LA, 1996—. Author: An Introduction to Music for the Blind Student Parts I & II; contbr. articles to profl. jours.; author: Introduction to the Piano for the Blind Student. Founder Music Edn. Network for The Visually Impaired, 1996. Recipient Ptnr. Sch. Award, Blend School-LAUSD, 1999. Mem.: ASCAP, Nat. Assn. of Schools of Music, Nat. Braille Assn. Roman Catholic. Achievements include development of Cal Transcribers and Educators of the Visually Handicapped music committee; developed curriculum for teaching of braille music. Avocations: hiking, amateur radio. Office: SCCM Braille Music Divsn 8230 Fall Brook Ave W Canoga Park CA 91304 Office Phone: 818-704-3819.

**TAFLOVE, ALLEN**, electrical engineer, educator, researcher, consultant; s. Harry and Leah T.; m. Sylvia Hinda Friedman, Nov. 6, 1977; children: Michael Lee, Nathan Brent. BS with highest distinction, Northwestern U., 1971, MS, 1972, PhD Cabell Fellow, 1975. Assoc. engr. IIT Rsch. Inst., Chgo., 1975-78; rsch. engr. 1978-81, sr. engr., 1981-84; assoc. prof. Northwestern U., Evanston, Ill., 1984-88, prof., 1988—, Charles Deering McCormick prof., 2000—03; member Lindgren/Slivka Residential Coll. Sci. & Engring., 2000—05. Author: Computational Electrodynamics: The Finite-Difference Time-Domain Method, 1995, 3rd edit., 2005; co-author: Computational Electromagnetics: Integral Equation Approach, 1993; editor: Advances in Computational Electrodynamics: The Finite-Difference Time-Domain Method, 1998. Fellow: IEEE. Achievements include pioneer of finite-difference time-domain method in computational electrodynamics. Office: Northwestern U Dept Elec Engring and Computer Sci 2145 Sheridan Rd Evanston IL 60208-0834 Office Phone: 847-491-4127. Business E-mail: taflove@ece.northwestern.edu.

**TAFOYA, MICHELE**, sports reporter; Talk show host Minn. Vikings Talk Radio, KFAN, 1993—94; reporter CBS Sports, 1994—2000, ESPN, 2000—, NBA on ABC, 2003; sideline reporter Sunday Night NFL, ESPN, 2002—04, Monday Night Football, ABC, 2004—.

**TAFT, BOB**, governor; b. Conn., Jan. 8, 1942; great grandson of William Howard Taft, 27th President of US; m. Hope Taft; 1 child, Anna. BA in Govt., Yale U., 1963; MA, Princeton U., 1967; JD, U. Cin., 1976. Pvt. practice;

---

mem. Ohio Ho. of Reps., Columbus, 1976-80; commr. Hamilton County, Ohio, 1981-90; sec. of state State of Ohio, Columbus, 1991-99, gov., 1999—. Vol. Peace Corps., E. Africa. Republican. Protestant. Office: Governor's Office 30th Fl 77 S High St Fl 30 Columbus OH 43215-6117 Office Fax: 614-466-9354.

**TAFT, EDMUND MORSE**, literature and language professor; s. Edmund Morse and Rita Day Taft; children: Anna Elizabeth, Patrick Keegan. BA, Duke U., Durham, NC, 1969; PhD, Penn State U., State College, 1982. Assoc. prof. English U. Nebr., Kearney, 1986—90; prof. Marshall U., Huntington, W.Va., 1990—. Contbr. articles to profl. jours. Lt. USN, 1970—75, Vietnam. Named Editor, W.Va. Shakespeare Conf., 1990—96, 2006. Mem.: Am. Fedn. Tchrs. (mem. exec. bd. 1997—2005), Shakespeare Assn. Am. Liberal. Roman Catholic. Avocations: golf, bridge, chess. Home: 1430 15th St Huntington WV 25701 Office: Marshall U One John Marshall Dr Huntington WV 25755-2646 Office Phone: 304-696-3155. Home Fax: 304-696-2448; Office Fax: 304-696-2448. Business E-mail: taft@marshall.edu.

**TAFT, SHELDON ASHLEY**, retired lawyer; b. Cleve., Mar. 2, 1937; s. Kingsley Arter and Louise Parsons (Dakin) T.; m. Rebecca Sue Rinehart, Dec. 26, 1962; children: Mariner R., Ashley A., Curtis N. BA, Amherst Coll., 1959; LLB, Harvard U., 1962. Bar: Ohio 1962. Assoc. Vorys, Sater, Seymour & Pease, Columbus, Ohio, 1965-69, 71-73; chief legal counsel Pub. Utilities Commn. Ohio, 1969-71; ptnr. Vorys, Sater, Seymour & Pease, Columbus, Ohio, 1974—2001, of counsel, 2002—04, ret., 2005. Ohio bd. advisors Chgo. Title Ins. Co., 1967-98. Rep. candidate for justice Ohio Supreme Ct., 1974; trustee Opera Columbus, 1989—, pres., 1991-93, life trustee, 1995—; trustee Columbus Bach Ensemble 2002—, pres. 2002-06; trustee Chamber Music Columbus, 2006—; councilor New England Hist. and Geneal. Soc., 2005—. 1st lt. USAF, 1963-65. Mem. Ohio State Bar Assn. (pres. pub. utilities com. 1984-87), Columbus Bar Assn. (pub. utilities com. 1962-2005), Ohio Camera Collectors Soc. (pres. 1985-87), Rocky Fork Hunt and Country Club, Hillsboro Club, 41 Club, Review Club. Congregationalist. Avocation: camera collecting. Business E-mail: staft@columbus.rr.com.

**TAFT, TIMOTHY NED**, orthopedist, surgeon, sports medicine physician; s. Samuel Milton and Helen Taft; m. Judith Ann Huffman, Sept. 13, 1971; children: Todd Daniel, Rebecca Lynn Fecher. AB, Princeton U., NJ, 1964; MD, U. Mo., Columbia, Mo., 1969. Diplomate Am. Bd. Orthopaedic Surgery, 1978, lic. physician N.C., 1978. Intern, resident in orthopedics U.N.C., NC, 1969—74, prof., 1974—, dir. sports medicine, 1991—2006. Mem. Red Cross, Chapel Hill, NC, 1999—2006. Mem.: Red Cross, Spl. Olympics N.C. Office: University of North Carolina 3154 Bioinformatics CB 7055 Chapel Hill NC 27599 Office Phone: 919-966-3340. Home Fax: 919-966-6730; Office Fax: 919-966-6730. Business E-mail: ttaft@med.unc.edu.

**TAFT, WILLIAM HOWARD, IV**, lawyer; b. Washington, Sept. 13, 1945; s. William Howard and Barbara Hoult (Bradfield) T.; m. Julia Vadala, May 4, 1974; Maria Consetta, William Howard V, Julia Harris. BA, Yale U., 1966; JD, Harvard U., 1969. Bar: D.C. 1969. Assoc. Winthrop, Stimson, Putnam & Roberts, NYC, 1969-70; atty.-advisor to chmn. FTC, Washington, 1970; prin. asst. to dep. dir. Office of Mgmt. and Budget, Washington, 1970-72, exec. asst. to dir., 1972-73; exec. asst. to sec. HEW, Washington, 1973-76, gen. counsel, 1976-77; ptnr. Leva, Hawes, Symington, Martin & Oppenheimer, Washington, 1977-81; gen. counsel US Dept. Def., Washington, 1981-84, dep. sec., 1984—89, acting sec., 1989; perm. rep. U.S. Mission to NATO, Brussels, 1989—92; legal adviser U.S. Dept. State, Washington, 2001—05; ptnr. Fried Frank Harris Shriver & Jacobson LLP, Washington, 1992—2001; of counsel Fried Frank Harris Shriver & Jacobson, 2005—. Recipient Disting. Service award HEW, 1975 Mem. D.C. Bar Assn., Lit. Soc. (Washington) Clubs: Cosmos (Washington), Leo (Washington). Republican. Office: Fried Frank Harris Shriver & Jacobson LLP 1001 Pennsylvania Ave NW Washington DC 20004 Business E-mail: taftwi@ffhsj.com.

**TAGATZ, GEORGE ELMO**, retired obstetrician, gynecologist, educator; b. Milw., Sept. 21, 1935; s. George Herman and Beth Elinore (Blain) T.; m. Susan Trunnell, Oct. 28, 1967; children: Jennifer Lynn, Kirsten Susan, Kathryn Elizabeth. AB, Oberlin Coll., 1957; MD, U. Chgo., 1961. Diplomate Am. Bd. Obstetricians and Gynecologists, Am. Bd. Reproductive Endocrinology (examiner, bd. reproductive endocrinology 1976-79). Rotating intern Univ. Hosps. of Cleve., 1961-62, resident in internal medicine, 1962-63; resident in ob-gyn U. Iowa, 1965-68; sr. research fellow in endocrinology U. Wash. dept. obstetrics and gynecology, 1968-70; from asst. prof. ob-gyn to prof. emeritus Med. Sch. U. Minn., 1970—2000, prof. emeritus Med. Sch., 2000—. Mem. fertility and maternal health adv. com. FDA, USPHS, HHS, 1982-86; cons. in field, 1986-87. Ad hoc editor: Am. Jour. Ob-Gyn, Fertility and Sterility; contbr. articles to profl. publs. Served with M.C. U.S. Army, 1963-65. Mem. AMA, Minn., Hennepin County med. socs., Minn. Obstet. and Gynecol. Soc., Am. Coll. Ob-Gyn (subcom. on reproductive endocrinology 1979-82), Endocrine Soc., Am. Fertility Soc., Central Assn. Obstetricians and Gynecologists, U. Iowa Ob-Gyn Alumni Soc. Home: 5828 Long Brake Trl Edina MN 55439-2622

**TAGGART, BRUCE M.**, library administrator; BS in pub. adminstrn., Nichols Coll., Mass.; M in pub. adminstrn., U. Conn., PhD in edn., 1993. Past assoc. dir. Computing Ctr. U. Conn.; exec. dir. Info. Tech. Portland State U., Oreg.; now vice provost Libr. and Tech. Svc. Lehigh U., Pa., 2000—. Mem. Educause, Gov.'s Telecom. Adv. Com., Oreg., N.W. Academic Computing Consortia, Lehigh Valley Econ. Devel. Corp. Office: Libr and Tech Svc Lehigh U 8A E Packer Ave Bethlehem PA 18015 Office Phone: 610-758-3025. E-mail: bmt2@lehigh.edu.*

**TAGGART, GANSON POWERS**, management consultant; b. Albany, N.Y., Aug. 16, 1918; s. Ralph Cone and Ruth Harriett (Townsend) T.; m. Paulett Long, June 30, 1945; children: H.Tee, Paulett Long, Cornelia V.C. BSchE, U. Mich., 1940, MSchE, 1941; postgrad., NE Sch. Advanced Mgmt., 1964. Registered engr., Mass. Mng. dir. Badger N.V., The Hague, Netherlands, 1965—70; v.p. world sales Badger Co., Cambridge, Mass., 1970—71; sr. v.p., dir. Badger Co. Inc., Cambridge, 1978—82; mgmt. cons. Devel. Scis. Inc., Sandwich, Mass., 1972—77; chmn. bd. Serapis Energy Inc., Boston, 1982—85, dir.; pres. Mgmt. Sys. Inc., 1984—. Chmn. bd. dirs. William K. Stout Pub. Co., 1995—; bd. dirs. E.F. Schumacher Soc. Contbr. articles to mags. Oil mem. Energy Facilities Siting Coun. Mass., Boston, 1979-82; mem. Winchester (Mass.) Planning Bd., 1971-77, Winchester Town Meeting, 1960-64; mem. exec. com. Internat. Sch. The Hague, 1965-70; trustee Ledges Condominium Assn., 1992-98, chmn., 1998; trustee USS Constn. Mus., 1989-95, treas. 1991-92; moderator Winchester Unitarian Soc., 1983-93; active Mus. Sci. Boston, Found. Global Cmty. Lt. (j.g.) USNR, 1944-48. Mem. AIChE (chmn. Boston sect. 1955, Order of Xiphias), Soc. Chem. Industry (London), Conservation Law Found., Am. Chem. Soc., World Bus. Acad., Inst. Noetic Scis., Chemists Club (N.Y.C.), Annisquam Yacht Club (Gloucester, Mass.), Harvard Club (Boston). Office: PO Box 516 7 Church St Winchester MA 01890-0516 *Hard work and flexibility in doing and thinking pays big dividends, as long as you are honest with yourself and others. I have always tried to see things from the other person's point of view, to give them the benefit of the doubt. I strive always to do the best I can and I do not spend a lot of time analyzing or criticizing what is wrong with others. And most important is a wonderful wife who accepts constructively life as it is dealt to you.*

**TAGGART, PAUL GORDON**, lawyer; b. Springfield, Mass., May 13, 1966; s. William P. Taggart and Marjorie Crawford; m. Sonia E. Mmaager, Aug. 13, 1995; children: Sophia G., Lukas A. BA in Econs., Calif. State U., Sacramento, 1988, JD, 1994. Bar: Calif. 1994, Nev. 1996. Law clk. U.S. Dept. Interior, Sacramento, 1993—94; environ. analyst U.S. Dept. Commerce, Washington, 1994—95; law clk. Nev. Supreme Ct., 1995—96, atty., 1996—97; dep. atty. gen. Nev. Atty. Gens. Office, 1997—2003; atty. King & Taggart, Carson City, 2003—. Bd. dirs. Nev. Bd. Bar Examiners, Brewery

---

Arts, Carson City. City atty. City of Fernley, Nev. Republican. Episcopalian. Avocations: running, swimming, bicycling, skiing, woodworking. Office: King & Taggart 108 Minnesota St Carson City NV 89703

**TAGGART, RICHARD J.**, corporate financial executive; BS, U. Wyo., 1967, MS in Agrl. Econs., 1970; grad. exec. mgmt. program, U. Wash. CPA. With ops. rsch. and systems devel. depts. Ford Motor Co., 1970—74; with Weyerhaeuser Co., Federal Way, Wash., 1974—, dir. investor rels., 1994—96, v.p. investor rels., 1996—98, v.p., treas., 1998—2001, v.p. fin., 2001—03, exec. v.p., CFO, 2003—. Office: Weyerhaeuser Co 33663 Weyerhaeuser Way S Federal Way WA 98063-9777*

**TAGGART, THOMAS MICHAEL**, lawyer; b. Sioux City, Iowa, Feb. 22, 1937; s. Palmer Robert and Lois Allette (Sedgwick) T.; m. Dolores Cecilia Baroway Renfro, Jan. 4, 1963; children: Thomas Michael Jr., Theodore Christopher; m. Mary Ann Gribben, Feb. 7, 1976. BA, Dartmouth Coll., 1959; JD, Harvard U., 1965. Bar: Ohio 1965, U.S. Dist. Ct. (so. dist.) Ohio 1967, U.S. Dist. Ct. (no. dist.) Ohio 1981, U.S. Supreme Ct. 1997. Ptnr. Vorys, Sater, Seymour & Pease, Columbus, Ohio, 1965—, now of counsel. Lectr. Ohio Legal Ctr. Inst., Ohio Mfrs. Assn., Capital U. Ctr. for Spl. and Continuing Legal Edn. Capt. USMC, 1959-63. Mem. ABA, Ohio Bar Assn. (bd. govs. 1991-99, liability ins. com. 1996-, pres. 1997-98, trustee Found. 1996-98, 2000—, pres 2005—, chair commn. on jud. evaluations 2000, Ohio Bar medal 1999), Columbus Bar Assn. (bd. govs., pres. 1989-90), Am. Bd. Trial Advocates, Columbus Area C. of C. Methodist. Home: 145 Stanbery Ave Columbus OH 43209-1465 Office: Vorys Sater Seymour & Pease 52 E Gay St Columbus OH 43215-3161 Office Phone: 614-464-6252. E-mail: tmtaggart@vssp.com.

**TAGIURI, CONSUELO KELLER**, child psychiatrist, educator; b. San Francisco; d. Cornelius H. and Adela (Rios) Keller; m. Renato Tagiuri; children: Robert, Peter, John. BA, U. Calif.-Berkeley; MD, U. Calif.-San Francisco. Diplomate Am. Bd. Psychiatry and Neurology. Resident psychiatry Mass. Gen. Hosp., Boston; staff psychiatrist Children's Hosp., Boston, 1951-59; med. dir. Gifford Sch., Weston, Mass., 1965-85; chief psychiatrist Cambridge (Mass.) Guidance Ctr., 1961-84; mem. faculty dept. psychiatry Harvard Med. Sch., 1965—2002; cons. early childhood program Children's Hosp., 1985—. Contbr. articles in field to books. Fellow Am. Orth. Psychiat. Assn., Mass. Med. Soc., New Eng. Coun. Child Psychiatry.

**TAGLIABUE, JOHN ANTHONY**, retired literature educator, poet; b. Cantù, Italy, July 1, 1923; arrived in U.S., 1927, naturalized; s. Battista and Adelaide (Boghi) Tagliabue; m. Grace Ten Eyck, Sept. 11, 1946; children: Fracesca, Dina. BA, Columbia U., 1944, MA, 1945. Lectr. Am. lit. Am. U., Beirut, 1945—46; lectr. English lit. State Coll. Wash., Pullman, 1946—47; asst. prof. English lit. Alfred U., NY, 1948—50; lectr. U. Pisa, Italy, 1950—52; prof. Bates Coll., Lewiston, Maine, 1953—89. Lectr. Tokyo (Japan) U., 1958—60, Fudan U., Shanghai, 1984, Indonesia U. Jakarta, 1993; dir. poetry reading series Bates Coll., dir. lit. mag.; numerous poetry readings. Author: Poems, 1959, A JapaneseJournal, 1966, The Buddha Uproar, 1970, The Doorless Door, 1970, The Great Day, 1984, New and Selected Poems: 1942-1997, 1998; contbr. more than 1500 poems, essays, prose to mags. and jours. Grantee (6), Fulbright Found. Mem.: PEN, Acad. Am. Poets, Phi Beta Kappa. Avocations: dance, arts. Home: 500 Angell St Apt 412 Providence RI 02906

**TAGLIABUE, PAUL JOHN**, retired national football league commissioner; b. Jersey City, Nov. 24, 1940; s. Charles and Mary Tagliabue; m. Chandler M. Minter, Aug. 28, 1965; children: Drew, Emily. BA, Georgetown U., 1962; JD, NYU, 1965; PhD. Humane Letters (hon.), Northeastern Univ., 1990; PhD of Laws (hon.), Colgate Univ., 2001. Bar: N.J. 1965, D.C. 1969. Atty. to sec. def. Dept. Def., Washington, 1966—69; assoc. Covington & Burling, Washington, 1969—74, ptnr., 1969—89; commr. NFL, NYC, 1989—2006. Bd. dir. Pro Football Hall of Fame; bd. dirs. Nat. Urban League; bd. govs. United Way of Am., 1990—99. Contbr. articles to profl. jours. Cofounder NFL Teacher of the Yr. Program, 1990. Co-recipient Stay Close Individual Leadership award, PFLAG, 2005; named Sports Industrialist of the Yr., Sports Business Daily, 2000, Sports Executive of the Yr., Sports Business Journal, 2001, Most Powerful Person in Sports, The Sporting News, 2001; recipient Humanitarians of the Yr. award, Comty. Anti-Drug Coalitions of Am., 2004, Ellis Island Family Heritage award, 2004; Gordon Grand Fellow, Yale U., 2001. Mem.: ABA (chmn. sports and entertainment industry com. antitrust sect. 1986), D.C. Bar Assn.*

**TAGLIAFERRI, LEE GENE**, investment banker; b. Mahanoy City, Pa., Aug. 14, 1931; s. Charles and Adele (Cirilli) Tagliaferri; m. Maryellen Stanton, Apr. 29, 1962; children: Mark, John, Maryann. BS, U. Pa., 1957; MBA, U. Chgo., 1958. Div. comptroller Campbell Soup Co., Camden, NJ, 1958—60; securities analyst Merrill, Lynch, Pierce, Fenner & Smith, Inc., N.Y.C., 1960—62; asst. v.p. U.S. Trust Co. of N.Y., 1962—71; v.p. corp. fin. div. Laidlaw & Co., Inc., N.Y.C., 1972—73; pres. Everest Corp., N.Y.C., 1973—. Dir. Fairfield Communities Inc., UEC, Inc., LRA, Inc., Industrialized Bldg. Systems, Inc. Past pres. West Windsor Cmty. Assn.; trustee Schuyler Hall, Columbia, Madison Sq. Boys Club. With AUS, 1953—55. Mem.: Princeton (N.Y.C.), Univ. Pa., K.C. Home: 77 Lillie St Princeton Junction NJ 08550-1307 Office: 1 Penn Plz New York NY 10119-0002

**TAGLIAPIETRA, ROBERT**, apparel designer; Grad., Parsons Sch. of Design. Co-owner, designer (with Jeffrey Costello) Costello Tagliapietra, 2004—. Work featured in Metropolitan Museum of Art's Costume Inst., Vogue, Elle, Bazaar, Style.com, Gloss, Maxim, Black Book. Recipient Ecco Domani Fashion Found. award, 2005. Office: Costello Tagliapietra 97 Second Pl 3Fl Brooklyn NY 11231*

**TAGLIENTE, JOSEPHINE MARLENE**, artist; b. Chisholm, Minn., Nov. 23, 1939; d. Joseph and Carmela (DeLuca) T.; m. Wayne W. Brown, May 28, 1960 (div. 1972); children: Michael Anthony, Troy Tagliente, Roben Tagliente, Angela Monique, Ninon Terese, Anina Maria (dec.). Student. Mpls. Coll. Art and Design, 1957-59, Mankato State Coll., 1966, Kansas City Art Inst., 1972; MFA, U. Guanajuato, Mex., 1974. Artist-in-residence Jewish Cmty. Ctr., Wilmington, 1969; illustration chairperson, mem. faculty Ray Coll. of Design, Chgo., 1980-87; adj. faculty Paradise Valley C.C., Phoenix; spkr. in field. One-woman exhbn. Natalini Gallery, Chgo., 1986; group exhbns. include Windbell Gallery, Wilmington, Del., Newark (Del.) Gallery, Galeria San Miguel, Mex., Galeria Osman, Mex., Galeria Condor, Mex., Torres Gallery, Albuquerque, Dartmouth Gallery, Albuquerque, Edith Lampert Gallery, Santa Fe, La Luna Nueva, Santa Fe, Herberger Theatre, Phoenix Little Theatre, Artesimo Gallery, Scottsdale, Ariz., Del. Art Mus., Wilmington, Sky Harbor Airport, 1994, Westaff, UK-Ariz., Canticles: Sight and Sound, 2002, others; represented in corp. collections Collins, Miller & Hutchins, Chgo., Mt. Sinai Hosp., N.Y.C.; also pvt. and pub. permanent collections; represented by Artisimo Gallery, Scottsdale; illustrations published in books; poetry published in anthologies; inventor garden products, office implements. Vol. art educator St. Anne's Intercity, Wilmington, 1967-68, Recreation Intercity, Chgo., 1978-79; cultural advocate for homeless Cultural Labor Party, Chgo., 1980-87, cultural advocate for minority concerns, 1985-88. Recipient Fine Art award Artist's Guild of Chgo., 1977, Print Drawing award, 1978, Educator/Svcs. award Sauk Area Career Ctr., 1984. Mem. Nat. Mus. Women in Arts, The Drawing Soc., Soc. Children's Book Writers and Illustrators, Statue of Liberty-Ellis Island Found. Social Democrat. Avocations: writing, digital painting, raising turtles and studying their habitat. E-mail: joyfulsunrise@qwest.net.

**TAGLIENTI, PAOLINA**, librarian; b. Huntington, NY, Nov. 5, 1967; d. Attilio and Loreta Taglienti; m. Gregg Luckner. BA in English, U. Del., 1989; MLS Queens Coll., 1995; M in Secondary English Edn., LI U., 1999. Serials coord. Pierpont Morgan Libr., NYC, 1989—95; cataloger, head of acquisitions LI U., Bklyn., 1995—2002; project libr. NY Acad. Medicine, NYC, 2002; head libr. Las Vegas Coll., 2004—. Symposium planning com. Assn.

Coll. and Rsch. Librs., NYC, 1999—2002. Contbr. articles to profl. jours., chapters to books. Mem.: Nev. Libr. Assn., ALA. Office: Las Vegas College 170 N Stephanie St Ste 145 Henderson NV 89074-8811 Office Phone: 702-567-1920. Business E-Mail: ptaglienti@cci.edu.

**TAGUCHI, KATSUYUKI,** science educator; BSc, Tokyo Inst. of Tech., Tokyo, Japan, 1989; MSc, Tokyo Inst. of Tech., 1991; PhD, U. Tsukuba, Tsukuba, Ibaraki, Japan, 2002. Sr. imaging scientist Toshiba Am. Med. Sys., Lincolnshire, Ill., 2002—05; instr. Johns Hopkins U., Balt., 2005—. Office: Johns Hopkins Univ 601 North Caroline St JHOC 4263 Baltimore MD 21287 Office Phone: 410-502-3934. Office Fax: 410-614-1977. Business E-Mail: ktaguchi@jhmi.edu.

**TAGUE, CHARLES FRANCIS,** retired engineering company executive, real estate company executive, construction executive; b. N.Y.C., Aug. 16, 1924; s. Charles and Isabelle (Carey) T.; m. Alicia Patricia Murtha, Aug. 6, 1949; children: Patrick, Charles, Thomas, Mary Alicia Haberman, James, Beth Anne Giuliano BS, Fordham U., 1952. Auditor Scovell, Wellington & Co., N.Y.C., 1951-57; comptroller Chem. Constrn. Corp., N.Y.C., 1957-75; contr. Burns and Roe, Inc., Oradell, NJ, 1975-81; fin. dir. Alfred Sanzari Enterprises, Hasbrouck Heights, NJ, 1981-84; v.p. fin. Alexander Summer Co., 1984-93; ret., 1993. Fin. advisor Cath. Cmty. at Seabrook Village. Mem. Colts Neck (N.J.) Sports Found.; active Boy scouts Am.; mem. Lacawac Sanctuary Steering Com.; pres. parish coun.; Ch. of Presentation; mem. pastoral coun. St. Thomas More Cath. Ch. With USNR, 1943-46, PTO, ETO, NATOUSA. Mem. Controllers Inst., Nat. Contract Mgmt. Assn., Assn. Govt. Accts., Scranton Club. Democrat. Roman Catholic. Address: 4 Appleby Ct Jackson NJ 08527

**TAGUE, JOHN P.,** air transportation executive; married; 2 children. Dir., then sr. v.p. Midway Airlines, 1985—91; with ATA Holdings, 1991—95; co-chmn., CEO The Pointe Group, 1995—97; pres., CEO ATA Holdings, 1993—2002; exec. v.p., customer United Airlines Corp., 2003—04, exec. v.p. mktg., sales and revenue, 2004—.

**TAHA, ASSAD M.,** surgeon; b. Nabatieh, Lebanon, Dec. 12, 1955; came to U.S. 1980; s. Muhyeddin S. and Hind (Jaber) T. BS, Am. U. Beirut, 1976, MD, 1980; PhD, Med. Coll. Ohio, Toledo, 1992. Diplomate Am. Bd. Surgery, Am. Bd. Surg. Critical Care. Surgery resident Good Samaritan Hosp., Cin., 1980-82, Med. Coll. Ohio, Toledo, 1982-85, attending surgeon, 1985-94, Am. U. of Beirut, 1994—, assoc. prof. surgery and physiology, 1994—. Dir. hyperbaric medicine Med. Coll. Hosp., Toledo, 1987—94, dir. surg. intensive care, 1988—94, assoc. prof. surgery; vis. surgeon surg. critical care Brigham & Women's Hosp., Harvard Med. Sch., Boston, 2000—01; vis. assoc. prof. Harvard U., 2000—01; vis. scholar trauma Ryder Trauma Ctr., Miami, Fla., 2003—04. Mem. editl. bd. European Jour. Emergency Surgery and Intensive Care; contbr. articles to profl. jours. Recipient AMA Physician Recognition award, 1987, 1991, 1997, 2000; grantee, Ohio Lions, 1987—92, Am. U.-Beirut U. Rsch. Bd., 1993—2000. Fellow ACS, AMA, Am. Heart Assn., Am. Physiologic Soc., Am. Soc. Gastrointestinal Endoscopy, European Assn. Trauma and Emergency Surgery, Royal Coll. Surgeons Can., Soc. Critical Care Medicine, Undersea and Hyperbaric Med. Soc., Am. Soc. Laser Medicine and Surgery, Am. Coll. Nutrition, Internat. Coll. Surgeons, Assn. Acad. Surgery, Shock Soc., European Soc. Intensive Care Medicine, World Assn. Disaster and Emergency Medicine, Soc. Am. GI Endoscopic Surgeons, World Med. Assn., Laser Inst. Am., Royal Soc. Medicine, Am. U. Beirut Alumni Assn., Am. Trauma Soc., Crit. Care Club, Disaster Med. Asst. Team; mem. AMA, AAUP. Avocations: chess, bridge. Office: Am U Beirut 3 Dag Hammarskjold Plz 8th Fl New York NY 10017-2303 Office Phone: 011-961-3628627, 305-468-2810. Office Fax: 212-583-7650, 011-961-1363291. Business E-Mail: at03@aub.edu.lb.

**TAHBAZ, CHRISTOPHER K.,** lawyer; b. Dec. 29, 1964; BA cum laude, Columbia U., 1986, JD, 1990. Bar: NY 1991. Assoc. Donovan Leisure Newton & Irvine; mem. Debevoise & Plimpton LLP, NYC, 1994—, ptnr. litig. dept., mem. ABA (immigr. Litig. & Antitrust Sects.), Urban Justice Ctr. (bd. dirs.), NY Lawyers Pub. Interest Inc. (vice chair, bd. dirs.), Internat. Bar Assn., Assn. Bar City NY. Office: Debevoise & Plimpton LLP 919 Third Ave New York NY 10022 Office Phone: 212-909-6543. E-mail: cktahbaz@debevoise.com.

**TAHERI, MARSHALL M.,** lawyer, educator; b. Iran, Dec. 29, 1934; came to U.S., 1963; children: Tara, Sara, Dara Jon. BBA, U. Houston, 1968; JD, So. Tex. Coll. Law, 1973; PhD of Law, Ministry Scis. and Higher Edn. Iran, 1974. Bar: Tex. 1974, N.Y. 1999, U.S. Supreme Ct. 1981, D.C. 1982, U.S. Ct. Internat. Trade 1989, U.S. Dist. Ct. (so. dist.) 1975, U.S. Ct. Appeals (5th cir.) 1975, U.S. Ct. Appeals (11th cir.) 1981, U.S. Ct. Appeals (9th cir.) 1986, U.S. Ct. Appeals (fed. cir.) 1991. Pvt. practice, Houston, 1974—. Adj. prof. internat. civil litig. South Tex. Coll. Law, Houston, 1980—; participant internat. bus. litig. and arbitration conf., N.Y.C., 2002. Fellow Houston Bar Found.; mem. ABA, ATLA, Tex. Bar Assn., State Bar Tex. (vice chmn. com. laws relating to immigration and nationality), Houston Bar Assn., Tex. Trial Lawyers Assn., Houston C. of C. (internat. bus. com., ad hoc immigration task force 1982, 87), World Trade Assn., Inst. Internat. Edn., Internat. Lawyers Assn., South Tex. Coll. Law Alumni Assn. (past pres.), Iran-Am. C. of C. (founder), Forum Club Office: PO Box 460165 Houston TX 77056-8165 Office Phone: 713-871-0000. Business E-Mail: taheri@marshalltaheri.com.

**TAHIR, MARY ELIZABETH (LIZ TAHIR),** marketing professional, consultant, writer; b. Greenwood, Miss., Dec. 14, 1933; d. Mahmoud Ibrahim and Mary Constance Tahir. Student, U. Miss., 1951-53. Cert. Profl. Cons., Acad. Profl. Cons. and Advisors. Mgmt. trainee Neiman-Marcus Co. Dallas, 1954-55, asst. buyer D.H. Holmes Co. Ltd., New Orleans, 1956-58, buyer, 1958-65, assoc. divisional mdse. mgr., 1965-67, divisional v.p., 1969-79, corp. v.p., gen. mdse. mgr., 1979-89; pres. Liz Tahir & Assocs., New Orleans, 1990—. Author: Mexico's Cosmetic and Fragrance Market: Past, Present and Future Opportunities, 1991, The Changing World of Mexican Retail Opportunities, 1991, Mexico: Window of Opportunity, 1991, Art of Negotiating, 1993, Negotiating More Profitable with Your Suppliers, Customers and Employees, 1994, Sizzling Customer Service, 1998. Bd. dirs. Vieux Carre Property Owners Assn., New Orleans, 1990, 2002, YWCA, 1996-2002. Recipient Role model award, YWCA, 1990, Woman Bus. Owner of Yr. award, 1996, Women of the Yr., City Bus. Pub. New Orleans, 2004, New Orleans Woman of Yr. award, 2001. Mem. Women's Profl. Coun. (pres. 1998, chmn. New Choices 1989), Fashion Group Internat. (Alpha award 1987-88, Lifetime Achievement award 1993), Nat. Spkrs. Assn., Am. Mktg. Assn. (bd. dirs. 1996—, pres. 1997), Am. Assn. Profl. Cons., Am. Mgmt. Assn., Fgn. Rels. Assn. (bd. dirs. 1992-2001, pres. bd. dirs. 1994-96), Nat. Retail Fedn. Avocations: art collecting, textiles collecting. Office: Liz Tahir & Assocs 201 Saint Charles Ave Ste 2500 New Orleans LA 70170-2500 Home: PO Box 8805 Metairie LA 70011-8805 Office Phone: 504-569-1670. Personal E-mail: liz@liztahir.com.

**TAI, ELIZABETH SHI-JUE LEE,** library director; b. Si-Ann, China, Aug. 12, 1942; arrived in U.S., 1965; d. Jun-Yee Lee and Fang-Yee Liu; m. Hsiang Tai, Dec. 29, 1969; children: Alan C., Victoria C., Brian C. BA in English Lang. and Lit., Nat. Cheng Kung U., Taiwan, 1965; M in Libr. and Info. Sci., Tex. Woman's U., 1967. Sr. libr. Queens (N.Y.) Borough Pub. Libr., 1967-73; asst. regional libr. Cin. Pub. Libr., Libr. for Blind and Physically Handicapped, 1973-75; libr. Ga. State Libr., Atlanta, 1975-78; dir. Poquoson (Va.) Pub. Libr., 1979—. Vol. ARC York County chpt., Va., 1980—; mem. York County Sch. Sys. Extend Program Coun., 1997; mem. Va. social svcs. bd. York County/City of Poquoson, 2002—; vice chmn. Peninsula Ret. Sr. Vol. Program Coun., Newport News, Va., 1994—99, chmn., 2000; bd. dir. Peninsula Ret. Sr. Vol. Program, 2001—, sec., 2002—. Named City Employee of Yr., City of Poquoson, Va., 1989; recipient Letter of Commendation, Va. Gov. James Gilmore III, 2001, Unsung Hero/Heroine award Nat. Cheng Kung U. N.Am. Alumni and Found., 2003. Mem. ALA, Va. Libr. Assn., Va. Pub. Libr. Dirs. Assn. (region 3 rep. 2003-05, treas., 2004—).

Outstanding Pub. Rels. award 1998, 2001, 02, 04, 06, Outstanding Facility award 1998, Outstanding Young Adult Program award 1999, Outstanding Children's Program award 1999, Outstanding Libr. Staff award 2003, Outstanding Va. Pub. Libr. Dir. award 2004), Va. Peninsula Chinese Am. Assn. (bd. mem. 2004—, pres. 2006—), Tidewater Area Libr. Dirs. Coun., Peninsula Chinese Am. Assn. (bd. dir. 2004—), Kiwanis Club (charter mem. Tabb chpt., chmn. youth program 2005—). Avocations: reading, gardening, swimming, tennis. Home: 129 Loblolly Dr Yorktown VA 23692-4254 Office: 500 City Hall Ave Poquoson VA 23662-1996 Office Phone: 757-868-3066. Business E-Mail: etai@ci.poquoson.va.us.

**TAI, TSZE CHENG,** aerodynamicist, researcher; b. Shaoxing, Chekiang, China, Apr. 29, 1933; arrived in U.S., 1963, naturalized, 1972; m. Shih Lin Sun, Aug. 27, 1965; children: Kuangheng, Kuangkai, Kuangshin. Diploma, Air Tech. Inst., Taiwan, Republic of China, 1957; MS, Clemson U., 1965; PhD, Va. Poly. Inst. and State U., 1968. Aircraft insp. Taoyuan Air Base, Taiwan, 1958—63; rsch. asst. Clemson U., 1963—65; grad. asst. Va. Poly. Inst. and State U., 1965—67, instr., 1967—68; sr. rsch. scientist Carderock divsn. Naval Surface Warfare Ctr., Bethesda, Md., 1968—2005. Chmn. panel US Navy Aero ballistics Com., Washington, 1978—81; Lectr. von Karman Inst. Fluid Dynamics, Belgium, 1980. Prin. Potomac Chinese Sch., Md., 1981—82; sci. officer fluid mechanics Office Naval Resch., 1985—86. Recipient Eugene Brooks award, Naval Ship R&D CTR., 1979. Fellow: AIAA (assoc.); mem.: Sigma Xi (pres. David Taylor chpt. 1989—90). Home: 10705 Tara Rd Potomac MD 20854-1356 Personal E-mail: tszetai@yahoo.com.

**TAIGANIDES, E. PAUL,** agricultural and environmental engineer, consultant; b. Polymylos, Macedonia, Greece, Oct. 6, 1934; s. Pavlos Theodorou and Sophia ((Elezidou) T.; m. Maro Taiganides, Dec. 25, 1961; children: Paul Anthony, Tasos E., Katerina. BS in Agri. Engring., U. Maine, 1957; MS in Soil and Water Engring., Iowa State U., 1961, D of Environ. Engring., 1963. Cert. engr., Iowa, Colo. Rsch. assoc., asst. prof. Iowa State U., Ames, 1957-65; prof. Ohio State U., Columbus, 1965-75; mgr., chief tech. adviser UN, FAO, Singapore, Singapore, 1975-84, mgr., chief engr., 1984-85, mgr., chief tech. adviser Kuala Lumpur, Malaysia, 1985-87; mgr., owner EPT Cons., Columbus, 1987—. Cons. EPD/Hong Kong, 1988-92, WHO, UN, Denmark, Poland, Czechoslovakia, 1972-75, Internat. Devel. Rsch. Ctr., Can., China, Asian, 1984-89, NAE, Thailand, 1990, FAO, Malaysia, Foxley & Co., Nu-Tek Foods; environ. advisor to Bertam Devel. Corp., Kuala Lampur, Malaysia, 1992—; waste cons. to U.S. Feed Grains Coun., Taiwan, Malaysia, 1992, Venezuela, 1993; pres. Fan Engring., (US) Inc., 1991—, Red Hill Farms, Ohio, 1992—. Author: (video) Waste Resources Recycle, 1985, Pig Waste Treatment and Recycle, 1992; editor: Animal Wastes, 1977; co-editor Agricultural Wastes/ Biological Wastes, 1979; contbr. articles to profl. jours. Bd. govs., v.p. Singapore Am. Sch., Singapore, 1978-83; clergy-leity congress Greek Orthodox Ch., Houston, 1974. Recipient rsch. awards EPA, 1971-75, Water Resources Inst., 1968-73; rsch. grantee UNDP, FAO, IDRC, GTZ, Asean, 1975-88. Fellow Am. Soc. Agrl. Engrs. (chmn. dept., A.W. Farral award 1974), Am. Assn. Environ. Engrs. (diplomate); mem. Am. Soc. Engring. Edn. (div. chmn.), Singapore Lawn Tennis Assn. (v.p. 1980-84), Am. Club (mgmt. com. 1980-85), Sigma Xi. Greek Orthodox. Avocations: tennis, classical music, folk dancing. Home and Office: 1800 Willow Forge Dr Columbus OH 43220-4414 E-mail: epaul@aol.com.

**TAI-SEALE, MING,** science educator, consultant; d. Jianzhong Tai and Xiouhua Zhao; m. Thomas Scott Seale, July 23, 1988; children: Sahar Marguerite, Arin Minghua. MPH, Emory U., Atlanta, Ga., 1988; PhD, UCLA, 1995. Asst. prof. Tex. A&M Health Sci. Ctr., College Station, 2001—02, assoc. prof., 2002—. Cons. to grant reviewers NIH, Bethesda, Md., 2001—. Recipient Mentored Scientist Career award, NIH, 2002—07. Mem.: Acad. Health (mem. advr. bd. health econs. interest group 2005—). Office: Taxes A&M Health Sci Ctr TAMU 1266 College Station TX 77843 Office Phone: 979-845-2387.

**TAISHOFF, LAWRENCE BRUCE,** publishing company executive; b. Washington, Aug. 30, 1933; s. Sol Joseph and Betty (Tash) T.; m. Nancy Lee Stuckey, Sept. 17, 1962 (div. 1979); children: Robert Paul, Randall Lawrence, Jonathan Bradford. AB, Duke U., 1955. Asst. dir. Sta. WTOP-TV, Washington, 1955-56; with Broadcasting Publs., Inc., Washington, 1958—91, pres., pub., 1971-91, chmn., 1991—95, also dir.; adviser Cahners Consumer/Entertainment Pub. divsn. Cahners Pub. Co., Washington, 1991—95; v.p. Jolar Corp., Washington, 1952-72, dir., 1958-72. Gen. ptnr. Jolar Assocs., Washington, 1972—; chmn. bd., pres. Graphictype, Inc., 1976-86, also dir.; chmn., pres. Solar Corp., 1982-86; chmn. Broadcasting-Taishoff Found., 1982-2001; chmn., CEO Chuckie Broadcasting, Ardmore, Okla., 1993—, Trustco, Washington, 1988—; CEO Solar Investments, Naples, Fla., 1996—. Co-author radio and TV segment Britannica Book of the Yr., 1983—. Trustee Washington Journalism Ctr., 1982-93. Nat. Press Found., 1993—, mem. adv. bd., 1993—; bd. dirs. Nat. Press Found., 1982—, mem. exec. com., 1990-94; mem. journalism and comms. exec. com. Capital Campaign for Arts and Scis., Duke U., 1984—, mem. athletic adv. bd., 1999—; bd. advisors Am. Journalism Ctr., Budapest, 1991-95; mem. White House Press Corps, 1983—; mem. Met. Washington Bd. Trade, 1970—; team capt. pubs. divsn. United Givers Fund drive, 1965; mem. admission adv. com. Duke Alumni Assn., 1968-70; mem. U.S. Senate and Ho. of Reps. Periodical Press Gallery, 1958-95; trustee Broadcast Pioneers Ednl. Fund Inc., 1985; judge VFW Voice of Democracy contest, 1978—; mem. bd. judges Peabody awards, 1985-91; mem. Am. U. Sch. Comms. Disting. Adv. Commn., 1985—; mem. Founders Soc. Duke U., 1985—, Duke Athletic Adv. Bd., The Mus. of TV and Radio Roundtable, 1988-89; bd. dirs. Ardissone, Naples, Fla., 1994-99; chmn., trustee Taishoff Family Found. With AUS, 1956-58. Mem. IEEE (sr.) Internat. Radio & TV Soc., Broadcast Pioneers (life, bd. dirs., exec. com. Broadcast Pioneers Libr.), Am. Sportscasters Assn. (exec. com. 1990—), White House Corrs. Assn., Nat. Press Club, Woodmont Country Club (Rockville, Md.), Cosmos Club (Washington), Sigma Delta Chi, Zeta Beta Tau. Jewish. Office Phone: 239-261-2660. E-mail: solarlc@earthlink.net.

**TAIT, JOHN REID,** lawyer; b. Toledo, Apr. 7, 1946; s. Paul Reid and Lucy Richardson (Rudderow) T.; m. Christina Ruth Bjornstad, Mar. 12, 1972; children: Gretchen, Mary. BA, Columbia U., 1968; JD, Vanderbilt U., 1974. Bar: Idaho 1974, U.S. Dist. Ct. Idaho 1974, U.S. Ct. Appeals (9th cir.) 1974. U.S. Supreme Ct., Nez Perce Tribal Ct. Assoc. Keeton & Tait, Lewiston, Idaho, 1974-76, ptnr., 1976-86, 89—, Keeton, Tait & Petrie, Lewiston, 1986-88. Chmn. bd. No. Rockies Action Group, Helena, Mont., 1985-86, bd. dirs., 1981-88; active Lewiston Hist. Preservation Commn., 1975-94, chmn., 1988-94; bd. dirs. Idaho Legal Aid Svcs., Boise, 1975-99, Idaho Housing Agy., Boise, 1984-91, St. Joseph Regional Med. Ctr. Found., Inc., 1989-94, Lewiston Ind. Found. for Edn., Inc., 1996—; Dem. precinct committeeman, 1976-86, state committeeman, 1977-94, 2000—; del. Dem. Nat. Conv., 1980, 84; regional coord. Idaho State Dem. Party, 1996-99; treas. Larry LaRocco for Congress, 1990, 92. With U.S. Army, 1968-71. Recipient Pro Bono Svc. award Idaho State Bar, 1988, Cmty. Recognition award Lewiston Intergovtl. Coun., 1992, Spl. Recognition award Idaho Legal Aid Svcs., 1993. Mem. ABA, ATLA, Idaho Trial Lawyers Assn. (regional dir. 1976-77, 86-88, 97-2003), Idaho State Bar (bd. dirs. worker's compensation sect. 2002—, chmn. 2004-06), Clearwater Bar Assn. (sec. 1974-76, pres. 1984-86), Consumer Attys. Calif., Workers Injury Law and Litig. Group (bd. dirs. 2002-). Office: Keeton & Tait PO Drawer E 312 Miller St Lewiston ID 83501-1944 Office Phone: 208-743-6231. Office Fax: 208-746-0962. Business E-Mail: lewlawus@lewiston.com.

**TAIT, ROBERT E.,** lawyer; b. Lima, Ohio, Sept. 3, 1946; s. Robert and Helen (Smith) T.; m. Donna G. Dome, June 22, 1968; children: Heather, Jennifer, Robert. BA, Kenyon Coll., 1968; JD, U. Mich., 1973. Bar: Ohio 1973, U.S. Dist. Ct. (so. dist.) Ohio 1976, U.S. Dist. Ct. (no. dist.) Ohio 1976, U.S. Dist. Ct. Md. 1980, U.S. Ct. Appeals (6th cir.) 1981, U.S. Supreme Ct. 1982. Ptnr. Vorys, Sater, Seymour & Pease, LLP, Columbus, Ohio, 1973— Staff counsel Govs. Select Com. on Prevention Indsl. Accidents, Columbus,

1977-78. Served with U.S. Army, 1969-70. Fellow Ohio Bar Found., Columbus (Ohio) Bar Found.; mem. ABA (litigation sect., products liability com.), Ohio Bar Assn. (worker's compensation com.), Columbus Bar Assn. (workers compensation and professionalism coms.), Def. Rsch. Inst. (workers compensation com.), Am. Bd. Trial Advocates, Assn. Def. Trial Attys. (exec. com. 1991-94, treas., 2002-), Fedn. Def. and Corp. Counsel (toxic torts com.). Home: 2045 Wickford Rd Columbus OH 43221-4223 Office: Vorys Sater Seymour & Pease PO Box 1008 52 E Gay St Columbus OH 43215-3161 Office Phone: 614-464-6341. Business E-Mail: retait@vssp.com.

**TAITT, EARL PAUL,** psychiatrist, military officer; b. LA, Nov. 6, 1956; s. Earl and Mary (Freitas) T.; m. Puruca Estepa, May 11, 1985; children: Anamaria, Earl. AA, East L.A. Coll., 1976; BS, U. Calif., Irvine, 1978; MD, Northwestern U., Chgo., 1984. Commd. capt. U.S. Army, 1984, advanced through grades to maj., 1991; intern in psychiatry Tripler Army Med. Ctr., Honolulu, 1984-85; resident in psychiatry Eisenhower Army Med. Ctr., Ft. Gordon, Ga., 1985-88; staff psychiatrist Community Mental Health Ctr., Ft. Gordon, Ga., 1988; div. psychiatrist, chief mental health 10th Mountain Div., Ft. Drum, N.Y., 1988-90; staff psychiatrist Community Mental Health Ctr., Ft. Meade, Md., 1990—; chief resident in psychiatry U.S. Army Hosp., Ft. Gordon, Ga., 1988. Cons. Army Drug and Alcohol Program, Ft. Drum, 1988-90, Installation Detention Facility, Ft. Meade, 1990—. Mem. San Gabriel (Calif.) Mission Parish Coun., 1975-76; pres. Medicai Soc., L.A., 1976. Mem. Assn. U.S. Army, Order of Green Key. Republican. Roman Catholic. Home: 14403 Altamaha Ct Orlando FL 32837-5425 Office Phone: 407-931-3001.

**TAKAGI, CAROL,** educational consultant; children: Jason, Kimberly. BA in Art and Anthropology, Calif. State U., L.A., 1972, MA in Edn., 1973, MS in Sch. Psychology and Counseling, 1976; PhD in Edn., Claremont U., Calif., 1989. Life std. multiple subject tchg. credential Calif., profl. adminstrv. credential Calif., single subject tchg. credential Calif. Sch. psychologist L.A. County Office Edn., Downey, Calif., 1976—89; spl. edn. coord. Ventura Unified Sch. Dist., 1989—90; program specialist Temple City Unified Sch. Dist., 1990—91; tchg. vice prin. Chino Unified Sch. Dist., 1991—94; elem. prin. San Luis Obispo Sch. Dist., 1994—97; dist. adminstrv. vice prin. San Miguel Joint Union Sch. Dist., 1997—2000; rsch. eval. and assessment cons. L.A. County Office Edn., 2000—. Mem. Orange County Pacific Symphony League, Costa Mesa, Calif., 2004—. Office: LA County Office Edn Divsn Rsch Eval Assessment 9300 Imperial Hwy Downey CA 90242-2813

**TAKAMURA, JEANETTE CHIYOKO,** dean; b. Honolulu, Aug. 1, 1947; d. Jiro and Jane Chiseko (Ishida) Chikamoto; m. Carl Takeshi Takamura, May 17, 1974; 1 child, Mari Leigh. BA, U. Hawaii, 1969, MSW, 1972; PhD, Brandeis U., 1985. Program dir. Moiliili Community Ctr., Honolulu, 1972-74; instr. sch. medicine and social work U. Hawaii, Honolulu, 1975-78, asst. prof., 1982-86; dir. exec. office on aging Office of Gov., Honolulu, 1987-94; dep. dir. State Dept. of Health, Honolulu, 1995-97; asst. sec. for aging U.S. Dept. HHS, Washington, 1997—2002; endowed chair in applied gerontology and pub. svc. Calif. State U., L.A., 2001—02; dean, Sch. Social Work Columbia U., N.Y.C., 2002—. Ptnr. Browne/Takamura, Honolulu, 1985-86. Contbr. articles to profl. jours. and chpts. to books; editorial bd.: Aging Today, 1991—. Adv. com. long term care Milbank Meml. Fund; adv. com. on aging issues World Econ. Forum. Grantee NIMH, 1982-84, U.S. Dept. HHS, 1985, 86, 89-90, 91. Mem. Nat. Assoc. State Units on Aging (2d v.p. 1991-92, bd. officer), Am. Soc. on Aging (program planning com. 1992-93, exec. com. 1996-, nat. adv. bd. White House Conf. on Aging, 1995), Gerontology Soc. Am., Futurist Soc. Congregationalist. Avocations: travel, reading, walking. Office: Columbia U Sch Social Work 1255 Amsterdam Rm 614 New York NY 10027 Personal E-mail: jctakamura@aol.com

**TAKAO, MOTOHARU,** physiologist; b. Takatsuki, Japan, Feb. 27, 1968; s. Takashi and Haruko Takao; m. Fusako Yagi; 1 child, Cay Raymond. PhD, Osaka U. Rsch. engr. Matsushita Refrigeration Co., Osaka, Japan, 1993—96; postdoctoral rsch. assoc. Brown U., 2000—. Postdoctoral Rsch. Fellowship on Abroad, Japan Soc. for the Promotion of Sci., 2002. Achievements include research in discovery of the intrinsic photosensitive retinal ganglion cell in mammalian retina. Office: Brown University 190 Thayer St Providence RI 02912 E-mail: takao@phys2.med.osaka-u.ac.jp.

**TAKEDA, YASUHIKO,** pathologist; b. Iiyama, Nagano, Japan, Mar. 16, 1927; arrived in U.S., 1953; s. Hideyoshi and Hanna Takeda; m. Tamako Kawai Takeda, May 5, 1958; children: James, Mary, Clara, Basil. MD, Chiba Sch. Medicine, Japan, 1952. Cert. physician Japan, 1953, lic. Colo., 1969, diplomate Am. Bd. Pathology 1970. Intern Bethesda Hosp., Cin., 1953—54; resident in anatomic pathology Sacred Heart Hosp., Spokane, Wash., 1954—56; resident in clin. pathology U. Colo. Hosp., Denver, 1956—58; resident fellow in dept. medicine U. Colo. Sch. Medicine, 1958—60; rsch. fellow Can. Rsch. Coun. McGill U. Med. Clinic, Montreal, 1960—63; instr. dept. medicine U. Colo., Denver, 1963—64, asst. prof., 1965—69, assoc. prof., 1969—78, prof., 1978—88, prof. emeritus medicine, 1988—, dir. immunoassay lab., 1972—86, dir. hematology lab., 1986—88, dir. Medicine 501 course, 1970—82. Reviewer manuscripts. Contbr. more than 60 articles to profl. jours. Recipient Career Devel. award, NIH, 1967—72; Rsch. fellow, Am. Heart Assn., 1964—66, Rsch. grantee, NIH, 1969—78. Fellow: Am. Soc. Clin. Pathologists, Coll. Am. Pathologists; mem.: Internat. Soc. Thrombosis and Hemostasis, Am. Physiol. Soc. Avocations: Go, gardening, ballroom dancing, fishing. Home: 635 Dexter St Denver CO 80220-5037 Office: Univ Colo Sch Medicine 4200 E 9th Ave Denver CO 80262

**TAKEI, GEORGE HOSATO,** actor; b. L.A., Apr. 20, 1937; s. Takekuma Norman and Fumiko Emily Takei, life ptnr. Brad Altman. BA, UCLA, 1960, MA, 1964. Dir., chmn. Golden Security Bancorp, Alhambra, Calif., 1981-. Appeared in films, including Green Beret, 1967, Star Trek I-VI, 1979-91, Return from the River Kwai, 1989, Blood Oath, 1990, Prisoners of the Sun, 1990, Live by the Fist, 1993, Oblivion, 1994, Chongbal, 1994, Oblivion 2: Backlash, 1996, Trekkies, 1997, Bug Buster, 1998, Mulan, 1998, Who Gets the House, 1999; plays include Equus, 2005, The Wash, 1990, Undertow, 1988, Year of the Dragon, 1974, Macbeth, 1972; TV shows include, Star Trek, 1966-69, Playhouse '90, 1959, Hercules, 1998; (TV movie) Kissinger and Nixon, 1995, The Best Bad Thing, 1997; announcer, radio personality, The Howard Stern Show, Sirius Satellite Radio, 2006-. Trustee, Japanese Am. Nat. Mus., L.A. Theatre Ctr., 1984—; dir., v.p. So. Calif. Rapid Transit Dist., L.A., 1973-84. Mem. Nat. Japanese-Am. Citizens League (cultural affairs chmn. 1970-73), SAG, Assn. of Asian Pacific Am. Artists, Am. Pub. Transit Assn. (v.p. 1978-80). Democrat. Buddhist. Avocations: running, architecture, historic preservation. Mailing: Hosato Enterprises Inc PMB 82 419 N Larchmont Blvd # 41 Los Angeles CA 90004-3013*

**TAKENAKA, TOSHIKO,** lawyer, educator; b. Tokyo, July 10, 1958; LLB, Seikei Univ., Tokyo, 1981; LLM, Univ. Wash., 1990, PhD, 1992. Bar: N.Y. 1993. Patent preparation analyst Texas Instruments Japan, 1981—86; assoc. Yamasaki Law & Patent Office, Tokyo, 1987—89; vis. rsch. assoc. Univ. Tokyo, 1999; adj. prof. George Washington Univ., 1998; vis. scholar U.S. Ct. Appeals Fed cir., 1998; assoc. prof. Univ. Washington Sch. Law, 1993—2003, W. Hunter Simpson prof., 2003—; dir. Ctr. Advanced Study & Rsch. Intellectual Property, Univ. Washington; vis. scholar Max Planck Inst., Munich; vis. prof. Wasenda Univ., Tokyo, 2003—. Contbr. articles to profl. jour. Mem.: Internat. Assn. for Advancement of Tchg. & Rsch. in Intellectual Property, Am. Intellectual Property Law Assn. (mem. exec. com., Intellectual Property sect.), N.Y. State Bar Assn., Assn. Am. Law Sch. Office: University of Washington Law School 1100 NE Campus Pky Seattle WA 98118

**TAKETOMI, SUSAMU,** physicist, researcher; b. Chiba City, Japan, Sept. 25, 1950; s. Manjiro and Kimie (Kida) T. B of Engring., U. Tokyo, 1975; DSc, Keio U., Yokohama, Japan, 1989. Rschr. Ctrl. Rsch. Lab. Fuji Elec. Co. Ltd., Yokosuka City, Japan, 1975-85; rschr. Matsumotoyushi Seiyaku Co. Ltd., Yao City, Japan, 1985—; vis. rschr. Keio U., Yokohama, Japan, 1985-89, Seikei U., Tokyo, 1990-95, U. Ctrl. Fla., 1995-96, U. Wash., Seattle, 1996-98, Kans.

State U., Manhattan, 1998-2000, Nat. Inst. Stds. and Tech., Gaithersburg, Md., 2001—03, Matsumoto Yeshi-Seiyaku Co. Ltd., Yao City, Japan, 2004—. Lectr. in field. Author: (book) Magnetic Fluids: Principle and Application, 1988, Magnetic Fluid Handbook, 1995. Mem. Am. Phys. Soc., Japan Phys. Soc., Japan Applied Phys. Soc. Avocation: playing violin. Office: Matsumoto Yushi-Seiyaku Co Ltd Shibukawa-Cho 581-0075 Japan Home: 710 6th Ave S #1042 Seattle WA 98104-3819 also: 1-1-4 # 201 Osakabe Yao City Osaka 581-0015 Japan Office Phone: 81 72 992 5268. Personal E-mail: staketomi@hotmail.com.

**TAKEUCHI, TETSUYA,** materials engineer; b. Okazaki, Aichi, Japan, Oct. 13, 1967; BS, Nagoya U. Japan, 1990; MS, Nagoya U., 1992; PhD, Meijo U., Japan, 1999. Tech. staff Hewlett Packard Lab., Kawasaki, Kanagawa, Japan, 1992—99; hardware engr. Agilent Technologies, Palo Alto, Calif., 1999—2003; sr. scientist Lumileds Lighting, San Jose, Calif., 2003—04; sr. engr. Canon, Atsugi, Japan, 2004—. Co-author: Properties, processing and applications of gallium nitride and related semiconductors, 1999, III-V Nitride Semiconductors: Applications and Devices, 2002. Recipient Young Rschrs. award, Japan Applied Physics Soc., 1999. Achievements include patents for group III-V semiconductor light emitting devices with reduced piezoelectric fields and increased efficiency, and method for obtaining high quality InGaN semiconductor devices. Avocation: guitar. Office: 5-1 Morinosato-Wakamiya Kanagawa 243-0193 Japan

**TAKIS, STEPHANIE,** retired state senator; Dem. rep. dist. 36 Colo. Ho. of Reps., 1996-2000; Dem. senator dist. 25 Colo. State Senate, 2000—; fin. specialist FEMA, Denver, 1992—94; rep. AtLarge City Coun., Aurora, Colo., 1989—93; mgmt. analyst U.S. Army, Aurora, Colo., 1983—92; congl. rels. Dept. Commerce, Washington, 1980—82; asst. to sen. Housing & Urban Devel. Com., Washington, 1979—80; ret. Mem. bus. affairs and labor and fin. coms. Colo. Ho. of Reps.; mem. legis. audit coms. Colo. State Senate, bus., labor com.; chair Trans com. Office: Colo State Senate State Capitol 200 E Colfax Denver CO 80203 Business E-Mail: stephanie.takis.senate@state.co.us.

**TAKUMI, ROY MITSUO,** state legislator; b. Honolulu, Oct. 13, 1952; m. Wanda A. Kutaka; children: Aisha, Jaron. BA, Friends World Coll., 1991; MPA, U. Hawaii, 1993. Cmty. organizer, Osaka, Japan, 1977-83; program dir. Am. Friends Svc. Com., Honolulu, 1984-90; polit. dir. Hawaii State AFL-CIO, Honolulu, 1990-92, comms. dir., 1992—. Rep. Ho. of Reps., Honolulu, 1992—. Office: State Ho Reps State Capitol Honolulu HI 96813 Office Phone: 808-586-6170. E-mail: reptakumi@capitol.hawaii.gov.

**TAL, JACOB,** electronics executive; b. Tiberias, Israel, Nov. 29, 1940; s. Refael and Seriora Tboul; m. Rivka Barlev; 1 child, Tomer. BS, Technion, Haifa, Israel, 1966; MS, U. Minn., 1968, PhD, 1970. Rsch. fellow U. Minn., Mpls., 1970-71; prof. elec. engring. U. Utah, Salt Lake City, 1971-78; rsch. engr. Hewlett Packard, Palo Alto, Calif., 1978-81; founder, owner Motion Control Seminar, Mountain View, Calif., 1981—90; founder, chmn. bd. dirs. Galil Motion Control, Mountain View, 1983—. Cons. Control Data, Mpls., 1970—75, Electro Craft, Mpls., 1970—78, Ford Motor Corp., Detroit, 1976—78, Burroughs Corp., Westlake, Calif., 1981—82. Author: Motion Control by Microprocessors, 1984, Motion Control Applications, 1989; author: (with others) Incremental Motion Control, 1978; contbr. articles to profl. jours. Mem.: IEEE, Electronic Motion Control Assn. Avocations: folk dancing, hiking, windsurfing. Office: Galil Motion Control 3750 Atherton Rd Rocklin CA 95765 Office Phone: 916-626-0101. E-mail: jacobt@galilmc.com.

**TALACHIAN, REZA,** filmmaker; b. Isfahan, Iran, Dec. 1, 1944; arrived in U.S., 1972; s. Ramezan Talachian and Taybeh Ajalouiean. BS in Motion Picture Prodn., So. Ill. U., 1977, MA in Pub. Visual Communication, 1981. Bank mgr. Bank Saderat, Shaikh-Bahiee, 1969—72; sales mgr. Southwestern Co., Franklin, Tenn., 1975—76; instr. Sch. Cinema and TV, Tehran, Iran, 1977—79; creative arts project coord. Sta. WSIU-TV, Carbondale, Ill., 1979—81; owner, prodr., editor Megatrend Visual Prodns., Hollywood, Calif., 1981—82. Screenwriter: (films) Darraab, 1977; Ashura, 1979; animator, editor: Graphic and Edn. Tech., 1978; co-prodr., writer: (films) How to count from 1 to 5, 1978; prodr., dir., editor Bazzar, 1979; author: (book) Brief Critical History and Survey Catalogue of Iranian Films from 1896 to 1975, 1981, Discover Your Mind, 1987, The Hidden Path, 1997. Home: 1831 8th Ave Apt 612 Seattle WA 98101

**TALALAY, PAUL,** pharmacologist, educator; b. Berlin, Mar. 31, 1923; arrived in U.S., 1940, naturalized, 1946; s. Joseph Anton and Sophie (Brosterman) Talalay; m. Pamela Judith Samuels, Jan. 11, 1953; children: Antony, Susan, Rachel, Sarah. SB, MIT, 1944; student, U. Chgo. Sch. Medicine, 1944—46; MD, Yale U., 1948; DSc (hon.), Acadia U., 1974. House officer, asst. resident surg. services Mass. Gen. Hosp., Boston, 1948—50; asst. prof. surgery U. Chgo., 1950—51, asst. prof. biochemistry, 1955—57, assoc. prof., then prof., 1957—63; asst. prof. Ben May Lab. Cancer Research, 1951—57, assoc. prof., then prof., 1957—63; John Jacob Abel prof., dir. dept., pharmacology and exptl. therapeutics Johns Hopkins Sch. Medicine, 1963—75, John Jacob Abel Distinguished Service prof., 1975—, Am. Cancer Soc. prof., 1958—63, 1977—. Sr. asst. surgeon USPHS, 1951—53; vis. prof. Guy's Hosp. Med. Sch., London, 1970, London, 1974—76; nat. adv. cancer coun. USPHS, 1967—71; vis. com. dept. biology MIT, 1964—67; bd. sci. advisers Jane Coffin Childs Meml. Fund for Cancer Rsch., 1971—80; bd. sci. consultants Sloan-Kettering Inst. Cancer Rsch., 1971—81. Hon. editl. adv. bd. Biochem. Pharmacology, 1963—68, editl. bd. Jour. Biol. Chemistry, 1961—66, Molecular Pharmacology, 1965—68, 1971—80, editor-in-chief, 1968—71. Recipient Premio Internationale la Madonnina Milan, 1978, Med. Alumni Disting. Svc. award, U. Chgo., 1978; fellow Guggenheim Meml., 1973—74; scholar Am. Cancer Soc., 1954—58. Fellow: Am. Acad. Arts and Scis.; mem.: NAS, AAAS (Theobald Smith award med. scis. 1957), Am. Soc. Pharm. and Exptl. Therpeutics, Am. Chem. Soc., Biochem. Soc., Am. Soc. Clin. Investigation, Am. Soc. Biochem. Molecular Biology, Am. Philos. Soc., Alpha Omega Alpha, Sigma Xi, Phi Beta Kappa. Home: 5512 Boxhill Ln Baltimore MD 21210-2039 Office: Johns Hopkins U Sch Medicine 725 N Wolfe St Baltimore MD 21205 Fax: 410-502-6818. Office Phone: 410-955-3499. Business E-Mail: ptalalay@jhmi.edu.

**TALAMO, JONATHAN HASKELL,** ophthalmologist, educator; b. Boston, Sept. 25, 1960; Student, Cornell U., 1978-80; AB, Johns Hopkins U., 1982, MD, 1986. Diplomate Am. Bd. Ophthalmology. Intern in medicine Children's Hosp. San Francisco-U. Calif., 1986—87; resident in ophthalmology Wilmer Ophthal. Inst., Johns Hopkins Hosp., 1987—90; clin. fellow ophthalmology, cornea and external disease Mass. Eye and Ear Infirmary-Harvard U. Med. Sch., Boston, 1990—91, asst. surgeon, 1992—95, sr. surgeon, 1995—, dir. gen. eye and cataract consultation svc., 1992—94, dir. keratorefractive surgery unit, 1992—95, acting dir. cornea svc., 1994—95, dir. cornea and external disease fellowship program, 1994—95; pvt. practice Providence, 1991—92, Boston, 1995—. Rsch. fellow in ophthalmology Harvard U. Med. Sch., 1984-85, clin. fellow in ophthalmology, 1990-91, instr. ophthalmology, 1992-94, asst. prof., 1994-95, asst. clin. prof., 1995-2005, assoc. clin. prof., 2005—; clin. fellow in ophthalmology Johns Hopkins U. Med. Sch., 1987-90; asst. clin. prof. surgery Brown U. Sch. Medicine, Providence, 1991-93; attending surgeon Miriam Hosp., Providence, 1991-93, R.I. Hosp., Providence, 1991-93; med. adv. bd. Intalage Corp., 2003—. Author: The Excimer Manual: a Clincians Guide to Excimer Laser Surgery, 1996; asst. editor jour. Refractive Surgery, 1994-99; mem. editl. bd. Ophthalmology Times, 1995—; contbr. 70 articles to profl. jours., chpts. to books. Tng. grantee USPHS, 1984, travel grantee Assn. for Rsch. in Vision and Ophthalmology, 1985, N.E. Corneal Transplant Rsch. Fund, 1993-94, Coherent Med., Inc., 1994-95; fellow Fight for Sight, 1985, Heed Ophthalmic Found., 1990. Mem. Am. Acad. Ophthalmology (Honor award 1998), Internat. Soc. Refractive Surgery (bd. dirs. 1995-2001), Am. Soc. Cataract and Refractive Surgery, Soc. Heed Fellows, New Eng. Ophthal. Soc., Mass. Soc. Eye Physician and Surgeons. Office Phone: 781-890-7797. Business E-Mail: jtalamo@lecb.com.

**TALAPATRA, DIPAK CHANDRA,** retired aerospace engineer; b. Laur, Bangladesh, Jan. 20, 1942; s. Upendra Chandra and Jalada Sundari Talapatra; m. Brigitte Hildegard Fischer; children: Indrani, Anika. B with honors, Indian Inst. Tech., Kharagpur, 1963; M in Engring., McGill U., 1968; PhD, U. BC, Vancouver, Can., 1972. Sr. scientist ENSCO Inc., Springfield, Va., 1972—77; sr. rsch. engr. Gen. Tire, Akron, Ohio, 1977—80; mech. engr. Naval Ordinance Sta., Indian Head, Md., 1980; aerospace engr. NASA, Goddard Space Flight Ctr., Greenbelt, Md., 1982—83, mgr. flight support sys., 1983—85, structural dynamics mgr., 1985—87; mgr. Can. programs NASA, Space Sta. Program Office, Reston, Va., 1987—92; mgr. NASA liaison in Can. Internat. Space Sta. Program, Montreal, Quebec, 1992—2005; ret., 2005. Patentee light weight arch type structures for large reflective mirrors for space and ground based telescopes (U.S. Patent #406634, 1977); contbr. articles to profl. jours. Presenter HS-Space Awareness Presentation, Montreal, Quebec, 2000, Internat. Tng. Environ. Leadership Group, Brazil Environ. Observations from Space, Montreal, 1995—. Recipient NRC of Can. Rsch. Assistantship, McGill U., 1966—68, U. BC, 1968—72, Exceptional Svc. medal, NASA, 2000. Mem.: ASME. Avocations: tennis, swimming, badminton, reading, art. Office: NASA International Space Station Program 2101 NASA Road 1 Houston TX 77058-3963 Office Fax: 450-926-4948. Personal E-mail: dipaktalapatra@yahoo.com.

**TALBERT, ARTHUR THOMAS,** music educator; b. Jackson, Miss., Aug. 29, 1925; s. Arthur William Talbert and Lucy Esther McIntosh. BA, Miss. Coll., 1948; MusM, La. State U., 1950; M of Sacred Music, Southwestern Bapt. Sem., 1954. Organist, choirmaster Cen. Bapt. Ch., NYC, 1954—56, 1st Bapt. Ch., Selma, Ala., 1955—56, 1st Meth. Ch., Booneville, 1956—59; instr. piano and organ N.E. Miss. Jr. Coll., Booneville, 1956—59; assoc. prof. Calif. Bapt. Coll., Riverside, 1960—69; organist, choirmaster Arlington Meth. Ch., Riverside, Calif., 1960—61, 1st Congl. Ch., San Bernardino, Calif. 1961—63, Lutheran Ch. of the Cross, Riverside, Calif., 1963—74; organist 1st Congrl. Ch., Corona, 1975—80, March Air Force Base, Riverside, 1980—82, St. Albans Episcopal Ch., Houston, 1992—94, Salem Luth. Ch., 1994—2000, 1st Ch. Christ Scientist, Bellaire, 2000—02, Spring, 2002—. Organist 9th Ch. of Christ Scientists, 2002—. Mem.: Am. Guild of Organists (assoc.). Home: 791 Bateswood Dr #121 Houston TX 77079 Office Phone: 281-589-8073.

**TALBERT, CHARLES HAROLD,** theologian, educator; b. Jackson, Miss., Mar. 19, 1934; s. Carl E. and Audrey (Hale) T.; m. Betty O'Neal Weaver, June 30, 1961; children: Caroline O'Neil, Charles Richard. BA, Samford U., 1956, LittD (hon.), 1990; BD, So. Bapt. Theol. Sem., Louisville, 1959; PhD, Vanderbilt U., 1963. Asst. prof. Wake Forest U., Winston-Salem, NC, 1963-68, assoc. prof., 1968-74, prof., 1974-89, Wake Forest prof., 1989-96; disting. prof. religion Baylor U., Waco, Tex., 1996—. Author: Reading Luke, 1982, Reading Corinthians, 1987, Learning Through Suffering, 1991, Reading John, 1992, The Apocalypse, 1994, Reading Acts, 1997, Romans, 2002, Reading Luke-Acts in its Mediterranean Milieu, 2003, Reading the Sermon on the Mount, 2004, Literary Patterns, Theological Themes and the Genre of Luke-Acts, 2005. Postdoctoral fellow U. N.C., 1968-69, Soc. for Values in Higher Edn., 1971-72. Mem. Soc. Bibl. Lit. (editor SBL Dissertation Series, N.T. 1984-86, 87-89, editorial bd. jour. 1984-89), Cath. Bibl. Assn. (assoc. editor Cath. Bibl. Quar. 1991-98, pres. 1999-00), Nat. Assn. Bapt. Profs. Religion (pres. 1985), Studiorum Novi Testamenti Societas. Independent. Baptist. Home: 9602 Old Farm Rd Waco TX 76712-6402 Office: Baylor Univ Dept Religion PO Box 97284 Waco TX 76798-7284 Business E-Mail: charles_talbert@baylor.edu.

**TALBERT, GEAL FUKUMOTO,** investment representative; b. Honolulu, Aug. 22, 1961; d. Alvin J. and Geraldine S. Fukumoto BBA, U. Hawaii, 1983. CFP, CLU, ChFC. Sales agt. Prudential, Long Beach, Calif., 1986-94; investment rep. Edward Jones, Kaneohe, Hawaii, 1994—2005; pres. Legacy Group Hawaii, Kaneohe, 2005—; mem. Fin. Planning Assn., 2003—. Mem. Kaneohe Bus. Group, 1994—, v.p., 1996, pres., 1998; mem. Edward Jones Grass Roots Task Force, 1997-2001, Edward Jones hiring team, 2000-2002. Vol. Jr. Achievement, 1994-98; bd. dirs. Nat. Fedn. Ind. Bus., 1997-99; mem. Hawaii Estate Planning Coun., 1996—. Mem. Am. Soc. CLUs (bd. dirs. Harbor chpt. 1992-94, chmn. continuing edn. 1992-93), Am. Bus. Womens Assn. (Ulupono charter chpt. 1994-98), Securities Industry Assn. of Hawaii (dir., govt. affairs chair 1999-2000, pres. 2002-2003), Small Bus. Hawaii (bd. dirs. 1999—), Rotary (Kaneohe chpt., chmn. youth svcs. 1996, sec. 1997-98, pres. 2000-2001), Investment Soc. Hawaii (bd. dirs. 1997-2000). Avocations: travel, reading. Office: Legacy Group Hawaii 45-1144 Kamehameha Hwy Ste 403 Kaneohe HI 96744-3226 Office Phone: 808-235-5100. Business E-Mail: geal@legacygrouphawaii.com.

**TALBERT, KENT DEAN,** federal agency administrator, lawyer; b. Greenwood, SC, 1960; BA magna cum laude, Erskine Coll., 1982; JD, USC, 1985. Staff mem., com. edn. and the workforce US Ho. of Reps.; staff mem., com. health edn. labor and pensions US Senate; staff mem. Office US Senator Strom Thurmond; atty. Columbia, SC; dep. gen. counsel, Divsn. Bus. Adminstrv. Affairs & Divsn. Legis. Counsel US Dept. Edn., Washington, 2001—06, acting gen. counsel, 2005—06, gen. counsel, 2006—. Republican. Office: US Dept Edn Office of Gen Counsel 400 Maryland Ave SW Rm 6E313 Washington DC 20202 Office Phone: 202-401-6000. E-mail: kent.talbert@ed.gov.*

**TALBERT, BLAKE STROTHERS,** retired urologist; b. Waynesville, Mo., Nov. 28, 1915; s. Charles Albert and Emma Pearl (Cugitt) Talbot; m. Margaret Noelke (div.); m. Peggy Jean Handley, Dec. 7, 1970; children: Gregory, Debra. BS in Medicine, U. Mo., Columbia, 1939; MD, U. Chgo., 1941. Commd. ensign USN, advanced through grades to capt., 1942, urologist, 1942—62; chief urologist numerous USN hosps., San Diego, 1947—62; ret., 1962. Assoc. clin. prof. urology U. Calif., San Diego, 1976. Mem.: ACS, Am. Urol. Assn. Avocation: sports. Home: 2620 2d Ave # 7D San Diego CA 92103

**TALBOT, DONALD ROY,** management consultant; b. Bridgeport, Conn., Jan. 23, 1931; s. Grant Edward and Elvera (Gilbert) T.; m. Beverly Rinebold, Aug. 15, 1953; children: Donna, Randall, Theodore, Timothy, Thomas. B in Marine Engring., N.Y. State Maritime Coll. Project engr. atomic power equipment div. GE, San Jose, Calif., 1952-58; mgr. nuclear labs., nuclear div. Martin Marietta Corp., Balt., 1958-62, project dir. nuclear div., 1962-67, dir. spl. studies Friendship, Md., 1967-71, project dir. environ. programs Balt., 1971-74, dir. environ. tech. ctr. Relay, Md., 1974-83, gen. mgr. environ. systems div. Columbia, Md., 1984-87; corp. v.p. Vexar, Inc., Springfield, Va., 1987-89; pres. R.E. Mgmt. Svc., Inc., Towson, Md., 1989—. Recipient Antarctica Svc. medal Civil Engrs. Corps USN, 1965, Cert. of Appreciation Sec. Dept. Commerce, 1975 Avocation: outdoor activities. Home: 712 Hickory Lot Rd Baltimore MD 21286-1427 Office: R E Mgmt Svcs Inc PO Box 10614 Baltimore MD 21285-0614 Office Phone: 410-583-1334, Personal E-mail: remsdrt@comcast.net.

**TALBOT, EMILE JOSEPH,** French language educator; b. Brunswick, Maine, Apr. 12, 1941; s. Joseph Emile and Flora Talbot; m. Elizabeth Mullen, Aug. 6, 1966; children: Marc, Paul. BA, St. Francis Coll., Biddeford, Maine, 1963; MA, Brown U., 1965, PhD, 1968. From instr. French to prof. U. Ill., Urbana, 1967—86, prof., 1986—2004, prof. emeritus, 2004—, head dept. French, 1988-94. Editor: (book) La Critique Stendhalienne, 1979; author: Stendhal and Romantic Esthetics, 1985, Stendhal Revisited, 1993, Reading Nelligan, 2002; rev. editor: The French Rev., 1979—82, Quebec Studies, 1988—93, mem. editl. bd.; 1993—96; mem. editl. bd. Quebec Studies, 2003—05; mem. editl. bd.: Nineteenth-Century French Studies, 1986—2003, La Revue Francophone, 1990—96, Etudes Francophones, 1996—2004, Nouvelles Etudes Francophones, 2004—; editor: Quebec Studies, 2004—. Decorated chevalier Ordre des Palmes Académiques (France); fellow, Ctr. Advanced Study U. Ill., 1973, Assoc., 1988, NEH, 1973—74, Camargo Found., France, 1976. Mem.: MLA, Am. Coun. Que. Studies (v.p. 1995—97, pres. 1997—99), Assn. Can. Studies in U.S., Am. Assn. Tchrs. French. Roman Catholic. Office: U Ill Dept French 707 S Mathews Ave Urbana IL 61801-3625 Office Phone: 217-244-2728.

**TALBOT, LEE MERRIAM,** ecologist, educator, director; b. New Bedford, Mass., Aug. 2, 1930; s. Murrell Williams and Zenaida (Merriam) T.; m. Martha Walcott Hayne, May 16, 1959; children: Lawrence Hayne, Russell Merriam. BA, U. Calif., Berkeley, 1953, MA, PhD, U. Calif., Berkeley, 1963. Biologist Arctic Research Lab., Point Barrow, Alaska, 1951; staff ecologist Internat. Union for Conservation, Brussels, 1954-56; ecologist, dir. East African ecol. research project Nat. Acad. Scis., Govts. of Kenya and Tanzania, 1959-63; wildlife advisor UN Spl. Fund, Africa, 1963-64; dir. S.E. Asia project Internat. Union for Conservation, 1964-65; resident ecologist, field rep. for internat. affairs Smithsonian Instn., Washington, 1966-70; sr. scientist, dir. internat. activities Pres.'s Council on Environ. Quality, Washington, 1970-78; sr. sci. advisor Internat. Council Sci. Unions, Paris, 1978-83; dir. conservation, spl. sci. advisor World Wildlife Fund Internat., Switzerland, 1978-80; dir. gen. Internat. Union for Conservation of Nature and Natural Resources, Gland, Switzerland, 1980-83; resident fellow Environ. and Policy Inst., East West Ctr., 1983-87; vis. fellow World Resources Inst., Washington, 1984-89; sr. environ. advisor World Bank, 1984—; pres. Lee Talbot Assocs. Internat., 1991—; sr. prof. environ. scis., internat. affairs and pub. policy George Mason U., Va., 1994—. Cons. UNESCO, World Bank, Asian Devel. Bank, Nat. Geog. Soc., Inter-Am. Devel. Bank, The Nature Conservancy, U.S. Govt., U. Calif., UN Spl. Fund, WHO, UN Environment Program, UN Univ., UN Devel. Programme, African and Asian Govts.; conservation coord. Internat. Biol. Program, 1965-70; bd. dirs. Defenders of Wildlife, Inst. Ecosys. Studies; mem. corp. NY Bot. Gardens; mem. sci. adv. coun. Nat. Pks. Conservation Assn.; founding trustee Inst. Ecosys. Studies, NY, 2006. Author 17 books and monographs; contbr. more than 270 articles to profl. jours. Active Boy Scouts Am., Geneva, 1980-82, Washington, 1987-95. With USMC, 1953-54. Decorated officer Order of Lion (Senegal); recipient Regents Lectureship award U. Calif., Santa Barbara, 1986, Pierre Chaleur prize French Acad. Scis., 1993, Festschrift Career Accomplishments award George Mason U., 2003, World Commn. Protected Areas East Asia award, 2005; named Disting. Alumnus, 1953 Officer Candidate Sch., USMC, 2003; Centenary Symposium named in his honor Bombay Natural History Soc., 2003 Fellow Royal Geog. Soc., Royal Soc. Arts, AAAS, N.Y. Zool. Soc.; mem. Am. Inst. Biol. Scis. (Disting. Scientist award 1979), Acad. Medicine, World Conservation Union (hon.), Am. Assn. for Club of Rome, Am. Soc. Mammalogists, Ecol. Soc., Wildlife Soc. (Outstanding Publ. award 1963), Soc. for Conservation Biology, Internat. Soc. for Ecol. Econs., Boone and Crockett Club (N.Y.C.), Explorers Club (N.Y.C.), Cosmos Club (Washington), Sigma Xi, Phi Kappa Sigma. Achievements include incorporation of ecological principles in international development; development of new principles for management of wild resources; biodiversity conservation; definition of ecosystem dynamics of tropical savannas including role of fire, feeding habits and migrations of wild herbivores; development and negotiation of national legislation and international agreements for environmental protection. Home: 6656 Chilton Ct Mc Lean VA 22101-4422 *My career is based on two premises: first, that our most important challenges are environmental issues which determine the earth's carrying capacity for human life and, equally important, the quality of that life; and second, that it is important to obtain direct experience in as much of the world as possible to understand the human ecological setting as a basis for action to improve it.*

**TALBOT, MARTHA HAYNE,** conservationist, biologist; b. San Francisco, Aug. 3, 1932; d. Francis Bourn and Anna (Walcott) Hayne; m. Lee Merriam Talbot, May 16, 1959; children: Lawrence Hayne, Russell Merriam. BA, Vassar Coll., 1954. Co-founder, asst. dir. student conservation program U.S. Nat. Parks, 1955-59; co-dir. East African Ecol. Rsch. Project, Kenya and Tanzania, 1959-63; asst. dir. S.E. Asia Project, Internat. Union for Conservation of Nature/Natural Resources, 1964-65; asst. coord. Internat. Biol. Programme, London, 1966; rsch. assoc. Smithsonian Instn., Washington, 1966-75; mem., treas. Fairfax County Park Authority, Fairfax, Va., 1973-77; sec-treas. Talbot Racing Assocs., McLean, Va., 1983—; owner, dir. Talbot Hayne Vineyard, St. Helena, Calif., 1988—; sec.-treas. Lee Talbot Assocs. Internat., McLean, 1991—. Bd. dir. Student Conservation Assn., 1966-78, 83-87, hon. dir., 1987— (Svc. Honor award), Defenders of Wildlife, 1974-77, Audubon Naturalist Soc., 1975-78, Rachel Carson Coun., 1975-94, treas., 1994-98, v.p., 1998—. Co-author: Introduction to the Landscape, East Africa, 1961; co-editor: Conservation in Tropical South East Asia, 1968; contbr. articles to profl. jours. Cub Scout troop leader Boy Scouts Am., Geneva, 1978-83, transp. coord., McLean, 1989-95. Recipient Outstanding Pub. award The Wildlife Soc., 1963, Cinema Golden Eagle award Documentary Film, 1968, Disting. Alumna award Katharine Branson Sch., 1981, Conservation Svc. award U.S. Dept. Interior, 1986, Bd. Tribute to co-founder, Student Conservation Assn., 1984, Resolution of Honor, 1999; N.Y. Zool. Soc. grantee, 1961; co-recipient World Comm. on Protected Areas East Asia award, 2005 Mem. Soc. Women Geographers (bd. dir. 1972-75, treas. 1984-89, treas. Washington group 1990-96), Napa Valley Grape Growers Assn., Rachels Network, Explorers Club Avocations: backpacking, hiking, bicycling, travel. Home: 6656 Chilton Ct Mc Lean VA 22101-4422

**TALBOT, MARY LEE,** minister; b. Cleve., Apr. 18, 1953; d. Richard William and Mary Helen (Jacobs) T. BA, Coll. Wooster, 1975; MDiv, Andover-Newton Theol. Sch., 1979; MPhil, Tchrs. Coll. Columbia U., 1990; PhD, Columbia U., 1997. Ordained to ministry Presbyterian Ch. (U.S.A.), 1981. Asst. in ministry Grace Congl. Ch., Framingham, Mass., 1975-78; resources coord. Women's Theol. Coalition, Boston, 1977-79; assoc. editor Youth Mag., Phila., 1979-80; co-dir. youth and young adult program Presbyn. Ch. U.S.A., NYC, 1981-88; cons. in religious edn. N.Y.C., 1988-90; dir. continuing edn. Pitts. Theol. Sem., Pitts., 1990—2001; interim pastor Hebron U.P. Ch., Clinton, 2002—03, supply pastor, 2004—. Bd. dirs. Christian Assn. U. Pa., 1979-81; mem. religion com. Chautauqua Inst., 1988-91. Author, editor Suicide and Youth, 1981, (newsletter) Trackings, 1986—88; editor: Racism and Anti-Racism, 1982, One Fantastic Book, 1982, My Identity: A Gift from God, 1987, A Guidebook for Presbyterian Youth Ministry, 1988, God's Gift of Sexuality, 1989, Celebrate Bible Study, 1990, The C.L.S.C. Banner Book, 2004; contbr. articles to popular mags., profl. jours. Bd. dirs. Christian Assoc. U. Pa., 1979-81. Recipient English award Bus. and Profl. Women, 1971. Mem. Assn. Presbyn. Ch. Educators, Assn. Presbyn. Clergywomen, Religious Edn. Assn. (bd. dirs. 1986-91), History of Edn. Soc., Kappa Delta Pi. Democrat. Office: 1767 Rte 30 Clinton PA 15026 Office Phone: 724-899-2620. Personal E-mail: mltalbot@aol.com.

**TALBOT, NYNA LUCILLE,** psychologist, writer; b. Warrington, Eng., May 24, 1954; d. John Robert Talbot and Lois June Snow. MA, Calif. Inst. Integral Studies, 1997, PhD, 2000; BA, Elmhurst Coll., 1976. Sr. tech. writer Hitachi Data Sys., Santa Clara, Calif., 1986—2006. Clin. psychology intern San Mateo County Emergency Response Team, 1990—91, San Mateo County Mental Health Svcs., Half Moon Bay, 2000—01. Clin. psychology intern mem. Red Cross, San Mateo, 1990—91. Mem.: Internat. Coun. Psychologists, Assn. Transpersonal Psychology, APA. Achievements include research in the relationship of companionship coupling in two significant populations. Avocations: painting, poetry. Office: Hitachi Data Sys 750 Central Expressway MS3288 Santa Clara CA 95050-2627 Personal E-mail: drnyna@yahoo.com. Business E-Mail: nyna.talbot@hds.com.

**TALBOT, PAMELA,** public relations executive; b. Chgo., Aug. 10, 1946; BA in English, Vassar Coll., 1968. Reporter Worcester, Mass. Telegram and Gazette, 1970—72; account exec. Daniel J. Edelman, Inc., Chgo., 1972—74, account supr., 1974—76, v.p.—78, sr. v.p., 1978—84, exec. v.p., gen. mgr., 1984—90; pres. Edelman West, Chgo., 1990—95; pres., CEO Edelman U.S., 1995—. Office: Edelman Pub Rels 200 E Randolph Dr Ste 6300 Chicago IL 60601-6436 E-mail: pam.talbot@edelman.com.

**TALBOT, PHILLIPS,** retired Asian affairs specialist; b. Pitts., June 7, 1915; s. Kenneth Hammet and Gertrude (Phillips) T.; m. Mildred Aleen Fisher, Aug. 18, 1943 (dec. June 20, 2004); children: Susan Talbot Jacox, Nancy, Bruce Kenneth (dec.). BA, U. Ill., 1936, BS in Journalism, 1936; student, London Sch. Oriental Studies, 1938—39, Aligarh Muslim U., India, 1939—40; PhD, U. Chgo., 1954; LLD (hon.), Mills Coll., 1963. Reporter Chgo. Daily News,

1936-38, corr. India and Pakistan, 1946-48, 49-50; assoc. Inst. Current World Affairs, 1938-41, 46-51; instr. U. Chgo., 1948-50, Columbia U., NYC, 1951; exec. dir. Am. Univs. Field Staff, 1951-61; asst. sec. Near Eastern and S. Asian affairs Dept. State, 1961-65; U.S. amb. to Greece, 1965-69; pres. Asia Soc., NYC, 1970-81, pres. emeritus, 1981—. Phi Beta Kappa vis. scholar, 1973-74. Author: (with S.L. Poplai) India and America, 1958, India in the 1980s, 1983; editor: South Asia in the World Today, 1950. Trustee emeritus Aspen Inst., U.S.-Japan Found.; counselor United Bd. for Christian Higher Edn. in Asia; elder Presbyn. Ch. 2d lt. cav. Officers Res. Corps, 1936; 1st lt. N.G., 1937-38; lt. comdr. USNR, 1941-46. Recipient Padma Shri honors, India, 2002, Bharatiya Shiromani Purskar award, 2006. Mem. Am. Acad. Diplomacy, Coun. Am. Ambs., Coun. Fgn. Rels., Century Assn., Cosmos Club. Address: 200 E 66th St New York NY 10021-9175 E-mail: talbotp@pipeline.com.

**TALBOT, PIERRE JOSEPH,** microbiologist, researcher; b. Quebec City, Que., Can., July 11, 1956; s. Arthur and Suzanne (Hudon) T.; m. France Ouellet, July 29, 1977; children: Natalie, Benoit, Dominic. BSc in Biochemistry, Laval U., Ste-Foy, Que., 1977; PhD in Biochemistry, U. B.C., Vancouver, 1981. Rsch. assoc. Scripps Clinic and Rsch. Found., La Jolla, Calif., 1981-84; asst. prof. Inst. Armand-Frappier U. Que., Laval, 1984-89; assoc. prof. Inst. Armand-Frappier, Laval, Que., 1989-92, prof., 1992—, dir. Human Health Rsch. Ctr., 1998—2001; dir. INRS Inst. Armand-Frappier, 2002—. Com. reviewer Med. Rsch. Coun., Ottawa, Ont., Can., 1989-96, 98-2000, Multiple Sclerosis Soc., Toronto, Ont., 1993-96, Nat. Sci. Engring. Res. Coun., Ottawa, 1999-2002, Can. Inst. Health Rsch., 1999—. Mem. editl. bd. Viral Immunology, San Antonio, 1990-99; contbr. articles to Virology, Jour. Virology, Annals Neurology, Jour. Immunology. Fonds de la Recherche en Santé du Que. scholar of exceptional merit, 1992-97. Mem. AAAS, Am. Soc. Virology, Am. Soc. Microbiology, Can. Soc. Microbiologists (Fisher Sci. award 1987, Roche Diagnostics award 2002), Can. Soc. Immunology, Assn. Can.-Francaise Pour L'Avancement des Scis., Internat. Soc. Neuroimmunology, Internat. Soc. Neurovirology. Achievements include research in immuno- and molecular biology of neurotropic coronaviruses and possible involvement in neurologic disease. Home: 38 59th Ave Laval PQ Canada H7V 2A9 Office: INRS Inst Armand-Frappier 531 Boul Des Prairies Laval PQ Canada H7V 1B7 Office Phone: 450-686-5515. E-mail: pierre.talbot@iaf.inrs.ca.

**TALBOTT, BEN JOHNSON, JR.,** lawyer; b. Louisville, May 2, 1940; s. Ben Johnson and Elizabeth (Farnsley) Talbott; m. Sandra Riehl, Oct. 19, 1963; children: Elizabeth, Betty, John, Ben, Sandra. AB magna cum laude, Xavier U., Cin., 1961; LLB, Harvard U., 1964. Bar: Ky. 1965, U.S. Ct. Appeals (6th cir.) 1967. Law clk. to presiding justice U.S. Dist. Ct. Ky., Louisville, 1964-65; assoc. Middleton, Reutlinger & Baird, Louisville, 1965-68, ptnr., 1968-80, Westfall, Talbott & Woods, Louisville, 1980-2000, Talbott & Talbott, PLLC, Louisville, 2000—04, Bardenwerper, Talbott & Roberts, PLLC, Louisville, 2004—. Atty. Stitzel-Weller Distillery, 1970—72, Louisville Gen. Hosp., 1974—83, Louisville and Jefferson County Bd. Health, 1974—80, U. Louisville, 1980—95. Mem. adv. bd. Louisville 15, Sta. WKPC-TV, bd. dirs., 1972—74, pres., 1974; past bd. dirs. U. Louisville Found., U. Louisville Med. Sch. Fund Orgn.; bd. dirs. Louisville Theatrical Assn., 1971—, pres., 1975—76, chmn., 1977—78; bd. dirs. Def. Enterprise Fund, 1994—, Macauley Theatre, 1975, TARC Adv. Com., 1971, Jefferson County Capital Constrn. Com., 1971, Louisville Orch., 1976—86, pres., 1979—81; bd. dirs. Ky. Ctr. Arts, 1983—, Louisville Lung Assn., 1974—75, treas., 1975; bd. dirs. Hist. Homes Found., 1972—78, 1995—97, 2000—01, 2002—, v.p., 1978, 2002—, advisor, atty., 1978—98; bd. regents Villarrial, 1993—2001; trustee U. Louisville, 1970—79, sec., 1974, vice chmn., 1975, chmn. fin. com., 1976. Named Outstanding Young Men of Louisville, Louisville Jaycees, 1976. Mem.: SAR, ABA, Louisville Bar Assn. (past mem. exec. com.), Def. Rsch. and Trial Lawyers Assn., Ky. Bar Assn. (chmn. 1989, Gen. Practice Session of CLE), Gulf Stream Bath and Tennis Club, Louisville Boat Club, Pendennis Club, Soc. Colonial Wars, Harvard Law Sch. Assn. Ky. (sec. 1965, pres. 1989—), Mayflower Soc., Filson Club, Louisville Country Club, U. Louisville Club, Big Sand Lake Club, Phi Kappa Phi (bd. dirs., treas. Louisville chpt. 1990—). Avocations: golf, tennis, skiing, fishing. Home: 566 Blankenbaker Ln Louisville KY 40207-1167 Office: Bardenwerper Talbott & Roberts PLLC 8311 Shelbyville Rd Louisville KY 40222 Office Phone: 502-426-6688. Business E-mail: lynn@bardlaw.net.

**TALBOTT, FRANK, III,** lawyer; b. Danville, Va., Mar. 26, 1929; s. Frank and Margaret (Jordan) Talbott; m. Mary Beverley Chewning, July 11, 1952; children: Beverley, Frank IV. BA, U. Va., 1951, LLB, 1953. Bar: Va. 1952. With firm Meade, Talbott & Tate, Danville, 1956—59, Talbott, Wheatley & Talbott, Danville, 1959—66; with Dan River Inc., 1966-76, v.p., gen. counsel, 1968-76; ptnr. firm Clement, Wheatley, Winston, Talbott & Majors, Danville, 1977-78; individual practice law Danville 1979-92; gen. counsel Va. Mfrs. Assn. Inc., 1983-92; of counsel Woods, Rogers PLC, Danville, Va., 1992—. Chmn. adv. bd. NationsBank, Danville, 1984-94. Vice-chmn. Danville Sch. Bd., 1964-70; trustee Va. Student Aid Found., 1963-68; bd. dirs. United Fund Danville, 1959-63, Meml. Hosp., Danville, 1977-90. Served with AUS, 1953-56. Decorated Commendation medal. Fellow Am. Bar Found. (life); mem. Va. Bar Assn. (v.p. 1965-66, exec. com. 1967-70), Danville Bar Assn. (pres. 1965-66), Am. Judicature Soc., Newcomen Soc., U. Va. Alumni Assn. (bd. mgrs.), Danville Golf Club, Farmington Country Club, Country Club Va., Country Club of North Carolina, Delta Psi, Phi Alpha Delta. Methodist. Home: 221 Salisbury Cir Danville VA 24541-5571 Office: 341 Main St Danville VA 24541

**TALBOTT, STROBE,** think-tank executive; b. Dayton, Ohio, Apr. 25, 1946; s. Nelson S. and Josephine (Large) T.; m. Brooke Lloyd Shearer, Nov. 14, 1971; children: Devin Lloyd, Adrian Nelson. BA, Yale U., 1968, MA (hon.), 1976. Mford Union, Eng. 1971. Past European corr. Time Mag., 1971-73, U.S. state dept. corr., 1973-75, white house corr., 1975-77, diplomatic corr., 1977-84, chief Washington bur. & fgn. affairs columnist, 1984-89, editor at large, 1989-91; amb. at large & spl. advisor to the Sec. of State on the new independent states U.S. Dept. State, Washington, 1993—94, dep. sec. state, 1994—2001; pres. Brookings Instn., Washington, 2002—. Editor, translator: Khrushchev Remembers, 1970, (with Edward Crankshaw) Khrushchev Remembers: The Last Testament, 1974, The Age of Terror: America & The World After September 11, 2001; author: Endgame: Inside Story of SALT II, 1979, Deadly Gambits: Reagan Administration & Arms Controls, 1984, The Russians and Reagan, 1984, Reagan and Gorbachev, 1987, The Master of the Game: Paul Nitze and the Nuclear Peace, 1988, (with Michael Beschloss) At the Highest Levels: The Inside Story of the End of the Cold War, 1993, The Russia Hand: A Memoir of Presidential Diplomacy, 2002, (with Robert L. Suettinger) Beyond Tiananmen: The Politics of U.S.-China Relations 1989-2000, 2003, Engaging India: Diplomacy, Democracy, and the Bomb, 2004. Trustee Yale U. 1976-82, Hotchkiss Sch., 1982-87; bd. dirs. Carnegie Endowment Internat. Peace; Council on Fgn. Relations. Recipient Edward Weintal Prize for Disting. Diplomatic Reporting Georgetown U., Overseas Press Club award, Stanley Hillman award. Office: The Brookings Instn 1775 Massachusetts Ave NW Washington DC 20036

**TALEN, BRUCE L.,** lawyer; s. James and Joyce Talen; m. Greta Volk, Feb. 0, 1989; children: Julia, Peter. BA, St. Olaf Coll., 1979; JD, Washington U., St. Louis, 1983. Cert. CFA Inst., 2004; bar: Ill. 1983, Mo. 1984, Minn. 1984. Market trust exec. Bank of Am., St. Louis, 2001—04; sr. counsel Commerce Trust Co., St. Louis, 2004—. Bd. dirs Eastwood Fin. Corp., Rochester, Minn. Bd. dirs. Rohan Woods Sch., St. Louis, 1999—2005. Mem.: Investment Co. Inst. Avocation: cycling. Office: Commerce Trust Co 8000 Forsyth Blvd Saint Louis MO 63105 Office Phone: 314-746-7338. Business E-mail: bruce.talen@commercebank.com.

**TALENT, JAMES MATTHES,** senator, former congressman, lawyer; b. Des Peres, Mo., Oct. 18, 1956; m. Brenda Lyons, 1984; children: Michael, Kathleen Marie, Christine. BA in Polit. Sci., Washington U., 1978; JD, U. Chgo. Law Sch., 1981. Law clk. 7th Ct. Appeals, 1981-82; adj. prof. law, 1982-84; mem. Mo. State Ho. Reps., 1984-93; minority leader, 1989-93; mem. 103rd-106th Congresses from 2nd Mo. Dist., 1993—2001, mem. edn.

and the workforce com., armed svcs. com., chmn. small bus. com., 1993—2001; US Senator from Mo., 2002—. Legislative Achievement award Mo. Hosp. Assn., 1989, Legis. of Yr. award Dept. Mo. Veterans Fgn. Wars, Spirit Enterprise award, Mo. C. of C., 1990, Nat. Public Policy award Nat. Assn. Women Bus. Owners, Lifetime Achievement award Vietnam Veterans of Am. 2000, Lawmaker of Yr. award Independent Electrical Contractors, Inc., 2004 Mem. Mo. Bar Assn. (Award for significant contbns. to adminstrv. justice 1989), Mo. C. of C. (Spirit of Enterprise award 1990), Order of the Coif. Republican. Presbyterian. Office: US Senate 493 Russell Senate Office Building Washington DC 20510 also: District Office 2nd Floor 122 E High St Jefferson City MO 65101-2960 Office Phone: 202-224-6154, 573-636-1070. Office Fax: 202-228-1518, 575-638-3891.*

**TALENTO-MILLER, EILEEN,** psychometrician; b. Naples, Italy, Oct. 30, 1970; d. Romualdo Diezmo and Scindia Velez Talento; m. James Brian Miller, Nov. 18, 1995; children: Elizabeth Amber Miller, James Zachary Miller. BA in Theatre and Math., Coll. William and Mary, 1992; MS in Edni. Psychology, Miss. State U., 2000, PhD in Edni. Psychology, 2004. Math. tchr. Virginia Beach (Va.) City Pub. Schs., 1992—98; rsch. studies mgr. Grad. Mgmt. Admission Coun., McLean, Va., 2003—. Actor: (play) Steel Magnolias, (musical) Godspell, West Side Story. Lector Sacred Heart Cath. Ch., Louisville, Miss., 2002—03. Nat. Hispanic scholar, 1988. Mem.: APA, Mid-South Edni. Rsch. Assn., Nat. Coun. on Measurement in Edn., Am. Edni. Rsch. Assn. Office Phone: 703-749-0131. Personal E-mail: lanietay@aol.com.

**TALESE, GAY,** writer; b. Ocean City, NJ, Feb. 7, 1932; s. Joseph Francis and Catherine (DiPaola) T.; m. Nan Ahearn, June 10, 1959; children— Pamela, Catherine. BA in Journalism, U. Ala., 1953. Staff writer N.Y. Times, N.Y.C., 1955-65; writer Esquire mag., N.Y.C., 1960. Author: New York - A Serendipiter's Journey, 1961, The Bridge, 1964, The Overreachers, 1965, The Kingdom and the Power, 1969, Fame and Obscurity, 1970, Honor Thy Father, 1971, Thy Neighbor's Wife, 1980, Unto the Sons, 1992, A Writer's Life, 2006; co-author: (with Barbara Lounsberry) The Literature of Reality, 1995; editor: Italians in America: A Celebration, 2001, The Gay Talese Reader, 2003; contbr. articles to Esquire mag., The New Yorker, others. Served to 1st lt. AUS, 1954-56. Mem. P.E.N. (v.p. 1984-87, bd. dir. 1980—), Phi Sigma Kappa. Home: 109 E 61st St New York NY 10021-8101 also: 154 E Atlantic Blvd Ocean City NJ 08226-4511 Office Phone: 212-753-3820.

**TALESE, NAN AHEARN,** freelance/self-employed publishing executive; b. NYC, Dec. 19, 1933; d. Thomas James and Suzanne Sherman (Russell) Ahearn; m. Gay Talese, June 10, 1959; children: Pamela Frances, Catherine Gay. BA, Manhattanville Coll. of Sacred Heart, 1955; LHD (hon.), Manhattanville, 2003. Fgn. exchange student 1st Nat. City Bank, London and Paris, 1956; editorial asst. Am. Eugenics Soc., NYC, 1957-58, Vogue mag., NYC, 1958-59; copy editor Random House Pub., NYC, 1959-64, assoc. editor, 1964-67, sr. editor, 1967-73, Simon & Schuster Pubs., NYC, 1974-81, v.p., 1979-81; exec. editor, v.p. Houghton Mifflin Co., NYC, 1981-83, v.p., editor-in-chief, 1984-86, v.p., pub., editor-in-chief, 1986-88; sr. v.p. Doubleday & Co., NYC, 1988—; pres., pub., editorial dir. Nan A. Talese Books, 1990—.*

**TALIAFERRO, ROBERT See BROOKE, TAL**

**TALL, CRAIG E.,** finance company executive; B in Econs., U. Pa.; postgrad., U. Calif., Berkeley. Former pres. Compensation Programs, Inc.; exec. v.p. WM Fin. Washington Mut., Inc., 1985—87, exec. v.p. corp. devel., 1987—99, mem. exec. team, 1990—, vice chair corp. devel., 1999—2002, vice chair for corp. devel. and strategic planning, 2002—. Founder, past pres. bd. trustees Seattle Acad. Arts and Scis.; former pres. bd. trustees Wash. chpt. Leukemia Soc. Am.; mem. corporate adv. coun. Puget Sound Blood Ctr. Office: Washington Mut Inc 1201 3d Ave Seattle WA 98101

**TALL, SONIA TERRY,** humanities educator, researcher; arrived in U.S., 1993; m. Abasse Tall; children: Amadou, Mouhamadou, Oumar, Billy. BA, U. Paris IV, 1981, PhD, 1991. Asst. prof. Roosevelt U., Chgo., 1995—2003, Kennedy-King Coll., Chgo., 2003—. Author: (literary criticism) Collective creation in Soyinka's Dance of the Forests, The New Negro Movement and the African Heritage, (film criticism) African Cinema as a Tool for Development. Recipient Peace Edn. award for St Mary Sch., Senegal, UNESCO, 1990. Mem.: Coll. Lang. Assn. Personal E-mail: tall_abasse@sbcglobal.net.

**TALL, SUSAN PORTER,** music educator; b. NYC, Apr. 16, 1942; m. Alan R. Tall, July 27, 1979; 1 child, Alexander A.; m. Burton F. Porter (div.); 1 child from previous marriage, Anastasia Porter. BA, Montclair State U., 1965; MA in Musicology, NYU, 1973; postgrad., U. Ill., 1978—80. Instr. music Am. Sch. London, 1966—68; instr. music, dir. inst. music Russell Sage Coll., Troy, NY, 1971—74; grad. asst. in conducting U. Ill., Champaigne-Urbana, 1978—79; mem. faculty music Tenafly Sch. Sys., NJ, 1980—. Dir. music, condr. Presbyn. Ch., Tenafly, 1980—90, 1995—2005, North Jersey Symphony Orch., Tenafly, 1984—89, Concerto Orch. N.J., Tenafly, 1986—88; guest condr. in field. Organizer, dir. Fanfare for Humanity, Tenafly, 2001, 2005, THS Chorus and Orch. Benefit, Tenafly, 2005. Nominee Disting. Secondary Sch. Tchg. award, Princeton U., 1990; named Tchr. of Yr., Tenafly Sch. Dist., 2002; recipient Disting. Tchg. award, Tenafly H.S., 2002, Tchr. Recognition award, Gov., N.J., 2002, Disting. Leadership in Arts Edn. award, Gov. of N.J., 1997. Mem.: N.J. Music Educators Assn. (Master Tchr. award 1997). Avocation: classical guitar. Home: PO Box 104 Cresskill NJ 07626 Office: Tenafly Sch Dist Dept Music 19 Columbus Dr Tenafly NJ 07626 Office Phone: 201-816-6621. Business E-Mail: stall@tenafly.k12.nj.us.

**TALLAPRAGADA, VIJAY KUMAR,** research scientist; b. Draksharama, Andhra Pradesh, India, July 3, 1971; arrived in U.S., 1999; s. Lakshmana Rao V. and Annapurna S. Tallapragada; m. Seshu V. Dinavahi, Apr. 30, 1998; 1 child, Lasya S. PhD, Andhra U., Visakhapatnam, India, 2000. Rsch. assoc. Fla. State U., Tallahassee, 1999—2006; scientist Nat. Ctrs. for Environ. Prediction/Environ. Modeling Ctr., Camp Springs, Md., 2006—. Achievements include first to improved typhoon forecasts from superensemble. Office: Environmental Modeling Center NCEP 5200 Auth Rd Camp Springs MD 20746 Office Phone: 301-763-8000. Business E-Mail: vijay.tallapragada@noaa.gov.

**TALLENT, HAMLIN B.,** career officer; BSEd, Southwest Mo. State U., 1972; Diploma, Indsl. Coll. of Armed Forces, 1991; MPA, George Washington U. Commd. ensign USN, 1973, advanced through ranks to rear adm.; various assignments to exec. officer, comdr. Ghostriders/USS Eisenhower, 1988-89; various to comdr. Tactical Tng. Group, Atlantic, 1997-98; head detailer for Naval Aviation Officers Bur. of Naval Personnel, 1998; asst. comdr. Navy Personnel Command.

**TALLENT, STEPHEN EDISON,** lawyer; b. Columbus, Nebr., Aug. 10, 1937; s. William E. and Helen Tallent; m. Martha Sutcliffe, Apr. 6, 1971; 1 child, Jennifer Diane. BA, Stanford U.; JD, U. Chgo.; LLD (hon.), Lincoln U. Bar: Calif. 1963, U.S. Dist. Ct. (so. and cen. dists.) Calif. 1965, U.S. Dist. Ct. (so. and ea. dists.) N.Y. 1989, U.S. Ct. Appeals (D.C. cir. 1981), U.S. Ct. Appeals (2d cir.) 1987, U.S. Ct. Appeals (3d. cir.) 1980, U.S. Ct. Appeals (4th cir.) 1982, U.S. Ct. Appeals (9th cir.) 1968, U.S. Ct. Mil. Appeals 1965, U.S. Supreme Ct. 1973. Ptnr. Gibson, Dunn & Crutcher, L.A., 1962-96; pvt. practice Washington, 1997—. Former adj. prof. Loyola Law Sch., L.A.; mem. vis. com. U. Chgo. Law Sch.; former mem. Calif. Atty. Gen.'s adv. com. for Evaluation of Anti-Organized Crime Programs; mem. L.A. Town Hall, L.A. World Affairs Council; mem. bd. visitors Stanford Law Sch.; founding dir. Am. Employment Law Coun., 1993—. Fellow Coll. Labor and Employment Lawyers (founding, pres. and gov. 1995—); mem. ABA (chair labor and employment law sect. 1998-99), Indsl. Rels. Rsch. Assn. Home: PO Box 512 Reedville VA 22539-0512 Office: 1050 Connecticut Ave NW Ste 900 Washington DC 20036-5320 Office Phone: 202-955-8552.

**TALLETT, ELIZABETH EDITH,** biopharmaceutical company executive; b. London, Apr. 2, 1949; d. Edward and Edith May (Vickers) Symons; m. James Edward Wavle Jr.; children: James Edward Tallett, Alexander Martin Tallett, Christopher Andrew Wavle. BS with honors, U. Nottingham (Eng.), 1970. Ops. rsch. analyst So. Gas Bd., 1970-73; mgmt. svcs. mgr. Warner-Lamber (UK), Eastleigh, England, 1973-77, strategic planning mgr., 1977-81; internat. dir. strategic planning Warner-Lambert, Morris Plains, NJ, 1981-82, corp. dir. strategic planning, 1982-84; dir. mktg. ops. Parke-Davis, Morris Plains, 1984-87; exec. v.p. therapeutic products Centocor, Malvern, Pa., 1987-89, pres. pharms. div., 1989-92; pres., CEO Transcell Techs., Inc., Monmouth Junction, NJ, 1992-96, Dioscor, Inc., Stockton, 1996—2003; prin. Hunter Ptnrs. LLC, 2002—. Bd. dirs. Prin. Fin. Group, Inc., Varian, Inc., Coventry Health Care, Inc., IntegraMed Am. Inc., Immunicon Inc., Varian Semi Conductor Equipment Assoc. Inc.; dir. Biotech. Coun. N.J., NJ Ctr. Life Sci. Contbr. articles to profl. jours. Avocations: acting, badminton, travel, skiing. Personal E-mail: dioscor@comcast.net.

**TALLEY, BRENDA S.,** performing arts center director, theatrical light designer; b. Las Vegas, Nev., Jan. 17, 1955; d. Wanda Marie and Milton Rex Linn; m. Donald P. Kennedy, June 19, 2001); m. Douglas L. Talley, Nov. 29, 2003; children: Ryan Rex Kennedy, Krista Marie Kennedy, Dawnie Rose Kennedy, Breanna (Annie) Linn Kennedy. AA in Gen. Studies, C.C. So. Nev., 1989; BA in Bus. Mgmt., St. Regis U., 2002. Ho. mgr. C.C. So. Nev. Performing Arts Ctr., 1996—2000; performing arts ctr. asst. dir. C.C. So. Nev., 2000—02, performing arts ctr. dir., 2002—. Mem. C.C. So. Nev. Lecture Com., 2000—; chmn. C.C. So. Nev. Honors Com., 2000—02, Campus Environment Coun., North Las Vegas, 2000—02; mem. Nev. C.C. Conf., 2001—02. V.p. Tule Springs Preservation Com., Las Vegas, 1998—2003; vice chair Congress of States Nat. Parent Tchr. Assn., Chgo., 1999—2001; pres. Nev. Parent Teachers Assn., Las Vegas, 1999—2001. Recipient Hon. Life Membership, Nat. PTA, 1994, Nev. PTA, 1996, Parent Hall of Fame, Clark County Sch. Dist., 1996, High Honors, Phi Theta Kappa, 1989. Mem.: AAUP (assoc.), Nev. Faculty Alliance (assoc.). Democrat. Latter Day Saint. Avocations: theater, rapelling, hiking, camping, music. Office: Community College Southern Nevada 3200 East Cheyenne Ave North Las Vegas NV 89030

**TALLEY, CHARLES RICHMOND,** retired bank executive; b. Richmond, Va., Dec. 23, 1925; s. Charles Edward and Marie (Thorckmorton) Talley; m. Anne Marie Smith, June 4, 1948; children: Laurie Anne, Charles Richmond Jr. BA in Econs, U. Richmond, 1949; postgrad., Rutgers U., 1959-61, Northwestern U., 1954-55; grad. exec. program U. Va., 1974. Asst. cashier 1st & Mchts. Nat. Bank, Richmond, 1955-57, asst. v.p., 1957-63, v.p.) 1963-69, sr. v.p., 1969-73, exec. v.p., 1973-84; corp. exec. officer Sovran Bank N.A., 1984-86, ret., 1986, 1986. Bd dirs Security Atlantic Life Ins Co; vpres, bd dirs Security Atlantic Ins Agency; bd dirs Sovran Properties Inc; vice chmn bd dirs Va Educ Loan Authority, 1983—87, chmn, 1988—91; vpres, mem exec comt Richmond Eye and Ear Hosp, pres, 1988—91. Pres Richmond Jr Cof C, 1960—61; treas Richmond chpt Nat Found, 1956—; pres Baptist Extension Bd Va, 1973—75; bd dirs Commonwealth Eye and Ear, 1986—89, Richmond Symphony Orchestra, Richmond Better Bus Bur. With USNR, 1944—46. Mem.: Richmond Clearing House Asn (pres 1977), Richmond Metropolitan CofC (bd dirs 1979—89), The Tartan Golf Course (Irvington, Va), Bull and Bear Club, Willow Oaks Country Club Richmond (pres 1971), Rotary (bd dirs Richmond 1981—83). Home: 4301 Stratford Rd Richmond VA 23225-1060 also: Bldg 2 Unit 2 The Green At Tides Lodge Irvington VA 22480

**TALLEY, HAYWARD LEROY,** communications executive; b. Nov. 3, 1923; s. Roy and Reta (Hayward) T.; m. Emma Mae Chandler, Sept. 2, 1950; children: Brian, Kevin. BS, U. Ill., 1948. Chief engr. Sta. WOKZ-AM-FM, Alton, Ill., 1948-50; pres., gen. mgr. Talley Broadcasting Corp. (sta. WSMI AM and FM), Litchfield, Ill., 1950—; pres. Talley Broadcasting Co. (sta. KBKB AM and FM), Ft. Madison, Iowa, 1960-99, North Cen. Iowa Broadcasting Co. (stas. KLSS, KSMN), Mason City, 1963-83, Talley Broadcasting Corp. (sta. WAOX), Staunton, Ill., 1999—. Chmn. ofcl. bd. Meth. Ch., 1961-63, 65-66, chmn. ch. coun., 2003-05; adv. bd. Lewis & Clark Coll., 1978—; adv. coun. St. Francis Hosp., 1992—. With Signal Corps, U.S. Army. Recipient Vincent T. Wasilewski Broadcaster of Yr. award, Ill. Broadcasters Assn., 2002. Mem.: Ill. Broadcasters Assn., Nat. Assn. Broadcasters, Am. Legion, Masons, Rotary (pres. Litchfield Club 1989—90). Home: 1414 N Harrison St Litchfield IL 62056-1209 Office: Sta WSMI PO Box 10 Litchfield IL 62056-0010

**TALLEY, JOSEPH EUGENE,** psychologist; b. Springfield, Mass., May 27, 1949; s. Joseph Addison and Miriam Louise (Ayers) T.; m. Vibeke Absalon, Jan. 3, 1981; children: Kirsten, David, Jonathan. BA, U. Richmond, 1971; MA, Radford Coll., 1973; PhD, U. Va., 1978. Diplomate Am. Bd. Profl. Psychology; lic. psychologist, N.C.; cert. health svc. provider, N.C. Clin. prof. med. psychology Duke U. Med. Ctr., Durham, NC, 1977—, asst. dir., counseling and psychol. svcs., 1979—; gen. practice psychotherapy Durham, 1980—. Author: Study Skills, 1981, Performance Prediciton of Law Enforcement Personnel, 1990, The Predictors of Successful Very Brief Psychotherapy, 1992, Seeking Something Sacred: Managing Our Frustrations, Losses and Fears, 2001; author, editor: Counseling and Psychotherapy Services, 1985, Counseling and Psychotherapy with College Students: A Guide to Treatment, 1986, Multicultural Needs Assessment with College and University Populations, 1995; contbr. articles to profl. jours. Bd. deacons Hillsborough Presbyn. Ch., N.C., 1983-85, chmn., 1985, bd. elders, 1987-94, 2002—, v.p. bd. trustees, 1992-94; bd. dirs. Orange County Mental Health Assn., Chapel Hill, N.C., 1982-83, mem. legis. com., 1983, site visitor for accreditation, Fellow APA (awards com. divsn. 17, 2002-05, chair awards com. 2006), Am. Acad. Clin. Psychology, Am. Acad. Counseling Psychology, Am. Acad. Counseling Psychology (pres. 1995-97, Disting. Svc. award 2002); mem. Am. Bd. Profl. Psychology (sec./treas. coun. of pres.'s psychology splty. acads. 1997-98, chmn./CEO 2000-03, spl. liaison to related groups 2003—, past chmn., CEO 2003-05, exec. bd. and spl. liaison to congress and related profl. groups, 2005—, Disting. Contbns. award 2002), N.C. Psychol. Assn., Nat. Soc. Clin. Hypnosis (cert. and approved cons., supr. and practitioner, ethics com. 1995-97), Phi Kappa Phi, Omicron Delta Kappa, Psi Chi, Phi Kappa Sigma. Democrat. Presbyterian. Home: 134 E Tryon St Hillsborough NC 27278-2550 Office: Duke U Counseling & Psychol Svcs PO Box 90955 214 Page Bldg Durham NC 27708-0955 Office Phone: 919-660-1000. Business E-mail: jtalley@duke.edu.

**TALLEY, MELVIN GARY,** academic administrator; b. West Chester, Pa., Feb. 26, 1945; s. Melvin G. and Alberta M. (Faddis) T.; m. Jolene Keller (div.); children: Kristin Jolene, Mark Gary. BS, Pa. State U., 1967; D (hon.), Bristol (Tenn.) Coll., 1988; MBA, U. Mo., 1998. Registered rep. DeHaven & Townsend, Phila., 1967-68; dir. Brown Mackie Coll., Salina and Overland Park, Kans., 1968-72, pres., 1972—94, emeritus, also bd. chmn.; mng. ptnr. ETG Partnership, LP, 2002—. Pres. Realty Mgmt. Investment Co., Salina, 1976—94; advisor region VI HEW, 1976-86, chmn. Region VII Adv. Proprietary Coun., 1989; mem. adv. bd. U.S. Office of Edn., 1988; chmn. region VII Coun. for Pvt. Career Colls. and Schs., 1989. Author: Reassessing Values in Postsecondary Edn., 1977. Bd. dirs. St. Francis Boys Home, Salina, 1975; trustee duPont, Hagley Mus. and Libr., 2004—. Mem. Pvt. Edn. Research Council, Inner Circle, Assn. Ind. Colls. and Schs. (bd. dirs.), Washington chpt. 1976-78), Claymont Savings and Loan Assn. (bd. dirs.), Hagley Mus. and Libr. (trustee, 2004—). Home: 4609 W 113th Terr Brittany Ct Leawood KS 66211 Office: ETG Partnership LP 4609 W 113th Terr Leawood KS 66217 Office Phone: 913-491-9348.

**TALLEY, NICHOLAS JOSEPH,** medical educator, research scientist, physician; b. Perth, Australia, Jan. 9, 1956; arrived in U.S., 2002; s. Nicholas Alexander and Irene Mary Talley; m. Catherine Elizabeth Davies, Dec. 30, 2004; children: Nicholas Stephen, Matthew Jonathon, Nicole Sarah. MB, BS, U. NSW, 1979; PhD, U. Sydney, 1987; MD, U. NSW, 1993, M in Med. Sci., 2003. Resident med. officer/registrar Prince of Wales Hosp., Sydney, 1979—83; rsch. fellow, prof. registrar Royal North Shore Hosp., Sydney,

1983—87; rsch. fellow Mayo Clinic, Rochester, Minn., 1987—88, asst. prof. medicine, 1988—91, assoc. prof., 1991—93; head divsn. medicine, prof. medicine Nepean Hosp., Sydney, 1993—2001; area dir. medicine Westworth Area Health Svc., Nepean Hosp., Sydney, 2001—02; prof. medicine, cons. Mayo Clinic, Rochester, 2003—. Author: (textbooks) Examination Medicine, 1985, 5th edit., 2006, Clinical Examination, 1988, 5th edit., 2006, Internal Medicine, 1990, 2d edit., 2000, Clinical Gastroenterology, 1996, 2d edit., 2006, Multiple Choice Questions in Clinical Examination, 1996, Pocket Clinical Examination, 1998, 2d edit., 2002, Conquering Irritable Bowel Syndrome, 2006, Conquering Lower Gastrointestinal Disorders, 2006; asst. editor Am. Jour. Gastroenterology, 1992-97; co-editor-in-chief, Am. Jour. Gastroenterology, 2004—; mem. editl. bd. Gastroenterology, 1993-98, Jour. Clin. Gstroenterology, 1994—, Alimentary Pharmacology and Therapeutics, 1995-2003, Jour. Gastroenterology and Hepatology, 1994-98, editor, 1998-2003; contbr. articles and revs. to profl. jours., chpts. to books. Pres. Miranda br. Young Liberals, Sydney, 1976; wing comdr. Royal Australia Air Force, 2000. Postgrad. rsch. scholar Nat. Health and Med. Rsch. Coun., Australia, 1984-85. Fellow ACP, Royal Australasian Coll. Physicians, Am. Coll. Gastroent., Australian Faculty Pub. Health Medicine (founding mem.), Royal Coll. Physicians; mem. Am. Gastroent. Assn., Gastroent. Soc. Australia, Brit. Soc. Gastroenterology, Functional Brain Gut Rsch. Group (pres.). Avocations: tennis, writing, travel, jogging, martial arts. Office: Mayo Clinic 200 First St SW PL-6 Rochester MN 55905 Office Phone: 507-266-1989. Business E-Mail: talley.nicholas@mayo.edu.

**TALLEY, RICHARD WOODROW**, accountant; b. Birmingham, Ala., Sept. 10, 1941; s. Alton Woodrow and Alta O. (Tittle) T.; m. Anita Marcell Moses, Jan. 14, 1966; children: Richard Woodrow Jr., Leah Michelle. BS in Commerce and Bus. Adminstrn., U. Ala., 1964. CPA Ala. Pres. Talley, Maulding & Peete, PC, Decatur, Ala., 1964—. Officer Boy Scouts Am. Decatur, Austin Band Boosters, Decatur, PTA, Decatur; mgr., coach Dixie Youth Baseball, Decatur; deacon Ch. of Christ. Served as sgt. USAR, 1964-70. Named Boss of Yr. Decatur Jaycees, 1980. Mem. AICPA, Tenn. Soc. CPAs, Ala. Soc. CPAs, Commerce Execs. Soc. U. Ala., Lions (sec. 1982-83, treas. 1985-86, sec.-treas. 1994-95). Avocations: genealogy, photography. Home: 1266 Brandywine Ln SE Decatur AL 35601-4582 Office: Talley Mauldin & Peete PC PO Box 2067 Decatur AL 35602-2067 Office Phone: 256-353-1421. Business E-Mail: richard@tmpcpa.com.

**TALLEY, ROBERT COCHRAN**, academic administrator, cardiologist; b. May 26, 1936; m. Katherine Ann Plocar; children: Andrew, Katherine, David. BS, U. Mich., 1958; MD, U. Chgo., 1962. Diplomate Nat. Bd. Med. Examiners (mem. medicine com. 1984-88, com. chair 1988-93). Asst. prof., dept. physiology and medicine U. Tex. Med. Sch., San Antonio, 1969—71, head, sect. cardiovascular diseases, 1971—75, assoc. prof., dept. medicine, 1971—75; acting chief medicine VA Hosp., San Antonio, 1974, chief cardiology svc., 1973—75; chmn. dept. internal medicine U. SD Sch. Medicine, Sioux Falls, 1975—87, Freeman prof. medicine, 1984—87, interim v.p., dean, 1986—87, v.p., dean, 1987—2004, dir. residency program, 2004—. Mem. liaison com. med. edn., 1998—; Contbr. articles to med. jours. Surgeon USPHS, 1966—68. Tchg. scholar, Am. Heart Assn. U. Chgo., 1972—75. Fellow: ACP, Am. Coll. Cardiology; mem.: AMA, Liaison Com. on Med. Edn., Assn. Am. Med. Coll. (mem. coun. deans new dean mentoring program, mem. adminstrn. bd. coun. deans 1999—2004), Am. Fedn. Clin. Rsch., Am. Heart Assn. (bd. dirs. Dakota affiliate). Home: 1305 Cedar Ln Sioux Falls SD 57103-4512 Office: U SD Sch Medicine 1400 W 22nd St Sioux Falls SD 57105-1505 Business E-Mail: rtalley@usd.edu.

**TALLEY, STEVEN K.**, lawyer; b. May 5, 1962; BS in Physics, Harvey Mudd Coll., 1984; JD, Univ. Calif., Berkeley, 1991. Former mgr., mgmt. info. systems for a mfg. co.; ptnr., corp. transactions and securities Gibson Dunn & Crutcher LLP, Denver, 2000—, and ptnr.-in-charge Denver office. Articles editor High Technology Law Jour., 1990—91. Mem.: Order of Coif. Office: Gibson Dunn & Crutcher LLP Ste 4100 1801 California St Denver CO 80202 Office Phone: 303-298-5775. Office Fax: 303-313-2840. Business E-Mail: stalley@gibsondunn.com.

**TALLEY, TRUMAN MACDONALD**, publisher; b. NYC, Feb. 3, 1925; s. Truman Hughes and Helen Nicholson (Macdonald) T.; m. Madelon DeVoe, Oct. 17, 1953 (dec. 1997); children: Melanie, Macdonald, Marina. Student, Buckley Sch., Deerfield Acad., Sorbonne, 1945—46; grad. cum laude, Princeton U., 1949. Assoc. editor New Am. Libr. of World Lit., N.Y.C., 1949-59, editl. v.p., 1959-64; pres., editl. dir. Weybright & Talley, N.Y.C., 1966-78; pub. Truman Talley Books with Times Books, 1978-82; with E.P. Dutton, 1983-98, St. Martin's Press, N.Y.C., 1998—. Trustee Clinton Hall Assn. Merc. Libr., N.Y.C. With AUS, 1943-46, ETO. Decorated Purple Heart. Mem.: PEN. Office: Truman Talley Books St Martin's Press 175 5th Ave New York NY 10010-7703 Business E-Mail: truman.talley@stmartin's.com.

**TALLEY, VERNON ANDREW**, museum administrator; b. Balt., Feb. 13, 1968; s. Kenneth Franklyn Talley; m. Nancy Rae Gerhart, Dec. 30, 1988; 1 child, Rhiannon Victoria. BA in Art History, Calif. State U., LA, 1996. Exhibit tech. Calif. African Am. Mus., LA, 1995—98, registrar interpretive collections, 1998—. Presenter ann. meeting Associated Hist. Socs. LA County, 2003—03; presenter ann. conf. Packing, Art Handling & Crating Info. Network, Portland, 2003—03. Mem. NAACP, Balt., 2004—06. Sgt. U.S. Army, 1989—91. Decorated Army Achievement medal US Army, Army Commondation medal; scholar, Calif. State U., LA, 1994; Joseph Uribe Meml. scholar, 1994. Mem.: Packing, Art Handling & Crating Info. Network, Am. Assn. Museums (registrar's com.), Phi Kappa Phi, Golden Key Nat. Honor Soc. Independent. Office: Calif African Am Mus 600 State Dr Exposition Pk Los Angeles CA 90037 Office Phone: 213-744-2023. Office Fax: 213-744-2050. E-mail: dtalley@caamuseum.org.

**TALLMAN, ANN MARIE**, lawyer; b. Iowa; BS in Psychology and Polit. Sci., with distinction and spl. honors, U. Iowa; JD, U. Calif. Berkeley, Boalt Hall Sch. Law. Atty. Kutak Rock, Denver; dep. dir. & head Planning and Community Develop. Agy. City and County of Denver; with Fannie Mae, Pasadena, Calif., 1994—2004; pres., CEO Fannie Mae Found., Washington, 1998—99; pres., gen. counsel MALDEF (Mexican Am. Legal Def. and Edn. Fund), LA, 2004—06. Bd. mem. MALDEF (Mexican Am. Legal Def. and Edn. Fund), 1998—2006; bd. dirs. J. C. Penney Company, Inc., 2006—. Founding bd. mem. Hispanic PAC USA; exec. dir. Colo. Hispanic League, 1990.

**TALLMAN, DENNIS EARL**, chemistry professor, research scientist; b. Bellefontaine, Ohio, Apr. 23, 1942; s. Maurice Earl and Mary Elizabeth Tallman. PhD, Ohio State U., Columbus, 1968. Postdoctoral rsch. assoc. Cornell U., Ithaca, NY, 1968—70; asst. prof. of chemistry N.D. State U., Fargo, 1970—73, assoc. prof. of chemistry, 1973—78, prof. of chemistry, 1978—. Co-dir. Corrosion/Coatings Rsch. Ctr. N.D. State U., Fargo, 2000—. Contbr. articles to profl. jours. (Fred Waldren Award for Outstanding Rsch., 2000); N.Am. editor: Jour. Solid State Electrochemistry, 1997—. Recipient postdoctoral fellowship, NIH, 1968—70, numerous rsch. grants, NSF, Dept. of Def., NIH, and EPA, 1970—. Mem.: Nat. Assn. of Corrosion Engrs., Electrochem. Soc., Am. Chem. Soc. (lobbied Congress for increases in fed. rsch. funding 2000—03), Soc. for Electroanalytical Chemistry (life; bd. dirs. 1998—2002), Phi Kappa Phi, Sigma Xi, Phi Lambda Upsilon. Achievements include patents pending for Direct Electrodeposition of Conducting Polymers on Active Metals. Avocations: four-wall handball, skiing, canoeing, biking, backpacking. Office: ND State U Dept Chemistry Fargo ND 58105-5516 Business E-Mail: dennis.tallman@ndsu.edu.

**TALLMAN, MARTIN STUART**, hematologist, oncologist; b. Chgo., July 6, 1954; m. Wendy S. Tallman; children: Sarah Chaya, Miriam Leah, Samuel Joseph, Jacob Ezra. BS, U. Mich., Ann Arbor, 1976; MD, Chgo. Med. Sch., 1980. Cert. Am. Bd. Internal Medicine, 1983, in Hematology 1987, in Med. Oncology 1988. Intern, internal medicine McGaw Med. Ctr., Evanston, Ill., 1980—81, resident, internal medicine, 1981—83, chief resident, dept. medi-

cine, 1983—84; asst. attending physician Evanston Hosp., Ill., 1983—84, adj. attending physician, divsn. hematology and oncology, 1989—93; fellow, hematology and oncology U. Wash., Fred Hutchinson Cancer Rsch. Ctr., Seattle, 1984—87; attending physician, divsn. oncology VA Med. Ctr., Seattle, 1987—88; attending physician Rehab. Inst. of Chgo., 1988—; attending physician, divsn. hematology & oncology Northwestern Meml. Hosp., Chgo., 1988—; adj. attending physician, divsn. hematology & oncology Lakeside VA Med. Ctr., Chgo., 1988—; mem. Robert H. Lurie Cancer Ctr., Northwestern U., Evanston, Ill., 1988—, co-chmn., edn. com. 1989—, dir., clin. leukemia rsch. program, 1990—, asst. dir., bone marrow transplant program, 1991—2000, dir., hematological malignancy program, 2001—; asst. prof., divsn. hematology & oncology Northwestern U. Feinberg Sch. Medicine, Evanston, Ill., 1988—96, assoc. prof., divsn. hematology & oncology, 1996—2002, prof., divsn. hematology & oncology, 2002—. Med. adv. bd. mem. Leukemia Rsch. Found., 1992—97, chmn., med. adv. bd. 1997—99; mem. leustatin adv. bd. Pharms. Rsch. Inst., Raritan, NJ, 1993—; mem., internat. adv. group Pharmacia, 1995—; mem., autologous bone marrow transplant adv. group U.S. Gen. Acctg. Office, Dept. Health and Human Svcs., 1995—; mem., med. adv. bd. Earl J. Goldberg Aplastic Anemia Found., 1995—; mem., hematology adv. bd. Chiron Therapeutics, Emerville, Calif., 1996—; mem., med. adv. bd. Hairy Cell Leukemia Rsch. Found., 1996—; mem., adv. bd. Supergen, 1997—; mem., safety bd. Can. Leukemia Study Group, 1999—; mem., adv. bd. Searle/Monsanto, 1999—, Wyeth-Ayerst Pharm., 1999—. Recipient John T. O'Connell award, Chgo. Med. Soc., 1992. Fellow: ACP; mem.: AAAS, Am. Soc. for Blood and Marrow Transplantation, Eastern Cooperative Oncology Group (mem., leukemia com. 1989—, mem., myeloma com. 1989—, mem., bone marrow transplant com. 1989—, mem., cytogenetics subcom. 1991—, co-chmn., leukemia com. 1993—97, mem., bone marrow transplant instl. rev. com. 1993—, mem., audit team 1995—, chair, leukemia com. 1997—), Am. Soc. Clin. Oncology, Ill. Med. Oncology Soc., Ill. Cancer Ctr., Am. Fedn. Clin. Rsch., Am. Cancer Soc., Am. Assn. Cancer Rsch., Internat. Soc. Exptl. Hematology, Internat. Soc. Hematology (mem., internat. sci. com. 1999—), Am. Soc. Hematology (mem., subcom. on neoplasia 1998—, mem., subcom. on publs. 2000—), Internat. Soc. Thrombosis and Haemostasis (mem., haemostasis and malignancy subcom. 1992—, chair, Ea. Coop. Oncology Group Leukemia Com., assoc. editor Blood Jour.). Office: Northwestern Univ Feinberg Sch Medicine Divsn Hematology/Oncology 676 N St Clair St #850 Chicago IL 60611 Office Phone: 312-695-6180. E-mail: m-tallman@northwestern.edu.

**TALLMAN, RENETTA DEREMER**, music educator; d. William Jay and Renetta Folk Deremer; m. James Albert Tallman, Dec. 27, 2003. BS, Ithaca Coll., 1998; MS, U. Albany, SUNY, 2005. Cert. tchr. music Pa. Orch. tchr. Shenendehowa Ctrl. Sch. Dist., Clifton Park, NY, 2002—; adminstrv. asst. Pitts. Symphony Orch., Pitts., 1998—99. Substitute cellist Schenectady Symphony Orch., Schenectady, NY, 2004—; sect. cellist Altoona Symphony Orch., Altoona, Pa., 1999—2002; cellist The Westwoods Ensemble, Windber, Pa., 2000—02, La Vergogna String Quartet, State College, Pa., 2000—02; sect. cellist Pa. Centre Chamber Orch., State Coll., Pa., 2001—02, North Pitts. Philharm., Pitts., 1998—99; cellist Romanza String Quartet, 1998—99. Recipient Television-Radio Faculty award, Ithaca Coll. TV-Radio Faculty, 1998, Oustanding Academic Achievement award, SUNY, Albany, 2005; Presdl. scholar, Ithaca Coll., 1994-1998, Beta Zeta scholar, SUNY, Albany, 2005. Democrat. Lutheran. Avocations: cello, piano, reading, counted cross stitch.

**TALLMAN, RICHARD C.**, federal judge, lawyer; b. Oakland, Calif., 1953; s. Kenneth A. and Jean M. Tallman; m. Cynthia Ostolaza, Nov. 14, 1981. BSc, U. Santa Clara, 1975; JD, Northwestern U., 1978. Bar: Calif. 1978, Wash. 1979, U.S. Dist. Ct. (no. dist.) Calif. 1979, U.S. Dist. Ct. (we. dist.) Wash. 1979, U.S. Dist. Ct. Hawaii 1986, U.S. Dist. Ct. (we. dist.) Wash. 1999, U.S. Ct. Appeals (9th cir.) 1979, U.S. Dist. Ct. (ea. dist.) Wash. 1999, U.S. Supreme Ct. 1997. Law clk. to Hon. Morrell E. Sharp U.S. Dist. Ct. (we. dist.) Wash., Seattle, 1978—79; trial atty. U.S. Dept. Justice, Washington, 1979—80; asst. U.S. atty. (we. dist.) Wash., Seattle, 1980—83; assoc., then ptnr. Schweppe, Krug & Tausend, PS, Seattle, 1983—89; mem. Bogle & Gates, PLLC, Seattle, 1990—99; ptnr. Tallman & Severin, LLP, Seattle, 1999—2000; apptd. U.S. cir. judge U.S. Ct. Appeals (9th cir.), 2000—. Chmn. western dist. Wash. Lawyer Reps. to Ninth Cir. Jud. Conf., 1996—97. Instr. Nat. Pk. Svc. Seasonal Ranger Acad., Everett and Mt. Vernon, Wash., 1983—93; chmn. Edmonds C.C. Found., Lynnwood, Wash., 1990—92; gen. counsel Seattle-King County Crime Stoppers, 1987—99; mem. exec. bd. Chief Seattle coun. Boy Scouts Am., 1997—. Mem.: Fed. Judges Assn. (bd. dirs. 2002—), King County Bar Assn., Fed. Bar Assn. (we. dist. trustee 1992—93, v.p. 1994, pres. 1995), Wash. Athletic Club, Rainier Club. Avocations: hunting, hiking, fishing. Office: Park Place Bldg 1200 Sixth Avenue 21st FL Seattle WA 98101-3123*

**TALLMAN, ROBERT HALL**, investment company executive; b. Creston, Iowa, Aug. 10, 1915; s. Ralph H. and Hazel Verne (Hall) T.; m. Elizabeth Childs, Sept. 19, 1938; children: Susan, Mary, Timothy. BS, U. Nebr., 1937. Trainee to dist. mgr. Firestone Tire & Rubber Co., Akron, Ohio, 1937-50; pres. Tallman Oil Co., Fargo, ND, 1950-80; chmn. bd. State Bank of Hawley, Minn., 1966-70, 1st Nat. Bank of Barnesville, Minn., 1965-88; pres. Tallman Investment Ent., Fargo, 1980—; pres., dir. Dak Tech. Inc. Dir. Bell Farms. Past pres. Fargo Bd. Edn., N.D. Petroleum Coun.; past pres. St. Lukes Hosp. Assn.; past chmn. trustees 1st Congl. Ch. of Fargo; trustee U. Nebr. Found., 1987—. Mem. Fargo C. of C. (past pres.), Am. Assn. Ret. Persons, Nat. Rifle Assn., N.D. State U. Teammakers Club (past pres.), Fargo Country Club, Kiwanis (past pres.), Masons, Shriners, Elks. Republican. Congregationalist. Avocations: golf, hunting, fishing, travel, photography. Office: Box 9886 2108 S University Dr Fargo ND 58103-5342 Home: 1200 Harwood Dr Apt 332 Fargo ND 58104-6294

**TALLMER, MARGOT SALLOP**, psychologist, gerontologist, psychoanalyst; b. N.Y.C., NY, Sept. 8, 1925; d. Harry and Mildred (Schifrin) Sallop; m. Jonathan Tallmer, Apr. 12, 1949 (dec.); children: Mary, Megan, Jill, Andrew. MS, NYU, 1948; MA, Yeshiva U., 1962, PhD, 1967; cert. in psychotherapy and psychoanalysis, NYU, 1976. Faculty dept. psychol. founds. Hunter Coll., NYC, 1969-76, assoc. prof. 1976-79, prof., emeritus; staff psychologist Mt. Sinai Hosp., NY, 1967-68; pvt. practice NYC, 1979—; faculty NY Ctr. for Psychoanalytic Tng., NY. Lectr. N.Y. Ctr. Psychoanalytic Tng. Author: Sex in Later Life, 1996; editor: Sex and Life Threatening Illness, HIV Testing Positive, The Child and Death, Sexuality and the Older Adult; co-author: Suicide in the Elderly; mem. editl. bd. Current Issues in Psychoanalysis, Psychoanalytic Rev.; contbr. chpts. to textbooks, articles to profl jours. Mem. APA, Boston Soc. Gerontologic Psychiatry, N.Y. State Psychol. Assn. (past pres. divsn. adult devel. and aging), Nat. Psychol. Assn. for Psychoanalysis (trustee 1972-2005, bd. dir. 1972—). Home: 515 E 85th St New York NY 10028-0246 Personal E-Mail: mamadoc4@n.y.c.rr.com.

**TALLON, DALE**, professional sports team executive; b. Oct. 19, 1950; m. Meg Tallon; 2 children. Player Vancouver Canucks, 1970—73, Chicago Blackhawks, 1973—78, Pittsburgh Penguins, 1978—80; color analyst Chicago Blackhawks, 1981—97, dir. of Player Personnel, 1998—2002, color analyst, 2002—03, asst. gen. mgr., 2003—, gen. mgr., 2005—. Named to NHL All-Star Team, 1971, 1972. Office: c/o Chicago Blackhawks 1901 W Madison St Chicago IL 60612

**TALLON, EDWARD JOSEPH**, social studies educator; b. Peoria, Ill., Dec. 6, 1962; s. Edward Joseph and Dorothy Margaret Tallon; m. Ellen Ruth Eason. BBA in Accountancy, U. Notre Dame, Ind., 1985; MS in History, Ill. State U., Normal, 2005. CPA Ill. Acct. Price Waterhouse, Seattle, 1985—88, Newark Electronics, Chgo., 1988—91; tchr. Peoria Notre Dame H.S., 1991—2001, Ill. Valley Ctrl. H.S., Chillicothe, 2001—. Office: Ill Valley Ctrl HS 1300 W Sycamore Chillicothe IL 61523

**TALMADGE, PHILIP ALBERT**, retired judge, retired state senator; b. Seattle, Apr. 23, 1952; s. Judson H., Jr. and Jeanne C. Talmadge; m. Darlene L. Nelson, Sept. 6, 1970; children: Adam, Matthew, Jessica, Jonathan,

Annemarie. BA magna cum laude, Yale U., 1973; JD, U. Wash., 1976. Bar: Wash. 1976. Atty. Karr Tuttle Campbell, 1976—89; pres. Talmadge & Cutler, P.S., 1989—95; senator State of Wash., 1979—94; justice Supreme Ct. Wash., 1995—2001; ptnr. Talmadge Law Group PLLC, 2001—. Author: The Nixon Doctrine and the Reaction of Three Asian Nations, 1973; editor: Law Rev., 1975—76; contbr. articles to profl. jours. Chair Senate Judiciary Com., 1981, 1983—87, Senate Health and Human Svcs. Com., 1992—95, Wash. Senate, 1978—94, ways and means com. Fellow: Am. Assn. Appellate Lawyers; mem.: Wash. Appellate Lawyers Assn., King County Bar Assn., Wash. State Bar Assn. Office: Talmadge Law Group PLLC 18010 Southcenter Pkwy Tukwila WA 98188

**TALMAGE, DAVID WILSON**, retired microbiologist, retired educator, retired dean; b. Kwangju, Korea, Sept. 15, 1919; s. John Van Talmage and Eliza (Emerson) Talmage; m. LaVeryn Marie Hunicke, June 23, 1944; children: Janet, Marilyn, David, Mark, Carol. Student, Maryville Coll., Tenn., 1937—38; BS, Davidson Coll., NC, 1941; MD, Washington U., St. Louis, 1944. Intern Ga. Baptist Hosp., 1944—45; resident medicine Barnes Hosp., St. Louis, 1948—50, fellow medicine, 1950—51; asst. prof. pathology U. Pitts., 1951—52; asst. prof., then assoc. prof. medicine U. Chgo., 1952—59; prof. medicine U. Colo., 1959—, prof. microbiology, 1960—86, disting. prof., 1986—, chmn. dept., 1963—65, assoc. dean, 1966—68, dean, 1969—71; dir. Webb-Waring Lung Inst., 1973—83, assoc. dean for rsch., 1983—86. Mem. nat. council Nat. Inst. Allergy and Infectious Diseases, NIH, 1963—66, 1973—77. Author (with John Cann): Chemistry of Immunity in Health and Disease; editor: Jour. Allergy, 1963—67; editor: (with M. Samter) Immunological Diseases. With M.C. AUS, 1945—48. Scholar Markle, 1955—60. Mem.: Am. Assn. Immunologists, Am. Acad. Allergy, Inst. Medicine, NAS, Alpha Omega Alpha, Phi Beta Kappa. Home Fax: 303-388-6955.

**TALMAGE, LANCE ALLEN**, obstetrician, gynecologist, military officer; b. Vandergrift, Pa., Feb. 23, 1938; s. Guy Wesley and Martha Lois (Bradstock) T.; m. Diana Elizabeth Heywood, June 23, 1962; children: Tamara, Lance Jr., Tenley. BS in Chem. Engring., U. Toledo, 1960; MD, U. Mich., 1964. Flight surgeon 24th Infantry Divsn. U.S. Army, Europe, 1966-69; resident U. Mich. Med. Ctr., Ann Arbor, 1969-73; clin. prof. Med. Univ. Ohio, Toledo, 1987—; med. dir. Ctr. for Women's Health, Toledo, 1987—2003. Brigadier gen. 112th Med. Brigage Ohio Army Nat. Guard, Columbus, 1995-97; pres. med. staff Toledo Hosp., 1989-91, chair dept. Ob-gyn., 1979-86; pres. Toledo Lucas County Acad. Medicine, 1994-95; mem. Toledo Hosp. Found. Bd., 2000-05, Ohio State Med. Bd., 1999—; supervising sec., 2003—. Cabinet mem. United Way, Toledo, 1994-96; hon. chmn. March of Dimes Mothers-March, Toledo, 1989; pres. Ottawa Hills (Ohio) Athletic Boosters, 1986-88, team physician, 1981-2003; trustee U. Toledo Found., 1999—. Decorated Legion of Merit; named to, Ohio Vets. Hall Fame, 2001; recipient Disting. Alumni award, Waite H.S., 1996, Garde Nationale Trophy, N.G. Assn. U.S., 1998, Outstanding Team Physician, Ohio H.S. Athletic Assn., 2002, Blue T award, U. Toledo, 2002, Outstanding Chem. Engr. Grad. award, 2002—03. Fellow ACS, Am. Coll. Obstetricians and Gynecologists (dist. chair 1996-99, v.p. 2000-01, Disting. Dist. Svc. award, 2004); mem. AMA (mem. ho. of dels.), Am. Soc. Reproductive Medicine, Ohio State Med. Assn. (pres. 1998-99), Pi Kappa Phi Alumni Assn. (Beta Iota chpt. Hall of Fame), U. Toledo Alumni Assn. (trustee 1996-2002, pres. 2000-01, athletic com., 2005—), Res. Officers Assn., Soc. Med. Cons. to Armed Forces, Am. Legion Post 335, Mil. Officers Assn. Am. (life), Assn. Mil. Surgeons U.S. (life), Nat. Guard Assn. U.S. (life). Republican. Lutheran. Office: The Toledo Hosp 2150 W Ctrl Ave Toledo OH 43606 Office Phone: 419-291-2193. Personal E-mail: latalmage@voyager.net.

**TALMI, YOAV**, conductor, composer; b. Kibbutz Merhavia, Israel, Apr. 28, 1943; m. Erella Gottesmann; 2 children. Diploma, Rubin Acad. Music, Tel Aviv; postgrad., Julliard Sch. Music; D (hon.), Laval U., 2001. Artistic dir., condr. Gelders Symphony Orch., Arnhem, 1974-80; prin. guest condr. Munich Philham. Orch., 1979-80; artistic dir. Israel Chamber Orch., 1984-88; music dir. New Israeli Opera, 1985-89, San Diego Symphony Orch., 1990-96, Waterloo Festival, NJ, 1994-95, Que. Symphony, Can., 1999—, Hamburg (Germany) Symphony, 2000—04. Guest condr. Berlin Philharm., Munich Philharm., London Philharm., Philharmonia, Royal Philharm., Concertgebouw, Paris Orch. Nat., Israel Philharm., NHK Symphony, Tokyo, New Japan Philharm., Vienna Symphony, St. Petersburg Philharm., Pitts. Symphony, Detroit Symphony, St. Louis Symphony, Houston Symphony, Dallas Symphony, Montreal Symphony, N.Y. Chamber Symphony, LA Chamber Orch., Oslo Philharm., Tonhalle Orch., Zurich, others. Composer: Dreams for choir a capella, Music for Flute and Strings; Overture on Mexican Themes (recorded), 3 Monologues for Flute Solo (pub.), Inaguuration Fanfare, Elegy for Strings, Timpani, and Accordion, 1997, Suite on Israeli Songs, The Double Marriage of Figaro; recs. include: Bruckner 9th Symphony (Oslo Philharm.), Tchaikovsky 1st Symphony (Quebec Symphony), Gliere 3d Symphony, Brahms Sextet/4 Serious Songs, Rachmaninov's Isle of the Dead, Berlioz: Symphonie Fantastique, Overtures, Harold in Italy, Romeo and Juliette, (San Diego Symphony), Tchaikovsky/Schoenberg, Bloch/Barber/Grieg/Puccini (Israel Chamber Orch.); (with Erella Talmi) works for flute and piano. Recipient Boskovitch prize for composition, Israel, 1965, Koussevitzky Meml. Conducting prize, Tanglewood, 1969, Ruppert Found. Condr. competition award, London, 1973, Ahad Ha'am award L.A. Ctr. Jewish Culture and the Am.-Israel Cultural Found., 1997. Home: PO Box 1384 Kefar Sava 44113 Israel Office: Michal Schmidt Artists Internat 59 E 54th St Ste 83 New York NY 10022 Office Phone: 212-421-8500. Home Fax: 972-9-765-6553. E-mail: talmi@netvision.net.il.

**TALPADE, RAJESH**, telecommunications industry executive; PhD, Ga. Inst. Tech., Atlanta, 1997; MBA, Columbia U., NYC, 2006. Cert. info. sys. security profl. ISC2. Rsch. dir. Telcordia Techs., Piscataway, NJ, 1997—. Grantee, U.S. Govt., 2000—06. Achievements include patents for IP Quality of Service; patents pending for IP network and security technologies; research in R&D in IP network and security technologies. Office: Telcordia Techs 1 Telcordia Dr Piscataway NJ 08854 Office Phone: 732-699-2832. E-mail: rtalpade@telcordia.com.

**TALSANIA, JAY S.**, orthopedist, surgeon; s. Suryakant J. and Betty Ann Talsania; m. Diana Kemp. BSMechE, Bucknell U., 1986; MD, Temple U., 1991. Diplomate in orthopedic surgery Nat. Bd. Med. Examiners, surgery of the hand Nat. Bd. Med. Examiners. Chief divsn. hand surgery Lehigh Valley Hosp., Allentown, Pa., 2004—. Office: Orthopaedic Associates Allentown 1243 S Cedarcrest Blvd Allentown PA 18103 Office Phone: 610-433-6045.

**TALUKDAR, ATANU**, electrical engineer; b. Burdwan, India, Aug. 18, 1973; s. Benoy and Sipra Talukdar; m. Suchita Shakraborty, Nov. 28, 1998; 1 child, Tathagata. B of Engring., Bengal Engring. Coll., Howrah, India, 1996; M of Engring., Jadarpur U., Kolkata, India, 1998. Scientist B, Integrated Test Range, Balasore, India, 1998—2001, scientist C, 2001—. Rschr. dept. engring. Indian Inst. Tech., Kharagpur, India, 2002—. Contbr. articles to profl. jours. With Nat. Cadet Corps, India, 1995—96. Integrated Guided Missile Devel. Program fellowship, Def. R&D Orgn., 1996—98. Avocations: nature watch, bicycling, photography, parties, reading. Home: Rabindra Sarani Bolpur India Office: Integrated Test Range Chandipur Balasore 756025 India Office Phone: +916782272231. E-mail: atanuxyz@yahoo.com.

**TALWALKAR, ABHI Y. (ABHIJIT Y. TALWALKAR)**, computer company executive; b. Pune, India, 1965; BEE, Oreg. State Univ., 1985. Sr. engring., mktg. mgmt. Sequent Computer Sys. (now part of IBM), Bipolar Integrated Tech. Inc., Lattice Semiconductor Inc.; with Intel Corp., Santa Clara, Calif., 1993—2005, various positions including v.p., gen. mgr., enterprise platform group, v.p., co-gen. mgr., digital enterprise group; pres., CEO, dir. LSI Logic Corp., Milpitas, Calif., 2005—. Office: LSI Logic Corp 1621 Barber Ln Milpitas CA 95035 Office Phone: 408-433-8000.*

**TALWANI, MANIK,** geophysicist, educator; b. Patiala, India, Aug. 22, 1933; came to U.S., 1954; m. Anni Fittler, Apr. 3, 1958; children: Rajeev Manik, Indira, Sanjay. BSc with honors, Delhi U., India, 1951, MSc, 1953; PhD, Columbia U., 1959; PhD (hon.), Oslo U., 1981. From rsch. scientist to assoc. prof. Lamont-Doherty Geol. Obs., Columbia U., N.Y.C., 1959-70, dir. obs., 1972-81; prof. Columbia U., N.Y.C., 1970-82; dir. Ctr. for Crustal Studies Gulf R & D Co., Pitts., 1981-83, chief scientist exploration div. Houston, 1983-85; Schlumberger prof. geophysics Rice U., Houston, 1985—; pres. Integrated Ocean Drilling Program-Mgmt. Internat., 2004—. Cons. Govt. of Iceland, 1982-92, Lockheed Martin, 1998-2000; dir. Geotech. Rsch. Inst., Houston Advanced Rsch. Ctr., Woodlands, 1985-98; Sackler disting. lectr. U. Tel Aviv, 1987; prin. investigator Apollo 17 first gravity measurements on moon. Co-author: Geophysical Atlas of the Norwegian Sea; editor 12 books on earth sci.; Maurice Ewing Meml. Symposium; co-editor: Geophysical Atlases of Indian, Atlantic and Pacific Oceans; contbr. over 150 papers to profl. jours. Recipient Krishnan award Indian Geophys. Union, 1964, Exceptional Sci. Achievement award NASA, 1973, Guggenheim award, 1974, Alfred Wegener medal European Union Geoscis., 1993; Fulbright-Hays fellow, 1974. Fellow: AAAS, Geol. Soc. Am. (George P. Woollard award 1984), Am. Geophys. Union (James B. Macelwane award 1964, Maurice Ewing award 1981), Geol. Soc. India (hon.); mem.: Houston Philos. Soc., Acad. Nat. Scis. Russian Fedn., Petroleum Club, Houston Geophys. Soc. (hon.), Norwegian Acad. Scis., Am. Assn. Petroleum Geologists, Soc. Exptl. Geophysicists, Cosmos Club, Sigma Xi. Home: 1111 Hermann Dr Apt 10 D Houston TX 77004-6929 Office: Rice U PO Box 1892 Houston TX 77251-1892 also: IODP-MI 815 Connecticut Ave NW Ste 210 Washington DC 20006

**TAM, SUNNY WING YEE,** physicist; s. Yin-Tso Tam and Yuk-Ying Sham Tam; m. Miho Ujimoto, Jan. 14, 1998; 1 child, Laurence Yoshina Ka-Ming. BA, U. of Calif., 1985-89; PhD, MIT, 1989—96. Rsch. asst. MIT, Cambridge, Mass., 1989—96, postdoctoral assoc., 1996—2000, rsch. scientist, 2000—. Prin. investigator of federally funded rsch. project NASA, 2003—, NSF, 2003—06; co-investigator of federally funded rsch. project NASA, 2000—03; co-principal investigator of federally funded rsch. projects NSF, 1996—2002; manuscript reviewer Geomagnetism and Aeronomy, 1996; invited lectr. solar & stellar physics seminar Harvard U., Cambridge, Mass., 1995; invited lectr. 1995 Cambridge Workshop on Multiscale Phenomena in Space Plasmas, Bermuda, 1995; rsch. proposal reviewer NASA, 2002—, NSF, 2002—, Natural Sciences and Engring. Rsch. Coun. of Can., 2003; guest editor, spl. issue on most recent advances in the new polar wind theory and observations Jour. of Atmospheric and Solar-Terrestrial Physics, 2004—; manuscript reviewer Jour. of Geophys. Rsch., 2001—, Multiscale Coupling of Sun-Earth Processes (Elsevier Pub.), 2004; invited mem., internat. team on polar wind rsch. Internat. Space Sci. Inst., Bern, Switzerland, 2000; spkr. in field. Contbr. scientific papers. Edward Frank Kraft scholar, U. Calif., Berkeley, 1986, James Monroe McDonald scholar, Physics Dept., U. Calif., Berkeley, 1988, Solar and Heliospheric Rsch. grantee, NASA, 2003 , Magnetospheric Physics Rsch. grantee, NSF, 2003—05. Mem.: Am. Geophys. Union (co-convener spl. session Fall mtg. 2005), Golden Key, Phi Beta Kappa Soc., Sigma Pi Sigma. Avocations: soccer, Scrabble, backgammon, fencing.

**TAMADDON, SINA,** information technology executive; b. Aug. 27, 1957; V.p. Advanced Tech. Software Alliance Inc.; v.p. profl. svcs. NeXT, 1994—96, v.p. Europe, 1996—97; sr. v.p. worldwide svc. and support Apple Computer Inc., v.p. and gen. mgr. Newton Group, sr. v.p. applications Cupertino, Calif., 1997—. Office: Apple Computer Inc 1 Infinite Loop Cupertino CA 95014 Office Phone: 408-996-1010.

**TAMARELLI, ALAN WAYNE,** venture capitalist; b. Wilkinsburg, Pa., Aug. 13, 1941; s. John Adam Tamarelli and Florence Eleanor (Heacock) T.; m. Carol Ann Crawford, Aug. 3, 1963; children: Robin Carol, Alan Wayne. BS, Carnegie Mellon U., 1963, MS, 1965, PhD, 1966; MBA, NYU, 1972. Engr. Exxon Corp., Linden, NJ, 1966, project leader, 1968-70; corp. planner Engelhard Minerals & Chem. Corp., Newark, 1970-71, asst. to exec. v.p., 1971-74, gen. mgr., 1974-77, v.p., 1977-79, group v.p., 1979-81; sr. v.p. Engelhard Corp., Iselin, NJ, 1981-83; chmn., chief exec. officer Dock Resins Corp, Linden, NJ, 1983—2000; pres. AWT Private Investments, 2000—. Mem. exec. com. nat. adv. coun. for environ. policy and tech. U.S. Dept. Environment Protection, Gov's. Econ. Task Force, N.J.; mem. exec. com. Alliance for Industrial Competitiveness; chmn. Jumpstart N.J., Joseph Priestley Soc. Capt. U.S. Army, 1966-68. NSF fellow, 1963-66 Mem. Synthetic Organic Chems. Mfrs. Assn. (chmn., vice chmn., bd. govs.), Am. Chem. Soc., N.Y. Paint and Coatings Assn. (chmn., pres., v.p., sec., treas., bd. dirs.), Chem. Industry Coun. (chmn., bd. dirs., exec. com.), N.J. Energy Rsch. Inst. (founding trustee), Am. Mgmt. Assn., N.Y. Acad. Scis., Scabbard and Blade, Rotary (pres., v.p., sec. Linden Club), Linden Indsl. Assn. (pres.), Joseph Priestley Soc. (chmn.), Shakespeare Theater of N.J. (bd. dirs.), Sigma Xi, Tau Beta Pi, Phi Kappa Phi, Omicron Delta Kappa. Home: 49 Wexford Way Basking Ridge NJ 07920-2432 Office Phone: 908-581-4308. E-mail: wayne@tamarelli.com.

**TAMAREN, MICHELE CAROL,** spiritual director, writer, retired special education educator, personal coach, presenter; b. Hartford, Conn., Aug. 2, 1947; d. Herman Harold and Betty (Leavitt) Liss; m. David Stephen Tamaren, June 8, 1968; 1 child, Scott. BS in Elem. Edn., U. Conn., 1969; MA in Spl. Edn., St. Joseph Coll., West Hartford, Conn., 1976; student, Claritas Inst. for Interspiritual Inquiry, Boulder, Colo., 2005—. Cert. elem. and spl. edn. tchr. Conn., Mass. Tchr. N.Y. Inst. Spl. Edn., Bronx, 1971-74; ednl. cons. Mvnbrook Sch., West Hartford, 1975-78; grad. instr. St. Joseph Coll., 1978; elem. tchr. Acton (Mass.) Pub. Schs., 1969-70, tchr. spl. edn., 1978-94, inclusion and behavioral specialist, 1996-2000; learning specialist and writer Educators Pub. Svc., Cambridge, Mass., 1994-96. Personal coach; cons. presenter in field. Author: (book) I Make a Difference, 1992; contbr. articles to profl. jours. Bd. dirs. United Way, Acton-Boxborough, 1996—99. Grantee, Mass. Gov.'s Alliance Against Drugs, 1992; Horace Mann grantee, Mass. Dept. Edn., 1987, 1988. Mem.: Kappa Delta Pi, Phi Kappa Phi. Avocations: travel, writing, reading, yoga, swimming. Home and Office: 34 Constitution Way Apt D Marblehead MA 01945-4652 Personal E-mail: to_life@earthlink.net.

**TAMARGO, MAURICIO J.,** federal agency administrator; b. Cuba; arrived in U.S., 1961; m. Tara Tamargo; 2 children. BA in History, U. Miami, 1985; JD, Samford U., 1989. Bar: Fla., D.C., U.S. Supreme Ct. Adminstrv. asst. Fla. State Rep. Ileana Ros-Lehtinen; legis. dir. Congresswoman Ileana Ros-Lehtinen; staff dir., counsel subcom. on internat. policy and trade House Internat. Rels. Com.; staff dir., counsel subcom. on Africa, staff dir. internat. ops. and human rights subcom.; chief of staff, legal counsel Congresswoman Ileana Ros-Lehtinen; chmn. Fgn. Claims Settlement Commn. U.S. Dept. Justice, Washington, 2002—. Republican. Office: US Dept Justice Fgn Claims Settlement Commn 600 E St NW Rm 6002 Washington DC 20579

**TAMARKIN, KATE,** conductor; b. Newport Beach, Calif. Student, Academia Musicale Chigiana, Siena, Italy; MusB magna cum laude, Chapman U.; MusM, Northwestern U.; MusD, Peabody Conservatory. Conducting fellow Tanglewood Music Festival, 1987; L.A. Philharm. Inst., 1988-89; music dir. Fox Valley Symphony, Appleton, Wis., 1982-90, Vt. Symphony Orch. Assn., Inc., Burlington. Music dir. E. Tex. Symphony Orch.; guest condr. Okla. City Philharm., Riverside Symphony N.J., Okla. Sinfonia, Tulsa Philharm., Grant Pk. Festival Orch., Chgo., others; vis. assoc. prof. orchestral studies U. Minn.; assoc. condr. Dallas Symphony, 1989-94; vis. condr. U. Minn. Sch. Music, 1997-98. Appeared in numerous TV prodns. including Christmas concerts, 1993, 94, CNN-TV, (CBS-TV) Today Show. Recipient Alumni Merit award Northwestern U., Alumni of Yr. award Chapman U., 1997. Office: Vt Symphony Orch Assn Inc 2 Church St Burlington VT 05401-4445

**TAMARO, GEORGE JOHN,** consulting engineer; b. Weehawken, N.J., Mar. 16, 1937; s. Giorgio Angelo and Giacomina T.; m. Rosemary Ann Volta, June 24, 1961; children: Peter Louis, Jean Marie, Paul Anthony, Mark Joseph. BCE, Manhattan Coll., 1959; MCE, Lehigh U., 1961; M of Archtl. Tech., Columbia U., 1969. Profl. engr., N.Y., N.J., D.C., Md., Pa., Calif., Ill., Tex., La., Wis., Wash., R.I., Ark., Mo., Miss., Idaho; structural engr., Ill., Mass.; geotech. engr., Calif.; chartered engr., U.K.; registered European engr. Staff engr. Port Authority of N.Y. & N.J., N.Y.C., 1961—71; v.p., chief engr. ICOS Corp. Am., N.Y.C., 1971—80; sr. ptnr. Mueser Rutledge Cons. Engrs., N.Y.C., 1980—. Patentee in field; author tech. papers. Chmn. Bergen County Planning Bd., N.J., 1978-82; vice-chair Leonia (N.J.) Planning Bd., 1971-89; mem. Bd. Adjustment, Leonia, 1974-76; councilman Borough Governing Body, Leonia, 1972. Recipient Lynn Beedle award, Lehigh U., 2005, NSPE award, 2006. Mem. ASCE (hon., Martin S. Kapp Found. Engr. award 1987, Homer Gage Balcom award 2002, Ralph B. Peck medal 2003, Friedman Profl. Recognition award 2003, OPAL award for engring. design 2004, Ernest E. Howard award 2006), NSPE (Annual award 2006), Am. Assn. Engring. Socs. (John Fritz medal 2005), Lehigh U.(Lynn Berdle award), Instn. Civil Engrs. U.K., Instn. Structural Engrs. U.K., Nat. Acad. Engring., Internat. Soc. Soil Mechs. and Found. Engrs., Deep Found. Inst. (Disting. Svc. award), The Moles (past pres., Outstanding Achievement in Constrn. award 2003, The Beavers' award for outstanding achievement in heavy engring. constrn. 2004), Coun. on Tall Bldgs. and Urban Habitat, Chi Épsilon (hon. mem. award 1990), Tau Beta Pi. Avocations: sailing, photography. Office: Mueser Rutledge Cons Engrs 225 W 34th St New York NY 10122-0002

**TAMBAKERAS, MARKOS I.,** machine tool manufacturer; BS, U. Witwatersrand, Johannesburg, South Africa. Various positions Honeywell Inc., 1984-92, v.p. mktg. and bus. ops., pres. indsl. automation and control bus., 1995-99; pres. Honeywell Asia Pacific, 1992-94; pres., CEO Kennametal Inc., Latrobe, Pa., 1999—2005, chmn., 1999—. Office: Kennametal Inc PO Box 231 1600 Technology Way Latrobe PA 15650-0231*

**TAMBLYN, AMBER ROSE,** actress; b. Santa Monica, Calif., May 14, 1983; d. Russ and Bonnie Tamblyn. Actor: (TV series) General Hospital, 1995—2001, Joan of Arcadia, 2003—; (films) Live Nude Girls, 1995, Rebellious, 1995, Johnny Mysto: Boy Wizard, 1996, The Ring, 2002, The Sisterhood of the Traveling Pants, 2005, (guest appearances) Buffy the Vampire Slayer, 2001, Boston Public, 2002, Twilight Zone, 2002, CSI: Miami, 2002, Without a Trace, 2003, Punk'd, 2003. Office: 8383 Wilshire Blvd Ste 530 Beverly Hills CA 90211

**TAMBOLI, DNYANESH CHANDRAKANT,** research scientist; s. Chandrakant and Jayashree Tamboli; m. Jyoti Tamboli, Dec. 18, 2002; 1 child, Gargee. BTech, Indian Inst. Tech., Mumbai, India, 1993; PhD, U. Ctrl. Fla., Orlando, 2000. Scientist Air Products and Chems., Allentown, Pa., 2000—. Contbr. articles to profl. jours. Recipient Marcel Pourbaix award, Nat. Corrosion Assn., 1999, First Pl. Paper award, 10th Internat. CMP User's Group Conf., 2005. Mem.: Electrochem. Soc., Am. Chem. Soc. Achievements include patents for; patents pending for. Office: Air Products & Chemicals 7201 Hamilton Blvd Allentown PA 18195 Office Phone: 610-481-3652. Personal E-mail: dctamboli@yahoo.com. Business E-Mail: tamboldc@airproducts.com.

**TAMBOR, JEFFREY,** actor, theater director, educator; b. San Francisco, July 8, 1944; m. Kasia Ostlun, Oct. 6, 2001. BA, San Francisco State; MFA, Wayne State U. Acting tchr. Milton Katselas' Acting Workshops, Beverly Hills, Calif. Actor (theatre) Sly Fox, 1976 (Broadway and L.A.), Measure for Measure, The Hands of the Enemy, Flea in Her Ear, American Mosaic; (films)...And Justice For All, 1979, Saturday the 14th, 1981, Dreamchasers, 1982, The Man Who Wasn't There, 1983, Mr. Mom, 1983, No Small Affair, 1984, Desert Hearts, 1985, Three O'Clock High, 1987, Brenda Starr, 1989, Lisa, 1990, City Slickers, 1991, Life Stinks, 1991, Pastime, 1991, Article 99, 1992, Crossing the Bridge, 1992, The Webbers, 1993, A House in the Hills, 1993, Radioland Murders, 1994, Heavyweights, 1995, My Teacher's Wife, 1995, Big Bully, 1996, Dr. Dolittle, 1998, There's Something About Mary, 1998, Meet Joe Black, 1998, Muppets From Space, 1999, Teaching Mrs. Tingle, 1999, Girl Interrupted, 1999, Pollock, 2000, How the Grinch Stole Christmas, 2000, Never Again, 2001, Get Well Soon, 2001, Scorched, 2002, The Freshman, 2002, Malibu's Most Wanted, 2003, My Boss's Daughter, 2003, Nobody's Perfect, 2004, Hellboy, 2004, Funky Monkey, 2004, (voice) The SpongeBob SquarePants Movie, 2004; (TV series) The Ropers, 1979-80, Hill Street Blues, 1981-87, 9 to 5, 1982, Mr. Sunshine, 1986, (voice) Jonny Quest, 1986, Max Headroom, 1987-88, Studio 5-B, 1989, American Dreamer, 1990, The Larry Sanders Show, 1992-98 (Emmy award nominee 1993), Me & George, 1998, (voice) The Lionhearts, 1998, Everything's Relative, 1999, The Lot, 1999, (voice) Sammy, 2000, That Was Then, 2002, 3-South, 2002, Hollywood Squares (announcer), 2002-03, Arrested Development, 2003—; (TV episodes) M*A*S*H, Barney Miller, L.A. Law, The Golden Girls, Empty Nest, Who's The Boss, Doogie Houser, M.D., Equal Justice, Murder She Wrote, Tales From The Crypt (Dead Right) (TV movies) Eddie and Herbert, 1977, Alcatraz: The Whole Shocking Story, 1980, A Gun in the House, 1981, The Star Maker, 1981, Pals, 1981, The Awakening of Candra, 1981, Take Your Best Shot, 1982, The Zertigo Diamond Caper, 1982, Cocaine: One Man's Seduction, 1983, Sadat, 1983, The Three Wishes of Billy Grier, 1984, Wildfire, 1986, A Quiet Little Neighborhood, a Perfect Little Murder, 1990, The Burden of Proof, 1992, 1775, 1992, (voice) Jonny's Golden Quest, 1993, Another Midnight Run, 1994, (voice) Jonny Quest vs. the Cyber Insects, 1995, The Man Who Captured Eichmann, 1996, Weapons of Mass Distraction, 1997, Eloise at the Plaza, 2003, Eloise at the Plaza, 2003, Eloise at Christmastime, 2003, The Muppets' Wonderful Wizard of Oz, 2005; (TV spls.) Living and Working in Space: The Countdown Has Begun; (TV miniseries) Robert Kennedy and His Times, 1985, dir. (in numerous theatre companies including Seattle Repertory Theatre, Actors Theatre of Louisville, Milw. Repertory Theatre, Acad. Festival Theatre, Chgo., San Diego Shakespeare Festival, South Coast Repertory Theatre, Loeb Drama Ctr., Cambridge, Mass., Sky Light Theatre, L.A. Office: Care The Gersh Agency c/o Leslie Siebert 232 N Canon Dr Beverly Hills CA 90210-5302

**TAMBORLANE, WILLIAM V., JR.,** pediatrician, educator; b. NYC, Aug. 25, 1946; s. William and Eleanor (Bernabo) T.; m. Kathleen Mary Blinn, Dec. 27, 1969; children: Melissa, Amy, James. BS, Georgetown U., 1968, MD, 1972. Diplomate Am. Bd. Pediatrics, Am. Bd. Pediatric Endocrinology. Attending physician Yale New Haven Hosp., 1977—. Asst. prof. pediatrics Yale U., New Haven, 1977-81, dir. Children's Diabetes Ctr., 1977-2004; assoc. prof. pediatrics Sch. Medicine, New Haven, 1982-83; chief pediatric endocrinology and diabetes Yale Sch. Medicine, 1985-, prof. pediatrics, 1986-; program dir. Yale Children's Clin. Rsch. Ctr., N.H., Conn., 1986-2004; chmn. Lawson Wilkens Diabetes Com., 1988-89; dir. Yale Pediatric Pharmacology Rsch. Unit, 1999-2004; chair steering com. Diabetes Rsch. Children Network, 2001-; dep. dir. Yale Gen. Clin. Rsch. Ctr., 2004-. Editor: Yale Guide to Children's Nutrition, 1997. Recipient Jonathan May award, Charles Best award Am. Diabetes Assn., 1979, Clin. Investigator award NIH, 1979-82, JDRF award for excellence in clin. rsch., 2006. Mem. Am. Fedn. Clin. Rsch., Am. Soc. Clin. Investigation, Endocrine Soc., Soc. Pediatric Rsch., Phi Beta Kappa. Office Phone: 203-785-4646. E-mail: william.tamborlane@yale.edu.

**TAMBS, LEWIS ARTHUR,** diplomat, educator, historian; b. San Diego, July 7, 1927; s. Fred B. and Marguerite Johanna (Tambs) Jones; m. Phyllis Ann Greer, 1982. BS, U. Calif., Berkeley, 1953; MA, U. Calif., Santa Barbara, 1962, PhD, 1967. Plant engr. Std. Brands, San Francisco, 1953—54; pipeline engr. Creole Petroleum Co., Caracas, Maracaibo, Venezuela, 1954—57; gen. mgr. Cacyp, Maracaibo, 1957—59; instr. Creighton U., 1965—67, asst. prof., 1967—69; prof. History Ariz. State U., Tempe, 1969—82, 1987—2002, dir. Ctr. L.Am. Studies, 1972—76; cons. NSC, 1982—83; U.S. ambassador to Colombia, 1983—85; U.S. amb. to Costa Rica, 1985—87; ret., 2002. Author: East European and Soviet Economic Affairs, 1975, Historiography, Method and History Teaching, 1975, Hitler's Spanish Legion, 1979; editor: United States Policy Toward Latin America, 1976, Inter-American Policy for the 80's; co-editor: Santa Fe IV, 2000, English translation of Karl Haushofer's Geopolitics of the Pacific, 2002; co-author periodical guides; contbr. articles to profl. jours. Bd. dirs. Ariz.-Mex. Commn., 1974-82, Coun. Inter-Am. Security, 1979-90. With U.S. Army, 1945-47, 50-51. Faculty grantee, Ariz. State U., 1970, 1971, 1974, 1978, 1979. Roman Catholic. E-mail: lewtambs@aol.com.

**TAMBUR, ANAT,** lab administrator; DMD, PhD, Hadassah Sch. Medicine, Jerusalem. Dir. transplant immunology lab. Northwestern U., Chgo., 2004—; dir. HLA lab. RUSH Med. Ctr. Pres. Am. Bd. Histocompatibility Immunogenetics, 2004—05. Office: Northwestern U Tarry 11 711 303 E Chicago Ave Chicago IL 60611 Office Phone: 312-503-2949. Office Fax: 312-503-3366.

**TAMBURINE, JEAN HELEN,** sculptor, painter, illustrator; b. Meriden, Conn., Feb. 20, 1930; m. Eugene E. Bertolli. Student, Art Students League, NYC, 1948-50; student of Jon Corbino, John Groth, Carlo Ciampaglia, Elisabeth Gordon Chandler. Exhibited group shows Rockport Art Assn., Mass., North Shore Arts Assn., Gloucester, Mass., George Walter Vincent Mus., Springfield, Mass., Hudson Valley Art Assn., NY, Pearl S. Buck Found., Phila., Am. Artists Profl. League, NY, Acad. Artists Assn., Springfield, Pen and Brush, NY; heritage bronze commd. by Wallingford Pub. Library, 1986, Conn.; represented in permanent collections Conn. State Library, Middletown, Nashville Pub. Library, Strong Sch., Hartford, Conn., L'Heure Joyeux, Paris; also pvt. collections; author, designer, illustrator: Almost Big Enough, 1963, I Think I Will Go to the Hospital, 1965, How Now, Brown Cow, 1967. Recipient Assoc. Members prize Acad. Artists, Founders prize Pen and Brush, 1981, 1st prize for sculpture Arts and Crafts Assn. of Meriden, Conn.; named to Meriden Hall of Fame. Mem. Rockport Art Assn. (Martha Moore Meml. award 1983), North Shore Arts Assn., Acad. Artists Assn., Salmagundi Club, Am. Artists Profl. League, Am. Medallic Sculpture Assn., FIDEM, Authors Guild. Home and Office: The Bertolli Studio 73 Reynolds Dr Meriden CT 06450-2532

**TAMBURRO, PETER JAMES, JR.,** secondary school educator; b. Hoboken, N.J., Jan. 20, 1947; s. Peter James and Rose Catherine (Verta) Tamburro; m. Andrea Everitt Huber, Aug. 21, 1976 (div. 1998); children: Peter James III, Christopher Harding, Matthew Everitt. BA in Polit. Sci. Dickinson Coll., 1969; MAT in Social Studies, Trenton State Coll., 1973. Cert. secondary sch. tchr., social studies N.J. Tchr. Morris Sch. Dist., Morristown, NJ, 1973-76, Hanover Park Regional H.S. Dist., East Hanover, NJ, 1976—. Cross country coach Hanover Park H.S., East Hanover, 1983—2003, volleyball coach, 1990—98, asst. basketball coach, 1990—2001; judge Bicentennial Com., NJ; asst. basketball coach Caldwell (N.J.) Coll., 1989—93; cons. Hist. Commn., East Hanover, 1989—92; cons. for developing Advanced Placement history programs, reader Advanced Placement exams ETS; mem. hist. com. Washington Twp., 1994—97, curriculum adv. com., 1996—97; adj. prof. William Paterson U., NJ, 1999—; spkr. in field. Author: (book) Gateway to Morris, 1993, Learn Chess from the Greats, 2000; editor (with Dale Brandreth): The Chess Diary of Rudolph Spielmann; editor: Atlantic Chess News, 1973—76, 2000—02; contbr. articles to chess mags.; nationally syndicated columnist: U.S. Chess Fedn., 1994—2001, columnist: Chessmates, Newark Star Ledger, 1997—; host internet radio show Openings for Amateurs, www.chess.fm. Mem. Hist. Commn., Washington Twp., NJ, 1994—96; scoutmaster Boy Scouts Am., 1994—97; team capt. Rep. Nat. Conv., 2000; Rep. County Committeeman Hanover Twp., NJ, 1984—88; legis. aide Assemblyman Robert Martin, Trenton, 1985—89; Rep. County Committeeman Morristown, NJ, 2002—03. Named N.J.'s Outstanding Tchr. History, DAR, 1990, Cross Country State Section Champions, 1987, 2000, 2001, 2002, Morris County Coach of the Yr., Cross Country, 2000; fellow Taft Inst. Two Party Govt., Fairleigh Dickinson U., 1984, Woodrow Wilson Found., 1991, Nat., Coun. Basic Edn., Washington, 1993; grantee, NSF, 1978, Dodge Found., Madison, N.J., 1987. Mem.: Chess Journalists Am. (v.p. 1990—99, pres. 1999—2003, awards 1995, 1996, 1997, 2002, 2003), U.S. Chess Fedn. (nat. chmn. hist. com. 1994—99), N.J. Edn. Assn., Hanover Park Regional Ednl. Assn. (v.p. 1994—95, pres. 1995—2001, chief negotiator 2003—), Morris County Hist. Soc., Nat. Coun. Social Studies. Avocations: rare books, chess. Home: 22 Budd St Morristown NJ 07960-5304 Office: Hanover Park High Sch 63 Mount Pleasant Ave East Hanover NJ 07936-2601 Office Phone: 201-887-0300.

**TAMIGI, PETER F.,** lawyer; s. Joseph and Rosa Tamigi; m. Tara Anne Maher, Aug. 3, 1990; 1 child, Rosemary. BA summa cum laud, Fordham U., 1985; JD, St. John's U., 1988. Bar: Conn. 1988, N.Y. 1989, D.C. 1989. Law clk. Judge Edward Re U.S. Ct. Internat. Trade, N.Y.C., 1988—90; assoc. Condon & Forsyth, N.Y.C., 1990—95; ptnr. Carole Burns & Assocs., Mineola, NY, 1995—2003; mng. ptnr. Burns, Russo, Tamigi & Reardon LLP, Garden City, NY, 2003—. Instr. legal rsch. and writing Lehman Coll., Bronx, NY, 1988—89. Editor-in-chief: St. John's Jour. Legal Commentary, 1987—88. Legis. aide N.Y. State Assembly, Albany, 1988. Recipient J. Mooney award, Fordham U., 1985. Mem.: Bronx County Bar Assn. (judiciary com. 1999—), N.Y. State Bar Assn. (chair trial lawyers subcom. on litig. 1998—99). Avocation: golf. Home: 4 The Hollows W East Norwich NY 11732 Office: Burns Russo Tamigi Reardon LLP 390 Old Country Rd Garden City NY 11530

**TAMILLOW, MICHAEL,** federal agency administrator; b. Brady, Tex., May 21, 1953; m. Kristie Jean McGuire, May 29, 1954; children: Richard Matthew, Megan Anne. Fire bn. chief Fairfax (Va.) County Fire and Rescue Dept. 1973—2002; urban search and rescue sect. chief DHS/FEMA, Washington, 2002—. Home: 11308 Field Cir Spotsylvania VA 22553 Office: Dhs/Fema 500 C St SW Washington DC 20472 Office Phone: 202-646-2549. Office Fax: 202-646-4684. Personal E-Mail: tamillowm@cs.com. Business E-Mail: mike.tamillow@dhs.gov.

**TAMIR, THEODOR,** electrophysics researcher, educator; b. Bucharest, Romania, Sept. 17, 1927; came to U.S., 1958, naturalized, 1968; s. Martin and Helena (Hart) Berman; m. Hadassah Cohen, Oct. 5, 1949; children: Jonathan, Yael. BS Technion, Israel Inst. Tech., 1953, Dipl. Ingenieur, 1954, MS, 1958; PhD, Poly. Inst. Bklyn., 1962. Instr. Technion Israel Inst. Tech., Haifa, 1956-58; mem. rsch. staff Poly. Inst., Bklyn., 1958-62; mem. faculty Poly. Univ., Bklyn., 1962—, head dept. elec. engring., 1974—79, prof. electrophysics, 1969—92, Univ. prof., 1992—. Sci. and engring. cons. to indsl. and govtl. labs. Editor, author: Integrated Optics, 1975 (transl. into Russian and Chinese), Guided Wave Optoelectronics, 1988 (transl. into Russian); co-editor: Springer Series in Optical Sciences, 1979-96; contbr. chpts. to books, articles to profl. jours. Served with Israeli Army, 1947-49. Awarded Instn. Premium, 1964, Electronics Premium, 1967, Instn. Elec. Engrs., London; citation for disting. research Polytechnic chpt. Sigma Xi, 1978. Fellow IEEE, Optical Soc. Am.; mem. Internat. Union Radio Sci., Sigma Xi. Home: 981 E Lawn Dr Teaneck NJ 07666-6604 Office: Polytechnic Univ Elec & Comp Engring Dept 5 MetroTech Ctr Brooklyn NY 11201 Office Phone: 718-260-3320. Business E-Mail: ttamir@duke.poly.edu.

**TAMKE, GEORGE WILLIAM,** venture capitalist; b. Beacon, NY, May 16, 1947; s. George William and Josephine Edna (Carbone) Tamke; m. Christine Barbara MacLeod, June 28, 1969; children: Kara Lee, Shannon. BSChemE, Vanderbilt U., 1969; MS in Mgmt. Sci., Stanford U., 1979. With IBM, N.Y., Fla., Calif., Ga., Minn., 1969—86, dir. orgn. planning and sec. to corp. mgmt. com. White Plains, NY, 1981—82, v.p. mfg. Communication Products div., 1982—83, v.p. display products Communication Products div., 1983—84, asst. group exec. Info Systems, Products Group, 1984—86; pres. Cullinet Software, Inc., Westwood, Mass., 1986—87, COO, 1987—88; exec. v.p. Emerson Electric Co., St. Louis, 1989—; principal Clayton, Dubilier & Rice, 2000—; CEO Kinkos, 2001, chmn., 2001—04, Culligan Internat., 2004, Hertz Corp., 2005—06. CEO Astec (BSR) Plc, Hong Kong, 1989—; bd. dir. Target Corp. Contbr. articles to profl. jours. Avocations: tennis, golf. Office: Clayton Dubilier & Rice 375 Park Ave 18th Fl New York NY 10152-1899*

**TAMKIN, CURTIS SLOANE,** real estate development company executive; b. Boston, Sept. 21, 1936; s. Hayward and Etta (Goldfarb) T.; m. Priscilla Martin, Oct. 18, 1975; 1 child, Curtis Sloane. BA in Econs., Stanford U., 1958. V.p., treas., dir. Hayward Tamkin & Co., mortgage bankers, L.A., 1963-70; mng. ptnr. Property Devel. Co., L.A., 1970-82; pres. The Tamkin Co., 1982—2000; chmn. Tamkin Capital Group L.L.C., 1999—. Mem. bd. govs. Music Ctr. L.A., 1974—98; pres. L.A. Master Chorale Assn. 1974—78; mem. vis. com. Stanford U. Librs., 1982—86; vice-chmn. bd. dirs., mem. exec. com. L.A. Philharm. Assn., 1985—, vice chmn. bd., 2004—, chmn. bd. overseers, 2001—. Lt. (j.g.) USNR, 1960—63. Mem.: Pacific Council Internat. Policy, L.A. Jr. C. of C. (dir. 1968—69), Founders League L.A. Music Ctr. (pres. 1988—98, chmn. emeritus 1998—), Hillcrest Country Club, Burlingame Country Club. Home: 1230 Stone Canyon Rd Los Angeles CA 90077-2920 Office: 9460 Wilshire Blvd Beverly Hills CA 90212-2732

**TAMKIN, S. JEROME,** manufacturing executive, consultant; b. LA, Apr. 19, 1926; s. William W. and Thelma (Brandel) T.; m. Judith Deborah, Mar. 23, 1963; children: Steven Marc, Windy Lynn, Gary William, Sherry Dawn. BS, U. So. Calif., 1950; MA, Fremont Coll., 1951, PhD, 1952; LL.D., St. Andrews U., London, 1954. Rsch. staff chemistry dept. U. Calif., LA, 1943; rsch. chemist, analyst supr. synthetic rubber div. U.S. Rubber Co., 1943-44; rsch. engr. Coll. Engring., U. So. Calif., 1946-48; gen. mgr. Pan Pacific Oil Co., Long Beach, Calif., 1948-55; plant mgr. indsl. sales and mfg., 1953-55; v.p., sales mgr. Wilco Co., LA, 1948-55, v.p charge indsl. sales and mfg., 1953-55; v.p., sales mgr. Unit Chem. Corp., LA, 1955-56; pres. Phillips Mfg. Co. (merger Instl. Food Equipment Corp.), LA, 1957-62, Waste King Corp. (subs. Instl. Food Equipment Corp.), 1962-67; also dir.; v.p., dir. Dyna Mfg. Co., LA, 1962-68; pres., dir. Profl. Rsch. Inc., LA, 1965-73; exec. v.p. Am. Med. Internat., Inc., Beverly Hills, Calif., 1966-71, dir., 1966-89; sec., dir. Rodger Young, Inc., L.A., 1971-77; pres., chmn. bd. TGT Petroleum Corp., Wichita, 1972—; pres., dir. Tamkin Cons. Corp., 1978—; owner, operator Tamkin Securities Co., 1979-86; vice chair bd., dir. Integrated Voice Solutions Inc., Chattanooga, 1991-96; bd. dirs. CAPP Care Inc., Newport Beach, Calif., 1991-99. Tech. cons. Daylin Inc., Beverly Hills, 1973-75; bd. dirs. Healthcare Decisions, Inc., Newport Beach, Calif., 1996-99. Contbr. articles to profl. jours.; patentee electronic gas detector, circuits for automatic control hazardous vapors. Cmty. warden W. Adams-Baldwin Hills Cmty. CD, 1950—52; bd. govs. West LA County coun. Boy Scouts Am., 1977—; bd. govs. Technion-Israel Inst. of Tech., 2001—; dep. sheriff L.A. County, 1949; city commr. L.A. Bd. Environ. Quality, 1972—78; founder Sunair Home Asthmatic Children, Recovery Found., Fund for Higher Edn., U. of Judaism, 1999—, UCLA Brain Mapping Found., 1999—, UCLA Ctr. on Aging, LA, 2005—; bd. visitors UCLA Sch. Medicine, 1990—; exec. com. adv. coun. crime prevention LA Police, 1985—; trustee, bd. visitors U. Calif.-Irvine Coll. Medicine, 1989—; trustee Morehouse Sch. Medicine, 1995—2005, Scripps Found. for Medicine and Sci., 1996—. Officer USNR, 1944—46. Mem. AIM, Am. Mgmt. Assn., Inst. Aero. Scis., Am. Soc. Naval Engrs., Soc. Am. Mil. Engrs., Am. Chem. Soc., IEEE, Soc. Motion Picture and TV Engrs., Am. Inst. Chem. Engrs., Soc. Advancement Mgmt., U.S. Naval Inst., Calif. Scholarship Fedn. (life), Nat. Eagle Scout Assn., Sunrise Country Club, The Springs Country Club, Malibu Riding and Tennis Club, Alpha Eta Rho. Office: 2100 Sawtelle Blvd Ste 201 Los Angeles CA 90025-6264

**TAMMELLEO, A. DAVID,** lawyer, editor, publisher; b. Providence, Aug. 9, 1935; s. Anthony and Kathleen (Gilleran) T.; m. Marylouise Kenney, Aug. 8, 1964; children: David A., Kathy. BA cum laude, Providence Coll., 1957; JD cum laude, Boston Coll., 1961. Bar: R.I. 1962, U.S. Dist. Ct. R.I., U.S. Ct. Appeals (1st cir.), U.S. Supreme Ct. Spl. investigative legal counsel State of R.I., Providence, 1961-69; sr. ptnr. A. David Tammelleo & Assocs., Providence, 1962—; chief trial counsel Monti & Monti, Providence, 1969-78; chief legal counsel Dept. Employment Security State of R.I., Providence, 1978-82; pres., pub. and CEO Medica Press Inc., Med. -Legal Pub. Co., Providence, 1984—2000; pub. Medica Press Inc., Providence, 1984—2004, editor-in-chief, 1984—2004; pres., pub. and CEO, editor-in-chief Medical Law Pub. Co., 2004—. Lectr. on hosp., med. and nursing law through U.S., 1984—; legal cons. Med. Econs. mag., 1984—. Editor: Nursing Law's Regan Report, 1984—; Hospital Law's Regan Report, 1984—, Medical Law's Regan Report, 1984—; mem. editl. bd. RN mag., 1984-94; contbg. editor RN Jour., 1984-2000; columnist Legally Speaking, Advice of Counsel, 1984—; contbr. articles to legal jours. Atty., mem. biomed. ethics commn. Diocese of Providence, 1984—. Fellow R.I. Bar Found. (editl. bd. R.I. Bar jour. 1975-90, R.I. Bar Assn. (med.-legal com., joint com. with R.I. Med. Soc.); mem. ABA, Am. Judicature Assn., Am. Acad. Hosp. Attys., Nat. Health Lawyers Assn., R.I. Bar Assn., Cath. Health Assn., New Eng. Conf. Cath. Health Assn., Boston Coll. Law Sch. Deans Coun., Boston Coll. Law Sch. Alumni Assn. Avocations: sailing, tennis, jogging, astronomy, aeronautics. Office: Crossroads Office Pk Ste 212 75 Sockanosset Cross Rd Cranston RI 02920-5558 E-mail: Adtlaw@aol.com.

**TAMMEUS, WILLIAM DAVID,** journalist, columnist; b. Woodstock, Ill., Jan. 18, 1945; s. W. H. and Bertha H. (Helander) T.; m. Marcia Bibens, Nov. 29, 1996; children: Lisen Tammeus Mann, Kate Tammeus Willaredt; stepchildren: Christopher L. Johnston, Daniel Bednarczyk, Kathryn B. Dandino, David Bednarczyk. BJ, U. Mo., Columbia, 1967; postgrad., U. Rochester, 1967-69. Reporter Rochester (N.Y.) Times-Union, 1967-70; reporter Kansas City (Mo.) Star, 1970-77, columnist, 1977—; syndicated columnist N.Y. Times News Svc., 1989-99, Knight Ridder/Tribune Info. Svcs., 2000—06; ret., 2006. Author: A Gift of Meaning, 2001; editor-at-large Presbyn. Outlook, 1993; contbg. editor Mo. Life mag., 1980-81; commentator Sta. KCPT-TV, 1979-90. Co-recipient Pulitzer prize for gen. local reporting of Hyatt Regency Hotel disaster, 1982; recipient 1st pl. opinion-editl. divsn. Heart of Am. award Kansas City Press Club, 1991, 93, 1st pl. column divsn., 1994, 1st pl. award best column/humor divsn. Mo. Press Assn., 1997, 2002, Best In-Depth Reporting on Religion award Am. Acad. Religion, 2001, David Steele Disting. Writer award Presbyn. Writers Guild, 2003, 1st pl. religion coverage Kans. Press Assn., 2004, Wilbur Column Writing award, Religion Communicators Coun., 2005, 1st pl. best feature column divsn. Mo. Press Assn. 2006. Mem. Nat. Soc. Newspaper Columnists (v.p. 1990-92, pres. 1992-94, 1st pl. items divsn. Writing award 1992, 3d place humor writing, 1999, 2000), Soc. Profl. Journalists. Presbyterian. Office Phone: 816-234-4437. E-mail: wtammeus@kc.rr.com.

**TAMONY, KATIE,** editor-in-chief; m. Patrick Tamony; children: Sara, Caitlin. BA in History, U. Calif., Berkeley, 1989. Mng. editor No. Calif. Home and Garden mag.; copy editor Sunset mag., N.Y.C., 1994—97, editl. dir., 1997—98, dir. custom pub., 1998, v.p., 1998, editor in chief, 2001—; Author: Your Second Pregnancy: What to Expect This Time, 1995. Dir. Custom Publishing.

**TAMPAS, JOHN P.,** radiologist; married; children: Jessica, Peter, Andrea, Christiana. BS, U. Vt., 1951, MD, 1954. Diplomate Am. Bd. Radiology. Radiology resident U. Vt., Burlington, 1957—60; teaching fellow pediat. radiology L.A. Children's Hosp., 1960—61; NIH Nat. Heart Inst. resident fellow cardiovascular radiology U. Ind., Indpls., 1961—62; attending radiology Med. Ctr. Hosp. Vt., Burlington, 1962—; asst. prof. radiology Coll. Medicine U. Vt., 1962—70; prof. & chmn. dept. radiology Med. Ctr. Hosp. Vt., Burlington, 1970—96. Contbr. articles to profl. jours. Recipient Karl Jefferson Thompson Meml. Excellence in Tchg. award, 1969, 1975; scholar, James Picker Found./NRC, 1962—65. Fellow: Am. Coll. Radiology (pres. 1987—88, bd. chancellors, emergency radiology com., accreditation com. chmn. mem. in. com., adminstrv. affairs commn.; radiologic practice commn., Gold medal 1996); mem.: AMA, Vt. Med. Soc., Vt. Radiol. Soc., Assn. Univ. Radiologists, Soc. Chmn. Acad. Radiology Depts., New Eng. Roentgen Ray Soc., Radiol. Soc. N.Am., Am. Roentgen-Ray Soc. (pres. 1982—83, Gold medal 1992), Soc. Pediat. Radiology, Alpha Omega Alpha. Office: Fletcher Allen Health Ctr 111 Colchester Ave Burlington VT 05401-1416 also: Hosp Vt Med Ctr Dept Radiology Burlington VT 05401

**TAMURA, CARY KAORU,** consultant; b. Honolulu, Jan. 9, 1944; s. Akira and Harue T.; m. Denise Jeanne Mitts, Oct. 17, 1987; children: Jennifer Joy, Matthew D. Student, U. Hawaii, 1961—63; BA in Philosophy, Nyack Coll., 1966; MA in Theology, Fuller Sem., 1986. Dir. svc. tng. ops. Fin. Adv. Clinic of Hawaii, Honolulu, 1972—76; dir. planned giving The Salvation Army, Honolulu, 1976—78, Portland, Oreg., 1981—85; cons. planned giving InterVarsity Christian Fellowship, Portland, 1978—80; account exec. Am. Income Life, Portland, 1980—81; dir. devel., planned giving U. So. Calif., 1985—90; dir. gift planning UniHealth America, Burbank, Calif., 1990—94; pvt. practice Brea, Calif., 1995—. Adv. com., adj. faculty UCLA Extension; lectr. in field. Bd. dirs. Nat. Com. on Planned Giving, Indpls., 1991-93, sec. exec. com., 1993; bd. dirs. Japanese Evang. Missionary Soc., 1990-95, 2003—, Simpson U., 1998—; deacons Evang. Free Ch., 1992-95. With U.S. Army, 1969-72. Mem. Planned Giving Round Table So. Calif. (pres. 1989-91, Pres.'s award 1992), Assn. of Fundraising Profls. (bd. dirs. Greater L.A. chpt. 1990-97, v.p. 1993, treas. 1996-97, Profl. Fund Raiser of Yr. award 1995). Republican. Avocations: photography, golf, travel. Office: PO Box 908 Brea CA 92822 E-mail: visionkeeper1@yahoo.com.

**TAMURA, LINDA GAYLE,** education educator; b. Hood River, Oreg., June 21, 1949; d. Harry and Chiyo Tamura. EdD, Oreg. State U., Corvallis, 1981. With Willamette Univ. Salem. Editl. adv. bd. Oreg. Hist. Soc., Portland, Oreg., 2002—; edn. adv. coun. World Affairs Coun. Oreg., Portland. Author: (book) Wrong Face, Wrong Name: The Return of Japanese American Veterans to Hood River, Oregon After WWII; co-editor: Turning Points in Teaching: Narrative Reflection on Profesional Practice, Willamette Jour. of the Liberal Arts; author: (book) The Hood River Issei: An Oral History of Japanese Settlers in Oregon's Hood River Valley; contbr. articles to profl. jours. Sr. fellow Am. Leadership Forum, Portland, 2001—06. Recipient Spl. Recognition award, Oreg. Multicultural Edn. Assn., 1995, Woman of Achievement, Salem YWCA, 1997, FACES Svc. Learning award, Willamette U., 2002—03, United Meth. award for Exemplary Tchg. and Svc. to U. and Cmty., 2003. Mem.: Phi Delta Kappa (bd. dirs. 2005—). Office: Willamette Univ 900 State St Salem OR 97062 Office Phone: 503-370-6430. Office Fax: 503-375-5453. Business E-Mail: ltamura@willamette.edu.

**TAN, ALSON,** computer scientist; b. July 1, 1974; BSc in Computer Sci.; MBA, Curtin U. of Tech., Perth, Australia, 2003. Sr. tech. cons., project mgr. Hewlett Packard, Singapore, 1992—97; sr. cons. Fiji Xerox, Singapore, 1997—2000; sr. cons. mgr. Infogain Inc., Calif., 2000—02; dir. IT IDS-Asia, 2002—.

**TAN, AMY RUTH,** writer; b. Oakland, Calif., Feb. 19, 1952; d. John Yueh-han and Daisy Ching (Tu) T.; m. Louis M. DeMattei, Apr. 6, 1974. Student, Linfield Coll., McMinnville, Oreg., San Jose (Calif.) City Coll.; BA in Linguistics and English with honors, San Jose (Calif.) State U., 1973, MA in Linguistics, 1974; LHD (hon.), Dominican Coll. San Rafael, 1991. Specialist lang. devel. Alameda County Assn. for Mentally Retarded, Oakland, 1976-80; project dir. M.O.R.E. Project, San Francisco, 1980-81; mng. editor Emergency Medicine Reports newsletter, San Francisco; freelance writer, 1981-88; literary editor West mag. LA Times. Author: (novels) The Joy Luck Club, 1989 (Nat. Book Critics Cir. award for best novel nomination 1989, LA Times Book award nomination 1989, Gold award for fiction Commonwealth Club 1990, Bay Area Book Reviewers award for best fiction 1990), The Kitchen God's Wife, 1991, The Hundred Secret Senses, 1995, The Bonesetter's Daughter, 2001, The Opposite of Fate: A Book of Musing, 2003, Saving Fish from Drowning, 2005; (children's books) The Moon Lady, 1992, The Chinese Siamese Cat, 1994; also numerous short stories and essays; screenwriter, prodr.: (film) The Joy Luck Club, 1993. Recipient Best Am. Essays award, 1991. Office: c/o Putnam Publicity 375 Hudson Street New York NY 10014*

**TAN, COLLEEN WOO,** communications educator; b. San Francisco, May 6, 1923; d. Mr. and Mrs. S.H. Nq Quinn; m. Lawrence K.J. Tan; children: Lawrence L., Lance C. BA in English/Am. Lit., Ind. U., 1950, MA in English, 1952; MA in Speech Arts, Whittier Coll., 1972; postgrad., U. Calif. Berkeley, 1952-53. Cert. secondary edn. tchr., K-12, community coll., Calif. Tchng. aide English U. Calif., Berkeley, 1952-53; tchr. English and Social Studies Whittier (Calif.) High Sch., 1957-60; prof. speech commn. Mt. San Antonio Coll., Walnut, Calif., 1960-94; dir. forensics, 1969-80; sen. acad. senate Mt. San Antonio Coll., Walnut, Calif., 1982-90, faculty rep., 1990—. Recipient Woman of Achievement Edn. award San Gabriel Valley, Calif. YWCA, 1995; named Outstanding Prof. Emeritus, Mt. San Antonio Coll. Found., 1994,Outstanding Alumnae, MaryKnoll Sisters Sch., 1997. Mem. AAUW (pres. Whittier Br. 1982, cultural interests chair Calif. state divsn. 1985-87, Fellowship award 1973-74, Las Distinguidas award 1992, Found. honoree Whittier br. 2004-05), Calif. Asian-Am. Faculty Assn., Delta Kappa Gamma, Phi Beta Kappa (Outstanding Educator of Am. award 1972), Alpha Delta Kappa (interim pres. 2003-04) Roman Catholic. Avocations: creative writing, reading fiction, attending theater, music, dance. Home: 13724 Sunrise Dr Whittier CA 90602-2547 Office: Mt San Antonio 1100 N Grand Ave Walnut CA 91789-1341

**TAN, ENG MENG,** immunologist, biomedical researcher; b. Seremban, Malaysia, Aug. 26, 1926; arrived in US, 1950; s. Ming Kee and Chooi Eng (Ang) T.; m. Liselotte Filippi, June 30, 1962; children: Philip, Peter. BA, Johns Hopkins U., 1952, MD, 1956. Intern Duke U., Durham, NC, 1956-57; resident, fellow Case-We. Res. U., Cleve., 1957-62; rsch. assoc. Rockefeller U., N.Y.C., Calif., 1962-65; asst. prof. Washington U. Sch. Medicine, St. Louis, Calif., 1965-67; assoc. mem. and mem. Scipps Rsch. Inst., LaJolla, Calif., 1967—77; prof. Scripps Rsch. Inst., LaJolla, Calif., 1982—, U. Colo. Sch. Medicine, Denver, 1977-82. Chmn. allergy & immunology rsch. com. NIH, Bethesda, Md., 1982-84; mem. nat. arthritis adv. bd. HHS, Washington, 1981-85; hon. prof. Shanghei (China) 2d Med. U. Contbr. chapters to books, articles to profl. jours. Named to Nat. Lupus Hall Fame, 1984; recipient US Sr. Scientist award, Humboldt Found., Germany, 1986, Ciba-Giegy-Internat. League against Rheumatism award, 1989, Carol Nachman award, Wiesbaden, Germany, 1989, Lee Howley Sr. award, Arthritis Found., 1989, Paul Klemperer award and medal, NY Acad. Medicine, 1993, City Medicine award, Durham, NC, 1996, Disting. Med. Alumnus award, Duke U., 2000, Mayo Soley award, Western Soc. Clin. Investigation, 2002, Japan Rheumatism Found. Internat. prize, 2003, Meritorious Svc. award, European League Against Rheumatism, 2005. Fellow AAAS; mem. Am. Coll. Rheumatology (pres. 1984-85, chmn. Blue Ribbon com. Future Acad. Rheumatology 1997-98, Disting. Investigator award 1991, Gold medal award 1998), Assn. Am. Physicians, Am. Soc. Clin. Investigation, Western Assn. Physicians (v.p. 1980-81), Am. Assn. Immunologists, Brazilian Soc. Rheumatology (hon.), Australian Rheumatism Assn. (hon.), Brit. Soc. Rheumatology (hon.), Mex. Nat. Acad. Medicine (hon.). Achievements include research on antibodies and antigens in cancer and in autoimmune diseases, systemic lupus erythematosus, scleroderma, Sjogren's syndrome, myositis and mixed connective tissue disease; relationship of autoantibodies to pathogenesis. Home: 8303 Sugarman Dr La Jolla CA 92037-2224 Office: Scripps Rsch Inst 10550 N Torrey Pines Rd La Jolla CA 92037-1000 Office Phone: 858-784-8686. Business E-Mail: emtan@scripps.edu.

**TAN, LI-SU LIN,** accountant, insurance company executive, consultant; b. Keelung, Taiwan, Republic of China, Mar. 7, 1956; arrived in US, 1985; d. I-Chang and Sung-Mei (Chen) Lin; m. Bert T. Tan, Aug. 19, 1985; children: Patricia Tan, Peter Puwen Tan, Lotus Tan. BBA, Nat. Taiwan U., 1978; MBA, Ill. Inst. Tech., Chgo., 1991. CPA, Ill., Taiwan; lic. ins. agt., Ill.; registered investment advisor. Asst. mgr. T.N. Soong & Co. (mem. firm Arthur Anderson & Co., SC), Taipei, 1978—85; practitioner Li-Su Lin, CPA, Taipei, 1981—85, Li-Su Lin Tan, CPA, Naperville, Ill., 1988—90; pres. Lisu L. Tan & Co., Ltd., CPAs, Naperville, 1990—; agt. Mut. Omaha Co., Lombard, Ill., 1991—94, Met. Life and Affiliated Cos., Bloomingdale, Ill., 1993—98, GE Fin. Assurance, Schaumburg, Ill., 1999—. Chair family Naperville Chinese Assn., 1990. Mem.: AICPA (tax divsn., quality control program), Ill. Soc. CPA, Amitabha Buddhist Libr. Chgo. (pres. 2003—, bd. dirs.), Buddha's Light Internat. Assn. (pres. Chgo. chpt. 2002—04, bd. dirs.), Chinese Am. Culture Found. (pres. 2001—, bd. dirs.), Nat. Taiwan U. Alumni Assn. Greater Chgo. (bd. dirs. 1999—2003), World Taiwanese C. of C. (dep. treas. 1998—99), Taiwanese C. of C. N.Am. (treas. 1998—99, bd. dirs.), Greater Chgo. Area Taiwanese Am. C. of C. (bd. dirs. 1995—2006), Taipei First Girls High Alumni Assn. (treas. 1990—94). Buddhist. Avocations: travel, art collecting, photography. Office: Lisu L Tan & Co Ltd CPAs 6S235 Steeple Run Dr #200 Naperville IL 60540-3754 Office Phone: 630-416-9422. Business E-Mail: lisu@lisutancpas.com.

**TAN, MARIA (MIA TAN),** music educator; arrived in US, 1962; d. Tjing Gich Tan and Kwan Nio Oei; divorced; children: Anita Thesen, Britt Thesen, Arne Thesen, Thomas Madison Flemming. MusB, U. Hawaii, 0196; postgrad., DePaul U., 1966—67; MusM in Piano Performance, U. Ill., 1970. Pres. Hawaii Piano Tchr. Assn., Honolulu, 1986—87; chmn. audition ctr. Nat. Guild Piano Tchrs.; chmn., jr. artist Hawaii Music Tchr. Assn., 1997—2000. Pres., founder Feng Shui Hawaii, Honolulu, 2003—; founder Amadeus concert competition Alexandria (Va.) Symphony, 1992. Scholar, East West Ctr. Cultural Exch., Honolulu, 1962—66, DePaul U., 1966—67, U. Ill., 1967—70. Mem.: Windward Music Tchr. Assn. (chmn. 2000—03), East West Ctr. Alumni Assn. (bd. dirs. 2001—05). Democrat. Avocation: floral designing.

**TAN, ROBERT C.,** music educator; b. Singapore, Oct. 8, 1936; arrived in U.S., 1959; s. Chin Khin and Lena Tan. BA, Union Coll., Lincoln, Nebr., 1963. Lic. tchg. Royal Sch. Music London, 1957, performance Royal Sch. Music London, 1958. Tchr. music Fortune Jr. Acad., Calif., 1965—68, Pleasant Hill Jr. Acad., 1968—82, Lodi Acad., 2002—2005; founder and dir. Lodi Children's Chorus, 1983—. Dir. English Oaks Seventh Day Adventist Ch. Choir, Lodi, Calif., 1983—, Zion Ref. Ch. Choir, 1983—. Recipient Instr. of Yr., Lodi Arts Commn., 1992, Tchr. of Yr., Lodi Acad., 1999, Mayor's Cmty. Svc. award, Lodi, Calif., 2002. Mem.: Am. Choral Dir. Assn., Twin Arbors Athletic Club. Republican. Adventist. Avocations: swimming, skiing, tennis, bodybuilding. Home: 1853 Songbird Pl Lodi CA 95240-7827

**TAN, TJIAUW-LING,** psychiatrist, educator; b. Pemalang, Java, Indonesia, June 2, 1935; came to U.S., 1967; naturalized, 1972; s. Ping-Hoey and Liep-Nio (Liem) T.; m. Esther Joyce Kho, June 2, 1961; children: Paul Budiman, Robert Yuling, Alice Ayling. BS, U. Indonesia Faculty Medicine, 1957, MD, 1961; postgrad., U. Indonesia, Jakarta, 1961-65, UCLA, 1967-71, Pa. State U., 1971-72. Diplomate Am. Bd. Psychiatry and Neurology, Gen. Psychiatry, Bd.Psychiatry & Neurology, Geriat. Psychiatry. Lectr. psychiatry U. Indonesia, Jakarta, 1965-67; psychiat. cons. Ctrl. Gen. Hosp., Jakarta, 1965-67; postdoctoral fellow UCLA Brain Rsch. Inst., 1967-69; asst. rsch. psychiatrist, dept. psychiatry Neuropsychiat. Inst., UCLA, 1969-70; asst. prof. psychiatry Pa. State U., 1972-87, assoc. prof. psychiatry, 1987-99, prof. psychiatry, 1999—. Chief inpatient psychiatry Univ. Hosp. Milton S. Hershey Med. Ctr., 1972-2005, dir. Behavioral Medicine Clinic, co-dir. Biofeedback Lab., 1975—2005; cons. psychiatry Family and Children's Svc. Lebanon County, Lebanon, Pa., 1971-79. Contbr. articles to profl. jours. Bd. dir. Retarded Children's Assn. Dauphin County, Inc., 1971—73. Fellow Am. Psychiat. Assn. (disting. life), Pa. Psychiat. Soc.; mem. Ctrl. Pa. Psychiat. Soc., Assn. Advancement Behavior Therapy, Assn. Applied Psychophysiology and Biofeedback, Soc. Behavioral Medicine, Assn. Psychophysiol. Study of Sleep, Am. Assn. for Geriat. Psychiatry, Am. Geriat. Soc. Democrat. Presbyterian. Home: 1478 Bradley Ave Hummelstown PA 17036-9143 Office: Pa State U Coll Medicine Dept Psychiatry 500 University Dr Hershey PA 17033-2390 Office Phone: 717-531-8207. Business E-Mail: lingtan@psu.edu.

**TAN, ZIXIANG,** education educator, researcher; s. Q. and P. Tan; m. Jin Zhou, Feb. 10, 1988; children: Elliot, Max. B and M, Tsinghua U., Beijing, China, 1978—85; M, Sussex U., Eng., 1989—90; PhD, Rutgers U., New Brunswick, N.J., 1992—96. Asst. prof. IST, Syracuse U., NY, 1996—2002, assoc. prof., 2002—06. Co-author (with M. Mueller): (book) China in the Information Age: Telecommunications and the Dilemmas of Reform, Washington, D.C./Westport in CT: the Center of Strategic and International Studies (CSIS), 1997. Office Phone: 1-315-443-2911.

**TANABE, CHARLES Y.,** lawyer; b. Denver, Nov. 27, 1951; BA cum laude, U. Colo., 1973; JD, U. Calif. Berkeley, 1976. Bar: Colo. 1976. Former atty. Sherman & Howard, L.L.C., Denver; sr. v.p., gen. counsel Liberty Media Corp., Englewood, Colo., 1999—, sec., 2001—. Mem. ABA, Phi Beta Kappa. Office: Liberty Media Corp 12300 Liberty Blvd Englewood CO 80112

**TANABE, NORIAKI,** library director; b. Shizuoka, Japan, Nov. 17, 1950; s. Sampei and Yoshie (Shinozuka) Tanabe; m. Yumi Inose. BA, Meiji U., Tokyo, 1975; cert. libr., Nat. Coll. Libr. Sci., Tokyo, 1976. Advisor to amb. Japanese Embassy, Jakarta, Indonesia, 1990—92; dep. gen. mgr. Tokyo Bankers Assn., 1992—97; chief libr. The Bankers Libr., Tokyo, 1997—. Avocation: rugby. Office: The Bankers Libr 3-1 Marunouchi 1-Chome Tokyo 100-8216 Japan Office Phone: (+81.3) 5252.3788. Office Fax: (+81.3) 5252.3797. Business E-Mail: tanabe@zenginkyo.or.jp.

**TANABE, PAULA,** nursing educator, researcher; m. Paula Geuss, Aug. 13, 1983. ADN, Coll. DuPage, Glen Ellyn, 1983; BS, Rush U., Chgo., 1987; MSN, Loyola U., Maywood, Ill., 1990; PhD, U. Ill., Chgo., 1996; MPH, Northwestern U., Chgo., 2006. Rsch. asst. prof. Northwestern U., Chgo., 2005—. Clin. nurse specialist Northwestern Meml. Hosp., Chgo., 2000—03. Fellow, Northwestern U., 2003—04, Agy. Healthcare Rsch. and Quality, 2003—04; grantee, 2005—06, Emergency Medicine and Emergency Nursing Found., 2005—06. Mem.: Emergency Nurses Assn. (state pres. 2000—00). Office: Northwestern U 259 E Erie Ste 100 Chicago IL 60611 Office Phone: 312-926-6483. Office Fax: 312-926-6274. E-mail: ptanabe2@nmff.org.

**TANAKA, KOUICHI ROBERT,** hematologist, educator; b. Fresno, Calif., Dec. 15, 1926; s. Kenjiro and Teru (Arai) T.; m. Grace Mutsuko Sakaguchi, Oct. 23, 1965; children: Anne M., Nancy K., David K. BS, Wayne State U., 1949, MD, 1952. Cert. in internal medicine Am. Bd. Internal Medicine, 1961, recertified in internal medicine Am. Bd. Internal Medicine, 1974, cert. in hematology Am. Bd. Internal Medicine, 1972. Intern Los Angeles County Gen. Hosp., 1952—53; resident, fellow Detroit Receiving Hosp., 1953—57; instr. Sch. Medicine UCLA, 1957—59, asst. prof. medicine, 1959—61, assoc. prof. medicine, 1961—68, prof. Sch. Medicine, 1968—97, prof. emeritus, 1998—. Chief hematology divsn. Harbor-UCLA, Torrance, Calif., 1961—97, chief hematology, 1998—2000. Author 136 rsch. publs. Served U.S. Army, 1946—48. Recipient Disting. Alumni Svc. award, Wayne St. U. Sch. Med. Alumni Assn., Med. Alumni Assn. Disting. Svc. award, UCLA. Master ACP (gov. So. Calif. region I 1993-97); mem. Am. Fedn. Med. Rsch., We. Soc. Clin. Investigation, Am. Soc. Hematology, Internat. Soc. Hematology, We. Assn. Physicians, Am. Soc. Clin. Investigation, Assn. Am. Physicians, Sigma Xi, Alpha Omega Alpha. Achievements include research on red cell metabolism. Home: 4 Cayuse Ln Rancho Palos Verdes CA 90275-5172 Office: Dept Med Box 400 Harbor-UCLA Med Ctr Torrance CA 90509 Office Phone: 310-222-3695.

**TANAKA, PATRICE AIKO,** public relations executive; b. Hawaii; BA, U. Hawaii, 1974. Editor Hawaii Press Newspapers, 1974-77; dir. pub. rels. Hotel Inter-Continental Maui, 1977-79; acct. exec. to sr. v.p. and creative dir. Jessica Dee Comm., NYC, 1979-87, exec. v.p., gen. mgr. 1987-90; CEO, creative dir. PT&Co., NYC, 1990—2005, CRT/tanaka, 2005—. Featured in books: American Dreamers, Visionaries and Entrepreneurs, 1995, The Art of Public Relations, 2002. Bd. dirs. Greater NY coun. Girl Scouts US, US Fund for UNICEF, Family Violence Prevention Fund, Asian Pacific Am. Women's Leadership Inst. Named one of nation's 500 Most Influential Asian Ams., Avenue mag., 1996; recipient Mothering That Works award, Working Mother mag., 1999, Women Mean Bus. award, Bus. and Profl. Women U.S.A., 1999, Paul M. Lund award for pub. svc., Pub. Rels. Soc. Am., 2002. Mem.: Asian Women in Bus. (bd. dirs.), Coun. Pub. Rels. Firms (founding bd. dirs.), Women Execs. in Pub. Rels., NY Women in Comm. (pres. 2001—02,

2002—03, Matrix award for pub. rels. 1996), Asian Pacific Am. Women's Leadership Inst. (founding bd. dirs.), Women's Forum NY, U. Hawaii Alumni Assn. (bd. dirs. NY chpt.). Office: CRT/tanaka 320 W 13th St Fl 7 New York NY 10014-1200

**TANAKA, RICHARD I.,** computer company executive; b. Sacramento, Dec. 17, 1928; s. G. and Kei Tanaka; m. Edith M. Arita, Aug. 18, 1951; children: Steven Richard, Jean Elizabeth, John Richard, Anne Mariko. BS with highest honors, U. Calif., Berkeley, 1950, MS, 1951; PhD, Calif. Inst. Tech., 1958. Sr. rsch. engr. N.Am. Aviation, Inc., 1951-54; mem. tech. staff Hughes Aircraft Co., 1954-57; dept. mgr., sr. mem. computer rsch. Lockheed Missiles & Space Co., Palo Alto, Calif., 1957-65; sr. v.p. Cal Comp (Calif. Computer Products, Inc.), Anaheim, 1966-77; pres. Internat. Tech. Resources Co., Tustin, Calif., 1977-80; pres., CEO Systonetics, Inc., Fullerton, Calif., 1980-86; pres. Lundy Electronics & Sys., Inc., Glen Head, NY, 1986-89; chmn., CEO, pres. Scan-Optics, Inc., Manchester, Conn., 1989-97; chmn., CEO V-Sys., Inc., San Juan Capistrano, Calif., 1999-2000; pres. ITR Co., Santa Ana, Calif., 2000—. Vis. prof. U. Calif., Berkeley, 1962 Author: Residue Arithmetic and Its Applications to Computer Technology, 1967. Hughes fellow Calif. Inst. Tech., 1955-57 Fellow IEEE (pres. computer soc. 1965-66, centennial medal, Golden Core award 1996); mem. Internat. Fedn. Info. Processing (pres. 1974-77, hon. life mem., U.S. del.), Am. Fedn. Info. Processing Socs. (pres. 1969-71, disting. service award 1983), Phi Beta Kappa, Tau Beta Pi, Eta Kappa Nu. Home: 10321 Shadyridge Dr Santa Ana CA 92705-1568 Personal E-mail: ritanaka@cox.net.

**TANAKA, RICHARD KOICHI, JR.,** architect, planner; b. San Jose, Calif., Oct. 16, 1931; s. Richard Inoru and Mae Yoshiko (Koga) T.; m. Barbara Hisako Kumagai, Oct. 7, 1961; children: Craig, Todd, Sandra, Trent. BArch, U. Mich., 1954; M in Urban Planning, Calif. State U., San Jose, 1978. Arch., planner Steinberg Group, San Jose, L.A., 1954. Chair, bd. dirs. Happi House Restaurants, Inc., 1972—. Author: American on Trial, 1988. Dir. Human Rels. Com., San Jose, 1969-73; dir., pres. Bicentennial Com., San Jose, 1974-77; bd. dirs. Santa Clara County Sch. Bd. Assn., 1980—; pres. Internment of Local Japanese Ams., San Jose, 1984—; past pres., trustee East Side H.S. Dist., San Jose, 1971-92, Japanese Am. Citizens League, San Jose; mem. bd. govs. Boy Scouts Am., San Jose, 1978—, NCCJ, San Jose, 1976—; past pres. Tapestry and Talent, 1976-80; trustee San Jose/Evergreen C.C., 1992—, pres., 1993-94, 97-98, 2001-02; bd. dirs. Calif. C.C. Trustees, 1993-2002, pres., 1997-98. Mem. AIA, Am. Planning Inst., Constrn. Specification Inst., Rotary. Avocations: golf, painting. Home: 14811 Whipple Ct San Jose CA 95127-2570 Office: 60 Pierce Ave San Jose CA 95110-2819 Office Phone: 408-251-6371. Personal E-mail: rktanaka@sbcglobal.net.

**TANANBAUM, JAMES,** medical engineering company executive; b. NYC, May 5, 1963; s. David J. and Elizebeth Zelda (Belfer) T. BS cum laude, Yale U., 1985; postgrad. health scis., tech. program, Harvard U. and MIT (joint), Boston, 1985-89; postgrad., Harvard Bus. Sch., Boston, 1989—. Rsch. asst. MIT, Cambridge, 1986—; chmn. Med. Engring. Devices, Inc., Boston, 1987—. Computer cons. Nat. Retirement Programs, Inc., N.Y.C., 1981—; Software Engring., Inc., N.Y.C. 1985, Clin. Computing Ctr., Inc., Boston, 1985—; student mem. Health, Scis., and Tech. Program, Harvard U. and MIT, 1986—. Mem. Sigma Xi. Office: Advanced Medical Inc 901Gateway Blvd South San Francisco CA 94080

**TANANBAUM, STEVEN ANDREW,** investment consultant; b. NYC, June 26, 1965; s. David Jay and Elizabeth (Belfer) Tananbaum. BA in Econs., Vassar Coll., 1987. Analyst Kidder, Peabody & Co., NYC, 1987-89; investment specialist MacKay Shields, NYC, 1989—91, head high yield grp., 1991—97, lead portfolio mgr. hedge fund area, 1997; sr. mng. mem., founding ptnr. GoldenTree Asset Mgmt., LP, NYC, 2000—, CEO, chief investment officer. Cons. Nat. Retirement Progs., 1987—89. Bd. dirs. Citymeals-on-Wheels, NYC; mem. corp. fund bd. John F. Kennedy Ctr. Performing Arts. Named one of Top 200 Collectors, ARTnews mag., 2006. Republican. Office: GoldenTree Asset Mgmt LP 300 Park Ave 21st Fl New York NY 10022*

**TANCER, EDWARD F.,** lawyer, utilities executive; b. 1961; BA, JD, Univ. Fla. Bar: Fla. 1985. Atty. through v.p. & gen. counsel FPL Energy, Juno Beach, Fla., 1988—2005; assoc. gen. counsel FPL Group, Juno Beach, Fla., 2003—05, v.p. & gen. counsel, 2005—. Office: FPL Group 700 Universe Blvd PO Box 14000 North Palm Beach FL 33408

**TANCER, ROBERT STEPHEN,** prosecutor, educator; b. NYC, Aug. 4, 1933; s. Manuel and Deborah Levy Tancer; m. Shoshana Baron Tancer, June 10, 1954; children: Sara Gordon, Manuel, Catherine Lawkowtiz, Cynthia. BA, U. Mich., 1957; LLM, Harvard U., 1960. Bar: Wash D.C. 1958, Ariz. 1970. Atty. Allenda y Braa, Buenos Aires, 1960—62; of counsel ABC Internat., NYC, 1962—65; capital divsn. officer A.I. D, Wash., DC, 1965—67, asst. dir., 1967—69; atty. O'Connor Cavanaugh, Phoenix, 1969—75; mng. ptnr Tancer Law Offices LLC, Phoenix, 1975—91; prof. Thunderbird Am. Grad. Sch., Glendale, Ariz., 1990—. Dir. Flagstaff Inst., Ariz., 1990—. Contbr. articles to profl. jours. Bd. mem. AZ Opera, 1993—, pres., 1999—2001; bd. mem. Darut Botanical Garden, Phoenix, 1999—2005, Mental Health Rsch., 2006—.

**TANCREDI, JAMES J.,** lawyer; b. Hartford, Conn., Apr. 1, 1954; s. Joseph I. and Angelina C. (Lanza) T.; children: Lauren, Jamie, Brian. BA in Urban Studies and Polit. Sci., Coll. Holy Cross, 1976; JD, U. Conn., 1979. Bar: Conn. 1979, U.S. Dist. Ct. Conn. 1979, U.S. Ct. Appeals (2d cir.) 1982, U.S. Dist. (so. dist.) N.Y. 1988, U.S. Supreme Ct., 1991; cert. comml. bankruptcy specialist. From assoc. to ptnr Day, Berry & Howard, Hartford, Conn., 1979—, ptnr., chmn. fin. restructuring group, 1996—. Editor: CT Bankruptcy Desk Book. Bd. dirs. Conn. Mental Health Assn., Hartford, 1986-89, 2001-04. Mem. ABA (bus. sect.), Am. Bankruptcy Inst., Conn. Bar Assn. (exec. com. mem. bankruptcy section), Hartford County Bar Assn. (dir., chair cmty. comml. law 1997-2004), Conn. Turnaround Assn. (dir. 2004—). Office: Day Berry & Howard LLP CityPlace I Hartford CT 06103 also: 875 Third Ave New York NY 10001 Office Phone: 212-829-3600. Business E-mail: jjtancredi@dbh.com.

**TANCREDI, LAURENCE RICHARD,** law educator, psychologist; b. Hershey, Pa., Oct. 15, 1940; s. Samuel N. and Alvesta (Pera) T. AB in English, Franklin and Marshall Coll., 1962; MD, U. Pa., 1966; JD, Yale U., 1972. Diplomate Am. Bd. Neurology and Psychiatry; Bar: N.Y. 1982. Sr. prof. assoc. Inst. Medicine, NAS, Washington, 1972-74; fellow in psychiatry Columbia U. Coll. Physicians and Surgeons, N.Y.C., 1974-75; postdoctoral fellow in psychiatry Yale U. Med. Sch., New Haven, 1975-77; assoc. prof. psychiatry Med. Sch. NYU, New Haven, 1977-84; Kraft Eidman prof. medicine and law U. Tex. Health Sci. Ctr., Houston, 1984-92, dir. health law program, 1983-92; clin. prof. psychiatry NYU, 1992—; clin. prof. health care scis. U. Calif., San Diego, 1993—2003; mem. staff Brookhaven Nat. Labs. Clin. Ctr., 1994-96; pvt. practice N.Y.C., 1994—. V.p., bd. dirs., pres.-elect Internat. Acad. Law and Mental Health, 1987—95, bd. dirs., 2002—, v.p., 2003—; mem. adv. com. on transplantations Health Care Fin. Adminstrn., Dept. Health and Human Svcs., 1981—84; mem. nat. adv. bd. NIMH Ctr. Study of Pub. Mental Health N.Y. State Office Mental Health, 1994—99; cmty. svcs. bd. Dept. Mental Health, Mental Retardation and Alcohol Svcs., City of N.Y., 1995—2001; mem. sci. adv. com. Am. Suicide Found., 1995—; cons. Commn. on Med. Profl. Liability; co-prin., investigator study ABA, 1978—80; cons. in field. Fellow: Am. Coll. Psychiatry, N.Y. Acad. Med. Office: 129B E 71st St New York NY 10021-4201 Personal E-mail: lrtancredi@aol.com.

**TANCREDO, THOMAS G.,** congressman; b. North Denver, Dec. 20, 1945; m. Jackie Tancredo; 2 children. BA, U. North Colo., 1968. Mem. Colo. State Ho. Reps., 1977-81; regional rep. U.S. Dept. Edn., 1981-93; mem. U.S. Congress from 6th Colo. dist., 1999—; mem. edn. and workforce, internat.

rels., and resources coms.; mem. Ho. Budget Com. Republican. Office: US Ho Reps 1130 Longworth Ho Office Bldg Washington DC 20515-0606 also: Dist Office Ste 200 6099 S Quebec St Centennial CO 80111-4547

**TANCS, LINDA ANN,** lawyer; b. Elizabeth, N.J., Sept. 27, 1963; d. Tibor Louis and Rose Tancs. Student, U. Warwick, Coventry, Eng., 1984; BA magna cum laude, Rutgers U., 1985; JD cum laude, Seton Hall U. Sch. Law, 1993. Bar: N.J. 1993, N.Y., 1994, U.S. Dist. Ct. (N.J.) 1993, U.S. Ct. Appeals (fed. cir.) 2001. Paralegal Fox and Fox, Counsellors at Law, Newark, 1985-88, Vol. Lawyers for Arts, N.Y.C., 1988; corp. paralegal Wilentz, Goldman & Spitzer, Woodbridge, N.J., 1988-90, assoc., 1993-96; staff atty. Muze, Inc., N.Y.C., 1996-97; atty. IMS Health, Inc., Totowa, NJ, 1997—99; sr. assoc. Norris, McLaughlin & Marcus, Somerville, NJ, 2000—05, ptnr., 2005—. V.p. Pro Agents, Inc., 1995-96; adj. prof. acctg. and legal studies dept. Middlesex County Coll., Edison, N.J., 1998-99; adj. prof. paralegal studies Fairleigh Dickenson U., 1999; councilwoman Borough of Roselle Park, 1999-2001. Assoc. editor Seton Hall Law Rev. Mem. ABA, N.J. Bar Assn., N.Y. State Bar Assn. (chair young entertainment lawyers com. 1994-96, co-chair motion pictures com. 2005-), Phi Beta Kappa, Phi Sigma Iota, Delta Phi Alpha. Office Phone: 908-252-4231. Business E-Mail: latancs@nmmlaw.com.

**TANDBERG, GERILYN GAY,** theater educator, costume designer; b. Rugby, ND, Aug. 23, 1942; d. Otto and Edna Tandberg; m. Maurice Berger, Aug. 2, 1980. BS in English, Minot State U., ND, 1963, BS in French, 1963, BS in Edn., 1963; PhD, U. Minn., Mpls., 1973. Cert. in tchg. State ND. Asst. prof. Minot State U., ND, 1966—73; costume designer and historian, dept. theatre La State U., Baton Rouge, 1973—. Critic Am. Coll. Theatre Festival, 1975—79; state chair La. Coll. Theatre Festival, 1976—80; costume designer Ctrl. State U., Okla., 1981—82; mem., theatre advisory bd. La. State Arts Coun., 1981, 82; costume designer U. Tulsa, Okla., 1986—87; reviewer, dress Jour. Am. Costume Soc., 1991—2003; co-chair, region 6 conf. Costume Soc. Am., New Orleans, 1996, bd. dir., region 6 conf., 96; v.p. Theatres La.; lectr. in field. Author: General Learning Press; state chair: National American Coll. Theatre Festival, 1976, 1991, 1997; Theatre Crafts, 1987; contbr. articles to profl. jours.; designed costumes for over 100 plays, musicals, operas. Officer pub. rels. flotilla 4-10 and regional divsn. iv Coast Guard Aux., Baton Rouge, New Orleans, 1980—2006. Recipient Outstanding Svc. citation, S.W. Theatre Assn., Gold Medallion, Am. Coll. Theatre Festival, 1984; grantee, Women's and Gender Studies Program, La. State U., 1995, Manship Found., 1996, The Student Tech. Fee, 2000—02. Mem.: Costume Soc. Am. (mem. bd. 1988—91, v.p. 1988—91). Democrat. Unitarian Universalist. Avocations: boating, reading, vintage clothing, vintage jewelry, photography. Office: Theatre La State Univ Hatcher Hall Rm 249 Baton Rouge LA 70836 Mailing: PO Box 2083 Baton Rouge LA 70821 Office Phone: 225-758-3809. Personal E-mail: gtandberg1@cox.net. Business E-Mail: gtandb1@lsu.edu.

**TANDLER, BERNARD,** cell biology educator; b. Bklyn., Feb. 18, 1933; s. Arthur and Pauline (Solomon) T.; m. Helen Weisman, Dec. 25, 1955 (dec. Aug. 14, 1986); children: Janice Dena, Evan Charles. BS, Bklyn. Coll., 1955; AM, Columbia U., 1957; PhD, Cornell U., 1961; DMD (hon.), U. Cagliari, 1997. Instr. anatomy NYU, NYC, 1962-63; assoc. Sloan Kettering Inst., 1963-67; asst. prof. cell biology Cornell U., NYC, 1965-67; assoc. prof. Case Western Res. U., Cleve., 1967-72, prof. oral biology, 1972-91, acting chmn. dept. oral biology, 1987-89. Affiliate prof. oral biology U. Wash., Seattle, 1993—; vis. prof. U. Copenhagen, 1973, U. Cagliari, 1983, Kyushu Dental Coll., 1994-98, bio. sci. Case We. Res. U., 2003—; sr. rsch. scientist Tex. Tech U., Lubbock, 1999-01; cons. NIH, NSF, VA. Author: (with C.L. Hoppel) Mitochondria, 1972; assoc. editor: Anatomical Record, 1974-98; guest editor: Microscopy Rsch. and Technique, 1993-94, European Jour. Morphology, 1995-2000, 02—; contbr. chpts. to books, articles to profl. jours. Recipient Disting. Alumnus award Bklyn. Coll., 1981, Robert E. Kennedy award for Acad. Freedom, Ohio chpt. AAUP, 1992, Disting. Scientist award Am. Assn. Dental Rsch., 1999; USPHS fellow, 1957-62. Mem. Am. Assn. Anatomists, Am. Soc. Cell Biology, Electron Microscopy Soc. Am., Japanese Soc. Oral Biology, Japanese Assn. Anatomists, Internat. Assn. Dental Rsch. (Disting. Scientist award 1999) Am. Soc. Mammalogists, Italian Soc. Anatomy (hon.), Sigma Xi. Office Phone: 216-368-0563. Business E-Mail: bernard.tandler@case.edu.

**TANDON, NARENDRA NATH,** research scientist, director; b. Moradabad, Uttar Pradesh, India, Sept. 20, 1946; arrived in US, 1976; s. Prakash Narain and Kamla Tandon; m. Ranjana Mehrotra, Jan. 28, 1974; children: Nandita, Nitin. BS, Agra U., Lucknow, India, 1965, MS, 1967, PhD in Organic Chemistry, 1975. Assoc. prof. clin. biochemistry King George Med. Coll., Lucknow, India, 1968—76; vis. scientist NIH, Bethesda, Md., 1976—78 FDA, Washington, 1978—80; sr. scientist ARC, Rockville, Md., 1980—96; dir. thrombosis rsch. Otsuka Md. Medicinal Labs., 1996—. Mem. editl. bd. Thrombosis Rsch. (jour.). Recipient Fujji award, Otsuka Pharm. Co., Japan, 2005. Mem.: Internat. Soc. Thrombosis and Hemostasis (corr.). Achievements include patents for Glycoprotein VI and its uses; patents pending for antithrombotic antibodies to GPVI. Office: Otsuka Md Medicinal Labs 9900 Med Ctr Dr Rockville MD 20850 Business E-Mail: narendrt@otsuka.com.

**TANDON, NEERAJ,** cardiologist, educator; b. New Delhi; arrived in U.S., 1994; MD, U. Delhi, India, 1992. Diplomate Am. Bd. Internal Medicine, cert. in internal medicine Am. Bd. Internal Medicine, 1997, in cardiovasc. disease Am. Bd. Internal Medicine, 2000, in interventional cardiology Am. Bd. Internal Medicine, 2001. Asst. prof. medicine La. State U. Health Scis. Ctr., Shreveport, 2001; chief sect. cardiology Overton Brooks VA Med. Ctr., Shreveport, 2003—. Assoc. dir. cardiology fellowship program La. State U. Health Scis. Ctr., Shreveport, 2001—. Fellow: Am. Coll. Cardiology, Soc. Cardiovasc. Angiography and Intervention. Office: Overton Brooks VA Med Ctr 510 E Stoner Ave Shreveport LA 71101 Office Phone: 318-424-6064.

**TANDON, RAJIV,** psychiatrist, educator; b. Kanpur, India, Aug. 3, 1956; came to U.S., 1984; s. Bhagwan Sarup and Usha (Mehrotra) T.; m. Chanchal Nammi Vohra; children: Neeraj, Anisha, Gitanjali. Student, St. Xavier's Coll., Bombay, India, 1974; BS, All India Inst., New Delhi, 1980; MD, Nat. Inst. of MH, India, 1983. Sr. resident Mental Health and Neuro-Scis., India, 1983-84; resident U. Mich. Hosps., Ann Arbor, 1984-87, attending psychiatrist, 1987-2000. Dir. schizophrenia program, dir. hosp. svcs. divsn. U. Mich., Ann Arbor, 1987—2000, assoc. prof., 1993—99, prof., 1999—; cons. Lenawee County Cmty. Mental Health, Adrian, Mich., 1985—99. Author: Biochemical Parameters of Mixed Affective States; Negative Schizophrenic Symptoms: Pathophysiology and Clinical Implications; contbr. over 120 articles to profl. jours. Recipient Young Scientist's award Biennial Winter workshop on Schizophrenia, 1990, 92, Travel award Am. Coll. Neuropsychopharmacology/Mead, 1990, Rsch. Excellence award Am. Assn. Psychiatrists from India, 1993, Sci. award, Best Drs. in Am. award, 1994-98, Gerald Klerman award for outstanding rsch. by a Nat. Alliance for Rsch. in Schizophrenia and Depression young investigator, 1995, FuturPsych award CINP, 1997. Mem. Am. Psychiat. Assn. (Wisniewski Young Psychiatrist Rschr. award 1993), World Fedn. Mental Health, Soc. for Neurosci., N.Y. Acad. Scis., Soc. Biol. Psychiatry, Mich. Psychiat. Soc. Democrat. Hindu. Office Phone: 850-921-0919. Business E-Mail: rtandon@umich.edu.

**TANDON, RAJIV,** training company executive; b. Allahabad, India, May 9, 1944; came to U.S., 1969; s. Jagdish Bihari and Vimla Devi (Mehrotra) T.; m. Priti Khanna, Sept. 1969; children: Ribhu Dev, Veeti. BTech with honors, Indian Inst. of Tech., 1966, MS in Ops. Rsch., 1972; MBA, U. Minn., 1972, PhD, 1987. Trainee Kumardhubi (India) Engring. Works, 1966-67, prodn. control officer, 1967-69; ops. rsch. analyst Nat. Car Rental, Mpls., 1971-72, mgr. ops. rsch., 1972-75, dir. fin. analysis, 1975-77, corp. v.p., MIS, 1977-81, corp. v.p., gen. mgr. car rental, 1981-86; dir. venture mgmt. U. St. Thomas, Mpls., 1988-93, dir. corp. venturing, 1993-95; pres., CEO Learning Byte Internat. (formerly Inst. for Advanced Tech.), Mpls., 1995—2001, Adayana, Inc., Mpls., 2001—. Mgmt. cons., 1986-95 Exec. editor New Venture Rev., 1985-90; contbr. articles to profl. jours. Pres. Planners League, 1978. Mem. Am. Mgmt. Assn., Inst. of Noetic Scis., Inst. of Mgmt. Scis. (sec. upper

Midwest chpt. 1975-76, v.p. 1976-77, pres. 1977-78). Avocations: reading, news. Home: 8109 Rhode Island Ave S Bloomington MN 55438-1146 Office: 4444 W 76th St Minneapolis MN 55435 E-mail: rtandon@adayana.com.

**TANDY, KAREN P.,** federal agency administrator; b. Ft. Worth, Tex. married; 2 children. Grad., Tex. Tech. U., Tex. Tech. Law Sch., 1977. Law clk. No. Dist. Tex.; asst. U.S. atty. ea. dist. Va., 1979—90; asst. U.S. atty. western dist. Wash., 1979—90; supr. dept. drug and forfeiture litig. Criminal Divsn. of Dept. Justice, 1990—99; assoc. dep. atty. gen., dir. Organized Crime Drug Enforcement Task Forces, 1999—2003, mgr. 2001—03; adminstr. Drug Enforcement Adminstrn., 2003—. Chief asset forfeiture unit U.S. Attys. Office Western Dist., Wash., 1988—90; clk. Chief Judge of No. Dist., Tex.; dep. chief Narcotics and Dangerous Drug Sect.; lectr. in field. Recipient Atty. Gens. award for disting. svc., Award for Extraordinary Achievement, Dept. Justice, Award for Superior Svc., U.S. Atty. Dir. Office: Drug Enforcement Adminstrn Mailstop AXS 2401 Jefferson Davis Hwy Alexandria VA 22301

**TANE, SUSAN JAFFE,** retired manufacturing company executive; b. NYC; d. Irving and Beatrice (Albert) J.; m. Irwin R. Tane; children by previous marriage: Robert Wayne, Stephen Mark. BS, Boston U., 1964; postgrad., Hofstra U., C.W. Post U. Elem. sch. tchr., Long Beach, NY, 1964-67; pres. Fashions by Appointment, Glen Cove, NY, 1967-71; adminstrv. asst. Peerless Sales Corp., Elmont, NY, 1967-71; from sales mgr. to mktg. dir. United Utensils Co., Inc., Port Washington, NY, 1973-78; v.p. ops. and control United Molded Products divsn. United Utensils Co., Inc., Port Washington, 1978-80; v.p. mktg. Utensco, Port Washington, 1980-88, Bd. dirs. Peerless Aerospace Corp. Co-inventor plastic container and handling assembly. Life mem. Ronald McDonald House; friend N.Y. Pub. Libr.; pres. Susan Jaffe Tane Found., Am. Jewish Congress, sr. v.p.; life mem. Hadassah; chair Commn. for Women's Equality/Am. Jewish Congress; bd. dirs. Poe Found. Mem. Boston U. Alumni Assn., Cornell Weil Med. Coll., Ptnrs. in Leadership, Shareholder ASsn. Rsch. and Edn. Leadership Coun., Poe Studies Assn. (sponsor), Boston U. (sponsor poetry workshop), Lotos Club.

**TANENBAUM, ALLAN JAY,** lawyer; b. Savannah, Ga., Aug. 9, 1946; s. Nathan and Gertrude Sadie (Palefsky) T.; m. Elaine Kruger, Aug. 8, 1971; children: Louis, Sharon, Stephen, Eric. BS in Econs., U. Pa., 1967; JD, U. Va., 1971. Bar: Ga. 1972. Ptnr. Frankel, Hardwick, Tanenbaum, Fink, P.C., Atlanta, 1972-96, Cohen Pollock Merlin Axelrod & Tanenbaum, 1996-2001; gen. counsel AFC Enterprises, Inc., 2001—; mng. dir. Lawyer Reference Svc. of Atlanta, 1977-87. Trustee Congregation B'nai Torah; sec., exec. com., bd. dirs. Jewish Family and Career Svcs., Inc. With USAR, 1968-74. Fellow Am. Bar Found.; mem. ABA (ho. of dels., chair gen. practice sect., spkr. young lawyers divsn., lawyer referral and info. svc., chair pub. edn. divsn., chair com. on scope and correlation of work, chair fellows young lawyers divsn., chair coun. fund for justice and edn. 2003—, nominating com. 2003—, Ga. state del. to ho. dels.), Atlanta Bar Assn. (past sec., del.), Lawyers Club Atlanta, Atlanta Council Younger Lawyers (past pres.). Office: Afc Enterprise Inc 5555 Glenridge Connector NE Ste 300 Atlanta GA 30342-4741 Office Phone: 770-353-3321. Business E-Mail: atanenbaum@afce.com.

**TANENBAUM, BASIL SAMUEL,** engineering educator; b. Providence, Dec. 1, 1934; s. Harry Milton and Rena Ada (Herr) Tanenbaum; m. Carol Binder, Aug. 26, 1956; children: Laurie, Stephen, David. BS summa cum laude, Brown U., 1956; MS, Yale U., 1957, PhD in Physics, 1960. Staff physicist Raytheon Co., Waltham, Mass., 1960—63; prof. engring. Case We. Res. U., Cleve., 1963—75; prof. Harvey Mudd Coll., Claremont, Calif., 1975—2003, dean faculty, 1975—93, Norman F. Sprague, Jr. prof. life scis., 1996—2003, prof. emeritus, 2003—; interim assoc. dean joint sci. dept. The Claremont Colls., 2003—05, adj. prof., 2005—. Vis. scientist Arecibo (P.R.) Obs. Cornell U., 1968—69; vis. assoc. prof. Northwestern U., Evanston, Ill., 1970; mem. sci. adv. com. Nat. Astronomy and Ionosphere Ctr., 1972—77; dir. Minority Engrs. Indsl. Opportunity Program, 1973—75; mem. sci. adv. com. Calif. Poly. Inst., Pomona, 1976—87; mem. engring. and sci. adv. com. Calif. State U., Fullerton, 1976—87; dir. summer sci. program Thacher Sch., Ojai, Calif., 1977—82; vis. scholar Beckman Laser Inst. U. Calif., Irvine, Calif., 1993—94, 1998, 2000—, mem. biomed. engring. adv. com., 2000—05; mem. nat. adv. com. Rowan Coll., Glassboro, NJ, 1993—2000; mem. Eisenhower adv. com. Calif. Postsecondary Edn. Com., 1993—97; pres.'s adv. coun. Olin Coll. Engring., Needham, Mass., 2001—, vice chmn., 2001, chmn., 2002—06; cons. in field. Author: Plasma Physics, 1967. Trustee Western U. Health Scis., Pomona, 1997—2004. Recipient Witke Tchg. award, Case We. Res. U., 1973; Woods Hole Oceanog. Inst. fellow, 1959, NSF fellow, Yale U., 1956—60, Sr. Sterling fellow, 1959. Mem.: AAUP, IEEE, AAAS, Am. Soc. Engring. Edn., Am. Phys. Soc., Sigma Xi (Rsch. award 1969). Home: 611 W Delaware Dr Claremont CA 91711-3458 Office Phone: 909-607-0776. Business E-Mail: sam_tanenbaum@hmc.edu.

**TANENBAUM, EDWARD,** lawyer; b. NYC, May 12, 1949; BA magna cum laude, Queens Coll., 1971; JD, Fordham Univ., 1974; LLM in Taxation, NYU, 1980. Bar: NY 1975. Ptnr., chmn., internat. tax group, mem., fed. income tax group Alston & Bird LLP, NYC. Mem.: ABA, Bar Assn. City NY, NY Bar Assn., Internat. Tax Inst. (past pres.), Nat. Coun., Internat. Fiscal Assn. Office: Alston & Bird LLP 90 Park Ave New York NY 10016-1387 Office Phone: 212-210-9425. Office Fax: 212-210-9444. Business E-Mail: etanenbaum@alston.com.

**TANENBAUM, JAY HARVEY,** lawyer; b. N.Y.C., Nov. 17, 1933; s. Leo Aaron and Regina (Stein) T.; m. Linda Goldman, May 28, 1961; children: Susan Hillary, Steven Eric. BA, Hobart and William Smith Colls., 1954; LLB, Union U., 1957, JD, 1961. Bar: N.Y. 1957, U.S. Dist. Ct. (so. dist.) N.Y. 1961, U.S. Supreme Ct. 1967. Chmn., internat. trader Associated Metals and Minerals Corp., N.Y.C., 1960-64; pvt. practice, N.Y.C., 1964—. Corp. counsel Internat. Gate Corp., Gen. Gate Corp. Named to Knighthood, His Royal Highness The Prince of Cittanova and His Royal Highness The Prince of Trabzon, 2001. Mem. N.Y. State Bar Assn., N.Y. Trial Lawyers Assn., Bronx County Bar Assn. Clubs: St. James (London), Le Club (N.Y.).

**TANENBAUM, JEFFREY L.,** lawyer; b. NYC, Apr. 2, 1952; BA cum laude, SUNY, Binghamton, 1973; JD with honors, SUNY, Buffalo, 1976. Bar: N.Y. 1977, U.S. Dist. Ct. (so., ea., and we. dists.) N.Y. 1977, U.S. Ct. Appeals (4th cir.) 1983, U.S. Ct. Appeals (11th cir.) 1984, U.S. Supreme Ct. 1986. Law clk. Appellate Divsn. 4th Dept., N.Y. 1976-78; joined Weil, Gotshal & Manges, NYC, 1978, ptnr. Tech. editor Buffalo Law Review, 1975-76. Mem. ABA, Am. Bankruptcy Inst., N.Y. State Bar Assn. (banking, corporation, bus., bankruptcy and antitrust sects., coun. on bankruptcy of the banking, corporation and bus. sect.), Phi Beta Kappa. Office: Weil Gotshal & Manges 767 5th Ave New York NY 10153-0119*

**TANENBAUM, JOEY,** real estate developer; m. Toby Tanenbaum. PhD (hon.), Ryerson U., 2003. Chmn., CEO Jay-M Enterprises Ltd., Jay-M Holdings Ltd. Trustee Royal Ontario Mus., Art Gallery of Ontario; hon. chmn. Can. Psychiat. Rsch. Found. Named one of Top 200 Collectors, ARTnews mag., 2003—06; recipient Order of Can. Avocation: Collector of 19-century European art; Cycladic and Neolithic art. Address: 317 Dundas St W Toronto ON M5T 1G4 Canada

**TANENBAUM, WILLIAM ALAN,** lawyer; b. Rochester, NY, Feb. 16, 1954; s. Burton David and Millicent (Kroll) T.; m. Judy Ellen Hertz, June 15, 1986. BA with highest honors, Brown U., 1976; JD, Cornell U., 1979. Ptnr. Kenyon & Kenyon, NYC, Rogers & Wells, NYC. Lectr. in field.; profl. assn. and confs. Co-author A Guide to European Data Protection and Privacy Laws for U.S. Companies, contbr. articles to profl. jours. Mem. ABA, NY State Bar Assn. (litigation com., intellectual property litigation com.), Intellectual Property Law Assn., Computer Law Assn. (founding co-chmn. ann. outsourcing conf., pres. 1995-96), NY Intellectual Property Law, Copyright Soc. USA,

Am. Arbitration Assn. (panel arbitrators), Phi Beta Kappa. Avocation: sailing. Office: Kaye Scholer LLP 425 Park Ave New York NY 10022 Office Phone: 212-836-7661. Business E-Mail: wtanenbaum@kayescholer.com.

**TANENHAUS, SAM,** editor; m. Kathryn Bonomi; 1 child. BA in English, Grinnell Coll., 1977; MA in English Lit., Yale U., 1978. With publicity Farrar, Straus and Giroux; with trade, acad., and crossover books Oxford Univ. Press, Chelsea House; asst. editor op-ed page N.Y. Times, 1997—99, editor book rev., 2004—; contbg. editor Vanity Fair, 1999—2004. Juror on biography Pulitzer Prize Com., 2000; affiliated writer Sch. Journalism NYU, 2002—03. Author: Literature Unbound: A Guide for the Common Reader, 1984, Louis Armstrong: Biography of a Musician, 1989, Whittaker Chambers: A Biography, 1997 (L.A. Times Book prize for biography, 1997, finalist Nat. Book award for nonfiction, 1997, finalist Pulitzer prize for biography, 1998); contbg. author: Wall St. Jour., Washington Post; contbg. author Boston Globe, LA Times, N.Y. Times Mag., Nat. Rev., New Criterion, N.Y. Rev. Books, New Republic, Am. Scholar, Commentary. Recipient award John M. Olin Found., Bradley Found.; grantee, NEH, 1997; Media fellow Hoover Instn., Stanford U., 2000, 2002. Mem.: Soc. Am. Historians (mem. exec. bd.). Office: The NY Times 229 W 43rd St New York NY 10036 Business E-Mail: tanenhaus@nytimes.com.

**TANEY, FRANCIS XAVIER, JR.,** lawyer; b. Camden, NJ, Aug. 31, 1970; s. Francis Xavier Sr. and Clara Mary Taney; m. Sheila Ann FitzPatrick, Oct. 26, 1996; children: Patrick Francis, Bridget Ann. BA in Econs. summa cum laude, Drew U., 1992; JD, Pa. U., 1995. Bar: Pa. 1995, NJ 1995, US Dist. Ct. (ea. dist.) Pa. 1995, US Dist. Ct. (NJ) 1995, US Ct. Appeals (3d cir.) 1996. Assoc. Klehr, Harrison, Harvey, Branzburg & Ellers, Cherry Hill, NJ, 1995—96, Piper & Marbuy LLP, Phila., 1996—97, Saul, Ewing, Remick & Saul LLP, Phila., 1997—2001, Buchanan Ingersoll and Rooney, P.C., Phila., 2001—03, shareholder, 2004—. Guest lectr. Pa. State U. Gt. Valley Campus, Malvern, 2004—; spkr. in field. Contbr. articles to profl. jours., chpt. to book.; editor: U. Pa. Law Sch. Law Rev., 1994—95. Recipient Pa. Rising Star (atty.), Law and Politics Mag./Phila. Mag., 2005. Mem.: ABA, Friendly Sons of St. Patrick, Drew U. Phila. Area Alumni Club (pres. steering com. 1999—2002), Phi Beta Kappa, Omicron Delta Epsilon. Avocations: tennis, music. Office: Buchanan Ingersoll and Rooney PC 1835 Market 14th Fl Philadelphia PA 19103 Office Phone: 215-665-3846. Office Fax: 215-665-8760. Business E-Mail: taneyfx@bipc.com.

**TANG, C. MARK,** investment banker, venture capitalist; b. Jiangyin, China, June 21, 1964; s. J.H. Tang and R.F. Kong; m. S. Sharon Guo, Jan. 20, 1994; children: Alexander, Gloria. BS in Biochemistry, Nanjing (China) U., 1985; PhD in Biochemistry and Molecular Biol., U. Calif., 1993; MBA in Fin., NYU, 2000. Postdoctoral rsch. assoc. Rockefeller U., N.Y.C., 1993-96; assoc. v.p. biotech., merchant banking and venture capital DH Blair Investment Banking Corp., N.Y.C., 1996-98; co-founder, CFO, vice chmn. Aegisoft Corp. (acquired by RealNetwork Inc.), Rockville, Md., 1998-2000; investment advisor UBS PaineWebber, Inc., N.Y.C., 1998-2000, Morgan Stanley, Jersey City, 2001—02; pres. World Tech. Ventures, LLC, 2002—. Author: The Essential Biotech Investment Guide, 2002; founding mng. editor, biotech. analyst Bio/Med. Tech. Stock Newsletter, 1994—98; contbr. articles to profl. jours. Mem.: Soc. Chinese Bioscientists in Am. Avocations: tennis, golf, volleyball, reading, writing. Office: PO Box 212 Jersey City NJ 07303 Office: World Tech Ventures One Exchange Pl # 1000 Jersey City NJ 07302 E-mail: cmtang311@ureach.com.

**TANG, CYRUS,** investment company executive; b. Chiangsu Province, China, 1930; arrived in US, 1950; married; 2 children. Attended, Widener U., Ill. Inst. Tech. CEO, pres., chmn. Tang Industries, Mt. Prospect, Ill. Office: 1650 W Jefferson Ave Trenton MI 48183-2136 Address: Tang Industries 3773 Howard Hughes Pkwy Ste 350N Las Vegas NV 89109

**TANG, ESTHER DON,** real estate developer, consultant, social worker; b. Tucson, Mar. 5, 1917; d. Don Wah and Yut (Gnan) Fok; m. David W. Tang, June 14, 1942; children: Patricia Karen Tang Crowley, Diana Cheryl Tang Simoes, David. Jr., Elizabeth Carol. Student, Draughn's Bus. Sch., San Antonio, 1936, U. Ariz., 1938-41, DHL, LHD, U. Ariz., 1992. Owner, operator supermarket, Tucson, 1940-66; exec. dir. Pio Decimo Ctr., Cath. Diocese, Tucson, 1966-85; cons., ptnr., vice chmn. bd. Netwest Devel. Corp., Tucson, 1985—. Prodr.: (video) Tapestry of Tucson (award winning). Mem. Tucson Airport Authority, 1975—; Pima County Crime and Pub. Safety Coun., 1999; chmn. Tucson-Taichung Sister Cities, 1979-91; chmn. Tucson Sister Cities Steering Com., 1984—; Sister Cities Assn. Tucson, 1990, Ariz. Pers. Bd.; chmn. bd. dirs Pima Community Coll., 1975-85; pres. bd. dirs. Pima Coun. on Aging, 1986-90; coord. US Bicentennial, Tucson; mem. adv. bd. Ariz. Dept. Econ. Security; master of ceremonies to welcome Pres. Clinton, City of Tuscon, 1999. Named Woman of Yr., City of Tuscon, 1955, Woman of Yr. in Adminstrn., 1968, Lady Comdr. the Holy Sepluchre Jerusalem; recipient Disting. Friend of the Humanities award Nat. Adv. Bd., 1989, Jefferson award Ariz. Daily Star, 1987, Svc. award Pima Coun. on Aging, 1987-89, Disting. Svc. award U. Pima CC Found., 1988, Roots and Wings Cmty. award, 1988, Rosie award So. Ariz. Ctr. Against Sexual Assault, 1990, Lifetime Achievement award YWCA, 1992, 93, La Doña de los Descendientes del Precido de Tucson, 1997-98, centennial alumni award U. Ariz., 1998, Pan-Asian Cmty. Leadership award, 1999, Arthritis Humanitarian award, 1999, Altrusa Women in Svc. award, 2000, Asia Am. Times Devel. Mgmt. Excellence award, 2000, Voices into the Millennium award Ariz. Border Patrol, Dynamic Duo—Pointing Lives in New Directions award Compass Health Care, Congl. Recognition, 2002, Lulac Nat. Presdl. citation, 2002, award Agave Ariz. Hist. Tape TV, 2002, Lifetime award U. Ariz. Coll. Agr. and Life Sci., 2002; Learning Svc. Bldg. and Gallery named in her honor, U. Ariz., 2001; named Ariz. History Maker State of Ariz. Hist. League, 2003, 15th annual Cath. Found. Honoring Esther Don Tang, 2004; featured as an active activist Foothills Publ., 2005. Mem. Soroptimist (hon., Women Who Helped Build Tucson award), Rotary Club Tucson (4 way test award 1998) Cath. Found. Diocese of Tucson (honorable mention, honoree Corner Stone Gala, 2004). Roman Catholic. Avocations: travel, cooking, golf. Home: 701 E Camino De Los Padres Tucson AZ 85718-1921

**TANG, GEORGE CHICKCHEE,** investment company executive; b. Hong Kong, Nov. 8, 1964; came to U.S., 1984; s. George and Margaret Tang. BS, Case Western Res. U., 1987; MS, Northwestern U., 1989. Registered securities rep., commodity rep., ins. agt., Ill.; CFA, CFP, portfolio mgr. investment mng. specialist, fin. planning specialist. With AT&T Bell Labs., Naperville, Ill., 1989-92; fin. advisor Smith Barney, Oakbrook, Ill., 1992—, 2d v.p. for investments, 1998-2000, v.p. for investments, 2000-01, 1st v.p. investments, 2001—05, 1st v.p. wealth mgmt., 2006—. Spkr., lectr. in field. Contbr. fin. columns to Chgo. Chinese Daily News, 1993—, Chinese Am. News, 1993—, China Jour., 1994-97. Writer ARC, Cleve., 1985-86; spkr. on environ. protection City Coun. Hong Kong, 1982. Recipient Champion of Wildlife Conservation award Hong Kong Std., 1982. Mem. Inst. CFA's (chartered), Assn. for Investment and Rsch., Orgn. Chinese Ams. (internal v.p. Chgo. chpt. 1994-95, pres. 1995-97). Avocations: tennis, swimming, bridge, art. Office: Smith Barney One Lincoln Ctr Ste 1300 Oakbrook Terrace IL 60181

**TANG, JOHN,** network technician, information scientist, educator; b. Hong Kong, Oct. 21, 1959; s. Chew Sang and Miu King Tang; m. Juana Teresita Enriquez, Mar. 15, 1990; 1 child, Jonathan Alexander. BA, San Francisco State U., 1981; MA, San Francisco State Univeristy, 1983; PhD, U. of Va., 1991. MIS mgr. Oakland Pvt. Industry Coun., Oakland, Calif., 1991—95; IT mgr. Western Human Nutrition Rsch. Ctr., San Francisco, 1995—98; network analyst Shaman Pharms., South San Francisco, Calif., 1995—98; instr. The Computer Learning Ctr., San Francisco, 1997—2001; adj. prof. City Coll. of San Francisco, 2000—; prof. DeVry U., Fremont, Calif., 2002—. Founder/pres. easyRE.net, Fremont, Calif., 2003—; founder, CEO Home Opportunities Inc., Oakland, Calif., 2003—. Contbr. articles to profl. jours., chpts. to books. Pres. Dance for Power, Oakland, 1993—98; mem. of bd. of advisors American-Viet League, Oakland, 1991—2003. Recipient Dupont

fellow, U. of Va., 1984—88, Grad. Achievement award, San Francisco State U., 1983. Roman Catholic. Avocations: creative writing, travel. Home: 6651 Gunn Dr Oakland CA 94611 Office: DeVry Univ 6600 Dumbarton Cir Fremont CA Personal E-mail: jltang@sbcglobal.net. Business E-Mail: jtang@fre.devry.edu.

**TANG, MEI,** psychology professor; b. Lanzhou, China, Oct. 19, 1965; arrived in U.S., 1988; d. Jifang Tang and Ziuhang Chen; m. Wei Zhang, May 14, 1991. MEd in English Edn., U. Ctrl. Okla., 1990; PhD in Counseling Psycholo0gy, U. Wis., Milw., 1996. Instr. Liao Ming Normal U., Dalian, China, 1985—88, U. Ctrl. Okla., Edmond, 1989—90; rsch. asst. U. Wis., Milw., 1990—96; prof. U. Cin., 1996—. Mem.: APA, Am. Counseling Assn. Home: 268 Glen Lake Rd Loveland OH 45140 Office: U Cin PO Box 210002 Cincinnati OH 45221-0002

**TANG, PAUL C.,** lawyer; b. Hong Kong, Oct. 4, 1952; m. Shirley Tang; children: Elizabeth, Margaret. BA, Harvard U., 1974; JD, Columbia U., 1977, MBA, 1978. Bar: (N.Y.) 1981, N.J. 1994. Tax acct. Deloitte & Touche, 1978—80; mem. Phillips Nizer, 1980—85, ptnr., 1985—87; co-founder law firm, 1987—89; ptnr. Reid & Priest, 1989—93; exec. v.p., gen. counsel, sec. Burlington (N.J.) Coat Factory Warehouse Corp., 1993—. Office: Burlington Coat Factory 1830 Rt 130 Burlington NJ 08016-3020 Business E-Mail: paul.tang@coat.com.

**TANG, PAUL CHI LUNG,** philosophy educator; b. Vancouver, B.C., Can., Jan. 23, 1944; came to U.S., 1971; s. Pei-sung and Violet (Wong) T. BSc with high distinction, U. B.C., 1966; MA in Edn., Simon Fraser U., Vancouver, 1971; MA, Washington U., St. Louis, 1975, PhD, 1982; cert. in bioethics, Kennedy Inst. Ethics, 1983; diploma in piano, Royal Conservatory Music, Toronto, 1962. Teaching asst. philosophy of edn. Simon Fraser U., 1969-71; instr. philosophy St. Louis C.C. at Meramec, Kirkwood, Mo., 1975-82; instr., lectr. philosophy Washington U., 1972-76; adj. asst. prof. Harris-Stowe State Coll., St. Louis, 1980-82; asst. prof. to assoc. prof. to prof. dept. philosophy Calif. State U., Long Beach, 1985—, chmn. dept. philosophy, 1988-94, acting chmn., 1998. Vis. lectr. philosophy So. Ill. U., Edwardsville, 1978-79. Editor: Philosophy of Sci. Assn. Newsletter, 1985—90; asst. editor: Philosophy of Sci. acad. jour., 1972—75, dep. editor: The Social Sci. Jour., 1999—; contbr. articles to profl. publs., revs. to profl. publs. Senator Internat. Parliament for Safety and Peace, Palermo, Italy. Decorated knight Templar Order of Jerusalem, knight Order Holy Cross of Jerusalem, knight comdr. Lofsenic Ursinius Order, chevalier Grand Croix de Milice du St. Sepulcre; recipient cert. of merit Student Philosophy Assn., 1988-90, 93-94, spl. award, 1992, Calif. State Senate Recognition award for commitment to edn., 1997; named faculty advisor of yr. Assoc. Students, 1987, 90, 91, 95, Highland Lord of Camster, Scotland, 1995; Paul Tang prize in philosophy named in his honor, 1996-99; fellow Washington U., 1971, summer rsch. fellow Calif. State U., 1988, 96, NEH fellow Harvard U., 1988, NEH Summer Seminar fellow, 1988; internat. scholar Phi Beta Delta, interdisciplinary scholar Phi Kappa Phi, 1993, Phi Beta Kappa, 2000, Phi Sigma Tau; grantee vis. philosophers program Coun. for Philos. Studies, 1987, 91, 92; Disting. Vis. Scholars and Artists Fund, Calif. State U., 1988, 89, rsch. grantee, 1995, 97, 99. Fellow: World Lit. Acad.; mem.: Maison Internat. des Intellectuels de l'Acad. Francaise, Soc. Philosophy and Psychology, Brit. Soc. Philosophy of Sci., Iowa Philos. Soc. (pres. 1985—86), Hastings Ctr., Kennedy Inst. Ethics, History of Sci. Soc., Philosophy of Sci. Assn., Am. Philos. Assn. (Excellence in Tchg. award 1995, 1997), numerous others, Order Internat. Fellowship (Eng.), Companion of Honour (Eng.), Golden Key Internat. Hon. Soc. (Internat. Man of Yr. 1995—96), Internat. Order Merit (Eng.). Avocations: hiking, tennis, chess, music, travel. Home: 5050 E Garford St Apt 228 Long Beach CA 90815-2859 Office: Calif State U Dept Philosophy 1250 N Bellflower Blvd Long Beach CA 90840-0006 E-mail: pcltang@csulb.edu.

**TANG, PHILIP W.,** engineer, educator; b. Sept. 12, 1964; s. Chung Chi Tang and Yuet Yee Cheng; m. Mary tang, May 27, 2000; 1 child, Chloe. BS in Aerospace Engring., SUNY Buffalo, 1986; MSEE, U. Ctrl. Fla., Orlando, 1994, PhD in Elec. Engring., 2002. Profl. engr. Fla., 1996. Engr. Fluids and Mech. br. UB-G2 NASA, Kennedy Space Ctr., Fla., sr. engr. Ajionics br. UB-G2. Sr. engr. NASA, Fla., 1986—; adj. prof. U. Ctrl. Fla., 1994—2000; profl. engr., cons., Orlando, 1996—. Author: tech. articles, NASA tech. briefs. Mem. industry adv. bd. U. Ctrl. Fla., 2005—. Mem.: IEEE. Achievements include member of return flight team after the Challenger and Columbia space shuttle accidents. Office: NASA Space Sta Ajionics Br UB-G2 Kennedy Space Center FL 32899 Business E-Mail: philip.w.tang@nasa.gov.

**TANG, TERRY,** editor, lawyer; BA, Yale U., 1980; JD, NYU, 1983. Atty. Preston Thorgrimson Ellis & Holman, Seattle, 1983; staff writer Seattle Weekly, 1984—89; editl. writer Seattle Times, 1989—97; mem. editl bd. New York Times, 1997—2000, Op-Ed page editor, 2000—03, dep. tech. editor, 2003—. Editor (mng.): Rev. of Law & Social Change, 1982—83. Nieman fellow, Harvard Univ., 1992—93. Office: New York Times 229 W 43d St New York NY 10036 Office Phone: 212-556-7745. Office Fax: 212-556-1448. Business E-Mail: tang@nytimes.com.*

**TANGHERLINI, FRANK ROBERT,** physics educator; b. Boston, Mar. 14, 1924; s. Emiliano Francesco Tangherlini and Rosa (Robinson) Leclaire; m. Jane Kjaergaard Kjems, Jan. 2, 1960 (div. 1979); children: Arne E.(dec.), Timothy R., Daniel M., Niels L. SB in Physics with honors, Harvard U., 1948; MS in Physics, U. Chgo., 1952; PhD in Physics, Stanford U., 1955. Rsch. engr. Convair-Gen. Dynamics, San Diego, 1958—59; postdoctoral fellow NSF, Copenhagen, Naples, 1959—60; rsch. assoc. U. NC, Chapel Hill, 1960-61; asst. prof. Duke U., Durham, 1961-64; assoc. prof. George Washington U., Washington, 1964-66; sci. assoc. Danish Space Rsch. Inst., Lyngby, Denmark, 1966-67; assoc. prof. Coll. of the Holy Cross, Worcester, Mass., 1967-94. Vis. scientist Internat. Ctr. Theoretical Physics, Trieste, Italy, 1973—74. Author: Introduction to the General Theory of Relativity, 1961; contbr. articles to profl. jours. Chmn. Cub Scouts Am., Auburn, Mass., 1975—77. With U.S. Army, 1943—46, ETO. Vis. scholar, Harvard U., 1988—89; Travel grantee, NSF, 1980, 1984. Mem.: AAUP, Am. Phys. Soc., Stanford Club San Diego, U. Chgo. Club San Diego, Harvard Club San Diego, Sigma Xi. Achievements include research in dimensionality of space, the classical electron, Snell's law, relativity, gravitation and cosmology. Office Phone: 858-638-7352. E-mail: frtan96@sbcglobal.net.

**TANGORA, MARTIN CHARLES,** mathematician, educator; b. N.Y.C., June 21, 1936; s. Albert and Virginia T.; m. Linda Perry, June 17, 1973; children: Charles, Elizabeth. BS, Calif. Inst. Tech., 1957; MS, Northwestern U., 1958, PhD, 1966. Instr. Northwestern U., Evanston, Ill., 1966—67, U. Chgo., 1967—69; asst. prof. U. Ill., Chgo., 1970—72, assoc. prof., 1972—2002, assoc. prof. emeritus, 2002—. Temp. lectr. U. Manchester, Eng., 1969-70; sr. vis. fellow U. Oxford, Eng., 1973-74. Author: Computing the Homology of the Lambda Algebra, 1985; co-author: Cohomology Operations and Applications in Homotopy Theory, 1968; editor: Computers in Algebra, 1988, Computers in Geometry and Topology, 1989, Algebraic Topology Oaxtepec 1991 (conf. proc.), 1993. Bd. dirs. Landmarks Preservation Coun. Ill., Chgo., pres., 1976, v.p. 1997-99; bd. dirs. Uptown Theatre and Ctr. for the Arts, chmn. bd., 2003-2005; bd. dirs. Civic Ballet of Chgo., 2005—. Mem. Math. Assn. Am., Am. Math. Soc. Office: U Ill Chgo Math M/C 249 851 S Morgan St Chicago IL 60607-7045 Business E-Mail: tangora@uic.edu.

**TANGUAY, JEANNE MARIE,** social worker; b. Flint, Mich., Sept. 1, 1939; d. Charles Frank and Mary Stella Ocenasek; m. Ray Tanguay (div.); children: Ray Eric, Michele Lynne. AA with high honors, Flint Jr. Coll., 1966; BA with high distinction, U. Mich., 1976. Mem. reservation dept. TWA Airlines, Los Angeles, 1980—81; travel agent Cardillo Travel, Commerce, Calif., 1982—83; sales agent Thrifty and Hertz, Scotts Valley, Calif., 1990—93; social worker Develop. Ctr., Ft. Walton Beach, Fla., 1995—96, Bridgeway, Ft. Walton Beach, Fla., 0196—1998; ret., 1998. Bd. mem. Tulsa Human Svcs., Okla., 1977. Polit. worker Dem. Party, Flint, Mich., 1962; council mem. Holy

Name Ch., Niceville, Fla., 2005, 2006; worker Dem. Party for John Kerry, Niceville, 2004. Mem.: Twin Cities Sr. Club, Pi Alpha. Democrat. Roman Cath. Avocations: reading, movies, Bingo.

**TANGUAY, PETER EUGENE,** child and adolescent psychiatry educator; b. Quebec City, Que., Can., Nov. 6, 1935; came to U.S., 1960, naturalized, 1971; s. Oscar E. and Marion L. (Grady) T.; m. Margaret Fife, Dec. 22, 1960; children: Heather Louise, Gretchen Marie. BA, U. Ottawa, Ont., Can., 1956, MD, 1960. Diplomate Am. Bd. Psychiatry and Neurology (com. for cert. in child and adolescent psychiatry 1981-87, written exam. com. for child and adolescent psychiatry 1981-87, chmn. 1985-87, dir. 1990—). Intern Harper Hosp., Detroit, 1960-61; resident in psychiatry UCLA Med. Ctr.-Harbor Gen. Hosp., 1961-64; registrar in psychiatry Kingsway Hosp., Derby, Eng., 1966-68; fellow in child psychiatry UCLA Ctr. for Health Scis., 1968-70, from asst. prof. to assoc. prof., 1970-8076, prof., 1980-94, dir. child psychiatry clin. rsch. ctr., 1977-87, assoc. chief div., 1984-91, acting chief, 1992-94; Ackerly prof. child psychiatry U. Louisville Sch. Medicine, 1994—2004, emeritus, 2004—. Tech. advisor Rainman, 1988; vis. prof. U. Tours, France, 1982, U. Hawaii, 1987, 90; Roy Grinker vis. prof. Michael Reese Hosp., Chgo., 1984; mem. gen. assembly Am. Bd. Med. Specialists, 1990—, rep. to Accreditation Coun. on Continuing Med. Edn., 1993—, mem. exec. com., 1994-96; bd. advisors Rieger Found., Santa Barbara, Calif., 1992—; mem. psychol. scis. rev. com. NIMH, 1976-80; lectr., presenter in field; editl. cons. EEG and Clin. Neurophysiology, 1979-85; numerous others. Author: (with Margaret Tanguay) Travel Adventure in Europe with Tent, Van or Motorhome, 1970; contbr. over 60 articles, abstracts and book revs. to sci. jours., over 20 chpts. to books. Mem. Clinton-Gore Nat. Leadership Coun., 1991-93. Recipient career sci. devel. award NIMH, 1970-75; grantee USPHS, 1977-87, 84-89, NIMH, 1980-95, MacArthur Found., 1983-88. Fellow Am. Psychiat. Assn. (coun. on rsch. 1980-95, vice chmn. 1981-94, mem. com. on chronically ill-emotionally handicapped child 1990-94), Am. Acad. Child and Adolescent Psychiatry (assoc. editor Jour. 1988—, co-chmn. task force on universal access to health care 1991—), Am. Coll. Psychiatry; mem. AMA, AAAS, Group for Advancement Psychiatry (chmn. child com. 1988—), Soc. for Rsch. in Child and Adolescent Psychopathology, Royal Coll. Psychiatry (Gt. Britain, affiliate). Democrat. Avocations: microcomputers, vegetable gardening, travel. Home: 1129 Cardinal Dr Louisville KY 40213-1363 Office: U Louisville Bingham Child Guidance Ctr 200 E Chestnut St Louisville KY 40202-1822 Personal E-mail: ptanky@aol.com.

**TANGUY-TRACEY, SHEILA ANNE,** artist, poet; b. Morristown, NJ, Dec. 19, 1955; d. Eugene Joseph and Francoise Marie-Thérèse Tracey; m. Abdul Aziz Hanif, Nov. 13, 1978 (div. Sept. 12, 1984); children: Aisha M. Hanif, Dianne Al Hady; m. Zafar Iqbal Kabli, Aug. 4, 1986 (div. 1992); children: John A. Tracey Kabli, Sammy F. Tracey Kabli. AA, Monterey Peninsula Coll., 1997; BA with distinction, Calif. State U., Monterey Bay, 2000. Gen. class lic. Grove Comm. Costume model Sunset Ctr., Carmel by the Sea, Calif., 1995—2005; art docent Monte Vista Sch., Monterey. Exhibitions include Maritime Mus., 2000, Borders' Books Inc., Sandy City, Calif., 2000—04, Intrim, Monterey, 2004—06, Dickman Ctr., New Monterey, Calif., 2004—05, Internat. League Pen Women, 2004—06. Recipient Editor's Choice award, Internat. Soc. Poetry, 2000, Cert. of Achievement, Resource Coun. Intrim, 2004—05; grantee Monterey Maritime Mus., 2000. Fellow: Internat. Soc. Poetry; mem.: Art Internat. League Pen Women (sec. 2004—06), Intrim Cmty. Coun. (coun. 2004—06). Avocation: sculpting. Home and Studio: Apt 4 5 Arkwright Ct Pacific Grove CA 93950 Personal E-mail: sheilah2597@sbcglobal.net.

**TANI, LLOYD YASUO,** pediatrician, educator; b. LA, Aug. 6, 1956; s. Lorraine Hiroko Tani; m. Yvette Friede Tani, May 30, 1990; children: Ryan Yasuo, Jaclyn Christine. BA in Biology, UCLA, 1978; MD, U. Calif., LA, 1982. Diplomate Nat. Bd. Med. Examiners, 1986, Am. Bd. Pediatrics, 1987, pediatric cardiology Am. Bd. Pediatrics, 1991, lic. Utah, 1989. Internship and residency pediatrics Baylor Coll. Medicine, 1982—86, fellowship pediatric cardiology, 1986—89; prof. pediat. Sch. Medicine U. Utah, Salt Lake City, 1989—, pediatric cardiologist Sch. Medicine, 1989—. Mem.: Utah Med. Assn., Am. Acad. Pediatrics, Am. Soc. Echocardiography, Am. Heart Assn. Office: University of Utah School of Medicine 100 N Medical Drive Salt Lake City UT 84113 Office Phone: 801-588-2600. Office Fax: 801-588-2612.

**TANIS, JAMES ROBERT,** library director, history professor, clergyman; b. Phillipsburg, NJ, June 26, 1928; s. John Christian and Bertha Marie (Tobiasson) T.; m. Florence Borgmann, June 26, 1963; children Justin Edward, James Tobiasson. BA, Yale, 1951; B.D., Union Theol. Sem., N.Y.C., 1954; Dr. Theol., U. Utrecht, Netherlands, 1967; LittD (hon.), Dickinson Coll., Carlisle, Pa., 1994. Ordained to ministry Presbyn. Ch., 1954. Co-pastor Greystone Presbyn. Ch., Elizabeth, NJ, 1954-55; librarian, mem. faculty Harvard Div. Sch., 1956-65; univ. librarian Yale U., 1965-68; mem. faculty Yale Div. Sch., 1968-69; dir. libraries, prof. history Bryn Mawr (Pa.) Coll., 1969-97; guest curator Phila. Mus. Art, 1997—2002; parish assoc. Valley Forge Presbyn. Ch., King of Prussia, Pa., 1973—2005. Author: Calvinistic Pietism in the Middle Colonies, 1967; co-author: Bookbinding in America, 1983, Images of Discord/De Tweedracht Verbeeld, 1993, Fantasy and Fashion, 1996, Leaves of Gold: Manuscript Illumination from Philadelphia Collections, 2001. Decorated officer Order Orange-Nassau. Home: 11302 Shannondell Dr Audubon PA 19403-5616 E-mail: jrtanis@sdlifestyle.com.

**TANKOOS, SANDRA MAXINE,** court reporting services executive; b. Bklyn., Nov. 12, 1936; d. Samuel J. and Ethel (Seltzer) Rich; m. Kenneth Robert Tankoos, Mar. 17, 1957; children: Robert Ian, Gary Russell, Jenine Sheryl. AA, Stenotype Inst., 1957; BA, Queens Coll., 1969; MA, C.W. Post Coll., 1973. Cert. stenotype reporter, 1959. Ct. reporter free lance, N.Y.C., 1957-70; tchr. Spanish various high schs., L.I., 1970-76; pres. Tankoos Reporting, N.Y.C., 1976—; Ar-Ti Recording, Mineola, N.Y., 1977—; Sterling Reporting Svc., 2000—. Author: (children's book) Ettie and the Evil Eye; contbr. articles to profl. jours. Past pres., bd. dirs. Temple Sinai, Roslyn Hts., N.Y., 1989-91; Am. Jewish Acad., West Hempstead, 1984-94, LWV, Roslyn, 1969-75, NOW, Nassau County, 1975-77, bd. dirs. Religious Action Ctr., Washington, 1995—, ARZA, 1997—. Avocations: writing, piano. Home: 77 Shepherd Ln Roslyn Heights NY 11577-2508 Office: Ar-Ti Recording Inc 142 Willis Ave Mineola NY 11501-2613 also: Tankoos Reporting Co 305 Madison Ave New York NY 10165 E-mail: sandra@tankoos.com.

**TANNA, ANGELO PETER,** ophthalmologist, educator; m. Carola Ann Tanna. BA, Johns Hopkins U., 1989; MD, Columbia U. Coll. of Physicians and Surgeons, 1994. Glaucoma Fellowship Johns Hopkins Hosp. / Md., 1999. Internship Grad. Hosp., Md., 1995; ophthalmology residency Wilmer Eye Inst., Md., 1998; attending ophthalmologist Johns Hopkins Bayview Med. Ctr., Baltimore, Md., 1998—99; dir., glaucoma svc. Northwestern Med. Faculty Found., Chicago, Ill., 1999—; asst. prof. of ophthalmology Northwestern U. Feinberg Sch. of Medicine, Chicago, Ill., 1999—. Dir., glaucoma svc. Northwestern Med. Faculty Found., Chicago, Ill., 1999—; editl. bd. mem. Survey of Ophthalmology, Brookline, Mass., 2000—. Contbr. articles various profl. jours. Recipient first prize in Engring., Northwestern U., 2003. Fellow: Am. Acad. of Ophthalmology; mem.: Am. Glaucoma Soc., Alpha Omega Alpha. Office: NW Med Faculty Found 675 N Saint Clair Ste 15-150 Chicago IL 60611 Office Phone: 312-908-8152.

**TANNEN, DEBORAH FRANCES,** writer; b. Bklyn., June 7, 1945; d. Eli S. and Dorothy (Rosen) T. BA, SUNY, Binghamton, 1966; MA, Wayne State U., 1970, U. Calif., Berkeley, 1976; PhD, U. Calif., 1979. English intr. Mercer County CC, Trenton, NJ, 1970-71; lectr. in acad. skills CUNY, Bronx, NY, 1971-74; asst. prof. Georgetown U., Washington, 1979-85, assoc. prof. linguistics, 1985-90, prof. linguistics, 1989-91, univ. prof., 1991—. McGraw disting. lectr. in writing Coun. for Humanities and dept. anthropology Princeton U., fall 1991; visitor Inst. for Advanced Study, Princeton, spring 1992; fellow Ctr. for Advanced Study in Behavioral Scis., Stanford, Calif., 1992-93. Author: Lilika Nakos, 1983, Conversational Style: Analyzing Talk Among Friends, 1984, That's Not What I Meant!: How Conversational Style Makes or Breaks Your Relations With Others, 1986, Talking Voices: Repetition, Dialogue and Imagery in Conversational Discourse, 1989, You Just Don't Understand: Women and Men in Conversation, 1990, Gender and Discourse, 1994, Talking From 9 to 5: Women and Men in the Workplace: Language, Sex and Power, 1994, The Argument Culture: Moving from Debate to Dialogue, 1998, The Argument Culture: Stopping America's War of Words, 1999, You're Wearing That? Understanding Mothers and Daughters in Conversation, 2006; editor: Analyzing Discourse: Text and Talk, 1982, Spoken and Written Language: Exploring Orality and Literacy, 1982, Coherence in Spoken and Written Discourse, 1984, Perspectives on Silence, 1985, Linguistics in Context: Connecting Observation and Understanding, 1988, Gender and Conversational Interaction, 1993, Framing In Discourse, 1993, (play) An Act of Devotion, 1994. Rockefeller Humanities fellow, 1982-83; grantee NEH, 1980, 83, 86; recipient Elizabeth Mills Crothers prize U. Calif. 1976, Dorothy Rosenberg Meml. prize U. Calif., 1977, Joan Lee Yang Meml. Poetry prize U. Calif., 1977, Shrout Short Story prize, 1978, Emily Chamberlain Cook prize, 1978. Office: Georgetown U Lang & Linguistics ICC Bldg Rm 471 37th & O St NW Washington DC 20057-0001 Office Phone: 202-687-5910. Business E-mail: tannend@georgetown.edu.*

**TANNEN, RICHARD LAURENCE,** nephrology educator; b. N.Y.C., Aug. 31, 1937; s. Harold and Fannie (Rosenberg) T.; m. Elizabeth Whitney Harriman, Aug. 8, 1964 (div. Apr. 1990); m. Vivien Baraban, Nov. 17, 1990; children: Bradford, Whitney, Jennifer, Alison, Julie. Student, Vanderbilt U., 1957; MD, U. Tenn., Memphis, 1960. Rsch. internist Walter Reed Inst. Rsch., Washington, 1966-69; assoc. prof., co-dir. nephrology unit U. Vt., Burlington, 1969-78; prof., chief nephrology divsn. U. Mich., Ann Arbor, 1978-88; prof., chmn. dept. medicine U. So. Calif., L.A., 1988-95; vice dean for rsch. U. Pa., Phila., 1995-97, prof. medicine, 1995—, sr. vice-dean, 1997—2002. Established investigator Am. Heart Assn., 1971-76. Co-editor: Fluids and Electrolytes, 1986, 3d edit., 1996; contbr. more than 130 sci. articles to profl. jours. Maj. U.S. Army, 1966-69. Recipient Merit award NIH, 1986-94, Disting. Alumnus award U. Tenn., 1991. Fellow ACP; mem. Am. Soc. Nephrology (pres. 1991-92), Am. Soc. Clin. Investigation, Assn. Am. Physicians, Nat. Kidney Found. (regional v.p. 1984-87, Pres.'s award 1986). Jewish. Avocations: tennis, travel. Office: U Pa Sch of Med 295 John Morgan Bldg Philadelphia PA 19104 Office Phone: 215-898-2270. Business E-Mail: tannen@mail.med.upenn.edu.

**TANNENBAUM, BERNICE SALPETER,** national religious organization executive; b. NYC; d. Isidore and May Franklin; 1 child, Richard Salpeter. BA, Bklyn. coll. Chmn. Commn. on the Status of Women of the World Jewish Congress; mem. exec. bd. Am. sect. World Jewish Congress; chmn. internat. affairs com.; mem. Zionist Gen. Coun.; active Exec. World Zionist Orgn. Bd. dirs., mem. gen. assembly Jewish Agy.; bd. dirs., v.p. United Israel Appeal; mem. exec. com. Am. Zionist Movement; former chair Hadassah mag.; nat. pres. Hadassah, 1976-80; nat. chmn. Hadassah Internat., 1984-95; liaison Hadassah Found.; sec. Jewish Telegraphic Agy.; bd. govs. Hebrew U. Office: Hadassah 50 W 58th St New York NY 10019-2590

**TANNENBAUM, HARVEY,** defense technology consultant; b. N.Y.C., June 26, 1923; s. Alfred and Ida (Kolbe) T.; m. Mildred Cohen, July 4, 1946; children: David Bruce, Mark Scott, Lynne Ellen. BS, NYU, 1946; postgrad., George Washington U., 1963-64. Chemist U.S. Army Chem. R & D Ctr., Aberdeen Proving Ground, Md., 1949-62, chief remote sensing, 1962-79; prin. staff engr. Honeywell, Inc., Clearwater, Fla., 1979-84; cons. Reistertown, Md., 1984—85; sr. program dir. SRI, Internat., 1985—88. Cons. EPA, CIA, Arms Control and Disarmament Agy., USAF, 1962-79; group chmn. NATO panel of experts on laser monitoring of atmosphere, Norway, 1976. Contbr. articles to profl. jours.; patentee in field. Served to cpl. USAF, 1942-45, ETO. Mem. Optical Soc. Am., Internat. Soc. Optical Engring., Infrared Symposia, Sigma Xi. Jewish. Achievements include patents in field. Avocations: bridge, photography. Home and Office: 12611 Mt Laurel Ct Reisterstown MD 21136-1801

**TANNENBAUM, MICHAEL J(AY),** physicist; b. N.Y.C., Mar. 10, 1939; s. Morris and Ann Tannenbaum; m. Barbara C. Moshinsky, July 15, 1973; children: Nina Fay, Lisa Marie. AB magna cum laude, Columbia U., N.Y.C., 1959, MA, 1960, PhD, 1965. Vis. scientist CERN, Geneva, 1965-66, 91, attache scientifique, 1973-84; from asst. prof. to assoc. prof. Harvard U., Cambridge, Mass., 1966-71; assoc. prof. Rockefeller U., N.Y.C., 1971-80; physicist Brookhaven Nat. Lab., Upton, NY, 1980-87, sr. physicist, 1987—, group leader, 2001—. Mem. sci. coun. Lab. Leprince-Ringuet, Ecole Polytechnique, France, 2002—05. Contbr. articles to profl. jours. Ernest Kempton Adams fellow, 1965, NSF fellow, 1959-63, 66, Alfred P. Sloan Found. fellow, 1967-69. Fellow: AAAS, Am. Phys. Soc.; mem.: NY Acad. Scis., Sigma Xi, Phi Beta Kappa. Home: 245 E 93rd St Apt 10F New York NY 10128-3965 Office: Physics Dept Brookhaven Nat Lab Bldg # 510C Upton NY 11973-5000 Office Phone: 631-344-3722. E-mail: mjt@bnl.gov.

**TANNENBAUM, MIKE (MICHAEL TANNENBAUM),** professional sports team executive; m. Michelle Tannenbaum; 1 child, Ella Morgan. BA in Acctg., Sports Mgmt., U. Mass., 1991; JD cum laude, Tulane Law Sch. Bar; Sports Law. Player personnel asst. New Orleans Saints, 1994, Cleve. Browns, 1995; with NY Jets, 1997—, team dir., pro. player devel., 2000, asst. gen. mgr., dir. pro. personnel, 2001—03, sr. v.p., football ops., asst. gen. mgr., 2003—06, gen. mgr., 2006—. Office: NY Jets 1000 Fulton Ave Hempstead NY 11550*

**TANNENBAUM, STEVEN ROBERT,** toxicologist, chemist; b. N.Y.C., Feb. 23, 1937; m. Carol Eigen, Sept. 6, 1959; children: Lisa, Mark. BS in Food Tech, MIT, 1958, PhD in Food Sci. and Tech, 1962. From asst. prof. to co-dir. Biol. Engring. Divsn. MIT, Cambridge, Mass., 1964—2002, co-dir. Biol. Engring. Divsn. 2000—03 Vis. prof. Hebrew U. of Jerusalem 1973-74; BASF vis. prof. U. Kaiserslautern, 1994; mem. adv. com. on biochemistry and chem. carcinogenesis Am. Cancer Soc., 1977-81, Inst. Medicine, Nat. Acad. Sci., 1996; bd. sci. advisors divsn. cancer etiology, NCI, 1994-95, Frederick Cancer Rsch. Facility, 1989—94, Nat. Cancer Inst., 1989-93; mem. cancer spl. program adv. com., 1979-82; mem. peer rev. com. Nat. Toxicology Program, 1983-85; founder, bd. dirs. Vicam, Ltd., Partnership; chmn. rev. homeland security safe bldg. program DHS, 2003; mem. sci. adv. bd. USAF, 1999. Editor: (with R.I. Mateles) Single-Cell Protein, 1968, (with D.I.C. Wang) Single-Cell Protein II, 1975, (with others) The Economics, Marketing and Technology of Fish Protein Concentrate, 1974, (with J.R. Whitaker) Food Proteins, 1977, Nutritional Safety Aspects of Food Processing, 1979, (with others) Gastrointestinal Cancer: Endogenous Factors, 1981, (with R.A. Scanlan) N-Nitroso Compounds, 1981; mem. editl. bd. Japanese Jour. Cancer Rsch., 1986—, Chem. Rsch. Toxicology, 1988-91, 95-98, Cancer Epidemiology, Prevention and Biomarkers, 1990—, Cancer Rsch., 1993-2001; contbr. over 350 articles to profl. jours. Fellow Japan Soc. Promotions Cancer Rsch.; mem. AAAS, Nat. Acad. Scis., Inst. Medicine, Am. Chem. Soc., Inst. Food Technologists (sect. councillor N.E. chpt. 1966-69, Samuel Cate Prescott Rsch. award 1970, Babcock Hart award 1980), editorial bd. sci. jour. 1970-73, Am. Inst. Nutrition, Am. Assn. Cancer Rsch., Soc. Toxicology, Oxygen Soc., Sigma Xi. Achievements include 11 U.S. patents. E-mail: srtcmit.edu. Office: MIT Div Biol Engring 77 Mass Ave Rm 56-731A Cambridge MA 02139-4307 Motto: Crisis equals danger plus opportunity.

**TANNENBERG, DIETER E.A.,** retired manufacturing executive; b. Chevy Chase, Md., Nov. 24, 1932; s. E.A. Wilhelm and Margarete Elizabeth (Mundhenk) T.; m. Ruth Hansen, Feb. 6, 1956; 1 child, Diana Sylvia Tannenberg BSME, Stevens Inst. Technology, Northwestern U., 1959. Registered profl. engr., N.Y., Ohio, Ill., Ind., Wis., N.J. Supervising engr. Flexonics div. Calumet & Hecla, Inc., Chgo., 1959-61, chief engr., 1961-63, program mgr. advanced space systems, 1963-65, dir. mfg. services, 1965-67; dir. mfg. engring. SCM Corp., Cortland, NY, 1967-69; tech. dir. internat. Singer Co. N.Y.C., 1969-71; v.p. ops. internat. div. Addressograph-Multigraph Corp., Cleve., 1971-74; mng. dir. Addressograph Multigraph GmbH, Frankfurt/Main, W. Ger., 1974-78; v.p., gen. mgr. Europe, Middle East, Africa AM Internat. Inc., Chgo., 1978-79; pres. AM Bruning div., 1979-82, AM Multigraphics Div., Mt. Prospect, Ill., 1982-86; corp. v.p. AM Internat., Inc., 1981-83, corp. sr. v.p.,

1983-86; chmn. bd. dirs., pres., chief exec. officer Sargent-Welch Sci. Co., Skokie, Ill., 1986-89; pres., CEO ExhibitGroup, Inc., Elk Grove Village, Ill., 1990-91, Bell & Howell Document Mgmt. Products Co., Chgo., 1991-94, Bell & Howell Postal Sys. Inc., Chgo., 1994-97; corp. v.p. Bell & Howell Co., Skokie, Ill., 1991-97. Chmn. AM Internat. GmbH, Frankfurt, 1977-86 Contbr. chpts. to handbooks, articles to tech., trade mags.; patentee in machinery field Served with M.I., U.S. Army, 1953-56 Named Man of Yr. Quick Print Mag., 1985 Mem. NSPE, ASME, Assn. Reprodn. Materials Mfrs. (bd. dirs. 1979-82, v.p. 1980-82), Nat. Assn. Quick Printers (bd. dirs. 1982-84), Nat. Printing Equipment and Supplies Mfg. Assn. (bd. dirs. 1983-86, chmn. govt. affairs com. 1985-86), Computer and Bus. Equipment Mfg. Assn. (bd. dirs. 1983-86, 91-93), Soc. Am. Value Engrs. (hon. v.p. 1985—), Value Found. (trustee 1985—), Pi Tau Sigma.

**TANNENWALD, PETER,** lawyer; b. Washington, Apr. 8, 1943; s. Judge Theodore and Selma (Peterfreund) T.; m. Carol B. Baum, May 25, 1969; 1 child, Jonathan Mark. AB, Brown U., 1964; LLB, Harvard U., 1967. Bar: U.S. Dist. Ct. D.C. 1968, U.S. Ct. Appeals (D.C. cir.) 1968, U.S. Supreme Ct. 1972. Assoc. Arent, Fox, Kintner, Plotkin & Kahn, Washington, 1967-74, ptnr., 1975-94; v.p. Irwin, Campbell & Tannenwald, P.C., Washington, 1995—. Columnist The LPTV Report, 1988-92. Mem. cmty. coun. Sta. WAMU-FM, Washington, 1986-93, 94-97, 2003—; dir. Brown Broadcasting Svc., Inc., Providence, 1970—; chmn. maj. law firms divsn. Nat. Capital Area affiliate United Way, 1977-79. Mem. Harvard Law Sch. Assn. D.C. (pres. 1979-80), Harvard Law Sch. Assn. (sec. 1982-84). Avocations: electronics, photography. Office: Irwin Campbell Tannenwald PC 1730 Rhode Island Ave NW Washington DC 20036-3101 Office Phone: 202-728-0400.

**TANNER, DANIEL,** education educator; b. NYC, Sept. 22, 1926; s. Jack and Lillian (Jupiter) T.; m. Laurel Nan Jacobson, July 11, 1948 (div. 1988). BS with honors, Mich. State U., 1949, MS, 1952; PhD, Ohio State U., 1955. Asst. prof. edn. San Francisco State Coll., 1955-60; coord. Midwest program on airborne TV instrn. Purdue U., 1960-62; assoc. prof. edn., assoc. dir. internat. program for edn. leaders Northwestern U., 1962-64; assoc. prof. rsch. divsn. tchr. edn. CUNY, 1964-66; prof. edn., dir. Ctr. for Urban Edn., U. Wis.-Milw. Sch. Edn., 1966-67; prof. edn., dir. grad. programs in curriculum theory and devel. Grad. Sch. Edn., Rutgers U., New Brunswick, NJ, 1967—, chmn. dept. curriculum and instrn., 1969-72, faculty rsch. fellow, 1974-75, 88-89. Vis. faculty U. Kansas City, 1956, Tehrs. Coll. Columbia, 1966, Emory U., 1968, SUNY, Binghamton, 1968, U. London, 1975, King Abdulaziz U., Saudi Arabia, 1992, U. Iowa, 1996; disting. lectr. ASCD, 1985, 86, Dewey Meml. lectr., 1984, Raths Meml. lectr., SUNY, 1984; Leadership Inst. lectr. U. Del., 1990; disting. lectr. Rider U., 1996; vis. scholar U. London Inst. Edn., 1974-75; rev. bd. coll. work-study program US Office Edn., 1965; mem. symposium on comparative curriculum history Inst. Sci. Edn. Kiel U., Fed. Republic Germany, 1989; del. leader Citizen Amb. Program, People-to-People Internat., Republic of South Africa, 1996, China, 1997, Dem. Citizenship Project Czech Republic, USIA, 1996-98; cons. U. Tex. Med. Ctr., 1961-62, Chgo. Sch. Survey, 1964-65, ctr. Urban Edn., NYC, 1964-65, West Chgo. Sch. Survey, 1963-64, Nat. Ednl. TV Ctr., NYC, 1963, Campbell County Sch. Survey, Va., 1970, Memphis Schs., 1977-78, Perth Amboy Schs., NJ, 1996-97; ASCD Commn. on Gen. Edn., 1980-81, West Orange, NJ, Curriculum Study, 1984, ASCD Commn. on Secondary Sch. Practices, 1985, ASCD Ednl. Policy Task Force, 1985, NASSP Curriculum Coun., 1985-95; SUNY Buffalo External Evaluation, 1988; dir. Nat. Curriculum Inst., Washington, 1987; delivered Founder's Day address Delaware Valley Coll., 1985, keynote address Nat. Conf. Citizen Edn., Palacky U., Czech Rep., 1998. Author: Schools for Youth: Change and Challenge in Secondary Education, 1965, Secondary Curriculum: Theory and Development, 1971, Secondary Education: Perspectives and Prospects, 1972, Using Behavioral Objectives in the Classroom, 1979, Supervision in Education, 1987, History of the School Curriculum, 1991, Crusade for Democracy: Progressive Education at the Crossroads, 1991, 2002; co-author: Teen Talk: Curriculum Materials in Communications, 1971, Curriculum Development Theory Into Practice, 4th edit., 2006; co-editor: Improving the School Curriculum, 1988, Restructuring for an Interdisciplinary Curriculum, 1992, Curriculum Issues and the New Century, 1995; founding editor, contbg. author: Rsch. Rev. for Sch. Leaders. 1996, 98, 2000, Philosophy Edn. Ency., 1996, Ency. Edn., 2d edit., 2003, Curriculum Issues, 87th Yearbook NSSE, 1988, 98th Yearbook, 1999, Ency. Ednl. Rsch., 5th edit., 1982, Readings in Edn. Psychology, 1965, Yearbook of the Assn. for Student Tchg., 1962, Great Debate, Our Schools in Crisis, 1959, Educational Issues in a Changing Society, 1964, Programs, Teachers and Machines, 1964, Views on American Schooling, 1964, Tng. America's Tchrs., 1975, Curriculum and Instruction, 1981, Experiencing Dewey, 2005, Intricate Palette, 2005; contbg. editor: Ednl. Leadership, 1969-74; mem. editl. bd. Tex. Tech. Jour. Edn., 1984-89, Tchg. Edn., 1986-90, Jour. Curriculum Supervision; editl. cons.: Ency. of Ednl. Rsch., 5th edit., 1982, Ency. of Edn., 2d edit., 2003, Jour. Ednl. Psychology; founding editor Rev. Rsch. for Sch. Leaders. Trustee Delaware Valley Coll., Doylestown, Pa., 1981-95; bd. dirs. Ohio State Alumni Assn. N.J., 1990-96. Recipient Excellence award, Edn. Press Am., 1989, Disting. Educator award, Rider U., 1996; grantee, Rutgers Rsch. Coun., 1988—89, 2000—01; Univ. scholar, Ohio State U., 1955. Fellow AAAS, John Dewey Soc. (bd. dirs. 1985-88, archivist 1989-, chmn. lectrs. commn. 1999-2004, pres. 2003-03); mem. AAUP, Am. Ednl. Rsch. Assn. (Lifetime Achievement award Divsn. B 2006), N.Y. Acad. Scis., Am. Polit. Scis. Assn., Am. Ednl. Studies Assn., Nat. Soc. Study Edn., Phi Kappa Phi, Phi Delta Kappa (sar. award 1957). Home: Highwood Rd Somerset NJ 08873 Office: Grad Sch Edn Rutgers U New Brunswick NJ 08901-1183 Fax: 732-732-6803. Personal E-mail: dantan@rci.rutgers.edu. The essential quality of education and life is growth. Hence problems must be seen as opportunities and not as limitations if solutions are to be found and progress is to be made.

**TANNER, DEE BOSHARD,** retired lawyer; b. Provo, Utah, Jan. 10, 1913; s. Myron Clark and Marie (Boshard) T.; m. Jane Barwick, Dec. 26, 1936 (div. Aug. 1962); children: Barry, Diane McDowell; m. Reeta Walker, Dec. 6, 1981. BA, U. Utah, 1935; LLB, Pacific Coast U., 1940; postgrad., Harvard U., 1936, Loyola U., L.A., 1937. Bar: Calif. 1943, US Dist. Ct. (so. dist.) Calif. 1944, US Ct. Appeals (9th cir.) 1947, ICC 1964, US Dist. Ct. (ea. dist.) Calif. 1969, US Supreme Ct. 1971. Assoc. Spray, Davis & Gould, LA, 1943-44; pvt. practice LA, 1944; assoc. Tanner and Sievers, LA, 1944-47, Tanner and Thornton, LA, 1947-54, Tanner, Hanson, Meyers, LA, 1954-64; ptnr. Tanner and Van Dyke, LA, 1964-65, Gallagher and Tanner, LA, 1965-70; pvt. practice Pasadena, Calif., 1970-95; ret., 1995. Mem.: LA Bar Assn., World Affairs Assn., LA Sheriff's Star Org., Harvard Law Sch. Assn., Lawyers' Club LA. Home and Office: 1720 Lombardy Rd Pasadena CA 91106-4127 Personal E-mail: rpltd@aol.com.

**TANNER, DOUGLAS ALAN,** lawyer; b. Palo Alto, Calif., Aug. 30, 1953; s. Bernard R. and Caroline (Orris) Tanner; m. Carol Scilacci, May 28, 1977; children: Lauren Elizabeth, Wynn Ann, Leigh Caroline. AB in History, Stanford U., 1974, MBA, JD, Stanford U., 1978. Bar: Calif. 1978, U.S. Dist. ct. (no. dist.) Calif. 1978, U.S. Ct. Appeals (9th cir.) 1979, N.Y. 1987. Law clk. to judge U.S. Ct. Appeals (9th cir.), San Francisco, 1978-79; assoc. Orrick, Herrington & Sutcliffe, San Francisco, 1979-83, ptnr. San Jose, Calif., 1984-86, N.Y., 1986-89, Milbank, Tweed, Hadley & McCloy, L.A., 1989-92, Hong Kong, 1992-2001, Palo Alto, Calif., 2001—04, NYC, 2004—, ptnr., head global securities group. Mem.: San Francisco Barristers (chmn. corps. com. 1981—82), Order of Coif, Phi Beta Kappa. Episcopalian. Office: Milbank Tweed Hadley & McCloy LLP 1 Chase Manhattan Plaza New York NY 10021 Office Fax: 212-530-5219. Business E-Mail: dtanner@milbank.com.

**TANNER, ERIC BENSON,** lawyer; b. St. Louis, Aug. 27, 1949; s. Robert H. and Delores (Benson) Tanner; m. Rosalind Grace Tanner, June 23, 1978; children: Jacob, Adam. BA, U. Mo., Columbia, 1971; JD, U. Mo., Kansas City, 1975; cert., Coll. Fin. Planning, Denver, 1988. Bar: Mo. 1975. Instr. paralegal program Avila Coll., Kansas City, Mo., 1982-84; staff atty. Legal Aid Western Mo., Kansas City, 1975-83; pvt. practice Kansas City, 1983-86, 1990—93, 2002—; asst. v.p. trust dept. United Mo. Bank, NA, Kansas City, 1986-90; v.p., trust counsel Commerce Bank, N.A., Kansas City,

1993—2002. CLE lectr. estate planning topics various bar assns. and univs., 1975—. Contbr. articles to profl. jours. Mem. planned giving com. Nat. Kidney Found., Kans., Kansas City, 1995—97; vol. Habitat for Humanity, 1997, 1999, 2002, 2004; bd. dirs. Prime Health, 1980—86, Marillac, 2003—, Investor Literacy Co., 2004—06. Mem.: Estate Planning Soc. Kansas City, Kansas City Corp. Fiduciaries Assn. (pres. 1997), Nat. Acad. Elder Law Attys., Kansas City Met. Bar Assn., Mo. Bar Assn. Office: 800 W 47th St Ste 320 Kansas City MO 64112 Office Phone: 816-931-7878.

**TANNER, ESTELLE NEWMAN,** oral historian; b. Chgo., Sept. 2, 1936; d. Albert Hardy and Sylvia (Laff) Newman; m. Harold Tanner, July 6, 1957; children: David Allen, James Michael, Karen Tanner Allen. BA, Wellesley Coll., 1957. Cert. oral history tchr. Wellesley (Mass.) Coll., 1982—, Assn. of Governing Bds. of Univs. and Colls., Washington, 1985-94. Trustee N.Y. State Archives Partnership Trust, Albany, 1994—, Ctr. Study of Philanthropy; dir. oral history project United Jewish Appeal Fedn., Jewish Philanthropists, N.Y., 1981-; chair WNYC Radio, Jewish Women's Archive. Contbr.: Women as Donors, Women as Philanthropists, 1993. Trustee Colonial Williamsburg (Va.) Found., 1991—, WNYC Found., N.Y.C., 1985-, Hebrew Union Coll., Jewish Inst. of Religion; bd. dirs. N.Y. Community Trust. Mem. Cosmopolitan Club, Harmonie Club. Office: NY Community Trust 909 Third Ave New York NY 10022*

**TANNER, HAROLD,** investment banker; b. N.Y.C., May 7, 1932; s. Irving and Pauline (Steinlauf) T.; m. Estelle Newman, July 6, 1957; children: David, James, Karen. BS, Cornell U., 1952; MBA, Harvard U., 1956. V.p., dir. Blyth & Co. Inc., N.Y.C., 1956-69; exec. v.p. New Court Securities Corp., N.Y.C., 1969-76, Blyth Eastman Dillon & Co., Inc., N.Y.C., 1977-80; ptnr. Salomon Bros. Inc., 1980-81, mng. dir., 1981-87; pres. Tanner & Co., Inc., N.Y.C., 1987—. Co-founder Vol. Urban Cons. Group. Pres. emeritus Am. Jewish Com.; former chmn. Transatlantic Inst.; chmn. Conf. Pres. Major Jewish Orgns.; chmn. bd. trustees emeritus Cornell U.; trustee Russell Sage Found., Revson Found., Classroom Inc. Lt. (j.g.) USNR, 1952—54. Mem. Coun. on Fgn. Rels., Century Country Club, Harmonie Club. Home: 2 Morris Ln Scarsdale NY 10583-6053 Office: Tanner & Co 950 Third Ave New York NY 10022-1029

**TANNER, HELEN HORNBECK,** historian, consultant; b. Northfield, Minn., July 5, 1916; d. John Wesley and Frances Cornelia (Wolfe) Hornbeck; m. Wilson P. Tanner, Jr., Nov. 22, 1940 (dec. 1977); children: Frances, Margaret Tanner Tewson, Wilson P., Robert (dec. 1983) AB with honors, Swarthmore Coll., 1937; MA, U. Fla., 1949; PhD, U. Mich., 1961. Asst. to dir. pub. rels. Kalamazoo Pub. Schs., 1937-39; with sales dept. Am. Airlines Inc., N.Y.C., 1940-43; tchg. fellow, then tchg. asst. U. Mich., Ann Arbor, 1949-53, 57-60, lectr. ext. svc., 1961-74, asst. dir. Ctr. Continuing Edn. for Women, 1964-68; project dir. Newberry Libr., Chgo., 1976-81, rsch. assoc., 1981-95, sr. rsch. fellow, 1995—. Expert witness in Indian treaty litig., 1963—; dir. D'Arcy McNickle Ctr. for Indian History, 1984-85; mem. Mich. Commn. Indian Affairs, 1966-70; cons. in field Author: Zespedes in East Florida 1784-1790, 1963, 89, General Green Visits St. Augustine, 1964, The Greeneville Treaty, 1974, The Territory of the Caddo Tribe of Oklahoma, 1974, The Ojibwas, 1992; editor: Atlas of Great Lakes Indian History, 1987, The Settling of North America: An Atlas, 1995. Named to Mich. Women's Hall of Fame, 2006; NEH grantee, 1976, fellow, 1989; ACLS grantee, 1990. Mem. Am. Soc. Ethnohistory (pres. 1982-83), St. Augustine Hist. Soc., Conf. L.Am. History, Soc. History Discoveries, Chgo. Map Soc., Hist. Soc. Mich. Home: 5178 Crystal Dr Beulah MI 49617-9618 Personal E-mail: hhtanner@charter.net.

**TANNER, JERRÉ E.,** composer, retired publishing executive; b. Lock Haven, Pa., Jan. 5, 1939; s. Roger P. Tanner and Mildred E. Catté. BA, U. Iowa, 1960; MA, San Francisco State U., 1970. Composer, Kailua-Kona, Hawaii, 1970—2003. Instr. music U. Hawaii, Hilo, 1965—67; West Hawaii arts coord. State Found. Culture and Arts, Hawaii, 1975—76; artistic dir. Opera Players Hawaii, Honolulu, 1978—79; pres., CEO Malama Arts, Inc., Kailua-Kona, Hawaii, 1979—2003. Composer: (opera) The Lei of God Kane, Boy with Goldfish, Heroic Fantasy For Soloists, Chorus, Orchestra, (choral symphony) The Naupaka Floret, (chamber opera) The Kona Coffee Cantata, (comic opera for youth) The Singing Snails, (choral symphony) No. 2: Keepers of the Land, (theme & variations for symphonic band) High Seas to High Shoals, (choral symphony) No. 3: Aumakua - Living Ancestors. Recipient Celia S. Buck award, Am. Composers & Conductors Assn., 1966, Std. Music award, A.S.C.A.P., 1967—2005; fellow Residence fellow, Huntington Hartford Found., 1963—64; Artist Music Composition fellow, Hawaii State Found. Culture & Arts, 1997, Margaret Fairbank Jory Copy Assistance grants, Am. Music Ctr., 1989, 1994, Assistance grants, Hawaii State Found. Culture & Arts, 1974, 1976, 1989, 1986. Mem.: Hawaii Chpt. Am. Choral Dirs. Assn., Iowa Composers Forum, Am. Music Ctr., Am. Composers Forum. Home: 159 La'imi Rd Honolulu HI 96817 E-mail: arsmusica@hawaiianet.net.

**TANNER, JIMMIE EUGENE,** retired dean; b. Hartford, Ark., Sept. 27, 1933; s. Alford C. and Hazel Ame (Anthony) Tanner; m. Carole Joy Yant, Aug. 28, 1958; children: Leslie Allison, Kevin Don. BA, Okla. Baptist U., 1955; MA, U. Okla., 1957, PhD, 1964. Prof. English Okla. Bapt. U., Shawnee, 1958—64, 1965—72; assoc. prof. Franklin Coll., Ind., 1964—65; v.p. acad. affairs Hardin-Simmons U., Abilene, Tex., 1972—78, La. Coll., Pineville, 1978—80; dean William Jewell Coll., Liberty, Mo., 1980—97, prof., 1997—2003, interm pres. 1993—94; ret. 2003. Contbg. author: The Annotated Bibliography of D. H. Lawrence, Vol. 1, 1982, Vol. 2, 1985. Mem. Shawnee Sch. Bd., 1966—72; elder. commn. So. Bapt. Conv., 1967—72; bd. dirs. Mo. Coun. for Humanities, 2003—, So. Fellowships Fund fellow, 1960—61, Danforth fellow, 1962—63. Mem.: SAR. Southern. Baptist. Avocations: tennis, photography. Home: 609 Lancelot Dr Liberty MO 64068-1023 As I reflect on my life, the thought that presses on me is my incredible luck at having been born in America in the 20th century, my good fortune in having the opportunity for education, for a satisfying career, for supportive family, friends, mentors at every stage of my life. I must recognize any accomplishment as communal as well as individual.

**TANNER, JOHN S.,** congressman, lawyer; b. Halls, Tenn., Sept. 22, 1944; s. E.B. and Edith (Sumners) Tanner; m. Betty Ann Portis, Sept. 2, 1967; children: Elizabeth Tanner Atkins, John Portis. BBA, U. Tenn., Knoxville, 1966; JD, U. Tenn. Law, 1968. Mem. Tenn. State Ho. Reps., 1976-88, US Congress from 8th Tenn. dist., 1989—, mem. nat. security com., 1989—97, mem. sci. com., 1989—97, mem. ways and means com., 1997—, mem. Sportsmen's Caucus. V.p. NATO Parliamentary Assembly. Active Obion County Cancer Soc.; bd. visitors US Naval Acad.; former mem. bd. visitors US Mil. Acad., USAF Acad. Lt. USN, 1968—73, col. Tenn. Army N.G., 1974—2000. Recipient Outdoor Life Conservation award, Pub. Svc., Silver Bayonet award, AMVETS. Mem. Obion County of C., Obion County Bar Assn., Rotary, Masons (32nd degree) Democrat. Mem. Christian Ch. (Disciples Of Christ). Avocations: golf, hunting. Office: US Ho Reps 1226 Longworth Ho Office Bldg Washington DC 20515-4208 Office Phone: 202-225-4714.*

**TANNER, JOSEPH RICHARD,** astronaut; b. Ill., 1950; married; 2 children. BSc in Mech. Engring., U. Ill., 1973, BS, 1973. Commd. ensign USNR, 1973, advanced through grades to comdr., 1988, pilot, 1975-89; astronaut NASA, Houston, 1992—. Astronaut Space Shuttle Atlantis (STS-66), 1994, Svc. to Hubble Space Telescope, Discovery (STS-82), 1997, ISS Assembly Flight 4A Endeavour (STS-97), 2000; astronaut, will perform spacewalks Space Shuttle Atlantis (STS-115), 2006. Recipient Outstanding Alumnus award, U. Ill., NASA Exceptional Svc. medal, NASA Space Flight medal, NASA Stuart M. Present Flight Achievement award. Avocations: swimming, camping, mountain climbing, time with family. Office: Astronaut Office CB NASA Johnson Space Ctr Houston TX 77058*

**TANNER, LAUREL NAN,** education educator; b. Detroit, Feb. 16, 1929; d. Howard Nicholas and Celia (Solovich) Jacobson; m. Daniel Tanner, July 11, 1948; m. Kenneth J. Rehage, Nov. 25, 1989. BS in Social Sci., Mich. State U., 1949, MA in Edn., 1953; EdD, Columbia U., 1967. Pub. sch. tchr., 1950-64; instr. tchr. edn. Hunter Coll., 1964-66, asst. prof., 1967-69; supr. Milw. Pub. Schs., 1966-67; mem. faculty Temple U., Phila., 1969—, prof. edn., 1974-89, prof. emerita, 1993—; prof. edn. U. Houston, 1989-96. Vis. professorial scholar U. London Inst. Edn., 1974—75; vis. scholar Stanford U., 1984—85, U. Chgo., 1988—89; curriculum cons., 1969—; disting. vis. prof. San Francisco State U., 1987. Author: Classroom Discipline for Effective Teaching and Learning, 1978, La Disciplina en la enseñanza y el Aprendizaje, 1980, Dewey's Laboratory School: Lessons for Today, 1997; co-author: Classroom Teaching and Learning, 1971, Curriculum Development: Theory into Practice, 1975, 4th edit., 2006, Supervision in Education: Problems and Practices, 1987, (with Daniel Tanner) History of the School Curriculum, 1990; editor Nat. Soc. Study Edn. Critical Issues in Curriculum, 87th yearbook, part 1, 1988. Faculty rsch. fellow Temple U., 1970, 80, 81; recipient John Dewey Rsch. award, 1981-82, Rsch. Excellence award U. Houston, 1992, Outstanding Writing award Am. Assn. Colls. Tchr. Edn., 1998; Spencer Found. rsch. grantee, 1992. Mem. ASCD (dir. 1982-84), Soc. Study Curriculum History (founder, 1st pres. 1978-79), Am. Edn. Rsch. Assn. (com. on role and status of women in edn. R & D 1994-97), Profs. Curriculum Assn. (Factotum 1983-84, chair membership com. 1994-95), Am. Ednl. Studies Assn., John Dewey Soc. (bd. dirs. 1989-91, pres. 2000-01), Alumni Coun. Tchrs. Coll. Columbia U. In my view, America has progressed over the years, and the best days are still to come. We have the single necessary resource to solve our most urgent problems and achieve our deepest moral values — human intelligence.

**TANNER, LYNN,** actress; b. NYC, Mar. 22, 1953; d. Harry J. and Barbara Sylvia (Hirschman) Maurer; m. Allen Barry Witz, Aug. 31, 1975. BS, NYU, 1975; JD, DePaul U., 1980. Bar: Ill. 1980. Actress, various, 1980—; chair, pres., CEO, Artists Funding Group, Inc. Actor: (films) Human Error, 1987, Another Time, Another Place, 1988, Twisted, 1995; (TV series, pilot) Hollywood Flat; (plays) Pack of Lies, Back at the Blue Dolphin Saloon, Toyer, Burying Rose, Dolores and Her Loved Ones, Final Placement, Facing the Dragon, The Workroom, Sign in Sidney Brusteins Window, Summer and Smoke, The Maids, Under Milkwood, Dark at the Top of the Stairs, Rosa; co-author: (screenplays) Wrong Turn, Tessa Deare, Reasons; co-prodr.: Hollywood Flat; dir.: (plays) Dickens, A Christmas Story, 2003. Pres./CEO Artists Funding Group Inc.; pres., CEO The Gambian Bridge to Hope. Mem. SAG, AFTRA, Actors Equity Assn., Women in Film, Women in Theatre, Ill. Bar Assn. Office Phone: 310-785-9079. E-mail: lynnjettstar@gmail.com.

**TANNER, MARTIN ABBA,** statistician, educator; b. Highland Park, Ill., Oct. 19, 1957; s. Meir and Esther Rose (Bauer) T.; m. Anat Talitman, Aug. 14, 1984; 1 child, Noam Ben. BA, U. Chgo., 1978, PhD, 1982. Asst. prof. stats. and human oncology U. Wis., Madison, 1982-87, assoc. prof., 1987-90; dir. lab., prof. and dept. biostatistics U. Rochester, 1990-94; prof. dept. statistics Northwestern U., 1994—. Cons. Kirkland & Ellis, 1980-82; mem. Nat. Inst. Allergy and Infectious diseases study sect., 1994-98; reviewer NIH, NSF, VA. Assoc. editor Jour. Am. Stat. Assn., 1987-99; editor Jour. Am. Statis. Assn., 1999-2003; contbr. articles to profl. jours. Recipient New Investigator Rsch. award NIH, 1984, Mortimer Spiegelman award Am. Pub. Health Assn., 1993; NSF grantee, 1983, 95, NIH grantee, 1986—. Fellow Royal Statis. Soc., Am. Statis. Assn. (Continuing Edn. Excellence award); mem. AAAS, Mensa, Sigma Xi. Avocations: classical guitar, medieval poetry. Office: Northwestern U 2006 Sheridan Rd Evanston IL 60208-0852 Office Phone: 847-491-2700. Business E-Mail: mat132@northwestern.edu.

**TANNER, PEGGY,** retired nurse; b. N.Y.C., N.Y., Sept. 9, 1929; d. Denis Michael Hegarty and Minnie Daly; m. Henry V. Tanner, Sept. 5, 1959; children: Denise Fontenelli, James. Student, Iona Coll., 1974. RN N.Y. Staff nurse Queen Mary's Hosp., Sidcup, Kent, England, 1950—53, Jewish Meml. Hosp., New York, NY, 1955—59; med. asst. Dr. Arthur Antenucci, N.Y.C., 1960—62; claimes examiner Am. Prog. Ins., Mount Vernon, NY, 1962—65; interviewer N.Y. State Unemployment Office, New Rochelle, NY, 1973—76; staff nurse New Rochelle Hosp., New Rochelle, 1977—92, ret., 1992. Author: Tales of Two Countries, 1997, The Joy of the Journey, 1999. Adv. com. Parks & Recreation, New Rochelle, 1971—75; oral history recorder Bicentennial Com., New Rochelle, 1975—76; dist. leader Rep. Party, New Rochelle, 1970—74. Mem.: Jersey Shore Writers Guild, Irish History Roundtable. Personal E-mail: pegoty4@aol.com.

**TANNER, W(ALTER) RHETT,** lawyer; b. Athens, Ga., May 16, 1938; s. Johnnie Bryson and Walterette (Arwood) T.; m. Carolyn Laverne Watson, Nov. 11, 1967; 1 child, Walter Rhett (dec. 1989). AB cum laude, U. Ga., 1960, JD cum laude, 1962. Bar: Ga. 1961; cert. neutral Ga. Office of Dispute Resolution. With Hansell & Post, Atlanta, 1964—89, Jones, Day, Reavis & Pogue, Atlanta, 1989—99. Panelist Am. Arbitration Assn., 1995—. Bd. dirs. Atlanta Symphony Orch., 1975—95, mem. exec. com., 1977—86, v.p., 1978, chmn. maj. gifts campaign, 1980, bd. counsellors, 1996—; mem. Leadership Atlanta, 1980, Leadership Ga., 1982; mem. bd. visitors Grady Meml. Hosp., 1983—92; trustee Ga. Legal History Found., 1986—, pres., 1996—; hon. chmn. Atlanta Decorators Show House, 2002; trustee Sr. Citizens Svc. Met. Atlanta, Inc., 2000—; Sr. Citizens Found., 2005—; bd. dirs. Highlands/Cashiers Chamber Music Festival, 2003—. Lt. comdr. USNR, ret. Mem. Atlanta Bar Assn. (bd. dirs. 1982-87, exec. com. 1983-87), State Bar Ga. (vice chmn. bar and media com. 1979-82), Atlanta Bar Found. (trustee 1985-91), U. Ga. Alumni (pres. chpt. 1973-74, chmn. Atlanta/Met. coun. 1975, mem. state bd. mgrs., v.p. 1976-78), Rotary Club, Gridiron, Capital City Club, Peachtree Racket Club, Phi Beta Kappa, Omicron Delta Kappa, Phi Kappa Phi, Phi Delta Phi, Delta Tau Delta. Home and Office: 2097 Bohler Rd NW Atlanta GA 30318-1515 E-mail: wtanner516@aol.com.

**TANNIAN, FRANCIS XAVIER,** economist, educator; b. Boston, Dec. 5, 1933; s. John Joseph and Marie (Killian) Tannian; m. Beatrix Laube, May 19, 1962; children— Monica, Margaret Joyce, Mark, Michele BA, Boston Coll., 1955, MA, 1959; PhD, U. Va., 1965. Bus. trainee GE Schenectady, 1955-56; asst. prof. econs. Duquesne U., Pitts., 1962-66; assoc. prof. econs. U. Del., Newark, 1967-72, prof. urban econs., 1972—91, assoc. dean, 1978-79, prof. emeritus, 1991—. Vis. prof. U. Stuttgart, Fed. Republic Germany, 1972-73, U. Karlsruhe, Fed. Republic Germany, 1982, San Diego State U., 1989, U. Nitra, Czechoslovakia, 1990, 96, 2001; cons. Fed. Water Pollution and Control Adminstrn., 1965-68, Deutsche Gesellschaft, Frankfurt, Fed. Republic Germany, 1982-83; lectr. urban studies US Dept State, Budapest, Bucharest, Belgrade, 1975; guest lectr. Czechoslovakian Acad. Scis., 1975. Editor: Externalities, 1972; contbr. articles to profl. jours. Mem. Del. Gov.'s Econ. Adv. Coun., 1969-72; bd. dirs. Del. OIC, Wilmington, 1970-78; bd. dirs. Parity Econ. Devel. Corpn., Wilmington, 1978-84; mem. Wilmington Mayor's Econ. Assn. Com., 1976-82. Served with U.S. Army, 1957-58 Mem. Am. Econ. Assn., So. Econ. Assn., Am. Real Estate and Urban Econs. Assn. Democrat. Roman Catholic. Office: U Del Coll Urban Affairs Newark DE 19711

**TANNO, JOHN W.,** university librarian; b. Bklyn., Sept. 28, 1939; s. John C. and Hildegarde (Whitaker) T.; children: Maria Elena, Luisa. AA, Phoenix Jr. Coll., 1959; MusB, Ariz. State U., 1963; MusM, U. So. Calif., 1965, MLS, 1970. Music librarian SUNY, Binghamton, 1965-68; order librarian Claremont Colls., Calif., 1970; music librarian U. Calif., Riverside, 1970-72, head monographs sect., 1972-78, asst. univ. librarian, 1978-83, assoc. univ. librarian, 1983—2002, univ. libr. Davis, 2002—. Mem. ops. com. So. Regional Library Facility, 1984—, task group Intercampus Transp., 1984, negotiating team CLSI, 1981-84, bldg. com. So. Regional Compact Shelving Facility, 1979-82, steering com. Univ. Bibliographic Access System, 1978-82; chair Systemwide Ops. and Planning Adv. Group, 2001-04. Editor Soundboard, 1976-80; contbr. articles to profl. jours. Mem. ALA, The Music Library Assn., Coll. Music Soc., Assn. Recorded Sound Collections, Guitar Found.

Am. (exec. com. 1976-80), Beta Phi Mu. Home: 130 Eastbrook Cir Sacramento CA 95835 Office: Gen Libr U Calif Davis 100 NorthWest Quad Davis CA 95616-5292 Office Phone: 530-752-2110. Business E-Mail: jwtanno@ucdavis.edu.

**TANNON, JAY MIDDLETON,** lawyer; b. Augusta, Ga., Feb. 24, 1956; BA summa cum laude, Univ. N.C., 1978; JD, U. Va., 1982; MBA cum laude, U. Louisville, 1983. Bar: Ky. 1982, DC. Ptnr. Brown, Todd & Heyburn, Louisville, 1982-2000; exec. committee Frost, Brown, Todd LLC, 2000—04; chmn. Kentucky WorldTrade Ctr., 1999—2004; ptnr., Corp. & Securities, Private Equity, Internat. practices, head DC & no. Va. Corp. & Securities group Pillsbury Winthrop LLP (now Pillsbury Winthrop Shaw Pittman), Washington, 2004—06; ptnr., co-chair Pvt. Equity Group DLA Piper, Washington, 2006—. Chmn., founder Comml. Dispute Resolution Inc., Louisville, 1986—90; chmn. Ky. Export Coun., 2001—04; svcs. adv. com. US Trade Rep., 2002—; internat. studies adv. bd. U. NC; exec. com. Evermore Investments LLC, 2000—04; mem. So. Tech. Coun., 2004—; mem. steering com. Internat. Bus. Exchange Coun., 2004—06. Contbg. author Ky. Bus. Acquisitions; contbr. articles to profl. jours. Bd. dirs. U. Louisville Sch. Bus., 1985-88, Independent Industries, Inc. 1988-95. Hearst Found. scholar, 1974, Johnston scholar U. N.C., 1976, Phillips scholar U. N.C., 1977, du Pont scholar U. Va., 1979; named one of Best Lawyers in Am. Woodward-White, Am.'s Leading Bus. Lawyers Chambers & Ptnrs. Mem. ABA, Internat. Bar Assn., Ky. Bar Assn., D.C. Bar Assn. Office: DLA Piper 1200 19th St NW Washington DC 20036 Office Phone: 202-861-3932. Business E-Mail: jay.tannon@dlapiper.com.

**TANOUE, DONNA A.,** bank executive, former federal agency administrator; BA, U. Hawaii, 1977; JD, Georgetown U., 1981. Spl. dep. atty. gen. Dept. Commerce and Consumer Affairs, Hawaii, 1981-83; commr. financial inst. State of Hawaii, 1983-87; ptnr. Goodsill Anderson Quinn & Stifel, Hawaii, 1987-98; chmn. FDIC, Washington, 1998—2002; vice chmn. Bank of Hawaii, 2002—. Office: PO Box 2900 Honolulu HI 96846-6000

**TANOUS, HELENE MARY,** radiologist, educator; b. Zanesville, Ohio, Oct. 22, 1939; d. Joseph and Rose Marie (Mokarzel) T.; m. John Camp, 1986 (dec. 1990). BA, Marymount Coll., 1961; MD, U. Tex., 1967. Diplomate Am. Bd. Radiology. Intern County Hosp., L.A., 1967-68; resident in radiology Cedars-Sinai Med. Ctr., L.A., 1968-69, U. So. Calif. Hosp., L.A., 1969-71; pvt. practice medicine specializing in radiology L.A., 1972-73; instr. radiology U. So. Calif. Med. Sch., L.A., 1971-72; asst. prof. diagnostic radiology Baylor Med. Sch., Houston, 1973-75; dir. med. student elective in diagnostic radiology Ben Taub Hosp., Houston, 1973-75; pvt. practice diagnostic radiology Largo, Fla., 1975—. Chief Radiology Diagnostic Clinic, Largo, Fla.; asst. prof. diagnostic radiology U. South Fla. Med. Sch., 1980—; asst. prof., dir. med. student edn. in diagnostic radiology U. Tex., Galveston, 1988-91. Pres., founder Children's Advs., Inc., 1977-85; bd. dirs. Fla. Endowment for Humanities, 1979-83. Decorated Chevalier des Palmes Academiques Govt. of France, 1988. Mem. AMA, So. Med. Assn., L'Alliance Francaise of Tampa (bd. dirs. 1984—, pres. 1985-87), Fedn. Alliances Francaises U.S.A. (bd. dirs. 1984—, pres. 1985-87). Home: 661 Bering Dr Unit 108 Houston TX 77057-2137 Office Phone: 713-785-3975. E-mail: helene@tanousladies.com.

**TANOUS, PETER JOSEPH,** investment advisor; b. NYC, May 21, 1938; s. Joseph Carrington and Rose Marie (Mokarzel) T.; m. Barbara Ann MacConnell, Aug. 18, 1962; children: Christopher, Helene, William. BA in Econs., Georgetown U., 1960. With Smith Barney & Co., Inc., N.Y.C., 1963-78, 2d v.p., mgr. Paris office, 1967, v.p., 1968-78, resident European sales mgr. in Paris, 1969-71, internat. sales mgr., 1971-78, 1st v.p., 1975-78; chmn. bd. Petra Capital Corp., N.Y.C., 1978-81; pres. Lynx Investment Advisory Inc., Washington, 1992—. Exec. v.p. Bank Audi (USA), N.Y.C., 1984—92; del. U.S.-Saudi Arabian Joint Econ. Commmn. Bus. Dialogue; bd. dirs. MPS Group, Inc. (formerly Modis Profl. Svcs., Inc.), Jacksonville, Fla., Christian Children's Fund, Worldcare Ltd., Cambridge, Mass. Author: Investment Gurus, 1997, The Wealth Equation, 1999, Investment Visionaries, 2003. Trustee Browning Sch., N.Y.C., 1987—93. Recipient Nat. Order of Cedar, Govt. of Lebanon, 2002. Office: 1100 Connecticut Ave NW Washington DC 20036-4101

**TANOV, ROMIL R.,** mechanical engineer, researcher; b. Rousse, Bulgaria, July 10, 1962; arrived in U.S.A., 96; s. Rayko I. Tanov and Ekaterina Y. Tanova; m. Nadya T. Georgieva, June 23, 1988; children: Radostin R., Srebrina R. Tanova. MSc, U. for Architecture, Civil Engring. and Geodesy, Sofia, Bulgaria, 1988; PhD, U. Cin., 2000. Asst. prof. U. Rousse, Bulgaria, 1989—96; rsch. asst. U. Cin., 1996—2000; applied mechanics engr. Ctr. Advanced Product Evaluation divsn. Ind. Mills & Mfg. Inc., Westfield, Ind., 2000—04; sr. engr. Abaqus Central, Inc., West Lafayette, Ind., 2004—. Reviewer Finite Elements in Analysis and Design, Internat. Jour. of Solids and Structures, AIAA Jour.; contbr. articles to sci. jours. R.T. Davis scholar, U. Cin., 2000. Mem.: ASME, Internat. Assn. for Computational Mechanics, U.S. Assn. for Computational Mechanics, Am. Soc. for Composites, Soc. Automative Engr. Office: ABAQUS Ctrl Cin Ste 410 9075 Centre Pointe Dr West Chester OH 45069 Office Phone: 513-275-1430. E-mail: rtanov@abaquscentral.com.

**TANPHAICHITR, KONGSAK,** rheumatologist, allergist, immunologist, internist; b. Bangkok, Feb. 22, 1946; came to U.S., 1971; s. Boonchoo and Hong (Nayakovit) T.; m. Sirirat Tareesung, June 17, 1973; children: Saksiri Marc, Marisa. Student, Mahidol U., Bangkok, Thailand, 1964-66, MD cum laude, 1970. Diplomate Am. Bd. Internal Medicine, Am. Bd. Rheumatology, Am. Bd. Allergy and Immunology; cert. Rheumatologist Royal Coll. Physicians Can. Student sta. med. intern Detroit Gen. Hosp.-Wayne State U., 1971-72; resident Barnes Hosp.-Washington U., St. Louis, 1972-74, fellow in rheumatology and immunology, 1974-76; instr. in medicine Washington U., 1976-77, asst. prof. medicine, 1977-97, assoc. prof. medicine 1997—2004, prof. clin. medicine, 2005—; attending physician Barnes Hosp., 1976—, Jewish Hosp. of St. Louis, 1981—. Dir. Allergy, Rheumatology & Immunology Specialists, St. Louis; cons. rheumatology Washington U., St. Louis, 1976—. Author: Amyloid Fibrils in Joint Fluid, 1976, Studies of Tolerance in NZB/NZW Mice, 1977, Vasculitis and Multiple Sclerosis, 1980, Buddhism and Science, 1987, Buddhism: Answers to Common Questions, 1990, Buddhism Answers Life, 1995, 2006, Mindfulness: The Key to Perfect One's Life, 1997, Mind and Universe, Mindfulness and Stress Management, 1998, Awakened Life for the New Millennium, 2000, Ethics and Morality, 2000, Parenting, 2000, Buddhism Beyond Non-Violence, 2001, Mom, 2001, The Best, the Worst and the Horrible of 9/11, 2001, Miracle of the Buddha's Wisdom, 2002, Mindfulness Amidst the Evolving World, 2003, Self-Awareness: The Neglected Essence of Life, 2003, Universal Language, Laws, and Community, 2004; editor: Vipassana 101, 2004, World Peace, 2004, Dependent Arising: Center of all Truths, 2004, Essence of Life: Mindfulness and Self-Awareness, 2005, Buddhism: The Ultimate Self-Improvement System, 2005, Science on Mind & Mindfulness, 2005, Buddhism and Qualia, 2006, Buddhism & Medicine, 2006; author: Pharma In Action, 2006. Dharma tchr., bd. dirs., sec. Wat Phrasriratanaram Buddhist Temple, St. Louis, 1983—; co-dir. Buddhist Coun., St. Louis, 1985-90; chmn. Buddhist Coun. Greater St. Louis, 1999—. Named Am.'s Top Physician, Consumers' Rsch. Coun. Am., 2003—. Fellow: ACP, Royal Coll. Physicians Can., Am. Coll. Rheumatology, Am. Acad. Allergy, Asthma, and Immunology; mem.: Thai-Am. Physicians Found. (treas., bd. dirs. 2004), Thai Physicians Assn. Am. (treas. Midwest chpt. 1994, sec. Midwest chpt. 1997, nat. treas. 1998, nat. bd. dirs. 1999—2001, nat. treas. 2000), UN Assn. Greater St. Louis (bd. dirs. 2004—), UN Assn. U.S.A., Thai Assn. Greater St. Louis (pres.), Thai Temple Karate Shorinryu Club (Black Belt). Avocations: Karate, karaoke, insight meditation. Home: 12413 Ladue Rd Saint Louis MO 63141-8100 Office: Allergy Rheum & Immun Specs 1115 New Halls Ferry Rd Florissant MO 63033-7613 Office Phone: 314-839-4339. Personal E-mail: kongsak@sbcglobal.net.

**TANSELLE, GEORGE THOMAS,** language educator, foundation administrator; b. Lebanon, Ind., Jan. 29, 1934; s. K. Edwin and Madge R. (Miller) T. BA magna cum laude, Yale U., 1955; MA, Northwestern U., 1956, PhD, 1959. Instr. Chgo. City Jr. Coll., 1958-60, U. Wis., Madison, 1960-61, asst. prof., 1961-63, assoc. professor, 1963-68, prof. English, 1968-78; v.p. John Simon Guggenheim Meml. Found., 1978—; adj. prof. English and comparative lit. Columbia U., 1980—. Mem. Planning Inst. Commn. on English, 1961; mem. exec. com. Ctr. for Edits. Am. Authors, 1970-73; mem. adv. com. for drama for bicentennial Kennedy Ctr., 1974-76; mem. Soviet-Am. symposium on editing Ind. U., 1976; mem. adv. com. Howells Meml., Kittery Point, 1976-78; exec. com. Ctr. for Scholarly Edits., 1976-81; mem. nat. adv. bd. Ctr. for Book, Libr. of Congress, 1978—; mem. adv. bd. Burton's Anatomy of Melancholy, 1978—, Pub. and Printing History, A Guide to Manuscript Resources in the U.S., 1980—; bd. dirs. Lit. Classics of U.S., Inc., 1979—; chmn. editl. standards com., 1979—, corp. sec., 1989—; mem. adv. com. N.Am. imprints program, 1980-92; Hanes lectr. U. N.C., 1981; mem. adv. coun. Rosenbach Mus. and Libr., 1980—; mem. adv. coun. Ind. U. Inst. Adv. Study, 1983—; mem. faculty Summer Rare Book Sch., Columbia U., 1984-87; mem. adv. bd. Ctr. for Am. Culture Studies, Columbia U., 1985-94; mem. adv. coun. Trust for the Brit. Libr., 1987—; Rosenbach lectr. U. Pa., 1987; mem. adv. coun. Am. Literary Manuscripts project, 1988—; bd. dirs. 18th Century Short-Title Catalogue/N.Am., Inc., 1988—, chmn., 1994—, Mark Twain Edition Project, 1991—; mem. vis. com. Lilly Libr., 1988-92; mem. adv. bd. Ctr. for Renaissance and Baroque Studies, U. Md., 1990—; mem. adv. com. Writings of J.F. Cooper, 1990—; Sandars lectr. Cambridge U., 1997; mem. adv. bd. Blake Archive, 1998—; bd. dirs. Am. Newspaper Repository, 1999—; mem. adv. bd. Cambridge edit. of Jonathan Swift, 2002--. Author: Royall Tyler, 1967, Guide to the Study of United States Imprints, 1971, A Checklist of Editions of Moby-Dick, 1976, Selected Studies in Bibliography, 1979, The History of Books as a Field of Study, 1981, Textual Criticism since Greg, 1987, expanded edit., 2005, A Rationale of Textual Criticism, 1989, Parkman Dexter Howe Library, Hawthorne and Melville, 1989, Textual Criticism and Scholarly Editing, 1990, Libraries, Museums, and Reading, 1991, A Description of Descriptive Bibliography, 1992, The Life and Work of Fredson Bowers, 1993, Literature and Artifacts, 1998, Italian transl., 2004, The Pleasures of Being a Scholar-Collector, 2006; co-editor: The Writings of Herman Melville, 1968—, Samuel Johnson's Translation of Sallust, 1993; editor: Library of Am. Melville, 1982-83, Books as a Way of Life: Essays by Gordon N. Ray, 1988, The Art Deco Book in France by Gordon N. Ray, 2005; mem. editorial bd. Contemporary Literature, 1962-91, Abstracts of English Studies, 1964-78, Papers of Bibliog. Soc. Am, 1968-80, Resources for American Literary Study, 1971—, Analytical and Enumerative Bibliography, 1977—, Review, 1978—, Am. Literature, 1979-82, Literary Research, 1986-90, Common Knowledge, 1991—, Book History, 1996—, Leviathan, 1998—; contbr. articles to books and profl. jours. Mem. coun. Friends of Columbia U. Librs., 1990-94; bd. dirs. Friends of Lilly Libr., 1990-92. Recipient Kiekhofer Teaching award U. Wis., 1963, Jenkins award for bibliography, 1973; Guggenheim fellow, 1969-70; Am. Council Learned Socs. fellow, 1973-74; Nat. Endowment for the Humanities fellow, 1977-78, Laureate award Am. Printing History Assn., 1987. Mem. MLA (mem. exec. com. bibliog. evidence group 1974-75, methods of lit. rsch. div. 1979-83, chmn. 1982, mem. Hubbell award Com. Am. lit. sect. 1978-82, chmn. 1982, mem. com. on prize for ind. scholars 1983-87, chmn. 1985-87, chmn. ad hoc com. on future of print record 1993-95), Modern Humanities Rsch. Assn., Bibliog. Soc. London (pres. Am. Friends 1992—), Bibliog. Soc. Australia, Bibliog. Soc. Am. (mem. council 1970-94, vice chmn. publs. com. 1974-76, chmn. 1981-84, sec. 1976-78, chmn. com. on regional groups, 1978-80, 2d v.p. 1978-80, 1st v.p. 1980-82, pres. 1984-88), Bibliog. Soc. U. Va. (pres. 1992—), Oxford, Cambridge, Edinburgh, Birmingham, No. Ill., Can. bibliog. socs. (mem. coun. 1996—), Soc. for Bibliography of Natural History, Printing Hist. Soc. (Am. corr. 1970-84), Am. Printing Hist. Assn. (trustee N.Y. chpt. 1979-85), Pvt. Librs. Assn., Ind. Rsch. Librs. Assn. (com. on standards for rare book cataloging in machine-readable form 1978-79), Fellows Morgan Libr., Manuscript Soc. (bd. dirs. 1974-79), Am. Pub. Libr. Film Project (bd. advisors 1993—), Am. Antiquarian Soc. (mem. publs. com. 1972-81, chmn. com. 1978-81, mem. coun. 1974-92, hon. councillor, 1992—, del. to Am. Coun. Learned Socs. 1978-93, exec. com. edits., 1987-89, chmn. exec. com. program on book in Am. culture 1983-89, com. on edns., 1982-85, chmn., 1983-85, chmn. com. on libr. 1988-91), Soc. Textual Scholarship (adv. bd. 1979—, pres. 1981-83), The Johnsonians (chmn. 1993), Melville Soc. (pres. 1982, Electronic Melville Com. 1997—), Book Club Calif., Typophiles, Guild Book Workers, Wis. Acad. Scis., Arts and Letters, Renaissance Soc. Am., Am. Soc. 18th-Century Studies, Renaissance English Text Soc., Assn. Documentary Editing (chmn. Julian Boyd award com. 1986, Boydston award com. 1995), Soc. Scholarly Pub., Assn. internationale de bibliophilie, Soc. History of Authorship, Reading and Pub. (bd. dirs. 1993—), Century Club, Yale Club, Caxton Club, Grolier Club (publs. com. 1979-82, 83-87, 97—, coun. 1980—, small exhbns. com. 1979-87, chmn. 1980-82, sec. 1982-86, chmn. libr. com. 1985-86, 90-2002, pres. 1986-90), Odd Volumes, Phi Beta Kappa. Office: John Simon Guggenheim Meml Found 90 Park Ave Fl 33 New York NY 10016-1301

**TANSEY, MARK,** painter; b. San Jose, Calif., 1949; One-man shows include Grace Borgenicht, 1982, 1984, John Berggruen Gallery, San Francisco, 1984, Contemporary Arts Mus., Houston, Tex., 1984, Curt Marcus Gallery, NY, 1986, 1990, 1993, 1997, 2000, Walker Art Ctr., Minn., 1990, Kohn/Abrams Gallery, 1993, Mus. Fine Art, Boston, 1994, Galleri Faurschou, Copenhagen, 1995, Gagosian Gallery, NY, 2004, Mus. Kurhaus, Kleve, Germany, 2005, exhibitions include Biennial, Whitney Mus. Am. Art, NYC, 1983, Aperto 86, Venice Biennale, Italy, 1986, Color and/or Monochrome, Nat. Mus. Modern Art, Tokyo, 1989, 10+10: Contemporary Soviet & Am. Painters, Corcoran Gallery Art, Washington, DC, 1989, The Charade of Mastery: Deciphering Modernism in Contemporary Art, Whitney Mus. Am. Art, 1990, Mountains of the Mind, Aspen Art Mus., Colo., 1994, Am. Kaleidoscope, Nat. Mus. Am. Art, Washington, DC, 1996, Double Trouble: The Patchett Collection, Mus. Contemporary Art, San Diego, 1998, Reality and Desire, Jóan Miro Found., Barcelona, 1999, The Burbs, DFN Gallery, NY, 2003, Perspectives @ 25: A Quarter Century of New Art in Houston, Contemporary Arts Mus., 2004, Am. Art of the 1980s, Washington U. Gallery Art, St. Louis, 2004. Mailing: 90 Warren St New York NY 10007*

**TANSILL, FREDERICK JOSEPH,** lawyer; b. Washington, Feb. 27, 1948; s. Frederick Riker and Mary Eileen (Loftus) T.; m. Joan Louise Trefsgar, July 10, 1971; children: Brendan Frederick, Brooke Charlotte, Charlotte Trefsgar. BA with honors, Brown U., 1970; JD, Georgetown U., 1974, LLM in Taxation, 1982. Bar: D.C. 1974, U.S. Tax Ct. 1976, Va. 1983. Assoc. Cross, Murphy & Smith, Washington, 1974-77; ptnr. Bird & Tansill, Washington, 1977-79; assoc. Ober, Grimes & Shriver, Washington, 1979-81; ptnr. Lewis, Mitchell & Moore, Vienna, Va., 1981-86; counsel Boothe, Prichard & Dudley, McLean, Va., 1986-87; ptnr. McGuire, Woods, Battle & Boothe, McLean, 1987-90; shareholder Verner, Liipfert, Bernhard, McPherson & Hand, Chartered, McLean, 1990-97; owner-mgr. Frederick J. Tansill & Assocs., LLC, McLean, 1997—. Gen. counsel No. Va. Cmty. Found., 1995-98, 1st v.p., 1998-99, pres. 1999-2000. Fellow Am. Coll. Trust and Estate Counsel; mem. ABA, Internat. Bus. Bar, Va. Bar Assn. (exec. coun. taxation sect. 1989-92, coun. and legis. com. wills sect. 1993-99—, trusts and estate sect. 1983-99, bd. govs. 1988-96, chmn. bd. govs. 1991-92, co-chmn. spl. task force lawyers as fiduciaries 1993-95), D.C. Bar Assn. (steering com. estates, trusts and probate law sect. 1995-97, co-chair 1997-99), Fairfax County Bar Assn. (will sect. 1986, chmn. tax sect. 1987-88, CLE com. 1988-89), No. Va. Estate Planning Coun. (exec. com. 1987-92, pres. 1990-91), Tower Club (bd. dirs. 1988—). Office: Frederick J Tansill & Assocs 1355 Beverly Rd Ste 215 Mc Lean VA 22101-3654 Office Phone: 703-847-1359. Office Fax: 703-847-1357. Business E-Mail: fred@fredtansill.com.

**TANSKI, SARAH PIATKO,** mathematics educator; b. Buffalo, Jan. 8, 1981; d. Michael Paul and Joanne Piatko; m. Scott Andrew Tanski, Aug. 6, 2005. M in Edn., State U. of NY Coll. at Buffalo, 2003. Math. educator West Seneca

West Sr. H.S., NY, 2003—. Lector 14 Holy Helpers Ch., West Seneca, NY, 2005—06. Office: West Seneca Ctrl Sch 3330 Seneca St West Seneca NY 14224 Personal E-mail: sarah@tanski.com.

**TANSKY, BURTON M.,** department store executive; b. 1938; married BA, U. Pitts., 1960. With Kaufmann's, 1961-67; from asst. store mgr. to mgr. Filenes, Boston, 1967-71; mdse. mgr. Rikes, Dayton, Ohio, 1971-74; v.p. Forbes and Wallace, Springfield, Ohio, 1974, I. Magnin, San Francisco, 1974-77; from sr. v.p. to exec. v.p. Saks and Co., N.Y.C., 1977-80, pres., 1980—94; chmn., CEO Saks & Co., N.Y.C., 1990—94, Neiman Marcus Stores, Dallas, 1994—98; exec. v.p. Neiman Marcus Group, Dallas, 1998, pres., COO, 1998—2001, pres., CEO, 2001—; interim CEO Bergdorf Goodman, 2004. Bd. dir. Internat. Flavors & Fragrances, 2003—. Named a Chevalier de la Legion d'Honneur, Govt. France, 2002. Office: Neiman Marcus Group One Marcus Sq 1618 Main St Dallas TX 75201-2581*

**TANSY, MARTIN F.,** dean; m. Margaret Tansy; children: Martin Jr., Margaret, Matthew. BS, Wilkes Coll.; MS, Thomas Jefferson Med. Coll.; PhD, 1964. From asst. to assoc. prof. physiology Temple U., Phila., 1964—72, prof., 1972—86, chmn. dept. physiology and biophysics in basic sciences, acting dean Sch. Dentistry, 1986, dean Sch. Dentistry, 1987—. Bd. dirs. Friends of the Nat. Inst. Dental and Craniofacial Rsch. Recipient Alumni Excellence Award in Edn. and Adminstrn., Wilkes U., 2000. Fellow: Internat. Coll. Dentists (hon.), Am. Coll. Dentists (hon.); mem.: Nat. Acad. Practices, Acad. Gen. Dentistry (hon.). Office: Temple U Sch Dentistry 333 Dental Sch Bldg 3223 N Broad St Philadelphia PA 19140 Office Phone: 215-707-2799. Office Fax: 215-707-3192. Business E-Mail: martintansy@temple.edu.*

**TANT, MARTIN RAY,** chemical engineer, biomedical engineer; b. Seneca, SC, Apr. 10, 1953; s. Larry Ray and Doris Jo Anne (Alexander) T. BS, Old Dominion U., 1975; MS, Va. Tech., 1979, PhD, 1986; postgrad. in Biomed. Sci., East Tenn. State U., 2003—. Chemist Naval Mine Engring. Facility, Yorktown, Va., 1975-76; chem. engr. Naval Surface Warfare Ctr., Dahlgren, Va., 1979—82; sr. rsch. engr. Dow Chem. USA, Freeport, Tex., 1986-88; rsch. assoc. Eastman Chem. Co., Kingsport, Tenn., 1988—. Co-editor Ionomers: Synthesis, Structure, Properties and Applications, 1997, High-Temperature Properties and Applications of Polymeric Materials, 1995, Structure and Properties of Glassy Polymers, 1998; contbr. over 50 publs. to books and profl. jours. Cunningham Dissertation fellow, 1985..Mem.: AIChE, Am. Assn. Pharm. Scientists, Am. Chem. Soc., Sigma Xi. Office: Eastman Chem Co PO Box 1972 Kingsport TN 37662-1972 Office Phone: 423-229-2147. Business E-Mail: tant@eastman.com.

**TANTRA, MULJADI,** corporate marketing professional; b. Selatpanjang, Riau, Indonesia, July 1, 1971; came to U.S., 1988; s. Pingardi and Lesmina Tantra; m. Vivi Effendy, Nov. 24, 1996; children: Vincent, Grace. BS, Iowa State U., 1992; MBA, San Diego State U., 1996. Ops. rsch. engr. Cymer, Inc., San Diego, 1996-98, mktg. analysis mgr., 1998-2000; dir. corp. mktg. Lam Rsch., Fremont, Calif., 2000—. Inventor, patentee in field. Mem. Sigma Xi (rsch. grantee 1995), Beta Gamma Sigma, Phi Beta Delta. Buddhist. Avocations: music, tennis, scuba diving, travel. Home: 2667 Torrey Ct Pleasanton CA 94588 Office: Lam Rsch 4650 Cushing Pky Fremont CA 94538 E-mail: muljadi.tantra@lamrc.com.

**TANTUM, JAMES KENT,** artist, publisher; b. Miami, Fla., Dec. 7, 1964; s. James Kent Tantum and Penelope Elaine Davis. BA, Temple U., 1990; MFA, San Francisco Art Inst., 2005. Facilitator, presenter World Game Inst., Phila., 1994—2001, asst. dir. mktg., 1996—2001; owner Tantum Mfg., San Francisco, 1998—; sr. fellow Cultural Studies and Analysis, Phila., 2002—06. Author: Teleological Expressionism, 1998, Time, Ontology, Reality, and Me, 2002; co-author: Sex Notes, 1998; author of short stories; photographer A Year in the Life of Rittenhouse Square Show, 1995; artist (calendar) Jim Calendar, 1997-2006; designer Pogany flatware, 1996, Wrax cd rack, 1995; creator, M.C., Jim's Ann. All-Invitational RoadRally, 1995—; featured Phila. Weekly, 2001; co-founder performance troupe Parsley, 2001; performer Phila. Fringe Festival 2001, 02, 03. Fellow Murphy fellow in the fine arts, San Francisco Found. Mem.: Golden Key. Avocation: travel. Home: PO Box 424 San Francisco CA 94104 Office: Tantum Mfg PO Box 424 San Francisco CA 94104 E-mail: TanTummfg@aol.com.

**TANUR, JUDITH MARK,** sociologist, educator; b. Jersey City, Aug. 12, 1935; d. Edward Mark and Libbie (Berman) Mark; m. Michael Isaac Tanur, June 2, 1957; children: Rachel Dorothy, Marcia Valerie. BS, Columbia U., 1957, MA, 1963; PhD, SUNY, Stony Brook, 1972. Analyst Biometrics Rsch., N.Y.C., 1955-67; lectr. SUNY, Stony Brook, 1967-71, from asst. prof. to prof. sociology, 1971-94, disting. teaching prof., 1994—. Cons. NBC, N.Y.C., 1976—89, Lang. of Data Project, Los Altos, Calif., 1980—89, Inst. for Rsch. on Learning, 1994—95; mem. com. on nat. stats. NAS, 1980—87, com. on applied and theoretical stats., 1997—2000; trustee NORC, U. Chgo., 1987—; bd. dirs. Social Sci. Rsch. Coun., 2000—; mem. adv. com. SBE, NSF, 2000—. Author: The Subjectivity of Scientists and the Bayesian Approach, 2001; editor: Statistics: A Guide to the Unknown, 1972, Internat. Encyclopedia of Statistics, 1978, Cognitive Aspects of Survey Methodology, 1984, Questions About Questions, 1991, Cognition and Survey Research, 1999, Internat. Ency. of Social Scis., 1963—67; contbr. articles to sci., stats., and social sci. jours. Bd. dirs. Vis. Nurse Svc., Great Neck, N.Y., 1970-2000; bd. govs. Gen. Soc. Survey, Chgo., 1989-92. Sr. rsch. fellow, Am. Statis. Assn./NSF/Bur. Labor Stats., 1988—89. Fellow AAAS, Am. Statis. Assn. (Founders award 1997); mem. Internat. Statis. Inst., Phi Beta Kappa. Home: PO Box 280 Montauk NY 11954 Office: SUNY Dept Sociology Stony Brook NY 11794-4356 Office Phone: 631-632-7738. Business E-Mail: jtanur@notes.cc.sunysb.edu.

**TAN VAN, See NGO, VAN**

**TANVEER, SALEH A.,** mathematics professor, researcher; b. Dhaka, Bangladesh, Feb. 8, 1956; s. Golam Gaffar and Sarah Chowdhury; m. Dilruba Sultana, Aug. 31, 1980; children: Mamun A., Tasnim N. BA, Pomona Coll., 1979; MA, Claremont Grad. Sh., 1979; MS in Civil Engring., Calif.-Tech.; PhD, Calif. Inst. Tech., Pasadena, 1983. Post-doctoral rsch. fellow Caltech, Pasadena, 1983—84; asst. prof. Va. Tech, Blacksburg, 1984—89; vis. assoc. Calif. Inst. Tech., Pasadena, 1986—87; assoc. prof. Ohio State U., Columbus, Ohio, 1989—95; vis. prof. U. Chgo., 1996—97; prof. Ohio State U., 1995—, vice chair, 2002—05; vis. fellow Inst. Math. Scis., Imperial Coll., London, 2005—. Cons. Inst. Computer Apps. Sci. and Engring., Hampton, Va., 1988—94; served on peer rev. panels Nat. Sci. Foundation and NASA. Contbr. over 50 archived jours. (Francois Frenkiel award, Am. Phys. Soceity, Divsn. of Fluid Dynamics, 1987); co-guest editor Co-Guest Editor, Journal of Fluid Mechanics. Basic Energy Scis. grant, Dept. Energy, 1992—95, Divsn. of Math. Sciences grant, NSF, 1987—93, 1995—, Microgravity Sciences Divsn. grant, NASA, 1993—2000, 2002—. Mem.: Am. Phys. Soc. Achievements include research in fundamental work in partial differential equations and fluid dynamics; research grant support from federal agencies since 1987. Office: Ohio State U Math Dept 231 West 18th Ave Columbus OH 43210 Office Phone: 614-292-5710. Office Fax: 614-292-1479. Business E-Mail: tanveer@math.ohio-state.edu.

**TANZI, RONALD THOMAS,** artist, educator; b. Brookline, Mass., Mar. 3, 1949; s. Henry Francis and Jennie (Vicenza) T.; m. Patricia Marie Morrill, Mar. 16, 1974 (div. Apr. 1990); children: Jennie Grace, Jacob Thomas. Student, Chapman Coll., Orange, Calif., 1968-70; BFA magna cum laude, U. Wash., 1984; MFA, U. Cin., 1986. Artist self-employed, Spokane, Boston, Seattle, 1970—; art editor Contbr.'s Copy Quar., Spokane, 1970-73; instr., lectr. U. Cin., 1984-86; instr. U. Wash., Seattle, 1986-87, Seattle Cmty. Colls. (North and Ctrl. campuses), 1987—, Edmonds (Wash.) C.C., 1992—96, Bellevue (Wash.) C.C., 1993—. Dir. R's Studio Gallery, Cheney, 1971-73; visual advisor Masque Theater Co., Everett, Wash., 1987-88; lectr. Seattle Art Mus., 1991, Seattle Art League, 1992, Bellevue Art Mus., 1995. Exhibited paintings in shows including Spokane

City Arts, 1971, Pacific Northwest Annual, 1976, N.W. Traditions: A Retrospective, 1987, King County Arts Commn., 1988, Seattle Ctrl. CC, 1994-2004, Faculty Art Shows, Bellevue CC, 1994, 95, 96, 97, 98, 99, Philip Howe Gallery, 1998; artist, pub. commn. Metro Bus Shelter Mural Program, 1991, Harborview Med. Ctr. Mural, 1995; represented in pvt. collections in U.S., Japan, Germany, Finland. Sgt. USAF, 1966-70, Vietnam. U. Cin. Grad. scholar, 1984, 85, 86. Mem. Coll. Art Assn., Am. Fedn. Tchrs., Wash. State Fedn. Tchrs., Seattle Art Mus., Phi Beta Kappa. Avocations: swimming, hiking, travel. Office: 219 NE 91st St Seattle WA 98115 E-mail: rtanzi@sccd.ctc.edu.

**TAO, DONGHUA,** health sciences librarian; BS, China Med. U., Sheng Yang, 1996; MA, postgrad., U. Mo. Med. editor editl. dept. Affiliated Beijing TongRen Hosp. of Capital U., Beijing, 1996—2001; resident Affiliated Beijing TongRen Hosp. of Capital U. of Med. Scis., Beijing, 1997; health scis. reference libr. Health Scis. Ctr. Libr., St. Louis U., 2005—. Contbr. articles and book chpts. to profl. publs. Recipient Grad. Curator's Grant-In-Aid award, U. of Mo.-Columbia, 2005, Spl. Contbn. Prize for two internat. congresses, Beijing TongRen Hosp. of Capital U. of Med. Scis. and Beijing Inst. of Otolaryngology, 1998, Dongyu scholarship, Dongyu Group, ShengY-ang, China, 1994, Grad. Student Paper Competition award, Mo. Libr. Assn., 2003, 2004; scholar, Chinese ALA, 2005. Mem.: ALA, Spl. Libr. Assn., Healthcare Info. and Mgmt. Sys. Soc., Am. Soc. for Info. Sci. and Tech., Med. Libr. Assn., Am. Med. Informatics Assn. Achievements include research in human information seeking behavior in medical environment, especially the effect of information seeking context on information seeking behavior. Avocations: travel, movies, cooking, making friends, swimming. Office: St Louis U Health Sci Ctr Libr 1402 S Grand Blvd Saint Louis MO 63104

**TAO, LIXIN,** computer science educator; arrived in USA, 1984; s. Xinhua Tao and Jinqian Zhang; m. Weilan Jiang, July 22, 1966; children: Michael Wenhan, Victor Wenhao. MSE in Computer Sci., East China Normal U., Shanghai, 1981, U. Pa., 1985, PhD in Computer Sci., 1988. Asst. prof. computer sci. Concordia U., Montreal, Que., Canada, 1988—93, assoc. prof. computer sci., 1993—2001; full prof.,computer sci. Pace U., Pleasantville, NY, 2001—. Contbr. articles to profl. jours. Grantee, Natural Sci. and Engring. Rsch. Coun./Can., 1989—91, 1991—94, Fonds pur la formation de chereheurs et l'aide á la recherche (FCAR)/ Que., Can., 1991—94, Strategic Tech. Program of Industry, Sci. and Tech. Can., 1993—95, Natural Sci. and Engring. Rsch. Coun. (NSERC)/Can., 1994—97, 1997—2001, 2001—. Mem.: IEEE (sr. mem. 2003), ACM. Achievements include research in parallel and distributed computing, Internet computing, and operations research. Office: Pace University CSIS 861 Bedford Rd Pleasantville NY 10570 Office Phone: 914-773-3449. Personal E-Mail: lixin@ieee.org. Business E-Mail: ltao@pace.edu.

**TAO, TERENCE CHI-SHEN,** mathematics professor; b. Adelaide, South Australia, Australia, July 17, 1975; arrived in U.S., 1992; s. Billy and Grace Tao; married. BSc with honors in Math., Flinders U., 1991, MSc in Math., 1992; PhD in Math., Princeton U., 1996. Asst. researcher Flinders Med. Centre, 1992—94; Princeton U., 1993—94; Hedrick asst. prof. UCLA, 1996—98, acting asst. prof., 1999, asst. prof., 2000, full prof., 2000—. Mem. Math. Sciences Rsch. Inst., 1997; vis. fellow U. NSW, Sydney, NSW, Australia, 1999—2000, vis. prof., 2000; long-term prize fellow Clay Math. Inst., Boston, 2001—03; hon. prof. Australian Nat. U., 2001—03; mem. scientific adv. bd. Australian Math. Sciences Inst., 2002—; mem. adv. bd. Internat. Math. Rsch. Surveys (IRMS), 2003—. Reviewer Zentralblatt Math., 1998—2005, assoc. editor J. Am. Math. Soc., 2002—04, full editor, 2004—06, assoc. editor Am. Jour. Math., 2002—, Dynamics of Partial Differential Equations, 2003—; author: Solving Mathematical Problems: A Personal Perspective, 1992, 2006, Analysis Vol. I, Analysis Vol. II, 2006. Co-recipient Levi L. Conant prize, Am. Math. Soc., 2005; recipient Bronze medal, Internat. Math. Olympiad, 1986, Silver medal, 1987, Gold medal, 1988, medal, Flinders U., 1992, Fulbright postgrad. award, Fulbright Assn., 1992—95, Salem prize, Salem Prize Com., 2000, medal, Australian Math. Soc., 2005, Bocher Meml. prize, Am. Math. Soc., 2002, Fields medal, Internat. Math. Union, 2006; Packard Found. fellow, David & Lucille Packard Found., 1999—; Rsch. fellow, Sloan Found., 1999—2001, MacArthur Fellow, John D. and Catherine T. MacArthur Found., 2006. Mem.: Australian Acad. Sci. (corr.). Office: UCLA Dept Math Math Sciences 5622 MS 6364 405 Hilgard Ave Los Angeles CA 90095-1555 Office Phone: 310-206-4844. Business E-Mail: tao@math.ucla.edu.*

**TAO, WILLIAM K.Y.,** retired education educator; b. Tientsin, China, Oct. 17, 1917; s. Sho Hsien Tao and Shu Hsien Fong; m. Anne Yu Tsai Kuo, July 4, 1943; children: David K.C., Richard K.D., Peter K.P. BS, Chekiang Univ., China, 1941; MS, Washington U., 1950, DSc (hon.), 1997. Prof. asst. Wash. Univ., St. Louis, 1950—75; chmn. CEO William Tao & Assoc., St. Louis, 1958—88; pres. Bldg. Sys. Cons., St. Louis, 1989—2002; ret. Contbr. articles pub. to over 30 profl. jour.; author: (textbook) Mechanical and Electrical Systems in Buildings, 1997, 2nd edit., 2000, 3rd edit., 2004. Bd. trustees Wash. Univ., St. Louis, 1978—89, emeritus trustees, 1990; emeritus dir. Goodwill Industries, 1992; adv. coun. U.N. Assn., St. Louis, 1984; emeritus trustee Mo. Botanical Garden, 1995. Fellow: ASHRAE (standard 100.3 com 1976—85, standard 90-75 com 1973—80, standard SSPC-90 com 1984—86), IEEE (life), Am. Cons. Engr. Coun. (energy com. 1979—81), Illuminating Engring. Soc. N.Amer. (sports lighting com. chmn. 1987—89), 1989—, bd. dirs. 1975—77); mem.: Mo. Soc. of Profl. Engr. (life). Achievements include patents for dynacoustic air mixing box; radial electric distribution analysis. Avocations: photography, tennis, golf, travel, writing. Office Phone: 314-446-0885.

**TAPELLA, GARY LOUIS,** manufacturing executive; b. Antioch, Calif. Sept. 1, 1943, s. Anthony M. and Mary (Lopez) T.; m. Karen Kent, June 24, 1967; children: Robert, Michael. BA in Internat. Rels., San Francisco State U., 1969. Staff asst. Rheem Mfg. Co., N.Y.C., 1969-71; plant mgr. Rheem Can., Vancouver, 1971-73, mktg. mgr. Toronto, 1973-79; regional sales mgr. Rheem Mfg. Co., New Orleans, 1979-80; mng. dir. Rheem Far East, Singapore, 1980-85; gen. mgr. Rheem Can., Toronto, 1985-89; corp. v.p. internat. Rheem Mfg. Co., N.Y.C., 1989-90, chief oper. officer, 1990-91, pres., chief exec. officer, 1991—. Dir. various Rheem Cos. With USN, 1961-63. Avocation: scuba diving. Office: Rheem Mfg Co 405 Lexington Ave Fl 22 New York NY 10174-0112

**TAPHORN, JOSEPH BERNARD,** lawyer; b. Beckemeyer, Ill., Oct. 9, 1921; s. Herman Henry and Marie (Gasser) T.; m. Anna Marie Klinge, June 25, 1944 (dec. Dec. 1991); children: Robert J., Joanne M., John F.; m. Joan Campen Klemmer, July 13, 1996. BS in Agr., U. Ill., 1943; BS in Engring., George Washington U., 1949, LLB, 1950. Bar: N.Y. 1952, D.C. 1952, U.S. Dist. Ct. (so. and ea. dists.) N.Y. 1952, U.S. Dist. Ct. (no. dist.) N.Y. 1991, U.S. Dist. Ct. D.C. 1952, U.S. Ct. Appeals (D.C. cir.) 1961, U.S. Ct. Appeals (fed. cir.) 1996, U.S. Supreme Ct. 1961. Patent examiner U.S. Patent Office, Washington, 1946-49, patent classifier, 1949-50; patent atty. Pollard and Johnston, N.Y.C., 1950-52; patent atty. IBM Corp., N.Y.C., 1952-59, patent mgr., counsel various locations, 1959-70, copyright counsel Armonk, NY, 1970-78, copyright and trademark counsel, 1978-88; pvt. practice Poughkeepsie, NY, 1989—. Chmn. bd. U.S. Dynamics, Yonkers, N.Y. 1975-77. Contbr. articles to profl. jours. Pres. Huntley Civic Assn., Eastchester, N.Y., 1958-59; trustee Copyright Soc. USA, N.Y.C., 1955-88. Capt. U.S. Army, 1943-46, ETO. Mem. ABA (com. chmn. 1983-87), N.Y. State Bar Assn., Dutchess County Bar Assn., Am. Intellectual Property Law Assn., N.Y. Intellectual Property Law Assn. (com. chmn. 1987-89), Ea. N.Y. Intellectual Property Law Assn., Dutchess Golf and Country Club, Americana Tennis Club, Germania Club. Republican. Roman Catholic. Avocations: hunting, fishing, tennis, skiing. Home and Office: 8 Scenic Dr Poughkeepsie NY 12603-5521 Office Phone: 845-462-3262. E-mail: jbtaphorn@prodigy.net.

**TAPIA, RICHARD ALFRED,** mathematics professor; b. Santa Monica, Calif., Mar. 25, 1939; s. Amado and Magda Tapia; m. Jean Rodriguez, July 25, 1959; children: Circee (dec.), Richard, Rebecca. BA, UCLA, 1961, MA,

1966, PhD, 1967. Asst. prof. math. rsch. ctr. U. Wis., Madison, 1968-70; asst. prof. math. scis. Rice U., Houston, 1970-72, assoc. prof., 1972-76, prof. math. scis., 1976—, chair dept. math. scis., 1978-83, assoc. dir. minority affairs Office Grad. Studies, 1989—. Vis. assoc. prof. ops. rsch. Stanford (Calif.) U., 1976-77. Author: Nonparametric Density Estimation; contbr. articles to profl. publs. Named one of 20 Most Influential in Minority Math. Edn., NSF, 1990, 50 Most Important Hispanics in Govt., Edn. Hispanic Engineer and Info. Tech. mag., 2005; recipient Nat. Achievement award for Edn. Hispanic Engring. Mag., 1990, A. Nico Habermann award Computer Rsch. Assn., 1994; named Prof. of Yr., Assn. Hispanic Sch. Adminstrs., 1994. Mem. NAE, Am. Math. Soc. (mem. com. on edn.), Soc. for Indsl. and Applied Math. (trustee, lectr. 1988), Math. Assn. Am., Math. Programming Soc., Soc. for Advancement of Chicanos and Native Ams. in Sci. Home: 5723 Portal Dr Houston TX 77006-6010 Office: Rice U Dept Math Scis PO Box 1892 Houston TX 77251-1892*

**TAPKEN, MICHELLE G.,** prosecutor; BA in Edn., U. SD, 1967, MA Psychology, 1970, JD, 1989. Bar: South Dakota; lic. Psychologist. Fed. law clerk, Lincoln, Nebr., 1989—90; prosecutor US Atty. Office, Sioux Falls, SD, 1990—2001; 1st asst. US atty. Dist. SD US Dept. Justice, 2001—, interim US atty. Dist. SD, 2005. Recipient Director's Award, US Dept. Justice, 1996. Office: US Attys Office 230 S Phillips Ave Ste 600 Sioux Falls SD 57104*

**TAPLETT, LLOYD MELVIN,** human resources specialist, consultant; b. Tyndall, SD, July 25, 1924; s. Herman Leopold and Emiley (Nedvidek) T.; m. Patricia Ann Sweeney, Aug. 21, 1958; children: Virginia Ann, Sharon Lorraine, Carla Jo, Carpatria Patricia, Catherine Marie, Colleen Elizabeth. BA, Augustana Coll., 1949; MA, U. Nebr., 1959; postgrad., S.D. State U., U.S.D., U. Iowa, Colo. State U. Accredited personnel dir.; prof. human resources; life cert. tchr. & counselor. Tchr. Sioux Falls Pub. Schs., SD, 1952—69; with All-Am. Transport Co., Sioux Falls, 1969—78, Am. Freight Sys., Inc., Overland Park, Kans., 1978—79; dir. human resources & pub. rels., corp. affirmative action Chippewa Motor Freight, Inc., Sioux Falls, 1979—80; cons. human resources & mgmt., 1980—81; mgr. Sioux Falls Job Svcs., 1981—85, Pioneer Enterprises, Inc., 1985—86; ops. mgr. ATE Environ., Inc., 1986—88; cons. Royal River Casino, 1988—90; acad. dean Huron U., Sioux Falls, 1990—91; instr. econs. Coll. Bus., 1992—98. Chmn. Chippewa Credit Union; mem. adv. bd. dirs. Nelson Labs., Sioux Falls, 1981-82; evening mgmt. instr. Nat. Coll., Sioux Falls, 1981-90, chmn. adv. com., 1984-90, Huron U., 1990-97, S.F. Washington H.S. Sports Heritage 1889-98; spkr. in field. Author: American Business, 2005; contbr. articles to popular mags. Past bd. dirs. Jr. Achievement, United Way, Sioux Vocat. Sch. Handicapped; past mem. Gov.'s Adv. Bd. Cmty. Adult Manpower Planning; chmn. bus. edn. adv. com. Sioux Falls Pub. Schs., 1982-85; chmn. adv. com. South East Area Vocat. Sch., 1982-85; mem. alumnae bd. Augustana Coll., 1985-88. Capt. USMC, 1943-46, 50-52, WWII, Korea. Recipient USMC Letter of Commendation award, 1944, Liberty Bell award S.D. Bar Assn., 1967, Sch. Bd. award NEA/Thom McAn Shoe Corp., 1966, S.D. Unsung Heroes Edn. Recognition award Sta. KSFV-TV, 1998; named Boss of Yr., Sioux Falls, 1977. Mem. NEA (life, Pacemaker award), Am. Soc. Pers. Adminstrn. (accredited pers. mgr., profl. human resources, life, S.D. dist. dir. 1980-84), Am. Trucking Assn. (pub. rels. coun.), S.D. Edn. Assn. (life), Sioux Falls Pers. Assn. (past pres.), Sales and Mktg. Club Sioux Falls, Sioux Falls Traffic Club, VFW (life, Nat. Polit. Action Recognition award 1990), Am. Legion, Toastmasters (past gov. dist. 41, Disting. Toastmaster award, Outstanding Toastmaster award dist. 41, Hall of Fame 1977), Elks. Republican. Roman Catholic. Office Phone: 605-332-8100.

**TAPLEY, BYRON DEAN,** aerospace engineer, educator; b. Charleston, Miss., Jan. 16, 1933; s. Ebbie Byron and Myrtle (Myers) T.; m. Sophia Philen, Aug. 28, 1959; children: Mark Byron, Craig Philen. BS in Mech. Engring., U. Tex., Austin, 1956, MS in Engring. Mechanics, 1958, PhD in Engring. Mechanics, 1960. Registered profl. engr., Tex. Engr. Structural Mechanics Rsch. Lab. U. Tex., Austin, 1954-58, instr. mech. engring., 1958, prof. aerospace engring. and engring. mechanics, 1960—, chmn. dept. aerospace engring. and engring. mechanics, 1966-77, Woolrich prof. engring., 1974-80, dir. Ctr. Space Rcsh., 1981—, Clare Cockrell Williams chair aerospace engring., 1984—; dir. Tex. Space Grant Consortium, 1990—. Mem. adv. com. on guidance control and nav. NASA, 1966-67, com. on space rsch., panel I, 1974-76, chmn. region IV, engring. coun. on profl. devel., 1974-76; chmn. geodesy com. NRC, 1981-84, mem. aeros. and space engring. bd., 1984-86, mem. space sci. bd., chmn. com. on earth studies, 1988-91; bd. dirs. Tex. Space Grant Consortium. Editor: Celestial Mech. Jour, 1976-79; assoc. editor: Jour. Guidance and Control, 1978-79; assoc. editor: Geophys. Revs, 1979-81. Recipient Exceptional Sci. Achievement medal, NASA, 1983, Pub. Svc. medal, 1995. Fellow: AAAS, AIAA (chmn. com. astrodynamics 1976—78, Mechanics and Control of Flight award 1989), Am. Geophys. Union (pres. geodesy sect. 1984—86, Charles A. Whitten medal 2001); mem.: Internat. Astron. Union, Soc. Engring. Sci., Am. Astronautical Soc. (pres. divsn. dynamic astronomy 1988—89, Dirk Brouwer award 1995), Am. Acad. Mechanics, IEEE, ASME, NAE, Tau Beta Pi, Phi Kappa Phi, Sigma Gamma Tau, Pi Tau Sigma, Sigma Xi. Office: Dept Aerospace Engring and Engring Mechanics U Tex 1 Univ Sta C0600 Austin TX 78712 E-mail: tapley@csr.utexas.edu.*

**TAPLIN, WINN LOWELL,** historian, retired federal agency administrator; b. Saint Albans, Vt., Oct. 3, 1925; s. Winn Lowell and Elinor (Cunningham) T.; m. Ellajean Allard, July 16, 1949; children: Leslie Taplin Baumann, Mark Allard. BSCE, U. Mich., 1946, AB, 1948, AM, 1950. PhD, 1956. Oper. officer CIA, Washington, Saigon, Bucharest, Geneva, Bangkok, 1955-81; cons. Stowe, Vt., 1981-94, Sarasota, Fla., 1994—. Author: Secret New England: Spies of the American Revolution, 1991, We Vermonters, 1992. Mem. U.S. del. to UN Commn. on Human Rights, 1969; pres. Vt. Hist. Soc., 1989-93, trustee, 1983-96; mem. Sarasota Geneal. Soc., v.p., 1999-2001, pres., 2001—03; pres. Mansfield View Water Corp., Stowe, 1989-92. 1st lt. USMC, 1943-46, 50-52, Korea. Decorated Bronze Star, Intelligence Medal of Merit. Mem. DAV, Central Intelligence Retirees Assn., Assn. Former Intelligence Officers, First Day Cover Soc., Am. Philatelic Assn., Soc. Mayflower Descendants (Sarasota Tilley chpt., dir. 2005-), Am. Legion, U. Mich. Club Sarasota (dir. 1994-04), Sigma Chi. Avocations: historical research, genealogy, classical music, stamp collecting/philately. Home: 4468 Calle Serena Sarasota FL 34238-5641 Personal E-mail: winn.ej@juno.com.

**TAPP, MAMIE PEARL,** educational association administrator; b. Aiken, SC, July 20, 1955; d. Willie Lee and Nancy (Madison) Garrett; m. Anthony Karl Tapp, Aug. 13, 1983; children: Anthony K. II, Barry Garrett, Myles Jarvis. BA, CUNY, 1977; MA, New Sch. for Social Rsch., 1984; student, Nova Southeastern U., 1994—2000. Flight attendant Capitol Airlines, Jamaica, N.Y., 1976-81; pers. assoc. Cmty. Svc. Soc., N.Y.C., 1982-83; pers. specialist Marriott Hotel, Tampa, Fla., 1983-84; dir. placement Tampa Coll., 1984-86, facility coord., 1986-87, compliance officer, 1987-88; career counselor Alpha House, Tampa, 1988-91; career specialist U. Tampa, 1991-96, adj. prof., 1992-93; career specialist Jr. Achievement Greater Tampa, Inc., Tampa, 1996—, tchr. asst. program adv. com. mem., 1996-98; area mgr. BBBS, Belcamp, Md., 2004—05. Tchr. asst. program adv. com. Hillsborough H.S., 1996-97; sr. edn. svc. mgr. Jr. Achievement, 1997-2004; faculty U. Phoenix, 2005. Author: (novels) Resumes, 1992, Cover Letters, 1991, Thank You Letters, 1992, (poetry) Inner Peace, 1999; co-editor: I Cried, 2001, Life, 2002. Bd. dirs. Children's Mus. Tampa, 1992-94; com. mem. United Way, Tampa, 1994-95; mem. bd. St. Peter Claver Cath. Sch., Tampa, 1995-99, exec. com. Glee Club, 1995; vol. Scout troop leader, 1997-98. Recipient Outstanding Bus. Woman award Am. Bus. Women's Assn., Tampa, 1987, Cmty. Svc. award Tampa Connections, 1993, Editor's Choice award Internat. Libr. of Poetry, 1999. Mem.: AAUW, Fla. Assn. Women in Edn., Am. Vocat. Assn. Roman Catholic. Avocations: reading, sewing. Office: Appollo Group Inc 4324 Marigold Ln Belcamp MD 21017 Personal E-mail: tapptbjpt@earthlink.net.

**TAPPÉ, ALBERT ANTHONY,** architect; b. Pitts., Aug. 12, 1928; s. Albert Anthony and Martha Ann (McKee) T.; m. Jean Bates, June 27, 1963; children: Eliza Bruce, Albert Anthony III. Student, William and Mary Coll., 1947-48, Fontainebleau Fine Art and Music Sch., 1951; BS, U. Va., 1952; M.Arch., MIT, 1958, M.City Planning. Designer McLeod & Ferrara (Architects), Washington, 1954-55; planner Boston City Planning Bd., 1957-58; architect, planner Architects Collaborative, Cambridge, Mass., 1958-61; ptnr. Huygens & Tappé, Inc. (architects and planners), Boston, 1962-80; pres. A. Anthony Tappé & Assocs., Inc., Boston, 1980—. Instr. dept. city planning MIT, 1959-60; instr. office exec. edn. Harvard U., 1989—; cons. architect Mass. Bur. Library Extension, 1965-76; chmn. bldg. commn., Brookline, Mass., 1977, mem. bd. examiners, Brookline; v.p. Guild Religious Architecture; mem. Back Bay Archtl. Commn.; bd. dirs. Boston Archtl. Center, 1980, bd. overseers, 2001-; vis. architect Am. Acad. Rome, 1997. mem. bd. trustees Fountain BCEA Assn., 2003-. Author: Guide to Planning a Library Building, 1967; important works include: Longy Concert Hall, Cambridge, Mass., Campus NH Coll., Franklin Park Zoo, Boston, Lynn Inst. for Savs., Interfaith Religious Ctr., Columbia, Md., student housing W.Va. Wesleyan Coll., Hotel, Costa Smeralda, Sardinia, Newton Pub. Libr., Beverly Pub. Libr., Am. Coll., Athens, Greece, Morse Inst. Library, Natick, Mass., Newton Public Library, Mass., Ctrl. Sch., Longmeadow, MA.; also residences in US, France, Switzerland, housing projects in New Eng. Served with AUS, 1946-47, 52-54. Recipient Prog. Architecture Design award, 1966, 1st place single family category Plywood Design Awards Program, 1973, award Merit, 1974 Fellow AIA (mem. nat. urban planning design com. 1975, citation, hon. mentions 1969, 1st honor award 1970, honor award New Eng. Regional Council 1976); mem. Mass. Assn. Architects (exec. com.), Boston Soc. Architects (dir., v.p. 1981-82, pres. 1982-83, award 1998), Am. Inst. Planners, Am. Planning Assn., Am. Inst. Cons. Planners, Ecoles D'Art Americaines Fontainebleau (trustee 2003), Harvard Travelers Club. Clubs: Union Boat (Boston), Eastern Point Yacht (Gloucester, Mass.), Harvard Club (Boston), Bass Rocks Golf Club (Gloucester, Mass.). Office: Tappe Assocs Inc 6 Edgerly Pl Boston MA 02116-5327 Business E-Mail: aatappe@tappe.com.

**TAPPER, LEONA (LEELA) SIFF,** artist; b. Akron, Ohio, Jan. 27, 1918; d. David M. and Dorothea (Rossen) Siff; m. William Tapper, Aug. 1942 (dec.); children: Bruce Elliot, Devore Tapper Treewater; m. Paul Revivi, Aug. 1984 (dec.). BA, U. Mich., 1938; postgrad., U. Wis., 1938—40; art student, Cleve. Inst. Art, 1944—48, Art Students League, N.Y.C., 1949—51, Han Hoffman, Provincetown, Mass., 1951—53; MA NYU, 1965. Pvt. art tchr., N.Y.C., 1952—58; art tchr. j.r. h.s., N.Y.C., 1958; pvt. art tchr. N.Y.C., 1959—62, Jaffa, Israel, 1962—93, Balt., 1993—99. Pvt. art therapist, N.Y.C., 1955—58. Exhibitions include Cleve. Art Mus., 1944, Denver Art Mus., Chappel Ho., 1948—49, Petrantonio Gallery, N.Y.C., 1956—61, Old City of Jaffa, Israel, 1965—93. Mem. mental health exec. com. Riverdale, N.Y.C., 1961—; mem. exec. com. Hosp. Joint Diseases, N.Y.C., 1956—58; UPA rep. New Lincoln Sch., N.Y.C., 1954—62, H.S. Music and Art, N.Y.C., 1954—62; mem. Denver Civic Symphony, 1942—45, Fla. String Quartet, 1949—51. Mem.: Artists Equity Assn. N.Y. Avocations: yoga, music, horseback riding, travel.

**TAQUEY, ANTONY,** accountant; b. Albert, Somme, France, Aug. 13, 1953; arrived in U.S., 1955; s. Charles Henri and Ruth McVitty Taquey; m. Karen Elizabeth Anderson, June 17, 2001. BA in Econs., New Eng. Coll., 1976; MS in Acctg. and Fin., Johns Hopkins U., 1997. Editor: War is Personal, 2001. Republican. Episcopalian. Home: PO Box 1751 Clemmons NC 27012

**TAR, LASZLO,** artist; b. Szabolcs, Hungary, June 9, 1922; arrived in U.S., 1956; s. Laszlo Tar; m. Olga Vida; children: Julia LaScalere, Leslie, Julius. BA, Royal Acad. Fine Arts, Budapest, 1948; apprentice, Italian master Giorgio Morandi, 1946; postgrad., New Sch., N.Y.C.; student, Art Students League, N.Y., 1971—77. Artist, 1927—; with WestPoint Pepperell, F. Schumacher & Co. Exhibitions include Washington Sq. Park Outdoor Art Show, maj. personal art works projects, Eng., France, Italy and Holland, 1977, 1995, exhibitions include Budapest Galeria, 1989, one-man shows include various locations throughout Hungary, Art Expo, N.Y.C., 1996, 1997, 1999, exhibitions include N.Y. Consulate of Republic of Hungary, 2000, Huntington Arts Counsel Art in the Atrium, 2001, Represented in permanent collections Budapest Mus. of Fine Art, Mcpl. Mus., Rome. Home: 3 Cliftwood Dr Huntington NY 11743 Office Phone: 631-223-2700. Personal E-mail: ltar@tarart.com

**TARABORELLI, JANICE CONTI,** humanities educator, academic administrator; d. Antonio and Pasqualina Conti; children: Michael A., Matthew A. BA, U. RI, Kingston, 1967, MA, 1975. Chmn. Sch. Arts Johnson & Wales U., Denver, 2000—. Home: 18459 E Columbia Cir Aurora CO 80013

**TARADASH, STACEY,** athletic trainer; b. New Hyde Park, N.Y., July 24, 1978; BS in Kinesiology, Pa. State U., State College, 2001; MS in Health Edn., Hofstra U., Hempstead, N.Y., 2003. Cert. athletic trainer Nat. Athletic Trainer's Assn., 2001. Athletic trainer Pa. State Summer Camps, State College, 2003—00, Maccabi Sports, Phila., 2006—; asst. athletic trainer Hofstra U., Hempstead, 2001—. Adj. prof. Hofstra U., 2003—. Mem.: Nat. Athletic Trainers Assn. (assoc.), Pa. State Alumni Assn. (life).

**TARAGIN, DAVIRA SPIRO,** curator; d. Herman Frank and Edith Mae Spiro; m. Marvin Maynard Taragin, June 22, 1975; 1 child, Charles Steven. BA, Barnard Coll., N.Y.C., 1973; MA, George Wash. U., Washington, 1975. Curator ednl. svcs. and grant rsch. Fayetteville (N.C.) Mus. of Art, 1976—77; curator, edn. coord. Mich. Artrain, Detroit, 1977—78; various positions ranging from rsch. assoc. to curator of 20th-century decorative arts and design Detroit Inst. of Arts, Detroit, 1978—90; curator 19th and 20th-century glass Toledo (Ohio) Mus. of Art, 1990—2002, dir. Ctr. for Design, 2001—02; dir. exhbns. and programs Racine (Wis.) Art Mus. Adviser Assn. Israel's Decorative Arts, N.Y.C., 2003—; contbr. to Web site Dale Chihuly Studio, Seattle, 2004—; mem. curatorial adv. panel New Art Forms Internat. Expn., Chgo., 1988—90. Exhbn. and publ., Design in America: The Cranbrook Vision 1925-1950 (Charles F. Montgomery prize, 1983), Contemporary Crafts and the Saxe Collection (Hon. Mention, AAM Publs. award, 1993), Furniture by Wendell Castle, The Alliance of Art and Industry: Toledo Designs for a Modern America (Hon. Mention, AAM Publs. award, 2002), exhbn. and brochure, Material Response: Michael James at RAM, exhbn. and catalog, Automobile and Culture-Detroit Style, Art to Art: Paley, Dine, Statom Respond to Toledo's Treasures, Contemporary Directions: The William and Maxine Block Collection, The Artist Responds: Albert Paley and Art Nouveau, Building the Bindings and Collections, exhbn., Drawing Out The Collection: John McQueen Responds to RAM. Bd. dirs. Toledo Modern Art Group, 1992—2000. Recipient Legal Issues in Mus. Adminstrn. scholarship, ALI-ABA, 2004, David Lloyd Kreeger award Hon. Mention, 1975, Internat. Partnership Among Museums grant, administered by Am. Assn. of Museums and funded by Dept. of State's Bur. of Ednl. and Cultural Affairs, 2003—05; grantee, Ctr. for Craft, Creativity and Design, U. of N.C., 2005—08. Mem.: Friends of Fiber Art, Soc. of North Am. Goldsmiths, Glass Art Soc. Office: Racine Art Mus PO Box 187 441 Main St Racine WI 53403 Office Phone: 262-638-8300. Office Fax: 262-898-1045. Business E-Mail: dtaragin@ramart.org.

**TARAKI, SHIRLEE,** librarian; b. Chgo., Apr. 25, 1922; d. Frank and Leah (Simon) Heda; m. Mohamed Rasul Taraki, June 3, 1944 (dec. Aug. 1972); children: Lisa, Yosuf. BA in Psychology, U. Chgo., 1943, MA in Edn., 1947. Instr. English, Ministry of Edn., Kabul, Afghanistan, 1947-65, materials technician, 1965-72; libr. asst. Northwestern U., Evanston, Ill., 1973-90; libr. Ctr. for Women's Health St. Francis Hosp., Evanston, 1990-95. Producer slide presentation An American Woman in Afghanistan, 1974—. Vol. Mather Pavilion at Wagner, Evanston, 1993—; mem. Evanston Comm. on Aging, 1999-2003. Mem. NOW (Evanston-North Shore chpt., founder), Circle Pines Ctr., Afghanistan Reconstrn. Support Com. (co-chair), Afghan Women's Task Force (founder, chair), Amnesty Internat., Phi Beta Kappa. Avocations: music, needlecrafts.

**TARAN, LEONARDO,** classicist, educator; b. Galarza, Argentina, Feb. 22, 1933; came to U.S., 1958, naturalized, 1976; s. Miguel and Liuba Taran; m. Judit Sofia Lida, Dec. 10, 1971; 1 child, Gabriel Andres. Legal degree, U. Buenos Aires, 1958; PhD in Classics, Princeton U., 1962. Jr. fellow Inst. Rsch. in Humanities, U. Wis., 1962-63, Ctr. Hellenic Studies, Washington, 1963-64; asst. prof. classics U. Calif., L.A., 1964-67; mem. faculty Columbia U., N.Y.C., 1967—; prof. Greek and Latin, 1971—; Jay prof. Greek and Latin, 1987—, chmn. dept., 1976-79; emeritus, 2004. Mem. Inst. Advanced Study, Princeton, N.J., 1966-67, 78-79; trustee Assn. Mems. Inst. Advanced Study, 1974-79; mem. mng. com. Am. Sch. Classical Studies, 1976-. Author: Parmenides, 1965, Asclepius of Tralles, Commentary to Nicomachus' Introduction to Arithmetic, 1969, Plato, Philip of Opus and the Pseudo-Platonic Epinomis, 1975, Anonymous Commentary on Aristotle's De Interpretatione, 1978, Speusippus of Athens, 1981, Collected Papers (1962-1999), 2001; co-author: Eraclito: Testimonianze e imitazioni, 1972; mem. editl. bd.: Columbia Studies in the Classical Tradition, 1976-80. Am. Coun. Learned Socs. fellow, 1966-67, 71-72, Guggenheim Found. fellow, 1975, NEH fellow, 1986-87; grantee Am. Philos. Soc., 1963, 71, 75, Am. Coun. Learned Socs., 1968, 72, NEH, 1985-87, 88-89. Mem. Am. Philol. Assn., Classical Assn. Atlantic States, Soc. Ancient Greek Philosophy, Assn. Guillaume Bude. Home: 39 Claremont Ave New York NY 10027-6802 Office: Columbia U 615 Hamilton Hall New York NY 10027 Business E-Mail: lt1@columbia.edu.

**TARANIK, JAMES VLADIMIR,** geologist, educator; b. LA, Apr. 23, 1940; s. Vladimir James and Jeanette Downing (Smith) T.; m. Colleen Sue Glessner, Dec. 4, 1971; children: Debra Lynn, Danny Lee. BSc in Geology, Stanford U., 1964; PhD, Colo. Sch. Mines, 1974. Chief remote sensing Iowa Geol. Survey, Iowa City, 1971-74; prin. remote sensing scientist Earth Resources Observation Systems Data Ctr., U.S. Geol. Survey, Sioux Falls, SD, 1975-79; chief non-renewable resources br., resource observation div. Office of Space and Terrestrial Applications, NASA Hdqrs., Washington, 1979-82; dean mines Mackay Sch. Mines U. Nev., Reno, 1982-87, prof. geology and geophysics, 1982—, Arthur Brant chair of geophysics, 1996—; pres. Desert Rsch. Inst., Univ. and C.C. Sys. Nev., 1987-98, Regents's prof. and pres. emeritus, 1998—; adj. prof. geology U. Iowa, 1971-79; vis. prof. civil engring. Iowa State U., 1972-74; adj. prof. earth sci. U. S.D., 1976-79; program scientist for space shuttle large format camera expt. for heat capacity mapping mission, liaison Geol. Scis. Bd., Nat. Acad. Scis., 1981-82; dir. NOAA Coop. Inst. Aerospace Sci. & Terrestrial Applications, 1986-94; program dir. NASA Space Grant consortium Univ. and C.C. Sys. Nev., Reno, 1991—2005, dir. NASA EPSCOR program, 1998—2005; dir. Great Basin Ctr. Geothermal Energy, 2000—03; acting dean Mackay Sch. Mines, 2003; dir. Mackay Sch. Earth Sci. and Engring., U. Nev., 2004—. Team mem. Shuttle Imaging Radar-B Sci. Team NASA, 1983-88, space applications adv. com., 1986-88; chmn. remote sensing subcom. SAAC, 1986-88; chmn. working group on civil space commercialization Dept. Commerce, 1982-84, mem. civil operational remote sensing satellite com., 1983-84; bd. dirs. Newmont Mining Corp., e-Quake, Inc.; adv. com. NASA Space Sci. and Applications Com., 1988-90, Nat. Def. Exec. Res., 1986-94, AF studies bd., com. on strategic relocatable targets, 1989-91; pre-launch rev. bd., NASA, Space Radar Lab., 1993-94; fed. lab. rev. task force, NASA, 1994-96; prin. investigator Japanese Earth Resources Satellite, 1991-94; environ. task force MEDEA, Mitre Corp., McLean, Va., 1993-98; mapping scis. com. Nat. Rsch. Coun., 2001-04; cons. Jet Propulsion Lab., Calif., Hughes Aircraft Corp., Lockheed-Marietta Corp., Mitre Corp., TRW; developer remote sensing program and remote sensing lab. for State of Iowa, ednl. program in remote sensing for Iowa univs. and U. Nev., Reno; program scientist for 2d space shuttle flight Office Space and Terrestrial Applications Program; mem. terrestrial geol. applications program NASA, 1981-82; co-investigator Can. Radarsat Program, 1995-97. Contbr. to profl. jours. Bd. dirs. Mountain States Legal Found., 2000-, Northwest Mining Assn., 2006—. Served with C.E. U.S. Army, 1965-67; mil. intelligence officer Res. Decorated Bronze Star medal; recipient Spl. Achievement award U.S. Geol. Survey, 1978, Exceptional Sci. Achievement medal NASA, 1982, NASA Group Achievement award Shuttle imaging radar, 1990, NASA Johnson Space Ctr. Group Achievement award for large format camera, 1985; NASA prin. investigator, 1973, 83-88, prin. investigator French Spot-1 Program to Evaluate Spot 1986-88; NDEA fellow, 1968-71. Fellow: AAAS, AIAA (assoc.), Am. Soc. Photogrammetry Remote Sensing, Explorers Club, Geol. Soc. Am.; mem.: IEEE (sr.), N.W. Mining Assn. (trustee 2005—), Mining and Metall. Soc. Am., Soc. Econ. Geologists, Am. Geol. Inst. Found. (trustee 1999—), Am. Astron. Soc. (sr.), Am. Inst. Metall. Engrs., Soc. Mining Engrs. Am., Am. Assn. Petroleum Geologists (chmn. rsch. com. 2000—), Am. Geophys. Union, Soc. Exploration Geophysicists, Internat. Acad. Astronautics, Bohemian Club San Francisco. Home: PO Box 7175 Reno NV 89510-7175 Office Phone: 775-784-6987. Business E-Mail: jvtaranik@cs.com. Business E-Mail: jtaranik@mines.unr.edu. *I have always been in awe of the universe in which we live and the little time we have on earth to perceive and understand it.*

**TARANTA, ANGELO (VISCA TARANTA),** physician, educator; b. Rome, 1927; came to U.S., 1952, naturalized, 1956; MD, U. Rome, 1949. Diplomate Am. Bd. Internal Medicine, also sub-bd. Rheumatology. Intern, dept. internal medicine and pediatrics Univ. Hosp., Rome, 1949-50, resident, 1950-52; resident in medicine St. Mary's Hosp., Rochester, NY, 1952-53; resident in cardiology Irvington (N.Y.) House, 1953-54, research assoc., 1955-59, research dir., 1959-62; assoc. dir. Irvington House Inst., N.Y.C., 1965-71; research fellow in microbiology NYU Sch. Medicine, 1955-56, instr. in microbiology, 1955-58, adj. asst. prof. microbiology, 1958-60, asst. prof. medicine, 1960-65, assoc. prof., 1965-75, on leave of absence, 1975-79; dir. medicine Cabrini Health Care Ctr., N.Y.C., 1973-93; prof. medicine, chief rheumatology and immunology div. N.Y. Med. Coll., 1979-85, chief div. humanities and ethics, 1985-88. Co-chmn. study group on heart disease in the young Inter-Soc. Commn. on Heart Disease Resources, 1972-78; bd. dirs. Am. Heart Assn., 1975-77; chmn. Council on Cardiovascular Disease in the Young, 1975-77; cons. in field. Author: (with M. Markowitz) Rheumatic Fever; editor (with E. Kaplan) Infectious Endocarditis; contbr. numerous articles to profl. publs. and textbooks. Fulbright travel grantee, 1952; recipient Terence Cardinal Cooke medal N.Y. Med. Coll., 1985. Master Am. Coll. Rheumatology; mem. Soc. Clin. Investigation, Am. Assn. Immunologists, N.Y. Acad. Medicine (chmn. sect. medicine 1980-87), Italian Rheumatology Soc. (hon.), Argentine Rheumatology Soc. (hon.). E-mail: angelissimo27@yahoo.com.

**TARANTINO, DAVID A., JR.,** military officer, emergency physician; b. Dec. 17, 1965; MD, Georgetown U., 1992. Surgeon Office Peace Keeping and Humanitarian Affairs, US Dept. Def., Washington; program dir. Civil, Military and Contingency Med. Affairs, Office Asst. Sec. Def. (Health Affairs). Lt. comdr. USN. Decorated medal Navy/Marine Corps; named regional finalist, White House Fellows Program, 2003—04; recipient Washingtonian Yr. award, Washingtonian Mag., 2001, Humanitarian Svc. medal, 2001, Medal Valor, AMA, 2003.*

**TARANTINO, DOMINIC A.,** retired professional services firm executive; b. San Francisco, Aug. 1, 1932; m. Leona Lazzareschi, July 24, 1954; children: John Robert, Stephen, Leanne. BS, U. San Francisco, 1954. With Price Waterhouse, 1957-98, mem. policy bd. and mgmt. com., 1979-93, vice chmn. tax svcs., 1982-88, co-chmn. bd., mng. ptnr., 1988-93; chmn. Price Waterhouse World Firm, 1995-98; ret., 1998. Mem. IRS Commr.'s Adv. Group, 1978. Trustee U. San Francisco, 1996-2005, chair bd. trustees, 1999-2003, chair Capital Campaign, 2003-; treas., bd. dirs. Bus. Opportunities for Leadership Diversity, 1988-. Recipient Delta Sigma Pi Career Achievement award, 1997. Mem. AICPA (bd. dirs. 1988-95, vice chair 1992-3, chmn. 1993-94, Dixon Meml. award 1990, Gold medal for disting. svc. 2000). Address: 549 Indian Field Rd Mead Point Greenwich CT 06830

**TARANTINO, LOUIS GERALD,** lawyer, management consultant; b. Bridgeport, Conn., Sept. 7, 1934; s. Louis Gerald and Mary Louise (Boyle) T. BA, U. Pa., 1955, LLB, 1958. Bar: Conn. 1958, N.Y. 1960. Assoc. Beekman & Bogue, 1959—67, ptnr., 1968—76; pres., bd. dirs. Berkeley Mgmt. Assocs., Inc., Boston, 1994—2003. Mem. enterprise adv. bd. Photonics Ctr.,

Boston U.; ptnr. Berkeley Investment Ptnrs., Boston, Wintzen Pharms, L.P., Netherlands, Early Stage Advisors., Boston; bd. dirs. Anyparty.com.Inc., Boston, Midnight Trader, Inc., Bethesda, Md. Mem. Bar Assn. City N.Y., N.Y. Bar Assn., Conn. Bar Assn., Huguenot Soc. Pa., St. Anthony Hall, Knickerbocker Club, India House N.Y.C., St. Anthony Club Phila. Home: One Devonshire Pl Apt PH309 Boston MA 02109

**TARANTINO, QUENTIN JEROME,** film director, scriptwriter; b. Knoxville, Tenn., Mar. 27, 1963; s. Tony and Connie Tarantino. Co-founder (with Lawrence Baker) A Band Apart Records. Actor: (films) My Best Friend's Birthday, 1987, Eddie Presley, 1993, (voice) The Coriolis Effect, 1994, Sleep With Me, 1994, Somebody to Love, 1994, Destiny Turns on the Radio, 1995, The Anatomy of Horror, 1995, Desperado, 1995, Girl 6, 1996, Steven Spielberg's Director's Chair, 1996, Full Tilt Boogie, 1997, Little Nicky, 2000, Planet of the Pits, 2004, Epreuves d'artistes, 2004; actor, writer & prodr.: From Dusk Till Dawn, 1996, writer (story): Natural Born Killers, 1994, writer & dir.: CSI: Crime Scene Investigation, episode 5.23, 2003, writer, dir. & prodr.: Kill Bill: Vol. 1, 2003, Kill Bill: Vol. 2, 2004, actor, writer & dir.: Reservoir Dogs, 1992, Pulp Fiction, 1994, actor (voice), writer & dir.: Jackie Brown, 1997, writer & prodr.: Curdled, 1996, actor, writer, prodr. & dir.: (with Alexandre Rockwell, Robert Rodriguez & Allision Anders) Four Rooms, 1995; exec. prodr.: God Said, 'Ha!", 1998, From Dusk Till Dawn 2: Tex. Blood Money, 1999, From Dusk Till Dawn 3: The Hangman's Daughter, 2000; exec. prodr.: Hostel, 2005, Daltry Calhoun, 2005, Freedom's Fury, 2006; prodr.: Siunin Wong Fei-hung tsi titmalau (aka Iron Monkey), 1993, released 2001; TV appearances Golden Girls, 1998, 1990, All-American Girl, The Muppets' Wonderful Wizard of Oz, 2005; dir.: (TV series) ER, episode 'Motherhood', 1994, Jimmy Kimmel Live, episode 5/18/2004. Named one of Time Mag. 100 Most Influential People, 2005; recipient Building Bridges award, Asian Excellence Awards, 2006. Home: 8439 W Sunset Blvd West Hollywood CA 90069-1921*

**TARANTO, DEBORAH JEAN,** literature and language professor, writer; b. Bklyn., N.Y., Aug. 6, 1956; d. Ralph Ruocco and Jean Tona; m. Brian Taranto, Aug. 2, 1981; children: Christina Marie, Brian Thomas, Alex William. MS in Edn., Wagner Coll., SI, NY, 1995. Lic. tchr. N.Y.C., 2000. Adj. prof. English SI (N.Y.) Coll., 2002, St. Johns' U., Staten Island, NY, 2002—. English tchr. St. John's Villa Acad. HS, Staten Island, NY, 1995—2002. Author: (novel) The Land of Crystals, 2005. Mem.: Pi Delta Epsilon. Liberal. Roman Catholic. Avocations: writing, chess, travel, gourmet cooking. Office: St John's Univ 300 Howard Ave Staten Island NY 10301 Office Phone: 1718 390-4500.

**TARANTO, MARIA ANTOINETTE,** psychology researcher and educator; b. Framingham, Mass., Dec. 28, 1941; d. Gaetano (Tom) Peter and Rose Marie (Busceme) T.; m. John Curtis Mahon, June 5, 1988. BA in Psychology, Bennington Coll., 1965; MA in Psychology, George Peabody Coll., 1968; M Philosophy in Psychology, Columbia U., 1981, PhD, 1985. Tchr. Head Start Pub Sch. System, Pitts., 1966-67; rsch. assoc. Hofstra U., Hempstead, NY, 1968-69, instr., 1969-72; co-dir. Inst. for Piagetian Studies, Hempstead, 1972-76; instr. Nassau C.C., Garden City, NY, 1976-78, asst. prof., 1978-85, assoc. prof. psychology, 1985-95, prof. emeritus, 1996—. Jour. reviewer Baywood Pub. Co., Long Island, N.Y., 1989, Karger, Basel, Switzerland, 1989. Contbr. articles to profl. jours. Mem. Union of Concerned Scientists, 1981—, Amnesty Internat., 1987—; sponsor Pearl S. Buck Found., 1984—; hon. pres. Eoliano Mus. Emigrazione, Salina, Italy. Recipient Mellon fellowship CUNY, N.Y.C., 1987, Woman of Yr. award Sicilia Mondo Soc., 2004. Mem. APA, Jean Piaget Soc., Gerontol. Soc., New Eng. Psychol. Assn., Filicudi Assn. (pres. 2002—) Avocations: hiking, gardening, picniking, cooking. Personal E-mail: minervasowl2@earthlink.net.

**TARAS, PAUL,** physicist, researcher; b. Tunis, Tunisia, May 12, 1941; emigrated to Can., 1957, naturalized, 1962; s. Wladimir and Benita (Koort) T.; m. Marja-Leena Malinen, Aug. 3, 1963; children— Lisa Helene, Michele Anne. BASc., U. Toronto, 1962, MA, 1963, PhD, 1965. Asst. prof. physics U. Montreal, Que., Canada, 1965-70, assoc. prof., 1970-76, prof., 1976—. Spokesman U. Montreal in rsch. projects. Helios, SDC, Babar. Rsch. on nuclear and particle physics; co-managed conception and constrn. of 8pi Spectrometer, Chalk River Nuclear Labs, 1984-86; contbr. articles to profl. jours.; presenter papers to profl. confs. U. Toronto, Province of Ont., U.K. Atomic Energy Authority fellowships; France-Que., NRC, Natural Scis. and Engring. Research Council Can. grantee. Mem. Am. Phys. Soc., Can. Assn. Physicists, Soc. Galilée (mem. exec. bd.), Babar Collaboration (bd. dirs.). Home: 1639 Norway Rd Montreal PQ Canada H4P 1Y3 Office: U Montreal Groupe Physique des Particules Montreal PQ Canada H3C 3J7 Business E-Mail: taras@lps.umontreal.ca.

**TARASI, LOUIS MICHAEL, JR.,** lawyer; b. Cheswick, Pa., Sept. 9, 1931; s. Louis Michael and Ruth Elizabeth (Records) T.; m. Patricia Ruth Finley, June 19, 1954; children: Susan, Louis Michael III, Elizabeth, Brian, Patricia, Matthew. BA, Miami U., Ohio, 1954; JD, U. Pa., 1959. Bar: Pa. 1960, U.S. Dist. Ct. (we. dist.) Pa. 1960, U.S. Ct. Appeals (3d cir.) 1964, U.S. Supreme Ct. 1969, U.S. Dist. Ct. (we. dist.) Tex. 1988, U.S. Ct. Appeals (5th cir.) 1989, U.S. Ct. Appeals (4th cir.) 1994, U.S. Ct. Fed. Claims 1987, U.S. Dist. Ct. Colo. 1998; cert. civil trial adv. Nat. Bd. Trial Advocacy. Assoc., owner Burgwin, Ruffin, Perry & Pohl, Pitts., 1960-68; ptnr. Conte, Courtney & Tarasi, Beaver County, Pa., 1968-78, Tarasi & Tighe, Pitts., 1978-82, Tarasi & Johnson, P.C., Pitts., 1982-95, Tarasi & Assocs., P.C., Pitts., 1995-99, The Tarasi Lawfirm, P.C., Pitts., 1997-2001, Tarasi & Tarasi, P.C., Pitts., 2001—. Mem. parish coun. St. James Ch., Sewickley, Pa.; mem. Sewickley Borough Allegheny Coun., 1978-1982. With U.S. Army, 1954-56. Fellow: Internat. Soc. Barristers; mem.: Am. Coll. Barristers (sr. counsel), Am. Bd. Trial Advs., Melvin Belli Soc., St. Thomas More Soc. (award 1991), West Pa. Trial Lawyers Assn. (pres. 1975), Pa. Bar Assn., Allegheny County Bar Assn., Acad. Trial Lawyers Allegheny County, Pa. Trial Lawyers Assn. (pres. 1979—80), Assn. Trial Lawyers Am. (gov., rep.). Democrat. Roman Catholic. Avocations: reading, golf, lecturing. Home: 1 Way Hollow Rd Sewickley PA 15143-1192 Office: Tarasi & Tarasi PC 510 3d Ave Pittsburgh PA 15219-2107 Office Phone: 412-391-7135. Business E-Mail: lmt@tarasilaw.com.

**TARAZA, DINU,** engineering educator, researcher; b. Bucharest, Romania, Oct. 10, 1936; s. Petre and Melania Valeria Taraza; m. Octaviana Croitoru, July 21, 1961; 1 child, Carmen Marina Mihai. BS in Mech. Engring., Poly. Inst. Bucharest, 1954—59, PhD in Mech. Engring., 1965—75. Mech. engr., Ministry Edn./Romania, 1959. Product engr. 23 Aug. Heavy Industry Plant, Bucharest, Romania, 1959—60; product devel. engr. Tech. Inst. of the Ministry of Transp., Bucharest, 1960—65; asst. Poly. Inst. of Bucharest, 1965—69, lectr., 1969—75, assoc. prof., 1975—90, prof., 1990—95; vis. prof. Darmstadt U. of Tech., Germany, 1991—92, Wayne State U., Detroit, 1995—97, prof. (tenure 2003), 1997—. Cons. Ministry Machine Bldg., Bucharest, 1977—95. Recipient Arch. T. Colwell Merit award, Soc. of Automotive Engineers (SAE), 1998. Fellow: Soc. Automotive Engineers; mem.: ASME, Am. Soc. for Engring. Edn. Christian Orthodox. Achievements include research and original contributions in the field of internal combustion engines, especially in engine dynamics. Avocations: travel, photography, skiing. Home: 415 Calvin Grosse Pointe Farms MI 48236 Office: Wayne State Univ 5050 Anthony Wayne Dr Detroit MI 48202 Office Phone: 313-577-3701. Business E-Mail: taraza@eng.wayne.edu.

**TARBI, WILLIAM RHEINLANDER,** secondary education educator, curriculum consultant, educational technology researcher; b. San Bernardino, Calif., Feb. 23, 1949; s. William Metro and Sue (Rheinlander) T.; m. Jenny Workman, Apr. 10, 1980 (div. 1985); m. Michele Hastings, July 4, 1990; children: Amy, Melissa. AA, Santa Barbara City Coll., 1969; BA in History, U. Calif., Santa Barbara, 1976; MA, U. Redlands, 1992. Cert. secondary edn. social studies tchr., Calif. Reporter AP, Santa Barbara, Calif., 1976-80, UPI, Seattle, 1980-85, Golden West Radio Network, Seattle, 1980-85; tchr.

Redlands (Calif.) Unified Sch. Dist., 1986—. Cons. IMCOM, Redlands, 1985—. Mem. E Clampus Vitus, Phi Delta Kappa. Avocations: painting, photography, writing, gardening, fencing. Personal E-mail: wtarbi@adelphia.net.

**TARBUCK, BARBARA JOAN,** actress; b. Detroit, Jan. 15, 1942; d. George and Ruth Erma (Fillmore) T.; m. James Denis Connolly, May 17, 1980; 1 child, Jennifer Lane. B of Philosophy, Wayne State U., 1963; MA, U. Mich., 1965; postgrad., Ind. U., 1965-66. Author: (children's play) Who Am I?, 1972; Author/actor: They Call Me Dr. Greer, 1994; actress: (TV movies) The Cracker Factory, 1979, Mrs. R's Daughter, 1979, A Christmas Without Snow, 1980, Between Two Loves, 1982, Victims for Victims: The Theresa Saldana Story, 1984, Out of Time, 1988, David, 1988, I Know My First Name Is Steven, 1989, Death of the Incredible Hulk, 1990, A House of Secrets and Lies, 1992, A Child Lost Forever: The Jerry Sherwood Story, 1992, Jack Reed: Badge of Honor, 1993, Moment of Truth: Eye of the Stalker, 1995, Seduced by Madness: The Diane Borchardt Story, 1996, Before He Wakes, 1998, Mr. Murder, 1998, Just Ask My Children, 1901; (films) Short Circuit, 1986, Big Trouble, 1986, Curly Sue, 1991, Midnight Witness, 1993, Scanner Cop II, 1995, Tie That Binds, 1995, Legend of Razorback, 2002, Tulse Luper Suitcases: The Moab Story, 2003, Walking Tall, 2004; guest appearances: (TV shows) include M*A*S*H*, 1982, Cagney & Lacey, 1983-84, Falcon Crest, 1986-87, The Golden Girls, 1997, Knots Landing, 1979, Quantum Leap, 1992, Picket Fences, 1992, The Practice, 1997 ER, 1999, CSI, 2000, Judging Amy, 2001, Crossing Jordan, 2001, Six Feet Under, 2002, Without a Trace, 2003, Cold Case, 2003; Broadway shows include Brighton Beach Memoirs, Water Engine, Landscape and Silence; nat. tours: Broadway Bound, America Hurrah!. Fulbright grantee, 1966-67; recipient L.A. Drama Critics award, 1985. Mem. Zeta Phi Eta, Democrat. E-mail: btarbuck@futurewest.ca.

**TARBUTTON, LLOYD T.,** hotel executive, consultant; Dr Comml. Sci. in Mktg., Pacific Western U. Grad. Realtors Inst.; cert. franchise exec., La. State U., cert. hotel adminstr. Divsn. sales mgr. Reuben H. Donnelley Corp. (advt. agy.), Norfolk, Va., 1953-58; chmn. bd., dir. Tarbutton Assocs., Inc., Norfolk, 1962—; founder, pres., chmn. bd. Econo Lodges of Am., Norfolk, 1967-83; chmn. bd. emeritus Econo Lodges of Am. (formerly Econ-Travel Motor Hotel Corp.), Norfolk, 1983—. Co-founder, chief judge Franchising Hall of Fame, Washington, 1979-82; co-founder, chmn. Coun. Franchise Suppliers, Washington, 1986-88. Author: Franchising--The How To Book, 1986. Trustee Edn. Found. Old Dominion U., 1979-86, chmn. bd. trustees Ctr. Econ. Edn., Old Dominion U., 1983-84. Recipient Hon. Tchr. award Maury High Sch., Norfolk, 1959. Mem. Internat. Franchise Assn. (hon. life, chmn. bd. dirs., chmn. 1st Asian Symposium on Franchising, Tokyo 1978, 1st European Symposium on Franchising, Amsterdam 1978, 1st So. Pacific Symposium on Franchising, Jakarta 1991; 1st Ea. Europe Franchise Symposiums (Varna, Bulgaria, 2000, inducted into Franchise Hall of Fame 2000), Internat. Coun. Hotel/Motel Mgmt., Realtor's Inst. Norfolk (chmn. 1965), Internat. Sales Execs. Club (Distinguished Sales award 1957), Internat. Platform Assn., Airplane Owners and Pilots Assn., Cavalier Golf and Yacht Club, Town Point Club, Registry Resort Tennis Club, The Club at Pelican Bay. Presbyterian. *I believe the greatest assist to my progress in business and personal life came when I became more aware of the "value of self" and thus others.*

**TARDE, JERRY (GERARD TARDE),** magazine executive; Editor-in-chief Golf Digest; chmn., editl. dir. The Golf Digest Co., Wilton, Conn., 2000—. Office: Golf Digest 20 Westport Rd Box 850 Wilton CT 06897 Office Phone: 203-761-5225.*

**TARDIFF, JILL ALEXANDRIA,** publishing executive, photographer; b. Morristown, N.J., Apr. 8, 1953; d. Howard James Tardiff and Jean Elizabeth Cook; m. Paul Edward Kozelka, Feb. 11, 1984. BA in liberal arts, Coll. St. Elizabeth, 1975. Cert. teacher, K-12 NJ, 1975. Mgr. retail Hallmark Cards Inc./Flagship, N.Y.C., 1976—81; mgr. mgr. Doubleday Book Shops/Flagship, N.Y.C., 1981—91; sales mgr./dir. of sales Tiffany & Co., N.Y.C., 1991—93; entrepreneur, self-propr. Bamboo River Assocs., Hoboken, NJ, 1993—; mng. editor/sr. rschr. Lintel Press, N.Y.C., 1993—94; assoc. editor BookWire Online, N.Y.C., 1995—98; contbg. editor/project mgr. Pubs. Weekly, N.Y.C., 1996—; mgr. advt. Persimmon, Asian Lit., Arts, and Culture Mag., N.Y.C., 1999—2002. Profl. spkr./tour facilitator Bamboo River Associates, Hoboken, 1991—; sec./bd. dirs. Contemporary Asian Culture Inc., N.Y.C., 1999—; adv. bd. mem. Women's Ink., N.Y.C., 1999—2004. Contbr. book Bob Vila's Guide to Historic Homes Series; reporter Shinbunka Weekly, Tokyo, 1995—2000. Mem.: AAUW (hon.), Internat. Women's Writing Guild (hon.), N.Y. Women in Comm. (assoc.), Women's Nat. Book Assn. (assoc.; main rep. UN DPI/NGO 2000—, nat. v.p., pres. elect 2002—04, nat. pres. 2004—06), Women's Nat. Book Assn. (assoc.; newsletter editor/v.p. N.Y.C. chpt. 1997—2000, pres. N.Y.C. chpt. 2000—, immediate past nat. pres. 2006—), Editl. Freelancers Assn. (assoc.), Diev Donné Papermill (assoc.), Japan Soc. (assoc.), Asia Soc. N.Y. (assoc.). Avocations: travel, photography, gardening, architecture, paper making. Office: Bamboo River Associates 45 Madison StSte 2 Hoboken NJ 07030-6305 Personal E-mail: jat-bambooriver@worldnet.att.net.

**TARDIO, THOMAS A.,** public relations executive; V.p. strategic planning and other positions Columbia Pictures Industries, 1979-88; CFO, v.p. adminstrn. Rogers & Cowan, Inc., L.A., 1988-89, exec. v.p. entertainment sect., 1989-91, pres., 1991-95; CEO Rogers & Cowan, L.A., 2002—; co-chmn., mng. dir. Rogers & Cowan, Inc., L.A., 1996—2000; pres. Shandwick, United States, L.A., 1998—2000; pres., COO, Weber Shandwick, Western Region, L.A., 1998—; CEO Shandwick Convergence, L.A., 2001—02. Mem. IBM mobile computing mktg. adv. bd. Mem. bd. visitors adv. bd. Loyola Law Sch. Mem. Pub. Rels. Soc. Am., Nat. Acad. Recording Arts and Scis., Pub. Communicators L.A. Contry Music Assn. Office: Rogers & Cowan 8687 Melrose Ave /th Fl Los Angeles CA 90069

**TAREN, JAMES ARTHUR,** neurosurgeon, educator; b. Toledo, Nov. 10, 1924; s. Joseph Clarence and Mary Frances (Walker) T. BS, U. Toledo, 1948; MD, U. Mich., 1952. Diplomate Am. Bd. Neurosurgery. Intern U. Mich. Hosp., Ann Arbor, 1952-53, resident in surgery, 1953-54, resident neurosurgery, 1955-57; clin. instr. U. Mich. Med. Sch., Ann Arbor, 1955-57, instr. neurosurgery, 1957-58, asst. prof., 1958-63, assoc. prof., 1963-67, prof. neurosurgery, 1967—, dir. neurobehavioral sci. program, 1975-78, assoc. dean acad. programs, 1978-87, dir. Brain Tumor Lab., 1985-88; dir. Integrated Acad. Info. Mgmt., 1988-89; dir. neuromodulation program U. Mich. Med. Sch., Ann Arbor, 1994-97. Neurosurgeon Wayne County Gen. Hosp., Eloise, Mich., 1957-71, VA Hosp., Ann Arbor, 1957-73; U.S.S Hope (Project Hope), Peru, 1962, Ecuador, 1963, Guinea, 1965; vis. prof. Hosp. Foch, Paris, 1966-67, St. Anne Hosp., Paris, 1981, Karolinski Inst., Stockholm, 1981, Haukland Sykehus, Bergen, Norway, 1984, Gumma U., Japan, 1989, Nihon U. Sch. Medicine, Tokyo, 1990. Author: dir. editor Correlative Neurosurgery, 1969, 3rd edit., 1982; contbr. articles to profl. jours. Dep. med. examiner Washtenaw County Dept. Health, Ann Arbor, 1962-90; pres. Hawaii Youth New Leadership Forum, 2000. Active U.S. Armed Forces, 1943-46, PTO. Fellow NIH, 1953; rsch. fellow in neurosurgery Boston Children's Hosp., Peter Bent Brigham Hosp., Boston, 1955. Fellow ACS; mem. AMA, Congress of Neuro. Surgeons, Am. Assn. Neuro. Surgery, Am. Assn. Med. Colls., Am. Soc. for Stereotactic and Functional Neurosurgery, Am. Neuromodulation Soc. (treas. 1994-98, v.p. 1998-99), Royal Soc. Medicine (affiliate), Brit. Med. Soc., Internat. Assn. Study of Pain, Ferrari Club Am. Personal E-mail: jtaren@ilhawaii.net.

**TARGOFF, MICHAEL BART,** space and communications company executive; b. NYC, July 20, 1944; s. Jerome H. and Tillie R. T.; m. Cheri Kamen, June 11, 1966; children: Ramie, Joshua, Jason, Hannah. AB, Brown U., 1966; JD cum laude, Columbia U., 1969. Bar: N.Y. 1969. Law clk. to presiding justice U.S. Dist. Ct. Mass., 1969-70; assoc. Willkie, Farr & Gallagher, NYC, 1970-76; ptnr. Willkie, Farr & Gallagher, NYC, 1976-80; gen. counsel, v.p. Savin Corp., Valhalla, NY, 1980-81; gen. counsel, sr. v.p., sec. Loral Corp., NYC, 1981-92, sr. v.p., 1992—96, also sec.; pres, COO

Loral Space and Communications, 1996—98; founder Michael B. Targoff & Co.; vice chmn. Loral Space and Communications, 2005—06, CEO, 2006—. Bd. dirs. Leap Wireless, 1998—, Globalstar Telecommunications Ltd., Infocrossing, Inc., 2001—06, Booksfree.com, ViaSat Inc., 2003—. Harlan Fiske Stone scholar, 1968-69. Mem. ABA, N.Y. State Bar Assn., Assn. of Bar of City of N.Y. Office: Loral Corp 600 3rd Ave Rm 3000A New York NY 10016-1901 Office Fax: 212-338-5662.*

**TARGOVNIK, SELMA E. KAPLAN,** retired dermatologist; b. NYC, Apr. 22, 1936; d. Harry A. and Helen (Goodstein) Kaplan; m. Jerome H. Targovnik, Dec. 2, 1961; children: Nina Rebecca, Labe Eric (dec.), Diane Michelle. BA, NYU, 1957; MD, Albert Einstein Col. Medicine, 1961. Diplomate Am. Bd. Dermatology. Intern Kaiser Found. Hosp., San Francisco, 1961-62; resident in internal medicine Bellevue Hosp., NYU Med. Ctr., 1962-63, U. Colo. Med. Ctr., Denver, 1963-64; rsch. fellow, resident in dermatology Boston U. Med. Ctr., 1964-66, mem. staff, 1968-69, NYU Med. Ctr., 1966-68, St. Joseph's Hosp., Phoenix, 1969—98, Good Samaritan Hosp., Phoenix, 1969—98; ret. Staff Carl Hayden VA Hosp., Phoenix, 1998—; mem. staff St. Joseph's Hosp., Phoenix, St. Luke's Hosp., Phoenix; chief divsn. dermatology Good Samaritan Hosp., Phoenix, 1985-90; adj. assoc. prof. Midwestern U. Coll. Medicine, Glendale, Ariz., 1998—; clin. assoc. prof. dermatology Kirksville Coll. Osteopathic Medicine, 2000—, clin. assoc. prof. dermatology, 1998. Bd. dirs. ACLU, Ariz., 1973-78, 83-94, Congregation Beth El, Phoenix, 1971-75, Flagstaff Festival of the Arts, 1984-86; active Jewish Nat. Fund. Fellow Am. Acad. Dermatology, Assocs. for the Weizmann Inst. Sci., Assocs. for the Technion Inst.; mem. Am. Technion Soc. (bd. dirs. 1988-92, pres. Ariz. divsn. 1990-92), Dermatology Found., Sonoran Dermatologic Soc., Southwestern Dermatologic Soc., Pacific Dermatological Soc., Noah Worcester Dermatol. Soc., Phi Beta Kappa, Mu Chi Sigma, Pi Delta Phi, Beta Lambda Sigma. Democrat. Jewish. Home: 3706 E Rancho Dr Paradise Valley AZ 85253 Office Phone: 602-954-8335. Personal E-mail: selmaderm@cox.net.

**TARINO, GARY EDWARD,** lawyer; b. Jersey City, Oct. 3, 1951; s. Edward G. and Veronica Tarino; m. Maureen Fitzpatrick, May 9, 1987. BA summa cum laude, Rutgers U., 1973, JD, 1976. Bar: N.J. 1976, U.S. Dist. Ct. N.J. 1976, D.C. Ct. Appeals 1978, U.S. Supreme Ct. 1980, N.Y. 1982, U.S. Dist. Ct. (so. dist.) N.Y. 1988, U.S. Dist. Ct. (ea. dist.) N.Y. 1990. Assoc. Winne, Banta, Rizzi & Harrington, Hackensack, N.J., 1976-79; asst. pros. Bergen County Pros. Office, Hackensack, 1979-83, chief organized crime squad, 1981-83; atty. Automatic Data Processing, Inc., Roseland, N.J., 1983—, assoc. gen. counsel, staff v.p., 1994—. Pub. defender Borough of Maywood, N.J., 1978; bd. dirs. N.J. Coun. Econ. Edn., 1990-2000; master Sidney Reitman Employment Law Am. Inn Ct., 1995-2000. Bd. dirs. Am. Heart Assn., N.J., 1976-81, Middlesex County (N.J.) chpt., 1973-81; trustee Integrity, Inc., 1991-97; grad. Leadership N.J., 1989; cubmaster pack III Boy Scouts Am., 2000-04; mem. oper. coun. N.J. Bus. Force, 2003—. Recipient cert. of appreciation U.S. Treasury Dept., 1983, letter of commondation PBA, 1983, Alumni Vol. Leadership award 1st Ann. Leadership N.J., 1991. Office: Automatic Data Processing 1 A D P Blvd Roseland NJ 07068-1786

**TARLETON, LARRY WILSON,** editor; b. Wadesboro, N.C., July 19, 1943; s. Harold Wilson and Martha (Roberson) T.; m. Judith Elaine Huntley, Sept. 8, 1963; children: Laurie Leigh, Larry Huntley. BA in Journalism, U. N.C., 1965. Reporter The Charlotte (N.C.) Observer, 1965-73; sports writer The Miami (Fla.) Herald, 1973-74; sports editor The Charlotte Observer, 1974-76; exec. sports editor, mng. editor, exec. editor The Dallas Times Herald, 1976-88, exec. editor, 1988—98; asst. pub. The Post and Courier, Charleston, SC, 1998—2000, pub., 2000—. Mem. Am. Soc. Newspaper Editors, S.C. Press Assn. (former pres.), Dallas Press Club (pres. 1988). AP Mng. editors, AP Sports Editors. Avocations: golf, travel. Home: 27 New St Charleston SC 29401-2405 Office: The Post and Courier 134 Columbus St Charleston SC 29403-4800 E-mail: Harleton@postandcourier.com.

**TARLOV, ALVIN RICHARD,** foundation administrator, physician, educator; b. Norwalk, Conn., July 11, 1929; s. Charles and Mae (Shelinsky) T.; m. Joan Hylton, June 12, 1956 (div. 1976); children: Richard, Elizabeth, Jane, Suzanne, David. BA, Dartmouth Coll., 1951; MD, U. Chgo., 1956. Intern Phila. Gen. Hosp., 1956-57; resident in medicine U. Chgo. Hosps., 1957-58, 62-63, research assoc., 1958-61; asst. prof. medicine U. Chgo., 1963-68, assoc. prof., 1968-70, prof., 1970-84, chmn. dept. medicine, 1981-90; chmn. grad. med. edn. nat. adv. com. HHS, Washington, 1980; pres. Henry J. Kaiser Family Found., Menlo Park, Calif., 1984-90; sr. scientist New Eng. Med. Ctr., Boston, 1990-99, exec. dir. The Health Inst., 1995-99; prof. of Pub. Health Harvard U., Boston, 1990-99; prof. of medicine Tufts U., 1990-99; dir. Tex. Inst. for Soc. and Health Rice U., Tex., 1999—. Dir. Tex. Program for Soc. and Health, James Baker III Inst. for Pub. Policy, Rice U. Pres. Med. Outcomes Trust, Inc., 1993-2000; chmn. bd., pres. Mass. Health Data Consortium, 1994-98. Served to capt. U.S. Army, 1958-61. Recipient Research Career Devel. award NIH, 1962-67; John and Mary Markle Found. scholar, 1966-71. Mem. ACP (master), Inst. Medicine of Nat. Acad. Scis. Office: Tex Program Soc & Health Rice U Baker Inst Pub Policy 6100 Main St Houston TX 77005 Home: 540 N State St Apt 3801 Chicago IL 60610-7240 E-mail: atarlov@rice.edu, atarlov@anet.com.

**TARN, NATHANIEL,** poet, educator, translator; b. Paris, June 30, 1928; s. Marcel and Yvonne (Suchar) T.; children: Andrea, Marc. BA with honors, Cambridge (Eng.), 1948, MA, 1952; postgrad., U. Sorbonne, U. Paris, 1949-51; MA, U. Chgo., 1952, PhD, 1957; postgrad., London Sch. Econs., 1953-58. Anthropologist, Guatemala, Burma, Alaska, and other locations, 1952—; prof. comparative lit. Rutgers U., 1970-85, prof. emeritus modern poetry, comparative lit, anthropology, 1985. Vis. prof. SUNY, Buffalo and Princeton, 1969-70. Author: Old Savage/Young City, 1964, Where Babylon Ends, 1968, The Beautiful Contradictions, 1969, October, 1969, A Nowhere for Vallejo, 1971, Lyrics for the Bride of God: Section: The Artemision, 1972, The Persephones, 1974, Lyrics for the Bride of God, 1975, The House of Leaves, 1976, Birdscapes, with Seaside, 1978, The Desert Mothers, 1985, At the Western Gates, 1985, Palenque, 1986, Seeing America First, 1989, Flying the Body, 1993, Multitude of One, 1995, Views from the Weaving Mountain: Selected Essays in Poetics and Anthropology, 1991, Scandals in the House of Birds: Shamans & Priests on Lake Atitlan, 1997, The Architextures, 2000, Three Letters From The City: The St. Petersburg Poems 1968-1998, 2000, Selected Poems 1950-2000, 2002, Dying Trees, 2003, Recollections of Being, 2004; co-author: (with Janet Rodney) The Forest, 1978, Atitlan/Alashka, 1979, The Ground of Our Great Admiration of Nature, 1978; contbg. author: Penguin Modern Poets No. Seven: Richard Murphy, Jon Silkin, Nathaniel Tarn, 1965, A.P.E.N. Anthology of Contemporary Poetry, 1966, The Penguin Book of Modern Verse Translation, 1966, Poems Addressed to Hugh MacDiarmid, 1967, Music and Sweet Poetry: A Verse Anthology, 1968, Frontier of Going: Anthology of Space Poetry, 1969, Shaking the Pumpkin, 1972, America: A Prophecy, 1973, Open Poetry, 1973, Active Anthology, 1974, Symposium of the Whole, 1983, Random House Book of Twentieth Century French Poetry, 1983, Beneath a Single Moon: Buddhism in American Poetry, 1991, American Poetry since 1950: Innovators and Outsiders, 1993; translator: The Heights of Macchu Picchu (Pablo Neruda), 1966, Stelae (Victor Segalen), 1969, Zapotec Struggles, 1993; editor, co-translator: Con Cuba: An Anthology of Cuban Poetry of the Last Sixty Years, 1969, Selected Poems (Pablo Neruda), 1970; editor Cape Edits. and founder-dir. Cape Goliard Press, J. Cape Ltd., 1967-69. Recipient Guinness prize for poetry, 1963. Office: PO Box 8187 Santa Fe NM 87504-8187

**TARNACKI, DUANE L.,** lawyer; b. Detroit, Dec. 21, 1953; s. Leo A. and Dorothy O. (Roginski) T.; m. Sheila Rimmel, July 28, 1994. BA in Psychology with high distinction and high honors, U. Mich., 1976; MBA with honors, JD cum laude, U. Notre Dame, 1980. Bar: Mich. 1980, U.S. Dist. Ct. (so. dist.) Mich., 1980. Ptnr., mem. Clark Hill P.L.C., Detroit, 1980—. Sec. for Creative Studies, 1991—; bd. dirs. Detroit Hist. Soc.; Juvenile Diabetes Found. Met. Detroit chpt., 1990-95, Acct. Aid Soc., 1990-96; gen. counsel Econ. Club of Detroit, 1995—; vice chmn. exec. com. Planned Giving Roundtable

of S.E. Mich., 1992-98. Author: Establishing a Charitable Foundation in Michigan, 1986, 3d edit., 1999, The Responsibilities of Service: A Guide for Directors of Nonprofit Organizations in Michigan, 1997, 99, 2003; co-author: The Michigan Community Foundation Legal Reference, 1993, 2d edit., 1996; assoc. editor Notre Dame Lawyer, 1977-80. Mem. increasing philanthropy and govt. rels. coms., Coun. Mich. Founds., planned giving com., Karmanos Cancer Inst., 1991-94; bd. dirs. Mich Supreme Court Hist. Soc. Inc., 1988-96; mem. legal adv. subcom. to cmty. found. com. Coun. on Founds., IRS Exempt Orgns. Liaison Group; trustee Thompson-McCully Found., 1999-2003, The Futures Found.; mem. adv. coun. Jr. League Detroit. Fellow: Mich. State Bar Found.; mem.: ABA (nonprofit corps. com., bus. law sect., real property, probate and trust law and tax sects., Outstanding Nonprofit Atty. award bus. law sect. 2003), Mich. Bar Assn. (nonprofit corp. com., bus. law sect., probate and estate planning law and tax sects.), Detroit Renaissance (bus. contbns. com.), Detroit Athletic Club (bd. dirs.), Econ. Club. Roman Catholic. Home: 39824 Woodside Dr N Northville MI 48167-3429 Office: 500 Woodward Ave Ste 3500 Detroit MI 48226-3435

**TARNOFF, JEROME,** lawyer; b. June 22, 1931; s. Meyer and Anne (Soshnick) T.; children: Marcy Jane, Margery Lynne; m. Nancy Radin, 1990. AB. Syracuse U., 1952; JD, Columbia U., 1957. Bar: NY 1957, U.S. Dist. Ct. (so. and ea. dists.) NY 1960, U.S. Ct. Appeals (2d cir.) 1961. Ptnr. Sheldon and Tarnoff, NYC, 1957-78, Feldesman, D'Atri, Tarnoff & Lubitz, NYC, 1978, Baskin and Sears, P.C., NYC, 1979-84, Baskin & Steingut P.C., 1984-85, Berger & Steingut, 1986-92, Morrison, Cohen LLP, NYC, 1993—. Contbr. articles to legal jours. Chmn. policy com. NY Dem. Party, 1975-78, vice chmn. NY County, 1978—; mem. com., 1980-88; mem. Cmty. Planning Bd. #8, 1966-75; bd. dirs. Grand St. Settlement, 1973—1981, Assoc. Y's of NY, 1972-88. With U.S. Army, 1952-54. Recipient Disting. Svc. award NAACP, 1975, Cert. Achievement, El Diario-La Prensa, 1977. Mem. ABA, NY State Bar Assn., Assn. Bar City of NY, N.T. County Lawyers, Am. Arbitration Assn. (nat. panel arbitrators), Phi Alpha Delta, Sunningdale Country Club (Scarsdale, NY), Harmonie Club (NYC), Audubon, Masons. Jewish. Office: Morrison Cohen LLP 909 Third Ave New York NY 10022 Office Phone: 212-735-8632. Business E-Mail: jtarnoff@morrisoncohen.com.

**TARNOFF, PETER,** federal agency administrator, consultant; b. NYC, Apr. 19, 1937; s. Norman Tarnoff and Henrietta (Goldfarb) Laing; m. Daniele Oudinot, Jan. 13, 1962 (div. Oct. 1981); children: Nicholas, Alexander; m. Mathea Falco, Dec. 24, 1981; 1 child, Benjamin. Student, U. Paris, 1956-57, postgrad., 60-61; BA, Colgate U., 1958; postgrad., U. Chgo., 1958-60. Joined Fgn. Svc., Dept. State, 1961; spl. asst. to amb. Am. Embassy, Bonn, Fed. Republic Germany, 1969; trainee Nat. Sch. Adminstrn., Paris, 1970; prin. officer Am. Consulate Gen., Lyon, France, 1971-73; dep. chief of mission Am. Embassy, Luxembourg, 1973-75; dir. Office Rsch. and Analysis for Western Europe Dept. State, Washington, 1975-76, exec. sec. Dept. State, 1977-81, fgn. affairs fellow San Francisco, 1981-82; exec. dir. World Affairs Coun. No. Calif., San Francisco, 1983-86; pres., dir. Coun. on Fgn. Rels., N.Y.C., 1986-93; under sec. state for polit. affairs Dept. State, Washington, 1993-97; pres. Internat. Adv. Corp., San Francisco, 1997—. Office: Internat Adv Corp 2028 Green St San Francisco CA 94123-4813 Office Phone: 415-440-7997. Personal E-mail: iacmail@aol.com.

**TARNOFSKY-OSTROFF, DAWN,** broadcast executive; BA in Journalism, Fla. Internat. U. Reporter WINZ (CBS affiliate), Miami; v.p. dev. Kushner-Locke Co., 1984-89; pres. Michael Jacobs Prodns.; sr. v.p. creative affairs 20th Century Fox TV, 1989-96; sr. v.p. programming, prodn. Lifetime TV, NYC, 1995-99, exec. v.p. entertainment, 1999—2002; pres. UPN Entertainment, LA, 2002—. Office: Lifetime TV 309 W 49th St Fl 16 New York NY 10019-7316

**TARNOPOL, MICHAEL LAZAR,** bank executive; b. 1936; s. Irving and Charlotte (Weber) T.; m. Lynne Lichtenstein, June 29, 1958; children: Lisa Silverman, Lori Moore. Gen. ptnr., sr. mng. dir., also bd. dirs. Lehman Bros. Inc., 1959-75; with Bear Stearns & Co. Inc., 1975—, vice-chmn., bd. dirs.; chmn. investment banking divsn., bd. dirs. Bear Stearns Internat. Mem. pres.'s coun. Solomon R. Guggenheim Found.; vice chmn. bd. trustees U. Pa., bd. overseers Wharton Sch.; bd. overseers, bd. mgrs. Meml. Sloan Kettering Cancer Ctr.; Bd. dirs. Cap Cure Found., U.S. Polo Tng. Found., Robert Steel Found., Inc. Mem. Palm Beach Country Club, Harmonie Club, East Hampton Tennis Club, Atlantic Golf Club, Quaker Ridge Golf Club, Trump Internat. Golf Club.

**TARNOVE, LORRAINE,** medical association executive; b. Atlantic City, July 26, 1947; d. Leonard Robert Tarnove and Jeanne Tarnove Yudkin; m. Steven B. Friedman, June 1, 1969; children: K. Brooke, Ari-Benjamin. BA, U. Md., 1969. Pres. Lorraine Tarnove Consulting, Columbia, Md., 1985-93; exec. dir. Am. Med. Dirs. Assn., Columbia. Contbr. chpt. to book. Office: AMDA 10840 Little Patuxent #760 Columbia MO 21044*

**TAROKH, VAHID,** engineering educator; PhD in Elec. Engring., U. Waterloo, 1995; AM (hon.), Harvard U., 2002; DSc (hon.), U. Windsor, 2003. Postdoctoral fellow U. Ill., Urbana-Champaign, 1995—96; tech. staff mem. AT&T Labs-Rsch., Florham Park, NJ, 1996—99, prin. tech. staff mem., 1999—2000, head dept. wireless comm. and signal processing, 2000; assoc. prof. Mass. Inst. Tech., Cambridge, Mass., 2000—02; Gordon-Mckay prof. elec. engring., Vinton Hayes sr. rsch. fellow Harvard U., 2002—. Co-founder Ctr. Comm. and Networking; mem. Harvard Broadband Comm. Lab. Author (with V.K. Bhargava, H. Vincent Poor and S. Yoon): (book) Communications Information and Network Security, 2002; contbr. articles to profl. jours. Named one of Top 100 Inventors of Yr., Tech. Rev. Mag., 1999—2002; recipient Gold Medal, Gov. Gen. Canada, 1995, Info. Theory Soc. Prize Paper award, IEEE, 1999, Alan T. Waterman award, NSF, 2001. Achievements include invention of space-time coding; design of efficient network protocols, wireless networks and algorithms for scheduling and switching; patents in field. Office: Divsn Engring and Applied Sci Harvard Univ 33 Oxford St Rm MD-347 Cambridge MA 02138 Office Phone: 617-384-5026. Office Fax: 617-496-6404. E-mail: vahid@deas.harvard.edu.

**TARONJI, JAIME, JR.,** lawyer; b. NYC, Nov. 20, 1944; s. Jaime and Ruth T.; m. Mary Taronji, May 16, 1970; children: Ian A., Mark N. Nicole V. BA, George Washington U., 1972; JD, Georgetown U., 1976. Bar: Va. 1977, DC 1978. Asst. to dep. staff dir. U.S. Commn. on Civil Rights, Washington, 1972-76; antitrust enforcement atty. FTC, Washington, 1976-79; antitrust counsel Westinghouse Electric Corp., Pitts., 1979-81; group legal counsel Dana Corp., Toledo, 1982-88; sr. gen. counsel Packaging Corp. Am. subs. Tenneco, Evanston, Ill., 1988-95; law v.p. NCR Corp., Dayton, 1996-99; v.p. gen. counsel, sec. Dayton Superior Corp., Dayton, 1999—2003; of counsel antitrust practice group Howrey LLP, Washington, 2004—. Mem. adv. bd. Corp. Counsel Inst., Georgetown U. Law Ctr. Author: The 1970 Census Undercount of Spanish Speaking Persons, 1974; editor: Puerto Ricans in the U.S., 1976. Capt. M.I., U.S. Army, 1965-70, Vietnam. Mem. ABA (antitrust sect.), Hispanic Nat. Bar Assn., Hispanic Bar Assn. DC. Democrat. Roman Catholic. Home: 20-A W Chapman St Alexandria VA 22301-2502 Office: Howrey LLP 1299 Pennsylvania Ave NW Washington DC 20004-2402 Office Phone: 202-383-7406. E-mail: taronjij@howrey.com.

**TARPEH-DOE, LINDA DIANE,** controller; b. Laramie, Wyo., Mar. 19, 1957; d. Leland Dean and Marilyn Lee (McClurg) Wheeler; m. Nyenpan Tarpeh-Doe, Jan. 16, 1982 (div. Nov. 1985); 1 child, Nyenpan Tarpeh-Doe II. BS in Acctg., U. Wyo., 1979. CPA, Cert. Govt. Fin. Mgr. Asst. auditor First Bank Holding Co., Lakewood, Colo., 1979-80; internal devel. intern USAID, Monrovia, Liberia, 1981-82; sys. acct. Washington, 1982-84, fin. analyst Kingston, Jamaica, 1984-88, macs coord. Washington, 1988-93, contr. Colombo, Sri Lanka, 1993-97, REDSO, Nairobi, Kenya, 1997-2000, USAID/Ethiopia, Addis Ababa, 2000—02, USAID, Jakarta, Indonesia, 2002—. Mem.: AICPA, Assn. Govt. Accts. Democrat. Methodist. Avocations:

music, reading. Home: 3851 Paseo Del Prado Boulder CO 80301-1527 Office: Am Embassy Jakarta Unit 8135 USAID Fpo AP 96520-8135 Office Phone: 62-21-3435-9445. Business E-Mail: Itarpeh-doe@usaid.gov.

**TARPLEY, JOHN R.,** lawyer; b. Lebanon, Tenn., Aug. 18, 1954; BS, U. Tenn., 1976, JD, 1980. Bar: Tenn. 1981. Law ckl. to Hon. Lewis H. Conner, Jr., Assoc. Judge, Tenn. Ct. Appeals, Mid. Divsn., 1981—82; asst. atty. gen. State of Tenn., 1982—89; atty. Lewis, King, Krieg & Waldrop, P.C., Nashville. Mem.: ABA (Young Lawyers divsn. long range planning com. 1986—89, editor Barrister 1987—89, Young Lawyers divsn. assembly clk. 1989—90, Young Lawyers exec. coun. 1989—91, standing com. on assn. comm. 1989—92, Young Lawyers divsn. assembly spkr. 1990—91, coun. mem. 1991—93, Ho. of Dels. 1997—2001, coun. mem. 1999—2002, revenue officer 1999—2002, torts and ins. practuce sect.), Nashville Bar Assn. (pres. Young Lawyers divsn. 1985, bd. dirs. Young Lawyers divsn. 1985—86, sec. 1989, bd. dirs. 1991—94, 1st v.p. 1994), Tenn. Bar Assn. (editor Young Lawyers Quar. 1984—86, bd. govs. 1984—90, moving v.p. 1986—87, pres.-elect 1987—88, bd. govs. 1987—89, pres. 1988—89, chairperson-elect 1989—90, chairperson 1990—91, treas. 1997—2000, v.p. 2001—02, pres.-elect 2002—03, Young Lawyers Conf., litigation coun.). Office: Lewis King Krieg and Waldrop Suntrust Bank Bldg 201 Fourth Ave N Ste 1500 Nashville TN 37219

**TARPY, THOMAS MICHAEL,** lawyer; b. Columbus, Ohio, Jan. 4, 1945; s. Thomas Michael and Catherine G. (Sharshal) T.; m. Mary Patricia Canna, Sept. 9, 1967; children: Joshua Michael, Megan Patricia, Thomas Canna, John Patrick. AB, John Carroll U., 1966; JD, Ohio State U., 1969. Bar: Ohio 1969, U.S. Dist. Ct. (so. dist.) Ohio 1972, U.S. Dist. Ct. (no. dist.) Ohio 1974, U.S. Ct. Appeals (6th cir.) 1982, U.S. Supreme Ct. 1997. Assoc. Vorys, Sater, Seymour & Pease LLP, Columbus, 1969-76, prinr., 1977—85, 1985—87, 1987—2005; v.p. Liebert Corp., Columbus, 1985-87. Chmn. Columbus Graphics Commn., 1980; mem. Columbus Area Leadership Program, 1975. With U.S. Army, 1969-75. Fellow Ocll. Labor and Employment Lawyers, Ohio Mgmt. Lawyers Assn. (founding mem.); mem. ABA, Ohio Bar Assn., Columbus Bar Assn. Office: Vorys Sater Seymour & Pease LLP PO Box 1008 52 E Gay St Columbus OH 43215-3161 E-mail: tmtarpy@vssp.com.

**TARR, CURTIS W.,** management consultant, educator; b. Stockton, Calif., Sept. 18, 1924; s. F.W. and Esther (Reed) T.; m. Elizabeth May Myers, 1955 (div. 1978); children: Pamela Elizabeth, Cynthia Leigh; m. Marilyn Van Stralen, 1979 (div. 1991); m. Mary Katherine Stegmiller, 1992. BA, Stanford U., 1948, PhD, 1962; MBA, Harvard U., 1950; L.H.D., Ripon Coll., 1965, Grinnell Coll., 1969, Lincoln Coll., 1980; LL.D., Lawrence U., 1974, Ill. Wesleyan U., 1980. Rsch. asst. instr. Harvard U., 1950-52; v.p. Sierra Tractor & Equipment Co., Chico, Calif., 1952-58; staff mem. 2d Hoover Commn., 1954-55; asst. dir. summer session Stanford U., 1961-62, dir., 1962-63, asst. dean humanities and scis., 1962-63, lectr. bus. sch., 1962-63; pres. Lawrence U., Appleton, Wis., 1963-69; asst. sec. for manpower and res. affairs Air Force, 1969-70; dir. SSS, Washington, 1970-72; under sec. state for security assistance, 1972-73; acting dep. under sec. for mgmt., 1973; from v.p. parts distbn. and matrials mgmt. to v.p. mgmt. devel. Deere & Co., Moline, Ill., 1973—83; dean, prof. Johnson Sch. Mgmt., Cornell U., 1984—89, prof. mgmt., 1989-90, dean emeritus, 1990—; vice chmn. Intermet Corp., 1992-95. Bd. dirs. Phyton Corp., Ithaca, N.Y., 1985-2002, State Farm Ins. Companies, 1985-98, Banta Corp. 1976-95, Intermet Corp., 1984-98; mem. Internat. Rsch. Coun. Ctr. for Strategic and Internat. Studies, Washington, 1989-92; adj. prof. mgmt. Emory U., 1991-93. Author: Private Soldier, 1976, By the Numbers, 1981, Youth, 1994. Trustee Inst. Paper Chemistry, 1963-69, Morehouse Sch. Medicine, Atlanta, 1994—2004; chmn. Task Force on Govt. Orgn., Fin. and Tax Distbn. for State Wis., 1967-69; chmn. Def. Manpower Commn., 1974-76, Ill. State Scholarship Commn., 1978-79, Quad Cities Grad. Study Ctr., 1982-84, Rep. candidate for Congress 2d Dist., Calif., 1958; trustee Am. Coll., Bryn Mawr, Pa., 1989-92; dir. Bethesda Home, Savannah, Ga., 1998-2003, The Mighty 8th Air Force Mus., Savannah, 1999-2004, Morehouse Sch. Medicine, Atlanta, 1999-2004. With AUS, 1943-46, ETO. Recipient Exceptional Civilian Service medal Air Force Dept., 1970; Distinguished Service award SSS, 1975 Mem. Univ. Club (Chgo.), Cosmos Club (Washington). Methodist. E-mail: curtis.tarr@sbcglobal.net.

**TARR, DAVID GERALD,** economist; b. Phila., Aug. 10, 1943; s. Morris and Esther P. (Martin) T.; m. Linda Haas, June 1971; children— Michael Eli, Adam Haas. B.A., Glassboro (N.J.) State Coll., 1965; M.A., Ohio U., 1967; Ph.D., Brown U., 1970. Instr., U. R.I. Kingston, 1969; asst. prof. Ohio State U., Columbus, 1970-74; sr. economist FTC, Washington, 1974-85; lead economist World Bank, 1985—. Authored over fifty peer reviewed professional journal articles and edited/wrote ten books/monographs. While at the World Bank, provided trade policy advice to governments in twenty countries. Have given seminars in an additional fifteen countries. Speak French well and good Russian. Recipient Disting. Alumnus of Yr. award, Rowan U., 1998. Mem.: Phia Kappa Psi, Pi Gammu Nu. Avocations: tennis. Personal E-mail: dgtarr@yahoo.com.

**TARR, JOEL ARTHUR,** historian, educator; b. Jersey City, May 8, 1934; s. Max Alfred and Florence (Levin) Tartalsky; m. Arlene Green, Sept. 2, 1956 (dec. June 1969); children: Michael Jay, Joanna Sue; m. Tova Brafman, Aug. 11, 1978; children: Maya Leah, Ilana Ariel. BS, Rutgers U., 1956, MA, 1957; PhD, Northwestern U., 1963. Asst. prof. Calif. State U., Long Beach, 1961-66; vis. prof. U. Calif., Santa Barbara, 1966-67; asst. prof. Carnegie Mellon U., Pitts., 1967-70, assoc. prof., 1969-72, prof. history and pub. policy, 1973-90, Richard S. Caliguiri prof. urban and environ. history and policy, 1990—2004, Richard S. Caliguiri univ. prof. history and pub. policy, 2004—, dir. program in tech. and soc., 1975-87, co-dir. program in applied history and social sci., 1978-86, acting dean Sch. Urban and Pub. Affairs, 1986, assoc. dean Coll. Humanities and Social Sci., 1988-91, acting dean Coll. Humanities and Social Sci., 1991-92, acting head dept. history, 1992-93, Univ. prof., 2004—. Author: A Study in Boss Politics, 1971; editor: Patterns of City Growth, 1974, Retrospective Technology Assessment, 1977, Transportation Innovation and Spatial Change in Pittsburgh, 1850-1934, 1978, Pittsburgh-Sheffield: Sister Cities, 1986, Technology and the Rise of the Networked City in Europe and America, 1988, The Search for the Ultimate Sink: Urban Pollution in Historic Perspective, 1996, Devastation and Renewal: An Environmental History of Pittsburgh and Its Region, 2003. Bd. dirs. Action Housing, Pitts., 1983; trustee Hist. Soc. Western Pa., 1993-2000. NEH fellow, 1969-70; grantee NSF, 1975-79, 78-80, 83-85, 95-98, NOAA, 1982-84; recipient Robert Doherty Prize for contbns. to excellence in edn. 1992, Choice Outstanding Acad. Book award, 1997, cert. Commendation Am. Soc. State and Local History, 2005. Mem. AAAS, Pub. Works Hist. Soc. (pres. 1982-83, Abel Wolman prize 1989), Orgn. Am. Historians, Pub. History Assn., Am. Soc. Environ. History, Soc. for the History of Tech., Urban History Assn. (pres. 1999). Democrat. Jewish. Home: 5418 Normlee Pl Pittsburgh PA 15217-1116 Office: Carnegie-Mellon U Schenley Pk Pittsburgh PA 15213 Office Phone: 412-268-2609. Business E-Mail: jt03@andrew.cmu.edu.

**TARR, KENNETH J.,** retired investment company executive; b. Mar. 1, 1945; s. Julius and Alice (Tamres) T.; 1 child, Alexandra Jennifer; m. Charlotte Kimball Kruesi, 1990 BA, U. Pa., 1967; MBA, Columbia U., 1971. With Chem. Bank, N.Y.C., 1971-72; asst. v.p. Standard and Poors/Inter Capital, N.Y.C., 1972-74; founder, mgr. S&P/Market Insights, N.Y.C., 1974-75; v.p. Kuhn Loeb and Co., N.Y.C., 1975-77; asst. v.p. Bessemer Trust Co., N.Y.C., 1977-80, v.p., 1980-82, sr. v.p., 1982-91; dir. rsch., 1984; pres., dir. Suisse Asset Mgmt., Inc., N.Y.C., 1991-93; mng. prin. Weiss, Peck & Greer, LLC, N.Y.C., 1994-97; exec. v.p., regional head pvt. banking Am.'s Deutsche Bank AG, N.Y.C., 1997-99; ret., 2000. Mem.: NY Yacht Club.

**TARR, RALPH WILLIAM,** lawyer, former federal government official; b. Bakersfield, Calif., Sept. 29, 1948; BA, Dartmouth Coll., 1970; MPA, Calif. State U., 1973; JD, U. Calif., Hastings, 1976. Extern to assoc. justice Calif. Supreme Ct., 1976; rsch. atty. to presiding justice Ct. Appeal (5th dist.) Calif., 1976-77; assoc. Baker, Manock & Jensen, Fresno, Calif., 1977-81, dir., mem.

exec. com., 1981-82; mem. adminstrv. com. Fed. Register, Washington, 1982-85; dep. asst. atty. gen. US Dept. Justice, Washington, 1982-84, acting asst. atty. gen., 1984-85; solicitor US Dept. Interior, Washington, 1985-89, counselor, 1989-90; pvt. practice LA, 1990—. Home: 24011 Alder Pl Calabasas CA 91302-2394 Office: Andrews Kurth LLP Ste 3700 601 S Figueroa St Los Angeles CA 90017-5742 Office Phone: 213-896-3136. Business E-Mail: rtarr@andrewskurth.com.

**TARR, ROBERT JOSEPH, JR.,** publishing executive, retail executive; b. Freeport, NY, Dec. 7, 1943; s. Robert Joseph and Janet Christman (Laughton) T.; m. Molly Worthington Upton, Feb. 28, 1970; children: William Upton, Robert Joseph, III, David Worthington. BS, U.S. Naval Acad., 1966; MBA, Harvard U., 1973; MA, Fletcher Sch. Law & Diplomacy, 1976. Asst. v.p. corp. fin. Paine Webber Jackson Curtis, Boston, 1973-75; dir. corp. planning, then v.p., treas. Gen. Cinema Corp., Chestnut Hill, Mass., 1976-78, sr. v.p., 1978-83, exec. v.p., COO, 1983-85, pres., COO, 1985—92; pres., CEO, COO Harcourt Gen., Inc. (Gen. Cinema Corp., 1993), Chestnut Hill, Mass., 1991-97; pres., spl. ptnr. Chartwell Investments, NYC, 2002—. Pres., CEO, COO The Neiman Marcus Group, Inc., 1987—92, pres., bd. dirs., CEO, COO, 1991—97; bd. dirs. WESCO Internat., Inc.; chmn., pres., CEO HomeRuns.com, Inc., 1999—2001. Lt. USN, 1966-71. Mem. Kiawah Island Club, Wianno Yacht Club, The Oyster Harbors Club, Briar's Creek Club, Sandwich Golf Club. Office: Chartwell Investments LLC 830 3d Ave 3d Fl New York NY 10022 Home: 58 River Marsh Ln Johns Island SC 29455-5202 Personal E-mail: rjtjr12@aol.com.

**TARRANCE, VERNON LANCE, JR.,** research and development company executive; b. Harlingen, Tex., Dec. 4, 1940; s. Vernon Lance Sr. and Mary Gilmore (Rea) T.; m. Eugenia Aline McCuistion, July 2, 1966; children: Vernon Lance III, Haloway McCuistion, Kyle Rea. BA, Washington & Lee U., 1962; postgrad., U. Mich., 1971; MA, Am. U., 1973; postgrad., Harvard U., 1973-74. Dir. rsch. Tex. Rep. Com., Austin, 1964-67, Rep. Nat. Com., Washington, 1969-70; spl. asst. to dir. U.S. Census Bur., Washington, 1970-73; v.p. Decision Making Info. Inc., Santa Ana, Calif., 1974-77; pres., founder Tarrance, Hill, Newport & Ryan, Houston, 1977-92; pres., mng. dir. Gallup China Ltd., Beijing, 1993-95; vis. prof. polit. sci. Tex. A&M U., College Station, 1995-96; scholar in residence Washington and Lee U., Va., 1996; mng. dir. Burson-Marsteller, Washington, 1997-99. Bd. dirs. Gallup Orgn., 1987-92; cons. Gallup Internat. Rsch. Ctr., Lincoln, Nebr.; co-chmn. adv. adjustment panel U.S. Census, 1990. Co-author: The Ticket Splitter, 1972, Checked and Balanced, 1998; editor: Texas Precinct Votes '66, '68, '70. Fellow John F. Kennedy Inst. Politics Harvard U., 1973-74; named one of 150 People Who Influence Fed. Govt. Nat. Jour. Mag., 1986. Mem.: Raleigh Tavern Philos. Soc. (founder), Am. Polit. Sci. Assn., Kappa Sigma. Avocations: mountain trekking, golf, aviculture, travel. E-mail: lanceterrancejr@aol.com.

**TARRANT, CHRISTINE GLORIA,** music educator; d. Nick and Bessie Boulos; m. Timothy Michael Tarrant, May 1, 2004; 1 stepchild, Joseph John 1 child, John Nicholas. BS, U. Ill., 1992, MS, 1997. Tchr. choral, music Marquardt Mid. Sch., Glendale Heights, Ill., 1992—98, Timber Ridge Mid. Sch., Plainfield, Ill., 1998—99, Heritage Grove Mid. Sch., Plainfield, Ill., 1999—2002, Drauden Point Mid. Sch., Plainfield, 2002—05. Children's choral dir. Hinsdale (Ill.) Children's Choir, 1997—97, United Meth. Ch., Downers Grove, Ill., 1997—99; youth choral dir. All Saints Greek Orthodox Ch., Joliet, Ill., 2000—03. Recipient Fine Arts award, Bloom Sch. Dist., 1988. Mem.: Am. Choral Dirs. Am., Alpha Delta Pi. Greek Orthodox. Avocations: reading, exercise.

**TARRANT, JAMES RICHARD, III,** music educator; b. Oak Ridge, Tenn., May 18, 1957; s. James Richard and Inice Carlisle Tarrant; m. Catherine Marie Tarrant, June 1, 1985; children: Sarah, Catherine, Brittany Grace. BA, Cumberland Coll., 1986; MusM, Eastern Ky. U., 1988; MusD, U. Memphis, 2001. Engr. Cmty. TV of Knoxville, Tenn., 1990—94; chmn., divsn. fine arts U. West Ala., 1994—95, asst. prof., 1994—95; music instr. U. Memphis, 1995—96; min. music edn. Glenwood Bapt. Ch., Oakridge, Tenn., 1996—98; asst. prof. Ottawa U., Kans., 1998—2004; assoc. prof. Southwest Bapt. U., Bolivar, Md., 2004—. Rep. Sumter Fine Arts Assn., Livingston, Ala., 1994—95; tchr. edn. coun. Southwest Bapt. U., Bolivar, 2004—. Dir. Sumter County Chorus, Livingston, Ala., 1994—95, Bolivar Cmty. Chorus, 2004—. Mem.: Music Eduators Nat. Conf, Am. Choral Dir. Assn., Nat. Assn. Tchrs. of Singing. Avocations: travel, antique cars, golf. Office: Southwest Bapt U 1600 University Ave Bolivar MO 65613

**TARRANT, RICHARD J(OHN),** classicist, educator; b. Bklyn., Apr. 4, 1945; s. John Joseph and Bertha (Slaney) T.; m. Jacqueline Brown, Sept. 14, 1968. BA, Fordham U., 1966; DPhil, Oxford U., 1972; AM (hon.), Harvard U., 1982. P.S Allen jr. research fellow Corpus Christi Coll., Oxford, England, 1968-70; lectr. Univ. Coll., Toronto, Ont., Canada, 1970-71, asst. prof., 1971-74, assoc. prof., 1974-79; prof. U. Toronto, 1979-82; prof. Greek and Latin Harvard U., Cambridge, Mass., 1982-87, Carl A. Pescosolido prof. Roman civilization, 1987-93, Pope prof. Latin language and Literature, 1993—, Harvard Coll. prof., 1999—2004, chmn. dept., 1988-94, acting dean Grad. Sch. Arts and Scis., 1995-96. Vis. Mellon prof. Inst. for Advanced Study, Princeton, 1991-92; vis. fellow Corpus Christi Coll. U. Oxford, 1992. Author: Greek and Latin Lyric Poetry in Translation: A Bibliographical Survey, 1972, Seneca, Agamemnon, 1976, (with others) Texts and Transmission: A Survey of the Latin Classics, 1983, Seneca's Thyestes, 1985, Ovid's Metamorphoses, 2004; editor Phoenix: Jour. Classical Assn. Can., 1978-82, Harvard Studies in Classical Philology, 1985-88, 93-94; editorial bd. Toronto Medieval Latin Texts, 1977—, Cambridge Classical Texts and Commentaries, 1992—; advisory bd. Transactions of the Soc. for Textual Scholarship, 1994—, Materiali e discussioni comitato scientifico, 2002—; contbr. articles to profl. jours. Cabot fellow, 1993—94, 2004—05. Marshall scholar, 1966—69. Mem. Am. Philol. Assn. (bd. dirs. 1987-89, v.p. publs. 1992-95), Cambridge Philol. Assn., Classical Assn. Can., Classical Assn. New Eng., Phi Beta Kappa. Office: Harvard U Dept Classics Boylston Hall 204 Cambridge MA 02138 Office Phone: 617-496-3611. Business E-Mail: tarrant@fas.harvard.edu.

**TARRANTS, WILLIAM EUGENE,** federal official; b. Liberty, Mo., Dec. 9, 1927; s. Joseph Eugene and Mildred Jane (Wright) Tarrants; m. Mary Jo Edman, Jan. 19, 1952 (div. 1981); children: James Timothy, Jennifer Lynn; m. Loma D. Lundberg, Sept. 24, 1988; stepchildren: David Murphy, Christine Walls, Janelle McCrea. B in Indsl. Engring., Ohio State U., 1951; MS in Indsl. Engring., 1959; PhD, NYU, 1963. Instr. indsl. engring. Ohio State U., Columbus, 1958-59; asst. prof., research asso. N.Y. U., 1959-64; chief accident research dir. Bur. Labor Stats., Dept. Labor, Washington, 1964-67; dir. manpower devel. div. Nat. Hwy. Traffic Safety Adminstrn., Dept. Transp., 1967-80; chief scientist Office of Program and Demonstration Evaluation, 1980-84; program analyst Office of Occupant Protection, 1984-87, program analyst evaluation staff, 1987-90, also chmn. sci. and tech. info. adv. bd., 1984-91. Cons. safety program evaluation Indsl. Commn. Ohio, 1959; instr. Johns Hopkins U., 1984—91, U. Md., 1991—92; planning and adminstrn. transp. safety mem. Transp. Rsch. Bd., NAS; mem. exec. com. Related Accreditation Commn., 1994—; accreditation bd. Engring. and Tech., Inc., 1994—. Co-author: A Selected Bibliography of Reference Materials in Safety Engineering and Related Fields, 1967, Selected Readings in Safety, 1973, Readings in Industrial Accident Prevention, 1980, Dictionary of Terms Used in the Safety Profession, 1971, Measurement of Safety Performance, 1980, Handbook of Occupational Safety and Health, 1987; contbr. articles to profl. jours.; mem. editl. bd. Jour. Safety Rsch., Accident Analysis and Prevention; editor-in-chief: Traffic Safety Evaluation Rsch. Rev. Region 8 rep. to bd. trustees E. Coast Conf., 1986—92; trustee, ch. chmn. Evang. Covent Ch., 1976—80, 1984—88. Capt. USAF, 1951—57. Named to Safety and Health Hall of Fame Internat., 1990; recipient Founder's Day award, NYU, 1963, 1st pl., Nat. Tech. Paper Awards, 1961, 1963, 1967, cert. for outstanding performance, Nat. Hwy. Traffic Safety Adminstrn., 1973, 1986, Disting. Svc. to Safety award, Nat. Safety Coun., 1989, Disting. Career Svc. award, U.S. Dept. or Transp., 1990. Fellow: Am. Soc. Safety Engrs. (dir., v.p. rsch. and

tech. devel., pres. 1977—78, chmn. acad. accreditation coun. 1978—97, chmn. profl. and ednl. stds. com. 1997—, fellow rev. bd. 1980—88, Pres.'s award 1996); mem.: AAAS, Nat. Safety Coun. (chmn. rsch. proejcts com. 1973—78, mem. exec. com. indsl. conf. 1977—78, Disting. Svc. award 1989), Soc. Risk Analysis, Am. Nat. Stds. Inst. (mem. stds. com.), Vets. Safety, Evaluation Rsch. Soc., Sys. Safety Soc., Human Factors Soc., Am. Inst. Indsl. Engrs., Am. Soc. Safety Rsch. (trsutee), Kappa Delta Pi, Alpha Pi Mu. Home: 606 Woodsmans Way Crownsville MD 21032-2317 Office: 400 7th St SW Washington DC 20590-0001 *We often look with awe at the successful person, much as we admire a well designed structure or a beautiful painting. Behind the finished product usually lies exhaustive effort, frustration, disappointment, and even failure which is obscured by the glow of accomplishment. Success is achieved by some ability, lots of hard work, perserverance, courage of convictions, help and support from others, a desire to reach a goal, self-discipline, and considerable personal sacrifice as we make choices concerning the use of our limited resources. The ability to bounce back from adversity is crucial. Most important of all is the strength and insight gained through prayer and the willingness to permit your life to be guided by Christian faith.*

**TARRIO, CHARLES,** physicist; b. Middletown, Conn., Dec. 20, 1960; s. Frank R. and Frances Baldwin Tarrio; m. Danielle Partello, Feb. 17, 1995; 1 child, Alyssa Partello Tarrio. BS, Bates Coll., Lewiston, Maine, 1982; PhD, U. of Va., Charlottesville, 1991. Physicist Nat. Inst. of Stds. and Tech., Gaithersburg, Md., 1991—. Recipient Dept. of Commerce Silver medal, U.S. Dept. of Commerce, 2004, Arthur S. Flemming award for applied sci., George Wash. U., 2003, Dept. of Commerce Bronze medal, U.S. Dept. of Commerce, 1994. Mem.: SPIE, Optical Soc. of Am. Office: Nat Inst Stds and Tech Stop 8410 100 Bureau Dr Rockville MD 20853 Office Phone: 301-975-3737.

**TARRO, GIULIO,** virologist; b. Messina, Italy, July 9, 1938; s. Emanuele and Emanuela (Iannello) Tarro. MD, U. Naples, 1962, postgrad. in nervous diseases, 1968, PhD in Virology, 1971; postgrad. in med. and biol. scis., Roman Acad., 1979; degree in medicine (hon.), U. Pro Deo, Albany, NY, 1989; degree in immunology (hon.), St. Theodora Acad., NY, 1991; degree in bioethics (hon.), Constantinian U., Cranston, R.I., 1996. Asst. in med. pathology Naples U., Italy, 1964-66; rsch. assoc. divsn. virology and cancer rsch. Children's Hosp., Cin., 1965-68; asst. prof. rsch. pediat. U. Cin. Coll. Medicine, 1968-69; rsch. fellow Nat. Rsch. Coun., Naples, 1966-74, rsch. chief, 1974; prof. oncologic virology Coll. Medicine U. Naples, 1971-85, prof. microbiology and immunology Sch. Specialization, 1972—; chief divsn. virology D. Cotugno Hosp. for Infectious Diseases, Naples, 1973—2006, pres. ethic com., 1998—, head dept. diagnostic labs., 2003—06, emeritus, 2006—; dean faculty natural and phys. scis. Nobile Accademia di Santa Teodora Imperatrice, Capua, Italy, 1993—; head dept. medicine Naples People U., 2000—. Sr. scientist Nat. Cancer Inst. Frederick Ctr., Md., 1973; project dir. Nat. Cancer Inst., Bethesda, Md., 1971-75; edn. min. rep. Zool. Sta., Naples, 1975-79; cons. Italian Pharmacotherapic Inst., Rome, 1980-88, sci. dir., 2006—; nat. com. on bioethics, 1993-98; ethics com. Basilicata Oncologic Hosp., 2005—; pres. De Beaumont Bonelli Found. for Cancer Rsch., Naples, 1978—, European Group Econ. Interest, Rsch. and Devel., Naples, 2003-06, Campania Tech. and Ecology Ctr., 2004—; sci. coord. extracorporeal hyperthermia in HCV patients First Circle Med., Mpls., 2000-03; vice chmn., gen. sec. sci. adv. bd. Unihart Biotech Pharm., London, 2005-. Author: Virologia Oncologica, 1979, Patologia dell'AIDS, 2001, Con il Cancro si Può Vivere, 1992, AIDS Cosa Possiamo Fare Cosa Dobbiamo Sapere, 1994, Pocket File Research Collection, 1997, 6th edit., 2003, To Prevent Is To Win, 1998, Bioethics and Culture of Prevention, 2001, Health Without Borders, 2004; editor-in-chief: Internat. Jour. Clin. Investigation, 2000—, Cotugno News, 2003—, Fratres, 2004—; contbr. over 360 articles to profl. jours. Pres. Sci. Cultural Com., Torre Annunziata, Italy, 1984, Tumor Prevention Assn. Rome, 1984; mem. acad. senate Constantinian U., Providence, 1990, U. Pro Deo, NY, 1994; hon. acad. U. Sancti Cyrilli, Valletta, Malta, 2001; mem. UNESCO-Hebrew U. Jerusalem Internat. Sch. Molecular Biology and Microbiology; hon. rector Ruggero II U., Fla., 2003. Maj. Italian Navy, 1982-84, lt. col., 1993-95. Decorated comdr. Nat. Order of Merit, Star of Europe, knight grand cross Sovereign Constantinian Order St. George, gt. officer Italian Republic; recipient Internat. Lenghi award Lincei Acad., 1969, Gold Microscope award Italian Health Min., 1973, Knights of Humanity award Internat. Register of Chivalry, Malta, 1978, Gold medal of culture award Pres. Italian Republic, 1975, Culture award, 1985, 1st prize in biomed. rsch., Italian Acad. Arts and Scis., 1987, Castello di Pietrarossa award, Italy, 1991, Gold Cesare award Padova, 1991, 20th Century award in Medicine, 1994, Gold Little Horse, Transnat. European Fedn., Rome 1996. King Manfredi award Manfredinia, 1999, Equestris Ordinis S. Sepulcri of Jerusalem, Rome, 1999, Gold medal of health Pres. Italian Republic, 1999, Saint Catherin award, Siena, 2003, Sorrento in the World award, 2004, Medal of Culture Ministry, 2005, Knight of Solidarity Internat. award Norman Acad., Rome, 2006, Saint Pio for Peace award City of Fiuggi, 2006, Tables of Law award Internat. Assn. Cath. Apostleship, Naples, 2006, others. Fellow: AAAS; mem.: Am. Chem. Soc., European Soc. Clin. Virology, Internat. Sch. for Molecular Biology and Microbiology, NY Acad. Scis., Nat. Order Journalists, AIDS Soc. Asia and the Pacific, Assn. Res. Prevention of Cancer (sci. com. 1995), Italian Assn. Viral Study and Rsch. (pres. 1995—), Italian Soc. Immuno-Oncology (v.p. 1975—, pres. 1990—), Internat. League Drs. for Abolition of Vivisection (pres. 1992—), Internat. Assn. Leukemias, Am. Assn. Cancer Rsch., Am. Soc. Microbiology, Rotary, Lions (pres. Pompei chpt. 1987—89, vice gov. dist. 1991—92, pres. com. fight cancer 1992—94, pres. com. sci. and life 1994—95, pres. com. fight drug addiction and AIDS 1995—97, pres. com. transplant and donations 1998—99, pres. com. oncology 2000—02, pres. com. on stem cells 2002—, dist. dir. operative area health and rsch. 2006—, pres. Pompei chpt. 2004—06, Melvin Jones fellow 1993, 2004). Roman Catholic. Achievements include patents in field; discovery of RSV virus in infant deaths in Naples and of tumor liberated protein as a tumor associated antigen, 100 kilodalton protein overexpressed in lung tumors and other epithelial adenocarcinomas. Home: 286 Posillipo 80123 Naples Italy Office: A O D Cotugno Hosp 54 Quagliariello 80131 Naples Italy Office Phone: +39-081-546-1300. Office Fax: +39-081-5463222. E-mail: gitarro@tin.it.

**TARR-WHELAN, LINDA,** policy center executive; b. Springfield, Mass., May 24, 1940; d. Albert and Jane Zack; m. Keith Tarr-Whelan; children: Scott, Melinda. BSN, Johns Hopkins U., 1963; MS, U. Md., 1967; PhD in Public Svc. (hon.), Chatham Coll. Program dir. AFSCME AFL-CIO, Washington, 1968-74, union area dir., 1974-76; adminstrn. dir. N.Y. State Labor Dept., Albany, N.Y., 1976-79; dep. asst. to pres. Carter White House, Washington, 1979-80; dir. govt. rels. NEA, Washington, 1980-86; CEO, pres. Ctr. for Policy Alternatives, Washington, 1986—2000, bd. dirs., 1985—; mng. dir. Tarr-Whelan Assoc. Inc., St. Helena Island, SC, 2000—. Apptd. U.S. rep. UN Commn. on Status of Women, 1996—. Bd. dirs. Benton Found., Adv. Inst., Ind. Sector; pres. State Issues Forum; mem. Freddie Mac Affordable Housing Adv. Bd. Recipient Disting. Grad. award Johns Hopkins U., 1981, Breaking the Glass Ceiling award, 1996; leadership fellow Japan Soc., 1987-88; named one of 50 Most Powerful Women in Washington, Ladies Home Journal. Democrat. Avocations: walking, travel. Home: Tarr-Whelan Assoc Inc PO Box 1012 Saint Helena Island SC 29920

**TARTAGLIA, RICHARD V.,** priest; b. White Plains, N.Y., Nov. 6, 1946; s. Valentine Tartaglia and Louise M. DiPopolo. BA, St. Mary's Coll., St. Mary, Ky., 1968; MDiv, Mt. St. Mary's Seminary, Emmitsburg, Md., 1972. Ordained priest St. John the Bapt. Cathedral, 1972. Deacon St. Clement Ch., Dover, NJ, 1971—72; assoc. pastor St. Andrew Ch., Clifton, NJ, 1972—73, Holy Family Ch., Forham Park, NJ, 1973—74, St. Mary Ch., Denville, NJ, 1974—; Advisor Juvenile Conf. Com., Denville, 1977—87. Mem.: KC (chaplain 1975—). Roman Catholic. Avocations: photography, tennis, baseball, electronics, military history. Home: 15 Myers Ave Denville NJ 07834 Office: St Marys Ch 15 Myers Ave Denville NJ 07834

**TARTER, CURTIS BRUCE,** physicist, science administrator; b. Louisville, Sept. 26, 1939; s. Curtis B. and Marian Turner (Cundiff) T.; divorced; 1 child, Shana Lee; m. Gabriela Odell, 2003. BS, MIT, 1961; PhD, Cornell U., 1967.

Tchg. asst. Cornell U., Ithaca, NY, 1961—63, rsch. asst., 1964—67; physicist, summers Lawrence Radiation Lab., Livermore, Calif., 1962—63; staff mem. theoretical physics divsn. U. Calif., Lawrence Livermore Nat. Lab., 1967—69, group leader macroscopic properties of matter, 1969—71, assoc. divsn. leader, 1971—74, group leader opacities, 1972—78, divsn. leader, 1974—84; dep. assoc. dir. for physics Lawrence Livermore Nat. Lab., 1984—88, assoc. dir. for physics, 1988—94, dep. dir., 1994, dir., 1994—2002, assoc. dir. at large, 2002—04, dir. emeritus, 2004—. Sr. scientist Applied Rsch. Labs. Aeronutronic divsn. Philco-Ford Corp.; cons. Hertz Found., field com. study on astronomy in the 80's, NRC, 1980; mem. Army Sci. Bd., Washington, 1989-96; adj. prof. appl. physical sci., U. Calif., Davis, 1999-; mem. Calif. Coun. on Sci. and Tech., 1996-2002, Pacific Coun. on Internat. Policy, 1998—, lab. opers. bd. DOE, 1998-2002, Nuc. Energy Rsch. Adv. Bd., 1999-2002, Coun. Fgn. Rels., 1999—; bd. dirs. Draper Lab. Contbr. numerous articles to profl. jours. Recipient Roosevelts Gold Medal award for sci., NNSA Gold medal for disting. svc., U.S. Dept. Energy Exceptional Pub. Svc. award, Sec. of Energy's Gold award. Fellow AAAS, Calif. Coun. Sci. and Tech., Am. Phys. Soc. (phys. policy com. 2002-05); mem. Am. Astron. Soc., Internat. Astron. Union. Avocations: golf, running, music. Office: Lawrence Livermore Nat Lab PO Box 808 Livermore CA 94551-0808 Office Phone: 925-422-4169. Business E-mail: tarter1@llnl.gov.

**TARTER, FRED BARRY,** advertising executive; b. Bklyn, Aug. 16, 1943; s. Irving and Edna (Kupferberg) T.; m. Lois; children: Scott Andrew, Heather Michelle, Megan Elizabeth. BS, CCNY, 1966. Pres. Jamie Publ. Hootenanny Enterprises, Inc., 1962-65; mdse. dir. Longines Symphonette Soc., 1965-67; with Universal Comm., Inc., NYC, 1967—, pres., CEO, 1969-74; exec. v.p. Deerfield Comma., Inc. NYC 1974-87 pres , CEO, 1977 88; pres. Deerfield Books, Inc., NYC, 1988-89; pub. S.E.W. mag., NYC, 1977-88; pres. The Rainbow Group Ltd., NYC, 1988—; chmn. Stagebill Mag., 1997-2001; pres., CEO The Lakeside Group of Co., 2001—. Exec. prodr. Joanne Carson's VIP's Miss Am. Teenager Pageant, 1972—73; prodr. Marriage Counselor, 1994, Spenser: Pale Kings & Princes, 1995, Spenser: A Savage Place, 1995, Spenser Judas Goat, 1995, Hearts Adrift, 1995, Ceremony, 1996, Wounded Heart, 1996, Reasons of the Heart, 1996, Lover's Leap, 1996; chmn. Stagebill Enterprises, LLC, 1997—2001; vice-chmn. Affinity Comm., Inc. 1997—2001, Inscap, LLC; pres., CEO The Telephone Co. LLC, 1999—2003; pres. The Programme Exch., U.K. Ltd.; bd. dirs. Asset Mgmt. Sys., LLC, Caribbean Internat. News Corp., Boardwalk Entertainment, Ltd., Lakeside Group, Inc. Home: 578 Westport Tpke Fairfield CT 06430-1670 Office: The Lakeside Group Ltd 210 E 39th St New York NY 10016-2754 Office Phone: 212-679-3800. Personal E-mail: ftarter@lakesideglobal.com. *An integral part of success is the capacity for failure. Persistence, combined with responsibility, has proven to be the winning combination time and again.*

**TARTER, JILL CORNELL,** science foundation director, astronomer, researcher; BEP, Cornell U. Sch. of Engring., 1966; attended, Cornell U. Grad. Sch. Theoretical Physics, 1965—67; MA in Astronomy, U. Calif., Berkeley, 1971, PhD in Astronomy, 1975. Teaching & rsch. asst. U. Calif., Berkeley, Calif., 1965—75; NRC resident rsch. assoc. postdoctoral fellow NASA Ames Rsch. Ctr., Moffett Field, Calif., 1975—77; asst. rsch. astronomer II-IV U. Calif. Space Sciences Lab, Berkeley, Calif., 1977—83, assoc. rsch. astronomer I, 1983—85; assoc. rsch. astronomer dept. of astronomony U. Calif., Berkeley, Calif., 1983—93; co-founder SETI Inst., Mountain View, Calif., 1984—, principal investigator, 1984—89, project scientist NASA SETI Microwave Observing Project & High Resolution Microwave Survey, 1989—93, dir. Project Phoenix, 1993—99, Bernard M. Oliver chair, 1997—; dir. SETI Research, Mountain View, Calif., 1999—2000, Ctr. for SETI Research, Mountain View, Calif., 2000—. Chair Internat. Acad. of Astronautics SETI Com., 1997—, Internat. Square Kilometer Arry Steering Com., 2002—; adv. bd. mem. Odyssey Mag., 1997—, Space.com, 2000—. Recipient Public Service medals, NASA, 1993, HRMS Group Achievement award, 1993, Chabot Observatory Person of Yr. award, 1997, Women's Fund Women of Achievement award, San Jose Mercury News, 1998. Fellow: Com. for Scientific Investigation of Claims of the Paranormal, Calif. Acad. Sci., Explorer's Club; mem.: AAAS (fellow 2002), World Tech. Network, Women in Aerospace (Lifetime Achievement award 1989), Internat. Soc. for Study of Origin of Life, Internat. Acad. of Astronautics, Internat. Radio Sci. Union (URSI Commn.), Internat. Astronomical Union, Am. Astronomical Soc. Office: Seti Institute 515 N Whisman Rd Mountain View CA 94043-2172

**TARTT, BLAKE,** lawyer; b. Houston, Mar. 16, 1929; s. Herbert Blake and Bernice (Schwalm) T.; m. Barbara Jean Moore, Jan. 30, 1960; children: Blake III, Courtnay Elias. BBA, So. Methodist U., 1949, JD cum laude, 1959. Bar: Tex. 1959. Assoc. Fulbright & Jaworski, Houston, 1959-70, ptnr., 1970-2000, Beirne, Maynard & Parsons, LLP, Houston, 2000—. Mem. Tex. Commn. on Jud. Conduct, 1996-2001; bd. dirs. Nat. Judicial Coll. Bd. dirs. Mus. Fine Arts, Houston; mem. bd. visitors Nat. Jud. Coll. Served to 1st lt. USAF, 1951-55, Korea. Decorated Air medal. Fellow Am. Bar Found. (chmn. fellows 1987, life), Tex. Bar Found. (chmn. bd. 1974-75, chmn. fellows 1978-79, life), Am. Coll. Trial Lawyers; mem. ABA (ho. of dels. 1976-99, state del. 1990-99, standing com. fed. jud. 1996-99, chair 1997, bd. govs. 2001-04), Am. Bd. Trial Advocates (advocate), Houston Bar Found. (life, chmn., bd. dirs. 1992), Fed. Bar Assn., Internat. Assn. Def. Counsel, Am. Judicature Soc. (bd. dirs. 1984-88), So. Conf. Bar Pres. (pres. 1984), State Bar Tex. (dir. 1972-75, exec. com. 1975-76, pres. elect 1982-83, pres. 1983-84), Houston Bar Assn., Law Inst., Tex. Jud. Commn., Citizens Commn. on the Tex. Judiciary, Tex. Commn. Jud. Conduct, Houston Philos. Soc., Coronado Club, Forest Club, Argyle Club (San Antonio), Reform Club (London), Delta Theta Phi, Alpha Tau Omega. Episcopalian. Office: Beirne Maynard & Parsons 1300 Post Oak Blvd Houston TX 77056-3028 Office Phone: 713-960-7331. E-mail: btartt@bmpllp.com

**TARUN, ROBERT WALTER,** lawyer; b. Lake Forest, Ill., Sept. 1, 1949; s. Donald Walter and Bonnie Jean (Cruickshank) T.; m. Helen J. McSweeney, May 1, 1987; children: Abigail Esch, Tyler Vincent, Parker Donald, Aimée Dakota. AB, Stanford U., 1971; JD, DePaul U., 1974; MBA, U. Chgo., 1982. Bar: Ill. 1974, Calif. 1975, U.S. Dist. Ct. (no. dist.) Ill. 1974, U.S. Dist. Ct. (we. dist.) Ark. 1986, U.S. Dist. Ct. (so. dist.) Ind. 1995, U.S. Dist. Ct. (no. dist.) Calif. 1995, U.S. Dist. Ct. (ea. dist.) Mich. 1996, U.S. Dist. Ct. (ea. dist.) Wis. 2000, U.S. Dist. Ct. (ctrl. dist.) Ill. 2001, U.S. Ct. Appeals (7th cir.) 1975, U.S. Ct. Appeals (5th cir.) 1992, U.S. Ct. Appeals (3d cir.) 1993, U.S. Ct. Appeals (Fed. cir.) 1995, U.S. Ct. Appeals (9th and 11th cirs.) 1996, U.S. Supreme Ct. 1978. Asst. atty. gen. State of Ill., Chgo., 1974-76; asst. U.S. atty. U.S. Dept. Justice, Chgo., 1976-79, dep. chief criminal div., 1979-82, exec. asst. U.S. atty. no. dist. Ill., 1982-85; ptnr. Reuben & Proctor, Chgo., 1985-86, Isham, Lincoln & Beale, Chgo., 1986-88, Winston & Strawn, Chgo., 1988—2003, Latham & Watkins LLP, Chgo., 2003—. Lectr. in law white collar criminal and bus. litig. U. Chgo. Law Sch., 2001—; adj. prof. Northwestern U. Sch. Law, 1999—2001; instr. Atty. Gen.'s Advocacy Inst., Washington, 1980—85, Nat. Inst. Trial Advs., 1990. Author (with Dan K. Webb): Corporate Internal Investigations, 1993—2005. Bd. dirs. Chgo. Ctrl. Area Com., 1993—2003. Named one of Best Lawyers in Am., Euroguide's Guide to World's Leading Litigators, Chambers USA Leading Bus. Lawyers. Fellow Am. Coll. Trial Lawyers (chair. fed. criminal procedure com. 2003-2004, admission to fellowship com. 1997-2000), bd. regents, 2004—; mem. ABA (white collar crime inst. 1997—, planning com.), Bar Assn. San Francisco, Chgo. Bar Assn., U. Chgo. Grad. Sch. Bus. Alumni Assn. (bd. dirs. 1986), Racquet Club, Wong Sun Soc. (San Francisco), Kenilworth Club, H.O.G. (Black Hills chpt.), Chgo. Stanford Assn. Presbyterian. Avocations: architecture, writing screenplays, motorcycling. Office: Latham & Watkins Sears Tower 5800 233 S Wacker Dr Chicago IL 60606 Home: 219 Leicester Rd Kenilworth IL 60043-1244 Office Phone: 312-876-7605.

**TARUSKIN, RICHARD FILLER,** musicologist, educator; b. N.Y., Apr. 2, 1945; s. Benjamin Joseph and Beatrice Filler Taruskin; m. Cathy Roebuck Taruskin, May 1, 1964; children: Paul Roebuck, Tessa Roebuck. BA, Columbia U., 1965, PhD, 1975; MusD (hon.), Grand Valley State U., 2000. Assoc. prof. music Columbia U., N.Y., 1975—86; prof. U. Calif., Berkeley, Calif., 1986—. Author: Opera and Drama in Russia, 1981, Music in the

Western World: A History in Documents, 1984, The Latin-Texted Works of Antoine Busnoys, 1990, Text and Act: Essays on Music and Performance, 1993, Stravinsky and the Russian Traditions, 1995 (medal Royal Philharm. Soc, 1997), Musorgsky: Eight Essays and an Epilogue, 1997, Oxford History of Western Music, 2004, 1996, Defining Russia Musically, 1997. Fellow: Am. Acad. Arts & Sciences; mem.: Internat. Musicological Soc., Am. Musicological Soc. (dir. 1983—86), Am. Philos. Soc. Jewish. Avocation: performing music. Home: 815 Galvin Drive El Cerrito CA 94530 Office: University of California at Berkeley Music Department/Morrison Hall Berkeley CA 94720 Office Phone: 510-642-2678. Office Fax: 510-642-8480. E-mail: taruskin@berkeley.edu.*

**TARVER, ANTONIO,** professional boxer; b. Orlando, Fla., Nov. 21, 1968; Former Olympic boxer, 1996; profl. boxer Internat. Boxing Fedn., 1997—. Named World Light Heavyweight Championship Belt, Internat. Boxing Fedn., World Boxing Assn., 2003, 2004—06. Achievements include standing record of 24-4 with 18 wins coming by way of knockout. Office: IBF 2d Fl 516 Main St East Orange NJ 07018*

**TARY-LEHMANN, MAGDALENA,** education educator; d. Endre and Magdolna Tary; m. Paul Viktor Lehmann, June 16, 1983; children: Iris Edith Lehmann, Alexander Andreas Lehmann. PhD, Tuebingen, Germany, 1988. Post doctoral tng. UCLA, Los Angeles, 1989—93; instr. Case Western Res. U., Cleve., 1993—95, asst. prof., 1997—2003, assoc. prof., 2003—. Cons. Cellular Tech. Ltd., Cleve., 1998. Grant, Am. Cancer Soc., 1995, Kidney Found. of Ohio, 1995, Mucos Ltd., 1995, Ireland Cancer Ctr., 1997, Am. Cancer Soc , 1997, Roche/NIH Steroid Withdrawal protocol, 1997, NIH, 1995, 1997, 2000, 2002, 2004, 2005. Mem.: CFAR, SDRC mem., Case Comprehensive Cancer Ctr., Am. Assn. of Immunologists, Clin. Immunology Soc. Achievements include research in ELISPOT work in immunology. Office: Case Western Reserve U 10900 Euclid Ave Cleveland OH 44106 Office Phone: 216-368-1298. Office Fax: 216-368-1357. Business E-Mail: mxt27@po.cwru.edu.

**TASH, BILL,** state senator; b. Dillon, Mont., Aug. 21, 1932; m. Marlene Tash. Student, Western Mont. Coll., Mont. State U. Rancher; Rep. rep. dist. 34 Mont. Ho. of Reps., 1992-2000; Rep. senator dist. 17 Mont. State Senate, 2000—. Mem. state administrn. com. Mont. State Senate, chair natural resources. With USN. Office: 240 Vista Dr Dillon MT 59725-3100 also: Mont State Senate Capitol Station Helena MT 59620

**TASH, MARTIN ELIAS,** publishing company executive; b. NYC, Jan. 24, 1941; s. David and Esther (Milch) T.; m. Arlene Sue Klein, June 23, 1962; children: Nathan, Faye, Jill. BBA, Baruch Sch. City Coll. N.Y., 1962. C.P.A. Staff accountant S.D. Leidesdorf & Co. (C.P.A.'s), N.Y.C., 1962-66; v.p. fin., dir. LMC Data Inc., N.Y.C., 1966-71; with Plenum Pub. Corp., N.Y.C., 1971-98, chmn. bd., pres., 1977-98; chmn. bd., pres., CEO Gradco Systems, Inc., 1990—. Office: Gradco Systems Inc 3753 Howard Hughes Pkwy Ste 200 Las Vegas NV 89109-0952

**TASH, PAUL CLIFFORD,** editor, publishing executive; b. South Bend, Ind., July 17, 1954; s. Robert N. and Barbara R. (Eller) T.; m. Karyn E. Krayer, Aug. 19, 1983; children: Kaley Marie, Kendyl Barbara. BA, Ind. U., 1976; LLB, Edinburgh (Scotland) U., 1978. Reporter St. Petersburg Times, 1978-83, city editor, 1983-86, metro editor, 1986-89, editor, pub. Fla. Trend Mag., 1990-91, Washington bur. chief, 1991-92, exec. editor, dep. chmn., 1992-2000, pres., editor, dep. chmn., 2000—. Bd. dirs. Times Pub. Co., Newspaper Assn. Am., Com. to Protect Journalists, Mich. Journalism Fellows, Fla. Trend Mag., Congressional Quar., Poynter Inst. Media Studies. Chmn. Fla. First Amendment Found.; mem. adv. bd. Ind. U. Sch. Journalism; bd. govs. Fla. C. of C. Marshall Aid Commemoration Commn. scholar, 1976-78. Mem.: Fla. First Amendment Found., Tampa Bay Area Com. on Fgn. Rels., Am. Soc. Newspaper Editors, Fla. C. of C. Home: 111 Bay Point Dr NE Saint Petersburg FL 33704-3805 Office: St Petersburg Times 490 1st Ave S Saint Petersburg FL 33701-4204 also: PO Box 1121 Saint Petersburg FL 33731-1121

**TASHIMA, ATSUSHI WALLACE,** federal judge; b. Santa Maria, Calif., June 24, 1934; s. Yasutaro and Aya (Sasaki) Tashima; m. Nora Kiyo Inadomi, Jan. 27, 1957; children: Catherine Y., Christopher I., Jonathan I. AB in Polit. Sci., UCLA, 1958; LLB, Harvard U., 1961. Bar: Calif. 1962. Dep. atty. gen. State of Calif., 1961—67; atty. Spreckels Sugar divsn. Amstar Corp., 1968—72, v.p., gen. atty. Spreckels Sugar divsn., 1972—77; ptnr. Morrison & Foerster, L.A., 1977—80; judge U.S. Dist. Ct. (ctrl. dist.), L.A., Calif., 1980—96, U.S. Ct. Appeals (9th cir.), Pasadena, Calif., 1996—2003, sr. judge, 2003—. Mem. Calif. Com. Bar Examiners, 1978—80. With USMC, 1953—56. Mem.: ABA, LA County Bar Assn. Democrat. Office: Richard A Chambers US Ct Appeals PO Box 91510 125 S Grand Ave Pasadena CA 91109-1510*

**TASHJIAN, BEATRICE CHARMIAN,** composer, educator; b. Detroit, Feb. 4, 1950; d. Berj Tashjian and Mildred Rasanen; m. L. Patrick McClure, July 4, 1975; children: Aric, Alana. Studied with Scott Willitis, Am. Conservatory Music, 1968—71; MusB, Northwestern U., 1971; MA, Stanford U., Calif., 1974; studied with M. William Karlins and Alan Stout, Northwestern U.; MusD, Nortwestern U., 1984; studied with Barry L. Vercoe, MIT, 1982; studied with Gyorgy Ligeti and John Chowning. Instr. Northwestern U., Evanston, Ill., 1977—78, 1982—83; adj. prof. Sch. Music Depaul U., Chgo., 1981—. Harper Coll. Instr. Columbia Coll., Chgo., 1984—88, Lake Forest Coll., Ill., 1998—99. Composer: (TV comml.) Nat. Heart Found., 1972; musician: Contemporary Music Ensemble; composer: (songs) Music for Flute, Harp, and Basic Drum, 1990, Armandohos, 1970, Antiphonies I, 1977, String Quartet, 1987, Chorus and Brass Sextet, 1989, Brass Quintet, 1991, Coalescences, 1993, Expressions of Youth, 1995, Songs of the Sea, 1997, others. Mem.: Am. String Tchrs. Assn., Am. Music Ctr., Broadcast Music Inc., Coll. Music Soc., Internat. Alliance Women in Music, Pi Kappa Lambda, Sigma Alpha Iota. Home: 1260 Meadow Lane Deerfield IL 60015

**TASMAN, ALICE LEA MAST,** not-for-profit fundraiser; d. Clarence Kurtz Mast and Florence Larue Barkley; m. William S. Tasman, Nov. 8, 1962; children: James B., W. Graham, Alice. BA, Barnard Coll., 1956; postgrad., U. Pa. Nat. Am. Cathedral, Paris, 1953—54; asst. dir. pub. rels. Phila. Art Mus., 1956—61; pub. rels. exec. WUHY-FM, 1976—77; cons. Franklin Mint, 1991—94. Author: Wedding Album: Customs & Lore Through the Ages, 1981, Adam, A Three Island Cat, 1984. Women's bd. Thomas Jefferson U. Hosp., 1983—; chmn. Art in City Hall, 1995—2003; fundraising com., spl. events Recording for Blind, 1993—95; devel. com., trustee Woodmere Art Mus., 1994—2003; mem. Associated Svcs. for Blind; originator, chmn. annual exhibit Form in Art, 1987—; vol. Phila. Mus. Art, 1991—; annual concert and ball com. Phila. Orch., 1972—75; libr. Chestnut Hill Acad. and Springside Sch., 1977—78; antiques show com. U. Pa., 1972—75; coord. long-term patient care Chestnut Hill Hosp., 1981; fundraising and publicity chair Project Orbis, 1982; fundraiser Am. Diabetes Assn., 1984; vol. Chestnut Hill Hosp., 1978—87; hon. chair fundraising Overbrook Sch. for Blind, 1989; fundraiser Am. Indian Fund, 1989; hon. chair symposium, fundraiser 1st Nat. Inst. Blind Artists, 1990; internat. ambassador City of Phila., 1993; assoc. trustee Sulgrave Manor, London; fundraising, corp. devel. exec. Wills Eye Hosp., 1996—, chair 17th ann. forum art exhbn.; co-organizer Haitian Arts Exhbn. Friends of Hosp. Albert Schweitzer, Haiti; bd. dirs. Chestnut Hill Presbyn. Ch., 1989—93, Nat. Exhibits by Blind Artists, 1987—, Chestnut Hill Women's Com. Phila. Orch., 1965—, Chestnut Hill Cmty. Ctr. and Women's Exchange, 1978—; bd. dirs. coun. visual arts Chestnut Hill Acad., 1997—; bd. dirs. Art in City Hall, 1993—2003, Hitchcock Found., 1982—83. Recipient Cert. of Appreciation. Phila. Arts Fest., 1959, Wills Eye Hosp., 1994, Overbrook Sch. for Blind award, 1989, Louis Braille award, Associated Svcs. for Blind, 1993, Founder's award, Nat. Exhibits by Blind Artists, Disting. Daughters of Pa. award, Gov. and Mrs. Tom Ridge, 1997, Lady of Dumbarton award, Nat. Soc. Colonial Dames, 1999, Lifetime Achievement award, Little Rock Found., 2001. Mem.: Friends Vielles Maisons Francaises,

Am. Ophthalmology Soc. (chair pres. dinner 1989—), Am. Bd. Ophthalmology (chair 75th anniversary dinner 1992), Am. Acad. Ophthalmology (chair Christian med. dental luncheon 1991—92, organizer 2nd Ann. Orbital Gala), French Huguenot Soc., Chestnut Hill Hist. Soc. (pres. 1972—74, program chair 1974—75, fundraising and spl. events chair 1981—), Nat. Soc. Colonial Dames Commonwealth Pa. (house com. 1980—89, garden com. 1987, house com. 1993—94, chair program com. 1993—96, first v.p. 1998—2002, co-chair capital campaign fund 1999—2001, pres. 2002—05, Alice Lea Mast Tasman ednl. chair), Rotary, Jr. League. Avocations: travel, skiing, painting, crafts, gardening.

**TASMAN, ALLAN,** psychiatry educator; b. Louisville, Feb. 8, 1947; s. Goodman and Zelda Tasman; m. Cathy Faye Goldstein, May 24, 1970. BA in Chemistry, Franklin and Marshall Coll., 1969; MD, U. Ky., 1973. Diplomate Am. Bd. Psychiatry and Neurology. Resident in psychiatry U. Ky. Med. Sch., Lexington, 1973-74, U. Cin. Med. Sch., 1974-76; asst. prof. psychiatry U. Conn. Med. Sch., Farmington, 1976-82, assoc. prof. psychiatry, 1982-88, prof. psychiatry, 1988-91; prof. psychiatry and behavioral scis., tenure and chmn. U. Louisville Sch. Medicine, 1991—. Editor: Annual Review of Psychiatry, 1989-92, Clinical Challenges in Psychiatry, 1993, Less Time to Do More, 1993; sr. editor: Textbook of Psychiatry, 1997, 2d edit., 2003; assoc. editor Am. Jour. Psychotherapy, 1999—; founding dep. editor Jour. Psychotherapy Practice and Rsch., 1992-99. Recipient Alpha Omega Alpha Faculty award, 2002, Pres.'s Disting. Faculty award for svc. to the profession, U. Louisville, 2003. Fellow Am. Psychiat. Assn. (v.p. 1996-98, pres.-elect 1998-99, pres. 1999-2000, Nancy Roeske award for excellence in med. student edn. 1991, Irma Bland award for excellence in resident tchg. 2005); mem. Am. Assn. Dirs. of Psychiat. Residency Tng. (pres. 1993-94), Assn. Acad. Psychiatry (pres. 1993-94, Educator of Yr. award 2000), Am. Assn. Chmn. Depts. Psychiatry (pres. 1996-97, 97-98), World Psychiat. Assn. (bd. dirs. 2002—, sec. for edn. 2005—), Royal Coll. Psychiatrists, Pacific Rim Coll. Psychiatrists (pres.-elect 2004—). Office: U Louisville Sch Medicine Dept Psychiatry Behavioral Scis Louisville KY 40292-0001

**TASMAN, WILLIAM SAMUEL,** ophthalmologist, educator; b. Phila., 1929; MD, Temple U., 1955. Intern Phila. Gen. Hosp., 1955-56; resident in ophthalmology Wills Eye Hosp., Phila., 1959-61; fellow Mass. Eye and Ear Infirmary, Boston, 1961-62; prof., chmn. dept. ophthalmology Jefferson Med. Coll., Phila., 1985—; attending surgeon Wills Eye Hosp., Phila., 1974—, ophthalmologist-in-chief, 1985—. Mem. AMA, Am. Acad. Ophthalmologists (sec. ann. meeting 1992-97, pres. elect. 1998, pres. 1999), Pa. Acad. Ophthalmologists, Am. Ophthal. Soc. (pres. 1999). Office: Wills Eye Hosp 840 Walnut St Ste 1510 Philadelphia PA 19107-5109

**TASOOJI, MICHAEL B.,** retail executive; m. Linda Tasooji; 3 children. BS in internat. trade and quantitative bus. analysis, U. So. Calif., MBA in internat. fin. and bus. econ. With Getty Oil Co., Columbia Pictures Studio; v.p. application systems Bergen Brunswig Corp.; v.p., info. svcs. Disneyland, 1995—2000; sr. v.p., CIO Walt Disney Attractions, 2000, Walt Disney Co., 2000—03; exec. v.p., CIO Gap, Inc., 2003—. Office: Gap Inc 2 Folsom St San Francisco CA 94105

**TASSÉ, ROGER,** lawyer, former Canadian government official; b. Montreal, Que., Can., 1931; BA, Coll. St. Marie, Montreal, 1952; Lic. in Law, U. Montreal, 1955; diploma d'Etudes Superieures, U. Ottawa, Ont., Can., 1957. Bar: Que. 1956, Ont. 1986; called to Queens Counsel 1971. Joined Dept. Justice, 1956, civil law counsel for Can. govt., from 1957, supt. bankruptcy, 1965-68, asst. dep. min. consumer and corp. affairs, 1968-72; dep. min. Dept. of Solicitor Gen., 1972-77; dep. min. of justice, atty. gen. of Can., 1977-85; ptnr. Land Michener Lash Johnston, Toronto and Ottawa, Noel Décary Aubry & Assocs., Hull, Que., 1985-88; exec. v.p. legal and environ. affairs Bell Can., 1988-91; of counsel Fraser & Beatty, Toronto, 1992-95, Gowling, Lafleur & Henderson, Ottawa, 1995—. Prin. constl. advisor to Spl. Joint Com. of the Senate and the House of Commons on a Renewed Can., 1991-92. Mem. Citizens' Forum on Canada's Future, 1990; co-chair task force Can. Mags., 1993; mem. DTH Panel, 1995. Decorated officer Order of Can. Avocations: skiing, tennis. Office: Gowling Lafleur Henderson LLP 160 Elgin St Ste 2600 Ottawa ON Canada K1P 1C3 Fax: (613) 563-9869. Office Phone: 813-786-0208. E-mail: roger.tasse@gowlings.com

**TASSINARI, MELISSA SHERMAN,** reproductive toxicologist; b. Lawrence, Mass., Sept. 26, 1953; m. R. Peter Tassinari; children: Michael, Emily, Sara. AB, Mt. Holyoke Coll., 1975; postgrad., U. St. Andrews, Scotland, 1973-74; PhD, Med. Coll. Wis., 1979. Diplomate Am. Bd. Toxicology. Rsch. asst. in orthopedic surgery, Lab. Human Biochemistry Children's Hosp. Med. Ctr., Boston, 1981-83; rsch. affiliate in toxicology Forsyth Dental Ctr., Boston, 1983-86, staff assoc. dept. toxicology, 1986-89; asst. prof. cell biology U. Mass. Med. Ctr., Worcester, 1989-91; head reproductive and developmental toxicology Pfizer Global R&D, Groton/New London, Conn., 1991—99, group dir. worldwide safety scis., 2001—04, sr. dir. regulatory policy and intelligence, 2004—. Rsch. fellow oral biology Harvard Sch. Dental Medicine, Boston, 1978-81, instr. oral biology and pathophysiology, 1981-83; asst. prof. biol. scis. Wellesley Coll., Mass., 1985-91, biology Simmons Coll., Boston, 1986-87. Contbr. abstracts, articles to profl. jours. Mem. Teratology Soc. (coun. 2000—, v.p. 2004, pres. 2005—), Neurobehavioral Teratology Soc., Mid. Atlantic Reprodn. and Teratology Assn. (steering com. 1994), Midwest Teratology Assn., Soc. Toxicology. Office: Pfizer Inc 50 Pequot Ave New London CT 06320

**TASSLER, NINA,** broadcast executive; Pres. CBS Entertainment, 2004—. Mailing: CBS Entertainment CBS Television City 7800 Beverly Blvd Los Angeles CA 90036*

**TASSONE, GELSOMINA (GESSIE TASSONE),** metal products executive; b. NYC, July 8, 1944; d. Enrico and A. Cira (Petriccione) Gargiulo; children: Ann Marie, Margaret, Theresa, Christine; m. Armando Tassone, Mar. 20, 1978. Student, Orange County Community Coll., 1975-79, Iona Coll., 1980—. Head bookkeeper Gargiulo Bros. Builders, N.Y.C., 1968-72; pres., owner A&T Iron Works Inc., New Rochelle, NY, 1973—. Recipient Profl. Image award Contractors Coun. Greater N.Y.C., 1986; named Businessowner of Yr., Contractors Coun. Greater N.Y.C., 1985, N.Y. State Small Bus. Person of Yr., 1988, Entrepreneur of Yr. Inc. mag., 1990; company named a Successful Small Bus. Co. Westchester County C. of C./BSBA, 1986-88. Mem. Nat. Ornamental and Miscellaneous Metal Assn., Builders Inst. Westchester and Putnam County, Westchester Assn. Women Bus. Owners, Profl. Women in Constrn., New Rochelle C. of C. Office: A&T Iron Works Inc 25 Cliff St New Rochelle NY 10801-6803 Office Phone: 914-632-8992. Personal E-mail: gesjames@aol.com. Business E-Mail: info@atironworks.com

**TASSONE, REBECCA C.,** elementary school educator; d. Anthony D. and Laura B. Tassone. BS in Elem. Edn., Millersville U., Pa., 2000. Libr. asst. Kaltreider Libr., Red Lion, Pa., 1994—95; dir. pub. rels. A.C.M.O., Millersville, 1999—2000; tutor Red Lion Area Sch., 2000—04, tchr., 2000—; cons. Mary Kay, 2004—. Coach, tutor Red Lion Schs., 2001—02, mem. sch. spirit com., 2003—, mem. bldg. coms., 2000—, chair writing conf., 2000—02. Dancer One Mo' Time, 2003; singer: Cat's Meow, 2004. Active Heifer Internat., Little Rock, 2000—; United Way, York, Pa., 2000—; mem. Food for Thought, 2005—. Scholar, Millersville U., 2000. Mem.: ASCD, Internat. Reading Assn., Phi Delta Kappa, Phi Kappa Phi. Avocations: reading, writing, acting.

**TASUMI, MASAHIRO,** science educator; s. Kozo and Michiko Tasumi; m. Nao Nao Mizutani, Dec. 24, 2003; 1 child, Maho Mizutani. BS in Environ. Sci., Tottori U., Japan, 1996, MS in Environ. Sci., 1999; PhD in Bio and Agrl. Engring., U. Idaho, Moscow, 2003. Vis. rschr. Internat. Water Mgmt. Inst., Colombo, Sri Lanka, 1997—98; postdoctoral fellow U. of Idaho, Kimberly, 2003—05, asst. prof., 2005—. Recipient Outstanding Jour. Paper award, Paddy and Water Environment, 2003. Mem.: Remote Sensing Soc. of Japan,

Japanese Soc. of Irrigation, Drainage and Reclamation Engring., Environ. and Water Resources Inst. of the ASCE, U.S. Com. on Irrigation, Drainage and Flood Control. Office: U Idaho 3793n 3600e Kimberly ID 83341 Office Phone: 208-423-6669. E-mail: tasumi@kimberly.uidaho.edu.

**TATA, GIOVANNI,** publishing executive; b. Taranto, Italy, Apr. 26, 1954; came to U.S., 1974, naturalized, 1982; s. Vito and Angela (Colucci) T.; m. Brenda Susan Smith, Feb. 14, 1978; children: Elizabeth Ariana, Katherine Allison, Margaret Anne, Michael Anthony, Hanna Amelia. BS cum laude, Brigham Young U., 1977, MA, 1980; grad. cert. area studies, U. Utah, 1980, PhD, 1986; postgrad., U. Turin, Italy, 1980-81. Archaeologist Utah State Hist. Soc., Salt Lake City, 1979; instr. dept. langs. U. Utah, Salt Lake City, 1983-85; Mediterranean specialist Soc. Early Hist. Archaeology, Provo, Utah, 1978-91; rsch. fellow Direzione Gen. Cooperazione Sci. Culturale e Technica, Rome, 1980-81; mus. curator Pioneer Trail State Park, Salt Lake City, 1982-83; instr. dept. art Brigham Young U., Provo, 1982-84, dir. creative works, 1996—; rsch. curator Utah Mus. Fine Arts, Salt Lake City, 1985-87; pres. Mus. Info. Sys., 1987-93, Transoft Internat., Inc., 1988—. Chmn. 35th Ann. Symposium on the Archaeology of the Scriptures, 1986, Taras Devel. Corp., 1994—97, MuseMedia, Inc., 1995—2000. Patentee method and system for computerized learning, response, and evaluation. Brigham Young U. scholar. Mem.: Intellectual Property Owners Assn., Assn. Univ. Tech. Mgrs., Nat. Coun. Museums, Am. Assn. Museums. Republican. Mem. Ch. Jesus Christ of Latter-day Saints. Office Phone: 801-422-3724. Business E-Mail: giovanni_tata@byu.edu. E-mail: tata@lexinet.com.

**TATA, ROBERT JOSEPH,** retired geographer, educator; b. New Britain, Conn., Mar. 3, 1935; s. Rosario and Anna Marie Tata; m. Maryann Hanson; children: Virginia Tata-Phillips, Amy Tata-Winslow, Steven. AB in Geography, Syracuse U., 1957, MA in Geography, 1961, PhD in Geography, 1968; MA in Econs., Fla. Atlantic U., 1975. Asst. prof. Fla. Atlantic U., Boca Raton, 1964—67, assoc. prof., 1968—80, chair geography, 1970—76, prof., 1980—99, prof. emeritus, 1999—. Cons. faculty U.S. Army Command and Gen. Staff, Ft. Leavenworth, Kans., 1967—80; cons. Pan Am Inst. Geography & History, 1974—75; reviewer NSF, Washington, 1982—98. Author: (book) Structural Changes in Puerto Rico's Economy, 1980, Haiti: Land of Poverty, 1982; editl. bd.: The Southeastern Geographer, 1968—72; contbr. articles to profl. jours. Col. U.S. Army, 1957—86. Rsch. grantee, U.S. Army Engr. Rsch. Inst. Mem.: Assn. Am. Geographers, Fla. Soc. Geographers (past. v.p., past pres. 1977—79, Profl. Cartography award 1966), Mil. Officers' Assn., Sigma Xi. Avocations: reading, travel, fishing, baseball, wine. Home: 2350 Harbour Oaks Dr Longboat Key FL 34228 Home Fax: 941-387-8958. Personal E-mail: b33bacchus@verizon.net.

**TATÁR, ANNA,** library director; Grad., DePauw U.; MLS, U. Mich. Dir. San Diego Pub. Libr. Named one of 50 People to Watch in 2003, San Diego Mag. Mem.: ALA. Office: San Diego Pub Libr Ctrl Div 820 E St San Diego CA 92101-6478 Office Phone: 619-236-5870. E-mail: atatar@sandiego.gov.*

**TATAR, JEROME F.,** business products executive; V.p., operating officer Mead Corp., Dayton, Ohio, 1994—96, pres., COO, 1996—97, chmn., CEO, 1997—2002; chmn. MeadWestvaco Corp., 2002. Bd. mem. Robbins & Myers Inc., Nat. City Corp., Bartech Group Inc. Office: Mead Corp Courthouse Plz NE Dayton OH 45463-0001

**TATARSKII, VALERIAN IL'ICH,** physics researcher; b. Kharkov, USSR, Oct. 13, 1929; s. Il'ya A. and Elizabeth A. (Lapis) T.; m. Maia S. Granovskaia, Dec. 22, 1955; 1 child, Viatcheslav V. MS, Moscow State U., 1952; PhD, Acoustical Inst. Acad. Scis., 1957; DSc, Gorky State U., 1962. Scientific rschr. Geophys. Inst. Acad. Sci. USSR, Moscow, 1953-56, Inst. Atmospheric Physics, Acad. Sci. USSR, Moscow, 1956-59, sr. scientific rschr., 1959-78, head lab., 1978-90; head dept. Lebedev. Phys. Inst. Acad. Sci., Moscow, 1990-91; sr. rsch. assoc. U. Colo. Coop. Inst. for Rsch. in Environ. Sci., Boulder, 1991—2001; sr. rsch. scientist Zel Techs. and NOAA/PSD, Boulder, 2001—. Author: Wave Propagation in a Turbulent Medium, 1961, 67, The Effect of the Turbulent Atmosphere on Wave Propagation, 1971, Principles of Statistical Radiophysics, 1989; contbr. articles to profl. jours. Recipient of Max Born award, 1994, Optical Soc. of Am., USSR State prize, 1990. Fellow Optical Soc. Am. (Max Born award 1994), Inst. of Physics; mem. Russian Acad. Sci., U.S.A. Nat. Acad. Engring., N.Y. Acad. Sci. Avocations: classical music, kayaking. Office: Zel Tech/NOAA PSD 325 Broadway St Boulder CO 80305-3328 Office Phone: 303-497-3668. E-mail: vtatarskii@hotmail.com.

**TATAVARTHY, APARNA,** biologist, researcher; arrived in U.S., 1997; d. Subbarao and Manikyalakshmi Kavuru; m. Viswanadh R. Tatavarthy, Oct. 25, 1997; 1 child, Anjali M. BS, Mas. A.V.N. Coll., 1995; MS, Andhra U., 1997; PhD, U. South Fla., Tampa, 2003. Tchg. asst. dept. biology U. South Fla., Tampa, 2000—02, rsch. asst. Ctr. for Biol. Def., 2002—. Contbr. articles to profl. jours.

**TATE, DEBORAH TAYLOR,** commissioner; b. Murfreesboro, Tenn. d. Louis Carlton Taylor; m. William H. Tate; children: Will, Taylor, Carlton. BA, JD, U. Tenn.; attended, Vanderbilt U. Cert.: Tenn. Supreme Ct. (Rule 31 Mediator). Atty., sr. policy advisor to Gov. Lamar Alexander and Gov. Don Sundquist, Tenn.; dir. Tenn. Regulatory Authority, 2000—06, chmn., 2003—04; commr. FCC, Washington, 2006—. Former dir. state and local policy ctr. Vanderbilt Inst. for Pub. Policy Studies; guest lectr. Vanderbilt U. Fellow: Nashville Bar Found.; mem.: Lawyer's Assn. for Women, Nashville Bar Assn. Office: FCC 445 12th St SW Washington DC 20554

**TATE, HAROLD SIMMONS, JR.,** lawyer; b. Taylors, S.C., Sept. 19, 1930; s. Harold Simmons and Cleone (Clayton) T.; m. Elizabeth Anne Coker, Dec. 22, 1952; children— Mary Elizabeth Anne, Martha Coker, Virginia Clayton. Degree in Internat. Law and Rels. cum laude, Harvard U., 1951, postgrad., 1954, JD, 1956; MA, U. SC, 2005. Bar: S.C. 1956. Ptnr. Haynsworth Sinkler Boyd, PA, Columbia, SC, 1962—. Chmn. U.S. Dist. Ct. (S.C.) Adv. Com., 1984—; lectr. Am. Law Inst.-ABA seminars; adv. com. on rules and procedures U.S. Ct. Appeals (4th cir.), 1990-95. Co-author: South Carolina Appellate Practice, 1985; bd. editors Federal Litigation Guide Reporter, 1985—; co-draftsman S.C. Rules of Evidence, 1995; contbr. articles and book revs. to profl. jours. Chmn. Richland County Mental Health Ctr., 1965-66; co-chmn. Columbia Hearing and Speech Ctr., 1962-64; mem. admission and scholarship com. Harvard U., 1961—; within. subcom. on legislation, legislation and fin. study commn. Gov.'s Adv. Group on Mental Health Planning, 1963-65; chmn. Columbia Bd. Supervisory of Registration, 1961-70; pres. Columbia Philharm. Orch., 1966-67, Town Theatre, 1967-70; bd. trustee Richland County Pub. Libr., 1973-78, Hist. Columbia Found., 1971-75, Caroliniana Soc., 1978—, Bostick Charitable Trust, 1968—, Archaeol. Rsch. Trust, 2000—; bd. mgrs. S.C. Hist. Soc., 1993-99, 2002—; commr. S.C. Commn. of Archives and History, 1995—. Capt. U.S. Army, 1951-53. Recipient DuRant award Disting Pub. Svc., 2001. Fellow Am. Coll. Trial Lawyers; mem. ABA, Am. Law Inst., Am. Judicature Soc., S.C. Bar Assn., Assn. Bar City N.Y., Richland County Bar Assn., Harvard Law Sch. Assn. S.C. (sec.-treas. 1968-70, pres. 1988—), Forest Lake Country Club, Columbia Drama Club (pres. 1963-64), Palmetto Club (sec: 1963-70, pres. 1973-76), The Forum Club, Harvard Club (N.Y.C.), Harvard Club S.C., Carolina Yacht Club. Episcopalian. Home: 15 Gibbes Ct Columbia SC 29201-3923 Office: Haynsworth Sinkler Boyd PA Fl 22 1201 Main St Ste 2200 Columbia SC 29201-3232 Office Phone: 803-779-3080. Business E-Mail: state@hsblawfirm.com.

**TATE, JAMES VINCENT,** poet, English educator; b. Kansas City, Mo., Dec. 8, 1943; s. Samuel Vincent Appleby and Betty Jean Whitsitt. BA, Kans. State Coll., 1965; MFA, U. Iowa, 1967. Instr. U. Iowa, Iowa City, 1966-67; vis. lectr. U. Calif., Berkeley, 1967-68; asst. prof. English Columbia U., NYC, 1969-71; from assoc. prof. to dist. univ. prof English U. Mass., Amherst, 1971—. Poet-in-residence Emerson Coll., 1970-71; cons. Coord. Coun. Literary Mags., 1971-74, Ky. Arts Commn., 1979; mem. Bollingen Prize Com., 1974-75; poetry editor Dickinson Rev., 1967-76; trustee, assoc. editor

Pym-Randall Pr., 1968-80; assoc. editor Barn Dream Pr. Author: (poems) Cages, 1966, The Destination, 1967, The Lost Pilot, 1967 (Yale Younger Poets award 1966), Notes of Woe, 1968, Camping in the Valley, 1968, Mystics in Chicago, 1968, The Torches, 1968, Row with Your Hair, 1969, Is There Anything?, 1969, Shepherds of the Mist, 1969, Amnesia People, 1970, Are You Ready Mary Baker Eddy, 1970, Deaf Girl Playing, 1970, The Oblivion Ha-Ha, 1970, Wrong Songs, 1970, Hints to Pilgrims, 1971, Nobody Goes to Visit the Insane Anymore, 1971, Absences, 1972, Apology for Eating Geoffrey Movius' Hyacinth, 1972, A Dime Found in the Snow, 1973, Hottentot Ossuary, 1974, Marfa, 1974, Suffering Bastards, 1975, Who Gets the Bitterroot?, 1976, Viper Jazz, 1976, Riven Doggeries, 1979, The Rustling of Foliage, the Memory of Caresses, 1979, If It Would All Please Hurray, 1980, Land of Little Sticks, 1981, Constant Defender, 1983, Just Shades, 1985, Reckoner, 1986, Distance from Loved Ones, 1990, Selected Poems, 1991 (Pulitzer Prize for poetry 1992), Worshipful Company of Fletchers, 1993 (Nat. Book Award for Poetry 1994), Shroud of the Gnome, 1997, Return to the City of White Donkeys, 2004, Memoirs of the Hawk, 2005; (novel) Lucky Darryl, 1977. Named Poet of Yr. by Phi Beta Kappa, 1972; recipient Nat. Inst. Arts and Letters award for poetry, 1974; Mass. Arts and Humanities fellow, 1975, Guggenheim fellow, 1976, Nat. Endowment for the Arts fellow, 1980. Office: U Mass Bartlette Hall Dept English Amherst MA 01003-0515

**TATE, JOHN TORRENCE,** mathematics professor, researcher; b. Mpls., Mar. 13, 1925; BA, Harvard U., 1946; PhD, Princeton U., 1950. Sid W. Richardson chair math. U. Tex., Austin, 1990—. Co-recipient Leroy P. Steele prize Am. Math. Soc., 1995, Cole prize in number theory, 1956, Wolf prize in math. Wolf Found., Israel, 2003. Mem. Nat. Acad. Scis., Academie des Scis. (Paris), mem. London Mathematical Society. Office: Univ Texas at Austin Dept Math 1 University Station C1200 Austin TX 78712-0257 Office Phone: 512-471-7121, 512-471-7711. Office Fax: 512-471-9038. E-mail: tate@math.utexas.edu.*

**TATE, JOHN WILLIAM,** consumer products company executive, former food products executive; BA in Econs., U. Tex., 1972. Various fin. and gen. mgmt. positions Dole Food Co. Inc., Westlake Village, Calif.; CFO fresh vegetables divsn. Dole Food Co., 1993-96, CFO Dole Europe Paris, CFO Westlake Village, Calif., 1998—2000, Krispy Kreme Doughnuts, Inc., Winston-Salem, NC, 2000—02; COO Krispy Kreme Doughnuts Inc., Winston-Salem, NC, 2002—04; exec. v.p., COO Restoration Hardware, Inc., Corte Madera, Calif., 2004—. With USAF, 1973-79. Office: Restoration Hardware Inc 15 Koch Rd Ste J Corte Madera CA 94925

**TATE, LARENZ,** actor; b. Chgo., Ill., Sept. 8, 1975; Actor: (TV series) The Twilight Zone, 1985, Hunter, 1987, Amen, 1988, 21 Jump Street, 1989, The Wonder Years, 1989, Matlock, 1989, New Attitude, 1990, Family Matters, 1990—91, The Royal Family, 1991, Fresh Prince of Bel-Air, 1992, South Central, 1994, Love Monkey, 2006; (TV films) The Women of Brewster Place, 1989, Seeds of Tragedy, 1991; (films) Menace II Society, 1993, The Inkwell, 1994, Dead Presidents, 1995, Love Jones, 1997, The Postman, 1997, Why Do Fools Fall in Love, 1998, Love Come Down, 2000, Biker Boyz, 2003, A Man Apart, 2003, Crash, 2004 (recipient, Outstanding Performance, SAG awards, 2006), Ray, 2004, Waist Deep, 2006. Office: Lions Gate Entertainment 555 Brooksbank Ave Vancouver BC V7J 355 Canada*

**TATE, NANCY JANE,** secondary school educator; b. Texarkana, Ark., Aug. 3, 1954; d. Robert Ellis and Pauline (McAfee) DeFee; m. William Tate, June 6, 1974 (dec. 1993); children: William, Christina. BS in Edn., U. Ark., 1976, MA, 1981. Tchr. Liberty-Eylau Ind. Sch. Dist., Texarkana, 1977—. Dir. dist. alt. ednl. program Libery-Eylau Ind. Sch. Dist., Texarkana, Tex., 2005—06. Named Dist. Tchr. of Yr., 2000. Republican. Avocation: travel. Home: 3206 WIlliamsburg Ln Texarkana TX 75503 Office: Liberty-Eylau ISD 2905 Leopard Dr Texarkana TX 75501-7817 Office Phone: 903-838-9959.

**TATE, SHEILA BURKE,** public relations executive; b. Washington, Mar. 3, 1942; d. Eugene L. and Mary J. (Doherty) Burke; m. William J. Tate, May 2, 1981 (dec. Aug. 1998); children: Hager Burke Patton, Courtney Paige Patton Manzel; m. John K. Yovel, Nov. 26, 2005. BA in Journalism, Duquesne U., 1964; postgrad. in mass comm., U. Denver, 1975—76. Rsch. asst. Westinghouse Air Brake Co.; asst. account exec. Falhgren and Assocs.; copywriter Ketchum, MacLeod and Grove, 1964—66; account exec. Burson-Marsteller Assocs., Pitts., 1967; sr. v.p. Washington, 1985—87; pub. rels. mgr. Colo. Nat. Bank, Denver, 1967—70; account exec. Hill and Knowlton, Inc., Houston, 1977—78, v.p. Washington, 1978—81; dep. to the chmn. Hill and Knowlton Inc., Washington, 1987—88; press sec. to First Lady White House, Washington, 1981—85; press sec. George Bush for Pres. Campaign, 1988; press sec. to Pres.-elect George Bush, 1988—89; vice chmn. Cassidy and Assocs. Pub. Affairs, Washington, 1989—91; pres. Powell Tate, Washington, 1991—99, vice-chmn., 1999—. Bd. dirs., former mem. Corp. for Pub. Broadcasting, vice chmn., 1990—92, chmn., 1992—94; bd. dirs. Ethics Resource Ctr., Washington, Guest Svcs. Corp., Fairfax, Va. Mem. nat. adv. bd. The Salvation Army; adv. bd. Am. Acad. Family Physicians, Kansas City, Kans. Mem.: Nat. Press Club, Belfair Club, Farmington Country Club, Washington Golf and Country Club, Duquesne U. Century Club. Office: Powell Tate 700 13th St NW Ste 1000 Washington DC 20005-5926 Business E-Mail: state@webershandwick.com.

**TATE, STANLEY G.,** diversified business executive, expert witness; b. N.Y., Apr. 25, 1928; s. Jack A. and Anna B. Tatelman; m. Joanne Marilyn Greenwood, Sept. 10, 1949; children: J. Kenneth, James David, Linda Sue Tate Best. BA, U. Fla. 1946, BS, 1948, postgrad., 1949, Columbia U., NYU; B of Arts and Scis. (hon.), Miami Dade Coll., 2005. Nat. cert appraiser; lic. gen. contractor, Fla.; cert. in forensic documentaton Am. Bd. Forensic Examiners. Founder Stanley Tate Builders, Inc., North Miami, Fla., 1954—, Investment Diversified Ltd., North Miami, Fla., 1964—, High Point of Delray Builders, Inc., North Miami, 1969—, Tate Enterprises, North Miami, 1986—. Chmn. bd. Envirocivil Engring. Corp.; receiver for real estate devels. and other bus. entitites throughout U.S.; expert witness in fed. and state cts. on real estate matters in litig., before U.S. Ho. of Reps. and Senate coms. on fed. legis. in housing and banking areas; pres., COO, King Internat. Corp., 1985-86, CEO Assoc. Mortgage Investors, 1971-81; past dir., chmn. region I adv. bd. Nat. Bd. Resolution Trust Corp.; past mem. adv. bd. BlueStone Capital Ptnrs., N.Y.C., BlueStone Capital Online, Inc.; bd. dirs. KFx, Inc.; charter mem. adv. coun. U. Fla. Sch. Bldg. Constrn.; hon mem. adv. staff Apt. and Constrn. News; guest lectr. U.Miami Bus. Sch.; guest spkr., lectr.; participant numerous industry-related seminars and programs; dir. Team Fla./Free Trade Ams. Contbr. numerous articles on gen. real estate and condominium develing, mktg. and Property devel. to profl. publs. Past bd. dirs. Miami Heart Inst., Fla. League Cities; past trustee pub. health trust Met. Dade County, Fla.; also past mem. exec. com.; past mem. Performing Arts Ctr. Trust, Inc., Dade County; past mem. and vice chmn. bd. Fla. Endowment Fund for Higher Edn.; past pres. Temple Israel, Miami, now trustee; past bd. dirs. and mem. exec. com. Miami City Ballet; past chmn. Metro Dade County Housing Oversight Com.; past bd. dirs. and vice chmn. Magnet Ednl. Choice Assn., Inc.; past chmn. Dade County Housing and Urban Devel. Adv. Bd.; past mem. adv. exec. com. YWCA Miami; mem. campaign cabinet United Way Dade County; trustee Fla. Taxwatch, Inc., James E. Scott Cmty. Assn., Mt. Sinai Med. Ctr.; bd. dirs. Miami Jewish Home and Hosp. for Aged, Keep Dade Beautiful, Dade County unit Am. Cancer Soc., Miami-Dade C.C. Found., Fla. Coun. of 100, Fla. Coun. on Econ. Edn., Easter Seals Dade County; trustee Thomas U., Kids Voting U.S.A., United Way Dade County; mem. family counseling svcs. adv. bd. Family Svc. Found., Inc.; mem., chmn. Fla. Prepaid Postsecondary Edn. Expense Bd., 1st chmn., 1987-; mem., chmn. Fla. Prepaid Coll. Found.; mem. cmty. adv. bd. Jr. League Miami; mem. exec. com. Fla. Guardian Ad Litem Program for 11th Jud. Cir.; hon. trustee Miami Children's Mus.; mem. program coordinating com. Dade County Family Self Sufficiency Program; mem. adv. coun. Voices for Children; past asst. mayor and mayor City of Bay Harbor Islands, Fla.; endowed tchg. chair Miami-Dade C.C. Med. Campus; pres. bd. dirs. Elephant Forum; mem. Ptnrs. in Productivity Task Force; mem. Fannie Mae's Nat. Housing Impact Adv. Coun.; mem. Miami-Dade adv. bd. Gulf Coast Jewish Family Svcs. (non-custodial

parent employment program); mem. Assn. Governing Bds. of Univs., Am. Nurses Credentialing Ctr.; mem. adv. coun. Fla. Bd. Edn.; bd. govs. Rep. Jewish Coalition. Recipient Shalom award State of Israel, 1971, Ben Gurion award, spl. honoree Israel Bonds Campaign and Greater Miami Jewish Fedn., Cmty. Star award Family Counslng Svcs. Greater Miami, 1991, award for devoted outstanding cmty. svc. B'nai B'rith, 1992, Dorothy Shula award United Way, 1996, Unsung Hero award Youth Law Ctr., 1996, Most Valuable Protector Vol. award Voices for Children, 1999, Disting. Svc. award Coll. Savs. Plan-USA Network, 1999, Eagle award for Outstanding Cmty. Svc., Miami-Dade Republican Pub. Party, 2001, Disting. Svc. award Fla. Student Assn., 2002, Arete award, Vol. Adv. Of Yr., Miami-Dade County Commn. on Ethics and Pub. Trust, 2003; recipient Outstanding Citizen award and named hon. Dade County Mayor, 1998; named Bus. Assoc. of Yr., Hurricane chpt. Am. Bus. Women's Assn., 1988, hon. treas. State of Ala., 1989; named one of Twelve Good Men, Ronald McDonald House, 2004. Fellow Am. Coll. Forensic Examiners; mem. Nat. Assn. Home Builders, Nat. Assn. Real Estate Appraisers (cert.), Nat. Assn. Rev. Appraisers and Mortgage Underwriters (cert.), Internat. Real Estate Inst., Latin Builders Assn., Hispanic-Am. Builders Assn. (bd. dirs.), Home Builders Assn. South Fla. (past dir., named to Hall of Fame 1994), Am. Israel Pub. Affairs (nat. exec. com.), Jewish Nat. Fund (investment com.), U.S. Senatorial Trust, Westview Country Club (past 1st v.p. and dir.), Bankers Club, Hound Ears Lodge and Club, Jockey Club Republican. Jewish. Avocations: golf, tennis. Office: Tate Enterprises 1175 NE 125th St Ste 102 North Miami FL 33161 Office Phone: 305-891-1106. Business E-Mail: stan@tateenterprises.com.

**TATE, STONEWALL SHEPHERD,** lawyer; b. Memphis, Dec. 19, 1917; m. Janet Graf; children: Adele Shepherd, Shepherd Davis, Janet Reid Walker. BA, Southwestern at Memphis (now Rhodes Coll.), 1939; JD, U. Va., 1942; LLD (hon.), Samford U., 1979, Suffolk U., 1982, Capital U., 1989, Rhodes Coll., 1993. Bar: Va. 1941, Tenn. 1942. Chmn. bd. Martin, Tate, Morrow & Marston, P.C. (and predecessor firms), Memphis, 1947—. Chmn. pres.'s coun. Rhodes Coll., 1995-96, sec. bd. trustees, 1967-77, 80-84. Pres. Episcopal Churchmen of Tenn., 1961-62; sec. standing com. Episcopal Diocese of Tenn., 1969-71; pres. Chickasaw Coun. Boy Scouts Am., 1967-78. With USNR, 1942-46; comdr. USNR; ret. Decorated Order of Cloud Banner (China); recipient Silver Beaver award Boy Scouts Am., 1963, Disting. Eagle Scout award, 1980, Disting. Svc. medal Rhodes Coll., 1978, Disting. Alumni award, 1991, Lawyers' Lawyer award Memphis Bar Assn., 1990; Memphis Rotary Club Civic Recognition award, 1983, Paul Harris fellow, 1985. Fellow Am. Bar Found., Am. Coll. Trust and Estate Counsel, Internat. Acad. Estate and Trust Law, Coll. Law Practice Mgmt. (hon.), Tenn. Bar Found., Memphis Bar Found. (Benjamin L. Hooks award 2003), Shelby County Bar Found.; mem. ABA (chmn. standing com. on profl. discipline 1973-76, chmn. standing com. on scope and correlation of work 1977, chmn. task force on lawyer advt. 1977, pres. ABA 1978-79, chmn. standing com. on lawyer competence 1986-92, mem. coun. sr. lawyers divsn. 1997-2001, 2004-), Am. Judicature Soc. (past bd. dirs.), Am. Law Inst., Lawyer-Pilots Bar Assn., Tenn. Bar Assn. (pres. 1963-64), Memphis and Shelby County Bar Assn. (pres. 1959-60), Nat. Conf. Bar Pres. (pres. 1972-73, Alumnus of Yr. 1996), U.S. 6th Cir. Jud. Conf. (life), U. Va. Law Sch. Alumni Assn. (mem. exec. coun. 1974-77), Rhodes Coll. Alumni Assn. (pres. 1951-53), Rotary (pres. 1982-83, bd. dirs. 1974, 80-84, 89-90), Raven Soc., Order of Coif, Phi Beta Kappa, Omicron Delta Kappa, Phi Delta Phi, Sigma Alpha Epsilon (highest effort award N.Y.C. Alumni Assn. 1979). Office: Martin Tate Morrow & Marston PC 6410 Poplar Ave Ste 1000 Memphis TN 38119-4843 Office Phone: 901-522-9000. Business E-Mail: sstate@martintate.com.

**TATE, WENDY K.,** risk management specialist; b. Elizabeth, NJ, Nov. 11, 1961; d. William Henry Jr. and Catherine Lillian (Fulton) Knight; 1 child, Faith Corinne. Student, U. Warwick, Eng., 1981—82; BA, Duke U., 1983; M in health admin., U.N.C., 2003. Cert. ins. counselor, assoc. in risk mgmt.; CPCU. V.p., client exect. Marsh, Inc., Charlotte, NC, 2003—05; practice leader risk mgmt. divsn. Hartfort Ins. Group, 2005—06; dir. risk mgmt. insurance svcs. Southern States Cooperative, 2006—. Former bd. dirs. Human Rels. Commn., City of Winston-Salem; chmn. New Horizons Fair Housing Com., Winston-Salem, 1999-2000. Mem. CPCU Soc., Am. Coll. Healthcare Execs., Soc. Cert. Ins. Counselors. Democrat. Episcopalian. Avocations: camping, tennis. Home: 9312 Springmount Terr Chesterfield VA 23832 Office Phone: 804-281-1581. Business E-Mail: wendy.tate@sscoop.com.

**TATE, WILLIAM FLEMING, IV,** mathematics educator; b. Chgo., Aug. 28, 1961; s. William Fleming and Melva Jean (DeBerry) T. BS, No. Ill. U., 1982; MA, U. Tex., Dallas, 1987; PhD, U. Md., 1991. Tchr. math. Dallas Ind. Sch. Dist., 1983-85, math curriculum specialist, 1985-87; asst. prof. math. Prince Georges County Community Coll., Largo, Md., 1988-89; rsch. asst. math. U. Md., College Park, 1988—; asst., then assoc. prof. math. edn. U. Wis., Madison, 1991—. Co-editor Am. Ednl. Rsch. Jour.; contbr. articles to profl. jours. Mem. St. Paul A.M.E. Ch. Patricia Robert Harris fellow, 1989-91, Cooper fellow, 1991—. Mem. Nat. Coun. Tchrs. Math. (nat. task force reaching all students with mathematics 1989—, rsch. adv. com. 1991—). Home: 3606 Blackwood Ct Richardson TX 75082-3730

**TATEL, DAVID STEPHEN,** federal judge; b. Washington, Mar. 16, 1942; s. Howard Edwin and Molly (Abramowitz) Tatel; m. Edith Sara Bassichis, Aug. 29, 1965; children: Rebecca, Stephanie, Joshua, Emily. BA, U. Mich., 1963; JD, U. Chgo., 1966. Bar: Ill. 1966. Instr. U. Mich., Ann Arbor, 1966—67; assoc. Sidley & Austin, Chgo. and Washington, 1967—69, 1970—72; dir. Chgo. Lawyer's Com., 1969—70. Nat. Lawyers Commn. for Civil Rights Under Law, Washington, 1972—74; assoc. Hogan & Hartson, Washington, 1974—77, ptnr., 1979—94; dir. Office for Civil Rights US Dept. Health Edn. & Welfare, Washington, 1977—79; judge U.S. Ct. Appeals (D.C. cir.), Washington, 1994—. Lectr. Stanford U. Law Sch., 1991—92; co-chmn. Nat. Lawyers Com. for Civil Rights Under Law, Washington, 1989—91; chmn., bd. dirs. Spencer Found., Chgo., 1990—97. Bd. dirs. Carnegie Found. for Advancement in Tchg., Stanford, Calif., 1997—. Office: US Ct Appeals 333 Constitution Ave NW US Courthouse Washington DC 20001-2866*

**TATERA, JAMES FRANK,** chemist; b. Milw., June 27, 1946; s. Harry Frank and Agnes Rose (Szymanowski) T.; m. Kaaren Marie Piekarski, Sept. 9, 1972; children: Patrick, Monica, David. BS in Chemistry and Math., U. Wis., Oshkosh, 1968; postgrad., U. Minn., 1968, 71-73; MBA, Cen. Mich. U., 1982. Cert. specialist in analytical tech. Tchg. rsch. assoc. chemistry dept. U. Minn., Mpls., 1968, 71-73; analytical chemist Dow Corning Corp., Midland, Mich., 1973-76, scale up engr. new products commercialization, 1976-78, prodn. bldg. supt. prodn. dept., 1978-80; analytical systems specialist project and plant engring. Dow Corning Ltd., Barry, Wales, 1981-84; analytical systems supr. plant engring. & maintenance Dow Corning Corp., Carrollton, Ky., 1984-85, analytical systems specialist plant engring. and maintenance, 1985-87, sr. analytical and control specialist project engring., 1988-90, sr. analytical systems specialist strategic change program, 1991-98, sr. analytical sys. specialist Process Analysis Expertise Ctr., 1998-2000; ret., 2000; sr. process analysis cons. Tatera & Assocs. Inc., Madison, Ind., 2001—. U.S. nat. com. Internat. Electrotech. Commn., Paris, 1993, Milan, 94, Montreal, 96, Houston, 98, Beijing, 2002, Madrid, 03, Ottowa, Canada, 2005—; session developer, panelist, course instr., presenter in field. Mem. editl. adv. bd.: InTech Jour., 1998—; contbr. articles to profl. jours., chpts. to books; author, presenter: internat. process analysis courses. 1st It. U.S. Army, 1969-71. Decorated Bronze Star, Bronze Star with oak leaf cluster. Fellow: Instrumentation Sys. and Automation Soc. (formerly Instrument Soc. Am.) (various sect. offices 1976—79, pres. N.E. Mich. sect. 1979—80, chmn. SP 76 stds. com. 1991—96, dir.-elect, sec.-treas. analysis divsn. 1994—96, Louisville sect. del. 1995—96, dir. 1996—98, com. mem 1998—, various divsns. and dept. positions 1998—, dir. on stds. and practices bd. 2005—); mem.: Air and Waste Mgmt. Assn. (com. on enhanced monitoring 1993—99, optical sensing divsn. indsl. issues and applications), Am. Chem. Soc. (sect. careers program and nat. chemistry week com. 1992—99, Louisville sect. chmn.-elect 1998—99, Louisville sect. chair 1999—2001, sect. careers program and nat. chemistry week com. 2001—, soc. councilor 2003—, soc. com. mem.

2004—, rep. vol. in pub. outreach program), KC, VFW, Elks, Am. Legion, Sigma Iota Epsilon, Phi Lambda Upsilon, Delta Sigma Phi. Roman Catholic. Home and Office: 2038 Ridgewood Dr Madison IN 47250-2729 Office Phone: 812-265-2301. E-mail: jtatera@seidata.com.

**TATHAM, DAVID FREDERIC,** art historian, educator; b. Wellesley, Mass., Nov. 29, 1932; s. Richard Merton and Florence Elizabeth (Mallette) T.; m. Cleota Reed, Dec. 12, 1979. AB, U. Mass., 1954; MA, Syracuse U., 1960, PhD, 1970. Dean students Syracuse (N.Y.) U., 1966-71, assoc. prof. fine arts, 1972-78, chmn. dept. fine arts, 1980-86, prof., 1978—2002, prof. emeritus, 2002—. Author: The Lure of the Striped Pig, 1973, Prints and Printmakers of New York State, 1986, Winslow Homer and the Art of the Book, 1990, Winslow Homer and the Illustrated Book, 1992, Fishing in the North Woods, 1995, Winslow Homer in the Adirondacks, 1996, Winslow Homer and the Pictorial Press, 2002 North American Prints 1913-47:An Examination, 2006, (exhbn. catalogs) Winslow Homer Drawings, 1979, Art, Artists and Museums, 1980, Bolton Brown, 1981, Abraham Tuthill, 1983, Winslow Homer: Masterworks from the Adirondacks, 2004; contbr. articles to profl. jours. Served with U.S. Army, 1956. Daniels research fellow, 1974; Am. Philos. Soc. grantee, 1980, 86, 98; Am. Art Jour. award for outstanding scholarship, 1984; NEH grantee, 1987-88, Newman Prize, 2004. Fellow Athenaeum of Phila., Royal Soc. Arts; mem. Am. Antiquarian Soc. (rec. sec. 1988-93), Coll. Art Assn. Home: 329 Westcott St Syracuse NY 13210-2107 Office: Syracuse U Dept Fine Arts Bowne Hall Syracuse NY 13244-1200 E-mail: dftatham@syr.edu.

**TATLOCK, ANNE M.,** trust company executive; b. White Plains, NY, July 1, 1939; d. John and Kathleen (McGrath) McNiff; m. William Tatlock, Apr. 29, 1967; children: Julina, Kerry, Christopher. BA, Vassar Coll., 1961; MA in Econs., NYU, 1968. 1st v.p. Smith Barney Harris Upham, NYC, 1962-84; exec. v.p. Fiduciary Trust Internat., NYC, 1984-94, pres., 1994—99, pres., CEO, 1999—2000, chmn., CEO, 2000—. Bd. dirs. Fortune Brands, Deerfield, Ill., 1996—, Franklin Resources, San Mateo, Calif., 2001—, Merck, NJ, 2000—. Trustee Am. Ballet Theatre, NYC, 1994-, pres., 1999-2001; trustee Vassar Coll., 1994—, The Teagle Found., NYC, 1995—; trustee Andrew W. Mellon Found., NYC, 1995—, chmn., 2003—; trustee Cultural Instns. Retirement Sys., NYC, 1989-2005, chmn., 1995-99; trustee Howard Hughes Med. Inst., Md., 2000—, The Conf. Bd., NYC, 2001—, Mayo Found., Minn., 2002—, World Trade Ctr. Meml. Found., 2005-; mem. Coun. Fgn. Rels. Fellow: Am. Acad. Arts and Scis. (elected 2004).

**TATLOW, GARY ARTHUR,** lawyer; b. Huntington Park, Calif., Mar. 11, 1939; s. Chester A. and Rosa May (Hallmark) T.; m. Marilyn Rose Silvey, June 2, 1962 (dec. Feb. 19, 2005); children: Jennifer Gay, Phillip Arthur, Rebecca Jane. BA, U. Mo., 1961; JD, U. Mo., 1964. Bar: Mo. 1964, U.S. Ct. Appeals Mo. 1964, U.S. Dist. Ct. Mo. 1964, Asst. atty. gen. State of Mo., 1964-65; city atty. City of Moberly, 1965-80; spl. asst. Mo. atty. gen., 1967-69, spl. pros. atty., 1970-71; ptnr. Hulen, Hulen, Tatlow & Gump, Moberly, Mo., 1968—. Mem. strategic planning coun., 2001-, U. Mo., legis. info. network, 2000-. Bd. dirs., chpt. chmn. ARC, Randolph County, 1968-69; mem. nat. campaign bd. U. Mo.; trustee Woodhaven Learning Ctr.; bd. dirs. Mo. Symphony Soc., Great River City Coun. Boy Scouts Am. Recipient Atty. Gen.'s Outstanding Citizenship award, 1968. Mem. Assn. Trial Lawyers Am., Randolph County Bar Assn. (pres. 1972-73, Mo. Bar Assn., ABA, Mo. Mcpl. Attys. Assn., Mo. Assn. Trial Attys. (past bd. mem.), U. Mo. Alumni Assn. (chmn. Randolph County chpt.), Phi Delta Phi. Clubs: Rotary (past pres.). Office: Tatlow Gump & Faiella 110 N 5th St Moberly MO 65270-1506 Office Phone: 660-263-3100. E-mail: gtatlow@tgflaw.com.

**TATOM, JOHN ANTHONY,** economist; b. Little Rock, Dec. 8, 1945; s. Vaughn L. and Dorothy L. (Huggins) T.; m. Cecelia A. Chamberlain, Aug. 20, 1966 (div. 1982); children: Shawn, Sharon, Sydney; m. Kathleen I. Rudd, July 3, 1986; 1 stepchild, Todd K. Hentschel. BA, U. Dallas, 1967; MA, U. Chgo., 1968; PhD, Tex. A&M U., 1971. Asst. prof. econs. Albion (Mich.) Coll., 1971-73, U. Redlands (Calif.), 1973-75, U. Ga., Athens, 1975-76; sr. economist Fed. Res. Bank of St. Louis, 1976-82, rsch. officer, 1982-84, asst. v.p., 1984-95; v.p. Union Bank of Switzerland, 1995—98, exec. dir., 1998—2000; exec.-in-residence DePaul U., Chgo., 2000—03, vis. prof., 2003—05; dir. rsch. Networks Fin. Inst., 2005—. Adj. assoc. prof. Washington U., St. Louis, 1985-87; sr. fellow Tax Found., 2003-04; assoc. prof. Ind. State U., 2005—. Editorial adv. bd. Jour. Econs. and Bus., 1985-95; contbr. articles to profl. jours. Mem. Am. Econ. Assn., Nat. Assn. Bus. Economists (chpt. v.p. 1990-91, pres. 1991-92), Missouri Valley Econs. Assn. (bd. dirs. 1983-85, pres. 1993-94), Western Econs. Assn. Home: 8633 Gordonshire Dr Indianapolis IN 46278 Office: Networks Fin Inst 2902 N MeridianSt Indianapolis IN 46208 Office Phone: 317-536-0281. Business E-Mail: john.tatom@isunetworks.org.

**TATREAU, (DOLORES) MAXINE,** artist; b. Minden, Iowa, Sept. 6, 1929; d. Charles Ross Teninty and Hester Evaline Peterson Teninty Hadfield; m. Donald Max Tatreau, Aug. 18, 1949; children: Douglas M., Dean M., Kevin L. Student, U. No. Iowa, 1947, Iowa State Tchrs. Coll, U. Nebr., Omaha. Receptionist, typesetter Neola (Iowa) Gazette Newspaper, 1946—47; rural sch. tchr. Neola, 1947—48; office worker Orchard and Wilhelm Furniture Co., Omaha, 1948—50; comptometer operator Western Elec., Omaha, 1950—53; office worker Western Elec. (AT&T Tech.), Omaha, 1969—86; artist Tatreau Studio, 1972—; represented by Wickwire Gallery, Hendersonville, NC, Carolina Gallery Art, Spartenburg, SC. Pres. Art League Henderson County, 2004. Exhibitions include Kans. Watercolor Soc. Competition (Purchase award), Rocky Mountain Nat. Watercolor Soc., Phi Theta Kappa Six State Regional Competition, Brand Libr. and Art Gallery, Glendale, Calif., Passageway Gallery, Omaha, Asheville Gallery of Art, 2000—04, Aberdale, Wales, 2004, many others, invitational exhibitions, Edina Art Ctr., Mpls., Conn Gallery, Landrum, SC, Wichita Art Gallery, Kans, Grandview Gallery, Lincoln, Nebr., many others, numerous corp. and pvt. collections in US and Europe. Den mother Boys Scouts Am., Omaha; wedding coord. 1st Luth. Ch., Omaha, Sunday sch. tchr., children's summer bible sch. leader, circle leader. Mem.: Kans. Watercolor Soc. (signature), So. Watercolor Soc., Upstate Visual Arts Greenville, SC, Watercolor Soc. NC (Purchase award), Tryon Painters and Sculptors, Nat. Watercolor Soc., Art League Henderson County, Internat. Soc. Exptl. Artists (signature), Nat. Mus. Women (charter). Lutheran. Avocations: golf, bridge, jewelry making, quilting, church choir. Home and Studio: 2701 Kalmia Ln Hendersonville NC 28791-1838

**TATSCH, JACKI LYNN,** music educator, diversified financial services company executive; b. Wilimantic, Conn., Mar. 11, 1971; d. Jack Adrian and Ellen Ann Wallis; m. Clinton Edward Tatsch, Aug. 7, 1993; 1 child, Bryan Edward. BS in Music Edn., E. Nazarene Coll., 1993. Cert. tchr. K-9 and 5-12 Mass., 1993. Pvt. music instr., Lynchburg, Va., 1994—99; music tchr. Nazarene Christian Sch., Asheville, NC, 1999—2001, Biltmore Bapt. Sch. Music, Arden, NC, 2000—03; pvt. music instr. Arden, 1999—2001, Asheville, 2001—03, Hendersonville, NC, 2003—; prin., owner Hart Lane Enterprises Inc., 2005—. Music tchr. AIMA Ctrl., Va., 1994—96; saxophonist Land Sky Concert Band, Asheville, 2002—03; saxophonist and clarinetist Bathtub Gin, Little Switzerland, 2002—03, Nouveau-Passe Orch., Hendersonville, 2004—; clarinetist Hendersonville Cmty. Band, 2004—05; freelance musician. Mem.: Internat. Clarinet Assn., Nat. Assn. Music Educators, U.S. Amateur Ballroom Dance Assn. Home: 28 Hart Ln Hendersonville NC 28792 Personal E-mail: jackitatsch@hotmail.com.

**TATUM, ARTHUR, III,** lexicographer, educator, pianist; b. Sumpter, S.C., July 7, 1935; s. Art Tatum and Lillie Bell. Cert. tchr. Prin. Youth in Action, N.Y.C., 1964-67; prin. tutor Cmty. Action, N.Y.C., 1968-72; performer Jazz Hall of Fame, L.A., 1975-79; music tutor Morgan Coll., Balt., 1980-83, Coppin State Coll., Balt., 1985-90, lang. tutor. Author: (Ebonese dictionary) Afro American Language, 1994, (gospel in ebonese) Gospel According to St. Matthew, 1996, Sula-Harmonic Systems (original method for reading and writing music). Lang. tutor Neighborhood Youth Corp., Charles Villa Balt., 1995-97. Avocations: sand-lot baseball, golf, table-tennis. Office Phone: 410-362-6388. E-mail: arthurtatum@webtv.net.

**TATUM, BEVERLY DANIEL,** psychology and education educator; b. Tallahassee, Sept. 27, 1954; d. Robert Alphonse and Catherine Faith (Maxwell) Daniel; m. Travis James Tatum, July 28, 1979; children: Travis Jonathan Daniel, David Alexander Daniel. BA, Wesleyan U., Middletown, Conn., 1975; MA in Psychology, U. Mich., 1976, PhD, 1984. Lic. clin. psychologist. From asst. prof. to assoc. prof. dept. psychology Westfield (Mass.) State Coll., 1983-89; assoc. prof. dept. psychology and edn. Mt. Holyoke Coll., South Hadley, Mass., 1989—; pvt. practice Northampton, Mass., 1989—. Lectr. dept. black studies U. Calif., Santa Barbara, 1983-89, counseling psychologist, 1979-83; vis. scholar Stone Ctr., Wellesley (Mass.) Coll., 1991-92; chair, bd. dirs. Equity Inst., Emeryville, Calif., 1987-89. Author: Assimilation Blues, 1987. Predoctoral fellow APA Minority Program, 1976-79, dissertation fellow U. Calif., 1980-81, postdoctoral fellow Ford Found., 1991. Mem. APA, Am. Psychol. Soc., Ea. Psychol. Assn., Mass. Psychol. Assn., Assn. Women in Psychology, Assn. Black Psychologists. Office: Mount Holyoke College Dept Psychology And Ed South Hadley MA 01075

**TATUM, DAVID ALAN,** music minister; b. Abilene, Tex., Mar. 10, 1967; s. Delton Vaughn and Ann Kathleen Tatum; m. Robin Denise Watson, July 8, 1995; children: Garrett Andrew, Tyson Graham, Kenzie Leigh. MusB, Hardin-Simmons U., 1989; MusM, Southwestern Bapt. Theological Sem., 1997. Choral music tchr. Temple Ind. Sch. Dist., Temple, Tex., 1989—95; min. music edn. First Bapt. Ch., Electra, 1995—99, Ft. Stockton, 1997—99, Madisonville, 1999—2003; assoc. pastor music Coulter Rd. Bapt. Ch., Amarillo, 2003—. Author: (study workbook) Worship, 1999. Mem.: Tex. Music Educators Assn., Am. Choral Dir. Assn., Tex. Choral Dir. Assn., Panhandle Singing Men of Tex., Singing Men of South East Tex., Phi Mu Alph. Avocation: woodworking. Home: 7909 Simpson Amarillo TX 79121 Office: Coulter Rd Bapt Ch 4108 Coulter Amarillo TX 79109 Business E-Mail: tatum.david@sbcglobal.net.

**TATUM, JERRY LEE,** researcher; m. Carmen Stretch; 1 child, Hannah. AA, St. Leo U., Fla., 1994—97, BA, 1994—98; MBA, Am. Intercontinental U., Ill., 2003—04. Assoc. Booz Allen Hamilton, Norfolk, Va., 2002; grad. rsch. asst. Coll. William & Mary, Williamsburg, Va., 2005—. 1st lt. U.S. Army, 1994—2003. Decorated Kosovo Campaign medal NATO, AF Commendation medal USAF. Personal E-mail: jltatu@wm.edu.

**TATUM, VALORIE,** elementary school educator, pharmacist; d. Louis Joe and Ruth (Gary) Tatum. Cert. in pharmacology, Kennedy King Coll., 1990; BA in Elem. Edn., Nat. Lewis U., 1994. Lic. pharmacist tech. Ill.; cert. tchr. Ill. Pharmacist technician Watson Pharmacies, Chgo., 1987—94; tchr. Chgo. Bd. Edn., Chgo., 1995—. Spl. edn. head tchr. McAuliffe Elem., Chgo., 1997—99. Author: Rita Rabbit and the Runaway Pie, 2006. Adminstrv. coun. Rust Meml. United Meth. Ch., Chgo., 2000—03, Sunday sch. tchr., 2002—, pastor parish rels. com., 2003—. Nominee Golden Apple award, 2003, Tchr. of Yr., Ill., 2006; recipient Wall of Tolerance award, 2004, Poet of the Year, Internat. Library of Poetry, 2004; Bilingual Mini grant, Chgo. Bd. Edn., 2003. Democrat. Methodist. Avocations: reading, writing, movies. Office Phone: 773-875-1032.

**TATYREK, ALFRED FRANK,** retired chemist, environmental engineer; b. Hillside, N.J., Jan. 23, 1930; s. Frank Peter and Frances (Luxa) T. BS, Seton Hall U., 1954; postgrad., Rutgers U., 1956—57. Rsch. chemist Bakelite div. Union Carbide, Bloomfield, NJ, 1958—58; rsch. chemist Bakelite divsn. U.S. Radium Corp., Morristown, NJ, 1958—62; analytical chemist insp. Chem. Procurement Dist. U.S. Army, N.Y.C., 1962—64, rsch. chemist Picatinny Arsenal Dover, NJ, 1964—73; chem. materials engr. U.S. Army Armament Rsch., Devel. and Engring. Ctr., NJ, 1973—95; ret. Cons. pyrotechnics, polymer materials and environ. chemistry. Patentee pyrotechnic compositions, chemiluminescent compounds and processes, crank case oil vacuum purification sys. for internal combustion engines, method for the removal of thermoset potting compound from the electronics package of a munitions item; lectr., contbr. publ. on mountaineering expdns. and adventures in the great mountain ranges of N.Am., S.Am., Europe and Africa to mags.; contbr. more than 50 sci. and tech. publs. 1st aid instr. ARC, Essex County, N.J., 1969-82; chief 1st aid Maplewood (N.J.) CD, 1971-91; patrol dir. Nat. Ski Patrol, Phoenicia, N.Y., 1978-84, sr. status, 1979-, lifetime Nat. Ski patroller So. N.Y. and N.J. region, 1993-; life mem. Blood Ctr. N.J. Staff sgt. N.J. Air N.G., 1948-57. Recipient comdr.'s award for pub. svc. Dept. of Army, 1996. Mem. Nat. Soc. Inventors, Sci. Rsch. Soc. (pres. Picatinny chpt. 1974-75, 79-80, 85-86), Nat. Assn. Underwater Instrs. (cert. basic and advanced diver and underwater photographer 1971-, cert. Nitrox diving 1999), Magicians Roundtable, Internat. Magicians Soc. (life), Alpine Club Can. (life mem.), N.J. Animal Rights Alliance, Appalachian Mountain Club (life mem., wildlife leader), Sierra Club, Sigma Xi. Roman Catholic. Climbed 15,771 feet Mt. Blanc, highest mountain peak in Europe; climbed to highest summit on Point Uruhu on 19,730 feet on Mt. Kilimanjaro, highest mountain peak in Africa, 1972; leader of climb on Matterhorn and Monte Rosa, Switzerland's highest peak; participant in numerous mountain expdns. in U.S. and Can., including 3 first ascents in No. Cascades of Wash. (S.E. ridge of Mt. Goode, Aug. 1963, Peak 7732 via the Snow Chute, Aug. 1964, East ridge of Bear Mountain Aug. 1964); numerous undersea photography expeditions to Caribbean and South Pacific coral reefs. Home: 27 Orchard Rd Maplewood NJ 07040-1919 Personal E-mail: atatyrek@att.net. *"God has given us a world rich in physical and intellectual beauty as well as intriguing scientific discovery. To earn these rewards we must seek out and meet the challenges of life, not as distasteful burdens, but as true opportunities upon which to build where others have failed or left off, using all the infinite resources which God has given to all of us".*

**TAUB, EDWARD,** psychology researcher; b. Bklyn., Oct. 21, 1931; s. Samuel Hart and Ida Pearl (Kimmel) T.; m. Mildred Allen Taub, Aug. 13, 1959. BA, Bklyn. Coll., 1953; MA, Columbia U., 1959; PhD, NYU, 1969. Rsch. asst. Columbia U., N.Y.C., 1956; rsch. asst. exptl. neurology Jewish Chronic Disease Hosp., N.Y.C., 1957-60, rsch. assoc., 1960-68; dir. Behavioral Biology Ctr., Inst. for Behavioral Rsch., 1968-83; assoc. dir. Inst. for Behavioral Rsch., 1978-83; univ. prof. psychology U. Ala., Birmingham, 1986—2000, 2000—; standing guest prof. U. Konstanz, Germany, 1995—; guest prof. U. Jena, Germany, 1996—. Asst. prof. dept. psychiatry Johns Hopkins U., Balt., 1972-82; vis. rsch. prof. grad. program dept. psychology CUNY, 1984-85; vis. prof. U. Tuebingen, U. Muenster, Humboldt U., Germany, 1993—2001. Contbr. articles to profl. jours. Recipient Pioneering Rsch. Contbn. award, 1989, Disting. Scientist of 1998 award, Assn. of Applied Psychophysiology and Biofeedback, Ireland prize for scholarly distinction, U. Ala., Birmingham, 1997, Humboldt Rsch. award, 2000; fellow Guggenheim Found., 1983—84. Fellow AAAS, APA (exec. com. divsn. 6, Disting. Sci. award for the applications of psychology 2004), Soc. for Behavioral Medicine, Am. Psychol. Soc. (charter, William James Fellow award 1997); mem. Soc. for Neurosci., Biofeedback Soc. Am. (pres. 1978-79, Outstanding Rsch. Contbn. award 1988), Am. Physiol. Soc. (exec. com. neurosci. 1988-91). Achievements include invention of technique of thermal biofeedback, 1970-71; constraint-induced movement therapy for rehabilitation for stroke, traumatic brain injury, spinal cord injury and other motor disorders due to neurological injury. Office: U Ala at Birmingham 712 CPM 1530 3d Ave S Birmingham AL 35294-0018 Office Phone: 205-934-2471. Business E-Mail: etaub@uab.edu.

**TAUB, JESSE J.,** electrical engineering researcher; b. N.Y.C., Apr. 27, 1927; s. Julius and Ida (Orlansky) T.; m. Eva Pollack, Dec. 24, 1955 (dec. Nov. 1973); children: Richard Lawrence, Jocelyn Cara, Suzanne Mara; m. Naomi Etta Trachtenberg, June 30, 1974. BEE, CCNY, 1948; MEE, Poly. U., 1949. Group leader microwave electronics, Material Lab. USN, Bklyn., 1949-55; engr. Airborne Instruments Lab., Mineola, NY, 1955-58, sect. leader, 1958-61, engring. cons., 1961-75; chief scientist AIL Systems Inc., Melville, NY, 1975-93; cons., 1993—. Mem. engring. adv. bd. N.Y. Tech., Hofstra U. Author: (with others) Microwave Measurements, 1963; contbr. numerous papers to profl. publs.; patentee microwave techniques With USN, 1945-46. Fellow IEEE (Centennial medal 1984, 3rd Millenium medal 2000, C.A.

Fowler award 1993, Region 1 William Terry award 2001, adminstrv. com. 1972-74, program chmn. microwave symposium, steering com., chmn. L.I. sect. awards, USAB Divsn. award 2002); mem. Archaeology Inst. Am. Democrat. Jewish. Avocations: classical music, contract bridge, archaeology. Home and Office: 115 Northgate Cir Melville NY 11747-3045 Personal E-mail: jjtaub@aol.com.

**TAUB, RICHARD PAUL,** social sciences educator; b. Bklyn., Apr. 16, 1937; s. Martin Glynn and Frances (Israel) T.; m. Doris Susan Leventhal, Aug. 14, 1961 (dec. Feb. 1996); children: Neela Robin, Zachariah Jacob; m. Betty G. Farrell, June 21, 2000. BA, U. Mich., 1959; MA, Harvard U., 1962, PhD in Social Relations, 1966. Asst. prof. sociology Brown U., Providence, 1965-69; from asst. prof. to Paul Klapper prof. of social scis. U. Chgo., 1969—, assoc. dean Coll. of Univ., 1982-86, chmn. dept. comparative human devel., 2000—. Adv. bd. Neighborhood Preservation Initiative, 1993-2000; chair adv. bd. Nat. Comty. Devel. Initiative, 1991-95; dir. South Ark. Rural Devel. Study, 1988-96; Disting. visitor Mac Arthur Found., 1998. Author: Bureaucrats Under Stress, 1969, (with D. Garth Taylor and Jan Dunham) Paths of Neighborhood Change, 1984, Community Capitalism, 1988, (with Doris L. Taub) Entrepreneurship in India's Small Scale Industries, 1989, Doing Development in Arkansas, 2004, (with Julius Wilson) There Goes the Neighborhood, 2006; editor: (with Doris L. Taub) American Society in Tocqueville's Time and Today, 1974; contbr. articles to profl. jours. Chmn. bd. St. Thomas the Apostle Sch., Chgo., 1983-86; bd. dirs. Hyde Park Kenwood Cmty. Conf., Chgo., 1972-75; bd. seminary Coop Bookstore, Chgo., 1994—. Angell scholar U. Mich., 1956; Woodrow Wilson fellow Harvard U., 1959-60, W.E.B. DuBois Inst. fellow, 1997-98; grantee Am. Inst. Indian Studies, Ford Found., MacArthur Found., NSF, Wieboldt Found., Nat. Inst. Justice; recipient Quantrell award U. Chgo., 1976, Outstanding Grad. Tchg. award U. Chgo., 2004. Mem. Am. Sociol. Assn., Midwest Sociol. Soc., Assn. for Asian Studies. Avocations: bicycling, music. Office: Univ Chgo 5730 S Woodlawn Ave Chicago IL 60637 Office Phone: 773-702-3971. Business E-Mail: rpt2@uchicago.edu.

**TAUB, ROBERT ALLAN,** lawyer; b. Denver, Nov. 25, 1923; s. Clarence Arthur and Mary Frances (Jones) T.; m. Doris Irene Schroeder, Dec. 22, 1945; children: Amanda, Jonathan, Barbara. BA, U. Chgo., 1944, JD, 1947. Bar: Ill. 1947. Legal staff Marshall Field & Co., Chgo., 1947-50; mgr. exec. compensation Ford Motor Co., Dearborn, Mich., 1950-63, asst. sect., 1963-74, dir. corp. affairs planning, 1974-98. Pres. Dearborn Community Arts Council, 1971-72; trustee Internat. Mus. Photography, George Eastman House, Rochester, N.Y., 1976-2006, chmn., 1979-82; mem. adv. bd. U. Mich. Dearborn, 1980—, Met. Mus. Art, N.Y.C., 1987—; trustee Henry Ford Hosp., Detroit, 1983-2006; chmn. Dearborn Pub. Libr., 1986—; bd. dirs., mem. exec. com., chmn. fin. com., Health Alliance Plan, 1992-2006. Mem. ABA, Ill. Bar Assn., Art Inst. Chicago, 1998—. Presbyterian. Home: 1824 Hawthorne St Dearborn MI 48128-1448 E-mail: robert@rataub.org.

**TAUBENBERGER, JEFFERY KARL,** pathologist, molecular biologist; b. Landstuhl, Germany, Sept. 23, 1961; BS in Biology, George Mason U., 1982; MD, Med. Coll. Va., 1986, PhD, 1987. Diplomate Nat. Bd. Med. Examiners; diplomate in anat. pathology Am. Bd. Pathology, diplomate in molecular genetics Am. Bd. Med. Genetics. Staff surg. pathologist Nat. Cancer Inst., Bethesda, Md., 1991-93; co-dir. molecular diagnostics lab. Armed Forces Inst. Pathology, Washington, 1993, chief divsn. molecular pathology, 1994—. Cons. Nat. Cancer Inst., 1993—; vis. scientist Nat. Inst. Allergy and Infectious Diseases, Bethesda, 1993—; affiliate asst. prof. dept. anatomy Med. Coll. Va., Richmond, 1993—. Contbr. articles to profl. jours.; featured in Secrets of the Dead: Killer Flu, PBS, 2005 Recipient Benjamin Castleman awrd U.S. and Can. Acad. Pathology, 1998, WIRED Rave award-Medicine, 2006 Mem. Assn. for Molecular Pathology. Achievements include being principal investigator on project to genetically characterize the 1918 Spanish Influenza virus. Office: Armed Forces Inst Pathology Annex Dept Molecular Biology Bldg 101 Rm 1057D 1414 Research Blvd Rockville MD 20850 Address: Armed Forces Inst Pathology 6825 16th St NW Washington DC 20306-6000 Office Phone: 301-319-0323. Office Fax: 301-295-9507. Business E-Mail: taubenberger@afip.osd.mil.*

**TAUBENFELD, HARRY S.,** lawyer; b. Bklyn., June 27, 1929; s. Marcus Isaac and Anna (Engelhart) T.; m. Florence Spatz, June 17, 1956; children: Anne Gail Weisbrod, Stephen Marshall. BA, Bklyn. Coll., 1951; JD, Columbia U., 1954. Bar: NY 1955, U.S. Supreme Ct. 1965, U.S. Dist. Ct. (so. and ea. dists.) NY 1976. Assoc. Benjamin H. Schor, Bklyn., 1955-58; ptnr. Zuckerbrod & Taubenfeld, Cedarhurst, NY, 1958—. Village atty. Village of Cedarhurst, 1977-88, trustee, 1989-2001; mem. bd. Downtown Cedarhurst Bus. Improvement Dist., 1993; legis. chmn., counsel Nassau County Village Ofcls., 1979-86, v.p., 1991-93, pres., 1993-94, mem. exec. com., 1989-99, chmn. intergovtl. liaison com., 1991-93; mem. legis. com. NY State Conf. Mayors, 1979-87, 92-93; mem. exec. bd. Tri-County Village Ofcls., 1991-95, pres., 1993-94; arbitrator Am. Arbitration Assn. Dist. Ct. Nassau County, 1980—; Assessment Rev. Panel, Supreme Ct., Nassau County, 1981—; mem. Constl. Bicentennial Com., 1987-89; adv. bd. First Am. Title Ins. Co. of N.Y., 2004-. Del. World Zionist Congress, 1977, 82, 87; mem. Zionist Gen. Coun., 1977-83; assoc. chmn. Am. Zionist Fedn., 1985-87; pres. Herut Zionists Am., 1977-79; v.p. Hartman YMHA, 1983-87; hon. trustee Cong. Beth Shalom, Lawrence, N.Y., 1990-2001; mem. bd. dir. Zionist Orgn. Am.; bd. govs. Jewish Agy., 1983-92; mem. assoc. com. World Zionist Orgn., 1983-92; trustee United Jewish Appeal, 1986-91; bd. dir. United Israel Appeal, 1986-91; hon. vice chmn., bd. dir. Jewish Nat. Fund, 1987-89; nat. bd. dir. Am. for a Safe Israel; hon. pres. World Coun. Herut Hatzoa, Jerusalem, Internat. Bd. Youthtown of Israel. Recipient Centenial award Jabotinsky Found. 1981, Betar Youth award World Betar 1982, award Internat League for Repatriation of Russian Jewry 1971, Youth Towns of Israel Leadership award 1973, Israel Bonds Leadership award 1976, Life Time Achievement award Israel Bonds 1991, Defender of Jerusalem award 1991, Israel Bonds Menachem Begin Leadership award, 1999. Mem.: Internat. Assn. Jewish Lawyers and Jurists, Beth El Synagogue Ctr., Zionist Orgn. Am. (nat. bd. 1996—), Jewish War Vets., B'nai B'rith, Nordau Circle Club. Home: 21 N Chatsworth Ave Larchmont NY 10538 Office: 575 Chestnut St Cedarhurst NY 11516-2223 Personal E-mail: handf21n@verizon.net.

**TAUBER, MARK J.,** lawyer; b. Detroit, Mar. 25, 1949; s. Max M. and Beatrice R. (Roth) T.; m. Anita L. Tilben, June 23, 1970; children: Melissa A., Benjamin M., Allison B. BA with honors, U. Mich., 1970; JD with honors, George Washington U., 1973. Bar: D.C. 1973, Md. 1974, US Dist. Ct. (DC, MD. dist.), US Ct. Appeals (1st, 3d, 4th, 7th, 11th, DC cir.), US Supreme Ct. 1980. From assoc. to ptnr. Pierson, Ball & Dowd, Washington, 1973—82; ptnr. Piper & Marbury, Washington, 1982-99, Piper, Marbury, Rudnick & Wolfe, Washington, 1999—2002; ptnr. chair comm. practice group Piper Rudnick LLP, Washington, 2002—04; ptnr., chair comm., e-commerce and privacy practice group DLA Piper Rudnick Gray Cary US LLP, Washington, 2005—. Assoc. editor: George Washington Law Rev., 1972—73. Mem.: Fed. Comm. Bar Assn. Home: 110 St Martin Dr Palm Beach Gardens FL 33418 Office: DLA Piper Rudnick Gray Cary US LLP 1200 19th St NW Washington DC 20036-2430 Office Phone: 202-861-3913. Office Fax: 202-689-7626. Business E-Mail: mark.tauber@dlapiper.com.

**TAUBIN, DAWN,** film company executive; Staff prodr., cable television programming Warner Amex Cable Comms., Ohio; dir. publicity and promotion Nat. Amusements Inc., Boston, 1983—85; west coast regional publicity/promotion rep. to v.p., publicity MGM, 1985—89; v.p., publicity Warner Bros. Pictures, 1989—93, v.p., advt. and publicity 1993—96, sr. v.p., advt. and publicity, 1996—99, exec. v.p., mktg., 1999—2001, pres., domestic mktg., 2001—. Named an 100 Most Powerful Women in Entertainment, Hollywood Reporter, 2005; named one of Top 100 women. Office: Warner Bros Pictures 4000 Warner Blvd Burbank CA 91522-0001*

**TAUBMAN, A. ALFRED,** real estate developer; b. Pontiac, Mich., Jan. 31, 1924; s. Philip and Fannie Ester (Blustin) T.; m. Reva Kolodney, Dec. 1, 1949 (div. July 1977); children: Gayle Kalisman, Robert S., William S.; m. Judith

Mazor, June 17, 1982. Student, U. Mich., 1945-48, LLD (hon.), 1991; student, Lawrence Inst. Tech., 1948-49, DArch (hon.), 1985; D in Bus. (hon.), Eastern Mich. U., 1984; D in Edn. (hon.), Mich. State U., 1993; HHD (hon.), No. Mich. U., 1995. Chmn. The Taubman Co., Bloomfield Hills, Mich., 1950—, Taubman Ctrs., Inc., Bloomfield Hills, Mich., 1992—. Prin. shareholder Sotheby's Holdings, Inc., N.Y.C., 1983-2001. Trustee Ctr. for Creative Studies, Detroit, Harper-Grace Hosps., Detroit; chmn. emeritus Archives Am. Art Smithsonian Inst., Washington, U. Pa. Wharton Real Estate Ctr., Phila.; pres. Arts Commn. of Detroit; mem. nat. bd. Smithsonian Assocs.; established Taubman Ctr. for State and Local Govt. Harvard U., Cambridge, Mass., chmn. Mich. Partnership for New Edn., Program in Am. Instns., U. Mich., Brown U.'s Pub. Policy and Am. Instns. Program; prin. benefactor A. Alfred Taubman Health Care Ctr. and A. Alfred Taubman Med. Libr., U. Mich.; bd. dirs. Detroit Renaissance, Inc., Friends of Art and Preservation in Embassies, Washington; active State of Mich. Gaming Commn. Recipient Bus. Statesman award Harvard Bus. Sch. Club of Detroit, 1983, Sportsman of Yr. award United Found. Detroit, SE Mich. Chpt. March of Dimes Birth Defects, 1983; named Michiganian of Yr. The Detroit News, 1983; named one of Forbes' Richest Americans, 2006 Mem. Urban Land Inst. (trustee), Nat. Realty Com. (bd. dirs.).*

**TAUBMAN, CLAUDIA,** gynecologist; b. N.Y.C., Sept. 5, 1949; m. Walter Borek; 1 child, Elijah Borek. BS, Syracuse U., N.Y., 1971; MA, Am. U., Washington, 1974; MD, Georgetown U., Washington, 1982. Intern Washington Hosp. Ctr., 1983, resident, 1983—86; obstetrican-gynecologist Dickman, Taubman, Ladd, Maggid, Rockville, Md., 1986—98, Capital Women's Care, Rockville, 1998—2004, Ob-Gyn Assocs., Silver Spring, Md., 2004—. Fellow: ACOG; mem.: Montgomery County Med. Soc., Md. Med. Soc. Office: Ob-Gyn Assocs 1400 Forest Glen Rd Silver Spring MD 20910

**TAUBMAN, JANE ANDELMAN,** literature and language professor; b. Boston, Oct. 23, 1942; d. Hyman M. and Esther (Rosenthal) Andelman; m. William Chase Taubman; children: Alexander, Phoebe. BA, Radcliffe Coll., 1964; MA, Yale U., 1968, PhD, 1972. Instr. Russian Smith Coll., Northampton, Mass., 1968-72; asst. prof. Russian Amherst (Mass.) Coll., 1973-83, assoc. prof. Russian, 1983-89, prof. Russian, 1989—. Author: A Life Through Poetry: Marina Tsvetaeva's Lyric Diary, 1989, Russian transl., 2000, Cinetek: Asthenic Syndrome, 2000, Kira Muratova, 2004; co-author: Moscow Spring, 1989; co-editor: Marina Tsvetaeva: One Hundred Years, 1994. Woodrow Wilson Found. fellow, 1964—, Am. Coun. Learned Socs.-SSRC, 1974, trustee-faculty fellow Amherst Coll., 1978, fellow Nat. Def. Title VI, 1965-68; grantee Am. Philos. Soc., 1975, Amherst Coll., 1991, 94, IREX grantee USSR, 1988. Mem. AAUP, Am. Assn. Tchrs. Slavic and East European Langs., Am. Assn. Slavic Studies, Am. Coun. Tchrs. of Russian. Office: Amherst Coll Dept Russian Amherst MA 01002 Office Phone: 413-542-2047. Business E-Mail: jataubman@amherst.edu.

**TAUBMAN, MARTIN ARNOLD,** immunologist, educator; b. N.Y.C., July 10, 1940; s. Herman and Betty (Berger) T.; m. Joan Petra Mikelbank, May 30, 1965; children: Benjamin Abby, Joel David. BS, Bklyn. Coll., 1961; DDS, Columbia U., 1965; PhD, SUNY, Buffalo, 1970; MA (hon.), Harvard U., 1997. Asst. mem. staff Forsyth Dental Ctr., Boston, 1970—, head immunology dept., 1972—, assoc. mem. staff, 1974-80; sr. staff mem. The Forsyth Inst., 1980—; asst. clin. prof. oral biology and pathophysiology Harvard U. Sch. Dental Medicine, 1976-79, assoc. clin. prof., 1979-97, prof. dept. oral and devel. biology, 1997—2005, prof. dept. devel. biology, 2005—. Mem. oral biology and medicine study sect. NIH, 1980-84. Editor: (with J. Slots) Contemporary Microbiology and Immunology; assoc. editor: Jour. Den Res., 2004—; contbr. articles to profl. jours, chpts. to books. Recipient Rsch. Career Devel. award, 1971-76, Fred Birnberg Alumni award for disting. dental rsch. Columbia U. Assn. Dental Alumni, Disting. Faculty award Harvard Sch. Dental Medicine, 1990, MERIT award NIH, 1991-2000; USPHS fellow, 1962-63; postdoctoral fellow, 1966-70. Mem. Am. Soc. Microbiology, Soc. Mucosal Immunology, Internat. Assn. Dental Rsch. (Oral Biology award 1991), Am. Assn. Immunologists, Am. Assn. Dental Rsch. (v.p. 1987—, pres.-elect 1988, pres. 1989). Office: The Forsyth Inst 140 Fenway Boston MA 02115-3799 E-mail: mtaubman@forsyth.org.

**TAUBMAN, NICHOLAS F.,** ambassador; m. Jenny Taubman. BS in Economics, U. Pa.; degree (hon.), Hollins U., 2005. Dir. Shenandoah Life Ins. Co.; chmn., dir. Advance Auto Parts; pres. Mozart Investments, Roanoke, Va.; US amb. to Romania US Dept. State, Bucharest, 2005—. Mem. Roanoke City Coun., 1976—78. Former dir. of various organizations including Ctrl. YMCA, Roanoke, Va., Va. Coll. Fund, Richmond, Blue Ridge Mountains Coun. Am. Boy Scouts, Roanoke Valley Industries, Roanoke Merchants Assn.; fomer trustee Va. Hist. Soc., Burrell Meml. Hosp. With U.S. Army, 1957—58, with U.S. Army, 1960—61. Recipient Disting. Svc. award, Roaoke Jaycees, 1978, Brotherhood Citation, Nat. Conf. of Christians and Jews, 1981. Office: Am Embassy 5260 Bucharest Pl Washington DC 20521*

**TAUBMAN, PHILIP,** publishing executive; s. Howard Taubman; m. Felicity Barringer. BA, Stanford U., 1971. Reporter NY Times, 1979, Moscow bur. chief, 1986—88, Washington (DC) editor, 1989—92, dep. nat. editor, 1993—94, asst. editorial page editor, 1994—2002, dep. editorial page editor, 2002—03, Washington (DC) bur. chief, 2003—. Author: Secret Empire: Eisenhower, the CIA & the Hidden Story of America's Space Espionage, 2003. Recipient George Polk award, 1981, 1983. Office: NY Times Washington Bur 7th Fl 1627 I St Washington DC 20006 Office Phone: 202-862-0300. Office Fax: 202-862-0340. E-mail: taubman@nytimes.com.*

**TAUBMAN, ROBERT S.,** real estate developer; b. Detroit, Dec. 27, 1953; s. A. Alfred and Reva (Kolodney) T.; m. Julie Reyes, Aug. 27, 1999; 1 child, Alexander Alfred. BS in Econs., Boston U., MA. With Taubman Co. Inc., Bloomfield Hills, Mich., 1976—, exec. v.p., 1984—, exec. v.p., chief oper. officer, 1988-90; pres. chief exec. officer, 1990—. Bd. dirs. Taubman Ctrs. Inc., Comerica, Inc., Sotheby's Holdings, Inc., fashionmall.com. Chmn. Mich. campaign drive UNCF; bd. dirs. Beaumont Hosp.; trustee Cranbrook Ednl. Cmty. Mem. Nat. Sssn. Real Estate Investment Trusts (bd. govs.), Real Estate Roundtable (bd. dirs.), Urban Land Inst. (trustee, chmn. Detroit regional dist. coun.). Office: Taubman Co Inc 200 E Long Lake Rd Bloomfield Hills MI 48304-2360

**TAUBMAN, WILLIAM CHASE,** political science professor, writer; b. N.Y.C., Nov. 13, 1941; s. Howard and Nora (Stern) T.; m. Jane Dea Andelman, May 18, 1969; children: Alexander, Phoebe. AB, Harvard U., 1962; MA, Columbia U., 1965, cert. of Russian Inst., 1965, PhD, 1969; MA (hon.), Amherst Coll., Mass., 1978. Instr. Amherst Coll., 1967-69, asst. prof., 1969-73, assoc. prof., 1973-78, prof. polit. sci., 1978-83, Bertrand Snell prof., 1983—. Mem. planning staff U.S. Dept. State, Washington, 1970-71; mem. bd. Internat. Rsch. and Exch. Bd., N.Y.C., 1971-74, mem. selection com., 1984-85; vis. assoc. prof. Yale U., New Haven, spring 1975; chmn. adv. com. Cold War Internat. History Project, Woodrow Wilson Ctr., Washington, 1993—; mem. Internat. Acad. Adv. Group, Russian Fgn. Ministry Archives, 1992-97; assoc. Davis Ctr. for Russian Studies, Harvard U. Author: The View from Lenin Hills, 1967; Governing Soviet Cities, 1973; Stalin's American Policy, 1982, Khrushchev: The Man and His Era, 2003 (Nat. Book Critics Circle award, 2004, Pulitzer Prize for biography, 2004, Wayne S. Vucinich Book prize Am. Assn. for Advancement of Slavic Studies 2004, Robert H. Ferrell Book prize 2004); co-author: (with Jane Taubman) Moscow Spring, 1989; editor, translator: Khrushchev on Khrushchev (Sergei N. Khrushchev), 1990; editor: Globalism and Its Critics, 1973; co-editor: Nikita Khrushchev, 2000. Named Alumnus of Yr., Harriman Inst., Columbia U., 2003; fellow Woodrow Wilson Nat. Found., 1962, Ford Found., 1963-67, Coun. Fgn. Rels., 1970-71, Rockefeller Found., 1983, Columbia U. Harriman Inst., 1987, Fulbright-Hays Found., 1988, NEH, 1992, Woodrow Wilson Internat. Ctr. for Scholars, 2000, Guggenheim Found., 2006; grantee Nat. Coun. Soviet and East European Rsch., 1984 Mem. Coun. Fgn. Rels., Authors Guild. Home: 43 Hitchcock Rd Amherst MA 01002 Office: Amherst Coll Dept Polit Sci Amherst MA 01002 Office Phone: 413-542-2420. E-mail: wctaubman@amherst.edu.

**TAUC, JAN,** retired physics professor; b. Pardubice, Czechoslovakia, Apr. 15, 1922; arrived in US, 1969, naturalized, 1978; s. Jan and Josefa (Semonska) T.; m. Vera Koubelova, Oct. 18, 1947; children: Elena (Mrs. Milan Kokta), Jan. Ing.Dr. in Elec. Engring., Tech. U. Prague, 1949; RNDr., Charles U., 1956; Dr.Sc. in Physics, Czechoslovak Acad. Scis., 1956. Scientist microwave research Sci. and Tech. Research Inst., Tanvald and Prague, 1949-52; head semiconductor dept. Inst. Solid State Physics, Czechoslovak Acad. Scis., 1953-69; prof. exptl. physics Charles U., 1964-69, dir. Inst. Physics, 1968-69; mem. tech. staff Bell Telephone Labs., Murray Hill, NJ, 1969-70; prof. engring. and physics Brown U., 1970-83, L. Herbert Ballou prof. engring. and physics, 1983-92, L. Herbert Ballou prof. emeritus, 1992—, dir. material research lab., 1983-88. Dir. E. Fermi Summer Sch., Varenna, Italy, 1965; vis. prof. U. Paris, 1969, Stanford U., 1977, Max Planck Inst. Solid State Research, Stuttgart, Germany, 1982; UNESCO fellow, Harvard, 1961-62 Author: Photo and Thermoelectric Effects in Semiconductors, 1962, also numerous articles; editor: The Optical Properties of Solids, 1966, Amorphous and Liquid Semiconductors, 1974; co-editor: Solid State Communications, 1963-92. Recipient Nat. prize Czechoslovak Govt., 1955, 69; Sr. U.S. Scientist award Humboldt Found., 1981, Silver medal Union of Czechoslovak Mathematicians and Physicists, 1992; Jan Tauc Grad. Fellowship in Engring. at Brown U. in his honor, 2003. Fellow AAAS, Am. Phys. Soc. (Frank Isakson prize 1982, David Adler award 1988); mem. NAS, European Phys. Soc. (founding), Czechoslovak Acad. Scis. (corr. 1963-71, 90-91, fgn. 1991-92, Hlavka medal 1992, de Scientia et Humanitate Optime Meritis medal 2003), Czech Learned Soc. (hon.). Office: Brown U Divsn Engring Providence RI 02912-0001 Office Phone: 401-863-1409. Business E-Mail: jan.tauc@brown.edu.

**TAUKE, THOMAS JOSEPH,** telecommunications company executive, former congressman; b. Dubuque, Iowa, Oct. 11, 1950; s. Joseph A. and Esther M. (Reicher) Tauke; m. Beverly Tauke, 2 children. BA magna cum laude, Loras Coll., 1972; JD, U. Iowa, 1974. Bar: Iowa 1974. Mem. Curran, Fitzsimmons, Schilling and Tauke, Dubuque, 1976-79, Iowa Gen. Assembly, 1975-79, US Congress from 2nd Iowa dist., 1979—91; v.p. govt. affairs NYNEX, Washington, 1991—97, exec. v.p. govt. affairs, 1991—97; sr. v.p. govt. rels. Bell Atlantic Corpn., 1997—2000; sr. v.p. pub. policy & external affairs Verizon Comm. Inc., 2000, exec. v.p. pub. affairs, policy and comm., 2004—. Del. Rep. Nat. Conv., 1976; chmn. 2nd Congl. Dist. of Iowa Rep. Party, 1974-77; mem. Iowa Rep. Ctrl. Com., 1974-77; chmn. Dubuque County Rep. Party, 1972-74 Mem. pastoral coun. Roman Catholic Archdiocese of Dubuque, 1971-73; trustee Mt. Mercy Coll., Cedar Rapids, Iowa. Mem. ABA, Iowa Bar Assn., Dubuque County Bar Assn., Dubuque C. of C., Cedar Rapids Area C. of C. Clubs: Rotary, Junipera Serra. Office: Verizon Comm Inc 1095 Ave Americas New York NY 10036

**TAULBEE, THOMAS LESTER,** psychotherapist, educator; b. Normal, Ill., June 12, 1947; s. Marion L. and Marjorie S. T. BS, Ill. State U., 1970; MS, Tex. A&M U., 1971, EdD, 1973. Cert. marriage and family therapist; cert. sports counselor; ordained min. Psychotherapist Human Resource Devel. Ctr., Dallas, 1974-76; prof. psychology Richland Coll., Dallas, 1976—, prof. history, 1994—. North Tex. regl. dir. Nat. Inst. Sports, 2000-2003, nat. coord. of divsn. chmn., 2002-03; bd. advisors Revival Fires Ministries, Branson West, Mo., 1997-99, bd. dirs. Sports Sys. Internat., 2001-2003, mem. sports chaplaincy adv. com. U.S. Coun. for Sports Chaplaincy, 2002-2003, exec. dir., exec. v.p., chief orgnl. officer, 2003; pres., founder Internat. Escorted Tour Svc., 2004—; internat. tour guide, with nat. and internat. cos., 1980—. Co-author: Psychology from a Personal Perspective, 1992, rev. edit., 1997; editor, co -author: Personal Applications of Psychology, 1997. Dir. Superior Student Roundtable, Parker, Tex., 1993, 1996—; bd. dirs. U.S. Coun. for Sports Chaplaincy, 2003—. Recipient Nat. Inst. for Staff and Orgnl. Devel. excellence award U. Tex., 2004; Ctr. for Behavioral Studies U. North Tex., Denton, 1971-74; named Baseball All-Am., Ill. State U., 1969; named to Ill. State U. Athletic Hall of Fame. Mem. Tex. Jr. Coll. Teachers Assn. Nat. Assn. Scholars, Assn. Behavior Analysis. Avocations: world travel, scuba diving, cooking. Office: Richland Coll 12800 Abrams Rd Dallas TX 75243-2173 E-mail: taulbee@verizon.net.

**TAUPENOT, LAURENT,** medical educator, researcher; BS in Cell Biology, Biochemistry and Physiology cum laude, U. Burgundy, Dijon, France, 1988; MS in Physiology cum laude, U. Burgundy, 1989; postgrad. degree in molecular and cellular biology, U. Louis Pasteur, Strasbourg, France, 1990; PhD in Molecular and Cellular Neurobiology summa cum laude, U. Louis Pasteur, 1995. Postdoctoral rsch. fellow U. Calif.-San Diego, La Jolla, 1995—2001, asst. rsch. scientist, 2001—03, asst. prof. medicine, 2003—. Recipient Scholarship award, French Ministry Edn. and Rsch., 1989, Rsch. Scientist Devel. award, NIH, 2001, 2004, Faculty Devel. award, Young Investigator award, 9th Internat. Symposium on Chromaffin Cell Biology, 1997; grantee, NIH, 2005; predoctoral fellow, Nat. Sci. Rsch. Ctr. (CNRS)/DRET, 1991—95, postdoctoral fellow, Nat. Kidney Found., 1996, 1998. Office: U Calif at San Diego 9500 Gilman Dr # 0838 La Jolla CA 92093-0838 Office Phone: 858-534-0670. Office Fax: 858-534-0626. E-mail: ltaupenot@ucsd.edu.

**TAURASI, DIANA,** college basketball player; Grad. U. Conn., 2004—. Guard women's basketball U. Conn., 2000—04; profl. basketball player Phoenix Mercury, WNBA, 2004—. Player USA Senior Nat. Team, 2004. Named Big East Preseason Rookie of the Yr., 2000—01, Most Outstanding Player of the NCAA East Region, 2000—01, Big East Championship Most Outstanding Player, 2000—01, Kodak All-Am. and AP Second Team All Am., 2001—02, Naismith Player of the Yr., 2001—02, 2003, NCAA Final Four and East Regional Most Outstanding Player, 2003, USBWA Nat. Player of the Yr., 2003, Big East First Team Performer, 2002—03, Preseason All-Am., 2003, WNBA Rookie of the Yr., 2004; named to Big East All-Rookie Team, 2000—01, NCAA Mideast Region All-Tournament Team, 2001—02, All Big-East First Team, 2002, Big East All Tournament Team, 2002, Big East All-Tournament Team, 2003; recipient Honda award for Women's Basketball Finalist, 2001—02, Honda Trophy Award, 2003, Wade Trophy, 2003, Espy Award for Best Female College Athlete, ESPN, 2003, 2004, Espy Award for Best Female Athlete, 2004. Office: c/o Phoenix Mercury 201 East Jefferson St Phoenix AZ 85004

**TAUREL, SIDNEY,** pharmaceutical executive; b. Casablanca, Morocco, Feb. 9, 1949; came to U.S., 1986; US citizen, 1999; s. Jose and Marjorie (Afriat) T.; m. Kathryn H. Fleischmann, Mar. 22, 1977; children: Alexis, Patrick, Olivia. BSBA, Ecole des Hautes Etudes Commerciales, Paris, 1969; MBA, Columbia U., 1971. Mktg. assoc. Eli Lilly Internat. Corp., Indpls., 1971-72; mktg. planning mgr. Eli Lilly Do Brasil Limitada, Sao Paulo, Brazil, 1972-75, gen. mgr., 1981—83; mgr. pharm. ops. Eastern Europe Eli Lilly and Elanco Gesmbh, Vienna, 1976; sales mgr. pharm. Eli Lilly France SA, Paris, 1977-79, mktg. dir. pharm., 1980-81; v.p. Europe Lilly European ops., London, 1983—85; pres. Eli Lilly Internat. Corp., Indpls., 1986-91, exec. v.p. pharm. divsn., 1991; exec. v.p. Eli Lilly and Co., 1993—98, pres. pharm. divsn., 1993, COO, 1996—98, pres., 1996—2005, CEO, 1998—, chmn., 1999—. Eli Lilly and Co., McGraw-Hill, Cies, IBM, ITT Industries; bd. overseers Columbia Bus. Sch. Bd. dirs. RCA Tennis Championships. Recipient Ellis Island medal of honor, 2000; named a chevalier (Knight) of the French Legion of Honor, 2001. Mem. Pharm. Rsch. and Mfrs. Assn. (PhRMA), Bus. Coun., Bus. Roundtable, President's Homeland Security Adv. Coun., 2002, President's Export Coun., 2003; trustee, Indpls. Mus. Art Avocations: tennis, music. Office: Eli Lilly and Co Lilly Corporate Ctr Indianapolis IN 46285 E-mail: staurel@lilly.com.*

**TAURMAN, JOHN DAVID,** lawyer; b. Charleston, W.Va., May 22, 1946; s. Ralph and Mikanna Elizabeth (Clark) T.; m. Donna Jill Naroff, June 13, 1981; children: Devon Elliott, Kyra Justine, Quinn Juliet. BA magna cum laude, Duke U., 1968; JD cum laude, Harvard U., 1971. Bar: D.C. 1971, U.S. Supreme Ct. 1981, Tex. 1984, U.S. Ct. Appeals (D.C., fed., 3d, 5th, 9th and 10th cirs.), U.S. Dist. Ct. D.C., U.S. Dist. Ct. (so., no. and ea. dists.) Tex., U.S. Ct. Fed. Claims. Assoc. Covington & Burling, Washington, 1971-78, Vinson & Elkins, Washington, 1979-82, ptnr. Houston, 1982-90, Washington,

1990—. Lectr. State Bar Inst. Tex., 1983. Editor Harvard Law Rev., 1969-71. Mem. ABA, State Bar Tex., D.C. Bar Assn., Phi Beta Kappa. Office: Vinson & Elkins Willard Office Bldg 1455 Pennsylvania Ave NW Fl 7 Washington DC 20004-1013 E-mail: jtaurman@velaw.com. Notable cases include: ETSI vs. Burlington No., Ea. Dist. Tex., antitrust jury trial; Bank United v. U.S., Ct. Fed. Claims, breach of contract trial; First Nationwide Bank v. U.S., Ct. Fed. Claims, breach of contract; United Investors v. Waddell & Reed, Ala. state ct., tortious interference jury trial; David's Supermarkets v. Fleming, Tex. state ct., fraud jury trial.

**TAURO, JOSEPH LOUIS,** federal judge; b. Winchester, Mass., Sept. 26, 1931; s. G. Joseph and Helen Maria (Petrossi) T.; m. Elizabeth Mary Quinlan, Feb. 7, 1959 (dec. 1978); children—Joseph L., Elizabeth H., Christopher M.; m. Ann Lefavour Jones, July 12, 1980. AB, Brown U., 1953; LLB, Cornell U., 1956; JD (hon.), U. Mass., 1985, Suffolk U., 1986, Northeastern U., 1990, New Eng. Sch. Law, 1992, Boston U., 1997, Brown U., 1998. Bar: Mass. 1956, D.C. 1960. Assoc. Tauro & Tauro, Lynn, Mass., 1958-59; asst. U.S. atty. Dept. Justice, Boston, 1959-60; ptnr. Jaffee & Tauro, Boston and Lynn, Mass., 1960-71; chief legal counsel Gov. of Mass., Boston, 1965-68; U.S. atty. Dept. Justice, Boston, 1972; judge U.S. Dist. Ct., Boston, 1972—; chief judge U.S. Dist. Ct., Mass., 1992-99. Mem. exec. com. Cornell Law Assn., Ithaca, N.Y., 1968-71; mem. adv. coun. Cornell Law Sch., Ithaca, 1975-80; vis. prof. law Boston U. Law Sch., 1977—; mem. Jud. Conf. U.S., 1994-97, mem. com. on operation of jury sys., 1979-86, mem. adv. com. on codes of conduct, 1988-94. Trustee Brown U., 1978—, Mass. Gen. Hosp., Boston, 1968-72, Children's Hosp. Med. Ctr., Boston, 1979-94. 1st lt. U.S. Army, 1956-58. Recipient Disting. Alumnus award Cornell U. Law Sch., 1992, Brown Bear award Brown U., 1993; named one of 10 Outstanding Young Men, Greater Boston Jaycees, 1966. Fellow Am. Bar Found.; mem. Mass. Bar Assn., Boston Bar Assn. (coun. 1968-71), D.C. Bar Assn., Boston Yacht Club (Marblehead, Mass.). Republican. Roman Catholic. Avocations: sports, reading, music, films, theater. Office: 1 Courthouse Way Ste 7110 Boston MA 02210-3009 Office Phone: 617-748-8787.

**TAUSAN, CAROL A.,** music educator; b. Holyoke, Mass., Mar. 14, 1958; d. Eugene A. and Margaret M. Miller; m. Jon Criss Tausan, June 20, 1994. MA, Chapman U., Colorado Springs, Colo., 1994; MusB, Nebr. Wesleyan U., 1980. Cert. tchr. Fla., 1996. Music tchr. Mary Our Queen Sch., Omaha, 1980—86, Panorama Mid. Sch., Colorado Springs, 1987—94, Turman Elem. Sch., Colorado Springs, 1994—96, Garden Elem. Sch., Venice, Fla., 1996—. Choir dir. Panorama Mid. Sch., Colorado Springs, Colo., 1987—94, gifted and talented coord., 1988—92; mem. authentic assessment com. Harrison Sch. Dist. #2, Colorado Springs, Colo., 1989—90; mem. coun. Curriculum, Instrn. and Assessment Coun., Colorado Springs, Colo., 1990—92; choir dir. Turman Elem. Sch., Colorado Springs, Colo., 1994—96, Garden Elem. Sch., Venice, Fla., 1996—, mem. faculty leadership com., 1996—; team leader Garden Elem., Venice, Fla., 1999—; mem. lang. arts com. Garden Elem. Sch., Venice, Fla., 1999—2002, bldg. rep. Sarasota Classified/Tchrs. Assn., 2001—02, sr. bldg. rep., 2002—; mem. com. Cmty./Schs. Partnership for Arts, Sarasota, Fla., 1997—, Renaissance Com., Venice, Fla., 2001—03; mem.music textbook adoption com. Sch. Bd. of Sarasota County, Fla., 2002—03. Choir dir. (performance) St. Mary's Cath. Ch., Bellevue, Nebr., 1982—84, All-City Eighth Grade Chorus, Sun Fiesta Parade (Best Edn. Entry, 1997), Venetian Holiday Festival. Grantee Sing out for Am., The Edn. Found. of Sarasota, 1997—98, The Magnificent 7, Edn. Found. of Sarasota, 1998—99, Hooray for the Red, White and Blue, 1998—99, All Am. Celebration, 1999—2000, Rockin' and Readin', 2000—01, Young Americans and Proud of It, 2000—01, True to the Red, White, and Blue, 2002—03, Rockin' and Readin', Cmty. Found. of Sarasota County, 2000-2001, The Merry Minstrel, 2002-2003, Recorders - An instrumental Opportunity, 2002-2003, Create and Communicate with Recorders, 2003-2004, You Can BEAT This!, 2003-2004, Got Recorders?, 2004—05; African Artist-in-Residence, Arts for a Complete Edn./Fla. Alliance for Arts Edn., 1998—99. Mem.: Colo. Music Educators Assn., Sarasota Area Music Educators, Fla. Music Educators Assn., Music Educators Nat. Conf. Home: 427 Pebble Creek Ct Venice FL 34285 Office: Garden Elem Sch 700 Center Rd Venice FL 34285 Personal E-mail: candcofppcc@comcast.net.

**TAUSCHER, ELLEN O.,** congresswoman; b. Newark, 1951; 1 child, Katherine. BS in early Childhood Edn., Seton Hall U., 1974. With Bache Securities, NYC, NY Stock Exch.; dir. Saton Found.; mem. US Congress from 10th Calif. dist., 1997—; mem. ho. armed svcs. com., ho. transp. com. US Ho. Reps. Founder The ChildCare Registry; bd. regents Seton Hall U.; co-chair Dianne Feinstein, US Senate Campaign, 1994; transp. and infrastructure com., surface transp. and water resources and environ. Author: The ChildCare Sourcebook, 1996. Chair New Dem. Coalition, Bipartisan Freshman Campaign Fin. Reform Task Force, House Career Awareness Working Group, Congl. Caucus on the Arts; co-chair Congl. Iraqi Women's Caucus; vice-chair Calif. Dem. Del., Dem. Leadership Coun. Democrat. Roman Catholic.

**TAUSSIG, LYNN MAX,** healthcare administrator, pulmonologist, pediatrician, educator; b. Milw., July 19, 1942; m. Lisa Peter; children: Heather, Jennifer. AB cum laude, Harvard U., 1964; MD, Washington U., St. Louis, 1968. Diplomate Am. Bd. Pediat., Nat. Bd. Med. Examiners, Am. Bd. Pediat. Pulmonary. Rsch. asst. dept. neuroanatomy Marquette U., Milw., 1965; intern in pediat. St. Louis Children's Hosp., 1968-69; resident in pediat. U. Colo. Med. Ctr., Denver, 1969-70; clin. assoc. pediat. metabolism br. Nat. Inst. Arthritis, Metabolism, and Digestive Diseases, NIH, Bethesda, Md., 1970-72; pulmonary fellow Montreal (Que., Can.) Children's Hosp., 1972-74; asst. prof. pediat. Ariz. Health Scis. Ctr., Tucson, 1974-77, cystic fibrosis ctr. dir., 1974-85, assoc. chief pulmonary function labs., 1974-85, dir. pulmonary sect., 1974-85, asst. dir. divsn. respiratory scis., 1976-92, assoc. prof. pediat., 1977-81, assoc. head dept. pediat., 1979-84, prof., 1981-93, head dept. pediat., 1985-93, dir. Steele Meml. Children's Rsch. Ctr., 1986-93; prof. pediats. U. Colo. Health Scis. Ctr., Denver, 1993—; pres., CEO Nat. Jewish Med. and Rsch. Ctr., Denver, 1993—. Frank Stevenson vis. prof. U. Con., 1977, 82; Robert Chinnock Meml. lectr. Loma Linda U., Calif., 1983; Jour. Pediats. vis. prof. U. Chgo., 1984; Brennenman lectr. L.A. Pediat. Soc., 1988, 94; Danis Meml. lectr. St. Louis U., 1989; Talamo Meml. lectr. Johns Hopkins U., Balt., 1989; Anna Zager vis. lectr. in pediats. Technion U., Haifa, Israel, 1990; Sir Clavering Fison vis. prof. Inst. Child Health, U. London, 1992; Benjamin Meaker vis. prof. U. Bristol, Eng., 1992; Ben Kagan vis. lectr. Cedars-Sinai Hosp., L.A., 1993. Mem. editl. bd. Chest, 1983-88, Am. Rev. Respiratory Diseases, 1983-89; contbr. articles to profl. jours. Trustee Congregation Anshei Israel, 1978-80; bd. dirs. Jerwish Cmty. Ctr., 1982-90, sec., 1984-86; v.p., 1987-89; mem. allocations com. Jewish Fedn. So. Ariz., 1985, 88, Allied Jewish Fedn. Denver, 1996—; bd. dirs. Colo. Biomed. Venture Ctr., 1994—; Congregation Rodef Shalom, 1996—; active Martin Luther King Jr. Minority Scholarship Program, 1994—; Colo. Concern, 1995—; Cystic Fibrosis Found. Clin. fellow, 1972-74, Sr. Internat. fellow Fogarty Internat. Ctr., 1980-81; Young Investigator Pulmonary Rsch. grantee Nat. Heart and Lung Inst., 1974-76, and numerous other med. grants; Pfizer Labs. Med. scholar, 1966; recipient Lange Med. Book award, 1966 Mem. Am. Acad. Pediat. (mem. exec. com. sect. on diseases of chest 1978-80, mem. ad hoc com. for pediat. pulmonary bds., sect. on diseases of chest 1978-85), Am. Pediat. Soc., Am. Thoracic Soc. (mem. com. to advise pres. 1975-76, sec. sci. assembly for pediats. 1975-77, mem. respiratory care com. 1976-78, mem. nominating com. 1977, 84-85, chmn. prograom com. 1979-81, mem. ann. meeting com. 1979-81, mem. rsch. rev. com. 1981-82, chmn. publs. policy com. 1988-89, 90-92, mem. exec. com. 1989-90, sec.-treas. 1989-90, active many other coms.), Am. Coll. Chest Physicians (mem. steering group for com. on cardiopulmonary diseases in children 1977-79), Ariz. Pediat. Soc., Ariz. Lung Assn., Pima County Pediat. Soc., Soc. Pediat. Rsch. (founder Lung Club 1985), Western Soc. Pediat. Rsch. (mem. nominating com. 1979-80, elected to coun. 1994—), Rotary, Harvard Club of So. Ariz. (schs. com. 1982-93, sec.-treas. 1989-93), Harvard Club of Colo., Alpha Omega Alpha. Office: Nat Jewish Med & Rsch Ctr 1400 Jackson St Denver CO 80206-2761

**TAUZIN, BILLY, II, (WILBERT JOSEPH TAUZIN II),** trade association executive, former congressman; b. Chackbay, La., June 14, 1943; s. Wilbert Joseph and Enola (Martinez) T.; m. Cecile Bergeron, May 29, 1993; children: Kristie René, Wilbert J. III, John Ashton, Thomas Nicholas, Michael James. BA, Nicholls State U., 1964; JD, La. State U., 1967. Bar: La. 1967. Practice, Houma and Thibodaux, La., 1967-80; ptnr. Marcel Marcel Fanguy & Tauzin, 1967-72; mem. firm Tauzin-Sonnier, 1972-80; mem. La. Ho. of Reps., 1971-80, house floor leader, 1974-79, chmn. Teche Clearinghouse Rev. Bd., 1975-78, chmn. house natural resources com., 1975-80; mem. U.S. Congress from 3d La. Dist., 1980—2005; mem. commerce com., mem. resources com.; chmn. energy & commerce com., 2001—04; pres., CEO Pharm. Rsch. & Manufacturers of Am. (PhRMA), Washington, 2005—. Mem. Thibodaux Playhouse, 1967-75; mem. Criminal Justice Inst. Recipient Thibodaux Outstanding Young Man award, 1971, Watchdogs of the Treasury award, Nat. Assn. Broadcasters, 1994, Golden Plow award Nat. Farm Bur.; Named Legis. Conservationist of the Yr. La. Wildlife Fedn., 1979; Named to Hall of Fame, Nicholls State U., 1964 Mem. ABA, La. State Bar Assn., Lafourche Parish Bar Assn. (past pres.), Chackbay-Choupic Jr. C. of C. (past pres.), Nicholls Alumni Council (v.p.) Lodges: Kiwanis; K.C. Republican. Office: Pharm Rsch & Manufacturers of Am 1100 15th St NW Ste 900 Washington DC 20005*

**TAVALIN, FERN,** educational consultant; b. Plainfield, N.J., Feb. 10, 1953; d. Marian Dorothy Higgins and Lester Amos Pagano; m. Peter Robert Tavalin, Apr. 11, 1981; children: Kuna Leya, Julian Zoe. BA, Franklin and Marshall Coll., Lancaster, Pa., 1976; EdD, U. Mass, Amherst, 1994. Tchr. English and social studies Putney Ctrl. Sch., Vt., 1987—93; grad. asst. U. Mass., Amherst, 1992—93; dir. Vt. Arts Assessment Initiative, Montpelier, 1993—96, exec. dir. The WEB Project, Vt., 1995—; project dir. The Flow of History, Vt., 2002—. Steering com. mem. framework of stds. Vt. Dept. of Edn., Montpelier, Vt., 1993—96; adv. coun. IBM Reinventing Edn. Software Devel., Essex Junction, Vt., 1995—99; cons. Spaulding Cmty. Svc. Learning, Barre, Vt., 2002—; program presenter Tech. Innovation in Edn.; dir. The WEB Exch.: Using Multimedia and Telecomm. to Improve Student Learning; spkr. at profl. confs. Contbg. writer: Putney: World's Best Known Small Town; author: (learning guide) Collaborative Learning: A Guide to Inquiry-Based Study Groups; co-author: Improving Student Learning through Multimedia Projects (ASCD book pick, 2002); prodr.(and dir.): (videos) Vt. MIDI Project, Art Responding through Tech., From Inside Out: Creating Dance in a Pub. Sch., We Can Work It Out: Using Students as Mediators, Taking a Stand in Cyberspace; dir.: Artifacts, History, and the World Wide Web; contbr. chapters to books, articles to profl. jours. Founding bd. mem. Strolling of the Heifers, Brattleboro, Vt., 2000—05. Named Promising Tech. Program, U.S. Dept. Edn., Putney Person of Yr., 2004; recipient Gov. and Commr. award Contrbn. to Tech. Avocations: photography, videography, international travel, house building, gardening. Office Phone: 802-387-4277. E-mail: ftavalin@bellsouth.net.

**TAVARES, SAMANTHA,** psychologist, educator; b. Bahia, Brazil, Oct. 23, 1968; arrived in U.S., 1984; d. Jose and Clarice Maria Tavares; 1 adopted child, Satyana Lua 1 child, Titus Sol. BA in Chinese Lang. Studies, Taipei, 1988; BA in Asian Studies, UCLA, 1990; M in Psychology, Forest Inst. Profl. Psychology, 1993; MA in Ea. Religion, U. Hawaii, 2000; PhD in Clin. Psychology, Am. Schs. Profl. Psychology, 1995. Lic. psychologist Hawaii, 1996, cert. hypnotherapist 1994, level II cert. Eye Movement Desensitization and Reprocessing. 1998, cert. holistic therapist 2000. Sch. counselor Han Guan Inst., China, 1986—88; pvt. practice clin. psychology Honolulu, Kailua, Hawaii, 1995—; clin. psychologist Dept. Health, Honolulu, 1996—98; clin. supr. Alaka'I Na Keiki, Inc., 1996—; clin. psychologist evaluator Dept. Edn. Dist. Hawaii, 1997—2000; assoc. prof. Holos U. Grad. Seminary, 2000—; faculty staff Inst. for Sci. Med. Intuition, 2000—04. Co-founder Samba Axe Hawaii, 1993—; dance instr., performer, 1993—; project dir. Support Adoption Hawaii, 2005—; exec. dir. Hawaii Hearts Helping Adoptions, 2005. Author: (compact disk, cassette tape) Transformative Liberation, 2005. Avocations: dance, yoga, meditation, running, surfing. Office: 43 Oneawa St Kailua HI Office Phone: 808-261-3731. E-mail: dr.tavaressam@yahoo.com.

**TAVARES, SAMIA COSTA,** economics professor; BA in Econs. with highest honors, U. Fla., Gainesville, 1996, MA in Econs., 1999, PhD in Econs., 2002. Asst. prof. econs. Rochester Inst. Tech., NY, 2003—. Faculty search com. dept. econs. Rochester Inst. Tech., 2003—04, elections com. mem. Coll. Liberal Arts, 2004—, webmaster dept. econs., 2004—; vis. scholar Carleton U., Ottawa, Canada, 2004, Bar-Ilan U., Ramat Gan, Israel, 2005. Recipient Cert. on Achievement in study of German, German Consulate-General, 1994, 1995, Cert. Academic Excellence, Coll. Bus. Adminstrn., U. Fla., 1996, Walter-Lanzillotti Dissertation award, Robert F. Lanzillotti Pub. Policy Rsch. Ctr., U. Fla., 2000—01, 2001—02; Fla. Academic scholar, State of Fla., 1993—96, Challenger Meml. scholar, 1993—96, Valedictorian scholar, U. Fla., 1993, Fla. AP State scholar, Coll. Bd., 1993, Grad. Rsch. Assistantship, Bur. Econs. and Bus. Rsch., U. Fla., 1997—98, Grad. Assistantship, Dept. Econs., U. Fla., 1998—2002, Travel grantee, Ctr. for Internat. Bus. Edn. and Rsch., U. Fla., 2001. Mem.: European Pub. Choice Soc., Phi Sigma Iota, Phi Kappa Phi, Golden Key, Beta Gamma Sigma, Phi Beta Kappa. Office Phone: (585) 475-4647.

**TAVEGGIA, THOMAS CHARLES,** management consultant; b. Oak Lawn, Ill., June 15, 1943; s. Thomas Angelo and Eunice Louise (Harris) Taveggia; m. Brigitte I. Adams, Jan. 23, 1965; children: Michaela, Francesca. BS, Ill. Inst. Technology, 1965; MA, U. Oreg., 1968, PhD, 1971. Prof. U. Oreg., Eugene, 1970, U. B.C., Vancouver, Can., 1970-73, U. Calif., Irvine, 1973-74, Ill. Inst. Technology, Chgo., 1974-77; mgmt. cons. Towers, Perrin, Forster, & Crosby, Chgo., 1977-80; ptnr. Manplan Cons., Chgo. 1980-81, Coopers & Lybrand, San Francisco, 1981-86, Touche Ross, San Francisco, 1986-88, prof. Calif. Sch. Profl. Psychology, Berkeley, 1988-98, U. Ariz., Tucson, 2000—05. Author: (with Dubin and Arends) From Family and School to Work, 1967; (with Dubin) The Teaching-Learning Paradox: A Comparative Analysis of College Teaching Methods, 1968; (with Dubin and Hedley) The Medium May Be Related to the Message: College Instruction by TV, 1969; contbr. articles to profl. jours. Grantee, Calif. Sch. Profl. Psychology, 1993—98; NDEA Title IV fellow, 1967—71, U. B.C. faculty rsch. grantee, 1970, 1971, 1973. Home: 3622 Edgewater Dr Enid OK 73703 Office Phone: 580-234-6097. Personal E-mail: taveg@aol.com.

**TAVEL, MARK KIVEY,** finance company executive, economist; b. Cambridge, Mass., May 9, 1945; s. Bernard Benjamin and Elizabeth (Rogers) T.; m. Susana Sara Doño, Dec. 14, 1980; children: Sarah Emily, Rachel Florence, Amanda Victoria, Nathaniel Benjamin, Roberto Aaron Doño. BA cum laude, Harvard U., 1967; MBA, Columbia U., 1968. Sr. mng. dir. Rothschild Asset Mgmt., Inc., N.Y.C. Trustee, treas. Trevor Day Sch., N.Y.C. Mem. Harvard Club (N.Y.C.). Home: 110 Riverside Dr New York NY 10024-3715 Office: Rothschild Inc 44th Fl 1251 Ave of the Americas New York NY 10020-1193

**TAVELLA, ELISE SHANNON,** librarian; b. Galveston, Tex., Feb. 7, 1950; d. William Landless Shannon and Mildred (Erlingheuser) Shannon Cooke; m. John Louis Tavella, May 27, 1972; children: Jennifer, Mark, Molly. BA in English with honors, U. of Pacific, 1971; MLS, San Jose State U., 1977. Asst. libr. San Jose (Calif.) State U., 1977; libr. dept. edn. Planned Parenthood Santa Clara County, San Jose, 1977-81; libr. San Jose Pub. Libr. 1980—. Author: The Ghosts of California: Master's Bibliography, 1977. Mem. Kappa Alpha Theta. Democrat. Episcopalian. Avocations: reading, writing, travel.

**TAVERNER, PAMELA JOHNSON,** secondary school educator; b. Benton, Ill., July 3, 1948; d. Elmer Ellsworth and Ruth Elizabeth (Claybourn) Johnson; m. Clyde K. Taverner, June 29, 1990. AB, Friends U., 1971; M in Comm., Wichita State U., 1981. Cert. tchr. Kans. No. Tchr. Elk Valley H.S., Longton, Kans., 1971—72, Summersville H.S., Mo., 1972—75, Clearwater H.S., Kans., 1975—. Comm. coun. Fourth Est. Corp., Wichita, 1989—93; mem. bd. examiners Nat. Coun. Accreditation Tchr. Edn., 2002—. Named Outstanding Tchr./Dir., Assn. Kans. Theatre, 1993. Mem.: NEA (exec. com.

---

1991—92, 2001—), Kans. Edn. Assn. (treas. S. Ctrl. Kans., pres. S. Ctrl. Kans., bd. dirs. 1989—95,), Kans. Exemplary Educators Network, Clearwater Tchrs. Assn. (pres. 1977—78, 2001, Oustanding Mem. 1990), Nat. Coun. Tchrs. English, Parents-FLAG (bd. dirs. Wichita chpt. 1993—95). Democrat. Mem. Soc. Of Friends. Avocations: victorian restoration, needlecrafts, gourmet cooking. Home: 1551 Fairview St Wichita KS 67203-2635 Office: Clearwater High Sch PO Box 248 Clearwater KS 67026-9176 Office Phone: 620-584-2361.

**TAVERNISE, SABRINA,** journalist; Reporter NY Times. Named Honorable Mention Kurt Schork award for Internat. Journalism, 2003. Office: New York Times 229 W 43rd St New York NY 10036 Office Phone: 202-556-1251. Office Fax: 212-556-3690.*

**TAVLI, BULENT,** communications engineer, researcher; b. Istanbul, Turkey, Jan. 2, 1975; arrived in U.S., 1999; s. Nuri and Emine Tavli. BSc, Mid. East Tech. U., Ankara, Turkey, 1996; MSc, Baskent U., Ankara, Turkey, 1998; M.Sc., U. Rochester, Rochester, N.Y., 2001, PhD, 2005. Rsrch. asst. U. Rochester, 1999—2005, rschr., 2005—. Author: Mobile Ad Hoc Networks: Energy-Efficient Real-Time Data Communications, 2006. Pvt. infantary Turkish Army, 2006. Recipient Bronze medal, Turkish Ministery Edn., 1989, Rsch. Mentoring award, U. Rochester, 2004; scholar, Baskent U., 1996—99, U. Rochester, 1999—2005. Mem.: IEEE (assoc.). Islam. Achievements include patents for protocol architectures for mobile ad hoc networks; research in energy efficient real time data communications in mobile ad hoc networks; ultrasound imaging. Avocation: travel. Home: 60 Crittenden Blvd 518 Rochester NY 14620 Office: University of Rochester Hopeman 327 Box 270126 Rochester NY 14620 Office Phone: 585-330-3850. Office Fax: 585-273-4919. Personal E-mail: btavli@yahoo.com. Business E-mail: tavli@ece.rochester.edu.

**TAVLIN, MICHAEL JOHN,** real estate company executive, manufacturing executive; b. Lincoln, Nebr., Dec. 16, 1946; BEd, Oklahoma City U., 1970; JD, U. Nebr., 1973; LLM in Taxation, Washington U., St. Louis, 1977. Bar: Nebr. 1973, Mo. 1974. Ptnr. Nelson & Harding, Lincoln, 1973-77; sr. tax mgr. Deloitte & Touche, Lincoln and Tulsa, 1979-84, PriceWaterhouseCoopers, Tulsa, 1984-86; v.p., treas., sec. Aliant Comm. Inc. and subs., Lincoln, 1986-99; sr. v.p., CFO, treas., sec Interactive Intelligence, Inc. and subs., Indpls., 1999—2001; CFO, gen. counsel Speedway Motors, Inc. and Speedway Properties, Lincoln, 2001—. Bd. dirs., treas. Cmty. Health Endowment, Lincoln, 1998-2004; bd. dirs. Woods Charitable Fund, Lincoln, 2000—, pres., 2005—. Named Disting. Alumnus Oklahoma City U., 1995. Office: Speedway Motors Inc PO Box 81906 Lincoln NE 68501 Office Phone: 402-323-3122.

**TAVROW, RICHARD LAWRENCE,** lawyer; b. Syracuse, NY, Feb. 3, 1935; s. Harry and Ida Mary (Hodess) T.; m. Barbara J. Silver, Mar. 22, 1972; children— Joshua Michael, Sara Hallie. AB magna cum laude, Harvard U., 1957, LL.B., 1960, LL.M., 1961; postgrad., U. Copenhagen, 1961-62, U. Luxembourg, 1962. Bar: N.Y. bar 1961, U.S. Supreme Ct. bar 1969, Calif. bar 1978. Atty. W.R. Grace & Co., NYC, 1962-66; asst. chief counsel Gen. Dynamics Corp., NYC, 1966-68; chief counsel office of fgn. direct investments U.S. Dept. Commerce, Washington, 1969-71; ptnr. Schaeffer, Dale, Vogel & Tavrow, NYC, 1971-75; v.p., sec., gen. counsel Prudential Lines, Inc., NYC, 1975-78, also bd. dirs.; v.p., sec., gen. counsel Am. Pres. Lines, Ltd., Oakland, Calif., 1978-80, sr. v.p., sec., gen. counsel, 1980-91, also bd. dirs.; sr. v.p., sec., gen. counsel Am. Pres. Cos., Ltd., Oakland, Calif., 1983-91, also bd. dirs.; sr. ptnr. Law Offices of R.L. Tavrow, 1991—; chmn., pres., CEO Diabetes Healthcare & Life Enhancement Ltd., 2000—. Instr. Harvard Coll., 1959-61; lectr. Am. Mgmt. Assn., Practising Law Inst.; other assns. Recipient Silver Medal award Dept. Commerce, 1970; Fulbright scholar, 1961-62 Mem. ABA, State Bar Calif., Internat. Bar Assn., Am. Soc. Internat. Law, Am. Corp. Counsel Assn., Am. Soc. Corp. Secs. Inc., Harvard Law Sch. Assn., Harvard Club (N.Y.C.).

**TAW, DUDLEY JOSEPH,** sales executive, director; b. Cleve., Mar. 11, 1916; s. William C. and Ella (Gedeon) T.; m. Louise E. Forshey, Sept. 10, 1938; children: Judith (Mrs. William W. Beck, Jr.), Dudley Joseph. Student, Hiram Coll., 1938. With McKesson & Robbins, Inc. (pharm. co.), after 1937, sales mgr. Boston, 1947, v.p. sales N.Y.C., 1953-60; v.p. Revlon, Inc., N.Y.C., 1960-64; v.p. mktg. East Ohio Gas Co., Cleve., 1964-74, pres., 1975-81, chmn., 1981-82, Middtaw, Inc., 1982. Bd. dirs. No. New England Gas Corp., First Union Mgmt. Co., Biskind Devel. Co., Vt. Gas Systems Inc. Mem. Better Bus. Bur., Cleve., chmn., 1973; trustee Lakewood Hosp.; treas. Salvation Army, Cleve. With USNR, 1946-47. Named Sales Exec. of Year Sales and Mktg. Execs. Cleve., 1966, Man of Year, 1977 Mem. Sales and Mktg. Execs. Cleve. (pres. 1969-70), Westwood Country Club, Union Club, Pepper Pike Club, Rotary (pres. Cleve. 1972-73). Methodist. Home: Apt 302 22500 Lake Rd Cleveland OH 44116-1025

**TAWEEL, JANICE M.,** artist, art educator; b. Ennis, Tex., Nov. 24, 1950; d. Josh H. and Evelyn M. Rivers; m. George M. Taweel, Nov. 24, 1973 (dec. Aug. 21, 1996); 1 child, Lorie M. BS, Lamar U., Beaumont, Tex., 1976. Cert. Tchg. Tex. Edn. Agy./Austin, Tex., 1976, Elem. Edn. Tex. Edn. Agy./Austin, Tex., 1990, All Level Art Tex. Edn. Agy./ Austin, Tex., 1976. Florist Designs by Delle Florist, Houston, 1968—69; credit/ billing lead Rogers Enterprises, Beaumont, Tex., 1976—90; owner Jan's Art, Beaumont, Tex., 1980—90; co-owner George's Boot and Shoe Repair, Beaumont, Tex., 1980—90; art educator Dallas Ind. Sch. Dist., Dallas, 1991—; owner The Artist Paper Trail, Dallas, 2004—. Sch. site coord. ArtsPartners, Dallas, 1999—, Crayola Dream-Makers, Dallas 1999—; academic art sponsor Adamson H.S. Academic Fair, Dallas, 1999—; sch. site coord. Dallas Mus. of Art/ Go Van Gogh, Dallas, 1999—. Prin. works include Mushrooms, Iris, The Villiage, Nature on the Lake, White Whooping Crane, Orchid. Sponsor Future Educators, Dallas, 2005. Grantee, Hispanic Salute North Tex. Ford Dealers, 2001, Jr. League of Dallas, 2002, 2003. Mem.: Dallas Art Educator Assn. (assoc.). Independent. Bapt. Avocations: painting, travel, photography, arts, crafts. Office: The Artist Paper Trail 8229 Cr 3823 Murchison TX 75778 Office Phone: 214-207-1293. Business E-Mail: jrserendipity@aol.com.

**TAYLER, DAVID S.,** musician; s. Edward W. Tayler; m. Hanneke van Proosdij, Jan. 4, 1996; 1 child, Kellan Tej Tayler McGuire. BA, BS, Hunter Coll., MA, U. Calif., Berkeley; PhD, U. Calif. Condr. Amherst Early Music, NYC, San Francisco Early Music Soc.; dir. Ensemble Pandora, El Cerrito, Calif. Recipient Eisner prize, U. Calif., Berkeley, 1985, Disting. Tchr. award, 1986. Mem.: Phi Beta Kappa. Address: 6919 Gladys Ave El Cerrito CA 94530

**TAYLER, IRENE,** English literature educator; b. Abilene, Tex., July 13, 1934; d. B. Brown Smith and Madeline (Bowron); m. Edward W. Tayler, June 3, 1961 (div. 1971); children: Edward Jr., Jesse; m. Saul Touster, Jan. 14, 1978. BA in Philosophy, Stanford U., 1956, MA in Am. Lit., 1961, PhD in English Lit., 1968. Tchr. Breadloaf Sch. of Eng., Middlebury, Vt., 1970, 71, 75, 76; teaching asst. Stanford U., Calif., 1958-60; lectr. Columbia U., N.Y., 1961-71; asst. prof. CUNY, 1971-73, assoc. prof., 1973-76, MIT, Cambridge, 1976-82, prof., 1982-96, sec. of the faculty, 1993-95, retired, 1996. Chair gov. com. The English Inst., 1981. Author: Blake's Illustrations to the Poems of Gray, 1971, Holy Ghosts: The Male Muses of Emily and Charlotte Bronte 1990; editor: Samuel Bak: Between Worlds, Paintings and Drawings from 1946 to 2001, 2002; contbr. articles to profl. jours. Internat. Rotary fellow, U. Munich, 1957-58; Wilson fellow Stanford U., 1961-62; NEH sr. scholar fellow, 1980; Mac Vicar faculty fellow MIT, 1993-2003; ACLS study grantee, 1968-69; Faculty Rsch. Found. grantee CUNY, 1972-73; first occupant Thomas Meloy chair rhetoric MIT, 1979-83. Mem.: St. Botolph Club (Boston) (pres. 2000—03). Business E-Mail: itayler@mit.edu.

**TAYLOR, ALANDYA NATASHA,** elementary school educator; b. Saginaw, Mich., June 3, 1958; d. Slaughter and Lucinda Taylor. AA, Delta Coll., University Center, Mich., 1998; BA, Saginaw Valley State U., 2001, University

---

Center, 2002. Sec. Saginaw Pub. Schs., Mich., 1987—2002, tchr., 2002—. Mem. adv. bd. Sloan Mus., Flint, Mich., 2001—02. Mem.: Phi Delta Kappa. Democrat. Methodist. Avocations: reading, bowling, Bingo.

**TAYLOR, ALEXANDER A.,** information technology analyst, freelance/self-employed musician; b. Hackensack, N.J., Feb. 12, 1948; s. Thomas Smith and Flora Acheson Taylor; m. Regina T. Riccio, Apr. 6, 1973 (div.); 1 child, Matthew Moen; m. Debra E. Fox, Nov. 7, 1981; children: Sandra Lynn, Timothy Fox. BS, Ithaca Coll., NY, 1970; diploma, Chubb Inst., Parsippany, NJ, 1987. Cert. tchr. music K-12 N.J. Asst. band dir. Pequannock Twp. H.S., Pompton Plains, NJ, 1971—78; band dir. Parsippany Hills (N.J.) H.S., 1978—87; programmer AT&T, NJ, 1988—2003; info. tech. analyst Sussex County Superior Ct., Newton, NJ, 2004—. Freelance profl. trombonist. Staff sgt. N.Y. N.G., 1970—76. Recipient Stanbury award, Am. Sch. Band Dirs. Assn., 1975, Disting. Am. Bandmaster award, First Chair Am. 1981. Mem.: Ridgewood Concert Band (prin. trombonist). Avocations: Civil War, bicycling, railroads. Home: 21 Matthew Ct Landing NJ 07850 E-mail: alext@alextaylor.us.

**TAYLOR, ALLAN BERT,** lawyer; b. Cin., June 28, 1948; s. H Ralph and Henrietta Irene (Medalia) Taylor; m. Sally Ann Silverstein, June 6, 1971; children: Rachel Elizabeth, Karen Ruth. AB, Harvard U., 1970, M in Pub. Policy, 1975, JD, 1975. Bar: Conn 1975, US Ct Appeals (DC cir) 1977, US Dist Ct (so dist) NY 1979, US Ct Appeals (2d cir) 1979, US Supreme Ct 1979, US Ct Appeals (1st and 10th cirs) 1991. Law clk. to J. Skelly Wright D.C. Cir., Washington, 1975-76; law clk. to Thurgood Marshall U.S. Supreme Ct., Washington, 1976-77; assoc. Day, Berry & Howard, Hartford, Conn., 1977-83, ptnr., 1983—. Overseer Bushnell Meml Hall Corp, Hartford, 1992—. Bd. dirs. Hartford Infant Action Project, 1990—2006, pres., 1999—2005; elected mem Hartford City Coun, 1981—87; mem. Hartford Bd. Edn., 1989—93, v.p., 1991—93; mem. State Bd. Edn., Hartford, 1994—2005, chair, 2005—; chmn. charter revision comns. City of Hartford, 1999—2002; bd dirs Conn Asn Bds Educ, Hartford, 1989—93, Hartford Stage Co. 1993—2001. Mem.: ABA, Hartford Bar Assn, Conn Bar Assn, Phi Beta Kappa. Democrat. Jewish. Avocation: reading. Home: 238 Whitney St Hartford CT 06105-2270 Office: Day Berry & Howard City Place Hartford CT 06103 E-mail: abtaylor@dbh.com.

**TAYLOR, ALLAN RICHARD,** retired banker; b. Prince Albert, Sask., Can., Sept. 14, 1932; s. Norman and Anna Lydia (Norbeck) T.; m. Shirley Irene Ruston, Oct. 5, 1957; children: Rodney Allan, Leslie Ann. LLD (hon.), U. Regina, Sask., 1987, Concordia U., Montreal, Can., 1988; DBA (hon.), Laval U., Quebec City, Can., 1990; LLD (hon.), Queen's U., Kingston, Ont., 1991; Doctorate of Univ. (hon.), U. Ottawa, 1992. With Royal Bank of Can., Toronto, Ont., 1949-95, pres., COO, dir., 1983-86, chmn., CEO, dir., 1986-94, chmn., 1994-95, ret., 1995. Bd. dirs. Can. Inst. Advanced Rsch., Toronto, NeuroSci. Can. Found., Montreal; mem. adv. coun. Can. Exec. Svc. Overseas; former chmn. Can. Bankers Assn.; past pres. Internat. Monetary Conf. Former chmn. corp. program IMAGINE; mem. adv. bd. Can. Found. AIDS Rsch.; chmn. hon. adv. bd. Can. Assn. for Cmty. Living. Decorated officer Order of Can. Address: 200 Bay St 18th Fl North Tower Toronto ON Canada M5J 2J5 E-mail: allan.taylor@rbc.com.

**TAYLOR, AMANDA DEANNE,** elementary school educator; b. El Paso, Tex., Nov. 29, 1979; d. Austin Yearwood and Dee Cunningham; m. Ben Taylor, July 17, 2004. BS in Elem. Edn., Centenary Coll. La., Shreveport, 2002. Nat. cons. Chi Omega Frat., Memphis, 2002—03; tchr. 2d grade El Paso Ind. Sch. Dist., 2003—04, Wash. Elem. Sch. Dist., Phoenix, 2004—. Student coun. advisor Lookout Mountain Elem. Sch., 2005. Grantee, Wash. Elem. Found., 2006. Mem.: Pi Lambda Theta (assoc.), Chi Omega (life; recruitment chair, new mem. educator 1999—2001, alumnae advisor 2005, Peggy Roundtree award 2002). Office: Lookout Mountain School 15 W Coral Gables Phoenix AZ 85023 Office Phone: 602-896-5928. E-mail: ataylor@lm.wesd.k12.az.us.

**TAYLOR, ANDREW C.,** rental and leasing company executive; b. 1947; BSBA, Denver U., 1970. With RLM Leasing Co., San Francisco, 1970—73, Enterprise Rent-A-Car, St. Louis, 1973—, pres., COO, 1980—91, CEO, 1991—, chmn., 2001—. Dir. Anheuser Busch Co., Commerce Bancshares; pres., CEO Crawford Group. Trustee, conference co-chair National Urban League; trustee Washington U., St. Louis Symphony Orch.; bd. dirs. United Way Greater St. Louis; life trustee Mo. Bot. Garden. Office: Enterprise Rent-A-Car 600 Corporate Park Dr Saint Louis MO 63105-4204*

**TAYLOR, ANDREW T., JR.,** radiologist, educator; b. Jackson, Tenn., Jan. 14, 1942; MD, Duke U., 1968. Cert. nuclear medicine Splty. Bd. 1, internal medicine Splty. Bd. 2. Resident U. Hosp.-U.C.S.D., San Diego, 1970, 1972—74, intern, 1969; co-dir. nuc. medicine Emory U. Sch. Med., prof. radiology, 2002—. Mem.: Am. Bd. of Nuclear Medicine (past chair). Office: Emory U Sch of Medicine Radiology 1440 Clifton Rd Atlanta GA 30322

**TAYLOR, ANGELO,** Olympic athlete; b. Albany, Ga., Dec. 29, 1978; Student, Ga. Inst. Tech. Champion 400 meter hurdles NCAA Championship, 1998; 2nd place U.S. Championships, 1998; winner 1st nat. title; co-winner Gold Medal 4X400 relay World Championships, 1999; winner Gold Medal 400 meter hurdles and gold medal 4x400m relay Sydney, 2000; IAAF Grand Prix overall and GP final champion, 2000; Jesse Owens award winner for top U.S. male track and field athlete, 2001; world outdoor champs gold medalist in 4x400m relay, 1999; 3 time US champion, 1999—2001; US indoor 400m champion, 1999; NCAA 400H champion, 1998. Named Collegiate Athlete of the Yr. T&FN, 1998, ranked no. 3 400 meter hurdler. Office: USA Track and Field Team One RCA Dome Ste 140 Indianapolis IN 46225

**TAYLOR, ANN,** artist; b. Rochester, N.Y., Mar. 23, 1941; Student, Vassar Coll., 1958-61; BA, The New Sch. U., 1962. Pvt. practice, Scottsdale, Ariz. One-woman shows include Carl Solway Gallery, Cin., 1964, York Gallery, N.Y.C., 1967-69, Hunter Gallery, Aspen, Colo., 1970, Christopher Gallery, N.Y.C., 1975, 77, Miller Gallery, Cin., 1978, 83, Munson Gallery, Santa Fe., 1980, Oxford Gallery, Rochester, 1965-95, C.G. Rein Galleries, Mpls., 1981, Scottsdale, Ariz., 1982, 85, Houston, 1983, Yuma (Ariz.) Art Ctr., 1984, Gallery Henoch, N.Y.C., 1984. Scottsdale Ctr. for Arts, 1985, Kauffman Galleries, Houston, 1986, Marilyn Butler Fine Art, Scottsdale, 1987, others; solo exhibition or solo traveling exhibition: Rochester Mus. and Scis. Ctr., 1984-85, Palm Springs Desert Mus., 1984-85, Yuma Art Ctr., 1984-85, Reed Whipple Cultural Ctr., 1984-85, Scottsdale Ctr. for the Arts, 1984-85, Beaumont Art Mus., 1984-85; exhibited in group shows at Indpls. Ctr. for Contemporary Art, Gallery of Modern Art, N.Y.C., Fine Art Ctr., Tempe, Ariz., Everson Mus., Syracuse, N.Y., Walton-Gilbert Galleries, San Francisco, Adelle M. Fine Art, Dallas, Janet Fleischer Gallery, Phila., Peter M. David Gallery, Mpls., Mickelson Gallery, Washington, Julia Black Gallery, Taos, N.Mex., Palm Springs Desert Mus., Scottsdale Ctr. for the Arts, Ariz. State U.; represented in permanent collections Eastman Kodak Co., Bank of Am., Houston, Am. Express, Phoenix, Bausch & Lomb, Inc., Rochester, A.C. Nielsen Corp., Chgo., 1st Interstate Bank, Phoenix, Honeywell, Inc., Mpls., Xerox, Rochester, Lincoln Chase Trust Co., Rochester, Third Nat. Bank, Dayton, Ohio, Cen. Trust Co., Cin., Valley Nat. Bank, Phoenix, Butterfield Savs. & Loan, Santa Ana, Calif., Sohio Petroleum Co., Houston, A.C. Neilsen Corp., Chgo., others. E-mail: atltd@mindspring.com.

**TAYLOR, ANN,** human resources specialist, educator; b. Gordonville, Pa., Feb. 28, 1940; d. Gideon S. and Elizabeth L. Stoltzfus; m. James R. Taylor III, Feb. 18, 1983 (dec. Sept. 1994). BA, Ea. Mennonite U., 1966; MEd, Millersville (Pa.) U., 1979; EdD, Temple U. 1995. Caseworker Lancaster (Pa.) Welfare Dept., 1969-72, Rockingham County Welfare Dept., 1966—67, Lancaster County Probation Parole Dept., 1967-69; parole agent Pa. Bd. Probation, Parole, Harrisburg, 1972-85; human resource cons., trainer Taylor Assocs., Lancaster, 1985—. Adj. prof. bus. mgmt. Pa. State U., Lancaster, 1979-2000; spkr. in field; free lance trainer Hamilton Bank, Lancaster, 1985-91, Armstrong World Industries, Lancaster, 1987, 91, adv. com. staff trainer Vantage Drug and Alcohol Facility, Lancaster, 1983-85. Co-author: Fire Up Your Brilliance; co-author articles to profl. jours. Vol. Lancaster County Mental Health Ctr., 1983-94; seminar leader Fulton County (Pa.) C. of C., 1985-86, York County (Pa.) C. of C., 1985-86, Lancaster County C. of C., 1985-88. Mem.: Am. Counseling Assn. Democrat. Episcopalian. Avocations: travel, reading, gardening, hiking. Office: 214 E King St Lancaster PA 17602 Office Phone: 717-394-6859. Personal E-mail: brilliance@comcast.net.

**TAYLOR, ANNA DIGGS,** federal judge; b. Washington, Dec. 9, 1932; d. Virginius Douglass and Hazel (Bramlette) Johnston; m. S. Martin Taylor, May 22, 1976; children: Douglass Johnston Diggs, Carla Cecile Diggs. BA, Barnard Coll., 1954; LLB, Yale U., 1957. Bar: D.C. 1957, Mich. 1961. Atty. Office Solicitor Gen. US Dept. Labor, 1957-60; asst. prosecutor Wayne County, Mich., 1961-62; asst. US atty. (ea. dist.) Mich. US Dept. Justice, 1966; ptnr. Zwerdling, Maurer, Diggs & Papp, Detroit, 1970-75; asst. corp. counsel City of Detroit, 1975-79; judge US Dist. Ct. (ea. dist.) Mich., Detroit, 1979—. Hon. chair United Way, Cmty. Found., S.E. Mich.; trustee emeritus Detroit Inst. Arts; co-chair, vol. Leadership Coun.; vice-chair Henry Ford Health Sys. Mem. Fed. Bar Assn., State Bar Mich., Wolverine Bar Assn. (v.p.), Yale Law Assn. Episcopalian. Office: US Dist Ct 740 US Courthouse 231 W Lafayette Blvd Detroit MI 48226-2700

**TAYLOR, ANNE WILKERSON,** elementary school educator; b. DeFuniack Springs, Fla., Oct. 10, 1950; d. Coston Ingram Wilkerson and Lelan Irene Blair; m. William Henry Taylor, Nov. 9, 1968; children: Matthew Allen, Randall Henry, William Jason. BS in Elem. Ed., Troy U., Ala., 1979; M in Elem. Ed., U. South Ala., 1991, administrv. degree, 2001. Cert. Project CRISS trainer. 6th grade tchr. Escatawpa (Miss.) Elem. Sch., 1985—88; 5th and 6th grade tchr. Castlen Elem. Sch., Grand Bay, Ala., 1988—98; 6th and 8th grade tchr. Grand Bay Mid. Sch., 1998—; 4th grade tchr. Dauphin Island Elem., Ala., 2005—. Title I parenting coord., staff dev. coord. Grand Bay Mid. Sch., 2003—. Named Tchr. of Yr., Castlen Elem. Sch. and Grand Bay Mid. Sch., 1997, 2004. Home: 10428 Knoke Ave Grand Bay AL 36541 Office Phone: 251-861-3864. Personal E-mail: wmhbilltaylor@aol.com.

**TAYLOR, BARBARA ALDEN,** public relations executive; b. Dallas, Aug. 21, 1943; d. Harold Earl and Sally Alden (Howard) T. BA, Smith Coll., 1965; MA, Antioch Coll., 1971. Vol. Peace Corps., India, 1966-68; tchr. Upper Merion Sch. Dist., King of Prussia, Pa., 1969-70, Cheltenham Sch. Dist., Elkins Park, Pa., 1970-74; pub. rels. dir. Princess Hotels Internat., N.Y.C., 1974-75; chmn. Taylor & Hammond Ltd., N.Y.C., 1975-84; pres. Doremus/Marketshare, 1984-86; exec. v.p. Porter/Novelli, N.Y.C., 1986-90; sr. v.p. Hill and Knowlton, Inc., N.Y.C., 1990-93; sr. v.p. corp. comm. Lancaster Group Worldwide, 1993-95; sr. v.p. Coty Inc. and Benckiser Group, 1995-97; exec. v.p. Edelman Pub. Rels. Worldwide, N.Y.C., 1997—. Bd. dirs. Madison Square Boys' and Girls' Club N.Y., 1978—, also mem. women's bd. Boys' Club N.Y. Named to Acad. of Women Achievers YWCA, 1985; bd. dirs. Up With People, Tucson, 1990—; trustee Smith Coll., 1999—. Mem. Women in Comms., Pub. Rels. Soc. Am. (counselors acad.), Internat. Women's Forum, Advt. Women N.Y., Cosmetic Exec. Women, Fashio Group, Doubles Internat., Smith Coll. Alumnae Assn. (bd. dirs. 1993-96), Club N.Y., Lyford Cay Club, Jr. League City N.Y. Avocations: tennis, walking, bridge. Office: Edelman Pub Rels Worldwide 1500 Broadway Ste 504 New York NY 10036-4048

**TAYLOR, BARBARA ANN OLIN,** writer, educational consultant; b. St. Louis, Feb. 8, 1933; d. Spencer Truman and Ann Amelia (Whitney) Olin; m. F. Morgan Taylor Jr., Apr. 5, 1954; children: Spencer O., James W., John F., Frederick Morgan. AB, Smith Coll., 1954; MBA, Northwestern U., 1978, PhD, 1984; LHD, U. New Haven, 1995. Mem. faculty Hamden (Conn.) Hall Country Day Sch., 1972-74; cons. Booz, Allen & Hamilton, Inc., Chgo., 1979; program assoc. Northwestern U., Evanston, Ill., 1982; co-founder, exec. dir. Nat. Ctr. Effective Schs. R&D, Okemos, Mich., 1986-89; rsch. assoc., 1987; chmn. Nat. Ctr. for Effective Schs. Resource and Devel. Found., 2002—03; cons. on effective schs. rsch. and reform Nat. Ctr. Effective Schs. R&D U. Wis., Madison, 1990-96; pres. Excelsior! Found., Chgo., 1994—. Mem. exec. com. Hudson Inst. New Am. Schs. Devel. Corp. Design Team, 1990—94; Danforth Disting. lectr. U. Nebr., Omaha, 1993. Co-author: (book) Making School Reform Happen, 1993, Keepers of the Dream, 1994, The Revolution Revisited: Effective Schools and Systemic Reform, 1995; editor: Case Studies in Effective Schools Research, 1990; contbr. articles to profl. jours. Co-chair Coalition Housing and Human Resources, Hartford-New Haven, 1970—73; co-chair steering com. Day Care Conn., Hartford, 1971—73; trustee U. New Haven, 1961—71, Smith Coll., Northampton, Mass., 1984—90, Choate Rosemary Hall Sch., 1973—78, Lake Forest Coll., 1996—, Hudson Inst., 1989—97, Northwestern U., 1998—2002; pres. Jr. League New Haven, 1967—69, NCCJ, New Haven, 1971—73. Recipient Humanitarian award, Mt. Calvary Bapt. Ch., 1988, Oustanding Alumna award, John Burroughs Sch., 1994, Pres.'s award, U. New Haven, Alumni Merit award, Northwestern U., 2004. Mem.: ASCD, Nat. Staff Devel. Coun., Nat. Commn. Citizens Ed. (bd. dirs. 1980—86), Phi Delta Kappa (Internat. award Outstanding Svc. 2000). Episcopalian. Office: Nat Ctr Effective Schs Rsch & Devel 1124 Lake Rd Lake Forest IL 60045-1723

**TAYLOR, BARBARA MAE HELM,** artist, educator; b. Salina, Kans. Aug. 4, 1940; d. Wilber John and Mildred Mae (Walters) Helm; m. Walter Luther Taylor, II, Feb. 11, 1957; children: Walter Luther III, Natalie Sue Taylor Estes, Laura Marie, Toby Clark. AA, East Ark. C.C., Forrest City, 1990; BFA, Ark. State U., Jonesboro, 1992, MA, 1994. Portrait painter Barbara Taylor Art Studio, Palestine, Ark., 1992—. Adj. prof. Mid South C.C., West Memphis, Ark., 1996—98, East Ark. C.C., Forrest City, Ark., 1998—2006. Author: Every One and Me; numerous shows. Country fiddle player Ark. Gospel Assn., Forrest City, 1994—; violin player Midway Bapt. Ch., Palestine, 1988—. Mem.: Smithsonian Soc., Audubon Soc., Little Rock Art Links, Am. Soc. Portrait Artists (assoc.), Ark. Artist Registry (life), Delta Art Soc. (v.p. 1999—2000), Memphis Art Links, St. Francis Art Club (life; founder, pres. 2000—), Gamma Beta Phi (life). Avocation: birdwatching. Home: 523 Saint Francis 867 Palestine AR 72372 Office: Barbara Taylor Art Studio 493 St Francis Co 867 Palestine AR 72372-8936 Office Phone: 870-581-3890. Business E-mail: barbhelmtaylor@arkansas.net.

**TAYLOR, BARRY LLEWELLYN,** microbiologist, educator; b. Sydney, Australia, May 7, 1937; arrived in US, 1967; s. Fredrick Llewelyn and Vera Lavina (Clarke) T.; m. Desmyrna Ruth Tolhurst, Jan. 4, 1961; children: Lyndon, Nerida, Darrin. BA, Avondale Coll., Cooranbong, New South Wales, 1959; BSc with honors, U. New South Wales, Sydney, 1966; PhD, Case Western Res. U., 1973; postgrad., U. Calif., Berkeley, 1973-75. Vis. postdoctoral fellow Australian Nat. U., Canberra, 1975-76; asst. prof. biochemistry Loma Linda (Calif.) U., 1976-78, assoc. prof. biochemistry, 1978-83, prof. biochemistry, 1983—, prof., chmn. dept. microbiology and molecular genetics, 1988-2000, interim dir. Ctr. for Molecular Biology, 1989-94, 96-98, v.p. for rsch. affairs, 2000—. Contbr. articles to profl. publs. Rsch. grantee Am. Heart Assn., 1978-85, NIH, 1981—. Mem. Am. Soc. Microbiology, Am. Soc. Biochemistry and Molecular Biology. Office: Loma Linda U VP Rsch Affairs Loma Linda CA 92350-0001

**TAYLOR, BARRY NORMAN,** physicist; b. Phila., Mar. 27, 1936; s. Morris and Sarah (Weiss) T.; m. Sheila Anne Cohen, Dec. 28, 1958; children: Deborah Susan, David Joel, Denise Beth. AB, Temple U., Phila., 1957; MS, U. Pa., 1960, PhD, 1963. Instr., then asst. prof. physics U. Pa., 1963-66; mem. tech. staff RCA Rsch. Labs., 1966-70; chief absolute elec. measurements sect. Nat. Bur. Standards (name changed to Nat. Inst. of Standards and Tech. 1988), Gaithersburg, Md., 1970-74, administr. NIST Precision Measurement Grants Program, 1974-2000, chief electricity divsn., 1974-89; mgr. Fundamental Cons. Data Ctr., Gaithersburg, Md., 1989-2001, scientist emeritus, 2001—. Instr. Rider Coll., Trenton, N.J., 1969-70; mem., chairperson nat. and internat. tech. coms. Co-author: Fundamental Constants and Quantum Electrodynamics, 1969; Co-editor: Precision Measurement and Fundamental Constants, 1971; Co-editor: Precision Measurement and Fundamental Constants II,

1984; contbr. articles to sci. jours. Recipient Silver medal U.S. Dept. Commerce, 1975, Gold medal, 1989, John Price Wetherill medal Franklin Inst., 1975, Codata prize, 2000, Disting. Exec. award Sr. Exec. Svc. of USA U.S. Pres., 2000. Fellow IEEE, Am. Phys. Soc. (chair topical group on fundamental constants and precise tests of phys. laws Inst. Physics 1990-92); mem. Acad. Metrology Russian Fedn. (disting. fgn. mem.), Sigma Xi. Office: Nat Inst of Stds and Tech 100 Bureau Dr Stop 8420 Gaithersburg MD 20899-8401 E-mail: barry.taylor@nist.gov.

**TAYLOR, BRYCE B,** music educator, consultant; b. Edinburg, Tex., Feb. 12, 1925; s. Charles B and Cecile B Taylor; m. Diana Olivia Rodriguez, Apr. 4, 1946; children: Scott Lee, David Kim, Cynthia Diane, Richard Kerry. MusB, Tex. A&I, 1951, M of music edn., 1955. Music band instr. 3 Rivers Tex. Pub. Schools, 1951—61; music supr./band dir. Alice Ind. Sch. Dist., Alice, Tex., 1961—91, music cons., 1991—; music edn. prof. Tex. A&M Kingsville, 1993—; condr./music dir. Corpus Christi Wind Symphony, 1986—. Music cons. U. Interscholastic League, 1960—; adjudicator Tex. Music Adjudicators Assn., 1958—. Cpl. USMC, 1942—46, Pearl Harbor. Recipient Outstanding Music Educator, Nat. Fedn. Music Assn., 1991, Tchr. of the Yr., 1982, Bandmaster of the Yr., Tex. Bandmasters Assn., 1983. Mem.: Am. Concert Band Assn., Am. Bandmasters Assn. (past pres., bd. mem. 1999—2000), Tex. Music Educators Assn. (past. pres., divsn. chair 1962—64), Phi Beta Mu Nat. Band Assn. Independent. Cath. Avocations: golf, auto restoration, guest conducting. Home: 1001 Lincoln Alice TX 78332 Personal E-mail: dbtaylor1001@sbc.global.net.

**TAYLOR, BYRON KEITH,** industrial engineer; b. Portsmouth, Va., July 9, 1955; s. Robert Lee and Joyce Sue (Cox) T.; m. Barbara Sue Keene, Aug. 27, 1977; 1 child, Joshua Lee. BS in Indsl. Engring., Va. Poly. Inst. and State U., 1980; MBA, Ariz. State U., 2002. Indsl. engr. Deere & Co. (Harvester), East Moline, Ill., 1980-81, 83-84, product engr., 1981-83, prodn. engr., 1984-90, module owner, 1990-93; sr. engr. new product devel., 1993-95; supr. engring. John Deere, Davenport (Iowa) Works, 1995-97; mgr. loader fabrications John Deere, Davenport Works, 1995-97; mgr. header and sheet metal mfg. John Deere Harvester Works, East Moline, Ill., 1998-99, mgr. supply mgmt., 1999—2001, mgr. mfg., 2001—04; dir. quality worldwide agrl. divsn. Deere and Co. World Hdqs., Moline, Ill., 2005—. Mem. engring. curriculum devel. panel Black Hawk Coll., Moline, Ill., 1989; tech. del. conf. Citizen's Amb. program Soviet Union, 1990. Program chmn. Meth. Mens Club, Colona, Ill., 1985; advisor Jr. Achievement, East Moline, 1986-87, cons., 1988; bd. dirs. Handicapped Devel. Ctr., Davenport, 2000—; dir. Deere Harvester Credit Union, East Moline, 2000—. Named Young Engr. of Yr. Quad-Cities Engring. and Sci. Coun., 1989-90. Mem. Inst. Indsl. Engrs. (sr., dir. pub. rels. chpt. 46, 1986-87, pres.-elect 1988-89, pres. 1989-90). Republican. Avocation: golf. Home: 3110 Halcyon Dr Bettendorf IA 52722 Office: Deere & Co World Hdqs One John Deere Pl Moline IL 61265

**TAYLOR, CARSON WILLIAM,** retired electrical engineer; b. Superior, Wis., May 24, 1942; s. William Stanley and Elizabeth Marie (Christophersen) T.; m. Gudrun Renate Leistner, Dec. 28, 1966; 1 child, Natasha Marie. BSEE, U. Wis., 1965; M in Engring., Rensselaer Poly. Inst., 1969. Elec. engr. U.S. Bur. Reclamation, Billings, Mont., 1967-68, Bonneville Power Adminstrn., Portland, Oreg., 1969-89, prin. engr., 1989—2006; ret. Prin. Carson Taylor Seminars, Portland, 1986—. Author: Power System Voltage Stability, 1994; contbr. papers to profl. publs.; patentee in field. Lt. U.S. Army, 1965-67. Lt. U.S. Army, 1965-67. Fellow IEEE (chmn. subcom. 1982—); mem. NAE, Conférence Internationale des Grands Réseaux Electriques a Haute Tension (CIGRE, disting. mem.), Eta Kappa Nu. Lutheran. Avocations: fishing, hunting, woodworking, reading, computers.

**TAYLOR, CELIANNA ISLEY,** information systems specialist; b. Youngstown, Ohio; d. Paul Thornton and Florence (Jacobs) Isley; divorced; children: Polly, Jerry, Jim. BA in Philosophy, Denison U., 1939; MLS, Western Res. U., 1942. Worked in several pub. librs. and univ. librs., 1939-50; head Libr. Cataloging Dept. Battelle Mem. Inst., Columbus, Ohio, 1951-53; head pers. office, assoc. prof. libr. adminstrn. Ohio State U. Librs., Columbus, 1954-65; coord. info. svcs., assoc. prof. libr. adminstrn. Nat. Ctr. for Rsch. in Vocat. Edn., Ohio State U., Columbus, 1966-70; sr. rsch. assoc., adminstrv. assoc., assoc. prof. libr. adminstrn. dept. computer and info. sci. Ohio State U., Columbus, 1970-86, assoc. prof. emeritus Univ. Librs., 1986—. Mem. Task Force on a Spl. Collections Database, Ohio State U. Librs., Columbus, 1988-89, comm. systems and recs. coord. Ohio State U. Retirees Assn., Columbus, 1992-93, info. specialist, MacForum, Ohio State U., Columbus, 2001-2004; cons. profl. orgns. including Ernst & Ernst CPA's and Oreg. State Sys. of Higher Edn., 1961-82. Author: (with J. Magisos) Guide for State Voc-Tech Edn. Dissemination Systems 1971; editor: (with A.E. Petrarca, and R.S. Kohn) Info. Interaction 1982; Highlights-Coun. for Ethics in Econs., 1997—; contbr. several articles to profl. jours.; designer info. sys.: CALL Sys., 1977-82, Channel 2000 Proj. Home Info. Svc., 1980-81, Continuing Education Info. Ctr., 1989-90, Human Resources (HUR) Sys., 1976-77,1979-82, DECOS, 1975-86, Computer-asst. libr. Sys., Optical Scan Sys., 1972-73, ERIC Clearinghouse for vocat. edn., 1966-70. Chmn. subcom. on design, info. and ref. com. Columbus United Cmty. Coun., 1972-73; bd. dir. Columbus Reg. Info. Svc., 1974-78, Cmty. Info. Referral Svc., Inc. 1975-81; dir. Computer Utility for Pub. Info. Columbus, 1975-81; acct. coord. Greater Columbus Free-net, 1994-98; info. specialist, coord. LWV Met. Columbus Website Com., 2001-02; judge Laws of Life Ohio Statewide H.S. Essay Contest, 2005—; mem. interprofessional pub. policy panel on tech. and ethics Interprofessional Commn. Ohio, 2006—. Mem. ALA, Assn. Computing Machinery (Ctrl. Ohio chpt.), Am. Soc. Info. Sci. and Tech., Assn. Faculty and Profl. Women Ohio State U., Columbus Metro Club, Coun. for Ethics in Econs., World Future Soc., Olympic Indoor Tennis Club. Avocations: bird watching, gourmet cooking, tennis, water aerobics. Home and Office: 3471 Greenbank Ct Columbus OH 43221-4724 Office Phone: 614-876-0069.

**TAYLOR, CHARLES,** law educator; b. McGill U.; MA, PhD, Oxford U. Prof. McGill U., Montreal; Bd. of Trustees Prof. law and philosophy Northwestern U., Chgo., 2002—. Contbr. articles to profl. jours. Named grand officer de l'Ordre national du Quebec, 2000; recipient Prix Léon-Gérin, 1992. Fellow: British Acad., Royal Soc. Can.; mem.: Am. Acad. Arts & Scis.

**TAYLOR, CHARLES ELLETT,** biologist, educator; b. Chgo., Sept. 9, 1945; s. Stewart Ferguson and Barbara (Ellett) Taylor; m. Minna Glushien, June 22, 1969. AB, U. Calif., 1968; PhD, SUNY, Stony Brook, 1973. Prof. U. Calif., Riverside, 1974-80, UCLA, 1980—. Cons. artificial life and population genetics; dir. UCLA Cognitive Sci. Rsch. Program, 1990—99; mem. adv. bd. Computer Mus. Fishtank. Co-author: Artifical Life II, 1992, Artifical Life VI, 1998; editor: Artificial Life, 1997—2001; assoc. editor: IEEE Transactions on Evolutionary Computing, 1997—99; assoc. editor Artifical Life and Robotics, 1999—, Artificial Life, 2002—; mem. editl. bd.: Internat. Jour. Distributed Sensor Networks, 2004—; contbr. articles to profl. publs. Office: Dept Ecology and Evolutionary Biology UCLA Box 951606 Los Angeles CA 90095-1606 Office Phone: 310-825-6850. E-mail: ctaylor@ucla.edu.

**TAYLOR, CHARLES HART,** congressman; b. Brevard, NC, Jan. 3, 1941; m. Elizabeth Owen; 3 children. BA, Wake Forest U., 1963, JD, 1966. Owner-operator Transylvania Tree Farms, Brevard, NC; founder, chmn. bd. Blue Ridge Savings Bank, Asheville, NC; dir. Fin. Guaranty Corpn.; mem. NC State Ho. Reps., Raleigh, 1967—73, minority leader, 1969—73; mem. NC State Senate, Raleigh, 1973—75, minority leader, 1973—75; mem. US Congress from 11th NC dist., 1991—; mem. appropriations com., chmn. interior, environment and related agencies subcommittee. Bd. visitors US Mil. Acad. West Point. Named to Congl. Honor Roll, Seniors' Coalition; recipient Golden Bulldog award, Watchdogs of the Treasury, 1997—98, Guardian of Small Bus. award, Nat. Fedn. Ind. Bus., 1997—98, Voting Achievement award, Nat. Farmers Union, 1997—98, Friend of the Taxpayer award, Ams. for Tax Reform, Nat. Environ. Edn Leadership award, Nat. Environ. Edn. and Tng. Found., 2005. Mem.: Western NC Environ. Coun. (vice chair), NC Pks.

and Recreation Coun. (chair), NC Energy Policy Coun., NC Bd. Transp. Republican. Baptist. Office: US Ho Reps 339 Cannon Ho Office Bldg Washington DC 20515 Office Phone: 202-225-6401.*

**TAYLOR, CHARLES HENRY,** psychoanalyst, educator; b. Boston, Oct. 2, 1928; s. Charles Henry and Rosamond (Stewardson) T.; m. Diana Burgess, 1950; children: Stephen, Diana Beth, Charles S., Eleanor; m. Patricia Finley, 1988. BA, Yale U., 1950, MA, 1952, PhD, 1955; postgrad., Cambridge U., Eng., 1950-51. From instr. to asst. prof. English Ind. U., 1955-61; from asst. dean to assoc. dean, also assoc. prof. English Yale U., 1961-63, acting provost, 1963-64, provost, prof. English, 1964-72, pres. rep., 1972-76; grad. C.G. Jung Inst., NY, 1979; pvt. practice, 1976—. Bd. dirs. Meridian Audio, Ltd. Author: The Early Collected Editions of Shelley's Poems, 1958, (with Patricia Finley) Images of the Journey in Dante's Divine Comedy, 1997; editor: Essays on the Odyssey, 1963; contbr. articles to profl. jours. Mem. com. on libr. Yale U. Coun., 1990-95; trustee Hampshire Coll., 1988-93, 99—, chair, 2000-04. Mem. Internat. Assn. Analytical Psychology, Archive for Rsch. in Archetypal Symbolism (pres. 1987-93, treas. 1993—), N.Y. Assn. Analytical Psychology, Nat. Assn. for Advancement Psychoanalysis, Phi Beta Kappa.

**TAYLOR, CHRISTINE,** actress; b. Allentown, Pa., July 30, 1971; d. Skip and Joan Taylor; m. Ben Stiller, May 13, 2000; children: Ella Olivia, Quinlin Dempsey. Actor: (films) Calendar Girl, 1993, Showdown, 1993, The Brady Bunch Movie, 1995, Breaking Free, 1995, The Craft, 1996, A Very Brady Sequel, 1996, Cat Swallows Parakeet and Speaks, 1996, Campfire Tales, 1997, The Wedding Singer, 1998, Overnight Delivery, 1998, Denial, 1998, Kiss Toledo Goodbye, 1999, Desperate But Not Serious, 1999, Zoolander, 2001, Dodgeball: A True Underdog Story, 2004; (TV films) Here Come the Munsters, 1995, To the Ends of Time, 1996, Heat Vision and Jack, 1999. Office: United Talent Agy 9560 Wilshire Blvd Ste 500 Beverly Hills CA 90212

**TAYLOR, CLIFFORD OTIS,** retired principal; b. Ft. Pierce, Fla., Jan. 4, 1926; s. Thomas Archie and Margaret Emeline (Tyler) T.; m. Dorothy Ann Pearce, Dec. 27, 1952. BA, Fla. State U., 1950; MEd, U. Ill., Urbana, 1954; postgrad., U. Miami, Appalachian State U. Cert. tchr., prin. Tchr. Fairlawn Sch., St. Lucie County, Ft. Pierce, North Grade Sch., Palm Beach County Bd. Edn., West Palm Beach, Fla.; prin. South Grade Sch., Palm Beach County Bd. Edn., West Palm Beach, Fla., Kirklane Elem. Sch., Palm Beach County Bd. Edn., West Palm Beach, Fla., ret., 1991. Hon. mem. state and nat. PTA. With USN, 1944-46. Kirklane Elem. Sch. renamed Clifford O. Taylor/ Kirklane Elem. Sch. in his honor. Mem. ASCD, NAESP, Palm Beach County Prins. Assn., So. Assn. Schs. and Colls., Fla. Assn. Sch. Adminstrs., Retired Educators Assn., Lions, Phi Delta Kappa. Episcopalian. Home: 1811 N J Ter Lake Worth FL 33460-6523

**TAYLOR, CLIFFORD WOODWORTH,** state supreme court justice; b. Delaware, Ohio, Nov. 9, 1942; s. Alexander E. and Carolyn (Clifford) T.; m. Lucille Taylor; 2 children. BA, U. Mich., 1964; JD, George Washington U., 1967. Asst. prosecuting atty. Ingham County, 1971-72; ptnr. Denfield, Timmer & Taylor, 1972-92; judge Mich. Ct. of Appeals, 1992-97; justice Mich. Supreme Ct., 1997—, chief justice, 2005—. Mem. standing com. on professionalism Mich. State Bar, 1992. Bd. dirs. Mich. Dyslexia Inst., 1991—, Friends of the Gov.'s Residence, 1991—; mem. St. Thomas Aquinas Ch. With USN, 1967-71. Fellow Mich. State Bar Found.; mem. Mich. Supreme Ct. Hist. Soc., Federalist Soc., Cath. Lawyers Guild, State Bar. Home: 9760 Sunny Point Dr Laingsburg MI 48848 Office: Mich Supreme Ct PO Box 300052 Lansing MI 48909*

**TAYLOR, CORA HODGE,** social worker; b. Fayetteville, N.C., Nov. 25, 1942; d. John Marlin and Cora Louise (Mitchell) Hodge; m. Charles L. Taylor, June 26, 1965; children: Charles L., John M. BS, N.C. Coll., Durham, 1963; MSW, U. N.C., Chapel Hill, 1965. Clin. social worker VA Hosp., Bedford, Mass., 1965-68, 73-79; chief social worker Regional Health Center, Wilmington, Mass., 1978-79; clin. social worker VA Hosp., Bedford, Mass., 1979-91, supervisory social worker geriatrics and long term care, 1991—2000, coord. contract programs, 1993—. Field instr. Boston U. Sch. Social Work, 1979-87, Smith Coll. Sch. of Social Work, 1986-89; instr., cons. primary care residents Tufts U. Med. Sch., Regional Health Center, Wilmington, Mass., 1978-79. Mem. Town Meeting, Billerica, Mass., 1981-2000; precinct clk., 1981, 82, 89, precinct chmn., 1984, 85, 86; deacon first Congl. Ch., 1986—; women vets. coord. VA Bedford; Social Work Leadership Tng. program, 1998; mem. bd. commrs. Housing Authority Atlantic Beach, SC, 2003-04. Mem. LWC (dir. 1970-73), Acad. Cert. Social Workers, Nat. Assn. Social Workers.

**TAYLOR, DANIEL J.,** film company executive; Sr. tax mgr. Arthur Andersen & Co.; exec. Tracinda Corp.; with Metro-Goldwyn-Mayer Inc (MGM), LA, 1985—91, exec. v.p.-corp. fin., 1997, sr. exec. v.p., CFO, 1997—2005, pres., 2005—. Office: MGM 10250 Constellation Blvd Los Angeles CA 90067 Office Phone: 310-449-3000.

**TAYLOR, DANIEL RUSSELL,** lawyer; b. Clarksville, Tenn., July 6, 1946; s. Daniel Russell Taylor and Effie Mae Winslow; m. Gwynne Stephens Taylor; May 24, 1975; children: Edward Winslow, William Brinson. Grad., U.S. Mil. Acad., West Point, NY, 1968; JD, Wake Forest U., Winston-Salem, N.C., 1976. Sr. ptnr. Kilpatrick Stockton, LLP, Winston-Salem, 1978—. With U.S. Army, 1968—73. Home: 700 Arbor Road Winston Salem NC 27104 Office: Kilpatrick Stockton LLP 1001 W Fourth Street Winston Salem NC 27101 Office Phone: 336-607-7330. Business E-Mail: dantaylor@kilpatrickstockton.com.

**TAYLOR, DARRELL RICHARD,** art gallery director, artist; b. Nashville, Jan. 10, 1961; s. Melvin Richard Taylor and Nancy Ledbetter (Taylor) Briggs; m. Christina Moose Taylor (div.); 1 child, Matthew Harrison; life ptnr. Mark Stephen McCusker. BFA, U. Iowa, 1996, MA, 1998, MFA, 1999. Co-artistic dir. Habeas Corpus, Iowa City, 1997—; prodn. assist. dance dept. U. Iowa, Iowa City, 1998—2001; acting dir. UNI Gallery of Art, U. No. Iowa, Cedar Falls, 2001—02, art gallery dir., 2003—. Standing mem. art and architecture com. U. No. Iowa, 2001—, mem. mus. adv. bd., 2004—. Author: (exhbn. catalog) Transformations in the Nervepool: The Rituals and Zoacodes of Ebon Fisher, 2005. Sec. Cedar Valley Cultural Alliance, Cedar Falls, 2005; tenor sect. leader Nashville Symphony Chorus, 1990. Recipient Charles Massey award, Mid. Tenn. State U., 1992; grantee, Iowa Arts Coun., 2002, 2004; Mendieta Meml. scholar, U. Iowa, 1997. Mem.: Coll. Art Assn., NE Iowa Print Club. Democrat. Avocation: dance. Home: 439 Peterson St Iowa City IA 52245 Office: UNI Gallery of Art U No Iowa 104 KAB Cedar Falls IA 50614 Office Phone: 319-273-6134. Office Fax: 319-273-7333. Business E-Mail: galleryofart@uni.edu.

**TAYLOR, DAVE,** former professional sports team executive, retired professional hockey player; b. Levack, Ont., Can., Dec. 4, 1955; m. Beth Duken, July 11, 1981; children: Jamie, Katie Ann. Hockey player LA Kings, 1977—94, mem. front office, 1993—97, gen. mgr., 1997—2006. Recipient Bill Masterton Meml. Trophy, 1991, King Clancy Meml. Trophy, 1991.*

**TAYLOR, DAVID GEORGE,** retired banker; b. Charlevoix, Mich., July 29, 1929; s. Frank Flagg and Bessie (Strayer) Taylor; m. Robyne T. McCarthy, July 28, 1990; children from previous marriage: David, Amy, Jeanine. BS, Denison U., 1951; MBA, Northwestern U., 1953. With Continental Ill. Nat. Bank and Trust Co. Chgo., 1958—86, asst. cashier, 1961—64, 2d v.p., 1964—66, v.p., 1966—72, sr. v.p., 1972—74, exec. v.p., 1974—80, exec. v.p., treas., 1980—83, vice chmn., 1983—84, chmn., CEO, 1984; vice chmn. Irving Trust Co. N.Y.C., 1986—89; group exec. Chem. Bank, N.Y.C., 1989—94; ret., 1994. Mem. Dealer Bank Assn. Com. on Glass-Steagall Reform, 1985—86; bd. dirs. CNA Income Shares. Author: Bajan's Tale. Bd. dirs. Evanston Hosp., Glenbrook Hosp.; trustee Art Inst. Chgo., 1981—86; advisor J.L. Kellogg Grad. Sch. Mgmt., Northwestern U., 1984—. Served to lt. USN, 1953—56. Mem.: Assn. Ret. City Bankers (asset/liability com.; govt. rels. com. 1983—), Govt. and Fed. Agys. Securities Com. (chmn. bd. dirs. 1982—83), Pub. Securities Assn. (chmn. 1977, bd. dirs. 1977—78, treas. 1978). Republican. Presbyterian. Personal E-mail: caldave110@aol.com.

**TAYLOR, DAVID KERR,** international business educator, consultant; b. Oxford, N.C., Oct. 11, 1928; s. David Kerr and Myrtle Norman (Shamburger) T.; m. Isabel de Sousa Botelho de Albuquerque, Apr. 23, 1960; children: Anne de Albuquerque Taylor Grave, Katherine Rowena Taylor. BA, Duke U., 1947, JD, 1949. Bar: N.Y., N.C. Atty. Ins. Co. N.Am., N.Y.C., 1949-51, Milbank, Tweed, Hadley & McCloy, N.Y.C., 1954-55; internat. exec. Mobil Corp., N.Y.C., Washington, Can., Portugal, Nigeria, France, others, 1955-86; adj. prof. internat. affairs, sr. fellow internat. bus. Georgetown U. Sch. Fgn. Svc., Washington, 1987-2000. Pres. Luso-Am. Bus. Coun., 1987-89; bd. visitors Duke U. Law Sch. 1st lt. U.S. Army, 1951-54, Germany. Mem. Am. Portuguese Soc. (bd. dirs., pres. 1968-70, 76-80), Washington Export Coun., Washington Inst. Fgn. Affairs, Dacor Bacon House, Cosmos Club, Phi Beta Kappa. Avocation: singing. Home: 2737 Devonshire Pl NW Washington DC 20008-3479

**TAYLOR, DAVID MICHAEL,** elementary school educator; b. Clarksville, Tenn., July 10, 1974; s. Gregory Alan Dixon and Sherry Lee Sanborn; m. Jennifer Lynn Taylor, June 2, 1999; children: Emily Noel, Dylan Matthew. AA, Owensboro C.C., Ky., 2002; BA, Western Ky. U., Bowling Green, 2004. Cert. middle school tchr. Tchr. social studies Ohio County Mid. Sch., Hartford, Ky.; tchr. sci. and social studies Render Edn. Ctr., Hartford. Spl. teams coord. varsity football team Ohio County H.S., Hartford. With U.S. Army. Mem. NEA, Hope Lodge #4. Avocations: cooking, Blues. Office: Render Education Ctr 100 Render St Hartford KY 42347

**TAYLOR, DAVID WYATT AIKEN,** retired clergyman; b. Tsingkiangpu, Kiangsu, China, Dec. 13, 1925; s. Hugh Kerr and Fanny Bland (Graham) T.; m. Lillian Ross McCulloch, Aug. 25, 1951; children: Frances Bland, David Wyatt. BA, Vanderbilt U., 1949; B.D. cum laude, Union Theol. Sem. Va., 1952; Th.M., Princeton Theol. Sem., 1953; D.D. (hon.), King Coll., Bristol, Tenn., 1959. Ordained to ministry Presbyn. Ch. U.S., 1952. Pastor chs., Elkton, Va., 1953-55, Bristol, Va., 1955-62; ednl. sec. bd. world missions Presbyn. Ch. U.S., 1962-68, program div. dir., 1968-73, ecumenical officer gen. assembly mission bd. Atlanta, 1973-82; pastor Orange Park Presbyn. Ch., Orange Park, Fla., 1982-86; gen. sec. for strategy and interpretation Consultation on Ch. Union, Princeton, NJ, 1986-88, gen. sec., 1988-93; ret., 1993. Interim Bible Presbyn. Jr. Coll., Maxton, N.C., 1951; mem. program bd., div. Christian edn. Nat. Council Chs., 1965-69, bd. mgrs., dept. edn. for mission, 1962-68, mem. program bd., div. overseas ministries, 1968-78, mem. governing bd., 1976-80, chmn. governing bd. credentials com., 1978; chmn. Church World Service, Inc., 1973-75; mem. adminstrn. and fin. com. Nat. Council Chs., 1973-75, mem. commn. on faith and order, 1978-93; mem. commn. on interchurch aid World Council Chs., 1973-75; mem. 5th Assembly, 1975; rep. Presbyn. Ch. U.S. to World Alliance Ref. Chs., 1976-82; bd. dirs. Presbyn. Survey mag., 1963-68; mem. Consultation on Ch. Union, 1974-93; chmn. Nat. Ecumenical Officers Assn., 1978-81; exec. coun. NC Coun. Chs., 2003—. Bd. dirs. Abingdon Presbytery's Children's Home, Wytheville, Va., 1958-62. Served with AUS, 1944-46, PTO. Mem. Sigma Chi. Presbyterian. Home: 3113 Glenhope Ct Cary NC 27511 Personal E-mail: taylor3@mindspring.com.

**TAYLOR, DIANA LANCASTER,** state official; b. Summit, N.J., Feb. 6, 1955; d. Edwin Douglas and Lois Johnston (O'Neill) T. AB, Dartmouth Coll., 1977; MBA, Columbia U., 1979-81. Analyst N.Y. State Dept. Soc. Service, N.Y.C., 1977-79; assoc. Smith, Barney, Harris, Upham, N.Y.C., 1981-82, Lehman Brothers Kuhn Loeb, N.Y.C., 1982-83, v.p., 1983-84, Donaldson, Lufkin & Jenrette, N.Y.C., 1984-86, sr. v.p., mgr. short-term banking, 1987-88, sr. v.p., mgr. edn. fin. group, 1987-88; founding prin. M.R. Beal & Co., 1988—90, pres., 1990—93; exec. v.p., head capital markets Muriel Siebert & Co., 1993—95; sr. v.p. pub. fin. Smith Mitchell Investment Group Inc., 1996—99; asst. sec. for pub. authorities State of NY, 1999; v.p. governmental and regulatory affairs KeySpan Energy, N.Y.C., 2000—; CFO LI Power Authority, NY, 2001—02; dep. sec. for state authorities State of NY, 2002—03, dep. sec. for fin. & housing, 2003, supt. banks, 2003—. Bd. dirs. YMCA Greater NYC, Hudson River Park Trust, The After Sch. Corp., NYC Transit Mus., Bklyn. Acad. Music. Office: Supt Banks NY State Banking Dept One State St New York NY 10004-1417 Office Phone: 212-709-3501.

**TAYLOR, DONALD,** retired manufacturing executive; b. Worcester, Mass., June 2, 1927; s. John A. B. and Alice M. (Weaver) T.; m. Ruth L. Partridge, June 24, 1950; children: Linda Taylor Robertson, Donald, Mark, John. BSME, Worcester Poly. Inst., 1949; grad., Northeastern U. Mgmt. Devel. Program, 1962, Harvard Bus. Sch. Advanced Mgmt. Program, 1979. Registered profl. engr., Mass. With George J. Meyer Mfg. Co., Milw., 1954-69; pres. mfg. div. A-T-O, Inc., 1969; exec. v.p. Nordberg div. Rex Chainbelt, Inc., Milw., 1969-73; v.p. ops. Rexnord Inc., Brookfield, Wis., pres., chief operating officer, 1978-85, chief exec. officer, from 1985, chmn., 1985-88; pres. Nordberg Machinery Group, Milw., 1973-78. With USNR, 1951—54. Mem. ASME, Alunagui C. of C., Milw. Country Club, Milw. Town Club, Univ. Club, Masons. Office: 1 Runnymede Dr North Hampton NH 03862-2328

**TAYLOR, DOUGLAS HOWARD,** translator; b. Washington, Apr. 4, 1961; s. Richard Powell and Barbara Jo Anne (Harris) T. BA, Amherst Coll., 1984; MA, Am. U., 1990. Freelance Russian translator, Germantown, Md., 1988—. Editor-in-chief Landon News, 1979—80; editor mag. Nat. Soc. for Children of Am. Revolution, 1979—80. Contbr. articles to profl. jours. Vol. Reagan/Bush Campaign, Potomac, 1980; mem. to chmn. Md. Bush/Quayle Campaign, Bethesda, 1988. Mem.: Phi Beta Kappa. Republican. Episcopalian. Avocations: coin collecting/numismatics, bowling, tennis, running, reading. Home and Office: 14914 Spring Meadows Dr Germantown MD 20874-3444

**TAYLOR, DUNCAN PAUL,** pharmacologist, researcher; b. Bremerton, Wash., Feb. 4, 1949; s. Alan Earl and Barbara Eleanor (Thiel) T.; m. Jeanne Louise Damgaard, Apr. 8, 1972; 1 child; Jack Xander. BS in Chemistry, Calif. Inst. Tech., 1971; PhD in Biochemistry, Oreg. State U., 1977. Technician analytical svcs. Carnation Co. Rsch. Labs., Van Nuys, Calif., 1967-70; Peace Corps vol. Princess Margaret Secondary Sch., St. Johns, Antigua & Barbuda, 1971-73; grad. tchg. and rsch. asst. biochemistry and biophysics Oreg. State U., Corvallis, 1973-77; rsch. assoc. sect. biochemistry and pharmacology NIMH, Bethesda, Md., 1977-79; scientist, neuropharmacologist, rsch. assoc. Pharm. divsn. Mead Johnson & Co., Evansville, Ind., 1979-80; sr. scientist, group leader Pharm. div. Mead Johnson & Co., Evansville, Ind., 1980-82; sr. scientist, group leader, neuropharmacologist Pharm. R & D divsn. Bristol-Myers Co., Evansville, 1982-83, sr. rsch. scientist, mgr., 1983-85, rsch. fellow preclin. ctrl. nervous sys. rsch., 1985-89; sr. rsch. fellow preclin. ctrl. nervous sys. rsch. Pharm. Rsch. Inst. Bristol-Myers Squibb Co., Wallingford, Conn., 1989-94; dir. pharmacology Symphony Pharms., Malvern, Pa., 1994-95; cons., 1995-96; analyst bus. devel. Pharmacia & Upjohn, Kalamazoo, 1996-98, dir. strategic rsch. assessment, 1998—2003; prin. MT Enterprises, Kalamazoo, 2003—04; dir. strategic rsch. assessment Biovail Techs., Ltd., Bridgewater, NJ, 2004—05; sr. dir. strategic intelligence Biovail Pharms., Inc., Bridgewater, 2005—. Mem. external adv. bd. dept. chemistry U. So. Miss.; grant reviewer NSF, 1981, 82, Med. Rsch. Coun. Can., 1987, 88; frequent presenter to profl. confs.; cons. in field. Contbr. numerous articles and abstracts to profl. jours. Bd. dirs. Posey County chpt. Am. Cancer Soc., 1983—85; mem. Tri-State Cursillo Cmty.; mentor Horizons Leadership Acad., Evansville-Venderburgh Sch. Corp., 1985; cons. Project Bus. Jr. Achievement, 1988; mem. chancel choir 1st United Meth. Ch., Mt. Vernon, Ind., 1976—86; mem. adult choir South Congl. Ch., Middletown, Conn., 1986—96, deacon, 1987—90, 1995—96, co-chmn., 1989—90, 1996, mem. coun., 1989—90, mem. task force on long-range planning, 1989—90; mem. adult choir 2d Reformed Ch., Kalamazoo, 1997—2004, mem. handbell choir, 1997—2004, mem. worship coun.

1997—99, elder, 1998—2001, consistory mem., 1998—2001, ch. outreach coun., 2000—01; active Grace United Ch. of Christ, Clinton, NJ, 2005—. Scholar Carnation Co., 1967-70, Calif. State scholar, 1967-68, 70; rsch. fellow NSF, 1970, Cold Spring Harbor Labs., 1974. Fellow: Am. Inst. Chemists; mem.: AAAS, Soc. Competitive Intelligence Profls., Internat. Brain Rsch. Orgn.-World Fedn. Neuroscientists, Fedn. Am. Socs. for Exptl. Biology, European Brain and Behavior Soc., Brit. Brain Rsch. Assn, Soc. for Neurosci. (v.p. Conn. chpt. 1989—93), Am. Soc. for Pharmacology and Exptl. Therapeutics, Am. Chem. Soc., Phi Lambda Upsilon, Sigma Xi. Democrat. Achievements include patent for method and treatment of ischemia in the brain; made significant efforts in identification and development of new antipsychotics and antidepressants; identification of potential mechanism of action of the antipsychotic BMY14802; research in receptors, in etiology, expression and pharmacotherapy of psychiatric disorders. Home: 11 Jockey Ln Flemington NJ 08822-1599 Office: Biovail Pharms Inc 700 Route 202/206 North PO Box 6935 Bridgewater NJ 08807 Office Phone: 908-927-1797. Business E-mail: duncan.taylor@biovail.com.

**TAYLOR, E. JANE,** lawyer; b. Niagra Falls, N.Y., Dec. 16, 1954; BA cum laude, Kent State U., 1977; JD, U. Akron, 1980. Bar: Ohio 1981, U.S. Dist. Ct. No. Dist. Ohio 1981, U.S. Ct. Appeals (6th cir.) 1985, U.S. Dist. Ct. So. Dist. Ohio 2002. Assoc. atty. Guy Lemmert & Towne, Akron, Ohio, 1981—90, ptnr., 1990—. Mem. Akron Law Rev., 1979—80. Mem. bd. trustees United Way Summit County, 1995—2002, past chair svc. rev. team, mem. cmty. investment coun., chair portfolio coun. improving health and wellness, past mem. planning and allocations com., co-chair task force multi-yr. funding. Named one of 100 Women of Distinction, Akron Area YWCA, 2001. Mem.: ABA, Comml. Law League Am., Ohio Women's Bar Assn., Nat. Conf. Bar Presidents, Ohio State Bar Assn. (mem. bd. govs. 2000—03, mem. coun. delegates 1996—2003, pres.-elect 2004—), Akron Bar Assn. (pres. 1994—95, v.p. 1993—94, bd. trustees 1990—93, chair bar applicants and students com. 1988—90, mem. bankruptcy and comml. law sect. 1989—, outstanding com. chairperson 1997—98). Office: Guy Lammert & Towne 2210 First Nat Twr 106 S Main St Akron OH 44308 Office Phone: 330-535-2151. Office Fax: 330-535-9048. E-mail: guylaw2210@aol.com.

**TAYLOR, EDWARD A.,** lawyer; b. SI, Jan. 25, 1958; BA, Fordham U., 1980, JD, 1983. Bar: NY 1984, US Dist. Ct. So. Dist. NY, US Dist. Ct. Ea. Dist. NY. Ptnr. Wilson, Elser, Moskowitz, Edelman & Dicker LLP, NYC. Mem.: ABA (torts & ins. practice sect., govt. & regulatory affairs divsn.), NY State Bar Assn. (ins. practice sect.). Office: Wilson Elser Moskowitz Edelman & Dicker LLP 150 E 42nd St 23rd Fl New York NY 10017-5639 Office Phone: 212-490-3000 ext. 2386. Office Fax: 212-490-3038. Business E-mail: taylore@wemed.com.

**TAYLOR, EDWARD CURTIS,** chemistry professor; b. Springfield, Mass., Aug. 3, 1923; s. Edward Curtis and Margaret Louise (Anderson) T.; m. Virginia Dion Crouse, June 29, 1946; children: Edward Newton, Susan Raines. Student, Hamilton Coll., 1942-44, DSc (hon.), 1969; AB, Cornell U., 1946, PhD, 1949. Postdoctoral fellow Nat. Acad. Scis., Zurich, Switzerland, 1949-50; DuPont postdoctoral fellow chemistry U. Ill., 1950-51, faculty, 1951-54, asst. prof. organic chemistry, 1952-54; faculty Princeton U., 1954—, prof. chemistry, 1964—, A. Barton Hepburn prof. organic chemistry, 1966—, A. Barton Hepburn prof. organic chemistry emeritus, 1997—, chmn. dept. chemistry, 1974-79, sr. rsch. scientist, 1997—. Vis. prof. Technische Hochschule, Stuttgart, Fed. Republic Germany, 1960, U. East Anglia, 1969, 71; Disting. vis. prof. U. Buffalo, 1968, U. Wyo., 1977; Backer lectr. U. Groningen, Holland, 1969; mem. chemistry adv. com. Office Sci. Research, USAF, 1962-73, Cancer Chemotherapy Nat. Service Ctr., 1958-62; mem. internat. adv. bd. Ctr. Medicinal Chemistry, Bar-Ilan U., Israel, 1994—; cons. rsch. divs. Parke-Davis Co., 1951-56, Procter & Gamble, 1953-80, Smith Kline & French, 1956-62, Eastman Kodak Co., 1965-83, Tenn. Eastman Co., 1968-83, Eli Lilly & Co., 1962-2002, Burroughs Wellcome Co., 1983-95, E.I. duPont de Nemours & Co., 1986-90, Polaroid Corp., 1986-2001, Dow Elanco Co., 1989-96, DuPont Merck Pharm. Co., 1990-97, Dow AgroScis., 1997-2003, DuPont Pharms. Co., 1997-2001. Author: (with McKillop) Chemistry of Cyclic Enaminonitriles and o-Aminonitriles, 1970, Principles of Heterocyclic Chemistry; film and audio courses, 1974; editor (with Raphael and Wynberg) Advances in Organic Chemistry, vols I-V, 1960-65, (with Wynberg) Vol VI, 1969, vols. VII-IX, 1970-79 (with W. Pfleiderer) Pteridine Chemistry, 1964, The Chemistry of Heterocyclic Compounds, 1968—, General Heterocyclic Chemistry, 1968—; organic chemistry editl. advisor John Wiley & Sons, Inc., 1968—; mem. editl. adv. bd. Jour. Medicinal Chemistry, 1962-66, Jour. Organic Chemistry, 1971-75, Synthetic Communications, 1971—, Heterocycles, 1973—, Chm. Substructure Index, 1971—, Advances in Heterocyclic Chemistry, 1983—, Pteridines, 1989—. Recipient rsch. awards, SmithKline and French Found., 1955, Hoffmann-LaRoche Foun., 1964—65, Ciba Found., 1971, Disting. Hamilton award, 1977, U.S. Sr. Scientist prize, Alexander von Humboldt Found., 1983, Disting. Alumni medal, Hamilton Coll., 1990, F. Gowland Hopkins medal, 1993, Thomas Alva Edison award, R&D Coun. NJ, 2004; sr. faculty fellow, Harvard U., 1959, Guggenheim fellow, 1979—80. Fellow N.Y. Acad. Scis., Am. Inst. Chemists; mem. Am. Chem. Soc. (award for creative work in synthetic organic chemistry, 1974, chmn. organic chemistry div. 1976-77, Arthur C. Cope scholar award 1994, Heroes of Chemistry award 2006), German Chem. Soc., Royal Soc. London, Internat. Soc. Heterocyclic Chemistry (5th Internat. award 1989), Phi Beta Kappa, Sigma Xi, Phi Kappa Phi. Achievements include pattern for Alimta. Home: 288 Western Way Princeton NJ 08540-5337 Office Phone: 609-258-3914. Business E-Mail: etaylor@princeton.edu.

**TAYLOR, EDWARD STEWART,** obstetrician, educator; b. Hecla, SD, Aug. 20, 1911; s. Robert Stewart and Sylvia Frances (Dewey) T.; m. Ruth Catherine; June 13, 1940; children: Edward Stewart, Elizabeth Dewey Taylor Bryant, Catherine Wells Taylor. BA, U. Iowa, 1933, MD, 1936. Diplomate Am. Bd. Ob-Gyn (dir. 1962-69). Intern. Hurley Hosp., Flint, Mich., 1936-37; splty. tng. ob-gyn L.I. Coll. Hosp., 1937-41; prof. ob-gyn, chmn. dept. Sch. Medicine, U. Colo., 1947-76, clin. prof., 1976-81, prof., chmn. emeritus, 1981—. Nat. cons. ob-gyn to surg. gen. USAF, 1958-62. Author: Manual of Gynecology, 1952, Essentials of Gynecology, 4th edit.; editor: Beck's Obstetrical Practice, 10th edit.; editor-in-chief for obstetrics: Obstetrical and Gynecol. Survey, 1967-92. Trustee Denver Symphony Orch., 1979-85. Served to lt. col. AUS, 1942-45. Endowed ob-gyn. chair U. Colo., 1999. Fellow ACS, Am. Coll. Obstetricians and Gynecologists (Disting. Svc. award 1984); mem. AMA, Am. Gynecol. Soc. (v.p. 1974-75), Am. Assn. Obstetricians and Gynecologists (pres. 1970-71), Ctrl. Assn. Obstetricians and Gynecologists, S.W. Obstet. and Gynecol. Soc. (hon.), Am. Gynecol. and Obstet. Soc., Assn. Profs. Ob-Gyn (pres. 1974-75), Western Surg. Soc., Finnish Gynecol. Soc. (hon.), University Club (Denver), Alpha Omega Alpha. Clubs: University (Denver). Congregationalist. Home: 80 S Dexter St Denver CO 80246-1051

**TAYLOR, EDWIN R.,** music director; b. Port Huron, Mich., Sept. 4, 1952; s. Leroy E. and Virgene M. Taylor; m. Faith A. Ferry, Sept. 28, 1996; children: Jenelle F. Ferry, Jordan W. Ferry, Colton W. Ferry. MusB, Westminster Choir Coll., Princeton, NJ, 1975, MusM, 1979; postgrad., UCLA, 1996. Music dir. Covenant Presbyn. Ch., Fort Myers, Fla., 1984—98; co-dir. Gulf Coast Opera Co., Fort Myers, Fla., 1996—2001; chorus master SW Fla. Symphony Chorus, Fort Myers, 1997—98; music dir. Venice (Fla.) United Ch. Of Christ, 1998—2001; min. music, music dir. The First Congl. Ch., Ridgefield, Conn., 2001—. Adj. prof. Fla. Gulf Coast Opera Co., Fort Myers, 1999—2001; concert series dir. The First Congl. Ch., Ridgefield, 2001—; guest condr. Wapping Cmty. Ch., South Windsor, Conn., 2004—; singer Yale Camerata, New Haven, 2005—. Composer: (anthem for choir, organ, brass, percussion) Sing Praise To God Who Reigns Above, (anthem for male chorus) In The Bleak Midwinter, (hymntune) Farmer, Crown Chase, Simpson, Keddy, Faithsong, Sluyter, King's Crown, Harding, Emory, Spring Hill Lane, (work for brass quintet) Lo, How A Rose E'er Blooming, Angels We Have Heard On High, (set of songs without words for piano) Songs Of Home; arranger: anthem for choir, organ, brass, percussion O Praise Ye The Lord, work for brass, organ, percussion Feierlicher Einzug, work for handbells, organ, brass,

percussion The Great Gate of Kiev, work for brass and organ Processional March, Rigaudon, Trumpet Tune, Prelude. Mem.: Westminster Choir Coll. Alumni Assn. (class agt. 1984—90, alumni coun. mem. 1994—96), Choristers Guild (v.p. 2006), Fairfield-West Chpt. Am. Guild Organists (mem. exec. bd. 2002—05, dean 2006—), Aircraft Owners and Pilots Assn. Republican. Congregationalist. Achievements include first to Conduct the modern-day premiere of Sousa's The Last Crusade, the first performance since the work's premiere under Sousa's direction; Conducted the Southwest Florida premiere of numerous choral/orchestral works. Avocations: flying, writing, cooking, travel. Home: 34 Spring Hill Ln Bethel CT 06801-2724 Office: The First Congregational Church 103 Main St Ridgefield CT 06877 Office Phone: 203-438-8077. Office Fax: 203-438-9678. Personal E-mail: fafert@sbcglobal.net. Business E-Mail: music@firstcongregational.com.

**TAYLOR, ELIZABETH (DAME ELIZABETH ROSEMOND TAYLOR),** actress; b. London, Feb. 27, 1932; d. Francis Lenn and Sara Viola (Warmbrodt) Taylor; m. Conrad Nicholas Hilton Jr., May 6, 1950 (div. Feb. 1, 1951); m. Michael Wilding, Feb. 21, 1952 (div. Jan. 30, 1957); children: Christopher Edward, Michael Howard; m. Michael Todd, Feb. 2, 1957 (dec. Mar. 22, 1958); 1 child, Elizabeth Frances; m. Eddie Fisher, May 12, 1959 (div. Mar. 6, 1964); m. Richard Burton, Mar. 15, 1964 (div. June 26, 1974); 1 adopted child, Maria; m. Richard Burton, Oct. 10, 1975 (div. Aug. 1, 1976); m. John W. Warner, Dec. 4, 1976 (div. Nov. 7, 1982); m. Larry Fortensky, Oct. 6, 1991 (div. Oct. 31, 1996). Student, Byron House, Hawthorne Sch., Metro-Goldwyn-Mayer Sch. Ptnr., cons. House of Taylor Jewelry, Inc, 2005—. Actress: (films) There's One Born Every Minute, 1942; Lassie Come Home, 1943; The White Cliffs of Dover, 1944; Jane Eyre, 1944; National Velvet, 1944; Courage of Lassie, 1946; Cynthia, 1947; Life with Father, 1947; A Date with Judy, 1948; Julia Misbehaves, 1948; Little Women, 1950; Conspirator, 1950; The Big Hangover, 1950; Father of the Bride, 1950; Quo Vadis, 1951; Father's Little Dividend, 1951; A Place in the Sun, 1951; Callaway Went Thataway, 1951; Lover is Better Than Ever, 1952; Ivanhoe, 1952; The Girl Who Had Everything, 1953; Elephant Walk, 1954; Rhapsody, 1954; Beau Brummel, 1954; The Last Time I Saw Paris, 1954; Giant, 1956; Raintree County, 1957; Cat on a Hot Tin Roof, 1958; Suddenly, Last Summer, 1959; Scent of Mystery, 1960; Butterfield 8, 1960 (Acad. award for Best Actress, 1960); Cleopatra, 1963; The V.I.P.'s, 1963; The Sandpiper, 1965; Who's Afraid of Virginia Woolf?, 1966 (Acad. award for Best Actress, 1966); The Comedians, 1967; Reflections in a Golden Eye, 1967; Dr. Faustus, 1967; Boom!, 1968; Secret Ceremony, 1968; Anne of the Thousand Days, 1969; The Only Game in Town, 1970; Under Mildwood, 1971; X, Y and Zee, 1972; Hammersmith is Out, 1972; Night Watch, 1973; Ash Wednesday, 1973; That's Entertainment, 1974; The Driver's Seat, 1974; Blue Bird, 1975; Winter Kills, 1977; A Little Night Music, 1977; The Mirror Crack'd, 1980; Young Toscanini, 1987; The Flintstones, 1994; Actress, prodr. The Taming of the Shrew, 1967; Actress: (TV films) Divorce His-Divorce Hers, 1973; Victory at Entebbe, 1977; Return Engagement, 1979; Between Friends, 1982; Malice in Wonderland, 1986; There Must Be a Pony, 1986; Poker Alice, 1987; Sweet Bird of Youth, 1989; These Old Broads, 2001; (TV miniseries) North and South, 1985; (TV series) General Hospital, 1981; All My Children, 1984; Hotel, 1984; The Simpsons, 1993; The Nanny, 1996; Murphy Brown, 1996; High Society, 1996; theatre appearances include: (Broadway plays) The Little Foxes, 1981; Private Lives, 1983; narrator: (documentaries) Genocide, 1981; exec. prodr.: (films) Number 13, 1962; exec. prodr.: (films) Oz, 1997; assoc. prodr.: (films) The Caretaker, 1963; author: (autobiography) Elizabeth Taylor, 1965, Elizabeth Taylor Takes Off: On Weight Gain, Weight Loss, Self Esteem and Self Image, 1988, Elizabeth Taylor: My Love Affair with Jewelry, 2002; co-author (with Richard Burton): (novels) World Enough and Time, 1964; lic. (fragrances) Elizabeth Taylor's Passion, Passion for Men, White Diamonds/Elizabeth Taylor, Elizabeth Taylor's Diamonds & Emeralds, Diamonds and Rubies, Diamonds & Sapphires, Elizabeth Taylor Black Pearls. Active philanthropic, relief, charitable causes internationally, including Israeli War Victims Fund for the Chaim Sheba Hosp., 1976, UNICEF, various children's hosps., med. clinics, Botswana; initiated Ben Gurion U. - Elizabeth Taylor Fund for Children of the Negev; supporter AIDS Project, L.A., 1985; founder, nat. chmn. Am. Found. for AIDS Rsch. (AmFAR), 1985—, internat. fund, 1985—; founder Elizabeth Taylor AIDS Found., 1991—. Named a Kennedy Ctr. Honoree, John F. Kennedy Ctr. for the Performing Arts, 2002; named Comdr. Arts Letters, France, 1985, an honoree with dedication of Elizabeth Taylor Med. Ctr. Whitman - Walker Clinic, Washington, 1993, Dame Comdr. of Order of British Empire, 1999; recipient Legion of Honor for work with AmFAR, France, 1987, Aristotle S. Onassis Found., 1988, Jean Hersholt Humanitarian Acad. award (for work as AIDS advocate), 1993, Life Achievement award, Am. Film Inst., 1993, BAFTA Fellowship Award, British Acad. Film and Television Arts, 1999, Presdl. Citizen's Medal, 2001. Address: Elizabeth Taylor AIDS Found PO Box 55995 Sherman Oaks CA 91413

**TAYLOR, ELIZABETH,** secondary school educator; BA, Georgetown Coll., 1949; MA, U. Ky., 1953; edn. specialist, Ea. Ky. U., 1956. Lic. real estate Ky. Bd. Realtors. Tchr. Russell County Bd. Edn., Jamestown, Ky., 1947—48; acct. Fayette Crutcher Clothing Bus., Frankfort, 1957—63; tchr. Ky. State U., Frankfort, 1958—64, Franklin County Bd. Edn., Frankfort, 1949—89; banker Farmers Bank and Trust Co., Frankfort, 1980—90; realtor Rector Hayden, Lexington, Ky., 1990—91; tchr. Woodford County Bd. Edn., Versailles, Ky., 1992—2005. Rep. Internat. Mission Bd., 1992—. Author: Prayer-A Link to God's Power, 2001; writer: lyrics Trust the Invisible God, 2002. Mem. mainland adv. coun. Hawaii Bapt. Acad., 2005; vol. emergency rm. St. Joseph Hosp., Lexington; active Ky. Disaster Relief. Mem.: NEA, Ky. Edn. Assn. Baptist. Avocations: travel, music, sports, walking, hiking. Home: 115 S Hill Versailles KY 40383

**TAYLOR, ELIZABETH JANE,** investment advisor, real estate company executive, marketing executive; b. Tiffin, Ohio, Oct. 27, 1941; d. Albert Joseph Lucas and Mary Jane Siebenaller-Swander; m. Gaylen Lloyd Taylor, July 11, 1977. Student, Heidelberg Coll., 1961, Austin CC, Tex., 1983-84; grad., Real Estate Edn. Ctr., 1984, Inst. Real Estate, 1988, Real Estate Inst., 1989; Tex. Realtors Inst., 1989; student, Rockhurst Coll., 1991-92. Dir. regional mktg. Sibrow, Inc., Ottawa, Can., 1981-83; realtor assoc. Alliance Sales, Austin, 1985-88; assoc. Broadway Comml. Investments, 1988-91; prin. Taylor & Assocs. Internat. Mktg. & Bus. Devel., 1980-98. Cons. Hypnosis Conn., Ohio, Tex. and Ariz., 1967—; tchr. mktg. and bus. devel., 1980-96. Author: Letters from Home, 1986, Unfinished Business, 2001, Reflections and Dreams, 2002, Unfinished Business, 2002, Southwest Celebration, 2003, A Dark and Stormy Night, 2003, Soul's Music, 2003, A Christmas Collection, 2003, Sourdough & More, 2003, Joy of Poetry, 2004, A Treasury of Poetry, 2005, Marketing Yourself As a Freelance Writer, 2005; contbr. Best New Poets of 1986, American Poetry Anthology, vol. VI., #3, 1986; columnist Austin Women Mag., 1984-86. V.p. Am. Congress on Real Estate, 1982-83; arbitrator Better Bus. Bur., 1984-89, sr. arbitrator, Austin, 1989-95; spkrs. bur. Austin Women Ctr., 1985-88; v.p. Austin World Affairs Coun., 1984-94; adv. panel Austin Woman Mag., 1984-86. Nominee to Tex. Womens Hall of Fame, 1984. Mem. NAFE (network dir. 1980-88), Am. Biog. Inst. Rsch. (hon., bd. advisors 1988). Avocations: writing, behavior research. Home: 3926 E Cherokee St Phoenix AZ 85044-3827 Personal E-mail: elizabethlucastaylor@yahoo.com.

**TAYLOR, ERROL BANCROFT,** lawyer; b. Kingston, Jamaica, Nov. 24, 1955; s. Samuel George and Etta Maud (Champagnie) T.; m. Paula Whitfield, July 8, 1989; children: Bradford Russell, Kyle Bancroft. BA in Biology, SUNY, Oswego, 1977; JD, NY Law Sch., 1987. Bar: NY 1988, US Dist. Ct. (So. and Ea. Dists.) NY 1988, US Ct. Appeals (Fed. Cir.) 1991. Sr. rsch. assoc. Squibb Corp., New Brunswick, NJ, 1977-81, asst. rsch investigator, 1981-87; assoc. atty. Fitzpatrick, Cella, Harper & Scinto, NYC, 1987-93, ptnr., 1994—2004, Milbank, Tweed, Hadley & McCloy, LLP, NYC, 2004—. Lectr. in field. Bd. dirs. Oswego Coll. Found., 1997—. Named one of Top 10 Litigators, Nat. law Jour., 2003. Mem. ABA, Am. Intellectual Property Law Assn., Fed. Cir. Bar. Assn., Nat. Bar Assn., N.Y. Intellectual Property Law

Assn., Assn. Bar for the City N.Y. (patent com. 1994-97). Office: Milbank, Tweed, Hadley & McCloy LLP 1 Chase Manhattan Plz New York NY 10005-1413 Office Phone: 212-530-5545. Office Fax: 212-822-5545. Business E-Mail: etaylor@milbank.com.

**TAYLOR, ESTELLE WORMLEY,** language educator, dean; b. Washington, Jan. 12, 1924; d. Luther Charles and Wilhelmina Wormley; m. Ivan Earle Taylor, Dec. 26, 1953. BS magna cum laude, Miner Tchrs. Coll. 1945; MA, Howard U., 1947; PhD, Cath. U. Am., 1969. Instr. English Howard U. 1947-52; tchr. Langley Jr. H.S., Washington, 1952-55, Eastern Sr. H.S., Washington, 1955-63; from instr. to prof. D.C. Tchrs. Coll., 1963—76; assoc. provost Fed. City Coll., Washington, 1974-75; prof. Howard U., 1976-91, chmn. dept. English, 1976-85, assoc. dean Coll. Liberal Arts, 1985-86, dir. expository writing program Grad. Sch. Arts and Scis., 1988-91, prof. emeritus, 1991. Mem., sec. Edn. Licensure Commn. of D.C., 1993—; mem. Commn. on Higher Edn., Mid. States Assn. Colls. and Schs., 1984-87, 88-90, co-chair steering com. to revise Characteristics of Excellence, 1992-93; mem. ctrl. exec. com. Folger Inst. Renaissance and 18th Century Studies, 1982-91; adv. bd. Humanities Inst. Montgomery Coll., 1997—. Contbg. editor A Howard Reader, 1997. 1st v.p. Order Daus. of King Episc. Ch. Diocese, Washington, 1994-98; commr. Edn. Licensure Com. of D.C., 1993—, also sec., vice chmn., 1995—; trustee U. D.C., 1979-83, vice chmn., 1983; mem. D.C. Cmty. Humanities Coun., 1990-91; co-chmn. planning com. Centennial Celebration of the Andrew Rankin Chapel Howard U., 1994; adv. bd. Coll. Arts and Svcs., Howard U., 2002—; mem. selection bd. Fgn. Agrl. Svc., 2002. Named Disting. Alumni, Howard U., 1995, Alumni award for Disting. Postgrad. Achievement in Edn. and Lit., 1997; So. fellow, 1968-69; Rockefeller/Aspen Inst. fellow, 1978-79. Mem. MLA (del. assembly 1994—), Nat. Assn. for Equal Opportunity in Higher Edn., Coll. Lang. Assn., Shakespeare Assn. Am., Pub. Mems. Assn. Fgn. Svc. Dept. of State, Links (v.p. Capital City chpt. 1979-81, corr. sec. 1989, rec. sec. 1991-93, 95—). Democrat. Home: 3221 20th St NE Washington DC 20018-2421 *Throughout my career I have been climbing a giant ladder, invisible to all but me. The challenging but humbling feature of this ladder is that whenever I get the feeling that I have almost reached the top, several additional rungs attach themselves to my Jacob's Ladder. Thus, that thing called success is for me forever a goal to be reached. As long as I continue to feel a restlessness and a yearning to climb another rung, I shall know that I am alive.*

**TAYLOR, FELICIA,** newscaster; BS in Comm., Northwestern U. Prodr., field reporter WLS-TV, Chgo.; anchor, prodr., writer Fin. News Network; anchor bus. shows Fin. Times; London corr. CNBC, Ft. Lee, N.J., 1992-93, co-anchor Today's Bus., anchor This Morning's Bus., 1993—98, co-anchor MarketWatch; co-anchor Weekend Today in New York NewsChannel4, N.Y.C., NY, 1998—2003, co-anchor NewsChannel 4 at 6 and 11, 2003—. Office: NBC News 30 Rockefeller Plaza New York NY 10112

**TAYLOR, FLORIETTA,** retired music educator, composer, retired social worker; d. Alfred Leroy and Anna Eliza Diggs; m. John Lawrence Taylor, Dec. 24, 1953; children: Sonja Joy Gore, Rhonna Lynn, Vicki Ann Bass. MusB in Edn., Howard U., Washington, 1952; MS in Edn., Jacksonville State U., 1974. Cert. music tchr. Ala. Organist Quinn Chapel AME Ch., Frederick, Md., 1944—48; pianist Hallelujah Gospel Chorus, Frederick, Md., 1944—48; cottage supr. N.J. State Home for Girls, Trenton, 1955—56; music instr., choral dir. Talladega County Bd. of Edn., Ala., 1957—72; social worker Dept. of Pensions and Security, Talladega, Ala., 1974—88; founder, dir., and organist Mt. Canaan Bapt. Ch. Inspirational Choir, Talladega, Ala., 1975—88; chapel musician, contract worker Fed. Correctional Instn., Talladega, Ala., 1981—82; min. of music First AME Ch., Gaithersburg, Md., 1988—90. 2d trumpet Howard U. Marching and Symphonic Band, Washington, 1948—52; piano instr., Talladega, Ala., 1957—; music dir. of youth choir Mt. Cannan Bapt. Ch., Talladega, Ala., 1959—65; mem. Talladega County Assn. for the Deaf, Blind and Handicapped, Ala., 1976—88, Ala. State Child Abuse and Neglect Bd., Montgomery, 1978—80, Ala. Gerontol. Soc., Montgomery, 1978—88; chmn. Cmty. Housing Resource Bd. of Housing and Urban Devel., Talladega, Ala., 1982—84; mem. Talladega Improvement Assn., Ala., 1984—88; guest spkr. Phyllis Wheatly H.S. All Class Reunion, Childersburg, Ala., 1985—85; mem. Wendell P. Whalum Cmty. Chorus, Atlanta, 1990—, Met. Atlanta Musicians Assn., Inc., 1990—; music dir./organist Sr./Retirees Group of St. Philip African Meth. Episcopal Ch., Atlanta, 1994—; pres. Met. Atlanta Musicians Assn., Inc., Atlanta, 1999—2004; choir participant Brazeal Dennard Choral Ensembles with tDetroit Symphony Civic Orch., 2002—02; music instr. Talladega Coll., 1952—54; pianist (christmas season) South DeKalb Mall. Composer: (four part composition) Hear My Pray'r, O Lord; musician (arranger): (musical compositions) Halleluia, Jesus the Lord is Risen Today; composer: (children's series) Treasure of Inspiration. Musician and advisor Soapstone Sa. Group, Decatur, Ga., 1993—2004; bd. dirs. Chapel Pk. Condominium Assn., Decatur, Ga., 1995—97; celebration participant Met. Atlanta Task Force for Homeless, 1996—96; pres. Taladega County Dem. Conf., Ala., 1980—88; alt. del. Ala. Dem. Party, Talladega County, 1984, del. Talladega County, 1988; music dir. youth choir Mt. Cannan Bapt. Ch., Talladega, Ala., 1959—65; interim choir dir. St. Philip African Meth. Episcopal Ch., Atlanta, 1991—93; mem. choir, European Concert Tour, Ebenezer Bapt. Ch., Atlanta, 2004. Recipient Outstanding Leadership and Svc. award, Talladega County Dem. Conf., 1982, 1983, 1988, Cmty. Svc. award, Gov. George Wallace, 1983, Office of Sec. of State, Ala., 1983, Lyndon Baines Johnson Leadership award, Ala. Dem. Conf., 1985, Outstanding Leadership and Svc. award, Talladega County Bd. Commrs., 1988, Outstanding Leadership award, Superior Ct. Judge William Sullivan, 1988, Outstanding Cmty. Svc. award, Etowah County Voters League, Ala., 1985, 1988, Talladega Mayor and City Coun., 1988, Office of Lt. Gov., Ala., 1988, Talladega County Dem. Exec. Com., 1988, Speakin' Out Newspaper, Ala., 1988. Mem.: Nat. Assn. of Negro Musicians (exec. bd. dirs. 2002—04), Ga. Music Educators Assn., Star Dusters Social Club (sec., v.p. and pres. 1980—88), Delta Sigma Theta (life). Democrat. Methodist. Avocations: working with humanitarian agencies, traveling, research and writing.

**TAYLOR, FOSTER JAY,** retired university president; b. Gibsland, La., Aug. 9, 1923; s. Lawrence Foster and Marcia Aline (Jay) T.; m. Lou Kavanaugh; 1 son, Terry Jay. Student, La. Poly. Inst., 1940-42; BA, U. Calif., Santa Barbara, 1948; MA, Claremont Grad. Sch., Calif., 1949; PhD, Tulane U., 1952. Assoc. prof. history, dean men. La. Coll., Pineville, 1952-56, prof., 1956-62, dean coll., 1960-62; pres. La. Tech. U., Ruston, 1962-87, pres. emeritus, 1987—. Past chmn. La. Labor Mediation Bd.; arbitrator Am. Arbitration Assn., Fed. Mediation and Counciliation Svc.; former mem. La. Adv. Coun. on Vocat.-Tecy. Edn.; bd. dirs. First Guaranty Bank. Author: The United States and the Spanish Civil War, 1936-39, 1956, Reluctant Rebel, The Secret Diary of Robert Patrick, 1861-1865, 1959. Served to lt. comdr., aviator USNR, 1942-46. Mem. Am. Hist. Assn., Miss. Valley Hist. Assn., So. Hist. Assn., Nat. Acad. Arbitrators., Phi Alpha Theta. Clubs: Rotary. Home: 500 Audubon Dr Ruston LA 71270-7800 Office Phone: 318-251-1790.

**TAYLOR, FRANCIS MICHAEL,** auditor, municipal official; b. Munich, 1960; came to the U.S., 1961; BS, Va. Tech., 1982. CPA Va., cert. internal auditor. Pub. acct., Roanoke, Va., 1982-84; controller ARC Roanoke, Inc., Roanoke, 1984-87; audit supr. City of Roanoke, 1987-94; city auditor City of Stockton (Calif.), 1994—. Nat. coord. com. Key Nat. Indicators Initiative. Mem. AICPA, Nat. Assn. Local Govt. Auditors (past pres.), Calif. Soc. CPAs, Inst. Internal Auditors, Govt. Fin. Officers Assn., Info. Sys. Audit and Control Assn., Bay Area Local Govt. Auditors. Office: 22 E Weber Ave Ste 325 Stockton CA 95202-1951

**TAYLOR, FRANCIS X.,** former federal agency administrator, retired military officer; BA in Govt. and Internat. Studies, U. Notre Dame, 1970, MA in Govt. and Internat. Studies, 1971; grad., Squadron Officer Sch., 1975, Air Command and Staff Coll., 1980, Armed Forces Staff Coll., 1984, Air War Coll., 1988. Commd. 2d lt. USAF, 1970, advanced through grades to brigadier gen., 1996, ret.; 2001; analyst, Mid. E, Africa, & S Asia divsn., Analysis & Dissemination Branch, Counterintelligence Divsn. Hdqs. Air Force Office of Spl. Investigations, Washington, 1970—72, area supr. Acquisition & Analysis

Divsn., Directorate of Personnel, 1974—76; chief counterintelligence acquisition and analysis br. Air Force Office of Spl. Investigations Dist. 69, Ankara, Turkey, 1976-77; comdr. Air Force Office of Spl. Investigations Detachment 411, Bolling AFB, D.C., 1977-79; chief resource career mgmt. divsn. Directorate of Pers. Hdqs. Air Force Office of Spl. Investigations, Bolling AFB, 1979-80, comdr. Hdqs. Squadron sect., asst. exec. to comdr., 1980-83; dep. dir. for ops. Dir. Counterintelligence/Invest. Programs Office of Dep. Under Sec. of Def. for Policy, The Pentagon, Washington, 1984-87; dep. comdr. 487th Combat Support Group, Comiso Air Station, Italy, 1988-90; comdr. Air Force Office of Spl. Investigations Dist. 45, Osan Air Base, South Korea, 1999-92, dir Air Force Office of Spl. Investigations Region 2, Langley AFB, Va., 1992-94; dir. mission guidance Hdqs. Air Force Office of Spl. Investigations, Bolling AFB, 1994-95; dir. spl. investigations Office of Inspector Gen. Office of Sec. of Air Force, The Pentagon, Washington, 1995-96; comdr. Hdqs. Air Force Office of Spl. Investigations, Bolling AFB, 1996-98, Andrews AFB, Md., 1998—2001; coord. for counterterrorism US Dept. State, Washington, 2001—02, asst. sec. for diplomatic security, dir. Office Fgn. Missions, 2002—05. Decorated Disting. Svc. medal, Def. Superior Svc. medal, Legion of Merit, Meritorious Svc. medal with 3 oak leaf clusters, Air Force Commendation medal with two oak leaf clusters, Air Force Achievement medal with oak leaf cluster; Named Outstanding Advocate for Women, Women in Fed. Law Enforcement, 2000

**TAYLOR, FRED,** professional football player; b. Belle Glade, Fla., June 27, 1976; m. Andrea Taylor; children: Nataajah, Inari. BS in Sociology, U. Fla. Running back Jacksonville Jaguars, Fla., 1998—. Spokesman Leukemia Soc. Am., Lymphoma Soc. Am., Glades Asthma Project. Achievements include ranks fourth on U. Fla. all-time rushing list; played in 3 college bowl games; team was 14-0 in games in which he had over 100 yards rushing. Office: Jacksonville Jaguars 1 Alltel Stadium Pl Jacksonville FL 32202-1917*

**TAYLOR, FREDERICK R.,** health facility administrator; s. Hildegaarde M Taylor; m. Jill J Jensen, Sept. 2, 1972; children: Michael K, Anne L. MD, U. of N.Mex SOM, 1973—77. Cert. Am. Bd. Neurology and Psychiatry, 1985, Am. Bd. of Electrodiagnostic Medicine, 1989, Nat. Bd. for Certification in Headache Mgmt., 2001. Active cons. Pk. Nicollet Health Svcs., Mpls., 1985—; headache clinic dir. Pk. Nicollet Headache Clinic and Rsch. Ctr., Mpls., 1996—. Assoc. editor Cochrane Collaborative, Oxford, England, 2004—. Contbr. book chpts., numerous articles to med. jours. Recipient Educator of the Yr., Pk. Nicollet Inst. for Rsch. and Edn., 1997, Migraine Innovators, AstraZeneca, 2003. Mem.: Am. Acad. of Neurology, Internat. Headache Soc., Am. Heaache Soc., Am. Coun. for Headache Edn. (bd. mem. 2002—04). Office: Park Nicollet Health Services 6490 Excelsior Boulevard E-500 Minneapolis MN 55426 Office Phone: 952-993-3639. Office Fax: 952-993-2701.

**TAYLOR, FREDERICK WILLIAM, JR., (FRITZ TAYLOR),** lawyer; b. Cleve., Oct. 21, 1933; s. Frederick William Sr. and Marguerite Elizabeth (Kistler) T.; m. Mary Phyllis Osborne, June 1, 1985; children: Frederick III, Ellen, Christopher, Stephanie, Andrew, Susan, Sarah Beth, Derek, Douglas. BA in History, U. Fla., 1957; MA in Near East Studies, U. Mich., 1959; JD cum laude, NYU, 1967. Bar: N.Y. 1968, Calif. 1969, U.S. Dist. Ct. (cen. dist.) Calif. 1969. Govt. rels. rep. Arabian Am. Oil Co., Dhahran, Saudi Arabia, 1959-63, oil supply coord. N.Y.C., 1963-68, sr. counsel Dhahran, 1969-71, gen. mgr. govt. rels. orgn., 1971-74, v.p indsl. rels., 1974-78; assoc. O'Melveny & Myers, L.A., 1968-69; ptnr. Burt & Taylor, Marblehead, Mass., 1978-80; pres., chief exec. officer Nat. Med. Enterprises Internat. Group, L.A., 1980-82; counsel Chadbourne, Parke & Afridi, United Arab Emirates, 1982-84; ptnr. Sidley & Austin, Cairo, 1984-87, Singapore, 1987-93; spl. counsel Heller Ehrman White & McAuliffe, L.A. and Singapore, 1993-95; legal advisor, corp. counsel law divsn. Lucent Techs. Internat. Inc., Riyadh, Saudi Arabia, 1995—2003; dir. MEA strategy and bus. ops., 2003—04; corp. counsel labor, litigation and employment Lucent Law Divsn., Murray Hill, NJ, 2004—. Contbr. articles to profl. jours. Mem. ABA, Calif. Bar Assn., Order of Coif, Singapore Cricket Club, Tanglin Club, Changi Sailing Club, Singapore Am. Club, Dirab Golf Club. Home: 9875 E Shadowlake Ct Claremore OK 74017-1444 Office: Lucent Techs Int Inc PO Box 44770 Abu Dhabi United Arab Emirates Office Phone: 908-582-4323. Business E-Mail: taylorf@lucent.com.

**TAYLOR, GAVIN HALL,** music educator; s. Mary Elizabeth and LeRoy Gerald Taylor. MusB, Jacksonville U., 1981—84; MusM, Hartt Sch. Music, U. Hartford, 1984—86. Adj. asst. prof. music Jacksonville U., Jacksonville, Fla., 1989—; piano dept. chmn. Douglas Anderson Sch. Arts, Jacksonville, 1998—99; dir. music/organist Ft. Caroline Presbyn. Ch., Jacksonville, 1990—2000; asst. min. music Arlington United Meth. Ch., Jacksonville, 2000—. Accompanist Bel Canto Nat. Opera Auditions, Jacksonville, Fla., 1994—94; accompanist for masterclasses, auditions, Delius festivals, faculty and student recitals Jacksonville U., Jacksonville, Fla.; guest recitalist Edwards Waters Coll., Jacksonville, Fla., 1991—91; pvt. piano studio tchr., Jacksonville, Fla., 1989—; pub. radio broadcasts/ wjct stereo 90 Jacksonville U. Faculty Recital Series, Jacksonville, Fla., 1990—2000. Recipient Omicron Delta Kappa Hon. Frat., Pi Kappa Lambda Hon. Music Frat. Mem.: Fla. Fedn. Music Clubs/St. Johns Dist. (dir. comm. 1998—2003), Nat. Guild Piano Teachers, Fla. Music Teachers Assn. Office: Jacksonville U 2800 University Blvd N Jacksonville FL 32211

**TAYLOR, GENE (GARY EUGENE TAYLOR),** congressman; b. New Orleans, Sept. 17, 1953; m. Margaret Gordon; children: Sarah, Emily, Gary. BA, Tulane U., New Orleans, 1976; student, U. So. Miss., Hattiesburg. Sales rep. Stone Container Corp.; city councilman Bay St. Louis, Miss., 1981—83; mem. Miss. State Senate, 1984-89, US Congress from 4th Miss. dist., 1989—, mem. house armed svcs. com., mem. transp. and infrastructure com., ranking mem. subcommittee on projection forces, co-chair Shipbuilding Caucus, Nat. Guard and Res. Caucus, Coast Guard Caucus and Expeditionary Warfare Caucus; mem. Conservative Democrats' Blue Dog Coalition. With USCGR, 1971-1984. Mem.: Rotary, Lions, Kappa Sigma. Democrat. Roman Catholic. Office: US House of Reps 2311 Rayburn House Office Bldg Washington DC 20515-2405*

**TAYLOR, GENE,** bank executive; m. Kathy Taylor; 3 children. BS in Fin., Fla. State U. Credit analyst Bank Am. Corpn., 1969, pres. Florida bank, 1990, pres. NationsBank, 1993, pres. merged NationsBank and Barnett Bank, 1997, head consumer and comml. banking ops. Western US, 1998, pres. consumer and comml. banking, 2001, head global bus. and fin. svcs., 2004, vice chmn., pres. global corp. and investment banking, 2005—, mem. risk and capital com. Bank Am. Corpn., mem. mgmt. operating com. Office: Bank Am Corp Ctr 100 N Tryon St Fl 58 Charlotte NC 28255-0001*

**TAYLOR, GEORGE B., JR.,** lawyer; BEE, Ga. Inst. Tech., 1975, MSEE, 1976; MBA, Ga. State U., 1984, JD, 1994. Bar: Ga. 1995. Planning engr. Oglethorpe Power Corp., Tucker, Ga., 1976—79, sec. mgr. Power Supply, 1979—84, dept. mgr. Power Contracts, 1984—86, sr. negotiator, 1986—92, mgr. Regulatory Compliance, 1992—96, legal advisor to CEO, 1996—2003, v.p., 2003—05, sr. v.p. strategic initiatives, 2005—. Office: Oglethorpe Power Corp PO Box 1349 Tucker GA 30085-1349 Office Phone: 770-270-7600. E-mail: george.taylor@opc.com.

**TAYLOR, GEORGE FREDERICK,** newspaper publisher, editor; b. Portland, Oreg., Feb. 28, 1928; s. George Noble and Ida Louise (Dixon) T.; m. Georga Bray, Oct. 6, 1951; children— Amelia Ruth, Rose Noble. BS, U. Oreg., 1950. Reporter Astoria (Oreg.) Budget, 1950-52, Portland Oregonian, 1952-54; copy reader Wall St. Jour., 1955-57, reporter, 1957-59, Detroit Bur. chief, 1959-64, Washington corr., 1964-68, asst. mng. editor San Francisco, 1968-69, mng. editor N.Y.C., 1970-77, exec. editor, 1977-86; pub. North Bend (Oreg.) News, 1981-86, Prime Time, 1987—, Coquille Valley Sentinel, 1989-2000. Lt. USAF, 1955-57. Mem. Oregon Newspaper Publishers Assn. (bd. dirs. 1997-2000). E-mail: Ftaylor@harborside.com.

**TAYLOR, GEORGE KIMBROUGH, JR.,** lawyer; b. Atlanta, Aug. 28, 1939; s. George Kimbrough and Helen Whiteside (Shepard) T.; m. Carol Ann McKinney, July 1, 1961 (div. 1976); children: George Kimbrough III, Thomas Haynes; m. Triska Ashley Drake, Oct. 2, 1981. BA, Emory U., 1961; LLB, U. Va., 1964. Bar: Ga. 1964, U.S. Dist. Ct. (no. dist.) Ga. 1964, U.S. Ct. Appeals (11th cir.) 1964. Assoc. Kilpatrick & Cody, Atlanta, 1964-70, ptnr., 1970-96, Kilpatrick Stockton LLP (formerly Kilpatrick & Cody), 1997—. Bd. dirs. Ont. Reins. Co. Ltd., Atlanta; chmn., bd. dirs. MFI Am., Inc., Atlanta, 2003—06. Chmn. bd. dirs. Spl. Audiences, Inc., Atlanta, 1985-87; bd. dirs. Atlanta Symphony Orch., 1986—; trustee Woodruff Arts Ctr., Atlanta, 1997—; bd. dirs. Atlanta Opera, 1995—, Ga. Humanities Coun., Atlanta, 1986-93, Ga. Conservancy, 1979-85; bd. dirs. Ga. Trust for Hist. Preservation, 2002—, vice chair, 2004—; bd. dirs. Ga. Coun. Internat. Visitors, Atlanta, 1987-94, pres., 1993; bd. dirs. Brit.-Am. Bus. Group, 1989-95, pres., 1994; bd. visitors Emory U., Atlanta, 1993-96, Brit.-Am. Bus. Coun., 1997—; chmn. 1997-98; mem. alumni coun. U. Va. Law Sch., 1995-98; active Leadership Atlanta. Woodrow Wilson fellow, 1961. Mem. ABA, Internat. Bar Assn., Atlanta Bar Assn., Order of Coif, Soc. Internat. Bus. Fellows, Capital City Club, Phi Beta Kappa, Omicron Delta Kappa. Democrat. Avocations: sailing, skiing. Office: Kilpatrick Stockton LLP 1100 Peachtree St NE Ste 2800 Atlanta GA 30309-4530 Office Phone: 404-815-6500. Business E-Mail: ktaylor@kilpatrickstockton.com.

**TAYLOR, GEORGE PEACH, JR.,** career military officer; b. Birmingham, Ala. BA in Physics and Russian Language, Rice U., Houston, Tex., 1975; MD, Baylor Coll. Medicine, 1978; MPH, Harvard Sch. Pub. Health, Boston, Mass., 1984; attended, Nat. War Coll., Fort Lesley J. McNair, Washington, DC, 1992—93. Lic. Tex. Capt. advanced through grades to gen. USAF, 1979—2002; resident USAF Sch. of Aerospace Medicine, Brooks AFB, Tex., 1984—85; chief flight medicine, squadron flight surgeon USAF Clinic, Kadena AFB, Japan, 1979—81; chief aerospace medicine Detachment 3 Air Force Flight Test Ctr., Henderson, Nev., 1981—83; chief aerospace medicine, comdr. air transportable hosp. USAF Hosp., Torrejon AFB, Spain, 1985—88; med. inspector active duty forces Air Force Inspection and Safety Ctr., Norton AFB, Calif., 1988—90; chief aerospace medicine USAF Hosp., Air Force Flight Test Ctr., Edwards AFB, Calif., 1990—92; comdr. and dir. base med. svcs. 75th med. group Ogden Air Logistics Ctr., Hill AFB, Utah, 1993—95; chief aerospace med. divsn., later dep. dir. Air Force Med. Ops. Agy., Bolling AFB, Washington, 1995—96; assoc. dir. to dir. med. programs and resources Office of Surgeon Gen., 1996—97; command surgeon USAF, Ramstein AFB, Germany, 1997—2000, Hdqs. Air Combat Command, Langley AFB, Va., 2000—02; asst. surgeon gen. expeditionary ops., sci. and tech. Office of Surgeon Gen., Bolling AFB, Washington, 2002, spl. asst. to surgeon gen. Air Force, 2002; surgeon gen. USAF, Washington, 2002—. Chmn., base realignment and closure Joint Med. Cross Svc. Group, 2002—05; disting. prof. mil./emergency medicine Uniformed Svcs. U. Health Svcs. Decorated Disting. Svc. medal, Def. Superior Svc. medal, Legion of Merit with oak leaf cluster, Bronze Star medal, Meritorious Svc. medal with four oak leaf clusters, Air Force Commendation medal, Air Force Achievement medal, Air Force Recognition Ribbon, Gold Cross of Honor of the Bundeswehr Germany; recipient Malcom C. Grow award for Air Force Flight Surgeon of Yr. Fellow: Aerospace Med. Assn. (former coun. mem.), Am. Coll. Preventive Medicine; mem.: AMA (Air Force delegate), Soc. US Air Force Flight Surgeons (former pres.), Am. Military Surgeons of U.S. (life Founders Medal), Am. Soc. Aerospace Medicine Specialists (former pres.).*

**TAYLOR, GLEN A.,** direct mail and technology executive, professional sports team executive; Grad., Minn. State U., 1962. State sen. Minn. Senate, 1980—90; chmn., CEO Taylor Corp., Mankato, Minn., 1975—2001, chmn. only, 2001—; owner Minn. Timberwolves and Minn. Lynx, Mpls., 1994—. Named one of Forbes' Richest Americans, 2006. Office: Taylor Corp 1725 Roe Crest Dr Mankato MN 56003-1807 also: Minnesota Timberwolves Target Ctr 600 1st Ave N Minneapolis MN 55403-1416*

**TAYLOR, GLORIA A.,** minister, educator; d. Walter Hedland and Margaret Rose Atkinson; m. Frederic Edward Taylor, Feb. 23, 1947; children: Greg Eugene, Lance Norman, Brett Jack, Scott Frederic, Penny Gay. Ordination, Diocesan Sch. Faith & Ministry, 1989. Ordained Diocese No. Ind., 1989. Chairperson Episcopal AIDS Ministry, South Bend, Ind., 1989—99; deacon St. Paul Episcopal Ch., Munster, Ind., 1989—93, Trinity Ch., Mich. City, Ind., 1993—. Support groups for people with HIV/AIDS and mothers, South Bend, 1988—99; provider pastoral care for women in all walks of life. Conservative. Episcopal. Achievements include being the first woman ordained in the 100 year old diocese in 1989. Avocations: travel, watercolor. Home: 1809 Holly Lane Munster IN 46321 Office Phone: 219-874-4355. Personal E-mail: gataylor89@aol.com.

**TAYLOR, HAROLD ALLEN, JR.,** industrial minerals consultant; b. San Jose, Calif., June 27, 1936; s. Harold Allen and Marie Anna (Briody) T.; m. Theresa Josephine Kustritz, Aug. 29, 1963; children: Harold Allen III, Ruth F., Jonathan L.E. BA, Brown U., 1958; MA, U. Minn., 1968. Project leader Office Mineral Supply, U.S. Bur. Mines, Mpls., 1968-70, commodity specialist divsn. ferrous metals Washington, 1970-74; commodity analyst U.S. internat. Trade Commn., Washington, 1974-80; sr. commodity specialist br. indsl. minerals U.S. Bur. Mines, Washington, 1980-95; pres. Basics Mines, Summit Point, W.Va., 1995—. Pub., editor Dimension Stone Advocate News, Graphite Advocate News, Bismuth Advocate News, Indium Advocate News, 2000—; contbr. articles to profl. jours. Pres. Arlington (Va.) Interfaith Coun., 1994, 95. Mem. AIME (sec 1983-84, 1st vice chmn. 1984-85, chmn. 1985-86, exec. adv. bd. mineral econs. subsect. 1981-83, 87-91), ASTM (chmn. subcom. nomenclature of com. on dimension stone 1987-2004, sec. of com. 1990-95). Soc. Govt. Economists (chmn. materials policy panels, 1979-84), Capitol Metals Forum (steering com. 1979-85), Toastmasters (pres. 1978-81, 87, 91, asst. area gov. 1978-79, area gov. 1979-80, dep. divsn. lt. gov. 1989-90), Sigma Gamma Epsilon Address: PO Box 185 Summit Point WV 25446-0185 Office Phone: 304-725-6619. E-mail: bmhtayl@earthlink.net.

**TAYLOR, HARRIS C.,** endocrinologist, consultant; b. Bklyn., Apr. 30, 1940; s. William and Florence Ruth T.; m. Diana Kahn, Sept. 3, 1962; children: Brian David, Rebecca Lynn. BS, Queens Coll., 1961; MD, U. Chgo., 1965. Diplomate Am. Bd. Internal Medicine, Am. Bd. Endocrinology and Metabolism. Cons. endocrinologist Kaiser Found., Cleve., 1972-86; chief divsn. endocrinology Luth. Med. Ctr., Cleve., 1977-96, dir. endocrinology & radioimmunoassay lab., 1978-96, dir. internal medicine residency, 1985-94, dir. rsch., internal medicine residency program Fairview Health Sys., 1996—. Sr. clin. instr. Case We. Res. U. Sch. Medicine, Cleve., 1977-81, clin. asst. prof., 1981-88, clin. assoc. prof. medicine in endocrinology, 1988-2003, clin. prof., 2003—; prin. investigator NIH, 2006—. Contbr. articles to profl. jours. Chmn. program com. Diabetes Assn. Cleve., 1976-81, exec. com., 1978-85, pres.-elect, 1981-82, pres., 1982-84. Sr. asst. surgeon USPHS, 1966-68. Named One of Best Drs. in Cleve., Cleve. Mag., 1998, 2002, 2004. Fellow: ACP (reviewer Annals of Internal Medicine 1986—), Master Tchr. award 2001), Am. Coll. Endocrinology (editl. bd. Endocrine Practice 1997—2004); mem.: Endocrine Soc., Am. Assn. Clin. Endocrinologists, Phi Beta Kappa. Jewish. Avocations: stamp collecting/philately, classical music. Office: Case Western Reserve Univ Sch of Medicine-Div of Endocrinology 2109 Adelbert Rd Cleveland OH 44106 Office Phone: 216-368-6129.

**TAYLOR, HEATHER MARIE,** director; b. Park Ridge, Ill., May 21, 1974; d. Kent Emil and Rebecca Jo Buchholz; m. Christopher Lee Taylor, Jan. 13, 2001. BA in English and Secondary Edn., No. Ill. U., 1996; MS in Integrated Mktg. Comm. summa cum laude, Roosevelt U., 2000. Writer corp. comm. 360 Comm., Chgo., 1995—96; tchg. asst. No. Ill. U., DeKalb, 1995—96; tchr. Streamwood (Ill.) H.S., 1996—97; sr. mktg. mgr. Hanley-Wood, LLC, Addison, Ill., 1997—2002; owner, pres. Pro Writer Ltd., Portage, Ind., 2000—; dir. comms. for admissions, fin. aid and mktg. Valparaiso (Ind.) U., 2002—; adj. prof., 2004—. Adj. prof. Roosevelt U., Chgo., 2001—. Contbr. Of Diamonds and Rust, 1989, Great Poems of the Western World Vol. 2, 1990, articles to profl. jours. Mem.: NEA, Am. Mktg. Assn., Roosevelt Adj. Faculty Orgn., Sigma Tau Delta, Phi Kappa Phi, Golden Key. Lutheran. Avocations:

photography, writing, travel. Home: 5683 Dovedale Ave Portage IN 46368 Office: Valparaiso U 1700 Chapel Dr Valparaiso IN 46383 Office Phone: 219-464-5011. Business E-Mail: heather.taylor@valpo.edu.

**TAYLOR, HENRY SPLAWN**, retired literature educator, poet; b. Loudoun County, Va., June 21, 1942; s. Thomas Edward and Mary Marshall (Splawn) Taylor; m. Mooshe Taylor, 2002. BA, U. Va., 1965; MA, Hollins Coll., Va., 1966. Instr. English Roanoke Coll., Va., 1966—68; asst. prof. U. Utah, 1968—71; faculty Am. U., Washington, 1971—2003, prof. lit., 1976—2003, co-dir. MFA program in creative writing, 1982—2003, dir. Am. studies program, 1983—84. Dir. writer's conf. U. Utah, 1970—72; writer-in-residence Hollins Coll., 1978; poet-in-residence Wichita State U., 1994, Randolph-Macon Woman's Coll., 1997; prof. poetry U. Cin., 2002. Author: (poetry) The Horse Show at Midnight, 1966, Breakings, 1971, An Afternoon of Pocket Billiards, 1975, Desperado, 1979, The Flying Change, 1985 (Pulitzer prize, 86), Crooked Run, 2006, Poetry: Points of Departure, 1974; editor: The Water of Light: A Miscellany in Honor of Brewster Ghiselin, 1976; author: Compulsory Figures: Essays on Recent American Poets, 1992, Understanding Fiction: Poems 1986-96, 1996, Brief Candles: 101 Clerihews, 2000, (cassette) Landscape with Tractor, 1985; contbg. editor: Hollins Critic, 1971—78, 1997—; editl. cons.: Magill's Literary Annual, 1972—90, adv. editor: Bellingham Rev., New Va. Rev., 2000—, cons. editor: Poet Lore, 1977—84; translator (with others): The Children of Herakles, 1981; translator: Plautus' The Weevil, 1995, Sophocles' Electra, 1998. Recipient Pulitzer Prize, Poetry, 1986, Michael Braude award for light verse, Am. Acad. Arts and Letters, 2002, Aiken Taylor award in Modern Am. Poetry, 2004; fellow, Nat. Endowment Arts, 1978, 1986; grantee, NEH, 1980 81. Mem.: PEN, Am. Lit. Translators Assn. Democrat. Mem.Soc.Of Friends. Office: Am U Dept Lit Washington DC 20016-8047

**TAYLOR, HUBERT G.**, lawyer; b. July 16, 1973; s. Hubert L. and Aurelia Glosser Taylor; m. Rebekah Leigh Tatum, Dec. 18, 1999. BA, Birmingham So. Coll., 1995; JD, U. Ala. Sch. Law, 1999. Bar: Ala. 1999, US Dist. Ct. (mid. and no. dist.) Ala. 1999, US Ct. Appeals (11th cir.) 2004. Atty. David Cromwell Johnson, Birmingham, 1999—2003, Leitman, Siegal & Payne, P.C., 2003—04. Performer: (Operas) The Marriage of Figaro, La Traviata, Orpheus and Eurydice, Carmen, The Magic Flute, Rigoletto and Aida. Bd. dirs., treas. P.E.E.R., Inc., 2003—05; bd. trustees East Lake United Meth. Ch., 2004; bd. dirs. Birmingham Boys Choir, 2004—05. Mem.: Birmingham Bar Assn., ABA, Nat. Assn. Criminal Def. Lawyers. Avocation: opera. Office Phone: 205-251-5900. Office Fax: 205-328-2098. Business E-Mail: hgt@lsppc.com.

**TAYLOR, HUMPHREY JOHN FAUSITT**, information technology executive; b. Meshed, Iran, Sept. 6, 1934; came to U.S., 1976; s. Geoffrey Fausitt and Frances Margaret (Kenyon) T.; m. Penelope Helen Taylor, Dec. 19, 1970; children: Zanthe, Helena. BA with honors, Cambridge (Eng.) U., 1958. Dist. officer Govt. of Tanganyika, 1959-62; mktg. and opinion researcher Nat. Opinion Poll, Eng., 1963-66; mng. dir. Opinion Rsch. Ctr., Eng., 1966-76; with Louis Harris and Assocs., N.Y.C., 1976-81; pres. Harris Interactive Inc., N.Y.C., 1981-98, CEO, 1992-98; chmn. The Harris Poll, N.Y.C., 1997—. Trustee U.S. com. UNICEF, N.Y.C., 1981—87; trustee Overseas Devel. Coun., Washington, 1987—2001; trustee, chmn. Am. Health Found., 1988—91; trustee Royal Soc. Medicine Found., 1992—; Albert and Mary Lasker Found., 2004—; mem. Coun. on Grad. Med. Edn., 2000—. 2d lt. Brit. Army, 1953—55. Fellow: Am. Acad. Ophthalmology (hon.; trustee); mem.: Nat. Coun. Pub. Polls (chmn.). Avocations: history, biographies, skiing, tennis, travel. Address: Harris Interactive 111 5th Ave Fl 8 New York NY 10003-1005 Office Phone: 212-539-9657.

**TAYLOR, IAN LOGAN**, dean; b. Eng. MD, PhD, Liverpool Med. Sch. Fellow in gastrointestinal rsch. UCLA, mem. Wadsworth V.A. Tng. Program, various positions, prof. medicine; chief of gastroenterology Duke U., 1986—89, dir. Sarah W. Stedman Ctr. for Nutritional Studies, 1989—90, prof. physiology, dept. cell biology, 1990—93; prof. and chmn. dept. medicine Med. U. S.C., 1993—2001, pres. U. Med. Assocs., 1999—2001; dean Sch. Medicine Tulane U., 2001—05; dean Coll. Medicine SUNY Health Sci. Ctr., Bklyn., 2006—. Office: Coll Medicine SUNY Health Sci Ctr 470 Clarkson Ave Brooklyn NY 11203*

**TAYLOR, J. MARY (JOCELYN MARY TAYLOR)**, museum director, educator, zoologist; b. Portland, Oreg., May 30, 1931; d. Arnold Llewellyn and Kathleen Mary (Yorke) T.; m. Joseph William Kamp, Mar. 18, 1972 (dec.); m. Wesley Kingston Whitten, Mar. 20, 2001. BA, Smith Coll., 1952; MA, U. Calif., Berkeley, 1953, PhD, 1959. Instr. zoology Wellesley Coll., 1959-61, asst. prof. zoology, 1961-65; assoc. prof. zoology U. B.C., 1965-74; dir. Cowan Vertebrate Mus., 1965-82, prof. dept. zoology, 1974-82; collaborative scientist Oreg. Regional Primate Research Ctr., 1983-87; (courtesy) dept. fisheries and wildlife Oreg. State U., 1984-95; dir. Cleve. Mus. Nat. History, 1987-96, dir. emerita, 1996—. Adj. mbr. dept. biology Case Western Res. U., 1987-96. Assoc. editor Jour. Mammalogy, 1981-82. Contbr. numerous articles to sci. jours. Trustee Benjamin Rose Inst., 1988-93, Western Res. Acad., 1989-94, U. Circle, Inc., 1987-96, The Cleve. Aquarium, 1990-93, Cleve. Access to the Arts, 1992-96; corp. bd. Holden Arboretum, 1988-98, The Cleve. Mus. Natural History, 1996—, The Catlin Gabel Sch., 1998-2000, The Inst. for the Northwest, 1999—2001. Recipient Lake County Environ. award, Lake county metro parks.; Fulbright scholar, 1954-55; Lalor Found. grantee, 1962-63; NSF grantee, 1963-71; NRC Can. grantee, 1966-84; Killam Sr. Rsch. fellow, 1978-79 Mem.: Rodent Specialist Group of Species Survival Commn. (chmn. 1989—93), Assn. Sci. Mus. Dirs. (v.p. 1990—93), Cooper Ornithol., Australian Mammal Soc. (hon. life), Am. Soc. Mammalogists (1st v.p. 1978—82, pres. 1982—84, hon. life, Hartley T. Jackson award 1993), Soc. Women Geographers, Sigma Xi. Home: 2718 SW Old Orchard Rd Portland OR 97201-1637 E-mail: taylorjm@teleport.com.

**TAYLOR, JACK C.**, rental and leasing company executive; b. 1922; With Lindburg Cadillac, St. Louis, 1944-50, Forrest Cadillac, St. Louis, 1951-56; chmn. bd. Enterprise Rent-A-Car, St. Louis, 1980—2001, chmn. emeritus, 2001—. With USN, ret. Named one of Forbes Richest Americans, 2006. Office: Enterprise Rent-A-Car 600 Corporate Park Dr Saint Louis MO 63105-4204

**TAYLOR, JACK P.**, lumber company executive; BS in Biology, U. Wash., 1966. With Weyerhaeuser Co., 1969—, Far East forester, raw materials ops. mgr. Indonesia, 1975—78, raw materials ops. mgr. Coos Bay, Oreg., 1978—83, woods and raw materials mgr., 1983—87, Coos Bay ops. mgr., 1987—92, gen. mgr. S.W. Oreg. ops., 1992—96, v.p., dir. ops. Western Timberlands, 1996—2003, sr. v.p. Timberlands Federal Way, Wash., 2003—. Bd. dirs. Keep Oreg. Green; past pres., former bd. dirs. Pacific Lumber Inspection Bur.; former bd. dirs. Oreg. Forest Industries Coun.; former mem. S.W. Oreg. Region Forest Practices Com. Office: Weyerhaeuser Co 33663 Weyerhaeuser Way S Federal Way WA 98063-9777

**TAYLOR, JAMES, JR.**, lawyer; b. Florence, S.C., Dec. 6, 1942; s. James and Thelma (Baker) T.; m. Jayne S.C. Bridge, May 19, 1974; children: James Robson, Ashley Baker. BA cum laude, U. of the South, 1965; JD, Georgetown U., 1973. Bar: D.C. 1973, U.S. Ct. Internat. Trade 1977, U.S. Ct. Appeals (fed. cir.) 1982, U.S. Supreme Ct. 1978. Assoc. Busby Rivkin Sherman Levy and Rehm, Washington, 1973-76, Busby and Rehm, Washington, 1977-78; ptnr. Busby Rehm and Leonard, Washington, 1979-87, Dorsey & Whitney, Washington, 1988-92, Stroock & Stroock & Lavan, Washington, 1992-95, Ablondi, Foster, Sobin & Davidow, P.C., Washington, 1996—2004, Adduci, Mastriani & Schaumberg LLP, Washington, 2001—. Lt. USN, 1967-70; Vietnam. Mem. ABA, D.C. Bar Assn., Club Interallié (Paris). Episcopalian. Avocations: sailing, fishing, languages. Office: Adduci Mastriani & Schaumberg LLP 1200 17th St NW Washington DC 20036

**TAYLOR, JAMES A.**, music educator; b. Martinsville, Va., May 11, 1951; s. James Albert and Lucy Belle Taylor; m. Della Sue Sandridge, Aug. 18, 1972; children: Katherine Antis, Sandra Anzuini, Robbie. MusB in Edn., Madison Coll., 1972; Masters in Music Edn., James Madison U., 1976. Lic. postgrad. profl. Commonwealth of Va., 2002. Tchr. Page County Pub. Schs., Luray, Va., 1973—79, Augusta County Pub. Schs., Fishersville, Va., 1979—. Dir. Augusta County Honors Band, 1985, 89, 93. Active Meth. Missions, Blackstone, Va., 1994—; bd. mem. Calvary United Meth. Ch., Stuarts Draft, 1983—, choir dir., 1986—94, lay leader, 1996—, lay spkr., 2000—. Recipient Outstanding Young Educator of Page County, Jaycees, 1976, Outstanding Leaders in Elem. and Secondary Edn., 1976. Mem.: NEA, Music Educators Nat. Conf., Augusta County Edn. Assn., Va. Choral Dir. Assn., Va. Band and Orch. Dir. Assn. Jaycees, Alpha Phi Omega (chaplain, sargent at arms, vp, pres., alumni pres. 1970—74, pres Madison Coll. chpt. 1972—73), Theta Chi. Avocations: swimming, scuba diving, woodworking. Office: Stuarts Draft HS 1028 Augusta Farms Rd Stuarts Draft VA 24477 Office Phone: 540-946-7602. E-mail: sornegl@adelphia.net.

**TAYLOR, JAMES C.**, writer; b. Nashville, Oct. 17, 1924; s. James Custer Taylor and Winnie Olive Duncan. AB in Journalism and Psychology, U. Ky., 1941; postgrad., Vanderbilt U., 1941, Notre Dame U., Ind., 1942, Kans. U., 1942. Sports writer Topeka State Jour., Kans., 1950—52; reporter, editor Kansas City Star, Mo., 1953—57; sr. editor TV Guide Mag., 1957—82; fgn. corr. Internat. Am., various locations, 1982—2000; ret., 2000. Guest columnist CDL Report, World Intelligence Rev.; lectr. in field. Author: (book) Dubious Duty, 1976, Pearl Harbor II, 1978, Khadafy, Man or Myth, 1984. Referee H.S. football games, Ariz., 1980—2000. With French Foriegn Legion, Algeria, lt. comdr. USNR, 1941 61. Recipient Outstanding Book award, Mark Twain Soc., St. Louis, 1958, Del Oro award, Fria Ord, Stockholm, 1982. Republican. Roman Catholic. Home: 5519 N 77th Pl Scottsdale AZ 85250

**TAYLOR, JAMES FRANCIS**, marketing professional; b. Detroit, Sept. 5, 1951; s. Harold James and Mary Frances (Law) T.; m. Janet Elizabeth Joss, May 21, 1977; children: Jonathan Harold, Jessica Frances, Jenna Leigh, Jeanette Mary. BA in Polit. Sci., Mich. State U., 1976; postgrad., Thomas Cooley Law Sch., 1979. Product mgr. Gen. Aluminum Products, Charlotte, Mich., 1975-77; sales mgr. Empire Metal Products, Columbus, Ohio, 1978; bus. mgr. Law Offices of Paul Martin, Lansing, Mich., 1978-79; dir. mktg. and sales Feather-Lite Mfg. Co., Troy, Mich., 1979-81; v.p. mktg. and sales Innovative Products Corp., Madison Heights, Mich., 1981-82; pres. J.F. Taylor Assocs., Inc., Durham, N.C., 1982—, Meadowcrest Group, Inc., 1989—; pres., bd. dirs. The Taylor-Grant-Joss Found., Durham, N.C.; COO C.J. Woodmaster, Inc., Durham, 1998—. Corp. sec., bd. dirs., CFO of All Corps. Unifinished Furniture Express, Inc., 1997—, Durham, N.C., C.J. Woodmaster of Raleigh, Inc.; CFO C.J. Woodmaster of Cary, Inc., 1999—; CFO, corp. sec. C.J. Woodmaster Devel., Inc., Durham, N.C., C.J. Woodmaster of Fayetteville, Inc. Mem.: Hope Valley Country Club, Rotary. Republican. Roman Cath. Home: 4 Roswell Ct Durham NC 27707-5070 Office: PO Box 51280 Durham NC 27717 Personal E-mail: cjwoodmaster@cjwoodmaster.org.

**TAYLOR, JAMES JOHN**, finance educator; b. Mpls., July 26, 1940; s. James John and Mary Elizabeth (Mason) T.; m. Margaret Claire Zacha, Dec. 28, 1976; children: Jerry William, John Allen. Ba, Oblate Coll. of S.W., 1966; MEd, St. Louis U., 1969, MBA in Fin., 1972; cert. of advanced studies, Harvard U., 1977; PhD in Adminstrn., Curriculum and Instrn, U. Nebr., 2002. Dept. head, tchr. Althoff High Sch., Belleville, Ill., 1966-71; asst. to controller U. of South Fla., Tampa, 1972-79; project mgr. W.Va. Bd. of Regents, Morgantown, 1979-83; prin., project dir. Am. Mgmt. Systems, Arlington, Va., 1983-90; mng. cons. Taylor Mgmt. Group, Arlington, 1990-91; v.p. bus. and fin. Guam C.C., 1991—2005; assoc. prof. fin. and econs. U. Guam, 2005—. Founder, treas. Guam Ednl. Radio Found., KPRG-FM, 1992-99; organizer Chief Bus. Officers of the Pacific, 1997, 98, 99; sec., trustee Govt. Guam Retirement Bd., 2004—; trustee, bd. govs. Guam C.C. Found., 1996—. Mem. adv. com. on spl. edn. Arlington Sch. Bd., 1981-83; founder, producer St. Louis High Sch. Film Makers Festival, 1968-72; contbr. articles to profl. jours. Bd. trustees Govt. Guam Retirement Fund, 2004. Founding mem. Harvard Club at Nat. Press Club; mem. Rotary. Avocations: photography, bridge, scuba diving. Home: 180 G Cruz Hts Talofofo GU 96915-3736

**TAYLOR, JAMES SHEPPARD**, communications educator; b. Montgomery, Ala., Dec. 15, 1943; s. Elbert Ruppert and Mary Pinckard (Bryan) T.; m. Mary Ann Luck, Mar. 30, 1972; children: John Brinson Overstreet, Laura Luck Biering. BA in Speech, Auburn U., 1965, MA in Speech, 1966; PhD in Rhetoric and Pub. Address, Fla. State U., 1968. Grad. asst. Auburn (Ala.) U., 1965-66, asst. prof. speech, 1969-73; grad. asst. Fla. State U., Tallahassee, 1966-68; asst. prof. speech N.C. State U., Raleigh, 1968-69; assoc. prof., chair comms. Houston Bapt. U., 1973-94, prof., chair comms., assoc. dean arts and humanities, 1994-98, dean arts and humanities, 1998—. Editl. assoc. So. Speech Jour., 1967-68; mem. editl. bd. N.C. Jour. Speech, 1966-69; news and notions editor So. Speech Comm. Jour., 1972-75. Recipient Tchg. Excellence and Campus Leadership award Sears-Roebuck Found., 1989-90. Mem. Tex. Speech Comm. Assn., So. States Comm. Assn., Speech Comm. Assn. (ERIC evaluator 1973-76), Phi Kappa Phi, Phi Delta Kappa, Kappa Delta Pi, Omicron Delta Kappa. Democrat. Methodist. Avocations: golf, running, tennis, hiking, reading. Office: Houston Bapt U 7502 Fondren Rd Houston TX 77074-3298 Office Phone: 281-649-3337. Personal E-Mail: sheptaylor@msn.com. Business E-Mail: jtaylor@hbu.edu.

**TAYLOR, JAMES WALTER**, business and management educator; b. St. Cloud, Minn., Feb. 15, 1933; s. James T. and Nina C. Taylor; m. Joanne Eylitte, Feb. 3, 1956; children: Theodore Iann, Samuel Daniel, Christopher John. BBA, U. Minn., 1957; MBA, NYU, 1960; DBA, U. So. Calif., 1975. Mgr. rsch. divsn. Atlantic Refining, Phila., 1960-65; dir. new product devel. Hunt-Wesson Foods, Fullerton, Calif., 1965-72; mng. dir. Digital Workbook Internat., LLC, Laguna Beach, Calif., 1975—. Vis. prof. U. Calif., Irvine; cons. Smithkline Beecham Corp., Tokyo, Govt. of Portugal, Lisbon, Austrade, Govt. of Australia, Hagenfeldt-Affarerna AB, Stockholm. Author: Profitable New Product Strategies, 1984, How to Create a Winning Business Plan, 1986, Competitive Marketing Strategies, 1986, The 101 Best Performing Companies in America, 1987, The Complete Manual for Developing Winning Strategic Plans, 1988, Every Manager's Survival Guide, 1989, Developing Winning Strategic Plans, 1990, How to Develop Successful Advertising Plans, 1993, Marketing Planning: A Step by Step Guide, 1997, The Marketing Strategy and Planning Workbook, 2004. Fulbright scholar Ministry of Industry, Lisbon, Portugal, 1986-87, U. We. Sydney, Australia, 1989-90; recipient Merit award Calif. State U., 1986-90. Home: 5317 Honoiki Rd Princeville HI 96722

**TAYLOR, JASON PAUL**, professional football player; b. Pittsburgh, PA, Sept. 1, 1974; m. Katina Taylor; 2 children. BA political science, criminal justice, U. of Akron, 1997. Defensive End Miami Dolphins, 1997—. Founder Jason Taylor Found., 2004—. Named to AFC Pro Bowl Team, 2000, 2002, 2004—05. Office: c/o Miami Dolphins 7500 SW 30th St Davie FL 33314*

**TAYLOR, JEAN ELLEN**, mathematics professor, researcher; d. Richard and Donna Taylor; m. John Mark Guckenheimer, Apr. 18, 1969 (div.); m. Frederick J. Almgren, Oct. 6, 1973 (dec. 1997); 1 child, Karen Taylor Almgren stepchildren: Ann Almgren, Robert Almgren; m. William T. Golden, July 8, 2001 (div.). AB summa cum laude, Mt. Holyoke Coll., 1966, DSc (hon.), 2001; MS in Chemistry, U. Calif., Berkeley, 1968; MS in Math., U. Warwick, Coventry, Eng., 1971; PhD, Princeton U., 1973. Instr. MIT, Cambridge, Mass., 1972-73; asst. prof. Rutgers U., New Brunswick, N.J., 1973-77, assoc. prof., 1977-82, prof., 1982-87, prof. II, 1987—2004, prof. emeritus, 2002—; vis. scholar Courant Inst., NYU, 2002—. Mem. Inst. for Advanced Study, Princeton, N.J., 1974-75, 77-78, 85, 95-96; Miller vis. prof. U. Calif., Berkeley, 1999; vis. scholar Stanford (Calif.) U., 1989; visitor Princeton U., 1980-81; mem. Geometry Computing Group (permanent faculty of the Nat. Sci. and Tech. Ctr. for Computational and Visualization of Geometric Structures); cons. Nat. Bur. Standards, Gaithersburg, Md.; guest expert 3-2-1 Contact program Children's TV Workshop, 1978; mem. exec. com. Conf. Bd. of the Math. Scis., 2000-2002; lectr. in field. Contbr. articles in math., physics and materials sci. to profl. jours. Recipient Presdl. Pub. Svc. award Rutgers Coll. Class of 1962, 1999, Sloan Found. fellow, 1976-78; NSF grad. fellow, 1966-72, hon. fellow Woodrow Wilson Found.; rsch. grantee NSF, 1973—97, Air Force Office Sci. Rsch., 1987-94. Fellow: AAAS (bd. dir. 1995—99, chair sect. 2004—05), Assn. for Women in Sci., Am. Acad. Arts and Scis.; mem.: Soc. for Indsl. and Applied Math., Assn. for Women in Math. (pres. 1999—2001, nominating com. chair 2003—04), Math Assn. Am., Materials Rsch. Soc., Am. Math. Soc. (nominating com. 1977—78, coun. 1984—89, exec. com. 1985—88, v.p. 1994—97, trustee 2003—, chair bd. trustees 2006—), Assn. Princeton Grad. Alumni (governing bd. 1999—2003), Phi Beta Kappa. Democrat. Achievements include proof, in the context of Geometric Measure Theory, that the singular set in a mathematical model for soap bubble clusters and soap films on wire frames is what is physcally observed, thereby solving a 100 year old problem; development of mathematical models for treating shapes of surfaces and interfaces for crystalline materials and use of them to model crystal growth. Office: Courant Inst 251 Mercer St New York NY 10012 Business E-Mail: jtaylor@cims.nyu.edu.

**TAYLOR, JEFF**, reporter, editor; Reporter Kansas City Star; asst. mng. editor Detroit Free Press. Recipient Pulitzer prize for nat. reporting, 1992, Sigma Delta Chi award, George Polk award. Office: Detroit Free Press 600 W Lafayette Blvd Detroit MI 48226-2703

**TAYLOR, JEFF**, Internet company executive; Degree, U. Mass. at Amherst; certificate, Owner/Pres. Mgmt. (OPM) Program, Exec. Edn., Harvard Bus. Sch. Head recruitment ad agency Adion; founder, chief monster Monster Board (formerly Monster.com now Monster, purchased by TMP Worldwide Inc. in 1995, now Monster Worldwide, Inc.), 1994—2005; advisor Monster, 2005—. Spkr. in field. Bd. dir. Nat. Jr. Achievement, Mass. Jr. Achievement, Wang Ctr. for Performing Arts, Boston. Achievements include helped pioneer job searching on the internet. Office: Monster 5 Clock Tower Place Maynard MA 01754 Address: Monster Worldwide Inc 622 3rd Ave 39th Fl New York NY 10017*

**TAYLOR, JIM**, scriptwriter, film director; MFA, NYU. Dir., writer: Memory Lane, 1995, The Lost Cause, 2004, writer: screenplays Citizen Ruth, 1996, Election, 1999, Jurassic Park III, 2001, About Schmidt, 2002, Sideways, 2004 (Academy award for best adapted screenplay, 2005); dir.: (films) Living Will, 1999. Office: Twentieth Century Fox Twentieth Century House 31-32 Soho Square London W1D 3AP England

**TAYLOR, JIMMY LYNN**, retired family practice physician, administrator; b. Franklin County, NC, May 11, 1936; s. Herman Benjamin and Ruby Lynn (Perry) T.; m. Dorothy Keenum, Sept. 4, 1960; children: Gregory Scott, Sonya Lynn Taylor Loper. AA, Mars Hill Coll., 1956; BS, Wake Forest U., 1958; MD, Wake Forest U. Sch. Medicine, 1962. Postdoctoral fellow Greenville (S.C.) Gen. Hosp., 1962-63; staff physician USPHS Indian Hosp., Pine Ridge, SD, 1963-65, chief of obstetrics, 1964-65; family physician, co-founder Monroe (N.C.) Family Med. Ctr., 1965; family physician, ptnr., 1965-95; student physician Wingate (N.C.) U., 1987-94; med. dir. Brian Ctr. Nursing Facility, Monroe, 1992-95. H.S. team physician, 1965—75. Lt. comdr. USPHS, 1963-65. Recipient Head Start Child Care Achievement award N.C. Head Start Assn., 1990. Fellow Am. Acad. Family Physicians; mem. Am. Bd. Family Practice (diplomate), N.C. Acad. Family Physicians, N.C. Med. Soc., Union County Med. Soc. (pres. 1976-77). Republican. Baptist. Avocations: golf, fishing, gardening, bridge, collecting autographed first edition books. Home: 1657 Pageland Hwy Monroe NC 28112-8737 Office: Monroe Family Med Ctr PA 1420 E Franklin St Monroe NC 28112-5160 Personal E-mail: jtaylor628412@yahoo.com, jtaylorb@carolina.rr.com.

**TAYLOR, JOB, III**, lawyer; b. N.Y.C., Feb. 18, 1942; s. Job II and Anne Harrison (Flinchbaugh) T.; m. Nancy C. August, Oct. 24, 1964 (div. 1978); children: Whitney August, Job IV; m. Sally Lawson, May 31, 1980; 1 child, Alexandra Anne. BA, Washington & Jefferson Coll., 1964; JD, Coll. William and Mary, 1971. Bar: N.Y. 1972, Mass. 2003, U.S. Dist. Ct. (no., so. ea. and we. dists.) N.Y. 1973, U.S. Ct. Appeals (2d cir.) 1973, U.S. Ct. Claims 1974, U.S. Tax Ct. 1974, U.S. Supreme Ct. 1975, U.S. Ct. Appeals (9th cir.) 1976, U.S. Ct. Mil. Appeals 1977, U.S. Ct. Appeals (D.C. and 10th cirs.) 1977, D.C. 1981, U.S. Ct. Internat. Trade 1981, U.S. Ct. Appeals (fed. cir.) 1982, U.S. Dist. Ct. (no. dist.) Calif. 1983, U.S. Ct. Appeals (6th cir.) U.S. Dist. Ct., 1987, U.S. Ct. Appeals (3d cir.) 1990, U.S. Dist. Ct. Conn. 1996. Ptnr. Olwine, Connelly, Chase, O'Donnell & Weyher, N.Y.C., 1971-85, Latham & Watkins, N.Y.C., 1985—. Served to lt. USN, 1964-68. Mem. ABA, Assn. Bar City N.Y., La Confrerie des Chevaliers du Tastevin, Racquet and Tennis Club, Wee Burn Country Club (Darien, Conn.). Republican. Episcopalian. Avocations: squash, tennis, golf, reading. Office Phone: 508-240-3069. Personal E-mail: job.taylor@lw.com.

**TAYLOR, JOEL SANFORD**, government agency administrator; b. Hazleton, Pa., Oct. 8, 1942; s. Robert Joseph and Alice Josephine (Sanford) T.; m. Donna Rae Caron, Mar. 26, 1967; children: Jason, Adam, Jeremy. BA in Polit. Sci. and Internat. Rels., Swarthmore Coll., 1965; LLB, Columbia U., 1968. Bar: N.Y. 1969, U.S. Ct. Appeals (2d cir.) 1970, U.S. Dist. Ct. (no. dist.) Ohio 1974, U.S. Supreme Ct. 1974, U.S. Dist. Ct. (so. dist.) Ohio 1975, U.S. Ct. Appeals (6th cir.) 1975, U.S. Dist. Ct. (we. dist.) Ky 1979. Law clk. hon. Constance B. Motley US Dist. Ct., NYC, 1968-69; assoc. Paul, Weiss, Rifkind, Wharton & Garrison, NYC, 1969-72; exec. asst. Ohio Office Budget and Mgmt., Columbus, 1972-74; asst. atty. gen. Ohio Atty. Gen., Columbus, 1974-83, chief counsel, 1983-91; ptnr. Dinsmore & Shohl, Columbus, 1991-2000; dir. fin. and mgmt. City of Columbus, 2000—. Pres. Ohio Sundry Claims Bd., Columbus, 1972-74, Ohio State Controlling Bd., Columbus, 1973-74; mem., bd. trustees Ohio State Tchrs. Retirement Sys., Columbus, 1986-91, Solid Waste Authority Ctrl. Ohio, 2001—. Mem.: Govt. Fin. Officers Assn., Nature Conservancy, Nat. Wildlife Fedn., Columbia Law Alumni Assn. Office: City Hall 90 W Broad St Columbus OH 43215-9000 Office Phone: 614-645-7036. E-mail: jstaylor@columbus.gov.

**TAYLOR, JOHN BRIAN**, former federal agency administrator; b. Yonkers, N.Y., Dec. 8, 1946; s. John Joseph and Lorraine (Crowley) T.; m. Raye Allyn Price, Dec. 30, 1972; children: Jennifer Lynn, John Andrew. AB in Econs. summa cum laude, Princeton U., 1968; PhD, Stanford U., 1973. Asst. prof. econs. Columbia U., N.Y.C., 1973-77, assoc. prof., 1977-79, prof., 1979-80; prof. econs. and pub. affairs Princeton U., 1980-84; prof. econs. Stanford U., 1984—, dir. Ctr. for Econ. Policy Rsch., 1994-97; dir. Introductory Econs. Ctr., 1997-2001; under sec. for internat. affairs U.S. Dept. Treasury, Washington, 2001—05. Sr. staff economist Pres.'s Coun. Econ. Advisers, 1976—77, mem., 1989—91; econometric cons. Townsend-Greenspan and Co., NY, 1978—81; rsch. advisor Fed. Res. Bank, Phila., 1981—84; rsch. assoc. Nat. Bur. Econ. Rsch. 1980—; rsch. economist Bank of Japan, Tokyo, 1987, hon. adviser, 1994—2001; panel of econ. advisers Congl. Budget Office, 1995—2001. Author: (non-fiction) Macroeconomics, 1986, Macroeconomic Policy in the World Economy, 1993, Economics, 1995, Unemployment, Inflation, and Monetary Policy, 1998, Monetary Policy Rules, 1999, Handbook of Macroeconomics, 2000; co-editor: Am. Econ. Rev., 1985—89; editor (assoc.): Econometrica, 1981—85, (jour.) Jour. Econ. Dynamics and Control, 1978—85, Jour. Monetary Econs., 1978—83, Jour. Econ. Perspectives, 1997—2001; mng. editor: Internat. Jour. Cntrl. Banking, 2005—; contbr. articles to profl. jours. NSF grantee, 1979-81, 81-83, 83-86, 86-89, 92-95; Guggenheim Found. fellow, 1983-84; sr. fellow Hoover Instn., 1996—. Fellow Econometric Soc., Am. Acad. of Arts and Sci.; mem. Am. Econ. Assn. (exec. com. 1991-94, v.p. 2000-01). Office Phone: 650-723-9677. E-mail: John.Taylor@stanford.edu.

**TAYLOR, JOHN CALVIN,** dentist; b. Cin., July 22, 1914; s. John Calvin Taylor V and Magdala Elizabeth Siehl; m. Adah Packard Boggs, Mar. 7, 1941; children: Sarah, Margaret, Virginia, John, Frederick, Alison, Carla. BSc, Muskingum Coll., 1937; BD, Cedarville Sem., 1939; DDS, U. Pitts., 1949; cert. excellence in Hindi and Urdu, Lang. Sch., Landour, India, 1940, 41. Diploma Acad. Gen. Dentistry. Missionary Reformed Presbyn. Synod, Roorkee, India, 1939-46; moderator, pastor Reformed Presbyn., Pitts.-Fairview, Pa., 1946-47; nat. missions missionary Presbyn. Bd. Home Missions, Pitts., Tyre, Pa., 1947-52; missionary dentist United Presbyn., Pitts.-Seattle, 1953-59; dir. Meth. Mission Hosp. Dental Clinic, Bariely, India, 1954—55; founder Dental Clinic Landour Cmty. Hosp., Mussoorie, India, 1955-59; pres. Rotary Club Internat., Mount Union, Pa., 1964-65; pastor 3 chs. Mt. Union, Johnsonburg and St. Mary areas, 1964-68; founder Shanta Bhawan Hosp. Dental Clinic, Katmandu, Nepal, 1968, Missionary Dentist, Inc., 1977; dental missionary svc. E.L.W.A. Hosp., Liberia, 1977, Tank Hosp., Pakistan, 1980—81, Sahiwal Hosp., Pakistan, 1981, Shell Clinics, Ecuador, 1983; provider free dental care India, 1778—2001; founder Oral Clinic Ctr., Dera Dun, India, 1981—. Tchr. emergency dentistry Vellore (India) Med. Coll., 1958; dentist Youth With a Mission, Mercy Ship, Hawaii, 1985. Author: Wildlife in India's Tiger Kingdom, 1980, Face the Devil's Roar, 1995, God's Kingdom helps Animal Kingdoms, 2005 Co-founder, life mem. Wildlife Preservation Soc., Dehra-Dun, India, 1954—, organizer, founder Rajpur Wildlife Park, 1954—. Recipient Cert. of Honor for 50 Yrs. of Dedicated Svc. to Dentistry, ADA, 1999. Mem. Herminie Lions Club (fgn. chmn., Lions Hat award 1993), N.Am. Hunting Club, NRA. Republican. Presbyterian. Avocations: zoology, hunting, taxidermy, photography, music. Office Phone: 724-446-7732. Personal E-mail: tgrtlr@juno.com.

**TAYLOR, JOHN CHESTNUT, III,** lawyer; b. NYC, Jan. 7, 1928; s. John Chestnut and Jean Elizabeth (Willis) T.; m. Dolores Yvonne Sunstrom, Nov. 17, 1950; children: Jane Willis, John Sunstrom, Anne Holliday. BA, Princeton U., 1947; LL.B. Yale U., 1950. Bar: N.Y. 1950, D.C. 1972. Assoc. Paul, Weiss, Rifkind, Wharton & Garrison, N.Y.C., 1950, 52-60, ptnr., 1961-85, 87-91, of counsel, 1986-87, 92—; exec. v.p., dir. AEA Investors Inc., N.Y.C., 1985-86, pres., 1986-87. Bd. dirs. AFS Intercultural Programs Inc., N.Y.C., 1972-80, trustee, 1973-79, chmn., 1975-79; trustee Carnegie Corp. N.Y., N.Y.C., 1975-84, chmn., 1979-84; trustee, mem. exec. com. Devereux Found., 1992-2003, vice chmn., 1994-2003. Served to capt. JAGC, AUS, 1950-52. Mem. Assn. of Bar of City of N.Y., Order of Coif, Phi Beta Kappa, Phi Delta Phi. Democrat. Home: 64 Meadow Lakes Hightstown NJ 08520 Office: Paul Weiss Rifkind Wharton & Garrison 1285 Avenue Of The Americas New York NY 10019-6064 E-mail: budsunny@verizon.net.

**TAYLOR, JOHN E.,** foundation administrator, lawyer; BA, Northeastern U., 1973, JD, 1980. Pres., CEO Nat. Cmty. Reinvestment Coalition. Chmn. Nat. Neighbors; appointee to Cmty. Devel. Fin. Insts. (CDFI) Fund; mem. bd. dirs. Rainbow/PUSH Coalition, Leadership Conf. for Civil Rights; past bd. mem. Consumer Adv. Coun., Fed. Reserve Bank Bd., Fannie Mae Housing Impact Div., Freddie Mac Housing Adv. Bd.; spkr. in field. Guest coor. ABC's Nightline, CBS, Fox news, CNN, CSPAN, Chgo. Tribune, NY Times, Washington Post; contbr. articles to profl. jours. Recipient Martin Luther King, Jr. Peace Award, US Congl. Citation Award, Award for Excellence in Cmty. Econ. Devel., State of Mass. Office: Nat Cmty Reinvestment Coalition Ste 900 727 15th St Washington DC 20005 Office Phone: 202-628-8866. Office Fax: 202-628-9800. E-mail: jtaylor@ncrc.org.*

**TAYLOR, JOHN JACKSON (JAY TAYLOR),** writer, retired diplomat; b. Little Rock, Dec. 4, 1931; s. Alfred Wesley and Annie Laurie (Cain) T.; m. Elizabeth Rose, July 9, 1954; children: John Jr., Laurie, Amy, Cynthia. BA, Vanderbilt U., 1952; MA, U. Mich., 1968. 3d sec. U.S. Fgn. Svc., Accra, Ghana, 1957-59, 2d sec. Taichung and Taipei, China, 1960-65; Chinese affairs analyst Dept. State, Washington, 1966-67; staff assoc. Ctr. for Chinese Studies, U. Mich., Ann Arbor, 1967-68; U.S. consul Sarawak, Sabah and Brunei, Kuching, Malaysia, 1968-70; chief external affairs reporting U.S. Consulate Gen., Hong Kong, 1970-74; officer-in-charge Chinese affairs Dept. State, Washington, 1974-75; staff mem. E. Asian affairs Nat. Security Coun., Washington, 1975-77; polit. counselor U.S. Embassy, Pretoria/Capetown, 1977-80, polit. cons. Peking, 1980-82; rsch. fellow Fairbank Ctr. for East Asian Studies Harvard U., Cambridge, Mass., 1982-83; dir. East Asian analysis Dept. State, Washington, 1983-85; dep. asst. sec. state Bur. Intelligence and Rsch., Dept. State, Washington, 1986-87; chief of mission U.S. Interests Sect., Havana, Cuba, 1987-90; diplomat in residence Carter Presdl. Ctr., Emory U., 1990-92; sr. mem. State Task Force 2000, 1992-93; sr. assoc. Global Bus. Access; assoc. in rsch. Fairbank Ctr. for East Asian Studies, Harvard U.; prodr., writer, dir. ?Why Prodns. Guest faculty Emory U. and Spelman Coll. Author: China and Southeast Asia, 1974, 1976, The Dragon and the Wild Goose, 1987, 1990, The Rise and Fall of Totalitarianism, 1993, The Generalissimo's Son, 2000, (documentary) Ubuntu, African and Afrikaner, 2000; contbr. China and National Security, 1985, columns in newspapers Washington Post, L.A. Times, N.Y. Times. Served as Naval Aviator with USMC, 1953-57. Mem.: Wash. Inst. Fgn. Affairs, Fgn. Svc. Assn. E-mail: jaytaylor888@sprintmail.com.

**TAYLOR, JOHN JOSEPH,** nuclear engineer, researcher; b. Hackensack, NJ, Feb. 27, 1922; s. John J.D. and Johanna F. (Thibideau) T.; m. Lorraine Crowley, Feb. 5, 1943; children: John B., Nancy M., Susan M. BA, St. John's U., Jamaica, NY, 1942, DSc (hon.), 1975; MS, U. Notre Dame, 1947. Mathematician Bendix Aviation Corp., Teterboro, NJ, 1946-47; engr. Kellex Corp., N.Y.C., 1947-50; v.p. water reactor divsn. Westinghouse Electric Corp., Pitts., 1950-81; v.p. nuc. power Electric Power Rsch. Inst., Palo Alto, Calif., 1981-95; energy cons., 1995—. Mem. adv. com. Oak Ridge (Tenn.) Nat. Lab., 1973-83, Brookhaven Nat. Lab., Upton, N.Y., 1986-92, Inst. for Nuc. Power Ops., 1988-95; mem. adv. com. Argonne (Ill.), Nat. Lab., 1980-86, bd. dirs.; cons. Office Tech. Assessment, Washington, 1975-93; mem. internat. adv. group IAEA, Vienna, Austria, 1992-95; mem. nuc. rsch. rev. com. NRC, 1995-97; mem. U.S.-Russian Commn. on Weapons Plutonium Disposition, 1996-2001, Nat. Acad. Bd. Radioactive Waste Mgmt., 1998-2001, DOE Nuc. Energy Rsch. Adv. Bd., 1998-2002; co-chair Adams for Peace Study, Livermore Lab., 2003-04; mem. on rev. of Dept. Energy Nuclear Energy R&D, Nat. Acad., 2006—. Co-author: Reactor Shielding Manual, 1953, Naval Reactor Physics Manual, 1956, Nuclear Power, Policy and Prospects, 1987, Management and Disposition of Excess Weapons Plutonium, 1995; contbr. articles to profl. jours. Bd. regents emeritus St. Mary's Coll., Moraga, Calif., Bd of Regents, St. Patrick's U. Calif. Lt. (j.g.) USN, 1942—45. Recipient Order of Merit Westinghouse Electric Corp., 1957, George Westinghouse Gold medal ASME, 1990. Fellow AAAS, Am. Phys. Soc., Am. Nuc. Soc. (bd. dirs., Walter Zinn award 1993); mem. NAE (chair), Elec. Power/Energy Sys. Engrs., Cosmos Club (Washington). Republican. Roman Catholic. Office: Electric Power Rsch Inst PO Box 10412 3412 Hillview Ave Palo Alto CA 94304-1344 Home: 620 Sand Hill Rd Apt 303b Palo Alto CA 94304-2069

**TAYLOR, JOHN LOCKHART,** retired municipal official; b. N.Y.C., Nov. 4, 1927; s. Floyd and Marian (Lockhart) T.; m. Barbara Becker, July 19, 1952; children: Catherine Fair, Robert, William, Susan. AB, Middlebury Coll., 1952; M.Govtl. Adminstrn., U. Pa., 1956. Reporter Providence Jour.-Bull., 1952-54; adminstrv. intern City of Xenia, Ohio, 1955-56; mcpl. mgr. Borough of Narberth, Pa., 1956-60; Town of Lakewood, N.J., 1960-64; asst. city mgr. Fresno, Calif., 1964-65; city mgr., 1965-68, Kansas City, Mo., 1968-74, Berkeley, Calif., 1974-76; lectr. U. Pa., 1957-58, Golden Gate U. 1977; sr. urban mgmt. specialist Stanford Research Inst., 1977-80; dir. Internat. Devel. Center, 1980-82; clk. of bd. suprs. City of San Francisco 1982-98, spl. asst., 1998—. Pres. Calif. Clks. Bd. Suprs. Assn., 1988-89. Served with USN, 1945-48. Mem. Internat. City Mgrs. Assn., Mcpl. Execs. Assn. (pres. 1991-93, 98). Address: 1005 Creston Rd Berkeley CA 94708-1503 E-mail: misterclerk@sbcglobal.net.

**TAYLOR, JOHN MCKOWEN,** lawyer; b. Baton Rouge, Jan. 20, 1924; s. Benjamin Brown and May (McKowen) T.; 1 child, John McKowen. BA, La. State U., 1948, JD, 1950. Bar: La. 1950, U.S. Ct. Appeals (5th cir.) 1959, U.S.

Supreme Ct. 1960. Assoc. Taylor, Porter, Brooks, Fuller & Phillips, Baton Rouge, 1950-55, Huckaby, Seale, Kelton & Hayes, Baton Rouge, 1955-58; ptnr. Kelton & Taylor, Baton Rouge, 1958-61; pvt. practice, Baton Rouge, 1961—. With AUS, 1943—46, maj. USAR, 1946—, ATO, ETO, PTO. Mem. ABA, AAAS, La. State Bar Assn., Baton Rouge Bar Assn., Mil. Order of World Wars, Am. Radio Relay League, Baton Rouge Country Club, City Club of Baton Rouge, Baton Rouge Amateur Radio Club, Camelot Club, SAR, Sigma Chi, Pi Gamma Mu, Phi Delta Phi. Republican. Presbyterian. Home and Office: 2150 Kleinert Ave Baton Rouge LA 70806-6712 Office Phone: 225-343-1928. E-mail: jmcktaylor@cox.net.

**TAYLOR, JOHN PAUL,** music educator, minister; b. Montgomery, Ala., Nov. 28, 1971; s. Tommy Joe and Barbara Alice Taylor; m. Cecilia Lee Sanders, June 25, 1994; children: Timothy Zechariah-Lotz, William Anderson. B Music Edn., Troy State U., 1995. Band dir. Malone (Fla.) HS, 1995—98, Houston County HS, Columbia, Ala., 1998—2000, Headland (Ala.) HS, 2002—; office mgr. Baten Internat., Wicksburg, Ala., 2000—02. Pastor Pine Hills Free Will Bapt. Ch., Dothan, Ala., 1998—. Mem.: Ala. Bandmasters Assn., Nat. Music Educators Conf., Lions Club. Home: 2201 Antenna Ave Dothan AL 36301 Office: Headland HS 8 Sporman St Headland AL 36345

**TAYLOR, JOSEPH EVANS,** law educator; Student, Calif. State U., Sacramento; JD, Loyola U., L.A., 1961; MBA, Pepperdine U., Malibu, Calif., 1986. Bar: Calif. 1962. Asst. chief dep. Sacramento Dist. Atty.'s Office, 1964-79; sr. atty. Ventura Dist. Atty.'s Office, 1979-86; counsel Lagerlof, Senecal, Drescher & Swift, Ventura, L.A., Calif., 1987; pub. defender County of Riverside, Calif., 1987-92; prof. law McGeorge Sch. Law, 1992—; judge pro tem Sacramento County Superior Ct., 1993—. Co-author trial practice cases. Named Prof. of Yr., U. Pacific McGeorge Sch. Law, 2005. Mem. Sacramento County Mgmt. Assn. (co-founder, v.p., past pres.), Calif. Dist. Attys. Assn. Office: McGeorge Sch Law 3200 5th Ave Sacramento CA 95817-2799

**TAYLOR, JOSEPH HOOTON, JR.,** radio astronomer, physicist; b. Phila., Mar. 29, 1941; s. Joseph Hooton and Sylvia Hathaway (Evans) T.; m. Marietta Bisson, Jan. 3, 1976. BA in Physics, Haverford Coll., 1963; PhD in Astronomy, Harvard U., 1968; DSc (hon., U. Chgo., 1985, U. Mass., 1994. Research fellow, lectr. Harvard U., 1968-69; asst. prof. astronomy U. Mass., Amherst, 1969-72, assoc. prof., 1973-77, 1977-81; prof. physics Princeton U., 1980—; James McDonnell Disting. prof. physics, 1986—, dean of faculty, 1997—2003. Author: Pulsars, 1977. Recipient Dannie Heineman prize in astrophysics, Am. Inst. Physics/Am. Astron. Soc., 1980, prize in gravitation and cosmology, Tomalla Found., 1985, Magellanic Premium award, Am. Philos. Soc., 1990, Einstein prize laureate, Albert Einstein Found., 1993, Wolf prize in physics, Wolf Found., Israel, 1992, Nobel Prize in Physics, Nobel Found., 1993, Carty Award for Advancement of Scis., Schwartzchild Medal; fellow MacArthur fellow, 1981. Fellow: Am. Phys. Soc., Am. Acad. Arts and Scis.; mem.: Internat. Astron. Union, Internat. Sci. Radio Union, Am. Astron. Soc., Am. Philos. Soc., NAS (Draper Medal). Mem. Soc. Of Friends. Achievements include discovery of first binary pulsar - a twin star system that provides a rare natural laboratory in which to test Albert Einstein's prediction that moving objects emit gravitational waves. Home: 272 Hartley Ave Princeton NJ 08540-5656 Office: Princeton U Dept Physics 215 Jadwin Hall PO Box 708 Princeton NJ 08544-0001 Business E-Mail: joe@pulsar.princeton.edu.*

**TAYLOR, JUNE RUTH,** retired minister; b. Annapolis, Md., June 27, 1932; d. Benjamin and Naomi Medora (Dill) Michaelson; m. Thomas Wayne Taylor, Mar. 20, 1954; children: Rebecca Susan Taylor DeLameter, Michael Steven. AB, Goucher Coll., 1952; MRE, Presbyn. Sch. of Christian Edn., Richmond, Va., 1954; MDiv., McCormick Theol. Sem., 1978. Ordained to ministry Presbyn. Ch. (U.S.A.), 1976. Min. Christian Edn. Congl. United Ch. of Christ, Arlington Heights, Ill., 1974-79; dir. pastoral svcs. Presbyn. U. Hosp., Pitts., 1979-89; dir. chaplaincy svcs. Ephrata (Pa.) Community Hosp., 1991-96; ret., 1996; interim pastor Kreutz Creek Presbyn. Ch., Hellam, Pa., 2001; interim parish vis. Highland Presbyn. Ch., Lancaster, Pa., 2004. Chaplain Rush-Presbyn. St. Luke's Med. Ctr., Chgo., 1976-78; chair exec. com. Presbyn. Assn. Specialized Pastoral Ministries, Louisville, 1987-89; bd. dirs. Cocalico Place. Book reviewer in field. Fellow Coll. Chaplains (sec. exec. com. 1985-87); mem. Soc. Chaplains, Hosp. Assn. Pa. (pres. 1983), Assn. Profl. Chaplains (cert.), Assn. Mental Health Clergy, Assn. for Clin. Pastoral Edn. (clin.), Rotary (liaison to Boys and Girls Club S.W. Pitts. chpt. 1990-91, v.p., program chair Denver-Adamstown club 1996-97, pres.-elect 1997-98), York North Rotary Club (chmn. vocation svc. 2003-2005), Mental Health Assn. York County (bd. dirs. 1999—2005), Gamma Phi Beta Alumnae Club (pres. 1990-91).

**TAYLOR, KAREN LYNN,** biology educator; b. Monroe, Mich., Dec. 24, 1961; d. John Arthur and Louella Jean Rieger; m. Jon Thomas Taylor, Aug. 28, 1969; children: Jaron Jaye, Jasper Lynkon. BS in Biol. Scis., Mich. Technol. U., Houghton, 1985; MA in Sci. Edn., Western Mich. U., Kalamazoo, 1992. Cert. secondary continuing edn. Mich., 1988, provisional edn. Mich., 1985. Physics, biology, math. tchr. Tecumseh H.S., Mich., 1985—86; biology, math. tchr. Galesburg Augusta H.S., Mich., 1986—92; tech. edn. sci. tchr. Portage Ctrl. Mid. Sch., Mich., 1992—93; biology tchr. Portage Ctrl. H.S., 1993—. Bd. of youth mast St. Michael Luth. Ch., Portage, 1998—2002. Fellow Princeton Tchg. Program award, Woodrow Wilson Nat. Fellowship Found., Princeton U. Woodrow Wilson Tchg. fellow, Woodrow Wilson Nat. Fellowship Found., 1992; Toyota Tapestry grant, Toyota, NSTA, Kalamazoo Coll. Summer Rsch. fellow, NSF, 1989, 1990. Mem.: Nat. Assn. Biology Tchrs. Office: Portage Ctrl HS 8135 South Westnedge Ave Portage MI 49002 Office Phone: 269-323-5217. E-mail: ktaylor@portageps.org.

**TAYLOR, KATHLEEN (CHRISTINE TAYLOR),** physical chemist, researcher; b. Cambridge, Mass., Mar. 16, 1942; d. John F. and Anna M. T. BA in Chemistry, Douglass Coll., New Brunswick, N.J., 1964; PhD in Phys. Chemistry, Northwestern U., 1968. Postdoctoral fellow U. Edinburgh, Scotland, 1968-70; assoc. sr. rsch. chemist Gen. Motors Rsch. Labs., Warren, Mich., 1970-74, sr. rsch. chemist, 1974-75, asst. phys. chemistry dept. head, 1975-83, environ. sci. dept. head, 1983-85, phys. chemistry dept. head, 1985-96; physics and phys. chemistry dept. head Gen. Motors Global Rsch. & Devel. Operations, Warren, Mich., 1995-98, materials and processes dir., 1998—2002. Recipient Mich. Sci. Trailblazer award Detroit Sci. Ctr., 1986. Fellow AAAS, Soc. Automotive Engrs. Internat.; mem. NAE, Am. Chem. Soc. (Garvan medal 1989), Materials Rsch. Soc. (treas. 1984, 2d v.p. 1985, 1st v.p. 1986, pres. 1987), N.Am. Catalysis Soc., Am. Acad. Arts Sci, Sigma Xi.

**TAYLOR, KATHY,** mayor; d. Jim and Lola Taylor; m. Bill Lobeck; 1 child. BA in Journalism, Okla. U., JD, 1981. Atty. pvt. practice; v.p., gen. counsel Thrifty Car Rental, 1988—2003; sec. Dept. Commerce State of Okla., 2003—05; mayor City of Tulsa, 2006—. Office: Office of Mayor City Hall 200 Civic Ctr 11th Fl Tulsa OK 74103 Office Phone: 918-596-7411. Office Fax: 918-596-9010.*

**TAYLOR, KENNETH GRANT,** chemistry professor; b. Paterson, N.J., May 12, 1936; s. Ulysses Grant and Susan (De Haan) T.; m. Carla May Rydell, June 17, 1961; children: Koren Lynn, Kevin Grant, Kaylyn Jo. BA, Calvin Coll., 1957; PhD, Wayne State U., 1963. Rsch. assoc. MIT, Cambridge, 1963-64; sr. rsch. assoc. Wayne State U., Detroit, 1964-66; from asst. to assoc. prof. chemistry U. Louisville, Louisville, 1966-73; prof., 1974—, acting chmn., 1973-74, vice chmn., 1976-78, chmn., 1978-87, assoc. dean. Rsch. Arts and Scis., 1991-97. Prof. associé Univ. de Nancy I, France, 1974-75, 83; vis. prof. U. Lund, Sweden, 1991, Ecole Nationale de Chimie-Montpellier, France, 1997. Contbr. numerous articles to profl. jours.; co-author, presentor numerous papers at sci. meetings. Rsch. and teaching grantee NIH, NSF, Am. Cancer

Soc., Am. Chem. Soc., Dept. Interior, U. Louisville, 1966—. Fellow AAAS; mem. Am. Chem. Soc., Ky. Acad. Sci. Democrat. Presbyterian. Home: 1838 Yale Dr Louisville KY 40205-2031 Office: U Louisville Dept Chemistry Louisville KY 40292-0001

**TAYLOR, KENNETH LAPHAM,** science educator; b. L.A., Calif., May 16, 1941; s. Angus Ellis and Mary Kathleen (Lapham) T.; m. Melva Lee Johnson, Aug. 28, 1969; children: Melissa, Benjamin, Nathaniel. AB, Harvard U., 1962, AM, 1965, PhD, 1968. Asst. prof. U. Okla., Norman, Okla., 1967-72, assoc. prof., 1972-86, dept. chair history sci., 1979-92, 99, prof., 1986—. Contbr. articles to profl. jours. Postdoctoral Rsch. fellow Centre Nat. de la Recherche Scientifique, Paris, 1973-74, Vis. Scholar, Ecole des Hautes Etudes en Sciences Sociales, Paris, 2001. Mem. Internat. Commn. for History Geol. Scis. (v.p. N.Am. 2004—), U.S. Nat. Com. for History Geology (chair 1990-93), History of Earth Scis. Soc. (pres. 1997-98), History of Sci. Soc. (vis. lectr. 1990-92), Geol. Soc. Am. (chair Hist. Geology divsn. 1999), Geol. Soc. London (Sue Tyler Friedman medal 1998). Home: 718 W Timberdell Rd Norman OK 73072-6323 Office: U Okla Dept History Sci Norman OK 73019-3106 Office Phone: 405-325-5416. Business E-Mail: ktaylor@ou.edu.

**TAYLOR, KOKO,** singer; b. Memphis, Sept. 28, 1935; m. Robert "Pops" Taylor (dec.). Singer: (albums) I Got What It Takes, 1975, The Earthshaker, 1978, From the Heart of a Woman, 1981, Queen of the Blues, 1985, Live from Chgo.: An Audience with the Queen, 1987, Jump for Joy, 1990, Force of Nature, 1993, Royal Blue, 2000, Deluxe Edition, 2002. Named to Blues Hall of Fame, 1997; recipient Legend of Yr., Clearly Canadian, 1993, Howlin' Wolf award, 1996, Outstanding Generosity award, Children's Brittle Bone Found., 1997; Nat. Heritage Fellowship, NEA, 2004. Achievements include 2 Grammy awards, 8 Grammy nominations; March 3, 1993 declared by mayor "Koko Taylor Day" in Chgo. Office: Alligator Records care Nora Kinnally PO Box 60234 Chicago IL 60660-0234

**TAYLOR, KRISTIE LEIGH,** performing arts educator, actor; d. Gary Robert Belles and Gloria Diane Patterson; m. Christopher Charles Taylor, July 29, 2000. BSEd in Comm. Arts, BFA in Theater, Clarion U. of Pa., 2000. Cert. tchr. Pa. Tchr. English and comm. Patrick Henry HS, Ashland, Va., 2001—03; English tchr. Brookville Jr./Sr. HS, Pa., 2003—04; drama and English tchr. Clarion-Limestone HS, 2004—. Dir., actor Brookville Cmty. Theatre, 2000—. Deacon Brookville Presbyn. Ch., 2005—. Named Outstanding Am. Tchr., NHR, 2005—06. Mem.: NEA. Avocations: mosaic tiling, home renovation, singing. Office: Carion Limestone Jr/Sr HS 4091 Clarion Limestone School Rd Strattanville PA 16258

**TAYLOR, LANCE JEROME,** economics professor; b. Montpelier, Idaho, May 25, 1940; s. Walter Jerome and Ruth (Robinson) T.; m. Yvonne S.M. Johnsson, May 31, 1963; children: Ian Lance, Signe Marguerite. BS with honors, Calif. Inst. Tech., 1962; PhD, Harvard U., 1968. Instr. econs. Harvard U., Cambridge, Mass., 1967-68, asst. prof., assoc. prof., 1970-74; research assoc. MIT, Cambridge, 1968-70, prof. econs., 1974-93, New Sch. for Social Rsch., N.Y.C., 1993—. Vis. prof. U. Brasilia, 1974, Pontifical Cath. U. Rio de Janeiro, 1981, U. Delhi, 1987-88, Stockholm Sch. Econs., 1990; Marshall lectr. Cambridge U., 1986-87; cons. World Bank, UN, various fgn. govts. Author: Macro Models for Developing Countries, 1979, Models of Growth and Distribution for Brazil, 1980, Structuralist Macroeconomics, 1983, Varieties of Stabilization Experience, 1988, Income Distribution, Inflation, and Growth, 1991, The Market Meets its Match: Restructuring the Economies of Eastern Europe, 1994, Global Finance at Risk, 2000, Restructuring Macroeconomics: Structuralist Proposals and Critiques of the Mainstream, 2004. Fulbright fellow, 1962-63 Mem. Am. Econ. Assn., Royal Econ. Soc. Home: PO Box 378 Washington ME 04574-0378 Office: New School for Social Rsch Grad Faculty 65 5th Ave New York NY 10003-3089 E-mail: lance@blacklocust.com.

**TAYLOR, LARRY D.,** lawyer; b. Montgomery, W.Va., Nov. 16, 1934; 2 children. BA, W.Va. U., Morgantown, 1956, JD, 1962. Bar: W.Va. 1962. Asst. atty. gen. Atty. Gen's. Office, Charleston, W.Va., 1964-70; pvt. practice, Charleston, 1970-98; atty. W.Va. Bur. Employment Program Legal Svcs., Charleston, 1998—2006. Mediator U.S. Dist. Ct. for W.Va., 1992—, W.Va. State Bar, 1995—, Kanawha County Circuit Ct. Mem. W.Va. Bar Assn. Democrat. Roman Catholic. Avocations: travel, golf, gardening. Home: 1237 Edgewood Dr Charleston WV 25302-2903

**TAYLOR, LEIGH HERBERT,** dean; b. Chgo., Oct. 23, 1941; s. Herbert and Leona Taylor; m. Nancy E. Young; children: Jennifer, Jeremiah. BA, U. Tulsa, 1964, JD, 1966; LLM, NYU, 1969. Bar: Okla. 1966, Ill. 1976. Trial atty. Civil Rights div. Dept. Justice, Washington, 1966-68; prof. DePaul U. Coll. Law, Chgo., 1969-77, asst. dean, 1972-73, assoc. dean, 1973-77; dean Coll. Law, Ohio No. U., Ada, 1977-78, Sch. Law Southwestern U., LA, 1978—2005, dean emeritus, prof. law emeritus, 2005—. Mem. adv. bd. 1st Woman's Bank of L.A., 1981-85; dir. Law Sch. Admissions Svcs., Inc., 1982-86; chmn. audit com. Law Sch. Admissions Coun., 1989-91, trustee, 1991-98, chair-elect, 1994-95, chair, 1995-97; mem. bd. trustees Coun. on Legal Edn. Opportunity, 1993-96, NALP Found., 1999—, chair-elect, 2002—. Editor-in-chief Tulsa Law Jour., 1966; author: Strategies for Law-Focused Education, 1977; (with others) Law in a New Land, 1972; mem. editorial bd. Family Law Quarterly, 1977-78. Bd. dirs. Criminal Def. Consortium Cook County (Ill.), Inc., 1975-77, L.A. Press Club Found., NALP Found., 1999—. With AUS, 1959. Fellow Am. Bar Found.; mem. ABA (accreditation com. 1991-95), Law in Am. Soc. Found., Ill. Bar Assn., Chgo. Bar Assn. (rec. sec.), L.A. County Bar Assn., Okla. Bar Assn. Office: Southwestern U Sch Law Office of Dean 675 S Westmoreland Ave Los Angeles CA 90005-3905 E-mail: ltaylor@swlaw.edu.

**TAYLOR, LELAND BARIDON,** lawyer; b. Poughkeepsie, N.Y., July 5, 1920; s. Alexander J. and Elsie Jane (Van Wyck) T.; m. Rosemary Olcott Coon, June 24, 1945; children: Barry Eugene, Craig Cameron, Mark Alexander, Meg Olcott Taylor Casey. BS, Syracuse U., 1942, JD, 1948. Bar: N.Y. 1948, U.S. Dist. Ct. (no. dist.) N.Y. 1954, U.S. Supreme Ct. 1958. Ptnr. Fitzgerald, Taylor, Pomeroy & Armstrong and predecessor, Cortland, NY, 1948-2000; of counsel Pomeroy, Armstrong & Casullo, Cortland, NY, 2000—. Judge City of Cortland, 1952-57; bd. dirs. First Nat. Bank of Dryden. Trustee Cortland Free Libr., 1950—. With Supply Corps, USNR, 1942-45. Named Cortland County Jr. C. of C. Young Man of Yr., 1952, N.Y. State Young Man of Yr., N.Y. State Jaycees, 1953, Syracuse U. Letterman of Distinction, 1977. Fellow N.Y. Bar Found., Am. Bar Found.; mem. ABA, N.Y. State Bar Assn. (v.p. 1974-76, sec. 1976-79, chmn. fin. com. 1979-84), Cortland County Bar Assn., Rotary (Paul Harris fellow), Masons. Presbyterian. Address: 16 Tompkins St Cortland NY 13045-2541 Office Phone: 607-756-7501.

**TAYLOR, LEONARD STUART,** engineering educator, consultant; b. N.Y.C., Dec. 28, 1928; m. Lillian Rachel Schlang, Apr. 12, 1954; children: Robin Jolie, Allyn Lise. AB, Harvard Coll., 1951; MSc, N.Mex. State U., 1955, PhD, 1960. Microwave engr. Raytheon Mfg. Co., Bedford, Mass., 1950-55; research physicist Gen. Electric Co., Phila., 1960-63; assoc. prof. Case Western Res. U., Cleve., 1964-67; prof. U. Md., College Park, Md., 1967-96, prof. emeritus, 1996—. Cons. UN, Silver Spring, Md., 1967-96. Contbr. articles to profl. jours; inventor Microwave Scalpel, Implantable Microwave Hyperthermia Applicator and numerous others. Recipient Disting. Alumni award, N.Mex. State U., 1975, Outstanding Contbn. award, U. Md. Coll. Engring., 2002. Fellow IEEE (life), Am. Soc. for Laser Medicine and Surgery; mem. Am. Phys. Soc., Optical Soc. of Am., Bioelectromagnetics Soc. Avocations: tennis, music. Office: U Md Dept Ee College Park MD 20742-0001 Office Phone: 301-405-3741. Business E-Mail: taylor@umd.edu.

**TAYLOR, LEWIS JEROME, JR.,** retired priest; b. Norfolk, Va., Feb. 22, 1923; s. Lewis Jerome and Roberta Page (Newton) T.; m. Pauline Rector Green, Nov. 24, 1945; children: Lewis J. III, Michael R., John B., Mary F., Joan E. BS in Engring., U.S. Naval Acad., 1944; MDiv., Seabury-Western

Theol. Sem., Evanston, Ill., 1961; PhD in Religion, Duke U., 1972. Ordained priest Episcopal Ch., 1962. With George R. Green, Inc., White Post, Va., 1949-52, Travelers Ins. Co., Norfolk, 1956-58; chaplain Coll. William and Mary, Williamsburg, Va., 1961-63; curate Bruton Parish Ch., Williamsburg, Va., 1961—63; rector St. Aidan's Episc. Ch., Virginia Beach, Va., 1963-68; prof. theology St. Andrews Sem., Manila, 1971-76; rector Ch. of the Messiah, Chester, NJ, 1978-86; interim rector of various parishes Diocese of Southern Va., 1986-93; instnl. chaplain Indian Creek Correctional Ctr., Chesapeake, Va., 1993-98. Mem. Dept. Missions Diocese of Newark, 1965-68, Commn. on Ministry, Newark, 1979-82; dean Lay Sch. of Christian Studies, Newark, 1977-82; chmn. Commn. on Racism, Southern Va., 1992-95. Author: In Search of Self: Life, Death, and Walker Percy, 1985; contbr. articles to profl. jours. Bd. dirs. Samaritan House, Virginia Beach, 1995—. Deck divsn. officer USN, 1944—45, Pacific War Zone, naval aviator USN, 1947, US Naval Base, Pensacola, Fla., naval aviator USN, 1947—04; Quonset Point, RI, active duty USNR, 1952—56, Korean War / PTO. Trinity Inst. grantee, 1986. Mem.: Rotary (pres. 1985—86). Democrat. Avocations: travel, camping, reading, writing. Home: 985 Fleet Dr Apt 269 Virginia Beach VA 23454-7391

**TAYLOR, LILI,** actress; b. Chgo., Feb. 20, 1967; Appeared in films Mystic Pizza, Say Anything, Born on the Fourth of July, Bright Angel, Dogfight, Watch It, Household Saints, Short Cuts, Rudy, Arizona Dream, Mrs. Parker and the Vicious Circle, Ready to Wear, The Addiction, Cold Fever, I Shot Andy Warhol, Girls Town, Ransom, Cosas Que Nunca te Deve, 1996, Letters Not About Love, 1997, Kicked in the Head, 1997, O.K. Garage, 1998, Pecker, 1998, The Impostors, 1998, Spring Forward, 1999, A Life Slipping Down, 1999, Janis, 1999, The Haunting, 1999, High Fidelity, 2000, Julie Johnson, 2001, Gaudi Afternoon, 2001, Casa de los Babys, 2003, Factotum, 2005; broadway plays include What Did He See, Aven U Boys; regional plays include Mud, The Love Talker, Fun.; TV appearance in (films) Subway Stories: Tales from the Underground, 1997, Deadline, 2000, Anne Frank: The Whole Story, 2001, Live From Baghdad, 2002, (TV series) Six Feet Under, 2002-2005. Office: c/o William Morris Agy 151 S El Camino Dr Beverly Hills CA 90212-2704

**TAYLOR, LINDSAY DAVID, JR.,** healthcare executive, bank executive, federal agency administrator; b. Balt., Dec. 15, 1945; s. Lindsay David Sr. and Lillian Helen (Wagner) T.; children: Sarah Ruth, John David, Margaret Katherine. B in Mech. Engring., Rensselaer Poly. Inst., 1967; MBA, Dartmouth Coll., 1969. Bus. assoc. U.S. Steel Corp., Pitts., 1968-70; spl. asst. to asst. sec. for health HEW, Washington, 1970-71, mgr. operational planning, 1971-74, dep. asst. sec. mgmt., 1977-79; programming officer World Bank, Washington, 1974-76; dir. exams. and supervision Fed. Home Loan Bank Bd., Washington, 1979-81; exec. v.p. Perpetual Bank, Alexandria, Va., 1981-89; pres., CEO Columbia (Md.)-FreeState Health Sys., 1989-91, Preferred Health Network, 1992-96; CEO Alpha Health Plan, 1997-99; COO NPD, LLC, Bethesda, Md., 1999—, Nat. Assn. Cmty. Health Ctrs., Washington, 2001—. Cons. Nat. Acad. Pub. Adminstrn., Washington, 1985—86, Ctr. for Advancement of Health, Washington, 1988—89, Diabetex Corp., Balt., 1996—2003, Latin Am. Youth Ctr., 2003—04; trustee Md. Sci. Ctr., 1996—2000; co-chair Greater Balt. Health Care Coun., 1996—2001, Leadership Md., 1996; mem. bd. advisors Found. for Island Health, 2001—06; mem. adv. bd. WAMU Pub. Radio, 1985—88; bd. dirs. Hospice No. Va., 1984—88; chmn. Washington Employers Coalition on Day Care, 1983—90; chair CHC Funding, LLP, 2002—06; bd. dirs. Capital Link, 2003—06. Recipient Mgmt. Improvement award Pres. U.S., 1973, 77; Edward Tuck scholar. Mem. Ctr. for Excellence in Govt. (prin. 1986-95), Washington Coun. Govts. (devel. policy com. 1986-89, mem. editl. adv. bd. Managed Care 1989-95), Tau Beta Pi, Pi Tau Sigma. Avocations: photography, folk music instruments, travel, wilderness, coaching youth baseball and basketball. Office: 4800 Montgomery Ln Ste 1000 Bethesda MD 20814-3472 also: Ste 210 7200 Wisconsin Ave Bethesda MD 20814 E-mail: LDavidTaylor@yahoo.com.

**TAYLOR, MARGARET TURNER,** clothing designer, architectural designer, economist, writer, planner; b. Wilmington, N.C., May 7, 1944. A.B. in Econs., Smith Coll., 1966; M.A. in Econ. History, U. Pa., 1970, now Ph.D candidate in City and Regional Planning. Tchr. Jefferson Jr. High Sch., New Orleans, 1966-69; instr. econs. U. Tex.-El Paso, 1974-75; adj. prof. econs., Salisbury State U., Md., 1976-78; prin. mgr., designer Margaret Norriss, women's clothing, Salisbury, Md., 1980-95; owner Functional Design Ideas, Inc., 1995—; planner at Wharton Ctr. Applied Research, Phila., 1985-86; planning cons., writer.

**TAYLOR, MARGARET WISCHMEYER,** retired language educator; b. Terre Haute, Ind., Aug. 5, 1920; d. Carl and Grace (Riehle) Wischmeyer; m. John Edward Taylor, Sept. 5, 1942 (dec. 1988); children: Deborah Ann, Tobin Edward (dec. 2002), Mary Leesa. BA magna cum laude, Duke U., 1941; MA, John Carroll U., Cleve., 1973. Feature writer Dayton (Ohio) Daily News, 1945-53; freelance writer Cleve., 1953—; asst. to Dr. Joseph B. Rhine Duke U. Parapsychology Lab., Durham, NC, 1941; asst. prof. English and journalism Ea. Campus, Cuyahoga CC, Cleve., 1973-92, prof. emeritus, 1992—; advisor campus newspaper, 1973-84, dir. Writers Conf., 1975-90. Writing cons., editor various cos. and pubs., Cleve., 1973—; founder, operator Grammar Hot Line, 1987-92. Author: Crystal Lake Reflections, 1985, English 101 Can Be Fun, 1991, The Basic English Handbook, 1995. Recipient top state honors Ohio Newspaper Women's Assn., 1947, award for best ednl., best overall stories Am. Heart Assn., 1970, Besse award for tchg. excellence, 1980, Profl. Excellence award, 1985, Provost's Pride award, 1987, Nat. Tchg. Excellence award Coun. for Advancement and Support of Edn., 1989; named Ohio Outstanding Citizen, Ohio Ho. Reps., 1987, 89, Innovator of Yr., League for Innovations in C.C.s, 1988, Pres.'s award Cuyahoga C.C., 1992. Mem. Mensa, Phi Beta Kappa, Pi Beta Phi. Presbyterian. Avocations: grammar consulting, reading, writing. Home: 21900 Fairmount Blvd Cleveland OH 44124-4616 Personal E-mail: taylorstock@gmail.com.

**TAYLOR, MARILYN JORDAN,** architectural firm executive; m. Brainerd O. Taylor; children: Brainerd I., Alexis. Degree in govt. and urban affairs, Harvard Coll., 1969; MArch, U. Calif., Berkeley; postgrad., MIT. Joined Skidmore, Owings and Merrill LLP, Washington, 1971, urban designer, dir. design stations program of N.E. Corridor Improvement Project, 1978—85, chief urban design and planning practice NYC, 1985—2001, ptnr., 1987—, chmn., 2001—04. Past pres. N.Y.C. chpt. AIA; chmn. Nat. AIA Regional and Urban Design Com.; vis. prof. Harvard Grad. Sch. Design; David Rockefeller fellow N.Y.C. Partnership, fellows adv. com. Key projects include N.J. Performing Arts Ctr., Newark, Riverside South, Manhattan, NYNEX Hdqs., Battery Park City, Penn Sta. Redevelopment Project, various airports, many others. Chmn. Urban Land Inst., 2005—; bd. dirs. NYC Bldg. Congress (chmn. 2002-04), Comml. Real Estate Women N.Y., Inst. for Urban Design. Named Woman of Yr., Comml. Real Estate Women N.Y., 1998; named one of Most Influential Women in Am. Real Estate, GRID mag., 2001; named to List of Most Influential Women, Crain's N.Y., 1996, 2000; recipient Profl. Leadership award, Profl. Women in Constrn., 2001. Office: Skidmore Owings and Merrill LLP 14 Wall St New York NY 10005*

**TAYLOR, MARK,** lieutenant governor; b. Atlanta, May 7, 1957; m. Sacha Taylor; 1 child. Degree in polit. sci., Emory U.; degree in law, U. Ga. Exec. Fred Taylor Co., Albany; mem. Ga. Senate, Atlanta, 1987—; asst. adminstrn. floor leader then adminstrn. floor leader Gov. Zell Miller; sec. transp. com.; mem. appropriations, ethics, ins. and labor, rules coms.; also reapportionment com.; lt. gov. State of Ga., Atlanta, 1999—. Mem. bd. dirs. March of Dimes, Albany/Dougherty 2000 Partnership, Thronateeska Heritage Found. Mem. Ga. Bar Assn., Dougherty County Bar Assn., Leadership Albany (charter), Artesian City Sertoma Club (past pres.), Rotary. Democrat. Office: Office Lt Governor 240 State Capitol Atlanta GA 30334 Office Phone: 404-656-5030. Office Fax: 404-656-6739. E-mail: mtaylorx@legis.state.ga.us.*

**TAYLOR, MARK DOUGLAS,** publishing executive; b. Geneva, Ill., Jan. 16, 1951; s. Kenneth Nathaniel and Margaret Louise (West) T.; m. Carol E. Rogers, May 28, 1973; children: Jeremy Peter, Kristen Elizabeth, Margaret Louise, Rebecca Cynthia, Stephen Rogers. BA, Duke U., 1973. Exec. dir.

Tyndale House Found., Wheaton, Ill., 1973-78, pres., CEO, 2004—; v.p. Tyndale House Pubs., Wheaton, Ill., 1978-84, pres., chief exec. officer, 1984—. Dir. Living Bibles Internat., Naperville, Ill., 1972-92; trustee Taylor U., 1998—. Author The Complete Book of Bible Literacy, 1992. Mem. Wheaton Liquor Control Commn., 1986—, chmn., 1994—; chmn. bd. dirs. Outreach Cmty. Ctr., 1986-93. Mem. Internat. Bible Soc. (bd. dirs. 1992-96). Office: Tyndale House Publishers Inc PO Box 80 Wheaton IL 60189-0080 *What we accomplish in life is soon forgotten. Our best legacy is to pass on to our children and grandchildren our positive values.*

**TAYLOR, MARK LYMAN,** music educator; b. Longmont, Colo., Oct. 26, 1955; s. Gaylord Lyman and Florence Stratton Taylor; m. Sandra Lynn Curneal, Nov. 15, 1958. MusB, Cornerstone U., 1978; MusM, Mich. State U., 1981; PhD, Case Western Res. U., 1995. Music tchr. First Bapt. Christian Sch., Elyria, Ohio, 1982—85; dir. of music Parma (Ohio) South Presbyn. Ch., 1991—94; asst. prof. of music Northwestern Coll., Orange City, Iowa, 1994—95; assoc. prof. of music Houghton (N.Y.) Coll., 1995—2001, Cornerstone U., Grand Rapids, Mich., 2002—; dir. Met. Choir of Praise, Grand Rapids. Com. mem. N.Y. State Tchr. Certification Examination-Content Adv. Com. for Music, Albany, NY, 2001—02; music dir. Wellsville (N.Y.) Performing Arts Orch., 1999—2002; founder & dir. Allegany Youth Wind Symphony, Houghton, NY, 1999—2001; headmaster's adv. coun. mem. Houghton (N.Y.) Acad., 1998—2002; spkr. in field. Mem.: ASCD, Mich. Sch. Band and Orch. Assn., Mich. Sch. Vocal Music Assn., N.Y. State Coun. of Music Tchr. Edn. Programs (sec. 1998—2002), Coll. Music Soc., Music Educators Nat. Conf., Phi Delta Kappn. Avocations: baseball, reading. Office: Cornerstone University 1001 East Beltline Avenue NE Grand Rapids MI 49525 E-mail: mark_l_taylor@cornerstone.edu.

**TAYLOR, MARTHA SUE,** librarian; b. Sweetwater, Tex., Aug. 16, 1947; d. John Neville Shipley and Erma Hall Shipley Neeper; m. Linn Bryant Taylor, May 22, 1981; children: Mark Bryant, Melissa Anne. BA in English and Govt., Tex. Tech U., 1969, MA in English, 1971; postgrad. in Libr. Sci., U. Tex., 1973. Tchr. English Sweetwater Ind. Sch. Dist., 1971-73, supr. elem. libr., 1973-78, tchr. govt. and English, 1978-83, libr. high sch., 1983—. Mem. dist. improvement coun. Sweetwater Ind. Sch. Dist., 1991-94, 95—, sec., 1993-94, v.p., 1995-96, mem. H.S. campus improvement com., 1991—; instr. govt. Western Tex. Coll., Snyder, 1983-88; com. to draw up new state libr. standards, 2001-03. Sec. adminstrv. bd. 1st United Meth. Ch., 1978-83, organist, 1979—. Mem. AAUW (pres. 1971-73, 1st v.p. 1985-87, treas. 1989-90), Tex. State Tchrs. Assn. (pres. 1987-88), Tex. Libr. Assn. Methodist. Avocations: organ, piano. Home: 1632 Morris Ave Sweetwater TX 79556-2646 Office: Sweetwater High Sch 1205 Ragland St Sweetwater TX 79556-2438

**TAYLOR, MATTHEW ALAN,** publishing executive, editor, mediator; b. Charlottesville, Va., June 11, 1974; s. Ronald Paul and Andrea Taylor. Cert. mediator East Bay Cmty. Mediation Calif., 2005. Editor IDG Comm./GamePro, Oakland, Calif., 1990—94; CEO, founder Vs. Books, Alameda, Calif., 1996—2002. Mediator East Bay Cmty. Mediation, Berkeley, Calif., 2005—; co-founder, editor PeacePower Mag., Berkeley, 2005—; mem. Transcend, 2005—; co-founder, mediator Conflict Resolution & Transformation Ctr., Berkeley. Contbr. articles to mags. Lit. editor Dean For Am., Burlington, Vt., 2005—05; canvassing coord. Matt Gonzalez for Mayor, San Francisco, 2005—05. Grantee Doreen Townsend Human Rights Fellowship, Townsend Ctr., UC Berkeley, 2005. Fellow: Order of Golden Bear. Green Party. Judaism. Avocations: travel, skiing, bicycling, cooking. Home: 2135 Cedar St Berkeley CA 94709 Personal E-mail: mtaylor@matthewtaylor.net.

**TAYLOR, MICHAEL J.,** shipbuilding company executive; Assembler programmer, 1967; info. tech. mgmt. positions Gen. Foods, 1972; chief info. officer Precision Castparts Corp., Portland, Oreg., 1976, Todd Pacific Shipyards Corp., Seattle, 1998—. Named one of Premier 100 IT Leaders, Computerworld, 2005. Office: Todd Pacific Shipyards Corp PO Box 3806 Seattle WA 98124 Office Phone: 206-623-1635. Office Fax: 206-442-8505.*

**TAYLOR, MILDRED D.,** author; b. Jackson, Miss., Sept. 13, 1943; d. Wilbert Lee and Deletha Marie (Davis) Taylor. BA in Edn., U Toledo, 1965; MA, U Colo., 1969. Vol. tchr. English and history Peace Corps, Ethiopia, 1965-67, then recruiter U.S., 1967-68; study skills coord. black edn. program U Colo., 1969-71. Author: (children's fiction) Song of the Trees, 1975 (Coun. on Interracial Books for Children award 1975), Roll of Thunder, Hear My Cry, 1976 (Newbery medal, 1977), Let the Circle Be Unbroken, 1981, The Gold Cadillac, 1987 (Christopher award), The Friendship and Other Stories, 1987, Mississippi Bridge, 1990 (Christopher award), The Road to Memphis, 1990, The Well, 1995 (winner Jane Addams book award, 1996), The Land, 2001 (Coretta Scott King award, L.A. Times Book award, Scott O'Dell award, Pen USA award). Address: care Dial Books For Young Readers 375 Hudson St New York NY 10014-3658

**TAYLOR, MILLICENT RUTH,** elementary school educator; b. Kingston, Jamaica, Nov. 18, 1944; came to U.S., 1981; m. Henry Taylor; children: T'ousant, Howard, Annette, Kerry-Ann. BE, U. West Indies, 1981; MS, U. Miami, 1991. Cert. elem. edn. tchr., secondary social sci. tchr., Fla.; nat. bd. cert. tchr., 2004. Chairperson dept. history Mays Middle Sch., Miami, Fla., 1987—, peer tchr., 1987—; clin. tchr., 1990—; seminar presenter Mays Middle Sch., Miami, Fla., 1987-88, clin. tchr., 1990—. Leader, trainer Global Edn., Miami, Fla. 1989, sponsor History Bee, Miami, 1988-90, Geography Bee, 1988-90, 2003. Recipient State award for tchg. econs. Dade County Sch., 1992, Nat. award for tchg. econs. Joint Coun. Econ. Edn., 1991, State award for Gov. Award for Excellence, 1993, Nat. award for tchg. econs., Nat. Coun. Econ. Edn., 1995. Mem. ASCD, Seventh Day Adventist. Avocations: reading, travel, sewing, photography. Home: 19834 SW 118th Ave Miami FL 33177-4435 Office: Mays Middle Sch Goulds FL 33170

**TAYLOR, MINNA,** lawyer; b. Washington, Jan. 25, 1947; d. Morris P. and Anne (Williams) Glushien; m. Charles Ellett Taylor, June 22, 1969; 1 child, Amy Caroline. BA, SUNY, Stony Brook, 1969; MA, SUNY, 1973; JD, U. So. Calif., 1977. Bar: Calif. 1977, U.S. Dist. Ct. (cen. dist.) Calif. 1978. Extern to presiding justice Calif. Supreme Ct., 1977; field atty. NLRB, L.A., 1977-82; dir. employee rels., legal svcs. Paramount Pictures Corp., L.A., 1982-85, v.p. employee rels. legal svcs., 1985-89; dir. bus. and legal affairs Wilshire Ct. Prodns., L.A., 1989-91; sr. counsel Fox Broadcasting Co., L.A., 1991-92, v.p. legal affairs, 1992-97, sr. v.p. legal affairs, 1997—. Webmaster www.ifcome-.com, 2001—. Editor notes and articles: U. So. Calif. Law Rev., 1976-77. Mentor MOSTE, L.A., 1986-87, 88-89; pres. Beverly Hills chpt. ACLU, LA, 1985; mem. Jr. League LA, 2003-, sec. 2006-07. Fellow ABA, Calif. State Bar (mem. copyright subcom. 1994-95), L.A. County Bar Assn.; mem. Beverly Hills Bar Assn., L.A. Bead Soc. (membership sec. 1992-94, mem. bd. dirs. 1994-95), Order of Coif. Office: Fox Broadcasting Co 10201 W Pico Blvd Los Angeles CA 90064-2606

**TAYLOR, NANCY ELIZABETH,** lawyer; b. Salt Lake City, Apr. 6, 1956; d. Calvin Walker and Dorothy (Cope) Taylor; m. Christopher Robbins Bowen, Jan. 22, 1978; children: Elizabeth Grant Bowen, Alexandra Taylor Bowen. BS, U. Utah, 1978; JD, Cath. U., 1988. Health policy dir. Senate Com. on Labor and Human Resources, Washington, 1981-91; ptnr. Law Offices of Deborah Steelman, Washington, 1991-93; prin. shareholder, nat. co-chair health law dept. Greenberg Traurig LLP, Washington, 1993—. Testimony presentor Rep. Nat. Conf., 1992. Recipient Commr. award FDA, 1989. Mem. Nat. Health Lawyers, Women & Gov. Rels., Food and Drug Law Inst. Republican. Mem. Lds Ch. Office: Greenberg Traurig LLP Ste 500 800 Connecticut Ave NW Washington DC 20006 Office Phone: 202-331-3100. Office Fax: 202-331-3101. Business E-Mail: taylorn@gtlaw.com.

**TAYLOR, NATHALEE BRITTON,** retired nutritionist, freelance/self-employed writer; b. Lubbock, Tex., June 8, 1941; d. Nathaniel E. and Dessie Pauline (Moss) Britton; children by previous marriage: Clay H., Bret N.

Courtney. BS in Home Econs., Tex. Tech U., 1963. Home economist Pioneer Gas, Lubbock, Tex., 1963-65; dietitian Tex. Tech U., Lubbock, 1966-71; home economist South Plains Electric Co-op., Lubbock, 1986; mgr. quality control Rip Griffins Enterprises, Lubbock, Tex., 1987; sales rep. Time Chem., Lubbock, 1987—2003; with Sentry, Lubbock; mktg. rep. Dodson Group Ins., Lubbock, Farmers Ins., Lubbock, Southwestern Bell Wireless; ret., 2003. Ranch Historian. Co-author: From Our House to Yours, 1975; columnist: Lubbock Lights mag., Ranch Record; presenter TV show Southwestern Cooking Sta. KTXT; contbr. articles to profl. publs. Bd. dirs. Am. Heart Assn., Lubbock, 1985-87; mem. Home Economist in Bus., pres. Lubbock chpt., 1985; culinary co-chmn. Lubbock C. of C. Arts Festival, 1982, 83, 84. Named Lincoln County Fair Queen. Mem. Tech. Home Econs. Alums (sec./treas.), Am. Home Econs. Assn. (v.p., sec./treas.), Bd.-Cove, Soroptomist (v.p. Lubbock club). Democrat. Avocations: gardening, writing, cooking, horseback riding. Personal E-mail: nathaleet@door.com.

**TAYLOR, NELLIE RUBY,** artist, poet; b. Lundale, W.Va., Apr. 18, 1946; d. John Otis and Blanche L. (Wright) Taylor; m. Ivan Lee Hurt, July 31, 1965 (div. Nov. 1982); children: Ivan Lee Hurt Jr., Bradley Allen Hurt. MA, 1995. Adminstr. Cleve. Sch., Cleve., 1987—; nursing Mary Farmers Nurses, Cleve. Heights, Ohio, 1987—2002; agent A.L. Williams Ins., Athens, Ohio, 1984—87; tchr. Manor-Care, Mayfield Heights, Ohio, 2002—. Author: (book) Mental Education; inventor Hopter-Copter; prodr., dir., host: (television) In Time Like These; founder & pres. (corporation) The Mean Corporation; Represented in permanent collections Portrait of Bill Clinton, Presdl. Libr., Ark. Recipient Award of Excellence, Ohio Sch. Bd. Assn. 1985—87, Lifetime Congl. award, U.S. Congress 11th Dist., 1998. Mem.: Am. Federation of Teachers. Achievements include represented as permanent leader, justice, tolerance new civil rights mem. ctr. with Rosa Parks, Montgomery, Ala. Avocations: writing, travel, poetry, drama. Home: 2826 E 130th Unit # 102 Shaker Heights Cleveland OH 44120

**TAYLOR, NICHOLAS C.,** lawyer, state agency administrator, energy executive; b. Washington, Sept. 18, 1937; s. James Spear Taylor and Helen Livingston MacGregor Strauss; m. Catherine Blaffer, d. Jan. 1,1999; children: Nicholas Van Campen, Katherine C., Christie. AB, Harvard U., 1959; JD, Georgetown U., 1963. Bar: DC 64, NY 66, Tex. 71. Assoc. Wilson, Woods & Villalon, Washington, 1964-65, Shearman & Sterling, N.Y.C., 1965-70, Locke, Liddell, Sapp, Dallas, 1970-74; shareholder Stubbeman, McRae, Sealy, Laughlin & Browder, Inc., Midland, Tex., 1974-93; atty. Midland, 1993—; pres. Mexco Energy Corp., Midland, 1983—; chmn., mem. State Securities Bd. of Tex., 1995—2003. Pres. Mexco Energy Corp., 1983—2003. Mem. Tex. Jud. Coun., 1990-95. Recipient Am. Jurisprudence prizes for constnl. law, oil, and gas taxation So. Meth. U. Law Sch. Mem. Natural Gas Prodrs. Assn., Permian Basin Petroleum Assn. (bds. dirs. 2002-03). Episcopalian. Office: 214 W Texas Ave Ste 1101 Midland TX 79701-4616 E-mail: mexco@msn.com.

**TAYLOR, NICOLE RENÉE (NIKI TAYLOR),** model, shop owner; b. Miami, Fla., Mar. 5, 1975; d. Ken and Barbara Taylor; m. Matt Martinez (div.); 2 children. With Tri Star Sports and Entertainment Group, Brentwood, 2006—; owner Abbie and Jesse's, Cool Springs, Tenn., 2006—, Franklin, Tenn., 2006—. Contracts with L'Oreal, 1990-92, Cover Girl Makeup; appeared in Seventeen (cover girl) 1989, Vogue, Elle, Mademoiselle, Harper's Bazaar; modeled for Yves Saint Laurent, Karl Lagerfeld; modeled swimsuit Sports Illus., 1997, cover Sports Illus. Calendar, 1998. Founder Begin Found. Achievements include appearing on over 320 magazine covers worldwide; youngest model to appear on the cover of Vogue; holds the world record for being the youngest model to receive a six figure deal. Office: TriStar Entertainment Group Suite 200 215 Ward Circle Brentwood TN 37027 Office Phone: 615-309-0969. Business E-Mail: tristar@tristarse.com.

**TAYLOR, P. CRAIG,** physics professor; b. Paterson, N.J., Mar. 17, 1942; s. Philip D. and Elizabeth E. Taylor; m. Muriel A. Allison, Dec. 20, 1969; children: Allison T. Severson, Heather M. Porecca. BA, Carleton Coll., 1964; PhD, Brown U., 1969. Postdoctoral rsch. assoc. NAS, Washington, 1969—71; rsch. physicist Naval Rsch. Lab., Washington, 1971—80, supervisory rsch. physicist, 1980—82; prof. physics U. Utah, Salt Lake City, 1982—2001, chmn. Dept. Physics, 1989—98, disting. prof. physics, 2001—05; prof. physics Colo. Sch. Mines, Golden, Colo., 2005—. Dir. Dixon Laser Inst., Salt Lake City, 1990—2005; assoc. dir. Colo. Energy Rsch. Inst., Golden. Recipient Rsch. Publ. award, Naval Rsch. Lab., 1975, Oustanding Profl. Contributions medal, Brown U., 1992, Disting. Rsch. award, U. Utah, 2002. Fellow: Am. Phys. Soc. (chmn. four-corners sect. 2000—02); mem.: AAAS, Materials Rsch. Soc., Am. Assn. Physics Tchrs. Office: Colorado School of Mines 1523 Illinois Street Golden CO 80401-1887 Office Phone: 303-273-3586. Home Fax: 303-273-3919; Office Fax: 303-272-3919. Business E-Mail: pctaylor@mines.edu.

**TAYLOR, P. MARK,** mathematics professor; b. St. Louis, Mo., July 6, 1967; s. Daniel R. and Beth M. Taylor. BA, Westminster Coll., 1989; MS, U. Mo., 1993, PhD, 2001. Math. tchr. Jefferson Jr. H.S., Columbia, Mo., 1989—90, Jefferson City H.S., 1990—91, Wright City H.S., 1993—96; adj. instr. St. Charles County Cmty. Coll., St. Peters, Mo., 1996; tchg. asst. U. Mo. 1991—93, doctoral asst., 1996—97; prof. math. U. Tenn., 2001—. Contbr. articles to profl. jours. Founding bd. pres. Delta Ctr. for Ind. Living, St. Charles, Mo., 1997. Mem.: Am. Ednl. Rsch. Assn., Assn. Math. Teachers Educators, Nat. Coun. Teachers of Math. Republican. Christian. Office: Assn Prof Math Edn U Tenn A423 Claxton Complex Knoxville TN 37996

**TAYLOR, PALMER W.,** pharmacology educator; m. Susan Serota; three children. BS in Pharmacy, U. Wis., 1960, PhD in Phys. Pharmacy, 1964. Rsch. assoc. pharmacology-toxicoogy assoc. program Lab. Chem. Pharmacology, 1965-68; NIH fellow molecular pharmacology unit Med. Rsch. Coun., Cambridge, Eng., 1968-70; NIH fellow Max Planck Inst. for Phys. Chemistry, Gottingen, Germany, 1970; asst. prof. divsn. pharmacology dept. medicine U. Calif., San Diego, 1971-74, assoc. prof. divsn. pharmacology dept. medicine, 1974-78, prof. divsn. pharmacology dept. medicine, 1978-87, head divsn. pharmacology dept. medicine, 1979-87, prof., chair dept. pharmacology, 1987—2003, Sandra & Monroe Trout endowed chair pharmacology, 1994—2002, dean Skaggs Sch. Pharmacy and Pharm. Scis., assoc. vice chancellor health scis. Mem. pharmacology study sect. NIH, 1974-78; mem. study sect. on chemotherapeutic agts. Multiple Sclerosis Soc., 1974-86; co-chmn. conf. on membrane receptors and diseases NIH-NIGMS, Bethesda, Md., 1978; participant Nat. Acad. Scis. Pharmacology Symposium, 1979; co-chair ASPET Symposium on Application of Molecular Pharmacology to Therapeutic Considerations, 1980; mem. pharmacol. scis. rev. com. NIH, 1980-85; vis. fellow Darwin Coll., U. Cambridge, 1980-81; Sterling Drug Co. vis. prof. U. Mich., 1985, U. Oreg., 1990; nat. adv. coun. mem. Nat. Inst. Gen. Med. Scis., 1988-92; vice chair, chair Gordon Conf. on Molecular Pharmacology, 1987-89; Krantz Meml. lectr. U. Md., 1989; Harold C. Hodge lectr. U. Rochester Med. Ctr., 1992; vis. prof., lectr. series Coll. de France, 1999, Tyler lectr. series Purdue U., bd. trustees Gordon Rsch. Confs., 1999—; Rene Couteaux lectr. XI Internat. Symposium on Cholinergic Mechanisms, 2002. Co-editor: (with W.B. Pratt) Principles of Drug Action, 3d edit., 1990, (with A.G. Gilman, T.W. Rall and A.S. Nies) Goodman and Gilman's Pharmacological Basis of Therapeutics, 8th edit., 1990; assoc. editor Molecular Pharmacology, 1971-75; mem. editl. bd. Jour. Biol. Chemistry, 1981-86, 92-98, Molecular Pharmacology, 1983—, Trends in Pharmacol. Scis., 1983-90, Jour. Molecular Medicine, 1992-98, Pharm. News, 1997—; cons. editor Jour. Clin. Investigation, 1992-98; contbr. articles to profl. jours. Recipient Borden award, Phi Lambda Upsilon award in pharm. chemistry, Toral Tollmann award in pharmacology, 2003, 700 Yr. award for rsch. in the cholinesterases Perugia U., 1994; Fogarty fellow U. Cambridge, 1980-81. Mem. FASEB (fin. com. 2000—), NAS-Inst. Medicine, Internat. Union Pharmacology (del. 1995—), Am. Soc. for Clin. Investigation (hon.), Am. Soc. for Pharmacology and Exptl. Therapeutics (councillor 1987-90, pres.-elect 1994-95, pres. 1995-96), Am. Soc. for Biochemistry and Molecular Biology, Am. Assn. for Med. Sch. Pharmacology, Fedn. Exptl. Biologists (bd. mem. 1995-99), Croatian-Slovenian Biochem. Soc. (hon.). Office: Dept Pharmacology Basic Sci Bldg 9500 Gilman Dr La Jolla CA 92093-0636 Business E-Mail: pwtaylor@ucsd.edu.*

**TAYLOR, PATRICIA,** director; b. Balt. Aug. 30, 1959; d. Roger Kirkbride and Katherine Heller Taylor; m. Augusto Hacthoun, July 10, 1984; 1 child, Katherine Ariadne Hacthoun. BA, Wheaton Coll., Norton, MA, 1982; M of Internat. Affairs, Columbia U., NYC, 1991, MPhil, 1995. Dir. prestigious fellowships Fordham U. Bronx, NY, 1998—2000; grad. sch. and fellowship adv. Marist Coll., Poughkeepsie, NY, 2004—. Internat. Predissertation fellow, Social Sci. Rsch. Coun., 1992—93, Cordier fellow, Columbia U., 1995—96. Mem.: Nat. Assn. Fellowship Advisors, Phi Beta Kappa. Avocations: cooking, reading, travel. Office: Marist Coll 3399 North Rd/Library 332 Poughkeepsie NY 12601 Office Phone: 845-575-3547. Business E-Mail: pat.taylor@marist.edu.

**TAYLOR, PATRICK LAWRENCE,** lawyer, educator; s. Jerome and Carol Taylor; m. Deirdre Roney, Feb. 18, 1989; 1 child, Nathaniel Liam. BA with honors, U. Wis., Madison, 1981; JD, Columbia U., 1986. Assoc. atty. Cravath, Swaine & Moore, NYC, 1986—88; asst. counsel NYC Office of the Corp. Counsel, NYC, 1988—91; asst. counsel Gov. Mario M. Cuomo, Albany, 1991—94; chief of staff-edn., sr. counsel NY State Assembly, Albany, 1994—96; sr. v.p., gen. counsel Albany Med. Ctr. Coll. and Hosp., 1996—2001; dep. gen. counsel, chief counsel rsch. affairs Children's Hosp. Boston, 2001—; lectr. Harvard Med. Sch., Boston, 2005—. Adj. prof. Albany Med. Coll., 1999—2001; adj. clin. prof. Albany Law Sch., 1999—2001; referee- reviewer Sci. and Engring. Ethics, Guildford, United Kingdom, 2005—; reviewer Trends in Biotechnology, London, 2006—. Editor: (photo-history) Children's Hospital Boston; contbr. articles to profl. jours. Founder Greater Boston Karma Kagyu Study Group, Boston, 2001—06; trustee, sec., counsel, mem. exec. and fin. com. Doane Stuart Sch., Albany, 1999—2002; counsel Karma Kagyu Inst., Woodstock, 1998—2004, Raktrul Found., Red Hook, 1999—2006. Recipient Prize for Outstanding Achievement, Assn. Bar of NYC, 1991; Tchg. Fellow, Columbia U. Law Sch., 1984, Harlan Fiske Stone Scholar, 1984, 1985, 1986. Mem.: NY State Bar Assn. (vice chair legis. com. 1997—98, chmn. in house counsel com. 1998—2001, mem. exec. com. 1998—2001), Phi Beta Kappa. Independent. Buddhist. Office: Children's Hosp Boston 300 Longwood Ave Boston MA 02115 Office Phone: 617-355-4935. Business E-Mail: patrick.taylor@childrens.harvard.edu.

**TAYLOR, PAUL B.,** choreographer; b. Allegheny County, Pa., July 29, 1930; s. Paul B. and Elizabeth (Pendleton) Taylor. Student, Syracuse U., 1949—52, Juilliard Sch. Music, 1952—53; PhD (hon.), Duke U., 1983, Conn. Coll., 1983, Syracuse U., 1986, Juilliard, 1988, SUNY, Purchase, 1988, Calif. Inst. Arts, 1989, Skidmore Coll., 1995. Artistic dir. Paul Taylor Dance Co. 1954. Dancer Merce Cunningham Co., 1954, Martha Graham, 1955—62, Paul Taylor Dance Co. 1954—74. Dancer Paul Taylor Dance Co. has performed in over 450 U.S. cities and 60 countries, PBS TV Dance in Am., Live From the Am. Dance Festival, Two Landmark Dances, Three Modern Classics, The Wrecker's Ball, The Taylor Co.: Recent Dances, Am. Masters, Paul Taylor, Dancemaker, Acts of Ardour, choreographer (partial list) Aureole, 1962, Private Domain, 1969, Esplanade, 1975, Cloven Kingdom, 1976, Airs, 1978, Le Sacre du Printemps (the Rehearsal), 1980, Arden Court, 1981, Mercuric Tidings, 1982, Sunset, 1983, Roses, 1985, Last Look, 1985, Musical Offering, 1986, Ab Ovo Usque ad Mala, 1986, Syzygy, 1987, Speaking in Tongues, 1988, Company B, 1991, Funny Papers, 1994, Offenbach Overtures, 1995, Eventide, 1996, Piazzolla Caldera, 1997, The Word, 1998, Cascade, 1999, Arabesque, 1999, Black Tuesday, 2001, Promethian Fire, 2002, Dante Variations, 2004, Klezmerbluegrass, 2004, Spring Rounds, 2005, Banquet of Vultures, 2005; author (autobiography): Private Domain, 1987 (Nat. Book Critics Cir. award for biography, 1987). Decorated Chevalier des Arts et Lettres, elevated to Officier France, Comdr. Legion of Honor; named Dancer of Yr., London's Dance and Dancers, 1965; named to Nat. Mus. Dance Hall of Fame, 1995; recipient Internat. Cir. of Criticism for Artistic Rsch. and Cultural Exch. award, Festival Nations, Paris, 1962, Best Fgn. Attraction prize, Critics of Chile, 1966, Capezio Dance award, 1967, Creative Arts award, Brandeis U., 1978, Dance Mag. award, 1980, Samuel H. Scripps Am. Dance Festival award, 1983, Arts award, State N.Y., 1987, Lions of Performing Arts award, N.Y. Pub. Libr., 1989, Emmy award, Speaking in Tongues, 1992, Kennedy Ctr. Honors award, 1992; Guggenheim fellow, 1961, 1966, 1983, MacArthur Found. fellow, 1985. Office: Paul Taylor Dance Co 552 Broadway New York NY 10012-3922 Office Phone: 212-431-5562.*

**TAYLOR, PAUL PEAK,** pediatric dentist, educator; b. Childress, Tex., May 11, 1921; s. Noah Peak and Lois C. (Vinson) T.; m. LaVerne Countryman, Aug. 11, 1945; chi dren: Scott, Peri Ann. Student, W. Tex. State Coll., 1938-40; DDS, Baylor U., 1944; MS, U. Mich., 1951. Diplomate Am. Bd. Pediatric Dentistry (examining mem. 1977-84, chair 1983). Prof. Baylor U. Coll. Dentistry, Dallas, 1958-86, chmn. grad. pediatric dentistry, 1960-69, chmn. dept. pediatric dentistry, 1969-86, prof. emeritus, 1986—; dir. dental svcs. Children's Med. Ctr., Dallas, 1965-86, dir. emeritus dental svcs. 1986—; dir. dental svcs. Tex. Scottish Rite Hosp. for Children, Dallas, 1965-86, dir. emeritus dental svcs., 1986—. Contbr. articles to Jour. of Dentistry for Children, 1960-82; author (with others) Pediatric Dentistry, 1986, Current Therapy in Pediatric Infectious Disease, 1989; mem. edtl. and publs. com. Jour. Dentistry for Children. Capt. U.S. Army, 1951-53. Named to Baylor Coll. Dentistry Hall of Fame, 1999; Mott Found. fellow, 1949-51. Fellow Am. Coll. of Dentists (life); mem. ADA (life), Tex. Dental Assn., Dallas County Dental Assn. (Dentist of Yr. 1999, Lifetime Achievement award 2002), Masons (life, 32d degree, KCCH), Shriners. Episcopalian. Avocation: golf. Home: 2615 Briarcove Dr Plano TX 75074-4905

**TAYLOR, PETER J.,** diversified financial services company executive; Grad., UCLA; MS in pub. policy analysis, Claremont Grad. U. Mem. staff Calif. State Assembly; exec. dir. Coro Found.; mgr. GTE Calif.; now mng. dir. Lehman Bros., LA. Mem. bd. James Irvine Found., 2000—; mem. bd. trustees J. Paul Getty Trust, LA, 2005—. Office: Lehman Bros 25th Fl 10250 Constellation Blvd Los Angeles CA 90067*

**TAYLOR, PETER VAN VOORHEES,** advertising and public relations consultant; b. Montclair, N.J., Aug. 25, 1934; s. John Coard and Mildred (McLaughlin) T.; m. Janet Kristine Kirkebo, Nov. 4, 1978; 1 child, John Coard III. BA in English, Duke U., 1956. Announcer Sta. WQAM, Miami, Fla., 1956; announcer, music dir. Sta. KHVH, Honolulu, 1959-61; promotion mgr. Sta. KPEN, San Francisco, 1962; with Kaiser Broadcasting, 1962-74, GE Broadcasting Co., 1974-78; program and ops. mgr. Sta. KFOG, San Francisco, 1962-66; mgr. Sta. WXHR-AM-FM, Cambridge, Mass., 1966-67; gen. mgr. Sta. WJIB, Boston, 1967-70; v.p., mgr. FM divsn. Kaiser Broadcasting, 1969-72; v.p., gen. mgr. Sta. KFOG, San Francisco, 1970-78; pres. Taylor Commn., 1978-90, 97—, Baggott & Taylor, Inc., 1990-91, Taylor Advt. & Pub. Rels., 1991-96, No. Calif. Broadcasters Assn., 1974-76, Broadcast Skills Bank, 1975-96. Pres. Roast Host, 1993—96. Trustee WDBS, Inc. Duke U., 1974-80; bd. dirs. San Francisco BBB, 1976-78, 89-94, Calif. Broadcasters Assn., 1972-88, KCRH Chabot Coll., 1982-83, San Francisco Boys and Girls Club, 1991-93, Coast Guard Found., 1991-2000, Leukemia Soc., San Francisco, 1992-93, Duke Devel. Coun., 1992-96; bd. dirs. Commencement Bay Rowing Club, sec., 1997-98, v.p. 1998-99, pres., 1999-2000; mem. exec. bd., Scandinavian Culture Coun., 2001-04, v.p., 2002-03, pres., 2003-04; bd. dirs. Lindquist Children's Dental Clinic, 2004—. Lt. USCGR, 1957—63. Mem. Nat. Radio Club, Internat. Radio Club, Long Wave Radio Club, Worldwide TV-FM Dx Assn., Rotary (bd. dirs. Sta 5150 1986-89, comd. chmn. 1990, area rep. 1992-93, dist. gov. nominee 1995-96, pub. rels. chair Tacoma 2002-03, auction chair 2005-, bd. dirs. 2004—, pres.-elect 2005-06, pres. 2006—). Home: 6002 Bayview Dr NE Tacoma WA 98422-1227 E-mail: taytac@comcast.net.

**TAYLOR, PEYTON TROY, JR.,** oncologist, educator; b. Tuscaloosa, Ala., July 21, 1941; s. Peyton Troy, Sr. and Frances (Sutter) Taylor; m. Helena Ström, Sept. 23, 1967; children: Annika, Karin, Sarah. BS, U. Ala., 1963, MS,

1968; MD, Med. Coll. Ala., 1968. Intern U. Va. Hosp., Charlottesville, 1968-69, resident, 1969-70, 72-75; asst. prof. ob-gyn. U. Va., Charlottesville, 1976-79, assoc. prof., dir. divsn. ob-gyn. Health Scis. Ctr., 1981-87, Richard N. and Louise R. Crockett prof., 1987—, med. dir. Cancer Ctr., 1996—; clin. assoc. surgery Nat. Cancer Inst., Bethesda, Md., 1970-72. Assoc. prof. U. Ala., Birmingham, 1979—81. Contbr. articles to profl. jours. With USPHS, 1970—72. Recipient Disting. Alumnus, U. Ala. Med. Alumni Assn., 2000. Fellow: ACS, Am. Coll. Obstetricians and Gynecologists; mem.: So. Surg. Assn., Internat. Gynecol. Cancer Soc., Am. Assn. Cancer Rsch., Am. Soc. Clin. Oncology, Soc. Surg. Oncology, Soc. Gynecol. Oncologists, Assn. Acad. Surgeons. Episcopalian. Avocations: sports, travel. Office Phone: 434-924-9933. Business E-Mail: ptt9y@virginia.edu.

**TAYLOR, PHILIP RAYMOND,** lawyer; b. Dublin, Ga., Nov. 1, 1933; s. Evan Augustus and Eula Bush Taylor; m. Elizabeth Lester Taylor (div.); children: Emily Taylor Fendig, Lester Taylor Odachowski. AB, Mercer U., Macon, Ga., 1955, JD, 1957. Bar: Ga. Ptnr. Harris, Watkins, Taylor & Davis, Macon, Ga., 1958—80, Fendig, McLemore, Taylor, Whitworth & Durham, Brunswick, Ga., 1980—2001; sr. ptnr. Taylor, Odachowski, Sperry & Crossland, St. Simons, Ga., 2001—. Bd. visitors Mercer U. Law Sch., Macon, Ga., 1998—2004, chmn. bd. visitors, 2002—04. Mem. editl. bd Mercer Law Rev., 1956—57. Mem. Ga. State Ho. of Reps., Atlanta, 1961—62; chmn. Macon-Bibb County Dem. Exec. Com., Macon, Ga., 1964—68, Macon-Bibb County Bd. of Elections, Macon, Ga., 1969—80. Capt. USAR, 1962—78. Fellow: Am. Coll. Trial Lawyers, Am. Bd. Trial Lawyers; mem.: ABA, Am. Acad. Healthcare Attys., Def. Rsch. Inst., Ga. Soc. Hosp. Attys., Brunswick-Glynn County Bar Assn., Ga. Def. Lawyers Assn. (bd. dirs. 1967), Delta Theta Phi. Avocations: travel, fishing, hunting. Office: Taylor Odachowski Sperry & Crossland 3300 Oak St Ste 200 Saint Simons Island GA 31522 Office Phone: 912-634-0955. Business E-Mail: ptaylor@toslaw.com.

**TAYLOR, PHYLLIS MILLER,** energy executive; m. Patrick F. Taylor (dec. 2004). Grad., U. S.W. La.; LLB, Tulane U. Law clerk for Supreme Ct. La., Orleans Parish Civil Dist. Ct.; in-house counsel for John W. Mecom, Sr., 1972; exec. v.p., bd. mem. Taylor Energy Co. LLC, New Orleans, 1979—2004, chmn., CEO, 2004—. Chmn., pres. Patrick F. Taylor Found. Named an Forbes' Richest Americans, 2006. Office: Taylor Energy Co LLC 1615 Poydras St New Orleans LA 70112 Office Phone: 504-581-5491.*

**TAYLOR, R. EUGENE,** bank executive; B in fin., Fla. State U. Credit analyst Bank Am. Corp., 1969—86, pres. Fla. bank, 1986—93, pres. cons. and comml. banking, 2000—04, pres. global bus. and fin. svcs., 2004—05, vice chmn., pres. global corp. and investment banking, 2005—; pres. NationsBank Mid Atlantic, 1993—97. Office: Bank of America Corp 100 N Tryon St Charlotte NC 28255

**TAYLOR, RALPH ARTHUR, JR.,** lawyer; b. Washington, Jan. 19, 1948; s. Ralph Arthur Sr. and Mary Florence Taylor; m. Joanna Lamb Moorhead, Jan. 30, 1988; children: Alison M., John Duncan. BS in Engring. with honors, Princeton, 1970; JD, U. Va., 1975. Bar: Va. 1975, D.C. 1976, Md. 1989, U.S. Dist. Ct. D.C. 1977, U.S. Dist. Cts. (ea. and we. dists.) Va. 1986, U.S. Dist. Ct. Md. 1988, U.S. Dist. Ct. Colo. 1998, U.S. Ct. Appeals (4th cir.) 1991, U.S. Ct. Appeals (D.C. cir.) 1977, U.S. Ct. Appeals (6th cir.) 1991, U.S. Ct. Claims 1985, U.S. Supreme Ct. 1980. Program advisor US EPA, Boston, 1970-72; assoc. Steptoe & Johnson, Washington, 1975-84, Shaw, Pittman, Potts, & Trowbridge, Washington, 1984-86, ptnr., 1986—2000, leader tech. and intellectual property litigation group, co-leader Yr. 2000 practice group; ptnr. Dorsey & Whitney, LLP, Washington, 2000—05, co-chair intellectual prop-erty litig. group, 2000—03, chair intellectual property litig. group, 2003—05; ptnr., litig., intellectual property groups Arent Fox PLLC, Washington, 2005—. Assoc. editor Litigation News, 1985-99, exec. editor, 1999-2004; notes editor Va. Law Rev., 1974-75; contbg. author: International Technology Transfers, 1995; co-chair com. newsletters com. ABA Litigation Sect., 2004—. Pres. Cloisters West Homeowners Assn., Washington, 1989, 1990, 1625 Q St. Condo. Assn., Washington, 1982—86; bd. dirs. Am. Liver Found. nat. capital chpt., pres., 2004—; mem. grad. bd. trustees Princeton Quad-rangle Club. Lt. USPHS, 1970—72. Mem. Order of the Coif, Met. Club (Washington), Barristers, Princeton Club (Washington), Chevy Chase Club, Lawyers Club Protestant. Avocations: sailing, skiing, tennis, golf. Office: Arent Fox PLLC 1050 Connecticut Ave NW Washington DC 20036-5339

**TAYLOR, RALPH ORIEN, JR.,** real estate developer, investor; b. Kansas City, Mo., Jan. 6, 1919; s. Ralph Orien Sr. and Genevieve (Sturgeon) T.; m. Betty Boswell, Dec. 7, 1940 (dec. Oct. 1959); children: Ralph Bradley, Nancy Virginia Stevens; m. Deborah Rosemary Berger, Oct. 10, 1982. BS in Bus. and Pub. Adminstrn., U. Mo., 1940. Ptnr. Sturgeon & Taylor, Kansas City, Mo., 1940-42; chmn., pres. Sturgeon & Taylor, Inc., Kansas City, Prairie Village (Kans.), 1946, Sturgeon & Taylor Devel. Co., Inc., Prairie Village, Kans., 1949—. Sturgeon & Taylor Co., Prairie Village, Kans., 1955-90; ptnr., co-founder ScripTpro LLC, Pharmacy Robotics & Automation, Mission, Kans., 1994, Orien Rose, LLC. Lt. comdr. USNR, 1942-46, PTO, ETO. Decorated Bronze Star with combat V; recipient Alumnus of Yr. award, Phi Delta Theta Fraternity, 2000, Ralph and Debbie Taylor Phi Delta Theta Baseball Stadium dedicated in his honor, U. Mo., 2000. Charter mem. Nat. Assn. Home Builders (life bd. dirs.), Home Builders Assn. Greater Kansas City (pres. 1951-52, life bd. dirs.), Builder of Yr. award 1979); mem., Ft. Lauderdale Country Clu b, Phi Delta Theta (Raymond L. Gardner Alumnus of Yr. award 2000). Republican. Mem. Christian Ch. Avocations: golf, boating. Home: 1050 Seminole Dr PHB Fort Lauderdale FL 33304-3225 Office Phone: 954-648-1164. E-mail: ralphotaylor@aol.com.

**TAYLOR, RAYMOND DEAN,** physicist; b. Okemah, Okla., Aug. 18, 1928; s. H. Ray and Vera M. (Bay) T.; m. Janis Dexter, June 24, 1961; children: Scott E., Kay S. Miller. BS, Pittsburg State U., Kans., 1950; PhD, Rice U., Houston, 1954. Mem. staff Los Alamos Nat. Lab., N.Mex., 1954-90, cons. N.Mex., 1990—. Cons. U. Cologne (Germany), 1995, 97; co-investigator U.S.-Israel Binational Sci. Found., 1989—2003. Contbr. over 240 articles to profl. jours. Humble Oil fellow Rice U., 1952-54. Mem. Am. Phys. Soc. Avocations: skiing, photography, fishing, travel. Home: 210 Navajo Rd Los Alamos NM 87544-2620 Office: Los Alamos Nat Lab # Ms-k764 Los Alamos NM 87545-0001 Office Phone: 505-667-4729. Personal E-mail: deantaylor@comcast.net. Business E-Mail: rdt@lanl.gov.

**TAYLOR, REGINA,** actress; b. Dallas, Aug. 22, 1960; d. Nell Taylor. Student, So. Meth. U. TV appearances include (movies) Crisis at Central High, 1981, Howard Beach: Making the Case for Murder, 1989, Children of the Dust, 1995, Hostile Waters, 1997, The Third Twin, 1997, Strange Justice, 1999, Cora Unashamed, 2000. In from the Night, 2006, (TV series) I'll Fly Away, 1991-93 (Emmy award nominee best actress in a drama 1993, Golden Globe award), Feds, 1997, The Education of Max Bickford, 2001-02, The Unit, 2006-; films include Lean on Me, 1989, Losing Isaiah, 1995, Clockers, 1995, The Keeper, 1995, Spirit Lost, 1996, A Family Thing, 1996, Courage Under Fire, 1996, The Negotiator, 1998; stage appearances include Romeo and Juliet, 1986, King Lear, 1987, The Tempest, 1988, one-woman show Escape From Paradise, 1994. Office: c/o William Morris Agency 1350 Avenue Of The Americas New York NY 10019-4702*

**TAYLOR, RENEE,** actress, writer; b. NYC, Mar. 19, 1933; m. Joseph Bologna, 1965; 1 child, Gabriel. Grad., Acad. Dramatic Arts; doctorate (hon.), Hofstra U. Actress (films) The Errand Boy, 1961, The Detective, 1968, A New Leaf, 1971, Last of the Red Hot Lovers, 1972, Lovesick, 1983, White Palace, 1990, Delirious, 1991, End of Innocence, 1990, All I Want for Christmas, 1991, Forever, 1992, Love Is All There Is, 1996, Dying on the Edge, 2001, 61*, 2001, Dr. Dolittle 2 (voice), 2001, Returning Mickey Stern, 2002, Lady Killers, 2003, Alfie, 2004, Kalamazoo?, 2005, A-List, 2006, Boynton Beach Club, 2006, Ice Age: The Meltdown, 2006, Kalamazoo?, 2006, (TV series) Dream On, 1992-94, Daddy Dearest, 1993, The Nanny, 1993-99, (stage) Three Sisters, Machinal, Annie Get Your Gun, Li'l Abner, Wish You Were

Here; writer (film) Lovers and Other Strangers (Academy award nomination), (TV) Paradise, (HBO spl.) Bedrooms (Writers Guild award); author: My Life On A Diet. Address: 16830 Ventura Blvd Ste 326 Encino CA 91436-1725*

**TAYLOR, RICHARD CORDIA,** mathematics educator; b. Wichita, Kans., May 4, 1958; s. Cordia James Taylor and Janice Taylor Thomas, McKinley Thomas (Stepfather); m. Rosalind Beth Matlow, Aug. 7, 1988; children: Ryan Maxwell, Justin Patrick, Christina Michelle. BA in Physics with high honors, U. Calif., Berkeley, 1980; MEd, UCLA, 1986; MBA, Stanford U., 1993. Tchg. credential in math. Calif. Dept. Edn. Rsch. assoc. U. Calif., Berkeley, 1979—82; math. tchr. East Side Union H.S. Dist., San Jose, Calif., 1984—. Math. team coach William C. Overfelt H.S., San Jose, 1986—91, site pres. East Side Tchrs. Assn., Calif. Tchrs. Assn., NEA, 1989—91; advisor MESA (Math., Engring., Sci. Achievement), San Jose, 1988—90; grant writer voluntary integration program East Side Union H.S. Dist., San Jose, 1997—98, mem. Dist. Math. Curriculum Com., 2002—03. Mem.: Stanford Grad. Sch. of Bus. Alumni Assn. (life). Achievements include research in improved efficiency of extreme ultraviolet cameras; development of curricu-lum for engineering mathematics course. Avocations: music, electronics and robotics, writing. Office: Santa Teresa HS 6150 Snell Ave San Jose CA 95123 Office Phone: 408-347-6200.

**TAYLOR, RICHARD EDWARD,** physicist, researcher; b. Medicine Hat, Alta., Can., Nov. 2, 1929; arrived in U.S., 1952; s. Clarence Richard and Delia Alena (Brunsdale) Taylor; m. Rita Jean Bonneau, Aug. 25, 1951; 1 child, Norman Edward. BS, U. Alta., 1950, MS, 1952; PhD, Stanford U., 1962; DHC (hon.), U. Paris-Sud, 1980; DSc, U. Alta., 1991; LLD (hon.), U. Calgary, Alta., 1993; DSc (hon.), U. Lethbridge, Alta., 1993, U. Victoria, B.C., Can., 1995; DHC (hon.), U. Blaise Pascal, 1997; DSc (hon.), Carleton U., Ottawa, Ont., 1999, U. Liverpool, U.K. 1999, Queen's U. Kingston, Ont., 2000. Boursier Lab. de l'Accelerateur Lineaire, Orsay, France, 1958—61; physicist Lawrence Berkeley Lab., Berkeley, Calif., 1961—62; staff mem. Stanford Linear Accelerator Ctr., 1962—68, assoc. prof., 1968—70, prof., 1970—2003, assoc. dir., 1982—86, Lewis M. Terman Prof., 1993—99, emeritus prof., 2003—. Recipient Nobel prize in Physics, 1990; fellow Guggenheim Found., 1971—72, von Humboldt Found., 1982. Fellow: AAAS, Royal Soc. London, Royal Soc. Can., Am. Acad. Arts and Scis.; mem.: NAS (fgn. assoc.), Can. Assn. Physicists, Am. Phys. Soc. (W.K.H. Panofsky prize divsn. particles and fields 1989). Achievements include first to conduct investigations concerning deep inelastic scattering of electrons on protons and bound neutrons, which have been of essential importance for the development of quark model in particle physics. Office: Stanford Linear Accelerator Ctr M/S 43 2575 Sand Hill Rd Menlo Park CA 94025-7015 E-mail: retaylor@slac.stanford.edu.

**TAYLOR, RICHARD WILLIAM,** investment banker, portfolio manager; b. Toledo, Sept. 16, 1926; s. Everett Ellsworth and Hazel (Broer) T.; m. Lyn Westerlund, Sept. 11, 1954; children: Julie Everett, Richard William, Alison Nichols, Jennifer Broer, Liane Westerlund. BS, U.S. Naval Acad., 1949; postgrad., U. Calif., 1952. Mem. Ohio Ho. of Reps. (100th gen. assembly from 9th Dist.); asst. mgr. Navy sales Martin Aircraft, Balt., 1953-56; with McKinsey & Co. (mgmt. cons.), N.Y.C., 1956-60; asst. to v.p. Cerro Corp., N.Y.C., 1960-62, spl. asst. to pres., 1965; pres. Cerro Aluminum Co., N.Y.C., 1962-65; successively v.p., exec. v.p., pres. and CEO Carter, Walker & Co., Inc., 1967-69; pres., CEO Burton, Dana, Westerlund, Inc., N.Y.C., 1969—; v.p. Sterling, Grace & Co., Inc., 1971-74; v.p. corp. fin., 1980-81; v.p. corp. fin. Moseley, Hallgarten, Estabrook & Weeden Inc., 1975-80; v.p. Kidder, Peabody & Co. Inc., 1981-93; dir. investments, pvt. client divsn. Oppenhe-imer & Co., 1993—. Bd. dirs., pres., chmn. fin. com. YWCA Retirement Fund, Inc. With USN, 1944-52. Decorated Air medal, Navy Commendation medal. Mem. U.S. Naval Acad. Alumni Assn., U.S. Naval Inst. Home: Apt D 132 Heritage Hill Rd New Canaan CT 06840-4631 Office: Oppenheimer & Co Inc 200 Park Ave New York NY 10166 Office Phone: 212-667-4022. E-mail: richard.taylor@opco.com.

**TAYLOR, RICHARD WIRTH,** retired political science professor; b. Cleve., Jan. 15, 1923; s. Robert and Irmgard (Wirth) T.; m. Sadie White, Sept. 19, 1946; children: Peter, Karla, Mark, Stephen. BA, U. Ill., 1947, MA, 1948, PhD, 1950. Instr. polit. sci. U. Minn., Mpls., 1950-52; asst. prof. polit. sci. Lehigh U., Bethlehem, Pa., 1952-55, Wis. State U., Stevens Point, 1955-56; vis. asst. prof. Northwestern U., Evanston, Ill., 1956-57; assoc. prof. Coe Coll., Cedar Rapids, Iowa, 1957-60, chmn., prof., 1960-67; prof. polit. sci. Kent State U., Ohio, 1967-92, prof. emeritus Ohio, 1992—, chmn. Ohio, 1974-82. Vis. prof. Karl-Marx-Universität, Leipzig, Fed. Republic Germany, 1990. Co-exec. editor Peace and Change, 1986-87. Policy com. Friends Com. Nat. Legis., Washington, 1964-85, exec. com., 1986-87; acad. adv. com., ombudsman com. Internat. Bar Assn., Edmonton Alta., Can., 1980—; active Friends World Com. on Consultation, 1991-98, Am. Friends Svc. Com., 2000—, clk. Lake Erie Yearly Meeting, 1977-79. Home: 115 Kendal Dr Oberlin OH 44074-1905 E-mail: sadiewithers@aol.com.

**TAYLOR, ROBERT BROWN,** physician, educator, writer; b. Elmira, NY, May 31, 1936; s. Olaf C. Taylor and Elizabeth (Place) Brown; m. Anita Dopico; children: Diana Taylor Root, Sharon Taylor Oliverio. Student, Bucknell U., 1954-57; MD, Temple U., 1961. Diplomate Am. Bd. Family Medicine. Gen. practice medicine, New Paltz, NY, 1964-78; faculty physician Sch. Medicine Wake Forest U., Winston-Salem, NC, 1978-84; prof. dept. family medicine Oreg. Health Scis. U. Sch. Medicine, Portland, 1984—, chmn., 1984-98, prof. emeritus family medicine, 1998—. Mem. comprehen-sive part II com. Nat. Bd. Med. Examiners, Phila., 1986-91. Author: Common Problems in Office Practice, 1972, The Practical Art of Medicine, 1974; editor: Family Medicine: Principles and Practice, 1978, 6th edit., 2003, Health Promotion: Principles and Clinical Applications, 1982, Difficult Diagnosis, 1985, Difficult Medical Management, 1991, Difficult Diagnosis II, 1992, Fundamentals of Family Medicine, 1996, 3rd edit, 2003, Manual of Family Practice, 1997, 2d edit., 2002, Taylor's Review of Family Medicine, 1998, Manual of Ten-Minute Diagnosis, 2000, The Clinician's Guide to Medical Writing, 2004, Taylor's Diagnostic and Therapeutic Challenges, 2005, Taylor's Cardiovascular Diseases, 2006, Academic Medicine: A Guide for Clinicians, 2006; contbg. editor Physicians Mgmt. Mag., 1972-99; editl. bd. The Family Practice Rsch. Jour., 1980-90, The Female Patient, 1984—, Am. Family Physician, 1990-98, Jour. of Family Practice, 1990-93, Med. Tribune, 1993-99. Served as surgeon USPHS, 1961-64. Fellow Am. Acad. Family Physicians (sci. program com., Thomas Johnson award, bd. curators found. archives, John G. Walsh Lifetime Achievement award); mem. Soc. Tchrs. Family Medicine (bd. dirs., cert. of excellence), Assn. Am. Med. Colls., Am. Assn. for Study Headache, World Orgn. Family Doctors (chmn. sci. program com.), Portland City Club, Multnomah Athletic Club, Phi Beta Kappa, Alpha Omega Alpha. Home: 1414 SW 3rd Ave Apt 2904 Portland OR 97201-6629 Office: Oreg Health Sci U Sch Medicine Mail Code FM 3181 SW Sam Jackson Park Rd Portland OR 97239-3098 Office Phone: 503-494-6611.

**TAYLOR, ROBERT LARRY,** freelance/self-employed writer; b. Abilene, Tex., July 22, 1940; s. Larry Thornton and Virginia (Kerby) T.; life ptnr. Theodore Thomas Nowick, June 22, 1975. BA in Journalism, Tex. Tech U., 1962. Editor NHSC Newsletter, Nat. Home Study Coun., Washington, 1968-72; asst. editor Music Educators Jour., Music Educators Nat. Conf., Washington, 1972-76; editor Transp. USA mag. U.S. Dept. Transp., Washington, 1976-80; dep. text editor Am. Illustrated mag. USIA, Washington, 1980-86; freelance writer and author. 1986—. Affiliate scholar Oberlin Coll., 2004—. Author: (novels) The Innocent, 1997, All We Have Is Now, 2002, Whose Eye Is On Which Sparrow?, 2004 (winner Ind. Pub. Book award, 2005), All We Have Is Now, 2006, (short stories) Revelation and Other Stories, 2002; contbg. author: Gay Pride: Photographs from Stonewall to Today, 1994; contbg. author I Do / I Don't: Queers on Marriage, 2004; contbr. short stories to publs. Mem. nat. coun. Am. Speaks Out, 2001—04; trustee Pierre Monteux Meml. Found., treas., 1994—97, exec. com., 1997—2002, v.p., 2002—; trustee Bill Long Found., 2005—, sec., 2006—; bd. dirs. Down East AIDS Network, 2003—04. With U.S. Army, 1962—67. Decorated

Bronze Star; recipient Blue Pencil award as 1st place for best mag. Nat. Assn. Govt. Communicators, 1980, Outstanding Alumnus award Tex. Tech U. Sch. Mass Comm., 1986. Mem.: Authors Guild. Democrat. Avocations: singing, making handmade books. Home: Kendal at Oberlin Oberlin OH 44074 E-mail: kailuum@oberlin.net.

**TAYLOR, ROBERT LEWIS,** finance educator; b. Pitts., Dec. 10, 1939; s. Robert William and Elinor (Miller) T.; m. Linda Taylor Shapiro, Oct. 28, 1988; 1 step child, Kara; children by previous marriage: Rob, Mike. AB in Am. Studies, cum laude, Allegheny Coll., 1961; MBA, Ohio State U., 1966; D in Bus. Adminstrn., Mgmt., Ind. U., 1972. Asst. prof. in. rsch. USAF Acad., Colorado Springs, Colo., 1971-77, assoc. prof., dir. instrn. dept. econ., geography, mgmt., 1977-79, prof. mgmt., head dept. econs., geography, mgmt., 1980-81; assoc. dean Coll. Letters and Sci., head div. Bus. and Econs., Carl N. Jacobs Prof. of Bus. U. Wis., Stevens Point, 1981-84; dean Coll. Bus. Pub. Adminstrn. U. Louisville, 1984—2003, dean emeritus and prof. of mgmt., 2003—. Chmn. bd. dirs. Ky. Wood Floors, Louisville, 1988-98, AACSB: Internat., Tampa, Fla., 1999-2000; bd. advisors Rawlings Co. Louisville; bd. dirs. Stock Yards Bancorp; cons., advisor Kellogg Nat. Fellowship program Kellogg Found., Battle Creek, Mich., 1985-89. Co-editor: Contemporary Issues in Leadership, 1984, 6th edit., 2006, Leadership Challenges for Today's Manager, 1988, Military Leadership: In Pursuit of Excellence, 5th edit., 2005; contbr. articles to profl. jours. Chmn. Mayor's Strategic Planning Group, Louisville, 1986—; mem. Gov.'s Econ. Devel. Com., Frankfort, Ky., 1987-89, exec. com. Bus. Advs., 1988-92, task force on econ. devel. Ky. Legis. Rsch. Coun., 1991, Leadership Louisville, 1986, Leadership Ky., 1987; bd. dirs. Metro United Way, 1999—, Ctr. Nonprofit Excellence, 2005—; Pub. Radio Partnership, 2006—; bd. trustees Jewish Hosp. Healthcare Svcs., Louisville, 2000—; active St. Michael Orthodox Ch. Mem. Acad. Mgmt. (proceedings editor 1976-77, newsletter editor 1983-86), Louisville C. of C. (bd. dirs., exec. com 1990-94), Sigma Xi, Beta Gamma Sigma, Pi Gamma Mu. Avocations: travel, walking, stamp collecting/philately, reading. Home: 1516 Sylvan Way Louisville KY 40205-2408 Office: U Louisville 375 College of Bus Louisville KY 40292-0001 Personal E-mail: tayl1450@bellsouth.net. Business E-Mail: rltayl01@gwise.louisville.edu.

**TAYLOR, ROBERT M.,** minister; b. Englewood, N.J., Mar. 5, 1932; s. Robert M. and Irene Maude T.; m. Anna Elizabeth Taylor, Dec. 27, 1953 (dec. Sept. 1970); m. Beverly Ann Taylor, Nov. 7, 1971; children: Robert M., William Harrison, Joanne Elizabeth, Susan Ruth. BA cum laude, Lafayette Coll., 1953; MDiv, Princeton Sem., 1956. Ordained min. Presbyn. Ch., 1956. Pastor Mahoning Presbyn. Ch., Danville, Pa., 1956—59; asst. pastor Harundale Presbyn. Ch., Glen Burnie, Md., 1959—62; pastor Ctrl. Presbyn. Ch., Downingtown, Pa., 1962—69; sr. pastor The Presbyn. Ch., New Brunswick, NJ, 1969—75, Rosedale Gardens Presbyn. Ch., Livonia, Mich., 1975—79, Immanuel Presbyn. Ch., Albuquerque, 1979—85; interim pastor Cmty. Presbyn. Ch., Mountainside, NJ, 1985—86; interim sr. pastor First Presbyn. Ch., Matawan, NJ, 1986—88; pastor Christ Ch. on Quaker Hill, Pawling, NY, 1988—94, Hope Presbyn. Ch., Lakewood, NJ, 1994—97; ret., 1997. Commr. Gen. Assembly/Presbyn. Ch., Mpls., 1968; supr. Princeton Sem. Tchg. Ch., New Brunswick, N.J., 1969-75; v.p. Inter-Ch. Coalition on Mission in Southwest, Phoenix, 1984; mem. Interfaith Clergy Coun.; bd. dirs., v.p. Cmty. Resource Ctr. Pawling, 1988-94. Mem. bd. govs. United Fund, Downingtown, 1969, Citizen's Adv. Com., 1969, Mayor's Youth Adv. Com., East Brunswick, 1973; sec. Coll. Scholarship Found., 1975. Fellow in Pastoral Leadership Devel., Princeton Theol. Seminary, 1973. Mem. Rotary, Alpha Chi Rho (pres. 1952-53). Home: 1500 Bishop Estates Rd Villa 13B Jacksonville FL 32259 *Life is a marvelous journey of caring and sharing with continual opportunities for growth. The challenge is to remain open to God's leading, even when the necessary hurdles are many.*

**TAYLOR, ROBERT MORGAN,** electronics executive; b. Orange, N.J., May 13, 1941; s. Morgan H. M. Taylor and Grace Anna (Bonynge) Loding; m. Sandra Ruth Cox, Sept. 11, 1965; children: Scott Joseph, Karen Lynne. BA in Chemistry, Williams Coll., 1963; PhD in Chemistry, Pa. State U., 1968; MBA, Drexel U., 1973. Scientist Leeds & Northrup Co., North Wales, Pa., 1968-70, sr. scientist, 1970-72, prin. scientist, 1972-84, corp. scientist, 1984-85, dir. R&D, 1985-92, dir. analytical mktg., 1990-93; v.p. The Capital Controls Group, Colmar, Pa., 1993-99; pres. RMT Cons., Lansdale, Pa., 1999—. Contbr. articles to profl. jours. Chmn. indsl. com. Montgomery County (Pa.) Sci. Rsch. Competition, 1987-99. Mem. IEEE, Electrochem. Soc. (fin. com. 1971-73, controlling mems. com. 1977), Am. Chem. Soc., Instrument Soc. Am. (sr.), Indsl. Rsch. Inst. (rep.). Achievements include patents for for water analysis (5). Personal E-mail: rmtconsulting@comcast.net.

**TAYLOR, ROBERT N.,** medical researcher, department chairman; s. Dotty Louise Warne; m. Martha Ann Miller, June 21, 1980; children: Christopher Brion, Patrick Phinney. MD, Baylor Coll. Medicine, Houston, Tex., 1975, PhD, 1981. Diplomate reproductive endocrinology and infertility Am. Bd. of Obstetrics and Gynecology, 1997. Dir., ctr. reproductive scis. U. Calif., San Francisco Sch. of Medicine, 2000—05; vice chair rsch. Emory U. Sch. Medicine, Atlanta, 2005—. Sci. adv. mem. World Endometriosis Soc., Quebec City, Canada, 2005. Fellow: Am. Coll. OB-GYN. Epic. Achievements include research in cellular pathogenesis of endometriosis and pre-eclampsia. Office: Emory U Sch Medicine 1639 Pierce Dr 4217-WMB Atlanta GA 30322 Office Phone: 404-727-9106. Office Fax: 404-727-8609. Business E-Mail: robert.n.taylor@emory.edu.

**TAYLOR, ROBERT SAXTON,** retired dean; b. Ithaca, NY, June 15, 1918; s. James Barnaby and Flora Estelle (Brown) Taylor; m. Leni Reichenberger (dec.); m. Fay Ann Golden, Aug. 22, 1998. BA, Cornell U., 1940; MS, Columbia U., 1950; MA, Lehigh U., 1954. Asst. libr., dir., info. scis. Lehigh U., Bethlehem, Pa., 1950—67; dir., libr. ctr. Hampshire Coll., Amherst, Mass., 1967—72; dean, prof. Syracuse U. Sch. of Info. Studies, Syracuse, NY, 1972—83; ret., 1983; Fulbright lectr. Delft Tekniske Hogeschole, Netherlands, 1956—57. Reviewer Nat. Sci. Found., 1965—77; com. medin. info. sci. Nat. Inst. of Health, Bethesda, Md., 1965—76; reviewer US Office of Edn., 1970—76. Author: Making of a Library, 1972 (Am. Soc. for Info. Sci. Best Book, 1972), Value Added Processes in Information Systems, 1986. Co-founder, mem. governing com. Chamber Music Society, Bethlehem, Pa., 1952—67. With U.S. Army, 1942—44. Decorated Bronze star. Mem: Am. Soc. for Info. Sci. (pres. 1968). Home: 5085 Skyline Dr Syracuse NY 13215 E-mail: rtaylor1@twcny.rr.com.

**TAYLOR, ROBERT SUNDLING,** language educator, critic; b. Newton, Mass., Jan. 19, 1925; s. Frank Millikan and Elsie (Sundling) T.; m. Brenda K. Slattery, June 20, 1964; children: Gillian, Douglas. AB, Colgate U., 1947; postgrad., Brown U. Art, music, film and theatre critic Boston Herald, 1948-67; editor publs. Inst. Contemporary Art, Boston, 1967; art critic Boston Globe, 1967-90, arts editor, 1973-76, book columnist, 1978—. Prof. English, Wheaton Coll., Norton, Mass., 1961-96; fiction coord. Ea. States Writers Conf., Salem (Mass.) State Coll., 1979-80. Author: (novel) In Red Weather, 1961, Saranac: America's Magic Mountain, 1986, Fred Allen: His Life and Wit, 1989, New England: The Home Front, WWII, 1991; co-author: Treasures of New England, 1976. Trustee, Abbot Public Library, Marblehead, Mass., 1980-83. Served with USN, 1943-46. Mem. Mass. Hist. Soc. Clubs: St. Botolph (Boston). Home: 1 Thomas Cir Marblehead MA 01945-1203 Office: Wheaton Coll Norton MA 02766

**TAYLOR, ROBERT WILSON,** military officer, publishing executive; b. Cambridge, Mass., Sept. 7, 1926; s. Walter Denzelo and Lucy Goudie Taylor; m. Shirley Hosmer, Apr. 3, 1948; children: Tobey Lee, David Alan, Stephen Hosmer. AA Polit. Sci., Syracuse U., 1959. With U.S. Army and USAF, 1945; advanced through grades to Sgt. Maj. USAF, 1965; asst. v.p. Skaneateles Savs. Bank, NY, 1965—78; land and residential appraiser Pomeroy Appraisal Assoc., Syracuse, 1978—88; co-owner Family Rm. Miniatures, Skaneateles, 1980—95; owner Romance Lives Publ. Co., Marcellus, NY, 2004—. Pres.

consortium N.Y. savs. banks N.Y. State Savs. Banks Study Group, N.Y.C., 1977—78; instr. Syracuse U. Coll. Liberal Arts, 1954—59. Author: The Secret Life of William Roberts, Ancora, por favore (not Rome), The Hosmer Family Footprints in History, The Memories of a Change Islands Childhood, Twenty Years in Business: Remembering Those Days. Fund originator, bd. mgmt. United Ch. of Change Islands, Newfoundland, 2000—; charter pres. Kiwanis Club We. Onondaga County, Skaneateles, 1974—77. Mem.: Small Pub. Assn. N.Am., Syracuse U. Alumni Club Ctrl. NY, Am. Legion. Republican. Presbyterian. Avocations: writing, gardening, literature. Home: 2474 Roman Ave Marcellus NY 13108 Office: Romance Lives Publ Co PO Box 134 Marcellus NY 13108 Office Phone: 315-673-0788. Office Fax: 315-673-0788. Personal E-mail: bobtaylor@mailstation.com.

**TAYLOR, ROGER LEE,** academic administrator, lawyer; b. Canton, Ill., Apr. 6, 1941; s. Ivan and Pauline Helen (Mahr) T.; m. E. Anne Zweifel, June 13, 1964. BA, Knox Coll., 1963; JD cum laude, Northwestern U., 1971. Bar: Ill. 1971, U.S. Dist. Ct. (no. dist.) Ill. 1971, U.S. Dist. Ct. (no. dist.) Tex. 1975, U.S. Ct. Appeals (7th cir.) 1972, U.S. Ct. Appeals (5th and 11th cirs.) 1981, U.S. Supreme Ct. 1975. Assoc. Kirkland & Ellis, Chgo., 1971-78, ptnr., 1978—; pres. Knox Coll., Galesburg, Ill., 2002—. Trustee Knox Coll., pres. 2002; trustee Ill. Hist. Preservation Agy., dir. Assoc. Coll. of Midwest, dir. Assoc. Coll. of Ill. Mem. Order of Coif, Univ. Club, Soangetaha Country Club (Galesburg, Ill.). Office: Knox College Galesburg IL 61401

**TAYLOR, RONALD DEAN,** retired psychologist, educator; b. Granite, Okla., Sept. 4, 1943; s. Roger Lafayette and Dortha Lee (Snow) T.; m. JoAnn Edith Irvine (div. Dec. 1984); 1 child, Tracy Kristin; m. Terry Susan Summers, Jan. 3, 1990; 1 child, Brian Sears. BS, Troy State Coll., 1966, MS, 1969; EdD, U. Houston, 1984. Guidance counselor Marathon (Fla.) Schs., 1966-69, Enterprise (Ala.) H.S., 1969-71; adminstr. ednl. programs Tex. Dept. Corrections, Huntsville, 1971-81; tng. cons. Houston, 1981-84; doctoral resident, tchg. asst., rsch. assoc. U. Houston, 1982-84, 86-88; asst. prof. psychology Dickinson (N.D.) State Coll., 1984-86; rsch. assoc. U. Houston, 1986-88; asst. prof. psychology Columbia (Mo.) Coll., 1988—92, assoc. prof., 1992—97, prof., 1997—2004, prof. emeritus, 2004—. Vis. lectr. U. Houston, 1984-93, N.D. State U., Dickinson, 1984-86; cons. Priem Group, Dickinson, 1985-86; judge ann. rsch. forum U. Mo., Columbia, 1990, 94—2004. Author: A Time to Forget--Remembered, 1974; contbr. numerous articles to profl. jours. Named Hon. Lt. Col. Gov. Ala., 1969; recipient Award for Excellence in Tchg. Gov. Mo., 1994, T.A. Abbott award Tchg. Excellence Cert. Recognition, 2001. Mem. Am. Ednl. Rsch. Assn., Phi Delta Kappa. Unitarian Universalist. Avocations: reading, riflery.

**TAYLOR, RONALD LEE,** academic administrator; b. Urbana, Ill., Nov. 11, 1943; s. Lee R. and Katherine L. (Becker) Taylor; m. Patricia D. Fitzsimmons, Mar. 10, 1973; children: Jamie, Lara, Meredith, Dana. AB, Harvard U., 1966; MBA, Stanford U., 1971. Asst. contr. Bell & Howell, Chgo., 1971-73, pres., CEO DeVry Inc., Chgo., 1973—2004, CEO, 2004—. Bd. dirs. La Petite Acad., Inc.; trustee Higher Learning Commn., North Ctrl. Assn. Colls. and Schs., 1985—. Trustee Rehabilitation Inst. Chgo.; mem. mgmt. bd. Stanford U. Sch. Bus., 2005. Achievements include feature in Crain's Mag. Chgo., 2006. Office: DeVry Inc 1 Tower Ln Ste 1000 Oakbrook Terrace IL 60181-4663 Business E-Mail: rtaylor@devry.com.

**TAYLOR, RONALD LEWIS,** sociology educator; b. St. Petersburg, Fla., Feb. 27, 1941; s. David T. and Lillian (Bell) Miller; m. Bernice E. Chavis, Dec. 24, 1967; children: Kevin, Darryl. BA, Bethune-Cookman Coll., 1962; MA, Howard U., 1964; PhD, Boston U., 1973. Dean of men Bethune-Cookman Coll., Daytona Beach, Fla., 1964-65, dir. fin. aid, 1965-67; instr., lectr. Boston U., 1967-70; rsch. assoc., cons. Army Bur. Rsch., Ft. Devens, Mass., 1971-73; asst. prof. U. Conn., Storrs, 1972-78, assoc. prof., 1978-90, chair dept. sociology, 1981-86, prof. sociology, 1990—, dir. Inst. African-Am. Studies, 1993-99, vice provost multicultural and internat. affairs, 1999—. Nat. adv. bd. Ctr. Nat. Policy, Washington, 1991—; grant review panel Ctrs. for Disease Control, Atlanta, 1991-93. Editor: Black Youth in America, 1990, Minority Families in the U.S., 1994, African-American Youth, 1995; co-editor: The Black Male in America, 1977; mem. editl. bd. Jour. African-Am. Male Studies, 1991-93; editor Race and Soc. Assn. Black Sociologists, 1995-2003 Mem. AAUP (U. Conn. chpt. pres. 1993-94), Am. Sociol. Assn. (com. on coms. 1991-93, nominations com. 1994-96), Eastern Sociol. Soc. (chair elections 1991-93, v.p. 2003-04) Business E-Mail: ronald.taylor@uconn.edu.

**TAYLOR, RONALD LOUIS,** lawyer; b. Memphis, July 18, 1942; s. George Festus and Ina Dell (Sanderson) T.; m. Elsa Juanita Parker, Dec. 28, 1969; children: Anna-Kathryn, Benjamin Louis. BA magna cum laude, Miss. State U., 1964; JD, U. Miss., 1970. Bar: Miss. 1970, U.S. Ct. Appeals (5th cir.) 1976, U.S. Supreme Ct. 1976. Assoc. B.G. Perry, Southaven, Miss., 1970-71; ptnr. Perry & Taylor, Southaven, 1971-73, Perry, Taylor & Whitwell, Southaven, 1973-75, Taylor & Whitwell, Southaven, 1976-85, Taylor, Jones, Alexander, Seale & Ryan, Ltd., Southaven, 1985-89, Taylor, Jones Alexander & Sorrell Ltd., Southaven, 1994—2003, Taylor, Jones & Alexander Ltd., Southaven, 2003—. Mcpl. judge City of Horn Lake, Miss., 1975-77; city atty. City of Southaven, 1982—. Vice chmn. Southaven Libr. Bd., 1973-76. Lt. col. USAR, 1964-2002, ret. Fellow Miss. Bar Found.; mem. ATLA, Miss. Trial Lawyers (bd. govs. 1980), DeSoto County Bar Assn. (pres. 1978, 86), Exch. Club (pres. 1973), Lions, Rotary Club (Paul Harris Fellow), Masons (32d degree), Shriner (Al Chymia Shrine Temple), Rotary (chmn. Southaven Spring Fest). Republican. Baptist. Office: Taylor Jones & Alexander Ltd PO Box 188 961 Main St Southaven MS 38671-0188 Home: 5115 Meadow Point Dr Southaven MS 38671 Office Phone: 662-342-1306.

**TAYLOR, ROY LEWIS,** botanist, educator; b. Olds, Alta., Can., Apr. 12, 1932; s. Martin Gilbert and Crystal (Thomas) T. B.Sc., Sir George Williams U., Montreal, Que., Can., 1957; PhD, U. Calif. at Berkeley, 1962; DSc (hon.), U. B.C., Vancouver, Can., 1997. Pub. sch. tchr. Olds Sch. Div., 1949-52; jr. high sch. tchr. Calgary Sch. Bd., Alta., Canada, 1953-55; chief taxonomy sect., research br. Can. Agrl. Dept., Ottawa, Ont., Canada, 1962-68; dir. Bot. Garden, prof. botany, prof. plant scis. U. B.C., Vancouver, 1968-85; pres., CEO Chgo. Hort. Soc., 1985-94; dir. Chgo. Bot. Garden, Glencoe, Ill., 1985-94; exec. dir. Rancho Santa Ana Bot. Garden, Claremont, Calif., 1994-99; prof. botany, chmn. botany program Claremont Grad. U., 1994-99, dir. emeritus, 1999. Pres. Western Bot. Svcs. Ltd. Author: The Evolution of Canada's Flora, 1966, Flora of the Queen Charlotte Islands, Vols. I and II, 1968, Vascular Plants of British Columbia: A Descriptive Resource Inventory, 1977; The Rare Plants of British Columbia, 1985; assoc. editor Pacific Horticulture, 2001—. Mem. State of Ill. Bd. Natural Resources and Conservation, 1987-94; trustee Nature Ill. Found., 1990-94, Elisabeth C. Miller Bot. Garden Trust, Seattle, 1994—, Elisabeth C. Miller Bot. Garden Endowment, 2001—, The Arbor Fund, Seattle, 1997—, chmn., 2002—; bd. dirs. Milner Gardens and Woodland Soc., Qualicum Beach, B.C., Can., 2000—, chmn., 2002—. Fellow Linnean Soc. London (hon.); mem. Can. Bot. Assn. (pres. 1967-68), Biol. Coun. Can. (pres. 1973-74), Am. Assn. Mus. (accreditation com. 1980-85, chmn. 1985-91, chmn. ethics commn. 1991-93, Centennial Honor Roll award, 2006), Am. Assn. Bot. Gardens and Arboreta (hon. life; pres. 1976, 77, award of merit 1987), Am. Soc. Bot. Artists (bd. dirs. 1997—2003), Claremont C. of C. (bd. dirs. 1995-98), Ottawa Valley Curling Assn. (pres. 1968-69), Milner Gardens and Woodland Soc. (bd. dirs. 2000—, chmn. 2002—), B.C. Soc. Landscape Archs. (hon.), U.B.C. Bot. Garden (hon.), Chgo. Hort. Soc. (life, medal 1994), Gov. Gen.'s Curling Club Can. (life), Wood Acres Strat Corp (pres., 2005—). Home Fax: 250-390-0860. E-mail: taylor.rl@shaw.ca.

**TAYLOR, RUSSELL BENTON,** mining executive; b. Eskridge, Kans., May 16, 1925; s. Bayard Charles and Eva May (Russell) T.; m. Arlene Marie Krebiel, Aug. 14, 1959; 1 child, Bruce Charles. BSBA, U. Kans., 1949; JD, U. Kans., 1951. Asst. cashier Eskridge (Kans.) State Bank, 1951-57, cashier, 1957, pres., 1958-69, chmn., 1969-78; v.p., dir South Standard Mining Co., Salt Lake City, 1978-96. Mayor City of Eskridge, Kans., 1959. Decorated

Purple Heart. Mem. Kans. Bar Assn., Kiwanis, Masonic, Arab Shrine. Republican. Methodist. Avocations: travel, ranching. Home and Office: 18213 Sanford Rd Eskridge KS 66423 E-mail: r7b9t@earthlink.net.

**TAYLOR, RUTH ARLEEN LESHER,** marketing educator; b. Riverton, Iowa, Mar. 7, 1941; d. Clyde Almond and Bernice Emogene (Graves) Lesher; m. Leslie (Milburn) Taylor, Aug. 10, 1963; children: Treg Anthony, John Leslie II. BS in Home Econs. Edn. magna cum laude, U. Houston, 1975; MEd, Tex. Christian U., 1977; PhD, U. N. Tex., 1981; PhD (hon.), U. Nat. Mayor de San Marcos, Lima, Peru, 2006. Prof. mktg. Tarrant County C.C. Ft. Worth, 1977-78, North Tex. State U., Denton, 1978-81, Southwestern U., Georgetown, Tex., 1982-87, S.W. Tex. State U., San Marcos, 1981-82, 87—; hon. prof. mktg. U. Nat. Mayor de San Marcos, Lima, Peru, 2006—. Dir. travel to China, Japan, Hong Kong, Costa Rica, Morocco, Europe, Eng., Mex., Dominican Republic, Venezuela, Chile, Peru; faculty intern Tex. Dept. Econ. Devel. and Tex. Sec. of State Office; collaborator STAT-USA and Internat. Catalog Exhbn. U.S. Dept. Commerce; dir. study program, Washington. Author: Text Maps Study Guides, 1994—; contbg. author: The Psychology of Fashion, 1985, Ethics in Accounting, 1994; contbr. articles to profl. jours. Mem. Lost Creek Garden Club, Austin, Tex., 1985—, v.p.; vol. Bob Bullock State Hist. Mus. Recipient Tchg. award McCoy Coll. Bus., 2005, N.Am. Small Bus. Trade Educators award 2005; nominated Gary Woods Rsch. award 2005; grantee Merrick Found., 1991; Fulbright sr. specialist, Peru, 2006. Mem.: DAR, Am. Soc. for Competitiveness, Winthrop Soc., French Huguenot Soc., Colonial Dames, Internat. Hospitality Coun. (bd. dirs.), Mayflower Soc., Mktg. Mgmt. Assn., Western Mktg. Educators Assn., Am. Mktg. Assn., Alpha Mu Alpha, Alpha Kappa Psi, Phi Delta Kappa, Phi Epsilon Omicron, Beta Gamma Sigma. Avocations: travel, gardening, reading, entertaining. Office: Texas State University 601 University Dr San Marcos TX 78666-4685 E-mail: rt01@txstate.edu.

**TAYLOR, S. BROOKE,** lawyer; b. Port Angeles, Wash. BA in Polit. Sci., Stanford U., 1965; JD, U. Va., 1968. Bar: Wash. 1968. Dep. prosecuting atty. Clallam County, 1969—70, prosecuting atty., 1970—75; co-owner, ptnr. Taylor & Taylor P.S., Port Angeles, 1975—90, Platt Irwin Taylor, Port Angeles, 1991—. Spkr. in field. Dir., pres. Clallam County Family YMCA; dir. G.M. Lauridsen Found.; dir., pres. Clallam County Cmty. Mental Health Ctr.; mem., dir. Port Angeles C. of C.; mem. Penninsula Coll. Found. Named Citizen of Yr., Clallam County, 1999. Mem.: ABA, Assn. Trial Lawyers Am., Wash. State Trial Lawyers Assn., Clallam County Bar Assn. (pres. 1981), Wash. State Bar Assn. (mem. bd. govs. 2000—02, treas. 2001—02, chmn. facilities com. 2001—, liaison dist. and mcpl. ct. judges assn. 2003—04, pres.-elect 2004—), Kiwanis Club (dir.). Achievements include contributions to the Washington State Bar Association's "Diversity Amendment" (later called the "Taylor Draft") which expanded the Association's definition of diversity and led to the creation of three governor-at-large positions. Office: Platt Irwin Taylor 403 S Peabody Port Angeles WA 98362 Office Phone: 360-457-3327. Office Fax: 360-452-5010.

**TAYLOR, SATOMI IZUMI,** education educator; d. Jinsaku and Umeno Izumi; m. John William Taylor, Sept. 14, 1972. PhD, Va. Poly. Inst. and State U., 1992. Asst. educator Ft. Valley State U., Ga., 1992—93; assoc. prof. U. Memphis, 1993—. Consulting editor Internat. Jour. of Early Childhood, Goteborg, Sweden, 2000—, Tenn.'s Children, Memphis, 2004—; bd. mem. Memphis Assn. for the Edn. of Young Children. Prodr.: (18 online video conferencing sessions) Constructivism in Higher Education; contbr. articles to profl. jours. Recipient Disting. Rsch. award, Assn. of Tchr. Educators, 1996-1997, Outstanding Svc. award, Profl. Devel. Schs. Partnership, 1997, Outstanding Award for Rsch., U. Memphis, 2003, Dean's Excellence Award in Tchg., 2004, Dean's Excellence Award in Mentoring, 2005. Mem.: Japan Soc. of Rsch. on Early Childhood Care and Edn., Am. Ednl. Rsch. Assn., Nat. Assn. for the Edn. of Young Children (life; profl. devel. panel 2005—). Achievements include research in publishing cross-cultural studies. Office Phone: 901-678-5363.

**TAYLOR, SENICA DUWAYNE,** music educator; b. New Albany, Ind., Dec. 3, 1976; s. Earnest Ellis and Leighanne Taylor; m. Veronica Lee Taylor, July 31, 1999. MusB, Ky. Wesleyan Coll., 1998; MusM, Ea. Ky. U., 2001, MA in Tchg., 2002. Music instr. Model Lab. Sch. Ea. Ky. U., Richmond, Ky., 2002—04, Garrard Mid. Sch., 2004—. Mem.: Ky. Music Educators Assn., Nat. Assn. Music Edn. Office: 324 W Maple Ave Lancaster KY 40444

**TAYLOR, SHANNON,** lawyer, not-for-profit developer; b. Passaic, NJ, June 14, 1955; s. Michael and Rita Taylor; m. Judith Ann Bernz. BA magna cum laude, Tufts U., 1976; attended, Hebrew U. Law, 1977; JD, Temple U., 1979. Bar: NJ 1979, NY 1980, No. Dist. 1980, US Dist. Ct. 1980, Ea. Dist. 1981. Ct. atty. to Hon. David Follender, Supreme Ct.-Civil Term, Hackensack, NJ, 1979—80; assoc. comml. litigation Goetz & Fitzpatrick, NYC, 1981—85; assoc. Nathan Cyperstein & Paul Gerstner, Bklyn., 1985—90; prin. ct. atty. to Hon. Jerome Hornblass, NY State Supreme Ct.-Criminal Term, 1992—96; ct. atty. NY State Criminal Ct., Housing Ct., Kings County, 1997—. Exec. dir. Blacks and Jews in Conversation, Inc., NYC, 1993—; pub. rels. and press coord., photographer, chronicler Not Just Blacks and Jews in Conversation, 1994—, stand-up comic, 1998—; adminstrv. law judge NYC Taxi and Limousine Commn., 1997—; radio show co-host, NYC, 1983—88; guest news commentator/panelist radio and TV news, NYC, 1990—. Photojournalist (for TV, newspapers, films, and mag.), contbr. columnist. Prodr., promoter comedy-celebrity workshops fundraiser Not-for-Profit Religious and Health Instns., internationally and in N.Y.C., 1990—. Recipient Most Productive Cmty. Assistance Orgn., YWCA, 1999. Mem.: NY Drama League, NYC Bar Animal Rights Divsn., NY Jewish Lawyers Guild, Tufts U. Law Alumni, NY Players Club, NY Friars Club. Avocations: percussionist, table tennis, mineralogy. Home: 123 W 83rd St 3 L New York NY 10024 Office: NYC Criminal Ct Law Dept 120 Schermerhorn St Brooklyn NY 11201 Office Phone: 917-374-3623.

**TAYLOR, SHELLEY E.,** psychology researcher, educator; b. Mt. Kisco, NY, Sept. 10, 1946; d. Charles Fox and Pearl May (Harvey) T.; m. Mervyn Francis Fernandes, May 1, 1972; children: Sara F, Charles F. AB magna cum laude in Psychology, Conn. Coll., 1968; PhD in Social Psychology, Yale U., 1972. Asst. prof. psychology and social rels. Harvard U., Cambridge, Mass., 1972-77, assoc. prof., 1977-79; assoc. prof. psychology UCLA, 1979-81, prof., 1981—. vis. faculty dept. adminstrv. scis. Yale U., New Haven, 1971-72, vis. Sloane fellow, 1978; mem. basic sociocultural rsch. rev. com. NIH, 1979-83; Katz-Newcomb lectr. U. Mich., 1982; cons. to pub. houses and TV producers. Author: Social Cognition, 1986, 2d edit., 1991, Health Psychology, 1986, 3d edit., 1995, 5th edit., 2002. Positive Illusions: Creative Self-Deception and the Healthy Mind, 1989, The Tending Instinct: How Nurturing is Essential to Who We Are and How We Live, 2002; contbr. numerous articles to sci. publs. Active numerous charitable and fund-raising orgns. including Curtis Sch. PTA and U. So. Calif./Norris Cancer Ctr. Recipient Rsch. Scientist Devel. award NIMH, 1981-86, 86-91, MERIT award, 1987, Donald Campbell award for disting. sci. contbn. to sociology, 1995; numerous rsch. grants in field; Winthrop scholar, 1967; Woodrow Wilson fellow, 1968, NIMH fellow, 1968-72. Fellow APA (Sci. Weekend lectr. 1988, Disting. Sci. award 1980, Outstanding Sci.Contbn. award Divsn. 38, 1994), Brit. Psychol. Soc. (flying fellow), Acad. Behavioral Medicine Rsch., Soc. Psychol. Study Social Issues, Soc. Behavioral Medicine; mem. AAAS, Soc. Exptl. Social Psychology, Western Psychol. Assn. (pres. 1993-94), Inst. Medicine. Office: UCLA Dept Psychology Franz 4611 Box 951563 Los Angeles CA 90095-1563

**TAYLOR, SHERRI JOI,** psychology professor; b. Athens, Ga., May 7, 1962; d. Benjamin Harris and Johnnie Kate Knight; m. Patrick Oscar Taylor, Oct. 6, 2001; children: Bryan Patrick, Ashley Lauren. BA, Auburn U., Ala.; MS, Troy State U., Dothan, Ala.; EdD, Nova Southeastern U., Ft. Lauderdale, Fla. Cert. paralegal Ctr. for Legal Studies Golden Colo. at Auburn U., Myers-Briggs Type Indicator Ctr. for Applications of Psychol. Type, Gainesville, Fla. Asst. prof. psychology Andrew Coll., Cuthbert, Ga., 2002—, dir. focus program; counselor/psychology instr. Wallace Coll.-Sparks Campus,

Eufaula, Ala.; habilitation treatment specialist and psychol. assoc. Eufaula Adolescent Ctr.-State of Ala. Dept. Mental Health, Eufaula, Ala. Group study exch. team mem. Internat. Rotary Assn., Eufaula; mem. exec. bd. Eufaula/Barbour County C. of C., 1996—2001; vol. Lakeview Cmty. Hospice, Eufaula; mem. Mainstreet Eufaula, Eufaula H.S. High Hopes, Ala. Gov.'s Conf. for Emerging Young Leaders, Montgomery, Barbour County Children's Policy Coun., Eufaula; vol. Ala. Coop. Ext. Svc., Eufaula; bd. mem. Friends of the Carnegie Libr., Eufaula, Ala.; mem. Eufaula Heritage Assn.; youth dir. St James' Episcopal Ch., Eufaula. Recipient Citizen of Yr., Eufaula Tribune, 2000, Vol. of Yr., Eufaula/Barbour County C. of C., 2000, James H. Woodall, Jr. award for Excellence in Tchg., Andrew Coll., 2006. Mem.: Learning Disability Assn. Am. (assoc.), AHEAD (assoc.), Auburn U. Alumni Assn. (assoc.), Delta Kappa Gamma (assoc.). R-Liberal. Episcopalian. Office Phone: 229-732-5908.

**TAYLOR, SHERRIL WIGHTMAN,** broadcast executive; b. Salt Lake City, Jan. 4, 1924; s. Kenneth E. and Florence May (Wightman) T.; m. Josephine Vermillion, May 2, 1970; 1 child by previous marriage, Sarah. Student, U. Utah, 1943-46; BJ, U. Mo., 1947; postgrad., Yale U. Promotion mgr. KSL Radio, Salt Lake City, 1947-51; sales promotion mgr. CBS, Hollywood, Calif., 1951-53, CBS radio sales N.Y.C., 1953-56; dir. sales promotion and advt. CBS Radio, N.Y.C.; also v.p. Radio Advt. Bur., N.Y.C., 1956-58; sr. group head J. Walter Thompson, Chgo., 1958-61; ind. TV producer Kukla, Fran, and Ollie Show, N.Y.C., 1961-64; v.p. Nat. Assn. Broadcasters, Washington, 1964-67, dir., 1969-78; v.p. affiliate relations CBS, 1967-79. Cons. Bonneville Internat. Corp., 1979-85; pres. Taylor Co., 1985-91; vice chmn. Coltrin & Assoc., 1991—; pvt. sector coordinator USIA, Washington, 1982, cons., 1982—; chmn. adv. com. Voice of Am., Washington, 1989—; vis. lectr. Brigham Young U., Provo, Utah, 1980—, Emerson Coll., Boston, Mich. Central U., Southern Vt. Coll.; adv. faculty-industry seminar, 1980, 81; bd. dirs. Am. Communications Inc., Utica-Rome TV Svcs. Inc., 1988—. Author: Radio Programming in Action, 1967. Mem. Carnegie Hall com. for Utah Symphony, Park Avenue Preservation Com.; past trustee The Helene Toolen Inst. Med. Rsch., Bennington, Vt., 1985—; mem. futures com. Bennington Mus., 1985—; bd. dirs. Nautical Ventures Inc., N.Y.C., 1987—; chmn. bd. Cmty. Action Network-N.Y., 2000-01. Recipient Nat. Assn. Broadcasters Ann. Com. Am. Broadcast Pioneer award, 1998. Mem. Internat. Radio and TV Soc. (v.p., bd. dirs., pres., chmn., bd. dirs. found.), Broadcasters' Found. (dir.), Food and Wine Soc. (N.Y. chpt.), Yale Club of N.Y., Sigma Chi (Significant Sig award 2000). Episcopalian. Home: PO Box 4004 Bennington VT 05201 Office: Yale Club of NY 50 Vanderbilt Ave Box 35 New York NY 10017 Office Phone: 727-403-9018. Personal E-mail: swt3@verizon.net.

**TAYLOR, STEPHEN LLOYD,** toxicologist, educator, food scientist; b. Portland, Oreg., July 19, 1946; s. Lloyd Emerson and Frances Hattie (Hanson); m. Susan Annette Kerns, June 23, 1973; children: Amanda, Andrew. BS in Food Sci. Tech., Oreg. State U., 1968, MS in Food Sci. Tech., 1969; PhD in Biochemistry, U. Calif., Davis, 1973. Research assoc. U. Calif., Davis, 1973-74, research fellow, 1974-75; chief food toxicology Letterman Army Inst., San Francisco, 1975-78; asst. prof. food toxicology U. Wis., Madison, 1978-83, assoc. prof., 1983-87; head dept. food sci. technology, dir. Food Processing Ctr. U. Nebr., Lincoln, 1987—2004, prof. dept. food sci. tech., 2004—. Cons. in field. Contbr. articles to profl. jours. Fellow: Inst. Food Technologists (divsn. chmn. 1981—82, sect. chmn. 1984—85, exec. com. 1988—91), Nat. Acad. Scis. (Food Forum); mem.: Soc. Toxicology, Am. Chem. Soc., Am. Acad. Allergy, Asthma and Immunology. Democrat. Presbyterian. Home: 941 Evergreen Dr Lincoln NE 68510-4131 Office: U Nebr Dept Food Sci Tech Lincoln NE 68583-0919 Office Phone: 402-472-2833. Business E-Mail: staylor2@unl.edu.

**TAYLOR, STEVE HENRY,** zoologist; b. Inglewood, Calif., Mar. 18, 1947; s. Raymond Marten and Ardath (Metz) T.; 1 child, Michael Travis; m. Sarah Margaret Young, May 14, 1993. BA in Biology, U. Calif.-Irvine, 1969. Animal keeper Los Angeles Zoo, 1972-75, assoc. curator, 1975-76; children's zoo mgr. San Francisco Zoo, 1976-81; zoo dir. Sacramento Zoo, 1981-88; dir. Cleve. Met. Zoo, 1989—. Bd. dirs. Sacramento Soc. Prevention Cruelty to Animals, 1983-87, Sacramento Red Cross, 1988-89, Conv. and Visitor Bur. of Greater Cleve., 1995-03, 06-, Leadership Cleve. Class 1997; mem. admissions com. United Way, 1999. Recipient Robert P. Bergman Impact award Convention & Visitors Bur. Greater Cleve., 2000. Fellow Am. Assn. Zool. Parks and Aquariums (infant care diet advisor 1979, 85, bd. dirs. 1987-93, pres. 1991-92, chmn. pub. edn. com. 1987-89, bd. regents, mgmt. sch., chmn. accreditation com. 1998, 99, Outstanding Svc. award 1979, 85, 88, 89, 91, 95, 98, 99, 2001); mem. Conservation Breeding Specialist Group, World Assn. Zoos and Aquariums, Sierra Club, Audubon Soc. Democrat. Home: 1265 Elmwood Rd Rocky River OH 44116-2236 Office: Cleveland Metroparks Zoo 3900 Wildlife Way Cleveland OH 44109-3132 Office Phone: 216-635-3331. Business E-Mail: sht@clevelandmetroparks.com.

**TAYLOR, STEVEN D.,** music educator; s. Norman Floyd and Peggy Cox Taylor; m. Gail Ann Burger, Dec. 18, 1976; children: Jeremy, Kevin, Chelsie. MusEdB, Youngstown State U., Ohio, 1978. Lic. tchr. music K-12 Ohio, 1978. Tchr. and chair music dept. Hillsdale Local Schs., Jeromesville, Ohio, 1978—. Adjudicator Ohio Music Edn. Assn.; officer Hillsdale Edn. Assn., 1986—. Named Tchr. of Yr., Hillsdale Schs., 1985, 1994. Mem.: Music Educators Nat. Conf., Am. Fedn. Musicians, Phi Beta Mu. Avocations: bicycling, camping.

**TAYLOR, STEVEN W.,** state supreme court justice; b. Henryetta, Okla., June 7, 1949; m. Mary Taylor; 1 child. BA in Political sci., Okla. State U., 1971; JD, U. Okla. Coll. of Law, 1974. Atty. Gotcher, Gotcher & Taylor, Okla., 1978—84; councilman McAlester City, Okla., 1980—82, elected mayor Okla., 1982—84; judge Okla. Dist. Ct., 1984—94; dist. judge, chief judge 18th Jud. Dist., 1994—2004; presiding judge E. Central Jud. Administrative Dist., 1997—2003; justice Okla. Supreme Ct., 2004—. Pres. Okla. Jud. Conference, 1990. Mem. bd. dirs Okla. Heritage Assn., Okla. Medical Rsch. Found. Served atty. & judge USMC, 1970—78. Mem.: Pittsburg County Bar Assn., Okla. Bar Assn. (Jud. Excellence award 2003, Outstanding Okla. Judge of Yr. 2004). Office: Okla Supreme Ct Rm 200 State Capital Bldg Oklahoma City OK 73105 Office Phone: 405-521-3844. Business E-Mail: steven.taylor@oscn.net.

**TAYLOR, STUART ROSS,** geochemist, writer; b. Ashburton, New Zealand, Nov. 26, 1925; s. Thomas Stuart and Anne Grace (Lloyd) T.; m. Noel Elvie White, May 21, 1958; children: Susanna, Judith, Helen. BSc, U. New Zealand, 1948, MSc, 1951; PhD, Ind. U., 1954; DSc, Oxford U., 1978. Lectr. U. Oxford, Eng., 1954-58; sr. lectr. U. Cape Town, South Africa, 1958-60; professorial fellow Australian Nat. U., Canberra, 1961-90, vis. fellow, 1990-99, prof. emeritus, 1997; prof. U. Vienna, 1992, 96. Vis. scientist Lunar and Planetary Inst., Houston, 1969-90. Author: Lunar Science: Post-Apollo View, 1975, Planetary Science, 1982, Solar System Evolution, 1992, (with others) Continental Crust, 1985, Destiny or Chance: Our Solar System and Its Place in the Cosmos, 1998, Solar System Evolution, 2d edit., 2001; contbr. more than 220 articles to profl. jours. Recipient Goldschmidt medal Geochem. Soc., 1993, Gilbert award Geol. Soc. Am., 1994, Bucher medal Am. Geophys. Union, 2002; Asteroid 5670 named Rosstaylor, 1997. Fellow Royal Soc. New Zealand (hon.), Australian Acad. Sci., Geol. Soc. London (hon.), Geol. Soc. India (hon.); mem. NAS (fgn. assoc.), Meteoritical Soc. (pres. 1989-90, Leonard medal 1998). Office: Australian Nat U Dept Geology Canberra 0200 Australia E-mail: ross.taylor@anu.edu.au.

**TAYLOR, SUSAN L.,** magazine editor; b. N.Y.C., Jan. 23, 1946; d. Lawrency and Violet (Weekes) T.; m. William Bowles (div.); 1 child, Shana-Nequai; m. Khephra Burns, 1989-. BA in Sociology, Fordham U., 1991, postgrad.; doctorate (hon.), Spelman Coll., Bennett Coll., Del. State, Fisk U., Lincoln U. Founder, rschr. and developer of a line of customized cosmetics and natural skin care line Nequai Cosmetics, 1970—81; freelance beauty editor to fashion Essence Mag., NYC, 1971-81; editor-in-chief Essence Comm., Inc, NYC, 1981—2000, v.p, 1986—93, sr. v.p., 1993, editl.

dir., 2000—, also bd. dir. Host, exec. prodr. weekly tv show Essence, 1983-87; exec. prodr. and driving force behind Essence Awards and Essence Music Festival; served on Comm. on Rsch. in Black Edn. through the Assn. Ednl. Rsch. Assn; spkr. in field. Author: In the Spirit: The Inspirational Writings of Susan L. Taylor, 1993, Lessons in Living, 1995; co-author with husband Confirmation: The Spiritual Wisdom That Has Shaped Our Lives, 1997; co-editor of several books. Co-chair Danny Glover for Shared Interest (to raise money to build housing in rural areas of S. Africa); bd. dir. Joint Ctr. for Polit. and Econ. Studies, Washington; mem. adv. bd. Black Adminstr. in Child Welfare; mem. La. Recovery Authority; committed to serving and empowering the poor and work with disadvantaged women and teenagers to encourage them take charge of their lives. Recipient Henry Johnson Fisher award, 1998, President's award, NAACP Image award, 2006. Mem.: Women in Communications, Am. Soc. Mag. Editors (inducted into Hall of Fame 2002), Nat. Assn. Black Journalists. Office: Essence Comm Inc 135 W 50th St 4th Fl New York NY 10020*

**TAYLOR, SUSAN M.,** museum director; Dir. Davis Mus. and Cultural Ctr., Wellesley Coll., Mass., Princeton U. Art Mus., NJ, 2000—. Office: Princeton U Art Mus Mc Cormick Hall Princeton NJ 08544 Office Phone: 609-258-3788.

**TAYLOR, SUSAN SEROTA,** biochemist, researcher; b. Racine, Wis., June 20, 1942; d. Rudolph M. and Helen L. (Vohs) S.; m. Palmer William Taylor, July 3, 1965; children: Tasha Katherine, Ashton David, Palmer Andrew. BS, U. Wis., 1964; PhD, Johns Hopkins U., 1968. Postdoctoral fellow MRC Lab. Molecular Biology, Cambridge, England, 1969—71, U. Calif. San Diego, La Jolla, 1971-72, asst. prof. chemistry, 1972-79, assoc. prof., 1979-85, prof. chemistry, biochemistry, 1985—, prof. pharmacology dept. chemistry, biochemistry, 2004. Investigator Howard Hughes Med. Inst., 1997—; mem. adv. coun. GM Cancer Rsch. Found. Recipient Career Devel. award NIH, postdoctoral fellow NIH 1969-72, Fogarty Internat. Fellow NIH, 1981-82. Mem. Am. Chem. Soc., AAAS, NAS, Inst. Medicine, Am. Soc. Biochemistry and Molecular Biology (mem. coun. 1989-92, pres. 1995-96). Office: U Calif San Diego Dept Chemistry MC 0654 La Jolla CA 92093-0654 Business E-Mail: staylor@ucsd.edu.

**TAYLOR, SUZONNE BERRY STEWART,** real estate broker; b. Memphis, Sept. 27, 1926; d. Andrew George and Sue Hodge (Berry) Stewart; m. Robert Allen Taylor, Sr., June 15, 1946; children: Robert A. Jr., Suzonne Stewart Taylor Davids. Student, Rhodes Coll., 1948, U. S.C., 1969. Cert. residential specialist CRS Coun., 1996; grad. Realtors Inst.; cert. real estate broker; accredited buyer's rep. Am. Bd. Realtors. Sales agt. E. Roy Stone Realtors, Greenville, SC, 1967—69; real estate broker Aven Assoc. Realtors, Dover, Del., 1970—80, Emerson & Co. Realtors, Dover 1980—2000; realtor ERA Harrington Realty, 1996—. Active Crest Music Club, Greenville, 1955, Wildwood Garden Club, Greenville, 1960; mem., costume chmn. Greenville Little Theater, Jr. League Greenville, 1956-66, sustaining mem., 1966—, Jr. League Wilmington, Del., 1999—, dir., 1999. Recipient Beyond Excellence award, ERA, 2004, 2005. Mem. Nat. Bd. Realtors, Del. Bd. Realtors, Kent County Bd. Realtors, Del. Hist. Soc., Biggs Mus., Alpha Omicron Pi. Republican. Episcopalian. Home: 517 Greenhill Rd Dover DE 19901-3766 Office: ERA Harrington Realty 1404 Forest Ave Dover DE 19904 Office Phone: 302-674-4663. Business E-Mail: staylor@harringtonera.com.

**TAYLOR, TERRY R.,** editor, educator; b. Valley Forge, Pa., Oct. 4, 1952; d. Thomas R. and Anna P. (Bystrek) T. BA in Journalism, Temple U., 1974. Reporter gen. assignments, sch. news Charlotte (N.C.) News, 1974-77; supr., writer AP, Phila., 1977-81, supr., writer sports desk N.Y.C., 1981-85, asst. editor sports, 1985-87, dep. editor sports, 1987-91, asst. chief bur., 1991-92, editor sports, 1992—; asst. editor sports N.Y. Times, 1991. Assoc. in journalism Columbia U., N.Y.C., 1991-95; adv. bd. Honda Awards, 1996—. Recipient John A. Domino Meml. award St. Bonaventure U., 1996. Founder's award Temple U., 1999; inductee Delaware County Sports Hall of Fame, 1998. Roman Catholic. Achievements include first woman sports editor at the AP. Office: AP Sports 50 Rockefeller Plz New York NY 10020-1605

**TAYLOR, THEODORE LANGHANS,** retired author; b. Statesville, N.C., June 23, 1921; s. Edward Riley and Elnora Alma (Langhans) T.; m. Gweneth Ann Goodwin, Oct. 25, 1946; children: Mark, Wendy, Michael; m. Flora Gray Schoenleber, Apr. 18, 1981. Student, Fork Union Mil. Acad., 1939-40, US Mcht. Marine Acad., 1942-44. Reporter Portsmouth (Va.) Star, 1941-42, Bluefield (W.Va.) News, 1946-47; sportswriter NBC-Radio, N.Y.C., 1942; asst. dir. pub. relations N.Y.U., 1947-48; dir. pub. relations YMCA Schs. and Colls., N.Y.C., 1948-50; publicist Paramount Pictures, Hollywood, Calif., 1955-56; assoc. producer Perlberg-Seaton Prodns., Hollywood, 1956-61; ret., 1961. Free lance writer 1961—; author: The Magnificent Mitscher, 1954, Fire on the Beaches, 1957, People Who Make Movies, 1968, The Cay, 1969 (Jane Addam's Children's Book award 1970), The Children's War, 1971, Air Raid: Pearl Harbor, 1971, The Maldonado Miracle, 1973, Rebellion Town, 1973, Showdown, 1973, Teetoncey, 1974, Teetoncey and Ben O'Neal, 1975, Battle in the Arctic Seas, 1976, The Odyssey of Ben O'Neal, 1977, A Shepherd Watches, A Shepherd Sings, 1977, Jule, 1979, Battle of Midway Island, 1981, The Trouble with Tuck, 1981, Sweet Friday Island, 1981, HMS Hood vs Bismarck, 1982, Battle in the English Channel, 1983, The Cats of Shambala, Rocket Island, 1985, Walking Up a Rainbow, 1986, The Stalker, 1987, The Hostage, 1988, Monocolo, 1989, Sniper, 1989, Tuck Triumphant, 1991, The Wierdo, 1991, Maria, 1992, To Kill the Leopard, 1993, Timothy of the Cay, 1993, The Bomb, 1995, Rogue Wave, 1996, The Flight of Jesse Leroy Brown, 1998, A Sailor Returns, 2000, The Boy Who Could Fly Without A Motor, 2002, Lord of The Kill, 2002, Hello, Artic, 2002, Ice Drift, 2005, Making Love to Typewriters, 2005, Billy the Kid, 2005, The Magnificent Mitscher, 2006. Served with USNR, 1945-46, 50-55. Recipient Lewis Carroll Shelf award, 1970, Silver medal Commonwealth Club, 1970, Best Book award So. Calif. Coun. on Children's Lit., 1970, Best Book award U. Calif. at Irvine, 1970, 74, Best Non-Fiction award Western Writers Am., 1977, Young Reader's Medal Calif. Reading Assn., 1984, 92, Edgar Allan Poe award, 1992, Utah Young Adult Book award, 1993, Md. Children's Book award, 1994, Scott O'Dell Best Hist. Fiction award, 1995, The Kerlan Body of Work award, 1997. Mem. Calif. Writers Guild, Acad. Motion Picture Arts and Scis., Screen Writers Guild. Republican. Lutheran. Address: 1856 Catalina Laguna Beach CA 92651-3340

**TAYLOR, T(HOMAS) ROGER,** educational consultant, educator; b. Urbana, Ill., May 31, 1945; s. Thomas and Ora Wilma Taylor; m. Beverly Milam, Dec. 19, 1981; 1 child, Whitney Brinson. BS, U. Ill., 1967; MA, So. Ill. U., 1972, PhD, 1980. Tchr. Mt. Vernon (Ill.) Schs., 1967-71; cons. Ill. Dept. State, 1971-74; dir. Area Svc. Ctr. for Gifted Children, South Cook County, Ill., 1975-79; prof. urban edn. Govs. State U., 1975-79; cons. Ednl. Cons. Assocs., Denver, 1977-82, also dir. Pres. Curriculum Design for Excellence, Oak Brook, Ill.; former sr. ptnr. T & H Investments, Hinsdale, Ill. V.p. Mt. Vernon C.C. Orch. Named Ky. Col., 1979, Outstanding Young Men of Am., YMCA, 1980, Best of the Best, IDEA Fellows Program, 1992, 93. Mem. NRA, NEA, Ill. Edn. Assn. (bd. dirs.), Nat. Assn. Gifted Children, World Coun. for Gifted, Assn. Childhood Edn. Internat., U. Ill. Alumni Assn. (dir. 1967-71), Profl. Assn. Diving Instrs., Demolay Club, Phi Delta Kappa. Home: 1907 Midwest Club Pkwy Oak Brook IL 60523-2525 Office: PO Box 4505 Hinsdale IL 60522-4505

**TAYLOR, THOMAS WILLIAM,** lawyer; b. Columbus, Ind., Feb. 11, 1943; s. Virgil W. and Margaret Emma (Voiles) T.; m. Linda Kay Followell, Jan. 1, 1964; children: Pamela Kay, William Lansing. AB with honors, Ind. U., 1965; LLB cum laude, Harvard U., 1968. Bar: Mass. 1968, U.S. Dist. Ct. Mass. 1969. Assoc. Ropes & Gray, Boston, 1968-78, ptnr., 1978-98, of counsel, 1999—; Lectr. Pres.'s urban policy program seminars U.S. Coun. of Mayors, 1982; chmn. tax panel nat. workshop Coun. of Infrastructure Financing Authorities, 1993; vol. astronomer Chaco Obs., Chaco Culture Nat. Hist. Park, 2000, 2006, prin. astronomer, 2001, 2005. Vol. Wilderness First Responder, 2002—; snowboard instr. Nashoba Valley Ski Area, 1999—2005,

staff trainer, 2003—05. Mem. Nat. Assn. Bond Lawyers (opinions com., chmn. securities law panel Washington workshop 1992, lectr. atty.'s workshop Chgo. 1983-97), Am. Coll. Bond Counsel (founding fellow), Appalachian Mountain Club Stewardship Soc. Avocations: rock climbing, orienteering, trumpet playing. Office: Ropes & Gray 1 International Pl Fl 4 Boston MA 02110-2624

**TAYLOR, TIMOTHY JOSEPH ANDREW,** social studies educator; s. Andrew and Eva Taylor. AA, Pensacola Jr. Coll., 1976; BA, U. West Fla., Pensacola, 1978. Cert. social studies tchr. Fla. Tchr. Santa Rosa Sch. Dist., Milton, Fla., 1988—. Named Tchr. of Yr., VFW, Milton, 2006, VFW Ladies Aux., Milton, 2006. Mem.: US Chess Fedn.

**TAYLOR, TOM,** marketing executive; Assoc. Outside Garden Dept. Home Depot, Inc., Miami, dept. head to asst. store mgr. to mgr., dist. mgr., regional v.p. S.W. Divsn., 1996, merchandising v.p. N.W. Divsn., 1999, divsn. pres. N.W., sr. v.p. PRO Bus., 2001—02, pres. Ea. Divsn., 2002—05, exec. v.p. Home Depot stores, exec. v.p. merchandising and mktg. Atlanta, 2005—. Named one of Top 20 Southerners to Watch, The Fin. Times, 2003. Office: Home Depot Inc 2455 Paces Ferry Rd Atlanta GA 30339*

**TAYLOR, TRENT E.,** retail executive; BS in information sci., Northeastern Ill. Univ., Schaumburg, Ill., 1984. Sr. programmer, analyst Motorola, Inc., 1984; cons. Ernst & Young, Chgo.; mgr. info sys. Walgreens, 1992—95, dir. infrastructure, architecture, 1995—99, divsn. v.p., CIO, 1999—2002, corp. v.p., CIO, 2000—, sr. v.p., 2002—05, exec. v.p., 2005—. Home: Walgreens 200 Wilmot Rd Deerfield IL 60015*

**TAYLOR, VICTORIA,** real estate rehabilitator, sculptor; b. Toronto, Ont., Can., Oct. 18, 1935; arrived in U.S., 1978; d. Alberto A. Equable and Evelyn McLaughlin; children: James R., Joseph J., Sherry L., Vincent A. AA, Fla. Keys C.C., 1989. Owner, operator Spring Dale Nursing Home, Peterborough, Ont., Canada, 1973—78, Sun & Surf Motel, Key West, Fla., 1978—79, Dairy Queen, Key West, 1979—82; real estate salesman/broker Key West, 1983—96. Mem.: Nat. Sculpture Soc. Home: 15A E Circle Dr Key West FL 33040-4013 Office Phone: 305-745-1363.

**TAYLOR, WATSON ROBBINS,** construction company executive; b. Wetumpka, Ala., Sept. 7, 1925; s. Henry Watson and Helen Robbins Taylor; m. Ernestine Jenkins, Sept. 10, 1949; children: Jane Albright, W. Robbins Jr., George Lewis. BS, U. Ala., 1948; DSc (hon.), Auburn (Ala.) U., 1986. Estimator Std. Roofing Co., Montgomery, Ala., 1948—52, v.p., 1952—66, pres., CEO, 1966—97, CEO, chmn. bd., 1997—; chmn., pres. Std.-Taylor Industries Inc., Montgomery, 1979—. Chmn. bd. Union Bank and Trust Co., Montgomery, 1980—94. Chmn. bd., founding chmn. Auburn U., Montgomery, 1967-80; dir. Ala. Shakespeare Festival, 1995—, Ala. State Docks, Mobile, 1992—. Lt. j.g. USN, 1943-45. Named Contractor of Yr. RSI mag., 1999; named univ. ctr. in his honor, Watson Robbins Taylor Ctr. Auburn U., 1999. Republican. Episcopalian. Avocations: golf, hunting. Home: PO Box 1 Letohatchee AL 36047-0001 Office: Std Roofing Co 516 N Mcdonough St Montgomery AL 36104-2645 Office Phone: 334-265-1262. Business E-Mail: r.taylor@standardtaylor.com.

**TAYLOR, WATSON ROBBINS, JR.,** investment banker; b. Montgomery, Ala., Mar. 16, 1956; s. Watson Robbins and Ernestine (Jenkins) T.; m. Davis Anne Denson, July 12, 1980; children: Watson Robbins III, Caroline Davis, Davis Denson. BS, Auburn U., 1979, MBA, 1982. Ranch foreman Johnston & Sons, Letohatchee, Ala., 1975-76; estimator Standard Roofing Co., Montgomery, Ala., 1976-78, v.p., 1978-84; pres. Standard Roofing USA, Inc., Montgomery, 1984-93, Standard-Taylor Industries, 1990-93; ptnr. First Commerce Capital, Inc., Montgomery, 1993-98; mgr. agribus. and middle market fin. group Morgan Keegan, Montgomery, 1998-99; pres. W.R. Taylor & Co., LLC, Montgomery, 1999—. Bd. dirs. Auburn U. Sch. Bus., Montgomery, Montgomery Acad. Fin. chmn. Ala. Rep. Com., Birmingham, 1989; trustee YMCA Endowment Found., Montgomery, 1989; bd. dirs. ARC, 1989, Montgomery coun. Boy Scouts Am., 1989. Mem. Montgomery Area C. of C. (bd. dirs. 1989-92), Ala. Alliance Bus. and Industry (bd. dirs. 1989-92), Rotary (past dir.), Young Pres.'s Assn. (Rebel chpt.), Montgomery Country Club, Ocean Reef Club. Methodist. Avocations: tennis, fishing, travel. Home: 9415 Dunleith Dr Montgomery AL 36117-5106 E-mail: rtaylor@wrtayco.com.

**TAYLOR, WESLEY BAYARD, JR.,** retired army officer; b. Covington, Ky., June 5, 1944; s. Wesley B. Sr. and Varina Martha (Morgan) T.; m. Linda L. Taylor, June 2, 1967; children: Kathleen C., Clint C. BS, U.S. Mil. Acad., 1965; MA in Internat. Rels., U. Calif., Santa Barbara, 1973; student, U.S. Army War Coll., 1985-86. Commd. 2d lt. U.S. Army, 1965, advanced through grades to brig. gen., 1990; asst. bn. advisor, sr. bn. advisor Airborne Divsn. Adv. Detachment, U.S. Mil. Assitance Command, Vietnam, 1967-68; staff officer Dept. of Army, Washington, 1980-81; bn. comdr. 3rd Bn., 5th Inf. U.S. Army, Republic of Panama, 1981-83; bn. comdr. 1st Ranger Bn. Hunter Army Airfield, Ga., 1983-85; strategic fellow U.S. Army War Coll., Carlisle Barracks, Pa., 1986-87; regimental comdr. 75th Ranger Regiment, Ft. Benning, Ga., 1987-89; asst. divsn. comdr. 1st Armored Divsn., Germany, 1989-91; dep. dir. ops, readiness and mobilization Dept. of Army, Washington, 1991-92; dep. asst. sec. of def. for policy and missions Office Sec. of Def., Washington 1992-94; pres., CEO Cal Farley's Boys Ranch & Affiliates, U.S.A.. Amarillo, Tex., 1995-99, Family & Childrens Ctr, Mishawaka, Ind., 2000—05, George C. Marshall Found., Lexington, Va., 2006—. Dist. commr. Boy Scouts Am., Germany, 1989-91. Decorated DSM, Def. Superior Svc. medal, Silver Star, Legion of Merit, Def. Meritorious Svc. medal, Bronze Star medal with oak leaf cluster, Air medals. Mem. Assn. U.S. Army, U.S. Army Ranger Assn., 75th Ranger Regiment Assn., Soc. Vietnamese Airborne Advisors, Soc. 173rd Airborne Brigade. Methodist. Avocations: fishing, hunting. Office: George C Marshall Found PO Drawer 1600 VMI Parad Lexington VA 24450 Personal E-mail: trextayl@comcast.net.

**TAYLOR, WILLARD B.,** lawyer; b. NYC, 1940; BA, Yale U., 1962, LLB, 1965. Bar: N.Y. 1966. Ptnr. with firm Sullivan & Cromwell, N.Y.C. Adj. faculty NYU Law Sch. Trustee North European Oil Royalty Trust. Mem. N.Y. State Bar Assn. (chair tax sect. 1983-84), Am. Law Inst. Office: Sullivan & Cromwell 125 Broad St New York NY 10004-2489

**TAYLOR, WILLIAM AL,** church administrator; b. Danville, Va., Sept. 26, 1938; s. Preston Floyd and Helen Elizabeth (Doss) T.; m. Brenda Flo Owen, June 4, 1961 (dec. 1996); children: Fawnia Rae Ricks, Albert Todd, Athena Dawn Jarman; m. Norma S. Pierce, June 28, 1997. AA, Lee Coll., 1957; postgrad., U. Calif., Santa Barbara, 1980. Br. mgr. Gerbico Britannica, Greensboro, NC, 1960-62, divsn. trainer Mpls., 1963; dist. mgr. Omaha, 1964-72; adminstrv. asst. Forward in Faith Internat. Broadcast, Cleveland, Tenn., 1972-80; gen. mgr. Sta. WQNE-FM, Cleveland, 1980—; cons. stewardship Ch. of God Internat. Offices, Cleveland, 1980—2004. Pres. Pathway Credit Union, Cleveland, 1985-2005, Vision Found., Cleveland, 1985—; exec. dir., 1979-80; chmn. Internat. Commn. on Prayer, Cleveland, 1986—. Author: Proving God, 1991, Days of Heaven on Earth, 1993, Stewardship Masterplanning, 1993, The Power of Vision, 2003. Pres. Clean Water Soc., Gastonia, N.C., 1974-75; speaker Citizens Against Legalized Liquor, Bradley County, Tenn., 1973, 75; advisor Mothers on March, Cleveland, 1976; active Nat. Conf. on Drug Abuse, Washington, 1978; master of ceremonies Nat. Religious Leaders Conf. on Alcohol and Drug Abuse, 1979; pres. Ch. of God Found., 2002. Recipient Mass Communications award Ch. of God Media Ministries, 1980, Stephen award Ch. of God Lay Ministries, 1990. Mem. Nat. Assn. Evangelicals (bd. adminstrs. 1985-98, chmn. stewardship commn. 1985-89), Christian Stewardship Assn. (bd. dirs. 1990-96, nat. prayer com. 1999—), Best of the Best Faculty award 1999, Outstanding Stewardship Profl. award 2000). Mem. Ch. Of God. Avocations: flying, travel, racquetball. Office: Ch of God Dept Stewardship 2490 Keith St NW Cleveland TN 37311-1309 Business E-Mail: ataylor@cogwm.org. E-mail: stewardcog@mindspring.com. *We are all spending the precious gift of life.*

*and we have been given the privilege to decide upon what we shall spend it. I have found the most worthy and fulfilling investment of life is God's stated purpose, "that we be conformed to the image of His son Jesus Christ.".*

**TAYLOR, WILLIAM B., JR.,** ambassador; married; 2 children. Grad., U.S. Mil. Acad., 1969; MA in Pub. Policy, Harvard U., 1977. Dir. Office Emergency Preparedness Dept. Energy; mem. staff Senator Bill Bradley; dir. Def. Dept., Washington; spl. dep. def. adv. U.S. Ambassador to NATO, Brussels, 1987—92; corrd. U.S. Assistance to Europe and Eurasia U.S. Dept. State, Washington, 1992—2002, spl. rep. Donor Assistance to Afghanistan Kabul, 2002—03, Afghanistan coord., 2003, dir. Iraq Reconstruction Mgmt. Office Baghdad, Iraq, 2004—05, mem. Quartet Spl. Envoy Jerusalem, 2005—06, US amb. to Ukraine Kiev, 2006—. Infantry officer U.S. Army, 1969—75, Vietnam and Germany. Office: DOS Amb 5850 Kiev Pl Washington DC 20521-5850*

**TAYLOR, WILLIAM COLTON,** physician, educator; b. Boston, Jan. 25, 1948; s. Manuel and Marjorie Taylor; m. Julia Katherine Landau, Dec. 4, 1983; children: Rachel, Hannah, Daniel, Benjamin, Jessica. BA, Yale U., New Haven, Conn., 1970; MD, U. Pa., Phila., 1974. Cert. bd. Am. Bd. of Internal Medicine, 1977. Sr. physician Beth Israel Deaconess Med. Ctr., Boston, 1996—; assoc. prof. medicine and assoc. prof. ambulatory care and prevention Harvard Med. Sch., Boston, 2006—.

**TAYLOR, WILLIAM JAMES (ZAK TAYLOR),** lawyer; b. Milw., Jan. 26, 1948; s. William Elmer and Elizabeth Emily (Lupinski) T.; m. Marlou Belyea, Sept. 20, 1975; children: Danielle Belyea, James Zachary Belyea. BA in Econs., Yale U., 1970; JD, Harvard U., 1976. Bar: Calif. 1976, U.S. Dist. Ct. (cen. dist.) Calif. 1976, U.S. Dist. Ct. (no. dist.) Calif. 1977, U.S. Ct. Appeals (9th cir.) 1977, U.S. Dist. Ct. (ea. dist.) Calif. 1980, U.S. Supreme Ct. 1980, U.S. Tax Ct. 1988. Law clk. to hon. Shirley M. Hufstedler U.S. Ct. Appeals (9th cir.), L.A., 1976-77; assoc. Broebeck, Phleger & Harrison, San Francisco, 1977-83; ptnr. Broebeck, Phleger and Harrison, San Francisco, 1983-95; shareholder Taylor & Jenkins, P.C., Oakland, Calif., 1995-96, Chilvers & Taylor, P.C., Oakland, 1996-99; of counsel Brobeck, Phleger & Harrison, LLP, San Francisco, 2000—03, Morgan Lewis & Bockius, LLP, San Francisco, 2003—04, ptnr., 2004—. Bd. dirs. Berkeley (Calif.) Law Found., 1988-91, Legal Svcs. for Children (recipient Jean Waldman Child Advocacy award, San Francisco 1988), 1983-89; co-chmn. Attys. Task Force for Children, San Francisco 1983-89. Editor-in-chief Harvard Civil Rights, Civil Liberties Law Rev., 1976; bd. editors No. Dist. Calif. Digest, 1978-83; co-author: California Antitrust Law, 1991; contbg. editor: Calif. Bus. Law Reporter, 1995—, Antitrust Law Developments, 1997, 4th edit., 2002. With U.S. Army, 1970-73. Mem. ABA, Bar Assn. San Francisco (bd. dirs. 1986-87, chair antitrust sect. 1987, chair fed. cts. sect. 1995-97), Am. Bus. Trial Lawyers Assn., Am. Health Lawyers Assn., Calif. Soc. Healthcare Attys., Barristers of San Francisco (bd. dirs. 1980-82, v.p. 1982-83). Democrat. Office: Morgan Lewis & Bockius LLP 1 Market Spear Tower San Francisco CA 94105-1420 Office Phone: 415-442-1315. Business E-Mail: wtaylor@morganlewis.com. E-mail: william.taylor@sbcglobal.net.

**TAYLOR, WILLIAM JAPE,** physician; b. Booneville, Miss., Sept. 5, 1924; s. William Melton and Cora Leona (Smith) T.; m. Audrey Y. Dennison, Jan. 31, 1948; children: J. Holley, Andrew D., Richard M., D. Lee. BS, Yale U., 1944; MD, Harvard U., 1947. Intern in internal medicine Boston City Hosp., 1947-48; resident in internal medicine Duke U. Hosp., 1948-50, fellow in cardiology, 1950-52, 54-55; instr. Duke U. Med. Sch., 1954-55, U. Pitts. Med. Sch., 1955-58; mem. faculty U. Fla. Coll. Medicine, Gainesville, 1958-95, prof. medicine, 1964-74, chief cardiology, 1958-74, disting. service prof. medicine, 1974-95; emeritus, 1995—. Vis. prof. U. Ife (Nigeria) Med. Sch., 1974-75; bd. dirs. PSRO, Fla. Area II, 1977-81 Author papers on human rights and health, human rights and peace, chpts. in books. Mem. human rights advocacy com. mentally retarded Fla. Dist. III, 1977-81; bd. dirs. Gainesville-Matagalpa Sister City, 1988-00, Gainesville UNA, 1999-01; mem. adv. coun. Ctr. African Studies, U. Fla., 1981-96. Fellow ACP (rsch. fellow 1950-51), Am. Coll. Cardiology; mem. Assn. U. Cardiologists, Am. Heart Assn. (fellow coun. clin. cardiology), Am. Fedn. Clin. Rsch., So. Soc. Clin. Investigation (pres. 1972-73), Fla. Heart Assn. (Disting. Svc. award 1975), Am. Soc. Tropical Medicine and Hygiene, Physicians for Social Responsibility (ho. of dels. 1985-90), Physicians for a Nat. Health Program, Sierra Club (exec. com. Suwannee/St. Johns Program 2002-04). Democrat. Home: 500 NW 80th Blvd Gainesville FL 32607-1531

**TAYLOR, WILLIAM JESSE, JR.,** international security studies educator, research institute senior advisor; b. Florence, S.C., Dec. 28, 1933; s. William J. and Dorothy (Byrd) T.; m. Louise Inger Haegerstrom, Apr. 9, 1977; 1 child, Nicolaus; children by previous marriage: Juliana C., William J. III, L. Scott, Christopher B., Helen B. BS, U. Md., 1962; MA, Am. U., 1964, PhD, 1967. Enlisted U.S. Army, commd. 2d lt., 1955, advanced through grades to col., 1976; prof. U.S. Mil. Acad., West Point, N.Y., 1970-81; vis. prof. U.S. Nat. War Coll., 1975-76; ret. col. U.S. Army, 1981; sr. exec. Ctr. for Strategic and Internat. Studies, Washington, 1981—2001, sr. v.p. internat. security programs, 1987—99; pres. Taylor Assocs. Inc., 1984—2006. Internat. lectr., debater, T.V. and radio mil. analyst, 1970—. Author: Future of Conflict: U.S. Interests, 1982, Future of Conflict into the 21st Century, 1987; co-author: American National Security: Policy and Process, 1981, 83, 89, 93, 99; co-editor: Defense Manpower Planning, 1980, The Future of Conflict in the 1980's, 1982, Strategic Requirements for the Army to the Year 2000, 1983, Strategic Responses to Conflict in the 1980's, 1984, Nordic Defense: Comparative Decisionmaking, 1985, Strategic Dimensions of Military Manpower, 1987, The Future of U.S.-Republic of Korea Security Ties, 1989, The Korean Peninsula: Prospects for Arms Control, 1990, Korea 1991: The Road to Peace, 1991, Elvis in The Army, 1995, 97. Mem. Presiding Bishop's Nat. Episc. Roundtable, 1983-86. Decorated Bronze Star with oak leaf cluster, Legion of Merit (2), Air Medal (3), Air medal for valor, Vietnam Cross of Gallantry, Combat Infantry Badge; recipient Pitman Potter Medal Am. U., 1964; named to Infantry Officer Hall of Fame, 1976; named Disting. Alumnus, Episcopal Acad., 1995, Disting. Alumnus, CSIS, 2001. Mem. St. Anthony Club. Republican. Episcopalian. Home: 6010 Maiden Ln Bethesda MD 20817-6261 Office Phone: 202-775-3203. E-mail: wjtaylor44@aol.com.

**TAYLOR, WILLIAM WOODRUFF, III,** lawyer; b. Richmond, Va., July 30, 1944; s. William Woodruff Jr. and Ida (Winstead) T.; m. Susan Broadhurst, Sept. 29, 1984; children: Katherine Lowell, Matthew Gordon. AB, U. N.C. 1966; LLB, Yale U. 1969. Bar: N.C. 1969, D.C. 1970, U.S. Ct. Appeals (2nd, 4th, 5th and 11th cirs.), U.S. Supreme Ct. Law clk. to judge U.S. Dist. Ct. Del., Wilmington, 1969-70; staff atty. Pub. Defender Service, Washington, 1970-75; assoc. Ginsburg, Feldman and Bress, Washington, 1975-78; ptnr. Zuckerman Spaeder LLP, Washington, 1978—. Instr. dept. forensic sci. George Washington U., Washington, 1973-74; adj. prof. Columbus Sch. Law, Cath. U. Am., Washington, 1973-76; mem. D.C. Commn. on Jud. Disabilities and Tenure, 1978-83, chmn., 1979-83; vis. prof. U. N.C. Law Sch., fall 1991. Named one of 75 Best Lawyers in Washington, Washingtonian survey amg., 2002. Fellow Am. Coll. Trial Lawyers; mem. ABA (criminal justice sect., vice chmn. for govtl. affairs 1989-92, chair criminal justice sect. 1996-97), Nat. Inst. for Trial Advocacy (faculty 1978—, chmn. pub. defender svc. assn. 1984-89), Jud. Conf. Adv. Com. on Rules of Evidence, Ctr. Death Penalty Litig., DC Com. on Jud. Disabilities and Tenure. Episcopalian. Avocations: fly fishing, tennis. Office: Zuckerman Spaeder LLP 1800 M St NW #1000 Washington DC 20036-5802 Office Phone: 202-778-1810. Business E-Mail: wwtaylor@zuckerman.com.

**TAYLOR, WILSON H.,** retired diversified financial company executive; Grad., Trinity Coll., With Conn. Gen., 1964—82; v.p. Aetna Ins. Co., 1975; exec. v.p., CFO Cigna Corp., Phila., 1982-88, pres. property casualty group, 1983-88, COO, 1988, pres., chief exec. officer, 1988—2000; ret., 2000. Phi Beta Kappa.

**TAYLOR-ANDERSON, JILL,** reading specialist; b. Oakland, Calif., Feb. 21, 1962; d. Allen Isaac and Phyllis Evelyn Taylor; 1 child, Christopher M. Anderson. BA in Liberal Studies, Calif. State Poly. U., 1984, MA in Edn., 1989. Reading specialist credential Calif. 6th grade tchr. Hacienda La Puente Unified Sch. Dist., Calif., 1984—88; kindergarten tchr. Riverside Unified Sch. Dist., Calif., 1988—95; reading specialist Corona-Norco Unified Sch. Dist., Norco, 1995—. Cub scout leader Boy Scouts Am., Grand Terrace, Calif., 1997—. Named Tchr. of Yr., Riverview Elem. Sch., 2003—04; recipient Celebrate Reading award, Inland Empire Reading Assn., 1997—2001, Founders' Day award, Riverview Elem. PTA, 2003. Mem.: Calif. Reading Assn., Internat. Reading Assn. Republican. Avocations: quilting, reading.

**TAYLOR CLAUD, ANDREA,** retired educational consultant; b. Warrenton, Va., Nov. 5, 1952; d. Andrew Earl and Catherine (Dennis) Taylor. BS, Norfolk State U., 1974, MA, 1983; postgrad., Old Dominion U., 1975-76, 89; MA in Cmty. Counseling, Regent U., 2000. Profl. collegiate cert. in learning disabilities, mentally handicapped, emotionally handicapped and technology stds. Classrm. tchr. Facquier County Sch. System, Warrenton, Va., 1974-75; child devel. specialist, team leader Norfolk Pub. Schs., Norfolk, Va., 1976-82, ednl. diagnostician, 1982-87; ednl. cons. Va. State Dept. Edn., Norfolk, 1987—2004; v.p. A Taylor of Hope, Inc., 2004—; pres. Perfect Storm, L.L.C., 2004—. V.p. DECAA Enterprises, Norfolk, 1983—. Active Nat. Kidney Found. of Va., Hampton Rds., Lindenwood Civic League, Norfolk; coord. bereavement ministry Pleasant Grove Bapt. Ch., Va. Beach, 2003, coun. mem., 2004; troop leader Girl Scouts U.S.A., Norfolk, 1977-79. Named Outstanding Young Women of Am., 1983; recipient Apple for Tchr. award, Iota Soroity, Inc., 1997, Outstanding Renal Healthcare Profl. Yr. award, Nat. Kidney Found. of Va., 1998, Sch. Bell award, Norfolk Pub. Sch., 2003. Mem. AARP, ACA, NEA, NAFE, Va. Edn. Assn., Norfolk Edn. Assn., Coun. Exceptional Children, Assn. Supervision and Curriculum Devel., Nat. Counseling Assn., Commonwealth Va. Notary, Delta Sigma Theta. Democrat. Avocations: travel, reading, listening to music, fishing.

**TAYLOR-HINES, REGINA ANITA,** civilian military employee; life ptnr. Daryl Lee Hines, May 17, 1989. MPA, Troy State U., Norfolk, Va., 1991—94. Cert. contracting officer rep. US Govt., 2001, general court mediator Va. Supreme Ct., 2004, juvenile dist. court mediator Va. Supreme Ct., 2005. Supply officer, contracting officer, techncial rep. NSF Diego Garcia, US Govt., England, 2001—02; contracting officer/bus. improvement officer Norfolk Naval Shipyard, Portsmouth, 2002—. V.p. Women's Veterans Svcs. Inc., Richmond, 2002—03. Vol. Girl Scouts Am., Inc., Driver, Va., 2004—06; vol. gen. & JD ct. mediator Cmty. Mediation Ctr., Norfolk, 2004—06. Lt. comdr. USN, 2002—06, Portsmouth. Decorated Def. Meritous Svc. award Def. Fin. & Acctg. Svc. Mem.: Nat. Orgn. Human Svcs. (assoc.). Independent. Protestant. Achievements include instituting the use of highly technical temporary labor for public shipyards. Avocations: furniture repair, gardening, travel. Home: 816 Shell Rd Chesapeake VA 23323-4105 Personal E-mail: rathines@cox.net.

**TAYLOR-WHITE-GRIGSBY, QUEEN DELORES,** minister, consultant; b. Oklahoma City, Aug. 21, 1948; d. Barnett C., Sr. and M. Bedell Boles Dewitt Taylor; m. Walter Thomas White II, Nov. 26, 1966 (div. June 1976); children: Walter Thomas III, Orlando Robin Orlando; m. James O. Grigsby, Sept. 19, 1976 (dec. Dec. 1976); 1 child, James Jumaané. BS, Howard U., 1970; M in Counseling, Liberty U., 1986. RN J. Sargent Reynolds U.; ordained to ministry Ray Deliverance Found., 1989. Housing cons. Montgomery County, Rockville, Md., 1971—73; founder, pres. Taylor & Co., Phoenix, Richmond, Va., Atlanta, and others, 1973—; assoc. cons. Trust Inc., Richmond, Va., 1973—80, Orgnl. Devel. Cons., Richmond, 1979—81; founder, pastor Tangible Substance God Is Love Ch., 1985—; founder, min. Man Child Ministries, Phoenix, 1988—. Cons. CETA, 1976, MARTA Atlanta, 1978-79, Frederick County, Md., 1973, Richmond Pub. Sch. System, 1977, Black Police Officers, Tulsa, 1986. Author: numerous poems. Advocate child and adult welfare Dept. of Corrections, Commonwealth of Va., 1974-76, Phoenix, 1990, advocate tchr. rights, 1991; active tchr. rights Phoenix Pub. Sch. System, 1992; supr. elections County Election Bd., Maricopa County, Ariz., 1987; trainer, developer internat. transactional analysis counseling model for abused women and their families in YWCA residential housing programs, 1992; coord. Y-Splash program Maricopa YWCA, Glendale Recreation Dept., 1992; active food programs and ministry Internat. Healing Cathedral/Hall of Deliverance Found. and Desert Moon Mission, 1985-; active children and youth program Phoenix Women's League, 1991-92; cons. Glendale Recreation Dept., 1997—; active Las Guias Heard Mus. Guild, 1990-93; docent Okla. Zoo., 2004—; vol. VA, 2004—, Column Writers, 2005. Lucille McMahn scholar, 1965, Nellie Green scholar, 1965, Philip Morris scholar, 1983; recipient Danforth Leadership award, 1965, Golden Poet award, 1991; named Internat. Woman of Yr., 2000-04. Mem. Soc. Tng. and Devel. (cert. housing specialist), Housing Specialist Inst. Independent Republican. Avocations: reading, swimming, hunting, fishing, camping. Office: Taylor & Co 1138 N Bath Ave Oklahoma City OK 73117-2602 Personal E-mail: taylorwhitegrigsby@webtv.net.

**TAYMOR, BETTY,** political science professor; b. Balt., Md., Mar. 22, 1921; d. William and Tillie (Blum) Bernstein; m. Melvin Lester Taymor, June 7, 1942; children: Michael, Laurie, Julie. AB, Goucher Coll., Towson, Md., 1942; MA in Am. Govt., Boston U., 1967; LHD (hon.), Goucher Coll., Towson, Md., 2001. Dir. program for women in politics and govt. Boston Coll., 1970-92; instr. in govt. Northeastern U., Boston, 1969-71; cons. office of pres. U. Mass., Boston, 1973-74; instr. MA in Urban Affairs program Boston U., 1967-68; instr. in politics & govt. McCormack Inst., Boston, 1973-92; coord. Boston Network for Women in Politics & Govt. U. Mass.-Boston 1992-94; dir. spl. projects Ctr. for Women in Politics & Pub. Policy U. Mass.-Boston, 1992—. Author: Running Against the Wind: The Struggle of Women in Massachusetts Politics, 2000. Mem. US nat. commn. UNESCO, 1966; mem. New Eng. Bd. Higher Edn., 1985—89; mem. adv. com. John F. Kennedy Libr.; state committeewoman Dem. State Com., Boston, 1956—92, nat. committeewoman Washington, 1976—96; bd. dirs. Univ. Hosp., Boston, 1989—91. Elizabeth King Ellicott fellow Goucher Coll., 1959-60; recipient Abigail Adams award Mass. Women's Polit. Caucus, 1989. Avocations: tennis, reading, theater. Home: 975 Memorial Dr Apt 601A Cambridge MA 02138-5803

**TAYMOR, JULIE,** theater, film and opera director and designer; b. Newton, Mass., 1952; d. Melvin L. and Betty Taymor. BA in folklore and mythology, Oberlin Coll., 1974; attended, L'Ecole Mimet Theatre in Paris, France, Herbert Berghof Studio, N.Y.C. Founder Teatr Loh. Dir. Way of Snow, The Transposed Heads, 1984, The Tempest, 1986, Liberty's Taken, 1985, Juan Darién, 1988, Fool's Fire, 1992, Titus Andronicus, 1994, Oedipus Rex, 1992, The Magic Flute, Salomé, The Flying Dutchman, The Lion King, 1997. (Tony awards for best director and costume design 1998), operas, classical plays and exptl. theater projects; prodr. Shakespeare plays and operas; designer puppets, masks, imaginative costumes and other visual elements. MacArthur grantee, Watson fellow, 1974-79, Obie awards, 1988.

**TAZELAAR, HENRY DALE,** physician, educator; s. Henry and Evelyn Teresa Tazelaar; m. Peggy Jean Ritsema, June 6, 1978; children: Andrew, Jeffrey. BA, Calvin Coll, Grand Rapids, Mich., 1978; MD, Rush U., Chgo., 1983. Bd. cert. in anatomic pathology Am. Bd. Pathology. Intern Stanford U. Med. Sch., Calif., 1983—84, resident, 1984—85, fellow, NIH, 1985—86, fellow, 1986—87, instr., 1987—88; asst. to full prof. Mayo Clinic Coll. Medicine, Rochester, Minn., 1988—, cons., 1988—. Vice chair edn. dept. Lab. Medicine and Pathology, 2002—05; mem. edn. com. US and Can. Acad. Pathology, Augusta, Ga., 2003—; chair anatomic pathology divsn. Mayo Clinic, Ariz., 2006—. Author: Pathology and Genetics of Tumors in the Lung, Pleura, Thymus and Heart, 2004; author, editor Lung Pathology, 2005. Bd. mem. Ransom Fellowship, Rochester, 1990—. Fellow: Am. Coll. Chest Physicians, Coll. Am. Pathologists; mem.: Pulmonary Pathology Soc. (pres. 2004—). Presbyterian. Avocations: hiking, scuba diving, backpacking, classical organ performance, choral arts. Office: Mayo Clinic 13400 E Shea Blvd Scottsdale AZ 85259

**TCHAIKOVSKY, LESLIE J.,** federal judge; b. 1943; BA, Calif. State Univ., Hayward, 1967; JD, Univ. of Calif., Berkeley, 1976. Law clk. to Hon. John Mowbray Nev. Supreme Ct., 1976-77; with Dinkelspiel, Steefel, Leavitt & Weiss, 1977-80, Gordon, Peitzman & Lopes, 1981, Dinkelspiel, Donovan & Reder, 1981-88; bankruptcy judge U.S. Bankruptcy Ct. (Calif. no. dist.), 9th circuit, Oakland, 1988—. Office: US Courthouse 1300 Clay St Oakland CA 94612-1425

**TCHAMENGO, MATHIAS NGOUFI,** energy executive, mathematician; b. Douala, Cameroon, Jan. 1, 1971; s. Joseph Ndjoumngwe and Marthe Kamkwe; m. Nicole Martin, Sept. 23, 1995; 1 child, Landry Ngoufi. Ingenieur Civil des Mines, Ecole des Mines de St-Etienne, France, 1994; PhD in Math., U. Bourgogne, Dijon, France, 1998. Quantitative analyst Dresdner Kleinwort Benson, Paris, 1995—97, Schroders Structured Products, London, 1997—98; sr. quantitative analyst Koch Energy Trading, Houston, 1998—2000, Shell Trading, Houston, 2000—. Mem.: Bachelier Fin. Soc., Internat. Assn. Fin. Engrs., Soc. for Indsl. and Applied Math. Achievements include research in Static strategies in finance: Provide means to reduce the risk induced by a liability through discrete transactions on other financial vehicle; patents pending for Means to describe prices of future contracts on seasonal commodities: electricity, natural gas, cocoa. Home: 2226 Blue Rose Dr Missouri City TX 77459 Personal E-mail: mtchamengo@yahoo.com. E-mail: mtchamengo@equiva.com.

**TCHERNEV, VELIZAR TZVETANOV,** physician, research scientist; b. Sofia, Bulgaria, Oct. 29, 1969; arrived in US, 1994; s. Lilia Zaharieva Jeleva and Tzvetan Vasilev Tchernev; m. Ralitza Vladislavova Gueorguieva; children: Alexander Velizar, Liliana Velizar. Cert. in tropical medicine, Higher Med. Inst., Sofia, Bulgaria, 1992, MD, 1993; cert. in biotechnology, U. Fla., 1994, PhD, 1998. Rsch. asst. dept. pathology, immunology and lab. medicine U. Fla., Gainesville, 1994—98; rsch. scientist discovery dept. CuraGen Corp., Alachua Fla. and Branford, Conn., 1998—2001; rsch. scientist Molecular Staging Inc., New Haven, 2001—03, sr. rsch. scientist, 2003—04; dir. clin. rsch. Genomas Inc., Hartford, Conn., 2005—. Contbr. articles to profl. jours. Recipient award, Am. Fedn. for Clin. Rsch., 1996; Scholarship, Internat. Mammalian Genome Soc., 1998, Fellowship for Excellent Academic Performance, Higher Med. Inst. Sofia, Bulgaria, 1988—93. Mem.: AAAS. Achievements include diplomas for translations of med. lit. to Eng. lang. and German lang; more than 50 patents pending in field. Home: 45 Jefferson Rd #3-12 Branford CT 06405 Personal E-mail: vtchernev@hotmail.com.

**TCHOUMAK, ADELINA,** corporate financial executive; b. Chishinau, Moldavia, Feb. 16, 1974; arrived in U.S., 1990; d. Mercuriu and Olga Ciumac. BBA in Econs. summa cum laude, U. Anchorage, 1996. Performance analyst Clay Finlay Inc., NYC, 1996—2000; asst. v.p. Oppenheimer Capital, 2000—02; sr. performance analyst Citigroup N.A., 2002—. Sponsor Children Internat., Honduras, 2002—. Atheist. Avocations: reading, yoga. Home: 223 Dean St #2 Brooklyn NY 11217 Office: Citigroup NA 111 Wall St 14th Fl New York NY 10005 Office Phone: 212-657-7924. Personal E-mail: tadelina@hotmail.com.

**TCHOUNWOU, PAUL BERNARD,** environmental health specialist, toxicologist, educator; b. Bangou, Cameroon, Aug. 14, 1960; came to U.S., 1985; s. Maurice and Christine (Kouanang) Seumo; m. Martha Namondo Mondoa, Aug. 3, 1990; children: Christine K., Hervey M., Solange S. BSc, U. Yaounde, Cameroon, 1983, MSc, 1984; MS in Pub. Health, Tulane U., 1986, ScD, 1990. Cert. toxicologist Nat. Environ. Health Assn.; registered sanitarian La. State Bd. Examiners for Sanitarians. Tchg. asst. Tulane Sch. Pub. Health, New Orleans, 1988—90; med. rschr. Inst. Med. Rsch., Yaounde, 1991—94; asst. prof. Faculty Medicine, Yaounde, 1992—94; rsch. assoc. Xavier and Tulane Univs., New Orleans, 1994—96; assoc. prof., dir. environ. sci. PhD program Jackson State U., 1996—; adj. assoc. prof. sch. pub. health Tulane U., 1999—2005; prof., dir. environ. sci. doctoral program Jackson State U., 2001—, dep. dir. Ctr. for Environ. Health, 2003—, chair dept. biology, 2004—. Adj. prof. Tulane U. Sch. Pub. Health, 2005—; environ. health cons. Orstom & UNICEF, Yaounde, 1992-93, U.S. AID, Kaele, 1991-93; rsch. supr. Tulane Sch. Pub. Health, New Orleans, 1994—; tng. and rsch. fellow U.S. AID, Washington, 1985-90; adj. assoc. prof. environ. health scis. Tulane U. Sch. Pub. Health and Tropical Medicine, 1999—. Editor-in-chief: Internat. Jour. of Environ. Rsch. and Pub. Health, 2003—, mem. editl. bd.: Internat. Jour. Environ. Toxicology and Water Quality, 1994—, guest editor: Internat. Jour. Molecular Scis., 2002—, regional editor: USA-Environ. Toxicology, 2002—, mem. overseas editl. bd.: Jour. Environ. Biology, 2002—; contbr. articles to profl. jours.; editor-in-chief: Environmental Toxicology, 2006—, mem. editl. bd.: Revs. on Environ. Health, 2003—. Grantee, Internat. Devel. Rsch. Ctr., 1992—93, Nat. Aeronautics and Space Adminstrn., 1977—99, NIH, 1998—, Nat. Oceanic and Atmospheric Adminstrn., 2001—, Dept. Army, 2002—03. Mem. APHA, AAUP, AAAS, Am. Cancer Rsch., Water Environ. Fedn., Cameroon Bioscis. Soc., Cameroon Assn. Epidemiology, Nat. Environ. Health Assn., N.Y. Acad. Scis., Miss. Acad. Sci., Soc. Environ. Toxicology and Chemistry, Soc. Toxicology, Delta Omega. Roman Catholic. Avocations: travel, playing tennis, watching tv sport programs. Home: 230 Clark Farms Rd Madison MS 39110-8112 Office: Jackson State U Sch Sci & Tech PO Box 18540 Jackson MS 39217

**TEACHOUT, TERRY,** writer, critic; b. Cape Girardeau, Mo., Feb. 6, 1956; s. H.H. and Evelyn (Crosno) Teachout. BS in Music and Journalism, William Jewell Coll., 1979. Sr. editor Harper's Mag., N.Y.C., 1985-87; editl. writer Daily News, N.Y.C., 1987-93, classical music and dance critic, 1993-2000; music critic Commentary Mag., N.Y.C., 1995—; contbr. Time Mag., N.Y.C., 1998—2001; arts columnist Washington Post, 1999—2005; drama critic Wall St. Jour., 2003—. Mem. Nat. Coun. on the Arts Nat. Endowment for the Arts, 2005—. Author: City Limits, 1991, The Skeptic: A Life of H.L. Mencken, 2002, A Terry Teachout Reader, 2003, All in the Dances: A Brief Life of George Balanchine, 2004; editor: Ghosts on the Roof: Selected Journalism of Whittaker Chambers, 1989, Beyond the Boom, 1990, A Second Mencken Chrestomathy, 1995. Office: 68 W 82nd St New York NY 10024-4660 E-mail: terryteachout@earthlink.net.*

**TEAGAN, JOHN GERARD,** publishing executive; b. Detroit, Sept. 23, 1947; s. Stanley John and Margaret Suzanne (Sullivan) T.; m. Carla Kay Eurich, Sept. 13, 1975; 1 child, Elizabeth Margaret. BBA, U. Notre Dame, 1969. CPA Mich. Audit supr. Ernst & Whinney (C.P.A.s), Detroit, 1969-73; acctg. mgr. Detroit Free Press, 1973-77, treas., controller, 1977-83, v.p. fin., treas. 1983-89, v.p., bus. mgr. 1989—2005; CFO Duluth News Tribune, 2005—. Adv. bd. Providence Hosp., Southfield, Mich., 1984-93, sec., 1989, vice chmn. 1990, chmn., 1991; trustee Grosse Pointe (Mich.) Acad., 1990-96, Children's Home Detroit, Grosse Pointe, 1997-2005; bd. dirs., treas. Free Press Charities, Inc.; bd. dirs. Providence Hosp. and Med. Ctrs., Southfield, 1998-2005; Metro Detroit bd. dirs. Am. Heart Assn., 1999-2005, chair, 2004-05; bd. dirs. Holy Cross Children's Svcs., 2001-05; mem. adv. bd. Knight Found., 2002-05. Mem. AICPA, Internat. Newspaper Fin. Execs., Mich. Assn. CPAs, Grosse Pointe Yacht Club. Roman Catholic. Business E-Mail: jteagan@duluthnews.com

**TEAGLE, DAVID BRYAN,** manufacturing executive; b. Abilene, Tex., Nov. 18, 1956; s. Ollie Bryan Teagle and Carolyn Ann Dorr; m. Colinda Jean Torrez, Sept. 17, 1999; 1 child from previous marriage, Kezia Anne. BBA, Abilene Christian U., 1979, MBA, 1980. With energy svcs. divsn. NCR Corp., 1980—81; landman ARCO Exploration/ARCO Oil, 1981—84; with Burroughs Sys., 1985—86, Continental Airlines, 1986—92; actor, 1992—2002; pres. Am. Ventilation Equipment Co., 2002—03; freelance photographer Cowboy mag., 1992—2002, Tex. State Troopers Assn. mag., Denver Post. Author: Fallen Angels of Sans Espair, 1997; photography represented in permanent collections William J. Clinton Presdl. Libr., Rock and Roll Hall of Fame Mus., Hist. Mus. So. Fla., Miami. Finalist Ernest Hemingway 1st Book award. Mem.: World Affairs Coun., Zuma Press, Bldg. Engineers Assn., Nat.

Def. Industry Assn., Nat. Press Photographer Assn. Achievements include patents for Enviroblower, emergency portable ventilation and capture equipment for chemical and biological containment. E-mail: enviroblower@earthlink.net.

**TEAGUE, BERNICE RITA,** accountant; b. Lowell, Mass., Nov. 1, 1957; d. Francis Joseph and Agnes Lena (Laferriere) T. Grad. h.s., Lowell, Mass. Student aide Hanscom AFB, Bedford, Mass., 1974; sec. asst. Family Svcs. of Greater Lowell, 1975—; asst. bookkeeper, 1976-86, bookkeeper, 1986, asst. bus. mgr., 1987-88, prin. acct., 1988-89; bus. mgr., 1989-99; acctg. clk., billing rep. Med Life Pharmacy, N. Billerica, Mass., 2000—01. Democrat. Roman Catholic. Avocations: embroidery, crafts, reading, fishing, gardening. Home: 163 A St Lowell MA 01851-4117

**TEAGUE, CHARLES PORTER,** academic administrator; b. Swannanoa, NC, May 6, 1945; s. Harry Walton and Bernie Elizabeth Teague; m. Daune Ward Teague, June 1, 1968; 1 child, Julie Renee. AA, Brevard Coll., 1966; BA, High Point Coll., 1968; MDiv, Emory U., 1971, D of Ministry, 1979. Ordained elder We. NC Ann. Conf. of United Meth. ch. Min. Avery's Creek United Meth. Ch., Arden, NC, 1971—72; chaplain, assoc. prof. religion dept. High Point U., High Point NC, 1972—84; sr. v.p. and coll. dean Brevard Coll., NC, 1984—97; pres. Spartanburg Meth. Coll., SC, 1997—. Avocations: golf, fishing, woodcarving. Office: Spartanburg Meth Coll 1000 Powell Mill Rd Spartanburg SC 29301

**TEAGUE, CHARLES WOODROW,** lawyer; b. Thomasville, N.C., May 27, 1913; s. Lonnie Edwards and Dora Mae (Lassiter) T.; m. Jessie Randle Perry (div. 1976); m. Julia Brent Byrum, July 25, 1980; children: Kathy Randle Teague Jennings, Penny Randle Teague Eubanks, Charles W. Teague Jr. LLB, Wake Forest U., Winston-Salem, N.C., 1934. Bar: N.C. 1934, U.S. dist. Ct. (ea. and mid. dists.) N.C., U.S. Ct. Appeals (4th cir.), U.S. Supreme Ct. Claims atty. Liberty Mut. Ins. Co., Boston, 1934-35, High Point, N.C., 1936-38, Lumber Mut. Casualty Ins. Co., Raleigh, N.C., 1938-42; ptnr. Teague, Campbell, Dennis & Gorham, Raleigh, 1946—. Sec. N.C. R.R., Raleigh, 1960-64. Chmn. bd. elections Wake County, Raleigh, 1960-64. Lt. comdr. USN, 1942-46, PTO. Mem. N.C. Bar Assn. (chmn., bd. govs. 1960-64, councilor 1968-76, pres. 1977-78)), ABA (del. 1980-85), Carolina Country Club, Country Club of N.C., Elk River Club, Kiwanis. Democrat. Presbyterian. Avocation: golf. Office: Teague Campbell Dennis & Gorham 4800 Six Forks Rd Raleigh NC 27619-9207 Office Phone: 919-873-0166.

**TEAGUE, LAVETTE COX, JR.,** systems educator, consultant; b. Birmingham, Ala., Oct. 8, 1934; s. Lavette Cox and Caroline Green (Stokes) T. Student, Auburn U., 1951-54; BArch, MIT, 1957, MSCE, 1965, PhD, 1968; MDiv with distinction, Ch. Div. Sch. Pacific, 1979. Cert. computer profl. Inst. Cert. Computer Profls. Archtl. designer Carroll C. Harmon, Birmingham, 1957, Fred Renneker, Jr., Birmingham, 1958-59; architect Rust Engring. Co., Birmingham, 1959-62, Synergetics, Inc., Raleigh, N.C. 1962-64, Rust Engring. Co., Birmingham, 1964-68; rsch. asst., instr., rsch. assoc. MIT, Cambridge, 1964-68; dir. computer svcs. Skidmore Owings & Merrill, San Francisco, Chgo., 1968-74; postdoctoral fellow UCLA, 1972; adj. assoc. prof. arch. and civil engring. Carnegie-Mellon U., Pitts., 1973-74; archtl. systems cons. Chgo., 1974-75, Berkeley, Calif., 1975-80, Pasadena, 1980-82, Altadena, Calif., 1982—. Lectr. info. systems Calif. State Poly. U., Pomona, 1980-81, prof., 1981-98, prof. emeritus, 1998—, asst. chair, 1990-91, chair, 1991-93, 96-98; Fulbright lectr., Uruguay, 1985; lectr. Peking U., 2004. Author: Event-Based Analysis and Design: An Introduction to Structured Methods, 2000; co-author: Structured Analysis Methods for Computer Information Systems, 1985, Object-Oriented Systems Analysis and Design with UML, 2005, Chinese edit., 2005. Mem. adv. bd. Ch. Div. Sch. of the Pacific. Recipient Tucker-Voss award MIT, 1967; Fulbright scholar, 1985. Mem. AIA (Arnold W. Brunner scholar 1966), Assn. Computing Machinery, Sigma Xi, Phi Eta Sigma, Scarab, Scabbard and Blade, Tau Beta Pi, Chi Epsilon, Beta Gamma Sigma. Episcopalian. Home: 1696 N Altadena Dr Altadena CA 91001-3623 Office: 3801 W Temple Ave Pomona CA 91768-2557 Business E-mail: lcteague@csupomona.edu.

**TEAGUE, RANDAL CORNELL, SR.,** lawyer; b. Durham, N.C., May 19, 1944; s. Roy M. Sr. and Lottie (Rhew) T.; children: R. Cornell, R. Townsend, Mary Robb Durham, James K.B. BA, Am. U., 1967; JD, George Washington U., 1971, LLM with highest honors, 1972; LLD (hon.), Allen U., 1973. Bar: Fla. 1972, D.C. 1972, U.S. Dist. Ct. D.C. 1972, U.S. Tax Ct. 1972, U.S. Ct. Mil. Appeals 1972, U.S. Ct. Appeals (D.C. and fed. cirs.) 1972, U.S. Ct. Appeals (5th cir.) 1973, U.S. Supreme Ct. 1975. Mass. 1979, U.S. Ct. Appeals (1st cir.) 1979, U.S. Dist. Ct. Mass. 1979, U.S. Ct. Internat. Trade. Coord. policy devel. Exec. Office of Pre. of U.S., Washington, 1971-73; chief of staff, legis. counsel to Rep. Jack F. Kemp Ho. of Reps., Washington, 1973-79; div. counsel Cabot Corp., 1979-81; counsel Vorys, Sater, Seymour & Pease LLP, Washington, 1981-83, ptnr., 1984—. Pres. Internat. Exch. Coun., 1984—; trustee Fund Am. Studies, Washington, 1976—, chmn. 1998—; trustee, dir. Air Force Acad. Found., Colorado Springs, Colo., 1983—; mem. adv. com. voluntary aid U.S. AID, 1987-91; trustee Earth U., Costa Rica, 1987—; councillor Atlantic Coun. of U.S., 1990—; co-founder Am. Inst. on Polit. and Econ. Sys., Charles U., Prague, 1993—; founder Internat. Inst. Polit. and Econ. Studies, Athens, Greece, 1996—; dir. Salzburg Seminar, 1997—. Named one of Outstanding Young Men Am., 1973; recipient George Washington medal Freedoms Found., 1978. Mem. Fla. Bar Assn., Mass. Bar Assn., D.C. Bar Assn., Univ. Club (Washington). Republican. Episcopalian. Office: Vorys Sater Seymour & Pease LLP 1828 L St NW Fl 11 Washington DC 20036-5109 Office Phone: 202-467-8817. Business E-mail: rcteague@vssp.com.

**TEAGUE, ROBERT COLE,** physician; b. Waxahachie, Tex., June 13, 1930; s. Isaac Lawson and Frances (Cole) Teague; m. Virginia M. Teague, Nov. 11, 1960 (dec. May 1, 2005); children: Patrick, Michael. BA in Chemistry, Baylor U., Waco, Tex., 1951; MD, U. Tex., Galveston, 1955. Lic. physician Ariz. Intern McLaren Hosp., Flint, Mich., 1955—56; med. officer, active duty USNR, 1956—58; physician family practice LaJolla, Calif., 1958—63, Phoenix, 1963—. Med. dir., pres. Vis. Nurse Svc., Phoenix; chmn. Family Practice Humana Hosp., 1984—86, past chmn.; chmn. Family Practice Good Samaritan Hosp., 1990—91. Fellow Am. Acad. Family Physicians (charter); mem. Ariz. Acad. Family Physicians (pres. 1988). Republican. Episcopalian. Avocations: golf, travel. Office: 5501 N 19th Ave Ste 106 Phoenix AZ 85015-2451

**TEAL, ARABELLA W.,** lawyer, former state attorney general; b. NYC, Jan. 1961; m. Gary Teal; 2 children. BA, Harvard Coll., 1984; JD, Georgetown U. Law Ctr., 1987. Law clerk for sr. judges D.C. Superior Court, 1987—88; section chief General Litigation Section I, 1996—99; acting prin. dep. corp. counsel D.C., 1999—2000, prin. dep. corp. counsel, 2000—02, interim corp. counsel, 2002—03; atty. McCabe & Mack LLP, Poughkeepsie, 2003—. Office: McCabe & Mack LLP 63 Washington St PO Box 509 Poughkeepsie NY 12602-0509

**TEAL, GILBERT EARLE, II,** lawyer, coast guard officer; b. Lafayette, Ind., May 1, 1959; s. Gilbert Earle and Evangeline Maxine (Piper) T.; m. Mary Anne Liwoch, Oct. 3, 1987. AS, Western Conn. State U., 1979; BS, USCG Acad., 1983; MPA, George Mason U., 1988; JD, Coll. William and Mary, 1991. Bar: Va. 1991, U.S. Mil. Ct. Appeals 1991, U.S. Ct. Appeals (4th cir.) 1991, D.C. 1992, U.S. Ct. Claims 1992, U.S. Ct. Appeals (fed. cir.) 1992, U.S. Tax Ct. 1998, Alaska 1998, U.S. Dist. Ct. Alaska 1998, U.S. Ct. Appeals (9th cir.) 1998, U.S. Supreme Ct. 1998; designated mil. judge, 2001; appellate judge Coast Guard Ct. Criminal Appeals, 2004. Commd. ensign USCG, 1983, advanced through grades to capt., 2004; assigned to USCG Cutter Vigorous (WMEC 627), New London, Conn., 1983-85; intelligence officer COMDT (G-OIS-3) Hdqrs. USCG, Washington, 1985-88; law clk. to chief trial judge Capt. Thomas Snook, USCG, N.Y.C., 1989; law clk. USCG RTC Yorktown, 1990; staff atty. Maintenance and Logistics Command Atlantic, Governors Island, N.Y., 1991-94; legal officer USCG Support Ctr., Kodiak, Alaska,

1994-97; br. legal officer 17th Coast Guard Dist., spl. asst. U.S. Atty., Dist. of Alaska, Anchorage, 1997—2001; dep. judge adv. Maintenance and Logistics Command Atlantic, Norfolk, Va., 2001—04; chief legal policy and program devel., spl. asst. judge adv. gen. USCG Hdqrs., Washington, 2004—. Recipient Dirs. award for outstanding performance as spl. asst. U.S. atty. Dept. Justice, Exec. Office for U.S. Attys., 1998, Lawrence R. Schneider award U.S. Dept. Transp., 1999, Cert. of Commendation, Dept. of Justice Environ. Natural Resources Divsn., 2000. Mem. ABA, FBA, Va. State Bar, Va. Bar Assn., D.C. Bar, AK Bar Assn., Jud. Advs. Assn. (life), U.S. Naval Inst. (life), Nat. Eagle Scout Assn. (life), Army and Navy Club (Washington), Army-Navy Country Club (Arlington, Va.), Trout Unltd. (life), Coastal Conservation Assn. (life), Fedn. Fly Fishers (life), Masons, Shriners, Phi Delta Phi (life), Phi Delta Kappa. Avocations: fishing, dog sport. Office: COMDT G-LPD 2100 2nd St SW Washington DC 20593 Home: 3104 London Company Way Williamsburg VA 23185-7928 Business E-Mail: gteal@comdt.uscg.mil.

**TEAMER, CHARLES CARL, SR.,** former fraternal organization administrator; b. Shelby, NC, May 20, 1933; s. Boyd and Mary (Wilkins) Teamer; m. Mary Alice Dixon, Aug. 3, 1957; children: Charles Carl, Roderic F., Cheryl R. BA, Clark Coll., 1952; postgrad., U. Omaha, 1962—63, Tulane U., 1965—66. Acct. SC State Coll., Orangeburg, 1955—56; asst. bus. mgr. Tenn. State U., Nashville, 1958—62; bus. mgr. Wiley Coll., Marshall, Tex., 1962—65; v.p. fiscal affairs Dillard U., New Orleans, 1965; pres. World Trade Ctr., New Orleans, 2004—. Dir. New Orleans Public Service Co.; bd. dirs. Common Fund, Ochner Med. Found., Children's Hosp., Greater New Orleans Regional Found.; past pres. United Way, New Orleans; commr. Port of New Orleans. With U.S. Army, 1956—58. Named one of Most Influential Black Americans, Ebony mag., 2006; recipient Silver Beaver award, Boy Scouts Am., 1968, 10 Outstanding Citizens of New Orleans, 1979. Mem.: Am. Assn. Blacks in Energy, So. Assn. Coll. and Univ. Bus. Officers, Nat. Assn. Coll. and Univ. Bus. Officers, C. of C. New Orleans, Shriners, Masons, Sigma Pi Phi (Grand Sire Archon 2004—06, Immediate Past Grand Sire Archon 2006—), Alpha Phi Alpha (life). Office: WTC Exec Offices 2 Canal St, Ste 2900 New Orleans LA 70130*

**TEARE, RICHARD WALLACE,** retired foreign service officer; b. Cleve., Feb. 21, 1937; m. Jeanie Walter; 3 children. BA, Harvard U., 1958; diploma, Nat. War Coll., 1978. Joined Fgn. Svc., 1959; vice consul U.S. Consulate, Bridgetown, Barbados, 1960-62; consular officer U.S. Embassy, Manila, 1962-64, polit. officer Saigon, Vietnam, 1965-67, Mexico City, 1971-74, counselor for polit. affairs Vientiane, Laos, 1974-76, dep. chief mission Wellington, New Zealand, 1983-86, Canberra, Australia, 1986-89; dep. and acting prin. officer U.S. Consulate Gen., Nha Trang, Vietnam, 1973; intelligence and rsch. specialist Dept. State, 1967-69, desk officer Vietnam Working Group, 1969-71, spl. asst. to asst. sec. for East Asian and Pacific Affairs, 1976-77, dep. dir. Office Philippine Affairs, 1978-80, dep. and acting U.S. rep. for Micronesian Status Negotiations, 1980-83, dir. Office of Indonesia, Malaysia, Brunei and Singapore Affairs, 1989-92, spl. projects officer Office of Dir. Gen., 1992-93, U.S. amb. to Papua New Guinea, Solomon Islands and Vanuatu, 1993-96; fgn. policy advisor to the Commander in Chief U.S. Pacific Command, Camp Smith, Hawaii, 1996-98; dir. Ctr. Australian and New Zealand studies Sch. Fgn. Svc., Georgetown U., 1998—2004, sr. fellow, 2004—. Mem.: Australian and New Zealand Studies Assn. N.Am. (past pres.), U.S.-New Zealand Coun. (bd. dirs.), Am. Fgn. Svc. Assn., Historic Chevy Chase DC. Address: 3111 Oliver St NW Washington DC 20015-1654

**TEAS, RICHARD HARPER,** lawyer; b. Streator, Ill., Sept. 24, 1930; s. Bert H. and Audrey C. Teas; m. Janice K. Eikenmeyer, July 29, 1960 (dec.); children: Catherine L. Teas-Rogers, Amelia H. AB, U. Ill., 1957, LLB, 1960. Bar: Ill. 1960, U.S. Dist. Ct. (so. dist.) Ill. 1960. Probate administr. Continental Nat. Bank and Trust Co. of Chgo., 1960-66; ptnr. Tracy, Johnson, & Wilson Law Offices, Joliet, Ill., 1966—. Comdr. USNR, 1952-69. Mem. Ill. State Bar Assn. (trust and estates sect. coun., chair, 2002-03, standing com. on legislation, task force on unauthorized practice of law), Will County Bar Assn. (probate com.), Am. Coll. of Trust and Estate Counsel, Estate Planning Coun. of Greater Joliet (pres. 1976) Avocations: tennis, golf. Home: 20853 Rock Run Dr Joliet IL 60431-9323 Office: Tracy Johnson & Wilson 2801 Black Rd Fl 2 Joliet IL 60435 Office Phone: 815-723-8500.

**TEASDALE, KENNETH FULBRIGHT,** lawyer; b. St. Louis, Nov. 8, 1934; s. Kenneth and Ann (Fulbright) T.; m. Elizabeth Driscol Langdon, June 13, 1964; children: Caroline, Doug, Cindy. AB, Amherst Coll., 1956; LLB, Washington U., St. Louis, 1961. Bar: Mo. 1961. Atty. antitrust div. U.S. Dept. Justice, Washington, 1961-62; asst. counsel Dem. Policy Com. U.S. Senate, Washington, 1962-63, gen. counsel Dem. Policy Com., asst. to majority leader, 1963-64; assoc. Armstrong, Teasdale, Kramer & Vaughan, St. Louis, 1964-67, ptnr., 1967-86; mng. ptnr. Armstrong, Teasdale, Schlafly & Davis, St. Louis, 1986-93, chmn. of firm, 1993—. Trustee United Way Greater St. Louis, Sci. Ctr. St. Louis, St. Louis Art Mus.; trustee, chmn. bd. regents St. Louis U.; mem. nat. coun. Washington U. Law Sch., 1988—. Mem. ABA, Bar Assn. Mo., Bar Assn. St. Louis, St. Louis Coalition for Plant and Life Scis., Racquet Club, Noonday Club, Old Warson Country Club. Episcopalian. Office: Armstrong Teasdale LLP Ste 2600 One Metropolitan Sq Saint Louis MO 63102-2733 Office Phone: 314-621-5070.

**TEATER, DOROTHY SEATH,** retired county official; b. Manhattan, Kans., Feb. 11, 1931; d. Dwight Moody and Martha (Stahnke) Seath; m. Robert Woodson Teater, May 24, 1952; children: David Dwight, James Stanley, Donald Robert, Andrew Scott. BS, U. Ky., 1951; MS, Ohio State U., 1954. Home econs. tchr. Georgetown (Ky.) City Schs., 1951-53; extension specialist Ohio Coop. Extension, Columbus, 1967-73; consumer affairs administr. City of Columbus, 1974-79, Bank One Columbus NA, 1980-85; councilmember Columbus City Coun., 1980-85; commr. Franklin County, Columbus, Ohio, 1985-2000; ret. Mem. Columbus Met. Area Cmty. Action Orgn.; mem. adv. bd. Ohio Housing Trust; chairwoman Franklin County Children's Cabinet; pub. mem. Ohio Bd. Pharmacy, 2000—. Bd. dirs. BBB;; Silesian Boys and Girls Club, Rickenbacker-Woods Mus.; mem. hon. adv. bd. Girl Scouts. Recipient Outstanding Alumnus award U. Ky., 1989, Women of Achievement award YWCA, 1995, Disting. Svc. award Ohio State U., 1997; named Disting. Alumni, Ohio State U., 1977. Mem. County Commrs. Assn. Ohio (pres. 1994), Columbus Met. Club, Greater Columbus C. of C. (Columbus award 1997). Republican. Methodist. Avocations: gardening, sewing.

**TEBBETS, GARY DUANE,** music educator; b. Kansas Clty, Mo., Apr. 2, 1948; s. Gilbert Dean and Bernice Ruth (Belk) Tebbets; m. Anna Marie Feagins, May 29, 1999; m. Roxanne Cox (div.); 1 child, Gary Duane Jr. B of Music Edn., U. Mo., 1975, B of Piano Music, 1978, B of Vocal Music, 1980; MusM in Theory, Pittsburg State U., Kans., 1997. Tchr. Jayhawk-Linn High Sch., Mound City, Kans., 2001—03; prof. Allen County C.C., Iola, 2004—. Adj. instr. Ft. Scott C.C., Ft. Scott, Kans.; dir. music First Christian Ch., 1998—. Mem. Jackson County Rep. Com., Kansas City, 1978—84; candidate Mo. State Legis., 1980, 1982; founder, dir. Ft. Scott Cmty. Chorus, Kans., 1997—. Mem.: Am Choral Dirs. Assn., Music Educators Nat. Conf., Music Tchrs. Nat. Assn. Avocations: crossword puzzles, reading. Home: PO Box 128 Fort Scott KS 66701 Office: Allen County CC 1801 N Cottonwood Iola KS 66749 Office Phone: 620-365-5116 258. Personal E-mail: garann@Wcomputingplas.biz. E-mail: tebbets@allencc.edu.

**TEBBI, CAMERON K,** hematologist, oncologist; b. Hamadan, Iran, Oct. 9, 1943; s. Mehdi and Iren A. Tebbi; m. Judith H Dautch, Apr. 22, 1982; children: Michael Lewis, David Nathan. MD, U. Tehran, Iran, 1968. Lic. MD 1974. Med. dir., adolescent unit Roswell Pk. Meml. Inst., Buffalo, 1979—90; med. dir., pediatric hematology/oncology Tampa Children's Hosp., Fla., 1990—. Sci. rev. bd. Nat. Cancer Inst., Washington, 1998—. Fouder Children Cancer Rsch. Group, Tampa, 2004. Recipient Medal Of Honor In Medicine, U. Tehran, 1968. Mem.: Am. Soc. of Clin. Oncology. Jewish. Office: Tampa Children's Hosp 3001 W ML King Blvd Tampa FL 33607 Office Phone: 813-870-4252. Office Fax: 813-554-8167. E-mail: cameron.tebbi@baycare.org.

**TEBBS, CAROL ANN,** secondary school educator, academic administrator; b. Columbus, Ohio, Sept. 9, 1939; d. John Arthur and Ann Laurie (Wickham) Williams; m. Ronald Daniel Tebbs, Mar. 31, 1957; children: Kimberly Ann, Ronald Dan. BA in English, Whittier Coll., 1963, MA in English and Edn., 1972. Cert. tchr. K-adult Calif. Tchr. art and English Hacienda La Puente Unified Sch. Dist., Hacienda Heights, Calif., 1963-84; tchr. advanced placement English, acad. decathlon advisor, yearbook advisor Glen A. Wilson H.S., Hacienda Heights, 1984—2000. Mentor tchr. Hacienda La Puente Sch. Dist., Hacienda Heights, 1988—2000; reader, tchr. trainer advanced placement English Coll. Bd., 2000—; bd. dirs. Kepler Coll., Lynnwood, Wash., pres., 2003—; bd. dirs., tchr. Online Coll., 2000—. Contbr. articles to profl. jours. Named Tchr. of the Yr., Nat. Walmart Stores Found., 1998; recipient D. Fedderson Cmty. Svc. award, PTA, 1970, Teacher of the Year, 1971, Glen A. Wilson Faculty Tchr. of Yr. award, 1999—2000. Mem.: United Astrology Congress (program chair 1986, 1989, 1992, coord. 1995, bd. chmn. 1995—99, co-founder), Internat. Soc. Astrol. Rsch. (pres. 1988—95, bd. dirs. 1995—2004), Delta Kappa Gamma. Methodist. Home: 56870 Jack Nicklaus Blvd La Quinta CA 92253-5074 Office: 4630 200th St SW Ste A-1 Lynnwood WA 98036 Office Phone: 425-673-4292. Personal E-mail: caroltebbs@aol.com.

**TEBEDO, MARYANNE,** state legislator; b. Denver, Oct. 30, 1936; m. Don Tebedo; children: Kevin, Ronald, Linda, Thomas, Christine. Profl. registered parliamentarian. Mem. Colo. Ho. of Reps., Denver, 1982-88, Colo. Senate, Denver, 1988—2001; owner, pres. Colo. Mediation and Parliamentary Profls., Colorado Springs. Mediator 4th Jud. Dist. Colo. Mem.: Nat. Assn. Parliamentarians, Colo. Assn. Parliamentarians (pres.). Republican. Office Phone: 719-471-2561. E-mail: matebedo@isp.com.

**TEBOH-EWUNGKEM, MIRANDA IJANG,** education educator; d. Aaron Bagen and Christiana Enih Teboh; m. Julius Ewungwo Ewungkem, July 31, 1998; 1 child, Julius Jr. Ewungwo Ewungkem. BS in Math., U. Buea, 1996, MS in Math., 1998; PhD in Math., Lehigh U., 2003, MS in Stats, 2003. Tchg. asst. U. Of Buea, Cameroon, 1997—98; dean's fellow Lehigh U., Bethlehem, Pa., 1998—99, tchg. asst., 1999—2003, hsiung vis. asst. prof., 2003—04; vis. post doc U. Mich., 2004—04; vis. asst. prof. Lafayette Coll., Easton, Pa., 2004—. Author: (conference book of abstracts) International Conference for Mathematics in Biology and Medicine, International Conference on Applied Math, International Conference on Mathematical Biology; contbr. articles to jours. Landahl student travel grant, Soc. of Math. Biology, 2002, Travel grant, AWM, 2004, Reidler grant, Lehigh U., 2003, SMB Travel grant, SMB, 2004, Commonwealth scholarship, Commonwealth group, 1998. Mem.: Soc. of Indsl. and Applied Mathematicians, Soc. for Math. Biology, Am. Math. Soc., Assn. for Women in Math. Christian. Avocations: reading, tennis. Office: Lafayette Coll Pardee Hall 225A Easton PA 18042 Office Phone: 610 330 5328. Office Fax: 610 330 5721. Business E-Mail: tebohewm@lafayette.edu.

**TECCO, ROMUALD GILBERT LOUIS JOSEPH,** violinist, concertmaster; b. Toulon, Var, France, May 1, 1941; came to U.S. 1960; s. Raymond Charles and Angele (Cornille) T. Student, Paris Conservatoire, 1954-60; diploma, postgrad. diploma, Juilliard Sch. Music, 1967-68. Mem. N.Y. String Quartet, 1969-72; concertmaster Juilliard Ensemble, N.Y.C., 1969-72, St. Paul Chamber Orch., 1972-98; soloist Chgo. Symphony, Bavarian Radio Orch., Orch. of Mex., Orchestre Colonne, Paris, Rotterdam Philharm.; performer numerous festivals, Sweden, Finland, France, Italy, U.S. Recs. with Aaron Copland and Lou Harrison Chamber Music. Served with French Navy, 1964-65, NATO hdqrs. Recipient first prize in violin Conservatoire Paris; recipient first prize chamber music Conservatoire Paris Mem. St. Paul Univ. Club.

**TECHAR, FRANK J.,** bank executive; b. Minn. BS in engring., Princeton U., 1978; MBA, U. Denver, 1983; exec. program, USC, 1992. Various banking positions First Interstate Bank, Denver; various engring. positions USG Corp., Oakfield, NY; sr. v.p., gen. mgr. BMO Fin. Group, London; acct. officer, corp. banking Bk. of Montreal, Denver, 1984, mgr. dir., corp. banking Houston, 1993—95, exec. v.p., small bus. banking Canada, 1999—2002; pres., CEO Harris Bankcorp, Toronto, Canada, 2002—06; pres., CEO Personal & Comml. Banking Canada BMO Fin. Group, 2006—. Mem.: Northwestern U. Bus. Sch. Adv. Coun., Chicagoland C.of.C. (bd. mem.), Exec. Club Chgo. (bd. mem.), U. Club, Chgo. Club, Econ. Club, Comml. Club of Chgo. Office: BMO Fin Group 1 First Canadian Pl M5X 1H3 Toronto ON Canada*

**TEDDER, THOMAS FLETCHER,** immunology educator, researcher; b. Chateauroux, France, May 14, 1956; came to U.S. 1959; s. Raymond Percy and Barbara (Hagemann) T. AA, Okaloosa-Walton C.C., Niceville, Fla., 1976; BS with honors, U. Fla., 1978, MS, 1980; PhD, U. Ala., Birmingham, 1984. Rsch. fellow in pathology Harvard Med. Sch., Boston, 1984-85, instr. pathology, 1986-88, asst. prof. pathology, 1988-93; assoc. prof. pathology Harvard U. Med. Sch., Boston, 1993; prof. immunology Duke U. Med. Ctr., Durham, NC, 1993—, chmn. dept. immunology, 1993—. Alter Geller prof. rsch. in immunology Duke U. Med. Ctr., 1997—; co-founder Angelica Therapeutics, Inc.; cons. in field. Assoc. editor Jour. Immunology, 1989-93, sect. editor, 1993-98, dep. editor, 2004—; contbr. numerous articles to med. jours., including Jour. Immunology, Nature, Lancet, Immunity. Recipient LeRoy Collins Disting. Alumnus award Fla. Assn. C.C.'s; named 25th Anniversary Disting. Alumnus, Okaloosa-Walton C.C., 1989; Damon Runyon-Walter Winchell rsch. fellow, 1985-87; scholar Leukemia Soc. Am., 1991-96, Stohlman scholar, 1995-96. Mem. Am. Soc. for Microbiology (Pres. fellow 1982), Am. Assn. Immunologists, Sigma Xi, Phi Kappa Phi. Achievements include identification and determination of structure and function of many human B lymphocyte cell-surface molecules. Office: Duke U Med Ctr Dept Immunology PO Box 3010 Durham NC 27710-0001 Office Phone: 919-684-3578. E-mail: thomas.tedder@duke.edu.

**TEDESCHI, GEORGE,** labor union administrator; Journeyman newspaper pressman Newsday, Long Island, NY; mem. Graphic Commn. Internat. Union, 1959—; v.p. & sec.-treas. Local 406C Graphic Comm. Internat. Union, pres. Nassau County 406C, 1972—2000, pres., 2000—. Mem. from Atlantic region gen. bd. Graphic Comm. Internat. Union, 1983—2000, pres. N.Am. Newspaper Conf., 1979—2000, sec. Ea. Conf.; exec. bd. Long Island Fedn. Labor, AFL-CIO. Dir. and sec. United Way of Long Island; bd. dir. Union Labor Life Ins. Co. (ULLICO). Office: Graphic Comm Internat Union 1900 L St NW Washington DC 20036 Office Phone: 202-462-1400.*

**TEDESCHI, JOHN ALFRED,** historian, educator, librarian; b. Modena, Italy, July 17, 1931; came to U.S. 1939, naturalized, 1944; s. Caesar George and Piera (Forti) T.; m. Anne Wood Christian, Sept. 8, 1957; children: Martha, Philip, Sara. BA, Harvard U., 1954, MA, 1960, PhD, 1966. Bibliographer European history and lit. Newberry Library, Chgo., 1965-84, curator rare books and manuscripts, head dept. spl. collections, 1970-82, dir. Ctr. Renaissance Studies, 1979-84; curator rare books and spl. collections Meml. Library U. Wis.-Madison, 1984-96; ret., 1996. Lectr. history U. Chgo., 1969—71; vis. prof. U. Wis.-Madison, 1972-73, adj. prof., 1979—84. Co-editor: (series) Corpus Reformatorum Italicorum, 1968-96; editor-in-chief: Bibliographie Internat. de L'Humanisme et de la Renaissance, 1977-82; editor: Italian Reformation Studies in Honor of Laelius Socinus, 1965, (with Anthony Molho) Renaissance Studies in Honor of Hans Baron, 1971, (with Gustav Henningsen) The Inquisition in Early Modern Europe: Studies on Sources and Methods, 1986, The Prosecution of Heresy: Collected Studies on the Inquisition in Early Modern Italy, 1991 (transl. into Italian 1997), Tommaso Sassetti, Il Massacro di San Bartolomeo, 1995, The Italian Reformation of the Sixteenth Century and the Diffusion of Renaissance Culture: A Bibliography of the Secondary Literature (c. 1750-1997), 2000, The correspondence of Roland H. Bainton and Delio Cantimori, 1932-66, 2002; translator: (with Anne Tedeschi) The Cheese and the Worms. The Cosmos of a Sixteenth-Century Miller (Carlo Ginzburg), 1980 (named an Outstanding Acad. Book by Choice mag.), The Night Battles. Witchcraft and Agrarian Cults in the Sixteenth and Seventeenth Centuries (Carlo Ginzburg), 1983, Clues, Myths, and the Historical Method (Carlo Ginzburg), 1989, Hans Urs von Balthasar: A Theological Style (Angelo Scola), 1995, Domenico Scandella Known as Menocchio: His Trials Before the Inquisition (1583-1599) (Andrea Del Col), 1996, The Protestant Reformation in Sixteenth-Century Italy (Salvatore Caponetto), 1999, Books of the Body: Anatomical Ritual and Renaissance Learning (Andrea Carlino), 1999, The Jews in Mussolini's Italy (Michele Sarfatti), 2006; mem. editl. com.: Index des Livres Interdits (Sherbrooke), Collected Works of Erasmus (Toronto); mem. editl. bd.: Studi e Testi per la Storia Religiosa Italiana del '500 (Florence), The Peter Martyr Libr. (Kirksville, Mo.); contbr. articles to profl. jours. Served with U.S. Army, 1954-56. Grantee Am. Philos. Soc., 1961; grantee NEH, 1967; Old Dominion fellow Harvard U. Ctr. Renaissance Studies, Florence, Italy, 1967-68; fellow Inst. Research in Humanities, U. Wis.-Madison, 1976-77; Huntington Library fellow, 1984. Mem. Am. Soc. Reformation Research (pres. 1972), Renaissance Soc. Am. (exec. bd. 1971-96), 16th Century Studies Conf. (pres. 1987), Archive of Congregation for the Doctrine of the Faith (Vatican City; pres. 1999-2002, scholarly adv. com.), Univ. Trieste, Congregation for the Doctrine of the Faith (the Vatican), Gen. Adminstrn. for Archives (Rome; pres. scholarly adv. com. for collaborative project to catalogue electronically dispersed Inquisitorial sources, 2004-; Livorno, Italy scholary adv. com. to plan for 4th centenary of elevation to status of a city, 2004—), Am. Hist. Assn., Am. Cath. Hist. Assn. Home: 57211 Rush Creek Rd Ferryville WI 54628 E-mail: tede@mwt.net.

**TEDESCHI, THOMAS E., JR.,** music educator; b. Chgo., Dec. 18, 1965; s. Thomas E. and Antoinette Tedeschi; m. Carol M. Krusec, June 20, 1992; children: Daniel T, Samuel E. MusB in Edn., DePaul U., 1990; MusM in Edn., VanderCook Coll. Music, 2000, degree in Med Adminstrn., No. Ill. U., 2001. Tchr. music Chgo. (Ill.) Pub. Schs., 1991—92, Ctr. Cass Sch. Dist. 66, Downers Grove, Ill., 1992—, dir. bands, 1992—. Dir. camp band Am. Band Camp, River Forest, Ill., 1998—; freelance musician. Mem.: Nat. Assn. Music Educators, Ill. Grade Sch. Music Assn., Ill. Music Educators Assn. Avocations: travel, golf, bowling. Home: 1901 Harcourt Dr Woodridge IL 60517 Office: Center Cass School District 66 701 Plainfield Rd Downers Grove IL 60516 Office Phone: 630-783-5124. Office Fax: 630-985-1545. Business E-Mail: ttedeschi@ccsd66.org.

**TEDESCO, FRANCIS JOSEPH,** retired academic administrator, medical educator; b. Derby, Conn., Mar. 8, 1944; s. Lena (Tufano) Tedesco; m. Luann Lee Ekern, Aug. 1, 1970; 1 child, Jennifer Nicole. BS cum laude, Fairfield U., 1965; MD cum laude, St. Louis U., 1969. Asst. instr. Hosp. of U. Pa., Phila., 1971-72; asst. prof. Washington U. Sch. Medicine, St. Louis, 1974-75, U. Miami (Fla.) Sch. Medicine, 1975-77, co-dir. clin. research, 1976-74, assoc. prof., 1977-78, Med. Coll. Ga., Augusta, 1978-81, chief of gastroenterology dept., 1978-88, prof., 1981—, acting v.p. clin. activities, 1984, v.p. for clin. activities, 1984-88, Interim dean Sch. of Medicine, 1986-88, pres., 1988—2001, pres. emeritus, 2001—. Cons. Med.-Letter/AMA divsn. drugs, Dwight D. Eisenhower Army Med. Ctr., Ft. Gordon, Ga., VA Med. Ctr., Augusta, Walter Reed Army Med. Ctr., Washington; mem. gastroenterology spl. study sect. NIH, Washington, 1982—, mem. nat. digestive disease adv. bd., 1985-88, vice chmn., 1986-87, chmn., 1987-88; mem. Ty Cobb Found. Scholarship Bd., 1998—. Contbr. numerous articles to profl. jours. Bd. dirs. Augusta Country Day Sch., 1981-83, Am. Cancer Soc., Augusta, 1985—, v.p., 1986—; bd. dirs., exec. com. Ga. Coalition for Health, 1995-2002; chmn. Gov.'s Health Strategies Coun., 1992-2002; bd. visitors CDC, 1998—; nat. adv. bd. Ga. Acad. Sci., Math. and Engring., 1998—; mem. Ty Cobb Fedn. Bd., 1998—. Recipient Eddie Palmer award for gastrointestinal endoscopy, 1983, cert. of appreciation Am. Cancer Soc., 1986, Outstanding Faculty award Med. Coll. Ga. Sch. Medicine, 1988, Profl. Achievement award Fairfield U., 1993, alumni merit award St. Louis U. Sch. Medicine, 1996, Avalon Found. scholar St. Louis U., 1968-69, Paul Harris fellow Rotary, 1990, Spirit of Ga. award Ga. Econ. Devel. Assn., 1998. Fellow ACP, Am. Fedn. Clin. Investigation, Am. Gastroent. Assn., Am. Soc. Gastrointestinal Endoscopy (treas. 1981-84, pres.-elect 1984-85, pres. 1985-86, Rudolph Schindler award 1993); mem. Am. Coll. Gastroenterology, So. Soc. Clin. Investigation, Richmond County Med. Soc., Med. Assn. Ga. Roman Catholic. Avocations: reading, swimming. Home: 2810 Peachtree Pl Augusta GA 30909 Office: Med Coll Ga Office Pres 1120 15th St Augusta GA 30912-0006 Business E-Mail: frant@mcg.edu.

**TEDESCO, PAUL HERBERT,** humanities educator; b. Nashua, NH, Dec. 28, 1928; s. Steven R. and Ruth (Weaver) T.; m. Eleanor Martha Hollis, Jan. 24, 1953; children: Steven Anthony, Sara Adams Tagget, James Beattie. AB in History, Harvard Coll., 1952; AM in History, Boston U., 1955, PhD in History, 1970; CAGS in Adminstrn., Northeastern U., Boston, 1974. Instr. humanities Mich. State U., East Lansing, 1955—60; tchr. history Great Neck North H.S., NY, 1960—62; chmn. dept. social studies Canton H.S., Mass., 1962—65; prof., chmn. edn. Northeastern U., Boston, 1965—87; Fulbright prof. history Peking U., Beijing, 1988—89; historian-in-residence City of Haverhill, Mass., 1989—90; lectr. bus., history, govt. edn. Asian divsn. U. Md., Korea, Japan, Guam, 1990—94; team leader, lectr. Joint Siberian-Am. Faculty Irkutsk State U., Russia, 1994—95; edn. coord. Asian divsn. U. Md., 1995—97, prof. European divsn., 1997—. Nat. dir. BHelp Bus., History and Econ. Life Program, Boston, 1968—; cons. in field Author: Teaching with Case Studies, 1978, A New England City: Haverhill Massachusetts, 1987, Attleboro, Massachusetts: The Hub of the Jewelry Industry, 1979, Protection, Patriotism and Prosperity: James M. Swank, the AISA, and the Tariff, 1872-1913, 1985; author, editor: The Creative Social Science Teacher, 1970, The Thunder of the Mills, 1981, Images of America: Dover, 2002 Mem. Town Fin. Com., Canton, Mass., 1966—; mem. long-range planning com. St. Dunstan, 1968-70; commr. Dover Hist. Comm., 2001—; Dover Hazardous Waste coord., 2003—. With U.S. Army, 1952-54. Recipient FEI Nat. collegiate award, 1985, Freedoms Found. George Washington medal for econ. edn., 1984. Mem. New Eng. History Tchrs. Assn. (past pres., Kidger award 1975), Dover Hist. Soc. (pres. 2000—). E-mail: pht52@aol.com.

**TEDFORD, DEBORAH J.,** lawyer; b. Dec. 1950; Grad. cum laude, Yale U., 1972; grad., Boston U., 1976. Ptnr. Tedford, Gianni & Jensen, P.C., Mystic, Conn. Bd. dirs. Hospice Southeastern Conn. Fellow: Conn. Bar Found., Am. Coll. Trust and Estate Counsel; mem.: Southeastern Conn. Estate and Tax Planning Coun. (past pres.), Conn. Bar Assn. (chair legal problems of the elderly 1990—92, chair estates and probate sect. 1997—, sec. 1999—2000, pres. 2002—03, founding editor Estates and Probate Newsletter), Mystic Rotary Club (past pres.). Office: PO Box 350 30 Bank St New Britain CT 06050

**TEDFORD, JACK NOWLAN, III,** construction executive, small business owner; b. Reno, Jan. 1, 1943; s. Jack Nowlan Jr. and Elizabeth (Kolhoss) T.; m. Nancy Joanne Stiles, Feb. 27, 1971; children: Jack Nowlan IV, James Nathan. BS, U. Nev., 1966, MBA, 1969. Bus. mgr. Los Angeles Bapt. Coll., Newhall, Calif., 1969-71; v.p. Jack N. Tedford, Inc., Fallon, Nev., 1971-98; owner/broker Tedford Realty, Fallon, 1974-94; owner/mgr. Tedford Bus. Systems, Fallon, 1978-94; pres. JNT, Inc., Incline Village, Nev., 1994—. Pres., Jack N. Tedford, Inc., 1998—. Author numerous computer programs. Mem. Selective Svc. Local Bd., Fallon, 1971-76; chmn. City of Fallon Bd. Adjustment, 1972-95, chmn. Churchill Co. Reps., Fallon, 1976-80; mem. ctrl. com. Nev. Reps., 1976-2002; del. Nat. Conv., Detroit, 1980, Dallas, 1984; former coun. ofcls. Western Nev. Devel. Dist.; former treas. Lahontan Valley Environ. Alliance. Mem. Assn. Gen. Contractors (past pres., former v.p., treas. Nev. chpt., dir.), Nat. Bd. Realtors, State Bd. Realtors, Incline Village Bd. Realtors, CEDA Bus. Coun. (bd. dirs. 1991-97), Rotary (bd. dirs. 1980-81), Master's Coll. (bd. dirs. 1971-95), Slavic Gospel Assn. (bd. dirs.), Nat. Assn. Gen. Contractors (bd. dirs. open shop com., closely held bus. com.), Fellowship of Cos. for Christ Internat. Republican. Baptist. Avocations: computers, golf. Home and Office: PO Box 7937 Incline Village NV 89452 Business E-Mail: jnt@jntinc.com.

**TEDFORD, JEFF,** college football coach; b. Lynwood, California, Nov. 2, 1961; BS in physical edn., Fresno State U., 1983. Profl. football player Hamilton, Calgary, Saskatchewan, and Winnipeg (CFL), 1983—87; volunteer asst. coach Fresno State U., 1987—88; coached Calgary Stampede (CFL),

1989—91; quarterback coach Fresno State U., 1992—97; offensive coord. U. Oregon, 1998—2001; head coach U. Calif. Golden Bears, 2002—. Named Pac-10 coach of the year, 2002. Achievements include winning the Insight Bowl (2003), Las Vegas Bowl (2005); creating a team that earned the school's highest national ranking (No. 4) since 1952 and registered its best regular-season record (10-1) in 54 years. Office: UC Berkeley Intercollegiate Athletics 209 Memorial Stadium Berkeley CA 94720 Office Phone: 510-642-3857.*

**TEDLOCK, BARBARA HELEN,** anthropologist, educator, academic administrator; b. Battle Creek, Mich., Sept. 9, 1942; d. Byron Taylor and Mona Gerteresse (O'Connor) McGrath; m. Dennis E. Tedlock, July 19, 1968. BA in Rhetoric, U. Calif., Berkeley, 1967; MA in Anthropology, Wesleyan U., 1973; PhD in Anthropology, SUNY, Albany, 1978. Lectr. in music Tufts U., Medford, Mass., 1977-78, asst. prof. anthropology, 1978-82, assoc. prof., 1982-87; assoc. prof. anthropology SUNY, Buffalo, 1987-89, prof. anthropology, 1989—, disting. prof., 2003, chair dept. anthropology, 1998—2000, 2002—03, assoc. dean undergrad. edn., 2000—01. Vis. mem. Inst. for Advanced Study, Princeton, 1986. Author: Time and the Highland Maya, 1982, The Beautiful and the Dangerous Encounters with Zuni Indians, 1992, The Woman in the Shaman's Body: Reclaiming the Feminine in Religion and Medicine, 2003; editor: Dreaming: Anthropological and Psychological Interpretations, 1987; co-editor: Teaching From the American Earth, 1975; assoc. editor Jour. of Anthropol. Rsch., 1987-93; sr. editor Dreaming, 1990-95; assoc. editor Latin Am. Rsch. Rev., 1992—; mem. editl. adv. bd. Encyc. Cultural Anthropology, 1993-95, Handbook of Qualitative Research, 1998—. Adv. bd. Mus. of Indian Arts, Santa Fe, 1991-95; mem. Royerofters at large East Aururra, N.Y., 1989—; mem. Cultural Survival, 1980—; mem. humanities panel WGBH, Boston, 1983-84; judge pottery Southwestern Assn. on Indian Affairs, Santa Fe, 1981-83. Fellowships NEH, 1986, 93, sr. fellowship Am. Coun. of Learned Socs., 1994, Weatherhead fellowship Sch. of Am. Rsch., 1980, sr. fellowship Ctr. for the Study of World Religions/Harvard U., 1998; Sabbatical fellow Am. Philos. Soc., 2002-03; recipient Charles Bordon, Geoffrey Bushnell Juan Cosmos prize in linguistics Internat. Congress of Americanists, 1979. Fellow Am. Anthropol. Assn. (bd. dirs. 1991-93, editor-in-chief Am. Anthropologist 1994-98, Pres.'s award for leadership 1997), Soc. for Cultural Anthropology, Am. Philosophical Soc.; mem. AAUW, PEN (elected), Soc. for Humanistic Anthropology (pres. 1991-93, Writing prize 1986), Soc. for Psychol. Anthropology (bd. dirs. 1993-96), Assn. for Study of Dreams (bd. dirs. 1990-95), Soc. for Ethnohistory (exec. bd. 1980-82), Am. Studies Assn. (exec. bd. 1983-85), Assn. on Am. Indian Affairs. Avocations: skiing, running, swimming, dance, videoing. Office: SUNY Buffalo Dept Anthropology Buffalo NY 14261-0001 E-mail: tedlockb@acsu.buffalo.edu.

**TEDRICK, DEBORAH LYNNE,** singer, actress, educator; b. Detroit, May 1, 1964; d. Alan Lee Tedrick and Janice Marie Leonard; m. Scott Ackerman (div.). MusB in Vocal Performance, Calif. State U., LA; postgrad., U. Tex., U. Mich., U. Ctrl. Fla. Owner InterACT Entertainment, Detroit. Vocal instr. Novi (Mich.) Cmty. Edn.; dir., music dir., accompanist, drama tchr., playwright The Cmty. Ho., Birmingham, Mich.; dir., music dir., accompanist, choreographer, playwright The Farmington Players Barn, Farmington Hills, Marquis Theater, Northville, Mich.; choreographer, accompanist Popcorn Players, Birmingham; dir., music dir., accompanist, choreographer Dougherty Arts Ctr., Austin, Tex.; music dir., accompanist Dearborn (Mich.) Youth Theater, Rising Stars Repertory Ensemble, Bloomfield Hills, Mich., Dominican HS, Detroit; music dir., accompanist, choreographer Oakland Theater Guild, Waterford, Mich.; dir., accompanist Austin State Sch. for Mental Retardation; motivational spkr. Home: 29555 Mullane Dr Farmington Hills MI 48334 E-mail: debbietedrick@aol.com.

**TEDROW, JOHN CHARLES FREMONT,** soils educator; b. Rockwood, Pa., Apr. 21, 1917; s. John Wesley and Emma Grace (Younkin) T.; m. Mary Jane Lough, Mar. 20, 1943 (dec. Mar. 1991); children: John Charles Fremont, Thomas Lough (dec.). BS, Pa. State U., 1939; MS, Mich. State U., 1940; PhD, Rutgers U., 1950. Jr. soil technologist Dept. Agr., 1941-42, soil scientist, 1946-47; instr. Rutgers U., New Brunswick, N.J., 1947-50, asst. prof., 1950-53, assoc. prof., 1953-57, prof. soils, 1957—73, prof. II, soils, 1973—84, prof. emeritus, 1984—. Cons. N.S. Research Found., 1949—; sr. pedologist Boston U., 1953—; prin. investigator Arctic Inst. N.Am., Washington, 1955-68, NSF, 1961-62, Atomic Energy Commn., Washington, 1961-63; cons. to govt. and industry. Author: (with R.C. Murray) Forensic Geology: Earth Sciences and Criminal Investigation, 1974, Soils of the Polar Landscapes, 1977, (with K.A. Linell) Soil and Permafrost Surveys in the Arctic, 1981, Soils of New Jersey, 1986, (with R.C. Murray) Forensic Geology, 1991; editor in chief Soil Science, 1978-79; editor: Antarctic Soils and Soil Forming Processes, 1966. Lt. USN, 1942-46. Recipient Lindback Research award Rutgers U., 1978, Antarctic Service medal. Fellow Am. Soc. Agronomy, Soil Sci. Soc. Am., Arctic Inst. N.Am.; mem. Internat. Soc. Soil Sci., Am. Geophys. Union, Sigma Xi, Alpha Zeta (hon.), Phi Mu Delta. Achievements include investigation of polar soils in Alaska, Can., Greenland, Scandinavia, Siberia and Antarctica. Home: 5 Bluebird Ct Edison NJ 08820-3677 Office: Rutgers U Ecology Evolution and Natural Resources PO Box 231 New Brunswick NJ 08903-0231

**TEEGARDEN, NICOLEE,** artist, consultant, retired art educator; d. Charles Whitney and Mary Lucille (Neiman) Webster; m. Ernest Allen Teegarden, Sept. 2, 1962 (div. May 1970); m. Joseph John Rozman, Jr., Dec. 26, 1973 (div. July 1986); m. Clark Love, Aug. 1986 (div. Dec. 1989). BFA in Art Edn., Drake U., 1967; MS in Painting, U. Wis., 1972, MFA in Painting, 1980. Relief house parent Evang. Children's Home, St. Louis, 1962; ward clk., male neurosurg. ward U. Ill., Neuropsych Inst. Rsch. and Edn. Hosp., Chgo., 1963; dental acct., office mgr. Des Moines, Iowa, 1963; tissue technician, INH sponsored arteriosclerosis rsch. lab. Coll. of Osteopathy, Des Moines, Iowa, 1963; med. records clk. Broadlawns County Hosp., Des Moines, 1963—66; elem. art specialist Kenosha (Wis.) Unified Sch. Dist., 1969—71; tchr. Tremper H.S., 1971—2000, chair dept. art, 1978—79; sabbatical leave, 1979—80; chair dept. art Tremper H.S., Kenosha, Wis., 1984—99; instr. drawing Advanced Placement Studio Art, 1992—2000; instr. advanced drawing Kenosha Inst. Arts, 2002—03; pres. N.Am. Sintered Metal Corp., Kenosha, 2003—; Havencrest Garden Studio, Racine, Wis., 2005—. Instr. Coll. Lake County, Grayslake, Ill., 1970; mem. steering com. Nat. Scholastic Art Awards, Washington, 1993—94; artist in residence Havencrest Studio Gardens, Racine, Wis., 2005—. One-woman shows include Carthage Coll. Art Gallery, Kenosha, 1971, Daken Gallery, Waukegan, Ill., 1971, David Barnett Gallery, Milw., 1972, U. Wis. Fine Arts Gallery, 1972, Marine Bank Gallery, 1980, Upstairs/Downstairs Gallery, Kenosha, 1980, Ctr. City Espresso, Racine, Wis., 1991, Racine St. Visitors and Conv. Bur., 1996, Hist. 6th St. Art Walk, Christian Sci. Reading Room, 2006. Regional Scholastic Art Awards adv. com. Milw. Art Mus., 1980—94; com. chair, 1990—94. Named Scholastic Art Awards Disting. Alumni, Milw. Art Mus., 1993; recipient Lakefront Festival Arts award of excellence, 1981; Nat. Art Inst. scholar, Alliance Inst. Colls. Art and Design Study, U.Wis./UC, 1988. Home: 1701 Wisconsin Ave Racine WI 53403 Office Phone: 262-634-8256.

**TEEGUARDEN, DENNIS EARL,** forest economist, educator; b. Gary, Ind., Aug. 21, 1931; s. Gary Leon and Mary Dessa (Purciful) T.; m. Sally Annette Gleason, Dec. 23, 1954; children: Jason Earl, Julie Annette, Justin Gary. BS in Forestry with honors, Mich. Tech. U., Houghton, 1953; M.Forestry, U. Calif., Berkeley, 1958, PhD in Agrl. Econs. (Bidwell research fellow 1962-63), 1964. Rsch. aid U.S. Forest Service, 1957; asst. rsch. specialist U. Calif., Berkeley, 1958-63, mem. faculty, 1963-91, prof. forestry econs. Sch. Forestry, 1963-91, S.J. Hall prof. forest econs., 1989-91, prof. emeritus, 1991—, chmn. dept. forestry and resource mgmt., 1978-86, acting dir. forest products lab., 1987-88, assoc. dean for acad. affairs, 1990-92, assoc. dean rsch. and extension, 1992-93. Mem. Calif. Commn. on Agr. and Higher Edn., 1993-95, com. scientists Dept. Agr., 1977-80; cons. in field; mem. adv. bd. U. Calif. Forest Products Lab., 1994-98; mem. adv. coun. Alberta Heritage Found. for Sci. and Engring. Rsch., 2001-03. Co-author: Forest Resource Management: Decision-Making Principles and Cases, 1979; contbr. articles to profl. jours. Trustee Mich. Tech. Fund, Mich. Tech. U., Houghton, 1994-2004,

life trustee, 2004—. Lt. USNR, 1953-57, Korea. Recipient Outstanding Alumnus award Mich. Tech. U., 1993, Berkeley citation U. Calif., Berkeley, 1994; grantee U.S. Forest Svc., Bur. Land Mgmt.; named to Honor Acad. Sch. Forestry and Wood Products, Mich. Tech. U., 1995. Fellow Soc. Am. Foresters; mem. Western Forest Economists, Calif. Water Fowl Assn. Home: 4732 Westwood Ct Richmond CA 94803-2441 Office: U Calif Coll Natural Resources Berkeley CA 94720-0001

**TEEL, JOYCE RALEY,** retail executive; b. 1930; m. James Teel. Dir. Raley's, West Sacramento, 1950—; co-chmn. bd. dirs. Raley's, Bel Air Markets, Food Source, Nob Hill Foods, No. Calif., Nev., NMex., 1991—. Dir. non-profit Food for Families. Named one of Forbes' Richest Americans, 2006. Office: Raleys & Belaire 500 W Capitol Ave West Sacramento CA 95605-2696*

**TEELEY, KEVIN,** educational association administrator; b. Detroit, 1954; BA in Sociology and Elem. Edn., U. Wash., 1978. Tchr. 5th and 6th grade gifted students Lake Washington Sch. Dist., Redmond, Wash., 1978—91, curriculum/staff devel. specialist, 1994—95; pres. Lake Washington Edn. Assn., Redmond, 1991—94, 1996—. Mem.: NEA (mem. profl. stds. and practice com. 1996—2002, del. Edn. Internat. World Congress 1998, 2001, 2004, rep. goodwill mission to Russia 2000), Nat. Bd. for Profl. Tchg. Stds. (bd. mem.). Office: Lake Washington Edn Assn 10628 NE 37t Cir Kirkland WA 98033 Office Phone: 425-822-9898.

**TEEM, PAUL LLOYD, JR.,** bank executive; b. Gastonia, N.C., Mar. 10, 1948; s. Paul Lloyd Sr. and Ruth Elaine (Bennett) T. BA, U. N.C., 1970; Cert., Inst. Fin. Edn., Chgo., 1984, Diploma, 1985. Degree of Distinction, 1989. Cert. tchr. N.C., cert. consumer credit exec.; lic. real estate broker; lic. lay Eucharistic minister. Exec. v.p., sec. Citizens South Bank, Gastonia, NC, 1983—; exec. v.p., sec. bd. dirs. Citizens South Fin. Svcs. Inc., Gastonia, 1988—; exec. v.p., sec. Citizens South Holdings, Mut. Holding Co., Gastonia, 1998—2002, Citizens South Banking Corp., Gastonia, 1998—. Bd. dirs. Gastonia Mchts. Assn., Inc., 1981-83; lay reader, lay eucharistic min. Episcopal Ch. Decorated Order Purple Cross, Legion of Honor. Fellow Soc. Cert. Credit Execs.; mem. Nat. Soc. Sons and Daus. of Pilgrims, SAR, Sons of Confederate Vets., Mil. Order of Stars and Bars, Masons (32d degree, bd. dirs., Disting. Svc. award 1987, Gold Honor award 1988, Active Legion of Honor 1989, Order of the Purple Cross of York 1990), Shriners, KT, Royal Order of Scotland, Hon. Order Ky. Cols., Phi Alpha Theta. Democrat. Avocation: genealogy. Home: 1208 Poston Cir Gastonia NC 28054-4634 Office: Citizens South Bank PO Box 2249 Gastonia NC 28053-2249 Office Phone: 704-884-2262. Business E-Mail: paul.teem@citizenssouth.com.

**TEEPEN, THOMAS HENRY,** editor, journalist; b. Nashville, Jan. 19, 1935; s. Albert George and Elizabeth Blanche (Winfree) T.; m. Nancy Irene Roux, Feb. 2, 1957 (div. 1974); children— Kristina Lynn, Jeremy Roux; m. Sandra Jean Richards, May 14, 1975; 1 stepchild, Jennifer Koerlin BS in Journalism, Ohio U., 1957. Reporter Urbana (Ohio) Daily Citizen, 1957-58; asst. editor Kettering-Oakwood Times, Dayton, Ohio, 1958-59; from reporter to editorial writer Dayton Daily News, 1959-68, editorial page editor, 1968-82, Atlanta Constitution, 1982-92; nat. corr. Cox Newspapers, Atlanta, 1992-2000, columnist, 2000—. Contbg. columnist Liberal Opinion Week. Former pres. Joel Chandler Harris Assn., Atlanta; mem. Atlanta Opera, 1985—, Joint Internat. Observer Group, Ethiopian Elections, 1992; mem. internat. adv. com. The African-Am. Inst., N.Y.C., 1985-97; bd. trustees Freedom to Read Found., Chgo; active Mayor's Cmty. Cultural Steering Com., Atlanta. Profl. journalism fellow Stanford Univ., 1967 Home and Office: 900 Charles Allen Dr NE Atlanta GA 30308-1722 Office Phone: 404-874-1421. E-mail: tteepen@earthlink.net, teepencolumn@coxnews.com.

**TEERLINK, J(OSEPH) LELAND,** real estate developer; b. Salt Lake City, July 16, 1935; s. Nicholas John and Mary Luella (Love) T.; m. Leslie Dowdle, Nov. 5, 1957; children: Steven, David, Andrew, Suzanne, Benjamin. Student, U. Utah, Salt Lake City, 1953-55. Sales rep. Eastman Kodak Co., Salt Lake City, 1960-69; founder Graphic Systems, Inc., Salt Lake City, 1969-82, pres., 1969-79, chmn. bd., 1979-82; founder Graphic Ink Co., Salt Lake City, 1973, pres., 1975-79, chmn. bd., 1979-82; founder G.S.I. Leasing Co., Salt Lake City, 1975, pres., 1975-82; chmn. bd. Graphic Sys. Holding Co., Inc., Salt Lake City, 1978-82; dir. leasing and acquisitions Terra Industries, Inc., real estate developers, 1982-86, ptnr., 1986—. Bd. dirs. ARC, Salt Lake City, 1979-82; co-founder, dir. Hope Living Ctr. Found. for Mothers and Children, 1993-99; vice consulate of the Netherlands for Utah, 1977-92; mem. active corps of execs., SBA, 1979-83; adv. bd. House of Hope Mothers and Children Utah Alcoholism Found., 1992-94. Recipient Masters award Salt Lake Bd. Realtors, 1993; named Small Businessman of Yr. for Utah, SBA, 1978 Mem. Graphic Arts Equipment and Supply Dealers of Am. (dir. 1978-82), Printing Industry of Am., Nat. Assn. Indsl. and Office Parks (pres. Utah chpt. 1986-87), Nat. Fedn. Ind. Businessman, Million Dollar Club (life). Republican. Mem.Lds Ch. Home: 2984 Thackeray Pl Salt Lake City UT 84108-2517 Office: 6925 Union Park Ctr Midvale UT 84047-4135 Business E-Mail: receptionist@terrautah.com.

**TEES, RICHARD CHISHOLM,** psychology professor, researcher; b. Montreal, Que., Can., Oct. 31, 1940; s. Ralph Charles and Helen Winnifred (Chisholm) T.; m. Kathleen F. Coleman, Sept. 1, 1962; children: Susan M., Carolyn V. BA, McGill U., 1961; PhD, U. Chgo., 1965. Asst. prof. U. B.C., Vancouver, Canada, 1965-67, assoc. prof., 1969-75, prof. psychology 1975—, head dept. psychology, 1984—94, 1999—2004, U. B.C. Okanogan transition mgmt. exec., 2004—, acting dep. vice chancellor, acad. v.p., 2006—. Rsch prof. U. Sussex, Brighton, Eng., 1972-73, 77-78; chmn. grant selection panel Nat. Scis. and Engring. Rsch. Coun. Can., Ottawa, 1993-96, B.C. Health Care Rsch. Found., Vancouver, 1984-87; chmn. studentship com. Med. Rsch. Coun., Ottawa, 1985-92; chmn. Can. Coun. Dept. Psychology, 1987-93; mem. B.C. Degree Quality Assessment Bd., 2006—; chair bd. dirs. Cetacea Networks Corp., 2005—. Author: (with Kolb) Cerebral Cortex of the Rat, 1990; mem. editl. bd. Can. Jour. Exptl. Psychology, 1975-84, 87—; contbr. articles to profl. jours., chpts. to books. Rsch. fellow Killam Found., 1972-73, 77-78; Rsch. fellow Can. Coun., 1972-73. Fellow APA, Am. Psychol. Soc., Can. Psychol. Assn.; mem. Soc. for Neurosci., Psychonomic Soc., Can. Soc. Brain, Behaviour, and Cognitive Sci. (pres. 1997-98, Richard C. Tees Leadership award, 2004), A.B.C. Senate, Nat. Ctr. Excellence Can. Stroke Network. Office: U BC Dept Psychology Vancouver BC Canada V6T 1Z4 Home: 4506 W 14th Ave Vancouver BC V6R 2Y4 Canada Office Phone: 604-822-3245. Business E-Mail: rtees@psych.ubc.ca.

**TEETER, DWIGHT LELAND, JR.,** journalism educator; b. L.A., Jan. 6, 1935; s. Dwight Leland and Ruth Elizabeth (Sauer) T.; m. Letitia Ruth Thoreson, July 7, 1956; children: Susan Letitia Hall, John Thoreson, William Weston. AB in Journalism, U. Calif.-Berkeley, 1956, M.J., 1959; PhD in Mass Communications, U. Wis., 1966. Reporter Waterloo Daily Courier, Iowa, 1957-60; asst. prof. Iowa State U., Ames, 1964-66; asst. to assoc. prof. U. Wis., Madison, 1966-72; assoc.prof. to prof. U. Ky., Lexington, 1972-77, dir. journalism dept., 1975-77; prof. journalism, chmn. dept. journalism U. Tex., Austin, 1977-84, William P. Hobby Centennial prof. communication, 1983-87; prof. dept. mass communications U. Wis., Milw., 1987-91; dean Coll. Communications U. Tenn., Knoxville, 1991—2002; prof. journalism, 2002—. Vis. assoc. prof. U. Wash., Seattle, 1969-70; treas. Journalism Council, Inc., N.Y.C., 1972-81 Author: (with Bill Loving) Law of Mass Communications, 11th edit., 2004, (with Jean L. Folkerts) Voices of a Nation: A History of Media in the United States, 4th edit., 2002, (with Lorman A. Ratner) Fanatics and Fire-Eaters: Newspaper Publications Leading to Civil War, 2003; contbr. articles to legal, hist., comm. jours. Chair Headliners Club of Tex. Media Contest, 1979-83; judge Tex. Bar Assn. Media Contest, 1981-85; mem. pub. affairs com. Tex. State Bar, 1985-87. Recipient Tex. Excellence in Teaching award Tex. Ex-Students' Assn., 1983, Harold L. Nelson award U. Wis., 1985, Outstanding Faculty Rsch. award, Tenn. Coll. Communication Info., 2005. Mem. Assn. for Edn. in Journalism and Mass Comm. (chmn. prof. freedom and responsibility com. 1971-73, pres. 1985-86, Disting. Svc. award 2001,

Disting. Rsch. award, 2005), Soc. Profl. Journalists (Disting. Tchr. award 1991), Phi Kappa Phi, Kappa Tau Alpha. Office: U Tenn 430 Communication Knoxville TN 37996-0330 Office Phone: 865-974-5139. Business E-Mail: teeter@utk.edu.

**TEETERS, LINDA MARIE,** retired educator; b. Cin., Aug. 22, 1945; d. Irvin Louis and Shirley H. (Huenefeld) T. Cert. dental asst. U. N.C., 1973. Pharmacy intern Edward W. Wolff Pharmacy, 1963-67; dental asst. to various dentists, 1967-73; coordinator dental asst. clinics Hamilton County (Ohio) Bd. Health, 1973-76; dental coordinator Western Hills Vocat. High Sch., Cin., 1976-94, chmn. adv. bd. for dental program, 1976-94; mem. Ohio Commn. Dental Assisting Certs., 1981-93. Mem. Delhi Civic Assn., 1988—. Mem. Am. Dental Assts. Assn. (3d dist. trustee 1984-86), Ohio Dental Assts. Assn. (pres. 1982-83, editor newsletter 1979-84), Cin. Dental Assts. Assn. (pres. 1971-72, 77-78). Democrat. Roman Catholic. Club: Internationally Yours (pres. local chpt. 1985-89, 93-97, historian internat. chpt. 1986-93, 1st v.p. internat. bd. 1987-89, internat. pres. 1989-93, 95-2001). Home: 267 Anderson Ferry Rd Cincinnati OH 45238-5632

**TEETERS, NANCY HAYS,** economist, director; b. Marion, Ind., July 29, 1930; d. S. Edgar and Mabel (Drake) Hays; m. Robert Duane Teeters, June 7, 1952; children: Ann, James, John. AB in Econs., Oberlin Coll., 1952, LLD, 1979; MA in Econs., U. Mich., 1954, postgrad., 1956—57, LLD (hon.), 1983, Bates Coll., 1981, Mt. Holyoke Coll., 1983. Tchg. fellow U. Mich., Ann Arbor, 1954—55, instr., 1956—57, U. Md. Overseas, Germany, 1955—56; staff economist govt. fin. sect. Bd. Govs. of FRS, Washington, 1957—66, mem. bd., 1979—84; economist (on loan) Coun. Econ. Advrs., 1962—63; economist Bur. Budget, 1966—70; sr. fellow Brookings Instn., 1970—73; sr. specialist Congl. Rsch. Svc., Library Congress, Washington, 1973—74; asst. dir., chief economist Ho. of Reps. Com. on Budget, 1974—78; v.p., chief economist IBM, Armonk, NY, 1984—90. Author: (with others) Setting National Priorities: The 1972 Budget, 1971, Setting National Priorities: The 1973 Budget, 1972, Setting National Priorities: The 1974 Budget, 1973; contbr. articles to profl. publs. Recipient Comfort Starr award in econs. Oberlin Coll., 1952; Disting. Alumnus award U. Mich., 1980 Mem. Nat. Economists Club (v.p. 1973-74, pres. 1974-75, chmn. bd. 1975-76, gov. 1976-79), Am. Econ. Assn. (com. on status of women 1975-78), Am. Fin. Assn. (dir. 1969-71) Democrat. Home: 77 3rd St C-8 Stamford CT 06905

**TEETS, PETER B.,** former civilian military employee; b. Feb. 1942; BS, U. Colo., 1963, MS in Applied Math., 1965, DSc (hon.), 1990; MS in Mgmt., MIT, 1978. Engr. Martin Marietta Denver Aerospace, Colo., 1963—70, mgr., Titan IIIC inertial guidance system Colo., 1970—75, program mgr. Transtage Project & dir. Space Systems Colo., 1975—80, v.p. bus. devel. Colo., 1980—82, v.p., gen. mgr. aerospace strategic & launch systems divsn. Colo., 1982—85, pres. Colo., 1985—93, Martin Marietta Space Group, Bethesda, Md., 1993—95; pres., COO Lockheed Martin Info. & Services, Bethesda, Md., 1995—97, Lockheed Martin Corp., Bethesda, Md., 1997—99; under sec. USAF US Dept. Def., Washington, 2001—05, acting sec., 2005; dir. Nat. Reconnaissance Office, Washington, 2001—05. Bd. trustees The Aerospace Corp, El Segundo, Calif., 2005—. Recipient Sloan Fellow Award, W. Stuart Symington award, 2004. Fellow: Am. Astronautical Society, Am. Institute of Aeronautics and Astronautics; mem.: Nat. Acad. Engring.

**TEETS, WALTER RALPH,** accounting educator; b. Boulder, Colo., Oct. 1, 1950; s. Otis E. and Elsie (Purchase) T.; m. Mary Anne Clougherty; stepchildren: Katherine Kuder, Elizabeth Wierman B in Music Edn., U. Colo., 1973; MMus, U. Wis., Madison, 1976; MS in Edn., U. Wis., Whitewater 1981, MS in Acctg., 1985; PhD, U. Chgo., 1989. Asst. prof. Wash. U., St. Louis, 1986-89, U. Ill., Urbana-Champaign, Ill., 1989-94, Gonzaga U., Spokane, Wash., 1994-99, assoc. prof., 1999—. Continuing profl. edn. expert Gonzaga U., 1996—2006, Wash. Soc. CPAs, numerous others; vis. assoc. prof. U. Notre Dame, 2000. Editor Fin. Reporting Jour., 1998—2002, spl. guest editor Issues in Acctg. Edn., 2001—03, assoc. editor Jour. Derivatives Acctg., 2003—; contbr. articles to profl. jours. Recipient Outstanding Acctg. Educator award Wash. Soc. CPAs, 1998-99; Acad. acctg. fellow Office of Chief Acct., U.S. SEC, 1997-98. Mem. Am. Acctg. Assn. (editor Fin. Reporting Jour. newsletter Fin. Acctg. and Reporting sect. 1998—02), Wash. Soc. CPAs (bd. dirs. Spokane chpt.), K.C. (fin. sec. 1990-93, 99-2003, treas. 2005—) Avocations: music, cross country skiing, four-wheeling. Office: Gonzaga Univ 502 E Boone Ave Spokane WA 99258-0001 Office Phone: 509-323-3416. Office Fax: 509-323-5811. Business E-Mail: teets@gem.gonzaga.edu.

**TEEVAN, JAIME,** application developer, researcher; b. Stanford, Calif., Sept. 5, 1976; d. James Ripley and Connie Monroe Teevan; m. Alexander Marliave Hehmeyer, June 15, 2002; 1 child, Griffin Alexander Teevan Hehmeyer. BS, Yale U., New Haven, Conn., 1998; M, MIT, Cambridge, Mass., 2001; student, MIT, 2001—. Financial Technology Option MIT Sloan Sch., 2003. Software engr. Infoseek Corp., Sunnyvale, Calif., 1998—99; rsch. asst. MIT, Cambridge, Mass., 1999—; rsch. intern Microsoft Rsch., Redmond, Wash., 2004. Grad. student coun. rep. MIT, Cambridge, Mass., 2002—03, inst. rep., faculty com. on the libr. sys., 2003—05. Recipient J. Edward Meeker prize, Yale U., 1995, Bloch prize, 1995, Master's Cup, Timothy Dwight Coll., 1998; Grad. Rsch. fellowship, NSF, 1999—2003. Mem.: Spl. Interest Group on Computer-Human Interaction, Spl. Interest Group on Info. Retrieval, Assn. for Computing Machinery. Achievements include patents pending for systems, methods, and interfaces for providing personalized search and information access; research in personalized search and personal information management. Office: Mass Inst of Tech 32 Vassar St G472 Cambridge MA 02139 Office Phone: 617-253-1611. E-mail: teevan@mit.edu.

**TEEVAN, RICHARD COLLIER,** retired psychology professor; b. Shelton, Conn., June 12, 1919; s. Daniel Joseph and Elizabeth (Halliwell) T.; m. Virginia Agnes Stehle, July 28, 1945; children— Jan Elizabeth, Kim Ellen, Clay Collier, Allison Tracy. BA, Wesleyan U., Middletown, Conn., 1951; MA, U. Mich., 1952, PhD, 1955. Rubber buffer Sponge Rubber Product Co., Derby, Conn., 1939-41; with U. Mich., 1951-57, teaching fellow, 1951-53, instr., 1953-57; asst. prof. Smith Coll., 1957-60; assoc. prof. Bucknell U., 1960-64, prof., 1964-69; chmn. psychology, prof. to prof. emeritus SUNY-Albany, 1969—; pres. Teevan Assocs., Cons., 1991—. Cons. on coll. teaching, 1989—. Author: Reinforcement, 1961, Instinct, 1961, Color Vision, 1961, Measuring Human Motivation, 1962, Theories of Motivation in Learning, 1964, Theories of Motivation in Personality and Social Psychology, 1964, Motivation, 1967, Fear of Failure, 1969, Readings in Elementary Psychology, 1973; contbr. articles to sci. jours. Served to capt. AUS, 1941-47; prisoner of war 1943-45, Ger. Office Naval Research grantee, 1958-72; recipient Lindbach award Bucknell U., 1966 Mem. AAAS, AAUP, Am. Psychol. Assn. (Disting. visitor 1981-85), Eastern Psychol. Assn., Phi Beta Kappa, Sigma Xi. Office: SUNY Dept Psychology 1400 Washington Ave Albany NY 12222-0100*

**TEFFT, JOHN F.,** b. Madison, Wis. m. Mariella Cellitti; children: Christine, Cathleen. BA, Marquette Univ.; MA in History, Georgetown Univ. Various positions to rank of min./counselor US Sr. Fgn. Svc., 1972—; internat. affairs adv. Nat. War Coll., Washington, 2003—04; dep. chief US Mission to Moscow US Dept. State, 1996—99, charge d'affaires Moscow, 1996—97, US amb. to Lithuania, 2000—03, dep. asst. sec. state European and Eurasian Affairs, 2004—05, US amb. to Georgia, 2005—. Recipient Disting. Honor award, US Dept. of State. Office: US Dept State 7060 Tbilisi Pl Washington DC 20521-7060

**TEGGE, PATRICIA ANN,** retired administrative assistant; b. Milw., Oct. 25, 1922; d. Edmund Finegan and Norma Berthe (Kussel) Jones; m. Lloyd Frederick Tegge, Oct. 23, 1946 (dec. 1990); 1 child, Mark. B in Philosophy and Journalism, Marquette U., 1945. Adminstrv. sec. Family Svc. of Waukesha, Wis., 1966-91; ret., 1991. Mem. adv. bd. Salvation Army, past chmn. Recipient Outstanding Svcs. award Salvation Army 1983-85. Mem. DAR,

Women in Communications (Southeastern Wis. chpt.), Nat. Assn. Parliamentarians (past pres. Wis. chpt.), Wis. Regional Writer's Assn. (chmn.), Wis. Soc. (recording sec. 1989—), Altrusa Club of Waukesha, Waukesha Women's Club (past pres.), Wis. Fedn. Women's Clubs (dist. pres. 1990—), Waukesha County Geneal. Soc. (newsletter editor 1997-2000). Republican. Lutheran.

**TEGNELIA, JAMES A.,** federal agency administrator; b. Monessen, Pa., 1942; BS in Physics, Georgetown U.; MS in Engring., George Washington U., 1975; PhD in Physics, Catholic U. Am. Supr. rsch. physicist to mgr. US Army Night Vision Lab., 1971—76; asst. under sec., acting. dep. under sec. Office Undersecretary Defense Rsch. Engring. US Dept Def., 1982—85; program mgr. and officer dir. Defense Advance Rsch. Projects Agy., 1976, dep. dir., 1985, acting dir.; v.p. engring. Martin Marietta Corp., v.p. bus. devel. Electronics Group; v.p. bus. devel., Energy and Environment Sector Lockheed Martin Corp., 1995, pres., Advanced Environ. Systems, Inc., 1996—98; exec. v.p., dep. dir. Sandia Nat. Lab., 1993, v.p. defense programs; dir. US Strategic Command Ctr. Combating Weapons Mass Destruction, 2004—, Defense Threat Reduction Agy., Ft. Belvoir, Va., 2004—. Mem. exec. coun., bd. dirs. Albuquerque C. of C., 1994—95; bd. dirs. Anderson Sch. U. N.Mex., Sandia Sci. and Tech. Pk., Tech. Ventures Corp., Laguna Industries, Inc.; bd. adv. George Washington U. Sch. Engring.; chmn. Greater Albuquerque US Saving Bond Campaign, 1996; chmn. Army Sci. Bd.; co-chmn. Nat. Lab. Nat. Security Adv. Panel; campaign chmn. United Way Ctrl. N.Mex., 1996. Served with U.S. Army, 1968—71, one yr. tour Vietnam. Recipient Bronze Star Medal, Civilian Meritorious Svc. Medal, Sr. Exec. Svc. Meritorious Svc. award. Mem.: Soc. Sigma Xi. Office: Defense Threat Reduction Agy 8725 John J Kingman Rd Stop 6201 Fort Belvoir VA 22060-6201*

**TEGTMEYER, JORDAN MICHAEL,** financial analyst; b. Hammond, Ind., Oct. 26, 1977; s. Roger Tegtmeyer and Laurie Falco. BS, Shippensburg (Pa.) U., 2000; MBA, U. Ill., 2003. Budget analyst NORC U. Chgo., 2000—03, fin. analyst NORC, 2003—05; fin. analyst, acct. U. Pa., Phila., 2005—. Home: 4425 Walnut Street Apt 2 Philadelphia PA 19104 Office Phone: 215-573-4940. Business E-Mail: jtegtmey@pobox.upenn.edu.

**TEI, TAKURI,** accountant; b. Korea, Feb. 25, 1924; s. Gangen and Isun (Song) T.; came to U.S., 1952, naturalized, 1972; diploma Concordia Theol. Sem., 1959; B.D., Eden Theol. Sem., 1965; M.Ed., U. Mo., 1972; m. Maria M. Ottwaska, Dec. 1, 1969; 1 dau., Sun Kyung Lee. Partner, Madeleine Ottwaska & Assos., St. Louis, 1968—; pres. TMS Tei Enterprises Inc., Webster Groves, Mo., 1969—; instr. Forest Park Community Coll. Mem. Am. Coll. Enrolled Agts. (pres. 1976—), Am. Accounting Assn., Am. Taxation Assn., Assn. Asian Studies, NAACP. Republican. Lutheran. Home and Office: 7529 Big Bend Blvd Saint Louis MO 63119-2103

**TEICH, ALBERT HARRIS,** professional society administrator; b. Chgo., Dec. 17, 1942; s. Maurice and Ina (Szuldiner) T.; m. Carolyn R. Richmond, June 3, 1965 (div. 1987); children: Mitchell Craig, Kenneth David; m. Jill H. Pace, Jan. 29, 1989; 1 child, Samantha Lynne. BS, MIT, 1964, PhD, 1969. Rsch. fellow Syracuse (N.Y.) U. Rsch. Corp., 1969-71, dir., sci. and tech. studies, 1971-73; coord. rsch. SUNY, Binghamton, 1973-74; dir. rsch. SUNY Inst. for Pub. Policy Alternatives, Albany, 1974-76; assoc. prof. pub. affairs and dep. dir., grad. program sci. tech. and pub. policy George Washington U., 1976-79; spl. policy studies AAAS, Washington, 1980-84, head, office of pub. sector programs 1984-89, dir. sci. and policy programs, 1989—. Cons. NAS, Office of Tech. Assessment, Washington, 1976-95, Orgn. Econ. Cooperation and Devel., Paris, 1994—96, Hertz Found., 2003; chmn. SRS adv. com. NSF, Washington, 1988-90; pres. Technosci. Assocs., Inc., Silver Spring, Md., 1977-82; chair Ga. Inst. Tech., Sch. Pub. Bd., 2001-2005; mem. bd. govs. US-Israel Binational Sci Found., 2001—, vice chmn., 2004-05, chmn., 2005-06; mem. rsch. adv. bd. U. Calif., Davis, 2003—; mem. rsch. and tech. coord. com. Nat. Rsch. Coun., 2003—. Editor: Science and Technology in the U.S.A., 1986, Technology and the Future, 10th edit., 2005; editor, author: Scientists and Public Affairs, 1974; mem. editl. bd. Science Communication, 1991—, Science, Technology and Human Values, 1994—, Prometheus, 1999—, Renewable Resources Jour., 2005-. Recipient Sci. Achievement award, Wash. Acad. Scis., 2004. Fellow AAAS (chmn. sect. X 1988); mem. Tech. Transfer Soc. (v.p. 1985-91), Soc. for Social Studies of Scis., Washington Acad. Scis., Nat. Press Club, Sigma Xi. Avocations: swimming, photography, travel writing. Office: AAAS 1200 New York Ave NW Washington DC 20005-3941 Office Phone: 202-326-6600. Business E-Mail: ateich@aaas.org.

**TEICH, HOWARD BERNARD,** lawyer, volunteer, public information officer; b. Huntington, N.Y., Nov. 1, 1946; s. Samuel and Beatrice Ann (Kay) T. AB, U. Pa., 1967; JD, Boston U., 1970. Bar: N.Y., 1971, U.S. Dist. Ct. (so. dist.) N.Y. 1984. Counsel N.Y. State Senator Emanuel Gold, N.Y.C., 1971-72; law sec. N.Y. State Supreme Ct. Justin Martin Evans, N.Y.C., 1972-75; assoc. pub. Firehouse mag., N.Y.C., 1975-79; pub. Midtown South Bus., N.Y.C., 1985-87; prin. Law Offices Howard B. Teich, N.Y.C., 1980—; sr. cons. The Kamber Group, Washington, 1995—; sr. counsel McLaughlin & Stein, P.C., N.Y.C., 1997—. Founder, chair New Dem. Dimensions, N.Y.C., 1981-91, Nat. Task Force on Life Safety for Handicapped, Washington, 1979-81; bd. dirs. Boys Choir of Harlem, N.Y.C., 1983-85, Assn. on Am. Indian Affairs, 1990-97, adv. bd., 1997—; chmn. New Leadership of Israel Bonds, N.Y.C., 1977-79; pres. Am. Jewish Congress Met. Region N.Y.C., 1992—, past nat. v.p.; bd. dirs. Jewish Comty. Rels. Coun., N.Y., 1995—; v.p. 1995-98; co-chair Jewish Heritage, N.Y.C., 1997—; dep. dir. N.Y. state citizens com. McGovern for Pres., 1972, Samuels for Gov., 1974, Carey for Gov., 1974; dep. dir. N.Y. state primary campaign Carter for Pres., 1980; co-chair N.Y. state citizens com. Glenn for Pres., 1984, Mondale/Ferraro '84, 1984; bd. dirs. Manhattan Playhouse. Recipient Robert Briscoe award Emerald Isle Immigration Soc., 1996, Israel Leadership award Israel Bonds, 1979, Martin Luther King Jr. Living-the-Dream award, Gov. George Pataki, N.Y., 1999. Mem. AJ Congress Met Region (pres. 1992—), U. Pa. Club, Assn. on Am. Indian Affairs (bd. dirs., nat. adv. bd.). Democrat. Jewish. Avocations: softball, tennis, reading, theater, dance. Home: 185 E 85th St New York NY 10028-2140 Office: 260 Madison Ave New York NY 10016-2401

**TEICH, MALVIN CARL,** electrical engineering educator; b. NYC, May 4, 1939; s. Sidney R. and Loretta K. Teich SB in Physics, MIT, 1961; MSEE, Stanford U., 1962; PhD in Quantum Electronics, Cornell U., 1966. Research scientist MIT Lincoln Lab., Lexington, Mass., 1966-67; prof. engring. sci. Columbia U., N.Y.C., 1967-96, prof. emeritus, 1996—, chmn. dept. elec. engring., 1978-80, mem. Columbia Radiation Lab., faculty applied physics dept. N.Y.C.; prof. elec. computer engring., biomed. engring., physics Boston U., 1995—. Mem. Photonics Ctr., Boston U., also Ctr. Adaptive Sys., Hearing Rsch. Ctr.; mem. sci. bd. Inst. Physics, Czech Acad. Scis., Prague. Author: (with B.E.A. Saleh) Fundamentals of Photonics, 1991, (with S.B. Lowen) Fractal Based Point Processes; dep. editor Quantum Optics, 1988-92; bd. editors Jour. Visual Comm. and Image Representation, 1989-92, Jemná Mechanika a Optika, 1994—; contbr. articles to profl. jours.; patentee in field; expert in patent and trade secret litigation. Recipient Citation Classic award Inst. for Sci. Info., 1981; Meml. Gold medal of Palacky U., Czech Republic, 1992; Guggenheim Meml. Found. fellow, 1973. Fellow AAAS, IEEE (Browder J. Thompson Meml. prize 1969, Morris E. Leeds award 1997), Optical Soc. Am. (editl. adv. panel Optics Letters 1977-79), Am. Phys. Soc., Acoustical Soc. Am.; mem. Sigma Xi, Tau Beta Pi. Office: Boston U Dept Elec and Computer Engr 8 Saint Mary's St Boston MA 02215-2421 Office Phone: 617-353-1236. Business E-Mail: teich@bu.edu.

**TEICHGRAEBER, RICHARD D.,** electrical engineer researcher; b. Hutchinson, Kans., Dec. 20, 1941; s. Robert Arthur and Rosanna Frances (Sandberg) T.; m. Viki Lyn Isbell, June 30, 1989; 1 child, Bryan R. BSEE, Kans. State U., 1964, MSEE, 1966, PhD in Elec. Engring., 1969. Registered profl. engr.; Tex. Draftsman Garwin Inc., Wichita, Kans., 1959-61; elec. draftsman Beech Aircraft Corp., Wichita, 1962-63; engr. Boeing Airplane Co., Wichita, 1964, 65; instr. Dept. Elec. Engring. Kans. State U., Manhattan, 1968-69; embedded software specialist, sr. staff program mgr. Gen.

Dynamics/Lockheed, Ft. Worth, 1969—. Contbr. 20 articles to profl. jours. Elder Univ. Christian Ch., Ft. Worth, chmn. men's fellowship, 1993-94; substitute tchr. Adopt-A-Sch., Ft. Worth, 1980-91; spl. friend Learning Ctr., Ft. Worth, 1988-90. Recipient tuition scholarship Wichita Univ., 1959-61, Rice Univ. Grad. Fellowship, Houston, 1964-65, NASA Traineeship Kans. State Univ., Manhattan, 1965-68, Disting. lectr. award Coll. Engring., Kans. State U., 2006. Mem. IEEE (sr., life), Soc. Photo-Instrumentation Engrs., Tex. Soc. Profl. Engrs. (treas. 1980-81, dir. 1980-95), Lnad Grand Legacy Soc., Toastmasters Internat. (pres. 1987), Sigma Tau, Eta Kappa Nu. Republican. Avocations: ice skating, skiing, golf, gardening. Home: 9005 Little Reata Tr Benbrook TX 76126 Office: Lockheed Martin Aeronautics Co PO Box 748 Mail Zone 2411 Fort Worth TX 76101-0748 Office Phone: 817-763-7509. E-mail: r.teichgraeber@ieee.org.

**TEICHLER, STEPHEN LIN,** lawyer; b. Charleston, W.Va., Jan. 30, 1952; s. Alfred H. and Marjorie R. (Dunbar) Teichler; m. Dana Ruth Hegerle, Aug. 6, 1977; children: Adam Reed, Ryan Stephen. BA, U. Va., 1974, JD, 1977. Bar: Va. 1977, DC 1979, US Supreme Ct., Supreme Ct. Va., US Ct. Appeals 1st, 2nd, 4th, 5th, 6th, 11th & Fed. Circuits, US Dist. Ct. DC, US Dist. Ct. Ea. Dist. Va. Atty. Dept. Air Force Office of Gen. Counsel, Washington, 1977-80; assoc. Baker & Botts LLP, Washington, 1980—88, ptnr., 1988—95, Metzger, Hollis, Gordon & Alprin, Washington, 1995-97, Duane Morris LLP, Washington, 1997—, chair firm energy and resources practice group, 2003—. Capt. USAF, 1977-80. Mem.: Energy Bar Assn., Va. State Bar Assn., DC Bar. Lutheran. Office: Duane Morris LLP 1667 K St NW Washington DC 20006-1608 Office Phone: 202-776-7830. Office Fax: 202-776-7801. Business E-Mail: slteichler@duanemorris.com.

**TEICHNER, LESTER,** general management executive; b. Chgo., Apr. 21, 1944; s. Ben Bernard and Eva Bertha (Weinberg) T.; m. Barbara Rae Bush, Jan. 30, 1966 (div. Aug. 1969); m. Doris Jean Ayres, Jan. 31, 1980; children: Lauren Ayres, Caroline Ayres. BSEE, U. Ill., 1965; MBA in Mktg. and Fin., U. Chgo., 1969. Sales engr. Westinghouse Electric Corp., Chgo., 1965-69; v.p. ops. Intec Inc., Chgo., 1969-74; pres., CEO The Chgo. Group Inc., 1974—2000, Guttermonster, LLC, 2005—; pres., COO Republic Window & Doors, 2000—05. Bd. dirs. Golub & Co., Inc., Strategic Processing Inc., NYC, Dees Comms. Ltd., Vancouver, B.C., Maxcor Mfg. Co., Colorado Springs; CEO, bd. dirs. Axcess Worldwide Ltd., Coal Gasification, Inc., Chgo.; guest lectr. U. Chgo. Grad. Sch. Bus., 1982-95. Co-inventor U.S. patent electronic marketplace; contbr. articles to profl. publs. Mem. The Chgo. Forum, 1976—; bd. dirs. Am. Israeli C. of C. Mem. Am. Mgmt. Assn., Am. Mktg. Assn., Midwest Planning Assn. (bd. dirs. 1981). Republican. Jewish. Avocations: astronomy, skiing. Home: 2230 N Seminary Ave Chicago IL 60614-3507 Office: The Chicago Group Inc 2230 N Seminary Ave Chicago IL 60614-3507 Office Phone: 773-371-0357. Personal E-mail: lteichner@aol.com.

**TEIG, MARLOWE GILMAN,** investment banker; b. Fargo, N.D., Sept. 13, 1938; s. Julius Berner Teig and Inez (Hedlund) Teig-Erickson; m. Carole Lynne Werner, Nov. 25, 1961; children: Jennifer Lynne, Alan Gilman. BA, U. Mich., 1961; postgrad., CCNY, 1962-64. With Harcourt Brace Jovanovich, 1964-80, Houghton Mifflin Co., 1980-87, Macmillan, Inc., 1987-88; mng. dir. Berkery, Noyes & Co., Newton, Mass., 1990—. Home: 40 Kirkstall Rd Newton MA 02460-2218 Office Phone: 617-969-7935. Business E-Mail: marlowe.teig@berkerynoyes.com.

**TEIGER, DAVID,** management consultant; b. Newark, June 13, 1929; s. Samuel and Fannie (Ginsburg) Teiger; children: Lauren, Douglas. BS, Cornell U., 1951. Ptnr. Samuel Teiger & Co., Newark, 1953-59, Ira Haupt & Co., NYC, 1959-64, Bache & Co., NYC, 1964-65; exec. v.p Shearson, Hammill & Co., Inc., NYC, 1965-73; chmn., CEO United Rsch. Co., Morristown, NJ, 1973-90; chmn. Gemini Consulting, Morristown, NJ, 1990-95. Hon. trustee Mus. Modern Art, NYC. Served to lt. U.S. Army, 1951—53. Named one of Top 200 Collectors, ARTnews mag., 2006. Mem.: Meadowood; Mountain Ridge. Office: Teiger Inc 51 Peachcroft Dr Bernardsville NJ 07924-1006

**TEILLON, LOUIS PIERRE, JR.,** lawyer; b. NYC, Nov. 15, 1943; AB, Yale U., 1965; LLB, Columbia U., 1968. Bar: Pa. 1968. Mem. Heckscher, Teillon, Terrill & Sager, P.C., West Conshohocken, Pa. Mem. Am. Coll. Trust and Estate Counsel, Pa. Bar Assn. (real property, probate and trust sects.), Phila. Bar Assn. (past chmn. probate sect.). Office: Heckscher Teillon Terrill & Sager 100 Four Falls Corp Ctr Ste 300 West Conshohocken PA 19428 Fax: 610-940-6042. Office Phone: 610-940-4169. E-mail: perry@htts.com.

**TEIMAN, RICHARD BARRY,** lawyer; b. Bklyn., May 19, 1938; s. AB, Princeton U., 1959; LLB, Harvard U., 1962. Bar: N.Y. 1963. Ptnr. Winston & Strawn LLP and predecessor Cole & Deitz, NYC, 1968—. Trustee Citizens Budget Commn., 1993—. Mem. Assn. Bar City N.Y. (com. admiralty 1975-78, 87, chair 1988-91, 03-06), Maritime Law Assn. (com. maritime financing 1980—, chmn. subcom. Recodification U.S. Ship Mortgage Act 1986-91, chmn. subcom. USCG, citizenship and related matters 1988-94), Phi Beta Kappa. Home: 5 Pryer Ln Larchmont NY 10538-4012 Office: Winston & Strawn LLP 200 Park Ave Rm 4100 New York NY 10166-4193 Office Phone: 212-294-6730. Business E-Mail: rteiman@winston.com.

**TEIN, JENN-YUN,** psychologist, researcher; arrived in U.S., 1980; d. Ji-Wu and Tsai-Jing Huang Tein; m. Chi-sheng Wang. BA, Nat. Chung-Hsing U., Taichung, Taiwan, 1977; MEd, U. Tex., 1982; PhD, Ohio State U., 1989. Co-primary investigator Prevention Rsch. Ctr. Ariz. State U., Tempe, 1988—. Preventive intervention program evaluator/cons., Tempe, 2001—; bd. dirs. Mountain Park Health Ctr., Phoenix. Mem. Asian Am. Faculty/Staff Assn., Ariz. State U., Tempe, 1995—96; v.p., bd. dirs. Chinese-Am. Profls. Assn. Ariz., Phoenix, 1995—97; pres. Asian Women Assn., Tempe, 1993—94. Mem.: Am. Evaluation Assn., Psychometric Soc., Soc. for Prevention Rsch.

**TEITELBAUM, PHILIP,** psychologist; b. Bklyn., Oct. 9, 1928; s. Bernard and Betty (Schechter) T.; m. Osnat Boné; children: Benjamin, Daniel, David, Jonathan, Gideon. BS, CCNY, 1950; MA, Johns Hopkins U., 1952, PhD, 1954. Instr., asst. prof. physical. psychology Harvard U., 1954-59; assoc. prof. psychology U. Pa., Phila., 1959-63, prof., 1963-73; prof. psychology U. Ill.-Urbana-Champaign, 1973-85, emeritus prof., 1985—, Disting. prof. Ctr. Advanced Studies, 1980-85; grad. research prof. U. Fla., Gainesville, 1984—. Author: Fundamental Principles of Physiological Psychology, 1967; editor: (with E. Satinoff) Motivation: Handbook Behavioral Neurobiology, 1983. Contbr. chpts. to books, articles to profl. jours. Fellow Ctr. for Advanced Study in Behavorial Scis., Stanford U., 1975-76, Fulbright fellow Tel Aviv U., 1978-79, Guggenheim fellow, 1984-85, Carnegie Found. fellow Inst. Neurol. Scis., U. Pa. Med. Sch., 1958-59. Fellow APA (pres. div. physiol. psychology, disting. sci. contbr. award 1978), Am. Psychol. Soc. (William James fellow); mem. NAS, AAAS, Am. Physiol. Soc., Soc. for Neurosci., Soc. Exptl. Psychology. Home: 2239 NW 17th Ave Gainesville FL 32605-3909 Office Phone: 352-392-0615. Personal E-mail: teitelb@hotmail.com.

**TEITELBAUM, STEVEN LAZARUS,** pathology educator; b. Bklyn., June 29, 1938; s. Hyman and Rose Leah (Harnick) T.; m. Marilyn Ruth Schaffner; children: Caren Beth, Aaron Michael, Rebecca Lee. BA, Columbia U., 1960; MD, Washington U., St. Louis, 1964; DSc (hon.), CUNY SI Coll., 2004. Intern Washington U. Sch. Medicine, St. Louis, 1964-65, 3d. yr. asst. resident, ACS clin. fellow, 1967-68; intern NYU, 1965-66, 2d yr. resident, 1966-67; assoc. pathologist Jewish Hosp. at Washington U. Med. Ctr., St. Louis, 1969-89, pathologist-in-chief, 1987-96; assoc. pathologist Barnes-Jewish Hosp., St. Louis, 1986—; pathologist St. Louis Shriners Hosp. for Crippled Children, 1986—; Wilma and Roswell Messing prof. pathology Washington U. Sch. Medicine, St. Louis, 1987—. Mem. Orthopedics and Musculoskeletal Study Sect. NIH, 1983-87; adv. counsel NIH, 2003—. Contbr. numerous sci. articles to med. jours., 12 chpts. to med. books and texts, 1976—; mem. editorial bd. Calcified Tissue Internat., 1980-85, 89-91, Human Pathology; mem. bd. assoc. editors Jour. Orthopaedic Rsch., Jour. Cellular Biochemistry. Recipient 2nd Century award, Washington U. Sch. Medicine,

2004. Mem. Am. Soc. Clin. Investigation, Assn. Am. Physicians, Am. Acad. Orthopaedic Surgeons (Ann Doner Vaughan Kappa Delta award 1988), Paget's Disease Found. (adv. panel), Am. Soc. for Bone and Mineral Rsch. (pres. 1993, William F. Neuman award 1998), Fed. Am. Soc. Expl. Biology (bd. dirs. 1997—, pres. 2002--). Office: Washington U Sch Medicine 216 S Kingshighway Blvd Saint Louis MO 63110-1026 E-mail: teitelbs@medicine.wustl.edu.

**TEITELL, CONRAD LAURENCE,** lawyer, writer; b. N.Y.C., Nov. 8, 1932; s. Benson and Belle (Altman) T.; m. Adele Mary Crummins, May 26, 1957; children: Beth Mary, Mark Lewis. AB, U. Mich., 1954; LL.B., Columbia U., 1957; LL.M., N.Y. U., 1968. Bar: N.Y. 1958, D.C., 1968. Mem. Prerau & Teitell, N.Y.C. and White Plains, NY, 1964-96, Cummings & Lockwood, Stamford, Conn., 1996—. Dir. Philanthropy Tax Inst., Old Greenwich, Conn., 1964—; adj. prof. U. Miami Law Sch., 1980—. Author: Philanthropy and Taxation, 5 vols., 1993-2006; editor, pub. Taxwise Giving, 1964—; contbr. articles to legal jours. Served with U.S. Army, 1957. Recipient Disting. Svc. to Higher Edn. award Am. Coll. Pub. Relations Assn., 1970, Disting. Svc. award Nat. Com. on Planned Giving, 1990, Harrison Tweed Spl. Merit award Am. Law Inst./ABA, 1992. Fellow Am. Coll. Trust and Estate Counsel; mem. ABA (former co-chmn. com. charitable giving, trusts, founds.), Assn. of Bar of City of N.Y. Home: 16 Marlow Ct Riverside CT 06878-2614 Office: Cummings & Lockwood 6 Landmark Sq Stamford CT 06901 also: PO Box 299 Old Greenwich CT 06870-0299 Office Phone: 203-351-4164. Business E-Mail: cteitell@cl-law.com.

**TEITELMAN, RICHARD B.,** state supreme court judge; BA in Math., U. Pa., 1969; JD, Washington U., 1973. Bar: Mo. 1974. Pvt. practice, St. Louis, 1974-75; staff atty. Legal Svcs. Ea. Mo., St. Louis, 1975-76, mng. atty., 1976-80, exec. dir., gen. counsel, 1980—; judge Mo. Ct. Appeals (ea. dist.), 1997—2000, Mo. Supreme Ct., 2002—. Bd. dirs. Citizens for Mo.'s Children, St. Louis, 1988—. Recipient Durward K. McDaniel award Am. Coun. of Blind, 1986. Mem. The Mo. Bar, Kansas City Met. Bar Assn., Mound City Bar Assn., Lawyers Assn., St. Louis, Women Lawyers' Assn. Greater St. Louis, St. Louis County Bar Assn., Bi-State Lawyers Assn., Am. Judicature Soc. (bd. dirs. 1986-2005), St. Louis Bar Found., Leadership St. Louis. Office: Mo Supreme Court PO Box 150 Jefferson City MO 65102 Office Phone: 573-751-1004. Business E-Mail: rteitelm@courts.mo.gov.*

**TEITZ, RICHARD STUART,** museum director, educator; b. Fall River, Mass., July 18, 1942; s. Alexander George and Lucille T.; m. Elaine Tallmadge Osborn, 1962; children: Rebecca Eve, Jessica Ann. Alexander Osborn. AB, Yale U., 1963; MA, Harvard U., 1965. Asst. curator Fogg Art Mus., Harvard U., 1964-65; curatorial asst. Worcester (Mass.) Art Mus., 1965-67, asst. dir., 1969-70, dir., 1970-81, Hood Mus. of Art, Dartmouth Coll., Hanover, N.H., 1981-84, Denver Art Mus., 1984—. Dir. Wichita Art Mus., 1967-69; lectr. Boston Archtl. Center, 1964-65; instr. Clark U., 1966-67; assoc. dir. Etruscan Found., Siena, 1965, 66—; prof. art Dartmouth Coll., 1981-84; bd. dirs. Ava Gallery, N.H. Visual Artists Coalition Author: Masterpieces of Etruscan Art, 1967, Art of the Victorian Era, 1969; also articles. Mem. Assn. Art Mus. Dirs., Archaeol. Inst. Am., Internat. Council Mus., Coll. Art Assn. Clubs: Yale (N.Y.C. and Colo.), Denver Athletic. Office: Denver Art Mus 1000 W 14th Ave Denver CO 80204-2525

**TEIXEIRA, ARTHUR ALVES,** food engineer, educator, consultant; b. Fall River, Mass., Jan. 30, 1944; s. Arthur Araujo and Emelia (Alves) T.; m. Jean E. Lamb, Dec. 26, 1966 (dec. Dec. 1983); children: A. Allan, Scott C.; m. Marjorie St. John, June 28, 1986; 1 stepchild, Craig St. John. PhD, U. Mass., 1971. Registered profl. engr., Fla., Mass. Rsch. engr. Ross Labs., Columbus, Ohio, 1971-73, R&D group leader, 1973-77; sr. cons. Arthur D. Little, Inc. Cambridge, Mass., 1977-82; assoc. prof. U. Fla., Gainesville, 1982-89, prof., 1989—. Sci. advisor Escola Superior de Biotecnologia, Porto, Portugal, 1991-96, FMC Corp., Santa Clara, Calif., 1989-92; internat. cons., Australia, Belgium, Brazil, Bulgaria, Chile, Cuba, Eng., France, Germany, Hungary, Indonesia, Ireland, Israel, Kenya, Netherlands, Poland, Portugal, Peru, Romania, South Africa, Spain; reviewer USDA, Washington, 1991—. Author: Computerized Food Processing Operations, 1989; contbr. 12 chpts. to books, 70 articles to profl. jours. Judge Internat. Sci. Fair, Orlando, Fla., 1991. Recipient Fulbright scholar award, Portugal, 1990—91, Golden Retort award of Merit, IFTPS, 1994, Sr. Faculty award, U. Fla. chpt. Gamma Sigma Delta, 1996, Tchr. of Yr. award, U. Fla. Coll. Engring., 1996, Fulbright scholar award, Peru, 2000, Disting. Food Engr. award, IAFIS/FPEI/ASAE, 2001, Marvin Tung Achievement award, 2005. Fellow Am. Soc. Agrl. Engrs. (dir. 1988-90, Paper awards 1988-89, 2001, assoc. editor Transactions of ASAE 1985—); mem. AIChE, Am. Soc. Agr. and Biol. Engrs., Inst. Food Technologists (mem. editl. bd. 1980-83, 2003—), Am. Soc. Engring. Edn., Inst. Thermal Process Specialists, Coun. on Agrl. Sci. and Tech., R & D Assocs. Gamma Sigma Delta (chpt. pres. U. Fla. 1999-2000), Sigma Xi, Alpha Epsilon, Tau Beta Pi. Roman Catholic. Achievements include design of on-line process control system to assure safety of sterilized canned foods; tech. and economic feasiblity for radiation sterilization of disposable feeding devices; research in computer optimization and control of food sterilization processes, mathematical modelling of bacterial spore population dynamics in processed foods, and anaerobic composting for solid waste management on long-term NASA space missions. Office: U Fla Rogers Hall Gainesville FL 32611-0570 Office Phone: 352-392-1864. E-mail: aateixeira@mail.ifas.ufl.edu.

**TEIXEIRA, MARK,** professional baseball player; b. Annapolis, Md, Apr. 11, 1980; Attended, Ga. Tech. First baseman Texas Rangers, 2003. Mem. Team USA, World Baseball Classic, 2006. Named to Am. League All-Star Team, 2005; recipient Silver Slugger award, MLB, 2005, A.L. Gold Glove, 2005. Office: Ameriquest Ball Park 1000 Ballpark Way Arlington TX 76002*

**TEJADA, FRANCISCO,** physician, educator; b. Moyobamba, San Martin, Peru, July 25, 1942; s. Francisco Tejada and Semiramis Reatequi; m. Barbara Ann Kotowski, Feb. 1, 1970; children: Anamaria, Semiramis, Barbara Lee, Francisco, James. BS, U. Nacional Mayor de San Marcos, Lima, Peru, 1961; MD, U. Peruana Cayetano Heredia, Lima, 1967. Diplomate Am. Bd. Internal Medicine, Am. Bd. Oncology. Resident in medicine Johns Hopkins U., Balt., 1969-72; sr. cancer rsch. Nat. Cancer Inst., NIH, Bethesda, Md., 1972-75; asst. clin. dir. Comprehensive Cancer Ctr. Fla., Miami, Fla., 1975-80; asst. prof. U. Miami, 1975-79, assoc. prof., 1979-85, prof., 1985—; vis. prof. U. Peruana Cayetano Heredia, Lima, 1994—; sr. ptnr. Oncology Assocs., Miami, 1980-85; chief cancer control Papanicolaou Cancer Ctr., Miami, 1984-86; assoc. dir. AMC Cancer Rsch. Ctr., Denver, 1986-87; pres. Am. Oncology Ctrs., Miami, 1985—; prof. U. San Agustin, Arequipa, Peru, 1992—, U. Peruana Cayetano Heredia, Lima, Peru, 1994—; clin. rsch. scientist UM/Sylvester Comprehensive Cancer Ctr., 2001—; investigator Lovelace Rsch. Svcs., Inc., 2002—. Oncology expert Pan Am. Health Orgn., Washington, 1975-85, Nat. Cancer Inst., Bethesda, Md., 1984-86; dir. Miami Cancer Inst., 1980—; dir. Peruvian-Am. Endowment Inc., 1993-99, v.p., 1995-97; bd. dirs. Integrated Med. Svcs. Fla. Keys, Key West, 1997-2000; dir. oncology dept. Clinica Ricardo Palma, Lima, Peru, 1991-99; med. dir. Fla. Comprehensive Cancer Control Initiative, 2000-03; dir. CureMeDoctor Inc., 2002-2002. Editor Miami Health Letter, 1986—; inventor cancer risk assessment. Mem. Beacon Coun., Miami, 1984, Latin Am. Cancer Info., Washington, 1976, Hispanic Cancer Rsch. Network, Washington, 1990; chpt. pres. Peruvian Am. Med. Soc., Miami, 1986; trustee Miami-Dade County Pub. Health Trust, 2002-05; bd. dirs. Miami-Dade County Policy Health Authority, 2002-03. Lt. Peruvian Army, 1966-67. Decorated comendador Orden Sociedad, Peruvian U. Cayetano Heredia; recipient Gold Medal Merit award Ministry of Edn., Lima, 1959, Hipolito Unanue award Hipolito Unanue Inst., Lima, 1968. Fellow ACP, Johns Hopkins U., Nat. Cancer Inst.; mem. Colegio Medico del Perú, Am. Assn. Cancer Rsch., Am. Soc. Clin. Oncology, Am. Soc. Hematology, Bolivian Cancer Soc. (hon.), Peruvian Cancer Soc. (hon.), Chilean Soc. Cancer (hon.), Argentinian Soc. Head and Neck Pathology (hon.) Roman Catholic. Avocations: hiking, photography, reading. Office: 1801 NW 9th Ave Rm 200F Miami FL 33136 Office Phone: 305-251-4540. Personal E-mail: ftejadamd@gmail.com.

**TEJADA, MIGUEL,** professional baseball player; b. Bani, Dominican Republic, May 25, 1976; Shortstop Oakland (Calif.) Athletics, 1997—2003, Balt. (Md.) Orioles, 2004—. Named Most Valuable Player, Am. League, 2002, MLB All-Star Game, 2005; named to Am. League All-Star Team, 2002, 2004, 2005; recipient Silver Slugger award, MLB, 2005. Achievements include won All-Star home run derby, 2004; led Am. League in RBI's (149), 2004. Office: 333 West Camden St Baltimore MD 21201

**TE KANAWA, KIRI,** opera and concert singer; b. Gisborne, N.Z., Mar. 6, 1944; d. Thomas and Eleanor Te Kanawa; m. Desmond Park, Aug. 30, 1967 (div. 1997); children— Antonia Aroha, Thomas Desmond. Student, St. Mary's Coll., Auckland, N.Z., 1957-60, London Opera Centre, 1966-69; DMus (hon.), Oxford U., Dundee U., 1983, Warwick U., Auckland U., Waikato U., Nottingham U., Chgo. U., Durham U., Cambridge U. Joined Royal Opera House, London, 1971; appeared in role of Countess in Le Nozze di Figaro, 1971; U.S. debut in Santa Fe Festival, 1971; Met. Opera debut as Desdemona in Otello, 1974; appearances with all major European and Am. opera houses, including Australian opera cos., Royal Opera House, Covent Garden, London, Paris Opera, Munich Opera, La Scala, others; opera appearences include Boris Gudonov, Carmen, Don Giovanni, the Magic Flute, Eugene Onegin, La Boheme, Manon Lescaut, many others; appeared in film Don Giovanni as Elvira, 1979; recs. include Blue Skies, 1986, Kiri Sings Gershwin, 1987, Kiri Te Kanawa: Italian Opera Arias, 1991, Kiri Her Greatest Hits, Ave Maria, Kiri on Broadway, The Kiri Selection, Kiri Side Tracks, My Fair Lady, Maori Songs; PBS appearance: Great Performances: West Side Story, 1985; author: Land of the Long White Cloud, 1989, Opera for Lovers, 1996. Decorated comdr. Order Brit. Empire, 1973, Dame Comdr. Brit. Empire, 1983, Order of Australia, 1990, Order of New Zealand, 1995. Mem.: Royal Acad. Music (hon.).

**TEKER, KASIF,** engineering educator; m. Fatma Teker; children: Asude, Tarik, Berire. MS, Ohio State U., Columbus, 1996; PhD, Case Western Res. U., Cleve., 2001. Engr. IQE, Inc., Bethlehem, Pa., 2001—03; asst. prof. Frostburg State U., Md., 2005—. Fellow, U. Del., Newark, 2003—05. Achievements include discovery of applications of carbon nanotubes for cancer research. Office: Frostburg State University 101 Braddock Rd Compton Science Center Frostburg MD 21532 Office Phone: 301-687-4339. E-mail: kteker@frostburg.edu.

**TELEANU, FLORIN I.,** risk management consultant, financial analyst; b. Slanic, Romania, May 16, 1980; s. Lizica Elena and Ion Teleanu. B in Econ., Acad. of Economics, Bucharest, Romania, 2002; MA in Internat. Economics and Fin., Brandeis U., Waltham, Mass., 2005. Fin. analyst, mergers and acquisitions DDP Cons. Group, Bucharest, Romania, 2001—02; analyst, fin. services group KPMG, Bucharest, Romania, 2002—03; asset backed securities, fin. analyst State St. Rsch. and Mgmt., Boston, 2004—05; fixed income analyst, risk mgmt. BlackRock, NYC, 2005—. Cmty. advisor Brandeis U., Waltham, Mass., 2004—05; v.p. Liberal Party - Youth Org., Ploiesti, Romania, 2000—02. Mem.: CFA Inst. (assoc.). Christian. Avocations: long distance running, travel. Home: 158 E 82nd St Apt 2B New York NY 10028 Office: BlackRock Park Ave Plaza 55 East 52nd Street New York NY 10055 Office Phone: 212-810-5997.

**TELEGDI, ANDREW,** member of parliament; b. Budapest, Hungary, May 28, 1946; arrived in Can., 1957; s. Alexander Sandor and Elenora Maria (Friedrich) T.; m. Nancy Curtin; 1 child, Erin. Student, U. Waterloo. Mem. Waterloo City Coun., 1985-93, Waterloo Regional Coun., 1988-93; mem. parliament Waterloo Ho. of Commons, 1993—2006, vice chair on human rights com., 1994-95, vice chair pub. accts. com., 1995-96; mem. justice com. Ho. of Commons, 1997-98, mem. caucus com. on postsecondary edn. 1996—, vice chair, regional licensing com., assoc. mem. fin., environ., and industry coms., 1993—2002, M.P. for Kitchener-Waterloo, chmn. standing com. on citizenship and immigration, chmn. liberal caucus SW Ontario, 2004—05. Exec. dir. Youth in Conflict with the Law, 1976-93; coord. Justice Week, Waterloo, 1979-83; pres. Fedn. of Students, U. Waterloo, 1973-75; advisor to Prime Min., Budapest Conf. on Security and Coop. in Europe, 1994; standing com. on citizenship and immigration, Ho. of Commons, Ottawa, 1998-2000; parliamentary sec. to Minister of Citizenship and Immigration, 1998-2000; parliamentary sec. to Prime Min. with spl. emphasis on aboriginal affairs, 2004; standing com. aboriginal affairs, no. devel. and natural resources, standing com. on citizenship and immigration, 2004-. Bd. dirs. The Working Centre and St. John's Soup Kitchen, 1986-93, Kitchener House, 1979—; pres. K.W. Multicultural Centre, 1987-89; chair Conestoga Coll. Basic Job Readiness Tng. Adv. Group, 1980-84; mem. clin. adv. com. Cath. Family Counseling Centre, 1986-87, family violence com.; chair People, Working and Learning Inc., 1984-86; mem. Senate U. Waterloo; mem. bd. govs. Wilfrid Laurier U., 1990-93. Mem. Waterloo Uptown Bus. Assn., Kitchener-Waterloo C. of C. (bus. edn. com.). Libr. Com. Mem. Avocations: fishing, golf, chess, reading. Office: House of Commons 285 Confederation Bldg Ottawa ON Canada K1A 0A6 E-mail: telega@parl.gc.ca.

**TELEMAN, SILVIU,** mathematician, educator; b. Corbeni, Romania, Aug. 21, 1931; arrived in U.S., 1986; m. Ecaterina Cioranescu, May 15, 1962; children: Calin Nicolae Stefan, Constantin. BS, M. Eminescu H.S., 1950; MS in Math., U. Bucharest, 1957, PhD of Math., 1968. Editor Inst. Romanian-Soviet Studies Romanian Acad. Sci., Bucharest, 1960—62; reader, chmn., lectr., dean Pedagogical Inst., Pitesti, Romania, 1962—68; lectr. Inst. Math. Romanian Acad. Scis., Bucharest, 1968—86; vis. prof. dept. math. Ind. U., Bloomington, 1986—87; Otto Szasz vis. prof. dept. math. U. Cin., 1987—88; vis. prof. dept. math. U. Mich., Ann Arbor, 1988—89; assoc. prof. Dept. Math. U. P.R., San Juan, 1989—95, prof. Dept. Math., 1995—. Author: Theory of Harmonic Algebras, with Applications to Von Neumann Algebras and Cohomology of Locally Compact Spaces (de Ilham's Theorem), 1971 (Gh. Tziteica award, 1971), An Introduction to Choquet Theory, with Applications to Reduction Theory, 1980; contbr. articles to profl. jours. Recipient Order of Work 3d Class, Pres. Romania, 1967, Rep. Presdl. Legion of Merit, Rep. Presdl. Legion Exec. Bd., 1997, Rep. Sen. Medal of Freedom, Rep. mem. of U.S. Senate, 1999. Mem.: AAAS, N.Y. Acad. Scis., Math. Assn. Am., Am. Math. Soc. Avocation: music. Home: 221 Calle Emmanuelli #2 Hato Rey San Juan PR 00917-4103 Office: Univ Puerto Rico Dept Math Rio Piedras Campus PO Box 23355 San Juan PR 00931 Office Phone: 787-764-0000 ext. 4699. Personal E-mail: ecaterinateleman@yahoo.com.

**TELENGATOR, ALEXANDER M.,** engineer; b. Samara, Russia, Jan. 11, 1972; MS with honors, Samara State Tech. U., 1994; PhD, U. Calif., La Jolla, 2000. Rsch. engr. Samara State Tech. U., 1994—96; grad. student rschr. dept. mech. and aerospace engring. U. Calif., La Jolla, 1996—2000; engring. scientist Ctr. for Energy Rsch. U. Calif. San Diego, La Jolla, 2000—. Contbr. articles to profl. jours. Recipient The Stipend of the Pres. of Russia, Russian Ministry of Higher Edn., 1995, Silver Medal for Student Sci. Rsch., 1994; Friends of the Internat. Ctr. scholar, U. Calif. La Jolla, 2000—. Mem.: AIAA, The Combustion Inst. Office: Univ Calif San Diego 9500 Gilman Dr La Jolla CA 92093-0417 Office Phone: 858-534-6617.

**TELESETSKY, WALTER,** federal agency administrator; b. Boston, Jan. 22, 1938; s. Keril and Nellie (Krelka) T.; m. Sharron-Dawn Lamp, July 15, 1961; children: Stephanie Ann, Anastasia Marie. BS in Mech. Engring., Northeastern U., 1960; MBA, U. Chgo., 1961; postgrad., Harvard U., 1977. Engr. trainee Chrysler Corp., Detroit, 1956-59; rsch. asst. Microtech Rsch. Co., Cambridge, Mass., 1959-60; engr. Allis Chalmers Mfg. Co., Milw., 1960-61; mem. tech. staff The Mitre Corp., Bedford, Mass., 1962-68; sr. mem. tech. staff Data Dynamics, Inc., Washington, 1969; phys. scientist NOAA, Rockville, Md., 1970-71, U.S. Gate Project coord., 1972-74, dir. U.S. Global Weather Experiment Project Office, 1974, dir. Program Integration Office, 1975-77, dir. Programs and Tech. Devel. Office, 1977-79, dir. Programs and Internat. Activities Office, 1979-81; dep. assoc. dir. for tech. svcs., chief AFOS ops. div. Nat. Weather Svc., Silver Spring, Md., 1981-86, dir. Office of Systems Ops., 1986-2000, dir. Office Operational Sys., 2000—02. Liaison to NAS coms. on atmospheric scis., geophysics studies and internat. environ. programs, 1975-81; U.S. coord. U.S./Japan Coop. Program in Natural Resources, 1980-88; chmn. U.S.-Japan Marine Resources and Engring. Coordination Com., 1980-88; U.S. del. governing coun. UN Environ. Program and World Meteorol. Orgn.; mem. commn. for Basic Systems World Meteorol. Orgn., 1988-2002; speaker in field. Contbr. articles to profl. publs. Recipient Silver medal Dept. Commerce, 1975, Gold medal Dept. Commerce, 1998. Mem. AAAS, Am. Geophys. Union, Am. Meteorol. Soc., Am. Soc. Mech. Engrs., Marine Tech. Soc. Home: 16 Eton Overlook Rockville MD 20850-3003

**TELFER, MARGARET CLARE,** internist, hematologist, oncologist; b. Manila, Apr. 9, 1939; came to U.S., 1941; d. James Gavin and Margaret Adele (Baldwin) T. BA, Stanford U., 1961; MD, Washington U., St. Louis, 1965. Diplomate Am. Bd. Internal Medicine, Am. Bd. Oncology; lic. Ill., Mo. Resident in medicine Michael Reese Hosp., Chgo., 1968, fellow in hematology and oncology, 1970, assoc. attending physician, 1970-72, dir. Hemophilia Ctr., 1971—; interim dir. div. hematology and oncology, 1971-74, 81-84, 89—, attending physician, 1972—, Rush-Presbyn. St. Luke's Hosp., 1999—; Olympia Fields (Ill.) Hosp., 1999—, Cook County Hosp., Chgo., 2000—, dir. hematology/oncology fellowship, 2002—; asst. prof. medicine U. Chgo., 1975-80, assoc. prof. medicine, 1980-85, assoc. prof. clin. medicine, 1985-89; assoc. prof. medicine U. Ill., Chgo., 1990-2001, Rush U., Chgo., 2001—. Mem. med. adv. bd. Hemophilia Found. Ill., 1971, chmn., 1972—83, lectr. annual symposium, 1978—84; mem. med. adv. bd. State of Ill. Hemophilia Program; dir. hematology-oncology fellowship program Michael Reese Hosp., 1971—75, 1981—84, 1989—2000, dir. Cook County Fellowship Program, 2004—, mem. numerous coms.; lectr. in field. Contbr. articles to profl. jours. Fellow ACP; mem. Am. Soc. Clin. Oncology, Am. Assn. Med. Culls., Am. Soc. Hematology, World Fedn. Hemophilia, Blood Club (Chgo.), Thrombosis Club (Chgo.). Office: Stroger Cook County Hosp Rm 750 Adminstrn Bldg 1900 W Polk Chicago IL 60612 Office Phone: 312-864-7250. Business E-Mail: mtelfer@ccbhs.org.

**TELLEEN, JUDY,** counselor; b. Chgo., Dec. 13, 1942; d. Kurt Theodore and Gertrude Lillian Lockwood Johnson; m. David Roger Telleen, June 15, 1964; children: Karin, Kirstin, Erik. BA, Lawrence U., 1964; MA, U. Mich., 1967, PhD, 1970. Program dir. counseling svcs. Asian Human Svcs., Chgo., 1994-95, coord. of counseling svcs., 1995-96, coord. of case mgmt., 1997-98; adj. prof. Gov.'s State Univ., University Park, Ill., 1995-99; counselor Arlington Heights, Ill., 1999—. Adv. com. mem. Bd. Suprs. and Sch. Bd., Va., 1993; mem. Pub. Policy and Legis. com. Ill. Counseling Assn., 1994, mem. governing coun., 2000—. Author: (book) A Predictive Model of the Cumulative Academic Achievement of Indian Students, 1970, (monograph) Guidance Factors Influencing Indian Students to Attend the University of Michigan, 1971; mem. editl. bd. (periodical) Ill. Counseling Assn. Quarterly, 1995—98. Youth adv. Bridge Youth & Family Svcs., Palatine, Ill., 1994—96; chairperson learning com. All Saints Luth. Ch., Palatine, 1993—2001. Mem. Am. Counselor's Assn., Ill. Counselor's Assn., Ill. Assn. of Couples & Family Couns. (pres.), Ill. Assn. for Multicultural Counseling, Ill. Assn. Mental Health Counselors, Assn. for Multicultural Counseling Develop., Internat. Assn. Marriage & Family Counselors, Internat. Assn. Addictions & Offender Counselors, Pi Lambda Theta, Phi Kappa Phi. Lutheran. Office: Ste 102 1040 S Arlington Heights Rd Arlington Heights IL 60005-3162

**TELLEM, NANCY REISS,** broadcast executive; b. Danville, Calif., Dec. 13, 1953; m. Arn Tellem; children: Michael, Matthew, Eric. BA in Polit. Sci., U. Calif., Berkeley, 1975; JD, Hastings Coll. Law, 1979. Intern to Congressman Ron Dullums, Washington, 1974; with legal affairs dept. Lorimar TV; joined Warner Bros. TV, 1987, exec. v.p. bus. and fin. affairs; exec. v.p. bus. affairs CBS Entertainment, exec. v.p. CBS Prodns. CBS, 1997—98, pres. CBS Entertainment, 1998—2004; pres. CBS Paramount Network TV Entertainment Group, 2004—. Bd. dirs. ThirdAge Media. Named one of 100 Most Powerful Women in Entertainment, Hollywood Reporter, 2005—06. Avocations: tennis, yoga, hiking, photography. Office: CBS Entertainment 7800 Beverly Blvd Los Angeles CA 90036*

**TELLEM, SUSAN MARY,** public relations executive; b. NYC, May 23, 1945; d. John F. and Rita C. (Lietz) Cain; m. Marshall R.B. Thompson; children: Tori, John, Daniel. BS, Mt. St. Mary's Coll., L.A., 1967. Cert. pub. health nurse; RN. Pres. Tellem Pub. Rels. Agy., Marina del Rey, Calif., 1977-80, Rowland Grody Tellem, L.A., 1980-90; chmn. The Rowland Co., L.A., 1990—; pres., CEO Tellem, Inc., L.A., 1992-93. Instr. UCLA Extension, 1983-97; adj. prof. Pepperdine U., 1999—; speaker numerous seminars and confs. on pub. rels. Editor: Sports Medicine for the '80's, Sports Medicine Digest, 1982-84. Bd. dirs. Marymount High Sch., 1984-87, pres., 1984-86; bd. dirs. L.A. Police Dept. Booster Assn., 1984-87; mem. Cath. Press Coun.; mem. pres.'s coun. Mus. Sci. and Industry. Mem. Am. Soc. Hosp. Mktg. and Pub. Rels., Healthcare Mktg. and Pub. Rels. Assn., Pub. Rels. Soc. Am. (bd. dirs. 1994—), L.A. Counselors, PETA, Am. Lung Assn. (chair comm. com. L.A. chpt.) Soc. for Prevention of Cruelty to Animals (chair PetSet), Sports Club (L.A.). Roman Catholic. Avocations: reading, tennis, aerobics. Office: 23852 Pacific Coast Hwy # 928 Malibu CA 90265-4879 Fax: 310-589-6101. Office Phone: 310-479-6111. Business E-Mail: stellem@tellem.com.

**TELLER, ADAM J.,** lawyer; b. Manchester, Conn., Jan. 12, 1963; s. Samuel H. and Joan D. Teller; m. Catherine E. Cushman. BA, Harvard U., 1984, JD, 1987. Bar: Conn. 1988, Mass. 1987, U.S. Ct. Mass. 1988, Conn. 1988, U.S. Ct. Appeals (2d cir.) 1997. Law clk. Judge Peter Dorsey U.S. Dist. Ct., Hartford, Conn., 1987-89; dept. asst. pub. defender Office Pub. Defender, Enfield, Conn., 1989-92; assoc. Leone Throwe & Nagle, East Hartford, Conn., 1992-96; ptnr. Leone Throwe Teller & Nagle, East Hartford, 1996—. Mem. Town of Bolton Planning and Zoning Commn., 2003—; chair Bolton Dem. Town Com., 2003—; sec. Town of Bolton Planning and Zoning Commn., 2001—03. Office: 33 Connecticut Blvd East Hartford CT 06128-0225 Office Phone: 860-528-2145.

**TELLER, ALAN,** museum program director, photographer, educator; b. NYC, Sept. 13, 1946; s. Nat Teller and Jeanette Zirlin; m. Jerri Zbiral, Nov. 8, 1980; children: Max Zbiral-Teller, Emma Zbiral-Teller. BA in Anthropology, Queens Coll., Flushing, NY, 1967. Founder, dir. Inner-City Photo Workshop, Chgo., 1969—74; photographic rschr. Field Mus. Natural History, Chgo., 1977—80; ptnr. The Collected Image, Evanston, Ill., 1978—; pres. Teller Madsen, Chgo., 1988—. Adj. faculty Lake Forest Coll., Ill., 2004—. Photographic exhbns., Union League Show, Sacred Art, others; dir.: (films) In the Shadow of Memory (Cine Golden Eagle, 2000), It's OK (Bush in 30 Seconds finalist/YouTube most discussed video, 2006); exhibit designer (exhibitions) The Mall of History/Lake County Museum (Best Exhibit award, 2002), An Uncommon Man/Herbert Hoover Presidential Library. Bd. mem. The Savoyaires, Evanston, 2004—06. Democrat. Jewish. Avocation: swimming. Home: 806 Monroe Evanston IL 60202 Office: Teller Madsen 5751 N Ravenswood Chicago IL 60660 Office Phone: 773-728-7887. Home Fax: 847-328-7010; Office Fax: 773-728-7915. Personal E-mail: teller@lfc.edu. Business E-Mail: ateller@tmexhibits.com.

**TELLES, CYNTHIA ANN,** psychologist; b. El Paso, Tex., Aug. 10, 1952; d. Raymond Lawrence and Delfina Telles; m. David Jimenez (div. Aug. 1991); 1 child, Raymond Jimenez. BA, Smith Coll., Northampton, Mass., 1974; PhD, Boston U., 1982. Cert. psychologist, Calif. Postdoctoral U. Hosp. Boston U. Med. Ctr., 1977-78; rsch. fellow psychology dept. Spanish Speaking Mental Health Rsch. Ctr. UCLA, 1978-79, co-investigator, rsch. diagnostician dept. psychiatry, 1982-84, investigator and mgr. Spanish instrument tng. Dept. Psychiatry, 1981-87; clin. project dir., co-investigator NIMH, 1984-86, investigator, 1986-90; project dir., co-prin. investigator Calif. State Dept. Mental Health, 1986—; psychologist adult outpatient dept. UCLA Neuropsychiat. Inst., 1979-80; co-dir. UCLA Spanish Speaking Psychosocial Clinic, 1980-87, dir., 1988—. Media psychologist for TV and radio; cons. Boston City Police, 1975, Boulder County Community Mental Health Ctr., 1978, Spl. Svc. for Groups, L.A., 1982, Ministry of Health, Lima, Peru, 1982, NIMH, 1984—, L.A. County Dept. Mental Health, 1985—, Calif. Sch. Profl. Psychology, 1986—; presenter in field; teaching fellow Boston U.

Sch. Medicine, 1975-78; lectr. dept. psychiatry UCLA, 1980-85, asst. clin. prof., 1986-96, assoc. clin. prof., 1996-, mem. faculty adv. com. Chicano Studies Rsch. Ctr., 1988—. Author: (with others) Psychiatric Epidemiology and Prevention: The Possibilities, 1985, Violence and Homicide in Hispanic Communities, 1988; contbr. articles to profl. jours.; mem. editorial bd. Hispanic Jour. Behavioral Scis., 1978-79; ad hoc reviewer Psychology of Women Quar., 1986-87. Bd. dirs. Coalition Pro-Salud Hispana, Boston, 1977-78, Nat. Hispanic Psychol. Assn., 1984-86, Ctr. for Study of Youth in Groups/Teen Line, Dept. of Psychiatry, Cedars-Sinai Med. Ctr., 1986-88, NCCJ, Southern Calif., 1990—, El Centro Human Svcs. Corp., 1988-90, Calif. Endowment, 2001-, bd. chair, 2004-; mem. Nat. Adv. Com. on Hispanic Women and AIDS, Ctrs. for Disease Control and Hispanic Designers Inc., 1989—; pres., founder Hispanic Health Found., 1988-98. Boston U. Grad. scholar, 1975-79, APA Minority fellow, 1975-79; recipient Humanitarian award East L.A. Coll., 1988, Civic and Community Leadership award Nat. Network of Hispanic Women, 1989, First Annual Achievement award for mental health pub. svc. APA Minority Fellowship Program, 1989. Mem. Nat. Hispanic Psychol. Assn. (charter), APA. Roman Catholic. Office: UCLA Dept Psychiatry 300 Ucla Medical Plz Los Angeles CA 90095-8346

**TÉLLEZ KUENZLER, LUIS,** former government official, investment banker; b. Mexico City, Mex., 1958; Grad., Inst. Tech.; PhD in Econs., MIT. Gen. dir. fin. & planning Sec. Fin. & Pub. Credit, 1988; undersec. planning Sec. Agrl. & Hydraulic Resources, chief staff of Pres. of Mex., 1996—97; sec. Energy, Mines & Parastatal Industry Govt. Mexico, Mexico, 1997—2000; exec. v.p., CEO Desc, S.A. de C.V., Mexico, 2001—03; mng. dir. The Carlyle Group, S. de R.L. de C.V., Mexico City. Dir. Fomento Economico Mexicano, S.A. de C.V., 2001—. Named Global Leader of Tomorrow, World Econ. Forum, Leader for the New Millennium, Time mag. Office: The Carlyle Group Montes Urales 720 Col Lomas de Chapultepec 11000 Mexico Office Phone: 52 55 52498020. Office Fax: 52 55 52498030. Business E-Mail: mexico@carlyle.com.*

**TELLIER, HENRI,** retired Canadian military officer; b. Montreal, Que., Can., Sept. 1, 1918; s. Henry Joseph and Jeanne (St. Cyr) T.; m. Virginia Wright, July 23, 1945; children: Pierre, Michele, Suzanne, John, Nicole. Student, U. Montreal, 1935-40, U. Ottawa, 1946-47, Canadian Army Staff Coll., 1942-43, Imperial Def. Coll., London, Eng., 1966, Dept. Def. Computer Inst., Washington, 1968; PhD in mil. sci., H.C. With Robert Howard & Co. (ins. brokers), Montreal, 1937-40; commd. 2d lt. Canadian Army, 1940, advanced through grades to lt. gen., 1973; asst. sec. to minister (Nat. Def.), 1945-48; comdg. officer (Royal 22d Regt.), 1948-51; instr. (Canadian Army Staff Coll.), 1951-54; army mem. (Joint Intelligence Staff), 1954-57; mil. adviser Vietnam, 1957-58; chief of staff (Que. Mil. Dist.), 1958-60; mil attache Rome, 1960- 63; dir. mil. ops. and plans Army, 1963-64, dir. internat. plans, 1964-65; comdr. (Canadian Contingent), Cyprus, 1965-66; dir. gen. plans (Forces Hdqrs.), Ottawa, Ont., 1967-70, chief plans, 1970-71; Canadian mil. rep. to mil. com. (NATO Hdqrs.), Brussels, 1971-73; ret., 1973. Assoc. nat. commr. Canadian Red Cross Soc., Toronto, Ont., 1973-75, nat. commr., 1975, sec.-gen., 1981-83, hon. v.p.; pvt. mem. Refugee Bd., 1984-89; chmn. Canadian sect. Mil. Coop. Com. Can.-U.S., Joint Permanent Bd. Def. Can.-U.S.; commr. Commn. for Strategic and Internat. Studies; mem. adv. council Can. Exec. Services Orgn. Decorated mem. Order of Canada; Disting. Service Order (Canada); Queens medal Netherlands; comdr. Order of Merit (Italy); companion Order of Red Cross. Mem. Canadian Inst. Internat. Affairs., Can. Exec. Svc. Orgn., Inst. Assn. Execs., Royal 22 Regiment Assn., UN Assn. Home: The Redwoods 703-2604 Draper Ave Ottawa ON Canada K2H 9B1

**TELLIER, RICHARD DAVIS,** management educator; b. Darby, Pa., Feb. 18, 1942; s. Joseph Campbell and Jane Grace (Davis) T.; m. Susan Gammon, June 10, 1974; children: John-Jo and Tiekka (twins). BSEE, Drexel U., 1967; MBA, Fla. State U., 1971, DBA, 1973. Elec. engr. Philco-Ford Corp., Phila., 1960-67; aerospace sys. engr. GE, Cape Canaveral, Fla., 1967-70; lectr. Fla. State U., Tallahassee, 1970-73; prof. mgmt. Calif. State U., Fresno, 1973-2000, chmn. dept. mgmt. and mktg., 1979-84, assoc. dean Sch. Bus., 1984-85, asst. dean, 1990-92, assoc. provost acad. resources, 1995-99, prof. emeritus, 2000—. Cons. ops. mgmt., market rsch. orgnl. behavior. Author: Operations Management: Fundamental Concepts and Methods, 1978, Production and Operations Management Test Bank, 1990; contbr. articles to profl. jours. Grantee 1975; recipient Meritorious Performance award, 1987, 88, 90. Mem. Ops. Research Soc. Am., Phi Kappa Phi. Home: 8294 N Academy Ave Clovis CA 93619-9454 Office: Calif State U Shaw and Maple Ave Fresno CA 93740-0001 Business E-Mail: rickt@csufresno.edu.

**TELNAES, ANN,** cartoonist; b. Stockholm, 1960; m. David Lloyd. BFA, Calif. Inst. Arts. Animator and layout designer for various animation studios in London, L.A., Taiwan and N.Y.C., Warner Bros., Walt Disney Imagineering; editorial cartoonist. Bd. dirs. Cartoonists Rights Network. Named Best Cartoonist, Population Inst. XVIIth Global Media awards, 1996, Best Editl. Cartoonist, 6th Ann. Environ. Media Awards, 1996; recipient Nat. Headliner award for Editl. Cartoons, 1997, Pulitzer prize, 2001, Berryman award, Nat. Press. Found., 2003. Mem.: Assn. Am. Editl. Cartoonists (past v.p.).

**TEMA-LYN, LAURIE,** management consultant; b. Bklyn., Mar. 25, 1951; d. Morton and Jeanne (Lite) Carlin. BA, Bklyn. Coll., 1972. Mgmt. supr. Rapp & Collins, Inc., N.Y.C., 1972-78, v.p., 1978-80; assoc. Synectics, Cambridge, Mass., 1980-83; founder, gen. ptnr. IdeaScope Assocs., Cambridge, 1983-95; prin. Practical Imagination Enterprises, Carlisle, Mass., 1995—. Presenter European Conf. on Innovation and Creativity, 1987, 94. Performer: VOICES Chorale; contbr. articles to profl. jours. Bd. dirs. Arica Inst., N.Y.C., 1979-80; pres. bd. dirs. Savoyand Light Opera Co.; bd. mem., performer Voices Chorale; mem. Heartland Cir., Hunterdon Radio Theater. Mem. Creative Problem Solving Inst. (presenter, leader), Am. Mktg. Assn., Direct Mktg. Assn. (presenter), Product Devel. Mgmt. Assn., Creative Edn. Found., New Eng. Bus. Assn. for Social Responsibility, Qualitative Rsch. Cons. Assn., Boston Womens Network, Mgmt. Roundtable, Sharing a New Song, Heartland Cir., Hunterdon Radio Theater. Office: Practical Imagination Enterprises 18 Losey Rd Ringoes NJ 08551-1206 Office Phone: 908-237-2246. E-mail: laurie@practical-imagination.com.

**TEMAM, ROGER M.,** mathematician, educator; b. Tunis, Tunisia, May 19, 1940; s. Ange M. and Elise (Ganem) T.; m. Claudette Cukorja, Aug. 21, 1962; children: David, Olivier, Emmanuele. M in Math., U. Paris, 1962, DSc, 1967. Asst. prof. math. U. Paris, 1960-67, prof., 1967—2003, prof. emeritus, 2003—; dir. Inst. for Sci. Computing and Applied Math. Ind. U., Bloomington, 1986—. Prof. Ecole Polytechnique, Paris, 1968-85. Author: Numerical Analysis, 1969, Navier-Stokes Equations, 1977, rev. edit., 2001, Mathematical Problems in Plasticity, 1983, Infinite Dimensional Dynamical Systems in Mechanics and Physics, 1988, 2nd edit., 1997; co-author: Convex Analysis and Variational Problems, 1976, rev. edit., 1999, Dynamic Multilevel Methods and the Numerical Simulation of Turbulence, 1999, Navier-Stokes Equations and Turbulence, 2001; assoc. editor: profl. jours.; contbr. articles to profl. jours. Recipient several prizes. Mem. AAAS, Am. Math. Soc., Am. Phys. Soc., Soc. Indsl. and Applied Math. (first pres. French chpt. 1983-87), NY Acad. Scis. Office: Ind U Dept Math Rawles Hall Bloomington IN 47405

**TEMARES, STEVEN H.,** retail executive; BA, Rutgers U., 1980; JD, U. Pa., 1983. Assoc. Real Estate Group Schulte Roth & Zabel LLP, N.Y.C., 1983—85; counsel Universal Maritime Svc. Corp., N.Y.C., 1986—88; atty. Real Estate Group Riker Danzig Scheler Hyland & Perretti, Morristown, NJ, 1988—92; from dir. real estate, gen. counsel to exec. v.p. Bed, Bath & Beyond Inc., Union, NJ, 1992—97, exec. v.p., COO, 1997—99, pres., COO, 1999—2003, pres., CEO, 2003—. Office: Bed Bath & Beyond Inc 650 Liberty Ave Union NJ 07083*

**TEMBREULL, MICHAEL A.,** automotive executive; Gen. mgr. PACCAR, Inc., 1985—90, sr. v.p., 1990-92, exec. v.p., 1992-95, dir., 1994—, vice chmn., 1995—. Office: PACCAR Inc Paccar Bldg 777 106th Ave NE PO Box 1518 Bellevue WA 98009*

**TEMERLIN, LIENER,** advertising executive; b. Ardmore, Okla., Mar. 27, 1928; s. Pincus and Julie (Kahn) T.; m. Karla Samuelsohn, July 23, 1950; children: Dana Temerlin Crawford, Lisa Temerlin Gottesman, Hayden Crawford, Sandy Gottesman. BFA, U. Okla., 1950. Assoc. editor Sponsor Mag., N.Y.C., 1950-51; from copywriter to COO Glenn Advt. Inc., Dallas, 1952—74; pres. Glenn, Bozell & Jacobs, Inc., 1974-79; chmn. bd. dirs. Bozell & Jacobs Inc., 1979-86, Bozell, Jacobs, Kenyon & Eckhardt, Dallas, 1986-89; chmn. Bozell, 1989-92, Temerlin McClain, Irving, Tex., 1992—2001; pres. Temerlin Cons., 2001—. Bd. dirs. East/West Inst. Chmn. Winston Churchill Found. award dinner, 1986; chmn. Dallas Symphony Assn., 1986-88, pres., 1984-86, bd. govs., 1982-84, pres. coun., 1989—; mem. Blair House Restoration Com., 1987-88; vice-chmn. Am. Film Inst., 1992-93, trustee 1992-2000, hon. trustee, 2000; bd. dirs. United Way of Met. Dallas Exec. Com., 1986-89, Dallas Bus. Com. for Arts, 1989, Dallas Citizen's Coun., 1984-86, 92; trustee Southwestern Med. Found., 1988—, mem. adv. com., 2003—; trustee com. univ. devel. So. Meth. U., mem. exec. bd., 1990-91, bd. dirs. Tate lectr. series, 2002—; trustee and chmn. of devel. com. Dallas Mus. Art, 1993-96; steering com. Susan G. Komen Found., 1989-91, art acquisition com. Meyerson Symphony Ctr., 1989-92, exec. coun. Daytop/Dallas, 1989—; chmn. grand opening fortnight Morton H. Meyerson Symphony Ctr., 1989; active Madison Coun. Libr. Congress, Washington, 1991-2002; hon. chair rsch. dinner Am. Lung Assn. Tex., 1996; corp. chmn. Sr. Citizens Greater Dallas for Spirit of Generations Award to Stanley Marcus, 1997; fundraising campaign chmn. Lieberman Rsch. Bldg., Baylor Med. Ctr., 1997; hon. chmn. ann. dinner Make A Wish Found., 1998; exec. bd. Meadows Sch. Arts, So. Meth. U., 2001; co-chair ann. fundraising event Vogel Alcove Child Care Ctr. for the Homeless, 2001; adv. cons. Dallas Ctr. Performing Arts, 2003-; founder, chmn. Am. Film Inst./Dallas Internat. Film Festival, 2006—. Lt. field arty. U.S. Army, Korea. Decorated Bronze Star; recipient Bill D. Kerss award Dallas Advt. League, 1983, Brotherhood award NCCJ, 1984, Susan G. Komen Found. for Breast Cancer Rsch. Cmty. award, 1989, Neiman Marcus (formerly James K. Wilson) Silver Cup award, 1990, Linz award 1990, Silver Medal award Dallas Advt. League, 1991, Vol. Fundraiser of Yr. award Nat. Soc. Fundraising Execs., 1991, Inst. Human Rels. award Am. Jewish Commn., Dallas, 2003; named Dallas Father of Yr., 1991, Best Man in Advt. award McCall's Mag., 1992; named Temerlin Advt. Inst. for Edn. and Rsch. in his honor So. Meth. U. Sch. Advt., 2001; inducted into Am. Advt. Hall Fame, 2004. Business E-Mail: connie.beebe@temerlinconsulting.com.

**TEMES, GABOR CHARLES,** electrical engineering educator; s. Erno and Rozsa (Angyal) Wohl-Temes; m. Ibi Kutasi-Temes, Feb. 6, 1954; children: Roy Thomas, Carla Andrea. Dipl.Eng., Tech. U. Budapest, 1952, DSc (hon.), 1991; Dipl. Phys., Eotvos U., Budapest, 1954; PhD, U. Ottawa, Ont., Can., 1961. Asst. prof. Tech. U. Budapest, 1952-56; project engr. Measurement Engring. Ltd., 1956-59; dept. head No. Electric Co. Ltd., 1959-64; group leader Stanford Linear Accelerator Center, 1964-66; corp. cons. Ampex Corp., 1966-69; prof. elec. engring. UCLA, 1969-90, chmn. dept., 1975-80; dept. head Oreg. State U., Corvallis, 1990—. Cons. Xerox Corp., ANT GmbH Author: (with others) Introduction to Circuit Synthesis and Design, 1977, Analog MOS Integrated Circuits for Signal Processing, 1986; assoc. editor: (with others) Jour. Franklin Inst, 1971-82; co-editor, contbg. author: (with others) Modern Filter Theory and Design, 1973, Oversampling Delta-Sigma Data Converters, 1991. Recipient Western Electric Fund award Am. Soc. Engring. Edn., 1982, Humboldt Sr. Rsch. award, 1991; NSF grantee, 1970—Fellow IEEE (life, editor Transactions on Circuit Theory 1969-71 Best Paper award 1969, 81, 85, Centennial medal 1984, Edn. award 1987, Tech. Achievement award 1989, Grad. Tchg. award 1998, Millenium medal 2000, CAS Golden Jubilee medal 2000, Gustav Robert Kirchhoff award 2006). Home: 7100 NW Grandview Dr Corvallis OR 97330-2708 Office: Oreg State U Dept Elec Engring Corvallis OR 97331 Personal E-Mail: temes@ieee.org. Business E-Mail: temes@ece.orst.edu.

**TEMIN, MICHAEL LEHMAN,** lawyer; b. Phila., July 18, 1933; s. Henry and Annette (Lehman) T.; children: Aaron Lehman, Seth Lehman; m. Anne L. Hearn, 2000. BA magna cum laude, Yale U., 1954; LL.B. cum laude, U. Pa., 1957. Bar: Pa. 1958, Del. 2000, U.S. Ct. Appeals (3d cir.) 1958, U.S. Supreme Ct. 1969, U.S. Ct. Appeals (2d cir.) 1986, U.S. Ct. Appeals (9th cir.) 1992, U.S. Ct. Appeals (11th cir.) 2002. Asst. U.S. atty. U.S. Atty.'s Office, Phila., 1958-59; assoc. Wolf, Block, Schorr and Solis-Cohen, Phila., 1959-66, ptnr., 1966—2006, of counsel, 2006—. Lectr. Law Sch., U. Pa., Phila., 1982-90, adj. prof., 1990-93, 94-95, 2002—; Thomas A. O'Boyle vis. disting. practitioner, 1985, I. Grant Irey lectr., 1988, 2003-04; vice chmn. Ea. Dist. Pa. Bankruptcy Conf., 1994-95, chmn., 1995-96. Editor U. Pa. Law Rev., 1955-57 Vice chmn. Ednl. Nominating Panel, Phila., 1981-83; bd. dirs. Citizens Com. in Pub. Edn., Phila., 1970-96, pres. 1980-82. Fellow: Am. Coll. Bankruptcy (recipient 1997—2003), scholar in residence 2005—); mem.: ABA (chmn. rules subcom. 1985—92, vice chmn. chpt. 11 subcom. 1992—96, bus. bankruptcy com. of sect. corp. banking and bus. law), Pa. Bar Assn. (ho. of dels. 1985—89, 1990—, co-chmn. legal ethics and profl. responsibility com. 2004—), Phila. Bar Assn. (mem. sect. corp. banking and bus. law 1979—86, chmn. profl. guidance com. 1985, sec. sect. corp. banking and bus. law 1985, treas. sect. corp. banking and bus. law 1986, vice chmn. sect. corp. banking and bus. law 1987, chmn. sect. corp. banking and bus. law 1988), Order of Coif. Jewish. Office: Wolf Block Schort & Solis-Cohen LLP 22d Fl 1650 Arch St Philadelphia PA 19103-2097 Office Phone: 215-977-2256. Business E-Mail: mtemin@wolfblock.com.

**TEMIRKANOV, YURI KHATUEVICH,** conductor, music director; b. Nal'chik, Russia, Dec. 10, 1938; s. Khatu Sagidovich and Polina (Petrovna) Temirkanov; m. Irina Guseva; 1 child. Grad., Leningrad Conservatory, Russia, 1966. Condr. Maly Opera and Ballet Theatre, Leningrad, 1966; chief condr. Leningrad Philharm. Orch., 1967—76, Kirov Opera and Ballet Theatre Orch., 1976—88; prof. Leningrad Conservatory, 1979; artistic dir. Leningrad Symphony Orch. (now St. Petersburg Philharm.), 1988; mus. dir., prin. condr. St. Petersburg Philharm.; condr. Baltimore Symphony Orch., Md., 1992, Md., 1995, Md., 1998—2000, dir. music Md., 2000—06. Chief guest condr. London Royal Philharm. Orch., 1992; guest condr. Berlin Philharm., Vienna Philharm., l'Orch. Paris, Dresden Staatskapelle, Amsterdam's Royal Concertgebouw, NY Philharm., Phila. Orch., Boston Symphony, Chgo. Symphony, San Francisco Symphony Orch., LA Philharm., Calif., Danish Nat. Radio Symphony; condr. laureate Royal Philharm., London; Rec. artists BMG/RCA, 1988. Musical dir. (Operas) Peter I (Petrov), 1975, War and Peace (Prokofiev), 1976, Dead Souls (Schedrin), 1978, Pushkin (Petrov), 1979, Queen of Spades (Tchaikovsky), 1979. Vice chmn. bd. All-Russian Theatrical Soc. Named People's Artist of Kabardino-Balkarian Autonomous Republic, People's Artist of Russian Soviet Fed. Socialist Republic; recipient 1st prize, USSR Contest for Condrs., 1967, USSR State Prize, 1976. Home: 1 Teatralnaya Ploschad Saint Petersburg Russia Office: Leningrad Symphony Orch Ul Brodskogo 2 Saint Petersburg Russia*

**TEMKIN, HARVEY L.,** lawyer; b. Madison, Wis., Jan. 1, 1952; s. Joe L. and Sylvia Temkin; m. Barbara, June 13, 1976; children: James, Daniel, Eli. BA, U. Wis., 1974; JD, U. Ill., 1978. Bar: Wis. 1978. Assoc. Foley & Lardner, Madison, 1978—83; prof. Tulane Law Sch., New Orleans, 1983-87; ptnr. Foley & Lardner, Madison, 1987—2002; shareholder Reinhart Boerner Van Deuren, s.c., Madison, 2002—. Lectr. U. Wis. Law Sch., 1990-93; mem. U.S. Senator Feingold's Bus. Adv. Group. First v.p. Hillel Found., Madison, 1982-83, bd. dirs., 1987-95; chmn. edn. com. Beth Israel Synagogue, Madison 1980-82; chmn. Jewish edn. panel Madison Jewish Cmty. Coun., 1993-98, bd. dirs., 1998-03; bd. dirs. Hospice Care, Inc. Fellow Am. Coll. Real Estate Lawyers; mem. ABA (real property probate and trust sect., reporter significant legis. panel 1983-85, significant lit. panel 1985-87),

Downtown Madison, Inc. (chmn. 1989-91), Friends of Overture Ctr; Hospice Care Inc. (bd. dirs.). Office: Reinhart Boerner Van Deuren 22 East Mifflin St PO Box 2018 Madison WI 53701-2018 E-mail: htemkin@reinhartlaw.com.

**TEMKIN, ROBERT HARVEY,** accountant; b. Boston, Oct. 21, 1943; s. Max and Lillian (Giller) T.; m. Ellen Phyllis Band, Sept. 25, 1966; 1 child, Aron; m. Debra Gottlieb, Oct. 3, 1998; 1 child, Rachel; m. Dianne Moore, Feb. 28, 1999; 1 child, Joshua. BBA, U. Mass., 1964. CPA, Mass. With Ernst & Young LLP, 1964—72, 1973—2002, ptnr., 1976—2002, nat. dir. auditing standards, 1980-88; prin. Robert H. Temkin, CPA, 2002—. Assoc. prof. NYU, 1982. Bd. dirs. Jewish Home for Elderly of Fairfield County, 1979—, pres., 1985-87; mem. Bd. Edn., Weston, Conn., 1983-87; dir. United Synagogue of Conservative Judaism, 1984-99, 2004—; mem. bus. adv. coun. U. Mass.; bd. dirs., chmn. bd. dirs. Jewish Cmty. Ctrs. of Greater Boston; mem. exec. com. Combined Jewish Philanthropies of Greater Boston, 1995-99, 2000—, bd. dirs. 1993—; treas. Synagogue Coun., Mass., 1988-93; dir. Hillel Found., U. Mass., 1992-99. Recipient Acctg. Alumni award U. Mass., 1978, Alumnus Award Sch. Mgmt. U. Mass., 1986; Cmtys. of Excellence award Combined Jewish Philanthropies, 2003. Mem. AICPA (staff dir. commn. on auditors responsibilities 1976-78, peer rev. com. 1982-84, auditing stds. bd. 1984-88, chmn. internat. auditing task force 1988-90), Mass. Soc. CPAs (Silver medal 1964), N.Y. State Soc. CPAs, Mass. Bd. Pub. Accountancy (sec. 1996, 2001, chmn. 1997, 2002, 06). Assoc. mem., Hyannis Yacht Club. Office: 3217 Main St PO Box 255 Barnstable MA 02630 Home: 294 Millway Barnstable MA 02630 Office Phone: 508-362-5518. Personal E-Mail: bobtemkin@rn.com.

**TEMKO, STANLEY LEONARD,** lawyer; b. N.Y.C., Jan. 4, 1920; s. Emanuel and Betty (Alderman) T.; m. Francine Marie Salzman, Mar. 4, 1944 (dec. Dec. 1998); children: Richard J., Edward J., William D. AB, Columbia U., 1940, LLB, 1943. Bar: N.Y. 1943, D.C. 1951. Practice in, N.Y.C., 1943, 46-47; law clk. Mr. Justice Wiley Rutledge, U.S. Supreme Ct., Washington, 1947-48; legal counsel Econ. Coop. Adminstrn., 1948-49; assoc. Covington & Burling, Washington, 1949-55, ptnr., 1955-90, sr. counsel, 1990—. Editor-in-chief: Columbia Law Rev, 1942-43. Trustee Beauvoir Sch., 1963-69; trustee Columbia U., 1980-91, trustee emeritus, 1991—, mem. bd. visitors Sch. Law, 1961-98, mem. emeritus, 1999—; mem. bd. govs. St. Albans Sch., 1967-73, chmn., 1971-73. 2nd lt. U.S. Army, 1943-46. Decorated Bronze Star; recipient medal for conspicuous alumni svc. Columbia U., 1979, Excellence medal Columbia U. Law Sch., 2004. Fellow Am. Bar Found. (chmn. rsch. com. 1970-72); mem. ABA, Am. Law Inst., D.C. Bar Assn., Columbia U. Sch. Law Alumni Assn. (pres. 1982-84), Met. Club, Nat. Press Club, Phi Beta Kappa. Home: Apt 618 700 New Hampshire AVe NW Washington DC 20037 Office: Covington & Burling 1201 Pennsylvania Ave NW Washington DC 20004-2401 Office Phone: 202-662-5514. Business E-Mail: stemko@cov.com.

**TEMME, MARCIA E. See HARDCASTLE, MARCIA E.**

**TEMONS, MARK JOSEPH,** science educator; b. Lock Haven, Pa., Jan. 14, 1954; s. James Garrison and Helen Louise Temons; m. Pamela Robin Haines, Oct. 19, 1986; children: Mark Joseph II, Colleen Marie, Sean Garrison, Laura Frances, Daniel Patrick. BS in Secondary Edn. and Social Sci., Lock Haven State Coll., 1975, cert. in biology and gen. sci., 1986; MS in Biology, Bloomsburg U., 1994. Sci. dept. chair Bishop Neumann H.S., Williamsport, Pa., 1983—93; lead sci. tchr. Muncy (Pa.) H.S., 1993—. Adj. faculty Pa. Coll. Tech., Williamsport, 1991, 92, 2001, Susouehanna U., Selinsgrove, Pa., 1996, varsity softball coach, 1993—, varisty field hockey coach, 2003—. Mem. adv. bd.: your World Biotechnology adn You, 2004—. Biotechnology framework com. PA Dept. of Edn. Recipient Biology Tchr. of the Yr. for Pa., 2000. Mem.: Nat. Assn. of Biology Tchrs., Nat. Sch. Tchrs. Assn., KC, Am. Legion. Republican. Roman Catholic. Home: 1300 St David's Rd Williamsport PA 17701 Office: Muncy High Sch 200 W Penn St Muncy PA 17756 Office Phone: 570-546-3127. Business E-Mail: mtemons@muncysd.org.

**TEMPEL, EUGENE RAYMOND (GENE TEMPEL),** foundation administrator, speaker, researcher; b. St. Meinrad, Ind., Mar. 30, 1947; s. Charles Xavier and Bernadette Scholastica (Otto) Tempel; m. Mary Ekerle, May 24, 1969; children: Jonathan, Jason, Zachary. BA, St. Benedict Coll., 1970; MA in English, Ind. U., 1973, EdD in Higher Edn., 1985. Asst. prof. English Vincennes U., Ind., 1970—77; dir. Jasper Ctr., 1973—77; v.p., dean of faculty Three Rivers CC, Poplar Bluff, Mo., 1977—80; dir. external affairs Coll. Arts & Scis. Ind. U., Bloomington, 1980—83; asst. prof. higher edn. Ind. U.-Purdue U. Indpls., 1985, vice chancellor external affairs, 1988; chmn. adv. com. Ind. U. Ctr. on Philanthropy, 1987, exec. dir., 1997—. Bd. dirs. Marian Heights Acad., Ferdinand, Ind., 1973; exec. dir. Indpls. Ind. U. Found., 1983—85, v.p., 1985; devel. cons. Ind. Agrl. Inst., Indpls., 1985. Co-author: Fund Raisers: Their Careers, Stories, Concerns and Accomplishments, 1996; editor: Achieving Excellence in Fund Raising. Vice chmn. bd. overseers St. Meinrad Sem., 1986; bd. dirs. Cath. Cmty. Found., 1988. Mem.: NSFRE, Nat. Soc. Fund Raising Execs., Am. Assn. Higher Edn., Coun. for Advancement and Support Edn., Indpls. C. of C. Roman Cath. Avocations: sailing, soccer. Home: 8079 Heyward Dr Indianapolis IN 46250-4226 Office: Ctr on Philanthropy at Ind U 550 W North St, Ste 301 Indianapolis IN 46202-3272 Office Phone: 317-274-4200.*

**TEMPELIS, CONSTANTINE HARRY,** immunologist, educator; b. Superior, Wis., Aug. 27, 1927; s. Harry and Thelma Marie (Hoff) T.; m. Nancy Louise Foster, Aug. 27, 1955; children: William H., Daniel S. BS, U. Wis.-Superior, 1950; MS, U. Wis.-Madison, 1953, PhD, 1955. Project assoc. immunology U. Wis.-Madison, 1955-57; instr. immunology U. W.Va., Morgantown, 1957-58; asst. rsch. immunologist U. Calif., Berkeley, 1958-66, assoc. prof. immunology, 1966-72, prof., 1972-95, prof. emeritus, 1995—; prof. grad. sch., 1996—. Vis. scientist Wellcome Rsch. Labs., Beckenham, Kent, Eng., 1977-78, U. Innsbruck, Austria, 1985, 90, 91; cons. in field. Contbr. articles to profl. jours. Served with USNR, 1945-46. Recipient Rsch. Career Devel. award, 1965-70; Fogarty sr. internat. fellow NIH, 1977-78 Mem. AAAS, Am. Assn. Immunologists, Fedn. Am. Soc. Exptl. Biology, Sigma Xi. Office: U Calif Sch Pub Health Berkeley CA 94720-0001 Business E-Mail: chtemp@berkeley.edu.

**TEMPLE, DONALD,** retired allergist, dermatologist; b. Chgo., May 21, 1933; s. Samuel Leonard and Matilda Eve (Riff) T.; m. Sarah Rachel Katz, Sept. 29, 1957; children: Michael A., Matthew D., Madeline B. AB in Biology cum laude, Harvard U., 1954; MD, U. Chgo., 1958. Diplomate Am. Bd. Allergy and Immunology, Am. Bd. Dermatology, Nat. Bd. Med. Examiners. lic. Intern Michael Reese Hosp., Chgo., 1958-59; resident in dermatology U. Chgo. Hosps., 1959-62; clin. asst., dept. dermatology Boston U. Sch. Medicine, 1963-64; clin. instr. dermatology Stanford U. Sch. Medicine, 1965; preceptee in allergy Offices of Leon Unger, M.D., and Donald Unger, M.D., Chgo., 1965-69; pvt. practice Des Plaines, Ill., 1969-70; with allergy dept. Glen Ellyn (Ill.) Clinic, 1972-97; ret., 1997. Dermatology and allergy staff Louis A. Weiss Hosp., Chgo., 1965-73, allergy sect. Loyola U. Med. Ctr., Maywood, Ill., 1977-80, exec. and contract medicine coms. Glen Ellyn; clin. asst. prof. dermatology Abraham Lincoln Sch. Medicine, U. Ill., 1977-85; clin. asst. prof. medicine sect. allergy and dermatology, Loyola U., 1977-85; mem. staff Cen. DuPage Hosp., Winfield, Ill., 1973-97, Glen Oaks Med. Ctr., Glendale Heights, Ill., Glendale Heights Cmty. Hosp., 1980-92. Contbr. articles to profl. jours. Bd. dirs. Am. Lung Assn., DuPage, McHenry counties, 1980-91; chmn. Contract Medicine, HMO Com., Glen Ellyn Clinic, 1985, mem. exec. com., 1988-92. Fellow Am. Coll. Chest Physicians, Am. Assn. Cert. Allergists, Am. Coll. Allergists, Am. Acad. Allergy, Ill. Soc. Allergy and Clin. Immunology, Chgo. Dermatol. Soc.; mem. AMA, Ill. State Med. Soc., DuPage County Med. Soc., Chgo. Med. Soc., Fla. Med. Assn. Collier County Med. Soc. Jewish. Avocations: sailing, investing. Home: 6585 Nicholas Blvd Ph 3 Naples FL 34108-7210 E-mail: don.temple@postharvard.edu.

**TEMPLE, DONALD EDWARD,** medical association administrator; b. N.Y.C., Nov. 28, 1946; s. James Edward and Helen Louise (Gannon) Temple; m. Lucy Chirinos de Lorentzen, Feb. 23, 1974 (div. 1989); 1 child, Gail

Marie. BBA, St. Francis Coll., Bklyn., 1968. Vol. U.S. Peace Corps, Lima, Peru, 1968-72; asst. to pres., gen. mgr. Barrons Ednl. Series, Inc., Hauppauge, NY, 1973-78; dir. supply svc. Am. Lung Assn., NYC, 1978-84; bus. mgr. Am. Jour. Respiratory and Critical Care Medicine, NYC, 1985—, Am. Jour. Respiratory Cell and Molecular Biology, 1989—, Procs. Am. Thoracic Soc., NYC, 2004—; dir. bus. affairs Am. Lung Assn., NYC, 1985-89, dep. mng. dir. bus. affairs, 1990-94; dir. bus. affairs Am. Thoracic Soc., 1994—. Mem. mailers tech. adv. com. U.S. Postal Svc., Washington, 1987—93. Vol. L.I. Assn. AIDS Care, 1994—98. Recipient Merit award, Soc. Tech. Communication, 1990. Mem.: N.Y. Soc. Assn. Execs., Healthcare Mktg. Commun. Coun., Am. Soc. Assn. Execs., Alliance Non-Profit Mailers (bd. dirs., chmn. tech. com. 1986—94, v.p. 1990—94), Soc. Scholarly Pub. Home: 63 Vanderwater St Farmingdale NY 11735-5235 Office: Am Thoracic Soc 61 Broadway New York NY 10006-2755 Business E-Mail: dtemple@thoracic.org.

TEMPLE, ELISE, neuroscientist; b. Carmel, Calif., Sept. 28, 1966; d. James Bryson and Anne Temple; m. Gregory Nox Connelly, Nov. 13, 1965; children: Dylan Walker, Chloe Anna Connelly. BS, U. Oreg., 1997; PhD, Stanford U., Calif., 2001. Asst. prof. human devel. Cornell U., Ithaca, NY, 2001—. Achievements include research in neural basis for development dyslexia. Office: Cornell U Dept Human Devel MVR Hall Ithaca NY 14853 Office Phone: 607-255-9640. Business E-Mail: et62@cornell.edu.

TEMPLE, JOHN BLAKE, mathematics professor; b. Cleve., June 5, 1951; s. Paul Blake and Louise Elizabeth Temple; m. Nancy June Wendel, July 8, 1978; children: Nathan Blake, Anne Louise. PhD, U. Mich., Ann Arbor, 1980. Prof. math U. Calif., Davis, Calif., 1990—, chair, grad. group applied math., 2004—. Postdoctoral rsch. fellow Rockefeller U., N.Y.C., 1980—82; vis. mem. Courant Inst. Math. Scis., N.Y.C., 1982—83; rsch. assoc. Math. Rsch. Ctr., Wis., 1983—84; Van Vleck asst. prof. U. Wis., Madison, Wis. 1984—86; lectr. in field. Author: Proceedings of the National Academy of Sciences (Guggenheim Fellow, 1994); contbr. articles various profl. jours. City commr. City of Davis, Calif., 1998—2004. Office: UC-Davis Dept Math 1 Shields Ave Davis CA 95616 Office Phone: 530-752-2214. Business E-Mail: temple@math.ucdavis.edu.

TEMPLE, LARRY EUGENE, lawyer; b. Plainview, Tex., Dec. 26, 1935; s. Herman Edward and Grace Eileen (Ivey) T.; m. Laura Louann Atkins, Feb. 23, 1963; children: Laura Allison, John Lawrence. BBA, U. Tex., 1957, LLB with honors, 1959; LLD (hon.), Lamar U., 1985. Bar: Tex., U.S. Dist. Ct. (we. dist.) Tex., U.S. Ct. Appeals (5th cir.), U.S. Supreme Ct. Law clk. to justice Tom Clark U.S. Supreme Ct., Washington, 1959-60; assoc. Powell, Rauhut, McGinnis, Reavley & Lochridge, Austin, Tex., 1960-63; legal adminstrn. asst., exec. asst. (chief of staff) Tex. Gov. John B. Connally, Austin, 1963-67; spl. counsel to pres. Lyndon Baines Johnson, Washington, 1967-69; pvt. practice Austin, 1969—. Bd. dirs. Temple-Inland, Inc., Guaranty Bank. Mem. U. Tex. Cancer Found., Houston, 1978-84, U. Tex. Devel. Bd., Austin, 1980-85, 90—, chmn., 1993-95; pres. U. Tex. Ex-Students Assn., 1997-98; mem. Tex. Higher Edn. Coordinating Bd., Austin, 1983-89, chmn., 1983-87; chmn. Select Com. for Higher Edn., Austin, 1985-87; bd. dirs. Lyndon B. Johnson Found., 1986—, vice chmn., 1989-2000, pres., 2000—; trustee U. Tex. Law Sch. Found., 1989—. Recipient Faculty award U. Tex. Law Sch., 1987, Humanitarian award Austin region NCCJ, 1988, Santa Rita award U. Tex. System, 1989, Disting. Alumnus award U. Tex., Austin, 1990, Outstanding Alumnus award U. Tex. Law Sch., 1999, Leon Green award Tex. Law Rev., 2003, Disting. Lawyer award Austin Bar Assn., 2004. Fellow: Tex. Bar Found.; mem.: ABA, Tex. Bar Assn. (chmn. legis. com. 1980, 1983—86), Tex. Jr. Bar Assn. (chmn. bd. dirs. 1967), Austin Bar Assn. (pres. 1962—63). Democrat. Episcopalian. Home: 2606 Escondido Cv Austin TX 78703-1610 Office: 400 W 15th St Ste 1510 Austin TX 78701-1648 Office Phone: 512-477-4467. Business E-Mail: letemple@onr.com.

TEMPLE, MARK ALLEN, adult education educator, consultant; b. West Monroe, La., Oct. 18, 1962; s. Floyd Aaron and Doris Burdeaux Temple; m. Adrian Renae Na, June 25, 1974. BS, N.E. La. U., 1980—85, MS in Edn., 1985—87; PhD, So. Ill. U. Carbondale, 1992—96. Asst. prof. Ill. State U., 1997—, Tex. Tech U., 1996—98; hiv, aids edn. coord. Jackson County Heath Dept., Murphysboro, Ill., 1992—94; tchr., coach West Ouachita H.S., Calhoun, La., 1987—90. Co-director Ill. HIV Prevention Edn. Project, Normal, Ill., 1999—2002. Author: (journal article) Opinions of Ill. Voters About Coordinated Sch. Health Programs (Am. Sch. Health Assn. Disting. Svc. Award, 2002); contbr. numerous articles in profl. jours. Advocacy chair Am. Sch. Health Assn., Kent, Ohio, 2001—; mem., Ill. Sch. Health Adv Bd. Ill. Dept. of Human Services, Springfield, 2000—03; Am. Sch. Health Assn. rep. Coalition of Nat. Health Edn. Organizations, Washington, 1998—2003; pres. Ill. Sch. Health Assn., Chgo., 2000—01, Grantee Nat. Sch. Health Coord. Leadership Inst., Am. Cancer Soc., 2002. Mem.: APHA (sect. counselor 2002—03), Am. Assn. for Health Edn., Am. Sch. Health Assn. (advocacy chair, exec. com. 1999—, Disting. Svc. Award 2002), Eta Sigma Gamma. Democrat. Avocations: endurance sports, martial arts, reading contemporary philosophy. Office: Illinois State University Campus Mail 5220 Normal IL 61790-5220 Home: 49 Whites Place Bloomington IL 61701 E-mail: matempl@ilstu.edu.

TEMPLE, ROBERT, physician, federal agency administrator; b. NYC, July 18, 1941; s. Samuel A. and Judith (Coslow) T.; m. Bonnie Streifer, Oct. 27, 1963; 1 child, James. BA magna cum laude, Harvard U., 1963; MD, NYU, 1967. Diplomate Am. Bd. Internal Medicine, Am. Bd. Clin. Pharmacology. Intern Columbia-Presbyn. Med. Ctr., N.Y.C., 1967-68, resident, 1968-69; clin. assoc. Nat. Inst. Arthritis and Metabolic Disease, NIH, Bethesda, Md., 1969-72; med. officer FDA, Rockville, Md., 1972-74, asst. to dir., bur. of drugs, 1974-76, dir. div. cardio-renal drug products, 1976-82, dir. office drug research and rev., 1982-84, dir. office of drug evaluation I, 1984—. Mem. coop. studies rev. com. VA, 1977-80. Contbr. articles to profl. jours. Served with USPHS, 1969-72. Recipient Disting. Alumni award NYU Sch. Medicine, N.Y. 1987; Pub. HealthSuperior Svc. award HHS, 1986, Disting. Svc. award, 1991; NORD Ann. Tribute, 2001; Outstanding Svc. award Drug Info. Assn., 2001, Disting. Svc. and Leadership award FDLI, 2002. Fellow Am. Coll. Clin. Pharmacology (hon.); mem. Soc. Clin. Trials (bd. dirs. 1983, v.p. 1986, pres. 1987), Am. Soc. Clin. Phrmacology and Therapeutics (bd. dirs. 1987-90, 92—), Rawls-Palmer Progress in Medicine lecture and award 2001), Alpha Omega Alpha. Democrat. Jewish. Avocations: model trains, tennis, gardening, cooking. Home: 3325 Rowland Pl NW Washington DC 20008-3226 Office: FDA 5600 Fishers Ln Rockville MD 20857 Office Phone: 301-443-5296. Business E-Mail: temple@cder.fda.gov.

TEMPLE, ROBERT WINFIELD, chemical company executive; b. New Albany, Ind., Feb. 25, 1934; s. Edgar Winfield and Kathryn (Rady) T.; m. Katrina Voorhis, Jan. 4, 1954 (div. Oct. 1970); children: James V., Robert K., Jennifer Anne; m. Katharine Ann Stobbs, Apr. 29, 1977 (div. June 1985); children: Andrew, Philip; m. Angela J. Temple, Aug. 5, 1986; 1 child, Sarah Louise. BSChemE, MIT, 1955, BS in Indsl. Mgmt., 1955, postgrad., 1955, NYU, 1955—58, Columbia U., 1966. Dist. sales mgr. ACF Industries, 1955-59; sr. staff cons. Arthur D. Little, Inc., 1959-64; dir. planning and devel. Am. Cryogenics, Inc., Atlanta, 1964-69; v.p. Williams Bros. Co., Atlanta, 1969; pres. Lang Engring., Coral Gables, Fla., 1970-74; CEO Western Process Co., Geneva and Houston, 1974—87; head agribus and biotechnology Brit.-Am. Tobacco Co., London, 1988—91; pres. TMR-Viterra Interant., Ltd., 1989-92; CEO Gulfcrest Internat., 1987—, Newco Internat., 1999—2001; sr. advisor Bacteria Bar Codes Inc., 1998—2001, Synthecon, 1999—2001; CEO Surface BioSolutions Inc., 2001—02; sr. adv. dir. Telerad Inc., 2002—03; ptnr. Roteva Advisors, 2002—03. Dir. World Congress on Super Conductivity, Global Econ. Action Inst. Coal. on African Devel.; dir. MIT Enterprise Forum (former chmn.); spkr. on mgmt. and mktg. various seminars. Contbr. articles to profl. jours. Fellow Am. Inst. Chemists and Chem. Engrs.; mem. Am. Chem. Soc., Am. Mgmt. Assn., Chem. Mktg. Rsch. Assn., Internat. Food Technologists (chmn. seminars on food irradiation 1995, 99), MIT Alumni Assn. (past regional pres., adv. bd.), Houston Fresh Fruit

and Vegetable Assn. (dir., past pres.), Sigma Chi Alumni Assn. Presbyterian. Home: 14134 Bluebird Ln Houston TX 77079-6836 Office: Gulfcrest Internat PO Box 19435 Houston TX 77224-9435

TEMPLE, WAYNE CALHOUN, historian, writer; b. nr. Richwood, Ohio, Feb. 5, 1924; s. Howard M. and Ruby March (Calhoun) T.; m. Lois Marjorie Bridges, Sept. 22, 1956 (dec. Apr. 1978); m. Sunderine Wilson, Apr. 9, 1979; stepson, James C. Mohn. AB cum laude, U. Ill., 1949, AM, 1951, PhD, 1956. Rsch. asst. history U. Ill., 1949-53, tchg. asst., 1953-54; curator ethnohistory Ill. State Mus., 1954-58; editor-in-chief Lincoln Herald, Lincoln Meml. U., 1958-73, assoc. editor, 1973—, also dir. dept. Lincolniana, dir. univ. press, John Wingate Weeks prof. history, 1958-64; with Ill. State Archives, 1964—, now chief dep. dir. Lectr. U.S. Mil. Acad., 1975; sec.-treas. Nat. Lincoln-Civil War Council, 1958-64; mem. bibliography com. Lincoln Lore, 1958—; hon. mem. Lincoln Sesquicentennial Commn., 1959-60; advisory council U.S. Civil War Centennial Commn., 1960-66; maj. Civil War Press Corps, 1962—; pres. Midwest Conf. Masonic Edn., 1985; mem. adv. com. Abraham Lincoln Bicentennial Commn., 2000—. Author: Indian Villages of the Illinois Country: Historic Tribes, 1958, rev. edits., 1966, 77, 87, Lincoln the Railsplitter, 1961, Abraham Lincoln and Others at the St. Nicholas, 1968, Alexander Williamson-Tutor to the Lincoln Boys, 1971, (with others) First Steps to Victory: Grant's March to Naples, 1977, Lincoln and Grant: Illinois Militiamen, 1981, Stephen A. Douglas: Freemason, 1982, Lincoln as a Lecturer, 1982, By Square and Compasses: The Building of Lincoln's Home and Its Saga, 1984, Lincoln's Connections with the Illinois and Michigan Canal, 1986, Dr. Anson G. Henry: Personal Physician to the Lincolns, 1988, Abraham Lincoln: From Skeptic to Prophet, 1995, Thomas and Abraham Lincoln as Farmers, 1996, Alexander Williamson: Friend of the Lincolns, 1998, By Square and Compass: Saga of the Lincoln Home, 2002, The Taste Is In My Mouth a Little...Lincoln's Victuals and Potables, 2004, Abraham Lincoln and Illinois' Fifth Capitol, 2006, Abraham Lincoln's Travels on the River Queen, 2006; co-author: Illinois's Fifth Capitol: The House that Lincoln Built, 1988; contbg. author: Capitol Centennial Papers, 1988; editor: Campaigning with Grant, 1961, 72, The Civil War Letters of Henry C. Bear, 1961; 71 radio scripts A. Lincoln 1809-1959, Indian Villages of the Illinois Country: Atlas Supplement, 1975; editorial advisory bd. Am. Biog. Inst., 1971—, Ency. Indians of Ams., 1973—; contbr. articles to profl. jours., encys. Sponsor Abraham Lincoln Bay, Washington Nat. Cathedral; mem. adv. com. Abraham Lincoln Bicentennial Commn.; mem. Ill. State Flag Commn., 1969—; trustee, regent Lincoln Acad. Ill., 1970-82; bd. govs. St. Louis unit Shriners Hosps. for Crippled Children, 1975-81; mem. commissioning com. hon. crew mem. and plank owner USS Springfield submarine. 1990—; hon. crew mem. USS Abraham Lincoln aircraft carrier, 1989—. With U.S. Army, 1943-46, gen. Res. (ret.). Decorated Bronze Star Medal, Silver Citizenship medal SAR, 1993, Literary Merit Gold medal Ill. Lodge of Rsch., 1993; recipient Order of Arrow Boy Scouts Am., 1957, Scouters award, 1960, Scouter's Key, also medallion, 1967, Lincoln medallion Lincoln Sesquicentennial Commn., 1960, award of Achievement U.S. Civil War Centennial Commn., 1965, Algernon Sydney Sullivan medallion, 1969, Distinguished Service award Ill. State Hist. Library, 1969, 77, I.H. Dural Distinguished Service award, 1971, legion of honor Internat. Supreme Council, Order of De Molay, 1972, Disting. Service award Civil War Round Table of Chgo., 1983, 91, Cert. Excellence Ill. State Hist. Soc., 1985, Archbishop Richard Chenevix Trench award, 1999;Lincoln Diploma Honor, Lincoln Meml. U., Harrogate, Tenn., 1963, Lifetime Achievement award 2001; named Hon. Ky. Col., Marshal of Okla. Territory. Fellow Royal Soc. Arts (life); mem. NRA, KT (Red Cross Constantine), Lincoln Group D.C. (hon.), U. Ill. Alumni Assn., Ill. State Hist. Soc., Board of Advisors, The Lincoln Forum, Ill. Profl. Land Surveyors Assn., Ill. State Dental Soc. (citation plague 1966), Res. Officers Assn., Lincoln Fellowship of Wis., Iron Brigade Assn. (hon. life), Mil. Order Loyal Legion U.S. (hon. companion), Mil. Order Fgn. Wars U.S., Army and Navy Union, Masons (33 degree, Meritorious Svc. award, grand rep. from Grand Lodge of Colo.), Shriners, Kappa Delta Pi, Phi Alpha, Phi Alpha Theta (Scholarship Key award), Chi Gamma Iota, Phi Beta Kappa, Tau Kappa Alpha, Alpha Psi Omega, Sigma Pi Beta (Headmaster), Sigma Tau Delta (Gold Honor Key award for editorial writing), Zeta Psi. Presbyterian (elder). Home: 1121 S 4th Street Ct Springfield IL 62703-2200 Office: Ill State Archives Springfield IL 62756-0001 *Only in America could a poor farm boy from Ohio work his way through a great university, like the University of Illinois, and receive a doctor's degree. Life has been kind to me, and I have tried hard and worked hard. I am proud to be an American.*

TEMPLEMAN, LYDIA, retired assistant principal; b. Sydney, Australia, 1913; arrived in U.S., 1946; d. Giuseppe and Maria Concetta Lo Schiavo; m. Bruce Liscum Templeman, May 20, 1950; 1 child, Geoffrey. BA, Sydney U., 1934, diploma in Edn., 1935; grad., Royal Acad. London, 1935; MA, U. Mich., 0950, B of Econs., 1956. Tchr. NSW Dept. Edn., Sydney, Australia, 1936—46, Jackson, Mich. Edn. Dept., 1947—91; asst. prof. Fullerton, Calif. Dept. Edn., 1967—91; ret., 1991. Owner, operator Bren Travel Svcs., Calif., 1965—88. Author: Travel Agency Operation, 1988, Dollars and Sense, 2004; tour dir. Europe, 1956—80. Mem.: Calif. Ret. Tchrs. Assn. Democrat. Roman Catholic. Avocations: sailing, motor boats.

TEMPLETON, ALAN ROBERT, biology professor; b. Litchfield, Ill., Feb. 28, 1947; s. John Smith and Lois Arlene (McCormick) T.; m. Bonnie A. Altman, Dec. 20, 1969; children: Jeremy Alan, Jeffrey Alan. BA, Washington U., 1969; MS in Stats., U. Mich., 1972, PhD in Genetics, 1972. Jr. fellow Mich. Soc. Fellows, Ann Arbor, 1972-74; asst. prof. U. Tex., Austin, 1974-77; assoc. prof. Washington U., St. Louis, 1977-81, prof., 1981—, Charles Rebstock prof. biology, 2001—. Cons. St. Louis Zool. Park, 1979—. Editor: Theoretical Population Biology, 1981-91; mem. editl. bd. Molecular Phylogenetics & Evolution, 1991—, Brazilian Jour. Genetics, 1991-97, Genetics and Molecular Biology, 1998-2001, Animal Conservation, 2004—, Evolutionary Bioinformatics Online, 2005—; assoc. editor Am. Naturalist, 2002-05; contbr. numerous article to profl. jours. Grantee NSF, 1974-80, 90—, NIH, 1980—, Nixon Griffis Fund for Zool. Rsch., 1986-87, Burroughs Welcome Fund for Functional Genomics, 2000—04. Fellow AAAS; mem. Soc. for Study Evolution (v.p. 1982, pres. 1996-97), Soc. Conservation Biology (bd. dirs. 1985-88), Nature Conservancy (trustee Mo. chpt. 1988—, v.p. 1996-2000). Avocations: hiking, caving, ethnomusicology, scuba diving, flying. Office: Washington U Dept Biology Saint Louis MO 63130-4899

TEMPLETON, DENNIS J., research scientist, pathologist; b. McCook, Nebr., Mar. 18, 1955; s. Dorothy Farrar Templeton; m. Jeanne M. Bono; children: Thaddeus Albert, Talitha Eve, Martha Grace. BA, Claremont McKenna Coll., 1977; PhD, U. Calif., San Diego, 1981, MD, 1983. Diplomate Am. Bd. Pathology. Fellow in pathology Harvard Med. Sch., Boston, 1984—86; fellow Whitehead Inst. MIT, Cambridge, 1986—91; prof. pathology and oncology Case Western Res. U., Cleve., 1991—2001; Walter Reed prof., chmn. pathology U. Va., Charlottesville, 2001—. Office: Univ Va MR5 3001 415 Lane Rd Charlottesville VA 22908 Office Phone: 434-924-1946. Office Fax: 434-924-9312. Business E-Mail: dtempleton@virginia.edu.

TEMPLETON, FIONA, poet, playwright, director, performance artist; Performances include The Later Medead, 2005, L'Ile, 2003, Recognition, 1996, She Held Her Peace: 'Twas Strange!, 1994, Realities/Metamorphosis, 1992, Articulate Architecture, 1992, Be Our Guest, 1992, Where on Earth, 1990, Delirium of Interpretations, 1990, 91, You-The City, 1988—, Strange to Relate, 1989, Experiments in the Destruction of Time, 1983, Thought/Death, 1980, Defense, 1982, Cupid and Psyche, 1981, Out of My Way, 1988, A/Version, 1985, Against Agreement, 1981-82, Under Paper Spells, 1981-82, The Seven Deadly Jealousies, 1981-82, There Was Absent Achilles, 1981-82, The Hypothetical Third Person, 1987, Out of the Mouths, 1984, The New Three-Act Piece, 1983; co-founder, Theatre of Mistakes, London, 1975; author: Elements of Performance Art, 1976, London, 1984, You-The City, 1990, Cells of Release, 1997, Oops the Join, 1999, Delirium of Interpretations, 2003; co-editor: Shattered Anatomies, 1995, Mum in Airdrie, 2005. Home: 100 Saint Marks Pl Apt 7 New York NY 10009-5822

TEMPLETON, JOHN MARKS, investment counsel, financial analyst; b. Winchester, Tenn., Nov. 29, 1912; s. Harvey Maxwell and Vella (Handly) T.; m. Judith Dudley Folk, Apr. 7, 1937 (dec. Feb. 1951); children: John Marks, Anne Dudley, Christopher Winston; m. Irene Reynolds Butler, Dec. 31, 1958 (dec. Nov. 1993). AB, Yale U., 1934; MA (law) (Rhodes scholar), Balliol Coll., Oxford, Eng., 1936; LLD (hon.), Beaver Coll., 1965, Marquette U., 1980, Jamestown Coll., 1983, Maryville Coll., 1984, Babson Coll., 1992, Rhodes Coll., 1992, U. Rochester, 1992, La. Coll., 1993, Moravian Coll., 1994; D.Litt. (hon.), Wilson Coll., 1974; D.D. (hon.), Buena Vista Coll., 1979; D.C.L. (hon.), U. of South, 1984; DLitt (hon.), Manhattan Coll., 1990; LHD, U. Dubuque, 1992, Fla. Southern Coll., 1992; DLitt (hon.), Campbell U., 1993; LLD, Moravian Coll., 1994; DPhil (hon.), Stonehill Coll., 1995; LHD (hon.), Furman U., 1995; LLD (hon.), Notre Dame U., 1996, Methodist Coll., 1997; LHD (hon.), Brigham Young U., 1998, Queens Coll., 1999; LHD (hon.), Johns Hopkins U., 2006. CFA. Sec.-treas., v.p., dir. Nat. Geophys. Co., Dallas and N.Y.C., 1937-41; pres., dir. Templeton, Dobbrow & Vance, Inc., NYC, 1941-65; chmn. Templeton Damroth Corp., 1959-62; v.p., dir. First Trust Bank Ltd., Bahamas, 1963—; pres., dir. Templeton Funds Inc., 1977-86, Templeton Global Funds Inc., 1981-86, Templeton Growth Fund Can., Ltd., Toronto, 1954-85; chmn Templeton Galbraith & Hansberger Ltd, 1986-92. Author: The Humble Approach, 1981; co-author: The Templeton Touch, 1985, The Templeton Plan, 1987, Global Investing, 1988, The God Who Would Be Known, 1989, Riches for the Mind and Spirit, 1990, Looking Forward, 1993, Discovering the Laws of Life, 1994, Is God the Only Reality?, 1994, Evidence of Purpose, 1994, Future Agenda, 1995; contbr. articles to fin. publs. Past pres. Lyford Cay (Bahamas) Property Owners Assn.; chmn. YMCA Bergen County, 1952-54; dir., campaign chmn. Englewood Community Chest, 1953-54; trustee Englewood Hosp., 1953-56, Soc. for Promoting Christian Knowledge, 1984-87, Balliol Coll. Endowments (Oxford), Templeton Project Trust (Eng.); chmn. bd. trustees Princeton Theol. Sem., 1967-73, 79-85, trustee for restoration of Westminster Abbey, 1991—; trustee Wilson Coll., 1941-73, Buena Vista Coll., 1981—, Templeton Found. Inc., 1952—, John Templeton Found. Inc., 1987—, council on theol. sems. United Presbyn. Ch. U.S.A., 1946-83; mem. Ctr. Theol. Inquiry, 1979-92, Commn. on Ecumenical Mission, 1961-70; bd. corporators Presbyn. Ministers Fund. Inc., 1960-93; bd. visitors Harvard Div. Sch., 1981-88; adv. bd. Harvard Ctr. for the study of World Religions, 1975-89; bd. mgrs. Am. Bible Soc., 1972-92; mgmt. Council Templeton Coll. (Oxford); pres. Templeton Theol. Sem., Bahamas, 1984-88; hon. rector Dubuque U., 1982-92. Decorated knight Order of Brit. Empire, Knight of St. John; recipient Churchman of Yr. award Religious Heritage Am., 1979, Internat. Churchman of Yr. award, 1981, Ecumenical Patriarch's Hon. Order of Mt. Athos, Free Enterprise award Palm Beach Atlantic Coll., 1984, Centennial medal NY Mayflower Soc., 1987, award USA Today, 1991, award for excellence in investment mgmt., 1991, Benjamin Franklin award Royal Soc. Arts, 1994, Lifetime Achievement award Laymans Nat. Bible Assn., 1995, Nat. Bus. Hall of Fame award Jr. Achievement Assn., 1996, Interfaith gold medallion Internat. Coun. Christians and Jews, 1997, Abraham Lincoln award, 1997, Ind. award Brown U., 1998, Alexis de Tocqueville award Ind. Inst., Calif., 1998, Faith and Freedom award Action Inst., 2000, Faith and Fredom award Action Inst., 2000; named to Wall Street Week Hall of Fame, 1990. Mem. Soc. Security Analysts, World Pres. Orgn., Chief Execs. Orgn. (pres. 1968-69), Bahamas C. of C. (bd. dirs. 1976-79), Internat. Acad. Religious Scis., Mt. Pelerin Soc., Elihu Club, Elizabethan Club (New Haven), Yale Club, University Club (NYC), Lyford Cay Club of Bahamas (dep. chmn. 1980-86), Lansdowne Club, Royal Overseas League, Athenaeum (Eng.), United Oxford and Cambridge Univs. Club (Eng.), White's Club (Eng.), Rotary (Bahamas), Phi Beta Kappa., Zeta Psi. Office: Box N7776 Nassau The Bahamas Mailing: John Templeton Found 300 Conshohocken State Rd, Ste 500 West Conshohocken PA 19428 Office Phone: 242-362-4904.

TEMPLETON, JOHN MARKS, JR., retired pediatric surgeon, foundation administrator; b. NYC, Feb. 19, 1940; s. John Marks and Judith Dudley (Folk) T.; m. Josephine J. Gargiulo, Aug. 2, 1970; children: Heather Erin, Jennifer Ann. BA, Yale Coll., 1962; MD, Harvard U., 1968; degree (hon.), Beaver Coll., Buena Vista U., Va. Commonwealth U., Alvernia Coll. Intern Med. Coll. Va., Richmond, 1968-69, resident, 1969-73; dir. trauma program U. Pa. and Children's Hosp. Phila., 1989—95, prof. pediat. surgery, 1995. Chmn. bd. Templeton Growth Fund, Ltd. Assoc. editor: Textbook of Pediatric Emergencies, 1993; pub. 6000 Name Geneology, 1997, A Searcher's Life, 1999, Thrift and Generosity, 2004. Chmn. health and safety, exec. bd. Coll. of Physicians of Phila., Cradle of Liberty coun. Boy Scouts Am.; mem. exec. bd. Eastern U., Fgn. Policy Rsch. Inst., Nat. Recreation Found., Melmark Charitable Found.; nat. bd. dirs., pres. Pa. divsn. Am. Trauma Soc.; bd. dirs. Nat. Bible Assn., Nat. Liberty Mus., Phila.; elder Proclamation Presbyn. Ch.; pres. John Templeton Found. With M.C., USNR, 1975-77. Barclay fellow Templeton Coll., Oxford U., Eisenhower Exch. fellow, fellow George H. Gallup Internat. Inst.; mem. Order of Charlemagne. Mem. ACS, AMA, Am. Pediat. Surg. Assn., Am. Acad. Pediats., Am. Assn. Surgery Trauma, Ea. Assn. Surgery Trauma, Phila. Coll. Physicians, Union League, Lyford Cay Club, Merion Cricket Club, Athenaeum Club London, Rotary Internat., White's London, United Oxford and Cambridge U. Club (London). Republican. Evangelical. Office: U Pa and Children's Hosp Ste 500 300 Conshohocken State Rd West Conshohocken PA 19428 Business E-Mail: bmcgraw@templeton.org.

TEMPLETON, MATT AARON, art educator; b. Jackson, Mich., May 20, 1975; s. John and Patricia Templeton; m. Katryn Ada Diatoit, July 27, 2001. BFA, Art Inst. Boston, 2000; MFA, Slade Sch. Fine Arts, 2003. Prof. New Eng. Sch. Art and Design, Boston, 2004—06, Wentmouth Inst. Tech., Boston, 2005—06. Presenter Boston U., 2005, Art Inst. Boston, 2005. Author: I Went to the Slade and All I Got Was This F...ing Dictionary, 2003, Format.05, 2005. Recipient Burgundy Leisure award, London, 2003, Adrian Carruthers Meml Studio award, 2003, Project award, Slade Sch., 2003; scholar, Art Inst. Boston, 1998, Gissings Cons. Svc., London, 2001—02. Mem.: Coll. Arts Assn., United South End Artists, Ft. Point Arts Cmty. Democrat. Methodist. Avocations: surfing, skiing, running, travel.

TEMPLETON, RICHARD (RICH) K., electronics company executive; BSEE, Union Coll., NY, 1980. Various positions Tex. Instruments, Inc., Dallas, 1980—91, v.p., semiconductor group, 1991—94, mgr., worldwide application specific prods., 1993—96, sr. v.p., semiconductor group, 1994—96, exec. v.p., pres. semiconductor group, 1996—2004, COO, 2000—04, pres., CEO, 2004—. Mem. bd. dirs. Tex. Instruments, 2003—, Semiconductor Industry Assn. Mem. Bus. Roundtable, Dallas Chief Executive Roundtable. Office: Texas Instruments Inc 12500 TI Blvd Dallas TX 75266-4136*

TEMPLIN, DONALD C., lawyer; b. Jacksonville, Fla., Nov. 10, 1945; BA, Yale U., 1967; JD, U. Okla., 1970. Bar: Okla. 1970, Tex. 1972, admitted to practice: US Supreme Ct., US Ct. Appeals (Fed. Cir.), US Ct. Appeals (5th Cir.), US Ct. Appeals (9th Cir.), US Ct. Appeals (10th Cir.). Ptnr., Intellectual Property Litig. Group Haynes and Boone LLP, Dallas, head, Litig. Sect. Lectr. in field, article and book rev. editor Okla. Law Rev., 1968—69. Chmn., exec. com. March of Dimes Birth Defect Found. of North Tex., 1998—99. Capt. USMC, 1971—73. Mem.: ABA (Intellectual Property Sect.), Tex. Assn. Def. Counsel, Okla. Bar Assn., Am. Bd. Trial Adv., Order of Coif. Office: Haynes and Boone LLP 3100 NationsBank Plz 901 Main St Ste 3100 Dallas TX 75202-3789 Office Phone: 214-651-5591. Office Fax: 214-200-0593. Business E-Mail: don.templin@haynesboone.com.

TEMPLIN, KENNETH ELWOOD, paper company executive; b. Mason City, Nebr., Jan. 26, 1927; s. Otto Rudolph and Marianna (Graf) T.; m. Harriet Elaine Ressel, Aug. 24, 1951; children: Steven, David, Daniel, Benjamin, Elizabeth. BS in Bus. Adminstrn, U. Nebr., 1950; MBA, Wayne State U., Detroit, 1961. Fin. analyst Ford Motor Co., 1950-54; fin. analyst, corp. staff Chrysler Corp., 1955-60, div. controller marine engine div., 1961-63, gen. sales mgr., 1964-65; v.p. Marsh and Templin, N.Y.C., 1966-69; v.p., gen. mgr. operating group Saxon Industries, N.Y.C., 1970-79, group v.p., 1979-82, sr. v.p., c.o.o., 1982-85; v.p.-converting Paper Corp. Am., Wayne, Pa., 1985-86;

exec. v.p. Quality Park Products Inc., St. Paul, 1986-88, 1986-88, pres., 1988-96, ret., 1996. Mem. exec. com. Single Service Inst., 1971-79 Regional chmn. Minn. devel. com. Nat. Multiple Sclerosis Soc., 1970-71; co-pres. Home and Sch. Assn., Bernardsville, N.J., 1975-76; bd. dirs. West Hennepin Counseling Svcs., Inc., 1996-2000, Brain Injury Assn. Minn., 1997-2001; mem. Svc. Corps Ret. Execs. (SCORE), 1996—, chmn. Mpls. chpt. 1999-2000; bd. dirs. Hennepin History Mus., 2000-06. With U.S. Army, 1945-47, 50-51. Mem. Envelope Mfrs. Assn. Am. (postal affairs com. 1989-96, fin. com. chmn. 1989-95, bd. dirs. 1990-91, 93-95). Presbyterian. Office Phone: 612-339-5200. E-mail: templink@aol.com.

**TEMPLIN, ROY,** corporate financial executive; B acctg., Indiana Univ., Bloomington. CPA. V.p. fin., chief acctg. officer Kimball Internat. Inc.; corp. v.p., controller Whirlpool Corp., Benton Harbor, Mich., 2003—04, exec. v.p., CFO, mem. exec. com., 2004—. Office: Whirlpool Corp 200 North M63 Benton Harbor MI 49022-2692*

**TENANTY, JANE ELIZABETH,** secondary school educator; b. Knoxville, May 23, 1956; d. Evan Philip and Mary Adelia (Blanc) Comer; m. Bruce Allen Beckner (div. 1985); m. Robert Michael Tenanty, Mar. 6, 1997; 1 stepchild, Robert Michael Jr. BS in Edn., Bloomsburg U., 1979; student, William Mitchell Coll. Law, 1986—87. Cert. K-12 reading tchr. State of Md. Bd. Edn., K-8 regular tchr. State of Md. Bd. Edn. Legal sec. various pvt. law firms, 1979—93; legal asst. Office of Atty. Gen., Annapolis, Md., 1993—96; substitute tchr. several counties in Md., 1996—2001; reading and math. tchr. Sylvan Learning Ctr., Easton, Md., 2003—04; facilitator distance learning Chesapeake Coll., Cambridge, Md., 2004—. Tutor Laubach Literacy, Red Wing, Minn., 1982—84, Project READ Adult, Cambridge, 2000—01. Contbr. poems to lit. mags. and anthologies. Vol. ARC, Red Wing, Minn., 1982—84, Hosp. Aux., Red Wing, Minn., 1982—84. Democrat. Avocations: writing, reading, outdoor activities, singing. Home: 714 Glasgow St Cambridge MD 21613-1738

**TENDLER, DAVID,** investment company executive; b. NYC, Jan. 15, 1938; s. Philip and Pearl (Berman) T.; m. Beatrice Weisberg, Oct. 11, 1958; children: Pearl, Karen. BBA in Internat. Econs., CCNY, 1959. With Philipp Bros. Co., 1960—, mgr. Far Eastern ops., 1968-75, pres. N.Y.C., 1975—; dir. parent corp. Engelhard Minerals & Chems. Corp. (name changed to Phibro Corp. 1981), N.Y.C., 1975-85, vice chmn. bd., 1979-81, chmn. bd., CEO, 1981—; co-chmn., co-CEO Phibro-Salomon Inc., N.Y.C., 1983-84; ptnr. Tendler Beretz, L.L.C. Ltd., N.Y.C., 1985—. Chmn. subcom. trade U.S.-German Dem. Rep. Trade and Econ. Coun., 1978—84; bd. dirs., mem. exec. com. U.S./USSR Trade and Econ. Coun., 1979—85, U.S.-China Bus. Coun., 1983—94, 1994—2005; bd. dirs. V.I. Techs., Inc., Watertown, Mass., Savient Pharm., East Brunswick, NJ, Agrifos Fertilizer Inc., Pasadena, Tex. Mem. bd. overseers NYU Grad. Sch. Bus., 1981-85; trustee Lenox Hill Hosp., 1981-94; trustee, mem. exec. com. N.Y. Blood Ctr., 1987—; bd. dirs., mem. exec. com. Fgn. Policy Assn., 1983-96; bd. dirs. Ctr. for the Advancement of Women, N.Y.C., 1999—; mem. adv. coun. Weissman Ctr. for Internat. Bus., Baruch Coll., 2001. Recipient Torch of Liberty award metals and metal products divsn. Anti-Defamation League, 1976, Edith and Herbert Lehman award Henry St. Settlement, 1982; named Man of Yr. Fgn. Trade Soc., Baruch Coll., CUNY, 1985. Office: Tendler Beretz LLC 150 E 52nd St New York NY 10022-6017 Office Phone: 212-593-0550. Personal E-mail: tenchan@aol.com.

**TENDLER, PAUL MARC,** lawyer; b. N.Y.C., Oct. 22, 1943; s. Leonard and Gladys (Steisel) T.; m. Elaine Lynn Isaacson, Mar. 28, 1971; children: Jamie Meredith, Seth Evan. B.A., Queens Coll., N.Y.C., 1965; M.S., So. Ill. U., Carbondale, 1966; J.D., Howard U., 1969; postgrad. U. Pitts., 1969-70. Bar: D.C. 1980. Press asst to Congressman Begich, Washington, 1971; legis. asst. to Congressman Halpern, Washington, 1972, Congressman Rinaldo, 1973; dir. legis. rsch. Cost of Living Council, Washington, 1973-74; asst. dir. govt. affairs Am. Nurses Assn., Washington, 1974-75; pres. Paul Tendler Assocs., Washington, 1975—; mng. ptnr. Tendler & Biggins, 1982-89; ptnr. Tendler, Goldberg, Biggins & Geltzer, 1989—; adj. prof. Georgetown U., 1980-83, asst. prof., 1975-80; dir. bus. program Trinity Coll., Washington, 1983-86. Author: The Federal Government at Work, 1976; An LPNs Guide to the Federal Government, 1978, 84. Ford Found. scholar, 1967-69. Mem. D.C. Bar Assn., Am. Arbitration Assn., ABA, Assn. Trial Lawyers Am., Delta Sigma Rho, Tau Kappa Alpha. Democrat. Jewish. Home and Office: 1090 Vermont Ave NW Washington DC 20005-4905*

**TENENBAUM, ANN G.,** art association administrator; b. Savannah, Ga., June 1961; m. Thomas H. Lee; children: Stephen Zachary, Robert Schiff. Grad., Sarah Lawrence Coll. Mem. vis. com. dept. photogs. Met. Mus. Art, 1996—2005, trustee, 2005—; vice chmn. bd. trustees Dia Art Found., NYC, 1994—2006. Co-pres. bd. trustees Film Soc. Lincoln Ctr. for Performing Arts; founding mem. bd. govs. Bard Coll. Ctr. Curatorial Studies; bd. dirs. Sarah Lawrence Coll., Channel 13/WNET, Studio Mus., Harlem, Second Stage Theatre, Guild Hall East Hampton; mem. chmn.'s coun. Mus. Modern Art. Named one of Top 200 Collectors, ARTnews mag., 2003—06; recipient Leo award, Ind. Curators Internat., 2003, Child Advocacy award, NYU Child Study Ctr., 2003. Avocation: Collector of Modern and contemporary art; Egyptian art. Office: c/o Met Mus Art 1000 5th Ave New York NY 10028*

**TENENBAUM, BERNARD HIRSH,** entrepreneur, educator; b. Long Beach, N.Y., Dec. 23, 1954; s. Abraham Benjamin and Helen Pearl (Wahrhaft) T. BA, Columbia Coll., 1976; postgrad., Stanford U., Calif., 1976-77; MBA, U. Pa., Phila., 1981. Mgr. Lido Beach (N.Y.) Hotel, 1976-77; gen. mgr. Sound Spectrum, Huntington, N.Y., 1977-78; dir. Small Bus. Ctr., Phila., 1980-84; asst. dir. Entre Ctr., Phila., 1984-85, assoc. dir., 1986-88; prof. entrepreneurial studies. dir. Fairleigh Dickinson U. Madison, N.J., 1988-93; v.p. corp. devel. Russ Berrie & Co., Inc., 1993-97; pres. Children's Leisure Products Group, The Jordan Co., N.Y.C., 1997—2003. Cons. Phila. Phillies, 1984-85; bd. dirs. Syms, Unger Global. Del. Securities Exchange Commn. on Small Bus. Capital Formation, 1984-86; vice chmn. Small Bus. Devel. Ctr. adv. bd., Phila., 1983—; bd. dirs. Pvt. Industry Council, Phila., 1983-88; chmn. Small Bus. Fair, Phila., 1983-88. Mem. Phila. C. of C. (vice chmn. small bus. coun. 1982-86, chmn. 1986-88), Venture Assn. N.J. (v.p.). Democrat. Jewish. Avocations: swimming, sports cars, music, literature, films. Office: Chldns Leisure Products LLC 71 Tamarack Cir Skillman NJ 08558 E-mail: bernie@btenenbaum.com.

**TENENBAUM, INEZ MOORE,** school system administrator; b. Hawkinsville, GA; m. Samuel J. Tenenbaum. Bsc, U. Ga., 1972, MEd, 1974; JD, U. S.C., 1986. Tchr. Elementary Sch.; dir. rsch. S.C. House Reps., 1977-83; attorney Sinkler & Boye, P.A., 1986-92; supt. edn. S.C. Dept. Edn., Columbia, 1999—. Founder S.C. Ctr. Family Policy. Office: South Carolina Dept Edn Rutledge Bldg 1429 Senate St Columbia SC 29201-3730

**TENENBAUM, JEFFREY S.,** lawyer; b. Boston, Oct. 29, 1968; BA, Univ. Pa., 1990; JD, Catholic Univ. Am., 1996. Bar: DC. Legis. asst. U.S. Ho. Reps., 1990—93; legal sect. mgr., govt. affairs analyst Am. Soc. Assn. Exec., Washington, 1993—95; of counsel Venable LLP, Washington, 1999—2003, ptnr., Nonprofit Assns., Trade & Profl. Assns. practices, 2003—. Spkr. in field. Author: Association Tax Compliance Guide; contbr. articles to profl. jours., magazines, newspapers; mem. editl. adv. bd. Assns. Law & Policy, 2000—, Nonprofit Tax & Financial Strategies, 1996—2002. Bd. dir. Fed. City Club Found. Named a Top Washington Lawyer, Washington Bus. Jour., 2004; named Outstanding Nonprofit Lawyer of the Year, ABA, Bus. Law section, 2006; recipient Chairman's award, Greater Washington Soc. Assn. Exec., 1997, Ctr. for Assn. Leadership, 2004. Mem.: Am. Soc. Assn. Execs. Office: Venable LLP 575 7th St NW Washington DC 20004 Office Phone: 202-344-8138. Office Fax: 202-344-8300. Business E-mail: jstenenbaum@venable.com.

**TENENBAUM, JOSEPH,** cardiologist; b. Neptune, NJ, Feb. 11, 1946; s. Sol and Marilyn Tenenbaum; m. Marilou Faith Jones, May 19, 1978; 1 child, Mollie Rodriguez. BA, Brandeis U., 1968; MD, Harvard U., 1974. Diplomate Am. Bd. Internal Medicine, Am. Bd. Cardiology. Edgar Leifer clin. prof. medicine Columbia U., NYC, 1979—; attending physician, interim chair dept. medicine Presbyn. Hosp., NYC, 2001—03. Fellow Am. Coll. Cardiology; mem. Columbia Faculty Practice Orgn. (chmn. 2000-03) Office: 161 Fort Washington Ave New York NY 10032-3713 Office Phone: 212-305-5288. Business E-Mail: jt7@columbia.edu.

**TENER, CAROL JOAN,** retired secondary school educator, consultant; b. Cleve., Feb. 10, 1935; d. Peter Paul and Mamie Christine (Dombrowski) Manusack; m. Dale Keith Tener, Feb. 13, 1958 (div. Aug. 1991); children: Dean Robert, Susan Dawn Tener Belair. Student, Cleve. Mus. Art, 1948-53, Cleve. Art Inst., 1953-54; BS in Edn. cum laude, Kent State U., 1957; MS in Supervision, Akron U., 1974; postgrad., Kent State U., 1964, 81, 88-90, Akron U., 1975, 79, John Carroll U., 1982, 83, 85-86, Ohio U., 1987, Baldwin Wallace Coll., 1989. Cert. permanent K-12 tchr., Ohio; cert. vol. counselor for Ohio sr. health ins. Ohio Dept. Ins. Stenographer Equitable Life Iowa, Cleve., 1953-54; tchr. elem. art Cuyahoga Falls (Ohio) Bd. Edn., 1957-58, 62-63, 65-68, tchr. jr. high sch., 1968-69; tchr. high sch. Brecksville (Ohio)-Broadview Heights Sch. Dist., 1969-94; chmn. dept. art Brecksville-Broadview Heights (Ohio) HS, 1979—94, chmn. curriculum devel., 1982, 1989, quality deployment team employee recognition district- wide bd. level, 1993—94; ret., 1994. Instr. for children Kent State U., 1956; advisor, prodr. cmty. svc. in art Brecksville Broadview Heights Bd. of Edn., 1969-94; former tchr. recreation and adult art edn. City of Cuyahoga Falls, 1967-68; com. mem. North Ctrl. evaluation com. Nordonia H.S., Nordonia City, Ohio, 1978, Solon H.S., Solon City, Ohio, 1989; chmn. north ctrl. evaluation com. Garfield Heights H.S., 1991; chair pilot program curriculum devel. com. in art/econs. Brecksville-Broadview Heights H.S., 1985-86, 86-87; spkr. in field. Contbr. articles to newspapers, brochures, mags.; commd. artist for mural Brecksville City's Kids Quarters, 1994, Christopher Columbus/John Glen portraits in relief commemorating Columbus Day, 1961, Wooster (Ohio) Products Co.; editor Greater Cleve. chpt. Ohio Ret. Tchrs. Assn., 1998-2002; contbr. to Resources for You, 2003, Ohio Sr. Health Ins. Info. Program, Ohio Dept. Ins., 2001—. Chmn. Artmart Invitational Exhibit PTA, 1982-94; active Meals on Wheels program in Brecksville and Broadview Hts., 1995-98, Heart Disease collection, 1995, Stow-Glen Assisted Living Visitations, 1994-95, NCR Assisted Living transp. provision to hosps. and dr. in neighboring county; trustee, sec. Gettysburg Devel. Block Group Parma, 1995-96, Kids Quarters, 1994; Med Save fraud vol. Cuyahoga County Dept. Sr. and Adult Svcs., 2000-2002, spkrs. bur.; sr. health ins. info. program, cert. vol. counselor of OSHIIP under the Dept. of Insurance, Ohio Dept. Ins., 2001-04—, vol. coord. spkr. and healthfair mktg., OSHIIP, 2004-05. Recipient Ohio Coun. on Econ. Edn. award, 1985-86, award for significant svc. to cmty. Ret. and Sr. Vol. Program of USA, 1996, Svc. award Greater Cleve. Chpt./Ohio Ret. Tchrs. Assn., 1998, Outstanding Svc. award Sr. Medicare Patrol Projects, Cert. of Appreciation, U.S. Dept. Health and Human Svcs. Adminstrn. on Aging, 2002; Pres.'s scholar Kent State U., 1954-57; Resolution to thank a Med-Save Project Vol. signed by Cuyahoga County Commrs. Tim McCormack, pres., Jimmy Dimora, v.p., and Peter Lawson Jones, commr. Mem.: NAFE, ASCD, NEA (life), AAUW, S.W. Area Ret. Educators (co-chair 1996—98, program chair 1996—98, program coord. 1999—2000), Nat. Mus. Women in Arts, Cleve. Mus. Art, Acad. Econ. Edn., Brecksville Edn. Assn., Internat. Platform Assn., Nat. Art Edn. Assn., Ohio Ret. Tchrs. Assn. (life; registration chair 1997—98, pres.-elect Cleve. chpt. 1998, program chair 1998, interim editor 1998, circulation mgr. 1998—2002, chpt. pres. 1999, editor 1999—2002, trustee 2000, guest spkr. on newsletter writing and pub. 2000, nominating chair 2000—01, by-law chair 2000—01, Pub. Rels. awards 1999—2002), Phi Delta Kappa Pi. Roman Catholic. Avocations: photography, collecting books on architecture, painting. Home: 7301 Sagamore Rd Parma OH 44134-5732 Office Phone: 440-885-2231.

**TENET, GEORGE JOHN,** diplomacy professor, former CIA director; b. Flushing, N.Y., Jan. 5, 1953; m. A. Stephanie Glakas; 1 child. BS in Fgn. Svc., Georgetown U., 1976; MIA, Columbia U., 1978. Legis. asst. to Sen. H. John Heinz III Senate Select Com. on Intelligence, Washington, 1985-86, designee to vice chair Sen. Patrick J. Leahy, 1986-89; dir. oversight of arms control negotiations Soviet Union/US, 1989-93, staff dir. to chmn. Senator David Boren, 1993; mem. presdl. transition team Nat. Security Coun., Washington, 1993-95, spl. asst. to pres., sr. dir. intelligence programs, 1995-97; dep. dir. CIA, Washington, 1995-96, acting dir., 1996-97, dir., 1997—2004; prof. diplomacy Georgetown U., Washington, 2004—; bd. dir. Viisage, 2005—. Author: The Ability of U.S. Intelligence to Monitor the Intermediate Nuclear Force Treaty. Recipient Presdl. Medal of Freedom, Pres. George W. Bush, 2004. Office: Inst for the Study of Diplomacy 1316 36th St NW Washington DC 20007 Office Phone: 202-687-8209.

**TEN EYCK, DOROTHEA FARISS,** real estate agent; b. Pulaski County, Va., Dec. 2, 1923; d. Orel Crook and Esther Mildred (Rexrode) Fariss; m. George Ten Eyck, Jan. 4, 1949 (dec.); m. John S. Kreeger, Aug. 27, 1965 (dec.); m. Robert L. Ten Eyck, Oct. 30, 1994; 4 children Student, Ind. U. Market rsch. Proctor & Gamble, Cin., 1944-47; ptnr. Santee Builders, 1960—63; sales real estate Lockwood Doeuch, Cin., 1963-65. Pres. women's com. Cin. Art Mus., mem. adv. com., docent emeritus; mem. Elder Indian Hill Ch. Independent. Presbyterian. Avocations: golf, gardening, travel, volunteerism. Home: 3032 Alpine Ter Cincinnati OH 45208-2925

**TENG, FRANCIS W.,** surgeon; b. Kong Kong, July 29, 1961; arrived in U.S., 1966; s. Chuck L. and Stella K. Teng. MD, U. Nev., Reno, 1991. Chief surgery Mt. View Hosp., Las Vegas, 2001—. Mem. critical care com. Mt. View Hosp., 2003—. Fellow: Am. Coll. Surgeons; mem.: Am. Soc. Bariatric Surgeons. Office: 3150 N Tenaya Way Ste 680 Las Vegas NV 89128-0461

**TENHOEVE, THOMAS,** academic administrator; b. Bklyn., Oct. 1, 1935; s. Thomas and Adeline Ruth (Vander Hill) T.; m. Suzanne Underwood, June 7, 1957; children: Thomas III, Carol, Timothy. AB, Hope Coll., 1956; MA, U. Mich., 1957; PhD, U. Toledo, 1965; postgrad., U. Western Mich.; EdD (hon.), Northwestern Coll., 1995. Biology tchr. South Haven. Mich. Pub. Schs., 1957-58; biology instr. Northwestern Coll., Orange City, Iowa, 1958-63; supr. biology student tchrs. U. Toledo, Ohio, 1963-65; acad. dean, acting pres. Northwestern Coll., Orange City, 1965-70; pres. Butler (Pa.) County Community Coll., 1970-84, Oakton Community Coll., Des Plaines, Ill., 1984-95. Dir. CoVest Banc, 1987—99. Bd. dirs. Sister Cities Internat., 1986-95, 1998-2004, nat. v.p., treas., 2001-04; trustee Northwestern Coll., 1988-95; mem. Ill. C.C. State Found. Bd., 1993-95, Ill. Math. and Sci. Acad. Selection Bd., 1986, 87, Cook County Sheriff's Scholarship Panel, 1995-96. Golden Corridor, 1986-92; vol. Good Samaritan Ministries, 2001-. Recipient Pacesetter award Nat. Coun. for Community Rels., 1986, Orchard Village award, Skyway Conf. Hall of Fame. Mem. Am. Coun. on Internat. Intercultural Edn. (chmn. 1992-95), Coun. North Ctrl. Two-Yr. Colls. (state rep. 1988-92, exec. bd. 1989-95, 2d v.p. 1990-91, 1st v.p. 1991-92, pres. 1992-93).

**TENHOLDER, EDWARD J.,** pharmaceutical executive; Sr. v.p. client svcs. and ops. Right Choice Managed Care, Inc., 1994—97; exec. v.p., COO Blue Cross and Blue Shield Mo., 1997—2000; sr. v.p., chief info. officer Express Scripts, Inc., Maryland Heights, Mo., 2000—, chief adminstrn. officer, 2003—. Office: Express Scripts Inc 13900 Riverport Dr Maryland Heights MO 63043

**TENNANT, JOHN RANDALL,** management consultant; b. North Bend, Wash., Aug. 23, 1940; s. Maurice Andrew and Jane Downing (Vinnede) T.; m. Nikki Mae Ferris, July 17, 1965 (div.); children: Ann Elizabeth, Randall Warren; m. Deborah Ann Francis, Oct. 25, 1986 (div.); 1 child, Alyssa Jane; m. Carol A. McDonnell, Feb. 2, 2005. BS in Indsl. Engring., Stanford U., 1962; MBA, U. Wash., 1966. Registered profl. engr., Wash. Sr. rsch. engr. Boeing Co., Seattle, 1962-68; mgr. Price Waterhouse, Seattle, 1968-73, ptnr. Tokyo, 1973-79, Los Angeles, 1979-89; founder, CEO, Manex, Inc., Newport

Beach, Calif., 1989—; dir. subs. Price Waterhouse Assocs., Pacific region, 1975-79. Mem. John Tracy Clinic Men's Com., Santa Catalina Island Conservacy, pres., 1985-87; capt. Long Beach Mounted Police. Mem. NSPE, Japan Computer Assn. (founder, pres. 1976-77), Japan Modapts Assn. (founder), Japan Am. Soc., Inst. Mgmt. Cons., Am. Inst. Indsl. Engrs. (pres. Seattle chpt. 1970-71), Data Processing Mgmt. Assn., Tokyo Lawn and Tennis Club, L.A. Country Club, Jonathan Club, Empty Saddle Club, Los Rancheros Visitadores Club, Los Caballeros Club. Home: 332 Sunset Ct Oak View CA 93022 Office Phone: 310-618-0299. Personal E-mail: tennantrjohn@aol.com.

**TENNANT, THOMAS MICHAEL,** lawyer; b. Anniston, Ala., July 23, 1948; s. Thomas Edward and Mary Eugenia (Warren) T.; m. Sharon Leigh Ebert, Mar. 21, 1970; children: Sharon Michelle, Michael Ebert. BS, Auburn U., 1970; JD, Walter F. George Sch. Law, 1973. Assoc. Webb, Fowler & Tanner, Lawrenceville, Ga., 1973-76, ptnr., 1976-77; mng. ptnr. Tennant, Andersen & Davidson, P.C., Lawrenceville, 1978-81, Tennant, Andersen, Davidson & Edmondson, P.C., Lawrenceville, 1982-85, Tennant, Davidson & Edmondson, P.C., Lawrenceville, 1985-86, Tennant, Davidson & Thompson, P.C., Lawrenceville, 1986-87, Tennant, Davidson, Thompson & Sweeny, Lawrenceville, 1987-89, Tennant, Thompson & Sweeny, 1990; ptnr., environ. land use group Alston & Bird LLP, Atlanta, 1991—. Judge Recorder's Ct., Lawrenceville, 1979-80; mem. State Disciplinary Bd., 1988-91. Chmn. bd. trustees Leadership Gwinnett; bd. dirs. Rsch. Atlanta, Inc., Regional Leadership Found., Cmty. Found. N.E. Ga., Inc., Lawrenceville, 1984—. Served to 1st lt. U.S. Army, 1970—78. Mem. Atlanta Bar Assn., State Bar Ga. (chmn. lawyer ethics com. young lawyers sect. 1979-80, bd. govs. 1986-92), Gwinnett County Bar Assn. (pres. 1978), Atlanta Lawyers Club, Gwinnett County C. of C. (pres. 1986). Presbyterian. Office: Alston & Bird One Atlantic Ctr 1201 Peachtree St Atlanta GA 30309-3400 Office Phone: 404-881-7838. E-mail: mtennant@alston.com.

**TENNANT-SNYDER, NANCY,** appliance company executive; BA in Sociology, West Va. U., 1980, MS in Indsl. Rels., 1981; Doctorate degree in orgn. behavior, George Washington U., 1996. Various mgmt. positions in orgn. development Kaiser Aluminum; with Whirlpool Corp., 1986—, corp. dir., organizational leadership development, 1994—99, corp. dir., strategic process, 1999—2000, v.p., strategic innovation and knowledge mgmt., 2000—01, corp. v.p. strategic competencies and leadership, 2001—. Spkr. in field; adj. prof. in exec. edn. U. Notre Dame. Author of numerous publs.; co-author: Mastering Virtual Teams and Strategiv Innovation. Bd. dir. First Tee, Benton Harbor, Mich. Named one of 25 Masters of Innovation, BusinessWeek. Office: Whirlpool Corp 2000 N M-63 Benton Harbor MI 49022-2692 Business E-Mail: nancy_t_snyder@whirlpool.com.

**TENNEN, LESLIE IRWIN,** lawyer, consultant; b. Toronto, Aug. 26, 1952; came to U.S., 1961; s. Edward and Elsie (Liberbaum) T. BA with distinction, U. Ariz., 1973, JD, 1976; Mount Scopus, Hebrew U., Jerusalem, 1975. Bar: Ariz. 1977, U.S. Dist. Ct. Ariz. 1979. Sole practice, Tucson, 1977—79; ptnr. Sterns and Tennen, Phoenix, 1979—. Cons. internat. law and aerospace activities; lectr. univs., colls. and law schs.; mem. Ariz. Space Commn., 1994-2000, also profl. aviation and aerospace congresses and seminars in N.Am., Europe, Asia, S.Am., Australia; judge Jessup Internat. Moot Court Competition, 1982, 83, 85, 92; dir., treas. Assn. U.S. Mems. Internat. Inst. Space Law; com. mem. U. Belarusian Culture Internat. Orgn. Mem. editl bd. Space Regulations Libr.; contbr. Ariz. Law Rev., 1975-76; contbr. articles to profl. jours. Precinct committeeman State Dem. Conv., 1972-73. Received highest score Ariz. Bar Exam., Feb. 1977. Mem. AIAA (sr.), Ariz. Bar Found., Internat. Eurasian Acad. Scis., Internat. Inst. Space Law (Appreciation award (with Patricia Margaret Sterns) 1998), Internat. Acad. Astronautics, Am. Soc. Internat. Law, Soc. Aerospace Communicators Inc., Internat. Law Assn., Planetary Soc., Fedn. Aerospace Socs. in Tucson (exec. bd.). Office: 849 N 3rd Ave Phoenix AZ 85003-1408 Office Phone: 602-254-5197. E-mail: LTennen@astrolaw.com.

**TENNEY, DUDLEY BRADSTREET,** retired lawyer; b. N.Y.C., July 13, 1918; s. Parker Gillespie and Josephine (Keeler) T.; m. Margaret Carter, June 13, 1941 (div. Oct. 1977); children: Ann, Janet Greene; m. Dorothy Walsh, Jan. 7, 1978 (dec. Sept. 1982); m. Joyce McPherson, Jan. 4, 1986. AB summa cum laude, Oberlin Coll., 1939; JD magna cum laude, Harvard U., 1942. Bar: N.Y. 1948. Assoc. firm Cahill, Gordon & Reindel, N.Y.C., 1946-54, ptnr., 1955-86. Pres.: Harvard U. Law Rev., 1941-42. Served to maj. AUS, 1942-46, CBI. Mem. ABA, Assn. Bar City of N.Y., World Trade Ctr. Club (N.Y.C.), Manhasset Bay Yacht Club (Port Washington, N.Y.). Home: 25 Wood Rd Sands Point NY 11050-2625 Office: Cahill Gordon & Reindel 80 Pine St Fl 17 New York NY 10005-1790

**TENNEY, FRANK PUTNAM,** marketing executive; b. Orono, Maine, Oct. 6, 1937; s. Carl Bither and Velma May (Williamson) T.; m. Margaret Anne Seymour, Apr. 23, 1960; children: Jane Dossiere, Carl B., Janet M., Alan F., Janice M. Lovell. Cert. notary public, Maine. Nat. sales mgr. Shaw & Tenney Oar & Paddle Co., Orono, Maine, 1958—68; sales mgr. George B. Wetherill, Phila., 1968—69; with R.M. Flagg, Veazie, Maine, 1968—69; salesman DuBois Chem., Cin., 1969—76; Maine sales mgr. Rochester Midland Co., NY, 1976—82; with H.A. Manning Co., Bellows Falls, Vt., 1982—86; dist. sales mgr. U.S. West Mktg. Resources, Loveland, Colo., 1986—90; sales mgr. City Directory, Inc., Belmond, Iowa, 1990—93; with RAK Industries, 1993; v.p. Maine Mktg. Resources, Brewer, Maine, 1994—. Adv. bd. Salvation Army. Tech. sgt. Maine ANG, 1955-87, ret. Mem.: KC (past grand knight Pine Cone coun., 4th degree, past faithful navigator Pine Cone assembly), VFW (pub. chmn., sr. vice comdr.), Greater Bangor C. of C., Golden Cir. (Averill plaque), 40/8, Profl. Sales Club Bangor, Am. Legion (Americanism officer 1997, post comdr. 1999—2000, ADF 2001—, past vice comdr. VFW), 1. patriotic instr. VFW). Republican. Roman Catholic. Office Phone: 207-942-6241.

**TENNEY, JANE MORRIS,** real estate developer; d. Mendel Morris and Floreine Welch; m. Mark William Tenney, June 1, 1974; m. Daniel Marston Shepherd, Mar. 16, 1957 (div.); children: Daniel Vincent Shepherd, David Morris Shepherd. BS, U. Ky., 1962. Sales rep. IBM, South Bend, 1975—80; pres. Technivest, Inc., South Bend, Ind., 1980—88; mgr. bus. incubator Control Data, South Bend, 1984—89; owner, pres. Tenney Assocs., Inc, Niles, Mich., 1992—. Land developer Longmeadow Residential and Comml. Cmty., Niles, Mich., 1997—. Elected del. White Ho. Conf. of Small Bus., Washington, 1984—84. Recipient Demonstration Project on Watershed Devel. Design, Conservation Fund, 1997, Women of Yr., Four Flags C. of C., 2003. Mem.: Nat. Assn. of Realtor, Nat. Home Builders Assn. Office: Tenney Assocs Inc 126 Churchill Ln Niles MI 49120 E-mail: sales@longmeadow.info.

**TENNEY, SARAH G.,** music educator; b. N.Y.C., Apr. 30, 1948; d. John Wool Griswold and Margaret Brett Tenney. BA, Bennington Coll., 1971; MusM, New Eng. Conservatory, 1976. Founder Spectrum Young Audiences Trio, Boston, 1976-80; marimba, percussion tchr. Rivers Music Sch., Weston, Mass., 1976-80, 85—, St. Ann's Sch., Bklyn., 1980-85; founder, dir. Marimba Magic, Weston, 1987—; tchr. improvisation Northeastern U., Boston, 1991-95. Percussionist on 6 Revel records; percussionist/timpanist in Christmas Revels, 1996—; presenter in field. Composer: (composition/musical) Gamelon Dream, 1989, Mysterious Waltz, 1991, Whole Tone Dream, 1996, Adventures, 1999, Machines, 2000, Jaja Mani Dreams, 2001, Drum Circle, 2002, 3 Canons, 2003, Moving Music, 2004, More Moving Music, 2005. Concert performer Concerts for Children, 1976-80, Cambridge World's Fair, 1997, 98, Clarimba Duo, 2002—03, WCRB Cartoonfest, Symphony Hall, 2005. Recipient Am. Composers Forum grant. Mem. Music Tchrs. Nat. Assn. (conf. presenter 1991) Musicians Union, Music Educators Nat. Conf. (presenter ea. conf. 1992, 96), Percussive Arts Soc. (presenter internat. conv. 1989, 97), Orff Schulwerk Assn. (presenter nat. conf. 1996) presenter European Piano Tchrs. Assn., Internat. Conf., Budapest, 2000, Internat. Marimba Conf., Belgium, 1992. Office: The Rivers Music Sch 337 Winter St Weston MA 02493-1072 Office Phone: 781-235-6840.

**TENNIES, ROBERT HUNTER,** headmaster; b. Bogotá, Colombia, Aug. 19, 1952; s. Leo C. and Ruth (Winston) T.; m. Ruth Ellen Fischer, June 14, 1975; children: Debbie, Julie. BS, Wheaton (Ill.) Coll., 1973; MA, U. South Fla., 1975; EdS, Fla. Atlantic U., 1978, EdD, 1982. Sci. tchr. Cypress Lake Middle Sch., Ft. Myers, Fla., 1973-77, Boca Raton (Fla.) Christian Sch., 1977-78, asst. administr., 1978-84, headmaster, 1984—, min. of children, 1984-90; interim. min. of edn., 1991-93. Spkr. Internat. Conf. Religious Edn. Petrozavodsk, Russia; mem. Nat. Rev. Panel Blue Ribbon Schs., 1999. Recipient Excellence in Edn. award Nat. Assn. Elem. Prins., 1990, 97. Mem. Nat. Sci. Tchrs. Assn., Assn. of Christian Schs. Internat. (chair Fla. accreditation commn.), Nat. Assn. Elem. Sch. Prins. Avocation: camping. Home: 2415 NW 30th Rd Boca Raton FL 33431-6214 Office: Boca Raton Christian Sch 315 NW 4th St Boca Raton FL 33432-3739 E-mail: Tennies_r@popmail.firn.edu, bocachristian@bocachristian.org.

**TENNIMON, DANNIE EARL,** academic administrator, educator; b. Selma, Ala., Mar. 15, 1947; s. Earl and Mary Tennimon; m. Lori Dee Krehbiel, Feb. 7, 1991; m. Kathy Leann McCowan, Aug. 31, 1968 (div. Feb. 1, 1991); children: Tara Lee Faulkner, Shelby Danielle, Brandi Kay Miller, Shandon Earl. BA, Auburn U., Ala., 1970; MEd, Boston U., 1975; MA in Tchg., Troy State U., 1995. Commd. lt. U.S. Army, 1970, advanced through grades to lt. col., 1988, ret., 1994; asst. to pres. Troy State U., Montgomery, Ala., 1996—2004; coord. instl. rsch., effectiveness and planning Troy U., Montgomery, 2004—. Adj. instr. history Troy U., Montgomery, 1998—; presenter in field. Deacon Millbrook (Ala.) Presbyn. Ch., 1996—2001, ruling elder, 2001—05. Decorated Bronze Star with 1oak leaf cluster U.S. Army, Meritorious Svc. award wuth 1 oak leaf cluster, Joint Svc. Meritorious Svc. award. Mem.: Soc. Coll. and U. Planning (assoc.), Assn. Instnl. Rsch. (assoc.), So. Assn. Instnl. Rsch. (assoc.), Ala. Assn. Instnl. Rsch. (assoc.; pres. 2003—04), Gamma Beta Phi (assoc.). Avocations: travel, backpacking, military history. Home: 46 Pine Mountain Court Millbrook AL 36054 Office: Troy University PO Drawer 4419 Montgomery AL 36103-4419 Office Phone: 334-241-9536. Home Fax: 334-285-1257; Office Fax: 334-241-8619. Personal E-mail: ltennimon@aol.com. Business E-Mail: dtennimon@troy.edu.

**TENNYSON, PETER JOSEPH,** lawyer; b. Winona, Minn., Mar. 18, 1946; s. Richard Harvey and Sylvia Josephine (Jadrich) T.; m. Mary Eileen Fay, Jan. 3, 1970; children: Mark Christian, Rachel Christine, Matthew Patrick, Erica Ruth. BA, Purdue U., 1968; JD, U. Va., 1975. Bar: Calif. Assoc. attys. O'Melveny & Myers, LA, 1975-82; v.p., gen. counsel Cannon Mills Co., Kannapolis, NC, 1982-84; ptnr. Stradling, Yocca, Newport Beach, Calif., 1984-89, Jones, Day, Reavis & Pogue, Irvine, Calif., 1990-95, Paul, Hastings, Janofsky & Walker, Costa Mesa, Calif., 1995—. Mem. Calif. Commn. on Future of Legal Profession and State Bar, 1994; lectr. in field. Mem. adv. bd. St. Joseph Hosp., Orange, Calif., 1987-; bd. dirs. Lincoln Club Orange County, 1991-93, South Coast Symphony, 1989-92; mem. found. bd. Orange County H.S. Arts. Capt. U.S. Army, 1968—72. Recipient Attys. of Yr. award, Calif. Lawyer, 2003. Mem.: Orange County Bar Assn., South Coast Repertory Silver Circle, Performing Arts Bus. Alliance. Roman Catholic. Avocations: downhill skiing, swimming. Home: 19 Monaco Newport Beach CA 92660 Office: Paul Hastings Janofsky & Walker LLP 695 Town Center Dr Fl 17 Costa Mesa CA 92626-1924 Office Phone: 714-668-6237. Business E-Mail: petertennyson@paulhastings.com.

**TENORIO, PEDRO A.,** resident representative; b. Saipan; BA in Geology, U. Hawaii, MS in Hydrology. Sen. for Northern Marianas Congress of Micronesia, 1972—74; mem. Northern Marianas Polit. Status Commn., 1973—76; exec. dir. Northern Marianas Office Transition Studies and Planning, 1975—77, Marianas Pub. Land Corp., 1977—81; legis. adv. 1st Commonwealth of Northern Mariana Islands (CNMI) Legislature, 1977—81; lt. gov. CNMI, 1981—89; resident rep. CNMI U.S. Ho of Reps., Washington, 2001—. Mem. Rep. Nat. Com. and Presdl. Victory Team. Mem.: Nat. Rep. Club Capitol Hill, Lions Club East Manoa. Republican. Office: Resident Rep US Ho of Reps 2121 R St NW Washington DC 20008 also: PO Box 504959 Saipan MP MP 96950*

**TENPAS, RONALD J.,** prosecutor, lawyer; m. Kathryn Dunn; children: Nathaniel, William. BA with hons., Mich. State U., 1985; degree in Philosophy, Politics and Econs., Oxford U., Eng., 1987; JD, U. Va., 1990. Law clk. U.S. Dist. Ct. (ea. dist.) Pa., 1990—91; law clk. to Chief Justice William H. Rehnquist U.S. Supreme Ct., Washington, 1991—92; law clk. Iran-U.S. Claims Tribunal The Hague, Netherlands, 1992—93; assoc. Carlton, Fields Law Firm, Tampa, Fla., 1993—97; asst. US atty. (mid. dist.) Fla. US Dept. Justice, 1997—99, asst. U.S. atty. Md., 1999—2003, branch chief Dist. Md. So. Divsn., 2001—03, interim US atty. (so. dist.) Ill., 2003—05, US atty. (so. dist.) Ill., 2005, assoc. dep. atty. gen., 2005—. Editor: Va. Law Rev. Rhodes scholarship, 1985—87, Hardy Cross Dillard scholarship, 1987—90. Office: US Attorneys Office So Dist Ill Nine Executive Dr Ste 300 Fairview Heights IL 62208 Office Phone: 618-628-3700.*

**TENTZERIS, EMMANOUIL MANOS,** engineering educator, researcher; b. Athens, Greece, Mar. 20, 1970; came to U.S., 1992; s. Markos E. Tentzeris and Irene M. Tentzeri. Diploma summa cum laude, Nat. Tech. U. Athens, 1992; MSc, U. Mich., 1993, PhD, 1998. Assoc. Ga. Inst. Tech., Atlanta, 1998—2004. Invited prof. Tech. U. Munich, Germany, 2002; assoc. dir. for RF rsch. and RF Alliance Leader NSF-GT-Packaging Rsch. Ctr., 1998; broadband tech. hardware, subthrust leader Ga. Electronics Design Ctr. Initiative of State of Ga., 2000; chair CEM-TD Symposium, 2005; tech. program co-chair Automatic Radio Frequency Techniques Group, Atlanta, 1999; vice-chair IEEE-Components Packaging and Mfg. Tech. Tech. Com. 16 Radio Frequency/Wireless. Author: (with others) Advances Computational EM, 1990, Electronic Packaging, 2000, The RF and Microwave Handbook, 2001, Microwave and RF Product Applications, 2003, Encyclopedia of RF Microwave, 2004, Si RF Handbook, 2005; reviewer in field. Recipient Best Paper award, Internat. Microelectronics and Packaging Soc. Symposium, 1997, Applied Computational Electromagnetics Soc. Symposium, 2001, 2002, Career award NSF, 2000, Ga. Tech.-ECE Outstanding Jr. Faculty award 2002; Greek Acad. Excellence fellow Greek Dept. Edn., 1988-92; Papastavridios Greek Math Excellence fellow Greek Govt., 1989. Mem. IEEE (sr., Outstanding Young Engr. award 2003, MTT-AP Atlanta chpt., chmn. bd. com. 2002, tech. session chair 1996, 2000-2005, chair steering com.1998), Ga. Tech. Wireless Inst., Tech. Chamber of Greece. Avocations: sports, history books, travel. Home: 195 14th St #1208 Atlanta GA 30309 Office: Ga Inst Tech tech ECE 777 Atlantic Dr Atlanta GA 30332-0250 Office Phone: 404-385-0378.

**TENUTA, LUIGIA,** lawyer; b. Madison, Wis., June 4, 1954; d. Eugene P. and Nancy (Gardner) T. AB in Internat. Studies with honors, Miami U., Oxford, Ohio, 1976; JD, Capital U., 1981; postgrad., Pontifical Coll. Josephinum, 1987-88. Bar: Ohio 1981. With internat. mktg. dept. Dresser Industries, Columbus, Ohio, 1976-80, analyst strategic planning, 1980, mgr. internat bus. planning Stratford, Conn., 1981; pvt. practice law Columbus, 1981—. Former mem. devel. com. Miami U. Mem. Ohio Bar Assn., Columbus Bar Assn. Roman Catholic. Office: 6400 Riverside Dr Dublin OH 43017-5197

**TEOLIS, MICHAEL FRANCIS,** music educator, musician, conductor, composer; b. Chgo., Aug. 25, 1953; s. Matthew Felix and Arlene Mary; m. Cynthia Louise Zakrzewski; children: Giovanna Marie, Adrianna Elizabeth. MusB, DePaul U., 1975; MusM, Vandercook Coll., 1991. Music educator Archdiocese of Chgo., 1974—89; freelance musician various, Chgo., 1973—; music dir. St. Benedict Ch., Chgo., 1975—83, Latin Sch., Chgo., 1989—. Assoc. dir. William Ferris Chorale, Chgo., 1973—; mem. adv. bd. St. Benedict HS; mem. alumni bd. VanderCook Coll. Music. Pub. (piano accompaniment) Beautiful Dreamer, If You've Only Got a Moustache, (handbell duet) Two for Two. Mem.: ASCAP, Nat. Cath. Bandmasters Assn., Music Educators Nat. Conf., Ill. Music Educators Assn., Ill. Music Assn., VanderCook Coll. Alumni Assn., KC Roman Catholic. Office: Latin Sch Chgo 59 W North Blvd Chicago IL 60610

**TEPLOW, THEODORE HERZL,** retired valve company executive; b. Brockton, Mass., Apr. 14, 1928; s. Edward Abraham and Evelyn (Stone) T.; m. Charlotte Leah Savitz, June 14, 1953; children: Rachel P., David I., Deborah R., Evan S., Jonathan P. BS, U.S. Mcht. Marine Acd., 1950; MBA, Harvard U., 1953; DHL honoris causa, Hebrew Coll., 1999; PhD honoris causa, Weizmann Inst. Sci., 2002. Mgmt. trainee to pres. Crosby Valve Inc. a Tyco Internat. Ltd. Co., Wrentham, Mass., 1953-82, cons., 1982—2001; dir. Emerson Investment Mgmt., Inc., Boston, 1985—. Cons. Firesafe Products Corp., N.Y.C., 1982-96; pres. Gateway Investment Corp., 2003—. Trustee Am. Mcht. Marine Mus. Found., Kings Point, N.Y., 1988-98, Rofeh Internat., Boston, 1990—, Hebrew Coll., Newton Center, Mass., 1971—, chmn., 1992-99; chmn. Hebrew Coll. Bd. Mgrs. of Trust Property, 1999—; trustee Kings Point Challenge, 1997—, U.S. Mcht. Marine Acad., Kings Point, N.Y., 2002—; v.p., bd. dirs. Internat. Catacomb Soc., Boston, 1982-99; bd. dirs. Cong. Beth El-Atereth Israel, Newton Center, Mass., 1975-85, Beth El Cmty. Hebrew Sch., Newton Center, 1965-85, USMMA Alumni Found., Kings Point, 1957—; asst. treas., dir. Am. Com. for Weizmann Inst. Sci., N.Y., 1987-2002, vice chair fin. and adminstrn., dir., 2002—; gov. Weizmann Inst. Sci., Rehovoth, Israel, 1991—; bd. dirs. Wilstein Inst. Jewish Policy Studies, L.A., Boston, 1993—, Stone Charitable Found., 1982-99; dir. Archives for Hist. Documentation, Boston, 1994—. Comdr. USNR, ret. Recipient Outstanding Profl. Achievement award U.S. Mcht. Marine Acad. Alumni Assn., 1970, Meritorious Alumni Svc. award, 1990, Disting. Svc. award, 1995. Democrat.

**TEPPER, CLIFFORD,** allergist, immunologist, educator; b. Schenectady, N.Y., Oct. 26, 1922; s. Solomon B. and Annette (Lifset) T.; m. Cynthia S. Tepper; children: Stewart, Nancy, Henry, Audrey. Chief allergy dept. Ellis Hosp., Schenectady, 1990—; allergist allergy asthma immunology ctr. Albany (N.Y.) Med. Coll., 1992—, prof. pediats., 1973—. Co-dir. Schenectady Vol. Physicians Free Clinic; cons. in field. Trustee Schenectady Mus., 1987-99, Schenectady Pub. Libr., 1985—; pres. Antismoking Acad. Schenectady County; co-dir. Vol. Physician Clinic, Shcenectady County. Mem. Coll. Allergy and Immunology, Am. Acad. Pediatrics, Am. Acad. Allergy and Immunology, New Eng. Soc. Allergy (pres. 1990-92), N.Y. State Allergy Soc. (treas. 1993-95), Eastern Allergy Soc. (exec. com.), Physicians for Social Responsibility. Avocations: bird watching, art history. Home: 2216 Stoneridge Rd Niskayuna NY 12309-5524 Office: Allergy Asthma Immunology Ctr Albany Med Coll 1201 Washihngton Ave Ext Albany NY 12205 Fax: 518 452 2683. E-mail: tepperc@mail.amc.edu.

**TEPPER, DAVID A.,** hedge fund manager; b. Pitts., 1958; m. Marlene Tepper; 3 children. BA, U. Pitts., 1978; MBA, Carnegie Mellon U., 1982. Credit & securities analyst Equibank, Pitts., 1978—80; with treas. dept. Republic Steel, Ohio, 1982—84; with Keystone Mutual Funds, Boston, 1984—85; credit analyst Goldman Sachs, NYC, 1985, head trader at high-yield desk, 1985—92; pres. & co-founder Appaloosa Mgmt., Chatham, NJ, 1993—. Mem. bus. bd. advisors Carnegie Mellon U. Tepper Sch. Bus. Named one of 400 Richest Americans, Forbes, 2005, 2006, World's Richest People, 2006. Office: Appaloosa Mgmt 26 Main St Chatham NJ 07928 Office Phone: 973-701-7000.*

**TEPPER, H. MARC,** lawyer; b. Vineland, N.J., Mar. 11, 1960; 2 children. BS, Ithaca Coll., N.Y., 1982; JD, New Eng. Sch. Law, Boston, 1986. Bar: Pa., N.J., Washington. Ptnr. Margolis Edelstein, Phila., 1995—96, Clark Ladner, 1996; ptnr., shareholder Buchanan Ingersoll PC, 1996—. Chair Ins. & Reinsurance Group/Buchanan Ingersoll PC, 2001—, Ins. Coverage Group/Buchanan Ingersoll PC, 2001—. Author: Legal Strategies for the Insurance Industry: Leading Lawyers on Handling Risks, Regulations, Litigation and More, 2005. Mem.: Am.-Israel C.of C., Waington DC Bar Assn., N.J. Bar Assn., Phila. Bar Assn., N.Y. Bar Assn. Achievements include ran N.Y., Phila. and Marine Corps. marathons. Avocation: marathon running. Home: 6 Hunters Ave Cherry Hill NJ 08003 Office: Buchanan Ingersoll PC 1835 Market St 14th Flr Philadelphia PA 19103 Office Phone: 215-665-3864. Business E-Mail: tepperhm@bipc.com.

**TEPPER, LLOYD BARTON,** preventive medicine physician, educator; b. L.A., Dec. 21, 1931; m. Lamonte Leverage; children: Jeffrey Hamilton, Evan Clothier. AB, Dartmouth Coll., 1954; MD, Harvard U., 1957, MPH, 1960, ScD in Hygiene, 1962. Diplomate Am. Bd. Preventive Medicine (trustee, vice chair, 1986-94), Am. Bd. Occupl. Medicine. Intern U. Calif., San Francisco, 1957—58; resident Harvard Sch. Pub. Health, 1959—62; rsch. fellow Harvard Med. Sch., Boston, 1958-59; clin. fellow Mass. Gen. Hosp., Boston, 1958-60; rsch. assoc. MIT, Cambridge, 1959-61; physician U.S. AEC, Washington, 1962-65; prof. environ. health U. Cin., 1965-72; assoc. dir. Kettering Lab., Cin., 1965-72; assoc. commr. U.S. FDA, Washington, 1972-76; corp. med. dir. Air Products and Chems., Inc., Allentown, Pa., 1976-97; adj. prof. medicine Jefferson Med. Coll., 1984—2001. Adj. prof. emergency medicine occupl. and environ. medicine U. Pa., 2000—. Editor: Jour. Occupl. Medicine, 1979—91. Fellow: Am. Acad. Occupl. Medicine (pres. 1980—81), Am. Coll. Occupl. and Environ. Medicine. Office Phone: 610-527-8918. E-mail: lbtepper@icdc.com.

**TEPPER, LYNN MARSHA,** gerontologist, educator; b. NYC, Mar. 16, 1946; m. William Chester Tepper, Aug. 27, 1967; children: Sharon Joy, Michelle Dawn. BS, SUNY, Buffalo, 1967; MA, Wayne State U., 1971; MS, Columbia U., 1977, EdM, 1978, EdD, 1980. Instr. John F. Kennedy Sch., Berlin, 1967-68, ednl. counselor, 1968-69; ednl. coordinator Army Edn. Ctr., Berlin, 1969-71; psychologist U.S. Dept. Def., Berlin, 1971-73; prof. gerontology L.I. U., 1979—2000, Mercy Coll., Dobbs Ferry, 1979—, Columbia U., NYC, 1982—. Cons. NATO, Naples, Italy, 1969-71, SHAPE, Brussels, 1969-71, Found. for Long Term Care, 1992—, others; dir. Gerontology Resource Ctr., Ctr. for Geriatrics and Gerontology, Columbia U., NYC, 1980-85, dir. Behavioral Sci. Program, 1982—; del. White House Conf. on Aging, 1980; clin. prof. Columbia U., 1982—. Author: (textbooks) Long Term Care, 1993, Respite Care, 1993, Multidisciplinary Perspectives on Aging, 2004; contbr. articles to profl. jours., chpts. to books. Advisor Office on Aging, State of N.Y., Albany, 1980-90; dir. Mercy Coll., Inst. Gerontology, 1990—; trustee, St. Cabrini Nursing Home, 1988-98, Morningside Nursing Home, 1998—; bd. dirs. Found. Long Term Care. Brookdale Inst. on Aging fellow, 1983; rsch. grantee NIH, Nat. Inst. on Aging, Nat. Inst. Gen. Med. Sci., U.S. Dept. Edn., U.S. Bur. Health Professions, interdisciplinary geriat. tng. U.S. Dept. Health Resources Svcs. Adminstrn. Fellow Gerontol. Soc. Am.; mem. Am. Psychol. Assn. Avocations: exercise, hiking. Office: Columbia U Med Campus Box 20 630 W 168th St New York NY 10032-3702

**TEPPER, MARCY ELIZABETH,** drug education director; b. Salt Lake City, Aug. 22, 1949; d. Warren Roswell and Rosemary Tepper. PhD, U. Ariz., Tucson, Ariz., 1983; MEd, U. Utah, Salt Lake City, Utah, 1972; Filosfia Y Letras, U. Valencia, Valencia, Spain, 1971; BA, San Francisco Coll. for Women, San Francisco, Calif., 1971. Cert. principal, mathematics, spanish tchr. 1990. Adjunct asst. prof. U. Arizona, Tucson, 1983—86; dir., owner 1.2.1 Tutoring, Tucson, 1984—90; counselor Teton County Sch. Dist., Jackson, Wyo., 1990—94; lectr. Ariz. State U., Tempe, Ariz., 1995—98; tchr. Santa Fe Public Schools, Santa Fe, 1998—99; coun. Safe Sch. Healthy Students Grant, Ethete, Wyo., 1999—2001; mid. sch. coord. Fremont County Schools #14, Ethete, Wyo., 2001—. Bd. mem. Ariz. Women Mathematics Sci., Tempe, 1997—98. Recipient Nat. Outdoor Leadership Sch. (NOLS) scholarship, 2003. Mem.: Interagy. Coord. Coalition (v.p. 2000—01, pres. 2001—03), Teton County Task Force (bd. 1992—94). Office: Wyoming Indian Sch 638 Blue Sky Highway Ethete WY 82520 Personal E-mail: marcyet@mail.trib.com. Business E-Mail: marcyt@fremont14.k12.wy.us.

**TEPPER, R(OBERT) BRUCE, JR.,** lawyer; b. Long Branch, NJ, Apr. 1, 1949; s. Robert Bruce and Elaine (Ogus) T.; m. Belinda Wilkins, Nov. 26, 1971; children: Laura Katherine, Jacob Wilkins. AB in HIstory, Dartmouth Coll., Hanover, N.H., 1971; JD cum laude, St. Louis U., 1976, MA in Urban Affairs, 1976. Bar: Mo. 1976, Calif. 1977, Ill. 1978, U.S.Ct. Appeals (7th cir.) 1978, (8th cir.) 1976, (9th cir.) 1978, U.S. Dist. Ct. (ctrl., no., so. and east dists.) Calif. 1978, U.S. Supreme Ct. 1991. Asst. gen. counsel St. Louis

Redevel. Authority, 1976-77; assoc. Goldstein & Price, St. Louis, 1977-78, Loo, Merideth & McMillan, L.A., 1978-82; sole practice L.A., 1982-84; sr. prin., CFO Kane, Ballmer and Berkman, L.A., 1984—2001; with R. Bruce Tepper, ALC, 2002—. Litigation counsel to San Diego, Santa Barbara, Huntington Beach, Anaheim, Culver City, L.A., Lynwood, Norwalk, Redondo Beach, Oceanside, Ontario, Oxnard, Pasadena, Moreno Valley, Grover Beach, Glendale, Hawthorne,and Calif. City; spl. counsel Castaic Lake Water Agy., 1993—; Friant Water Authority, Hyundai, 2002-. San Diego State U, 2002; judge pro tempore Los Angeles County Mcpl. Ct., 1983—95; grader State Bar Calif., 1980-84; lectr. in land use and environ. issues Assoc. editor St. Louis U. Law Jour., 1974-76; mem. editl. bd. L.A. Lawyer; contbr. articles to legal jours. Mem. ABA, Los Angeles County Bar Assn. (com. on jud. evaluations), Assn. Bus. Trial Lawyers, So. Calif. Dartmouth Club (bd. dirs. 1989-), L.A. Athletic. Republican. Jewish. Home: 10966 Wrightwood Ln Studio City CA 91604-3957 Office: 1880 Century Pk E Ste 615 Los Angeles CA 90067-1622 Office Phone: 310-551-6590. Business E-Mail: tap@rbtlaw.com.

**TEPPER MADOVER, ARIELLE,** theater producer; d. Martin Tepper and Susan Levin. BFA, Syracuse U., 1996. Bd. govs. League Am. Theaters and Producers; founder Summer Play Festival, 2004; panelist Coll. Visual and Performing Arts Drama Dept. Prodr: (Broadway plays) Harlem Song, A Class Act (5 Tony award nominations), James Joyce's The Dead (Tony award), Freak (2 Tony award nominations), Sandra Bernhard's I'm Still Here...Damn It, A Raisin in The Sun (4 Tony nominations), Jumpers (4 Tony award nominations), Hollywood Arms (Tony award), Monty Python's SPAMALOT, The Pillowman, West End: Guys and Dolls, (off-Broadway plays) The Last Five Years (2 Drama Desk awards), De La Guarda Villa Villa, Goodnight Children Everywhere (Olivier award for best play, 2000), Transpotting; (films) 30 Days, 2000, (off-Broadway) Bounce, The Moonlight Room. Bd. trustees Syracuse U.; mem. adv. bd. Coll. Visual and Performing Arts; bd. trustees The Dalton Sch. Office: 1501 Broadway Ste 1301 New York NY 10036

**TERAUDS, JURIS,** retired science educator, research scientist; b. Jelgava, Latvia, Oct. 15, 1936; s. Janis Hermanis and Tatijana (Odins) Terauds; m. Shirley Jean Henry, Apr. 1, 1961 (div. Oct. 15, 1986); children: Jeffry Juris, Dana Kelly, Kimberly Kirsten. BS, Univ. Dubuque, Dubuque, IA, 1961; MS, Biomechanics, LA State Univ., Lost Angeles, CA, 1965; PhD (hon.), Univ. Md., College Park, MD, 1972. Instr. Univ. Md., College Park, Md., 1968—72; assoc. prof. Univ. Tex., Odessa, 1972—75; prof. Univ. Alta., Edmonton, Alberta, Canada, 1975—80; adj. prof. San Diego State Univ., San Diego, 1981—86; prof./dept. head Colo. State Univ., Fort Collins, 1986—90, prof. emeritus, 1991—. Pres. Internat. Soc. of Biomechanics Sports, San Diego, 1978—85, Rsch. Ctr. for Sports, San Diego and Fort Collins, Colo., 1978—; ceo X-Iser Industries, Fort Collins, Colo., 1991—. Author: 13 books on biomechanics, over 80 articles. Editor IAF Internat. Olympic Com., London, England, 1978—90, IAAF Internat. Olympic Cmte., London, England, 1978—90; rsch. dir. Olympics of Montreal, Montreal, Canada, 1976; chmn. SPIE Photooptical Instruments, 1982; chmn. photooptical instruments SPIE, 1982. Recipient Superior Contbn., Internat. Olympic Cmte., 1976, Profl. Achievement, Univ. Dubuque, IA, 1999; fellow, Internat. Soc. of Biomechanics in Sports, 1998. Fellow: Internat. Soc. of Biomechanics in Sports (dir. 1978—2002); mem.: Internat. High Speed Cinematography & Videography (chmn. 1982—88). Achievements include invention of Stepping Exercise Machine, 1977-2002. Avocations: reading, digital motion analysis, photography, videography. Home: 3319 Lone Jack Rd Encinitas CA 92024-7014 Office: X-Iser Industries RCS 1501 West Lake Fort Collins CO 80521

**TERBURG, BART PAUL,** physicist, industrial engineer; b. Leidschendam, Zuid-Holland, Netherlands, July 6, 1969; arrived in US, 1992; s. Anton Lambertus and Hendriena Maria Terburg. Degree in Engring., Delft U. Tech., The Netherlands, 1992; MS in Physics, U. Ill., 1993, PhD in Physics, 1999. Mgr. global regulations GE Consumer and Indsl. Automotive Lighting, Cleve., 1999—, lead systems engr., 1999—. Chmn. SAE Internat. Lighting Standards Com., Warrandale, Pa., 2004—; vice-chmn. working group Group de Travail Bruxelles, 2004—. Contbr. articles to profl. jours. Recipient Thesis prize, S.E. U. Rsch. Assn., 1999; grantee, Netherlands Fulbright Com., 1992; Felix T. Adler fellowship, The U. Ill. Physics Dept., 1999. Mem.: Royal Dutch Inst. Engrs., Soc. Automotive Engrs. (Young Engrs. award 2004). Achievements include patents pending for tungsten halogen lamp with optimized silicon hydride fill; automotive headlamps with improved beam chromaticity. Office: GE Consumer and Industrial - Lighting 1975 Noble Road MD 334D Cleveland OH 44143 Office Phone: 216-266-9070. Personal E-mail: terburg@n2net.net.

**TERESI, JOSEPH,** publishing executive; b. Mpls., Mar. 13, 1941; s. Cliff I.A. and Helen Ione (Leslie) (dec.); 1 child, Nicholas (dec.). CEO Jammer Cycle Products Inc., Burbank, Calif., 1968—80, Paisano Pubs. LLC, Agoura Hills, Calif., 1970—; chmn. bd., CEO V-Twin Expo, Agoura Hills, Calif., 1998—. Promoter motorcycle events; prodr. Easyriders Video mag.; owner Teresi Dyno Drags. Pub. (mags.) Easyriders, 1971—, In the Wind, 1974—, Biker, 1986—, Tattoo, 1986—, Am. Rodder, 1987-2001, Womens Enterprise, 1987-89, V-Twin News, 1989—, V-Twin, 1989, Tattoo Flash, 1993—, Tattoo Savage, 1993—, VQ, 1994—, Early-Riders, 1994-96, Quick Throttle, 1995-99, Roadware, 1995—, Tailgate, 2000, Tattoo Industry, 2000, Highbeams, 2003, Street Customs, 2004, Am. Choppers, 2004, Cable TV Prodr., 2004. Achievements include holding the world speed record for motorcycles set at 322 miles per hour, 1990. Office: Paisano Pubs LLC PO Box 3000 Agoura Hills CA 91376-3000

**TER HORST, JERALD FRANKLIN,** public affairs counselor; b. Grand Rapids, Mich., July 11, 1922; s. John Henry and Maude (Van Strien) ter H.; m. Louise Jeffers Roth, Jan. 20, 1945; children: Karen Dayens Morris, Margaret Fulton Robinson, Peter Roth, Martha Morgan Lubin. Student, Mich. State U., 1941-42; AB, U. Mich., 1947. Reporter Grand Rapids Press, 1946-51; mem. staff Detroit News, 1953-74, city and state polit. writer, 1953-57, Washington corr., 1958-60; chief Detroit News (Washington bur.), 1961-74; White House press sec. to Pres., 1974; columnist Detroit News/Universal Press Syndicate, 1974-81; dir. nat. pub. affairs Ford Motor Co., 1981-91; fgn. assignments include Berlin crisis, 1959; assignments in Vietnam, Israel, Germany, USSR, Latin Am. Writer N.Am. Newspaper Alliance, 1958-74 Author: Gerald Ford and Future of the Presidency, 1974, The Flying White House: The Story of Air Force One, 1979; contbr. to mags. and TV documentaries. Bd. dirs. Nat. Press Found., 1982-98, WETA-TV (Channel 26), 1988-99, Brady Campaign to Prevent Gun Violence, 1992-2002; chmn. Gridiron Club, 1978-2005, Grad. Sch. Polit. Mgmt., George Washington U., 1985-96. Officer USMCR, 1943-46, 51-52. Mem. Pub. Rels. Soc. Am., Soc. Profl. Journalists, Psi Upsilon. Presbyterian (elder). Clubs: Gridiron, Nat. Press. Overseas Writers. Office Phone: 703-765-8056. Personal E-mail: jterhorst@aol.com.

**TERKEL, STUDS (LOUIS TERKEL),** writer, journalist; b. NYC, May 16, 1912; s. Samuel and Anna (Finkel) T.; m. Ida Goldberg, July 2, 1939; 1 son, Dan. PhB, U. Chgo., 1932, JD, 1934. Disting. Scholar in Residence, Chgo. Hist. Soc., 1998—. Stage appearances include Detective Story, 1950, A View From the Bridge, 1958, Light Up the Sky, 1959, The Cave Dwellers, 1960; moderator: (TV program) Studs Place, 1950-53, (radio programs) Wax Museum, 1945— (Ohio State Univ. award 1959, UNESCO Prix Italia award 1962), Studs Terkel Almanac, 1952—, Studs Terkel Show, Sta. WFMT-FM, Chgo.; actor (films) Beginning to Date, 1953, Eight Men Out, 1988; (TV movies) The Dollmaker, 1984; master of ceremonies Newport Folk Festival, 1959, 60, Ravinia Music Festival, 1959, U. Chgo. Folk Festival, 1961, others; panel moderator, lectr., narrator films; Author: Giants of Jazz, 1957, Division Street: America, 1967, Hard Times: An Oral History of the Great Depression, 1970, Working: People Talk About What They Do All Day and How They Feel about What They Do, 1974 (Nat. Book award nomination 1975), Talking to Myself: A Memoir of My Times, 1977, American Dreams: Lost and Found, 1980, The Good War: An Oral History of World War II (Pulitzer prize for Non-fiction 1985), Chicago, 1986, The Great Divide: Second Thoughts On The American Dream, 1988, Race: How Blacks and Whites Think and Feel

About the American Obsession, 1992, Coming of Age, 1995, My American Century, 1997, Spectator, 1999, Will the Circle Be Unbroken, 2001, And They All Sang: Adventures of an Electric Disc Jockey, 2005; (play) Amazing Grace, 1959; also short stories. Named Communicator of Yr. U. Chgo. Alumni Assn., 1969; recipient Nat. Humanities Medal, 1997, Nat. Book Critics Circle Lifetime Achievement award, 2004, Dayton Lit. Peace prize, 2006. Office: Disting Scholar in Residence Chgo Hist Soc Clark St at North Ave Chicago IL 60614

**TERMAN, LEWIS MADISON,** retired electrical engineer, researcher, director; b. San Francisco, Aug. 26, 1935; s. Frederick Emmons and Sibyl (Walcott) T.; m. Barbara Chertok, Aug. 28, 1958. BS in Physics, Stanford U., 1956, MSEE, 1958, PhD, 1961. Mem. rsch. staff T.J. Watson Rsch. Ctr., IBM, Yorktown Heights, NJ, 1961-89, sr. mgr., 1989-91, sr. mem. tech. planning staff, 1991-93; mgr. VLSI processor design IBM Rsch. Ctr., Yorktown Heights, NY, 1993-94, rsch. staff T.J. Watson Rsch. Ctr., 1994—2001, assoc. dir. Sys. Dept., 2003—06, rschr. emeritus, 2006—; pres. IBM Acad. Tech., Yorktown Heights, 2001—03. Co-chmn. Symposium on Very Large Scale Integrated Technology, Systems and Application, Taiwan, 1989, 91, 93, 95, 97, 99, 01, 03, 05, tech. program co-chmn., 1985, 87; tech. program chmn. Internat. Solid State Cirs. Conf., N.Y.C., 1983; chmn. Symposium on Very Large-Scale Integrated Tech., Kobe, Japan, 1985, San Diego, 1986, Symposium on Very Large-Scale Integrated Cirs., Karuizawa, Japan, 1988, Kyoto, Japan, 1989, Symposium on Low Power Electronics, San Diego, 1994; mem. tech. coun. IBM Acad. Tech., 1995-98. Contbr. articles to profl. jours. Pres. Twin Lakes Water Works Corp., S. Salem, N.Y., 1980—. Recipient IEEE Solid-State Cirs. Tech. Field award, 1995. Fellow: IEEE (chmn. tech. mtgs. coun. 1993—94, tech. activites bd. treas. 1995—98, chair strategic planning and rev. com. 1999—2000, v.p. elect tech. activities bd. 2000, v.p. tech. activities bd. 2001, treas. publs., svcs. and products bd. 2003, divsn. one dir., mem. bd. dirs. 2004—05), AAAS; mem.: Nat. Acad. Engring., Circuits and Sys. Soc. of IEEE (adminstrv. com. 1981—83), IEEE Solid-State Circuits Soc. (editor jour. 1974—77, treas. 1988—89, v.p. 1996—97, pres. 1998—99), IEEE Electron Devices Soc. (v.p. 1988—89, pres. 1990—91, Disting. Svc. award 1995), IBM Acad. Tech. (co-chair tech. program com. 1996, chair components and processes com., tech. coun. 1996—98, pres. 2001—03, past pres. 2003—05). Achievements include patents in field. Avocations: music, theater, opera, hiking. Home: 61 Twin Lakes Rd South Salem NY 10590-1012 Office: IBM TJ Watson Rsch Ctr 1101 Kitchawan Rd PO Box 218 Yorktown Heights NY 10598

**TERMEER, HENRICUS ADRIANUS,** pharmaceutical executive; b. Tilburg, Holland, Feb. 28, 1946; came to U.S., 1971, naturalized, 1999; s. Jacques and Mary (Van Gorp) T. Student, Economisch Hogeschool (Erasmus U.), Rotterdam, The Netherlands, 1969; MBA, Darden Sch., U. Va., 1973. Mgr. mgmt. svcs. Norvic Co., Norwich, England, 1969-71; mgr. internat. product planning Baxter Travenol, Inc., Deerfield, Ill., 1973-74, internat. mktg. mgr., 1975-76; gen. mgr. Travenol GMBH, Munich, 1976-79; v.p. Hyland Therapeutics divsn. Baxter Travenol, Glendale, Calif., 1979-81, exec. v.p., 1981-83; pres. Genzyme Corp., Inc., Boston, 1983—, COO, 1983-85, CEO, 1985—, chmn., 1988—. Bd. dir. Abiomed, Inc., Biotech. Industry Orgn., Pharma. Rsch. and Manufactures Am., Mass. High Tech. Coun., Mass. Gen. Hosp.; trustee Hambrecht & Quist Lifescis. Fund, Hambrecht & Quist Health Care Investors Fund; bd. associates Whitehead Inst. for Biomedical Rsch.; mem. adv. bd. of the Dean of Harvard Med. Sch.; mem. MIT Corp. vis. com. dept. biology; chmn. New England Healthcare Inst., 2002-2006. Trustee Darden Bus. Adminstrn. Sch.; trustee Boston Mus. Sci., Harvard Med. Sch. Bd. Fellows, Biomedical Sci. Careers Project, 1994-, dir. 1995; bd. dir. Project Hope; Served to 1st lt. Netherlands Royal Air Force, 1966-67. Named Entrepreneur of Yr., Merrill Lynch and Ernst & Young, Inc., 1992, Renegade of Yr., Success Mag., 1995, Humanitarian of Yr., Cardinal Cushing Sch. for Exceptional Children, 1997; recipient Torch of Liberty award, Anti-Defamation League, New England Region, 1995, The Governor's New Am. Appreciation award, 1997, Golden Door award, Internat. Inst. Boston, 1999, Genetic Disease Found. Humanitarian award, 1999, Franklin Delano Roosevelt Humanitarian award, March of Dimes, 2003, Cor Vitae award, Am. Heart Assn., 2003. Fellow: Am. Acad. Arts & Sciences, Royal Coll. Physicians (hon.). Office: Genzyme Corp 500 Kendall St Cambridge MA 02142

**TERNAR, MINE Y.,** artist, art educator; b. Istanbul, Turkey, Apr. 18, 1961; d. Orhan Ternar and Gulbun Tok; 1 child, Dilara Ilayda Nur Ternar Kal. Student, State Acad. Fine Arts, Istanbul, 1979—80; BA in Liberal Arts, Bennington Coll., Vt., 1984; MA in Painting and Serigraphy, Mimar Sinan U., Istanbul, 1986; MFA in Art Practice, U. Calif., Berkeley, 1991. C.c. instr. credential fine and applied arts Bd. Govs. Calif. Cmty. Colls.; tchg. credential adult edn. art Commn. Tchr. Credentialing. Papermaking and painting asst. to artist Sophie Healy Trout Paper, Eagle Bridge, NY, 1980—81; copywriter, illustrator Radar Advt. Agy., Istanbul, 1985—86; curatorial asst., intern Phoebe A. Hearst Mus. Anthropology, U. Calif., Berkeley, 1989—91, intern Berkeley Art Mus., 1990—91; vol. coord. Pro Arts Gallery, Oakland, Calif., 1991—92; mem. adj. faculty Calif. Coll. Arts, Oakland, 1992—93, San Francisco Art Inst., 1992—93; asst. dir. Cartoon Art Mus., San Francisco, 1993—94; cmty. outreach coord. Dean Lesher Regional Ctr. Arts, Walnut Creek, Calif., 1994—97; mem. adj. faculty dept. visual arts Cabrillo Coll., Aptos, Calif., 1994—98; mem. faculty dept. art City Coll. San Francisco, 1996—. Vol. outreach coord. Gilles Peres photo installation New Langton Arts, San Francisco, 1994; freelance designer, computer graphics Golden Touch Design, Berkeley, 1996—2000; intranet webmaster Coherent Laser Co., Santa Clara, Calif., 1997—98; faculty advisor Diego Rivera website City Coll. San Francisco, 1997—98, gallery dir., curator City Arts Gallery, 1998—, mem. works of art sub-com., acad. senate, 2002—. Author co-prodr., collaborator (film/video) Conversations Across the Bosphorus, 1995; one-man shows include Osman Hamdi Hall, Mimar Sinan U., Istanbul, 1986, exhibitions include Lutfu Gunay Studio, Turkish-Am. Cultural Assn., Ankara, Turkey, 1978, Adnan Coker Studio, Istanbul State Gallery Fine Arts, 1985, Berkeley Art Mus., 1991, Worth Ryder Gallery, U. Calif., Berkeley, 1991, Walter/McBean Gallery, San Francisco Art Inst., 1992—93, KALA Artists Exhbn., 1997—98, Kala Artists' Ann., 1998—99, exhibited in group shows at Harcourts Modern and Contemporary Art Gallery, San Francisco, 1989, Berkeley Art Ctr., 1998, PRO ARTS Open Studios, 1996, Cabrillo College Gallery, 1997. Recipient Winning design, Health Through Art: Signs of Recovery, Alameda County Cmty. Project, 1996—2000; fellow, Calif. Student Aid Commn., 1990—91, KALA Art Inst., Berkeley, 1997; grantee, City Coll. San Francisco, 1997—98; scholar, Univ. per Stranieri, Perugia, Italy, 1979, Bennington Coll., 1980—84. Mem.: Coll. Art Assn. Am., Turkish-Am. Assn. Calif. (assoc.; bd. dirs., dir. arts and culture 1994—97), U. Calif. Alumni Assn. (life), YMCA. Avocations: reading, swimming, films, music, travel. Office: City Coll San Francisco Art Dept 50 Phelan Ave San Francisco CA 94112 Office Phone: 415-239-3157, 415-452-5354. Office Fax: 415-239-3131. Business E-Mail: mternar@ccsf.edu.

**TERNBERG, JESSIE LAMOIN,** pediatric surgeon, educator; b. Corning, Calif., May 28, 1924; d. Eric G. and Alta M. (Jones) T. AB, Grinnell Coll., Iowa, 1946, ScD (hon.), 1970; PhD, U. Tex., Austin, 1950; MD, Washington U., St. Louis, 1953; ScD (hon.), U. Mo., St. Louis, 1981. Diplomate: Am. Bd. Surgery. Intern Boston City Hosp., 1953—54; asst. resident in surgery Barnes Hosp., St. Louis, 1954-57, resident in surgery, 1958-59; rsch. fellow Washington U. Sch. Medicine, 1957-58; practice medicine specializing in pediatric surgery St. Louis, 1966—; instr., DGMS trainee in surgery Washington U., 1959-62, asst. prof. surgery, 1962-65, assoc. prof. surgery, prof., 1965-71, prof. surgery, 1971-96, chief divsn. pediatric surgery, 1972-90, prof. emeritus, 1996—; mem. staff Barnes Hosp., 1959—90; surgeon in chief Children's Hosp. of St. Louis, 1974-90. Mem. staff Children's Hosp., dir. pediatric surgery, 1972-90. Contbr. numerous articles on pediatric surgery to profl. jours. Trustee Grinnell Coll., 1984—. Recipient Alumni award Grinnell Coll., 1966, Faculty/Alumni award Washington U. Sch. Medicine, 1991, 2nd Century award 2006, 1st Aphrodite Jannopaulo Hofsommer award, 1993, Local Legend Changing the Face of Medicine award AMWA. Fellow AAAS; mem. SIOP, Am. Pediatric Surg. Assn., We. Surg. Assn. (2d v.p. 1984-85), St.

Louis Med. Soc., Soc. Surgery of the Alimentary Tract, Am. Acad. Pediatrics, Soc. Pelvic Surgeons (v.p. 1991-92), Brit. Assn. Paediatric Surgeons, Assn. Women Surgeons (charter mem. 1995), Mo. State Surg. Soc., St. Louis Surg. Soc. (pres. 1980-81), St. Louis Pediatric Soc., Soc. Surg. Oncology, Pediatric Oncology Group (chmn. surg. discipline 1983-96), St. Louis Childrens Hosp. Soc. (pres. 1979-80), Acad. Sci. St. Louis (Trustees award 2002), St. Louis Met. Med. Soc. (hon., councilor, trustee), Barnes Hosp. Soc., Phi Beta Kappa, Sigma Xi, Iota Sigma Pi, Alpha Omega Alpha. Office: St Louis Childrens Hosp 1 Childrens Pl Saint Louis MO 63110-1002 Business E-Mail: ternbergj@wudosis.wustl.edu.

**TERNUS, MARSHA K.,** state supreme court chief justice; b. Vinton, Iowa, May 30, 1951; married; 3 children. BA, U. Iowa, 1972; JD, Drake U., 1977. Bar: Iowa 1977, Ariz. 1984. With Bradshaw, Fowler, Proctor & Fairgrave, Des Moines, 1977—93; justice Iowa Supreme Ct., Des Moines, 1993—, chief justice, 2006—. Former mem. Iowa Jury Instructions Com.; former bd. mem. Polk County Legal Aid Soc.; pres. bd. of counselors Drake U. Law Sch.; former mem. Iowa Supreme Ct. Commn. on Planning for the 21st Century, MultiState Perf. Test Policy Com., Nat. Conf. of Bar Examiners. Editor-in-chief: Drake Law Rev., 1976—77. Mem.: Iowa State Bar Assn. (bd. governors), Polk County Bar Assn. (pres. 1984—85), Order of Coif, Phi Beta Kappa. Office: Iowa Supreme Ct Jud Branch Bldg 1111 E Ct Ave Des Moines IA 50319-0001*

**TERP, THOMAS THOMSEN,** lawyer; b. Fountain Hill, Pa., Aug. 12, 1947; s. Norman T. and Josephine (Uhran) T.; m. Pamela Robinson; children: Stephanie, Brian, Adam; step-children: Taylor Mefford, Grace Mefford. BA, Albion (Mich.) Coll., 1969; JD, Coll. of William and Mary, 1973. Bar: Ohio 1973, U.S. Dist. Ct. (so dist.) Ohio 1973, U.S. Ct. Appeals (6th cir.) 1973, U.S. Supreme Ct. 1979. Assoc. Taft, Stettinius & Hollister, Cin., 1973-80, ptnr., 1981—. Bd. dirs. Starflo Corp., Orangeburg, S.C., Attorneys' Liability Assurance Soc., Ltd., Hamilton, Bermuda, ALAS, Inc., Chgo. Editor-in-chief William & Mary Law Rev., 1972-73; mem. bd. editors Jour. of Environ. Hazards, 1988—, Environ. Law Jour. of Ohio, 1989—. Mem. Cin. Athletic Club, Camargo Club, Epworth Assembly (Ludington, Mich.), Lincoln Hills Golf Club (Ludington), Queen City Club. Avocations: tennis, golf, travel. Office Phone: 513-357-9354. Business E-Mail: terp@taftlaw.com.

**TERPELUK, PETER G., JR.,** former ambassador; b. Pa., Feb. 1948; Bachelors Degree, LaSalle Coll.; MPA, Rider Coll. Founder Terpeluk and Assocs., 1986—93; prin. Wojdak and Assocs., Washington, 1989—93; mng. dir. Am. Continental Group, 1994—2002; U.S. amb. to Luxembourg US Dept. State, Washington, 2002—05. Active U.S. SBA, 1981—84; bd. dirs. Pa. Ave. Devel. Commn.; town mgr. Pa., 1972.

**TERPENING, VIRGINIA ANN,** artist; b. Lewistown, Mo., July 17, 1917; d. Floyd Raymond and Bertha Edda (Rodifer) Shoup; m. Charles W. Terpening, July 5, 1951; 1 child by previous marriage, V'Ann Baltzelle Deatrick. Student, William Woods Coll., Fulton, Mo., 1936-37, Washington U. Sch. Fine Arts, 1937-40. Lectr. on art; jurist for selection of art for exhibits Labelle (Mo.) Centennial, 1972; chmn. Centennial Art Show, Lewistown, 1971, Bicentennial, 1976; dir. exhibit high sch. student for N.E. Mo. State U., 1974; supt. ann. art show Lewis County (Mo.) Fair, 1975-90. One-woman shows include Culver-Stockton Coll., Canton, Mo., 1956, Creative Gallery, N.Y.C., 1968, The Breakers, Palm Beach, Fla., 1976, others; group shows include Mo. Ann. Show, City Art Mus., St. Louis, 1956, 65, Madison Gallery, N.Y.C., 1960, Ligoa Duncan Gallery, N.Y.C., 1964, 78, Two Flags Festival of Art, Douglas, Ariz., 1975, 78-79, Internat. Art Exhibit, El Centro, Calif., 1977, 78, Salon des Nations, Paris, 1985, UN World Conf. of Women, Narobi, Kenya, 1985, William Woods Coll., Fulton, Mo., 1992-95, La Junta Coll. Art League Internat., 1992, 94, Coffret Musée, Paris, 1995; represented in permanent collection Nat. Mus. of Women in Art, 1990; executed Mississippi RiverBoat oil painting presented to Pres. Carter by Lewis County Dem. Com., Canton, 1979. Mem. Lewistown Bicentennial Hist. Soc.; charter mem. Canton Area Arts Coun. of N.E. Mo. Recipient Cert. of Merit Latham Found., 1960-63, Mo. Women's Festival of Art, 1974, Bertrand Russell Peace Found., 1973, Gold Medallion award Two flags Festival of Art, 1975, Safeco purchase award El Centro (Calif.) Internat. Art Exhibit, 1977, 1st Pl. award LaJunta (Colo.) Fine Arts League, 1981, diploma Univ. Delle Arti, Parma, Italy, 1981, Purchase award Two Flags Art Festival, 1981, award Assn. Conservation and Mo. Dept. Conservation Art Exhibit, 1982, Purchase award Canton Area Arts Coun., 1988, Colorado Springs Art Festival, 1989; paintings selected for Competition '84 Guide by Nat. Art Appreciation Soc., 1984, 1st Pl. award New Orleans Internat. Art Exhibit, 1984, Two Flags Festival of Art, 1986, Sunflower Judges award Harlin Mus. West Plains, Mo., 1994, Key to City, Lifetime award, 1998; named artist laureate, Nepenthe Mondi Soc., 1984. Mem. Artist Equity Assn., Internat. Soc. Artists, Internat. Platform Assn., Nat. Mus. Women in Art (charter), Animal Protection Inst. Mem. Christian Ch. (Disciples Of Christ). Address: 105 S Vine St PO Box 117 Lewistown MO 63452-0117

**TERR, LENORE CAGEN,** psychiatrist, writer; b. NYC, Mar. 27, 1936; d. Samuel Lawrence and Esther (Hirsch) Cagen; m. Abba I. Terr; children: David; Julia. AB magna cum laude, Case Western Res. U., 1957; MD with honors, U. Mich., 1961. Diplomate Am. Bd. Psychiatry and Neurology (subspecialty bd. child and adolescent psychiatry). Intern U. Mich. Med. Ctr., Ann Arbor, 1961-62; resident Neuropsychiat. Inst. U. Mich., Ann Arbor, 1962-64, fellow Children's Psychiat. Hosp., 1964-66; from instr. to asst. prof. Case Western Res. U. Med. Sch., Cleve., 1966-71; pvt. practice Terr Med. Corp., San Francisco, 1971—; from asst. clin. prof. to clin. prof. psychiatry Sch. Medicine U. Calif., San Francisco, 1971—. Lectr. law, psychiatry U. Calif., Berkeley, 1971—90, Davis, 1974—88; dir. Am. Bd. Psychiatry and Neurology, 1988—96, chair psychiatry coun., 1996. Author: Too Scared to Cry, 1990, Unchained Memories, 1994, Beyond Love and Work, 1999; contbr. articles to profl. jours.; exhibited works in art show at Canessa Gallery, San Francisco 2002. Named to Cleveland Heights H.S. Disting Alumni Hall of Fame, 2003; recipient Career Tchr. award, NIMH, 1967—69, Child Advocacy award, APA, 1994; grantee project, Rosenberg Found., 1977, William T. Grant Found., 1986—87, Leon Lowenstein Found., 2002; scholar-in-residence, Rockefeller Found., Italy, 1981, 1988. Fellow: Am. Acad. Child and Adolescent Psychiatry (coun. 1984—87), Am. Coll. Psychiatrists (program chair 1991—92, Bowis award 1993), Am. Psychiat. Assn. (Child Psychiatry Rsch. award 1984, Clin. Rsch. award 1987, Marmor Sci. award 2002); mem.: Phi Bet Kappa, Alpha Omega Alpha. Avocations: piano, walking, travel, gardening, needlepoint. Office Phone: 415-433-7800.

**TERRACCIANO, ANTONIO,** psychologist, researcher; b. Napoli, Italy, Apr. 21, 1974; s. Giuseppe Terracciano and Giuseppina Varriale. PhD, Seconda Universita' di Napoli, 1999. Vis. rsch. fellow NIH, Balt., 1999—2006, staff scientist, 2006—. Cons. editor, ad hoc reviewer several jours. Contbr. articles to profl. jours. Mem.: APA (local circuit program com. 2005), Assn. Psychol. Sci. Radical Party. Achievements include research in stereotypes of national character are inaccurate; personality traits development; personality traits associated with smoking status; cross-cultural differences in personality traits; sequencing human genome, candidate genes, and linkage analysis for complex traits; sex differences across cultures on personality traits and emotions. Office Phone: 410-558-8358. Business E-Mail: terraccianoa@grc.nia.nih.gov.

**TERRACINA, ROY DAVID,** entrepreneur; b. Chgo., Aug. 24, 1946; s. Angelo R. and Josephine T.; divorced; children: Joseph, Vincent, Angela Peter, Paul. BS in Fin., Marquette U., 1968, MBA, 1972. Officer First Wis. Nat. Bank, Milw., 1968-71; account exec. Robert W. Baird Co., Milw., 1971-74; v.p. mktg. Midwest Retail Group, Milw., 1974-76; mgmt. cons. Anderson-Roethke, Milw., 1976-77; v.p., treas. Farm House Foods Corp., Milw., 1977-84; pres. Sterling Foods, Inc., San Antonio, 1984-93, pvt. investor, 1994—. Instr. personal fin. Marquette U.; instr. fin. Trinity U.; bd. dir. US Global Investors, JP Morgan Chase, San Antonio. Roman Catholic. Office: 7900 Callaghan Rd San Antonio TX 78229-2327

**TERRAGNO, PAUL JAMES,** information industry executive; b. Ogden, Utah, May 17, 1938; s. Charles L. and Florence E. (Gabardi) T.; m. Nancy Robinson, Aug. 26, 1961; children— Thomas C., Paul A., Teresa A. BA, U. Utah, 1960; MS, U. Wyo., 1962. Vice pres. Westat, Inc., Rockville, Md., 1962-70; vice pres. Remac Information, Gaithersburg, Md., 1970-76; dir. U.S. Patent Office, Washington, 1976-80; v.p. Pergamon Internat., McLean, Va., 1980-84; pres. Pergamon InfoLine, McLean, Va., 1984-87, Pergamon ORBIT InfoLine, McLean, 1987-89, Maxwell Online, Inc., 1989-92. Pres. Pergamon Orbit InfoLine, Ltd., London, 1984-89, Pergabase, Inc., Gainesville, Fla., 1985-92, pres. Topate Info. Svcs. Inc., 1992-97; dir. Eagle Design and Mgmt., Inc., Bethesda, Md. Contbr. articles to various publs. Mem. Am. Soc. Info. Sci. Roman Catholic. Office: 7830 Old Georgetown Rd Bethesda MD 20814-2432 Home: 1002 Elmcroft Blvd Apt 401 Rockville MD 20850-6657 E-mail: terragno@comcast.net.

**TERRAS, VICTOR,** literature and language professor; b. Poltsamaa, Estonia, Jan. 21, 1921; arrived in US, 1952, naturalized, 1956; s. Evald and Elena (Rosenberger) T.; m. Rita Schubert, 1951; 1 child, Alexander. MPhil, U. Tartu, Estonia, 1942; PhD, U. Chgo., 1963. Lectr. U. Tartu, 1943-44; instr. to assoc. prof. U. Ill., Urbana, 1959-64; prof. Slavic langs., 1965-66; prof. U. Wis., Madison, 1966-70; prof. Slavic langs. and comparative lit. Brown U., Providence, 1970-88, prof. emeritus, 1988—. Author: The Young Dostoevsky: A Critical Study, 1969, Belinskij and Russian Literary Criticism, 1974, A Karamazov Companion, 1981, 2d edit. 2002, Vladimir Mayakovsky, 1983; editor: Handbook of Russian Literature, 1984, The Idiot: An Interpretation, 1990, A History of Russian Literature, 1991, Russian Poetry of the Silver Age, 1998, Reading Dostoevsky, 1998. Mem. Am. Assn. Advancement Slavic and East European Studies, Am. Assn. Tchrs. Slavic and East European Langs. (pres. 1981-82), Internat. Dostoevsky Soc. (v.p. 1983—). Office: Brown U Box E Providence RI 02912

**TERRASSA, JACQUELINE,** museum director; MFA, U. Chgo., 1994. Staff mem. Columbia Coll., Chgo.; edn. dir. Hyde Park Art Ctr., David and Alfred Smart Mus. Art, U. Chgo., 1998—, interim dir., 2004—05, established SmART Explorers sch. program, dep. dir. collections, programs, & interpretation, 2005—. Office: Smart Mus Art U Chgo 5550 S Greenwood Ave Chicago IL 60637*

**TERREL, JAMES E.,** controller; b. Elyria, Ohio, June 28, 1949; BS in Acctg., Miami U., 1971, MBA in Fin. & Acctg., 1972. CPA 1972. Sr. acct. Ernst & Whinney, 1972—76; fin. acct. Internat. Harvester Co., 1976—77, sr. ops. analyst, 1977—78; mgr. fin. components group, 1978—81, mgr. spl. fin. projects, 1981, mgr. mfg. analysis, 1981—83; dir. external reporting Ga. Pacific, Atlanta, 1983—84, controller fin. reporting, 1984—87, group controller, 1987—89, v.p., controller, 1989—91, 1991—. Mem.: AICPA, Inst. Mgmt. Accts., Ga. Soc. CPA's, Fin. Execs. Internat. (mem. nat. com. corp. reporting). Office: GA Pacific 133 Peachtree St NE Atlanta GA 30303

**TERRELL, G. IRVIN,** lawyer; b. Houston, Sept. 28, 1946; s. George I. and Adella (Weichert) T.; m. Karen Steenberg, Jan. 8, 1984; 1 child, Katharine. BA, U. Tex., 1968, JD, 1972. Bar: Tex., US Supreme Ct., US Ct. Appeals (3d and 5th cirs.), US Dist. Ct. (so., no. and ea. dists.) Tex., US Dist. Ct. (we. dist.) Pa, US Dist. Ct. (so. dist.) NY. Assoc. Baker & Botts LLP, Houston, 1972-79, ptnr., 1980—. Mem. ABA, Houston Bar Assn., Internat. Soc. Barristers. Office Phone: 713-229-1231. Business E-Mail: irv.terrell@bakerbotts.com.

**TERRELL, HELLENNA L.,** education educator; d. Ernestine Robinson and Herman L. Terrell. BS, Spelman Coll., Atlanta, 1986; MS, Jacksonville State U., Ala., 1995; EdD, U. Ala., Tuscaloosa, 1999. Dir. alumni affairs/pub. rels. Mary Holmes Coll., West Point, Miss., 1986—88; project dir. U.S. Dept. of Agr., Washington, 1988—91; asst. to exec. v.p. Talladega (Ala.) Coll., 1991—93; dean student life Tex. Coll., Tyler, 1993—95; dean multicultural initiatives U. Tenn., Chattanooga, 1997—2004; v.p. for student affairs St. Augustine's Coll., Raleigh, NC, 2004—. Mem. Raleigh Rotary Club, 2006, Chattanooga Area Food Bank, 1997—2004, Chattanooga Theater Ctr., 1997—2004. Mem.: So. Assn. for Coll. Student Affairs, Nat. Assn. of Student Pers. Administrs., Am. Assn. Univ. Pers., Am. Assn. Univ. Women. Office Phone: 919-516-4117. Personal E-mail: hlterrell@bellsouth.net. Business E-Mail: hlterrell@st-aug.edu.

**TERRELL, J. ANTHONY,** lawyer; b. NYC, Sept. 20, 1943; s. Claude M. and Kathleen L. (Prevost) Terrell; m. Karen E. Terrell; 1 child, Elizabeth S. BA, NYU, 1965, LLM in Taxation, 1975; JD, Villanova U., 1968. Bar: NY. With Frueauff, Farrell, Sullivan & Bryan, NYC, 1970—74, ptnr., 1977; assoc. Thelen Reid & Priest LLP, NYC, 1974—76, ptnr., 1977; now ptnr. Dewey Ballantine LLP, NYC. Named one of Am.'s Leading Lawyers for Bus., Chambers USA, 2005, Best Lawyers in Am., 2006. Mem.: ABA, Nat. Assn. Bond Lawyers, Internat. Bar Assn., Coral Beach and Tennis Club, Met. Club, Belle Haven Club. Office: Dewey Ballantine LLP 1301 Avenue of the Americas New York NY 10019-6092 Office Phone: 212-259-7070. Office Fax: 212-259-6333. E-mail: jterrell@deweyballantine.com.*

**TERRELL, JAMES (NELSON JAMES TERRELL),** physicist; b. Houston, Aug. 15, 1923; s. Nelson James Sr. and Gladys Delphine (Stevens) T.; m. Elizabeth Anne Pearson, June 9, 1945; children— Anne (dec.), Barbara, Jean BA, Rice U., 1944, MA, 1947, PhD, 1950. Rsch. asst. Rice U., Houston, 1950; asst. prof. physics We. Res. U., Cleve., 1950—51; mem. staff Los Alamos Nat. Lab., U. Calif., 1951—89, assoc., 1989—94; affiliate, 1994—2005; ret., 2005. Producer (computer generated movie) The X-Ray Sky, 1969-76; contbr. articles to profl. jours. and encys. Served to 1st lt. AUS, 1944-46 Graham Baker scholar Rice U., 1943-44; fellow Rice U., 1946-48, AEC, 1948-50 Fellow Am. Phys. Soc., AAAS; mem. Am. Astron. Soc., Internat. Astron. Union, Phi Beta Kappa, Sigma Xi Achievements include research in relativity, quasars, x-ray and gamma ray astronomy, nuclear physics, lasers. Home: 85 Obsidian Loop Los Alamos NM 87544-2528

**TERRELL, WILLIAM GLENN,** university president emeritus; b. Tallahassee, May 24, 1920; s. William Glenn and Esther (Collins) T.; m. Gail Strandberg Terrell; children by previous marriage: Francine Elizabeth, William Glenn III. BA, Davidson Coll., 1942, LLD (hon.), 1969; MS, Fla. State U., 1948; PhD, State U. Iowa, 1952; LLD (hon.), Gonzaga U., 1984, Seattle U., 1985. Instr., then asst. prof. Fla. State U., Tallahassee, 1948-55; asst. prof., then assoc. prof., chmn. dept. psychology U. Colo., Boulder, 1955—63, asst. dean Coll. Arts and Scis., 1963-65; prof. psychology, dean Coll. Liberal Arts and Scis., U. Ill. at Chgo., 1963-65, dean faculties, 1965-67; pres. Wash. State U., Pullman, 1967-85, pres. emeritus, 1985—. Pres. Nat. Assn. State Univs. and Land-Grant Colls., 1977-78; cons. The Pacific Inst., Seattle, 1987—. Author The Ministry of Leadership, 2002; Contbr. articles to profl. jours. Served to capt. inf. U.S. Army, 1942-46, ETO. Recipient Disting. Alumnus award U. Iowa, 1985; Disting. Grad. Dept. Psychology, U. Iowa, 1996. Fellow APA, AAAS; mem. Soc. Rsch. in Child Devel., Sigma Xi, Phi Kappa Phi. Avocations: golf, reading, travel. Home: 2438 36th Ave W Seattle WA 98199-3704 Office: The Pacific Inst 1709 Harbor Ave SW Seattle WA 98126-2073 Office Phone: 206-628-4800. Personal E-mail: glennterrell@aol.com. Business E-Mail: gterrell@pac-inst.com.

**TERRILL, ROSS GLADWIN,** writer, educator; b. Melbourne, Australia; arrived in U.S., 1965, naturalized, 1979; s. Frank and Miriel (Lloyd) Terrill. BA with honors, U. Melbourne; PhD, Harvard U., 1970. Tutor in polit. sci. U. Melbourne, 1962-63; staff sec. Australian Student Christian Movement, 1964-65; tchg. fellow Harvard U., 1968-70, lectr. govt., 1970-73, assoc. prof., 1974-78, rsch. assoc. E. Asian studies, 1970—, dir. student programs Ctr. Internat. Affairs, 1974-78; contbg. editor Atlantic Monthly, 1970-84; rsch. fellow Asia Soc., 1977—79. Vis. prof. U. Tex., Austin, 1999—. Author: China Profile, 1969, China and Ourselves, 1971, 800,000,000: The Real China, 1972, R. H. Tawney and His Times, 1973, Flowers on an Iron Tree, 1975, The Future of China, 1978, The China Difference, 1979, Mao: A Biography, 1980, rev., 2000, White-Boned Demon, 1984, The Australians, 1987, Madam Mao, 1992, rev., 1999, China in Our Time, 1992, The Australians: How We Live

Now, 2000, The New Chinese Empire, 2003; contbr. articles to Foreign Affairs, National Geographic, New Republic, Weekly Standard, New York Review of Books, others. Recipient Sumner prize, 1970, Nat. Mag. award, 1972, George Polk Meml. award outstanding mag. reporting, 1972, Book prize, L.A. Times, 2003. Mem.: PEN, Authors Guild, Harvard Club (N.Y.C.). Home: PO Box 230772 Astor Station Boston MA 02123-0772 Office Phone: 617-445-2542. E-mail: RT5789@cs.com.

**TERRIS, ALBERT,** metal sculptor; b. N.Y.C., Nov. 10, 1916; s. Aaron and Fania Teraspulsky; children: Susan, Abby, David, Enoch. BSS, CCNY, 1939; postgrad., NYU Inst. Fine Arts, 1939-42. Lectr. Met. Mus. Art, 1941-42; tchr. fine arts N.Y.C. High Sch. System, 1947-54; prof. emeritus Bklyn. Coll., 1947-86. Steel sculptures include Non-Fixed Relationship, 1948, Homely Cosmology, 1948, Anti-Gravity, 1950, Giraffes, 1953, Short Art, 1953, Pro-Gravity Chains, 1956, Tools, 1956, Crushed Sculpture, 1956, Words, 1957, Discursive-Illegible-Boustrophedon, 1975, Plates of Charlemagne, 1975, Fireharps, 1975, Cycle of Life, 1977, Wipes, 1996, Quantum Photography, 1995, Meals, 1998, Visitors, 1998, Twigs Door Music, 2001; one-man shows: Saidenberg, 1955, Duveen-Graham, 1958, Carnegie Internats., 1958, 62, Bklyn. L.I Artists Bklyn. Mus. (awarded first prize), 1960, Allan Stone, 1962, Critics Choice, 1972, Artists Space, 1975, Gloria Cortella, 1977, (retrospective) The Artist in the Civil Service Bklyn. Coll. Gallery, 1985, Queensborough C. C., 2005; exhibited in group shows at Tanager Gallery, 1952-61, Stable Anns., 1952-60, Mus. Modern Art, N.Y.C., 1962, others; represented in permanent collections: Stephen Paine, Boston, Arnold Maremont, Evanston, G. David Thompson Estate, NBC-TV, others Served with 1st Allied Airborne, 1942-45. Home: 25 Coleman Place Red Bank NJ 07701

**TERRIS, LILLIAN DICK,** psychologist, health facility administrator; b. Blooomfield, N.J., May 5, 1914; d. Alexander Blaikie and Herminia (Doscher) Dick; m. Louis Long, Apr. 22, 1935 (dec. Sept. 1968); 1 son, Alexander Blaikie Long; m. Milton Terris, Feb. 6, 1971 (dec. Oct. 2002). BA, Barnard Coll., 1935; PhD, Columbia U., 1941. Diplomate Am. Bd. Examiners in Profl. Psychology. Instr. psychology Sarah Lawrence Coll., Bronxville, NY, 1937-40; jr. pers. tech. SSA, Washington, 1941; sr. pers. clk. OWI, N.Y.C., 1941-43; dir. profl. examination svc. Am. Pub. Health assn., N.Y.C., 1943-70; pres., 1970-79; pres. emeritus, 1979—. Assoc. editor Jour. Pub. Health Policy, 1979—; contbr. articles to profl. jours. Recipient Nat. Environ. Health assn. award, 1976, Cert. Svc. award Bd. Preventive Medicine, 1979. Fellow Am. Psychol. Assn., Am. Coll. Hosp. Adminstrs. (hon.); mem. Am. Pub. Health Assn., N.Y. State Psychol. Assn., Phi Beta Kappa, Sigma Xi. Home: 1450 Post St 506 San Francisco CA 94109 Office: 475 Riverside Dr New York NY 10115-0122 E-mail: jphpterris@aol.com.

**TERRIS, SUSAN,** physician, cardiologist, researcher; b. Morristown, N.J., Sept. 5, 1944; d. Albert and Virginia Terris. BA in History, U. Chgo., 1967, PhD in Biochemistry, 1975, MD, 1976. Diplomate in internal medicine, endocrinology and metabolism, cardiovasc. disease Am. Bd. Internal Medicine. Resident in internal medicine Washington U., Barnes Hosp., St. Louis, 1976-78; fellow in endocrinology and metabolism U. Chgo., 1978-80, fellow cardiology, 1980-83, U. Mich., Ann Arbor, 1983-85, instr. cardiology, 1985-86; head cardiac catheterization lab., head cardiology Westland (Mich.) Med. Ctr., 1985. Contbr. articles to Jour. Biol. Chemistry, Am. Jour. Physiology, Am. Jour. Cardiology, Jour. Clin. Investigation, other profl. publs. Grantee Juvenile Diabetes Found., 1978-80, NIH, 1978-79. Mem. AAAS, Am. Heart Assn., N.Y. Acad. Sci. Achievements include rsch. demonstrating dependence of intracellular degradation of insulin upon its prior adsorptive pinocytotic uptake by liver; studies on the electrophysiologie effect of cathecholamines on sheep Parkinje fibers and on the hemodynamic effects of various drugs on the human circulatory system.

**TERRITO, MARY C.,** health facility administrator, hematologist, educator; BS in Biology, Wayne State U., 1965, MD, 1968. Intern/resident in internal medicine Parkland Hosp., Dallas, 1971-73; fellow in hematology/oncology Harbor-U. Calif., L.A., 1973-74, UCLA, 1974-75; rsch. assoc. Wadsworth VA Hosp., L.A., 1975-81; asst. prof. dept. medicine UCLA, 1975-81, assoc. prof., 1981-96, prof., 1996—; dir. bone marrow transplant program Ctr. Health Scis., 1981—. Contbr. articles to profl. jours. Office: UCLA Bone Marrow Transplantation Program Ctr 42-121 CHS 10833 Le Conte Ave Los Angeles CA 90095-3075

**TERRY, ANNE CURTIS,** lawyer, writer; d. Charles and Florine Curtis; m. Edward H. Terry; children: Edward, Ellyn. BA, Fla. State U., 1970; MA, U. Tex., 1972; JD, U. Fla., 1978. Bar: Fla. 1979. Tchg. asst./lectr. dept. geography U. Tex., Austin, 1972—74; appellate law clk. 1st Dist. Ct. of Appeals, Tallahassee, 1978—79; asst. atty. gen. Office of Fla. Atty. Gen., Tallahassee, 1980—86; staff counsel Fla. Legislature, Tallahassee, 1986—89; solo practitioner/firm owner Law Office of Anne Curtis Terry, Tallahassee, 1993—. Author: (non-fiction, hist. biography) The Spirit in the South, 2006, (over 100 opinions) Annual Report of the Attorney General of Florida. NDEA Title VI fellowship, Inst. of Latin Am. Studies, U. Tex., 1971-1972. Mem.: Phi Kappa Phi. Independent. Methodist. Achievements include represented Southern Christian Leadership Conference in First Amendment litigation; represented numerous plaintiffs in employment discrimination cases, based on disability, race and gender. Avocations: travel, photography, poetry, cooking, gardening. Office: Law Office of Anne Curtis Terry 6209 Verdura Way Tallahassee FL 32311 Office Phone: 850-878-2168.

**TERRY, CAROLE COSGROVE,** small business owner, historian, researcher; b. San Francisco, Jan. 5, 1938; d. John Charles and Emile Dohrmann Cosgrove; m. Norman Berkley Terry, Feb. 14, 1970; children: Emilie Terry Melnadler, Brenda Jane. BA, Stanford U., Calif., 1959, MA, U. Nevada, Las Vegas, 2000, PhD candidate, 2001—. Cert. Merit Katharine Gibbs Sch., N.Y., 1960. Sec. asst. Hon. Herbert Hoover, NYC, 1959—60; exec. sec. E.F. Hutton & Co. Inc., LA, 1960—71; interim alumnae dir. Marlborough Sch., LA, 1991—92; owner, v.p., CFO Galleria Travel, Inc., Glendale, 1976—93. Co-author (with Emilie D. Cosgrove): California Potpourri 1852-1936, 1966; co-author: (pamphlet) The History of Chinatown, 1971; contbr. articles to profl. jour., scientific papers. Treas. bd. mem. San City Quilters, 2002—05; stewardship team chair St. Andrew Luth. Ch., 2004—05, stewardship, counting chair, 1996—99; treas. bd. mem. Jr. League Las Vegas Sustainers, 2001—05; sec. bd. mem. Jr. League Las Vegas Endowment Bd., 2002—; bd. mem., treas. Costume Coun., L.A. County Mus. Art, 1992—95. E-mail: terrynandc@cox.net.

**TERRY, CLIFFORD LEWIS,** journalist; b. Highland Park, Ill., Jan. 19, 1937; s. Clifford Lewis and Isabelle (Marlow) T.; m. Patricia West Dickelman, Sept. 1, 1966; children: Christopher West, Scott Marlow. Student, Carleton Coll., Northfield, Minn., 1954-55; BA, Trinity Coll., Hartford, Conn., 1958; postgrad., Columbia U., 1962-63. Tchr., English and history Mt. Hermon (Mass.) Sch., 1958-59; police reporter City News Bur. Chgo., 1959-60; mem. staff Chgo. Tribune, 1960-94, movie critic, 1965-70; assoc. editor Chgo. Tribune (Sunday mag.), 1970-82, feature writer, 1982-85, TV critic, 1985-89, arts feature writer, 1989-94; ind. writer, 1994—. Author: Chicago: Off the Beaten Path, 2000. Served with AUS, 1960. Nieman fellow Harvard U., 1969-70 Mem. Phi Beta Kappa.

**TERRY, EDWIN WELLINGTON,** college librarian; b. Bklyn., Dec. 4, 1918; s. Edwin Wellington Roberts Terry and Ursaline Whittle McClane; m. Natalie Johnston (dec.); children: Brian Paul, Francesca Natalie. BA, Bklyn. Coll., 1941, MA, 1968; BSc with honors, Columbia U., 1946; MA, Columbia Tchrs. Coll., 1948; PhD, St. John's U., 1971. Cert. pub. libr. SUNY Dept. Edn., 1967. Cataloger Columbia U. Libr., NYC, 1946—47; acquisition asst. Queens Coll., Flushing, NY, 1948—59; dir. Dillard U. Libr., New Orleans, 1947—48, Nassau CC Libr., Garden City, 1960—67, Bronx CC Libr., 1967—78, staff mem., 1978—88; adj. libr. Bronx CC, 1988—93, Manhattan CC, NYC, 1993—2000. Chair two yr. coll. chief libres. SUNY, 1965; mem. ad hoc com. Nassau County Ctrl. Libr., 1965—66; pres. Nassau County Lib. Assn., 1965—66; chair profl. status com. Libr. Assn. of CUNY, 1978—80,

chair publ. com., 1980—88; mem. adv. com. minority fellowship Queens Coll. Libr. Sch., 1966—90; mem. Middle States Assn. Colls. and Acad. Schs. Editor: Urban Academic Librarian, 1983—88; contbr. articles to profl. jours.; co-author: Cure Collection in Nursing and Allied Heath Sciences, 1990. Mem. Friends of U. Calif. San Diego Libr., 2004. Staff sgt. U.S. Army, 1943. Recipient Cert. of Svc., Bronx CC Student Coun., 1968, Cert. of Merit, Bronx CC, 1988. Mem.: Archons of Colophon, Beta Phi Mu. Democrat.

**TERRY, ELIZABETH HAYS,** artist, small business owner; b. Bryn Mawr, Pa., July 29, 1935; d. James Franklin and Mary Ellen (Carmichael) Hays; m. Charles L. Terry, III, Feb. 8, 1958; children: Elizabeth Harllee Carmichael Terry Moran, Charles L. IV. AB, Smith Coll., 1957. Asst. to profs. Harvard U., Cambridge, Mass., 1957-58; art tchr. Exeter (N.H.) Day Sch., 1968-72; asst. editor Phillips Exeter Acad. Alumni Quarterly, 1972-75, dir. alumni records, 1975-85; owner Elizabeth Terry, Calligraphy, Illumination and Needlepoint Design, Exeter, NH, 1980—. Tchr. needlepoint Guild of Strawbery Banke, Portsmouth, N.H. Dir. for Town of Exeter-Save Our Shores, 1972. Mem. Smith Coll. Class of 1957 (class fund agt. 1972-77, alumnae fund com. 1977-80, class bequest chair 1982—, com. on deferred giving 1990—), N.H. Colonial Dames (pres. 1989-92, nat. historian 1992-94, nat. v.p. 1994-2000). Episcopalian. Avocations: tennis, needlepoint, historic preservation. Home and Office: 77 Brookside Dr Stratham NH 03885-2128 Office Phone: 603-772-8942. E-mail: ceterry@verizon.net.

**TERRY, ELIZABETH HUDSON,** personal care industry executive, realtor; d. Otis Hudson and (Russell) Evelena; m. Lester Terry; 1 child, Darric. Student, Clark Coll., Atlanta, 1966; BA business, Atlanta Sch. Bus., 1968; student, Dekalb Perimeter Coll., Decatur, Ga., 1978—83; cert. enterpreneurship program, U. Ga., 1993; cert., Speak Easy Sch., Atlanta, 1993. Lic. real estate salesperson Ga., 1996. Asst. dir. Count Jackson Studio, Atlanta, 1968—72; mgr. BellSouth Corp., Atlanta, 1970—97, Bank of Am., Atlanta, 1999—; wedding dir., cons. Weddings by Liz, Decatur, Ga., 1980—; realtor, sales assoc. Coldwell Banker Buckhead Brokers, Tucker, 1996—2000, Quest Realty Inc., Decatur, 2000—. Notary, Decatur; featured in numerous newspapers and mags.; guest appearances on several t.v. and radio shows. Author: Just Think About It, 1993. Mem. Veracruz Homeowners Assn., Decatur, 2001—, Nat. Coalition of 100 Black Women's Assn., NAACP, United Negro Coll. Fund; pub. rels. advisor Uptown Social Club, Atlanta; vol. Habitat for Humanity, Atlanta; asst. dir. The Colored People Prodn., Atlanta; program dir. Azusa St. Revival Prodn., 1995; asst. dir., program dir. Fix Me Jesus Prodn., Atlanta; mem. Jr. Achievement Mentoring Program, 1990—96; founding mem. Nat. Campaign Tolerance, 2005; mem. Beulah Bapt. Ch., Decatur; adv. bd., bd. dirs. Suncrest Resources, Inc., Stone Mountain, Ga., 1986. Recipient Pearl award, Diamond award, Ruby award, Emerald award, Gold award. Mem.: Midnight Expression Orgn., Chamber of Commerce, Rainbow Internat. chpt. (Am. Bus. Women's Assn.) (founder 1985—86, v.p. 1985—86, pres. 1986—87, chmn. Program Com., Woman of the Year 1985—86) Sphnix chpt. (Am. Bus. Women's Assn.) (exec. bd. secy. 1984, chmn. Extension Com., Woman of the Year 1984—85, Woman of Quarter 1985, Hand of Friendship award), St. Peter and Paul Parent-Teacher Assn., United Coun. for Negro Women Assn., Am. Bus. Women's Assn. (chpt. chmn. adminstrv. bd. 1986—88, chmn. mem. com., chmn. bus. assn. com., chmn. edn./scholarship com.), Starwood Vistana Vacation Assn., Toastmasters (v.p. edn. 2003—04, pres. Bank of Am. 2004—, Competent Toastmaster award 2004, Competent Leadership award). Avocation: writing. Office Phone: 770-374-4900.

**TERRY, FREDERICK ARTHUR, JR.,** lawyer; b. Buffalo, May 24, 1932; s. Frederick Arthur and Agnes Elizabeth (Tranter) T.; m. Barbara (Anderson). BA, Williams Coll., 1953; LLB, Columbia U., 1956. Bar: N.Y. 1957, U.S. Dist Ct. (so., no., and ea. dist.), N.Y., U.S. Tax Ct., U.S. Supreme Ct. Law clk. to hon. Sterry R. Waterman U.S. Ct. Appeals (2d cir.), 1956—57; assoc. Sullivan and Cromwell, N.Y.C., 1957—64, ptnr., 1965—99, sr. counsel, 2000—. Trustee Harold K. Hochschild Found.; chmn. Flagler Found.; bd. dir. Natural Resources Def. Coun., Rockefeller U., McIntosh Found., Weinman Found.; trustees coun. Nat. Gallery of Art. Mem. ABA, N.Y. State Bar Assn., Assn. Bar City of N.Y., River Club, Union Club, India House, Maidstone Club, The Bathing Corp Office: Sullivan and Cromwell 125 Broad St Fl 25 New York NY 10004-2400 Office Phone: 212-558-3923.

**TERRY, GARY A.,** lawyer, director, former trade association executive; b. Ogden, Utah, Apr. 2, 1935; s. Hyrum Aceal and Viola (Sorenson) T.; m. Carole Ann Eitel, June 23, 1962; children— Stephanie Ann, Brendan Gary BA in Polit. Sci., UCLA, 1964; JD, George Washington U., 1968. Bar: N.Y. 1969 D.C. 1969. Mem. staff U.S. Ho. of Reps., Washington, 1964-65; Washington staff Bethlehem Steel Corp., 1965-69; atty. HUD, Washington, 1969; exec. v.p. Am. Land Devel. Assn. (now Am. Resort Devel. Assn.), Washington, 1969-82, pres., 1982-91, also dir.; with Jones, Waldo, Holbrook & McDonough, Washington, 1991-95, St. George, 1995-97. Dir. Internat. Found. for Timesharing, Washington, 1981-91, mem. consultative council Nat. Inst. Bldg. Scis., Washington, 1982-85; U.S. rep. land use and town planning com. Internat. Real Estate Fedn., Brussels, 1984-91; mem. Found. for Internat. Meetings, Washington, 1984-92; del. Lincoln Inst. Land Policy, Harvard U., 1984, 85 Contbr. articles to profl. jours. Asst. to exec. dir. Presdl. Inaugural Com., 1969-70; mem. adv. bd. NOAA, Washington, 1972; bd. dirs. Zacchaeus Free Med. and Legal Clinics, Washington, 1991-95, co-chair lawyers com., 1992-95; bd. dirs. Celebrity Concert Series, St. George 1999—, pres., 2004—; chmn. Pioneer Ctr. for the Arts Found., St. George, 2000-02, bd. trustees, 1998-2003. Seved with USN, 1953-56. Decorated Am. Spirit of Honor medal. Mem. Va. Bar Assn., D.C. Bar Assn. Mem. Lds Ch. Avocations: music, literature, flying, art, travel. Home: 952 Lizzie Ln Saint George UT 84790-2255 E-mail: gaterry@earthlink.net.

**TERRY, JACK CHATTERSON,** lawyer; b. Monett, Mo., Nov. 23, 1919; s. Jacob E. and Florence V. (Chatterson) T.; m. Susan W. Terry, June 7, 1941; children: Susan L. Terry Galewaler, Philip C. BA in History and Govt., U. Mo., Kansas City, 1949, JD, 1952. Bar: Mo. 1952, U.S. Supreme Ct. 1961. Sole practice, Independence, Mo., 1952—. Mem. Mo. Legislature, 1955-56; legis. liaison officer Jackson County (Mo.), 1967-68; atty. Inter-City Fire Protection Dist., 1955-74; city atty. City of Blue Summit (Mo.), 1971-76; atty. Jackson County (Mo.) Bd. Election Commrs., 1974—. Pres. Independence Good Govt. League, 1961-63, Jackson County League Better Govt., 1962-66. Served as officer USAAF, 1941-46, PTO. Decorated Purple Heart, Air medal. Mem. ABA, Mo. Bar Assn., Kansas City Bar Assn., Inter-City Kiwanis (pres. 1967), Masons, Shriners. Democrat. Mem. Christian Ch. (Disciples Of Christ). Home: 614 Bellevista Dr Independence MO 64055-1746 Office Phone: 816-254-6070.

**TERRY, JAMES JOSEPH, JR.,** lawyer; b. Yonkers, N.Y., July 2, 1952; s. James Joseph Sr. and Marie Catherine (O'Boyle) T.; m. Marguerite Mary O'Connor, Sept. 29, 1985; 1 child, James Daniel. BA, NYU, 1974; JD, Columbia U., 1977. Bar: N.Y. 1978, U.S. Dist. Ct. (so. and ea. dists.) N.Y. 1978, U.S. Ct. Appeals (2d cir.) 1981, U.S. Ct. Appeals (3d cir.) 1989, U.S. Supreme Ct. 2000. Assoc. Cole & Deitz, N.Y.C., 1977-89; ptnr. Winston & Strawn (formerly Cole & Deitz), N.Y.C., 1989—2002; v.p., gen. counsel FJ Sciame Constrn. Co., Inc., N.Y.C., 2002—. Mem. ABA, N.Y. State Bar Assn. N.Y. County Lawyers Assn. Democrat. Roman Catholic. Avocations: fishing, reading. Home: 190 Kneeland Ave Yonkers NY 10705-2713 Office: Sciame Constrn Co Inc 80 South St New York NY 10038 Office Phone: 212-232-2200. E-mail: jterry@fjsciame.com.

**TERRY, JOHN ALFRED,** judge; b. Utica, NY, May 6, 1933; s. Robert Samuel and Julia Berenice (Collins) T. BA magna cum laude, Yale U., 1954; JD, Georgetown U., 1960. Bar: D.C. 1960. Asst. U.S. atty. for D.C. US Dept. Justice, 1962-67; staff atty. Nat. Commn. Reform of Fed. Criminal Laws, Washington, 1967-68; pvt. practice law Washington, 1968-69; chief appellate divsn. U.S. Atty.'s Office for D.C. US Dept. Justice, 1969-82. Criminal Appeals, 1982—2006, sr. judge, 2006—. Mem. D.C. Bar (bd. govs. 1977-82), ABA, Phi Beta Kappa. Office: DC Ct Appeals 500 Indiana Ave NW Washington DC 20001-2138

**TERRY, JOHN FRANKLIN, JR.,** secondary school educator; b. Inglewood, Calif., Apr. 25, 1976; s. John Franklin, Sr. and Lois Francis Terry; m. Sonja Cecilia Quinones, Aug. 25, 2001; 1 child, John Franklin III. BA in social sci., Calif. State, LA, 1999; Masters in Ednl. Adminstrn., Calif. State U., LA, 2005. Edn. cons. Prentice, Sacramento; secondary tchr. LA Unified Sch. Dist. Mem.: Calif. Council of Social Studies, Assn. for Suspension of Curriculum Devel., Nat. Council for Social Studies. Avocations: reading, gardening, sports. Personal E-mail: jterryjr76@aol.com.

**TERRY, JOHN JOSEPH,** transportation investor; b. Chgo., July 29, 1937; s. Michael Parnell and Honore (Ryan) T.; m. Terese Rose Mulkern, Dec. 31, 1960; children: Michael P., Gregory, Deirdre BS, Loyola U., Chgo., 1959; postgrad., U. So. Fla., 1967. C.P.A., Ill. With Touche, Ross & Co., 1959-65; v.p. Nat. City Lines, Denver, 1965-71; v.p. fin. Pepsico Transp., Inc., Tulsa, 1971-74; v.p. U.S. Rwy. Assn., Washington, 1974-76; chmn. P.I.E. Transport Europe, 1976-79; exec. v.p. IU Internat. Corp., Wilmington, Del., 1976-85; pres. Transp. Mgmt. Investment Group, Inc., Phila., 1985—. V.p.-at-large Am. Trucking Assn., Washington, 1984-85, chmn., internat. competitiveness task force, 1991, tax policy com., 1987—; bd. dirs. Caldwell Freight Lines, Lenoir, N.C., Basin Western, Inc., Roosevelt; cons. freight transp. World Bank and European Bank for Reconstrn. and Devel., 1986—. Served with U.S. Army, 1960-63 Recipient Best Motor Carrier Rsch. award Transp. Rsch. Forum, 1991. Office: Transp Mgmt Investment Group Inc 210 Locust St Apt 11B Philadelphia PA 19106-3923

**TERRY, KAREN ELIZABETH,** lawyer; b. Miami, Fla., June 13, 1970; d. Edmund and Barbara Terry. AB, Duke U., 1991; JD and M in Mass Comm., U. Fla., 1994. Bar: Fla. 1995. Atty. Judge Walter Colbath, West Palm Beach, Fla., 1994; ptnr. Searcy Denney, West Palm Beach, 1995—. Author: Violence, Regulation, and First Amendment, 1995, So. Fla. Legal Guide, Trend Mag. Top Lawyers Named one of Top Ten Litigators in South Fla. Under Age 40, Fla. Trend Mag., 2003, 2005. Mem. ABA, Acad. Fla. Trial Lawyers (eagle mem.). Palm Beach County Bar Assn., Assn. Trial Lawyers Am., Million Dollar Adv. Avocations: rock climbing, scuba diving, tennis, golf. Home: 11337 Lost Tree Way North Palm Beach FL 33408 Office: Searcy Denney Scarola Barnhart & Shipley PA PO Drawer 3626 West Palm Beach FL 33409-3626 Office Phone: 561-686-6300. Business E-Mail: ket@searcylaw.com.

**TERRY, LEE RAYMOND,** congressman, lawyer; b. Omaha, Jan. 29, 1962; s. Leland R. Terry; m. Robyn L. Terry, Feb. 14, 1992; children: Nolan E., Ryan, Jack. BA in Polit. Sci., U. Nebr., Lincoln, 1984; JD, Creighton U. Sch. Law, Omaha, 1987. Bar: Nebr. 1987, US Dist. Ct. Nebr. 1987. Staff atty. Schrempp & Salerno, Omaha, 1987-92; ptnr. Schrempp, Salerno & Terry, Omaha, 1992-93, Terry & Kratville, Omaha, 1993-98; mem. City Coun., Omaha, 1991—98, US Congress from 2nd Nebr. dist., 1999—, mem. energy & commerce com. Co-author: Trying the Soft Tissue Case in Nebraska, 1995. V.p. Omaha City Coun., 1993-94, pres., 1995-97; chair elect Am. Diabetes Assn., Great Plains, 1996-97, chair Nebr. area, 1997-99; co-chmn. Impact Aid Coalition. Named One of Ten Outstanding Young Omahans, Omaha Jaycees, 1994, Outstanding Young Nebraskan Nebr. Jaycees, 1997; recipient Spirit of Enterprise award US C. of C., 2002 Mem. Nebr. Assn. Trial Attys. (dir. 1995), Suburban Rotary. Republican. Meth. Avocations: travel, playing, spending time with family. Office: US Ho Reps 1524 Longworth House Office Bldg Washington DC 20515-2702 Office Phone: 202-225-4155.*

**TERRY, LEON CASS,** neurologist, educator; b. Dec. 22, 1940; s. Leon Herbert and Zella Irene (Boyd) T.; m. Suzanne Martinson, June 27, 1964; children: Kristin, Sean. Pharm. D., U. Mich., 1964; MD, Marquette U., 1969; PhD, McGill U., 1982; MBA, U. So. Fla., 1994. Diplomate Am. Bd. Psychiatry and Neurology, Am. Bd. Med. Mgmt. Intern U. Rochester, NY, 1969-70; staff assoc. NIH, 1970-72; resident in neurology McGill U., Montreal, Que., Canada, 1972-75; MRC fellow, 1975-78; assoc. prof. U. Tenn., Memphis, 1978-81; prof. neurology U. Mich., Ann Arbor, 1981-89; assoc. prof. physiology, 1982-89; asst. chief neurology VA Med. Ctr., Ann Arbor, 1982-89; chmn. dept. neurology Med. Coll. of Wis., Milw., 1989—2000, prof. neurology and physiology, 1989—2003; chief med. officer Nexostherapeuticals, 2003—; pres., CEO Neurologic Cons., LLP, 2004—, Longevitech, 2004—. Dir. clin neurosci. ctr. and multiple sclerosis clinic, Med. Coll. Wis.; assoc. dean for amb. care, 1996-98; vice chief of staff Froedtert Hosp., 1994-97; chief of staff, 1997-98; chief med. officer cenegenics, 1997-98. Contbr. articles to profl. jours, chpts. to books. Served to lt. comdr. USPHS, 1970-72. NIH grantee, 1981-92; VA grantee, 1980-92 VA Clin. Investigator award, 1980-81. Mem. AMA, Am. Soc. Clin. Investigation, Cen. Soc. Clin. Investigation, Am. Neurol. Assn., Am. Coll. Physician Execs. (vice chmn. academic health ctr. soc. 1994-95, chair, 1995-98, leader forum health care delivery 1995-98), Am. Coll. Healthcare Execs., Endocrine Soc., Am. Acad. Neurology, Internat. Soc. Neuroendocrinilogy, Internat. Soc. Psychoeuroendocrinilogy, Soc. Neurosci., Soc. Rsch. Biol. Rhythms, Milw. Acad. Physicians, Wis. Neurol. Assn., Wis. State Med. Soc. (del.-elect 1995-96), Med. Soc. Milw. County, Milw. Neuropsychiatric Soc. (pres.-elect.). Avocations: pilot, skiing, scuba diving, computers. Office: Neurologic Consultnats LLP Suite 209 1009 W Glen Oaks Lane Mequon WI 53092 Office Phone: 262-241-8512. E-mail: cass@cass-terry.com, drcassterry@wi.rr.com.

**TERRY, LINDA FAYE,** librarian; b. Paducah, Ky., June 26, 1947; d. John Rodman and Frances B. (Clark) Tomlinson; m. Steven Lynn Terry, June 8, 1974; children: Elizabeth Lynn, Matthew Lee. BS, Western Ky. U., 1970, MA in Reading, 1971; MLS, Ind. U., 1991. Cert. tchr., Ky., Ind.; Ind. Student asst. Coll. Hgts. Found., Western Ky. U., Bowling Green, 1966-69; tchr. elem. Waddell Ave. Elem. Sch., Madisonville, Ky., 1969-70; bookkeeper asst. City County Hosp., Bowling Green, 1970, grad. asst. reading Western Ky. U., Bowling Green, 1970-71; cons. reading tchr. Greater Clark County Schs. Jeffersonville, Ind., 1971-75; reading tchr. Crittenden (Ky.) Elem. Sch., 1975; children dir., asst. dir. Brownsburg (Ind.) Pub. Libr., 1979-82, bookkeeper, treas., 1984-87, jr. high tchr., 1990; project cons. Ind. State Libr., Indpls., 1991-92, pub. libr. svcs. cons., 1993—. Treas. Floyd-Clark County I.R.A., Jeffersonville, Ind., 1971-73; treas.-pres. Hendricks County I.R.A., Brownsburg, 1980-85, membership com., 1988-92; family involvement com. Ind. State Reading Coun., Indpls., 1985-88. Leader Girl Scouts of Am., Brownsburg, 1982-84; parent support group Brownsburg Jr. High Sch., 1988-90, Brownsburg High Sch., 1990-92, band boosters, 1990—. Named Libr. Employee of Yr., Ind. State, 2006. Mem. ALA, ASCD, Internat. Reading Assn., Am. Assn. Sch. Librs., Pub. Libr. Assn., Hendricks County Reading Coun. (pres. 1980—), Assn. Ind. Media Educators, Ind. Reading Assn. Southern Baptist. Office: Ind State Libr 140 N Senate Ave Indianapolis IN 46204-2207 Office Phone: 317-232-1938. E-mail: fayeterry626@yahoo.com.

**TERRY, MARSHALL NORTHWAY, JR.,** language educator, writer; b. Cleve., Feb. 7, 1931; s. Marshall Northway and Margaret Louise (Carpenter) T.; m. Antoinette Barksdale, Sept. 5, 1953; children: Antoinette Terry Bryant, Mary Marshall Terry Benton. Student, Amherst Coll., 1949-50, Kenyon Coll., 1950-51; BA, So. Meth. U., 1953, MA, 1954. Teaching fellow English So. Meth. U., Dallas, 1954, dir. pub. relations, lectr. English, 1957-64, instr. English, 1956, 65-67, asst. prof., English, assoc. prof., 1969-71, prof. English, 1972—, chmn. dept., 1971-75, 79-82, dir. creative writing program. Book critic Dallas News, 1970-75; pres. faculty senate So. Meth. U., 1993-94, assoc. provost, 1994-98, E.A. Lilly prof. Eng. 1998—. Author: Old Liberty, 1961, Tom Northway, 1968, Dallas Stories, 1986, Ringer, 1987, My Father's Hands, 1993, Land of Hope and Glory, 1996, Angels Prostate Fall, 2001, Tex Rex, 2003, The Memorialist, 2006; contbr. short stories to various jours. and mags.; editor Prize Stories, 1986. Past trustee Incarnate Word Coll., San Antonio; sec. bd. trustees Fort Burgwin Research Ctr., Ranchos de Taos, N.Mex. Recipient Jesse H. Jones Distinguished award Tex. Inst. Letters, 1968, Best Short Story award S.W. Rev., 1973, S.W. Writer of Yr. award, 1988, Willis M. Tate award So. Meth. U., 1990, 94, Lon Tinkle award for continuing excellence in Letters, Tex. Inst. Letters, 1991, Disting. Alumnus award, So. Meth. U., 2003. Mem. AAUP (chpt. pres. 1971), Coll. Conf. Tchrs. English, South Central MLA, Tex. Inst. Letters (pres. 1977-79, councilor 1980—)

Democrat. Methodist. Home: 2717 Lovers Ln Dallas TX 75225-7905 Office: So Meth Univ Dept English Dallas TX 75275-0001 Office Phone: 214-768-2952. Business E-Mail: mterry@smu.edu.

**TERRY, MICHAEL W.,** elementary school educator; b. Portales, N.Mex., Sept. 6, 1961; s. H.R. and Nona Faye Terry; m. Kristie Kent, June 19, 1991; children: Teegan, Braden, Micah. M in Adminstrn., ENMU. Tchr. James Elem., Portales, N.Mex., 1988—92, Valencia Elem., 1992—97. Office: R M James Elementary 701 West 18th Street Portales NM 88130 Office Phone: 505-356-8431. Office Fax: 505-356-4852. E-mail: mterry61@hotmail.com.

**TERRY, NICHOLAS P.,** law educator; b. London, Eng., Dec. 5, 1952; BA, Kingston Univ., U.K., 1975; LLM, Univ. Cambridge, 1977. Lectr. Univ. Exeter, England; prof. Saint Louis Univ. Sch. Law, 1980—; co-dir. Ctr. Health Studies, Saint Louis Univ., 2000—; prof. Saint Louis Univ. Sch. Public Health, 2003—. Vis. prof. Univ. Mo. Columbia Sch. Law, 1986—87, Washington Univ. Sch. Law, 1986—99; dir. Legal Edn. LEXIS-NEXIS, Dayton, Ohio, 1996—97; sr. fellow Melbourne Law Sch., Australia, 2001—. Co-author: Cases, Materials and Problems in the Law of Torts, 2002, Products Liability, Cases, Material, Problems, 2002; contbr. articles to profl. jour.; co-editor (in-chief): Jour. Health Law, 2000—. Mem. ed. bd. dir. Ctr. for Computer Assisted Legal Instruction, 1998—; mem. editl. bd. Jour. Medical Internet. Rsch., 2000—; mem. internat. bd. adv. Medical Law Rev., Oxford Univ. Press, 1992—; mem. ed. adv. Melbourne Law Sch., Australia, 2001—. Mem.: ABA, Am. Health Lawyers Assn., Am. Soc. Law & Medicine (mem. bd. dir.), Health Law Tchr. Assn. Office: Saint Louis University School of Law 3700 Lindell Blvd Saint Louis MO 63108

**TERRY, PATRICIA HART,** dietician, educator; b. Tuscaloosa, Ala., Oct. 19, 1949; d. James A. and Gloria Creel; m. Bobby S. Terry, Mar. 22, 2002; children: Jennifer Wendorf, Taylor Hart, Brent, Jean Cullen. BS, U. Ala., Tuscaloosa, 1972, MS, 1975; PhD, Tex. Woman's U., Denton, 1987. Registered dietitian Am. Dietetic Assn., 1973, lic. State of Ala. Bd. of Examiners, 1990. Chief nutritionist Children and Youth Project, U. Ala., Birmingham, 1975—76; nutritionist Fgn. Mission Bd., Caracas, Venezuela, 1978—89; nutrition tng. coord. Jefferson County Dept. of Health, Birmingham, Ala., 1989—90; dir. didactic program in dietetics Samford U., Birmingham, Ala., 1990—, assoc. prof., 1990—; free lance corr. The Birmingham News, Ala., 1992—. Mem. Bapt. World Alliance, Falls Church, Va., 2005—. Author: (book) Made for Paradise: God's Original Plan for Healthy Eating, Physical Activity and Rest, (weekly newspaper column) In Season; contbr. articles to profl. jours. Leadership coun. Am. Diabetes Assn., Birmingham, Ala., 2004; mem. mission team Havana, Cuba, 2001; mem. visioning team Woman's Missionary Union, Kishinev, Moldova, 2003—06; chair food svc. com. Dawson Meml. Bapt. Ch., Birmingham, Ala., 2006—. Recipient Jack Davis Profl. Achievement award, U. Ala., 1994, Pat Terry Scholarship in Nutrition and Dietetics, Samford U., 2006; Latin Am. scholar, 2006. Mem.: Birmingham Dietetic Assn. (licentiate; exec. bd. 1991—, Outstanding Dietitian 1998), Ala. Dietetic Assn. (licentiate; bd. dirs. 1993—2001), Am. Dietetic Assn. (licentiate; dietetic educators of practitioners 1990—, Mead Johnson scholarship 1971), Am. Assn. of Family and Consumer Scis. (assoc.; del. 2003—06), Bapt. Nursing Fellowship (assoc.), Nat. Fellowship of Bapt. Educators (assoc.), Nat. Rural Health Assn. (assoc.), Kappa Omicron Nu, Phi Kappa Phi, Phi Upsilon Omicron, Mortar Bd., Hypatia Honor Soc., Alpha Sigma Lambda. Office: Samford Univ 800 Lakeshore Dr Birmingham AL 35229 Office Phone: 205-726-2930. Office Fax: 205-726-4483.

**TERRY, RICHARD EDWARD,** public utility holding company executive; b. Green Bay, Wis., July 7, 1937; s. Joseph Edward and Arleen (Agamet) T.; m. Catherine Lombardo, Nov. 19, 1966; children— Angela, Edward BA, St. Norbert's Coll., West DePere, Wis. 1959; LLB, U. Wis., 1964; postgrad., Harvard U., 1986. Assoc. Ross & Hardies, Chgo., 1964-72; atty. Peoples Energy Corp., Chgo., 1972-79, asst. gen. counsel, 1979-81, v.p. gen. counsel, 1981-84; exec. v.p. People's Energy Corp., Peoples Gas Light & Coke Co. and North Shore Gas Co., 1984-87, pres., COO, 1987-90, chair, CEO Chgo., 1990—. Bd. dirs. Peoples Energy Corp., Peoples Gas Light, North Shore Gas Co., Harris Bancorp, Harris Trust & Savs., Amsted Industries. Bd. dirs. Mus. Sci. & Ind., 1991—, Inst. Gas Tech., 1987—, Ill. Coun. on Econ. Edn., 1987—, Big Shoulders, 1991—; mem. Chgo. Area Ctrl. Com., 1991—; mem. bus. adv. coun. Chgo. Urban League, 1991—; prin. Chgo. United, 1991—; trustee St. Xavier U., 1989—, St. Norbert Coll., 1982—, DePaul U., 1992—. 1st lt. U.S. Army, 1959-61. Mem. Am. Gas Assn. (bd. dirs. 1991—), Nat. Petroleum Coun., Chgo. C. of C. (bd. dirs. 1988—), Univ. Club, Mid-Am. Club, Chgo. Club, Econ. Club, Comml. Club Chgo. (mem. civic com. 1991—). Avocations: golf, fishing, reading.

**TERRY, ROBERT BROOKS,** food products executive, lawyer; b. Kansas City, Mo., July 7, 1956; s. Frank R. and Susan S. (Smart) T.; m. Penny Susan Kanterman, July 2, 1987; children: Ryan, Kevin, Erin. Student, Vanderbilt U., 1974-75; BS in Acctg., U. Mo., 1978, JD, 1981. Bar: Mo. 1981, U.S. Dist. ct. (we. dist.) Mo. 1981, U.S. ct. Appeals (8th and 10th circs.) 1983. Assoc. Spencer, Fane, Britt & Browne, Kansas City, Mo., 1981—89; v.p., gen. counsel Farmland Industries, Inc., Kansas City, 1993—, pres., CEO, 2002—. Mem. ABA, Kansas City Mo. Bar Assn., Lawyers' Assn. Kansas City, Order of Coif. Avocation: baseball. Home: 4952 W 132nd Ter Leawood KS 66209-3460

**TERRY, ROBERT DAVIS,** neuropathologist, educator; b. Hartford, Conn., Jan. 13, 1924; m. Patricia Ann Blech, June 27, 1952; 1 son, Nicolas Saul. AB, Williams Coll., 1946, DSc (hon.), 1991; MD, Albany Med. Coll., NY, 1950. Diplomate: Am. Bd. Pathology, Am. Bd. Neuropathology. Postdoctoral tng. St. Francis Hosp., Hartford, 1950, Bellevue Hosp., N.Y.C., 1951, Montefiore Hosp., N.Y.C., 1952-53, 54-55, Inst. Recherches sur le Cancer, Paris, 1953-54, sr. postdoctoral fellow, 1965-66; asst. pathologist Montefiore Hosp., 1955-59; assoc. prof. dept. pathology Einstein Coll. Medicine, Bronx, NY, 1959-64, prof., 1964-84, acting chmn. dept. pathology, 1969-70, chmn., 1970-84; prof. depts. neuroscis. and pathology U. Calif.-San Diego, 1984-94, prof. emeritus, 1994—. Mem. study sect. pathology NIH, 1964-68; study sects. Nat. Multiple Sclerosis Soc., 1964-72, 74-78; mem. bd. sci. counselors Nat. Inst. Neurol. and Communicative Disorders and Stroke, NIH, 1976-80, chmn., 1977-80; mem. nat. sci. coun. Huntington's Disease Assn., 1978-81; mem. med. sci. adv. bd. Alzheimer Assn., 1978-88; mem. sci. adv. bd. Max Planck Inst., Martinsried, 1990-96. Mem. editorial adv. bd. Jour. Neuropathology and Exptl. Neurology, 1963-83, 85-88, Lab. Investigation, 1967-77, Revue Neurologique, 1977-87, Annals of Neurology, 1978-82, Ultrastructural Pathology, 1978-86, Am. Jour. Pathology, 1985-89. Served with U.S. Army, 1943-46. ETO. Recipient Potamkin prize for Alzheimer Rsch., 1988, Met. Life Found. award, 1991, Irving Wright award Am. Fedn. Aging Rsch., 2006. Fellow AAAS, Am. Acad. Arts and Sci.; mem. Am. Assn. Neuropathologists (pres. 1969-70, Meritorious Contbn. award 1989), N.Y. Path. Soc. (v.p. 1969-70, pres. 1971-73), Am. Assn. Pathologists, Am. Neurol. Assn., Am. Acad. Neurology. Achievements include research and publications on Alzheimer disease and Tay Sachs disease.

**TERRY, ROBERT MEREDITH,** foreign language educator; b. Danville, Va., Dec. 16, 1939; s. Willard Terry and Martha Willeford; m. Anne Reynolds Beggarly, Jan. 30, 1965; children: Michael Reynolds, Christopher Robert, Meredith Anne. BA in French, Randolph-Macon Coll., Ashland, Va., 1962; PhD in Romance Langs., Duke U., Durham. N.C., 1966. Asst. prof. French U. Fla., Gainesville, Fla., 1966-68; assoc. prof. U. Richmond, Richmond, Va., 1968-83, prof., 1983—. Pres. Am. Coun. on Tchg. Fgn. Langs., 1994, mem. exec. coun., 1983-85, 2000-04. Co-author: Accent: Conversational French I, 1980, Vous Y Etes!, 1990, Intersections, 1997; editor Dimension, So. Conf. Lang. Tchg., 1991-97; assoc. editor ACTFL Foreign Language Education Series, 1994, 96, 98, 99, 2000; editor N.E. Conf. Report, 2000; articles editor NECTFL Rev., 2002—; contbr. articles to profl. jours. Recipient Stephen A. Freeman award N.E. Conf. on Teaching Fgn. Lang., 1990, Robert J. Ludwig Nat. Fgn. Lang. Leadership award, 1995, Florence Steiner award for Leadership in Fgn. Lang. Teaching Post-Secondary Edn., 2004. Mem. Am. Coun. on Tchg. Fgn. Langs., Fgn. Lang. Assn. Va., Am. Assn. Tchrs. French, So. Conf.

on Lang. Tchg. Home: 1504 Cloister Dr Richmond VA 23238 Office: Univ Richmond PO Box 25 28 Westhampton Way Richmond VA 23173-0025 Office Phone: 804-289-8117. Business E-Mail: rterry@richmond.edu.

**TERRY, ROGER,** retired pathologist, consultant; b. Waterville, NY, May 8, 1917; s. Orrin and Mary Isabelle (Kennedy) T.; m. Eleanor Virginia Wallace, Dec. 13, 1942; children: Robin, Orrin. AB magna cum laude, Colgate U., 1939; MD, U. Rochester, 1944. Cert. anatomic pathologist. Intern then resident Strong Meml. Hosp., Rochester, NY, 1944-51; asst. prof. U. Rochester Sch. Medicine, 1951-56, assoc. prof., 1956-61, prof. pathology, 1961-69, U. So. Calif. Sch. Medicine, Los Angeles, 1969-82; pathologist San Gabriel (Calif.) Valley Med. Ctr., 1982—2003; ret., 2003. Exec. dir. Calif. Tumor Tissue Registry, L.A., 1969-84. Contbr. articles to profl. jours. Served to capt. USAF, 1954-56. Fellow Am. Soc. Clin. Pathologists, Coll. Am. Pathologists; mem. AMA, Internat. Acad. Pathology (councilor 1973-76), Am. Soc. Investigative Pathology, L.A. Soc. Pathologists (pres. 1974, Lifetime Achievement award 2006), Am. Soc. Cytopathology, Internat. Soc. Dermatopathology, Phi Beta Kappa, Sigma Xi, Alpha Omega Alpha. Republican. Episcopalian. Avocations: ballroom dancing, snorkeling, bicycling. Home: 2841 Shakespeare Dr San Marino CA 91108-2230

**TERRY, THEO B., III,** technology executive; b. Elizabethtown, Ky., Feb. 16, 1962; s. Theo Bennett Terry, Jr and Ester Leona Terry; m. Robin Joy McCabe, May 3, 1991; children: Andrew Richards Hawkins, Theo Bennett IV, Emma Grace. BS, Western Ky. U., 1985. Sanitarian Ky. Sr. environmentalist Lincoln Trail Dist. Health Dept., Elizabethtown, 1985—92, environ. health supr., 1992—97; exec. v.p. Zabel Environ. Tech., Crestwood, Ky., 1997—2005; mgr. tech. Ring Indsl. Group, Oakland, Tenn., 2005—. Mem. JWW com. NSF Internat., Ann Arbor, Mich., 2005—. Pres. Lincoln Days Celebration, Inc., Hodgenville, Ky., 1989—90; city councilman City Coun., Hodgenville, 2005—06; bd. dirs. Lincoln Mus. Inc. Hodgenville, 1991—93, Hodgenville Main St. Assn., 2004—05. Recipient Steve Sandlin award, KAMFES, Inc 1988. Mem.: Ky. Assn. of Milk, Food and Environ. Sanitarians, Ga. Onsite Wastewater Assn. (bd. dirs. 1997—99), Nat. Onsite Wastewater Recycling Assn. (bd. dirs. 1996—99), Ky. Onsite Wastewater Assn. (pres. 1994—96, bd. dirs. 1990—96), Assn. for Installers and Mfrs. (pres. 1999—2001). Achievements include patents in field; patents pending for. Office: Ring Indsl Group 65 Industrial Park Rd Oakland TN 38060 Office Phone: 800-649-0253. Office Fax: 866-279-9203. Business E-Mail: theo.terry@ringindustrial.com.

**TERRY, TIMOTHY P.,** lawyer; b. Aug. 11, 1965; BA, U. Tex., Austin, 1986; grad. studies in Internat. Transactions, George Mason U., 1993; JD, U. Calif. Hastings Coll. Law, 1999. Bar: Calif. 2000. Worked on Subcom. on Commerce US Ho. of Reps, 1987—88; legis. asst. & press sec. US Rep. Gus Yatron, 1988—90; legis. dir. US Rep. Vic Fazio, 1990—95; prin. Ferguson Co., Washington, 1995—96; law clk./assoc. Abramson & Smith, San Francisco; assoc. Leboeuf, Lamb, Greene & MacRae, LA, Sonnenschein Nath & Rosenthal LLP, LA. Chmn. bd. dirs. The Fed. Tech. Ctr., Sacramento. Mem.: ABA. Office: Sonnenschein Nath & Rosenthal LLP 601 S Figueroa St, Ste 1500 Los Angeles CA 90017 Office Phone: 213-892-5073. Office Fax: 213-623-9924. Business E-Mail: tterry@sonnenschein.com.

**TERRY, W. BURKS,** lawyer; b. Balt., Dec. 12, 1950; BA in Econ. and Philosophy, U. Calif., Berkeley, 1973; JD, U. Notre Dame, 1976. Bar: Calif. From program counsel and contracts mgr. to v.p. dep. gen. counsel Northrop Grumman Corp., LA, 1976—99, corp. v.p., gen. counsel, 2000—. Mem.: ABA, Ill. Bar Assn. Office: Northrop Grumman Corp 1840 Century Park E Los Angeles CA 90067-2199

**TERRY, WAYNE GILBERT,** healthcare educator, hospital administrator; b. Plymouth, Mass., Oct. 2, 1932; s. Lawrence Arthur and Betty Frances (Bouteman) Terry; m. Barbara Bromwell, Sept. 20, 1980; children: Karleton Wayne, Dale Duane, Kendrick Shane, Kristen Alayne, Tammye Van Clief, Wade Bromwell Delk. AA in Gen. Adminstrn., Allan Hancock Coll., 1960; BBA in Bus. Mgmt., U. Hawaii, 1966; MHA, Med. Coll. Va., 1973; PhD in Health Svcs. Mgmt., LaSalle U., 1999. Commd. 2d lt. USAF Med. Svc. Corps, 1967, advanced through grades to maj., 1976; asst. adminstr. for registrar activities USAF Hosp., Orlando AFB, Fla., 1966-67; assoc. adminstr. aeromed. evacuation activities USAF, Hickam AFB, Hawaii, 1967-71; adminstrv. resident USAF Regional Hosp., Langley AFB, Va., 1972-73; CEO USAF Hosp., Columbus AFB, Miss., 1973-75; nat. health edn. and tng. program advisor Office of Surgeon Gen., Dept. of Air Force, Washington, 1975-78; dir. health professions pers. planning and policy divsn. Office of Asst. Sec. Def. for Health Affairs, The Pentagon, Washington, 1978-80; dep. project mgr./adminstrv. dir. King Faisal U. Teaching Hosp., Al-Khobar, Saudi Arabia, 1980-82; dep. project mgr.; hosp. dir. North Yemen Healthcare Project, As-Salem Hosp., Sadah, Yemen Arab Republic, 1982-83; hosp. dir., CEO western area Armed Forces Hosps., Khamis Mushayt, Saudi Arabia, 1983-84; chief adminstr./commissioning team chief Orbit Summit Health, Ltd., Riyadh, Saudi Arabia, 1984-85; hosp. dir., adminstrv. dir. Truk State Dept. Health Svcs., Moen, Federated States of Micronesia, 1985-87; assoc. adminstr. support svcs. King Fahad Hosp., Saudi Arabian N.G., Riyadh, 1987-90; project mgr., CEO N.W. Armed Forces Hosps. Program, Tabuk, Saudi Arabia, 1990-98, cons. in health svcs. mgmt., 1998-99; cons., mediator in health svcs. mgmt. Crozet, Va., 1999-2000; exec. dir., CEO Southside Area Health Edn. Ctr. Longwood U., Farmville, Va., 2000—. Apptd. mil. cons. healthcare planning to the Air Force Surgeon Gen., 1979; apptd. preceptor program in healthcare adminstrn. U. Mich. for adminstrv. residents at N.W. Armed Forces Hosps. Programs, Tabuk, Saudi Arabia, 1993; supervisory bd. Royal Coll. Surgeons in Ireland, Dublin, 1990-98; cert. sr. grant specialist, reviewer, cons.; lectr., cons. in field. Contbr. articles to profl. jours. Warden to Am. Cmty. N.W. Region of Yemen Arab Republic to Am. Embassy in Sanaa, 1982-83, warden to Am. Cmty. N.W. Region of Saudi Arabia to Am. Embassy in Riyadh, 1990-99; mem. Internat. Sys. Coord. Com., Tabuk, 1990-99; bd. dirs. Taif Sch. Dist. Sys., Saudi Arabia, 1981-82; chmn., exec. com., bd. dirs. Ctrl. Va. Health Planning Agy., Richmond, Va., 2001—; bd. dirs. Va. Tobacco Settlement Found., Regional Adv. Bd., Richmond, Va., 2001—, Southside Area Health Edn. Ctr., Longwood U., Farmville, 2001—; leadership and planning group Nat. Area Health Edn. Ctr. Assn., Balt., 2003-04. Decorated Def. Meritorious Svc. medal, Air Force Meritorious Svc. medal with 3 oak leaf clusters, Air medal with 2 oak leaf clusters, Air Force Commendation medal with 2 oak leaf clusters, Republic of Vietnam Gallantry Cross with palm, Republic of Vietnam Svc. medal with 11 svc. stars, Korean Def. Svc. medal, Sec. of Def. Svc. medal/badge, Air Staff badge Dept. Air Force, Air Force Chief Med. Svc. Corps badge; recipient Citation of Appreciation Nat. Coun. Social Welfare, Seoul, Republic of Korea, 1963, Citation of Appreciation award Suchan Province Gov., Choong Nam, Republic of Korea, 1963, award of merit Pacific Air Forces Command, Hickam AFB, Hawaii, 1965, Outstanding Jr. Officer in 22nd Air Force, USAF, 1970, Outstanding Rsch. award Med. Coll. Va., 1973, Personality of the South award, 1975, Men of Achievement award, Cambridge, Eng., 1982, Citation of Appreciation Gov. Truk State, Federated States of Micronesia, 1987, Citation of Merit Internat. Red Cross Comman., Bern, Switzerland, 1991, N.W. Armed Forces Hosps., Ministry Def. and Aviation, Tabuk, 1991, Citation of Appreciation Presidency of Gen. Staff Hdqs., Ministry of Def. and Aviation, Tabuk, 1992-93, 95-99, Disting. Alumni award Allan Hancock Coll., Santa Maria, 2000, Citation of Appreciation Longwood U., Va., 2006. Fellow Am. Coll. Healthcare Execs., Royal Soc. Health; mem. Am. Hosp. Assn., Am. Mgmt. Assn., Air Force Med. Svc. Corps Assn. (membership and awards com. 2003—), bd. dirs., newsletter editor 2005—), Assn. Mil. Surgeons of U.S., Air Force Assn. Republican. Baptist. Avocations: tennis, coin collecting/numismatics, hiking. Office: Southside Area Health Edn Ctr Longwood Univ 201 High St Farmville VA 23909 Office Phone: 434-395-2862. Business E-Mail: terrywg@longwood.edu.

**TERSCHAN, FRANK ROBERT,** lawyer; b. Dec. 25, 1949; s. Frank Joseph and Margaret Anna (Heidt) T.; m. Barbara Elizabeth Keily, Dec. 28, 1974; 1 child, Frank Martin. BA, Syracuse U., 1972; JD, U. Wis., 1975. Bar: Wis. 1976, U.S. Dist. Ct. (ea. and we. dists.) Wis. 1976, U.S. Ct. Appeals (7th cir.)

1979, U.S. Ct. Appeals (10th cir.) 1989, U.S. Supreme Ct. 1992. From assoc. to ptnr. Frisch, Dudek & Slattery Ltd., Milw., 1975-88; ptnr. Slattery and Hausman Ltd., Milw., 1988-94, Terschan & Steinle Ltd., Milw., 1994-96, Terschan, Steinle & Ness, Milw., 1996—. Chmn. MBA Fee Adminstrn. Com., 2000—; mem. Wis. Jud. Conduct Adv. Com., 2002—. Treas., sec. Ville du Park Homeowners Assn., Mequon, Wis., 1985-86; cubmaster Boy Scouts Am., 1989-90, asst. scoutmaster, 1991-93. Mem. ABA, Am. Bd. Trial Advocates, Wis. Bar Assn., Milw. Bar Assn., Assn. Trial Lawyers Am., Wis. Acad. Trial Lawyers (bd. dirs. 1996—), 7th Cir. Bar Assn., Order of Coif. Republican. Lutheran. Avocations: swimming, coin collecting/numismatics, reading, outdoor activities. Home: 10143 N Lake Shore Dr Mequon WI 53092-6109 Office: 309 N Water St Ste 215 Milwaukee WI 53202 Office Phone: 414-258-1010. Business E-Mail: frt@tsn-law.com.

**TERSINE, BRENDA L.,** funeral director; b. Punxsutawney, Pa., June 2, 1948; d. G.J. and Mary V. tersine; m. Bill Goichberg, Feb. 20, 1993. BS in Edn., Indiana U. Pa., 1970; Diploma, Pitts. Inst. Mortuary Sci., 1971; MA, SUNY, Albany, 1985. Lic. funeral dir., N.Y., Pa. Embalmer, funeral dir., Punxsutawney, 1971-75; embalmer, funeral dir. Oliver H Bair, Phila., 1976-80; per diem substitute Phila. Bd. Edn., 1978-80; embalmer, anatomical gifts Albany Med. Coll., 1980-90; asst. prof. mortuary sci. Hudson Valley C.C., Troy, N.Y., 1980-90; funeral dir., embalmer Salisbury Mills, N.Y., 1990—. Contbg. author: Embalming History, Theory and Practice, 1990. Vice pres. adv. bd. Continental Chess, Salisbury Mills, 1991—; supportive counseling/crisis intervention YWCA, Troy, 1989-91. Mem. Acad. Profl. Funeral Svc. Practice (life), Funeral Svc. Ednl. Found., Nat. Funeral Dirs. Assn., Cath. daus. of Am. Democrat. Roman Catholic. Avocation: organizing chess tournaments. Home: PO Box 240 Salisbury Mills NY 12577-0240

**TERSOFF, JERRY DAVID,** physicist; BA in Physics, Swarthmore Coll., 1977; PhD in Physics, U. Calif., Berkeley, 1982. Postdoctoral fellow Bell Labs., Murray Hill, NJ, 1982-84; mem. rsch. staff IBM T.J. Watson Rsch. Ctr., Yorktown Heights, NY, 1984—. Contbr. numerous articles on solid state physics to scholarly and profl. jours. Fellow Am. Physical Soc. (Davisson Germer prize 1997); mem. Materials Rsch. Soc. (MRS medal 1996), Am. Vacuum Soc. (Peter Mark award 1988). Achievements include theoretical advances in the understanding of scanning tunneling microscopy; heterojunction band offsets and Schottky barriers; epitaxial growth and carbon nanotube electronic devices. Office: IBM TJ Watson Rsch Ctr PO Box 218 Yorktown Heights NY 10598-0218

**TERTELING-PAYNE, CAROLYN ANN,** city official; b. Buhl, Idaho, Dec. 20, 1936; d. Carl Treva and Ann Christine (Witt) Edwards; m. Joseph Loyd Terteling, June 20, 1959 (div. Sept. 1991); children: Joseph Nixon, Steven Loyd, Thomas Edward, Andrew James; m. Frank Adrian Payne, May 13, 1995. BA with highest honors, U. Idaho, Moscow, 1959. Grad. tchg. asst. Ariz. State U., Phoenix, 1959-60; mem. Boise City Coun., 1993—, pres., 1996—2003; mayor City of Boise, Idaho, 2003—. Sustainer Boise Jr. League; mem. Collector's Forum, Boise Art Mus.; trustee, mem. exec. com., mem. bldg. and planning com. St. Lukes Regional Med. Ctr.; pres. Boise Pub. Libr. Found.; dir., past pres. U. Idaho Found.; dir. Fundsy Charitable Found., Boise River Festival; mem. adv. bd. Lit. Lab, Warm Springs Counseling Ctr.; hon. bd. Idaho Zool. Soc.; emeritus dir. Boise Philharmonic; past dir. Boise Mus. Art, Boise Bicentennial Commn., Boise Sch. Vols., Idaho Hist. Preservation Coun., Morriso Ctr. for Ars, Endowment Dr., Women's Life at St. Lukes, Idaho Law Found.; mem. adv. bd. Children at Risk Evaluative Svcs.; past dir. area coun. 11 Western states, Assn. Jr. Leagues Am.; past pres. St. Lukes Hosp. Aux., U. Idaho Found., Boise Jr. League; past chair symposium Albertson Coll. Idaho, Grand Opening of Morrison Ctr. for Arts, Sun valley, Arts and Humanities Benefit, Alternate Mobility Adventure Seekers, Boise State U. Named Idaho Statesman Disting. Citizen, 1979, Woman of Yr., C. of C., 1986; recipient Woman of Today and Tomorrow award Girl Scouts, 1992, Disting. Svc. award Idaho State Bar, 1992, Cultural Heritage award Coll. Letters and Sci. U. Idaho, 1994. Mem. U. Idaho Alumni Assn., Hillcrest Country Club (past dir.), PEO, Phi Beta Kappa, Gamma Phi Beta. Avocations: golf, tennis, gardening, reading. Home: 2050 Table Rock Rd Boise ID 83712-6663 Office: City Hall 150 N Capitol Blvd Boise ID 83702-5920

**TERVALON, JOSEPHINE M.,** psychotherapist, social worker; b. Pender County, N.C., Oct. 9, 1939; d. Joseph Samuel and Dorothy Ann (Messick) Merritt; m. William F. Cunningham Jr. (div.); children: Charles F. Cunningham, Steven Troy Cunningham; m. Albert T. Tervalon, Mar. 20, 1999; stepchildren: Albert L. III, Mark, Brett, Tasha. BS, Tuskegee Inst., 1961; MSW, Smith Coll., 1963. Diplomate Am. Bd. Examiners in Clin. Social Work; LCSW Tex. State Bd. Examiners, cert. Registry of Cert. Group Psychotherapists N.Y., profl. coach Grow Tng. Inst. Sr. psychiatric social worker Cmty. Guidance Ctr., San Antonio; dir. outpatient svc., chief social worker San Antonio Children's Ctr.; program coord. adolescent ctr. Houston Internat. Hosp.; dir. social svcs., coord. adolescent unit W.Oaks Hosp., Houston; dir. unit programs Psychiatric Inst. Houston; pvt. practice Houston. Cons., Houston; practicum asst. prof. Worden Sch. Social Svcs., Our Lady of Lake U., 1975—80; clin. instr. Baylor Coll. Medicine, 1981—2000; adj. asst. prof. Smith Coll. Sch. Social Work, 1985—. Mem.: Nat. Assn. Female Exec. (workshop presenter 1990—92), Tex. Soc. Clin. Social Work (keynote spkr. 2001). Office: Cunningham Tervalon Assoc 4801 Woodway Dr Ste 350W Houston TX 77056

**TERWILLEGAR, JANE CUSACK,** librarian, educator; b. Warsaw, N.Y., Nov. 7, 1935; d. James Scott and Estella B. (Ackerman) Cusack; m. Gordon H. Terwillegar, July 26, 1958 (div. Mar. 1989); children: Sarah Ann Terwillegar Smedley, Arne Matthew. BA, Elmira Coll., NY, 1957; MLS, SUNY, Geneseo, 1960; EdS, U. Ga., 1977. Cert. tchr., Fla. Instr. U. Ga., Athens, 1975-81; libr. Palm beach County Libr., West Palm Beach, Fla., 1981-83, Palm Beach County Schs., Royal Palm Beach, Fla., 1983-94, dist. libr. media svcs. mgr. West Palm Beach, 1994—2000; dir. Lake Park Public Libr., 2000—. Lectr. Sch. Libr. and Info. Sci., U. South Fla., Tampa, 1987—; Nova U., Ft. Lauderdale, Fla., 1995—; task force mem. SUNLINK project Fla. Dept. Edn., 1995-2000; mem. adv. coun. Fla. Sch. and Tech. Act., 1999—. Co-author: Commonsense Cataloging, 3d edit. 1983, 4th edit. 1990; reviewer Sch. Libr. Jour., 1986—; contbr. articles to profl. jours. Pres. Staff Assn. Palm Beach Sch. Dist., 1997-99. Mem. ALA, AAUW (pres. No. Palm Beach br. 2001-05), Am. Assn. Sch. Librs. (exec. bd. 1990-94), Assn. for Libr. Svc. to Children (Newbery com. 1988-89), Fla. Assn. Media in Edn. (sec. 1988-89, bd. dirs. 1997—, pres. 1999-2001), Ednl. Media Assn. Fla. (pres. 1988), Kiwanis Club of Lake Park, Phi Beta Kappa, Phi Delta Kappa. Avocations: scuba diving, sports cars. Home: 911 Oak Harbour Dr Juno Beach FL 33408-2173 Office: Lake Park Public Libr 529 Park Ave West Palm Beach FL 33403- Office Phone: 561-881-3330.

**TERWILLIGER, J. RONALD,** real estate company executive; Grad., US Naval Acad.; MBA (hon.), Harvard U. Pres., COO Sea Pines Plantation Co., Hilton Head (S.C.) Plantation Co.; chmn., CEO Trammell Crow Residential, Atlanta, 1986—. Chmn. emeritus Wharton Real Estate Ctr.; mem. Fannie Mae Adv. Coun. Mem. internat. bd. dirs. Habitat for Humanity; vice chmn. Atlanta Neighborhood Devel. Partnership; dir. Naval Acad. Found. Baker scholar, Harvard Grad. Sch. Bus. Mem.: Real Estate Roundtable, Urban Land Inst. (immediate past chmn.). Office: Trammell Crow Residential Ste 1100 2859 Paces Ferry Rd Atlanta GA 30339

**TERZIAN, GRACE PAINE,** communications executive; b. Boston, Oct. 19, 1952; d. Thomas Fite and Grace Hillman (Benedict) Paine; m. Philip Henry Terzian, Oct. 20, 1979; children: William Thomas Hillman, Grace Benedict Paine. BA in Art History, Williams Coll., 1974. Art dir. The New Republic, Washington, 1976-78; asst. editor The Chronicle of Higher Edn., Washington, 1978-79; rsch. editor Archtl. Digest, L.A., 1982-85; pub The Women's Quar., Arlington, Va., 1994—2004; exec. dir. Allergy and Asthma Network Mothers of Asthmatics, 2004—06; v.p. for comm. Hudson Inst., 2006—. Editor Ex Femina, 1996—2004; sr. v.p. Ind. Women's Forum, 1998-2004. Mem. Soc.

Colonial Dames in Am., Phi Beta Kappa. Episcopalian. Home: 10505 Adel Rd Oakton VA 22124-1605 Office Phone: 202-974-2400. Personal E-mail: gterzian@cox.net. Business E-mail: gracet@hudson.org.

**TERZIAN, PHILIP HENRY,** journalist; b. Kensington, Md., July 5, 1950; s. L. A. and Louise (Anderson) Terzian; m. Grace Barrett Paine, Oct. 20, 1979; children: William Thomas Hillman, Grace Benedict Paine. BA in English, Villanova U., 1973; DTS, Episcopal Theol. Sem., Va., 1995; postgrad., Oxford (Eng.) U., 1976. Desk editor Reuters, Washington, 1973, U.S. News & World Report, Washington, 1973-74; asst. editor The New Republic, Washington, 1974-78; mem. policy planning staff Dept. State, Washington, 1978-79; asst. editor Anniston (Ala.) Star, 1979-80; assoc. editor Lexington (Ky.) Herald, 1980-82; asst. editor of editl. pages L.A. Times, 1982-86; editor of editl. pages Providence Jour., 1986-92, assoc. editor, syndicated columnist, 1992—2005; books and arts editor The Weekly Standard, Washington, 2005—. Panelist Washington Wk. in Rev., C-SPAN, Fox News, Nat. Pub. Radio. Contbr. articles to newspapers and jours. Pres. Providence Com. Fgn. Rels., 1989—92. Named finalist Disting. Commentary, Pulitzer Prize, 1991; recipient Edn. Writers award, Edn. Writers Am., 1981, Svc. to Preservation award, Ida Lee Willis Found., 1982, juror, Pulitzer Prize, 1994—95; Media fellow, Hoover Instn., Stanford U., 2002, 2004, 2005, 2006. Fellow: Am. Journalism Found.; mem.: Va. Hist. Soc., Am. Coun. on Germany, Assn. Literary Scholars and Critics, Order Hosp. St. John of Jerusalem, Soc. King Charles the Martyr, St. Andrew's Soc. Washington, Sons of Union Vets. of Civil War, Wolver Beagles (hon. whip), Univ. Club, Nat. Beagle Club. Republican. Episcopalian. Home: 10505 Adel Rd Oakton VA 22124-1605 Office: The Weekly Standard 1150 17th St NW Washington DC 20036 Office Phone: 202-293-4900. E-mail: pterzian@weeklystandard.com.

**TERZIC, PETAR,** mathematician, educator; b. Podgorica, Montenegro, Serbia-Monteneg (Yugoslavia), July 9, 1944; arrived in U.S., 1994; s. Vojin and Koviljka Terzic; m. Slavka Kaludjerovic, Jan. 28, 1950; children: Balsa, Katarina Terzic Conrad. BS, U. of Montenegro, Podgorica, 1974; MS, U. of Belgrade, Yugoslavia, 1985; MA, Liberty Theol. Sem., Lynchburg, Va., 2001; Bible cert., Liberty Bible Inst., Lynchburg, Va., 1996. Math. tchr. Dusan Vlahovic Agrl. H.S., Bar, Montenegro, 1973—74; instr. elec. engring. E. T. C. Nikola Tesla, Belgrade, 1974—80; comm. adminstr. City of Belgrade, 1980—90; profl. of elec. engring. Mil. Acad., Belgrade, Serbia, Yugoslavia, 1990—94; instr. of math. Liberty U., Lynchburg, 1997—. Author: (book) Einstein's Picture of the World, 1996, Philosophy of Nature, 1996, (5-vol. book) Famous Military Leaders of the World, 1992—93 (2nd Pl. award Internat. Book Fair, Belgrade, 1993). Recipient Recognition for excellence in tchg., State of Montenegro, 1974, 2nd Pl. award at the European Vet.'s Athletic Competition, European Recreation Assn., 1989, 3rd Pl. award at the amateur chess competition in Belgrade, Chess Assn. of Belgrade, 1977, 1st Pl. award in shot put in the jr. competition, Athletic Assn. of Montenegro, 1961. Mem.: Am. Math. Assn., Nikola Tesla Amateur Radio Club (bd. dirs. 1980—90). Avocation: recreation. Office: Liberty U 1971 University Blvd Lynchburg VA 24506 Office Phone: 434-582-2199. Personal E-mail: pterzic@liberty.edu.

**TESAR, JENNY ELIZABETH,** freelance/self-employed writer, freelance/self-employed editor; b. Rockville Centre, NY, Mar. 24, 1937; d. Joseph Anthony and Mary Elizabeth (Schedlbower) T. BS, Cornell U., 1959; MS, Oreg. State U., 1964. Sci. tchr. Oceanside (N.Y.) Pub. Schs., 1959-60; sci. tchr., chmn. sci. dept. Monterey (Calif) Pub. Schs., 1960-65; editor Grolier Inc., N.Y.C., 1969-74; mng. editor The Stonehouse Press, N.Y.C., 1975-77; founding editor Columbia Today Simmons-Boardman, N.Y.C., 1975-77; freelance writer and editor Tesar Communications, N.Y.C., 1977-80, Bethel, Conn., 1980—. Cons. product devel. Program Design, Inc., Greenwich, Conn., 1979-83; cons. sci. Sci. Rsch. Assocs., 1977, cons. product devel. Sci. Pub, 1985—. Author: Introduction to Animals, 1980, Preparing for the SAT and Other Aptitude Tests, 1982, Parents as Teachers, 1987, Scientific Crime Investigation, 1991, Global Warming, 1991, The Waste Crisis, 1991, Shrinking Forests, 1991, Endangered Habitats, 1992, Threatened Oceans, 1991, Food and Water: Threats, Shortages and Solutions, 1992, Green Plants, 1993, Insects, 1993, Mammals, 1993, The New Webster's Computer Handbook, 1993, Spiders, 1993, Fungi, 1994, Humans, 1994, Patterns in Nature, 1994, What on Earth...is a Booby?, 1994, What on Earth...is a Meerkat?, 1994, What on Earth...is a Sea Squirt?, 1994, What on Earth...is a Tuatara?, 1994, The New View Almanac, 1995, What on Earth...is an Echidna?, 1995, What on Earth...is a Nudibranch?, 1995, America's Top Ten Cities, 1997, America's Top Ten Mountains, 1997, America's Top Ten Natural Curiosities, 1997, America's Top Ten National Parks, 1997, America's Top Ten Rivers, 1997, What on Earth...is a Bustard?, 1997, What on Earth...is a Quokka?, 1997, The Moon, 1998, The Planets, 1998, Space Travel, 1998, The Sun, 1998, Kidbits, 1999, Science on the Edge-Stem Cells, 2003; co-author: America's Top 100, 2000, The Penguin Desk Encyclopedia of Science and Mathematics, 2000, The Blackbirch Encyclopedia of Science and Invention, 2001, Discover Science Almanac, 2003; author (software) Alphabet Arcade (Arcade awards cert. of merit 1983), others; contbr. articles jours. Bd. dirs. Chestnut Hill Village Assn., Bethel, 1981—; bd. dirs. Friends of Bethel Pub. Libr., 1995—. Mem. Nat. Assn. Sci. Writers, Cornell Assn. Class Officers (class of 1959 officer 1972—), Toastmasters (pres. West-Conn. chpt. 1988). Avocations: music, travel, photography. Office: Tesar Communications 97 A Chestnut St Bethel CT 06801-2663 Office Phone: 203-792-8237. Business E-Mail: jet24@cornell.edu.

**TESAREK, DENNIS GEORGE,** retired business consultant, writer, educator; b. Chgo., Jan. 2, 1935; s. George Joseph and Mary (Basl) T.; m. Caroline Arrena Myers, Jan. 1956 (div. Oct. 1968); children: William Paul, Dianne, Peter Bond; m. Kathleen Leigh Holm, Nov. 26, 1969; children: Philip Shawn, Leigh-Anne. BA in Math., U. Mo., 1956; postgrad., Systems Rsch. Inst., 1966, UCLA, 1984, Harvard U., 1985, MIT, 1986. Saleman Conn. Mut. Life Ins. Co., Dallas, 1959-61; systems engr. IBM, Phoenix, 1961-66, instr. L.A., 1966-68, mgr. Houston, 1968-74, industry mgr. White Plains, NY, 1974-76, project mgr. L.A., 1976-78, planning cons. Houston, 1978-84, cons. in bus. transformation, planning and gen. mgmt., 1984-97; owner Tesarek Enterprises (Consulting and Investments), 1997—. Adj. prof. Ariz. State U., 1963-65; guest lectr. U. Houston, 1980, 81, 83, 87. Author: Distributed Information Systems Planning Methodology, 1982, Information Systems Management Effectiveness Assessment, 1983, Business Systems Planning for Competitive Advantage Methodology, 1986, Executive Strategy Session Methodology, 1987, Management Planning Session Methodology, 1987, Steps in Strategic Investment Methodology, 1989. Tutor Vols. in Pub. Schs., Houston Ind. Sch. Dist., 1972-74, 80-82. 1st lt. USMC, 1956-59. Republican. Mem. Christian Sci. Ch. Avocations: color photography and printing, wood working, reading, jogging. E-mail: dtesarek@earthlink.net.

**TESCHNER, DOUGLASS PAUL,** project administrator; b. Cambridge, Mass., Oct. 29, 1949; s. Douglass P. Teschner and Mary Elizabeth (Bernt) Teschner Zeller; m. Martha Weaver, Sept. 26, 1981. BS in Forestry, U. Mass., 1971, EdD in Adminstrn., 1985; MS in Botany, U. Vt., 1978. Land surveyor Lincoln Engring. and Burnell Land Surveying, 1974, 78; tchr. White Mountain Sch., 1976; dir. Inst. Exptl. Studies, various locations, 1984-87; fin. officer Becket Acad., East Haddam, Conn., 1984-85; project dir. Riverbend Cmty. Mental Health, Concord, 1987—2002; state rep. N.H. Ho. of Reps., Concord, 1988—88, 2000—02; project dir. Rwanda Parliament Support Project, Kigali, 2002—04; project dir. Morocco Parliament Support Project USAID, 2004—. Co-editor: Wilderness Challenge: Outdoor Education Alternatives for Youth in Need, 1984; contbr. articles to profl. jours. Mem. Haverhill Hist. Soc.; vol. Peace Corps, 1971-73, Haverhill Congl. Ch. Mem.: Appalachian Mountain Club. Avocations: mountain climbing, hiking, rock and ice climbing, skiing. Home: 2100 Brushwood Rd Pike NH 03780-9706

**TESELLE, EUGENE ARTHUR, JR.,** religion educator; b. Ames, Iowa, Aug. 8, 1931; s. Eugene Arthur and Hildegarde (Flynn) TeS.; m. Sallie McFague, Sept. 12, 1959 (div. Oct. 1976); children: Elizabeth, John; m. Penelope Saunders, Mar. 4, 1978; children: William, James, Thomas. BA, U. Colo., 1952; BD, Princeton Theol. Sem., 1955; MA, Yale U., 1960, PhD,

1963. Commr. to gen. assembly Presbyn. Ch. in U.S.A., 1993. Issues analyst Witherspoon Soc., 1987-93, 99—, pres., 1996-99; chmn. global missions com. Presbytery Mid. Tenn., 1989-93, mem. nominating com., 2002-05. Author: Augustine, the Theologian, 1970, Augustine's Strategy as an Apologist, 1974, Christ in Context, 1975, Thomas Aquinas: Faith and Reason, 1988, Living in Two Cities: Augustinian Trajectories in Political Thought, 1998. Incorporator Belmont-Hillsboro Neighbors, Nashville, 1971, Consumer Coalition for Health, Nashville, 1980, Nashville Local, Dem. Socialists Am., 1983, Cen. Am. Solidarity Assn., Nashville, 1986. Presbyn. Grad. fellow, 1958, Rockefeller doctoral fellow, 1960, Kent fellow, 1961; recipient Thomas Jefferson award Vanderbilt U., 1996. Mem. Am. Acad. Religion, Am. Soc. Ch. History, Soc. for Values in Higher Edn., Workgroup on Constructive Christian Theology, Witherspoon Soc. (pres. 1995—99), Phi Beta Kappa. Home: 2007 Linden Ave Nashville TN 37212-5021 Personal E-mail: teselle@bellsouth.net.

**TESH, ROBERT BRADFIELD,** epidemiologist, educator; s. Robert Christian and Edith Bradfield Tesh; m. Hilda Guzman; children: Diana, Carolyn, Natalia. BS, Franklin Marshall Coll., 1957; MD, Jefferson U., 1961; MS, Tulane U., 1967. George Dock disting. prof. pathology UTMB. Intern San Francisco (Calif.) Gen. Hosp., 1961—62; resident in pediats. Gorgas Hosp., Canal Zone, Panama, 1962—63; physician Peace Corps. USPH, Recife, Brazil, 1963—65; fellow infectious diseases Tulane U., New Orleans, 1965—67; head Epidemiology Unit Mid. Am. Rsch. Unit, Canal Zone, 1967—72; rsch. physician Pacific Rsch. Unit, Honolulu, 1973—80; from assoc. prof. to prof. Med. Sch. Yale U., New Haven, 1980—95, prof., 1995, U. Tex. Med. Br., Galveston, Tex., 1995—. Mem. adv. com. Am. Type Culture Collection, Manassas, Va., NIH, USAID; cons. Pan Am. Health Org., Washington. Mem. editl. bd.: Am. Jour. Tropical Medicine and Hygiene, 1990—, Vector-Borne and Zoonotic Diseases, 2001—; contbr. articles to profl. jours. Fellow: AAAS. Avocations: travel, swimming, history. Office: Dept Pathology Univ Texas Med Branch 301 University Blvd Galveston TX 77555-0609 Office Phone: 409-747-2431. Business E-Mail: rtesh@utmb.edu.

**TESK, JOHN ALOYSIUS,** materials scientist; b. Chgo., Oct. 19, 1934; s. John August and Theresa Mary (Mattea) T.; m. Regina Sophia Budzyn, Dec. 10, 1960; 1 child, John A.W. BS in Engring. Sci., Northwestern U., 1957, MS in Metallurgy, 1960, PhD in Materials Sci., 1963. Asst. prof. U. Ill., Chgo., 1964-67; cons. Argonne (Ill.) Nat. Lab., 1964-67, asst. metallurgist, 1967-70; dir. rsch. Dental, Howmedica Inc., Chgo., 1970-77; dir. edn. svcs. Inst. Gas. Tech., Chgo., 1977-78; gen. phys. scientist, group leader, biomaterials coord. polymers divsn., sr. tech. advisor, indsl. liaison dir.'s office Nat. Inst. Stds. & Tech., Gaithersburg, Md., 1978—2005; cons. in biomed. materials and devices, 2005—. Mem. bioengineered materials applications bd. Nat. Acads., 2001-03; cons. Dentsply Internat., York, Pa., 1977-78; mem. review bd. Dental Sch. Case Western Res. U., Cleve., 1987-88, Biomaterials Program, Clemson U., 1972-74, Dental Sch., Tokushima U., Japan, 1997; mem. orthopaedic adv. bd. Clemson U., 1999-2001; mem. adv. bd. Industry/Univ. Ctr. of NSF, U. Buffalo, 2002-03; chmn. dental stds. ADA, Chgo., 1980-86; leader U.S. Del. Internat. Stds. Orgn., 1980-86; organizer confs. Holder 8 patents; mem. editl. bd. Jour. Dental Materials, 1988-91, Jour. Oral Implantology, 1984-2000, Biomaterials Forum, 1996—2005, Applied Biomaterials, 1998—; mem. editl. rev. bd. Nat. Inst. Stds. and Tech., 1996-2001; contbr. chpts. to books, articles to profl. jours. Mem. bldg. com. Divine Savior Parish, Downers Grove, Ill., 1971-72; chmn. troop 737 Cub Scouts, Highland, Md., 1980; adult supr. youth group Saint Louis Parish, Highland, 1982-83. Fellow Acad. Dental Materials (exec. com. 1987-94); mem. ASTM (exec. com. 2000—), Am. Phys. Soc., Am. Soc. Metals (exec. com. Chgo. chpt. 1964-67, 78), Biomaterials Soc. (founding mem., charter, nominating com. 1987, 96, editl. bd. Applied Biomaterials 1998—, stds. com. 1995—2004, contbg. editor Biomaterials Forum, co-chmn. reference materials/reference data com., coun. 1996-2003, liaison com. 1996-98, program com. 1999), Internat. Assn. Dental Rsch. (treas. dental materials group 1987-94), Tech. Materials Soc. (exec. com. Chgo chpt. 1965), Japanese Soc. for Dental Materials (hon.). Roman Catholic. Avocations: gardening, boating, travel, walking. Home: 6759 Cortina Dr Highland MD 20777-9501 Office: Nat Inst Stds & Tech Rm A143 Bldg 224 Gaithersburg MD 20899-0001 Office Phone: 301-854-9727. Personal E-mail: jatesk@erols.com. Business E-Mail: john.tesk@nist.gov.

**TESKE, RACHEL,** professional golfer; b. Port Macquarie, Australia, Apr. 23, 1972; m. Teske Dean Teske, May 22, 1998. Attended, Fla. State U. Winner First Union Betsy King Classic, 1998, Chick-fil-A Charity Championship, 1999, City of Hope Myrtle Beach Classic, 1999, Evian Masters, 2001, PING Banner Health, 2002, Jamie Farr Kroger Classic, 2002, Giant Eagle LPGA Classic, 2003, Wegmans Rochester LPGA, 2003; second place finish British Open, 2004, Australian Open, 2004. Winner New South Wales Jr. Championships, 1989, 90, 91, 92; mem. Australian Tasman Cup Team, 1989, 91, 93; winner NSW Amateur Open, 1992. Avocations: music, movies, hiking. Office: c/o LPGA 100 International Golf Dr Daytona Beach FL 32124-1092

**TESMER, NANCY ANN STUTLER,** retired librarian; b. Aug. 25, 1934; d. Ernest Lynn and Sophrona Rebecca (Pepper) Stutler; m. John A. Tesmer, Sept. 10, 1980. Student, U. Akron, 1952—54; BA, Kent State U., 1956. Jr. asst. libr. E. Br. Libr., Akron, 1956—59; hosp. libr. VA Hosp., Northampton, Mass., 1959—61, med. libr. Brecksville, Ohio, 1961—65, chief libr., 1965—73, assoc. chief libr. Cleve., 1973—75, chief libr., 1975—. Chief Regional Libr. Svc., 1986—90. Mem.: N.E. Ohio Med. Libr. Assn., Med. Libr. Assn., Zeta Tau Alpha. Home: 8537 SW 90th Pl Unit G Ocala FL 34481-7516 E-mail: nst0825@aol.com.

**TESON, FERNANDO ROBERTO,** law educator, consultant; b. Buenos Aires, Aug. 3, 1950; s. Roberto Julio and Marta (Grun) T.; m. Maria Teresa Martinez, Nov. 11, 1976 (div. Feb. 1992); children: Fernando, Marcelo; m. Bettina C. Rauleder, Oct. 11, 1996; 1 child, Carolina. Grad., U. Buenos Aires, 1975; lic. internat. law, U. Libre de Bruxelles, Brussels, 1982; SJD, Northwestern U., 1987. Assoc. prof. law Ariz. State U., Tempe, 1984-88, prof. law, 1988—2002; prof. Fla. State U. Sch. Law, Tallahassee, 2002—. Vis. prof. San Diego Summer Program, Mex., 1987, Dublin, Ireland, 1988, Paris, 1990, 93, Hastings Law Sch., San Francisco, Spring 1990, Cardozo Law Sch., N.Y.C., Fall 1992, Ind. U., Bloomington, Spring 1993, Cornell U., Ithaca, N.Y., 1994-95; permanent vis. prof. Di Tella U., Buenos Aires, 1996—; career diplomate Argentina Govt., Buenos Aires, 1977-81; prof. George Washington/Oxford U. Internat. Human Rights Program, New College, Oxford, 1999, 2001. Author: A Philosophy of International Law, Humanitarian Intervention: An Inquiry into Law and Morality, 3rd edit.; contbr. articles to profl. jours. James N. Raymond fellow Northwestern U., 1982-83; Tobias Simon Eminent scholar Fla. State U. Sch. Law, 2002. Mem. Am. Soc. Internat. Law, Am. Soc. Social and Polit. Philosophy. Avocations: music, bridge, food. Office: Fla State U Coll of Law Tallahassee FL 32306-1601 Office Phone: 850-644-4287.

**TESORI, JEANINE,** composer; b. 1961; m. Michael Rafter; 1 child. Composer: (Broadway plays) How to Succeed in Business Without Really Trying, 1995, Violet, 1997, Dream, 1997, Twelfth Night, 1998 (Tony nom. best original musical score, 1999), Swing!, 1999, Thoroughly Modern Millie, 2002 (Tony nom. best original musical score, 2002), Caroline, or Change, 2004 (Tony nom. best original musical score, 2004, Drama Desk award best musical score, 2004, Obie award, 2004). Office: Eugene O'Neill Theatre 230 W 49th St New York NY 10019

**TESSEMA, GEORGE,** mathematician, educator; b. Addis Ababa, Ethiopia, May 20, 1942; arrived in U.S., 1985; s. Tessema Garedew and Woodnesh Tessema; m. Tafesech Mengistu; children: Thomas, Michael. BSc, Addis Ababa U., Ethiopia, 1966; MSc, Fla. State U., Tallahassee, Fla., 1970; PhD, SUNY, Albany, N.Y., 1991. Tchr. math. Ras Darghe H.S., Assela, Ethiopia, 1967—70; prof. math. Ketobe Coll. Tchr. Edn., Addis Ababa, 1971—85, Armstrong Atlantic State U., Savannah, Ga., 1993—94, Savannah State U., 1994—, coord., 1994—. Mem.: Am. Math. Assn. Avocations: walking, ping pong/table tennis, soccer, reading. Office: Savannah State Univ Savannah GA 31404

**TESSENEER-STREET, SUSAN,** photographer, artist, writer; b. Murray, Ky., Dec. 14, 1939; d. Ralph Athen and Susan Geneva (Kirkland) Tesseneer; m. Robert Beni Street Sr., Jan. 16, 1939 (div.); children: Robert Beni II, Ralph Calvin Sr. Student, Blue Mountain Coll. for Women, 1959—61, Memphis State U., 1963—66; BA, S.E. Mo. U., 1974; student, Harvard U., 2002. Tchr., 1974-79; bus. owner, 1977-85; writer, 1984-86; photographer, 1990—; artist, 1998—. Author: (book) Gift in Celebration of Women. Mem. Sikeston Art League, 1980—, pres., 1990-94; sec., treas., organizer Cmty. Concert, Sikeston, 1989. Mem. AAUW (charter), Profl. Photographers Am., Am. Soc. Portrait Artists, Hemingway Soc., Nat. Writers Club, Women in the Arts (charter), Am. Soc. Portrait Painters, Impressionist Soc., Nat. Writers Assn., Hemingway Soc., Nat. Assn. Women Writers, Nat. Women's History Mus. (charter).

**TESSER, DOROTHY,** artist; b. Bklyn., Mar. 11, 1926; d. Max and Ethel Weber; m. Jack Tesser, Oct. 12, 1947; children: Clifford Charles(dec.), Jean Karasic, Barbara Campbell. Degree in graphic art, Pratt Inst.; cert. art therapist, New Sch. U., 1983. Artist Famous Studios, N.Y.C.; owner, artist and prodr. D&J Films Animation, N.Y.C.; freelance artist All Animation Studios, N.Y.C.; art dir. D&R Animation, N.Y.C., Storyboard, N.Y.C. N.J. Ctr. Healing Arts, Freehold Area Hosp. Pediat. Ward; author: (biography) Darkness to Light (subtitle) Drawing from Pain, 2002. Mem.: Ladies Aux. War Vets. (pres. 2001—03, v.p., Pres. of Yr. award 2001—02). Mailing: 525 Ocean Blvd Apt 307 Long Branch NJ 07740-8910

**TESSIER-LAVIGNE, MARC TREVOR,** neurobiologist, researcher; b. Trenton, Ont., Can., Dec. 18, 1959; arrived in US, 1987; s. Yves Jacques and Sheila Christine (Midgley) Tessier-L.; m. Mary Alanna Hynes, Feb. 4, 1989; children: Christian, Kyle, Ella. BSc, McGill U., 1980; BA, Oxford U., 1982; PhD, U. London, 1986. Exec. dir. Can. Student Pugwash Orgn., Ottawa, Ont., 1982-83; rsch. fellow devel. neurobiology unit Med. Rsch. Coun., London, 1986-87; rsch. fellow Ctr. for Neurobiology, Columbia U., N.Y.C., 1987-91; asst. prof. dept. anatomy U. Calif., San Francisco, 1991-95, assoc. prof. dept. anatomy, 1995-97, prof. dept. anatomy and dept. biochemistry and biophysics, 1997—2000; Susan B. Ford prof. dept. biol. scis. Sch. Humanities and Scis. Stanford U., 2000—03; sr. v.p. rsch. drug discovery Genentech Inc., 2003—. Asst. investigator Howard Hughes Med. Inst., 1994-97; investigator Howard Hughes Med. Inst., 1997—. Contbr. articles on neurobiology to profl. jours. Recipient McKnight Investigator award, 1994, Karl Judson Herrick award for comparative neurology Am. Assn. Anatomists, 1994, Ameritec prize for significant contbn. in basic rsch. towards cure for paralysis, 1995, Ipsen prize for neuronal plasticity, 1996, Viktor Hamburger award in devel. neurobiology Internat. Jour. Devel. Neurosci., Young Investigator award Soc. for Neurosci., 1997, Wakeman award, 1998, Rober Dow award, 2003; Rhodes scholar, 1980, Commonwealth scholar, 1983, Markey scholar, 1989, Searle scholar, 1991, McKnight scholar, 1991; Klingenstein fellow, 1992. Fellow: AAAS, Royal Soc. of Can., The Royal Soc. (London); mem.: NAS, Soc. for Neuroscience (nominating com. 2000—02). Office: Genentech Inc 1 DNA Way South San Francisco CA 94080-4990

**TESSING, LOUISE SCIRE,** graphic designer; b. Chgo., May 13, 1946; d. Rocco Roy and Ruth Louise (Knueppel) Scire; m. Arvid Victor Tessing, Jan. 18, 1975. BS in Visual Design, Ill. Inst. Tech., 1968; MBA in Mktg., Loyola U., Chgo., 1986. Jr. designer Field Mus. Natural History, Chgo., 1968—69, Charles MacMurray & Assocs., Chgo., 1969—74; designer, art dir. Grant-Jacoby Inc., Chgo., 1974—76, Playboy Enterprises Inc., Chgo., 1976—78, Stevens Biondi Decicco Inc., Chgo., 1978—80; prin., owner Tessing Design Inc., Chgo., 1980—. Lobby treas. Ill. Women's Agenda, Chgo., 1990-92. Mem.: Soc. Typographic Arts (v.p. 2000—05), Internat. Assn. Bus. Communicators (v.p. comm. and design 1998—2002), Am. Ctr. for Design (bd. dirs. 1971—77, pres. 1976—77), Women in Design Chgo. (founder 1977, pres. 1977—78, 1991—93, Friend award 1990, Founder award 1997). Home and Office: Tessing Design Inc 3822 N Seeley Ave Chicago IL 60618-3912 Office Phone: 773-525-7704. E-mail: tess46@comcast.net.

**TESSMAN, WES,** secondary school educator; b. Grand Rapids, Minn., Aug. 24, 1956; s. Wes and Sonia Tessman; m. Toni Murray Tessman; children: Amy, Kelly, Wes. AAS, Itasca CC, Grand Rapids, Minn., 0976; BS, Bemidji State U., Minn., 1979; MEd, S.W. State U., Marshall, Minn., 2000. Social studies tchr. Amboy-Good Thunder Sch. Dist., Amboy, Minn., Graceville Sch. Dist., Esko Sch. Dist., St. Louis County Schs., Orr, Minnewaska Area Schs., Glenwood. Mem.: NEA, Minn. Wrestling Coaches Assn., Nat. Coun. Social Studies, Minnewaska Tchrs.' Assn., Minn. Edn. Assn. Office: Minnewaska Area HS 25122 State Hwy 28 Glenwood MN 56334

**TESTA, JOSEPH R.,** cytogeneticist; b. Norwalk, Conn., Apr. 28, 1947; PhD, Fordham U., 1976. Diplomate Am. Bd. Clin. Cytogenetics. With tumor cytogenetics U. Chgo., 1976-80; sr. geneticist Fox Chase Cancer Ctr., Phila., dir. sect. molecular cytogenetics, dir. Human Genetics Program. Mem. AAAS, ASGH, Am. Assn. Cancer Rsch., Am. Soc. Hematology. Office: Fox Chase Cancer Ctr 333 Cottman Ave Philadelphia PA 19111-2497 Office Phone: 215-728-2610. Fax: 215-214-1623. E-mail: Joseph.Testa@fccc.edu.*

**TESTA, MICHAEL HAROLD,** lawyer; b. NYC, 1939; m. Carol Waldenberg, 1962; 2 children. BS summa cum laude, NYU, 1958, LLB cum laude, 1961, LLM in Taxation, 1967. Bar: NY 1961. Assoc. White & Case, N.Y.C., 1962-71, Skadden, Arps, Slate, Meagher & Flom, N.Y.C., 1971-72, ptnr., 1972-91; conservation lawyer, sole practitioner Michael H. Testa, N.Y.C., 1992—. Advisor U.S. del. to UN Conf. on Straddling Fish Stocks and Highly Migratory Fish Stocks, 1994-95, U.S. del. to Kyoto Internat. Conf. on Sustainable Contribution of Fisheries to Food Security, 1995, to N.W. Atlantic Fisheries Orgn., 1996, 98, to 22d Session of FAO Com. on Fisheries, 1997, to Western and Ctrl. Pacific Fisheries Conf., 1998-2001; adj. assoc. prof. law NYU Law Sch., 1986; mem. consultative com. to secs. state and commerce N.W. Atlantic Fisheries Conv., 1996-2002. Assoc. editor, contbr.: NYU Law Rev., 1960-61; contbr. articles to legal jours. Mem. planning bd. Town of Tuxedo (N.Y.), 1971-76. Served to capt. USAFR, 1961-72. Root-Tilden-Snow scholar, 1958-61. Mem. Order of Coif. Home: 860 UN Plz New York NY 10017 Office: Ste 28-424 4 Times Square New York NY 10036-6522

**TESTA, SHEILA M.,** manufacturing executive; MBA, Harvard U., Cambridge, Mass. Prin. Tex. Transaction Mgmt. Co., Fair Winds Corp., Houston, 1990—. Chpt. 11 trustee, 1997-99; pres., CEO Bristol Resources Corp., 2000. Mailing: PO Box 27433 Houston TX 77227 Office Phone: 713-409-4933. E-mail: sheilamtesta@yahoo.com.

**TESTAVERDE, VINCENT FRANK (VINNY TESTAVERDE),** professional football player; b. Bklyn., Nov. 13, 1963; m. Mitzi Testaverde; children: Alicia Marie, Vincent Jr. Student, U. Miami, Fla. Quarterback Tampa Bay (Fla.) Buccaneers, 1987—92, Cleve. Browns, 1993—95, Balt. Ravens, 1996—98, N.Y. Jets, Hempstead, NY, 1998—2004, 2005—, Dallas Cowboys, 2004. Named Coll. Football Player of Yr., The Sporting News, 1986; named to NFL Pro-Bowl, 1996, 1998; recipient Heisman trophy, 1986. Achievements include Passing for over 40,000 yards.*

**TESTER, LEONARD WAYNE,** psychology professor; b. Nampa, Idaho, Aug. 21, 1933; s. Walter Vernon and Dora Dorothy (Peters) T. BTh, Kansas City Coll., 1957; MA, Abilene Christian Coll. (now Abilene Christian U.), 1961; STB, Harvard U., 1969; EdM, Columbia U., 1971, EdD, 1976, MPhil, 1979, PhD, 1981. Lic. psychologist, N.Y. 1983. Mgr. pers. Boston Safe Deposit & Trust Co., 1966—69; adj. instr. clin. counseling N.Y. Inst. Tech., Westbury, 1971—80, adj. assoc. prof., 1980—84, sr. counselor, 1980—92, assoc. prof., 1984—92, prof., 1992—, prof., chmn. 1992—95. Cons., grad. asst. Bus. Sch. and Tchrs. Coll. Columbia U. 1977-81. Contbr. articles to profl. jours.; presenter workshops in field. Founder, convenor Spiritual-Growth Ctr. (formerly Earth-Human Ctr.), N.Y.C.; exec. dir. Ho. of Carpenter, Boston, 1967-68; bd. dirs. Pierre (S.D.) Coun. of Arts, Counseling Ctr. Episcopal Ch., Great Neck, N.Y., Tech. Sch. N.Y.C. William Wayne Jackson honors scholar Harvard Div. Sch. Fellow Am. Orthopsychiat. Assn.; mem. APA, N.Y. Soc. Clin. Psychologists, N.Y. Soc. Hypnosis and Psychotherapy Home: PO Box 20107 New York NY 10023-1477 Office: NY Inst Tech 1855 Broadway New York NY 10023-7692

**TESTY, KELLYE,** dean; BA cum laude, Ind. U., 1982; JD grad. minor in Women's Studies, Ind. U. Sch. Law, 1991. Clk. to Hon. Jesse E. Eschbach US Ct. Appeals (7th Cir.); prof. Seattle U. Sch. Law, 1992—, Patricia Wismer prof., 2001—03, dean, 2005—. Lectr. in field; co-founder Access to Justice Inst.; founding adv. Seattle Jour. Social Justice. Editor-in-chief Ind. Law Jour. John H. Edwards Fellow, Chancellor's Scholar. Mem.: Order Coif. Office: Seattle U Sch Law Office of Dean 901 12th Ave PO Box 222000 Seattle WA 98122-1090 Office Phone: 206-398-4309. E-mail: ktesty@seattleu.edu.

**TETER, HANNAH,** Olympic athlete; b. Belmont, VT, Jan. 27, 1987; Profl. snowboarder Burton Snowboarding team, 2002—; snowboarder US Olympic Team, Torino, Italy, 2006. Named Competitor of the Yr., N.A. Snowsports Journalists Assoc., 2004; recipient Winner Halfpipe Event, World Cup, 2003, 2004, 2005, Halfpipe award, Vans Triph Crown, 2003, 2004, 2005, ESPY award Best Female Action Sports Athlete, 2006. Achievements include halfpipe Jr. World Champion, 2002; winner, World halfpipe Championship, 2003-2004, Vans Triple Crown halfpipe, 2003, US Snowboard Overall Grand Prix Champion, 2004; winner, Gold Medal, Winter X Games, 2004; winner, Gold Medal, halfpipe, Torino Olympic Games, 2006. Office: c/o USOC 1 Olympic Plaza Colorado Springs CO 80909

**TETHER, ANTHONY JOHN,** aerospace executive; b. Middletown, N.Y., Nov. 28, 1941; s. John Arthur and Antoinette Rose (Gesualdo) T.; m. Nancy Engle Pierson, Dec. 27, 1963 (div. July 1971); 1 child, Jennifer; m. Carol Suzanne Dunbar, Mar. 3, 1973; 1 child, Michael. AAS, Orange County C.C., N.Y., 1961; BS, Rensselaer Poly Inst., 1963; MSEE, Stanford (Calif.) U., 1965, PhD, 1969. V.p., gen. mgr. Sys. Control Inc., Palo Alto, Calif., 1968-78; dir. nat. intelligence Office Sec. of Def., Washington, 1978-82; dir. strategic tech. DARPA, Washington, 1982-86; corp. v.p. Ford Aerospace, Newport Beach, Calif., 1986-90, LORAL, Newport Beach, 1990-92; corp. v.p., gen. mgr. Sci. Application Internat., Inc., San Diego, 1992-94; CEO Dynamics Tech. Inc., Torrance, Calif., 1994-96; CEO, pres. Sequoia Group, Newport Beach, Calif., 1996-2001; dir. def. advanced rsch. project agy. Office of Sec. of Def., Washington, 2001—. Bd. dirs. Condyne Tech., Inc., Orlando, Fla., 1990—92, chmn., 1990—92; dir. Orincon, La Jolla, Calif., 1996—99, Evans & Sutherland, Salt Lake City, 2001; mem. def. sci. bd. Army Sci. Bd. Task Forces, 1998—2002; cons. Army Sci. Bd., Def. Sci. Bd. Contbr. articles to profl. jours.; mem. editl. adv. bd. Scientific American. Recipient Nat. Intelligence medal DCI, 1986, Civilian Meritorious medal U.S. Sec. Def., 1986. Mem. IEEE, Cosmos Club, Sigma Xi, Eta Kappa Nu, Tau Beta Pi. Avocations: amateur radio, skiing, golf. Home: 6400 Lyric Ln Falls Church VA 22044 Personal E-mail: ttether@aol.com.

**TETI, LOUIS NICHOLAS,** lawyer; b. Bryn Mawr, Pa., May 29, 1950; BA, Dickinson Coll., 1972; JD, Temple U., 1976, LLM in Taxation, 1981. Bar: Pa. 1976. Ptnr. MacElree Harvey, Ltd., West Chester and Kennett Square, Pa. Mem. disciplinary bd. Supreme Ct. Pa., 2000-, chair, 2004-05. Fellow Am. Coll. Trust and Estate Counsel; mem. ABA (ho. dels. 1985-91, 99-2001), Pa. Bar Assn. (young lawyers divsn. 1982-85, 91-94, 97-2001, pres. 1999-2000), Chester County Bar Assn. (sec. 1979-82, 86-88, v.p. 1989, pres.-elect 1990, pres. 1991, chair young lawyers sect. 1977, bd. dirs. 1977-92), Chester County Estate Planning Coun. (pres. 1988-89). Office: MacElree Harvey Ltd 17 W Miner St PO Box 660 West Chester PA 19381-0660 Fax: 610-429-4486. Office Phone: 610-840-0300. E-mail: lteti@macelree.com.

**TETOR, DAVID R.,** agriculturist, consultant; b. Montour Falls, N.Y., Dec. 16, 1943; s. Donald Booth and Margaret Eva (Howell) Tetor; m. Louise Anne Weeks, Apr. 23, 1966; children: Brian David, Michael James, Eric John. BS, Cornell U., 1965. Cert. pesticide applicator/trainer N.Y. Dept. Environ. Conservation. Student trainee USDA Soil Conservation Svc., summers, 1962—64, soil scientist Rochester, NY, 1965; systems analyst Cornell Coop. Ext., Ithaca, NY, 1970; agr. program leader Herkimer (N.Y.) County Cornell Coop. Ext., 1970—72, Dutchess County Cornell Coop. Ext., Millbrook, NY, 1972—2000. Agr. cons.; pres. N.Y. State Assn. County Agrl. Agts., NY, 1972—, Cornell Coll. Agr. Alumni, Ithaca, NY, 1990—2000; co-chair Dutchess County Tourism Bd., Poughkeepsie, NY, 1998—2000. Treas. adv. bd. Pine Plains Future Farmers Am., 1976—; supr. Town of Stanford, NY, 1992—95; pres. Pine Plains (N.Y.) Sch. Bd., 1982—87; bd. dirs. Dutchess County Indsl. Devel. Agy., Poughkeepsie, 1990—, Stanford Town Bd., 2002—; mem. coun. Cornell U., 2002—. Capt. U.S. Army, 1965—69. Named Outstanding Young Agt., Nat. Assn. County Agrl. Agts., 1979; named to Alumni Honor Roll, SUNY, 2000; recipient Disting. Svc. award, Nat. Assn. County Agrl. Agts., 1984, Outstanding Alumni award, Coll. of Agr. and Life Scis., Cornell U., 2002. Mem.: Dutchess County Farm Bur. (bd. dirs. 1990—), Dutchess County Agrl. Soc., N.Y. State Agrl. Soc. (bd. dirs. 2002—), Grange. Republican. Avocations: attending NASCAR races, coin collecting/numismatics, stamp collecting/philately, camping. Home: 5626 Rt 82 Clinton Corners NY 12514 Office: Dave Tetor Agr Cons PO Box 46 Stanfordville NY 12581

**TETTE, SHARAN FLYNN,** writer; b. PennYan, NY; d. Howard Paul Flynn and Margaret Louise Ansley; m. James Patrick Tette; children: Mark Patrick, Monica Helene, Matthew Raymon. BA cum laude, Nazareth Coll. Rochester, 1959—63. Elem. tchr. Blessed Sacrament Sch., Kenmore, NY, 1963—64; motivational spkr., libr. aid Gorham Free Libr., 1980—90; freelance writer. Contbr. articles. Chmn. Operation Merry Christmas, Geneva, NY, 1972; parish coun. mem. St. Michael's Ch., Penn Yan, NY, 2003; founding mem., bd. mem. Geneva Ctr. of Concern, 1973; bd. mem. United Cmty. Coalition, Geneva, NY. Mem.: Up Country Writers, Red Jacket Writers Group. Avocations: swimming, walking, reading, painting. Home: 14755 Keuka Village Rd Dundee NY 14837 Business E-Mail: jpt1@nysaes.cornell.edu.

**TETTEH, EMMANUEL,** director; 3 children. B of Profl. Studies, Met. Coll. N.Y., 2000, MS in Adminstrn., 2001; Phd, Sch. of Mgmt. Klalden Univ., 2004—. Ordination Mt. Calvary Holy Ch. of Am., N.Y., 1995, Internat. Evangelism Crusades, 1993, Internat. Ever-Living Praise Tabernacle of CGEM, Ghana, 1988; School Certificate and General Certificate of Education West African Exam. Coun., Ghana, 1986. Assoc. min. Mt. Calvary Holy Ch. of Am., Staten Island, NY, 1994—; learning ctr. tutor Met. Coll. NY, 1999—2000, adminstrv. asst., 1999—2000, asst. to v.p. for student fin., 2000—. Ch. missions Internat. Evangelism Crusaders/Internat. Coun. of Cmty. Churches, Bklyn., 1991—94; ch. devel. Praise Tabernacle Ch./Ever-Prevailing Word Ch., Osu-Accra, Ghana, 1988—91; pastoral services Christian Growth Ch., 1986—88; adj. prof. Met. Coll. NY, N.Y.C., 2001—. Author: (instructional outlines/study guide) Classes (Purpose) I, V, VII, & A (Constructive Action) Lesson Outlines, (instructional computer lesson manual) 4) How to Create Labels and to Build a Database, (instruc. computer literacy lesson manual) 3) How to Construct an Eco-Map and to Build a Database, (biblical studies) 1) The Importance of Christian Fellowship, (biblical studies) 2) The Principles of Obtaining the Exaltation of God, Theories of Democratic Governance in the Institutions of Higher Education, 2004. Rsch. svc. learning Service-Learning in Higher Edn., Staten Island, 2000; min. religion Mt. Calvary Holy Ch., 1996. Recipient Disting. recognition as mem. of the Honor and Crystal Societies, Met. Coll. NY, 1998—2001, Dean's List, 1998—2001; College's Presdl. scholar, 1998—2001, Juanita Blake Meml. scholar, 1999, 2000. Mem.: ASPA (life), Soc. Human Ecology (corr.), Am. Ednl. Rsch. Assn. (corr.), Am. Assn. Christian Counselors (life), Nat. Orgn. Human Svc. Edn. (life). Democrat. Achievements include discovery of At the epilogue of my Masters' degree research project, I emerged with the discovery of a metaphorical concept that I called Communal Photosynthesis based on this discovery and; commitment to scientific rsch., I have established The Ctr. for Communal Photosynthesis Rsch. Avocation: travel.

**TETTLEBAUM, HARVEY M.,** lawyer; m. Ann Safier; children: Marianne, Benjamin. AB, Dartmouth Coll., 1964; JD, Washington U. Sch. Law, 1968, AM in History, 1968. Asst. dean Washington U. Sch. Law, 1969-77; asst. atty. gne., chief counsel Consumer Protection and Anti-Trust Div., 1970-77; pvt. practice Jefferson City, Mo., 1977-90; mem., chmn. health law practice group Husch & Eppenberger, LLC, Jefferson City, Mo., 1990—. Contbr. articles to profl. jours. Treas. Mo. Rep. State Com., 1976—2004; v.p. Moniteau County R-1 Sch. Dist. Bd., 1991-95, pres., 1995-96; mem. Calif. R-1 Sch. Bd., 1990-96, v.p., 1993-95, pres., 1995-96. Mem. Am. Health Lawyers Assn. (bd. dirs. 1993-99, co-chair long-term care and the law program 1993-01, chair 2001—, chair long-term care and law program 2001—, former chair long term care practice group 1997-01), Mo. Bar Assn. (health and hosp. law com., chmn. adminstrv. law com., vice chair delivery of legal svc. com., Mo. statewide legal svc. com.), Am. Health Care Assn. (legal subcom. 1994—, chair 2004-06), Rep. Nat. Lawyers Assn. (bd. dirs. 1998-, 1st v.p. 2002—, pres. 2003-). Home: 56295 Little Moniteau Rd California MO 65018-3069 Office: Husch & Eppenberger LLC Monroe House Ste 300 235 E High St PO Box 1251 Jefferson City MO 65102-1251 Office Phone: 573-761-1107. Business E-Mail: harvey.tettlebaum@husch.com.

**TETZELI, RICK,** editor; With FORTUNE Mag., 1990—93, assoc. editor, 1993—95, editor, 1996—97, sr. editor, 1997—99, asst. mng. editor, 1999, exec. dir., 2000, asst. mng. editor, 2001; mng. editor Entertainment Weekly, NYC, 2002—. Office: Entertainment Weekly 1675 Broadway New York NY 10019 Office Fax: 212-522-6104, 212-522-8350.*

**TETZLAFF, CHRISTIAN,** violinist; b. Hamburg, Germany, 1966; married; 3 children. Soloist Berlin Philharmonics, Vienna Philharmonic, Royal Concertgebouw Orch., NHK Symphony Orch., Tokyo, Cleve. Orch., Phila. Orch., Minn. Orch., London Symphony Orch., Lincoln Ctr., NY Philharmonic, numerous others. Musician: (albums) Sibelius: Complete works for violin and orchestra, Bartók, Weill, Janácek Violin Concertos & Sonatas, Haydn: 3 Violin Concertos, 1991, Romantic Moments from the Classics, 1994, Bach: Sonatas and Partitas for solo violin, 1994, Mozart: The 5 Violin Concertos, 1996, Beethoven for Children, 2000, Mozart: Violin Concertos Nos. 1, 3, and 5, 2000, Mozart: Violin Concertos Nos. 2 and 4, 2001, Dvorák: Violin Concerto Lalo: Symphonie espagnole, 2001, Haydn: Violin Concertos, 2002, Bach: Sonatas and Partitas for solo violin Cello Suites, 2004, Bartók: Violin Sonatas, 2004, others. Named Instrumentalist of Yr., Musical Am. Internat. Dir. Performing Arts, 2005.

**TETZLAFF, JOHN EDWIN,** physician; b. N.Y.C., N.Y., Feb. 26, 1953; m. Susan Joan Harrison, May 21, 1982; children: Roger, John, Glen, Laura, James, Christopher, Emily. MD, St. Louis U., 1979. Anesthesiologist Cleve. Clinic, 1988—2003; prof. anesthesiology Cleve. Clinic Lerner Coll. of Medicine of Case Western Reserve U. Author: (text book) Orthopedic Anesthesiology, 1995, Clinical Pharmacology of Local Anesthetics, 1999. Lcdr USN, 1975—88. Office: The Cleve Clin Found E-30 9500 Euclid Ave Cleveland OH 44195

**TETZLAFF, THEODORE R.,** lawyer; b. Saukville, Wis., Feb. 27, 1944; AB magna cum laude, Princeton U., 1966; LLB, Yale U., 1969. Bar: Ind. 1969, D.C. 1969, Ill. 1974. Legis. asst. to Congressman John Brademas, 1970; exec. dir. Nat. Conf. Police Community Rels., 1970-71; acting dir. US Office Legal Svcs., Office Econ. Opportunity, Washington, 1972-73; counsel, Com. Judiciary US Ho. of Reps., Washington, 1974; v.p., legal and external affairs Cummins Engine Co., 1980-82; gen. counsel Tenneco, Inc., Greenwich, Conn., 1992-99; ptnr. Jenner & Block, Chgo., 1976—80, 1982—2001, McGuireWoods LLP, Chgo., 2002—05, mng. ptnr. Chgo. office; gen. counsel Peoples Energy, 2003—; ptnr. Ungaretti & Harris LLP, Chgo., 2005—. Bd. dirs. Continental Materials Corp., Chgo. Pres. Chgo. area Found. Legal Svcs., 1983—; commr. Pub. Bldg. Commn. Chgo., 1990-2005; chmn. Met. Pier and Expo Authority, 2005—. Reginald Heber Smith fellow, 1969-70. Mem. ABA (chair sect. litigation 1991-92), Ill. State Bar Assn., Ind. State Bar Assn., D.C. Bar. Office: Ungaretti & Harris LLP 3500 Three First Nat Plz Chicago IL 60602 also: Peoples Energy 130 E Randolph Dr Chicago IL 60601 Office Phone: 312-977-4150. Business E-Mail: tedt@mycingular.blackberry.net.

**TEUBER, WILLIAM J, JR.,** corporate financial executive; B, Coll. of the Holy Cross; MBA, Babson Coll.; MS in taxation, Bentley Coll. V.p., contr. EMC Corp., 1995—97, v.p., CFO, 1997—2000, sr. v.p., CFO, 2000—01, exec. v.p., CFO, 2002—06, vice-chmn., CFO, 2006—. Ptnr. Coopers & Lybrand. Office: EMC 171 South St Hopkinton MA 01748-9103*

**TEUBNER, FERDINAND CARY, JR.,** retired publishing executive; b. Phila., Sept. 22, 1921; s. Ferdinand Cary Teubner and Esther Roslyn (Test) Alperstein; m. Ruth May Hazen, Nov. 1, 1953; 1 child, Janell Caron Teubner Crispyn. Student, U. Pa., 1940-41; grad., Charles Morris Price Sch. Advt. and Journalism, 1949. Rep. W.H. Hoedt Studios, Inc., Phila., 1945-52; account exec. Patterson Prodns., Inc., Phila., 1955-56, v.p., 1956-57; staff exec. Am. Assn. Advt. Agys., N.Y.C., 1957-59; rep. W.H. Martin & Co., Inc., N.Y.C., 1959-62; advt. salesman Editor & Pub. Co., Inc., N.Y.C., 1962-65, advt. mgr., 1965-76, gen. mgr., treas., 1976-78, treas., pub., 1978-95, dir., 1969-95; sec.-treas., dir. E & P Research, Inc., N.Y.C., 1985-95, ret., 1995. Served with USAAF, 1942-45, ETO; served with U.S. Army, 1952-55, Korea, ret. maj. AUS, 1981. Decorated Purple Heart; recipient Silver Shovel award Internat. Newspaper Mktg. Assn., 1993, David Paul Hegg II Lifetime Achievement award Episcopal Diocese Newark, 2003. Mem. Sales Execs. Club N.Y.C., Res. Officer Assn. Clubs: Union League, Lake Valhalla Country. Episcopalian. Home: 18 Lenape Dr Montville NJ 07045-9795

**TEUFEL, WILLIAM LOCKWOOD,** emergency physician; b. Cleve., Mar. 21, 1941; s. William John and Dorothy Margaret (Lockwood) T.; m. Margaret Ong, June 28, 1969 (div. Sept. 1980); 1 child, Drew William; m. Zoe Ann Zimmerman (dec. Oct. 1999); children: Thea Anna, Kallie Abra. BS in Chemistry, Denison U., 1963; MD, U. Cin., 1967. Resident in gen. surgery Highland Hosp., Oakland, Calif., 1968—69; resident in emergency medicine U. Cin., 1971—73; from asst. dir. to dir. emergency svc. Highland Gen. Hosp., Oakland, 1973—76, San Francisco Gen. Hosp., 1976—80; ptnr. Calif. Emergency Physicians Med. Group, Oakland, 1980—90; med. dir. emergency svc. Marin Gen. Hosp., Greenbrae, Calif., 1986—89; sr. ptnr. Calif. Emergency Physicians Med. Group, Oakland, 1990—2005, emeritus ptnr., 2006—; med. dir. Coastal Valleys Emergency Svc. Agy., Santa Rosa, Calif., 1999—, Marin Emergency Svc. Agy., 2004—. Oral examiner Am. Bd. Emergency Medicine, Lansing, Mich., 1981—; health coun. County of Marin, San Rafael, Calif., 1997-2002. Lt. comdr. USNR, 1964—74. Fellow Am. Acad. Emergency Medicine (bd. dir. Calif. chpt. 1998—2002). Avocations: motorcycling, native plant gardening. Office: Calif Emergency Physicians 2100 Powell St Ste 920 Emeryville CA 94608-1803 Home: PO Box 471 437 Meadow Way San Geronimo CA 94963-0471 Office Phone: 510-350-2777. E-mail: wlteufel@comcast.net.

**TEUSCHER, SIMON HANS,** history professor, researcher; b. Bern, Switzerland, Apr. 26, 1967; arrived in U.S., 2000; s. Hans Gottfried Teuscher and Denise Claire Lehmann. MA, U. of Zurich, Switzerland, 1995, PhD, 1997, Habilitation, 2005. Assoc. prof. U. of Zurich, 1995—99; vis. prof. U. Neuchâtel, Switzerland, 2001—02, Ecole des Hautes Etudes en Sciences Sociales, Paris, 2002; mem. Inst. for Advanced Study, Sch. of Hist. Studies, Princeton, NJ, 2004—05; vis. asst. prof. UCLA, 2000—; univ. prof. U. Zurich, 2006—. Author: (book) Bekannte—Klienten—Verwandte. Soziabilität und Politik in der Stadt Bern um 1500; contbr. articles to profl. jours. Office Phone: 310-825-8333. Business E-Mail: teuscher@history.ucla.edu.

**TEUTUL, PAUL, SR.,** television personality, mechanic; b. Yonkers, NY, May 1, 1949; children: Paul Jr., Michael. Owner Orange County Iron Works, Inc., 1973—, Orange County Choppers, 1999—. Co-star (TV series) Amercian Chopper: The Series, 2003—. Office: Orange County Choppers 10 Factory St Montgomery NY 12549 Office Phone: 845-457-1992. Office Fax: 845-457-4529.*

**TEVANIAN, AVADIS, JR.,** information technology executive; BA in math., U. Rochester; MS in computer sci., PhD in computer sci., Carnegie Mellon U. Principal designer and engr. Mach operating system Carnegie Mellon U.; engr. to engr. NEXTSTEP, NeXT, 1988—95; v.p. engring. NeXT, 1995—97; sr. v.p. software engring. Apple Computer Inc., 1997—2003, chief software tech. officer, 2003—06. Bd. dir. Tellme Networks, 2006—.

**TEVRIZIAN, DICKRAN M., JR.,** judge; b. LA, Aug. 4, 1940; s. Dickran and Rose Tevrizian; m. Geraldine Tevrizian, Aug. 22, 1964; children: Allyson Tracy, Leslie Sara. BS, U. So. Calif., 1962, JD, 1965. Tax acct. Arthur Andersen and Co., LA, 1965-66; atty., ptnr. Kirtland and Packard, LA, 1966-72; judge LA Mcpl. Ct., 1972-78, State of Calif. Superior Ct., LA, 1978-82; ptnr. Manatt, Phelps, Rothenberg & Tunney, LA, 1982-85, Lewis, D'Amato, Brisbois & Bisgaard, LA, 1985-86; judge U.S. Dist. Ct., LA, 1986—. Adv. dir. UCLA Sch. Pub. Policy. Recipient Peter the Great Gold Medal of Honor Russian Acad. Natural Scis., 1998, Ellis Island Medal of Honor award, 1999, Disting. Pub. Svc. award Orange County Fed. Bar Assn., 2003. Mem. Calif. Trial Lawyers Assn. (Trial Judge of Yr. 1987), LA County Bar Assn. (Trial Judge of Yr. 1994-95), Malibu Bar Assn. (fed. ct. trial judge of yr. 1998, Maynard Toll award 2002, Jud. Svcs. award DSR Emil Gumpert ADR, 2005, Justice Armand Arabian Leaders in Pub. Svc. award 2005). Office: US Dist Ct Royal Federal Bldg 255 E Temple St Los Angeles CA 90012-3332

**TEW, E. JAMES, JR.,** management services company executive; b. Dallas, July 7, 1933; s. Elmer James and Bessie Fay (Bennett) T.; children: Teresa Annette, Linda Diane, Brian James. Student, Arlington State Jr. Coll., 1955—57; BBA in Indsl. Mgmt., So. Meth. U., 1969; MS in Quality Systems, U. Dallas, 1972, MBA in Mgmt., 1975; EdD in Adult Edn., Nova U., 1986. Registered profl. engr., Calif. Mgr. quality assurance ops. Tex. Instruments Inc., Dallas, 1957-98; chmn. corp. metric implementation com. Texins Credit Union, co-chmn. credit com. Adj. faculty Richland Coll. Mountain View Coll., LeTourneau U.; precinct chmn., election judge, del. several county and state convs.; bus. computer info. systems adv. bd. U. North Tex.; bd. dirs. ctr. for quality and productivity U. North Tex.; bd. examiners Malcolm Baldridge Nat. Quality award, U.S. Dept. Commerce, Nat. Inst. Standard and Tech., 1988, 89, 90, 91, 95, 96; chmn. panel judges, fellow Tex. Quality Award, 1993-2001; cons. nat. quality award Govt. Singapore, 1994; spkr. in field; bd. examiners Presdl. Quality Award, 1994-96, judge 1997-2000; quality examiner U.S. Army, 1996—; sr. quality examiner USAF, 1995-98, postdoctoral edn. in mediation and arbitration edn., 1998, 99; vol. mediator for dispute mediation svc., 1998—. Spkr. in field. Contbr. articles to profl jours. Decorated Army Commendation medal with oak leaf cluster, Meritorious Svc. medal, Legion of Merit. Fellow Am. Soc. Quality Control (cert. quality auditor, cert. quality mgr., cert. as quality and reliability engr., chmn. Dallas-Ft. Worth sect. 1974-75). Fellow U.S. Metric Assn. (cert., chmn. cert. bd. 1986-87); mem. U.S. Res. Officers Assn., Dallas C. of C. (chmn. world mfg. com. 1974-77, chmn. spl. tasl force career edn. adv. bd. 1973-74), Mensa (mem. air force blue ribbon commn. on assesments and evaluations 1996-98), Sigma Iota Epsilon, Phi Delta Kappa. Baptist. Clubs: Texins Rod and Gun (pres. 1969-70), Texins Flying, Masons (32 degree). Office Fax: 214-349-3686. Personal E-mail: ejtew@swbell.net.

**TEWARSON, REGINALD PRABHAKAR,** retired mathematics educator, consultant; b. Pauri, Garhwal, India, Nov. 17, 1939; came to U.S., 1957; s. Seth Narottam and Chand (Mani) Tewarson; m. Hedi Thomann, July 1, 1960 (div. Nov. 1990); children: Anita Jasmine, Monique Shanti; m. Ghenwah Albarazi, Apr. 16, 2003. MA, Agra U., 1952; PhD, Boston U., 1961. Lectr. Lucknow U., India, 1951—57; sr. mathematicisn Honeywell EDP, Wellesley Hills, Mass., 1960—64; leading prof. applied math. and stats. SUNY, Stony Brook, 1964—2000, leading prof. physiology and biophysics dept., 1964—2000, leading prof. emeritus, 2001—. Cons. NIH, Washington, 1971-74. Author: Sparse Matrices, 1973; mem. editorial bd. Applied Math. Letters, 1986-2004, Math. Computer Modeling, 1991-2004, Pan. Am. Math. Jour., 1991-2004; contbr. articles to profl. jours. Centenary scholar Govt. of India, 1946-50, Crusade scholar U.S. Coun. Chs., 1957-59; rsch. grantee NIH, 1973-97, Air Force Office Sch. Rsch. Math. and Info. Scis., 1983-85, NSF, 1993-95. Mem. Am. Math. Soc., Soc. Indsl. and Applied Math., Soc. for Math. Biology. Democrat. Achievements include pioneering research on sparse matrices based largely on own research; co-development of mathematical model of kidney concentrating mechanism, of computer model of neuronal function. Home: 22 Night Heron Dr Stony Brook NY 11790-1108 Office: SUNY Dept Applied Math And Stats Stony Brook NY 11794-0001 Office Phone: 631-632-8370. Personal E-mail: tewarson@optonline.net. E-mail: tewarson@ams.sunysb.edu.

**TEWELL, JOSEPH ROBERT, JR.,** retired electrical engineer; b. Albany, NY, May 19, 1934; s. Joseph Robert and Florence Edna Tewell; m. Barbara Ann Johnson, Nov. 20, 1960; children: Patricia Ann, Donna Lynn, Joseph Robert, III. B.E.E., Rensselaer Poly. Inst., 1955, M.E.E., 1958. Rsch. engr. N.Am. Aviation, Inc., Downey, Calif., 1955; assoc. rsch. engr. Lockheed Aircraft Corp., Burbank, Calif., 1956; instr. Rensselaer Poly. Inst., 1957-64; sr. rsch. scientist Martin Marietta Corp., Denver, 1964-79, mgr. advanced programs Michoud, La., 1979-87, mgr. shuttle-C project, 1988-90, mgr. computer-aided productivity, 1991-93, mgr. sys. engring., 1994-96; ret., 1996. Cons. in field. Contbr. articles to profl. jours. Founding sponsor Challenger Ctr. Served with Army Security Agy., 1957. Recipient NASA Manned Awareness citation, 1970, NASA Skylab Achievement award, 1974, NASA New Tech. award, 1976, Tech. Achievement award Martin Marietta Corp., 1977, Sustained Performance award Martin Marietta Corp., 1981, NASA cert. of recognition, 1977, Author of Yr. award, 1986, also 38 publ. awards, 1965—. Fellow Explorers Club; mem. AIAA, Smithsonian Assocs., Air and Space Mus., Unmanned Vehicle Sys., Nat. Audubon Soc., Sigma Xi, Eta Kappa Nu, Tau Beta Pi, Theta Chi. Achievements include invention of dual action single drive actuator; spacecraft docking and retrieval mechanism. Home and Office: 619 Legendre Dr Slidell LA 70460-3427

**TEXAS, SAM FAYAD,** small business owner, political activist; b. Monrovia, Liberia, Oct. 20, 1958; came to U.S., 1979; naturalized; s. Moufid and Elizabeth (Mowad) Fayad. Student, U. Houston, 1977-80. Handler pub. complaints against govt. agencies, 1980-90; owner, mgr. Texas Sam Import/Export, Houston, 1990—. Contbr. articles to jours. and newspapers. Vol. Bib Brothers, Houston, 1990—, Human Rights Watch, Houston, 1990—, Amnesty Internat., Houston, 1990—, Habitat for Humanity, Houston, 1990—, ARC; precinct judge, Houston, 1990, 91; del. to state and nat. Rep. and Dem. convs., 1992; mgr. local polit. campaigns, 1990; investigator genicide in Bosnia, 1996; Dem. nominee for Tex. Ho. of Reps., 1992, Named Outstanding Citizen, Mayor of Tex. and Gov. of Tex., 1988, 90, 92, 93; recipient outstanding vol. award Amnesty Internat., 1994. Republican. Roman Catholic. Avocations: prison ministry, councillor for needy, teaching sunday school, counseling youth. Home: PO Box 55707 Houston TX 77255-5707 E-mail: samtexas@samtexas.simplenet.com.

**TEXTOR, ROBERT BAYARD,** cultural anthropology educator, writer, consultant; b. Cloquet, Minn., Mar. 13, 1923; s. Clinton Kenney and Lillian (Nickles) T.; divorced; children: Alexander Robertson, Marisa Elizabeth. Student, Lafayette Coll., 1940—41, Antioch Coll., 1941—43; BA in Asian Studies, U. Mich., 1945; PhD in Cultural Anthropology, Cornell U., 1960. Civil info. and edn. officer Mil. Govt., Kyoto-Wakayama, Japan, 1946-48; rsch. fellow anthropology and S.E. Asia studies Yale U., 1959-60, assoc., 1960-61; rsch. fellow in stats. Harvard U., 1962-64; assoc. prof. edn. and anthropology Stanford U., 1964-68, prof. edn. and anthropology, 1968-86, prof. anthropology, 1986-90, prof. anthropology emeritus, 1990—; sr. scholar Ctr. to Bridge the Digital Divide, Wash. State U., 2005—. Vis. prof. U. Saar, Saarbrücken, Germany, 1984-85; cons. Motorola, Inc., 1991-2001, Ministry of Planning, Kuwait, 1999; mem. S.E. Asia Coun., 1974-77; cons. cultural anthropology to govt. agys., 1957-58, 61-62. Author: Roster of the Gods: An Ethnography of The Supernatural in a Thai Village, 6 vols., 1973, Austria 2005: Projected Sociocultural Effects of the Microelectronic Revolution, 1983, Anticipatory Anthropology, 1985, (with Sippanondha Ketudat) The

Middle Path for the Future of Thailand, 1990, (with others) Uncompromising Integrity: Motorola's Global Challenge, 1998; editor: Margaret Mead and the World Ahead: An Anthropologist Anticipates the Future, 2005, (with Eugene Veselsky and others) The Austrian Future: Chances and Risess in the Age of Nanotechnology, German edit., 2006; editor, commentator; assoc. editor Jour. Conflict Resolution, 1965-70; mem. editl. bd. Human Orgn., 1966-71, Jour. Cultural Futures, 1979-87; adv. editor Behavior Sci. Rsch., 1974-86. Bd. dirs. Vols. in Asia, Stanford, Calif., 1968-73; mem. Metro Portland Future Vision Commn., 1993-95; mem. Portland, Oreg., Organizing Com. for Lewis and Clark Bicentennial, 1996-97. Served with U.S. Army, 1943-46. Fellow Rockefeller Found., 1951-52, fgn. area tng. fellow Ford Found., Thailand 1955-58, Carnegie fellow, 1958-59, Fulbright West Europe rsch. fellow, 1984-85, East-West Ctr. fellow, 1988-90; NSF grantee, Thailand, U.S. 1969-73, Volkswagen Found. grantee, Thailand and Germany, 1984. Fellow Am. Anthrop. Assn. (life, chair resource devel. com. 2003-04), Soc. Applied Anthropology; mem. Siam Soc. (life), Assn. Asian Studies (life), Council on Anthropology and Edn. (pres. 1974-75), AAUP (pres. Stanford chpt. 1975-76), Phi Kappa Phi.

**TEYAN, FREDERICK GENE,** pediatrician; b. NYC, Sept. 16, 1938; s. Jack H. and Pearl A. (Chernesky) T.; m. Dec. 18, 1965; children: Frederick II, Julie, Jonathan. AB, St. Peter's Coll., 1960; MD, Seton Hall, 1964. Diplomate Am. Bd. Pediatrics. Intern Kings County Hosp., Bklyn., 1964-65, resident in pediat., 1969-70, L.I. Jewish Hosp., New Hyde Park, NY, 1970-71; pvt. practice, Rockville Centre, NY, 1971—. Major U.S. Army, 1966-69. Fellow Am. Acad. Pediatrics; mem. Nassau Pediatric Soc. Roman Catholic. Office: 36 Lincoln Ave Rockville Centre NY 11570-5768 Office Phone: 516-766-2602. Personal E-mail: fgjteyan@ix.netcom.com.

**TEYTELMAN, DMITRY,** physicist; b. Minsk, Belorussia, USSR, May 6, 1971; s. Boris L'vovich and Raisa Naumovna Teytelman; m. Eugenia Anisimovich, Aug. 5, 1999; 1 child. Lev. BS in Engring. Sci., BS in Applied Physics, CUNY, S.I., N.Y., 1993; MSEE, Stanford U., Calif., 1995, PhD in Elec. Engring., 2003. Accelerator physicist Stanford Linear Accelerator Ctr., Menlo Park, Calif., 2001—. Recipient Outstanding Doctoral Thesis Rsch. in Beam Physics award, 2004. Mem.: IEEE, Am. Phys. Soc. Achievements include research in architectures and algorithms for control and diagnostics of coupled-bunch instabilities in circular accelerators. Home: 1407 Hess Rd Redwood City CA 94061 Office: Stanford Linear Accelerator Ctr 2575 Sand Hill Rd Menlo Park CA 94025 Office Phone: 650-926-8532.

**TEZANOS-PINTO, ROSA,** Hispanic American literature educator; d. Alfredo Tezanos Pinto and Enriqueta Otiniano Tezanos Pinto; m. Jose L. Vargas Vila, Aug. 6, 1993; children: Sebastian Martin Valverde, Isabel Maria Valverde. BA, U. Miami, 1979, MA, 1994, PhD, 2002. Cons. and test evaluator U. Fla., Tampa, 1985—99; pres. Sigma Delta Pi, Miami, 1988—91; coord. symposia Michel de Certeau Ur. for Critical Studies, Coral Gables, Fla., 1990—92; lectr. U. Miami, Coral Gables, 1992—99; dir. John Adams Pub. Co., Coral Gables, 1994—97; prof. of hispanic Am. lit. Lebanon Valley Coll., Annville, Pa., 1999—; dir. Alroquema Pub., Miami, 1999—; coord. youth scholars program in Spanish Lebanon Valley Coll., Annville, 2000—; advisor Spanish club, 2001—; advisor Spanish majors and minors, open majors, 2001—; dir. Asociación de Poetas de América, Buenos Aires, 2000—; coord., meeting hispanic authors program Lebanon Valley Coll., Annville, 2001—; advisor Nat. Assn. of Fellowships Advisors, 2002—. Rschr. Alroquema Pub. Co., Miami, 2003—. Editor: Redimiendo la Infancia en la estructura póetica, 2004, Nation and Narration in The LUSO - Hispanic World, 2005. Recipient Jayanca Disting. Visitor Diploma, Chiclayo, Peru, 2002, Comodoro Rivadavia Book Fair Plaque, Comodoro Rivadavia Book Fair (Argentina), 2001; Profl. grant, Lebanon Valley Coll., 2001—03. Mem.: Latin Am. Inst. Pa. (pres.), Assn. Cervantistas, Colloquium Com., Diversity Adv. Com., Círculo Panamericano, Instituto Literario y Cultural Hispánico, Casa del Poeta del Perú, Am. Assn. of Teachers of Spanish and Portuguese, Nat. Assn. of Fellowships Advisors, Grad. Fellowship Com., Sigma Delta Pi, Phi Sigma Iota. Achievements include research in the relationship in form and practice of poetic language and the Freudian psychoanalytic language; the hidden text of Infancy in the Poetic works of Ester de Izaguirre and Loreina Santos Silva and testimonial literature; publications in the USA, France, Spain, Argentina, Peru, Paraguay, Brazil, Puerto Rico, India, etc; presented papers at USA, Chile, Venezuela, Guatemala, Puerto Rico, Australia, Peru, Colombia, Paraguay, Argentina, Spain, France, India, Mexico and Brazil. Office: Lebanon Valley College 101 North College Ave Annville PA 17003 Office Phone: 717-867-6257. E-mail: tezanos@lvc.edu.

**TEZLA, ALBERT,** language educator; b. S. Bend, Ind., Dec. 13, 1915; s. Mihály and Lucza (Szénási) Tezla; m. Olive Anna Fox, July 26, 1941; children: Michael William, Kathy Elaine. BA, U. Chgo., 1941, MA, 1947, PhD, 1952. Instr. Ind. U. Ext., S. Bend, 1946-48; from instr. to assoc. prof. U. Minn., Duluth, 1949-61, prof., 1961-82, prof. emeritus 1982—. Vis. prof. Hungarian lit. Columbia U., N.Y.C., 1966, cons., 1966-71, 77-81, vis. scholar, 1975; cons. U. Minn., Mpls., 1968-83; project reviewer NEH, Washington, 1979-82; vis. prof. Hungarian lit. U. Minn., Duluth, 1998. Author: An Introductory Bibliography to the Study of Hungarian Literature, 1964, Hungarian Authors: A Bibliographical Handbook, 1970, The Hazardous Quest: Hungarian Immigrants in the United States, 1895-1920, 1993; co-author: Academic American Encyclopedia, 1980, World Authors, 1975-1980, 1985, Benét's Readers Encyclopedia, 1987, World Authors, 1980-85, 1991; editor, contbg. translator: Ocean at the Window: Hungarian Prose and Poetry since 1945, 1980, Three Contemporary Hungarian Plays, 1992, contbg. translator: Hungarian Short Stories, 1983, The Kiss: 20th Century Hungarian Short Stories, 1993; translator: God in the Wagon: Ten Short Stories (Ferenc Sánta), 1985 (Hungarian pubs. award, 1985), The Fifth Seal (Ferenc Sánta), 1986 (Hungarian pubs. award, 1986), Somewhere in a Distant Fabled Land, 1980 (Hungarian pubs. award, 1986); author: Modern Hungarian Poetry, American Hungarians, 1895-1920, 1987, On the Balcony: Selected Short Stories (Iván Mándy), 1988 (Hungarian pubs. award, 1988), Hungary: A Brief History (István Lázár), 1990, An Illustrated History of Hungary (István Lázár), 1992, Memoir of Hungary, 1944-48 (Sándor Máral), 1996, Once There Was a Central Europe: Selected Short Stories and Other Writings (Miklós Máazoly), 1997, A Wartime Memoir, Hungary, 1944-45 (Alaine Polcz), 1998, Authoring, Barbering and Other Occupations, 2002, With One Heart in Two Homelands, 2005; editl. cons. Holmes and Meier Pubs., 1996. Lt. (s.g.) USN, 1942-46, PTO. Recipient Diplome d'honeur, Inst. Cultural Rels., Hungary, 1970, Commemorative medal, 1970, Endre Ady Medallion, Presidium Hungarian PEN Ctr., 1986, Pro Cultura Hungarica award, Rep. Hungary, 1996, Abraham Lincoln award, Am. Hungarian Found., 1998; fellow Fulbright Rsch. fellow, Associated Bd. Rsch. Coun., 1959—60, Rsch. fellow, Internat. Co. Traveling Grants, 1963—64, Internat. Rsch. and Exchs. Bd., 1978; grantee Rsch. grantee, Am. Coun. Learned Socs., 1961, 1968, NEH, 1978—82. Mem. Internat. Assn. Hungarian Studies (mem. exec. com. 1978-83, John Lotz Meml. award 1986), Am. Hungarian Educators' Assn., Fulbright Assn. Democrat. Avocations: gardening, physical fitness, reading, classical films. Home: 5412 London Rd Duluth MN 55804-2511 E-mail: atezla@d.umn.edu.

**THACH, WILLIAM THOMAS, JR.,** neurologist, educator; b. Okla. City, Jan. 3, 1937; s. William Thomas and Mary Elizabeth T.; m. Emily Ransom Otis, June 30, 1963 (div. 1979); children: Sarah Brill, James Otis, William Thomas III. AB in Biology magna cum laude, Princeton U., 1959; MD cum laude, Harvard U., 1964. Diplomate Am. Bd. Psychiatry and Neurology (in Neurology). Intern Mass. Gen. Hosp., Boston, 1964-65, asst. residency, 1965-66; staff assoc. physiology sect. lab. clin. sci. NIMH, Bethesda, Md., 1966-69; neurology resident, clin. and rsch. fellow Mass. Gen. Hosp., 1969-71; from asst. prof. neurology to assoc. prof. neurology Yale U. Sch. Medicine, New Haven, Conn., 1971-75; assoc. prof. neurobiology and neurology dept. anatomy and neurobiology Washington U. Sch. Medicine, St. Louis, 1975-80, prof. neurobiology and neurology dept. anatomy and neurobiology, 1980—, chief divsn. neurorehab. dept. neurology, 1992—. Acting dir. Irene Walter Johnson Rehab. Inst. Washington U. Sch. Medicine, 1989-91, dir., 1991-92; attending neurologist Barnes Hosp., med. dir. dept. rehab.; attending neurologist Jewish Hosp., St. Louis Regional Hosp.; bd. sci.

counselors NINCDS, 1988-92; mem. NIH Study Sect. Neurology A, 1981-85. Assoc. editor Somatosenory and Motor Research; contbr. numerous articles to profl. jours. Fulbright grantee U. Melbourne, Australia, 1959-60; NIH grantee, 1971— Mem. Physiol. Soc., Am. Acad. Neurology, Soc. Neurosci., Am. Neurol. Assn., Am. Soc. Neurorehab., Phi Beta Kappa, Sigma Xi, Alpha Omega Alpha. Achievements include research on brain control of movement and motor learning, roles of the basal ganglia and the cerebellum in health and disease. Home: 7520 Clayton Rd Saint Louis MO 63117-1418 Office: Washington Univ Dept Anatomy & Neurobiol 600 S Euclid Ave Dept Anatomy& Saint Louis MO 63110-1010 E-mail: thachw@peg.wustl.edu.

**THACKER, CHARLES P.,** computer engineer, engineering executive; m. Karen Thacker; 2 children. BA, U. Calif., 1967; D (hon.), Swiss Fed. Inst. of Tech. Engr. U. Calif., Berkeley, 1967-68; project leader Berkeley Computer Corp., 1969-71; mem. rsch. staff Xerox Palo Alto (Calif.) Rsch. Ctr., 1971-75, mgr. processor architecture sys. devel. divsn., 1975-77, mgr. digital processor develop. electronics divsn., 1977-79, prin. engr., 1979-80, rsch. fellow, 1980-82, sr. rsch. fellow, 1982-83; sr. cons. engr. Digital Equipment Corp. Sys. Rsch. Ctr., Palo Alto, 1983-89, corp. cons. engr., 1989—97; dir. advanced systems Microsoft Rsch., Cambridge, England, 1997—99; disting. engr., emerging tech. group Microsoft Corp., 1999—. Named a Disting. Alumnus, U. Calif.; recipient Charles Stark Draper prize NAE, 2004, 2004. Fellow: Am. Acad. Arts and Sciences, Assn. Computer Machinery (Software System award 1984); mem.: IEEE, NAE. Achievements include research in in digital computer development. Mailing: c/o Microsoft Research Thames Valley Park Reading RG6 1WG England*

**THACKER, KIRK DAVID,** secondary school educator; b. Richmond, Mo., Feb. 25, 1968; s. Melvin Lee and Kathleen Thacker; m. Lisa Kay Taylor, Aug. 11, 2000; children: Carly Elizabeth, Dalton Lee. BA in History, William Jewell Coll., Liberty, Mo., 1992, tchr. cert., 1996; M in Secondary Sch. Adminstrn., Ctrl. Mo. State U., Warrensburg, 2003. Cert. tchr. Mo. Tchr. Oak Grove (Mo.) Mid. Sch., 1996—2000, Hardin-Ctrl. H.S., Mo., 2000—. Mem. Ray County Dems., Richmond, Mo., 2006—06. Mem.: Kappa Alpha. Democrat. Baptist. Personal E-mail: kthacker@hardincentral.k12.mo.us.

**THACKER, STEPHEN BRADY,** medical association administrator, epidemiologist; b. Independence, Mo., Dec. 30, 1947; m. 1976; 2 children. AB, Princeton U., 1969; MD, Mt. Sinai Sch. Medicine, 1973; MSc, London Sch. Hygiene and Tropical Medicine, 1984. Chief consolidated surveillance and commn. activity epidemiol. program office Ctrs. Disease Control and Prevention, Atlanta, 1978-83, dir. surveillance and epidemiol. studies, 1983-86, dir. epidemiol. program office, 1989—2004, acting dep. dir., 1998, acting dir. Nat. Ctr. Injury Prevention and Control, 1999-2000, acting dir. Nat. Ctr. Environ. Health, 1993-95, dir. Office of Workforce and Career Devel., 2004—; asst. dir. sci. Ctr. Environ. Health and Injury Control, Atlanta, 1986-89. Mem. steering com. Assn. Behavioral Sci. Med. Edn., 1971-74; assoc. Dept. Cmty. Medicine, Med. Ctr. Duke U., Durham, N.C., 1975-76; lectr. Cmty. Ctr. Mt. Sinai Sch. Medicine, N.Y.C., 1978—; Sch. Medicine Emory U., Atlanta, 1985-86; cons. epidemiology Arab Republic Egypt, 1979-91; clin. asst. prof. cmty. health Sch. Medicine Emory U., 1986-91; adj. prof. Emory U. Sch. Pub. Health, 1992— Editor: Epidemiologic Revs., 1990-2003. Clin. scholar Robert Wood Johnson Found., 1974-75; recipient Mosby Book award for excellence, 1973, Pub. Health Svc. Outstanding Svc. medal, 1987, Pub. Health Svc. Meritorious Svc. medal, 1988, 2002, Saul Horowitz Jr. Meml. award, 1990, Supervisory award for contbr. advantage of women, 1991, Pub. Health Svc. Commendation medal, 1991, Pub. Health Svc. Disting. Svc. medal, 1993, 2006, Pub. Health Svc. Surgeon Gen.'s Exemplary Svc. medal, 1993, Pub. Health Svc. Disting. Svc. medal, 1997, Medal of Excellence William C. Watson, Jr., 1996, Ray E. Brown award Assn. Mil. Surgeons of U.S., 2003. Achievements include rsch. public health surveillance, infectious disease, environ. health, injury prevention, alcohol abuse, health care delivery, meta-analysis, technology assessment. Office: Ctrs for Disease Control and Prevention MS E94 1600 Clifton Rd NE Atlanta GA 30333 Business E-Mail: sbt1@cdc.gov.

**THACKERAY, FRANK W.,** history professor; b. Pitts., Mar. 16, 1943; s. Frank E. Thackeray and Lucille D. Schneider; m. Katherine Margit Lukacs, Nov. 27, 1971; children: Alexander James, Drew Max. BA, Dickinson Coll., 1965; MA, Temple U., 1971, PhD, 1977. Prof. history Ind. U. S.E., New Albany, 1977—. Author: (book) Antecedents of Revolution, 1981; editor: Events That Changed the World, 1995, Events That Changed Germany, 2004. With USAR, 1966—72. Recipient Fulbright Rsch. award, U.S. Govt., 1972—74. Mem.: Fulbright Alumni Assn., Louisville Com. on Fgn. Rels. Avocations: tennis, reading. Office: Ind Univ SE Dept History Grant Line Rd New Albany IN 47150 Office Phone: 812-941-2299. Business E-Mail: fthacker@ius.edu.

**THACKERAY, JONATHAN E.,** lawyer; b. Athens, Ohio, July 30, 1936; s. Joseph Eugene and Betty Rutherford (Boright) T.; m. Sandra Ann McMahon; children: Jennifer, Sara, Amy, Jonathan. AB cum laude, Harvard U., 1958, JD, 1961. Bar: Ohio 1961, U.S. Dist. Ct. (no. dist.) Ohio 1961, U.S. Supreme Ct. 1972, U.S. Ct. Appeals (6th cir.) 1973, U.S. Ct. Appeals (9th cir.) 1982, N.Y. 1993. Assoc. Vorys, Sater, Seymour & Pease, Columbus, Ohio, 1961, Baker & Hostetler, Cleve., 1965-72, ptnr., 1973-93; v.p., gen. counsel The Hearst Corp., N.Y.C., 1993—2003; ret., 2003. Served to lt. USNR, 1961-65. Mem. ABA, Ohio Bar Assn., Cleve. Bar Assn., Am. Law Inst. Office: Hearst 959 Eighth Ave New York NY 10019 Notable cases include: administrative proceedings leading to approval of joint newspaper operating agreements in Cincinnati, Seattle and Las Vegas; litigation of newspaper antitrust cases in Memphis, Trenton and Dallas.

**THACKER-ESTRADA, ELIZABETH LORELEI,** librarian, historian; b. Burbank, Calif., Nov. 29, 1957; d. Ernest Wichman and Mariam Lorelei (Ihrig) Thacker; m. Hedwing José Estrada, Nov. 29, 1997. BA summa cum laude, U. Calif., Santa Barbara, 1979; M in Libr. and Info. Studies, U. Calif., Berkeley, 1986. Part-time reference libr. Advanced Info. Mgmt., Mountain View, Calif., 1987—93; head libr. Inst. Transpersonal Psychology, Menlo Park, Calif., 1988—90; part-time faculty Foothill Coll., Los Altos Hills, Calif., 1990; interim campus libr. San Jose (Calif.) State U., Salinas, 1991, part-time reference libr. San Jose, 1994; reference libr. San Francisco (Calif.) Pub. Libr., 1993—95, collection devel. libr., 1995—2000, unit mgr., 2000—02, spl. projects mgr., 2002—04, govt. info. ctr. dir., 2004—. Editl. bd. mem., cons. Nat. First Ladies Libr., Canton, Ohio, 2003—. Mem. editl. bd.: White House Studies; contbr. chpts. to books, encycs., articles to profl. jours. Chair missions and social outreach team Burlingame (Calif.) United Meth. Ch., 2003—. H. W. Wilson Found. scholar, U. Calif., Berkeley, 1985. Mem.: ALA, Inst. Hist. Study, Western Social Sci. Assn. (conf. panelist 2000—02), Govt. Docs. Round Table, Libr. History Round Table, Am. Hist. Assn., Sch. Info. Mgmt. and Systems Alumni Assn. (life), Calif. Alumni Assn. (life), Sierra Club (life), Mortar Bd. / Pi Sigma Alpha (life). Democrat. Methodist. Office: San Francisco Public Library 100 Larkin St San Francisco CA 94102-4733 Office Phone: 415-557-4201. Office Fax: 415-557-4475. Business E-Mail: ethacker@sfpl.org.

**THACKRAY, ARNOLD WILFRID,** historian, educator, foundation administrator; b. Eng., July 30, 1939; came to U.S., 1967, naturalized, 1982; s. Wilfred Cecil and Mary (Clarke) T.; m. Barbara Hughes (Wed. div. 1990); children: Helen Mary, Gillian Winifrid, Timothy Arnold; m. Diana Schueler, 1994; 1 stepchild, Gregory Jordan. B.Sc., Bristol U., Eng., 1960; MA, Cambridge U., Eng., 1965, PhD, 1966. Research chemist Robert Dempster and Co., Yorkshire, Eng., 1960-61; research fellow Churchill Coll., Cambridge U., 1965-68; prof. history and sociology of sci. U. Pa., Phila., 1968-96, Joseph Priestley prof. emeritus history/sociology of sci., 1996—, chmn. dept., 1970-77, dir. Beckman Ctr. for History of Chemistry, 1982-96; prof. history, prof. chemistry, dean grad. studies and research U. Md., 1985-86. Exec. dir. libr. chem. Chemical Found., 1987-96, pres., 1996—; vis. lectr. Harvard U., 1967-68; vis. fellow All Souls Coll., Oxford, Eng., 1977-78; mem. Inst. Advanced Study, 1980. Editor: Isis, an Internat. Rev. of History of Science and its Cultural Influences, 1978-85, Osiris, 1985-94, Science After '40, 1992,

Constructing Knowledge in the History of Science, 1995, Private Science, 1998, (with others) Science and Values, 1974, Toward a Metric of Science, 1978; author: Atoms and Powers, 1970, John Dalton, 1972, (with others) Gentlemen of Science, 1981-82, Chemistry in America, 1985, (with others) Arnold O. Beckman, 2000; contbr. articles to profl. jours. Recipient Gladstone Essay prize, also pub. speaking prize Churchill Coll., Cambridge U.; Guggenheim fellow, 1971-72, 85-86; Ctr. for Advanced Study in Behavioral Scis. fellow, 1973-74, 83-84 Fellow AAAS, Am. Acad. Arts and Scis., Royal Hist. Soc., Royal Chem. Soc.; mem. Am. Chem. Soc. (Dexter award 1983), Am. Hist. Assn., Manchester Lit. and Philos. Soc. (corr.), History of Sci. Soc., Am. Coun. Learned Socs. (bd. dirs., treas. 1985-96), Soc. for Social Studies of Sci. (pres. 1981-83), Am. Coun. on Edn. (bd. dirs. 1987), Société Chimie (bd. dirs. 1997-2005), Cosmos Club (Washington); trustee U. Pa. Press, Chem. Edn. Found. Episcopalian.

**THACKSTON, EDWARD LEE,** civil engineering educator; b. Nashville, Apr. 29, 1937; s. Guy Carleton and Sydney Virginia (Adams) T.; m. Betty Tucker, Mar. 19, 1961; children: Guy Carleton Thackston Nixon, Leah Virginia Thackston Hawkins. BE summa cum laude, Vanderbilt U., 1961; MS, U. Ill., 1963; PhD, Vanderbilt U., 1966. Registered profl. engr., Tenn. City engr. City of Lebanon, Tenn., 1959; design engr. City of Nashville, 1961-62; instr. Vanderbilt U., Nashville, 1965-66, asst. prof., 1966-69, assoc. prof., 1969-75, prof. engring., 1975-2000, chmn. dept. civil and environ. engring., 1980-99. Asst. to gov. for environ. affairs, State of Tenn., 1972-74; cons. in field. Author book, tech. reports; contbr. to profl. publs. Bd. dirs. Tenn. Environ. Coun., Nashville, 1971-76; bd. dirs. Tenn. Conservation League, Nashville, 1974-2003, v.p., 1977, pres., 1978-80; trustee Cumberland Mus., Nashville, 1986-92; trustee Cumberland U., Lebanon, 1996—, mem. exec. com., 1996-2002, 04—, sec.-treas., 2000-02, 04—. Recipient Tenn. Lifetime Environ./Conservation Stewardship award State Tenn. 1996, Engr. of Yr. Mid. Tenn. Tenn. Soc. Prof. Engring., 2001, Landmark Paper award Assn. Environ. Engring. and Sci. Profs., 2001; named Tenn. Conservationist of Yr., 1974. Fellow ASCE; mem. Am. Water Works Assn. (life), Water Environ. Fedn. (life), Environ. Engring. Profs. (emeritus, Landmark Paper award 2001), Tenn. Hist. Soc., Hillwood Country Club, Tau Beta Pi, Chi Epsilon. Republican. Episcopalian. Avocations: genealogy, history, photography, weightlifting. Business E-Mail: elt@vuse.vanderbilt.edu.

**THADANI, UDHO,** physician, cardiologist; b. Hyderabad, India, Apr. 1, 1941; came to U.S., 1980; s. Vensimal Mulchand and Gopi Thadani; m. Dorothy Ann Thadani, 1974; 1 child, Emma Sarala. MBBS, All India Inst. Med. Scis., New Delhi, 1964. Lic. physician, Okla., Ont., Can., Eng., India; cert. internal medicine, U.K., Can.; cert. cardiology, Can.; diplomate in internal medicine and cardiovasc. diseases Am. Bd. Internal Medicine. Intern All India Inst. Med. Scis., New Delhi, 1964-65, house physician, surgeon, 1965-66; house physician in medicine Joyce Green Hosp., Dartford, Kent, England, 1966-67; sr. house physician in medicine Kingston Gen. Hosp., Hull, England, 1967-69, registrar, rsch. fellow in medicine and cardiology, 1969-71, U. Leeds (Eng.), The Gen. Infirmary at Leeds, 1971-75; sr. rsch. fellow, clin. asst. medicine Queen's U., Kingston Gen. Hosp., Ont., Canada, 1975-78; asst. prof. medicine Queen's U., Kingston, 1978-80; staff physician Kingston Gen. Hosp., 1978-80; assoc. prof. medicine U. Okla. Health Scis. Ctr., Oklahoma City, 1980-83; prof. medicine Okla. U. Health Scis. Ctr., Oklahoma City, 1983—2001, prof. emeritus medicine, 2001, mem. cardiology fellowship com., 1980-82; dir. clin. cardiology Okla. U. Health Scis. Ctr. and VA Med. Ctr., Oklahoma City, 1980-87, cons., 1980—, vice chief cardiovasc. sect., 1981-99, dir. clin. rsch., 1987-99. Vice-chmn. rsch. and devel. com. VA Med. Ctr., Oklahoma City, 1989-92, chmn. physiology-pharmacology categorical rev. com., 1989-94, chmn. rsch. and devel. com., VA Med. Ctr. Oklahoma City, 1992-94, 2003-05; sr. rsch. fellow Ont. Heart Found., 1978-80, rsch. fellow, 1976-78; rsch. fellow dept. medicine Queen's U., Kingston, Ont., 1975-76; rsch. fellow U. Leeds, Pub. Health and Ciba Found., dept. medicine and cardiovasc. sect. Leeds Gen. Infirmary, 1971-75. Editor: Medical Therapy of Ischemic Heart Disease, 1992, Nitrates Updated, 1996; mem. editl. bd. panel Cardiology Drug Facts and Comparison, 1989; contbg. rev. panel Drug Facts and Comparisons, 1989—; mem. editl. bd. Internat. Jour. Cardiology, 1987-93, Cardiovascular Drugs and Therapy, 1987-2004, Heart Diseases, 1999-2004, Am. Jour. Pharmacology, 2000-04, Am. Jour. Cardiovasc. Drugs, 2003—, Cardiology, 2005—; reviewer Circulation, Jour. Am. Coll. Cardiology, Am. Jour. Cardiology, Brit. Heart Jour., Internat. Jour. Cardiology, Can. Jour. Cardiology, European Heart Jour., Annals of Internal Medicine, New Eng. Jour. Medicine, Archives of Internal Medicine, Cardiovasc. Drugs and Therapy, Drugs, European Jour. Pharmacology, Clin. Pharmacology and Therapeutics; contbr. over 200 articles to profl. jours., chpts. to books. Recipient Provost Rsch. award, OUHSC, 1995, James F. Hammarsten award for physicians of excellence award, VA Med. Ctr., Okla., 2003. Fellow: Coun. Clin. Cardiology Am. Heart Assn. (coun. rep. Okla. 1989—2000), Am. Coll. Cardiology (mem. cardiovasc. drug com. 1990—94), Royal Soc. Medicine London; mem.: Can. Cardiovasc. Soc., Royal Coll. Physicians U.K., Phi Kappa Phi (mem. FDA cardiovasc. and renal drugs adv. com. 1995—99). Avocations: gardening, tennis, travel. Office: Okla U Health Sci Ctr Cardiology Sect 920 SL Young WP 3120 Oklahoma City OK 73104 Office Phone: 405-271-4742. Business E-Mail: udho-thadani@ouhsc.edu.

**THADDEUS, PATRICK,** physicist, researcher; b. Wilmington, Del., June 6, 1932; s. Victor and Elizabeth (Ross) T.; m. Janice Petherbridge Farrar, Apr. 6, 1963 (dec. Dec. 2001); children: Eva, Michael; m. Valerie McCollom, Nov. 1, 2003. B.Sc., U. Del., 1953; MA, Oxford U., Eng., 1955; PhD, Columbia U., 1960; DSc (hon.), U. Chgo., 2003. Research assoc. Columbia Radiation Lab., 1960-61; research assoc. Goddard Inst. Space Studies, N.Y.C., 1961-63, mem. sci. staff, 1963-86; mem. faculty Columbia U., 1965-86, adj. prof. physics, 1971-86; prof. astronomy and applied physics Harvard U., 1986-2000, Robert Wheeler Willson prof. applied astronomy, 2000—; mem. sci. staff Smithsonian Astrophys. Obs., 1986—. Vis. com. Nat. Radio Astronomy Obs. 1973-76, 91-94; mem. Astronomy Survey Com., 1978-80, 89-90; chair task group on Space Astronomy and Astrophysics, 1996-97; Fairchild Disting. Scholar Calif. Inst. Tech., 1994; Russell Marker lectr. Pa. State U., 1989; vis. fellow Inst. Astronomy, Cambridge, Eng. 1983. Author papers on microwave spectroscopy, optical and radio astronomy. Recipient Exceptional Sci. Achievement medal NASA, 1970, 85; John C. Lindsay Meml. award Goddard Space Flight Center, 1976; Alexander von Humboldt award, 1983; Herschel medal Royal Astron. Soc., 2001; Fulbright fellow, 1953-55. Fellow Am. Phys. Soc.; mem. Am. Astron. Soc., Am. Acad. Arts and Scis., Nat. Acad. Scis., Internat. Astronomical Union, Saturday Club, Sigma Xi. Address: 58 Garfield St Cambridge MA 02138-1802

**THADEN, EDWARD CARL,** history professor; b. Seattle, Apr. 24, 1922; s. Edward Carl and Astrid (Engvik) T.; m. Marianna Theresia Forster, Aug. 7, 1952. BA, U. Wash., 1944; student, U. Zurich, Switzerland, 1948; PhD, U. Paris, 1950. Instr. Russian history Pa. State U., 1952-55, asst. prof., 1955-58, assoc. prof., 1958-64, prof., 1964-68, U. Ill., 1968—92, chmn. dept. history, 1971—73, prof. emeritus 1992—. Vis. prof. Ind. U., 1957, U. Marburg, 1965, U. Ill., Urbana, 1980, U. Halle, Germany, 1988, U. Helsinki, Finland, 1990; editl. cons. Can. Rev. Studies in Nationalism, 1973—78; vis. rsch. scholar USSR Acad. Scis., 1975, 88, 90; project prin. rschr. Ford Found., 1975—78; U.S. rep. Internat. Congress of Hist. Scis., 1980; project dir. NEH grant, 1980—82. Author: Conservative Nationalism in Nineteenth-Century Russia, 1964, Russia and the Balken Alliance of 1912, 1965, Russia Since 1801: The Making of a New Society, 1971, Russia's Western Borderlands, 1710-1870, 1984, Interpreting History: collected Essays on Russia's Relations with Europe, 1990, Essays in Russian and East European History: Festschrift in Honor of Edward C. Thaden, 1995, The Rise of Historicism in Russia, 1999; co-author, editor: Russification in the Baltic Provinces and Finland, 1855-1914, 1981; co-editor: Finland and the Baltic Provinces in the Russian Empire, 1984; mem. editorial bd. Jour. Baltic Studies, 1984-93, assoc. editor, 1987-93, East European Quarterly, 1968—. Served to lt. (j.g.) USNR, 1943-46. Carnegie Inter-Univ. Com. travel grantee to USSR, 1956; Fulbright rsch. grantee Finland, 1957-58, Germany, 1965, Poland and Finland, 1968; Soc. Sci. Rsch. Coun. grantee, 1957; Am. Coun.

Learned Socs. grantee, 1963, 65-66; fellow Woodrow Wilson Internat. Ctr. for Scholars, 1980 Mem. Am. Hist. Assn. (life), Nat. History Ctr. (founding mem.), Am. Assn. for Advancement Slavic Studies (pres. Midwest br. 1975-76, exec. sec. 1980-82), Chgo. Consortium for Slavic and Ea. European Studies (pres. 1982-84), Baltische Historische Kommission, Göttingen (corr. mem. 1985—), Commn. Internat. des Etudes Historiques Slaves (v.p. 1985-95, pres. 1995-2000, pres.d'honneur 2000—). Office: U Ill Dept History 913 UH (M/C 198) 601 S Morgan St Chicago IL 60607-7100

**THAIN, JOHN A.,** stock exchange executive; b. Antioch, Ill., May 26, 1955; BS, MIT, 1977; MBA, Harvard U., 1979. CFO, head of ops., tech. & fin. The Goldman Sachs Group, L.P., 1994—99, co-CEO European ops., 1995—97, pres, co-COO, 1999; co-COO The Goldman Sachs Group, Inc., NYC, 1999—2003, pres., 1999—2004, COO, 2003—04; CEO NY Stock Exch., NYC, 2004—06; NYSE Group, Inc., NYC. Bd. dirs. The Goldman Sachs Group, Inc., 1998—2004, NYSE Group, Inc., 2006—; mem. MIT Corp., 2000—, MIT Sloan Sch. Mgmt. dean's adv. coun., INSEAD US Nat. Adv. Bd., Fed. Res. Bank NY Internat. Capital Markets Adv. Com., BritishAmerican Bus. Inc. Mem. James Madison Coun. Libr. Congress; gen. trustee Howard U.; trustee NY-Presbyn. Hosp.; gov. NY Presbyn. Found., Inc.; mem. adv. coun. MIT Sloan Sch. Mgmt. Mem.: Trilateral Commn., French Am. Found. Office: NYSE Group Inc 11 Wall St New York NY 10005*

**THAI-TANG, HAU,** automotive engineer; b. Saigon, Vietnam, Sept. 12, 1966; m. Jenny Thai-Tang. BS in mech. engring., Carnegie-Mellon U.; MBA, U. Mich. Ford Coll. grad. trainee Ford Motor Co., 1988, vehicle engring. mgr. Mustang line, Ford N. Am. car chief engr. Thunderbird, Mustang, and Windstar lines, vehicle engring. mgr. 2000 Lincoln LS, 1997—99. Race engr. Nigel Mansell's CART team Ford Racing, 1993, race engr. Newman-Haas Racing team, 93, race engr. Mario Andretti Racing team; lead recruiter for Ford Motor Co. Carnegie-Mellon U.; leader/tchr. New Bus. Leader program Ford, 2000. Recipient Young Leadership and Excellence award, Automotive Hall Fame, Dearborn, Mich., 2001. Achievements include Lincoln LS earned Motor Trend Car Yr. award, Autoweek's Ten Best award, Consumer Report's "Promising" rating, and was named best driving domestic sedan, Road and Track mag; led the devel. and launch of 2001 Mustang GT, V-6, Cobra and Bullitt GT models for Ford Motor Co; responsible for devel. of Nigel Ansell's and Mario Andretti's race cars. Office: Ford Motor Co PO Box 6248 Dearborn MI 48126

**THAKOR, NITISH VYOMESH,** biomedical engineering educator; b. Nagpur, India, Feb. 9, 1952; came to U.S., 1976; s. Vyomesh H. and Jayshree V. Thakor; m. Ruchira N. Thakor, Dec. 17, 1983; children: Mitali N., Milan N., Jai N., Vir N. B of Tech., Indian Inst. Tech., Bombay, 1974; PhD, U. Wis., 1981. Engr. Philips India Ltd., Bombay, 1974-76; rsch. asst. U. Wis., Madison, 1977-81; asst. prof. Northwestern U., Evanston, Ill., 1981-83, Johns Hopkins U., Balt., 1984-87, assoc. prof., 1987-94, prof., 1994—. Cons. Biomed. Instrumentation, 1984—. Mem. editl. bd. Jour. Ambulatory Monitoring, Med. Design and Material, 1978—, IEEE Jour. Transactions on Biomed. Engring., IEEE Transactions Info. Tech. Biomedicine, 1988-92, Jour. Biol. Sys., 1993-97; contbr. over 130 articles to profl. jours.; patentee in field. Recipient Presdl. Young Investigator award 1985, NIH Rsch. Career Devel. award Centennial medal U. Wis. Sch. Engring.; Fulbright scholar 1987; grantee NSF, NIH, Dept. Edn. Fellow IEEE, Am. Inst. Med. and Biol. Engring.; mem. Sigma Xi. Achievements include devel. of micro-computer-based ambulatory ECG monitor; techniques for arryhythmia detection in implantable pacemakers and defibrillators, neurological signal processing and monitoring instrumentation, medical microsystems and nanotechnology. Home: 12010 Misty Rise Ct Clarksville MD 21029-1256 Office: Johns Hopkins U Med Sch Biomed Engring Dept 720 Rutland Ave Baltimore MD 21205-2109 E-mail: nthakor@bme.jhu.edu.

**THAL, STEVEN HENRY,** lawyer, consultant; b. NYC, Nov. 16, 1942; s. Michael and Mildred (Hirsch) T.; 1 child, Eric Alexander. BA, U. Mich., 1964, JD, 1967; postgrad., U. Tubingen, Fed. Republic Germany, 1967-68, New Sch. Social Rsch., N.Y.C., 1971-72. Bar: N.Y. 1968, U.S. Ct. Appeals (2d cir.) 1969, U.S. Dist. Ct. (so. and ea. dists.) N.Y. 1969, U.S. Supreme Ct. 1973; cert. District Ct., Frankfurt, Germany. Assoc. Donovan, Leisure, Newton & Irvine, N.Y.C., 1968-69, Handler, Kleiman & Sukenik, N.Y.C., 1969-72; ptnr. Thal & Youtt, N.Y.C., 1972-84, Kaplan, Russin & Vecchi, N.Y.C., 1984-88, Summit, Rovins & Feldesman, N.Y.C., 1988-90, Oppenheimer Wolff & Donnelly, N.Y.C., 1990-94, LeBoeuf Lamb Greene & MacRae, N.Y.C., 1994—2003, Latham & Watkins, N.Y.C., 2003—. Pres. Export Assist Corp., Ft. Lee, N.J., 1988-94; trusted atty., Consulate Gen. of Fed. Republic Germany, N.Y.C., 1986—; Austrian Trade Commn., N.Y.C., 1988—; fgn. legal cons., Frankfurt, Germany, 1991; counsel German-Am. Partnership Program, 1998—. Fulbright scholar, 1967-68; grantee Ford Found., 1967-68, Deutsche Akademisches Austauchdienst, 1967-68. Mem. Internat. Bar Assn., N.Y. State Bar Assn. (internat. law com.), Assn. Bar City N.Y., German Am. Lawyers Assn., Gesellschaft fuer Rechtsvergleichung. Avocations: boating, fishing, camping. Office: Latham & Watkins 885 Third Ave Ste 100 New York NY 10022 Office Phone: 212-906-1671. Business E-Mail: steven.thal@lw.com. E-mail: stesq17@hotmail.com.

**THALACKER, ARBIE ROBERT,** lawyer, director; b. Marquette, Mich., Apr. 17, 1935; s. Arbie Otto and Jeanne (Emmett) T.; m. Rita Annette Skaaren, Sept. 11, 1956 (div. July 1992); children: Marc Emmett, Christopher Paul, Robert Skaaren; m. Deborah B. Garrett, Jan. 10, 1998. AB, Princeton U., 1957; JD, U. Mich., 1960. Bar: NY 1961, U.S. Ct. Appeals (2d cir.) 1962. Assoc. Shearman & Sterling, N.Y.C., 1960—68, ptnr., 1968—2000, of counsel, 2001—. Dir. Detrex Corp., Detroit, 1981—, chmn. bd., 1993-96. Leader Rep. Dist. Com., 1966-68; v.p., trustee Greenwich Village Soc. for Hist. Preservation; trustee Naropa Univ.; bd. dirs. Meredith Monk House Found., Shambhala Internat. Mem. ABA, N.Y. Bar Assn., Assn. Bar City N.Y. (securities regulatory comm.), ITF (Tennis), Wine and Food Soc. (bd. dirs. 1976-78, 85-93, 94-2006), Chevaliers du Tastevin, Commanderie de Bordeaux, Siwanoy Country Club (bd. govs. 1976-79), Derby Club, Links Club, Verbank Hunting and Fishing Club. Home: 17 Commerce St New York NY 10014-3763 Office: Shearman & Sterling 599 Lexington Ave Fl C2 New York NY 10022-6069

**THALDEN, BARRY R.,** architect; b. Chgo., July 5, 1942; s. Joseph and Sibyl (Goodwin) Hechtenthal; m. Irene L. Mittleman, June 23, 1966 (div. 1989); 1 child, Stacey; m. Kathyn McKnight, Sept. 1996. BArch, U. Ill., 1965; M in Land Architecture, U. Mich., 1969. Landscape architect Hellmuth, Obata, Kassebaum, St. Louis, 1969-70; dir. landscape architecture PGAV Architects, St. Louis, 1970-71; pres. Thalden Corp. Architects, St. Louis, 1971—; ptnr. Thalden-Boyd Architects, 1998—. Prin. works include Rock Hill Park, 1975 (AIA award, 1977), Wilson Residence, 1983 (AIA award), Nat. Bowling Hall of Fame, 1983 (St. Louis RCGA award, 1984), Village Bogey Hills (Home Builders award, 1985, St. Louis ASLA award, 1994), St. Louis U. Campus Mall (St. Louis ASLA award, 1989), Horizon Casino Resort, Lake Tahoe, Nev., St. Louis Airport's Radisson Hotel, Lady Luck, Treasure Bay, Palace Casinos, Biloxi, Miss., Boomtown Casino, New Orleans, Pres. Casino on the Admiral, St. Louis, Plaza of Champions, Busch Stadium, Ho Chunk Casino, Wisconsin Dells (ABC award Best Bldg. in Wis., 2000), Potowatomi Casino, Milw., Terrible's Casino, Las Vegas, Chumash Casino Resort, Santa Ynez, Calif., Casino Morongo, Palm Springs, Calif. Bd. dirs. St. Louis Open Space Coun., 1973—83, St. Louis Art., Ednl. Coun.; bd. trustees Las Vegas Art Mus.; apptd. Mo. Lands Architect Coun., 1990—94. Named Architect of Yr. Builder Architect mag., 1986. Fellow ASLA, Am. Soc. Landscape Architects (nat. v.p. 1979-81, pres. St. Louis chpt. 1975, trustee 1976-79, nat. conv. chair 1991); mem. AIA, World Future Soc. (pres. St. Louis chpt. 1984-94, keynote conf. spkr. 1995). Avocations: painting, gardening, tennis, guitar. Home: 2204 Chatsworth Ct Henderson NV 89074-5307 Office: Thalden Corp 8085 Manchester Rd Saint Louis MO 63144

**THALER, LINDA KAPLAN,** advertising executive; m. Fred Thaler; children: Michael, Emily. BA magna cum laude, CCNY, MA in music. Former music instr. CCNY; with J. Walter Thompson, most recently as exec. v.p., exec. group creative dir.; exec. v.p., exec. creative dir. Wells Rich Greene BDDP, 1994—97; founder, CEO, chief creative officer Kaplan Thaler Group Ltd., NYC, 1997—. Former mem. comedy improv troupe. Author: (jingle) I Don't Want to Grow Up, I'm a Toys 'R' Us Kid, Eastman Kodak-Because Time Goes By, (book) BANG! Getting Your Message Head in a Noisy World, 2003. Named Advertising Women of Yr., Advertising Women of NY, 2001; recipient 13 Clio awards. Office: Kaplan Thaler Group Ltd 825 Eighth Ave - 34Fl New York NY 10019-7498 Office Phone: 212-474-5000. Office Fax: 212-474-5702. E-mail: kaplanthalergroup@kaplanthaler.com.

**THALER, RICHARD WINSTON, JR.,** investment banker; b. Boston, Apr. 9, 1951; s. Richard Winston and Victoria Louise (Sears) T.; m. Mary Alice Gast, June 28, 1980; children: Julia Davis, Sarah Sears, Hannah Warren. BA in Am. Polit. History cum laude, Princeton U., 1973; MBA, Harvard U., 1978. Salesman Media Networks, N.Y.C., 1973-74; banker Bank of Boston, Rio de Janeiro, 1975-77, Boston, 1978-80; mng. dir. investment banking Lehman Bros., N.Y.C., 1980-96; mng. dir. investment banking, vice chmn. Deutsche Bank Securities, N.Y.C., 1996—. Spl. gifts solicitor Princeton U. Ann. Giving, N.Y.C., 1987—88, 1997—98, 2002—03, class agt., 1988—93; trustee Daily Princetonian, 1989—, pres. bd., 2004—; trustee Episc. Divinity Sch., Cambridge, Mass., 1995—2004, Plimoth Plantation, Plymouth, Mass., 1995—; del. Dem. Nat. Conv., 1996; active Dem. Leadership Coun.; mem. vestry Chapel of St. James the Fisherman, Wellfleet, Mass. Mem. Mass. Soc. Mayflower Descs., Harvard Club, Siwanoy Country Club, Univ. Cottage Club. Democrat. Episcopalian. Avocations: gardening, sailing, American political history, travel. Personal E-mail: richard.thaler@db.com.

**THALL, BURNETT MURRAY,** retired newspaper executive; b. Toronto, Ont., Can., Sept. 27, 1922; s. Henry and Selina (Harris) Rosenthal; m. Eleanor Langbord, Sept. 23, 1945; children: Nelson Spencer, Martin Evan BASc., U. Toronto, 1945, MASc., 1947, PhD, 1949. Registered profl. engr., Ont. Spl. lectr. applied sci. and engring. U. Toronto, 1947; cons. engr., then prodn. engr. Toronto Star, 1947-50, v.p., 1958-68, sr. v.p., 1968-96, also dir. Chmn. Toronto Star Newspapers Ltd., elected chmn. bd., 1996-99 Trustee Atkinson Charitable Found.; hon. trustee Women's Coll. Hosp. Urgent Care Ctr.; founding trustee Princess Margaret Hosp. Urgent Care Centre named in his honour Women's Coll. Hosp., 1989 Mem. Assn. Profl. Engrs. Ont. (Citizenship medal 1991) Home: 15 Rosemary Ln Toronto ON Canada M5P 3E7 Office: 1 Yonge St Toronto ON Canada M5E 1E5

**THALL, ROBERT,** photographer, educator; b. Chgo., Dec. 6, 1948; BA in Design, U. Ill., 1972, MFA in Photography, 1986. Prof. photography Columbia Coll., Chgo., 1976—, chmn. Photography Dept. Vis. artist U. Ill., Chgo., 1975, adj. asst. prof. art, 80; lectr. in field. One-man shows include Evanston (Ill.) Art Ctr., 1980, Moming Art and Dance Ctr., Chgo., 1980, Edwynn Houk Gallery, 1984, Art Inst. Chgo., 1994, Ehlers Caudill Gallery, Chgo., 1995, City of Chgo. Photography Gallery at Water Tower, 1999, Mus. Contemporary Photography, 1999, exhibited in group shows at Hodges Taylor Gallery, Charlotte, N.C., 1996, Mus. Contemporary Art, Chgo., 1996, Mus. Van Bommel-Van Dam, Venlo, The Netherlands, 1997, Milw. Art Mus., 1999, others; curated exhbns. include Truman Coll., 1980, Chgo. Ctr. Contemporary Photography, Columbia Coll., 1983; commns. include, Historic Bldgs. Iowa, 1976, Ctrl. Mfg. Dist., 1983, Midway Airport Pub. Art Competition, 1999, others, Represented in permanent collections Art Inst. Chgo., Calif. Mus. Photography, Riverside, Calif., Can. Ctr. Arch., Montreal, Chgo. Hist. Soc., Getty Ctr. History Art and Humanities, Santa Monica, Calif., Hallmark Collection, Kansas City, Mo., Milw. Art Mus., Mus. Fine Art, Houston, Mus. Folkwang, Essen, Germany, Mus. Modern Art, N.Y.C., Seagram Collection, Victoria and Albert Mus., London, others; book and exhbn. reviewer Exposure and New Art Examiner, 1980—83; author: The Perfect City, 1994; The New American Village, 1999, City Spaces, 2002. Grantee Project Completion grantee, Ill. Arts Coun., 1980; Graham Found. grantee, 1998, John Simon Guggenheim Meml. Found. fellow, 1998. Office: Columbia Coll Dept Photography 600 S Michigan Ave Chicago IL 60605-1900

**THALLANDER, MARK ALAN,** music educator; b. Grand Forks, N.D., Aug. 9, 1950; s. Wilfred Lasse and Mae Bernice Thallander. BA, Vanguard U., 1972; MA, Calif. State U., Long Beach, 1974; postgrad., U. So. Calif. Asst. dir. music Crystal Cathedral, Garden Grove, Calif., 1976—93; assoc. min. worship Menlo Park (Calif.) Presbyn. Ch., 1993—95; dir. music Lake Ave. Ch., Pasadena, Calif., 1995—98; assoc. prof. music Vanguard U., Costa Mesa, Calif., 1998—2002; organ editor Fred Bock Music Co., Tarzana, Calif., 1998—. Adj. prof. music Glendale (Calif.) Coll., 2002—. Editor: Encore! Encore!, 2000; author, arranger: Cathedral Hymns, 1993, Organ Hymns of Faith, Vol. 1, 1997, Vol. 2, 1999, Vol. 3, 2004. Pres. Mark Thallander Found., Pasadena, 2004—; organist Glendale Presbyn. Ch., 1998—2001. Recipient Crystal Wave award, Crystal Cathedral, 2004. Mem.: Nat. Assn. Ch. Musicians, Am. Guild Organists (dean Orange County chpt. 1987—90). Office: Glendale CC 1500 N Verdugo Rd Glendale CA 91208-2894 Personal E-mail: markthallander@aol.com.

**THALLER, SETH RAY,** plastic surgeon; b. N.Y.C., June 22, 1949; m. Patricia Thaller; children: Cody, Lexi. BA, Lafayette Coll., 1971; MD, U. Louisville, 1975; DMD, Boston Sch. Dentistry, 1978; resident gen. surgery, St. Vincent's Hosp., 1978-80. Intern in internal medicine SUNY, Buffalo, 1975-76; resident in gen. surgery St. Vincent's Hosp., N.Y.C., 1978-80; resident otalaryngology/head and neck surgery Mass. Eye and Ear Infirmary, 1980-83; resident in plastic surgery Albert Einstein Coll. Medicine Affiliated Hosps., 1983—85; craniofacial fellowship UCLA Sch. Medicine, 1986; clin. instr. NYU Sch. Dentistry, N.Y.C., 1984-86; adj. asst. prof. plastic surgery U. Calif., L.A., 1986, asst. prof. plastic surgery, 1987-93, acting chief divsn. plastic surgery, 1989, assoc. prof. plastic surgery Davis, 1993-95; prof. and chief divsn. plastic surgery U. Miami/Jackson Meml. Hosp., 1995—. Mem.: Florida Soc. Plastic Surgeons, Inc, ACS, Am. Assn Plastic Surgeons, Assn. Academic Chmn. Plastic Surgeons, Am. Soc. Maxillofacial Surgeons, Am. Soc. Plastic & Reconstructive Surgeons, Am. Cleft Palate Craniofacial Assn., Am. Society for Aesthetic Plastic Surgery, Am. Acad. Pediatrics, AMA. Home: 11010 Paradela St Coral Gables FL 33156-4244 Office: Univ Miami Jackson Meml Hospital PO Box 16960 Miami FL 33101-6960

**THAMAN, MICHAEL H.,** building material systems executive; BSEE, Princeton U., BS in Computer Sci. V.p. Mercer Mgmt. Cons., N.Y.C., 1986—92; dir. corp. devel. Owens Corning, 1992-94, plant mgr. Toronto insulation facility, 1994-96, gen. mgr. OEM solutions group Louisville, 1996-97, v.p., pres. engineered pipe systems bus. Brussels, 1997-99, v.p., pres. exterior systems bus., 1999-2000, sr. v.p., CFO Toledo, 2000—, bd. chmn., 2002—. Bd. dir. FPL Group. Office: Owens Corning One Owens Corning Pkwy Toledo OH 43659*

**THAMES, LEE DAVIS,** lawyer; b. Vicksburg, Miss., July 24, 1936; s. James D. and Susan (Davis) T.; m. Jane Andrews; children: Hampton D., Kendall Thames Nelson, Mary Louise Thames Bexley, Amzi, Marshall, Holley Thames Biedenharn, Lee Davis. BA with honors, U. Miss., 1958, LLB with honors, 1960. Bar: Miss. 1960, U.S. Dist. Ct. (so. dist.) Miss. 1960, U.S. Ct. Mil. Appeals 1960, U.S. Ct. Appeals (5th cir.) 1964, U.S. Dist. Ct. (no. dist.) Miss. 1965, U.S. Supreme Ct. 1969, U.S. Ct. Appeals (11th cir.) 1983, U.S. Ct. Appeals (9th cir.) 1988, U.S. Ct. Appeals (2d cir.) 1992, U.S. Ct. Appeals (6th cir.) 1994, U.S. Ct. Appeals (4th cir.) 1996, U.S. Ct. Appeals (D.C. cir.) 2000. Ptnr. Vollor & Thames, Vicksburg, 1962-70, Ramsey, Bodron, Thames & Robinson, Vicksburg, 1970-81, Butler, Snow, O'Mara, Stevens & Cannada, Jackson, Miss., 1981—. Part time U.S. Magistrate, So. Dist. Miss., 1968-75; speaker trial tactics subjects Def. Rsch. Inst., Miss. Def. Lawyers Assn. and other orgns. Contbr. to book; contbr. articles to profl. jours. Sec. Standing Commn. on Peace Episcopal Ch., USA, 1986-91; lectr. Episcopal Diocese of Miss., 1983-85, 90-92, v.p., 1990, 91, mem. standing com., 1986-89, sec., 1987, dep. gen. conv., 1988, 91, 94, 97, alt., 1985, Peace Commn., 1982-87, chmn., 1985-87, Div. of Youth, Edn. for Ministry, Living

into our Baptism, Cursillo; pres. Vicksburg Jaycees, Vicksburg-Warren County United Givers Fund, Vicksburg Theater Guild; chmn. Vicksburg Bd. Archtl. Rev.; bd. dirs. Jackson Symphony. Brig. gen. USAR, ret. Decorated D.S.M., Army Res. Components Achievement medal with oak leaf cluster, Army Res. medal with 10-year device, Army Res. Components Overseas Tng. Ribbon with numeral 2, Air Assault-Badge. Fellow Am. Coll. Trial Lawyers, Miss. Bar Found.; mem. ABA, Fed. Bar Assn., Internat. Assn. Def. Counsel, Products Liability Adv. Coun., Miss. State Bar Assn. (bd. bar commrs., complaint tribunal), Hinds County Bar Assn., Warren County Bar Assn. (pres.), Warren County Jr. Bar Assn. (pres.), Vicksburg C. of C. Office: PO Box 22567 Jackson MS 39225-2567 Office Phone: 601-985-4517. Business E-Mail: lee.davis.thames@butlersnow.com.

**THAMES, RICK,** publishing executive, editor; b. Laurinburg, NC; m. Debbie Thames; children: Nathan, Hunter, Lucy. AB in English, Pfeiffer Coll., Misenheimer, NC; MS in Comm., U. Tenn., Knoxville. Reporter The Fayetteville Observer, NC, 1978—80; various positions including mng. editor Miami News, 1980—88; various positions including govt. editor, city editor, assist. mng. editor, public editor The Charlotte Observer, 1988—96; editor The Wichita Eagle, Kans., 1997—2004; v.p., editor The Charlotte Observer, 2004—. Chmn. adv. bd. Elliot Sch. of Comm., Wichita State U. Mem.: Am. Soc. of Newspaper Editors (mem. Freedom of Info. Com.), Kansas Press Assn. (bd. dirs.). Office: The Charlotte Observer PO Box 32188 600 S Tryon St Charlotte NC 28232

**THAMM, JOCHEN WALTER,** library director; b. Magdeburg, Germany, Jan. 11, 1952; s. Walter and Anna (Goldmann) T.; m. Gabriele Neumann, Apr. 16, 1977; children: Ute, Stephan, Anna. Diplom in math., Tech. U., Merseburg, German Dem. Republic, 1974; Fachbibliothekar, U. Berlin, German Dem. Republic, 1985. Mathematician various cos., 1974-83; dir. libr. Deutsche Akademie der Naturforscher Leopoldina, Halle, 1985—. Office: Dt Akademie Naturforscher Bibliothek A-Bebel-Str 50a D 06108 Halle Sachsen-Anhalt Germany E-mail: thamm@leopoldina-halle.de.

**THAMPI, MOHAN VARGHESE,** environmental health and civil engineer; b. Kuching, Sarawak, Malaysia, Mar. 25, 1960; s. Padmanabha Ramachandran and Sosamma (Varghese) T. Gen. Cert. Edn., Cambridge U., 1976; B in Tech. with honors, Indian Inst. Tech., Kharagpur, India, 1983; MS in Engring., U. Tex., 1985; DSc (hon.), London Inst. Applied Rsch., 1992. Registered profl. engr., Tex., Fla., registered environ. mgr.; cert. safety tng. OSHA; cert. Nat. Coun. Examiners for Engrs. and Surveyors. Assoc. engr. Brown & Caldwell, Dallas, 1985-87, project mgr. Orlando, 1987-88, Stottler Stagg & Assocs., Cape Canaveral, Fla., 1988-91; sr. project engr. Chastain-Skillman, Inc., Lakeland, Fla., 1991-93; project mgr. Glace & Radcliffe, Inc., Winter Park, Fla., 1993-94; mgr. FDEP, West Palm Beach, Fla., 1995-96; project mgr. Office of Capital Projects Mgmt., Naples, Fla., 1996—2004; projects engring. mgr. Project Mgmt., Bradenton, Fla., 2004—. Author: Ultraviolet Disinfection Studies in a Teflon-Tube Reactor, 1985; contbr. articles to profl. jours. Active Rep. Pres.'s Citizens Adv. Commn., 1992. Recipient Cert. of Cont. Profl. Devel. award Fla. Engring. Soc., 1992. Mem. NRA, NSPE, ASCE (assoc.), Project Mgmt. Inst., Internat. Assn. Water Pollution Rsch. and Control, Am. Mensa, Am. Water Works Assn., Water Pollution Control Fedn. (com. for preparing design practice manuals 1989—), Internat. Freelance Photographers Assn., Internat. Platform Assn., Internat. Assn. Air Travel Couriers, Am. Mgmt. Assn., Am. Smokers Alliance, Am. Gunsmithing Assn., Smithsonian Instn., Nat. Geog. Soc., Nat. Registry Environ. Professionals, U. Tex. Ex-Students Assn., Wine Soc. Am., Nat. Family Opinion, Internat. Deep Purple Appreciation Soc., Wilson Ctr. Assocs., I.I.T. Kharagpur Tech. Found., NASA Tech Briefs Reader Opinion Panel, Chemical Engring. Jour. Product Rsch. Panel, Nat. Rifle Assn., Plant Engring. Editl. Quality Panel, Kharagpur Tech. Alumni Found., N.Am. Hunting Club, Knight Order of Templars (Jerusalem), PC Bug Computer Club. Mar Thoma Syrian Christian. Avocations: photography, music, travel, sports. Home: PO Box 11954 Naples FL 34101-2954 Personal E-mail: thampimv@juno.com.

**THANDAPANI, ETHIRAJ,** mathematics professor; PhD, Madras U., Chennai, India, 1980. Prof. of math. Periyar U., Salem, Tamil Nadu, 2001—. Contbr. articles to profl. jours. Office: Periyar U Bangalore Main Rd Tamil Nadu Salem 636011 India Office Phone: +914272345766. Office Fax: +914272345124. E-mail: ethandapani@yahoo.co.in.

**THAPAR, AMUL R.,** prosecutor; b. Troy, Mich., 1969; m. Kimberly Ann Thapar; children: Zachary, Carmen, Nicholas. Grad., Boston Coll., 1991; JD, U. Calif. Berkeley, 1994. Law clk. to Hon. S. Arthur Spiegel US Dist. Ct. (so. dist.) OH, 1994—96; law clk. to Hon. Nathaniel R. Jones US Ct. Appeals (6th Cir.); assoc. Squire, Sanders & Dempsey, Cin., Williams & Connolly, Washington; asst. US atty. DC US Dept. Justice, Washington, 1999—2001, asst. US atty. (so. dist.) OH Cin., 2002—06, US atty. (ea. dist.) Ky. Lexington, 2006—. Founder Street Law Inc., Cin., 1995; adj. prof. law George University Law Ctr., U. Cin. Coll. Law. Office: US Attys Office 110 W Vine St Ste 400 Lexington KY 40507*

**THARALDSON, GARY DEAN,** hotel developer, owner; b. Valley City, N.D., Oct. 17, 1945; BA in Phys. Edn., Valley City State U.; postgrad., N.D. State U. Tchr., Leonard, N.D.; ins. agt., agy. owner, 1969-89; owner of 350 hotels, Valley City, 1982; pres. Tharaldson Enterprises, Fargo, N.D., 1982—. Office: Tharaldson Enterprises 1202 Westrac Dr Fargo ND 58103-2344

**THARNEY, LEONARD JOHN,** education educator, consultant; b. New Haven, Nov. 6, 1929; s. Lillian A. Batey; m. Denise A. Gauvin, June 20, 1981; children: Karen L., Linda L. BS, Trenton (N.J.) State Coll., 1954; MEd, Rutgers U., 1959; postgrad., Lehigh U., Bethlehem, Pa., 1963-70, Columbia U.; grad., Command & Gen. Staff Coll., Ft. Leavenworth, Kans., 1972. Cert. secondary math. and sci. tchr., elem. tchr. Tchr. (elem. demonstration) Trenton State Coll., NJ, 1954-60; tchr. (jr. high demonstration) Ewing Twp. Sch., NJ, 1960-63; cons., evaluator Am. Coun. on Edn., Washington, 1975-95, field coord., 1995—2003; cons., evaluator Mid. States Assn., Phila., 1987—; prof. Trenton State Coll., 1963-92, dept. chmn., 1988-92, prof. emeritus, 1993—; cons., evaluator Nat. Assn. Indsl. Tech., Ann Arbor, 2003—. Cons. to internat. sch. for curriculum or sci. edn., Monrovia, Accra, Athens, Mogadishu, Cairo, Alexandria, Aleppo, Damascus, 1975—; tchr. grad. courses in curriculum and ednl. rsch. at overseas sites, Spain, Cyprus, Saudi Arabia, Syria, 1981—; exch. prof., Worcester Coll. Higher Edn., Eng., 1984-85; presenter sci. edn. workshops, AISA Internat. Conf., Nairobi, 1987; rep. from Coll. to Prins. Tng. Ctr., London, 1994; bd. dir. Trenton, NJ chpt. People to People Internat., 1995-98, chpt. pres., 1998—; NJ del. Worldwide Conf. of People to People Internat., Chester, Eng., 1998, Hong Kong, 2000, Aalborg, Denmark, 2001, Kansas City, Mo., 2002, Stockholm, 2002, Roman, Romania, 2003; internat. trustee, 2000-; 15th World Wide Conf. del., Kansas City, Mo., 2002, 16th World Wide Conf. del., Milan, 2004; mem. Accrediting Commn. of the Distance Education and Training Council, Wash., DC, 2000—. Co-author 7 manuals for uniform constrn. codes. Col. AUS, 1947-81. Decorated Meritorious Svc. medal; recipient ACE award for outstanding svc. in mil. evaluations, 1987; cert. of appreciation, presdl. citation, 1989, spl. plaque award, Outstanding Svc. and Support award 112th FA Assn., 1998; Alumni Assn. award, Distinguished Svc., Coll. N.J., 2005, People to People Internat. Outstanding Leadership award, Seoul, Republic of Korea, 2005, others. Mem.: ASCD, Nat. Coun. Social Studies, Assn. for Edn. Tchrs. in Sci., Assn. Tchr. Educators, Am. Air Mus. in Britain (founding mem.), Torch Club Internat., the Trenton Club (bd. dir. 1998—2001, v.p. 2001—02, pres. 2002—03). Home: 20 Lawrenceville-Penning Rd Lawrenceville NJ 08648-1648 E-mail: ljmt.afa@att.net.

**THARNISH, ROSE MARIES LEHMAN,** veterinarian; b. Greenville, Miss., Sept. 23, 1942; d. Isadore Hyman Lehman and Leatha Josephine Haynes; m. Robert Earley (div.); m. Larry Leslie Tharnish, Feb. 3, 1981. Student, N.W. Jr. Coll., Delta State U.; B, Memphis State U. N.Y.; JD, U.

Tenn. Pres., owner Faith Ministry, Walls, Miss. Chmn. adv. bd. Rep. Nat. Com.; pres., bd. dirs. ACLU. Mem. Gardening Club, Audio Club, Book Club, Sierra Club, VFW, NAPCA. Avocation: scuba diving. Home: 5491 Adams Cir Walls MS 38680-8935

**THAROOR, SHASHI,** international organization official; b. London, Mar. 9, 1956; came to the U.S., 1975; s. Chandran and Lily (Menon) T.; m. Tilottama Tharoor; children: (twins) Ishaan, Kanishk. BA with honors, Delhi U., 1975; MA, Tufts U., 1976, MA in Law and Diplomacy, 1977, PhD, 1978. External affairs officer UN High Commn. for Refugees, Geneva, 1978-81, head sub-office and rep. Singapore, 1981-84, dep. chief of secretariat Geneva, 1985-87, exec. asst. to the dep. high commr., 1987-89; spl. asst. to under-sec.-gen. for peace-keeping UN, N.Y.C., 1989—96, prin. officer dept. peace-keeping ops., 1995-96, exec. asst. to the sec-gen., 1997-98; dir. comm. and spl. projects Office of Sec.-Gen., 1998—2001; interim head of dept. of public information UN, 2001—02, under-sec. gen. for communications and public information, 2002—. Author: Reasons of State, 1981, The Great Indian Novel, 1989 (Best Book of the Yr., Fedn. Indian Pubs. 1990, Best Book Eurasian region Commonwealth Writers prize 1990), Show Business, 1992, India: From Midnight to the Millennium, 1997, Riot, 2001, (with M.F. Husain) Kerala: God's Own Country, 2002, (short story collection) The Five-Dollar Smile, 1990, 93; columnist The Hindu, contbg. editor, Newsweek Internat.; book reviewer Washington Post, The N.Y. Times, others; contbr. articles to profl. jours. Named Global Leader of Tomorrow, World Econ. Forum, Davos, Switzerland, 1998. Fellow N.Y. Inst. of the Humanities; mem. Internat. Inst. Strategic Studies (keynote spkr. 1995), Indian Internat. Ctr. Hindu. Avocations: reading, writing, cricket, theater. Office: UN Room S-1027A New York NY 10017*

**THARP, ROLAND GEORGE,** psychology professor; b. Galveston, Tex., June 6, 1930; s. Oswald Roland and Berma Lucille (Keefer) T.; m. Stephanie Dalton; children: Donald Martin, Thomas Roland, David Michael, Julie. Student, Middlebury Coll., 1956, 60; BA cum laude, U. Houston, 1957; MA, U. Mich., 1958, PhD, 1961. Cert. Am. Bd. Examiners in Profl. Psychology. Reporter Tex. City Sun, 1946-47; mgr. Tharp Lumber Co., LaMarque, Tex., 1949-54; intern VA Hosp., Menlo Park, Calif.; 1960; asst. prof. U. Ariz., Tucson, 1961-65, assoc. prof., 1965-68; prof., dir. clin. studies, dir. multicultural ctr. for higher edn. U. Hawaii, Honolulu, 1968-87; provost and v.p. for acad. affairs U.S. Internat. U., San Diego, 1987-89; prof. edn., psychology U. Calif., Santa Cruz, 1990—; dir. Nat. Rsch. Ctr. for Diversity, 1995—. Dir. Ctr. for Rsch. on Edn., Diversity and Excellence, 1996—; prin. investigator Kamehameha Early Edn. Program, Honolulu, 1969-89; field selection officer Peace Corps, Washington, 1965-67. Author: (poetry) Highland Station, 1978; co-author: Behavior Modification in the Natural Environment, 1969, Self-Directed Behavior, 1980, Rousing Minds to Life, 1988, Teaching Transformed, 2000; writer, producer, dir. film Scenes from the Life, 1981 (Purchase prize The Contemporary Mus. 1981). Mem. Bd. Psychologist Examiners, Ariz., 1964-67; pres. Hawaii Literary Arts Coun., Honolulu, 1982. Robert Frost fellow Middlebury Coll., 1960; recipient Am. Film Mag. award for filmmaking Hawaii Internat. Film Festival, 1990, Grawemeyer award edn., 1993. Mem. Am. Ednl. Rsch. Assn., Am. Anthropol. Assn. Episcopalian. Avocations: tennis, painting. Office: 560 N St SW Apt N702 Washington DC 20024-4621 E-mail: tharp@ucsc.edu.

**THARP, TWYLA,** dancer; b. Portland, Ind., July 1, 1941; m. Peter Young (div.); m. Robert Huot (div.); 1 child, Jesse Huot. Student, Pomona Coll.; BA in Art History, Barnard Coll., 1963; D of Performing Arts (hon.), Calif. Inst. Arts, 1978, Brown U., 1981, Bard Coll. 1981; LHD, Ind. U., 1987; DFA, Pomona Coll., 1987; studied with Richard Thomas, Merce Cunningham, Igor Schwezoff, Louis Mattox, Paul Taylor, Margaret Craske, Erick Hawkins. Dancer Paul Taylor Dance Co., 1963-65; freelance choreographer with own modern dance troupe and various other cos. including Joffrey Ballet and Am. Ballet Theatre, 1965-87; founder, choreographer Twyla Tharp Dance Found., N.Y.C., 1965-87; artistic assoc., resident choreographer Am. Ballet Theatre, N.Y.C., 1987-91; teaching residencies various colls. and univs. including U. Mass., Oberlin Coll., Walker Art Ctr., Boston U. Choreographer White Oak Dance Project. Choreographer Tank Dive, 1965, Re-Moves, 1966, One Two Three, 1966, Forevermore, 1967, Generation, 1968, Medley, 1969, After Suite, 1969, Dancing in the Streets of London and Paris, 1969, The One Hundreds, 1970, The Fugue, 1970, The Bix Pieces, 1971, Eight Jelly Rolls, 1971, The Raggedy Dances, 1972, Deuce Coupe, 1973, As Time Goes By, 1974, Sue's Leg, 1975, Ocean's Motion, 1975, Push Comes to Shove, 1976, Once More Frank, 1976, Mud, 1977, Baker's Dozen, 1979, When We Were Very Young, 1980, Nine Sinatra Songs, 1982, The Catherine Wheel, 1982, Bach Partita, 1984, The Little Ballet, 1984, with Jerome Robbins Brahms Handel, 1988, At the Supermarket, 1984, In the Upper Room, 1987, Ballare, 1987, Stations of the Crossed, 1988, Everlast, 1989, Quartet, 1989, Bum's Rush, 1989, The Rules of the Game, 1990, Brief Fling, 1990, Grand Pas: Rhythm of the Saints, 1991, Deuce Coupe II, 1992, The Men's Piece, 1992, with Mikhail Baryshnikov Cutting Up, 1992—93, Demeter and Persephone, 1993, Waterbaby Bagatelles, 1994, Demeter and Persephone, 1994, Red, White & Blues, 1995, How Near Heaven, 1995, I Remember Clifford, 1995, Jump Start, 1995, Americans We, 1995, Movin' Out, 1998 (Touring Broadway awards, best choreography, 2005), The Times They Are A-Changin', 2006, (films) Hair, 1979, Ragtime, 1981, Amadeus, 1984, White Nights, 1985, Valmont, 1989, I'll Do Anything, 1994, video spls. Making Television Dance, 1977, CBS Cable Confessions of a Corner Maker, 1980, (Broadway plays) Sorrow Floats, 1985, Singin' in the Rain, 1985, TV Baryshnikov by Tharp, 1985 (Emmy award for Outstanding Choreography, 1985, Emmy award for Outstanding Writing of Classical Music/Dance Programming, 1985), The Catherine Wheel, 1982 (Emmy award nomination for Outstanding Choreography, 1982); author (autobiography): When Push Comes to Shove, 1987. Recipient Creative Arts award, Brandeis U., 1972, Dance Mag. award, 1981, Univ. Excellence medal, Columbia U., 1987, Lions of the Performing Arts award, N.Y. Pub. Libr., 1989, Samuel M. Scripps award, Am. Dance Festival, 1990; MacArthur Found. fellow, 1992.

**THARPE, DON L.,** foundation administrator; b. Jan. 1952; m. Linda Tharpe; children: Justin, Adrienne. BS, Murray State U., 1974, MS, 1975; PhD in Edn. Adminstrn., Va. Polytechnic & State U. Dir. trade and vocational edn. Mo. State Dept. Edn.; with Am. Vocational Assn.; dir. profl. programs Assn. of Sch. Bus. Officials Internat., Reston, Va., 1985—89, acting exec. dir., 1989—90, exec. dir., 1990—2002; exec. v.p., COO Coun. on Founds., Washington, 2002—06; pres., CEO Congl. Black Caucus Found., Inc., Washington, 2005—. Former mem. Nat. Policy Bd. for Ednl. Adminstrn. Contbr. articles to profl. jours. Recipient Disting. Alumnus, Murry State U., 2005. Mem.: Am. Soc. Assn. Execs. (former vice chair, fellow), Greater Washington Soc. Assn. Execs., Alpha Phi Alpha. Office: Congl Black Caucus Found 1720 Massachusetts Ave NW Washington DC 20036 Office Phone: 202-263-2800. Office Fax: 202-775-0773.*

**THARPE, FRAZIER EUGENE,** journalist; b. Panama City, Fla., Jan. 10, 1941; s. Henry Clayton and Margaret Jane (Jenkins) T.; m. Barbara Ann Hembree, Oct. 30, 1971. BA in Polit. Sci. and History, Vanderbilt U., Nashville, 1963. Reporter Miami (Fla.) News, 1963; reporter U.P.I., Atlanta and Columbia, SC, 1964; pub. relations exec. Atlanta, 1965-69; fin. editor Atlanta Constn., 1969-73. Editl. assoc., columnist, 1974-83, columnist Helpline, ConsumerWatch, 1983-98; editor Homefinder, 1999-2002.

**THATCHER, GEORGE ROBERT,** banker, writer, journalist, columnist; b. Austin, Pa., Sept. 18, 1922; S. Walter Robert and Roberta Estelle (Bernard) T.; widowed; children: Georgia Anne Thatcher Faneca, James Estelle Thatcher Holmes, Walter Wimberly. BA, U. Miss., 1948. Pvt. U.S. Army, 1942, infantry maj., 1948, ret., 1952; ptnr. Rand-Thatcher Advt. Agy., Gulfport, Miss., 1948—67; pres. coast devel. Magnolia Fed. Bank, Gulfport, 1981-92; councilman City of Gulfport, 1989; hon. canon St. Peter's Cathedral, Likoma Island, Malawi, 1997—; daily columnist The Sun Herald, Biloxi, Miss., 1997—; commentator Pub. Radio Miss. 2006. Trustee U.S. Senate Art Preservation Bd., 2005—. Author: Misrepresentation in MS, 1954, Beach Walks, 1998, 2d edit., 1999, Beach Walks II, 2000, Scenes From the Beach,

2003. Chmn. Miss. Arts Commn., 1991-2000; past chmn. United Way, Harrison County Libr.; past pres. Episcopal Laymen of Miss., Miss. Hist. Assn. Decorated Bronze Star; named Outstanding Citizen Miss. Coast C. of C., 1998. Mem. Gulfport Rotary Club (pres. 1995-96, Citizen of Yr. 1993, Paul Harris fellow), Century Club (pres.), Gulfport Yacht Club, Coast Tennis Club, Great So. Club. Republican. Roman Catholic. Avocations: tennis, chess, reading, classical music. Home: 1302 2nd St Gulfport MS 39501-2219 Office: Regions Bank 2200 14th St Gulfport MS 39501-2005 E-mail: fishcrow@aol.com.

**THATCHER, JANET SOLVERSON,** financial advisor, writer; b. Sept. 24, 1946; m. John G. Thatcher, Mar. 20, 1976. BA, U. Wis., 1968, MBA, 1976, PhD, 1979. Svc. rep. Wis. Telephone Co., Beloit, 1968-71; trust dept. Baraboo (Wis.) Nat. Bank, 1971-73; pension, profit sharing trust dept. US Bank, Madison, Wis., 1973—74; asst. prof. fin. Va. Tech., Blacksburg, 1978-82, Clarkson U., Potsdam, N.Y., 1982-86; prof. U. Wis., Whitewater, 1986—2001. Contbr. articles to profl. jours. including Jour. Fin., Fin. Mgmt., Jour. Fin. Rsch., Jour. Fin. Rsch., Fin. Rev; columnist Plus Mag. Home: 4546 Wavertree St San Luis Obispo CA 93401-7831

**THATSNEYAKUL, YAOVARES,** pediatrician, consultant; b. Bangkok; m. Michael Pulaski, 1975. MD, Siriraj Med. Sch., Bangkok. Diplomate Am. Bd. Pediatrics. Cons. Dept. Human Svcs., State of N.J., 1985—. Office: Divsn Med Assistance and Health Svcs PO Box 712 Trenton NJ 08625-0712 Business E-Mail: yaovares.thatsneyakul@dhs.state.nj.us.

**THATTASSERY, EMIL GEORGE,** internist; b. Washington, Mar. 19, 1977; s. Pious and Jacie Thattassery. BS, Johns Hopkins U., 1997; MD, U. Md., 2003; MPH, Columbia U., 2006. Rsch. intern Walter Reed Army Inst. Rsch., Washington, 1993—97; software engr. Genesis Med. Tech., Balt., 1998—99, Trilogy Software, Austin, Tex., 1999; resident in internal medicine Northwestern Meml. Hosp., Chgo., 2003—06; mem. rapid response team Meml. Sloan Kettering Cancer Ctr., Chgo., 2006—. Contbr. articles to med. jours. Pres. Cir. K, Johns Hopkins U., Balt., 1996—97; pres. student coun. U. Md. Med. Sch., Balt., 2000—01. Mem.: AMA, Tau Beta Pi. Office: Meml Sloan Kettering Cancer Ctr 1275 York Ave New York NY 10021 Office Phone: 312-926-2000. E-mail: ethat001@hotmail.com.

**THAU, WILLIAM ALBERT,** lawyer; b. St. Louis, June 22, 1940; s. William Albert and Irene Elizabeth (Mundy) T.; m. Jane Hancock, Sept. 7, 1961; children: William Albert, Caroline Jane, Jennifer Elizabeth. BS in Indsl. Mgmt., Ga. Inst. Tech., 1962; JD, U. Tex., 1965. Bar: Tex. 1965. Ptnr., head of real estate sect. Jenkens & Gilchrist, Dallas, 1965—2002. Chmn. real estate developer/builder symposium S.W. Legal Found, 1975-79; bd. dirs. Southwestern Film Archives, So. Meth. U.; lectr. Practicing Law Inst. Author: Negotiating the Purchase and Sale of Real Estate, 1975, Non-Recourse, 2004, The Source and Code, 2006; editor Tex. State Bar Assn. Newsletter on Real Estate, Probate and Trust Law, 1978-81; contbr. articles to Real Estate Rev., 1983—. Bd. dirs. St. Philips Sch., Dallas, 1988, So. Meth. U.; trustee Dallas Can. Acad., 1987-88. Mem. ABA, Tex. State Bar Assn. (chmn. real estate, probate, trust law sect.), Am. Coll. Real Estate Lawyers. Republican. Office: 140 Tanglewood Rd Saint Simons Island GA 31522 Personal E-Mail: wthau@aol.com.

**THAWLEY, MICHAEL,** diplomat; b. Eng., 1950; arrived in Australia, 1960; m. Deborah Wilkins; children: Samuel, Thomas, Cosimo. BA with honors, Australian Nat. U., 1971; postgrad. diploma in Russian, Surrey (Eng.) U., 1980. Joined Australian Fgn. Svc., 1972, first asst. sec. Prime Mins. Dept., 1993-96; nat. security advisor Prime Min. Australia, 1996; dep. sec. dept. fgn. affairs and trade; Australian amb. to the U.S. Washington, 2000—. Avocations: reading, music, gardening. Office: Embassy of Australia 1601 Massachusetts Ave NW Washington DC 20036-2273 Fax: 202-797-3209.

**THAYER, CHARLES JAMES,** investment banker; b. Abilene, Kans., Feb. 28, 1944; s. Bruce V. and Neoma (Obermeyer) T.; 1 child, Travis J. Grad., U. Kans., 1967. Exec. v.p., CFO Citizens Fidelity Bank, Louisville, 1977—87; exec. v.p. fin. PNC Bank Corp., Pitts., 1987—89; chmn., mng. dir. Chartwell Capital Ltd., Ft. Lauderdale, Fla., 1989—; interim chmn., CEO Sunbeam-Oster, Providence, 1993. Adv. dir. Louisville Cmty. Devel. Bank, 1997—; Keefe Mgrs., Inc., NYC, 1990-02; mem. adv. bd. Am. Assn. Bank Dirs.; bd. dirs. BB&T Bank, Fla., Republic Bank, St. Petersburg, Fla., 1999-04 Trustee Cystic Fibrosis Found., Washington, 1980—; chmn. Cystic Fibrosis Svcs., Washington, 1994-04. Mem. Nat. Assn. Corp. Dirs. (Fla. bd. dirs. 2005). Avocation: sailing. Office: Chartwell Capital Ltd 420 Isle Of Capri Dr Fort Lauderdale FL 33301-2438 Business E-Mail: cjt@chartwellcapital.com.

**THAYER, CYNTHIA A.,** farmer, writer; b. N.Y.C., Apr. 11, 1944; d. Charles Coll and Margaret M. (Mac Willie) Underwood; m. William H. Thayer, Feb. 23, 1937; children: Thomas, Robin. BA, Bridgewater (Mass.) State Coll., 1972. Cert. secondary English tchr. Owner, operator Darthia Farm, Gouldsboro, Maine; owner, operator weaving bus. Tch. Bridgewater and Raynhanm, Mass., 1972-76, Sumner Adult Edn., Sullivan, Maine. Tchr. Summer Adult Edn., Sullivan, Maine; author: Strong for Potatoes, 1998, A Certain Slant of Light, 2000, A Brief Lunacy, 2005. Pres. Schoodic Futures, Prospect Harbor, Maine, 1997-98. Author: Starong for Potatoes, 1998 (Discover award 1998). Mem. Maine Organic Farmers and Gardeners Assn. (bd. dirs.), Schoodic Pen C. of C. (pres. 1995-97), Maine Won't Discriminate, Directions-Crafts Orgn. (pres. 1990—). Avocations: bagpiping, spinning, reading, swimming, bookeeping. Home and Office: Box 520 Gouldsboro ME 04607

**THAYER, EDNA LOUISE,** health facility administrator; b. Madelia, Minn., May 21, 1936; d. Walter William Arthur and Hilda Engel Emily Ann (Geistfeld) Wilke; m. David LeRoy Thayer, Aug. 30, 1958; children: Scott, Tamara, Brenda. Diploma in nursing, Bethesda Luth., 1956; BS in Nursing Edn., U. Minn., 1960; MSN, Washington U., St. Louis, 1966; MS in Counseling, Mankato (Minn.) State U., 1972. Cert. nursing adminstr. advanced ANA. Nurse Bethesda Luth. Hosp., St. Paul, 1956-58, U. Minn. Hosp., Mpls., 1958; from nurse to asst. head nurse supr., edn. dir. Fairmont (Minn.) Community Hosp., 1959-63; instr. Alton (Ill.) Meml. Hosp., 1963-66; from nursing instr. to assoc. prof. and dean Sch. Nursing Mankato State U., 1966-77; asst. adminstr. Rice County Dist. One Hosp., Faribault, Minn., 1977-89; RN, adminstrv. supr. St. Peter (Minn.) Regional Treatment Ctr., 1990-96; spkr., 1996—. Nurse surveyor Minn. Dept. Tech. Edn., St. Paul, 1980-93; mem. adv. co. LPN and MA programs Tech. Inst., Faribault, 1977-2001. Co-author (with Mary Huntley and Linda Beer): Celebrating the First Fifty Years, 2003; co-author: (with Mary Huntley) A Mirthful Spirit: Embracing Laughter for Wellness, 2006. Mem. Rice County Ext. Bd., Faribault, 1986-91, adult leader 4-H Rice County and St. Paul, 1971-97; advisor Med. Explorers, Faribault, 1977-89; mem. Rep. Rodosovich Health Com., Faribault, 1984-94; coun. mem. Our Savior's Luth. Ch., Faribault, 1984-87; mem. Rep. Boudreau Health Care Adv. Com., 1996-2001. Recipient alumni award Nat. 4-H Club, 1983, Disting. Friend of Nursing award Mankato State U., 1995. Mem. Minn. Orgn. Nurse Execs. (bd. dirs. 1987-89), Dist. F Nursing Svc. Adminstrs. (pres. 1980-82), Minn. Nurses Assn. (bd. dirs. 1982-87, Pres.'s award 1983, pres. 5th dist. 1974, 75, pres. 13th dist. 1984-86), AAUW, Sigma Theta Tau, Delta Kappa Gamma (pres. Pi chptr. 1982-84, Woman of Achievement award 1985), Hosp. Aux., Legion Aux. Republican. Avocations: crafts, volunteer work, theater, plays. Home: 7 Roots Beach Ln Elysian MN 56028-9731 Office Phone: 507-267-4588. Personal E-mail: dethayer@myclearwave.net.

**THAYER, GAYLORD BERTRAM, JR.,** retired electronics executive, investor; b. Jamestown, NY, July 2, 1944; s. Gaylord Bertram and Marion Brown (Klock) T. BSME, U. Rochester, 1966; MBA, Harvard U., 1968. Asst. to contr. Teradyne, Inc., Boston, 1968-70, mgr. MIS, 1970-72, sales engr., 1972-76, product mgr., 1976-84, divsn. mgr., 1984-91, mktg. dir., 1991-98; pvt. investor, 1998—. Exec.-in-residence entrepreneurship program Babson Coll., 2003—; adv. bd. Lexent Techs., Lexington, Mass., 1999—, Simply Media Inc., Lincoln, Mass.; gubernatorial appt. to Mass. Pub. Health Coun.

Policy Bd. State Dept. of Pub. Health, 2003. Bd. dirs. New Eng. divsn. Am. Cancer Soc., Boston; elected town meeting mem., 2003—; bd. trustees Boston Collegiate Charter Sch. Mem.: Nat. Assembly Am. Cancer Soc. Avocations: cooking, reading, travel, flying. Home: 52 Royalston Rd Wellesley MA 02481-1244

**THAYER, PAUL WILLIAM,** psychology educator, consultant; b. Birmingham, Ala., July 18, 1927; s. Hugh Olin and Margaret Elizabeth (Young) T.; m. Bjorg Magda Skoklefald, June 12, 1951; children: Scott, Lisa, Christina. BS, U.S. Mcht. Marine Acad., 1950, Pa. State U., 1950; PhD, Ohio State U., 1954. From asst. program dir. to sr. v.p. Life Ins. Mktg. & Rsch. Assn., Hartford, Conn., 1956-77; prof. psychology, head dept. N.C. State U., Raleigh, 1977-93, prof. emeritus, 1993—. Author: Training in Business and Industry, 1961; also numerous articles and book chpts. Fellow AAAS, APA, Assn. for Psychol. Sci. (treas. 1994-2000), Soc. for Indsl. and Orgnl. Psychology (sec.-tres. 1974-76, pres. 1976-77, Disting. Profl. Practice award 1987, Disting. Svc. award 1990), SIOP Found. (pres. 2004-). Home: 117 Duncansby Ct Cary NC 27511-6403 Personal E-mail: pthayer@mindspring.com.

**THAYER, ROBERT WILCOX,** music educator; b. Detroit, Oct. 26, 1927; s. Willard Charles and Eva Stuart (Missildine) T.; m. Norma Jean Boyd, Dec. 19, 1954; children: Douglas Boyd, Stephen Bruce. B.Music, U. Rochester, 1949; M.M.E., Wichita State U., 1955; Ph.D., U. Iowa, 1971. Elem. and secondary music tchr. pub. and pvt. schs. Waterford Pa., Wichita, Kans., Clearwater, Kans., 1949-53; asst. prof. music Friends U., Wichita, 1953-58; assoc. prof. music Cornell Coll., Mt. Vernon, Iowa, 1958-72; assoc. prof. music SUNY-Potsdam, 1972-73, assoc. dean music, 1973-76, dean music, 1976-82; dean music Coll. Musical Arts Bowling Green State U., Ohio, 1983-93, devel. officer, 1993-96, dean emeritus and trustee prof., 1993; musician French horn and tuben Rochester Philharm. Orch., N.Y., 1949, French horn Erie Philharm. Orch., Pa., 1949-50; solo French horn Wichita Symphony Orch., Kans., 1950-58, Cedar Rapids Symphony Orch., Iowa, 1958-70; adj. instr. horn Wichita State U., 1955-58; cons. Nat. Assn. Schs. Music, Reston, Va., 1978—, accreditation evaluator, 1975-93, grad. commn., 1979-85, mem. task force on State Certification, 1981-82, chmn. commn. on non-degree granting instns., 1988-93, cons., 1996—, hon. mem., 1995; planner, adminstr. Olympic ceremonial music by Crane Sch. Music 1980 Winter Olympic Games, Lake Placid, N.Y., 1980; cons. music edn. Republic of China, 1981, 88, 91, 92. Contbr. articles to profl. jours. Mem. Music Educators Nat. Conf., Coll. Music Soc., Phi Mu Alpha Sinfonia (sec. Wichita alumni chpt. 1955-58). Democrat. Club: Torch (Toledo). Office: Bowling Green State U Coll Music Arts Bowling Green OH 43403-0001 Office Phone: 920-832-6614. E-mail: thayerr@bgnet.bgsu.edu.

**THAYER, RUSSELL, III,** air transportation executive; b. Phila., Dec. 5, 1922; s. Russell and Shelby Wentworth (Johnson) T.; m. Elizabeth Wright Mifflin, June 12, 1947; children: Elizabeth, Dixon, Shelby, Samuel, David. Student, St. George's Sch., 1937-42; AB, Princeton U., 1949. Mgmt. trainee Eastern Air Lines, 1949-52; mgr. cargo sales and service Am. Airlines, Los Angeles, 1952-63; v.p. mktg. Seaboard World Airlines, N.Y.C., 1963-70; sr. v.p. Braniff Airways, Inc., Dallas, 1970-72, exec. v.p., 1972-77, pres., chief oper. officer, 1977-80, vice chmn., 1981-82; dir. (Braniff Airways, Inc.), 1971-82; v.p. Pan Am. World Airways, Inc., N.Y.C., 1982-84, sr. v.p., 1984-88, Airline Econs., Inc., Washington, 1988—, also bd. dirs., 1988—. Dir. Ft. Worth Nat. Bank, 1977-82; vice chmn. Airline Capital Assn.; bd. dirs. Kiwi Internat. Airlines, Inc., World Aux. Power Corp. Mem. Trinity Ch. Ushers Guild, Princeton, N.J., 1968—; Trustee Aviation Hall of Fame N.J. Served with USAAF, 1942-45, ETO. Decorated D.F.C. Air medal with 11 oak leaf clusters. Mem. Am. Aviation Hist. Assn., Air Force Assn., Exptl. Aircraft Assn., Nat. Aeros. Assn., Ivy Club (Princeton), Pretty Brook Tennis Club (Princeton), Bay Head (N.J.) Yacht Club, Nassau Club (Princeton), Princeton Club (N.Y.C.), Phila. Club, Delta Psi. Home: Hulfish St Apt 17-I Princeton NJ 08542-3706 Office: Airline Capital Associates Inc 545 5th Ave Rm 1009 New York NY 10017-3655 Office Phone: 609-252-9675.

**THAYER, THOMAS MANOR, JR.,** artist; b. Lansing, Mich., Apr. 8, 1958; BFA, U. Mich., 1981. Owner, lead artist Alexander Raymond Thomas Qaulity Fine Art, Camano Island, Wash., 1996—. Instr. Art Workshop, 1999—. One-man shows include Mountlake Terrace Civic Ctr. Gallery, Mountlake Terrace, Wash., 1999, Edmonds C.C., Edmonds, Wash., 1996, PACCAR Corp., Bellevue, Wash., 1995, Mountlake Terrace Libr., 1995, Cascade Estates Winery, Seattle, 1992, exhibited in group shows at The Artist's Mag. Competition, 2001, 2002, Washington State Ducks Unlimited, 1997 (2d pl. award Artist of Yr., 1997), Northwest Color III Exhbn., Seattle, Statements DC 207 Exhbn., 2001, The Colored Pencil Soc. of Am., 2d Ann. Internat. Exhbn., Portland, 1994, 4th Ann. Internat. Exhbn., San Diego, 1996, 8th Ann. Internat. Exhbn., Birmingham, Mich., 2000, 9th Ann. Internat. Exhbn., San Francisco, 2001 (Cippy Best of Show award), 10th Ann. Internat. Exhbn., Dallas, 2002, New Art Internat., 2004, Arts of the Terrace, 2004 (Best Show, 2d pl., 2004), numerous others, including the Points of Color DC 207 Exhbn., Bothell, Wash., 2000; contbr. artwork and articles to mags.; contbr. (books) Best of Colored Pencil, 1994, 1997, Creative Colored Pencil, 1995, Creative Colored Pencil Portraits, 1996, Exploring Colored Pencil, 1999; Exhibited in group shows at Edmonds Art Festival, 2002 (1st pl. award, 2002, 1995, 2d pl. award, 1996, 1st pl. award, 1998), 2003 (1st pl. award, 2003). Mem.: Am. Soc. of Classical Realism, Colored Pencil Soc. of Am. Avocation: collecting and restoring classic cars of the 1960s and 1970s, snow skiing. Home: 1633 Hemlock Dr Camano Island WA 98282

**THEALL, DONALD FRANCIS,** retired university president; b. Mt. Vernon, N.Y., Oct. 13, 1928; s. Harold A. and Helen (Donaldson) T.; m. Joan Ada Benedict, June 14, 1950; children: Thomas, Margaret, John. Harold, Lawrence, Michael. BA with honors, Yale U., 1950; MA with 1st class honors, U. Toronto, 1951, PhD with 1st class honors, 1954. Teaching fellow U. Toronto, 1950-52, mem. faculty, 1952-65, prof. English, chmn. joint depts. English, 1964-65; dir. communication studies York U., also prof. English and communications, 1965-66; dir. English division Atkinson Coll., 1965-66; mem. faculty McGill U., Montreal, Que., Canada, 1966-79, prof. English, 1966-79, chmn. dept., 1966-74, Molson prof., 1972-79, dir. grad. program in communications, 1976-79, adj. prof. grad. comm. Montreal, Que., Canada, 1989-91; pres., vice chancellor, prof. English and cultural studies Trent U., Peterborough, Ont., 1980-87, univ. prof., 1987-94, univ. prof. emeritus, 1994—. Cultural exch. prof. Govt. of Can. and China, 1991, mem. adv. bd. Semiotic Inquiry, 1982—; cons. in field. Author: (with Robinson and Wevers) Let's Speak English, 4 vols., 1960-61, The Medium Is the Rear View Mirror: Understanding McLuhan, 1971, (with G.J. Robinson) Studies in Canadian Communications, 1975, Beyond the Word: Reconstructing Sense in the Joyce Era of Technology, Culture, and Communication, 1995 (short-listed Harold Adams Innis prize 1997), James Joyce's Techno-Poetics, 1997, The Virtual Marshall McLuhan, 2001; mem. editl. bd. Sci. Fiction Studies, 1976—, Can. Jour. Comm., 1979—, Jour. Can. Studies, 1980-87. Mem. Greater Peterborough Econ. Council, 1982-87; mem. fed. adv. council to minister employment and immigration for Peterborough area, 1986-87. Recipient awards Social Sci. and Humanities Rsch. Coun., 1991-94, 94-97, 97-2000, 2000—, Can. Fedn. Humanities-Aid to Scholarly Publs., 1994, 96, 2000; grantee Humanities Rsch. Coun. Can., 1954-56, 73-76, Ont. Dept. Edn., 1956-59, 91, Atkinson Found., 1960, CBC, 1961, Can. Coun., 1966-68, 73-76, Eastman Kodak Corp., Nat. Film Bd. Can., Can. Dept. Industry, Can. Dept. Trade and Commerce, Can. Ctrl. Mortgage and Housing, 1967-69, Que. Ministry Comm., 1977; sr. leave fellow Can. Coun., 1975. Corr. fellow Acad. Medicine (Toronto); mem. Internat. Communications Assn. (dir. 1978-81), Can. Communications Assn. (chmn. com. to investigate formation 1978, pres. 1979-80), MLA, Philol. Soc. Gt. Britain, Can. Assn. Chmn. English (founding chmn. 1971-74), Assn. Can. Univ. Tchrs. English, Internat. Inst. Communications, Soc. Arts Publs. (v.p. 1967-68), Sci. Fiction Research Assn., Elizabethan Club of Toronto, Yale Club (Toronto), McGill Faculty Club, Elizabethan Club (Yale). Office: Trent Univ Grad Methodologies Program Peterborough ON Canada K9J 7B8 E-mail: dtheall@trentu.ca, dtheall@cogeco.ca.

**THEALL, MICHAEL,** education educator, director; b. Manchester, N.H., Feb. 16, 1942; s. John William and Doris Claire Theall; m. Louise Cecile Provencher, Aug. 21, 1971; children: Adam M., Eric J., Luke R. BA in English, St. Anselm Coll., Manchester, N.H., 1963; postgrad., Boston U., 1970—71; MS in Instrnl. Tech., Syracuse U., 1976, PhD in Instrnl. Design, Devel. and Evaluation, 1980. Tchr. Weare (N.H.) HS, 1963—65, Salem (N.H.) HS, 1971—72, Manchester W. HS, 1972—74; media prodn. specialist Northeastern U., 1976—82, coord. rsch., devel. & evaluation, 1982—84, mgr. Office Instrnl. Devel. and Evaluation, 1984—90; assoc. prof., dir. Tchg. and Learning Ctr. U. Ala., Birmingham, 1990—96; assoc. prof. ednl. adminstrn. dir. Ctr. Tchg. and Learning U. Ill., Springfield, 1996—2001, assoc. prof. liberal studies, dir. On-Line Writing Assistance Project, 2001—02; assoc. prof. edn., dir. Ctr. Advancement Tchg. and Learning Youngstown State U., 2002—. Reviewer Innovative Higher Edn., Jour. Higher Edn., Rev. Higher Edn., Jour. Excellence in Coll. Tchr., 2000—; presenter in field; cons. in field. Mem. editl. bd., sect. editor Tech. Source, 1997—2002; sect. editor: Nat. Tchg. and Learning Forum; exec. prodr.: Effective Use of Time in the College Classroom; contbr. articles to profl. jours.; prodr.: 4 documentary videotapes. Cub scout leader Boy Scouts Am.; pres. Jr. HS PTA; mem. tech. com. Rochester Sch. Dist.; mem. Rochester Schs. Band Boosters. Capt. USAF, 1965—69. Recipient W.J. McKeachie Career Achievement award, Am. Rsch. Assn., 2002, Disting. Acad. Achievement award, St. Anselm Coll. Alumni Assn., 2003, Integrative Scholarship award, Am. Ednl. Rsch. Assn., 2005; grantee, Mass. Dept. Employment Security, 1978, Fund Improvement Postsecondary Edn., 1985—88, Jennings Found., 2003, Ctrl. Ill. Higher Edn. Consortium, 1996, 1998, 1999, Ill. Bd. Higher Edn., 2000, 2001; NSF grantee, Northeastern U., 1979—82. Mem.: Timberlane Music Assn. (exec. bd.), Profl. and Orgnl. Devel. Network, Am. Ednl. Rsch. Assn. (mem. exec. bd. 1981—82, mem. SIG faculty evaluation and devel. 1981—, sec./treas. 1989—93, program chair 1993, 1994, chmn. spl. interest group 1994—96, sec./treas. 2000—02, chmn. spl. interest group 2001, treas. 2002—). Roman Catholic. Avocations: music, acting, reading, movies, photography. Home: 3409 Swallow Hollow Dr Youngstown OH 44514 Office: Youngstown State U CATALYST Tod B 139 One University Plz Youngstown OH 44555 Office Phone: 330-941-1320. Business E-Mail: mtheall@ysu.edu.

**THE EDGE, (DAVID HOWELL EVANS),** musician; b. Ireland, Aug. 8, 1961; children: Holly, Aaron, Blue Angel, Cian. Guitarist U2, 1978—. Albums include U2:3, 1979, Boy, 1980, October, 1981, War, 1983, Under A Blood Red Sky, 1983, Unforgettable Fire, 1984, Wide Awake in America, 1985, Joshua Tree, 1987 (Grammy awards for best rock performance by a duo or group with vocals, album of yr., 1988, MTV Music Video award for viewers choice for With or Without You 1987, best performance music video for Where the Streets Have No Name 1989), Rattle and Hum, 1988 (MTV Music Video award for best video from film for When Love Comes to Town with B.B. King 1989, Grammy award for best rock performance by a duo or group with vocal for Desire 1989), Achtung Baby, 1991 (Grammy award for prodr. yr. 1991, MTV Music Video awards for best group video, best spl. effects in a video for Even Better Than the Real Thing 1992), Zooropa, 1993 (Grammy award for alternative album of yr. 1993), Pop, 1997, All That You Can't Leave Behind, 2000 (Grammy awards: album of the year, best pop performance, best rock performance, best rock album, 2001), The Best of 1990-2000, 2002, How to Dismantle an Atomic Bomb, 2004 (Grammy awards: best rock album, album of yr., best rock group performance & song of yr. for Sometimes You Can't Make it On Your Own, best rock song for City of Blinding Lights, 2005). Co-founder Music Rising initiative, 2005. U2 named Best-Selling Irish Artist of Yr., World Music Awards, 1993, 1998, World's Best-Selling Rock Act, World Music awards, 2006; named to VH1: Greatest Artists of Rock & Roll, 1998; co-recipient (with U2) Ambassador of Conscience award, Amnesty Internat., 2005; recipient Brit. Record Industry award for best internat. group, 1988, 89. Achievements include inducted into Rock and Roll Hall of Fame as mem. U2, 2005. Address: Interscope Records 2220 Colorado Ave Santa Monica CA 90404*

**THEILMANN, MICHAEL T.,** human resources specialist; m. Nancy Theilmann; 3 children. Grad., Gustavus Adolphus Coll.; MS, U. Nebr. With human resources dept. Burger King, Grand Metropolitan; various positions in human resources PepsiCo and Yum! Brands, Inc., 1993—2000; v.p. human resources Europe ops. Yum! Brands, Inc., 2000—02, sr. v.p. human resources, chief people officer internat. bus., 2002—05; exec. v.p., chief human resources and adminstrn. officer JC Penney Company, Inc., 2005—. Office: JC Penney Co Inc 6501 Legacy Dr Plano TX 75024-3698 Office Phone: 972-431-1000. Office Fax: 972-431-1362.

**THEIS, MARTIN,** neuroscientist, researcher; b. Hueckeswagen, North Rhine Westphalia, Germany, Sept. 5, 1969; arrived in U.S., 2001; s. Bernd and Marianne Theis; m. Heidi Kirschner, July 1, 1973; children: Elisabeth, Nico Paolo Connor. D of Natural Scis., U. of Bonn, Germany, 2001; diploma, U. of Cologne, Germany, 1996. Predoctoral rsch. scientist U. of Bonn, North Rhine Westphalia, 1996—2001; postdoctoral rsch. scientist Columbia U., N.Y.C., 2001—. Recipient TILL Photonics Tech. prize, 2005, Siemens Westinghouse Disting. Mentor Recognition award, 2004. Mem.: German Neurosci. Soc. Achievements include research in New technique in mouse transgenics: Columbia Univ 1051 Riverside Dr New York NY 10032 Office Phone: 212-543-5249. Office Fax: 212-543-5474. Business E-Mail: mt2050@columbia.edu.

**THEIS, PETER GEORGE,** retired classicist; b. Milw., Dec. 18, 1930; s. Peter Joseph and Laura Gertrude (Kornely) T.; m. Jane Elizabeth Grattan, Aug. 12, 1961; children: Peter Leo, Paul Joseph, Mary Ellen Brune, Thomas George. BA magna cum laude, Marquette U., 1952; AM, U. Chgo., 1957. Part-time instr. U. Wis., Milw., 1956; instr. Rockhurst U., Kansas City, Mo., 1960-61; instr., then asst. prof. classics Marquette U., Milw., 1961-90; ret., 1990. Mem. editl. bd. Holy Family Cath. Ch., Whitefish Bay, Wis., 1974-75; troop fundraising chmn. Boy Scouts Am., Whitefish Bay, 1976-77; pres. Post-Polio Resource Group of Southeastern Wis., Wauwatosa, 1987, Milw. Area Latin Tchrs. Assn., 1963-64, Fox River Valley Classical Assn., Milw., 1970-71, Wis. Latin Tchrs. Assn., Milw., 1976-78. Cpl. U.S. Army, 1953-55. NEH grantee, 1973. Mem. AAUP, Am. Classical League, Am. Philological Assn., Classical Assn. of the Mid. West and South, Wis. Assn. Fgn. Lang. Tchrs. (pres. 1980-82, Recognition award 1989), Paralyzed Vets. Am. (life), Disabled Am. Vets. (life), Wis. Latin Tchrs. Assn., Marquette U. Retirees Assn. Avocations: reading, puzzles. Home: 2328 W Apple Tree Rd Milwaukee WI 53209-3312

**THEISMANN, JOSEPH ROBERT (JOE THEISMANN),** former professional football player, announcer; b. New Brunswick, N.J., Sept. 9, 1949; s. Joseph James and Olga (Tobias) T.; m. Robin Smith, Dec. 5, 1970 (div.); children: Joseph Winton, Amy Lynn, Patrick James. BA in Sociology, U. Notre Dame, 1971. With Toronto Argonauts, CFL, 1971-74, Washington Redskins, 1974-86, punt returner, 1974-79, starting quarterback, 1979-86; analyst CBS Nat. Football League broadcasts, 1987-88, ESPN Nat. Football League broadcasts, 1988—; announcer, Monday Night Football ESPN, 2006—. Pres., CEO JRT Assocs.; tchr. Offense-Def. Football Camp; Superstar participant, 1979-80, played in Pro-Bowl, 1983-84; mem. Pres.'s Athletic Adv. Com., 1993; active Pres. Nat. Svc. Adv. Com., 1993. Author: Quarter Backing. Mem. corp. bd. Children's Hosp. Nat. Med. Center, Washington; participant benefits for Multiple Sclerosis children's hosps., Armed Forces Christmas benefits. High sch. All-Am. Football, 1967; All-Am. Coll., 1971; Acad.-All-Am.; All-Pro UPI; recipient Brian Piccolo award; played in Pro Bowl, 1982, 83; mem. Super Bowl XVII Championship Team, 1982; cable Ace award, Best Sports Commentator-Analyst, 1994. Mem. Nat. Football Players Assn. Republican. Methodist. Office: ESPN 935 Middle St Bristol CT 06010*

**THEISS, RICHARD EDWARD,** electrical engineer, applications engineer; b. Nyack, N.Y., July 30, 1965; s. Joseph Francis and Lorraine Anita Theiss; m. Janet Grace Heapes, Apr. 9, 1994; children: Steven Richard, Nicole Grace, Andrew Joseph. BSEE, Boston U., 1987; MBA, Iona Coll. Hagen Sch. of Bus., N.Y., 1994. Tech. support engr. IPC Automation, Riverdale, NJ, 1987—92; applications engr. LeCroy Corp., Chestnut Ridge, NY, 1992—95, applications engring. supr., 1995—98, product mgr., 1998—2001; sr. applications engr. Boonton Electronics (Wireless Telecom Group Co.), Parsippany, NJ, 2001—05, product mgr., sr. applications engr., 2005—. Lecroy corporate rep. PXI Sys. Alliance, San Diego, 2000—01. Author: (web seminar) Wireless OEM Design Expo. Coach Monroe Woodbury PTA Basketball, Central Valley, NY, 2002—06; mgr. Monroe (N.Y.) Woodbury Little League, 2004; coach St. Patricks CYO Basketball, Highland Mills, NY, 2005—06. Liberal. Avocations: coaching, running, travel, baseball, football. Home: 7 Country Hollow Highland Mills NY 10930 Office: Boonton Electronics (Wireless Telecom Group Co) 25 Eastmans Rd Parsippany NJ 07054-3702 Office Phone: 973-386-9696. Business E-Mail: rtheiss@boonton.com.

**THELANDER, BEVERLY,** oil company executive; BS, UCLA, MBA in Fin. Variuos fin. positions ARCO, 1981-98, v.p. comm. pub. affairs & investor rels. L.A., 1998—. Office: ARCO 4 Centerpointe Dr La Palma CA 90623-2502

**THELEN, BRUCE CYRIL,** lawyer; b. St. Johns, Mich., Nov. 24, 1951; BA, Mich. State U., 1973; JD, U. Mich., 1977. Bar: N.Y. 1978, Mich. 1980, Ill. 1992. Assoc. Dewey, Ballantine, Bushby, Palmer & Wood, N.Y.C., 1977-80; ptnr. Dickinson, Wright, Moon, Van Dusen & Freeman, Detroit, 1981-83, Dickinson Wright PLLC, Detroit, 1984—. Mem. U.S. Dept. Commerce-Mich. Dist. Export Coun., 1995—. Contbr. articles to profl. jours. Mem. allocation panel, mem. spkrs. bur., chmn. rsch. and info. svcs. com., mem. strategic planning com. and cmty. leaders coun. United Way Cmty. Svcs., 1987—; mem. Mich. Task Force Internat. Trade, Lansing, 1990, Detroit Com. Fgn. Rels., Greater Detroit-Windsor Japan Am. Soc.; mem. adv. coun. Ctr. Internat. Bus. Edn., U. Mich. Sch. Bus. Decorated Order of Merit Germany. Mem.: Econ. Club Detroit, World Trade Club and Internat. Bus. Coun. (mem. exec. com. 1992—), Internat. Inst. Detroit (bd. dirs. 1997—99, v.p. 1999—2000), Ill. Bar Assn. (internat. law sect.), Am. Soc. Internat. Law, Internat. Bar Assn. (chmn. fin. aspects internat. sales subcom. 2003—05, vice chmn. internat. sales com. 2006—), State Bar Mich. (chmn. internat. law sect. 1990—91), N.Y. Bar Assn. (internat. law sect.), Wayne State U. Mentors and Internat. Bridge Coun. (bd. vis. internat. programs), Mich. Israel C. of C. (bd. dirs. 1997—2001), German Am. C. of C. Midwest (bd. dirs. 1992—, pres. Mich. chpt. 1994—2004, chmn. 2004—), French-Am. C. of C. Detroit, Greater Detroit C. of C. (chmn. European mission com. 1991—92, mem. export com. 1992—95, chmn. European mission com. 1995, mem. Leadership Detroit VIII program 1996—97), Detroit Athletic Club. Office: Dickinson Wright PLLC 500 Woodward Ave Ste 4000 Detroit MI 48226-3416 Office Phone: 313-223-3624.

**THELEN, EDMUND,** research executive; b. Berkeley, Calif, May 8, 1913; s. Paul and Alice (Arnold) T.; m. Helen Naomi Betton, Oct. 30, 1965; children: Nancy Anne, Joan Arnold Thelen Hanson, BS, U. Calif., Berkeley, 1934. Asst. chemist Certain-Teed Products Corp., Richmond, Calif., 1934-35; chemist O. C. Field Gasoline Corp., Santa Maria, Calif., 1936-41; asst. mgr. Eclipse Pioneer divsn. Bendix Corp., Teterboro, NJ, 1946-47; sr. rsch. chemist Franklin Inst. Rsch. Labs., Phila., 1947-51, mgr. colloids and polymers br., 1951-74, v.p., dir. phys. and life scis. dept., 1974-76, Inst. fellow, sec. com. on sci. and the arts, 1976-82, mem., 1982-2001, emeritus, 2001—. Pres. Safety Surface Corp., 1983-88; mem. Coun. for Delivery of Dental Care, 1970-85; bd. govs. Franklin-Hahnemann Inst. Occupl. and Environ. Health, 1975-80, Mayor's. Sci. and Tech. Adv. Com. on Environment, 1973-80; instr. dental medicine Hahnemann Med. Coll. and Hosp., 1964-74; v.p., dir. Pa. Environ. Coun., 1974-85; treas. Home Health Svcs. of Chester County and Vicinity, 1981-86. Co-author: (book) Porous Pavement for Runoff Control, 1978; editor Am. Assn. Ret. Persons, Eastern Chester County newsletter, 1994-97; contbr. papers to tech. publs. Bd. dir. Neighborhood Vis. Nurse Assn., 1987-93. With USN, 1941-45; comdr. USNR, 1941-66. Recipient spl. recognition award Am. Soc. Landscape Archs., 1974. Mem. Franklin Inst., Sierra Club (ea. Pa. group chmn. 1968, Atlantic chpt. vice-chmn. 1971-73, founding chmn. Pa. chpt. 1974), Ret. Officers Assn. (treas. Valley Forge chpt. 1980-85, v.p. 1987, pres. 1988-89, sec. 1994-97), Toastmasters Internat. (dist. gov. 1960-61), Sunday Breakfast Spkr. Club (pres. 1960-61), Sigma Xi, mem., Nat. Resources Defense Coun., Southern Poverty Law Ctr. Home: 658 Davis Ln Wayne PA 19087-5418 Office Phone: 610-687-3958. E-mail: ked92@earthlink.net.

**THELEN, GIL,** publishing executive; b. Chgo. s. Gilbert Carl and Violet (Okonn) T.; m. Carol Abernathy, July 1966 (div. Apr. 1978); children: Deborah Brooke, Todd Foster; m. Cynthia Jane Struby, Sept. 2, 1979; children: Matthew David, Jonathan Whitfield. BA, Duke U., 1960. Reporter Milw. Jour., 1960-61, AP, Washington, 1965-72; writer Consumer Reports, Mt. Vernon, N.Y., 1972-77; reporter Chgo. Daily News, 1977-78; asst. met. editor Charlotte (N.C.) Observer, 1978-82, met. editor, 1982-83, asst. mng. editor, 1983-87; editor The Sun News, Myrtle Beach, S.C., 1987-90; exec. editor The State, 1990-97; cons. editor Knight-Ridder, Inc., Columbia, S.C., 1997-98; exec. editor The Tampa Tribune, 1998—2003, pub., 2003—. Adj. prof. U. S.C., Aiken, 1989-98. Pres. Montgomery County Big Bros., Bethesda, Md., 1967-69; co-founder Valley Group, Myrtle Beach, S.C., 1989. Mem. Am. Soc. Newspaper Editors, Fla. Soc. Newspaper Editors, Leadership S.C., Leadership Columbia, Leadership Tampa, Phi Beta Kappa, Omicron Delta Kappa. Methodist. Avocations: golf, reading, classical music. Office: 200 S Parker St Tampa FL 33606-2308 also: Tampa Tribune PO Box 191 Tampa FL 33601 E-mail: gthelen@tampatrib.com.

**THELIN, JOHN ROBERT,** historian, educator, researcher; b. West Newton, Mass., Oct. 15, 1947; s. George Willard and Rozalija Katherine (Komarec) T.; m. Anna Sharon Blackburn, June 24, 1978. AB cum laude, Brown U., 1969; MA, U. Calif., Berkeley, 1972, PhD, 1973. Rsch. asst. Brown U., Providence, 1968-69; rschr., lectr. U. Calif., Berkeley, 1972-74; asst. prof. U. Ky., Lexington, 1974-77; asst. dean Pomona Coll., Claremont, Calif., 1977-79; from asst. dir. to rsch. dir. Assn. Ind. Calif. Colls. and Univs., Santa Ana, 1979-81; chancellor prof. Coll. William and Mary, Williamsburg, Va., 1981-93, pres. faculty assembly, 1990-91; prof. higher edn. and philanthropy Ind. U., Bloomington, 1993-96; prof. ednl. policy and history U. Ky., Lexington, 1996—, disting. univ. rsch. prof., 2001—. Vis. prof. grad. sch. Claremont U., 1978—81; vis. scholar U. Calif., Berkeley, 1995; curator Marquandia Soc., 1971—2006; essay rev. editor Rev. of Higher Edn., 1979—91; rsch. cons. NSF, Washington, 1991; mem. faculty senate U. Ky., 1997—; guest faculty Club. Bus. Mgmt. Inst., 1998—2006; chair social sci. com. Grad. Coun., U.K., 1998—2001; rsch. cons. Am. Enterprise Inst., 2005—06; keynote spkr. Author: Higher Education and Its Useful Past, 1982, The Cultivation of Ivy, 1976, Higher Education and Public Policy, 1991, Games Colleges Play, 1994, A History of American Higher Education, 2004; author: (with others) The Old College Try, 1989, One Hundred Classic Books About Higher Education, 2000; assoc. editor (jour.) Higher Edn.: Theory and Rsch., 1983—91, guest columnist Lexington Herald-Leader, 2001. Pres., bd. dirs. United Way, Williamsburg, 1987-89; pres. Friends of Williamsburg Libr., 1989. Grantee Spencer Found., 1989-91, 99-2001, Ky. Humanities Coun., 2003-05; Regents fellow U. Calif., 1972; recipient Outstanding Faculty Rsch. award Coll. of Edn., U. Ky., 2000, Great Tchrs. award U. Ky., 2004, Provost's Tchg. award U. Ky., 2006, State Local History Rsch. award Ky. Hist. Soc., 2006. Mem. Assn. for Study of Higher Edn. (bd. dirs. 1988-90, keynote spkr. 1994, pres. 1999-2000), History of Edn. Soc. (editl. bd. 1988-91), Order of Ky. Cols., Lexington Club, Phi Beta Kappa (Faculty award for advancement of scholarship Alpha of Va. 1986, Alpha of R.I. 1969), Omicron Delta Kappa. Avocations: long-distance running, history of Los Angeles and California, sports history. Home: 1745 Richmond Rd Lexington KY 40502 Office: U Ky Edn Policy Studies Lexington KY 40506-1 Office Phone: 859-257-4996. Business E-Mail: jthelin@uky.edu.

**THELIN, STEPHEN RUSSELL,** lawyer; b. Warren, Pa., Oct. 2, 1961; s. Russell Perry and Ruth Carolyn Thelin; m. Lisa Ann Matheis; children: Benjamin Stephen, Emily Katherine. BA, Wittenberg U., Springfield, Ohio, 1983; JD, Dickinson Sch. Law, Carlisle, Pa., 1986; advanced cert. Acctg., Mercyhurst Coll., Erie, Pa., 1998. Bar: Pa. 1986, U.S. Cir. Cts. (3d cir.) 1987. Assoc., then ptnr. MacDonald, Illig, Jones & Britton, Erie, Pa., 1986—99; assoc. Kooman Law Firm, Clarion, 1999—2001; assoc. gen. counsel Erie Ins. Group, 2001—. Author: Case Note, 1985, Comment, 1985. Dir. Lutheran Affiliated Svcs., Cranberry Tree, Pa., 2000—04. Mem.: ABA, Pa. Bar Assn. Office: Erie Ins Group 100 Erie Insurance Pl Erie PA 16530

**THEOBALD, EDWARD ROBERT,** lawyer; b. Chgo., Feb. 10, 1947; BA, So. Ill. U., 1969; JD, Ill. Inst. Tech., 1974. Bar: Ill. 1974, U.S. Dist. Ct. (no. dist.) Ill. 1974. Asst. state's atty. Cook County, Chgo., 1974-79, supr. felony trial divsn., 1980-81; assoc. Conklin, Leahy & Eisenberg, Chgo., 1977; ptnr. Boharic & Theobald, Chgo., 1981-83, owner, ptnr., 1983—. Legal adv. Sheriff of Cook County, Ill., 1986-89; spl. state's atty. U.S. Dist. Ct. no. dist. Ill., 1989-91, Cook County, Ill., 2002-06; apptd. spl. corp. counsel City of Chgo., 1994. Mem. Parent adv. bd. Downers Grove (Ill.) South H.S., 1992-94. Named Number One Trial Atty. in Felony Trial Divsn. of Office of Cook County State's Atty., Felony Trial Divsn. Suprs., 1979. Mem. ABA (sect. on tort and ins. law, sect. on labor and employment law, chmn. com. on sentencing alternatives young lawyers sect. 1982-83, tort and ins. practice sect., labor and employment law sect.), ATLA, Chgo. Bar Assn. (mem. bd. mgrs. 1985-87, mem. labor and employment law com. 1983—2002, mem. com. on coms. 1990-94, mem. membership com. 1990-95, vice chair judicial evaluation com. 1999-2000), Ill. Bar Assn. Roman Catholic. Office: Three First Nat Plaza 70 W Masdison Ste 2030 Chicago IL 60602 Office Phone: 312-346-9246. Personal E-mail: bears51@aol.com.

**THEOBALD, THOMAS CHARLES,** banker; b. Cin., May 5, 1937; m. Gigi Mahon, Jan. 1987 AB in Econs., Coll. Holy Cross, 1958; MBA in Fin. with high distinction, Harvard U., 1960. With Citibank, N.A. div. Citicorp, 1960-87; vice-chmn. Citicorp, N.Y.C., 1982-87; CEO, chmn. Continental Bank Corp., Chgo., 1987-94; chmn. bd. dirs. Continental Bank N.A., Chgo., 1987-94; mng. dir. Blair Capital Ptnrs., Chgo., 1994—. Bd. dir. Jones, Lang LaSalle US Realty Income & Growth Fund, Anixter Internat., Liberty Funds, MONY Group, Ambac Financial Group; bd. chmn. Columbia Mutual Funds. Trustee Northwestern U.; bd. dirs. MacArthur Found.; bd. of adv. Harvard Bus. Sch. Office: William Blair Capital Partners 222 W Adams St Chicago IL 60606-5307*

**THEODORE, ARES NICHOLAS,** chemist, researcher; b. Kalamata, Greece, Oct. 28, 1933; came to U.S., 1954; s. Nicholas A. and Angeliki (Myseros) Theodoracopulos; m. Peggy Salvarakis, Sept. 3, 1961; children: Nicholas A., Angie A. BA cum laude, Westminster Coll., Salt Lake City, 1958; MS, U. Utah, 1961; postgrad., Case Western Res. U., 1967-68. Asst. prof. chemistry Westminster Coll., 1961-64; sr. rsch. chemist Diamond Shamrock Corp., Cleve., 1964-69; rsch. scientist Ford Motor Co., Detroit, 1969-73, sr. rsch. scientist, 1973-84, prin. rsch. scientist, 1984—2000. Contbr. articles to profl. jours. Mem. ch. bd. Holy Cross Greek Orthodox Ch., Farmington Hills, Mich., 1986-88; campaigner Farmington Hills Dem. Com., 1986-88; mem. bus. coun. Boston Dem. Com., 1988—, Nat. Dem. Com., 1988—. Fellow, NSF, 1964; U. Utah fellow, 1958—61. Mem. Am. Chem. Soc. (treas. 1967), Ahepa (bd. govs. Dearborn, Mich. 1985-86). Achievements include patents in field. Avocations: swimming, golf, photography. Home: 34974 Valley Forge Dr Farmington Hills MI 48331-3210

**THEODORE, DAVID,** research scientist; MS in Materials Sci. and Engring., Northwestern U., 1986; PhD in Materials Sci. and Engring., Cornell U., 1991. Sun Certified Programmer For Java 2 Platform Sun Microsystems, Inc., 2003. Staff scientist Advanced Custom Technologies Motorola Inc., Mesa, Ariz., 1990—91, sr. staff scientist Advanced Custom Technologies, 1991—92, prin. staff scientist Materials Rsch. & Strategic Technologies, 1992—96, mem. tech. staff, rsch. scientist and tech. mgr. Ctr. for Integrated Systems Devel., 1997—99, mem. tech. staff, tech. mgr. and rsch. scientist Materials Rsch. & Strategic Technologies, 1999—2001, disting. mem. tech. staff, tech. mgr. and rsch. scientist Advanced Products R&D Labs. Tempe, Ariz., 2001—04; disting. mem. tech. staff Freescale Semiconductor Inc., Tempe, 2005—, mgr. tech., 2005—, rsch. scientist advanced products R&D Labs., 2005—06, rsch. scientist wireless and packaging sys. lab., 2006—. Contbr. articles to profl. jours. Vol. tchr. 5th-6th grade kids, Mesa, 1995—2004. Mem.: Materials Rsch. Soc. Achievements include patents in field; patents pending in field. Office: Freescale Semiconductor Inc Wireless and Packaging Sys Lab 2100 East Elliot Rd Tempe AZ 85284 Personal E-mail: femtophysicist@yahoo.com.

**THEODORE, EUSTACE D.,** educational association administrator, consultant; b. Marietta, Ohio, Aug. 4, 1941; s. Demetrios E. and Nicoletta D. T.; m. Carol Nagy, June 13, 1964; children: Kyle James, Graham Clark. BA, Yale U., 1963; MA, Cornell U., 1965, PhD, 1967. Mem. faculty Hollins Coll., Roanoke, Va., 1967-71, Mt. Holyoke Coll., South Hadley, Mass., 1971-72; dean Calhoun Coll., Yale U., New Haven, 1972-81; exec. dir. Assn. Yale Alumni, 1981-97; pres. Coun. for Advancement and Support of Edn., Washington, 1997-2000; prin. eAdvancement.org, 2000—. Mgmt. and ednl. cons., 1965—. Contbr. articles to jours. Office: eAdvancement 1301 21st St NW Washington DC 20036-1503 Office Phone: 202-463-7310. Business E-Mail: theodore@eadvancement.org.

**THEODORE, JOSE,** professional hockey player; b. Sept. 13, 1976; Goalie Montreal Canadiens, 1995—2006, Colo. Avalanche, 2006—. Player NHL All-star game, 2002, 04; mem. Team Can., World Cup of Hockey, 2004. Named Player of Week, Nat. Hockey League, 1999, Fredericton's Player of Yr., Am. Hockey League; named to World Hockey Championship 2nd All-Star team, 2000; recipient Vezina Trophy, 2002, Hart Meml. Trophy, 2002. Achievements include being a member of World Cup Champion Team Canada, 2004. Office: c/o Colorado Avalanche Pepsi Ctr 100 Chopper Circle Denver CO 80204-1743*

**THEODORESCU, RADU AMZA SERBAN,** mathematician, educator; b. Bucharest, Romania, Apr. 12, 1933; emigrated to Can., 1968, naturalized, 1975; s. Dan and Ortensia Maria (Butoianu) T.; children: Dan, Paul, Anne; m. Marie-José Michiels. BSc, U. Bucharest, 1954, DSc, 1967; PhD, Acad. Romania, 1958. Asst. prof. Inst. Math. of Acad., 1954-57, sr. asst. prof., 1957-60, assoc. prof., sci. sec., 1960-64; prof., head dept. Center Math. Statistics, 1964-68; prof. U. Bucharest, 1968-69, Laval U., Quebec, Canada, 1969-2000, prof. emeritus, 2000—; guest prof., lectr. univs. in Europe, N.Am. and Australia. Author: (with G. Ciucu) Processes with Complete Connections, 1960, (with S. Guiasu) Mathematical Information Theory, 1968, Uncertainty and Information, 1971, (with M. Iosifescu) Random Processes and Learning, 1969, (with W. Hengartner) Concentration Functions, 1973, 2d edit., 1980, Monte-Carlo Methods, 1978, (with E. Bertin and I. Cuculescu) Unimodality of Probability Measures, 1997; mem. editl. bd. Annales des Sciences Mathématiques du Québec, 1976-99, Optimization, 1970-2000, Statistics and Decisions, 1981-2003, Revstat, 2002—; contbr. articles to profl. jours. Mem. bd. European Orgn. Quality Control, 1966-69. Recipient prize Acad. Romania, 1960 Fellow Inst. Math. Stats., Am. Stat. Quality; mem. Statis. Soc. Can. (hon.), Statis. Soc. Romania (hon.), Am. Math. Soc., Internat. Statis. Inst. Home: Apt 1603 9 Jardins Mérici Quebec City PQ Canada G1S 4S8 Office: Laval U Dept Math and Stats Quebec City PQ Canada G1K 7P4 Office Phone: 418-656-3057. Business E-Mail: radutheo@mat.ulaval.ca.

**THEODORIDIS, GEORGE CONSTANTIN,** biomedical engineering educator, researcher; b. Braila, Romania, Dec. 3, 1935; came to U.S. 1959; s. Constantin George and Anastasia (Haritopoulos) T.; m. Lilly Kate Hyman, Sept. 20, 1975; 1 child. Alexander. BS in Mechanical and Elec. Engring., Nat. Tech. U. Athens, 1959; DSc, MIT, Cambridge, Mass., 1964. Rsch. assoc. MIT, Cambridge, Mass., 1964; sr. scientist Am. Sci. Engring., Cambridge, Mass., 1964-68; assoc. prof. in residence U. Calif., Berkeley, 1968-70; biomedical engring. U.Va., Charlottesville, 1970—; prof. elec. engring. U. Patras, Greece, 1976-83. Cons. Food and Drug Adminstrn., Washington, 1975-76, Applied Physics Lab, Columbia, Md., 1978-79. Author: Applied Math, 1983; contbr. articles to profl. jours. Den leader Boy Scouts Am.,

Charlottesville, Va., 1984-85. Fulbright fellow U.S. Govt., MIT, 1959-60; Nato fellow NATO, MIT, 1961-64; Spl. fellow NIH, U. Calif., 1968-70; recipient teaching award GE, MIT, 1963. Mem. Inst. Elec. and Electronics Engrs., Sigma Xi. Greek Orthodox. Avocations: history, travel. Home: 1817 Fendall Ave Charlottesville VA 22903-1613 Office: U Va Dept Biomed Engring PO Box 377 Charlottesville VA 22902-0377 Office Phone: 434-924-8885. Business E-Mail: gct@virginia.edu.

**THEODOSIUS,** retired leader of the Orthodox Church in America; b. Canonsburg, P.A., 1933; Grad., Washington and Jefferson Coll., Washington, PA; M of Divinity, Saint Vladimir Orthodox Theological Seminary, 1960. Ordained to the diaconate & priesthood Orthodox Church in Amer., 1961; bishop Diocese of Sitka and Alaska, 1967—72, Diocese of Pittsburgh, Pa., 1972—77; metropolitan of Amer., Canada Orthodox Church of Amer., 1977—2002; archbishop of Washington, 1977—2002. Office: Orthodox Ch in Am PO Box 675 Syosset NY 11791-0675

**THEON, JOHN SPERIDON,** meteorologist, researcher; b. Washington, Dec. 12, 1934; s. Lewis and Merope Theon; m. Joanne Edens, July 31, 1965; children: Christopher James, Catherine. BS in Aero. Engring, U. Md., 1957; BS in Meteorology, Pa. State U., 1959, MS, 1962; PhD in Engring. Sci. and Mechanics, U. Tenn., 1985. Aero. engr. Douglas Aircraft Co., Santa Monica, Calif., 1957-58; engr. U.S. Naval Ordnance Lab., White Oak, Md., 1962; rsch. meterologist, 1962-74; head meterology br. NASA Goddard Space Flight Center, Greenbelt, Md., 1974-77; asst. chief lab. Atmospheric Scis., 1977-78, Nimbus project scientist, 1972—78; program scientist Global Weather Rsch. Pogram NASA Hdqrs, Washington, 1978—82, chief atmospheric dynamics and radiation program, program scientist Spacelab 3 program, 1982—87, program scientist tropical rainfall measuring mission, 1984—95, chief climate process rsch. program, 1987—94, exec. sec. interagency task force on observations and data mgmt., 1994—95. Cons. Orbital Scis. Corp., 1995—96, Inst. Global Environ. Strategies, 1995—2005, Cal Tech Jet Propulsion Lab., 1997—99, George Washington U., Washington, 2005—. Contbr. articles to profl. jours. With USAF, 1958—60. Named Disting. Alumnus, U. Tenn., 1989; recipient Goddard Exceptional Performance award, 1978, Exceptional Performance award, NASA, 1986, Radio Wave award, Ministry of Posts & Telecom. Japan, 1995. Fellow: Am. Meterol. Soc. Presbyterian. Home and Office: 6801 Lupine Ln Mc Lean VA 22101-1518

**THERIOT, EDWARD C.,** museum director; BS in Zoology, La. State U., Baton Rouge, 1975, MS in Fisheries Biology, 1978; PhD, U. Mich. Sch. Natural Resources, 1983. V.p. biodiversity and evolution Acad. Natural Scis., Phila.; dir. Tex. Meml. Mus., Austin; prof. molecular evolution U. Tex., Austin. Nat. bd. dirs. Assn Systematics Collections, 1995—97, past pres. nat. bd. dirs., 1997—99; com. mem. Species Concepts, Systematics Agenda, 2000; adv. panel Nat. Sci. Found. Biol. Databases and Informatics, 2000. Editl. bd. Phycological Soc. Am., 1988—90, assoc. editor, 1991—93, editl. bd. Molecular Phylogenetics and Evolution, 1992—2000. Office: Tex Meml Mus 2400 Trinity St Austin TX 78705-5730

**THERIOT, JULIE,** microbiologist, medical educator; BS, MIT, 1988; PhD in Cell Biology, U. Calif. San Francisco, 1993; predoctoral fellow, Howard Hughes Med. Inst., 1988—93; fellow, Whitehead Inst.for Biomedical Rsch., 1993—97. Asst. prof., biochemistry, microbiology and immunology Stanford U. Sch. Medicine, Calif., 1997—. Author of numerous articles pub. in such acad. jour. as Nature, Proceedings of the Nat.l Acad. of Sci. USA, and Jour. of Cell Biology. Office: Theriot Lab Beckman Ctr Dept Biochemistry Stanford Univ Med Sch Stanford CA 94305*

**THERNSTROM, ABIGAIL,** federal agency administrator, writer; b. NYC, Sept. 14, 1936; d. Ferdinand and Helen Mann; m. Stephan Thernstrom, Jan. 3, 1959; children: Melanie, Samuel. BA, Barnard Coll., N.Y.C., 1958; MA, Harvard U., 1961; PhD, 1975. Lectr. Harvard U., Cambridge, Mass., 1975-78; project dir. The Twentieth Century Fund, N.Y.C., 1981-86; vis. lectr. Harvard U., Cambridge, Mass., 1988-89, Boston Coll., 1990; stringer The Economist, London, 1988-92; adj. prof. Sch. Edn. Boston U., 1991—93; sr. fellow The Manhattan Inst., N.Y.C., 1993—. Domestic strategy group Aspen (Colo.) Inst., 1992-97; edn. policy com. Hudson Inst., 1994-97; bd. dirs. Inst. for Justice, Washington; adv. bd. Am. Friends Inst. for Justice, London, 1993-2003; mem. Mass. State Bd. Edn., 1995—; commr. US Commn. on Civil Rights, 2001—, vice-chair, 2004—. Author: Whose Votes Count?: Affirmative Action and Minority Voting Rights, 1987, School Choice in Massachusetts, 1991; co-author: (with Stephan Thernstrom) America in Black and White: One Nation Indivisible, 1997, No Excuses: Closing the Racial Gap in Learning, 2003; editor: A Democracy Reader, 1992; co-editor: Beyond the Color Line: New Perspectives on Race and Ethnicity in America, 2002; contbr. articles to profl. jours. Mem. Citizen's Initiative on Race and Ethnicity, 1998—2002; vice chair U.S. Commn. on Civil Rights, 2004—; mem. bd. advisors U.S. Election Assistance Commn., 2006—. Recipient Anisfield Wolf Book award, 1987, Am. Bar Assn. cert. merit, 1988, Best Policy Book award Polit. Studies Orgn., 1987, Benchmark Book award Ctr. for Judicial Studies, 1987. Am. Polit. Sci. Assn. Home and Office: 1445 Massachusetts Ave Lexington MA 02420-3810 Office Phone: 781-861-7634. Business E-Mail: thernstr@fas.harvard.edu.

**THERNSTROM, STEPHAN,** historian, educator; b. Port Huron, Mich., Nov. 5, 1934; s. Albert George and Bernadene (Robbins) T.; m. Abigail Mann, Jan. 3, 1959; children— Melanie Rachel, Samuel Altgeld. BS, Northwestern U., 1956; A.M., Harvard, 1958, PhD, 1962. Instr. history Harvard U., Cambridge, Mass., 1962-66, asst. prof., 1966-67, prof., 1973-81, Winthrop prof., 1981—, chmn. com. on higher degrees in history of Am. civilization, 1985-92; prof. Brandeis U., 1967-69, UCLA, 1969-73; Pitt. prof. Am. history and instns. Cambridge U., 1978-79; dir. Charles Warren Ctr. for Research in Am. History, 1980-83. Author: Poverty and Progress, 1964, Poverty, Planning and Politics in the New Boston, 1969, The Other Bostonians, 1973, History of the American People, 1984, 88; co-author: America in Black and White, 1997, Reflections on The Shape of the River, 1999, No Excuses: Closing the Racial Gap in Learning, 2003; editor: Harvard Ency. Am. Ethnic Groups; co-editor: Harvard Studies in Urban History; Cambridge Interdisciplinary Perspectives on Modern History Series, Beyond the Color Line, 2001. Recipient Bancroft prize, R.R. Hawkins award, Faculty prize Harvard U. Press, Waldo G. Leland prize; Guggenheim fellow, John M. Olin fellow, ACLS fellow, sr. fellow Manhattan inst., 1998—, Nat. Humanities Coun., 2003. Office: Harvard U Robinson Hall Cambridge MA 02138 Office Phone: 617-495-3035. Business E-Mail: thernstr@fas.harvard.edu.

**THERON, CHARLIZE,** actress; b. Benoni, South Africa, Aug. 7, 1975; d. Charles and Gerda Theron. Studied dance, Joffrey Ballet, N.Y.C. TV and print ad representative for J'Adore perfume Christian Dior, 2004—. Actor: (films) Children of the Corn III, 1995, 2 Days in the Valley, 1996, That Thing You Do!, 1996, The Devil's Advocate, 1997, Trial and Error, 1997, Celebrity, 1998, Mighty Joe Young, 1998, The Astronaut's Wife, 1999, The Cider House Rules, 1999, Reindeer Games, 2000, The Yards, 2000, Men of Honor, 2000, The Legend of Bagger Vance, 2000, Sweet November, 2001, 15 Minutes, 2001, The Curse of the Jade Scorpion, 2001, Trapped, 2002, Waking Up in Reno, 2002, The Italian Job, 2003, (also prodr.) Monster, 2003 (Golden Globe for best dramatic actress, 2004, Screen Actors Guild Award for best actress, 2004, Acad. Award for best actress, 2004), Head in the Clouds, 2004, North Country, 2005, Aeon Flux, 2005; (TV films) The Life and Death of Peter Sellers, 2004, Hollywood Confidential, 1997, (guest appearance): (TV series) Arrested Development, 2005—. Named one of 50 Most Beautiful People, People Mag., 2000; recipient Best Performance by a Human-Female (In Aeon Flux), Spike TV Video Game awards, 2005, Spirit of Independence award, LA Film Festival, 2006. Address: United Talent Agy Ste 500 9560 Wilshire Blvd Beverly Hills CA 90212*

**THEROUX, DAVID JON,** economist, educator, research and development company executive; b. Lansing, Mich., May 25, 1949; s. Paul Richard and Marjorie Erma (Withrow) Theroux; m. Elaine Laconia Shipp, 1976 (div.

1991); children: Paul Jacques, Drake Emeri; m. Mary Lyn Garvey, 1991. AB in Applied Math., U. Calif., Berkeley, 1973, BSME, 1973, MSME, 1974; MBA, U. Chgo., 1977. Rsch. asst. Richmond Field Sta., U. Calif., Berkeley, 1974, U. Chgo., 1976; project engr. Exxon Co. U.S.A., 1975-76; dir. vis. lectr. program in econ. sci. U. Chgo., 1977; v.p., dir. acad. affairs, dir. pub. policy studies Cato Inst., San Francisco, 1977—79; pres., dir. Pacific Rsch. Inst. Pub. Policy, San Francisco, 1979—86, Ind. Inst., Oakland, Calif., 1986—90; pres., gen. ptnr. LTN Ptnrs., 1986—90; pub., editor LibertyTree Network, 1986—; pub. Independent Review: A Journal of Political Economy. Adv. bd. No. Calif. Econ. Seminars, 1981—; bd. dirs. Grocery Express, Ltd., 1986—; mem. Coun. for Monetary Reform. Sr. editor Policy Report, 1978—79; editor: Cato Papers, 1978—79, The Energy Crisis: Government Policy and the Economy, 1978; editor: (with P. Truluck) Private Rights and Public Lands, 1983; editor: Politics and Tyranny: Lessons in Pursuit of Freedom, 1985. Trustee William Koch Found., 1978—79; mem. Mencken award book com. Free Press Assn., 1990—; exec. com. Templeton Honor Roll for Higher Edn. in a Free Soc. With USAF, 1967—72. Recipient George Washington Honor medal for excellence, Freedoms Found., 1983, Mencken award for Best Book, Free Press Assn., 1988. Mem.: Pub. Choice Soc., Nat. Assn. Bus. Economists, So. Econ. Assn., Western Econ. Assn., Royal Econ. Soc., Am. Econ. Assn., John Randolph Club, Omicron Delta Epsilon, Pi Tau Sigma. Home: 11990 Skyline Blvd Oakland CA 94619-2421 Office: 100 Swan Way Oakland CA 94621-1428

**THEROUX, PAUL EDWARD,** author; b. Medford, Mass., Apr. 10, 1941; s. Albert Eugene and Anne (Dittami) T.; m. Anne Castle, Dec. 4, 1967 (div. 1993); children: Marcel, Louis; m. Sheila Donnelly, Nov. 18, 1995. BA, U. Mass., Amherst, DLitt, 1988, Trinity Coll., Washington, 1980, Tufts U., 1980. Lectr. U. Urbino, Italy, 1963, Soche Hill Coll., Malawi, 1963-65; faculty English dept. Makerere U., Uganda, 1965-68, U. Singapore, 1968-71; vis. lectr. U. Va., 1972-73. Author: (fiction) Waldo, 1967, Fong and the Indians, 1968, Girls at Play, 1969, Murder in Mt. Holly, 1969, Jungle Lovers, 1971, Sinning with Annie, 1972, Saint Jack, 1973, The Black House, 1974, The Family Arsenal, 1976, The Consul's File, 1977, Picture Palace, 1978 (Whitbread prize for fiction), A Christmas Card, 1978, London Snow, 1980, World's End, 1980, The Mosquito Coast, 1981, The London Embassy, 1982, Half Moon Street, 1984, O-Zone, 1986, My Secret History, 1988, Chicago Loop, 1990, Millroy and the Magician, 1993, My Other Life, 1996, Kowloon Tong, 1997, Collected Stories, 1997, Collected Short Novels, 1998, Hotel Honolulu, 2001, The Stranger at the Palazzo d'Oro, 2003, Blinding Light, 2005; (nonfiction) V.S. Naipaul, 1973, The Great Railway Bazaar, 1975, The Old Patagonian Express, 1979, The Kingdom by the Sea, 1983, Sailing Through China, 1983, Sunrise with Sea Monsters, 1985, The White Man's Burden, 1987, Riding the Iron Rooster, 1988, The Happy Isles of Oceania, 1992, The Pillars of Hercules, 1995, Sir Vidia's Shadow, 1998, Fresh Air Fiend, 2000, Nurse Wolf and Dr. Sacks, 2001, Dark Star Safari, 2002; (film script) Saint Jack, 1979, Chinese Box, 1998. Recipient Editorial award Playboy mag., 1972, 76, 77, 79, Lit. award AAAL, 1977, James Tait Black award, 1982, Yorkshire Post Best Novel award, 1982, Thomas Cook Travel Book prize, 1989. Fellow Royal Soc. Lit., Royal Geog. Soc.; mem. AAAL.

**THEROUX, WILLIAM GERARD,** lawyer; b. Morristown, N.J., May 6, 1959; s. William E. and Mary T. (Conroy) T. BA magna cum laude, Montclair State Coll., 1981; JD cum laude, Seton Hall Law Sch., 1984. Bar: N.J. 1984, U.S. Dist. Ct. (N.J.) 1984; cert. civil trial atty. Corp. atty. Hannoch Weisman, Roseland, N.J., 1984-86; litigation atty. Francis & Berry, Morristown, 1986—96, Jackson & Buckley, PC, 1996—98, Buckley & Theroux, LLC, 1998—. Mem. N.J. State Bar Assn. Roman Catholic. Avocation: reading. Office: Buckley & Theroux LLC 932 State Rd Princeton NJ 08540 Office Phone: 609-924-9099. Business E-Mail: bill@buckleytheroux.com.

**THERRIEN, FRANCOIS XAVIER, JR.,** business and tax consultant; b. Amesbury, Mass. June 6, 1928; s. Francis Xavier and Doris Alma (Cote) T.; BS, U.S. Mil. Acad., 1950; MS, U. Ariz., 1962; Cert. tax profl., tax advisor, enrolled agt., environ. inspector, bd. cert. bus. appraiser; m. Yoshiko Kashima, July 22, 1969; children: Francois Xavier, Norman, Sakura, Izumi. Commd. 2d lt., U.S. Army, 1950, advanced through grades to lt. col., 1965, ret., 1970; dist. dir. R. J. Carroll Assoc., Inc., Atlanta, 1970-71; with Treasure Lake, Atlanta, 1971; pres. Identiseal of Fla., Orlando, 1972-74; owner Yoshiko Enterprises, Winter Park, Fla., 1974-87, bd. dirs., pres., 1988—; instr. Seminole Community Coll., 1974-79; regional rep. H.D. Vest Investment Securities, Inc., Irving, Tex., 1989—. Decorated Army Commendation medals (2), Air medal, Bronze Star medal, Silver Star, Croix DeGuerre with palm. Mem. Nat. Assn. Enrolled Agts. Roman Catholic. Office: 2265 Lee Rd Ste 223 Winter Park FL 32789-1858

**THERRIEN, MICHEL,** former professional hockey coach; b. Nov. 4, 1963; m. Genevieve Therrien; children: Élizabeth, Charles. Coach Lvaal Titan, Granby Predateurs; 1st head coach Quebec Citadelles, 1999—2000; head coach Montreal Canadiens, 2000—03, Wilkes-Barre/Scranton Penguins (AHL), 2003—05, Pittsburgh Penguins, 2005—. Office: c/o Pittsburgh Penguins 66 Mario Lemieux Place Pittsburgh PA 15219

**THEUER, CHARLES P.,** pharmaceutical executive, researcher; MD, U. Calif., San Francisco, 1989; PhD, U. Calif., Irvine, 2002. Cert. Am. Bd. of Surgery, 1997. Chief med. officer TargeGen, San Diego, 2004—06; CEO Tracon Pharma, San Diego, 2006—. Lt. US Pub. Health Svc., 1991—93. Office: Tracon Pharma 4510 Executive Dr San Diego CA 92121 Office Phone: 858-550-0780. Business E-Mail: ctheuer@traconpharma.com.

**THEURER, BYRON W.,** aerospace engineer, business owner; b. Glendale, Calif., July 1, 1939; s. William Louis and Roberta Cecilia (Sturgiss) T.; m. Sue Ann McKay, Sept. 15, 1962 (div. 1980); children: Karen Marie, William Thomas, Alison Lee; m. Patricia Ann Pilcher, Nov. 2, 2002 BS in Engring. Sci., USAF Acad., 1961; MS in Aero. Sci., U. Calif., Berkeley, 1965; MBA, U. Redlands, 1991. Commd. USAF, 1961, advanced through grades to lt. col., ret., 1978; project officer Space Shuttle Devel. Prog., Houston, 1971-76; chief of test F-15 Systems Prog. Office Wright Patterson AFB, Ohio, 1976-78; sr. engr. Veda, Inc., Dayton, Ohio, 1979-81, Logicon Inc., Dayton, 1981-83; project mgr. Support Systems Assocs., Inc., Dayton, 1983-84, CTA Inc., Ridgecrest, Calif., 1985-89; owner, operator The Princeton Rev. of Ctrl. Calif., Ridgecrest, 1989-92, San Luis Obispo, 1993—2002; counselor Svc. Corps. Ret. Execs., 2002—. Cons. in field. Counselor SCORE. Decorated Silver Star, D.F.C., Air Medals (16); named Officer of the Yr., Air Force Flight Test Ctr., Edwards AFB, 1970 Mem. Air Force Assn., Assn. Old Crows, USAF Acad. Assn. Grads. (nat. bd. dirs. 1972-75, chpt. pres. 1981-83), Svc. Corps Ret. Execs. Republican. Episcopalian. Avocation: walking. Home and Office: 387 E 800 S Ivins UT 84738

**THEVENET, PATRICIA CONFREY,** social studies educator; b. Norwich, Conn., Apr. 16, 1924; d. John George and Gertrude Pauline (Doolittle) Confrey; m. Rubén Thevenet, Dec. 15, 1945 (dec. Mar. 1983); chldren: Susanne, Gregory, Richard, R. James. BS, U. Conn., 1944; AM, U. Chgo., 1945; EdM, Columbia U., 1992, EdD, 1994. Cert. elem. tchr., N.J. Counselor testing and guidance U. Chgo., 1945; home economist Western Mass. Electric Co., Pittsfield, 1946; tchr. Unquowa Sch., Fairfield, Conn., 1950-53, Alpine (N.J.) Sch., 1968-86; program asst. soc. studies Tchrs. Coll. Columbia U., N.Y.C., 1987-93; ret., 1993. Historian Borough Northvale, N.J., 1987-94; participant summer seminar Smithsonian Instn., Washington, 1984. Del. 2d dist. rep. Town Mtg., Trumbull, Conn., 1954-56; pres., trustee Northvale Pub. Libr. Assn., 1957-63; trustee Northvale Bd. Edn., 1963-72, pres. Northvale Bd. Edn., 1969-70; exec. bd. mem. Bergen County (N.J.) County Bds. Edn., 1965-72; mem. Evening Sch. Comm. No. Valley Regional Dist., Bergen County, 1976-83; trustee Voluntown Libr., 1997-2001. Mem. Voluntown Hist. Soc., Friends of Slater Mus., DAR. Home: 88 N Shore Rd # B Voluntown CT 06384-1719

**THEVENOT, MAUDE TRAVIS,** retired home economist; b. Many, La., Dec. 31, 1914; d. Rennie L. and Fairy D. (Minter) Travis; m. Aubrey J. Thevenot, July 4, 1952 (dec. Sept. 1981); 1 stepchild, Peter A. BA, Northwestern State U., 1939; MS, La. State U., 1963. Tchr. home econs. Bienville Parish High Sch., Jamestown, La., 1940-41; parish home mgmt. supr. Farmers Home Adminstrn., USDA, Natchitoches, Oak Grove, Winnefield, La., 1942-47, state home mgmt. supr. Alexandria, La., 1948-52; social worker La. Dept. Pub. Welfare, New Roads, Alexandria, Marksville, La., 1952-56; home economist La. State U.-La. Coop. Extension Svc., Makrsville, Alexandria, 1957-74, specialist expanded food & nutrition edn. program Baton Rouge, 1975-79. Co-advisor in home econs. Ptnrs. of Am. La./El Savador and La. Home Econs., 1975. Author: Central District Louisiana Home Economics Association, 1984 Louisiana Federation of Chapters of the National Association of Retired Federal Workers, 1989; co-author: A Taste of Yesterday, 1988. Mem. Kent Plantation House, Inc., Alexandria, 1970—, com. mem. for orgn., 1970, exec. bd., 1985-88, cookbook chmn., 1985-90; mem. Friendship House-Adult Day Care Ctr., Alexandria, 1982-90, exec. bd., 1982-88, organizer, pres. vol. orgn., 1978-90; advisor Anchors as Pilot Club of Alexandria Outreach Com., Anchor Club of Pineville (La.) High Sch., 1978-90; mem. La. Avoyelles & Rapides Parish Farm Bur., Marksville, Alexandria, 1967-90, Avoyelles & Rapides Cowbelles, Alexandria, Marksville, 1967-70; mem. Calvary Bapt. Ch., leader Sunday Sch. class, mem. sr. group decoration com. for monthly luncheons, leader Dottie Hayes Bible Study Group. Recipient Plaque for Svc. Rapides Parish Coun. on Aging, Alexandria, 1971, Plaque for Outstanding Leadership & Svc., Rapides Parish Homemakers Coun., Alexandria, 1974, Plaque of Appreciation as Coord. Expanded Food and Nutrition Ednl. Program La. State U., Baton Rouge, 1978, 11 Certs. of Appreciation, Anchor Club of Pineville High Sch., 1980-90, Cert. of Recognition (3) Friendship House-Day Care for Adults, 1983, 84, 85, Plaque for Outstanding Svc., Rapides Coun. on Aging 20th Am., 1967-87. Mem. Internat. Fedn. Home Econs., Am. Assn. Family and Consumer Sci., La. Home Econs. Assn. (v.p. 1972-73, Disting. Home Economist 1979-80), Am. Assn. Family and Consumer Svcs. (Wiley-Berger award 1995), Cen. Dist. Home Econs. (pres. 1972-73, Disting. Svc. award 1967, hon. mem. 1985), Nat. Assn. Extension Home Economist, La. Assn. Extension Home Economist, AAUW, La. Assn. Nat. Assn. Retired Fed. Employees (past pres., v.p. region VI, Meritorious Svc. plaque and cert. of citation 1988-89, Meritorious Svc. award 1992-93, life), CENLA (past pres.), Am. Assn. Retired Persons, La. State U. Alumni, La. State U. Home Econs. Retiree, Northwestern State U. Alumni, La. Retired Tchrs. Assn. (life), Pilot Club Internat., Epsilon Sigma Phi (life), Gamma Sigma Delta (Extension award of merit 1978). Democrat. Avocations: travel, voluntary activities. Home: 507 Tanglewood Dr Alexandria LA 71303-3354

**THEWLIS, DAVID,** actor; b. Blackpool, Eng., Mar. 20, 1963; m. Sara Sugarman, 1992 (div. 1993). Grad., Guildhall Sch. Music and Drama. Actor: (films) Little Dorrit, 1988, Resurrected, 1989, Afraid of the Dark, 1991, Life Is Sweet, 1991, Damage, 1992, Naked, 1993 (Cannes Internat. Film Festival Best Actor), The Trial, 1993, Black Beauty, 1994, Restoration, 1994, Total Eclipse, 1995, Dragonheart, 1996, The Island of Dr. Moreau, 1996, American Perfekt, 1997, Seven Years in Tibet, 1997, Besieged, 1999, Whatever Happened to Harold Smith?, 1999, Gangster No. 1, 2000, Goodbye Charlie Bright, 2001, Timeline, 2003, Harry Potter and the Prisoner of Askaban, 2004, Kingdom of Heaven, 2005, All the Invisible Children, 2005, The New World, 2005, Basic Instinct 2, 2006, The Omen, 2006; (TV series) Valentine Park, 1985, A Bit of a Do, 1989; (TV films) The Short and Curlies, 1987, Skulduggery, 1989, Oranges Are Not the Only Fruit, 1990, Journey to Knock, 1991, Afraid of the Dark, 1991, Black and Blue, 1992, Prime Suspect 3, 1993, Love Story, 1999, (voice) The Miracle Maker, 2000, (voice) Hamilton Mattress, 2001; writer, dir.: (films) Hello, Hello, Hello, 1995, Cheeky, 2003.*

**THEYSKENS, OLIVIER,** apparel designer; b. Brussels, Jan. 4, 1977; Attended, Ecole Nationale Superieure des Arts Visuels de la Cambre. Designer, owner Olivier Theyskens Collection, Belgium, 1997—; artistic dir. Rochas, France, 2002—. Office: Olivier Theyskens 19 rue de la Concorde 1050 Brussels Belgium also: Rochas 33 rue Francois 1er 75008 Paris France*

**THIBADEAU, EUGENE FRANCIS,** education educator, consultant; b. N.Y.C., May 18, 1933; s. Eugene Servanis and Lillian (Archer) T.; 1 child, Christine. BA, NYU, 1959, MA, 1967, MA, 1968, PhD, 1973. Tchr. NYU, N.Y.C., 1968; lectr. in philosophy Dowling Coll., Oakdale, 1968-70; prof. edn. Indiana U. of Pa., 1970—. Vis. assoc. prof. Adelphi U., Garden City, N.Y., 1974-75; vis. scholar N.Y. U., N.Y.C., 1984-85; vis. prof. Hofstra U. Hempstead, 1974-75, 84, 86, Fudan U., Shanghai, China, 2000; cons. Central Bur. of Ednl. Visits, London, 1980-81, Commonwealth Speakers Bur., Harrisburg, Pa., 1983-85, U.S. Dept. Edn., Washington, 1983-85, Pa. Dept. Edn., Harrisburg, 1988—. Author: Opening Up Edn.-In Theory and Practice, 1976, Curriculum Theory, 1988, Existentialism in the Classroom, 1994; rev. editor: Focus on Learning, 1973-77, editor, 1977-84; contbg. editor: Internat. Ency. of Edn., 2d edit., Internat. Ency.of Teaching and Tchr. Edn., 2nd edit., Internat. Ency. of Social and Behavioral Scis.; contbr. articles to profl. jours. Active United Way, Indiana, Pa., 1980—, NAACP, Indiana, 1985—, Red Cross, Indiana, 1985—. Fulbright sr. lectr. Thames Polytechnic, London, 1978-79, Fulbright sr. scholar Janus Pannonius U., Peces, Hungary, 1990-91; foreign expert Shanghai (China) Tchrs. U., 1988; designated faculty rsch. assoc. Inst. for Applied Rsch. and Pub. Policy, Indiana U. Pa., 1989; named Commonwealth Teaching fellow and Cert. Excellence in Teaching, Pa. State Colls. and Univ. Disting. Faculty Awards Com., 1976; recipient Founder's Day award, NYU, 1973, Outstanding Prof. award Ind. U. Pa.-Pa. State Edn. Assn., 1993. Fellow Am. Philosophy Edn. Soc.; mem. AAUP, ASCD, Am. Ednl. Studies Assn., The S.W. Philosophy Edn. Soc. Avocations: travel, skiing, tennis, reading, chess. Home: 534 Chestnut Ridge Rd Penn Run PA 15703 Office: Indiana Univ Pa 131 Stouffer Hall Indiana PA 15705 Office Phone: 724-357-4543. Business E-Mail: eft@iup.edu.

**THIBAULT, GEORGE EDWIN,** medical educator, non-profit healthcare organization administrator; b. 1943; Degree, Georgetown U., 1965; MD, Harvard Med. Sch., 1969. Resident internal med. Mass. Gen. Hosp., 1971, 1974, chief med. resident, 1975, fellow cardiology, 1976, dir. med. practices evaluation unit, dept. med., 1977, dir. ICU/CCU, 1977, dir. tng. program internal med., 1978, assoc. chief; fellow cardiology Nat. Heart & Lung Inst., Bethesda, Md., 1973; chief med. svcs. Brockton/West Roxbury VA Med. Ctr., Mass., 1988; vice chmn. med. Brigham and Women's Hosp., 1988—95, chief med. officer, 1995—99; v.p. clin. affairs Partners HealthCare System Inc., Boston, 1999—; prof. med. Harvard Med. Sch., dir. The Academy, 2001—. Chmn. special med. adv. group Dept. Vet. Affairs, Boston. Office: Partners HealthCare Sys Inc Prudential Tower 800 Boylston St Ste 1150 Boston MA 02199-8001

**THIBERT, ROGER JOSEPH,** clinical chemist, educator; b. Tecumseh, Ont., Can. Aug. 29, 1929; s. Charles and Violet (Hebert) T.; m. Audrey M. Wissler, July 10, 1954; children: Mark Roger, Robert Francis. BA, U. Western Ont., 1951; MS, U. Detroit, 1954; PhD, Wayne State U., 1958, DSc, U. Windsor, 2004. Diplomate: Am. Bd. Clin. Chemistry (past bd. dirs.). Mem. faculty U. Windsor, Ont., Canada, 1953—, prof. chemistry Ont., 1967-94, dir. clin. chemistry Ont., 1972-94, prof. emeritus Ont., 1994—; prof. pathology Med. Sch. Wayne State U. Detroit, 1972-94; assoc. divsn. head, clin. chemistry Detroit Receiving Hosp., Univ. Health Ctr., 1973-94, mem. med. staff, 1973-94. Cons. med. biochemistry Med. Labs. Windsor, Ont., Can., 1995-2000; sci. dir. Med. Labs., Windsor, 2000-2005. Contbr. articles on chemistry, biochemistry, analytical chemistry, clin. chemistry to profl. jours. Recipient Smith Kline award Am. Assn. Clin. Chemistry, 1980, Tchg. award Ont. Confedn. Univ. Faculty Assns., 1990, Beckman Edn. Excellence award Canadian Soc. Clin. Chemists, 1992, Alumni Tchg. award U. Windsor, 1988, Alumni award of merit, 1994, alumni excellence in mentoring award, 2003; Chem. Inst. Can. fellow, 1968—; Nat. Acad. Clin. Biochemistry fellow, 1978—; grantee Natural Scis. and Engring. Rsch. Coun., Can., award Union Carbide, Chem. Inst. Can., 1978. Fellow AAAS, Can. Acad. Clin. Biochemistry; mem. Am. Chem. Soc., Chem. Inst. Can., Assn. Chem. Profession Ont., Am. Assn. Clin. Chemistry, Nat. Acad. Clin. Biochemistry, Can. Soc. Clin.

Chemists (Ames award 1988), Ont. Soc. Clin. Chemists, Am. Soc. for Biochemistry and Molecular Biology, Fedn. Am. Socs. Exptl. Biology, Can. Soc. Biochemistry and Molecular Biology, Can. Fedn. Biol. Scis., Can. Soc. for Chemistry, Sigma Xi. Roman Catholic. Home: 4612 Dali Ct Windsor ON Canada N9G 2M8 Office: U Windsor Dept Chemistry/Biochemistry Windsor ON Canada N9B 3P4

**THIBODEAU, GARY ARTHUR,** academic administrator; b. Sioux City, Iowa, Sept. 26, 1938; m. Emogene J. McCarville, Aug. 1, 1964; children: Douglas James (dec.), Beth Ann. BS, Creighton U., 1962; MS, S.D. State U., 1967, MS, 1970, PhD, 1971. Profl. service rep. Baxter Lab., Inc., Deerfield, Ill., 1963-65; tchr., researcher dept. biology S.D. State U., Brookings, 1965-76, asst. to v.p. for acad. affairs, 1976-80, v.p. for adminstrn., 1980-85; chancellor U. Wis., River Falls, 1985-2000; sr. v.p. acad. affairs U. Wis. Sys., 2000—01. Mem. investment com. U. Wis., River Falls Found.; trustee W. Cen. Wis. Consortium U. Wis. System; bd. dirs. U. Wis. at River Falls Found.; mem Phi Kappa Phi nat. budget rev. and adv. comm., Phi Kappa Phi Found. investment comm., commm. on Agrl. and Rural Devel., steering commn. Coun. of Rural Colls. and Univs., Joint Coun. on Food and Agrl. Scis., USDA. Author: Basic Concepts in Anatomy and Physiology, 1983, Athletic Injury Assessment, 1994, Textbook of Anatomy and Physiology, 2006, Structure and Function of the Body, 2004, The Human Body in Health and Disease, 2005, Anatomy and Physiology, 2006. Mem. AAAS, Am. Assn. Anatomists, Am. Assn. Clin. Anatomists, Human Anatomy and Physiology Soc., Sigma Xi, Phi Kappa Phi, Gamma Sigma Delta, Gamma Alpha. Office: U Wis 116 N Hall River Falls WI 54022

**THIBODEAU, JOAN MARIE SERAFIN,** writer, educator; b. Raynham, Mass., May 8, 1934; d. Michael Joseph and Mary Rose (Shurgot) Serafin; m. Philip Joseph Thibodeau, Sept. 20, 1975 (dec. Mar. 1994). BA, Annhurst Coll., 1956; MA, U. Notre Dame, 1965, PhD, 1968. Mem. faculty St. Bernard's H.S., New London, Conn., 1956-65; adj. faculty U. Hartford, Conn., 1968-69; assoc. prof. Capital Cmty. & Tech. Coll., 1969-72, dean of faculty, 1970-72; interim dir. Conn. Cmty. Colls. Instrnl. TV, 1972; writer-in-residence Killingly Meml. Sch., Danielson, Conn., 1995-96, mem. pub. rels. com., 1996—. Dir. lit. poetry discussion group Ctr. for Optimum Care, Danielson, 1993—; mentor U. Notre Dame, 1997—. Author: Faulker's Uses of the Classics, 1983. Avocations: poetry, writing, reading, community projects. Home and Office: 111 Westcott Rd Danielson CT 06239-2929 Office Phone: 860-774-5062. E-mail: drjoant@sbcglobal.net.

**THIBODEAUX, RUBY See PRIVAT, RUBY**

**THIE, JOSEPH ANTHONY,** nuclear engineer; s. Joseph Aloysius Thie and Veronica Veneranda Thie (nee Volk); m. Frances Morris Thie, Dec. 30, 1967. BS in Physics, U. Notre Dame, Ind., 1947; PhD in Nuc. Physics, U. Notre Dame, Notre Dame, IN, 1951; DSc (hon.), U. Indpls., 2004. Registered profl. engr., Wis.; Q-clearance AEC. Chief physicist Argonne (Ill.) Nat. Lab., 1953—60; ind. nuc. reactor and medicine cons. Knoxville, 1960—; adj. prof. nuc. engring. U. Tenn., Knoxville, 1989—. Chmn. nuc. reactor safety rev. com. Dairyland Power, LaCrosse, Wis., 1967—; mem., dir.'s adv. com. Oak Ridge (Tenn.) Nat. Lab., 1974—78; lectr. in field. Author: Power Reactor Noise, 1981, Reactor Noise, 1963, Heavy Water Exponential Experiments using ThO2 and UO2, 1961; mem. editl. adv. bd. Jour. Nuc. Medicine, 2003; contbr. articles to profl. jours. Trustee cath. edn. trust fund Roman Cath. Diocese Knoxville, 2004—06. Postdoc. fellow, US AEC, 1951—52. Mem.: Soc. Nuc. Medicine, Am. Nuc. Soc. (life). Achievements include pioneer in first commercial reactors and in analysis of their random phenomena. Avocation: electronic music. Office Phone: 865-966-4041.

**THIEBAUD, WAYNE MORTON,** artist; b. Mesa, Ariz., Nov. 15, 1920; s. Morton J. and Alice Eugenia (LeBaro) T.; m. Betty Jean Carr, Dec. 11, 1959; children: Twinka, Mallary Ann, Paul LeBaron. BA, Sacramento State Coll., 1951, MA, 1952; MFA (hon.), Calif. Coll. Arts and Crafts, 1975. Art dir., N.Y.C.; also Hollywood, 1946-49; chmn. art dept. Sacramento City Coll., 1951; design cons. Calif. State Fair and Expn.; guest instr. San Francisco Art Inst., 1958; assoc. prof. art U. Calif. at Davis, now prof., Faculty Research lectr., from 1973. Vis. artist Cornell U., U. Hawaii, U. Wis., U. Utah, U. Ill., Yale U., U. Va., Bradley U.; tchr. Sacramento City Coll., 1951—61, U. Calif., 1960—76. Author: Etching Delights, 1965, Prints, 1970-71, Seven Still Lifes and a Rabbit; one-man shows include Crocker Art Gallery, Sacramento, Calif., 1952, Artists Coop. Gallery, Sacramento, Calif., 1954, DeYoung Mus., San Francisco, 1962, Allan Stone Gallery, N.Y.C., 1962—70, Stanford, 1965, Sao Paulo Biennale, 1966, Galleria Schwarz, Milan, 1963, San Francisco Mus., 1967, Pasadena Mus. Art, 1967—68, Whitney Mus., 1972, Indocu-menta, 1972, Boston Inst. Contemporary Art, 1976, Walker Art Ctr., Mpls., 1981, Ft. Worth Art Mus., 1981, Mus. Fine Arts, St. Petersburg, Fla., 1981, museums, U.S., Toronto, The Hague, Vienna, Berlin, Hong Kong, S.Am., Oakland Mus., Phoenix Mus., U. So. Calif., Des Moines Mus., one-man shows include organized by Mus. Modern Art for 50th Ann. Wayne Thiebaud exhibn., Newport, R.I., 1985, Milw., 1985, Columbus, 1985, Kansas City, 1985, exhibited in group shows at Santa Barbara (Calif.) Mus. Art, 1980, Bklyn. Mus., 1980, 1981, Whitney Mus. Am. Art, 1981, San Antonio Mus. Art, 1981, Indpls. Mus. Art, 1981, Inst. Contemporary Art, U. Pa., Phila., 1981, Carnegie Inst., Pitts., 1981, Allan Stone Gallery, N.Y.C., 1982, Represented in permanent collections Mus. Modern Art, Whitney Mus. Am. Art, Albright Knox Mus., Wadsworth Athenaeum, Libr. Congress, Woodward Found., Rose Art Mus., Brandeis U., Stanford, Sheldon Meml. Art Gallery U. Nebr., Fines Arts Mus., San Francisco, Utah Mus. Fine Arts U. Utah, Kemper Mus. Contemporary Art, U. Maine Mus. Art, Spencer Mus. Art U. Kans., Nat. Mus. Am. Art, Washington, Crown Point Press, also numerous pvt. collections, commns. include fountain mobile sculpture Calif. State Fair, 1952, paintings Wimbledon Tennis Tournament, 1968, woodblock prints Crown Point Press, Kyoto, Japan, 1987, Yosemite Ridge Line for Bicentennial Exhibn., 1976, 42 works on paper Arts Club Chgo., 1987; prodr., dir.: 12 ednl. motion pictures (1st prize Art Film Festival, 1956, award for Space Golden Reel Film Festival Calif. State Fair, 1956, named Univ. Art Studio Tchr. of Yr. Coll. Art Assn. Am., 1981, Faculty Research medal U. Calif., Davis., 1984, Award of Distinction Nat. Art Schs. Assn., 1984, Spl. Citation Nat. Assn. Schs. Art and Design, 1984). With USAF, 1942—45. Recipient Cyril Magnin award, San Francisco, 1987, Golden Plate award, Am. Acad. Achievement, 1987, Nat. Medal Arts, 1994. Mem.: Nat. Acad. Design (academician), Am. Acad. and Inst. Arts and Letters. Office: co Paul Thiebaud Gallery 631 Union St San Francisco CA 94133

**THIEL, DAVID BRIAN,** physician assistant; b. Cin., July 2, 1956; s. Joseph Lee and Mary Jane (Otting) T. BA, Wabash Coll. Crawfordsville, Ind., 1978; AS with honors, Kettering Coll. Med. Arts, 1980. Cert. physician asst. Resident Los Angeles County-U. So. Calif. Med. Ctr., L.A., 1985-86; physician asst. in orthopedic surgery Ketchikan, Alaska, 1980-85; physician asst. in phys. medicine and electrodiagnostic medicine New Orleans, 1987—2004; physician asst. USCG, 2004—. In-svc. lectr. HealthSouth Rehab., Harahan, La., 1990—. Tannenbaum scholar, 1974-78; recipient Orchid award Paphiopedilum Mystic Jewel, David's Dream, Highly Commended Cert. Am. Orchid Soc., 2003. Fellow: Sigma Xi (numerous Orchid awards); mem.: Internat. High IQ Soc. Republican. Avocations: swimming, skiing, sailing, orchid growing, bicycling. Address: 106 Sawmill Crrek Rd Pearl River LA 70452 E-mail: cynicno@hotmail.com.

**THIEL, JOHN ROBERT,** history professor; b. Lansing, Mich., Sept. 5, 1976; s. John M. and Barbara J. Thiel; m. Amanda Louise Thiel, July 7, 2001; 1 child, Jackson R. MA in History, Mich. State U., East Lansing, 2000. Instr. History Kirtland CC, Roscommon, Mich., 2001—. Bd. mem. River Ho. Shelter Domestic Violence and Homelessness, Grayling, Mich., 2005. Recipient Outstanding Faculty award, Mich. Campus Compact, 2005. Mem.: Orgn. Am. Historians, Am. Hist. Assn. Office: Kirtland CC 10775 N St Helen Rd Roscommon MI 48653 Office Phone: 989-275-5000 278.

**THIEL, PETER,** social sciences educator; s. Ernest Thiel and Heidi Bauer; m. Maria Magdalena Ahumada, Jan. 30, 1969; children: Helena, Alexander. BSBA, U.S. Internat. U., Calif., 1983; MSc in Ednl. Leadership, Fla. Internat. U., Miami, 1987; DA in Econs., Ill. State U., Normal, 1995. Prodn. mgr. Thiel-Tex, S.A., Mexico City, 1980—83; bus. software cons. Tecnicas Electronicas Administrativas, Mexico City; tchr. math. Instituto Tecnologico de Monterrey, Queretaro, Mexico, 1984—87, mem. faculty econs., 1987—91, Ill. State U., Normal, 1992—95, Pardise Valley C.C., Phoenix, 1995—. Home: 4715 E Gatewood Rd Phoenix AZ 85050 Office: Paradise Valley Community Coll 18401 N 32nd St Phoenix AZ 85032 Office Phone: 602-787-7294. Business E-Mail: peter.thiel@pvmail.maricopa.edu.

**THIEL, PETER A.,** investment company executive; BA, JD, Stanford U. Securities law atty. Sullivan & Cromwell; derivatives trader CS Fin. Products; founder, head Thiel Capital Mgmt. LLC; chmn., CEO Confinity, Inc; co-founder PayPal, Inc., 1998, chmn., CEO, 1998—2002; founder, pres., chmn. Investment Com. Clarium Capital Mgmt. LLC, 2003—. Rsch. fellow, bd. dirs. Independent Inst.; bd. dirs. Pacific Rsch. Inst. Co-author: The Diversity Myth, 1998. Bd. visitors Stanford Law Sch. Office: Clarium Capital Mgmt LLC Ste 4360 555 California St San Francisco CA 94104 Office Phone: 415-248-5140. Office Fax: 415-248-5141.*

**THIEL, PHILIP,** design educator; b. Bklyn., Dec. 20, 1920; s. Philip and Alma Theone (Meyer) T.; m. Midori Kono, 1955; children: Philip Kenji, Nancy Tamiko, Susan Akiko, Peter Akira (dec.) BSc, Webb Inst. Naval Architecture, 1943; MSc, U. Mich., 1948; BArch, MIT, 1952. Registered arch., Wash. Instr. naval architecture MIT, Cambridge, 1949—50; instr. architecture U. Calif., Berkeley, 1954—56, asst. prof., 1956—60; assoc. prof. U. Wash., Seattle, 1961—66, prof. visual design and experiential notation, 1966—91; guest prof. Tokyo Inst. Tech., 1976—78; vis. prof. Sapporo Sch. Arts, Japan, 1992—98. Lectr., U.S., Can., Japan, Norway, Denmark, Sweden, Eng., Austria, Switzerland, Peru, Bolivia, Korea; cons. FAO, Rome, 1952; co-founder Environment and Behavior, 1969; founder Ctr. for Exptl. Notation, Seattle, 1981 Author: Freehand Drawing, 1965, Visual Awareness and Design, 1981, People, Paths and Purposes, 1997; patentee in field. Soc. Naval Architects and Marine Engrs. scholar, 1947; Rehmann scholar AIA, 1960; grantee NIMH, 1967, Nat. Endowment for Arts, 1969, Graham Found., 1995 Mem. Soc. Naval Archs. and Marine Engrs. (assoc.), Phi Beta Kappa, Sigma Xi

**THIELE, DWAIN LOUIS,** medical educator, department chairman; b. Kingsville, Tex., Dec. 22, 1952; s. Louis and Olivia Thiele; m. Elizabeth Crosser, Oct. 30, 1954; children: Alan, Kyle. BA, Rice U., 1974; MD, Baylor Coll. Medicine, 1977. Diplomate Am. Bd. Internal Medicine, 1980, in gastroenterology Am. Bd. Internal Medicine, 1983. Internship, residency Duke U. Med. Ctr., 1977—80; fellow gastroenterology, hepatologn U. Tex. Southwestern Med. Ctr., Dallas, 1980—83, from asst. prof. internal medicine to prof., 1983—95, prof. internal medicine, 1995—, chief hepatology, 1998—2005, interim chief digestive, liver diseases, 2002—05, vice chair internal medicine, 2005—. Mem.: Assn. Am. Physicians, Am. Soc. Clin. Investigation. Office: University of Texas Southwestern Med Ctr 5323 Harry Hines Blvd Dallas TX 75390 Office Phone: 214-648-4570. Office Fax: 214-648-5607. E-mail: dwain.thiele@utsouthwestern.edu.

**THIELE, GLORIA DAY,** librarian, small business owner; b. L.A., Sept. 4, 1931; d. Russell Day Plummer and Dorothy Ruby (Day) Plummer Thi; m. Donald Edward Cools, June 13, 1953 (div.); children: Michael, Ramona, Naomi, Lawrence, Nancy, Rebecca, Eugene, Maria, Charles. MusB, Mt. St. Mary's Coll., L.A., 1953. Libr. asst. Anaheim (Calif.) Pub. Libr., 1970-73, head Biblioteca de la Comunidad, 1973-74, children's libr. asst., 1974-76, childre's br. specialist, 1976-78, children's librr., 1978-81; head children's svcs. SantaM Maria (Calif.) Pub. Libr., 1981-85; cons. Organizationsl Ch.-Sch. Libr., L.A., 1980; owner, founder Discovery Garden, Grass Valley, Calif., 1989-93. Guest lectr. children's lit. Allan Hancock Coll., Santa Maria, 1981-85; cons. children's libr. programs, 1986—; profl. storyteller, 1989—. Contbr. poems to Amherst Soc.'s Am. Poetry Ann., 1988. Libr. liaison Casa Amistad Cmty. Svc. Group, Anaheim, 1973-74; mem. outreach com. Santiago Libr. System, Orange County, 1973-74, mem. children's svcs. com., 1971-81; mem. Cmty. Svcs. Coord. Coun., Santa Maria, 1982-85; chair children's svcs. com. Black Gold Libr. System, 1983-84; Allegro Alliance vol. for music in mountains, 1994-98; vol. Oasis Sr. Ctr., 1998-2002; mem. steering com. Cmty. Svcs. Dist. Status, Orcutt, 1999-2002; rep. 4th supervisorial dist. adv. com. Santa Barbara County Libr., 1999-2002. Mem. So. Calif. Coun. Lit. for Children and Young People, Kiwanis (sec., publicity chair, newsletter editor 1996-98, sec. Orcutt 1999-2000, Central Coast Winds & Waves, 2000—, bd. dirs. 2000-2001), Orcutt Friends of Libr. (v.p. 1999-2000, pres. 2000), P.E.O. Sisterhood (rec. sec. chpt. VZ 2002-03), Delta Epsilon Sigma. Republican. Roman Catholic.

**THIELE, HOWARD NELLIS, JR.,** lawyer; b. Dayton, Ohio, June 22, 1930; s. Howard Nellis and Irma Laura (Scheibe) T.; m. Alma Kuhn, Oct. 14, 1995; children: Leslie, Howard III, Craig. AB, Miami U., Oxford, Ohio, 1952; JD with distinction, U. Mich., 1955. Bar: Ohio 1955. Assoc., ptnr. Smith & Schnacke, LPA, Dayton, Ohio, 1957-89; ptnr. Thompson, Hine & Flory, Dayton, 1989-95; ret., 1995. Pres. Dayton Art Inst., 1981-85; bd. dirs. Dayton Area chpt. ARC, 1983—, 1st vice chmn., 1990-91, chmn., 1992-94. Capt. USAF, 1955-57. Mem.: Phi Beta Kappa, Order of the Coif. Republican. Lutheran.

**THIEM, JON EDGAR,** literature educator; b. Cin., Oct. 9, 1946; s. John Rudolph and Virginia Clare Thiem; m. Barbara von Haimberger, Apr. 15, 1973; children: Nathaniel Edgar, Benjamin Silvio. PhD, Ind. U., 1975; AB, Dickinson Coll., 1968. Peace corps lectr. U.S. Peace Corps, Ghana, 1968—70; asst. prof. U. Tex. at Dallas, Richardson, 1975—79; prof. Colo. State U., Fort Collins, 1979—. Rschr. local history, Ft. Collins, 1997—2005. Translator (poet): (scholarly edit. and trans.) Lorenzo de' Medici: Selected Poems and Prose (short listed Columbia Transl. Ctr. Transl. prize, 1991); poet (book of poems) Book of the Mermaid (with Ralph Slotten and Bettie Anne Doebler); Nine Waves (with Ralph Slotten and Bettie Anne Doebler); editor (co-editor with Patrick McKee): (anthology of short stories) Real Life: Ten Stories of Aging. Peace Corps fellow, Ind. U., 1971-72. Mem.: Sierra Club (assoc.). Achievements include research in anti-intellectualism and the epigone in literature, published in such journals as Journal of the History of Ideas, Comparative Literature, Sincronie, Translation and Literature, and Cadmos. Avocations: hiking, history, ice skating, bicycling, travel. Office: English 1773 Colo State U Fort Collins CO 80523

**THIEMANN, RONALD FRANK,** dean, religious studies educator; b. St. Louis, Oct. 4, 1946; s. Frank Joseph and Marie Magdalene (Graeser) T.; m. Beth Arlene Barkow, June 15, 1968; children: Sarah Elizabeth, Laura Kristen. BA magna cum laude, Concordia Sr. Coll., Fort Wayne, Ind., 1968; MDiv, Concordia Sem., St. Louis, 1972; MA, Yale U., 1973, MPhil, 1974, PhD, 1976; postgrad., Eberhard-Karls Universitat, Tubingen, W.Ger., 1974-75. Asst. prof. dept. religion Haverford Coll., Pa., 1976-82, assoc. prof. dept. religion Pa., 1982-85, prof. dept. religion Pa., 1985-86, acting provost Pa., 1985, acting pres. Pa., 1986; dean Div. Sch. Harvard U., Cambridge, Mass., 1986-98, John Lord O'Brian prof. divinity, 1986-98, prof. theology, religion & soc., 1998—, faculty fellow Harvard U., 1986—; vis. prof. history program Villanova U., 1981; vis. asst. prof. Luth. Theol. Sem., Phila., 1977; mem. Ctr. Theol. Inquiry, Princeton, N.J., 1982-83; mem. consultation on Christianity and Marxism, U.S.A. nat. coun. with Luth. World Fedn., 1979-83, mem. consultation on civil religion, 1983-86, mem. consultation on problem of common good, 1985-88; bd. dirs. Trinity Press Internat.; mem. exec. com. Assn. Theol. Schs., 1994-2000; faculty mem. Hanser Ctr. JFK Sch. Govt. Harvard U., 1998—. Author: Revelation and Theology, 1985, Constructing a Public Theology: The Church in a Pluralistic Culture, 1991, Religion in Public Life: A Dilemma for Democracy, 1995, Who Will Provide? The Changing Role of Religion in American Social Welfare, 2001; editor: The Legacy of H. Richard Niebuhr, 1991, Why Are We Here? Everyday Questions and the Christian Life, 1998, Where Shall My Wandering Soul Begin: The

Landscape of Evangelical Piety and Thought, 2000; mem. editl. bd.: Dialog, 1987—; contbr. numerous articles to profl. jours. Mem. bd. trustees Buckingham Browne & Nichols Schs., 1988-90; mem. task force on theol. education, Evang. Luth. Ch. in Am., 1989-91, task force on Luth.-Reformed Conversations, Evang. Luth. Ch. Am., 1988-92. Recipient Disting. Teaching award Lindback Found., 1982, Lilly Scholars award, 1988-99; Mellon Found. fellow, 1982-83; Deutscher Akademischer Austauschdienst fellow, 1974-75. Mem. Am. Acad. Religion. (chmn. narrative interpretation and theology group 1982-86), Soc. Christian Ethics, Am. Theol. Soc. Avocations: tennis, squash, piano. Home: 186 Shadyside Ave Concord MA 01742-2740 Office: Harvard Div Sch 45 Francis Ave Cambridge MA 02138-1911

**THIEMENS, MARK H.,** chemistry professor; b. St. Louis, Jan. 6, 1950; m. Nasrin Thiemens; 2 children. BS, U. Miami, 1972; MS, Old Dominion U., 1974; postgrad., Fla. Inst. Technology, 1974-75; PhD, Fla. State U., 1977. Grad. rsch. asst. dept. oceanography Old Dominion U., Norfolk, Va., 1972-74; grad. rsch. asst. dept. physics Fla. Inst. Technology, Melbourne, 1974-75; participant trace element aerosol rsch. program Fla. State U., Tallahassee, 1975-76; researcher dept. atmospheric chemistry Brookhaven Nat. Labs., Upton, N.Y., 1976-77; postdoctoral fellow Enrico Fermi Inst. U. Chgo., 1977-80; vis. prof. dept. chemistry U. Calif., San Diego, La Jolla, 1980-81, asst. prof. step II dept. chemistry, 1981-83, asst. prof. step IV dept. chemistry, 1983-85, assoc. prof. step I dept. chemistry, 1985-87, assoc. prof. dept. chemistry step II, 1987-88, assoc. prof. step II dept. chemistry, 1988-89, prof. step I dept. chemistry, 1989-91, prof. step II dept. chemistry, 1991-93, prof. step III dept. chemistry, 1993-95, prof. step VII dept. chemistry, 1996-2000, prof. step IX dept. chemistry, 2000—, chair dept. chemistry, 1996-99, dean divsn. phys. sci., 1999—. Dir. Cr. Environ Rsch. and Tng. U. Calif., San Diego, 1996—, mem. Ctr. Astrophysics and Space Sci., 1980—, Scripps Inst. Oceanography, 1996—; mem. workshop panel Origins of Solar Sys. NASA, 1989, mem. panel cosmochemistry divsn. group b isotope geochemistry, 1996—, cosmochemistry rev. panel Johnson Space Ctr., 1997; organizer, convenor 1997 Informal Symposium on Kinetic and Photochemical Processes in the Atmosphere, 1997. Contbr. numerous articles to profl. jours. Alexander von Humboldt fellow Inst. Phys. Chemistry U. Göttingen (Germany), 1990-91, 93; Camille and Henry Dreyfus tchg. scholar, 1984-89; recipient Ernest Orlando Lawrence Meml. award US Dept. of Energy, 1999, Disting. Scientist of Yr. award Am. Chem. Soc., 2002. Fellow Meteoritical Soc.; mem. Am. Acad. Arts Scis., NAS. Achievements include development of analytical capability to measure stable isotope variations at ultra-high precision in sulfur, oxygen, carbon and nitrogen to use in development of experimental programs in varying research fields including atmospheric chemistry, physical chemistry of gas phase photochemical eractions, electrical plasmas, early solar system history, and gas-solid conversion mechanisms; development of the ability to measure sulfur isotopic in meteoritic and lunr material to a precision greater than an order-of-magnitude over previous laboratory determination to determine the nature of pre-solar sulfur chemistry, cosmic-ray-spallation, and nucleosynthetic inputs; development of rocket borne atmospheric sampling and analysis. Office: U Calif Chem & Biochem Dept Urey Hall 9500 Gilman Dr La Jolla CA 92093-5004 E-mail: mthiemens@ucsd.edu.*

**THIENEMAN, MICHAEL D.,** manufacturing executive; b. Louisville; BA in Physics, Bellarmine Coll., 1970; MS, PhD in Physics, U. Ky., 1977; MBA, U. Evansville, 1981. Former project engr. Whirlpool Corp., former pres., CEO Inglis Ltd. subs., former pres. Whirlpool Compressor Ops. Riva di Chieri, Italy, former corp. v.p. global procurement ops., exec. v.p. N.Am. region, 1997—, chief tech. officer, 2000—. Chair fund devel. com. Harbor Habitat for Humanity; trustee Whirlpool Found., 1997—. Office: Whirlpool Corp 2000 N M-63 Benton Harbor MI 49022 Business E-Mail: michael_d_thieneman@whirlpool.com.

**THIEN-STASKO, VICKI LYNN,** civil engineer; b. Scott AFB, Ill., Apr. 22, 1953; d. Cordell Albert Knepper and Erna Rose (Studnicka) Knepper; m. Michael Lee Stasko, Nov. 19, 1988; stepchildren: Julie Stasko, Elliott Stasko; m. William Frederick Thien, Mar. 12, 1971 (div.); 1 child, Kyle Thien. Associates of Arch., Belleville Area Coll., 1982, Associates of Applied Sci., 1988; BSc cum laude, Greenville Coll., 1998. Civil engr. tech. St. Clair County Hwy. Dept., Belleville, Ill., 1982—; part-time real estate agent Better Homes & Gardens /Strano, Belleville, Ill., 1993—94. Census enumerator U.S. Dept. Commerce, Belleville, 2000—01; co-chmn. Operation Bag-It, Belleville, 1998—2002; owner, designer Bagapalooza Purse Co., 2004—. Exhibitions include Not a Creature was Stirring, 1996 (Best of Show, 1996), Nuts Anyone?, 1997 (Merchant's award, 1997), Frosty the Gingerbread Snowman, 1998 (Downtown Merchant's award, 1998), Crayola Factory, 2002 (first place profl. divsn.), 2003 (Best of Show, 2000). Precinct committeewoman Dem. Party, Belleville, 1978—91; sec. Belleville Dem. Orgn., Belleville, 1979—91; mayoral appointment/mem. Belleville Re-develop. Com., Belleville, 1982—84; member St. Clair County Hist. Soc., Belleville, 2000—02; ch. sch. bd. mem., tchr. Christ United Ch. of Christ, Belleville, 1987—91. Recipient Ill. Gov's Hometown award, State of Ill., 1999. Avocations: gardening, remodeling, travel. Office: St Clair County Hwy Dept 1415 N Belt W Belleville IL 62226

**THIER, SAMUEL OSIAH,** physician, educator; b. Bklyn., June 23, 1937; s. Sidney and May Henrietta Thier; m. Paula Dell Finkelstein, June 28, 1958; children: Audrey Lauren, Stephanie Ellen, Sara Leslie. Student, Cornell U., 1953—56; MD, SUNY, Syracuse, 1960, DSc (hon.), 1987, Tufts U., 1988, George Washington U., 1988, Mt. Sinai Sch. Med., 1989, Hahnemann U., 1989; DSc (hon.), U. Pa., 1994, Dartmouth Coll., 1996; LHD (hon.), Rush U., 1988, Va. Commonwealth U., 1992, Med. Coll. Pa., 1992; LHD (hon.), Brandeis U., 1994. Diplomate Am. Bd. Internal Medicine. Intern Mass. Gen. Hosp., Boston, 1960—61, asst. resident, 1961—62, sr. resident, 1964—65, clin. and research fellow, 1965, chief resident, 1966; clin. asso. Nat. Inst. Arthritis and Metabolic Diseases, 1962—64; from instr. to asst. prof. medicine Harvard U. Med. Sch., 1967—69; prof. medicine, health care policy Harvard Med. Sch., 1994—; asst. in medicine, chief renal unit Mass. Gen. Hosp., Boston, 1967—69; asso. prof., then prof. medicine U. Pa. Med. Sch., 1969—72, vice chmn. dept., 1971—74; assoc. dir. med. svcs. Hosp. U. Pa., 1969—71; David Paige Smith prof. medicine Yale U. Sch. Medicine, 1978—81, Sterling prof. medicine, 1981—85, chmn. dept., 1975—85; pres. Inst. Medicine NAS, Washington, 1985—91; pres., Univ. prof. Brandeis U., Waltham, Mass., 1991—94; pres. Mass. Gen. Hosp., Boston, 1994—97, Ptnrs. HealthCare Sys., Inc., Boston, 1994—96, 1997—2002, CEO, 1996—2002. Chief medicine Yale-New Haven Hosp., 1975—85, trustee, 1978—85; dir. chir. Conn. Hospice, Inc., 1976—82; dir. Am. Bd. Internal Medicine, 1977—85, exec. com., 1981—85, chmn., 1984—85. Mem. editl. bd.: New Eng. Jour. Medicine, 1978—81; contbr. articles to med. jours. Mem. adv. com. to the dir. NIH, 1980—85. With USPHS, 1962—64. Recipient Christian R. and Mary F. Lindback Found. Disting. Tchg. award, 1971. Mem.: ACP (bd. regents 1982—85), Interurban Clin. Club, Assn. Am. Physicians, Assn. Profs. Medicine, Internat. Soc. Nephrology, Am. Physiol. Soc., Am. Soc. Nephrology, Am. Fedn. Clin. Rsch. (pres. 1976—77), John Morgan Soc., Assn. Am. Med. Colls. (adminstrv. bd. coun. acad. socs.), Alpha Omega Alpha. Home: 99-20 Florence St # 8 Chestnut Hill MA 02467-1927

**THIES, RICHARD BRIAN,** lawyer; b. Chgo., Dec. 14, 1943; s. Fred W. and Loraine C. (Mannix) T.; m. Anita Marie Rees, Aug. 5, 1972; children: Emily Marie, Richard Clarke. BA, Miami U., 1966; JD, Loyola U., 1974. Bar: (Ill. 1974), (Ohio U.S. Tax Ct.). Assoc. Wilson & McIlvaine, Chgo., 1974-78; assoc.-ptnr. Isham, Lincoln & Beale, Chgo., 1978-88; ptnr. Wildman, Harrold, Allen & Dixon, Chgo., 1988—2005, mem. exec. com., 1999—2005; pvt. ptnr. Bd. govs. Chgo. Heart Assn., 1980-87, exec. com., 1982-87; bd. dirs. Juvenile Protective Assn., Chgo., 1984—; v.p. Samaritan Counseling Ctr., Evanston, 1989-94, pres., 1994. Mem. ABA, Chgo. Bar Assn., Chgo. Estate Planning Coun. Avocations: photography, music. Home: 305 Driftwood Ln Wilmette IL 60091-3441 Office: Ste 3800 200 S Wacker Dr Chicago IL 60606 Office Phone: 312-650-8620.

**THIESSEN, DELBERT DUANE,** psychologist; b. Julesberg, Colo., Aug. 13, 1932; s. David and Eva Peters (Wetherby) T.; children: Trevor, Theron, Kendell Courtney. BA in Psychology with distinction, San Jose State Coll., Calif., 1958; PhD, U. Calif., Berkeley, 1963. Extension instr. U. Calif., La Jolla, fall 1964; asst. sect. med. psychology, divsn. psychiatry and neurology Scripps Clinic and Research Found., La Jolla, 1962-65; faculty U. Tex., Austin, 1965-2000, prof. psychology, 1971-2000, prof. emeritus Austin, 2000—. Rsch. cons. NIMH. Author: Gene Organization and Behavior, 1972, The Evolution and Biochemistry of Aggression, 1976, Bitter-Sweet Destiny: The Stormy Evolution of Human Behavior, 1996, Universal Desires and Fears: The Deep History of Sociobiology, 1997, Survival of the Fittest: The Darwinian Diet and Exercise Program, 1998, Night of the Dagger: A Historical Voodoo Novel, 2005; contbr. articles and chpts. to books. With AUS, 1952-54, Korea. Fellow USPHS, 1960-61; recipient Career Devel. award NIMH, 1967-72, grantee, 1967-78; grantee Russel Sage Found., NSF, U. Tex. Rsch. Inst. Fellow AAAS, APA; mem. Alumni Assn. Roscoe B. Jackson Meml. Lab., Am. Genetic Assn., Psychonomic Soc., Animal Behavior Soc., Southwestern Psychol. Assn., Behavior Genetics Assn., Sigma Xi, Phi Kappa Phi, Psi Chi. Business E-mail: wolf@delthiessen.com.

**THIGPEN, ALTON HILL,** transportation executive; b. Kinston, N.C., Feb. 3, 1927; s. Kirby Alton and Alice (Hill) T.; m. Rebecca Ann Braswell, May 16, 1953; children: David Alton, Jennifer Ann, Steven Roy. BS in Indsl. Engring., N.C. State U., 1950. With Assoc. Transport, Inc., Burlington, NC, 1950-71, engr., 1950-57, asst. terminal mgr. Phila., 1957-58, terminal mgr. Knoxville, Tenn., 1959, regional mgr. Valley region, 1960-62, South region, 1962-68, v.p.,dir. So. divsns., 1968-71; v.p. R.S. Braswell Co. Inc., Kannapolis, NC, 1971-80, pres., 1980—, Hartford Motor Inn Inc., North Myrtle Beach, SC, 1982—, A.T. Developers, Inc., North Myrtle Beach, 1982—. Pres. Cherokee 2 Inc., Shelby, N.C., 1986-95, bd. dirs.; bd. dirs. Wachovia Bank, Earl Ownsby Studios Inc., Shelby. Bd. regents Berkshire Christian Coll., Lenox, Mass., 1975—; mem. adv. bd. Salvation Army, chmn. adv. bd., 1997-99. Served with USNR, 1945-46. Mem. Motor Carriers Va. (pres. 1967-68), N.C. Motor Carriers Assn. (dir. 1968-), Masons (32d degree), Lions, Sigma Chi, Tau Beta Pi. Mem. Advent Christian Ch. Home: 5395 Mooresville Rd Kannapolis NC 28081-8726 Office: PO Box 1197 Kannapolis NC 28082-1197 Office Phone: 704-933-2269.

**THIGPEN, JAMES TATE,** oncologist, educator; b. Columbia, Miss., June 6, 1944; m. Louisa Berdie Kessler, June 14, 1969; children: Monroe Tate, James Howard, Samuel Calvin, Richard Allen, David Albert. BS U. Miss., 1964, MD, 1969. Intern Strong Meml. Hosp., U. Rochester, N.Y., 1969-70; resident U. Miss. Sch. Medicine, 1970-71, prof., dir. divsn. med. oncology dept. internal medicine, 1973—; also prof. ob-gyn. Nat. med. del. from Miss. Am. Cancer Soc., 1983-85, nat. pub. issues com., 1983-85; cancer clin. investigations rev. com. Nat. Cancer Inst., 1990-95, chmn., 1993-95. Nat. bd. govs. ARC, 1981-87. Fellow divsn. hematology/oncology dept. medicine, 1971-73. Fellow ACP; mem. AMA, Miss. Med. Assn., Ctrl. Med. Soc., Jackson Acad. Medicine, Miss. Acad. Scis., SW Oncology Group, Gynecologic Oncology Group (group vice chmn. sci. 1988—), Am. Fedn. Clin. Rsch., Am. Assn. Cancer Edn., Am. Soc. Clin. Oncology, Am. Assn. cancer Rsch., Am. Soc. Hematology, Soc. Gynecologic Oncologists, Soc. Assn. Oncology (pres. 1988-90), Am. Radium Soc., Optimists (internat. v.p. 1983-84, internat. pres. 1990-91). Baptist. (deacon 1978—, Sunday sch. tchr. 1979-85). Home: 3601 Kings Hwy Jackson MS 39216-3322 Office: Miss Oncology Assocs 2500 N State St Jackson MS 39216-4500 Office Phone: 601-984-5590. Personal E-mail: jtthigpen@att.net.

**THIGPEN, RICHARD ELTON, JR.,** retired lawyer; b. Washington, Dec. 29, 1930; s. Richard Elton and Dorathy (Dotger) Thigpen; m. Nancy H. Shand, Dec. 15, 1951; children: Susan B., Richard M. AB, Duke U., 1951; LLB, U. N.C., 1956. Bar: NC 1956, U.S. Ct. Appeals (4th cir.) 1960, U.S. Ct. Appeals (5th cir.) 1960, U.S. Ct. Appeals (10th cir.) 1974, U.S. Tax Ct. 1958, U.S. Ct. Claims 1978, U.S. Supreme Ct. 2003. Lawyer FTC, Washington, 1956-58, Thigpen & Hines, Charlotte, NC, 1958-84, Moore & Van Allen, Charlotte, 1984-88, Poyner & Spruill, Charlotte, 1988-93; gen. counsel Richardson Sports, 1994-98; ret. Bd. dirs. O.L. Miller Rsch. Inst., 2001—, Charlotte-Mecklenburg YMCA, 1964—88, Heineman Med. Rsch. Ctr., Charlotte, 1970—, Charlotte C. of C., 1982—85. Lt. USNR, 1951—53. Fellow: Am. Coll. Tax Counsel (regent 1989—95, vice chmn. 1992, chmn. 1993—94); mem.: ABA, Sports Lawyers Assn. (bd. dirs. 1995—, pres. 2003—05), N.C. Bar Assn. (chmn. tax sect. 1976—80, pres. 1988—89), N.C. State Bar. Avocations: golf, travel. Office: 1100 Kenilworth Ave Ste 200 Charlotte NC 28204-2943 Office Phone: 704-332-8000.

**THIGPEN, STEPHEN P.,** horticulture products company executive; b. 1956; BS in Plant and Soil summa cum laude, U. Mass.; PhD in Plant Physiology, U. Calif., Davis. Joined Weyerhauser Co., 1981, gen. mgr. Vacaville nursery, 1985; pres., CEO Hines Horticulture, Inc., Irvine, Calif., 1995—, chmn. bd., 2000—. Bd. dirs. Coun. for a Green Environment. Office: Hines Horticulture Inc 12621 Jeffrey Rd Irvine CA 92620 Office Fax: 949-786-0968.

**THILMANY, DAWN DENISE,** economist, educator; b. Cedar Rapids, Iowa, Aug. 3, 1968; d. Lumir Emil and Sara Mae Dostal; m. David Scott Thilmany, Dec. 29, 1990; 1 child, Elizabeth. PhD, U. Calif., Davis, 1994; BS in Pub. Svc. and Adminstrn. in Agr. and Internat. Agr., Iowa State U., 0100. Asst prof. Utah State U., Logan, 1994—97; assoc. prof. Colo. State U., Fort Collins, 1997—. Nat. program leader USDA-Coop. State Rsch. Extension and Edn. Svc., Washington, 2006—. Sec.-treas. Western Agrl. Econs. Assn., Fort Collins, Colo., 2001—04. Recipient Faculty award of Merit, Gamma Sigma Delta, 2004. Mem.: Agr. Appl. Econs. Assn. (found. bd. 2005—06). Home: 1070 Rosemary Ct Fort Collins CO 80524 Office: Colorado State University B325 Clark Fort Collins CO 80523-1172 Office Phone: 970-491-7220. Personal E-mail: thilmany@lamar.colostate.edu.

**THIM, FRANK,** physicist, astronomer; b. Immenhausen, Germany, Aug. 5, 1963; s. Josef and Franziska Thim; life ptnr. Christa Heckelmann; 1 child, Wega Heckelmann. MSc in Physics, U. Freiburg, Germany, 1994; Dr., U. Basel, Switzerland, 2001. Customer engr. Applied Materials, Munich, 1995; rsch. assoc. U. Basel, 1995—2001, Nat. Optical Astronomy Obs., Tucson, 2001—04; physicist Software Co., Paderborn, Germany, 2004—. Played in concerts, various cities including Berlin, Munich, Heidelberg, Kassel, Germany; played with bands Paranoid, Paran, others. Grantee, European So. Obs., 2001—02. Achievements include research in distances to spiral galaxies; magnetic structure of solar pores; discovery of new variable stars. Avocations: music, sports, science, reading, travel. Home: Querweg 65 Paderborn 33098 Germany Office: Brandenburg GmbH Technologiepark 19 Paderborn 33100 Germany Office Phone: 0049-5251-681644. Personal E-mail: fthim@web.de. E-mail: thim@brandenburg-gmbh.de.

**THIMMIG, DIANA M.,** lawyer; b. Germany, May 5, 1959; BA cum laude, John Carroll U., 1980; JD, Cleve. State U., 1982. Bar: Ohio 1983, U.S. Dist. Ct. (no. dist.) Ohio 1983, U.S. Ct. Appeals (6th cir.) 1983, U.S. Supreme Ct. 1983, U.S. Ct. Appeals (3d cir. 1996); cert. Am. Bankruptcy Bd. for Consumer and Bus. Bankruptcy. Ptnr. Roetzel & Andress, Cleve. Contbr. articles to profl. jours. Hon. counsul of Germany, 1988—; trustee Geauga United Way Svcs. Coun., 1992-96, Altenheim, 1992-97, Internat. Svcs. Ctr., 1998-04; trustee Cuyahoga County Bar Assn., 1995-05, pres., 2003-05; trustee Legal Aid Soc., 1998—, pres., 2003-05. Mem. Women's City Club Cleve. (pres. 1997-99). Office: Roetzel & Andress 1375 East Ninth St One Cleveland Ctr Ninth Floor Cleveland OH 44114 Office Phone: 216-696-7078. Business E-Mail: dthimmig@ralaw.com.

**THIMOTHEOSE, KADAKAMPALLIL GEORGE,** psychologist; b. Karipuza, India, Feb. 11, 1938; came to the U.S., 1976; s. K.G. and Mariamma Varghese; m. Mariamma Thimotheose, May 20, 1968; children: Geebee, Sonia T. Andrews. MA in Psychology, ME.D 1st class & rank, Kerala U., India, 1967, B in Edn., 1960, MA in Sociology, 1969, MA

in History, 1975, PhD in Psychology, 1975; D Therapeutic Philosophy (hon.), World U., 1989. Lic. psychologist, marriage and family therapist, Mich.; diplomate Am. Bd. Med. Psychotherapists, Am. Bd. Psychotherapy, Am. Bd. Sexology, Am. Bd. Forensic Examiners, Am. Bd. Forensic Medicine, Am. Bd. Psychol. Specialities. Lectr., head dept. ednl. psychology S.N. Tchrs. Coll., Trivandrum, India; clin./adminstrv. dir. Alexandrine House, Inc., Detroit, 1976-81; chief exec. officer Cen. Therapeutic Svcs., Inc., Southfield, Mich., 1981—. Adv. bd. Trivandrum Med. Coll. Hosps., 1969-75; edn. faculty mem. U. Calicut, Kerala, India, 1969-75; v.p. forum ednl. rsch. and studies Kerala U., 1969-73. Author: Educational Psychology for B.Ed. Students, 1970; editor: Kerala University Journal of Education, 1969-73. Fellow Am. Bd. Med. Psychotherapists, Am. Acad. Clin. Sexologists. Am. Coll. Forensic Examiners, Am. Coll. Advanced Practice Psychologists; mem. APA, Am. Coll. Sexologists (sexologist), Am. Bd. Sexology (clin. supr.), World U. Round Table (hon. cultural doctorate in therapeutic philosophy); diplomate Am. Bd. Psychological Specialities. Republican. Avocations: photography, travel, reading, sightseeing. Home: 3048 Brewster West Bloomfield MI 48322-2471 Office: Cen Therapeutic Svcs Inc 17600 W 8 Mile Rd Ste 7 Southfield MI 48075-4316 Office Phone: 248-559-4340.

**THIRLBY, RICHARD COLLER,** surgeon; b. Traverse City, Mich., Aug. 30, 1952; s. Richard Leeson Thirlby; m. Patricia Rosso, July 17, 1976; children: Marjorie Rose, David Ryan. BA, Dartmouth U., Hanover, NH, 1974; MD, U. Mich., Ann Arbor, 1978. Contbr. articles to profl. jours. Mem.: ACS (pres. Wash. State chpt. 2003—04), Am. Bd. Surgery (bd. dirs. 2006—), Western Surg. Assn. (pres. 2005—06). Office: Virginia Mason Med Ctr 1100 9th Ave Mailstop C6-GSUR Seattle WA 98111 Office Phone: 206-223-6636.

**THIRSK, ROBERT BRENT,** astronaut; b. New Westminister, Brit. Columbia, Canada, Aug. 17, 1953; m. Brenda Biasutti; 3 children. BSc in Mech. Engring., U. Calgary, 1976; MSc in Mech. Engring., MIT, 1978; MD, McGill U., 1982; MBA, MIT, 1998. Resident Queen Elizabeth Hosp., Montreal, Canada, 1982—83; astronaut Can. Astronaut Program, 1984—; sabbatical yr. Victoria, B.C., Canada, 1994—95; chief astronaut Can. Space Agy., 1996—98; astronaut NASA, Houston, 1998—. Dir. Can. Found. Internat. Space U., 1992—; crew comdr. CAPSULS mission, 1994; astronaut Space Shuttle mission STS-78, 1996; crew comdr. NEEMO 7 undersea mission, 2004; backup astronaut STS-41G space shuttle mission, 1984, Soyuz 10 S taxi mission, 2005. Recipient Disting. Alumni award, U. Calgary, 1985. Mem.: Coll. Physicians and Surgeons B.C., Coll. Physicians & Surgeons Ontario, Aerospace Med. Assn., Can. Aeronautics & Space Inst., Can. Coll. Family Physicians, Assn. Profl. Engrs. Ontario (Gold Medal award 1997). Avocations: hockey, squash, playing the piano. Office: Astronaut Office CB NASA Johnson Space Center Houston TX 77058

**THIRY, KENT J.,** health products executive; BA in Polit. Sci., Stanford U., 1978; MBA with honors, Harvard U., 1983. Sr. cons. Andersen Consulting, 1978-81; ptnr., v.p. Bain & Co., 1983—91; pres., COO Vivra, Inc., San Francisco, 1991-92, pres., CEO, 1992-97; chmn., CEO Vivra Holdings Inc., 1997—99, Da Vita Inc., El Segundo, Calif., 1999—. Dir. Oxford Health Plans, 1998—2004, chmn., 2002—04. Bd. dirs. Vol. Ctr. San Mateo County. Mem. Phi Beta Kappa. Office: 601 Hawaii St El Segundo CA 90245-4814*

**THISTED, RONALD AARON,** statistician, educator, consultant; b. L.A., Mar. 2, 1951; s. Dale Owen and Barbara Jean (Walker) T.; m. Linda Jeane Soder, Dec. 30, 1972; 1 child, Walker. BA, Pomona Coll., 1972; PhD, Stanford U., 1977. Asst. prof. statistics U. Chgo., 1976-82, assoc. prof. statistics, 1982-92, assoc. prof. anesthesia and critical care, 1989-92, prof. stats. and anesthesia and critical care, 1992—, prof. health studies, 1996—, chmn. health studies, 1999—. Co-dir. Clin. Rsch. Training Program, 1999—. Author: Elements of Statistical Computing, 1988; contbr. more than 90 articles to profl. jours. Fellow AAAS, Am. Statis. Assn.; mem. Assn. for Computing Machinery, Inst. for Math. Stats. Office: U Chgo MC 2007 5841 S Maryland Ave Chicago IL 60637-1463 Office Phone: 773-834-1242.

**THISTLETHWAITE, DAVID RICHARD,** architect; b. Burlington, Iowa, Aug. 24, 1947; s. Robert and Nona (Binder) T.; m. Carol Anne Armstrong, Aug. 22, 1970. BArch, Iowa State U., 1971. Registered arch., Calif., 1979, Minn., 1975; registered nat. Coun. Archtl. Registration Bds., 1978; cert. Health Care arch., Am. Coll. Healthcare Archs., 2000. Designer Morrison Architects, St. Paul, 1971-73, Times Architects, Mpls., 1973-74; project architect Bentz/Thompson Assocs., Mpls., 1974-77; project mgr. Setter Leach Lindstrom, Mpls., 1977-78; project architect Wurster Bernardi Emmons, San Francisco, 1978-79, Strotz & Assocs., Tiburon, Calif., 1979-81, Hood Miller Assoc., San Francisco, 1981-84; prin., ptnr. R S T Architects, San Francisco, 1984-88; prin. Thistlethwaite Archtl. Group, San Francisco, 1988—. Contbr. articles to profl. jours. Mem. AIA (nat. profl. devel. com. 1983-86, treas. San Francisco chpt. 1985-86, chmn. Calif. coun. health facilities com. 1994-96, chmn. design com. Acad. Architecture for Health, 1994-96, Calif. coun. ins. bd. trustees 1988-2002, Calif. coun. legis. com. 1996-98) Am. Coll. Healthcare Archs. (mem. pub. rels. com. 2004-05), Am. Soc. Healthcare Engring., Design Profls. Safety Assn. (bd. dirs.). Office: 355 Bryant St Ste 210 San Francisco CA 94107

**THISTLETHWAITE, SUSAN BROOKS,** religious organization administrator; BA, Smith Coll.; MDiv summa cum laude, Duke Div. Sch.; PhD, Duke Univ. Ordained minister United Ch. Christ, 1974—; former prof. theol. Chgo. Theol. Sem., former dir., PhD ctr., pres., 1999—. Translator two translations of Bible; leadership adv. com. Assn. of Theol. Schools, 2000—; adv. com. Lilly Endowment, 2000—; bd. dir. Medill Ctr. for Religion and the News Media, Northwestern Univ., 2001—. Author: Metaphors for the Contemporary Church, 1983, Sex, Race and God: Christian Feminism in Black and White, 1989; co-author (with Rita Nakashima Brock): Casting Stones: Prostitution and Liberation in Asia and the US, 1996; co-author: (with Mary Potter Engel) Lift Every Voice: Constructing Christian Theologies from the Underside, 1998; contbg. editor: Adam, Eve and the Genome: The Human Genome Project and Theology, 2003; editorial bd.: Theology Today, 1993—. Named one of Chicago's Most Influential Women, Crain's Chicago Business mag., 2004. Office: Office of President Chgo Theol Seminary 5757 S Univ Ave Chicago IL 60637

**THOEN, DORIS RAE,** retired small business owner; b. Corvallis, Oreg., Feb. 1, 1925; d. Birt F. and Alice M. (Maxfield) Read; m. Monte Len Thoen, Oct. 22, 1950; children: David Allen, Rick Lee. BA, Oreg. State U., 1947. Sec. State of Oreg., Salem, Oreg., 1947—48; home loan closer Porland Fed. Bk., Portland, Oreg., 1949—50; head of personnel dept. Bur. of Reclamation, Klamath Falls, Oreg., 1950—52; ptnr. Thoen Truck Rentals, Portland, Oreg., 1954—94; ret., 1994. Regional v.p. Oreg. Parent Tchrs. Assn., Portland, Oreg., 1960—75. State pres. Oreg. Federation of Rep. Women, Portland, Oreg., 1973—75; nat. awards chmn. Nat. Federation of Rep. Women, Wash. DC, 1976—80; state treas. Oreg. Rep. Party, Salem, Oreg., 1975—78; vol. Portland Art Mus, 1995—, Pacific Northwest Truck Mus., 1992—, Am. Cancer Soc., 1959—2005. Recipient Nat. Vol. award, Am. Cancer Soc., 1987, Life Membership award, Oreg. Partn Tchrs. Assn., 1960. Mem.: AAUW, DAR, Wash. County Hist. Soc., Benton County Hist. Soc., Am. Truck Hist. Soc., Sunset Valley Family and Cmty. Edn. (treas. 1959—), Beaverton West Slope Rep. Women (treas. 1998—), Daughters of the Colony, Delta Zeta. Republican. Avocations: travel, volunteering. Home: 13124 NW Sue St Portland OR 97229

**THOM, RICHARD DAVID,** retired electronics executive; b. St. Louis, Oct. 4, 1944; s. Reginald James and Vlasta (Koukl) T.; m. Linda Marie Hunt, Sept. 9, 1967; children: Elizabeth Marie, Robert James. BS in Physics, U. Mo., Rolla, 1967. MSEE, UCLA, 1971. Co-op engr. McDonnell Aircraft Corp., St. Louis, 1962-67; head advanced tech. group IR systems dept., aerospace group Hughes Aircraft Co., Culver City, Calif., 1967-72; mem. tech. staff Santa Barbara Rsch. Ctr., Hughes Aircraft Co., Goleta, Calif., 1972-76, assoc. mgr. R&D Lab., 1976-80, mgr. advanced applications, 1980-83, chief engr., 1984-86, chief scientist 1986-90, dir. tech., 1990-95; tech. program exec.

Hughes Aircraft Co., Goleta, Calif., 1995-98; asst. mgr. Raytheon Santa Barbara Rsch. Ctr., Goleta, Calif., 1998-99; ret. Contbr. articles to profl. jours.; patentee in field. Recipient Hughes Group Patent award for pioneering contbns. in infrared detector tech., 1990. Mem. IEEE, Tau Beta Pi, Sigma Pi Sigma, Delta Sigma Phi. Republican. Avocations: freelance travel writing and photography, specializing in railway travel around the world. Home: 38 Fawn Run Pl PO Box 326 Coupeville WA 98239-0326 Personal E-mail: richthommail@aol.com.

**THOMA, RICHARD WILLIAM,** chemical safety and waste management consultant; b. Milw., Dec. 7, 1921; s. Joseph Donath and Margaret Mary (Murphy) T.; m. Ida Mary Scharfschwerdt, Mar. 15, 1952; children: Adele, Richard W., Joseph O., John C. AA, U. Chgo., 1941; BS, U. Wis., Madison, 1947, MS in Biochemistry, 1949, PhD, 1951. R&D fermentation E.R. Squibb & Sons, Inc., New Brunswick, NJ, 1951-82; dir. process devel. New Brunswick Sci. Co., Inc., Edison, 1982-84, cons., 1984—. Safety officer Harbor br. Oceanographic Inst. St. Lucie County, Fla., 1988—96. Contbr. articles to profl. jours.; patentee microbiol. transformation of steroids. Commr. Somerset County Bd. Elections, 1981-84; mem. Bridgewater Town Coun., 1975-81, Environ. Commn., 1974-75, Sewerage Authority, 1975-76, Police Commn., 1977-81; chmn. Birdgewater Dem. Mcpl. Com., 1980-87; alderman St. Lucie Village, 1996-98. With AUS, 1942-46. Mem. VFW, Am. Chem. Soc., Am. Soc. Microbiology, Am. Acad. Microbiology, Phi Beta Kappa, Sigma Xi, Phi Lambda Upsilon. Home and Office: 3772 Outrigger Ct Fort Pierce FL 34946-1911 E-mail: rthoma3772@aol.com.

**THOMAJAN, ROBERT,** lawyer, management consultant; b. N.Y.C., May 4, 1941; s. Leon and Fay T. BS, NYU, 1962; JD, St. John's U., 1965. Bar: N.Y. 1965, Tex. 1987, U.S. Ct. Internat. Trade 1975, U.S. Supreme Ct. 1975, U.S. Ct. Appeals (9th cir.) 1976, U.S. Dist. Ct. (we. dist.) Tex. 1979. Atty. Nixon, Mudge, Rose, Guthrie, Alexander & Mitchell, N.Y.C., 1965—68; ptnr. Milgrim, Thomajan & Lee, N.Y.C., 1968-90; exec. dir. Richco, Inc., 1990—93; pres. Eterna Investments, Austin, Tex., 1995—. Arbitrator Civil Ct., N.Y., 1981-86; mem. adv. bd. Ronald McDonald House, 1988-90; bd. dirs. Big Bros./Big Sisters, 1988-90; mem. World Econ. Forum, 1990-93. Mem. Am. Soc. Internat. Law, Internat. Law Assn.

**THOMAN, G. RICHARD,** corporate financial executive; b. Tuscaloosa, Ala., June 25, 1944; s. Richard S. and Evelyn (Zumwalt) Thoman; m. Wenke Helina Brier, Aug. 25, 1966 (div. Dec. 1987); children: Camille, Alexis; m. Lynn Susan Bendheim, Sept. 16, 1989; children: Kylie, Max, Amy, Eric. BA with honors, McGill U., 1966; MA, Grad. Inst. Internat. Studies, Geneva, 1968; MA in Internat. Econs., Tufts U., 1967, MA in Law and Diplomacy, 1969, PhD in Internat. Econs., 1971. Exec. trainee Citicorp, NYC, 1968-69; sr. fin. analyst Exxon Corp., NYC, 1970-72; sr. assoc. McKinsey and Co., NYC and Paris, 1972-79; exec. v.p., CFO Am. Express Travel Related Svcs., NYC, 1979-85, pres., Travel Related Svcs. Internat., 1985-89, chmn., CEO, 1989-92; pres., CEO Nabisco Internat. RJR Nabisco, Inc., NYC, 1992-94; sr. v.p., group exec. IBM Corp., Somers, NY, 1994-95, sr. v.p., CFO Armonk, NY, 1995-97; pres., COO Xerox Corp., 1997-99, pres., CEO, 1999-2000, also bd. dirs.; pvt. investor; sr. advisor Evercore Ptnrs., NYC, 2001—02; mng. ptnr. Corporate Perspectives, NYC, 2002—; adj. prof. Columbia U., 2003—; vis. prof. Fletcher Sch., 2005—. Bd. dirs. Union Bancaire Privee, Geneva; mem. US adv. bd. INSEAD; mem. adv. bd. Mid Oceanic Capital Ptnrs. Bd. dirs. Americas Soc., NYC, 1990—, French-Am. Found.; bd. advisors Fletcher Sch. Law and Diplomacy, Tufts U., Medford, Mass., 1990—; mem. adv. bd. Sch. Mgmt. McGill U., Montreal, Bus. Coun.; US chair TransAtlantic Bus. Dialogue. Recipient Legion of Honors, Govt. of France, 1992. Mem.: Trilateral Commn., Coun. on Fgn. Rels., River Club, Links Club. Avocations: tennis, reading, jogging, travel. Office: Corp Perspectives 126 E 56th St Fl 9 New York NY 10022 Office Phone: 212-813-0323.

**THOMAN, HENRY NIXON,** lawyer; b. Cin., May 5, 1957; s. Richard B. and Barbara (Lutz) Thoman; m. Anne Davies, May 25, 2002; children: Victoria E., Nicholas B. BA, Duke U., 1979; JD, U. Chgo., 1982. Bar: Ohio 1982, U.S. Dist. Ct. (so. dist.) Ohio, 1982. With Taft, Stettinius & Hollister, Cin., 1982-88; sr. atty. John Morrell & Co., Cin., 1988-90; sr. counsel Chiquita Brands Internat. Inc., Cin., 1990-91, corp. planner, 1991-92; sr. dir. CTP ops. Chiquita Brands, Inc., Cin., 1993-94, chief adminstrv. officer Armuelles divsn., 1994-95; corp. counsel The Loewen Group, Covington, Ky., 1995-97; assist. chief counsel, asst. v.p. The Midland Co., Amelia, Ohio, 1997-99; v.p. orgnl. devel. Kendle Internat. Inc., 1999-2000, v.p. complementary ops., 2000—02; pvt. atty., 2002—; exec. dir. Madisonville Edn. and Assistance Ctr., 2004—; dir. acquisitions Unifund CCR Ptnrs., 2004—. Mem. counselors com. U.S. Swimming, Colo., 1983-89; bd. dirs. Friends of Cin. Parks, 1990-93, 96-98, Starshine Children's Hospice, 1996-99, Cinci. Aquatic Club, 1997-2002, Kids Helping Kids, 2000-2001, Mariemont Aquatic Club, v.p., 1992-93; pres. Club Atletico Y Socialde Chiriqui, 1994-95. Mem. ABA, Ohio State Bar, Cin. Bar Assn. E-mail: thoman.henry@fuse.net.

**THOMAN, MARK EDWARD,** pediatrician; b. Chgo., Feb. 15, 1936; s. John Charles and Tasula Mark (Petrakis) T.; m. Theresa Thompson, 1984; children: Marlisa Rae, Susan Kay, Edward Kim, Nancy Lynn, Janet Lea, David Mark. AA, Graceland Coll., 1956; BA, U. Mo., 1958, MD, 1962. Diplomate Am. Bd. Pediat., Am. Coll. Toxicology (examiner), 1975-90. Intern U. Mo. at Columbia, 1962—63; resident in pediat. Blank Meml. Children's Hosp., Des Moines, 1963—65; cons. in toxicology USPHS, Washington, 1965—66; chief dept. pediat. Shiprock (N.Mex.) Navajo Indian Hosp., 1966—67; dir. N.D. Poison Info. Ctr.; also practice medicine specializing in pediat. Quain & Ramstad Clinic, Bismarck, ND, 1967—69; dir. Iowa Poison Info. Ctr., Des Moines, 1969—99; mem. pediat. exec. com. Broadlawns Med. Ctr., Des Moines, 1969—2000, pres. med. staff, 2000—01. Accident investigator FAA, 1976—2005, sr. aviation examiner, 1977—2000; sr. cons. in field; lectr. aviation seminars, 1977—; mem. faculty Des Moines U., 1969—2005, dir. cystic fibrosis clin., 1973—82; dir. Mid-Iowa Drug Abuse Program, 1972—76; mem. med. adv. bd. La Leche League Internat., 1965—; chief med. officer Broadlawns Med. Ctr., Des Moines, 2000—02; sci. rev. panel Nat. Libr. Medicine, 2003—; med. cons., expert witness Office Hearings and Appeals Social Security Adminstrn., 2003—. Editor-in-chief AACTION, 1975-90; monthly columnist Aviation Medicine Twin and Turbine Mag., 2005-06. Bd. dirs. Polk County Pub. Health Nurses Assn., 1969-77, Des Moines Speech and Hearing Ctr., 1974-79, Ecumenical Coun. Iowa, 1990-99; bd. govs. Mo. U. Sch. Medicine Alumni, 1988—. With USMCR, 1954-59; lt. comdr. USPHS, 1965-67; capt. USNR, 1988-96, ret. 1996; dir. Dept. Health Svcs. USNR. Recipient N.D. Gov.'s award of merit, 1969, Cystic Fibrosis Rsch. Found. award, 1975, Am. Psychiat. Assn. Thesis award, 1962. Fellow Am. Coll. Med. Toxicology (diplomate 1996), Acad. Clin. Toxicology; mem. AMA (del. 1970-88), APHA, NRA (life), Assn. Am. Physicians & Surgeons (chief of staff, pres. Broadlawns Polk County Med. Ctr. 2000-02), Polk County Med. Soc., Iowa State Med. Assn., Aerospace Med. Assn., Res. Officers Assn., Civil Aviation Med. Assn., Soc. Adolescent Medicine, Inst. Clin. Toxicology, Internat. Soc. Pediat., Am. Acad. Pediat. (chmn. accident prevention com. Iowa chpt. 1975-2000), Cystic Fibrosis Club, Am. Acad. Clin. Toxicology (trustee 1969-90, pres. 1982-84), Am. Assn. Poison Control Ctrs., Am. Coll. Physician Execs., U.S. Naval Inst., Flying Physicians Club, Aircraft Owners and Pilots Assn, Nat. Pilots Assn. (Safe Pilot award). Republican. Greek Orthodox. Home: 5355 Crane Ave E Port Orchard WA 98366 Office Phone: 360-871-2219. Office Fax: 360-871-4436. Personal E-mail: paro1795@aol.com.

**THOMAN, ROY EDWARD,** political scientist, educator; b. Evansville, Ind., Mar. 11, 1938; s. Joseph Henry and Nell Yates Thoman; m. Judith Ann Schiff, May 20, 1967 (div. Apr. 18, 1985); 1 child, Mark; m. Jan Brister, May 21, 2005. BA magna cum laude, U. Evansville, 1960; MA, Ind. U., 1964; PhD, U. Ky., 1967. Asst. prof. West Tex. A&M U., Canyon, 1969—70, assoc. prof., 1970—76, prof., 1976—. Contbr. articles to profl. jours.; consulting editor World Affairs, 1979—82. Recipient scholarship medal, Pi Gamma Mu, 2000, endowed scholarship in his name, Phi Eta Sigma, 2000; grantee, Tex. Ednl. Assn., 1972—75. Mem.: KC, Am. Polit. Sci. Assn. Republican. Roman

Catholic. Office: West Tex A&M U WT Box 725 Canyon TX 79016 Home: 3816 Doris Dr Amarillo TX 79109-5505 Office Phone: 806-352-6140. Business E-mail: rthoman@mail.wtamu.edu.

**THOMAS, ABLE MABLE,** communications executive, state legislator, councilwoman; b. Atlanta, Nov. 8, 1957; d. Bernard and Madie Thomas. BS in Pub. Adminstrn., Ga. State U., 1982, postgrad., 1983—. With acctg. dept. Trust Co. Bank, Atlanta, 1977; recreation supr. Sutton Cmty. Sch., Atlanta, 1977-78; data transcriber Ga. Dept. Natural Resources, Atlanta, 1978-79; clk. U.S. Census Bur., Atlanta, 1980; laborer City of Atlanta Parks and Recreation, 1980-81; student assn. Ga. State U., Atlanta, 1981-82; pres. Master Comms. Inc., Atlanta, 1992—; city councilwoman, chair com. on council Dist 1 CityWide, Atlanta, 1998—2001; mem. city coun., citywide rep. City of Atlanta; mem., Dist. 55 Ga. Ho. Reps., Atlanta, 2003—. Mem. exec. com. Ga. Legis. Black Caucus, Atlanta, 1985—. Mem. adv. youth coun. Salvation Army Bellwood Club, 1975; founder, pres. Greater Vine City Opportunities Program Inc., 1990; founder Vine City Cmty. improvement Assn., Atlanta, 1985; mem. neighborhood planning unit adv. bd. of comprehensive youth svcs. Ga. State U., 1988—; mem. Nat. Black Woman's Health Project, Ga. Housing Coalition; bd. dirs. Ga. Coalition Black Women, 1996, Am. Cancer Soc., 1988—. Recipient Bronze Jubilee award City of Atlanta Cultural Affairs, 1984, Disting Svc. award Grady Hosp., 1985, Human Svc. award for cmty. and polit. leadership for disadvantaged, 1986, Exceptional Svc. award Young Cmty. Leaders, 1986, Citizenship award Salvation Army Club, Leadership and Achievement award Ga. Breast Cancer Prevention Coalition, 1994, Adopt a Sch. Appreciation award Atlanta Pub. Schs., 1996; named Outstanding Freshman Legislator, 1986, one of Outstanding Young People of Atlanta, 1987. Mem. Nat. Polit. Congress Black Women (bd. dirs., Fannie Lou Hamer award Phila. chpt. 1995, 2005), Conf. Minority Pub. Adminstrn. (Outstanding Svc. award), Ga. Assn. Black Elected Ofcls. (mem. housing and econ. devel. com.). Democrat. Methodist. Office: 765 Jones Ave NW Atlanta GA 30314 also: State Capitol Rm 611 Legislative Office Bldg Atlanta GA 30334 Office Phone: 404-656-0314. Office Fax: 404-588-9159. E-mail: mthomas949@aol.com.

**THOMAS, ADRIAN WESLEY,** research scientist, director, retired science educator; b. Edgefield, S.C., June 23, 1939; s. Hasting Adrian and Nancy Azalena (Bridges) T.; m. Martha Elizabeth McAllister, July 12, 1964; children: Wesley Adrian, Andrea Elizabeth. BS in Agrl. Engring., Clemson U., 1962, MS in Agrl. Engring., 1965; PhD, Colo. State U., 1972. Rsch. scientist USDA-Agrl. Rsch. Svc., Tifton, Ga., 1965-69, Fort Collins, Colo., 1969-72, rsch. leader Walkinsville, Ga., 1972-89, lab. dir. Tifton, 1989-98, retired, 1998. Mem. acad. faculty Colo. State U., Ft. Collins, 1969—72; acad. faculty U. Ga., Athens, 1973—, grad. faculty, 1988—2002, adj. prof., 2004—. Contbr. agrl. rsch. articles to profl. jours. With U.S. Army, 1962-63. Mem. Am. Soc. Agrl. Engrs., Am. Soc. Agronomy, Soil and Water Conservation Soc. Am., Soil Sci. Soc. Am., Sigma Xi, Alpha Epsilon, Gamma Sigma Delta, Phi Kappa Phi. Lutheran. Avocations: reading, gardening, yard care, remodeling home, sports. Personal E-mail: awthomas39@hotmail.com.

**THOMAS, ALLEN LLOYD,** lawyer, private investor; b. Orange, NJ, Sept. 15, 1939; s. Richard Lloyd and Dorothy (Carr) Thomas; m. Virginia Dehnert, June 24, 1961 (div. 1974); children: Sarah Ann, Anne Marjorie; m. Barbara Singer, Mar. 12, 1978 (div. 2001); 1 child, Allen Lloyd. BA, Wesleyan U., 1961; LLB, Yale U., 1964. Bar: N.Y. 1965, U.S. Ct. Appeals (D.C. cir.) 1981; solicitor, Eng. and Wales, 1996. Ptnr. Paul Weiss Rifkind Wharton & Garrison, N.Y.C., 1973—92; resident ptnr. Hong Kong, 1983-87; dir. gen. counsel Gerard Atkins & Co. Ltd., 1992-94; gen. counsel Gen. Atlantic Group Ltd., 1992-94; chmn. Highway Insurance Holdings, PLC, 1996—2002, Forney, Inc., 2005—. Gov. English Nat. Ballet Sch.; chmn. The Cathy Marston Project. Chmn. Urban Bus. Assis. Corp., N.Y.C., 1971-82; chmn. Hong Kong Ballet, 1985-87; co-chmn. Internat. Com., N.Y.C. Ballet, 1986-91; pres. Internat. Salzburg Assn. Am., 1987-92; dir., mem. exec. com., gen. counsel Child Care Action Campaign, 1990-92. Mem. River Club (NY), Boodle's, Met. Club of Washington, Hong Kong Club, Hong Kong Jockey Club, Lenox Club, Buck's Club. Home: 3 Chester St London SW1X 7BB England E-mail: allenlloydthomas@hotmail.com.

**THOMAS, ANDREA B.,** food products executive; Bachelor's degree, U. Utah; MBA, Brigham Young U., Provo, Utah. Dir., new product mktg. Pizza Hut, Inc.; v.p., retail mktg. and promotions, Fritos and Tostitos brands Frito-Lay, Inc., v.p., innovation; v.p. global chocolate Hershey Co., 2006—. Named one of 25 Masters of Innovation, BusinessWeek. Office: Hershey Co 100 Crystal A Dr Hershey PA 17033-0810*

**THOMAS, ANDREW S.W.,** astronaut; b. Adelaide, South Australia, Dec. 18, 1951; s. Adrian C. and Mary E. Thomas. B with hon. in Mech. Engring. (with First Class Honors), U. Adelaide, South Australia, 1973; PhD in Mech. Engring., U. Adelaide, 1978. Rsch. scientist Lockheed Aero. Sys. Co., Marietta, Ga., 1977—80, principal aerodynamic scientist, 1980—83, head, advanced flight sciences dept., 1983—87, mgr. flight sci. divsn., 1987—89; with Jet Propulsion Lab., Pasadena, Calif., 1989—92, NASA, Houston, 1992—93, astronaut, mission specialist, 1993—. Payload comdr. Endeavour Space Shuttle STS-77, 1996; bd. engr. 2, STS-89, returned with crew of STS-91 Space Shuttle Endeavor, Russian Space Sta. Mir, 1998; with space flight STS-102, 2001; dep. chief astronaut office NASA, 2001—03; mission specialist 3 (MS-3) STS-114 (Discovery) Return to Flight mission during which the crew will test & evaluate new procedures for flight safety & shuttle inspection & repair techniques, 2005. Fellow: Institution of Engrs. Australia (hon.). Achievements include first Australian citizen in space. Avocations: horseback riding, mountain biking, running, wind surfing, playing classical guitar. Office: Astronaut Office CB NASA Johnson Space Ctr Houston TX 77058

**THOMAS, ANN VAN WYNEN,** retired law educator; b. The Netherlands, May 27, 1919; arrived in U.S., 1921, naturalized, 1926; d. Cornelius and Cora Jacoba (Daansen) Van Wynen; m. A. J. Thomas, Jr., Sept. 10, 1948. AB with distinction, U. Rochester, 1940; JD, U. Tex., 1943; degree, So. Meth. U., 1952. U.S. fgn. svc. officer, Johannesburg, London, The Hague, The Netherlands, 1943-47; rsch. atty. Southwestern Legal Found. So. Meth. U. Sch. Law, Dallas, 1952-67, asst. prof. polit. sci., 1968-73, assoc. prof., 1973-76, prof., 1976-85, prof. emeritus, 1985—. Author: Communism versus International Law, 1953, Non-Intervention - The Law and Its Import in the Americas, 1956, OAS: The Organization of American States, 1962, International Legal Aspects of Civil War in Spain, 1936-1939, 1967, Legal Limitations on Chemical and Biological Weapons, 1970, The Concept of Aggression, 1972, An International Rule of Law - Problems and Prospects, 1974, Presidential War Making Power: Constitutional and International Law Aspects, 1981; author: (with A. J. Thomas, Jr.) International Treaties, 1950. Chmn. time capsule com. Grayson County Commn. Tex. Sesquicentennial, 1986—88; co-chmn. Grayson County Commn. Bicentennial U.S. Constn., 1988—93, Grayson County Commn. Millenium, 1997—; co-chmn. com. Grayson County Sesquicentennial, 1994—97. Recipient Am. medal, Nat. DAR, 1992. Mem.: Grayson County Bar Assn., Am. Bar Assn., Tex. Law, Tex. Bar Assn. Home: Spaniel Hall 374 Coffee Cir Pottsboro TX 75076-3164

**THOMAS, ANNE MOREAU,** former newspaper owner; b. Trenton, N.J., May 23, 1930; d. Daniel Howard and Lillis Dale (Simmonds) Moreau; m. Henry Seely Thomas, Jr., June 14, 1952 (dec. Aug. 1994); children: Catherine, John Martin II, Howard Moreau. BA, Middlebury Coll., 1951; DHL, Rutgers U., 1999; AA (hon.), Raritan Valley C.C. Tchr. North Hunterdon H.S., Annandale, N.J., 1951-52, Hunterdon Adult Sch., Flemington, N.J., 1953-70; home and food editor Hunterdon County Democrat, Flemington, 1954-99, owner, bd. sec., 1985-94, owner, chmn. bd., 1994—2001. Trustee Rutgers U., New Brunswick, N.J., 1985-2005, bd. govs., 1991-2005, chmn. bd. govs., 1995-98, trustee emerita, 2005—; trustee Bloomfield Coll., 2005—, Hunterdon Healthcare Sys.; mem. N.J. Commn. Higher Edn., Trenton, 1995-98. Recipient N.J. Food Communicator of Yr. award N.J. Dept. Agr., 1981, Golden award for cmty. svc. Hunterdon County C. of C., 1990, Eagle Leadership award Ctr./Urban cmty. Leadership, 1996, Hunterdon Disting

Citizen award Ctrl. N.J. Coun. Boy Scouts Am., 1999-2000; named Woman of Yr., Hunterdon County YMCA, 1997. Mem. N.J. Press Assn. (bd. dirs. 1977-85, pres. 1984, chmn. 1985), DAR, Copper Hill Country Club, N.J. Mus. Agr. (trustee). Republican. Presbyn. Avocations: restoration of circa 1750 Cape Cod family homestead, gardening, cooking. Home: 38 Pennsylvania Ave Flemington NJ 08822-1222

**THOMAS, ARCHIBALD JOHNS, III,** lawyer; b. Jacksonville, Fla., Apr. 27, 1952; s. Archibald Johns and Jean (Snodgrass) T.; m. Martha Ann Marconi, Sept. 1, 1973. BA, U. So. Fla., 1973; JD, Stetson U., 1977. Bar: Fla. 1977, U.S. Dist. Ct. (mid. dist.) Fla. 1977, U.S. Ct. Appeals (11th cir.) 1981, U.S. Supreme Ct. 1981, U.S. Claims Ct. 1990; cert. labor and employment law, Fla. Law clk. to U.S. magistrate U.S. Dist. Ct., Tampa, Fla., 1977-78; 1st asst. fed. pub. defender U.S. dist. Ct., Jacksonville, 1978-84; sr. ptnr. Thomas & Skinner, P.A., Jacksonville, 1984-89; pvt. practice Jacksonville, 1990—. Faculty mem. Stetson U. Coll. Law, 1999—; mem. labor and employment law cert. com. Fla. Bar, 2002—. Mem.: ATLA (employment rights sect.), Jacksonville Bar Assn., Fla. Nat. Employment Lawyers Assn. (pres. 2002), Nat. Employment Lawyers Assn. (co-chmn. Fla. chpt. 1992), Fed. Bar Assn., Fla. Bar Assn. (co-chmn. individual rights com. 2001, exec. coun. labor and employment law sect. 2006—, chmn. current legal events com. 2006—). Democrat. Avocation: sailing. Home: 708 Mccollum Cir Neptune Beach FL 32266-3789 Office: Riverplace Tower 1301 Riverplace Blvd Ste 1640 Jacksonville FL 32207 Office Phone: 904-396-2322. E-mail: archibald@job-rights.com.

**THOMAS, BARBARA L.,** not-for-profit executive; 2 children. With CBS. Named one of Most Influential Black Americans, Ebony mag., 2006. Mem.: Nat. Black MBA Assn. (life; pres. Boston Chpt., v.p. fin. and administrn., CFO, interim pres., CEO 2003—04, pres., CEO 2004—). Office: NBMBAA Ste 1400 180 N Michigan Ave Chicago IL 60601 Office Phone: 312-236-2622. Office Fax: 312-236-0990.*

**THOMAS, BETTY,** director, actress; b. St. Louis, July 24, 1948; BFA, Ohio U., 1969. Former sch. tchr.; co-star Hill St. Blues, from 1981. Joined Second City Workshop, Chgo.; appeared on Second City TV, 1984; appeared in after sch. spl. The Gift of Love, 1985, Prison of Children, 1986. Appeared in The Fun Factory game show, 1976; (TV films) Outside Chance, 1978, Nashville Grab, 1981, When Your Lover Leaves, 1983, The Late Shift, 1996 (Dirs. Guild Am. dramatic spl. award 1996); star TV series Hill Street Blues, 1981-87 (Emmy nominations 1981, 82, 83), (Emmy award, 1985); dir.: (TV) Hooperman, 1987, Doogie Howser, M.D., 1989, Mancuso, FBI, 1989, Shannon's Deal, 1990, Dream On: "For Peter's Sake" (Emmy award, Outstanding Individual Achievement in Directing in a Comedy Series, 1993), 1993, Parenthood, 1990, Sons and Daughters, 1991, On the Air, 1992, My Breast, 1994, Couples, 1994, The Late Shift, 1996, The Loop, 2006-; (films) Troop Beverly Hills, 1989, The Brady Bunch Movie, 1995, Private Parts, 1997, Doctor Dolittle, 1998, 28 Days, 2000, I Spy, 2002, R3, 2003, John Tucker Must Die, 2006; prodr.: Can't Hardly Wait, 1998, Surviving Christmas, 2004; exec. prodr. (films) Charlie's Angels, 2000, Guess Who, 2005, (TV films) Silicon Follies, 2001. Recipient Women in Film Crystal award, 2001.*

**THOMAS, BROOKS,** publishing executive, director; b. Phila., Nov. 28, 1931; s. Walter Horstman and Ruth Sterling (Boomer) Thomas; m. Galen Pinckard Clark, Apr. 25, 1969 (div. 1973); m. Kiono Tucciarone, Oct. 7, 2004. BA, Yale U., 1953, LLB, 1956; grad. Advanced Mgmt. Program, Harvard U. 1973. Bar: Pa. 1957, N.Y. 1960. With law firm Winthrop, Stimson, Putnam & Roberts, N.Y.C., 1960—68; sec., gen. counsel Harper & Row, Pubs., Inc., N.Y.C., 1968—69, v.p., gen. counsel, 1969—73, exec. v.p., 1973—79, CEO 1977—81, pres., 1979—87, CEO, 1981—87, chmn. bd., 1986—87. Chmn. bd. dirs. Harper & Row, Ltd., London, 1973—87; bd. dirs. Harper & Row, Pty. Ltd., Australia, Harla S.A. de C.V., Mexico, Harper & Row Pubs. Asia, Pty. Ltd., Singapore. Trustee Outward Bound USA, 1980—, vice chmn., 1983—84, chmn., 1984—87, Nat. Book Awards, 1984—85, bd. dirs., 1985—87, Outward Bound Internat., 1997—2003, Outward Bound Expenditionary Learning, 2000—; pres., bd. dirs. Butterfield House, 1968—72; trustee, bd. dirs. RADG, Inc., 1987—89; bd. dirs. Thomason Island Outward Bound Edn. Ctr., 1987—96, Colo. Outward Bound Sch., 1990—96, bd. govs., 1996—; bd. dirs. Young Audiences, Inc., 1977—, chmn., 1985—, Vail Valley Inst., 1989—; trustee Episcopal Acad., 2000—, sec., 2002—; mem. devel. bd. Yale U., 1985—89, adv. bd. Sch. Orgn. and Mgmt., 1987—96. Lt. (j.g.) USNR, 1956—59. Mem.: ABA, Assn. Am. Pubs. (bd. dirs. 1980—85, chmn. 1983—85), Assn. Bar City of N.Y., Yale U. Alumni Assn. (law sch. rep. 1980—83), Coun. Fgn. Rels., Essex Yacht Club (Conn.), N.Y. Yacht Club (N.Y.C.), Univ. Club (N.Y.C.), Yale Club (N.Y.C.), Century Club (N.Y.C.), Merion Cricket Club (Phila.). Home: 5 Tudor City Pl New York NY 10017-6853 also: 141 Saybrook Rd Essex CT 06426-1412

**THOMAS, CAL,** syndicated columnist; m. Ray Thomas; 4 children. B., Am. Univ. Formerly with NBC, CNBC, PBS; now polit. commentator Fox News. Syndicated columnist, host (TV show) After Hours with Cal Thomas, Fox News; author: A Freedom Dream, 1977, Public Persons and Private Lives, 1979, Book Burning, 1983, Liberals for Lunch, 1985, The Death of Ethics in America, 1988, Occupied Territory, 1989, Things That Matter Most, 1994, Blinded by Might: Can the Religious Right Save America?, 1999, The Wit & Wisdom of Cal Thomas, 2001. Office: Fox News Network LLC 1211 Ave Of The Americas New York NY 10036 Address: Tribune Media Svcs Ste 1500 435 N Michigan Ave Chicago IL 60611 Business E-mail: Afterhours@foxnews.com.

**THOMAS, CHARLES ALLEN, JR.,** molecular biologist, educator; b. Dayton, Ohio, July 7, 1927; s. Charles Allen and Margaret Stoddard (Talbott) T.; m. Margaret M. Gay, July 7, 1951; children: Linda Carrick, Stephen Gay. AB, Princeton (N.J.) U., 1950; PhD, Harvard U., 1954. Rsch. scientist Eli Lilly Co., Indpls., 1954-55; NCR fellow U. Mich., Ann Arbor, 1955-57; prof. biophysics Johns Hopkins U., Balt., 1957-67; prof. biol. chemistry Med. Sch. Harvard U., Boston, 1967-78; chmn. dept. cellular biology Scripps Clinic & Rsch. Found., La Jolla, Calif., 1978-81; pres., dir. Helicon Found., San Diego, 1981—; founder, CEO The Syntro Corp., San Diego, 1981-82; founder, CEO, now dir. of R & D Pantox Corp., San Diego, 1989—. Mem. genetics study sect. NIH, 1968-72; mem. rsch. grants com. Am. Cancer Soc., 1972-76, 79-85. Mem. editl. bd. Virology, 1967-73, Jour. Molecular Biology, 1968-72, BioPhysics Jour., 1965-68, Chromosoma, 1969-79, Analytic Biochemistry, 1970-79, Biochim Biophys. ACTA, 1973-79, Plasmid, 1977—. With USNR, 1945-46. NRC fellow, 1965-66. Mem. AAAS, Am. Acad. Arts and Scis., Am. Fedn. Biol. Chemists, Genetics Soc. Am., Am. Chem. Soc. Achievements include research in genetic and structural organization of chromosomes and development of a practical assessment of the antioxidant defense system by analytical biochemistry. Home: 1640 El Paso Real La Jolla CA 92037-6304 E-mail: cathomas@pantox.com.

**THOMAS, CHERRYL T.,** former federal agency administrator; b. Oct. 31, 1946; BS Biology & Chem., Marquette U.; MS Physiology, U. Illinois, Chicago. Dir., mgmt. services Dept. Aviation, 1989; dir., personnel policy & utilization Dept. Water, 1989—92; deputy chief of staff Mayor Richard M. Daley City of Chgo., 1992—94, commr. Dept. Bldgs., 1994-98, chmn. U.S. Railroad Retirement Bd., 1998—2003. Mem., bd. trustees U. Chgo., 2000—. Home: 5020 S Lake Shore Dr Apt 2716N Chicago IL 60615-3220

**THOMAS, CHERYL SHANKS,** public health service officer; d. Charles Ray and Martha Jorene Davis; m. Darrell Jackson Thomas, Jan. 1, 2000; children: Albert Agustus Shanks, Chandan Aubah Shanks. AS in Nursing, Troy State U., 1978; BS in Edn., Valdosta State U., 1998; MS in Mgmt., Troy State U., 2002. RN Ala.; cert. tchr. Ala, Ga. Health occupations instr. Autauga County Area Vocat. Ctr., Prattville, Ala., 1983—89, Robert E. Lee H.S., Montgomery, Ala., 1991—93, Westover H.S., Dougherty County Bd. of Edn., Albany, Ga., 1989—91; dir. Alzheimer's program Atria Halcyon Assisted

Living Facility, Montgomery, 1998—99; asst. don Prattville Bapt. Nursing Ctr., Prattville, Ala., 2000—03; case mgr. Gentiva Home Health Svcs., Montgomery, 1999—2000; asst. dir. nursing Beverly Healthcare, Tyson Manor, Montgomery, 2003; dir. nursing Sunbridge at Merry Wood, Elmore, Ala., 2003; collaborative practices insp. Ala. Bd. of Med. Examiners, Montgomery, 2003—. Author: (poetry) Wishing Wells, 1992 (Nat. Poet Laureate award, 1991). Cub scout pack leader Boy Scouts Am., Millbrook, Ala., 1988—96, mem. com., 1996—2000; mem. choir First United Meth. Ch., Millbrook, 1990—. Recipient Nat. Poet Laureate, Iliad Poetry, 1991, 2003.

**THOMAS, CHRISTOPHER YANCEY, III,** surgeon, educator; b. Kansas City, Mo., Oct. 27, 1923; s. Christopher Yancey and Dorothea Louise (Engel) T.; m. Barbara Ann Barcroft, June 27, 1946; children: Christopher, Gregg, Jeffrey, Anne Student, U. Colo., 1942-44; MD, U. Kans., 1948. Diplomate Am. Bd. Surgery. Intern U. Utah Hosp., Salt Lake City, 1948-49; resident in surgery Cleve. Clinic Found., 1949-52; pvt. practice specializing in surgery Kansas City, Mo., 1954-89. Mem. staff St. Luke's Hosp., chief surgery, 1969-70; mem. staff Children's Mercy Hosp.; clin. prof. surgery U. Mo., Kansas City Med. Sch.; pres. St. Luke's Hosp. Edn. Found., 1977-83, Med. Plaza Corp., 1977-79; pres. Midwest Organ Bank, 1977-82. Editor IMTRAC investment adv. letter, 1978-2000. Served to capt. M.C., U.S. Army, 1952-54 Fellow ACS; mem. AMA, Southwestern Surg. Congress, Central Surg. Assn., Mo. State Med. Soc., Kansas City Surg. Soc. (pres. 1968), Jackson County Med. Soc. (pres. 1971) Clubs: Kansas City Country. Republican. Methodist. Home: 50 Coventry Ct Shawnee Mission KS 66208-5225 Personal E-mail: christhomas5452@sbcglobal.net.

**THOMAS, CLARA MCCANDLESS,** retired literature educator; b. Strathroy, Ont., Can., May 22, 1919; d. Basil and Mabel (Sullivan) McCandless; m. Morley Keith Thomas, May 23, 1942; children: Stephen, John. BA, U. Western Ont., London, 1941, MA, 1944; PhD, U. Toronto, 1962; DLitt (hon.), York U., 1986, Trent U., 1991; LLD (hon.), Brock U., 1992. Instr. English U. Western Ont., London, 1947-61, U. Toronto, 1958-61; asst. prof. English York U., Toronto, 1961-68, prof., 1969-84, prof. emeritus, 1984—. Librs. Can. Studies Rsch. fellow, 1984—; acad. adv. panel Social Scis. and Humanities Research Council, 1981-84; mem. Killam Awards Selection Bd., 1978-81; rsch. fellow York U. Librs. Can. Studies, 1984—. Author biography of Anna Jameson, 1967, of Egerton Ryerson, 1969, of Margaret Laurence, 1969, 75, (with John Lennox) of William Arthur Deacon, 1982; Literary criticism (Can.), 1946, 72, 94, Memoir, 1999; mem. editl. bd. Literary History of Can., 1980—, Collected Works of Northrop Frye, 1995—. Recipient Internat. Coun. of Can. Studies prize No. Telecom., 1989; grantee Can. Coun., 1967, 73, Social Sci. and Humanities Rsch. Coun. Can., 1978-80, Clara Thomas Archives and Spl. Collections, York U., 2005. Fellow Royal Soc. Can.; mem. Assn. Can. Univs., Tchrs. English (pres. 1971-72), Assn. Can. and Que. Lit., Bus. and Profl. Women's Club, Assn. for Can. Studies. New Democratic. Office: York U 305 Scott Libr 4700 Keele St North York ON Canada M3J 1P3 Office Phone: 416-736-2100 22374.

**THOMAS, CLARENCE,** United States Supreme Court Justice; b. Pin Point, Ga., June 23, 1948; s. M.C. Thomas and Leola Anderson (Williams); m. Kathy Grace Ambush, 1971 (div. 1984); 1 child, Jamal Adeen; m. Virginia Lamp, May 30, 1987. Student, Immaculate Conception Sem., 1967—68; BA, Holy Cross Coll., 1971; JD, Yale U., 1974. Bar: Mo. Asst. atty. gen. State of Mo., Jefferson City, 1974—77; legal counsel Monsanto Co., St. Louis, 1977—79; legis. asst. to Sen. John C. Danforth US Senate, Washington, 1979—81; asst. sec. for civil rights U.S. Dept. Edn., Washington, 1981—82; chmn. EEOC, Washington, 1982—90; judge U.S. Ct. Appeals (DC cir.), Washington, 1990—91; assoc. justice U.S. Supreme Ct., Washington, 1991—. Mem. bd trustees Holy Cross Coll.; bd. advisors DC Cases. Mem.: Internat. Churchill Soc. Office: US Supreme Court One First St NE Washington DC 20543-0001*

**THOMAS, CLAUDEWELL SIDNEY,** psychiatrist, educator; b. NYC, Oct. 5, 1932; s. Humphrey Sidney and Frances Elizabeth (Collins) T.; m. Carolyn Pauline Rozansky, Sept. 6, 1958; children: Jeffrey Evan, Julie-Anne Elizabeth, Jessica Edith. BA, Columbia U., 1952; MD, SUNY, Downstate Med. Ctr., 1956; MPH, Yale U., 1964. Diplomate Nat. Bd. Med. Examiners, Am. Bd. Psychiatry, Am. Bd. Forensic Medicine, Am. Bd. Psychol. Specialties. From instr. to assoc. prof. Yale U., New Haven, 1963-68, dir. Yale tng. program in social community psychiatry, 1967-70; dir. div. mental health service programs NIMH, Washington, 1970-73; chmn. dept. psychiatry U.M.D.N.J., Newark, 1973-83; prof. dept. psychiatry Drew Med. Sch., 1983—, chmn. dept. psychiatry, 1983-93; prof. dept. psychiatry UCLA, 1983-94, vice chmn. dept. psychiatry, 1983-93, prof. emeritus dept. psychiatry, 1994—; med. dir. Tokanui Hosp., TeAwamutu, N.Z., 1996. Cons. A.K. Rice Inst., Washington, 1978—80, SAMSA/PHS Cons., 1991—99, L.A. County Homeless Outreach Program, 2001—04; mem. LA County Superior Ct. Psychol. Panel, 1991—97; cons. psychiatrist L.A. County AB2034 Homeless Outreach Program (Skid Row Dual Diagnoses), 2001—04. Author: (with B. Bergen) Issues and Problems in Social Psychiatry, 1966; editor (with R. Bryce LaPorte) Alienation in Contemporary Society, 1976, (with J. Lindenthal) Psychiatry and Mental Health Science Handbook; mem. editl. bd. Internat. Jour. Mental Health, Adminstrn. In Mental Health. Bd. dirs. Bay Area Found., 1987—. Served to capt. USAF. 1959-61. Fellow APHA, Am. Psychoanalytic Assn. (hon.), Am. Psychiat. Assn. (disting. life), NY Acad. Sci., NY Acad. Medicine; mem. Am. Sociol. Assn., Am. Coll. Mental Health Adminstrs., Am. Coll. Psychiatrists (emeritus), Sigma Xi. Avocations: tennis, racquetball, violin, piano. Office: 30676 Palos Verdes Dr E Palos Verdes Peninsula CA 90275-6354 Business E-mail: cysid32@ucla.edu. E-mail: Thomas@sigmaxi.org. *Personal philosophy: Integrity sooner or later calls upon courage. If courage is not home integrity goes away.*

**THOMAS, CLAUDIA LYNN,** orthopedic surgeon; b. N.Y.C., Feb. 28, 1950; d. Charles Mitchell and Daisy Mae T; m. Maxwell Delaine Carty, Aug. 24, 1985. BA, Vassar Coll., 1971; MD, Johns Hopkins U., 1975. Diplomate Am. Bd. Orthopedic Surgery. Intern Yale-New Haven Hosp., 1975-76, resident in surgery, 1976-77, resident in orthopaedic surgery, 1977-80; orthopaedic trauma fellow Md. Inst. Emergency Med. Services Systems, Balt., 1980; asst. prof. orthopaedic surgery Johns Hopkins Hosp., 1981-85, Balt. City Hosp., 1981-85; mem. staff Children's Hosp., Provident Hosp. (both Balt.). Mem. AMA, Eastern Orthopaedic Assn., Yale Orthopaedic Assn., Newington Alumni Assn., Nat. Med. Assn., Monumental Med. Assn. (v.p. 1983-85), Johns Hopkins Minority Faculty Assn. (pres. 1983-85). Author: (with A.A. White, M.M. Panjabi) Clinical Biomechanics of the Spine, 1978; (with P. Leppert, E. Siff, C. Thomas) Being a Woman: Your Body and Birth Control, 1979. First black female orthopedic surgeon; contbr. articles to profl. jours. Democrat.

**THOMAS, CRAIG,** senator; m. Susan Roberts; children: Peter, Paul, Patrick, Alexis. BS, U. Wyo., 1955; LLB, La Salle U., 1963. V.p. Wyo. Farm Bur., Laramie, 1959-66; with Am. Farm Bur., 1966-75; gen. mgr. Wyo. Rural Elec. Assn., 1975-89; mem. Wyo. Ho. of Reps., 1985—88, US Congress, Washington, 1989—95; US Senator from Wyo. Washington, 1995—. Mem. energy and natural resources com., environment and pub. works com., fin. com., Indian affairs com. Former chmn. Natrona County (Wyo.) Rep. Com.; state rep. Natrona County Dist.; del. Rep. Nat. Conv., 1980. Capt. USMC. Mem. Am. Soc. Trade Execs., Masons. Republican. Methodist. Office: US Senate 307 Dirksen Senate Office Bldg Washington DC 20510-0001 Office Phone: 202-224-6441.

**THOMAS, DANIEL FOLEY,** retired diversified financial services company executive; b. Washington, Aug. 24, 1950; s. Richard Kenneth and Margaret (Foley) T.; m. Barbara Jane Clark, June 30, 1973; 1 child, Alison Clark. BS in Acctg., Mt. St. Mary's Coll., 1972. CPA, Va. Auditor Deloitte & Touche, Washington, 1972-74; various fin. positions Comsat: Satellite Corp., Washington, 1974-78, asst. treas., 1984-85, treas., 1986-87, contlr., 1987-89, Comsat Telesystems, Washington, 1978-79; mgr. acctg. and taxes Satellite Bus. Systems, McLean, Va., 1979-81, treas., 1981-84; v.p. fin. Comsat Tech. Products, Inc., Washington, 1985-86, Comsat Video Enterprises, Inc., Washington, 1989-90; exec. v.p. Leasetec Corp., Boulder, Colo., 1990—2002; ret., 2002. Instr. acctg. Colo. State U., 2003—05, U. Colo., 2003—. Active cmty. svc. activities. Mem. AICPA, Va. Jaycees (life), Great Falls Jaycees (pres. 1978). Roman Catholic. Avocations: running, golf. Home: 36495 Peak to Peak Hwy Nederland CO 80466 Office Phone: 303-808-1181. E-mail: dfthomas@aol.com.

**THOMAS, DAVID ALBERT,** law educator, director; b. LA, Feb. 4, 1944; s. Albert Rees and Betty Lou (Adams) T.; m. Paula Rasmussen, Aug. 7, 1967; children: Rebecca, David R., John H., Matthew A., Susannah, Amanda, Christina, Erin. BA, Brigham Young U., 1967; JD, Duke U., 1972; MLS, Brigham Young U., 1977. Jud. clk. U.S. Dist. Ct. Utah, Salt Lake City, 1972-73; pvt. practice, 1973-74; asst. prof. Law Sch. Brigham Young U., Provo, 1974-76, dir. law libr. Law Sch., 1974-80, assoc. prof. Law Sch., 1976-79, prof. Law Sch., 1979—, Rex E. Lee endowed chair, prof. law, 2005—. Accreditation site insp. ABA, Chgo., 1978—. Author: Utah Civil Procedure, 1980, (with others) A Practical Guide to Disputes Between Adjoining Landowners, 1989, Utah Civil Practice, 1992, 4th edit., 2005, (with others) Thomas and Backman on Utah Real Property Law, 1999, 2d edit., 2005; prin. author, editor-in-chief: Thompson on Real Property, Thomas Edition, 1995, 1994; contbr. articles to profl. jours. With U.S. Army, 1969-71, Vietnam. Mem. ABA (mem. sect. coun., chmn. real property probate and trust sect.) Office: Brigham Young U Law Sch Provo UT 84602 Business E-Mail: david_thomas@byu.edu.

**THOMAS, DAVID CLIFTON,** music educator; s. Donald and Glenon Thomas; m. Kathie Weeks Thomas. AAS, Onondaga C.C., 1981; B of Music, Syracuse U., 1983; MusM, Ithaca Coll., 1989. Tchr. music Onteora Jr./Sr. High Sch., Boiceville, NY, 1984—. Sgt. USAF, 1969—99. Home: 31 Church St Great Barrington MA 01230 Office: Onteora Jr/Sr High Sch Rte 28 Boiceville NY 12412 Office Phone: 845-657-2373. Business E-Mail: dkthomas31@verizon.net.

**THOMAS, DAVID LINDSEY,** lawyer, state senator; b. Washington, D.C., Jan. 14, 1962; s. Lindsey Kay and Nancy ruth Thomas; m. Lynn Stosich Thomas, Apr. 21, 1987; children: Tyler, Tristan, Richard, Gwendolyn. BS in Fin., Brigham Young U., Salt Lake City, 1986; JD, Coll. William and Mary, Williamsburg, Va., 1990. Vice chmn. Utah Comm. Agy.Network, West Valley City, Utah, 1999—; chief civil dep. Summit County Atty., Utah; state sen., 2003—. Mem. Utah Tech. Commn., 2003—; chmn. Standing Commn. Edn. Utah State Senate, Salt Lake City, Judiciary Interim Com. Utah State Senate, Exec. Offices and Criminal Justice Appropriations Com. Utah State Senate. Contbr. articles to law jours. Planning commr., South Weber, Utah, 2000; city councilman, 2001—02. Maj. U.S. Army, 1990—99. Recipient Profl. Merit award, ABA, 1991, Exec. Dirs. award, Utah Sheriff's Assn. Mem.: Nat. Assn. Bond Attys., Am. Legion. Home: 60 N Main Coalville UT 84017

**THOMAS, DAVID LLEWELLYN,** physician; b. Clinton, Iowa, June 11, 1948; s. Marvin Llewellyn and Marjorie Emma (Mayer) Thomas; m. Sheryl L. Miller, 2002; children: Tana, Paige, Drew, Aleksandr. BA in Zoology, U. Iowa, 1970, MD, 1974. Diplomate Am. Bd. Family Practice, Am. Bd. Geriatric Medicine. Resident in family medicine U. Ill., Rockford, 1977; pvt. practice Marshalltown, Iowa, 1977—; family physician McFarland Clinic, PC, Marshalltown, 1994, also bd. dirs., v.p., 1995—98, treas., 1999—. Clin. lectr. U. Iowa Coll. Medicine, Iowa City, 1981—. Bd. dirs. Iowa Found. Med. Care, Des Moines, 1986—2001, Iowa Ctrl. Agrl. Safety and Health, 1995—97; trustee Marshalltown Med. and Surg. Ctr., 1998—2003. Mem.: Am. Health Quality Assn. (bd. dirs. 1995, v.p. 1997—2000, pres. 2000—03). Republican. Episcopalian. Office: McFarland Clinic 303 Nicholas Dr Ste 1 Marshalltown IA 50158-4443 Office Phone: 641-752-0099. Business E-Mail: dthomas@mcfarlandclinic.com.

**THOMAS, DAVID LLOYD,** accountant, consultant; b. Atlanta, May 10, 1942; s. Elbert and Evelyn Thomas; m. Mary Jo Ann Matney, June 25, 1966; children: Christine, Michael. BSBA, U. N.C., 1964. CPA, N.C. Auditor Price Waterhouse, N.Y.C., 1964, Atlanta, 1969-70; divsn. contr. Dart Industries, Atlanta, 1971; contr. Ithaca Industries, Inc., Wilkesboro, N.C., 1971-82, sec.-treas., 1982-91, CFO, bd. dirs., 1983-91; pres. David L. Thomas, CPA, 1991—. CFO Wilkes Regional Med. Ctr., 1993-2000, v.p., 1996-2000; sec. N.W. Health Care, 1994-95. Bd. dirs., mem. Wilkes Art Gallery, 1985-91; bd. dirs. Wilkes Edn. Found., 1988-91, N.C. Citizens for Bus. and Industry, 1989-92, John A. Walker Cmty. Ctr., 1996-02, mem. exec. com., 1999-02, v.p., 2000-01, pres., 2001-02; mem. adv. bd. Wilkes C.C., 1989-97, vice chair, 1994-96, chmn., 1996-97, mem. vision 2010 cultural and quality of life com., 2001; mem. maj. firms calling com. Wilkes United Way, 1994-02; lectr., mem. fin. com. First Meth. Ch., North Wilkesboro, 2005—. Capt. MSC, U.S. Army, 1965-68. Fellow: N.C. Assn. CPAs (sec. Catawba Valley chpt. 1982—83); mem.: U. N.C. Alumni Assn. (reunion vice chmn. 2004), Wilkes C of C. (bd. dirs. 1979—81, v.p. 1982, trustee found. 1983—90, v.p. 1986, bd. dirs. 1990—92, v.p. 1991), Kiwanis (co-chmn. interclub visitation com. 2003—04, dir. 2004—, treas. 2004—). Republican. Methodist. Home and Office: 172 Walnut Pl Wilkesboro NC 28697-8775

**THOMAS, DAVID MANNING,** secondary school educator; b. Youngstown, Ohio, Nov. 6, 1954; s. Willie J and Willetta H Thomas; children: Ruyshannia, Leandria, Imani. BS in music edn., Case Western Reserve, 1981; M in music, Cleve. State U., 1993 Tchr. E. Cleve. Bd. Edn. 1987—93 Cleve Bd Edn 1993—. Adj. music instr. Cleveland State U., 1989—98; performing musician and music dir. Southeast 7th Day Aventist Ch., 2002—. Co-author: (book) A Child's First Book of African-American Spirituals "All Night All Day", 1991, composer orchestral compositions and choral pieces. Recipient Tchr. of the Yr., East Cleve. Bd. Edn., 1993, Loretta Scott King award, 1992. Mem.: Music Educators Nat. Conf., Phi Delta Kappa Internat. Home: 15932 Brewster Rd Cleveland OH 44112 Office: Cleve Bd Edn JFK H S Cleveland OH 44112 Office Phone: 216-371-0500. Business E-Mail: stthomas@en.com.

**THOMAS, DAVID SNOW,** plastic surgeon; b. Chgo., Feb. 7, 1951; s. Allan Perry and Verna Bea (Snow) T.; m. Becky Williams Thomas, Aug. 25, 1973; children: Nathan David, Abigail, Elizabeth. BA, U. Utah, 1974, MD, 1978. Diplomate Am. Bd. Plastic Surgery, Am. Bd. Surgery. Resident surgery UCLA, 1978-83, resident plastic surgery, 1983-85, fellow craniofacial surgery, 1985; pvt. practice Salt Lake City, 1986—; chief plastic surgery Primary Childrens Med. Ctr., Salt Lake City, 1988-90, LDS Hosp., 1993-99. Clin. asst. prof. U. Utah Plastic Surgeons, Salt Lake City, 1986-89, assoc. prof. surgery, 1990-93, clin. assoc. prof., 1993—. Bd. Dirs. AMICUS, Salt Lake City, Utah, 1990-92. Fellow ACS; mem. Am. Soc. Plastic and Reconstructive Surgery, Am. Soc. Maxillofacial Surgery, Am. Cleft Palate Craniofacial Assn., Am. Soc. Aesthetic Plastic Surgery, Interplast (pres. Salt Lake City, 1992—, bd. dirs. Palo Alto, Calif., 1992—), The Country Club (Salt Lake City), Alta Club (sec.). Office: 370 9th Ave Ste 200 Salt Lake City UT 84103-3185 Office Phone: 801-355-0731. Business E-Mail: dst@davidsthomasmd.com.

**THOMAS, DEBI (DEBRA J. THOMAS),** ice skater; b. Poughkeepsie, N.Y., Mar. 25, 1967; d. McKinley and Janice Thomas; m. Christopher Bequette, Nov. 1996; children: Christopher Jules II, Luc. BS, Stanford U.; MD, Northwestern U., 1997; grad., Charles R. Drew U., 2005. Competitive figure skater, 1976-88. Winner U.S. Figure Skating Championship, 1986, 88, World Figure Skating Championship, 1986, World Profl. Figure Skating Championship, 1988, 89, 91. Recipient Am. Black Achievement Award, Ebony mag., named Women Athlete of Yr., 1986; winner Bronze medal Olympic Games, 1988; named to U.S. Figure Skating Hall of Fame, San Jose Sports Hall of Fame. Address: Mentor Mgmt 5610 Town Center Dr # 5 Granger IN 46530-

**THOMAS, DENE KAY,** academic administrator, educator; 3 children. B Lit., S.W. State U., cert. in secondary edn., 1978; PhD English, U. Minn., 1984; course, Bryn Mawr's Women in Higher Edn. Adminstrn. program, 1990. Vice provost acad. affairs to tchr., dept. chmn., dean U. Idaho; pres. Lewis-Clark State Coll., 2001—. Office: Lewis-Clark State Coll 500 8th Ave Lewiston ID 83501

**THOMAS, DENNIS,** retired paper company executive, retired federal official; b. Balt., Dec. 8, 1943; s. George Crosby and Justa Mae (Witherspoon) T.; m. Dawn Frances Haines, 1965; 1 son, William David. BS, Frostburg State Coll., 1965; MSW., U. Md., 1967. Asst. to Hon. J. Glenn Beall, Jr. U.S. Ho. of Reps., Washington, 1969-71; spl. asst., 1971-73, 1973-77, adminstrv. asst. to Hon. William V. Roth, Jr., 1977-81; asst. sec. legis. affairs Dept. Treasury, Washington, 1981-83; dep. asst. to Pres. for legis. affairs White House, Washington, 1983-85; ptnr. Touche Ross and Co., Inc., 1985; asst. to Pres., The White House, 1985-87; sr. v.p. pub. affairs and comm. Internat. Paper Co., Stamford, Conn., 1987—. Republican. Office: Internat Paper 400 Atlantic St Stamford CT 06921

**THOMAS, DEONA LEE,** music educator; b. Nashville, Dec. 15, 1955; d. Joseph Benjamin and Frances Lee (Gwaltney) Thomas. BMus in Edn., Belmont Coll., Nashville, 1978; MusM in Edn., Peabody Coll. Vanderbilt U., Nashville, 1980. Cert. tchr. Tenn., 1978. Pvt. practice tchr. music, Carthage, Tenn., 1982—2001. Dir. Women's Missionary Union, 1980—; coord. North Ctrl. Region Children's Bible Drill, 2000—. Mem.: DAR (historian Carey Fork chpt.), Am. Orff Schulwerk Assn., Am. Guild Organists, Am. Coll. Musicians, Hist. and Geneological Soc., Sigma Alpha Iota, Beta Sigma Phi. Baptist. Avocations: sewing, church activities. Home: 220 Jenkins Hill Rd Alexandria TN 37012

**THOMAS, DONALD LEE,** construction technology educator; b. Hampton, Va., Jan. 28, 1964; s. Lloyd Jene Thomas Sr. and Elsie Marie Thomas, Senior. Cert. in project planning and cost estimating, Old Dominion U., 1989, cert. in purchasing and supply chain mgmt., 2002; B in Mgmt., Calif. Coast U., Santa Ana, 2006; cert. in Bus. Info. Tech., No. Va. C.C., Woodbridge, Virginia, 2000—00; cert. in Paralegal studies, Old Dominion U., Ctr. for Global Bus. & Exec. Edn., Norfolk, Virginia, 1993—93. Cert. quality assurance sys. Def. Logistics Agy. Quality assurance specialist Def. Logistics Agy., Richmond, Va., 2001—; instr. constrn. tech. No. Va. C.C., Woodbridge, Va., 2000—. Germanna C.C., Fredericksburg, Va., 2002—; bldg. inspector nat. office IRS, Washington. Author: (instrn. manual) Reading Construction Prints, Student Supplement. Mem.: Am. Soc. Mil. Comptrs., Intellectual Property Owners Assn. (corr.; apptd. com. mem. small bus. affairs 2004—). Achievements include invention of Building Energy Saving Equipment. E-mail: inventors@hamptonsroad.com.

**THOMAS, DOROTHY,** indexing consultant, writer; b. N.Y.C., Mar. 3, 1923; d. Hyman and Clara (Lond) Fisch; student Hunter Coll., 1940-43; cert. N.Y. U. Sch. Bus., 1944; m. Sidney Thomashower, Sept. 2, 1944; children: William Jay, James Evan. Personnel troubleshooter W.P.B., 1943; employment mgr. Emerson Radio & Phonograph Corp., 1943-47; editor, author, 1947—; indexer, cons., N.Y.C., 1960—; biographer, lectr., radio producer and moderator; specialist in history of women in legal profession; dir. spl. projects Found. Continuing Legal Edn.; dir. Documentation Abstracts Inc., lectr. colls., clubs, orgns. Active legis. reform and women's movement; mem. Nat. Women's Polit. Caucus, NOW. Mem. AFTRA, Am. Soc. Indexers (pres. elect 1982-83, pres. 1983-84, dir.), Coalition of Labor Union Women, Friends of Columbia Libraries, Friends of Schlesinger Library of Harvard U., N.Y. Hist. Soc. Ind. Democrat. Club: Women's City (N.Y.C.). Author: Women Lawyers in the U.S., 1957; Women, The Bench and The Bar, in preparation; contbr. articles and biographies to Notable American Women, 1607-1950, 1971, Law Book Indexing, 1983; author: Wigmore on Evidence, Vol. XI, 1985, also other indexes and tables. Home and Office: 123 W 74th St New York NY 10023-2209

**THOMAS, DUKE WINSTON,** lawyer; b. Scuddy, Ky., Jan. 25, 1937; s. William E. and Grace T. Thomas; m. Jill Staples, Oct. 24, 1964; children: Deborah L., William E. II, Judith A. BSBA, Ohio State U., 1959, JD, 1964. Bar: Ohio 1964, U.S. Dist. Ct. Ohio 1966, U.S. Ct. Appeals (3d cir.) 1971, U.S. Ct. Appeals (6th cir.) 1972, U.S. Supreme Ct. 1973, U.S. Ct. Appeals (7th cir.) 1979. Ptnr. Vorys, Sater, Seymour and Pease, LLP, Columbus, Ohio, 1964—2005. Chmn. bd. dirs. Ohio Bar Liability Ins. Co. Fellow: Columbus Bar Found., Ohio Bar Found., Am. Coll. Trial Lawyers (chmn. Ohio joint select com. jud. compensation 1987), Internat. Soc. Barristers, Am. Bar Found. (life); mem.: ABA (ho. of dels. 1985—99, state del. 1989—95, bd. govs. 1995—98), Columbus Bar Assn. (pres. 1978), Ohio Bar Assn. (pres. 1985), The Golf Club, Columbus Athletic Club, Pres.'s Club Ohio State U. Home: 2090 Sheringham Rd Columbus OH 43220-4358 Office: Vorys Sater Seymour & Pease LLP PO Box 1008 52 E Gay St Columbus OH 43215-3161 Office Phone: 614-464-6263. Business E-Mail: dwthomas@vssp.com.

**THOMAS, DWIGHT REMBERT,** writer; b. Savannah, Ga., Dec. 8, 1944; s. Huguenin and Alma (Sanders) Thomas. BA in English with honors, Emory U., 1967; PhD in Am. Lit., U. Pa., 1978. Fellow English dept. U. Pa., Phila., 1971-78; writer Savannah, 1979—. Cons. Film Odyssey, Washington, 1988—89. Author: (book) The Poe Log: A Documentary Life of Edgar Allan Poe, 1987. Dir. Edgar Allan Poe Mus., Richmond, 1988—96. With U.S. Army, 1969—71. Mem.: MLA, Am. Med. Writers Assn., Mensa (treas. Savannah area 1985—88, local sec. 1989—90), Phi Beta Kappa. Roman Catholic. Avocations: German language, current cinema, bicycling. Home: 7 E Gordon St Savannah GA 31401-4925

**THOMAS, DYNDA A.,** lawyer; b. Springfield, Ill., 1959; BA magna cum laude, Miami U., 1982; JD, U. Cin., 1986. Bar: Ohio 1986. Ptnr. Squire, Sanders & Dempsey LLP, Cleve., co-chmn., Project Fin. Practice Group. Mem.: ABA (global infrastructure com., Pub. Utility, Comm. & Transp. Law Sect.), Cleve. Bar Assn. (Real Property, Probate & Trust Law Sect.). Office: Squire Sanders & Dempsey LLP 4900 Key Tower 127 Public Sq Cleveland OH 44114-1304 Office Phone: 216-479-8583. Office Fax: 216-479-8780. Business E-Mail: dthomas@ssd.com.

**THOMAS, EDWARD DONNALL,** internist, hematologist, retired medical educator; b. Mart, Tex., Mar. 15, 1920; m. Dorothy Thomas; 3 children. BA, U. Tex., 1941, MA, 1943; MD, Harvard U., 1946; MD (hon.), U. Cagliari, Sardinia, 1981, U. Verona, Italy, 1991, U. Parma, 1992, U. Barcelona, Spain, 1994, U. Warsaw, Poland, 1996, U. Jagiellonski, Cracow, Poland, 1996. Lic. physician Mass., N.Y., Wash., diplomate Am. Bd. Internal Medicine. Intern in medicine Peter Bent Brigham Hosp., Boston, 1946—47, rsch. fellow hematology, 1947—48; NRC postdoctoral fellow in medicine dept. biology MIT, Cambridge, 1950—51; chief med. resident, sr. asst. resident Peter Bent Brigham Hosp., 1951—53, hematologist, 1953—55; instr. medicine Harvard Med. Sch., Boston, 1953—55; rsch. assoc. Cancer Rsch. Found. Children's Med. Ctr., Boston, 1953—55; physician-in-chief Mary Imogene Bassett Hosp., Cooperstown, NY, 1955—63; assoc. clin. prof. medicine Coll. Physicians and Surgeons Columbia U., N.Y.C., 1955—63; attending physician U. Wash. Hosp., Seattle, 1963—90; prof. medicine Sch. Medicine U. Wash., Seattle, 1963—90, head divsn. oncology Sch. Medicine, 1963—85, prof. emeritus medicine Sch. Medicine, 1990—; dir. med. oncology Fred Hutchinson Cancer Rsch. Ctr., Seattle, 1974—89, assoc. dir. clin. rsch. programs, 1982—89, mem., 1974—. Mem. hematology study sect. NIH, 1965—69; mem. bd. trustees and med. sci. adv. com. Leukemia Soc. Am., Inc., 1969—73; mem. clin. cancer investigation rev. com. NCI, 1970—74; 1st ann. Eugene C. Eppinger lectr. Peter Bent Brigham Hosp. and Harvard Med. Sch., 1974; Lilly lectr. RCP, London, 1977; Stratton lectr. Internat. Soc. Hematology, 1982; Paul Aggeler lectr. U. Calif., San Francisco, 1982; 65th Mellon lectr. U. Pitts. Sch. Medicine, 1984; Stanley Wright Meml. lectr. Western Soc. Pediat. Rsch., 1985; Adolfo Ferrata lectr. Italian Soc. Hematology, Verona, Italy, 1991. Mem. editl. bd. Blood, 1962—75, 1977—82, Transplantation, 1970—76, Proc. of Soc. for Exptl. Biology and Medicine,

1974—81, Leukemia Rsch., 1977—87, Hematological Oncology, 1982—87, Jour. Clin. Immunology, 1982—87, Am. Jour. Hematology, 1985—. Bone Marrow Transplantation, 1986—. With U.S. Army, 1948—50. Recipient A. Ross McIntyre award, U. Nebr. Med. Ctr., 1975, Philip Levine award, Am. Soc. Clin. Pathologists, 1979, Disting. Svc. in Basic Rsch. award, Am. Cancer Soc., 1980, Kettering prize, GM Cancer Rsch. Found., 1981, Spl. Keynote Address award, Am. Soc. Therapeutic Radiologists, 1981, Robert Roesler de Villiers award, Leukemia Soc. Am., 1983, Karl Landsteiner Meml. award, Am. Assn. Blood Banks, 1987, Terry Fox award, Can., 1990, Internat. award, Gairdner Found., 1990, Hong Kong prize, N.Am. Med. Assn., 1990, Nobel Prize in Medicine, 1990, Presdl. medal of sci., NSF, 1990, Lifetime Achievement award, Am. Soc. Blood and Marrow Transplantation, 2004. Mem.: NAS, Soc. Exptl. Biology and Medicine, Western Assn. Physicians, Am. Soc. Clin. Investigation, Am. Soc. Clin. Oncology (David A. Karnoksky Meml. lectr. 1983), Am. Fedn. Clin. Rsch., Assn. Am. Physicians (Kober medal 1992), Am. Assn. Cancer Rsch., Academie Royale de Medicine de Belgique (corr.), Nat. Acad. Medicine Mex. (hon.), Royal Coll. Physicians and Surgeons Can. (hon.), Swedish Soc. Hematology (hon.). Office: Fred Hutchinson Cancer Ctr 1100 Fairview Ave N D5-100 PO Box 19024 Seattle WA 98109-1024 Office Phone: 206-667-4319. Business E-Mail: ethomas@fhcrc.org.

**THOMAS, EDWARD LABELLE,** company executive; b. Milw., Dec. 13, 1951; s. Edward L. and Dorothy H. (Goggans) T.; m. Kay S. Olm, Aug. 8, 1972 (div. May 1986); 1 child, Johanna O.; m. Katharine E. Teeter, Oct. 4, 1986; children: Carlos, Marisol, Giancarlo. BA in Philosophy, Lakeland Coll., 1975; postgrad., Harvard Div. Sch., 1975; MBA, Bentley Grad. Sch. Bus., 2000. Radio engr. Sta. WBUR-FM, Boston, 1983-85; sr. audio engr. Bose Corp., Framingham, Mass., 1985-88; radio engr. Sta. WGHB-FM, Boston, 1988-90; tech. dir. Monitor Radio, Boston, 1988-97; tech. dir. religious prodn. Christian Sci. Pub. Soc., Boston, 1997—2000; dir. fin. and adminstrn. Peace Games, Inc., Boston, 2000—01; prin. Thomas Assocs., 2000—01; COO, CFO United Leaders, Cambridge, Mass., 2002—03; v.p. fin. & adminstrn. New Eng. Sch. Acupuncture, 2003—; v.p. ops. and compliance crispus attucks Children's Ctr., Dorchester, Mass., 2004—. Bd. dors. Boston Urban Gardeners, 1979-80, Boston Citizens Elder Affairs, 1979-80; house facilitator Shared Living House, Boston, 1980-82. Fund For Theol. Edn. fellow, 1975-76. Home: 16 1/2 Woodbridge St Cambridge MA 02140-1220 Personal E-mail: thomas.edward@comcast.net.

**THOMAS, ELIZABETH MARSHALL,** writer; b. Boston, Sept. 13, 1931; d. Laurence K. and Lorna (McLean) Marshall; m. Stephen Thomas, 1956; children: Stephanie, Ramsay. Student, Smith Coll.; BA in English, Radcliffe Coll., 1954. Writer, 1954—. Author: The Harmless People, 1959, Warrior Herdsmen, 1965, Reindeer Moon, 1987, The Animal Wife, 1990, The Hidden Life of Dogs, 1993, The Tribe of Tiger, 1994, Certain Poor Shepherds, 1998, The Social Lives of Dogs, 2000. Office: 80 E Mountain Rd Peterborough NH 03458-2318

**THOMAS, ELLEN LOUISE,** school system administrator; b. Doylestown, Pa., Nov. 30, 1940; d. Edward Martin and Evelyn Graham (Axenroth) Happ; m. Eugene Greene Leffever, June 30, 1963 (dec. Nov. 1978); children: Eugene Greene II, Jeanette Ellen Dellaripa; m. William Dewey Thomas, Sept. 15, 1981; 1 child, Jeremiah David. BA in Edn., Immaculata (Pa.) Coll., 1962; postgrad., Pa. State U., 1962-67. Pvt. practice tutor, Doylestown, 1958-65; tchr. Cen. Bucks Sch. System, Doylestown, 1962-65; adminstr. The Curiosity Shoppe, Doylestown, 1965—, The Toddler Ctr., Doylestown, 1979—; exec. dir. Camp Curiosity, Doylestown, 1984—, Thomas Lea Equestrian Ctr., Doylestown, 1988—. Tchr. trainer Confortunity of Christian Doctrine, Doylestown, 1965-78; cons. early childhood Am. Sch. in Hong Kong, 1981-84; lectr. in early childhood Bucks County Community Ctr., Newtown, Pa., 1978-90; workshop facilitator Head Start, Phila., 1990; cons. day care Cen. Bucks C. of C., Doylestown, 1989-90; ednl. coord. Forest Grove Presbyn. Ch., 1984-90. Mem. U.S.C. of C., Washington, Bucks County C. of C., Doylestown, Nat. Fedn. of Ind. Bus., Washington; children's ministry coord. Jesus Focus Ministry, 1995—; trainer Pa. Child Care, 1995—; past pres. Pa. Day Camp Assn., 1998-2001; Sunday sch. tchr. Hilltown Bapt. Ch., 1995-2000; mem. Am. Camping Assn., 1994-, Plumstead Christian Sch. Bd., 1995-2001; varsity tennis coach, Plumstead Christian Sch.-boys, 1998-, girls, 2001-; children's chmn. Central Bucks Village Fair, 2001-03; mem. Quality Child Care Coun., Pa. Keystone Stars; bd. dirs., ednl. chair Plumstead Christian Sch., 2002-05. Mem. ASCD, Assn. for Childhood Edn. Internat., United Pvt. Acad. Schs. Assn., Bucks County Assn. Edn. Young Children (pres. 1974-78). Office: The Curiosity Shoppe 4425 Landisville Rd Doylestown PA 18901-1134 E-mail: FaxThomdew@aol.com.

**THOMAS, ESTHER MERLENE,** elementary and adult education educator; b. San Diego, Oct. 16, 1945; d. Merton Alfred and Nellie Lida (Von Pilz) T. *Great-great-great-grandfather, James Thomas, fought in the American Revolutionary War. He was from Great Britain. He married Mary Hughes from Warren County, Tennessee. Their children were James P. Thomas (b. 1807), and Polly Thomas, who married John Henderson son of Pleasant Ree Henderson and Agnes Robards of Warren County. Pleasant's father was Samuel Henderson Jr., whose brothers were Richard and Pleasant Henderson. They formed the Transylvania Land Company who bought out of most of Kentucky and middle Tennessee from the Cherokee. The town of Henderson was named for Col. Richard Henderson.* AA with honors, Grossmont Coll., 1966; BA with honors, San Diego State U., 1969; MA, U. Redlands, 1977. Cert. elem. and adult edn. tchr.; cert. in crossculturul lang. and acad. devel., English lang. devel. Tchr. Cajon Valley Union Sch. Dist., El Cajon, 1969 ; sci. fair coord. Flying Hills Sch. Tchr. Hopi and Navajo Native Americans, Ariz., Utah, 1964-74, Goose and Gander Nursery Sch., Lakeside, Calif., 1964-66; dir., supt. Bible and Sunday schs. various chs., Lakeside, 1961-87; mem. sci. coun., math. coun. Cajon Valley Union Sch. Dist., 1990-91, libr. com., 1997-98. Author: Individualized Curriculum in the Affective Domain; co-author: Campbell County, The Treasured Years, 1990, Legends of the Lakeside; songwriter: songs Never Trouble Trouble, Old Glory, Jesus Is Our Lord, Daniel's Prayer, There Lay Jesus, God's Hands, Washing Machine Charlie, Playmates, The Kid in the Hall, Spring Time on the Blue Ridge, Christ's DNA, If You Need Me, Chances (Four Star award, 2003), Blame, The Star of Bethlehem, Where the Eagle Flies, Born to Win, Happy Birthday Dear Jesus, Christmas Lights, Walk the Line, You Don't Know What Repentance Is, I'm Asking You, Clear the Path Lord, Aqua Forte, In the Volume of the Book, Home is Where the Heart Is, You Don't Even Know Who I Am, No Place to Cry, To Walk With God, Ixnay, If You Never Loved Me, for Columbine Records Corp., Life of A Single Woman, Take This Pain Away, We Can Keep In Touch, Let Me Know, A Letter Is A Letter, The Battle, 2004; contbr. articles to profl. jours., newspapers, chpts. to books. Treo. U.S. Senatorial Club, Washington, 1984—; Conservative Caucus, Inc., Washington, 1988—, Ronald Reagan Presdl. Found., Ronald Reagan Rep. Ctr., 1988, Rep. Presdl. Citizen's Adv. Commn., 1989—, Rep. Platform Planning Com., Calif., 1992, at-large del. representing dist. #45, Lakeside, Calif., 1992, 1995—, Am. Security Coun., Washington, 1994, Congressman Hunter's Off Road Adv. Coun., El Cajon, Calif., 1994, Century Club, San Diego Rep. Century Club, 1995; mem. health articulation com. project AIDS, Cajon Valley Union Sch. Dist., 1988—, Nacurit Depot Hist. Mus., San Diego, 1989, Citizen's Drug Free Am., Calif., 1989—, The Heritage Found., 1988—; charter mem. Marine Corps Mus.; life mem. San Diego Aerospace Mus.; mem. Lakeside Centennial Com., 1985-86; hon. mem. Presdl. Task Force, Washington, 1986; del. Calif. Rep. Senatorial Mid-Term Conv., Washington, 1994; mus. curator Lakeside Hist. Soc., 1992-93, life mem.; mem. Rep. Nat. Com., Washington, 2003 Recipient Outstanding Svc. award PTA, 1972-74, Outstanding Svc. award KYXY Radio, San Diego, 1999, Dream Classroom award KSWB-TV, San Diego, 2005; recognized for various contbns. including Hats Off to Tchr. recognition for music Comdg. Post Gen., San Diego Bd. Edn., 1989. Mem. NRA, Tchrs. Assn., Calif. Tchrs. Assn., Cajon Valley Educators Assn. (faculty advisor, rep. 1980-82, 84-86, 87-88), Nat. Trust for Hist. Preservation, Christian Bus. and Profl. Women,

Trust for Hist. Preservation, Nat. WWII Memml. (life, charter), Ridgecrest Golden Terrace Park Assn. (pres. 1998-99), Nashville Songwriters Assn., Capitol Hill Women's Club, Am. Ctr. for Law and Justice, Internat. Christian Women's Club (Christian amb. to Taiwan, Korea, 1974), Paul Revere Soc. Republican. Avocations: travel, vocal music, piano, guitar. Home: 13594 Hwy 8 # 3 Lakeside CA 92040-5235 Office: Flying Hills Elem Sch 1251 Finch St El Cajon CA 92020-1433

**THOMAS, ETAN,** professional basketball player, poet; b. Harlem, N.Y., Apr. 1, 1978; BS in Bus. Mgmt., Syracuse Univ., 2000. Profl. basketball player Wash. Wizard, 2001—. Political spkr. and activist. Author: (volume of poetry) More Than an Athlete, 2005. Achievements include hon. mention All-America, AP, 2000; named to first team All-Big East Conf., 2000; two-time Big East Defensive Player Yr. Office: Washington Wizards MCI Ctr 601 F St NW Washington DC 20004*

**THOMAS, EVELYN B.,** agricultural products supplier; Sec., treas. book-keeper Brandt Fertilizer, Pleasant Plains, Ill., 1953—; co-owner Har Brand, 1963-67, Brandt Chemical, 1967; sec./treas. Brandt Consolidated, Pleasant Plains, Ill. Office: Brandt Consolidated PO Box 350 Pleasant Plains IL 62677-0277 Fax: 217-626-1927. E-mail: bcadmin@brandtconsolidated.com.

**THOMAS, FAYE EVELYN J.,** elementary and secondary school educator; b. Summerfield, La., Aug. 3, 1933; d. Reginald Felton and Atlee (Hunter) Johnson; m. Archie Taylor Thomas, Sept. 8, 1960; 1 child, Dwayne Andre. BA, So. U., 1954; student, Tuskegee Inst., 1958, student, 1969, U. Detroit, 1961, student, 1962, student, 1963, Ctrl. Mich. U., 1965; MS, U. Ctrl. Ark., 1971, Cleve. State U., 1979. Tchr. Cullen (La.) Elem. Sch., 1957; tchr. English and social studies Charles Brown H.S., Springhill, La., 1957—70; tchr. English, Upward Bound Program, Grambling State U., 1968; tchr. English, Springhill H.S., 1970; elem. intermediate tchr. Riveredge Elem. Sch., Berea, Ohio, 1971—93; tchr. 7th grade English, Ford Mid. Sch., 1993—94; program dir. First Bapt. Ch. Teen Pregnancy Prevention Program, Cullen, La., 2003—04. Tchr. asst. elem. coun. curriculum and instrn. Berea Sch. Dist., 1984—85. Author: When the Time Is Right, Move On, 2002, A Journey to the Mountain Top, 2003. Dir. teen pregnancy prevention program Firt Bapt. Ch., Cullen, La., 2003—04. Grantee, EDPA, 1970—71, Internat. Paper Found., 1958, 1960, NDEA, 1965; scholar Martha Holden Jennings scholar, 1984—85. Mem.: ASCD, NEA, N.E. Ohio Tchrs. Assn., Berea Edn. Assn., Ohio Edn. Assn., Black Caucus NEA, People United to Save Humanity, Toastmasters, Order Eastern Star. Democrat. Baptist. Office: 311 Henrietta White Blvd Springhill LA 71075-8407

**THOMAS, FLORIAN PATRICK,** physician, researcher; b. Frankfurt, Germany, Mar. 15, 1957; children: Tristan Simon Konrad, Cosima Raffaela, Immanuel Jacob, Oscar, Peter Matthew. MD, U. Bonn, Germany, 1982, MA in Psychology, 1983; PhD, McGill U., Canada, 1995. Cert. Neurology. Resident Case Western Reserve U., Cleve., 1983—87; Fellow Columbia U., N.Y.C., 1987—90, McGill U., Montreal, Quebec, Canada, 1991—95; assoc. prof. St. Louis U., 1995—2005; prof. St Louis U., 2005—; dir. Spinal Cord Injury Unit St. Louis VA Hosp., 2005—, assoc. chief of staff, 2005—. Mng. editor eMedicine, 2000—; bd. dirs. Nat. Multiple Sclerosis Soc., 2005—. Capt. German mil., 1982—84. Office: Saint Louis Univ 3635 Vista Ave Saint Louis MO 63110-0250 Business E-Mail: thomasfp@slu.edu.

**THOMAS, FRANK EDWARD,** professional baseball player; b. Columbus, Ga., May 27, 1968; Student, Auburn U. With Chgo. White Sox, 1990—2006, Oakland Athletics, 2006—. Named Maj. League Player of Yr., Sporting News, 1993; named to All-Star Club. All Am. team, 1989, All-Star Team, 1991, 1993—94, Am. League, 1993—95; recipient Silver Slugger award, 1991, 1993, 1994, Most Valuable Player award, Am. League, 1994. Office: Oakland Athletics 7000 Coliseum Way Oakland CA 94621*

**THOMAS, FRANK M., JR.,** lawyer; b. Feb. 20, 1947; BA, Amherst Coll., 1969; M in City Planning, Harvard U., 1973; JD, U. Pa., 1977. Bar: Pa. 1977, U.S. Supreme Ct. 1983. Ptnr. Morgan, Lewis & Bockius, Phila., 1987—2002; pvt. practice Phila., 2002—.

**THOMAS, FRANKLIN A., III,** lawyer; b. Charleston, W.Va., Oct. 17, 1948; BA, U. Va., 1970, MA, 1971. Bar: Va. 1974, U.S. Tax Ct. 1974, U.S. Ct. Appeals (4th cir.) 1974. Atty. Shackelford, Thomas & Gregg, PLC, Orange, Va. Fellow: Am. Bar Found., Am. Coll. Trust and Estate Counsel; mem.: ABA, Order of Coif, Va. State Bar (bd. govs. trust and estates sect. 1983—90, chmn. 1988—89), Va. Bar Assn. (chair sect. wills, trusts and estates 1997—98, pres.-elect 2002, pres. 2003). Office: Shackelford Thomas and Gregg PO Box 871 149 W Main St Orange VA 22960

**THOMAS, FRANKLIN AUGUSTINE,** lawyer, consultant; b. Bklyn., May 27, 1934; s. James and Viola (Atherley) T.; div.; children: Keith, Hillary, Kerrie, Kevin. BA, Columbia U., 1956, LL.B., 1963; LL.D. (hon.), Yale U., 1970, Fordham U., 1972, Pratt Inst., 1974, Pace U., 1977, Columbia U., 1979, New School U., 2002. Bar: N.Y. 1964. Atty. Fed. Housing and Home Finance Agy., N.Y.C., 1963-64; asst. U.S. atty. for So. Dist. N.Y., 1964-65; dep. police commr. charge legal matters N.Y.C., 1965-67; pres., chief exec. officer Bedford Stuyvesant Restoration Corp., Bklyn., 1967-77; pres. The Ford Found., 1979-96; atty., cons., 1996—. Bd. dirs. ALCOA, Citigroup, Lucent Techs., PepsiCo, Inc. Trustee Columbia U., 1969-75. Served with USAF, 1956-60. Recipient LBJ Found. award for contbn. to betterment of urban life, 1974, medal of excellence Columbia U., 1976, Alexander Hamilton award Columbia U., 1983 Office Phone: 212-557-3004.

**THOMAS, FREDERICK BRADLEY,** lawyer; b. Evanston, Ill., Aug. 13, 1949; s. Frederick Bradley and Katherine Kidder (Bingham) T.; m. Elizabeth Maxwell, Oct. 25, 1975; children: Bradley Bingham, Stephens Maxwell, Rosa Macaulay. AB, Dartmouth Coll., 1971; JD, U. Chgo., 1974. Bar: Ill. 1974, Law clk. to hon. judge John C. Godbold U.S. Ct. Appeals (5th cir.), Montgomery, Ala., 1974-75; assoc. Mayer, Brown, Rowe & Maw, LLP, Chgo., 1975—80, ptnr., 1981—. Bd. trustees La Rabida Children's Hosp., 1990—; bd. mgrs. YMCA Met. Chgo., 2002—. Mem.: ABA, Chgo. Coun. Lawyers. Republican. Episcopalian. Office: Mayer Brown Rowe & Maw LLP 71 South Wacker Dr Chicago IL 60606-4637

**THOMAS, GARNETT JETT,** accountant; b. Farmington, Ky., July 27, 1920; s. Pinkney Madison and Ethel (Drinkard) T.; m. Katherine Gardner, Mary. 26, 1948 (dec. Sept. 1979); m. Nell Penton, May 23, 1981; stepchildren: Vernon Bice, Michael Bice, Gina Black. BS, Lambuth U., 1947; MS, Miss. State U., 1949. Clk., acct. Ill. Cen. R.R., Paducah, Ky., 1941-42; mgr. Coll. Bookstore Lambuth U., Jackson, Tenn., 1946-47; acct. Miss. Agrl. and Forestry Expt. Sta., Mississippi State, 1948-60, chief acct., 1960-75, administrv. officer and chief acct., 1975-85; administrv. officer emeritus, 1985—; pres. PBR Corp., Starksville, Miss., 1974-84. Fin. adminstr. seed tech., rsch. internat. programs Brazil, India, Guatemala, Columbia, Thailand, Kenya, 1958-85; fin. adminstr. seed tech. research internat. programs Brazil, India, Guatemala, Columbia, Thailand, Kenya, 1958-85 bd. dirs. Govt. Employees Credit Union, 1967-86, pres., 1969-73. With USN, 1942-46. Decorated Bronze Star with oak leaf cluster. Mem. Nat. Assn. Accts., Asn. Govt. Accts., Am. Assn Accts., Acad. Acctg. Historians, So. Assn. Agrl. Scientists, Rotary (pres., 1959-90, dist. 682 gov. 1977-78, adv. com. to pres. 1979-80, dist. chmn. Poloplus, 1987-90). Republican. Methodist. Home: 114 Grand Ridge Rd Starkville MS 39759-4112

**THOMAS, GARY L.,** retired academic administrator; b. Willows, Calif., May 12, 1937; s. Leonel Richard and Myrtle Blanch (Moncur) T.; m. Margaret Anderson, Aug. 11, 1960 (div. 1975); children: Katelin, Elizabeth Ann, Derek Alan. AA, Modesto Jr. Coll., 1958; BS in Elec. Engring., U. Calif., Berkeley, 1960, MA in Physics, 1962, PhD in Elec. and Computer Engring., 1967. Acting asst. prof. U. Calif., Berkeley, 1967; asst. prof. elec.

engring. SUNY, Stony Brook, 1967-70, assoc. prof. elec. engring., 1970-73, assoc. dean grad. sch., 1973-74, chairperson, prof. elec. engring., 1975-79; congl. fellow A.A.A.S., Washington, 1974-75; provost, v.p. acad. affairs N.J. Inst. Tech., Newark, 1980-98, prof. elec. and computer engring., 1980-2000; chancellor U. Missouri-Rolla, Rolla, Mo., 2000—05. Student asst. bd. Dept. Higher Edn., N.J., 1980-97; chairperson rsch. adv. bd. PSE & G, Newark, 1986-90, Regional Transp. Rsch. Bd., N.Y. and N.J., 1987-90; bd. dirs. Kessler Inst. for Rehab., West Orange, N.J., 1988—; chair bd. dirs. Kessler Med. Rehab. Rsch. & Edn. Corp., 1997-2002. Author, editor: Fundamentals of Electrical and Computer Engineering, 1983. State of Calif. scholar, 1960, Schumberger scholar, 1961; NSF grantee, 1973-79. Home: 7 Vosseler Ct West Orange NJ 07052-3911

**THOMAS, GARY LYNN,** information technology executive; b. Port Vue, Pa., May 15, 1942; s. Willis L. and Luella M. (Rorabaugh) T.; m. Sharen A. Gibbons, May 13, 1967; children: Gregory Scott, Tara Elizabeth. BS in Bus. Adminstrn. Pa. State U., 1964; grad., Sch. Bank Adminstrn., U. Wis., 1973. CPA, Pa. Sr. auditor Arthur Andersen & Co., Los Angeles and Pitts., 1964-69; v.p. and dep. comptroller Pitts. Nat. Bank, 1969-77; v.p. and treas. Md. Nat. Corp., Balt., 1977-80; v.p., mgr. corp. fin. div. Md. Nat. Bank, Balt.; exec. v.p. adminstrn. Peterson, Howell & Heather, Hunt Valley, Md., 1980-82; v.p. fin. Am. TeleServices, Inc, a Metromedia co., Balt., 1983-85; chief fin. officer First Cellular Group, Inc., Balt., 1985-88. Schelle, Warner, Murray & Thomas, Inc., Balt., 1988—95. Mng. dir. Schelle Cellular Group, Inc., 1989—; pres. Ruxton Capital Group, Inc., 1989-95; chief fin. officer Am. Personal Communications, Inc., Balt. and D.C., 1990-98; adj. instr. Sch. Bank Adminstrn., U. Wis., 1975-80; speaker 14th annu. Bank Tax Inst., 1978. Mem. adv. bd., fin. com. St. Joseph Hosp., Balt., 1979-1982; bd. dirs. industry luncheon club Towson State U., 1980-1985. Served with USAR, 1965-1971. Inducted into McKeesport H.S. Hall of Fame, 1994. Mem. AICPA, Pa. Inst. CPAs, Md. Assn. CPAs (prior chmn. mems. in industry com.), Greater Naples Leadership Program, Conservancy of SW Fla.(bd. dirs.). Republican. Methodist. Home: 575 18th Ave S Naples FL 34102-7536

**THOMAS, GEOFFREY L.,** lawyer; b. Lindsay, Calif., May 12, 1944; AB cum laude, Harvard U., 1967; JD, Stanford, 1971. Bar: Calif. 1972. Ptnr. Paul, Hastings, Janofsky & Walker LLP, L.A., gen. counsel, chmn. profl. responsibility com. Mem. bd. editors Stanford Law Rev., 1970—71. Contbr. (chapter) Examining Witnesses to Civil Procedure During Trial. Office: Paul Hastings Janofsky & Walker LLP 515 S Flower St Los Angeles CA 90071-2228 Office Phone: 213-683-6149. Office Fax: 213-627-0705. Business E-Mail: geoffreythomas@paulhastings.com.

**THOMAS, GREGG DARROW,** lawyer; b. Jacksonville, Fla., July 31, 1951; BA magna cum laude, Vanderbilt U., 1972; JD with honors, U. Fla., 1976. Bar: Fla. 1976, D.C. 1978. Law clk. U.S. Dist. Ct. (mid. dist.) Fla., 1976-79; mem. Holland & Knight, Tampa, Fla., 1979—; ptnr., 1983—. Exec. editor U. Fla. Law Rev., 1975-76. Bd. dirs. Vol. Lawyer's Resource Ctr., 1990-95; trustee Tampa Mus. of Art, 1993—, vice chmn., 1998, chair, 1999-2001. Mem. ABA (mem. forum com. comm. law 1983—), Am. Judicature Soc., Fla. Bar (co-chair Fla. bar media and comm. com. 1987-88, mem. grievance com. 1988, chmn. 1989-91), Fla. Bar Found. (mem. legal assistance to poor com. 1988-91) Hillsborough Bar Assn., D.C. Bar, Phi Beta Kappa. Office: Holland & Knight 100 N Tampa St Ste 4100 Tampa FL 33602-3644 Office Phone: 813-227-6611. Business E-Mail: gthomas@khlaw.com.

**THOMAS, GREGORY HALL,** psychology professor; b. Ocala, Fla., May 17, 1957; s. Karon William and Virginia Mae Thomas; BA, U. Ctrl. Okla., 1979; MA, Angelo State U., 1994; PhD, U. Okla., Oklahoma City, 2000. Adj. instr. Cameron U., Lawton, Okla., 1995—96, instr., 1997—98; psychol. intern U. Fla. Counseling Ctr., Gainesville, Fla., 1996—97; psychometrist Mental Health Ctr., Newport News, Va., 1998—99; counselor Garden City (Kans.) C.C., Kans., 1999—2000, instr. psychology and sociology, 2000—. Faculty senate mem. Garden City C.C., 2001—. Contbr. articles to profl. jours. Grant writer Habitat for Humanities, Garden City, 2001; Sunday sch. tchr. Bible Christian Ch., Garden City, 2002; active Garden Valley Ch., 2003—; bd. mem. Big Bros./Big Sisters, Garden City, 2001—02. Mem.: Assn. for Pro Basketball Rsch., Pro Football Rschrs. Assn. Home: 909 Amy St Garden City KS 67846 Office: Garden City CC 801 Campus Dr Garden City KS 67846

**THOMAS, HARRY K., JR.,** former ambassador; m. Ericka O. Smith-Thomas; 1 child, Casey Merie Eunice. Grad., Coll. Holy Cross; postgrad., Columbia U. With U.S. Fgn. Svc., New Delhi, Harare, Kaduna, and Lima, 1984; staff asst. Asst. U.S. Sec. for African Affairs; spl. asst. Under Sec. Polit. Affairs; dep. dir. to dir. Ops. Ctr. US State Dept., sr. watch officer; dir. for South Asia Nat. Security Coun., White House, Washington, 2001—02; US amb. to Bangladesh US Dept. State, Dhaka, Bangladesh, 2003—05.*

**THOMAS, HAYWARD,** manufacturing executive; b. LA, Aug. 9, 1921; s. Charles Sparks and Julia (Hayward) T.; m. Phyllis Mary Wilson, July 1, 1943; children: H. David, Steven T. BS, U. Calif., Berkeley, 1943. Registered profl. engr. Staff engr. Joshua Hendy Corp., Los Angeles, 1946-50; prodn. mgr. Byron Jackson Co., Los Angeles, 1950-55; mgr. mfg. Frigidaire div. Gen. Motors Corp., Dayton, Ohio, 1955-70; group v.p. White Motor Corp., Cleve., 1971-73; sr. v.p. Broan Mfg. Co., Hartford, Wis., 1973-85; pres. Jensen Industries, Los Angeles, 1985-87; retired, 1987. Served to lt. USNR, 1943-46. Mem. Soc. Mfg. Engrs. (chmn. mfg. mgmt. council 1984-86). Republican. Episcopalian. Avocations: tennis, fishing. Home: 1320 Granvia Altamira Palos Verdes Peninsula CA 90274-2006

**THOMAS, HAZEL BEATRICE,** state official; b. Franklin, Tenn. d. William Henry Fuller and Mattie Betty (Covington) Fuller Young; m. Charles B. Thomas (dec. 1969); children: Charles Bradford Jr., Deborah Carlotta (dec.). BA, Fisk U., 1946; MA, Tenn. State U., 1972. Cert. elem. and secondary tchr., Tenn. Tchr. elem. Met.-Nashville Sch., 1954—87; rsch. assoc. Johns Hopkins U., Balt. 1978—79, Marquette U., Milw., 1979—86; exec. asst. to commr. edn. Tenn. Dept. Edn., Nashville, 1987—. Cons. Peer Mediated Learning System, Nashville, 1980-82; instr. Met. Sch. Tchr. Ctr., Nashville, 1985-87; mem. tech. assistance team for high sch. that work, So. Regional Edn. Bd., 1998-99; nat. disseminator student team learning rsch. project, Johns Hopkins U., 1978-1979. Author training modules Substitute Teaching, Tchr. Aides. Pres. Davidson County Dem. Women, Nashville, 1985-87; v.p. Tenn. Fedn. Dem. Women, 1989-91, pres., 2001—; pres. elect Nashville Women's Polit. Caucus, 1991—; pres. Tenn. Women's Polit. Caucus 1994-95; mem. administrv. com. of bd. Nat. Women's Polit. Caucus, 1993-95, v.p., 1995—, v.p. edn. and tng., 2001—; mem. Tenn. Leadership, Inc., 1992—; spkr., polit. trainer U.S. Info. Agy., Nairobi, Kenya, 1997; mem. exec. bd. Citizen's Com. for Ann. Gov.'s Prayer Breakfast, 1992—; mem. exec. com. Tenn. Dem. Party, 2001—; mem. exec. com. Bellevue C. of C.; pres. Tenn. Fedn. Dem. Women, 2001-03; v.p. Nat. Fedn. Dem. Women, 2002-05, 3d v.p., 2005—; mem. pub. edn. and govt. com. Metro. Govt. Nashville, Tenn., 2002-03; apptd. to pub. ednl. and govt. access oversight com. Nashville Mayor Purcell, 2003—; apptd. to pub. edn. govt. com. Metro Nashville City Coun., 2002 Recipient Svc. to Edn. and Teaching Profession award Nat. Coun. Negro Women, 1988; Nat. Def. Edn. Act scholar, 1965, 67. Mem. Am. Bus. Womens Assn. (charter), Tenn. Edn. Assn. (pres. dept. classroom tchr. 1974-75, state dept. affiliate, pres. 1988-Ed. c90), Bellevue C. of C. (bd. govs. 1990-91, edn. chair 2002-03), Assn. Classroom Tchrs. (pres. S.E. region 1975-76), Met. Nashville Edn. Assn. (exec. bd. 1971-77), Bellevue Sertoma Club (life, pres. 1990-91), Nat. Women's Polit. Caucus (v.p. 1995—), Nat. Assn. Dem. Women (v.p., 2003-05, named Woman of Distinction for Tenn., 2002, 03), Nat. Fedn. Dem. Women (v.p. 2003). Baptist. Avocations: reading, bridge. Office: Tenn Dept Edn Andrew Johnson Tower 710 James Robertson Pkwy Nashville TN 37243-1219 Office Phone: 615-532-5740. E-mail: hazel.thomas@state.tn.us.

**THOMAS, HELEN AMELIA (MRS. DOUGLAS B. CORNELL),** editor-in-chief, former White House correspondent; b. Winchester, Ky., Aug. 4, 1920; d. George and Mary (Thomas) T.; m. Douglas B. Cornell. BA, Wayne

State U., 1942; BA in Law, Mount Vernon Coll., 1999; LHD, Wayne State U., 1974, U. Detroit, 1979; LLD, Ea. Mich. State U., 1972, Ferris State Coll., 1978; LLD (hon.), Brown U., 1986, St. Bonaventure U., 1988, Franklin Marshall U., 1989, No. Mich. U., 1989, Northeastern U., 1990, Skidmore Coll., 1992, Susquehanna U., 1993, Sage Coll., 1994, U. Mo., 1994, Franklin Coll., 1995, Mich. State U., 1996, Potsdam U., 1998, A Willenberg Univ., 1999, Milliken U., 2002, Am. U. Beirut, 2003, Western Ky. U., 2005, Cabrini Coll., 2005; LittD, Ohio Dominican U., 2004. With United Press Radio, UPI, 1943-2000, wire svc. reporter Washington, 1943-74; White House corr. Washington, 1970; White House bur. chief UPI, Washington, 1974-2000; columnist Hearst Newspapers, 2000—. Author: Dateline White House, Front Row at the White House: My Life and Times, 1999, Thanks for the Memories Mr. President: Wit and Wisdom from the Front Row at the White House, 2002, Watchdogs of Democracy?: The Waning Washington Press Corps and How It Has Failed the Public, 2006; columnist Hearst Newspapers. Named one of the 25 Most Influential Women in Am., World Almanac; recipient Woman of Yr. in Comm. award, Ladies Home Jour., 1975, 4th Estate award, Nat. Press Club, 1984, Journalism award, U. Mo., Al Newharth award, 1990, Ralph McGill award, 1995, Lifetime award, Internat. Media Found., Internat. Women's Press Found., 1996, Lowell Thomas award, Marist Coll., 2001, Kahlil Gibran award, 2003, NOW award, 2003, Torch Bearer award, Planned Parenthood award, Physician Social Responsibility award, Utah Am. Women of Yr., 2004, Eleanor Roosevelt Legacy award, 2004, Lifetime Achievement award, Glamour mag. Mem. Women's Nat. Press Club (pres. 1959-60, William Allen White Journalism award), Am. Newspaper Women's Club (past v.p.), White House Corrs. Assn. (pres. 1976, Helen Thomas Lifetime Achievement award 1998), Nat. Newspaper Assn. (Lifetime award 2002), Gridiron Club (pres. 1993), Sigma Delta Chi (fellow, Hall of Fame), Delta Sigma Phi (hon.). Achievements include fighting hard for women's representation in the fields of journalism and politics, and in clubs and organizations where they had been excluded; the first women officer of the National Press Club, the White House Correspondents Association, and first women member of the Gridiron Club; entered into political reporting in 1961, when she began filing stories about the Kennedy administration. She has covered nine presidents; only woman print journalist to go on President Nixon's historic trip to China and traveled with presidents Ford, Carter, Reagan, Bush, Sr., Clinton, & Bush; first female White House chief of a wire service in 1974; considered the "dean of Washington press corps" and she was allowed to ask the first question at the presdl. conferences; referred to as "The First Lady of the Press"; at the end of her first presidential press conference in 1961, she said "Thank you, Mr. President", following a tradition, which recently ended in 2003; covered every presdl. econ. summit until 1999. Office: Hearst Corp 959 8th Ave New York NY 10019 Office Phone: 202-263-6437. Business E-Mail: helent@hearstdc.com.

**THOMAS, HOWARD,** business educator; b. Jan. 31, 1943; BSc, London U., 1964, MSc, 1965; MBA, U. Chgo., 1966; PhD, Edinburgh U., 1970. From prof. dept. bus. adminstrn. to dean emeritus U. Ill., Urbana-Champaign, 1980—2001, dean emeritus Commerce and Bus. Adminstrn., 2001—; dean Warwick Bus. Sch. U. Warwick, Coventry, U.K., 2000—. Vis. prof. MIT, 1986-87, Northwestern U., 1990. Office: Warwick Bus Sch U Warwick Coventry CV4 7AL England Office Phone: 44-2476-524534. E-mail: Howard.Thomas@wbs.ac.uk.

**THOMAS, HOWARD PAUL,** civil engineer, consultant; b. Cambridge, Mass., Aug. 20, 1942; s. Charles Calvin and Helen Elizabeth (Hook) T.; m. Ingrid Nybo, Jan. 4, 1969; children: Kent Michael, Lisa Karen, Karina Michelle. BS in Engring., U. Mich., 1965, MS in Engring., 1966. Registered profl. engr., Alaska, Calif. Engr. Ove Arup & Ptnrs., London, 1966-67; project engr. Woodward-Clyde Cons., San Francisco, 1967-73, assoc. Anchorage, 1975-89; spl. cons. Cowiconsult Cons., Copenhagen, 1973-75; prin. engr. Harding-Lawson Assocs., Anchorage, 1989-90; v.p., chief engr. EMCON Alaska, Inc., Anchorage, 1991-94; gen. mgr. Internat. Tech. Corp., Anchorage, 1994-96; assoc. GeoEngrs., Inc., Anchorage, 1996—2002; prin. engr. CH2M Hill, Anchorage, 2001—; mem. Anchorage Mayor's Geotech. Adv. Commn., 1997—2003. Chmn. Nat. Tech. Coun. Cold Regions Engring., 1988-89, chmn. com. program and publs., 1982-84; chmn. 4th Internat. Conf. Cold Regions Engring., Anchorage, 1986; liaison NAS/Nat. Rsch. Coun. Polar Rsch. Bd., 1989-99. Contbr. articles to profl. jours. Fellow ASCE (pres. Anchorage chpt. 1985-86, chair mgmt. group A 1996-97, pres. Alaska sect. 1998-99, mem. nat. policy com. 2005—, named Alaskan Engr. of Yr. 1986, Harold R. Peyton award 2002); mem. Internat. Soc. for Soil Mechanics and Geotech. Engring., Cons. Engrs. Coun. Alaska (pres. 1989-90), Am. Cons. Engrs. Coun. (nat. dir. 1990-91), Project Mgmt. Inst. (v.p. Alaska chpt. 1991-95), Toastmasters (pres. Anchorage club 1984), Sons of Norway (pres. Anchorage lodge 2000-02). Lutheran. Avocations: french horn, travel, skiing, sailing, album collecting. Home: PO Box 1235 Metrotown RPO Burnaby BC V5H 4J8 Canada Personal E-mail: hthomas@ch2m.com.

**THOMAS, HUW FRANCIS,** dean, dental educator; BDS, U. London; Guy's Hosp., 1975; MS in Dental Rsch., U. Rochester, 1978; PhD in Biomedical Sci., U. Conn., 1986. Cert. pediatric dentistry Eastman Dental Ctr., U. Rochester, 1978. Postdoctoral fellow. NIH, 1980—84; asst. prof. pediatric dentistry U. Tex. Health Sci. Ctr., San Antonio, 1978—80; assoc. prof. pediatric dentistry dept. U. Conn. Health Ctr., Conn., 1980—92; prof., chmn. dept. pediatric dentistry U. Tex. Health Sci. Ctr., San Antonio, 1992—2003, prof. dept. pediat. & cellular and structural biology; prof., dean Sch. Dentistry, U. Ala., Birmingham, 2004—. Sci. cons. ADA Commn. on Dental Accreditation. Reviewer: American Journal of Anatomy, Archives of Oral Biology, Journal of Dental Education. Recipient New Investigator Research award, NIH, 1985. Fellow: Internat. Coll. Dentists, Am. Coll. Dentists, Am. Acad. Pediat. Dentistry; mem.: AAAS (mem. at large sec. on dentistry and oral health sci.), Am. Assn. Dental Rsch. (mem. nominating com.), Am. Acad. Pediat. (mem. exec. com. pediat. dentistry sect.), Omicron Kappa Upsilon. Office: U Ala Birmingham Sch Dentistry SDB 406 1530 3rd Ave S Birmingham AL 35294-0007 Office Phone: 205-934-4720. Office Fax: 205-975-6544. Business E-Mail: hft@uab.edu.

**THOMAS, IRV,** writer, journalist; b. San Francisco, Apr. 14, 1927; s. David Goldstein and Minnie Resnick; m. Vivian Laura Allen, Nov. 30, 1956; life ptnr.: Alice Joy. BA, U. Wash., 1990. Pub./editor Black Bart Brigade/Yin Times, Canyon, Calif., 1971-83; editor Earthstewards jour./newsletter, Bainbridge Island, Wash., 1985-89; pub./editor Ripening Seasons Jour., Seattle, 1995—2003. Tchr., workshop organizer Finding a Way Out, San Francisco, 1971-75; presenter World Futurist Conf., Toronto, Ont., 1980, Assn. for Humanistic Psychology Conv., Estes Park, Colo., 1976, Calif. Life. Assn. Conv., Disneyland, 1972. Author, illustrator: Innocence Abroad, 1994, rev. edit., 2001, Derelict Days..., 2004, A Seasoned Life, 2006; contbr. anthology: Alternative Papers, 1982; contbr. articles to profl. jours. Housing activist Seattle Sr. Housing Program Advocates, 1996-99; co-founder Afterlife.org, 2001. Avocation: hitchhiking. Home: 6545 Ravenna Ave NE #307 Seattle WA 98115 Personal E-mail: irvthom1@comcast.net.

**THOMAS, ISIAH LORD, III,** professional basketball coach, professional sports team executive, retired professional basketball player; b. Chgo., Apr. 30, 1961; s. Mary Thomas; m. Lynn Kendall, 1985; children: Joshua, Lauren. BA in Criminal Justice, Ind. U., 1987. Profl. basketball player Detroit Pistons, 1981—94; pres. NBA Players Assn., 1989—94; v.p. Toronto Raptors, 1994—97, co-owner, exec. v.p. basketball ops., 1994—98; sportscaster NBC Sports, N.Y.C., 1997—2000; owner, chmn., CEO Continental Basketball Assn., 1999—2001; founder Enlighten Sports, Inc., 1999—; head coach Ind. Pacers, Indpls., 2000—03; pres. basketball ops. NY Knicks, 2003—, head coach, 2006—. Named Michiganian of the Yr., 1985; named to NBA All-Rookie team, 1982, All-Star Team, 1982—93, All NBA First Team, 1984, 1985, 1986, Basketball Hall of Fame, 2000; recipient All-Star Team MVP award, 1984, 1986, NBA Playoff MVP award, 1990, NBA Finals MVP, 1990. Achievements include being a mem. of U.S. Olympic Basketball Team, 1980; playing on NBA Championship Teams, 1989-90. Office: NY Knicks Two Pennsylvania Plz New York NY 10121-0091*

**THOMAS, J. EARL,** retired physicist; b. Seattle, Sept. 7, 1918; s. Jacob Earl and Ursula May (Johnson) T.; m. Margaret Louise Johnston, June 15, 1977; children— Richard Bruce, Jacob Earl, John Calvin, James Hayden, Denise May, Stillman Jefferson. AB, Johns Hopkins U., 1939; PhD, Calif. Inst. Tech., 1943. Group leader rocket devel. Calif. Inst. Tech., Pasadena, 1942-45; group leader Manhattan Project, U. Calif., Los Alamos, 1945-46; asst. prof. elec. engring. M.I.T., Cambridge, 1946-51; mem. tech. staff Bell Telephone Labs., Murray Hill, NJ, 1951-52; group leader M.I.T. Lincoln Labs., Lexington, 1952-55; prof., chmn. dept. physics Wayne State U., Detroit, 1955-59; dir. research Sylvania Electric, Woburn, Mass., 1959-62; mgr. solid state devel. IBM, Poughkeepsie, NY, 1962-64; mgr. new product devel. Gen. Instrument Co., Newark, 1964-67; v.p. Carman Sapphire Co., Reseda, Calif., 1967-70; cons. Warnecke Electron Tubes, Des Plaines, Ill., 1970-71; dir. components research Victor Comptometer Co., Des Plaines, 1971-75; mgr. advanced devel. NCR Corp., Ithaca, NY, 1975-84. Cons. pvt. cos. and govt. agys. Contbr. articles to sci. jours.; patentee in field. Active S.E. Asian refugee resettlement program. Recipient Service award U.S. Office Sci. Research and Devel., 1946 Fellow: IEEE (Millennium medal), Am. PHys. Soc.; mem.: Tau Beta Pi, Phi Beta Kappa, Sigma Xi. Democrat. Presbyterian. Home: 323 Savage Farm Dr Ithaca NY 14850-6503 E-mail: ethomas4@twcny.rr.com.

**THOMAS, J. MARK,** sociologist, educator, minister; b. Ft. Worth, Dec. 20, 1947; s. Jacob Gillespie and Eleanor Rose (Geivett) T.; m. Jacquelyn Higby, Sept. 2, 1978; children: Megan Lane, Drew Martin. BA, Tex. Christian U., 1971, MDiv, 1974; PhD, U. Chgo., 1983. Ordained to ministry United Ch. of Christ, 1974. Asst. prof. philosophy and religion, chaplain Drury Coll., Springfield, Mo., 1983-85; adj. asst. prof. religion, chaplain Ripon (Wis.) Coll., 1985-87; vis. asst. prof. philosophy and religion Beloit (Wis.) Coll., 1987-89; sr. rsch. fellow Au Sable Inst. Environ. Studies, Mancelona, Mich., 1989—. Sociology instr., chair dept. social sci. Madison Area Tech. Coll. Author: Ethics and Technoculture, 1987, (with others) Being and Doing, 1987, Philosophy and Technology, Vol. 10, 1990, Religion in the New Millennium, 2001, Encyclopedia of Science, Technology and Ethics, 2005; editor: Paul Tillich, The Spiritual Situation in Our Technical Society, 1988, God and Capitalism, 1991, Religion in the New Millennium, 2001. Chmn. planning com. Congress of Sci., Tech. and Religion for the Parliament of World Religion, 1993. Recipient Disting. Tchr. Yr., Madison Area Tech. Coll., 1999. Mem. Midwest Sociol. Soc., Communitarian Network. Democrat. Mem. United Ch. of Christ. Home: 816 Lincoln St Madison WI 53711-2163 Office: Madison Area Tech Coll Downtown Edn Ctr 211 N Carroll St Madison WI 53703-2211 E-mail: jmarkthomas@charter.net.

**THOMAS, JACQUELYN MAY,** librarian; b. Mechanicsburg, Pa., Jan. 26, 1932; d. William John and Gladys Elizabeth (Warren) Harvey; m. David Edward Thomas, Aug. 28, 1954; children: Lesley J., Courtenay J., Hilary A. BA summa cum laude, Gettysburg Coll., 1954; student, U. N.C., 1969; MEd, U. N.H., 1971. Libr. Phillips Exeter Acad., Exeter, NH, 1971-77, acad. libr., 1977—. Chair governing bd. Child Care Ctr., 1987-91; chair Com. to Enhance Status of Women, Exeter, 1981-84; chair Loewenstein Com., Exeter, 1982—; pres. Cum Laude Soc., Exeter, 1984-86; James H. Ottaway Jr. prof., 1990—; mem. bldg. com. Exeter Pub. Libr., 1980s. Author: No New Eng. Coun. for Women in Ind. Schs., 1985-87; chmn. Lamont Poetry Program, Exeter, 1984-86. Editor: The Design of the Library: A Guide to Sources of Information, 1981, Rarities of Our Time: The Special Collections of the Phillips Exeter Academy Library; pub.: Memorial Minutes, Phillips Exeter Academy, 1936-2002, Friends of the Academy Library, Collected Letters Book, Class of 1945 special collections brochure, other Phillips Exeter materials. Libr. trustee, treas. Exeter Day Sch., 1965-69; bd. Exeter Hosp. Vols., 1954-59; mem. Exeter Hosp. Corp., 1978—; bd. dirs. Greater Portsmouth Cmty. Found., 1990—; active AAC&U, On Campus with Women, Wellesley Coll. Ctr. for Rsch. on Women; mem. People to People Amb. Program, sch. and youth svcs. libr. del. to People's Rep. China, 1998. Grantee N.H. Coun. for Humanities, 1981-82, NEH, 1982; recipient Lillian Radford trust award, 1989. Mem. ALA, Internat. Assn. Sch. Librs., New Eng. Libr. Assn., N.J., Ednl. Media Assn., New Eng. Assn. Ind. Sch. Librs., Am. Assn. Sch. Libris (chmn. non-pub. sch. sect.), Phi Beta Kappa. Home: 17 Eagle Dr Newmarket NH 03857 Office: Class of 1945 Libr Phillips Exeter Acad 20 Main St Exeter NH 03833-2460 Office Phone: 603-777-3328. Office Fax: 603-777-4389. Business E-Mail: jthomas@exeter.edu.

**THOMAS, JAMES BERT, JR.,** retired federal agency administrator; b. Tallahassee, Mar. 16, 1935; s. James Bert and Stella E. (Lewis) T.; m. Sharon Mae Kelly, June 16, 1962; children: James Bert III, Mary Elizabeth, John Christopher. BS, Fla. State U., 1957. C.P.A., Fla. Spl. auditor Office State Comptr., Jacksonville, Fla., 1958; jr. auditor J.D.A. Holley & Co., C.P.A.'s, Tallahassee, 1959; sr. auditor Office of the State Auditor, Tallahassee, 1959-60; trainee, audit dir. HUD audit divsn., Washington, 1960-71; asst. dir. Bur. Accounts ICC, Washington, 1972-75; dir. Bur. Accounts, 1977-80; insp. gen. U.S. Dept. HUD, Washington, 1975-77, U.S. Dept. Edn., Washington, 1980-95; dir. auditing Office of the Gov., State of Fla., Tallahassee, 1995—2004; ret., 2004. Mem. Pres.'s Coun. Integrity and Efficiency, chmn. audit stds. subcom., 1984-95, chmn. audit com., 1989-90. Mem. AICPA (strategic planning com. 1987-90, chmn. govt. auditing stds. adv. coun. 1991—), Inst. Internal Auditors (trustee Rsch. Found. 1991-92), Assn. Govt. Accts. (chmn. fin. mgmt. stds. bd. 1985-86), Accts. Roundtable. Roman Catholic. Home: 4737 Tory Sound Ln Unit 601 Tallahassee FL 32309-2266 Office: Exec Office of Governor Rm 2107 The Capitol Tallahassee FL 32399-0001

**THOMAS, JAMES EDWARD,** accountant; b. Darlington, S.C., Oct. 18, 1944; s. Willie Thomas and Cleola (Sawyer) T.; m. Joan Yvette Grant, Mar. 15, 1945; 1 child, James E. II. BS in Acctg., Johnson C. Smith Coll., Charlotte, N.C., 1966; MA in Fin., C.W. Post Coll., Greenvale, N.Y., 1980; PhD in Fdn. Fordham U., 1996, MBA, Pace U., 1976. Cert. paralegal. Asst. mgr. Mfrs. Hanover Trust, N.Y.C., 1970-78, Met. Savs. Bank, N.Y.C., 1978-81; auditor N.Y. State Dept. Social Svcs., N.Y.C., 1981-83; acct. N.Y.C. Bd. Edn., 1983-86; acct., agt. IRS, N.Y.C., 1987-99; dir. fin. N.Y.C. Dept. Design and Constrn., Long Island City, 1999—. Instr. Katherine L. Gibbs, Inc., N.Y.C., 1987-89. Mem.: Internat. Platform Assn., Nat. Soc. Pub. Accts., Nat. Assn. Sch. Bus. Ofcls., Am. Mgmt. Assn., Assn. MBA Execs., Sigma Rho Sigma. Avocations: woodworking, basketball, baseball, track, reading. Home: 99-72 66th Rd# 3R Rego Park NY 11374

**THOMAS, JAMES EDWARD, JR.,** brokerage house executive; b. Atlanta, Apr. 23, 1950; s. James Edward and Dortha Jean (White) Thomas; m. Leslie Ann Stagmaier, Sept. 6, 1975; children: Steele Stagmaier, Katherine Mills. BA magna cum laude, U. Ga., 1972, JD cum laude, 1975. Mgr. Genuine Parts Co., Atlanta, 1975-77; v.p. Robinson Humphrey Co., Atlanta, 1977-94; ptnr. J.C. Bradford and Co., Atlanta, 1994—2000; mng. dir. Wachovia Securities, Ga., 2000—02; chmn., CEO Stillpoint Advisors, Inc., 2003—. Bd. dirs. Enstar Comm. Corp., The Kinston Group, Inc., Atlanta, Tophat Soccer Club, Atlanta, Hall's Boathouse, Inc., Lakemont, Ga., Vista Environ. Info., Inc., San Diego. Pres. Castlewood Civic Orgn., Inc., Atlanta; mem. Lake Rabun Homeowners Assn., Lakemont, Ga.; mem. bd. advisors U. Ga., Habitat for Humanity. Mem. Internat. Platform Assn., Ga. Bar Assn., La Societe des Tetes Grandes, Capital City Club, U. Ga. LEADS Adv. Bd., Ga Tennis Found. (treas., trustee). Republican. Episcopalian. Avocations: boating, tennis, golf.

**THOMAS, JAMES PATRICK,** special education educator; b. Chgo., Sept. 24, 1946; s. Jacque Anthony and Dorothy Lucille (Brown) T.; m. Cathy E. Hanks, Sept. 29, 1979 (div. Aug. 1990); 1 child, Nicholas Jacque. BA in History and Polit. Sci., Drake U., 1973; MS in Pub. Adminstrn., Troy State U., 1983; MS in Spl. Educ., Johns Hopkins U., 1994, cert. advanced grad. studies, 1994. cert. spl. educator. Commd. 2nd lt. USAF, 1973, advanced through grades to maj., 1985; missile launch officer, instr., crew comdr., contr. 91st Strategic Missile Wing, Minot, N.D., 1974-78; exec. officer, asst. ops. officer, resource advisor 6916th Electronic Security Squadron, Hellenikon Air Base, Greece, 1978-81; chief programs br. 6940th Electronic Security Wing, Ft. Meade, Md., 1981-82; program mgr. USAF Ops. Security Hq USAF/XOEO Directorate of Electronic Combat, Washington, 1982-85; intelligence collection activities mgr./chief Hdqrs. U.S. European Command, Stuttgart, Germany, 1986-88; signals intelligence planning staff officer Nat. Security Agy., Ft. Meade, 1988-90; cons. spl. edn. Balt., 1991—. Adj. faculty mem. Catonsville (Md.) C.C., 1991—; spl. educator Howard County Sch. System, Columbia, 1992-94, Boonsborro (Md.) Middle Sch., 1994-96, Hiatt Mid. Sch., Des Moines, 1996-98, Johnston (Iowa) Mid. Sch., 1998-99, Johnston H.S., 1999-2000, Variety Sch., Las Vegas, Nev., 2000-04, spl. edn. instrnl. facilitator Victoria Fertitta Mid. Sch., 2004-05, C.J. Lawrence Mid. Sch., 2005—. Author: (pamphlet) Your Rights to Legal Advice, 1994; co-author: The Outcome of a Services Evaluation for Families of Vietnam Vets. with Children with Disabilities in the Balt. Met. Area, 1995. Pres. Cath. Men Parish Athens, Greece, 1979—81, Minot AFB, ND, 1975—78. With USN, 1964—73. Decorated Purple Heart, 2 Def. Meritorious Svc. medals, Meritorious Svc. medals, Air Force Commendation medal, Air medal, Air Force Achievement medal, Navy Combat Action Ribbon, Vietnam Gallantry Cross. Mem.: KC, VFW (life), Swiftboat Sailors Assn. Inc. (pres. 1995—2002), Am. Legion China Post 1, Assn. Air Force Missileers (life), Vets. Vietnam War (life), Navy League (life), Mil. Order Purple Heart (life), Ret. Officers Assn. (life), Air Force Assn. (life), Disabled Am. Vets. (life), Phoenix Soc., Soaring Assn. Am., Phi Delta Gamma. Roman Catholic. Avocations: pilot of sailplanes, sailing, snorkeling, golf, running. Home: 1929 High Mesa Dr Henderson NV 89012-6182

**THOMAS, JAMES WILLIAM,** lawyer; b. N.Y.C., May 12, 1949; s. Howard and Alice (Brennan) T.; m. Cecilia Coleman Goad, July 7, 1973; children: James William, Brennan McKinney. BS, U. Dayton, 1971; JD, Ohio No. U., 1974. Bar: Ohio 1974. U.S. Dist. Ct. Ohio 1976 Ptnr Farley & Thomas, Eaton, Ohio, 1974-89; pvt. practice Eaton, 1989—. Village solicitor Village of Lewisburg (Ohio), 1977-81, Village of Verona (Ohio), 1979-81; asst. pros. atty. Preble County (Ohio), 1980-81. Mem. Preble County Cmty. Corrections Planing Bd. Fellow Ohio State Bar Found.; mem. ABA, Ohio State Bar Assn., Ohio State Bar Coll., Ohio Acad. Trial Lawyers, Ohio Assn. Criminal Def. Lawyers, Preble county Bar Assn. (pres. 1982-84), Comm. Improvement Corp., Eaton Country Club, Rotary (dir. 1980-87, pres. 1987-88). Republican. Roman Catholic. Avocations: boating, tennis. Home: 761 Vinland Cv Eaton OH 45320-2536 Office: 112 N Barron St Eaton OH 45320-1702

**THOMAS, JANET Y.,** political science professor, researcher; d. Enoch Thornton and Florence Rose Thomas. BA, Norfolk State U., 1991; EdM, Widener U., 1997; PhD, U. Ill., 2000. Rsch. assoc. Hahnemann U., Phila., 1995—97; assoc. rsch. scientist Johns Hopkins U., Balt., 2000—03; with dept. academic support programs Office of Dir. Provost, U. Pa., Phila., 2003—. Author: Educating Drug-Exposed Children, 2004. Mem.: Am. Edn. Assn., Am. Edn. Rsch., Kappa Delta Pi, Phi Delta Kappa. Office: 220 S 40th St Ste 240 Philadelphia PA 19106 Business E-Mail: janety@pobox.upenn.edu.

**THOMAS, JEFFREY CONE,** financial executive, consultant; b. New Orleans, Oct. 10, 1941; s. Eads Poitevent and Virginia Lee (King) T.; m. Brenda Gayle Ballard, June 7, 1969 (div. Mar. 1972). BA, La. State U., 1965. CLU; ChFC; CFP; CFS. Mgmt. trainee Am. Bank and Trust Co., Baton Rouge, 1965—68; supr. Travelers Ins. Co., Baton Rouge, 1968—71; dist. dir. Conn. Gen. Life Ins. Co., Baton Rouge, 1971—74; pres., CEO Pension & Profit Sharing Cons., Baton Rouge, 1974—77; pres. Fin. Advisor & Cons., Baton Rouge, 1977—. Adj. instr. adult eve. classes Coll. Fin. Planning, 1987-92; cons. Ethyl Corp., Baton Rouge, 1982, Dow Chem., Plaquemine, La., 1986. Vol. ARC, Baton Rouge, 1965—69; mem. adminstrv. bd. First Meth. Ch., Baton Rouge, 1987—89. Avocations: golf, tennis, fishing, gardening. Office: Fin Advisor & Cons PO Box 65238 Baton Rouge LA 70896-5238 Office Phone: 225-293-1035.

**THOMAS, JEFFREY T.,** lawyer; b. Nov. 15, 1957; BA in Polit. sci., Univ. Calif., San Diego, 1979; JD magna cum laude, Univ. San Diego, 1982. Bar: Calif. 1982. Law clk. Hon. Gerald Brown Calif. Ct. of Appeals (4th dist.), 1982—83; joined Gibson Dunn & Crutcher LLP, Orange County, Calif., 1983—, former co-ptnr-in-charge, Orange County office, ptnr.-in-charge and co-chair litig. practice group, 1999—. Comments editor San Diego Law Rev., 1981—82; co-author: Intellectual Property Law, Damages and Remedies, 2000. Mem.: Orange County Bar Assn., Calif. Bar Assn., Pacific Legal Found. (bd. trustees), San Diego Sch. of Law Bd. Dir., Chapman Univ. Exec. Fellows (bd. dir.), Orange County Bus. Coun. (bd. dir.), Assn. for Corp. Growth (Orange County chapter) (bd. dir.). Office: Gibson Dunn & Crutcher LLP Jamboree Ctr Ste 1400 4 Park Plz Irvine CA 92614-8557 Office Phone: 949-451-3967. Office Fax: 949-475-4670. Business E-Mail: jtthomas@gibsondunn.com.

**THOMAS, JENNIE See ORR, JENNIE**

**THOMAS, JEREMIAH LINDSAY, III,** lawyer; b. Wilmington, Del., June 20, 1946; s. Jeremiah Lindsay Jr. and Dorothy Eleanor (Conway) T.; m. Clara Ewing Ruthrauff, Oct. 17, 1981; children: Catherine Ewing, Lindsay Barlow. BA, U. Va., 1968, JD, 1972. Bar: N.Y. 1973. Assoc. Simpson Thacher & Bartlett, N.Y.C., 1972-79, ptnr., 1979—. Mem. Met. Golf Assn. (legal counsel 1984—, exec. com. 1992—98, dir. Found. 1992—98), Assn. Bar of City of N.Y., N.Y. State Bar Assn. Office: Simpson Thacher & Bartlett 425 Lexington Ave Fl 28 New York NY 10017-3954 Office Phone: 212-455-7110. Business E-Mail: jthomas@stblaw.com.

**THOMAS, JERRY ARTHUR,** soil scientist; b. Logansport, Ind., Mar. 5, 1942; s. Purnal Kidd and Dorothy Helen (Smith) T.; m. Virginia Amy York, Oct. 17, 1964; 1 child, Clark. Edward. BS in Agronomy and Soil Chemistry, Purdue U., 1965; MS in Soil Fertility, Pa. State U., 1969. Fin. chemistry dept. Purdue Univ., West Lafayette, Ind., 1963, tech. aid USDA, ARS, agronomy dept., 1963-65; grad. teaching asst. agronomy dept. Pa. State U., University Park, 1965-67; soil scientist USDA Soil Conservation Svc., Indpls., 1967-85, Ind. State Bd. Health, Indpls., 1985—. Com. mem. Ind. State 4-H Rabbit com., West Lafayette, 1976-2000. Author publs. in field including Classification of the Sloping Soils of the West Baden Group in Monroe County, Ind., 1978, Soil Survey of Monroe County, Ind., 1981, Soil Survey of Lawrence County, Ind., 1985, Availability of Conservation Tillage Planting Systems for Northwestern Ind., 1985. Asst. scoutmaster Boy Scouts Am., Rensselaer, Ind., 1982-92. Recipient Innovative award Coun. State Govts., 1988; named Environ. Health Specialist of Yr., Environ. Health Assn., 1993. Mem. Am. Soc. Agronomy, Soil Sci. Soc. Am., Soil and Water Conservation Soc. Am., Ind. Acad. Sci., Ind. Environ. Health Assn. Profl. Soil Classifiers, Ind. Environtl. Health Assn., Masons, Eastern Star. Mem. Christian Ch. (Disciples Of Christ). Home: 301 S Park Ave Rensselaer IN 47978-3037 Office: Ind State Bd Health Divsn Sanitary Engring 5E 2 N Meridian St Indianapolis IN 46204-3003 Office Phone: 317-233-7177. Business E-Mail: jthomas@isdh.in.gov.

**THOMAS, JIM GUS,** music educator; b. El Paso, Tex., July 10, 1945; s. Gus Demetrios Thomopoulos and Antigone Mourgelas; m. Evi Deligianni Thomas, Aug. 15, 1970 (div. May 18, 1998); children: Gus James, Georgianna. Bachelor Music Edn., Ariz. State U., Tempe, AZ, 1969, MA, 1975. Music educator Creighton Sch. Dist., Phoenix, Ariz., 1970—; choral, gen. music educator Isaac Sch. Dist., Phoenix, Ariz., 1972—76; founder, orchestral strings educator Paradise Valley Sch. Dist., Phoenix, Ariz., 1976—79; music educator Cartwright Sch. Dist., Phoenix, Ariz., 1979—. Dir., educator Summer Music Camp, Prescott, Ariz., 1993—; instr. Honors String Orch., 2002—, The Funky Fiddlers, 2002—; music curriculum coord. Cartwright Sch. Dist., Phoenix, 2002—; adminstrv. asst. to dist. music cons., 2002—. Composer: (greek folk dance for clarinet trio) Pentozalis. Mem.: Ariz. Music Educators Assn. (O.M. Hartsell Excellence Tchg. Music award 2002), Am. String Teachers Assn., Music Educators Nat. Conf. D-Liberal. Greek Orthodox. Achievements include two tours to Europe with music students. Avocations: biking, travel, learning and performing multicultural music and instruments. Home: 4905 E Robin Lane Phoenix AZ 85054 Office: Peracta Elementary School 7125 West Encanto Phoenix AZ 85033

**THOMAS, JIMMY LYNN,** retired treasurer; b. Mayfield, Ky., Aug. 3, 1941; s. Alben Stanley and Emma Laura (Alexander) T.; m. Kristin H. Kent, Oct. 1986; children: James Nelson, Carter Danforth. BS, U. Ky., 1963; MBA, Columbia U., 1964. Fin. analyst Ford Motor Co., Detroit, 1964-66; asst. treas. Joel Dean Assocs., N.Y.C., 1966-67; asst. contr. Trans World Airlines, N.Y.C., 1967-73; sr. v.p. fin. svcs., treas. Gannett Co., Inc., Arlington, Va., 1973-98. Bd. dirs. HSBC, Rochester, Tremont Ptnrs. Fundraiser United Negro Coll. Fund; bd. trustees, treas. Harley Sch., Rochester, N.Y.; bd. overseers Strong Meml. Hosp., Rochester; bd. govs. Genesee Hosp., Rochester; bd. dirs. Arlington Cmty. Found., Nat. Press Club Bldg., Washington. With U.S. Army, 1966-72. Ashland Oil Co. scholar, 1959-63, McKinsey scholar 1964; Samuel Bronfman fellow, 1963-64. Mem. Nat. Assn. Corp. Treas., U. Ky. Alumni Assn., Columbia U. Alumni Assn., Country Club of Rochester, Genessee Valley Club, Beta Gamma Sigma, Omicron Delta Kappa, Sigma Alpha Epsilon. Democrat. Mem. Christian Ch. (Disciples Of Christ). Home: 9700 Jennings Rd Eden NY 14057-9518 Office Phone: 716-992-9935.

**THOMAS, JO,** journalist, educator; b. Long Beach, Calif., Dec. 7, 1943; d. Guy O'Neil DeYoung, Jr. and Josephine (Bradley) DeYoung; m. William L. Thomas III (Sept. 1969); m. William Thomas III, June 12, 1965 (div. Sept. 1969); m. William F. Kelleher Jr., Dec. 19, 1985; children: Susan Elizabeth Kelleher, Kathleen DeYoung Kelleher. BA summa cum laude, Wake Forest U., 1965; MA, U. N.C., 1967. Reporter Cin. Post and Times-Star, 1966—70, Detroit Free Press, 1971—77; from Washington corr. to writer N.Y. Times, 1977—2001, writer, 2001—02; assoc. prof. U. Ill., Urbana, 1987—94, asst. chancellor, 2003—04; assoc. chancellor Syracuse U., NY, 2004—, prof. journalism, 2004—. Contbr. articles to newspapers and mags. Bd. dirs. Cir. Cmty. Alternatives. Recipient Outstanding Reporting award Detroit Press Club, 1974-75, Robert F. Kennedy award, 1973; Nieman fellow Harvard U., 1970-71; mem NY Times staff team winning Pulitzer prize, 2002. Mem. Phi Beta Kappa, Kappa Tau Alpha. Office Phone: 315-443-3793. Personal E-mail: jothom@gmail.com.

**THOMAS, JOAB LANGSTON,** retired academic administrator, biologist, educator; b. Holt, Ala., Feb. 14, 1933; s. Ralph Cage and Chamintney Elizabeth (Stovall) Thomas; m. Marly A. Dukes, Dec. 22, 1954; children: Catherine, David, Jennifer, Frances. AB, Harvard U., 1955, MA, 1957, PhD, 1959; DSc (hon.), U. Ala., 1981; LLD (hon.), Stillman Coll., 1987; LHD (hon.), Tri-State U., 1994; LHD (hon.), N.C. State U., 1998. Cytotaxonomist Arnold Aboretum, Harvard, 1959—61; prof. biology U. Ala., University, 1966—76, 1988—91, asst. dean Coll. Arts and Scis., 1964—65, 1969, dean for student devel., 1969—74, v.p., 1974—76, dir. Herbarium, 1961—76, dir. Arboretum, 1964—69, pres. Tuscaloosa, 1981—88; chancellor N.C. State U., Raleigh, 1976—81; pres. Pa. State U., University Park, 1990—95, pres. emeritus, 1995. Intern acad. adminstrn. Am. Coun. on Edn., 1971. Author: A Monographic Study of the Cyrillaceae, 1960, Wildflowers of Alabama and Adjoining States, 1973, The Rising South, 1976, Poisonous Plants and Venomous Animals of Alabama and Adjoining States, 1990. Bd. dirs. Internat. Potato Ctr., 1977—83, chmn., 1982—83; bd. dirs. Internat. Svc. for Nat. Agrl. Rsch., 1985—91. Named Citizen of Yr., City of Tuscaloosa, 1987; recipient Ala. Acad. Honor, 1983, Palmer Mus. Art medal, Coll. Pres.'s award, All-Am. Football Found., 1997, Spl. Recognition award, Assn. for Continuing Higher Edn., 1998. Mem.: Golden Key, Phi Kappa Phi, Omicron Delta Kappa (Laurel Crowned Circle award 2001), Sigma Xi, Phi Beta Kappa. Office: Univ Ala 413 Sci Collections Bldg Tuscaloosa AL 35487-0001 Business E-Mail: jlthomas@dbtech.net.

**THOMAS, JOE CARROLL,** retired human resources director; b. Belmont, NC, Nov. 2, 1931; m. Ruth Stone, June 17, 1951; children: Joe(dec.), Jerry, Angela. BA, Belmont Abbey Coll., 1954; MS, Cornell U., 1961; postgrad., U. NC, 1985. Diplomate in profl. counseling; cert. Sr. Profl. in Human Resources. Terr. salesman Gen. Foods Corp., Charlotte, NC, 1954—59, adminstrv. asst. to dist. mgr. Atlanta, 1960, mgr. terr. sales San Antonio, 1962; asst. dir. personnel textiles divsn. Kendall Co., Charlotte, NC, 1962-64; dir. personnel S.E. region Gifford Hill & Co., Charlotte, 1964-71; dir. mgmt. svcs. Ervin Industries, Charlotte, 1971-75; v.p. indsl. rels. Crompton & Knowles, Charlotte, 1975-76; exec. v.p. dir. human resources Barclays Group Inc., Charlotte, 1976-97; ret., 1997. Mem. adv. coun. Sch. Bus., Western Carolina U., Cullowhee, NC, 1980-84; mem. bd. arbitrators NASD Dispute Resolution, Inc., 2001; bd. adv. Belmont Abbey Coll., 2005 Vice chmn. bd. trustees Belmont Abbey Coll., 1982-88, bd. adv., 2005-; chmn. fundraising campaign Charlotte chpt. Am. Heart Assn., 1984; mem. bd. visitors mercy Hosp., Charlotte, 1984-87; bd. dirs. mercy Health Svcs., Charlotte, 1988-96; bd. dirs. Jr. Achievement Charlotte, 1985-88, INROADS divsn. Charlotte, Inc., 1987-88; bd. visitors Johnson C. Smith Univ., 1989-92 Mem. Soc. Human Resource Mgmt., Employers Assn. (bd. dirs. 1993-99, exec. com. 1995-99), Charlotte Athletic Club (pres. 1982-83), Charlotte Rotary, Charlotte C. of C. (bd. advisors 1992-97, Aldersgate bd. advisors 2000—, Aldersgate bd. dirs. 2003—, bd. dirs. chair elect 2005-2006) Republican. Personal E-mail: carrolleth@aol.com.

**THOMAS, JOHN,** mechanical engineer, artist; b. Tiruvalla, Kerala, India, Jan. 2, 1946; arrived in U.S., 1974; s. Munnencheril Varghese and Rachel (Mathai) Thomas; m. Mary Parapat Varghese, Apr. 28, 1975; children: Joel George, Sayana Rachel. BSMechE, Birla Inst. Tech., Ranchi, India, 1969; MSMechE, U. Waterloo, Ont., Can., 1974. Registered profl. engr., Wis. Lectr. mech. engring. U. Kerala, 1970-71; design engr. Combustion Engring., Inc., Springfield, Ohio, 1974-76; mech. engr. Ingersoll-Rand Co., Painted Post, NY, 1977-80; engr. Allis-Chalmers Corp., Milw., 1980-82; pvt. practice engring. cons. Milw., 1982-84; sr. technology devel. engr. Cross & Trecker divsn. Kearney & Trecker Corp., Milw., 1984-87; ptnr. John Thomas & Assocs., Brookfield, Wis., 1988-90; sr. product engr. N.W. Water Group, Pub. Ltd. Corp. (now U.S. Filter Corp.), Waukesha, Wis., 1989-94; pres. Thomas Products Co., Brookfield, Wis., 1995—; staff engr. Milsco Mfg. Co. unit of Jason Inc., Milw., 1997—2003. Mem.: ASME, U. Waterloo Alumni Assn. Achievements include patents in field. Avocations: photography, golf. Home: 18330 Benington Brookfield WI 53045-5419 Office: Thomas Products Co The Nature Arts Gallery PO Box 401 Brookfield WI 53008-0401

**THOMAS, JOHN ARLEN,** pharmacologist, educator, science administrator; b. LaCrosse, Wis., Apr. 6, 1933; s. John M. and Eva Hazel (Nelson) T.; m. Barbara A. Fisler, June 22, 1957; children: Michael J., Jane L. BS in Sci. Edn., U. Wis., 1956; MA in Physiology, U. Iowa, 1958, PhD in Physiology, 1961. Diplomate Am. Acad. Toxicologic Sci. Instr. U. Iowa, Iowa City, 1961; asst. prof. U. Va., Charlottesville, 1961-64; assoc. prof. Creighton U., Omaha, 1964-67, W.Va. U., Morgantown, 1968-69, prof. pharmacology, 1970-80; asst. dean W.Va. Sch. Medicine, Morgantown, 1973-75, assoc. dean, 1973-80; v.p. corp. rsch. Baxter Internat. Travenol Labs., Round Lake, Ill., 1980-87; v.p. acad. svcs. U. Tex. Health Sci. Ctr., San Antonio, 1988-99, prof. emeritus pharmacology dept. toxicology, 1988—. Chmn. expert adv. com. Can. Network Toxicol. Ctr., 1999-02; mem. sci. adv. bd. USAF, 2002-05, FDA, 2003—; adj. prof. pharmacology Ind. U. Sch. Medicine, Indpls., 2005; cons. to NIH, Inst. of Medicine, NRC, NAS. Author (with M.G. Mawhinney): Synopsis of Endocrine Pharmacology, 1978; author: (with E.J. Keenan) Principles of Endocrine Pharmacology, 1986; editor (with others): Basic and Clinical Toxicology of Lead, 1985; editor: Endocrine Toxicology, 1985, 1996, Drugs Athletes & Physical Performance, 1988, Biotechnology and Safety Assessment, 1993; editor: (with Laurie A. Myers) Biotechnology and Safety Assessment 2d edit., 1981; editor: (with Roy L. Fuchs) Biotechnology and Safety Assessment, 3d edit., 2002; editor: Endocrine Methods, 1996, Toxic Substances Mechanism Jour.; contbr. articles to profl. jours. Sgt. U.S. Army, 1951-53. Recipient Cert. Svc. U.S. EPA, 1977; named Outstanding Tchr., W.Va. U., 1971, 73, 79, Outstanding alumnus U. Wis.-La Crosse, 1978. Disting. Alumni, U. Iowa, 1997; named to Hall of Excellence-LaCrosse, 2002. Fellow Acad. Toxicol. Sci. (pres. 2001); mem. Endocrine Soc., Soc. Toxicology (councilor, Merit award 1998), Am. Soc. Pharmacology and Exptl. Therapeutics, Am. Coll. Toxicology (councilor, pres., disting. fellow 2004, Disting. Svc. award), Teratology Soc., Am. Acad. Vet. Pharmacology, Am. Chem. Soc. (pres. chem. toxicology pathology), Tex. Soc. Biomed. Rsch.

(bd. sci. advisors 1989-99, Disting. Svc. award 1996), Russian Acad. Med. Sci. (fgn. fellow-elect 1995). Home: 7258 Pymbroke Cir Fishers IN 46038 Office Phone: 317-845-5224. Personal E-mail: jat-tox@sbcglobal.net.

**THOMAS, JOHN CHARLES,** lawyer; b. Norfolk, Va., Sept. 18, 1950; s. John and Floretta V. (Sears) T.; m. Pearl Walden, Oct. 9, 1982; children: John Charles Jr., Ruby Virginia, Lewis LeGrant. BA in Am. Govt. with distinction, U. Va., 1972, JD, 1975. Bar: Va. 1975, U.S. Dist. Ct. (ea. and we. dists.) 1976, U.S. Ct. Appeals (4th cir.) 1976, U.S. Supreme Ct. 1979, U.S. Ct. Appeals (D.C. cir.) 1980, U.S. Ct. Appeals (10th cir.) 1991, U.S. Ct. Appeals (11th cir.) 1992. Assoc. Hunton & Williams, Richmond, Va., 1975-82, ptnr., 1982-83, 89—; justice Supreme Ct. of Va., Richmond, 1983-89. Former mem. adv. con. on appellate rules U.S. Jud. Conf., permanent mem. 4th cir. Hon. dir. U. Va. Law Sch. Found. Fellow Am. Bar Found., Va. Bar Found.; mem. ABA (former co-chair nat. conf. lawyers and reps. of media, coun. appellate lawyers), Ct. Arbitration for Sport, Am. Acad. Appellate Lawyers, Va. State Bar, Va. Bar Assn., Bar Assn. City of Richmond, Old Dominion Bar Assn., Omega Psi Phi, Sigma Pi Phi Office: Hunton & Williams Riverfront Plz East Tower PO Box 1535 Richmond VA 23218-1535 Office Phone: 804-788-8522. Business E-Mail: jcthomas@hunton.com.

**THOMAS, JOHN DAVID,** composer, musician, compact disc artist, photographer, music and arts business owner; b. Muncie, Ind., Mar. 30, 1951; s. John Charles and Phyllis Lorraine (Wear) T.; m. Rosalie Faith Baldwin, July 27, 1974 (div. 1990); children: Bethany Carol, Mark David. Student, Purdue U., 1969-71, Jordan Coll. of Music, Indpls., 1961-65; BS in Music Theory and Composition, Ball State U., 1976. Musician, composer, 1955—; digital and film photographer, graphic designer Have Camera Will Travel, 1956—; cellist The Howe String Quartet (with Ann Pinney, Mary Ann Tilford, Anne Wuster), Indpls., 1967-68; keyboardist, vocalist, cellist Fire and The Rebel Kind rock bands, Indpls., 1967-69, Good Conduct rock band, Muncie, Ind., 1972-73; pianist The Pavillion at Olde Towne, Los Gatos, Calif., 1969; radio announcer John David's Late Night Rock Show WCCR-AM, West Lafayette, Ind., 1969-70; photographer Indpls., 1964-84, 1991—2000; budget analyst Office of Comptr. USAFAC, Indpls., 1976-84; co-leader, keyboardist, composer, arranger, vocalist, sound technician Jetstream band, Carmel, Indpls., Kokomo, Columbus, Bloomington, Ind., 1979-83; co-leader, keyboardist, vocalist, sound technician The Thomas Bros., King's Crown Inn, Kokomo, 1979; sound/audio visual technician Valley Cathedral Ch., Phoenix, 1987. Pianist, synthesist Paul Thomas and Night and Day, The Tim Barnett Band, Indpls. Mus. Art, 1992, Radisson Hotel and Broadmoor Country Club, Indpls., 1991, Highland Country Club, Indpls., The Ritz Charles Hotel and Summertrace, Carmel, Ind., Stonehenge Resort, Bedford, Ind., 1991; solo pianist Terranova Mansion, Paradise Valley, Ariz., 1987, Wrigley Mansion, Phoenix, 1988, Boulders Resort, Carefree, Ariz., 1987, Clarion Inn/McCormick's Ranch Resort, Scottsdale, Ariz., 1986, China Gate, Phoenix, 1988, Victor's, Phoenix, 1988, Cascade Club, Everett, Wash., 1990; keyboardist, synthesist, key bassist, The Gulch Gang, Pinnacle Peak Patio, Scottsdale, 1984, Dee Dee Ryan, The Longhorn Saloon, Apache Junction, Ariz., 1984-86, The Last Straw Band, Country City saloon, Mesa, Ariz., 1986; keyboardist, pianist, vocalist with Peter, Paul and John, Anderson (Ind.) Coll., 1977; CEO, owner, composer, photographer, arranger, prodr., musician, engr., graphic designer, computer operator, John David Thomas Prodns., Indpls., 1993—; CEO, owner JD Thomas Music Co., 1999—, Monolith Records, 1999-2001, JDT Records, 2001—, Serious Bizness Music Co., 2002—, Global Concept Music Co., 2002—, Silky Rd. Music Co., 2002—, Spirit Realm Music Co., 2002—, Mega Modern Music Co., 2002—, Dark Horse Music Co., 2005-; rec. artist CD label mp3.com, 2000-2004, CD label besonic.com, Europe, 2002-, JDT Records, 2001- Composer, lyricist of over 350 classical, religious, comml., rock, jazz, popular and avante garde/futuristic compositions, including Infinity, 1970-71, Death of Rock and Roll, 1970, Night Visions, 1972, First Things First, 1972, Two Nudes and a Fire Hydrant, 1972-73, Chant for Orchestra, 1972, 2001, Love Theme in D, 1972, 98, Zeitgeist: The Spirit of the Time, 1974, The Little Prince, 1973, 2001, When We Dead Awaken, 1973, Pray, 1972, Apogee, 1974, Chinese Baby, 1973, Alabama DA (Top Forty recording), 1973, Angel, 1974, Music for French Horn, Cello, and Piano, 1976, Cruising Beyond, 1979, Jetstream Theme, 1979, Chrissy, 1979, Love Theme in B Minor, 1979, In Your Heart, 1983, Future Music, 1987, The Recurrent New Millenium Orchestral Olympic Disco Festival Dance, 1989, Jubilee in F, 1989, Praise Him, The King Liveth, 1989, Love Flowers: Reflections and Meditations on Beauty and Truth, 1990, Sheena's Theme, 1992, I Want You Forever You're My Miracle, 1992, My Pseudo-Erotic, Sensual, Exotic Musical Fantasy and Romance for Our Heavenly Nocturnal Starry-Skied Carpet Ride to Paradise in Istanbul and Constantinople, 1992, I'm in Love with Someone Beautiful, 1992, Improvisations for Sheena, 1992, Musical Essences, 1994, 2002, Mystery World #1, 1994, Mystery World #2, 1994, Orient, 1994, Orchestral #17, 1994, Drums and Percussion Music, 1994, My Renaissance Brass Music, 1994, Postlude, 1994, Music for Baritone Vocal and String Orch., 1995, Meditations for Pipe Organ and Male Choir, 1996, Trumpet Voluntary in F, 1996, Pathway to Love, 1996, Majestic Brass Music in F#, 1997, J.D.'s Theme, 1998, The Road to Tomorrow, 1999, Let Me Be the One, 2000, God and the Everlasting, 2000, Sunshine, 2000, Love Theme, 2000, Dreaming, 2000, Together, 2000, Love You, 2000, The Road of Life, 2000, Desires of the Heart, 2000, The Open Sky, 2000, Just Me and You, 2000, In the Spirit of Mozart, 2001, God and the Everlasting, 2001, From Me to You, 2001, Ostinato for Double Reeds, 2001, God 1, 2001, God 2, 2001, Randy's Theme, 2002, Music for Suzy, 2003, Music for Beautiful Women, 2003, over 140 short piano compositions, 1999-2003; (albums) The Journey of Life, Destiny's Calling: Improvisations, 1994, 2002; (cd's) The Journey of Life, 1994, 2002, Musical Essences, 1994, 2002, Music for Bethany, 2002, The Avant-Garde of John David Thomas, 2002, From Me to You, 2002, Desires of the Heart, 2002, Spirit Music, 2002, The Seen and the Unseen, 2000, John David Thomas at the Piano, 2005, Romantic Abstract for the Modern Woman in Love with this Composer, 2005, Pathway to Love, 2005, Desires of the Heart, 2005, Early Songs and Jazz of John David Thomas: 1970-1987, 2005, Potpourri: Music for the World, 2000, Music for the World, vol. 2, 2000, (broadcast) Hometown Hour, Sta. WFBQ-FM, Indpls., 1979-80, Music for Kelly, Judy, Karyn, and Stacey, 2003; performed orginal composition, Someday, WFBM-TV, Indpls., 1969; designer automotive concepts and popular fashions; recordings of over 120 original songs and compositions including Love Theme in D, 1972, 98, Majestic Brass Music in F# for Bethany and Mark, 1997, J.D.'s Theme, 1998; plus over 90 recordings on CD's; author numerous poems. Musician, vocalist, composer Downey Ave. Christian Ch., Indpls., 1961-69, Univ. Presbyn. Ch., West Lafayette, Ind., 1969-71, Castleview Bapt. Ch., Indpls., 1974-84, Valley Cathedral Ch., Phoenix, 1986-87, Edmonds (Wash.) Christian Ch., 1988-90, Edmonds United Meth. Ch., 1989-90; page to speaker Ho. of Reps. Ind. State Legislature, 1963; active All Souls Unitarian Ch., Indpls., 1994-96. GM scholar Purdue U., 1969-70, Hoosier scholar, 1969, Palmer Meml. Music scholar Ball State U., 1971-74; named to Ind. All-State Orch. (cellist), 1968; recipient 1st place award (cellist) Ind. State Music Contest, 1968, God and Country award, 1965, Outstanding Musician award Irvington Music Club, Indpls., 1969, Purdue U. Symphonette, 1970, Hometown Hour award WFBQ-FM Radio Sta., Indpls., 1979. Mem. ASCAP, NARAS, Am. Fedn. Musicians local 47, Audio Engring. Soc., Recording Musicians Assn. LA, Mensa. Avocations: reading, computers, music, photography, bridge. Home: c/o Simone Hotel Box 401 520 San Julian Los Angeles CA 90013 Personal E-mail: composerandartsamn@excite.com.

**THOMAS, JOHN HOWARD,** astrophysicist, mechanical engineer, educator; b. Chgo., Apr. 9, 1941; s. William Whitney and Dorothy Loretta (Derris) T.; m. Lois Ruth Moffit, Aug. 11, 1962; children: Jeffrey, Laura. BS in Engring. Sci., Purdue U., 1962, MS in Engring. Sci., 1964, PhD in Engring. Sci., 1966. Lic. profl. engr., NY. NATO postdoctoral fellow U. Cambridge, Eng., 1966-67; asst. prof. mech. and aerospace sci. U. Rochester, 1967-73, assoc. prof., 1973-81, prof., 1981—prof. astronomy, 1986—, assoc. dean for grad. studies Coll. Engring. and Applied Sci., 1981-83, univ. dean grad. studies, 1983-91. Vis. astronomer Nat. Solar Obs., Sunspot, N.Mex., 1971, 81; vis. scientist Max-Planck Inst. for Physics and Astrophysics, Munich, 1973—74, High Altitude Obs., Boulder, Colo., 1985; vis. fellow Worcester

Coll., vis. prof. dept. theoretical physics U. Oxford, England, 1987—88; affiliate scientist Nat. Ctr. for Atmospheric Rsch., Boulder, 1989—; vis. prof. Rsch. Ctr. for Theoretical Astrophysics U. Sydney, Australia, 1991, Sch. Math. and Stats., 1993; vis. fellow Clare Hall, vis. prof. dept. applied math. and theoretical physics U. Cambridge, England, 2002, sr. fellow Isaac Newton Inst., 04; prin. investigator NASA, NSF, USAF, Office Naval Rsch. Editor: Physics of Sunspots, 1981, Sunspots: Theory and Observations, 1992; assoc. editor Astrophys. Jour., 1993—96, sci. editor, 1996—2002, author articles on astrophysics, solar physics and fluid dynamics. NSF fellow, 1963-66; Guggenheim fellow, 1993-94. Fellow Am. Phys. Soc.; mem. AAAS, Am. Astron. Soc. (chair solar physics divsn. 1995-97), Internat. Astron. Union, Am. Geophys. Union, Royal Astron. Soc. (UK), Sigma Xi, Tau Beta Pi, Sigma Delta Chi.

**THOMAS, JOHN MELVIN,** retired surgeon; b. Carmarthen, U.K., Apr. 26, 1933; U.S. 1958; s. Morgan and Margaret (Morgan) T.; m. Betty Ann Mayo, Nov. 3, 1958; children: James, Hugh, Pamela. MB, BChir, U. Coll. Wales, U. Edinburgh, 1958. Intern Robert Packer Hosp., Sayre, Pa., 1958-59, chief surg. resident, 1963, pres. med. staff, 1968; assoc. surgeon Guthrie Clinic Ltd., Sayre, 1963-69, chmn. dept. surgery, 1969-91; vice chmn. Guthrie Healthcare System, 1995—99. Pres. bd. dirs. Guthrie Clinic Ltd., 1972-89; pres. bd. dirs. Donald Guthrie Found., 1983-95; chmn. Chemung Springwater Co.; trustee Robert Packer Hosp.; chmn. exec. com. Guthrie Healthcare Sys., 1990-92, dir., 1994-2001; guest examiner Am. Bd. Surgery, 1979, 81, 85; bd. dirs. Measurement Innovations Corp., Mansfield, Pa., Trianalytics Corp., First Citizens Nat Bank; cons. The Hunter Group, 1993-96; interim pres., Citizen Fin. Bank, 2003—; arbitrator Nat. Assn. Securities Dealers, 2005—. Bd. dirs. Donald Guthrie Found. for Rsch., pres., 1983-94; bd. dirs. Pa. Trauma Sys. Found., 1984-90, pres., 1988, 89; chmn. licensure and accountability Gov.'s Conf., 1974; bd. dirs. Vol. Hosps. Am., 1993-95; trustee Mansfield (Pa.) U. Found., 1991-98; trustee Mansfield Univ. Found., 1991-95. Fellow ACS (gov. 1985-91); mem. AMA, Am. Group Practice Assn., Soc. for Surgery Alimentary Tract, Pa. Med. Soc., Bradford County Med. Soc., Cen. NY Surg. Soc., Internat. Soc. Surgery, Soc. Surgery Alimentary Tract, Ea. Vascular Soc., Ithaca Country Club, Whitchurch Golf Club, Country Club Naples, Tower Club (Ft. Lauderdale). Presbyterian. Home: Cap Ferrat 6597 Nicholas Blvd #701 Naples FL 34108 E-mail: jthoma8422@aol.com.

**THOMAS, JOHN THIEME,** management consultant; b. Detroit, Aug. 21, 1935; s. John Shepherd and Florence Leona (Thieme) T.; m. Ellen Linden Taylor, June 27, 1959; children: Johnson Taylor, Evan Thurston. BBA, U. Mich., 1957, MBA, 1958. Mfg. dept. mgr. Procter & Gamble Co., Cin., 1958-60, brand mgr., 1960-63; sr. cons. Glendinning Cos. Inc., Westport, Conn., 1964-66, v.p. London, 1967-69, exec. v.p. Westport, 1970-74, also bd. dirs.; exec. v.p., chief operating officer Ero Industries, Chgo., 1974-76; v.p. Lamalie Assocs. Inc., Chgo., 1977-81; pres. Wilkins & Thomas Inc., Chgo., 1981-87; ptnr. Ward Howell Internat., Chgo., 1987—, mng. dir., cons. practice, 1992-98, chief of staff, 1995-98; also bd. dirs.; cons. ret. LAI Ward Howell, Chgo., 1999—, El Jefe, Thomas Ent. Inc., 1999—. Exec. dir. Procter & Gamble Alumni Assn., Chgo., 1981—. Pub. Procter & Gamble Mktg. Alumni directory, 1981—; author articles in profl. jours. Chmn. bd. dirs. Winnetka (Ill.) Youth Orgn., 1986—2005; chmn. United Way Winnetka, 2001—, United Way North Shore; bd. dirs. No. Ill. Girl Scouts Coun., 2002—; mem. planning commn. City Winnetka, 2003—05; selector Winnetka Town Coun., 1978, 1980, 1984, Winnetka Caucus Exec. Com., 1997—2001, Winnetka Zoning Bd., 2002—05; commr. Winnetka Pks., 2005—. Mem. Nat. Assn. Corp. & Profl. Recruiters, Assn. Exec. Search Cons., Am. Soc. Pers. Adminstrn. Clubs: Fairfield (Conn.) Hunt (treas. 1971-74). Avocations: gardening, music, playing tuba. Home and Office: 525 Ash St Winnetka IL 60093-2601 Office Phone: 847-446-5401. E-mail: enjthomas@aol.com, pngalumni@aol.com.

**THOMAS, JOHN VAL,** architect; b. San Diego, Feb. 26, 1943; Grad arch., Rice Univ., Houston; MArch, MCP, U. Pa. Prin. Val Thomas Inc., Seattle, 1985—; devel. mgr. Pike Pl. Market Preservation and Devel. Authority, Seattle, 1974. Cons. ptnr. Cardwell/Thomas & Assoc., Seattle. Conversion, W. Queen Anne Sch. (Award for Excellence, Nat. Endowment for the Arts). Fellow: Am. Inst. Arch.; mem.: Housing Comm. of the Greater Seattle Chamber of Commerce, Univ. of Wash. Profl. Coun. for the Sch. of Urban Planning, Seattle Planning Commission (chrmn.). Democrat. Episcopalian. Achievements include development of Thomas Incorporated; headed the development team for the new headquarters building of the Fremont Public Association on North 45th Street. Avocations: skiing, aerobics, painting, gardening. Office: Thomas Inc 1221 2nd Ave Ste 480 Seattle WA 98101 Office Phone: 206-621-1221.

**THOMAS, JOSEPH FLESHMAN,** retired architect; b. Oak Hill, W.Va., Mar. 23, 1915; s. Robert Russel and Effie (Fleshman) T.; m. Margaret Ruth Lively, Feb. 28, 1939 (dec.); children: Anita Carol, Joseph Stephen; m. Dorothy Francene Root, Apr. 29, 1967 (div.); m. Bonnie Abbott Buckley, June 15, 1991 (dec.). Student, Duke U., 1931—32; BArch, Carnegie-Mellon U., 1938. Practice architecture various firms, W.Va., Va., Tenn., Calif., 1938-49; staff arch. Calif. Divsn. Architecture, L.A., 1949-52; prin. Joseph F. Thomas, Arch., Pasadena, Calif., 1952-53; pres. Neptune & Thomas (archs.-engrs.), Pasadena and San Diego, 1953-78; architect NTO Stechler, 2006—. Mem. Pasadena Planning Commn., 1956-64, chmn., 1963-64; pres. Citizens Coun. for Planning, Pasadena, 1966-67; steering com. Pasadena NOW, 1970-74; mem. Pasadena Design Com., 1979-86; adv. bd. Calif. Office Architecture and Constrn., 1970-72; archtl. adv. com. Calif. State U. Sys., 1981-84; adv. coun. Sch. Environ. Design Calif. Poly. Inst., 1983-2002; outreach for architecture com. Carnegie Mellon U., 1989-95, pres.'s devel. com., 1991-95. Prin. works include Meth. Hosp., Arcadia, Calif., Foothill Presbyn. Hosp., Glendora, Calif., master plans and bldgs., Citrus Coll., Azusa, Calif., Riverside (Calif.) Coll., Westmont Coll., Monticeto, Calif., Northrop Inst. Tech., Inglewood, Calif, Indian Valley Coll., Marin County, Calif., Pepperdine U., Malibu, Calif., UCLA, U. Calif., San Diego, Long Beach (Calif.) State U., Calif. Inst. Tech., Pasadena, Pacific Tel. Co., Pasadena, LA County Superior Ct. Bldg., U.S. Naval Hosp., San Diego, others Trustee Almansor Edn. Ctr., 1986-92; bd. dirs., co-founder Syncor Internat., 1973-83; founding dir. Bank of Pasadena, 1962-65. Lt. (j.g.) USNR, 1943-46. Recipient Svc. award, City of Pasadena, 1964, Disting. Svc. award, Calif. Dept. Gen. Svcs., 1972, Gold Crown award, Pasadena Arts Coun., 1981. Fellow AIA (4 awards honor, 13 awards merit 1957-78, dir. Calif. coun. 1966-68, exec. com. 1974-77, pres. Pasadena chpt. 1967, chmn. Calif. sch. facilities com. 1970-72, mem. nat. jud. bd. 1973-74, nat. dir. 1974-77, treas. 1977-79, exec. com., planning com., chmn. finance com.); mem. Breakfast Forum (chmn. 1983), Annandale Golf Club, Pi Kappa Alpha. Republican. Methodist. Home: 330 San Miguel Rd Pasadena CA 91105-1446

**THOMAS, JOSEPH WINAND,** lawyer; b. New Orleans, Aug. 2, 1940; s. Gerald Henry and Edith Louise (Winand) T.; m. Claudette Condoll, Aug. 2, 1960 (div. Nov. 1985); children: Jeffery J., Anthony M.; m. Shawn B. Watkins, May 26, 1986 (div. June 1989); children: Adelle, Anne; m. Sandra J. Green, May 17, 1992; children: Winand, Elizabeth, Alice, Shepard, Julia. BS, Loyola U., Chgo., 1967; JD, Loyola U., New Orleans, 1973; MBA, Tulane U., 1984. Bar: La. 1973, U.S. Dist. Ct. (ea. dist.) La. 1973, U.S. Ct. Appeals (5th cir.) 1973, U.S. Supreme Ct. 1976, D.C. 1990. Staff atty. New Orleans Legal Assistance Corp., 1973-74; asst. atty. gen. State of La., 1974-80; pvt. practice New Orleans, 1980—. Pres., bd. dirs. New Orleans Legal Assistance Corp. Active NAACP, New Orleans, 1987-89; bd. dirs. Urban League, New Orleans. Mem. ABA, Louis Martinet Legal Soc., New Orleans Bar Assn., La. Bar Assn. Democrat. Roman Catholic. Office: Ste 1295 1615 Poydras St New Orleans LA 70112 E-mail: jthomas@bellsouth.net.

**THOMAS, JUDY JANET,** reporter, public health service officer; b. Detroit, Mich., Feb. 28, 1964; d. J.W. and Geneva Anna Thomas; children: Robert A., Arrelle R. BA, U. of D Mercy, Detroit, MI; Associates, Wayne County Coll., Detroit, MI. Job developer U. D Mercy, Detroit, 1999—2000; mgr. Alstate Glass Co., Detroit, 2000; reporter Metroplex Newspaper, Detroit, 2002—;

cmty. svc. Doctors Ho. Svc., Detroit, 2002—. Dir. sr. organ Consortium, Detroit. Mem. Voice Wrtiers Orgn., Detroit, 2001—01. Liberal. Avocations: reading, writing, banking, art. Home: 19144 Robson Detroit MI 48235 Office: Doctors House Call Service 17117 W 9 Mile Road Southfield MI Office Phone: (313) 864-7062.

**THOMAS, KENNETH GLYNDWR,** mining executive; b. Llanelli, Wales, June 25, 1944; arrived in Can., 1980; m. Elizabeth June Hickman, Sept. 25, 1976; children: Louise June, Kelly Jane. BSc in Metallurgy, U. Wales, Cardiff, 1970; MSc in Mgmt. Sci., U. London, 1971; PhD in Tech. Sci., U. of Delft, The Netherlands, 1994. Chartered engr., U.K.; registered profl. engr., Ont., Can. Metallurgist Brit. Steel Corp., Wales, 1959-67, Anglo Am. Corp., Kitwe, Zambia, 1971-75, plant supt. Klerksdorp, South Africa, 1975-80; design metallurgist Kilborn Engring., Toronto, Ont., 1980-85; mill supt. Giant Yellowknife (Can.) Mines Ltd., N.W.T., 1985-87; sr. v.p. metallurgy and constrn. Barrick Gold Corp., Toronto, 1987-95, sr. v.p. tech. svcs., 1995-2001; mng. dir. mining and mineral processing Hatch, Mississauga, Ont., 2001—02; mng. dir. We. Australia, 2002—03; COO, exec. v.p. Crystallex Internat. Corp., Toronto, 2003—05; mng. dir. Hatch, Mississauga, 2006—. Contbr. articles to tech. jours.; co-patentee in field. Fellow Inst. Materials, Minerals & Mining (U.K.), Can. Inst. Mining, Metallurgy and Petroleum (Mill Man of Yr. award 1990, Airey award 1999, Selwyn G. Blaylock medal 2001). Office Phone: 905-403-3908. Business E-Mail: kentomas@rogers.com.

**THOMAS, LAWRENCE ELDON,** mathematics professor; b. Columbus, Ohio, Mar. 15, 1942; s. Bertram D. and Glorian (Butler) T.; m. Rebecca Nolan, June 13, 1970; children: David Nolan, Kathleen Rebecca. BS, U. Mich., 1964; PhD, Yale U., 1970. Rsch. asst. math. dept. Swiss Fed. Inst. Tech., Zurich, 1970-72; rsch. asst. physics dept. U. Geneva, 1972-74; asst. prof. math. U. Va., Charlottesville, 1974-76, assoc. prof., 1976-82, prof., 1982—, chmn. dept., 1989-93. Contbr. articles on theory of Schrodinger operators, statis. mechanics and stochastic processes to profl. jours. Mem. Am. Math. Soc., Am. Physics Soc., Internat. Nat. Math. Physics, Phi Beta Kappa. Avocations: sailing, tennis. Office: U Va Dept Math Cabell Dr Charlottesville VA 22903

**THOMAS, LEE MULLER,** former paper company executive, former government offical; b. Ridgeway, SC, June 13, 1944; s. Robert Walton and Laura (Muller) Thomas; m. Dixie Gay Smily, June 20, 1981; children: Jordan, Braden; children: Lee, Elliott. BA, U. of South, 1967; M.Ed., U. S.C., 1971. Exec. dir. criminal justice program Office Gov., Columbia, SC, 1972-77, dir. pub. safety programs, 1979-81; ind. cons. Criminal Justice Planning, 1977-79; assoc. dir. state and local programs and support FEMA, Washington, 1981-82, dep. dir., 1982-83; asst. adminstr. EPA, Washington, 1983-85, adminstr., 1985-89; chmn., chief exec. officer Law Environmental Inc., Atlanta, 1989—93; with Georgia Pacific Corp., Atlanta, 1993—, sr. v.p. paper, 1995—96, exec. v.p. paper & chemicals, 1997—2000, exec. v.p. consumer products, 2000—02, pres. bldg. products & distribution, 2002, pres., 2002—03, pres., COO, 2003—05. Bd. dir. Airgas Inc., Resolve Inc., Rayonier Inc., Regal Entertainment Inc., Fed. Reserve Bank, Atlanta. Bd. dir. World Resources Inst., Washington, Nat. Merit Scholarship Corp., Ga. Environ. Facilities Authority. Mem.: SC Law Enforcement Officers Assn., SC Corrections Assn., Nat. Criminal Justice Assn. (chmn. 1979—81), Sigma Nu.*

**THOMAS, LEONA MARLENE,** healthcare educator; b. Rock Springs, Wyo., Jan. 15, 1933; d. Leonard H. and Opal (Wright) Francis; children: Peter, Paul, Patrick, Alexis. BA, Govs. State U., University Park, Ill., 1982, MHS, 1986; cert. med. records adminstr., U. Colo., 1954. Asst. prof. Chgo. State U., 1984—, acting dir. health info. adminstrn. program, 1991-92; acting dir. health info. Internat. Coll., Naples, Fla., 1994; dir. Chgo. State U., 1994—. Chairperson dept. health info. adminstrn. Chgo. State U., 1994—. Mem. adv. com. Wellness Ctr., mem. adv. com. occupl. therapy program Chgo. State U. Mem. Assembly on Edn., Am. Health Info. Mgmt. Assn., APHA, Chgo. and Vicinity Med. Records Assn., Ill. Assn. Allied Health Profls., Gov.'s State Alumni Assn. Democrat. Methodist. Home: 6340 Americana Dr Apt 1101 Willowbrook IL 60527 Office: Chgo State U Coll Health Scis 95th at King Dr Chicago IL 60628 Personal E-mail: lthomas@msn.com.

**THOMAS, LESTENE,** nurse; b. Hampton, Ark., May 1, 1956; d. James Earnest Moore and Alma Lee Moore-Penny; m. Emile Garth Thomas; children: Learie D., Stephen J.R. AAS in Nursing, U. Ark. Little Rock, 1978. RN; notary public, Ark. Nurse U. Hosp., Little Rock, 1978-82, Vets. Hosp., Little Rock, 1982-86, Ctrl. Ark. Home Health Agy., Little Rock, 1986-89, St. Vincent Infirmary, Little Rock, 1989-90, Jefferson Regional Med. Ctr., Pine Bluff, Ark., 1990-94, Ark. Convalescent Nursing Home, Pine Bluff, 1996-97, Pulaski County Regional Detention Facility, Little Rock, 1998—2002, Maxim Health Svcs., 2002—, Parkview Rehab. and Health Care, 2003—. Mem. Angel Flight, UAM, Monticello, Ark., 1975—76. 2d lt. Ark. NG, 1984—86. Mem.: Nat. Alliance for Mentally Ill, Zeta Phi Beta. Baptist. Avocations: calligraphy, photography, music, international pen-friends. Home: 8501 Dreher Ln Apt 25 Little Rock AR 72209

**THOMAS, LINDSEY KAY, JR.,** research ecology biologist, educator, consultant; b. Salt Lake City, Apr. 16, 1931; s. Lindsey Kay and Naomi Lurie (Biesinger) T.; m. Nancy Ruth Van Dyke, Aug. 24, 1956; children: Elizabeth Nan Thomas Cardinale, David Lindsey, Wayne Hal, Dorothy Ann Thomas Brown. BS, Utah State Agrl. Coll., 1953; MS, Brigham Young U., 1958; PhD, Duke U., 1974. Park naturalist Nat. Capital Pks., Nat. Pk. Svc., Washington, 1957—62, pk. naturalist (rschr.) Region 6, 1962—63, rsch. pk. naturalist Nat. Capital Region, 1963—66; rsch. biologist S.E. Temperate Forest Pk. Areas, Washington, 1966, Durham, NC, 1966—67, Great Falls, Md., 1967—71, Nat. Capital Pks., Great Falls, 1971—74, Nat. Capital Region, Triangle, Va., 1974—93, Washington, 1985—93, Nat. Biol. Svc., Washington, Triangle, 1993—96; resource mgmt. specialist Balt.-Washington Pkwy., Greenbelt, Md., 1996, Nat. Capital Region, Nat. Park Svc., 1998—. Bd. dirs. Prince William County (Va.) Svc. Authority, 1996-2004; adj. prof. George Mason U., Fairfax, Va., 1988—, George Washington U., Washington, 1992-98; instr. Dept. Agr. Grad. Sch., 1964-66; aquatic ecol. cons. Fairfax County (Va.) Fedn. Citizens Assns., 1970-71; guest lectr. Washington Tech. Inst. (now U. DC), 1976; cons. in field, Natural Resources divsn. Arlington County, Va., 2004—. Contbr. articles to profl. jours. Wildlife mgmt. cons. Girl Scouts Am., Loudoun County, Va., 1958; preservation and mgmt. cons. McAtean Magnolia Bogs, Save Araby, Mattawoman and Mason Springs in Charles County, Md., 2002-06, Nat. Resources Divsn., Arlington County, Va., 2004—; asst. scoutmaster, scoutmaster, merit badges counselor Boy Scouts Am., 1958—, Scouters Tng. award, 1961. Recipient Incentive award Nat. Park Svc., 1962, Superior Performance award, 1989; Rsch. grant Washington Biologists' Field Club, 1977, 82. Mem.: AAAS, Md. Native Plant Soc., Nat. Trust for Historic Preservation, Washington Biologists' Field Club, So. Appalachian Bot. Soc., Soc. for Early Hist. Archaeology, The Nature Conservancy, George Wright Soc., Ecol. Soc. Am., Phi Beta Kappa, Sigma Xi. Mem. Lds Ch. Home: 13854 Delaney Rd Woodbridge VA 22193-4654 Office: Prince William Forest Park 18100 Park Hdqrs Rd Triangle VA 22172

**THOMAS, LIZANNE,** lawyer; BA, Furman U., 1979; JD, Washington & Lee, 1982. Bar: Ga. 1982. Ptnr. bus. practice group Jones Day, Atlanta, firmwide adminstrv. ptnr., 2003—. Lectr. corp. fin. U. Calif., Berkeley and Davis; pres. Law Alumni Assn. Washington and Lee U., 2001—05; mem. Krispy Kreme Doughnuts, 2004—. Recurring panelist Directors' Inst. of the Conf. Bd. Mem. adv. bd. Salvation Army Metro Atlanta Advisory Bd. Mem. Sp. A. G. C. of C. Mem.: State Bar of Ga. Office: Jones Day 1420 Peachtree St NE Atlanta GA 30309-3053 Office Phone: 404-581-8411. Office Fax: 404-581-8330. Business E-Mail: lthomas@jonesday.com.

**THOMAS, LLOYD BREWSTER,** economics professor; b. Columbia, Mo., Oct. 22, 1941; s. Lloyd B. and Marianne (Moon) T.; m. Sally Leach, Aug. 11, 1963; 1 child, Elizabeth. AB, U. Mo., 1963, AM, 1964; PhD, Northwestern U., 1970. Instr. Northwestern U., Evanston, Ill., 1966-68; asst. prof. econs. Kan. State U., Manhattan, 1968-72, assoc. prof., 1974-81; asst. prof. Fla. State U., Tallahassee, 1973-74; prof. Kan. State U., Manhattan, 1983—; head of dept. Fla. State U., Tallahassee, 2004—. Vis. prof. U. Calif., Berkeley, 1981-82, U. Del., 1993, U. Ind., Bloomington, 1997-98, Adelaide U., 2002; prof., chair dept. econs. U. Idaho, 1989. Author: Money, Banking and Economic Activity, 3d edit., 1986, Principles of Economics, 2d edit, 1993, Principles of Macroeconomics, 2d edit, 1993, Principles of Microeconomics, 2d edit, 1993, Money, Banking and Financial Markets, 2006; contbr. articles to profl. jours. Mem. Am. Econs. Assn., Midwest Econs. Assn., Phi Kappa Phi. Avocations: tennis, classical music. Home: 1501 N 10th St Manhattan KS 66502-4607 Office Phone: 785-532-4584. Business E-Mail: lbt@ksu.edu.

**THOMAS, LOIS BASKERVILLE,** retired language educator; b. Montclair, NJ, Dec. 22, 1931; d. Charles William Sr. and Ruth Gladys (Smith) Baskerville; children: Richard, Rodney, Octavia. BA, Howard U., 1953; MA, Trenton State Coll., 1979. H.S. tchr. Newark Sch. Sys., 1964—65; tchr. Mahwah (NJ) Jr./Sr. H.S., 1965—68, West Side H.S., Newark, 1968—99, chmn. dept. world langs.; ret., 1999. Contbr. numerous articles to profl. publs.; author (booklet) Victim by Heritage, 1969. Vol. Job Corps, Darby, Mont., 1970. Avocations: writing, art, painting, piano. Home: 545 Berkeley Ave Orange NJ 07050

**THOMAS, LOIS C.,** musician, educator, religious organization administrator, composer; b. Ft. Worth, Oct. 15, 1932; d. Walter Scott and Margaret Alice Dawn Cook; m. Richard Wallace Thomas, Nov. 5, 1988. BA in Organ Performance, Tex. Christian U., 1966; postgrad., SWBT Sem. Organist Western Hills Bapt. Ch., Ft. Worth, 1959-69, 1st Ch. of Christ, Scientist, Ft. Worth, 1969-84, First Congl. Ch., Ft. Worth, 1985-87; organist, dir. Anglican Ch. St. Charles the Martyr, Grand Prairie, Tex., 1999—99; organist, dir., assoc. rector Anglican Ch. St. Raphael, the Archangel, Grand Prairie, 2002—04. Deacon United Cath. Ch., 1996; priest Communion Evang. Episcopal Chs., 1997; fin. officer USCG Aux., Grapevine, Tex., 1989—95, sec., Grand Prairie, Tex., 1995. Commd.: hymnal Diocese St. Paul, the Apostle, 2000. Mem.: Music Tchr.'s Nat. Assn., Tex. Music Tchr.'s Assn., Arlington Music Tchr.'s Assn. (phone com.), Guild Organists (phone com., svc. playing cert.). Home: 1501 Connally Ter Arlington TX 76010-4514

**THOMAS, LOWELL, JR.,** writer, retired military officer, retired state senator; b. London, Oct. 6, 1923; s. Lowell Jackson and Frances (Ryan) T.; m. Mary Taylor Pryor, May 20, 1950; children: Anne Frazier, David Lowell. Student, Taft Sch., 1942; BA, Dartmouth Coll., 1948; postgrad., Princeton Sch. Pub. and Internat. Affairs, 1952. Asst. cameraman Fox Movietone News, S.Am., 1939, Bradford Washburn Alaskan mountaineering expdn., 1940; illustrated lecturer, 1946—; asst. economist, photographer with Max Weston Thornburg, Turkey, 1947, Iran, 1948; film prodn. Iran, 1949; Tibet expdn. with Lowell Thomas, Sr., 1949; field work Cinerama, S.Am., Africa, Asia, 1951-52; travels by small airplane with wife, writing and filming Europe, Africa, Middle East, 1954-55; mem. Rockwell Polar Flight, first flight around the world over both poles, Nov., 1965; mem. Alaska State Senate, 1967-74; lt. gov. State of Alaska, 1974-79; owner Talkeetna Air Taxi, Inc., air contract carrier, Anchorage, Alaska, 1980-94. Producer series of films Flight to Adventure, NBC-TV, 1956; producer, writer TV series High Adventure, 1957-59; producer documentary film Adaq, King of Alaskan Seas, 1960; producer two films on Alaska, 1962, 63, film on U. Alaska, 1964, South Pacific travel documentary, 1965, film on Arctic oil exploration, Atlantic-Richfield Co., 1969. Author: Out of this World, A Journey to Tibet, 1950, (with Mrs. Lowell Thomas, Jr.) Our Flight to Adventure, 1956, The Silent War in Tibet, 1959, The Dalai Lama, 1961, The Trail of Ninety-Eight, 1962, (with Lowell Thomas Sr.) More Great True Adventures, 1963, Famous First Flights that Changed History, 1968. Past pres. Western Alaska coun. Boys Scouts Am.; bd. dirs. Anchorage unit Salvation Army, Alaska Conservation Found. 1st lt. USAAF, 1943-45. Mem. Nat. Parks and Conservation Assn. (bd. dirs.), Alaska C. of C., Aircraft Owners and Pilots Assn. Clubs: Explorers, Marco Polo, Dutch Treat (N.Y.C.), Rotary, (Anchorage), Press (Anchorage); Dartmouth Outing; American Alpine. Address: 10800 Hideaway Lake Dr Anchorage AK 99507-6139

**THOMAS, LUCILLE COLE,** librarian; b. Dunn, NC, Oct. 1, 1921; d. Collie and Minnie (Lee) Cole; m. George Browne Thomas, May 24, 1943; children: Ronald C., Beverly G. BA, Bennett Coll., 1941; DHL (hon.), Benentt Coll., 1996; MA, NYU, 1955; MS, Columbia U., 1957. Tchr. Bibb County Bd. Edn., Macon, Ga., 1947—55; libr. Bklyn. Pub. Libr., 1955—56, NYC Bd. Edn., Bklyn., 1956—68, supr. librs., 1968—77, dir. elem. sch. librs., 1977—83; program dir. Weston Woods Inst., Weston, Conn., 1984—85; adj. prof. libr. sci. Queens Coll., CUNY, 1986—89; libr. cons., 1989—. Prof. libr. sci. St. John's U., 1986, Pratt Inst., 1989; founder Sch. Libr. Media Day, NY State, 1983. Jour. Sch. Libr. Media Month, 1985; cons. Putnam Pub. Group, NYC, 1983; bd. examiners NY City Bd. Edn., 1983—91; adv. bd. Regents' Adv. Council on Learning Tech., Albany, NY, 1982—88; reviewer U.S. Office Ednl. Rsch. & Improvement, 1988—90; coord. UNESCO/Internat. Assn. Sch. Librarianship Book Program for devel. countries, 1980—89; chair seminar for librs. from devel. countries, Spain, 1993; trustee NY Met. Ref. and Rsch. Libr. Agy., NYC, 1979—83; liaison Freedom to Read Found., 1986—88; 1st v.p. Shomburg Corp., 1983—85. Contbr. articles to profl. jours.; editor: Insight, 1974, Cultural Heritage Through Literature, 1993. Del. White House Conf. Libr. and Info. Svcs., 1979, World Conf. on Edn. for all in Jamtien, Thailand, 1990; hon. del. White House Conf. Libr. and Info. Svcs., 1991; treas. Bklyn. Home for Aged Commn., 1967—; del. NY Gov's. Conf. on Librs., 1978, 1990; adv. bd. Books Kids, 1989—; mem. libr. sect. Nat. Martin Luther King, Jr. Commn., 1990—95; trustee Bklyn. Pub. Libr., 1993—, v.p., 2000—03, pres., 2003—06; pres. bd. trustees St. Mark's Day Sch., 2001—; trustee Trustee of Leroy Merritt Humanitarian Award, 2005—; vestry mem. St. John's Episcopal Ch., Bklyn., 1988—90, chair stewardship com., 1987—90; active St. Mark's Ch., Bklyn., 1969—85, 1990—; bd. dirs. NY Is Book Country, 1991—96. Named Woman on the Move, State Sen. Carl Andrews, 2003; recipient Disting. Alumna award, Bennett Coll., 1981, Edn. award, Bus. and Profl. Women's Club, 1983, program v.p., Merit award, Bklyn. Coun. Suprs., 1983, Achievement award, Columbia U. Sch. Libr. Svcs., 1987, Grolier Found. award, 1988, Disting. Pub. Svc. award, SUNY, Albany, 1989, Svc. award, North Queens, NY, 1993, Disting. Svc. award, St. Mark's Ch., 2003, Achievement award, Consortium of Doctors, 2004, NY Black Librs., 2004, citation, Bklyn. Borough Pres., 2005, Letter of Commendation, First Lady Laura Bush, 2005, Faithful Servant award, Concord Bapt. Ch., 2006. Mem.: ALA (hon.), Internat. Sch. Librarianship (pres. 1989—93), Internat. Fedn. Libr. Assn. (sec. 1985—96, chair sch. librs. sect. 1989—93, ofcl. rep. UN and UNICEF 1991—94, chair planning and implementation com.), NYC Sch. Librs. Assn. (pres. 1970—72, chair sch. librs. sect. 1989—93), Bklyn. Pub. Libr. Found., Schomburg Commn. (1st v.p. 1986—90), Bklyn. Hist. Soc. (named one of outstanding women of Bklyn. 1985), Women's City of NYC Club (bd. dirs. 1986—2000, vice chmn. 1987—89, chair edn. com. 1989—92, v.p. 1992—93), NY Libr. Club (v.p. 1976—77, pres. 1977—93), Alpha Kappa

Alpha (Pi Phi Omega chpt. parliamentarian 1990—92, v.p. 1990—94, pres. 1994—2000, mem.-at-large 2004—, v.p. 1992—94, co-coord. 1996—2000). Democrat. Home: 1184 Union St Brooklyn NY 11225-1512 Personal E-mail: lucillecthomas@aol.com.

**THOMAS, M. ANN,** bank executive; m. Tony Singer, Aug. 31, 2001. JD, Ohio No. U., 1985. Atty. Bracewell & Patterson; exec. v.p. Woodforest Nat. Bank, Houston, 1995—99, COO, 1999—2001, pres., COO, 2001—. Named one of 25 Women to Watch, US Banker Mag., 2003. Office: Woodforest Nat Bank 13301 E Fwy Houston TX 77015

**THOMAS, MARCIA MARKOWITZ,** library director, educator; b. Fort Worth, Dec. 2, 1944; d. Samuel and Davida Shosid Markowitz; m. Rickard James Thomas, Sept. 1, 1978 (div. July 1982); children: Aaron, James; m. John Katchmarik, Dec. 2, 1994. BA, U. Mo., 1968, MA, 1975. Libr. asst. Kansas City (Mo.) Pub. Libr., 1968—73; libr. dir. Ruth R. Cleveland Meml. Libr., Kansas City, 1976—. Chair instl. rev. bd. Cleve. Chiropractic Coll., Kansas City, Mo., 1979—, prof. human biology, 1996—, faculty coun. pres., 1993—95, 2005—06, 1997—99, 2001—03. Co-author: Chiropractic: An Annotated Bibliography, 2000; contbr. articles to profl. jours. Rep. Southtown Neighborhood Coun., Kansas City; campus coord. Heart of Am. United Way, 1999—; bd. dirs. Astor Place Homes Assn., Kansas City, pres., 2004—; mem. task force sch. governance Kansas City Consensus. Mem.: ALA, MLA (chiropractic librs. sect., chair, program chair, bylaws com.), Chiropractic Libr. Consortium (pres., treas., sec.), Kansas City Libr. Network (treas., archivist), Midwest Bioethics Ctr., Med. Libr. Assn. (sect. coun. rep.). Liberal. Jewish. Avocations: bioethics, music, neighborhood advocacy. Office: Ruth R Cleveland Meml Libr 6401 Rockhill Rd Kansas City MO 64131 Office Phone: 816-501-0142. E-mail: marcia.thomas@cleveland.edu.

**THOMAS, MARIANNA,** volunteer community activist, writer, speaker; b. Greenville, Ohio, Dec. 9, 1927; d. John Darl and Eva Jane (Hill) Munn; m. Harold D. Krickenbarger, Aug. 31, 1947 (div.); children: Harold Krickenbarger Jr., Jane Krickenbarger, Marryln Krickenbarger, John Krickenbarger; m. Lowell J. Thomas, Jan. 5, 1977 (dec.); 1 stepchild, Lowell J. Student, Dayton (Ohio) Art Inst.; MA (hon.), Union (Ky.) Coll., 1978. Farmer Holstein Show Herd, Arcanum, Ohio, 1947-68; advt., broadcasting sta. work and writing positions Arcanum Times; sales and decorating positions Lowe Bros., Greenville, Ohio; exec. dir./fundraising Help for Children in the Holy Land/Spafford Children's Ctr., NYC, 1969-76. Author: Catitudes, 1987, The Second Mrs. Lowell Thomas, 2000; mem. bd. contbrs. Dayton Daily News. Founder Citizens for Moral War peace orgn., 1967—70; mem. coun. Freedoms Found. Valley Forge, 1982—84; founder, chmn. US Civil Responsibilities, Dayton, 1988—93; nat. bd. dirs. Family Svc. Assocs. Am., NYC, 1979—85, Am. Judicature Soc., 1978—80. Mem.: Dayton Engrs. Club (hon.). Avocations: painting, poetry, swimming, cooking. Home: PO Box 626 Dayton OH 45405-0626

**THOMAS, MARLIN ULUESS,** industrial engineer, educator, academic administrator; b. Middlesboro, Ky., June 28, 1942; s. Elmer Vernon and Helen Lavada (Banks) T.; m. Susan Kay Stoner, Jan. 18, 1963; children: Pamela Claire Thomas Davis, Martin Phillip. BSE, U. Mich., Dearborn, 1967; MSE, U. Mich., Ann Arbor, 1968, PhD, 1971. Registered profl. engr., Mich. Asst. and assoc. prof. dept. ops. rsch. Naval Postgrad. Sch., Monterey, Calif., 1971-76; assoc. prof. systems design dept. U. Wis., Milw., 1976-78; mgr. tech. planning and analysis vehicle quality-reliability Chrysler Corp., Detroit, 1978-79; prof. dept. indsl. engring. U. Mo., Columbia, 1979-82; prof. indsl. engring., chmn. dept. Cleve State U., 1982-88, acting dir. Advanced Mfg. Ctr., 1984-85; prof., chmn. indsl. engring. Lehigh U., Bethlehem, Pa., 1988-93; prof., head Sch. Indsl. Engring. Purdue U., West Lafayette, Ind., 1993-98; dir. Inst. Interdisciplinary Engring. Studies, West Lafayette, 1998—. Program dir. NSF, Washington, 1987-88. Contbr. numerous articles to indsl. engring. and ops. rsch. to profl. jours. With USN, 1958-62; capt. USNR, 1971—. Named Outstanding Tchr., U. Mo. Coll. Engring., 1980, Coll. Man of Yr, Cleve. State U. Coll. Engring., 1985, Disting. Alumnus of Yr., U. Mich.-Dearborn, 1996, Engr. Excell Engagement Svc. award, Purdue U., 2003, IIE Holzman Disting. Educator award, 2004. Fellow Inst. Indsl. Engrs. (past pres., recipient Frank Groseclose Medallion award, 2005), Am. Soc. for Quality, Inst. for Ops. Rsch. and Mgmt. Scis.; mem. Am. Soc. for Engring. Edn., Am. Indian Sci. and Engr. Soc., VFW, Seabee Vet. Am. Office: Sch Indsl Engring Purdue Univ 315 N Grant St West Lafayette IN 47907-2023 Office Fax: 765-494-1299. Business E-Mail: muthomas@ecn.purdue.edu.

**THOMAS, MARLO (MARGARET JULIA THOMAS),** actress; b. Detroit, Nov. 21, 1943; d. Danny and Rose Marie (Cassani) T.; m. Phil Donahue, May 21, 1980. Ed., U. So. Calif. Theatrical appearances in Thieves, Broadway, 1974, Barefoot in the Park, London, Social Security, Broadway, 1986, The Shadow Box, Broadway, 1994, Two Goldsteins on Acid, 1999; star: TV series That Girl, 1966-71 (Golden Globe award Best TV actress, 1967); appeared in TV films: The Body Human: Facts for Girls (Emmy award Best Performer Children's Program), 1981, The Last Honor of Kathryn Beck, 1984 (also exec. prodr.), Consenting Adults, 1985, Nobody's Child, 1986 (Emmy Best Dramatic Actress), Held Hostage: The Sis and Jerry Levin Story, 1991, Ultimate Betrayal, 1994, Reunion, 1994, A Century of Women, 1994, Playing Mona Lisa, 2000; TV movies: Two Against Time, 2002, Our Heroes, Ourselves, 2002, Deceit, 2004; TV appearances include Friends, 1996, 2002, Roseanne, 1996, Ally McBeal, 2000, Law & Order: Special Victims Unit, 2004; conceived book and record, starred in TV spl. Free to Be...You and Me, 1974 (Emmy for best children's show); films include Jenny, 1963, Thieves, 1977, In the Spirit, 1991, The Real Blonde, 1997, Startucker, 1998; conceived book, record and TV spl. Free to Be A Family (Emmy Best Children's Show). Recipient 4 Emmys, Golden Globe award, George Foster Peabody award, Tom Paine award Nat. Emergency Civil Liberties Com.; inducted into Broadcasting & Cable Hall of Fame. Mem. Ms. Found., Nat. Women's Polit. Caucus. Address: William Morris Agy 151 El Camino Dr Beverly Hills CA 90212 also: Creative Artists Agy 9830 Wilshire Blvd Beverly Hills CA 90211 Office: Kerner Entertainment 8522 National Blvd Ste 109 Culver City CA 90232-2454

**THOMAS, MARY ANN MCCRARY,** counselor, school system administrator; b. Washington, Feb. 11, 1935; d. Frank Robert and Mary (Davison) McCrary; m. John Ralph Thomas, Sept. 30, 1961; children: Robert Davison, John Shannon, Kristen Aldridge. BA, U. So. Calif., Berkley, 1956; MA, UCLA, 1959. Cert. tchr., Calif. Supr. Pacific Bell, San Francisco, 1962-67; advisor gifted, talented San Rafael (Calif.) City Schs., 1973—, counselor, 1973—, dir. student affairs, 1982—. Pres. San Rafael PTA Coun., 1981-84, outstanding svc. award, 1983, 86, 89, San Rafael High Sch. Site Coun., 1985; pres. bd. dirs. Marin Wildlife Ctr., 1979-85. Recipient Golden Bell award, Marin Community Found., 1987, Outstanding Student Activities program state award, 1992; named Pub. Schoolmaster of Yr., 1993. Mem. Calif. Assn. Gifted, Calif. Assn. Tchrs. English. Republican. Episcopalian. Avocations: reading, gardening. Home: 70 Windsor Ave San Rafael CA 94901-1068 Office: Davidson Mid Sch 280 Woodland Ave San Rafael CA 94901-5097

**THOMAS, MARY AUGUSTA,** library administrator; b. Washington, Mar. 15, 1951; d. Abram Henry and Mary Agnes Rosenfeld; m. George D. Thomas Jr., Nov. 9, 1991. AB cum laude, Mt. Holyoke Coll., South Hadley, Mass., 1973; MSLS, Cath. U., Washington, 1978. From rare book libr. to mgr. planning and adminstrn. Smithsonian Libr., Washington, 1976-91, asst. dir. 1991—2002, assoc. dir., 2002—. Author: An Odyssey in Print: Adventures in the Smithsonian Libraries/ Smithsonian Press, 2002; editor: Information Imagineering, 1998; contbr. mags. to librs. Recipient Smithsonian Inst. Sec.'s award for Excellence in Equal Employment Opportunity, 2000. Mem. ALA (chair editl. adv. bd., councilor 1999-2003, 05—, mem. com. orgn., 2004—), DC Libr. Assn. (pres. 1999, Disting. Svc. award 2001), Fed. Librs. and Info. Ctrs. (adv. bd. 1997-99), DC Libr. Adminstrn. and Mgmt. (chair, vice chair, and fiscal officer discussion group 1998—, chair, editl. adv. bd. LA&M 1998-2002), Beta Phi Mu. Avocations: cooking, writing. Office: Smithsonian Librs Nhb 22 Washington DC 20560-0001 Business E-Mail: thomasm@si.edu.

**THOMAS, MARY LEE,** property manager; d. Louis and Virgie Mae Bedford; children: Tamara Simone Times, Bobbi Makeda. A in Liberal Arts, S.W. Ill. Coll., 2003; B in Bus. Adminstrn., Lindenwood U., 2005. Mgmt. intern program East St. Louis Housing Authority, 1992, cert. earned income dissallowance specialist Nan Mckay And Assoc., 2003, pub. housing rent calculation specialist Nan Mckay And Assoc., 2004, universal phys. condition stds. specialist Nan McKay & Assocs., 2005. Property mgr. East St. Louis (Ill.) Housing Authority, 1990—2004, asset mgr., 2004—; uniform phys. condition stds. specialist Nan McKay and Assocs., 2005—. Mem.: Nat. Assn. Housing Redevelopment Orgn. (cert. pub. housing mgr. 1992). Democrat. Baptist. Achievements include received award for providing inspiration to co-workers and residents by singing at various functions within the housing authority and the community. Avocations: singing, cycling, walking, tae-bo, skating. Home: 718 Country Meadow Ln Belleville IL 62221 Office: E St Louis Housing Authority 700 N 20th St East Saint Louis IL 62205 Office Phone: 618-646-7321. Business E-Mail: mthomas@elsha.org.

**THOMAS, MICHAEL J.,** secondary school educator; children: Michael, Nathan, Samuel, Mathew. BS in Biology, No. Ariz. U., Flagstaff; MA in Edn., No. Ariz. U. Tchr. Needles Unified Sch. Dist., 1988—. Tchr. Grace Luth., Needles. Mem.: Elks (assoc.). Democrat. Office: Needles HS 1800 Washington Ave Needles CA 92363 Office Phone: 760-326-2191.

**THOMAS, MORY,** chef; b. Garden City, Kans. Grad., Conrad N. Hilton Coll. for Hotel and Restaurant Mgmt., U. Houston, Inst. Culinary Edn., NYC. Chef JoJo, NYC; recipe tester Food Network. Avocation: cooking. Office: Home of Food Network 75 9th Ave New York NY 10011*

**THOMAS, NANCY HINCKLEY,** special education educator; b. L.A., Mar. 7, 1939; d. Barton Armin and Helen (Ferguson) Hinckley; children: Gregory Dean, Garold Daniel, Deanna Nancy, Barton William, Deborah Hinckley, Bryan Joseph. AB, Stanford U., Calif., 1959. Resource Specialist Calif. Dept. head K-Mart Corp., Petaluma, Calif., 1982—89; spl. edn. tchr. R-House, Santa Rosa, Calif., 1994—2005, resource specialist, 1998—, St. Rose Sch., 2005—. Resource specialist St. Rose Sch., Santa Rosa, Calif., 2005—06. Mem. Commonwealth Club, San Francisco, 1996—2004. Mem.: AAUW (treas. 1965—67), Smithsonian Instn. Avocations: reading, gardening. Home: 724 Bassett St Petaluma CA 94952

**THOMAS, ORVILLE C.,** retired allergist; b. Haynesville, La., Aug. 23, 1915; children— David, Diane, Cody Pre-med. Student, Marian Mil. Inst., 1932-33, Tulane U., 1933, MD, 1939. Diplomate Am. Bd. Pediatrics. Diplomate Am. Bd. Allergy and Immunology. Intern Shreveport Charity Hosp., La., 1939-40; asst. resident in pediatrics Children's Meml. Hosp., Chgo., 1946-47, resident in pediatrics, 1947, chief resident in pediatrics, 1948; active staff Tex. Children's Hosp., Houston, 1962—, fellow pediatric allergy, 1963-65, chief allergy sect., 1973-78; fellow in pediatric allergy Baylor Coll. Medicine, 1963-65; chief pediatrics Schumpert Meml. Hosp., Shreveport, La., 1958-61, chief of staff, 1958; sr. staff pediatrics Confederate Meml. Hosp., Shreveport, La., 1948-61; active staff Highland Hosp., Shreveport, La., 1948-61, North La. Hosp., Shreveport, La., 1948-61, Physicians and Surgeons Hosp., Shreveport, La., 1948-61, Ben Taub Gen. Hosp., Houston, 1962—, Hermann Hosp., Houston, 1966-69; hon. staff St. Luke's Hosp., Houston, 1962—; cons. staff Meth. Hosp., Houston, 1962—, St. Joseph Hosp., Houston, 1966—, Bellaire (Tex.) Gen. Hosp., 1966-86, Rosewood Gen. Hosp., Houston, 1967—, Meml. Bapt. Hosp., Houston, 1968—, Pasadena Bayshore Hosp., Pasadena, Tex., 1970—; instr. pediatrics Northwestern U. Sch. Medicine, Chgo., 1948; assoc. prof. pediatrics La. State U. Postgrad. Sch. Medicine, 1956-61; clin. instr. pediatrics Baylor Coll. Medicine, Houston, 1961-66, asst. clin. prof. pediatrics, 1966-76, assoc. clin. prof. pediatrics, 1977—. Assoc. clin. prof. allergy and immunology U. Tex. Grad. Sch. Biomed. Scis., Houston, 1970—. Book reviewer: Venom Diseases; Aspects of Allergy and Applied Immunology. Contbr. articles to profl. jours. Served to maj. USMC AUS, 1942-46. Fellow Am. Coll. Allergy and Immunology (pediatrics com. 1964—, pres. 1978), Am. Acad. Allergy and Immunology, Am. Assn. Cert. Allergists (bd. govs. 1974, pres. 1979); mem. AMA, Am. Acad. Pediatrics. So. Med. Assn. (chmn. allergy sect. 1970-71), Tex. Allergy Research Found. Houston(research and edn. com. 1966-86, chmn. sci. adv. council 1973—), Tex. Pediatric Soc., Harris County Med. Soc., Tex. Med. Assn. (chmn. allergy sect. 1976-77), Am. Assn. for Inhalation Therapy (awards com. 1969-72, spl. edn. com. 1969-72), Greater Houston Allergy Soc. (pres. 1977), Joint Council of Allergy and Immunology, Internat. Assn. of Allergology and Clin. Immunology (U.S. rep. 1981-85). Home: 651 Bering Dr Unit 902 Houston TX 77057

**THOMAS, PATRICIA ANNE,** retired law librarian; b. Cleve., Aug. 21, 1927; d. Richard Joseph and Marietta Bernadette (Teevans) T. BA, Case Western Res. U., 1949; JD, 1951. Bar: Ohio 1951, U.S. Supreme Ct. 1980. Libr. Arter & Hadden, Cleve., 1951-62; asst. libr. IRS, Washington, 1962-78; libr. dir. Adminstrv. Office U.S. Cts., 1978-93; ret., 1993. Mem. Am. Assn. Law Librs., Soc. D.C. (pres. 1967-69), Soc. Benchers (Case Western Res. Law Sch.)

**THOMAS, PATRICIA GOODNOW,** journalist; b. Framingham, Mass., Dec. 28, 1924; d. Charles Frederick and Dorothy (Eaton) G.; m. Roy Condit Thomas, Oct. 7, 1961. BS, Simmons Coll., 1946; MAT, Rollins Coll., 1971. News reporter-writer Radio Station WCOP, Boston, 1946-52; editorial specialist Central Intelligence Agy., Washington, 1952-54; asst. editor Hood Milk Corp., Boston, 1954-55; sr. writer/editor Voice of America, Washington, 1955-61; writer Orlando Mag. Orlando, Fla. 1964-72; tchr. French, Eng. Oviedo (Fla.) H.S., 1965-66; prof. of journalism Seminole Cmty. Coll., Sanford, Fla., 1972-88; freelance writer Blairsville, Ga., 1988—. Editor: From Sky to Sea, 1993; contbr. articles to profl. jours. Mem. Fla. Freelance Writers Assn., Kappa Delta Pi. Personal E-Mail: rpthomas@alltel.net.

**THOMAS, PATRICIA JOANNE,** journalist, writer; b. Kenosha, Wis., July 17, 1948; d. Leatrice Shuman Magic and Russell Morton Maxwell (Stepfather); life ptnr. Meriwether Burrusse Rhodes. BA, U. of Calif., Berkeley, 1967—69; MA, Stanford U., 1969—70. Vis. scholar, knight ctr. for sci. and med. journalism Boston U., Boston, 2002—03; editor, harvard health letter Harvard Med. Sch., Boston, 1991—97. Mem., bd. of advisors Am. Bd. of Internal Medicine, Philadelphia, Pa., 1992—98. Author: (non-fiction book) Big Shot: Passion, Politics, and the Struggle for an AIDS Vaccine (Leonard Silk Journalism fellowship, 1998). Elected mem. Town Meeting, Arlington, Mass., 1992—2002. Fellow Knight Sci. Journalism Fellowship, MIT, 1986-1987. Mem.: Nat. Assn. Sci. Writers. Avocations: tennis, standard poodles. Home: 775 Riverhill Dr Athens GA 30606-4049 Personal E-mail: pthomasauthor@yahoo.com.

**THOMAS, PATRICK,** Native American tribal leader; Vice chmn. Blackfeet Nation, 2004—05, chmn., 2005—. Office: Blackfeet Tribe PO Box 850 Browning MT 59417 Office Phone: 406-338-7521. Office Fax: 406-338-7530.*

**THOMAS, PATRICK ROBERT MAXWELL,** oncologist, educator, academic administrator; b. Exmouth, Devon, Eng., Feb. 23, 1943; came to U.S., 1976; s. Christopher Codrington and Aileen Daphne (Gordon) T.; m. Linda Sharon Rich, June 23, 1986 (dec. 1987); m. Geraldine M. Jacobson, Mar. 2, 1996 (div. 1999); m. Frances Aquino, Feb. 19, 2005. Diploma in biochemistry, London U., 1965, MB, BS, 1968. Lectr. Inst. Cancer Rsch., London, 1974-76; assoc. chief clinician Roswell Park Meml. Inst., Buffalo, 1976-79; asst. prof. Washington U., St. Louis, 1979-83, assoc. prof., 1983-89, prof., 1989-90; prof., chmn. Temple U., Phila., 1991-98; radiation oncologist Pinellas (Fla.) Radiation Oncology Assocs., 1998—; prof. radiation oncology Pa. State U., 2004—, Pa. State U., 2006—. Extramural bd. PDQ, Bethesda, Md., 1989—; mem. in-svc. exam. com. Am. Coll. Radiology, Reston, Va., 1990-97; examiner Am. Bd. Radiology, Louisville, 1990—. Mem. editl. adv. bd.: Med. and Pediatric

Oncology, 2002—. Fellow Am. Coll. Radiologists, Royal Coll. Physicians of London; mem. Internat. Soc. Pediatric Oncology (sci. com. 2000—). Office: 100 Beach Dr NE Saint Petersburg FL 33701

**THOMAS, PAUL AUGUSTUS, JR.,** retired thoracic surgeon; b. Berlin, NH, Dec. 6, 1923; s. Paul Augustus and Madge M. (Murphy) Thomas; m. Loretta Hardin-Thomas (div.); m. Eva Cuna Hernandez-Thomas, May 22, 1979; children: Paul A., Marian K., John H., Laura A., Robert F., Susan L., Renyann T. MD, George Wash. U., 1952. Clin. assoc. prof. surgery Jefferson U., Lankenau Hosp., Phila., 1970—75; clin. prof. surgery U. Ill. Dept. Surgery, Chgo., 1975—95; chief staff, chief surgery VA West Side Med. Ctr. Contbr. articles various profl. jours. Elected rep., pres. Village Libr. Bd., Western Springs, Ill., 1996—2001; state ctrl. com. Rep. Party, Ill., 1998—2002. Col. U.S. Army, 1952—70. Various grants, VA Adminstrn. Republican. Roman Cath. Avocations: politics, music, golf. Home: 5127 Ellington Ave Western Springs IL 60558

**THOMAS, PAUL D.,** human resources specialist, metal products executive; V.p. Alcoa, Inc., Pitts., 1998—2004, pres. engineered products, 1998—2001, pres. mill products, 2001—03, group pres. N.Am. fabricated products, 2003—04, exec. v.p., 2004—, exec. v.p. people, ABS and culture, 2004—. Bd. dirs. Aloca Found., Aluminum Assn., Inc. Office: Alcoa Inc 201 Isabella St Pittsburgh PA 15212-5858 Office Phone: 412-553-4545.

**THOMAS, PAUL LINDSLEY,** composer, musician, director; b. N.Y.C., Mar. 18, 1929; s. Richard Banks and Virginia Bartholomew (Carrington) T.; m. Joyce Robertshaw, Sept. 3, 1955; 1 child, Craig Carrington. BA, Trinity Coll., Hartford, Conn., 1950; diploma, Am. Conservatory, Fontainbleau, France, 1954; MusB, Yale U., 1957, MusM, 1958; D of Musical Arts, U. North Tex., 1979. Organist, choirmaster St. George's-by-the-River, Rumson, NJ, 1950-55; St. James Episcopal Ch., West Hartford, Conn., 1955-60; organist Wesleyan U., Middletown, Conn., 1958-60; dir. Apollo Glee Club, Yale U., New Haven, 1958-60; instr. in organ So. Meth. U., Dallas, 1960-65; music dir., organist St. Michael and All Angels Ch., Dallas, 1960-97; composer in residence, music dir. emeritus, 1997—; music dir. Trinity Epis. Ch., Dallas, 1998—. Chmn. liturgy and music commn. Episcopal Diocese of Dallas, 1992—98. Composer (opera) Everyman, 1986; composer ch. anthems and organ music. Named Canon of Ch. Music, Episcopal Diocese of Dallas, 1980; recording grantee Stemmons Found., Dallas, 1995; Joyce and Paul Thomas Music Wing named in his honor St. Michael and All Angels, Dallas, 1994. Fellow Am. Guild Organists (dean Dallas chpt. 1967-69, gen. chmn. nat. conv. 1972, nat. coun. 1972-75); mem. Assn. Anglican Musicians, Am. Choral Dirs. Assn. Republican. Episcopalian. Home: 6822 Northwood Rd Dallas TX 75225-2538 Office: Trinity Episcopal Ch 12727 Hillcrest Rd Dallas TX 75230-2007

**THOMAS, PAUL MILTON,** retired science educator; b. Sligo, Pa., Dec. 1, 1929; s. Milton Ivan and Maude, Hazel Thomas; m. Dorothy Marie McGinnett; 1 child, Mona Lee Callahan. BA, Allegheny Coll., 1958; MEd, U. Mich. 1959, MA, 1962, PhD, 1964; DMin, Drew U., 1980. Instr. biology Houghton Coll., NY, 1959—62; asst. prof. Point Loma Coll., San Diego, 1964—66; rsch. fellow Calif. Inst. Tech., Pasadena, 1967—68; vis. prof. Johns Hopkins U., Baltimore, 1968; prof., chmn. dept. biology Edinboro U., Pa., 1968—90; pastor United Ch. of Christ, Greensburg, 1993—2006. Vis. scholar Harvard U., Cambridge, Mass., 1993. Contbr. articles to profl. jours.; author: (books) W. Edwards Deming: Improving Quality in Colleges and Universities, Easter Urges Us to Look at Death, A Christian Looks at Death, Pennsylvania Fish Commission, Fishes of Erie County, Fishes of Pymatuning. Mem. Sch. Bd., Union City, Pa., 1969—75. Mem.: Audubon Soc., Sigma Xi, Phi Kappa Phi. R-Consevative. United Church Of Christ. Avocations: hiking, world traveling. Home: 87 West High St Union City PA 16438-1239 Personal E-mail: pthomas@velocity.net.

**THOMAS, PETER CHARLES,** psychologist, educator; b. Houston, Sept. 24, 1947; s. Stephen and Eileen S. (Steyn) T.; m. Beverly J. Call, Aug. 30, 1969; children: Jonathan, Stephen, Katherine. BA in Psychology, Emory U., 1969; MEd in Sch. Psychology, Ga. State U., 1970, PhD in Sch. Psychology, 1978. Instr. Ga. State U., Atlanta, 1970-72; cons. Ga. Dept. Edn., Atlanta, 1972-73; field coord. U.S. Office Edn.: Exemplary Racial Discrimination Project, N.C., 1974; psychologist Dekalb County Sch. System, Atlanta, 1973-82; pvt. practice Atlanta, 1982—. Cons. Decatur City Sch. Sys., 1982-86, Ga. Spl. Olympics Program, Atlanta, 1987, Fulton County Sch. Sys., 1984-87, Needs Assessment Panel for Psychological Svcs. Fayette County Schs., 2001; mem. adv. bd. Village of St. Joseph, Gables Acad., 1981-94, AIDS and Drug adv. bd. Met. Regional Ednl. Svc. Agy., Atlanta, The Howard Schs.; bd. dirs. Profl. Acad. Custody Evaluators, Doylestown Borough, Pa., 1993—, bd. mem. Internat. Dyslexia Assn. (Ga. br.), 2005—. Bd. dirs. Briarcliff Woods Civic Assn., Atlanta, 1982-84, North Atlanta Parents Coun., 1990—; bd. dirs., pres. Briarcliff Woods Beach Club, Atlanta, 1980-82, 85-87; mem. profl. adv. bd. L.D. Adults of Ga., 2002—; mem. bd. Internat. Dyslexia Assn., Ga., 2005-. Recipient Service award Down Syndrome Assn. of Atlanta, 1986. Fellow Ga. Psychol. Assn. (Divsn. G chmn. 1985-87, 96-97, treas. 1996-99, mem. ethics com. 2000—, v.p. 2005—; Cert. of Merit for Outstanding Contbn. to Profession of Psychology, 1987, Pres. award 1999); mem. APA, Nat. Acad. Neuropsychology, Soc. Personality Assessment, Assn. Children with Learning Disabilities, Ga. Assn. Sch. Psychologists (bd. mem. 1982-83). Avocations: swimming, ballroom dancing, home remodeling. Home: 1821 Morris Landers Dr NE Atlanta GA 30345-4103 Office: Ste 775 3500 Piedmont Rd NE Atlanta GA 30303 Office Phone: 404-633-3725. E-mail: pctfocus@bellsouth.net.

**THOMAS, PHILIP STANLEY,** economist, educator; b. Hinsdale, Ill., Oct. 23, 1928; s. Roy Kehl and Pauline (Grafton) Thomas; m. Carol Morris, Dec. 27, 1950; children: Lindsey Carol, Daniel Kyle, Lauren Louise, Gay Richardson. BA, Oberlin Coll., 1950; MA, U. Mich., 1951, PhD, 1961; postgrad., Delhi U., 1953—54. Instr. U. Mich., 1956-57; asst. prof. Grinnell (Iowa) Coll., 1957-63, assoc. prof., 1963-65; assoc. prof. econs. Kalamazoo Coll., 1965-68, prof. econs., 1968-94, prof. emeritus, 1994—. Econ. advisor Pakistan Inst. Devel. Econs., 1963—64, USAID, 1965—68, 1971, Planning Commn.. Pakistan, 1969—70, Ctrl. Bank Swaziland, 1974—75, Ministry Planning, Kenya, 1980—81, 1983—85, 1986—88, Ministry Fin., Swaziland, 1990, Kenya, 91, 92, Ministry Indsl. Devel., Sri Lanka, 1997, Res. Bank Malawi, 1998—99, Jordan-U.S. Bus. Partnership, 2000—01. Contbr. articles to profl. jours. Mem. alumni coun. Oberlin Coll., 1961—63, 1974—76, 1983—88, 1995—2001, treas. alumni coun., 2004—06. With AUS, 1954—56. Fellow Overseas, Ford Found., 1953—54; scholar Fulbright. Mem.: Am. Econs. Assn., Phi Beta Kappa. Home and Office: 313A S Shabwasung St Northport MI 49670-9604 E-mail: pcthomas@charter.net.

**THOMAS, PHILLIP,** music educator, department chairman, musician; b. Huntington, W.Va., July 16, 1954; s. Francis E. and Nettie Thomas; m. Dale Frith, Aug. 13, 1977; 1 child, Shannon N. BA in Music, Lee Coll., 1976; MusM, Peabody Conservatory of Johns Hopkins U., 1977; PhD, U. Cin., 1996. Prof. music, chair dept. instrumental music Lee U., Cleveland, Tenn., 1977—. Staff pianist Chattanooga Symphony Orch., 1977—83; tchg. asst. Coll. Conservatory Music U. Cin., 1984—85; min. music East Ridge Ch. of God, Chattanooga, 1985—94; staff pianist Mt. Paran North Ch. of God, Marietta, Ga., 1995—; conducting fellow Inst. Musical de Provence-Aubagne, 2001. Condr., prodr. (musical recording) Lee U. Chamber Orch. Organizer, devel. cmty./univ. orch. program Lee U. Named prize winner, George Gershwin Piano Competition, Tenn.; scholar Grad. Fellowship, U. of Cin., 1983-85. Mem.: Music Tchrs. Nat. Assn. (profl. cert. piano 1989, cert. chair Tenn. chpt. 1993—98), Coll. Music Soc., Am. Musicological Soc., Pi Kappa Lambda. Office: Lee U Sch Music 1020 N Ocoee St Cleveland TN 37320-3450 Office Phone: 423-614-8264. E-mail: pthomas@leeuniversity.edu.

**THOMAS, RALPH CHARLES, III,** federal official; b. Roanoke, Va., Apr. 10, 1949; s. Ralph C. Jr. and Dorothy (Easley) T. BA, U. Calif., Berkeley, 1975; JD, Harvard U., 1978. Assoc. Bergson, Borkland, Margolis & Adler, Washington, 1978-80; sr. ptnr. Thomas, John & Everett, Washington, 1980-85; clin. instr. in Law Sch. George Washington U., Washington, 1982-83; exec. dir. Nat. Assn. Minority Contractors, Washington, 1985-92; assoc. adminstr. for small/disadvantaged bus. utilization NASA, Washington, 1992—. Adj. instr. U. Va., Charlottesville, 1989—91; chmn. Fed. Small Bus. Dirs. Interagy. Coun., 2001—03; bd. dirs. Sr. Execs. Assn., 2002—05. Author: Extreme Flashbacks, 1997; contbr. articles to profl. jours. Mem. Pres.'s Interagy. Working Group on Minority Bus. Devel., 1995. Staff sgt. USAF, 1967-71, Vietnam. Recipient Spl. Honor award, World Assn. Small and Medium Enterprises, 1999, Presdl. Rank for Disting. Exec. award, 2001, Minority Bus. Entrepreneur Adv. of Yr. award, Asian Enterprise mag., 2004, Man of Yr. award, Minority Enterprise Adv. Mag., 2005. Mem. Fed. Bar Assn. (chair govt. contracts sect. 2002-03). Office: NASA Small & Disadvantaged Bus Utilization 300 E St SW Code K Washington DC 20546-0005

**THOMAS, RANDALL STUART,** lawyer, educator; b. Princeton, N.J., Nov. 25, 1955; s. John Bowman and Eleanor (Graefe) T.; m. Cheri D. Ferrari; children: Cameron Stuart, Cortland Andrew, Colin Duncan, Carson F. Thomas. BA, Haverford Coll., 1977; MA, U. Mich., 1979, PhD, 1983, JD, 1985. Bar: Del. 1987, U.S. Dist. Ct. Del. 1987. Economist U. Mich., Ann Arbor, 1979-83; law clk. Fed. Dist. Ct. (ea. dist.) Mich., Ann Arbor, 1985; assoc. Potter, Anderson & Corroon, Wilmington, Del., 1986, Skadden, Arps, Slate, Meagher & Flom, Wilmington, 1987-90; assoc. prof. law U. Iowa, 1990-94, prof. law, 1994—, Vanderbilt Univ., 2000—, John Beasley prof. law and bus., 2003—. Vis. prof. Boston U. Law Sch., 1995, U. Mich. Law Sch., 1996, Duke U. Sch. Law, 1999. Rackham fellow U. Mich., 1982-83. Mem.: Order of Coif. Democrat. Methodist. Office: Vanderbilt Univ Sch Law 131 21st Ave S Nashville TN 37203-1120 Office Phone: 615-343-3814. Business E-Mail: Randall.Thomas@law.vanderbilt.edu.

**THOMAS, REGENA L.,** former state official; b. Clinton, Ky., Oct. 31, 1957; BA in U. Studies, Morehead State U. Cons. Dem. Gov.'s Assn.; legislative analyst Legislative Research Commn., KY State Legislature, 1980—85; ptnr. IEM Mesage mgmt., Inc.; served Torricelli for Senate, 1996, McGreevey for Gov., 1997, Corzine for Senate, 2000; sec. state State of N.J., Trenton, 2002—06. Prin. liaison non-govtl. orgns., key Dem. constituencies; dep., dir. Constituent Svcs. Govt. Dist. Columbia; legis. analyst Legis. Rsch. Commn. Ky. State Legislature; with Nat. Rainbow Coalition and its founder, Rev. Jesse L. Jackson.*

**THOMAS, RICHARD,** actor; b. NYC, June 13, 1951; s. Richard and Barbara (Fallis) T.; m. Alma Gonzalez, Feb. 14, 1975 (div. 1993); children: Richard F., Barbara, Gwyneth and Pilar (triplets); m. Georgiana Bischoff, Nov. 20, 1995; 1 child, Montana; children from previous marriage: Brooke, Kendra. Student, Columbia U. Owner, prin. Melpomene Prodns. Actor: (broadway debut at age 7 in) Sunrise at Campobello, 1958, A Naked Girl on the Appian Way, 2005; (regular on children's series) One, Two, Three-Go!, 1961-62, regular (TV series) The Waltons, 1972—77 (Emmy award, 1973, Golden Globe nominee); dir.: (TV series) The Waltons, 1972; actor: (films) Strange Interlude, 1962, The Playroom, 1965, Winning, 1969, Last Summer, 1969, You Can't Have Everything, 1970, Red Sky at Morning, 1971, The Todd Killings, 1971, Cactus in the Snow, 1971, You'll Like My Mother, 1972, 9/30/55, 1977, Battle Beyond the Star, 1980, Wonder Boys, 2000, Fortune Hunters, 2000; (stage appearances) Sunrise at Campobello, 1958, Whose Life Is It Anyway?, 1980, The Fifth of July, 1981, The Sea Gull, 1984, The Count of Monte Cristo, 1985, Citizen Tom Paine, 1986, The Front Page, 1986, Hamlet, 1987, Peer Gynt, 1989, Love Letters, 1989-90, Square One, 1990, Lisbon Traviata, 1990, Danton's Death, 1992, Richard II, 1993, Richard III, 1994, Tiny Alice, 1998, 2000, Measure for Measure, 1999, A Midsummer's Night's Dream, 1999, stage appearances ART (West End), 2000, 2001, A Distant Country Called Youth, 2002, The Stendahl Syndrome, 2004, Democracy, 2004; stage appearances: A Naked Girl on the Appian Way, 2005, Twelve Angry Men, 2006—; author: (poems) Poems by Richard Thomas, Vols. I and 2, 1974; actor: (TV dramatic spl. and movies) The Homecoming-A Christmas Story, 1971, The Red Badge of Courage, 1974, The Silence, 1975, All Quiet on the Eastern Front, 1979, The Hank Williams Jr. Story, 1983, Hobson's Choice, 1984, The Master of Ballantrae, 1984, Getting Married, No Other Love, 5th of July, 1981, Common Ground, Glory!, Glory!, 1990, Andre's Mother, 1990, It, 1990, Mission of the Shark, 1991, Yes, Virginia There Is a Santa Claus, 1991, A Walton's Thanksgiving Reunion, 1993, Death in Small Doses, 1993, Linda, 1993, A Walton Wedding, 1995, A Christmas Box, 1995, What Love Sees, 1996, A Walton Easter, 1998, Swiss Family Robinson, 1997, 1,000 Men and a Baby, 1997, Swiss Family Robinson, 1997, 1,000 Men and a Baby, 1997, Flood: A River's Rampage, 1997, Down Out and Dangerous, 1997, Big and Hairy, 1998, Beyond the Prairie, 2000, In the Name of the People, 2000, It's a Miracle, 1999-2000, The Christmas Secret, 2000, Miracle of the Cards, 2001, Beyond the Grave II, 2002, Anna's Dream, 2002, Annie's Point, 2005, Wild Hearts, 2005, Nightmaers and Dreamscapes, 2006, (host children's spl.) H.M.S. Pinafore, 1973; (TV series) Touched By an Angel, 1994, Promised Land, 1996, The Practice, 1997, Law & Order: Special Victims Unit, 1999, Just Cause, 2002—host: It's a Miracle. Nat. chmn. Better Hearing Inst., 1987. Office: care Springer Assoc 1501 Broadway Ste 506 New York NY 10036-5601 Office Phone: 212-354-4660.

**THOMAS, RICHARD STEPHEN,** construction executive; b. Mason City, Iowa, June 5, 1949; s. H. Idris and Mildred (Keen) T.; m. Pamela Jane Chipka, Sept. 11, 1982. AA, No. Iowa C.C., 1969; BA, U. No. Iowa, 1971, BLS, 1991; MBA, U. Calif., Berkeley, 1991. Cost acct. Boise Cascade, Mason City, Iowa, 1971-72, cost acct. mgr. Shippensburg, Pa., 1973-74; staff acct. Grumman Corp., Williamsport, Pa., 1974-76; acctg. mgr. Pullman Power Products, Williamsport, 1976-79; treas, controller Schweizer Dipple Inc., Cleve., 1979-87; treas., corp. controller Langenau Mfg. Co., Cleve., 1987-92, chief fin. officer, 1987-92; sec.-treas. World Trade Wins Inc., Cleve., 1987-92; v.p. fin. and CFO Norris Bros. Co., Inc., Cleve., 1992—. Mem. employer adv. com. Ohio Job Svc., Greater Cleve. Growth Assn., Westlake Ohio Sch. Bd. Mem. Inst. Mgmt. Accts. (contr.'s coun. 1985), Constrn. Fin. Mgmt. Assn. (pres. 1995-2002, state dir., nat. dir.), Am. Coun. for Constrn. Edn. (fin. comm. 1997-98), Constrn. Industry Liason Comm. (chmn.), Cleve. Treas.'s Assn., Cleve. Engring. Soc., Associated Builders and Contractors, Constrn. Employers Assn., Cleve. World Trade Assn., Masons (local treas. 1984), York Rite Bodies, City Club of Cleve., U. Club, Cleve. Athletic Club, Phi Beta Lambda. Republican. Avocations: skiing, photography, sailing. Home: 1663 Settlers Reserve Way Westlake OH 44145-2042 Office: Norris Bros Co Inc 2138 Davenport Ave Cleveland OH 44114-3791 Office Phone: 216-771-2233. Personal E-mail: rsthomas49@netzero.com.

**THOMAS, RITCHIE TUCKER,** lawyer; b. Cleve., Aug. 12, 1936; s. Myron F. and Marjorie (Ritchie) T.; m. Elizabeth Blackwell Hanes Main, Jan. 1, 1994. BA, Cornell U., 1959; JD, Case-Western Res. U., 1964. Bar: Ohio 1964, U.S. Dist. Ct. (no. dist.) Ohio 1964, U.S. Ct. Appeals (D.C. cir.) 1971, U.S. Ct. Appeals (fed. cir.) 1973, U.S. Ct. Fed. Claims 1973, U.S. Ct. Internat. Trade 1976, U.S. Ct. Appeals (9th cir.) 1985. Assoc. office of gen. counsel U.S. Tariff Commn., Washington, 1964-67; assoc. Squire, Sanders & Dempsey, Cleve., 1967-69, Cox, Langford & Brown, Washington, 1969-74; ptnr. Squire, Sanders & Dempsey, Washington, 1974—. Mem. exec. com. Meridian House Internat., Washington, 1977-94. Assoc. editor Western Res. U. Law Rev., 1964; columnist Commerce Germany; contbr. articles to profl. jours. Mem. Waring Prize Com., Western Res. Acad., 1996—; mem. Bretton Woods Com., Washington, 2003— Recipient Book award West Pub. Co., 1964 Mem. Fed. Bar Assn., D.C. Bar Assn., Belgian American Assn. (v.p. bd. dirs. 1989—), Am. C. of C. (Washington rep. 1984—), Order of Coif. Home 620 Bradley Blvd Bethesda MD 20817-3045 Office: Squire Sanders & Dempsey 1201 Pennsylvania Ave NW PO Box 407 Washington DC 20044-0407 Business E-Mail: rtthomas@ssd.com.

**THOMAS, ROB (ROBERT KELLY THOMAS),** singer, songwriter; b. Landstuhl, Germany, Feb. 14, 1972; m. Marisol Maldonado, 1999; 1 child from previous relationship, Maison Avery William. Co-founder, band mem. Tabitha's Secret, 1993—95; lead singer, pianist Matchbox Twenty, 1996—. Singer: (albums) Yourself or Someone Like You, 1996, Mad Season, 2000, More Than You Think You Are, 2002, Something to Be, 2005, Ever the Same, 2005, (songs) Smooth (with Carlos Santana), 1999 (Grammy awards: Record of the Year, 1999, Song of the Year, 1999, Best Pop Collaboration with Vocals, 1999); vocals: (albums) The Great Divide (with Willie Nelson), 2002, background vocals: (albums) Goddess in the Doorway (with Mick Jagger), 2001, Broken Promises (with Rusty Truck), 2003. Recipient Starlight award, Songwriters Hall of Fame, 2004.

**THOMAS, ROBERT EGGLESTON,** retired manufacturing executive; b. Cuyahoga Falls, Ohio, July 28, 1914; s. Talbott E. and Jane S. (Eggleston) T.; 1 child, Barbara Ann. BS in Econs, U. Pa., 1936. Asst. to gen. mgr., sec., mgr. r.r. investments Keystone Custodian Funds, Boston, 1936-53; v.p. Pennroad Corp., NYC, 1953-59; chmn. exec. com., dir. M.A.- T. R.R., 1956-65; mem. exec. com. MAPCO Inc., 1960-84, dir., chief exec. officer, 1960-80, pres., 1960-76, chmn. bd., 1973-84. Bd. dir. BancOkla. Corp. Mem.: Newcomen Soc., Nat. Mining Assn. (hon. dir.), Am. Petroleum Inst. (hon. dir.), Desert Horizons Country Club (Indian Wells, Calif.), San Diego Yacht Club, Summit Club (Tulsa), So. Hills Country Club (Tulsa), Chgo. Club. Episcopalian. Office: Williams Cos PO Box 4679 Tulsa OK 74159-0679 Office Phone: 918-573-8100. E-mail: Robert.Thomas@williams.com.

**THOMAS, ROBERT JAY,** music educator, musician; b. Wheeling, W.Va., Dec. 11, 1947; s. Robert John and Edna Mae Thomas; m. Mary Lane Fahnestock-Thomas, May 20, 1984; children: Mary Elizabeth Fahnestock, Robert George Fahnestock. MusB, W.Va. U., 1969; MusM, Ind. U., 1974, MusD, 1979. Cert. tchr. music Nashville Tchrs. Nat. Assn., 1980. Instr. music DePauw U., Greencastle, Ill., 1977—79, asst. prof. music, 1979—82, Miami U., 1982—87, assoc. prof. music, 1987—97, prof. music, 1997—. Musician: Weinbrennersaal, Kurhaus, Church St. Martin-in-the-Fields, Weill Recital Hall of Carnegie Hall, National Radio Broadcast Dame Myra Hess Memorial Concerts series, National Radio Broadcast from WFMT-FM Robert Schumann, Live, series, Xavier U. Classical Piano Series. Specialist U.S. Army, 1970—73, Seoul, South Korea. Mem.: Am. Fedn. Musicians, Music Tchrs. Nat. Assn., European Piano Tchrs. Assn. (assoc.; recitals at confs.). Episcopalian. Avocations: hiking, running, traveling. Office: Miami University Oxford OH 45056 Office Phone: 513-529-3078. Office Fax: 513-529-3027. Business E-Mail: thomasrj@muohio.edu.

**THOMAS, ROBERT L.,** retired manufacturing company executive; b. Atlanta, Aug. 1, 1941; s. Orville Kermit Smith and Ina Evelyn (Farris) Peterson; m. Karen Degenhardt, Dec. 4, 1960 (div. Apr. 1978); children: John Harding, Gregory James, Kristen Ann; m. Mary Ellen Seaman, May 2, 1981; children: Lindsey Marian, Mark Gordon. BA in History, Queens Coll., 1968. Buyer J.C. Penney Co. Inc., NYC, 1964-70; sales mgr. Avon Products Inc., Atlanta, 1970-72; pres. Saul Bros. & Co. Inc., Atlanta, 1973—2002; founder, pres., CEO RLT Enterprises, LLC, Atlanta, 2004—. Bd. dirs. Murphey Candler Little League, Atlanta, 1972, also bd. trustees; bd. dirs. Leukemia Soc., Atlanta, 1988—; mem. Dekalb County Exec. Com. Rep. Party, Atlanta, 1970-74; del. State Convention Rep. Party, Atlanta, 1972. Established scholarship Michael Daniel and Alexander Tyler Smith Scholarship Found., U. S.C., 1995—. Mem. South East Textile and Apparel Mfrs., U.S. Polo Assn., Atlanta Polo Club, Gulfstream Polo Club (West Palm Beach), N.Y. Athletic Club (N.Y.C.), Country Club of the South (Alpharetta, Ga.). Republican. Roman Catholic. Home: 4095 Big Creek Overlook Alpharetta GA 30005-4213 Office Phone: 678-296-6409. E-mail: rthomas93@comcast.net.

**THOMAS, ROBERT MCGUFFEY,** automotive executive, educator; b. Newcastle, Pa., Jan. 7, 1917; s. Trevor Thomas and Clara Belle Speer; m. Millie Reddy, Jan. 7, 1945 (div. Apr. 11, 1962); children: Trevor, Diane, Robert; m. Natalie Khorandf, Apr. 10, 1964. Degree in Music (hon.), Music Master, Sharon, Pa. 1938. Exec. stalist Ford Motor Co., Dearborn, Mich., 1965—74; piano tchr. and band leader San Diego, 1975—95; sign painter Penny Co. Sharon. Author: How To Play Piano, 1984, War Is Hell, 1985, Life Is Life, 1995. With U.S. Army, 1940—45. Europe. Mem.: Piano Club. Avocation: piano. Home: 10539 Caminito Pollo San Diego CA 92126

**THOMAS, ROBERT MORTON, JR.,** lawyer; b. Kansas City, Kans., Jan. 1, 1941; s. Robert Morton Sr. and Arlowyne Edith (Arganbright) T.; m. Rebecca Ann Myers, Aug. 21, 1965; children: Brooke J., Austin B. BA, U. Kans., 1962; LLB, Harvard U., 1966. Bar: NY, 1970, US Dist. Ct. (so. dist.) NY, 1970, US Ct. Appeals (2d cir.), 1970. Local govt. advisor Republic of Botswana, Gaborone, 1966, dist. officer Serowe, 1967, dist. commr. Maun, 1968; assoc. Sullivan & Cromwell, LLP, NYC, 1969-75, ptnr., 1975—, ptnr.-in-charge London, 1979-82, mng. ptnr. gen. practice group NYC, 1986-91. Mem. exec. bd. Manhattan coun. Boy Scouts Am.; trustee U. Kans. Endowment Assn., Helen Keller Internat. Mem. ABA, NY State Bar Assn., Assn. Bar City of NY, Internat. Bar Assn., Am. Club Beijing, Harvard Club, Mill Reef Club, Verbank Hunting and Fishing Club, Knickerbocker Club, Beijing Am. Club, Am. C. of C. in China/Beijing, Confrerie des Chevaliers de Tastevin, Bentley Drivers Club, Vintage Sports Car Club Am. Republican. Presbyterian. Office: Sullivan & Cromwell LLP China World Trade Ctr Tower 1 One Jianguo Menwai Ave Ste 501 Beijing 100004 China

**THOMAS, ROBERT PAIGE,** lawyer; b. Columbus, Ohio, July 31, 1941; s. Charles Marion and Elsie (Cavanaugh) T.; children: Paige Cason, Park Cavanaugh. B.A., Vanderbilt U., 1963, M.A., 1965, J.D. 1970. Bar: Tenn. 1970, U.S. Dist. Ct. (mid. dist.) Tenn. 1970, U.S. Ct. Appeals (6th cir.) 1977. Assoc. Boult, Cummings, Conners & Berry, Nashville, 1970-74, ptnr., 1974—, mng. ptnr., 1977-84. chmn. Tenn. Dem. Party; Mem. Bill Clinton's Nat. Fin. Com.; fin. chmn. Sen. Jim Sasser. Mem. ABA, Tenn. Bar Assn., Nashville Bar Assn. Democrat. Episcopalian. Clubs: Yale of N.Y.C.; Belle Meade Country. Office: PO Box 340025 Nashville TN 37203 Office Phone: 615-252-2314. Business E-Mail: bthomas@boultcummings.com.

**THOMAS, ROBERT R.,** state supreme court justice; b. Rochester, NY, Aug. 7, 1952; m. Maggie Thomas; 3 children. BA in govt., U. Notre Dame, 1974; JD, Loyola U., 1981. Cir. ct. judge DuPage County, 1988, acting chief judge, 1989—94; appellate Ct. Second Dist., 1994—2000; justice Ill. Supreme Ct., 2000—, chief justice, 2006—. Named to Academic All-Am. Hall of Fame; recipient NCAA Silver Anniversary award, 1999. Mem.: DuPage County Bar Assn., Acad. All-Am. Hall of Fame (life NCAA Silver Ann. Award 1999). Office: Illinois Supreme Ct 160 N LaSalle St Chicago IL 60601*

**THOMAS, ROGER MERIWETHER,** lawyer; b. Hartford, Conn., Feb. 28, 1930; s. Frederick Metcalf and Helen Meriwether (Lewis) T.; m. Mary Dorothea Wyman, Dec. 4, 1965; children— Donald Wyman, Helen Dorothea. AB, Princeton U., 1952; LL.B., Va., 1957; LL.M., Boston U., 1964. Bar: N.Y. 1958, Mass. 1960, U.S. Dist. Ct. (Mass) 1965, U.S. Tax Ct. 1965, U.S. Supreme Ct. 1967. Assoc. Angulo, Cooney, Marsh & Ouchterloney, N.Y.C., 1957-60; assoc., then ptnr. Gaston & Snow, Boston 1960-91; counsel Condit & Assocs., P.C., Boston, 1992-94. Outline author and lectr. Mass. Continued Legal Edn., Inc., Boston; past panelist New Eng. Law Inst. Estate Planning Forums, Boston. Trustee Buckingham Browne & Nichols Sch., Cambridge, Mass., 1967-69. 1st lt. U.S. Army, 1952-54, Korea. Mem. Am. Coll. Trust and Estate Counsel, Boston Bar Assn., Mass. Bar Assn. Avocations: reading, sports, old movies. Home: 40 Byron Rd Weston MA 02493-2229

**THOMAS, ROGER WARREN,** lawyer; b. South Weymouth, Mass., Sept. 17, 1937; s. Clement Rogers and Beatrice (Merritt) T.; m. Maria Sava Brenner, July 5, 1968; children: Caroline, Andrew, Phillip. BA, U. N.H., 1959; postgrad. (Rotary Internat. fellow), Free U. Berlin, 1960; LLB (Root-Tilden scholar), NYU, 1963, LLM (Ford Found. grantee), 1965;

postgrad., U. Chile, Santiago, 1965. Bar: N.Y. 1964. Assoc. Cleary, Gottlieb, Steen and Hamilton, N.Y.C., 1965-66, 69-74, partner, 1974—. Mem. Harvard-Chile Tax Reform Project, 1966-68, head project in Chile, 1968-69; cons. to UN, Santiago, 1969; adj. prof. taxation NYU, 1974-96. Co-author: El Impuesto a la Renta, 1969. Bd. dirs. Spanish Repertory Theatre, Fundacion Chile; chmn. UNH Found. Mem. ABA, Am. Fgn. Lawyers Assn., N.Y. State Bar Assn., N.Am.-Chilean C. of C. (pres. 1984-96), Am. Soc., Coun. of Am., Knickerbocker Club. Home: 1150 5th Ave New York NY 10128-0724 Office: 1 Liberty Plz New York NY 10006-1404

**THOMAS, RONALD ROBERT,** English literature educator, writer; b. Orange, NJ, Jan. 29, 1949; s. Robert Louis and Doris Josephine (Rambo) T.; m. Mary Domingo, June 15, 1991. BA in English, Wheaton Coll., 1971; MA in English and Am. Lit., Brandeis U., 1978, PhD in English and Am. Lit., 1983. Asst. prof. English lit. U. Chgo., 1982-90; assoc. prof. Trinity Coll., Hartford, Conn., 1990—2003, chmn. dept. English, 1993—2003, chief of staff, v.p., 1998—2001, acting pres., 2001—02; pres. Univ Puget Sound, Tacoma, 2003—. Author: Dreams of Authority: Freud and the Fictions of the Unconscious, 1990, Detective Fiction and the Rise of Froensic Science, 1999; co-editor: Nineteenth-Century Geographics: The Transformation of Space from the Victorian Age to the American Century, 2002; contbr. articles to profl. jours., chpt. to Columbia History of Brit. Novel. Andrew Mellon fellow Harvard U., 1991-92. Mem. MLA, Dickens Soc., Soc. for Study of Narrative Lit., N.E. Victorian Assn., Interdisciplinary 19th-Century Studies Assn., Phi Beta Kappa. Office: Univ Puget Sound 1500 North Warner Tacoma WA 98416 Business E-mail: president@ups.edu.

**THOMAS, SARAH E.,** librarian; AB, Smith Coll., 1970; MS in Libr. Sci., Simmons Coll., 1973; PhD in German, Johns Hopkins U., 1982; student, Universität Hamburg, Germany, 1968—69, Albert-Ludwigs Universität, 1971, Johann Wolfgang Goethe Universität, 1977—78. Preliminary cataloger Widener Libr., Harvard U., Cambridge, Mass., 1970—71, catalog intern & reference libr., 1971—73, original cataloger Germanic languages, 1973, head departmental libr. cataloging sect., 1974, head computer-based cataloging, 1974—75; instr. elem. German Johns Hopkins U., Balt., 1976—77, instr. intermediate German, 1978—79, sr. cataloger Eisenhower Libr., 1978—79; libr. coord. Rsch. Libraries Group, Stanford, Calif., 1979—80, mgr. libr. coordination, 1980—83; Coun. Libr. Resources academic libr. mgmt. intern U. Ga., Athens, 1983—84; assoc. dir. tech. services Nat. Agrl. Libr., Beltsville, Md., 1984—92; dir. cataloging Libr. Congress, Washington, 1992—94, acting dir. pub. services and collection mgmt., 1995, acting dir. public svc. collections, 1995—96; Carl A. Korch U. Libr. Cornell U., Ithaca, NY, 1996—, adj. prof. German dept. modern languages, 1996—. Faculty adv. bd. on info. tech. Cornell U., 1996—; corp. vis. com. for the libraries of MIT, 1997—; bd. governors Cornell Inst. for Social and Econ. Rsch., 1997—; vis. com. Carnegie Mellon Libr., 1999—; overseers' com. to visit the libr. Harvard U., 1999—; chair exec. com. Smith Coll. Libraries, 2002—; chair adv. bd. Project Euclid, 2002—; ctrl. adv. bd. PubMed, 2003—; adminstrv. bd. Cornell U. Coun. Named Online Computer Libr. Ctr. Disting. Scholar, 2000; recipient Cert. Merit, Nat. Agrl. Libr., 1989, Superior Svc. Award, USDA, 1990; Deutscher Akademischer Austauschdienst Fellowship, 1977—78. Mem.: ALA (life), Assn. Libr. Collections and Tech. Services, Assn. Coll. & Rsch. Libraries, Assn. Rsch. Libraries (bd. mem. 1999—, pres. 2003—04, membership com. 2003—, chair nominating com. 2003—), Grolier Club. Office: Cornell U 201 Olin Libr Ithaca NY 14853 Office Phone: 607-255-3689. Office Fax: 607-255-6788. Business E-mail: set9@cornell.edu.*

**THOMAS, SARAH ELAINE,** music educator; b. Little Rock, Aug. 8, 1947; d. William and Madie Murle (Stout) Collins; m. Gary Wayne Thomas Aug. 8, 1970 (dec. Nov. 1991). MusB in Edn., U. N. Tex., 1970; M in Ednl. Adminstrn., Dallas Bapt. U., 1997. Cert. tchr.-all-levels, Tex., prin. Music tchr. Winnetka Elem., Dallas, 1970-82, L. K. Hall Elem. Dallas, 1982-94, Kleberg Elem. Dallas, 1994—2001, Pleasant Grove Elem., 2001—05; supr. elem. fine arts Lincoln Instrnl. Ctr., 2005—. Staff. devel. presenter Dallas Ind. Sch. Dist., 1977-97, 97-2005; workshop presenter Tex. Arts Coun., Austin, 1990-94. Bd. dirs. Dallas PTA, 1980-82; bd. dirs. Dallas All-City Elem. Choir, chair, 1991—, dir., 1999-2004. Named Class Act Teacher, Sta. KDFW-TV, Dallas, 1992. Mem. PTA (life), Am. Fedn. Tchrs., Tex. Music Educators Assn., Dallas Music Educators Assn. (v.p. 1992), Am. Orff-Schulwerk Assn., Music Educators Nat. Conf., Rotary (Svc. Above Self award 2003). Avocations: cooking, sewing, gardening, travel. Home: 2407 Norwich Ct Arlington TX 76015-3262 Office: Lincoln Instrnl Ctr 5000 S Malcom X Blvd Rm 104 Dallas TX 75215 Office Phone: 972-749-2545. Personal E-mail: elainethomas3@comcast.net. Business E-mail: elthomas@dallasisd.org.

**THOMAS, SCOTT E.,** lawyer, former commissioner; b. Buffalo, Wyo., Mar. 5, 1953; s. Ralph E. and Bonnie E. Thomas; m. Elena W. King, Apr. 28, 1984. BA, Stanford U., 1974; JD, Georgetown U., 1977. Bar: D.C. 1977, U.S. Ct. Appeals (9th cir.) 1980, U.S. Supreme Ct. 1981. Atty. Office of Gen. Counsel, Fed. Election Commn., Washington, 1977-80; asst. gen. counsel for enforcement Fed. Election Commn., Washington, 1980-83, exec. asst. to commr., 1983-86, commr., 1986—2006, vice chmn., 1992, 1998, chmn., 1987, 1993, 1999, 2005; of counsel Pub. Policy & Law Group Dickstein Shapiro Morin & Oshinsky LLP, Washington, 2006—. Mem. D.C. Bar Assn. Office: Dickstein Shapiro Morin & Oshinsky LLP 2101 L St NW Washington DC 20037 E-mail: ThomasS@dsmo.com.*

**THOMAS, SIDNEY,** fine arts educator, researcher; b. NYC, Dec. 21, 1915; s. Hyman and Rose (Samilowitz) T.; m. Rae Dinkowitz, May 26, 1940; children: David Phillip, Deborah Rose. BA, CCNY, 1935; MA, Columbia U., 1938, PhD, 1943. Tutor in English CCNY, N.Y.C., 1939-43; instr. English Queens Coll., N.Y.C., 1946-54, 54-56; employed on editor, 1954-58; assoc. editor Merriam-Webster, Springfield, Mass., 1958-61; assoc. prof. fine arts Syracuse U. (N.Y.), 1961-66, prof., 1966-85, prof. emeritus, 1985—, dir. humanities doctoral program, 1964-72, chmn. dept. fine arts, 1969-73. Bibliographer Shakespeare Assn., N.Y.C., 1949-54 Author: The Antic Hamlet, 1943; co-editor: The Nature of Art, 1964; editor: Images of Man, 1972. Served to sgt., inf. U.S. Army, 1943-45, ETO. Research fellow Folger Shakespeare Library, Washington, 1947-48 Mem.: AAUP (pres. Syracuse U. chpt. 1974), ACLU, MLA (life), Shakespeare Assn. Am., Phi Beta Kappa. Office: Syracuse U Dept Fine Arts Syracuse NY 13210

**THOMAS, SIDNEY R.,** federal judge; b. Bozeman, Mont., Aug. 14, 1953; m. Martha Sheehy. BA in Speech-Comm., Mont. State U., 1975, JD cum laude, 1978; D (hon.), Rocky Mountain Coll., 1998. Bar: Mont. 1978, U.S. Dist. Ct. Mont. 1978, U.S. Ct. Appeals (9th cir.) 1980, U.S. Dist. Ct. (9th cir.) 1980, U.S. Ct. Fed. Claims 1986, U.S. Supreme Ct. 1994. Shareholder Moulton, Bellimgham, Longo and Mather, P.C., Billings, Mont., 1978—96; judge U.S. Ct. Appeals 9th Cir., Billings, 1996—. Adj. instr. Rocky Mountain Coll., Billings, 1982—95. Contbr. articles to profl. jours. Recipient Gov.'s award for Pub. Svc., 1978, Outstanding Faculty award, Rocky Mountain Coll., 1988. Mem. ABA, Yellowstone County Bar Assn., State Bar Mont. Office: US Ct Appeals Ninth Circuit PO Box 31478 Billings MT 59107-1478*

**THOMAS, STEPHEN,** retired industrial engineer; b. NYC, Aug. 29, 1923; s. Peter and Amelia Thomas; m. Jane Anne Broderick, July 3, 1948; children: Barbara Gail, Jessica Lynne, Susan Amelia. BS in Indsl. Mech. Engring., U. Mich., 1951. From foreman to personnel supr. EI du Pont, Buffalo, Wilmington, Del. and Brevard, NC, 1951—84, personnel supr., 1970—84, ret., 1984. Asst. chem. lab. U. Mich., Ann Arbor, 1948, asst. metalurgical lab. 1948—51; instr. Blue Ridge C.C., Hendersonville, NC, 1970—75; cons. human rels. EI du Pont, Brevard, NC, 1984—91. Chmn. Mayor's Com. for Handicapped, Henderson County, 1980; bd. dirs. Cmty Found. Henderson County, 1986—88; mem. PTA (life). Laurel Park (NC) Alcohol Beverage Control Bd., 1983—99; mediator Dispute Settlement Ctr. Henderson County, 1984—2002; arbitrator BBB, Asheville, NC, 1986—2002; mem. bd. dirs. Dispute Settlement Ctr. Henderson County, 2001—02; treas. Rep. Party,

Henderson County, NC; mem. bd. dirs. Western Carolina Cmty. Action, Henderson County, 1970, Western NC Tomorrow, 1986—94, Margaret R. Pardee Meml. Hosp., Henderson County, 1981—94. 2d lt. transp. corp U.S. Army, 1945—46.

**THOMAS, STEPHEN JAY,** anesthesiologist; b. Washington, 1943; MD, Jefferson Med. Col., 1968. Intern San Francisco Gen. Hosp., 1968-69; resident in anesthesiology Mass. Gen. Hosp., Boston, 1971-73, fellow, 1973-74; assoc. prof. NYU Med. Ctr.; vice chmn., Topkins-Van Poznak prof. dept. anesthesiology N.Y. Presbyn. Weill Cornell Ctr., 1989—; pres. Am. Soc. Anesthesiology, 2001—. Office: NY Presbyn Weill Cornell Ctr Dept Anesthesiology 525 E 68th St New York NY 10021-4870*

**THOMAS, STEPHEN PAUL,** lawyer; b. Bloomington, Ill., July 30, 1938; s. Owen Wilson and Mary Katherine (Paulsen) T.; m. Marieanne Sauer, Dec. 7, 1963 (dec. June 1984); 1 child, Catherine Marie; m. Marcia Aldrich Toomey, May 28, 1988; 1 child, Ellen Antonia. BA, U. Ill., 1959; LLB, Harvard U., 1962; student in MLA Program, U. Chi, 2005—. Bar: Ill. 1962; cert. naturalist Morton Arboretum, 2001, treekeeper Openlands Found., 2004. Vol. Peace Corps, Malawi, Africa, 1963-65; assoc. Sidley Austin LLP, Chgo., 1965-70, ptnr., 1970-2000. Lectr. on law Malawi Inst. Pub. Adminstrn., 1963-65. Pres. Hyde Park-Kenwood Cmty. Conf., Chgo., 1988-90; life trustee Chgo. Acad. for Arts, chmn., 1992-97; life trustee Union League Civic and Arts Found., Chgo., 1999—. Recipient Paul Cornell award Hyde Park Hist. Soc., 1981. Mem. ABA, Chgo. Bar Assn., Chgo. Fedn. Musicians, Ill. State Hist. Soc., Union League Club Chgo., Chgo. Lit. Club, Ill. Geog. Soc. Democrat. Roman Catholic. Avocations: jazz piano playing, naturalist studies. Home: 9756 S Longwood Dr Chicago IL 60643-1610 Office: Sidley Austin LLP One S Dearborn St Ste 900 Chicago IL 60603 Office Phone: 312-853-7516. Business E-mail: sthomas@sidley.com.

**THOMAS, STEPHEN S.,** health facility administrator; BBA and Econs., Ind. Ctrl. U., 1977. Various mgmt. positions Burroughs Corp., 1978—83, Digital Equipment Corp., 1978—83; pres. Datapro Info. Svcs. Group divsn. McGraw-Hill Cos., 1993—97; exec. v.p., pres. Cardinal's Pyxis Corp.; exec. v.p. Cardinal Health, Inc., 1999—, group pres. automation and info. svcs., 1999—. Bd. dirs. SupplyPro, San Diego. Mem.: Honor Soc. Nursing Indpls., Sigma Theta Tau (mem. adv. group). Office: Cardinal Health Inc 7000 Cardinal Pl Dublin OH 43017

**THOMAS, STEVE,** professional hockey player; b. Stockport, Eng., July 15, 1963; m. Lori Thomas; children: Lauren, Christian. Left wing Toronto Mapleleafs, 1984—87, 1998—, Chgo. Black Hawks, 1987—92, N.Y. Islanders, 1992—95, N.J. Devils, 1995—98. Capt. Team Can. World Hockey Championships, Vienna. Recipient MVP award, SportsChannel, Nystrom award, 1992—93.

**THOMAS, SUZANNE CHARISE,** artist, educator; b. Okla. City, Okla., Dec. 7, 1964; d. Irs and Donna Thomas. MFA, So. Ill. U., Carbondale, Ill., 1994. Prof. art Rose State Coll., Midwest City, Okla., 1997—. Set designer Rose State Coll. Midwest City, Okla., 2006; tchr. art Okla. City Arts Coun., Okla. City, 2002—. Fellow, So. Ill. U., Carbondale, 1992—93. Mem.: Coll. Arts Assn. (assoc.). Office: Rose State College 6420 SE 15th Midwest City OK 73110 Office Phone: 405-733-7515. Business E-mail: sthomas@rose.edu.

**THOMAS, TED, JR.,** Drummer, producer, composer; b. Portsmouth, Va. s. Ted Thomas Sr. and Charletta Thomas. Attended, Norfolk State U. Toured with Orthea Barnes, Earl Klugh. Musician: (songs) Power!, (off-Broadway) Your Arms Are Too Short To Box With God; prodr.: (albums) Who Is Jill Scott? Words and Sounds Vol. 1, 2000; prodr.: (songs) Be Ready, 2001; prodr., composer (songs) Salvador Bahia, Doc Gibbs, 2002; musician (musician, writer): Emeril Live Band. Achievements include touring and producing with many accomplished artists all over the world.*

**THOMAS, TERESA ANN,** microbiologist, educator; d. Sam Charles and Edna Thomas. BS cum laude, Coll. Misericordia, 1961; MS in Biology, Am. U., Beirut, 1965; MS in Microbiology, U. So. Calif., 1973; cert. in ednl. tech., U. Calif., San Diego, 1998. Tchr., sci. supr., curriculum coord. Meyers H.S., Wilkes-Barre, 1962-64, Wilkes-Barre Area Pub. Schs., 1961-66; rsch. assoc. Proctor Found. Rsch. in Ophthalmology U. Calif. Med. Ctr., San Francisco, 1966-68; instr. Robert Coll. of Istanbul, Turkey, 1968-71, Am. Edn. in Luxembourg, 1971-72, Bosco Tech. Inst., Rosemead, Calif., 1973-74, San Diego C.C. Dist., 1974-80; prof. microbiology and ecology Sch. Math Sci. and Engring. Southwestern Coll., Chula Vista, Calif., 1980—2005, prof. emeritus, 2005—; mem. Vecinos Baja Studies EcoMundo team internat. program Southwestern Coll. Pres. acad. senate, 1984-85, del., 1986-89; chmn., coord., steering com. project Cultural Rsch. Ednl. and Trade Exch., 1991-2000. Southwestern Coll.-Shanghai Inst. Fgn. Trade; coord. Southwestern Coll. Great Tchg. Seminar, 1987, 88, 89, coord. scholars program, 1988-90; steering com. Southwestern Coll.; exec. coun. Acad. Senate for Calif. C.C.s, 1985-86, Chancellor of Calif. C.C.s Adv. and Rev. Coun. Fund for Instrnl. Improvement, 1984-86; co-project dir. statewide, coord. So. Calif. Biotech. Edn. Consortium, 1993-95, steering com., 1993-98; adj. asst. prof. Chapman Coll., San Diego, 1974-83, San Diego State U., 1977-79; chmn. Am. Colls. Istanbul Sci. Week, 1969-71; adv. bd. Chapman Coll. Cmty. Ctr., 1978-81; cons. sci. curriculum Calif. Dept. Edn., 1986-89; pres. Internat. Rels. Club, 1959-61; mem. San Francisco World Affairs Coun., 1966-68, San Diego World Affairs Coun., 1992—; v.p. Palomar Palace Estates Home Owners Assn., 1983-85, pres., 1994-99, 2003-2004, v.p., 1999—; mem. Rsch. Conf. on Undergrad. Microbiology Edn., Conn. Coll., 1999; bd. dirs. US Orgn. Med. Ednl. Needs, US Internat. Boundary and Water Commn Citizens Forum Bd., mem. South Bay Networking Group, 2006—; presenter in field. Emeritus mem. edilt. rev. bd.: Jour. of Coll. Sci. Tchg. Life mem. Chula Vista Nature Ctr.; mem. Internat. Friendship Commn., Chula Vista, 1985-95, vice chmn., 1989-90, chmn., 1990-92; mem. US-Mex. Sister Cities Assn., nat. bd. dirs., 1992-94, gen. chair 30th nat. conv., 1993; founding pres. Chula Vista-Odawara Sister Cities Assn., 1993—; mem. City of Chula Vista Resource Conservation Commn., 1996-2005, chmn. 2002-04; mem. Chula Vista Bd. Ethics, 1999-2000, County San Diego Solid Waste Hearing Panel, 2000-05; co-organizer Chula Vista People-to-People Sister City Dels. to Odawara City, Japan, 1991, 94, 99; cmty. adv. com. San Diego Mus. Man, 2000-03; citizens forum bd. U.S. Internat. Boundary and Water Commn., 2001—; steering com. Chula Vista Gen. Plan Update, 2002—05; com. mem. Chula Vista Environ., Open Space and Sustainable Devel., 2002-05; alt. del. citizens adv. com. Port of San Diego and City Chula Vista Bayfront Master Plan, 2003-06; assoc. mem. Calif. Local Govts. Commn., 2005— mem. Sister Cities Internat. 50th Anniversary Cir. of Disting. Vols., 2006; docent Bonita Mus. and Cultural Ctr., 2006—; mem. Northwest Chula Vista Civic Assn., 2006. Grantee Pa. Heart Assn., 1962; fellow NSF, 1965, USPHS, 1972-73; recipient Nat. Tchg. Excellence award Nat. Inst. Staff and Orgnl. Devel., 1989; named Southwestern Coll. Woman of Distinction, 1987, Hon. Coach Southwestern Coll. Ladies Basketball Apaches, 2001, Jaguars Basketball Team, 2003, Chula Vista Environmentalist of Yr., 2005, 50th Anniversary Cir. Dist. Vol. award Sister Cities Internat., 2006. Mem.: NIH (mentor Bridges to the Future program Southwestern Coll. and San Diego 1993—98, steering com.), NSTA (life; coord. internat. honors exch. lectr. competition 1986, internat. com.), NEA (life), South Bay Networking Group, Faculty Assn. Calif. C.C.s (state policy com. 2003—05), Am. Assn. Cmty. and Jr. Colls., Am. Soc. Microbiology (So. Calif. MicrobeDiscovery Team 1995—99), Calif. Sci. Tchrs. Assn. (life), Calif. Tchrs. Assn. (life), Nat. Assn. Biology Tchrs. (life), Chula Vista C. of C. (life), Chula Vista-Odawara (Japan) Sister Cities Assn. (founding pres. 1993—), Am.-Lebanese Assn. San Diego (1st v.p. 1984—91, pres. 1988—93, chmn. scholarship com., hon. life mem. 2006), Japanese Am. Hist. Soc. (life), Chula Vista Nature Ctr. (life), San Diego Zool. Soc., Am. U. Beirut Alumni and Friends of San Diego (1st v.p. 1984—91), Japan Soc. San Diego and Tijuana (life), Am. Lebanese Syrian Ladies Club (pres. 1982—83), Lions Internat. (bull. editor 1991—93, 2d v.p. 1992—93, 1st v.p. 1993—94, editor Roaring Times Newsletter 1993—94, chmn. dist. internat. rels. and cooperations com. 1993—95, pub. rels. 1997—98, S.W.

San Diego County v.p. 2006—, Best Bull. award 1992—93, S.W. San Diego County Lion of Yr. 2000), Delta Kappa Gamma (Gamma Omicron chpt. corr. sec. 2006—, Outstanding Pub. Svc. award Gamma Omicron chpt. 2003), Phi Theta Kappa, Sigma Phi Sigma, Kappa Gamma Pi (pres. Wilkes-Barre chpt. 1963—64, pres. San Francisco chpt. 1967—68)), Alpha Pi Epsilon (life; advisor Southwestern Coll. chpt. 1989—90, founder). Office Phone: 619-427-3181. Personal E-mail: terrytom@ix.netcom.com.

**THOMAS, TIM,** professional basketball player; b. Paterson, N.J., Feb. 26, 1977; Student, Villanova U., Pa., 1997. Basketball player Phila. 76ers, 1997—99, Milw. Bucks, 1998—2004, New York Knicks, 2004—05, Chgo. Bulls, 2005—. Named All-Rookie 2nd Team, 1997—98. Office: Chgo Bulls United Ctr 1901 W Madison St Chicago IL 60612*

**THOMAS, TOM,** retired plastics company executive; b. Malang, Java, Indonesia, Feb. 15, 1932; arrived in Can., 1954; s. Ferdinand and Elfrieda Emma (Macht) T.; m. Jannie Chine Sneep, Jan. 19, 1956; children: Gregory John, Renée Sonja Elfrieda, Michael Grant, Thomas. Grad. high sch., The Hague, Holland. Jr. mgr. Lever Bros. Ltd., Toronto, Ont., Canada, 1954-60; sr. mgr. Impac & Somerville Plastics, Toronto, Ont., Canada, 1960-64; founder, C.E.O. Can. Cup Inc., Toronto, Ont., Canada, 1964—, also bd. dirs., 1964-93; ret., 1993. Inventor in field. Trustee Frazer Inst., Vancouver, B.C., Can., 1977-93; gov. Massey and Roy Thomson Hall, Toronto, 1991-92; bd. dirs. Toronto Symphony, 1986-92, mem. Maestro's Club, 1984, mem. pres.'s coun. Can. Opera Co., 1980, adv. coun. Toronto Symphony, 1995-2000, pres. Coun. Can. Opera, 1980-95. Avocations: sailing, history, classical music, chess.

**THOMAS, TONY,** producer; Prodr., ptnr. Witt-Thomas Prodns., L.A., 1976-81; ptnr. Witt-Thomas-Harris Prodns., 1981—. Exec. prodr. (with others) (TV series) Fay, 1975-76, Loves Me, Loves Me Not, 1977, Soap (Emmy award nominations best nighttime and primetime comedy series, 1978, 80, Emmy award best primetime comedy series 1981), Benson, 1979, It's a Living, 1980-81, Making a Living, 1982, It Takes Two, 1982-83, Condo, 1983; exec. prodr. (TV series), The Golden Girls, 1985-92 (Emmy awards best primetime comedy series 1986, 87), Beauty and the Beast, 1987, Empty Nest, 1988-95, Nurses, 1991, Herman's Head, 1991, Blossom, 1991-95, The John Larroquette Show, 1993-97; prod. (TV movies) Bloodsport, 1973, Snatched, 1973, Griffin and Phoenix: A Love Story, 1976; co-exec. prodr. (TV movies) Satan's Triangle, 1975; assoc. prodr. (TV movies) Brian's Song, 1971, No Place to Run, 1972, Home for the Holidays, 1972, The Letters, 1973, A Cold Night's Death, 1973, Remember When, 1974, The Gun and the Pulpit, 1974, High Risk, 1993; co-prodr. (films) Firstborn, 1984, Dead Poets Society, 1989, Final Analysis, 1992. Office: Witt-Thomas Prods 11240 Magnolia Blvd Ste 201 North Hollywood CA 91601-3790

**THOMAS, TRACEY WILLIAMS,** researcher; b. Birmingham, Ala., Nov. 14, 1971; d. Donald Randolph and Mary Hunter Williams; m. Stephen Wesley Thomas, Feb. 18, 1971. BA, Hampton U., 1994; PhD, Howard U., 2000. Postdoctoral rsch. fellow Johns Hopkins Sch. of Medicine, Balt., 2000—03; aaas sci. policy fellow U.S. EPA, Washington, 2003—. Founder, CEO TWThomas Solutions, LLC, Wash., DC; officer Postdoctoral Assn., Johns Hopkins Sch. of Medicine, Balt., 2001—03; rsch. supr. BioTechnical Inst. of Md., Balt., 2002—; CEO Columbia Consultants and Govt. Solutions Group LLC, Ellicott City, Md., 2006—; sr. bioscience cons. Boez Allen Hamilton, Abingdon, Md., 2004—06. Contbr. articles various profl. jours. Team leader Greater DC Cares, Youth Impact, Wash., DC, 1995—98; mem. Joint Steering Com. for Pub. Policy, Bethesda, Md., 2002—04. Recipient Predoctoral and Postdoctoral Travel awards, Am. Soc. of Cell Biology, 1998-2000, XIV Internat. Conf. on AIDS Young Sci. Investigator award, Conf. Com., 2002; Postdoctoral fellowship Funding, NIH, 2001-2003, Sci. Policy fellowship, AAAS, 2003-2004. Mem.: AAAS, Am. Soc. of Cell Biology, Assn. of Women in Sci. (assoc.). Democrat. Roman Catholic. Achievements include research in calcium release mechanism in eggs of a protostome; posttranslational modification mutation of a G-Protein coupled receptor involved in HIV. Avocations: travel, reading. Home: 105 Autumnwood Ave York PA 17404 Personal E-mail: twthomas20@hotmaill.com.

**THOMAS, TROY D.,** banking executive; B in computer info. sciences, Cleve. State U., 1986. Cert. data processor 1988. Joined Ameritrust Corp., 1986, Society Corp., 1989, sr. programmer customer info. dept.; (Society Corp. merged with KeyCorp, 1994); dept. mgr. Hogan CIS dept. KeyCorp, 1994—96, divsn. mgr. customer warehouse divsn., 1996—98, sr. v.p. customer info., 1998—99, acting group mgr. customer info. warehouse group, 1999, group mgr. tech. process group, 1999—2001, exec. v.p enterprise mgmt. services, 2001—, also chief info. security officer. Named one of Premier 100 IT Leaders, Computerworld, 2005. Office: KeyCorp 127 Public Sq Cleveland OH 44114-1306*

**THOMAS, VIOLETA DE LOS ANGELES,** real estate broker; b. Buenos Aires, Dec. 21, 1949; came to U.S., 1967; d. Angel and Lola (Andino) de Rios; m. Jess Thomas, Dec. 23, 1974; 1 child, Victor Justin. Student, Harvard U. and U. Buenos Aires, 1967—73. Mgr. book div. Time-Life, N.Y.C., 1985-94; real estate broker First Marin Realty, Inc., Mill Valley, Calif., 1996-97; assoc. broker Trump Corp., N.Y.C., 1997—, Brown Harris Stevens, N.Y.C., 1997—. Rep. N.Y.C. Bd. dirs. Alliance Francaise, St. Louis, 1995-96, City of Tuburon, Calif., 1987-93, Art and Heritage Commn., Tiburon. Named Woman of Yr., City of Buenos Aires, 1977, Broker of Yr., Marin County and San Francisco, 1987-92. Mem. Principia Coll. Club (pres. 1997—). Office: Brown Harris Stevens 60 Windmill Ln Southampton NY 11968

**THOMAS, WAYNE LEE,** lawyer; b. Sept. 22, 1945; s. W. M. and June F. Thomas; m. Patricia H. Thomas, Mar. 16, 1968; children: Brigitte Elisabeth Williams, Kate Adelaide Culpepper. BA, U. Fla., 1967, JD cum laude, 1971. Bar: Fla. 1971, U.S. Supreme Ct. 1975, U.S. Ct. Appeals (5th cir.) 1975, U.S. Ct. Appeals (11th cir.) 1981, U.S. Ct. Claims 1976, U.S. Dist. Ct. (mid. dist.) Fla. 1973, U.S. Dist. Ct. (so. dist. trial bar) Fla. 1975; cert. mediator and arbitrator. Law clk. U.S. Dist. Ct. (mid. dist.) Fla., 1971—73; assoc. Trenam, Simmons, Kemker, Scharf, Barkin, Frye & O'Neill, PA, Tampa, 1973—77, ptnr., 1978—81; founder, pres. McKay & Thomas, PA, Tampa, 1981—89; ptnr. Carlton, Fields, Ward, Emmanuel, Smith & Cutler, PA, 1989—95; pvt. practice Tampa, 1995—. Mem. ABA, Fla. Bar (chmn. sect. gen. practice 1981-83, ethics com., vice chmn. unauthorized practice law com. 1994-98, 2000-04, chmn. 2004-06, vice chmn. fed. practice com. 1995-96, chmn. 1996-97, bd. bar examiners 1986-91, chmn. 1990-91, chmn. unauthorized practice law com. 13A 1998-2001), Nat. Conf. Bar Examiners (multistate profl. responsibility exam. policy com. 1994-2004), Hillsborough County Bar Assn. (chmn. grievance com. 1985-86), Order of Coif, J.C. Cheatwood Am. Inn of Ct., Fla. Blue Key, Phi Kappa Phi, Omicron Delta Kappa. Democrat. Office: 707 N Franklin St Fl 10 Tampa FL 33602-4430

**THOMAS, WENDY EVELYN,** biomedical engineer, educator; b. Urbana, Ill., Apr. 24, 1965; d. C. Gomer and Patricia S. Thomas, E. Jane Cameron (Stepmother); life ptnr. Deborah de Armas. BA in Molecular Biology, Princeton U., N.J., 1987; MS in Applied Math., PhD in Bioengring., U. Wash., Seattle, 2003. Postdoctoral fellow U. Wash., Seattle, 2003—04, asst. prof. bioengring., 2004—. Mem.: Biophysical Soc., ASME, Biomed. Engring. Soc., Soc. Women Engrs. Office: Univ Washington Box 355061 Seattle WA 98195-5061 Office Phone: 206-616-3947. Office Fax: 206-685-3300. Business E-mail: wendyt@u.washington.edu.

**THOMAS, WILLIAM DANIEL,** journalist; b. Salem, Va., July 24, 1974; s. William Claude Thomas and Judith Ann McDonald. BA in Econs. and Journalism, Coll. William and Mary, Va., 1994, U. NC, Chapel Hill, 1996. Reporter, photographer The Daily News, Eden, NC, 1996—97; sportswriter The Vail Trial, Colo., 1997—99, Tahoe Daily Tribune/Swift Publicity, South Lake Tahoe, Calif., 1999—2000; writer, editor The Summit Daily News/Swift Publicity, Frisco, Colo., 2000—03; copy editor The Rutland Herald, Rutland, Va., 2003—04, The Post Ind., Glenwood Springs, Colo., 2004—05, The

Aspen Times, Colo., 2005—. Recipient 2d Pl. for sports column, Colo. Press Assn., 1999. Mem.: Am. Assn. Snowboard Instrs., Am. MENSA. Independent. Avocations: snowboarding, mountain biking. Home: 431A Park Cir Aspen CO 81611 Personal E-mail: heel_side@hotmail.com.

**THOMAS, WILLIAM GRIFFITH,** lawyer; b. Washington, Nov. 1, 1939; s. Henry Phineas and Margaret Wilson (Carr) T.; m. Suzanne Campbell Foster, June 7, 1963. Student, Williams Coll., 1957-59, Richmond Coll., 1960; JD, U. Richmond, 1963. Bar: Va. 1963. With Hazel & Thomas (combined with Reed Smith in 1999), 1973—99; ptnr. Reed Smith LLP, Falls Church, Va., 1999—, mem. exec. com. Dir. Va. Elective and Power Co., Richmond, 1987-2000. Sec. Va. Dem. Com., 1968-70, chmn., 1970-72. Mem. ABA, Va. State Bar Assn., Am. Law Inst., Am. Coll. Real Estate Lawyers. Office: Reed Smith LLP 3110 Fairview Park Dr Ste 1400 Falls Church VA 22042-4503 Office Phone: 703-641-4238. Business E-Mail: wthomas@reedsmith.com.

**THOMAS, WILLIAM H.,** anthropologist, director; b. Youngstown, Ohio, Aug. 16, 1954; PhD, Ariz. State U., Tempe, 1990—99. Asst. prof. Marquette U., Milw., 2000—02; dir. NJ Sch. Conservation, Branchville, NJ, 2002—. Dir. Forest Stewards Initiative, Wanakipa, Southern Highlands Province, Papua New Guinea, 2002—. Fellow: Explores Club. Office: NJ Sch Conservation 1 Wapalanne Rd Branchville NJ 07826 Office Fax: 973-948-5131. Personal E-mail: pngexplore@aol.com. Business E-Mail: thomasw@mail.montclair.edu.

**THOMAS, WILLIAM MARSHALL (BILL THOMAS),** congressman; b. Wallace, Idaho, Dec. 6, 1941; s. Virgil and Gertrude Thomas; m. Sharon Lynn Hamilton, Jan. 1968; children: Christopher, Amelia. Student, Santa Anna CC, 1961; BA, San Francisco State U., 1963, MA, 1965. Mem. faculty dept. Am. govt. Bakersfield (Calif.) Coll., 1965-74, prof., 1965-74; mem. Calif. State Assembly, 1974-78, U.S. Congress from 22nd Calif. dist. (formerly 21st), 1979—; chmn. ways and means com., 2001—; chmn. Com. on House Oversight, 1995-2001. Mem. del. to Soviet Union, by Am. Council Young Polit. Leaders, 1977; chmn. Kern County Republican Central Com., 1972-74; mem. Calif. Rep. Com., 1972-80; del. Republican Party Nat. Conv., 1980, 84, 88; mem. Rep. Leader's Task Force on Health Care Reform. Recipient James Madison award Am. Library Assn. 1993, Legis. Svc. award, Pharm. Care Mgmt. Assn., 2000, Congl. award, Small Bus. Coun. Am., 2001 Republican. Office: US Ho Reps 2208 Rayburn Ho Office Bldg Washington DC 20515-0522

**THOMAS, WILLIAM SCOTT,** lawyer; b. Joliet, Ill., Aug. 16, 1949; AB, Stanford U., 1971; JD, U. Calif., Hastings, 1974; LLM in Taxation, Golden Gate U., 1981. Bar: Calif. 1975, U.S. Dist. Ct. (no. dist.) Calif. 1975, U.S. Tax Ct. 1982. Tax editor Internat. Bur. Fiscal Documentation, Amsterdam, Holland, 1974-75; tax atty. Chevron Corp., San Francisco, 1975-77; from assoc. to ptnr. Brobeck, Phleger & Harrison, San Francisco, 1978—2003; ptnr. Morgan Lewis & Bockius, San Francisco, 2003. Mem. ABA (taxation sect.), Calif. Bar Assn. (exec. com. taxation sect. 1984-89, chmn. 1987-88). Office: Morgan Lewis & Bockius 1 Market Plz Ste 2900 San Francisco CA 94105 Office Phone: 415-442-1000. Business E-Mail: wthomas@morganlewis.com.

**THOMAS, WILLIAM SCOTT,** physician; b. Cumberland, Md., Feb. 24, 1974; s. William Grant and Virginia Darlene Thomas; m. Paula Marie Schwerdt, June 2, 2001; 1 child, Lennon Paul. AA in Biology, Potomac State Coll., 1994; BA in Biology, W.Va. U., 1996, MD, 2001. Lic. physician W.Va., 2005. Chief resident family medicine Residency Program W.Va. U., Morgantown, W.Va., 2004—.

**THOMAS, ZACH MICHAEL,** professional football player; b. Pampa, Tex., Sept. 1, 1973; BS in Exercise Science, Tex. Tech, 1996. Linebacker Miami Dolphins, 1996—. Opened health and fitness club Zach's Club 54, Amarillo, Tex. Mem. Crunch on Paralysis team. Named First Team All-American, 1995; named to Pro-Bowl, 1999—2003, 2005. Avocations: weightlifting, basketball. Office: Miami Dolphins Tng Facility 7500 SW 30th St Davie FL 33314*

**THOMAS, ZACHARY ADAM,** music director, educator; b. Dayton, Ohio, May 31, 1976; s. Fred George and Melissa Sue Thomas. B in Music Edn., Bowling Green State U., Ohio, 1999. Dir. bands Liberty Benton Local Schs., Findlay, Ohio, 1999—. Mem.: Music Educators Nat. Conf., Ohio Music Edn. Assn. Home: 229 E Eagle St Findlay OH 45840

**THOMASCH, ROGER PAUL,** lawyer; b. NYC, Nov. 7, 1942; s. Gordon J. and Margaret (Molloy) T.; children: Laura Leigh, Paul Butler. BA, Coll. William and Mary, 1964; LLB, Duke U., 1967. Bar: Conn. 1967, Colo. 1974. Assoc. atty. Cummings & Lockwood, Stamford, Conn., 1967-70; trial atty. U.S. Dept. Justice, Washington, 1970-73; ptnr. Roath & Brega, Denver, 1975-87; mng. ptnr. Denver office of Ballard, Spahr, Andrews & Ingersoll LLP, 1987—, chmn. litigation practice, 2005—. Vis. assoc. prof. of law Drake U. Sch. Law, Des Moines, 1973-74; frequent lectr. in field, U.S. and Can.; adj. faculty mem. U. Denver Coll. Law, 1976-80. Recipient Leland Forrest Outstanding Prof. award, Drake U. Sch. Law, 1973. Fellow Am. Coll. of Trial Lawyers, Am. Bar Found., Colo. Bar Found. mem. ABA, Colo. Bar Assn., Denver Country Club, Univ. Club. Office: Ballard Spahr Andrews & Ingersoll LLP 1225 17th St Ste 2300 Denver CO 80202-5535 Office Phone: 303-299-7301. E-mail: Thomasch@BallardSpahr.com.

**THOMAS-GRAHAM, PAMELA,** apparel executive; b. Detroit, 1963; d. Albert and Marian Thomas; m. Lawrence Otis Graham; 3 children. Grad., AB, Harvard Coll., MBA, Harvard Bus. Sch.; JD, Harvard Law Sch. With McKinsey & Co., 1989—99, ptnr., 1995—99; pres., CEO CNBC.com, 1999—2001, CNBC, Ft. Lee, NJ, 2001—05, chmn., 2005; group pres. Liz Claiborne, Inc., NYC, 2005—. Editor: Harvard Law Rev.; author: Ivy League Mystery Series, (novels) A Darker Shade of Crimson, 1998, Blue Blood, 1999, Orange Crushed, 2004. Bd. dirs. Clorox, Idenix Pharms., NYC Opera. Named Woman of Yr., Finl. Women's Assn.; named one of Forty Under Forty Rising Young Bus. Leaders, Crain's N.Y. Bus., Top 20 Women in Fin., Global Fin. Mag., Top 10 Cons. in Am., Cons. Mag.; recipient Matrix award, N.Y. Women Comm., 2001. Mem.: Phi Beta Kappa.

**THOMASHOW, LINDA SUZANNE,** microbiologist; b. Norwood, Mass. d. John Michael and E. Jean (Cole) Ravinski. BS, U. Mass., 1968; PhD, UCLA, 1979. Asst. prof. Wash. State U., Pullman, 1983-84; rsch. geneticist USDA Agrl. Rsch. Svc., Pullman, 1985—. Adj. prof. dept. plant pathology Wash. State U. Editorial bd. Applied & Environ. Microbiology, Washington, 1990-98; contbr. articles to profl. jours. Mem. Am. Soc. Microbiology, Am. Phytopathol. Soc. (Ruth Allen award 1997), Internat. Soc. for Molecular Plant-Microbe Interactions. Achievements include research in production of antibiotics by beneficial bacteria that live in association with the roots of plants, structure, function and regulation of genes involved in antibiotic synthesis by bacteria, the ecological significance of antibiotic production in natural environments. Office: Wash State Univ PO Box 646430 Dept Plant Pathology Pullman WA 99164-6430

**THOMASHOW, STEVEN ROY,** military officer, intelligence officer; b. Bronx, Jan. 27, 1957; s. Isaac Tom and Dorothy (Cuilino Bodsky) T. Accredited, U.S. Mil. Acad. Commd. United States of the World, adm., with spl. ops., 1988—; served with Israeli War USN, served with Gulf War. Recipient Pres. Nat. Medal of Patriotism; named to Am. Fedn. Police Assn., 1996. Fellow Nat. Law Enforcement Acad. (hon.); mem. Am. Fedn. Police. Avocations: Karate (black belt), torah studies, boxing, reading. Home and Office: United States of the World Recon One 4644 Myrtle Ln West Palm Beach FL 33417-5316 Fax: 561-689-3149.

**THOMASON, DUSTIN,** writer; b. 1976; BS in Anthropology & Medicine, Harvard U., 1998; MD, MBA, Columbia U., 2003. Co-author: (novels) (with Ian Caldwell) The Rule of Four, 2004 (Publishers Weekly bestseller list, 2004, NY Times bestseller list, 2004, San Francisco Chronicle bestseller list, 2004,

Boston Globe bestseller list, 2004, NY Post bestseller list, 2004). Office: c/o Dial Books 375 Hudson St New York NY 10014

**THOMASON, MORIAH ELIZABETH,** neuroscientist; BA, U. Calif., Berkeley, 1998; PhD, Stanford U., 2006. Rsch. assoc. Princeton Rev., N.Y.C., 1991—96; contract rsch. intern Covance Periapproval Svcs. Inc., Walnut Creek, Calif., 1996—97; social sci. rschr. Gabrieli Neuroimaging Lab., Stanford, Calif., 1999—2001. Contbr. scientific papers to profl. jours. Recipient James W. Lyons Svc. award, Stanford U., 2005; fellow, Summer Inst. Cognitive Neuroscience Dartmouth Coll., 2002, Summer Inst. Cognitive Neuroscience Squaw Valley, 2003; Mead Clark & Senator Herbert W. Slater scholar, 1994, Will & Ruth Craig scholar, 1994, Travel fellow, Internat. Soc. Magnetic Resonance Medicine, 2004. Office: Dept Brain and Cognitive Sci 43 Vassar St Bldg 46-4037 Cambridge MA 02139 Personal E-mail: moriah@stanford.edu.

**THOMASON, NOLA FAYE,** emergency physician; b. East St. Louis, Ill., May 23, 1957; d. Noel Noble and Dorothy Bernice (Burkett) Manring; m. Paul David Thomason, Mar. 23, 1979; children: Paula Faye, Rachel Elisabeth. ADN, Frontier C.C., Fairfield, Ill., 1986; Mobile Intensive Care Nurse/Emergency Care RN, Good Samaritan Hosp., Mt. Vernon, 1992; Trauma Nurse Specialist, Carbondale Meml. Hosp., 1996; EMT Basic, Frontier C.C., 1997. Cert. mobile intensive care nurse, mobile intensive care instr., emergency nursing care pediatric core curriculum, 1997. Charge nurse Rest Haven Manor, Albion, Ill., 1986—; staff nurse Kimberly Quality Care, Belleville, 1986—87; staff nurse emergency room Clay County Hosp., Flora, 1987—88; RN, supr. Good Samaritan Hosp., Mt. Vernon, 1990—92, Crossroads Cmty. Hosp., 1988—91; night supr. Fairfield (Ill.) Meml. Hosp., 1993—. Home: RR 3 Box 86 Fairfield IL 62837

**THOMASON, SANDRA LEE,** elementary school educator; d. Eugene LeRoy Ducat and Jean Frances Miller-Ducat; 1 child, Eric Christopher. EdB, U. Toledo, 1968, MEd, 1974. Permanent Tchg. Cert. Ohio State Dept. Edn., 1993, Reading Cert. K-12 Ohio State Dept. of Edn., 1993. Primary edn. tchr. Wash. Local Schs., Toledo, 1968—75, Sylvania (Ohio) schs., 1985—2000; vis. prof. U. Toledo, 1999—2003; reading instr. Ohio State Dept. of Edn., Perrysburg, Ohio, 1999—2003, Sylvania, 1999—2003, Toledo, 1999—2003; guest tchr. Lourdes Coll., Sylvania, Ohio, 2000; literacy specialist Sylvania Schs., 2003; reading cons., tchr., trainer NW Ohio Regional Profl. Devel. Ctr., Toledo, 2000—03; literacy support tchr., mid. sch. Olentangy Local Schs., Powell, Ohio, 2003—. Program administr. Summer Fun Summer Play Sch., Toledo, 1979; literacy specialist Ohio State Dept. of Edn., 1999—2003; counseling support group leader U. Toledo Counseling Ctr., 1982—84; youth enrichment seminar tchr. Sylvania Schs., Sylvania, 1996—97, 1996—97; spkr. Lourdes Coll., 1997—98; presenter, integrated curriculum with a lit. base, k-4 Patrick-Henry Local Schs., Deshler, Ohio, 1995—96; cons. in field. Dir.: (exhbn.) Developmentally Appropriate and Integrated Activities Across the Curriculum; contbr. articles to popular mags. Sect. leader Toledo 20/20 City Initiative. Mem.: ASCD, Ohio Coun. of the Tchrs. Lang. Arts, Internat. Reading Assn., Pi Lambda Theta (hon.), Phi Delta Kappa (hon.). Achievements include development of curriculum for primary grade children, balanced literacy curriculum for elementary and middle school students; design of edn. programs for summer sch. students in presch. and primary grades. Office: Olentangy Local Schs 814 Shanahan Rd Ste 300 Lewis Center OH 43035 Office Phone: 740-657-4050. Business E-Mail: sandra_thomason@olentangy.k12.oh.us.

**THOMASON, SCOTT,** automobile executive; b. 1953; BS, U of Oreg., Portland. Prin. Thomason Toyota, Gladstone; pres. Dee A. Thomason Ford Co., Gladstone, 1974—2002, Thomason Nissan Inc., Gladstone, 1990—2002, Heritage Auto Ctr. Inc., Kirkland, Wash., 1991—2002, Thomason Auto Group, Portland, Oreg., Barber Auto Group, Bakersfield, Calif., 2003—. Office: Barber Auto Group 4600 Wible Rd Bakersfield CA 93313

**THOMASOS, DENYSE,** artist; b. Trinidad, 1964; BA in Painting and Art History, U. Toronto, 1987; student, Skowheggan Sch., 1988; MFA in Painting and Sculpture, Yale U., 1989. Asst. prof. painting Tyler Sch. Art Temple U., Phila., 1990—95; asst. prof. painting visual and performing arts Rutgers U., Newark, 1995—. One-woman shows include Fleisher Art Meml. Gallery, Phila., 1993, Olga Korper Gallery, Toronto, Ont., Can., 1994, 1998, Queens (N.Y.) Mus. Art, Bulova Corp. Ctr., 1997, Lennon, Weinberg Gallery, N.Y.C., 1997, 1999, exhibited in group shows at Alpha Gallery, Boston, 1989, A Space, Toronto, 1992, Vox Populi, Phila., 1993, Mercer Union, Toronto, 1994, Ottawa (Ont.) Art Gallery, 1994, Lennon, Weinberg Gallery, N.Y.C., 1996, 1998, Newhouse Ctr. Contemporary Art, Snug Harbor Cultural Ctr., S.I., 1997, Art Gallery North York, N.Y., 1997, Fine Arts Ctr. Galleries, U. R.I. Kingston, 1999, Works on Paper, Global Art Source, Zurich, Switzerland, 2002—03, others; curator (exhibitions) Art in Gen., Gallery 6, N.Y., 1998; one-woman shows include St. Vincent Univ. Gallery, Halifax, NS, 2004. Recipient Joan Mitchell Found. award, 1998; grantee Exploration grantee, Can. Coun., 1990, "B" Nat. grantee, 1994, Visual Arts fellow in painting, Pa. Coun. on Arts, Phila., 1994, Mid-Atlantic Regional grantee, NEA, 1994; Pew fellow in Arts, Phila., 1995, Guggenheim Found. fellow, 1997. Office: Lennon Weinberg Inc 514 W 25th St New York NY 10001-5585 Fax: 212-941-0098.

**THOMAS-RAZZA, CONSTANCE,** retired elementary school educator; b. Balt., Dec. 28, 1935; d. Arthur and Bertha Crippen Thomas; m. Joseph C. Razza, Jr., Oct. 29, 1969; children: Joseph C. Razza III, Constance Miriam Razza, Renata Joy Razza; m. Garnett George Adam (div. 1968). BA, Coppin State Tchrs. Sch. Fine Arts, Balt., 1957, U. Mich., Ann Arbor, 1962. Cert. tchr. Balt., Md., 1957, Washington, DC, 1962. Tchr. Balt. City Pub. Schs., 1957—62, DC Pub. Schs., 1962—96; tchr. ESL Peace Corps, Cape Verde, West Africa, 2000—02. Lectr. Am. U., Washington, 1973. Author: (book) My Mother's Love Life, 1998; prodr.: (theatre) Spedjo, 2001. Sec. LeDroit Park Civic Assn., Washington, 1990, 2005; vol. Smithsonian Instn., Washington, 1996—98; protestor No War on Cuba, 2002—. Named Outstanding Newsletter Publisher, DC Fedn. Civic Assns., 1986, Outstanding Educator, Potomac LINKS, 2005. Democrat. Buddhist. Avocations: beading, writing, gardening. Home: 501 T St NW Washington DC 20001 Personal E-mail: ctrazza05@verizon.net.

**THOMASON, DAN KING,** newspaper executive, columnist; b. Shelbyville, Ind., Dec. 22, 1933; s. Hubert Lee and Mary Margaret (King) T.; m. Laqueta Forducey, Sept. 1, 1958; children: Scot, Lisa, Sean, Patrick. BS, Ind. U., 1956; postgrad., Colo. U., 1959. Reporter, editor Indpls. Star, 1956; reporter Lawton (Okla.) Constitution, 1957-58, The Rocky Mountain News, Denver, 1959-64; corr. Scripps Howard Newspapers, Washington, 1964-74, asst. mng. editor, 1974-76; mng. editor Scripps Howard News Svc., Washington, 1976-80, editor, 1980—; v.p. news Scripps Howard Newspapers, Cin., 1986—; v.p. E.W. Scripps Co., 1996—. Weill vis. prof. Nat. U., 1999; vis. prof. Hampton U., 2000. Pres. Raymond Clapper Found., Washington, 1980-2004; bd. dirs. Scripps Howard Found., Cin., 1987-2003, v.p., 1994; trustee Franklin Coll., 1990—; nat. mat. adv. com. E.W. Scripps Sch. Journalism, 1990, Ohio U., 1990, Nat. Pub. Affairs Coun., Ind. U., 1990—; bd. visitors Inst. Polit. Journalism Georgetown U., 1990—. With U.S. Army, 1956-58. Presdl. fellow Trinity Coll., Hartford, 2000; media fellow Hoover Instn., 2001, 2002, 2003; Louis Weill scholar Ind. U., 1999; named Man of Yr., Shelbyville, Ind. C. of C., 1970, Indiana Journalism Hall of Fame, 1993; elected Ind. Acad., 1993; named to Ind. Journalism Hall of Fame, 1997. Mem. Am. Soc. Newspaper Editors, White House Corrs. Assn., Gridiron Club of Washington, Overseas Press Club, Nat. Press Club, Univ. Club of Washington, Washington Golf and Country Club (Arlington, Va.), Bohemian Club (San Francisco), Sigma Delta Chi. Home: 3729 Morningside Dr Fairfax VA 22031-3317 Office: Scripps Howard 1090 Vermont Ave NW Ste 1000 Washington DC 20005-4906 Business E-Mail: thomason@shns.com.

**THOMASSON, KATHRYN AMBLER,** chemistry educator, researcher; b. Richmond, Va., Nov. 20, 1959; d. John Nelson and Joan (Holbeeck) T. PhD, Iowa State U., 1990. Rsch. assoc. Biosym Techs., Inc., San Diego, 1990-91;

Dreyfus postdoctoral fellow Tenn. Technol. U., Cookeville, Tenn., 1991-93; assoc. prof. chemistry U. N.D., Grand Forks, 1993—. Contbr. articles to profl. jours. Mem. Am. Chem. Soc. (Red River Valley sect. bd. dirs. 1999-2000, Sigma Xi (U. N.D. chpt. pres. 1999-2000), Iota Sigma Pi (coord. members-at-large). Office: Univ ND Dept Chemistry PO Box 9024 Grand Forks ND 58202-9024 Fax: 701 777-2331. E-mail: kthomasson@chem.und.edu.

**THOME, JIM,** professional baseball player; b. Peoria, Ill., Aug. 27, 1970; m. Andrea Pacione; 1 child. Student Illinois Central College. Player Cleve. Indians, 1991—2002, Philadelphia Phillies, 2003—05, Chgo. White Sox, 2005—. Honorary Co-Chmn. United Way Home Run Derby. Named to Am. League All-Star Team, 1997—99, Nat. League All-Star Team, 2004. Achievements include led Nat. League in Home Runs (47), 2003; hit 400th career Home Run, June 13, 2004. Office: Cellular One Field 333 W 35th St Chicago IL 60616*

**THOMFORDE, CHRISTOPHER MEREDITH,** minister; b. Cleve., Jan. 25, 1947; s. Fredrich Henry and Marie (Meredith) T.; m. Christine Elizabeth Stone Huber, June 10, 1972; children: Christopher, Rebecca, Sarah, Jonathan. BA, Princeton U., 1969; MDiv, Yale U., 1974. Ordained to ministry Luth. Ch. in am., 1976. Asst. chaplain Colgate U., Hamilton, N.Y., 1974-78; pastor St. Paul's Luth. Ch., Dansville, N.Y., 1978-86; chaplain Susquehanna U., Selinsgrove, Pa., 1986—. Pres. Dansville Ministerium, 1979-81. Sec. ARC, Danville, 1983-86. Named Citizen of Yr., Dansville, 1986. Office: Susquehanna U Chaplain's Office Selinsgrove PA 17870 Home: 1215 Saint Olaf Ave Northfield MN 55057-1534

**THOMLINSON, RALPH,** demographer, educator; b. St. Louis, Feb. 12, 1925; s. Ralph and Ora Lee (Barr) T.; m. Margaret Mary Willits, Dec. 21, 1946; children: Elizabeth Barr, William Lockwood. BA, Oberlin Coll., 1948; postgrad., U. Pitts., 1943-44, Harvard U., 1948; MA, Yale U., 1949; PhD, Columbia U., 1960. Asst. town planner, Montclair, N.J., 1949-50; asst. city planner Paterson, N.J., 1950; research asst. Bur. Applied Social Research, N.Y.C., 1952; med. statistics asst. actuarial dept. Met. Life Ins. Co., N.Y.C., 1952-53; instr. statistics and population U. Wis., 1953-56; instr. sociology and anthropology Denison U., Granville, Ohio, 1956-59; asst. prof. sociology Calif. State U., L.A., 1959-62, assoc. prof., 1962-65, prof., 1965-88, prof. emeritus, 1988—, chmn. dept. sociology, 1967-69; vis. prof. sociology U. Alta., Can., 1966; vis. prof. biostatistics U. N.C., Chapel Hill, 1972-73; demographic adviser Inst. Population Studies, Chulalongkorn U., Bangkok, Thailand, 1969-71; cons. Nat. Family Planning Program, Thailand, Census of Thailand, 1970-71, Population/Food Fund, 1977-79, also various research centers abroad, 1969-73. Cons. to fourteen book pubs., 1965—; field assoc. Population Coun., N.Y.C., 1969-71; rsch. adviser Ctr. for Rsch. and Demographic Studies, Rabat, Morocco, 1972-73; acad. visitor Population Investigation Com., London Sch. Econs., 1973; vis. scholar Nat. Inst. Demographic Studies, Paris, 1973-74 Author: A Mathematical Model for Migration, 1960, Population Dynamics, 2d edit, 1976, Sociological Concepts and Research, 1965, Demographic Problems, 2d edit, 1975, Urban Structure, 1969, Thailand's Population, 1971, (with others) The Methodology of the Longitudinal Study of Social, Economic and Demographic Change, 1971; editor: (with Visid Prachuabmoh) The Potharam Study, 1971; adv. editor: Social. Abstracts, 1963-67, Sociology Quar., 1978-84; cons. editor: As-Soukan, 1972-73; assoc. editor: Pacific Social. Rev, 1976-83; Social. Perspective, 1983-85; chmn. editorial bd. Calif. Sociologist, 1981-84; cons.: Dictionary of Modern Sociology, 1969; contbr. to: Dictionary of Demography, 5 vols., 1985-86; books, profl. jours. Served with AUS, 1943-45, ETO. Mem. Population Assn. Am., Internat. Union for Sci. Study Population, Am. Sociol. Assn., Internat. Assn. Survey Statisticians, Assn. Asian Studies. Home: 201 Chadbourne Ave Apt 218 Millbrae CA 94030

**THOMOPOULOS, MICHAEL,** music educator; b. Lowell, Mass., Apr. 24, 1953; s. George and Doris Thomopoulos. MusB, The New Eng. Conservatory of Music, Boston, 1975; MusM, The Juilliard Sch., N.Y.C., 1977. Founder, music dir. Palisades Chamber Players, Ft. Lee, NJ, 1979—. Founder, dir., tchr. Palisades Sch. Music. Recipient Morris Loeb Meml. prize, Internat. Concert Artist Guild, 1977. Avocations: private piloting, scuba diving, politics, travel. Office: The Palisades Sch of Music 196 Washington Ave Fort Lee NJ 07024 Office Phone: 201-944-1311. Office Fax: 201-944-1311. E-mail: mthomopoulos@yahoo.com.

**THOMOPOULOS, GREGS G.,** consulting engineering company executive; b. Benin City, Nigeria, May 16, 1942; s. Aristoteles and Christiana E. (Ogiamien) Thomopulos; m. Patricia Walker, Sept. 4, 1966 (div. 1974); 1 child, Lisa; m. Mettie L. Williams, May 28, 1976; children: Nicole, Euphemia. BSCE with highest distinction, U. Kans., 1965; MS in Structural Engring., U. Calif., Berkeley, 1966; PhD (hon.), Teikyo Marycrest U., 1996. Sr. v.p. internat. div Stanley Cons., Inc., Muscatine, Iowa, 1978-84, sr. v.p. project divsn., 1984-87; pres., CEO Stanley Consultants, Inc., Muscatine, Iowa, 1987—; exec. v.p. SC Co., Inc., Muscatine, 1992-98; pres., COO, 1998-99; pres., CEO, 2000—; also bd. dirs. SC Co., Inc., Muscatine; chmn., CEO Stanley Environ., Inc., Chgo. 1991—; also bd. dirs.; chmn., CEO SC Power Devel., Inc., 1992—. Chmn., CEO Stanley Design-Build, Inc., 1995—; bd. dirs. Stanley Cons., Inc., Muscatine, Wellmark, Inc., Blue Cross Blue Shield Iowa and S.D., 1999—; mem. adv. bd. U. Kans. Sch. Engring., 2002—; mem. industry adv. panel U.S. Dept. State. Mem. adv. bd. Coll. Engring. U. Iowa, 1992-2000, Hydraulics Inst., 2000-06. Fellow ASCE, Am. Coun. Engring. Cos.; mem. NSPE, Internat. Fedn. Cons. Engrs. (exec. com.), US Dept. of State, Industry Adv. Panel, 33 Club (pres. 1987), Rotary. Presbyterian. Avocations: tennis, computers, music. Home: 25 Shagbark Ct Iowa City IA 52246-2786 Office: Stanley Cons Inc 225 Iowa Ave Muscatine IA 52761-3765 Personal E-mail: thomopoulos@home.com. Business E-Mail: thomopulosg@stanleygroup.com.

**THOMPSON, ADAM CLAY,** reporter; Sr. writer San Francisco Bay Guardian, Calif. Recipient Pub. Svc. award, N. Calif. Ch. Soc. Professional Journalists, 2004, George Polk award for local reporting, 2006. Office: San Francisco Bay Guardian 135 Mississippi St San Francisco CA 94107 Office Phone: 415-255-3100. Office Fax: 415-255-8762.*

**THOMPSON, ALAN ERIC,** economics professor; b. Sept. 16, 1924; s. Eric Joseph and Florence Thompson; m. Mary Heather Long, 1960; 4 children. MA, U. Edinburgh, 1949, MA with 1st class honors, 1951, PhD, 1953. Asst. in polit. econ. U. Edinburgh, 1952-53, lectr. econs., 1953-59, 64-71; prof. econs. of govt. Heriot-Watt U., Edinburgh, 1972—. Adviser to Scottish TV, 1966-76; Scottish gov. BBC, 1976-79; vis. prof. Grad. Sch. Bus., Stanford U. (Calif.), 1966, 68; chmn. adv. bd. econs. edn. Esmee Fairbairn Rsch. Project, 1970-76. Author: (with others) Development of Economic Doctrine, 1980; contbr. articles to profl. jours. M.P. Labour Party, Dunfermline, 1959-64; mem. Scottish Com. Pub. Schs. Commn., 1969-70; mem. Joint Mil. Edn. Com. Edinburgh and Heriot-Watt Univs., 1975—, local govt. boundary commn. for Scotland, 1975-82; chmn. No. Offshore Resources Study, 1974-84; mem. bd. govs. Newbattle Abbey Coll., 1980-82; bd. govs. Leigh Nautical Coll., 1981-87; trustee Bell's Nautical Trust, 1981-87; parliamentary adviser Pharm. Gen. Coun., 1985-2000; bd. dirs. Scottish AIDS Rsch. Found., 1992; adv. Robert Burns Meml. Trust, 1995—99; advisor Robert Burns Meml. Trust, 1995-2000. With Brit. Army, WWII. Carnegie Rsch. scholar, 1951-52. Fellow Royal Soc. Arts, Soc. Antiquaries (Scotland); mem. Assn. Nazi War Camp Survivors (v.p. 1960—), Edinburgh Amenity and Transport Assn. (pres. 1970-75), New Club, Loch Earn Sailing Club.

**THOMPSON, ANDREA,** television personality, retired newscaster, actress; b. Dayton, Ohio, 1959; m. David Guc, 1987 (div. 1990); m. Jerry Doyle, 1995 (div. 1997); 1 child, Alec. Correspondent KRQE-TV, Albuquerque, 2000—01; news anchor, Headline News CNN, 2001—02. Films include Wall Street, 1987, Doin' Time on Planet Earth, 1988, Delirious, 1991, Lost Valley, 1998, A Gun, A Car, A Blonde, 1998, Rocket's Red Glare, 2000; TV series include Falcon Crest, 1989-90, Babylon 5, 1994-95, JAG, 1995-96, NYPD Blue, 1996-2000; host: Court TV, Saturday Night Line Up, 2002.

**THOMPSON, ANNE KATHLEEN,** entertainment journalist; b. NYC, Aug. 10, 1954; d. Charles Torrington Thompson and Eleanor Josephine (Callahan) Dekins; m. David Christopher Chute, Oct. 23, 1983; 1 child, Nora Thompson Chute. BA in Cinema Studies, NYU, 1976. Asst. mgr. Bleecker St. Cinema, NYC, 1975—76; publicist United Artists, NYC, 1976—79; account exec. P/M/K Pub. Rels., NYC, 1979—81; assoc. editor Film Comment Mag., NYC, 1981-82, west coast editor, 1982-96; publicity dir. Twentieth Century Fox Pictures, 1983-85; wrote column Risky Bus. LA Weekly, LA Times Syndicate, 1985-93; columnist Inside Film, 1988-90; U.S. editor Empire Mag., London, 1989-91; sr. writer Entertainment Weekly, 1993-96; west coast editor Premier Mag., 1996—2002; contbr. Premiere, Filmmaker, Wired, NY Times, Washington Post, NY mag., London Observer; dep. film editor The Hollywood Reporter, LA, 2005—. Mem. Nat. Writer's Union, Women in Film. Office: The Hollywood Reporter 5055 Wilshire Blvd Los Angeles CA 90036-4396

**THOMPSON, ANNIE FIGUEROA,** retired academic administrator; b. Río Piedras, P.R., June 7, 1941; d. Antonio Figueroa-Colón and Ana Isabel Laugier; m. Donald P. Thompson, Jan. 23, 1972; 1 child, John Anthony. BA, Baylor U., 1962; MSLS, U. So. Calif., 1965; AMD, Fla. State U., 1978, PhD, 1980. Educator Mayan Sch., Guatemala City, Guatemala, 1962-63; cataloger libr. sys. U. P.R., Río Piedras, 1965-67, head music libr., 1967-81, assoc. prof. librarianship, 1981-85, dir. grad. sch. libr. info. sci. Rio Piedras, 1986-93, prof., 1986-96; ret., 1996. Author: An Annotated Bibliography About Music in Puerto Rico, 1975; co-author: Music and Dance in Puerto Rico from the Age of Columbus to Modern Times, An Annotated Bibliography, 1991; contbr. articles to profl. jours.; performed song recitals Inst. of P.R. Culture and U. P.R. Artist Series, 1974-78; soloist with P.R. Symphony Orch., San Juan, 1978; performed in opera, on radio and TV, San Juan, 1968-81. Sec. P.R. Symphony Orch League, San Juan, 1982-84; mem. pub. libr. adv. com. Adminstrn. for Devel. of Arts and Culture, P.R., 1982-84, Pub. Libr. Adv. Bd., 1989-94. Recipient Lauro a la Instrucción Bibliotecaria Sociedad de Bibliotecarios de P.R., 1985, Lauro a la Bibliografía Puertorriqueña, 1993. Mem. Sarasota Rotary (bd. dirs. 2000-02), Sociedad de Bibliotecarios de P.R. (pres. 1994-96), Music Libr. Assn. (bd. dirs. 1982-84, asst. conv. mgr. 2002-04, conv. mgr. 2004-06), Sarasota Rotary Found. (bd. dirs.), Sigma Delta Kappa, Mu Phi Epsilon, Beta Phi Mu. Episcopalian. Home: 435 S Gulfstream Ave Sarasota FL 34236-6736 Personal E-mail: annietmla@aol.com.

**THOMPSON, ANNIE LAURA (LAURA ANNE THOMPSON),** foreign language educator; b. Henderson, Tenn., July 8, 1937; d. Wesley Sylvester and Letha Irene (Jones) T.; m. Edward L. Patterson, June 7, 1980. BA, U. Ala., 1959; MA, Duke U., 1961; PhD, Tulane U., 1973. Instr. Spanish lang. U. Miss., Oxford, 1960-64; instr. Auburn (Ala.) U., 1964-66; tchg. asst. Tulane U., New Orleans, 1966-70; prof. Spanish lang. Delgado C.C., New Orleans, 1970—. Instr. Spanish for Physicians and Med. Persons Tulane U., La. State U. Med. Eye Ctr., Ochsner Clinic and Hosp. Author: Religious Elements in the Quijote, 1960, The Attempt of Spanish Intellectuals to Create a New Spain, 1930-36, 1973, The Generation of 1898: Intellectual Politicians; asst. editor The Crusader, 1961-64. Rep. candidate for gov. State of La., 1991, 95, for 1st Dist. U.S. Congress, 1992; alt. mem. La. Coastal Commn., 1984—; del. Women's State Rep. Conv., 1987, La. State Rep. Conv., 1990, 93, La. Coastal Adv. Coun., 1988, Pan Am. Commn., 1992-95; v.p. pub. rels. Alliance for Good Govt., 1990; candidate State Senate La., 1994; mem. DAR (Vieux Carré chpt.), 2000. Recipient Outstanding Tchr. award Delgado Coll. Student Govt. Assn., 1974; Woodoow Wilson fellow, 1959-60, NDEA fellow, 1968-69. Mem. AAUP, DAR, Pachyderm Club, Women's Rep. Club, Phi Beta Kappa, Phi Alpha Theta, Sigma Delta Pi. Republican. Mem. Ch. of Christ.

**THOMPSON, ANTHONY WAYNE,** metallurgist, educator, consultant; b. Burbank, Calif., Mar. 6, 1940; s. William Lyman and Mary Adelaide (Nisbet) T.; m. Mary Ruth Cummings, Aug. 24, 1963; children: Campbell Lyman, Michael Anthony. BS, Stanford U., 1962; MS, U. Wash., 1965; PhD, MIT, 1970. Research engr. Jet Propulsion Lab., Pasadena, Calif., 1962-63; mem. tech. staff Sandia Labs., Livermore, Calif., 1970-73, Rockwell Sci. Ctr., Thousand Oaks, Calif., 1973-77; assoc. prof. Carnegie Mellon U., Pitts., 1977-79, prof., 1980-94, dept. head, 1987-90; staff scientist Lawrence Berkeley Lab., Berkeley, Calif., 1994-99; rsch. engr. U. Calif., Berkeley, Calif., 1995—. Vis. scientist U. Cambridge, Eng., 1983, Risø, Denmark, 1987, U. Calif., 1991; cons. Sandia Labs., 1977—1998, GE, 1988-2000. Editor: Work Hardening, 1976, Metall. Transactions, 1983-88, Signature Press Book Pubs., 1993–; co-editor: Hydrogen in Metals, 1974, Hydrogen Conf. Proc., 1976, 81, 89, 94, 2002; mem. editl. bd. Internat. Metals Revs., 1980-88; contbr. articles to profl. jours. Overseas fellow Churchill Coll. Cambridge U., 1982 Fellow Am. Soc. Metals; mem. Clubs: Sierra, Nat. Model R.R. Assn. Democrat. Home: 2906 Forest Ave Berkeley CA 94705 Office: Lawrence Berkeley Lab Material Sci Divsn Berkeley CA 94720-0001

**THOMPSON, AUGUSTINE CRAIG,** priest, historian; b. Mineola, N.Y., 1954; s. Arthur Thomas and Anna Dean Thompson. BA, MA, Johns Hopkins U., 1976; MDiv, St. Albert's Coll., 1985; PhD, U. Calif., Berkeley, 1988. Ordained priest Cath. Ch., 1985. Asst. prof., then assoc. prof. religious history U. Oreg., Eugene, 1990—99, chmn. dept. religious studies, 1996—99; assoc. prof. religious studies and hsitiry U. Va., Charlottesville, 1999—2006, dir. grad. studies in religion, 2004—, prof. religious studies and history, 2006—. Pastor Cath. Ctr. So. (Oreg.) State Coll., Ashland, 1995—96. Author: Revival Preachers & Politics in 13th Century Italy, 1992, Cities of God: Religion in the Italian Communes 1125-1325, 2005; translator: Gratian/ Treatise on Laws, 1993. Provincial councillor We. Dominican Province, Oakland, Calif., 1996—2001. Mem.: Medieval Acad. Am., Am. Cath. Hist. Assn., Am. Hist. Assn. Roman Catholic. Office: Univ Virginia Religious Studies Dept Charlottesville VA 22904

**THOMPSON, B. LOLANA,** archivist; b. Harlingen, Tex., Dec. 8, 1953, d. John M. and Betty E. Lummus; m. Foye Lynn Thompson, May 15, 1976; children: Jay Alan, Amy Kay. BA in History, U. Tex., Austin, 1975; MA in History, Tex. Tech U., Lubbock, 1982. Cert. archivist Acad. Cert. Archivists, 2005, in archival adminstrn. U. Tex., 1999. Archival asst. SW Collection, Tex. Tech U., Lubbock, 1976—79; libr. asst. Tex. Tech U. Libr., 1983—84; acquisitions asst. Dallas Theol. Sem., 1992—2001, archivist, 2003—. Local program spkr. SW Area Theol. Libr. Assn., 2004. Mem.: Soc. SW Archivists, Soc. Am. Archivists. Office: Dallas Theol Seminary 3909 Swiss Ave Dallas TX 75204

**THOMPSON, BARBARA ANN,** principal, educator; d. Glenn and Mary Jane Arrasmith; children: Vitaly Ivanyuk Winker, Aliya Rakhmetova Winker, Ramil Miroshnikov Winker. BS, Kent State U., Ohio, 1977; MA, Ohio State U., Columbus, 1981; PhD, The George Wash. U., DC, 2005. Tchr. State of Ohio, Columbus, 1977—81, Prince William County Pub. Schs., Manassas, Va., 1981—84; spl. edn. tchr. Arlington Pub. Schs., Va., 1984—94, spl. edn. vocat. coord., 1994—2003, asst. dir., 2003—05, HS prin., 2005—. Adj. prof. special edn. and pschology Marymount U., Arlington, 2005—. Sec. SOC, Inc, Arlington, 1994—96. Mem.: ASCD, Arlington Sch. Adminstrs., Coun. Exceptional Children. Avocations: sailing, swimming. Home: 2323 N Burlington St Arlington VA 22207-2520 Office: Arlington Mill HS 4975 Columbia Pike Arlington VA 22204 Office Phone: 703-228-5350. Business E-Mail: bthompso@arlington.k12.va.us.

**THOMPSON, BARBARA STORCK,** state official; b. McFarland, Wis., Oct. 15, 1924; d. John Casper and Marie Ann (Kassabaum) Storck; m. Glenn T. Thompson, July 1, 1944; children—David C., James T. BS, Wis. State U., 1956; MS, U. Wis., 1959, PhD, 1969; L.H.D. (hon.), Carroll Coll., 1974. Tchr. pub. schs., West Dane County, Mt. Horeb, Wis., 1944-56; instr. Green County Tchrs. Coll., Monroe, Wis., 1956-57; coordinator curriculum Monroe Pub. Schs., 1957-60; instr. U. Wis., Platteville, 1960; supr. schs. Waukesha County Schs., Wis., 1960-63, supt. schs., 1963-65; prin. Fairview Elem. Schs., Brookfield, Wis., 1962-64; adminstrv. cons. Wis. Dept. Pub. Instrn., Madison, 1964-72, state coordinator, 1971-72; instr. U. Wis., Madison and Green Bay, 1972; supt. pub. instrn. Madison Wis., 1973—81. Mem. Wis. State Bd. Vocat. Edn., 1973-81, Wis. Edn. Comm. Bd. 1973-81, Univ. Wis. Sys. Bd. Regents,

1973-1981. Author: A Candid Discussion of Critical Issues, 1975; mem. editorial bd.: The Education Digest, 1975—; contbr. articles to profl. jours. Mem. White House Conf. Children, 1970, Gov.'s Com. State Conf. Children and Youth, 1969-70, Manpower Council, 1973-81; bd. dirs. Vocational, Tech. and Adult Edn., 1973-81, Ednl. Communications, 1973-81, Higher Edn. Aids, 1973-81, Agy. Instructional TV, 1975-81; mem. nat. panel on SAT score decline; bd. regents U. Wis., 1973-81, U.S. office f Edn. Visiting Sch. Team - England, GErmany, Sweden, Poland, Iran, Syria, India, and Japan. Recipient State Conservation award Madison Lions CLub, 1956; Waukesha Freeman award, 1961 Mem. Nat. Coun. Adminstrv. Women in Edn. (named Woman of Year 1974), Nat. Coun. State Cons. in Elem. Edn. (pres. 1974-75), Wis. Assn. Sch. Dist. Adminstrs., Assn. Supervision and Curriculum Devel., Wis. Assn. Supervision and Curriculum Devel., Southwestern Wis. Assn. Supervision and Curriculum Devel., Southeastern Wis. Assn. Supervision and Curriculum Devel. (mem. exec. council 1972-73), Dept. Elem. Sch. Prins., Wis. Elementary Sch. Prins. Assn., NEA, Wis. Edn. Assn. (pres. local chpt 1970-71); life mem. So. Wis. Edn. Assn., Wis. Ednl. Rsch. Assn., Dept. Elem.-Kindergarten-Nursery Edn., Assn. Childhood Edn. Internat., Assn. Childhood Edn., Coun. Chief State Sch. Officers, Edn. Commn. of States, Nat. Coun. State Cons. in Elem. Edn. (pres. 1974-75), Am. Assn. Sch. Dist. Adminstrs. (chmn. policy com. 1963-81), Madison Ctrl. Internat. Lions Club, U. Wis. Alumni Orgn. (Sarasota, Fla. and Madison), U. Wis. League (Madison chpt.), Delta Kappa Gamma, Pi Lambda Theta. Office: Apt 123 325 S Yellowstone Dr Madison WI 53705-4301

**THOMPSON, BENJAMIN K.B.,** financial analyst; b. Koforidua, Ghana, Nov. 25, 1958; arrived in US, 1981; s Benjamin Kwaku Boyc Thompson and Alice Narkie; m. Cynthia Korankye Thompson, Oct. 4, 2001. BS in Econ., U. Tex., Arlington, 1987; MBA in Fin., Dallas Baptist. U., 1990; postgrad., Walden U., 2005—. Fin. analyst PrimeCo Personal Comm., West Lake, Tex., 1996—99, Dallas Morning News, 1994—2000; adv. fin. analyst Evercom Sys., Irving, Tex., 2000—02. Media dir. Fellowship of Joy, Arlington, 2005. Mem.: Soc. Indsl. Leaders. Avocations: reading, basketball. E-mail: bkbthompson@lycos.com.

**THOMPSON, BENNIE G.,** congressman; b. Bolton, Miss., Jan. 28, 1948; m. London Johnson; 1 child, BendaLonne. BA in Polit. Sci., Tougaloo Coll., Miss., 1968; MS in Ednl. Adminstrn., Jackson State U., Miss., 1972; grad., U. So. Miss. Alderman, Bolton, Miss., 1969—73; mayor, 1973—79; supr. Hinds County, Miss., 1980-93; mem. US Congress from 2nd Miss. dist., 1993—, former mem. budget com., agr. com. and small bus. com., ranking mem. homeland security com. Presdl. appointee Nat. Coun. Health Planning and Devel. Bd. trustees Tougaloo Coll.; bd. dirs. So. Regional Coun., Housing Assistance Coun. Named one of 100 Most Influential Black Americans, Ebony mag., 2006. Mem.: Miss. Assn. Black Suprs. (founding mem.), Miss. Assn. Black Mayors (founding mem.). Democrat. Methodist. Original plaintiff in 1975 Ayers case. Office: 2432 Rayburn House Office Bldg Washington DC 20515-0001*

**THOMPSON, BERT ALLEN,** retired librarian; b. Bloomington, Ind., Dec. 13, 1930; s. James Albert and Dorothy Fern (Myers) T.; m. Martha Ellen Palmer; children— John Carter II, Anne Palmer, Paul Julian. BS, Ball State Tchrs. Coll., 1953; AM, Ind. U., 1960; certificate in archival adm., U. Denver, 1967. Tchr., libr. Ind. pub. schs., 1953-55; ref. asst. Indpls. Pub. Libr., 1956-59; head ref. svc. Mankato (Minn.) State U., 1959-61; instr. Grad. Libr. Sch. No. Ill. U., Dekalb, 1961-63; dir. libs., asst. prof. ednl. media U. Nebr. at Kearney, 1963-69; dir. libr. svc. Benedictine I., Lisle, Ill., 1969-90, spl. collections libr., 1990-92. Mem. exec. bd. Ill. regional Libr. Coun., 1976-79. Recipient 1st Melvin R. George LIBRAS award for Outstanding Svc. to Libr. Cooperation, 1993. Mem. Ill. (de Lafayette Reid Research scholar 1976), Cath. Libr. Assn. (treas. Ill. chpt. 1973-75, nat. sec.-treas. coll./univ. sect. 1981-85, nat. bd. dirs. 1987-93), Nebr. Libr. Assn. (chmn. coll. and univ. sect. 1963-64) Episcopalian. Home: 1808 Caxton Dr Wheaton IL 60187-6140

**THOMPSON, BERTHA BOYA,** retired education educator; b. New Castle, Pa., Jan. 31, 1917; d. Frank L. and Kathryn Belle (Park) Boya; m. John L. Thompson, Mar. 27, 1942; children: Kay Lynn Thompson Koolage, Scott McClain. BS in Elem. & Secondary Edn., Slippery Rock State Coll., 1940; MA in Geography and History, Miami U., 1954; EdD, Ind. U., 1961. Cert. elem. and secondary edn. tchr. Elem. tchr., reading specialist New Castle (Pa.) Sch. System, 1940-45; tchr., chmn. social studies Talawanda Sch. System, Oxford, Ohio, 1954-63; assoc. prof. psychology and geography, chair edn. dept. Western Coll. for Women, Oxford, 1963-74; assoc. prof. edn., reading clinic Miami U., Oxford, 1974-78, prof. emeritus, 1978—. Contbr. articles to profl. jours. Folk art com. Miami U. Art Mus., Oxford, 1974—76; adv. com. Smith libr., Oxford Pub. Libr., 1978—81. Mem. AAUP, Nat. Coun. Geographic Edn. (exec. bd. dirs. 1966-69), Nat. Soc. for Study Edn., Assn. Am. Geographers, Soc. Women Geographers, Nat. Coun. for the Social Studies, Pi Lambda Theta, Zeta Tau Alpha, Pi Gamma Mu, Gamma Theta Upsilon, Kappa Delta Pi. Avocations: antiques, reading, travel, tennis. Home: 6073 Contreras Rd Oxford OH 45056-9708

**THOMPSON, BRADFORD,** chef; b. Wilmington, Del., 1969; Grad., U. Rochester, NY. Garde mgr. Max on Main, Hartford, Conn., line cook, pastry chef; chef Camelback, Phoenix, Café Boulud, NYC, DB Bistro Moderne, NYC; mgr. private dinning Daniel, NYC; exec. chef Mary Elaine's, The Phoenician, Scottsdale, Ariz. Author: two cookbooks. Named one of Top 10 Best New Chefs in Am., Food & Wine Mag., 2004; recipient Best Chef: Southwest award, James Beard Found., 2006. Achievements include cuisine featured on Today Show and Food Network. Office: The Phoenician Mary Elaine's 6000 E Camelback Rd Scottsdale AZ 85251 Office Phone: 480-423-2530.*

**THOMPSON, BRIAN JOHN,** academic administrator, optics scientist, educator; b. Glossop, Eng., June 10, 1932; came to U.S., 1962; s. Alexander William and Edna May (Gould) T.; m. Joyce Emily Cheshire, Mar. 31, 1956; children: Karen Joyce, Andrew Derrick. B of Sci. Tech., U. Manchester, Eng., 1955, PhD, 1959. Demonstrator in physics dept. tech. U. Manchester, 1955-56, asst. lectr. dept. tech., 1957-59; lectr. physics U. Leeds, England, 1959-62; sr. physicist Tech. Optics, Inc., Burlington, Mass., 1963-65, dir. dept. optics, 1966-67; mgr. tech. ops. west, tech. dir. Beckman and Whitley, Mountainview, Calif., 1967-68; prof. Inst. Optics U. Rochester, NY, 1968-94, dir. Inst. Optics NY, 1968-75, dean Coll. Engring. and Applied Scis. NY, 1975-84, Wm. F. May prof. engring. NY, 1982-85, provost NY, 1984-94, provost emeritus, prof. of optics emeritus, Disting. U. prof. NY, 1994—. Editor Optics and Laser Tech., 1969-96; assoc. editor: Optical Engring., 1972-76, Optics Comm., 1979-86; editor Optica Acta, 1981-85, Optical Engring. Series, vols. 1-116, 1980—; mem. editl. bd. Laser Focus, 1970-84, Particle Characterization, 1984-95, Optics and Lasers in Engring., 1985, Milestone Series of Selected Papers, vols. 1-182, 1985-2006, Optical Engring., 1991-98; chmn. adv. bd. Marquis Who's Who Directory Optical Scientists and Engrs., 1983-86; contbr. articles to profl. jours. With Brit. Army, 1950-52. Fellow: Inst. Physics and Phys. Soc. (Gt. Britain), Optical Soc. Am. (bd. dirs. 1969—72, exec. com. 1970—73, assoc. editor jour. 1966—77), Soc. Photo-Optical Instrumentation Engrs. (life; pres. 1974—76, editor jour. 1991—98, Pres.'s award 1967, Pezzuto award 1978, Kingslake medal 1978, Gold medal 1986, Dir. award 1998); mem.: AAAS, Am. Phys. Soc. Home and Office: 9 Esternay Ln Pittsford NY 14534-1014

**THOMPSON, BUZZ (BARTON H. THOMPSON JR.),** law educator; b. 1951; AB in Economics, Stanford U., 1972, MBA, JD, Stanford U., 1976. Law clk. to Judge Joseph T. Sneed US Ct. Appeals 9th Cir., San Francisco, 1976—77; law clk. to Justice William H. Rehnquist US Supreme Ct., 1977—78; assoc. O'Melveny & Myers, LA, 1978—83, ptnr., 1984—86; mem. faculty Stanford Law Sch., 1986—, Robert E. Paradise fellow, 1993—95, Robert E Paradise prof. natural resources law, 1996—, vice dean, 2000—04; co-dir. Stanford Inst. for the Environment, 2004—. Instr. water resources UCLA, 1980—83; vis. fellow Hoover Instn. for War, Revolution,

and Peace Stanford U., 1999. Bd. dirs. Nat. Heritage Inst. Office: Stanford Law Sch Crown Quadrangle 559 Nathan Abbott Way Stanford CA 94305-8610 Office Phone: 650-723-2518. Office Fax: 650-725-8509. Business E-Mail: buzzt@stanford.edu.

**THOMPSON, CARLYNN JEAN,** information scientist; b. San Saba, Tex., Nov. 8, 1952; d. Joe Paul and Andragene Grumbles; m. David John Thompson, May 27, 1972; children: Lessa Anne, Kira Jo. MLS, U. of Md., 1976. Libr. in phys. sciences and engring. Def. Tech. Info. Ctr., Ft. Belvoir, Va., 1976—79, adminstrv. libr., 1979—82, tech. info. specialist, 1982—85, divsn. chief info. rsch. and tech., 1986—91, dir. component info. support, 1991—. Chmn. World Wide Web Fed. Consortium, Arlington, Va., 1996—98; def. sci. bd. summer study on Dept. of Def. roles and missions in homeland security Dept. of Def., Arlington, 2003; elected mem. Internat. Coun. for Sci. and Tech. Info., Paris, 2004—. Complimentary music dir. Village Bapt. Ch., Bowie, Md., 1999—2006. Named Fed. Libr. of Yr., 2001; recipient Leadership award, Assn. for Fed. Info. Resources Mgmt., 1998, Exceptional Civilian Svc. award, Def. Info. Sys. Agy., 2003, Svc. citation, L. Paul Bremer, III, Coalition Provisional Authority, Iraq, 2004, Fed. Computer Week Fed. 100 award, 1999. Mem.: Am. Soc. for Info. Sci. and Tech. Bapist. Office: Def Tech Info Ctr 8725 John J Kingman Rd Fort Belvoir VA 22060 Office Phone: 703-767-9170. Office Fax: 703-767-9174. Business E-Mail: cthompson@dtic.mil.

**THOMPSON, CATHY JOANNE,** nursing educator, consultant, critical care nurse; b. NYC, Feb. 17, 1959; AS in Nursing, Mesa Coll., 1984; BSN, U. Tex., Houston, 1990, MSN, 1991; PhD, Tex. Woman's U., Denton, 1997. Cert. critical care nurse specialist. Staff nurse Tex. Heart Inst. St. Luke's Episcopal Hosp., Houston, 1984—94; asst. prof. Health Sci. Ctr., Sch. of Nursing U. Tex., Houston, 1994—96; asst. prof. Sch. for Health Care Professions Dept. of Nursing Regis U., Denver, 1996—98; asst. prof. Health Scis. Ctr. Sch. of Nursing U. Colo., Denver, 1998—2005, assoc. prof. Health Scis. Ctr. Sch. Nursing, 2005—. Instr. clin. nursing Houston Health Sci. Ctr. Sch. Nursing U. Tex., Houston, 1991—94. Mem. editl. bd.: The Internet Jour. of Advanced Nursing Practice, 1996—, Critical Care Nursing Clinics of N.Am., 1999—; contbr. articles to profl. jours. Mem.: Nat. Assn. Clin. Nurse Specialists, AACN Certification Corp. (bd. mem. 1997—99), Am. Heart Assn. (nat. adv. coun. Mended Heart Orgn. 1996—2000), Western Inst. Nursing Rsch., Soc. Critical Care Medicine, Am. Assn. Critical-Care Nurses (mem. various coms. 1986—, bd. mem. 1996—99, AACN Svc. Appreciation award 1999), Sigma Theta Tau Internat. Lutheran. Achievements include research in the area of research utilization, critical care, evidence-based practice, pain, and end-of-life care. Office: University of Colorado School of Nursing 4200 E Ninth Ave Box C288 Denver CO 80262 E-mail: cathy.thompson@uchsc.edu.

**THOMPSON, CHARLES KERRY,** company executive; b. Chgo., Sept. 11, 1943; s. Charles Edward and Rose Elizabeth (Peacock) T.; children: Charles Edward, Tiffany Shaffer, Rebecca Lynn. Student, Parsons Coll., 1961-62. Pres. Am. Woman, Inc., Richardson, Tex., 1976-79; zone mgr. The Southland Corp., Dallas, 1979-86; pres. Printelligence Inc. (formerly Graphic Telesis, Inc.), Dallas, 1986-92; ptnr. Cybersearch-U.S., Inc., 1995—; mktg. dir. Nova Internet Svcs., Inc., 1996—. Contbr. articles to profl. jours. Chmn. Muscular Dystrophy, Southland, N. Tex., 1982-86. Republican. Home: 14588 Berklee Dr Addison TX 75001-3532 E-mail: chuck@chuck_thompson.com.

**THOMPSON, CHARLES MURRAY,** lawyer; b. Childress, Tex., Oct. 13, 1942; s. Walter Lee and Lois S. (Sheehan) T.; children: Murray, McLean. BS with honors, Colo. State U., 1965; JD cum laude, U.S.D., 1969, LLD (hon.), 1995. Bar: S.D. 1969, U.S. Dist. Ct. S.D. 1969, U.S. Ct. Claims 1989, U.S. Ct. Appeals (8th cir.) 1972, U.S. Supreme Ct. 1973. Ptnr. May, Adam, Gerdes & Thompson, Pierre, SD, 1969—. Bd. dirs. Bank West, Pierre, SD; past pres. Delta Trust, Pierre; spkr. in field. Editor S.D. Law Rev., 1969 Pres. S.D. Council Sch. Attys., 1984-86. Fellow Am. Bar Found. (chmn. 1991-92, bd. dirs. 1989-92), Coll. Law Practice Mgmt., Am. Coll. Trial Lawyers; mem. ABA (ho. of dels. 1978-2002, bd. govs. 1983-86, standing com. on fed. judiciary 2004—), ATLA, Am. Bd. Trial Advs., Am. Counsel Assn., Am. Judicature Soc. (bd. dirs. 1981-85), Am. Bar Endowment (bd. dirs. 1991—, pres. 2000-02), Nat. Conf. Bar Pres.'s (exec. coun. 1986-94, pres. 1992-93), State Bar S.D. (pres. young lawyers sect. 1974-75, pres. 1986-87), S.D. Bar Found. (pres. 1991), S.D. Trial Lawyers Assn. (pres. 1980-81), Jackrabbit Bar Assn. (chancellor 1981-82), S.D. Cmty. Found., Kiwanis (pres. local club 1977). Democrat. Avocations: flying, ranching. Home and Office: PO Box 160 Pierre SD 57501-0160 Office Phone: 605-224-8803.

**THOMPSON, CHARLES SPURGEON,** retired music educator, retired conductor; b. Radford, Va., Aug. 18, 1942; s. Nathaniel A. and Mollie Harris Thompson, Jr.; m. Billie Sue Pietsch, June 1, 1968; children: Charles Spurgeon II, William Nathaniel. BA in History, U. Memphis, 1965; BA in Sacred Music, Moody Bible Inst., 1968; MusM, Am. Conservatory Music, 1979. Tchr. Millington Ctrl. HS, Tenn., 1968—69; music dir. studio prodn. Trans World Radio, Bonaire, Netherlands Antilles, 1969—77; asst. pastor, min. music First Bapt. Ch., Wheaton, Ill., 1979—83; prof. sacred music Moody Bible Inst., Chgo., 1982—2005; ret., 2005. Condr. Women's Concert Choir and Bell Ensemble, Chgo., 1982—2005. Composer: Carol of the Straw Child. Bd. mem. cottager com. Cedar Lake Bible Conf. Ctr., Ind., 1999—2005, chmn. cottager com., 1982—2005. Recipient Faculty Citation award, Moody Bible Inst., 2005. Mem.: Nat. Assn. Tchrs. Singing, Am. Guild English Handbell Ringers, Am. Choral Dirs. Assn., R-Conservative Baptist. Avocations: music, bicycling, photography, hiking. Home: PO Box 8237 Asheville NC 28814

**THOMPSON, CHARLES WILLIAM SYDNOR See THOMPSON, SYDNOR JR.**

**THOMPSON, CHARLOTTE ELLIS,** pediatrician, educator, writer; d. Robert and Ann Ellis; divorced; children: Jennifer Ann, Geoffrey Graeme. BA, Stanford U., 1950, MD, 1954. Diplomate Am. Bd. Pediat. Intern Children's Hosp., San Francisco, 1953-54; resident UCLA, 1960-61, L.A. Children's Hosp., 1962-63; pvt. practice La Jolla, Calif., 1963-75; dir. Muscle Disease Clinic Univ. Hosp.-U. Calif. Sch. Medicine, San Diego, 1969-80, asst. clin. prof. pediat., 1969—; founder, dir. Ctr. for Handicapped Children and Teenagers, San Francisco, 1981—2004. Cons. U.S. Naval Hosp., San Diego, 1970-91; dep. dir. Santa Clara County Child Health and Disability, Santa Clara, Calif., 1974-75; dir. Ctr. for Multiple Handicaps, Oakland, Calif., 1976-81; co-dir. Muscle Clinic Children's Hosp., San Diego, 1963-69; dir. muscle program U. Rochester, 1957-60. Author: Raising a Handicapped Child: A Helpful Guide for Parents of the Physically Disabled, 1986, 4th edit., 1991, rev., expanded edit., 2000, Allein leben: Ein umfassendes Handbuch für Frauen, 1993, Making Wise Choices: A Guide for Women, 1993, Raising a Child with a Neuromuscular Disorder, 1999, Raising A Handicapped Child, 1999, 101 Ways to the Best Medical Care, 2006; contbr. articles to med. jours., including Clin. Pediat., New Eng. Jour. Medicine, Neurology, Jour. Family Practice, Mothering, Jour. Pediatric Orthopedics, Pediatrician, Am. Baby, Pediatric News, also chpts. to books. Mem. Calif. Children's Svc. Com., 1977—. Fellow: Am. Acad. Pediat. Avocations: tennis, ice skating, opera. Office: 8070 La Jolla Shores Dr # 514 La Jolla CA 92037-3296 Personal E-mail: cetmd@earthlink.net.

**THOMPSON, CHERYL BAGLEY,** nursing educator, director; m. Mark Neal Thompson; children: Shannon Elizabeth Johnson, Sarah Ann Cooke. BSN, Creighton U., 1977; M Nursing, U. Wash., 1979; PhD, U. Nebr., 1992. RN Registered Nurse, Nebr. Dir. clin. informatics U. Utah Coll. Nursing, Salt Lake City, 1992—2001; assoc. prof. U. Nebr. Med. Ctr. Coll. Nursing, Omaha, 2001—, dir. health informatics, 2004—. Sr U Nebr Med Ctr Coll Nursing 985330 Nebraska Medical Center Omaha NE 68198 Office Phone: 402-559-3645. Business E-Mail: cbthompson@unmc.edu.

**THOMPSON, CHRISTINA ELIZABETH,** music educator, musician; b. Petersburg, Va., Oct. 17, 1980; d. John Bernard Thompson, Jr. and Kathleen Morrissette Thompson. MusB, East Carolina U., 2002. Office assoc. J. B. Thompson and Assocs., Colonial Heights, Va., 1996—98; delivery driver Pizza Hut, Colonial Heights, 1999—2000; stage mgr. East Carolina U. Sch. Music, Greenville, NC, 2001—02; intern East Millbrook Magnet Mid. Sch., Raleigh, NC, 2002—02; pvt. music instr. MARS Music, Raleigh, 2002—02; band and music educator Wake Forest (N.C.) Elem. Sch., 2002—. Pvt. trombone instr., Raleigh, NC, 2001—; trombonist Raleigh Civic Symphony and Chamber Orch., 2002—, Brass on the Slide, Chapel Hill, 2003—, Armand and Bluesology, Chapel Hill, 2004—, Spoonful of Soul, 2005—, Via Mandingue, 2005—. Musician: Exercises in Breathing; musician: (composer) Harlem Timeshare. Organizer clothing drive for hurricane floyd victims, Greenville, NC, 1999—2000; pub. info. sec. Narcotics Anonymous, Raleigh, 2004—05; vol. Ten Thousand Villages, 2005—; pub. outreach Voice Women's Orgn., Greenville, 2001—02; entertainer Hillside Nursing Home, Wake Forest, 2004—05. Scholar, East Carolina U. Sch. Music, 1999—2002. Mem.: NEA, Music Educators Nat. Conf., Internat. Assn. for Jazz Edn., Phi Kappa Phi, Pi Kappa Lambda, Nat. Soc. Collegiate Scholars. Democrat. Avocations: yoga, reading, walking, writing. Office: Wake Forest Elementary School 136 West Sycamore St Wake Forest NC 27587 Home: 7657 Summerglen Dr Raleigh NC 27615 Office Phone: 919-554-8655. Personal E-mail: lil_cx@hotmail.com. Business E-Mail: cethompson@wcpss.net.

**THOMPSON, CLAIRE LOUISA,** nurse, educator, consultant; b. Columbus, Ohio, Sept. 29, 1938; d. Harry Edgar and Clara Etta (Brackenbusch) McKeever; m. Roger Lee Thompson, Dec. 20, 1958 (div. 1988); children: Jeffrey, Michael. Diploma, Bethesda Hosp. Sch. Nursing, Cin., 1959; student, Ball State, 1970, Ind. U., 1981, Purdue U., 1982-83. RN, Ohio, Ind., Calif.; cert. ins. rehab. specialist, case mgr.; cert. health occupl. level tchr., Ind. Oper. rm./emergency rm. nurse Greene Meml. Hosp., Xenia, Ohio, 1959-60; med.-surg. nurse, charge nurse Bethesda Hosp., 1960-64; med.-surg. nurse Porter Meml. Hosp., Valparaiso, Ind., 1965-66; staff and charge nurse Mercy Hosp., Elwood, Ind., 1968-74; gen. practice nurse W. A. Scea, MD, Elwood, 1970-74; exec. dir. Vis. Nurse Assn., Elwood, 1974-78; analyst Blue Cross/Blue Shield of Indpls., 1978; supr. Meth. Hosp. Clinic, Indpls., 1979-80; DON Upjohn Health Care, Indpls., 1980; staff nurse Americana Health Care Ctr., Indpls., 1981; instr. health occups. Washington Twp. Schs., Indpls., 1981-84; br. mgr. health & rehab. Crawford & Co., Indpls., 1984-88, regional med. svcs. advisor western region San Francisco, 1988-92; br. mgr. Crawford & Co., Health Care Mgmt., Modesto, Calif., 1992-94; ret., 1994. Developer in case mgmt. nursing svcs., 1974-94. Founder Meals on Wheels, Elwood, 1975, Vis. Nurses Assn., Elwood, 1976; mem. altar guild, lay eucharist min. Episcopal Ch.; vol. H.E.B. Hosp., 2004—. Mem. NLN, Assn. Rehab. Nurses (pres. Ind. chpt. 1987-88), Nat. Ins. Womens Assn., Case Mgmt. Soc. Am., San Francisco Ins. Womens Assn., Rehab. Ins. Nurses Group. Avocations: the arts, photography.

**THOMPSON, CLIFTON C.,** retired chemistry professor, academic administrator; b. Franklin, Tenn., Aug. 16, 1939; s. Clifton C. and Ruby M. Thompson; m. Sarah Ellen Gaunt, Dec. 1, 1970; children: Brenda Kay, Victoria Lea. BS, Middle Tenn. State U., 1961; PhD, U. Miss., 1964. Asst. prof. Rutgers U., New Brunswick, NJ, 1965, Marshall U., Huntington, W.Va., 1965-66; assoc. prof. Middle Tenn. State U., Murfreesboro, 1966-68, U. Memphis, 1968—74; prof. chemistry, dept. head, dean Coll. Sci. and Math., dir. Ctr. for Sci. Rsch., assoc. v.p. for grad. studies and rsch. Mo. State U., Springfield, 1974-96, prof. emeritus, 1996—; prof. chemistry Cen. Mich. U., Mt. Pleasant, 1996-98. Rsrch. assoc. U. Tex., Austin, 1964-65; rschr. Oak Ridge Nat. Lab., 1968; cons. Mid-South Research Assocs., Memphis, 1969-71; mem. med. tech. rev. com. Nat. Accrediting Agy. for Clin. Lab. Sci., Chgo., 1974-80; vis. prof. So. Ill. U., Carbondale, 1995. Author: Ultraviolet-Visible Absorption Spectroscopy, 1974; contbr. articles to profl. jours. Mem. health care com. Springfield C. of C., 1978-79, mem. econ. devel. com., 1983-89; bd. dirs. United Hebrew Congregation, Springfield, 1983-86, United Hebrew Found., Inc., 1994-96. NSF fellow, 1961-64; Sigma Xi grantee-in-aide, 1970; NSF sr. fgn. scientist grantee, 1971; NSF coop-coll. sch. sci. grantee, 1972; Higher Edn. Applied Projects grantee, 1987-90. Mem. Am. Chem. Soc., Royal Soc. Chemistry, Sigma Xi, Phi Kappa Phi. Office: Mo State U Dept Chemistry Springfield MO 65804

**THOMPSON, CRAIG B.,** physician; b. Cambridge, Mass., Feb. 9, 1953; m. Tullia Lindsten; children: Kajsa, Nicklas. AB summa cum laude, Dartmouth Coll., 1973, BS with honors, 1975; MD, U. Pa., 1977. Asst. prof. Uniformed Svcs. U. Health Scis., Bethesda, Md., 1982-87; asst. investigator Howard Hughes Med. Inst., Ann Arbor, Mich., 1987-89; asst. prof. U. Mich., Ann Arbor, 1987-89, assoc. prof., 1989-92; assoc. investigator Howard Hughes Med. Inst., Ann Arbor, 1989-93, investigator, 1993; prof. U. Chgo., 1993—99; scientific dir. Abramson Family Cancer Rsch. Inst., 1999—; chair dept. cancer biology U. Pa. Recipient Clinical Investigator award, Am. Soc. Clinical Investigation, 2003, Mosby Book award, Merck award, Int. Acad. award, Alpha Omega Alpha. Mem.: Am. Acad. Arts Sciences, IOM, NAS. Office: Abramson Inst 451 BRB II/III 421 Curie Blvd Philadelphia PA 19104-6160*

**THOMPSON, CRAIG SNOVER,** corporate communications executive; b. Bklyn., May 24, 1932; s. Craig F. and Edith (Williams) T.; m. Masae Sugizaki, Feb. 21, 1957; children: Lee Anne, Jane Laura. Grad., Valley Forge Mil. Acad., 1951; BA, Johns Hopkins U., 1954. Newspaper and radio reporter Easton (Pa.) Express, 1954-55, 57-59, Wall St. Jour., 1959-60; account exec. Moore, Meldrum & Assocs., 1960; mgr. pub. relations Cen. Nat. Bank of Cleve., 1961-62; account exec. Edward Howard & Co., Cleve., 1962-67, v.p., 1967-69, sr. v.p., 1969-71; dir. pub. relations White Motor Corp., Cleve., 1971-76; v.p. pub. relations No. Telecom Inc., Nashville, 1976-77, White Motor Corp., Farmington Hills, Mich., 1977-80, v.p. corp. communications, 1980-81; dir. exec. communications Rockwell Internat. Corp., Pitts., 1981-86, El Segundo, Calif., 1986-91, Seal Beach, Calif., 1992-97, sr. communications exec., 1997; pres. Craig S. Thompson, Inc., 1997—. Bd. dirs. Shaker Lakes Regional Nature Center, 1970-73. Served to 1st lt., inf. U.S. Army, 1955-57. Mem. Pub. Rels. Soc. Am. (accredited), Alumni Assn. Valley Forge Mil. Acad. (bd. dirs. 1988-94).

**THOMPSON, DANIEL EMERSON,** vending machine service company executive; b. Fairbanks, Alaska, Jan. 24, 1947; s. George Edmond and Emma Jean (Burns) T.; m. Yvette Clarice Brazeau, Aug. 16, 1980. Student, U. Notre Dame, 1965-67. Vice-pres. Music Inc., Fairbanks, 1965—67; pres. Music Inc. (doing bus. as Alaska Music Co.), Fairbanks, 1967—81, 1987—; sec. Music Inc. (doing bus. as Vend Alaska-Fairbanks), Fairbanks, 1984—87; pres. Vend Inc. (doing bus. as Vend Alaska-Anchorage), Anchorage, 1984—. Bd. dirs. Music Inc., Fairbanks, Vend Inc., Anchorage, Denali State Bank, Fairbanks; ptnr. Thompson Investment Co., Fairbanks, 1976—. Trustee Hi Pow, Fairbanks, 1972—; pres. Fairbanks Downtown Assn., 1987-88, bd. dirs., 1984-94; bd. dirs. Alaska State Devel. Corp., Juneau, 1971-82, Monroe Found., Fairbanks, 1991-2000, North Star Dance Found., 2002—; vocatonal edn. adv. com. Fairbanks North Star Borough Sch. Dist., 1993—. Mem. Amusement Music Operators Am., Nat. Automatic Merchandising Assn., N.W. Automatic Vending Assn. (bd. govs. 1983—). Rotary, Fairbanks C. of C. Roman Catholic. Office: 1810 Burgess Ave Fairbanks AK 99709-5516

**THOMPSON, DARLENE BENNETT,** realtor, musician; b. Simpson, La., June 28, 1931; d. Odis Pharon and Carrie Josephine (Knight) Blackwell; m. Elmo Bennett (dec.); children: Debra Kathleen Bennett, Eric Blane Bennett, Denise Darlene Bennett; m. Mitchell Glenn Thompson, Dec. 28, 1990. BS, Northwestern State U., Natchitoches, La., 1952, EdM, 1959, EdD, May1963, EdD, 1981. Tchr. K-12 Vernon Parish Sch. Bd., Leesville, La., 1952—82; dir. alternative sch. Vidor (Tex.) Ind. Sch. Dist., 1982—85; reading specialist Burkville (Tex.) Ind. Sch. Dist., 1986—2000; realtor ERA Broker, Leesville, 2003—. Dir. music Simpson Ch. of God, Simpson Assembly of God; organist Pok Episcopal Ch., St. Michael's Cath. Ch. Mem.: Ret. Tchrs. La., Piano Tchrs. La., Music Educators La., Pilot Club Leesville, Phi Delta Kappa. Home: 554 Alexandria Hwy Leesville LA 71446

**THOMPSON, DAVID ALFRED,** industrial engineer; b. Chgo., Sept. 9, 1929; s. Clifford James and Christobel Eliza (Sawin) T.; children: Nancy, Brooke, Lynda, Diane, Kristy. B.M.E., U. Va., 1951; BS in Indsl. Enrging. U. Fla., 1955, MS in Engring. 1956; PhD, Stanford U., 1961. Registered profl. engr., Calif; cert. profl. ergonomist; bd. cert. diplomate in forensic engring. Research asst. U. Fla. Engring. and Industries Exptl. Sta., Gainesville, 1955-56; instr. indsl. engring. Stanford U., 1956-58, acting asst. prof., 1958-61, asst. prof., 1961-64, asso. prof., 1964-72, prof., 1972-83, prof., asso. chmn. dept. indsl. engring., 1972-73, prof. emeritus, 1983—; clin. faculty occupational medicine U. Calif. Med. Sch., San Francisco, 1985—; pres., chief scientist Portola Assocs., Palo Alto, Calif., 1962—97, Incline Village, Nev., 1997—; prin. investigator NASA Ames Rsch. Ctr., Moffatt Field, Calif., 1974-77. Cons. Dept. State, Fed. EEO Commn., maj. U.S. and fgn. cos.; cons. emergency commn. ctr. design Santa Clara County Criminal Justice Bd., 1974, Bay Area Rapid Transit Control Ctr., 1977, Govt. of Mex., 1978, Amadahl Corp., 1978-79, Kerr-McGee Corp., 1979, Chase Manhattan Bank, 1980, St. Regis Paper Co., 1980-82, Pacific Gas & Electric, 1983-85, Pacific Bell, 1984-86, 89-93, IBM, 1988-91, Hewlett-Packard, 1990-91, 98-99, Reuter's News Svc., 1990-92, Safeway Corp., 1992-94, New United Motors Mfg., 1993-95, Sun Microsys., 1993-94, Microsoft, 1995-00; mem. com. for office computers Calif. OSHA. Dir., editor: documentary film Rapid Answers for Rapid Transit, Dept. Transp., 1974; mem. editorial adv. bd. Computers and Graphics, 1970-85; reviewer Indsl. Engring. and IEEE Transactions, 1972-86; contbr. articles to profl. jours. Served to lt. USNR, 1951-58. HEW grantee, 1967-70 Fellow Nat. Assn. Forensic Engrs.; mem. IEEE, Am. Inst. Indsl. Engrs., Human Factors and Ergonomics Soc., Am. Soc. Safety Engrs., Soc. Forensic Engrs. and Scientists, Am. Assn. Forensic Scientists. Home: PO Box 6685 Incline Village NV 89450-6685 Address: PO Box 6088 Incline Village NV 89450-6088 Office Phone: 775-833-3304. Personal E-mail: davidthompson@pyramid.net. Business E-Mail: davidthompson@humanfactors.org.

**THOMPSON, DAVID O'NEAL,** retired basketball player; b. Shelby, N.C., July 13, 1954; BS in Sociology, N.C. State U., 1975. With Denver Nuggets, 1975-82, Seattle SuperSonics, 1982-84. Named Athlete of Yr., ACC, 1973, 75, Player of Yr., ACC, 1973-75, Most Valuable Player, NCAA Tournament, Player of Yr., Naismith, 1975, Rupp, 1975, AP, 1975, UPI, 1975, Eastman Kodak, 1975, The Sporting News, 1975, Most Valuable Player ABA All-Star, 1976, MBA Rookie of Yr., 1976, N.C. Sports Hall of Fame, 1982, Most Valuable Player, 1979 All-Star Game, Basketball Hall of Fame, 1996, Colo. Sports Hall of Fame, 1996, Sport Mag. Performer of Yr./Basketball, 1978; voted to Best 5 in History of Coll. Basketball, AP Coll. Player of Yr., 1974, 75; recipient Joe Mallamo Humanitarian award 1994, others; Naismith Basketball Hall of Fame inductee, 1996, voted All Time ABA top 30 team, 1997. Achievements include three-time First-Team All-Am., Three-time All-ACC selection; mem. Championship Team, 1974, NCAA All-Decade Team, 1970's; First Team All-NBA selection, 1977, 78, four-time NBA All-Star.

**THOMPSON, DAVID RENWICK,** federal judge; b. 1930; BS in Bus., U. So. Calif., 1952, LLB, 1955. Pvt. practice Thompson & Thompson (and predecessor firms), 1957—85; judge U.S. Ct. Appeals (9th cir.), 1985—98, sr. judge, 1998—. With USN, 1955—57. Mem.: ABA, Am. Bd. Trial Lawyers (sec. San Diego chpt. 1983, v.p. 1984, Pres. 1985), San Diego County Bar Assn. Office: US Ct Appeals 940 Front St Rm 2193 San Diego CA 92101-8919*

**THOMPSON, DAVID RUSSELL,** engineering educator, dean; b. Cleve., Apr. 4, 1944; s. Dwight L. and Ella Caroline (Wolff) T.; m. Janet Ann Schall, Aug. 27, 1966; children: Devin Mathew, Colleen Michelle, Darin Michael. BS in Agrl. Engring., Purdue U., 1966, MS in Agrl. Engring., 1967; PhD in Agrl. Engring., Mich. State U., 1970. Asst. prof. agrl. engring., food sci. and nutrition depts. U. Minn., St. Paul, 1970-75, assoc. prof., 1975-81, prof., 1981-85; prof. agrl. engring., head dept. Okla. State U., Stillwater, 1985-91, assoc. dean Coll. Engring., Architecture and Tech., 1991—. Engr. ops. dept. Green Giant Co., La Sueur, Minn., 1978-79; reviewer Colo. State U., Coop. State Rsch. Svc., USDA, Ft. Collins, 1989, foods, feeds and prodn. cluster U. Mo., Columbia, 1989, 93, dept. agrl. engring. Pa. State U., University Park, 1990, Tex. A&M U., College Station, 1992, Utah State U., Logan, 1993, USAF, Tyndall, Fla. and San Angelo, Tex., 1994-95, 97, Wash. State U., Pullman, 1995, U. Ga., Athens, 1996, S.D. State U., 1997, U. Fla., 1998, U. Del., 1998, U. Neb., 1999, U. Wis., 2000, U. Idaho, 2001, Rutgers U., 2003, Lake Superior State U., Sault St. Marie, 2003, Auburn U., 2004, U. Tenn., 2005, Western New Eng. Coll., 2005, So. Ill. U., Carbondale, 2006, St. Petersburg Coll., 2006, U. of the Pacific, 2006, others; reviewer USDA, 1983; vis. scholar Va. Poly. Inst. and State U., Blaksburg. Author: The Influence of Materials Properties on the Freezing of Sweet Corn, 1984, Mathematical Model for Predicting Lysine and Methionine Losses During Thermal Processing of Fortified Foods; contbr. over 50 articles to profl. jours. including Jour. Food Sci. Fellow Am. Soc. Agrl. Engrs. (div. chmn. 1976-77, bd. dirs. 1981-84, 87-89, v.p. 1994-98, stds. coun. chmn. 1997-98, Farm and Indsl. Equip. Inst., Young Rschr. award 1983, Pres.'s citation 1989, 98); mem. ASHRAE, NSPE (chair Okla. mid-north sect. 1994-95), Okla. Soc. Profl. Engrs. (v.p. 2000-01), Inst. Food Technologists (program com. 1982-85, state officer 1987-89), Am. Soc. Engring. Edn. (chair Midwest sect. 1994-95), Engring. Accreditation Commn. Accreditation Bd. Engring. and Tech., Sigma Xi, Phi Kappa Phi, Tau Beta Pi, Alpha Epsilon, Phi Eta Sigma, Gamma Sigma Delta. Office: Okla State U Coll Engring Arch & Tech 201 Adv Tech Rsch Ctr Stillwater OK 74078-5010 Office Phone: 405-744-5140. Business E-Mail: dthomps@okstate.edu.

**THOMPSON, DAVID W.,** retail executive; V.p. Value City Furniture, Columbus, Ohio, pres., 1993—. Bd. dirs. Am. Eagle Outfitters, Inc. Office: Value City Furniture 1800 Moler Rd Columbus OH 43207

**THOMPSON, DAVID WALKER,** astronautics company executive; b. Phila., Mar. 21, 1954; s. Robert H. and Nancy S. (Walker) T.; m. Catherine K. Ahulii, April 16, 1983. BS in Aeronautics and Astronautics, MIT, 1976; MS, Calif. Inst. Tech., 1977; MBA, Harvard U., 1981. Project engr. Jet Propulsion Lab., Pasadena, Calif., 1976; aerospace engr. NASA, Houston, 1977, project mgr. Huntsville, Ala., 1977-79; spl. asst. to pres. Hughes Aircraft Co., Los Angeles, 1981-82; pres., chief exec. officer Orbital Scis. Corp., Dulles, Va., 1982—. Cons. Rockwell Internat., Thousand Oaks, Calif., 1980-81, Rand Corp., Santa Monica, Calif., 1982. Recipient Nat. award Space Found., Houston, 1981, Nat. Medal Tech. U.S Dept. Commerce Tech. Adminstrn., 1991; Nat. Air and Space Mus. Trophy, 1990; fellow Hertz Found., 1976, NSF fellow, 1976, Rockwell Internat. fellow, Harvard U. fellow, 1979; named Va. Industrial of Yr., 1991, Satellite Exec. of Yr., 1990, George M. Low Space Transportation award, Am. Inst. of Aeronautics and Astronautics, 1994 Fellow AIAA (assoc., Young Engr./Scientist Yr. award 1984, George M. Low Space Trans. award 1994), mem. Nat. Spac. Club. Office: Orbital Sciences Corp 21839 Atlantic Blvd Sterling VA 20166-6850

**THOMPSON, DEAN ALLAN,** cattleman; b. Peru, Ind., Jan. 29, 1934; s. Paul Franklin and Pauline St. Clair (Thrush) T.; m. Shirley Roach Anerson, May 25, 2003. Student Purdue U., 1952-54. Mgr. Thompson Farms, breeders registered Hereford cattle, Peru, 1956-69; owner Thompson Farms, Wartrace, Tenn. and Peru, 1970-87, Dean Thompson Prodns., Wartrace, Wartrace Records; chmn. bd. Instant Copy and Printing, Inc., Monterrey, Calif., 1976-86, Trenton Energy Inc., 1977-83, Bloomfield, Ind.; v.p., dir. 5B Cattle Co., Twin Bridges, Mont., 1986-87; ptnr., Brann-Thompson Ltd.; internat. beef cattle judge; dir. Maine Manna, Gorham, Mt. Bd. Fair Comnrs. Bd. dirs. Thrush-Thompson Found. (formerly H.A. Thrush Found.), Peru; trustee Middle Tenn. State U. Found., 1981-83, 85-89, chmn. fin. com., 1982-83, 85-87, exec. com., 1983-89, sec. 1988, pres.-elect, 1989; precinct committeeman, chmn. Miami County (Ind.) Young Republican Club, 1962-67; elder Presbyn. Ch., 1986-88. With U.S. Army, 1955-56. Mem. Nat. Western (dir.), Ind. (dir. 1958-68, pres. 1960) Polled Hereford Assns., Ind. Cattleman's Assn. (founding dir.), Ind. Livestock Breeders Assn., Am. Hereford Assn. (v.p.

pres.'s coun. 1981, pres. 1982), Tenn. Hereford Assn. (dir. 1977-81, 93-97, v.p. 1979, pres. 1980-81, 97), Toastmasters (pres., area gov.), Columbia Club. Home and Office: 900 19th Ave S Apt 1201 Nashville TN 37212-2155

**THOMPSON, DEAN M., II,** marketing executive; BA, U. NC, Greensboro. Dir. mktg. and MIS Stockton Bates LLP, Phila., 1992—99; chief mktg. officer, co-founder MoveMedia, Inc., Norristown, Pa., 1999—2000; v.p. strategic devel. Wired Vines, Inc., Plymouth Meeting, Pa., 2000; dir. mktg. and comm. Cmty. Options, Inc., Princeton, NJ, 2003—. CEO Knowledge Shark, Trenton, NJ, 2000—; bd. adv. Practice Devel. Inst., Inc., Pub. Interest Law Ctr., Phila.; internet initiative project mem. Rutgers U., NJ. Mem.: Legal Mktg. Assn., Assn. Acctg. Mktg., Am. Mktg. Assn.

**THOMPSON, DEBORAH J.,** mathematics educator; b. Louisville, Sept. 18, 1956; d. Harold and Marlene Burnett; m. Rock E. Thompson, June 10, 1978; children: Christopher, Katherine, Benjamin. BS, U. Ky., 1978; MEd, U. Louisville, 1983. Cert. tchr. Ky., 1978. Tchr. Oldham County H.S., Buckner, Ky., 1992—. Recipient Pyramid award, Oldham County Edn. Found.; scholar, Scottish Rites, 2004, 2005. Mem.: Consortium for Rsch. on Ednl. Accountability and Tchr. Evaluation, Am. Ednl. Rsch. Assn., Nat. Coun. Tchrs. Math. Office: Oldham County High Sch PO Box 187/1150 N Hwy 393 Buckner KY 40010 Office Phone: 502-222-9461.

**THOMPSON, DENNIS FRANK,** political science professor, consultant; b. Hamilton, Ohio, May 12, 1940; s. Frank and Florence (Downs) T.; m. Carol Thompson, June 22, 1963; children: Eric, David. BA, Coll. of William and Mary, 1962, Oxford U., 1964, MA, 1968; PhD, Harvard U., 1968; LHD (hon.), Coll. of William and Mary, 1990. Instr. govt. Harvard U., Cambridge, Mass., 1967-68, Alfred North Whitehead prof., 1986—, dir. univ. ctr. for ethics, 1986—, assoc. provost, 1996—2002, sr. advisor to the pres., 2002—05; prof. politics Princeton (N.J.) U., 1968—75, prof., 1975—86, chmn. Dept. Politics, 1976—79, 1982—83. Cons. to spl. counsel U.S. Senate Select Com. on Ethics, 1990-91, U.S. Dept. HHS, 1980, FDA, 1993. Author: The Democratic Citizen, 1970, John Stuart Mill and Representative Government, 1976, Political Ethics and Public Office, 1987, Ethics in Congress, 1995, (with A. Gutmann) Democracy and Disagreement, 1996, Ethics and Politics: Cases and Comments, 4th edit., 2005, Just Elections, 2002, (with A. Gutmann) Why Deliberative Democracy, 2004, Restoring Responsibility, 2005; mem. editl. bd. Polit. Theory, 1974—, Philosophy and Pub. Affairs, 1971—, Am. Polit. Sci. Rev., 1985-88. Trustee Smith Coll., 1994-2004. Fellow Am. Acad. Arts and Scis.; mem. Am. Soc. Legal and Polit. Philosophy (v.p. 1977-80, pres. 1986-89). Home: 9 Shady Hill Sq Cambridge MA 02138-2035 Office: Harvard U Edmond J Safra Found Ctr for Ethics 202 Taubman 79 JFK St Cambridge MA 02138-5801

**THOMPSON, DENNIS PETERS,** plastic surgeon; b. Chgo., Mar. 18, 1937; s. David John and Ruth Dorothy (Peters) T.; m. Virginia Louise Williams, June 17, 1961; children: Laura Faye, Victoria Ruth, Elizabeth Jan. BS, U. Ill., 1957, BS in Medicine, 1959, MS in Physiology, 1961, MD, 1961. Diplomate Am. Bd. Surgery, Am. Bd. Plastic Surgery. Intern Presbyn.-St. Lukes Hosp., Chgo., 1961—62; resident in gen. surgery Mayo Clinic, Rochester, Minn., 1964—66, fellow in gen. surgery, 1964—66; resident in gen. surgery Harbor Gen. Hosp., L.A., 1968—70; resident in plastic surgery UCLA, 1971—73, clin. instr. plastic surgery, 1975—82, asst. clin. prof. surgery, 1982—97, assoc. clin. prof. surgery, 1998—. Practice medicine specializing in plastic and reconstructive surgery, LA, 1974-78, Santa Monica, Calif., 1978—; chmn. plastic surgery sect. St. John's Hosp., Santa Monica, 1986-91; mem. staff Olive View Hosp.; chmn. dept. surgery Beverly Glen Hosp., 1978-79; pres. Coop. of Am. Physicians Credit Union, 1978-80, bd. dirs., 1980-97, chmn. membership devel. com., 1983-97, treas., 1985-97. Contbr. articles to med. jours. Moderator Congl. Ch. of Northridge (Calif.), 1975-76, chmn. bd. trustees, 1973-74, 80-82; bd. dirs. L.A. Bus. Coun., 1987-90. Am. Tobacco Inst. rsch. grantee, 1959-60. Fellow ACS; mem. AMA (Physicians Recognition award 1971, 74, 77, 81, 84, 87, 90, 93, 96, 99, 2002, 05), Calif. Med. Assn., L.A. County Med. Assn. (chmn. 1979-80, chmn. ethics com. 1980-81, 2000-01, sec.-treas. dist. 5 1982-83, program chmn. 1983-84, pres. 1985-86, councilor 1988-96, 2001-03, councilor-at-large 2004—, v.p. 1999-2000), Pan-Pacific Surg. Assn., Am. Soc. Plastic Surgeons, Calif. Soc. Plastic Surgeons (chmn. bylaws com. 1982-83, chmn. liability com. 1983-85, councilor 1988-91, sec. 1993-95, v.p. 1995-96, pres.-elect 1996-97, pres. 1997-98), L.A. Soc. Plastic Surgeons (sec. 1980-82, pres. 1982-97), Lipoplasty Soc. N.Am., UCLA Plastic Surgery Soc. (treas. 1983-84, v.p. 1996-98, pres. 1998-2005, 03-05), Am. Soc. Aesthetic Plastic Surgery, Internat. Soc. Clin. Plastic Surgeons (bd. dirs. 1999—, pres. 2004-06), Am. Assn. Accreditation of Ambulatory Surg. Facilities (bd. dirs. 1995-97, 2002-, ofcl. observer to AMA ho. of dels. 1999—), Western L.A. Regional C. of C. (bd. dirs. 1981-84, 86-89, chmn. legis. action com. 1978-80), Phi Beta Kappa, Alpha Omega Alpha, Nu Sigma Nu, Phi Kappa Phi, Delta Sigma Delta, Omega Beta Pi, Phi Eta Sigma. Republican. Office: 1301 20th St # 460 Santa Monica CA 90404-2102 Office Phone: 310-829-6876. Business E-Mail: dthompso@ucla.edu.

**THOMPSON, DIDI CASTLE (MARY BENNETT),** writer, editor; b. Terre Haute, Ind., Feb. 7, 1918; d. Robert Langley Bennett and Marjorie Rose (Tyler) Castle; student U. Ill., Champaign, 1935-36, U. Ky., 1936-39; m. Jamie Campbell Thompson, Jr., June 24, 1939; children— Jamie III, Julia King Balko, Langley Stewart Ruede. News editor Glen-Echoes, Glencoe, Ill., 1930; columnist Ky. Kernel, U. Ky., Lexington, 1937-39; radio script writer Modern Am. Music, 1940-42; asst. pub. relations dir. Salem Coll., Winston-Salem, N.C., 1945; pub. relations chmn. Barrington (Ill.) Horse Show, 1959-67; staff writer, columnist Barrington Press Newspapers, 1958-84; editor ECHO, Defenders of the Fox River, Inc. newsletter, 1970-80; travel editor Barrington Press Newspapers, 1973-84; columnist The Daily Herald, Paddock Publs., 1984-86; columnist Rapid City (S.D.) Journal, 1990-95; freelance writer, 1943—. Past bd. mem. Barrington chpt. Lyric Opera Guild Chgo., Barrington Sr. Center, Infant Welfare Soc. Chgo., Art Inst. Chgo., Barrington Assos.; elected trustee Village of Barrington Hills, 1969-73, health, pub. relations chmn., 1969-73; mem. Barrington Hills Plan Commn., 1986. Mem. DAR, Women in Communications (past dir.), Citizens for Conservation (past dir.), Barrington Countryside Assn. (past dir.), Barrington Hist. Soc., Spring Creek Basset Hounds Club, Barrington Hills Riding Club (past dir.), Pan Hellenic Coun., Gulf Shore Lit. Soc., Conservancy S.W. Fla. (Naples), Chgo. Press Club, Chi Omega. Episcopalian.

**THOMPSON, DON,** food products executive; m. Elizabeth Thompson; children: Xavier, Mung MA. BSc in elec. engring., Purdue U. Engr. specialist, def. systems divsn. Northrop Corp., Rolling Meadows, Ill.; restaurant systems engr. McDonald's Corp., 1990—91, project mgr., 1991—93, staff dir., then dir. ops. for Denver region, 1993, regional v.p., San Diego region, 1998, sr. v.p., restaurant support officer, Midwest divsn., 1998—2000; pres., Midwest divsn. McDonald's USA, 2000—; pres., West divsn. McDonald's Corp., 2001—04, exec. v.p. restaurant Solutions, 2004—05, exec. v.p., COO McDonald's USA, 2005—06, pres. McDonald's USA. Office: McDonald's Corp McDonald's Plaza Oak Brook IL 60523*

**THOMPSON, DONALD RAYMOND,** film producer, playwright; b. Long Beach, Calif., Oct. 19, 1956; s. Norman Allen and Margie Ann Thompson; m. Diana Misa Takata, June 24, 1984. BA, MA, U. Calif., L.A., Calif., 1984. Dir.(prodr., writer): (films) Clouds (Best New Dir. award Bklyn. (N.Y.) Internat. Film Festival, 1999); co-prodr.: Singing The Bones (named Ofcl. Selection, Montreal (Can.) Internat. Film Festival, 2001), Through The Hollow Bamboo: Tibet In Song; author: (plays) Democracy: A Work In Progress, Tibet Does Not Exist, L.A. Book Of The Dead; co-editor: Your Life Is A Movie: The Best of SnitPix, 2002-2005. Mem.: Ind. Feature Project. Democrat. Office: nextPix Productions LLC 295 Greenwich Street #348 New York NY 10007 Office Phone: 212-465-3125. Home Fax: 212-658-9627; Office Fax: 212-658-9627. Business E-Mail: don@nextpix.com.

**THOMPSON, DOROTHY BARNARD,** elementary school educator; b. Flushing, NY, Aug. 14, 1933; d. Henry Clay and Cecelia Minnie Theresa (La Pardo) Barnard; m. Norman Earl Thompson, Aug. 12, 1956 (dec.); children: Greg, Scot, Henry, Marc (dec.), Matthew. BSEd, SUNY, New Paltz, 1953; MS, Hofstra U., Hempstead, N.Y., 1984. Cert. elem. tchr. K-6th grades, reading specialist K-12th grades, NY. Adjunct prof. Suffolk Community Coll., Brentwood, NY, 1987—; adj. prof. Nassau Cmty. Coll., Uniondale, NY, 1986—; adj. instr. Ctr. for Acad. Achievement Long Isl. U., Greenvale, NY, 1984-92; tchr. reading, 1st and 2nd grades Long Beach Pub. Sch., NY, 1988—2005; ret., 2005. Mem. founding group Parent/Tchr., The Learning Tree, Garden City, NY, 1971; founder parent coop. Happy Day Nursery Sch., Bellmore, NY, 1975; parent-tchr. Commonwealth Sch., Bay Shore, Oakdale, 1976-82. Office Phone: 516-582-1335. Personal E-mail: anetco01@aol.com.

**THOMPSON, EARL ALBERT,** economics professor; b. L.A., Oct. 15, 1938; s. Hyman Harry and Sue (Field) T.; m. Velma Montoya, June 9, 1961; 1 son, Bret. BA, UCLA, 1959; MA (fellow), Harvard U., 1961, PhD, 1961. Asst. prof. econs. Stanford (Calif.) U., 1962-65, UCLA, 1965-68, assoc. prof., 1968-70, prof., 1970—. Grantee NSF, Lily Found., Found. Rsch. in Econs. and Edn. Mem. Am. Econ. Assn. Home: 6970 Los Tilos Rd Los Angeles CA 90068-3107 E-mail: thompson@econ.ucla.edu.

**THOMPSON, ELIZABETH,** bank executive; Comptroller First Regional Bancorp, 1998—2003, CFO, 2003—. Office: First Regional Bancorp 1801 Century Park East Los Angeles CA 90067

**THOMPSON, ELLEN ANN,** elementary school educator; b. Newton, Mass., Mar. 23, 1955; d. Arthur Malachi and Eva Louise (Harris) T.; m. John A. Rasys, Nov. 30, 1980 (div. Apr. 1987); 1 child, Christopher Michael Rasys; m. James E. Holzschuh, July 1, 1995. BS in Edn., U. Vt., 1977, MEd, 1986, postgrad. Cert. elem. tchr., spl. edn. tchr., Vt.; nat. bd. cert. tchr. early childhood generalist. Title I tchr. remedial reading grades 1-3 Colchester (Vt.) Sch. Dist., 1977-78; title I readiness rm. tchr. Union Meml Sch., Colchester, 1978-79, tchr. grade 2 transitional grade, 1979-81, classroom tchr. grades 1-3 multiage, 1981-99; adj. instr. dept. grad. edn. U. Vt., Burlington, 1987—; adj. instr. undergrad. edn. program Trinity Coll., Burlington, 1992-94. Presenter N.E. Whole Lang. Conf., Johnson (Vt.) State Coll., 1987-97, resource agt. tchr. insvc. programs Vt. Dept. Edn., 1988—; resource cons. Vt. Writing Portfolio Assessment Program, 1990—; network leader # 16, 1991-95; conf. presenter, adj. instr. Am. Inst. for Creative Edn., Augusta, Maine, 1988-92; art cons. Within the Forest, Sci. Rsch. Assocs., 1991—; ednl. cons., presenter Soc. for Devel. Edn., Peterborough, N.H.; teaching fellow regional lab. Rural Small Sch. Network, 1991-92; pres. Ellen A. Thompson, Inc., 1999—; reading lang. arts cons., Vt. Dept. Ed., 1999-2000; adj. prof. U. Vt., Undergrad. Sch. Edn., literacy cons. Reading Excellence Award Grant Program, Winooski, Vt., Gloucester, Mass., 2000—. Author: (videos) The Nuts and Bolts of Multiage Classrooms, 1994, How to Teach in a Multiage Classroom, 1994, (book) I Teach First Grade!, 2001. Recipient State Teacher of the Yr. awd., Vermont, Coun. of Chief State School Offices, 1993. Mem. ASCD, Nat. Coun. Tchrs. English (presenter 1991, 92), Internat. Reading Assn. (presenter annual conf. 1991, Leaders of Readers award 1990), Vt. Coun. on Reading (newsletter editor and conf. presenter 1988—, pres. 1991-92), Vt. Tchrs. Applying Whole Lang., Colchester Edn. Assn. (internal newsletter 1987-89, newsletter editor 1988-89, 96-98), Phi Delta Kappa. Mailing: Univ Vermont Education Dept Waterman Bldg Burlington VT 05405 Office Phone: 802-656-3356. E-mail: Ellen.Thompson@uvm.edu.

**THOMPSON, EMILY,** historian; b. Pitts., Feb. 20, 1962; d. George John and Majorie Haseman Thompson. BS in Physics, Rochester Inst. of Tech., 1980—84; PhD in History, Princeton U., 1992. Sr. tech. assoc. Bell Lab., Holmdel, NJ, 1985—86; vis. asst. prof. Rensselaer Poly. Inst., Troy, NY, 1992—93; post doctoral fellow Harvard U, Cambridge, Mass., 1993—94; asst. prof. Iowa State U., Ames, Iowa, 1994—95, U Pa., Philadelphia, Pa., 1995—2002; sr. fellow Dibner Inst. for History of Sci. and Tech., Cambridge, Mass., 2002—03; assoc. prof. history U. Calif., San Diego, 2005—. Asst. prodr. (albums) Carl Arter, Songs From Afar, 1984; co-editor: The Architecture of Sci., 1999; author: The Soundscape of Modernity, 2002. Recipient Derek Price Prize, History of Sci. Soc., 2000, John Hope Franklin prize, Am. Studies Assn., 2003, Sci. Writing prize, Acoustical Soc. Am., 2002; John Slater Fellow, Am. Philos. Soc., 1989—90, Rsch. Fellow, NSF, 1998—2001, NEH, 2004, MacArthur Fellow, John D. and Catherine T. MacArthur Found., 2005. Mem.: Am., Studies Assn., Soc. For the History of Tech., History of Sci. Soc. Office: Univ Calif San Diego History 0104 9500 Gilman Dr La Jolla CA 92093-0104 Office Phone: 858-822-1532. Office Fax: 858-534-7283. E-mail: emilyt@ucsd.edu.*

**THOMPSON, EMMA,** actress; b. London, Apr. 15, 1959; d. Eric Thompson and Phyllida Law; m. Kenneth Branaugh, Aug. 20, 1989 (div. Oct. 1995); m. Greg Wise, July 29, 2003, 1 child Gaia Romilly Wise Student of English, Cambridge U., Eng. Performances include: (films) Henry V, 1989, The Tall Guy, 1989, Dead Again, 1991, Impromptu, 1991, Howard's End, 1992 (Acad. award for best actress 1993), Peter's Friends, 1992, Much Ado About Nothing, 1993, The Remains of the Day, 1993 (Acad. award nominee for best actress 1993), In the Name of the Father, 1993 (Acad. award nominee for best supporting actress 1993), My Father, the Hero, 1994, Junior, 1994, Carrington, 1995 (Best Actress award Nat. Bd. Rev. 1995), Sense and Sensibility, 1995 (Golden Globe award nominee for best actress in film 1996, Acad. award nominee for best actress 1996), Winter Guest, 1996, Primary Colors, 1998, Judas Kiss, 1998, Maybe Baby, 2000, Treasure Planet (voice), 2002, Love Actually, 2003, Imagining Argentina, 2003, Harry Potter and the Prisoner of Azbakan, 2004, Nanny McPhee, 2005; (TV films) Al Fresco, Up For Grabs (a.k.a. Sexually Transmitted), Tutti Frutti, Fortunes of War, 1987, Cheers, 1991, Wit, 2001; (miniseries) Angels in America, 2003; (London stage) Me and My Girl, Look Back In Anger, also writer screen adaptation. Sense and Sensibility, (Jane Austin), 1995 (Best Screenplay award N.Y. Film Critics 1995, L.A. Film Critics 1995, Boston Film Critics 1995, Golden Globe award for best adapted screenplay 1996, Acad. award for best adapted screenplay 1996, BAFTA Best Actress award 1996), Nanny McPhee, 2005. Active in Footlights Theatrical Group, Cambridge, Eng. Office: William Morris Agy 151 S El Camino Dr Beverly Hills CA 90212-2775*

**THOMPSON, EWA M.,** foreign language educator; b. Kaunas, Lithuania; came to U.S., 1963; d. Jozef and Maria Majewski; m. James R. Thompson. BA in English and Russian, U. Warsaw, Poland, 1963; MFA in Piano, Sopot Conservatory Music, 1963; MA in English, Ohio U., 1964; PhD in Comparative Lit., Vanderbilt U., 1967. Instr. Vanderbilt U., Nashville, Tenn., 1964-67; asst. prof. Ind. State U., Terre Haute, 1967-68, Ind. U., 1968-70, Rice U., Houston, 1967-73, assoc. prof., 1974-79, prof., 1979—, chair, 1987-90; assoc. prof. U. Va., Charlottesville, 1973-74. Cons. NEH, 1973—. The John D. and Catherine T. MacArthur Found., The John Simon Guggenheim Found., U.S. Dept. Edn.; vis. cons. Tex. A&M U.; seminar dir. NEH Summer Inst., Southeastern La. U., 1990; chair Russian lit. conf. Rice U., 1989; lectr. various colls. and univs. Author: Russian Formalism and Anglo-American New Criticism: A Comparative Study, 1971, Witold Gombrowicz, 1979, Polish transl., 2002, Understanding Russia: The Holy Fool in Russian Culture, 1987 (Chinese transl. 1995, 2nd Chinese edit. 1998), The Search for Self-Definition in Russian Literature, 1991, Imperial Knowledge: Russian Literature and Colonialism, 2000, Polish transl. 2000; editor the Sarmatian Rev., 1988—; contbr. articles to profl. jours., chpts. to books. Recipient Silver Thistle award Poland's Scottish Heritage Found, 1988; Mellon grantee, 1990, Rice U. grantee, 1990, Internat. Rsch. and Exchanges Sr. Scholar grantee, 1991; Hoover Inst. fellow, 1988; Vanderbilt U. scholar, 1964-67, Will Herberg award, ISI, 2003. Roman Catholic. Office: Sarmatian Rev PO Box 73119 Houston TX 77279-9119 Office Phone: 713-467-5836.

**THOMPSON, FRANCES MCBROOM,** mathematics professor, writer; BS in Edn., Abilene Christian U., Tex., 1963; MA, U. Tex., Austin, 1967; EdD, U. Ga., Athens, 1973. Math. cons., tchr., 1963—84; math. prof. Tex. Woman's U., Denton, 1984—. Author: (tchr. resource books) Hands on Math for Grades 4-8, 1994, Hands on Algebra for Grades 7-12, 1998, Math Proficiency Lessons and Activities, Fourth Grade, 2003, Math Essentials, Middle School Level, 2005, Math Essentials, High School Level, 2005. Bible class coord.; tchr., 1982—95. Recipient Mary Mason Lyon Jr. Faculty award, Tex. Woman's U., 1992, Alumni Citation for achievement, Abilene Christian U., 1998, Grover C. Morlan Outstanding Educator award, 2005, Distinction in Svc. award, Tex. Woman's U., 2006. Mem.: Rsch. Coun. for Math. Learning, Tex. Coun. Tchrs. Math., Tex. Assn. Suprs. Math., Math. Assn. Am., Nat. Coun. Tchrs. Math. Office: Tex Woman's U PO Box 425886 Denton TX 76204-5886 Office Phone: 940-898-2157. Business E-Mail: fthompson@twu.edu.

**THOMPSON, FRANK JOSEPH,** political science professor; b. New Ulm, Minn., Mar. 21, 1944; s. Joseph Mariem and Alice Louise (Lindquist) T.; m. Benna Miriam, June 15, 1944; children: Samuel, Aliza, Elizabeth. BA in Polit. Sci., U. Chgo., 1966; MA in Polit. Sci., U. Calif., Berkeley, 1967, PhD in Polit. Sci., 1973. Asst. prof. polit. sci. Calif. State U., Long Beach, 1971-72; asst. prof. U. Ga., Athens, 1972-78, assoc. prof., 1978-83, prof., 1983-88, head dept., 1982-87; prof. pub. administrn., policy, polit. sci. and pub. health SUNY, Albany, 1987—, dean Grad. Sch. of Pub. Affairs, 1988—97, assoc. provost, 1990-97, interim provost, 1998—2000; dean Rockefeller Coll., 2000—. Analyst HEW, Washington, 1968, City Govt. Oakland, Calif., 1968-71; cons. USPHS, 1976-79, 82, U.S. Pres.'s Commn. for Nat. Agenda for 80's, 1980, Am. Pub. Welfare Assn., 1981-83; publ. cons. U.S. Adv. Commn. on Intergovtl. Rels., 1983; mem. task force on exec. and mgmt. devel. U.S. Office Pers. Mgmt., 1990; exec. dir. Nat. Commn. on the State and Local Pub. Svc., 1991-97. Author: Personnel Policy in the City, 1975, Health Policy and the Bureaucracy, 1981, Public Administration: Challenges, Choices, Consequences, 1990; editor: Classics of Public Personnel Policy, 1979, 3d edit., 2003, Revitalizing State and Local Public Service, 1993, Medicaid and Devolution: A View from the States, 1998; contbr. articles to profl. jours. Bd. dirs. Upper Hudson Planned Parenthood, 1990-96, Albany-Tula Alliance, 1998-2003. Pub. administrn. fellow U.S. Pub. Health Service, 1975-76, NSF fellow, 1970-71; recipient Simon award Internat. Jour. Pub. Adminstrn., 1981. Fellow Nat. Acad. Pub. Adminstrn.; mem. Assn. for Pub. Policy Analysis and Mgmt., Am. Soc. for Pub. Adminstrn. (publs. com. 1982-84, William E. Mosher award 1983), Am. Polit. Sci. Assn. (chmn. departmental services com. 1985-87, exec. com. sect. pub. adminstrn. 1985-87, 89, 91, 96—98, chair sect. pub. adminstrn. 1990-91, chair Gaus award com. 1991-92), Nat. Assn. Schs. Pub. Affairs and Adminstrn. (peer rev. com. 1984-86, 1st chmn. commn. on peer rev. and accreditation 1986-87, chmn. task force on revitalizing the pub. svc., v.p. 1990-91, pres. 1991-92, chmn. com. advancement of pub. adminstrn. 1996-98), N.Y. State Acad. Pub. Adminstrn. (bd. dirs. 1994—98). Home: 9 Harvard Ave Albany NY 12208-2019 Office: SUNY Rockefeller Coll Milne 102 Albany NY 12222-0001 E-mail: thompson@albany.edu.

**THOMPSON, FRANKIE MAZIE,** school psychologist; b. Montgomery County, Ga., Dec. 17, 1944; d. Freeman Franklin and Emmer May Fountain Thompson; children: Ursula Fran Tyson, Elizabeth Louise Boswell. BS in Edn., Ga. So. U., 1966, MEd, 1970, EdS, 1972; postgrad., U. S.C., 1987, Valdosta State U., 2004. Lic. sch. psychology Ga., sch. counselor Ga., spl. edn. tchr. Ga., dir. spl. edn. Ga., gifted edn. Ga. Tchr. mid. grades Savannah (Ga.) Christian Sch., 1966—67; tchr. reading Baxterville (Mass.) Attendance Ctr., 1967—68; tchr. mid. grades math. Petal (Miss) Jr. H.S., 1968—69; head resident counselor Ga. So. U., Statesboro, 1969—72; tchr. of gifted, counselor Wadley (Ga.) H.S., 1972—76; tchr. spl. edn. S. Madison Mid. Sch., Colbert, Ga., 1978—79, Brookley (Ga.) Mid. Sch., 1976—78; tchr. h.s. spl. edn. Appling County H.S., Baxley, Ga., 1979—81; tchr. spl. edn. Claxton (Ga.) H.S., 1981—86, Glennville (Ga.) Mid. Sch., 1986—91, Hinesville (Ga.) Mid. Sch., 1991—96; sch. psychologist Liberty County Sch. Sys., Hinesville, 1996—98; sch. psychologist dept. def. Diamond Elem. Sch., Ft. Stewart, Ga., 1998—. Author: (bi-weekly newspaper column) Frankly Speaking (Outstanding Educators of Am. award, 1972). Ct-apptd. spl. adviser CASA, Hinesville, 2006. Named Tchr. of Yr., Glennville Mid. Sch., 1988. Mem.: NEA (life), Ga. Assn. of Educators (life), First Families of Ga. (life; libr. gen. 1998—2000). Methodist. Avocations: Scrabble competitions, sewing, gardening, travel, cooking. Home: 815 Barrington Dr Hinesville GA 31313 Office: Diamond Elem Dept Def 482 Davis Avenue Fort Stewart GA 31315 Office Phone: 912-876-5798. Office Fax: 912-876-8350. Personal E-mail: fmthompson84@coastalnow.net. E-mail: frankie.thompson@am.dodea.edu.

**THOMPSON, FRED DALTON,** actor, former senator; b. Sheffield, Ala., Aug. 19, 1942; m. Sarah Lindsey, 1959; children: Tony, Daniel, Elizabeth Betsy Panici(dec.); m. Jeri Kahn, 2002; 1 child, Hayden. BS, Memphis State U., 1964; JD, Vanderbilt U., 1967. Asst. U.S. atty. Mid. Tenn., 1969-72; min. counsel Senate Watergate Com., 1973-74; pvt. practice, 1975-94; spl. counsel U.S. Senate Fgn. Rels. Coms., 1980, Senate Intelligence Com., 1982; atty. Arent, Fox, Kintner, Plotkin & Kahn, 1991-94; U.S. senator from Tenn., 1994—2002. Chmn. senate govtl. affairs com., 1997-2001. Actor: (films) A True Story, 1985, No Way Out, 1987, Feds, 1988, Fat Man and Little Boy, 1989, The Hunt for Red October, 1990, Days of Thunder,1990, Die Hard 2: Die Harder, 1990, Flight of the Intruder,1991, Class Action, 1991, Necessary Roughness, 1991, Curly Sue, 1991, Cape Fear, 1991, Aces: Iron Eagle III, 1992, Thunderheart, 1992, White Sands, 1992, Born Yesterday, 1993, In the Line of Fire, 1993, Baby's Day Out, 1994, Download This, 2002, (voice) Racing Stripes, 2005; (TV movies) Unholy Matrimony, 1988, Bed of Lies, 1992, Stay the Night, 1992, Keep the Change, 1992, Barbarians at the Gate, 1993, Evil Knieval, 2004; TV guest appearances include: Wiseguy, 1988, China Beach, 1989, Roseanne, 1989, Matlock, 1989, Law & Order: Special Victims Unit, 2003; (TV series) Law and Order, 2002-; author: At That Point In Time, 1975. Republican. Address: PO Box 143 Hermitage TN 37076-0143

**THOMPSON, GEORGE ALBERT,** geophysics prof., educator; b. Swissvale, Pa., June 5, 1919; s. George Albert Sr. and Maude Alice (Harkness) T.; m. Anita Kimmell, July 20, 1944; children: Albert J., Dan A., David C. BS, Pa. State U., 1941; MS, MIT, 1942; PhD, Stanford U., 1949. Geologist, geophysicist U.S. Geol. Survey, Menlo Park, Calif., 1942-49; asst. prof. Stanford (Calif.) U., 1949-55, assoc. prof., 1955-60, prof. geophysics, 1960—, chmn. geophysics dept., 1967-86, chmn. geology dept., 1979-82, Otto N. Miller prof. earth scis., 1980-89, dean in earth scis., 1987-89. Part-time geologist U.S. Geol. Survey, Menlo Park, 1949-76; cons. adv. com. on reactor safeguards Nuclear Regulation Commn., Washington, 1974-94; mem. bd. earth sci. NRC, 1986-88, vice chmn. Yucca Mountain Hydrology-tectonics panel NRC, 1990-92; mem. exec. com. Inc. Rsch. Inst. for Seismology, Washington, 1990-92; mem. sr. external events rev. com. Lawrence Livermore Nat. Lab., 1989-93; mem. Coun. on Continental Sci. Drilling, 1990-94; cons. Los Alamos Nat. Lab. on volcano-tectonic processes, 1993-96, S.W. Rsch. Inst., 1993; chair com. to review sci. issues NRC, Ward Valley, Calif., 1994-95, 2004-; mem. panel on probabalistic volcanic hazard analysis Geomatrix Cons., Inc., 1995-96, 2005— Author over 100 research papers. With USNR, 1944-46. Recipient G.K. Gilbert award in seismic geology, 1964, John Wesley Powell award U.S. Geol. Survey, 1999; NSF postdoctoral fellow, 1956-57; Guggenheim Found. fellow, 1963-64 Fellow AAAS, Geol. Soc. Am. (coun. mem. 1983-86, George P. Woollard award 1983, v.p. 1995, pres. 1996), Am. Geophys. Union; mem. NAS (chair geology sect. 2000-03), Seismol. Soc. Am., Soc. Exploration Geophysicists. Avocation: forestry. Home: 421 Adobe Pl Palo Alto CA 94306-4501 Office: Stanford U Geophysics Dept Stanford CA 94305-2215 Office Phone: 650-723-3714. Business E-Mail: thompson@pangea.stanford.edu.

**THOMPSON, GEORGE FLETCHER,** editor, publishing executive; b. Denver, Colo., Jan. 4, 1954; s. Richard Potter and Alasee Payne Thompson; m. Cynthia Ann Roberts, Sept. 2, 1978; 1 child, Haley Ellen. Attended, U. Pa., 1971—73; BA in English, U. Ala., 1977; MA in Landscape Arch., U. Wis.-Madison, 1990. Vice pres. John Hopkins U. Press, Balt., 1984—89; pres. Ctr. for Am. Places, Santa Fe and Staunton, Va., 1990—. Editor: Landscape in America (Notable Book of 1995); co-editor: Ecological Design and Planning, 1997; co-author: Registered Places of New Mexico, 1995, Beyond the Great Divide, 1992; editor, curator publ.: Chicago Portfolio: Where Geography and Photography Meet, 2006. Recipient Publs.

award, Assn. Am. Geographers, 2000, Publs. citation, Vernacular Architecture Forum, 2002, Comms. award, Coun. Educators in Landscape Architecture, 2005. Mem.: Sigma Lamda Alpha. Independent. Avocations: reading, gardening, travel, photography, music. Office: Ctr For Am Places 101 W Frederick St Ste 309 Staunton VA 24401 Office Phone: 540-885-1180. Office Fax: 540-886-5263. E-mail: editors@americanplaces.org.

**THOMPSON, GEORGE LEE,** retail executive, consultant; b. Denver, June 12, 1933; s. George H. and Frances M. (Murphy) Thompson; m. Patricia M. Mackenzie, Sept. 25, 1993; children: Shannon, Tracy, Bradley. BS in Bus., U. Colo., 1957; degree in Advanced Mgmt., NYU, 1969. With GTE Sylvania, Danvers, Mass., 1957-65, nat. sales mgr., 1965-67, mktg. mgr., 1967-68; v.p. sales entertainment products Batavia, NY, 1968-73; dir. corp. mktg. Stamford, Conn., 1973-74; v.p. mktg. Servomation Corp., NYC, 1974-76, exec. v.p., 1976-78, Singer Co., Edison, NJ, 1978-81, pres., 1981-83; pres. consumer products SCM Corp., NYC, 1983-86; pres., CEO Smith-Corona Corp., New Canaan, Conn., 1986-89, chmn., CEO, 1989-93; pres. Mackenzie-Thompson Assocs., Essex, Conn., 1995—. Bd. dirs. Vol. Products, Inc.; chair Sweet P's, Essex, Conn., 1998—; dir. Conn. State Tourism Coun., 2003-. Chmn. Standards Com. U.S. Dept. Commerce; mem. bus. alumni adv. coun. U. Colo., 1989—94; mem. bd. overseers Sch. Bus. U. Conn., 1993—96; mem. Pres.'s Export Coun., 1991—93; mem. bd. advisors Jr. League; vice chmn. Essex Econ. Devel. Commn., Conn., 2003—; chmn. Main Street renovation com. City of Essex; bd. dirs. Internat. Tennis Hall of Fame, Am. Jr. Golf Found., 1986—89, Am. Jr. Golf Assn., 1986—2000, United Way of New Canaan, 1989—93; pres. Essex Bd. Trade, 2005—. Recipient Disting. Bus. Alumni award, U. Colo., 1990. Mem. Computer and Bus Equipment Mfg. Assn. (bd. dirs. 1992-94), Sales and Mktg. Execs. Internat. (trustee), Am. Mgmt. Assn. (trustee, exec. com. chmn., gen. mgmt. coun. 1989-99), St. John Assn. (bd. dirs., pres. 1983-93), Woodway Country Club, Club at Seabrook Island, Wilton Riding Club (bd. govs. 1980-83), Navesink Country Club (bd. govs. 1983-86), Harbour Ridge Yacht and Country Club, Essex Yacht Club, Old Lyme Country Club, Chi Psi. Episcopalian. Office: Mackenzie Thompson Assocs 51 Main St Essex CT 06426-1150 also: Sweet P's LLC Griswold Sq Essex CT 06426 Office Phone: 860-767-7805. Personal E-mail: leethompson51@sbcglobal.net.

**THOMPSON, GERALDINE KELLEHER RICHTER,** retired orthopedist; b. Tokyo, Aug. 22, 1948; (parents Am. citizens); d. Edward Elkins and Marguerite Geraldine Kelleher; m. Wayne Wray Thompson, Dec. 30, 2000; m. Paul S. Richter (div.); children: Karl Kelleher Richter, Brian Kelleher Richter, Kelly Kelleher Richter. BA with high honors, Wellesley Coll., Mass., 1969; MD, Georgetown U., Washington, 1973. Intern internal medicine Georgetown U. Hosp., Washington, 1973—74, residency orthop. surgery, 1974—78; pvt. practice orthop. surgery Fairfax and Manassas, Va., 1978—2002; assoc. prof. orthop. surgery Georgetown U., Washington, 1978—2002; fellow Am. Acad. Orthop. Surgery, 1981—2001. Pres. Prince William Med. Soc., 1999—2000. Parent leader Boy Scouts Am., 1990—99; mem. parents assn. St. Albans Sch., Washington, Nat. Cathedral Sch. Girls. Fellow: Am. Acad. Orthop. Surgeons; mem.: Wellesley Literary Cir., AOA, Sigma Xi, Phi Beta Kappa. Avocations: art history, literature, cultural history, history of medicine. Home: 2720 N Quincy St Arlington VA 22207-5055 *three successful children-Karl 27- St. Albans and MIT, capt. MIT crew team - current micro chip analysts San Francisco; Brian 24, MS from UCSD-internat. econs. and Asian studies, currently at Fed Reserve; Kelly 21 will graduate from U. Chgo. this June in three years Dean's List plans to go in to med. sch.*

**THOMPSON, GORDON, JR.,** federal judge; b. San Diego, Dec. 28, 1929; s. Gordon and Garnet (Meese) T.; m. Jean Peters, Mar. 17, 1951; children-John M., Peter Renwick, Gordon III. Grad., U. So. Calif., 1951, Southwestern U. Sch. Law, Los Angeles, 1956. Bar: Calif. 1956. With Dist. Atty.'s Office, County of San Diego, 1957-60; partner firm Thompson & Thompson, San Diego, 1960-70; U.S. dist. judge So. Dist. Calif., San Diego, 1970—, chief judge, 1984-91; sr. judge, 1994—. Mem. ABA, Am. Bd. Trial Advocates, San Diego County Bar Assn. (v.p. 1970), San Diego Yacht Club, Delta Chi. Office: US Dist Ct 940 Front St San Diego CA 92101-8994

**THOMPSON, GREGORY LEE,** social sciences educator; b. Huntington Park, Calif., June 14, 1946; s. Karl Windsor and Virginia Alice (Hanna) T. AB in Geography, U. Calif., Davis, 1968; M of City Planning, U. Calif., Berkeley, 1970; PhD in Social Scis., U. Calif., Irvine, 1987. Transp. planner City of Edmonton (Alberta) Transit Sys., 1970-72; transp. analyst Can. Transport Commn., Ottawa, Ontario, 1972-73; transp. coord. City of Berkeley (Calif.) Planning Dept., 1973-74; sr. transp. planner San Diego County, 1974-77, Met. Transp. Devel. Bd., San Diego, 1977-80; sr. cons. Mass Transit, Calif. Assembly, Sacramento, 1980-81; rsch. fellow Hagley Mus. & Libr., Wilmington, Del., 1987-88; asst. prof. Fla. State U., Tallahassee, 1988-94, assoc. prof., 1994—2003, prof., 2003—. Author: The Passenger Train in the Motor Age: California 1910-1941, 1993; contbr. articles to profl. jours. Organizer, pres. Citizens of Rail Calif., San Diego, 1976—80. Named Advanced Rsch. fellow Andrew W. Mellon/NEH, 1987-88, Disting. Student scholar Sch. Engring. U. Calif., Irvine, 1983. Mem. Am. Planning Assn. (sect. dir. San Diego), Soc. for History of Technology, Econ. History Assn., Bus. History Assn., Planning History Assn., Am. Inst. Cert. Planners. Democrat. Avocations: photography, swimming. Home: 418 E Georgia St Tallahassee FL 32301 Office: Fla State U Dept Urban Regional Pl Tallahassee FL 32306 Office Phone: 850-644-8514.

**THOMPSON, HERBERT ALDEN,** microbiologist, public health scientist; s. Otto Anous and Carmen Louise Thompson; m. Donna Rae Burrhus, June 13, 1964; 1 child, Bradley Alden. BA, Drake U. Des Moines, 1961; MA, Drake U., 1966, PhD, U. Kans., Lawrence, 1971. From asst. to full prof. W.Va. U., Morgantown, 1976—2000; microbiologist Ctrs. for Disease Control and Prevention, Atlanta, 2000—02, chief viral and rickettsial zoonoses br., 2000—06. Contbr. articles to profl. jours. Pres., treas., newsletter editor Trout Unlimited, Morgantown, 1982—88. Named Outstanding Tchr., W.Va. U., 1980; recipient MacLachlan award, W.Va. U. Sch. Medicine; grantee, NIH, 1997—99, NSF, 1980—86. Mem.: Am. Biol. Safety Assn. (corr.), Am. Soc. Rickettsiology (corr.), Soc. Gen. Microbiology (corr.), Sigma Xi (corr.). Avocations: physical fitness, physical rehabilitation, fly fishing, carpentry, astronomy. Home: 7075 Northgreen Dr NE Sandy Springs GA 30328 Office: Ctrs for Disease Control and Prevention 1600 Clifton Rd NE Atlanta GA 30333 Office Phone: 404-639-1083. Home Fax: 770-804-0446; Office Fax: 404-639-4436. Personal E-mail: thompson5544@bellsouth.net. E-mail: hct2@cdc.gov.

**THOMPSON, HOLLEY MARKER,** lawyer, consultant, marketing professional; b. Jamestown, NY, Jan. 30, 1947; d. Burdette James and Mary (Novitske) Marker; m. Lawrence D. Thompson; children: Jennifer Kristen Simos, Kendra Elise Blair, Jennifer Lynn, Stephanie Lynn. AAS, Jamestown C.C., 1966; BS, Ohio U., 1969; MA, W.Va. U., 1974, JD, 1980. Bar: W.Va. 1980, U.S. Dist. Ct. (so. dist.) W.Va. 1980, Pa. 1982, U.S. Dist. Ct. (we. dist.) Pa. 1982. Tchr. math. various pub. schs., Santa Ana (Calif.) Lakewood (N.Y.) and Morgantown (W.Va.), 1970-77; atty. for students W.Va. U., Morgantown, 1980; assoc. libr., lectr. W.Va. U. Law, Morgantown, 1980-83; assoc. libr. Jackson, Kelly, Holt & O'Farrell, Charleston, W.Va., 1983-86; cons. Hildebrandt, Inc., Somerville, NJ, 1986-94; sr. v.p. mktg. and preference markets LexisNexis, Dayton, Ohio, 1994—2006; ptnr. The Sterling Group 925, Springboro, Ohio, 2006—. Spkr. in field. Contbr. articles to profl. jours. Mem.: Am. Assn. Law Librs., Phi Delta Phi. Personal E-mail: holleymthompson@aol.com.

**THOMPSON, HORACE A., III, (TOPPER THOMPSON),** commissioner, lawyer; b. New Orleans, 1942; m. Susan Thompson; children: Clarke, Jeffery. BA, Tulane U., 1965, JD, 1968. Bar: La. 1968, Miss. 1998, Ark. 1988, U.S. Ct. Appeals (5th cir.) 1979, U.S. Supreme Ct. 1977, U.S. Dist. Ct. (ea., we. and mid. dists.) La. 1968. Adminstrv. leader labor and employment law sect. Jones, Walker, Waechter, Poitevent, Carrere & Denegre LLP; founding ptnr. McCalla, Thompson, Pyburn, Hymowitz & Shapiro, LLP, 1976—2001; ptnr., co-chair labor and employment law practice group Watkins Ludlam Winter & Stennis, P.A., 2001—; commr. Occupational Safety and Health Rev. Commn., 2006—. Fellow: Am. Coll. Labor Rels. and Employment Lawyers; mem.: ABA, La. Bar Assn., Miss. Bar Assn., New Orleans Met. Safety Coun., La. Assn. Bus. and Industry, La. Restaurant Assn. Office: One Lafayette Ctr 1120 20th St 9th Fl Washington DC 20036-3457 also: Watkings Ludlam Winter & Stennis PA 1310 27th Ave 2d Fl Post Office Drawer 160 Gulfport MS 39502 Office Phone: 202-606-5390, 228-864-3094. Office Fax: 202-606-5050, 228-864-0516. E-mail: tthompson@watkinsludlam.com.*

**THOMPSON, HUGH P.,** state supreme court justice; b. Montezuma, Ga., July 7, 1943; married; 2 children. JD, Mercer U., 1969. Bar: Ga. 1970. Pvt. practice, Milledgeville, Ga., 1970—71; judge Recorder's Ct. of Milledgeville, 1971—79, Baldwin County Ct., 1973—78, Superior Ct. of Ga., 1979—94; chief judge Ocmulgee Jud. Cir., 1987—94; justice Ga. Supreme Ct., Atlanta, 1994—. Instr. bus. law Ga. Coll., 1971—72; pres. Coun. Superior Ct. Judges, 1993—94. Communicant St. Stephen's Episcopal Ch. Named Outstanding Young Man of Baldwin County, 1972; recipient Disting. Svc. award, Baldwin County Jaycees, 1972, Outstanding Alumnus award, Mercer U. Law Sch., 1994, Disting. Svc. award, Ga. Coll. and State U., 2002. Mem.: ABA, Bleckley Inn of Ct., Ga. Bar Found., State Bar Ga., Charles Longstreet Weltner Family Law Inn of Ct., Old War Horse Lawyers Club, Lawyers Club Atlanta. Avocations: hunting, gardening, golf, fishing. Office: Supreme Ct Ga State Judicial Bldg 244 Washington St SW Rm 572 Atlanta GA 30334-9007*

**THOMPSON, HUGH WALTER,** chemistry professor; b. N.Y.C., Dec. 7, 1936; s. Will S. and Myra M. Thompson; m. Elizabeth Barnes, Mar. 4, 1961; 1 child, Victoria. AB, Cornell U., Ithaca, N.Y., 1958; PhD, MIT, Cambridge, 1963; postgrad., Columbia U., 1962-64. Asst. prof., assoc. prof., prof. chemistry dept. Rutgers U., Newark, 1964—. Contbr. articles to profl. jours. Mem. Am. Chem. Soc., Sigma Xi. Office: Rutgers U Chemistry Dept 73 Warren St Newark NJ 07102-1811

**THOMPSON, J. ANDY,** bank executive; b. Ft. Worth, Sept. 21, 1943; s. Fredrick Dickson and Mary Alice (Rhea) T.; m. Nancy Sealy, Jan. 15, 1966; children: J. Andrew Jr., Christopher Sealy. BBA, U. Tex., 1965. Exec. v.p. Internat. Svc. Ins. Co., Ft. Worth, 1968-83, Ctrl. Bancorp. Inc., Ft. Worth, 1984-86, pres., 1986-88, chmn., chief exec. officer, 1988-97, Cen. Bank & Trust, Ft. Worth, 1988-97, North Ft. Worth Bank, 1988-92. Adv. bd. Policy Mgmt. Systems, Columbia, S.C., 1975-83; bd. dirs. Ft. Worth C. of C., 1989-91; chmn., trustee Tex. Health Resources. Mem. adminstrv. bd. First Meth. Ch.; trustee, chmn. Harris Meth. Hosp., Ft. Worth, Harris Meth. Health System, Harris Meth. Health Found.; bd. dirs. Lena Pope Home for Children, James L. West Presbyn. Spl. Care Ctr.; vice chair Ft. Worth Mus. Sci. & History; bd. trustees Lean Pope Home Found. Capt. U.S. Army, 1966-68, Vietnam. Mem. Tex. Banker's Assn., Am. Banker's Assn., Ft. Worth Club (pres. 1993-96, mem. bd. govs.), Rotary Internat. Republican. Methodist. Avocations: tennis, sailing, golf.

**THOMPSON, JACK EDWARD,** mining company executive; b. Central City, Nebr., Nov. 17, 1924; s. Ray Elbert and Bessie Fay (Davis) T.; m. Maria del Carmen Larrea, May 8, 1948; children: Jack Edward, Ray Anthony, Robert Davis. Student, Northwestern U., 1942-43, Colo. Sch. Mines, 1943-45, D of Engring. (hon.), 1993. V.p. Cía. Química Comercial de Cuba S.A., 1946-60, Cía. de Fomento Químico S.A., 1946-60; with Newmont Mining Corp., N.Y.C., 1960-86, asst. to pres., 1964-67, v.p., 1967-71, dir., 1969-86, exec. v.p., 1971-74, pres., 1974-85, vice chmn., 1985-86, cons., 1986-90. Chmn. bd. trustees Minerals Industry Ednl. Found. Recipient Distinguished Achievement medal Colo. Sch. Mines, 1974 Mem. AIME, Mining and Metall. Soc. Am., Mining Found. of S.W. (past pres., bd. govs.), Tucson Country Club. E-mail: rayonera@aol.com.

**THOMPSON, JAMES ALEXANDER, JR.,** lawyer; b. Providence, July 18, 1945; s. James Alexander and Agnes Florence (Bainton) T.; m. Cheryl Ann Martin, Mar. 6, 1971; children: Scott Alexander, Jeffrey Martin. BA, U. Pa., 1967; JD, George Washington U., 1973. Bar: Mass. 1974, D.C. 1983, Conn. 1989. Atty.-advisor Region 1 U.S. EPA, Boston, 1974-76, asst. regional counsel Region 1, 1976-79, regional counsel Region 8 Denver, 1979-82; ptnr. Wickwire, Gavin & Gibbs, P.C., Washington, 1982-86, Pepe & Hazard, Hartford, Conn., 1986-94, LeBoeuf, Lamb, Greene & MacRae, LLP, Conn., 1994—. Mem. exec. com. LeBoeuf, Lamb, Greene & MacRae, LLP, chmn. nat. and internat. Environ. Health and Safety Practice Group. Contbg. author: Environmental Law and Planning, 1973. Soccer coach Hartwell Sports Club, Glastonbury, Conn., 1986—89; basketball coach Youth Basketball Assn., Glastonbury, 1990; chmn. bd. trustees Talcott Mountain Sci. Ctr., Avon, Conn., 1991—2003. 1st lt. U.S. Army, 1969—73. Mem. ABA (natural resources sect.), Conn. Bar Assn. (environ. quality sect.). Avocations: running, skiing, tennis, architecture. Office: LeBoeuf Lamb Greene & MacRae LLP Goodwin Sq 225 Asylum St Hartford CT 06103-1516 Office Phone: 860-293-3507. Office Fax: 860-293-3555. Business E-mail: jthompso@llgm.com.

**THOMPSON, JAMES E.,** lawyer; BA, U. Mich., 1983, JD, 1986. Bar: Ill. DC. Law clk. stagiaire Court of Justice of European Communities, Luxembourg; atty. Jones, Day, Reavis & Pogue, 1987—95; chief legal officer innovations bus. unit Alticor, Inc., assoc. gen. counsel internat. legal dept.; group v.p., gen. counsel, sec. McLeodUSA Inc.; sr. v.p., chief compliance officer Chiquita Brands Internat., Inc., 2006—. Office: Chiquita Brands Internat Inc Chiquita Ctr 250 E Fifth St Cincinnati OH 45202 Office Phone: 513-784-8000. Office Fax: 513-784-8030.*

**THOMPSON, JAMES HOWARD,** historian, librarian; b. Memphis, Aug. 20, 1934; s. Curtis Barnabas and Clara (Terry) T.; m. Margaretta Ortenblad, Nov. 24, 1961; children— Ralph, Anna, Howard. BA in History, Rhodes Coll., Memphis, 1955; MA, U. N.C., Chapel Hill, 1957, PhD in History, 1961; MS in LS, U. Ill., 1963. Teaching fellow U.N.C., Chapel Hill, 1955-56, departmental asst., 1956-57, reference asst., 1959-61, dir. undergrad. library, lectr. in history, 1968-70; circulation asst. U. Ill., 1961-63; asst. Center for Russian Area and Lang. Studies, 1962-63; cataloger Duke U., 1963-65; asst. prof. history U. S.W. La., 1965-66; assoc. prof. U. Colo., 1966-68; dir. libraries, prof. history U. N.C., Greensboro, 1970-94; ret., 1994. Bd. dirs. Southeastern Library Network, 1979-82, treas., 1981-82 Contbr. articles, revs. to profl. jours. Ford Found. research fellow, 1957-58; U. Colo. grantee, 1967; U. N.C. at Greensboro grantee, 1977-78, 89. Mem. Phi Beta Kappa (chpt. pres. 1979-80), Beta Phi Mu, Phi Alpha Theta, Chi Beta Phi. Episcopalian. Home: 4020 Crown Hill Dr Durham NC 27707-5393 Personal E-mail: jaytee34@earthlink.net.

**THOMPSON, JAMES LEE,** lawyer; b. L.I., N.Y., Sept. 9, 1941; s. Robert Luther and Marjorie Emma (Jones) T.; m. Diana Dill Stevenson, June 29, 1963; children: James C., Thomas J. BA, Yale U., 1963; JD, U. Va., 1966. Bar: Va. 1966, Md. 1966, U.S. Ct. Mil. Appeals 1968, U.S. Dist. Ct. Md. 1972, U.S. Supreme Ct. 1978. Ptnr. Miller & Canby, Rockville, Md., 1970—, head litigation, 1975—. Mem. jud. conf. U.S. Ct. Appeals (4th cir.). Mem. Thousand Acres Assn., Deep Creek Lake, Md., 1985-87. Capt. JAGC, USMC, 1966-70. Decorated D.S.M. Fellow Am. Coll. Trial Lawyers; mem. ABA, Md. State Bar Assn. (bd. govs. 1975, 78, 79, 83, 89, 94, sec. 1995, pres. 1999-00), Montgomery County Bar Assn. (pres. 1987-88, Cert. of Merit 1985), Nat. Conf. Bar Pres., Md. Bar Found., Montgomery County Bar Found. (pres. 1988-89), Loophole Club (pres. 1978-79), Phi Delta Phi. Democrat. Episcopalian. Avocations: sailing, skiing, tennis, golf, gardening. Home: 419 Russell Ave Apt 110 Gaithersburg MD 20877-2836 Office: Miller & Canby 200 Monroe St Ste B Rockville MD 20850-4423 Office Phone: 301-762-5212. Business E-mail: jlthompson@mmcanby.com.

**THOMPSON, JAMES LYNN,** music educator; b. Louisville, Jan. 27, 1963; s. Mildred Louise and James Aried Thompson. MusB, U. Louisville, 1987, MusM, 1992; postgrad., U. Cin. Asst. prof. St. Catharine (Ky.) Coll., 1994—96, Western Ill. U., Macomb, 1996—. Dir. music St. George's

Episcopal Ch., Macomb, Ill., 1996—. Singer (co-artistic director): (performance ensemble) Ars Vocalis. Recipient Norman Treigle Meml. prize, NYC Opera, 1992—93. Mem.: Nat. Assn. Tchrs. Singing (chpt. pres. 2006—). Liberal Episcopalian. Home: 245 S Chestnut St PO BOX 110 Good Hope IL 61439-0110 Office: Western Illinois Univ 1 University Circle Macomb IL 61455 Office Phone: 309-298-1065. Office Fax: 309-298-1968. Personal E-mail: james.thompson1@mchsi.com. Business E-Mail: l-thompson@wiu.edu.

**THOMPSON, JAMES NICHOLAS,** medical association administrator; b. Cin., Oct. 20, 1944; m. Carol Washburn; children: Carrie, David, Victoria, Deborah. BA, DePauw U., 1966; MD, Ohio State U., 1971. Lic. otolaryngologist NC, diplomate Am. Bd. Otolaryngology. Intern Mercy Hosp., Pitts., 1971—72, resident in gen. surgery, 1972—73, resident in otolaryngology, 1973—76; fellow in otolaryngology U. Calif., Irvine, 1976—77; asst. prof. surg. scis., otolaryngology Bowman Gray Sch Medicine, Winston-Salem, NC, 1979—81, assoc. prof. surg. scis., otolaryngology, 1981—88, dep. assoc. dean, 1986—87, assoc. dean, 1987—94, prof. surg. scis., otolaryngology, 1988—2002, assoc. sports medicine, 1989—2002, assoc. pediat., 1991—2002, dean, 1994—97; v.p., dean Wake Forest U. Sch. Medicine, 1997—2001, spl. adv. to exec. v.p. for health affairs, 2001—02, dean emeritus, 2002—, prof. emeritus, 2002—; pres., CEO Fedn. of State Med. Bds. of U.S., Inc., Dallas, 2002—. Libr. and learning resources com. Wake Forest U. Sch. Medicine, 1981—82, clin. skills workshops and rev., 1982, 84, admissions and pre-med. rels. com., 1984—86, clin. faculty adv. coun., 1985—2001, chair dept. clinics computer adv. com., 1985—87, faculty exec. coun., 1986—2002, vice chair, 1993—94, chair, 1994—2001, clin. svcs. coord. com., 1988—89, chair clin. scis. bldg. com., 1988; profl. ins. com. Risk and Ins. Mgmt. Adv. Coun., 1989—2001, affirmative action com., 1990—2001, 50th anniversary com., 1990—91, compliance com., 1999—2001; acad. coun. Wake Forest U., 1987, adminstrv. coun., 87, affirmative action com., 90, long range planning standing com., 93, intra-univ. ops. com., 2001, exec. coun., 1994, univ. ofcl. for animal care, 97, audit and compliance com., 99; clin. prof. otolaryngology U. Tex. S.W. Med. Ctr., Dallas, 2002; composite com. U.S. Med. Licensing Exam., 2002—, budget com., 2002—. Contbr. chapters to books, articles to profl. jours. Chair med. adv. com. Wake Forest U. Sch. Medicine/VA Med. Ctr., Salisbury, NC, 1995—2001; med. audit/utilization rev. com. NC Bapt. Hosp., 1982—84, capital equipment com., 1984—92, chiefs of profl. svcs. com., 1984—2001; bd. trustees The Med. Found., 1984—2001, Wake Forest Sch. Medicine, 1984—2001, NC Bapt. Hosp., 1984—2001, Arts Coun. Winston-Salem and Forsyth County, 1992; bd. visitors Wake Forest U. Bapt. Med. Ctr., 1997—2001; internat. med. edn. cons. to China China Med. Bd. N.Y., Inc., 2000; bd. govs. Bermuda Run Country Club, 1982—84; disting. citizens dinner steering com. Old Hickory Coun. Boy Scouts Am., 1994, 1997, 2000; indsl. devel. and econ. authority City of Winston-Salem, 1998—99; mem. planning com. Crosby Golf Classic, Bermuda Run, NC, 1987; bd. advisors Here's Life Winston-Salem, 1985—87; corp. recruitment chair Juvenile Diabetes Found. Winston-Salem, 2000; mem. Leadship Winston-Salem, 1987—88, health and human svc. day com., 1988—89, co-chair health and human svc. day com., 1991—92; dinner of champions com. Nat. Multiple Sclerosis Soc., Ctrl. NC chpt., 1999; campaign coord. surgery dept. otolaryngology sect. United Way Forsyth County, 1983—84, mem. med. ctr. com., 1987, health care campaign divsn. chair, 1989, vice chmn. divsn. III, 1992, mem. campaign cabinet, 1997—99, cmty. chair Forsyth County Cmty. Campaign, 2001—02, bd. dirs. Forsyth County, 2001—02; bd. dirs. Forsyth County Day Sch., 1987—90, Greater Winston-Salem C. of C., 1995—97. With USAR, 1972—78. Mem.: Tex. Med. Assn., Dallas County Med. Soc., Am. Acad. Med. Ethics, Am. Coll. Physician Execs., Am. Acad. Med. Dirs., Am. Laryngological, Rhinological and Otological Soc., Am. Acad. Otolaryngology, Head and Neck Surgery, So. Med. Assn., Christian Soc. Otolaryngology, Head and Neck Surgeons, Christian Med. and Dental Assns., Bapt. Med./Dental Fellowship. Office: Fedn State Med Bds of the US Inc PO Box 619850 Dallas TX 75261-9850 Office Phone: 817-868-4000. E-mail: jthompson@fsmb.org.

**THOMPSON, JAMES ROBERT, JR.,** lawyer, former governor; b. Chgo., May 8, 1936; s. James Robert and Agnes Josephine (Swanson) T.; m. Jayne Carr, 1976; 1 child, Samantha Jayne. Student, U. Ill., Chgo., 1953-55, Washington U., St. Louis, 1955-56; JD, Northwestern U., 1959. Bar: Ill. 1959, U.S. Supreme Ct. 1964. Asst. state's atty., Cook County, Ill., 1959-64; assoc. prof. law Northwestern U. Law Sch., 1964-69; asst. atty. gen. State of Ill., 1969-70; chief criminal divsn., 1969; chief dept. law enforcement and pub. protection, 1969-70; 1st asst. U.S. atty. (No. dist.) Ill. US Dept. Justice, 1970-71, U.S. atty., 1971-75; counsel Winston & Strawn LLP, Chgo., 1975-77, ptnr., 1991—, chmn., CEO, 1993—2006, chmn. exec. com., 1991—2006, head gov. rels. practice; gov. State of Ill., Springfield, Ill., 1977-91. Chmn. Rep. Govs. Assn., 1982, Nat. Govs. Assn., Midwest Govs. Assn., Coun. Gt. Lakes Govs., 1985, Pres.' Intelligence Oversight Bd., 1989—93; adv. bd. Fed. Emergency Mgmt. Agy., 1991—93; bd. govs. Chgo. Bd. Trade; mem. ABA Commn. on Separation of Powers & Jud. Independence, 1996—97; commr. The Nat. Commn. on Terrorist Attacks Upon the U.S. (The 9-11 Commn.), 2002—04; bd. dirs. FMC Corp., FMC Tech., Inc., Navigant Cons. Inc., Maximus, Inc. Co-author: Cases and Comments on Criminal Justice, 1974, Criminal Law and Its Adminstration. Bd. dirs. Civic Com., Comml. Club Chgo. Mem. ABA, Ill. Bar Assn., Chgo. Bar Assn. Republican. Office: Winston & Strawn LLP 35 W Wacker Dr Ste 4200 Chicago IL 60601-9703 Office Phone: 312-558-7400. Fax: 312-558-5700. E-mail: jthompson@winston.com.

**THOMPSON, JAMES WILLIAM,** lawyer; b. Dallas, Oct. 22, 1936; s. John Charles and Frances (Van Slyke) Thompson; m. Marie Hertz, June 26, 1965 (dec. 1995); children: Elizabeth, Margaret, John; m. Linda Ball Dozier, May 2, 1998. BS, U. Mont., 1958, JD, 1962. Bar: Mont. 1962; CPA, Mont. Acct. Arthur Young & Co., NYC, 1959; instr. bus. adminstrn. Ea. Mont. Coll., Billings, 1959-60, U. Mont., Missoula, 1960-61; assoc. Cooke, Moulton, Bellingham & Longo, Billings, 1962-64, James R. Felt, Billings, 1964-65; asst. atty. City of Billings, 1963-64, atty., 1964-66; ptnr. Felt, Speare & Thompson, Billings, 1966-72, McNamer, Thompson & Cashmore, 1973-86, McNamer & Thompson Law Firm PC, 1986-89, McNamer, Thompson, Werner & Stanley, P.C., 1990-93, McNamer Thompson Law Firm PC 1993-98, Wright Tolliver Guthals Law Firm PC, Billings, Mont., 1999—2003, Guthals Hunnes Reuss Thompson PC, Billings, 2004—. Bd. dirs. Associated Employers of Mont., Inc., 1989—98; mem. adv. coun. Sch. Fine Arts, U. Mont., 1997—2001. Mem. Billings Zoning Commn., 1966—69; v.p. Billings Cmty. Action Program (now Dist. 7 Human Resources Devel. Coun.), 1968—70, pres., 1970—75, bd. trustees, 1975—; mem. Yellowstone County Legal Svcs. Bd., 1969—70, City-County Air Pollution Control Bd., 1969—70; pres. Billings Symphony Soc., 1970—72; bd. dirs. Billings Studio Theater, 1967—73, United Way Billings, 1973—81, Mont. Inst. Arts Found., 1986—89, Downtown Billings Assn., 1986—90, Billings Area Bus. Incubator, Inc., 1991—94, Found. of Mont. State U, Billings, 1992—98, Our Mont., Inc., 1997—, pres., 2000—; bd. dirs. Rimrock Opera Co., 1998—, treas., 1998—2002; mem. Billings Transit Commn., 1971—73, City Devel. Agy., 1972—73; Diocesan Exec. Coun., 1972—75. Mem. ABA, Am. Acad. Estate Planning Attys., Nat. Acad. Elder Law Attys., State Bar Mont., Yellowstone Area Bar Assn. (bd. dirs. 1983-87, pres. 1985-86), Elks, Kiwanis (pres. Yellowstone chpt. 1974-75), Sigma Chi (pres. Billings alumni assn. 1963-65). Episcopalian. Home: 123 Lewis Ave Billings MT 59101-6034 Office: 10 N 27th St PO Box 1977 Billings MT 59103-1977 Office Phone: 406-245-3071. Personal E-mail: jwtldt@aol.com.

**THOMPSON, JAYNE CARR,** public relations and communications executive, lawyer; b. Oak Park, Ill., Apr. 7, 1946; d. Robert Edward and Laurette (Rentner) Carr; m. James R. Thompson, June 19, 1976; 1 child, Samantha Jayne. BA, U. Ill., Chgo., 1967; JD, Northwestern U., 1970; degree (hon.), Lincoln (Ill.) Coll., 1990. St. Xavier U., Chgo., 1995, Ill. Coll., 1995. Assoc. in litigation McDermott, Will & Emery, Chgo., 1970; asst. atty. gen. State of Ill., Chgo., 1970-77, chief of criminal appeals divsn., 1972-77, dep. chief prosecution assistance bur., 1975-76, dep. chief criminal divsn., 1976-77,

acting chief criminal divsn., 1977; of counsel Brown, Hay & Stephens, Springfield, Ill., 1977-78, Silets & Martin, Chgo., 1983-84; house counsel and v.p. devel. Nat. Coll. Edn., Evanston, Ill., 1984-85; atty. Lydon & Griffin, Chgo., 1989-91; prin. Dilenschneider Group Inc., Chgo., 1999-2000, mng. prin., 2000—02; CEO, pres. Jayne Thompson and Assocs. Ltd., 2002—. Contbr. chpt. to book, articles to profl. jours. First Lady of Ill., Springfield, 1977-91; mem. Ill. Commn. on Status of Women, 1997-2001; pres. bd. dirs. Chgo. Pub. Libr., 1998—; mem. women's bd. Northwestern U., 1998—; bd. dirs. Chgo. Pub. Libr. Found., 1998—; mem. adv. bd. for Ill. Treas. for Women's Issues, 2002—; mem. chmn.'s adv. coun. Lincoln Pk. Zoo, 2002—; mem. Met. Planning Coun., 2002—. Mem. Ill. State Bar Assn., Execs. Club (Chgo.), Coun. on Fgn. Rels. (Chgo. com.), Econ. Club (Chgo.). Avocations: reading, cooking, tennis. Office: Jayne Thompson & Assocs Ltd 33 N Dearborn St Ste 2200 Chicago IL 60602 E-mail: jthompson@jaynethompson.com.

**THOMPSON, JEAN TANNER,** retired librarian; b. San Luis Obispo, Calif., June 15, 1929; d. Chester Corey and Mildred (Orr) T.; 1 child, Anne Marie Miller Student, Whitworth Coll., Spokane, Wash., 1946-49; AB, Boston U., 1951; postgrad., U. Wis., Eau Claire, 1964-67; MS.L.S., Columbia U., 1973; Ed.M., U. Va., Charlottesville, 1978. Asst. social sci. librarian Univ. Libraries Va. Polytechnic Inst. and State U., Blacksburg, 1973-77, head social sci. dept. Univ. Libraries, 1977-83; head reference dept. Meml. Library U. Wis., Madison, 1983-86, asst. dir. reference and info. svcs., 1986-91, ret. Contbg. editor: ALA Guide to Information Access, 1994; mem. editorial bd. RQ, 1984-89. Mem. ALA, Assn. Coll. and Research Libraries (edn. and behavioral sci. sect. vice chmn. 1985-86, chmn. 1986-87), Wis. Library Assn., Wis. Assn. of Acad. Librarians. Presbyterian. Home: 4929 High Grove Rd Tallahassee FL 32309-2957

**THOMPSON, JENNIFER B.,** Olympic swimmer; b. Dover, N.H., Feb. 26, 1973; BS in Human Bio., Stanford Univ., 1995; student in Med. Sch., Columbia U. Mem. U.S. Olympic Swim Team, Barcelona, 1992, Atlanta, 1996, Sydney, 2000, Athens, 2004. Active Swim Across Am. Named Sportswoman of Yr., Women's Sports Found., 2000, Swimmer of Yr., USA Swimming, 1993, 1998, 10-time USA Swimming All-Star; recipient Spring Nationals Kiphuth award, 1993, Performance of Yr. award, USA Swimming, 1999. Achievements include being the most decorated olympic female athlete in U.S. history; winning gold medal in 4x100m medley relay, 4x100m free relay, Olympic Games, 1992, 1996, 2000, 4x200m free relay, 1996, 2000; winnning 8 career Olympic Gold medals, 3 Silver, 1 Bronze; being World Champion in 4x100m free relay, winning World Championships in 1991, 1998, 2003, 4x100m medley relay, 1991, 1998, 100m butterfly, 1998, 2003, 100m free, 1998; winning 36 career Pan Pacific titles; winning 26 US National titles.

**THOMPSON, JENNIFER LEE,** lawyer; b. Towson, Md., Nov. 2, 1974; d. Armstead Brian Thompson. BS, Rochester Inst. Tech., 2001; JD, SUNY, Buffalo, 2004. Bar: Md. 2004, Minn. 2005, D.C. 2006, Calif. 2006. Paramedic Rural Metro Med. Svcs., Rochester, NY, 1995—2002; tissue recovery specialist Rochester Eye and Human Parts Bank, 2001—03; atty.-at-law Janet Jenner & Suggs, Balt., 2004, Lopez Hodes Restaino, et al, Newport Beach, Calif., 2004—. Author: (book) Bonadonna Interval, 1995; editor: EZ Rules for Property, 2002. Mem.: ATLA. Office: Lopez Hodes Restaino et al 2d Fl 450 Newport Center Dr Newport Beach CA 92660

**THOMPSON, JENNIFER LYNN,** lawyer; b. Jan. 2, 1964; BS, U. Tenn., 1986, JD, 1996. Bar: Tenn. 1996, U.S. Dist. Ct. (mid. dist.) Tenn. 1968, U.S. Ct. Appeals (6th cir.) 2003. Clk. for judge Tenn. Ct. Criminal Appeals, Knoxville, 1996—97; assoc. Blackburn, Slobey Freeman & Happled, Nashville, 1997—98; pvt. practice Nashville, 1998—. Office: Attorney at Law 1208 17th Ave S Nashville TN 37212 Office Phone: 615-320-4344. E-mail: iltfdb@hotmail.com.

**THOMPSON, JEROME LAFAYETTE,** curator; b. Ames, Iowa, Apr. 30, 1952; s. Louis Milton Thompson, Sr and Margaret Stromberg Thompson; m. Gretchen Lynn Mlinar, June 28, 1975; 1 child, Grant Lafayette. BA, Iowa State U., 1974; MA, Tex. Tech. U., Lubbock, 1977. Site adminstr. Ter. Hill, Des Moines; hist. sites coord. State Hist. Soc. of Iowa, Des Moines, 1982—86, mus. dir., 1986—2004, state curator, 2004—. Recipient Disting. Svc. award, Art Educators of Iowa, 1993. Mem.: Ter. Hill Soc., Iowa Mus. Assn. (pres. 1991—93, bd. dirs. 1994—). Avocations: Tae Kwon Do, hunting, fishing, cooking, travel. Office: State Hist Soc of Iowa 600 E Locust Des Moines IA 50319 Office Phone: 515-281-4221. Office Fax: 515-281-6975. E-mail: jerome.thompson@iowa.gov.

**THOMPSON, JERRY E.,** oil industry executive; BS, Colo. Sch. Mines. V.p. refining CITGO Petroleum Corp., 1987—98, sr. v.p., 1998—2003, COO, 2003—06; pres., CEO TEPPCO Partners LLP, Houston, 2006—. V.p., past chmn. Nat. Petrochemical & Refiners Assn. Office: TEPPCO Partners 2929 Allen Pkwy Houston TX 77019*

**THOMPSON, JESSE ELDON,** vascular surgeon; b. Laredo, Tex., Apr. 7, 1919; s. Jesse Eathel and Sara Gail (Bolton) T.; m. Madeleine Jane Curtis, Sept. 18, 1944; children: Sally C., Jesse E., Janet E., Diane B. BA, U. Tex., 1939; MD, Harvard U., 1943; Rhodes scholar, Oxford U., 1949-50. Intern Mass. Gen. Hosp., Boston, 1943, resident in surgery, 1944-48; practice medicine specializing in surgery, tchr. surgery Boston U., 1949-54; practice medicine specializing in surgery, tchr. vascular surgery Baylor Hosp., Dallas, 1954—, chief vascular surgery, 1980-86. Clin. prof. surgery U. Tex. Southwestern Med. Sch., Dallas; attending surgeon Baylor Hosp., 1954-92, hon. surgeon, 1992—, chief vascular surgery Baylor Hosp., Dallas, 1982-86; Harm Ark. and Dist. Rhodes Scholar Selection Coms. Author: Surgery for Cerebrovascular Insufficiency, 1968; mem. editl. bd. Surgery, 1975-89, Jour. Cardiovasc. Surgery, 1975—; sr. editor Jour. Vascular Surgery, 1984-86; contbr. over 200 articles to profl. jours. Served to capt. M.C. AUS, 1945-47. Fulbright sr. fellow, 1949-50 Fellow ACS (treas., pres. N. Tex. chpt. 1961); mem. Am. Surg. Assn., So. Surg. Assn., Tex. Surg. Soc. (pres. 1972), Soc. Vascular Surgery (pres. 1977), Internat. Cardiovascular Soc. (pres. N.Am. chpt. 1973), Internat. Soc. Surgery, So. Assn. for Vascular Surgery (pres. 1986-87), Dallas Country Club, Dallas Petroleum Club. Methodist. Home: 3705 Stanford Ave Dallas TX 75225-7204

**THOMPSON, JEWEL TAYLOR,** music educator; b. Kinsale, Va., Oct. 27, 1935; d. Waverly Edward and Ella Joyce (Holman) Taylor; m. Leon Everette Thompson, June 10, 1961 (dec. June 1983); children: Sonca Patrice, Miya Kateri. BS, Va. State U., 1956; MA, Eastman Sch. of Music, 1960, PhD, 1982. Asst. prof. Va. State U., Petersburg, 1960-62, W.Va. State Coll., Institute, 1967-68, W.Va. Inst. Tech., Montgomery, 1968-72; adj. asst. prof. Hunter Coll., CUNY, 1972-85, asst. prof., 1985-90, assoc. prof., 1990-96, prof., 1997—. Organist Abyssinian Bapt. Ch., N.Y.C., 1978-83, minister of music, choirmaster, 1983—; ea. area music dir. Links, Inc., 1995-2003, nat. music dir., 2004—. Author: Samuel Coleridge-Taylor, 1994; composer and arranger numerous compositions; contbr. Internat. Dictionary of Black Composers 1999. Scholarship selection com. United Negro Coll. Fund; chair art program Links, Inc., 1989-93; music dir. at area and nat. levels; mem. Am. Music Ctr., Inc. Named Dame of Honour, Knights of Malta, 1982; recipient Hunter Coll. Presdl. award for excellence in svc., 1998, Outstanding Ministry award, Coun. Chs. of NYC, 2005; Hattie M. Strong Found. fellow, 1959—60, Ford Found. fellow, 1974—77, Prince Hall Masons grantee, 1977—78. Mem. ASCAP, Am. Women Composers, Inc., Music Theory Soc. N.Y. State. Avocations: travel, art. Home: 1425 Lozier Pl Teaneck NJ 07666-5106 Office: CUNY Hunter Coll 695 Park Ave New York NY 10021-5024 Office Phone: 212-650-3608.

**THOMPSON, JOAN (JO),** anthropologist; b. Colo. B in Psychology and Sociology, Wittenberg Univ., Ohio, 1978; M in Anthropology, Univ. Colo., 1992; PhD in Biological Anthropology and Primatology, Univ. Oxford, Eng., 1997. Founder, dir. Lukuru Wildlife Research Project, Democratic Republic of Congo, 1992–98; fund-raiser LWRP, Colo. (due to unrest in DRC). Named an assoc. laureate, Rolex award for Enterprise, 2004. Achievements include 13 years of conducting biological field rsch., community-based conservation and wildlife edn. in the Dem. Republic of the Congo on behalf of human and primate populations, particularly bonobos. Office: Lukuru Wildlife Rsch Found PO Box 1284 La Grande OR 97850-6284 Business E-Mail: jat434@aol.com.

**THOMPSON, JOCELYN PHARR,** organist, director, music educator; b. Peekskill, NY, Mar. 30, 1956; d. Ernest Eugene and Jonsie (Crawford) Pharr; m. Sherman Bradford Thompson, Oct. 12, 1985. MusB, U. NC, Greensboro, 1978, MusM in Edn., 1980, M in Spl. Edn., 1986. Cert. K-12 music, K-12 in spl. edn. Tchrs. aide Clay St. Elem., Gastonia, NC, 1980—81; tchr. Eckerd Family Youth Alternatives, Candor, NC, 1981—85, ednl. coord., 1985—89; choral tchr. Providence Sr. HS, Charlotte, NC, 1989—94; asst. dir., prin. accompanist Carolina Voices, 1994—2001, dir. mainstage choir, 2001—02; asst. dir. music Meml. Presbyn. Ch., 1990—96, dir. music, organist, 1996—; choral tchr. West Charlotte Sr. HS, 1992—. Asst. dir., accompanist Charlotte Contemporary Ensemble, Charlotte, 2002—; dir. Martin Luther King Mass Choir, Gaston County Orgn. for Cmty. Concern, 1997—. Mass choir dir. Nat. Bapt. Conf., Charlotte, 2001, World Gathering Presbyn. Women, Louisville, 2003—. Recipient Cmty. Svc. award, Black Women's Caucus, Charlotte, 2002, Heritage award, Cultural Calendar, Charlotte, 2001, Person of Tear, Gaston County Orgn. for Cmty. Concern, NC, 2005. Mem.: Am. Music Choral Dirs. Assn., Music Educators Nat. Conf., Links Inc., Alpha Kappa Alpha. Democrat. Avocations: reading plays, tennis, piano, movies. Office: West Charlotte Sr HS 2219 Senior Dr Charlotte NC 28216

**THOMPSON, JOE D.,** physicist; BS in Physics, 1969, PhD in Physics, 1975. Postdoctoral Cryogenics Group Los Alamos Nat. Lab., N.Mex., 1975—77, tech. staff mem. Condensed Matter and Thermal Physics Group, 1977—2001, dep. group leader, 1989—92, group leader, 1992—2001, Lab. fellow, 2001—. Fellow: AAAS, Am. Phys. Soc. Office: Los Alamos Nat Lab MSK-764 PO Box 1663 Los Alamos NM 87545

**THOMPSON, JOE FLOYD,** aerospace engineer, researcher; b. Grenada, Miss., Apr. 13, 1939; s. Joe Floyd and Bernice Thompson; m. Emilie Kay Wilson, June 1, 1974; children: Mardi, Douglass. BS, Miss. State U., 1961, MS, 1963; PhD, Ga. Inst. Tech., 1971. Aerospace engr. NASA Marshall, Huntsville, Ala., 1963-64; prof. Miss. State U., Starkville, 1964—, Disting. prof. aerospace engring., 1995—. Mem. tech. rev. bd. Army Rsch. Lab., Adelphi, Md., 1993-95; dir. computer code Nat. Grid Project 1993-96; dir. NSF Engring. Rsch. Ctr. for Computational Field Simulation, 1990-95; dir. acad. team Dept. of Def. Cewes Major Shared Resource Ctr., 1996—; mem. Pres.'s Info. Tech. Adv. Com., 1997—. Author: Numerical Grid Generation, 1985, (computer code) Eagle Grid System, 1987; sr. assoc. editor Applied Math. and Computation, 1985-94; assoc. editor Numerical Heat Transfer, 1989—; mem. edit. bd. Computational Fluid Dynamics Jour., 1993—, Jour. Computational Physics, 1995—. Recipient Commdr.'s award Army Waterways Exp. Sta., Vicksburg, Miss., 1992. Mem. IEEE Computer Soc., AIAA (Aerodynamics award 1992), Assn. for Computing Machinery. Presbyterian. Achievements include establishment of NSF Engineering Research Center; pioneering work in field of numerical grid generation; led academic team in winning competition for programming environment and training support at three of the four Dept. of Defense Major Shared Resource Center. Home: Miss State U PO Box 255 Mississippi State MS 39762-0255 Office: Miss State U PO Box 9627 Mississippi State MS 39762

**THOMPSON, JOHN ALBERT, JR.,** dermatologist; b. Austin, Tex., June 5, 1942; s. J. Albert Sr. and Elizabeth (Brady) T. BA, Georgetown U., 1963; MD, Bowman Gray Sch. Medicine, 1967; Dermatology Fellowship, U. N.C., 1971-73. Diplomate Am. Bd. Dermatology. Resident in internal medicine N.C. Baptist Hosp., Winston-Salem, NC, 1967-69; resident in dermatology N.C. Meml. Hosp., Chapel Hill, NC, 1971-73; pvt. practice Charlotte, NC, 1974—; clin. prof. dermatology Dept. Dermatology, U. N.C. Sch. Medicine, Chapel Hill, 1974—. Author profl. papers. Lt. comdr. USNR, 1969-71, Vietnam. Mem. Am. Acad. Dermatology (chmn. subcom. for sch. health edn. 1976-79, task force--nat. health ins.), Carolinas-Va. Dermatology Assn. (adv. bd. council rep. 1976-79), Charlotte Dermatology Assn., Mecklenburg County Med. Soc., N.C. Med. Soc., North Am. Clin. Dermatology Soc. Southern Med. Assn., Southeastern Consortium for Continuing Dermatol. Edn. (steering com. 1983—2003), South Cen. Dermatol. Congress (organizing com. 1982-86), Am. Soc. Dermatol. Surgery, Am. Dermatol. Soc. Allergy and Immunology, Am. Soc. Laser Medicine and Surgery, Am. Democrat. Episcopalian. Home: 2633 Richardson Dr Apt 8A Charlotte NC 28211-3346 Office: Dermatol Laser Ctr Dermatologic Laser Ctr 2310 Randolph Rd Charlotte NC 28207-1526 Office Phone: 704-376-9849.

**THOMPSON, JOHN DOUGLAS,** corporate financial executive; b. Montreal, Que., Can., Sept. 28, 1934; s. William Douglas and Anne F. (Whebby) T.; children: Jacqueline, Catherine, Peter, Anne Marie, Francois. B, McGill U., 1957; MBA, U. We. Ont., 1960. Dep. chmn. bd. Montreal Trustco Inc. Past chmn. bd. dirs. Trust Cos. Assn. of Can.; bd. dir. Air Transat, Shermag Inc., Nat. Trust Co., Scotia Mortgage Corp., Scotia Life Ins. Co., Scotia Gen. Ins. Co., The Bank of N.S. Trust Co., The Mortgage Ins. Co. of Can, Victoria and Grey Corp. Bd. dirs. MacDonald Stewart Found., Windsor Found., mem. audit com. McGill U.; past pres. St. Mary's Hosp. Found.; gov., past pres. St. Mary's Hosp. Mt. Royal Club, Montreal, Royal Montreal Golf Club, Mt. Bruno Country Club, Inc., The Forest and Stream Club. Roman Catholic. Office: Montreal Trust 4th Fl 1002 Sherbrooke West Montreal PQ Canada H3A 3L6 Office Phone: 514-499-5517.

**THOMPSON, JOHN H,** research and development company executive; b. Washington, June 9, 1951; s. Edwin Hubert and Edna Claire Thompson; m. Bonnie Jean Horrigan, June 30, 1973; children: Lowell, Meredith, John. BS in math, Va. Tech., 1973, MS in math, 1975. Rsch. U.S. Bur. Census, Washington, 1975—97, assoc. dir., 1997—2001, prin. assoc. dir., 2001—02; exec. vice pres. Nat. Opinion Rsch. Ctr., Chgo., 2002—. Recipient Gold medal, Dept. of Commerce, 2000, Disting. Exec. award, The White House, 2001. Fellow: Am. Statis. Assn.; mem.: Sr. Exec. Svc., Am. Statis. Assn. Achievements include directed the 2000 Decennial Census on time and on budget. Office: Nat Opinion Rsch Ctr 55 E Monroe St Chicago IL 60603

**THOMPSON, JOHN HERD,** history professor; b. Winnipeg, Man., Can., Sept. 18, 1946; came to U.S. 1989; s. Joseph Whyte and Gladys Kate T.; m. Katrin Ann Partelpoeg, Jan. 15, 1977 (div. Sept. 2001); children: Anne Marie, Mark Thomas; m. Janet J. Ewald, May 2002. BA with honors, U. Winnipeg, 1968; MA, U. Man., 1969; PhD, Queens U., Kingston, Ont., 1975. Faculty Duke U., Durham, NC, 1989—, chair dept. history, 2000—. Author: Harvests of War, 1978, Decades of Discord: Canada 1922-1939, 1985, Canada and the United States: Ambivalent Allies, 1994, 2d edit., 1997, 3d edit., 2002, Forging the Prairie West, 1998, British Columbia: Land of Promises, 2005. Mem. Am. Hist. Assn., Can. Hist. Assn., Soc. for Am. Baseball Rsch., Assn. for Can. Studies in the U.S. Avocation: baseball.

**THOMPSON, JOHN W.,** information technology executive; b. Ft. Dix, NJ, Apr. 24, 1949; s. John H. and Eunice Thompson; m. Sandi Thompson; children: John E., Ayanna. BBA, Fla. A&M U., 1971; MBA in Mgmt. Sci., MIT's Sloan School of Mngmt., 1982. Sales rep. IBM, 1971—75, branch office mgr., 1975—79, regional adminstrv. asst., regional mktg. dir., 1980—84, asst. to CEO, 1984, dir. Midwest ops., 1990—93, head mktg. US ops., 1993, gen. mgr. personal software products, 1994—98; gen. mgr. IBM Americas, 1997—99; chmn., pres., CEO Symantec Corp., Cupertino, Calif., 1999—. Bd. dirs. UPS, 2000—, NiSource, Inc., Seagate Tech., 2004—, Crystal Decisions; appt. mem. Nat. Infrastructure Adv. Coun., Washington, 2002—; chair Silicon Valley Blue Ribbon Task Force on Aviation Security & Tech.; mem., Worldwide Mgmt. Coun. IBM; spkr. in field. Chmn. Fla. A&M U. Cluster; Ill. Gov's human resource adv. coun. Office: Symantec Corp 20330 Stevens Creek Blvd Cupertino CA 95014*

**THOMPSON, JON L.,** retired oil industry executive; BS in geology, MS in geology, U. Fla. Geologist Exxon Co. U.S.A., New Orleans, 1962; v.p. Exxon Corp., 1992—99; pres. Exxon Exploration Co., 1992—99; v.p. ExxonMobil Corp., 2000—; pres. ExxonMobil Exploration Co., 2000—. Office: Exxon-Mobil Exploration Co Ste 1241 233 Benmar St Houston TX 77066-3105

**THOMPSON, JOSEPH PAUL,** retired systems administrator; b. Denver, Colo., Apr. 11, 1949; s. James Paul Thompson and Emma Lucinda Neal; m. Nola Ann Schlorholtz (div.). Planner data analyst Colo. Dept. of Transp., Denver, 1974—2001. Adv. bd. mem. Nat. Ctr. for Voice and Speech, Denver. Mem.: Toastmasters Internat. (lt. gov. edn. and tng. 2002—03, dist gov-elect 2003—). Libertarian. Avocations: reading, bicycling. Home: 7474 E Arkansas Ave #3010 Denver CO 80231

**THOMPSON, JOSEPH T., JR.,** health facility administrator; b. Cranston, R.I., Jan. 13, 1946; s. Joseph T. Thompson Sr. and Frances R. (Marshall); m. Sidney Carla Lopez, June 22, 1986; children: Endre J., Paige Nicole. BS, La Salle U., 1999. Cert. CCFC, LADAC, S.A.P. Case mgr. San Juan Youth Shelter, Aztec, N.Mex., 1998—99; DWI counselor San Juan County DWI Detention/Treatment Facility, Farmington, N.Mex., 1999—2001; intake co-ord. Four Winds Recovery Ctr., Farmington, N.Mex., 2001—; dir., owner White Eagle Counseling & Edn. Svc., Farmington, N.Mex., 2001—; with dept. behavioral health svcs. Navajo Nation, 2001. Adj. faculty San Juan Coll., Farmington, N.Mex., 1999—; prin. substance abuse counselor Dept. Behavioral Health Navajo Nation, 2001—. Chief petty officer USN, 1964—86. Mem.: Am. Coll. Cert. Forensic Counselors, NAADAC. Avocations: fishing, hunting, camping. Office: White Eagle Counseling 605 N Butler Ave Farmington NM 87401

**THOMPSON, JOSHUA M.,** music educator; b. Milw., June 6, 1973; s. Bert R. and Kathryn D. Thompson; m. Ruthie A. Shoberg, Feb. 12, 1970; children: Jack Grady, Kate Linnea, Dane Anders. B of Music Edn., Northwestern U., Evanston, Ill., 1995; M of Music History, Vandercook Coll. of Music, Chgo., 2004. Band dir. Kankakee Schs., Ill., 1995—97; and dir. Lake Zurich H.S., Ill., 1997—. Musician: Disneyland All Am. Coll. Band. Mem.: IAJE, MENC. Avocations: woodworking, jazz. Office: Lake Zurich HS 300 Church St Lake Zurich IL 60047 Office Phone: 847-438-5155. Office Fax: 847-438-5989. Business E-Mail: josh.thompson@lz95.org.

**THOMPSON, JUDITH KASTRUP,** nursing researcher; b. Marstal, Denmark, Oct. 1, 1933; came to the U.S., 1951; d. Edward Kastrup and Anna Hansa (Knudsen) Pedersen; m. Richard Frederick Thompson, May 22, 1960; children: Kathryn Marr, Elizabeth Kastrup, Virginia St. Claire. BS, RN, U. Oreg., Corvallis, 1958; MSN, U. Oreg., 1963. RN, Calif., Oreg. Staff nurse U. Oreg. Med. Sch., Eugene, 1957-58, Portland, 1958-61, head staff nurse, 1960-61; instr. psychiat. nursing U. Oreg. Sch. Nursing, Portland, 1963-64; rsch. asst. U. Oreg. Med. Sch., Portland, 1964-65, U. Calif., Irvine, 1971-72; rsch. assoc. Stanford (Calif.) U., 1982-87; rsch. asst. Harvard U., Cambridge, Mass., 1973-74; rsch. assoc. U. So. Calif., L.A., 1987—. Contbg. author: Behavioral Control and Role of Sensory Biofeedback, 1976; contbr. articles to profl. jours. Treas. LWV, Newport Beach, Calif., 1970-74; scout leader Girl Scouts Am., Newport Beach, 1970-78. Named Citizen of Yr. State of Oreg., 1966. Mem. Soc. for Neurosci., Am. Psychol. Soc. (charter), ANA, Oreg. Nurses Assn. Republican. Lutheran. Avocations: art collecting, travel, tennis. Home: 28 Sky Sail Dr Corona Del Mar CA 92625-1436 Office: U So Calif University Park Los Angeles CA 90089-0001 Office Phone: 213-740-7350. Business E-Mail: judith@usc.edu.

**THOMPSON, KATHLEEN SHAMBAUGH,** marriage and family counselor; b. Bakersfield, Calif., Oct. 22, 1945; d. Stephen W. and Marilyn L. Shambaugh; m. John W. Thompson, June 10, 1967 (dec. Mar. 1971); children: Stephen, Charles. Student, Colo. Women's Coll., 1964; BA in English, U. Colo., 1968; MA in Counseling, U. Denver, 1976. Tchg. credential U. Colo. 1971, lic. marriage and family counselor Denver, Colo., Calif., 1978. Tchr., Denver, 1971—78; marriage, family and child counselor, 1982—. Editor, proofreader, 1977—80. Author: An American Girl in Canada, 2002, Going Through Life-Poems and Short Works, 2004, Coping with Grief and the Death of Loved Ones, 2004, A Life Filled With Poetry, 2004, Professional Guides: The Case Study, Human Sexuality in Marriage, Crime and Rehabilitation, Introducing the Gap Theory, 2004, Counseling Helps, 2005, The Surgery Experience, 2005, Writers and Writing, 2005, Landscaping Any Small Lot, 2005, Gina's Rehabilitation, 2006, The Equal Personage of the Child, 2005, Going Through Life, 2005, Brown Flowers in Gloucester, 2006, I Care For My Cats, 2006, Charlie and Mom Cat, 2006, Travellers, 2006, Getting Through Life--Other Poems and Short Works, 2006, Funeral Planning, Memorial Services, and Coping with Death, 2006. Named one of Best Poets of 2000, Internat. Libr. Poetry, 2001, 2005. Mem.: Internat. Soc. Poets (Internat. Poet Merit 2000), Delta Delta Delta. Presbyterian/Swedenborgian. Avocations: stamp collecting/philately, doll collecting, art, literature, gardening. Home and Office: 1655 W Ajo Way # 170 Tucson AZ 85713

**THOMPSON, KATHY C.,** bank executive; From. sr. v.p. to exec. v.p. Stock Yards Bancorp Inc, Louisville, 1992—96, exec. v.p., 1996—. Named No. 3 Fast Tracker in the Industry, U.S. Bankers Mag., 2003. Office: Stock Yards Bancorp Inc 1040 East Main St Louisville KY 40206

**THOMPSON, KEN (G. KENNEDY THOMPSON),** bank executive; b. Rocky Mount, N.C., Nov. 25, 1950; BA in Am. Studies, U.N.C., Chapel Hill; MBA, Wake Forest Fu. With First Union Corp., Charlotte, NC, 1976—, head S.E. divsn., mgr. mid. market dept., mgr. N.Y. loan prodn. office, pres. First Union-Ga., sr. v.p., head human resources, pres. First Union-Fla., vice chmn. corp., head global capital markets, 1998—99, pres. CEO, 1999—2001, Wachovia Corp. (merger of First Union and Wachovia Corp.), 2001—, chmn., 2001—. Bd. dirs. N.Y. Clearing House; mem. Fin. Services Roundtable Fin. Svcs. Forum, chmn.-elect. Bd. visitors U.N.C., Chapel Hill, Babcock Grad. Sch. Mgmt., Wake Forest U.; bd. dirs. N.C. Blumenthal Performing Arts Ctr., Charlotte Latin Sch., United Way, Charlotte, Teach for Am., Carolinas Healthcare Sys., Charlotte Inst. Tech. Innovation; mem. met. bd. YMCA Morehead scholar U. N.C. Office: Wachovia Corp 301 S College St Charlotte NC 28288*

**THOMPSON, KENNETH,** software engineer; b. New Orleans, 1943; BSEE, U. Calif., Berkeley, 1965, MSEE, 1966. With Computer Scis. Rsch. Ctr. Bell Labs/Lucent Technologies, Murray Hill, NJ, 1966—2000; disting. mem. tech. staff Bell Labs/Lucent Techs, Murray Hill, NJ; fellow Entrisphere, Inc. Vis. prof. U. Calif., Berkeley, 1975—76, U. Sydney, Australia, 1988. Co-recipient U.S. Nat. Medal of Tech., 1999, C&C prize, NEC, 1989; named Bell Labs Fellow, 1983; recipient Fellow award, Computer History Mus., 1997, Emmanuel R. Piore award, IEEE, Richard Hamming medal, Harold Pender Award, Sch. Engring. and Applied Sci., U. Pa., 2003. Mem.: Assn. Computing Machinery (Turing award and software sys. award 1983), NAE, NAS, IEEE Computer Soc. (Tsutomu Kanai award 1999). Achievements include patents for computer technology; research in operating systems, programming languages, software for voice and data communications, security, computer games and digital music distribution; co-developer of UNIX operating system in 1969; with J.H. Condon was involved with the development of Belle, a chess computer, which won the US and World Computing Chess Championships in 1980.*

**THOMPSON, KENNETH W(INFRED),** educational association administrator, writer, editor, social sciences educator; b. Des Moines, Aug. 29, 1921; s. Thor Carlyle and Agnes (Rorbeck) T.; m. Betty Bergquist (dec.); m. Beverly Bourret (dec.); children: Kenneth Carlyle, Paul Andrew, James David, Carolyn Cordry. AB, Augustana Coll., 1943, LHD (hon.), 1986, LLD, 1986; MA, U. Chgo., 1948, PhD, 1950; LLD, U. Notre Dame, 1964, Bowdoin Coll., 1972, St. Michael's Coll., 1973, St. Olaf Coll., 1974, U. Denver, 1983; L.H.D., W.Va. Wesleyan U., 1970; LHD, Nebr. Wesleyan Coll., 1971. Lectr. social scis. U. Chgo., 1948, asst. prof. polit. sci., 1951-53; from asst. prof. to assoc. prof. polit. sci. Northwestern U., 1949-55, chmn. internat. relations

com., 1951-55; asst. dir. social scis Rockefeller Found., 1955-57, from assoc. dir. social scis. to v.p., 1957-73; dir. higher edn. for devel. Internat. Council for Ednl. Devel., 1974-76; Commonwealth prof. govt. and fgn. affairs U. Va., 1975-78, White Burkett Miller prof. govt. and fgn. affairs, 1979-86; J. Wilson Newman prof. govt. and fgn. affairs, 1986—; dir. White Burkett Miller Ctr. Pub. Affairs, 1978-98; dir. emeritus Miller Ctr., 1999—. Riverside Meml. lectr. Riverside Ch., N.Y.C., 1958; Lilly lectr. Duke, 1959; James Stokes lectr. N.Y.U., 1962; Rockwell lectr. Rice U., 1965; Ernest Griffith lectr. Am. U.; Andrew Cecil lectr. U. Tex., 1983; Stuber lectr. U. Rochester, 1984; Morgenthau Meml. lectr., N.Y.C., Mike Mansfield Ctr. lectr., U. Mont.; dir. Inst. Study World Politics, N.Y.C., 1975-01; cons. in field. Author, editor: Principles and Problems of International Politics, 1951, 82, Man and Modern Society, 1953, Christian Ethics and the Dilemmas of Foreign Policy, 1959, 81, Conflict and Cooperation Among Nations, 1960, Political Realism and the Crisis of World Politics, 1960, 82, American Diplomacy and Emergent Problems, 1962, 82, Foreign Policies in a World of Change, 1964, The Moral Issue in Statecraft, 1966, Reconstituting the Human Community, 1972, Foreign Assistance: A View From Private Sector, 1972, 82, Higher Education for National Development, 1972, Understanding World Politics, 1975, Higher Edn. and Social Change, 1976, World Politics, 1976, Truth and Tragedy, 1977, Ethics and Foreign Policy, 1978, Interpreters and Critics of the Cold War, 1978, Foreign Policy and the Democratic Process, 1978, Ethics, Functionalism and Power, 1979, Morality and Foreign Policy, 1980, Masters of International Thought, 1980, The Virginia Papers, vols. 1-30, 1979-96, The President and the Public Philosophy, 1981, Cold War Theories: World Polarization, 1944-53, Vol. I, 1981,91. Winston S. Churchill's World View, 1983, 89, Toynbees's World Politics and History, 1985, Moralism and Morality, 1985, Ethics and International Relations, 1985, Theory and Practice of International Relations, 1987, Arms Control and Foreign Policy, 1990, Traditions and Values in Politics and Diplomacy, 1992, Fathers of International Thought, 1994, Schools of Thought in International Relations, 1996, Politics Among Nations, expanded and updated, 2005; editor: Am. Values Series, Vols. I-XX, Presdl. Nominating Process, Vols. I-IV, Portraits of American Presidents, Vols. I-IX, Herbert Butterfield: The Ethics of History; The American Presidency, Vols. I-XVI, 1982-83, Ethics and International Relations, 1985, Moral Dimensions of American Foreign Policy, 1985, 94, The Credibility of Leadership and Institutions, Vols. I-XX, 1983-86, Rhetoric and Political Discourse, Vols.I-XX, Governance, Vols. I-VII, 1990-97, Constitutionalism, Vols. I-VII, 1989-91, Presidency and Science Advising, Vols. I-VIII, 1986-90, Political Transitions and Foreign Policy, Vols. I-IX, 1985-91, A World in Change, Vols. I-XI, 1989-96, Presidential Disability, Vols. I-IV, 1989-96, A New World Order, Vols. I-VI, 1991-97, Great American Presidents, 1994, Defeated Presidential Candidates, 1994, Statesmen Who Were Never President, 1996; bd. editors Society, Ethics and International Affairs, Interpretation, The Rev. of Politics; contbr. articles to profl. jours. Pres. Dist. of Scarsdale and Mamaroneck (N.Y.) Bd. Edn., 1965-68; trustee Union Theol. Sem., 1967-71, Dillard U., 1975-96, Social Sci. Found., U. Denver, 1974-94, Compton Found., 1975-98. 1st lt. AUS, 1943-46. Named Va. laureate, 1981; recipient Phi Beta Kappa and Va. Coll. Stores prizes, Va. Social Sci. Assn. ann. award, English Speaking Union award.Spl. Edward Weintal prize Georgetown U. Acad. Diplomacy, 1999. Fellow Soc. Religion Higher Edn., Am. Acad. Arts and Scis.; mem. Century Club, Scarsdale Town Club, Raven Soc. (ann. award U. Va.), Phi Beta Kappa (pres.), Omicron Delta Phi. Office: Univ Va Miller Ctr PO Box 400406 Charlottesville VA 22904-4406 Office Phone: 434-924-6051. Business E-Mail: kwt.8b@virginia.edu.

**THOMPSON, KIP RUSSELL,** education educator, researcher; s. Billy G. and Carroll S. Thompson; m. Becky L. McQuerter, May 27, 1989. PhD, U. South Ala., Mobile, 2000. Cert. tchr. Mo., Ala. Coord. life sci. instrn. Ozarks Tech. CC, Springfield, Mo., 2000—. Contbr. articles to profl. jours. Capt. M.C. U.S. Army, 2001—06. Grantee, Miss. Ala. Sea Grant Consortium, 1993—95, Mo. State U., 1992—93. Mem.: North Am. Assn. Environ. Educators, Am. Fisheries Soc., Am. Soc. of Ichtyologists and Herpetologists, Lambda Chi Alpha. Avocations: bicycling, running, swimming. Office: Ozarks Tech Cmty Coll 1001 E Chestnut Expressway Springfield MO 65802 Office Phone: 417-447-8246. Office Fax: 417-447-8204. Business E-Mail: thompsok@otc.edu.

**THOMPSON, KIRK,** transportation executive; CPA, Ark. With J.B. Hunt Transport Svcs., Inc., Lowell, Ark., 1973-78, v.p. fin., 1979-84, exec. v.p., CFO, 1984-85, pres., CEO, 1986-87, 1987—. Office: JB Hunt Transport Svcs Inc 615 JB Hunt Corporate Dr Lowell AR 72745

**THOMPSON, LARRY ANGELO,** film and television producer, lawyer, motivational speaker, writer; b. Clarksdale, Miss., Aug. 1, 1944; s. Angelo and Ann (Tuminello) T.; m. Kelly Ann LeBlanc, 1999; children: Taylor Ann, Trevor Lorenzo. BBA, U. Miss., 1966, JD, 1968. Bar: Miss. 1968, Calif. 1970. In-house counsel Capitol Records, Hollywood, Calif., 1969-71; sr. ptnr. in entertainment law Thompson, Shankman, Bond and Moss, Beverly Hills, Calif., 1971-77; pres. Larry A. Thompson Orgn., Inc., 1977—. Co-owner New World Pictures, 1983-85; lectr. in entertainment bus. UCLA, U. So. Calif., Southwestern U. Law Sch., The Learning Annex; founder Project Rise and Shine, 2004. Author: How to Make a Record Deal and Have Your Songs Recorded, 1975, Prime Time Crime, 1982, Shine: A Powerful 4-Step For Becoming a Star in Anything You Do, 2005; prodr.: (TV) Jim Nabors Show, 1977 (Emmy nominee), Mickey Spillane's Margin for Murder, 1981, Bring 'Em Back Alive, 1982, Mickey Spillane's Murder Me, Murder You, 1982, The Other Lover, 1985, Convicted, 1986, Intimate Encounters, 1986, Eagle and My Bear, 1987, The Woman He Loved, 1988 (Emmy nominee, Golden Globe nominee), Original Sin, 1989, Class Cruise, 1989, Little White Lies, 1989 Moon in the Middle, 1989, Lucy and Desi: Before the Laughter, 1990 (Emmy nominee), Broken Promises, 1993, Separated By Murder, 1994, Face of Evil, 1996, Replacing Dad, 1998, Tonight @ House of Blues, 1998, The Beat Goes On: The Sonny and Cher Story, 1999 (Emmy nominee), Murder in the Mirror, 2000, Iron Chef USA: Showdown in Las Vegas, 2001, Iron Chef USA: Holiday Showdown, 2001, Celebrity Home Video, 2003, A Date with Darkness: The Trial of Andrew Luster, 2003, Little Girl Lost: The Delimar Vera Story, 2005; (film) Crimes of Passion, 1984, Fraternity Vacation, 1985, Quiet Cool, 1987, My Demon Lover, 1987, Breaking the Rules, 1992. Co-chmn. Rep. Nat. Entertainment Com.; apptd. by Gov. of Calif. to Calif. Entertainment Commn.; mem. Inauguration of Thompson Ctr. for Fine Arts in Clarksdale, 1986. Served with JAGC, U.S. Army, 1966-72. Recipient Show Bus. Atty. of Yr. award Capitol Records, 1971, Vision award, 1993; named Showman of Yr., U.S. TV Fan Assn., 1997. Mem. ABA, Miss. Bar Assn., Calif. Bar Assn., Inter-Am. Bar Assn., Hon. Order Ky. Cols., Am. Film Inst., Nat. Acad. Rec. Arts and Scis., Acad. TV Arts and Scis. Republican. Roman Catholic. Office: Larry A Thompson Orgn 9663 Santa Monica Blvd Ste 801 Beverly Hills CA 90210-4303 Home: 1348 Club View Dr Los Angeles CA 90024-5304 Office Phone: 310-288-0700. E-mail: ltbeverlyhills@aol.com.

**THOMPSON, LARRY DEAN,** lawyer, former federal agency administrator; b. Hannibal, Mo., Nov. 15, 1945; s. Ezra W. and Ruth L. (Robinson) T.; m. Brenda Anne Taggart, June 26, 1970; children: Larry Dean, Gary E. BA cum laude, Culver-Stockton Coll., Canton, Mo., 1967; MA, Mich. State U., 1969; JD, U. Mich., 1974. Bar: Mo. 1974, Ga. 1978. Indsl. rels. rep. Ford Motor Co., Birmingham, Mich., 1969-71; atty. Monsanto Co., St. Louis, 1974-77, King & Spalding, Atlanta, 1977, ptnr., 1986—2001; U.S. atty. (no. dist.) Ga. U.S. Dept. Justice, 1982-86; dep. atty. gen. U.S. Dept Justice, Washington, 2001—03; sr. fellow Brookings Instn., Washington, 2003—04; sr. v.p. govt. affairs, gen. counsel, sec. PepsiCo, Inc., Purchase, NY, 2005—. Mem. 11th Cir. Commn. on Lawyer Qualifications and Conduct; ind. counsel HUD investigation, 1995, visiting prof., U. Ga Sch. of Law, 2004; mem. Ga. Bd. Bar Examiners; bd. dirs. Delta Air Lines Inc., 2003-. Editor: Jury Instructions in Criminal Antitrust Cases 1976-80, 1982. Chmn. Atlanta Urban League; mem. Ga. Bd. Edn., 1997; bd. dirs. Ga. Rep. Found. Recipient Outstanding Achievement award FBA, 1992. Mem. ABA, Nat. Bar Assn. Republican. Presbyterian. Office: PepsiCo Inc 700 Anderson Hill Rd Purchase NY 10577*

**THOMPSON, LARRY JAMES,** retired gifted and social studies education educator; b. Savannah, Ga., May 14, 1948; s. James Howell and Dorothy (Hendley) T. BA, Armstrong Atlantic State U., 1970; MAT, Tulane U., 1974; EdD, Ga. U., 1986. Cert. tchr., instrnl. supr., adminstr., Ga. Tchr. social studies Chatham County Bd. Edn., Savannah, 1970-71, 75-87, adminstrv. coord. social studies, 1987-97, gifted, talented educator, 1997-2001; ret., 2001. With USNR, 1971-73. Mem. Nat. Coun. Social Studies, Ga. Ret. Educators Assn., Ga. Hist. Soc., Phi Delta Kappa. Home: 18 E Deerwood Rd Savannah GA 31410-3171 E-mail: ljthompson514@comcast.net.

**THOMPSON, LAURA KEY,** school system administrator; b. Macon, Ga., June 18, 1962; d. Guerry R. and Shelba P. Key; m. Frank Thompson, Aug. 21, 1982; children: Jake, Katherine, Benjamin. BS in Home Econs., U. Ga., 1984; MEd, Ga. Coll., 1995. Cert. tchr. Ga. Tchr. Gatewood Schs., Eatonton, Ga., 1984—89, 1990—99, 2000—01, head sch., 2001—; dir. Stepping Stones Learning Ctr., Eatonton, 1999—2000. Mem. Eatonton Svc. League, 1985—99, Leadership Putnam, Eatonton, 2000, Women's Leadership Forum, Milledgeville, Ga., 2004—05. Named Mem. of the Yr., Eatonton Svc. League, 1989, 1997, Citizen of the Yr., Eatonton-Putnam C. of C., 1990. Mem.: ASCD, Profl. Assn. Ga. Educators. Baptist. Avocations: reading, walking. Office: Gatewood Schs 139 Phillips Dr Eatonton GA 31024 Personal E-mail: lthompson4gw@yahoo.com.

**THOMPSON, LAWRENCE HYDE,** federal agency official; b. Hamilton, Ohio, Oct. 6, 1943; s. William Hayton and Evelyn (Covault) T.; m. Catherine Crosby, Feb. 3, 1973; children: Bradford Stephen, Sarah Catherine. BS, Iowa State U., 1964; MBA, U. Pa., 1966; PhD, U. Mich., 1971. Economist Office Sec. Health, Edn. and Welfare, Washington, 1974-77, dir. Soc. Security Planning, 1977-79; assoc. commr. Social Security Adminstrn., Washington, 1979-81, dir. rsch., 1981-83; chief economist Gen. Acctg. Office, Washington, 1983-89, asst. comptroller gen., 1989-93; prin. dep. commr. Social Security Admnistrn., 1993-95; sr. fellow The Urban Inst., Washington, 1996—. Contbr. articles to pubs., books. Mem. Am. Economic Assn., Nat. Acad. Social Ins. (dir. 1985-96, sec. 1997-99, pres. 1999-2003). Avocations: racquetball, choral singing. Office: The Urban Inst 2100 M St NW Ste 401 Washington DC 20037-1264 Business E-Mail: lthompso@ui.urban.org.

**THOMPSON, LEE (MORRIS THOMPSON),** lawyer; b. Hutchinson, Kans., Nov. 29, 1946; s. Morris J. and Ruth W. (Smith) T.; m. M. Susan Morgan, May 26, 1974; children: Deborah, Erin, Andrew, Christopher. BA, Wichita State U., 1968; MA, Emporia State U., 1970; JD, George Washington U., 1974. Bar: Kans., 1974, U.S. Dist. Ct. Kans., 1974, U.S. Ct. Appeals (10th cir.) 1976, U.S. Supreme Ct., 1978. Instr., lectr. Emporia State U., Kans., 1969-70; lctr. in speech George Washington U., Washington, 1970-71; asst. to Senator James Pearson Washington, 1971-75; assoc. Martin, Pringle, et al., Wichita, Kans., 1976-78, ptnr., 1979-89; U.S. atty. for dist. of Kans., Dept. Justice, Wichita, 1993-95; ptnr. Triplett, Woolf & Garrets, LLC, Wichita, 1993—2001; mng. mem. Thompson Law Firm, LLP (previously Thompson Stout & Goering LLC), Wichita, 2001—. Treas. Kansans for Kassebaum, Wichita, 1978-88; mem. Kans. State Rep. Cen. Com., Topeka, 1978-79, 88-90; candidate U.S. Ho. of Reps., Kans., 1988; crimn. civil issues subcom. Atty. Gen.'s Adv. Com. of U.S. Attys., 1992-93. Mem. Kans. Bar Assn. (pres. criminal law sect. 1994-95). Methodist. Office: Thompson Law Firm 106 E 2nd St Wichita KS 67202 Office Phone: 316-267-3933. Office Fax: 316-267-3901. E-mail: lthompson@tslawfirm.com.*

**THOMPSON, LOHREN MATTHEW,** oil company executive; b. Sutherland, Nebr., Jan. 21, 1926; s. John M. and Anna (Ecklund) T.; children: Terence M., Sheila M., Clark M. Ed., U. Denver. Spl. rep. Standard Oil Co., Omaha, 1948-56; sales mgr. Frontier REF. Co., 1956-67, v.p. mktg., 1967-68; mgr. mktg. U.S. region Husky Oil Co., Denver, 1968-72; v.p. Westar Stas. Inc., Denver, 1972-77; chmn. bd. Colo. Petroleum, Denver, 1971—. Served with USAAF, 1944-46 Mem. Colo. Petroleum Council, Am. Petroleum Inst., Am. Legion Clubs: Denver Petroleum, Denver Oilman's, Lodges: Lions. Lutheran. Home: 2410 Spruce Ave Estes Park CO 80517-7146 Office: Colo Petroleum 4080 Globeville Rd Denver CO 80216-4906

**THOMPSON, LONDON (WILLIAM LONDON EVANS-THOMPSON),** recording industry executive, publishing executive, sound recording engineer, executive film producer; b. Phila., June 26, 1970; s. Samuel London Evans and Anne Mayo Thompson; m. Antonina Vassilkovsky; children: Jordan Profitt-Thompson, Alexander London. Diploma, Trevor G. Browne HS, Phoenix, 1988. Pres. BlissTunes Rec. Corp., LA, 1998—, Pure Bliss Pub., LA, 1998—. Dancer I Spirit; exec. prodr.: Music Inspired by the film Sugar Valentine, Music Inspired by the film Nora's Hair Salon, Music Inspired by the film County General, Music Inspired by the film Brothers in Arms; music dir.: B2K Scream 2 Tour, music dir.: TRL Tour: Destiny's Child, mixer, engr., vocalist: (film underscore and soundtrack) Master of Disguise, composer, mixer, engr.: (album) B2K: Santa Hooked Me Up; (album), My Destiny, Listen: Our Life In Music, Pure Bliss (Best Male R&B Artist, Ariz. Music Awards, 1996); mixer, engr.: albums B2K: Pandamonium; B2K: Greatest Hits, B2K: The Remixes, MH: Marques Houston. Pres. Black Student Union, Phoenix Coll., 1994—95. Republican. Avocations: skiing, soccer, football. Office Phone: 323-962-8863. Personal E-mail: london@blisstunes.com.

**THOMPSON, LORIN ANDREW III,** chemist; b. Lexington, Ky., Nov. 19, 1970; s. William Oxley and Joan Homel Thompson; m. Patricia Beron Thompson, July 16, 1994; children: Connor William, Andrew Forrest. PhD, U Calif., Berkeley, 1997; BS, U. NC, Chapel Hill, 1992. Prin. rsch. scientst DuPont Merck Pharmaceuticals, Wilmington, Del., 2000—02; group leader Bristol-Myers Squibb, Wallingford, Conn., 2002—. Mem.: Soc. for Neurosci. Achievements include patents in field. Office Phone: 203-677-5967.

**THOMPSON, LORING MOORE,** retired college administrator, writer; b. Newton, Mass., Feb. 17, 1918; s. Henry E. and Ella (Gould) T.; m. Pearl E. Judiesch, Dec. 30, 1949 (dec. May 2002); children: Bruce C., Douglas P. (dec.). BS in Indsl. Engring. Northeastern U., 1940; MS, U. RI, 1947; PhD, U. Chgo., 1956. Instr. U. RI, 1946; asst. to pres. Assn. Colls. Upper NY, 1947-49; assoc. prof. U. Toledo, 1952-59, asst. dean acad. adminstrn., 1958-59; dir. univ. planning Northeastern U., Boston, 1959-63, dean adult programs, 1964-66, v.p. planning, 1967-80, emeritus, 1980—; faculty assoc. continuing edn. Ariz. State U., 1982-84. Cons. in field. Author: (with others) Business Communication, 1949; contbr. articles to profl. jours. Bd. dirs. Back Bay Assn., Boston, 1961-63, v.p., 1963; trustee Huntington Gen. Hosp., Boston, 1970-80; mem. Fenway Project Area Com., 1973-76; mem. Mass. conf. ch. and edn. com. United Ch. of Christ, 1972-78, chairperson, 1973-74, mem. task force on ch. growth, 1978-80; mem. Chandler Area Coun., 1988-89; sec. Interfaith Coun. Greater Sun Lakes, 1993-96. Lt. USNR, 1942-45. Mem. Inst. Noetic Scis., Tau Beta Pi. Home: 25408 S Sedona Dr Sun Lakes AZ 85248-6636

**THOMPSON, LOUIS MILTON,** agronomy educator, researcher; b. Throckmorton, Tex., May 15, 1914; s. Aubrey Lafayette and Lola Terry (Frazier) T.; m. Margaret Stromberg, July 10, 1937 (dec. Nov. 1972); children: Louis Milton, Margaret Ann, Glenda Ray (dec.), Carolyn Terry, Jerome Lafayette; m. Ruth Hiatt Phipps, July 7, 1990. BS, Tex. A&M U., 1947, PhD, 1950. Soil surveyor, Tex., 1935-36, 39-40; instr. Tex. A&M U., 1936-39, 40-42; asst. prof. soils Iowa State U., Ames, 1947-50, prof. soils, head farm operation curriculum, 1950-58, assoc. dean agr. charge resident instrn., 1958-83, emeritus prof. agronomy, 1983—, assoc. dean emeritus, 1984—. Author: Soils and Soil Fertility, rev. edit., 1957; co-author: rev. edit., 1978, 1983; contbr. articles on weather-crop yield models and climate change to profl. jours. Elder Presbyn. Ch. With AUS, 1942-46; col. Res. (ret.). Recipient Henry A. Wallace Award for Disting. Svc. to Agr., 1982, Faculty citation Iowa State U. Alumni Assn., 1990, Disting. Achievement citation, 1993, Alumni Recognition medal, 1996, Disting. Iowa Scientist Award Iowa Acad. Sci., 1991, Agr. Innovator award Iowa State U. Agr. Alumni Soc., 1992, Friends of Agrl. award Iowa Dept. Agr. and Nat. Agrl. Mktg. Assn., 1993,

Disting. Svc. to Iowa Agr. award Iowa Farm Bur., 1995, Disting. Svc. to Agr. award Iowa chpt. Am. Soc. Farm Mgrs. and Rural Appraisers, 2000; named one of 150 Iowans Who Made a Difference, Iowa Farm Bur., 1996. Fellow AAAS, Am. Soc. Agronomy, Soil Sci. Soc. Am., Soil and Water Conservation Soc, (pres.'s citation); mem. Farm House (hon.), Rotary (past local pres., Paul Harris fellow), Sigma Xi, Alpha Zeta (Tall Corn award 1957), Gamma Sigma Delta (nat. pres. 1956-58), Phi Kappa Phi (chpt. pres. 1961, Centennial medal 1997). Home: 2214 Hamilton Dr Ames IA 50014-8287 *To succeed in an academic community one must become an authority on a subject and be able to communicate it.*

**THOMPSON, LOUIS MILTON, JR.,** investment company executive, consultant; b. Bryan, Tex., Sept. 21, 1938; s. Louis Milton and Margaret (Stromberg) T.; m. Anne Strand, Aug. 5, 1961 (div. Feb. 1992); children: Louis Milton III, Eric Norman, Christopher Scott, Mary Margaret, Mary Elizabeth; m. Emily Allan, Helen Aubrey. BS, Iowa State U., 1961, MS with honors, 1969. News editor, anchor Sta. WOI-TV-AM-FM, Ames, Iowa, 1960-61; commd. 2d lt. U.S. Army, 1961, resigned, 1974; advanced through grades to lt. col. USAR, 1981; asst. press sec. The White House, Washington, 1974-75; asst. to pres. Am. Enterprise Inst., Washington, 1975-76; dir. pub. affairs Nonprescription Drug Mfrs. Assn., Washington, 1976-78; sr. v.p. Nat. Assn. Home Builders, Washington, 1978-82; pres., CEO, Nat. Investor Rels. Inst., Vienna, Va., 1982—. Individual investor adv. com. NY Stock Exch., NYC, 1990—92, NYC, 2004—; new founds. working group Harvard U. John F. Kennedy Sch. Cambridge, Mass., 1992—94; consumer affairs adv. com. SEC, Washington, 1996—99; chmn. adv. coun. Greenlee Sch. Journalism and Comm., Iowa State U., Ames, 2005—, liberal arts and scis. dean's coun., 2001—. Author: The Handbook of Investor Relations, 1989; contbr. articles to profl. jours. Va. chmn. U.S. Equestrian Team, Gladstone, NJ, 1978—82; dressage judge Am. Horse Shows Assn., Lexington, Ky., 1979—86; bd. dirs. Nat. Coun. Econ. Edn., 2001—04. Recipient Disting. Svc. award, Investment Edn. Inst., 1987, Investor Rels. Mag. and Barron's lifetime achievement award, 2000, J.W. Schwartz award, Iowa State U., 2001. Mem. Investor Rels. Assn., Internat. Investor Rels. Fedn., Am. Hanoverian Soc. (disting. mem., pres. 1988-94), Univ. Club, Phi Kappa Phi. Avocations: equestrian sports, golf, wine collecting, breeding horses. Home and Office: Home Again Farm 11539 Spicers Mill Rd Orange VA 22960-2103

**THOMPSON, MACK EUGENE,** historian, educator; b. Burley, Idaho, Feb. 24, 1921; s. Eugene and Nora (McFate) T.; m. Helen Goldhamer, Oct. 30, 1945. AB, Queen's Coll., CUNY, 1948; MA, Brown U., 1951, PhD, 1955. Instr. history Brown U., 1954-55; asst. prof. Calif. Inst. Tech., 1955-56, U. Calif. at Riverside, 1956-62, asso. prof., 1962-66, prof., 1966-77; emeritus prof., 1977—; chmn. div. humanities U. Calif. at Riverside, 1961-63, asso. univ. dean acad. planning, 1965-66, dean, div. undergrad. studies, 1971-74; exec dir. Am. Hist. Assn., Washington, 1974-81. Chmn. editorial bd. Experiment and Innovation: New Directions in Edn., U. Calif., 1966-68 Author: The Ward-Hopkins Controversy and the American Revolution in Rhode Island: An Interpretation, 1959, Moses Brown, Reluctant Reformer, 1962, Causes and Circumstances of the Du Pont Family's Emigration, 1969. Bd. dirs. Harry S. Truman Libr. Inst., 1974-81. With AUS, 1942-45. Home: 1378 River Oaks Ct Oldsmar FL 34677-4828

**THOMPSON, MARGARET M.,** physical education educator; b. Merrifield, Va., Aug. 1, 1921; d. Lesley L. and Madeline (Shawen) T. BS, Mary Washington Coll., 1941; MA, George Washington U., 1947; PhD, U. Iowa, 1961. Tchr., supr. phys. edn. Staunton (Va.) City Schs., 1941-44; tchr. jr. high sch. phys. edn. Arlington County, Va., 1944-47; instr. women's phys. edn. Fla. State U., Tallahassee, 1947-51; instr., asst. prof., assoc. prof. phys. edn. Purdue U., Lafayette, Ind., 1951-65, dir. gross motor therapy lab., 1963-65; assoc. prof. phys. edn. U. Mo., Columbia, 1965-68, prof., 1968-71, dir. Cinematography and Motor Learning Lab. Dept. Health and Phys. Edn., 1965-71; prof. phys. edn. U. Ill., Champaign-Urbana, 1971-87, prof. emeritus, 1987—. Vis. prof. Escola de Educação Física, U. de São Paulo, Brazil, 1985; vis. prof. phy. edn. Inst. Bioscis. de Rio Claro, U. Estadual Paulista, Brazil, 1991. Author: (with Barbara B. Godfrey) Movement Pattern Checklists, 1966, (with Chappelle Arnett) Perceptual Motor and Motor Test Battery for Children, 1968, (with Barbara Mann) An Holistic Approach to Physical Education Curriculum: Objectives Classification System for Elementary Schools, 1977, Gross Motor Inventory, 1976, revised edit., 1980, Developing the Curriculum, 1980, Setting the Learning Environment, 1980, Sex Stereotyping and Human Development, 1980; also film strips, articles. Mem.: AAHPER. Home and Office: 1311 Wildwood Ln Mahomet IL 61853-9770

**THOMPSON, MARGIE ANN,** artist; b. L.A., Nov. 5, 1934; d. John William Jr. and Odessa Addie Meek; m. Donald Leroy Thompson, June 29, 1956; children: Mark(dec.), Laurie, Donna, Lee. Grad. high. sch. Various office positions, Calif., 1952—80; freelance graphic designer Saugus, Calif., 1980—88; advt. designer The Signal, Saugus, 1988—89; watercolor artist Quartz Hill, Calif., 1990—. Mem.: Antelope Valley Allied Arts Assn. (various positions 1990—97). Republican. Personal E-mail: donandmargie@adelphia.net.

**THOMPSON, MARIAN NELL,** poetry, historical, non-fiction and fiction writer, educator, poet; b. Birmingham, Ala., Aug. 30, 1938; d. Euclid Derring and Gena Grace Meadows; m. Claude Thompson, Aug. 2, 1962; children: Steven Claude, Shirley Nell. BS, Samford U., Homewood, AL, 1959. Salesperson Darling Shoppe, Birmingham, Ala., 1955—56; student asst. Samford Libr., East Lake, Ala., 1956—59; youth dir. various churches, Birmingham, Ala., Ocilla, Ga., and Flint, Mich.; educator Atherton Elem. Sch., Flint, Mich., 1959—61; writer, student libr. asst. New Orleans Seminary Libr., New Orleans, 1961—62; educator Chalmette El. Sch., Chalmette, La., 1962—63; preschool dir. Golden Acres Bapt. Ch., Pasadena, Tex., 1979—88; educator St. Pias Parochial Sch., Pasadena, Tex., 1970—74; Richey E & South Shaver Elem. Schools, Pasadena, 1989—98. Substitute tchr. Pasadena Schools, Pasadena, Tex., 1970—74; vol. Golden Acres Sch. Libraries, Pasadena, Tex., 1970—79. Author short stories, (chapbook) Thank God For His Creations, (poetry) Wheels of Thoughts, Strong Foundations Building for a Proud Future, 2003, Wonderful But Troublesome Times, The James Family Moving to Texas, Transforming in the Firm Foundation, 2003. Sustaining and life membership Rep. Party, 2001, 2002. Recipient Life Membership, Internat. Libr. of Photography, 2001. Mem.: AARP, Golden Vista Ext. for Home Edn. R-Consevative. Baptist. Avocations: music, reading, writing, photography. Office: Read Writing of MYNE 2722 Randolph Road Pasadena TX 77503-4244 E-mail: Marian_Tho@msn.com.

**THOMPSON, MARK S.,** electronics executive; BS in Chemistry, SUNY; PhD in Inorganic Chemistry, Univ. NC. V.p. OEM group Raychem Electronics; v.p.; gen. mgr. power components divsn. Tyco Electronics; CEO Big Bear Networks, 2001—04; exec. v.p. mfg. and tech. group Fairchild Semiconductor Internat., Portland, Maine, 2004—05, pres., CEO, dir., 2005—. Bd. dir. Big Bear Networks. Office: Fairchild Semiconductor 82 Running Hill Rd South Portland ME 04106 Office Phone: 207-775-8100.

**THOMPSON, MARTIN CHRISTIAN,** retired news executive; b. Council Bluffs, Iowa, Oct. 25, 1938; s. Ross Kenneth and Mary Ellen (Pierce) T.; m. Janet Ann Morrow, Aug. 4, 1962; children: Chris Michael, Sean Martin. BA in Communications, U. Wash., 1960. Newsman Sta. KEDO, Longview, Wash., 1960-61; news dir. Sta. KREW, Sunnyside, Wash., 1961-66; newsman AP, Seattle, 1966-68, corr. Reno, 1968-70, newsman San Francisco, 1970-72, news editor, 1972-75, chief of bur. San Francisco, 1975-86, Los Angeles, 1986-88, mng. editor N.Y.C., 1989-92, dir. state news, 1992—2003; ret., 2003. Presbyterian.

**THOMPSON, MARTYN PHILIP,** political and literary studies educator, translator; b. Hitchin, Gt. Britain and No. Ireland, Nov. 13, 1945; arrived in U.S., 1991; s. Philip John and Doris Primrose Thompson; m. Penelope Ann Burden, Jan. 15, 1972; 1 child, Daniel. BS in Econs., London Sch. Econs.,

1967; PhD, London U., 1974; Dr. phil. habil., Tübingen (Germany) U., 1984. Lectr. in polit. studies London U., 1971-74; lectr. Tübingen, 1974-76, asst. prof., 1976-85, assoc. prof., 1985-87, prof. lit. and intellectual history, 1987-91; prof. polit. theory Tulane U., 1991—. Founder, mem. exec. com. German Soc. Study of Polit. Thought, Münster, 1989; vice chmn. Conf. for Study of Polit. Thought, 1991-96, chmn., 1996; mem. nat. screening com. for Fulbright Awards, Inst. Internat. Edn., N.Y.C., 2000—. Author: Ideas of Contract in the Age of John Locke, 1987; editor: Locke and Kant: Historical Reception and Contemporary Relevance, 1991, co-editor Yearbook of German Political Thought, 11 vols., 1991—; contbr. articles to profl. jours. Huntington Libr. and Art Gallery fellow, 1980; fellow commoner Churchill Coll., Cambridge U., Eng., 1985—; recipient Mellon fellowship William Andrews Clark Meml. Libr., UCLA, 1981. Mem. Am. Polit. Sci. Assn., Polit. Studies Assn. Gt. Britain, Inst. Hist. Rsch. U.K., Collingwood Soc. UK (hon. life), Deutsche Gesellschaft zur Erforschung des politischen Denkens (exec. com. 1989-2001). Avocations: travel, chess, non-pedigree dogs. Office: Tulane Univ Dept Polit Sci St Charles Ave New Orleans LA 70118-5698 E-mail: martynpt@aol.com, mpt@tulane.edu.

**THOMPSON, MARY ELIZABETH,** application developer; d. William Reid Jones and Mildred Faye King; 1 child, Barbara Chancee Craig. MA, St. Mary Coll., 1995; BFA, U. of Kans., 1963. Cert. Computer Programming and Operations Ga., 1980; supr. devel. program for higher edn. Art dir. Quantico Va. Dependents Sch. Sys., Quantico, Va., 1964—65, Camp LeJeune NC Dependents Sch. Sys., Camp Lejeune, NC, 1965—67; computer programmer analyst Bank of the South, Atlanta, 1980—82, Hanes Corp., Atlanta, 1982—82; computer programming instr. Cobb County Cmty. Sch. Sys., Marietta, Ga., 1983—83; computer info. sys. instr. Johnson County C.C., Overland Park, Kans., 1987—88; computer info. sys. sr. prof. DeVry U., Kansas City, Mo., 1988—, suprv. devel. program, 2005—. Kansas designer craftsman show, (Charles Rombold Art Award, 1963), philharmonic showhouse book. Mem. Jr. Women's Philharm. Assn., Kansas City, Mo., 1970—73; chairperson Alpha Phi Help Lick Heart Disease, Kansas City, Mo., 1974; mem. Jr. League of Johnson County, Overland Park, Kans., 1998—99. Recipient New Prof. Prime Addition award, DeVry U., 1988, Mo. Governor's award for Excellence in Tchg. and Performance Excellence in Edn., The State of Mo., 2004. Mem.: Kans. City Profl. Devel. Coun., Micro Focus User Group, Assn. of Info. Tech. Profls., Alpha Phi Sorority (life; alumni rep. 1963—63). Achievements include development of faculty adv. for portfolio devel; exploring teamwork in the classroom seminar; textbook selection chairperson; assessment faculty adv. com; development of mentor to new faculty. Home: 10801 W 115th St Overland Park KS 66210 Office: DeVry U 11224 Holmes Rd Kansas City MO 64131 Office Phone: 816-941-0430. E-mail: mbthompson@kc.devry.edu.

**THOMPSON, MARY KOLETA,** small business owner, not-for-profit developer; b. Portsmouth, Va., Dec. 27, 1938; m. James Burton Thompson, May 5, 1957; children: Burt, Suzan, Kate, Jon. BFA, U. Tex., 1982; postgrad., Boston U.; MA in Philanthropy and Devel., St. Mary's U. Minn., 1999. Cert. non-profit mgmt. Pres., CEO The Planning Resource People, Burnet, Tex., 1990—; Tex. fin. devel. specialist ARC Tex., 1994-98; devel. dir. Very Spl. Arts Tex., 1991-92; dir. devel. ARC, Austin, 1992-94; pub. affairs adminstr. Pink Palace Mus. and Memphis Mus. Inc., Memphis, 1998; CEO Lamapasas C. of C., Lampasas, TX, 1998-99; pres., CEO Assn. Non-Profit Orgns., 1998—, Tex. Assn. Bed and Breakfast Innkeepers, 1998; pres. A Little Cottage B&B, 1999—2004; owner Heritage Sta. Antiques, 1999—. Dir. Tex. Children's Mus., Fredericksburg, 1987-88, Internat. Hdqrs. SHAPE Command Arts and Crafts Ctr., 1985-86; com. chmn. Symposium for Encouragement Women in Math. and Natural Sci., U. Tex., Austin, 1990; instr. nonprofit mgmt., fin. devel. bd. leadership, grant proposal writing Ctrl. Tex. Coll., 2002—. Sculptor portrait busts. Bd. dirs. Teenage Parent Coun., Austin, 1990-92, ARC. Named U.S. Vol. of Yr., NATO-Shape Belgium Cmty. Svcs., 1986; grantee, NEA, 1988. Mem.: AAUW (life; pres. 1990—92), Women in Comm. (co-chmn. SW regional conf.), Lometa Lions Club (pub. rels. com. 1999—), Heritage Station Antique Vehicle Show (founder), Heritage Station Antiques Show and Sale (founder), Leadership Tex. (life), U. Tex. Ex-Student Assn. (life), Heritage Station Antiques Forum (founder), Raleigh Tavern Soc. (founder), Leadership Tex. Alumnae Assn. (bd. dir.), Tex. Hist. Found (life). Avocations: writing, lecturing, meeting and strategic planning.

**THOMPSON, MICHAEL,** lawyer; b. Des Moines, Aug. 2, 1951; s. Harold L. and Carolyn Annette (Yacinich) T.; m. Barbara Ann Haafke, Oct. 29, 1977 (div. Oct. 1984). BA, U. No. Iowa, 1973; JD, U. Iowa, 1976, MA, 1977. Bar: Iowa 1976, N.Y. 1979, Mo. 1980, Tex. 1994, Ill. 1999, U.S. Ct. Appeals (2d cir.) 1980, U.S. Ct. Appeals (7th cir.) 1982, U.S. Ct. Appeals (D.C. cir.) 1981, U.S. Ct. Appeals (fed. cir.) 1988, U.S. Ct. Internat. Trade 1988, U.S. Supreme Ct. 1984. Asst. atty. gen. Iowa Dept. Justice, Des Moines, 1976; economist Iowa Commerce Commn., Des Moines, 1976-77; spl. asst. N.Y. Pub. Svc. Commn., Albany, 1977-80; commerce counsel Mo. Pacific R.R., St. Louis, 1980-83; atty. Southwestern Bell Corp., St. Louis, 1983—86; exec. v.p., gen. counsel SBC Internat. Devel. Corp., 1986—2000; pvt. practice Chgo., 2000—. Adj. instr. corp. fin. Drake U., Des Moines, 1977; lectr. U. Chgo. Law Sch., 2006—. Mem.: ABA, Caxton Club (pres. 2003—05), Union League Club, Arts Club Chgo., Grolier Club, Houston Yacht Club, Chgo. Yacht Club. Republican. Office: 401 N Michigan Ave Ste 1200 Chicago IL 60611 E-mail: michaelthompsonlaw@earthlink.net.

**THOMPSON, MICHAEL DAVID,** physician; b. Toronto, Canada, July 3, 1961; s. Samuel John Thompson and Dorothy Gwendolyn Armstrong; m. Angela Mary Nervi, June 7, 1996; children: Mary Claire, Matthew Christopher. BS in Engring., U. Mass., 1983; MSEE, Univ. So. Calif., LA, 1985; MD, U. Mass., 1993. Diplomate Nat. Bd. of Med. Examiners, 1995, Am. Bd. of Surgery, 1999, Am. Bd. of Plastic Surgery, 2002. Systems engr. Hughes Aircraft Corp., LA, 1983—88; physician New Eng. Plastic Surgery, Fallon Clinic, Worcester, Mass., 2001—. Author: (abstract presentation) Internat. Ultrasonic Imaging Conf. Vol. Canton Youth Hockey, Canton, Mass., 2005—06. Recipient Ann. Housestaff Tchg. award, Dartmouth Med. Sch., 1997, Outstanding Med. Educator, Worcester Med. Ctr., 2003, 2004; Fellowship, Howard Hughes Found., 1983—85. Mem.: Mass. Med. Soc., ACS, New Eng. Soc. of Plastic and Reconstructive Surgeons, Am. Soc. of Plastic Surgeons, Am. Soc. for Aesthetic Plastic Surgery (assoc.). Roman Catholic. Avocations: airplane pilot, hockey, travel. Office: New England Plastic Surgery 123 Summer St #570 Worcester MA 01608-1312 Office Phone: 508-368-3199. Office Fax: 508-368-3902.

**THOMPSON, MIKE (C. MICHAEL THOMPSON),** congressman; b. St. Helene, Calif., Jan. 24, 1951; s. Charles Thompson and Beverly (Forni) Powell; m. Janet Thompson, Mar. 8, 1982; children: Christopher, Jon. BA in Political Sci., Calif. State U., Chico, 1982, MA in Public Admin., 1996. Owner, maintenance supr. Beringer Winery; mem. Calif. State Senate, 1991—98, U.S. Congress from 1st Calif. dist., 1999—; mem. armed svcs. com., agr. com. Former chair select com. on Calif.'s Wine Industry; former chair Calif. Senate budget com.; former vice chair Calif. Senate natural resources com.; lectr. San Francisco State U., Calif. State U., Chico. Co-founder, co-chair Congl. Wine Caucus; co-vice chair Congl. Sportsmen's Caucus; mem. New Dem. Coalition, Blue Dog Coalition. Staff sgt. U.S. Army, Vietnam. Decorated Purple Heart. Named Freshman Legislator of the Yr. Calif. Sch. Bds. Assn., 1990, Legislatorof the Yr. Calif. Abortion Rights Action League, Legislator of the Yr. Calif. Assn. Persons with Handicaps, Legislator of the Yr. Police Officers Rsch. Assn. Calif., Legislator of the Yr. Disabled in State Svc., 1994, Senator of the Yr. Calif. Assn. Homes and Svcs. for Aging, 1995; Recipient Disting. Svc. award Calif. State Assn. Counties, Disting. Svc. award Calif. Assn. Hosps., Legis. Leadership award Calif. Assn. Health Svcs. Home, 1994, Disting. Svc. award Aids Project L.A., 1995, Outstanding Senator award Planned Parenthood Affiliates Calif., 1996, Outstanding Senator of the Yr. award Calif. Sch. Bds. Assn., 1996, Outstanding Senator of the Yr. award Calif. Profl. Firefighters, 1996 Democrat. Roman Catholic. Office: US Ho Reps 231 Cannon Ho Office Bldg Washington DC 20515-0501

**THOMPSON, NEIL DANIEL,** retired lawyer; b. Calexico, Calif., Feb. 21, 1935; s. Francis Marion Thompson and Leah Harriet Howell. AB with honors, UCLA, 1957; PhD, Columbia U., 1963; LLB, Harvard U., 1963. Bar: N.Y. 1964, U.S. Dist. Ct. (so. dist.) N.Y. 1965, U.S. Customs Ct. 1967, U. S. Ct. Appeals (2d cir.) 1971, U.S. Supreme Ct. 1973. Assoc. Jas. Maxwell Fassett, N.Y.C., 1964-65, Doman & Ablondi, N.Y.C., 1965-69, Pollack & Kaminsky, N.Y.C., 1969-80; pvt. practice N.Y.C., 1980-86; rsch. cons. Salt Lake City 1986—. Author: Family of Bartholomew Stovall, 1993; editor The Genealogist, 1980-96; contbr. articles to profl. jours. Trustee Bd. for Cert. of Genealogists, 1977-89, pres., 1983-86. Fellow Am. Soc. Genealogists (pres. 1992-95), Soc. Genealogists (London), Utah Geneal. Assn. (bd. dirs. 1988-89); mem. Phi Beta Kappa, Phi Mu Alpha. Democrat. Mem. Lds Ch. Avocations: music, stamp collecting/philately, book collecting. Home: 255 N 200 W Salt Lake City UT 84103-4545 Office Phone: 801-521-4732. Personal E-mail: gryphon801@aol.com.

**THOMPSON, N(ORMAN) DAVID,** insurance company executive; b. Rockville Centre, N.Y., July 30, 1934; s. Norman J. and Laurel H. (Johnson) T.; m. Joyce L. Angeletti, June 7, 1958; children: John L., Jennifer L., Sarah S. BA with distinction, Wesleyan U., 1956; LLB, Columbia U., 1959; postgrad., Harvard U., 1973. Bar: N.Y. Pvt. practice law, N.Y.C., 1961-62; corp. sec. Gen. Reins. Corp., N.Y.C., 1964-69, v.p. Greenwich, Conn., 1969, v.p., gen. counsel, sec., 1976-77; exec. v.p. N.Am. Reins. Corp., N.Y.C., 1977-78, pres., 1978-92; chmn., CEO Swiss Reins. Am. Corp. (formerly N.Am. Reins.), 1992-95, Swiss Re Am. Holding Corp. (formerly SwissRe Holding Co.), 1992-97; chmn. SwissRe Group Cos. (U.S.), 1992-95. Dir. Nat. Legal Ctr. for Pub. Interest, chmn., 1992-95; trustee Coll. Ins., 1992, 98. With U.S. Army, 1959-60. Mem. Reins Assn. Am. (chmn. 1982-83), Nat. Assn. Casualty and Surety Execs. (pres. 1986-87), Am. Arbitration Assn. (bd. dirs., chmn. fin. com. 1992-93), Am. Inst. Property and Casualty Underwriters (trustee, 1992-98), Univ. Club (N.Y.C.), Saugatuck Harbor Yacht Club (Westport, Conn.). Home: 47 Kettle Creek Rd Weston CT 06883-2208

**THOMPSON, NORMAN WINSLOW,** surgeon, educator; b. Boston, July 12, 1932; s. Herman Chandler and Evelyn Millicent (Palmer) T.; m. Marcia Ann Veldman, June 12, 1956; children: Robert, Karen, Susan, Jennifer. BA, Hope Coll., 1953; MD, U. Mich., 1957; MD (hon.), U. Linköping, Sweden, 1995. Diplomate Am. Bd. Surgery. From intern to prof. emeritus surgery U. Mich., Ann Arbor, Mich., 1957–2001, prof. emeritus surgery, 2001—. Contbr. articles to profl. jours. Trustee Hope Coll., Holland, Mich., 1973-88. Fellow Royal Australasian Coll. Surgeons (hon.), Royal Coll. Physicians and Surgeons of Glasgow; mem. ACS (gov. 1979-85), Ctrl. Surg. Assn., Western Surg. Assn. (1st v.p. 1992-93, pres. 1994-95), F.A. Coller Surg. Soc. (pres. 1986), Am. Surg. Assn., Am. Thyroid Assn., Soc. Surg. Alimentary Tract, Internat. Assn. Endocrine Surgeons (pres. 1989-91), Internat. Soc. Surgeons (v.p. 1995—), Am. Assn. Endocrine Surgeons (pres. 1980-81, 81-82), Royal Soc. Medicine, Brit. Assn. Endocrine Surgeons, Spanish Assn. Surgeons (hon.), Assn. French Endocrine Surgeons, Scandanavian Surg. Soc., Soc. Surg. Oncology, Turkish Assn. Endocrine Surgeons, Spanish Soc. Surgeons (hon.), Alpha Omega Alpha. Home: 465 Hillspur Rd Ann Arbor MI 48105-1048 Office: Surgery Faculty 1327 Jones Dr Ste 201 Ann Arbor MI 48105 Office Phone: 734-998-0167. Office Fax: 774-998-0173. Business E-Mail: normant@med.umich.edu.

**THOMPSON, OMAR,** art educator, artist; BA in Art Edn., Fla. A&M U., 1977; MFA in Ceramics, Ohio State U., 1980. Asst. prof. art Fla. A&M U., Tallahassee, 1980—81, 2003—, Hampton (Va.) U., 1982—85, The New World Sch. of the Arts/Miami Dade C.C., Fla., 1987—90; adj. prof. Parsons Sch. Design and Cooper Union Sch. Art, NYC, 1992—94; asst. prof. art Atlanta Pub. Schs., 1994—99; Marist Sch., Atlanta, 1999—2003. One-man shows include Fla. A&M U., 1980, 2003, Stanford U., 1990, Emory U., Atlanta, 1995; Birmingham (Ala.) Civil Rights Inst., 2003, Ala. State U., 2004, Fla. State U., 2006, Gadsden Art Ctr., Quincy, Fla., 2004, Tallahassee C.C., 2006, Art-Park Gallery, NYC, 2006, exhibited in group shows at Ga. Coun. Arts and Humanities, 1980, Atlanta Life Ins. Co., 1982 (2d pl. purchase award), 1991 (1st pl. purchase award), High Mus. Art, Atlanta, 1983, Arts Festival of Atlanta, 1990, Nat. Black Arts Festival, Atlanta, Coconut Grove Arts Festival, Miami, Parsons Sch. Design, The New Sch., NYC, 1993, Ga. State U., 1996, Charles H. Wright Mus. African Am. History, Detroit, 2000, Thelma Harris Art Gallery, Oakland, Calif., LaGrange (Ga.) Nat. Biennial, 2002, The Contemporary Art Ctr., Atlanta, 2003, South Cobb Arts Alliance, 2003 (1st pl. award), Fla. State U., 2004, Agnes Scott Coll., 2004, Valentine NY Mag., 2004 (1st pl. mixed media, finalist Arts of Y.), Creative Tallahassee 2005 (1st pl.), Represented in permanent collections Atlanta Life Ins. Co., Martin Luther King Jr. Ctr., John Hope Sch., Atlanta, C. of C., Miami, Fla. A&M U. Libr./Credit Union, Atlanta City Employees Credit Union, Harlem C. of C., NYC, numerous pvt. collections. Address: 1887-A Darryl Dr Tallahassee FL 32301 E-mail: carlton.thompson@famu.edu.

**THOMPSON, OTHO M.,** lawyer, former solicitor; b. Md., Sept. 4, 1945; BA, Morgan State U., 1967; JD, U. Md., 1971. Bar: Md. 1972, Md. Ct. Appeals, US Dist. Ct. (Md.), US Ct. Appeals (4th cir.). US Supreme Ct. Asst. solicitor City of Balt., 1975—93, city solicitor, 1993—96, city solicitor, 1996-2000; ptnr., State & Local Govt. practice Venable LLP, Balt., 2000—. Chmn. authored com. report Citizens' Ad Hoc Com. for Children at Risk, Anne Arundel County Public Schools, 1988—90; mem. Anne Arundel County Pub. Sch. Parents Council, 1988—90, Anne Arundel County Children's Council, 1988—90. Served to major USAR, 1972—81. Mem.: Nat. Bar Assn., Md. Volunteer Lawyers Assn., Internat. Mcpl. Lawyers Assn., Md. State Bar Assn., Anne Arundel County Bar Assn. Saltworks Cmty. Assn., Balt. Assn. for Retarded Citizens, Anne Arundel County YMCA. Office: Venable LLP 1800 Mercantile Bank & Trust Bldg 2 Hopkins Plaza Baltimore MD 21201 Office Phone: 410-244-7452. Office Fax: 410-244-7742. Business E-Mail: omthompson@venable.com.

**THOMPSON, PAMELA PADWICK,** public relations executive; b. Columbus, Ohio, June 13, 1943; d. Frank John and Tiami Judith (Padwick) T.; stepfather, James William Bampton; m. Fairman Rogers Thompson, Jan. 10, 1942; children: Ryder McNeal, Darby McNeal. BA, U. Louisville, 1994; MA, U. Dayton, 1998. Ptnr. Crutcher, Kelly and Assocs., Louisville, 1979-83; owner Transl. Co., Louisville, 1981-83, Technigraphics, Louisville, 1984-87; v.p. dir. individual support Grtr. Louisville Fund for the Arts, Louisville, 1989-92; v.p. comms. John Templeton Found., Radnor, Pa., 1997—. Adj. prof. U. Louisville, 1997. Contbr. articles to profl. jours. including Small Group Behavior. Chair pub. rels. com. Keene Valley Libr., 2000-01; bd. dirs. Louisville Nature Ctr., 1996-97; mem. ad hoc com. State Ky. Biodiversity Coun., Louisville, 1996-97; city commr. City of Rolling Fields, Louisville, 1991-94; alliance bd. dirs. J.B. Speed Art Mus., Louisville, 1986-92. Mem. APA, Soc. for Consumer Psychology, Pub. Rels. Soc. Am., Jr. League Phila., Cosmo. Club Phila., Ausable Club. Episcopalian. Avocations: hiking, gardening, tennis, travel. Home: 4 Porter Ln Rose Valley PA 19086 Office: John Templeton Foundation 300 Conshohocken State Rd Ste 500 Conshohocken PA 19428-3801 Fax: (610) 687-8961. Office Phone: 610-941-5194. Business E-Mail: pthompson@templeton.org.

**THOMPSON, PATRICK S.,** lawyer; b. Muskegon, Mich., July 24, 1967; BA, U. Mich., 1989; JD, Harvard Law Sch., 1992. Bar: Calif. 1992. Ptnr., antitrust, telecom., complex litig. Pillsbury Winthrop LLP, San Francisco. Editor: Antitrust Law Jour., 1996—2002. Chmn. bd. dirs. Calif. Pacific Med. Ctr., dir., 1996—; exec. com. bd. trustees Am. Conservatory Theater; bd. dirs. Francis of Assisi Cmty. Named one of Am. Top Black Attys., Black Enterprise, 2003, Top 20 Lawyers Under Age 40, Daily Jour., Calif., 2004. Mem.: ABA (mem. antitrust section), State Bar Calif. (mem. exec. com. antitrust and unfair competition section). Office: Pillsbury Winthrop LLP 50 Fremont St San Francisco CA 94105-2228 Office Phone: 415-983-1511. Home Fax: 415-983-1200. Business E-Mail: pthompson@pillsburywinthrop.com.

**THOMPSON, PAUL C.,** labor union administrator; m. Roberta Thompson; 2 children. Fireman Atchison, Topeka & Santa Fe Railway, 1959; with Kans. City Southern; pres. Local 298, United Transp. Union, 1968—70, chairperson, 1970—82; internat. v.p. United Transp. Union, 1983—99, gen. sec., treas., 1999—2001, asst. pres., 2001—04, internat. pres., 2004—. Labor rep. to Pres. Clinton's Sch./Work program com., 1993. Office: UTU 14600 Detroit Ave Cleveland OH 44107-4250 Office Phone: 216-228-9400. Business E-Mail: President@utu.org.*

**THOMPSON, PAUL MATTHEW,** neuroscientist; b. York, Eng., June 13, 1971; s. Derek and Cynthia (Jenkinson) T.; m. Lynn Lee Hodges, Sept. 9, 1995. BA in Classical Langs., Oxford (Eng.) U., 1991, MA in Math., 1993; PhD in Neurosci., UCLA, 1998. Rsch. scholar Oxford U., 1989-93; Fulbright scholar Brain Mapping divsn. UCLA, 1993-98; fellow Howard Hughes Med. Inst., Bethesda, Md., 1993-98; prof. neurology UCLA Brain Rsch. Inst., 1998—. Cons. Nathan Kline Inst., N.Y.C., 1998—; sci. investigator NIH Neuro-Imaging Resource, L.A., 1996—, NSF, Bethesda, 1998—. Contbr. over 70 articles to profl. jours. Recipient SPIE Medical Imaging award, 1997, Outstanding Grad. Student of the Yr., UCLA Chancello's Svc. award, 1998, Eiduson award for Neuroscience Rsch., 1998, Di Chiro Outstanding Scientific Paper award, 1998; Rsch. grantee Nat. Ctr. for Rsch. Resources, 1998—, NIH, 1998—, NINDS, 1998—, NSF, 1998—. Mem. U. Calif. Alumni Assn. Achievements include design of new algorithms for brain image analysis and pathology detection; developed new strategies for analyzing brain image data bases and for brain mapping in large human populations; creation of systems to detect and map alterations in brain structure and function; developed system to map growth patterns in brain development. Office: Lab of Neuro Imaging UCLA Sch Med 635 Charles E Young Dr S Ste 225E Los Angeles CA 90095 E-mail: thompson@loni.ucla.edu.*

**THOMPSON, PAUL MICHAEL,** lawyer; b. Dubuque, Iowa, Aug. 30, 1935; s. Frank W. and Genevieve (Cassutt) T.; m. Mary Jacqueline McManus, Jan. 30, 1960; children: Anne, Tricia, Paul, Tim, Jim. BA magna cum laude, Loras Coll., 1957; LL.B., Georgetown U., 1959. Bar: Iowa 1959, DC 1959, Va. 1966. Atty. appellate ct. br. NLRB, Washington, 1962-66; assoc. Hunton & Williams, Richmond, Va., 1966-71, ptnr., 1971—. Adj. prof. The T.C. Williams Sch. Law U. Richmond; adj. prof. law sch. Coll. William and Mary Sch. Law. Served with JAGC, USAF, 1960-62. Mem. ABA, Va. State Bar, Va. Bar Assn., Internat. Bar Assn., Commonwealth Club. Roman Catholic. Office: The TC Williams School Law University of Richmond Richmond VA 23173 Office Phone: 804-289-8856. Personal E-mail: thompmerrypoint@aol.com. Business E-Mail: pthomps3@richmond.edu.

**THOMPSON, PETER J.,** manufacturing executive; Pres. U.S. opers. Schweitzer-Mauduit Internat., Inc., Alpharetta, Ga., 1995—. Office: Schweitzer-Mauduit Internat Inc 100 N Point Ctr E Ste 600 Alpharetta GA 30022-8263

**THOMPSON, PETER JOHN,** music educator, director; b. Milw., Jan. 23, 1963; s. John and Ruth Thompson; m. Susan Beth Schoenemann, June 16, 1988; 1 child, Laurel Ann. BFA in Music Edn., U. Wis., 1986; MusM in Edn., Vandercook U., 1993. Cert. educator Wis., 1986. Dir. bands Elcho (Wis.) H.S., 1987—89, Cath. Meml. H.S., Waukesha, Wis., 1990—98, Adams-Friendship (Wis.) H.S., 1998—99, South Milw. (Wis.) H.S., 1999—. Mem.: Internat. Assn. Jazz Educators, Nat. Band Assn., Wis. Bandmasters' Assn. Avocations: flying, golf, bicycling. Home: 2962 South 80th Street West Allis WI 53219 Office: South Milwaukee High School 801 15th Avenue South Milwaukee WI 53172 Office Phone: 414-766-5176. Personal E-mail: jazz8888@ameritech.net. Business E-Mail: pthompson@sdsm.k12.wi.us.

**THOMPSON, PETER L.,** lawyer; s. David D. and Lynn P. Thompson; m. Amy A. Aldredge, Sept. 12, 1987; children: Elizabeth R., Bernard D., Miles M. BS, Bowdoin Coll., 1991; JD, U. Maine, 1994. Cert.: Maine 1994. Atty. Law Offices of Peter L. Thompson, Portland, Maine, 1994—. Dir. Consumer Health Law Program, Augusta, Maine, 1997—. Active Million Dollar Advocates Forum, 2004—; bd. dirs. Brain Injury Assn. Maine, Augusta, 2001—, Disability Rights Ctr., Augusta, 2004—. Mem.: Am. Trial Lawyers Am., Maine Employment Lawyers Assn., Maine Bar Assn., Maine Trial Lawyers Assn. Office: Law Offices of Peter L Thompson 217 Commercial St Unit 200 Portland ME 04101 Office Phone: 207-874-0909. Business E-Mail: peter@ptlawoffice.com.

**THOMPSON, PETER LAYARD HAILEY, SR.,** landscape and golf course architect, architectural firm executive; b. Modesto, Calif., Apr. 26, 1939; BS in East Asian Studies, U. Oreg., 1962, B in Landscape Architecture, 1971, M in Urban Planning, 1971; postgrad., U. Calif., Berkeley, 1975, Nat. U. Registered landscape arch., Calif., Oreg., Wash., Nev. With Oreg. Planning Commn., Lane County, 1965-70, commr. Eugene, 1981-83; sr. assoc. Ruff, Cameron, Lacoss, Eugene, 1971-75; prin. Peter L. H. Thompson & Assocs., Eugene, 1975-83, John H. Midby & Assocs., Las Vegas, Nev., 1983-86, Thompson-Wihlborg, Ltd., Corte Madera, Calif., 1982-89, Thompson Planning Group (now Thompson Golf Planning), Ltd., Novato, Calif., 1989—. With Oreg. Planning Commn., commr., 1981-83, Novato, Calif. Planning Commn., commr 1989-93, pres. 1989-93; spkr. Oreg. Home Builders Conf., 1980, Pacific Coast Builders Conf., 1984, Tacoma Country Club Pro-Pres. Tournament, 1991, Marodna Links Men's Golf Club, 1991, Twin Lakes Country Club Pro-Pres. Tournament, 1992, Golf Expo, Palm Springs, Calif., 1993, 95, Golf Expo, Nashville, 1993, Golf Expo, Monterey, Calif., 1994, others. Contbr. articles to mags. Mem. citizen's adv. bd. City of Eugene, Oreg., City of Las Vegas. Mem. USGA, Am. Soc. Landscape Archs., Am. Assn. Planners Nat. Golf Found, Urban Land Inst., Rotary Internat. Office: Thompson Golf Planning Ltd 1510 Grant Ave Ste 305 Novato CA 94945-3146 Office Phone: 415-878-2020.

**THOMPSON, PETER M.,** retired food products executive; b. Australia; Student, Oxford U.; Columbia U. Regional v.p. for Brazil Pepsi-Cola Internat., 1980—83; CEO Grand Met. PLC, 1984—94; pres. Snack Ventures Europe, Walkers Snack Foods Pepsi-Cola Internat., 1994—96, pres., COO, 1996—98, pres., CEO, 1998—2001, Pepsico Beverages Internat., Pepsico, Inc., Purchase, NY, 2001—04; ret., 2004. Office: Pepsico Beverages Internat 700 Anderson Hill Rd Purchase NY 10577

**THOMPSON, PHILIP C.,** lawyer, investment advisor, educator; b. Balt., Oct. 21, 1945; s. Earl Clinton and Virginia (Baugh) Thompson; m. Julie Ann Young, June 10, 1948; children: Kathryn Adair, Julia Hamilton, Philip Clinton Jr. BA, Washington and Lee U., 1967, BS, 1968, JD, 1971. Bar: Ga. 1973, U.S. Dist. Ct. (no. dist.) Ga. 1973. Ptnr. Jones, Day, Reavis & Pogue, Atlanta, 1973—86, Dow, Lohnes & Albertson, Atlanta, 1986—94, Arnall, Golden, Gregory LLP, Atlanta, 1994—2004, Duane Morris LLP, Atlanta, 2004—. Adj. prof. Emory U., Atlanta, 2003—. Capt. U.S. Army, 1972—73. Mem.: Capital City Club. Republican. Reformed Anglican. Avocations: youth programs, gardening, running, tennis, chess. Office Phone: 404-253-6920. Business E-Mail: philip.thompson@duanemorris.com.

**THOMPSON, PHYLLIS D.,** judge, lawyer; b. Washington, Oct. 1, 1952; BA in Anthropology, with distinction, George Washington U., 1974; MA in Religion (focus in Ethics), Princeton U., 1976; JD with high honors, George Washington U., 1981. Bar: DC 1981. Instr., lectr. Georgetown U., Washington, 1977-81; joined Covington & Burling, Washington, 1982—, now ptnr., fed. benefits programs practice group; assoc. judge DC Ct. Appeals, Washington, 2006—. Instr. & lectr. - Theology Dept. Georgetown U., Washington, 1977—81. Co-author (with Susan L. Burke): Analysis Has Its Privileges: Compliance Rev. May Be Protected From Discovery, 1999. Mem.: Am. Health Lawyers Assn., DC Bar Assn. (steering com. affairs divsn.). Office: Covington & Burling 1201 Pennsylvania Ave NW PO Box 7566 Washington DC 20044-7566 also: DC Ct of Appeals Moultrie Courthouse 500 Indiana Ave NW Washington DC 20001 Office Phone: 202-662-5668. Office Fax: 202-662-6291. Business E-Mail: pthompson@cov.com.*

**THOMPSON, RALPH GORDON,** federal judge; b. Oklahoma City, Dec. 15, 1934; m. Barbara Irene Hencke, Sept. 5, 1964; children: Lisa, Elaine, Maria. BBA, U. Okla., 1956, JD, 1961. Bar: Okla. 1961. Spl. agt. Office of Spl. Investigations, USAF, 1957—60; ptnr. Thompson, Thompson, Harbour & Selph (and predecessors), Oklahoma City, 1961-75; judge U.S. Dist. Ct. for Western Dist. Okla., Oklahoma City, 1975—; chief judge U.S. Dist. Ct. (we. dist.) Okla., 1986-93. Mem. Okla. Ho. of Reps., 1966-70, asst. minority floor leader, 1969-70; spl. justice Supreme Ct. Okla., 1970-71; tchr. Harvard Law Sch. Trial Advocacy Workshop, 1981—; apptd. by chief justice of U.S. to U.S. Fgn. Intelligence Surveillance Ct., 1990-97; elected to jud. conf. of the U.S., 1997; apptd. to Edward J. Devitt Disting. Svc. Justice award selection com., 1997-99; apptd. by chief justice of U.S. to exec. com. of Jud. Conf. of the U.S., 1998-2000; coord. Long Range Planning for Fed. Judiciary, 1999-2000. Co-author: Bryce Harlow: Mr. Integrity, Bob Burke and Ralph G. Thompson, 2000. Rep. nominee for lt. gov., Okla., 1970; chmn. bd. ARC, Oklahoma City, 1970-72; chmn. pres. Okla. Young Lawyers Conf., 1965; mem. bd. visitors U. Okla., 1975-78. Lt. USAF, 1957-60, col. Res., ret. Decorated Legion of Merit; named Oklahoma City's Outstanding Young Man, Oklahoma City Jaycees, 1967, Outstanding Young Oklahoman, Okla. State Jr. C. of C., 1968, Outstanding Fed. Trial Judge, Okla. Trial Lawyers Assn., 1980; recipient Regents Alumni award U. Okla., 1990, Disting. Svc. award, 1993, Jour. Record Pub. Co. award for Disting. Svc., 2001, Humanitarian award Oklahoma City Pub. Schs. Found., 2003; inducted Okla. Hall of Fame, 1995, Fellow Am. Bar Found.; mem. ABA, Fed. Bar Assn., Okla. Bar Assn. (chmn. sect. internat. law and gen. practice 1974-75), Oklahoma County Bar Assn. (Jud. Svc. award 1988), Jud. Conf. U.S. (com. on ct. adminstrn. 1981-89, com. on fed-state jurisdiction 1988-91), U.S Dist. Judges Assn. 10th Cir. (pres. 1992-94), Rotary (hon.), Order of Coif, Am. Inns of Ct. (pres. XXIII 1995-96), Phi Beta Kappa (pres. chpt. 1985-86, Phi Beta Kappa of Yr. 1991), Beta Theta Pi, Phi Alpha Delta. Episcopalian. Office: US Dist Ct 200 NW 4th St Oklahoma City OK 73102-3027

**THOMPSON, RALPH NEWELL,** former chemical corporation executive; b. Boston, Mar. 4, 1918; s. Ralph and Lillian May (Davenport) T.; m. Virginia Kenniston, Jan. 31, 1942; children: Pamela, Nicholas, Diana. BS, MIT, 1940. Research engr. Middlesex Products Co., Cambridge, Mass., 1940-42; tech. dir. Falulah Paper Co., Fitchburg, Mass., 1945-48; staff engr. to v.p., div. gen. mgr. Calgon Corp., Pitts., 1948-70; v.p. mktg., corp. devel. Pa. Indsl. Chem. Corp., Clairton, 1970-74; gen. mgr. chem. div. Thiokol Corp., Trenton, NJ, 1974-76, group v.p.-chem. Newtown, Pa., 1976-82; marine artist, specializing in lighthouses and historic sailing vessels, 1982—. Dir. Mulford Co. Inc., Mass., 1956-82, Thiokol Can. Ltd., 1975-82, Thiokol Chems., Ltd., Eng., 1976-82, Toray Thiokol Co. Ltd., Japan, 1976-82, Nisso-Ventron K.K., Japan, 1977-82, S.W. Chem. Services Inc., Tex., 1978-82, S.W. Plastics Europe (S.A.), Belgium, 1978-82, Dynachem. Corp., Calif., 1979-82, Carstab Corp., Ohio, 1980-82 Patentee in field. Mem. Mt. Lebanon (Pa.) Civic League, 1950-74. Served with USNR, 1942-45. Recipient Goodreau Meml. Fund medal in chemistry, 1936 Fellow Am. Inst. Chemists; mem. TAPPI (contributor monograph series 1950-65), N.Y. Acad. Scis., Soc. Chem. Industry, Nat. Maritime Soc., Am. Soc. Marine Artists, Mil. Order World Wars, Pa. Soc., Soc. Descs. Colonial Clergy. Republican. Presbyterian. E-mail: thompsonrn@verizon.net.

**THOMPSON, RAYMOND HARRIS,** retired anthropologist, educator; b. Portland, Maine, May 10, 1924; s. Raymond and Eloise (MacIntyre) T.; m. Molly Kendall, Sept. 9, 1948; children: Margaret Kelsey Luchetta, Mary Frances. BS, Tufts U., 1947; A.M., Harvard U., 1950, PhD, 1955. Fellow div. hist. research Carnegie Instn., Washington, 1950-52; asst. prof. anthropology, curator Mus. Anthropology, U. Ky., 1952-56; faculty U. Ariz., 1956-97, prof. anthropology, 1964—, Riecker Disting. prof., 1980-97, head dept., 1964-80; emeritus, 1997; dir. Ariz. State Mus., 1964-97; emeritus, 1997. Mem. adv. panel program in anthropology NSF, 1963-64, mem. mus. collections program, 1983-85; mem. NSF grad. fellowship panel Nat. Acad. Scis.-NRC, 1964-66; mem. research in nursing in patient care rev. com. USPHS, 1967-69; com. on social sci. comm. edn. in agr. and natural resources Nat. Acad. Scis., 1968-69; mem. anthropology com. examiners Grad. Record Exam., 1967-70, chmn., 1969-70; mem. com. recovery archaeol. remains, 1972-77, chmn., 1973-77; collaborator Nat. Park Service, 1972-76; mem. Ariz. Hist. Adv. Commn., 1966-97, chmn., 1971-74, chmn. hist. sites rev. com., 1971-83; chmn. Ariz. Humanities Council, 1973-77, mem., 1979-85; adv. bd. Ariz. Hist. Recors, 1976-84; mem. research review panel for archaeology NEH, 1976-77, mem. rev. panel for museums, 1978, Ariz. Archaeology Adv. Commn., 1985-97; cons. task force on archaeology Adv. Council on Historic Preservation, 1978. Author: Modern Yucatecan Maya Pottery Making, 1958; editor: Migrations in New World Culture History, 1958, When is a Kiva, 1990; mem. editl. bd. Science, 1972-77. Trustee Mus. No. Ariz., 1969-84, 86-90; bd. dirs. Tucson Art Mus., 1974-77; cons. Nat. Mus. Act Coun., 1984-86. Served with USNR, 1944-45, PTO. Named Raymond H. Thompson award in his name, Dept. Anthrop., U. Ariz., 2006; recipient Pub. Svc. award, Dept. Interior, 1990. Fellow AAAS (chmn. sect. H 1977-78), Tree-Ring Soc., Am. Anthrop. Assn. (Disting. Svc. award 1980); mem. Soc. Am. Archaeology (editor 1958-62, exec. com. 1963-64, pres. 1976-77, disting. svc. award 1998), Am. Soc. Conservation Archaeology (Conservation award 1980), Seminario de Cultura Maya, Am. Assn. Museums (accreditation vis. com. 1972, 82-90, cons. mus. assessment program 1983-89, repatriation task force 1987, steering com. mus. data collection program 1988-93), Internat. Coun. Museums (assoc.), Coun. Mus. Anthropology (dir. 1978-79, pres. 1980-83), Assn. Sci. Mus. Dirs. (sec.-treas. 1978-80), Ariz. Acad. Sci., Ariz. Archaeol. and Hist. Soc. (Byron Cummings award 1993), Mus. Assn. Ariz. (pres. 1983, 84), Phi Beta Kappa, Sigma Xi. Office: Univ Ariz Ariz State Museum Tucson AZ 85721-0026

**THOMPSON, RICHARD,** psychologist; s. Ralph and Miriam Thompson; m. Sherise Ferguson, Aug. 9, 2005. BA, Acadia U., Wolfville, 1993; PhD, McGill U., Montreal, 2000. Lic. Clin. Psychologist Ill. 2003. Rsch. associated U. Pa., Phila., 1999—2003; assoc. prof. U. Ill., Chgo., 2005—06; dir. of rsch. Juvenile Protective Assn., Chgo., 2003—. Contbr. articles to numerous profl. jour. Mem.: APA. Achievements include research in Longitudinal studies on child abuse and neglect. Office: Juvenile Protective Assn 1333 N Kingsbury Ste 306 Chicago IL 60610 Business E-Mail: rthompson@juvenile.org.

**THOMPSON, RICHARD DICKSON,** lawyer; b. Lexington, Ky., Aug. 14, 1955; s. Lawrence Sidney and Algernon Smith (Dickson) T.; m. Bobbi Dale Magidoff, Aug. 3, 1980; children: Anne Katherine, Harrison Asher, Tracey Ruth. AB, Harvard U., 1977; JD, Stanford U., 1980. Bar: Calif. 1980, U.S. Dist. Ct. (so. dist.) Calif. 1980. Assoc. Rosenfeld Meyer & Susman, Beverly Hills, Calif., 1980-83, Silverberg Rosen Leon & Behr, L.A., 1983-86, assoc. ptnr., 1986-89; ptnr. Silverberg Katz Thompson & Braun, L.A., 1989-95, Bloom, Hergott, Diemer, & Cook, Beverly Hills, Calif., 1995—2000; sr. v.p., corp. devel. then COO The Brodia Group, San Francisco, 2000—02; of counsel Bloom, Hergott Diemer Rosenthal & LaViolette, LLP, Beverly Hills, Calif., 2002—. Former bd. trustees L.A. Copyright Soc. (former pres.). Mem. Order of the Coif, Phi beta Kappa. Office: Bloom Hergott et al 150 S Rodeo Dr Beverly Hills CA 90212 Office Phone: 310-859-6839. E-mail: rdt@bhdrl.com.

**THOMPSON, RICHARD FREDERICK,** psychologist, educator, neuroscientist; b. Portland, Oreg., 1930; s. Frederick Albert and Margaret St. Clair (Marr) T.; m. Judith K. Pedersen, May 22, 1960; children: Kathryn M., Elizabeth K., Virginia St. C. BA, Reed Coll., 1952; MS, U. Wis., 1953, PhD, 1956. Asst. prof. med. psychology Med. Sch. U. Oreg., Portland, 1959-63, assoc. prof., 1963-65, prof., 1965-67; prof. psychobiology U. Calif., Irvine, 1967-73, 75-80; prof. psychology Harvard U., Cambridge, Mass., 1973-74, Lashley chair prof., 1973; prof. psychology, Bing prof. human biology Stanford U., Palo Alto, Calif., 1980-87; Keck prof. psychology and biol. scis. U. So. Calif., L.A., 1987—; dir. neuroscience program, 1989—. Author: Foundations of Physiological Psychology, 1967, (with others) Psychology, 1971, Introduction to Physiological Psychology, 1975; Psychology editor (with others), W.H. Freeman & Co. publs., chief editor, Behavioral Neurosci.,

1983—; editor: Jour. Comparative and Physiol. Psychology, 1981-83; regional editor: (with others) Physiology and Behavior; contbr. (with others) articles to profl. jours. Fellow AAAS, APA (Disting. Sci. Contbn. award 1974, governing coun. 1974—), Soc. Neurosci. (councilor 1972-76); mem. NAS, Am. Acad. Arts and Scis., Internat. Brain Rsch. Orgn., Nat. Sci. Bd., Am. Philos. Soc., Psychonomic Soc. (gov. 1972-77, chmn. 1976), Am. Psychol. Soc. (pres. 1994-96), Western Psychol. Assn. (pres. 1994-95), Soc. Exptl. Psychology (Warren award). Office: Univ of So Calif Neuroscis Program HNB 122 Univ Park Los Angeles CA 90007 Office Phone: 213-740-7350. Business E-Mail: thompson@usc.edu.

THOMPSON, RICHARD LEON, pharmaceutical executive, lawyer; b. Rochester, N.Y., Dec. 5, 1944; s. Leslie L. and Marion (Cosad) T.; m. Catherine Jean Terry, July 6, 1974; children: Kristin Anne, Catherine Elizabeth. AB cum laude, SUNY, Albany, 1966; MA, Syracuse U., 1967; JD, Cath. U., 1975. Staff dir., counsel U.S. Ho. of Reps., Washington, 1973-78; dir. Abbott Labs., Washington, 1978-83; v.p. Squibb Corp., Washington, 1983-89, Bristol-Myers Squibb Corp., Washington, 1989—2001, sr. v.p. policy and govt. affairs, 2001—. Chmn. legis. adv. com. Proprietary Assn., Washington, 1984; bd. dirs. Bus. Govt. Rels. Coun. Mem. com. on changing enrollments Fairfax (Va.) County Pub. Sch., 1983-84, supts. adv. com., 1984-85, mem., 1988-98; mem. Fed. City Coun., 1992; chmn. legis. com. P.R.-U.S.A. Found., 1985-95; co-chair Edn. in 2010; bd. dirs. D.C. Hospice, Bryce Harlow Found., 1990-95; bd. dirs. Ford Theater, 2000—, chmn. 2000-06; chmn. governance com. Meridian Internat. Ctr., 2000-02 1st lt. U.S. Army, 1968-69, Vietnam. Named one of Outstanding Young Men of Am., Jaycees, 1976. Mem. ABA, D.C. Bar Assn., Pharm. Mfrs. Assn. (chmn. Washington reps. com.1988), Congl. Country Club, City Club. Office Phone: 202-783-8609.

THOMPSON, RICHARD LLOYD, retired pastor; b. Lansing, Mich., May 8, 1939; s. Lloyd Walter and Gladys V. (Gates) T.; m. Dianne Lee Tuttle, Nov. 14, 1958; children: Matthew, Beth Anne, Douglas. BA, Azusa Pacific U., 1969; MDiv, Concordia Theol. Sem., 1973; DD, Concordia U., Mequon, Wis., 1997. Aerospace industry test engr. Hycon Mfg. Co., Monrovia, Calif., 1961-69; pastor Trinity Luth. Ch., Cedar Rapids, Iowa, 1973-84, Billings, Mont., 1984-94, Good Shepherd Luth. Ch., Watertown, Wis., 1994—2001; ret., 2001. Chmn. mission com. Iowa E. dist. Luth. Ch. Mo. Synod, 1979-81, 2nd v.p. Iowa dist. E, Cedar Rapids, 1981-84, cir. counselor so. cir. and 2d v.p. Mont. dist., bd. mgr. Concordia plans, St. Louis, 1983-86, bd. dirs., St. Louis, 1986-98, chmn. bd. dirs., 1992-98, mem. commn. on theology and ch. rels., 2001; chmn. bd. dirs. Ambs. and Reconciliation, 2005—; served on various task forces and coms. dealing with structure and vision setting for chs. at local, dist. and nat. level, 1975—. Mem. Nat. Exch. Club, Cedar Rapids, 1982-84, Billings, 1986; pro tem com. structure Commn. Doctrinal Rev., 2001—. With USN, 1957-61. Mem. Kiwanis. Lutheran. Avocations: attending auctions, yard work, travel, exercise activity. Personal E-mail: diarich39@msn.com, rlt50@hotmail.com.

THOMPSON, RICHARD S., lawyer, former prosecutor; b. Jacksonville, Fla., Nov. 26, 1957; m. Jennifer Darby; children: Loree Ann, Darby. BA cum laude, Mercer U., 1979, JD, 1982. Bar: Ga. Asst. dist. atty. Douglas County, Ga.; asst. atty. gen. State of Ga., 1986—88; pvt. practice Statesboro and Vidalia, 1989—95; ptnr. McNatt, Greene & Thompson, Vidalia, Ga., 1995—2001; U.S. atty. so. dist. Ga. US Dept. Justice, 2001—04; ptnr. Weidner & Thompson, LLC, Clarksville, Ga., 2004—. Mem.: Ga. Def. Lawyers Assn. Office: So Dist Ga PO Box 8999 Savannah GA 31412 also: Weidner & Thompson LLC 146 Professional Park Dr PO Box 2017 Clarkesville GA 30523 Office Phone: 706-754-9000. Office Fax: 706-754-0098.

THOMPSON, RICHARD STEPHEN, management consultant; b. Des Moines, Oct. 14, 1931; s. Richard Stephen and Mary Ellen (Dailey) T.; m. Nancy Ann Jensen, Apr. 17, 1954; children—Traci Nan, Gregory Christian, Jonathan Richard BSc, State U. Iowa, 1953; MBA, Ind. U., 1960. Regional dir. Bristol Myers Co., N.Y.C., 1969-75; regional dir. Warner Lambert Co., Morris Plains, NJ, 1975-78; exec. v.p. Milton Bradley Co., Milton Bradley Internat., Inc., Springfield, Mass., 1979-83, pres., 1983-84; sr. v.p. internat., dir. Hasbro, Inc., Pawtucket, RI, 1984-89; pres. Richard Thompson Assocs., London, 1989—. Served to 1st lt. USAF, 1954-55 Mem.: Chatham Beach Tennis (Mass.); Pilgrims (London and N.Y.); American (London); Roehampton (London). Republican. Avocations: tennis, hiking, skiing, reading.

THOMPSON, RICHARD THOMAS, academic administrator; b. Buffalo, Oct. 11, 1939; m. Nancy A. Streeter, July 29, 1959; children: Elizabeth Thompson Grapentine, Richard Thomas Jr., David Bryant. BA, Ea. Mich. U., 1961, MA, 1963; LLD (hon.), Walsh Coll., 2000. Cert. tchr. Mich. Tchr. Warren Consol. Sch., Mich., 1961—66; dean, pres. Highland Lake campus Oakland C.C., Union Lake, 1966—75, pres. Orchard Ridge campus Farmington, 1975—84, v.p. Bloomfield, 1984—88, vice chancellor, 1988—91, chancellor, 1996—2004, pres. Auburn Hills campus, 1995—96, chancellor emeritus, 2004. Arbitrator Better Bus. Bur., Detroit, 1987—; bd. dirs., past chair Providence Hosp., Southfield; cons. examiner North Ctrl. Assn. Commn. Higher Learning, 1988—2004. Contbr. articles to profl. jours. Pres. Oakway Symphony Orch., Livonia, Mich., 1981—85; chair Oakland Literacy Coun., Pontiac, 1988—2002. Recipient Leadership award, Oakland County C. of C., 1987, Tricounty Disting. Svc. award, Detroit Coll. Bus., 1996, Shirley B. Gordon award Distinction, Phi Theta Kappa Internat., 2001. Mem.: Phi Delta Kappa. Home: 6868 W Harbor Dr Elk Rapids MI 49629

THOMPSON, ROB ROY, legislator, writer; b. Rochester, NY, Mar. 29, 1964; s. Robert M. and Elaine M. Thompson. AA, We. Nev. CC, Fallon, Nevada, 1982—86. Homeless social worker Clavary St. Ministry, Memphis, 1989—96; polit. dir. Amb Alan Keyes, Manchester, NH, 1997—2000; legislator NH Ho. Reps, Concord, 2000—02. Author: (books) On Eagles Wings: The Fight for Christian America, Ashley Bay, Nevada Wind. Dir. Alan Keyes NH Presidential Primary, 2000; lobbyist Christian Coalition, Concord, 2002—05. Conservative-R. Anglican. Avocations: writing, history. Home: 83 S Main Box H Concord NH 03301

THOMPSON, ROBERT ALLAN, aerospace engineer; b. Cleve., June 10, 1937; s. Roy Henry and Viola Alverta (Nehls) T.; m. Louise Alberta Saari, Nov. 27, 1970. BSEE, Case Western Reserve U., 1958; postgrad. studies, Cleve. State U., 1959, John Marshall Law Sch., 1970; PhD, Union Inst., 1979. Registered profl. engr., Ohio, Wis., Conn., R.I. Tchr. Cleve. Bd. Edn., 1958-65; rsch. engr. Sohio Satellite Tracking Sta., Standard Oil Rsch. Lab., Cleve., 1958-63, acting dir., 1964-65; dir. Warrensville Hghts. (Ohio) Planetarium and Space Sci Program, 1964-65; tchr. spl. programs faculty Case Inst. Tech., Cleve., 1965; dir. planning phase sci. divsn. Cleve. Supplementary Edn. Ctr., 1965-66; dir. James A Lovell Regional Space Ctr., Milw., 1967-73; engring. and edn. cons. Chgo., 1973-78, Mystic, Conn., 1978—; pres., chmn. bd. Spatialworld Corp., 1982—. Chmn. secondary math. curriculum com. Cleve. Pub. Schs., 1963-64; mem. Wis. Aerospace Edn. Commn., 1968-71; lectr. U. Wis., Milw., 1968-71; sec. Friends of Space Ctr., 1968-75. Author: The New Egoshell: An Individualized Space Age Realty; co-author (with L. Thompson) Egoshell-Planetary Individualism Balanced within Planetary Interdependence, 1987; contbr. articles to profl. jours. Kiwanian faculty adv. Collinwood Key Club, 1959—64. Recipient Leadership award, NE Cleve. Kiwanis, 1961; Goodwin Watson fellow, Union Inst., 1978—79. Fellow: Brit. Interplanetary Assn.; mem.: AIAA (chmn. Wis. sect. 1969—70, sr. mem. Conn. sect., coun. 1984—85, disting. lectr. 1987—89), AAAS, IEEE (sr. life) (chmn. membership com. Cleve. sect. 1965—66, exec. com.), Cleve. Astron. Soc. (exec. com. 1966—67), Cleve. Engring. Soc., Inst. Planetary Egology (pres. 1988—), Union Inst. Alumni Assn., Case Alumni Assn. Home: PO Box 624 Mystic CT 06355-0624 Office: PO Box 2001 Mystic CT 06355-0624 Office Phone: 860-572-0145. Personal E-mail: egoshell@aol.com.

THOMPSON, ROBERT CHARLES, lawyer; b. Council, Idaho, Apr. 20, 1942; s. Ernest Lavelle and Evangeline Montgomery (Carlson) T.; m. Marilyn Anne Wilcox, Jan. 17, 1960 (dec. Mar. 1962); m. Patricia Joan Price, June 1, 1963 (div. 1969); m. Jan Nesbitt, June 29, 1973 (dec. May 1998); m. Shari Lewis, Feb. 7, 1999; children: Christopher, Eric, Tanya, Carrie AB, Harvard U., Cambridge, Mass., 1963, LLB, 1967. Bar: Mass. 1967, Calif. 1983, U.S. Dist. Ct. (ea. dist.) Mass. 1975, U.S. Ct. Appeals (1st cir.) 1976, U.S. Ct. Appeals (9th cir.) 1984, U.S. Dist. Ct. (no. dist.) Calif. 1983, U.S. Dist. Ct. (ea. dist.) Calif., 1996. Assoc. Choate, Hall & Stewart, Boston, 1967-73; asst. regional counsel EPA, Boston, 1973-75, regional counsel, 1975-82, assoc. gen. counsel, 1979-82, regional counsel San Francisco, 1982-84; ptnr. Graham & James, San Francisco, 1984-91, LeBoeuf, Lamb, Greene & MacRae LLP, San Francisco, 1992—, of counsel, 2000—. Contbr. articles to profl. jours. Bd. dirs. Peninsula Indsl. and Bus. Assn., Palo Alto, Calif. 1986-98, chmn. Cambridge Conservation Commn., Mass., 1972-74; cochmn. The Clift Confs. on Environ. Law, 1983-98; assoc. mem. Bay Conservation and Devel. Commn., 1998-2000. John Russell Shaw traveling fellow Harvard Coll., 1963-64; recipient Regional Administs. Bronze medal EPA, 1976, 84. Mem. ABA (chmn. natural resources sect., chmn. com. native Am. natural resources law, spl. com. mktg.), HumanRights Watch, Internat. Pub. What You Pay Campaign, Human RightsFirst, OxFan Am., Phi Beta Kappa. Democrat. Episcopalian. Avocations: yoga, antiques, cooking, gardening. Office: LeBoeuf Lamb Greene & MacRae One Embarcadero Ctr San Francisco CA 94111 E-mail: thomps925@aol.com.

THOMPSON, ROBERT L., JR., pharmaceutical executive, lawyer; b. St. Paul, Aug. 19, 1944; s. Robert L. and Dorothy R. (Bergstrom) T.; m. Carolyn H. Foss, Aug. 4, 1973; children: Sarah, Kathryn, Jill. BA, Macalester Coll., St. Paul, 1967; JD, U. Oreg., 1973; LLM, NYU, 1988. Bar: Minn. 1973, U.S. Dist. Ct. Minn. 1978, N.Y. 1984. Corp. counsel Northrup King Co., Mpls., 1974-84; assoc. gen. counsel Sandoz Corp., N.Y.C., 1984-88, v.p., gen. counsel, sec., 1989-96; exec. v.p., gen. counsel Novartis Corp., N.Y.C., 1997-2001; vice chmn., pres., mng. dir. Novartis India, Ltd., Bombay, 2001—02; v.p., gen. counsel Novartis Insts. for BioMed. Rsch., Inc., 2002—. Mem. adv. bd. FM Global Ins. Co., N.Y.C., 1990-2001; mem. bd. visitors U. Oreg. Law Sch., 1995-2001. 1st lt. U.S. Army, 1968-70. Mem. ABA, Assn. Bar City N.Y. Republican. Presbyterian. Office: Novartis Insts for BioMed Rsch Inc 400 Technology Sq Cambridge MA 02139

THOMPSON, ROBERT LEE, agricultural economist, educator; b. Canton, N.Y., Apr. 25, 1945; s. Robert M. and Esther Louise (Weatherup) T.; m. Karen Hansen, Aug. 9, 1968; children: Kristina Marie, Eric Robert. BS, Cornell U., Ithaca, N.Y., 1967; MS, Purdue U., West Lafayette, Ind., 1969, PhD, 1974; LLD, Dalhousie U., 1999; DSc honoris causa, Pa. State U., 1999. Vol. agriculturalist Internat. Vol. Service, Pakse and Vientiane, Laos, 1968-70; vis. prof. Fed. Univ. Vicosa, Brazil, 1972-73; prof. Purdue U., West Lafayette, Ind., 1974-93, dean of agr., 1987-93; rsch. scholar Internat. Inst. for Applied Systems Analysis, Laxenburg, Austria, 1983; sr. staff economist Coun. Econ. Advisers, Washington, 1983-85; asst. sec. econs. U.S. Dept. Agr., Washington, 1985-87; pres., CEO Winrock Internat. Inst. Agrl. Devel., 1993-98; sr. advisor World Bank, Washington, 1998-99; dir. rural devel., 1999—2002; sr. advisor Ctr. for Strategic and Internat. Studies, 1998—99, Nat. Ctr. for Food and Agr. Policy, Washington, 2003—; Gardner prof. agr. policy U. Ill., Urbana, 2004—. Vis. prof. Econ. Rsch. Svc., USDA, 1979-80; chmn. adv. coun. Nat. Ctr. Food and Agrl. Policy, Washington, 1987-92; mem. Ind. Commn. on Agr. and Rural Devel., 1989-93, Nat. Commn. on Agrl. Trade and Export Policy, 1985-86, Nat. Commn. Internat. Trade, Devel., and Cooperation, 1996-97; mem. bd. agr. NRC, 1987-92; mem. Internat. Policy Coun. on Agr. and Trade, 1987—, chmn., 2000—; mem. USDA Joint Coun. on Food and Agrl. Scis., 1994-96; cons. USAID, OECD, Agr. Can., Ford Found., Brazilian Agr. Ministry, FAO, World Bank, Internat. Food Policy Rsch. Inst., Internat. Maize and Wheat Improvement Ctr., U.S. Feed Grains Coun., Nat. Planning Assn., USIA, Centre for Internat. Econs., Canberra, Club d'Experts en Economie Agricole Internat., Paris, Danish Coun. Rsch. Policy, FAO, Rome; bd. dirs. Cordell Hull Inst., Washington; mem. agrl. policy adv. coun. trade, USDA and US Trade Rep., 2005—. Contbr. numerous articles to profl. publs. Author monographs, book chpts. Bd. dirs. Ind. 4-H Found., Ind. Inst. Agr. Food and Nutrition, 1987-93, Inst. for Sci. in Soc., 1991-93, USDA Grad. Sch., Washington, 1985-87; mem. nat. adv. com. Minorities in Agr., Natural Resources and Related Sci.; bd. dirs. Farm Found., 1987-92, chmn. 1991-92. Recipient Agrl. Rsch. award Purdue U. 1983, Outstanding Alumni award Cornell U., 1988, Superior Svc. award USDA, 1989, Justin Smith Morrill award, 1995, Nat. 4-H Alumni award, 1992, Chgo. Farmers Agriculturalist of Yr. award, 1992, Bob Pim Agrl. Vision award Nat. Forum Agr., 1997; named Humanitarian of Yr., Am. Coll. Nutrition, 1999. Fellow AAAS, Am. Agrl. Econs. Assn. (editl. coun. 1983-85, quality com. award 1979, 91, 93); mem. Internat. Agribus Mgmt. Assn., Am. Econ. Assn., Internat. Assn. Agrl. Economists (pres. 1993-96), Chgo. (Ill.) Coun. Fgn. Rels., Bretton Woods Com., Royal Swedish Acad. Agr. and Forestry (1), Ukrainian Acad. Agrl. Scis., Cosmos Club (Washington), Sigma Xi, Alpha Gamma Rho, Alpha Zeta (Centennial Honor Role award 1997), Gamma Sigma Delta. Republican. Avocation: foreign language study. Office: 412 Mumford Hall MC-710 1301 W Gregory Dr Urbana IL 61801-3608 Office Phone: 217-333-1313. Business E-Mail: rlt@uiuc.edu.

THOMPSON, ROBERT SAMUEL, retired lawyer; b. Cleve., Nov. 2, 1930; s. Wayne Charles Thompson and Cornelia Irene (Anderson) Thompson Baker; m. JoAnne Courtney; children: Robert Dale, Richard Wayne. BA, Hamilton Coll., 1953; JD, U. Mich., 1956; postgrad., Air Command and Staff Coll., Montgomery, Ala., 1967-68. Bar: Mich. 1956, Ohio 1962, U.S. Supreme Ct. 1962, Oreg. 1973. Judge advocate USAF, 1956-77; pvt. practice McMinnville, Oreg., 1977—2003; ret., 2003. Judge mcpl. ct. 1977-2003. Mem. Oreg. Soc. SAR (pres. 1989-90), Oreg. Mcpl. Judges Assn. (pres. 1992-93), Rotary (bd. dirs. McMinnville chpt. 1989), Am. Legion, Masons. Home and Office: 127 NW 19th St Mcminnville OR 97128-2611

THOMPSON, ROBY CALVIN, JR., orthopedic surgeon, educator, department chairman; b. Winchester, Ky., May 1, 1934; s. Roby Calvin and Mary Davis (Guerrant) T.; m. Jane Elizabeth Searcy, May 2, 1959; children: Searcy Lee, Roby Calvin, III, Mary Alexandria. BA, Va. Mil. Inst., 1955; MD, U. Va., 1959. Diplomate Am. Bd. Orthopaedic Surgery (mem. bd. 1983). Intern Columbia Presbyn. Med. Center, N.Y.C., 1959-60, asst. resident, then resident in orthopedic surgery, 1963-67; instr. orthopaedic surgery Coll. Phys. and Surg. Columbia U., 1967-68; mem. faculty Med. Sch. U. Va., 1968-74, prof. orthopaedic surgery, vice chmn. dept. Med. Sch., 1973—94; prof., chmn. dept. Med. Sch. U. Minn., 1974—94; chief med. officer U. Minn. Health Sys., 1995-96, v.p. clin. and acad. affairs, 1996—2001; sr. assoc. dean clin. affairs U. Minn. Sch. Medicine, 1996—. Merit rev. bd. VA, 1977-80; study sect. on applied physiology and orthopedics NIH, 1980-83; adv. coun. NIH, Nat. Inst. Arthritis, Musculoskeletal Disease and Skin, 1987-91; chmn. bd. dirs. U. Minn. Physicians, 2001-05, CEO, 2001—. Trustee Jour. Bone and Joint Surgery, 1988-94, chmn. bd. trustees, 1991-94; contbr. articles to med. jours. Capt. M.C. USAR, 1960-61. Grantee John Hartford Found., NIH Mem. ACS, Orthopaedic Rsch. and Edn. Found. (bd. trustees 1990-96), Am. Acad. Orthopaedic Surgeons (bd. dirs. 1975-76, 83-90, pres. 1986), Orthopaedic Rsch. Soc. (pres. 1978), Am. Orthopaedic Assn., Musculoskeletal Tumor Soc. (pres. 1988-89), U. Va. Med. Alumni Assn. (bd. dirs. 1979-84), Woodhill Club (Wayzata). Republican. Presbyterian. Office: U Minn MMC 293 420 Delaware St SE Minneapolis MN 55455-0374

THOMPSON, RONALD EDWARD, lawyer; b. Bremerton, Wash., May 24, 1931; s. Melville Herbert and Clara Mildred (Griggs) T.; m. Marilyn Christine Woods, Dec. 15, 1956; children: Donald Jeffery, Karen, Susan, Nancy, Sally, Claire BA, U. Wash., 1953, JD, 1958. Bar: Wash. 1959. Asst. city atty. City of Tacoma, 1960—61; pres. firm Thompson, Krilich, LaPorte, West & Lockner, P.S., Tacoma, 1961—99. Judge pro tem Mcpl. Ct., City of Tacoma, Pierce County Dist., 1972—; Pierce County Superior Ct., 1973—. Chmn. housing and social welfare com. City of Tacoma, 1965-69; mem. Tacoma Bd. Adjustment, 1967-71, chmn., 1968; mem. Tacoma Com. Future Devel., 1961-64, Tacoma Planning Commn., 1971-72; bd. dirs., pres. Mcpl. League

Tacoma; bd. dirs. Pres. Tacoma Rescue Mission, Tacoma Pierce County Cancer Soc., Tacoma-Pierce County Heart Assn., Tacoma Grand Cinema, Tacoma-Pierce County Coun. for Arts, Econ. Devel. Coun. Puget Sound, Tacoma Youth Symphony, Kleiner Group Home, Tacoma C.C. Found., Pierce County Econ. Devel. Corp., Wash. Transp. Policy Inst.; Coalition to Keep Wash. Moving, precinct committeeman Rep. party, 1969-73. With AUS, 1953-55; col. Res. Recipient Internat. Cmty. Svc. award Optimist Club, 1970, Patriotism award Am. Fedn. Police, 1974, citation for cmty. svc. HUD, 1974, Disting. Citizen award Mcpl. League Tacoma-Pierce County, 1985; named Lawyer of the Yr. Pierce County Legal Secs. Assn., 1992. Mem. ATLA, Am. Arbitration Assn. (panel of arbitrators), ABA, Wash. State Bar Assn. (Local Hero award 2002), Tacoma-Pierce County Bar Assn. (sec. 1964, pres. 1979, mem. cts. and judiciary com. 1981-82), Wash. State Trial Lawyers Assn., Tacoma-Pierce County C. of C. (bd. dirs., exec. com., chmn.), Downtown Tacoma Assn. (com. chmn., bd. dirs. exec. com., chmn.), Variety Club (Seattle), Lawn Tennis Club, Tacoma Club, Optimist (Tacoma, internat. pres. 1973-74), Phi Delta Phi, Sigma Nu. Roman Catholic. Home: 3101 E Bay Dr NW Gig Harbor WA 98335-7610 Office: PO Box 2091 4411 Point Fosdick Dr Ste 207 Gig Harbor WA 98333-4091 Office Phone: 253-853-7449. Personal E-mail: retpllc@att.net.

THOMPSON, RONELLE KAY HILDEBRANDT, library director; b. Brookings, S.D., Apr. 21, 1954; d. Earl E. and Maxine R. (Taplin) Hildebrandt; m. Harry Floyd Thompson II, Dec. 24, 1976; children: Clarissa, Harry III. BA in Humanities magna cum laude, Houghton Coll., 1976; MLS, Syracuse U., 1976; postgrad., U. Rochester, 1980, 81; cert., Miami U., 1990. Libr. asst. Norwalk (Conn.) Pub. Libr., 1977; elem. libr. Moriah Ctrl. Schs., Port Henry, NY, 1977—78; divsn. coord. pediat. gastroenterology and nutrition U. Rochester (N.Y.) Med. Ctr., 1978—81, cons., pediat. housestaff libr. com., 1980—81; dir. Medford Libr. U. S.C., Lancaster, 1981—83; dir. Mikkelsen Libr., Libr. Assocs., Ctr. for Western Studies, mem. libr. com. Augustana Coll., Sioux Falls, SD, 1983—, adminstrv. pers. coun., 1989—94, 1997—2004. Presenter in field. Contbr. articles to profl. jours. Mem. S.D. Symphony; advisor pers. dept. City of Sioux Falls. Recipient leader award YWCA, 1991; Gaylord Co. scholar Syracuse U., 1976; named S.D. Libr. of Yr., 1998. Mem. ALA, AAUW, Assn. Coll. and Rsch. Librs. (nat. adv. coun. coll. librs. sect. 1987—), Mountain Plains Libr. Assn. (chair acad. sect., nominating com. 1988, pres. 1993-94), S.D. Libr. Assn. (chair interlibr. coop. task force 1986-87, pres. 1987-88, chair recommended minimum salary task force 1988, chair local arrangements com. 1989-90, 2002-03), S.D. Libr. Network (adv. coun. 1986—; exec. com. 1992-96, 1998-2000, chair adv. coun. 1994-96, 98-2000). Office: Augustana Coll Mikkelsen Libr 29th & Smt Sioux Falls SD 57197-0001 Office Phone: 605-274-4921. Business E-Mail: ronelle.thompson@augie.edu.

THOMPSON, SALLY ANN, editor; b. Hillsboro, N.D., Apr. 10, 1943; d. C. Hilman and Blanche E. (Bjerkan) Swenson; m. Arthur G. Thompson, July 1, 1965 (dec. Mar. 1990); 1 child, Laurie Kate Beth. Student, Concordia Coll., Moorhead, Minn., 1961-65. Reporter Valley Jour., Halstad, Minn., 1979-84; contbg. editor Prairie West Publs., Wahpeton, ND, 1982-84; editor Hillsboro Banner, Hillsboro, ND, 1984-95. Sun Newspapers, Eden Prairie, Minn., 1995—. Lectr. Career Day Mayville State U., ND, 1985—92. Bd. dirs. Trail County Hist. Soc., 1979—95, Hillsboro Forestry Bd., 1990—93; mem. commns. com. Eastern N.D. Synod ELCA, 1990—93. Recipient numerous journalism awards. Lutheran. Avocations: photography, collages, reading, history. Home: 1805 Highway 101 Apt 203 Plymouth MN 55447-2715 Office: Sun Newspapers 10917 Valley View Rd Eden Prairie MN 55344 Office Phone: 952-392-7668. Personal E-mail: sally_thompson@hotmail.com.

THOMPSON, SAMUEL DONALD, assemblyman; b. Mobile, Ala., July 31, 1935; m. Jacqueline Thompson; children: Shaun, Vanessa, Richard. BS in Chemistry and Math, U. of Ark., 1960; PhD in Phys. Chemistry, La. State U., 1965. Del. Rep. Nat. Con., 1988, 1992, 1996, 2000, alt. del., 2004; dir. planning, analysis, and govt. rels. N.J. Turnpike Authority, 1994—97; assemblyman N.J. Gen. Assembly, 1998—; chmn. Old Bridge Rep. County Com., 2001. Rsch. scientist E.I. duPont de Nemours, 1965—68, J.P. Stevens and Co., 1968—71; dir. clin. lab improvement svc. N.J. State Dept. of Health, 1972—94; chmn. Middlesex County Rep. Com., 1986—94; mem. Old Bridge Twp. Environ. Commn., 1983, Old Bridge Twp. Planning Bd., 1983, U.S. Armed Forces Epidemiological Bd., 1983—90; co-chair Govs. Edn. Task Force, 1994. Mem. Task Force on Adolescent Violence, 1983, Commn. on Elder Care, 1999—2001. Republican. Baptist. Office: 725 Hwy 34 Matawan NJ 07747 Office Phone: 732-583-5558. Business E-Mail: AsmThompson@njleg.org.

THOMPSON, SANDRA GUERRA, lawyer, educator; BA, Yale Univ. 1985, JD, 1988. Asst. dist. atty. N.Y. County, 1988—90; prof. Univ. Houston Law Ctr., 1990—; dir. Criminal Justice Inst., Univ. Houston. Co-author: The Law of Asset Forfeiture; contbr. articles to prof. jour. Mem.: Assn. Am. Law Sch. (chair, Criminal Justice sect. 2001), Hispanic Bar Assn. (mem. bd. dir.), Houston Bar Assn., Am. Law Inst. (mem. bd. adv. Model Penal Code: Sentencing project). Office: Criminal Justice Institute 100 Law Ctr 4800 Calhoun Rd Houston TX 77204

THOMPSON, SANDRA LEE, library administrator; b. Dover, Ohio, Jan. 23, 1968; d. Robert Leonard and Gwendolyn Ruth Stewart; m. Alan McKinney Thompson, Sept. 9, 1990; children: LeeAnna, Alisha, James. BS in Edn., Ohio U., 1989; M of Libr. Info. Sci., U. S.C., 2001. Tchr. Harrison Hills City Sch. Dist., Hopedale, Ohio, 1989-90; asst. dir. Puskarich Pub. Libr. Cadiz, Ohio, 1990-97, dir., 1998—. Mem. Ohio Libr. Coun., Columbus, 1994—; bd. dirs. Southeastern Ohio Libr. Orgn., Caldwell, 1997—, Ohio Pub. Libr. Info. Network. Mem.: Cadiz Rotary Assocs. (trustee), Am. Libr. Assn. Office: Puskarich Pub Libr 200 E Market St Cadiz OH 43907-1200 E-mail: sthompson@oplin.org.

THOMPSON, SCOTT L., automotive executive; BBA, Stephen F. Austin State U. CPA. Exec. v.p., oper. and fin. KSA Ind., Inc., 1991—96; sr. v.p., CFO, treas. Group1 Automotive, Houston, 1996—2002, exec. v.p., CFO, treas., 2002—. Office: Group 1 Automotive Inc 950 Echo Ln Ste 100 Houston TX 77024

THOMPSON, SHERWOOD, academic program director, consultant; b. Greenville, S.C., Jan. 7, 1952; s. Carolyn Harris; children: Malik K., Aminah M. BA, U. S.C., 1979; MEd, U. Mass., 1989, EdD, 1990. Cons. NUWorld Comms., Inc., Lawrence, Kans., 1978-83; dir. Third World Affairs Office U. Mass., Amherst, 1983-91; dir. office minortiy affairs, adj. faculty sch. edn. U. Kans., Lawrence, 1991—. Coord. minority programs Assn. Coll. Unions Internat. Region 1, 1986-88; faculty fellow U. Okla. Health Scis. Ctr., 1996. Vol. block grant program City of Greenville, 1975-76. Recipient Appreciation award City of Greenville, 1975. Mem. Nat. Black Meeting Planners. Democrat. Methodist. Avocation: rare books.

THOMPSON, SHIRLEY WILLIAMS, mathematics professor; b. Laurens, SC, Oct. 12, 1941; d. Spellman and Lula Mae SR Williams; m. Joseph Earl Thompson, Nov. 27, 1969; children: Shirley Elizabeth Thompson Marshall, Joseph Earl Jr., Amber Gale Thompson Ramsey. BS, Johnson C. Smith U., Charlotte, NC, 1963; MEd, U. NC, 1971; MS, Atlanta U., 1988; PhD, Ga. State U., 1980. Adminstrv. specialist Ga. State U., Atlanta, 1976—77; asst. prof. math. Morehouse Coll., Atlanta, 1980—84, assoc. prof. math., 1984—. Nat. Inst. Assn. Mathematicians, Balt., 1996—2000, Excellence in Edn. Barry Goldwater Scholarship, Phoenix, 1990—; program rev. com. Presdl. Scholars, Washington, 1995—. Field reader Jack Kent Cooke Found., Washington, 2002—. Mem.: Math. Assn. Am., Beta Kappa Chi, Pi Mu Epsilon, Kappa Delta Psi. Presbyterian. Achievements include first to receive master's degree in mathematics from U. NC. Avocations: travel, reading, art history. Home: 4793 Carlene Way SW Lilburn GA 30047 Office: Morehouse Coll 830 Westview Dr Atlanta GA 30314 Business E-Mail: sthompson@morehouse.edu.

**THOMPSON, STANLEY B.,** church administrator; Pres., CEO, dir. The Free Meth. Found., Spring Arbor, Mich.; chmn., CEO, dir. King Trust Co., N.A.; CEO, chmn., dir. King Trust Charitable Gift Fund; ret., 2003. Office: Free Methodist Foundation PO Box 580 Spring Arbor MI 49283-0580 Home: PO Box 284 Spring Arbor MI 49283-0284 E-mail: stanleythompson@comcast.net.

**THOMPSON, STEVE ALLAN,** writer; b. Mpls., Sept. 10, 1951; s. John Thomas and Charlotte Joan (Ellis) T.; m. Michele Rae Jones, July 16, 1983; 1 child, Kent Lloyd. Student, U. Minn., 1969-73. Dept. supr. Hennepin County Libr., Edina, Minn., 1973-87; writer, 1987—. Cons. Okefenokee Glee & Perloo Inc., L.A., 1988—. Waycross/Ware County (Ga.) C. of C., 1990—. Phipps Ctr. for Arts, Hudson, Wis., 1996. Author: Walt Kelly Collector's Guide, 2d edit., 2004; co-author: Pogo Files for Pogophiles, 1992; editor The Fort Mudge Most 1988—; editl. bd. of Internatl. Jour. of Comic Art; contrb. articles to profl. jours. Mem. Internat. Soc. for Humor Studies, Bibliographical Soc. Am., Walt Kelly Soc. (pres. 1987—), Lewis Carroll Soc., Baker Street Irregulars, Grand Comics Database Project, Comics Scholars Consortium. Achievements include international recognized on life and career of Walt Kelly. Home: 6908 Wentworth Ave Richfield MN 55423-2363 E-mail: thompson_s@epi.umn.edu, thomp034@tc.umn.edu.

**THOMPSON, SYDNOR, JR., (CHARLES WILLIAM SYDNOR THOMPSON JR.),** lawyer, mediator, arbitrator; b. Balt., Feb. 18, 1924; s. Charles William Sydnor Thompson and Helen Josephine Layne; m. Harriette Line, June 2, 1947; children: Darcy T. Howard, Charles William Sydnor III, Harriet T. Moore, Brenneman L., Mary Katherine Line T. Kelly. AB, Syracuse U., 1947; LLB, Harvard U., 1950; student, St. Andrews U., Scotland, 1945, Manchester U., Eng., 1950, London Sch. Econs., 1951. Cert.: N.C. Dispute Resolution Commn. (mediator), EEOC, Am. Arbitration Assn. (arbitrator), Nat. Assn. Securities Dealers. Assoc. Davis Polk & Wardwell, N.Y.C., 1951—54; ptnr. Parker Poe Thompson Bernstein Gage & Preston, Charlotte, NC, 1954—94; judge N.C. Ct. Appeals, Raleigh, NC, 1994; of counsel Parker, Poe, Adams & Bernstein, LLP, Charlotte, 1995—; prin. Mediation, Inc., Winston-Salem, NC, 1995—. Author: The Sydnor Family Saga, 2000, A Collection of Ad Hominem Verse, 2002; contrb. articles to law revs. Pres. Charlotte Symphony Orch., 1958—61, Charlotte Opera Assn., 1971—75; vice chair N.C. Arts Coun., Raleigh, 1981—84; pres. Mecklenburg Ministries, 1987—89, Wing Haven Found., 2001—02; chmn. Mecklenburg County Dem. Party, 1977—81. With U.S. Army, 1943—46, ETO. Decorated Bronze star; Fulbright scholar, 1950, 1951. Master: William H. Bobbitt Inn of Ct.; mem.: ABA (chmn. circuits subcom. 1977—95), Mecklenburg Bar Assn. (pres. 1990), N.C. Bar Assn. (chmn. appellate rules study com. 1989—91, chmn. local bar svcs. com. 1991—93), Old Catawba Soc., Horace Williams Philosophy Club, English Speaking Union, Charlotte City Club, Sporadic Book Club, Charlotte Country Club. Avocations: genealogy, writing, tennis, acting. Office: Parker Poe Adams & Bernstein LLP Ste 3000 401 S Tryon St Charlotte NC 28202 Office Phone: 704-372-9000. Business E-mail: sydnorthompson@parkerpoe.com.

**THOMPSON, TERENCE WILLIAM,** lawyer; b. Moberly, Mo., July 3, 1952; s. Donald Gene and Carolyn (Stringer) T.; m. Caryn Elizabeth Hildebrand, Aug. 30, 1975; children: Cory Elizabeth, Christopher William, Tyler Madison. BA in Govt. with honors and high distinction, U. Ariz., 1974; JD, Harvard U., 1977. Bar: Ariz. 1977, U.S. Dist. Ct. Ariz. 1977, U.S. Tax Ct. 1979. Assoc. Brown & Bain P.A., Phoenix, 1977-83, ptnr., 1983-92, Gallagher and Kennedy, P.A., Phoenix, 1992—. Legis. aide Rep. Richard Burgess, Ariz. Ho. of Reps., 1974; mem. bus. adv. bd. Citibank Ariz. (formerly Great Western Bank & Trust, Phoenix), 1985-86. Mem. staff Harvard Law Record, 1974-75; tech. editor Harvard Internat. Law Jour.,1976; lead author, editor-in-chief: Arizona Corporate Practice, 1996—; contrb. articles to profl. jours. Mem. Phoenix Mayor's Youth Adv. Bd. 1968-70, Phoenix Internat.; active 20-30 Club, 1978-81, sec. 1978-80, Valley Leadership, Phoenix, 1983-84, citizens task force future financing needs City of Phoenix, 1985-86; exec. coun. Boys and Girls Clubs of Met. Phoenix, 1990-2000, sr. coun. 2000—; bd. dirs. Phoenix Boys Choir, 1992-94; deacon Shepherd of Hills Congl. Ch., Phoenix, 1984-85; pres. Maricopa County Young Dems., 1982-83, Ariz. Young Dems., 1983-84, sec. 1981-82, v.p. 1982-83; exec. dir. Young Dems. Am., 1985, exec. com. 1983-85; others. Recipient Best of Ariz. State Bar, Ariz. Bus. Jour., 2004. Fellow Ariz. Bar Found.; mem. State Bar Ariz. (vice chmn. internt. law sect. 1978, sec. securities law sect. 1990-91, vice chmn. sect. 1991-92, chmn.-elect 1992-93, chmn. 1993-94, exec. coun. 1988-96, sec. bus. law sect. 1992-93, vice chmn. 1993-94, chmn. 1994-95, exec. coun. 1996-98), Nat. Assn. Bond Lawyers, Nat. Health Lawyers, Select Com. of State Bars, Greater Phoenix Black C. of C. (bd. dirs. 1999-2001), Blue Key, Phi Beta Kappa, Phi Kappa Phi, Phi Eta Sigma. Home: 202 W Lawrence Rd Phoenix AZ 85013-1226 Office: Gallagher & Kennedy PA 2575 E Camelback Rd Phoenix AZ 85016-9225 Office Phone: 602-530-8515. Business E-Mail: twt@gknet.com.

**THOMPSON, THELMA BARNABY,** university president, classical languages educator; b. Balaclava, Jamaica, West Indies, July 22, 1940; d. Claude Noel and Elaine Jordan (Robertson) Barnaby; m. Winston Lloyd Thompson, June 15, 1976; 1 child, Lisa Valdeen. BA, Howard U., Washington, D.C., 1970; MA, Howard U., 1972, PhD, 1978; diploma, Bethlehem Tchrs. Coll., Malvern, Jamaica, West Indies, 1960. Lectr. CUNY, 1972—74; asst. prof. Bowie (Md.) State Coll., 1974—76; assoc. prof., asst. chmn. English dept. U. DC, Washington, 1976—88, assoc. dean, 1988—90; dean Sch. Arts and Letters Norfolk State U., 1990—98, v.p. acad. affairs, 1998—2002; pres. U. Md. Ea. Shore, Princess Anne, 2002—. Author: The Seventeenth Century English Hymn; also articles. Named one of Md.'s 100 Outstanding Women, 2004, Women Shaping the World, Essence Mag., 2005; recipient Bethlehem Coll. Medal of Distinction, scholarship and grad. fellowship award for outstanding accomplishment in field of edn., Howard U., 2005, Best of St. Bess award, Jamaica, West Indies, 2003. Mem. MLA, Coll. Lang. Assn., South Atlantic MLA, Middle Atlantic Writers, Phi Beta Kappa, Phi Delta Kappa (award for disting. svc. and commitment to excellence in edn. 1991). Achievements include extensive outreach work in Africa and the Caribbean. Office: U Md Eastern Shore JT Williams Hall Rm 2117 Princess Anne MD 21853 Office Phone: 410-651-6101. Business E-Mail: tbthompson@umes.edu.

**THOMPSON, THEODORE ROBERT,** pediatric educator; b. Dayton, Ohio, July 18, 1943; s. Theodore Roosevelt and Helen (Casey) J.; m. Lynette Joanne Shenk; 1 child, S. Beth. BS, Wittenberg U., 1965; MD, U. Pa., 1969. Diplomate Am. Bd. Pediatrics (Neonatal, Perinatal Medicine). Resident in pediat. U. Minn. Hosp., Mpls., 1969—72, chief resident in pediat., 1971—72, fellow neonatal, perinatal, 1974—75, asst. prof., 1975—80, dir. divsn. neonatology and newborn intensive care unit, 1977—91, assoc. prof., 1980—85, prof., 1985—, co-dir. Med. Outreach, 1988—91, med. dir. med. outreach, 1991—2000, assoc. chief pediat. svcs., 1988—2003, assoc. head pediat. edn. and cmty. programs, 2003—04, assoc. head cmty. affairs, 2004—; med. dir. outreach, bd. dirs. U. Minn. Physicians, 1992—. Med. exec. com., sec.-treas. U. Minn. Med. Ctr., Fairview, 2002—04, chief of staff elect, 2004—. Editor: Newborn Intensive Care: A Practical Manual, 1983. Bd. dirs. Life Link III, St. Paul, 1987—; cons. Maternal and Child Health, Minn. Bd. Health, 1975-94; bd. dirs. Minn. Maternal and Child Health, Minn. 1995-99. With USPHS. 1972-74. Recipient Avocacy award, U. Minn. Med. Sch., Pres.'s award for outstanding svc., U. Minn. Fellow: Am. Acad. Pediats.; mem.: Acad. Med. Educators, Gt. Plains Orgn. for Perinatal Health Care (Sioux Falls, SD Kunshe award 1989, Pres.'s Outstanding Svc. award 2006). Lutheran. Office: MMC 39 420 Delaware St SE Minneapolis MN 55455-0374 Office Phone: 612-626-2841. Business E-Mail: thomp005@umn.edu.

**THOMPSON, THOMAS MARTIN,** lawyer; b. Albion, Pa., Jan. 7, 1943; s. Donald C. and Mabel Louise (Martin) T.; m. Judith E. Daucher; children: Reid, Chad, Matthew, Molly. AB, Grove City Coll., 1965; JD cum laude, Harvard U., 1968. Bar: Pa. 1968. Ptnr. Buchanan Ingersoll, Pitts., 1968—. Adj. prof. law U. Pitts.; past chairperson, dir. Pa. Lawyer Trust Acct. Bd. Past pres. Neighborhood Legal Svcs. Assn.; trustee emeritus Pitts. Pub. Theater.

---

Mem. ABA, Pa. Bar Assn. (chair bus. law sect., Pro Bono award 1989), Allegheny County Bar Assn. (past chmn. pub. svc. com., past chmn. bus. law coun., past chair PBA legal opinion steering com.), Assn. for Corp. Growth (past pres. Pitts. chpt.). Democrat. Home: 1142 Dartmouth Rd Pittsburgh PA 15205-1705 Office: Buchanan Ingersoll One Oxford Ctr 301 Grant St Fl 20 Pittsburgh PA 15219-1410 Office Phone: 412-562-8855. E-mail: thompsontm@bipc.com.

**THOMPSON, TINA MARIE,** professional basketball player; b. LA, Feb. 10, 1975; B in sociology, U. So. Calif., 1997. Basketball player U. So. Calif., 1993—97; profl. basketball player Houston Comets, WNBA, 1997—. Named All-Star Game MVP, WNBA, 2000; named to First Team All-WNBA, 1997, 1998, WNBA All-Star Team, 1999, 2000, 2001, 2002, 2004. Achievements include No. 1 draft pick in 1997, the first WNBA draftee in the history of the league; mem. Houston Comets WNBA Championship Teams, 1997, 98, 99, 2000; mem. US Women's Basketball Team, Athens Olympics, 2004.

**THOMPSON, TOMMY (THOMAS GEORGE THOMPSON),** lawyer, former secretary of health and human services; b. Elroy, Wis., Nov. 19, 1941; s. Allan and Julia (Dutton) T.; m. Sue Ann Mashak, 1969; children: Kelli Sue, Tommi, Jason. BS in Polit. Sci. and History, U. Wis., 1963, JD, 1966. Polit. intern U.S. Rep. Thomson, 1963; legis. messenger Wis. State Senate, 1964-66; sole practice Elroy and Mauston, Wis., 1966-87; mem. Dist. 87 Wis. State Assembly, 1966-87, asst. minority leader, 1972-81, floor leader, 1981-87; self-employed real estate broker Mauston, 1970—; gov. State of Wis., 1987-2001; sec. U.S. Dept. Health & Human Services, Washington, 2001 05; pres. Logistics Health Inc., 2005—, ptnr. Akin Gump Strauss Hauer & Feld LLP, 2005—; independent chmn., sr. advisor Deloitte Ctr for Health Solutions Deloitte & Touche USA LLP, 2005—. Alt. del. Rep. Nat. Conv., 1976; chmn. Intergovtl. Policy Adv. Commn. to U.S. Trade Rep.; chmn. Nat. Govs. Assn., 1995-96, mem. nat. govs. assn. exec. com., AGA Med. Corp.; chmn. bd. dirs., Amtrak, 1998-2001; mem. bd. dirs. C.R. Bard, Inc., 2005-, Certere Corp., 2005-; pres. Logistics Health, 2005-. Served with USAR. Recipient med. award for Legis. Wis. Acad. Gen. Practice, Thomas Jefferson Freedon award Am. Legis. Exchange Coun., 1991, Most Valuable Pub. Official award City and State Mag., 1991, Governance award Free Congress Found., 1992, Governing Mag. Public Ofcl. of the Year, 1997, recipient Horatio Alger award, 1998, USA Mex. C of C, Good Neighbor award., 1999. Mem. ABA, Wis. Bar Assn., Rep. Govs. Assn., Phi Delta Phi. Republican. Roman Catholic. Office: Akin Gump Robert Stauss Bldg 1333 New Hampshire Ave NW Washington DC 20036-1564

**THOMPSON, TRACY MICHELLE,** lawyer; d. Owen Lamar Lynn and Rosemary Knight; m. Stephen Thompson; 1 child, Victoria. BA in English and Polit. Sci. summa cum laude, U. Ala., 1994; JD, Yale U., 1997. Bar: Ala. 1997. Ptnr. Bradley Arant Rose & White LLP, Birmingham, Ala., 1997—. Sr. editor Yale Law Jour., 1996. Mem. Project Corp. Leadership C. of C., Birmingham, 2000—01; chmn. U. Ala. Honors Coll. Bd. of Visitors, Tuscaloosa, 2005—; chmn. bd. dirs. child care ctr. Highlands United Meth. Ch., Birmingham, 2004—, trustee, 2005—, sec., 2003—. Vulcan scholar, U. Ala. Mem.: ABA, Birmingham Bar Assn. (bus. law sect.), Ala. State Bar, Newcomen Soc., Birmingham Venture Club, Phi Kappa Phi, Phi Beta Kappa. Office: Bradley Arant Rose & White LLP 1819 5th Ave N Birmingham AL 35203

**THOMPSON, VERITA JEAN,** music educator; b. Sept. 20, 1963; d. Garvester Hardy Thompson, Sr. and Jean Salter Thompson. Degree in Music, Hampton U., Va., 1988. Pvt. piano instr., Norfolk, Va., 1983—. Musician, dir. choir St. Mary's Cath. Ch., Tidewater, Va., 1996—. Dir.: 80 children's and youth choirs, 1989—94. Recipient Plaque, St. Mary Cath. Ch., 2002. Mem.: Hampton Rds. Choir Dirs. and Organists Guild (chaplain 2004—, pres. 2003—). Home: 558 Briar Hill Rd Norfolk VA 23502

**THOMPSON, VERN,** political organization executive; b. Maddock, N.D., Aug. 23, 1956; m. Cindy; one child, Will. Former city councilman; former twp. supr.; rep. N.D. State, 1989-91, state senator, 1997—2000. Exec. dir. ND Dem. Party, 2001—. Recipient N.D. Weekly N.D. POI. Figure of the Yr., 1995, Minnewaukan Citizen of the Yr., 1996. Democrat. Home: 2214 Victoria Rose Dr S Fargo ND 58104-6813

**THOMPSON, VETTA LYNN SANDERS,** psychologist, educator; b. Birmingham, Ala., Sept. 7, 1959; d. Grover and Vera Lee (King) S.; m. Cavelli Andre Thompson, May 27, 1990; children: Olajuwon, Malik Rashad, Kemberlyn, Assata Iyana. BA, Harvard U., 1981; MA, Duke U., 1984, PhD, 1988. Cert. psychologist and health svc. provider, State of Mo. Com. Psychology intern Malcolm Bliss Mental Health Ctr., St. Louis, 1985-86; psychotherapist, testing coord. Washington U. Child Guidance Clinic, St. Louis, 1986-87; psychologist, treatment team coord. Hawthorn Children's Psychiatric Hosp., St. Louis, 1987-89; asst. prof. U. Mo., St. Louis, 1989-95, assoc. prof., coord. black studies, 1995—. Tchg. asst. Duke U., Durham, N.C., 1982-84, rsch. asst., 1984-85; chair monitoring com. crisis access sys. Ea. Regional Adv. Coun. Dept. Mental Health, St. Louis, 1995-97; chair African Am. Task Force on Mental Health, Jefferson City, Mo., 1995-97; chair budget and planning com. Ea. Regional Adv. Coun., Dept. Mental Health, St. Louis, 1996-97, pres. Ea. Regional Adv. Coun.; mem. children's mental health planning group St. Louis Mental Health Bd., 1996-97. Mem. editl. adv. bd. A Turbulent Voyage: Readings in African American Studies, 1995-96; mem. bd. editl. advisors Gt. Plains Rsch.; contrb. articles to profl. jours. Mem. adv. com. on violence prevention and investment in youth Mo. House, Jefferson City, 1995; mem. managed care steering com. Dept. Mental Health, Jefferson City, 1995—96, mem. strategic planning adv. coun., 1997; mem. Mo Dd for Respiratory Care, 1997, mem, state com. for psychologist Mo., 1997—; chair Mo., 2000—02; sec., chair discipline com. Mo., 1999—2000; bd. dirs. St. Louis Mental Health Assn., sec., 2000—02, chair planning com., 2002, 2d v.p., 2002, pres., 2003. Kellogg Found.-Mo. Youth Initiative fellow, 1991-93; Ctr. for Great Plains Studies fellow U. Nebr., 1995—; recipient Disting. Svc. award Mental Health Assn. St. Louis, 1998, 99. Mem. APA (divsns. 1, 45), Assn. Black Psychologists, Am. Orthopsychiat. Assn. Methodist. Avocations: aerobics, walking, jazz.

**THOMPSON, WADE FRANCIS BRUCE,** manufacturing executive; b. Wellington, New Zealand, July 23, 1940; came to U.S., 1961, naturalized, 1990. m. Angela Ellen Barry, Jan. 20, 1967; children: Amanda and Charles (twins). B in Commerce, Cert. Acctg., Victoria U., Wellington, 1961; MSc, NYU, 1963. Dir. diversification Sperry & Hutchinson, N.Y.C., 1967-72; v.p. Texstar Corp., N.Y.C., 1972-77; chmn. Hi-Lo Trailer Co., Butler, Ohio, 1977—2003; chmn., pres., chief exec. officer Thor Industries Inc., Jackson Center, Ohio, 1980—. Trustee Mystic Seaport Mus., Conn., 1984—; trustee Wade F.B. Thompson Charitable Found. Inc., 1985—, Mcpl. Art Soc., N.Y.C., 1993—, Seventh Regiment Armory Conservancy, N.Y.C., 1997—; founder The Drive Against Prostate Cancer. Mem. Union Club, N.Y. Yacht Club (N.Y.C.). Avocations: tennis, collecting contemporary art. Office: Thor Industries Inc PO Box 629 Jackson Center OH 45334-0629

**THOMPSON, WALLACE REEVES, III,** physical education educator; b. Atlanta, Oct. 17, 1950; s. Wallace Reeves II and Annie Mae (Neal) T.; m. Sherrilyn Winkfield, Aug. 19, 1976 (div. 1985); 1 child, Sherrilyn M. m. Sandra Hicks, Feb. 28, 1994; 3 children: Garry C., Keneisha R., Ira. BA, Morehouse Coll., 1973. Cert. phys. edn. tchr., Ga. Phys. edn. tchr. Atlanta Pub. Schs., 1974—. Coach Saturday Sch. for the Arts, Atlanta, 1979-81. Vol. Nat. Black Arts Festival, Atlanta, 1990—, Ga. State Games, Atlanta, 1992—; coach Butler St. YMCA, Atlanta, 1982-85, AAU-Jr. Olympics, Atlanta, 1977-82, Centennial Olympics, Sports Video Viewing Room, Atlanta, 1996. Mem. AAHPERD. Baptist. Home: 119 Anderson Ave NW Atlanta GA 30314-1852

**THOMPSON, WALTER DAVID, JR.,** systems analyst; b. Leakesville, N.C., Sept. 8, 1952; s. Walter David Sr. and Rachel Henderlite (Jones) T. Student, St. Andrews Coll., 1970-75. Beverage distributor N.Y. Seltzer,

---

N.Y.C., 1975-76; restaurant mgr. Fountainhead Cafe, N.Y.C., 1976-77; newspaper delivery Greensboro (N.C.) Daily News, 1978-80; computer programmer Gary Brown Assocs., Greensboro, 1980-82; pvt. cons. Thompson Software Systems, Greensboro, 1982-86; asst. treas. corp. trust Bankers Trust, N.Y.C., 1987-88; computer analyst bond funds Merrill Lynch, N.Y.C., 1988; team leader, cons. corp. fin. Citibank, N.Y.C., 1988-89; v.p., sr. systems analyst Kidder, Peabody & Co., Inc., Manakin-Sabot, Va., 1989-94; dir. MIS James River Capital Corp., Manakin-Sabot, Va., 1995—. Rsch. grantee NSF, 1971. Mem. Am. Mensa Ltd. (membership coord. 1990-91). Office: James River Capital Corp 58 Broad Street Rd Manakin Sabot VA 23103-2213

**THOMPSON, WAYNE WRAY,** historian; b. Wichita, Jan. 30, 1945; s. Clarence William and Elaine Maxine (Wray) T.; m. Lillian Evelyn Hurlburt, June 28, 1969 (div. 1999); m. Geraldine Kelleher Richter, Dec. 30 2000. BA, Union Coll., Schenectady, 1967; student, U. St. Andrews, Scotland, 1965-66; PhD, U. Calif., San Diego, 1975. Historian USAF, 1975—2004, Checkmate Air Campaign Planning Group, 1990—2004; sr. hist. advisor Gulf War Air Power Survey, 1991-93. Contrb. Congress Investigates (Arthur M. Schlesinger Jr. and Roger Bruns, editors), 1975; editor Air Leadership, 1986; contbr. War in the Pacific (Bernard Nalty, editor), 1991; contbr.: Winged Shield, Winged Sword, 1997; author: To Hanoi and Back, 2000. Served with AUS, 1971-72. Mem. Am. Hist. Assn., Orgn. Am. Historians, Air Force Hist. Found., Air Force Assn., Soc. Historians Am. Fgn. Rels., Soc. Mil. History, US Commn. Mil. History, Inter-Univ. Seminar Armed Forces, Assn. Asian Studies, Asia Soc., World History Assn., Phi Beta Kappa. Home: 2720 N Quincy St Arlington VA 22207

**THOMPSON, WILLARD SCOTT (W. SCOTT THOMPSON),** social sciences educator; b. Providence, Jan. 1, 1942; s. Francis Willard and Loretta Bell Thompson; m. Phyllis Arina Nitze, Dec. 28, 1968 (div. May 1982); children: Phyllis Elizabeth Pratt, Nicholas Edwin Scott, Heidi Alexandra Nitze. BA with honors, Stanford U., 1963; PhD, Oxford U., Eng., 1967. Assoc. profl. internat. politics Fletcher Sch. Law and Diplomacy, Medford, Mass., 1967—93; asst. to sec. of def. Dept. Def., Washington, 1975—76; assoc. dir. U.S. Info. Agy. U.S. Govt., Washington, 1981—84; rsch. adj. prof. internat. politics Fletcher Sch. Law and Diplomacy, Medford, Mass., 2001—. Vis. prof. Asian Inst. Mgmt., Manila, 2001—; chair Universal Trading and Investment Co., Boston, 1993—. Internat. Ctr. for Instnl. Develop., Berkeley, Calif., 2000—. Author: Ghana's Foreign Policy, 1969; co-author (with Nicholas Thompson): The Baobab and The Mango Tree, 2000, The Philippines in Crisis, 1992; contrb. articles to profl. jours. Co-chair Ams. for Effective Pres., Boston, 1980, Mass. Tomorrow, Boston, 1972—78; pres. Inst. Internat. Rels., Stanford U., 1962—63. Rhodes scholar, 1963, Fulbright fellow, Manila, 1989, Danforth fellow, 1965—67, White House fellow, 1975—76. Mem.: Coun. on Fgn. Affairs, Internat. Inst. for Strategic Studies. Avocations: gardening, films, marathons, writing fiction. Home: 14398 Storybook Ln Amissville VA 20106 Office: Policy Ctr Asian Inst Mgmt Paseo de Roxas Makati Philippines Address: Villa Kusuma Seri Sukuwati, Bali Indonesia E-mail: thompsonwscott@yahoo.com.

**THOMPSON, WILLIAM, JR.,** engineering educator; b. Hyannis, Mass., Dec. 4, 1936; s. William and Dinella Helen (Szeliga) T.; m. Martha Marion Cate, July 4, 1959; children: Melanie A., Sharon E., Jennifer L., Keith W. SB, MIT, 1958; MS, Northeastern U., 1963; PhD, Pa. State U., 1971. Staff engr. Raytheon Co., Wayland, Mass., 1958-60; sr. engr. Cambridge (Mass.) Acoustical Assocs., 1960-66; rsch. asst. Applied Rsch. Lab., State College, Pa., 1966-72; asst. prof. engring. sci. Pa. State U., University Park, 1972-78, assoc. prof., 1978-85, prof., 1985-2001, prof. emeritus, 2001—. Head transducer group Applied Rsch. Lab., State College, 1971-80; sabbatical leave Naval Rsch. Lab., Orlando, Fla., 1988-89; chairperson IBM Master Tchrs. Team, 1997-98. Contbr. articles to profl. jours.; patentee in field. Bd. dirs., treas., past pres. Nittany Mountain chpt. Am. Diabetes Assn., State College, 1979-92; bd. dirs., asst. treas., treas. Mid-Pa. affiliate, Bethlehem, 1980-90; bd. dirs. Sight-Loss Support Group of Ctrl. Pa., 1999, treas. 2000-05. Recipient Disting. Svc. citation Mid-Pa. Affiliate Am. Diabetes Assn., 1981, and Affiliate Svc. award, 1988, J.R. Cardenuto award, Sight-Loss Support Group of Ctrl. Pa., 1998. Fellow Acoustical Soc. Am. (patent reviewer of soc. jour. 1990-); mem. Soc. Engring. Sci., Lions (pres. State College 1981-82, 89-90, sec.-treas. 1984-88, 90-92, treas. 1992-2005, dist. diabetes chmn. 1983-88, 94-2005, chmn. Ctr. Lions Foresight Commn. 1992-2004, Melvin Jones fellow 1991, internat. leadership award 1998, dist. chmn. Habitat for Humanity Project, 2001-04), Cen. Pa. Ballroom Dancers Assn. (pres.-elect 1997-98, pres. 1998-99). Republican. Avocations: sports, reading, photography, ballroom dancing. Home: 1245-62 Westerly Pky State College PA 16801 Office: Pa State U Dept of Engring Sci and Mechanics 212 Earth and Engring Scis University Park PA 16802-6812 Business E-Mail: W1TESM@engr.psu.edu.

**THOMPSON, WILLIAM C., JR.,** school system administrator; b. Bklyn. BA in Polit. Sci., Tufts U., 1974; LHD (hon.), Mercy Coll., 1998. Chief of staff Congressman Fred Richmond, Bklyn.; dep. borough pres. Borough of Bklyn., 1983—92; Bklyn. rep. NYC Bd. Edn., 1994—96, pres., 1996; comptroller NYC, 2002—. Cons. investment banking svcs. to states, municipalities and pub. benefit corps. in N.Y., Health Care industry, non-profit orgns. Bd. dirs. Bedford Stuyvesant Restoration Corp., City Parks Found., Bklyn. Union Gas Co; trustee Tufts U. Office: Office of the Comptroller c/o Karen Crowe 1 Centre St Room 526 New York NY 10007 Fax: 718-935-3157.*

**THOMPSON, WILLIAM DAVID,** minister, educator; b. Chgo., Jan. 11, 1929; s. Robert Ayre and Mary Elizabeth (McDowell) T.; m. Linda Brady Stevenson, Nov. 2, 1968; children: Tammy, Kirk, Lisa, Rebecca, Gwyneth. AB, Wheaton Coll., Ill. 1950; BD, No. Bapt. Sem. 1954; MA, Northwestern U., 1955, PhD, 1960. Ordained to ministry Am. Baptist Ch., 1954. Instr. speech Wheaton Coll., 1952-55; pastor Raymond Baptist Ch., Chgo., 1956-58; assoc. prof. homiletics No. Bapt. Sem., Chgo., 1958-62; mem. faculty Eastern Bapt. Sem., Phila., 1962-87, prof. preaching, 1969-87; minister 1st Bapt. Ch., Phila., 1983-90. Pres. Thompson Comm., 1988-98, prin. The Spirited Workplace, 1998—, Thompson Properties, 1999-. Author: A Listener's Guide to Preaching, 1966, Recent Homiletical Thought, 1967, Dialogue Preaching, 1969, Preaching Biblically, 1981, Listening on Sunday for Sharing on Monday, 1983, Philadelphia's First Baptists, 1989, Public Speaking for Pleasure and Profit, 1997, On the Job Prayers, 2005; editor Abingdon Preachers Libr., 12 vols., Essence of Public Speaking series, 10 vols. Mem. Phila. Hist. Commn., 1984-92, Ctr. for Baptismal Living Bd., 1999-, Singing City Bd., 2003-. Vis. fellow Cambridge U., 1968-69. Mem. Nat. Speakers Assn., Mid-Atlantic Speakers Assn. (pres. 1995), Acad. Homiletics (pres. 1973, Lifetime Achievement award 2005), Religious Speech Comm. Assn. (v.p. 1983, pres. 1984), Union League Club, Wheaton Coll. Scholastic Honor Soc. Democrat. Home: 765 Ormond Ave Drexel Hill PA 19026-2417 Personal E-mail: Thompcom@aol.com.

**THOMPSON, WILLIAM IRWIN,** writer, educator; b. Chgo., July 16, 1938; s. Chester Andrew and Lillian Margaret (Fahey) Thompson; m. Gail Joan Gordon, Feb. 3, 1960 (div. Jan. 1979); children: Evan Timothy, Hilary Joan, Andrew Rhys; m. Beatrice Madeleine Rudin, Mar. 1, 1979. BA in Philosophy, Pomona Coll., 1962; MA (Woodrow Wilson fellow), Cornell U. 1964, PhD (Woodrow Wilson dissertation fellow), 1966. From instr. to asst. prof. humanities MIT, Cambridge, 1965—67, assoc. prof., 1968, Old Dominion fellow, 1967; assoc. prof. York U., Toronto, Ont., Canada, 1968-72, prof., 1973; founding dir. Lindisfarne Assocs., 1972—97; curriculum designer, faculty cons. Ross Sch., East Hampton, N.Y, 1995—2000. Vis. prof. religion Syracuse (N.Y.) U., 1973; vis. scholar in polit. sci. U. Hawaii, 1981, vis. prof., 85; vis. prof. Celtic studies U. Toronto, 1984; mentor, cons. Ross Sch., East Hampton, NY, 1995—; Lindisfarne scholar-in-residence Crestone Mt. Zen Ctr. Author: (book) Imagination of an Insurrection: Dublin, Easter 1916, 1967, At the Edge of History, 1971, Passages about Earth, 1974, Evil and World Order, 1976, Darkness and Scattered Light, 1978, The Time Falling Bodies Take to Light, 1981, From Nation to Emanation, 1981, Blue Jade from the Morning Star, 1983, Islands Out of Time, 1985, Pacific Shift, 1986, GAIA: A Way of Knowing, 1987, Imaginary Landscape, 1989, Selected

Poems, 1959–89, GAIA TWO: Emergence, the New Science of Becoming, 1991, Reimagination of the World, 1991, The American Replacement of Nature, 1991, Coming into Being, 1996, Worlds Interpenetrating and Apart, 1997, Transforming History, 2001, Self and Society, 2004. Hon. colleague, Lindisfarne scholar Cathedral St. John the Divine, NYC, 1972–97. Recipient Obstfelder prize, Oslo Internat. Poetry Festival, 1986; grantee, Laurance S Rockefeller, 1992—98; Rockefeller scholar, Calif. Inst. Integral Studies, 1992—95. Address: Lindisfanne Fellows House PO Box 130 Crestone CO 81131

**THOMPSON, WILLIAM MOREAU,** radiologist, educator; b. Phila., Oct. 20, 1943; s. Charles Moreau and Aileen (Haddon) T.; m. Judy Ann Seel, July 27, 1968; children: Christopher Moreau, Thayer Haddon. BA, Colgate U., 1965; MD, U. Pa., 1969. Diplomate Am. Bd. Radiology. Intern Case Western Res. U., Cleve., 1969-70; resident in radiology Duke U., Durham, NC, 1972-75, from asst. prof. Med. Ctr. to prof., 1975—2001, prof. radiology Med. Ctr., 2001—, The Reed and Martha Rice Disting. prof. radiology Med. Ctr., 2004—; chmn. Dept. Radiology U. Minn. Hosp. and Clinic, Mpls., 1986-2000, Vilhelmina and Eugene Gedgared chair radiology, 1986—2001, prof. radiology, dir. imaging rsch., 2000-01. Contbr. chpts. to books and articles to profl. jours. Served with USPHS, 1970-72. Recipient James Picker Found. Scholar in Acad. Medicine award, 1975-79, Disting. Scientist award, Armed Forces Inst. Pathology, Washington, 2001-02; R & D grantee VA, 1977-86. Fellow Am. Coll. Radiology; mem. AMA, Radiology Soc. N.Am. (program chmn. 1994-97), Minn. Med. Soc., Am. Roentgen Ray Soc., Assn. Univ. Radiologists (pres. 1989-90, Gold medal 2001), Soc. Gastrointestinal Radiology (pres. 1994-95, Cannon medal 2001), Assn. Program Dirs. (pres. 1995, Achievement award 2001), Soc. Chairs of Acad. Radiology Depts. (pres. 1997-98), Sigma Xi. Republican. Presbyterian. Home: 225 Galway Dr Chapel Hill NC 27517-6558 Office: PO Box 3808 Durham NC 27702-3808 Office Phone: 919-684-7448. Business E-Mail: thomp132@nc.duke.edu.

**THOMPSON, WINFRED LEE,** academic administrator, lawyer; b. Little Rock, July 28, 1945; s. Vester Lee and Willow Mae (Mills) T.; m. Carmen Angeles Tiongson; children: Emily, Michael. BA, U. Ark., 1967; MA, U. Chgo., 1970, PhD, 1987; JD, George Washington U., 1976, LLM, 1978. Congl. aide U.S. Ho. of Reps., Washington, 1973-77; exec. asst. to asst. sec. labor U.S. Dept. Labor, Washington, 1977-78; atty. Hatfield and Thompson, Searcy, Ark., 1978-81; dir. devel. U. Ark. State U., Jonesboro, 1981-82, v.p. for planning and devel., 1982-84; v.p. for fin. and adminstrn. U. Ark. System, Fayetteville, 1984-85; vice chancellor for fin. and adminstrn. U. Ark, Fayetteville, 1985-87; pres. U. Cen. Ark., Conway, 1988—2001; chancellor Am. U. of Sharjah, United Arab Emirates, 2002—. Bd. dirs. Ark. Sci. and Tech. Authority, Little Rock, 1984-89. Bd. dirs Ark. Symphony Orch., 1991-94; mem. U.S. Peace Corps, The Philippines, 1967-69. 2d lt. USAR. Woodrow Wilson fellow U. Chgo., 1969-70. Mem. Phi Beta Kappa. Office: U Ctrl Ark Office of the President 201 Donaghey Ave Conway AR 72035-5001 Home: 1022 Oak St Conway AR 72032-4353

**THOMPSON, WINSTON MARK OBED,** entomologist, consultant, writer; s. Samuel Frendo and Iris Agatha Thompson. BSc, U. Guyana, S.Am., 1989; M of Agr., Oreg. State U., 1994; PhD, U. Greenwich, Eng., 2001. Rsch. asst. Nat. Agrl. Rsch. Inst., Georgetown, Guyana, 1989—92, rsch. scientist virology, 1994—98, rsch. scientist, 2001—03; rsch. fellow Internat. Inst. for Biol. Control, Curepe, Trinidad and Tobago, 1991, Caribbean Agrl. R&D Inst., Bridgetown, Barbados, 1991; lectr. entomology Guyana Sch. Agr., Georgetown, 1995—98; pvt. cons. and author Bellevue, Wash., 2004—. Keynote spkr. Ministry of Agr., Guyana, 1989—90; nat. agrl. rsch. inst.'s rep. Guyana's Vegetable Quality Assurance Com., Georgetown, 1996—98; mem. rev. team Caribbean Jour. Agr. and Natural Resources, Georgetown, 1997—98, Internat. Jour. Tropical insect Sci., 2005—. Contbr. articles to profl. jours. V.p. Ebenezer Luther League, New Amsterdam, Berbice, Guyana, 1983—83; music dir. Ebenezer Music Group, New Amsterdam, Berbice, Guyana, 1995—98. Recipient Pub. Svc. Ministry award, Govt. Guyana, 1985-1989, 9 Acad. awards, U. Guyana, 1986-1989; Commonwealth scholar, Assn. of Commonwealth Univs., 1998-2001, FAO of UN fellow, 1992-1994. Mem.: Guyana Assn. Profl. Agriculturists, Entomol. Soc. Am., Internat. Soc. for Pest Info. (corr.) Achievements include research recognized by other professionals; research recognized by the United States Dept. of Justice as an Alien of Extraordinary Ability for the O visa; a visa category exclusive for nobel prize winners or persons of international acclaim; research recognized by the Food and Agricultural Organization of the United Nations in 1995 as the only Plant Virologist In Guyana, South America; research recognized and selected by the Inter-American Institute for Cooperation on Agriculture to participate in a Caribbean Regional Workshop on Citrus Budwood Certification. Avocations: reading, guitar, piano. Office: PO Box 7226 Bellevue WA 98008 Office Phone: 425-562-3482. Personal E-mail: winston_thompson@hotmail.com.

**THOMPSON, ZACHARY,** city health department administrator; AS, El Centro Coll.; BS in Social Work, U. Tex., Arlington; MS, Amberton U., Garland, Tex. With W. Dallas Cmty. Ctr.; dep. dir. Dallas Co. Dept. Health and Human Svcs., Dallas, 1997—2004, dir., 2004—. Office: Dallas Co Dept Health and Human Svcs 2377 N Stemmons Fwy Dallas TX 75207-2710*

**THOMPSON-CHRISTIE, HEATHER MARIE,** adult education educator; b. Saginaw, Mich., Jan. 31, 1980; d. Thomas George and Linda Marie Thompson; m. Scott Robert Christie, Sept. 27, 2003; stepchildren: Adam Scott Christie, Caleb Michael Christie children: Jasmine Marie Thompson, Jenna Catherine Thompson. MA of Psychology, U. of Mich., Flint, 2000—02, MA in Edn., 2002—03. Lic. CAC Mich., 2001. Instr. ARC, Saginaw, Mich., 1999—; rschr. U. Mich., Flint, 2000—03; adult edn. Mich. Works, Port Huron, Mich., 2003; mgr. edn. Sylvan Edn. Solutions, Phila., 2003—. Author: (research) Everybody says I love you, Chivalry and sexism, Reaction in Witnesses of Fatal Construction Accidents. Recipient Saginaw County Hero Award, ARC, 2002; grantee Beatrice and William Caldwell Rsch. Fund, U. Of Mich., 2003. Mem.: ARC (life; chair of logistics 2001—02). R-Consevative. Bapt. Avocations: horse back riding, music playing, researching. Home: 8565 Dorwood Rd Birch Run MI 48415 Personal E-mail: collegegirluofm@yahoo.com. Business E-Mail: hethomps@umflint.edu.

**THOMPSON CORNWALL, LONIETA AURORA,** music educator, consultant; b. Newark, June 13, 1944; d. Wilmore and Hattie Stewart Thompson; children: Ronald Pearson Cornwall Jr. children: Arminta Morant Cornwall, Ronald Pearson Cornwall. MusB, Manhattan Sch. Music, N.Y.C., 1962, MusM, 1966; M of Sacred Music, Union Theol. Sem., Sch. of Sacred Music, N.Y.C., 1973; EdD in Coll. Tchg. of Music, Teachers Coll., Columbia U., N.Y.C., 2006. Music tchr. Bd. Edn., N.Y.C., 1966—70; instr. music Shaw U., Raleigh, NC, 1984—. Organist Abyssinian Bapt. Ch., N.Y.C., 1965—68; dir. music Holy Trinity Luth. Ch., Hollis/Queens, NY, 1970—75; min. music First Bapt. Ch., Raleigh, NC, 1981—95; organist Christian Faith Bapt. Ch., Raleigh, 1999—2001; dir. music First Bapt. Ch. of Cary, Cary, NC, 2001—. Composer: (musical score) Canticles for the Soul, Hebrews 25 Let us Encourage One Another, 2004, The African American Art Song: A Continuum In the Art of Song, 2006; presentor Nat. Assn. Negro Mus., 2006; contbr. scientific papers. Participant US EPA, Raleigh, NC, 2002, NC State Workers/Dr. Martin Luther King Holiday Observance, Raleigh, 2000—04; missionary to Zambia, South Africa Operation Reachback, Redlands, Calif. 2000; chair Gethsemane Seventh-day Adventist Ch. Sch., Raleigh, NC, 1995—2000; musical cons. Dr. Martin Luther King Celebration Com. Raleigh, 1995—2004. Recipient H.B. Caple Humanitarian award, The Shaw Players/Shaw U., 1997—98, The Crystal award, Women's Ministries/South Atlantic Conf. of Seventh-day Adventists, 1999, Lamplighter -Music Outreach award, Radio One-Hunter Industries, 2002. Mem.: Nat. Assn. Negro Musicians, Raleigh Chamber Music Guild (bd. dirs. 1994—95, 2006—), N.C. Bach Festival (bd. dirs. 1990—94), Am. Guild of Organists, Alpha Chi. Seventh-Day Adventist. Avocations: writing (religius), walking, travel. Home: 2304 Foxtrot Rd Raleigh NC 27610 Office: Shaw Univ 118 East South St Raleigh NC 27601 Office Phone: 919-546-8412. Personal E-mail: lonieta@aol.com. E-mail: lcornwal@shawu.edu.

**THOMS, CHRISTOPHER MICHAEL,** elementary school educator; s. Betty Ann Thoms; m. Raenelle Leigh Walgren, Nov. 6, 2004; 1 child, Ashton Leigh. BA in Edn., Wayne State Coll., Nebr., 1997. Cert. tchr. K-12 health and phys. edn. Nebr., 1997. Tchr. k-12 health and phys. edn. Clarks (Nebr.) Pub. Schs., 1998—2000, High Plains Cmty. Schs., Polk, Nebr., 2000—04, Lakeview Cmty. Schs., Columbus, Nebr., 2004—. Mem.: Nebr. State Edn. Assn. (assoc.; negotiator 2004—06). Home: 1114 3rd Street Columbus NE 68601 Office Phone: 402-564-8518. Personal E-mail: cthoms@hotmail.com. Business E-Mail: cthoms@esu7.org.

**THOMS, DAVID MOORE,** lawyer; b. NYC, Apr. 28, 1948; s. Theodore Clark and Elizabeth Augusta (Moore) T.; m. Susan Rebecca Stuckey, Dec. 16, 1972. BA, Kalamazoo Coll., 1970; M in Urban Planning, Wayne State U., 1975, LLM in Taxation, 1988; JD, U. Detroit, 1979. Bar: Mich. 1980, NY 1995. Planner City of Detroit, 1971-75; atty. Rockwell and Kotz, P.C., Detroit, 1980-87; pvt. practice David M. Thoms & Assocs., P.C., Detroit, 1987—2002, Miller Canfield Paddock and Stone, P.L.C., 2002—. Adj. assoc. prof. Madonna U., 1993—; presenter NYU Tax Inst. Editor Case and Comment U. of Detroit Law Rev., 1978-79. Mem. program com. Fin. and Estate Planning Coun. Detroit, 1980—; mem. adv. bd., chmn. nominating com., mem. exec. com. Met. Detroit Salvation Army, 1980—, sec.-treas., vice chmn., 1994-95, chmn., 1995-96; bd. dirs. bylaws and property com., mem. nominating com., devel. com., exec. com. Mich. chpt. ARC; bd. dirs. L'Alliance Française de Grosse Pointe, 1980-2004, 05—, pres., 1985-88, 94-95; bd. dirs. French Festival of Detroit, Inc., 1986-89, 91-94, pres.; bd. dirs. Fedn. of Alliances Français, 1989-95, 97-2002, also past treas., v.p., chmn. fin. com., pres., 2000-01; bd. dirs. Vis. Nurse Assn., 2003—, sec., 2004—; bd. dirs. Detroit Symphony Orch. Hall, Inc., 1996-97; trustee Kalamazoo Coll., 1993-97, mem. exec. com., 1995-97; trustee Henry M. Selden Charitable Trust, 2003—, Mich. Colls Found., 2004—; dir. vis. com. European art DIA, 1995-97. Decorated officier Ordre des Palmes Academiques, knight Order of Salvador (Salvador Dali Mus.); recipient Prix Schonberger/ Burton scholar U. Detroit, 1979; named to Best Lawyers in Am., 2005. Mem. ABA (chmn. subcom. on probate and estate planning, mem. charitable trust com.), Fed. Bar Assn., Oakland County Bar Assn., Detroit Bar Assn., State Bar Mich., NY Bar Assn., Bar Assn. of City of NY, Am. Planning Assn. (Mich. chpt.), The Grosse Pointe Club. Mem. United Church of Christ. Avocations: tennis, architecture, music, travel, art history. Office: 840 W Long Lake Rd Ste 200 Troy MI 48098 Office Phone: 248-267-3242. Business E-Mail: thoms@millercanfield.com.

**THOMS, JOSEPHINE BOWERS,** artist; b. Lansing, Mich., Sept. 14, 1922; d. Raymon Lyon and Adele (Hammond) Bowers; m. Bert Thoms, June 4, 1945 (dec.); 1 child, Adele Lucile Thoms; m. Peter Blackford Lauck, May 10, 1983. BA, Hillsdale Coll., 1944; MA, Md. Inst. Art, 1977. Instr. modern dance Hillsdale (Mich.) Coll., 1943-44; artist-in-residence St. John's Coll., Annapolis, Md., 1953-55, 68-70; instr. art Washington and Jefferson Coll., Washington, Pa., 1956, Bethany (W.Va.) Coll., 1963-65; illustrator Md. Dept. Natural Resources, Annapolis, 1977-95. Joint owner Onset Bay Gallery and Studio, Onset, Mass., portrait artist, colorist; instr. Washington Art Assn., 1958-69; art dir. Md. Fedn. Art, Annapolis, 1970-72, pres., 1972-74. Illustrator: Federal Prose, 1947; executed murals: History of Electricity, Hillsdale, 1942, The Harbor at Annapolis, Crownsville, Md., 1989. Mem. Caritas Soc. at St. John's Coll., 1969—, Md. Peace Action, Annapolis, 1983—. Recipient 1st prize for Exhbn. of Nature-Related Art, Adkins Arboretum, Tuckahoe State Pk., Denton, Md., 1995. Mem. Md. Soc. Portrait Painters (cert., exhibits chairperson 1995—), Annapolis Watercolor Club (1st prize 1993). Democrat. Episcopalian. Avocations: swimming, aerobics, piano, needlepoint design. Home: 61 Southgate Ave Annapolis MD 21401-2829

**THOMS, LINDA CHATMAN,** federal agency administrator; d. William C. Chatman; m. Steuart Hill Thomsen, Oct. 16, 1982. BA, Smith Coll., 1976; JD, Harvard U. Atty. Davis Polk & Wardwell, Washington, NYC; asst. U.S. atty. Dist. Md. US Dept. Justice; asst. chief litigation counsel SEC, Washington, 1995—97; asst. dir. Divsn. Enforcement, SEC, Washington, 1997—2000, assoc. dir., 2000—02, dep. dir., 2002—05, dir., 2005—. Named one of 50 Women to Watch, Wall St. Journal, 2005. Office: SEC 450 Fifth St NW Washington DC 20549*

**THOMSON, BASIL HENRY, JR.,** lawyer; b. Amarillo, Tex., Jan. 17, 1945; m. Margaret Shepard, May 4, 1985; children: Christopher, Matthew, Robert. BBA, Baylor U., 1968, JD, 1973. Bar: Tex. 1974, U.S. Ct. Mil. Appeals 1974, U.S. Supreme Ct. 1977, U.S. Dist. Ct. (we. dist) Tex. 1988, U.S. Ct. Appeals (fed. cir.) 1990. Oil title analyst Hunt Oil Co., Dallas, 1971-73; atty., advisor Regulations and Adminstrv. Law divsn. Office of Chief Counsel USCG, Washington, 1973-77; dir. estate planning devel. dept. Baylor U., Waco, Tex., 1977-80, gen. counsel, 1980—2002; ret., 2002; assoc. gen. counsel So. Meth. U., Dallas, 2002—. Adj. prof. law Baylor U.; lobbyist legis. Ind. Higher Edn., 71st Session of Tex. Legislature; mem. legis. com. Gov.'s Task Force on Drug Abuse; dir. govtl. rels. Baylor U.; spkr. at meetings of coll. and univ. adminstrs.; assisted in drafting legis. for Texan's War on Drugs Tex. Legislature; mem. legal adv. com. United Educators Ins. Risk Retention Group, 1994-96. Active Longhorn Coun. Boy Scouts of Am.; mem. planning and zoning commn. City of Woodway, 2004—, mem. bd. adjustment, 1998—2004; bd. dirs. Heart of Tex. Coun. on Alcohol and Drug Abuse, 1987—91. Recipient Pres.'s award Ind. Colls. and Univs. of Tex., 1994, Dist. award of merit Boy Scouts Am. Fellow Coll. State Bar Tex.; mem. ABA, FBA, Nat. Assn. Coll. and Univ. Attys. (fin., nominations and elections coms. 1994-95, bd. dirs. 1988-91, 2000—, pres. 2004-05), Nat. Assn. Ind. Colls. and Univs. (mem. legal svcs. rev. panel), Tex. Bar Assn., Waco Bar Assn., McLennan County Bar Assn., Owners Assn. of Sugar Creek, Inc. (bd. dirs. 1991-95). Baptist. Avocations: backpacking, running, environmental concerns, historical reinactment. Home: 100 Sugar Creek Pl Waco TX 76712-3410 Office: So Meth U PO Box 750132 Dallas TX 75275-0137 Office Phone: 214-768-3233. Business E-Mail: bthomson@smu.edu.

**THOMSON, CAROLINE HELEN,** artist; b. Takapuna, New Zealand, Jan. 12, 1945; d. William Harvey Thomson and Phyllis Alwyn Morgan. Artist Provincetown Art Assn. and Mus. One-woman shows include Eye of Horus Gallery, Provincetown, 1993-94, Bangs St. Gallery, Provincetown, Mass., 1995-99; exhibited in group shows at Bangs St. Gallery, Provincetown, 1995-99, David Armstrong, Susanna Coffey, Jack Pierson, Caroline Thomson, 2000, two person exhbn., Susanna Coffey, Caroline Thomson, 1996-99, Provincetown Art Assn. and Mus., 1999, selections from the permanent collection, juried exhbn., Provincetown Art Assn. and Mus., 1989-97, Invitational exhbns., PAAM, 1989-98. Exhbn. include Charles Hawthorne, Varujan Boghosian, Lily Harmon, Provincetown Art Assn. and Mus. Documentary film based on the life of Caroline Thomson, London, 1967, directed by Sheldon Rochlin and Diane Rochlin. Avocations: singer-song writer, wildlife rehabilitation. Home Fax: 508-349-7922. Personal E-mail: dmschachter2000@yahoo.com.

**THOMSON, DAVID K.R.,** publishing executive; s. Kenneth Thomson. Grad., Upper Can. Coll.; MA in hist., Selwyn Coll., Cambridge, 1978. With Hudson's Bay Co.; pres. Zellers and Simpsons, 1980—90; dep. chmn. Woodbridge Co. Ltd., 1990—; mem. bd. dirs. The Thomson Corp., Toronto, 1988—, chmn., 2002—. Named one of Top 200 Collectors, ARTnews Mag., 2004. Avocation: Collector of Constable; Italian Futurism; Contemporary art. Office: Thomson Corp Toronto-Dominion Bank Tower, 66 Wellington St W Toronto ON M5K 1A1 Canada Office Phone: 416-360-8700.

**THOMSON, DONALD ARTHUR,** education educator; b. Detroit, Apr. 9, 1932; s. Arthur and Theresa Rita (Stasin) T.; m. M. Jenean Gruner, Apr. 6, 1957; children: Erin, Kurt, Lisa, Madelon. BS, U. Mich., 1955, MS, 1957; PhD, U. Hawaii, 1963. Asst. prof., curator of fishes dir. mar. sci. to prof. U. Ariz., Tucson, 1963-98, prof. emeritus, 1998—. Author: Reef Fishes of the Sea of Cortez, 2000, Fishwater's Guide to the Gulf of Calif., 1976, Tide

Calendar for the Northern Gulf of Calif., 1967-2003; contbr. articles to profl. jour. Democrat. Avocations: photography, fly fishing, aquaria, dogs. Office: Dept Ecol/Evol Biol Univ Ariz Tucson AZ 85721-0001 E-mail: dat@u.arizona.edu.

**THOMSON, DONNA R,** primary school educator, researcher; b. Alton, Ill., July 7, 1947; d. Cecil Clyde and Mary Alice Hodge; m. William Eugene Thomson, June 7, 1968; 1 child, Philip Andrew. BSc, Tex. Christian U., 1972; MSc, Tex. Wesleyan U., 1987. Tchr. Ft. Worth Sch. Dist., Tex., 1972—2001; adminstr./prin. Tower Christian Acad., 2001—03; tchg. asst./rschr. U. North Tex., 2004—05. Mem. missions bd. Houston First Ch. of God, 2004—05. Recipient Outstanding Doctoral student in early childhood, U. North Tex., 1999. Mem.: Am. Ednl. Rsch. Assn., Phi Delta Kappa. Home: 9911 Burntfork Houston TX 77064 Personal E-mail: donnarb54321@aol.com.

**THOMSON, GERALD EDMUND,** physician, educator; b. N.Y.C., 1932; s. Lloyd and Sybil (Gilbourne) T.; m. Carolyn Webber; children: Gregory, Karen. MD, Howard U., 1959; DSc (hon.), Morehouse Med. Coll., 1997. Diplomate Am. Bd. Internal Medicine (bd. govs. 1985-92, exec. com. 1988-91, chmn.-elect 1990-91, chmn. 1991-92). Resident in medicine SUNY-Kings County Hosp. Center, 1959-62, chief resident, 1962-63, N.Y. Heart Assn. fellow in nephrology, 1964-65, asst. vis. physician, 1963-70, clin. dir. dialysis unit, 1965-67; practice medicine specializing in internal medicine N.Y.C., 1963-64; attending physician SUNY Med. Bklyn. Hosp., 1966-70; instr. in medicine SUNY, Bklyn., 1963-68, clin. asst. prof. medicine, 1968-70; asso. chief med. services Coney Island Hosp., Bklyn., 1967-70; attending physician Presbyn. Hosp., 1970—; dir. nephrology Harlem Hosp. Center, N.Y.C., 1970-71; dir. med. services, 1971-85, pres. med. bd., 1976-78; assoc. prof. medicine Columbia Coll. Physicians and Surgeons, 1970-72, prof., 1972—, Samuel Lambert prof. medicine, 1980—, Robert Sonneborn prof. medicine, 1997—; exec. v.p. for profl. affairs, chief of staff Columbia-Presbyn. Med. Ctr., 1985-90; sr. assoc. dean Coll. Physicians and Surgeons, Columbia U., N.Y.C., 1990—. Mem. Health Rsch. Coun. City N.Y., 1972-75; mem. med. adv. bd. N.Y. Kidney Found., 1971-82; mem. Health Rsch. Coun., State N.Y., 1975-81; mem. hypertension info. and edn. adv. com. NIH, 1973-74, N.Y. State Adv. Com. on Hypertension, 1977-80; com. on nonpharm. treatment of hypertension Inst. of Medicine, Nat. Acad. Scis., 1980; mem. med. adv. bd. Nat. Assn. Patients on Hemodialysis and Transplantation, 1973-83; mem. adv. bd. Sch. Biomed. Edn., CUNY, 1979-83, Med. News Network, 1993-95; mem. com. on mild hypertension Nat. Heart and Lung Inst., 1976, mem. clin. trials rev. com., 1980-85, mem. rev. panel, 1979; bd. dirs. N.Y. Heart Assn., 1973-81, chmn. com. high blood pressure, 1976-81; bd. dirs. Primary Care Devel. Corp.; chmn. com. hypertension N.Y. Met. Regional Med. Program, 1974-76; mem. adv. com. Heart and Hypertension Inst. of N.Y. State, 1984; mem. N.Y. Gov.'s Health Adv. Coun., 1981-84, pub. Health Coun., N.Y., 1983-95, Joint Nat. Com. High Blood Pressure NIH, 1983-84, 87-88, mem. rev. panel hypertension detection and monitoring bd. study cardiovasc. risk factors in young Nat. Heart, Lung and Blood Inst., 1984-90; mem. panel on receiving and withholding med. treatment ACLU, 1984-88; mem. Grad. Med. Edn. Commn., State of N.Y., 1984-86, mem. Commn. on End-State Renal Disease, 1985, 89-90; pres. Washington Heights-Inwood Ambulatory Care Network Corp., 1986-91; bd. dirs. Primary Care Devel. Corp., 1993—. Mem. adv. bd. Jour. Urban Health, 1974-80, Med. News Network, 1993-94. Chmn. ad hoc com. on access to nursing homes Pub. Health Coun. State of N.Y., 1982-96; pres. Washington Heights-Inwood Ambulatory Care Network Corp., 1986-91; mem. Mayor's Commn. Health and Hosps. Corp.; dir. Harlem Ctr. for Health Promotion and Disease Prevention, 1993-95. Recipient Nat. Med. award Nat. Kidney Found., N.Y., 1984, Outstanding Alumnus award Howard U., 1987, Disting. Alumnus award, 1998, Dean's Outstanding Tchg. award Coll. Physicians and Surgeons Columbia U., 1986, Columbia U. Pres. award Outstanding Tchg., 2002, Nickens award, Soc. General Internal Med., 2004. Fellow ACP (Gov.'s coun. downstate region 1982-89, chmn. com. health pub. policy N.Y. chpt. 1982-89, health care professions com. 1987-90, bd. regents 1990-97, chmn. nat. health and pub. policy com. 1993-94, pres.-elect 1994-95, pres. 1995-96), N.Y. Acad. Medicine (mem. com. medicine in soc. 1974-76, chmn. com. medicine in soc. 1997-98, bd. trustees, 2000-, sec., 2003-); mem. AAAS, N.Y. Soc. Nephrology (pres. 1973-74), Am. Fedn. Clin. Rsch., Federated Coun. for Internal Medicine (chmn. 1991-92, 95-96), Soc. Urban Physicians (pres. 1972-73), Am. Soc. Artificial Internal Organs (adv. bd., 1998-2002, chmn. bd. trustees, 2002-), Assn. Program Dirs. in Internal Medicine, Pub. Health Assn. N.Y.C. (dir. 1983-86), Physicians for Social Responsibility of N.Y. (dir. 1983), Physicians Human Rights (co-chmn., 2001-03, bd. trustees, 2005-) Assn. Acad. Minority Physicians (pres. 1988-90), Inst. of Medicine, Nat. Acad. Scis. Home: Premium Pt New Rochelle NY 10801-5327 Office: Coll Physicians & Surgeons Columbia U New York NY 10032

**THOMSON, HELEN LOUISE,** retired artist; b. Lewiston, Ill., Nov. 28, 1928; d. Clyde Arthur Pomeroy and Myrtle Lynch Cluney; m. William Edward Thomson, 1950; children: Persephone Ann, Lucinda Renee, Cynthia Louise. Student, Western Ill. U., 1972, 78, 85, U. Ill., 1972; diploma, North Light Art Sch. Artist, Table Grove, Ill., 1970—. Adj. prof. Western Ill. U., Macomb, 1985-94; mem. spkrs. roster Spoon River Coll., Canton, Ill., 1986-94; exec. dir. Two Rivers Arts Coun., Macomb, 1985-94. Exhibited in numerous one woman and group exhbns.; contbr. art to calendars United Fed. Savs. & Loan, 1980, 86. Pres. Spoon River Coll. Found., Canton, Ill., 1979-85, Fulton County Arts Coun., Canton, 1973-83; bd. dirs. Regional Arts Adv. Coun., Western Ill. U., 1978-85; mem. adv. panel Ill. Arts Coun., Chgo., 1980-83; officer PTA, Table Grove, 1957-85. Recipient Ruth Watts Svc. award Performing Arts Soc., Western Ill. U., 1994, award Two Rivers Arts Coun., 1994; selected for feature stories on pub. TV via. WMEC, 1997, Canton Daily Ledger, Macomb Jour., Peoria (Ill.) Jour. Mem.: Chgo. Art Inst., Galesburg Civic Art Ctr. (exhbn. awards), Ill. Watercolor Soc., Ill. Art League (exhbn. awards), PEO Sisterhood (pres., sec., chaplain, v.p.). Avocations: antiques, antique dolls, family history, travel. Home: 404 S Broadway St PO Box 163 Table Grove IL 61482-0163

**THOMSON, IAIN DONALD,** philosopher, educator; s. Captane Peter and Helen McLeod Thomson; m. Kirsten Millinor Krebs, Apr. 27, 1996; 1 child, Darian Skye. PhD magna cum laude in Philosophy, U. Calif. San Diego, La Jolla, Calif., 1999. Assoc. prof. Dept. Philosophy U. N.Mex., Albuquerque, 2000—05, assoc. prof. Dept. Philosophy, 2005—. Author: Heidegger on Ontotheology: Technology and the Politics of Education. Recipient Gunter Starkey Tchg. Excellence award, U. N.Mex. Coll. Arts and Scis., 2003. Fellow: Phi Beta Kappa. Office: University of New Mexico Department of Philosophy — MSCO3 2140 Albuquerque NM 87131-0001 Personal E-mail: ithomson@unm.edu.

**THOMSON, JAMES ALAN,** think-tank executive; b. Boston, Jan. 21, 1945; s. James Alan and Mary Elizabeth (Pluff) T.; m. Darlene Thomson; children: Kristen Ann, David Alan. BS, U. N.H., 1967; MS, Purdue U., 1970, PhD, 1972, DSc (hon.), 1992; LLD (hon.), Pepperdine U., 1996. Research fellow U. Wis., Madison, 1972-74; systems analyst Office Sec. Def., U.S. Dept. Def., Washington, 1974-77; staff mem. Nat. Security Council, White House, Washington, 1977-81; v.p. RAND, Santa Monica, Calif., 1981-89, chief exec. officer, 1989—. Bd. dirs. L.A. World Affairs Coun., AK Steel Holding Corp., Encysive Pharms., Object Reservoir. Contbr. articles to profl. jours. and chpts. to books. Mem. Internat. Inst. for Strategic Studies (coun. 1985-99), Coun. Fgn. Rels. Office: RAND 1776 Main St Santa Monica CA 90401-3297 Office Phone: 310-451-6936. Business E-Mail: thomson@rand.org.

**THOMSON, JAMES ALEXANDER,** molecular biologist, educator; b. Chgo., Dec. 20, 1968; married; 2 children. BS in Biophysics, U. Ill., 1981; DVM magna cum laude, U.Pa., 1985, DS in molecular biology, 1988. Cert. Am. Coll. Veterinary Pathologists. Joined U. Wis., Madison, 1991, assoc. veterinarian, chief pathologist Wis. Regional Primate Rsch. Ctr.; John D. McArthur Prof., dept. anatomy U. Wis.-Madison Med. Sch. Named a finalist for World Tech. award in health and medicine, The Economist, London, 1999; recipient Ill. Gen. Assembly award, 1978, Eastman Kodak award in Biol.

Scis., 1979, Golden Plate award, Am. Acad. Achievement, 1999, Frank Annunzio award, Christopher Columbus Fellowship Found., 2003; fellow Undergrad. Rsch. Participation, Princeton U., N.J., 1979; scholar Nat. Merit, 1977. Mem.: Phi Zeta, Phi Beta Kappa. Achievements include first to isolate and culture nonhuman primate embryonic stem cells in 1995, and human ES cells in 1998. Office: Univ Wisconsin Primate Rsch Ctr 1220 Capitol Ct Madison WI 53715 E-mail: thomson@primate.wisc.edu.

**THOMSON, JOHN ALISTAIR,** music educator; b. Hewall, Cheshire, Eng., Apr. 4, 1963; U.S. s. William Alexander Thomson and Nora Hillary Lyons Thomson; m. Jean Soo Hahn, July 30, 1991; children: Alexa, Sean. Prof. U. S.D., Vermillion. Office: U SD 414 E Clark St Vermillion SD 57069

**THOMSON, JOHN ANSEL ARMSTRONG,** biochemist; b. Detroit, Nov. 23, 1911; s. John Russell and Florence (Antisdel) T.; m. June Anna Mae Hummel, June 24, 1938; children: Sheryll Linn, Patrisha Diane, Robert Royce. AA, Pasadena (Calif.) City Coll., 1935; AB cum laude, U. So. Calif., 1957; BGS (hon.), Calif. Poly. State U., 1961; MA, PhD, Columbia Pacific U., 1978, 79; DA, Internat. Inst. Advanced Studies, Clayton, Mo., 1979. Cert. secondary tchr., Calif. Chemist J.A. Thomson Bio-Organic Chemist, L.A., 1938, Vitamin Inst. (formerly J.A. Thomson Bio-Organic Chemist), L.A. and North Hollywood, Calif., 1939—. Vocat. edn. instr. U.S. War Manpower Commn., 1943-44; chmn. activities coun. World Coun. of Youth, L.A., 1932; pres. Coun. of Young Men's Divsns. Athletic Commns., YMCA Pasadena area, 1931, chmn. exec. coun., 1932; dist. officer Boy Scouts Am., San Fernando Valley coun., 1954-64, del. to nat. conf., 1959, and others. Author: (booklets) Whose Are the Myths?, 1949, Open Eyes, Illegalize Agency Abuses, 1968, Non-toxic Vitamins-hormones Answers to Environmental, Public Problems, 1972, Lobby Interest Goals to Sequester Nutrients Among Those Rarely Educated in Them, 1973, Support of Pressures to Homeostasis, Normality, 1990, Minimization of Toxics in Agriculture, 1991, Need for Recognition and Reversal of Rapid Decline of Heritage of American and World Children 1995, 1996; contbr. articles to jours. Prog. leader United Meth. Men Quadrennial Conf., Lafayette, Ind., 1982, instr. United Methodist Ch. nat. seminar for profls., Nashville, Tenn., 1983, pres. United Meth. Men, 1979-80, mem. adminstv. bd., 1952—, chmn. commn. ch. and soc., 1938—, First United Meth. Ch., North Hollywood; mem. Rep. county ctrl. Com. L.A. County, 1941-50, chmn. 63d assembly dist., 1948-50, Rep. state ctrl. com., Calif. 1948-50. Recipient Sci. and Industry award San Francisco Internat. Expn., 1940, various scouting leadership awards Boy Scouts Am., Civic Svc. award State of Calif., 1949, others. Mem. AAAS (life), Am. Inst. Biol. Scis., N.Y. Acad. Scis., Am. Hort. Soc., Am. Chem. Soc., Internat. Acad. Nutrition and Preventive Medicine, Am. Forestry Assn., Garden Writers Assn. Am., Profl. Grounds Mgmt. Soc., Internat. Soc. Hort. Sci., Nat. Recreation and Parks Assn., Nat. Nutritional Foods Assn. (Pioneer Svc. award 1970), Nat. Health Fedn. (life), Nat. Resources Def. Coun., Lawn and Garden Mktg. and Distbn. Assn. (Lifetime Achievement award 2005, 06), Am. Nursery and Landscape Assn., Am. Nurseries adn Garden Ctrs., China Soc. of So. Claif. (pres., 1990-1991), Com. for Nuc. Responsibility, Inst. for Health Freedom, Internat. Union of Pure and Applied Chemistry, Perennial Plant Assn., So. Calif. Pub. Health Assn., Tree Care Industry Assn., Universal City-North Hollywood C. of C., Sierra Club, Soc. Colonial Wars (life), Kiwanis (projects panelist internat. confs. 1987, 91, pres. N. Hollywood club 1996-97), Friends of the Earth, Negative Population Growth, Amnesty Internat., U. So. Calif. Gen. Alumni Assn. (life), Life Extension Found., Am. Assn. for Health Freedom, Union of Concerned Scientists, U.S. C. of C., Am. Acad. of Anti-Aging. Republican. Achievements include origination of a high proportion of known uses for horticultural hormones, with first products, many of them via solely-invented and produced Hormes 4, 1 and 2, Superthrive, Cutstart and Seedyield, multiple vitamins-hormones, distributed worldwide; development of highest known efficacies in plant activating, reviving, transplanting, growing, perfecting, rooting and seed invigoration; creation of water-miscible multiple vitamins powder Auzon, for humans; creation of more than 300 core formula products. Office: Vitamin Inst 12610 Saticoy St S North Hollywood CA 91605-4313 Office Phone: 323-877-5186.

**THOMSON, KEITH STEWART,** biologist, author; b. Heanor, Eng., July 29, 1938; s. Ronald William and Marian Adelaide (Coster) T.; m. Linda Gailbreath Price, Sept. 27, 1963; children: Jessica Adelaide, Elizabeth Rose. B.Sc. with honors, U. Birmingham, Eng., 1960; A.M., Harvard U., 1961, PhD (NATO fellow), 1963. NATO postdoctoral fellow Univ. Coll., London U., 1963-65; asst. prof. to prof. biology Yale U., 1965-87, dean Grad. Sch., 1979-87; dir. Peabody Mus. Natural History, 1976-79; pres. Acad. Natural Scis., Phila., 1987-95; disting. scientist-in-residence New Sch Social Rsch., N.Y.C., 1996-98; prof., dir. Mus. Natural History Oxford U., 1998—2003, prof. emeritus, 2003—; sr. rsch. fellow Am. Philos. Soc., Phila., 2003—. Dir. Sears Found. Marine Rsch. and Oceanographic History; hon. rsch. fellow Australian Nat. U., 1967; trustee, mem. corp. Woods Hole Oceanographic Inst.; bd. dirs. Wistar Inst., Ctrl. Phila. Devel. Corp., Wetlands Inst., Phila. Cultural Alliance, Charles Darwin Trust; rschr. in vertebrate evolution. Mem. editl. bd. Paleobiology, Jour. Morphology, 1988, Aspects of Lower Vertebrate Evolution, 1968, Origin of Terrestrial Vertebrates, 1968, Saltwater Fishes of Conn., 1971, 88, Priorities and Needs in Systematic Biology, 1981, Morphogenesis and Evolution, 1988, Living Fossil, 1991, The Common But Less Frequent Loon and Other Essays, 1993, HMS Beagle, 1995, 2003, Treasures on Earth, 2002, Before Darwin: Reconciling Science and Religion, 2005, Fossils, A Very Short Introduction, 2005. Fellow Linnean Soc. London, Zool. Soc. London; mem. Soc. Vertebrate Palaeontology, Sigma Xi.

**THOMSON, PAUL RICE, JR.,** lawyer; b. Syracuse, NY, Dec. 28, 1941; s. Paul Rice and Marcella Elizabeth (Shea) T.; m. Elizabeth Ann Cutliff, Aug. 21, 1965; children: Paul R. III, Pamela Judeth. BA in History, Va. Mil. Inst., 1960, JD, Washington and Lee U., 1966. Bar: Va. 1966, US Dist. Ct. (we. dist.) Va. 1966, US Ct. Mil. Appeals 1967, US Ct. Appeals (4th cir.) 1972, US Ct. Appeals (11th cir.) 2004. Assoc. Clement, Wheatley, Winston & Ingram, Danville, Va., 1969-71; asst. U.S. atty. Western Dist. Va., Roanoke, 1971-75, U.S. atty., 1975-79; gen. counsel natural resources The Pittston Co., Lebanon, Va., 1980—87; dep. asst. adminstr. EPA, Washington, 1987—90; ptnr. Woods Rogers PLC, Roanoke, Va., 1990—. Pres. Roanoke Valley Law Enforcement Coun., 1975-76; mem. Fed.-State Law Enforcement Coun., 1975-79; trustee Ea. Mineral Law Found., Pitts., 1980-82; adj. prof. Washington & Lee U., 1981-99. V.p. Danville Jr. C. of C., 1971. Capt. JAGC USMC, 1966—69. Recipient Spl. Achievement award Dept. Justice, 1974, Silver Beaver award, Boy Scouts Am., Blue Ridge Mountains Coun., 2004. Mem. ABA, Va. Bar Assn., Fed. Bar Assn. (pres. local chpt. 1979), NRA, Trout Unltd. Roman Catholic. Avocations: fly fishing, bird hunting, raising labrador retrievers. Office: Woods Rogers PLC 10 S Jefferson St Roanoke VA 24011 Office Phone: 540-983-7742. Business E-Mail: thomson@woodsrogers.com.

**THOMSON, RICHARD MURRAY,** retired bank executive; b. Winnipeg, Man., Can., Aug. 14, 1933; s. H.W. and Mary Thomson. BASC in Engring., U. Toronto, 1955; MBA, Harvard U., 1957; fellow course in banking. Queen's U., 1958. From mem. staff to pres., CEO Toronto Dominion Bank, Ont., Canada, 1957—77, pres., CEO 1977—78, chmn., 1978—98, CEO, 1978—97, ret., 1998. Bd. dirs. S.C. Johnson & Son Inc., The Thomson Corp., Trizec Properties, Inc., Nexen Inc. Office: The Toronto Dominion Bank 66 Wellington St W 10th Fl TD Bank Tow POB 1 Toronto Dominion Ctr Toronto ON Canada M5K 1A2

**THOMSON, ROGER F.,** lawyer; b. Detroit, Apr. 4, 1949; m. Carol M. Barger. BA, Miami U., Oxford, OH, 1971; JD, So. Meth. U., Dallas, 1974. Bar: Tex. 1974, US Dist. Ct. No. Dist. Tex., US Ct. Appeals 5th Cir. Legal counsel S&A Restaurant Corp., Dallas, 1978—80, corp. counsel, 1980—82, v.p., gen. counsel, 1982—83, v.p., gen. counsel sec., 1983—84, sr. v.p., gen. counsel, sec., 1984—85, exec. v.p., gen. counsel, sec., 1985—88; sr. v.p., gen. counsel Burger King Corp., Miami, Fla., 1988—93; sr. v.p., gen. counsel, sec. Brinker Internat. Inc., Dallas, 1993—94, dir., 1993—95, exec. v.p., gen. counsel, sec., 1994—; chief adminstrv. officer, 1996—. Mem.: State Bar Tex. Office: Brinker Internat Inc 6820 LBJ Fwy Dallas TX 75240

**THOMSON, THYRA GODFREY,** former state official; b. Florence, Colo., July 30, 1916; d. John and Rosalie (Altman) Godfrey; m. Keith Thomson, Aug. 6, 1939 (dec. Dec. 1960); children— William John, Bruce Godfrey, Keith Coffey. BA cum laude, U. Wyo., 1939. With dept. agronomy and agrl. econs. U. Wyo.,1938-39; writer weekly column Watching Washington pub. in 14 papers, Wyo., 1955-60; planning chmn. Nat. Fedn. Republican Women, Washington, 1961; sec. state Wyo. Cheyenne, 1962-86. Mem. Marshall Scholarships Com. for Pacific region, 1964-68; del. 72d Wilton Park Conf., Eng., 1965; mem. youth commn. UNESCO, 1970-71, Allied Health Professions Council HEW, 1971-72; del. U.S.-Republic of China Trade Conf., Taipei, Taiwan, 1983; mem. lt. gov.'s trade and fact-finding mission to Saudi Arabia, Jordan, and Egypt, 1985 Bd. dirs. Buffalo Bill Mus., Cody, Wyo., 1987—; adv. bd. Coll. Arts and Scis., U. Wyo., 1989, Cheyenne Symphony Orch. Found., 1990—. Recipient Disting. Alumni award U. Wyo., 1969, Disting. U. Wyo. Arts and Scis. Alumna award, 1987, citation Omicron Delta Epsilon, 1965, citation Beta Gamma Sigma, 1968, citation Delta Kappa Gamma, 1973, citation Wyo. Commn. Women, 1986; named Internat. Woman of Distinction, Alpha Delta Kappa, Keith and Thyra Honors Convocation in her honor Coll. of Arts and Scis. U. Wyo., 1997. Mem. N.Am. Securities Adminstrs. (pres. 1973-74), Nat. Assn. Secs. of State, Council State Govts. (chmn. natural resources com. Western states 1966-68), Nat. Conf. Lt. Govs. (exec. com. 1976-79) Republican. Home: 3102 Sunrise Rd Cheyenne WY 82001-6136

**THOMSON, TODD STUART,** investment company executive; b. Stanford, Calif., Jan. 30, 1961; s. Scott Dayton and Margaret Elaine (Guice) T.; m. Melissa Kay McKeithen, May 22, 1988. BA in Econs., Davidson Coll., 1983; MBA with distinction, U. Pa., 1987. With Barents Group LLC, cons., sr. cons. Booz Allen & Hamilton, Bethesda, Md., 1983-85; cons., mgr. Bain & Co., Boston, 1986-91; sr. v.p. strategic planning & bus. devel. GE Capital Sevices; sr. v.p.-global devel. Travelers Group, NYC, 1998; sr. v.p. strategy & bus. devel. Citigroup Inc., NYC, 1998—2000, exec. v.p. fin., ops. & strategy, CFO, 2000—04; chmn., CEO Smith Barney, NYC, 2004—. Office: Smith Barney 388 Greenwich St New York NY 10013

**THOMSON, VIRGINIA WINBOURN,** humanities educator, writer; b. Oakland, Calif., Aug. 6, 1930; d. Harry Linn and Jennie Cook (Vineyard) Thomson. AA, San Mateo Coll., 1949; BA, San Jose State Coll., 1951; MA, U. Calif., Berkeley, 1952. Cert. secondary tchr. Calif. Tchr. social sci. Capuchino H.S., San Bruno, Calif., 1952—54, Watsonville H.S., Calif., 1954—87. Saleswoman, storyteller Home Interiors, San Mateo, 1963—64. Author: The Lion Desk, 1965, Short Talks Around the Lord's Table, 1985, Lawson's Castle, 2001, numerous poems. Mem.: AAUW (life), Nat. Geog. Soc. (life), Calif. Alumni Assn. (life), Calif. Writer's Club (life), Homer Honor Soc., Internat. Poets, Phi Alpha Theta. Republican.

**THONGBOONKERD, VISITH,** nephrologist, researcher; b. Phichit, Thailand, Nov. 13, 1971; MD with first class honors (hon.), Chiang Mai U., Thailand, 1994. Diplomate Thai Board of Nephrology Nephrology Soc. of Thailand. Clin. nephrology fellow Chiang Mai U., 1998—2000; Internat. Soc. of Nephrology fellow U. Louisville, 2000—. Recipient Best Fellow's Poster award, Internat. Soc. Nephrology, 2001. Office: U Louisville Proteomics Lab 570 South Preston St Ste 102 Louisville KY 40202

**THONGSAK, VAJEEPRASEE THOMAS,** finance company executive; b. Udonthani, Thailand, Feb. 10, 1935; came to U.S., 1970; s. Chanmar and Pee Vajeeprasee; m. Somchit; 1 child, Rosarine. BS in Sociology, BA in Philosophy, Mahamakut U., Bangkok, 1968; MA in Edn., Kean Coll. N.J., 1976; MA in Philosophy, NYU, 1989; PhD in Mgmt., AMA Mgmt. Inst., 1987. Cert. cash mgr. Tchr. Machimavas Sch., Udonthani, 1958-65; spl. instr. Chana Songkram Sch., Bangkok, 1965-68; tchrs. staff Thai Sripratoom U., Bangkok, 1968-70; salesman Met. Life of N.Y., 1974-76; rep. Mut. Life of N.Y., 1976-78; agt. Equitable Life Ins., N.Y.C., 1983-84; insp. IBI Security Svc. Inc., L.I., 1979-85; security police insp. Brandeis U., Waltham, Mass., 1985-86; U.S. chief legal investigator, pvt. investigator U.S. Legal Investigation, Inc., U.S. Bur.'s Security Agy., Boston, N.Y.C., Fresno, Calif., 1987—; chmn. Worldwide Bank Assocs. Investment, 2000—. Advisor Thai N.E. Assn., N.Y.C., 1980—, Rep. Nat. Com., Washingotn, 1980—; state advisor U.S. Congl. Adv., Washington, 1980; assoc. mem. Nat. Security Ctr., Citizen's Adv. Coun., Washington, 1989; pres., chief security agt. U.S. Bur. Security Agy., 1991; mem. Pres. Pvt. Sector Survey on Cost Control, Washington, 1989—; adv. bd. Am. Security Coun., Washington, 1983-88. Mem. G.O.P. Republican Conservative Party (recommendation pres. Gerald R. Ford 1977), 1977—, Nat. Republican Congl. Com. Victory Fund, Washington, 1982—, Republican Presdl. Task Force and Comsn. (recommendation chmn. Nat. Republican Senatorial Com. 1982, 93), 1982—, Am. Security Coun. Found., 1978—, Defense Dept., Defense Inst., 1982—, Nat. Rep. Senatorial Com., Washington, Chiefs of Police Nat. Drug Task Force, 1982—, Nat. Law Enforcement Officers Meml. Fund, Washington, 1982—, Natl. Wildlife Fedn., 1982—; apptd. state advisor U.S. Congl. Adv. Bd., 1979, 93; priest asst. U.S.A. Buddhayaram Temple, Bronx, 1970—; pres. S.E. Asia Found., 1970; mem. Citizens Against Govt. Waste, Washington; mem. U.S. Def. Com., Washington, 1982-86; sec. Wat Buddhamonthol United Buddhist Meditation Ctr., 1992—. Recipient Presdl. Seal, Rep. Orgn., 1983, 84, Rep. Presdl. Legion of Merit highest level of Govts. for Lifetime, 1999. Mem.: ANA, Nat. Constitution Ctr. (Pa. signer), Navy League U.S., Internat. Assn. Chiefs of Police, Rep. Presdl. Legion of Merit, Am. Fedn. Police (life), Sen.'s Club, Pres.'s Club. Office Phone: 212-430-9536.

**'T HOOFT, GERARDUS (GERARD 'T HOOFT),** physicist, researcher; b. Den Helder, The Netherlands, July 5, 1946; s. Hendrik 't Hooft and Margaretha Agnes (van Kampen) t' Hooft; m. Albertha Anje Schik, July 1, 1972; children: Saskia Anne, Ellen Marga. Student Utrecht U., The Netherlands; doctoraalexamen Theoretical Physics, Rijksuniversiteit Utrecht, The Netherlands, 1969, PhD, 1972; DSc (hon.), U. Chgo., 1981, U. Louvain, 1996, U. Bologna, 1998, Eurasian U., Astana, Kazakjstan, 2000, U. Western Cape, South Africa, 2001; D Humane Letters honoris causa, Hofstra U., 2001; Doctorat de Scences honoris causa, U. Mediterranee, 2001; Dsc honoris causa, Ohio State U., 2003; Doctorate (hon.), U. Sci. and Tech. China, 2004. Fellow European Ctr. Nuc. Rsch., Geneva, 1972—74; lectr., asst. prof. physics U. Utrecht, The Netherlands, 1974—77, prof., 1977—. Loeb lectr. Harvard U., Cambridge, Mass., 1976; Fairchild disting. scholar Calif. Inst. Tech., Pasadena, 1981; assoc. etranger Acad. des Scis., Paris, 1995; guest prof. Boston U., 1998, Duke U., 1989; hon. prof. Nanjing U., China, 2002, Zhejiang U., China, 2004. Assoc. editor Nuc. Physics B; contbr. articles to profl. jours. Decorated officer Legion of Honor France, comdr. Order Ned. Leeuw; recipient Dannie Heineman prize, Am. Phys. Soc., 1979, Am. Inst. Physics, N.Y.C., 1979, Wolf prize in physics, Wolf Found., Israel, 1981, Piou XI medal, Pontifica Accademia delle Sci. John Paul II, Vatican City, 1983, Spinoza premium, NWO, 1995, Franklin medal, Phila., 1995, Gian Carlo Wick commn. medal, Lausanne, 1997, HEP prize, European Phys. Soc., 1999, Nobel prize in physics, 1999, Osker Kein Silver medal, Royal Acad. Sweden, 1999, Hon. medal, Astana, Kazakhstan, 2000. Mem.: Academie des Scis. Paris, Koninklijke Nederlandse Academie voor Wetenschappen (Lorentz medal 1986), Am. Acad. Arts and Scis. (hon.), U.S. Nat. Acad. Scis. (assoc.). Office: Spinoza Inst Leuvenlaan 4 PO Box 80 195 NL3508TD Utrecht Netherlands E-mail: g.thooft@phys.uu.nl.*

**THOPPIL, PRASAD,** oceanographer, researcher; m. Shelley A. Thoppil, Nov. 9, 1999. BSc, Mahatma Gandhi U., Kayamgore, India, 1989; MSc, Cochin U. Sci. and Tech., Kochi, India, 1991; PhD, Hokkaido U., Sapporo, Japan, 2001. Rsch. assoc. Naval Postgraduate Sch. Monterey, Calif., 2002—05; rsch. scientist U So. Miss., Stennis Space Ctr., Miss., 2005—. Contbr. articles to profl. jours. Monbusho scholar, Japanese Govt., 1999—2001.

**THOR, IRA P.,** sports director; b. Paterson, N.J., Jan. 20, 1977; s. Hilary S. and Karen B. M. Thor; m. Kathryn J. Bual, July 9, 2000. BA in Com., William Paterson U., 2001. Promotions asst. Sta. WQHT-FM, N.Y.C., 1997—2000; staff writer Bergen Record, Hackensack, NJ, 1999—2000; sports writer Worrall Cmty. Newspapers, Union, NJ, 2000; sports info. dir. N.J. City U.

Athletics, Jersey City, 2000—. Sports info. dir. N.E. Collegiate Volleyball Assn., Mahwah, NJ, 2002—; divsn. II/III coord. N.J. Collegiate Baseball Assn., New Brunswick, NJ, 2004—. Bd. trustees Camelot at Woodhaven Homeowners Assn., Old Bridge, NJ, 2003—04. Recipient 2d pl. Outstanding Sports Writing Weekly Newspapers, Soc. Profl. Journalists, N.J. chpt., 2000, 1st pl. Outstanding Sports Writing Weekly Newspapers, 2000, V.P.'s Excellence in Svc. award, N.J. City U., Divsn. Student Affairs, 2003—04, Grant Burger Media award, Region SID of Yr., Am. Volleyball Coaches Assn., 2004—05. Mem.: Eastern Coll. Athletic Conf. Sports Info. Dirs. Am., Coll. Sports Info. Dir. Am. Independent. Jewish. Avocations: golf, tennis, beach volleyball, collecting/listening to music, travel. Home: 36 Cannon Rd Old Bridge NJ 08857-4247 Office: New Jersey City Univ Athletics 2039 Kennedy Blvd Jersey City NJ 07305-1597 Office Phone: 201-200-3301. Office Fax: 201-200-2365. Personal E-mail: irapthor@optonline.net. E-mail: ithor@njcu.edu.

**THOR, LINDA M.,** college president; BA, Pepperdine U., 1971, EdD, 1986; MPA, Calif. State U., L.A., 1980. Dir. pub. info. Pepperdine U., Los Angeles, 1971-73; pub. info. officer L.A. C.C. Dist., 1974-75, dir. comm., 1975-81, dir. edn. svcs., 1981-82, dir. high tech., 1982-83, sr. dir. occupl. and tech. edn., 1983-86; pres. West Los Angeles Coll., Culver City, Calif., 1986-90, Rio Salado Coll., Phoenix, 1990—. Contbr. articles to profl. jours. Active Continuous Quality Improvement Network for Cmty. Colls., 1991—; mem. Ariz. Gov.'s Adv. Coun. on Quality, 1992—97; pres. Ariz. Cmty. Coll. Pres.'s Coun., 1995—96; bd. dirs. Coun. for Adult and Experiential Learning, 1990—2005, C.C. Baccalaureate Assn., 2000—, Ariz. Town Hall, 2005—, Nana's Children Mental Health Found., 2003—. Friends of Pub. Radio Ariz. Named Woman of the Yr., Culver City Bus. and Profl. Women, 1988, Pacesetter of Yr., Nat. Coun. Mktg. and Pub. Rels., 1998; recipient Delores award, Pepperdine U., 1986, Alumni Medal of Honor, 1987, Outstanding Achievement award Women's Bus. Network, 1989, Shirley B. Gordon award of distinction, Phi Theta Kappa Internat. Honor Soc., 2000, Paul A. Elsner Excellence in Leadership award, Chair Acad., 2003. Office: 2323 W 14th St Tempe AZ 85281-6950 Business E-Mail: linda.thor@riomail.maricopa.edu.

**THORBECKE, ERIK,** economics professor; b. Berlin, Feb. 17, 1929; s. William and Madelaine (Salisbury) T.; m. Charla J. Westerberg, Oct. 17, 1954; children: Erik Charles, Willem, Jon. Student, Netherlands Sch. Econs., Rotterdam, 1948-51; PhD, U. Calif., 1957; doctorate (hon.), U. Ghent, 1981. Asst. prof. econs. Iowa State U., 1957-60, assoc. prof., 1960-63, prof., 1963-73, Cornell U., 1974—, chmn. dept. econs., 1975-78, H.E. Babcock prof. econs. and food econs., 1978—. Econ. adviser Nat. Planning Inst., Lima, Peru, 1963-64; asso. asst. adminstr. for program policy AID, Washington, 1966-68, mem. research advisory com., 1976-81; sr. economist world employment program Internat. Labor Office, Geneva, 1972-73; vis. prof. Erasmus U., Rotterdam, 1980-81; mem. com. on internat. nutritional programs NRC-NAS, 1979-81; dir. program on comparative econ. devel., Cornell U., 1988—; sr. rsch. fellow USAID Inst. Policy Reform, 1990—. Author: The Tendency Towards Regionalization in International Trade, 1960, (with Irma Adelman) Theory and Design of Economic Development, 1966, (with K. Fox, J. Sengupta) Theory of Quantitative Economic Policy, 1968, Role of Agriculture in Economic Development, 1968, (with G. Pyatt) Planning Techniques for a Better Future, 1976; (with J. Defourny) Structural Path Analysis and Multiplier Decomposition within a Social Matrix, 1984, (with J. Foster, J. Greer) A Class of Decomposable Poverty Measures, 1984, (with J. Lecaillon, C. Morrisson) Economic Policies and Agricultural Performance of Low Income Countries, 1987, Planning Techniques for Social Justice In: The Balance between Industry and Agriculture in Economic Development, vol. 4, 1989, (with I. Adelman) The Role of Institutions in Economic Development, Special Issue of World Development, 1989, (with others) Adjustment and Equity in Indonesia, 1992, (with D. Berrian) Budgetary Rules to Minimize Societal Poverty in a General Equilibrium Context, 1992, (with T. van der Pluijm) Rural Indonesia: Socio-economic Development in a Changing Environment, 1993, (with A. de Janvry and E. Sadoulet) Impact of State and Civil Institutions on the Operation of Rural Market and Non-Market Configurations In: State, Market and civil Organizations: New Theories, New Practices, and Their Implications for Rural Development, 1995, (with A. Parikh) Impact of Rural Industrialization on Village Life and Economy: A Social Accounting Matrix, 1996, (with H-S Jung) A Multiplier Decomposition Method to Analyze Poverty Alleviation, 1996, (with others) Methods of Interregional and Regional Analysis, 1998, (with H. Wan) Taiwan's Development Experience: Lessons on Roles of Government and Market, 1999, (with C. Charumilind) Economic Inequality and its Socio-economic Impact, 2002; contbr. articles to profl. jours. Mem. Am. Econ. Assn., Am. Assn. Agrl. Econs. (Nat. award for best pub. research 1970) Office: Cornell U Dept Econs Ithaca NY 14853 Office Phone: 607-255-2066. Business E-Mail: et17@cornell.edu.

**THORBECKE, WILLEM HENRY,** manufacturing executive, consultant; b. Paris, July 4, 1924; s. Willem Johan Rudolf and Madelaine (Salisbury) T.; m. Sonya Stokowski, June 8, 1946; children: Noel Evangeline, Johan Rudolf, Willem Leif, Christine Louise. BS in Engring., MIT, 1948, BSBA, 1948. Exec. Royal Dutch Shell, NYC, London, Tokyo, 1948-60, Mobil Corp., NYC, 1960-69; cons. various cos., NYC, Chgo., Houston, 1969-75; pres. Dravo Internat., Pitts., 1975-82, W.H. Thorbecke Assocs., Sewickley, Pa., 1982—. Chmn., chief exec. officer Energy Support Svcs. Inc., Coraopolis, Pa., 1982-87, dir., 1987-90; founder, chmn., CEO Thorbecke Enterprises, Inc., Sewickley, 1996—. Dir. World Affairs Coun., Pitts. 1978—; chmn. MIT Enterprise Forum, Pitts., 1987-93, 93-94. Flight lt. RAF. Named Tri-State Area Entrepreneur of Yr. Venture Mag., Ernst & Young, 1987. Mem. Am. Mgmt. Assn. (internat. coun. 1977-83), Nat. Assn. Corp. Dirs., Duquesne Club (Pitts.), Haagse Club (The Netherlands). Republican. Episcopalian. Home: Deer Haven Farm Stonedale Rd Sewickley PA 15143 Office Phone: 412-741-6521. E-mail: whthorbecke@aol.com.

**THORBURN, DAVID,** literature educator; b. NYC, Aug. 14, 1940; s. Frank and Claire (Feller) T.; m. Barbara Ellen Levitan, June 30, 1963; children: Daniel, Adam. Rachel. AB, Princeton U., 1962; MA, Stanford U., 1966, PhD, 1968. Instr., asst. prof., then assoc. prof. dept. English, Yale U., New Haven, 1966-76; prof. lit., dir. film and media studies MIT, Cambridge, 1976—, dir. cultural studies project and comm. forum, 1985—. Vis. appointments include U. Calif., Santa Barbara, U. Ill. Author: Conrad's Romanticism, 1974; contbr. articles to profl. jours.; editor scholarly collections; gen. editor Media and Popular Culture, 1986-90, Media in Transition, 2001— (book series). Fulbright fellow, Morse fellow, Woodrow Wilson fellow and Rockefeller fellow, 1966-77. Mem. MLA, Popular Culture Assn., Am. Studies Assn., Soc. for Cinema Studies. Democrat. Avocation: basketball. Office: MIT 14N-335 Lit Faculty Cambridge MA 02139

**THORDARSON, WILLIAM,** retired hydrogeologist; b. NYC, Mar. 14, 1929; s. William and Lillian (Hirsch) T. BA, Columbia U., 1950; postgrad., U. Kans., 1953—55; MA, U. Colo., 1987. Hydrogeologist U.S. Geol. Survey, Denver, 1955—94; ret., 1994. Author: Perched Groundwater, Nevada, 1965, Hydrogeology of Test Wells, 1975, Hydrogeology of South-Central Great Basin, 1983, Hydrogeologic Monitoring, Nevada, 1985, Hydrogeology of Anhydrite, 1989. Served with U.S. Army, 1950-52. Mem. Nat. Geog. Soc., Colo. Ground Water Assn., Colo. Sci. Soc., Geol. Soc. Wash. Home: 1453 Belcourt Lane Mount Pleasant SC 29466-8103

**THOREEN, MARY LOUISE,** elementary school educator, consultant; b. Fort Walton Beach, Fla., Oct. 3, 1959; d. James Leonard and Norma Jean Thoreen; m. James L. Young, June 14, 1997. BS in Math., Fla. State U., 1981, MS in Higher Edn., 1982. Cert. early adolescence math. Nat. Bd. for Profl. Tchg. Stds., 1999, math. grades 6-12 Fla., 2002, math. grades 5-9 Fla., 2002, gifted edn. Fla. Dir. student activities Mars Hill (N.C.) Coll., 1982—84; program dir. Va. Tech, Blacksburg, 1987; asst. dir. U. Ctr. U. South Fla., Tampa, 1987—89; consulting analyst The Omnia Group, Tampa, 1989—94; math. tchr. Sch. Dist. Hillsborough County, Tampa, 1994—. On-air tutor math. homework hotline The Edn. Channel, Tampa, 2004—. Finalist Dist. Tchr. of Yr., Sch. Dist. Hillsborough County, 1999; recipient Nat. Educator award, Milken Family Found., 2003. Mem.: Nat. Coun. Tchrs. Math., Phi Delta Kappa. Lutheran. Avocations: hiking, bicycling, music. Office Phone: 813-276-5682. Personal E-mail: tampathor@aol.com.

**THORELLI, SARAH V.,** economist, researcher; b. Atlanta, Dec. 30, 1922; m. Hans B. Thorelli; children: Irene, Tom. AB, U. Ga., 1944; MA, U. Ala., 1945; Ph.Lic., U. Stockholm, 1954. Free-lance researcher and scholar; v.p. Intopia, Inc. Cons. FTC, NSF, Sears, Roebuck and Co.; ofcl. translator legal documents Swedish Fgn. Office, Stockholm; intelligence rsch. analyst U.S. Dept. State; overseas rep. Equifax Co.; account exec. J. Walter Thompson Advt. Agy., N.Y.C. Co-author: Consumer Information Handbook: Europe and North America, Consumer Information Systems and Consumer Policy; contbr. articles to profl. jours. Mem. Ind. U. Women's Club, AAUW, Network Career Women, Local Coun. Women, Psi Iota Xi. Home and Office: 2604 E 2nd St Apt F Bloomington IN 47401-5351 Office Phone: 812-333-3174.

**THORGEIRSSON, SNORRI SVEINN,** medical researcher; b. Iceland, Dec. 1, 1941; came to U.S., 1972, naturalized, 1980; d. Thorgeir Jonsson and Sigurlina Sigujonsdottir; M.D., U. Iceland, 1968; Ph.D., U. London, 1971; m. Unnur Thorgeirsson, Sept. 5, 1969; children— Sif, Christian. Intern, Univ. Hosp., Reykjavik, Iceland, 1968-69; registrar, research fellow dept. clin. pharmacology Royal Postgrad. Med. Sch., London, 1969-71; vis. fellow Lab. Chem. Pharmacology, Nat. Heart and Lung Inst., NIH, Bethesda, Md., 1972-73, vis. scientist sect. devel. pharmacology, Neonatal and Pediatric Medicine br. Nat. Inst. Child Health and Human Devel., 1974-75, chief sect. on molecular toxicology devel. pharmacology br., 1975-76; head biochem. pharmacology sect. Lab. Chem. Pharmacology, Nat. Cancer Inst., 1976-81, chief Lab. Exptl. Carcinogenesis, 1981—, also head Cellular and Molecular Biology Sect.; mem. Chem. Selection Working Group, 1978—; mem. Com. on Occupational Carcinogenesis, 1979; mem. com. on amines Nat. Acad. Scis., 1979-80; co-chmn. Internat. Conf. on Carcinogenic and Mutagenic N-Substituted Aryl Compounds, NIH, Bethesda, 1979; preceptor Pharmacology Research Assoc. Program, Nat. Inst. Gen. Med. Scis., 1977—; mem. biol. response modifiers decision network com. Nat. Cancer Inst., 1980; lectr. in field. Mem. Am. Assn. Cancer Research, AAAS, Am. Soc. Exptl. Pharmacology and Exptl. Therapeutics, Am. Chem. Soc., N.Y. Acad. Scis., Environ. Mutagen Soc., Soc. Toxicology, European Assn. Cancer Research. Contbr. numerous articles, chpts. to profl. publs.; research in mechanisms of chem. carcinogenesis, control of differentiation in neo-plastic cells. Office: Nat Cancer Inst Lab Exptl Carcinogenesis Bldg 37 Rm 4146A 37 Convent Dr Bethesda MD 20892-4262 Office Phone: 301-496-1935. Office Fax: 301-496-0734. E-mail: snorri_thorgeirsson@nih.gov.*

**THORHAUG, ANITRA L.,** environmental scientist, educator; d. Thorlief Harald and Helene Heman Thorhaug; m. Richard George Bader, May 11, 1972 (dec. Oct. 31, 1974). Student, Smith Coll., Northhampton, Mass., 1958—59, U. Olso, Norway, 1960—61; BS, U. Miami, 1963, MS, 1965; postgrad., Stanford U., Pacific Grove, Calif., 1967; PhD, U. Miami, 1968; PhD (hon.), Phillipines Women's U., Manila, 1992. With Weizmann Inst. Scis., Rehovoth, Israel, 1970; rsch. scientist dept. fisheries and estuarine ecology U. Miami, 1971—72, rsch. asst. prof. dept. microbiology, 1973—78; rsch. prof. dept. biol. scis. Fla. Internat. U., 1978—92; mem. rsch. faculty Yale U., Sch. Forestry and Environ. Studies, New Haven, 2001—. Cons. World Bank, Washington, 1989—94, UN Food and Agrl. Orgn., Rome, 1984—87, UNDP, NYC, 1987—89, UN UNESCO IOC, Paris, 1991—92, Us Erda, Washington, 1974—84; vis. prof. U. Calif., Donner Labs., Brkeley, Calif., 1969—70. Contbr. articles to profl. jours. Fellow, NOAA, Miami, 1969; grantee, Aec/ Erda, 1969—77, US EPA, 1969—71, NSF, 1974—76, US State Dept., 1980—86, Mobil Found., 1980—89, FAO, 1984—87, UNEP, 1985—86. Mem.: Bot. Soc. Am. (life; chair physiol. sect. 2004—, Diamond award 1975), Club Rome, USA Club Rome (pres. 2005—, Lifetime Achievement award 2006). Achievements include research in use thermal standards and policy for emmissions into the coastal and nearshore tropical waters for UNESCO and for US and Caribbean nations; invention of reflectance signatures for remote sensing mapping of tropical coastal habitats; technical process for examining ion fluxes under gradients across giant plant cell membranes; first to use spectral reflectance for stress measurements in marine macroplants; use membrane and photosynthetic indicators for examining whole plant populations in field stress conditions; discovery of fragility of tropical ecosystems to high temperature stress; invention of large scale seagrass restoration; development of policy for rehabilitating damaged estuaries around the world; instructions how to rehabilitate fish nurseries for Asian, African and Latin American Ministry of Fisheries. Avocations: scuba diving, flying. Office Phone: 305-490-0074.

**THORIN, SUZANNE E.,** dean, university librarian; BA in music edn., N. Park Coll., Chgo., 1963; MA in music history, lit., Univ. Mich., 1964, MLS, 1968. With Libr. Cong., Washington, 1980—96, chief of staff, 1992—96; Ruth Lilly univ. dean of univ. libr. and assoc. v.p. digital libr. devel. Ind. Univ., 1996—2005; univ. libr., dean of libr. Syracuse Univ., 2005—. Office: Dean of Libr Syracuse Univ 221 E S Bird Libr 2573 Syracuse NY 13244 Office Phone: 315-443-2573. Business E-Mail: sethorin@syr.edu.*

**THORN, ROBERT CHARLES,** lawyer; b. Albany, Ga., Mar. 4, 1955; s. Robert H. and June I. (Slater) T.; children: Robert Jacob, Wayne Franklin, Evan Charles, Nathan Colin. BA in Polit. Sci., San Diego State U., 1977; JD, Calif. Western Sch. Law, 1980. Bar: Calif. 1981, U.S. Dist. Ct. (so. dist.) Calif. 1981. Pvt. practice, San Diego, 1982-87; mng. atty. Kimball, Tirey & St. John, San Diego, 1987-95, ptnr., 1995—. Mem. Pi Alpha Delta. Republican. Avocations: golf, scuba diving, racquetball. Office: Kimball Tirey & St John 1202 Kettner Blvd Fl 5 San Diego CA 92101-3353 E-mail: Robert.Thorn@kts-law.com.

**THORN, STUART WALLACE,** marketing and financial executive; b. Glen Cove, N.Y., Mar. 20, 1956; s. Benjamin Chessman and Nancy Elizabeth (Libby) T.; m. Jean Marie Gillis, Oct. 7, 1979 (div.); children: Alexander Chessman, Jason Keane, Tyler Steven; m. Sharon Elizabeth Foreman, June, 2003. BS in Econs. magna cum laude, U. Pa., 1978, MBA in Fin., 1979. Market rsch. intern People's Savs. Bank, Bridgeport, Conn., 1987-88; fin. analyst, corp. control S.C. Johnson & Son, Inc., Racine, Wis., 1979-80, cost mgmt. analyst, prodn. support, 1980-81; project supur. Johnson Worldwide Assocs., S.C. Johnson & Son, Racine, 1982-83; fin. mgr. Porelon, Inc., Cookeville, Tenn., 1983-86; corp. acquistions dir. S.C. Johnson & Son, Inc., Racine, 1986-87, regional controller Africa and Nr. East Frimley, Eng., 1987-90, internat. mktg. assoc. Racine, 1990-91, dir. fin. N.Am. consumer products, 1991-94; v.p. internat. fin. Campbell Soup Co., 1994—; CFO Beaulieu of Am., 1995—2001; pres., CEO Southwire Co., Carrollton, Ga., 2001—. Solicitor United Way, Racine; bd. dirs. Explorers, Boy Scouts Am., 1986-87; bd. dirs. Racine County Opportunity Ctr., 1991—. Named Nat. Champion Nat. Collegiate Racing Assoc. Avocations: tennis, windsurfing, golf. Office: Southwire Co 1 Southwire Dr Carrollton GA 30119*

**THORN, SUSAN HOWE,** interior designer; b. Washington, Apr. 22, 1941; d. James Bennett Cowdin and Lois (Fiesinger) Howe; m. William D. Thorn, June 22, 1963; children: Melissa Ann, William David. Lighting design, Parsons Sch. Design, 1975—77; BA, Syracuse U., 1962; AB, N.Y. Sch. Interior Design, 1995. Owner, designer Susan Thorn Interiors, Inc., Cross River, NY, 1965—. Designer total bldg. Cooper Labs, Bedford Hills, N.Y., 1973, total redesign Nycrest Corp., Cold Spring, N.Y., 1973-75, showrooms, model rooms stylist and coordinator France Voiles Co. Inc., N.Y.C., 1976, total design new corp. hdqrs. in Gen. Dynamics Bldg. (with Marjorie Borradaile Helsel), Robert E. Eastman Co., N.Y.C., 1967, Cummin & Friedland Capital Corp., 1982; designer offices, stores employee areas comml., public, residential clients, including Waccabuc (N.Y.) Country Club, 1969, S. Salem (N.Y.) Library, St. Vincent's Hosp., N.Y.C., 1996; instr. adult edn. dept. John Jay High Sch.; spkr. civic orgns. Mem. Am. Soc. Interior Designers (profl.), Internat. Assn. Lighting Designers (assoc.), Decorators Club, Club of N.Y., Waccabuc Country Club. Episcopalian. Home: 88 N Salem Rd Cross River NY 10518 Office Phone: 914-763-1210. Business E-Mail: thorninteriors@earthlink.net.

**THORN, TERENCE HASTINGS,** energy executive, consultant, writer; b. Takoma, Md., July 6, 1946; s. John Hastings and Norine R. (Freytag) T.; m. Judith Carol Bailey, Aug. 15, 1970; children: Kristin Lynn, Matthew Hastings. BA, U. Md., 1969, MA, 1973. Dir. congl. rels. Am. Gas Assn., Arlington, Va., 1975-79; dir. govt. rels. J. Walter Thompson Co., Washington, 1979-81; v.p. govt. rels. Houston Natural Gas Co., Washington, 1981-85; exec. v.p., chmn. bd. Mojave Pipeline Co., Houston, 1986-89; pres., CEO Transwestern Pipeline Co., Houston, 1993—; sr. v.p., exec. mgmt. com. bd. Enron Corp., Houston, 1993-98, exec. v.p. internat. govt. rels. and environ. affairs, 1998—2001, mng. dir. Middle East, 2001; cons. Houston Tex. Energy, Environment, Tech.; pres. JKM Cons., Houston, 2001—. Cons. in field. Contbr. articles to profl. jours. Bd. dirs. Houston Pops, 1989-90, Pin Oak Charities, Houston, 1991-93, Greater Houston chpt. YMCA, 1994; city alderman, 1992-93; mem. Hermann Soc., 1993—, Energy Industry Sector Adv. Com. U.S. Dept. Commerce; prin. liason Pres.'s Coun. Sustainable Devel.; chmn. internat. com. Bus. Coun. of Sustainable Devel.; mem. adv. com. Commn. for Environ. Cooperation; trustee Tomas Rivera Policy Inst.; chmn. Internat. Gas Ctr. Mem. Pacific Coast Gas Assn. (chmn. 1994-95), Internat. Gas Union (chmn. com. 9), U.S.C. of C. (mem. internat. policy com.), Coun. of the Ams. (adv. com.), Wildlife Conservation Soc. (trustee), Nature Conservancy (trustee). Avocation: writing.

**THORNBERRY, MAC (WILLIAM MCCLELLAN THORNBERRY),** congressman; b. Clarendon, Tex., July 15, 1958; m. Sally Thornberry; 2 children. BA summa cum laude in Hist., Tex. Tech U., Lubbock, 1980; JD, U. Tex. Law Sch., 1983. Legis. coun. Staff of US Rep. Tom Loeffler of Tex., 1983-85; chief of staff Staff of US Rep. Larry Combest of Tex., 1985-88; dep. asst. sec. legis. affairs US State Dept., 1988-89; def. atty. Peterson, Farris, Doores & Jones, Amarillo, Tex., 1989-94; mem. US Congress from 13th Tex. dist., 1995—. Mem. armed svcs. com. US Congress, mem. permanent select com. on intelligence, chair oversight subcommittee. Mem. Tex. and Southwestern Cattle Raisers Assn. Republican. Presbyterian. Office: US Ho Reps 2457 Rayburn Ho Office Bldg Washington DC 20515-4313 Office Phone: 202-225-3706.*

**THORNBRO, WILLIAM GRADEN,** writer; b. Muncie, Ind., July 8, 1952; s. William Wesley Thornbro and Bonnie Ather Marcum; m. Janice Kay Waters, Aug. 7, 1976; children: Christopher Wesley, Nicholas Dale. BS, Ball State U., 1978. Author: (book) An Uncertain Justice, A Question of Conspiracy, numerous poems. Mem.: Natural Resources Def. Coun., Environ. Def., Planetary Soc., Sierra Club. Democrat. Avocations: reading /research, gardening. Home: 212 S Pasture Ln Muncie IN 47304-4120 Personal E-mail: wmthornbro@sbcglobal.net.

**THORNBURG, FREDERICK FLETCHER,** lawyer; b. South Bend, Ind., Feb. 10, 1940; s. James F. and Margaret R. (Major) T.; children: James Brian, Charles Kevin, Christian Sean, Christopher Herndon; m. Patricia J. Malloy, Dec. 4, 1981. AB, DePauw U., 1963; postgrad., U. Notre Dame, 1965; JD magna cum laude, ind. U., 1968. Bar: Ind. 1968, U.S. Tax Ct. 1970, U.S. Ct. Appeals (7th cir.) 1970, U.S. Supreme Ct. 1971. Tchr., coach U.S. Peace Corps, Colombia, 1963-65; law clk. to chief judge U.S. Ct. Appeals (7th cir.), 1968-69; assoc. Thornburg, McGill, Deahl, Harman, Carey & Murray, South Bend, 1969-75, ptnr., 1975-80; v.p. systems and svcs. group The Wackenhut Corp., Coral Gables, Fla., 1981-82, sr. v.p. adminstrn., 1982-86, exec. v.p., 1986-88, also bd. dirs.; pres. Wackenhut Internat. Corp. and Wackenhut Svcs., Inc.; v.p., legal counsel St. Thomas U., 1988-90, adj. prof. law, 1989-90; pres., CEO PropServ, Inc., 1991-94; pres. EPS Ltd., 1995—; CEO Practice Resources Corp., 1996-97; CEO, of counsel Stephens, Lynn, Klien & McNicholas, P.A., 1998-2000. Cons. MSC, Am. Tel. Corp.; legal and mgmt. cons., mem. bd. advisors Publix Supermarkets, Inc., 1994—95, St. Thomas U., 1990—95, 2001—06; bd. dirs., pres. Doral Park Country Club; bd. dirs., mem. exec. com., trustee RFBD, Inc.; bd. dirs. YEI, Inc., Carlos Albizu U. Found., 2002—; trustee U. Cmty. Hosp. Found., 1991—94; adj. prof. bus. St. Mary's Coll., 1975—78; vis. prof. CTA, 1985—95; vice chmn., pvt. sec. adv. coun. Fla. Sec. of State, 1985—90; chair ethics com. Miami-Dade County Pub. Schs., 2002—; legal and mgmt. cons., mem., chair bd. advisors WLRN-PBS Radio and TV, 2003—; adj. prof. bus. St. Thomas U. Law Sch., 1999—2000, Carlos Albizu U., 2004, chair Bus. Sch. Adv. Bd., 2003—04. Assoc. editor in chief Ind. Law Jour., 1967-68; contbr. articles to legal and bus. jours. Mem. Civic Ctr. Found., 1976—80; pres. Jaycees, 1974; trustee RFD&D, Inc.; former bd. dirs. Michiana YMCA, Channel 34, Symphony Orch. Assn., 1974—80, Boy Scouts of U.S.A., 2000—02; bd. dirs., mem. exec. com. Doral and West Airport C. of C.; bd. dirs. Miami-Dade (Fla.) County Ethics Coalition. Fulbright selectee, Halleck scholar. Mem. ABA, Ind. Bar Assn., Greater Miami C. of C. (former corp. rep. trustee), Doral Park Golf and Country Club (bd. dirs.), Order of Coif, Phi Delta Phi, Alpha Delta Sigma, Lambda Phi Gamma Delta (Disting. Alumni award) Office: 10005 NW 52nd Ter Miami FL 33178-2608 Fax: 305-591-6560. Office Phone: 305-591-1898. Personal E-mail: MrFPT@aol.com.

**THORNBURG, GARRETT, JR.,** finance company executive; BA, Williams Coll.; MBA, Harvard Univ. CFO NY State Urban Develop. Corp.; limited ptnr., founding mem. pub. fin. dept. Bear Stearns & Co., NYC; sole dir. Thornburg Investment Mgmt. Inc., 1982—, Thornburg Securities Corp.; founder, chmn., CEO Thornburg Mortgage Inc., Santa Fe, 1993—. Bd. gov. Investment Co. Inst., Nat. Assn. REIT Inc. Bd. mem. Nat. Dance Inst. N. Mex.; trustee Coll. Santa Fe. Office: Thornburg Mortgage Inc Ste 302 150 Washington Ave Santa Fe NM 87501*

**THORNBURG, LACY HERMAN,** federal judge; b. Charlotte, NC, Dec. 20, 1929; s. Jesse Lafayette and Sarah Ann (Ziegler) T.; m. Dorothy Todd, Sept. 6, 1953; children— Sara Thornburg Evans, Lacy Eugene, Jesse Todd, Alan Ziegler. AA, Mars Hill Coll., 1950; BA, U. N.C., 1951, JD, 1954. Bar: U.S. Dist. Ct. (we. dist.) N.C. Practiced law, Webster, NC, 1954-67; superior ct. judge State of N.C., 1967-83, atty. gen Raleigh, 1985-92; emergency judge N.C. Superior Ct., Webster, 1993-94; mem. Nat. Indian Gaming Commn., 1994-95; judge U.S. Dist. Ct. for N.C., Asheville, 1995—. Mem. staff Congressman Taylor, Sylva, NC, 1960, Congressman David Hall, Sylva, 1959-60; mem. N.C. Ho. of Reps., 1961-65; mem. NC Cts. Commn., NC Criminal Code Commn., Capital Planning Commn., Raleigh Chmn. Jackson County Bd. of Health, Sylva, 1965-84; commr. Tryon Palace, New Bern, N.C. Served with U.S. Army, 1947-48. Mem. Lions, Masons, Shriners. Democrat. Avocations: fly fishing, skeet shooting. Office: US Dist Ct 200 US Courthouse 100 Otis St Asheville NC 28801-2611 Office Phone: 828-771-7250. Business E-Mail: lacythornburg@ncwd.uscourts.gov.

**THORNBURG, LEE ELLIS,** film executive, director; b. Houston, Feb. 16, 1942; s. Richard Ellis and Lucyle (Comstock) T.; m. Jane Kaiser (div. 1981); children: Janette Mattas, Deanne Waddell; m. Patricia Ann Kirkham, June 16, 1987. Tech. svc. engr. Dresser Industries, Houston, 1970-76; pres. Lone Star Pictures Internat., Inc., Dallas, 1976—. Bd. dirs. TCJ Wholesale. Dir. films including Hollywood High Part II, 1981, 6-Pack, 1991, Southwest, 1996, Memo, 1996; prodr. films including Kings of the Hill, 1976, Mr. Mean, 1978. Mem. Am. Film Market Assn. Republican. Methodist. Office: Lone Star Pictures 700 E Route 66 #77 Glendora CA 91740-3510 Office Phone: 214-522-2389. E-mail: lonestarpictures@aol.com.

**THORNBURG, LINDA A.,** writer; b. Denver, Aug. 8, 1949; d. William J.R. Thornburg and Marjory Smith. BA, U. Colo., 1973. Pres., prin. Word Wizards, Fredericksburg, Va., 1990—. Author: (book series) Cool Careers for Girls, 1999—2004; editor: iLinx, Society for Human Resource Management, 2000—03, Staffing Management, Society for Human Resource Management, 2004—05, ADA Compliance Guide, 2006, Section 504 Compliance Handbook, 2006. Mem.: AAUW (br. sec. 2000—02, br. program chair 2004), Washington Ind. Writers. Personal E-mail: wordwzrds@aol.com.

**THORNBURG, RON,** editor; BA in Polit. Sci., Purdue U., 1971. Reporter Jour. and Courier, Lafayette, Ind., 1972-73; mng. editor The Evening Times, Melbourne, Fla., 1973-75; met. editor, asst. news editor, copy editor, bur.

chief Today, Melbourne, 1975-78; mng. editor, 1978-80; exec. editor News Press, Fort Myers, Fla., 1980-86; news exec. Cmty. Newspapers, Gannet Co., Inc., Rosslyn, Va., 1986-88; editor Burlington (Vt.) Free Press, 1988-94; mng. editor Standard Examiner, Ogden, Utah, 1994—2003, editor circulation and news, 2003—. Office: Standard Examiner 332 S Ward Ave PO Box 12790 Ogden UT 84412-2790 E-mail: rthornburg@standard.net.

**THORNBURGH, DANIEL ESTON,** retired university administrator, journalism educator; b. Terre Haute, Ind., Sept. 17, 1930; s. Lester D. and Dorothy (Green) T.; m. Adrianne Ames, Aug. 11, 1956; children: Debra Kay Thornburgh Considine, Stewart Beckett, Malcolm Noble. BS, Ind. State U., 1952; MA, U. Iowa, 1957; EdD, Ind. U., 1980. Reporter Terre Haute Star, 1952; publicity dir. Simpson Coll., Indianola, Iowa, 1955; info. dir. Marshall U., Huntington, W.Va., 1957—59, Ea. Ill. U., Charleston, 1959—65, chmn., prof. journalism, 1965—84, dir. univ. rels., 1992; ret. Vis. prof. U. Hawaii, 1982—83, U. Fla., 1993—94, Millikin U., 1996; mem. Gov.'s Coun. Health and Phys. Fitness, 1987—2003; pub. Casey Banner Times, Ill., 1967—69. Editor: (with others) Interpretative Reporting Workbook, 1982. Mem. Charleston City Coun., 1973-77; active Ill. Recreation Coun., Springfield, 1979-85; pres. Coles Hist. Soc., Charleston, 1972-74, 1992, trustee, 2004—; pres., trustee Five Mile House Found., 1998—; trustee Lincoln and Sargent Farm Found., 1999-2004; chmn. higher edn. and campus min. com. Meth. Ch., 2000-02. With U.S. Army, 1952—54. Named Outstanding Advisor, Coun. Coll. Publs. Advisors, 1971. Mem. Charleston C. of C. (Area Man of Yr. award 1971), Assn. Edn. Journalism and Mass Comm., Pub. Rels. Soc. Am., Soc. Profl. Journalists, Coun. Advancement and Support Edn. (Ea. Ill. U. PRSSA chpt.), Assn. Preservation Hist. Coles County (Merit award 2003), Masons (Cmty. Builder award 1997), Elks, Rotary (pres. Charleston 1976-77, dist. gov. 6490 2000-01, dist. Hall of Fame 2004, pres. chpt. Charitable Found. 2004—), Charleston Country Club. Methodist. Avocation: writing. Home: 1405 Buchanan Ave Charleston IL 61920-2924 Personal E-mail: adthorn@consolidated.net.

**THORNBURGH, DICK (RICHARD L. THORNBURGH),** lawyer, former United States attorney general; b. Pitts., July 16, 1932; s. Charles Garland and Alice (Sanborn) T.; m. Virginia Walton Judson, Oct. 12, 1963; children: John, David, Peter, William. B in Engring., Yale, 1954; LLB, U. Pitts., 1957; degrees (hon.). Bar: Pa. 1958, US Supreme Ct. 1965, DC 1998. Atty. Kirkpatrick Lockhart, Nicholson Graham LLP, Pitts., 1959-69, 77-79, 87-88, 91-92, 94—; US atty. (we. dist.) Pa. US Dept. Justice, Pitts., 1969-75, asst. atty. gen. criminal divsn. Washington, 1975-77; gov. State of Pa., Harrisburg, 1979-87; dir. Inst. Politics John F. Kennedy Sch. Govt., Harvard U., 1987-88; atty. gen. US Dept. Justice, Washington, 1988-91; under-sec.-gen. for adminstrn. & mgmt. UN, NYC, 1992-93; of counsel Kirkpatrick Lockhart, Nicholson Graham LLP, Washington. Del. Pa. Constl. Conv., 1967-68; vice-chair World Com. on Disability; bd. dirs. Nat. Mus. Indsl. History, Gettysburg. Author: (autobiography) Where the Evidence Leads: The Autobiography of Dick Thornburgh, 2003. Trustee Urban Inst., U. Pitts. Recipient Spl. Medallion award, Drug Enforcement Adminstrn., 1973, Disting. Svc. medal, Am. Legion, 1992, Lifetime Achievement award, Am. Lawyer mag., 2006. Fellow Am. Bar Found.; mem. Am. Judicature Soc., Coun. Fgn. Rels., Am. Law Inst. Republican. Office: Kirkpatrick & Lockhart Nicholson Graham LLP 1601 K St NW Washington DC 20006-1600 Office Phone: 202-778-9080. Office Fax: 202-778-9100.

**THORNBURGH, RICHARD EDWARD,** bank executive; b. Cin., July 9, 1952; s. Robert Wesley and Frances (Cowing) Thornburgh; m. Cornelia Parsons, Aug. 6, 1983; children: Ainsley Frances, Katrina Parsons. BBA cum laude, U. Cin., 1974; MBA, Harvard U., Boston, 1976. Assoc. The First Boston Corp., N.Y.C., 1976-81, v.p., 1983-86, mng. dir. L.A., 1987—88; mng. dir., various roles including head global fin. institutions group Credit Suisse First Boston (formerly The First Boston Corp.), 1989—95; exec. bd, CFO Credit Suisse First Boston, 1995—96; CFO Credit Suisse Group, 1997—99; vice chmn. exec. bd Credit Suisse First Boston, 1999—2002, CFO, 2000—02; chief risk officer Credit Suisse Group, 2003—, mem. com. exec. bd., 2004—, mem. oper. com. Credit Suisse First Boston, 2002—. Bd. dirs. L.A. Chamber Orch., 1989-91, First Congregational Ch. of Darien (Conn.), 1990-91. Mem. Harvard Club of N.Y.C., Racquet and Tennis Club, The Calif. Club, The Links. Avocations: sailing, golf, racquet sports, skiing. Office: Credit Suisse Group 11 Madison Ave New York NY 10010-3629

**THORNBURGH, RON E.,** state official; b. Burlingame, Kans., Dec. 31, 1962; m. Annette Thornburgh. BA in Criminal Justice, Washburn U., 1985. Dep. asst. sec. of state, then asst. sec. of state State of Kans., Topeka, 1985-87, asst. sec. of state, 1991-95, sec. of state, 1995—. Vice chairperson blue ribbon panel on ethical conduct State of Kans., 1989. Mem. Kids Voting Kans. Exec. Com.; mem. adv. com. United Way. Toll fellow Henry Toll Fellowship Program, 1995, Digital Gov Agent of Change Award, MIT, 2002, Lee Ann Elliott Election Excellence Award, Kids Voting USA, 2004. Mem. Washburn U. Alumni Bd., 20/30 Club Internat. Republican. Methodist. Office: Office Sec of State Memorial Hall First Floor 120 SW 10th Ave Topeka KS 66612-1504 Office Phone: 785-296-4575. Office Fax: 785-368-8033.

**THORNBURY, JOHN ROUSSEAU,** radiologist, physician; b. Cleve., Mar. 16, 1929; s. Purla Lee and Gertrude (Glidden) T.; m. Julia Lee McGregor, Mar. 20, 1955; children: Lee Allison, John McGregor. AB cum laude, Miami U., Oxford, Ohio, 1950; MD, Ohio State U., 1955. Diplomate: Am. Bd. Radiology. Intern Hurley Hosp., Flint, Mich., 1955-56; resident U. Iowa Hosps., Iowa City, 1958-61; instr., asst. prof. radiology U. Colo. Med. Center, Denver, 1962-63; practice medicine specializing in radiology Denver, 1962-63, Iowa City, 1963-66, Seattle, 1966-68, Ann Arbor, Mich., 1968-79, Albuquerque, 1979-84, Rochester, NY, 1984-89, Madison, Wis., 1989-94. Mem. staff U. Wis. Hosp., Madison; prof. radiology, chief sect. body imaging, U. Wis. Med. Sch., 1989-94, prof. emeritus, 1994—; asst. prof. radiology U. Iowa Hosps., 1963-66, U. Wash. Hosp., Seattle, 1966-68; assoc. prof. radiology U. Mich. Med. Ctr., 1968-71, prof., 1971-79, chief uroradiology sect., 1971-79; prof. radiology, chief divsn. diagnostic radiology Sch. Medicine, U. N.Mex., 1979-84; prof. radiology U. Rochester Sch. Medicine, 1984-89, acting chmn., 1985-87; chmn. sci. com. on efficacy studies Nat. Coun. on Radiation Protection, 1980-95; rapporteur/mem. sci. group on indications/limitations of x-ray diagnostic procedures WHO, 1983; cons. com. on efficacy of magnetic resonance nat. health rsch. dir. panel Australian Inst. Health, 1986; invited U.S. cons. MRI program, Nijmegen, The Netherlands, 1992; mem. planning group Low Back Pain Collaboration at Nat. Congress, Inst. for Health Care Improvement, 1997-98; mem. methodologic rsch. issues working group NIH and Pub. Health Svc.-Office of Women's Health, 1998; cons. spkr. Royal Australasian Coll. Radiologists, Melbourne, Australia, 1997; cons. tech. assessment and outcomes rsch., 1994—; cons. in tech. assessment and outcomes rsch. to dept. neuroradiology Loma Linda Med. Ctr., 2002—; cons. to Am. Soc. Neuroradiology, 1995-2000; lectr. in field. Co-author/cons. Clin. Efficacy Assessment Project, Am. Coll. Physicians, 1986-89; assoc. editor: Yearbook of Radiology, 1971-82; mem. editl. bd.: Contemporary Diagnostic Radiology, 1977-84, Urologic Radiology, 1977-84 Bd. dirs. Sally Jobe Found., Denver, 1996—. Capt., M.C. USAF, 1956-58. Recipient Dist. Svc. award Am. Bd. Radiology, 2000, Alumni Achievement award Ohio State U. Coll. Medicine, 2000, Gold medal Assn. Univ. Radiologists, 2002, Gold medal Soc. Uroradiology, 2005; grantee Agy. Health Care Policy and Rsch., 1986-91, U. Rochester, 1986-89, U. Wis., Madison, 1989-91 Fellow Am. Coll. Radiology (mem. emeritus); mem. Am. Coll. Radiology Imaging Network (outcomes and quality of life subcom., urology com., NIH, 1999-2002), Soc. Uroradiology (pres. 1976-77, dir. 1977-79, gold medal 2005), Assn. Univ. Radiologists (pres. 1980-81), Radiol. Soc. N.Am., Am. Roentgen Ray Soc. (Caldwell medal 1993), Soc. for Health Svcs. Rsch. in Radiology (adv. com. to bd. dirs. 1998—), Coll. Radiology, Phi Beta Kappa, Delta Tau Delta, Omicron Delta Kappa, Phi Chi. Republican. Episc. Home: 1340 Forest Park Cir #16 Lafayette CO 80026 *"Mooring Post" relationships and sharing have been essential to success and achievements in* *my multi-disciplinary research. "Mooring Post" persons range from expert mentors and stellar colleagues, to the bedrock of a loving and supportive family. Further, to me, Rule One in medicine has always been, "The patient comes first.".*

**THORNDIKE, EDWARD HARMON,** physicist; b. Pasadena, Calif., Aug. 2, 1934; s. Edward Moulton and Louise (Harmon) T.; m. Elizabeth H. Wenger, Sept. 8, 1955; children: Susan Lee, Patricia Lynn, Edward Harmon Jr. AB, Wesleyan U., Middletown, Conn., 1956; MS, Stanford U., 1957; PhD, Harvard U., 1960. Rsch. fellow Harvard U., Cambridge, Mass., 1960-61; mem. faculty U. Rochester, NY, 1961—, asso. prof. physics, 1965-72, prof., 1972—. Vis. prof. U. Geneva, 1969-70; vis. scientist CERN, Geneva, 1969-70; mem. adv. coun. Ctr. Environ. Info., Rochester, 1974-93; mem. adv. com. Stanford Linear Accelerator Ctr. Exptl. Program, 1987-89; mem. vis. com. for Fermilab, Univs. Rsch. Assn., 1993-95. Author: Energy and Environment, a Primer for Scientists and Engineers, 1976; contbr. articles to profl. jours. Recipient W.K.H. Panofsky prize, 1999; NSF fellow, 1970, Guggenheim fellow, 1987-88. Fellow Am. Phys. Soc. Office: U Rochester Dept Physics/Astronomy Rochester NY 14627

**THORNE, CARL F.,** gas industry executive; b. 1940; BS in Petroleum Engring., U. Tex.; JD, Baylor U. Bar: Tex. 1967. Dir. Sedco Inc., Dallas, 1986—, pres., CEO, 1987—, chmn. bd. dirs., 1987—; dir. Crescent Op., Inc., chmn. compensation com.; CEO, dir. Blocker Energy Corp., 1987—; ptnr. BEC Ventures; former pres. Sedco-Forex; pres., CEO ENSCO Internat. Inc., Dallas, 1987—, chmn. bd., 1987—. Mem. Nat. Ocean Industries Assn. (dir.). Office: ENSCO 500 N Akard St Ste 4300 Dallas TX 75201-3331

**THORNE, FRANCIS,** composer; b. Bay Shore, NY, June 23, 1922; s. Francis Burritt and Hildegarde (Kobbé) T.; m. Ann Cobb, Dec. 9, 1942; children: Ann Boughton (Mrs. William F. Niles), Wendy Oakleigh (Mrs. William H. Forsyth, Jr.), Candace Kobbé (Mrs. Anthony M. Canton). BA in Music Theory, Yale U., 1942. Founder, pres. Thorne Music Fund Inc., 1965-75; pub. Edward B. Marks Music Corp., 1963—, Gen. Music Pub. Co., 1971—, G. Schirmer/AMP, 1985—, Theodore Presser Co., 1989—. Exec. dir. Lenox Arts Ctr., 1972-76, Am. Composers Alliance, 1975-85; co-founder, pres. Am. Composers Orch., 1976— Composer: Elegy for Orch., 1964, Burlesque Overture, 1966, Lyric Variations for Orch., 1967, Symphony No. 1, 1963, No. II, 1966, No. III, 1970, No. IV, 1977, Fortuna, 1961-62, Liebesrock, 1969, Sonar Plexus, 1969, Six Set-Pieces, 1969, Contra Band Music, 1970, Antiphonies, 1970, Simultaneities, 1971, Quartessence, 1971, Fanfare, Fugue and Funk, 1972, Lyric Variations II, 1972, Piano Sonata, 1972, Lyric Variations III, 1973, Cantata Sauce, 1973, Evensongs, 1973, Cello Concerto, 1974, Piano Concerto, 1974, Violin Concerto, 1975, String Quartet 1, 1960, 2, 1967, 3, 1976, 4, 1983, Spoon River Overture, 1976, Grand Duo, 1976, Five Set Pieces, 1976, Love's Variations, 1976, Pop Partita, 1978, The Eternal Light for Soprano and Orchestra, 1979, Divertimento for Flute, Strings and Percussion, 1979, Lyric Variations IV for Solo Violin, 1980, Divertimento 2 for Bassoon and Stringed Instruments, 1980, Eine Kleine Meyermusik, 1980, Gems From Spoon River, 1980, Lyric Variations No. 6 for solo clarinet, 1981, Divertimento No. 3, 1982, Praise and Thanksgiving, 1983, Lyric Variations No. 5 for Orch., 1980-81, Symphony No. 5, 1984, Concerto Concertante, 1985, Rhapsodic Variations, No. 2, 1985, Humoresque for Orch., 1985, Rhapsodic Variations No. 3 for Oboe and Strings, 1986, The Affirming Flame for Soprano and Chamber Ensemble, 1987; seven simple syncopations for Piano solo, 1987, Rhapsodic Variations No. 4 for Viol Solo, 1987, Rhapsodic Variations No. 5 for Violins and Piano, 1988, Money Matters for Tenor and Chamber Ensemble, 1988, Piano Concerto No. 3, 1989, Remembering Dizzy for Brass Quintet, 1990, Pop Partita No. 2 for woodwinds and strings, 1991, Mario and The Magician, opera after Thomas Mann, in Prologue and 1 Act, 1991, Symphony No. 6 for Strings, 1992, Symphony No. 7 Along the Hudson for chorus and orch., 1994, Cello Concerto No. 2, 1995, Echo for Soprano and Mixed Chorus, 1996, Clarinet Concerto, 1997, Rhapsodic Variations No. 7 for Solo Piano, 1998, Lyric Variations No. 8, 1999, Flash Dances for Orchestra, 1999, Oboe Concerto, 1999-2000, SONG To Mark Stand's Poem, 2000, Concerto for Orchestra, 2000-01, The Four Seasons, for mezzo and string trio, 2002, Triple Concerto for English Horn, Bass Clarinet, Viola and Orchestra, 2004, Lyric Variations No. 9 for Solo Piano, 2004, Songs and Dances for Orchestra, 2005; recs. on Composers' Recs., Inc., Serenus, Owl, Louisville Opus One and New World Trustee Am. Symphony Orchestra League, Manhattan Sch. Music, Am. Music Center, MacDowell Colony, Walter W. Naumburg Found., Contemporary Music Soc., Theater Devel. Fund, Group for Contemporary Music., Am. Brass Quintet. Lt. USNR, 1942-45. Nat. Endowment Arts grantee, 1966, 73; fellow, 1976, 79; Nat. Inst. Arts and Letters grantee, 1968; N.Y. State Arts Council ballet commn., 1973 Mem. AAAL, BMI, Contemporary Music Soc. (bd. dirs.), Am. Composers Alliance, League Composers. Clubs: Century Assn. Home: Geer Village #104 77 S Canaan Rd Canaan CT 06018 Office Phone: 860-824-2650. E-mail: aco@americancomposers.org. *Having spent ten years as a businessman, I have been privileged to serve my composer colleagues as an administrator for musical organizations. The practical experience has also served me well as a creative artist in having instilled the virtues of discipline. Serving music as composer and administrator gives the highest sense of satisfaction, from participating in this life-giving world in a total comprehensive way.*

**THORNE, JOHN,** lawyer; b. Milw., Dec. 7, 1956; s. John Farley and Ann Thorne, Jr.; m. Sara Marie Sherman, Nov. 14, 1986; children: Elizabeth Marie, John Farley Thorne IV, Walter Joseph, Samuel Taylor. BA, Kenyon Coll., 1978; JD, Northwestern U., 1981. Bar: DC, Ill. Sr. v.p., dep. gen. counsel Verizon Comm. Inc., Arlington, Va., 1988—. Adj. faculty Columbia Law Sch., N.Y.C., 1996—. Contbr. articles various profl. jours. and speeches. Mem. capital campaign steering com. St. Alban's Parish, Washington, 2002-04 Mem. Math Assn Am. Am Math Soc. At its [illegible] in [illegible] patents for electronic mail security. Home: 1920 Plymouth St NW Washington DC 20012 Office: Verizon Comm Inc 1515 N Courthouse Rd Fifth Fl Arlington VA 22201 Office Phone: 703-351-3900. E-mail: john.thorne@verizon.com.

**THORNE, JOHN REINECKE,** finance educator, venture capitalist; b. Pitts., Mar. 25, 1926; s. John Mueller and Louise (Reinecke) T.; m. Barbara Siebert, Aug. 31, 1951 (dec. Feb. 1995); children: John S., Barbara L., Richard W.; m. Helen L. Totzke, Dec. 29, 1999. BS, Brown U., 1947; MSEE, U. Pitts., 1949; MS in Indsl. Adminstrn., Carnegie Mellon U., 1952. Devel. engr. Westinghouse Elec. Corp., Pitts., 1947-50; mgr. fin. analysis Hughes Aircraft Co., L.A., 1952—57; dir. computer systems lab. Litton Industries, L.A., 1957—63; founder, chmn., pres. The Scionics Corp., L.A., 1963—69; cons., L.A., 1969-72; prof. bus. Carnegie-Mellon U., Pitts., 1972—2003, Morgenthaler prof. entrepreneurship, 1987—2003, Morganthaler emeritus prof. entrepreneurship, 2003—, dir. Donald H. Jones Ctr. for Entrepreneurship, 1990—2000; founder, chmn. Enterprise Corp. Pitts., 1983-98; gen. ptnr. Pitts. Seed Fund, 1986—2004. Contbr. articles to profl. jours. Named Named Fin. Svcs. Adv. of Yr., SBA, 1988. Mem.: Rolling Rock Club, Duquesne Club. Unitarian Universalist. Home: 137 Furnace Run Ln Laughlintown PA 15655-0369 Office: Tepper Sch Bus Carnegie-Mellon U Pittsburgh PA 15213 Office Phone: 412-268-2263. Business E-Mail: thorne@andrew.cmu.edu.

**THORNE, JOHN WATSON, III,** advertising and marketing executive; b. Washington, Jan. 16, 1934; s. John Watson, Jr. and Mary Washington (Tucker) T.; m. Joan Kramer Vail, Mar. 2, 1957; children: Vail Tucker, Tracy Tucker, John Watson, IV. BA in Polit. Sci., George Washington U., 1955; MA in Sociology, The New Sch., N.Y.C., 1974. Asst. account exec. Young & Rubicam, Inc., N.Y.C., 1957-59; advt. mgr. GE, Decatur, Ill., 1959-63; dir. advt. promotion Brand Names Found., N.Y.C., 1963-66; account exec. Tatham-Laird & Kudner (advt.), N.Y.C., 1966-67; v.p., mgmt. supr. Wells, Rich, Greene, Inc., N.Y.C., 1973-76; v.p., account supr. Batten, Barton, Durstine & Osborn, Inc., N.Y.C., 1967-73, sr. v.p., mgmt. supr., 1976-81, exec. v.p., 1981-87, also dir. mem. super. com.; chmn. Thorne & Assocs., Newtown, Pa., 1987—; pres., CEO Telerx Mktg., Spring House, Pa., 1991-95; chmn., CEO Alliance Mktg. Svcs. Group, Inc., Jamison, Pa., 1995—2004, Alliance Healthcare Info., Inc., Ivyland, Pa., 2004—. Mem. bus.

program com. Proprietary Assn., Washington; adj. prof. advt. Syracuse (N.Y.) U. Pres. Hastings-on-Hudson (N.Y.) Bd. Edn.; bd. dirs. Young Concert Artists, N.Y.C.; mem. comm. coms. Nat. Urban League, Carnegie Hall. Served as 1st lt. USMCR, 1955-57. Mem.: Lotos Club (NYC), Buckingham Racquet Club. Republican. Roman Catholic. Home: 100 Stoney Brook Rd Ivyland PA 18940-2506 Office: Alliance Healthcare Info Inc One Ivybrook Blvd Ste 100 Ivyland PA 18974

**THORNE, KIP STEPHEN,** physicist, researcher; b. Logan, Utah, June 1, 1940; s. David Wynne and Alison (Comish) T.; m. Linda Jeanne Peterson, Sept. 12, 1960 (div. 1977); children: Kares Anne, Bret Carter; m. Carolee Joyce Winstein, July 7, 1984. BS in Physics, Calif. Inst. Tech., 1962; A.M. in Physics (Woodrow Wilson fellow, Danforth Found. fellow), Princeton U., 1963, PhD in Physics (Danforth Found. fellow, NSF fellow), 1965, postgrad. (NSF postdoctoral fellow), 1965-66; D.Sc. (hon.), Ill. Coll., 1979; Dr.h.c., Moscow U., 1981; D.Sc. (hon.), Utah State U., 2000, U. Glasgow, 2001; D.H.L. (hon.), Claremont Grad. U., 2002. Research fellow Calif. Inst. Tech., 1966-67, assoc. prof. theoretical physics, 1967-70, prof., 1970—, William R. Kenan, Jr. prof., 1981-91, Feynman prof. theoretical physics, 1991—. Fulbright lectr., France, 1966; vis. assoc. prof. U. Chgo., 1968; vis. prof. Moscow U., 1969, 75, 78, 82, 83, 86, 88, 90, 98; vis. sr. rsch. assoc. Cornell U., 1977, A.D. White prof.-at-large, 1968-92; adj. prof. U. Utah, 1971-98; mem. Internat. Com. on Gen. Relativity and Gravitation, 1971-80, 92-01, Com. on U.S.-USSR Coop. in Physics, 1978-79, Space Sci. Bd., NASA, 1980-83; co-founder, chair steering com. LIGO, 1984-87. Co-author: Gravitation Theory and Gravitational Collapse, 1965, Gravitation, 1973, Black Holes: The Membrane Paradigm, 1986, Black Holes and Time Warps: Einstein's Outrageous Legacy, 1994. Alfred P. Sloan Found. Rsch. fellow, 1966-68; John Simon Guggenheim fellow, 1967; recipient Sci. Writing award in physics and astronomy Am. Inst. Physics, 1969, 94, P.A.M. Dirac Meml. lectureship Cambridge U., 1995, Karl Schwarzschild medal Astron. Soc. Germany, 1996, J. Robert Oppenheimer Meml. lectureship U. Calif., 1999, Charles Darwin Meml. Lectureship Royal Astron. Soc., 2000, Arthur Holly Compton Meml. lectureship Washington U., 2001, Herzberg Meml. Lectureship Can. Assn. Physicists, 2001; recipient, Common Wealth award, Sci Invention, 2005; Robinson Prize in Cosmology, U. Newcastle, 2002. Fellow Am. Phys. Soc. (Julius Edgar Lilienfeld prize 1996, chair topical group in gravity 1997-98); mem. Am. Philosophical Soc., Nat. Acad. Scis., Am. Acad. Arts and Scis., Am. Astron. Soc., Internat. Astron. Union, AAAS, Russian Acad. Scis., Ligo Sci. Collaboration, Lisa Internat. Sci. Team, Sigma Xi, Tau Beta Pi. Office: California Inst Tech 130-33 Theoretical Astrophysics 1200 E California Blvd Pasadena CA 91125

**THORNE, RICHARD MANSERGH,** physicist; b. Birmingham, Eng., July 25, 1942; s. Robert George and Dorothy Lena (Goodchild) T.; children: Peter Baring, Michael Thomas, Thomas Mansergh. BSc, Birmingham U., 1963; PhD, MIT, 1968. Grad. asst. M.I.T., 1963-68; asst. prof. dept. atmospheric scis. UCLA, 1968-71, asso. prof., 1971-75, prof., 1975—, chmn. dept., 1976-79. Vis. fellow St. Edmund's Coll., Cambridge (Eng.) U., 1986-87, 92; cons. NATO Adv. Group for Aerospace R&D, 1973, Jet Propulsion Lab., Aerospace Corp. Contbr. articles to profl. jours. Recipient numerous grants NSF, NASA, NATO, Jet Propulsion Lab.; Fulbright scholar, 1963-70; fellow Royal Norwegian Coun. for Sci. and Indsl. Rsch., 1973, sr. vis. fellow U. Sussex, 1979-80, rsch. fellow Royal Soc. London, 1986-87. Fellow Am. Geophys. Union; mem. Internat. Union Radio Scis. Home: 10390 Caribou Ln Los Angeles CA 90077 Office: UCLA Dept Atmospheric and Oceanic Scis Los Angeles CA 90095-1565 Business E-Mail: rmt@atmos.ucla.edu.

**THORNE, STEPHEN H.,** research scientist; s. Peter H. and Barbara A. Thorne; m. Rebecca J. Critchley, Nov. 6, 2004. BSc, Oxford U., Eng., 1993; PhD, Imperial Coll., London, 1997. Rsch. assoc. Stanford (Calif.) U., 2002—. Dir. viral rsch. Jennerex Biotherapeutics, San Francisco. Mem.: Am. Assn. Cancer Rsch. (assoc.).

**THORNELL, JACK RANDOLPH,** photographer; b. Vicksburg, Miss., Aug. 29, 1939; s. Benjamin O. and Myrtice (Jones) T.; divorced; children—Candice, Jay Randolph. Student pub. schs. Photographer Jackson (Miss.) Daily News, 1960-64; with A.P., 1964—, assigned Dominican Republic, 1965, Selma, Ala., 1965, Democratic Nat. Conv., 1968. Served with AUS, 1958-60. Recipient Pulitzer prize for news photography of shooting of James Meredith, 1967; Headliners Photography award, 1967 Office: 3800 Howard Ave New Orleans LA 70125-1429

**THORNER, MICHAEL OLIVER,** medical educator; b. Beaconsfield, Eng., Jan. 14, 1945; came to U.S., 1977; s. Hans and Ilse T.; m. Prudence Maria Ross, July 7, 1966; children— Benjamin Bruno, Anna Rosa MB, BChir, U. London, 1970. Intern, resident Middlesex Hosp., St. Bartholomew's Hosp., London; lectr. chem. pathology St. Bartholomews Hosp., London, 1974, research fellow, 1974-75, lectr. medicine, 1975-77; assoc. prof. medicine U. Va., Charlottesville, 1977-82, prof. medicine, 1982-90, head div. endocrinology and metabolism, 1986-98, dir. Clin. Research Ctr., 1984-97, assoc. dir. CRC, 1981-84, Kenneth R. Crispell prof. in internal medicine, 1990-98, Henry B. Mulholland prof. internal medicine, 1998—. Chmn. dept. internal medicine U. Va., 1997—. Contbr. articles to profl. jours. Recipient Albion O. Bernstein award, 1984, Virginia Scientist of Yr. award, 1985, Gen. Clin. Rsch. Ctrs. program award, 1995, The Pituitary Soc. Annual award for contbns. to understanding pituitary disease, 1995, Theodore E. Woodward Award 1996. Fellow Royal Coll. Physicians, ACP (John Phillips Meml. award 1999); master Am. Coll. of Physicians; mem. AAAS, Soc. Endocrinology, Endocrine Soc. (Edwin B. Astwood award 1992), Assn. Am. Physicians, Am. Soc. Clin. Investigations. Office: U Va Health Sys Dept Internal Medicine Endocrinology PO Box 801411 Charlottesville VA 22908 Home: PO Box 315 North Garden VA 22959-0335 Fax: 804-979-4967. E-mail: mot@virginia.edu.

**THORNHILL, ARTHUR H., JR.,** retired publishing executive; b. Boston, Jan. 1, 1924; s. Arthur Horace and Mary Josephine (Peterson) T.; m. Dorothy M. Matheis, Oct. 28, 1944; children: Sandra Susanne Thornhill Brushart, Arthur Horace. AB magna cum laude, Princeton U., 1948. With Little, Brown & Co., Inc., Boston, 1948-88, v.p., 1955-58, gen. mgr., 1960-87, chief exec. officer, pres., 1962-87, chmn. bd., 1970-87; chmn., pres., dir. Little, Brown & Co. (Can.), Ltd., 1955-84; v.p. Time, Inc., 1968-87; vice chmn. Time-Life Books, Inc., 1976-86. Mem. adv. council history dept. Princeton U., 1964-85; trustee, treas. Princeton U. Press, 1972-85; chmn. N.Y. Graphic Soc., 1974-79. Trustee Bennington Coll., 1969-76; fellow emeritus Ctr. for Creative Photography U. Ariz.; bd. dirs. Am. Book Pubs. Council, 1964-67. Served to 1st lt. USAAF, World War II. Decorated Air medal; recipient Princeton U. Press medal, 1985, Disting. Alumni award Dwight-Englewood Sch., 1998. Mem. Assn. Am. Pubs. (bd. dirs. 1978-81), Edgartown Yacht Club, Edgartown Reading Room (pres. 1990-92), Union Club (N.Y.C.), Princeton Club (N.Y.C.), Century Club (N.Y.C.), Publs. Lunch Club (N.Y.C.), Union Club (Boston), St. Botolph (Boston). Home: Apt 5303 250 Pantops Mountain Rd Charlottesville VA 22911-8703

**THORNHILL, M. JERRY,** mathematics professor; b. Columbia, La., Feb. 13, 1943; s. Marcus and Elsie Thornhill; m. G. Jane Hayes; 1 child, Tresa Gail Henry. BS, La. Poly. Inst., Ruston, 1965; MS, Clemson U., SC, 1968. Assoc. prof. math. SW Va. C.C., Richlands, 1972—. Tailtwister Lions Club, Lebanon, Va. Named William T. Lowry Tchr. of Yr., Va. Coun. Tchrs. Math., 2006; recipient Emmet F. Low Tchg. award, SW Va. Coun. Tchrs. Math., 2005, Excellence award, NISOD, 2000, 2004. Mem.: Va. Math. Assn. for 2-Yr. Colls. (v.p. 1995—97), Am. math. Assn. for 20-Yr. Colls., Math Assn. Am. Office: SW Va CC PO Box SVCC Richlands VA 24641-1101 Office Phone: 276-964-7328. E-mail: jerry.thornhill@sw.edu.

**THORNSBERRY, CLYDE,** microbiologist; b. Pippa Passes, Ky., June 20, 1930; s. Columbus B. and Ollie Mae (Sparkman) T.; m. Glenda L. Martin, May 13, 1952; children: Teresa, David, Robert. BS, U. Ky., 1958, PhD, 1966. Chief Antimicrobial Investigations Br. Ctrs. for Disease Control, Atlanta, 1966-89; dir. Inst. for Microbiol. Rsch., Franklin, Tenn., 1989-93, Focus

BioInova, Inc., Franklin, 1993— Lectr. in field; chmn., vice-chmn. Intersci. Conf. Anti-Agts., Washington, 1989-94; adv. bd. several pharm. cos., 1980—. Contbr. articles to profl. jours. Recipient awards USPHS, Washington, 1982, 87. Fellow Infectious Disease Soc. of Am.; mem. Am. Soc. Microbiology (BD award for Rsch. in Clin. Microbiology 2003), Am. Acad. Microbiology, N.Y. Acad. Scis., WHO Coms. on Antibiotics, Nat. Com. Clin. Lab. Stds. Democrat. Achievements include patent-use of antimicrobial agts. to sterilize tissue for implanting; study of antimicrobials, antimicrobial resistance, and in vitro testing of antimicrobial activity; lab. was designated a WHO lab. for antimicrobial agts. Home: 5182 Waddell Hollow Rd Franklin TN 37064-9436 Office: Focus Diagnostics Inc 5182 Waddell Hollow Rd Franklin TN 37064 Office Phone: 615-794-7011. Business E-Mail: cthornsberry@focusbioinova.com.

**THORNSBERRY, WILLIS LEE, JR.,** chemist; b. Sturgis, Ky., Aug. 10, 1940; s. Willis Lee and Jane (Hall) T.; m. Mary Elizabeth Gaswint, June 19, 1965; children: Brian, Michele B., Murray State U., 1963; MS, U. Ark., 1967; PhD, Tulane U., 1974. Rsch. chemist Freeport-McMoran Inc., Belle Chasse, La., 1967—74, sr. rsch. chemist, 1974—82; pres. Tech. Devel. Svcs. Inc., Sturgis, Ky., 1995—. Contbr. articles to profl. jours. Coach, leader for youth groups Jefferson Parish Playgrounds, Gretna, La., 1970-84, Boy Scouts Am., Gretna, 1975-82. 1st lt. U.S. Army, 1963-65. Mem. Am. Chem. Soc. (sect. chmn. 1982), Sigma Xi. Democrat. Achievements include numerous patents for process for uranium recovery from phosphoric acid, recovery of silica from hydrofluorosilicic acid, stabilization of gypsum for construction purposes, preparation and use of fertilizer additives. Office: 1024 N Main St Sturgis KY 42459-1245 Office Phone: 270-333-2243. Personal E-mail: mwthorns@bellsouth.net.

**THORNTON, ANDREW JOHN,** minister; b. Ukiah, Calif., Oct. 20, 1977; s. Gary Evan and Sandra Sue Thornton; m. Sarah Rebecca Ensor. BS in Christian Ministries, Southwestern Bapt. U., Bolivar, Mo., 1996—2000; MA in Bibl. Theology, Luther Rice Theol. Sem., Atlanta, 2000—02, MA in Christian counseling, 2000—02. Summer missionary Mo. Bapt. Conv., Jefferson City, Mo., 1994—96; asst. min. students Golden Ave. Bapt. Ch., Springfield, Mo., 1996—98, assoc. pastor, 1999—2003; min. students First Bapt. Ch. of Ozark, Ozark, Mo., 2003—. Conservative. Baptist. Avocations: basketball officiating, reading, public speaking. Office: First Baptist Ch of Ozark 1400 W Jackson Ozark MO 65721 Home: 1329 N Washington Ave Springfield MO 65802-1935 E-mail: andy@fbcostudents.com.

**THORNTON, BILLY BOB,** actor, film producer; b. Hot Springs, Ark., Aug. 4, 1955; s. Billy Ray and Virginia Thornton; m. Melissa Lee Gatlin, 1978 (div. 1980); 1 child; m. Toni Lawrence, 1986 (div. 1988); m. Cynda Williams, 1990 (div. 1992); m. Pietra Dawn Cherniak, Feb. 18, 1993 (div. Apr. 1997); 2 children; m. Angelina Jolie, May 5, 2000 (div. May 27, 2003); 1 child. Actor: (films) For the Boys, 1991, Indecent Proposal, 1993, Tombstone, 1993, On Deadly Ground, 1994, Floundering, 1994, Dead Man, 1995, The Winner, 1996, A Gun, A Car, A Blonde, 1997, U-Turn, 1997, A Thousand Miles, 1997, The Apostle, 1997, Primary Colors, 1998, Homegrown, 1998, Armageddon, 1998, A Simple Plan, 1998, Pushing Tin, 1999, The Last Real Cowboys, 2000, South of Heaven, West of Hell, 2000, Monster's Ball, 2001, Bandists, 2001, The Man Who Wasn't There, 2001, Waking up in Reno, 2002, The Badge, 2002, Intolerable Cruelty, 2003, Love Actually, 2003, Levity, 2003, Bad Santa, 2003, The Alamo, 2004, Friday Night Lights, 2004, Bad News Bears, 2005, The Ice Harvest, 2005; dir., actor, writer (films) Sling Blade, 1996 (Acad. award Best Adapted Screenplay), Daddy and Them, 2001, dir., prodr. All the Pretty Horses, 2000, actor, writer One False Move, 1992, The Gift, 2000, (screenplays) Trouble Bound, 1993, Some Folks Call It a Slingblade, 1994, A Family Thing, 1996; actor: (TV films) The Man Who Broke 1,000 Chains, 1987, Circus, 1988, Out There, 1995, Don't Look Back, 1996; (TV series) The Outsiders, 1988, Hearts A Fire, 1992; TV appearances include Matlock, 1987, Evening Shade, 1990, Knots Landing, 1990, Ellen, 1997, (voice) King of the Hill, 1998. Office: Rogers Cowan 8687 Melrose Ave Ste G700 West Hollywood CA 90069-5721*

**THORNTON, CAMERON MITCHELL,** financial planner; b. L.A., Sept. 30, 1954; s. H. Walter and Naomi L. (Brown) T.; m. Jane Kubasak, June 18, 1978; children: Mitchell, Kathryn, Andrew. BA, U. So. Calif., L.A., 1976; MBA, U. La Verne, 1983. CFP. Planner Lockheed Calif. Co., Burbank, 1980-84; adv. assoc. Fin. Network Investment Corp., Burbank, 1983—, fin. cons., 1983—, prin., br. mgr. 1997—; prin. Cameron Thornton Assocs., Burbank, 1982—; prin. lic. charitable gift planner Renaissance Inc., 1992-99. Author: (manual) Computer Aided Planning System, 1982-83. Vice chair St. Joseph Med. Ctr. Found., 1988-92, chmn. planned giving dept., 1991-92; mem. planned giving dept. Mater Dolorosa Passionist Retreat Ctr., Sierra Madre, Calif., 2000—; chair Burbank Police Commn., 1981-85, Burbank Planning Commn., 1989-93; active ARC, Burbank, 1984-88, chmn. 1987-88; asst. scoutmaster Boy Scouts of Am., Burbank, 1994-97, 2001—05, scoutmaster, 1997-2000. Named Friend of Campfire, Camp Fire Coun., Pasadena, Calif., 1989; named to Bloomberg's Top Wealth Mgr. List, 2001-06; Fin. Advisor Top Ria Ranking, 2006. Mem. Fin. Planning Assn., Cert. Fin. Planner Bd. Standards, Burbank C. of C. Republican. Roman Catholic. Avocations: fishing, reading, skiing. Office: Cameron Thornton Assocs 290 E Verdugo Ave Ste 205 Burbank CA 91502-1342

**THORNTON, CHARLES VICTOR,** metals executive; b. Salt Lake City, Feb. 8, 1915; s. Charles Victor and Winnie May (Fitts) T.; m. Margaret Louise Wiggins, Apr. 17, 1937; children: Charles Victor III, Carolyn Louise (Mrs. John J. Moorhouse), David Frank. BS in Civil Engring., U. Utah, 1935; HHD, Ind. Inst. Tech., 1972. Registered prof. engr., Ohio, Tex. Engr. Truscon Steel Co., Youngstown, Ohio, 1935-37, dist. engr. Washington, 1937-40; chief engr. Jo. Iron Works, Inc., Alexandria, Va., 1940-45, pres. Thornton Industries, Inc., Ft. Worth, 1945-75, chmn. bd., 1975-88. Bd. dirs. Bank Commerce and Comml. Fin. Corp.; chmn. bd. dirs. Southview Corp. Mem.: American Association of Private Railroad Car Owners Roster of Private R.R. Cars, 1991, Autobiography, 1993, Charlie, 1994, Winnie, 1994. Chmn. bd. Southview Corp., 1980—, comm. investments Shriners Hosps. for Children; mem. nat. adv. coun. U. Utah, 1985-96; chmn. investment com. Longhorn coun. Boy Scouts Am., 1985-88; v.p. campaign chmn. Ft. Worth Arts United, 1989; v.p. Tarrant County Arts Coun., 1989; pres. Tarrant County Water Bd., 1984-88; mem. policy com. Dallas-Ft. Worth Railtran, 1991-98; pres. Ft. Worth chpt. Internat. Good Neighbor Coun., 1991-92; bd. dirs. Ft. Worth Opera, 1997—; mem. World Affairs Coun. Ft. Worth, 1996, bd. dirs., 1997—, treas., 1998. Recipient Salesman of Yr. award Ft. Worth Sales and Mktg. Execs., 1984, Good Neighbor of Yr. award Internat. Good Neighbor Coun., 1984, Merit of Honor award U. Utah, 1986; holder airplane speed record Dallas to Wichita, Kans., 1969. Mem. ASCE (life) (Tex. sect. Svc. to People award 1995), Tex. Assn. Bus. (life), Ft. Worth C. of C. (pres. 1960), Am. Assn. Pvt. R.R. Car Owners (pres. 1982-83), Petroleum Club, Fort Worth Club, City Club, Exch. Club of Fort Worth (past pres.), La Cima Club, Oxford Club, Grand Coun. (Fort Worth chpt. Confrerie Saint Etienne), Masons (33 degree s.r.), Shriners (past imperial potentate), Kiwanis (past pres.), Elks, Petroleum Club, Tau Beta Pi. Home: 5301 Bryant Irvin Rd Fort Worth TX 76132-4030 Home Fax: 817-237-0100.

**THORNTON, CHARLES VICTOR,** lawyer; b. Takoma Park, Md., July 18, 1942; s. Charles Victor and Margaret Louise (Wiggins) T.; m. Suzanne Thorne, May 16, 1970; children: Christopher, Matthew, Joshua, Jeremy. AB, Cornell U., 1964; JD, U. Mich., 1967. Bar: Calif. 1969, U.S. Dist. Ct. (ctrl. dist.) Calif. 1969. Instr. U. Pa. Law Sch., Phila., 1967-68; assoc. Paul, Hastings, Janofsky & Walker, L.A., 1968-74, ptnr., 1975—, mng. ptnr. L.A. office, 1992-96, mng. ptnr. San Francisco office, 1997-2000. Contbr. articles to publs. Pres. Info. and Referral Fedn. L.A. County, 1988-95; mem. exec. com. L.A. County United Way, 1998-92. Named Bd. Vol. of Yr. United Way, 1986, Bd. Vol. of Yr. YMCA, 2004. Mem. Calif. Club, LA Country Club, San Francisco YMCA (bd. dirs., 1998—, chmn. bd., 2006-). Avocations: running, golf. Office: Paul Hastings Janofsky & Walker 24th Flr 55 Second St San Francisco CA 94105 Office Phone: 415-856-7001. Business E-Mail: charlesthornton@paulhastings.com.

**THORNTON, CHARLIE MAE,** secondary school educator; b. Idabel, Okla., Oct. 7, 1947; d. Juanita Cotton; children: Kimberly, Joel. BA in English Edn., East Cen. State U., Ada, Okla., 1968; MEd, Northeastern State U., Tahlequah, Okla., 1979. Cert. reading specialist Okla. Tchr. 6th grade reading Tulsa (Okla.) Pub. Schs., Tulsa, 1973—. Sec. Friends of Rudisill North Regional Libr., Tulsa. Mem. NEA, Internat. Reading Assn., Okla. Reading Assn., Okla. Edn. Assn., Tulsa County Reading Coun., Tulsa Classroom Tchrs. Assn., Alpha Kappa Alpha, Phi Delta Kappa Democrat. Mem. Ch. Of Christ. Avocation: reading. Home: 2205 W Reading Pl Tulsa OK 74127-2238 Office: Wilson Mid Sch 1127 S Columbia Tulsa OK 74104 Office Phone: 918-833-9340. Business E-Mail: thornch@tulsaschools.org.

**THORNTON, CLARENCE GOULD,** electronics executive, civilian military employee; b. Detroit, Aug. 3, 1925; s. Lorenzo C. and Violet (Gould) T.; m. Gloria Fuchs, June 18, 1949; children: Susan Carol, Richard Scott. BS, U. Mich., 1949, MS, 1950, PhD, 1952. Project engr. Sylvania Electric Co., Woburn, Mass., 1951-52; sect. head to dir. Semiconductor div. Philco Corp., Lansdale, Pa., 1952-60; dir. R&D Philco Corp., Blue Bell, Pa., 1960-72; dir. Electronics Technology and Devices Lab., U.S. Army, Fort Monmouth, NJ, 1972-92; directorate exec. Army Rsch. Lab., 1992-95. Mem. Commn. on Engring. and Tech. Sys. Bd. on Army Sci. and Tech., Nat. Rsch. Coun., 1995—; sci., tech., bus. cons. 1995—; vol. lab. dir. emeritus U.S. Commn. Electronics Rsch., Devel. and Engring. Ctr., 2003-05. Contbr. articles to profl. jours.; patentee in field of electronics. Mem. Colts Neck Bd. Health, 1974-79. Served with USN, 1944-46. Recipient Local Svc. award Boy Scouts Am., 1963, Sci. Conf. award Dept. Army, 1976, Rsch. and Devel. Achievement award, 1976, Lab. of Yr. award, 1980, 83, 88, Lab. Excellence award, 1981, 85, 86, Sr. Exec. award, 1980-93, Gold medal Armed Forces Comms. and Electronics Assn., 1983, Handicapped Adv. Coun. award of achievement, 1985, Exceptional Civilian Svc. medal Dept. Army, 1985, Presdl. Rank award of Meritorious Svc., 1986, Presdl. Rank award of Disting. Sr. Exec., 1987, Crozier award, 1990, Superior Civilian Svc. medal, 1995, Exceptional Civilian Svc. medal, 1995. Fellow IEEE (Centennial medal 1994, Third Millennium medal 2000, Engring. Leadership Recognition award 1994, Joint Logistics Comdrs. award 1994); mem. AAAS, Nat. Def. Indsl. Assn., Assn. U.S. Army, Armed Forces Electronics Assn., Sr. Execs. Assn. (Exec. Achievement award 1994), Am. Defense Preparedness Assn., Alpha Chi Sigma, Phi Kappa Phi, Phi Lambda Upsilon. Mem. Reformed Ch. Home: 28 Glenwood Rd Colts Neck NJ 07722-1015 Office: AMSRL-EP Fort Monmouth NJ 07703

**THORNTON, D. MCCARTY (MAC THORNTON),** lawyer; b. Wilmington, Del., Sept. 6, 1947; m. Molly F. Carr, July 7, 1996. BA, Stanford U., 1969, JD with high honors, 1972. Bar: Calif. 1973, DC 1973, US Supreme Ct. 1977. Trial atty. Bur. Consumer Protection FTC, Washington, 1972-78, dep. asst. dir., 1978; prosecutor fraud sect., criminal divsn. US Dept. Justice, Washington, 1978-82; assoc. Cole & Corette, Washington, 1982-83; chief of litigation Office of Insp. Gen., US Dept. HHS, Washington, 1983-90, chief counsel to Insp. Gen., 1990—2002; ptnr., health care group Sonnenschein Nath & Rosenthal LLP, Washington, 2003—. Founder, chmn. bd. W.Va. Rivers Coalition, Elkins, 1989-97. Mem. The Potomac Conservancy (founder, chair 1992-95, vice chair 1995-99), Am. Health Lawyers Assn. (bd. dirs. 1991-97), Health Care Compliance Assn. Avocation: whitewater kayaking. Office: Sonnenschein Nath & Rosenthal LLP Ste 600 East Tower 1301 K St NW Washington DC 20005 Office Phone: 202-408-6432. Office Fax: 202-408-6399. Business E-Mail: mthornton@sonnenschein.com.

**THORNTON, EDMUND B.,** philanthropist; b. Chgo., Mar. 9, 1930; s. George A. and Suzanne W. Thornton; children from previous marriage: Thomas, Jonathan, Susan, Amanda; m. Susan Feldhaus; 1 child, Taylor. BA, Yale U., 1954. With No. Trust Co., Chgo., 1957-59; asst. sec., asst. treas. Ottawa (Ill.) Silica Co., 1959-61, v.p. corp. devel., 1961-62, pres., CEO, 1962-75, chmn. bd., CEO, 1975-83, chmn. bd., 1983-86; dir., v.p. Ottawa Nat. Bank. Author various articles on historic preservation, history and military subjects. Del. Rep. Nat. Conv., 1964-88, precinct committeeman, 1978-92; chmn. LaSalle County Rep. Ctrl. Com., 1980-92, Ill. and Mich. Canal Nat. Heritage Commn., 1985-2004; pres. Ottawa Silica Co. Found., Edmund B. Thornton Found., Ottawa, 1986— 1st lt. USMC, 1954—56. Recipient Conservation Svc. award U.S. Dept. Interior, 1973. Mem. NRA (life), Nat. Assn. Mfrs., U.S. C. of C., Nat. Indsl. Sand Assn. (dir. 1968-73), Ill. Mfrs.' Assn. (dir. 1969-75, chmn. 1975), Ill. State C. of C. (dir. 1972-78), Explorers Club, Univ. Club (Chgo.), Elks. Republican. Congregationalist. Home: PO Box 1 Ottawa IL 61350-0001 Office: PO Box 949 Ottawa IL 61350-0949 Office Phone: 815-434-6664.

**THORNTON, FELICIA D.,** food service company executive; BSc Econs., Santa Clara U.; MBA Corp. Fin., Mktg., U. So. Calif. V.p., corp. planning and acctg. Ralphs Grocery Co., v.p., admin., 1998, group v.p., fin. and adminstrn., 1999—2001; group v.p. retail ops. Kroger Co., 2000—01; exec. v.p., CFO Albertson's, Inc., 2001—. Office: Albertson's Inc 250 Parkcenter Blvd Boise ID 83706*

**THORNTON, GLENDA ANN,** librarian; b. Chickasha, Okla., Aug. 11, 1949; d. G. Van and Clara Maude (Lister) Long; m. Phillip Wynn Thornton, Sept. 18, 1970; children: Edward D., Jonathan C. BA, U. Okla., 1971, MLS, 1973; PhD, U. North Tex., 1993. Reference libr. Aurora (Colo.) Pub. Libr., 1974-75; tech. svcs. libr. Adams State Coll., Alamosa, Colo., 1975-80; collection devel. libr. Henderson State U., Arkadelphia, Ark., 1980-85, acting dir. libr., 1984; head material acquisitions libr. U. North Tex., Denton, 1985-91; assoc. dir. libr. svc. Auraria Libr. U. Colo., Denver, 1991—98; dir. Cleve. State U. Libr., 1998—. Co-author: AHE Vendor Directory, 1988; editor: Collection Management, vols. 26-27, 2000-03, mem. editl. bd. vol. 28, 2004—, revs. editor vol. 29, 2005—; revs. editor Tech. Svcs. Quar., 1997—; contbr. articles to profl. jours. Mem. Ohio LINK Libr. Adv. Coun., 1998—. Mem. ALA, Libr. Adminstrn. and Mgmt. Assn., Assn. Coll. and Rsch. Librs., Acad. Libr. Assn. Ohio, Cleve. Area Met. Libr. Assn. (bd. dirs. 2002-06), Beta Phi Mu. Avocation: gardening. Office: 2121 Euclid Ave RT 501 Cleveland OH 44115-2214 Office Phone: 216-687-2475. Business E-Mail: g.thornton@csuohio.edu.

**THORNTON, H MONTE,** textiles executive; Pres. Hollytex Inc., 1984—90, Mohawk Industries (previously Karastan Bigelow), 1990—2000; pre. fashion and performance divsn. Mohawk Industries, 2000—01, pres., carpet group, 2001—. Office: Mohawk Industries P O Box 12069 Calhoun GA 30703-7002

**THORNTON, J. DUKE,** lawyer; b. Murray, Ky., July 11, 1944; s. Arthur Lee and Ruth Maxine (Billings) T.; m. Carol Caceres, Dec. 26, 1966 (dec.); children: Jennifer, Carey. BBA, U. N.Mex., Albuquerque, 1966, JD, 1969. Bar: N.Mex. 1969, U.S. Ct. Appeals (10th cir.) 1969, N.Y. 1985, U.S. Supreme Ct. 1992. With Butt, Thornton & Baehr, P.C., Albuquerque, 1971—, now chmn. bd. Legal counsel N.Mex. Jaycees, 1972; clk. N.Mex. Supreme Ct., Santa Fe, 1969; mem. com. N.Mex. Uniform Jury Instructions, 1987-88. Author: Trial Handbook for New Mexico Lawyers, 1992. Bd. dirs. N.Mex. Bd. of Dentistry, Santa Fe, 1987-88; commr. N.Mex. Racing Commn., Albuquerque, 1988-95. Mem. ABA, Am. Bd. Trial Advs., Albuquerque Bar Assn. (bd. dirs. 1978-79), Nat. Collegiate Athletic Assn. (agt.). Avocation: pilot. Office: Butt Thornton & Baehr PC PO Box 3170 Albuquerque NM 87190-3170

**THORNTON, J. RONALD,** technology consultant; b. Fayetteville, Tenn., Aug. 19, 1939; s. James Alanda and Thelma White (McGee) T.; m. Mary Beth Packard, June 14, 1964 (div. Apr. 1975); 1 child, Nancy Carole; m. Martha Klemann, Jan. 23, 1976 (div. Apr. 1982); 1 child, Trey; m. Bernice McKinney, Feb. 14, 1986; 1 child, Paul Leon. BS in Physics and Math., Berry Coll. 1961; MA in Physics, Wake Forest Coll., 1964; postgrad., U. Ala., 1965-66, Rollins Coll., 1970. Rsch. physicist Brown Engring. Co., Huntsville, Ala., 1963-66; sr. staff engr. Martin Marietta Corp., Orlando, Fla., 1966-75; dep. dir. NASA, Washington, 1976-77; exec. asst. Congressman Louis Frey, Jr.,

Orlando, 1978; pres. Tens Tec, Inc., Orlando, 1978-79; dir. So. Tech. Applications Ctr. U. Fla., Gainesville, Fla., 1979—2002. Bd. dirs., treas. North Fla. Tech. Innovation Ctr., 1994—2004; mem. light wave tech. com. Fla. High Tech. and Indsl. Coun., Tallahassee, 1986—93, NASA Tech. Transfer Exec. Com., Washington, 1987—, Javits Fellowship Bd., Washington, 1986—91, Gov.'s New Porduct Award Com., Tallahassee, 1988—94, Fla. K-12 Math., Sci. and Computer Sci. Edn. Quality Improvement Adv. Coun., 1989—94, Fla. Sci. Edn. Improvement Adv.Com., 1991—92; bd. dirs. North Fla. Enterprise Corp., 2001—04. Pres. Orange County Young Rep. Club, Orlando, 1970-71; treas. Fla. Fedn. Young Reps., Orlando, 1971-72; chmn. Fla. Fedn. Young Reps., Orlando, 1972-74; pres. Gainesville Area Innovation Network, 1988-89; mem. Berry Coll. Alumni Coun., 2006—. Named Engr. Exhibiting Tech. Excellence and Accomplishment ctrl. Fla. chpt. Fla. Engring. Soc., 1975, Achievement award NASA, 1977; named to Berry Coll. Hall of Fame, 2005. Mem. IEEE, Soc. Mfg. Engrs., Tech. Transfer Soc. (pres. 1999, bd. dirs. 1996—2001, Thomas Jefferson award 1999), Nat. Assn. Mgmt. and Tech. Assistance Ctrs. (bd. dirs. 1988, pres. 1992). Republican. Avocations: music, travel, reading, golf. Home and Office: 17829 NW 20th Ave Newberry FL 32669-2143 Office Phone: 352-472-6026. Personal E-Mail: ronthornton@cox.net.

**THORNTON, JOE,** professional hockey player; b. London, Ont., Can., July 2, 1979; Player Boston Bruins, 1997—2005, HC Davos, Switzerland, 2004—05, San Jose Sharks, 2005—. Mem. Team Can., World Championships, 2001, 05, Team Can., World Cup of Hockey, 2004, Team Can. Olympic Games, Torino, Italy, 2006; player NHL All-Star Game, 2002, 03, 04. Named to Second All-Star Team, NHL, 2003, First All-Start Team, 2006; recipient Art Ross Trophy, 2006, Hart Meml. Trophy, 2006. Achievements include being a member of World Cup Champion Team Canada, 2004. Office: c/o San Jose Sharks 525 W Santa Clara St San Jose CA 95113*

**THORNTON, JOHN CHRISTOPHER,** music educator; b. Marphysboro, Ill. s. Johnie Lynn and Martha Kay Thornton. MusB, Murray State U., 2003. Music tchr. Heath Elem. Sch., Paducah, Ky., 2004—. Musician: The Egyptian Combo, 1994—, pianist: Milburn Chapel, 2005—. Recipient Jr. Citizen of Yr., City of Herrin, Ill., 1996, Key to the City, Herrin, Ill., 2004. Mem.: Phi Mu Alpha Sinfonia. Avocation: scuba diving.

**THORNTON, JOHN EDWIN,** social studies educator; b. Schenectady, N.Y., Sept. 3, 1943; s. Gordon Edwin and Marguerite Elizabeth Thornton; m. Nancy Kohlhaas Thornton, Aug. 10, 1974; children: Tammara, Robert. BA in History, Doane Coll., Crete, Nebr., 1963—66; MA in Secondary Edn., U. Nebr., Lincoln, 1971—72. Tchr. English/social studies R.J. Barr Jr. High, Grand Island, Nebr., 1966—79; tchr., social studies Kuemper HS, Carroll, Iowa, 1979—85, Valley HS, W. Des Moines, Iowa, 1986—. Adj. instr. Des Moines Area CC, Carroll, 1982—84, W. Des Moines, 2003—. Recipient Sallie Mae Tchr. award, 1991. Office: Valley HS 1140 Valley West Dr West Des Moines IA 50266

**THORNTON, JOHN L.,** former diversified financial services company executive; AB in History, Harvard U., 1976; BA, MA in Jurisprudence, Oxford U., 1978; MPPM, Yale U., 1980. With Goldman Sachs Group, Inc., 1980—88, ptnr., 1988—95, co-CEO Goldman Sachs Internat., 1995—96, chmn. Goldman Sachs Asia, 1996—98, pres., co-COO 1999—2003, sr. adv., 2003—; spl. adv. on China to Pres. Richard C. Levin Yale U., 2003; prof., dir. Global Leadership prog. Tsinghua U., Beijing, 2003—. Bd. dirs. Ford Motor Corp., 1996—, Pacific Century Group, Intel Corp., 2003—, News Corp., 2004—, China Netcom, 2004—; mem. adv. bd. Yale Univ. Sch. Mgmt. Trustee Brookings Institution, 2000—, chmn., 2003—; trustee, bd. pres. Hotchkiss Sch.; trustee Asia Soc., China Inst., Eisenhower Fellowships, Morehouse Coll., Tsinghua U. Sch. Econ. & Mgmt., The Hotchkiss Sch. Mem.: Asia Soc., Coun. Fgn. Rels. Office: Tsinghua U Beijing 100084 China*

**THORNTON, JOSEPH SCOTT,** research and development company executive, materials scientist; b. Sewickley, Pa., Feb. 6, 1936; s. Joseph Scott and Evelyn (Miller) T.; divorced; children: Joseph Scott III, Chris P. BSME, U. Tex., 1957, PhD, 1969; MSMetE, Carnegie Mellon U., 1962. Engr. Walworth Valve Co., Boston, 1958; metall. engr. Westinghouse Astronuclear Lab., Large, Pa., 1962-64; instr., teaching assoc. U. Tex., Austin, 1964-67; group leader Tracor Inc., Austin, 1967-69, dept. dir., 1973-75; dept. mgr. Horizons Rsch., Inc., Cleve., 1969-73; chmn., chief exec. officer Tex. Rsch. Internat., Inc. (formerly Tex. Rsch. Inst., Inc.), Austin, 1975—. Contbr. numerous tech. papers to profl. publs.; editor: WANL Materials Manual, 2 vols., 1964; patentee in field. Founder, chmn., program dir. Vols. at the Creek, Austin. Recipient IGS award, 2002; fellow Alcoa, Austin, 1964, RC Baker Found., 1967. Mem.: ASTM, Internat. Geosynthetics Soc. (award 2002), Adhesion Soc., Am. Soc. Metals Internat. (exec. com. 1965—66). Office: Tex Rsch Internat Inc 9063 Bee Caves Rd Austin TX 78733-6201 Office Phone: 512-263-2101. E-mail: jst@tri-intl.com.

**THORNTON, KATHRYN C.,** physicist, astronaut; b. Montgomery, Ala., Aug. 17, 1952; d. William C. and Elsie Cordell; m. Stephen T. Thornton; children: Carol Elizabeth, Laura Lee, Susan Annette; stepchildren: Kenneth, Michael. BS in Physics, Auburn U., 1974; MS in Physics, U. Va., 1977, PhD, 1979. Physicist U.S. Army Fgn. Sci. & Tech. Ctr., Charlottesville, Va., 1980-84; with NASA, 1984—; astronaut Lyndon B. Johnson Space Ctr. Houston, 1985—, mission specialist Space Shuttle Discovery flight STS-33, 1989-96; prof. University of Virginia Sch of Engineering, VA, 1996—. Aboard maiden flight Space Shuttle Endeavor, 1992. Nato post-doctoral fellow Max Planck Inst. Nuclear Physics, 1979-80. Mem. AAAS, Am. Phys. Soc., Sigma Xi, Phi Kappa Phi.

**THORNTON, MARY LEITA,** musician, educator; b. Oconomowoc, Wis., Nov. 27, 1969; d. John William and Margaret Thornton. MusB, Rice U., 1991; MusM, Cleve. Inst. Music, 1993; MusD, U. Wis., 2002. Musician Green Bay (Wis.) Symphony, 1993—, Madison (Wis.) Symphony, 1995—96; instr. Del Mar Coll., Corpus Christi, 2001—; musician Victoria Symphony, 2002—, Corpus Christi (Tex.) Symphony, 2002—. Adj. instr. Tex. A&M U., Corpus Christi, Tex., 2005—. Musician (composer: Bernofsky): (songs) Concerto for Trumpet and Orchestra, 2001; musician: (composer: Flory) Four Pieces for Trumpet and Percussion, 2005; musician: (comoser: Bernofsky) Trio for Brass. Mem.: Am. Fedn. Musician, Tex. Music Educator's Assn., Internat. Trumpet Guild. Office Phone: 361-698-1602.

**THORNTON, MICHAEL B.,** federal judge; b. Hattiesburg, Miss., Feb. 9, 1954; BS in accounting, So Miss U., 1976, MS in accounting, 1977; MA in English Lit., U. Tenn., 1979; JD, Duke U., 1982. Bar: DC 1982. Law clk. to Hon. Charles Clark US Ct. Appeals (5th cir.), 1983—84; assoc. Sutherland, Asbill & Brennan, Washington, 1982—83, Miller & Chevalier, Washington, 1985—88; tax counsel US Ho. Com. on Ways & Means, Washington, 1988—93, chief minority tax counsel, 1995; atty. advisor US Dept. Treasury, Washington, 1995, dep. tax legis. counsel, Office Tax Policy, 1995—98; judge U.S. Tax Ct., Washington, 1998—. Mem. editl. bd. Duke U. Law Journ., 1981—82. Recipient Treasury Sec.'s Annual award, US Dept. Treasury, 1997, Meritorious Svc. award, 1998. Mem.: Order of the Coif. Office: US Tax Ct 400 2D St NW Washington DC 20217-0001

**THORNTON, RAY,** retired state supreme court justice, former congressman; b. Conway, AR, July 16, 1928; s. R.H. and Wilma (Stephens) Thornton; m. Betty Jo Mann, Jan. 27, 1956; children: Nancy, Mary Jo, Stephanie. BA, Yale U., 1950; JD, U. Ark., 1956. Bar: Ark. 1956, U.S. Supreme Ct. 1956. Pvt. practice in, Sheridan and Little Rock, 1956—70; atty. gen. Ark., 1971—73; mem. 93d-95th Congresses from 4th Ark. dist.; exec. dir. Quachita Bapt. U./Henderson State U. Joint Ednl. Consortium, Arkadelphia, Ark., 1979—80; pres. Ark. State U., Jonesboro and Beebe, 1984—89, U. Ark. Sys., Fayetteville, Little Rock, Pine Bluff, Monticello, 1984—89; mem. 102nd-104th Congresses from 2d Ark. dist., 1991—96; assoc. justice Ark. Supreme Ct.,

1997—2004. Chmn. Ark. Bd. Law Examiners, 1967—70; del. 7th Ark. Constl. Conv., 1969—70. Chmn. pres.'s devel. coun. Harding Coll., Searcy, Ark., 1971—73. With USN, 1951—54, Korea. Mem.: AAAS (chmn. com. on sci., engring. and pub. policy 1980).

**THORNTON, SPENCER P.,** ophthalmologist, educator; b. West Palm Beach, Fla., Sept. 16, 1929; s. Ray Spencer and Mae (Phillips) T.; m. Annie Glenn Cooper, Oct. 6, 1956; children: Steven Pitts, David Spencer, Ray Cooper, Beth Ellen. BS, Wake Forest Coll., 1951, MD, 1954. Diplomate: Am. Bd. Ophthalmology. Intern Ga. Bapt. Hosp., Atlanta, 1954-55; resident gen. surgery U. Ala. Med. Center, 1955-56; resident ophthalmology Vanderbilt U. Sch. Medicine, 1960-63; practice medicine specializing in ophthalmic surgery Nashville, 1960—; med. dir. Thornton Eye Ctr., 1995-99; clin. prof. ophthalmology U. Tenn., Memphis, 2002. Disting. vis. prof. dept. ophthalmology U. Tenn., Memphis 2001, Ridley medal lectr., 2001; mem. staff Bapt. Hosp., chief ophthalmology svc., 1982-87; guest prof., vis. lectr. U. Toronto, 1990-92, U. Paris, 1989, Rothchilds Inst., Paris, 1992, 94, U. Pretoria, 1991, 93, others; instr. Moscow Inst. Eye Microsurgery, 1981; instr. ophthalmic surgery Am. Acad. Ophthalmology Ann. Courses; lectr. lens implant symposiums Eng., Spain, Australia, Switzerland, Can., Sweden, Greece, Germany, France, Republic of South Africa, Japan; Berzelius lectr. U. Lund, Sweden, 1992; P.J. Hay Gold medal lectr. North of Eng. Ophthal. Soc., Scarborough, 1992; pres. Biosyntrx Inc., 2002—. King Features syndicated newspaper columnist, 1959-60, feature writer, NBC radio and TV, 1958-60; author, co-author textbooks on cataract and refractive surgery; mem. editl. bd. Jour. Refractive and Corneal Surgery, Jour. Cataract and Refractive Surgery, Video Jour. Ophthalmology, Ocular Surgery News (Ophthalmologist of Yr. 1996), Ophthalmic Practice (Can.), Eye Care Tech. Mag. (Lifetime Achievement award 1996); contbr. articles to profl. jours.; inventor instruments and devices for refractive and lens implant surgery. Named one of 100 Best Ophthalmologists in Am., Ophthalmology Times mag., 1996; recipient Honor award Can. Implant Assn., 1993, Outstanding Achievement award Bowman Gray Sch. Medicine, 1995, Ridley medal U. Tenn., Memphis, Tenn., 2001, Epstein medal lectr. Durban S. Africa, 2005. Fellow: ACS (life), Am. Coll. Nutritional Medicine (pres. 2000—), Am. Acad. Ophthalmology (honor award 1995); mem.: Am. Soc. Cataract and Refractive Surgery (pres. 1997—99), Can. Implant Soc. (life), South African Intraocular Implant Soc. (life), Am. Med. Soc. Vienna (life), Delta Kappa Alpha, Phi Rho Sigma. Baptist. Home and Office: 5070 Villa Crest Dr Nashville TN 37220-1425 Business E-Mail: sthornton@biosyntrx.com.

**THORNTON, THOMAS E.,** literature and language educator; s. Thomas B. and Eileen M. Thornton; m. Kathleen M. Kenneally, 1992; children: Michael, Ian, Kyra; m. Kathleen K. Thornton (div.). BA, SUNY, 1970; MA, SUNY, Albany, 1974. Cert. tchr. N.Y. State Edn. Dept., 1974. Tchr. English dept. Columbia HS, East Greenbush, NY, 1974—, curriculum specialist, 2002—. Contbr. poetry to jour.; co-author: (poetry) Teachers on Teaching, 2001. Mem.: Albany Police Pipes and Drums (drummer 2001—). Avocations: golf, writing, travel, music, cartooning. Home: 2072 Brookview Rd Castleton On Hudson NY 12033 Office: Columbia HS Luther Rd East Greenbush NY 12061

**THORNTON, THOMAS NOEL,** publishing executive; b. Marceline, Mo., Apr. 23, 1950; s. Bernard F. and Helen F. (Kelley) T.; m. Cynthia L. Murray, Nov. 26, 1971; children: T. Zachary, Timothy. B.J., U. Mo., 1972. Asst. to editor Universal Press Syndicate, Kansas City, Mo., 1972, v.p., 1974, dir. mktg., 1976; v.p., mktg. Universal Press Syndicate and Andrews McMeel Pub., Kansas City, 1976-87; pres., COO Andrews McMeel Pub., 1987—2002, pres., CEO, 2003—. Bd. dirs. Andrews McMeel Universal. Office: Universal Press Syndicate 4520 Main St Ste 700 Kansas City MO 64111-7701 Office Phone: 816-932-6700. Business E-Mail: tthornton@amuniversal.com.

**THORNTON, YVONNE SHIRLEY,** obstetrician, writer, musician; b. N.Y.C., Nov. 21, 1947; d. Donald E. and Itasker F. (Edmonds) T.; m. Shearwood McClelland, June 8, 1974; children: Shearwood III, Kimberly Itaska. BS in Biology, Monmouth Coll., 1969; MD, Columbia U., 1973, MPH, 1996; DSc (hon.), Tuskegee U., 2003. Diplomate Am. Bd. Ob-gyn. Resident in ob-gyn Roosevelt Hosp., N.Y.C., 1973-77; fellow maternal-fetal medicine Columbia-Presbyn. Med. Center, N.Y.C., 1977-79; commd. lt. comdr. M.C. USN, 1979; asst. prof. ob-gyn Uniformed Svcs. U. Health Scis., 1979-82; assoc. prof. Cornell U. Med. Coll., N.Y.C., 1989-92; dir. clin. svcs. dept. ob-gyn N.Y. Hosp.-Cornell Med. Center, 1982-88; asst. attending N.Y. Lying-In Hosp., 1982-89; assoc. clin. prof. ob-gyn. Columbia P&S, 1995-98, assoc. clin. prof., 2001—02; clin. prof. ob-gyn. U. Medicine and Dentistry N.J., 1998-2000; prof. clin. ob-gyn. Med. Coll. Cornell U., 2003—05. Dir. Chorionic Villus Sampling Program, 1984-92; divsn. maternal-fetal medicine St Luke's Roosevelt Hosp. Ctr., 2000-02; vice chair ob-gyn, dir. maternal-fetal medicine, Jamaica Hosp. Med. Ctr., 2002-05; staff Nat. Naval Med. Ctr. Bethesda, Md.; saxophonist Thornton Sisters ensemble, 1955-76; vis. assoc. physician The Rockefeller U. Med., 1986-96; prof. clinical OB/GYN Cornell U. Med. Coll., 2003-05; examiner Am. Bd. Ob-Gyn, 1997—; vice chmn. Dept. Ob-Gyn. Jamaica Hosp. Med. Ctr.; bd. dirs Integra Med Am., 2006. Author: The Ditchdigger's Daughter, 1995, (named best books for young adults ALA, Excellence in Lit. award, N.J. Edn. Assn., One Book N.J., N.J. Libr. Assn., 2006, nominated Pulitzer Prize 1995) Primary Care for the Obstetrician and Gynecologist, 1997, Woman to Woman, 1997. Recipient Excellence in Literature award, N.J. Edn. Assn., 1996, winner Daniel Webster Oratorical Competition, Internat. Platform Assn., 1996; nominated Pulitzer Prize, 1995. Fellow: ACOG, ACS; mem.: AMA, Am. Fedn. Musicians, Soc. Maternal-Fetal Medicine, Assn. Women Surgeons, N.Y. Acad. Medicine. Democrat. Baptist. Office Phone: 201-570-8181. Business E-Mail: thornton@carroll.com.

**THORON, GRAY,** lawyer, educator; b. Danvers, Mass., July 14, 1916; s. Ward and Louisa Chapin (Hooper) T.; m. Pattie Porter Holmes, Dec. 30, 1971 (dec. 2000); children from previous marriage: Claire, Louisa, Grenville C., Molly D., Thomas G. AB, Harvard U., 1938, LLB, 1941. Bar: N.Y. 1942. Assoc. Sullivan & Cromwell, N.Y.C., 1941-42, 45-48; assoc. prof. law U. Tex., 1948-50, prof. law, 1950-56; dean Law Sch. Cornell U., Ithaca, N.Y., 1956-63, prof. law, 1956-87, prof. emeritus, 1987—. Vis. prof. law U. Mich., 1951, U. Tex., 1970; faculty Salzburg Seminar in Am. Studies, 1959; asst. to solicitor gen. Dept. Justice, Washington, 1954-56; mem. NY State Laporte Legis. Ethics Com., 1964; spl. asst. atty. gen. NY State, 1965. Del. Rep. Nat. Conv., 1952; trustee Concord Acad., 1958-61. Served with AUS, 1942-45. Decorated silver star, bronze star, purple heart with oak leaf cluster. Fellow Am. Bar Found. (life); mem. ABA, Am. Law Inst. (life), N.Y. State Bar Assn. (chmn. spl. com. to rev. code of profl. responsibility 1974-77, com. profl. ethics 1965-87, vice chmn 1973-83, emeritus 1987—), Am. Arbitration Assn. (arbitrator 1965-90), Assn. Bar City NY, Lawyers Com. Civil Rights Under Law (trustee 1965-97), Phi Alpha Delta, Phi Kappa Phi, Century Assn., Harvard Club (NYC). Address: Savage Farm Dr Ithaca NY 14853

**THORP, BENJAMIN A., III,** retired paper company executive; b. Albany, N.Y., May 31, 1938; s. Benjamin Jr. and Anna C. (Head) T.; m. Barbara Sue Tellock, Aug. 1, 1964 (div. Mar. 1986); 1 child, Benjamin A. IV; m. Laurie Diane Murdock, Oct. 25, 1987. Student in elec. engring., Rensselaer Poly. Inst., 1956-61, postgrad. in mgmt., 1967-68; BS in Physics, U. Md., 1964; postgrad. in engring., U. Bridgeport, 1966; postgrad. in mktg., U. Tenn., 1970. Product devel. mgr. Huyck Formex div. Huyck Corp., Wake Forest, NC, 1969-71, mktg. mgr., 1971-73; v.p. gen. mgr., 1973-75, Huytech Systems div., Wake Forest, NC, 1975-78; v.p., dir. research Huyck Corp., Rensselaer, NY, 1978-80; pres. Benjamin A. Thorp Inc., Albany, 1980-82, POYRY-BEK Inc., Raleigh, NC, 1982-84; v.p. engring. BE&K Inc., Birmingham, Ala., 1984-85, James River Corp., Richmond, Va., 1984-95; v.p. mfg. tech. Chesapeake Corp., Richmond, Va., 1996-97; dir. pulp and paper engring. Ga. Pacific, Atlanta, 1998—2004, ret., 2004. Mem. exec. com. Pulp and Paper Found. Bd., Ga. Inst. Tech., 1991-95, pres. 1993-95; mem. indsl. adv. bd. Forest Web.com, 2000—, MTCI, Balt., Md., 2001-2003, Peregrine Energy, Greenville, S.C., 2002—; chmn. bd. Besicorp-Empire Newsprint LLC,

2004—; bd. mem. K.P. Products. Co-author: Pulp and Paper Energy Best Practice Guidebook, 2d edit., 2006; tech. editor Paper Machine Operations, Vol. 7, 3d edit., 1991; contbr. more than 100 articles to profl. jours.; patentee in field. Bd. dirs. Richmond Math. and Sci. Ctr., 1987-93, Sci. Mus. of Va. Found., 1989-98; chmn. papermaking project adv. com. Inst. Paper Sci. and Tech., 1990-94. Fellow TAPPI (chmn. papermakers com. 1984-86, vice chmn. paper and bd. divsns. 1988-90, chmn. 1990-92, bd. dir., Leadership award 1994); mem. Paper Industry Mgmt. Assn. (pres. 1996-97, chmn. bd. trustees 1999—2003, Glen T. Rinnegar award 1999), PIMA-CPBIS Mgmt. Excellence award 2003, Exptl. Aircraft Assn., Meadowbrook Estates Civic Assn. (bd. dirs. 1996-98, pres. 2003-04), Meadowbrook Country Club (bd. dirs. 2005—). Presbyterian. E-mail: bathorp@comcast.net.

**THORP, EDWARD OAKLEY,** investment management company executive; b. Chgo., Aug. 14, 1932; s. Oakley Glenn and Josephine (Gebert) T.; m. Vivian Sinetar, Jan. 28, 1956; children: Raun, Karen, Jeffrey. BA in Physics, UCLA, 1953, MA, 1955, PhD in Math., 1958. C.L.E. Moore instr. MIT, Cambridge, Mass., 1959—61; asst. prof. N.Mex. State U., 1961—63, assoc. prof. math., 1963—65, U. Calif., Irvine, 1965—67, prof. math., 1967—77, prof. fin., 1977—82, regents lectr., 1992—93; gen. ptnr. Edward O. Thorp & Assocs., LP, Newport Beach, 1989—. Vis. prof. UCLA, 1991; chmn. Oakley Sutton Mgmt. Corp., Newport Beach, Calif., 1972-91; mng. gen. ptnr. Princeton/Newport Ptnrs., Newport Beach, 1969-91, OSM Ptnrs., MIDAS Advisors, Newport Beach, 1986-89; gen. ptnr. Ridgeline Ptnrs., Newport Beach, 1994-2002; portfolio mgr.-cons. Glenwood Investment Corp., Chgo., 1992-94; prin., cons. Grosvenor Capital Mgmt., Chgo., 1992-93; pres. Noesis Corp. 1994-2002, UCI Found. Bd., 2004— Author: Beat the Dealer: A Winning Strategy for the Game of Twenty-One, 1962, rev. edit., 1966, Elementary Probability, 1966, The Mathematics of Gambling, 1984; co-author: Beat The Market, 1967, The Gambling Times Guide to Blackjack, 1984; columnist Gambling Times, 1979-84, Wilmott 2002—. Grantee NSF, 1954-55, 62-64, Air Force Office Sci. Rsch., 1964-73. Fellow NSF, Inst. Math. Stats.; mem. Phi Beta Kappa, Sigma Xi. Avocation: astronomy. Office: Edward O Thorp & Assocs LP 610 Newport Center Dr Ste 1240 Newport Beach CA 92660-6436

**THORP, STEVEN MARK,** music educator; s. Donald G. and Maud O. Thorp; m. Vanda Dee Bishop, Nov. 27, 1981; children: Lauren, Mara. MusB, Ea. N.Mex U., 1981, MusM, 1989. Choral dir. Roswell H.S., N.Mex., 1985—97; choral dir. and music dept. chair N. Mex Mil. Inst., Roswell N.Mex., 1997—. Mem.: Music Educators Nat. Conf. Southern Baptist. Office Phone: 505-624-8443.

**THORPE, GEOGORY B.,** lawyer; b. LA, 1953; BA cum laude, U. Calif., Santa Barbara, 1977; JD cum laude, Loyola Marymount U., 1982. Bar: Calif. 1982. Ptnr., real estate and natural resources practice O'Melveny & Myers LLP, Santa Barbara, Calif., 1982—, chair, project development and fin. practice group. Staff mem. and chief article editor Loyola LA Law Review, 1980—82. Mem.: LA County Bar Assn. (mem. general real property subsection), ABA (mem. real property sect.), St. Thomas More Law Soc. Office: O'Melveny & Myers LLP 400 S Hope St Los Angeles CA 90071-2899 Office Phone: 213-430-6593. Office Fax: 213-430-6407. Business E-Mail: gthorpe@omm.com.

**THORPE, JAMES,** retired researcher; b. Aiken, S.C., Aug. 17, 1915; s. J. Ernest and Ruby (Holloway) T.; m. Elizabeth McLean Daniells, July 19, 1941; children: James III (dec.), John D., Sally Jans-Thorpe. AB, The Citadel, 1936, LL.D., 1971; MA, U. N.C., 1937; PhD, Harvard U., 1941; Litt.D., Occidental Coll., 1968; L.H.D., Claremont Grad. Sch., 1968; H.H.D., U. Toledo, 1977. Instr. to prof. English Princeton, 1946-66; dir. Huntington Libr., Art Gallery and Bot. Gardens, San Marino, Calif., 1966-83; sr. research assoc. Huntington Libr., San Marino, Calif., 1966-99; ret., 1999. Author: Bibliography of the Writings of George Lyman Kittredge, 1948, Milton Criticism, 1950, Rochester's Poems on Several Occasions, 1950, Poems of Sir George Etherege, 1963, Aims and Methods of Scholarship, 1963, 70, Literary Scholarship, 1964, Relations of Literary Study, 1967, Bunyan's Grace Abounding and Pilgrim's Progress, 1969, Principles of Textual Criticism, 1972, 2d edit., 1979, Use of Manuscripts in Literary Research, 1974, 2d edit., 1979, Gifts of Genius, 1980, A Word to the Wise, 1982, John Milton: The Inner Life, 1983, The Sense of Style: Reading English Prose, 1987, Henry Edwards Huntington: A Biography, 1994, H.E. Huntington: A Short Biography, 1996, A Pleasure of Proverbs, 1996, Proverbs for Friends, 1997, Proverbs for Thinkers, 1998, The Gutenberg Bible, 1999, Poems Written at the Huntington Library, 2000, Proverbs for Our Time, 2003, Proverbs for the Future, 2004. Served to col. USAAF, 1941-46. Decorated Bronze Star medal.; Guggenheim fellow, 1949-50, 65-66. Fellow Am. Acad. Arts and Scis., Am. Philos. Soc.; mem. MLA, Am. Antiquarian Soc., Soc. for Textual Scholarship. Democrat. Episcopalian. Home: 20 Loeffler Rd Apt T320 Bloomfield CT 06002-2277

**THORPE, JANE FUGATE,** lawyer; b. Hazard, Ky., 1954; BA, Univ. Ga., 1976, JD, 1979. Bar: Ga. 1979. Ptnr., food, drug, device products liability group Alston & Bird LLP, Atlanta. Frequent contbr. to profl. journals, frequent lectr. on scientific evidence; co-author: Court-Appointed Experts and Technical Advisors, 2000, Science and Expert Testimony: A Response to the Attack Upon Judge Jones and the Hall Opinion. Mem.: Internat. Assn. Defense Counsel. Office: Alston & Bird LLP One Atlantic Ctr 1201 W Peachtree St NW Atlanta GA 30309-3424 Office Phone: 404-881-7822. Office Fax: 404-881-7777. Business E-Mail: jthorpe@alston.com.

**THORPE, JANET CLAIRE,** judge; b. Bklyn., Dec. 8, 1953; d. Burton Walter and Phyllis Claire (Read) T.; m. David Frank Palmer, Aug. 26, 1978 (div. 1988); children: Katherine Elaine, Jennifer Claire; m. James Francis Box, June 29, 1991; children: Melissa Richelle, Maergrethe Cashel. Student, Boston U., 1972-74; BA in Polit. Sci. & History with honors, Union Coll., 1975; postgrad., Western New Eng. Sch. Law, 1975-76; JD, Emory U., 1978. Bar: Ga. 1978, U.S. Ct. Appeals (5th and 11th circs.) 1978, 80, Fla. 1987, U.S. Dist. Ct. (mid. dist.) Fla. 1987. Law clk. to judge U.S. Dist. Ct., Atlanta, 1978; regional atty. Comptroller of Curency, Atlanta, 1978-80; assoc. corp. counsel Trust Co. Ga., Atlanta, 1980-86; dir. Trusco Properties, Inc., Atlanta, 1981-86; gen. counsel, corp. sec. SunTrust Banks Fla., Inc., Orlando, 1986-2000; gen. counsel SunTrust Bank N.A., Orlando, 1986-2000; group v.p. SunTrust Banks, Inc., 1995-2000; cir. ct. judge State of Fla. (9th cir.), Orlando, Fla., 2000—. Mem. Coun. Battered Women, Atlanta, 1983-86, bd. dirs., 1986; bd. visitors Cornell Mus. Fine Art, Rollins Coll., 1990-96; mem. bd. zoning variances City of Orlando, 1996-99; bd. dirs. Orange County Cmty. Alliance, 2000-03. Mem. Ga. Bar Assn., Fla. Bar Assn., Assn. Bank Holdings Cos. (corporate counsel com. 1983-90), Am. Corp. Counsel Assn. (bd. dirs. ctrl. Fla. chpt. 1991-99), Am. Diabetes Assn. (bd. dirs. Fla. chpt. 1989-97), Leadership Orlando. Episcopalian. Avocations: gardening, child rearing, house renovation, photography. Office: Orange County Courthouse 425 N Orange Ave Orlando FL 32801

**THORPE, JOHN MILTON,** lawyer; b. Hayward, Calif., Sept. 23, 1932; s. MIlton W. and Jennie A. (Schwab) T.; m. Paulette Nelson, June 19, 1955; 1 child, Nelson Victor. BS, Stanford U., 1954; LLB, U. Calif., 1957. Bar: Calif. 1957, U.S. Dist Ct. (dists. no. so. and ctrl.) Calif. 1957, U.S. Supreme Ct. 1973. Assoc. Sills & Sills, Hayward, Calif., 1958-63; pvt. practice Hayward, 1963—. Pres. Shorelands Corp., Hayward, 1982-91. Mem. Hesperian Found., Palo Alto, Calif., 1990; sponsor Hayward Ednl. Fund, 1992. Mem. Calif. Bar Assn., Alameda County Bar Assn. Democrat. Home: 41700 Parker Rd Castro Valley CA 94546-1224 Office: 21790 Hesperian Blvd Hayward CA 94541-7003 Office Phone: 510-783-3440.

**THORSEN, JAMES HUGH,** retired aviation director, retired airport manager; b. Evanston, Ill., Feb. 5, 1943; s. Chester A. and Mary Jane (Currie) T.; m. Nancy Dain, May 30, 1980. BA, Ripon Coll., 1965. FAA cert. comml. pilot, flight instr. airplanes and instruments. Bd. dirs. Internat. Northwest Aviation Coun. Pres. Thorsen Aviation Cons. Recipient Region Safety award FAA N.W. Mountain. Mem. Am. Assn. Airport Execs. (past pres. N.W. chpt., Disting. Svc. award 1999), Mensa, Idaho Falls W. Rotary Club (pres. 2002), Quiet Birdmen, Sigma Alpha Epsilon. Home: 334 Westmordand Dr Idaho Falls ID 83402-4607

**THORSEN, MARIE KRISTIN,** radiologist, educator; b. Milw., Aug. 1, 1947; d. Charles Christian and Margaret Josephine (Little) T.; m. James Lawrence Troy, Jan. 7, 1978; children: Katherine Marie, Megan Elizabeth. BA, U. Wis., 1969; MBA, George Washington U., 1971; MD, Columbia Coll. Physicians and Surgeons, 1977. Diplomate Am. Bd. Radiology. Intern. Columbia-Presbyn. med. Ctr., N.Y.C., 1977-78, resident dept. radiology, 1978-81; asst. prof. radiology Med. Coll. Wis., 1982-84, assoc. prof., 1984-89, prof., 1989-94; dir. computed tomography Waukesha Meml. Hosp., 1994—, Oconomowoc Meml. Hosp., 1994—. Contbr. articles to profl. jours. Fellow computed body tomography Med. Coll. Wisc., Milw, 1981-82; Am. Coll. Radiology, Radiol. Soc. N. Am., Wis. Radiologic Assn. (v.p. 2005). Office Phone: 262-928-2400. Personal E-mail: mkthorsen@aol.com.

**THORSEN, NANCY DAIN,** real estate broker; b. Edwardsville, Ill., 1944; d. Clifford Earl and Suzanne Eleanor (Kribs) Dain; m. David Massie, 1968 (div. 1975); 1 child, Suzanne Dain Massie; m. James Hugh Thorsen, May 30, 1980. BSc in Mktg., So. Ill. U., 1968, MSc in Bus. Edn., 1975; grad., Realtor Inst., Idaho, 1983. Cert. residential and investment specialist, fin. instr., luxury home mktg. specialist, 2004; designated real estate instr. State of Idaho; accredited buyer rep. Personnel officer J.H. Little & Co. Ltd., London, 1969-72; instr. in bus. edn. Spl. Sch. Dist. St. Louis, 1974-77; mgr. mktg./ops. Isis Foods, Inc., St. Louis, 1978-80; asst. mgr. store Stix, Baer & Fuller, St. Louis, 1980; assoc. broker Century 21 Sayer Realty, Inc., Idaho Falls, Idaho, 1981-88, RE/MAX Homestead Realty, 1989—. Spkr. in field; real estate fin. instr. State of Idaho Real Estate Commn., 1994; founder Nancy Thorsen Seminars, 1995; pres. S.E. Idaho Women's Coun. of Realtors, 2006 Bd. dirs. Idaho Vol.. Boise, 1981-84, Idaho Falls Symphony, 1982; pres. Friends of Idaho Falls Libr., 1981-83; chmn. Idaho Falls Mayor's Com. for Vol. Coordination, 1981-84; power leader Power Program, 1995; mem. Mtn. River Valley Red Cross, chair capital campaign, cmty. gifts chair ARC. Recipient Idaho Gov.'s award, 1982, cert. appreciation City of Idaho Falls/Mayor Campbell, 1982, 87, Civilian Disting. Pres. award, 1990, Bus. Women of the Yr. award C. of C., 1998; named to Two Million Dollar Club, 1987, 88, Four Million Dollar Club, 1989, 90, Top Investment Sales Person for Eastern Idaho, 1985, Realtor of Yr. Idaho Falls Bd. Realtors, 1990, Outstanding Realtors Active in Politics, Women of Yr. Am. Biog. Inst., 1991, Profiles of Top Prodrs. award Real Estate Bd. Assn., Above the Crowd award 1997; named Western Region Power Leader, Darryl Davis Seminars. Mem. Nat. Spkrs. Assn., Idaho Falls Bd. Realtors (chmn. Orientation 1982-83, chmn. edn. 1983, chmn. legis. com. 1989, 95—, chmn. program com. 1990, 91), Idaho assn. Realtors (pres. Million Dollar Club 1988-2001, edn. com. 1990-93, Mem. of Yr. 1991), Women's Coun. Realtors, Am. Bus. Women's Assn., So. Ill. U. Alumni Assn., Idaho Falls C. of C. (Bus. Woman of the Yr.-Professions, 1997), newcomers Club, Civitan (pres. Idaho Falls chpt. 1988-89, Civitan of Yr. 1986, 97, Outstanding Pres. award 1990, Hall of Fame 1998), Real Estate Educators Assn. Office: RE/MAX Homestead Inc 1301 E 17th St Ste 1 Idaho Falls ID 83404-6273 E-mail: thorsen@srv.net.

**THORSEN, STEVEN N.,** mathematics professor, military officer; s. Tom S. and Jean M. Thorsen; m. Colleen Alexandra Curven, Aug. 23, 1986; children: Brianna E., Nicole A., Marissa J., Grace I. AA, Palm Beach C.C., Lake Worth, Fla, 1988; BA, Fla. Atlantic U., Boca Raton, 1991; MA, East Carolina U., Greenville, N.C., 1997; PhD, Air Force Inst. Tech., Dayton, Ohio, 2005. Ops. plans officer 4th Fighter Wing, Seymour Johnson AFB, NC, 1994—97; exec. officer 53rd Wing, Eglin AFB, Fla., 1997—98, ops. analyst, 1998—99; instr. math. sci. US Air Force Acad., Colorado Springs, 1999—2001; asst. prof. Air Force Inst. Tech., Wright Patterson AFB, Ohio, 2005—. Author: A Description of Competing Fusion Systems. Maj. USAF. Fellow, USAF, 2001—05. Mem.: Pi Mu Epsilon. Christian. Achievements include research in receiver operating characteristics.

**THORSON, CONNIE CAPERS,** library educator; b. Dallas, July 25, 1940; d. Ewing Ashby and Constance (Romberg) Capers; m. James Llewellyn, June 6, 1970. BA, U. Ark., 1962, MA, 1964; PhD, U. N.Mex., 1970; MS in Library Sci., U. Ill., 1977. Instr. English S.E. Mo. State U., Cape Girardeau, 1963-67; with U. N.Mex., Albuquerque, 1970-71, 79-95, acquisitions libr., 1980-94, head reference, 1994-95, assoc. prof. libr., 1984-90, prof., 1990-95, prof. emerita, 1995—; prof., libr. dir. Allegheny Coll., Meadville, Pa., 1995—2000, ret., 2000—; fulbright, sr. scholar Belarus, 2005—. Author: The RFP Process: Effective Management of the Acquisition of Library Materials, 1998; editor: A Million Stars, 1981, Pocket Companion for Oxford, 1989. Scholar, Fulbright Found., 2005—. Mem. South Cen. Soc. for 18th Century Studies (pres. elect 1988-89, pres. 1989-90, 2002-2003), Modern Lang. Assn. Am., Am. Soc. for 18th Century Studies, ALA. Avocations: travel, reading, walking.

**THORSON, ERIC M.,** federal agency administrator; BS, USAF Acad. Chief investigator permanent subcom. U.S. Senate, spl. asst. to Rep. leader; sr. advisor U.S. Office Personnel Mgmt.; inspector gen. Small Bus. Adminstrn., 2006—. Served with USAF. Office: Small Bus Adminstrn 49 Third St SW Rm 7150 Washington DC 20416 Office Phone: 202-205-6586.*

**THORSON, STEVEN GREG,** lawyer; b. Van Nuys, Calif., Feb. 7, 1948; s. Robert G. and Ruth V.; m. Patricia Lynn LaPointe, Aug. 3, 1974; 1 child, Kai Johannes. BA, St. Olaf Coll., Northfield, Minn., 1977; JD, Hamline U., St. Paul, Minn., 1980. Bar: Minn. 1980, US Tax Ct. 1980, US Ct. Appeals (8th cir.) 1980, US Supreme Ct. 2003. Pres. Thorson & Berg, Maple Grove, Minn., 1990—99; shareholder Barna, Guzy & Steffen, Ltd. Attys. at Law, Mpls., 1999—. Lectr. continuing legal edn., 1986—; apptd. to Minn. State Bar Assn. Commn. on Unauthorized Practice of Law, 1990-92; atty. for Columbus Twp. (Anoka County), 1981-96; mem. residential real estate com. Minn. State Bar Assn., 1992—. Mem. ch. coun. Peace Luth. Ch. Named a Super Lawyer, Minn. Law and Politics Mag., 2000—06; named one of Minn. Super Lawyers, Mpls./St. Paul mag., 1998, 2000—06, Minns. Top 40 Real Property Attys., Minn. Law & Politics, 2004, 2005. Mem. ABA, Minn. State Bar Assn. (real property coun., chair publs. com. 2001—), Hennepin County Bar Assn. (chmn. purchase agreement com. 1986-88), Anoka County Bar Assn. (pres. real estate sect. 1988). Avocation: skiing. Office: 400 Northtown Fin Plz 200 Coon Rapids Blvd NW Ste 400 Minneapolis MN 55433-5894 Office Phone: 763-783-5124. Business E-Mail: sthorson@bgslaw.com.

**THORSTED, V. DARLEENE,** neonatal/perinatal nurse, community health nurse; b. Albuquerque, Dec. 4, 1944; d. Charles F. and Violet J. (Keefe) Perry; m. Lawrence H. Thorsted, Nov. 1, 1974; children: Melanie, Dennis, Deidra. ADN, Coll. So. Idaho, 1973; BSN, Boise State U., 1987. RN Idaho. Staff nurse Magic Valley Regional Med. Ctr., Twin Falls, Idaho, 1973; coord. med. care Intracorp, Missoula, Mont., 1987; case mgr. home care, primary nurse St. Luke's Regional Med. Ctr., Boise, Idaho, 1977-90, staff nurse neonatal ICU, 1977-90; exec. dir. Idaho Bd. Medicine, 1994—2000; RN Medicare coord. Boise Samaritan Village, 2000—. Mem.: Idaho Nurses Assn., Sigma Theta Tau. Home: 1881 Hendricks Ct Meridian ID 83642-1337 Office Phone: 208-343-7726.

**THORSTEINSSON, GUDNI,** physiatrist; b. Vestmannaeyjar, Iceland, Aug. 5, 1941 (out in U.S., 1971); s. Thorsteinn and A. G. Einarsson; m. Elin Klein, Apr. 10, 1965; children: Arnar Karl, Asdis Thora. BS, Reykjavik (Iceland) Coll., 1961; candidatus med. et chirurg., U. Iceland, Reykjavik, 1968; MS, U. Minn., 1976. Diplomate Am. Bd. Phys. Medicine and Rehab. Dist physician Icelandic Govt., Djupivogur, 1970-71; resident dept. phys. medicine and rehab. Mayo Found., Rochester, Minn., 1972-75. mem. consulting staff, 1975-80; chair dept. Nat. Hosp., Reykjavik, 1980-81; dir. rehab. Mayo Clinic/St. Mary's Hosp., Rochester, 1981-85; dir. out-patient rehab. Mayo Clinic, Rochester, 1985-88, chair dept., 1987-91, chair dept. phys. medicine and rehab. Jacksonville, Fla., 1991-99. Physiatrist cons. Mayo Clinic, Rochester, 81-91, Jacksonville, 1991—. Author: (with others) Efficacy of Transcutaneous Electrical Stimulation, 1977, Placebo Effect of Transcutaneous Electrical Stimulation, 1978, Electrical Stimulation for Anagesia, 1983, Management of Post Polio Syndrome, 1997. Mem. Am. Acad. Phys. Medicine and Rehab. Office: Mayo Clinic Jacksonville 4500 San Pablo Rd S Jacksonville FL 32224-1865

**THORSTENBERG, LAURENCE (JOHN L. THORSTENBERG),** oboe and English horn player; b. Salt Lake City, Dec. 6, 1925; s. Laurence Nathaniel and Alys Josephine (Blomquist) T. MusB, Curtis Inst. Music, Phila., 1951. Instrumental tchr., 1975-96, New Eng. Conservatory, Boston U., 1980-96; mem. Symphony Orch. Balt., 1951-52, Dallas Symphony Orch., 1952-54, Chgo. Symphony Orch., 1954-63, Boston Symphony Orch., 1964-93. Appeared summers, Marlboro (Vt.) Music Festival, 1952-54. With U.S. Army, 1944-46, ETO. Mem. Internat. Conf. Symphony and Opera Musicians (emeritus).

**THORSTENSEN, SHELLEY M.,** artist, educator; b. Ft. Sill, Okla., July 5, 1953; BFA cum laude, Syracuse U., 1975; MFA with honors, Temple U., 1987. Tchg. asst. Rutgers U., Camden U., 1978—83, adj. prof., 1987—88; tchg. asst. Fine Art Printmaking area Princeton U., 1980—86; tchg. asst. Tyler Sch. of Art of Temple U., 1985—87; asst. prof. Mpls. Coll. Art and Design, 1988—90; adj. prof., asst. prof. Marywood Coll., Scranton, Pa., 1990—92; adj. prof. Keystone Jr. Coll., La Plume, Pa., 1992; tchr. art, lit. and grammar The Father's Heart Urban Prep Sch., Trenton, NJ, 1992—97; adj. prof. Moore Coll. Art and Design, 1998—2001, vis. artist Pa., 1998. . Tchr. Women's Studio Workshop, Rosendale, NY, 1990—98, 2006, 06; artist residency Frans Masereel Centrum, Kasterlee, Belgium, 2004, 05; lectr. in field. One-woman shows include Pikeville (Ky.) Coll., 1990, U. Scranton, 1993, Marywood Coll., 1993, Edinboro (Pa.) U., 1993, Women's Studio Workshop, 1994, 2005, Quincy (Ill.) Coll., 1994, The Nassau Club, Princeton, 1997, River Run Gallery, Lambertville, 2002, The Free Pub. Libr. of Phila., 2002, Moore Coll. Art and Design, 2003, Myabi Gallery, Fukuoka, Japan, 2004, Gallery Recolte, Fukuoka, 2006, exhibited in group shows at Oreg. Book Artists Guild, 1991, U. Ctrl. Ark., 1991, Lycoming Coll., 1991, Boston Printmakers, 1991, The Sordoni Gallery of Wilkes U., 1991, Galeria Brita Prinz, Madrid, 1992, DOSHI Ctr. for Contemporary Art, Harrisburg, Pa., 1992, Purdue U. Gallery, 1993, Laura Craig Galleries, Scranton, 1993, Quick Ctr. for the Arts, Fairfield, Conn., 1994, Lore Degenstein Gallery, Susquehanna U., 1995, Waldorf Coll., 1998, Art Inst. for the Permian Basin, 1998, Williams Gallery, Princeton, 1999, Moore Coll. Art and Design, 2001, 2003, 2004, Univ. of the Arts Gallery, Phila., 2001, River Run Gallery, Lambertville, 2002, Chubb Atrium Gallery, Warren, NJ, 2002, Hunterdon Mus. Art, Clinton, NJ, 2002, Art Students League, NY, 2002, The Free Pub. Libr. of Phila., 2002, Muse Gallery, Phila., 2002, The Armory, 2003, 2004, Susan Teller Gallery, NYC, 2003, The Old Print Shop, 2004, Sabine Rose Gallery, Doylestown, PA, 2004, Tex. Tech U., 2005, Seattle Print Fair, 2006, many others, Represented in permanent collections Advent Internat., Boston, Aurora Capital, LA, Blank Rome Tenzer Greenblatt, NYC, Blue Cross/Blue Shield of Pa., Phila., Frans Masereel Centrum, Free Pub. Libr. of Phila., Mpls. Coll. Art and Design, Maywood Coll., NJ Coll. Medicine and Dentistry, Newark Pub. Libr., Oreg. Inst., Portland, Polymetaal, Netherlands, Royal Mus. Art, Antwerp, Belgium, Rembrandt Graphic Arts, Rosemont, NJ, Rutgers U., Tex. Tech U., U. Scranton, Women's Studio Workshop, Woodmere Art Mus., Phila. Recipient F. Lammot Belin Art Scholarship award, 1992—93, Purchase award, Soc. Am. Graphic Artists, 2003, Univ. Print Club award, Cleve. Mus. Art, 2005; grantee, The Puffin Found. through Isles, Inc., Trenton, 1997; faculty rsch. grantee, Mpls. Coll. Art and Design, 1998, IMI faculty rsch. grantee, Moore Coll. Art and Design, 2000, digital printmaking fellow, Silicon Gallery, Phila., 2004, Geraldine R. Dodge fellow, 2005. Mem.: Women's Studio Workshop, So. Graphics Coun., Soc. Am. Graphic Artists (elected coun.), Keisho Art Assn. (Tokyo), Phila. Print Collaborative (founding, steering com., planning com. Philagrafika Biennial 2010, Re-Print 2007), Coll. Art Assn. Address: 42 Perry St Lambertville NJ 08530 E-mail: jane_doe_press@yahoo.com.

**THORUD, DAVID B.,** academic administrator; BS in Forestry, U. Minn., 1958, MS in Forest Hydrology, 1960, PhD in Forest Hydrology, 1964. Asst. prof. U. Minn., 1961—66; assoc. prof. U. Ariz., 1966—72, head dept. watershed mgmt. Coll. Agr., 1972—74, dir. Sch. Renewable Natural Resources, 1974—77; asst. dir. Southeastern Forest Experiment Sta. USDA Forest Svc., 1977—78, prin. rsch. hydrologist Forest Environment Rsch., 1978—79, dir. Forest Expt. Sta., 1979—81; dir. govt. rels. U. Wash., Seattle, 1984—85, dean Coll. Forest Resources, 1981—94, acting provost, 1994—. Chair West Ctrl. Region Assn. State Coll. and Univ. Forestry Rsch. Orgns., 1972—74; chair U.S. Man and the Biosphere Project on Grazing Lands, 1976—78; pres. Internat. Soc. Tropical Foresters, 1982—83, Nat. Assn. Profl. Forestry Schs. and Colls., 1985—87; mem. U.S. Joint Coun. on Food and Agrl. Scis., 1987—89; mem. com. on forestry rsch. NRC, NAS, 1989—90, chair, 1990—91; trustee Ctr. for Internat. Forestry Rsch., 1994—97; chair bd. trustees Internat. Ctr. for Rsch. in Agro-forestry, 1994—97; bd. dirs. Evergreen Partnership, Port of Tacoma, Mountain to Sound Greenway. Contbr. articles to profl. jours. Fellow: Soc. Am. Foresters. Office: U Wash Office of the Provost 301 Gerberding Hall Box 351237 Seattle WA 98195-1237

**THORUD, JEFFREY SCOTT,** director, lawyer; b. Natrona Heights, Pa., Sept. 14, 1964; s. Carol Jean Guman. BA in Speech Comm., Edinboro U., Pa., 1986; MPA, Marywood U., Scranton, Pa., 1993; JD, Thomas Jefferson Sch. Law, San Diego, 1998; cert. in Intl. Human Rights Law, Oxford U., England, 1996. Prof. Kelsey-Jenney Coll., San Diego, 1998—2002; acquisitions assoc. Teligent Comm., 1999—2000; acquisitions mgr. Qwest Comm., 2000—02; pres. Oxford Pacific Lending, 2002—; dir. legal studies Maric Coll., 2003—2000—01, Maric Coll., 2003—. Contbr. articles to profl. jours. Mem.: Pi Kappa Delta, Alpha Phi Sigma. Office: Maric Coll 9055 Balboa Ave San Diego CA 92123 Office Phone: 858-654-3618. Business E-Mail: jthorud@mariccollege.edu.

**THOULESS, DAVID JAMES,** retired physicist, educator; b. Bearsden, Scotland, Sept. 21, 1934; arrived in U.S., 1979, naturalized, 1994; s. Robert Henry and Priscilla (Gorton) T.; m. Margaret Elizabeth Scrase, July 26, 1958; children: Michael, Christopher, Helen. BA, U. Cambridge, Eng., 1955, ScD, 1986; PhD, Cornell U., 1958. Physicist Lawrence Berkeley Lab., 1958-59; rsch. fellow U. Birmingham, England, 1959—61, prof. math. physics, 1965—78; lectr., fellow Churchill Coll. U. Cambridge, England, 1961—65; prof. physics Queen's U., Kingston, Ont., Canada, 1978; prof. applied sci. Yale U., New Haven, 1979-80; prof. physics U. Wash., Seattle, 1980—2003; ret. Author: Quantum Mechanics of Many Body Systems, 2d edit., 1972, Topological Quantum Numbers in Nonrelativistic Physics, 1998. Recipient Maxwell medal Inst. Physics, 1973, Holweck prize Soc. Francaise de Physique-Inst. Physics, 1980, Fritz London award for Low temperature physics, Fritz London Meml. Fund, 1984, Wolf prize in physics, Wolf Found., Israel, 1990, Paul Dirac medal Inst. Physics, 1993, Lars Onsager prize Am. Phys. Soc., 2000; Edwin Uehling disting. scholar U. Wash., 1988-89. Fellow: Royal Soc.; mem.: NAS. Office: U Wash PO Box 351560 Seattle WA 98195-1560 Business E-Mail: Thouless@u.washington.edu.

**THOYER, JUDITH REINHARDT,** lawyer; b. Mt. Vernon, NY, July 29, 1940; d. Edgar Allen and Florence (Mayer) Reinhardt; m. Michael E. Thoyer, June 30, 1963; children: Erinn Thoyer Rhodes, Michael John. AB with honors, U. Mich., 1961; LLB summa cum laude, Columbia U., 1965. Bar: N.Y. 1966, D.C. 1984. Law libr. U. Ghana, Accra, Africa, 1963-64; assoc. Paul, Weiss, Rifkind, Wharton & Garrison, N.Y.C., 1966-75, ptnr., 1975—. Mem. TriBar Opinion Com., 1995—. Bd. visitors Law Sch. Columbia U., N.Y.C., 1991—; bd. dirs. Women's Action Alliance, N.Y.C., 1975-89, pro bono counsel, 1975-97; mem. Women's Coun. Dem. Senatorial, campaign com., 1993-97; organizing com. Alumnae Columbia Law Sch., 1988—. Recipient medal for excellence, Columbia Law Sch., 2003. Mem. N.Y. County Lawyers Assn. (mem. securities and exchs. com. 1976-98), Assn. of Bar of City of N.Y. (mem. securities regulation com. 1976-79, mem.

recruitment of lawyers com. 1980-82, mem. com. on mergers, acquisitions and corp. control contests 1996—). Home: 1115 5th Ave Apt 3B New York NY 10128-0100 Office: Paul Weiss Rifkind Et Al 1285 Ave of Americas New York NY 10019-6028

**THRALL, ARTHUR ALVIN,** artist, educator; b. Milw., Mar. 18, 1926; s. Irving and Helen (Fabich) T.; m. Winifred Rogers, 1960; children: Grant, Wade, Sara, Jay. BS, Milw. State Tchrs. Coll., 1950; MS, U. Wis., Milw., 1954; postgrad. (fellow), U. Ill., 1954-55. Tchr. art Lincoln Jr. High Sch., Kenosha, Wis., 1951-54; asst. prof. SUNY, Geneseo, 1955-56; assoc. prof. Milw.-Downer Coll., Milwaukee, 1956-64; prof., Farrar-Marrs prof. fine arts Lawrence U., Appleton, Wis., 1964-90, prof. emeritus, 1990—. One-man shows include Smithsonian Instn., 1960, U. Dubuque, Iowa, 1993, Mt. Mary Coll., Milw., 1994, St. Norbert Coll, De Pere, Wis., 1995, Cardinal Stritch U., Milw., 1998, also others; group shows include Corcoran bienials, Washington, 1951, 53, 55, 57, 62, Bklyn. Mus. annuals, Mus. Modern Art, N.Y.C, NAD, N.Y.C, Audubon Artists, N.Y.C., 1985, S.A.G.A., N.Y.C., 1985, Charles Allis Art Mus., Milw., 1996, Miller Art Ctr., Sturgeon Bay, Wis., 1997, Elvehem Mus. Art, Madison, Wis., 1998, 99, Fairfield Gallery, Sturgeon Bay, Wis., 2001; represented in permanent collections Tate Gallery, Victoria and Alberta Mus., Brit. Mus., all London, Phila. Mus., Seattle Mus., Art Inst. Chgo., Bklyn. Mus., others. Served with U.S. Army, 1944-46, ETO. Recipient Bklyn. Mus. print awards 1952, 64; Pa. Acad. Arts award 1960; NAD awards 1956, 68; Louis Comfort Tiffany fellow, 1963 Mem. AAUP, Boston Printmakers (awards 1963, 65), Soc. Am. Graphic Artists (awards 1951-52, 60, 78, 2000), Audubon Artists Inc. (award 1977) Home: 4225 N Woodburn St Milwaukee WI 53211-1504

**THRALL, GORDON FISH,** publishing executive; b. Jamestown, N.Y., July 28, 1923; s. Clyde Lowell and Beulah Mae (Fish) T.; m. Betty Jane Roberts, Sept. 24, 1964 (dec. May 28, 2005); 1 dau., Jenifer Jane. A.B. in History and Polit. Sci., Alfred U., 1949; J.D., Baylor U., 1953. Bar: Tex. 1953, U.S. Supreme Ct. 1957, D.C. 1958, U.S. Ct. Appeals (D.C. cir.) 1958, U.S. Ct. Mil. Appeals 1958, U.S. Dist. Ct. (ea. dist.) Tex. 1976, U.S. Ct. Appeals (5th cir.) 1986. Law clk. U.S. Dist. Ct. (ea. dist.) Tex., 1953-54; asst. prosecutor Dallas County Dist. Atty., 1954-55; assoc. firm Phinney & Hallman, Dallas, 1955-56; asst. Tex. Atty. Gen., 1957; adviser, examiner ICC, Washington, 1957-59; asst. gen. counsel Tex. State Bar, Austin, 1959-61; county atty. Reagan County, Big Lake, Tex., 1961-72; ptnr. Norman, Thrall, Angle, Guy & Day, L.L.P., Jacksonville, Tex., 1972—2002; v.p. Heflin & Thrall Lang. Publs., Inc., 2002-. Mem. exec. com. Tex. Baptist Gen. Conv., 1965-70, adminstrv. bd., 1991-95; deacon So. Bapt. Ch.; chmn. Permian Basin dist. Concho Valley council Boy Scouts Am., Big Lake, 1965-66; chmn. Jacksonville United Fund Drive, 1987, pres., 1989; pres. Cherokee County Health Facilities Devel. Corp., 1982—; v.p., bd. dirs. Travis Towers Retirement Facility, Jacksonville, 1980-2003; co-trustee Summers A. Norman Found., 1988-2002; mem. Nan Travis Meml. Hosp. Found. Bd., 1994—; pres. bd. visitors Jacksonville Coll., 1998—2003. Mem. Tex. State Bar, Tex. Bar Found. (vice chmn. UPL com. 1964), Big Lake C. of C. (pres. 1963, 67), Jacksonville C. of C. (pres. 1979), Cherokee Country Club, (dir. 1981-83), Kiwanis (pres. 1978, lt. gov. div. 34 1982), Big Lake Lions (pres. 1969), Masons (32 degree). Republican. Home: 702 Fort Worth St Jacksonville TX 75766-2610 Office: Heflin and Thrall Lang Publs Inc PO Box 1724 Jacksonville TX 75766 Office Phone: 903-586-2445. Business E-Mail: jheflin@language-publications.com.

**THRALL, RICHARD CAMERON, JR.,** broadcast executive; b. Delaware, Ohio, Nov. 13, 1929; s. Richard Cameron and Pauline (Taylor) T.; m. Nancy Burrows, June 7, 1952 (div. Jan. 1962); children: Vallerie E. Alm, Cynthia L. Graser; m. Shirley Annette Sturgeon, Oct. 6, 1962; children: Laurie Jo Woodward, James W. Hochberg. BA, Miami U., Oxford, Ohio, 1951. Producer, dir. Sta. WBNS-TV, Columbus, Ohio, 1951-57, Sta. KDKA-TV, Pitts., 1957-59, pub. affairs dir. 1959-63, asst. program dir., 1963-67; program mgr. Sta. WLWC, Columbus, 1967-68; mgr. corp. TV Avco Broadcasting, Cin., 1968-70, mgr. TV programming 1970-76; v.p. programming Multimedia Broadcasting., Cin., 1976-82; sr. v.p. Multimedia Entertainment, Cin., 1982-84; sr. v.p., gen. mgr. Multimedia Entertainment of Tenn., Nashville, 1984-88; sr. v.p. programming 1994-96; ret., 1996. Freelance prodr., writer, program cons., 1996—. Writer numerous TV scripts and songs. Served with USN, 1947-48. Recipient Outstanding Country Special award Music City News, Nashville, 1983-87; named to Hon. Order Ky. Cols. Mem. Country Music Assn., NATAS (pres. Columbus/Dayton/Cin. chpt. 1980-83, bd. govs. MidSouth chpt. 1985-87, chmn. nat. awards com. 1989-2002, winner regional Emmys and Emmy cert.). Congregationalist. Avocations: fishing, boating, skiing, travel.

**THRASH, PATRICIA ANN,** retired educational association administrator; b. Grenada, Miss., May 4, 1929; d. Lewis Edgar and Weaver (Betts) T. BS, Delta State Coll., 1950; MA, Northwestern U., 1953, PhD, 1959; cert. Inst. Edn. Mgmt., Harvard U., 1983; EdD (hon.), Vincennes U., 1997; DHL, Drake U., 1997, Adrian Coll., 1998. Tchr. high sch. English, Clarksdale, Miss., 1950-52; head resident Northwestern U., 1953-55, asst. to dean women, 1955-58, asst. dean women, 1958-60, lectr. edn., 1959-65, dean women, 1960-69, assoc. prof. edn., 1965-72, assoc. dean students, 1969-71; asst. exec. sec. Commn. on Instns. Higher Edn., North Central Assn. Colls. and Schs., 1972-73, assoc. exec. dir., 1973-76, assoc. dir., 1976-87, exec. dir., 1987-96; exec. dir. emeritus, 1997—. Mem. adv. panel Am. Coun. on Edn., MIVER program evaluation nat. base program, 1991-94; mem. nat. adv. panel Nat. Ctr. Postsecondary Tchg., Learning & Assessment, 1991-95. Author (with others): Handbook of College and University Administration, 1970; editor Jour. Northwestern U. Inst. for Learning in Retirement, 2000-02, course coord., 2000—; contbr. articles to ednl. jours. Bd. dirs. Delta State U. Found., 2000-02. Mem. nat. Assn. Women Deans and Counselors (v.p. 1967-69, pres. 1972-73), Ill. Assn. Women Deans and Counselors (sec. 1961-63, pres. 1964-66), Am. Coll. Pers. Assn. (editl. bd. jour. 1971-74), Coun. Student Pers. Assns. in Higher Edn. (program nominations com. 1974-75, adv. panel Am. Coll. Testing Coll. Outcome Measures project 1977-78, staff Coun. on Postsecondary Accreditation project for evaluation nontraditional edn. 1977-78, mem. editl. bd. Jour. Higher Edn. 1975-80, guest editor Mar.-Apr. 1979, co-editor NCA Quar. 1988-96, vice-chair regional accrediting dirs. group 1993, exec. com. Nat. Policy Bd. for Higher Edn. Inst. 1993-95), Mortar Bd. (hon.), Phi Delta Theta, Pi Lambda Theta, Alpha Psi Omega, Alpha Lambda Delta. Methodist. Home: 2337 Hartrey Ave Evanston IL 60201-2552 Personal E-mail: patsy1941@comcast.net.

**THRASH, REBECCA C.,** theater educator, theater director; b. New Orleans, Apr. 13, 1952; d. L.O. (Tobe) Thrash and Mary Claire Illges; children: Kimen C. Allen, I. Marie Allen. BA, U. New Orleans, MFA, 1998. Prof. theatre, speech Rose State Coll., Midwest City, Okla., 2001—06. Sgt. U.S. Army, 1983—86. Decorated Army Achievement Good Conduct medal U.S. Army. Personal E-mail: rthrash@cox.net.

**THRASHER, DIANNE ELIZABETH,** mathematics educator, computer scientist, consultant; b. Brockton, Mass., July 11, 1945; m. George Thomas Thrasher, Jan. 28, 1967; children: Kimberly Elizabeth, Noelle Elizabeth. BA in Math., Bridgewater State Coll., 1967, post grad in computer sci., 1987. Cert. secondary math., history tchr. Tchr. math. Plymouth/Carver Regional Schs., Plymouth, Mass., 1976-78, Alden Sch. Duxbury, Mass., 1980-82, Marshfield (Mass.) H.S., 1982-84; computer cons. TC2I-Thrasher Computer Cons. and Instrn., Duxbury, Mass., 1988—; dir., owner Internat. Ednl. Franchise, 1991-95; owner Duxbury Math. Ctr. K-Adult, 1995—. Owner New Eng. Regional Kumon Ednl. Franchise, 1991-95, 2000—; Mass. State approved profl. point devel. provider for tchr. cert., 1996. Active U.S. Figure Skating Assn., Colorado Springs, 1978-85; 2d reader First Ch. Christ Scientist, Plymouth, 1971-73; bd. govs. Skating Club of Hingham, Mass., 1978-85, pres., 1983-85, dir. Learn to Skate program, 1983-85; active First Ch. Christ Scientist, Boston, 1964—; with New Eng. Regional Kumon Franchise Owners, 1991-95; charter mem. Nat. Adv. Coun. of the U.S. Navy Meml. Found., 1992, Mary Baker Eddy Libr. for the Betterment of Humanity,

Boston, 2002. Recipient Presdl. Nomination for Excellence in Tng. Math., NSF, 1992, Ed Taylor Meml. Vol. Svc. award Skating Club Hingham, 1995, Amateur Photo award Internat. Libr. Photography, 1999. Mem. NAFE, AAUW, Math. Assn. Am., Am. Math. Soc., Am. Nat. Coun. Tchrs. Math, Nat. Hist. Trust and Preservation Soc., Smithsonian, Internat. Soc. Photographers (Amateur Photo award 1999). Avocations: antiques, bicycling, skating, sailing. Home: 140 Toby Garden St Duxbury MA 02332-4945 Personal E-mail: sumizumi@aol.com.

**THRASHER, FAY C.,** clinical psychologist; b. Wynne, Ark., Dec. 17, 1935; d. Andrew J. and Joy M. (Charles) Thrasher; children: Jeffrey K. Mitchell, Sidney J. Guidroz Jr. MEd, McNeese State U., 1963; MA, La. State U., 1967, PhD, 1970. Lic. psychologist. Chief psychologist Cmty. Mental Health, Lake Charles, La., 1970-73; clin. psychologist VA Hosp., Salisbury, NC, 1973-76; chief psychologist VA Opt Clinic, San Antonio, 1976-77, Alvin C. York VA Med. Ctr., Murfreesboro, Tenn., 1977-87; clin. psychologist VA Med. Ctr., Alexandria, Va., 1990-95, chief psychologist, 1995—. Bd. dirs. Oasis Ministry, Pineville, La.; cons. to freedom cons., 1996—; bd. dirs. New Beginning Acad., Alexandria, treas., 1997—; cons. Bunkie Adolexcent Ctr., Bunkie Gen. Hosp., 1993—97. Chmn. Combined Fed. Campaign, Murfreesboro, 1985—86. Mem.: APA, Am. Coll. Forensic Examiners, Nat. Register. Avocations: bridge, antiques, art, music. Home: 303 Rain Tree Pl Pineville LA 71360-5472 Office: Freedom Counseling Ctr 2809 Donahue Ferry Rd Pineville LA 71360-4513 Office Phone: 318-473-0010 x 2626.

**THRASHER, KAREN HEWELL,** counseling administrator; b. Gainesville, Ga., June 12, 1967; d. Jimmie Carl Hewell and Linda Kay Keys; m. David Lamar Thrasher, Jan. 10, 1997; children: Sloane, Seth, Rylee, Kyle, Grace. A. Gainesville Coll., 1996; B, N. Ga. Coll., 1998; M in Edn., Ga. State U., 1999; specialist in Edn., Ga. State. U., 2001. Cert. sch. psychologist Ga. Sch. psychologist Hall County Bd. Edn., Gainesville, 2000—. Mem. bd. dirs. Family Relations Program, Gainesville; lead psychologist Hall County Bd. Edn. Sunday sch. tchr. Hopewell Bapt., Gainesville, 2002—. Named Most Outstanding Student, Gainesville Coll. Mem.: Ga. Assn. Sch. Psychologists, Nat. Assn. Sch. Psychologists. Republican. Bapt. Home: 5113 Presley Dr Flowery Branch GA 30542 Office: Hall County Bd Edn 711 Green St Ste 100 Gainesville GA 30504

**THRASHER, MARY AHLF MARCROFT,** educator, social worker; b. St. Louis, Apr. 25, 1923; d. Gustave and Florence Regina (Froelich) Ahlf; m. Keith R. Marcroft, Mar. 23, 1946 (div. 1969); children: Joanne Marcroft Williamson, Karen A. Marcroft; m. Hugh Riley Thrasher, June 28, 1989 (dec. Jan. 2006). BS, Ind. U., 1944; postgrad., U. Md., 1968-69, U. Evansville, 1971-72. Lic. tchr., Ind., Ky. Office mgr. U. Utah, Salt Lake City, 1946-48; sec. Brown Shoe Co., St. Louis, 1948-52; sch. tchr. Prince George's County Schs., Bowie, Md., 1965-70, Troy Twp. Sch. Corp., Tell City, Ind., 1970-73; sec. Perry County Extension Svc., Cannelton, Ind., 1973-75; caseworker Perry County Dept. Pub. Welfare, Cannelton, 1975—86. Composer, lyricist (musical play) ON MAIN STREET, 1988. Pres. Am. Legion Aux., 1986-87, Tell City Hist. Soc., 1987-89. Mem. AAUW, Order of Eastern Star. Mem. United Ch. of Christ. Avocations: choir member, church organist, accompanist to vocal and instrumental soloists, painter, gardener. Home: 225 11th St Tell City IN 47586-1907 E-mail: humathra@sbcglobal.net.

**THRASHER, ROSE MARIE,** critical care nurse, community health nurse; b. Urbana, Ohio, Jan. 19, 1948; d. Jesse and Anna Frances (Clark) T. Student, Mercy Med. Ctr. Sch. Med. Tech., 1966—67, Wittenberg U., 1969—70; BSN, Ohio State U., 1974, BA in Anthropology, 1994, BA in Art History, 1997, BA in Geography, 2002, postgrad., 2005—. RN, Ohio; bd. cert. cmty. health nurse ANA; cert. provider BCLS and ACLS, Am. Heart Assn., CCRN, AACN; cert. asthma mgmt. edn. Am. Lung Assn. Ohio. Critical care nurse Staff Builders Health Care Svc., Oakland, Calif., 1975—76; supr., case mgr. and home health nurse passport and intermittent care programs Interim Health Care, Columbus, Ohio, 1976—77, 1985—2004; pub. health nurse Columbus Health Dept., 1977—78; critical care nurse VA Med. Ctr., San Francisco, 1981, Staff Builders Health Care Svc., Oakland, 1981—85; IRP nurse Ohio State U. Hosps. East, 1999—2003; ind. home health nurse, provider med. svcs State of Ohio Dept. Human Svcs., 1999—2005; home health nurse Interim Health Care, Newark and Pataskala, Ohio, 2000—. Acad. scholar Wittenberg U., Ohio State U. Mem. AACN, ANA (coun. cmty. health nursing), AAUW, AAAS, Internat. Union Anthrop. and Ethnol. Scis., N.Y. Acad. Scis., Ohio Nurses Assn., Intravenous Nurses Assn., Ohio State U. Alumni Assn., Am. Anthrop. Assn., Midwest Art History Soc., Coll. Art Assn., Nat. Mus. Women in Arts, Nat. Women's Hall of Fame, Ohio Acad. Sci., Ohio State U. Coll. of Nursing Alumni Soc. Office: 112 International Dr Pataskala OH 43062 Business E-Mail: thrasher.2@osu.edu.

**THREEDY, DEBORA LYNN,** law educator; b. Chgo., June 10, 1951; d. Edward Clarence and Irene Frances (Palenik) T. BA, Beloit Coll., 1973; JD, Loyola U., 1980. Bar: Ill. Law clk. to Hon. Getzendanner U.S. Dist. Ct. (no. dist.) Ill., Chgo., 1980-82; assoc. Mayer Brown & Platt, Chgo., 1982-86; assoc. prof. law U. Utah, Salt Lake City, 1986—, prof. law, assoc. dean academic affairs, acting dean, 2004—. Contbr. articles to profl. jours. Bd. dirs. ACLU, Salt Lake City, 1990; trustee Theater Works West, Salt Lake City, 1990. McCormick Scholar Loyola U., 1980, Owens Scholar, 1980. Mem. Phi Beta Kappa. Office: U Utah Coll Law 332 South 1400 East Salt Lake City UT 84112-1107

**THREEFOOT, SAM ABRAHAM,** physician, educator; b. Meridian, Miss., Apr. 10, 1921; s. Sam Abraham and Ruth Frances (Lilienthal) Threefoot; m. Virginia Rush, Feb. 6, 1954; children: Barbara Jane Stockton Mattingly, Ginny Ruth Threefoot Lindberg, Tracyann Threefoot Esenstad, Shelley Ann. BS, Tulane U., New Orleans, 1943, MD, 1945. Diplomate: Am. Bd. Internal Medicine. Intern Michael Reese Hosp., Chgo., 1945-47; asst. vis. physician Charity Hosp. New Orleans, 1947-50, vis. physician, 1950-57, sr. vis. physician, 1957-69, cons., 1969-70, 76-91; clin. asst. dept. medicine Touro Infirmary, New Orleans, 1953-56, jr. asst., 1956-60, sr. asst., 1960-63, dir. med. edn., 1953-63, dir. research, 1953-70, sr. dept. medicine, 1963-70; fellow dept. medicine Tulane U., 1947-49, instr., 1948-53, asst. prof., 1953-59, assoc. prof., 1959-63, prof., 1963-70, 76-91, prof. emeritus, 1991—, asst. dean, 1979-91, adj. prof. emeritus Sch. Pub. Health & Tropical Medicine, 1993—; chief of staff VA Hosp. (Forest Hills div.), Augusta, Ga., 1970-76; asso. chief staff VA Hosp., New Orleans, 1976-79, chief of staff, 1979-91, cons., 1991—; asst. dean Med. Coll. Ga., 1970-76, prof. medicine, 1970-76. Cons. physician Lallie Kemp Charity Hosp., Independence, La., 1951-53 Editor: Lymphology, 1967-70, sr. mem. editl. bd.; Contbr. articles profl. jours. Served with AUS, 1943-45. La. Heart Assn. grantee, 1953-55; John A. Hartford Found. grantee, 1956-74; Am. Heart Assn. grantee, 1959-61; USPHS grantee, 1953 Fellow ACP, Am. Coll. Cardiology, NY Acad. Sci.; mem. Am. Heart Assn. (v.p. 1970, fellow council on circulation), Central Soc. Clin. Research, So. Soc. Clin. Investigation (pres. 1967), AAAS, Internat. Soc. Lymphology, Soc. Exptl. Biology and Medicine, Soc. Nuclear Medicine, Microcirculatory Conf., Inc., Am. Fedn. Clin. Research, La. Heart Assn. (pres. 1967), Nat. Assn. VA Chiefs of Staff (pres. 1987-88), Phi Beta Kappa, Sigma Xi. Jewish. Home: 1750 St Charles Ave Unit 616 New Orleans LA 70130 Office Phone: 504-524-3668. Personal E-mail: threefoot@bellsouth.net. Business E-Mail: sa3fta@tulane.edu. *I am one of those fortunate individuals who has been able to approach goals set early in life. Although my achievements are far short of my aspirations, at least I have had the opportunity. In dealing with both people and things, I have always felt that no detail was too small to receive attention.*

**THRELKELD, RICHARD DAVIS,** retired broadcast journalist; b. Cedar Rapids, Iowa, Nov. 30, 1937; s. Robert M. and Lou Jane (Davis) T.; m. Sharon A. Adams, June 11, 1960 (div. 1983); children: Susan Anne, Julia Lynn; m. Betsy Aaron, May 15, 1983. BA, Ripon Coll., 1959, LHD (hon.), 1989; MS in Journalism, Northwestern U., 1961. Editor Sta. WHAS-TV, Louisville, 1961; reporter Sta. WMT-TV, Cedar Rapids, Iowa, 1961-66; corr. CBS News, NYC and San Francisco, 1966-82, nat. corr., 1989-96, Moscow corr., 1996-98, ret., 1998; chief corr. ABC News NY, NYC, 1982-89. Author:

Dispatches From the Former Evil Empire, 2001; corr.: TV news report Rhodesia Remembered, 1980 (Overseas Press Club Award), Lebanon-Grenada, 1983 (Overseas Press Club Award), Vietnam Remembered, 1985 (Emmy Award); TV news documentary Defense of America, 1981 (Emmy Award); TV news series Status Reports, 1984 (Alfred I. Dupont-Columbia U. Award). Named to Hall of Achievement, Medill Sch. Journalism, Northwestern U., 2004; CBS News Fellow, 1964. Mem.: Soc. Profl. Journalists. Personal E-mail: threlkeldr@aol.com.

**THRO, WILLIAM EUGENE,** lawyer; b. Elizabethtown, Ky., Nov. 8, 1963; s. Ernest Guernsey and Joan (Young) T.; children: Sandra Lucinda Grace Edwards-Thro, William Thomas Daniel Edwards-Thro, Noah Christopher James Edwards-Thro.; m. Julie Urback, Sept. 04, 2004. BA, Hanover Coll., 1986; MA, U. Melbourne, Australia, 1988; JD, U. Va., 1990. Bar: Ky. 1990, Colo. 1991, Va. 1998, U.S. Dist. Ct. (we. dist.) Va. 1990, U.S. Dist. Ct. Colo. 1991, U.S. Ct. Appeals (6th and 10th cirs.) 1991, U.S. Ct. Appeals (3d cir.) 1993, U.S. Supreme Ct. 1993, U.S. Ct. Appeals (4th cir.) 1997, U.S. Dist. Ct. (ea. dist.) Va. 1998, U.S. Ct. (we. dist.) Va. 1998, U.S. Ct. Appeals (D.C. cir.) 1999, U.S. Bankruptcy Ct. (ea. and we. dists.) Va. 2002, U.S. Dist. Ct. (ea. dist.) Ky. 2003, U.S. Dist. Ct. (no. dist.) Ill. 2003, US CT. Appeals (7th cir.), 2005. Jud. clk. Judge Ronald E. Meredith, U.S. Dist. Ct. (we. dist.) Ky., Louisville, 1990-91; asst. atty. gen. State of Colo., Denver, 1991-97, Commonwealth of Va., Richmond, 1997—99; gen. counsel Christopher Newport U., Newport News, 2000—04; dep. state solicitor gen. Commonwealth Va., 2002—04, state solicitor gen., 2004—. Mem. authors' com. West's Edn. Law Reporter, St. Paul, 1992—. Author: Why You Cannot Sue State U: A Guide to Sovereign Immunity, 2001; co-author: Race Conscious Admissions and Financial Aid After the University of Michigan Decisions, 2004; co-editor: The NACUA Handbook for Lawyers New to Higher Education, 2003; contbg. author The Yearbook of Education Law, 2005—; mem. editl. bd. Jour. Coll. and Univ. Law, 2000—, vice chair, 2004-05, chair, 2005—; mem. editl. bd. Encyclopedia of Law, 2005—; contbr. articles to scholarly jours. Active LaCrosse Presbyn. Ch.; gen. counsel adv. bd. NCAA, 2001—04. Recipient Best Brief award, Nat. Assn. of Attys. Gen., 2003—04, Hardin County Sch. Disting. Alumni award, 2004; scholar U.S. Senate Youth scholar, Hearst Found., 1982, Harry S Truman scholar, Truman Scholarship Found., 1984, Rotary Internat. Ambassadorial scholar, Melbourne, 1987. Mem.: South Africa Edn. Law and Policy Assn., Am. Inns of Ct., Edn. Law Assn., Nat. Assn. Coll. and U. Attys., Ky. Bar Assn., Va. Bar Assn., Federalist Soc., Nat. Eagle Scout Assn., Hon. Order of Ky. Cols. Republican. Presbyn. Office: Office of Atty Gen 900 E Main St Richmond VA 23219 Mailing: 100 Bucktail Run Yorktown VA 23692 Office Phone: 804-786-2436. Personal E-mail: withro@cox.net. Business E-Mail: wthro@oag.state.va.us.

**THROCKMORTON, REX DENTON,** lawyer; b. Lima, Ohio, June 4, 1941; s. Francis and Jane (Corwin) T.; m. Barbara Catherine Poore, July 21, 1962; children: Scott, John. BS, Denison U., 1963; JD, Ohio State U., 1965. Bar: Ohio 1966, N. Mex. 1971, U.S. Dist. Ct. N. Mex. 1971, U.S. Ct. Appeals (10th cir.) 1973. Assoc. Squire, Sanders & Dempsey, Cleve., 1965-66; shareholder, bd. dirs. Rodey, Dickason, Sloan, Akin & Robb, P.A., Albuquerque, 1971—, ptnr., pres., mng. dir., 1999—2004. Editor Ohio State Law Jour., 1965. Pres. Albuquerque Civic Light Opera Assn., 1985; sec. Accion, N.Mex. Capt. JAGC, USAF, 1966-71. Named one of best lawyers in Am., 2003—04. Mem. ABA, N.Mex. Bar Assn. (bd. of bar commrs. 1990-98, sec.-treas. 1994, v.p. 1995, pres.-elect 1996, pres. 1997), Albuquerque Bar Assn. (pres. 1982). Republican. Avocations: golf, running. Office: Rodey Dickason Sloan Akin & Robb PO Box 1888 Albuquerque NM 87103-1888 Office Phone: 505-765-5900. Office Fax: 505-768-7395. Business E-Mail: rthrockmorton@rodey.com.

**THRODAHL, MARK CRANDALL,** medical products executive; b. Charleston, W.Va., Mar. 31, 1951; s. Monte Cordon and Josephine (Crandall) T.; m. Sudie Kenton, Oct. 21, 1978; children: Mary Elizabeth, Anne Katherine, Andrew Kenton. AB, Princeton U., 1973; MBA, Harvard U., Boston, 1975. Various positions Mallinckrodt, Inc., St. Louis, 1975-88; dir. corp. planning Becton Dickinson & Co., Franklin Lakes, NJ, 1988-91, pres. Nippon Becton Dickinson Tokyo, 1991-94, sector pres. Franklin Lakes, 1994-95, sr. v.p., 1995-2001; CEO Bespak Plc, London, 2001—. Mem. Old Warson Country Club, Ivy Club. Republican. Episcopalian. Home: 38 Carteret Rd Allendale NJ 07401-1850 Office: Bespak Plc Blackhill Dr Wolverton Mill So Milton Keynes MK12 5TS England Office Phone: 44 (0) 1908-525200. Business E-Mail: mark.throdahl@bespak.co.uk.

**THRONER, GUY CHARLES, JR.,** aerospace engineering executive, scientist, inventor, consultant; b. Mpls., Sept. 14, 1919; s. Guy Charles and Marie (Zechar) T.; m. Jean Holt, Dec. 5, 1943; children—Richard, Carol Anne, Steven BA, Oberlin Coll., 1943; postgrad., UCLA, 1960, 61. Registered profl. engr., Calif. Br. head Naval Weapon Ctr., China Lake, Calif., 1946-53; mgr. ordnance div., mgr. weapon systems div. Aerojet Gen. Corp., Azusa, Calif., 1953-64; v.p., div. mgr. FMC Corp., San Jose, Calif., 1964-74; research dir. Vacu Blast Corp., Belmont, Calif., 1976-78; v.p., devel. mfg. Dahlman, Inc., Braham, Minn., 1978-79; mgr. ordnance systems & tech. Battelle Meml. Inst., Columbus, Ohio, 1979-85; pres. Guy C. Throner & Assocs., tech. and mgmt. cons., 1985—. Dir. Omron Corp. Am., Chgo., 1976-77 Inventor, patentee indls., med. and mil. systems design Served as officer USNR, World War II Recipient Am. Order St. Barbara medal U.S. Army Arty, 1983, IR-100 award Indsl. Rsch. Mag., Chgo., 1971, Congl. Commendation, 1985, Commendation, State of Ohio Ho. of Reps., 1995, also various commendations. Mem. AIAA, Am. Def. Preparedness Assn. (Bronze medal 1974, Simon Silver medal 1985), Lake Wildwood Country Club, Sigma Xi. Republican. Avocations: astronomy, photography, golf. Home and Office: 17992 Jayhawk Dr Penn Valley CA 95946-9205 Office Phone: 330-432-1012. E-mail: jeannguy@comcast.net.

**THROWER, DANIEL NEPHI,** musician, composer, educator; b. Canyon, Tex., May 28, 1976; s. Woodrow Allen and Laura Jeanne (Maus) Thrower; m. Eden Dawn Guymon, June 11, 1999; children: Joseph Andrew, Adam Christian, Samuel Clark, Paul Kimball, Emily Danielle. MusB, Brigham Young U., 2001, MusM, 2002; postgrad., Ariz. State U., 2005—. Trumpet instr. Crescent Sch. of Music, American Fork, Utah, 1998—2002, Modern Sch. of Music, Orem, Utah, 2002—03; founder, dir., composer, instr. Utah Trumpet Guild, Orem, Utah, 2003—04; adj. prof. trumpet Brigham Young U., Rexburg, Idaho, 2003—04, prof. trumpet, 2004—05. Prin. trumpet Idaho Falls Symphony Brass Quintet, Idaho Falls, Idaho, 2004—05, Brigham Young U., Idaho Brass Quintet, Rexburg, Idaho, 2003—05; lead trumpet Brigham Young U., Idaho Faculty Jazz Ensemble, Rexburg, 2004—05. Composer, musician (trumpet) numerous CDs. Missionary The Ch. of Jesus Christ of Latter-Day Saints, Portugal, 1995—97; student ambassador People to People, Internat., Russia, 1992. Named Composer of the Month, Eighth Note Publications, 2005; recipient 1st Place award, Mayhew-Hinckley Composition Contest, 2001, 2d Place award, Internat. Trumpet Guild Composition Contest, 2006; Thomas E. Ricks grantee, 2004. Mem.: Idaho Falls Symphony, Internat. Trumpet Guild. Republican. Avocations: woodcarving, stamp collecting/philately, music composition. E-mail: daniel.throwerd@asu.edu.

**THROWER, RANDOLPH WILLIAM,** lawyer; b. Tampa, Fla., Sept. 5, 1913; s. Benjamin Key and Ora (Hammond) T.; m. Margaret Munroe, Feb. 2, 1939; children: Margaret MacCary, Patricia Barmeyer, Laura (Mrs. David T. Harris, Jr.), Randolph William, Mary (Mrs. George B. Wickham), Gail. BA, Ga. Mil. Acad., 1930; BPh, Emory U., 1934, JD, 1936. Bar: Ga. bar 1935, D.C. bar 1953. Partner Sutherland, Asbill & Brennan, Atlanta, Washington, 1947-69, 71—. Commr. internal revenue, 1969-71; Lectr. bar, legal meetings; spl. agt. FBI, 1942-43; mem. Arthur Andersen & Co. Bd. of Rev., 1974-80, Nat. Council on Organized Crime, mem. exec. com., 1970-71 Past Pres. Ga. Met. Atlanta mental health assns.; chmn. City of Atlanta Bd. Ethics 1981-93; past trustee Emory U., Clark Coll.; past chmn., trustee Wesleyan Coll.; bd. govs. Woodward Acad.; past chmn. bd. visitors Emory U. Served as capt. USMCR, 1944-45. Mem. Atlanta Legal Aid Soc. (past pres.), Emory U. Alumni Assn. (past pres.), ABA (chmn. spl. com. on survey local needs

1971-78, past chmn. sect. taxation, mem. ho. of dels. 1964-66, 74-89), Ga. Bar Assn., Atlanta Bar Assn. (past pres.), Am. Bar Found. (dir. 1980-88, pres. 1986-88, medal 1993), Am. Law Inst., Atlanta Lawyers Club (past pres.), U.S. Claims Ct. Bar Assn. (pres. 1987-88), Phi Delta Phi. Clubs: Commerce (Atlanta), Capital City (Atlanta), Piedmont Driving (Atlanta). Republican. Methodist. Home: 2240 Woodward Way NW Atlanta GA 30305-4043 Office: Sutherland Asbill & Brennan Ste 2300 999 Peachtree St NE Atlanta GA 30309 Office Phone: 404-853-8704. Business E-Mail: randolph.thrower@sablaw.com.

**THUEME, WILLIAM HAROLD,** secondary school educator, counselor, travel coordinator; b. St. Clair, Mich., Sept. 4, 1945; s. Harold Arthur and Delphine Betty (Buhl) Thueme; m. Katheen Koning, May 8, 1971; children: Benjamin William, Rebecca Kathleen, Jeffery William, Sarah Kathleen; m. Nora Thueme. Student, Port Huron Jr. Coll., 1963-64; BA, Mich. State U., 1967, MA, 1969; PhD in Counseling, Progressive Universal Life Ch., 1993, PhD in Motivation, 1997, PhD in Paranormal Psychology, 1997, PhD in Psychometrics, 1999; postgrad., Oakland U., 1971, San Francisco State U., 1975, U. Hawaii, 1975; student, Spring Arbor Coll., 1968; PhD in Reading Edn., U. Mich., 1977; PhD (hon.), Aspen U., 2003. Cert. tchr., Mich. Ordained min. Universal Life Tchr. pub. schs., Charlotte, Mich., 1967-69, Ann Arbor, Mich., 1969—. Fgn. travel coord.-Ambs. Abroad Program, Amsterdam, The Netherlands, 1968—; regional driver coord. for Southeastern Mich. Avis Rent-a-Car, 1983—; travel coord. domestic and fgn. Go Ahead Tours; worldwide travel coord. Air, Land and Sea Cruises. Active UN Children's Found., Mich. Sheriffs Ednl. Found., Feed the Children, Woods Rd. Assn., Normal Pk. Neighborhood Assn., US Legal Found., Found. for Nicaraguan Democracy, Habitat for Humanity Internat. (charter), Carter Ctr., Nat. Coun. Better Edn., participant Skyhook II Project; coord. Mich. Fraternal Order of Police BBB, Ea. Mass.; elections coord. Eaton County (Mich.) Rep. Party, 1968, nat. com., 1968—, nat. senatorial com.; troop com. Coun. Boy Scouts Am., Ypsilanti, merit badge counselor, 1988-89, cub scout summer camp instr.; Internat., Incorp. (life mem.). Shore Nat. Network of Poet's Soc. Wolverne Coun., 1987; coach of the angels Ypsilanti Am. Little League, 1988; parent adv. bd. The Childrens Devel. Lab. Ea. Mich. U., 1988-89; active Mich. United Conservation Clubs, Big Bros. Am., Charlotte, Mich., Human Rights Watch, Nat. Security Caucus US, 1988—, Heritage Found., 1988—, ofcl. sponsor Mandate for Leadership III, Policy Strategies for 1990's Project, Project Save Our Schs., 1988—, Citizens United for Better Edn., World Awareness, Inc., Group 61 Amnesty Internat., Legal Affairs Coun., Coun. for Inter-Am. Security, Am. Inst. for Econ. Rsch., Nicaraguan Resistance Edn. Found., Nat. Right to Work Legal Def. Found., Citizens Against Govt. Waste, Citizens Commn. for Ethics in Govt., Citizens for Decency Through Law, Inc., Nat. Consumers League, Participating Parents for Progress in Ypsilanti Pub. Schs.; parents adv. bd. Chapelle Elem. Sch., Ypsilanti, 1989-90, West Mid. Sch., Ypsilanti, 1991-92, Ypsilanti Pub. Schs., 1990—, Ypsilanti HS; charter sponsor Victory over Communism Project; nominated charter mem. Presdl. Task Force; participant Imperial Congress: Crisis in the Separation of Powers Project, line-item veto project Heritage Found., 1989, campaign to revise medicare catastrophic coverage law project Nat. Assn. Uniformed Svcs., 1989, repeal of catastrophic coverage act program Conservative Caucus Inc., 1989, Srs. Coal. Against the Tax, 1989; nat. adv. coun. Citizens Com. for Right to Bear Arms; jr. and sr. choir, Sunday sch. tchr. St. Paul's Luth. Ch., 1959-64 (Perfect Attendance award 8 yrs.), Marine city, Mich., 1960-63; youth Sunday sch. tchr., dir. youth min. coun. Lawrence Ave. Meth. Ch., Charlotte, Mich., 1967-69; assoc. mem. for Gentlemen of All Ages Second Amendment Sisters, 2003, Internat. Amb. Goodwill World Peace and Diplomacy Forum, founding cabinet, life mem., 2003, amb., 2004; senator seat for lifetime term World Nations Congress; mem. concert choir Mich. Mormon; vol. The Ctrl. Intelligence Agy., The USA, 1967-06, Homeland Security USA, 2005-; vol. missionary The Ch. of Jesus Christ of LDS, 1973-06; Sunday sch. sec., Mich.; Elder's Quorum instr., exec. sec., sec., High Priests Quorum Group Ypsilanti, Mich., Ann Arbor Stake Sunday Sch. sec.; Sunday sch. tchr. youth age grades 7-12. Recipient Spl. Recognition award Richard Nixon, 1968-79, Gerald Ford, 1974-76, Ronald Reagan, 1971-88, George Bush, 1988-92, Spl. Recognition award Reagan Presdl. Campaign, 1981, Bush Presdl. Campaign, 1988, Citizen of Yr. award Citizens Com. for Right to Bear Arms, 1988, cert. recognition US Justice Found., 1991, Hale Found., Am. Security Coun. 30th Anniversary Spl. Recognition cert., cert. appreciation 2d Amendment Found., 1988, Appreciation of Devoted and Valuable Svc. award Chapelle Elem. Sch., 1988-89, Merit Badge, Wolverine Coun.; Internat. Peace prize, United Cultural Conv., 2002, Outstanding contbns. to Literacy, Edn., Humanitarians and Peace, 2002, World medal of Freedom for hope, freedom and peace, 2006; letters from First Lady Nancy Reagan, First Lady Barbara Bush, Mich. Gov. John Engler, Nelson Mandella, Tchg. Excellence award, Cmty. Svc. award, Global Rels. award, 2002, others. Mem. NEA, NRA (life, endowment), Am. Inst. for Econ. Rsch., Lincoln Inst. for Rsch. Edn., United Conservatives of Am. (participant citizens against the catastrophic health act tax 1989), Mich. Edn. Assn., Internat. Reading Assn., Mich. Sheriffs Assn. (assoc.), Police Marksmanship Assn., Washtenaw Reading Coun., Southeastern Mich. Reading Assn., Mich. Reading Assn., Mich. ASCD, Ann Arbor Edn. Assn., Am. Security Coun., Am. Def. Inst., Found. for Christian Living, Am. Family Assn., Nat. Geog. Soc., Am. Film Inst., Internat. Freelance Photographers Orgn. (life, profl. photographer), Taxpayers Edn. Lobby, Gun Owners Am., Nat. Assn. Federally Lic. Firearms Dealers, Nat. Consumers League, Conservative Caucus, Inc., Ams. for Freedom, Tri-County Sportsman League, Mich. United Conservation Clubs, Mich. State U. Alumni Assn. (Blue Water chpt.), Mich. State U. Coll. Comm. Arts Alumni Assn., Cruise Lines Internat. Assn., Internat. Air Transport Assn., US Tour Operators Assn. of One Million Dollar Consumer Protection Plan, Mich. State U. Coll. Social Sci. Alumni Assn., Inventors Assistance League (life), San Francisco State U. Alumni Assn., Shore Nat. Network Poets Soc. (life), Group Leaders Am., Group Travel Bus. Inst., Ft. Gratiot, Lions Club (v.p. 1998—), Lions Club Internat., Washtenaw Sportsmen's Club (Ypsilanti), Internat. Optimist Club (v.p. Ann Arbor chpt., bd. dirs. 1975-78), Port Huron Noon Optimist Club, Judo Black Belt Fedn. Am., Sigma Alpha Eta. Evangelican Lutheran. Office Phone: 800-381-5111. Personal E-Mail: whthueme@yahoo.com.

**THUESEN, GERALD JORGEN,** industrial engineer, educator; b. Oklahoma City, July 20, 1938; s. Holger G. and Helen S. T.; m. Harriett M. Thuesen; children: Karen T. Hannah, Dyan T. Jacobus. BS, Stanford U., 1960, MS, 1961, PhD, 1968. Engr. Pacific Tel. Co., San Francisco, 1961-62, Atlantic Richfield Co., Dallas, 1962-63; asst. prof. indsl. engring. U. Tex., Arlington, 1963, 67-68; assoc. prof. indsl. and sys. engring. Ga. Inst. Tech., Atlanta, 1968-76, prof., 1976-, prof. emeritus, 1996—. Author: Engineering Economy, 4th edit., 1971, 5th edit., 1977, 6th edit., 1984, 7th edit., 1989, 8th edit., 1993, 9th edit., 2001, Economic Decision Analysis, 1974, 2nd edit., 1980, 3rd edit., 1998; assoc. editor: The Engring. Economist, 1974-80, editor, 1981-91. NASA/Am. Soc. Engring. Edn. summer faculty fellow, 1970. Fellow Inst. Indsl. Engrs. (dept. editor Trans. 1976-80, v.p. publs. 1979-80, divsn. dir. 1978-80, Wellington award 1989, Publs. award 1990, bd. trustees 1979-81), Am. Soc. Engring. Edn. (bd. dirs. 1977-79, Eugene L. Grant award 1977, 91); mem. Sigma Xi. Office: Ga Inst Tech Sch Indsl & Sys Engring Atlanta GA 30332-0205 Business E-Mail: gthuesen@isye.gatech.edu.

**THUESEN, PETER JOHANNES,** religious studies educator, writer; b. Hickory, NC, Sept. 18, 1971; s. Theodore Johannes and Mary Wise Thuesen; m. Jane Allen Kenyon, June 8, 1996; 3 children. BA, U. NC, Chapel Hill, 1993; MA, PhD, Princeton U., NJ, 1998. Asst. editor The Works of Jonathan Edwards, Yale U., New Haven, 1998—2001; asst. prof. of comparative religion Tufts U., Medford, Mass., 2001—04; assoc. prof. religious studies Ind. U.-Purdue U., Indpls., 2004—. Author: In Discordance with the Scriptures. Mem.: Am. Hist. Assn., Am. Soc. Ch. History (coun. mem. 2004—, Frank S. and Elizabeth D. Brewer prize 1998). Office: Ind U Purdue U Dept Religious Studies 425 University Blvd CA 335 Indianapolis IN 46202-5140 Office Phone: 317-274-5942. E-mail: pthuesen@iupui.edu.

**THUESON, DAVID OREL,** pharmaceutical executive, researcher, writer, educator; b. Twin Falls, Idaho, May 9, 1947; s. Orel Grover and Shirley Jean (Archer) T.; m. Sherrie Linn Lowe, June 14, 1969; children: Sean, Kirsten, Eric, Ryan, Todd. BS, Brigham Young U., 1971; PhD, U. Utah, 1976. Postdoctoral fellow U. Tex. Med. Br., Galveston, 1976-77, asst. prof., 1977-82; sr. rsch. assoc. Parke-Davis Pharms., Ann Arbor, Mich., 1982-88; dir. pharmacology Immunetech Pharms., San Diego, 1988-90; dir. immunopharmacology Tanabe Rsch. Labs., San Diego, 1990-92; v.p. discovery Cosmederm Techs., San Diego, 1992-97. Contbr. articles to profl. jours.; patentee in field. Scout leader Boy Scouts Am., Mich., Tex. and Calif., 1979—. NIH grantee, 1978-81. Mem. Am. Acad. Allergy and Clin. Immunology, Am. Assn. Immunologists, Am. Thoracic Soc. Republican. Mem. Lds Ch. Avocations: water-skiing, tennis, scuba diving. Home: 1356 Winchester Ave Mckinleyville CA 95519-8801 Office: 2330 Central Ave Ste 3 Mckinleyville CA 95519-3696 Office Phone: 707-840-0623. Business E-Mail: thueson@reninet.com.

**THULEAN, DONALD MYRON,** symphony conductor; b. Wenatchee, Wash., June 24, 1929; s. Elmer Edward and Mary (Myron) T.; m. Meryl Mary Parnell, Mar. 17, 1951; children— Dorcas Marie, Mark Myron, William Norton. BA, U. Wash., 1950, MA in Music, 1952; Mus.D. (hon.), Whitworth Coll., 1967. Faculty Pacific U., 1955-62; dean Pacific U. (Sch. Music), 1957-62. Assoc. conductor Portland (Ore.) Symphony, 1961-62, conductor, music dir. Spokane Symphony, 1962-84; v.p. profl. and artistic svcs. Am. Symphony Orch. League, 1983-99, condr. emeritus, 1998—; asst. conductor Seattle Symphony, 1966-69, chorus master, Aspen Music Festival, 1957-61; artistic cons. Title III project in performing arts, Wash., 1966-68, music dir. Tamarack Music Festival, 1971. Bd. dirs. Seattle Symphony, 2000—, Seattle Youth Symphonies, 2002--; mem. vis. com. U. Wash. Sch. Music, 2000--. Served with AUS, 1953-55. Unitarian (trustee). Personal E-mail: thulean2@comcast.net.

**THUMMA, SAMUEL ANDERSON,** lawyer; b. Emmetsburg, Iowa, May 2, 1962; s. H. Russell and Lanore Ava (Anderson) T.; m. Barbara J. Dawson. BS, Iowa State U., 1984; JD, U. Iowa, 1988. Bar: Iowa 1988, Ill. 1990, D.C. 1990, Ariz. 1992. Broadcaster Sta. WOI-AM, Ames, Iowa, 1982-84; print journalist Iowa Dept. Agr., Des Moines, 1985; law clk. to Hon. David R. Hansen, U.S. Dist. Ct. for No. Dist. Iowa, Cedar Rapids, 1988-90; assoc. Arnold & Porter, Washington, 1990-92; law clk. to Hon. Stanley G. Feldman, Ariz. Supreme Ct., 1992-93; mem. Brown & Bain, P.A., Phoenix, 1996, Perkins Coie Brown & Bain, P.A., Phoenix, 2004—. Adj. prof. Ariz. State U. Coll. Law, 2000. Contbr. articles to profl. jours. Western area Svc. Coun. Mem., American Red Cross, 2004-; ex officio bd. mem. and spl. transp. svcs. com. chair Grand Canyon chpt. ARC, 1998-99, bd. dirs., 1999-2004, chmn. bd., 2002-2004; bd. dirs., nat. conv. cabinet vice chair blood related activities ARC, 2000-2002; bd. dirs., purchasing coord. Gifts for Homeless, Inc., Washington, 1991-93; mem. study affairs devel. adv. coun. Iowa State U., 1993-96; mem. Paradise Valley Village Planning Com., 1994-96, sec., 1995-96; judge Nat. Chpt. award and Proficiency award Ariz. FFA, 1996-99, 2001. Harry S. Truman Found. scholar, 1982-87. Mem. ABA, Fed. Bar Assn., Am. Law Inst., State Bar of Ariz. (fee arbitration com. 1994—, chair 1997-2002, civil practice and procedure com. 1997—, vice chair 2001-2002, chair 2002—), Maricopa County Bar Assn. (task force on recruitment and retention of women and minorities 1999—, CLE com. 1995-99, barristers ball com. 1997-99), Ill. Bar Assn., D.C. Bar Assn., Iowa Bar Assn., Ariz. Bar Assn., Order of Coif. Republican. Methodist. Avocations: photography, travel, cooking. Office: Perkins Coie Brown & Bain PA PO Box 400 2901 N Central Ave Ste 2000 Phoenix AZ 85012-2788

**THUMMEL, ROSA,** artist; b. Des Moines, Apr. 17, 1916; d. Sposeto Frank and Victoria Jaquinta; m. John W. Thummel-Senneich (dec. Mar. 1988); children: Randolph, Carl, Gabriella Student, Drake U., U. Iowa. One woman shows include Swiss Ctr. Gallery, N.Y.C., 1975, Nat. Art Ctr., N.Y.C., 1979, Tosta Gallery, Coconut Grove, Fla., 1980-83, Corridor Gallery, Summit, N.J., 1981; exhibited in group shows at Montclair (N.J.) Pub. Libr., 1976, Summit Art Ctr., 1978, 80, 82 (Beth Born Portrait award 1978, Best in Show 1980, First prize 1982), Painters & Sculpters Soc., N.Y.C., 1976-79, N.J., 1980-83, Bergen County (N.J.) Artist Guild, 1980, Sheila Nussbaum Gallery, Millburn, N.J., Lever House, N.Y.C., 1984, others; represented in pvt. collections. Home: 1323 Friarcreek Houston TX 77055

**THUNE, JOHN RANDOLPH,** senator; b. Murdo, SD, Jan. 7, 1961; m. Kimberley Jo Weems, 1984; children: Brittany, Larissa. BBA, Biola U., Calif., 1983; MBA, U. SD, 1984. Legis. asst. to Senator James Abdnor US Senate, 1985-87; dep. staff dir. to the ranking rep. Senate Small Bus. Com., 1987-89; exec. dir. South Dakota Rep. Party, 1989-91; dir. railroad divsn. State of SD, 1991-93; exec. dir. SD Mcpl. League, 1993-96; founder The Thune Group LLC; mem. US Ho. Reps. from SD, 1997—2003; US Senator from SD, 2005—. Mem. com. armed services US Senate, com. environment and public works, com. small bus. and entrepreneurship, com. veterans affairs. Republican. Protestant. Avocations: basketball, pheasant hunting. Office: US Senate 383 Russell Senate Office Bldg Washington DC 20510 also: District Office 320 North Main Ave Sioux Falls SD 57104-6056 Office Phone: 202-224-2321, 605-334-9596. Office Fax: 202-228-5429, 605-334-2591.*

**THURBER, PETER PALMS,** lawyer; b. Detroit, Mar. 23, 1928; s. Cleveland and Marie Louise (Palms) T.; m. Ellen Bodley Stites, Apr. 16, 1955; children: Edith Bodley, Jane Chenoweth Thomas, Sarah Bodley. BA, Williams Coll., 1950; JD, Harvard U., 1953. Bar: Mich., 1954. With Miller, Canfield, Paddock and Stone, Detroit, 1953-93, of counsel, 1994—. Trustee McGregor Fund, Detroit, 1979-2003. Bd. dirs. Detroit Symphony Orch., Inc., 1974-93; trustee Community Found. for Southeastern Mich., 1990-2000, Coun. Mich. Founds., 1991-2000. With U.S. Army, 1953-55. Fellow Am. Bar Found.; mem. ABA, Mich. Bar Assn. Clubs: Country of Detroit (Grosse Pointe Farms, Mich.). Roman Catholic. Avocations: reading, travel, sports. Home: 28 Provencal Rd Grosse Pointe Farms MI 48236-3038 Office: Miller Canfield Paddock & Stone 150 W Jefferson Ave Ste 2500 Detroit MI 48226-4416

**THURBER, SHARON LEE,** elementary resource educator; d. Donald Lee and Alka Mae Shears; m. Donald Lee Thurber, Mar. 30, 1983. BE, Ind. State U., Terre Haute, 1971; MEd, Ind. U., Bloomington, 1976. Cert. in tchg. Alaska, Ind., Tex., Fla. Elem. tchr. grade 3 Martinsville Ind. Sch. Dist., 1971—81; elem. tchr. grade 6 Galena Pk. Sch. Dist., Houston, 1981—82; elem. tchr. grades 1 and 2 Burton Ind. Sch. Dist., Tex., 1982—84; elem. tchr. grades 4-6 Archer City Ind. Sch. Dist., Tex., 1984—88; elem. resource tchr. South Elem. Sch., Okeechobee, Fla., 1988—89, Ocala Springs Elem. Sch., Fla., 1989—90, Russian Jack Elem. Sch., Anchorage, 1991—. Named Highly Qualified Tchr., Anchorage Sch. Dist., 2004; nom. to Career Ladder Excellent Tchrs. Tex., 1984—88. Mem.: NEA, Educators Social Responsibility, Anchorage Edn. Assn. (bldg. rep. 1994—96). Office: Russian Jack Elem Sch 4420 E 20th Ave Anchorage AK 99508 Office Phone: 907-742-1300. Business E-Mail: thurb2r_sharon@asdk12.org.

**THURM, DAVID AARON,** lawyer, publishing executive; b. Winslow, Ariz., Dec. 5, 1953; s. Richard Henry and Evelyn Joyce (Boches) T.; m. Andrea Granoff, Mar. 29, 1981; children: Amanda Margot, Matthew Charles, James Richard. AB, Harvard U., 1975; JD, NYU, 1978. Bar: NY 1979, US Dist. Ct. (So. and Ea. Dists.) NY 1979. Assoc. Rogers & Wells, NYC, 1978-81; atty. The NY Times Co., NYC, 1982-87, sr. atty., 1988-89, dir. adminstrn., 1988—90; exec. dir. project devel. 1991—95, v.p. prodn., 1995—99; v.p. real estate develop. The NY Times Co. and NY Times, NYC, 2000—, chief information officer, 2004—; COO NY Times Digital, NYC, 1999—2000. Home: 10 Sherman Ave Bronxville NY 10708-4219 Office: The New York Times Co 229 W 43rd St New York NY 10036-3959

**THURMAIER, MARY JEAN,** educational association administrator; b. Delavan, Ill., Dec. 14, 1931; d. Emil Edward Pech and Grace May Creager; m. Roland J. Thurmaier, Oct. 22, 1955 (dec.); children: Kurt, Barbara, John, Matthew. B in edn., U. Iowa, 1960; M in Reading, U. Wis., Stevens Point, 1971. Mgr. City Bus. Sys., Stevens Point, 1974—78; office mgr. Carter/Mondale Campaign, Milw., 1980; exec. dir. Stevens Point Conv. and Vis. Bur., 1986—99; with NSBA Fed. Rels. Network, Washington, 1987—; chair bd. trustees Ins. Plan State, Madison, Wis., 1997—. Mem. bd. rev. City of Stevens Point; mem. Stevens Point Bd. Edn.; statutory chair Portage County Dem. Party, Stevens Point. Methodist.

**THURMAN, ANDREW EDWARD,** lawyer; b. Raleigh, N.C., May 11, 1954; s. William Gentry and Peggy Lou (Brown) T.; m. Patricia Thurman, May 19, 1979 (dec. 1989); children: Gentry Brown, Harrison Beauchamp, Andrew Guilford; m. Tracy Fletcher, Nov. 16, 1991; 1 child, Spencer Lee. BA, Columbia U., 1976; JD, Coll. William and Mary, 1979; MPH, U. Okla., 1984. Bar: Va. 1979, Okla. 1980, U.S. Ct. Appeals (10th cir.) 1981, U.S. Supreme Ct. 1985, Pa. 1988. Staff atty. Dept. of Human Svcs., Oklahoma City, 1979—80; counsel State of Okla. Tchg. Hosps., Oklahoma City, 1980—84; mem. Miller, Dollarhide, Dawson & Shaw, Oklahoma City, 1984—87; ptnr. Berkman, Ruslander, Pohl, Lieber & Engel, Pitts., 1988—89; of counsel Buchanan Ingersoll, Pitts., 1989; sr. v.p. and gen. counsel Forbes Health Sys., Pitts., 1989—96; sr. counsel Allegheny Health Edn. & Rsch. Found., Pitts., 1997—98; dep. gen. counsel Allegheny U. Hosps. West, 1998—99; asst. gen. counsel We. Pa. Allegheny Health Sys., 1999—2002; assoc. prof. Carnegie-Mellon U., 2000—; pvt. practice, 2002—; assoc. prof. U. Pitts., 2003—, assoc. dir. consortium ethics program, 2004—; asst. prof. Am. U. Caribbean, 2003—. Pres. Coun. Neighborhood Assns., Oklahoma City, 1984, Lincoln Terr. Neighborhood Assn., Oklahoma City, 1984; trustee Rader Trust, Oklahoma City, 1980—; treas. Bd. dirs. State Okla. Tchg. Hosps. Found., Oklahoma City, 1984-87, Newman Meml. Hosp., 1983-87, Willowview Hosp., Spencer, Okla., 1985-87, Allegheny U. Med. Ctrs., Allegheny U. Med. Ctr./Cannonsburg Ambulance Svc., 1997—, Allegheny U. Hosps. West, 1998—, Diversified Health Group, 1998-99, Allegheny Med. Practices Network, 1999—, Allegheny Speciality Practice Network, 1999—; chair HCWP Ethics Task Force, 1993-2000. Fellow Am. Health Lawyers Assn.; mem. St. Anthony Hall Club N.Y.C. (pres. 1976), Rivers Club. Democrat. Presbyterian. Avocation: reading detective novels. Home: 106 Richmond Dr Pittsburgh PA 15215-1039 Office: 1151 Freeport Rd # 391 Pittsburgh PA 15238 Office Phone: 412-252-2878. E-mail: andy@thurmanhealthlaw.com, andy@thurmans.net.

**THURMAN, CYNTHIA DENISE,** human services administrator; b. Ft. Myers, Fla., Mar. 14, 1970; children: Asia Naikee Garcia, Jai'ya Ja'V-ae Armani. Grad. high sch. Residential care coord. Sandy Pk. Redevelopment Ctr., North Fort Myers, Fla., 2001—; human services worker Gulf Coast Ctr., Ft. Myers, 2000-. Author: (poems) Soon. Recipient Shakespare Trophy of Excellence, Famous Poets Soc., 2004. Home: 4926 Gary Dr Fort Myers FL 33905 Office: Gulf Coast Center 5820 Buckingham Rd Fort Myers FL 33905 Office Phone: 239-694-2151 226. Personal E-mail: cind33905@aol.com.

**THURMAN, JOANN TRUAX,** educational consultant; b. Rome, N.Y., July 26, 1947; m. John Fulton: children: Winter Poppy Beefheart, Ezechial Z. Riff. BA in Math., SUNY, Buffalo, 1969; MA, S.E. Mo. State U., 1995. Cert. secondary math. tchr., Mo., ednl. cons., 2003. 9th grade tchr. Starpoint Ctrl. Sch., Lockport, N.Y., 1969-70; 8th grade tchr. Turner Unified Sch. Dist. 202, 1970-71; tchr., chairperson, math dept. East Carter H.S., Ellsinore, Mo., 1975—2001; ednl. cons., 2003—. Adj. instr. math. Three Rivers C.C., 1982-2000, off-campus liaison, 1988-95; math. revision curriculum com. East Carter R-2 Sch. Dist., chairperson, 1993-2002, steering com., career ladder com., 1988-2000, coord. Fed.funds, 1995-2002, central office admin. asst., 1997-2003, summer sch. dir., 1990-2002, curriculum dir., 1996—, grant writer, 1996—. Recipient Most Influential Tchr award U Mo., 1988-89, 89-90, Ednl. Excellence award Cmty. Tchrs. Assn., 2001. Mem. Mo. State Tchrs. Assn., Nat. Coun. Tchrs. Math., S.E. Mo. Coun. Tchrs. of Math. (pres. 1988-90, sec.-treas. 1992-05, Outstanding Sec. Math Educator award 1995-96), Mo. Coun. Tchrs. of Math. (v.p. secondary 1990-91, state exec. bd. dirs. 1988-91).

**THURMAN, KAREN L.,** former congresswoman, lobbyist; b. Rapid City, S.D., Jan. 12, 1951; d. Lee Searle and Donna (Altfillisch) Loveland; m. John Patrick Thurman, 1973; children: McLin Searl and Liberty Lee. BA, U. Fla., 1973. Mem. Dunnellon City Coun. (Fla.), 1975—83; mayor of Dunnellon Dunnellon, 1979-81; mem. Monroe Regional Med. Ctr. Governancy Com., Comprehensive Plan Tech. Adv. Com., Fla. State Senate, 1983—93, U.S. Congress from 5th Fla. dist., 1993—2002, ways and means com., 1996—2002, House agrl. comm., comm. on gov. reform and oversight; lobbyist eAppeals, Miami, 2004—, Freedom Healthcare, Hollywood, 2004—. Del. Fla. Dem. Conv., Dem. Nat. Conv., 1980; mem. Regional Energy Action com. Recipient Svc. Above Self award Dunnellon C. of C., 1980, Regional Coun. Appreciation for Svc. award. Mem. Dunnellon C. of C. (dir.), Fla. Horseman's Children's Soc. (charter). Democrat. Episcopalian.

**THURMAN, ROBERT A.F.,** theology studies educator, philosopher; m. Nena von Schlebrugge. BA, MA, PhD, Harvard Univ. Co-founder Am. Inst. Buddhist Studies, 1973—; founder Tibet House, NY, 1987—; scholar, activist, chair religion dept. Columbia U., N.Y.C., 1988—, prof. religion dept., now Jey Tsong Kappa Prof., Indo-Tibetan Studies. Author: The Central Philosophy of Tibet, 1991, Inner Revolution, 1999, Anger, the Seven Deadly Sins, 2004, Infinite Life: Seven Virtues for Living Well, 2004, The Jewel Tree of Tibet: The Enlightenment Engine of Tibetan Buddhism, 2005. Named One of the Most Influential Americans, Time Mag. Buddhist. Office: Rm 203 80 Claremont Columbia U New York NY 10027-7003 Office Phone: 212-851-4133. E-mail: tbt7@columbia.edu.

**THURMAN, UMA KARUNA,** actress; b. Boston, Apr. 29, 1970; d. Robert and Nena (von Schlebrugge) T.; m. Gary Oldman, Oct. 1990 (div. 1992); m. Ethan Hawke, May 1, 1998 (div. July 20, 2004); children: Maya Ray, Roan. Spokesperson Lancome cosmetics, 2000. Appeared in films Kaze no tani no Naushika, 1984, Kiss Daddy Good Night, 1988, Johnny Be Good, 1988, Dangerous Liaisons, 1988, The Adventures of Baron Munchausen, 1988, Where the Heart Is, 1990, Henry and June, 1990, Final Analysis, 1992, Jennifer Eight, 1992, Mad Dog and Glory, 1993, Even Cowgirls Get the Blues, 1993, Pulp Fiction, 1994 (Acad. award nom. Best Supporting Actress), A Month By the Lake, 1995, The Truth About Cats and Dogs, 1996, Beautiful Girls, 1996, Batman & Robin, 1997, Gattaca, 1997, Avengers, 1998, Les Miserables, 1998, Vatel, 1999, Sweet and Lowdown, 1999, Vatel, 2000, Tape, 2001, Chelsea Walls, 2001, Kill Bill: Volume 1, 2003, Paycheck, 2003, Kill Bill: Volume 2, 2004, Be Cool, 2005, Prime, 2005, The Producers, 2005, My Super Ex-Girlfriend, 2006; TV movies include Robin Hood, 1991, Duke of Groove, 1996, The Golden Bowl, 2000, Hysterical Blindness, 2002 (also exec. prodr.; Golden Globe for Best Performance by an Actress). Bd. dirs. Room to Grow. Named a knight in the Order of Arts & Letters, France, 2006. Office: Creative Artists Agy care Brian Lourd 9830 Wilshire Blvd Beverly Hills CA 90212-1804*

**THURMAN, VICTORIA L.,** school psychologist; d. Carl and Janet Weissert; m. Jason Thurman, Dec. 27, 2000; children: Madelyn, Logan. BS, SE Mo. State U., 1991; MS, SE. Mo. State U., 1997, specialist in sch. psychology, 1999. Cert. sch. psychologist Mo. Sch. psychologist BASSC, Belleville, 1999—2000; dist. sch. psychologist Pattonville Sch. Dist., St. Ann, Mo., 2000—. Mem.: Nat. Assn. Sch. Psychologists, Mo. Assn. Sch. Psychologists (membership chair 2004—06, regional rep. 2001—04). Office: Pattonville Sch Dist 11097 St Charles Rock Rd Saint Ann MO 63074 Office Phone: 314-213-8072.

**THURMER, ROBERT,** art gallery director; b. Vienna, Oct. 8, 1953; s. Robert and Helene (Vilim) T.; m. Nancy J. Clark, Aug. 2, 1973 (div. 1988); children: Kate E., Clayton R. BFA, Syracuse U., 1977; MA, U. Nebr., 1979;

MFA, RISD, 1981. Instr. SUNY, Oswego, 1982-83; designer Cleve. Mus. Art, 1983-88; curator Everson Mus. Art, Syracuse, N.Y., 1988-90; art gallery dir. Cleve. State U., 1990—. Supt. fine arts N.Y. State Fair, Syracuse, 1989-90; asst. dir. CCNY, N.Y.C., 1992-93; visual art review panelist Ohio Arts Coun., Columbus, 1992-95; instr. exhbn. design U. Calif., Berkeley, 1994. Exhbns. include Gallerie Satelite, Paris, 1999, Gallerie forum Kunst, Weilheimteck, Germany, 1999. Festival dir. Cleve. Performance Art Festival, 1997-99; trustee Performers and Artists for Nuclear Disarmament, 1999—. Avocations: mountain climbing, backpacking, skiing. Office: Cleve State U Art Gallery 2307 Chester Ave Cleveland OH 44114-3607

**THURMOND, GEORGE MURAT,** judge; b. Del Rio, Tex., Oct. 22, 1930; s. Roger H. and Day (Hamilton) T.; m. Elsiejean Davis, June 27, 1959; children: Carolyn Day, Georganna, Sarah Gail. BA, U. of the South, 1952; JD, U. Tex., 1955. Bar: Tex. 1955. Ptnr. Montague & Thurmond, Del Rio, 1955-69; judge Tex. Dist. Ct. (63rd dist.), Del Rio, 1970-2000, sr. judge, 2000—. Presiding judge 6th Adminstrv. Region, Del Rio, 1983-87; chmn. jud. sect. State Bar Tex., 1988-89. Staff: U. Tex. Law Review, 1955. Rep. Tex. Ho. of Reps., 1955-58. Mem.: ABA, Fifth US Ct. Appeals, Tex. Bar Assn. Republican. Anglican. Avocations: exercise, traditional jazz, model railroading. Business E-Mail: gthurmand@stx.rr.com.

**THURMOND, J. STROM, JR.,** lawyer, former prosecutor; b. S.C., Oct. 18, 1972; s. Strom and Nancy Thurmond; m. Heather Holland, 1998; 1 child, Strom III. BA in English, U. S.C., 1995, grad. in Law, 1998. Bar: S.C. Ptnr. Strom, Young & Thurmond, LLP, Columbia, SC, 1998—99; asst. solicitor S.C. 2d Jud. Cir., 1999—2001; U.S. atty. Dist. SC US Dept. Justice, 2001—05; ptnr. Smith, Massey, Brodie, and Thurmond LLP, 2005—. Chmn. dist. law enforcement coordinating com. Dist. S.C., mem. atty. gen.'s adv. coun. violent crime subcom.

**THURMOND, JOHN PETER, II,** bank executive, rancher, archaeologist; b. Elk City, Okla., Apr. 22, 1955; s. Arthur Leslie and Dorothea Jean (Lee) Thurmond; m. Susan Ide Smith, June 7, 1979; children: Katherine Anne, Allison Lee, Patrick Andrew. BA, U. Tex., 1976, MA, 1979. Pres., chmn. First Nat. Bank Leedey, Okla., 1984-92, Leedey Bancorporation, Inc., 1984-92, Thurmond Ranch, Inc., Cheyenne, Okla., 1982—. Pres., chmn. Dempsey Divide Rsch. Found., Inc., 2001—05; vis. rsch. assoc. Sam Noble Okla. Mus. Natural History, U. Okla., 2001—05; vice chmn. 1st Nat. Bank & Trust Co., Elk City, 1992—. Author: Archeology of the Cypress Basin, NE Texas, 1981, Late Paleoindian Utilization of the Dempsey Divide, 1990. EMT, sec. Leedey Ambulance Svc., Inc., 1981—88. Recipient Hist. Preservation award, Okla. Hist. Soc., 1991, 1997, Goodyear Conservationist award, 2000. Mem.: Okla. Hist. Soc. (dir. we. chpt. 2004—), Okla. Cattlemen's Assn., Geol. Soc. Am., Am. Quaternary Assn., Plains Anthrop. Soc., Tex. Archeol. Soc., Okla. Anthrop. Soc. (sec., treas. 1988—2006, Disting. Svc. award 1999), Cum Laude Soc., Phi Beta Kappa, Phi Kappa Phi. Personal E-Mail: dempseydiv@aol.com.

**THURNAUER, MARION CHARLOTTE,** chemist; d. Hans and Lotte Oettinger Thurnauer; m. Alexander Dimitrije Trifunac, June 23, 1967. BA, U. Chgo., 1968, MS, 1969, PhD, 1974. Sr. scientist Argonne Nat. Lab., Ill., 1991—2004, dir. chemistry divsn., 1995—2003. Sr. scientist, guest resident Argonne Nat. Lab., Ill., 2004—06, sr. scientist emeritus, 2006—. Recipient Agnes Fay Morgan Rsch. award, Iota Sigma Pi, 1987, Argonne Nat. Lab. Dir.'s award for extraordinary effort involved in organizing sci. careers in search of women Conf., Argonne Nat. Lab., 1990, Disting. Performance award at Argonne, U. Chgo., 1991, Outstanding Women Leaders of DuPage County award, YWCA, 1996, Francis P. Garvan-John M. Olin medal, Am. Chem. Soc., 2002. Fellow: AAAS; mem.: Internat. EPR Soc. (corr.), Assn. for Women in Sci. (corr.; Chgo. chpt. pres. 1987—87), Am. Chem. Soc. (corr.), Iota Sigma Pi (corr.). Achievements include research in Photochemical Energy Conversion in Photosynthesis; Time Resolved Electron Paramagnetic Resonance. Personal E-Mail: mariont@anl.gov.

**THURNER, HENRY,** retired writer; b. Ulm, Germany, Mar. 3, 1924; s. Charles and Charlotte Thurner; m. Trudy Cecilia Eder, Aug. 16, 1945; children: Claudia, Ritchie. BA cum laude, Syracuse U., Syracuse, NY, 1947—53. Counter intelligence agt. US War Dept., 1945—47; tech. writer / editor GE, Syracuse, NY, 1950—69. Author: (novels) The Man Who Knew God, GECKO, Rufus in Heaven, others. Sgt. US Army, 1946—50, France / Germany. Decorated Cert. of Appreciation Electronic Systems Divsn., Air Force Systems Command. Avocations: painting, wood carving, poetry.

**THURSBY, JERRY GILBERT,** economics professor, consultant, department chairman; b. Camp Le Jeune, NC, Aug. 6, 1947; s. Gilbert Earl and Mary Kathleen (Bailey) T.; m. Marie Sloan Currie, Mar. 11, 1972; children: James, Mary. AB, U. N.C., 1969, PhD, 1975. Asst. prof. Syracuse (N.Y.) U., 1975-78; from asst. to assoc. prof. Ohio State U., Columbus, 1978-88; prof. Purdue U., West Lafayette, Ind., 1988-01; prof. econs., chmn. dept. Emory U., Atlanta, 2001—. Contbr. articles to profl. jours. With U.S. Army, 1969-71. Home: 910 Springdale Rd NE Atlanta GA 30306-4620 Office: Emory U Dept Econs Rich Meml Bldg Atlanta GA 30322 Office Phone: 404-712-8688. Business E-Mail: jthursb@emory.edu.

**THURSFIELD, DAVID W.,** automotive executive; Plant mgr. Ford Motor Co., 1979—84, gen. mfg. mgr. and gen. ops. mgr. various locations in Europe, 1984—92, dir. body and assembly ops. Ford of Europe, mgr. vehicle ops. Ford automotive ops., 1996—98, v.p. vehicle ops. Ford automotive ops. 1998—2001, group v.p. internat. ops. and global purchasing, 2001, chmn., CEO, and pres. Ford of Europe, 2001—02, exec. v.p. and pres. internat. ops. and global purchasing, 2002—. Office: Ford Motor Co One American Rd Dearborn MI 48126-1899

**THURSFIELD, FRED FALCONER, II,** foundation administrator; b. Rochester, NY, Mar. 13, 1950; s. Richard Emmons and Alice (Hedges) T.; m. Kathi Suzanne Heathcote, Jan. 22, 1972 (div. Dec. 1996); children: Amy Christine Humphreys, Jennifer Anne Swain; m. Sara Garland Barr, Sept. 2, 1997; 1 stepchild, Shelby Blair Oktar. BA, U. Md., 1972. Cert. fund raising exec. Sales rep. Life of Va. Ins. Co., 1972-78; dir. alumni fund Johns Hopkins Med. Instns., Balt., 1978-82; major gift officer, dir. acad. programs Duke U., Durham, NC, 1982-92, asst. dir. devel. Sch. Environ, 1992-94; dir. ann. and capital programs Geisinger Found., Danville, Pa., 1994-95; assoc. dir. devel. Washington Hosp. Ctr. Found., 1995-97; exec. dir. Peninsula Regional Found., Salisbury, Md., 1997—2001, Health First Found., Melbourne, Fla., 2001—04, Upper Chesapeake Health Found., Inc., 2004—. Mem. coun. Wildlife Preservation Trust, Internat., 1994-99; bd. dirs. Harford County Econ. Devel., 2005—. Mem.: Harford County C. of C. (bd. mem. 2004—), Assn. Fund Raising Profls., Assn. Healthcare Philanthropy (regional sec. treas. 1998—99, chair elect 1999—2000, chair 2000—01, mem. Brevard County Zoo bd. 2002—04), U. Md. Alumni Assn. and Terrapin Club, Rotary. Methodist. Avocations: golf, reading, philately, art. Home: 1014 Hazel Ln Bel Air MD 21014 Office: 520 Upper Chesapeake Dr Bel Air MD 21014 Office Phone: 443-643-3460. Personal E-Mail: ffalconert@aol.com.

**THURSTON, BONNIE BOWMAN,** religious studies educator, minister, poet; b. Bluefield, W.Va., Oct. 5, 1952; d. Ernest Venoy and Eleanor Sabina (King) Bowman; m. Burton Bradford Thurston, May 29, 1980 (dec. Nov. 1990). BA summa cum laude, Bethany Coll., 1974; MA, U. Va., 1975, PhD, 1979; postgrad., Harvard Div. Sch., 1983, Eberhard Karls U., Germany, 1983—84, Ecole Biblique, Jerusalem, 1993. Ordained to ministry Disciples of Christ Ch., 1984. Instr., asst. dean U. Va., Charlottesville, 1977-80; adj. prof. Wheeling Coll. (now Wheeling Jesuit U.), W.Va., 1980—81, assoc. prof., chair dept. theology, 1985—95; asst. prof. Bethany Coll., W.Va., 1981—83; assoc. prof. N.T. Pitts. Theol. Sem., 1995—99, William F. Orr prof., chair, 1999—2002. Vis. scholar Harvard U. Div. Sch., Cambridge, Mass., 1983; tutor Inst. Study of Christian Origins, Tubingen, Germany, 1983—85. Author: (books) The Widows, 1989, Wait Here and Watch, 1989, Spiritual Life in the Early Church, 1993, Women in the NT, 1998, To

Everything a Season, 1999, Preaching Mark, 2002, Philippians and Philemon, 2004, (books of poetry) The Heart's Land, 2001, Hints and Glimpses, 2004; contbr. articles to profl. jours., poetry to jours. Mem.: Soc. for the Study of Christian Spirituality, Disciples Hist. Soc., Soc. for Buddhist-Christian Studies, Internat. Thomas Merton Soc., Soc. Bibl. Lit., Cath. Bibl. Assn. Avocations: gardening, music, cooking. Office: PO Box 2258 Wheeling WV 26003

**THURSTON, DONALD ALLEN,** broadcast executive; b. Gloucester, Mass., Apr. 2, 1930; s. Joseph Allen and Helen Ruth (Leach) T.; m. Oralie Alice Lane, Sept. 9, 1951; children: Corydon Leach, Carolie Lane. Grad., Mass. Radio and Telegraph, 1949; HHD (hon.), North Adams State Coll., Mass., 1977; LHD (hon.), Emerson Coll., 1995. Announcer, engr. Sta. WTWN, St. Johnsbury, Vt., 1949-52; v.p., gen. mgr. Sta. WIKE, Newport, Vt., 1952-60; v.p., treas., gen. mgr. Sta. WMNB, North Adams, 1960-66; pres., treas. Berkshire Broadcasting Co., Inc., North Adams, 1966—2003. Bd. dirs. Broadcast Capital Fund, Inc., 1980-96, chmn. bd., 1981-89; bd. dirs. Broadcast Music, Inc., N.Y.C., 1990-2005, chmn. bd., 1994-97. Pres. No. Berkshire Indsl. Devel. Corp., 1965-67; commr. Mass. Cmty. Antenna TV Commn., 1972-74; trustee Mass. Coll. Liberal Arts, 1991-2001, vice chmn. bd. trustees, 1993-96, chmn., 1996-2001. Recipient Laymen's award Vt. Tchrs. Assn., 1958; Laymen's award Mass. Tchrs. Assn., 1962; Abe Lincoln Merit award So. Baptist Radio and TV Commn., 1975; named Man of Yr. Vt. Assn. Broadcasters, 1978 Mem. North Adams C. of C. (Hayden award 1967, pres. 1964-67), Nat. Assn. Broadcasters (dir. 1965-69, 73-77, chmn. radio 1976-77, chmn. bd., chmn. exec. com. 1977-79, Disting. Svc. award 1980), Mass. Broadcasters Assn. (pres. 1964, Disting. Svc. award 1964, 71, 78), Taconic Golf Club (Williamstown, Mass.; bd. dirs. 1975-89). Republican. Methodist. Office: 61 Main St PO Box 386 North Adams MA 01247-0386 *My goals have been to better my community, profession and life in general because I was a positive participant, and to provide independence, a sense of responsibility and a love of humanity for my family.*

**THURSTON, GEORGE BUTTE,** mechanical and biomedical engineering educator; b. Austin, Tex., Oct. 8, 1924; s. Rudolph D. and Olivia Ruth (Lester) T.; m. Carol A. McWharter, Apr. 5, 1947; children— John Douglas, Mary Elizabeth. BS, U. Tex., Austin, 1944, MA, 1948, PhD, 1952. Registered profl. engr., Tex. Supr. hydroacoustics Def. Rsch. Lab., U. Tex., Austin, 1949-52; asst. prof. physics U. Wyo., Laramie, 1952-53, U. Ark., Fayetteville, 1953-54; physicist Naval Ordnance Test Sta., Inyokern, Calif., 1954-55; assoc. prof. Okla. U. Stillwater, 1954-59; rsch. physicist U. Mich., Ann Arbor, 1958-59; prof. Okla. State U., 1959-68; vis. scientist Centre de Recherche sur les Macromolecules, Strasbourg, France, 1963-64; prof. mech. engring. and biomed. engring. U. Tex., Austin, 1968—; pres. Vilastic Scientific, Inc. Vis. prof. Helmholtz Inst. fur Biomedizinsche Technik, Aachen, West Germany, 1975-76; cons. for govt., industry. Contbr. articles to profl. jours. Recipient Brown U. Calculus prize, 1942; Alexander von Humboldt Found. Sr. U.S. Scientist award, 1975; NSF faculty fellow, 1963-64; numerous grants. Fellow Am. Phys. Soc., Acoustical Soc. Am.; mem. ASME, Soc. Rheology, Internat. Soc. Biorheology, Brit. Soc. Rheology, Sigma Xi, Sigma Pi Sigma. Home: 1000 Madrone Rd Austin TX 78746-4320 Office: U Tex Dept Mech Engring Austin TX 78712

**THURSTON, REBECCA CLARK,** psychologist; BA, Stanford U., Palo Alto, Calif., 1996; PhD, Duke U., Durham, N.C., 2003. Scholar Harvard U., Cambridge, Mass., 2003—05; asst. prof. psychiatry and epidemiology Sch. Medicine U. Pitts. Sch., 2006—. Scholar, Robert Wood Johnson Found., 2003—05; James B. Duke fellow, Duke U., 1998—2003. Mem.: Phi Beta Kappa. Business E-Mail: thurstonrc@upmc.edu.

**THURSTON, SALLY A.,** lawyer; b. Glens Falls, N.Y., 1961; BS, Cornell U., 1983; JD, Harvard U., 1986. Bar: N.Y. 1987. Ptnr. Skadden, Arps, Slate, Meagher & Flom, N.Y.C.; v.p. tax counsel NBC, Inc., N.Y.C., 1994—. Office: Skadden Arps Slate Meagher & Flom LLP 4 Times Sq New York NY 10036-6595 Business E-Mail: sthursto@skadden.com.

**THURSTON, STEPHEN JOHN,** pastor; b. Chgo., July 20, 1952; s. John Lee and Ruth (Hall) T.; m. Joyce DeVonne Hand, June 18, 1977; children: Stephen John II, Nicole D'Vaugh, Teniece Rael, Christian Avery Elijah. BA in Religion, Bishop Coll., 1975; Hon. degree, Chgo. Baptist Inst., 1986. Co-pastor New Covenant Missionary Bapt. Ch., Chgo., 1975-79, pastor, 1979—; pres. National Baptist Convention, Inc. Third v.p. Nat. Bapt. Conv. Am., mem. exec. com. Christian Edn. Congress; pres. Ill. Nat. Bapt. State Conv.; mem. Christian Fellowship Dist. Assn.; lectr. various orgns.; instr. New Covenant Bapt. Ch., Fellowship Bapt. Ch. Co-chmn. religious affairs div. People United to Save Humanity (PUSH); bd. dir. nat. alumni assn. Bishop Coll.; active NAACP; trustee, fin. chmn. Chgo. Bapt. Inst. Named one of 100 Most Influential Black Americans, Ebony mag., 2006. Mem. Broadcast Ministers Alliance, Bapt. Ministers Conf. Chgo. (Ministerial Pioneer award). Clubs: Bishop Coll. (Chgo.). Office: New Cov Miss Baptist Church 740 E 77th St Chicago IL 60619-2553*

**THURSTON, THOM BUSTER,** economics professor, consultant; b. Kans. City, Mo., Sept. 11, 1943; s. Marion Foster and Virginia Buster Thurston; m. Yoko Katagiri Thurston, June 2, 2006; 1 child, Tobias Katagiri. BA, Harvard U., Cambridge, Mass., 1965; PhD in Econs., U. Calif., Berkeley, Calif., 1970. Prof. Queens Coll. CUNY, Flushing, NY, 1971—, exec. officer PhD Program NYC, 2000—. Contbr. articles to profl. jours. Capt. U.S. Army, 1972. Avocations: piano, running, languages. Office: Economics Program CUNY Graduate Cntr 365 5th Ave New York NY 10016 Office Phone: 212-817-8256. Business E-Mail: tthurston@gc.cuny.edu.

**THURSTON, WILLIAM PAUL,** mathematician; b. Washington, Oct. 30, 1946; s. Paul Ambrose and Margaret (Martt) Thurston; m. Karen T. Barris, Dec. 10, 1993; children: Hannah, Nathaniel, Dylan, Emily. BS, New Coll., Sarasota, Fla., 1967; PhD, U. Calif., Berkeley, 1972. Mem. Inst. Advanced Study, Princeton, NJ, 1972—73; asst. prof. Sloan fellow MIT, Cambridge, 1973—74; prof. math. Princeton (N.J.) U., 1974—91, U. Calif., Berkeley, 1991—96, dir. Math. Sci. Rsch. Inst., 1992—96, prof. math Davis, 1996—2003; prof. Dept. Math. & Faculty of Computing and Info. Sci. Cornell U., 2003—. Recipient Waterman award, NSF, Fields medal, IMU, 1982. Fellow: Am. Acad. Sci., Nat. Acad. Scis.; mem.: Am. Math. Soc. (Oswald Veblen Geometry Prize 1976). Democrat. E-mail: wpt@math.ucdavis.edu.

**THYDEN, JAMES ESKEL,** diplomat, educator, lecturer; b. LA, Apr. 10, 1939; s. Eskel A. and Mildred Aileene (Rock) T.; m. Patricia Irene Kelsey, Dec. 15, 1959; children: Teresa Lynn, Janice Kay, James Blaine. BA in Biology, Pepperdine U., 1961; MA in Scandinavian Area Studies, U. Wash., 1992. Tchr. Gompers Jr. High Sch., L.A., 1962-64; fgn. svc. officer U.S. Dept. State, Washington, 1964-90; rschr. U. Wash., Seattle, 1992-93; exec. dir. Seattle chpt. UN Assn. 1993-96; affiliat prof. internat. studies Jackson Sch. U. Wash., 2006—. Travel lectr. Cunard Lines' Royal Viking Sun, 1995, and Royal Caribbean's Splendour of the Seas, 1997. Editor govt. report, ann. human rights reports, 1983-86; author, editor in-house govt. reports, documents. Dir. Office of Human Rights, 1983-86; counselor Embassy for Polit. Affairs, Am. Embassy, Oslo, Norway, 1986-90. Named to Outstanding Young Men Am., 1969, Alumnus of Yr., Pepperdine U., 1984. Mem.: Edmonds Libr. Bd., Soc. Advancement of Scandinavian Studies, World Affairs Coun. Seattle, Am. Fgn. Svc. Assn. Avocations: travel, reading. Home: 5631 153rd Pl SW Edmonds WA 98026-4239

**THYM, JÜRGEN,** musicologist; b. Germany, July 2, 1943; came to U.S., 1969; s. Heinrich and Brunhilde T; m. Peggy Dettwiler, June 6, 1992. Diploma in Schulmusik, Berlin Hochschule für Musik, 1967; diploma in history, Berlin Freie U., 1969; PhD in Musicology, Case Western Reserve U., 1974. Vis. instr. Oberlin (Ohio) Coll., 1973-74; asst. prof., 1974-80, assoc. prof., 1980-89, chmn. dept. musicology, 1982-2000, prof. emeritus, 2003—.

Cons. Ednl. Testing Svc., Princeton, N.J., 1980-87. Co-translator: Kirnberger's Art of Strict Composition, 1982 (Deems-Taylor award ASCAP 1983), Schenker's Counterpoint, 1987, Luca Lombardi Construction of Freedom and Other Writings, 2006; editor: (scores) Schoenberg's Collected Works Vols. XIII and XIV, 100 Years of Eichendorff Songs, 1984; contbr. numerous articles on text-music rels., German Lied, Schubert, Schumann, Brahms, others to profl. jours. Mem. Am. Musicological Soc. (adv. coun. 1985-90, AMS '50 com. 1987-92), Word Music Assn., Lyrica. Episcopalian. Avocations: photography, travel. Office: Eastman Sch of Music 26 Gibbs St Rochester NY 14604-2599 Office Phone: 585-274-1450. Personal E-Mail: jthy@aol.com.

**TIAHRT, TODD (W. TODD TIAHRT),** congressman, former state senator; b. Vermillion, SD, June 15, 1951; s. Wilbur E. and Sara Ella Marcine (Steele) T.; m. Vicki Lyn Holland, Aug. 14, 1976; children: Jessica, John, Luke. Student, SD Sch. Mines & Tech., Rapid City, 1969-72; BA, Evangel Coll., 1975; MBA, S.W. Mo. State U., 1989. Property estimator Crawford & Co., Springfield, Mo., 1975-78; project engr. Zenith Electronics, Springfield, 1978-81; cost engr. Boeing, Wichita, Kans., 1981-94, proposal mgr., 1991-94; state senator State of Kans., Topeka, 1993—95; mem. US Congress from 4th Kans. dist., Washington, 1995—; mem. appropriations com., 1997—. Chmn. 4th dist. Rep. party, 1990-92; exec. com. Kans. Rep. party, 1990-92, nat. security com., sci. com. Mem. Pachyderm (bd. dirs. 1991-92), Delta Sigma Phi. Republican. Office: US Ho Reps 2441 Rayburn Ho Office Bldg Washington DC 20515-1604*

**TIAN, FEI-RAN,** mathematician, educator; BS in Math., Jinan U., China, 1984; MS in Math., Clarkson U., 1987; PhD in Math., Courant Inst., 1991. Assoc. prof. math. Ohio State U., 2002—; Dicikson instr. math. U. Chgo., 1991—93; postdoctoral staff MSRI, 1993—94; vis. mem. Courant Inst., 1994—95; asst. prof. math. Ohio State U., 1995—2002, assoc. prof. math., 2002—. Fellow, John Simon Guggenheim Meml. Found., 2003. Office: Ohio State Univ Dept Math 231 W 18th Ave Columbus OH 43210*

**TIAN, GANG,** mathematics professor; BS, Nanking U., 1982; MS, Beijing U., 1984; PhD, Harvard U., 1988. Asst. prof. math. Princeton U., NJ, 1988—90; assoc. prof. math. SUNY, Stony Brook, NY, 1990—91, NYU Courant Inst. Math. and Sci., NYC, 1991—92, prof. math., 1992-95, MIT, Cambridge, 1995—96, Simons prof. math., 1996—. Visiting mem. Institute for Advanced Study, Princeton, 1988—89, 1998, Inst. Hautes Etudes Sci., Paris, 1991; visiting prof. Stanford U., 1994; prof. Math. Inst. Academia Sinica, China, 1988—, Peking U., Beijing, 1991—. Editor Pacific Jour. Math., 1994-, Comm. in Analysis & Geometry, 1994-, Geometry & Topology, 1996-; assoc. editor Jour. Am. Math. Soc., 1995-, Internat. Math. Rsch. Notices, 1996-. Recipient Alfred P. Sloan Found. Doctoral Dissertation Fellowship, 1987, Alan T. Waterman award NSF, 1994, Velben Geometry prize Am. Math. Soc., 1996. Fellow: Am. Acad. Arts & Sciences. Office: MIT Dept Math 77 Massachusetts Ave Cambridge MA 02139-4307

**TIAN, HANQIN,** ecologist, educator; b. Jinyun, China, May 7, 1962; arrived in USA, 1991, permanent resident, 2006; s. Chen Tian and QiaoRui Chen; m. Shufen Pan, Dec. 14, 1988; children: Tina, Alex. BS, Zhejiang U., Hangzhou, China, 1982; MS, Chinese Acad. Agrl. Scis., Beijing, China, 1986; PhD, SUNY, Syracuse, 1996. Rsch. asst. Zhejiang Jinyun Inst. Agrl. Scis., Jinyun, 1982—83; asst. prof. China Nat. Rice Rsch. Inst., Hangzhou, 1986—88; rsch. asst. Beijing Forestry Inst., 1988—91; postdoctoral scientist Marine Biol. Lab., Woods Hole, Mass., 1995—98, staff scientist, 1998—2001; assoc. prof. The U. Kans., Lawrence, Kans., 2001—03; prof. Auburn U., Ala., 2003—. Mem.: Am. Assn. for Advancement Sci., Am. Geophysical Union, Ecological Soc. Am. Office: Auburn Univ 602 Duncan Dr Auburn AL 36849 Office Phone: 334-844-1059. Office Fax: 334-844-1084. Business E-Mail: tianhan@auburn.edu.

**TIAN, HONGQI,** application developer, researcher; arrived in U.S., 2001; s. Tao Tian and Fengkun Li; m. Yan Li; children: Annie Miao, Tony Run. BS, Huazhong U. Sci. Tech., Wuhan, 1982, Master, 1984, PhD, 1989. Rschr. Chiba (Japan) U., 1991—94; sr. rsch. engr. Seiko Instruments Inc., Chiba, 1994—96; sr. software engr. Digital Dispatch Sys., Richmond, BC, Canada, 1997—2000, Digital Control Inc., Kent, Wash., 2001—. Author: (book) Sliding Mode Control, 1994. Mem.: NY Acad. Sci. Achievements include patents for sliding mode control of magnetic bearing sys. Home: 14245 60th St SE Bellevue WA 98006 Personal E-Mail: hongqi_tian@hotmail.com.

**TIAN, LI,** computer company executive, educator; arrived in U.S., 1996; m. Min Shi, Apr. 20, 2001. B in Engring., Tsinghua U., Beijing, 1993; M in Engring., Beijing U. Aeronautics & Astronautics, 1996; MS in Info. Sys., George Mason U., 1999; MBA, U. Chgo., 2006—. Cert. sys. engr., database adminstr., solution developer Microsoft; project mgmt. profl. Project Mgmt. Inst. Gen. mgr. multimedia tech. Beijing Feitian Inst. New Tech., 1993—96; software engr. GTSI Corp., Chantilly, Va., 1998; project cons. MCI Comm. Corp., Pentagon City, Va., 1998; supr. systems/infrastructure Airlines Reporting Corp., Arlington, Va., 1998—; faculty U. Phoenix, 2002—; founder, CEO Dcom Solutions, Llc, Fairfax, Va., 2001—. Industry advisor and virtual mentor Mgmt. Leadership Tomorrow, N.Y.C., 2005—; dir. internat. Rsch. Assn., Cambridge, Mass., 2005—; treas. Fairfax Ctr. Recreation Assn., Inc., 2005—; team leader beta program Microsoft, 2001—; v.p. project mgmt. Inst. Diversity SIG, Newtown Sq., Pa., 2005—. Vol. Ctr. Internat. Disaster Info. Arlington, 2003—; pres. Washington organizing com. U.S.-China People Friendship Assn., Fairfax, 2005—. Recipient Software Excellence award, 1996. Mem.: IEEE (sr.), Project Mgmt. Inst., Assn. Computing Machinery (Spl. Interest Group MIS), PA SQL Server, IEEE Control Sys. Soc. (sr.), IEEE Info. Theory Soc. (sr.), IEEE Engring. Mgmt. Soc. (sr.), IEEE Edn. Soc. (sr.), IEEE Computer Soc. (sr.), IEEE Comm. Soc. (sr.). Achievements include development of GTSI.COM, GTSIEXPRESS.COM and MCI ISC Online; C/C++ class libraries for modeling and operation of dimensions and tolerances; computer aided road design system; multimedia general information management software system. Personal E-Mail: ltian01@gmail.com.

**TIANO, ANTHONY STEVEN,** television producer, publishing executive; b. Santa Fe, Mar. 27, 1941; s. Joseph A. and Marian (Adlesperger) T.; m. Kathleen O'Brien, Dec. 29, 1972; children: Mark A., A. Steven. BA, U. N.Mex., 1969, MA, 1971; LittD (hon.), Calif. Sch. Profl. Psychology, 1985. Dir. programming Sta. KNME-TV U. N.Mex., Albuquerque, 1968-72; sta. mgr. Sta. WHA-TV U. Wis., Madison, 1972-76; exec. dir. Sta. KETC-TV, St. Louis, 1976-78; pres., CEO KQED, Inc., San Francisco, 1978-93; chmn., CEO Santa Fe Ventures, Inc., San Francisco, 1993—2003; CEO Santa Fe Prodns., Inc., Albuquerque, 2003—. Vice-chair bd. dirs. Calif. Sch. Profl. Psychology, San Francisco, 1985-90. Mem. Nat. Assn. Pub. TV Stas. (vice chair bd. dirs. 1986). Office: Santa Fe Prodns Inc 83114 Calle Pizaflor NW Albuquerque NM 87120

**TIANO, LINDA V.,** lawyer; b. 1957; BA summa cum laude, U. Cin.; JD cum laude, Boston U. Assoc. Epstein Becker and Green, P.C., 1981—90, ptnr., stockholder, 1990—92; v.p. for legal and govt. affairs, gen counsel MVP Health Plan, 1992—95; sr. v.p., gen. counsel Empire BlueCross BlueShield, 1995—, WellChoice, Inc., 2002—. Office: WellChoice Inc 11 W 42nd St New York NY 10036

**TIBA, AMER,** research scientist; s. Abdul Razak Tiba and Badiah Arafah Sayd; m. Taghrid Horbol, Apr. 19, 1968; children: Al Maiden, Sarah. PhD, Ohio State U., Columbus, 1998. Rschr. Ea. Mich. U., Ypsilanti, 1989—91, Ohio State U., Columbus, 1991—98, Bisco Inc., Schaumburg, Ill., 1999—2000, Naval Rsch. Inst., Great Lakes, Ill., 2002—. Cons. Bosworth Co., Skokie, Ill., 2002—; reviewer, judge Mil. Medicine Mag. Contbr. articles to profl. pubs. Recipient Golden medal, Naval Rsch. Inst., 2006, Naval Med. Rsch., 2005, Rsch. Asst. scholarship, Ohio State U., 1992—98, tchg. scholarship, Ea. Mich. U., 1989—91. Mem.: Internat. Dental Rsch. Soc., Am. Dental Rsch. Soc. (assoc). Achievements include invention of Dental Dressing For War Fighters; development of AquaBondTM, Dental Bonding Agent; Gorilla Seal,

Dental Sealant; AELITE LS, Dental composite filling; Trauma Dental Splint. Home: 1002 W Washington Ave Lake Bluff IL 60044 Office: Naval Rsch Inst Bldg 1-H 310a B St Great Lakes IL 60088 Office Phone: 847-688-5647 189. Office Fax: 847-688-4279. Personal E-mail: amer.tiba@gmail.com. E-mail: atiba@nidbr.med.navy.mil.

**TIBBLE, DOUGLAS CLAIR,** lawyer; b. Joliet, Ill., May 26, 1952; BA, DePaul U., 1974; JD, Syracuse U., 1977. Bar: Ill., US Dist. Ct. (no. dist.) Ill., US Ct. Appeals (7th cir.), US Supreme Ct. Ptnr. McBride, Baker & Coles, Oakbrook Terrace, Ill., 1996—2003, Brooks, Adams and Tarulis, Naperville, Ill., 2003—. Mem. ABA, DuPage County Bar Assn., Illinois State Bar Assn. Office: Brooks Adams and Tarulis 101 N Washington St Naperville IL 60540-4511 Office Phone: 630-355-2101.

**TIBBS, MARTHA JANE PULLEN,** civic worker, retired social worker; b. Memphis, Feb. 12, 1932; d. John Thomas Jr. and Martha Frances (Gragg) Pullen; m. Eugene Edward Tibbs; children: Martha Katherine, Eugene Edward Jr. BSBA, U. Tenn., 1953; MA Edn., U. Memphis, 1958. Cert. tchr., social worker, Tenn. Tchr. Lausanne Sch., Memphis, 1954-55, Millington H.S., Memphis, 1955-56, Presbyn. Day Sch., Memphis, 1956-57, St. Mary's Episcopal Sch., Memphis, 1958-60; social worker Tenn. Dept. Pub. Welfare, Memphis, 1962-63. Author geneal. works. Mem. Memphis Vol. Svc. Bd., 1963-64; mem. Shelby County Hist. Comm., 1983-97, commr., 1983—; block worker Cancer, Kidney and Heart Fund, Memphis, 1984—.; sec., treas. Eastland Presbyterian Ch. Mem.: DAR (past chpt. regent, sec.-treas. regents coun.), AAUW, NEA, Tenn. Geneal. Soc., Tenn. Tchrs. Assn., Colonial Dames of Am., Memphis Scottish Soc., Sovereign Colonial Soc. Ams. Royal Descent, Tenn. State Dames of Ct. of Honor (pres. 2003—05, historian, 1st v.p., nat. def. chmn.), Cleve. Med. Aux. (sec./treas.), West Tenn. Hist. Soc., Chicasaw Dist. DAR Sch. (Tenn. state vice chmn. DAR schs., parliamentarian Zachariah Davies chpt., chmn. Zachariah Davies chpt.), Nat. Registrar Daus. of Founders and Patriots Am. (past Tenn. state registrar 2006—, v.p. Tenn. chpt.), Tenn. State Registrar Founders and Patriots (pres. 2003—), Nat. Soc. Colonial Dames XVII Century (1st v.p., pres. 2003—, 2d v.p. past treas. Chucaqua chpt.), Nat. Soc. So. Dames Am. (historian 2001—02, sec. 2002—, past pres. Memphis chpt., past state pres.), Colonial Dames Am., Tenn. State DAR (transp. chmn. 2001—), Cleve. Jr. Aux., Colonial Order of Crown, Soc. Descendants of Knights Most Noble Order of Garter, Family of Bruce Soc., Planetgenet Soc., Am. Clan Donald Soc., Am. Clan Gregor Soc., Tenn. Soc. Pres. Founders and Patriots of Am., Nat. Soc. Magna Charta Dames and Barons (past state sec. 2000—02, past Magna Carta sec. West Tenn. chpt. 2001—02, treas. West Tenn. chpt. 2002—04), Cleve. Garden Club (past pres.), U. Club Memphis, Early Settlers Shelby County (registrar 1988, bd. dirs. 1992—, sec. 1998—, pres. 2002—), Nineteenth Century Club (newsletter editor 1985—88, sec. 1993—95, corr. sec. 1999—), Racquet Club, Cleve. Women's Club, Alpha Omega Pi. Republican. Presbyterian. Avocations: art, genealogy, computers, dance, tennis. Home: 2008 Massey Rd Memphis TN 38119-6404 Personal E-mail: mtptmem@aol.com.

**TIBERI, PATRICK JOSEPH,** congressman, former state legislator; b. Columbus, Ohio, Oct. 21, 1962; m. Denice Tiberi; 1 child. BA in Journalism, Ohio State U., 1985; HHD (hon.), Capital U., 2005. Realtor ReMax Achievers; asst. dist. mgr. Staff of US Rep. John Kasich; mem. Ohio State Ho. Reps. from Dist. 26, 1993—2001, majority leader; mem. ins. and vets. affairs coms. Ohio Ho. Reps.; mem. US Congress from 12th Ohio dist., 2001—, mem. fin. svcs. com., mem. edn. and the workforce com., chmn. select edn. subcommittee. Mem. adv. bd. Columbus chpt. ARC, Columbus Italian Cultural Ctr.; pres., co-founder Windsor Terrace Learning Ctr. Recipient Pres.'s award Northland Cmty. Coun., Vet. Admin Commendation award, Svc. award ARC, Watchdog of Treas. award United Conservatives of Ohio, Giving from the Heart award Alzheimer's Assn. Ctrl. Ohio Chpt. Mem. Sons of Italy. Republican. Roman Catholic. Office: US Ho Reps 113 Cannon Ho Office Bldg Washington DC 20515-3512 Office Phone: 202-225-5355.*

**TIBERIO, RONALD SETH,** mathematics educator; s. Settimeo Joseph Tiberio and Grace Felicitas Altobelli; m. Sheila Lois Tiberio, Aug. 8, 1970; children: Stephanie Lee Thorpe, Ronald Seth Jr. BS, U. Mass., 1968. Math. instr. Wellesley (Mass.) HS, 1972—. Resident faculty mem. young scholars program Rutgers (NJ) U., 2001—04; vis. scholar Worcester Poly. Inst., 1989. With US Army, 1969—70, Vietnam. Decorated Army Commendation medal with oak leaf cluster US Army; recipient Redfield award, Wellesley HS, 1987, Crockett award for Excellence in Edn., 1991. Mem.: VFW (life), Am. Statis. Assn., Nat. Coun. Tchrs. Math., Math. Assn. of Am., Am. Math. Soc., Elks.

**TIBURZI, PAUL A.,** lawyer; b. Balt., May 28, 1955; BA, Loyola Coll., 1977; JD with honors, Univ. Md., 1980. Bar: Md. 1980. Law clk. Chief Judge Harrison L. Winter, US Ct. Appeals 4th cir.; ptnr., chmn. State Legis. & Public Policy practice group, office mng. ptnr. DLA Piper Rudnick Gray Cary, Balt. Editor (in chief): Md. Law Rev.; mem. adv. bd. Rev. of Md. Laws; contbr. articles to profl. jours. Mem. transition team for Md. Gov. William Donald Schaefer, 1986; chmn. Commn. to Revise Md. Adminstry. Procedure Act, 1991—92, Md. State Adv. Council on Adminstry. Hearings; mem. Md. Governor's Task Force on Self-Insurance, 1987, Animal Testing, 1989, Procurement Law, 1995—96, Regulatory Reform, 2000—01; mem. Md. Gen. Assembly Code Revision Com. for Public Ethics Law, 1995, for Pub. Svc. Commn. Law, 1998; chmn. Md. St. of C. Task Force on Md. Public Ethics Law. Mem.: Wranglers Law Club, Council on Mgmt. & Productivity, Order of the Coif. Office: DLA Piper Rudnick Gray Cary 6225 Smith Ave Baltimore MD 21209-3600 Office Phone: 410-580-4273. Office Fax: 410-580-3001. Business E-Mail: paul.tiburzi@dlapiper.com.

**TICE, BRADLEY SCOTT,** humanities educator; b. Palo Alto, Calif., Oct. 6, 1959; s. Lilburn Trent and Paula Nanette (Osborne) T. AA, De Anza Coll., Cupertino, Calif., 1983, AA, 1995; AA in Liberal Arts, West Valley Coll., 2003; BA in History, San Jose State U., 1987; PhD in Chemistry, Fairfax U., Baton Rouge, 1996; Diploma in Ayurvedic Medicine, The Ayurvedic Inst.; Diploma in Stress therapy, Internat. Yoga Sch.; LittD in Tchg., St. Clements Univ., The Carribean, 1998; PhD in Elec. Engring., Cambridge State U., 2001, Northwestern Internat. U., Denmark, 2003, PhD in Math., 2003, PhD in Telecomm., 2003, PhD (hon.) in Physics, 2003; M in Law, Northwestern Internat. U., 2003; JD, Northwestern Internat. U., Denmark, 2002; MBA, Suffield U., Twin Falls, Idaho, 2006, PhD in Molecular Biology, 2006. Cert. Cmty. Emergency Response Tng., Cupertino, Calif. Mem. staff Stanford Linear Accelerator Ctr., 1981-87, intern archives dept. Menlo Park, Calif., 1991; prof. Pacific Lang. Inst., Cupertino, Calif., 1992—; dir. rsch. Advanced Human Design, Cupertino, 1992—; CEO Tice Pharms., San Jose; intern Ames Rsch. Ctr. NASA, Moffett Field, Calif., 1997-98, mission specialist astronaut candidate, 2001—04; substitute instr. Palo Alto (Calif.) Unified Sch. Dist., 2001; assoc. Ames-NASA Rsch. Ctr., Moffett Field, Calif., 2003; instrnl. student asst. Calif. State U. Stanislaus, Turlock, 2004—05. Substitute libr. Robert Crown Law Libr. Stanford U., 1989; substitute instr. San Jose Unified Sch. Dist., 2002, Turlock Unified Sch. Dist., Calif., 2004—05; adj. prof. Sch. Arts and Scis. Nat. U., San Jose, 2000—01; adj. prof. Nat. Hispanic U., San Jose, 2000—03, mem. faculty senate; grand awards judge engring. Intel Internat. Sci. and Engring. Fair, Louisville, 2002; mem. staff San Jose Giants Baseball Club, 2002; substitute tchr. Turlock Unified Sch. Dist., 2004—05; instrnl. student asst. Calif. State U., Turlock, 2005. Editor: Jour. Pacific Lang. Inst., 1995—96; mem. editl. bd. The Story of Life; contbr. articles to profl. jours. With Boy Scouts Am., 1972—75; vol. De Young Mus., San Francisco, 1990, Mus. Modern Art, San Francisco, 1990, Calif. Acad. Scis., San Francisco 1990, Nat. Steinbeck Ctr., Salinas, Calif.; vol. guide Monterey Bay Aquarium, 1990; elected mem. Cupertino Pub. Safety Commn., 2000—02; mem. Santa Clara County Sheriff's Citizens Acad., San Jose, 2002; apptd. mem. Turlock City Arts Commn., 2004—06; candidate for bd. trustees Foothill-De Anza CC Dist., Los Altos Hills, Calif., 2002; grand awards judge in chemistry Intel Internat. Sci. and Engring. Fair, San Jose, 2001; investor in preservation Cupertino Computer History Mus., Moffett Field, Calif., 2001. Recipient Pres.'s award Nat. Author's Registry, 1996, editor's choice award (3), The Nat. Libr. of Poetry, 1995, (2), 1996, Cert. Merit for essay, Pharmacia Biotech and Sci. prize for young scientists, 1997, Commemorative

Medal Honor, Hallmark, 2000, Jr. Engr. award A.G. Spalding and Bros., 1965; elected Order of Internat. Ambs., 1999, Internat. Man of the Year (medal of hon.), 1996, 97, Man of the Year (commemorative medal award), 1997, Internat. Order Merit, 2000, Commemmorative medal of honor Hallmark, 2000, Noble Prize Outstanding Achievement and Contbns. to Humanity, United Cultural Conv., Raleigh, N.C., 2001. Fellow Am. Coll. Metaphys. Theology; em. ACS, IEEE, AIAA, COSPAR (mem. com. space rsch.), Am. Physical Soc., N.Y. Acad. Scis., Assn. Computing Machinery, Am. Soc. Microbiology, Internat. Assn. Tchrs. English as a Fgn. Lang., Internat. Soc. Poets, Mars Soc. (found. mem.), Calif. Assn. for Health, Phys. Edn., Recreation and Dance (v.p. elect for recreation 1999), Internat. Pankration Assn. (founder), Kurt Godel Soc. Avocations: weight training, fencing, bicycling, swimming, scuba diving.

**TICE, DOUGLAS OSCAR, JR.,** federal bankruptcy judge; b. Lexington, N.C., May 2, 1933; s. Douglas Oscar Sr. and Lila Clayton (Wright) T.; m. Janet N. Capps, Feb. 28, 1959 (div. Sept. 1976); children: Douglas Oscar III, Janet E.; m. Martha Murdoch Edwards, June 8, 1996. BS, U. N.C., 1955, JD, 1957. Bar: N.C. 1957, U.S. Ct. Appeals (4th cir.) 1964, Va. 1970, U.S. Dist. ct. (ea. dist.) Va. 1976, U.S. Bankruptcy Ct. (ea. dist.) Va. 1976. Exec. sec. N.C. Jud. Coun., Raleigh, 1958-59; assoc. Baucom & Adams, Raleigh, 1959-61; trial atty. Office Dist. Coun., IRS, Richmond, Va., 1961-70; corp. atty. Carlton Industries, Inc., Richmond, 1970-75; ptnr. Hubard, Tice, Marchant & Samuels, P.C., Richmond, 1975-87; judge U.S. Bankruptcy Ct. (ea. dist.) Richmond, Norfolk, Alexandria, Va., 1987-99, chief judge, 1999—. Co-author: Monument & Boulevard, Richmond's Grand Avenues, 1996; contbr. articles to profl. jours. Vice pres. Richmond Pub. Forum, 1976-80, com. chmn. Richmond Forum, Inc., 1986-2001; past pres. Richmond Civil War Roundtable, mem., 1965—; bd. dirs. Epilepsy Assn. Va., Inc., 1976-87. Capt. USAR, 1957-66. Fellow Am. Coll. Bankruptcy; mem. ABA, Va. Bar Assns., City of Richmond Bar Assn., Am. Bankruptcy Inst., Nat. Conf. Bankruptcy Judges (bd. govs.), So. Hist. Assn., Va. Hist. Soc., Old Dominion Sertoma (pres. Richmond chpt. 1967), Comml. Law League Am., Supreme Ct. Hist. Soc., State-Fed. Jud. Coun. Va., Am. Inn of Ct., Hist. Soc. of U.S. Dist. Ct. for Eastern Va. (assn. sec., bd. dir. mem. 2006—). Home: 5 Foxmere Dr Richmond VA 23238 Office: US Bankruptcy Ct 1100 E Main St Ste 339 Richmond VA 23219-3538 Office Phone: 804-916-2460. Personal E-mail: thetices2@comcast.net. Business E-Mail: douglas_tice@vaeb.uscourts.gov.

**TICE, GEORGE A(NDREW),** photographer; b. Newark, Oct. 13, 1938; s. William S. and Margaret T. (Robertson) T.; m. Joanna Blaylock, 1958; m. Marie Tremmel, 1960; children: Christopher, Loretta, Lisa, Lynn, Jennifer. DHL (hon.), William Paterson U., 2003. Instr. photography New Sch. Social Research, 1970-98. Photographer (one-man shows) Met. Mus. Art, 1972, internat. Ctr. Photography, 2002, Newark Mus., 2006, (group shows) Whitney Mus. Am. Art, 1974, Mus. Modern Art, 1979, (permanent collections), Met. Mus. Art, Art Inst. Chgo., Bibliotheque Nationale, Nihon U., Tokyo, books include Fields of Peace, 1970, Fields of Peace, reissued, 1998, Goodbye River, Goodbye, 1971, Paterson, 1972, Seacoast Maine, 1973, George A. Tice Photographs, 1953-73, 1975, Urban Landscapes, 1975, Artie Van Blarcum, 1977, Urban Romantic, 1982, Lincoln, 1984, Hometowns, 1988, Stone Walls, Grey Skies, 1991, George Tice: Selected Photographs, 1953-1999, 2001, George Tice: Urban Landscapes, 2002, Common Mementos, 2005, Paterson II, 2006. Served with USN, 1956-59. Recipient Grand prix for best photography book of Year Arles, France, 1973; Guggenheim Found. fellow, 1973-74, Nat. Endowment for Arts fellow, 1973—; Bradford fellow, Eng., 1990-91, N.J. State Coun. on the Arts fellow, 1998. Address: 581 Kings Hwy East Atlantic Highlands NJ 07716-2825 Office Phone: 732-706-3585.

**TICE, RAPHAEL DEAN,** military officer; b. Topeka, Kans., Dec. 4, 1927; s. Arthur Taylor and Mamie (McDonald) T.; m. Eunice Miriam Suddarth, Dec. 23, 1946; children: Karen Ann Tice Claterbos, William Dean. BS in Mil. Sci., U. Md., 1963; MSBA, George Washington U., 1970. Served as enlisted man U.S. Army, 1946-47; commd. 2d lt., 1947; advanced through grades to lt. gen., 1981; platoon leader and co. comdr. 1st Inf. div., W.Ger., 1949-52; co. comdr., regimental adj. 8th Inf. divsn., 1955-56; tng. advisor Vietnam, 1956-57; mem. staff Office of Dep. Chief of Staff for Pers., Dept. Army, 1960-63; chief pers. mgmt. divsn. Office of Under Sec. of Army, 1963-64; plans Officer So. Command, Panama, 1965-67; dep. comdr. 3rd Brig., 4th Inf. Divsn., 1967; comdr. 2nd Bn., 12th Inf. of 25th Inf. divsn., Vietnam, 1968; exec. for pers. procurement Office of Sec. Def. for Manpower and Res. Affairs, 1968-69; comdr. 1st Brig., 1st Inf. divsn., 1970, chief of staff, 1971; dep. dir. mil. pers. mgmt. Dept. Army, 1972-73; comdg. gen. Berlin Brigade, 1974-76; dep. chief of staff personnel U.S. Army Europe, 1976-77; comdg. gen. 3rd Inf. divsn., 1977-79; dep. asst. sec. Def. for mil. pers. and force mgmt. Dept. Def., 1979-85; exec. dir. Nat. Recreation and Pk. Assn., 1986—2001; ret., 2001. Spl. advisor Pres.'s Coun. on Phys. Fitness and Sports; bd. dirs. Sports Pub. LLC, Class 6 Kayak, Inc. Decorated Silver Star, Legion of Merit with 2 oak leaf clusters, Air medal with V and 7 oak leaf clusters, Bronze Star with V, Vietnam Cross of Gallantry with Palm, Purple Heart., Def. Disting. Service medal, Army Disting. Service medal Mem. Assn. U.S. Army, Am. Chess Found. (hon. pres.) Home: 18077 Clendenning Cir Round Hill VA 20141-2580 Personal E-mail: ticepunky@aol.com.

**TICHY, NOEL M.,** psychology professor, academic administrator; m. Patricia Stacey. BA in Psychology, Colgate U., Hamilton, N.Y., 1968; PhD in Social Psychology, Columbia U., N.Y., N.Y., 1972. Lic. psychologist N.Y. Personal asst., market rsch. asst. Bankers Trust Co., N.Y.C., 1966—67; rsch. asst. Social Psychology Program Tchr.'s Coll. Columbia U., N.Y.C., 1968—72, assoc. prof. Grad. Sch. Bus., 1972—80; assoc. Inst. Social Rsch. The U. Mich., Ann Arbor, 1980—85; prof. orgnl. devel. and human resource mgmt. chmn. and academic dir. global bus. partnership U. Mich. Ross Sch. Bus. Global Bus. Partnership, Ann Arbor, 1980—, academic dir. Bus. Sch., Exec. Edn. Ctr., 1982—90. Sr. ptnr. Action Learning Assocs.; specialist mgmt. and organl. devel. Hazard (Ky.) Family Health Svcs. Apalachian Regional Hosps., 1977—78; sr. rsch. assoc. Ctr. Policy Rsch., N.Y., 1970—80; mgr. Gen. Electric Co., Croton-on-Hudson, 1985—87; lectr. in field; mem. adv. bd. The Leadership Devel. Conf., Work in Am.; mem. editl. adv. bd. SMR, 1999—2002. Author: The Cycle of Leadership: How Great Leaders Teach Their Companies to Win, with Nancy Cardwell, Organization Design for Primary Health Care: The Case of the Dr. Martin Luther King, Jr. Health Center, "How to Hand on a Legacy of Leadership." Association for Quality and Participation, The Leadership Engine: How Winning Companies Create Leaders at All Levels, with Eli Cohen., Control Your Destiny or Someone Else Will: How Jack Welch is Making General Electric the World's Most Competitive Company, with Stratford Sherman, Global Corporate Citizenship, with Andrew R. McGill and Lynda St. Claire, The University of Michigan Business School's Guide to The Ethical Challenge: How to Lead With Unyielding Integrity, with Andy McGill, Every Business is a Growth Business, with Ram Charan., The Transformational Leader, Strategic Human Resource Management, with Charles J. Fombrun and Mary Anne Devanna, Managing Strategic Change: Technical, Political and Cultural Dynamics; editor: Human Resource Mgmt. Jour., 1981—90; mem. editl. bd.: Orgnl. Dynamics; contbr. chapters to books, articles to profl. jours. Recipient New Perspective on Exec. Leadership award, Johnson Smith & Knisley, 1987, Educator of Yr. award, Sales and Mktg. Executives Internat., 1994, Gifford Lectr. in Bus. Leadership award, Lynchburg Coll., 1994; fellow, Japan Soc., 1985. Fellow: Nat. Acad. Human Resources; mem.: APA, ASTD (bd. govs. 1985—88, Best Practice award 1993, grantee 1990—), Acad. Mgmt., Commonwealth Found. (academic advisor), Sigma Xi. Office: University of Michigan 701 Tappan Street Ann Arbor MI 48109-1234 Office Phone: 734-764-5134. Office Fax: 764-936-2196. Business E-Mail: tichy@umich.edu.

**TICK, JUDITH,** music historian, educator; Matthews Distinguished U. prof., dept. music Northeastern U., Boston, 1999—. Author: Women Making Music: The Western Art Tradition 1150-1950, 1986 (ASCAP Deems Taylor award (co-edited with Jane Bowers), 1987), Ruth Crawford Seeger: A Composer's Search for American Music, 1997 (Outstanding Academic Book,

1998, Named Best Book, Soc. Am. Music, 1998, ASCAP Deems Taylor award, 1998), articles on Charles Ives; assoc. editor for the Am. Music sect. Musical Quarterly, 1991—. Recipient Hon. Citation award for Svc., Am. Women Composer, Inc. (NY Chpt.), 1993. Mem.: Am. Acad. Arts and Scis. Office: Dept Music Northeastern U 351 Ryder Hall Boston MA 02115 Office Phone: 617-373-8537. Office Fax: 617-373-4129. Business E-Mail: j.tick@neu.edu.

**TICKNOR, CAROLYN M.,** computer company executive; BA in Psychology, U. Redlands, Calif.; MA in Indsl. Psychology, San Francisco State U.; MBA, Stanford U. From programming, ops. mgr. to pres., CEO Hewlett-Packard Co., Palo Alto, Calif., 1977-94, pres., CEO laser jet imaging sys., 1994—. Office: Hewlett Packard Co 300 Hanover St Palo Alto CA 94304

**TICOTIN, RACHEL,** actress; b. Bronx, NY, Nov. 1, 1958; m. David Caruso, 1983 (div. 1989); 1 child; m. Peter Strauss, Dec. 31, 1998. Actor: (films) King of the Gypsies, 1978, Fort Apache the Bronx, 1981, Critical Condition, 1987, Total Recall, 1990, One Good Cop, 1991, F/X2, 1991, Where the Day Takes You, 1992, Falling Down, 1993, Criminal Passion, 1994, Don Juan DeMarco, 1995, Steal Big Steal Little, 1995, Turbulence, 1997, Con Air, 1997, Civility, 2000, Can't Be Heaven, 2000, Desert Saints, 2002, Something's Gotta Give, 2003, Man on Fire, 2004, Sisterhood of the Traveling Pants, 2005, (TV films) Love, Mary, 1985, When the Bough Breaks, 1986, Rockabye, 1986, Spies, Lies & Naked Thighs, 1988, Prison Stories: Women on the Inside, 1991, Keep the Change, 1992, From the Files of Joseph Wambaugh: A Jury of One, 1992, Thicker Than Blood: The Larry McLinden Story, 1994, Deconstructing Sarah, 1994, The Wharf Rat, 1995, First Time Felon, 1997, Aftershock: Earthquake in New York, 1999, Warden of Red Rock, 2001, (TV series) For Love and Honor, 1983, Ohara, 1987-88, Crime and Punishment, 1993, (voice) Gargoyles, 1994-96, American Family, 2002-04, Skin, 2003.

**TIDBALL, CHARLES STANLEY,** computer scientist, educator; b. Geneva, Apr. 15, 1928; (parents Am. citizens); s. Charles Taylor and Adele (Desmaison) T.; m. Mary Elizabeth Peters, Oct. 25, 1952. BA, Wesleyan U., 1950; MS (Univ. scholar), U. Rochester, 1952; PhD, U. Wis., Madison, 1955; MD (Shattuck fellow, Van Noyes scholar), U. Chgo., 1958; LHD (hon.), Wilson Coll., 1994; DSc (hon.), Hood Coll., 1999. Rotating intern Madison (Wis.) Gen. Hosp., 1958-59; physician I Mendota State Hosp., Madison, 1959; asst. research prof. physiology dept. George Washington U. Med. Center, Washington, 1959-63, USPHS spl. fellow, 1960-61, asso. prof., acting chmn. dept., 1963-64, prof., 1964-65, chmn. dept., 1964-71, Henry D. Fry prof., 1965-84, research prof. med., 1972-80; dir. Office Computer Assisted Edn. George Washington U. Med. Ctr., 1973-75, dir. Office Computer Assisted Edn. and Svcs., 1975-78; Lucie Stern disting. vis. prof. natural scis. Mills Coll., 1980; prof. edn. George Washington U., 1982-84, dir. ednl. computing tech. program Sch. Edn., 1982-84, prof. computer medicine Med. Ctr., 1984-92, prof. emeritus computer medicine, 1992, prof. neurol. surgery, 1990-92, prof. emeritus neurol. surgery, 1992; civil surgeon Immigration and Naturalization Svc., Dept. Justice, Washington, 1986-89; disting. schol., co-dir. Tidball Ctr. for Study Ednl. Environments Hood Coll., Frederick, Md., 1994—. Trustee in residence Skidmore Coll., 1995. Co-author: Consolidated Index to For Thy Great Glory, 1993, Taking Women Seriously, 1999, Jesus, Lazarus, and the Messiah, 2005; editor: (with M. C. Shelesnyak) Frontiers in the Teaching of Physiology: Computer Literacy and Simulation, 1981; mem. editorial bd. Jour. Applied Physiology, 1966-69, Jour. Computer-Based Instrn., 1974-89, Am. Jour. Physiology; assoc. editor The Physiologist, 1979-85; contbr. articles to profl. jours. Trustee Cathedral Choral Soc., 1976-79, Wilson Coll., 1983-92, Everitt-Pomeroy, 1993-96, Population Reference Bur., 1987-94, 1996-2002, chmn. bd. trustees, 1992-94, sec., 1994-97; lay reader St. Albans Parish, 1965-67, Washington Nat. Cathedral, 1967-94, lay eucharist minister, 1994—, clergy asst., 1968—, homilist, 1977—, info. sys. specialist, 1986-93, vol. mgr. info. sys. program, 1993—; mem. comm. Episcopal Diocese Washington, 1964—; mem. com. mgmt. YMCA Camp Letts, 1968-96, chmn., 1972-75; dir., chmn. Endowment Fund, 1977-96; bd. dirs. Met. YMCA, Washington, 1972-84, trustees coun., 1984-91, fin. com., 1972-93, v.p. internat. program, 1974-75, asst. treas., 1975-77, v.p., treas., 1977-79, vice chmn., 1979-80, chmn., 1980-82, pres. of found., 1991-93; bd. dirs., treas. Woodley Ensemble, 1993-2003; bd. dirs. Mid-Atlantic Region YMCA, 1974-83; bd. dirs., vice-chmn. Cathedral West Condo., 1983-84, chmn., 1984-87, 91-93, fin. com., 1979-94; bd. dirs. Buckingham's Choice Residents' Assn., 2000-02, chmn. resident svcs. com., 2000-02, mem. fin. com., 2004—. Recipient award Washington Acad. Scis., 1967, Leader of Yr. award Met. YMCA, Washington, 1974, Red Triangle award, 1994, Service award, 1979; Dakota Indian name Am. Youth Found., 1976; Research Career Devel. award USPHS, 1961-63 Mem. Am. Physiol. Soc. (emeritus). Home: 3200 Baker Cir #I-235 Adamstown MD 21710 E-mail: ctidball@gwu.edu.

**TIDBALL, M. ELIZABETH PETERS,** physiologist, educator; b. Anderson, Ind., Oct. 15, 1929; d. John Winton and Beatrice (Ryan) Peters; m. Charles S. Tidball, Oct. 25, 1952. BA, Mt. Holyoke Coll., 1951, LHD, 1976; MS, U. Wis., 1955, PhD, 1959; MTS summa cum laude, Wesley Theol. Sem., 1990; DSc (hon.), Wilson Coll., 1973, Trinity Coll., 1974, Cedar Crest Coll., 1977, U. of South, 1978, Goucher Coll., 1979, St. Mary-of-The-Woods Coll., 1986; LittD (hon.), Regis Coll., 1980, Coll. St. Catherine, 1980, Alverno Coll., 1989; HHD (hon.), St. Mary's Coll., 1977, Hood Coll., 1982; LLD (hon.), St. Joseph Coll., 1983; LHD (hon.), Skidmore Coll., 1984, Marymount Coll., 1985, Converse Coll., 1985, Mt. Vernon Coll., 1986. Tchg. asst. physiology dept. U. Wis., 1952—55, rsch. asst. physiology dept., 1958—59; rsch. asst. anatomy dept. U. Chgo., 1955-56, rsch. asst. physiology dept., 1956-58; USPHS postdoctoral fellow NIH, Bethesda, Md., 1959-61; staff pharmacologist Hazleton Labs., Falls Church, Va., 1961, cons., 1962; assoc. in physiology George Washington U. Med. Ctr., 1960-62, asst. rsch. prof. dept. pharmacology, 1962-64, assoc. rsch. prof. dept. physiology, 1964-70, rsch. prof., 1970-71, prof., 1971-94, prof. emeritus, 1994—; asst. dir. M of Theol. Studies program Wesley Theol. Sem., 1993-94; disting. rsch. scholar Hood Coll., Frederick, Md., 1994—, co-dir. Tidball Ctr. for Study of Ednl. Environments, 1994—. Lucie Stern Disting. vis. prof. natural scis. Mills Coll., 1980; scholar in residence Coll. Preachers, 1984, Salem Coll., 1985, Wesley Theol. Sem., 1992; Disting. scholar in residence So. Meth. U., 1985; vis. trustee prof. Skidmore Coll., 1995; cons. FDA, 1966-67, assoc. sci. coord. sci. assocs. tng. programs, 1966-67; cons. on NIH tng. programs and fellowships NAS, 1972-75; faculty summer confs. Am. Youth Found., 1967-78; founder, dir. Summer Seminars Women Am. Youth Found., 1987-95; cons. for instl. rsch. Wellesley Coll., 1974-75; exec. sec. com. on edn. and employment women in sci. and engring. Commn. on Human Resources, NRC/NAS, 1974-75, vice-chmn., 1977-82; cons., staff officer NRC/NAS, 1974-75; cons. Woodrow Wilson Nat. Fellowship Found., 1975-99, NSF, 1974-91; bd. mentor Assn. Governing Bds. Univs. and Colls., 1991-2000, Gale Fund for the Study of Trusteeship Adv. Comm., 1992-98; cons. Women's Coll. Coalition Rsch. Adv. Com., 1992-2000; Single Gender Schooling Working Group, US Dept. Edn., 1992-94, Women's Colls. Round-table, 1998; rep. to DC Commn. on Status of Women, 1972-75; nat. panelist Am. Coun. on Edn., 1983-90; panel mem. Congl. Office Tech. Assessment, 1986-87; fellows selection com., fellows mentor Coll. Preachers, 1992-05. Lead author: Taking Women Seriously: Lessons and Legacies for Educating the Majority, American Council on Education Higher Education Series, 1999; columnist Trusteeship, 1993-95; mem. editl. bd. Jour. Higher Edn., 1979-84, cons. editor, 1984—; mem. editl. bd. Religion and Intellectual Life, 1988—; contbr. articles to profl. jours. Trustee Mt. Holyoke Coll., 1968-73, vice chmn., 1972-73, trustee fellow, 1988—; trustee Hood Coll., 1972-84, 86-92, exec. com., 1974-84, 89-92, trustee emerita, 1997—; overseer Sweet Briar Coll., 1978-85, dir. emerita, 2003—; trustee Cathedral Choral Soc., 1976-90, pres. bd. trustees, 1982-84, hon. trustee, 1991—; trustee Skidmore Coll., 1988—, mem. exec. com., 1993—, trustee Bishop Claggett Ctr., 2003—; mem. governing bd. Coll. of Preachers, 1979-85, chmn., 1983-85; mem. governing bd. Protestant Episcopal Cathedral Found., 1983-85, mem. exec. com., 1983-85; bd. vis. Salem Coll., 1986-93; ctr. assoc. Nat. Resource Ctr. Girls Club Am., 1983-90; mem. governing bd. Buckinham's Choice Residents' Assn., 1999-2002. Named Outstanding Grad., The Penn Hall Sch.,

1988; recipient Alumnae medal Honor, Mt. Holyoke Coll., 1971, Outstanding Svc. award, Am. Youth Found., 1975, Valuable Contbns. Gen. Alumni Assn. award, George Washington U., 1982, 1987, Pres.'s medal, 1999, Chestnut Hill medal Outstanding Achievement, Chestnut Hill Coll., Phila., 1987, Lifetime Svc. and Schoalrship award, Bd. Women's Coll. Coalition and Nation's Women's Coll. Presidents, 1998, Order of Merit, Cathedral Choral Soc., 2000, Shattuk fellowship, 1955—56, Mary E. Woolley fellowship, Mt. Holyoke Coll., 1958—59, postdoctoral fellowship, USPHS, 1959—61. Mem. AAAS, Am. Physiol. Soc. (chmn. task force on women in physiology 1973-80, com. on coms. 1977-80, mem. emeritus 1994—), Am. Assn. Higher Edn., Mt. Holyoke Alumnae Assn. (dir. 1966-70, 76-77), Histamine Club, Sigma Delta Epsilon, Sigma Xi. Episcopalian. Home: 4100 Cathedral Ave NW Washington DC 20016-3584 also: 3200 Baker Cir # I-235 Adamstown MD 21710 Personal E-mail: ctidball@gwu.edu.

**TIDSWELL, MARK,** medical educator; m. Stephanie Osiecki; children: Ben K., Anna J. BA, Reed Coll., Portland, Oreg., 1982. Asst. prof. U. Calif., San Francisco, 1994—98, Tufts U. Sch. Medicine, Boston, 1998—; critical care physician Baystate Med. Ctr., Springfield, 1999—. Rsch. Baystate Med. Ctr., Springfield, Mass., 2001—. Mem.: Soc. Critical Care Medicine, Am. Thoracic Soc. Achievements include research in acute lung injury and ARDS. Office Phone: 413-794-5439. E-mail: mark.tidswell@bhs.org.

**TIDWELL, CAROLYN HOLT,** elementary school educator; b. Memphis, Tenn., May 20, 1950; d. James Benjamin Holt and Frances Janette (Halford) Holman; m. Robert Harold Tidwell. BS in Elem. Edn., Memphis State U., 1973. Cert. elem. tchr. Tenn., sch. facilitator So. Assn. Colls. and Schs./Coun. on Accreditation and Sch. Improvement. Substitute tchr. Memphis City Sch., 1973; elem. tchr. First Assembly Christian Sch., Memphis, 1973—, elem. coord., 1998—. Chair various curriculum coms. So. Assn. Colls. and Schs., 1973—76; SACS coord., 1997—; coms. Sherman (Tex.) Assembly of God Sch., 1980; sci. fair coord., 2004, 05. Commn. mem. Memphis City Beautiful, 1984. Avocation: acting. Office Phone: 901-458-5543. Business E-Mail: ctidwell@facsmemphis.org.

**TIDWELL, RUSSELL MURRAY,** secondary school educator; b. Guymon, Okla., Aug. 23, 1968; s. David L and Connie Tidwell; m. Debborah Christine Ritter, June 29, 1991; 1 child, David Michael. BA, Okla. Panhandle State U., Goodwell, 1986—93. Lic. tchr. Kans. Dept. Edn., 1994. Speech, debate, and forensics tchr./coach Garden City HS, Kans., 1994—. Steering com. Debate Coaches' Invitational Tournament, Kans., 1999—; speech dept. instrnl. leader Garden City HS, Kans., 2000—; west kans. nfl com. mem. Nat. Forensic League, Ripon, Wis., 2003—. Musician (singer) (guitiar and mandolin) various Jam Sessions, festivals, and community opportunities. Ch. musician-guitarist First So. Bapt. Ch., Garden City, Kans., 2002—04; project mgr.-growth renovation project, 2005—05, deacon, 1998—2006; help with act selection and emcee Tumbleweed Music Festival, Garden City, 2004—06. Recipient Debate Coach of Yr., Debate Coaches Invitational, 2000—01, 2003—04. Mem.: Kans. Speech Communication Assn. (licentiate), Nat. Forensic League (life; wknfl com. mem. 2004—06, Double Diamond Coach 2005). Republican. Mem. Christian Ch. Avocations: music, string instrument lutherie, gardening, woodworking. Office: Garden City HS 1412 N Main Garden City KS 67846 Office Phone: 620-276-5281. Business E-Mail: rtidwell@gckschools.com.

**TIEDE, TOM ROBERT,** journalist; b. Huron, SD, Feb. 24, 1937; s. Leslie Albert and Rose (Allen) T.; children: Kristina Anne, Thomas Patrick. BA in Journalism, Wash. State U., 1959. Mem. staff Kalispell (Mont.) Daily Interlake, 1960-61, Daytona Beach (Fla.) News Jour., 1961-63; war corr. Newspaper Enterprise Assn., N.Y.C., 1966—. Lectr. in field. Author: Your Men at War, 1965, Coward, 1968, Calley: Soldier or Killer?, 1971, Welcome to Washington, Mr. Witherspoon, 1979, The Great Whale Rescue, 1986, American Tapestry: Eye Witness Accounts of the 1900's, 1988, The Man Who Discovered Pluto, 1990, Fosser, 1994, Self Help Nation, 2001; permanent collections Boston U. Libr. Served as lt., inf. AUS, 1960. Recipient Ernie Pyle Meml. award, 1965; Freedoms Found. award, 1966; George Washington medal, 1972 Mem. Internat. Platform Assn., Sigma Delta Chi, Lambda Chi Alpha. Clubs: Overseas Press, National Press, Nat. Headliners (award 1966 Atlantic City). Roman Catholic. Office: NEA 1090 Vermont Ave NW Washington DC 20005-4905 also: The Pinery 10599 Norwood Wingina VA 24599 Personal E-mail: ttiede@mindspring.com.

**TIEDEMANN, CHARLES WELCH (CHAD TIEDEMANN),** lawyer; b. Bronxville, NY, Jan. 30, 1956; AB, U. Notre Dame, 1978; JD, Catholic U. Am., 1981. Bar: DC 1981. Nat. chair, real estate sect. Holland & Knight LLP, Washington; former chmn., nat. real estate practice development task force; ptnr. Holland & Knight LLP, Washington, chair, United Way Campaign, chair, Christmas in April House Sponsorship. Mem.: Bldg. Industry Assn. (mem. real estate group, Washington. DC), ABA, DC Bar, U. Notre Dame Alumni Club (Washington, DC). Office: Holland & Knight LLP 2099 Pennsylvania Ave NW Ste 100 Washington DC 20006 Office Phone: 202-955-3000. Business E-Mail: chad.tiedemann@hklaw.com.

**TIEDGE-LAFRANIER, JEANNE MARIE,** editor; b. N.Y.C., July 24, 1960; d. Richard Frederick and Joan Jean (Gerardo) Tiedge; m. John Daniel Lewis Lafranier, Oct. 8, 1989; children: Katelyn Ellen, John Richard. BA, Drew U., 1982. Asst. Denise Marcil Lit. Agy., N.Y.C., 1982-84; sr. editor New Am. Libr., N.Y.C., 1984-87, Warner Books, N.Y.C., 1987-95; editor corp. comm. Disticor, Ajax, Ont., Can., 1995—. Avocations: marathoner, equestrian.

**TIEDJE, JAMES MICHAEL,** microbiologist, educator, ecologist; b. Newton, Iowa, Feb. 9, 1942; married, 1965; 3 children. BS, Iowa State U., 1964; MS, Cornell U., 1966, PhD in Soil Microbiology, 1968. From asst. prof. to prof. Mich. State U., 1968-78, disting. prof., 1991—; dir. sci. and tech. ctr. microbial ecology NSF, 1988—. Vis. assoc. prof. U. Ga., 1974-75; cons. NSF, 1974-77; vis. prof. U. Calif. Berkeley, 1981-82; mem. biotech. sci. adv. com. EPA, 1986-89, chair sci. adv. com. GPA, 1988-90. Editor: Applied Microbiology, 1974—, editor-in-chief, 1980-86. Recipient Carlos J. Finley prize, UNESCO, 1993. Mem. AAAS, Am. Soc. Agronomy (Soil Sci. award 1990), Internat. Inst. Biotech., Am. Soc. Microbiology (award in applied and environ. microbiology 1992), Soil Sci. Soc. Am., Ecol. Soc. Am., Internat. Soc. Soil Sci. (chair soil biology divsn.). Achievements include research in dentrification, microbial metabolism of organic pollutants, and molecular microbiol. ecology. Office: Michigan State U Microbial Ecology Ctr 540 Plant & Soil Scis Bldg East Lansing MI 48824-1325

**TIEFEL, VIRGINIA MAY,** librarian; b. Detroit, May 20, 1926; d. Karl and June Garland (Young) Brenkert; m. Paul Martin Tiefel, Jan. 25, 1947; children: Paul Martin Jr., Mark Gregory. BA in Elem. Edn., Wayne State U., 1962; MA in Library Sci., U. Mich., 1968. Librarian Birmingham Schs., Mich., 1967-68; librarian S. Euclid-Lyndhurst Schs., Cleve., 1968-69; acquisitions-reference librarian Hiram Coll., Ohio, 1969-77; head undergrad. libraries Ohio State U., Columbus, 1977-84, dir. library user edn., 1978-95, faculty outreach coord., 1995-98. Contbr. articles to profl. jours. Recipient Disting. Alumnus award, U. Mich. Sch. Info. and Libr. Studies, 1993. Mem. ALA (v.p. Ohio sect. 1973-74, pres. 1974-75, Miriam Dudley Bibliographic Instrn. Librarian of Yr. 1986), Acad. Library Assn. Ohio (Outstanding Ohio Acad. Librarian 1984), Assn. Coll. and Research Libraries (chmn. bibliographic instrn. sect. com. on research 1983-84, chmn. com. on performance measures 1984-90). Lutheran. Achievements include Excellence in Teaching award at Ohio State University Libraries established in her honor in 2004. Home: 4711 Oak Bluff Ct Eau Claire WI 54701 E-mail: vtiefel1@aol.com.

**TIEFEL, WILLIAM REGINALD,** hotel company executive; b. Rochester, NY, Mar. 30, 1934; s. William Reginald and Mary Hazel (Cross) T.; m. Vada Morell, Dec. 30, 1985 (dec. Apr. 1999); m. Norma Gewirz Kline, Nov. 25, 2000. Student, Williams Coll., 1952-54; BA with honors, Mich. State U., 1956; postgrad., Harvard Bus. Sch.; DBA in Hospitality Mgmt. (hon.),

Johnson and Wales U. Gen. mgr. Marriott Hotels, Arlington, Va., 1964-65; Saddle Brook, NJ, 1966-69, Newton, Mass., 1969-71, regional v.p. Washington, 1971-80; corp. v.p. Marriott Corp., Washington, 1976-89; exec. v.p. Marriott Hotels and Resorts, Washington, 1980-88; pres. Marriott Hotels, Resorts and Suites, 1988-92; exec. v.p., mem. exec. and growth coms. Marriott Corp., 1988—2002; pres. Marriott Lodging Group, 1992-98; vice chmn. Marriott Internat., 1998—2002; chmn. Ritz-Carlton Hotel Co. 1998—2002, chmn. emeritus, 2002—; dir. Bulgari Hotels and Resorts, 2001—. Bd. dirs. Carmax, chmn. nominating and performance com., 2002—; bd. dirs. NY Stock Exch.; dir. Lydian Pvt. Bank, 2005—. Bd. visitors Valle Forge Mil. Acad. and Jr. Coll., 1976-79, chmn., 1979, trustee, 1982-92; chmn. Campaign for Valley Forge, 1985-88, chmn. com. on trustees, 1989-91, hon. life trustee; trustee Johnson and Wales U., 2002—, Norton Mus. Art, 2004—, advancement com. chair; adv. coun. Wilmer Eye Inst., Johns Hopkins U. Mem. Am. Hotel and Lodging Assn. (dir. Ednl. Inst., Arthur Landstreet award 1997), Soc. of the Four Arts (Palm Beach), Kennedy Ctr. Internat. Com. on the Arts (Washington), Cosmos Club (Washington), Tavern Club (NYC). Republican. Roman Catholic. Home: 236 Via Las Brisas Palm Beach FL 33480-1643 E-mail: william.tiefel@ritzcarlton.com.

**TIEFENBRUNN, ALAN JAMES,** medical educator; b. St. Louis, Aug. 26, 1948; s. Kenneth Sylvester and Margaret Ann (Smith) T.; m. Sharon Kay Frost, June 3, 1972; children: Theresa, Curtis. AB cum laude, Washington U., St. Louis, 1970, MD, 1974. Intern, resident U. Calif., San Diego, 1974-77; fellow in cardiology Washington U., St. Louis, 1977-79, asst. prof. medicine 1980-86, assoc. prof. medicine, 1986—, asst. prof. radiology, 1980—; assoc. physician Barnes Hosp., St. Louis, 1980—. Mem. adv. bd. Nat. Registry Myocardial Infarction, 1991—; mem. sci. steering com. Advancent Nat. CHF Registry, 2002—; cons. in field. Contbr. articles to profl. jours. Fellow Am. Coll. Cardiology, Am. Heart Assn. (coun. clin.cardiology), Alpha Omega Alpha. Avocations: skiing, scuba diving, shotgun sports. Home: 6255 Wydown Blvd Saint Louis MO 63105-2306 Office: Washington U Box 8086 660 S Euclid Ave Saint Louis MO 63110-1093 E-mail: atiefenb@im.wustl.edu.

**TIEFENWERTH, WILLIAM PHILIP,** university program director; b. Bklyn., June 25, 1951; s. William Frederick and Catherine Florence (Klotz) T.; m. Karen Taylor, Aug. 15, 1977; 1 child, Casey Elizabeth. BS in Philosophy and Religion, Towson, U., 1973. Tchr., dept. dir. St. Mark Sch., Catonsville, Md., 1975-79; asst. to chaplain Johns Hopkins U., Balt., 1979-92, dir. vol. svcs., 1992-96, dir. cmty. rels., 1996—. Acad. advisor Johns Hopkins U., 1997, co-chairperson Mid-Atlantic region Am. Reads Regional Conf., 1997. Co-designer area mural (Balt.'s Best Mural award City Paper 1997). Founder cmty. ctr. Safe & Smart, 1990; bd. dirs. Homewood Literacy Adv., 1997, Charles Village Ben. Dist., Balt., 1996—; advisor Learn and Serve, Met. Balt., 1997, St. Paul St. Libr. Project, Balt., 1997; recruitment advisor Balt. Mentoring Partnership, 1997. Recipient award for Best Usage of Urban Property for Cmty. Use, 1994, 941st Point of Light award U.S. Pres. George Bush, Washington, 1992, Learning Loft award Abell Found., Balt., 1994. Mem. Md. Coun. Dirs. of Vol. Svcs., Student Affairs Adminstrs. Higher Edn. Democrat. Roman Catholic. Avocations: jazz, gardening, contemporary literature. Home: 2204 Grey Fox Ct Bel Air MD 21015-8905 Office: Johns Hopkins Univ 3400 N Charles St Baltimore MD 21218-2680

**TIELMAN, ROB A.P.,** social sciences educator; b. Hilversum, The Netherlands, Aug. 19, 1946; s. Albert Tielman and Tine Angenent. MA in Sociology, U. Utrecht, Netherlands, 1971; PhD in Social Sci., U. Utrecht, 1982. Mem. acad. staff U. Utrecht, 1971—, head Gay and Lesbian Studies dept., 1982—92, prof. humanist studies, 1987—. Chmn. adv. bd. WHO, Geneva, 1989—93; head humanist tchr. tng. Humanist Ethical Edn., Utrecht, 1993—99; sec. Study Ctr. Pub. Edn., Utrecht, 1994—; sr. advisor pub. edn. Gen. Pedagogic Ctr., Utrecht, 1994—2005; pres. ethics commn. Dutch Inst. Mental Health, Utrecht, 1975—97; pres. Pub. Schs. in the Netherlands, Utrecht, 1989—; v.p. European Platform on Edn., Alkmaar, 1994—2006; rep. of Internat. Humanist Ethical Union UNESCO, Paris, 1989—99, Coun. of Europe, Strasbourg, 1989—; rep. of European Humanist Fedn. EU, Brussels, 1991—99. Author: Homoseksualiteit in Nederland, 1982; editor: Bisexuality and HIV/AIDS, 1991, Third Pink Book, 1993. Sec.-gen. Dutch Gay and Lesbian Assn., Amsterdam, 1971—75; pres. Dutch Humanist Assn., Utrecht, 1977—87, Internat. Humanist Ethical Union, London, 1986—98, Humanist Archives, Utrecht, 1996—. Named Knight, Queen of the Netherlands, 1987. Fellow: Dutch Gay and Lesbian Profs. (sec. 1998—); mem.: European Humanist Profls. (pres. 1993—2000), Internat. Acad. Humanism. Dutch Labor Party. Humanist. Avocation: historical topography of the low countries and former Dutch colonies. Office: Universiteit Utrecht Heidelberglaan 2 3584 CS Utrecht Netherlands Business E-Mail: r.tielman@aps.nl.

**TIEMEYER, KAYLA SUE,** music educator; b. Superior, Nebr., Aug. 12, 1967; d. Roland Vernon and Norman Lee Doering; m. David Wayne Tiemeyer, July 31, 1993; children: Dylan, Colton, Jordyn. B, Bethany Coll., 1989. Cert. tchr. State of Kans. Vocal music tchr. Norton (Kans.) Jr. Sr. H.S. 1989—91; show choir dir. Atwood (Kans.) Elemo H.S., 1991—99; music tchr. Rawlins County Elem. Sch., Atwood, 2003—; vocal music dir. Rawlins County Jr. Sr. H.S., Atwood, 2004—. Show choir dir. Atwood H.S., 2002—; presch. tchr. God's Little St. Presch., Atwood, 1999—2004. Organist, choir accompanist Redeemer Luth. Ch., Atwood, 1991—. Mem.: Kans. Music Educators Assn., Music Club. Lutheran. Avocations: walking, scrapbooks, crocheting, singing, piano. E-mail: tiemeyer@ruraltel.net.

**TIEMSTRA, JOHN PETER,** economics professor; b. Chgo., July 15, 1950; s. Peter John and Margaret (Lamont) T.; m. Suzanne Spicer, Dec. 28, 1985; 1 child: Remi Spicer Rakipi. AB, Oberlin Coll., 1971; PhD, MIT, 1975. Asst. prof. econs. Calvin Coll., Grand Rapids, Mich., 1975-81, assoc. prof., 1981-85, prof., 1985—. Vis. prof. Potchefstroom U., South Africa, 1992. Author: Economics: A Developmental Approach, 1999; editor, co-author: Reforming Economics, 1990; contbr. articles to profl. jours. Dean Grand Rapids Am. Guild of Organists, 1990-91; pres. West Mich. Irish Heritage Soc., Grand Rapids, 1988-91, Forest Hills Condo Assn., Cascade, Mich., 1988—; organist St. Paul's Episcopal Ch., Grand Rapids, 1990-06, Working Group on Ethics and the Earth, Reformed Ch. in Am., 2002-04, St Michael's Episcopal Ch., Grand Rapids, Mich., 2006-. Mem. Assn. Social Econs. (v.p. 2005, pres.-elect 2006), Assn. Christian Economists, Am. Econ. Assn. Christian Reformed. Avocation: music. Office: Calvin Coll 1740 Knollcrest Cir SE Grand Rapids MI 49546-4301 Office Phone: 616-526-6192. Business E-Mail: tmst@calvin.edu.

**TIENDA, MARTA,** demographer, educator; b. Tex. BA in Spanish magna cum laude, Mich. State U., 1972; MA in Sociology, U. Tex., Austin, 1975, PhD in Sociology, 1977. From asst. prof. to prof. rural sociology U. Wis., Madison, 1976—87; vis. prof. Stanford U., 1987; Ralph Lewis prof. sociology U. Chgo., 1994—97, chmn. dept. sociology, 1994—96; prof. sociology and pub. affairs Princeton U., NJ, 1997—, dir. office population rsch., 1998—2002, Maruice P. During prof. demographic studies, 1999—. Rsch. assoc. office population rsch. Princeton U., 1997—; bd. dirs. Fed. Res. Bank N.Y. Co-author: Hispanics in the U.S. Economy, 1985, Hispanic Population of the United States, 1987, Divided Opportunities, 1988, The Color of Opportunity, 2001, Youth in Cities, 2002; editor: Ethnicity and Causal Mechanisms, 2005, Hispanics and the Furure of America, 2005, Multiple Origins, Uncertain Destinies: Hispanics and the American Future, 2005; contbr. articles to profl. jours. Trustee Corp. of Brown U., Jacobs Found. of Switzerland, Sloan Found.; bd. dirs. Princeton Med. Ctr. Named one of 80 Elite Hispanic Women, Hispanic Bus. Mag., 2003, Top 100 Influential Hispanics, 2003; recipient Lifetime Achievement award, Hispanic Bus. Inc., 2004; Guggenheim fellow. Fellow: AAAS, Am. Acad. Political Social Sci., Ctr. Advanced Study Behavioral Scis.; mem.: Internat. Union for Sci. Study of Population, Population Assn. Am. (past pres.), Am. Econ. Assn., Am. Sociol. Assn. Office: Office Population Rsch Princeton U 247 Wallace Hall Princeton NJ 08544-2091*

**TIENKEN, ARTHUR T.,** retired foreign service officer; b. Yonkers, N.Y., Aug. 5, 1922; BA, Princeton U., 1947, MA, 1949. With U.S. Fgn. Svc., 1949-87, dep. chief mission Tunis, Tunisia, 1973-75, Addis Ababa, Ethiopia, 1975-77; Ambassador to Gabonese Republic and Democratic Republic of Sao Tome and Principe, Libreville, Gabon, 1978-81; dir. Fgn. Svc. Assignments and Career devel. Dept. State, 1981-85, sr. insp., 1985-87, ret., 1987. Diplomat-in-residence Marquette U., 1972-73 Served with U.S. Army, 1943-46. Mem. Diplomatic and Consular Officers Ret. (bd. govs. 1999—2005).

**TIERNEY, BRIAN PATRICK,** publishing executive, former advertising and public relations executive; b. Bryn Mawr, Pa., Feb. 21, 1957; s. James Richard and Claire Ella (Springfield) T.; married; 2 children. BA, U. Pa., 1979; JD, Widener U., 1987. Field person Rep. Nat. Com., Washington, 1979-82, dir. incumbent programs, 1979-81, dep. dir. edn., 1981-82; polit. dir. GOPAC, Washington, 1982-83; asst. regional adminstr. Small Bus. Adminstrn., Bala Cynwyd, Pa., 1983-84; pres. Tierney & Co., Phila., 1984—; CEO Lewis, Gilman & Kynett Pub. Rels., Phila., 1986-89, Tierney Communications (formerly The Tierney Group), Phila., 1989—2000, Tierney & Ptnrs., Phila., 1994—98; chief mktg. officer Advanta Corp., 2004—05; CEO Phila. Media Holdings LLC, 2006—. Entrepreneur in resident Wharton Sch. Bus., 2002—03. Ann. giving chmn. Ingis House for Disabled Persons, Phila.; bd. dirs. Wilma Theater, Phila., Moore Coll. Art and Design, Phila., Sch. Bd. Archdiocese of Phila., Ave of Arts, Inc., Phila. Police Athletic League, Phila. coun. Boy Scouts Am., fund for Phila., Phila. Festival of Arts; chmn. Marian Anderson award City of Phila.; bd. dirs. Phila. Zool. Soc.; mem. bd. regional Performing Arts Ctr., Phila. Mem. ABA, Pa. Bar Assn., Phila. Bar Assn., Pub. Rels. Soc. Am., St. Anthony Club, Union League. Roman Catholic. Avocations: skydiving, gardening.*

**TIERNEY, GORDON PAUL,** real estate broker, genealogist; b. Ft. Wayne, Ind., Oct. 17, 1922; s. James Leonard and Ethele Lydia (Brown) T.; m. Carma Lillian Devine, Oct. 17, 1946; 1 child, Paul N Student, Ind. U., 1940—41, Cath. U. Am., 1941—42. Br. mgr. Bartlett-Collins Co., Chgo., 1956—84; prin., broker Kaiser-Tierney Real Estate, Inc., Palatine, Ill., 1984—89; pres. Tierney Real Estate, Newburgh, Ind. Author: Burgess/Bryan Connection, 1978; assoc. editor Colonial Genealogist Jour., 1976-85 With U.S. Army, 1943—45, China. Named Ky. Col Fellow Am. Coll. Genealogists (pres. 1977-2000); mem. SAR (life, v.p. gen. 1984-85, genealogist gen. 1981-83, Silver and Bronze medals 1978-80, Patriot medal 1976, Meritorious Svc. award 1983, Minutemen award 1984), Huguenot Soc. Ill. (state pres. 1978-80), Huguenot Soc. S.C., Nat. Huguenot Soc., Huguenot Soc. Ind. (pres. 1993-95), Nat. Geneal. Soc., Ind. Hist. Soc., Soc. Ind. Pioneers, First Families Ohio, Ohio Geneal. Soc., Va. Geneal. Soc., Md. Geneal. Soc., Augustan Soc., Gen. Soc. War 1812 (state pres. 1985), Sons and Daus. Pilgrims, Descs. Old Plymouth Colony, Md. Order Stars and Bars, Soc. Descs. Colonial Clergy, Sons Union Vets., Sons Confederate Vets., Pioneer Wis. Families, Welcome Soc. Pa., Pa. Geneal. Soc., Nat. Soc. Archivists, Soc. Colonial Wars in Ill. (life), Soc. Colonial Wars in Ind. (gov. 1992-94), Soc. Colonial Wars in Commonwealth Ky. (life), Sons Am. Colonists (nat. v.p. 1971-74), Mil. and Hospitalier Order St. Lazarus of Jerusalem, Clan Johnston/e in Am., Order Descs. Ancient Planters, Hump Pilots Assn., Nat. Bd. Realtors, Ill. Bd. Realtors, Sword Bunker Hill, Tri-State Geneal. Soc., Jamestowne Soc., Baronial Order Magna Charta, Royal Order Scotland, Masons, Shriners, Rolling Hill Country Club, Legion of Honor (comdr. 2001-02, decorated) Republican. Presbyterian. Home and Office: 8766 Hanover Dr Newburgh IN 47630-9327

**TIERNEY, JAMES EDWARD,** law educator, former state attorney general; b. Bklyn., Apr. 12, 1947; s. Charles J. and Agnes V. (Quinn) T.; m. Susan Webster, Jan. 26, 1969; children: Adam, Josie, Matthew, Daniel, Kate. BA with highest honors, U. Maine, 1969, JD, 1974. Bar: Maine 1974. Mem. Maine State Ho. Reps., 1972-80, majority leader, 1976-80; atty. gen. State of Maine, 1980-90; cons. state attys. gen., 1994—; lectr. Columbia Law Sch., NYC, 2000—, dir. Nat. State Atty. Gen. Program, 2004—. Bd. dirs. People for the Am. Way, Topsham, Maine, 1991-93; spl. prosecutor investigate Pa. Supreme Ct., 1992-93; mem. bd. commentators Courtroom TV Network. Wasserstein fellow Harvard Law Sch., 1992-93. Mem. Am. Judicature Soc. (bd. dirs.). Office: Columbia Law Sch 435 W 116 St Box B-26 New York NY 10027 E-mail: jtiern@law.columbia.edu.*

**TIERNEY, JOHN F.,** congressman, lawyer; b. Salem, Mass., Sept. 18, 1951; m. Patrice Tierney. BA, Salem State Coll., 1973; JD, Suffolk U., 1976. Ptnr. Tierney, Kalis, and Lucas, North Shore, Mass.; mem. US Congress from 6th Mass. dist., 1997—; mem. com. edn. and workforce, com. gov. reform, permanent select intelligence com. Pres. Salem C. of C. Democrat. Office: US Ho Reps 120 Cannon Ho Office Bldg Washington DC 20515-2106 Office Phone: 202-225-8020. Office Fax: 202-225-5915.*

**TIERNEY, JOHN MARION,** journalist, columnist, reporter; b. Elgin, Ill., Mar. 25, 1953; s. John William and Patricia Anne (O'Neill) Tierney; m. Dana Groseclose, June 10, 1995; 1 child. BA in Am. Studies cum laude, Yale U., 1976. Reporter Bergen Record, Bergen County, NJ, 1976-78, Washington Star, 1978-80; staff writer Science 81-85 mag., Washington, 1981-85; freelance writer, 1985-90; reporter NY Times, Washington, 1990—, Washington correspondent, 2002—03, 2003—05, Baghdad correspondent, 2003, op-ed columnist, 2005—. Staff writer, columnist N.Y. Times Mag., 1995—; contbr. articles to numerous mags. and newspapers including Atlantic, Discover, Esquire, Hippocrates, National Geographic Traveler, Newsweek, Outside, New York, N.Y. Times Mag., Playboy, Rolling Stone, Washington Monthly, The Wall Street Jour., Washington Post, Vogue; co-author, God Is My Broker; author, The Best-Case Scenario Handbook, 2002. Recipient Washington Monthly Journalism award, 1982, Am. Inst. of Physics-U.S. Steel Found. Sci. Writing award, 1984, AAAS/Westinghouse Sci. Journalism award, 1988; fellow Freedom Forum Media Studies Ctr., Columbia U., 1993-94. Office: NY Times 1627 I St NW Washington DC 20006*

**TIERNEY, KEVIN ALLEN,** elementary school educator; b. Castro Valley, Calif., Sept. 23, 1958; s. Robert James and Jacqueline Elizabeth Tierney; m. Karen Naomi Zimmer, Aug. 23, 1987. BA in History, San Francisco State U., 1990; MA in Edn. Curriculum and Instrn., Sacramento State U., Calif., 2002. Cert. profl.clear multiple subject tchg. credential Calif. Tchr. grade 4 Wagner Holt Elem. Sch., Stockton, Calif., 1991—92; tchr. grade 5 Silva Valley Elem. Sch., El Dorado Hills, 1992—98; tchr. history grade 7-8 Rolling Hills Mid. Sch., 1998. Trainer El Dorado County Office Edn., Placerville, Calif., 2001—; mentor trainer Buckeye Union Sch. Dist., Shingle Springs, 2000—. Com. mem. Cemetery Advisor Com., El Dorado County, 2002—. Named Most Influential Tchr., Oak Ridge H.S. students, 1999. Tchr. of Yr., Rolling Hills Mid. Sch., 2001, 2004, 2005; fellow, Colonial Williamsburg Tchr. Inst., 2001, Eurasia Excellence Tchg. fellow, U.S. Dept., 2004, Japan Fulbright Meml. Fund, 2005. Mem.: ASCD, Nat. Coun. Soc. Studies. Avocations: banjo, golf, fly fishing. Home: 5001 Gold Crest Ct Camino CA 95709 Office: Rolling Hills Mid Sch 7141 Silva Valley Pkwy El Dorado Hills CA 95762-7862 Office Phone: 530-676-2490 x 377. E-mail: katierne@mindspring.com.

**TIERNEY, KEVIN JOSEPH,** lawyer, arbitrator, mediator, director; b. Lowell, Mass., Dec. 13, 1951; s. Joseph Francis and Esther Rowena T. BS cum laude, Bowdoin Coll., 1973; JD, U. Maine, 1976. Bar: Maine 1976. Atty. Union Mutual Life Ins. Co., Portland, Maine, 1976-80, asst. counsel, 1980, 2d v.p., counsel, 1980-84, 2d v.p., counsel, corp. sec., 1984-86, UNUM Corp., Portland, 1986-89, v.p., corp. counsel, sec., 1989-91, gen. counsel, sr. v.p., sec., 1991-99; atty. in pvt. practice Falmouth, Maine, 1999—. Bd. dirs. Vesta Ins. Group, MLIG Variable Ins. Trust. Bd. dirs. Pine Tree Alcoholism Treatment Ctr., Maine, 1977-84, So. Regional Alcoholism and Drug Abuse Coun., Maine, 1982-85; mem. radiation therapy tech. adv. com. So. Me. Vocat. Tech. Inst., 1985; trustee Portland Symphony Orch., 1990-99; trustee, treas. Falmouth Med. Libr. Mem. ARIAS-U.S., Assn. Life Ins. Counsel, Maine State Bar Assn., Cumberland County (Maine) Bar Assn., ABA.

**TIERNEY, MAURA,** actress; b. Boston, Feb. 3, 1965; m. Billy Morrissette, 1994. Student, NYU, Cir. in the Sq. Theatre Sch. Actor: (TV series) 704 Hauser St., —, News Radio, 1995—2000, ER, 2000—; (TV films) Flying Blind, 1990—, Out of Darkness, —, Student Exchange, —, Crossing the Mob, —, (guest appearance): (TV series) Growing Pains; (TV films) Family Ties; (TV series) Law & Order, The Van Dyke Show,: (films) Dead Women in Lingerie, 1991, The Linguini Incident, 1991, White Sands, 1992, Fly By Night, 1993, The Temp, 1993, Primal Fear, 1996, Primary Colors, 1997, Liar, Liar, 1997, Primary Colors, 1998, Forces of Nature, 1999, Instinct, 1999, Welcome to Mooseport, 2004, Danny Roane: First Time Director, 2006; (plays) Some Girl(s), 2006. Office: c/o Creative Artists Agy 9830 Wilshire Blvd Beverly Hills CA 90212*

**TIERNEY, MICHAEL JOHN,** mathematics professor; b. St. Louis, Feb. 19, 1947; s. John Thomas and Alice Marie (Krieger) T.; m. Edith L. Echelmeyer, Nov. 21, 1975 (div. Sept. 1984); 1 child, John E.; m. Virginia Lee Christian, Apr. 6, 1985. BS, St. Louis U., 1969, MS, 1971, PhD, 1974; MS, U. Va., 1995. Prof. math. and actuarial sci. Maryville Coll., St. Louis, 1974-83; prof. math. and computer sci. Va. Mil. Inst., Lexington, 1983—, dept. chair, 1995—2004. Mem. AAUP, AAAS, Am. Math. Soc., Math. Assn. Am., Soc. Indsl. and AppliedMath., Assn. Computing Machinery, Sigma Xi. Presbyterian. Avocations: tennis, landscaping. Home: 819 Gwynne Ave Waynesboro VA 22980-3342 Office: Va Mil Inst Lexington VA 24450

**TIERNEY, THOMAS J.,** social entrepreneur; b. San Francisco, Mar. 5, 1954; s. Ralph Thomas and Eleanor Faye (Webart) T.; m. Joy Karen McGee, Sept. 23, 1984; children: Colin McGee, Braden Thomas. BA in Econs. with distinction, U. Calif., Davis, 1976, MBA with distinction, Harvard, 1980. Field engr. Bechtel Internat., Azrew, Algeria, 1976-78; cons. Bain & Co., San Francisco, 1980-82, mgr., 1982-83, v.p., 1983-87, mng. ptnr., 1987-92; pres. Bain & Co. Worldwide, San Francisco, 1992-2000, CEO, 1993-2000; founder & chmn. Bridgespan Group, 2000—; bd. dirs. eBay, Inc. Co-author: Aligning the Stars, 2002. Trustee Woods Hole Oceanographic Inst., The Hoover Inst., Harvard Bus. Sch. Social Enterprise; former bd. dirs. Nature Conservancy, Cath. Charities, WGBH, U. Calif.-Davis Alumni Assn., Bay Area United Way, United Way Mass. Bay, Stanford Bus. Sch.; bd. dirs. Inst. for Higher Edn., Nat. Acads. Recipient Winslow Meml. award U. Calif. Davis, 1976. Roman Catholic. Avocations: fishing, politics, non-profit sector. Home: 45 Old Farm Rd Wellesley MA 02481-1423 Office Phone: 617-572-3015. Business E-Mail: thomas.tierney@bridgespan.org.

**TIESENGA, MARVIN FRANCIS,** surgeon; b. Slayton, Minn., Apr. 3, 1929; s. Edward Tiesenga and Sieka Drenth-Tiesenga; m. Ardythe Rae Noorlag, Aug. 19, 1955; children: Jane, Edward, Mary, Frederick, Anne. BS, Roosevelt U., 1950; MD, U. Ill., 1954. Diplomate Am. Bd. Surgery. Intern Cook County Hosp., Chgo., 1954, resident gen. surgery, 1957—61; pres. med. staff West Suburban Hosp., Oak Park, Ill., 1986—88, chief surgery, 1989—. Contbr. articles to profl. jours. Mem. Elmhurst Christian Ref. Ch., 1971—. Capt. U.S. Army, 1955—57, Korea. Named Number one Dr., Crane's Chgo. Mag., 2000, 2001, 2002, 2003; recipient, 2004, Ken Douglas award for excellence, Citizens of Oak Park, 2000. Fellow: ACS; mem.: AMA, SAGES, Chgo. Med. Soc., Ill. Med. Soc., Am. Soc. Breast Surgeons, Am. Soc. Bariatric Surgery, Aux Planes Med. Soc., Christian Med. and Dental Assn. Avocations: boating, travel, history, collecting antique tractors. Office: 7411 Lake St Ste 2100 River Forest IL 60305

**TIESI, JOSEPH A.,** corporate financial executive; Grad., St. Francis Coll., 1980. With PricewaterhouseCoopers, 1980—86; sr. fin. analyst Altria Corp. Svcs., Inc., 1986—90, mgr. fin. reporting and analysis, 1990—95, dir. fin. reporting and analysis, 1995—98, asst. contr. fin. reporting and consolidation, 1998—99, v.p., contr., 1999—. Office: Altria Corp Svcs Inc 120 Park Ave New York NY 10017

**TIETKE, WILHELM,** gastroenterologist, educator; b. Niengraben, Germany, Oct. 15, 1938; came to U.S., 1969, naturalized, 1979; s. Wilhelm and Frieda (Schmeding) T.; m. Imme Schmidt, Oct. 15, 1965; children: Cornelia, Isabel. MD, U. Goettingen, Germany, 1968. Diplomate Am. Bd. Internal Medicine, Am. Bd. Gastroenterology. Intern Edward W. Sparrow Hosp., Lansing, Mich., 1970; resident in internal medicine Henry Ford Hosp., Detroit, 1971-73, fellow in gastroenterology, 1973-75; practice medicine specializing in gastroenterology Huntsville, Ala., 1975—. Mem. vol. faculty, cons. U. Ala., Huntsville, 1976; clin. assoc. prof. internal medicine, 1979—; v.p. Huntsville Gastroenterology Assocs., P.C., 1979—. Fellow Coll. Gastroenterology; mem. AMA, ACP, Ala. Med. Soc., Am. Soc. Gastrointestinal Endoscopy, Rotary. Lutheran. Home: 2707 Westminster Way SE Huntsville AL 35801-2241 Office: 119 Longwood Dr Huntsville AL 35801 Home: PO Box 2324 Birmingham AL 35201-2324

**TIFFANY, JOSEPH RAYMOND, II,** lawyer; b. Dayton, Ohio, Feb. 5, 1949; s. Forrest Fraser and Margaret Watson (Clark) T.; m. Terri Robbins, Dec. 1, 1984. AB magna cum laude, Harvard U., 1971; MS in Internat. Relations, London Sch. Econs., 1972; JD, U. Calif., Berkeley, 1975. Bar: U.S. Dist. Ct. (no. dist.) 1975, U.S. Dist. Ct. (ea. dist.) 1977, U.S. Ct. Appeals (9th cir.) 1982, U.S. Ct. Appeals (fed. cir.) 2004. Assoc. Pillsbury, Madison & Sutro, San Francisco, 1975-82, ptnr., 1983-2001, Pillsbury Winthrop LLP, Palo Alto, Calif., 2001—01, Pillsbury Winthrop Shaw Pittman LLP, 2005—. Mem. ABA (antitrust, litigation sects.), Calif. Bar Assn. (antitrust and unfair competition sect. Office: Pillsbury Winthrop Shaw Pittman LLP 2475 Hanover St Palo Alto CA 94304-1115 Office Phone: 650-233-4644. Business E-Mail: joseph.tiffany@pillsburylaw.com.

**TIFFORD, JOHN MARK,** lawyer; of Harry A. and Rose K. Tifford. BA, CCNY, N.Y.C., 1962; LLB, Cornell U., Ithaca, N.Y., 1965. Bar: D.C. 1978, N.Y. 1965, Va. 1977. Atty. Fed. Trade Commn., Washington, 1975—88; ptnr. DLA Piper LLP, Washington, 1988—. Presenter in field. Contbr. articles to profl. jours. With USAR, 1965—71. Mem.: ABA, D.C. Bar Assn., Va. Bar Assn., N.Y. State Bar Assn. Office: DLA Piper LLP 1775 Wiehle Ave Ste 400 Reston VA 20190 Office Phone: 703-773-4244. Office Fax: 703-773-5055. Business E-Mail: john.tifford@dlapiper.com.

**TIFFT, WILLIAM GRANT,** retired physics professor, scientist; b. Derby, Conn., Apr. 5, 1932; s. William Charles and Marguerite Howe (Hubbell) T.; m. Carol Ruth Nordquist, June 1, 1957 (div. July 1964); children: Jennifer, William John; m. Janet Ann Lindner Homewood, June 2, 1965; 1 child, Amy, stepchildren: Patricia, Susan, Hollis. AB, Harvard Coll., 1954; PhD, Calif. Inst. Tech., 1958. Postdoctoral fellow Australian Nat. U., Canberra, 1958-60; rsch. assoc. Vanderbilt U., Nashville, 1960-61; astronomer Lowell Obs., Flagstaff, Ariz., 1961-63; asst. prof. U. Ariz., Tucson, 1964-73, prof., 1973—2002, prof. emeritus, 2002—; prin. scientist Sci. Assn. Study of Time in Physics and Cosmology, 2000—. Joint author: Revised New General Catalog, 1973; joint editor: Modern Mathematical Models of Time and Their Applications to Physics and Cosmology, 1997; contbr. over 100 articles to profl. jours. NSF Predoctoral fellow, 1954-58, NSF Postdoctoral fellow, 1958-60; grantee NASA, NSF, ONR, Rsch. Corp. Fellow Am. Astron. Soc.; mem. Internat. Astron. Union, Sci. Assn. Study of Time in Physics and Cosmology (prin. scientist 2000-). Achievements include discovery of redshift quantization and correlations relating to it, including variability; first to detect voids in mapping of large scale supercluster structure; investigations of three-dimensional time in cosmology and particle physics. Office: U Arizona Dept Astronomy Tucson AZ 85721-0001

**TIFT, MARY LOUISE,** artist; b. Seattle, Jan. 2, 1913; d. John Howard and Wilhelmina (Pressler) Dreher; m. William Raymond Tift, Dec. 4, 1948. BFA cum laude, U. Wash., 1933; postgrad., Art Ctr. Coll., L.A., 1945-48, U. Calif., San Francisco, 1962-63. Art dir. Vaughn Shedd Advt., L.A., 1948; asst. prof. design Calif. Coll. Arts & Crafts, Oakland, Calif., 1949-59; coord. design dept. San Francisco Art Inst., 1959-62. Subject of cover story, Am. Artist mag., 1980, studio article, 1987; one-woman shows, Gumps Gallery, San Francisco, 1977, 1986, 90, Diane Gilson Gallery, Seattle, 1978, Oreg. State U., 1981, Univ. House, Seattle, Frye Art Mus., Seattle, 2000; exhibited in group shows including Brit. Biennale, Yorkshire, Eng., 1970, Grenchen Triennale, Switzerland, 1970, Polish Biennale, Crakow, 1972, Nat. Gallery, Washington, 1973, Madrid Biennale, 1980, U.S.-U.K. Impressions, Eng., 1988; represented in permanent collections, Phila. Mus. Art, Bklyn. Mus., Seattle Art Mus., Library Congress, Achenbach Print Collection, San Francisco Palace Legion of Honor, San Diego Mus. Art, U.S. Art in Embassies. Served to lt. USNR, 1943-45. Mem. Print Club Phila., World Print Council, Calif. Soc. Printmakers, Phi Beta Kappa, Lambda Rho. Christian Scientist. Studio: 4400 Stone Way N Apt 521 Seattle WA 98103-7487

**TIGAR, MICHAEL EDWARD,** law educator; b. Glendale, Calif., Jan. 18, 1941; s. Charles Henry and Margaret Elizabeth (Lang) T.; m. Pamet Ayer Jones, Sept. 21, 1961 (div. Mar. 1973); children: Jon Steven, Katherine Ayer; m. Amanda G. Birrell, Feb. 16, 1980 (div. Aug. 1996); 1 child, Elizabeth Torrey; m. Jane E. Blanksteen, Aug. 22, 1996. BA in Polit. Sci., U. Calif., Berkeley, 1962, JD, 1966. Bar: D.C. 1967, U.S. Ct. Appeals (2d, 4th, 5th, 6th, 7th, 8th, 9th, 10th, 11th, fed. and D.C. cirs.), U.S. Tax Ct., U.S. Supreme Ct. 1972, N.Y. 1993. Assoc. Williams & Connolly, Washington, 1966-69; editor-in-chief Selective Svc. Law Reporter, Washington, 1967-69; acting prof. law UCLA, 1969-71; pvt. practice law Grasse, France, 1972-74; assoc. William & Connolly, Washington, 1974, ptnr., 1975-77, Tigar & Buffone, Washington, 1977-84; prof. law U. Tex., Austin, 1984-87, Joseph D. Jamail Centennial prof. law, 1987-98; of counsel Haddon, Morgan & Foreman, Denver, 1996-98; prof. law, and Edwin A. Mooers, Sr., Scholar Am. U. Washington Coll. Law, Washington, 1998—; mem. Tiger Law Firm. Reporter 5th Cir. Pattern Jury Instrns., Austin, 1988-90. Author: Practice Manual Selective Service Law Reporter, 1968, Law and the Rise of Capitalism, 1977, (with Jane B. Tigar) Federal Appeals: Jurisdiction and Practice, 3d edit., 1999, Examining Witnesses, 1993, Persuasion: The Litigator's Art, 1999; contbr. articles to profl. jours. Mem. ABA (vice chair 1987-88, chair elect 1988-89, chair 1989-90 sect. litigation). Avocations: sailing, cooking. Office: Washington Coll Law 4801 Massachusetts Ave NW Washington DC 20016-8196 Office Phone: 202-549-4229.

**TIGER, IRA PAUL,** retired lawyer; b. Bklyn., Jan. 31, 1936; s. Sidney and Rebecca (Frankel) T.; m. Rosalind Silverman, July 4, 1957 (dec. Nov. 1972); children: Ruth, Lori; m. Ann Mae Gersh, May 5, 1974; stepchildren: Jimmie, Randy, Richard Riesenberg. BS in Econs., U. Pa., 1956, JD magna cum laude, 1959. Bar: Pa. 1960, U.S. Dist. Ct. (ea. dist.) Pa. 1960, U.S. Ct. Appeals (3d cir.) 1960, U.S. Supreme Ct. 1971, U.S. Ct. Appeals (7th cir.) 1996. Law clk. 3d cir., 1959-60; assoc. Schnader, Harrison, Segal & Lewis, Phila., 1960-67, ptnr., 1968—2002, chmn. litigation dept., 1986-90, chmn. standing com. on profl. conduct, 1992—2003, sr. counsel, 2003—04. Judge pro tem Phila. Ct. Common Pleas, 1994—2003; mediator U.S. Dist. Ct. (ea. dist.) Pa., 1991—2003. Rsch. editor U. Pa. Law Rev., 1958-59. Pres. Temple Sinai Synagogue, 1989-91, Elkins Park House Coun., 1996-98; mem. Planning Adv. Bd. Upper Dublin Twp., 1982-87, mem. edul. adv. com., 1976-78; legal counsel Phila. Jr. C. of C., 1963-64, bd. dirs., 1962-66, sec. Jewish campus activities bd., 1971-73; mem. citizens' adv. com. Cheltenham Twp., 2004—, vice-chmn., 2006—. Mem. ABA, Am. Judicature Soc., Inst. Jud. Adminstrn., Phila. Bar Assn. (chmn. fed. cts. com. 1985), Lawyers Club Phila., Order of Coif (exec. com. Pa. chpt. 1981-83), Beta Alpha Psi, Beta Gamma Sigma. Democrat. Office: Schnader Harrison 1600 Market St Ste 3600 Philadelphia PA 19103-7286 Business E-Mail: itiger@schnader.com.

**TIGER, LIONEL,** social scientist, anthropology consultant; b. Montreal, Que., Can., Feb. 5, 1937; s. Martin and Lillian (Schneider) T.; 1 child, Sebastian Benjamin. BA, McGill U., 1957, MA, 1959; PhD, U. London, 1963. Instr. anthropology U. Ghana, Accra, 1960; asst. prof. dept. anthropology and sociology U. B.C., Vancouver, Canada, 1963—68; assoc. prof. anthropology Rutgers U., New Brunswick, NJ, 1969—74, prof. anthropology, 1974—, Charles Darwin prof. anthropology, 1990—. Cons., rsch. dir. Harry F. Guggenheim Found., N.Y.C., 1972-84; chmn. bd. social scientists US News and World Report, 1968-88; sci. adv. bd. Am. Wine Inst., San Francisco; sr. rsch. assoc. Nat. Inst. Pub. Policy; mem. bd. advisors George Polk Awards, 2004—. Author: Men in Groups, 1969, 3d edit., 2004, (with Robin Fox) The Imperial Animal, 1971, 3d edit., 1998, (with Joseph Shepher) Women in the Kibbutz, 1975, Optimism: The Biology of Hope, 1979, 2d edit., 1994, China's Food, 1985, The Manufacture of Evil: Ethics, Evolution and the Industrial System, 1987; editor: Female Hierarchies, 1978, (with Michael Robinson) Man and Beast Revisited, 1992, The Pursuit of Pleasure, 1992, 2d edit., 2000, The Decline of Males, 1999, The Apes of New York, 2003; series editor: Anthropology and Human Nature, 2005; mem. editl. bd. Social Sci. Info., Ethology and Sociobiology jour., Jour. of Social Distress and the Homeless Cultural laureate N.Y.C. Landmarks Found., 1999. Recipient W.I. Susman award for excellence in tchg., 1985, McNaughton prize for creative writing; Guggenheim fellow, 1969, rsch. fellow ASDA Found., 1985, Can. Coun., fgn. area tng. fellow Ford Found., Can. Coun.-Killam fellow for interdisciplinary rsch., Rockefeller fellow Aspen Inst., 1979, H.F. Guggenheim Found. fellow, 1988-89; Inst. for Law and Behavioral Rsch. fellow; Govt. of Que. fellow, 2005-06. Mem. PEN (mem. exec. bd., treas. 1988-91, v.p. 1991-94), Am. Anthrop. Assn., Internat. Humanist Assn. (humanist laureate), Can. Humanists Assn. (hon.), Internat. Humanist Assn. (humanist laureate), Century Assn. for Study of Evolution, Century Assn. Home: 248 W 23rd St Fl 4 New York NY 10011-2304 also: PO Box 965 Millbrook NY 12545 Office: Rutgers U 131 George St New Brunswick NJ 08901-1414 Business E-Mail: ltiger@rcl.rutgers.edu.

**TIGERMAN, STANLEY,** architect, educator; b. Chgo., Sept. 20, 1930; s. Samuel Bernard and Emma Louise (Stern) T.; m. Margaret I. McCurry; children: Judson Joel, Tracy Leigh. Student, MIT, 1948-49; BArch, Yale U., 1960, MArch, 1961. Archtl. draftsman firm George Fred Keck, Chgo., 1949-30, Skidmore, Owings and Merrill, Chgo., 1957-59, Paul Rudolph, New Haven, 1959-61, Harry Weese, Chgo., 1961-62; partner firm Tigerman & Koglin, Chgo., 1962-64; prin. firm Stanley Tigerman & Assos., Chgo., 1964-82; ptnr. Tigerman Fugman McCurry, Chgo., 1982-88, Tigerman McCurry, 1988—. Prof. architecture U. Ill.-Chgo., 1967-71, 80-93, dir. Sch. Architecture, 1985-93; vis. lectr. Yale U., 1974, Cornell U., Ithaca, N.Y., 1963, Cooper Union, 1970, U. Calif. at Berkeley, 1968, Cardiff (Wales) Coll., 1965, Engring. U., Bangladesh, 1967; chmn AIA com. on design, coordinator exhbn. and book Chicago Architects, 1977; Charlotte Shepherd Davenport prof. architecture Yale U., 1979; architect-in-residence Am. Acad. in Rome, 1980; vis. prof. architecture Harvard U., 1982; William Henry Bishop Chair, prof. architecture Yale U., 1984, Sarrinen prof., 1993; dir. post-professional grad. program U. Ill.-Chgo.; co-founder Archeworks, Design Lab., Chgo., 1993; mem. adv. com. Princeton U., 1997. Prin. works include The Ounce of Prevention Educare Ctr., Chgo., Fukuoka Apt. Complex, Japan, The Power House, Zion, Ill., The Chgo. Children's Adv. Ctr.; author: Versus, 1982, Architecture of Exile, 1988, Stanley Tigerman: Buildings and Projects, 1966-89, 1989; contbr. Design of the Housing Site, 1966, Chicago on Foot, 1969, Art Today, 1969, New Direction in American Architecture, 1969, Contemporary Jewelry, 1970, Urban Structures for the Future, 1972, Spaces for Living, 1973, Chicago 1930-70, 1974, Interior Spaces Designed by Architects, 1976, 100 Years of Architecture in Chicago, 1976, 100 Years of Architecture in Chicago, 1986, Mies Reconsidered, 1986, Chicago Architecture 1872-1922, 1988, articles; exhibitions include Venice Biennale, 1976, 1980, Calif. Condition, 1982;, author essay; exhibitions include Chicago Architecture, The New Zeitgeist: In Search of Closure, 1989, 1989; author: (catalog) Chicago Architecture, The New Zeitgeist: In Search of Closure, 1989. Pres. Yale Arts Assn., 1969-70; mem. advisory com. Yale Archtl. Sch., 1976—; bd. dirs. Bangladesh Found. Served in USN, 1950-54. Recipient Alpha Rho Chi medal, Yale, 1961, Archtl. Record award 1970, Masonry award, 1974, Masonry gold medal, 1974, Alumni Art award, Yale U., 1985, Design award for Art Inst. Chgo. Schinkel Exhbn., Am. Soc. Interior Designers, 1995, Humanitarian award, Holocaust Meml. Foundtn. Ill. 2001, Grand award of Excellence, NAHB, 2001, 2003, Recognition award, World Trade Ctr. Meml., 2004, Cultures Achievement award, Univ. Club Chgo., 2004; grantee Advanced Studies in Fine Art, Graham Fedn., 1965. Fellow AIA (chmn. com. design 1976-77, adv. com., Disting. Svc. award Chgo. chpt. 1983, Chgo. Honor awards 1977-79, Nat. Honor award 1982, 84, 87, 91, 98, Nat. Modern Income Housing award 1970, Nat. Homes for Better Living award 1974, 75, Ill. award 1976, Nat. award of Merit 1970, 74, 75, named to Hall of Fame 1990, Disting. Bldg. award for pvt. residence Chgo. chpt. 1991, Chgo. Interior Archtl. Award of Excellence 1981, 83, 87, 91, 92, Nat. Interior Archtl. Award of Excellence 1992-93, Chgo. Disting. Bldg. award 1971, 73, 75, 77, 79, 81, 82, 84, 85, 86, 91, 94, Italian Ceramic Tile Design award 1995, Fukuoka Urban Beautification award 1995, 6 citations of merit Chgo. chpt. 1994, Interior Design award for A.I.C. Schinkel Exhibit 1996, Chgo. Interior Architecture award 1997, Chgo. Chpt. Arch. award 1998, Nat. Interior Architecture award 1998, Louis Sullivan award 2000), Ill./Ind. Masonry Coun. (Silver Award for Excellence in Masonry 2003); mem. Arts Club of Chgo., Yale Club of N.Y.C., Century Assn. Club, Phi Kappa Phi. Office: Tigerman & McCurry Ltd 444 N Wells St Ste 206 Chicago IL 60610-4522 Office Phone: 312-644-5880.

**TIGHE, MARY ANN,** real estate company executive; m. David Hidalgo; 1 child from previous marriage, Aaron. BA in art history, Cath. U.; MA in art history, U. Md. Staff mem. Smithsonian Instn.; arts adv. to v.p. Walter Mondale; dep. chmn. Nat. Endowment Arts; v.p. Am. Broadcasting Co.; sales assoc. Edward S. Gordon Inc. (name changed to Insignia/ESG Inc. 1997), 1984; exec. mng. dir. Insignia/ESG Inc., NYC, 1993—99, vice chmn., 1999—2002; pres., CEO NY Tri-State Region CB Richard Ellis, NYC, 2002—. Dir. Imperial Parking Corp. Bd. dirs. NYC Ballet, Parrish Art Mus., The New 42nd St., Joan's Legacy: The Joan Scarangello Found. to Conquer Lung Cancer. Recipient Woman Yr., Comml. Real Estate Women NY, 2001. Mem.: Real Estate Bd. NY (exec. com. bd. govs. 2001—), Henry Hart Rice award 1997, 2002, Robert T. Lawrence award 1992, 1998). Office: CB Richard Ellis Group Inc 200 Park Ave New York NY 10166

**TIGHE, THOMAS,** non-profit organization executive; Grad., U. Calif., 1982, JD, 1985; LLD (hon.), Hobart and William Smith Colls., 2003. Assoc. counsel com. veteran's affairs U.S. Senate, Washington, 1989—93; assoc. gen. counsel Peace Corps, 1993—95, chief of staff, COO, 1995—2000; pres., CEO Direct Relief Internat., Santa Barbara, Calif., 2000—. Vol. tchr. Peace Corps, Thailand, 1986—88; mem. Pacific Coun. Internat. Policy; dir. Dreamweaver Med. Found., Salt Lake City. Office: Direct Relief Internat 27 S La Paterna Ln Goleta CA 93117 Office Phone: 805-964-4767. Office Fax: 805-681-4838.

**TIGHE-MOORE, BARBARA JEANNE,** electronics executive; b. Wadsworth, Ohio, Jan. 12, 1961; d. Norton Raymond and Laura Alida (Frank) Tighe; m. Derek William Moore, June 26, 1982. Student summa cum laude, Hocking Tech. Coll., 1981; student, Sinclair Coll., 1986; BBA magna cum laude, Kent State U., 1988. Lic. amateur radio operator. Tech. writer computer dept. Sinclair Coll., Dayton, Ohio, 1983; project mgr. O'Neil & Assocs., Dayton, 1983-84; biomed., bio-acoustic real-time flight simulation tempest developer Systems Rsch. Labs., Dayton, 1984-86; computer specialist Kent State U. Press, 1987-88; mgmt. analyst Electronic Warfare Frontier Engring. Inc., 1988-89; supr. computer tech. svcs. Frontier Engring., Inc., 1989-90, project engr., 1990-92; ptnr., bd. dirs. MKCC, Dayton, 1990—, SDCC, Dayton, 1992—; regional mgr. User Tech. Assocs., Dayton, 1993-96; pres., owner Lida Ray Techs., Dayton, 1978—; prof. dept. computer sci. Nat. Coll. Bus. and Tech. Graphics steering com., mem. sanctioned UNIX software adv. team Aero. Sys. Divsn.; program chair IEEE Internat. Wireless LAN Conf.; pres. Engring. Application Support Environ. Security Working Group, 2000; proceedings chmn. Nat. Aerospace & Electronics Conf., 1995—97, pres., 2000; bd. dirs. MKCC, Dayton, Cin. Digital Women; spkr. in field. Author: Job Search Strategies for the 90's, 1993, Through the Glass Ceiling, 1997, Riding the 5:15, 2000, Convergence of Socio-Economic and Technology Factors, 2001; co-author: Women on a Wire, 1996, vol. 2, 2001; editor: Graphics Directions, 1990—91; pub.: Team Advisor, SDCC Cleaning Times, IEEE Update; author: numerous poems; contbr. articles to profl. jours. Counselor Kwam's Kinder Kamp; tchr. Bible Sch.; cook Meals on Wheels; organizer/cook funeral Svcs. Dinners. Recipient Vol. Citizen award Wadsworth C. of C, 1979, Ohio Essayist award, 1979, Virginia Perryman award, 1979, Disting. Leadership award, 1990-91 Mem.: IEEE (former treas., sec. Dayton sect., bd. dirs. 1995—97, chmn. bd. dirs. Dayton sect. 1999, region 2 chpt. coord. 2000—), Equestrian Team (point rider 1977—87), Armed Forces Comms. and Electronics Assn. (judge sci. fair western dist. 1992—), Internat. Film Soc. (pres. 1986—88), Assn. Internat. Students Econs. & Commerce (pres. 1986—87), Def. Planning Analysis Soc. (sec. 1987—), Assn. Computer Machinery, Data Processing Mgmt. Assn., Tech. and Soc. of IEEE, Engring. Mgmt. Soc. of IEEE, Computer Soc. of IEEE (sec. 1991—92, vice chmn. 1992—93, chmn. 1994—95), Mortar Bd., Fencing Club, Beta Gamma Sigma, Omicron Delta Kappa, Phi Theta Kappa. Avocations: travel, writing, equestrian show jumping, soccer, painting. Home: 729 Kyle Dr Tipp City OH 45371-1435 Office Phone: 937-667-4972. Business E-Mail: bjmoore@lidaray.com.

**TIJANI, HAKEEM IBIKUNLE,** history professor, researcher; m. Olubunmi Nurat Bello, Feb. 8, 2002; children: Funmi, Lola, Tunde, Toyosi, Gbolahan. BA in History with honors, Lagos State U., Nigeria, 1988; MA in History, U. Lagos, Nigeria, 1990; MPhil in History, U. London, 1998; PhD in History, U. South Africa, Johannesburg, 2005. Cert. pub. sch. tchr. Tex. Assoc. lectr. Coll. Edn., Jalingo, Nigeria, 1988—89; lectr. Lagos State U., 1989—98; tchr. Fort Worth Ind. Sch. Dist., Tex., 2001—04; vis. asst. prof. Henderson State U., Arkadelphia, Ark., 2004—05; asst. prof. St. Francis, Joliet, Ill., 2005—. Founder History and Polit. Sci. Newsletter, Joliet, Ill., 2005. Author: Britain, Leftist Nationalists and the Transfer of Power in Nigeria, 2005, Nigeria's Urban History, 2006. With USAR, 1990—2003. Decorated Blue Ribbon award U.S. Army, Disting. Svc. award; recipient U. St. Francis award 2005; Commonwealth scholar, 1994—97. Mem.: African Studies Assn., Am. Hist. Assn. (Schmidt Rsch. award 2005). Avocation: reading. Office: Univ St Francis 500 Wilcox St Joliet IL 60435

**TIJMANN, WILLEM BERT,** civil engineer, consultant; b. Semarang, Java, Indonesia, Oct. 19, 1929; came to the U.S., 1956; s. Johan Hendrik and Alida Catharina (Deylius) T.; m. Martha Vanderlaan, Oct. 21, 1958 (div. 1986); children: Sonya Maria, John (dec.); m. Mirna Aeschlimann, Aug. 18, 1991. BS, Poly. Coll., Amsterdam, The Netherlands, 1953, M in Civil Engring., 1955. Registered profl. engr., Europe. Sr. hydraulics engr. Olarte, Ospina Arias y Payan Ltda, Civil Engrs., Bogotá, Colombia, 1955-56; soils and materials engr. Fay Spofford, Boston, 1956-62; sr. project engr. Dames & Moore, San Francisco, 1962-76; v.p. Slope Indicator Co., Seattle, 1976-87; pres. E&T Instrumentation, Stoneham, Mass., 1987—, W.B.T. Cons., Edmonds, Wash., 1987—. Inventor: holds 4 patents in U.S. and Can. Mem. ASCE (hon.), ASTM (sr.), Internat. Soc. Soil Mechanics and Engring. Found., Assn. Engring. Geologists (affiliate). Avocations: certified professional diver, diving, sailing, tennis, hiking. Home: 101A Pond St Stoneham MA 02180-2804 Office: 10628 W Deanne DR Sun City AZ 85351-4451 E-mail: 70@yahoo.com.

**TIKALSKY, PAUL J.,** civil engineering educator, structural engineer; s. Lee J. and Marilyn A. Tikalsky; m. Julie A. Tikalsky; children: Peter, Daniel. BS in Civil and Environ. Engring., U. of Wis., 1983; MS in Structural Engring., U. of Tex., 1986, PhD in Structural Materials Engring., 1989. Lic. profl. engr., Calif. Housefellow U. of Wis., Madison, 1981—84, tchg. asst., 1984; tech. asst. U. of Tex., Austin, 1984—89; from asst. to assoc. prof. Santa Clara U., Calif., 1989—95; consulting engr. TEI and Assocs., Santa Clara, 1989—94; prof. Pa. State U., University Park, 1995—2006; chair and prof. U. Utah, Salt Lake City, 2006—. Prin. engr. Tikalsky Engring. Svcs., Sandy, Utah, 1993—. Contbr. scientific papers to profl. jours. Vice-chair, bd. mem. Habitat for Humanity, San Jose, Calif., 1992—95; dep. dir. Pa. Transp. Inst.; bd. dirs. Stand Together, State College, 1998—2000. Grantee, PennDOT, U.S. Dept. Edn., Pvt. Founds., 1990—2003. Fellow: Am. Concrete Inst. (chair coms., bd. dirs.); mem.: ASTM, ASCE, Sierra Club (life), Chi Epsilon (pres.). Achievements include research in development of 100-year highway program.

**TIKEKAR, RAHUL VASANT,** computer science educator; s. Vasant and Madhumalati Tikekar; m. Rupali Rahul Khandekar, Nov. 9, 1995; 1 child, Uma. PhD, Wayne State U., Detroit, 1997. Asst. prof. Augustana Coll., Sioux Falls, SD, 1990—91; mgr. info. systems TLG, U. Calif., Irvine, 1997—98; assoc. prof. So. Oreg. U., Ashland, 1998—. Vis. lectr. U. Waikato, Hamilton, New Zealand, 2005; cons. Maharashtra Knowledge Corp. Ltd., Pune, India, 2006. Recipient Best Project award, IEEE Bangalore Chpt., 1988; grantee So. Oreg. U., 1989—2005. Office: So Oreg U Dept Computer Sci Ashland OR 97520-5028 Office Phone: 541-552-6975. Office Fax: 541-552-6171. E-mail: tikekarr@sou.edu.

**TIKOSH, MARK AXENTE,** lawyer; b. Arad, Banat, Romania, Aug. 17, 1955; arrived in U.S., 1981; s. Axente and Elena Ticosh; m. Mary Victoria Rotarescu, Sept. 10, 1979. BBA in Acctg. summa cum laude, Calif. State U., Fullerton, 1989; JD, U. of the Pacific, 1992, LLM, 1993. Bar: Calif. 1993. Acct., auditor II Orange County Probation Dept., 1984-88; pvt. practice Sacramento, Calif., 1993-94, Long Beach, Calif., 1994—. Cons. U. Banat Acad. Found., Timisoara, Romania, 1997—. Editor: The Transnational Lawyer, 1991. Mem. Town Hall L.A., 2002—. Scholarship McGeorge Legal Edn. Endowment Found., 1989-90, Dana Found., 1992-93. Mem. Calif. State Bar Assn. (estate planning trust and probate law sect.), L.A. County Bar Assn., Cato Inst., Beta Gamma Sigma. Republican. Avocations: travel, history, philosophy.

**TILAAR, HENRY A.R.,** social sciences educator; b. Tondano, Indonesia, June 16, 1932; s. Kilala and Engelien (Mamuaya) T.; m. Martha Handana, Jan. 12, 1964; children: Bryan, Pingkan, Wulan, Kilala. MA in Edn., U. Indonesia, Jakarta, 1961; MSc in Edn., Ind. U., 1967, EdD, 1969. Prof. State U. Jakarta, 1969—97; mem. staff Nat. Devel. Office (Bappenas), Jakarta, 1970—93, asst. min., 1986-93; prof. U. Jakarta, 1987-98, prof. emeritus, 1997—. Dir. Inst. Mgmt. Devel. U. Jakarta, 1991—; mem. adv. bd. Indonesian Tchrs. Assn.; cons. in field. Author: Education in National Development, 1990, National Education Management, 1992, Indonesian Education Development, 1945-1995, A Policy Study, 1995, Human Resources Development, Vision and Mission for 2020, 1997, Agenda for Education Reform for 21st Century, 1998, Education, Culture, and Civil Society, 1999, New Paradigms of National Education, 2000, National Education Reconstruction, 2001, Social Change and Education, A Transformative Pedagogy for Indonesia, 2002, Power and Education, A Cultural Studies Perspective, 2003, Multicultural Education, 2004, National Education Manifesto, 2005. Chmn. bd. advisors Cath. U., Jakarta, 1995-99; mem. bd. advisors Acad. Mgmt., Jakarta, 1996. Recipient Grand medal of merit Republic of Indonesia, 1998. Mem. Nat. Rsch. Coun., Indonesian Soc. for Advancement of Social Scis., Indonesian Lectrs. Assn. Democrat. Roman Catholic. Avocations: gardening, jogging, watching soccer. Home: Jl Patra Kuningan Utara Blok L-VII No 4 Jakarta Indonesia Office: LPMP State U Jakarta Jl Rawamangun Muka Jakarta DKI Indonesia E-mail: hartilaar@marthatilaar.net.

**TILDEN, BRADLEY D.,** air transportation executive; b. Houston, Tex., 1960; Degree, Pacific Luth. U., 1983, U. Wash., 1997. From mem. staff to exec. v.p., CFO Alaska Air Group, Inc., Seattle, 1991—2000, CFO, 2000—, exec. v.p. fin., 2002—. Office: Alaska Air Group Inc 19300 Pacific Hwy south Seattle WA 98188

**TILDEN, WESLEY RODERICK,** writer, retired application developer; b. Saint Joseph, Mo., Jan. 19, 1922; s. Harry William and Grace Alida (Kinnaman) T.; m. Lorraine Henrietta Frederick, June 20, 1948 (dec. Mar. 1999). Grad., Navy Supply Corps Sch., 1945; BS, UCLA, 1948; BA, Park Coll., Mo., 1990. Purchasing agent Vortox Co., Claremont, Calif., 1951-61; lang. lab. dir. Mount San Antonio Coll., Walnut, Calif., 1962-65; computer programmer, operator General Dynamics, Pomona, Calif., 1967-70; ret., 1970. Author: Scota, The Egyptian Princess, 1994, Merit-Sekhet: Foster Mother of Moses?, 1996; photographer, textbooks, mags., newspaper, catalogs. Historian Claremont Sister City Assn., 1963-66. Lt. USNR, 1942-46 PTO. Recipient with Lorraine Tilden People to People award Reader's Digest Found., 1963-65; named Hon. Citizen Guanajuato, Mexico, 1963. Mem. Soc. Mayflower Descendants, Scottish Clans, UCLA Alumni Assn., Park Coll. Alumni Assn., Univ. Club of Claremont, The Scituate (Mass.) Hist. Soc. Republican. Avocations: history, genealogy, photography, gardening. Home: 351 Oakdale Dr Claremont CA 91711-5039

**TILESTON, JACKIE,** artist, educator; b. Manila, Philippines, Dec. 11, 1960; arrived in U.S., 1979; d. Peter Ayer and Margaret Doreen Tileston. BA in fine arts (painting) summa cum laude, Yale U., New Haven, Conn., 1983; MFA in painting, Ind. U., Bloomington, 1988. Faculty Glassell Sch. Art Mus. Fine Arts, Houston, 1990—98; asst. prof. painting U. N.Mex., Albuquerque, 1998—2000; asst. prof. fine arts U. Pa., Phila., 2000—. Adj. faculty mem. U. Houston, 1993—98; adj. faculty Rice U., 1997; faculty Glassell Sch. of Art, Mus. of Fine Arts, Houston, 1990—98. One-woman shows include W.A. Graham Gallery, Houston, 1990, 1992, Mus. Art, Longview, Tex., 1994, Lawing Gallery, Houston, 1997, Satellite Space, U. Tex., San Antonio, 1998, U. N.Mex., Albuquerque, 2000, Barbara Davis Gallery, Houston, 2003, 2006, Phila. Art Alliance, 2003, Zg Gallery, Chgo., 2005, Holly Johnson Gallery, Dallas, 2005, Not Always So, Barbara Davis Gallery, Houston, 2006, Chromatopia, Rowan U. Gallery, Glassboro, NJ, 2006, numerous group shows, Represented in permanent collections JP Morgan Chase, Mus. Fine Arts, Houston (Catalog). Named Bellagio resident, Rockefeller Found., 2005; recipient Fellowship Award in Painting, Mid-Am. Arts Alliance/Nat. Endowment for the Arts, 1994; fellow, John S. Guggenheim Meml. Found., 2006; Academic fellow, Ind. U., Bloomington, 1986—88, Core Fellowship resident, Mus. Fine Arts, Houston, 1988—90, PEW Found. fellow, Phila., 2004. Mem.: Coll. Art Assn., Phi Beta Kappa. Office: Fine Arts Univ Pa 100 Morgan Bldg 205 S 34th St Philadelphia PA 19104 Business E-Mail: tiletson@design.upenn.edu.

**TILEWICK, ROBERT,** lawyer; b. N.Y.C., Jan. 16, 1956; s. David and Helen (Fogel) T.; m. Susan Dara Tilewick; children: Naomi Seana, Benjamin Solomon. BA, Columbia U., 1977; JD, Temple U., 1985. Bar: N.Y. 1986, Ct. 1993, U.S. Dist. Ct. (so. and ea. dists.) N.Y. 1988, U.S. Ct. Appeals (2d cir.) 1989, U.S. Dist. Ct. Conn. 1991. Systems analyst, cons. Personnelmetrics, Inc., N.Y.C., 1977-80, 81-82; assoc. Cravath, Swaine & Moore, N.Y.C., 1985-87, Paul, Weiss, Rifkind, Wharton & Garrison, N.Y.C., 1987-91, 96-97, Wiggin & Dana, New Haven, Conn., 1991-96, Kalow, Springut & Bressler, N.Y.C., 1997-99, Graham & James, N.Y.C., 1999—. Co-designer race timing system for N.Y.C. Marathon, 1977-82. NIH grantee Marine Biol. Lab., Woods Hole, Mass, 1980. Mem. ABA, N.Y.C. Bar Assn., Conn. Bar Assn., Supreme Ct. Hist. Soc. Avocation: music. Office: 885 3rd Ave New York NY 10022-4834

**TILGHMAN, RICHARD CARMICHAEL, JR.,** lawyer; b. Balt., July 6, 1947; s. Richard Carmichael and Mary Donnell (Singer) T.; m. Beverly Oliver Wheeler, Sept. 11, 1975; 1 child, Elizabeth Lloyd. BA, Union Coll., 1969; JD with honors, U. Md., 1975. Bar: Md. 1975, U.S. Dist. Ct. Md. 1976. Law clk. to presiding justice Md. Ct. Appeals, Annapolis, 1975-76; assoc. Piper & Marbury, Balt., 1976-83, ptnr., 1983—2004; ptnr., co-chmn. Pub. Co. & Corp. Governance practice group DLA Piper Rudnick Gray Cary, Balt., 2005—. Asst. editor U. Md. Law Rev., 1975. Trustee Gilman Sch., Balt., Balt. City Life Mus.; bd. mem. Ruxton Country Sch., bd. mem. & past pres. Roland Park Country Sch.; served with USN, 1969-72. Mem. ABA, Md. Bar Assn., Md. Hist. Soc., Order of Coif. Clubs: Md., Elkridge (Balt.). Democrat. Episcopalian. Avocations: golf, squash. Office: DLA Piper Rudnick Gray Cary 6225 Smith Ave Baltimore MD 21209-3600 Office Phone: 410-580-4274. Office Fax: 410-580-3274. Business E-Mail: richard.tilghman@dlapiper.com.

**TILGHMAN, SHIRLEY MARIE,** academic administrator, biology professor; b. Toronto, Can., Sept. 17, 1946; 2 children. BSc in Chemistry with honors, Queen's U., Kingston, Ont., 1968, DSc (hon.), 2002; PhD in Biochemistry, Temple U., Phila., 1975; DSc (hon.), Oxford U., 2002, NYU,

2005; postgrad., NIH. Secondary sch. tchr., West Africa, Sierra Leone, 1968—70; Fogarty internat. fellow NIH, Bethesda, Md., 1975—77; investigator Inst. Cancer Rsch., Phila., 1979—86, Howard Hughes Med. Inst., Chevy Chase, 1988—2001; asst. prof., Fels Rsch Inst. Temple U., Phila., 1978—79; prof. molecular biology Princeton U., NJ, 1986—, Howard A. Prior prof. life scis., 1986—2001, chair Coun. Sci. and Tech., 1993—2000, pres., 2001—. Founding dir. Lewis-Sigler Inst. Integrative Genomics, 1998—2003; adj. assoc. prof. human genetics and biochemistry and biophysics U. Pa., 1980—86; adj. prof. Robert Wood Johnson Medical Sch., 1988—2001; sci. adv. bd. Whitehead Inst. for Biomedical Scis., MIT; founding mem. Nat. Adv. Coun. Human Genome Project Initiative NIH; founder Princeton Postdoctoral Tchg. fellow. Trustee The Jackson Lab., 1994—, Carnegie Endowment Internat. Peace, 2005—, Google Inc., Rockefeller U., Cold Spring Harbor Lab.; mem. Pew Charitable Trusts Scholars Prog., Biomedical Scis. Selection Com., Lucille P. Markey Charitable Trust Scholar Selection Com. Recipient Pres.'s award disting. tchg., Princeton U., 1996, L'Oréal-UNESCO Internat. Women in Sci. award, 2002, Lifetime Achievement award, Soc. Devel. Biology, 2003, Radcliffe Inst. medal, Harvard U., 2004, Presdl. Medal of Honor, Dillard U., 2006. Mem.: NAS, Am. Acad. Arts and Scis., Royal Soc. London, Inst. Medicine, Am. Philos. Soc. Achievements include first to identify the H19 gene in mice, an early example of parental imprinting; research in cloning the first mammalian gene. Office: Princeton U Office of Pres One Nassau Hall Princeton NJ 08544-0001 Office Phone: 609-258-6101.

**TILL, BRIAN D.,** finance educator, consultant; b. Ft. Leonard Wood, Mo., Nov. 3, 1960; s. Lee George and Nancy Carol Till. BS in Advt., U. Tex., Austin, 1982, MBA, 1985; PhD in Bus., U. S.C., Columbia, 1992. Brand mgr. Purina, St. Louis, 1985—88; asst. prof. Drexel U., Phila., 1993—95; assoc. prof. and chair mktg. St. Louis U., 1995—. Pres. Stella Maris Child Ctr., St. Louis, 2002—06. Named Outstanding Tchr., Beta Gamma Sigma, 1991, 2001, Disting. Prof., GBA-Drexel U., 1994, Great Tchr. in Mktg., Soc. Mktg. Advances, 1998; recipient Tchg. Excellence award, U. Tex., 1985, Outstanding Tchr., Beta Gamma Sigma, 2005. Libertarian. Home: 1811 Hickory Saint Louis MO 63104 Office: St Louis Univ 3674 Lindell Blvd Saint Louis MO 63108 Office Phone: 314-977-3863. Office Fax: 314-621-1741. Business E-Mail: tillbd@slu.edu.

**TILL, JAMES EDGAR,** medical educator, researcher; b. Lloydminster, Sask., Can., Aug. 25, 1931; s. William and Gertrude Ruth (Isaac) T.; m. Marion Joyce Sinclair, June 6, 1959; children: David William, Karen Sinclair, Susan Elizabeth. BA, U. Sask., 1952, MA, 1954; PhD, Yale U., 1957; DSc (hon.), U. Toronto, Can., 2004. Mem. physics divsn. Ont. Cancer Inst., Toronto, 1957-67, with divsn. biol. rsch., 1967-89, divsn. head, 1969-82, with divsn. epidemiology and stats., 1989—; assoc. dean U. Toronto, 1981-84, univ. prof., 1984-97, univ. prof. emeritus, 1997—. Contbr. articles to profl. jours. Recipient Gairdner Found. Internat. award, 1969, Order of Can., 1994, Albert Lasker award for Basic Med. Rsch., Lasker Found., 2005; named to Canadian Med. Hall Fame, 2004. Fellow Royal Soc. Can., Royal Soc. London. Achievements include research in biophysics, cell biology and cancer control research. Home: 182 Briar Hill Ave Toronto ON Canada M4R 1H9 Office: Princess Margaret Hosp 9th Fl Rm 416 610 University Ave Toronto ON Canada M5G 2M9 Office Phone: 416-946-2948. Business E-Mail: till@oci.utoronto.ca. *Albert Einstein said: "The most beautiful thing we can experience is the mysterious. It is the source of all true art and science." He also believed that concern for humanity must always form the chief interest of all technical endeavors—"in order that the creations of our mind shall be a blessing and not a curse to mankind." Is there a more eloquent summary of standards for the scientist than this?.*

**TILLACK, THOMAS WARNER,** pathologist, educator; b. Jacksonville, Fla., Nov. 16, 1937; s. Warner S. and Charlotte G. T.; m. Lynne Anne Beam, Oct. 30, 1970; children— Jonathan Allan, Allison Anne. BA, U. Rochester, 1959; MD, Yale U., 1963. Diplomate Am. Bd. Pathology. Intern Barnes Hosp., St. Louis, 1963-64, resident, 1964-66; staff assoc. NIH, Bethesda, Md., 1966-69, sr. staff fellow, 1969-71; asst. prof. pathology Washington U., St. Louis, 1971-73, assoc. prof., 1973-76; Walter Reed prof., chmn. dept. pathology U. Va. Med. Center, Charlottesville, 1976-2001; prof. U. Va. Health Sys., Charlottesville, 2001—. Served with USPHS, 1966-69. Mem. Am. Soc. Investigative Pathology, U.S. and Can. Acad. Pathology, Am. Soc. Cell Biology, Assn. Pathology Chairs, Phi Beta Kappa. Achievements include research in cell biology and pathology. Home: 491 Ednam Cir Charlottesville VA 22903-4607 Office: U Va Health Sys Dept Pathology PO Box 800214 Charlottesville VA 22908-0214

**TILLAPAUGH, DANIEL WESTON,** academic administrator; b. Cobleskill, N.Y., Apr. 7, 1979; s. Allan Leonard and Nancy Katherine Tillapaugh. MusB., Ithaca Coll., N.Y., 2001; MEd, U. of Md., 2005. Resident dir. Salem State Coll. Dept. of Residence Life, Salem, Mass., 2001—03; grad. asst. for resident edn. and leadership programs U. of Md. Dept. of Resident Life, College Park, Md., 2003—05; asst. dir. of student activities Goucher Coll., Balt., 2005—. Nat. pub. rels. coord. ACPA Standing Com. for LGBT Awareness, Washington, 2004—06. Office: Goucher College 1021 Dulaney Valley Rd Baltimore MD 21204 Office Phone: 410-337-6243.

**TILLER, EMERSON H.,** law educator; BA, Indiana U., 1984, JD with honors, 1987; PhD in Bus. and Pub. Policy, U. Calif., Berkeley. John M. Olin faculty fellow Yale Law Sch., 1997—98; asst. prof. bus., politics and law U. Tex. at Austin, McCombs Sch. Bus., 1994—99, assoc. prof., 1999—2003, co-dir. Ctr. for Bus., Tech. and Law, 1999—2003; vis. prof. law Northwestern U. Sch. Law, Chgo., 2002, prof. law, 2003—. Vis. asst. prof. U. Pa. Sch. Law, 1999; vis. prof. bus. and pub. policy U. Calif., Berkeley, 2002. Contbr. articles to profl. jours. Office: Northwestern U Sch Law 357 E Chicago Ave Chicago IL 60611 Office Phone: 312-503-4772. Office Fax: 312-503-5950. E-mail: tiller@law.northwestern.edu.

**TILLER, OLIVE MARIE,** retired church worker; b. St. Paul, Dec. 13, 1920; d. Otto William and Myrtle Alice (Brougham) Foerster; m. Carl William Tiller, June 21, 1940; children: Robert W., Jeanne L. Peterson; m. Edward J. Alo, Dec. 15, 2001. BS, U. Minn., 1940. Spl. edn. tchr., Prince Georges County, Md., 1955-63; spl. asst. for profl. svcs. Kendall Demonstration Elem. Sch., Gallaudet Coll., Washington, 1971-78; spl. asst. for program Ch. Women United, N.Y.C., 1979-80; exec. asst. to gen. sec. Nat. Coun. Chs. of Christ in U.S.A., 1981-87; dep. gen. sec. for coop. Christianity Am. Bapt. Chs. of U.S.A., Valley Forge, Pa., 1987-88. Author (with Carl W. Tiller): At Calvary, 1994. Mem. Human Rels. Commn. Prince George's County, 1967—73; bd. dirs. Am. Leprosy Missions, Greenville, SC, 1981—95, Bapt. Peace Fellowship of N.Am., Charlotte, NC, 1984—95; mem. Nat. Interreligious Svc. Bd. for Conscientious Objectors, 1991—98, treas., 1994—95, sec., 1997—98; mem. nat. coun. Fellowship of Reconciliation, 1985—88, 1996—97; mem. Study Commn. on Human Rights Bapt. World Alliance, 1995—2000, mem. Study Commn. on Freedom and Justice, 2000—05, mem. World Aid com., 2000—05; v.p. Am. Bapt. Chs. U.S.A., Valley Forge, 1976—77. Named to Hall of Fame, St. Paul Ctrl. H.S., 1993; recipient Dahlberg Peace award, Am. Bapt. Chs., 1991, Valiant Woman award, Ch. Women United, 1978, Meeker award, Ottawa U., 1995, Luke Mowbray Ecumenical award, Am. Bapt. Chs., 1999, Girls Dormitory at Ulaya Secondary Sch. in Tanzania named for Olive Marie Tiller. Baptist. Home: 283 Norman Dr Cranberry Township PA 16066-4235 Personal E-mail: olivet@zoominternet.net.

**TILLER, THOMAS C.,** manufacturing executive; BA, MIT, 1983; MBA, Harvard U., 1991; M in Mech. Engring., U. Vt. Engr. GE, 1983; mgr. GE Appliances; v.p.; gen. mgr. GE Silicones; pres., COO Polaris Industries Inc., Mpls., 1998—99, pres., CEO, 1999—. Office: Polaris Industries Inc 2100 Highway 55 Hamel MN 55340-9770*

**TILLERSON, REX W.,** oil company executive; b. Wichita Falls, Tex., Mar. 23, 1952; m. Renda St. Clair. BS in Civil Engring., U. Tex., Austin. Joined Exxon Co., U.S.A., 1975, various positions, prodn. dept., 1975—87, bus. devel. mgr., natural gas dept., 1987—89, gen. mgr., ctrl. prodn. divsn., 1989—92; prodn. adv. Exxon Corp., Dallas, 1992; coord., affiliate gas sales Exxon Co. Internat., Florham Park, NJ, 1992—95; pres. Exxon Yemen Inc., Esso Exploration and Prodn. Khorat Inc., 1995—98; v.p. Exxon Ventures Inc., 1998—99; pres. Exxon Neftegas Ltd., 1998—99; exec. v.p. ExxonMobil Devel. Co., 1999—2001; sr. v.p. Exxon Mobil Corp., 2001—04, pres., 2004—06, chmn., CEO, 2006—. Mem. adv. coun. Engring. Found., U. Tex. at Austin; bd. dirs. Exxon Mobil Corp., 2004—. Bd. trustee Ctr. for Strategic and Internat. Studies; mem. nat. exec. bd. Boy Scouts of Am.; mem. exec. bd. Circle Ten Coun.; mem. engring. found. advisory coun. U. Tex. Austin. Mem.: U.S.-Russia Bus. Coun. (dir.), Soc. Petroleum Engrs., Am. Petroleum Inst. Office: ExxonMobil Corp 5959 Las Colinas Blvd Irving TX 75039-2298*

**TILLEY, CAROLYN BITTNER,** information scientist; b. Washington, July 29, 1947; d. Klaud Kay and Margaret Louise (Hanson) Bittner; m. Frederick Edwin Dudley, June 18, 1985 BS, Am. U., 1975; M.L.S., U. Md., 1976. With NIH, 1965-71; statis. research asst. Health Manpower Edn., Bethesda, Md., 1971-72; tech. info. specialist Nat. Libr. Medicine, Bethesda, Md., 1972-81, head medlars (med. lit. analysis and retrieval sys.) mgmt. sect., 1981—2002, advisor for UMLS support, 2002. Mem. editl. bd. Med. Reference Svcs. Quar. Recipient Merit award NIH, 1984, Rogers award Nat. Libr. Medicine, 1991. Mem. Med. Libr. Assn., IEEE Libr. Adv. Coun. Presbyterian. Avocation: horseback riding. Office: Nat Libr Medicine 8600 Rockville Pike Bethesda MD 20894-0002

**TILLEY, JOHN LEWIS,** psychologist; b. Columbus, Aug. 13, 1974; s. Linda Gayle and John Lewis, Sr. Tilley; 1 child, Travis Linn. D in Psychology, U. Indpls., 2000. Lic. Psychology Ohio Bd. of Psychology, 2002. Chief clin. officer Behavioral Sci. Specialists, LLC, Columbus, 2001—; instr. Capital U., Columbus, 2001—; cons. Twin Valley Behavioral Healthcare, Columbus, 2002—; expert evaluator Franklin County Probate Ct., Columbus, 2003—; psychologist Ctrl. Ohio Mental Health Ctr., Delaware, Ohio, 2003—; expert evaluator Fairfield County Mcpl. Ct., Lancaster, Ohio, 2004—; bd. mem., chief psychologist Helping Hands Ctr. for Spl. Needs Children, Powell, Ohio, 2005—. Recipient Ohio Student Choice award, Capital U., 1996, Top Ranking in First in Class Doctoral Program, U. of Indpls., 2000; Challenge grant, Capital U., 1992, 1993, 1994, 1995, 1996. Mem.: Nat. Register for Health Svc. Providers in Psychology, Ctrl. Ohio Psychol. Assn., Ohio Psychol. Assn., APA, Am. Coll. of Forensic Examiners, Am. Mensa, Ltd. Office: Behavioral Science Specialists LLC 100 W 3rd Ave Ste 200 Columbus OH 43201 Office Phone: 614-291-7600. Office Fax: 614-291-3800. Business E-Mail: johntilley@behavioralsciencespecialists.com.

**TILLEY, NORWOOD CARLTON, JR.,** federal judge; b. Rock Hill, S.C., 1943; s. Norwood Carlton and Rebecca (Westbrook) Tilley. BA, Wake Forest U., 1966, JD, 1969. Bar: NC 1969, admitted to practice: US Dist. Ct. (Mid. Dist.) NC 1971. Law clk. to Hon. Eugene A Gordon, U.S. Dist. Judge US Dist. Ct. (Mid. Dist.) NC, 1969-71; ptnr. Osteen, Adams, Tilley & Walker, Greensboro, 1977-88; asst. US atty. US Dist. Ct. (Mid. Dist.) NC, Greensboro, 1971-73, US atty., 1974-77, dist. judge Durham, 1988—2000, chief judge, 2000—. Instr. Wake Forest U. Sch. Law, 1980. Office: US Dist Ct PO Box 3443 Greensboro NC 27402-3443

**TILLEY, TANA MARIE,** pharmaceutical executive; b. Athens, Ga., Dec. 28, 1955; d. Harry Sanford Pierce and Shirley Joanne Webster; m. Scott David Tilley, Aug. 28, 1977; children: Christopher Scott, Lauren Brooke. AD in Nursing, U.S.C., 1980, BS in Nursing cum laude, 1990. Asst. mgr. Brook's Fashions, 1975-78; staff nurse labor and delivery Spartanburg Regional Hosp., 1980-84, head nurse labor and delivery, 1984-89, staff nurse emergency rm., 1989-90; profl. sales rep. L'Nard & Assocs., 1989-90, TAP Pharm., 1990-92, regional hosp. liaison, 1992-95, dist. mgr., hosp. acct. execs., 1995-96, dist. mgr., 1996, 1997-2000, regional sales mgr., 2000—. Methodist. Home: 605 Shade Lake Ct Alpharetta GA 30004 Office: TAP Pharmaceuticals 1050 Crown Point Ste 1445 Atlanta GA 30338 E-mail: tanatilley@tap.com.

**TILLINGHAST, CHARLES CARPENTER, III,** retired marketing company executive; b. NYC, Nov. 16, 1936; s. Charles Carpenter, Jr. and Lisette (Micoleau) T.; m. Cynthia Branch, Sept. 28, 1974; children by previous marriage: Avery D., Charles W., David C. BS in Mech. Engring., Lehigh U., 1958; MBA, Harvard U., 1963. Asst. to dir. devel. Lehigh U., Bethlehem, Pa., 1958-61; adminstrv. asst. Boise Cascade Corp., Portland, Oreg., 1963; asst. to v.p. Boise (Idaho) Cascade Corp., 1964-65, gen. mgr. office supply divsn., 1965-67, gen. mgr. paper distbn. divsn., 1966, v.p. bus. products, 1967-69, sr. v.p. housing group, 1969-71, sr. v.p., 1971-73; pres. CRM divsn. Ziff-Davis Pub. Co., Inc., Del Mar, Calif., 1971-75; pres., treas. Value Communications, Inc., La Jolla, Calif., 1975-76; pres. Oak Tree Publs., Inc. San Diego, 1976-81; co-founder, pres. Advanced Mktg. Svcs. Inc., San Diego, 1982-94, chmn., 1994—2004, pres., CEO, 2004; ret., 2004. Served to 2d lt. AUS, 1959. Home: PO Box 503 207 Morning Star Rd Sun Valley ID 83353-0503

**TILLINGHAST, DAVID ROLLHAUS,** lawyer; b. NYC, Feb. 25, 1930; s. Charles Carpenter and Josephine Dorothy (Rollhaus) T.; m. Phyllis Van Horn, Sept. 24, 1955 (div. Jan. 1984); m. Lisa Sewell, Feb. 25, 1984; children: Gregory Barrett Sewell, Lauren Alexa. AB cum laude, Brown U., 1951; LLB cum laude, Yale U., 1954. Bar: N.Y. 1955, Oreg. 1956, U.S. Supreme Ct. 1978. Assoc. Hughes, Hubbard & Reed, N.Y.C., 1954-55, 57-61, ptnr., 1961-62, 65-90; assoc. King, Miller, Anderson, Nash & Yerke, Portland, Oreg., 1955-57; spl. asst. for internat. tax affairs U.S. Dept. Treasury, Washington, 1962-65; ptnr. Chadbourne & Parke, N.Y.C., 1990-99, Baker & McKenzie, N.Y.C., 1999—. Adj. prof. Sch. Law, NYU, 1977-87; cons. UN Ctr. on Transnat. Corps., 1978-87; reporter Am. Law Inst. Project on Internat. Aspects of U.S. Income Taxation, 1982-91; cons. to reporters Am. Law Inst. Revision of Restatement of Fgn. Relations Law of U.S., 1982-83. Author: Tax Aspects of Internat. Transactions, 1978, 2d edit., 1984; co-author: Income Tax Treaty Arbitration, 2004; contbr. articles to profl. publs. Mem. transition team Sec. of Treasury W. Michael Blumenthal, 1977. Established David R. Tillinghast lectureship on internat. taxation NYU Sch. Law. Mem.: Coun. Fgn. Rels., Tax Forum, Internat. Bar Assn. (vice chmn. com. on taxation bus. law sect. 1984—86), Internat. Fiscal Assn. (v.p. U.S. br. 1983—2000, permanent sci. com. 1983—2000, vice chmn. 1993—95, chmn. 1995—2000), Assn. of Bar of City of N.Y. (chmn. com. on taxation 1981—83). Democrat. Avocations: golf, tennis. Office: Baker & McKenzie 1114 Avenue of the Americas New York NY 10036 Office Phone: 212-891-3526. Business E-Mail: david.r.tillinghast@bakernet.com.

**TILLINGHAST, EDWARD HUDSON, III,** lawyer; b. Annapolis, Md., July 18, 1958; s. Edward H. Jr. and Eugenia (Cheshire) T.; m. Dorri Elaine Berry. BA with honors, Lake Forest Coll., 1980; JD, Chgo. Kent Coll. Law, 1983. Bar: Ill. 1983, N.Y. 1985, U.S. Dist. Ct. (so. and ea. dist.) N.Y., U.S. Dist. Ct. (no. dist.) N.Y. 1990, U.S. Ct. Appeals (3d cir.) 1987, U.S. Ct. Appeals (2d cir.) 1988, U.S. Supreme Ct. 1989. Asst. county atty. Suffolk County Dept. Law, Hauppauge, N.Y., 1984-86; assoc. Dreyer and Traub, N.Y.; ptnr., head Global Fin. Restructuring & Insolvency practice & mem. exec. bd. Coudert Bros. LLP, NYC. Mem. Chgo.-Kent Law Rev., 1981-83; contbr. articles to profl. jours. Mem. ABA, N.Y. State Bar Assn., Assn. of Bar of City of N.Y., Am. Bankruptcy Inst., INSOL, Univ. Club N.Y. Avocations: sailing, yachting, skiing. Office: Coudert Bros LLP 1114 Ave of the Americas New York NY 10036 Office Phone: 212-626-4744. Office Fax: 212-626-4120. Business E-Mail: tillinghaste@coudert.com.

**TILLINGHAST, JOHN AVERY,** utilities executive; b. N.Y.C., Apr. 30, 1927; s. Charles C. and Dorothy J. (Rollhaus) T.; m. Mabel Healy, Sept. 11, 1948; children: Katherine Brickley, Susan Trainor, Abigail Ryan. BSME, Columbia U., 1948, MS, 1949. With Am. Elec. Power Service Corp., N.Y.C., 1949-79, exec. v.p. engring. and constrn., 1967-72, sr. exec. v.p., vice chmn.

engring. and constrn., 1972-79; sr. v.p. tech. Wheelabrator-Frye Inc., Hampton, NH, 1979-83, Signal Advanced Tech. Group, The Signal Cos., Hampton, NH, 1983-85; sr. v.p. Allied-Signal Internat., Hampton, 1985-86, Sci. Applications Internat. Corp., San Diego, 1986-88; pres. TILTEC, Portsmouth, NH, 1987—; CEO, Great Bay Power Corp., Dover, NH, 1994-97; CEO BayCorp Holdings, Ltd., Dover, 1997-98, chmn. bd. Portsmouth, 1998—99. Patentee generating unit control system. Elder Reformed Ch., 1976-79. Served with USN, 1944-46. Fellow ASME; mem. IEEE, NAE, Sigma Xi, Tau Beta Pi. Office Phone: 603-964-7454. E-mail: jtillinghast@comcast.net.

**TILLMAN, EUGENE,** lawyer; b. LA, Oct. 9, 1950; BA in anthropology with honors, UCLA, 1973, JD, 1976. Bar: Calif. 1976, DC 1979. Staff atty. Office of Gen. Counsel, 1976—79; dep. dir. Office of Regulation Mgmt., Health Care Financing Adminstrn. HHS, 1979—80; with Reed Smith LLP, 1980—, now ptnr. DC office, dir. legal personnel, mem. exec. com. & mgmt. com. Mem.: DC Bar Assn., Calif. Bar Assn., Am. Health Lawyers Assn. (pres. 1996—97). Office: Reed Smith LLP 1301 K St NW, Ste 1100 Washington DC 20005-3317 Office Phone: 202-414-9244. Office Fax: 202-414-9299. Business E-Mail: etillman@reedsmith.com.

**TILLMAN, JOSEPH EDWARD,** elementary school educator; b. New Hampton, Iowa, May 16, 1951; s. Marcellus Hubert Tillman and Gertrude Elizabeth Fischbach; m. Claudia Sue Dutcher, Dec. 28, 1974; children: Marissa Tillman, Katie Tilliam, Maggie Tilliam. BS in Elem. Edn. and Phys. Edn., Upper Iowa Coll., Fayette, 1973. Cert. tchr. Iowa. 5th grade tchr. Forest City (Iowa) Cmty. Sch. Dist., 1973—80, 6th grade tchr., 1980—, girls basketball coach, 1980—82, 6th grade math bcc coach, 1993—98. Vol. Forest City Sesquicentennial Com., 2005, Am. Field Svc., Forest City, 1992—2003, host parent, 1995, 2003. Recipient Golden Apple award, KIMT-TV, Mason City, Iowa, 1995, 2001. Mem.: Forest City Edn. Assn. (treas. 1973—2006). Avocations: genealogy, fishing, hunting, bowling, woodworking. Home: 34975 180th Ave Forest City IA 50436

**TILLMAN, KAREN SUE,** lawyer; b. Garland, Tex., June 21, 1962; d. Franklin Willard and Mary Ruth Wright; m. Massie Tillman, July 2, 1993. BA, Baylor U., 1984, JD, 1986. Bar: U.S. Dist. Ct. (no. dist.) Tex. Law clk. U.S. Bankruptcy Ct., Ft. Worth, 1987—89; assoc. Hill & Gilstrap, Arlington, Tex., 1989—90; litig. atty. Radio Shack Corp., Ft. Worth, 1990—. Mem.: Ft. Worth Club. Republican. Baptist. Avocation: piano. Office: Radio Shack Riverfront Campus 300 Radio Shack Cir Mail Stop CF4-122 Fort Worth TX 76102-2847 Office Phone: 817-415-3767. E-mail: karen.tillman@radioshack.com.

**TILLMAN, MARY NORMAN,** urban affairs consultant; b. Atlanta, Jan. 31, 1926; d. Mary Nellie Shehee; m. James A. Tillman Jr., Apr. 11, 1952; children: James A., Gina G. BA, Morris Brown Coll., 1947; postgrad., U. Minn., 1964, Old Dominion U., 1975—. Asst. bus. mgr. Morris Brown Coll., Atlanta, 1947-53; race rels. and urban affairs cons. Tillman Assocs. Cons. Social Engrs., Atlanta and Syracuse, NY, 1963—, sr. ptnr., treas., from 1965, now pres. Bd. dirs. The Tillman Inst. of Human Rels., Inc.; clin. prof. United Theol. Sem., New Brighton, Minn.; adj. prof. Gordon-Conwell Theol. Sem., South Hamilton, Mass. Author: What is Your Racism Quotient?, 1964, A Common Sense Approach to Racism and Other Exclusivities, 1998, (with James A. Tillman, Jr.) Why America Needs Racism and Poverty, 1972, Black Intellectuals, White Liberals and Race Relations: An Analytic Overview, 1973; What is your Exclusivity Quotient, 1978, A Common Sense Approach to Racism and Other Exclusivities, 2001; contbr. articles to profl. jours. Adv. coun. to urban ministries dept. So. Bapt. Conv., Cmty. Rels. Commn., Atlanta; bd. dirs. Christian Coun. Met. Atlanta, Tillman Inst. Human Rels. Mem. Tidewater Assn. Pub. Adminstrs. (dir.), Am. Acad. Cons., Nat. Black Writers Consortium (v.p.), Joint Ctr. for Polit. Studies. Office: 1765 Glenview Dr SW Atlanta GA 30331-2307 Office Phone: 404-349-3668.

**TILLMAN, MASSIE MONROE,** mediator, arbitrator, art gallery owner, retired judge; b. Corpus Christi, Tex., Aug. 15, 1937; s. Clarence and Artie Lee (Stewart) T.; m. Karen Wright, July 2, 1993; children: Jeffrey Monroe, Holly. BBA, Baylor U., 1959, LLB, 1961. Bar: Tex. 1961, U.S. Dist. Ct. (no. dist.) Tex. 1961, U.S. Ct. Appeals (5th cir.) 1969, U.S. Supreme Ct. 1969, formerly bd. cert. personal injury law Tex., cert.: Tex. Edn. Agy. (hearing examiner). Ptnr. Herrick & Tillman, Ft. Worth, 1961-66; pvt. practice, Ft. Worth, 1966-70, 79-87; ptnr. Brown, Herman et al, Ft. Worth, 1970-78, Street, Swift et al, Ft. Worth, 1978-79; U.S. bankruptcy judge Ft. Worth divsn. No. Dist. Tex., 1987-2001; mediator, arbitrator, 2001—. Author: Tillman's Trial Guide, 1970, 2d edit 1985; comments editor, case notes editor; mem. editl. bd. Baylor Law Rev., 1960-61. Fellow Am. Bd. Trial Advocates, Tex. Bar Found.; mem. Ft. Worth/Tarrant County Bar (bd. dirs. 1969-70, v.p. 1970-71), Trial Attys. Am., Coll. State Bar Tex. Republican. Baptist. Avocation: hunting. Address: PO Box 20213 Fort Worth TX 76102 Personal E-mail: tillmanmediator@yahoo.com.

**TILLMAN, MERCIA V.,** musician; b. Chatham, Eng. Singer Sid Mills Band, London, 1932—39; club hostess, catering mgr. U.S. Mil. Officer Clubs, 1955—69; owner Mercia Tillman Wedding Cons. & Catering, Manassas, Va., 1972—73; dir. svcs. Innisbrook Resort, Tarpon Springs, Fla., 1975—76; columnist West Coast Publs., Largo, Fla., 1977—78; owner Mercia Tillman Prodns., 1996—. Author: (songs) Florida, My State of Dreams, 1996, Walk Around the Mall, 1996, Goodbye Little Princess, 1998, Hello, My Love, Hello, 2000; author and pub.: Little Gems, 2004. Named Ms. Fla. Sr. Am., 1996; recipient Vol. Woman of Yr., Soroptimist Internat., Fla., 1997, Blue Cross/Blue Shield Ageless Hero award, State of Fla., 1999, 2000, Inductee Sr. Hall of Fame, City of St. Petersburg, Fla., 2000, KFC Col.'s Way award, State of Fla., 2000. Mem. WWII Meml. fdn. (booster), Ms. Sr. Am. Fla. Council Club. Personal E-mail: merciatillman@att.net.

**TILLMAN, VICKIE A.,** financial information company executive; BA in comm., U. Pitts., MPA in fin. With Standard & Poor's, 1977—, exec. mng. dir. pub. fin. ratings dept., now v.p. structured fin. ratings, 1994—99, exec. v.p., 1999—, mem. exec. com. Office: Standard & Poor's 55 Water St New York NY 10041

**TILLY, JENNIFER,** actress; b. Harbor City, Calif., Sept. 16, 1958; m. Sam Simon, 1984 (div., 1991). Grad., Stephens Coll., 1979. TV series include: Shaping Up, 1984, Key West, 1993, Out of Practice, 2005-; TV movies include: Heads, 1994; films include: No Small Affair, 1984, Moving Violations, 1985, He's My Girl, 1987, Inside Out, 1987, Rented Lips, 1988, High Spirits, 1988, Johnny Be Good, 1988, Remote Control, 1988, The Fabulous Baker Boys, 1989, Let It Ride, 1989, Far From Home, 1989, Scorchers, 1991, Shadow of the Wolf, 1992, Made in America, 1993, At Home With the Webbers, 1993, Double Cross, 1994, Bullets Over Broadway, 1994 (Academy award nomination best supporting actress 1994), The Getaway, 1994, The Pompatus of Love, 1996, Liar, Liar, 1996, House Arrest, 1996, Edie & Pen, 1996, Bound, 1996, American Strays, 1996, Bride of Chucky, 1998, Music From Another Room, 1998, The Muse, 1999, Goodbye, 1999, Do Not Disturb, 1999, (voice) Bartok the Magnificent, 1999, (voice) Stuart Little, 1999, Play It to the Bone, 1999, Bruno, 2000, Cord, 2000, The Crew, 2000, The Cat's Meow, 2001, Monsters, Inc. (voice), 2001, Jericho Mansions, 2003, The Haunted Mansion, 2003, Home on the Range (voice), 2004, El Padrino, 2004, St. Ralph, 2004, Deluxe Combo Platter, 2004, Seed of Chucky, 2004, Bailey's Billion$, 2005, Lil' Pimp (voice), 2005, The Civilization of Maxwell Bright, 2005, Tideland, 2005. Achievements include won Ladies No-Limit Texas Hold'Em World Series of Poker Tournament, Las Vegas, 2005, World Poker Tour Ladies Night III, 2005. Home: Care Carrol Gettko 118 S Beverly Dr Beverly Hills CA 90212-3003

**TILLY, JONATHAN L.,** obstetrician, gynecologist, reproductive biologist; BS in Animal Scis., Rutgers U., 1984, MS in Animal Scis., 1987, PhD in Animal Scis., 1990. Postdoctoral tng., molecular biology Stanford U. Med. Ctr., Calif., 1993; asst. prof. reproductive biology John Hopkins U., Balt., 1993—95; assoc. dir. Vincent Ctr. for Reproductive Biology, Mass. Gen.

Hosp., Boston, 1995—98, dir. 1998—; biologist Vincent Obstetrics and Gynecology Svc., Boston, 1995—, chief, divsn. rsch., 1998—; assoc. prof., obstetrics, gynecology, and reproductive biology Harvard Med. Sch., Boston, 1995—; adj. assoc. prof., pathology and lab. medicine Boston U. Sch. Medicine, 1996—2003; investigator Dana-Farber/Harvard Cancer Ctr., 1999—. Mem. rsch. coun. Mass. General Hosp., 1995—98, mem. subcommittee on review of rsch. proposals, 1995—2003, exec. com. mem., dept. obstetrics/gynecology, 1997—2003, mem. small animal users group subcommittee, 2002—; organizer, chair Serono Symposium on Cell Death in Reproductive Physiology, Chgo., 1996, Symposium on Apoptosis in Reproduction and Infertility, 16th World Congress on Fertility and Sterility, San Francisco, 1998; ad-hoc reviewer Reproductive Biology Study sect., 96, 2001; site reviewer, population coun. NIH, 1996; scientific advisor Fed. Dist. Ct. Judge Richard G. Stearns, 1996—2000; panel mem. Internat. Life Sciences Inst. Workshop on the Evaluation and Interpretation of Reproductive Endpoints for Human Health Risk Assessment, Washington, 1997; lectr., apoptosis lab. course dir. NICHD/MBL Tng. Course on Frontiers in Reproduction, Marine Biological Lab., Wood Hole, Mass., 1998—2001; mem., Development-1 (DEV-1) study sect., 2004—. Editl. bd. mem. Endocrinology, 1996—99, Journal Endocrinology, 2000—, Cell Death & Differentiation, 2001—, editl. bd. adv. com. mem. Endocrine Journal, contbg. editor SAGE-KE; contbr. articles to peer-reviewed publs. Nominee Rave award in Medicine, WIRED, 2005; recipient Boston Coalition award for Disting. Achievement in Rsch., 2002, Richard E. Weitzman Meml. award, Endocrine Soc., 2002. Mem.: Am. Fedn. for Aging Rsch. (mem. Nat. Scientific Adv. Coun. 2003—). Office: Mass General Hosp The Vincent Ctr for Reproductive Biology 55 Fruit St VBK 137 Boston MA 02114 Office Phone: 617-724-2182. Office Fax: 617-726-7548. Business E-Mail: tilly.jonathan@mgh.harvard.edu.

**TILNEY, ELIZABETH A.,** marketing executive; B, U. Va; MBA, Dartmouth U. With media planning Benton & Bowles Advt., N.Y.C., 1979-81; with acct. mgmt. Ogilvy & Mather Advt., N.Y.C. and Houston, 1983-87; formerly with Russell Reynolds Assocs.; sr. v.p. mktg. comm. and adminstrn. Enron, Houston, 1996-99; sr. v.p. mktg. comm. and human resources Energy Svcs. subsidiary Enron, Houston, 1999—.

**TILSON, DANIEL,** elementary school educator; Tchr. Eastwood Elem. Sch., Roseburg, Oreg., 1985—2003, Jo Lane Mid. Sch., Roseburg, Oreg. Recipient Excellence in Sci. Tchg. award, 1990, Milken Nat. Edn. award, 1992, State Tchr. of Yr. elem. award Oreg., 1992; Christa McAuliffe fellow, 1988. Office: Jo Lane Mid Sch 2153 NE Vine Roseburg OR 97470 Business E-Mail: dtilson@roseburg.k12.or.us.

**TILSON, DOROTHY RUTH,** word processing executive; b. Bloomsburg, Pa., Mar. 24, 1918; d. Roy Earl and Mary Etta (Masteller) Derr; m. Irving Tilson, Sept. 1949. BS, Bloomsburg U., 1940. Tchr. Madison Consol. Sch., Jerseytown, Pa., 1940-42; gage checker Phila. Ordinance Gage Lab., 1942-43; tabulating asst. Remington Rand, Phila., N.Y.C., 1943-46; copy writer Sears Roebuck, Phila., N.Y.C., 1946-48; statis. asst. Ford Internat., N.Y.C., 1949-56; word processing adminstrv. asst. Coopers & Lybrand, N.Y.C., 1956-91; ret. Life mem. Rep. Senatorial Inner Circle, Washington, 1987—. Mem. Am. Movement for World Govt. (sec. 1991—), N.Y. Theosophical Soc. (libr. 1969—), UN Assn.-USA (mem. global policy project which includes internat. econ. governance and human rights). Home: 435 W 119th St # 9G New York NY 10027-7110 E-mail: dotttilson@netscape.net.

**TILSON, M(ARTIN) DAVID, III,** surgeon, scientist, educator; b. Texarkana, Tex., Aug. 25, 1941; s. M. David and Leta (Martin) Tilson; 3 children BA, Rice U., 1963; MD, Yale U., 1967, Diplomate Am. Bd. Surgery, Nat. Bd. Med. Examiners. Surg. intern Yale U., New Haven, 1967-68; resident in surgery U. New Haven, 1968-72; asst. to assoc. prof. Yale U., New Haven, 1974-83, prof., 1983-89; Ailsa Mellon Bruce prof. surgery Columbia U., N.Y.C., 1989—. Contbr. articles to profl. jours. Maj. USAF, 1972-74. Rsch. grantee, NIH, 1983—94, 1999—2003. Mem. ACS, Soc. Univ. Surgeons, Am. Surg. Assn., Soc. Vascular Surgery, Internat. Soc. Cadiovasc. Surgery, Halsted Soc. Home: 105 Garth Rd B2 Scarsdale NY 10583-2714 Office: St Lukes Roosevelt Hosp 1000 10th Ave New York NY 10019-1192 E-mail: mdt1@columbia.edu.

**TILSON THOMAS, MICHAEL,** conductor; music director; b. LA, Dec. 21, 1944; s. Theodor and Roberta Tilson Thomas. Studies with, Ingolf Dahl, U. So. Calif., others; student conducting, Berkshire Music Festival, Tanglewood, Mass.; student conducting (Koussevitsky prize 1968); LL.D., Hamilton Coll.; L.H.D. (hon.), D'Youville Coll., 1976. Asst. condr. Boston Symphony Orch., 1969, assoc. condr., 1970-72, prin. guest condr., 1972-74; also Berkshire Music Festival, summer 1970, 74; music dir., condr. Buffalo Philharmonic Orch., 1971-79; prin. guest condr. LA Philharm., 1981—85; music dir., prin. condr. Great Woods Ctr. for Performing Arts, 1985-88; founder, artistic dir. New World Symphony, Fla., 1988—; prin. condr. London Symphony Orch., 1988—95, prin. guest condr., 1995—; music dir. San Francisco Symphony, 1995—. Chief condr. Ojai Festival, 1967, condr., dir. N.Y. Philharm. Young People's Concerts CBS-TV, 1971—77, vis. condr. numerous orchs., U.S., Europe, Japan, dir. Ojai Festival, 1972—77, rec. artist Sony Classical/CBS Masterworks, 1973—, opera debut, Cin., 1975, condr. Am. premiere Lulu, Santa Fe Opera, 1979, prin. guest condr. Gershwin Festival London Symphony Orch., Barbcan Ctr., 1987; composer: Grace-A Song for Leonard Bernstein, 1988; composer: (for Empire Brass Quintet) Street Song, 1988; composer: (for orch. and narrator Audrey Hepburn and New World Sym-phony) From the Diary of Anne Frank, 1990; co-artistic dir. Pacific Music Festival, 1990—, commd. for Concerts for Life's European premiere UNICEF, 1991, conducted Mozart Requiem, —. Named Musician of Yr., Musical Am., 1970, Condr. of Yr., 1994; recipient Koussevitsky prize, 1968, Grammy award, Carmina Burana with Cleve. Orch., 1976, Gershwin Live with L.A. Philharm., 1983, Ditson award, 1994, Am. Music Ctr. award, 2001, Grammy award, Mahler Symphony No. 3 with San Francisco Symphony Orch., 2004, Classic FM Gramophone award for Artist of Yr., 2005. Fellow: Am. Acad. Arts and Sciences. Office: 888 7th Ave Fl 37 New York NY 10106-3799 Mailing: Van Walsum Mgmt 4 Addison Bridge Pl London W14 8XP England Office Phone: 212-246-7726.*

**TILTON, DAVID LLOYD,** savings and loan association executive; b. Santa Barbara, Calif., Sept. 21, 1926; s. Lloyd Irvine and Grace (Hart) T.; m. Mary Caroline Knudtson, June 6, 1953; children: Peter, Jennifer, Michael, Catharine. AB, Stanford U., 1949, MBA, 1951. With Santa Barbara Savs. & Loan Assn., 1951-90, pres., 1965-84; now pres. Fin. Corp., Santa Barbara. Trustee, chmn. Calif. Real Estate Investment Trust, 1988. Served with USNR, World War II. Mem. Calif. Savs. and Loan League (dir. 1980), Delta Chi. Home: 630 Oak Grove Dr Santa Barbara CA 93108-1402 Office: Fin Corp Santa Barbara 311 E Carillo St Santa Barbara CA 93101-2761 E-mail: dtilton@earthlink.net.

**TILTON, GLENN F.,** air transportation executive; b. Washington, Apr. 9, 1948; BA in Internat. Rels., U. S.C., 1970. Sales trainee U.S. div. ops. Texaco Inc., Washington, 1970, various assignments, 1970—76, div. supr. mktg. East Brunswick, NJ, 1976—78, area mgr. resale N.Y. div. N.Y.C., 1978, asst. to gen. mgr. northeastern region, 1978—79, mktg. mgr. resale Phila. div., 1979—81, staff coord. corp. planning and econs. dept. Harrison, NY, 1981—83; asst. gen. mgr. sales Texaco Europe, 1983—84, gen. mgr. mktg., 1984—87; v.p. mktg. Texaco U.S.A., Houston, 1984—88; pres. Texaco Refining and Mktg. Inc., Houston, 1988—91; v.p. Texaco Inc., 1989; chmn. Texaco Ltd., 1991—92; pres. Texaco Eruope, 1992—94, Texaco USA, Houston, 1994—2002; sr. v.p. Texaco Inc., 1995—2002; CEO Texaco, White Plains, NY, 2001; chmn., pres., CEO UAL Corp. and United Airlines, 2002—; pres. Texaco Global Bus. Unit. Mem.: bd. dirs., Chevron Texaco (chmn., 2002). Office: UAL PO Box 66100 Chicago IL 60666*

**TILTON, WEBSTER, JR.,** contractor; b. St. Louis, Sept. 11, 1922; s. Webster and Eleanor (Dozier) T.; m. Grace Drew Wilson, Feb. 14, 1948 (div. Oct. 1959); 1 child: Webster III; m. Nancy McBlair Payne, Jan. 5, 1963. Master brewers degree, U.S. Brewers Acad., 1949. Asst. brewing technologist F&M Schaffer Brewing Co., Bklyn., 1948—52; factory sales rep. Cole Steel Equipment Co., N.Y.C., 1957—68; dist. sales mgr. Scantlin Electronics, Inc., Wash., 1968—70; sales rep. Comml. Washer & Dryer Sales Co., Wash., 1970—72; propr. Webster Tilton, Jr., contractor, Wash., 1972—86. Chief mate Mcht. Marine Res. USNR, 1942—45. Episcopalian. Home: 309 Briar Hill Rd Cooperstown NY 13326-3905

**TILY, STEPHEN BROMLEY, III,** retired bank executive; b. Phila., July 7, 1937; s. Stephen Bromley Jr. and Edith Helen (Straub) T.; m. Janet Anita Walz, July 10, 1965; children: Deborah Powell, Stephen Bromley IV, James Charles II. BS in Econs., Washington and Jefferson Coll., 1960; postgrad., Temple U. Sch. Law, 1963. Trust officer Indsl. Valley Bank & Trust Co., Phila., 1968—71; v.p. Farmers Bank Del., Wilmington, 1971—77; exec. officer G&T, Inc., Ltd., Wilmington, 1977—80; pres., COO DCG&T Co., Wilmington, 1977—91, chmn., CEO, 1991—93, chmn. emeritus, 1993—. Chmn. The Declaration Group, Conshohocken, Pa., 1985-97; trustee Declaration Fund, 1988-99; tchr. Am. Inst. Banking, 1970-79. Capt. USAR, 1960-61. Mem. Fin. Analysts of Phila., Barnegat Light Yacht Club (commodore 1988-89, trustee 1989-92), Kimberton Fish and Game Assn., Waynesborough Country Club, John's Island Golf Club, Merion Golf Club, Ducks Unltd., The 200 Club. Republican. Episcopalian.

**TIMBALAND, (TIMOTHY Z. MOSLEY),** recording industry executive, rap artist; b. Norfolk, Va., Mar. 10, 1971; Mem. Timbaland & Magoo; founder, pres. Mosely Music Group/Geffen. Singer: (albums) Welcome to Our World, 1997, Tim's Bio, 1998, Indecent Proposal, 2001, Under Construction, Part II, 2003; prodr. (Jodeci) Diary of a Mad Band, 1993, The Show, The After Party, The Hotel, 1994, (Aaliyah) One in a Million, 1996, Aaliyah, 2001, I Care 4 U, 2002, (Ginuwine) The Bachelor, 1996, 100% Ginuwine, 1999, The Life, 2001, (Missy Elliot) Supa Dupa Fly, 1997, Miss E: So Addictive, 2001, Under Construction, 2002, This is Not a Test!, 2003, The Cookbook, 2005, (Jay-Z) Vol. 2: Hard Knock Life, 1998, Vol. 3: Life & Times of S Carter, 1999, The Blueprint, 2001, The Blueprint 2: The Gift & the Curse, 2002, The Black Album, 2003, (Beck) Mutations, 1998, (Nas) I Am, 1999, Nastradamus, 1999, (Snoop Dogg) The Last Meal, 2000, (Ludacris) Word of Mouf, 2001, Red Light District, 2004, (Limp Bizkit) New Old Song, 2001, (Destiny's Child) This is the Remix, 2002, (Justin Timberlake) Justified, 2002, FutureSex/LoveSounds, 2006, (TLC) 3D, 2002, (Fabolous) Ghetto Fabolous, 2001, Street Dreams, 2003, (Bubba Sparxxx) Dark Days, Bright Nights, 2001, Deliverance, 2003, (The Charm, 2006, (Alicia Keys) The Diary of Alicia Keys, 2003, (Lil Kim) La Bella Mafia, 2004, (Brandy) Afrodisiac, 2004, (LL Cool J) The DEFinition, 2004, (Jennifer Lopez) Rebirth, 2005, (Black Eyed Peas) Monkey Business, 2005, (Jamie Foxx) Unpredictable, 2005, (Nelly Furtado) Loose, 2006, (soundtracks) Sprung, 1996, Money Talks, 1997, Dr. Doolittle, 1998, Why Do Fools Fall in Love, 1998, The PJs, 1999, Austin Powers: The Spy Who Shagged Me, 1999, Romeo Must Die, 2000, Nutty Professor II: The Klumps, 2000, Exit Wounds, 2000, Lara Croft: Tomb Raider, 2001, Shark Tale, 2004. Co-recipient award for Most Performed Song from Motion Picture, ASCAP, 1999, 2001, 2002.*

**TIMBERLAKE, CHARLES EDWARD,** historian, educator; b. South Shore, Ky., Sept. 9, 1935; s. Howard Ellis and Mabel Viola (Collier) T.; m. Patricia Alice Perkins, Dec. 23, 1958; children: Mark Brewster, Daniel Edward, Eric Collier BA, Berea Coll., 1957; Calif. State Teaching Credential, Claremont Grad. Sch., 1958, MA, 1962; PhD, U. Wash., 1968. Tchr. Barstow H.S., Calif., 1959-60, Claremont City Sch., Calif., 1960-61; tchg., rsch. asst. U. Wash., Seattle, 1961-64; asst. prof. history U. Mo., Columbia, 1967-73, assoc. prof., 1973-81, prof. history, 1981—, Byler disting. prof., 1996, chmn. dept., 1996—2000, asst. dir. Honors Coll., 1988-90. Exch. prof. Moscow State U., 1985, U. Manchester, England, 1987—88; hon. prof. history Lanzou U., China, 1991; dir. edn. svcs. Leisure Voyages, 1992—2000; vis. prof. Joensuu (Finland) U., 1996, 98, 2000, 03, adj. prof. 2005—. Author: The Fate of Russian Orthodox Monasteries and Convents Since 1917, 1995; editor: Essays on Russian Liberalism, 1972, Detente: A Documentary Record, 1978, Religious and Secular Forces in Late Tsarist Russia, 1992, Profiles of Finland series, 1991-94, (microfiche) The St. Petersburg Collection of Zemstvo Publs., 1992—; contbr. chpts. to books, articles to profl. jours. Mem. Citizens Alliance for Progress, Columbia, Mo., 1969—75, pres., 1969—70; founding mem. High Edn. Rescue Operation, Mo., 1983—91; mem. Columbians Against Throw-Aways, 1980—83. Recipient Disting. Alumnus award Berea Coll., 2002; Fgn. Area fellow, 1965-66, fellow Internat. Rsch. and Exchs. Bd., 1971, 95, 2001, Am. Coun. Learned Socs., 1978-79, Fulbright-Hays fellow, 1995; grantee NEH, 1972, 79, 87; Am. Couns. for Internat. Edn. grantee, 2005. Mem. Am. Assn. Advancement Slavic Studies (bd. dirs. 1980-82, 84-86, chmn. council regional affiliates 1981-82, 85-86, chmn. permanent membership com. 1981-84), Western Slavic Conf., Am. Hist. Assn. (exec. council Conf. on Slavic and East European history 1987-89), Central Slavic Conf. (sec.-treas. 1967-68, pres. 1968-69, 76-77, 83-84, 88-89, 2001-02, exec. bd. 1972—; custodian archive 1972—), Mo. Conf. History (pres. 1992, sec.-treas. 1996-2000), State Hist. Soc. Mo., Fulbright Assn. (pres. Mo. chpt. 1997-2000). Avocations: hiking, travel. Office: Dept History U Mo 101 Read Hall Columbia MO 65211-0001 Office Phone: 573-442-4580. Business E-Mail: timberlakec@missouri.edu.

**TIMBERLAKE, JUSTIN,** vocalist; b. Memphis, Jan. 31, 1981; s. Randy Timberlake and Lynn Harless. Vocalist 'N Sync, 1996—2002; solo vocalist, 2002—. Launched William Rast clothing line (with Trace Ayala), 2005, restaurant co-owner (with Eytan Sugarman) Destino's, 2006. Singer (with 'N Sync): (albums) N Sync, 1998, Home for Christmas, 1998, No Strings Attached, 2000, Celebrity, 2001; singer: (solo albums) Justified, 2003 (Grammy awards: Best Male Pop Vocal Performance for song "Cry Me A River", 2003, Best Pop Vocal Album, 2003), FutureSex/LoveSounds, 2006; actor: (films) Longshot, 2000, Edison, 2005; (TV films) Model Behavior, 2000. Founder J. Timberlake Found.: Office: Jive Records 137-139 W 25th St 9th Floor New York NY 10012*

**TIMCENKO, LYDIA TEODORA,** secondary school educator, biochemist; b. Beograd, Yugoslavia, July 4, 1951; arrived in U.S., 1975; d. Teodor Pavle and Branislava (Spasojevic) Timcenko; m. Ghazi Youssef, June 16, 1980 (div. Oct. 1989); children: Ali Alexander Youssef, Kareem Misha Youssef; m. Peter Porzio, Mar. 11, 1996. BS in Chemistry, U. Belgrade, Yugoslavia, 1975; MS, Wayne State U., 1977, PhD, 1984. Grad. teaching asst. Wayne State U., 1976-78, 81-84, rsch. assoc., 1986—88, lectr. in chemistry, 1989; postdoctoral fellow Mich. Cancer Found., Detroit, 1985; postdoctoral fellow Sch. Medicine Wayne State U., 1986—88; lectr. in chemistry Lawrence Tech. U., Southfield, Mich., 1989, 90-91; biochemist Strohtech, Inc., Detroit, 1990—91; prof. chemistry Sussex County Coll., Newton, NJ, 1997—99; asst. prof. chemistry N.Y. Techol. Coll., City U. Bklyn., 1999—; sci. tchr. New Milford (NJ) H.S., 2002, Newton (N.J.) H.S., 2002—; adj. assoc. prof. organic chemistry Pace U., N.Y.C., 2004—05; tchr. chemistry, physics, biology Dwight Morrow H.S., Englewood, NJ, 2004—; sci. tchr. Jonathon Dayton H.S., Springfield, NJ, 2005—. Prin. investigator, rsch. scientist ICN Galenika Inst., Clin. Ctr. Serbia, Belgrade, 1991—96; rsch. technologist. cons. Huet Biol., Birmingham, Mich., 1987—91; adj. prof. chemistry Kean Coll.; adj. prof. dept. chemistry and chem. biology Stevens Inst. Tech., Castle Point on Hudson, Hoboken, NJ; adj. assoc. prof. organic chemistry Pace U., N.Y.C., 2004—04; adj. prof. in organic and biochemistry CUNY, 2004. Contbr. articles to profl. jours. Mem.: Am. Chem. Soc., Am. Soc. Microbiology, Phi Lambda Upsilon. Achievements include research in shigella toxin in shigella and E. coli; mitoch GPO in advenal cortex; liberation of labile sufur from ferredoxins; adhesion shigella to HCTH and HELA; localization of GST and GPO in adrenal. Home: 306 State Route 94 Columbia NJ 07832-2771 Personal E-mail: ltim51@cs.com. Business E-Mail: pjp@eclipse.net.

TIMCO, JOSEPH JUSTIN, elementary school educator; b. Fairview, OH, Sept. 26, 1975; s. Joseph John Timco and Andrea Turek; m. Melanie S. King, July 15, 2000; children: Joseph Andrew, Jonathon James. BSc in Edn., Sports Medicine, U. Akron, OH, 2003. Cert. tchr. Ohio, 2006. Tchr. Highland Local Schs., Medina, Ohio, 2003—. Soccer coach Highland Boys Soccer, Medina, Ohio, 2003—06; track coach Highland Mid. Sch., 2004—06. Mem.: OH Edn. Assn., Ednl. Leadership (assoc.), Phi Kappa Psi. Lutheran. Avocations: backpacking, photography, video production, sports. Office: Highland Local Schools 4880 Ridge Road Medina OH 44215 Office Phone: 330-239-1901.

TIMKEN, WARD J., JR., manufacturing executive; BA, Georgetown Univ.; MBA, Univ. Va. Mgr., Washington office McGough & Assoc. govt. affairs. cons.; with Timken Co., Canton, Ohio, 1992—, corp. v.p., 2000—03, bd. dir., 2002—, exec. v.p., pres. steel group, 2003—05, vice chmn., 2005, chmn., 2005—. Bd. mem. Am. Iron & Steel Inst.; bd. dir. Team NEO, Stark Devel. Bd., Henry & Louise Timken Found.; mem. Ohio Bus. Develop. Council. Bd. dir. Firestone Country Club. Office: Timken Company 1835 Dueber Ave SW Canton OH 44706-0932 Office Phone: 330-438-3000.*

TIMKEN, WILLIAM R., JR., (WILLIAM ROBERT TIMKEN JR.), ambassador, former manufacturing executive; b. 1938; m. Sue Timken; 6 children. BA, Stanford U., 1960; MBA, Harvard U., 1962. With Timken Co. (formerly The Timken Roller Bearing Co.), Canton, Ohio, 1962—2005, asst. v.p. sales, 1964-65, dir. corp. devel., 1965-68, v.p., 1968-73, vice-chmn. bd., chmn. fin com., 1973-75, chmn. bd., chmn. fin. com., 1975—2003, non-exec. chmn., 2004—05, also dir.; chmn. Securities Investor Protection Corp., Washington, 2003—05; US amb. to Germany US Dept. State, Berlin, 2005—. Named Ohio Bus. Statesman of Yr., Chevalier French Legion of Honor, hon. citizen, Colmar, France; recipient Henry Laurence Gantt medal, ASME, 2003, Woodrow Wilson award corp. citizenship, Adam Smith award, Ellis Island Medal of Honor, Ohio Governors award. Office: US Embassy 5090 Berlin Pl Washington DC 20521*

TIMKO, MAUREEN CECILIA, music educator; d. Eugene and Mary Catherine Baxter; m. John Michael Timko, Apr. 20, 1985; 1 child, Michael John. AS in Bus., SUNY, Cobleskill, 1980; MusB, SUNY, Potsdam, 1984. Pvt. piano and voice tchr. Timko Enterprises, Pt. Crane, NY, 1991—; piano and voice tchr. Cmty. Music Ctr., Binghamton, NY, 1991—97. Asst. dir. music Jan DeAngelo Prodn. Co., Endicott, NY, 1994—. Actor(musician): A Funny Thing Happened on the Way to the Forum; composer: (piano compositions) Petonia Lake Theme, Irish Mood, Seasonal Interludes; actor-(musician): Albert Herring, The Pajama Game. Choir mem., soprano St. James Cath. Ch., Johnson City, NY, 2000—06, cantor, 2005—. Mem.: Am. Coll. Musicians, Nat. Guild Piano Tchrs. Roman Catholic. Avocations: swimming, dance, hiking, travel, writing.

TIMLIN, JAMES CLIFFORD, bishop; b. Scranton, Pa., Aug. 5, 1927; s. James C. and Helen E. (Norton) T. AB, St. Mary's Sem., Balt., 1948; STB, Gregorian U., Rome, 1950. Ordained priest Roman Cath. Ch., 1951. Asst. pastor St. John the Evangelist Ch., Pittston, Pa., 1952—53, St. Peter's Cathedral, Scranton, 1953—66; asst. chancellor, sec. Diocese of Scranton, 1966—71, chancellor, 1971—77, aux. bishop, vicar gen., 1976—84, bishop, 1984—2003, bishop emeritus, 2003—; pastor Ch. of Nativity, Scranton, 1979—84. Roman Catholic. Address: 1600 Green Ridge St Dunmore PA 18509

TIMLIN, MIKE, professional baseball player; b. Midland, Tex., Mar. 10, 1966; Pitcher Toronto Blue Jays, 1991—96, Seattle Mariners, 1997—98, Balt. Orioles, 1999—2000, St. Louis Cardinals, 2000—02, Phila. Phillies, 2002, Boston Red Sox, 2003—. Achievements include mem. MLB Am. League All-Star Team, 2005. Office: Boston Red Sox 4 Yawkey Way Boston MA 02215-3496

TIMLIN, ROBERT J., judge; b. 1932; BA cum laude, Georgetown U., 1954, JD, 1959, LLM, 1964. Atty. Douglas, Obear and Campbell, 1960-61, Law Offices of A.L. Wheeler, 1961; with criminal divsn. U.S. Dept. Justice, 1961-64; atty. U.S. Atty. Office (ctrl. dist.) Calif., 1964-66, Hennigan, Ryneal and Butterwick, 1966-67; city atty. City of Corona, Calif., 1967-70; prin. Law Office of Robert J. Timlin, 1970-71, 75-76; ptnr. Hunt, Palladino and Timlin, 1971-74, Timlin and Coffin, 1974-75; judge Mcpl. Ct., Riverside Calif., 1976-80, Calif. Superior Ct., Riverside, 1980-90; assoc. justice Calif. Ct. Appeals, 1990-94; judge U.S. Dist. Ct. (ctrl. dist.) Calif., L.A., 1994—. Part-time U.S. Magistrate judge Ctrl. Dist. Calif., 1970-74. Served U.S. Army, 1955-57. Mem. Calif. Judges Assn. Office: US Dist Ct Central Dist Calif Western Divsn 312 N Spring St Los Angeles CA 90012 Office Phone: 213-894-5272.

TIMM, ROGER K., lawyer; b. Bay City, Mich., May 21, 1947; BS, U. Mich., 1969; JD, Harvard U., 1972. Bar: Mich. 1972. Mem. Dykema Gossett, Detroit. Mem.: ABA, State Bar Mich. Office: Dykema Gossett 400 Renaissance Ctr Detroit MI 48243-1668 Office Phone: 313-568-6597. E-mail: rtimm@dykema.com.

TIMMCKE, ALAN EDWARD, colon and rectal surgeon; b. Madison, Wis., July 7, 1949; s. Wesley Eugene Timmcke; m. Teresa Ann Watkins, Dec. 31, 1977; children: Gretchen Kristine, Alan Edward Jr. BS, Dickinson Coll., 1971; MD with honors, Temple U., 1975. Diplomate Am. Bd. Surgery, Am. Bd. Colon and Rectal Surgery; lic. physician, Pa., Maine, Mo., La. Intern in surgery Nat. Naval Med. Ctr., Bethesda, Md., 1975-76, resident in gen. surgery, 1976-79; rsch. fellow in colon and rectal surgery Jewish Hosp./Washington U. Med. Ctr., St. Louis, 1985-86, clin. fellow in colon and rectal surgery, 1986-87; asst. in surgery Washington U. Sch. Medicine, St. Louis, 1985-87; staff colon and rectal surgeon Ochsner Clinic, New Orleans, 1987—. Staff surgeon Nat. Naval Med. Ctr., Bethesda, 1979, Naval Regional Med. Ctr., Newport, R.I., 1979-82, dept. colon and rectal surgery Lahey Clinic Med. Ctr., Burlington, Mass., 1984-85; staff surgeon Rumford (Maine) Community Hosp., 1982-84, med. staff v.p., 1983-84; instr. surgery Uniformed Svcs. U. of Health Scis., Bethesda, 1978-79; lectr. in field. Assoc. editor Diseases of the Colon and Rectum, 2002—; contbr. articles and abstracts to profl. jours. Lt. comdr. M.C., USN, 1975-82. Recipient Harry E. Bacon Found. award for best original paper, 1987; NIH Summer Rsch. fellow, 1972. Fellow ACS, Am. Soc. Colon and Rectal Surgeons; mem. New Orleans Surg. Soc., Surg. Assn. of La., Internat. Soc. Univ. Colon and Rectal Surgeons, Soc. of Am. Gastrointestinal Endoscopic Surgeons, Am. Soc. Gastrointestinal Endoscopy, Alpha Omega Alpha. Office: Ochsner Clinic Dept Colon/Rectal Surgery 1514 Jefferson Hwy New Orleans LA 70121-2483 Office Phone: 504-842-4060. Personal E-mail: atimmcke@aol.com.

TIMMER, BARBARA, state agency administrator; b. Holland, Mich., Dec. 13, 1946; d. John Norman and Barbara Dee (Folensbee) T. BA, Hope Coll., Holland, Mich., 1969; JD, U. Mich., 1975. Bar: Mich. 1975, U.S. Supreme Ct. 1995. Assoc. McCrosky, Libner, VanLeuven, Muskegon, Mich., 1975-78; apptd. to Mich. Women Commn. by Gov., 1976-79; staff counsel subcom. commerce, consumer & monetary affairs Ho. Govt. Ops. Com., U.S. Ho. of Reps., 1979-82, 85-86; exec. v.p. NOW, 1982-84; legis. asst. to Rep. Geraldine Ferraro, 1984; atty. Office Gen. Counsel Fed. Home Loan Bank Bd., 1986-89; gen. counsel Com. on Banking, Fin. and Urban affairs U.S. Ho. of Reps., Washington, 1989-92; asst. gen. counsel, dir. govt. affairs ITT Corp., Washington, 1992-96; sr. v.p., dir. govt. rels. Home Savs. of Am., Irwindale, Calif., 1996-99; ptnr. Manatt, Phelps & Phillips, Washington, 1999—; gen. counsel MyPrimeTime, Inc., San Francisco, 2000-01; asst. sec. U.S. Senate, 2001—02, asst. sgt. at arms, 2003; chief info. officer Calif. Dept. Transp., Sacramento, 2003—. Mem. info. tech. coun. Women's Transp. Seminar, Calif., 2004—. Editor: Compliance With Lobbying Laws and Gift Rule Guide, 1996. Mem. Calif. State CIO Coun., 2004—05; bd. dirs. Women's High Tech Coalition. Named to Acad. of Women Achievers, YWCA, 1993; recipient Affordable Housing award, Nat. Assn. Real Estate Brokers, 1990, Disting. Alumni award, Hope Coll., 2003. Mem.: FBA (chair exec. coun. banking law com.), ABA (bus. law sect., electronic fin. svcs. subcom.), Bar of

D.C., Mich. Bar Assn., Supreme Ct. Hist. Soc., Supreme Ct. Bar Assn., Women in Housing and Fin. (bd. dirs. 1992—94, gen. counsel 1994—98), Exchequer Club. Episcopalian. Office: 2629 Main St PMB 115 Santa Monica CA 90405 E-mail: btimmerdc@earthlink.net.

TIMMER, MARGARET LOUISE (PEG TIMMER), art educator; b. Osmond, Nebr., July 4, 1942; d. John Henry and Julia Adeline (Schilling) Borgmann; m. Charles B. Timmer, May 23, 1964 (div. June 1990); children: Jill Marie, Mark Jon. AA, N.E. Community Coll., Norfolk, Nebr., 1987; BA in Edn., K-12 art endorsement, Wayne (Nebr.) State U., 1988; MEd, Bank Street Coll./Parsons Sch. Design, N.Y.C., 1992. Cert. tchr., Nebr. Bookkeeper Goeres Electric, Osmond, 1960-61; tel. operator Northwestern Bell, Norfolk, 1961-64; with want advt. dept. Washington Post, 1964-65; saleswoman Jeannes Fashion Fabrics, Norfolk, 1970-72, Tripps, Norfolk, 1986-87; office art tchr. Tim's Plumbing & Heating Inc., Norfolk, 1972-88; tchr. art Norfolk Cath. Schs., 1988—, mem. bd., 1985-88. Instr. art history N.E. Community Coll., 1992—; mem. youth art bd. Norfolk Art Ctr., 1988—; visual arts com.; del. Oxford (Eng.) Round Table, 2006. One-woman show Uptown Restaurant, Norfolk, 1993, Norfolk Art Ctr., 1996; exhibited in group shows Sioux City (Iowa) Art Ctr., 1988, Columbus (Nebr.) Art Ctr., 1993, Noyes Gallery, Lincoln Norfolk Art Ctr, Reeder Original Norfolk, 2003, 04. Mem. choir St. Mary's Cath. Ch., Norfolk, 1991—; mem. Norfolk Community Choir, 1991; bd. dirs. Norfolk Community Concerts Assn., 1984-87; treas. Norfolk Cath. Booster Club, 1985-86; leader 4-H, Madison County, 1973-78; judge art show Laurel (Nebr.) Women's Club, 1988; presenter Oxofrd Roundtable, Eng., 2006. Named outstanding profl. vol. Norfolk Art Ctr., 1996; recipient Crystal Apple award Norfolk (Nebr.) C. of C., 1999. Mem. N.E. Nebr. Art Assn., Nebr. Art Edn. Assn. (3d place award 1988). Avocations: painting, gardening, reading, gourmet cooking, sewing. Home: Rte 2 Box 239 55380 Warnerville Dr Norfolk NE 68701-9758 Office: Norfolk Cath Schs 2300 Madison Ave Norfolk NE 68701-4456 Personal E-mail: ptimmer@yahoo.com.

TIMMERHAUS, KLAUS DIETER, chemical engineering professor; b. Mpls., Sept. 10, 1924; s. Paul P. and Elsa L. (Bever) T.; m. Jean L. Mevis, Aug. 3, 1952; 1 dau., Carol Jane. BS in Chem. Engring. U. Ill., 1948, MS, 1949, PhD, 1951. Registered profl. engr., Colo. Process design engr. Calif. Rsch. Corp., Richmond, 1952-53; extension lectr. U. Calif., Berkeley, 1952; mem. faculty U. Colo., Boulder, 1953-95, prof. chem. engring., 1963—86, assoc. dean engring., 1963—86, dir. engring. rsch. ctr. coll. engring., 1983—86, chmn. aerospace dept., 1983—86, chmn. chem. engring. dept., 1986-89, Patten Chair Disting. prof., 1986-89, presdl. tchg. scholar, 1989—. Chem. engr. cryogenics lab. Nat. Bur. Standards, Boulder, summers 1955,57,59,61; lectr. U. Calif. at L.A., 1961-62; sect. head engring. div. NSF, 1972-73; cons. in field. Bd. dirs. Co. Engring. Expt. Sta., Inc., Engring. Measurements Co. Editor: Advances in Cryogenic Engineering, vols. 1-25, 1954-80; co-editor: Internat. Cryogenic Monograph Series, 1965-. Served with USNR, 1944-46. Recipient Disting. Svc. award Dept. Commerce, 1957, Samuel C. Collins award for outstanding contbns. to cryogenic tech., 1967, Meritorious Svc. award Cryogenic Engring. Conf., 1987, Disting. Pub. Svc. award NSF, 1984, Exemplary Contbr. award Cryogenic Engring. Conf., 2005; named CASE Colo. Prof. of Yr., 1993, Disting. Lectr., L-T Fan, 2001. Fellow AAAS (v.p. 1985, pres. 1986, Southwestern and Rocky Mountain divsn. Pres.'s award 1989), AIChE (v.p. 1975, pres. 1976, Alpha Chi Sigma award for chem. engring. rsch., 1968, Founders award 1978, Eminent Chem. Engring. award 1983, W.K. Lewis award 1987, F.J. Van Antwerpen award 1991, Inst. Lecture award 1995), Am. Soc. for Engring. Edn. (bd. dirs. 1986-88, George Westinghouse award 1968, 3M Chem. Engring. divsn. award 1980, Engring. Rsch. Coun. award 1990, Delos Svc. award 1991), Cryogenic Soc. Am.; mem. Internat. Inst. Refrigeration (v.p. 1979-87, pres. 1987-95, US nat. commn. 1983-, pres. 1983-86, W.T. Pentzer award 1989, hon. co-chair, IIR World Congress, 2003); mem. NAE, Am. Astron. Soc., Austrian Acad. Sci., Cryogenic Engring. Conf. (chmn. 1956-67, bd. dirs. 1967-), Internat. Cryocooler Conf. (bd. dirs. 1980-), Soc. Automotive Engrs. (Ralph Teetor award 1991), Sigma Xi (v.p. 1986-87, pres. 1987-88, bd. dirs. 1981-89), Verein Deutscher Ingenieure, Sigma Tau, Tau Beta Pi, Phi Lambda Upsilon. Home: 905 Brooklawn Dr Boulder CO 80303-2708 Business E-Mail: klaus.timmerhaus@colorado.edu.

TIMMERMAN, ANNE N., retired public relations executive; b. Evanston, Ill., May 10, 1910; d. Charles Edward and Agnes (Bateman) N.; m. John C. Timmerman, Sept. 30, 1933; 1 child, Jan LaTrobe. AB, U. S.C., 1930; postgrad., Hunter Coll., 1930-31, NYU, 1932-33. APR (Accredited Pub. Relations Practitioner). Editl. asst. Pictorial Rev. Mag., N.Y.C., 1930—32; copy asst. J. Walter Thompson Co., N.Y.C., 1932—33; sub editor Cosmopolitan Mag., N.Y.C., 1933—37; with Girl Scouts of U.S., N.Y.C., 1937—57, chief pub. rels. officer, 1945—57; dir. pub. info. edn. Nat. Recreation and Park Assn., 1957—66; spl. asst. gen. dir. Internat. Social Svc. Am. Br., N.Y.C., 1966—68; dir. devel. Nat. Accreditation Coun. for Agys. Serving Blind and Visually Handicapped, N.Y.C., 1969—78; pres. Timmerman & New Inc., Mamaroneck, NY, 1980—2001; ret., 2001. Cons. dept. pub. adminstrn. Baruch Coll., CUNY, 1987-94, Sch. Pub. Affairs, 1994-99. Author: Service For Givers, The Story of the National Information Bureau, 1983, Raise More Money for Your Nonprofit Organization, 1991; contbr. articles to profl. jours. Bd. dirs. Mamaroneck (N.Y.) United Fund, 1963-64; chair nominating com. LWV, Mamaroneck, 1988; warden emerita St. Thomas' Episc. Ch., Mamaroneck. Recipient Marzella Garland award for outstanding achievement in promotion of improved housing conditions in Mamaroneck Village, 1995. Mem. Pub. Rels. Soc. Am. (bd. dirs. N.Y. chpt. 1958-72), Women Execs. Pub. Rels. (sec. 1962-63), Assn. Fundraising Profls. (bd. dirs. Greater N.Y. chpt. 1978-84), Phi Beta Kappa. Democrat.

TIMMERMAN, WILLIAM B., utilities executive, accountant; b. Columbia, S.C., Nov. 12, 1946; s. William Bledsoe and Helen (Speissegger) T.; m. Janet Russell, Sept. 15, 1971; children: William III, Catherine Lucille. BA in Pub. Acctg., Duke U., 1968; postgrad., Harvard U., 1990. CPA, N.C. Auditor Arthur Andersen & Co., Charlotte, NC, 1968-78; sr. v.p. Carolina Energies, Inc., Columbia, 1978-82; v.p. S.C. Electric & Gas Co., Columbia, 1982-83, v.p., group exec., 1983-84; chief fin. officer, sr. v.p. SCANA Corp., Columbia, 1984—94, exec. v.p., CFO, contr., 1994—95, pres., 1995—, COO, 1996—97, chmn., CEO, 1997—. Exec. adv. com. Edison Electric Inst.; acctg. and fin. exec. com. Southeastern Electric Exchange; bd. dir. SCANA Corp., Liberty Corp., Preholding Inc., Palmetto Bus. Forum; past dir. Powertel Inc., SouthernNet/Telecom USA, Wachovia Bank SC, Palmetto Seed Corp.; chmn. bd. Standard Fed. Savs. Bank, Columbia; past chmn. SC Rsch. Authority. Trustee United Way of Midlands, Columbia, 1985—; vice chmn. fin. ARC, Columbia, 1986—; adv. bd. Sch. Bus. U. SC, 1985—, Duke Neighborhood Partnership; bd. dir. Duke U., the Fuqua Sch.; past dir. Benedict Coll., SC State Ports Authority. Served with USNR, 1968-72. Office: SCANA Corp 1426 Main St Ste 100 Columbia SC 29201-2834*

TIMMERMANN, ALLAN GILLING, management and economics professor; b. Skovlund, Denmark, Oct. 9, 1964; came to U.S., 1994; s. Viggo Nielsen and Gyda Bente (Gilling) T.; m. Solange Maria Ferreli Fortes, Feb. 1, 1992. MS, London Sch. Econs., 1988; PhD, U. Cambridge, England, 1992. Lectr. fin. econs. U. London, 1991-94; asst. prof. U. Calif., San Diego, 1994-98, assoc. prof., 1999—2001, prof., 2001—. Cons. Barclay's Global Investors, 1998, IMF, Fed. Res. Bd., European Cntrl. Bank; reviewer London Sch. Econs., 1998-99. Dept. editor Jour. of Forecasting, 2000-05; assoc. editor Jour. Bus. and Econ. Stats., 2001—, Jour. Fin. Econometrics, 2003—; contbr. articles to profl. jours. Hellman Faculty fellow, U. Calif., San Diego, 1997; British Coun. scholar, London, 1987; recipient Tress prize U. London, 1993. Mem. Am. Fin. Assn., Ctr. Econ. Policy Rsch. (rsch. fellow), Econometric Soc. Avocations: long distance running, tennis. Office Phone: 858-534-4860, 858-534-0894. Business E-Mail: atimmermn@ucsd.edu.

TIMMINS, ALLAN S., information technology manager, educator; s. Chester E. and Mildred I. Timmins; life ptnr. Gail N. Rein; children: Kim Angelique, Michael Antony. MS in Adminstrn. and Supervision, U. Lowell, Mass., 1974. Cert. profl. educator Fla., 1991. Classroom tchr. Bedford Pub.

Schs., Mass., 1967—90, Hernando County Pub. Schs., Brooksville, Fla., 1991—97, tech. coord. Spring Hill, 1997—. With U.S. Army, 1967—70, Vietnam. Mem.: AARP, NEA, Internat. Soc. Tech. Educators, Mass. Ret. Tchrs., Ret. State, County and Mcpl. Employee Assn. Independent. Avocations: travel, gardening, sports. Home: 8040 Spanish Oak Dr Spring Hill FL 34606 Office: Westside Elem Sch 5400 Applegate Dr Spring Hill FL 34606 Office Phone: 352-797-7080. Personal E-mail: timminsa60@earthlink.net.

TIMMINS, LOIS FAHS, lecturer, writer, consultant; b. NYC, July 3, 1914; d. Charles Harvey and Sophia (Lyon) Fahs; m. James W. Timmins, Aug. 12, 1942 (div.); children: Nancy Timmins Kirk, Kathy Fahs Timmins. BS in Edn., Northwestern U., 1935; MA, Columbia U., 1936, EdD, 1941. Instr., Mt. Allison U., Sackville, N.B., Can., 1936-39; asst. prof. Willimantic State Tchrs. Coll., Conn., 1941-43 (now named Eastern Conn. State U.); social dir. UNESCO, Mondsee, Austria, summer 1950; asst. prof. Tex. Woman's U., Denton, 1953-57; profl. staff Timberlawn Psychiat. Hosp., Dallas, 1957-80; dir. Communication Studies, Omaha, 1972—; profl. spkr., Dallas, 1980—; anti-racist resource mgr. S.W. dist. Unitarian Universalist Assn., 1994-2000; vol. Martin Luther King Jr. Libr., Dallas, 1980-2002, instr. AARP Tax Aide, Omaha, 2004, 05. Author: Swing Your Partner, 1939, Understanding Through Communication, 1972, Life Time Chart, 1978, Finding Words for Your Feelings, 1985; (cassettes) Making Friends with All Your Feelings, 1984, The Mirrors Inside You, 1984, Ambivalance, 1985, Our Secret World of Feelings, including Anger: The Primitive Emotion, Fear: The Toxic Emotion, Distress: The Paralyzing Emotion, Shame: The Social Emotion, Guilt: The Noble Emotion, and Joy: The Emotion Everyone Wants, 1986, (6 cassette album) Disappointment: Parent or Despair, 1989, Nostalgia: Yearning for the Yesterday that Never Was, 1991, (4 cassettes) The Pros and Cons of Growing Up Unitarian: Childhood, Money, The Social Action Imperative, Communication, 2004; contbr. 24 articles to profl. jours. Recipient citation Nat. Therapeutic Recreation Soc., 1976, Top Rating at Profl. Spkrs. Showcase Internat. Platform Assn., 1982. Home: 9220 Western Ave #213 Omaha NE 68114 Personal E-mail: drloistimmons@aol.com.

TIMMONS, DONNA FRANCES, music educator; b. Rockeville Centre, N.Y., June 11, 1953; d. Donald Francis and Eudrice (Freitag) Timmins. MusB, Juilliard Sch., 1975, MusM, 1977; cert. tchr., Adelphi U., 1980; DA, George Mason U., 2004. Cert. K-12 music tchr. N.Y., Va., S.C. Asst. in piano pedagogy, tchg. fellow Juilliard Sch., N.Y.C., 1975—76, piano class instr., tchg. fellow, 1975—78; piano class instr. Garden City (N.Y.) Adult Sch., 1977—81; pvt. piano tchr. Garden City, 1980—86; dir. Cathedral Inst. Acad. Music., Garden City, 1985—86; music dir. Cathedral Sch. St. Mary, Garden City, 1984—86; choral dir., gen. music tchr. Berkeley County Pub. Schs., Moncks Corner, SC, 1986—91; choral dir. Snenandoah County Pub. Schs., Woodstock, Va., 1991—98; tchg. intern Blue Ridge C.C., Weyers Cave, Va., 1997; choral dir. Loudoun County Pub. Schs., Ashburn, Va., 1998—, mentor, 2001—06. Organist, dir. adult and youth choirs Pinopolis (S.C.) United Meth. Ch., 1987—91; condr. Garden City Cmty. Orch., 1980—81; pres. FourTen Pub., Harrisonburg, Va., 1991—. Composer (lyricist, prodr.): (albums) Don't Be A Fool, Stay in School, 1988, Voices of the Heart; composer: (dir., host) (documentaries) Get Real - Virtually, 1996; composer: (plays) Top Secret, 2003; author: All Ye People in Theatre of The Mind, 2003, Musical Theater in the 21st Century Community College, 2004, THe Home of the Brave and the Free, 2005. Named Berkeley County (S.C.) Tchr. of Yr., 1988; recipient Magic Tchr. award, S.C. Mid. Sch. Assn., 1988, Outstanding Contbn. Sch. Prevention award, Berkeley County Commn. Alcohol and Drug Abuse, 1990, Distinction award, Communicator Awards, 1998, Crystal award of Excellence Communicator award, 2003, 2004, Seneca Ridge Mid. Sch. Tchr. of the Yr., 2005; fellow, Julliard Sch., 1975—77; grantee, S.C. Commn. Alcohol and Drug Abuse, 1990—91, Edn. Found., 1998, Washington Post, 1998; scholar, Julliard Sch., 1972—77, Julliard Pre-Coll. Div., 1962—71. Mem.: DAR, ASCAP (ASCAPLUS award 2003, 2004), NEA, Mid Valley Consortium for Tchr. Edn., Loudoun Edn. Assn., Va. Edn. Assn., Mayflower Soc., Delta Kappa Gamma. Avocations: gardening, flying, skeet shooting, reading.

TIMMONS, EVELYN DEERING, pharmacist; b. Durango, Colo., Sept. 29, 1926; d. Claude Elliot and Evelyn Allen (Gooch) Deering; m. Richard Palmer Timmons, Oct. 4, 1952 (div. 1968); children: Roderick Deering, Steven Palmer. BS in Chemistry and Pharmacy cum laude, U. Colo., 1948. Chief pharmacist Meml. Hosp., Phoenix, 1950—54; libr. med. lit. rsch. Hoffman-LaRoche, Inc., Nutley, NJ, 1956—57; staff pharmacist St. Joseph's Hosp., Phoenix, 1958—60; relief mgr. various ind. apothecaries, Phoenix, 1960—68; asst. then mgr., dir. compounding Profl. Pharmacies, Inc., Phoenix, 1968—72; mgr. Mt. View Pharmacy, 1972—76, owner/mgr., 1976—; pres. Ariz. Apothecaries, 1976—. Mem. profl. adv. bd., bereavement counselor Hospice of Valley, 1983-96; mem. profl. adv. bd. Upjohn Health Care and Svcs., Phoenix, 1984-86; bd. dirs. Am. coun. on Pharm. Edn., Chgo., 1986-92, v.p., 1988, 89, treas., 1990-91; mem. expert adv. bd. compounding pharms. U.S. Pharmacoepial Conv., 1992—; preceptor U. Ariz., 1965—, Midwestern Coll. Pharmacy, Ariz. Campus, 1998—; chief cons. bioidentical hormone replacement therapy and safety; disease mgmt. specialist; lectr. on NHRT and BHRT. Mem. editl. adv. bd. Internat. Jour. Pharm. Compounding, 1997-2000; author poetry; contbr. articles to profl. jours. Mem. Scottsdale (Ariz.) Fedn. Rep. Women, 1963-68; various other offices Rep. Fedn.; mem. platform com. State of Ariz., Nat. Rep. Conv., 1964; asst. sec. Young Rep. Nat. Fedn., 1963-65; active county and state Rep. coms.; adv. bd. Internat. Jour. of Pharm. Compounding, 1996-2001; fin. chmn. Internat. Leadership Symposium: Women in Pharmacy, London, 1987; treas. Leadership Internat. Women Pharmacy, 1991-2001; mem. founders circle Gladys Taylor McGarey Med. Found., 1996—. Named Outstanding Young Rep. of Yr., Nat. Fedn. Young Reps., 1965, Preceptor of Yr., U. Ariz./Syntex, 1984; recipient Disting. Pub. Svc. award Maricopa County Med. Soc., 1962, Disting. Alumni award Wasatch Acad., 1982, Career Achievement award Kappa Epsilon, 1983, Leadership and Achievement award Upjohn Labs., 1985-86, Outstanding Achievement in Profession award Merck, Sharp & Dohme, 1986, award of Merit Kappa Epsilon, 1988, Disting. Coloradoan award U. Colo., 1989, Vanguard award Kappa Epsilon, 1991, Unicorn award Kappa Epsilon, 1993, Compounding Pharmacist of the Yr. award Profl. Compounding Corp. of Am., 1994, 96, Healing Heart award Gladys Taylor McGarey Found., 1998, 50 Yr. Certificate U. Colo., 2000. Fellow Am. Coll. of Apothecaries (v.p. 1982-83, pres. elect 1983-84, pres. 1984-85, chmn. bd. 1985-86, adv. coun. 1986-92, Chmn. of Yr. 1980-81, Victor H. Morganroth award 1985, J. Leon Lascoff award 1990), Internat. Acad. of Compounding Pharmacists (bd. dirs. 1993-2000, hon. life fellow 2005); mem. Ariz. Soc. of Hosp. Pharmacists, Am. Pharm. Assn. (Daniel B. Smith award 1990), Ariz. Pharmacy Assn. (Svc. to Pharmacy award 1976, Pharmacist of Yr. 1981, Bowl of Hygeia 1989, 1st Innovative Pharmacy award 1994, 50 Yr. Practice and Membership award 2001), Maricopa County Pharmacy Assn. (pres. 1977, Svc. to Pharmacy award 1977), Am. Soc. of Hosp. Pharmacists, Am. Aircraft Owners and Pilots Assn., Air Safety Found., Nat. Assn. of Registered Parliamentarians, Civinettes (pres. Scottsdale chpt. 1960-61), Kappa Epsilon (recipient Career Achievement award 1986, Vanguard award 1991, Unicorn award 1993). Avocations: flying, skiing, swimming, hiking, writing. Office: Mt View Pharmacy 10565 N Tatum Blvd Ste B-118 Scottsdale AZ 85253-1095 Personal E-mail: evelyntimmons@cox.net.

TIMMONS, GORDON DAVID, economics professor, farmer; b. Elbert, Tex., May 21, 1919; s. Walter James and Ella Mae (McCarson) T.; m. Jean Betty Kulhanek, Feb. 11, 1947; children: Kathy, Linda, Scott, Jim, Tamara, Dallas, Timothy, Kelly, Susanna. Student, U. Tex., 1937-40. U. Mont., 1961-64; BS, Utah State U., 1955; MS, Mont. State U., 1958. Enlisted USAF, 1939, advanced through grades to col., ret., 1961; instr. Columbia Basin Coll., Pasco, Wash., 1966-86. Pres. Assn. Higher Edn., 1969-72. Decorated Legion of Merit, Croix de Guerre (France). Mem. Acad. Polit. Sci., N.W. Econ. Conf. Democrat. Avocation: horse breeding. Home and Office: Star Rte Box 39-A Olney TX 76374-0039 Office Phone: 940-862-5614. Business E-Mail: timmons@brazos.com.

**TIMMONS, ROBBIE,** news anchor; m. Jim Brandstatter. Grad., Ohio State U. Anchor WILX-TV, Lansing, Mich., 1972—76, WJBK-TV, Detroit, 1976—82, WXYZ-TV, Detroit, 1982—. Recipient numerous Emmy awards, Silver Cir. award, Nat. Acad. TV Arts and Scis., 1998, Most Powerful Woman in Mich., 2002. Achievements include being the first woman in the US to anchor TV news at 6 & 11pm. Office: WXYZ-TV 20777 W Ten Mile Rd Southfield MI 48037 E-mail: rtimmons@wxyz.com.

**TIMMONS, SEAN ABBOTT,** lawyer; b. Washington, Aug. 4, 1967; s. James Donald and Anita Abbott Timmons; m. Sheri Lynn Outlaw, June 8, 1996; children: Elizabeth Kelly Ross, Sean Abbott. BA, Williams Coll., 1989; JD, Duke U. Sch. Law, 1994. Bar: NC 1998, US Dist. Ct. (ea. dist.) NC 1998, US Ct. Appeals (4th cir.) 2001. Atty. Smith, Anderson, Blount, Dorsett, Mitchell & Jernigan, LLP, Raleigh, 1998—2006, ptnr., 2006—. Mem.: NC Bar Assn., Am. Health Lawyers Assn., ABA. Associate Home: 2902 Everett Ave Raleigh NC 27607 Office: Smith Anderson Blount Dorsett Mitchell & Jernigan LLP 2500 Wachovia Capitol Ctr PO Box 2611 Raleigh NC 27602-2611 Office Phone: 919-821-1220. Office Fax: 919-821-6800. Business E-Mail: stimmons@smithlaw.com.

**TIMMONS, SHARON L.,** retired elementary school educator; b. South Kansas City, Mo., July 25, 1949; d. Clyde George and Sarah Ethyl (Thrift) Manley; m. Joseph D. Timmons, June 6, 1970; children: Stacia, Matt. BSE, U. Kans., 1972; MA, U. Mo., Kansas City, 1980. Cert. elem., jr. high tchr., Mo; elem. tchr., Kans. Team tchr. elem. Loretto Acad., Kansas City, Mo., 1976—80; team tchr. lead med. sch. and block schedule programs, 8th grade, Ctr. Sch. Dist. 58, Kansas City, Mo., 1980—94; ret., 1994. Author: (Title II grants) For Indivdualized Math Program, Kansas City Rep. for Scientific Literacy. Mem. Sigma Kappa.

**TIMMONS, WILLIAM EVAN,** business executive; b. Chattanooga, Dec. 27, 1930; s. Owen Walter and Doris (Eckenrod) T.; m. Mimi Bakshian, Sept. 28, 1966; children: Karen Leigh, Kimberly Anne, William Evan. Grad., Baylor Mil. Acad., Chattanooga, 1949; BS in Fgn. Svc., Georgetown U., 1959; postgrad., George Washington U., 1959-61. Aide to U.S. Senator Alexander Wiley, 1955-62; adminstrv. asst. to U.S. Rep. William Brock, 1963-69; dep. asst. to Pres. Richard M. Nixon, 1969-70, asst., 1970-74; asst. to Pres. Gerald R. Ford, 1974; pres. Timmons & Co. Inc., 1975-86, chmn. exec. com., 1986—2002, chmn. emeritus, 2002—. Mem. Fed. Property Rev. Bd., 1972-75, Pres.'s Trade Adv. Com., 1975-80; U.S. del. to Internat. Conf. on Viet Nam, Paris, 1973. Presdl. appointee U.S.-Japan Adv. Commn., 1983—85; nat. conv. dir. Reagan for Pres. Com., Detroit, 1980, Dallas, 1984, nat. polit. dir., 1980; exec. dir. Tenn. Rep. Com., 1962; mgr. Brock campaigns, 1962, 1964, 1966, 1968; dir. congl. rels. Nixon-Agnew campaign, 1968; coord. Nixon for Pres.; active Rep. Nat. Conv., Miami, Fla., 1968, 1972, dir. Pres. Ford com. Kansas City, 1976; mem. adv. com. Rep. Nat. Com. Conv., New Orleans, 1988, San Diego, 1996; mem. exec. com. Nat. Young Reps., 1965—67; dep. dir. for transition Office of Pres.-Elect, 1980—81; mem. faculty Nat. REp. campaign workshops, 1963—69; sr. adviser Bush for Pres. Com., New Orleans, 1988, Dole for Pres. Com., 1996; mem. adv. com. Bush for Pres., Rep. Nat. Conv., Phila., 2000; adviser Bush-Cheney Transition, 2000—01; bd. dirs. Radio Free Europe/Liberty, 1975—82, Georgetown U. Ctr. Strategic and Internat. Studies, 1982—85. With USAF, 1951—55. Named Outstanding Young Rep. of Year Nat. Rep. Com., 1965; recipient 1970 Ann. Achievement award Georgetown Alumni Club; citation for Disting. Service Baylor Mil. Acad. Alumni Assn., 1970 Mem. SCV, SAR, Soc. of the Cin., Columbia Country Club, George Towne Club, City Club, St. Alban's Tennis Club, Masons (33d degree). Home: 4426 Garfield St NW Washington DC 20007-1142 Office: Timmons & Co 1875 Eye St NW Ste 400 Washington DC 20006 Office Phone: 202-331-1760. Personal E-mail: BTimmons@aol.com.

**TIMMONS, WILLIAM TODD,** chemical engineer, educator; b. Amarillo, Tex., Apr. 1, 1961; s. William Calvin and Martha Lynn Timmons; m. Rebecca Jo Lindsey; children: Lindsey Michelle, William Terry. BSChemE, Tex. Tech U., Lubbock, 1983, MS in Math., 1988; MA in History of Sci., U. Okla., Norman, 1996, PhD in History of Sci., 2002. Process engr. Diamond Shamrock Corp., Dumos, Tex., 1983—86; instr. U. Ark., Ft. Smith 1988—2001, asst. prof., 2002—03, assoc. prof., 2004—, adj. prof. history Little Rock, 2001. Presenter at confs. in field. Author: Science and Technology in 19th Century America, 2005. Mem. organizing com. nat. sci. quiz bowl competition Dept. Edn., 2005; mem. organizing com. BEST HS Robotics Competition, 2003; regional dir.HS math. contest Ark. Coun. Math. Tchrs., 2003—05; mem. organizing com. Sonia Kovalevsky Day, 2004; organizer poster session and lectures. Am. Heritage Week, 2005; youth soccer coach Western Ark. Soccer Assn. Mem.: Ark. Math. Assn. Two-Yr. Colls. (past pres.), History of Sci. Soc., Math. Assn. Am. Avocation: running. Office: U Ark Ft Smith 3620 Grand Ave Fort Smith AR 72913

**TIMMONS-GOODSON, PATRICIA,** state supreme court justice; b. Florence, SC, Sept. 18, 1954; d. Edward and Beulah Timmons; m. Ernest J. Goodson; 2 children. BA, U. NC, Chapel Hill, 1976, JD, 1979. Dist. mgr. U.S. Census, 1979—80; asst. dist. atty. Twelfth Prosecutorial Dist., NC, 1981—83; staff atty. Lumbee River Legal Services, Inc., Fayetteville, 1983—84; dist. ct. judge Twelfth Judicial Dist., NC, 1984—97; judge NC Ct. of Appeals, 1997—2005; assoc. justice NC Supreme Ct., 2006—. Former co-host and co-prodr. television program Dimensions of Justice. Mem. central selection com. Morehead Scholarship; bd. dirs. alumni assn. U. NC Mem.: ABA (mem. appellate judges conference exec. com.), NC Assn. of Black Lawyers, NC Bar Assn. Office: NC Supreme Ct PO Box 2448 Raleigh NC 27602*

**TIMONEY, PETER JOSEPH,** veterinarian, educator, virologist, consultant; b. Dublin, June 5, 1941; came to U.S., 1983; s. John Francis and Evelyn Norah (Whittle) T.; m. Katherine Mary Murphy, Sept. 11, 1971; children: Peter, Caroline, Sarah, David. MVB, Nat. U., Dublin, 1964; MS, U. Ill., 1966; PhD, U. Dublin, 1974. Rsch. assoc. U. Ill., Urbana, 1964-66; rsch. officer Vet. Rsch. Lab., Abbotstown, Ireland, 1966-72; sr. rsch. officer equine diseases sect. Veterinary Rsch. Lab., Abbotstown, Ireland, 1972-79; assoc. prof. diagnostic lab., dept. microbiology Cornell U., Ithaca, NY, 1979-81; sci. dir. Irish Equine Ctr., Johnstown, Ireland, 1981-83; assoc. prof. virology vet. sci. dept. U. Ky., Lexington, 1983-87, prof. virology, assoc. chair for rsch., 1987-89, Frederick Van Lennep chair, 1988—, acting chair, 1989-90, chair, 1990-99, 2002—. Cons. Daryl Labs., Inc., Santa Clara, Calif., 1981-86, Ft. Dodge (Iowa) Animal Health Lab., 1984-99. Fellow Royal Coll. Vet. Surgeons, World Equine Vet. Assn. (pres. 1995-99); mem. Am. Assn. Equine Practitioners, Am. Soc. Microbiology, Am. Soc. Virology, U.S. Animal Health Assn. Avocations: reading, gardening. Office: Gluck Equine Rsch Ctr 108 Gluck Ctr Lexington KY 40506-0099 Business E-Mail: ptimoney@uky.edu.

**TIMONI, STEPHEN ANTHONY,** lawyer, accountant; b. Elizabeth, N.J., July 15, 1954; s. Vincent A. and Jean E. (Petrone) T.; m. Cynthia A. Yarusi, May 24, 1987; children: Christina Marie, John Anthony. BS in Bus./Econs., Wagner Coll., 1976; JD, Seton Hall U., 1982. Bar: N.J. 1982, U.S. Dist. Ct. N.J. 1982, U.S. Tax Ct., U.S. Ct. Appeals (3d cir.) 1991; CPA, N.J., N.Y. Audit staff Touche Ross & Co. CPA's, Newark, 1976-78; tax assoc. Reydel Perter & Neral CPA's, Westfield, N.J., 1978-82; Price Waterhouse CPA's, N.Y.C., 1982-84; pvt. practice law Clark, N.J., 1984-87; ptnr. Galfy & Timoni, Clark, 1987-90, Galfy, Timoni, Rubino & Huttle, Clark; ptnr. & pro bono coord. Kirkpatrick & Lockhart Nicholson Graham LLP, Newark. Bd. govs. Rahway (N.J.) Hosp.; mem. N.J. Tech. Council Fellow N.J. Soc. CPAs; mem. ABA, N.J. Bar Assn. (real property and trust sect.), Catholic Health Assn. U.S., Am. Health Lawyers Assn., Union County Bar Assn., Assn. Trial Lawyers Am., N.J. Assn. Trial Lawyers, AICPA, Union County C. of C., Builders Assn. Met. N.J. Roman Catholic. Avocations: reading, travel, golf. Office: Kirkpatrick & Lockhart Nicholson Graham LLP 10th Fl 1 Newark Ctr Newark NJ 07102-5252 Office Phone: 973-848-4020. Office Fax: 973-848-4001. Business E-Mail: stimoni@klng.com.

**TIMONY, PETER EDWARD,** chemist, researcher; b. East Orange, N.J., Dec. 30, 1943; s. Peter B. and Tillie E. (Fedorha) T.; m. Pamela Dale Logan, June 11, 1966; children: Susan, Kathleen, Kristen, Jennifer. BA, Fairleigh Dickinson U., 1967; PhD, U. Notre Dame, 1972. Chemist Royal Lubricant, Hanover, NJ, 1965—67; rsch. chemist Stauffer Chem. Co., Dobbs Ferry, NY, 1971—75, sr. rsch. chemist, 1975—76, supr., 1976—79, asst. to rsch. dir., 1979—81, mgr. organic sect., 1981—88; dir. of rsch. Alcolac, Inc., Balt. 1988—90; dir. chem. technology Lonza, Inc., Annandale, NJ, 1990—99; mgr. chem. technology Uniqema, New Castle, Del., 1999—2005. Home: 328 Prospect Bay Dr W Grasonville MD 21638-1099 Personal E-mail: timonyp@aol.com.

**TIMOSHCHUK, VICTOR ARKADYEVICH,** research scientist; b. Mary, Turkmenistan, Sept. 20, 1946; s. Arkady and Raisa Timoshchuk; m. Margarita Sergievsky, Feb. 16, 1990; m. Ludmila Gumenyuk, Aug. 10, 1979 (div. Feb. 13, 1990); children: Vladislav, Kirill, Sergey. MS in Organic Chemistry, St. Petersburg State U., Russia, 1964—69; PhD in Organic Chemistry, Rsch. Inst. Bio-organic Chemistry, Belarus Acad. Scis., Minsk, 1971—75. Sr. rschr. Rsch. Inst. Bio-organic Chemistry, Minsk, Belarus, 1976—81, Rsch. Inst. Peat, Minsk, 1981—84; head, lab. Rsch. Inst. Microbiology and Epidemiology, Minsk, 1984—88; sr. rschr. Rsch. Inst. Radiation Medicine, Minsk, 1988—90; chief rschr. Belarus State U., Minsk, 1990—96; vis. rschr. Brigham Young U., Provo, Utah, vis. scientist, 1996—99; scientist TriLink Biotechnologies, Inc., San Diego, 1999—. Contbr. articles to profl. jours. Mem.: Internat. Soc. for Nucleosides, Nucleotides and Nucleic Acids. Achievements include discovery of a new type of isomery; patents for the syntheses of nucleosides of aberrent types. Office: TriLink BioTechnologies Inc 9955 Mesa Rim Rd San Diego CA 92121 Office Phone: 858-546-0004. Personal E-mail: vatimoshchuk@yahoo.com. Business E-Mail: vtimoshchuk@trilinkbiotech.com

**TIMOTHY, DAVID HARRY,** retired biology professor; b. Pitts., June 9, 1928; s. David Edgar and Harriett P. (Stein) T.; m. Marian Claire Whiteley, Sept. 5, 1953; children: Marjory J., M. Elisabeth, David W. BS, Pa. State U., 1952, MS, 1955; PhD, U. Minn., 1956. Asst. geneticist Rockefeller Found., Bogota, Colombia, 1956-58, assoc. geneticist, 1958-61; assoc. prof. N.C. State U., Raleigh, 1961-66, prof., 1966-93, prof. crop sci., botany and genetics emeritus, 1993—; ret. Cons. to fgn. and U.S. govts., also U.S. and internat. sci. orgns.; mem. USDA crop adv. com. on grasses, 1983-87, mem. policy adv. com., sci. and edn. grants program, 1982-84, chief scientist USDA Sci. and Edn. Competetive Rsch. Grants Office, 1985, 86; with Nat. Plant Genetic Resources Bd., 1984-91, vice chmn., 1991; bd. dirs., treas. Genetic Resources Comms. Sys., Inc., 1985-91, pres., 1991-93; mem. bd. on agr. NAS-NRC, work group on U.S. Nat. Plant Germplasm Sys., 1987-89. Co-author monographs; contbr. chpts. to books; contbr. articles to profl. jours. With AUS, 1946-48, PTO. Grantee NSF, 1965, 78, Rockefeller Found., 1968, 69, Pioneer Hi-Bred Internat., 1982, 83. Fellow AAAS (electorate nominating com., sect. O, Agr. 1988-90), Am. Soc. Agronomy, Crop Sci. Soc. Am. (editl. bd. 1982-84, assoc. editor Crop Sci. 1982-84, Frank N. Meyer medal for plant genetic resources 1994). Home: 13 Furches St Raleigh NC 27607-7048

**TIMPA, VICKI ANN,** government health program administrator; b. Houston, Aug. 20, 1955; d. Edmund Burke and Helen Kanosky Huber; m. John Gerrard Fewel, May 27, 2000; children: Julie Marie Fecht, Anthony Alan. BSN, U. Tex., 1977; MSN in Edn. Adminstrn. and Rsch., Tex. Woman's U., 1990, advanced nurse practitioner degree, 1993. Cert. ACLS, domestic prepardness for biol.-radiol.-chem. VA, neurosurg. cert., cert. prevention inst. instr.; critical care nurse; cert. Covey trainer, appraiser. Team leader cardiopulmonary shock trauma emergency ctr., nurse Ben Taub Emergency Ctr., Harris County Hosp. Dist., Houston, 1977; emergency rm. and GI lab staff nurse Mesquite Hosp., Tex., 1978—80; nurse Baylor U. Med. Ctr. Hosp. Sys., Dallas, 1980—90; rsch. nurse coord. VA, Dallas, 1990—93; dept. of edn. mgr. Meth. Hosps. of Dallas, 1993; patient health edn. coord. VA North Tex. Health Care Sys., Dallas, 1993—; peritoneal dialysis nurse Parkland Meml. Hosp., Dallas County Hosp. Dist. Coord. nat. rsch. studies VA, Dallas, 1990—92, nat. liaison for Nat. Ctr. for Health Promotion and Disease Prevention, Durham, NC, 2002—, congl. legis. cons., Washington, 2000—; ICU mock code creator and trainer Baylor U. Hosp. Sys., Dallas, 1980—90; cardiopulmonary resuscitation instr. Am. Heart Assn., Dallas, 1989—94; Plain Lang. Act cons. Exec. Br., Washington, 1995—. Contbr. articles to profl. jours. V.p. Miracle Wish Found., 2006. Named Most Valuable Person, VA Rsch., 1992; named one of Great 100 Nurses award, 1997; recipient Unsung Hero award, VA, 1993. Mem.: Sigma Theta Tau (fin. and fund raising com. 1993—2001, Academic Excellence and Rsch. Excellence awards 1993, 2001, Nat. Plank Owner award 2005). Roman Catholic. Avocations: travel, antiques and collectibles appraising. Home: 1307 High Ridge Dr Duncanville TX 75137 Office: VA 4500 S Lancaster Rd (141P) Dallas TX 75216 Office Phone: 214-857-1161. Fax: 972-572-5525. Personal E-mail: vickiern7@netzero.net. Business E-Mail: vicki.timpa@med.va.gov.

**TIMPERLAKE, EDWARD THOMAS,** writer; b. Perth Amboy, N.J., Nov. 22, 1946; s. James Elwood Timperlake Jr. and Joan Dorothy (Conkling) Maurer; m. Barbette Runckel, Aug. 10, 1969 (div. 1993); children: Tara, Kimberly; m. Cathryn Porcelli Gekas, Apr. 8, 2000. BS, U.S. Naval Acad., 1969; MBA, Cornell U., 1977. Commd. 2d lt. USMC, 1969, advanced through grades to lt. col., ret., 1993; asst. venture mgr. Exxon Enterprise, N.Y.C., 1977-78; sect. mgr. T.A.S.C., Arlington, Va., 1978-81; dep. dir. Nat. Dir. Vietnam Vets. Leadership Program, Action Agy., Washington, 1981-83; dir. mobilization plans and requirements Office of Sec. Def., Washington, 1984; campaign staff George Bush for Pres., 1988; asst. sec. Dept. Vets. Affairs, Washington, 1989-93; prog. T.Q. Group, 1993-95; profl. staff rules com. U.S. House of Reps., Washington, 1996—99; dir. tech. assessment internat. tech. security Office of the Sec. of Def., The Pentagon, Washington, 2003—. Author: Year of the Rat, 1998, Red Dragon Rising, 1999; contbr. articles to profl. jours. Mem.: Naval Acad. Alumni Assn., N.Y. Yacht Club, Army-Navy Club. Home: 1027 22d St Arlington VA 22202

**TIMS, ROBERT AUSTIN,** data processing official, pilot; b. Seattle, Dec. 21, 1942; s. Robert Mitchell Tims and Winifred Eileen (Dorgan) Bristol; m. Jane Moore, June 6, 1980. Student, Pacific Union Coll., 1960—61, Alpha Aviation Sch., 1976—77; BS in Computer Info. Sys. with honors, Ark. State U., 1998. Lic. comml. and instrument pilot; cert. flight instr. Engring. technician Tex. Instruments, Inc., Ridgecrest, Calif., 1966-67, various projects, Conn., N.Y. and N.J., 1967-70; homesteader Leslie, Ark., 1970-77; chief pilot/flight instr. Sharp Aviation Co., Jonesboro, Ark., 1977-79; chief pilot Pizza Inn of Ark., Jonesboro, 1979-83; data processing mgr., chief pilot Realty Assocs. Brokerage, Inc., Jonesboro, 1983-91, microanalyst, 1991-94. Pres., owner ABS Logic, Inc., computers and programming cons., Jonesboro, 1985—2005; programmer Jimco Lamp Mfg., Bono, Ark., 1998—99; programmer, analyst TEK Systems, Memphis, 2000—02; software engr. Northrop Grumman, Little Rock, 2003—04, Nextech, Memphis, 2003—04, Nucor Steel, Hickman, Ark., 2004—05, JD Resources, Memphis, 2005—05; sr. software engr. Rural Sourcing, Inc., Jonesboro, Ark., 2006—. Served with USN, 1962-66. Recipient Nat. Collegiate Bus. Merit award. Mem. CAP (squadron comdr. Jonesboro 1986-93), NRA, Am. Philatelic Soc., Planetary Soc., Nat. Space Soc., SETI Inst., Second Amendment Found., Gun Owners Am., Beta Gamma Sigma. Avocation: philately. Home and Office: 1616 Alonzo St Jonesboro AR 72401-4802 Office Phone: 870-680-4164. Business E-Mail: rtims@abslogic.com.

**TINBERG, HOWARD,** language educator; b. Portland, Oreg., Mar. 6, 1953; s. Leon Tinberg and Sophie Sandman; m. Toni Lenz, June 13, 1982; children: Miriam, Leah. BA, UCLA, 1975, MA, 1977; PhD, Brandeis U., 1980. Asst. prof. English Boston U., 1985-87; prof. English Bristol C.C., Fall River, Mass., 1987—, dir. writing lab, 1993—. Author: Border Talk: Writing and Knowing at the Two-Year College, 1997, Writing with Consequence: What Writing Does in the Disciplines, 2002; editor: Teaching English in the Two-Year College. Recipient Outstanding C.C. Prof. of Yr., Coun. for Advancement and Support of Edn. & Carnegie Found. for Advancement of Tchg., 2004. Mem. Nat. Coun. Tchrs. English (mem. editl. bd. Coll. English 1999—). Office: Bristol CC 777 Elsbree St Fall River MA 02720-7307

**TINCHER, WAYNE COLEMAN,** engineering educator; BA in Chemistry, David Lipscomb U., 1956; PhD in Physical Chemistry, Vanderbilt U., 1960. From rsch. chemist to rsch. group leader Monsanto Co., Research Triangle Park, NC, 1960-71; from assoc. prof. to prof. Ga. Inst. Technology, Atlanta, 1971—. Recipient Olney medal Am. Assn. of Textile Chemists and Colorists, 1996. Office: Ga Inst Tech Sch Textile & Fiber Engring 801 Ferst Dr Atlanta GA 30332-0295 Office Phone: 404-894-2197. E-mail: wayne.tincher@tfe.gatech.edu.

**TINDALL, GEORGE BROWN,** retired historian, educator; b. Greenville, S.C., Feb. 26, 1921; s. Goin Roscoe and Nellie Evelyn (Brown) Tindall; m. Carliss Blossom McGarrity, June 29, 1946; children: Bruce McGarrity, Blair Alston Mercer. AB, Furman U., 1942, LittD, 1971; MA, U. N.C., 1948, PhD, 1951. Asst. prof. history Ea. Ky. State Coll., 1950—51; asst. prof. U. Miss., 1951—52, U. N.C. Woman's Coll., 1952—53, La. State U., 1953—58; assoc. prof. U. N.C., Chapel Hill, 1958—64, prof., 1964—69, Kenan prof., 1969—90, Kenan prof. emeritus, 1990—; ret., 1990. Vis. prof. Coll. Charleston, 1951, Kyoto Am. Studies Sem., 1977; Fulbright guest prof. U. Vienna, 1967—68; mem. Inst. Advanced Study, 1963—64, Ctr. Advanced Study Behavioral Scis., 1979—80. Author: (book) South Carolina Negroes 1877-1900, 1952, The Emergence of the New South, 1913-1945, 1967 (Jules F. Landry award, 1968, Mayflower Cup, 1968, Lillian E. Smith award, 1968, Charles S. Syndor award, 1968), The disruption of the Solid South, 1972, The Persistent Tradition in New South Politics, 1975, The Ethnic Southerners, 1976, America: A Narrative History, 1984; author: (with David Shi), 1999; author: Natives and Newcomers: Ethnic Southerners and Southern Ethnics, 1995; editor: The Pursuit of Southern History, 1964, A Populist Reader, 1966. Fellow Guggenheim, 1957—58, Social Sci. Coun., 1959—60, Ctr. Advanced Study Behavioral Scis., 1979—80. Mem.: So. Hist. Assn. (pres. 1973), Orgn. Am. Historians, N.C. Lit. and Hist. Soc., Hist. Soc. N.C. (pres. 1990), Am. Hist. Assn. Home: Carol Woods 750 Weaver Dairy Rd Apt 242 Chapel Hill NC 27514 Personal E-Mail: historymill@nc.rr.com. Business E-Mail: tindall@email.unc.edu.

**TINDALL, ROBERT EMMETT,** lawyer, educator; b. NYC, Jan. 2, 1934; s. Robert E. and Alice (McGonigle) T.; children: Robert Emmett IV, Elizabeth. BS in Marine Engring., SUNY, 1955; postgrad., Georgetown U. Law Sch., 1960—61; LLB, U. Ariz., 1963; LLM, NYU, 1967; PhD, City U., London, 1975. Bar: Ariz. 1963. Mgmt. trainee GE, Schenectady, NY, Lynn, Mass., Glens Falls, NY, 1955-56, 58-60; law clk. Haight, Gardner, Poor and Havens, NYC, 1961; prin., mem. Robert Emmett Tindall & Assocs., Tucson, 1963—; assoc. prof. mgmt. U. Ariz., Tucson, 1969—. Vis. prof. Grad. Sch. of Law, Soochow U., China, 1972, Grad. Bus. Ctr., London, 1974, NYU, 1991—; dir. MBA program U. Ariz., Tucson, 1975-81, dir. entrepreneurship program, 1984-86; investment cons. Saudi Arabia, 1981—; lectr. USIA, Eng., India, Mid. East, 1974; lectr. bus. orgn. and regulatory laws Southwestern Legal Found.; Acad. Am. and Internat. Law, 1976-80. Actor cmty. theatres, Schenectady, 1955-56, Harrisburg, Pa., 1957-58, Tucson, 1961-71; appeared in films Rage, 1971, Showdown at OK Corral, 1971, Lost Horizon, 1972; appeared in TV programs Gunsmoke, 1972, Petrocelli, 1974; author: Multinational Enterprises, 1975; contbr. articles on domestic and internat. bus. to profl. jours. Served to lt. USN, 1956-58. Fellow Ford Found., 1965-67; grantee Asia Found., 1972-73. Mem. Strategic Mgmt. Soc., State Bar Ariz., Acad. Internat. Bus., SAG, Honourable Soc. of Mid. Temple (London), Phi Delta Phi, Beta Gamma Sigma, Assn. Corp. Growth, Royal Overseas League (London). Home: PO Box 42196 Tucson AZ 85733-2196 Office: Coll Bus & Public Adminstrn U Ariz Dept Mgmt & Policy Tucson AZ 85721-0001

**TINDALL, ROBERT J.,** architectural firm executive; Joined Callison Arch., Inc., Seattle, 1976—, COO, 1996—98, pres., 1998—. Acting exec. dir. Insight Alliance; spkr. in field. Mem.: adv. bd.: Retail Constrn. mag.; contbr. articles to profl. jours. Mem.: AIA (large firm roundtable), Urban Land Inst., Internat. Coun. on Shopping Ctrs. Office: Callison Arch Inc Ste 2400 1420 Fifth Ave Seattle WA 98101-2343

**TINDLE, CHARLES DWIGHT WOOD,** broadcast executive; b. Bryn Mawr, Pa., Jan. 13, 1950; s. Charles Wood and Nancy (Sapp) T. Student, Kenyon Coll., 1968-71. Pres. Dwight Karma Broadcasting, Mesa, Ariz., 1971-76, Natural Broadcasting System, Mesa, 1976-79; producer, fellow Am. Film Inst. Ctr. for Advanced Film Studies, 1978-79; pres. Network 30, Scottsdale, Ariz., 1985—. Owner Sta. KDKB-AM-FM, Mesa, Sta. KSML-FM, Lake Tahoe, Calif., Sta. KNOT-AM-FM, Prescott, Ariz., Sta. KBWA, Williams, Ariz. Recipient Peabody award U. Ga., 1976. Republican. Seventh Day Adventist. Office: 644 N Country Club Dr Mesa AZ 85201-4948 Home: 7662 E Minnezona Ave Scottsdale AZ 85251-2102 Office Phone: 480-951-1597. E-mail: dwtindle@qwest.net.

**TING, ALBERT CHIA,** biomedical engineer, researcher; b. Hong Kong, Sept. 7, 1950; came to U.S., 1957; s. William Su and Katherine Sung T.; m. Shirley Roung Wang, July 30, 1988. BA, UCLA, 1973; MS, Calif. State U., L.A., 1975, Calif. Inst. Tech., 1977; PhD, U. Calif., San Diego, 1983. Rsch. asst. Calif. Inst. Tech., Pasadena, 1975-77, U. Calif., San Diego, 1982-83; sr. staff engr. R&D Am. Med. Optics, Irvine, Calif., 1983-86; project engr., rsch. Allergan Med. Optics, Irvine, Calif., 1987-89, sr. project engr., rsch., 1989-92, sr. project engr., engring., 1993-94; bioengr. cons. Pharmacia Iovision, Inc., Irvine, Calif., 1995-97; sr. engr. D & E, 1997, sr. engr., project mgr., 1998-99; rsch. and devel. mgr., surg. Bausch & Lomb, Irvine, 1999—2001; R & D mgr. Visiogen, Inc., Irvine, 2001—02, sr. R & D mgr., 2002—. Inventor med. and optical devices, recipient patent awards 1988, 89, 91, 92, 93, 95, 2004, 05; contbr. articles to sci. jours. Mem. AAAS, Biomed. Engring. Soc., Assn. for Rsch. in Vision and Ophthalmology, Biomed. Optics Soc. Office: Visiogen Inc 4 Jenner St # 180 Irvine CA 92618 Office Phone: 949-341-0700.

**TING, JOHN M.,** dean, engineering educator; BEng, McGill U., Montreal, 1975; MS, Calif. Inst. of Tech., Pasadena, 1976; ScD, MIT, Cambridge, Mass., 1981. Registered profl. engr., Calif. Mem. faculty Calif. Inst. Tech., 1981—83, U. Toronto, 1983—90, U. Mass., Lowell, 1990—, dean engring., 2003—. Commr. Lowell Arena and Standard Commn. Office: U Mass Lowell One University Ave Lowell MA 01854 Home: Groton MA 01450 Office Phone: 978-934-2576.

**TING, ROBERT YEN-YING,** physicist; b. Kwei-yang, China, Mar. 8, 1942; arrived in U.S., 1965; s. Chi-yung and Shou-feng (Yang) T.; m. Teresa Yen-chun Ting, June 3, 1967; children: Paul H., Peggy Y. BS, Nat. Taiwan U., 1964; MS, MIT, 1967; PhD, U. Calif., San Diego, 1971. Rsch. engr. U.S. Naval Rsch. Lab., Washington, 1971-77, supervisory engr., 1977-80, supervisory physicist Orlando, Fla., 1980-97; prof. dept. chemistry U. Ctrl. Fla., Orlando, 1997—. Prof. George Washington U., 1972—80. Contbr. over 100 articles in rheology, polymer and acoustics to profl. jours. Fellow Acoustical Soc. Am.; mem. Am. chem. Soc., Am. Ceramics Soc., Am. Inst. Chem. Engrs. Office: U Ctrl Fla Dept Chem Orlando FL 32816-2366 Office Phone: 407-823-2246. Business E-Mail: rting@pegasus.cc.ucf.edu

**TING, SAMUEL CHAO CHUNG,** physicist, researcher; b. Ann Arbor, Mich., Jan. 27, 1936; s. Kuan H. and Jeanne (Wong) Ting; m. Susan Carol Marks, Apr. 28, 1985; children: Jeanne Min, Amy Min, Christopher M. BS in Engring., U. Mich., 1959, MS, 1960, PhD in Physics, 1962, ScD (hon.), 1978, Chinese U. Hong Kong, 1987, U. Bologna, Italy, 1988, Columbia U., 1990, U. Sci. and Tech., China, 1990, Moscow State U., 1991, U. Bucharest, Romania, 1993, Nat. Tsinghua U., Taiwan, 2002, Nat. Jiaotong U., 2003, Hong Kong Bapt. U., 2003, Rheinische Westfalsich Technische Hochschule, Aachen, Germany, 2004, Nat. Ctrl. U., 2005, Hong Kong U. Sci. and Tech., 2005. Ford Found. fellow CERN (European Orgn. Nuc. Rsch.), Geneva, 1963; instr. physics Columbia U., 1964, asst. prof., 1965—67; group leader Deutsches Elektronen-Synchrotron, Hamburg, Germany, 1966; assoc. prof.

physics MIT, Cambridge, 1967–68, prof., 1969—, Thomas Dudley Cabot Inst. prof., 1977—. Program cons. divsn. particles and fields Am. Phys. Soc., 1970; hon. prof. Beijing Normal Coll., 1987, Jiatong U., Shanghai, 1987, U. Bologna, Italy, 1988. Sci. editor Nuc. Physics B, 1970, editl. bd. Nuc. Instruments and Methods, Mathematical Modeling; contbr. articles to profl. jours. Recipient Nobel prize in Physics, 1976, De Gasperi prize in Sci., Italian Republic, 1988, Ernest Orlando Lawrence award, U.S. Govt., 1976, Gold medal in Sci., City of Brescia, Italy, 1988, Golden Leopard award, Town of Taormina, 1988, Forum Engelberg prize, 1996, Pub. Svc. medal, NASA, 2001; fellow Am. Acad. Arts and Scis., 1975; hon. fellow, Tata Inst. Fundamental Rsch., Mumbai, India (hon.); mem.: Inst. Fundamental Rsch. Mumbai India (hon.); mem.: NAS, Spanish Acad. Sci. (fgn. mem.), Royal Spanish Acad. Sci. (fgn. mem.), Chinese Acad. Sci. (fgn. mem.), Hungarian Acad. Sci., Deutsche Acad. Naturforscher Leopoldina (fgn. mem.), Russian Acad. Sci., Acad. Sinica, Pakistani Acad. Sci. Achievements include the discovery of a heavy elementary particle of a new kind. Office: MIT Dept Physics 51 Vassar St Cambridge MA 02139-4308 E-mail: ting@lns.mit.edu.

**TINGELSTAD, JON BUNDE,** retired pediatrician, educator; b. McVille, N.D., Jan. 15, 1935; s. Sophus B. and Mabelle (Bunde) T.; m. Marcia Ayers, Dec. 17, 1960; children: Paul, Catherine, David. BA, U. N.D., 1957, BS, 1958; MD, Harvard U., 1960. Diplomate Am. Bd. Pediatrics. Intern Children's Hosp. Med. Ctr., Boston, 1960-61, resident, 1961-62, U. Colo. Med. Ctr., Denver, 1962-63; fellow in pediatric cardiology Children's Hosp., Buffalo, 1965-67; asst. prof. pediatrics Med. Coll. Va., Richmond, 1967-71, assoc. prof., 1971-76; prof., vice chmn. pediatrics East Carolina U. Sch. Medicine, Greenville, NC, 1976-79; prof., chmn. pediatrics, 1977-2000. Mem. Greenville City Bd. Edn., 1978-82, chmn., 1981-82. Served to capt. USAF, 1963-65. Fellow Am. Acad. Pediatrics, Am. Coll. Cardiology; mem. Am. Bd. Pediatrics (emeritus), Phi Beta Kappa, Phi Eta Sigma. Home: 103 Providence Pl Chocowinity NC 27817-8940 Office: E Carolina U Sch Med Dept Pediatrics Greenville NC 27858-4354 E-mail: JonBTing1@msn.com.

**TINGLE, JAMES O'MALLEY,** retired lawyer; b. NYC, June 12, 1928; s. Thomas Jefferson and Mercedes (O'Malley) T. BS, U. Mont., 1950, BA, LL.B., U. Mont., 1952; LL.M., U. Mich., 1953, SJD, 1958. Bar: Calif. 1959, Mont. 1952, N.Y. 1961. Asst. prof. law U. Mont., Missoula, 1955-56; atty. Shell Oil Co., N.Y.C., 1957-62; assoc. Pillsbury, Madison & Sutro, San Francisco, 1962-68, ptnr., 1969-2000. Author: The Stockholder's Remedy of Corporate Dissolution, 1959; editor: State Antitrust Laws, 1974. Served to 1st lt. USAF, 1953—55. William W. Cook fellow U. Mich. Mem. Mont. Bar Assn., Calif. Bar Assn., ABA Democrat.

**TINGLER, MARLENE JOHANNSEN,** music educator, insurance agent; b. St. Louis, Aug. 22, 1948; d. Otto August and Charlotte (Sachse) Johannsen; m. Charles E. Tingler, June 19, 1971; 1 child, Matthew Johannsen. BS in Edn., William Jewell Coll., 1970; studied with Max Rabinovitsj, 1970—73; postgrad., Civil. Mo. State U., U. Mo., Kansas City. Cert. ins. Mo.; tchr. Mo. Pvt. violin tchr. St. Louis, Kansas City, 1971—; orch. dir., head dept. Berkeley (Mo.) Sch. Dist., 1971—73, Luth. Sch. Sys., Kansas City, 1989—2002; orch. dir. Parkway Schs., St. Louis, 1974—75; office mgr. Pa. Life Ins., Kansas City, 1976—84; mgr. Liberty (Mo.) Symphony Orch., 1977—85, BTI Ins. Co., Kansas City, 1985—88; v.p. Harry Loves Bess, Kansas City, 1999—. Instr. William Jewell Coll., Liberty, 1978—79; world judge, coach State Bal. Odyssey of the Mind. Musician: Jacksonville (Ill.) Symphony, St. Joseph (Mo.) Symphony, St. Louis Philharm. Recipient Outstanding Svc. award, Liberty Symphony, Hickman Mills, Mo. Sch. Dist. Mem.: Music Educators Nat. Conf., Delta Zeta (music dir. 1968—71), Sigma Alpha Iota (sec. 1968—71). Lutheran. Avocations: computers, travel. Personal E-mail: sniffer4@earthlink.net.

**TINGLEY, FLOYD WARREN,** retired internist; b. Charlotte, N.C., Nov. 22, 1933; s. Floyd Warren Sr. and Janie (Suggs) T.; m. Sandra Carpenter, Aug. 20, 1955 (div. Dec. 1984); children: Sheryl Tingley Hagen, David Alan; m. Johnette Hill, Apr. 5, 1985. BA in English, Emory U., 1955, MD, 1959. Diplomate Am. Bd. Internal Medicine (bd. govs. 1986-92). Intern USAF Hosp., Lackland AFB, Tex., 1959-60; resident in internal medicine Parkland Meml. Hosp., Dallas, 1963-65, fellow in cardiology, 1965-66; pvt. practice specializing in internal medicine Arlington, Tex., 1966-88; med. dir. southwestern region Met. Life Ins. Co., Irving, Tex., 1989-90; regional practice leader William M. Mercer Inc., 1990-91; v.p., sr. med. dir. Provident Life and Accident Co., Chattanooga, 1991-92; v.p., nat. med. dir. Travelers Ins. Cos., Hartford, Conn., 1992-94; v.p., chief med. officer Kemper Nat. Svcs., Plantation, Fla., 1995-2000; med. dir. Mednet Connect, 2005—. Apptd. Tex. Commn. on Health Care Reimbursement Alternatives, 1987; bd. dirs. Riverside Nat. Bank, Grand Prairie, Tex. Contbr. articles to profl. jours. Pres. Arlington YMCA, 1971; chmn. budget com. Family Services, Ft. Worth, 1973; participant Health Policy Agenda for Am. People, Chgo., 1984-87; trustee Tex. Med. Liability Trust, Austin, 1987-88. Capt. USAF, 1958-63. Fellow ACP (pres. Tex. chpt. 1981); mem. AMA (chmn. sect. coun. internal medicine, 1979-88), Am. Soc. Internal Medicine (pres. 1986-87), Tex. Med. Assn. (treas. 1978-85, alt. del. to AMA 1985-91, commendation 1985), Tarrant County Med. Soc. (pres. Arlington br. 1974, del. to Tex. Med. Assn., Community Svc. award 1983). Presbyterian. Avocations: photography, sailing, gardening, computer hobbies. Home: 2709 Park Place Ct Arlington TX 76016-5891

**TINGLEY, TYLER C.,** headmaster; m. Marcia Tingley; children: Chase, Morgan. AB cum laude, Harvard U., EdM, EdD, Harvard U. Former headmaster Kingswood-Oxford Sch., W. Hartford; head of sch. The Blake Sch., Minneapolis, 1991—97; headmaster Phillips Exeter Acad., Exeter, NH, 1997—. Former pres. Conn. Assn. of Independent Schools, Minn. Assn. of Independent Schools; former vice chmn. Minn. Independent Schools Fund; dir. Secondary Sch. Admissions Testing Bd. Mem.: Headmaster's Assn. (v.p.), Nat. Assn. of Independent Schools. Office: Phillips Exeter Acad 20 Main St Exeter NH 03833

**TINGSTRUM, NANCY ASH,** dietitian; d. Howard Wesley and Ruth Hamilton Ash; m. James Frederick Tingstrum, Oct. 22, 1988; 1 child, Michelle Martin Monts; m. Ralph K Martin (div.); 1 child, Noelle Lisa Vail. BS, Penn State U., 1964; MBA, George Mason U., 1988. Registered Dietitian Am. Dietitic Assn., 1972. Hosp. dietician RI Hosp., 1965—66; budget analyst Dept. of Def. Pentagon, Wash., DC, 1982—84, program analyst, 1995—2001, dept. team chief, program analyst, 2001—02; ret., 2002. Recipient Civilian Superior Svc. award, Dept. Army, Pentagon, Achievement medal for Commander's Award. Avocations: reading, exercise, gardening, quilting.

**TINGUS, STEVEN JAMES,** physiologist, researcher; b. Sacramento, Aug. 19, 1963; s. James George and Joanne Fotene (Kamilos) Tingus. BS in Biol. Sci., U. Calif., Davis, 1985, MS in Physiology, 1990, C.Phil. in Physiology, 1994. Dir. Nat. Inst. on Disability and Rehab. Rsch. US Dept. Edn., Washington, 2001—. Mem.: AAAS, Am. Assn. Polit. Cons. Republican, Greek Orthodox. Office: Dir Nat Inst on Disability and Rehab US Dept Edn 400 Maryland Ave SW Washington DC 20202 Office Phone: 202-245-7549. Personal E-mail: stingus@earthlink.net.

**TINIANOV, BRANDON DILLAN,** engineering executive, acoustical engineer; b. Cortez, Colo., Sept. 5, 1969; s. Martin Charles Tinianow and Virginia Anne Wallace; m. Stacey Leigh Vura, Oct. 9, 1999; children: Kendall Paige, Riley Sinclair. BS in Mech. Engring., Tulane U., New Orleans 1991; MS in Mech. Engring., U. Tex., Austin, 2000; PhD in Engring. Sys., Colo. Sch. Mines, Golden, 2004. Lic. profl. engr., Oreg. State Bd. Engrs., 2003, bd. cert. noise expert, Inst. Noise Control Engring. With Johns Manville, Littleton, Colo., 1996—2004; vp engring. Quiet Solution, Sunnyvale, Calif., 2004—. Mem.: Inst. Noise Control Engring. (bd. dir. 2003—05), Acoustical Soc. Am. (sec. tech. com. archtl. acoustics 2004—06). Achieve-

ments include patents in field; patents pending in field. Home: 647 Monroe St Santa Clara CA 95050 Office: Quiet Solution 1250 Elko Dr Sunnyvale CA 94089 Office Phone: 408-541-8012. Office Fax: 408-715-2560. E-mail: brandon@quietsolution.com.

**TINKELMAN, JOAN,** lawyer; b. St. Louis, Apr. 25, 1952; d. Philip and Elizabeth (Cohen) I.; m. David Tinkelman, Jan. 24, 1999. Student, Fleming Coll., Lugano, Switzerland, 1969-70, U. Colo., 1970-71; BS, RN, U. Mo. 1974; BS/RN, St. Louis U., 1976, JD cum laude, 1980. Bar: Mo. 1981, U.S. Dist. Ct. (ea. dist.) Mo. 1981, U.S. Ct. Appeals 1981, Ill. 1981, Colo. 1984, U.S. Dist. Ct. Colo. 1984. RN St. Louis Children's Hosp., 1976-77; assoc. Shepherd, Sandberg & Phoenix, St. Louis, 1980-82; risk mgr. Luth. Med. Ctr., Wheat Ridge, Colo., 1983-91; v.p. risk mgmt. Rose Health Care Systems, Denver, 1991—96; dir. risk mgmt. Denver Health and Hosp. Authority, 1997—99; ind. practice, 1999—. Named Outstanding Young Woman Am., 1984. Mem. ABA, Mo. Bar Assn., Colo. Bar Assn., Denver Bar Assn., Am. Acad. Hosp. Attys., Am. Soc. Healthcare Risk Mgmt., Colo. Health Lawyers Assn. (bd. dirs. 1984-85), Colo. Hosp. Assn. Risk Mgrs. (founder, pres. 1985). Jewish. Office Phone: 303-466-6744.

**TINKER, JOHN HEATH,** anesthesiologist, educator; b. Cin., May 18, 1941; s. Leonard Henry and Georgia (Reeves) T.; m. Martha Iuen (div. Jan., 1989); children: Deborah H. Lynne, Karen Sue, Juliette Kay; m. Bonnie Howard, Mar. 18, 1989. BS magna cum laude, U. Cin., 1964, MS summa cum laude, 1968. Diplomate Am. Bd. Anesthesiology (sr. examiner 1976—). Surg. intern, resident Harvard Med. Sch., Peter Bent Brigham Hosp., Boston, 1969-70, resident in anesthesiology, 1970-72; cons. anesthesiology Mayo Clinic, Rochester, Minn., 1974-83, chief cardiovascular anesthesiology, 1978-83; prof. anesthesiology U. Iowa Coll. Medicine, Iowa City, 1983-97, chmn. dept., 1983-97; prof., chmn. anesthesiology U. Nebr., Med. Ctr., Omaha, 1997—. Mem. pharm. scis. rev. com., NIH, Bethesda, Md., 1986—; dir. Matrix Med. Inc., Orchard Park, N.Y., 1988—; frequent guest lectr. Author: Controversies in Cardiopulmonary Bypass, 1989 (monograph award Soc. Cardiovascular Anesthsiologists); editor: Anesthesia and Analgesia, Jour. Internat. Anesthesiology Rsch. Soc., 1983—; contbr. over 185 articles to profl. jours. Maj. U.S. Army, 1972-74. NIH grantee, 1977-87. Fellow Royal Coll. Surgeons Australia; mem. Am. Soc. Anesthesiologists (active numerous coms. 1972—), Soc. Cardiovascular Anesthesiologists, Assn. Univ. Anesthetists. Avocations: fishing, golf, modeling ships and airplanes. Office: U Nebr 984455 Nebr Med Ctr Omaha NE 68198-0001

**TINKER, PAUL DAVID,** music educator; b. Butler, Pa., Feb. 18, 1956; s. Norman Everett and Gean Marie Tinker; m. Marilyn Ruth Cooper, July 26, 1998. M of Music Edn., La. Tech., Ruston, 1990. Educator Caddo Parish Sch. Bd., Shreveport, La., 1978—. Baptist. Home: 7431 Beebe Dr Greenwood LA 71033 Office: Walnut Hill Mid Sch 9360 Woolworth Rd Shreveport LA 71129 Office Phone: 318-687-6610.

**TINKER, THOMAS EATON,** retired headmaster; b. Providence, May 24, 1941; s. George Milan and Ruth (Eaton) T.; m. Roslyn May Silverman, Dec. 21, 1968. BA, Columbia U., 1963; MA, Brown U., 1968. English instr. Tabor Acad., Marion, Mass., 1964-66; history instr. Wheeler Sch., Providence, 1967-77; headmaster Broadmeadow Sch., Middletown, Del., 1977-82, St. Paul's Sch., Garden City, N.Y., 1982-89, The Barnard Sch., N.Y.C., 1989-93; assoc. head sch. Trevor Day Sch., N.Y.C., 1993—2003, head sch., 2003—05, ret., 2005. Evaluator Mid. State Assn. Colls. and Schs., Phila., 1978—. Trustee Barnard Sch. Found., 1993—; bd. dirs. Univ. Club L.I., 1984-86. With USAR, 1963-69. Mem. Nat. Assn. Ind. Schs., N.Y. State Assn. Ind. Schs., L.I. Episcopal Sch. Assn. (v.p./treas. 1984-89), Del. Assn. Ind. Schs. (sec. 1978-82). Episcopalian. Avocation: sailing. Home: Box 504 Jamestown RI 02835-0504

**TINKHAM, MICHAEL,** physicist, researcher; b. Green Lake County, Wis., Feb. 23, 1928; s. Clayton Harold and LaVerna (Krause) T.; m. Mary Stephanie Merin, June 24, 1961; children: Jeffrey Michael, Christopher Gillespie. AB, Ripon Coll., Wis., 1951, Sc.D. (hon.), 1976; MS, MIT, 1951; PhD, 1954; MA (hon.), Harvard, 1966; DSc (hon.), ETH Zurich, 1997. NSF postdoctoral fellow at Clarendon Lab., Oxford (Eng.) U., 1954-55; successively research physicist, lectr., asst. prof., asso. prof., prof. physics U. Calif. at Berkeley, 1955-66; Gordon McKay prof. applied physics Harvard U., 1966—, prof. physics, 1966-80, Rumford prof. physics, 1980—, chmn. physics dept., 1975-78. Cons. to industry, 1958—; participant internat. seminars and confs.; mem. commn. on very low temperatures Internat. Union Pure and applied Physics, 1972-78; vis. Miller rsch. prof. U. Calif.-Berkeley, 1987; vis. prof. Technical Univ., Delft, The Netherlands, 1993. Author: Group Theory and Quantum Mechanics, 1964, Superconductivity, 1965, Introduction to Superconductivity, 1975, 2d edit., 1996; contbr. articles to profl. jours. Served USNR, 1945-46. Recipient award Alexander von Humboldt Found. U. Karlsruhe, W. Ger., 1978-79, Fred E. Saalfeld award for lifetime achievement in sci., Office Naval Rsch., 2005; NSF sr. postdoctoral fellow Cavendish lab.; vis. fellow Clare Hall Cambridge (Eng.) U., 1971-72; Guggenheim fellow, 1963-64 Fellow Am. Phys. Soc. (chmn. div. solid state physics 1966-67, Buckley prize 1974, Richtmyer lectr. 1977), AAAS; mem. Am. Acad. Arts and Scis., Nat. Acad. Scis. Home: 98 Rutledge Rd Belmont MA 02478-2633 Office: Harvard Univ Physics Dept Lyman Lab of Physics 326 Cambridge MA 02138 Business E-Mail: tinkham@RSJ.harvard.edu.

**TINKHAM, THOMAS W.,** lawyer; b. Milw., June 29, 1944; s. Richard Perry and Helen (Savage) T.; m. Jackie Hauser; children: Tamara, Liza, Taylor. BS with honors, U. Wis., 1966; JD with honors, Harvard U., 1969. Bar: Minn. 1969. Ptnr. Dorsey & Whitney, Mpls., 1974—, now ptnr.-in-charge Mpls. off, chmn., commit. contract. litig. Mem. Minn. State Bar (pres. 1991), Hennepin County Bar Assn. (pres. 1980). Office: Dorsey & Whitney Ste 1500 50 S 6th St Minneapolis MN 55402-1498 Office Phone: 612-340-2829. Office Fax: 612-340-2868. Business E-Mail: tinkham.tom@dorsey.com.

**TINNEY, HARLE HOPE HANSON,** museum administrator; b. Providence, Apr. 15, 1941; d. Frederick Charles and Grace Alma (Williamson) Hanson; m. Donald Harold Tinney, Dec. 2, 1960. Student, Albion Coll., 1959—60, Brown U., 1960. Tour guide Belcourt Castle, Newport, RI, 1959-60, mus. ptnr., owner, 1972—; stained glass crafter St. Luke Studio, Providence, 1961-89; exec. dir. Royal Arts Found. at Belcourt Castle, Newport, 2000—. Sec. founder Royal Arts Found., Newport, 1969—, events planner, 1984—, treas., 1996—; donor svcs. Mosaic Club, Newport, 1984-2000, Shake-A-Leg, Newport, 1980-1989, Newport Music Festival, 1964—; ch. organist St. Declan Chapel, 1998-2001. Mem. Sovereign Order Knights Hospitaller St. John Jerusalem (asst. editor newsletter 1998—), Royal Arts Found. (exec. dir. 2002-). Avocations: music, cello, church organ, antique restoration. Home: Belcourt Castle 657 Bellevue Ave Newport RI 02840-4280 Office Phone: 401-846-0669. E-mail: royalarts@aol.com.

**TINNING, HERBERT PETER,** association executive; b. Hoboken, N.J., Apr. 17, 1928; s. Peter Christian and Emmy Asta (Andersen) T.; divorced; children: Christian, Kirsten; m. Adeline Augusta Falk, Aug. 13, 1990. Degree in mech. engring., Stevens Inst. Tech., 1952. Engr. Good Housekeeping Inst., N.Y.C., 1954-56; dir. membership and serets. Am. Soc. Refrigerating Engrs., N.Y.C., 1956-58; application and sales engr. Dunham Bush Inc., N.Y.C., 1958-61; dir. tech. svcs. ASHRAE, N.Y.C., 1961-69; asst. tech. dir. Assn. Home Appliance Mfrs., Chgo., 1969-71; regional coord., dir. socioecon. program Nat. Assn. Accts., N.Y.C., 1972-77; administrv. exec. Compressed Gas Assn., N.Y.C., 1977-79; group dir., tech. affairs ASME, N.Y.C., 1980-93; exec. dir. Devils Foot Soc., Millburn, N.J., 1982—. Chmn. heating, refrigeration and air conditioning stds. bd. Am. Nat. Stds. Inst., N.Y.C., 1968-69; presenter in field. Contbr. articles to various publs. Mem. current affairs com. Berkeley Square Svc. Assn., Arlington Heights, Ill., 1969-72; mem. pub. rels. and bylaws coms. Citizens Adv. Com., Arlington Heights, 1969-71; mem. mayor's action com. on drugs Village of Arlington Heights, 1970-71; mem. devel. com. Twp. of Weehawken, N.J., 1978-81; chmn. Brotherhood of

St. Andrew, Arlington Heights, 1970-72; trustee Seabury-Western Theol. Sem., Evanston, Ill., 1972-75; deacon Episcopal Ch., 1974; fund capt. Stevens Inst. Tech., Hoboken, 1982-87. Recipient award of excellence U.S. Dept. Commerce, 1977. Mem. Am. Soc. Assn. Execs. (life, cert.), N.Y. Soc. Assn. Execs. (life, chmn. awards com., mem. human resources com.), Palisades Nature Assn. (life), Baker Street Irregulars (Horace Harker award 1973), Sherlock Holmes Soc. London, Priory Scholars (hon.), Millburn Old Guard (citation 1995). Avocations: sherlockian studies, gardening, natural history, reading. Home and Office: 93 Sagamore Rd Millburn NJ 07041-2154

**TINSLEY, ADRIAN,** former college president; b. NYC, July 6, 1937; d. Theodore A. and Mary Ethel (White) Tinsley. AB, Bryn Mawr Coll., 1958; MA, U. Wash., 1962; PhD, Cornell U., 1969. Asst. prof. English U. Md., College Park, 1968-72; dean William James Coll., Grand Valley State, Allendale, Mich., 1972-87; assoc. vice chancellor acad. affairs Minn. State U., St. Paul, 1982-85; exec. v.p.; provost Glassboro (N.J.) State Coll., 1985-89; pres. Bridgewater (Mass.) State Coll., 1989—2002, pres. emerita, 2002—. Coord. women higher edn. administrn. Bryn Mawr & Hers Summer Inst., Bryn Mawr, Pa., 1977—. Editor: Women in Higher Education Administration, 1984. Office: Boyden Hall Bridgewater State Coll Bridgewater MA 02325-0001 Office Phone: 508-697-9656. Business E-Mail: atinsley@bridgew.edu.

**TINSLEY, BOYD CALVIN,** musician; b. Charlottesville, Va., May 16, 1964; s. George Franklin and Helen Carter Tinsley. Degree in History, U. Va.; studies violin with Isadore Saslav. Mem. Boyd Tinsley Band formerly Down Boy Down, 1987—92; mem. (violinist) Dave Matthews Band, 1992—. Musician (violinist with Dave Matthews Band): (albums) Remember Two Things, 1993, Crash, 1996, Live at Red Rocks 8.15.95, 1996, Before These Crowded Streets, 1998, Don't Drink the Water, 1998, Everyday, 2001, Busted Stuff, 2002, Central Park Concert, 2003, Gorge, 2004; musician: (violinist solo) True Reflections, 2003; musician: (violinst) Autopilot, The Samples, 1994, Kickin' & Screamin', Allgood, 1994, Best of Columbia Records Radio Hour, Vol. 2, Various Artists, 1996, Live on Letterman: Music from the Late Show, Various Artists, 1997, Scream 2 Original Soundtrack, 1997, Musical Chairs, Hootie & The Blowfish, 1998, Turnpike Diaries, The Getaway People, 2000, Return to Earth, The Samples, 2001, Wire, Third Day, 2004. Recipient (with Dave Matthews Band) Grammy award for Best Rock Performance by a Duo or Group with Vocal for So Much to Say, 1996, Chmns. award, NAACP Image Awards, 2004. Office: RCA Records 1540 Broadway New York NY 10036

**TINSLEY, NIKKI LEE RUSH,** federal agency administrator; b. Apr. 23, 1948; BS in Bus. Admistrn., Ohio State U./Va. Commonwealth U., 1970; MS in Bus. Admistrn., U. Colo./U. No. Colo., 1981. Ednl. program asst. Office of Edn., Wash., 1971; bookstore mgr. U.S. Govt. Printing Office, Denver, 1971-76; auditor U.S. GAO, Denver, 1976-82; supervisory auditor Dept. of Interior, Minerals Mgmt. Svc., Lakewood, Colo., 1982-90; divsnl. insp. gen. EPA, Kansas City, Kans., 1990—95, dep. insp. gen. Washington, 1995-96, acting insp. gen., 1997-98, insp. gen., 1998—. Chair human resources com. Pres.'s Coun. on Integrity and Efficiency, 2002—04; mem. Adv. Coun. on Govt. Auditing Stds., Comptroller Gen.'s Domestic Working Group. Recipient Bronze medal for commendable svc. EPA, 1995. Mem.: Colo. Soc. CPAs, Inst. Internal Auditors, Assn. Govt. Accts. (Disting. Fed. Leadership award 2004). Office: EPA MC 2410 1200 Pennsylvania Ave NW Washington DC 20460-0001 Office Phone: 202-566-0847. E-mail: tinsley.nikki@epa.gov.

**TINSTMAN, ROBERT ALLEN,** former construction company executive; BS, Mining Engring., Univ. Wisconsin, Platteville, 1968. Underground engr. Reynolds Mining Corp., Bauxite, Ark., 1966-68, stripping engr., 1968-71, asst. mine superintendant, 1971-73; sr. mine engr. Texasgulf, Aurora, N.C., 1973-74, Morrison Knudsen Corp., Boise, Idaho, 1974-75, asst. mgr., mining engr., 1975-77, dir. mining engring., 1977-79, v.p., gen. mgr. mining engring., 1979-85; exec. v.p. Morrison Knudsen Engineers, Inc., Boise, Idaho, 1985-88, pres., 1988-89; pres. mining group Morrison Knudsen Co., Inc., Boise, Idaho, 1989-95; pres, CEO Morrison Knudsen Corp., Boise, Idaho, 1995-99; pres. Tinstman and Assoc., 1999—. Exec. comm. mem. Morrison Knudsen bd. dirs.; mng. dir. MK Peru; dir., Centennial Engring. Inc.; dir. Natl. Projects Inc.; bd. dirs. Home Fed., Ida Corp., Home Fed.; chmn. bd. Contractorhub.com. Bd. dirs. St. Lukes. Mem. Natl. Soc. of Professional Engrs., Soc. of Mining Engrs.

**TINTLE, CARMEL JOSEPH,** public relations executive; b. Paterson, NJ, Sept. 25, 1924; s. Herbert J. and Agnes (Merna) T.; m. Alice M. Hayes, Sept. 1, 1948; children: Joseph, Alice Maureen. BS, Fordham U., 1951; postgrad., NYU. Editl. asst. Newsweek mag., NYC, 1946-50; news editor Beverage Retailer Weekly, NYC, 1950-52; city editor Paterson Sunday Eagle, 1950-52; staff writer Carl Byoir & Assocs., Inc., NYC, 1952-59, asst. account exec., 1959-64, assoc. account exec., 1964; account supr. Grey Pub. Rels., Inc., NYC, 1964; v.p. Schenley Affiliated Brands Corp., subs. Schenley Industries, NYC, 1964-72, sr. v.p., 1972-74; v.p. corp. affairs Am. Distilling Co., 1974—80; v.p. Banfi Vintners, Old Brookville, NY, 1980—90; CEO Vinum Comm., Inc., Old Brookville, NY, 1980-90; cons. corp. comm. Banfi Vintners, 1990—2002. Publicity dir. Jumby Bay Island, a Banfi resort property, Antigua, 1985-95. Vol. publicist Assumption Coll. Sis., Mendham, NJ, 2001—. Seaman, officer US Mcht. Marine, 1943-46. Mem. NY Press Club, SAR, KC, St. Patrick Guard of Honor NJ, US Mcht. Marine Vets., Irish-Am. Cultural Inst., Fordham Univ.'s Golden Rams. Home: 14 Potter Ct Upper Montclair NJ 07043-1514

**TINTURIN, PETER,** composer; b. Ekaterinoslav, Russia, June 1, 1910; arrived in U.S., 1929, naturalized; s. Leonid and Elizabeth Tinturin; m. Wela Davies, Sept. 1941 (dec.); children: Leonid, Glenn. Student, Vienna Conservatory Music, 1924—29; BA, U. Vienna, 1929; MusB cum laude, Chapman Coll., 1953. Former v.p. Advanced Pictures Corp., Hollywood; former pres. Fine Arts Recording Co., 1948. Composer, writer various films and plays; author: over 300 works publ.; prodr., writer (musical) Pardon My Ph.D. Pvt. U.S. Army, 1943—44. Mem.: ASCAP (award for outstanding compositions 1934, 1937, 1941).

**TIPLER, FRANK JENNINGS, III,** physicist; b. Andalusia, Ala., Feb. 1, 1947; s. Frank Jennings Jr. and Anne (Kearley) T.; m. Jolanta Rokicka; children: Allison Anne, Caroline Nicole. S.B., MIT, 1969; PhD, U. Md., 1976. Rsch. mathematician U. Calif., Berkeley, 1976-79; sr. rsch. fellow Oxford (Eng.) U., 1979; rsch. assoc. U. Tex., Austin, 1979-81; assoc. prof. physics and math. Tulane U., New Orleans, 1981-87, prof., 1987—. Vis. sr. scientist Max-Planck Inst. Astrophysics, Munich, 1987; vis. fellow U. Sussex, Brighton, Eng., 1987; vis. prof. Inst. Astrophysics, Liege, Belgium, 1988, U. Bern, Switzerland, 1988, U. Vienna, Austria, 1992. Author: l'Homme et le Cosmos, 1984, The Anthropic Cosmological Principle, 1986, The Physics of Immortality, 1994; editor: Essays in General Relativity, 1980; contbr. articles to profl. jour. Rsch. grantee NSF, 1984, 86. Libertarian. Office: Tulane Univ Physics Dept St Charles ave New Orleans LA 70118 Office Phone: 504-865-5727. Business E-Mail: tipler@tulane.edu.

**TIPPETT, DAVE,** professional hockey coach; m. Wendy Tippett; children: Nicole, Natalie. Player Hartford Whalers, Wash. Capitals, Pitts. Penguins, Phila. Flyers, 1984—95; capt. Can. Olympic Team, Sarajevo, 1984, mem. Albertville, France, 1992; player, asst. coach Houston Aeros, IHL, 1995—99, gen. mgr., head coach, 1999; asst. coach LA Kings, 1999—2002; head coach Dallas Stars, 2002—. Achievements include being a member of silver medal Canadian Hockey team, Albertville Olympic Games, 1992. Office: Dallas Stars 2601 Ave Of The Stars Ste 100 Frisco TX 75034-9016*

**TIPPING, WILLIAM MALCOLM,** social services administrator; b. Oak Park, Ill., Mar. 31, 1931; s. William McKinley and Evelyn Amelia (Freier) T.; m. Lois A. Grife, Sept. 18, 1954 (dec. May 1986); children: William, Barbara, Robert; m. Babette J. Cumming, Oct. 10, 1987; children: Christopher Cumming, Courtney Barone. BA, Carleton Coll., Northfield, Minn., 1954. Sales rep. Gen. Mills, Inc., Mpls., 1954-56; account exec. Campbell Mithun,

Inc., Mpls., 1956-63, v.p. mgmt., supr. Mpls. and Chgo., 1965-76; account supr., v.p. Lennen & Newell, Inc., N.Y.C., 1963-65; ptnr., mgr. Heidrick & Struggles, Inc., Chgo., 1976-88; exec. v.p., chief exec. officer Am. Cancer Soc., Atlanta, 1988-91; pres. Tipping and McRae, Inc., Atlanta, 1991-93; mng. dir. Ward Howell Internat., Inc., Atlanta, 1993-97. Trustee Carleton Coll., 1986-90; bd. dirs. Nat. Health Coun., N.Y.C., Ga. Conservancy, Families First; mem. fin. com. UICC, Geneva, 1990-91. Recipient Disting. Svc. award Carleton Coll., 1984. Mem. Capital City Club (Atlanta), Quechee (Vt.) Club, Commerce Club (Atlanta). Republican. Episcopalian.

TIPPY, MARGARET O'SHEA, psychologist; b. Glen Cove, May 20, 1970; d. Nicholas Francis and Kathleen McCann O'Shea; m. Gil Tippy, May 5, 2005; 1 stepchild, Glenn. BA, Hofstra U., N.Y.C., 1992; MS in Edn., Pace U., N.Y.C., 1995, PsyD, 2000. Psychologist Schneider Children's Hosp. L.I. Jewish Med. Ctr., New Hyde Park, NY, 1999—. Pvt. practice, Manhasset, NY. Office: #301 444 Comty Dr Manhasset NY 11030

TIPRE, DNYANESH NISHIKANT, pharmacist, researcher; arrived in US, 2002; s. Nishikant and Sandhya Tipre. BS in Pharmacy, Govt. Coll. Pharmacy, Karad, India, 1995; MS in Pharmacy, Nagpur U., India, 1998; PhD in Pharmacy, U. Mumbai, India, 2002. Rsch. fellow NIH, Bethesda, Md., 2002—06; sch. assoc. scientist Howard U. Hosp., Washington, 2006—. Cons. NIH. Vol. adminstrn. Shiva Vishnu Temple, Greenbelt, Md. Fellow, Fogarty Internat. Ctr., 2002—05. Mem.: Acad. Molecular Imaging (assoc. award 2006). Peace And Freedom. Hindu. Achievements include research in successful inhibition of defluorination of 18F-FCWAY radiotracer in a rat model. Avocations: travel, music. Home: 4604 Crekshore Dr Rockville MD 20852 Office: Howard Univ Hospital 2041 Georgia Ave NW Washington DC 20060 Personal E-mail: dnyanesht@yahoo.com

TIPSON, (LYNN) BAIRD, academic administrator, religious studies educator; b. Plainfield, N.J., Oct. 22, 1943; s. Lynn Baird Sr. and Yvonne (Gaston) T.; m. Sarah Oden, May 16, 1970; children: David, Elizabeth. AB, Princeton U., 1965; M in philosophy, Yale U., 1969, PhD in religious studies, 1972. Asst. prof. religious studies U. Va., Charlottesville, 1970-76; asst. prof. religion Cen. Mich. U., Mt. Pleasant, 1976-77, assoc. prof., acting chair, 1977-78, assoc. prof., acting asst. dean Sch. Arts and Scis., 1978-81, assoc. dean Coll. Arts and Scis., 1981-87; provost, prof. religion Gettysburg (Pa.) Coll., 1987—95, acting pres., fall 1988; pres. Wittenberg U., Springfield, Ohio, 1995—2004, Washington Coll., Chestertown, Md., 2004—. Pres. North Coast Athletic Conf. Contbr. articles to profl. jours., dictionaries, and encys. Pres., bd. dirs. Springfield Symphony Orch. Fulbright-Hays fellow, 1965-66, Woodrow Wilson fellow, 1966-67, Rockefeller Dissertation fellow, 1969-70, NEH summer seminar grantee, 1977. Mem. Am. Soc. Ch. History (presented paper at nat. conf. 1984), Hist. Soc. of Protestant Episcopal Ch., Inst. Early Am. History and Culture, Phi Beta Kappa. Lutheran. Office: Washington Coll 300 Washington Ave Chestertown MD 21620

TIPSORD, MICHAEL L., insurance company executive; b. Ill. B in Acctg., Ill. Wesleyan U.; JD, U. Ill. Urbana-Champaign. CPA; CLU 1991, CPCU 1995. Asst. tax counsel, 1988; with State Farm Ins. Cos., 1988—, dir. acctg., 1995—96, asst. controller, 1996—97, exec. asst., 1997—98, v.p., asst. treas., 1998—2001, v.p., treas., 2001—02, sr. v.p., CFO, 2002—04, vice chmn., CFO, 2004—. Bd. dir. State Farm Lloyds, Inc., Ins. Placement Svc., Inc., State Farm Investment Mgmt. Corp., State Farm V.P. Mgmt. Corp., State Farm Bank, FSB; trustee State Farm Mutual Fund Trust, State Farm Variable Product Trust, State Farm Assoc.'s Funds Trust, State Farm Ins. Co. Employee Retirement Trust, State Farm Ins. Co. Savings and Thrift Trust for US Employees; prof., dept. accountancy Univ. Ill., Urbana-Champaign. Bd. trustees Ill. Wesleyan U. Mem.: Ill. State Bar Assn., ABA. Office: State Farm Ins Cos 1 State Farm Plz Bloomington IL 61710-0001*

TIPTON, CLYDE RAYMOND, JR., communications and resources development consultant; b. Cin., Nov. 13, 1921; s. Clyde Raymond and Ida Marie (Molitor) Tipton; m. Marian Gertrude Beushausen, Aug. 16, 1942 (dec. Aug. 2, 2000); children: Marian Page Ashley, Robert Bruce. BS, U. Ky., Lexington, 1946, MS, 1947. Rsch. engr. Battelle Meml. Inst., Columbus, Ohio, 1947-49, sr. tech. adviser, 1951-62, coord. corp. comm., 1969-73, v.p. comm., 1973-75, asst. to pres., 1978-79, v.p., corp. dir. comm. and pub. affairs, 1979-86; staff mem. Los Alamos Sci. Lab., 1949-51; dir. research Basic, Inc., Bettsville, Ohio, 1962-64; asst. dir. Battelle Pacific N.W. Labs., Richland, Wash., 1964-69; pres., trustee Battelle Commons Co. for Cmty. Urban Redevel., Columbus, 1975-78; cons. bus. comm. and devel. Columbus, 1986—. Secretariat US del. 2d Internat. Conf. Peaceful Use Atomic Energy, Geneva, 1958; cons. U.S. AEC in Atoms for Peace Program, Tokyo, 1958, New Delhi, 1959—60, Rio de Janeiro, 1960. Author: (book) How to Change the World, 1982; editor: Jour. Soc. Nondestructive Testing, 1953—57, The Reactor Handbook, Reactor Materials, vol. 3, 1955, vol. 1, 1960, Learning to Live on a Small Planet, 1974. Past pres. Pilot Dogs, United Way Franklin County, Greater Columbus Arts Coun.; bd. dirs., treas. Pilot Guide Dog Found.; pres. emeritus Arhcs. Soc. Ohio Found.; bd. dirs., treas. Torch Club of Columbus; dir. Episc. Retirement Homes, Inc. With USAAF, 1943. Named to U. Ky. Engring. Hall of Distinction, 1997; Haggin fellow, U. Ky., 1947, Sr. fellow, Otterbein Coll., 1978. Fellow: NSPE (past pres., Outstanding Svc. award 1992); mem.: Ohio Soc. Profl. Engr. (past pres., award of distinction, Uncommon Man award, Outstanding Svc. award 1993, 1998), Am. Soc. Metals, Lions, Sigma Xi, Alpha Chi Sigma. Episcopalian. Achievements include patents in field. Home and Office: 2218 Aschinger Blvd Columbus OH 43212-4620 Office Phone: 614-424-6077.

TIPTON, JAMES D., retired military officer, education educator; b. Greeneville, Tenn., Jan. 8, 1937; s. P.H. and Ruby Tipton; 1 child, Dennis R. BA in Biology, Tusculum Coll., Tenn., 1958; MS in Logistic Mgmt., Air Force Inst. Tech., Dayton, Ohio, 1973; MS in Edn., Jacksonville State U., Ala., 1994. Cert. tchr. secondary edn. State of Ala., 1994. Commdg. officer U.S. Army, Washington, 1958—91. Adj. faculty Gadson State C.C., Anniston, Ala., 1994—98, Troy State U., Ft. Benning Campus, Ga., 2000—02, Columbus Tech. Coll., Ga., 2004—. Deacon, 1974—76. Col. (o6) U.S. Army, 1984—91, Ft. McClellan, Ala. Decorated Joint Superior Svc. medal, Bronze Star U.S. Army, Legion of Merit, Meritorious Svc. medals (5), Army Commendation medal U.S. Army Chem. Sch. Home: 1800 Lakewood Dr Apt F-1 Phenix City AL 36867 Office: Columbus Tech Coll Manchester Expressway Columbus GA 39104 Office Phone: 706-641-5282.

TIPTON, KENNETH WARREN, retired agricultural administrator, researcher; b. Belleville, Ill., Nov. 14, 1932; s. Roscoe Roy and Martha Pearl (Davis) T.; m. Barbara Adds, Mar. 2, 1957; children: Kenneth Warren Jr., Nancy Tipton O'Neal. BS, La. State U., 1955, MS, 1959; PhD, Miss. State U., 1969. Asst. prof. Agrl. Ctr., La. State U., Baton Rouge, 1959-70, assoc. prof., 1970-75, prof., 1975—, supt. Red River Rsch. Sta., La. Agrl. Expt. Sta. Bossier City, 1975-79, assoc. dir. La. Agrl. Expt. Sta. Baton Rouge, 1979-89, dir. La. Agrl. Expt. Sta., vice chancellor, 1989-96, vice chancellor, dir. emeritus, 1996—; ret. 1996. Mem. com. nine USDA/Coop. State Rsch. Svc., 1986-88; Expt. State Com. Orgn. Policy, 1988-91. Contbr. articles to Agronomy Jour., Jour. Econ. Entomology, Grain Sorghum Conf. Coach baseball program Am. Legion, 1969-74; scoutmaster Boy Scouts Am., Baton Rouge, 1970-75. Capt. USAF, 1955-58. Mem. Am. Soc. Agronomy, Crop Sci. Soc. Am., Coun. Agrl. Sci. Tech. Achievements include research on inheritance of fiber traits in cotton, resistance of grain sorghum hybrids to bird damage, tannin content of grain sorghum and effects of phosphorus on growth of sorghum. Home: 732 Baird Dr Baton Rouge LA 70808-5916 Personal E-mail: barkentip@aol.com.

TIPTON, MARGARET ANN, religious organization administrator, writer; b. Covington, Tenn., Sept. 25, 1937; d. Hurtell Tipton and Jennie Anna Williams; 1 child, Cheryl Ann Brown-Dunbar. BA, Trinity Coll., Deerfield, Ill., 1985; postgrad., Moody Grad. Sch., Chgo., 1996. Underwriter Motors Ins. Corp., Chgo., 1963—70; youth coord. Monument of Faith Ch., Chgo. 1964—70, pres. personal evang. ministry, 1964—; pres. founder Effectual

Door Bible Coll., Chgo., 1982—; editor, writer Beautiful for Him mag., Chgo., 1986—92; Christian edn. dir. Hope Tabernacle Ch., Chgo., 1988—91; pres., founder Jennie Williams Davis Found., Chgo., 2001—. Author: Personal Evangelism, 1-5, 1989, Mission, 2004, Most Misinterpreted Biblical Truths, 2004; host (cable TV program) The Margaret Tipton Show, Effectual Door Bible Coll. Radio Program, host (radio program) The EDBC Radio Teacher's Forum, 1985. Sec. Beat 322 Chgo. Alternative Policing Strategy Chgo. Police Dept., 1999—; pres. Bapt. Midwest Youth Conf., 1961—64; class leader Moody Bible Inst. Sch. Recipient Outstanding Svc. award, Midwest Youth Conf., 1982, Outstanding Cmty. Svc. award, Chgo. Police Dept., 2001. Mem.: NAACP, Nat. Black Evangel. Assn., Evangel. Tng. Assn., Nat. Urban League. Office: Effectual Door Bible Coll PO Box 20350 Chicago IL 60620

TIRANA, BARDYL RIFAT, lawyer; b. Geneva, Dec. 16, 1937; s. Rifat and Rosamond English (Walling) T.; m. Anne Prather, June 22, 1985; children by previous marriage: Kyra, Amina. AB, Princeton U., 1959; LL.B., Columbia U., 1962. Bar: D.C. 1962, Md. 1986, N.Y. 1986, Va. 1986, Pa. 1992. Trial atty. Dept. Justice, 1962-64; assoc. Amram, Hahn & Sundlun, Washington, 1965-68, ptnr., 1969-72; dir., sec. Exec. Jet Aviation, Inc., Columbus, Ohio, 1970-77, Technics, Inc., Alexandria, Va., 1971-77; ptnr. Sundlun, Tirana & Scher, Washington, 1972-77; dir. def. civil preparedness agy. Dept. Def., Washington, 1977-79; mem. armed forces policy coun., 1977-79; chmn. bd. Technics, Inc., San Jose, Calif., 1979-85; of counsel Silverstein and Mullens, Washington, 1982-84, ptnr., 1984-90; pvt. practice law Washington, 1991—. Mem.-at-large D.C. Bd. Edn., 1970-74; trustee Jimmy Carter Inaugural Trust, Washington, 1977-87; co-chmn. 1977 Presdl. Inaugural Com., 1976-77; mem. exec. adv. coun. Calif. Commn. Indsl. Innovation, 1981-82; pres. China/USA Edn. Fund, Inc., Washington, 1981-2002; trustee The Waltz Group of Washington, 2000—; dir. Rocky Mountain Inst., Snowmass Colo., 1982-95. Recipient medal for disting. pub. svc. Dept. Def., 1979, Fuess award Phillips Acad., 1991, Svc. Commendation award YWCA of Nat. Capital Area, 1991. Mem. N.Y.C. Racquet and Tennis Club, D.C. Met. Club, The Century Assn. (N.Y.C.). Home: 33 Mercer St Loft 5C New York NY 10013-2565 Office Phone: 212-966-7397. Personal E-mail: btirana@aol.com.

TIRAVANIJA, RIRKRIT, sculptor; b. Buenos Aires, 1961; Student, Ont. Coll. Art, Toronto, Can., 1981, Banff Ctr. Sch. Fine Arts, Can., 1984, Whitney Ind. Studies Program, N.Y.C., 1986, Sch. Art Inst. Chgo., 1985. Adj. asst. prof. Columbia U. Sch. Arts, N.Y.C. One-man shows include Paula Allen Gallery, N.Y.C., 1990, Randy Alexander Gallery, N.Y.C., 1991, 303 Gallery, N.Y.C., 1992, 95, Randolph St. Gallery, Chgo., 1993, Jack Hanley Gallery, San Francisco, 1994, Schipper & Krome, Koln, Germany, 1994, Kunsthalle St. Gallen, Switzerland, 1996, Kolnischer Kunstverien, Cologne, Germany, 1996, Mus. Modern Art, N.Y.C., 1997, Mus. for Gegenwartskunst, Zurich, 1998, Phila. Mus. Art, 1998, L.A. County Mus. Art, 1999, Gavin Brown's Enterprise, N.Y.C., 1999, Wexner Ctr. for the Arts, Columbus, Ohio, 1999, la Caixa, Barcelona, 1999, Galeria Emi Fontana, Milan, 2000, Galaria Salvador Diaz, Madrid, 2000; group shows at The New Mus. Contemporary Art, N.Y.C., 1991, Jack Tilton Gallery, N.Y.C., 1991, Ctr. Contemporary Arts, Ujazdowski Castle, Warsaw, Poland, 1991, 303 Gallery, N.Y.C., 1992, Goethe House, N.Y.C., 1992, Holly Solomon Gallery, N.Y.C., 1993, Aldrich Mus. Contemporary Art, Conn., 1993, Inst. Contemporary Arts, London, 1993, Musee d'Art Moderne de la Ville de Paris, 1994, Galerie Jennifer Flay, Paris, 1994, Whitney Mus. Am. Art, 1995, The Carnegie Mus. Art, Pitts., 1995, Walker Art Ctr., Mpls., 1995, CAPC Bordeaux, France, 1997, Wexner Ctr., Columbus, Ohio, 1999, The Ikon Gallery, Birmingham, Eng., 2003-04, Peace Tower, Day for Night, Whitney Biennial, 2006; film exhbns. include The New Film Maker, The Collective for Living Cinema, N.Y.C., 1985, Video Event, Tom Cugliani Gallery, N.Y.C., 1991; sculpture projects Munster, Germany, 1997, Venice Biennial, Italy, 1999. Fax: 212-941-9828.*

TIRICO, MIKE, sportscaster; b. Whitestone, N.Y., Dec. 13, 1966; married, 2 children. BA in Polit. Sci. and Broadcast Journalism, Syracuse U., 1988. Sports dir. WTVH-TV (affil. CBS), Syracuse, NY, 1987-91; reporter ESPN, Bristol, Conn., 1991—; host NFL Prime Monday, co-host GameDay ESPN Sports Radio, anchor SportsCenter, 1993—; announcer, Monday Night Football, 2006—; studio host, NBA broadcasts ABC, 2002—06. Spkr. in field All-American Talent & Celebrity Network. Actor: (films) Jerry Maguire, 1996. Named top local sportscaster Syracuse Jour., 1989; recipient A.P. N.Y. Broadcasters award. Office: ESPN Inc Comms Dept Espn Plz Bristol CT 06010-1099*

TIRMAN, JOHN, academic research director; Exec. dir. Winston Found. for World Peace, 1986—99; prog. dir. Social Sci. Rsch. Coun., 2001—04; exec. dir. MIT Ctr. Internat. Studies, Cambridge, Mass., 2004—. Author: Fallacy of Star Wars, 1984, Spoils of War, 1997, 100 Ways America is Screwing Up theWorld, 2006. Recipient U.N. Assn. Human Rights award; grantee Fulbright Sr. Scholar in Cypress, 1999—2000. Office: MIT Ctr Internat Studies E38-600 292 Main St Cambridge MA 02139 Office Phone: 617-253-9861. Business E-mail: tirman@mit.edu.*

TIRONE, BARBARA JEAN, retired health insurance administrator; b. Celina, Ohio, Nov. 19, 1943; d. Vincent James and Theresa Barbara (Goettermoeller) G. BA, Miami U., 1965; MBA, U. Chgo., 1977. Asst. dir. for internat. trade State of Ill., Chgo., Brussels, Hongkong and Sao Paulo, Brazil, 1973-76; dir. office of mgmt. and planning Office Human Devel. Svcs., Chgo., 1976-79; dep. regional adminstr. Health Care Financing Adminstrn., Chgo., 1979-82, regional adminstr., 1982-87, dir. bur. of prog. ops. Balt., 1987-92; dir. health stds. and quality bur. Health Care Fin. Adminstrn., Balt., 1992-96; pres, CEO AdminStar, Inc. Indpls. 1996-2001; ret. 2002 Recipient Presdl Disting. Rank award 1988, 94, Presdl. Mentorous Rank award 1987, 92; named Fed. Exec. of Yr., 1987. Home: 11212 Appaloosa Dr Reisterstown MD 21136 Office Phone: 410-833-5570. Personal E-mail: bgagel@comcast.net.

TIRRELL, DAVID A., research scientist, educator; b. Jan. 10, 1953; BS in Chemistry, MIT, 1974; MS in Polymer Sci. and Engring., U. Mass., 1976, PhD in Polymer Sci. and Engring., 1978; D honoris causa (hon.), Tech. Univ. Eindhoven, 2001. Rsch. assoc. Kyoto U., 1978; asst. prof. chemistry Carnegie-Mellon U., 1978-82, assoc. prof. chemistry, 1982-84; assoc. prof. polymer sci. and engring. U. Mass., 1984-87, prof. polymer sci. and engring., 1987-92, Barrett prof. polymer and sci. and engring., 1992-98; Ross McCollum-William H. Corcoran prof. Calif. Inst. Tech., 1998—, chair chemistry divsn. & chem. engring., 1999—. Mem. molecular and cellular biology faculty, 1990—; adj. prof. chemistry U. Mass., 1991; dir. NSF materials rsch. lab., 1991, NSF materials rsch. sci. and engring. ctr., 1994—; vis. prof. chemistry Queensland U., Australia, 1987, Inst. Charles Sadron, Strausbourg, Austria; mem. materials rsch. adv. com. NSF, 1988—91; chmn. com. on synthetic hierarchical structures Nat. Rsch. Coun., 1990—94, mem. panel on biomolecular materials, 1991—; mem. polymers in biosystems com. Naval Rsch. Lab., 1994; co-chmn. grad. polymer rsch. conf., State Coll., Pa., 1994; co-chmn. program com. IUPAC Macromolecular Symposium, 1994; chmn. Gordon Rsch. Conf. on Chemistry of Supramolecules and Assemblies, 1995; Fellow American Association for the Advancement of Science, 2003, 2003. Editor: (profl. jours.) Jour. of Polymer Sci., 1988—99; assoc. editor: New Polymeric Materials, 1986—87, editl. bd.: Indsl. and Engring. Chemistry, Product Rsch. and Devel., 1983—86, Jour. Bioactive and Compatible Polymers, 1986—, Biomaterials, 1986—, New Polymeric Materials, 1987, Jour. of Macromolecular Sci-Chemistry, 1990—, Progress in Polymer Sci., 1992—, Macromolecular Reports, 1992, Materials Sci. and Engring., 1993—, Chem. and Engring. News, 1995—; contbr. articles to profl. jours. Recipient Presdl. Young Investigator award, 1984—89, Fulbright Sr. scholar award, 1987, Chancellor's medal, Univ. Mass., 1997; fellow Univ., 1974—77, Alfred P. Sloan Rsch., 1982—84, Rothschild, Curie Inst., 1995—97. Fellow: Am. Inst. Med. & Biol. Engring., AAAS; mem.: NAS, Phi Lambda Upsilon, Materials Rsch. Soc., NY Acad. Scis., Am. Chem. Soc. (Harrison Howe award 1996, Carl S. Marvel Polymer Chem. award 1991, Polymer Chem. award 2001), Sigma Xi. Office: Calif Inst Tech Divsn Chemistry Mail Code 164-30 Pasadena CA 91125*

TIRRELL, JOHN ALBERT, organization executive, consultant; b. Boston, Feb. 11, 1934; s. George Howard and Helen Sarah (Hitchings) T.; m. Helga Ruth Eisenhauer, Jan. 29, 1966; children: Steffanie Ruth, Sabina Lisette, Monica Susanne. BA in Psychology, The King's Coll., Briarcliff Manor, N.Y., 1961; MEd, U. Ariz., Tucson, 1975. Various positions for several orgns., 1962-68; analyst instrnl.-ednl. systems GE, Daytona Beach, Fla., 1969-72; dir. curriculum and program devel. Brookdale C.C., Lincroft, NJ, 1972; dir. learning and faculty resources Pima C.C., Tucson, 1972-76; dir. human resources planning and devel. Miami divsn. Cyprus Copper Co., Claypool, Ariz., 1976-79; exec. dir. Calvary Missionary Fellowship, Tucson, 1983-85; interim pastor Sagauro Evang. Ch., Tucson, 1985-86; pastor Midvale Evangelical Ch., Tucson, 1986-87; founder, pres. The Jethro Consultancy, Birmingham, Mich., 1979—; v.p. mgmt. svc. AA Gage, Ferndale, Mich., 1987-88; pastor Desert Hills Bapt. Ch., Tucson, 1993-95. Mem. adv. bd. UIM Internat., Greeley, Colo., 1983-92, mem. fin. com., 1983-94, svc. support svcs. field bd., 1993-01, sec. bus. and devel. field bd., 2002-, sec., chmn. pers. com., 1997—, sec., 1998—, also bd. dirs., 1993—; mem. policy revision com., 2004-, v.p. internat. bd., 2005-, mem. search com., 2005-, vice pres., sec. 2005—, mem. bus. and devel. bd., chmn. nominating com., 2005-; assoc. faculty mem. Gila Pueblo Campus Ea. Ariz. Coll., Globe, 1978; adj. prof. Montclair State Coll., Upper Montclair, N.J., 1972; chmn. mgmt. and pers. com. Wildwood Ranch, Inc., Howell, Mich., 1989-92; interim pres., v.p. programs, v.p. devel. Detroit Rescue Mission Ministries, 1990-92; v.p. corp. planning, tng., productivity George Instrument Co., Royal Oak; mem. mgmt., comm., sociology So. Ariz. and Phoenix campuses U. Phoenix, 1997—; area chair for social scis., 2001-04; adj. faculty mem. psychology Pima County C.C., 1999-2002. Contbr. articles to profl. jours. Mem. Ariz. Coun. for Econ. Conversion, 1992-94; mem. facilities task force Grace Evang. Free Ch., Birmingham, 1989-90, chmn. bylaws revision com., 1989-90, chmn. property devel. com., 1990-92; interim pastor Desert Hills Bapt. Ch., Tucson, 1992-93; elder 1st Evang. Free Ch., Tucson, 1979-81, 86-87, 97, supt. Sunday sch., 1981-84, supr. adult Sunday sch., 1992-93, chmn. gen. bd., elder bd., 1979-82, short-term missions coord., missions bd., 1992-93; bd. dirs. S.W. Border dist. Evang. Free Ch. Am., 1996-00, mem. comm. com., 1996-01, chmn. comm. com., 1998-99; bd. dirs. Clearing House of Operational Resources for Christian Orgns., Royal Oak, Mich., 1991; bd. dirs. Shadow Roc Homeowners Assn., 1996-98, treas., 1997; v.p. parent-tchr. fellowship Palo Verde Christian Sch., Tucson, 1980-81. Staff sgt. USAF, 1952-56. Mem. ASTD (treas., Old Pueblo chpt. 1982, bd. dirs.-at-large 1983, Human Resources Devel. award Valley of the Sun chpt. 1977), Birmingham-Bloomfield C. of C. (mem. profl. devel. edn. com. 1987-91, mem. pub. rels. mktg. com. 1989), King's Coll. Alumni Assn. (class gov. 1988-95, 2000-03). Republican. Avocation: Bible teaching. Home and Office: 1205 E Deer Canyon Rd Tucson AZ 85718-1069 Office Phone: 520-544-9750. Personal E-mail: jack.tirrell@comcast.net.

TIRRELL, MATTHEW V., engineering educator; b. Phillipsburg, NJ, Sept. 5, 1950; s. Matthew Vincent Tirrell Jr. and Loraine (Wier) Gonsky; m. Pamela LaVigne, Aug. 1993. BS in chem. engring., Northwestern U., 1973; PhD in polymer sci. and engring., U. Mass., 1977. Mem. coop. edn. program Cin. Milacron Chem. Inc., 1970-72; tchg. and rsch. assist. U. Mass., Amherst, 1973-77; asst. prof. U. Minn., Mpls., 1977-81, assoc. prof., 1981-85, prof. chem. engring. and materials sci., 1985—99, Shell disting. chair. chem. engring., 1986-91, Earl E. Bakken Prof. Biomed. Engring., 1993—97, head chem. engring. and materials sci., 1995-99; dir. Biomed. Engring. Inst., 1995-98; dean Coll Engring. U. Calif., Santa Barbara, 1999—, Richard A. Auhll Prof., 1999—, also prof. materials engring.; venture ptnr. NGEN Partners, LLC. Mem. adv. panel Grad. Sch. Integrative Sciences and Engring. Nat. U. Singapore, 2003—05, vis. com. chem. and environ. engring., 2003—05; cons. Institut Francais du Petrole, 1982—, Kimberly-Clark Corp., 2000—, Edwards Lifesciences, 2000—, Santa Barbara Tech. Group, 2000—, bd. mem.; editl. adv. bd. Jour. Polymer Sci., Polymer Physics Edit., 1986—2000, Macromolecules, 1987—90, McGraw-Hill Chem. Engring. Series, 1987—98, Jour. Rheology, 1990—, Progress in Polymer Sci., 1992—97, Polymerica Acta, 1992—, Jour. Adhesion Sci. and Tech., 1993—96, Langmuir, 1995—, Current Opinion in Colloid and Interface Sci., 1996—, Oxford Univ. Press, Chem. Engring. Series, 1998—2000, Chemistry of Materials, 1998—, Gordon and Breach, 2000—; editl. bd. Jour. Chem. Physics, 1991—93; US editor Chem. Engring. Sci., 1988—91; assoc. editor Reviews in Macromolecular Sci., 1992—2000, editor, 2000—; Sci. and Tech. Panel U. Calif. Pres.'s Coun. for Nat. Lab. Adminstrn., 2000—; bd. dirs. Cottage Health Sys., Santa Barbara, 2000—; US Chair German-Am. Frontiers of Engring., 1999—. Author: Modeling of Polymerization Processes, 1995. Advisor Camille and Henry Dreyfus Found., 1998—. Named Outstanding Young Chem. Engr. of Minn., 1981; recipient Camille and Henry Dreyfus Tchr.-Scholar Award, 1980, George Taylor/IT Alumni Soc. Disting. Rsch. Award, U. Minn. Inst. Tech., 1981, Gordon Starr Outstanding Contribution Award, U. Minn., 1981, Presdl. Young Investigator Award, NSF, 1984, Chancellor's Medal, U. Mass. Amherst, 1987, Alumni Merit Award, Northwestern U., 1997; Alfred P. Sloan Found. Fellowship, 1982, John Simon Guggenheim Meml. Found. Fellowship, 1986. Mem. NAE, AIChE (assoc. editor jour. 1991—2001, inst. lectr. 2001, Allan P. Colburn award 1985, Profl. Progress award 1994, Charles M.A. Stine Award 1996), Am. Chem. Soc., Materials Rsch. Soc., Biomed. Engring. Soc., Controlled Release Soc., Soc. Biomaterials, Soc. Polymer Sci. Japan, Soc. Rheology; fellow AAAS, Am. Inst. Med. and Bio. Engineers, Am. Phys. Soc. (John H. Dillon Medal 1987). Avocations: gourmet cooking, movies, distance running. Office: U Calif Dean's Office Coll Engring Santa Barbara CA 93106-5080

TIRRO, FRANK PASCALE, music educator, composer, writer; b. Omaha, Sept. 20, 1935; s. Frank and Mary Carmela (Spensieri) T.; m. Charlene Rae Whitney Aug. 16, 1961; children: John Andrew, Cynthia Anne. B.M.E., U. Nebr., 1960; M.M., Northwestern U., 1961; Ph.D., U. Chgo., 1974. Chmn. lab. sch. U. Chgo., Ill., 1961—70; fellow of Villa I Tatti Harvard U., Florence, Italy, 1971—72; lectr. U. Kans., Lawrence, Kans., 1972—73; asst. prof. music Duke U., Durham, NC, 1973—74; dir. Southeastern Inst. Medieval and Renaissance Studies, Durham, NC, 1978—80; chmn., assoc. prof. music Duke U., Durham, NC, 1973—80; prof. Yale U., New Haven, 1980—, dean, 1980—89. Reader, cons. several univ. presses; jurist Parisot Internat. Cello Competition, Sao Paolo, Brazil, 1981. Author: Historia del Jazz Clásico, 2001, Historia del Jazz Moderno, 2001, Jazz: A History, 1977, rev. edit., 1993, Renaissance Choirbooks in the Archive of San Petronio in Bologna, 1986, Living With Jazz, 1996, (with others) The Humanities: Cultural Roots and Continuities, 2000, 7th edit., 2004; editor: Medieval and Renaissance Studies No. 9, 1982; mem. editl. bd. Am. Music, Wittenberg Rev.; composer American Jazz Mass, 1960; assoc. editor Am. Nat. Biography, 1994—. Bd. dirs. New Haven Symphony, 1980-89, Neighborhood Music Sch., New Haven, 1982-89, Chamber Orch. New Eng., 1980-82, Ctr. for Black Music Rsch., 1985-91. Recipient Standard Composer award Am. Soc. Composers, Authors and Pubs., 1966, 99, 2000-05, Gustavus Fine Arts medal, 1988, Duke Ellington Fellow medal, 1989, Disting. Alumnus award, U. Nebr., 2006; travel grantee Am. Coun. Learned Socs., 1967; rsch. grantee Duke U., 1978; named to Omaha Ctrl. H.S. Hall of Fame, 2002. Mem. Am. Musicol. Soc. (council 1978-80), Coll. Music Soc. (council 1980-82, mem. exec. bd. 1984-86), Nat. Assn. Schs. of Music, Internat. Soc. Jazz Research, Renaissance Soc. Am., Mory's Club, Yale Club (NYC). Republican. Lutheran. Office: Yale U Sch Music PO Box 208246 New Haven CT 06520-8246 Office Phone: 203-432-5989. E-mail: frank.tirro@yale.edu.

TIRUMALA, VIJAYA RAGHAVAN, materials scientist; s. Ranganathan and Kowsalya Tirumala; m. Veena S. Mellarkod, May 13, 2004. BTech in Chem. Engring., Jawaharlal Nehru Technol. U., Anantapur, India, 1999; PhD, Mich. Technol. U., Houghton, 2003. Cer. engring. prins. neutron diffraction, Oakridge Nat. Lab., 2001. Rsch. asst. Mich. Technol. U., Houghton, 1999—2002; grad. student Argonne (Ill.) Nat. Lab., 2001—02, rsch. aide, 1999—03, post-doctoral rschr., 2003—05; chem. engr. materials divsn. Nat. Inst. Standards and Tech., Gaithersburg, Md., 2005—. Vis. scholar polymer sci. and engring. U. Mass., Amherst, 2005—. Recipient Grad. Sch. award, Exptl. Facilities Divsn., Argonne Nat. Lab., 2002—03, Travel award, Neutron Scattering Soc. Am., 2004; Grad. fellow, Oakridge Associated U.,

2002. Mem.: AIChE, AAAS (assoc.), Am. Phys. Soc. (chair polymer gels and networks session March meeting 2006), Am. Chem. Soc. (assoc.). Achievements include patents for procedure by which polymers of any shape or size can be synthesized; invention of novel way to fabricate environmentally responsive nanostructures. Office: NIST 100 Bureau Drive Stop 8541 Gaithersburg MD 20899-8541 Office Phone: 301-975-6840. Personal E-mail: vijay.tirumala@nist.gov.

**TISCH, ANDREW HERBERT,** corporate executive; b. Asbury Park, N.J., Aug. 14, 1949; s. Laurence Alan and Wilma Zelda (Stein) T.; 2 children. BS, Cornell U., 1971; MBA, Harvard U., 1977. Brand mgr. Lorillard Co., NYC, 1971-75; mgr. operational analysis Loews Corp., NYC, 1977-79; pres. Bulova Corp., Woodside, NY, 1979—90, bd. dir.; past chmn.; chief exec. officer Lorillard Tobacco Co., NYC, 1990—95; chmn. exec. com. Loews Corp., NYC, 1998—, co-chmn. (with Jonathan Tisch), 2006—. Bd. dir. CNA Fin. Corp., 2006—. Contbr. articles to profl. jours. Mem. fgn. affairs com. Am. Jewish Com., N.Y.C., 1983—; bd. dirs. Outward Bound, Inc., Greenwich, Conn., 1983-88; trustee Central Synagogue, N.Y.C., 1984—; gen. chmn. United Jewish Appeal Fedn. of Jewish Philanthropies N.Y., vice chmn. United Jewish Appeal, chmn. Prime Minister's Coun.; bd. dirs. N.Y. Shakespeare Festival, K12; chmn. Children's Hearing Inst., 1988; bd. mem. N.Y.C. Sports Commn.; mem. vis. com. Harvard Bus. Sch.; pres. City Parks Found.; trustee Wildlife Conservation Soc., PENCIL Inc., NY City Police Found. Mem. 24 Karat Club N.Y., Century Country Club, Harmonie Club, Plumb Club, Achilles Track Club (bd. dirs.). Avocations: tennis, running. Office: Loews Corp 667 Madison Ave New York NY 10021-8087*

**TISCH, CARRIE CATHERINE,** elementary school educator; b. Chgo. Ridge, Ill., Dec. 11, 1974; d. Warren Edward and Cynthia Olga Ferst; m. John Michael Tisch, July 23, 2005. BS in Elem. Edn., St. Xavier U., 1997; MA in Curriculum and Instrn., Nat. Louis U., 2004; MA in Ednl. Adminstrn., Governors State U., 2005. Type 03 Elementary Education Ill., 1998. Veterans meml. md. sch. Dist. 130, Blue Island, Ill., 1999—. Volleyball, softball coach Bremen H.S. Athletics, Midlothian, Ill., 1998—2004; jr. varsity head softball coach St. Xavier U. Athletics, Chgo., 2001—04; varsity boys and girls volleyball coach Chgo. H.S. for Agrl. Sciences Athletics, 2004—. Athletic Softball scholarship, St. Xavier U., 1993—97. Home: 15505 Keating Ave Unit B Oak Forest IL 60452 Office: Veterans Meml Mid Sch 12320 Greenwood Ave Blue Island IL 60406 Office Phone: 708-385-6630. Personal E-mail: cferst12@comcast.net.

**TISCH, JAMES SOLOMON,** diversified holding company executive; b. Atlantic City, Jan. 2, 1953; s. Laurence A. and Wilma (Stein) Tisch; m. Merryl Hiat; children: Jessica, Benjamin, Samuel. BA, Cornell U., 1975; MBA, Wharton Grad. Sch., U. Pa., 1976. With Loews Corp., NYC, 1977—; exec. v.p., 1987-94, pres., COO, 1994-99, pres., CEO, 1999—, mem. office pres., 1999—. Chmn., CEO Diamond Offshore Drilling, Inc.; bd. dirs. CNA Fin., Vail Resorts, Inc., Loews Corp. Bd. dirs. Fedn. Employment and Guidance Svc., NYC, 1985; trustee NY Public Libr., Mt. Sinai Med. Ctr./NYU Med. Ctr., NYC, 1988—; past pres., UJA Fedn. NY; past chmn. Conf. Presidents Major Am. Jewish Organizations, United Jewish Communities; mem. bd. overseers, U. Pa. Wharton Sch. Bus.; mem. exec. com. Partnership for NYC. Mem.: Council on Fgn. Rels., Phi Beta Kappa. Office: Loews Corp 667 Madison Ave Fl 7 New York NY 10021-8087*

**TISCH, JONATHAN MARK,** hotel company executive; b. Atlantic City, Dec. 7, 1953; s. Preston Robert and Joan (Hyman) T. BA in Political Sci., Tufts U., 1976. Cinematographer, producer WBZ-TV, Boston, 1976-79; sales mgr. Loews Hotels, NYC, 1980-81, dir. devel., 1981-82, v.p., 1982-85, exec. v.p., 1985-86, pres., 1986, CEO, 1989—, chmn.; mem. office pres. Loews Corp., 1998—, co-chmn. (with Andrew Tisch), 2006—. Mem. mgmt. com. Loews Corp.; bd. dirs. N.Y. Giants, 1991—. Author (with Karl Weber): The Power of We: Succeeding Through Partnerships, 2004. Trustee Robert Steel Found., NYC, Gunnery Sch., Washington, Conn., 1983, Tufts U., Medford, Mass., 1986-, Vice Pres.'s Residence Found., 1994; chmn. NYC host com. for Grammys, 1988, 92, 94; bd. dirs. Pediatric AIDS found.; vice chair econ. devel. com. NYC Partnership, 1994—; chmn. NYC & Co. Recipient Disting. Alumni award, Tufts U., 1996. Mem. Am. Hotel and Motel Assn. (officer 1994-97), Travel Bus. Roundtable (chmn. 1995—, conf. chmn. 1995—), Friars Club. Avocations: golf, tennis, skiing. Office: Loews Hotels 667 Madison Ave New York NY 10021-8087*

**TISCH, STEVEN ELLIOT,** television and movie producer; b. Lakewood, N.J., Feb. 14, 1949; s. Preston Robert and Joan (Hyman) T.; m. Patricia Keast, Sept. 27, 1981 (div. July 1991); m. Jamie Alexander, 1996; 5 children BA, Tufts U., 1971. Pres. Tisch-Avnet Prodns., L.A., 1981-88, Steve Tisch Co., L.A., 1988—. Exec. prodr. (films) Deal of the Century, 1983, The Long Kiss Goodnight, 1996, American History X, 1997, Wild America, 1997, Lock, Stock and Two Smoking Barrels, 1998, Wayward Son, 1999, Snatch, 2000, Looking for an Echo, 2000, Alex and Emma, 2003; prodr. Outlaw Blues, 1977, Coast to Coast, 1980, Risky Business, 1983, Soul Man, 1986, Big Business, 1988, Hot To Trot, 1988, Heart of Dixie, 1989, Heart Condition, 1990, Bad Influence, 1990 Forrest Gump, 1994, Corrina, Corrina, 1994, Dear God, 1996, Wild America, 1997, The Postman, 1997, Nico the Unicorn, 1997; TV prodr. Homeward Bound, 1980, Prime Suspect, 1982, Dirty Dancing, 1988, Lies of the Heart, 1991; co-prodr. Evil in Clear River, 1988, Mission Extreme, 2000; assoc. prodr. The Missing Are Deadly, 1975; exec. prodr. No Other Love, 1979, Something So Right, 1982, Calendar Girl Murders, 1984, The Burning Bed, 1984, Triplecross, 1985, In Love and War, 1987, Out on the Edge, 1989, Judgement, 1990, Afterburn, 1992, Keep the Change, 1992, The People Next Door, 1996; actor; Cry Uncle!, 1971, Dear God, 1996 Chmn. AIDS Project L.A., 1992-94. Office: care Steve Tisch Co 10202 W Washington Blvd Culver City CA 90232-2715

**TISCH, WILMA STEIN,** foundation administrator; b. Asbury Park, N.J., June 25, 1927; d. Joseph F. and Rose E. (Liebesman) Stein; m. Laurence A. Tisch (dec. 2003); children: Andrew H., Daniel R., James S., Thomas J. BS, Skidmore Coll., Saratoga Springs, N.Y., 1948, LHD (hon.), 1990, Mt. Sinai Med. Sch., 1990, CUNY, 1990, NYU, 2006. Trustee Blythedal Children's Hosp., Valhalla, N.Y., 1964-71, Fedn. of Jewish Philanthropies, N.Y.C., 1971—, pres., 1980-83. Trustee Coun. Jewish Fedns., N.Y.C., 1980-87, Jewish Communal Fund; Am. Jewish Joint Distribution Com., N.Y., 1986-94, United Way N.Y.C., 1986—, Skidmore Coll., 1994—, Carnegie Corp., N.Y.C., 1994-98, WNYC Radio, N.Y.C., 1984—, pres., 1988-93; trustee coun. advisors Hunter Coll. Sch. Social Work, N.Y.C., 1986-97. Mem. N.Y. State Gov.'s Select Com. on Capital Health Care Needs, N.Y.C., 1983, Mayor's Transition Coun., N.Y.C., 1993, Carnegie Coun. on Adolescent Devel., N.Y.C., 1987—97; co-chmn. Task Force on Youth Devel. and Cmty. Programs, N.Y.C., 1990—94; chmn. transition adv. team Parks and Recreation—Cultural Affairs, N.Y.C., 1993; mem. policy bd. Sept. 11th Fund, 2001—04. Recipient Louis D. Marshall medal Jewish Theol. Sem., 1980; Milender fellow Brandeis U., 1982; named one of Forbes Richest Americans, 2006. Fellow: Am. Acad. Arts & Sciences. Jewish.

**TISCHLER, GARY,** critic, journalist; Arts and entertainment critic Washington Diplomat, Wheaton, Md.; art and entertainment critic Georgetowner, Washington. Office: Georgetowner 1054 Potomac St Washington DC 20007

**TISCHLER, GARY LOWELL,** psychiatrist, educator; b. N.Y.C., Oct. 30, 1935; s. Louis and Dorothy (Green) T.; m. Judith Post, Aug. 18, 1957; children: Laurie Dee, Marc David, Rachel Mara. AB, Hamilton Coll., 1957; MD, U. Pa., 1961; MS, Yale U., 1975. Intern Kings County Hosp., Bklyn., 1961-62; resident in psychiatry Yale U. Sch. Medicine, New Haven, 1962-65, asst. prof., 1967-70, assoc. prof., 1970-75, prof. psychiatry, 1975-90, chmn. dept. psychiatry, 1986-87; prof., chmn. dept. psychiatry and biobehavioral scis., dir. Neuropsychiatric Inst. UCLA Sch. Medicine, 1990-95; dir. Yale Psychiat. Inst., New Haven, 1978-87; chief psychiatry Yale-New Haven Hosp., 1986-87; clin. dir. Hill-West Haven divsn. Conn. Mental Health Ctr.,

New Haven, 1968-70, dir., 1970-77; prof. psychiatry UCLA, 1990-95, prof. emeritus, 1996—; prof., exec. vice chair dept. psychiatry, dir. Cornell U. Med. Coll., 1994—2002; dir. Westchester divsn., dir. mental health programs N.Y. Hosp., 1994-99, dir. Payne Whitney Clinic, 1996-97. Study dir. Pres.'s Commn. on Mental Health, Washington, 1977-79; cons. Arthur D. Little Inc., Boston, 1973-75, IBM Corp., Armonk, N.Y., 1986-87; mem. profl. adv. com. Am. Med. Internat., L.A., 1984-86; mem. bd. mental health and behavioral medicine Inst. Medicine, Washington, 1986—, com. on clin. evaluation, 1990-94. Author: Quality Assurance Thru Utilization and Peer Review, 1982; editor: Patient Care Evaluation in Mental Health, 1985, Diagnosis and Classification in Psychiatry, 1987; contbr. articles to profl. jours. Mem. Gov.'s transition staff on mental health, Conn., 1975; vice chmn. Bd. Mental Health State of Conn., 1986. Served to capt. U.S. Army, 1965-67, Vietnam. Fellow Am. Psychiat. Assn., Am. Coll. Mental Health Adminstrn., Am. Assn. for Social Psychiatry, Am. Coll. Psychiatry. Home: 36 Rock Hill Rd Bedford NY 10506-1522 E-mail: glt35@netscape.net.

**TISCHLER, JUDITH BLANCHE,** retired publishing executive; b. N.Y.C., May 14, 1933; d. Max and Anna (Drescher) Zucker; m. Alfred Tischler, Dec. 14, 1958; children: Marva, Mira, Gary. MA, CCNY, 1975; PhD, Jewish Theol. Sem., 1989. Editor, dir. Transcontinental Music Publs., N.Y.C., 1981—2000. Prof. music Jewish Theol. Sem., H.L. Miller Cantorial Sch. French hornist various concerts worldwide, 1952-71. Office: HL Miller Cantonal Sch Jewish Theol Sem of Am 3080 Broadway New York NY 10027 E-mail: tisch33@netvision.net.il, judithtischler@hotmail.com.

**TISCHMAN, MICHAEL BERNARD,** lawyer; b. Elizabeth, N.J., Oct. 8, 1937; s. Nathan and Ann (Goldberg) T.; m. Elinor Cohen, Aug. 16, 1959; children: David F., Susan F. BA, U. Pa., 1959; LLB, Harvard U., 1963; LLM in Taxation, NYU, 1968. Bar: N.J. 1964, Fla. 1979, N.Y. 1984. Law sec. Judge Walter J. Freund N.J. Appellate Div., 1963-64; assoc. Schiff, Cummis & Kent, Newark, 1964-67; ptnr. Cummis, Kent, Radin & Tischman, Newark, 1968-70, Sills, Beck, Cummis, Radin & Tischman, Newark, 1971-87, Sills, Cummis, Radin, Tischman, Epstein & Gross, Newark, 1988—2003; sr. counsel Sills, Cummis, Epstein & Gross, Newark, 2004—. Panel chmn. fee arbitration com. N.J. Supreme Ct. Dist. Essex County, 1987-91; mem. health law and policy program adv. bd. Seton Hall Law Sch., 1997—. Mem. Mayor's Performing Arts Ctr. Task Force, Newark, 1988-96. Mem. N.J. Bar Assn. (com. on ltd. partnership act revisions 1983-88), Phi Beta Kappa. Home: 8 Wedgewood Way Scotch Plains NJ 07076-2727 Office: Sills Cummis Epstein & Gross One Riverfront Pla Newark NJ 07102 Office Phone: 973-643-7000. Business E-mail: mtischman@sillscummis.com.

**TISCH SUSSMAN, LAURIE,** art gallery director; d. Preston Robert Tisch; 2 children from previous marriage. B, Duke U.; MFA, Catholic U. Chmn. Ctr. Arts Edn. Inc., Children's Mus. Manhattan; pres. Laurie Tisch Found.; cmmnr. NY City Dept. Cultural Affairs. Sec. Whitney Mus. Am. Art, bd. dir.; dir. Mattel Entertainment, Paramount Mem.: NY State Coun. Arts. Mailing: c/o Whitney Mus Am Art 945 Madison Ave New York NY 10021

**TISDALE, DOUGLAS MICHAEL,** lawyer; b. Detroit, May 3, 1949; s. Charles Walker and Violet Lucille (Battani) Tisdale; m. Patricia Claire Brennan, Dec. 29, 1972 (dec. Jan. 2004); children: Douglas Michael Jr., Sara Elizabeth, Margaret Patricia, Victoria Claire. BA in Psychology with honors, U. Mich., 1971, JD, 1975. Bar: Colo. 1975, U.S. Dist. Ct. Colo. 1975, U.S. Ct. Appeals (10th cir.) 1976, U.S. Supreme Ct. 1979. Law clk. to chief judge U.S. Dist. Ct., Denver, 1975-76; ptnr. Brownstein Hyatt & Farber, P.C., 1976—92; shareholder Popham, Haik, Schnobrich & Kaufman, Ltd., 1992-97, dir., 1995-97; ptnr. Baker & Hostetler LLP, Denver, 1997—2002; owner Tisdale & Assocs., Denver, 2002—. Chmn. bd. dirs. Eagle Health Care Ctr. Inc.; treas. Vail Valley Med. Ctr.; chmn. bd. dirs. Colo. Neurol. INst. City councilman Cherry Hills Village, 2000—; mayor pro-term, 2006—. Home: 4662 S Elizabeth Ct Cherry Hills Village CO 80113-7106 Office: Tisdale and Assocs LLC Colo State Bank Bldg Ste 2600 1600 Broadway Denver CO 80202-4989 Office Phone: 303-832-1800. Business E-mail: doug@tisdalelaw.com.

**TISDALE, THOMAS J.,** social studies educator; b. Eldore, Iowa, Feb. 18, 1947; s. Dale and Norene Tisdale; m. Raylene Tisdale, Aug. 24, 1968; children: Krista, Dorry. BS in Edn. with high honors, U. Ark., Fayetteville, 1969, MA in Geography, 1975. Tchr. Newton Cmty. Schs., Iowa, 1969—. Named Newton Tchr. of Yr., Newton Cmty. Bd. Found., 2001—02; recipient Don Taft Meml. Jr. High Football, 1996. Avocations: baseball, fishing. Home: 208 E 7th St S Newton IA 50208

**TISE, LARRY EDWARD,** historian, cultural organization administrator; b. Winston-Salem, N.C., Dec. 6, 1942; s. Russell Edward and Lena Irene (Norman) T.; children: Larry Edward, Nicholas Allen, William Zane. AB, Duke U., 1965, M.Div., 1968; PhD (Ford Found. fellow, 1970, Research Triangle fellow, 1971), U. N.C., 1974. Part-time editor John Fries Blair, Pub., Winston-Salem, 1969-72; teaching fellow history dept. U. N.C., Chapel Hill, 1971, instr., 1972-73; dir. hist. publs. N.C. Bicentennial Com., 1973-74; asst. dir. N.C. Div. Archives and History, Raleigh, 1974-75, dir., 1975-81, N.C. State Hist. Preservation officer, 1975-81; exec. dir. Pa. Hist. and Mus. Commn., 1981-87; Pa. State Hist. Preservation officer, 1981-87; dir. Am. Assn. for State and Local History, Nashville, 1987-89; exec. dir. Benjamin Franklin Nat. Meml., Phila., 1989-97; pres., CEO Internat. Congress of Disting. Awards, 1997—. Adj. prof. grad. sch. fine arts U. Pa., 1984-87; vis. prof. Vanderbilt U., 1988-89, Temple U., 1989-91; Willbur Orville Wright vis. disting. prof. E. Carolina U., 2000—; mem. Nat. Hist. Publs. and Records Commn., 1982-88 Author, co-author writings in fields of archives, hist. preservation, hist. sites and museums, history, society, religion; author: The Southern Experience in the American Revolution, 1978, The Monitor: Its Meaning and Future, 1978, Writing North Carolina History, 1979, A House Not Made with Hands, 1966, The Yadkin Melting Pot: Methodism and the Moravians in the Yadkin Valley, 1750-1850, 1968, Proslavery: The Defense of Slavery in America, 1987, A Book About Children, 1992, The American Counterrevolution, 1998, Keep on Running, 1998, Benjamin Franklin and Women, 2000, The Soaring Place: The Untold Story of Kitty Hawk, 2003, Benjamin Franklin, 2004, Hidden Images in the Wright Brothers Photographs, 1900-1911, 2005; gen. editor: writings in fields of archives, hist. preservation, hist. sites and museums, history, society, religion including Winston-Salem in History, 13 vols, 1976; edit. bd. The Public Historian, 1980-86; editor N.C. Hist. Rev., 1974-81, Pa. Heritage, 1981-87, History News, 1987-89, Franklin Gazette, 1989-97; contbr. articles to books, newsletters, publs. Recipient William R. Davie History award, 1979, Herbert L. Feis award, Am. Hist. Assn., 1989, Benjamin Franklin Nat. Meml. awards 1990, Best New Book in History, Ind. Book Pubs., 1999; Nat. Endowment for the Humanities fellow, 1992-93; faculty fellow NASA-Langley Rsch. Ctr., 2000-03. Mem. Am. Hist. Assn. (various coms.), Orgn. Am. Historians (chmn. coms.), So. Hist. Assn., Am. Assn. State and Local History (mem. coun. and coms.), Nat. Assn. State Archives and Records Adminstrs. (pres. 1980-81), Nat. Conf. State Hist. Preservation Officers (dir. 1976-79, pres. 1979-81), Nat. Coun. on Pub. History (bd. dirs., exec. com. 1979-83, pres. 1983-85), N.C. Hist. Commn. (sec. 1975-81), N.C. Lit. and Hist. Assn. (sec., treas. 1977-81), Pa. Fedn. Hist. Socs. (sec. 1981-87), Friends of Franklin, Inc. (exec. sec. 1989-97). Methodist. Office Phone: 215-765-1311. E-mail: ltise@attglobal.net.

**TISHER, CHARLES CRAIG,** nephrologist, educator, dean; MD, Wash. U., St. Louis, 1961. Resident Barnes Hosp., St. Louis, U. Wash. affiliated Hosps., Seattle; fellow in nephrology U. Wash., Seattle; positions at Walter Reed Hosp. and Walter Reed Army Inst. Rsch., Washington; joined faculty Duke U. Sch. Medicine, 1969; prof. medicine and pathology U. Fla. Coll. Medicine, Gainesville, Fla., 1980—, chief divsn. nephrology, hypertension and transplantation, 1980—87, named Ctrl. Fla. Kidney Ctr. Eminent Scholar Chair in Nephrology, 1989; prof. anatomy and cell biology, sr. assoc. dean, 1998—2002, Folke H. Peterson Disting. Professorship, 1999—, dean, 2002—; dir. Ctr. Clin. Trials Rsch U. Fla. Founding asst. editor Kidney Internat. jour.; chmn. med. adv. board Bioavailability Systems Inc., Cocoa

Beach, Fla. Recipient Faculty Rsch. Prize in Clin. Scis., U. Fla., 1985. Mem.: Internat. Soc. Nephrology, Am. Soc. Nephrology (pres. 1990—91, jour. editor 1996—2001, John P. Peters Award 2001). Office: U Fla Divsn Nephrology Box J224 JHMHC Gainesville FL 32610 also: U Fla PO Box 100215 Gainesville FL 32610-0215 Office Phone: 904-392-3859, 352-846-2473. Business E-mail: tisher@dean.med.ufl.edu.*

**TISHLER, RICHARD NORMAN,** lawyer; b. Jack Murray Allen Tishler and Dorothy Tishler Ziff; m. Jean Lawrence Tishler, Oct. 13, 1996; children: Amy, David. BS in Acctg., U. Ala., Tuscaloosa, 1986, JD, 1989; LLM in Taxation, NYU, N.Y.C., 1990. Bar: Ala. 1989, Mo. 1992. Atty. Lange Simpson, Birmingham, Ala., 1990—91, Riezman Berger, P.C., St. Louis, 1992—. Bd. trustees B'nai Amoona, 1999. Named to Ala. Law Rev., U. Ala. Law Sch., 1987; recipient Charles Parker Yarbrough award; Prime F. Osborn scholar, 1987, Hugo Black scholar. Mem.: ABA (coord. subcom. valuation issues sm. bus. 1993), Bar Assn. Met. St. Louis, Order of Coif. Avocation: exercise. Office: Riezman Berger PC 7700 Bonhomme 7th Fl Saint Louis MO 63105 Office Phone: 314-727-0101.

**TISHLER, WILLIAM HENRY,** landscape architect, educator; b. Baileys Harbor, Wis., June 22, 1936; s. William John and Mary Viola (Sarter) T.; m. Betsy Lehner, Sept. 23, 1961; children: William Phillip, Robin Elizabeth. BS in Landscape Architecture, U. Wis., 1960; M in Landscape Architecture, Harvard U., 1964. Urban planner City of Milw., 1961-62; mem. faculty dept. landscape architecture U. Wis., Madison, 1964—; assoc. Hugh A Dega & Assocs. (Landscape Archs.), 1964-66; prin. Land Plans Inc. (Land and Hist. Preservation Planning Cons.), Madison, 1966—. Advisor emeritus Nat. Trust for Hist. Preservation; bd. dirs. The Hubbard Ednl. Trust. Author: American Landscape Architecture: Designers and Places, 1989, Midwestern Landscape Architecture, 2000, Door County's Emerald Treasure: A History of Peninsula State Park, 2005; contbr. articles to profl. jours. With C.E., U.S. Army, 1960. Recipient Design Arts Program award NEA, 1981, Hawthorn award Friends of The Clearing, 1997, Outstanding Educator award Coun. Educators in Landscape Architecture, 1988; Attingham (Eng.) Program fellow Soc. Archtl. Historians, 1980; Dumbarton Oaks sr. fellow, 1990. Fellow Am. Soc. Landscape Archs. (Horace Cleve. vis. prof. U. Minn. 1993, nat. merit award 1971, 97, 99, honor award 1980, 89, Wis. chpt. Lifetime Achievement award 2000); mem. Assn. Preservation Tech., Wis. Acad. Arts, Letters and Scis., Pioneer Am. Soc. (Henry Douglas award), Hist. Madison (hon.), Vernacular Architecture Forum (past pres.), Madison Trust for Hist. Preservation, Alliance for Hist. Landscape Preservation (founder), The Clearing Landscape Inst. (founder, dir.), Phi Kappa Phi, Sigma Lambda Alpha, Gamma Sigma Delta, Sigma Nu. Meth. Home: 3925 Regent St Madison WI 53705-5222 Office: U Wis Dept Landscape Architecture Madison WI 53706

**TISHMAN, JOHN L.,** realty and construction company executive; b. N.Y.C., Jan. 24, 1926; s. Louis and Rose F. (Foreman) T.; m. Suzanne Weisberg; children: Daniel R., Katherine T. BS, U. Michigan. Chmn. bd. dirs., pres. Tishman Realty & Constrn. Co., Inc., N.Y.C., 1976—, CEO. Mem. bd. execs. Ronald McDonald House, NYU Med. Ctr., Pratt Inst., Carnegie Hall, Central Park Conservancy; chmn. bd. trustees New Sch. Univ., N.Y.C. Home: Mianus Riv Rd Bedford NY 10506 Office: Tishman Realty Const Corp NY 666 5th Ave Fl 36 New York NY 10103-0256*

**TISINGER, CATHERINE ANNE,** retired history professor; b. Winchester, Va., Apr. 6, 1936; d. Richard Martin and Irma Regina (Ohl) T. BA, Coll. Wooster, 1958; MA, U. Pa., 1962, PhD, 1970; LLD (hon.), Coll. of Elms, 1985. Provost Callison Coll., U. of Pacific, Stockton, Calif., 1971—72; v.p. Met. State U., St. Paul, 1972—75; v.p. academic affairs Southeast State U., Minn., 1975—77, interim pres., 1976—77; mem. gov.'s office staff State of Minn., 1979; dir. Ctr. for Econ. Edn., R.I. Coll., Providence, 1979—80; v.p. acad. affairs Ctrl. Mo. State U., Warrensburg, 1980—84; pres. North Adams State Coll., Mass., 1984—91; dean arts and scis. Shenandoah U., Winchester, Va., 1991—2001, prof. history and econs., 2001—04, disting. prof., 2001, prof. emerita, 2004—. Cons. North Cen. Assn. Colls. and Schs., 1980-84, New Eng. Assn. Schs. and Colls., 1978-79, 85-91, Minn. Acad. Family Physicians, 1973-77; mem. adv. bd. First Agrl. Bank, North Adams, 1985-91; pres. No. Berkshire Cooperating Colls., 1986-91; v.p. Coll. Consortium for Internat. Studies, 1989-90; cons. Inst. for Experiential Learning, 2002—; dean arts and scis. Zayed U., UAE, 2001-02. V.p. Med. Simulation Found., 1986-88; cons. historian, curator Shenandoah Ctr. for Heritage and Environment, 2002—, bd. dirs. 2004—; bd. dirs. Williamstown Concerts, 1988-91, Shawnee coun. Girl Scouts U.S.A., 1992-93, Parents' Choice, 1997-98, Parents Guide to Children's Media, Inc., 1998-2004, pres. 2004—. Mem. No. Berkshire C of C. (bd. dirs. 1984-89, v.p. 1986-89). Avocations: fiber and textile arts, photography. Office: Shenandoah U 1460 University Dr Winchester VA 22601-5195 E-mail: ctisinge@su.edu.

**TITCHENAL, CHARLES ALAN,** nutrition educator; b. Camp Shoemaker, Calif., Feb. 21, 1946; s. Robert Alden Titchenal and Barbara Annette Bitticks; m. Joan Clare Dobbs, June 2, 1987. BA, U. Hawaii, 1969; MS, U. Calif. at Davis, 1980, PhD, 1986. Cert. nutrition specialist Cert. Bd. Nutrition Specialists, 1995. Assoc. prof. U. Hawaii, Honolulu, 1991—. Author: (newspaper column) Health Options/Honolulu Star-Bulletin. Mem.: Nat. Strength and Conditioning Assn., Internat. Soc. of Sports Nutrition, Am. Med. Athletic Assn., Am. Dietetic Assn., Am. Coll. of Sports Medicine, Am. Coll. of Nutrition, Am. Soc. for Nutrition. Office: Human Nutrition - U of Hawaii 1955 East-West Rd Honolulu HI 96822 Office Phone: 808-956-7411. Office Fax: 808-956-4024.

**TITCOMB, CALDWELL,** music and theatre historian; b. Augusta, Maine, Aug. 16, 1926; s. Samuel and Lura Elizabeth (Smith) T. AB summa cum laude, Harvard U., 1947, MA, 1949, PhD, 1952. Univ. organist Brandeis U., Waltham, Mass., 1953-70, dir. undergrad. studies music, 1956-84, curator creative arts, libr., 1961-64, co-chmn. music dept., 1977-84, from instr. to prof. music, 1953-88, prof. emeritus, 1988—. Drama critic Harvard Crimson, 1953-82, Bay State Banner, 1975—, This Month on Stage, 1996-99, Totalth-eater.com, 2000—; trustee Charles Playhouse, Boston, 1966-71 Editor: The Art of Fine Prints, 1965, The Furies (Lucien Price), 1988; co-editor: Varieties of Black Experience at Harvard, 1986, Blacks at Harvard: A Documentary History of African-American Experience at Harvard and Radcliffe, 1993; contbr. articles to profl. jours., ency.; composer stage and film music scores. Bd. dirs. Cambridge (Mass.) Civic Symphony Orch., 1959-70; exec. bd. Mus. Fine Arts Friends Music, Boston, 1959-65; panelist Music Commn. Arts and Humanities, 1981-83; mem. selection com. Theater Hall of Fame, 1980—; juror Elliot Norton awards, 1985—; pres. Boston Theater Critics Assn., 1994—. With U.S. Army, 1944-46, PTO; with Mil. Intelligence Res., 1946-50. Mem. AAUP, Coll. Music Soc., Am. Theatre Critics Assn. (charter), New Eng. Theatre Conf. (adv. coun. 1961-81, coll. fellows 1981—), Am. Guild Organists, Am. Musicol. Soc. (coun. 1965-67), Soc. for Ethnomusicology, Eugene O'Neill Soc., Hist. Brass Soc., Signet Soc., Soc. for Am. Music, Phi Beta Kappa. Meth. Meth. Mass. 1984—). Avocations: philology, afro-american history and culture. E-mail: caldwell67@aol.com.

**TITLE, ALAN M.,** astrophysicist; BA in Math., UCLA, 1960; PhD in Physics, Calif. Inst. Tech., 1966. Rsch. assoc. Harvard U., 1967—71; scientist, sr. fellow Lockheed Martin Corp., 1971—; prin. investigator TRACE solar telescope project Lockheed Martin Space Systems Advanced Tech. Ctr., Palo Alto, prin. investigator Atmospheric Imaging Assembly, Solar Dynamics Observatory. Prof. physics Stanford U. Recipient Public Svc. award, NASA, Hale prize, Am. Astronomical Soc.; Nat. Acad. Scis. Rsch. fellow, Smithsonian Astrophysical Observatory. Mem.: Internat. Acad. Astronauts, Nat. Acad. Engring., NAS. Achievements include research in techniques and development of optical systems for observing the sun from orbiting spacecraft. Office: Lockheed Palo Alto Rsch Lab Dept 91-30 Bldg 252 3251 Hanover St Palo Alto CA 94304-1191

**TITLE, GAIL MIGDAL,** lawyer; b. Waldenberg, Germany; AB, Wellesley Coll.; JD, U. Calif., Berkeley. Bar: Calif. Mng. ptnr. Katten Muchin Rosenman, LLP, LA. Adj. prof. law Loyola U.; head Nat. Entertainment Litigation Practice; former trustee Ctr. for Law in the Pub. Interest, 1976-96; exec. com., bd. Pub. Counsel Law Ctr. & Constl. Rights Found; co-chair USDC Magistrate Selection Com., ctrl. Calif. Named a Woman of Distinction, Women's Lawyer's Assn. LA. Mem. ABA (litigation sect., forum com. entertainment), Assn. Bus. Trial Lawyers, State Bar Calif. (standing com. pub. interest law 1976—), Beverly Hills Bar Assn., LA Copyright Soc. (trustee). Office: Katten Muchin Rosenman LLP 2029 Century Park E Los Angeles CA 90067 Office Phone: 310-788-4727. Office Fax: 310-712-8427. Business E-Mail: gail.title@kattenlaw.com.

**TITLE, PETER STEPHEN,** lawyer; b. New Orleans, Nov. 24, 1950; s. Harold Benjamin and Beulah (Sterbcow) Title; m. Sheryl Gerber, June 14, 1981. BA, Columbia U., 1972; JD, Tulane U., 1975. Bar: La. 1975, U.S. Dist. Ct. (ea., we., mid. dists.) La., U.S. Ct. Appeals (5th cir.). Assoc. Session, Fishman & Nathan LLP, New Orleans, 1975—81, ptnr., 1982—. Instr. on property Tulane U., 1978; asst. examiner Com. on Admissions to Bar, 1980—88, examiner, 1988—; lectr. on real estate. Author: Louisiana Real Estate Transactions, 1991, 2000. Named to Best Lawyers in Am. (La. Real Estate). Mem.: ABA, Am. Judicature Soc., Am. Coll. Mortgage Attys., New Orleans Bar Assn. (chmn. title examinations com. 1992—93), La. Bar Assn. (chmn. sect. on trust estates, probate and immovable property law 1983—84), B'nai B'rith, Order of Coif, Phi Delta Phi. Jewish.

**TITLEY, SPENCER ROWE,** geology educator; b. Denver, Sept. 27, 1928; m. Clara Helen Ruxton, May 1951; children: Ronald, Jane, Jennifer. Geol. Engr., Colo. Sch. Mines, 1951; PhD in Geology, U. Ariz., 1958. Ops. geologist N.J. Zinc Co., Gilman, Colo., 1951, 53-55; instr. U. Ariz., Tucson, 1955-58; regional geologist S.W. N.J. Zinc Co., 1958-60; from asst. to full prof. geology U. Ariz., 1960—. Panel mem. NSF, Divsn. Biol., Math. and Geophysical Scis. and Engring., 1978-81; sec. Soc. Econ. Geologists Found., 1972-83; mem. Apollo Field Geology Investigation Team, U.S. Geol. Survey, 1969-72; pres. Ariz. Geol. Soc., 1973-74. Mem. editl. bd. Econ. Geology, 1970-75, Ore Geology Reviews, 1984-2003; editor 5 books; contbr. over 85 articles to profl. jours. With U.S. Army Corps Engrs., 1951-53, Korea. Decorated Bronze Star; recipient Disting. Achievement medal Colo. Sch. Mines, 1975, Excellence in Tchg. award Burlington No. Found., 1985, Creative Tchg. award U. Ariz. Found., 1986, D.C. Jackling award Soc. Mining, Mettalurgy and Exploration of AIME, 1997; Fulbright Sr. lectr. Fed. U. Para'Brazil, 1986, Phoebe Apperson Hearst Disting. lectr. U. Calif., Berkeley, 1988. Fellow Geol. Soc. Am., Soc. Econ. Geologists (councilor 1980-83, Thayer Lindsley lectr. 1985, Disting. lectr. 1995, Penrose medal 1996), Mineral. Soc. Am., Australasian Inst. Mining and Metallurgy; mem. Nat. Acad. Engring., Soc. Applied Geology Home: 6920 E Taos Pl Tucson AZ 85715-3343 Office: Univ Ariz Dept Geosciences Simpson Bldg Tucson AZ 85721-0001 Office Phone: 520-621-6018. Business E-Mail: stitley@geo.arizona.edu.

**TITMAN, SHERIDAN,** finance educator; b. Denver, May 23, 1954; s. William and Toby Titman; m. Margaret Fry Fry, Nov. 2, 1980; children: Trevor, Elliot, Gordon. PhD, Carnegie Mellon U., Pitts., 1980. Prof. UCLA, LA, 1980—93, Hong Kong U. Sci and Tech, 1993—94, Boston Coll., 1994—97, U. Tex., Austin, Tex., 1997—. Office: U Tex McCombs Sch Bus Austin TX 78712 E-mail: sheridan.titman@mccombs.utexas.edu.

**TITO, DENNIS ANTHONY,** former aerospace engineer, financial advisor; b. Queens, NY, Aug. 8, 1940; m. Suzanne Tito (div.); 3 children. BS in Astronautics and Aeronautics, NYC, 1962; MA in Engring., Rensselaer Polytechnic Inst., Troy, NY, 1964; DEng (hon.), Rensselaer Polytechnic Inst., 2002. Former engr. NASA, Jet Propulsion Lab., 1960—72; founder, CEO Wilshire Associates, Santa Monica, Calif., 1972—. Bd. commr. LA Dept. Water and Power, 1990. Achievements include being the world's first private space tourist to fly in space aboard the Soyuz TM32 to the International Space Station from the Baikonur Cosmodrome in Kazakhstan, Russia in April, 2001; first to pay for a trip to space. Office: Wilshire Associates 1299 Ocean Ave Ste 700 Santa Monica CA 90401*

**TITSWORTH, TOBIE RICHARD, III,** academic administrator; b. Henryetta, Okla., May 13, 1945; s. Tobie Richard II and Thelma Edith (Stephens) T.; m. Laura Jeanne Barnes, Dec. 24, 1966; children: Scottie Richard, Stephanie Ann Titsworth Alves. BS, Okla. State U., 1967, MS, 1973, EdD, 1976. Cert. tchr., supt., Okla. Vocat. agriculture instr. Miami (Okla.) Pub. Schs., 1971-74; grad. teach. asst. Okla. State U., Stillwater, 1974-75; asst. prof. Tex. A&M U., College Station, 1975-79; v.p. continuing and tech. edn. Rogers State Coll., Claremore, Okla., 1979-90, v.p. for academics, 1990-92; advisor USAFR, Wright-Patterson AFB, Ohio, 1992-95; sr. systems engr. Electronic Data Systems Corp., 1995; v.p. for acad. affairs Okla. State U., Okmulgee, 1995-98; asst. supt. bus. and industry svcs. Northeast Tech. Ctr., Pryor, Okla., 1998-2000, dept. supt., 2000—. Adj. faculty Wright State U., Dayton, Ohio, 1993-95; mem. adv. com. Sinclair C.C., Dayton, 1992-95; vis. lectr., cons. Air Force Inst. Tech., Wright-Patterson AFB, 1993-95. Contbr. chpt. to book and articles to profl. jours. Chair, vice chair Claremore Park Bd. Commrs., 1988-90; vice chair, bd. dirs. Claremore Area United Way, 1989-91; bd. dirs., divsn. v.p. Claremore Area C. of C., 1994, chmn., 2005; bd. dirs. Pryor Area C. of C., v.p., 1998-2001; leadership Pryor grad., 1999; leadership Vo-Tech III, 2000; mem. N.E. Okla. Region Workforce Investment Bd., 1999—2005; deacon, tchr. Adult Bible Study, Faith Bapt. Ch., 2000-04; min adm North Park Trinity Bapt. Ch., 2001 . With USAF, 1968—71, col. USAFR, 1998—. Named to Hall of Fame Muskogee Svc. League, 1991; decorated Legion of Merit, 1998. Mem. ASCD, Okla. Cmty. and Jr. Colls. (pres. 1987-88), Okla. Tech. Soc. (pres. 1986-87, pres. instrnl. adminstrn. 1986-87), Am. Tech. Edn. Assn., Okla. Vocational Assn., Assn. Career and Tech. Edn. Baptist. Avocations: woodworking, collecting, reading, walking. Office: Northeast Tech Ctr PO Box 487 Pryor OK 74362 Office Phone: 918-825-7040. E-mail: titsworth@netechcenters.com.

**TITTMANN, BERNHARD RAINER,** engineering science and mechanics educator; b. Moshi, Tanganjika, East Africa, Sept. 15, 1935; came to US, 1950, naturalized, 1956; s. Gustav and Hermine Marie (Polland) T.; m. Katharine Shower, Dec. 17, 1966; children: Christine M., Heidi E., Raymond J., Monica M., Brian P.F. BS, George Washington U., 1957; MS, UCLA, 1961, PhD, 1965. Mem. staff Hughes Aircraft Co., Culver City, Calif., 1957-65; asst. prof. UCLA, 1965-66; mem. staff Rockwell Internat., Thousand Oaks, Calif., 1966-79, dept. mgr., 1979-89; Schell prof. engring. Pa. State U., University Park, 1989—. Co-author 6 books; contbr. over 300 articles to profl. jours.; patentee in field. George Washington fellow George Washington U., 1953, Howard Hughes fellow Hughes Aircraft Co., 1957, Fulbright fellow, 1998. Fellow IEEE (life, adminstrv. com. for ultrasonics, ferrolectrics, frequency control, major awards chmn. 1999—, disting. lectr. 1998-99), Acoustical Soc. Am., Am. Soc. Materials, KC (4th degree); mem. Phi Beta Kappa. Home: 2466 Sassafras Ct State College PA 16803-3366 Office: Pa State U 212 Earth Engring Sci Bldg University Park PA 16802-6804 Office Phone: 814-865-7827. Business E-Mail: brt4@psu.edu.

**TITUS, BRUCE EARL,** lawyer; b. NYC, June 5, 1942; BA, Coll. William and Mary, 1964, JD, 1971. Bar: Va. 1971, D.C. 1972, Md. 1984. Asst. dir. torts by. civil divsn. U.S. Dept. Justice, 1971-82; mem. Jones, Waldo, Holbrook and McDonough, Washington; ptnr. Venable, Baetjer and Howard, LLP, McLean, Va., 1986—97; prin. Rees, Broome & Diaz P.C., Vienna, Va., 1997—. Exec. editor William & Mary Law Review, 1970-71. Mem. ABA, Va. State Bar, D.C. Bar, Fairfax Bar Assn. (pres. 1999-2000), Md. State Bar, Phi Delta Phi, Omicron Delta Kappa. Office: Rees Broome & Diaz PC 9th Fl 8133 Leesburg Pike Vienna VA 22182-2706 Office Phone: 703-790-1911.

**TITUS, CHRISTINA MARIA,** lawyer; b. Phila., Oct. 31, 1950; BA, NYU, 1972; JD, Georgetown U., 1977. Bar: N.Y. 1978, U.S. Dist. Ct. N.Y. (so. and ea. dists.) 1979. Assoc. Trubin Sillcocks Edelman & Knapp, N.Y.C., 1977-80; v.p.: counsel Merrill Lynch, Hubbard Inc., N.Y.C., 1980—. Recipient 1st prize Drexel Keyboard Competition, 1968. Mem. Assn. of Bar of City of N.Y.

**TITUS, JEFFREY BYRON,** pediatric neuropsychologist; b. St. Louis, Aug. 10, 1974; s. Robert Edmond and Janet L. (Elliott) Titus. BS, Evangel U., Springfield, Mo., 1997; MA, U. No. Colo., 1999; PhD, Ball State U., Muncie, Ind., 2002. Neuropsychology fellow Henry Ford Hosp., Detroit, 2002—04; pediat. neuropsychologist St. Louis Children's Hosp./Washington U. Sch. Medicine, St. Louis, 2004—. Contbr. articles to profl. jours., chapters to books. Recipient Thelma Hunt Rsch. award, Psi Chi, 2000. Mem.: APA, Nat. Acad. Neuropsychology, Internat. Neuropsychol. Soc.

**TITUS, ROGER WARREN,** judge; b. Washington, Dec. 16, 1941; s. George R. and Margaret Titus; m. Catherine Mary Gaughen, Aug. 16, 1961; children: Paula Titus Laboy, Richard Roger, Mark William. BA, Johns Hopkins U., 1963; JD, Georgetown U., 1966. Bar: Md. 1966, D.C. 1966, U.S. Dist. Ct. Md. 1966, D.C. Dist. 1966, U.S. Ct. Appeals (4th cir.) 1966, U.S. Supreme Ct. 1970. Ptnr. Titus & Glasgow, Rockville, Md., 1966-88, Venable, Baetjer & Howard, Rockville, 1998—2003; judge U.S. Dist. Ct. for the Dist. of Md., Greenbelt, Md., 2003—. Asst. city atty. City of Rockville, 1966-69, city atty., 1970-82; spl. asst. Md. State Bd. of Law Examiners, 1969-72; adj. prof. law Georgetown U., Washington, 1972-78; mem. inquiry com. Atty. Grievance Commn., Annapolis, Md., 1975-80; mem. Trial Cts. Judicial Nominating Commn Montgomery County, 1979 91; mem. standing com. on rules of practice and procedure Ct. of Appeals of Md., 1989-2003; mem. Appellate Jud. Nominating Commn., 1991-99 Trustee Suburban Hosp., Inc., Bethesda, Md., 1986-2000, chmn. bd., 1997-2000. Fellow: Am. Acad. Appellate Lawyers, Md. Bar Found. (bd. dirs. 1987—93, v.p. 1990—91, pres. 1991—93), Am. Bar Found., Am. Coll. Trial Lawyers; mem.: ABA (del. 1987—95), Montgomery County Bar Assn. (exec. com. 1983—84), Md. Mcpl. Attys. Assn. (pres. 1975), Am. Judicature Soc. (bd. dirs. 1995—2001), Md. Bar Assn. (sec. 1984—87, pres. 1988—89), Nat. Conf. Bar Pres. (mem. exec. coun. 1990—93). Office: US Dist Ct for Dist of Md 6500 Cherrywood Ln Greenbelt MD 20770

**TITUS, VICTOR ALLEN,** lawyer; b. Nevada, Mo., Sept. 2, 1956; s. Charles Allen and Viola Mae (Cliffman) T.; m. Laraine Carol Cook, Oct. 13, 1974 (div. Feb. 1982); 1 child, Matthew; m. Deborah Diane Carpenter, Apr. 10, 1984; 1 child, Jacquelynn. BS, BA, Ctrl. Mo. State U., 1978; JD, U. Mo., 1981. Bar: N.Mex. 1981, U.S. Dist. Ct. N.Mex. 1981, Mo. 1982, U.S. Ct. Appeals (10th cir. 1983), U.S. Supreme Ct. 1986, Colo. 1989, Ariz. 1995. Lawyer Jay L. Faurot, P.C., Farmington, N.Mex., 1981-83; ptnr. Faurot & Titus, P.C., Farmington, N.Mex., 1983-85; lawyer, sole proprietor Victor A. Titus, P.C., Farmington, N.Mex., 1985—. Arbitrator in civil disputes Alternative Dispute Resolution-Arbitration; liquor lic. hearing officer City of Farmington, 1989-94. Contbr. articles to profl. jours. Adult Behind Youth, Boys & Girls Club, Farmington, 1987—; mem. hosp. adv. bd. San Juan Regional Med. Ctr., Farmington, 1988-93. Recipient one of Best Lawyers in Am., 1995-96, 97—. Mem. ATLA, Am., N.Mex. Trial Lawyers (bd. dirs. 1983—, pres. 1993-94), State Bar of N.Mex. (disc plinary bd. 1997—2002, specialization com. 1992-98, legal advt. com. 1990), San Juan County Bar Assn. (pres. 1984), Nat. Assn. Criminal Def. Lawyers (life), Colo. Trial Lawyers. Democrat. Avocation: sports. Home: 5760 Pinehurst Farmington NM 87402-5078 Office: Victor A Titus PC 2021 E 20th St Farmington NM 87401-2516 Office Phone: 505-326-6503. E-mail: victor@titusmurphylaw.com.

**TITZE, INGO ROLAND,** physics professor; b. Hirschberg, Silesia, Germany, July 8, 1941; came to U.S. 1955; s. Kurt Herrmann and Marta Emma (Bettermann) T.; m. R. Katherine Pittard, July 19, 1969; children: Karin, Michael, Jason, Gregory BSEE, U. Utah, 1963, MS in Elec. Engring. and Physics, 1965; PhD in Physics, Brigham Young U., 1972. Rsch. engr. N. Am. Aviation, Tulsa, 1965-66, Boeing Co., Seattle, 1968-70; lectr. Calif. State Poly. U., Pomona, 1973-74; asst. prof. U. Petroleum and Minerals Dhahran, Saudi Arabia, 1974-76, Gallaudet Coll., Washington, 1976-79; disting. prof. speech sci. and voice U. Iowa, Iowa City, 1979—. Cons. Bell Labs., Murray Hill, N.J., 1977-78; exec. dir. Wilbur James Gould Voice Rsch. Ctr., Denver Ctr. Performing Arts, 1983—; pres. Voice Cons. Inc., 1985—; panelist, site visitor NRC-NAS, 1984—; regular cons. divsn. rsch. grants NIH, 1986—; chmn. task force on voice Nat. Inst. Deafness and Other Comm. Disorders, 1989; adj. prof. Westminster Choir Coll., Princeton, N.J., 1989-94; dir. Nat. Ctr. for Voice and Speech, 1990—. Author: Principles of Voice Production, 1993; editor: Vocal Fold Physiology: Biomechanics, Acoustics and Phonatory Control, 1985, Vocal Fold Physiology: Frontiers in Basic Science, 1992; assoc. editor Jour. of Voice; contbr. articles to profl. jours. Adv. bd. Voice Found., N.Y.C., 1980—; young men's pres. Latter Day Saints Ch. and Boy Scouts Am., Iowa City, 1982— Jacob Javits Neurosci. Investigator grantee NIH, 1984; recipient William and Harriot Gould Found. award, 1983, Claude Pepper award, 1989, Quintant award Voice Found., 1990, U. Iowa Regents award, 1995; ASHA fellow, 1992. Fellow Acoustical Soc. Am. (tech. coun., awards com. 1989), Am. Laryngological Assn. (hon.: award 1996); mem. Am. Speech-Hearing-Lang. Assn., Nat. Assn. Tchrs. Singing (rsch. coun. 1977—, editl. bd. 1986—), Internat. Assn. Rsch. Singing (dir. publs. 1982—), Am. Assn. Phonetic Scis., Internat. Assn. Logopedics and Phoniatrics, Collegium Medicorium Teatri. Republican. Avocations: singing, tennis, home building. Nat Ctr for Voice & Speech Univ of Iowa 330 Wjshc Iowa City IA 32242-1012 Home: 1551 Larimer St No 2301 Denver CO 80202

**TIZZIO, THOMAS RALPH,** brokerage house executive; b. Elmont, N.Y., Jan. 9, 1938; s. Anthony Thomas and Ann Marie (Pascale) T.; m. Mary Ann Gentile, Aug. 26, 1962; children: Anthony, Vincent, Thomas. BBA, Bklyn. Coll., 1962. Underwriter W.J. Roberts & Co., N.Y.C., 1957-65; sr. underwriter Atlantic Mut. Ins. Co., 1965-67; various positions AIG Am. Home Assurance Co., N.Y.C., 1967-74, sr. v.p. property underwriting, 1974-78; exec. v.p. AIG Transatlantic Reins. Co., N.Y.C., 1978-80, pres., 1980-82; sr. v.p. reins. Am. Internat. Group, Inc., N.Y.C., 1982-85, pres. domestic brokerage divsn., 1985-91, pres. Brokerage divsn., 1986-91, pres., 1991-97, sr. vice chmn., 1997—2006, honorary dir. and adviser, 2006—. Bd. dir. 21st Century Ins. Group, 2006—. Recipient Lifetime Achievement award, Nat. Italian American Found., 2003. Mem. Am. Inst. for Property and Liability Underwriters (trustee), Ins. Inst. Am. (trustee). Office: Am Internat Group Inc 175 Water St New York NY 10038-4918 Business E-Mail: yvonne.melfi@aig.com.

**TJOFLAT, GERALD BARD,** federal judge; b. Pitts., Dec. 6, 1929; s. Gerald Benjamin and Sarita (Romero-Hermoso) Tjoflat; m. Sarah Marie Pfohl, July 27, 1957 (dec.); children: Gerald Bard, Marie Elizabeth; m. Marcia Penman Parker, Feb. 21, 1998. Student, U. Va., 1947—50, U. Cin. 1950—52; LLB, Duke U., 1957; DCL (hon.), Jacksonville U., 1978; LLD (hon.), William Mitchell Coll., 1983. Bar: Fla. 1957. Pvt. practice, Jacksonville, Fla., 1957—68; judge 4th Jud. Cir. Ct., Fla., 1968—70, U.S. Dist. Ct. Mid. Dist., Jacksonville, 1970—75, U.S. Ct. Appeals 5th Cir., Jacksonville, 1975—81, U.S. Ct. Appeals 11th Cir., Jacksonville, 1981—, chief judge, 1989—96. Mem. Adv. Corrections Coun. U.S., 1975—87, Jud. Conf. U.S., 1989—96, mem. commn. adminstrn. probation sys., 1972—87, chmn., 1978—87; mem. Fed. Jud. Ct. Com on Sentencing, Probation and Pretrial Svcs., 1988—90; U.S. del. 6th and 7th UN Congress for Prevention of Crime and Treatment of Offenders. Hon. life mem., bd. visitors Duke U. Law Sch., 2000; pres. North Fla. coun. Boy Scouts Am., 1976—85, 2000—01, chmn., 1985—90; trustee Jacksonville Marine Inst., 1976—90, Episc. H.S., Jacksonville, 1975—90; mem. vestry St. Johns Cathedral, Jacksonville, 1969—71, 1973—75, 1977—79, 1981—83, 1985—87, 1993, 1995—96, sr. warden, 1975, 1983, 1987, 1991, 1992. With U.S. Army, 1953—55. Recipient Merit award, Duke U., 1990, Fordham-Stein prize, 1996. Mem.: ABA, Am. Judicature Soc., Am. Law Inst., Fla. Bar Assn. Episcopalian. Office: US Courthouse 300 N Hogan St Ste 14-200 Jacksonville FL 32202-4257 Office Phone: 904-301-6570.*

**TKACHEV, SERGEY NIKOLAYEVICH,** geophysicist; b. Izmail, Odessa Region, Ukraine, July 19, 1964; arrived in US, 1994; s. Nikolay Yefimovich and Liliya Ivanovna Tkachev; m. Maria Sarah Simmons, June 19, 1999. MS in Physics, Moscow State U., Russia, 1991; MS in Geology, U. Ill., Urbana, 1997; PhD in Geology and Geophysics, U. Hawaii, Honolulu, 2005. Rsch. physicist Inst. Exptl. Mineralogy Russian Acad. Scis., Chernogolovka, Russia, 1991—2001; rsch. asst. Dept. Geology U. Ill., Urbana, 1994—96, tchg. asst., 1996—97; rsch. scientist Hawaii Inst. Geophysics and Planetology, Honolulu, 1997—98; rsch. asst. Dept. Geology and Geophysics U. Hawaii, 1998—99, tchg. asst., 2000—05; postdoctoral rschr. Dept. Physics Colo. State U., Fort Collins, 2005—06; postdoctoral assoc. Geophys. Lab. Carnegie Instn., Washington, 2006—. Contbr. scientific papers, articles to profl. jours. Guard platoon sgt. Soviet Air Forces, 1982—84. Recipient Tuition Waiver award, Dean Grad. Divsn. U. Hawaii, 1999; J. Watumull Merit scholar, Dept. Geology and Geophysics U. Hawaii, 2002—03. Mem.: Am. Geophys. Union. Achievements include being first to characterize elastic moduli of the novel bulk superhard cubic BC2N phase (the hardest crystalline material after Diamond) by Brillouin scattering; research in situ Brillouin spectroscopic study of a pressure-induced apparent second order transition in a Silicate glass; Brillouin scattering study of pentane at high pressure; new experimental data on ice VI, ice VII and liquid water phase boundaries; characterization of current nonlinearly in semiconductors in weak electric fields; characterization of elastic properties of nc-TiN/a-Si3N4 nanocomposites films by surface Brillouin scattering; micro-Raman spectroscopy and X-ray diffraction studies of atomic-layer-deposited ZrO2 and HfO2 thin films; elastic and structural properties of Alkaline-Calcium Silica Hydrogels; hydrated and anhydrous Na2O-2SiO2 liquid and also glass to 8 GPa using Brillouin scattering; Characterization of Elastic Properties of Superhard Amorphous Carbon Pressure-Synthesized from C60 by Surface Brillouin Scattering; Brillouin spectroscopy studies of surface modes in thin-film Si3N4 on GaAs; determination of sound velocity and attenuation in stable and metastable liquid water to 1.2 GPa by Brillouin spectroscopy. Avocations: racquetball, tennis, hiking, swimming, camping. Home: 12053 Cherokee Park Rd Livermore CO 80536 Office: Carnegie Instn Washington 5251 Broad Branch Rd NW Washington DC 20015 Office Phone: 202-478-8926. Office Fax: 202-478-8901. E-mail: stkachev@gl.ciw.edu.

**TKACHUK, KEITH,** professional hockey player; b. Melrose, Mass., Mar. 28, 1972; With Phoenix Coyotes formerly Winnipeg (Canada) Jets, 1992—2001, St. Louis Blues, 2001—. Mem. Team U.S.A., World Cup of Hockey, 1996, 2004, U.S. Olympic Hockey Team, Nagano, Japan, 1998, Salt Lake City, 2002. Named NHL Second Team All-Star, 1995, 1998; named to NHL All-Star Game, 1997—99, 2004. Achievements include being a member of World Cup Champion Team USA, 1996. Office: St Louis Blues Savvis Ctr Saint Louis MO 63103

**TLOU, JOSIAH S.,** education educator; b. Zimbabwe, Dec. 31, 1935; s. Litsila and Mothatoho T.; m. Litha T., Sept. 3, 1959; children: Lee, Hla, Joy B., Leeto. BA, Luther Coll., 1968; MA, Ill. State U., 1969; EdD, U. Ill., 1972. Cons. curriculum Glencoe (Ill.) Pub. Schs.; specialist social studies USAID U. Botswana, Gaborone; prof. Va. Tech., Blacksburg; civic curriculum planner for U.S. AID project Creative Assocs. Internat./Harvard Inst. Internat. Devel., Malawi, 1996-98; dir. USAID/Malawi Govt. Projects UPIC, 1998—. Cert. tchr., Zimbabwe. Contbr. articles to profl. jours. Recipient Disting. Svc. award Luther Coll.; Luce-Bergeson rsch. grantee, African-Am., Scholars Coun. grantee, Creative Univ. Rsch. grantee, 1992-94, 94-95. Mem. ASCD, WCCI, Nat. Coun. Social Studies, ASA, AAPRDTW, Botswana Edn. Rsch. Assn., Phi Delta Kappa. E-mail: tlou@vt.edu.

**TLSTY, THEA DOROTHY,** research scientist, educator; b. Mobile, Ala., Jan. 28, 1952; d. Theodore H. and Josepine M. Tlsty. BS in zoology, U. South Fla., 1973; PhD in molecular biology, Washington U., 1980. Asst. prof. pathology U. N.C. Chapel Hill, 1985-92, mem. Lineberger Comprehensive Cancer Ctr., 1985—95, assoc. prof. pathology, 1992—95, U. Calif., San Francisco, 1995—96, dir. molecular pathology, 1995—96, mem. Cancer Rsch. Inst., 1995—96, prof. pathology, 1996—, dir. Ctr. for Translational Rsch. in the Molecular Genetics of Cancer, 1996—, dir. program cell cycling and signaling, Comprehensive Cancer Ctr., 1996—. Predoctoral fellow cellular and molecular biology program, Wash. U., St. Louis, 1976-80, postdoctoral fellow dept. microbiology and immunology, 1980-81; postdoctoral fellow/sr. rsch. assoc. dept. biological sciences, Stanford U., 1981-85; vis. scientist U. Geneva, 1982; vis. scholar U. Zimbabwe, 1992; cons. Bristol-Meyers Co., 1987, Glaxo, 1990—94, Geron, 1993—95, Oncormed, 1995-97, Onyx, 1997-98, Day Casebeer, 1999-2000, Pennie and Edmonds, 2001-02; mem. editl. bd. Molecular Carcinogenesis, 1992—, Carcinogenesis, 1993—, Cancer Rsch., 1995—, Environ. Health Perspectives, 1996—, Am. Jour. Pathology, 1997—; mem. adv. coun., GM Cancer Rsch. Found. Contbr. numerous articles to sci. jours. Recipient Gold Key Honor Soc. Award; Starter Grant Award, Pharmecutical Mfrs. Assn.; Avon Scholar, 2001-. Mem. AAAS, Am. Soc. Microbiology, Am. Assn. Cancer Rsch., Am. Soc. Biological Chemists and Molecular Biologists, Assn. for Women in Sci., Women in Cancer Rsch., Women in Cell Biology, Calif. Soc. Pathologists, Assn. Molecular Pathologists, Am. Soc. Investigative Pathology, Am. Soc. Cell Biology, Am. Soc. Biochemistry and Molecular Biology. Avocations: bicycling, sculpting, swimming. Office: U Calif Box 0506 San Francisco CA 94143-0506

**TO, STEPHEN EDWARD,** editor, writer; b. N.Y.C., July 5, 1963; s. Cho To and Lilly Fong Yee. BA in Biology, Purchase Coll., SUNY, 1985; MBA, Fordham U. Technician specialist Cornell U. Med. Coll., N.Y.C., 1986—88; rsch. biologist Rockefeller U., N.Y.C., 1988—97; med. project editor, writer AM Medica Comm., N.Y.C., 1998—98; mng. med. editor, writer IntraMed Ednl. Group, N.Y.C., 1999—. Freelance editor Nature Am., N.Y.C. 1998—99. Mem.: Regulatory Affairs Profl. Soc., Am. Med. Writers Assn. Avocations: sailing, travel. Home: 1539 Lexington Ave Apt 3E New York NY 10029 Office: Hoffman-La Roche Inc PDR Drug Reg Affairs 340 Kingsland St Nutley NJ 07110 Personal E-mail: sto1967@aol.com. Business E-Mail: stephen.to@roche.com.

**TOAL, JAMES FRANCIS,** academic administrator; b. NYC, June 7, 1932; s. John Joseph and Catherine (Whyte) T. MA, St. John's U., 1966; PhD, Fordham U., 1976. Cert. elem. tchr. N.Y. cert. supt., adminstrn. and supervision, English 7-12. Athletic dir., tchr. English St. Francis Prep. High Sch., N.Y.C., 1957-60; tchr. Bishop Ford High Sch., N.Y.C., 1960-66, chmn. dept. English; prin. St. Francis Central Summer High Sch., N.Y.S., 1966-73, St. Francis Prep. High Sch., N.Y.C., 1966-73; exec. v.p., assoc. prof. dept. edn. adminstrn. and supervision Grad. Sch. St. Bonaventure U., NY, 1976-83; pres., prof. Quincy U., Ill., 1983-97; v.p. Siena Coll., Loudonville, NY, 1997—; also bd. trustees. Mem. Springfield Diocesan Bd. of Edn., Provincial Bd. of Edn., Franciscan Friars of Chgo. and St. Louis. Trustee Siena Coll. Loudonville, N.Y., 1977-83; bd. advisors Jamestown Community Coll., Olean, N.Y., 1979-83; bd. dirs. Am. Cancer Soc., Olean, 1981-83; mem. Mental Health Assn., 1981-83; mem. state legis. com. Commn. of Ind. Colls. and Univs., Albany. N.Y., 1980-83; mem. bd. trustees Padua Franciscan High Sch. Grantee Colgate U., 1967; grantee SUNY-Plattsburg, 1968, St. Bonaventure U., 1980 Mem. Am. Coun. on Edn., Associated Colls. of Ill., Ill. Bus. and Edn. Forum, Assn. of Governing Bds., West Ctrl. Ill. Ednl. Telecomm. Corp. (bd. dirs. exec. com., fin. com.), Fedn. Ind. Ill. Colls. and Univs. (pub. rels. com.), Mid. States Accrediting Assn. (assoc., evaluation team for higher edn.), Nat. Assn. Secondary Sch. Prins., North Ctrl. Accrediting Assn. (evaluation team for higher edn., chair evaluation team 1986—), Soc. Coll. and U. Planning, Quincy C. of C. (transp. com. 1985-96, computer com. 1996—), Rotary, Univ. Club, KC, Phi Delta Kappa. Office: Siena Coll Office of VP Loudon Rd Loudonville NY 12211

**TOAL, JEAN HOEFER,** state supreme court chief justice; b. Columbia, S.C., Aug. 11, 1943; d. Herbert W. and Lilla (Farrell) Hoefer; m. William Thomas Toal; children: Jean Toal Eisen, Lilla Patrick. BA in Philosophy, Agnes Scott Coll., 1965; JD, U. S.C., 1968; LHD (hon.), Coll. Charleston, 1990; LLD (hon.), Columbia Coll., 1992, The Citadel, 1999, Francis Marion U., 1999, U. S.C., 2000. Bar: S.C. Assoc. Haynsworth, Perry, Bryant, Marum & Johnstone, 1968—70; ptnr. Belser, Baker, Barwick, Ravenel, Toal & Bender, Columbia, 1970—88; assoc. justice S.C. Supreme Ct., Columbia, 1988—2000, chief justice, 2000—. Mem. S.C. Human Affairs Commn. 1972-74; mem. S.C. Ho. of Reps., 1975-88, chmn. house rules com., constitutional laws subcom. house judiciary com.; mem. parish coun. and lector St. Joseph's Cath. Ch.; chair S.C. Juvenile Justice Task Force, 1992-94; chair S.C. Rhodes Scholar Selection Com., 1994; bd. dirs. Nat. Ctr. State Cts., 2005—; pres.-elect Conf. Chief Justices, 2006—. Mng. editor S.C. Law Rev., 1967—68. Bd. visitors Clemson U., 1978; trustee Columbia Mus. Art, 1980-85; bd. trustees Agnes Scott Coll., 1996—. Named Outstanding Legislator of Yr., Greenville News, 1976, Woman of Yr., U. S.C. Mortar Bd., 1989; named one of Top 25 Doers, Dreamers & Drivers, Govt. Tech. Mag., 2002; recipient Disting. Svc. award, S.C. Mcpl. Assn., 1980, U. Notre Dame award, 1991, Algernon Sydney Sullivan award, U. S.C., 1991, Agnes Scott Coll. Outstanding Alumna award, 1991, John W. Williams award, Richland County Bar Assn., 1995, Jean Galloway Bissell award, S.C. Women Lawyers Assn., 1995, Margaret Brent Women Lawyers of Achievement award, 2004. Mem. ABA, S.C. Women Lawyers Assn., S.C. Bar Assn., John Belton O'Neall Inn of Ct., Phi Beta Kappa, Mortar Bd., Order of the Coif Office: Supreme Ct SC PO Box 11330 Columbia SC 29211-2456 Business E-Mail: jtoal@sccourts.org.

**TOALE, THOMAS EDWARD,** school system administrator, minister; b. Independence, Iowa, Aug. 30, 1953; s. Francis Mark and Clara R. (DePaepe) T. BS in Biology, Loras Coll., 1975, MA in Edn. Adminstrn., 1986; MA in Theology, St. Paul Sem., 1980; PhD in Ednl. Adminstrn., U. Iowa, 1988. Ordained priest Roman Cath. Ch., 1981; cert. tchr., prin., supt., Iowa. Tchr. St. Joseph Key West, Dubuque, Iowa, 1975-77, Marquette High Sch., Bellevue, Iowa, 1981-84, prin., 1984-86; assoc. supt. Archdiocese of Dubuque, 1986-87, supt. schs., 1987—2006, vicar for edn., 2002—. Assoc. pastor St. Joseph Ch., Bellevue, 1981-84; pastor Sts. Peter and Paul Ch., Springbrook, Iowa, 1984-86, St. Peter, Temple Hill, Cascade, Iowa, 1986—. Mem. Nat. Cath. Edn. Assn. (pres., chief adminstrn Cath. edn.) Office: Archdiocese of Dubuque 1229 Mount Loretta Ave Dubuque IA 52003-7826

**TOAN, BARRETT N.,** health products executive; s. Winthrop A. and Edith Byrne Toan; m. Polly O'Brien; children: Elliot, Frannie. BA in history, Kenyon Coll., 1969; MBA, U. Pa., 1974. With budget bur. State of Ill., Springfield; positions with State of Pa.; cons. PriceWaterhouse, Washington; commr. divsn. social svcs. State of Ark., 1979—81; dir. dept. social svcs. State of Mo., 1981—85; exec. dir., COO Sanus Health Plan of St. Louis, 1985—91; pres. Express Scripts Inc., Maryland Heights, Mo., 1990—2002, CEO, 1992—2005, chmn., 2000—. Bd. dirs. Pharm. Care Mgmt. Assn., Sigma-Aldrich Corp. Mem. bd. dirs., treas. Mentor St. Louis. Named Entrepreneur of Yr. Inc. Mag., 1994. Office: Express Scripts 13900 Riverport Dr Maryland Heights MO 63043-4827*

**TOAY, THELMA M.,** columnist, poet; b. Anamosa, Iowa, Feb. 22, 1915; d. Frank Leroy and Edna May Stoughton; m. John S. Toay; 3 children. Student, St. Lukes Sch. Nursing, Davenport, IA, 1933, Highland Coll., 1966—67; AA in Journalism, N.E. Iowa C.C., Peosta, 1995—97; student, U. Iowa, 2001—03. Columnist: newspapers, Freeport, Ill., 1962—; contbr. Julien's Jour., Dubuque, Iowa, 1995—. Author: Bittersweet, 1979, Places for the Heart - Profiles of Life, 2001. Avocations: theater, music, reading, flower gardening.

**TOBACH, ETHEL,** retired curator; b. Miaskovka, USSR, Nov. 7, 1921; arrived in U.S., 1923; d. Ralph Wiener and Fanny (Schechterman) Wiener Idels; m. Charles Tobach, 1947 (dec. 1969). BA, Hunter Coll., 1949; MA, NYU, 1952, PhD, 1957; DSc (hon.), LI U., 1975. Lic. psychologist N.Y. Rsch. fellow Am. Mus. Natural History, N.Y.C., 1958-61, assoc. curator, 1964-69, curator, 1969-90, emerita curator; rsch. fellow NYU, N.Y.C., 1961-64, ret., 1990. Adj. prof. psychology and biology CUNY, N.Y.C., 1964—; disting. cons. faculty Saybrook Inst., San Francisco, 1998—; assoc. editor: Peace and Conflict: Jour. Peace Psychology, 1994—. Recipient NIHH Career Devel. award, 1964—74, Disting. Sci. Career, Assn. Women in Sci., 1974, Disting. Sci. Publ. Assn. Women in Psychology, 1982, Kurt Lewin award, Soc. Psychol. Study Social Issues, 1993, Gustavus Myers award for Outstanding Pub. Human Rights in N.Am., 1996, Lifetime Achievement Psychology in Pub. Interest Gold Medal award, Am. Psychol. Found., 2003. Fellow: APA (pres. comparative psychology divsn. 1985, peace psychology divsn. 2003, Leadership award Com. in Women in Psychology 2005); mem.: Soc. Study Peace, Conflict and Violence (pres. 2003, Lifetime Peace Activity award 1999), Psychologists for Social Responsibility, N.Y. Acad. Scis. (v.p. behavioral scis. 1973—76), Eastern Psychol. Assn. (pres. 1987, bd. dirs. 2001—, mem. exec. com. 2002—), Internat. Soc. Comparative Psychology (hon.; sec. 1988—92, pres.). Office: Am Mus Natural History Central Pkwy 79th St New York NY 10024-5192

**TOBACK, PAUL A.,** recreational facility executive; Atty. Katten Muchin & Zavis, Chgo.; dir. adminstrn. City of Chgo.; exec. asst. to Chief Staff The White House, Washington; COO Globetrotters Engring. Corp.; from exec. v.p., COO to pres., CEO Bally Total Fitness Holding Corp., Chgo., 1997—2002, pres.- 2002—, CEO, 2002—, chmn. bd. dirs. Office: Bally Total Fitness Holding Corp 8700 W Bryn Mawr Ave Chicago IL 60631*

**TOBE, STEPHEN SOLOMON,** zoology educator; b. Niagara-on-the-Lake, Ont., Can., Oct. 11, 1944; s. John Harold and Rose T. (Bolter) T.; m. Martha Reller. BSc, Queen's U., Kingston, Ont., 1967; MSc, York U. Toronto, Ont., 1969; PhD, McGill U., Montreal, Que., Can., 1972. Rsch. fellow U. Sussex, Eng., 1972-74; asst. prof. U. Toronto, 1974-78, assoc. prof., 1974-78, prof., 1982—, assoc. dean scis., faculty arts and sci., 1988-93, vice dean faculty arts and sci., 1995-96. Vis. prof. U. Calif., Berkeley, 1981, Nat. U. Singapore, 1987, 1993-94, U. Hawaii, 1988; mem. animal biology grant selection com. Natural Scis. and Engring. Rsch. Coun. Can., 1986-89, chair, 1988-89; lectr. Internat. Congress Entomology, Vancouver, B.C., Can., 1988; cons. in hydroponics. Editor Insect Biochemistry, 1987; mem. editl. bd. Jour. Insect Physiology, 1980—; Physiol. Entomology, 1985—, Life Scis. Advances, 1987—; Gen. and Comparative Endocrinology, 1995—; contbr. chpts. to books and articles to profl. jours. Recipient Pickford medal in comparative endocrinology, 1993; E.W.R. Steacie fellow Natural Scis. and Engring. Rsch. Coun. Can., 1982-84. Fellow Royal Soc. Can., Royal Entomol. Soc.; mem. AAAS, Entomol. Soc. Can. (C. Gordon Hewitt award 1982, gold medal 1990), Soc. Exptl. Biology. Avocations: amateur radio, gardening, hydroponics. Home: PO Box 695 Virgil ON Canada L0S 1T0 Office: U Toronto Dept Zoology 25 Harbord St Toronto ON Canada M5S 3G5 Business E-Mail: stephen.tobe@utoronto.ca.

**TOBEN, BRADLEY J. B.,** dean, law educator; m. Beth Toben; children: John, Sarah Beth. BA in Polit. Sci. with honors, U. Mo., St. Louis; JD with honors, Baylor U., 1977; LLM, Harvard U., 1981. Bar: Tex., Mo. Tchr. Ind. U. Sch. Law, Indpls.; of counsel Dawson & Sodd (Dallas and Corsicana); with faculty Baylor Law Sch., dean Law Sch., 1991—; Gov. Bill and Vara Faye Daniel prof. law, 1991—. Participant in accreditation and membership inspection of law schs. ABA, Assn. Am. Schs. Gov. apptd. Tex. commr. Nat. Conf. of Commrs. on Uniform State Laws. Mem. Am. Bar Found., Tex. Bar Found., State Bar of Tex. (active in bankruptcy specialization cert. program). Office: Baylor U PO Box 97288 Waco TX 76798-7288

**TOBEN, DOREEN A.,** telecommunications industry executive; b. Curacao; m. Ed Toben; 2 children. AB Polit. Sci., Rosemount Coll.; MBA Fin. and Mktg., Fairleigh Dickinson Univ. Dir. corp. planning AT&T, 1972; exec. dir. mktg. Bell Atlantic Enterprises Internat., Inc., 1989; various positions equipment engring., ops., and small bus. and consumer market mgmt. Bell Atlantic Inc., Pa.; dir. fin., 1983, divsn. mgr. strat. planning, 1984, asst. v.p.-comptroller, 1992, CFO, 1993, v.p. corp. fin., mem. com. - v.p., CFO telecom. network, 1997—99; v.p., controller Verizon Communications Inc., 1999—2000; sr. v.p., CFO telecom. group Verizon Communications, Inc., 2000—02, exec. v.p., CFO, 2002—. Bd. dirs. NY Times Co., 2004—. Named one of Most Powerful Women in Bus., Fortune mag., 2005, 10 Most Powerful Women in NJ Bus., Star-Ledger, 2006. Office: Verizon 1095 Avenue of Americas New York NY 10036*

**TOBER, BARBARA D. (MRS. DONALD GIBBS TOBER),** editor; b. Summit, NJ, Aug. 19, 1934; d. Rodney Fielding and Maude Starkey; m. Donald Gibbs Tober, Apr. 5, 1973. Student, Traphagen Sch. Fashion, 1954-56, Fashion Inst. Tech., 1956-58, N.Y. Sch. Interior Design, 1964. Copy editor Vogue Pattern Book, 1958-60; beauty editor Vogue mag., 1961; dir. women's services Bartell Media Corp., 1961-66; editor-in-chief Bride's mag., N.Y.C., 1966-94; chmn. Mus. Arts and Design; pres. Acronym, Inc., N.Y.C., 1995—, The Barbara Tober Found., 1995—. Sec.-treas., dir. Sugar Foods Corp.; adv. bd. Traphagen Sch.; coord. SBA awards; Am. Craft Coun., 1983—, benefit food com. chmn., 1984-87. Author: The ABC's of Beauty, 1963, China: A Cognizant Guide, 1980, The Wedding...The Marriage...And the Role of the Retailer, 1980, The Bride: A Celebration, 1984 Mem. Nat. Council on Family Relations, 1966; nat. council Lincoln Center Performing Arts, Met. Opera Guild; mem. NYU adv. bd. Women in Food Service, 1983; NYU Women's Health Symposium: Steering Com., 1983—. Recipient Alma award, 1968, Penney-Mo. award, 1972, Traphagen Alumni award, 1975, Diamond Jubilee award, 1983, Disting. Women award Northwood U., 1997. Mem. Fashion Group, Internat. Furnishings and Design Assn. (v.p., program chmn.), Am. Soc. Mag. Editors, Am. Soc. Interior Designers (press mem.), Intercorporate Group, Women in Communications (60 yrs. of success award N.Y. chpt. 1984), Nat. Assn. Underwater Instrs., Pan Pacific and S.E. Asia Women's Assn., Asia Soc., Japan Soc., China Inst., Internat. Side Saddle Orgn., Millbrook Hounds, Golden's Bridge Hounds, Wine and Food Soc., Chaines des Rotisseurs (chargée de press) (bd. dirs.), Dames d'Escoffier, Culinary Inst. Am. Home and Office: 620 Park Ave New York NY 10021-6591

**TOBER, STEPHEN LLOYD,** lawyer; b. Boston, May 27, 1949; s. Benjamin Arthur Tober and Lee (Hymoff) Fruman; m. Susan V. Schwartz, Dec. 22, 1973; children: Cary, Jamie. Grad., Syracuse U., 1971, JD, 1974. Bar: N.H. 1974, U.S. Dist. Ct. N.H. 1974, U.S. Supreme Ct. 1978, N.Y. 1981. Assoc. Flynn, McGuirk & Blanchard, Portsmouth, NH, 1974-79; sole practice Portsmouth, 1979-81; ptnr. Aeschliman & Tober, Portsmouth, 1981-91; prin. Tober Law Offices, P.A., Portsmouth, 1992—. Lectr. Franklin Pierce Law Ctr., Concord, N.H., 1978-80. Contbr. articles to profl. jours. Mem. Portsmouth Charter Commn., 1976, Portsmouth Planning Bd., 1977-81; del. N.H. Constl. Conv., Concord, 1984; city councilman, Portsmouth, 1977-81. Fellow: Internat. Acad. Trial Lawyers, Am. Bar Found. (chmn. ea. region 2003—); mem.: ATLA (gov. 1988—96), ABA (chmn. standing com. on fed. judiciary 2005—, state del., chmn. tech. and comms. com., chmn. credentials and admissions com.), N.H. Bd. Bar Examiners, N.H. Trial Lawyers Assn. (pres. 1977), N.H. Bar Assn. (pres. 1988—89, chmn. com. to redraft code of profl. responsibility, Disting. Svc. award 1986, 1994), New Eng. Bar Assn. (bd.dirs. 1988—91). Democrat. Jewish. Avocations: reading, tennis. Home: 55 T J Gamester Ave Portsmouth NH 03801-5871 Office: Tober Law Offices PA PO Box 1377 Portsmouth NH 03802-1377 Office Phone: 603-431-1003. Business E-Mail: stober@toberlaw.com.

**TOBEY, MARTIN ALAN,** cardiologist; b. Dallas, Sept. 24, 1947; s. Nathan Gene and Rose Marcus T.; m. Judith Helane Ross, Mar. 10, 1974; children: Daniel, Rachel. BS with highest distinction, U. Tex. Austin, 1968; MD, Jefferson Med. Coll., 1970. Diplomate Am. Bd. Internal Medicine, Am. Bd. Cardiovascular Diseases, Am. Bd. Interventional Cardiology. Intern Phila. Gen. Hosp., 1970-71; resident in internal medicine Parkland Meml. Hosp., Dallas, 1971-74; fellow in cardiology U. Tex. Southwestern Med. Sch., Dallas, 1976-78; cardiologist Fort Worth Heart, 1978—. Mem. med. bd. Harris Hosp. Meth., Ft. Worth, 1988-90, chmn. cardiology divsn., 1988-90. Author (software) Workshops in Coronary Angioplasty, 1984, Revolution: The New Practice of Medicine. Major U.S. Army, 1974-76. Fellow Am. Coll. Cardiology (regional rep. Tex. chpt. 1996-98), Am. Heart Assn., Alpha Omega Alpha. Avocations: classical music, computers, photography. Office: Cardiology Assocs Ft Worth 1300 W Rosedale St Fort Worth TX 76104-2802

**TOBEY, WILLIAM HAYWARD,** federal agency administrator, former investment banker; b. Decatur, Ill., Aug. 2, 1959; s. William Robert Jr. and Beverly Joy (Nilson) T.; m. Elizabeth Ness, Oct. 28, 1989; 1 child, Emma Channer. BS, Northwestern U., 1981; M of Pub. Policy, Harvard U., 1984. Presdl. mgmt. intern US Dept. Def., Washington, 1984-85; adv. U.S. Delegation to Nuclear and Space Talks, Geneva, 1985-86; dir. def. policy NSC, Washington, 1986-93; v.p. Smith Barney, NYC; gen. ptnr. Embryon Venture Capital, LLC, 1996; dir. counterproliferation strategy NSC, Washington; dep. adminstr. for def. nuclear nonproliferation Nat. Nuclear Security Adminstrn., US Dept. Energy, Washington, 2006—. Republican. Lutheran. Avocations: golf, squash, oenology. Office: Nat Nuclear Security Adminstrn US Dept Energy 1000 Independence Ave SW Washington DC 20585*

**TOBIAS, ANDREW PREVIN,** columnist, educator; b. N.Y.C., Apr. 20, 1947; s. Seth D. and Audrey J. (Landau) T. BA, Harvard U., 1968, MBA, 1972. Pres Harvard Agys Inc., Cambridge, Mass., 1967-68; v.p. Nat. Student Mktg. Corp., N.Y.C., 1969-70; contbg. editor N.Y. Mag., 1972-77, Esquire mag., 1977-83; columnist Playboy mag., 1982-86; contbr. Time mag., 1989-94, Worth mag., 1995—. Co-host Beyond Wall Street, PBS series, 1997; daily internet columnist, 1996-. Author: The Funny Money Game, 1972, (under pen name John Reid) The Best Little Boy in the World, 1973, Fire and Ice, 1976, The Only Investment Guide You'll Ever Need, 1978, rev. edit., 1996, Getting by on $100,000 a Year and (Other Sad Tales), 1980, The Invisible Bankers, 1982, (software) Managing Your Money, 1984-89; Money Angles, 1984, The Only Other Investment Guide You'll Ever Need, 1987, Kids Say Don't Smoke, 1991, Auto Insurance Alert!, 1993, My Vast Fortune, 1997, the Best Little Boy in the World Grows Up, 1998. Treas. Dem. Nat. Com., 1999—; co-founder Alliance to Revitalize Calif.; bd. mem. Human Right's Campaign. Recipient Gerald Loeb award, 1984, Consumer Fedn. of Am. Media Svc. award, 1993, GLSEN Valedictorian award, 1997, Smith-Weld prize Harvard Mag., 1998.

**TOBIAS, GEOFFREY,** otolaryngologist, plastic surgeon; b. Paterson, NJ, Dec. 20, 1947; MD, Tufts U., 1973. Intern Tufts New England Med. Ctr., 1973—76; resident Mt. Sinai Hosp., NYC, 1976—78; attending surgeon and instr. Mt. Sinai Hosp. and Sch. Medicine, NYC; assoc. chief head and neck surgery Englewood Hosp., NJ. Mem. sci. adv. bd. Longevity mag. Named one of Top Doctors in NY, NY Mag., 2004. Mem.: Am. Acad. Otolaryngology - Head and Neck Surgery, Am. Acad. Facial Plastic Surgery. Office: 214 Engle St Englewood NJ 07631-2418 also: 815 Park Ave New York NY 10021-3276 Office Phone: 201-567-7966. Office Fax: 201-567-6770.*

**TOBIAS, JOSEPH DREW,** pediatric anesthesiologist; b. St. Louis, Mo., Dec. 16, 1958; s. Sherwin Larue and Georgia Xenos Tobias; m. Julie Ann Turpin, Nov. 3, 2001. BA, U. Mo., Kansas City, 1981, MD, 1983. Diplomate Am. Bd. Pediat., Am. Bd. Anesthesiology, Am. Bd. Pediat. Critical Care, Am. Bd. Anesthesiology Critical Care Medicine, Am. Bd. Anesthesiology Pain Mgmt., cert. Am. Acad. Pain Mgmt. 1990. Chief pediatric anesthesiology, attending pediatric ICU St. Jude Children's Hosp., Memphis, 1990—91; assoc. dir., divsn. pediatric anesthesiology/critical care; assoc. prof. anesthesiology and pediat. Vanderbilt U., Nashville, 1991—95; chief pediatric anesthesiology/pediatric critical care, prof. anesthesiology and pediat. U. Mo., Columbia, 1995—, vice-chmn., dept. anesthesiology, 2001—. Home: 4112 Compton Rd Columbia MO 65203 Office: U Missouri One Hospital Dr - 3W27G HSC Columbia MO 65212 Office Phone: 573-882-7168. Business E-Mail: tobiasj@health.missouri.edu.

**TOBIAS, PAUL HENRY,** lawyer; b. Cin., Jan. 5, 1930; s. Charles H. and Charlotte (Westheimer) T.; 1 child, Eliza L. AB magna cum laude, Harvard U., 1951, LLB, 1958. Bar: Mass. 1958, Ohio 1962. Assoc. Stoneman & Chandler, Boston, 1958-61, Goldman & Putnick, Cin., 1962-75; ptnr. Tobias, Kraus and Torchia, Cin., 1976—. Instr. U. Cin. Law Sch., 1975-77. Author: Litigating Wrongful Discharge Claims, 1987; co-author: Job Rights and Survivor Strategies, a Handbook for Terminated Employees, 1997; contbr. articles to profl. jours. Mem. Cin. Bd. of Park Commrs., 1973-81, Cin. Human Rels. Commn., 1980-84, Cin. Hist. Conservation Bd., 1990-91. With U.S. Army, 1952-54. Mem. ABA, Nat. Employment Lawyers Assn. (founder), Nat. Employee Rights Inst. (chmn.; editor-in-chief Employee Rights quar. 2000-02), Ohio State Bar Assn., Cin. Bar Assn. (past chmn. legal aid com.), Phi Beta Kappa. Home: 15 Hill And Hollow Ln Cincinnati OH 45208-3317 Office: Tobias Kraus Torchia 911 Mercantile Libr Bldg Cincinnati OH 45202 Office Phone: 513-241-8137. Business E-Mail: tkt@tktlaw.com.

**TOBIAS, RANDALL LEE,** federal agency administrator, retired pharmaceutical company executive; b. Lafayette, Ind., Mar. 20, 1942; m. Marilyn Jane Salyer, Sept. 2, 1966 (dec. May 1994); children: Paige Noelle, Todd Christopher; m. Marianne Williams, July 15, 1995; stepchildren: James Russell Ullyot, Kathryn Lee Ullyot. BS in Mktg., Ind. U., 1964; LLD (hon.), Galuedette U.; D of Engring. (hon.), Rose Hulman Inst. Tech., Sagamore of the Wabash, Ind.; LLD (hon.), Ind. U., 1997. Numerous positions Ind. Bell, 1964-77, Ill. Bell, 1977-81; v.p. residence mktg. sales and service AT&T, 1981-82, pres. Am. Bell Consumer Products, 1983, pres. Consumer Products, 1983-84, sr. v.p., 1984-85; chmn., CEO AT&T Comm., N.Y.C., 1985-91, AT&T Internat., Basking Ridge, NJ, 1991-93; vice chmn. bd. AT&T, N.Y.C., 1986-93; chmn., CEO Eli Lilly & Co., Indpls., 1993-98, chmn. emeritus, 1999; coord., US Govt. Activities to Combat AIDS Globally US Dept. State, Washington, 2003—06, dir. fgn. assistance, 2006—; adminstr. USAID, Washington, 2006—. Bd. dirs. Kimberly-Clark, 1994-2003, ConocoPhillips Petroleum Co., 2002-03, Knight-Ridder, Inc. Co-Author: Put The Moose On The Table, 2003 Chmn. bd. trustees Duke U.; trustee Colonial Williamsburg Found.; bd. govs. Indpls. Mus. Art; bd. dirs. Indpls. Symphony Orch., Ind. U. Found. (hon.), Econ. Club Indpls. Named one of Top 25 Mgrs. of Yr., Bus. Week, 1997, Family Champion, Working Mothers Mag., 1997. Mem. Bus. Coun., Indpls. Corp. Cmty. Coun., Coun. Fgn. Rels., Meridian Hills Country Club (Indpls.), Woodstock Club (Indpls.), Columbia Club (Indpls.), Athletic Club (Indpls.), Univ. Club (Indpls.), Amwell Valley Conservancy (N.J.), Theta Chi. Avocations: skiing, fly fishing, shooting. Office: USAID Ronald Reagan Bldg 1300 Pennsylvania Ave NW Washington DC 20523*

**TOBIAS, ROBERT MAX,** labor leader, lawyer; b. Detroit, Aug. 4, 1943; BA, U. Mich., 1965, MBA, 1968; JD, George Washington U., 1969. Lawyer Nat. Treasury Employees Union, Washington, 1968-70, gen. counsel, 1970-79, exec. v.p. and gen. counsel, 1979-83, pres., 1983-99; disting. adj. prof. pub. adminstrn., dir. Inst. for Study of Pub. Policy Implementation, Am. U., Washington, 1999—, dir. pub. sector exec. edn., 2005—. Lectr. George Washington U. Law Sch., Washington, 1970-90; mem. IRS oversight bd., 2000—. Contbr. articles to law revs. Pres. Fed. Employee Edn. and Asst. Fund, Washington, 1986—. Fellow Nat. Acad. Pub. Adminstrn.; mem. ABA, Soc. for Labor Relations Profls. (1st Annual Union Leader award, 1987), Fed. Bar Assn. Democrat. Episcopalian. Office: Am U Sch Pub Affairs 4400 Massachusetts Ave Washington DC 20016-8070 E-mail: rtobias@american.edu.

**TOBIAS, STEPHEN C.,** rail transportation executive; b. Bogota, Colombia, Dec. 11, 1944; BA in History, Citadel, 1967; postgrad., Harvard U., 1986. Jr. engr. Pocahontas divsn. Norfolk and Western Rlwy. Co., 1969-70, asst. roadmaster Scioto divsn., 1970, asst. trainmaster Pitts. divsn., 1970-71, gen. yardmaster Pitts. divsn., 1971-73, trainmaster Bellevue terminal, 1973-74, asst. supt. Bellevue terminal, 1974-79, supt. Pitts. divsn., 1979-81, asst. gen. mgr. lake region, 1981, asst. gen. mgr. supt. eastern region, 1981-84, gen. mgr. eastern region Norfolk (Va.) So. Corp., 1984, gen. mgr. western lines, 1984-89, v.p. transp., 1989-92, v.p. strategic planning, 1992-93, sr. v.p. ops., 1993-94, exec. v.p. ops., 1994-98, vice chmn. and COO, 1998—. Trustee Norfolk Acad.; prin. Va. Bus. Coun.; bd. dirs. Plum Creek Timber Co., TTX Co., Inc. Dir. Va. law Enforcement Found.; mem. exec. adv. coun. Commonwealth Musical Stage. Capt. U.S. Army, 1967-69. Mem. Assn. Am. R.R.s. Office: Norfolk So Corp 3 Commercial Pl Norfolk VA 23510-2108

**TOBIASSEN, BARBARA SUE,** systems analyst, consultant, volunteer; b. Bklyn., Feb. 22, 1950; d. Vincent and Esther Alice (Hansen) M. BA in Math Edn., Rider Coll., 1972; postgrad., Montclair State U., 1973. Cert. secondary tchr., NJ. Math tchr. Westwood (NJ) H.S., 1973-80; programmer Prudential Ins. Co., Roseland, NJ, 1980-81; programmer, analyst Grand Union, Paramus, NJ, 1981-82; cons. Five Techs., Montvale, NJ, 1987-90; project mgr. Info. Sci., Inc., Montvale, 1982-84, cons., project mgr., 1987-90; pres. B. Maxwell Assoc., Inc., Westwood, 1990—; vol. Peace Corps; mem. Peace Corps., 2001—02; tchr. St. Paul's Luth., Accra, Ghana, 2002—03. Guest spkr. Info. Sci., Best of Am., Computer Assocs. B.A.C.; educator, Ghana W. Africa, 2002-. Contbr. articles to profl. jours. Vol. Peace Corps, 2001—02. Mem.: APA (v.p. N.J. chpt. 1996), NAFE, Am. Payroll Assn., N.J. Info. Republican. Lutheran. Avocations: travel, reading, gardening, hiking. E-mail: btobiassen2003@yahoo.com.

**TOBIN, BARBARA KAY,** minister; b. Davenport, Iowa, Oct. 9, 1943; d. Robert Thomas Myers and Frances Louella Davis; m. Richard James Tobin, Feb. 12, 1966; 1 child, Mary Beth Tobin Peter. B.Humanities, Social Sci. and Edn., Purdue U., 1966; BEd, Ball State U., 1968; MDiv, Colgate Rochester Div. Sch., 1994. Cert. tchr. N.Y., ordained to ministry Presbyn. Ch., 1994. Fgn. lang. tchr. West Irondequoit Schs., Rochester, NY, 1968—93; chaplain Strong Meml. Hosp., Rochester, 1993—94; pastor of visitation First Presbyn. Ch., Pittsford, NY, 1994—96; assoc. pastor Perinton Presbyn. Ch., Fairport, NY, 1995—2000; pastor Irondequoit Presbyn. Ch., Rochester, 2000—. Sec., bd. dirs. Irondequoit Sr. Transp. Ministry, Rochester, 2002—; mem. com. on prep. ministry Genesee Valley Presbytery, 2001—05; leader internat. study tours West Irondequoit Schs., 1983—88; leader student mission trips Perinton Presbyn. Ch., 1991—99. Mem. Irondequoit Youth Bureau Adv. Bd., 2004—; leader,youth mission trips, 1992—99. Mem.: N.Y. State Ret. Tchrs. Assn., Purdue U. Alumni Assn. (life; pres.'s coun. 1993—). Presbyterian. Avocations: reading, travel, sailing. Office: Irondequoit Presbyn Ch 2881 Culver Rd Rochester NY 14622 Office Phone: 585-266-3370. Personal E-Mail: pastorbobbi@rochester.rr.com.

**TOBIN, CALVIN JAY,** retired architect; b. Boston, Feb. 15, 1927; s. David and Bertha (Tanfield) T.; m. Joan Hope Fink, July 15, 1951; children—Michael Alan, Nancy Ann. B.Arch., U. Mich., 1949. Designer, draftsman Arlen & Lowenfish (architects), N.Y.C., 1949-51; with Samuel Arlen, N.Y.C., 1951-53, Skidmore, Owings & Merrill, N.Y.C., 1953; architect Loebl, Schlossman & Bennett (architects), Chgo., 1953-57, v.p., 1953-57, Loebl, Schlossman & Hackl, 1957—; ret., 1998. Chmn. Jewish United Fund Bldg. Trades Div., 1969; chmn. AIA and Chgo. Hosp. Council Com. of Hosp. Architecture, 1968-76; archtl. cons. Resurrection Healthcare Corp., 1998—. Archtl. works include Michael Reese Hosp. and Med. Ctr., 1954—, Prairie Shores Apt. Urban Redevel., 1957-62, Louis A. Weiss Meml. Hosp., Chgo., Chgo. State Hosp., Ctrl. Cmty. Hosp., Chgo., Gottlieb Meml. Hosp., Melrose Park, Ill., West Suburban Hosp., Oak Park, Ill., Thorek Hosp. and Med. Ctr., Chgo., Water Power Pl., Chgo., Christ Hosp., Oak Lawn, Greater Balt. Med. Ctr., Shriners Hosp. for Crippled Children, Chgo. Hinsdale (Ill.) Hosp., South Chgo. Cmty. Hosp., Chgo., Mt. Sinai Med. Ctr., Chgo., Alexian Bros. Med. Ctr., Elk Grove Village, Ill., Luth. Gen. Hosp., Park Ridge, Ill., Evanston (Ill.) Hosp., Resurrection Med. Ctr., Chgo., New Cook County Hosp., Chgo., also numerous apt., comml. and cmty. bldgs. Chmn. Highland Park (Ill.) Appearance Rev. Commn., 1972-73; mem. Highland Park Plan Commn., 1973-79; mem. Highland Park City Coun., 1974-89, mayor pro-tem, 1979-89; mem. Highland Park Environ. Commn., 1979-84; Highland Park Hist. Preservation Commn., 1982-89; bd. dir. Highland Park Hist. Soc., Young Men's Jewish Coun., 1953-67, pres., 1967; bd. dirs. Jewish Community Ctrs. Chgo., 1973-78, bd. dirs., 1989-93; Ill. Coun. Against Handgun Violence,

1989-94; trustee Ravinia Festival Assn., 1990-98; bd. govs. Highland Park Cmty. House, 1994—. With USNR, 1945-46. Recipient Boys Club Medallion award, Boys Club Am., 1968, Disting. Alumni award, Taubman Coll. Architecture and Urban Planning, U. Mich., 2004. Fellow AIA (2d v.p. Chgo. chpt.); mem. U. Mich. Alumni Soc. Coll. Architecture and Urban Planning (bd. govs. 1989-95), U. Mich. Alumni Assn. (bd. govs. 1990-95, v.p. 1993-95, pres. 1997-99, Disting. Alumni Svc. award 1996), Std. Club, Ravinia Green Country Club, Pi Lambda Phi. Jewish. Home: 814 Dean Ave Highland Park IL 60035-4749

**TOBIN, CRAIG DANIEL,** lawyer; b. Chgo., Aug. 17, 1954; s. Thomas Arthur and Lois (O'Connor) T. BA with honors, U. Ill., 1976; JD with high honors, Ill. Inst. Tech., 1980. Bar: Ill. 1980, U.S. Dist. Ct. (no. dist.) Ill. 1980, U.S. Dist. Ct. (no. dist.) Ind. 1986, U.S. Ct. Appeals (7th cir.) 1986, U.S. Supreme Ct. 1987. Trial atty. Cook County Pub. Defender, Chgo., 1980-82; trial atty. homicide task force Pub. Defender, Chgo., 1982-84; ptnr. Craig D. Tobin and Assocs., Chgo., 1984—. Lectr. Ill. Inst. for Continuing Legal Edn., Cook County Pub. Defender, Chgo., 1983, 92, Ill. Pub. Defender Assn., 1987; instr. Nat. Inst. Trial Advocacy. Recipient award for legal excellence Midwest Comm. Coun., 2002; named to Outstanding Young Men in Am., 1985. Mem. ABA, Chgo. Bar Assn., Nat. Assn. Criminal Def. Lawyers. Roman Catholic. Office: Tobin Petkus & Munoz LLC 3 First National Plz Chicago IL 60602 Home: 6622 N Longmeadow Ave Lincolnwood IL 60712-3208 Office Phone: 312-641-1321.

**TOBIN, DENNIS MICHAEL,** lawyer; b. Chgo., June 3, 1948; s. Thomas Arthur and Lois (O'Connor) T.; m. Sue Wynn Henslee, June 14, 1969 (div. 1977); m. Karen Thompson, Oct. 11, 1980; children: Kyle James, Daniel Patrick BA with honors, U. Ill., 1971; JD, Loyola U., Chgo., 1976. Bar: Ill. 1976, U.S. Dist. Ct (no. dist.) Ill. 1976, U.S. Ct. Appeals (7th cir.) 1985, U.S. Supreme Ct. 1985, Wis. 1989. Trial atty. Cook County Homicide Task Force, Chgo., 1976-84; prin. Dennis M. Tobin & Assocs., Chgo., 1984— Gen. counsel Forest Health Systems and Found., Ill., Miss., Hawaii, 1986—; Manages Behavioral Care Inc., Pits, Co. Am. Dir. Forest Health Systems Found.; mem. Chgo. Coun. on Fgn. Rels. Mem. ABA (forum on health law), Nat. Assn. Criminal Def. Attys., Chgo. Bar Assn. (com. on health law), Am. Soc. Law and Medicine, Ill. Assn. Criminal Def. Attys. (v.p. 1984-87), Ill. Attys. for Criminal Justice, Wis. Bar Assn., Ill. Assn. Hosp. Attys., Nat. Health Lawyers Assn., U.S. Sporting Clays Assn., Nat. Sporting Clays Assn., Gateway Gun Club. Roman Catholic. Office: 335 Frost Dr Williams Bay WI 53191-9716

**TOBIN, EUGENE MARC,** foundation administrator, retired academic administrator; b. Newark, Mar. 23, 1947; s. Hyman and Clara (Pekersky) Tobin; m. Beverly Stethem, May 26, 1979; children: David Gehm, Leslie, BA in History, Rutgers U., 1968; MA in History Am. Civilization, Brandeis U., 1970, PhD in History of Am. Civilization, 1972; LLD (hon.), Hamilton Coll. 1994. Vis. instr. history Jersey City State Coll., 1972—75; vis. asst. prof. Kutztown State Coll., Pa., 1975—76; NEH postdoctoral fellow Vanderbilt U., Nashville, 1976—77; vis. asst. prof. Miami U., Oxford, Ohio, 1977—79, Indiana U., Bloomington, 1979—80; asst. prof. history Hamilton Coll., Clinton, NY, 1980—83, assoc. prof. history, 1983—88, prof. history, 1988—; dir. Am. studies program 1983—88, chair dept. history, 1986—88, acting dean coll., 1988, dean faculty, 1989—93, pres., 1993—2003; sr. adv. Andrew W. Mellon Found., NYC, 2003—. Presenter in field. Co-author (with Michael H. Ebner): The Ape of Urban Reform: New Perspectives on the Progressive Era, 1977, Organize or Parish: America's Independent Progressives 1913-1933, 1986; co-author: (with Ann Fagan Ginger) The National Lawyers Guild: From Roosevelt Through Reagan, 1988; contbr. articles to profl. jours. With USAR, 1968—74. Recipient William Adee Whitehead award, N.J. Hist. Soc., 1976; fellow, NDEA, 1968—72; grantee rsch. grantee, Am. Philos. Soc., 1978—79, 1982—83. Mem.: Orgn. Am. Historians, Am. Hist. Assn. Office: Andrew W Mellon Found 140 E 62nd St New York NY 10023 Home: 50 E 89th St New York NY 10128-1225 E-mail: etobin@hamilton.edu.

**TOBIN, GARY ALLAN,** cultural and community organization educator; b. St. Louis, July 26, 1949; BA in History, Washington U., 1971; PhD in City and Regional Planning, U. Calif., Berkeley. Pres. Inst. for Jewish and Cmty. Rsch., San Francisco; dir. Abramson Program in Jewish Policy Rsch. U. Judaism, L.A.; former dir. Cohen Ctr. for Modern Jewish Studies Brandeis U., Waltham, Mass. Rsch. on antisemitism, racial and ethnic diversity, Jewish orgn. planning and philanthropy in Jewish Cmty. and Jewish Family Founds. Author: Jewish Perceptions of Antisemitism, Church and Synagogue Affiliation, Opening the Gates: How Proactive Conversion Can Revitalize the Jewish Community, Rabbis Talk About Intermarriage.

**TOBIN, JAMES MICHAEL,** lawyer; b. Santa Monica, Calif., Sept. 27, 1948; s. James Joseph and Glada Marie (Meisner); m. Kathleen Marie Espy, Sept. 14, 1985; children: Kristina Claire, Victoria Elizabeth Joy. BA with honors, U. Calif., Riverside, 1970; JD, Georgetown U., Washington, D.C., 1974. Bar: Calif. 1974, Mich. 1987. From atty. to gen. atty. So. Pacific Co., San Francisco, 1975-82; v.p. regulatory affairs So. Pacific Comm. Co., Washington, 1982-83; v.p. gen. counsel Lexitel Corp., Washington, 1983-85; v.p., gen. counsel, sec. ALC Comm. Corp., Birmingham, Mich., 1985-87, sr. v.p., gen. counsel, sec., 1987-88; of counsel Morrison & Foerster, San Francisco, 1988-90, ptnr., 1990—2005, Law Office of James M. Tobin, 2006—. Mem. ABA, Calif. Bar Assn., Fed. Comm. Bar Assn. Republican. Unitarian Universalist. Avocations: carpentry, travel. Home: 3134 Baker St San Francisco CA 94123-1805 Office: Two Embarcadero Ctr Ste 1800 San Francisco CA 94111 Office Phone: 415-732-1700. Business E-Mail: jim@tobinlaw.us

**TOBIN, JAMES ROBERT,** biomedical device manufacturing company executive; b. Lima, Ohio, Aug. 12, 1944; s. J. Robert and Doris L. (Hunt) T.; m. Janet Trafton, Dec. 30, 1971; children: James Robert III, Amanda Trafton. BA in Govt., Harvard U., 1966; MBA, Harvard U. Bus. Sch., 1968. Fin. analyst Baxter Internat., Inc., Deerfield, Ill., 1972-73, internat. contr., 1973-75, mng. dir. Japan, 1975-77, mng. dir. Spain, 1977-80, pres. IV Sys. Divsn., 1981—86, group v.p., 1984-88, exec. v.p. Deerfield, 1988-92, pres., COO, 1992-94, Biogen Inc., 1994-97, pres., CEO, 1997-98, Boston Sci. Corp., Natick, Mass., 1999—, also bd. dirs. Bd. dirs. Creative Biomolecules, Pathogenesis, PE Corp. Bd. dirs. Beth Israel Deaconess Med. Ctr., Inc., contbr. BioMedical Sci. Career Program. Served to lt. USN, 1968—72. Republican. Office: Boston Scientific 1 Boston Scientific Pl Natick MA 01760-1537*

**TOBIN, STEVE ROBERT,** artist; b. Phila., Feb. 10, 1957; B in Theoretical Mathematics, Tulane U., 1976—79. Rsch. asst. to Dr. Campbell Laird U Pa., 1975; tchr. glass sculpture Tokyo Glass Art Inst., Japan, 1985—86. One-man shows include Sculptured Glass, Bienville Gallery, New Orleans, 1979, Glasscapes, Spring Street Enamels Gallery, NY, 1980, Glass Portraits, Hanson Gallery, New Orleans, 1980, Glass Sculpture, Gallery 10, NY, 1982, Manhattan Bowls, Snyderman Gallery, Phila., 1985, Wheaton Ware, LaVaggi Gallery, NY, 1986, Glass for Tea Ceremony, Tazawa Gallery, Kyoto, Japan, 1987, The Glass Garden, Coll. Art & Design, Levy Gallery for Arts, Phila., 1988, Cocoons, Moore Coll. Art & Design, Phila., 1988, Transformations: Three Installations in Glass, Lehigh U., Wilson and Hall Gallery, Bethlehem, Pa., 1992, Retretti Art Centre, Punkaharju, Finland, 1993, Sanske Galerie, Zurich, Switzerland, 1994, Reconstructions, Philip and Muriel Berman Mus. Art, Ursinus Coll. Pa., 1995, Matzoh House, Gallery BAI, NY, 1996, Broadway River, NYU, 1997, Earth Bronzes, OK Harris, NY, 1998, Earth Bronze Trilogy-Part I, Buschlen-Mowatt Gallery, Vancouver, Can., 2001, Naked Earth, George C. Page Mus., LA, 2003, Lantern House on World Records for blowing world's largest glass bottle, 1995; speaks Spanish, Japanese, and Venetian dialect. Mailing: c/o Kouros Gallery 23 East 73rd St New York NY 10021

**TOBIN, THOMAS J.,** bishop; b. Pitts., Apr. 1, 1948; Grad., St. Mark. Sem. HS, Erie, Pa., St. Francis Coll., Loretto, 1969, PhD (hon.), 1997; studied, Gannon Coll., Erie, North Am. Coll., Rome, Gregorian U., Pontifical Liturgical Inst. of San Anselmo. Ordained priest, 1973; asst. pastor St. Vitus Parish, New Castle, Pa., 1973—79, St. Sebastian Parish, Ross Twp., Pa., 1979—84; adminstrv. sec. to bishop Diocese of Pitts., 1984—87, assoc. gen. sec., 1987—90, vicar gen. & gen. sec., 1990—92; ordained bishop, 1992; Auxiliary Bishop of Pitts., 1992—95; Bishop of Youngstown Ohio, 1996—2005; Bishop of Providence RI 2005—. Trustee Pontifical Coll. Josephinum, Columbus, Ohio; mem. episcopal adv. bd. Catholics United for the Faith. Mem.: US Conf. Cath. Bishops (mem. adminstrv. com.). Roman Catholic. Office: Diocese of Providence One Cathedral Sq Providence RI 02903

**TOBIN, VINCENT MICHAEL,** professional football coach, former sports team executive; b. Burlington Junction, Mo., Sept. 29, 1943; BE, U. Mo., 1965, M in Guidance and Counseling, 1966. Def. ends coach Missouri, 1967-70, def. coord., 1971-76, Brit. Columbia Lions CFL, 1977-82, Phila./Balt. Stars USFL, 1983-85, Chgo. Bears NFL, 1986-92, Indpls. Colts NFL, 1994-95; head coach Ariz. Cardinals, 1996—2000.

**TOBIN, WILLIAM JOSEPH,** newspaper editor; b. Joplin, Mo., July 28, 1927; s. John J. and Lucy T. (Shoppach) Tobin; m. Marjorie Stuhldreher, Apr. 26, 1952; children: Michael Gerard, David Joseph, James Patrick. BJ, Butler U., 1948; LLD (hon.), Gonzaga U., 2006. Staff writer AP, Indpls., 1947-52, news feature writer N.Y.C., 1952-54, regional membership exec. Louisville, 1954-56, corr. Juneau, Alaska, 1956-60, asst. chief bur. Balt., 1960-61, Helena, Mont., 1961-63; mng. editor Anchorage Times, 1963-73, assoc. editor, 1973-85, gen. mgr., 1974-85, v.p., editor-in-chief, 1985-89, editor editl. page, 1990, asst. pub., 1991; sr. editor Voice of the Times, 1991—. Mem. devel. com. Anchorage Winter Olympics, 1984-91, bd. dirs. Anchorage organizing com., 1985-91; bd. dirs. Alaska Coun. Econ. Edn., 1978-84, Boys Clubs Alaska, 1979-83, Anchotage Symphony Orch., 1986-87, Blue Cross Wash. and Alaska, 1987—, chmn., 1990-91; chmn. Premera Corp., 1994-99; mem. adv. bd. Providence Hosp., Anchorage, 1974-91, chmn., 1980-85. Sgt. U.S. Army, 1950-52. Mem. Alaska AP Mems. Assn. (pres. 1964), Anchorage C. of C. (bd. dirs. 1969-74, pres. 1972-73), Alaska World Affairs Coun. (pres. 1967-68), Alaska Press Club (pres. 1968-69), Commonwealth North Club (Anchorage). Home: 2130 Lord Baranof Dr Anchorage AK 99517-1257 Office: Anchorage Times PO Box 100040 Anchorage AK 99510-0040 Office Phone: 907-264-8193. Personal E-mail: wjt@alaska.life.net.

**TOBIS, JEROME SANFORD,** physician; b. Syracuse, NY, July 23, 1915; s. David George and Anna (Feinberg) T.; m. Hazel Weisbard, Sept. 18, 1938; children: David, Heather, Jonathan. BS, CCNY, 1936; MD, Chgo. Med. Sch., 1943. Diplomate Am. Bd. Phys. Medicine and Rehab. Intern Knickerbocker Hosp., 1943-44; resident Bronx VA Hosp., 1946-48; med. dir. state fever therapy unit USPHS, Brookhaven, Miss., 1944-46; practice medicine N.Y.C., 1948-70; prof. dir. dept. phys. medicine and rehab. N.Y. Med. Coll., Flower and Fifth Av. Hosps., 1948-61; prof. rehab. medicine Albert Einstein Coll. of Medicine, 1963-70; chief div. rehab. medicine Montefiore Hosp., 1961-70; dir. vis. physician Met., Bird S. Coler hosps., 1952-61; prof., chmn. dept. phys. medicine and rehab. Calif. Coll. Medicine, U. Calif. at Irvine, 1970-82, prof., dir. program in geriatric medicine and gerontology, 1980-86; mem. adv. com. Acad. Geriatric Resource program, 1984-86, 95—. Expert med. com. Am. Rehab. Found., 1961-70; cons. Dept. Health, NYC, Long Beach VA Hosp., 1970—, Fairview State Devel. Ctr., 1976—; adv. coun. phys. medicine and rehab. for appeals com. Calif. Med. Assn., 1971-74, adv. com. U. Calif. Acad. Geriatric Resource Program, 1995—; NIH Internat. Fogarty fellow, hon. lectr., dept. geriat. medicine U. Birmingham, 1979-80; rev. panel musculoskeletal diseases NIH, 1996; rsch. prof. dept. phys. medicine & rehab. U. Calif., Irvine, 1986—, dept. med. ethics com., 1986—; mem. Ctr. Health Policy Rsch. U. Calif., Davis, 1996—. Mem. editorial bd.: Heart and Lung, 1973-76, Geriatrics, 1975-80, Archives of Phys. Medicine and Rehab, 1958-73. Named Physician of the Year, 1957; recipient Distinguished Alumnus award Chgo. Med. Sch., 1972, Acad. award Nat. Inst. on Aging, 1981-86; named hon. faculty mem. Calif. Zeta chpt. Alpha Omega Alpha, 1981; Leavitt Meml. lectureship Baylor Coll. Medicine, 1983, Griffith Meml. lectureship Am. Geriatric Soc., 1984; Australian Coll. Rehabilitation Medicine, 1984; Jerome S. Tobis Ann. Conf. on Geriatric Medicine established in his name, U. Calif. at Irvine, 1986. Fellow ACP, Am. Coll. Cardiology, Am. Congress Rehab. Medicine (hon.); mem. AMA (mem. residency rev. com. Coun. Med. Edn. 1973), AAAS, Am. Acad. Cerebral Palsy, Am. Acad. Phys. Medicine and Rehab. (Disting. Clinician award 1993), Am. Congress Rehab. Medicine (pres. 1962), Calif. Coun. Gerontology and Geriatrics (bd. dirs. 1980-86, pres. 1985), N.Y. Acad. Medicine, N.Y. Acad. Sci., Orange County Med. Soc., Assn. U. Calif. Irvine (chair emeritae/i 1996-97). Home: 1115 Goldenrod Ave Corona Del Mar CA 92625-1508 Personal E-mail: jstobis@uci.edu.

**TOBISMAN, STUART PAUL,** lawyer; b. Detroit, June 5, 1942; s. Nathan and Beverly (Porvin) T.; m. Karen Sue Tobisman, Aug. 8, 1965; children: Cynthia Elaine, Neal Jay. BA, UCLA, 1966; JD, U. Calif., Berkeley, 1969. Bar: Calif. 1969. Assoc. O'Melveny & Myers, LA, 1969-77, ptnr., 1977—2006, Loeb & Loeb LLP, LA, 2006—. Contbr. articles to profl. jours. Trustee L.A. County Bar Assn., 1983-84. With USN, 1961-63. Fellow Am. Coll. Trust and Estate Counsel; mem. Phi Beta Kappa, Order of Coif. Office: Loeb & Loeb LLP 10100 Santa Monica Blvd Los Angeles CA 90067-4120

**TOBUREN, LARRY HOWARD,** physicist, researcher; b. Clay Center, Kans., July 9, 1940; s. Howard H. and Beulah (Boyd) T.; m. Lana L. Henry, June 16, 1962; children: Debra L., Tina L. BA, Emporia State U., 1962; PhD, Vanderbilt U., 1968. Rsch. scientist Battelle Northwest Lab., Richland, Wash., 1967-80, staff scientist, mgr. radiation physics and chemistry sect., 1980-93; sr. program officer NRC/NAS, Washington, 1993-95; prof. physics East Carolina U., Greenville, NC, 1995—, prof. Accelerator Lab., 1995—2002, dir. grad. studies in physics, 2000—06. Affiliate asst. prof. radiological physics U. Wash., 1982-91, affiliate assoc. prof. environ. health, 1991-94; adj. lectr. environ. scis. Wash. State U., 1991-94. Contbr. articles to profl. jours. Fellow Am. Phys. Soc.; mem. AAAS, Radiation Rsch. Soc. Office: East Carolina Univ Dept of Physics Greenville NC 27858-4353 Home: 1656 Wimbledon Dr Apt 204 Greenville NC 27858 Office Phone: 252-328-1861. E-mail: toburenl@ecu.edu

**TOBY, JACKSON,** sociologist, educator; b. N.Y.C., Sept. 10, 1925; m. Marcia Lifshitz, Aug. 1, 1952 (dec. Jan. 1997); children: Alan Steven, Gail Afriat (dec.). BA, Bklyn. Coll., 1946; MA in Econs, Harvard U., 1947, MA in Sociology, 1949, PhD in Sociology, 1950. Rsch. assoc. Lab. Social Relations, Harvard, 1950-51; mem. faculty Rutgers U., 1951—2002, prof. sociology, chmn. dept., 1961-68, prof. sociology emeritus, 2002, dir. Inst. for Criminological Rsch., 1969-94; vis. scholar Enterprise Inst., 2004—. Cons. Youth Devel. Program, Ford Found., 1959-63 Author: (with H.C. Bredemeier) Social Problems in America, 1960, 2d edit., 1971; Contemporary Society, 1964, 2d edit., 1971; contbr. numerous articles to profl. jours., pub. policy jours., N.Y. Times, Wall St. Jour., L.A. Times, Chgo. Tribune, Washington Post, The Weekly Standard, Nat. Rev., Sociol. Rsch. Cons., Pres.'s Commn. Law Enforcement and Adminstrn. Justice, 1966; trustee NAMI-N.J., 1997-2000. Recipient numerous research grants Mem. Am. Sociol. Assn., Sociol. Rsch. Assn., Am. Soc. Criminology, Nat. Assn. Scholars. Achievements include spl. research adolescent delinquency in U.S., Sweden, Japan, other countries, on violence and dropouts in Am. public schools. Home: 17 Harrison Ave Highland Park NJ 08904-1813 Office: Rutgers U Dept Sociology Lucy Stone Hall Livingston Campus New Brunswick NJ 08903 E-mail: jtoby@rci.rutgers.edu.

**TOBY, SIDNEY,** retired chemistry professor; b. London, May 30, 1930; arrived in U.S., 1957; s. Jack and Jennie Toby; m. Frina Sheila Schwartzman, Sept. 6, 1952; children: Brian Howard, Carole Leslie Rodenstein. BSc, Queen Mary Coll., London, England, 1952; PhD, McGill U., Montreal, Can., 1955. Postdoctoral fellow NRC, Ottawa, Ont., Canada, 1955—57; prof. Dept of

Chemsitry Rutgers U., New Brunswick, NJ, 1957—2000, chmn. Dept Chemistry, 1974—77, ret., 2000. Contbr. over 75 articles to profl. jours. Aircraftsman 1st class Royal Air Force, 1948—49. Named Tchr. of Yr., Rutgers U., 1990; grantee, NSF, 1962—72, Army Rsch. Office, Durham, 1962—72. Mem.: Am. Chem. Soc. (life). Achievements include patents in field. Office: Dept of Chemistry Rutgers University Taylor Road Piscataway NJ 08854 Office Phone: 732-445-4455. Business E-Mail: toby@rci.rutgers.edu.

**TOCCI, NEIL MICHAEL,** marketing executive, educator, corporate communications executive; b. Boston, Feb. 15, 1949; s. Nildo Neil and Irene Marie (Rioux) T.; m. Marlene Perscheid, Apr. 22, 1972; 1 child, Margaux. BS, Boston Coll., 1971; MBA in Mktg., Fairleigh Dickinson U., 1976; MA, Seton Hall U., 1999. Pres. Carrera Graphic Assocs. Inc., Newark, 1976-94, Carrera Digital, Newark, 1994-97; digital color specialist AOE Ricoh, Fairfield, NJ, 1997-99; mgr., mktg. and corp. comm. Kyocera Mita Am. Inc., Fairfield, 1999—2002; dir. mktg. Fuji Hunt Photog. Chem., Inc., Allendale, NJ, 2003—. Adj. prof. psychology William Paterson U., Wayne, NJ, 2000—; panel, cons. mktg. strategy Essex County Coll., Newark, 1990; panelist, cons. comms. skills Seton Hall U., South Orange, NJ, 1992. Active Wyckoff YMCA, 1999—, coach recreation league, Wyckoff, 2002—. Mem.: ACA, NJ Psychol. Assn., High Mountain Golf Club. Roman Catholic.

**TOCCO, ELAINE KAY,** insurance agent; b. Columbus, Ohio, May 20, 1957; d. Arthur Gene and Nancy Louise Lanker; m. Peter Joseph Tocco; children: Nicholas, Alexander; 1 child, Zachary. BA, Brescia U., 1981. Program cons. Disability Determination Svcs., Indpls., 1983—98; social ins. specialist Social Security Adminstrn., Balt., 1999—. Webelos leader Boy Scouts Am., Columbia, 1999—2001; coord. support group Multiple Sclerosis Soc., Indpls., 1985—86. Mem.: Nat. Assn. Disability Examiners, Mensa, Psy Chi, Alpha Chi. Roman Catholic. Avocations: reading, gardening. Office: Social Security Adminstrn 6401 Security Blvd Baltimore MD 21207 Personal E-mail: elaine_tocco@hotmail.com. Business E-mail: elaine.tocco@ssa.gov.

**TOCCO, JAMES,** pianist; b. Detroit, Sept. 21, 1943; s. Vincenzo and Rose (Tabbita) T.; 1 child, Rhoya. Prof. music Ind. U., Bloomington, 1977-91; eminent scholar, artist-in-residence U. Cin. Coll.-Conservatory Music, 1991—; prof. Musikhochschule, Lübeck, Ger., 1990—; artistic dir. Great Lakes Chamber Music Festival, 1994—; prof. Manhattan Sch. Music, 2002—. Debut with orch., Detroit, 1956, since appeared with symphony orchs. including Chgo. Symphony, Los Angeles Philharmonic, Cin. Symphony, Detroit Symphony, Nat. Symphony, Balt. Symphony, Atlanta Symphony, Denver Symphony, Montreal Symphony, London Symphony, London Philharm., BBC Orch., Berlin Philharm., Moscow Radio-TV Orch., Amsterdam Philharmonic, Munich Philharmonic, Bavarian Radio Orch., Royal Concertebouw Orch., also recitals, U.S. and abroad, and performances, CBS and NBC networks; guest performer, White House; Recs. include the complete preludes of Chopin, collected piano works of Leonard Bernstein, complete piano works of Charles Tomlinson Griffes, 4 piano sonatas of Edward MacDowell, selected piano works of Aaron Copland, complete Bach-Liszt organ transcriptions, piano works of John Corigliano. concertos of Igor Stravinsky, Leonard Bernstein, and John Corigliano. Recipient Bronze medal Tchaikovsky Competition, Moscow 1970, Bronze medal Queen Elisabeth of Belgium Competition, Brussels 1972, 1st prize Piano Competition of Americas, Rio de Janeiro 1973, 1st prize Munich Internat. Competition 1973. Office: U Cin Coll Conservatory Musi Cincinnati OH 45221-0001

**TODARO, GEORGE JOSEPH,** pathologist, researcher; b. NYC, July 1, 1937; s. George J. and Antoinette (Piccini) Todaro; m. Jane Lehv, Aug. 12, 1962; children: Wendy C., Thomas M., Anthony A. BS, Swarthmore Coll., 1958; MD, NYU, 1963. Intern NYU Sch. Medicine, N.Y.C., 1963—64, fellow in pathology, 1964—65, asst. prof. pathology, 1965—67; staff assoc. Viral Carcinogenesis br. Nat. Cancer Inst., Bethesda, Md., 1967—70, head molecular biology sect., 1969—70; chief Viral Carcinogenesis br. Nat. Cancer Inst. (Lab. Viral Carcinogenesis), 1970—83; sci. dir. pres. Oncogen, Seattle, 1987—90; sr. v.p. exploratory biomed. rsch. Bristol-Myers Squibb Pharm. Rsch. Inst., 1990; pres., CEO Cytokine Networks, Inc., Seattle, 1998—; now prof. pathobiology U. Wash., Seattle. Adj. prof. pathology U. Wash., Seattle, 1983—, past chmn. dept. pathobiology; sr. v.p., sci. dir. Pathogenesis Corp., Seattle, 1992—95; mem. Fred Hutchinson Cancer Rsch. Ctr., Seattle, 1991—93. Editor: Cancer Rsch., 1973—86, Archives of Virology, 1976—, Jour. Biol. Chemistry, 1979; contbr. articles to profl. jours. Med. officer USPHS, 1967—69. Named Walter Hubert lectr., Brit. Cancer Soc., 1977; recipient Borden Undergrad. Rsch. award, 1963, Career Devel. award, USPHS, 1967, HEW Superior Svc. award, 1971, Gustav Stern award for virology, 1972, Parke-Davis award in exptl. pathology, 1975. Mem.: Am. Soc. Clin. Investigation, Am. Soc. hemists, Soc. Exptl. Biology and Medicine, Am. Assn. Cancer Rsch., Am. Soc. Microbiology, NAS. Home: 1940 15th Ave E Seattle WA 98112-2829 Office Phone: 206-336-5572. E-mail: gtodaro@targetedgrowth.com.

**TODARO, MICHAEL PAUL,** economics professor, consultant; b. May 14, 1942; s. George Joseph and Annette (Piccini) Todaro; m. Donna Renee Crickenberger, June 17, 1974; 1 child, Lenora Jean. BA, Haverford Coll., 1964; MPhil, Yale U., 1966, PhD, 1967. Vis. lectr. Makerere U. Uganda, 1964—65; vis. sr. lectr. U. Nairobi, Kenya, 1968—70, 1974—76; assoc. dir. Rockefeller Found., N.Y.C., 1968—76; vis. prof. U. Calif., Santa Barbara, 1976—77; dep. dir. Population Coun., N.Y.C., 1977, sr. assoc., cons., 1978—; prof. econs. NYU, N.Y.C., 1977—97. Cons. Fund for Peace (Inst. for Study of World Politics), N.Y.C., 1979—. Author: Internal Migration in Developing Countries, 1976, Economics for a Developing World, 1991, Economic Development in the Third World, 2000; co-author: Economic Theory, 1969; mem. editl. bd.: Population and Devel. Rev., 1976—. Fellow, Woodrow Wilson Found., 1966, NDEA, 1966; grantee, Compton Found., 1981—84. Mem.: Population Assn. Am., Internat. Union for Sci. Study of Population, Am. Econ. Assn., Coun. on Fgn. Rels., Phi Beta Kappa. Roman Catholic. Office: Population Coun 1 Dag Hammarskjold Plz New York NY 10017

**TODARO, PETER M.,** lawyer; b. Easton, Pa., July 20, 1970; s. James M. and Bernice P. Todaro; m. Tanya M. Masri, Sept. 23, 1995; children: Isabella Marie, James Michael, Sofia Grace. BA in Econs. and Fgn. Affairs, U. Va., Charlottesville, 1992, JD, 1996. Bar: Va. 1996, US Ct. Appeals (4th cir.) 1996, DC 1997, US Ct. Appeals (DC cir.) 1998, US Ct. Appeals (7th cir.) 2001, US Ct. Appeals (3rd cir.) 2001, US Supreme Ct. 2002. Assoc. King & Spalding LLP, Washington, 1996—2004; ptnr. King & Spalding LLP, Washington, 2005—. Mem. editl. bd.: Va. Law Rev., 1994—96. Vol. Make-A-Wish Found. of Mid-Atlantic, 2006—, spkr., 2006—. Mem.: ABA (antitrust sect.), Va. Bar Assn., Order of the Coif. Avocation: skiing. Office: King & Spalding 1700 Pennsylvania Ave NW Washington DC 20006 Office Phone: 202-626-5518. Business E-Mail: ptodaro@kslaw.com.

**TODD, CAROL,** music educator; b. Paulding, Ohio, Apr. 2, 1942; d. Merle and Glendine Jeffery; m. Larry Todd, Aug. 15, 1964; children: Tara Michelle Lineweaver, Trista Lynn Todt. BS, Bowling Green State U., Ohio, 1963; MA, Ohio State U., 1968. Cert. music tchr. Ohio Edn. Dept., elem. tchr. Ohio Edn. Dept., kindergarten tchr. Ohio Edn. Dept. Music tchr. grades 1-12 Licking Heights Sch. Dist., Summit Station, Ohio, 1964—67; music tchr. grades 7-12 Hilliar City Schs., Ohio, 1967—69; music tchr. grades 9-12 Clark-Shawnee Local Schs., Springfield, Ohio, 1982—98; asst. prof. music Cedarville U., Ohio, 1998—2006, Wittenberg U., Springfield, 2000—. Dist. rep. curriculum course study Clark County, Ohio, 1988, Ohio, 93; guest condr. Springfield Symphony All-County Choir, 1992, Ohio Music Educators All-Dist. XII Women's Choir, Dayton, 1997, Clark County All-County Choir Festival, Springfield, 2001; adj. prof. music Clark State C.C., Springfield, 1996—2002; clinician Ohio Music Educators' State Conf., Columbus, Ohio, 2004, Cin., 05. Campaign collector March of Dimes, Springfield, 2000—; min. music Maumee United Meth. Ch., Ohio, 1972—74; leadership coun. Asbury United Meth. Ch., North Hampton, Ohio, 2000—10; active High Street United Meth. Ch., Springfield, 2004—. Recipient Tchr. Achievement award, Ashland Oil Co., 1993, 1995, 1997, Excellence in Tchg. award, Clark County News Assn.

1997. Mem.: Ohio Ret. Tchrs. Assn., Ohio Music Educators' Assn. (Ohio Music Educator 25+ Years award 1999), Am. Choral Dirs. Assn., Music Educators' Nat. Conf. (student chpt. advisor). Republican. Avocations: tennis, musical theater, singing, camping, bridge. Home: 3985 St James Ct Springfield OH 45502 Office: Wittenberg Univ Music Dept PO Box 720 Springfield OH 45501 Office Phone: 937-327-7341. Business E-Mail: ctodd@wittenberg.edu.

**TODD, CATHERINE JACKSON,** writer; b. L.A., Jan. 31, 1947; d. Hubert Edward and Carolyn Arden (Laws) Jackson; m. Timothy Gordon Todd, Aug. 24, 1968. AB cum laude, Occidental Coll., 1968; MA, Stanford U., 1969. Cert. tchr., Calif. Tchr. English, French Sequoia Union H.S., Redwood City, Calif., 1968-73, Country Day Sch., San José, Costa Rica, 1970-72; tchr. English Grossmont Union H.S., La Mesa, Calif., 1991-93; bus. svcs. writer San Diego, 1993—. Author: Bond of Honor, 1981, Marian, 1991, (as Elizabeth Jackson) A Brilliant Alliance, 1993, (as Elizabeth Jackson) Galatea's Revenge, 1993, (as Elizabeth Jackson) Rogue's Delight, 1995, Making Waves, 1997, Staying Cool, 1997, Exit Strategies, 2002, Secret Lives of Second Wives, 2003; contbr. articles to profl. jours. Mem. Authors Guild, Romance Writers Am., Phi Beta Kappa. E-mail: cathetoddbooks@aol.com.

**TODD, J. C. See COOPER, JANE**

**TODD, JAMES DALE,** federal judge; b. Scotts Hill, Tenn., May 20, 1943; s. James P. and Jeanette Grace (Duck) T.; m. Jeanie M. Todd, June 26, 1965; 2 children. BS, Lambuth Coll., 1965; M Combined Scis., U. Miss., 1968; JD, Memphis State U., 1972. Bar: Tenn. 1972, U.S. Dist. Ct. (we. dist.) Tenn. 1972, U.S. Ct. Appeals (6th cir.) 1973, U.S. Supreme Ct. 1975. Tchr. sci., chmn. sci. dept. Lyman High Sch., Longwood, Fla., 1965-68, Memphis U. Sch., 1968-72; ptnr. Waldrop, Farmer, Todd & Breen, P.A., 1972-83; cir. judge div. II 26th Jud. Dist., Jackson, Tenn., 1983-85; judge US Dist. Ct. (we. dist.) Tenn., Jackson, 1985-2001, chief judge, 2001—. Recipient Lifetime Achievement award Lambuth U., 2001; named Alumnus of Yr. Lambuth Coll. Alumni Assn., 1985. Fellow Tenn. Bar Found.; mem. Fed. Judges Assn. (bd. dirs. 1998-2002), Fed. Bar Assn., Jackson Madison County Bar Assn. (pres. 1978-79), Dist. Judges Assn. of 6th Cir. (pres. 2000-2001). Methodist. Office: US Dist Ct 111 S Highland Ave Jackson TN 38301-6107

**TODD, JAY MARLYN,** retired editor; b. Granger, Utah, July 28, 1936; s. Kenneth Christian and Gertrude A. (Viehweg) T.; m. Janet Cutrer, Mar. 20, 1964; children: Deborah, Jay Randall, Deanna, Jason Cutrer, Sarah Janet. BS, U. Utah, 1961. Staff writer Deseret News, Salt Lake City, 1960-61; tchr. Ch. Edn. Sys., various cities in Utah, Idaho, 1961-65; asst. editor, asst. mng. editor Improvement Era, Salt Lake City, 1966-70; mng. editor New Era, Salt Lake City, 1971-72, Ensign, Salt Lake City, 1972-2001. Author: Curtain Time USA: Ambassador of Inspiration, 1965, Saga of the Book of Abraham, 1968, (booklets) The Creed Haymond Story, 1979, A Historical Walking Tour of Holladay, 1996; editor: A Treasury of Edward J. Wood, 1983.

**TODD, JOE LEE,** historian; b. Bartlesville, Okla., Sept. 28, 1946; s. Harold Albert and Mildred Viola Todd. Student, Okla. State U., 1964-66; BA in Anthropology, U. Okla., 1974; postgrad. in Anthropology, U. Tex., Austin, 1979-81. Curator of collections Okla. Hist. Soc., Oklahoma City, 1971-76; dir. 45th Infantry div. mus., Oklahoma City, 1976-78; curator Ft. Hood (Tex.) Mus., 1978-82; oral historian, archivist Okla. Hist. Soc., Oklahoma City, 1982—. Cons. Confederate Air Force, Midland, Tex., 1990—, Andersonville (Ga.) POW Camp, 1991—. Author: Pipe-Tomahawks in the Oklahoma Historical Society, 1976, Native American Interviews, oral histories, 1985, USS Oklahoma, Remembrance of a Great Lady, 1990. Bd. dirs. Sacred Heart (Okla.) Indian Mission, 1989-95. With U.S. Army, 1966-69, Okla. Nat. Guard, 1975-78, Tex. Nat. Guard, 1978-83, USAR, 1983-96. Decorated Air medal; recipient Humanitarian Svc. medal U.S. Army, 1992, Vietnam Svc. medal, 1969, Kuwaiti Liberation medal, 1991. Republican. Episcopalian. Office: Okla Hist Soc 2100 N Lincoln Blvd Oklahoma City OK 73105-4907 Home: RR 5 Box 415 Bartlesville OK 74003-9315

**TODD, JOHN,** mathematician, educator; b. Carnacally, Ireland, May 16, 1911; came to U.S., 1947, naturalized, 1953; s. William Robert and Catherine (Stewart) T.; m. Olga Taussky, Sept. 29, 1938. BS, Queen's U., Belfast, Ireland, 1931; research student, St. John's Coll., Cambridge U., Eng., 1931-33. Lectr. Queen's U., 1933-37, King's Coll., London, 1937-49; chief computation lab., then chief numerical analysis Nat. Bur. Standards, 1947-57; prof. math. Calif. Inst. Tech., 1957—; Fulbright prof. Vienna, Austria, 1965. Hon. fellow Barbara Bodichon Found., Girton Coll., Cambridge (Eng.) U., 2005. Author, editor books on numerical analysis and tables; editor in chief: Numerische Mathematik, 1959—; assoc. editor Aequationes Mathematicae, 1967-85, 89-95, Jour. Approximation Theory, 1967-93. Mem. Am. Math. Soc., Soc. Indsl. and Applied Math., Math. Assn. Am. (gov. 1980-83) Office: Calif Inst Technology Mathematics 253 # 37 Pasadena CA 91125-3700 Fax: (626) 585-1728.

**TODD, JOHN DICKERSON, JR.,** retired lawyer; b. Macon, Ga., June 30, 1912; s. J.D. and Hazel (McManus) T.; m. Mellicent McWhorter, Mar. 7, 1943; children: Rosalind (Mrs. Jack Harding Tedards, Jr.), John D. Student, Va. Mil. Inst., 1930-32; LLB, U. Ga., 1935. Bar: S.C. 1935. With firm Hingson & Todd, 1935-51; partner firm Leatherwood, Walker, Todd & Mann, Greenville, SC, 1952-2000; sr. partner; judge Greenville City Ct., 1939; atty. County of Greenville, 1948-56; mem. bd. bar examiners State of S.C.; ret. Chmn. S.C. Judicial Study Commn., 1995. Served to maj. AUS, 1941-45. Mem.: ABA, Greenville County Bar (past pres.), Greenville Jr. C. of C. (pres.), S.C. Bar Assn. (bd. govs., pres. 1978—), 4th U.S. Cir. Jud. Conf., Am. Bar Found., Am. Coll. Trial Lawyers, Poinsett Club, Greenville Country Club (past pres.), Greenville Kiwanis (past pres.), Sigma Nu, Phi Delta Phi. Baptist. Home: 200 Riverside Dr Greenville SC 29605-1133

**TODD, JOHN EDWARD,** retired farmer; b. Waynesboro, Va., Feb. 8, 1924; s. Andrew James Todd and Clare Elizabeth Kennedy; m. Jessica Frances Swisher, June 8, 1946; children: John Jr., Cheryl, Jeffrey S., Darcel(dec.), Michell L. BS, U. Md., 1965; MEd, U. Va., 1973, D of Edn., 1976. Commd. lt. U.S. Army, 1952, advanced through grades to capt., 1957, sgt. air crew, 1942—47; sgt. supply specialist USAF, 1948—50; lt. airborne US Army, 1950—56, lt. spl. forces A team, 1956—57, capt. spl. forces, 1957—63, 1963—64, ret., 1964; owner beef cattle farm, 1966—98. Mem.: Reserve Officers Assn., Military Officer Assn. Am., Nat. Assn. Uniformed Svcs., Disabled Am. Vets., VFW, Am. Legion. Republican. Presbyterian. Home: 368 Poor Creek Ln Greenville VA 24440-1809

**TODD, JOHN JOSEPH,** lawyer; b. St. Paul, Mar. 16, 1927; s. John Alfred and Martha Agnes (Jagoe) T.; m. Dolores Jean Shanahan, Sept. 9, 1950; children: Richard M., Jane E., John P. Student, St. Thomas Coll., 1944, 46-47; B.Sci. and Law, U. Minn., 1949, LL.B., 1950. Bar: Minn. 1951. Practice in South St. Paul, Minn., 1951-72; partner Thuet and Todd, 1953-72; assoc. justice Minn. Supreme Ct., 1972-85; sole practice West St. Paul, 1985-92; of counsel Brenner & Glassman Ltd., Mpls., 1992—99, Orme & Assoc., Eagan, Minn., 1999—. With USNR, 1945—46. Mem. state bar assns., VFW. Home: 6689 Argenta Trl W Inver Grove Heights MN 55077-2208 Office: Orme & Associates 4040 Nicols Rd Eagan MN 55121 Office Phone: 651-688-7646. Personal E-Mail: jjbtodd@comcast.net. Business E-Mail: jtodd@ormelaw.com.

**TODD, KARYN L.,** lawyer; b. Milw., Feb. 28, 1970; d. Doyle Fred and Linda Kay (Croft) Todd. BA, Ea. Mich. U., 1994; JD, St. Thomas U., 1997. Bar: Fla. 1997, U.S. Dist. Ct., So. Dist. 1998. Atty. Law Offices of Karyn L. Todd, Miami, 2000—. Investigator Fla. Bar, Miami, 2001—05. Hon. chmn. Rep. Congl. Com. Small Bus., Miami, 2003. Recipient Bus. Woman of Yr., Nat. Rep. Congl. Com., 2003, Nat. Leadership award, 2003. Mem.: Fla. Bar Assn., Am. Immigration Lawyers Assn., ABA. Office: Law Offices of Karyn L Todd PA 80 SW 8th St Ste 2000 Miami FL 33130 Office Phone: 305-545-0000. Business E-Mail: karyn@viveamerica.com.

**TODD, LEE TROVER, JR.,** academic administrator, electrical engineer; b. Earlington, Ky., May 6, 1946; s. Lee T. Todd; m. Patricia Brantley; children: Troy, Kathryn. BSEE, U. Ky., 1968; MS, MIT, 1970, PhD in Elec. Engring., 1973. IBM postdoctoral fellow MIT, 1973-74; asst. prof. engring. U. Ky., Lexington, 1974-78, assoc. prof., 1978-87, pres., 2001—; chmn., chief exec. officer DataBeam Corp., Lexington, 1983—2000; v.p. Hughes Display Products, Lexington, 1993—93; sr. v.p. pres. Lotus Devel. Corp., 2000—01. Chmn. Ky. Sci. & Tech. Coun., Lexington, 1987—; mem. Ky. Epscor Com., 1985—, Ky. Acad. Sci., 1988; chair Southeastern Conf. Com. on Academic Initiatives; mem. Cou. of Edn. Commn. Contbr. articles to profl. jours. Chmn., deacon Calvary Bapt. Ch., Lexington, 1989; bd. dirs. Ky. Econ. Devel. Corp., Frankfort, Georgetown Coll., Ky. Named Entrepreneur of Yr., INC mag., 1989; recipient Outstanding Alumnus award U. Ky. Coll. Engring., 1989, Small Bus. of Yr. award Lexington C. of C., U.S. Gt. Tchr. award, 1983; Hertz Found. fellow, 1968-73. Mem. NSF, Ky. Soc. Profl. Engrs. (Award of Achievement 1990), U. Ky. Alumni Assn., Leadership Ky., Louisville Adv. Tech. Coun. Baptist. Achievements include patents in field. Office: Pres Office U Ky 101 Main Building Lexington KY 40506-0032 Office Phone: 859-257-1701. Office Fax: 859-257-1760. E-mail: ltodd@email.uky.edu.*

**TODD, LINDA MARIE,** nutrition researcher, circulation manager, financial consultant, pilot; b. LA, Mar. 30, 1948; d. Ithel Everette and Janet Marie Fredricks; m. William MacKenzie Cook, Jan. 11, 1982 (div. Oct. 1989); m. Robert Oswald Todd, Apr. 8, 1990; 1 child, Jesse MacKenzie Todd. BA in Psychology and Sociology, U. Colo., 1969; student in Psychology, U. No. Colo., 1970; ins. and estate planning courses, 1990—, mgmt. tng. programs, 2001—. Pilot lic., weather cert., FCC lic., Calif. life ins. lic., coll. teaching credential; registered with Nat. Assn. Securities Dealers. Counselor Jeffco Juvenile Detention Ctr., Golden, Colo., 1969-71; communications Elan Vital, Denver, 1971-81; legal sec. Fredman, Silverberg & Lewis, San Diego, 1980-82; escrow supr. Performance Mktg. Concepts, Olympic Valley, Calif., 1982-85; mgmt. commn. instr. Sierra Coll., Truckee, Calif., 1986-87; regional mgr. Primerica Fin. Svcs., Reno, 1987-91; air traffic, weather advisor Truckee Tahoe Airport Dist., Calif., 1986-96; circulation mgr. Tahoe World Newspaper, 2001—03, Sierra Sun, 2001—. Student tour leader, air show organizer Truckee (Calif.) Tahoe Airport, 1986-96; fin. cons. Primerica Fin. Svcs., Truckee, 1987-91; gen. agt. TTS Fin., 1992—; co-founder Todd Nutrition, 1995—; co-owner Todd Aero, 1990—; bd. dirs. Pacific Crest Fin. Corp., 1996—. Editor: (newsletter) Communications, 1975. Chorus mem. operas and musicals, 1960s-70s; prodn. crew Lake Tahoe Summer Music Festivals, 2000-03; sec. gen. Arapahoe H.S. Model UN, Littleton, Colo., 1965; del. State Model UN, Colo., 1966; conv. del. Elan Vital, The Ninety-Nines, Inc.; pub. affairs officer CAP. Univ. scholar Littleton (Colo.) Edn. Assn., 1966, flight scholar The Ninety-Nines Inc., Reno, 1990; named Recruiter of Month, Al Williams Primerica, Reno, 1987. Mem. CAP, Elan Vital, Plane Talkers, The Ninety Nines, Planetary Soc. Avocations: hiking, skiing, swimming, flying, soaring. Home and Office: PO Box 1303 Truckee CA 96160-1303 Personal E-Mail: toddaero@sbcglobal.net.

**TODD, MARGARET DONNELLAN,** librarian, director; MLS, U. So. Calif.; MBA, Pepperdine U. Sr. libr. mgr. Orange Pub. Libr., Calif.; dir. Whittier Pub. Libr., Calif., 1989—2001; county libr. County of LA Pub. Libr., Calif., 2001—. Mem.: Calif. Libr. Assn. Office: County of LA Pub Libr 7400 East Imperial Highway Downey CA 90241-7011 Office Phone: 562-940-8400. E-mail: mdtodd@gw.colapl.org.*

**TODD, MARY BETH,** oncologist, researcher; b. Tulsa, Okla., June 10, 1951; d. Earl K. and Edith (Beaty) T. BA, Okla. City U., 1972; postgrad., U. Tulsa, 1973-74; DO, Okla. State U., 1978. Assoc. rsch. scientist Yale Sch. Medicine, New Haven, 1984-86; dir. outpatient svc. Yale Medical Sch., New Haven, 1986-93; asst. prof. Sch. Medicine Yale U., New Haven, 1986-91, assoc. prof., 1991-93; assoc. prof. medicine UMDNJ-RWJMS, New Brunswick, 1993—2002, prof. medicine, 2002—; deputy dir. The Cancer Inst. N.J., New Brunswick, NJ, 1993—, COO, chief med. officer, 2005—. Scientific adv. panel for immunology svcs. Food & Drug Adminstrn., Washington, 1991-95; scientific adv. bd. HEM Pharmeceuticals Corp., 1991-93; external medical adv. bd. Conn. Hospice, 1990-92; co-chair N.J. Working Group to Improve Outcomes in Cancer Patients. Recipient grants Nat. Inst. Health, 1989-98. Mem. Am. Coll. Physicians, Am. Fedn. Clinical Rsch., Am. Soc. Clinical Oncology, Am. Assn. Cancer Rsch., Am. Soc. Hemetology, Internat. Soc. Interferon and Cytokine Rsch. Office: The Cancer Inst NJ 195 Little Albany St New Brunswick NJ 08903-2681

**TODD, NORMA ROSS,** retired government official; b. Butler, Pa., Oct. 3, 1920; d. William Bryson and Doris Mae (Ferguson) Ross; m. Alden Frank Miller, Jr., Apr. 16, 1940 (dec. Feb. 1975); 1 child, Alden Frank III; m. Jack R. Todd, Dec. 23, 1977 (dec. Sept. 1990). Student, Pa. State U., Donora, 1944—46, Yale U., New Haven, Conn., 1954-57. Exec. mgr. Donora C. of C., Pa., 1950-57, pres. Pa., 1972; exec. mgr. Donora Cmty. Chest, 1950-57; office mgr. Donora Golden Jubilee, 1951; staff writer Donora Herald-American, 1957, city editor, 1957-70; assoc. editor Daily Herald, Donora and Manongahela, 1970-73; svc. rep. Pitts. Telesvc. Ctr., Social Security Adminstrn., HHS, 1977-83. Mem. Mayor's Adv. Coun., Donora, 1965-69, Citizens' Adv. Coun., Donora, 1965-69; mem. Donora Bd. Edn., 1954-60, pres., 1960; mem. Donora Borough Coun., 1970-72; bd. dirs. Mon Valley chpt. ARC, 1964-99, sec. bd., 1964-97, chmn. bd. dirs., 1997-99, mem. lifetime adv. bd., 2000; bd. dirs. Washington County Tourism Agy., 1970-90, sec., 1972-90; bd. dirs. Washington County History and Landmarks Found., 1971-80, 91-92, sec., 1975-80, 91-93, hon. life mem., 1996; bd. dirs. Mon Valley YMCA, 1960-66, Mon Valley coun. Camp Fire Girls, 1965-79, Mon Valley Drug and Alcoholism Coun., 1971-78; hon. life mem. Pa. Congress PTAs; bd. dirs. United Way Mon Valley, 1973-82, chmn. pub. rels., 1973-74; rep. nat. com. Eisenhower Commn., 2005; Platinum mem. Presdl. Task Force, 2004-06; commr. Rep. Sen. Inner Cir., 2005. Recipient Fine Arts Festival of Pa. Poetry first prize award Fedn. Women's Clubs, 1987, 1st and 2d pl. awards for photography Washington County Fine Arts Festival, County Fedn. Women's Clubs, 1990, Disting. Svc. award Donora Rotary Club, 1997, Millenium Peace award, India, 2001, Two World Poets award J. Mark Press, 2002, U.S. Rep. Senatorial Medal of Freedom, 2003, 2006, Congl. Order Merit, 2003, Cert of Recognition U.S. Justice Found, 2004, cert. appreciation Ronald Reagan Presdl. Found., 2006; pub. in Best Poems of 1995 Nat. Libr. of Poetry, Best Poems of 1996, Best Poems of 1997, Outstanding Poets of 1998, Am. at the Millennium The Best Poets of the 20th Century, The Best Poems and Poets of 2001, The Best Poems and Poets of 2002, of 2003, 04, 05 and numerous anthologies in U.S., Italy, Great Britain and India. Mem. Svc. Corps Ret. Execs. (sec. 1998-2005), Pa. Soc. Newspaper Editors, Pitts. Press Club, Donora C. of C. (pres. 1971-72), DAR (regent Monongahela Valley chpt. 1974-77, treas. 1992-2001), Internat. Platform Assn. (finalist Acad. of Poets Competition, 2001), World Poetry Soc. Internat., Internat. Poets Acad., Famous Poet Soc., U.S. Poets, Metverse Muse (hon. life, India), Washington County Poetry Soc. (pres. 1967-69), Donora Hist. Soc. (curator 1990—), Family of Bruce Internat. Descs. of King Robert the Bruce of Scotland, Clan Ross Assn., Mt. Vernon Ladies Assn., Washington County Fedn. Women's Clubs (rec. sec. 1964-66, pub. rels chmn. 1990-92), Order Ea. Star (worthy matron 1966-67, treas. 1986-94, 98—2003, bd. dirs. Western Pa. Eastern Star Home 1997-98, adv. bd. Masonic Eastern Star Home-West 1998-2000), White Shrine of Jerusalem (high priestess 1973-74, treas. 1995-2001), Order of Amaranth (royal matron 1966, dist. dep. 3 times, grand rep. W.Va. 1979-80), Donora Forecast (pres. 1957-59), Donora Unidon (pres. 1965-66, 56-57). Avocation: genealogy. Home: Overlook Ter Donora PA 15033 also: 1310 Mckean Ave Donora PA 15033-2200

**TODD, ROBERT FRANKLIN, III,** oncologist, educator; b. Granville, Ohio, Apr. 16, 1948; m. Susan Erhard, 1977; children: Currier Nathaniel, Andrew Joseph. AB, Duke U., 1970, PhD, 1975, MD, 1976. Diplomate Am. Bd. Internal Medicine. Intern Peter Bent Brigham Hosp., Boston, 1976-77, resident, 1977-78; fellow in oncology Sidney Farber Cancer Inst., Boston, 1978-80; clin. fellow in medicine Harvard Med. Sch., Boston, 1978-81; postdoctoral fellow divsn. tumor immunology Sidney Farber Cancer Inst., Boston, 1979-81; asst. prof. medicine Harvard Med. Sch., Boston, 1981-84;

assoc. prof. internal medicine U. Mich., Ann Arbor, 1984-88, assoc. prof. cellular and molecular biology, 1985-88, assoc. dir. divsn. hematology-oncology internal medicine, 1987-91, prof. internal medicine, 1988—, assoc. chair for rsch. dept. internal medicine, 1989-91, assoc. chair dept. internal medicine, 1991-93, chief divsn. hematology-oncology dept. internal medicine, 1993—, assoc. v.p. rsch., 1999—2005, Frances and Victor Ginsberg prof. hematology/oncology, 1999—. Attending physician U. Mich. Hosps., 1984—. Contbr. numerous articles to profl. jours.; patentee in field. Mem.: Assn. Am. Physicians, Am. Soc. Clin. Investigation, S.W. Oncology Group, Ctrl. Soc. Clin. Rsch. (councilor 1997—, pres. 2001—02), Am. Fedn. Clin. Rsch. (councilor midwest chpt. 1986—89), Am. Soc. Hematology (councilor 2005—), Soc. Leukocyte Biology (councilor 1996—99), Am. Soc. Clin. Oncology, Am. Assn. Cancer Rsch., Am. Assn. Immunologists, ACP, Alpha Omega Alpha, Phi Beta Kappa. Office: U Mich Med Sch 1500 E Med Ctr Dr 7216 CCGC Ann Arbor MI 48109-0948 Business E-Mail: robtodd@umich.edu.

**TODD, RONALD GARY,** lawyer; b. Spokane, Wash., Dec. 12, 1946; s. Theodore H. and Dorothea I. (Swanson) T.; m. Natalie A., June 16, 1973; children: Russell E., Brian N., David E. AB, Cornell U., 1969; JD, Columbia U., 1972. Bar: N.Y. 1973, U.S. Dist. Ct. (so. and ea. dists.) N.Y. 1975, U.S. Ct. Appeals (2d cir.) 1975, U.S. Supreme Ct. 1976, D.C. 1993. Atty. Dewey Ballantine, N.Y.C., 1973-79, Simpson Thacher & Bartlett, N.Y.C., 1980-82; atty., ptnr. Golenbock & Barell, N.Y.C., 1982-89; ptnr. Reid & Priest (now Thelen Reid & Priest LLP), N.Y.C., 1989-2000; chief counsel J.P. Morgan Title Agy. LLC, 2000—05; asst. gen. counsel JP Morgan Chase & Co., 2000—05; v.p. First Am. Title Ins. Co. N.Y., N.Y.C., 2005—, counsel nat. underwriting, 2005—. Instr., guest lectr. NYU Sch. Continuing Edn., 1983-90; adv. bd. Commonwealth Land Title and TransAm. Title Ins. Co., N.Y.C., 1992-97. Contbr. articles to profl. jours. Pres., bd. dirs. Seven Bridges Field Club, 1982—85. Mem. ABA (real property sect. 1973—), N.Y. Bar Assn. (real property sect. 1973—), D.C. Bar Assn. (real property sect. 1992—). Avocations: instrumental music, tennis. Office: First Am Title Ins Co NY 633 Third Ave New York NY 10017 Business E-Mail: ronald.todd@jpmchase.com, rgtodd@firstam.com.

**TODD, SHIRLEY ANN,** school system administrator; b. May 23, 1935; d. William Leonard and Margaret Judy (Simmons) Brown; m. Thomas Byron Todd, July 7, 1962 (dec. July 1977). BS in Edn., Madison Coll., 1956; MEd, U. Va., 1971. Cert. tchr. Va. Elem. sch. tchr. Fairfax County Sch. Bd., Fairfax, Va., 1956—66, mid. sch. tchr., 1966—71; guidance counselor James F. Cooper Mid. Sch., McLean, Va., 1971—88, dir. guidance, 1988—96; chmn. mktg. Lake Anne Joint Venture, Falls Church, Va., 1979—81, mng. ptnr., 1980—82. Del. Fairfax County Rep. Conv., 1985. Fellow: Fairfax Edn. Assn. (bd. dirs. 1968—70, profl. rights and responsibilities commn. 1970—72); mem.: ASCD, NEA, Va. Sch. Counselors Assn., Va. Counselors Assn., Va. Counselors Assn. (exec. com. 1987), No. Va. Counselors Assn. (exec. bd. 1982—83, hospitality and social chmn.), Va. Edn. Assn. (state com. on local assns. and urban affairs 1969—70), Vintage Ladies of No. Va. (newsletter editor 2002—03), Women's Golf Assn. (pres. 1997—98), Welcome Club of No. Va. (pres. 2003—04), Chantilly Nat. Golf and Country Club (v.p. social 1981—82). Baptist. Avocations: golf, tennis. Home: 6543 Bay Tree Ct Falls Church VA 22041-1001

**TODD, VIRGIL HOLCOMB,** clergyman, theology studies educator; b. Jordonia, Tenn., June 22, 1921; s. George Thurman and Nellie Mai (Dutton) T.; m. Irene Rolman, Sept. 21, 1941; 1 child, Donald Edwin. BA, Bethel Coll., 1945; BD, Cumberland Presbyn. Sem., 1947; MA, Scarritt Coll., 1948; PhD, Vanderbilt U., 1956. Ordained to ministry Presbyn. Ch., 1944. Minister Cumberland Presbyn. Chs., Tenn. and Ky., 1943-52; assoc. prof. Bethel Coll., McKenzie, Tenn., 1952-54; prof. of Old Testament Memphis Theol. Sem., 1954-2001, ret., 2001. Interim minister Presbyn. chs. in Tenn., Ky. and Miss., 1952—; vice-moderator Gen. Assembly Cumberland Presbyn. Ch., 1984-85, moderator, 1985-86. Author: Prophet Without Portfolio (2d Isaiah), 1972, A New Look at an Old Prophet (Ezekiel), 1977, Biblical Eschatology, 1985. Active Shelby (County) United Neighbors, Memphis, 1973-74, United Way of Greater Memphis, 1974-82. Mem. Soc. Bibl. Lit., Memphis Ministers' Assn. Lodges: Civitan (chaplain, bd. dirs. local chpt.). Democrat. Presbyterian. Avocations: travel, golf. Home: 3095 E Glengarry Rd Memphis TN 38128-2911

**TODD, WILLIAM MICHAEL,** lawyer; b. Cleve., Dec. 13, 1952; s. William Charles and Jennie Ann (Diana) T. BA, U. Notre Dame, 1973; JD, Ohio State U., 1976. Bar: Ohio 1976, U.S. Dist. Ct. (so. dist.) Ohio 1977, U.S. Supreme Ct. 1987. Assoc. Porter, Wright, Morris & Arthur, Columbus, Ohio, 1976-82, ptnr., 1983-93, Squire, Sanders & Dempsey, Columbus, 1993—. Trustee Callvac Svcs., Columbus, Ohio, 1985—91, pres., 1988; trustee Opera Columbus, 2004—. Mem. ABA (governing com. forum on health law 1988-91), Ohio Bar Assn., Columbus Bar Assn., Am. Soc. Med. Assn. Counsel, Am. Bd. Trial Advocates, Ohio Soc. Healthcare Attys. (pres. 1999-2000), Am. Health Lawyers Assn., Rep. Nat. Lawyers Assn. (chmn. Ohio chpt. 2005—), Columbus Athletic Club. Roman Catholic. Avocations: music, recreational sports. Office: Squire Sanders & Dempsey 41 S High St Columbus OH 43215-6101 Office Phone: 614-365-2712. Business E-Mail: wtodd@ssd.com.

**TODD, ZANE GREY,** retired utilities executive; b. Hanson, Ky., Feb. 3, 1924; s. Marshall Elvin and Kate (McCormick) T.; m. Marysnow Stone, Feb. 8, 1950 (dec. 1983); m. Frances Z. Anderson, Jan. 6, 1984. Student, Evansville Coll., 1947-49; BS summa cum laude, Purdue U., 1951, DEng (hon.), 1979; postgrad., U. Mich., 1965; DHL, U. Indpls., 1993. Fingerprint classifier FBI, 1942-43; electric system planning engr. Indpls. Power & Light Co., 1951-56, spl. assignments supr., 1956-60, head elec. system planning, 1960-65, head substation design div., 1965-68, head distbn. engring. dept., 1968-70, asst. to v.p., 1970-72, v.p., 1972-74, exec. v.p., 1974-75, pres., 1975-81, chmn., chief exec. officer, 1976-89, dir., chmn. exec. com., 1989-94, chief exec. officer, 1981-89; chmn., pres. IPALCO Enterprises, Inc., Indpls., 1983-89, dir., chmn. exec. com., 1989-94; chmn. bd., chief exec. officer Mid-Am. Capital Resources, Inc. subs. IPALCO Enterprises, Inc., Indpls., 1984-89, also bd. dirs., 1984-94. Gen. mgr. Mooresville (Ind.) Pub. Svc. Co., Inc., 1956-60; bd. dirs. Nat. City Bank Ind. (formerly Merch. Nat. Corp.), 1975-94, Am. States Ins. Co., 1976-94; hon. dir. 500 Festival Assocs., Inc., pres. 1987. Originator probability analysis of power system reliability; contbr. articles to tech. jours. and mags. Past pres. adv. bd. St. Vincent Hosp.; past chmn., bd. trustees Ind. Cen. U. (now U. Indpls.); Nat. and Greater Indpls. adv. bds. Salvation Army, 1984-96; bd. govs. Associated Colls. of Ind. 1979-92. Sgt. AUS, 1943-47. Recipient William Booth award Salvation Army, 1994; named Disting. Engring. Alumnus Purdue U., 1976, Outstanding Elec. Engr. Purdue U., 1992, Knight of Malta, Order of St. John of Jerusalem, 1986. Fellow IEEE (past chmn. power sys. engring. com.); mem. ASME, NSPE, Power Engring. Soc., Ind. Fiscal Policy Inst. (bd. govs.), Ind. C. of C., Indpls. C. of C., Mooresville C. of C. (past pres.), PGA Nat. Country Club, Ulen Country Club, Indpls. Athletic Club (past bd. dirs.), Meridian Hills Country Club (past bd. dirs.), Skyline Club (bd. govs.), Newcomen Soc. (past chmn. Ind.), Rotary, Lions (past pres.), Eta Kappa Nu, Tau Beta Pi.

**TODD COPLEY, JUDITH A.,** engineering educator; b. Wakefield, West Yorkshire, Eng., Dec. 13, 1950; arrived in US, 1978; d. Marley and Joan Mary (Birkinshaw) Booth; m. David Michael Todd, June 17, 1972 (div. June 1981); m. Stephen Michael Copley, Aug. 3, 1984; 1 child, Amy Elizabeth. BA in Materials Sci., Cambridge U., Eng., 1972, MA, PhD in Metall./Materials Sci., 1976. Rsch. asst. Imperial Coll. Sci. and Tech., London, 1976-78; rsch. assoc. SUNY, Stonybrook, 1978; rsch. engr. U. Calif., Berkeley, 1979-81; asst. prof. materials sci. and mech. engring. U. So. Calif., L.A., 1982—90; assoc. prof. metall. and materials engring. Ill. Inst. Tech., Chgo., 1990-97, assoc. chair mech. materials and aerospace engring., 1995—2001, prof. materials and mech. engring., 1997—2002; assoc. dean rsch. Armour Coll. Engring. and Sci., 2001—02; P.B. Breneman dept. head chair dept. engring. sci. and mechanics Pa. State U., University Park, 2002—. Mem. task force Materials Property Coun., N.Y.C., 1979—89; prof. Iron and Steel Soc., 1996—2002;

mem. editl. bds. Contbr. articles to profl. jours.; patentee in field. Recipient Brit. Univs. Student Travel award, 1972, Brit. Fedn. Univ. Women award, 1972, Faculty Rsch. award Oak Ridge (Tenn.) Nat. Lab., 1986, Vanadium award British Inst. Materials, 1990; Kathryn Kingswell Meml. scholar, 1972, Julia Beveridge Award, IIT, 1998, Cert. Appreciation Am. Soc. Mech. Engrs., 1995, 97, Forging Industry Ednl. Rsch. Found., 1993, Booz-Allen and Hamilton Award for Tchg. and Svc., Ill. Inst. Tech., 1996, Mary Ewart Traveling Scholarship, Cambridge Univ., 1972, Sci. Rsch. Coun. Fellowship and Overseas Travel Award, 1972. Fellow ASM Internat., ASME Internat. (chmn. materials and fabrication com. 1993-97, pressure vessel and piping divsn. membership chair PVP divsn., 1997-2001, assoc. editor Jour. Pressure Vessel and Piping Tech. 1994-2001, exec. com. and publs. chair PVP divsn. 2001-05, v.p. mfg. group 2002-05, tech. program chair, 2004-05, tech. conf. chair 2005—, bd. on women and miniorites award 1997), Soc. Engring. Sci. (bd. dirs. 2006—), Assn. Women in Sci., ASM Internat. (chmn. LA chpt. 1986-87, coun. materials sci. divsn. 1984-89); mem. AIME (Rsch. award 1983), ASTM, AAUW, Soc. Women Engrs. (sr.) Electron Microscopy Soc., Electrochem. Soc., Hist. Metallurgy Soc., Nat. Soc. Corrosion Engrs. (Seed grant award 1983), Microbeam Analysis Soc., Soc. Mfg. Engrs. (sr.), Instn. Materials, Chartered (sr.) Engr. Status, Minerals, Metals, Materials Soc. of the Am. Inst. Mining, Metall. Petroleum Engrs., Am. Ceramics Soc., Ill. Microscopical Soc., Soc. Engring. Sci. (mem. bd. dirs.). Avocation: archaeology. Office: Pennsylvania State Univ Dept Engring Sci and Mechanics 212 Earth-Engring Sci Bldg University Park PA 16802-6812 Office Phone: 814-863-0771. E-mail: jtodd@psu.edu.

**TODHUNTER, JOHN ANTHONY,** toxicologist, consultant; b. Cali, Valle, Colombia, Oct. 9, 1949; s. John Arthur and Teresa Maria (Torres) T.; divorced, 1986; children: Jennifer, Julia; m. Holli Wilson, Apr. 19, 1986, 1 child, Jacqueline Rose. BSc, UCLA, 1971; MSc, Calif. State U., 1973; PhD, U. Calif., Santa Barbara, 1976. Diplomate Am. Bd. Toxicology, Am. Bd. Forensic Examiners. Instr. Calif. State U., L.A., 1972-73; rsch. asst. U. Calif., Santa Barbara, 1973-76; fellow Roche Inst. Molecular Biology, Nutley, NJ, 1976-78; asst. prof. Cath. U. Am., Washington, 1978-81, chmn. Biochemistry Program, 1980-81; asst. adminstr. U.S. EPA, Washington, 1981-83; cons. Sci. Regulatory Svcs. Internat., Washington, 1983-91; pres. SRS Internat. Corp., 1991—, SRS Internat. Health Care Group, 1995—; CEO OAM Pharmaceuticals, 2006—. Expert advisor European regional office WHO, Stockholm, 1984; mem. Hazardous Waste Siting Bd., Annapolis, Md., 1980-81. Contbr. articles to profl. jours. Bd. dirs. Reagan Alumni Assn., Washington, 1985—; vol. Am. Cancer Soc., Washington, 1988-93; mem. Presdl. Transition Team, Washington, 1980. U. Calif. Bd. Regents fellow, 1975, B.R. Baker Meml. fellow dept. chemistry U. Calif., Santa Barbara, 1976. Fellow Am. Inst. Chemists (dir. at large 1989-92, vice chmn. bd. 1992); mem. Soc. of Toxicology, Am. Chem. Soc., Soc. for Risk Analysis, N.Y. Acad. Sci. Business E-Mail: todhunter@srsinternational.com.

**TODMAN, MICHAEL A.,** manufacturing executive; b. St. Thomas, U.S. V.I. BBA, Georgetown U. Formerly with Price Waterhouse and Co., Wang Labs., Inc.; dir. fin. United Kingdom Whirlpool, Inc., 1993—95, from gen. mgr. No. Europe to v.p. consumer svcs. Whirlpool Europe, 1993—95, contr. N.Am., 1995—96, v.p. product mgmt., 1996—97, v.p. Sears sales and mktg., 1997—99, v.p. sales and mktg. N.Am., 1999—2001, corp. exec. v.p., mem. corp. exec. com., 2001, corp. exec. v.p., pres. Whirlpool Europe, 2001—. Office: Whirlpool Inc 2000 N M-63 Benton Harbor MI 49022

**TODREAS, NEIL EMMANUEL,** nuclear engineering educator; b. Peabody, Mass., Dec. 17, 1935; s. David and Anna (Gendleman) T.; m. Carol S. Schonberg, June 19, 1958; children: Timothy, Ian. BSM.E., MS, Cornell U., 1958; ScD in Nuc. Engring., MIT, 1966. Asst. prof. dept. nuc. engring. MIT, Cambridge, Mass., 1970-71, assoc. prof., 1971-75, prof., 1975—, Kepco prof. nuc. engring. and prof. mech. engring., 1992—, head dept. nuc. engring., 1981-89. Served to lt. (j.g.) USN, 1958-62. Named Disting. Tchr., Ruth and Joel Spira award MIT Sch. Engring., 1995. Fellow: ASME, Am. Nuc. Soc. (Tech. Achievement award for outstanding contbns. to thermal hydraulics 1994, Arthur Holly Compton award for outstanding educators in nuc. engring. 1995, Henry DeWolf-Smyth award 2005); mem.: Internat. Nuc. Energy Acad., Nat. Acad. Engring., Sigma Xi, Tau Beta Pi, Pi Tau Sigma. Office: MIT Bldg 24 Rm 205 77 Massachusetts Ave Cambridge MA 02139-4307 E-mail: todreas@mit.edu.

**TOEDT, D(ELL) C(HARLES), III,** lawyer; b. Maxwell AFB, Ala., Nov. 17, 1954; m. Maretta A. Comfort. BA with high honors, U. Tex., 1973, JD, 1981. Bar: Tex. 1982, U.S. Patent and Trademark Office 1983, U.S. Dist. Ct. (so. dist.) Tex. 1984, U.S. Ct. Appeals (fed. cir.) 1984, U.S. Supreme Ct. 1991, Calif. 1996. Atty. Schlanger, Cook, Cohn, Mills & Grossberg, Houston, 1982-83, Arnold, White & Durkee, Houston, 1983-99; v.p., gen. counsel BindView Corp., Houston, 1999—2006. Adj. prof. S. Tex. Coll. Law, 1988—90. Assoc. editor: Tex. Law Rev., 1981—82, author, editor: Licensing Law Handbook: Computer Software Issues, 1987; editor: Law and Bus. Computer Software, 1989—2002; contbr. articles to profl. jours. Served to lt. USN, 1974—79. mem.: ABA (chmn. computer-related coms. 1985—96, elected mem. coun. sect. intellectual property law 1999—2000). Office Phone: 713-893-3925. Personal E-mail: dc.toedt@toedt.com.

**TOEDT, MICHAEL EDGAR,** military officer, hospital administrator; s. Klaus Friederich and Gretel Toedt; m. Dominique Marie Gooby; children: Matthew Klaus, Daniel Robert. BS in Applied Physics, Ga. Inst. of Tech., 1991; MD, Uniformed Services U., Bethesda, MD, 1995. Board Certified in Family Medicine Am. Bd. of Family Medicine, 1999. Commd. officer USPHS, Cherokee, NC, 1991—; chief med. staff Cherokee Indian Hosp., NC, 2005—. Comdr. USPHS, 2004, Cherokee, NC. Recipient Rookie Physician of Yr., Indian Health Svc., 2001, Field Med. Readiness Badge, US Pub. Health Svc., 2003, Achievement medal, 2004, Crisis Response fire award, 2004, 2006, Fellowship in Obstetrics, Franklin Sq. Hosp. Ctr., Balt., MD, 1997. Fellow: Am. Acad. Family Practice; mem.: Commd. Officers Assn. of the USPHS (pres., cherokee br. 1999—2002). Office Phone: 828-497-9163.

**TOEDTMAN, JAMES SMITH,** journalist, editor; b. Dayton, Ohio, Dec. 1, 1941; s. James Christian and Ella Barnes (Smith) T.; m. Haydee N. Sicart, Aug. 23, 1969; children: Eric, Kristen. AB, Coll. Wooster, 1963; postgrad., U. Queensland, Brisbane, Australia, 1964; MSc in Journalism, Columbia U., 1967. Pub. dir. Coll. Wooster, Ohio, 1963, 65; reporter, city editor, Sunday news editor, mng. editor, Washington Bur. chief Newsday, LI, NY, 1967-79, 1986—2005; exec. editor Boston Herald Am., 1979-82; editor Balt. News Am., 1982-86, AARP Bulletin, 2005—. Adv. bd. comm. dept. Flagler Coll., 2003—. Recipient shared award Silurian Soc., Polk award, Pulitzer Prize, 1970, 92, 97, spl. citation Inter-Am. Press Assn., 1979, Best Editl. award Md.-Del.-D.C. Press Assn., 1984, 86; Rotary Found. fellow, 1964, Internat. fellow Columbia U., 1966-67. Mem.: Coll. Wooster Alumni Assn. (pres. 1980—81). Methodist. Home: 2604 Geneva Hill Ct Oakton VA 22124-1534 Office: 601 E St NW Washington DC 20049 Office Phone: 202-434-3357. Business E-Mail: jtoedtman@aarp.org.

**TOENNIES, JAN PETER,** research chemical physicist; b. Phila., May 3, 1930; arrived in Fed. Republic Germany, 1957; s. Gerrit and Dita (Jebens) T.; m. Monika Elisabeth Zelesnick; children: Susanne, Annette. BA in Physics, Amherst (Mass.) Coll., 1952; PhD in Chemistry, Brown U., Providence, 1957; D (hon.), U. Gothenburg, 2000. Rsch. asst. Bonn (Fed. Republic Germany) U., 1957-65, dozent, 1965-68; dir., sci. mem. Max Planck Inst. Fluid Mechanics, Göttingen, 1969—98. Adj. prof. Bonn U., 1971—; assoc. prof. Göttingen U., 1971—; vis. Miller Prof. Chemistry and Physics, U. Calif., Berkeley, 2005-06; cons. Uranit GmbH, Jülich, Fed. Republic Germany, 1977-89. Author: Chemical Reactions in Shock Waves, 1964; adv. editor Jour. Physics, 1973-78; editor monograph series, Springer Series in Chem. Physics, 1979—. Recipient Gold Heyrovsky medal Czechoslovak Acad. Sci., 1991, Alumni citation Brown U., 1988, Hewlett-Packard Europhysics prize for outstanding achievement in condensed matter rsch., 1992, Max Planck prize Deutsche Forschungsgemeinschaft and Alexander Humboldt Soc., 1992, Kotos medal Polish Chem. Soc., 2005, Benjamin Franklin medal in Physics, Franklin Inst., 2006. Fellow Am. Phys. Soc., World Innovation Found.; mem. European Phys. Soc., German Phys. Soc. (sect. chmn. 1977-80, Stern-Gerlach medal 2002, mem. atomic physics sect.), Göttingen Acad. Scis. (corr., Physics award 1964), Coun. European Phys. Soc., Acad. Sciences Czech Republic, World Cultural Coun. (mem. interdisciplinary bd.), Deutsche Akademie der Naturforscher Leopoldina. Home: Ewaldstrasse 7 D-37085 Göttingen Germany Office: Max Planck Inst for Dynamics and Self Orgn Bunsenstr 10 D-37073 Göttingen Germany Office Phone: 0049(0)5515176600. Business E-Mail: jtoenni@gwdg.de.

**TOENSING, VICTORIA,** lawyer; b. Colon, Panama, Oct. 16, 1941; d. Philip William and Victoria (Brady) Long; m. Trent David Toensing, Oct. 29, 1962 (div. 1976); children: Todd Robert, Brady Cronon, Amy Victoriana; m. Joseph E. diGenova, June 27, 1981. BS in Edn., Ind. U., 1962; JD cum laude, U. Detroit, 1975. Bar: Mich. 1976, D.C. 1978. Tchr. English, Milw., 1965-66; law clk. to presiding justice U.S. Ct. Appeals, Detroit, 1975-76; asst. U.S. atty. U.S. Atty.'s Office, Detroit, 1976-81; chief counsel U.S. Senate Intelligence Com., Washington, 1981-84; dep. asst. atty. gen. criminal div. Dept. Justice, Washington, 1984-88; spl. counsel Hughes Hubbard & Reed, Washington, 1988-90; ptnr. Cooter and Gell, Washington, 1990-91; ptnr., co-chmn. nat. white collar group Manatt, Phelps and Phillips, Washington, 1991-95; founding ptnr. diGenova & Toensing, Wasington, 1996—. Mem. working group on corp. sanctions U.S. Sentencing Commn., 1988-89; co-chairperson Coalition for Women's Appts. Justice Judiciary Task Force, 1988-92; spl. counsel for Teamsters investigation, U.S. Ho. of Reps., Subcom. on Oversight and Investigations of com. on Edn. and the Workforce, 1997-98. Author: Bringing Sanity to the Insanity Defense, 1983, Mens Rea: Insanity by Another Name, 1984; contbg. author: Fighting Back: Winning The War Against Terrorism, Desk Book on White Collar Crime, 1991; contbr. articles to profl. jours. Founder, chmn. Women's Orgn. To Meet Existing Needs, Mich., 1975-79; chmn. Republican Women's Task Force, 1979-81; bd. dirs. Project on Equal Edn. Rights, Mich., 1980-81, Nat. Hist. Intelligence Mus., 1987-95, America's Talking Legal Analyst, 1995; MSNBC legal analyst, 1998-99. Recipient spl. commendation Office U.S. Atty. Gen., 1980, agy. seal medallion CIA, 1986, award of achievement Alpha Chi Omega, 1992; featured on cover N.Y. Time Mag. for anti-terrorism work, April 1991. Mem. ABA (mem. standing com. on law and nat. security, mem. coun. criminal justice sect., mem. adv. com. complex crimes and litigation, vice chmn. white collar crime com., chmn. subcom. on corp. criminal liability). Office Phone: 202-289-7701.

**TOEPFER, SUSAN JILL,** editor-in-chief, editor; b. Rochester, Minn., Mar. 9, 1948; d. John Bernard and Helen Esther (Chapple) Toepfer; m. Lorenzo Gabriel Carcaterra, May 16, 1981; children: Katherine Marie, Nicholas Gabriel. BA, Bennington Coll., 1970. Mng. editor Photoplay Mag., N.Y.C., 1971-72; freelance writer N.Y.C., 1972-78; TV week editor N.Y. Daily News, N.Y.C., 1978-79, leisure editor, 1979-82, features editor, 1982-84, arts and entertainment editor, 1984-86, exec. mag. editor, 1986-87; sr. writer People Mag., N.Y.C., 1987-89, sr. editor, 1989-91, asst. mng. editor, 1991-94, exec. editor, 1994—2000, dep. mng. editor, 2000—02; editor-in-chief Rosie Mag., 2002, Devel. G+J USA, N.Y.C., 2003—04, Quick & Simple, N.Y.C., 2005—. Home: 225 7th Ave #10X New York NY 10001

**TOEVS, ALDEN LOUIS,** management consultant, researcher; b. American Falls, Idaho, Jan. 25, 1949; s. Alden Louis and Wilma Christen (Coffey) T. BS, Lewis and Clark Coll., 1971; PhD, Purdue U., 1975. NSF fellow MIT Energy Lab., Boston, 1975-76; prof. econs. La. State U., Baton Rouge, 1976-77, U. Oreg., Eugene, 1978-83; dir. mortgage rsch. Morgan Stanley and Co., N.Y.C., 1983-90; exec. v.p. First Manhattan Cons. Group, N.Y.C., 1990—. Vis. scholar Fed. Home Loan Bank, San Francisco, 1983, Fed. Reserve Bank, 1982; dir. capital market research U. Oreg., Eugene, 1982-83; instnl. investor All-Am. Rsch. Team, 1990. Author: Innovations in Bond Portfolio Managements, 1983, Winning the Credit Cycle Game, 1998; contbr. articles to profl. jours. Trustee Orch. St. Lukes, 1990—, Creative Glass Ctr. Am., Contemporary Glass Ctr. Am., 2004—. Recipient Graham and Dodd scroll Fin. Analysts Fed., 1983.

**TOFEL, RICHARD JEFFREY,** foundation administrator; b. NYC; s. Robert Leonard and Carol T.; m. Jeanne Helen Straus, Feb. 26, 1983; children: Rachel Straus, Colin Straus. AB, Harvard U., 1979; MPP, JFK Sch. Govt., 1983; JD, Harvard U., 1983. Bar: N.Y. 1984, U.S. Dist. Ct. (so. and ea. dists.) N.Y. 1984, U.S. Ct. Appeals (2d cir.) 1987, U.S. Dist. Ct. (no. dist.) N.Y. 1988, U.S. Supreme Ct. 1990. Assoc. Patterson, Belknap, Webb & Tyler, NYC, 1983—86; exec. dir. Mayor's Commn. Human Svcs. Reorganization, NYC, 1984—85; assoc. Gibson, Dunn & Crutcher, NYC, 1986—89; counsel Dow Jones & Co., NYC, 1989—91, asst. gen. counsel, 1991—92; asst. mng. editor Wall Street Jour., NYC, 1992—95; dir. internat. devel. and adminstrn. Dow Jones & Co., NYC, 1995—97, v.p. corp. comm., 1997—2000, v.p., asst. to publ. Wall Street Jour., 2000—02, v.p., asst. publ. Wall Street Jour., 2002—04; pres. The Internat. Freedom Ctr., World Trade Ctr. site, NYC, 2004—05; v.p., gen. counsel The Rockefeller Found., NYC, 2006—. Bd. dirs. Wildcat Svc. Corp. Author: A Legend in the Making: The New York Yankees in 1939, 2002, Vanishing Point: The Disappearance of Judge Crater, and the New York He Left Behind, 2004, Sounding the Trumpet: The Making of John F. Kennedy's Inaugural Address, 2005; contbr. articles to profl. jours. Democrat. Jewish. Office: The Rockefeller Found 420 Fifth Ave New York NY 10018 Business E-mail: r.tofel@rockfound.org. E-mail: dick_tofel@yahoo.com.

**TOFIAS, ALLAN,** retired accountant; b. Boston, Apr. 13, 1930; s. George I. and Anna (Seidel) T.; m. Arlene Shube, Aug. 30, 1981; children: Bradley Neil, Laura Jean Silver. BA, Colgate U., 1951; MBA, Harvard U., 1956. CPA, Mass. Sr. acct. Peat, Marwick, Mitchell & Co., Boston, 1956-61; mng. ptnr. Tofias, Fleishman, Shapiro & Co., P.C., Boston, 1960-96, chmn. bd., 1996-97. Bd. dir. Rowe Cos.; trustee Gannett, Welch & Kotler Mut. Funds, 1996-2002. Mem. Brookline (Mass.) Town Meeting, 1970-77, mem. fin. adv. bd., 1975-81; mem. New Eng. Bapt. Health Care Corp., 1985—, trustee, 1998—, chmn. fin. com., 1998-2002; bd. dir. West Newton YMCA, 1986-89; mem. exec. com. Boston Aid to Blind, bd. dir., 1988-97, pres., 1993-94. Lt. USNR, 1951-54. Mem. AICPA (coun. 1995-99), Mass. Soc. CPA's (pres. 1995-96), Nat. CPA Group (exec. com. 1983-88, vice chmn. 1985-88), BKR Internat. (world bd. dirs. 1988-97, chmn. 1994-96), Wightman Tennis Club (treas. 1974-76), Newton Squash and Tennis Club (bd. dirs. 1966-99), Masons. Home: 33 Glen Oak Dr Wayland MA 01778 Office: 167 Worcester St Wellesley MA 02481

**TOFTNER, RICHARD ORVILLE,** engineering executive; b. Warren, Minn., Mar. 5, 1935; s. Orville Gayhart and Cora Evelyn (Anderson) T.; m. Jeanne Bredine, June 26, 1960; children: Douglas, Scott, Kristine, Kimberly, Brian. BA, U. Minn., 1966; MBA, Xavier U., 1970. Registered environ. assessor Calif. Sr. economist Federated Dept. Stores, Inc., Cin., 1967-68; dep. dir. EPA, Washington and Cin., 1968-73; mgmt. cons. environ. affairs, products and mktg., 1973-74; prin. PEDCo Environ., Cin., 1974-80; trustee PEDCo trusts, 1974-80; pres. ROTA Mgmt., Inc., Cin., 1980-82; gen. mgr. CECOS, 1982-85; cons., 1985—; v.p. Smith, Stevens & Young, 1985-88; real estate developer, 1980—. Pres., CEO Toxitrol Internat., Inc., 1988-89; dir. Environ. Svcs. Belcan Engring. Group, Inc., Cin., 1989-92; prin. exec. cons. Resource Mgmt. Internat., Inc., 1994—; adj. prof. environ. engring. U. Cin., 1975-86; lectr. Grad. fellowship rev. panel Office of Edn., 1978-79; advisor, cabinet-level task force Office of Gov. of P.R., 1973; pvt. investor, 1991—; bd. dirs. EnviroAudit Svcs., Inc., pres., CEO, 1992—; mem. legis. com. Ohio Chem. Coun., 1995—; v.p. environ. engring. CSA Architects & Engrs., 1996-2001; client svc. mgr. Weston Solutions Inc. Environ. Cons., 2001—; subcom. Nat. Safety Coun., 1972; mem. exec. environ. briefing panels Andersen Consulting, 1991-92; nominee environ. PUCO, Ohio; chmn. Cin. City Waste Task Force, 1987-88; co-chair Hamilton County Resource Recovery Com., 1989—. Contbr. articles on mgmt. planning and environ. to periodicals, chpts. to books; inventor, developer Toxitrol Waste Minimization; inventor EnviroAudit. With AUS, 1954-57. Mem. U.S. Tennis Assn., Nat. Registry Environ. Profl. Rep., Engring. Soc. Cin., Assn. Corp. Environ.

Execs., Cin. C. of C., Global Assn. Corp. Environ. Execs. (charter). Republican. Lutheran. Home: 9175 Yellowwood Dr Cincinnati OH 45251-1948 Office: 4100 Executive Park Dr Ste 16 Cincinnati OH 45241-4026

**TOGAFAU, MALAETASI M. (SIALEGA MALAETASI MAUGA TOGAFAU),** attorney general, judge; b. Pago Pago, Am. Samoa, June 4, 1946; s. Sefulu Mauga Togafau and Femalua'i (Mauga) Sialo'i; m. Oreta Mapu, Dec. 10, 1977; children: Malaetasi Jr., Steve, June, Wayne, Heidi. BS, Peru Stat U., 1971; JD, Calif. Western Sch. of Law, 1974. Asst. pub. defender High Ct., Am. Samoa, 1974; legis. asst. Office of Del.-at-Large, Washington, 1975—80, U.S. Ho. of Reps., Washington, 1981—82; rep. Legislature of Am. Samoa, Am. Samoa, 1983—86; atty. Law Firm of Talalelei Tulafono, Am. Samoa, 1983—86; dist. ct. judge High Ct., Am. Samoa, 1986—93; atty. gen. Am. Samoa, 1993—96, 2005—. Chmn. budget com. Ho. of Reps., Am. Samoa, 1985—86; vice chmn., bd. dirs. Dem. Bank of Am. Samoa, 1985—86; legal counsel Dem. Party, Am. Samoa, 1985—86. Mem.: Nat. Jud. Coll., Am. Samoa Bar Assn. Democrat. Mem. Congregation Christian Church. Avocations: softball, long boat crew, farming. Office: American Samoa Govt Exec Office Bldg Utulei Territory of American Samoa Pago Pago AS 96799 Office Phone: 684-633-4163. Office Fax: 684-633-1838.*

**TOGASAKI, SHINOBU,** computer scientist; b. San Francisco, Aug. 17, 1932; s. Kikumatsu and Sugi (Hida) T.; m. Toshiko Kawaguchi, Nov. 24, 1959; children: John Shinobu, Ann Mariko. BS in Math., Duke U., 1954; postgrad., Stanford U., 1954—56. Math. programmer IBM, 1956—69, DB/DC arch., 1969—72, sr. programmer Palo Alto, Calif., 1970—87, mgr. Palo Alto sys. ctr., 1972—74, risk OS mgr., 1974—82, DB/DC mktg. cons., 1982—87; mgr. applications devel. Service Bur. Corp., Palo Alto, 1961—64, sr. analyst, 1964—68, systems architect devel. lab. San Jose, Calif., 1968-70; CFO. Robin Hood Ranch, Inc., 1976—86; mgr. architecture & strategy Hewlett Packard Corp., Cupertino, Calif., 1987-89, mgr. strategic planning, 1989—93; chief architect MFA Hewlett Packard, 1993—2002; strategic cons., 2002—. Mem. Am. Mgmt. Assn., AAAS, Am. Statis. Assn., Assn. Computing Machinery, Inst. Mgmt. Sci., Sigma Pi Sigma. Home: 2367 Booksin Ave San Jose CA 95125-4705 E-mail: togasaki@alumni.duke.edu.

**TOGNINO, JOHN NICHOLAS,** diversified financial services company executive; b. NYC, Sept. 20, 1938; s. Gennaro and Catherine (Barbieri) T.; m. Norma Lucille Borrelli, Nov. 7, 1959; children: Katherine Ann, John Nicholas Jr., Michael A. BA in Econs. summa cum laude, Fordham U., 1975. Instnl. sales trader A.G. Becker & Co., N.Y.C., 1970-72; trader Merill Lynch, N.Y.C., 1957-69, instnl. salesman, 1972-74, mgr. over-the-counter sales trading, 1974-83, dir. over-the-counter dept., 1983-87, dir. unlisted trading, 1983-90, mng. dir. non-dollar equities London, 1988-91, mng. dir. global equities, ret. N.Y.C., 1991-93; exec. v.p. Charles Schwab & Co., Inc., Jersey City, 1993-96; pres., CEO Security Traders Assn., N.Y.C., 1996-99, EVP NASDAQ, 1999—2001; chmn., CEO Pepper Fin. Group, 2001—. Bd. dirs. Nat. Assn. Security Dealers Automated Quotations Inc. Contbg. author: Market Maker Sponsorship: A Synergistic Package of Services, 1987. Mem. Ardlsey Bd. Edn., 1977—84, pres., 1979; v.p. Ardsley Sch. Dist. Bd., 1978, 1981; trustee, vice chmn. St. Barnabas Hosp., Bronx, 1996—; mem. health sci. adv. coun., Coll. of Phys. and Surgeons Columbia Presbyn. Med. Ctr., 1998—; pres. Ardsley Rep. Club, 1967—68; mem. exec. com. of laity Archdiocese of N.Y.C., 1988; trustee Fordham U., 2000—, chmn. bd. trustees, 2004—; dir. Muscular Dystrophy Assn., 2000—05; bd. dirs. Bus. Coun. for Internat. Understanding, 2000—01. Named Trader of Yr., Security Traders Monthly mag., 1984, Over-the-Counter Man of Yr., Equities mag., 1986; recipient lifetime achievement award Chgo. Stock Exch., 1997. Mem. Nat. Security Traders Assn. (various offices 1981-88, chmn. fin. com. Found. 1992—), Nat. Assn. Security Dealers (bus. conduct com. 1984-86), Security Traders Assn. N.Y. (various offices 1973-83, pres. 1980-81), St. Andrews Golf Club (Hastings, N.Y.), Alpha Sigma Lambda, Alpha Sigma Nu. Republican. Roman Catholic. Avocations: jogging, tennis, golf. Home: Two Stoneleigh Plz Apt 4H Bronxville NY 10708 Office: Pepper Fin Group PO Box 395 Waccabuc NY 10597 Office Phone: 914-234-4580. E-mail: jntog@aol.com.

**TOI, ZANG,** apparel designer; b. Kelantan, Malaysia, June 11, 1961; US, 1980; BFA, Parsons Sch. of Design, 1985. Apprenticed with Mary Jane Marcasiano and Ronaldus Shamask; owner, designer Toi House, 1989—; launched Zang Toi Couture Collection. Owner Zang Toi Boutiques, Malaysia. Decorated Knight Malaysia; recipient Mouton-Cadet Young Designers award, 1991. Office: Toi House 30 W 57th St New York NY 10019*

**TOIBIN, COLM,** writer, journalist; b. Enniscorthy, County Wexford, Ireland, 1955; s. Michael Tobin. BA, U. Coll. Dublin, 1975. Tchr. Dublin Sch. English, Barcelona, 1975—78; (returned to Ireland, 1978); writer Hibernia, The Sunday Tribune, In Dublin, features editor, 1981—82; editor Magill, 1982—85; journalist, columnist Dublin Sunday Ind., 1985—. Fellow Ctr. for Scholars and Writers NY Pub. Libr., 2000. Author: (fiction) The South, 1990, The Heather Blazing, 1992, The Story of the Night, 1996, Finbar's Hotel (collaborative novel), 1999, The Blackwater Lightship (made into TV film, 2004), 1999, The Master, 2004 (Internat. Impac Dublin Literary award, 2006), (non-fiction) Seeing is Believing: Moving Status in Ireland, 1985, The Trial of the Generals, 1990, Dubliners, 1990, Homage to Barcelona, 1990, The Sign of the Cross, 1994, Bad Blood, 1994, The Kilfenora Teaboy, 1997, The Irish Famine, 1999, Love in a Dark Time: Gay Lives from Wilde to Almodovar, 2001, Lady Gregory's Toothbrush, 2002, (plays) Beauty in a Broken Place, 2004; editor: SOHO Square VI: New Writing from Ireland, 1997, Enniscorthy: History & Heritage, 1998, The Modern Library: The 200 Best Novels in English since 1950, 1999, The Penguin Book of Irish Fiction, 2001. Recipient E.M. Forster Award, AAAL, 1995. Mem.: Aosdána.*

**TOKOFSKY, JERRY HERBERT,** film producer; b. N.Y.C., Apr. 14, 1936; s. Julius H. and Rose (Trager) T.; m. Myrna Weinstein, Feb. 21, 1968 (div.); children: David, Peter; m. Fiammetta Bettuzzi, 1970 (div.); 1 child, Tatianna; m. Karen Oliver, Oct. 4, 1981. BS in Journalism, NYU, 1956, LLD, 1959, M in Am. Lit., 1999. Talent agt. William Morris Agy., N.Y.C., 1953-59, v.p. L.A., 1959-64; exec. v.p. Columbia Pictures, L.A., 1964-69; v.p. Paramount Pictures, London, 1970; exec. v.p. MGM, London, 1971; pres. Jerry Tokofsky Prodns., L.A., 1972-82; exec. v.p. Zupnik Enterprises, L.A., 1982-92; pres. Jerry Tokofsky Entertainment, Encino, Calif., 1992—; CEO TKO Comm. Prof. Sch. TV and Film U. So. Calif. Sch. Bus. Prodr. films: Where's Poppa, 1971, Born to Win, 1972, Paternity, 1981, Dreamscape, 1985, Fear City, 1986, Wildfire, 1988, Glengarry Glen Ross, 1992, The Grass Harp, 1995, American Buffalo, 1995, Double Down, 1997, Life on Mars, 1998, John Steinbecks In Dubious Battle, 2004, Puccini, 2004, Daisy Winter, 2005, Gods House of Style, 2005, High Desert, 2005; exec. prodr. Easy Rider, Man for All Seasons, Funny Girl, Oliver, Born Free, Georgy Girl, Professionals. With U.S. Army, 1959, 63, res. 1959-63. Named Man of Yr. B'nai B'rith, 1981; recipient L.A. Resolution City of L.A., 1981. Mem. Variety Club Internat. Avocations: skiing, tennis, golf, chess. *Passion for family, life, work, with patience and intelligence and you have a chance to grab that winning ring.*

**TOKUHATA, GEORGE K.,** retired medical educator, epidemiologist, consultant; b. Matsue, Japan, Aug. 25, 1924; arrived in U.S., 1951; s. Yujiro and Hama Tokuhata; m. Sumiko Matsui, June 10, 1949. BA, Keio U., 1950; MA, Miami U., Oxford, Ohio, 1952; PhD, U. Iowa, 1955; Dr.PH, Johns Hopkins U., 1962. Chief epidemiology chronic disease divsn. USPHS, Washington, 1961—64; assoc. prof. preventive medicine U. Tenn., Memphis, 1965—67; dir. rsch. Pa. Dept. Health, Harrisburg, 1968—89; prof. behavioral sci. Pa. State U. Coll. Medicine, Hershey, 1970—90; prof. epidemiology U. Pitts., 1970—90; ret. 1990. Cons. product safety U.S. FDA, Washington, 1970—73; cons. maternal child health svcs. U.S. Children's Bur., 1974—77; cons. rsch. grant svcs. Nat. Cancer Inst., 1982—86. Contbr. chapters to books, articles over 100 articles to profl. jours. Grantee, USPHS, U.S. FDA. Fellow: APHA, Am. Coll. Epidemiology; mem.: Fgn. Policy Assn. (bd.dirs. 1995—2000), Torch Club Internat. (bd.dirs. 1999—2002). Achievements include first to find genetic role played in lung cancer; research in radiation, stress and health; first to new method of finding familial aggregation of chronic diseases; design of and execution of long-term cohort study of health effects of the Three Mile Island accident - first major episode among all commercial nuclear plants in the U.S. Avocations: classical music, landscape design, gardening. Home: 410 Rupley Rd Camp Hill PA 17011

**TOKUTANI, MASAO,** risk management educator; b. Tokyo, Nov. 1, 1940; s. Takeo and Matsu (Hagiwara) T. B, Chuo U., 1964, Dr., 1978; Mr., Waseda U., 1967. CPA, Tokyo. Asst. prof. Chiba U. Commerce, 1967-73; assoc. prof. Seikei U., Tokyo, 1974-78, full prof., 1979-2001, prof. emeritus, 2001—; prof. Grad. Sch. Internat. Acctg. Chuo U., 2002. Cons. in field. Author: Corporate Social Accounting, 1977, Risk Management, 1983. Mem. Japan Acctg. Assn., Secom Sci. and Tech. Found. (Risk Measurement and Bus. Behavior award 1983), Asian-Pacific Rsch. Ctr. Seikei U. Avocations: golf, fishing. Home: 63-25 Isshiki Hayama Miuragun, Kanagawa 240-0111 Japan Office: 1-19-403 Sakaecho-Kanagawku Yokohama 221-0052 Japan E-mail: mt@miraisitu.com

**TOLAR, ANNE MELTON,** minister, music educator; b. Geneva, Ala., Jan. 17, 1937; d. Ernest Lester and Lovie Hewett Melton; m. Robert F. Tolar, Apr. 21, 1966; children: Robert Jr., William, Sharon Tolar Stone, Ginny Tolar Knight. BA in English & Psychology, U. Ala., 1959; BA in Music/Piano, U. W. Fla., 1960. Teller/bookkeeper 1st Bank & Trust, Pensacola, Fla., 1952—56, collections & loan officer Atlanta; br. office asst. mgr. 1st Fed. Savings & Loan Assn., Atlanta, 1970—73; evangelist, musician, tchr. Fountain of Praise Ministries, St. Pauls, NC, 1972— presbyter, min. Missionary Ch. Internat., Columbia, SC, 1985—; music tchr. St. Pauls; tchr., musician, pastor Fountain of Praise Ch., Lumberton, NC, 2001—. Judge Mountain Gospel Music; v.p. Fountain of Praise Ministries, Missionary Ch. Internat., Lumberton, NC, 2001—; spkr. in field. Author: (book) Wilt Thou Be Made Whole?, 1988; songwriter: 106 songs and cantatas. Named Internat. Savings & Loan Speech Contest, Atla., 1972; recipient Mother of Yr. award, Fountain of Praise Ch., St. Pauls, N.C. 1998. Republican. Mem. Christian Ch. Office: Fountain of Praise Ministries Cedar St Lumberton NC 28358

**TOLBERT, BERT MILLS,** biochemist, educator; b. Twin Falls, Idaho, Jan. 15, 1921; s. Ed. and Helen (Mills) T.; m. Anne Grace Zweifler, July 20, 1959; children— Elizabeth Dawn, Margaret Anne, Caroline Joan, Sarah Helen. Student, Idaho State U., 1938-40; BS, U. Calif. at Berkeley, 1942, PhD, 1945; postgrad., Fed. Inst. Tech., Zurich, Switzerland, 1952-53. Chemist Lawrence Radiation Lab., Berkeley, 1944-57; faculty U. Colo., Boulder, 1957-89, prof., 1961-89, prof. emeritus, 1989—, assoc. chmn. dept. chemistry and biochemistry, 1980-88. Bd. dirs. Hauser Chem. Rsch., Boulder, 1983-99; dirs. Hauser Inc., Boulder, 1983-99, vis. prof. IAEA, Buenos Aires, Argentina, 1961-62; Biophysicist U.S. AEC, Washington, 1967-68; cons. pvt. cos, govt. agys. Author: (with others) Isotopic Carbon, 1948; contbr. (with others) articles to profl. jours. Fellow AAAS; mem. Am. Chem. Soc., Am. Soc. Biochemistry and Molecular Biology, Radiation Rsch. Soc., Soc. for Exptl. Biology and Medicine. Achievements include rsch. on organic chemistry, including use of isotopes in chemistry and biochemistry, radiation chemistry, radiation effects in protein, intermediary metabolism, metabolism of ascorbic acid, nutritional biochemistry, instrumentation in radioactivity. Home: 444 Kalmia Ave Boulder CO 80304-1732 Personal E-mail: bert.tolbert@colorado.edu.

**TOLBERT, BETH WILLDEN,** real estate company executive, real estate broker; b. Delta, Utah, Apr. 7, 1935; d. Delbert B. and Mildred (Twitchell) Willden; m. Stanley Tolbert, May 12, 1955; children: Keven, Tracy, Troy. Student, Brigham Young U., 1953-54. Cert. residential specialist. Realtor Harding Realty, Am. Fork, Utah, 1976-82; associate broker Pine Valley Realty, Alpine, Utah, 1982-97; prin., owner Beth Tolbert Realty Group, St. George, Utah, 1997—; ptnr., prin. broker Tolbert & Nielsen Realty Group, LLC, St. George, Utah, 2003—. Apptd. Utah Real Estate Commn., Salt Lake City, 1993—, chair 1993-94; bd. trustees Utah Valley State Coll., Orem, 1991—, chair 1996-97; pres. Nat. Womens Coun. Realtors, 1994; bd. trustees Leadership Dixie, 2000-01. Recipient Realtor of Yr. award Utah Assoc. Realtors, 1984, Distinguished Svc. award 1994, 97, Realtor of Yr. award Utah County Bd. Realtors, 1984. Home: 656 Country Ln Santa Clara UT 84765-5471

**TOLBERT, CLINTON JAME,** army officer, machinist; b. Auburn, Ala., Dec. 22, 1953; s. Clinton and Rosia Love (Fillmore) T.; m. Gloria Jean Fitzpatrick, Sept. 23, 1974; children: Christopher, Mark, Marcella. BS, Tukegee U., 1983; MBA, Troy State U., 1987, MS, 1990; AS in Applied Sci., So. U., Opelika, Ala., 1996. EMT U.S. Army, Fort Benning, Ga., 1972-75; machine operator West Point Pepperll, Inc., Valley, Ala., 1975-82; 1st lt. Army Nat. Guard, Roanoke, Ala., 1982-86, capt., 1986-92, major Montgomery, Ala., 1992-96; machinist Falk Corp., Auburn, Ala, 1996—. Elder Methodist Ch., Auburn, Ala., 1996— Named All- Am. Scholar, U.S. Achievement Acad., Lexington, Ky., 1996; recipient Minority Leadership award, U.S. Achievement Acad., Lexington, 1996. Mem. Nat. Guard Assn. Democrat. Avocations: reading, golf. Home: 989 Fitzpatric Rd Auburn AL 36830

**TOLBERT, CORNELIA EMMA,** music educator; b. St. Louis, Mo., Sept. 15, 1954; d. Cornelius and Morzell Tolbert. BA, St. Louis U., 1977. Cert. instrumental and vocal music tchr. grades K-12 Mo., 1982. Substitute tchr. St. Louis Pub. Schs., 1975—83, piano and voice tchr., 1976—78, vocal music tchr., 1985—95, asst. music tchr., 1997—2001, instrumental music asst. tchr., 2001—; pvt. piano and organ tchr. Ludwig Aeolian Music Store, 1982—85. Music choral dir. Meth. Ch., St. Louis, 1972—, asst. orgn., 1977—2003, pianist, 2003—. Vol. phone bank St. Louis Tchrs. Union, 2004; coord. for United Way St. Louis Pub. Schs., 2004, coord. William L. Clay Scholarship fund, 2004. Recipient Editor's Choice award, Internat. Soc. Poets, 2001. Mem.: St. Louis Univ. Alumni Assn., Internat. Soc. Poets, Am. Fedn. Tchrs., St. Louis Tchrs. Union Local 420, Nat. Music Educators Assn., Mo. Music Tchrs. Assn. Democrat. Methodist. Avocations: bowling, tennis, ping pong/table tennis, writing songs, gardening.

**TOLBERT, MARGARET A.,** geochemistry educator; AB in Chemistry, with honors, Grinnell Coll., 1979; MS in Chemistry, U. Calif., Berkeley, 1985; PhD in Chemistry, Calif. Inst. Tech., 1986. Postdoctoral fellow Stanford Rsch. Inst., 1986—87; rsch. asst. U. Calif., Berkeley, 1979—83, Calif. Inst. Tech., 1983—86; staff scientist, Chemistry Lab. SRI Internat., 1986—91, leader Atmospheric Chemistry Group, 1990—91; assoc. prof. Dept. Chemistry and Biochemistry U. Colo., 1991—98, prof., 1998—. Author: Stratispheric Ozone Depletion, 2000. Recipient James B. Macelwane Young Investigator medal Am. Geophys. Union, 1993. Fellow: Am. Geophysical Union (James B. Macelwane Young Investigator medal 1993); mem.: NAS. Office: U Colo CIRES 166 Campus Box 216 Boulder CO 80309-0216 Office Phone: 303-492-3179. Fax: 303-492-1149. Business E-Mail: tolbert@colorado.edu.*

**TOLCHIN, JOAN GUBIN,** psychiatrist, educator; b. NYC, Mar. 10, 1944; d. Harold and Bella (Newman) Gubin; m. Matthew Armin Tolchin, Sept. 1, 1966; 1 child, Benjamin. AB, Vassar Coll., 1964; MD, NYU, 1972. Diplomate Am. Bd. Psychiatry. Am. Bd. Child Psychiatry. Rsch. asst. Albert Einstein Coll. Medicine, N.Y.C., 1964-68; instr. psychiatry med. coll. Cornell U., N.Y.C., 1977-78, clin. instr. 1978-86, clin. asst. prof., 1986—2004, clin. assoc. prof., 2004—. Contbr. articles to profl. jours., chapters to books. Fellow: Am. Acad. Child and Adolescent Psychiatry; mem.: N.Y. Coun. Child and Adolescent Psychiatry (bd. dirs. 1992—96, pres. 1994—95, bd. advisors 2001—), Am. Acad. Psychoanalysis and Dynamic Psychiatry (sec. 1998—2001), Alpha Omega Alpha. Office: 35 E 84th St New York NY 10028-0871

**TOLCHIN, MARTIN,** journalist, writer; b. NYC, Sept. 20, 1928; s. Charles T. and Evelyn (Weisman) Tolchin; m. Susan Jane Goldsmith, Dec. 23, 1965; children: Karen. Student, U. Utah, 1947-49; LL.B., N.Y. Law Sch., 1951. Reporter N.Y. Times, N.Y.C., 1954—94; publisher and editor-in-chief The Hill, Washington, 1994—2002. Author (with Susan Jane Tolchin): To The Victor, 1971; author: Clout-Woman Power and Politics, 1974, Dismantling America-The Rush to Deregulate, 1983, Buying Into America: How Foreign Money is Changing the Face of Our Nation, 1988, Selling Our Security-The Erosion of American's Assets, 1992, Glass Houses: Congressional Ethics and the Politics of Venom, 2001, A World Ignited: How Apostles of Ethnic, Religious and Racial Hatred Torch the Globe, 2006. Served with U.S. Army, 1951-53. Recipient Schaeffer Gold Typewriter award E.M. Schaeffer Co., 1967; recipient Page One award Newspaper Guild N.Y., 1967, 69, 73, Citizens Budget Commn. award, 1967, Sigma Delta Chi award, 1973, Everett M. Dirksen award for disting. reporting of Congress, 1983; named to Journalism Hall Fame, Soc. Profl. Journalists, 2004. Mem. Nat. Press Club (Washington), Univ. Club. Jewish. Home: 3525 Winfield Ln NW Washington DC 20007-2378 Personal E-mail: mtolchin@aol.com.

**TOLCHIN, SUSAN JANE,** political science professor, writer; b. N.Y.C., Jan. 14, 1941; d. Jacob Nathan and Dorothy Ann (Markowitz) Goldsmith; m. Martin Tolchin, Dec. 23, 1965; 1 child, Karen Rebecca. BA, Bryn Mawr Coll., 1961; MA, U. Chgo., 1962; PhD, NYU, 1968. Lectr. in polit. sci. CCNY, N.Y.C., 1963-65; Bklyn. Coll., 1965-71; adj. asst. prof. polit. sci. Seton Hall U., South Orange, NJ, 1971-73; assoc. prof. polit. sci., dir. Inst. for Women and Politics, Mt. Vernon Coll., Washington, 1975-78; prof. pub. adminstrn. George Washington U., Washington, 1978-98; prof. pub. policy Sch. Pub. Policy George Mason U., Fairfax, Va., 1998—. Disting. lectr. Indsl. Coll. Armed Forces, 1994. Author: The Angry American: How Voter Rage is Changing the Nation, 1996, 2d edit., 1998; author: (with Martin Tolchin) To the Victor: Political Patronage from the Clubhouse to the White House, 1971, Clout--Womanpower and Politics, 1974, Dismantling America--The Rush to Deregulate, 1983, Buying Into America--How Foreign Money Is Changing the Face of Our Nation, 1988, Selling Our Securit--The Erosion of America's Assets, 1992, Glass Houses--Congressional Ethics and the Politics of Venom, 2001, A World Ignited: How Apostles of Ethnic, Religions and Racial Hatred Torch the Globe, 2006. Bd. dirs. Cystic Fibrosis Found., 1982-98; county committeewoman Dem. Party, Montclair, N.J., 1969-73. Recipient Founder's Day award NYU, 1968, Trachtenberg award for rsch. George Washington U., 1998; named Tchr. of Yr., Mt. Vernon Coll., 1978; Dilthey fellow George Washington U., 1983, Aspen Inst. fellow, 1979. Fellow Nat. Acad. Pub. Adminstrn.; mem. Am. Polit. Sci. Assn. (pres. Women's Caucus for Polit. Sci. 1977-78), Am. Soc. Pub. Adminstrn. (chair sect. natural resources and environ. adminstrn. 1982-83, Marshall Dimock award 1997). Democrat. Office: Sch Pub Policy George Mason U Fairfax VA 22030 Business E-Mail: tolchin@gmu.edu.

**TOLCHINSKY, PAUL DEAN,** organization design psychologist; b. Cleve., Sept. 30, 1946; s. Sanford Melvin and Frances (Klein) T.; m. Laurie S. Schermer, Nov. 3, 1968 (div. Jan. 1982); m. Kathy L. Dworkin, June 19, 1988; children: Heidi E., Dana M. BA, Bowling Green State U., 1971; PhD, Purdue U., 1978. Asst. br. mgr., tng. instr. Detroit Bank and Trust, 1971-73; mgr. tng. and devel. nuclear divsn. Babcock and Wilcox Co., Barberton, Ohio, 1973-75; internal cons. food products divsn. Gen. Foods Corp., West Lafayette, Ind., 1975-77; grad. tchg. asst. Krannert Grad. Sch. Mgmt. Purdue U., West Lafayette, 1975-78; asst. prof. mgmt. Coll. Bus. Adminstrn. Fla. State U., Tallahassee, 1978-79, U. Akron, Ohio, 1979-81; pres. Performance Devel. Assocs., Cleve., 1975—; ptnr. Dannemiller Tyson Assocs., Cleve., 1994-99; mng. ptnr. Performance Devel. Assocs., 2000—. Sr. lectr. Case Western Res. U., 2002—. Contbr. articles to profl. publs. Bd. dirs. Temple Tiferth Israel, Cleve., 95, Cleve. Jewish News, Jewish Family Svcs. Assn. Cleve. With U.S. Army, 1966-69, Vietnam. Mem. APA, Acad. Mgmt. Democrat. Jewish. Avocations: running, travel. Office: Performance Devel Assocs 50 Fox Glen Rd Moreland Hills OH 44022 Office Phone: 440-349-1990. Personal E-mail: kdtpdt@aol.com.

**TOLEDANO, RALPH DE,** columnist, writer, poet; b. Internat. Zone of Tangier, Aug. 17, 1916; m. Nora Romaine, July 6, 1938 (div. 1964); children: James, Paul Christopher; m. Eunice Marshall, Apr. 19, 1979 (dec. Aug. 1999). BA, Columbia Coll., 1938; postgrad., Cornell U., 1943. Founder, co-editor Cross-Town, 1932-33; Founder, co-editor Jazz Info., 1938-39; assoc. editor The New Leader, 1941-43; editor The Standard, 1946; mng. editor Plain Talk, 1946-47; pub. dir. Dress Joint Bd., Internat. Ladies Garment Workers Union, 1947-48; asst. editor Newsweek, 1948, nat. reports editor, 1950-60, asst. chief Washington Bur., 1956-60; syndicated columnist King Features, 1960-71, Nat. News Research Syndicate, 1971-74, Copley News Service, 1974-89, Heritage Features Syndicate, 1989-91, Creators Syndicate, 1991-98, Nat. News Rsch. Syndicate, 1998—; editor House Republican Leadership report Am. Mil. Strength and Strategy, 1960; chief Washington Bur., Taft Broadcasting Co., 1960-61; dir. polit. intelligence Goldwater Presdl. Campaign, 1963-64; contbg. editor Nat. Rev., 1960—2001; pres. Nat. News-Rsch., 1960—, Anthem Books, 1960—; editor-in-chief Washington World, 1961-62. Vice-chmn. Am. Conserva-Union, 1965-66; mem. 20th Century Fund Task Force on Freedom Press, 1971-72. Author: Seeds of Treason, 1950, Spies, Dupes and Diplomats, 1952, Day of Reckoning, 1955, Nixon, 1956, Lament for a Generation, 1960, The Greatest Plot in History, 1963, The Winning Side, 1963, The Goldwater Story, 1964, RFK: The Man Who Would be President, 1967, America, I-Love-You, 1968, One Man Alone: Richard M. Nixon, 1969, Claude Kirk: Man and Myth, 1970, Little Cesar, 1971, J. Edgar Hoover: The Man in His Time, 1973, Hit and Run: The Ralph Nader Story, 1975, Let Our Cities Burn, 1975, Poems: You & I, 1978, Devil Take Him, 1979, The Apocrypha of Limbo (poems), 1994, Notes from the Underground: The Chambers-Toledano Letters, 1997, Cry Havoc: The Secret War on America, 2006; editor: Frontiers of Jazz, 1947, Mark Twain on Practically Anything, 2001; co-editor: (with Melvin Laird) The Conservative Papers, 1962,; editor-in-chief: Political Success, 1968-69; mem. editl. bd. Yale Lit. Mag, 1981-86; contbg. editor Insight, Washington Times; contbr. articles to nat. mags. Bd. dirs. Americans for Constitutional Action, 1966-67, Constructive Action, 1990—2000 With OSS, AUS, 1943-46. Recipient Freedoms Found. award, 1950, 61, 74; Americanism award VFW, 1953; Disting. Journalism fellow Heritage Found. Mem. Internat. Mark Twain Soc., Bibl. Archeology Soc., Dutch Treat Club (N.Y.), Nat. Press Club, Naval and Mil. Club (London), Am. Legion (comdr. Pershing/NPC post), Sigma Delta Chi. Office: 500 23rd St NW Washington DC 20037-2828 E-mail: ralphdetoledano@aol.com.

**TOLEDO, ISABEL,** apparel designer; b. Cuba, 1961; m. Ruben Toledo. Grad., Fashion Inst. of Tech., NYC, Parsons Sch. of Design. Launched collection Isabel Toledo 1985—; opened first store The Lab, NYC, 2004—. Collaborator (with Ruben Toledo) on various art exhibits including A Marriage of Art and Fashion; designs shown in Victoria & Albert Museum, London, Mode Museum, Antwerp, Fashion Inst. of Tech., Kent State U. Museum, Ohio, Gallery of Museum of Otis Coll. of Art and Design, Los Angeles. Recipient Cooper Hewitt Design award, Fashion Design award Nat. Design Museum. Office: Isabel Toledo Ltd 277 5th Ave New York NY 10016*

**TOLEDO-PEREYRA, LUIS HORACIO,** transplant surgeon, researcher, historian educator; b. Nogales, Ariz., Oct. 19, 1943; s. Jose Horacio and Elia (Pereyra) Toledo; m. Marjean May Gilbert, Mar. 21, 1974; children: Alexander Horacio, Suzanne Elizabeth. BS magna cum laude, Regis Coll., 1960; MD, Nat. U. Mex., 1967, MS in Internal Medicine, 1970; PhD in Surgery, U. Minn., 1984. Intern Hosp. Juarez, Nat. U. Mex., 1966; resident in internal medicine Instituto Nacional de la Nutricions, Nat. U. Mex., 1968, 70; resident in surgery U. Minn., 1970-76; resident in thoracic and cardiovascular surgery U. Chgo., 1976-77; dir. surg. rsch. Henry Ford Hosp., Detroit, 1977-79; co-dir. transplantation, 1977-79; chief transplantation, dir. surg. rsch. Mt. Carmel Mercy Hosp., Detroit, 1979-89; chief transplantation, dir. rsch. Borgess Med. Ctr., Kalamazoo, 1990-99, 90—; clin. prof. surgery Mich. State U., 1993-96, prof. surgery, 1996—. Adj. prof. Sch. Health Sci. Mercy Coll., Detroit, 1983-91, history Western Mich. U., 1990—, biol. sci., 1991-96; prof. surgery Nat. U. Mex., 1990-96. Guest editor various med. and transplant jours.; mem. editl. bd. Dialysis and Transplantation, 1979—, Rsch. in Surgery, 1991—, Cirugia Iberoamericana, 1992—, clin. adv. bd. Transpl. Proc., 1993—; Medico Interamericano, 1993—, Cirugia Espanola, 1994—; assoc. editor Transplantology, 1990—; contbr. over 800 publs. on organ preservation, transplantation, other surg. and med. related areas, and the history of medicine to profl. jours. Recipient Outstanding Achievement award

U. Mex., 1961, 64, 67; Resident Rsch. award Assn. Acad. Surgery, 1974; Cecil Lehman Mayer Rsch. award Am. Coll. Chest Physicians, 1975, Surgery Rsch. Nat. award Mex. Assn. Gen. Surgery, 1993. Mem. AMA, Transplantation Soc., Assn. Acad. Surgery, Am. Soc. Transplant Surgery, Soc. Organ Sharing (pres., founder), Am. Assn. History Medicine, Am. Soc. Nephrology, Am. Assn. Immunologists, Am. Physiol. Soc., Soc. Exptl. Biology and Medicine, Am. Soc. Artificial Organs, Am. Diabetes Assn., European Soc. Study of Diabetes, No. Am. Soc. Dialysis Transplantation (pres., founder), Pan Am. Soc. Dialysis Transplantation (pres. elect, founder), Transplantation Soc. Mich. (pres., exec. bd.). Roman Catholic. Home: 3598 Whistling Ln Portage MI 49024-5545 Office: Borgess Med Ctr 1631 Gull Rd Ste 110 Kalamazoo MI 49048-1626

**TOLER, PENNY,** former professional basketball player, sports team executive; b. Mar. 24, 1966; B in Psychology, Long Beach State U., 1989. Guard, Montecchio, Italy, 1989—91, Pescara, Italy, 1991—94, Sporting Flash, Greece, 1994—96, Ramat HaSharon, Israel, 1996—97, Los Angeles Sparks, (WNBA), 1997—99; gen. mgr. L.A. Sparks, 1999—. Mem. U.S. Basketball Olympic Com., 1999—. Founder Points from Penny Program, 1998. Named All-Am. & Co-Player of Yr./Big West, 1988, 1989. Achievements include scored first ever basket in WNBA history. Avocations: ping pong/table tennis, tennis, craps. Office: LA Sparks Great Western Forum 555 N Nash St El Segundo CA 90245-2818

**TOLES, THOMAS GREGORY,** editorial cartoonist; b. Buffalo, Oct. 22, 1951; s. George Edward and Rose Elizabeth (Riehle) Toles; m. Gretchen Amanda Saarnijoki, May 26, 1973; children: Amanda Laurel, Seth August. BA in English, SUNY, Buffalo, 1973. Artist Buffalo Courier-Express, NY, 1973—80, cartoonist NY, 1980—82, Buffalo News, NY, 1982—2002, UPS, 1982—, US News & World Report, 1994—99, The New Republic, 2000—02, Washington Post, Wash., DC, 2002—. Author: My School Is Worse than Yours, 1997; cartoon collection, The Taxpayer's New Clothes, 1985, Mr. Gazoo: A Cartoon History of the Reagan Era, 1987, At Least Our Bombs Are Getting Smarter: A Cartoon Preview of the 1990's, 1991, My Elected Representatives Went to Washington, 1993, Duh, 1996, comic strip, Curious Avenue, 1992—94, Randolph Itch, 2a.m., 2000—02. Recipient John Fischetti Editorial Cartoon award, Columbia Coll., Chgo., 1984, Pulitzer Prize for editl. cartooning, 1990, Editl. Cartoonist of the Yr., 2002. Mem.: Am. Assn. Editorial Cartoonists. Office: Washington Post 1150 15th St NW Washington DC 20071

**TOLHURST, JEFFREY WAYNE,** science educator, information systems educator; s. Gene and Charlotte Tolhurst; children: Courtney, Taryn. BA, U. Calif., Santa Barbara, 1983; MS, Humboldt State U., Arcata, Calif., 1995; PhD, U. S.C., Columbia, 1999. Cert. phys. sci. tchr. Calif. Hydrologic technician U.S. Geol. Survey, Santa Barbara, Calif., 1983—86; sci. tchr. San Benito HS, Hollister, Calif., 1986—91, dept. chair, 1988—89; cons. hydrologist Trinity Restoration Assocs., Arcata, Calif., 1991—94; faculty geosci., geographic info. sys. High Sierra Inst. at Baker Sta., Yosemite C.C. Dist., Sonora, Calif., 2005—. Delta Sierra Sci. Project lead instr. San Joaquin County and Columbia Coll., Sonora, 2005—; grant proposal reviewer NSF, Arlington, Va., 1997—; mem. steering com. Bay Area Earth Sci. Inst., San Jose, 1989—91, Earth and Space Sci. Technol. Edn. Project, Boulder, Colo., 1995—96; planning team mem., presenter Nat. Assn. Geosci. Tchrs., Colorado Springs, 2000; author geosci. curriculum Monterey Bay Aquarium. Author (and tech. advisor): Aftershock: The Loma Prieta Earthquake and its Impact on San Benito County; contbr. articles to profl. jours. Recipient Excellence in Edn. award, Calif. Geog. Info. Assn., 2001; fellow Joseph Woolford, M.D. Student fellow, Eureka Rotary, 1992. Mem.: Geol. Soc. Am. (Excellence in Tchg. award 1989), Nat. Assn. Geology Tchrs., Nat. Assn. Geosci. Tchrs. (counsilor-at-large 2002—06, Outstanding Earth Sci. Tchr. 1989), Hollister Gem and Mineral Club (editor 1989—91, pres. 1989—91), San Benito Amateur Radio Club (sec. 1989—91). Office: Columbia College 11600 Columbia College Dr Sonora CA 95370 Home: 308 Bradley St Denton TX 76201

**TOLIA, VASUNDHARA K.,** pediatric gastroenterologist, educator; b. Calcutta, India; came to U.S., 1975; d. Rasiklal and Saroj (Kothari) Doshi; m. Kirit Tolia, May 30, 1975; children: Vinay, Sanjay. MBBS, Calcutta U., 1968-75. Intern, resident Children's Hosp. Mich., Detroit, 1976-79, fellow, 1979-81, dir. pediat. endoscopy unit, 1984-90, dir. pediat. gastroenterology and nutrition, 1990—2005. Instr. Wayne State U., Detroit, 1981—83, asst. prof., 1983—91, assoc. prof., 1991—97, prof., 1997—2005. Mem. editl. bd. Inflammatory Bowel Diseases, 1999— Am. Jour. Gastroenterology, 1999, Rev. of World Lit. in Pediatrics, 1999—, AAP Grand Rounds and Therapy, 2006—; contbr. articles to profl. jours. Named Woman of Distinction, Mich. chpt. Crohn's and Colitis Found. Am., 1991. Fellow Am. Coll. Gastroenterology (chair ad-hoc com. pediat. gastroenterology 1998-2000), Am. Acad. Pediats.; mem. Am. Gastroenterology Assn., N.Am. Soc. Pediat. Gastroenterology and Nutrition, Soc. Pediat. Rsch. Home: 4304 Copper Cliff Ct Bloomfield Hills MI 48302 Personal E-mail: vasu.tolia@gmail.com.

**TOLINS, ROGER ALAN,** lawyer; b. Bklyn., Jan. 25, 1936; s. Albert and Claire (Rothstein) T.; m. Doris Levine, May 15, 1960; children: Fran, Jonathan. AB with distinction, Dartmouth Coll., 1956; LLB, NYU, 1959, LLM in Taxation, 1961. Bar: N.Y. 1959. Assoc. Brennan, London & Buttenwieser, N.Y.C., 1961-67; ptnr. Goldfeld, Charak, Tolins & Lowenfels, N.Y.C., 1967-74, Tolins & Lowenfels, N.Y.C., 1975—. Guest lectr. in securities law Seton Hall U. Sch. Law, 1989—. With U.S. Army, 1959-60. Mem. ABA (sect. on taxation), N.Y. State Bar Assn. Office Phone: 212-421-1965. E-mail: roger@tolinslowenfels.com

**TOLIVER, LEE,** mechanical engineer; b. Wildhorse, Okla., Oct. 3, 1921; s. Clinton Leslie and Mary (O'Neall) T.; m. Barbara Anne O'Reilly, Jan. 24, 1942 (dec. Jan. 1999); children: Margaret Anne, Michael Edward. BSME, U. Okla., 1942. Engr. Douglas Aircraft Co., Santa Monica, Calif., 1942, Oklahoma City, 1942-44, Los Alamos (N.Mex.) Sci. Lab., 1946; instr. mech. engring. Ohio State U., Columbus, 1946-47; engr. Sandia Nat. Labs., Albuquerque, 1947-82; instr. computer sci. and math. U. N.Mex., Valencia County, 1982-84; number theory researcher Belen, N.Mex., 1982—. Author: Relations Between Prime and Relatively Prime Integers, 1998. With Manhattan Project (Atomic Bomb) U.S. Army, 1944-46. Home: 206 Howell St Belen NM 87002-6225

**TOLL, BARBARA ELIZABETH,** art gallery director; b. Phila., June 8, 1945; d. Joseph M. and Evelyn Toll BA, Goucher Coll., 1967; MFA, Pratt Inst., 1969. Asst. dir. jr. coun. Mus. Modern Art, N.Y.C., 1969-70; dir. Hundred Acres Gallery, N.Y.C., 1971-76; curator David Rockefeller Collection, N.Y.C., 1975-81; pres., dir. Barbara Toll Fine Arts, N.Y.C., 1981-94, dir., 1994—. Bd. dirs. Corp. Yaddo; curator Focus: Donald Judd Furniture, Parrish Art Mus., Southampton, NY, 1996, Friendships in Arcadia: Writers and Artists at Yaddo in the 90s, 2000, Follies: Fantasy in the Landscape, Parrish Art Mus., 2001, Reconfiguring Space: Blueprints for Art in Gen., 2003. Trustee Ind. Curators Internat.; nat. bd. dirs. ArtTable, 2001—04. Avocation: gardening. Office: 138 Prince St New York NY 10012-3135

**TOLL, BRUCE ELLIOT,** real estate developer; b. Phila., Apr. 29, 1943; s. Albert Arthur and Sylvia Toll; m. Robbi Stern; children: Michelle, Elizabeth, Wendy, Jennifer. BA in Acctg., U. Miami, 1965. Pres., dir., COO Toll Brothers Inc., Horsham, Pa., 1967—98, vice chmn., 1998—; founder, principal BET Investments. Bd. dir. UbiquiTel Inc., Home Builders Assn. Bucks & Montgomery Counties. Twp. commr. Abington Twp., Pa., 1985-87; bd. dirs. Abington Meml. Hosp., Pa. Nursing Home Loan Agy., 1983-91; chmn., past pres. Abington Jewish. Devel. Authority; bd. mem. Ben Franklin Tech Ctr. SE Pa., Phila. Mus. Art. Mem. Nat. Homebuilders Assn., Philmont Country Club, Equity. Republican. Office: Toll Brothers Inc 250 Gibraltar Rd Horsham PA 19044*

**TOLL, JOHN SAMPSON,** retired academic administrator, physics professor; b. Denver, Oct. 25, 1923; s. Oliver Wolcott and Merle d'Aubigne (Sampson) T.; m. Deborah Ann Taintor, Oct. 24, 1970; children: Dacia Merle Sampson, Caroline Taintor. BS with honors, Yale U., 1944; AM, Princeton U., 1948, PhD, 1952; DSc (hon.), U. Md., 1973, U. Wroclaw, Poland, 1975; LLD (hon.), Adelphi U., 1978; PhD (hon.), Fudan U., Peoples Republic China, 1987; LHD (hon.), SUNY, Stony Brook, 1990; LLD (hon.), U. Md., Eastern Shore, 1993. Mng. editor, acting chmn. Yale Sci. mag., 1943-44; with Princeton U., 1946-49, proctor fellow, 1948-49; Friends of Elementary Particle Theory Research grantee for study in France, 1950; theoretical physicist Los Alamos Sci. Lab., 1950-51; staff mem., assoc. dir. Project Matterhorn, Forrestal Rsch. Ctr., Princeton U., 1951-53; prof., chmn. physics and astronomy U. Md., 1953-65; pres., prof. physics SUNY, Stony Brook, 1965-78, U. Md., 1978-89, chancellor, 1988-89, chancellor emeritus, prof. physics, 1989—; pres. Univs. Rsch. Assn., Washington, 1989-94, Washington Coll., Chestertown, Md., 1995—. 1st dir. chancellor's panel on univ. pruposes SUNY, 1970; physics cons. to editl. staff Nat. Sci. Tchrs. Assn., 1957—61; U.S. del., head scientist, secretariat Internat. Conf. High Energy Physics, 1960; mem.-at-large U.S. Nat. Internat. Union Pure and Applied Physics, 1960—63; chmn. rsch. adv. com. on electrophysics NASA, 1961—65; mem. gov. Md. Sci. Resources Adv. Bd., 1963—65; mem., chmn. adv. panel for physics NSF, 1964—67; mem. N.Y. Gov.'s Adv. Com. Atomic Energy, 1966—70; mem. governing coun. Wye Faculty Seminar, 1997—; dir. Eastern Shore Assn. Coll. Pres., 1998—; mem. bd. dirs. Md. Ctr. Agro-Ecology, Inc., 1999—; vis. prof. Nordic Inst. Theoretical Physics, Niels Bohr Inst., Denmark, U. Lund, Sweden, 1975—76; mem. math. scis. edn. bd. NAS; mem. Higher Edn. Heritage Action Com., 2002—. Contbr. articles to profl. jours. Mem. adv. coun. Del-Mar-Va coun. Boy Scouts Am., 1999—; mem. Higher Edn. Heritage Action Com., 2002—; bd. dirs. Hodson Scholarship Found., 1996, Mid-Shore Cmty. Found., 2002—. Recipient Benjamin Barge prize in math. Yale U., 1943, George Beckwith medal for Proficiency in Astronomy, 1944, Outstanding Citizen award City of Denver, 1958, Outstanding Tchr. award U. Md. Men's League, 1965, Copernicus award govt. of Poland, 1973, Stony Brook Found. award for disting. contbns. to edn., 1979, Disting. Svc. award State of Md., 1981, Silver medal Sci. U. Tokyo, 1994, Internat. Landmark award U. Md., 1994, first recipient Lifetime Achievement award Md. Assn. for Higher Edn., 2000, Chief Exec. Leadership award Coun. for Advancement and Support Edn., 2000; named Washingtonian of Yr., 1985, Citizen of Yr. Chestertown Optimist Club, 1997, John S. Toll Physics Bldg., Univ. Md., 2001; John Simon Guggenheim Meml. Found. fellow Inst. Theoretical Physics U. Copenhagen, U. Lund, Sweden, 1958-59. Fellow AAAS, Am. Phys. Soc., Washington Acad. Scis. (pres. 1995-96), N.Y. Acad. Scis.; mem. NSTA, Am. Coun. Edn. (bd. dirs. 1986-89, NAACP (life), Am. Assn. Physics Tchrs., Fedn. Am. Scientists (chmn. 1961-62), Philos. Soc. Washington, Assn. Higher Edn., Yale U. Sci. and Engring. Assn. (award for disting. contbns. 1996), Cosmos Club, Hamilton St. Club, Baltimore, Univ. Club (Washington and N.Y.), Phi Beta Kappa, Phi Kappa Phi (disting., Marylander of Yr. 2000 award), Sigma Xi (Sci. Achievement award 1965), Omicron Delta Kappa (hon.), Sigma Pi Sigma. Achievements include research on elementary particle theory, scattering. Office: U Md Dept Physics College Park MD 20742-4111 also: Washington Coll Pres's Office Chestertown MD 21620 E-mail: johntoll@physics.umd.edu, jtoll2@washcoll.edu. *Throughout my life I have tried mainly to do whatever seemed most important and useful.*

**TOLL, LARRY ALLEN,** history professor; b. Muncie, Ind., Dec. 12, 1959; s. Paul Eugene and Bessie Toll; m. Mary Krewsen, Nov. 16, 1996; children: Zachary, Daniel. BA, Ball State U., Muncie, 1982, MA, 1984, PhD, 1990. Assoc. prof. history Brewton-Parker Coll., Mt. Vernon, Ga., 1991—. Named Tchr. of Yr., Brewton-Parker Coll., 1993; recipient, 1995, 2001. Mem.: So. Hist. Assn. Mem. Assemblies of God Avocation: Civil War reenacting. Office: Brewten-Parker Coll BPC # 2099 PO Box 197 Mount Vernon GA 30445

**TOLL, PERRY MARK,** lawyer, educator; b. Kansas City, Mo., Oct. 28, 1945; s. Mark Irving and Ruth (Parker) T.; m. Mary Anne Shottenkirk, Aug. 26, 1967; children: Andrea Lynne, Hillary Anne. BS in Polit. Sci. and Econs., U. Kans., 1967, JD, 1970. Bar: Mo. 1970 1970, U.S. Dist. Ct. (we. dist.) Mo. 1970, U.S. Tax. Ct. 1979, U.S. Supreme Ct. 1979. With Shughart, Thomson & Kilroy P.C., Kansas City, 1970—, pres., 1995—2006, past chmn. bus. dept. Asst. prof. deferred compensation U. Mo., Kansas City, 1979-83; bd. dirs., pres. Heart of Am. Tax Inst., Kansas City, 1975-87. Mem., chmn. Prairie Village (Kans.) Bd. Zoning Appeals, 1977-93. Mem., ABA, Mo. Bar Assn., Am. Health Lawyers Assn., Am. Agr. Law Assn., Mo. Merchants and Mfrs. Assn., Greater Kansas City Med. Mgrs. Assn., Lawyers Assn. Kansas City, Bant Kans. Estate Planning Coun. (bd. dirs., pres.), Phi Kappa Tau (bd. dirs. Beta Theta chpt.). Office: Shughart Thomson & Kilroy 12 Wyandotte Plz 120 W 12th St Ste 1500 Kansas City MO 64105-1929

**TOLL, ROBERT IRWIN,** home construction company executive; b. Elkins Park, Pa., Dec. 30, 1940; s. Albert A. and Sylvia (Steinberg) T.; m. Norma (div.); children: Laurie, Deborah; m. Jane Snyder; children: Rachel, Jacob; stepson, Joshua Goldfein. AB, Cornell U., 1963; LLB cum laude, U. Pa., 1966. Bar: Pa. 1967. Atty. Wolf, Block Schorr Solis-Cohen, Phila., 1966-67; founder Toll Bros., Huntingdon Valley, Pa., 1967, chmn., CEO, 1967—. Mem. Mayor's Coun. on Housing in Phila.; mem. bd. overseers U. Pa. Law Sch.; mem. real estate coun. Cornell U. Real Estate Coun. Bd. dirs. Pa. Campaign for Choice, Phila., Beth Sholom Synagogue, Elkins Park, Southeastern chpt. ARC, Seeds of Peace, NYC; sponsor Say Yes to Edn., Phila.; mem. bd. trustees Abington Meml. Hosp. Found. Named Profl. Builder of Yr., Builder Mag., 1988, America's Best Builder, Nat. Assn. Homebuilders and Builder Mag., 1996, Ernst & Young's Master Entrepreneur of Yr. Award, 1996; recipient Nat. Housing Quality Award, Nat. Assn. Home Builders, 1995, Bronze Award, CEO of Yr. Fin. World, 1996, Residential Building Industry's CEO Silver Award, Wall Street Transcript, 1996. Mem. Nat. Assn. Home Builders, Philmont Country Club (Huntingdon Valley), Equity Lodge 591. Avocations: racing j/35 sailboats, tennis, skiing. Office: Toll Brothers Inc 250 Gibraltar Rd Horsham PA 19044-2323*

**TOLL, SHELDON SAMUEL,** lawyer; b. Phila., June 6, 1940; s. Herman and Rose (Ornstein) T.; m. Roberta Darlene Pollack, Aug. 11, 1968; children: Candice Moore, John Maitland, Kevin Scott. BA, U. Pa., 1962; MA, Oxford (Eng.) U., 1964; JD, Harvard U., 1967. Bar: Pa. 1967, Mich. 1972, Ill. 1990, Tex. 1990, U.S. Dist. Ct. (ea. dist.) Pa. 1968, U.S. Ct. Appeals (3d cir.) 1970, U.S. Supreme Ct. 1971, Mich. 1972, U.S. Dist. Ct. (ea. dist.), U.S. Ct. Appeals (6th cir.) 1973, U.S. Ct. Appeals (5th cir.) 1978, U.S. Dist. Ct. (no. dist.) Calif. 1986, U.S. Ct. Appeals (9th cir.) 1987, U.S. Dist. Ct. (ea. dist.) Wis. 1989. Assoc. Montgomery McCracken et al, Phila., 1967-72; sr. ptnr. Honigman Miller Schwartz and Cohn, Detroit, 1972—2003; prin. Sheldon S. Toll PLLC, Southfield, Mich., 2003—. Panelist Bankruptcy Litigation Inst., N.Y.C., 1984-94. Author: Toll's Pennsylvania Crime Code, 2005, Bankruptcy Litigation Manual, 2004. Bd. dirs. Southeastern Mich. chpt. ARC, Detroit

Mem. Fed. Bar Assn. (past pres. Detroit chpt.), ABA, Pa. Bar Assn., Phila. Bar Assn., Franklin (Mich.) Hills Country Club, Mar-a-Lago Club (Palm Beach, Fla.), Phi Beta Kappa. Democrat. Jewish. Office: Sheldon S Toll PLLC 2000 Town Ctr Ste 2550 Southfield MI 48075 Office Phone: 248-358-2460. Business E-Mail: lawtoll@comcast.net.

**TOLLEFSON, BEN C.,** state legislator, retired utilities executive; b. Minot, N.D., June 14, 1927; s. Ben K. and Hannah G. (Espeseth) T.; m. Lila R. Adams, Apr. 11, 1949; children: Robb, LuAnn, David, Richard. Student, Minot State U., 1946-48. Advt. salesman Minot Daily News, 1956-57; utility salesman No. States Power Co., Minot, 1957-72, sales mgr., 1972-89; retired, 1989; advisor Ctrl. Venture Capital, Minot, 1990-95; mem. N.D. Ho. of Reps., Bismark, 1984-99, N.D. Senate from 38th dist., Bismark, 2001—. Pres. Minot Jaycees, 1957. Served with USN, 1945-47. Recipient Clara Barton Svc. award Am. Red Cross, 1969; named one of Outstanding Young Men Am., Minot Jaycees, 1958, State Ofcl. Yr., Nat. Assn. Home Builders, 1992. Mem. Kiwanis (Minot lt. gov. 1973, Outstanding Lt. Gov. 1973), Elks. Republican. Lutheran. Avocations: hunting, public speaking. Home: 500 Twenty Fourth St NW Minot ND 58701

**TOLLEFSON, LEE,** architect; BArch, U. Minn.; MArch, U. Pa. Adj. prof., design studio & N. Am. Indian architecture U. Minn., Mpls., 1970—; ptnr. Rafferty, Rafferty, Tollefson Archs., St. Paul, 1983—. Fellow: AIA. Office: CALA Ralph Rapson Hall 89 Church St SE Minneapolis MN 55455 E-mail: tolle001@umn.edu.

**TOLLEFSON, TERRENCE ALFRED,** education educator, consultant; b. Pontiac, Mich., May 1, 1938; s. Alfred and Iva Denice Tollefson; m. Bonnie Lou Bradley, 1961; children: Bradley Alfred, Michelle Suzanne Miller. BA in Edn. and Soc. Studies, U. Mich., Ann Arbor, 1961; PhD, U. Mich., 1975; MBA in Mktg., Mich. State U., East Lansing, 1963. Assoc. prof. dept. adult and C.C. edn. N.C. State U., Raleigh, 1989—97; interim chair dept. ednl. leadership and policy analysis East Tenn. State U., Johnson city, 1993—. Home: Unit H4 780 Hamilton Rd Blountville TN 37617 Office: East Tennessee State Univ Box 70550 Johnson City TN 37614-1707 Office Phone: 423-439-7617.

**TOLLEN, CYNTHIA JOYCE,** photographer, writer; b. Chester, Pa., May 31, 1949; d. Samuel M. and Miriam S. Tollen; life ptnr. A. Prengel. Student, San Francisco Art Inst., 1972—74; BA, U. Pa., 1971; cert. in mgmt., Harvard U., 1988. TV prodn. WGBH-TV, Boston; film editor WSBK-TV, Boston, 1975—78; freelance photographer, writer Boston, 1975—2006. Cons. Commonwealth Mass., Boston. Photographer, author to numerous newspapers, jours., books, exhbns. and stock photography. Statewide coord. Communication Access Tech., 1991—93; book cons. Friends of Pub. Librs.; nat. constituency coord. Dem. Nat. Presdl. Campaign, Boston, 1988; mem. Inst. Nat. Electricity and Electronics Project, Boumerdes, Algeria, 1978—80; founding mem. Friends of Fox Libr., Arlington, Arlington Coun. Disability. Grantee, Mass. Cultural Coun. and Arlington Cultural Coun., 2005. Mem.: Arlington Hist. Soc. Democrat. Avocations: art, travel, wildlife and nature, psychic phenomena. Home: 50 Fairmont St Arlington MA 02474-8718 E-mail: ctollen@hotmail.com.

**TOLLENAERE, LAWRENCE ROBERT,** retired industrial products company executive; b. Berwyn, Ill., Nov. 19, 1922; s. Cyrille and Modesta (Van Damme) T.; m. Mary Elizabeth Hansen, Aug. 14, 1948; children: Elizabeth Homer, Stephanie, Caswell, Mary Jennifer. BS in Engring., Iowa State U., 1944, MS in Engring., 1949; MBA, U. So. Calif., 1969; LLD (hon.), Claremont Grad. Sch., 1977. Specification engr. Alumnium Co. Am., Vernon, Calif., 1946-47; asst. prof. indsl. engring. Iowa State U., Ames, 1947-50; sales rep. Am. Pipe and Constrn. Co. (now AMERON), South Gate, Calif., 1950-53, spl. rep. S.Am., 1952-54, 2nd v.p., mgr. Columbian divsn. Bogota, S.Am., 1955-57, divsn. v.p., mgr. Calif., 1957-63, v.p. concrete pipe ops. Monterrey Park, Calif., 1963-65, pres. corp. hdqrs., 1965-67; pres., CEO Ameron Inc., Monterrey Park, Calif., 1967-89, CEO, pres. Pasadena, 1989-93, chmn. bd. dirs., 1989-94, ret., 1994. Trustee The Huntington Library, Art Gallery and Bot. Gardens; emeritus mem. bd. fellows Claremont U. Ctr.; bd. gov.'s Iowa State U. Found. Mem. Calif. C. of C. (bd. dirs. 1977-92), Calif. Club (past pres.), Jonathan Club, Bohemian Club, San Francisco Club, Beavers Club (past pres., hon. dir.), Alpha Tau Omega. Republican. Avocations: fishing, hunting, horseback riding, stamp collecting/philately. Office: 3452 E Foothill Blvd Ste 230 Pasadena CA 91107 Home: 650 Harrison Ave Claremont CA 91711-4538

**TOLLER, PAIGE W.,** philosopher, educator; b. Plainview, Nebr., Jan. 16, 1977; d. Bruce E. and Jodi R. Forbes; m. Stephen P. Toller, Dec. 13, 1997. PhD, U. Nebr., Lincoln, 2006. Instr. of comm. McMurry U., Abilene, Tex., 2000—02; asst. prof. U. Nebr., Omaha, 2006—. Lay min. First Christian Ch., Omaha, 2006. Presdl. fellow, U. Nebr., 2005—. Office Phone: 402-554-4856.

**TOLLES, BRYANT FRANKLIN, JR.,** historian, educator; b. Hartford, Conn., Mar. 14, 1939; s. Bryant Franklin and Grace Frances (Ludden) T.; m. Carolyn Coolidge Kimball, Sept. 15, 1962; children: Thayer Coolidge, Bryant Franklin III. BA, Yale U., 1961, MA in Tchg., 1962; PhD, Boston U., 1970. Instr. history King Sch., Stamford, Conn., 1962-63; tchr. history St. George's Sch., Newport, RI, 1963-65; instr., asst. dean Tufts U., Medford, Mass., 1965-71; asst. dir., libr., editor publs. N.H. Hist. Soc., Concord, 1972-74; exec. dir., libr. Essex Inst., Salem, Mass., 1974-84; dir. mus. studies program, prof. history and art history U. Del., Newark, 1984—2005, prof. emeritus, 2005—, chmn. art conservation dept, 1997 2000. Mem. Com. for a New Eng. Bibliography, Inc. Author: New Hampshire Architecture, 1979, Architecture in Salem, 1983, The Grand Resort Hotels of the White Mountains: A Vanishing Architectural Legacy, 1998, Summer Cottages in the White Mountains: The Architecture of Leisure and Recreation, 1870-1930, 2000, Resort Hotels of the Adirondacks: The Architecture of a Summer Paradise, 1840-1940, 2003; editor: Leadership for the Future, 1991; contbr. articles and book revs. to profl. jours. Trustee Mt. Washington Obs., N.H., N.H. Hist. Soc. Ford. Found. fellow Yale U., 1962. Mem. Am. Antiquarian Soc., Colonial Soc. Mass., Orgn. Am. Historians, Soc. Archtl. Historians, Soc. Indsl. Archaeology, Am. Assn. Mus., New Eng. Mus. Assn., Mid-Atlantic Mus. Assn., Am. Assn. for State and Local History, Wilmington Rowing Club, Appalachian Mountain Club. Home: 1002 Kent Rd Wilmington DE 19807-2820 Business E-Mail: bftolles@udel.edu.

**TOLLEY, AUBREY GRANVILLE,** psychiatrist, health facility administrator; b. Lynchburg, Va., Nov. 15, 1924; married. Student, Duke U., 1942—43, U. Va., 1946—48, MD, 1952. Diplomate Am. Bd. Psychiatry and Neurology. Intern St. Elizabeths Hosp., Washington, 1952-53; asst. resident psychiatry U. Va. Hosp., Charlottesville, 1953-54; resident psychiatry VA Hosp., Roanoke, Va., 1955-56; instr. U.N.C. Sch. Medicine, 1956-61, asst. prof., 1961-66, clin. asst. prof. psychiatry, 1966-72, clin. assoc. prof., 1972-76, clin. prof., 1976—; dir. psychotherapy Dorothea Dix Hosp., Raleigh, N.C., 1962-67, dir. hosp., 1973-78. Dir. resident tng. John Umstead Hosp., Butner, N.C., 1966-67; dir. profl. tng. and edn. N.C. Dept. Mental Health, Raleigh, 1967-72, asst. dir., 1972-73; prin. investigator USPHS grant, 1957-59; cons. VA Hosp., Fayetteville, N.C., 1957-78; sr. cons., supervising faculty, cmty. psychiatry sect. dept. psychiatry U.N.C. Sch. Medicine, 1971-88; exec. sec. Multiversity Group, 1968-73 Trustee Found. Hope, Raleigh, 1984—. Served with USNR, 1943-46. Recipient The Order of the Long Leaf Pine, state of N.C., 1982. Fellow Am. Psychiat. Assn. (disting. life; assembly rep. N.C. Dist. br. 1969-82, 86-2000, mem. joint commn. on pub. affairs 1984-87, mem. constl. membership com. 1990-96, mem. commn. on subspecialization 1990-94, Warren Williams award 1987), Am. Coll. Psychiatrists (life); mem. AMA, N.C. Med. Soc. (life), Durham-Orange County Med. Soc., N.C. Psychiat. Assn. (pres. 1984-85, Lifetime Disting. Svc. award 1999), N.C. Hosp. Assn. (life), George C. Ham Soc. (Disting. Alumni award 1992). Home and Office: 110 Laurel Hill Rd Chapel Hill NC 27514-4323

**TOLLEY, B. CARY, III,** lawyer; b. Washington, July 17, 1949; BA in Polit. Sci., Yale Univ., 1972; JD summa cum laude, Washington & Lee Univ., 1975; LLM in Taxation, Univ. Fla., 1978. Bar: Va. 1975, Fla. 1977, NY 1988. Ptnr., tax & ERISA practice Hunton & Williams LLP, NYC, and mem. exec. com. Exec. editor Washington & Lee Law Rev., 1974—75. Trustee Presbyn. Ch. USA Found., Presbyn. Investment Loan Program. Lt. JAG USNR, 1975—78. Mem.: ABA, Order of Coif. Office: Hunton & Williams LLP 43rd Fl 200 Park Ave New York NY 10166-0136 Office Phone: 212-309-1180. Office Fax: 212-309-1100. Business E-Mail: ctolley@hunton.com.

**TOLLEY, EDWARD DONALD,** lawyer; b. San Antonio, Jan. 31, 1950; s. Lyle Oren and Mary Theresa Tolley; m. Beth Dekle Tolley; 1 child, Edward Spencer. BBA, U. Ga., 1971, MBA, 1974, JD, 1975. Bar: Ga. 1975, U.S. Dist. Ct. (5th cir.) 1976, U.S. Supreme Ct. 1978, U.S. Ct. Appeals (11th cir.) 1981. Ptnr. Cook, Noell, Tolley Bates and Michael and predecessor firms, Athens, Ga., 1975—. Lectr. various colls., univs., civic and profl. groups. Mem. Family Counseling Assn. of Athens, Inc., mem. Gov.'s Comm. on Criminal Sanctions and Correctional Facilities, 1988-90; past bd. dirs. Am. Cancer Soc.; pres. Clarke County Bd. Edn., 1992-93. Recipient award for cmty. svc. Chief Justice Ga. Supreme Ct., 2000. Fellow Ga. Bar Found., Am. Bd. Criminal Lawyers (bd. dirs. 1987, pres. 1996); mem. Fed. Bar Assn. (sec. 1983, treas. 1985, pres. Macon chpt. 1997-98), State Bar Ga. (chmn. law office and econ. com., bd. govs. 1985—, formal adv. opinion bd., Professionalism award 2002), Ga. Trial Lawyers (v.p.), Ga. Assn. Criminal Def. Lawyers (pres. 1985, Indigent Def. award 1983, 88), Athens Bar Assn. (past pres.), Am. Judicature Soc., Order of Barristers (pres.). Svc. award Chief Justice Ga. Supreme Ct., 2000). Office: Cook Noell et al 304 E Washington St Athens GA 30601-2731 Office Phone: 706-549-6111.

**TOLLEY, JERRY RUSSELL,** academic administrator; b. Goldsboro, N.C., Nov. 6, 1942; s. Elva Russell Tolley and Clara (Smith) Tolley-Bunch; m. Joan Morrison, June 8, 1965; children: Jerry R. Jr., Justin Clay. BS, East Carolina U., 1965, MEd, 1966; EdD, U. N.C. Greensboro, 1982; exec. mgmt. courses, Duke U. Tchr., coach Fayetteville Sr. HS, NC, 1966; asst. football coach, head track and tennis coach Elon Coll., NC, 1967-77, head football coach, 1977-81, dir. athletic scholarship fund, 1982, dir. corp. and ann. resources, 1983, coordinator Pride II Capital Campaign, 1984, assoc. dir. devel., 1985, officer corp. and major gifts, maj. gifts officer, 1999, dir. ann. giving, 2003; asst. v.p. tng., nat. dir. tng. & pub. affairs Lab. Corp. of Am., Burlington, NC, 1986—. Author: Intercollegiate History of Athletics and Elon College, 1982, American Football Coaches Guidebook to Championship Football Drills, 1985, 101 Winning Football Drills -From the Legends of the Game, 2003, The Complete Book of Defensive Football Drills, 2005, co-author: 101 Winning Plays, 1977, Leadership Education: A Source Book, 1989; contbr. articles. Treas. Town of Elon Coll., 1984-87, mayor protem, 1988, mayor, 1990-98, 2006, mayor emeritus, 1998-2006, chmn. recreation commn.; mayor Town of Elon, 2006; convenor City County Govt. Assn., 1987-98, Alamance County, NC, 1986—; mem. exec. bd. dirs. Cherokee Coun. Boy Scouts Am., 1986, Thomas E. Powell Jr. Biology Found.; pres. Alamance Found.; exec. bd. NC Health & Fitness Found.; bd. visitors Elon Coll.; mem. exec. com. Alamance County Ptnrs. in Edn.; bd. govs. 2 Those Who Care; dir. Alamance Edn. Alliance; bd. dirs. Cmty. Found. Greensboro; chmn. Citizens for Schs.; mktg. advisory com. Village of Brookwood; bd. advisors Morris Plan Bank. Named one of Outstanding Young Men Am., 1980, Internat. Men of Achievement, 1990, Cmty. Leaders Am., 1990, Mayors Hall of Fame, 1995; recipient Dwight D. Eisenhower award Nat. Football Hall of Fame, 1980, 81, Nat. Collegiate Football Championship award Eastman Kodak, Meritorious Svc. award Tom Sawyer-Huck Finn Tennis Classic, 1986, Order of the Long Leaf Pine, 1997, Laurel Wreath award State of NC, 2002; named Nat. Football Coach of Yr., Nat. Assn. Intercollegiate Athletics, 1980, Elon Coll. Sports Hall of Fame, East Carolina U. Athletic Hall of Fame, 1991. Mem.: All-Am. Football Found. (Lifetime Achievement award 2003), Coun. Advancement of Edn., Am. Football Coaches Assn. (life), Omicron Delta Kappa, Phi Delta Kappa, Sigma Delta Psi. Avocations: writing, racquet sports, jogging. Home: 1322 Westbrook Ave Elon NC 27244-9358 Office: Elon Univ 2600 Campus Box # 2600 Elon NC 27244-2010 Office Phone: 336-278-7447. Business E-Mail: tolleyj@elon.edu.

**TOLLISON, COURTNEY L.,** history professor; b. Greenville, SC, Aug. 26, 1977; d. Charles David and Linda Surett Tollison. BA, Furman U., 1999; MA, U. SC., 2001, PhD, 2003. Rsch. asst. Smithsonian Instn., Nat. Mus. of Am. History, Washington, 1998—98; instr. history Columbia Coll., SC, 2001—01, Dalton State Coll., Ga., 2003—03; vis. adj. asst. prof. history Furman U., Greenville, SC, 2004—; dir. oral history project Office of Pres. David E. Shi, Furman U., Greenville, SC, 2004—. Advanced placement reader for us history advanced placement exam Ednl. Testing Svc., Princeton, NJ, 2004—05. Author: Furman University, 2004 (Matrix award Nat. Assn. Women in Comms., 2005); contbr. chapters to books. Head agt. class of 1999 Furman U. Devel. Office, Greenville, SC, 2004—05, class agt., coll. graduating class, 1999—2004; reunion com. co-chair Furman U., 2004. Named Communicator of Yr. award, Assn. Women in Comm., 2005; named one of 35 and Under Best and Brightest, Greenville Mag.; recipient Young Profl. Yr., Greenville, SC C. of C., 2006, Head Agy Yr. award, Furman U., 1999, 2005—06. Mem.: So. Assn. of Women Historians, SC. Hist. Assn., Orgn. of Am. Historians, Am. Hist. Assn., Phi Alpha Theta, Alpha Delta Pi (life; stds. chair 1997—98). Avocations: reading, swimming, travel, ballet. Office Phone: 864-294-2377. Personal E-Mail: courtneytollison@yahoo.com. Business E-Mail: courtney.tollison@furman.edu.

**TOLLISON, JOSEPH W.,** family practice physician; BS, Citadel Mil. Coll., S.C., 1963; MD, Med. Univ. S.C., 1967. Pres. Am. Bd. Family Practice, Lenington, Ky, 1997, dep. exec. dir. 1999—. Prof. Med. Coll. Ga. Office Am Bd Family Practice 2228 Young Dr Lexington KY 40505-4219

**TOLLIVER, DOROTHY,** librarian; b. N.Y.C., Apr. 10, 1937; d. Morris and Rose (Poliner) Lamm; m. Robert F. Tolliver, Sept. 3, 1956; children: Craig Lee, Marc Alan. BA, Ind. U., 1958; MSLS, U. Ill., Champaign-Urbana, 1973. Inter-libr., reference libr. L.A. County Libr., 1958-59; dir. libr. Temple City (Calif.) Pub. Libr., 1959-60; reference, young adult libr. Burbank (Calif.) Pub. Libr., 1960-62; PTA libr. Roselawn Elem. Sch., Danville, Ill., 1970-72; reference libr. Danville Area C.C., 1972-76, head libr., 1973—88; libr. dir. Kahului Pub. Libr., 1988—89; head libr. UH Maui C.C., Kahului, 1989—, unit head for outreach and acad. support, 2004—. Cons. Ill. Office Edn., 1980-88, Hawaii Dept. Edn., 1992—. Mem. Commn. Status of Women, 1992—98; sec. Maui County Com. Status of Women, 1991—96; dir. Jewish Arts and Edn. Coun. Maui, 1996—99; mem. Hawaii Book Acad., judge Ka Pala Pala Po'okela awards, 2002—; chair Maui County Women's Conf., 1993; vice chair Maui County Commn. Persons with Disabilities, 1996—2001; pres. S&M Katz Jewish Libr. of Maui, 1996—, Hawaii Ctr. for the Book, 2002—; bd. dirs. Congregation Gan Eden, 1990—, pres., 1991—95; bd. dirs. Congregation Israel, pres., 1983—91; bd. dirs. Maui Cmty. Theater, 1997—; actor, dir. Voices on the Wind Readers' Theater, 1992—. Recipient Little Red Schoolhouse award Danville Schs. Citizens Com., 1972, Hawaii State award for leadership in promoting postive soc. change, edu. and womens equity, 1997. Mem.: AAUW (pres. Maui chpt. 1993—97, state bd. dirs. 1993, Hawaii State award), ALA, Am. Coll. and Rsch. Librs., Maui County Libr. Assn. (pres. 1990—96), Hawaii Libr. Assn. (bd. dirs.), Phi Beta Mu (alpha chpt.). Jewish. Avocations: reading, theater, travel. Office: Maui Community Coll 310 W Kaahumanu Ave Kahului HI 96732-1617 Office Phone: 808-984-3583. E-mail: tolliver@hawaii.edu.

**TOLLIVER, GLENDA REEDER,** social worker; b. Tyler, Tex., May 12, 1949; d. Nathaniel and Jessie Mae Reeder; m. Cletis Frank Tolliver, Feb. 23, 1985; 1 stepchild, Cletis K. Student in psychology, Tyler Jr. Coll., 1967—69, Tex. So. U., 1969—71, student in psychology, 1975—77. LCSW. Day care counselor Neighborhood Ctr., Inc., Houston, 1973—77; child protective svc. specialist Tex. Dept. Protective and Regulatory Svcs., Houston, 1977—99, supr., child protective svcs., 1999—. Adv. mem. 5th Ward Enrichment Program, Houston, 1992. Mem.: NAACP, Nat. Black Child Devel., Inc. (pub.

rels. 1981—, Pres. award, Houston chpt. 1994), Nat. Coun. Negro Women (v.p. Houston chpt. 1982—83), Toastmasters (pin), Gamma Phi Delta (pres. 1985—91). Avocations: sign language, writing poetry and novellas, piano, reading, studying cultures.

**TOLLMAN, AARON PAUL,** military officer; b. Chadron, Nebr., Feb. 16, 1978; s. Rex F. and Julie Ann Tollman. Commd. lt. U.S. Army, advanced through grades to sgt., chaplain's asst. Fort Hood, Tex., 1997—99, noncommissioned officer in charge Installation Chaplain's Office Presidio of Monterey, Calif., 1999—2003, noncommissioned officer in charge phys. security Transp. Terminal Brigade Vellajo, Calif., 2003—03, patrol supr. Mil. Police Detachment Law and Order Baghdad, Iraq, 2004—. Decorated Army Achievement medal U.S. Army, Army Good Conduct Medal US Army, Iraq Campaign Medal, Global War on Terrorism Svc. medal U.S. Army, Nat. Def. Svc. medal U.S. Dept. Def., Overseas Svc. ribbon, Good Conduct medal U.S. Army, Achievement medal Def. Lang. Inst. Air Force Wing, Army Commendation medal Def. Lang. Inst. Fgn. Lang. Ctr., Commendation medal U.S. Army; recipient Global War on Terrorism Svc. medal, 2005, 2006. Republican. Roman Catholic. Home: 737 Indian Creek Road Lusk WY 82225 Office: 313th Military Police Detachment L & O 2901 East Sahara Avenue Las Vegas NV 89104-4123

**TOLMACH, JANE LOUISE,** community activist, municipal official; b. Havre, Mont., Nov. 12, 1921; d. Robert Francis and Veronica (Tracy) McCormick; m. Daniel Michael Tolmach (Dec.), Sept. 9, 1946; children: James, Richard, Eve Alice, Adam, Jonathan. AB, UCLA, 1943; M in Social Scis., Smith Coll., 1945; JD, S. We. U., L.A., 1981. Social worker ARC Field Svcs. Corona Naval Hosp., Norco, Calif., 1945-46; chmn. bd. dirs. Camarillo (Calif.) State Hosp., 1959-68; trustee Oxnard (Calif.) Union High Sch. Dist., 1965-72; mem. state reclamation bd. Calif., 1981-82; mem. bd. govs. Calif. C.C., 1982-87; mem. bd. St. John's Regional Hosp., Oxnard, 1986-89; mem. bd. of assessment appeals County of Ventura, Ventura, Calif., 1992—2002, transp. commr., 2002—05, mem. campaign fin. ethics commn., 2005—, mem. fin. ethics commn., 2006—. Chmn. fin. com. Ventura County Grand Jury, 1958; mem. Oxnard (Calif.) Planning Commn., 1957-62; exec. mem. So. Calif. Assn. Govts., L.A., 1975-76. Author: Smith Studies, 1945. Chmn. dem. com., Ventura County, 1959-62, mem. campaign fin. ethics commn., 2006—; alternate or del. Dem. Nat. Convs., 1960, 68, 76, 88, 92, alt. 1956, 64; Women'schm. S. Calif. Dem. Com., 1966-70; nominee state assembly, 36th dist., Ventura, Calif., 1976; elected Oxnard City Coun. 1970-78, mayor, 1973-74. Home: 656 Douglas Ave Oxnard CA 93030-4614 Personal E-mail: jane.tolmach@adelphia.net.

**TOLMAN, BRETT L.,** prosecutor; b. Provo, UT; BA, Brigham Young U., 1994, JD, 1998. Chief counsel for crime & terrorism, Judiciary com. US Senate, Salt Lake City, 2004—05; asst. US atty. Dist. UT US Dept. Justice, Salt Lake City, 2000—03, US atty., 2006—. Office: US Attys Office 185 S State St Ste 400 Salt Lake City UT 84111

**TOLMIE, KENNETH DONALD,** artist, writer; b. Halifax, N.S., Can., Sept. 18, 1941; s. Archibald and Mary Evelyn (Murray) T.; m. Ruth MacKenzie, Aug. 11, 1962; children: Sarah Katherine, Jane Marianna. B.F.A., Mt. Allison U., 1962. Owner Tolmie Film Prodns., Kendog Films, Tolmie Gallery, Toronto. Chmn. Visual Arts Ottawa, 1975-76; founding mem. Bridgetown and Area Hist. Soc., James House Mus. Author: (children's book) Tale of an Egg, 1974, (art book) A Rural Life: An Artist's Portrait, 1986; 3 TV documentary films produced on his work by CBC and by TV-Ont., producer, Tolmie films prodn. in assn. with CBC, 2002 (aired nat. on CBCTV, 2002); one-man shows include Dorothy Cameron Gallery, Toronto, 1963, Beckett Gallery, Hamilton, 1986, Kaspar Gallery, Toronto, 1988; Mt. Allison Univ. solo cross Can. touring exbn. Bridgetown Series, 1982-84; group shows include Banfer Gallery, N.Y.C., 1963, Nat. Gallery Can., Watercolors Prints and Drawing, 1964, 66, London Art Mus., Ont., 1966, Can. Soc. Graphic Art, 1973, Art Gallery N.S., 1980, 81, N.S. Art Bank, 1981; represented in permanent collections Nat. Gallery Can., Ottawa, Montreal Mus. Fine Arts, N.S. Art Bank, Art Gallery N.S., Confedn. Centre for Arts, Hirshhorn Collection, Washington, Owens Art Gallery, Mt. Allison U., Dofasco Ltd., Husky Oil Ltd., Procter & Gamble Ltd., Slater Steels Ltd., Crownx Ltd., Moving Products, Inc. Bd. dirs. Art Gallery N.S., 1979-81. Recipient prodn. grant Nova Scotia Film Devel. Corp., 1999. Mem. Visual Arts N.S., Visual Arts Ont., Visual Arts Ottawa (chmn. 1975-76), Bridgetown Hist. Soc. (hon. life) Address: 39 Kenneth Ave Toronto ON Canada M6P 1J1 E-mail: ken@kentolmie.com.

**TOLNICK CHAMPA, JUDITH ELLEN,** art gallery director, curator; b. Boston, Nov. 21, 1952; d. Bernard and Rita Snyder Tolnick; m. Kermit Swiler Champa, May 31, 2001 (dec.). Student, Lake Forest Coll., 1970—72; BA magna cum laude, Brandeis U., 1974; MA in History of Art, Brown U., 1979, postgrad., 1986—87. Art historian Swain Sch. Design, New Bedford, Mass., 1979—82; curator, assoc. dir. curatorial affairs Bell Gallery, Brown U., Providence, 1982—89; dir. Fine Arts Ctr. Galleries U.R.I, Kingston, 1991—. Honors program faculty U. R.I., Kingston, 1994—95; external recommender various profl. visual artists Guggenheim Found., N.Y.C., 2000—; invited critic printmaking dept. RISD, Providence, 2002, adj. faculty, 03; panelist, instnl. grant reviewer Conn. Commn. on the Arts, Hartford, 2003. Organizing curator, author (exhbn. catalogue) Over Hear: Meanderer, The First Exile, 1989, R.I. State House Centennial Exhbn., 1996, Translations/Transgressions, 2002. Recipient Quality award, U. R.I., 1993, Diversity Planning Com. award, 2001, Outreach award, 2001. Mem.: N.E. Mus. Assn. (bd. mem. 1985—91, ann. conf. organizer 1988), Coll. Art Assn., Am. Assn. Mus., Phi Sigma Iota. Democrat. Avocations: classical music, modern music. Home: 26 Old Tannery Rd Providence RI 02906 Office: U RI Fine Arts Ctr Galleries 105 Upper College Rd Ste 1 Kingston RI 02881-0820 Office Phone: 401-874-2775. Business E-mail: jtolnick@uri.edu.

**TOLO, VERNON THORPE,** orthopedist, educator; b. Onawa, Iowa; MD, Johns Hopkins U., 1968. Diplomate Am. Bd. Orthopaedic Surgery. Intern Johns Hopkins Hosp., Balt., 1969—70, resident orthop. surgery, 1972—75; fellow pediat. orthop. Hosp. Sick Children, Toronto, Canada, 1975—76; asst. prof. Johns Hopkins U. Sch. Medicine, Balt., 1976—82, assoc. prof., 1982—87; prof. U. So. Calif., L.A., 1987—. Attending physician Johns Hopkins Hosp., Balt., 1976—87, Children's Hosp., L.A., 1987—. Mem.: Scoliosis Rsch. Soc., Pediat. Orthopedics Soc., Am. Acad. Pediatricians, Am. Orthop. Assn., Am. Acad. Orthop. Surgeons (1st v.p. 2002—03, pres. 2002—03). Office: Children's Hosp 4650 W Sunset Blvd Los Angeles CA 90027-6062

**TOLON, MICHAEL ODED,** music educator, director; b. Midway City - Tinker AFB, Okla., Jan. 30, 1958; s. Oded and Mattie Loren Tolon; m. Joni Beth - Hamilton Tolon, Apr. 9, 1983; children: Cathryn Marye, Elizabeth Ashley, Joel David Michael, Rachel Ruth. BA, Columbia Christian Coll.; MSc in Music Edn., Portland State U., Oreg., 1988; postgrad., U. San Diego. Cert. tchr. Oreg., Wash., advanced placement music theory tchr., guitar instr. Levels I and II. Dir. of bands Marshall H.S., 1989—93, Tigard (Oreg.) HS, 1993—98, Parkrose HS, Portland, Oreg., 1998—. Adj. instr. Cascade Coll., Portland, 1997—. Ch. leader Metro Ch. of Christ, Gresham, Oreg., 1992—2002. Grantee, Guitar Workshops Ltd., 2001. Mem.: Oreg. Music Educator Assn. (assoc.). Republican. Avocations: church work, camping, fishing. Home: 3505 Southwest Victoria Place Gresham OR 97080 Office: Parkrose High School 12003 NE Shaver Street Portland OR 97220 Office Phone: 503-408-2605. Personal E-mail: michael_tolon@parkrose.k12.or.us. E-mail: mjtolon@yahoo.com.

**TOLOR, ALEXANDER,** psychologist, educator; b. Vienna, Oct. 21, 1928; s. Stanley and Josephine (Kellner) T.; m. Belle Simon, Sept. 2, 1951; children: Karen Beth, Lori Ann, Diana Susan. BA, NYU, 1949 MA, 1950, PhD, 1955. Diplomate Am. Bd. Profl. Psychologists. Grad. asst. NYU, 1950-52; intern Neurol. Inst., N.Y.C., 1952-53, clin. psychologist, 1953-55; sr. clin. psychologist Inst. of Living, Hartford, Conn., 1957-59; dir. psychol. services Fairfield

Hills Hosp., Newtown, Conn., 1959-64; clinic dir. Kennedy Center, Bridgeport, Conn., 1964-65; dir. Inst. Human Devel., Fairfield U., 1965-77, assoc. prof. psychology, 1965-68, research prof. psychology, 1968-75, prof. psychology, 1975-89, dir. school psychology div., 1975-77, dir. sch. and applied psychology program, 1982-86, prof. emeritus, 1989—; practice psychology Danbury, Conn., 1960-96; clin. instr. psychology Yale U., 1963-67. Cons. West Haven VA Hosp., 1962-66, Bridgeport Bd. Edn., Silver Hill Found., 1972-75, Fairfield Hills Hosp., 1973-94, Hallbrooke Hosp., 1975-92. Author: (with H.C. Schulberg) An Evaluation of the Bender-Gestalt Test, 1963, (with G.G. Brannigan) Research and Clinical Applications of the Bender-Gestalt Test, 1980, (with M. Deignan) Adjustment Problems in Children, 1984; editor: Effective Interviewing, 1985; adv. editor Jour. Cons. and Clin. Psychology; cons. editor Personality: An Internat. Jour.; contbr. articles to profl. jours. Served to 1st lt. USAF, 1955-57. Fellow Am. Psychol. Assn., Soc. Personality Assessment, Conn. Psychol. Assn. (mem. council 1964, pres. 1984); mem. Eastern Psychol. Assn., Psi Chi, Delta Phi Alpha, Beta Lambda Sigma, Phi Delta Kappa Home: 6 Brittania Dr Danbury CT 06811-2606 Personal E-mail: atbt51@aol.com.

**TOLSTEDT, CARRIE L.,** bank executive; BS in Bus. Adminstrn., U. Nebr.; degree in Banking, U. Wash. From credit tng. program to corp. banking officer United Bank Denver, corp. banking officer; from v.p. corp. banking to sr. v.p. downtown Omaha (Nebr.) retail banking Norwest Bank Nebr., Omaha, 1986—95; sr. v.p. corp. retail FirstMerit Corp., Akron, Ohio, 1995—96, pres., CEO Citizens Nat. Bank and Peoples Nat. Bank, 1996—98, exec. v.p., 1996—98; with Norwest Corp., 1998; regional pres. Ctrl. Calif. Wells Fargo & Co., San Francisco, 1998—2001, exec. v.p. regional banking, 2001—, bd. dirs. The Cmty. Coll. Found. Mem.: Consumer Bankers Assn. (bd. dirs.), U. Nebr. Alumni Assn. (bd. dirs.), Calif. C. of C. (bd. dirs.). Office: Wells Fargo & Co 420 Montgomery St San Francisco CA 94163

**TOLUIE, KAMRAN,** cardiologist, electrophysiologist; b. Tehran, Iran, June 29, 1961; arrived in U.S., 1991; s. Kiumars Toluie and Shahin Noor Bakhsh; m. Fereshteh Salim Shahshahani, June 14, 1990; children: Sherwin, Ava. MD, Tabriz (Iran) U., 1986. Diplomate Am. Bd. Internal Medicine, Am. Bd. Cardiovascular Diseases, Am. Bd. Cardiac Electrophysiology. Resident in internal medicine SUNY, Bklyn., 1993-96; cardiology fellow Metrohealth Med. Ctr./Mt. Sinai Med. Ctr., Cleve., 1996-98; electrophysiology fellow Hosp. U. Pa., Phila., 1998-2000; dir. cardiac electrophysiology dept. Kaiser Permanente Med. Ctr., L.A., 2000—. Translator: Introdction to ECG, 1990, Manual of Medical Procedures; contbr. chapters to books, articles to profl. jours. Fellow: ACP, Am. Coll. Cardiology. Achievements include performed first FDA-approved biventricular ICD in a non-clinical site in the U.S; performed first atrial fibrillation ablation under phased array intracardiac echocardiography guidance and 3-D electroanatomical mapping in Iowa; performed first biventricular pacer in Cedar Rapids, Iowa. Avocation: tennis. Home: 18100 Lake Encino Dr Encino CA 91316 Office: Kaiser Permanente LA Med Ctr 4867 Sunset Blvd 6th Fl Los Angeles CA 90027 Office Phone: 323-783-5850. Personal E-mail: ktoluie@pol.net.

**TOM, JAMES ROBERT,** accountant; b. Odessa, Tex., Apr. 21, 1939; s. George Ellison and Mattie Inez (Zimmerman) T.; m. Frances Kay Mackey, Sept. 16, 1961; children: Susan Kay, James Robert Jr., Emily Christian. Student, Tex. A&M U., 1957; BBA in Acctg., Tex. Tech. U., 1961; postgrad., Colo. State U., 1961—62. CPA Tex. Jr. acct. Peat, Marwick, Mitchell & Co., Midland, Tex., 1965; asst. trust officer 1st City Nat. Bank, Midland, 1966-67, v.p., trust officer, 1969-72; sr. acct. Main Hurdman, Midland, 1967-68; pres. Gibson Mfg. Co., Midland, 1972-73; exec. v.p., CEO Teraco, Inc., Midland, 1974-75, fin. cons., 1975-76, acct., 1976—. Bd. dirs. Am. Heart Assn., Midland, 1966, Arthritis Found., Midland, 1971-72, 75, Midland County Livestock Assn., Midland, 1966-72, ARC, Midland, 1970-80, Boys Club, Midland, 1971-72. 1st lt. U.S. Army, 1963-65. Mem.: AICPA, Permian Basin CPA, Tex. Soc. CPA. Republican. Roman Catholic. Avocations: fishing, hunting, reading. Home: 605 Sandy Oaks Dr Boerne TX 78015 Office: 130 Medical Dr Boerne TX 78006

**TOM, LAUREN,** actress, singer; b. Chgo., Aug. 4, 1959; d. Chan and Nancy (Dare) T.; m. Glenn Lau-Kee, Oct. 23, 1982. Student, Northwestern U., 1977; BA, NYU. Actress (Broadway plays) A Chorus Line, 1978—79, Doonesbury, 1983—84, Hurlyburly, 1985, (plays) The Music Lessons, 1980, Family Devotions, 1981, (films) Nothing Lasts Forever, 1982, Joy Luck Club, 1993, When a Man Loves a Woman, Mr. Jones, With Friends Like These, 1998, Catfish in Black Bean Sauce, Manhood, 2003, Synergy, Bad Santa, 2003, God's Waiting List, (TV series) The Facts of Life, 1982, Grace Under Fire, 1993, DAG, 2000, Friends, (one woman show) 25 Psychics (Dramalogue awards, best performance), actress (voice) Futurama, King of the Hill, Codename: Kids Next Door, 2002, Teacher's Pet, 2004, Rocket Power, Max Steel, Batman, Superman, Kim Possible, Clifford's Puppy Days, 2003, American Dragon, Mulan II, 2004. Supporter Asia Inst., Washington. Mem. Actors' Equity Assn., Screen Actors Guild, AFTRA. Office: c/o Kelly Garner Pop Art Films and Mgmt 9615 Brighton Way Ste 426 Beverly Hills CA 90210

**TOM, LAWRENCE,** technology executive; b. L.A., Jan. 21, 1950; BS, Harvey Mudd Coll., 1972; JD, Western State U., San Diego, 1978; spl. diploma, U. Calif., San Diego, 1991. Design engr. Rockwell Internat., L.A., 1972-73, Goodrich Corp. (formerly Rohr, Inc.), Chula Vista, Calif., 1973-76, sr. design engr., 1980, computer graphics engring. specialist, 1980-83, chief engring. svcs., 1989-91, chief engring. quality, 1991-93, project mgr., 1993-98, info. tech. specialist, 1998—2002. Sr. engr. Rohr Marine, Inc., Chula Vista, 1977-79; chief exec. officer Computer Aided Tech. Svcs., San Diego, 1983-87; software cons. Small Systems Software, San Diego, 1984-85; computer graphics engring. specialist TOM & ROMAN, San Diego, 1986-88; dir. Computervision Users Group, 1986-88, vice chmn. 1988-91, pres., 1991-93, exec. chmn., 1992-94; bd. dirs. Exec. Program for Scientists and Engrs.-Alumni Assn. U. Calif., San Diego, 1991—; CFO Global Peregrine Users Group, 2001-03; pres. Art to Art, San Diego, 1994-99; pres. SGL Computer Profls., San Diego, 1999—; cons. in field. George H. Mayr Found. scholar, 1971, Bates Found. Aero. Edn. scholar, 1970-72. Mem. Nat. Mgmt. Assn. (chpt. v.p.), Aircraft Owners and Pilots Assn., Infiniti Club. Office: 7770 Regents Rd Ste 113-190 San Diego CA 92112-1967 Office Phone: 619-985-9850. Business E-mail: larry.tom@sglpro.com.

**TOM, RANDOLPH L.,** corporate financial executive; s. Bell Kam and Choy Mee Tom; m. Linda K. Wong, May 28, 1988; children: Gwendolyn L., Jarrett L. BS, MBA, NYU, 1974, JD, MBA, 1978. Bar: N.Y. 1978, Calif. 1994, DC 1994. Sr. assoc. corp. securities Fulbright & Jaworski (formerly Reavis & McGrath), N.Y.C., 1978—85; gen. counsel, sec. AT&E Corp., San Francisco, 1985—91; chmn., CEO Dynasty Capital Svcs. LLC, Moraga, Calif., 1988—; pres. Asia Pacific AT&E Corp., San Francisco, 1989—91; securities ptnr., head Asia Pacific practice Oppenheimer Wolff & Donnelly LLP, Palo Alto, Calif., 1998—2000. Editor, pub.: bimonthly tech. perspective Dynasty Perspectives; author: (nat. law jour. spl. report) Internet May Offer Access to US Cash; contbr. bus. plans handbook. Bd. dirs. Cmty. Tech. Found. of Calif., San Francisco, 2004—05, U. of San Francisco Ctr. for the Pacific Rim, San Francisco, 2004—05. Recipient Gary scholarship, NYU, Book scholarship, Mgmt. Assn., N.Y.C., univ. scholarship, NYU, Law Ctr. scholarship, NYU. Sch. of Law, Marcus Nadler fellowship, Stern Grad. Sch. of Bus., George Baker scholar. Mem.: Beta Gamma Sigma, Phi Alpha Kappa. Office: Dynasty Capital Svcs LLC One Madsen Ct Moraga CA 94556 Office Phone: 925-377-5300. E-mail: dynasty@dynastycap.com.

**TOMA, J. DOUGLAS,** education executive; b. Mount Clemens, Mich., Dec. 16, 1963; s. John D. and Judith A. Toma; m. Linda P. Bachman, June 1996; 1 child, John Stephen. BA, Mich. State U., 1986; JD, U. Mich., 1989, MA, 1993, PhD, 1995. Asst. prof. U. Mo., Kansas City, 1995—2000; sr. fellow U. Pa., 2000—03; assoc. prof. Inst. Higher Edn. U. Ga., Athens, 2003—. Author: Football U.: Spectator Sports in the Life of the American University, 2003.

Mem. Airport Authority of Athens-Clarke County, Athens, Ga. Democrat. Avocations: travel, sports. Home: Rutherford Hall Athens GA 30609 Office: Institute of Higher Education 8 Meigs Hall Athens GA 30602 Business E-Mail: jdt@uga.edu.

**TOMAIN, JOSEPH PATRICK,** law educator, retired dean; b. Long Branch, N.J., Sept. 3, 1948; s. Joseph Pasquale and Bernice M. (Krzan) T.; m. Kathleen (Corcione), Aug. 1, 1971; children: Joseph Anthony, John Fiore. BA, U. Notre Dame, 1970; JD, George Washington U., 1974. Bar: NJ, Iowa. Assoc. Giordano and Halleran, Middletown, NJ, 1974-76; asst. to prof. law Drake U. Sch. Law, Des Moines, 1976-83; prof. law U. Cin., 1983—, acting dean, 1989—90, dean, 1990—2004, Nippert prof. law, 1990—, dean emeritus, 2004. Vis. prof. law U. Tex., Austin, 1986—87. Author: Energy Law in a Nutshell, 1981, Nuclear Power Transformation, 1987; co-author: Energy Decision Making, 1983, Energy Law and Policy, 1989, Energy and Natural Resources Law, 1992, Regulatory Law and Policy, 1993, 2d edit., 1998, 3rd edit., 2003, Energy, The Environment and the Global Economy, 2000. Trustee Ctr. for Chem. Addictions Treatment, Cin., Vol. Lawyers for Poor, Cin.; mem. steering com. BLAC/CBA Round Table, Cin.; chair Knowledge Works Found.; trustee Ohio State Bar Found., Ohio Legal Assitance Found.; gov. Greater Cin. Found. Served in USAR, 1970-76. Mem. ABA, Am. Law Inst., Ohio State Bar Assn. (del.), Mercantile Libr. Assn. (v.p.). Roman Catholic. Home: 3009 Springer Ave Cincinnati OH 45208-2440 Office: U Cin Coll Law Office Dean PO Box 210040 Cincinnati OH 45221-0040 Office Phone: 513-556-0067. Business E-Mail: joseph.tomain@uc.edu.

**TOMAINO, JOSEPH CARMINE,** former retail executive, former postal inspector; b. Danbury, Conn., Dec. 12, 1948; s. Joseph and Lena Marie (LaCava) T.; m. Eileen M. Pulver (div. Feb. 1978); m. Ann C. Underriner, Sept. 20, 1986; children: Joseph Richard, Robert John. BS, Western Conn. State U., 1970; MBA, Roosevelt U., 1978, MS in Acctg., 1986. Cert. fraud specialist; cert. fraud examiner; diplomate Am. Bd. Law Enforcement, Am. Coll. Forensic Examiners; expert, lic. pvt. investigator, Ill. Post office clk. U.S. Postal Svc., Ridgefield, Conn., 1970-71, postal inspector Chgo., 1971-80, supervisory postal inspector, 1980-93; mgr. we. ops. loss prevention dept. Walgreen Co., Deerfield, Ill., 1993-96; sr. mgr. litigation svcs. Altschuler, Melvoin & Glasser CPAs, Chgo., 1996-98; dir. litigation svcs. Altschuler, Melvoin & Glasser/Am. Express Co., Chgo., 1999-2000; ptnr. Altschuler, Melvoin & Glasser CPAs, Chgo., 2000—; mng. dir. Am. Express Tax & Bus. Svcs., Chgo., 2000—02; sr. mng. dir. Chgo. region Citigate G.I., 2002—05; ptnr. Smarts & Assocs., LLP, Chgo., 2005—. Mem. Am. Soc. Indsl. Security, Fed. Law Enforcement Officers Assn., Nat. Assn. Chiefs Police, Ill. Chiefs Police, Spl. Agts. Assn., Ill. Police Assn., Nat. Soc. Pub. Accts., Assn. Cert. Fraud Examiners, Am. Coll. Forensic Examiners, Assn. Cert. Anti-Money Laundering Specialists, Ill. Soc. CPAs. Office: Smarts and Assocs LLP 30 N LaSalle St 35th Fl Chicago IL 60602

**TOMAN, MARY ANN,** federal official; b. Pasadena, Calif., Mar. 31, 1954; d. John James and Mary Ann Zajec T.; m. Milton Allen Miller, Sept. 10, 1988; 1 child, Mary Ann III. BA with honors, Stanford U., Calif., 1976; MBA, Harvard U., 1981. Mgmt. cons. Bain and Co., Boston, 1976—77; mgr. brand Procter & Gamble Co., Cin., 1977—79; summer assoc. E.F. Hutton, N.Y.C., 1980; head corp. planning Burton Group, PLC, London, 1981—84; pres., founder Glenclair Ltd., London, 1984—86; pres. London Cons. Group, London, Beverly Hills, Calif., 1988; mem. U.S. Presdl. Transition Team, Bus. and Fin., 1988—89; dep. asst. sec. commerce, automotive affairs, consumer goods U.S. Dept. Commerce, Washington, 1989—93; commr., chmn. L.A. Indsl. Devel. Authority, 1993—95; dep. treas. State of Calif., Sacramento, 1995—99. Bd. dirs. U.S. Coun. of Devel. Fin. Agencies, 1994-97. Founder, chair Stanford U. Fundraising, London, 1983-88; chair Reps. Abroad Absentee Voter Registration, London, 1983-88; bd. dirs. Harvard Bus. Sch. Assn., London, 1984-87; vol. Bush-Quayle Campaign, 1988; trustee Bath Univ., Eng., 1988—; apptd. by Gov. Wilson to State of Calif. Econ. Devel. Adv. Coun., 1994-97. Jobs Tng. Coordinating Coun., 1998-2000; first vice chmn. Rep. Party L.A. County, 1996-99, chmn., 1999—; mem. exec. bd. Coun. Calif. County Chairmen, 1999—; mem. U.S. Presdl. Transition Team, 2000-2001; Rep. candidate for Calif. State Treas., 2002. Named Calif. Mother of Yr., 1997. Mem. Stanford Club U.K. (pres. 1983-88), Harvard Club N.Y., Harvard Club Washington, Harvard Club Boston, Nat. Assn. of Urban Rep. County Chmn. Roman Catholic. Home: 604 N Elm Dr Beverly Hills CA 90210-3421 Office: PO Box 71483 Los Angeles CA 90071-0483 Office Phone: 310-274-4822. Business E-Mail: tomanmail@aol.com.

**TOMAR, RICHARD THOMAS,** lawyer; b. Camden, N.J., Mar. 4, 1945; s. William and Bette (Brown) T.; children: Lindsay, Leanne Meryl, Daniel Gregory. BA, Columbia U., 1967; JD, U. Pa., 1970. Bar: DC 1971, N.J. 1971, Md. 1976. Pvt. practice, Washington, 1971-73; ptnr. Philipson, Mallios & Tomar, P.C., Washington, 1973—89; Margolius, Mallios, Davis, Rider & Tomar, LLP, Washington, 1989—2002; chair comml. litigation Karp, Frosh, Lapidus, Wigodsky & Norwind, PA, Rockville, Md., 2002—. Mem. D.C. Trial Lawyers Assn. (bd. dirs. 1980-89). Office: Karp Frosh Lapidus Wigodsky & Norwind PA 2273 Research Blvd Ste 200 Rockville MD 20850-3283 Home: 4801 Hampden Ln Apt 304 Bethesda MD 20814-6556 Office Phone: 301-948-3800. Office Fax: 301-948-5449. Business E-Mail: rtomar@karpfrosh.com.

**TOMAR, RUSSELL HERMAN,** pathologist, educator, researcher; b. Phila., Oct. 19, 1937; s. Julius and Ethel (Weinreb) T.; m. Karen J. Kent, Aug. 29, 1965; children: Elizabeth, David. BA in Journalism, George Washington U., 1959, MD, 1963. Diplomate Am. Bd. Pathology, Am. Bd. Allergy and Immunology, Am. Bd. Pathology, Immunopathology. Intern Barnes Hosp., Washington U. Sch. Medicine, 1963-64, resident in medicine, 1964-65; asst. prof. medicine SUNY, Syracuse, 1971-79, assoc. prof., 1979-88, assoc. prof. microbiology, 1980-84, prof., 1984-88, asst. prof. pathology, 1974-76, assoc. prof., 1976-83, prof., 1983-88, dir. immunopathology, 1974-88, attending physician immunodeficiency clinic, 1982-88, acting dir. microbiology, 1977-78, 82-83, interim dir. clin. pathology, 1986-87; prof. pathology and lab. medicine U. Wis. Ctr. for Health Scis., Madison, 1988—2003; dir. div. lab. medicine U. Wis., Madison, 1988-95, dir. immunopathology and diagnostic immunology, 1995-98, prof. population health scis., 1999—2003, vis. prof. population health scis., 2003—; chair dept. pathology Stroger Hosp. Cook County, Chgo., 1999—; prof. pathology Rush U., 1999—. Past mem. numerous coms. SUNY, Syracuse, U. Wis., Madison; mem. exec. com., chair and med. cons. AIDS Task Force Cen. N.Y., 1983-88. Assoc. editor Jour. Clin. Lab. Analysis; contbr. articles, rev. to profl. jours. Mem. pub. health com. Onondaga County Med. Soc., 1987-88. Lt. comdr. USPHS, 1965-67. Allergy and Immunology Div. fellow U. Pa. Fellow Coll. Am. Pathologists (diagnostics immunology rsch. com. 1993-2003, stds. com. 1995-97, commn. on clin. pathology 1997-2003), Am. Soc. Clin. Pathology (com. on continuing edn. immunopathology 1985-91, pathology data presentation com. 1976-79, pathology rep. coun. med. subspecialty socs. 2004—), Am. Acad. Allergy (penicillin hypersensitivity com. 1973-77); mem. AAAS, Am. Assn. Immunologists, Am. Assn. Pathology (chmn. 2002—), Acad. Clin. Lab. Physicians and Scientists (com. on rsch. 1979-81, chairperson immunology 1979), Clin. Immunology Soc. (clin. lab. immunology com., chair coun. 1991-96). Office: Stroger Cook County Dept Pathology 1901 W Harrison St Chicago IL 60612 Business E-Mail: russell.tomar@hektoen.org.

**TOMASELLI, FRED,** artist; b. Santa Monica, Calif., 1956; m. Laura Miller; 1 child. BA in Painting and Drawing, Calif. State U., Fullerton, 1982. One-man shows include Contemporary Arts Ctr., Cin., 1997, White Cube, London, 2001, Alright-Knox Gallery Art, N.Y.C., 2003, James Cohan Gallery, 2003, exhibited in group shows at Whitney Mus. Am. Art, 1997, The Barbican, London, 2001, Malborough Gallery, N.Y.C., 2003, Whitney Biennial, Whitney Mus. Am. Art, NY, 2004; co-author (with Michael Rush, Amy Cappellazzo): Fred Tomaselli: Ten Year Survey, 2003; co-author: (with Franz Ackerman, Eija-Liisa Ahtila, Dan Graham, John Boc) Parkett #68: Eija-Liisa Ahtila, 2003; co-author: (with Peter Buchanan-Smith and Rick Mooty) The Wilco Book, 2004. Named Invited Exhibitor, Biennial Exhbn., Whitney Mus.

Am. Art, N.Y.C., 2004; recipient Art Commn. award for excellence in design, City Hall, N.Y.C., 1993; Joan Mitchell Grant, 1998. Mailing: c/o James Cohan Gallery 533 West 26th St New York NY 10001

**TOMASH, ERWIN,** retired computer company executive; b. St. Paul, Nov. 17, 1921; s. Noah and Milka (Ehrlich) T.; m. Adelle Ruben, July 31, 1943; children: Judith Sarada Tomash Diffenbaugh, Barbara Ann Tomash Bussa. BS, U. Minn., 1943; MS, U. Md., 1950. Instr. elec. engring. U. Minn., 1946; assoc. dir. computer devel. Univac div. Remington Rand Corp., St. Paul, 1947-51; dir. West Coast ops. Univac div. Sperry Rand Corp., L.A., 1953-55; pres. Telemeter Magnetics, Inc., L.A., 1956-60; v.p. Ampex Corp., L.A., 1961; founder, pres. Dataproducts Corp., L.A., 1962-71, chmn. bd., 1971-80, chmn. exec. com., 1980-89; chmn. bd., dir. Newport Corp., Irvine, Calif., 1982-94. Founder, trustee, dir. Charles Babbage Found., U. Minn.; dir. and nat. gov. Coro Found., L.A. Served to capt. Signal Corps AUS, 1943-46. Decorated Bronze Star; recipient Outstanding Grad. award U. Minn., 1983. Mem. IEEE (sr., computer entrepeneur award 1988), Am. Soc. for Technion, History of Sci. Soc., Soc. for History of Tech., Assn. Internationale du Bibliophile. Home: 3918 Mainsail Pl Soquel CA 95073 Personal E-mail: etomash@ieee.org.

**TOMASI, DONALD CHARLES,** architect; b. Sacramento, Oct. 24, 1956; s. Thomas M. and Anita (Migliavacca) T.; m. Loretta Elaine Goveia, Feb. 1, 1986; children: Jeffrey, Genna, Michael. AB in Architecture with honors, U. Calif., Berkeley, 1979; MArch, U. Wash., 1982. Registered architect, Calif. Project mgr. Robert Wells and Assocs., Seattle, 1982-84, Milbrandt Architects, Seattle, 1984, T.M. Tomasi Architects, Santa Rosa, 1984-86; prin. Tomasi Architects, Santa Rosa, 1986-93, sr. prin.; prin. TLCD Architecture, Santa Rosa, 1993—. Grad. Leadership Santa Rosa, 1992; mem. design rev. com. Sonoma County, 1988-90; chmn. Santa Rosa Design Rev. Bd., 1990-97. Recipient Honor award Coalition for Adequate Sch. Housing, 1991, 93, 96, 99, 2000, 02, 04, Merit award, 1991. Mem. AIA (chpt. bd. dirs 1990-91, 98, v.p. 1999, pres. 2000, Calif. Coun. bd. dirs. 2002-03, Merit award 1986). Avocations: skiing, wine, travel. Office Phone: 707-525-5600. E-mail: don.tomasi@tlcd.com.

**TOMASKO, EDWARD A.,** financial planner; b. Stafford Springs, Conn., Sept. 18, 1943; s. Edward A. Sr. and Gertrude Ann (Burr) T.; m. Helen F. Flanagan, Oct. 18, 1969; children: Felicia, Joy. BA, Quinnipac Coll., 1966; MBA, Am. U., 1968. CFP. Direct mktg. & sales Iroquois Brands, Stamford, Conn., 1979-81; owner Tomasko Bus. Cons., Bethel, Conn., 1981-82; v.p. mktg. & consulting Excell Mktg., New Canaan, Conn., 1982; market mgr. Stauffer Chem., Westport, Conn., 1982-85; direct mktg. & sales Folz Vending, L.I., NY, 1986; registered rep. Moseley Securities, New Haven, 1987-88; Fahnestock & Co. Inc., Danbury, Conn., 1988; prin. Titan Value Equities, Hamden, Conn., 1990—. V.p. bd. govs. Quinnipac Coll.; chmn. pension and ins. commn. Town of Bethel, Conn. Mem.: FPA (pres. So. Conn. chpt. 1993—96, chmn. state conf. 1992—93, adv. coun. 1997—). Republican. Avocations: photography, choir singing. Home: 20 Spring Hill Ln Bethel CT 06801-2726 E-mail: edward_a_tomasko@sbcglobal.net.

**TOMASKY, SUSAN,** electric power industry executive; b. Morgantown, W.Va., Mar. 29, 1953; m. Ron Ungvarsky; 1 child, Victoria. BA cum laude, Univ. Ky., 1974; JD (hons.), George Washington Univ., 1979. Staff mem. House Com. Interstate and Fgn. Commerce, Washington, 1974—76; with Office Gen. Counsel Fed. Energy Regulatory Commn., Washington, 1979—81; assoc. Van Ness, Feldman & Curtin, Washington, 1981—86; ptnr. Van Ness, Feldman & Curtis, Washington, 1986—93; gen. coun. Fed. Energy Regulatory Commn., Washington, 1993—97; ptnr. Hogan & Harts, Washington, 1997-98; sr. v.p., gen. coun. & sec. Am. Electric Power Co., Columbus, Ohio, 1998—2000, exec. v.p., gen. counsel, sec., 2000—01, exec. v.p., CFO, 2001—06, exec. v.p. re. Shared Services, 2006—. Staff mem. George Washington U. Law Rev., 1979. Trustee Columbus Symphony Orch., Columbus Sch. for Girls; co-chair Keystone Energy Bd. Mem. Greater Columbus C. of C., Phi Beta Kappa. Office: American Electric Power 1 Riverside Plz Fl 30 Columbus OH 43215-2355*

**TOMASSETTI, BENJAMIN,** music educator; b. Fairfax, Va., July 12, 1962; s. Benjamin Anthony and Virginia Hart Tomassetti; m. Elizabeth Berg Tomassetti; children: Benjamin Anthony II, Chiara maria. MusB, Shenandoah Conservatory of Music, 1984; MusM, U. Oreg., 1987, MusD, 1995. Sabbatical replacement music instr. Eastern Oreg. U., LaGrande, Oreg., 1992—93; adj. music instr. Western Oreg. U., Monmouth, Oreg., 1993—94; music tech. instr. Treasure Valley C.C., Ontario, Oreg., 1995—97; music media instr. U. La., Lafayette, La., 1997—99; program dir. audio tech. Am. U., Wash., DC, 1999—2003; coord. music engring. tech. Hampton U., Hampton, Va., 2003—. Owner, engr. James River Music and Audio, Newport News, Va., 2004—. Author various musical compositions and articles in profl. jours. Mem.: Soc. of Composers, Inc., Coll. Music Soc., Audio Engring. Soc. Avocations: golf, cooking. Home: 110 James Landing Rd Newport News VA 23606 Office: Hampton U Music Dept Hampton VA 23668 Office Phone: 757-727-5404. E-mail: emidio.tomassetti@hampstonu.edu.

**TOMASSON, HELGI,** dancer, choreographer, dance company executive; b. Reykjavik, Iceland, 1942; m. Marlene Rizzo; children: Kristinn, Erik. Student, Sigridur Arman, Erik Bidsted, Vera Volkova, Sch. Am. Ballet, Tivoli Pantomime Theatre, Copenhagen. With Joffrey Ballet, 1961-64; prin. dancer Harkness Ballet, 1964-70, NYC Ballet, 1970-85; artistic dir. San Francisco Ballet, 1985—, also dir. Dancer debut Tivoli Pantomime Theatre, 1958, A Season of Hell, 1967, Stages and Reflections, 1968, La Favorita, 1969, The Goldberg Variations, 1971, Symphony in Three Movements, 1972, Coppelia, 1974, Dybbuk Variations, 1974, Chansons Madecasses, 1975, Introduction and Allegro, 1973, Allegro, 1973, Union Jack, 1976, Vienna Waltzes, 1977, choreographer Theme and Variations, Polonaise, Op. 65, 1982, Ballet d'Isoline, 1983, Menuetto, N.Y.C. Ballet, 1984, Beads of Memory, 1985, Swan Lake, 1988, Handel-a Celebration, 1989, Sleeping Beauty, 1990, Romeo and Juliet, 1994, Prism, 2000, Bartok Divertimento, 2002, Chi-Lin, 2002, Concerto Grosso, 2003, 7 for Eight, 2003. Decorated Knight Order of Falcon Iceland, Comdr. Order of Falcon; recipient Silver medal, Internat. Moscow Ballet Competition, 1969, Golden Plate award, Am. Acad. Achievement, 1992, Dance Mag. award, 1992, Disting. Citation, Commonwealth Club Calif., 1991. Office: San Francisco Ballet 455 Franklin St San Francisco CA 94102-4438*

**TOMASULO, PATRICIA A.,** medical librarian, plant pathologist, researcher; d. Vincent James and Helen Gloria Farrell Tomasulo; m. Michael McGann, Nov. 25, 2005. MLS, Pratt Inst., Bklyn., N.Y., 1977. Libr. dir. Downstate Dept. of Psychiatry Libr., Bklyn., 1977—84, Bellevue Med. Libr., N.Y.C., 1984—86, N.Y. Hosp.-Cornell Dept. of Psychiatry Libr., N.Y.C., 1986—94; info. svcs. libr. Weill Cornell Med. Libr., N.Y.C., 1994—2001; coord. info. resources and user svcs. NYU Ehrman Med. Libr., N.Y.C., 2001—04, coord. prod. and med., 2004—. Editor (select. editor): (jour.) Med. Reference Svcs. Quar. Sec. 529 Owners Corp., N.Y.C., 1999—2004, Ull Mor Br., Comhaltas Ceoltoiri Eireann, N.Y.-N.J.C., 1999—2005. Recipient Outstanding Achievement by Mem., NY-NJ Chpt./Med. Libr. Assn., 2000, 2003. Mem.: Evidence-Based Medicine Librs. Group, Med. Libr. Assn. (N.Y.-N.J. chpt. chair-elect/chair 1998—2000, chpt. coun. credentialing liaison 2004—07, mental health sect. coun. 1998—99, N.Y.-N.J. chpt. sec. 1995—97, chpt. coun. alt. rep. 2004—, Mental Health sect. award for disting. svc. 2000), Pi Delta Phi. Avocations: plant spirit medicine, Irish traditional music and dance, classical ballet. Office: NYU Sch of Medicine 550 First Ave New York NY 10016 Office Phone: 212-263-8497. E-mail: tomasp01@library.med.nyu.edu.

**TOMASULO, VIRGINIA MERRILLS,** retired lawyer; b. Belleville, Ill., Feb. 10, 1919; d. Frederick Emerson and Mary Eckert (Turner) Merrills; m. Nicholas Angelo Tomasulo, Sept. 30, 1952 (dec. May 3, 1986); m. Harmon I. Anthes, Mar. 5, 1988. BA, Wellesley Coll., 1940; LLB (now JD), Washington U., St. Louis, 1943. Bar: Mo. 1942, U.S. Ct. Appeals (D.C. cir.)

1958, Mich. 1974, U.S. Dist. Ct. (ea. dist) Mo. 1943, U.S. Supreme Ct. 1954, U.S. Tax Ct. 1974, U.S. Ct. Appeals (6th cir.) 1976. Atty. Dept. of Agr., Office of Solicitor, St. Louis and Washington, 1943-48; chief counsel's office IRS, Washington and Detroit, 1949-75; assoc. Baker & Hostetler, Washington, 1977-82, ptnr., 1982-89, of counsel, 1989, ret., 1989. Sec. S.W. Day Care Assn., Washington, 1971—73; state bd. mem., dir. region IV Fla. Life Care Residents Assn., 2002—04; mem. adv. bd. Brede-Wilkins Scholarship Found., 2002—. Mem.: ABA, Mo. Bar, Village on the Green Residents Assn. (mem. coun. 1998—2000, chair health care com. 1999—2001, chair fin. com. 2004—05; mem. fin. coun.), Wellesley Club (Ctrl. Fla.). Episcopalian. Home: 570 Village Pl Apt 300 Longwood FL 32779-6037

**TOMASZEWSKI, RICHARD PAUL,** market representation executive; b. Flushing, NY, Jan. 8, 1958; s. Francis Richard and Agatha Jean (Corsaro) T.; m. Joann L. Turone, Aug. 2, 1980; children: Elizabeth Jean, Annamaria Concetta. BA in Econs. and Polit. sci. cum laude, Union Coll., Schenectady, N.Y., 1980; MBA in Mktg., Fin., Syracuse U., 1982. Grad. asst. Syracuse (N.Y.) U., 1981; field ops. analyst Ford Motor Co., Charlotte, N.C., 1982-83, zone mgr., 1983-93, mkt. representation specialist Atlanta, 1993-98, nat. employee involvement rep. Atlanta region, 1994-98, mkt. representation mgr., 1998—. Mem. Ford Motor Co. Polit. Action Com., Atlanta, 1993, Cmty. Rels. Com., 1999-2002. Tidmarsh scholar Union Coll., Schenectady, 1977; co-recipient Total Market Representation award, 1997, 99-2005. Mem. Union Coll. Alumni Assn., Syracuse U. Alumni Assn., U.S. Tennis Assn., Atlanta Lawn Tennis Assn., Wynterhall Swim and Tennis Club (chmn. tennis com. 2003-05, co-capt., 2002—), Omicron Delta Epsilon, Alpha Mu Alpha. Republican. Roman Catholic. Avocations: tennis, swimming, chess, walking. Office: Ford Motor Co 1455 Lincoln Pkwy E Ste 530 Atlanta GA 30346-2288 Business E-Mail: rtomasze@ford.com.

**TOMBLIN, EARL RAY,** state legislator, lieutenant governor; b. Logan County, W.Va., Mar. 15, 1952; s. Earl and Freda (Jarrell) T.; m. Joanne Jaeger, Sept. 8, 1979; 1 child, Brent Jaeger. BS, W.Va. U.; MBA, Marshall U.; postgrad., U. Charleston. Former sch. tchr.; businessman; mem. W.Va. Ho. Dels., 1974-80, W.Va. State Senate, 1980—, pres., 1995—; lt. gov. State of W.Va., Charleston, 2000—. Chmn. So. Legis. Conf. Former pres., bd. dirs. Appalachia Ednl. Lab., Inc.; mem. Logan County Devel. Authority. Mem. Kappa Alpha. Democrat. Presbyterian. Office: Capitol Bldg Rm 229M Charleston WV 25305 Address: PO Box 116 Chapmanville WV 25508-0116

**TOMBLINSON, JAMES EDMOND,** architect; b. Flint, Mich., Feb. 12, 1927; s. Carl and Edna Ethel (Spears) T.; m. Betsy Kinley, Sept. 26, 1959; children: Amy Lisa, John Timothy (dec.). B.Arch., U. Mich., 1951. Draftsman firms in Detroit, 1951-53, Flint, 1953-54, 56-57, San Francisco, 1955-56; field engr. Atlas Constructors, Morocco, 1952-53; architect Tomblinson, Harburn, & Assocs., Inc. (and predecessors), Flint, 1958—, pres., 1969-95; chmn. bd. Tomblinson, Harburn & Assocs., Inc. (and predecessors), 1995—2001; chmn. Mich. Bd. Registration Architects, 1975-77; sec. Mundy Twp. Planning Commn., 1974-85, Grand Blanc Planning Commn., City of Mich., 1985—; chmn., 1988—. Pres. Flint Beautification Commn., 1968-69; bd. dirs. Grand Blanc Beautification Commn., 1969-84; founding mem. bd. dirs. Flint YMCA, 1969-75, chmn. camp com., 1971-75; founding mem. bd. dirs. Flint Environ. Action Team, 1971-77, v.p., 1971-73; elder First Presbyn. Ch. Flint, 1983, trustee, 1986-99; exec. com. Tall Pine council Boy Scouts Am., 1975—; bd. dirs. New Paths, 1994-2004, pres., 1985-86, 94—; trustee Grand Blanc Cmty. Found., 1997-2004; mem. vestry St. Christopher's Ch., 2004—. Served with AUS, 1945-46. Recipient various civic service awards. Fellow AIA; mem. Mich. Soc. Architects, Flint Area C. of C. Clubs: Greater Flint Jaycees (dir. 1957-63, v.p. 1963), Flint City, U. Mich. (pres. Flint chpt. 1980—). Lodges: Rotary (pres. 1984-85). Home: 686 Applegate Ln Grand Blanc MI 48439-1669 Office: THA Architects Engrs 817 E Kearsley St Flint MI 48503-2076 Office Phone: 810-767-5600. Personal E-mail: jetomblinson@aol.com. E-mail: jtomblinson@tha-flint.com.

**TOMBRELLO, THOMAS ANTHONY, JR.,** physics professor; b. Austin, Tex., Sept. 20, 1936; s. Thomas Anthony and Jeanette Lilian (Marcuse) T.; m. Esther Ann Hall, May 30, 1957 (div. Jan. 1976); children: Christopher Thomas, Susan Elaine, Karen Elizabeth; m. Stephanie Carhart Merton, Jan. 15, 1977; 1 stepchild, Kerstin Arusha. BA in Physics, Rice U., 1958, MA, 1960, PhD, 1961; PhD (hon.), Uppsala U., Sweden, 1997. Rsch. fellow in physics Calif. Inst. Tech., Pasadena, 1961-62, 64-65, asst. prof. Physics, 1965-67, assoc. prof., 1967-71, prof., 1971—, William R. Kenan Jr. prof., 1997—; tech. assessment officer, 1996—, chair divsn. physics, math. and astronomy, 1998—; asst. prof. Yale U., New Haven, 1963. Cons. in field: disting. vis. prof. U. Calif.-Davis, 1984; v.p., dir. rsch. Schlumberger-Doll Rsch., Ridgefield, Conn., 1987-89; mem. U.S. V.P.'s Space Policy Adv. Bd., 1992; mem. sci. adv. bd. Ctr. of Nanoscale Sci. and Tech., Rice U., 1995—; bd. dirs. Schlumberger Tech. Corp., Schlumberger Found., 1987-89. Assoc. editor Nuc. Physics, 1971-91, Applications Nuc. Physics, 1980-89, Radiation Effects, 1985-88, Nuc. Instruments and Methods B, 1993-96; mem. editl. bd. Blue Origin, 2003—, Applied Minds, 2004—, Arrowhead Rsch., 2005—, Form Factor, 2005—, Trilience Rsch., 2005— Recipient Alexander von Humboldt award von Humboldt Stiftung, U. Frankfurt, Germany, 1984-85; named Disting. Alumnus, Rice U., 1998; NSF fellow Calif. Inst. Tech., 1961-62, A.P. Sloan fellow, 1971-73. Fellow Am. Phys. Soc.; mem. AAAS, Phi Beta Kappa, Sigma Xi, Delta Phi Alpha. Democrat. Avocations: reading, jogging. Office: Calif Inst Tech Dept Physics Mail Code 200 36 Pasadena CA 91125-0001 Office Phone: 626-395-4241. Business E-Mail: tat@caltech.edu.

**TOMBROS, PETER GEORGE,** pharmaceutical executive; b. Oak Hill, W.Va., June 12, 1942; s. George P. and Mary Jane (Boliski) T.; m. Ann Riblett Cullen, June 12, 1965. BS, Pa. State U., 1964, MS, 1966; MBA, U. Pa., 1968. Mktg. asst. Pfizer Labs. div. Pfizer Inc., N.Y.C., 1968; asst. product mgr. Pfizer Inc., N.Y.C., 1969, product mgr., 1970-71, group product mgr., 1972-74, v.p. mktg., 1975-80; sr. v.p., gen. mgr. Roerig div. Pfizer Inc., N.Y.C., 1980-86; exec. v.p. Pfizer Pharms. div. Pfizer Inc., N.Y.C., 1986-90, v.p. corp. strategic planning, 1990-94; also corp. officer Pfizer Inc., N.Y.C.; ret. pres., CEO Enzon, Inc., Piscataway, 1994—2001, also bd. dirs.; chmn., CEO VivoQuest Inc., 2001—05; dir. Cambrex Corp., East Rutherford; prof., exec. in residence Pa. State U., 2005—; dir. Dendrite Internat., Bedminster, NJ, 2005—. Alumni fellow Pa. State U., 1993; bd. dirs. Alpharma Inc., Oslo, Norway, NPS Pharm., Inc., Salt Lake City, Protalex, Inc., New Hope, Pa Bd. dirs. Dendrite Internat., Bedminster, NJ, Am. Found. Pharm. Edn., North Plainfield, NJ, 1980-01, past chmn.; trustee Fisk U., Nashville, 1986-96, Dominican Coll., Orangeburg, NY, 1987-02; trustee Bklyn. Borough Hall Restoration, 1987-92; mem. corp. devel. com. Cen. Park Conservancy, NYC, 1986-94; bd. dirs. Vote America, 1990; bd. dirs. Cancer Care; chmn. bd. dirs. NJ Tech. Coun., 2001-03. Recipient Disting. Alumnus award, Pa. State U., 2006. Mem. Pharm. Mfrs. Assn. (past chmn. mktg. steering com., 1986-1992), Links Club, Blind Brook Club, Masons. Avocations: marathon running, golf, tennis, skiing, bridge.

**TOMCZAK, PATRICIA ANN,** dean, archivist; b. Detroit, June 8, 1957; d. Raymond and Veronica Tomczak. BA in History, Wayne State U., 1979; MS in Libr. Sci., Wayne State U., Detroit, 1982. Ref. libr. Quincy Pub. Libr., Quincy, Ill., 1986—88; reference libr. Quincy U., Quincy, Ill., 1988—2000, dean of lit. and info. resources, 2000—. Contbr. digitized, online exhibit, digitized online exhibit. Mem.: Soc. of Am. Archivists, Ill. Libr. Assn., ALA, Colonial Williamsburg Found. Roman Catholic. Avocations: travel, visiting historical sites, reading, theater. Office: Quincy University 1800 College Ave Quincy IL 62301 Office Phone: 217-228-5351. E-mail: Tomczakp@aol.com.

**TOME, CAROL B.,** corporate financial executive; b. Jackson, Wyo. BS in Comm., U. Wyo.; MBA in Fin., U. Denver. Comml. lender United Bank Denver (now Wells Fargo); dir. banking Johns-Manville Corpn.; v.p., treas. Riverwood Internat. Corpn., 1992—95, Home Depot, 1995—2000, sr. v.p. fin., 2000—01, exec. v.p., CFO Atlanta, 2001—. Bd. dirs. United Parcel Svc., 2003—. Bd. dirs. Girls Inc.; trustee Ga. Substance Abuse Adv. Coun., Home Fund; chair and bd. Met. Atlanta Arts Fund. Office: Home Depot Inc 2455 Paces Ferry Rd Atlanta GA 30339-4029*

**TOMÉ, WOLFGANG AXEL,** physicist, researcher, educator; b. Ludwigsburg, Fed. Republic Germany, May 15, 1962; arrived in U.S., 1987, naturalized, 2004; s. Kurt Wolfgang and Monika Else (Bub) T.; m. Marie-Jacqueline Lamoth, Aug. 24, 1990; children: Anne-Sophie, Marie-Hélène. Vordiplom in Physik, Eberhard-Karls U., Tuebingen, Fed. Republic of Germany, 1986; MS in Physics, U. Denver, 1989; PhD in Physics, U. Fla., Gainesville, 1995. Diplomate Am. Bd. Radiology, Am. Bd. Therapeutic Radiol. Physics. Grad. teaching asst. U. Denver, 1987-89, grad. rsch. asst., 1988, U. Fla., Gainesville, 1989-95, postdoctoral assoc. in med. physics 1995-98, asst. prof. human oncology and med. physics, 1998—2003, assoc. prof. human oncology and med. physics, 2003—. Author: Path Integrals on Group Manifolds, 1998; contbr. articles to Founds. of Physics, Jour. Math. Physics, Acta Physics Polonica, Annales Inst. Henri Poincaré, Med. Physics, Physics in Medicine and Biology, Internat. Jour. Radiation Oncology, Biology and Physics, Radiotherapy and Oncology, Acfa Oncologica, Internat. Jour. of Cancer, Med. Dosimetry, Tech. in Cancer Rsch. and Treatment, others Doctoral fellow Studienstipud der deutschen Volkes, 1992; fellow Studienstiftung des deutschen Volkes, 1986. Mem. Am. Soc. for Therapeutic Radiology and Oncology, Am. Assn. Physicists in Medicine, Internat. Assn. Math. Physics, Am. Coll. Med. Physics, European Soc. for Therapeutic Radiology and Oncology, Sigma Xi Rsch. Soc., Alpha Nu Sigma, Pi Mu Epsilon, Phi Beta Delta. Office: U Wis Dept Human Oncology Madison WI 53792 Office Phone: 608-263-8510. Business E-Mail: tome@humonc.wisc.edu.

**TOMEI, CAROLYN,** state representative; m. Gary Michael. BS in Psychology, Portland State U., MSW. State rep., dist. 41 Oreg. House Rep., Salem, 2001—; mayor City of Milwaukie, Oreg.; child devel. specialist Portland Pub. Schs. Vice-chair Health and Human Svcs. Com.; mem. Water Com.; instr. Portland C.C. Democrat. Office: 900 Court St NE H-388 Salem OR 97301 Office Phone: 503-986-1441. E-mail: rep.carolyntomei@state.or.us.

**TOMEI, MARISA,** actress; b. Bklyn., Dec. 4, 1964; d. Gary and Patricia Tomei. TV appearances include (series) As the World Turns, 1983-88, A Different World, 1987, Only Love, 1998, My Own Country, 1998, Since You've Been Gone, 1998, (films) The Flamingo Kid, 1984, Playing for Keeps, 1986, Parker Kane, 1990, Oscar, 1991, Zandalee, 1991, My Cousin Vinny, 1992 (Acad. award best supporting actress 1993), Chaplin, 1992, Untamed Heart, 1993, Equinox, 1993, The Paper, 1994, Only You, 1994, The Perez Family, 1994, Four Rooms, 1995, Unhook the Stars, 1996, What Women Want, 2000, Dirk and Betty, 2000, Driven, 2000, King of the Jungle, 2000, In the Bedroom, 2001 (ShoWest award best supporting actress, 2002), Someone Like You, 2001, The Guru, 2002, The Wild Thornberrys Movie (voice), 2002, Anger Management, 2003, Loverboy, 2004, Alfie, 2004; theatre appearances include Slavs! Thinking About the Longstanding Problems of Virtue and Happiness, 1994, Welcome to Sarajevo, 1997, This Is How It Goes, 2005. Office: United Talent Agy 9560 Wilshire Blvd Ste 500 Beverly Hills CA 90212

**TOMEK, WILLIAM GOODRICH,** agricultural economist; b. Table Rock, Nebr., Sept. 20, 1932; s. John and Ruth Genevieve (Goodrich) T. BS, U. Nebr., 1956, MA, 1957; PhD, U. Minn., 1961. Asst. prof. Cornell U., Ithaca, NY, 1961-66, NSF fellow, 1965, assoc. prof. agrl. econs., 1966-70, prof., 1970-99, grad. sch. prof., 2000—, chmn. dept. agrl. econs., 1988-93. Vis. econ. USDA, 1978-79; vis. fellow Stanford U., 1968-69, U. New Eng., Australia, 1988; mem. adv. panel Rev. Agrl. Econs., 1996-98; mem. adv. bd. Rev. Futures Markets, 2005-. Author: Agricultural Product Prices, 2003; editor: Am. Jour. Agrl. Econs., 1975-77; co-editor: Chgo. Bd. Trade Rsch. Symposia, 1993-2001; mem. editl. bd. Jour. Futures Markets, 1992-95; contbr. articles to profl. jours. Served with U.S. Army, 1953-55. Recipient Earl Combs Jr. award Chgo. Bd. Trade Found. Mem. Am. Agrl. Econs. Assn. (pres. 1985-86), Am. Econ. Assn., Econometric Soc., Northeastern Agrl. Econs. Assn., Am. Agrl. Econs. Assn. (awards 1981, 89, 97, fellow), Gamma Sigma Delta (rsch. award 1994). Democrat. Methodist. Office: Cornell U Warren Hall Ithaca NY 14853-7801 Office Phone: 607-255-2189. E-mail: wgt1@cornell.edu.

**TOMICH, LILLIAN,** lawyer; b. LA; d. Peter S. and Yovanka P. (Ivanovic) T. AA, Pasadena City Coll., 1954; BA in Polit. Sci., UCLA, 1956, cert. secondary tchg., 1957, MA, 1958; JD, U. So. Calif., 1961. Bar: Calif., U.S. Ct. Appeals (9th Cir.) 1978, 2002. Sole practice, 1961-66; house counsel Mfrs. Bank, L.A., 1966; assoc. Hurley, Shaw & Tomich, San Marino, Calif., 1968-76, Driscoll & Tomich, San Marino, Calif., 1976—2005, Conway & Tomich, San Marino, Calif., 2005—. Dir. Continental Culture Specialists Inc., Glendale, Calif. Trustee St. Sava Serbian Orthodox Ch., San Gabriel, Calif. Recipient Episcopal Gramata award Serbian Orthodox Met. of Midwestern Am., 1993, Episcopal Gramata award Serbian Orthodox Bishop of Western Am., 1996, 2002; Charles Fletcher Scott fellow, 1957; U. So. Calif. Law Sch. scholar, 1958. Mem.: ABA, ATLA, Women Lawyers Assn., Los Angeles County Bar Assn., Calif. Bar Assn., Order Mast and Dagger, San Marino C. of C., UCLA Alumni Assn., Town Hall and World Affairs Coun., Pi Kappa Delta, Alpha Gamma Sigma, Iota Tau Tau. Office: 2460 Huntington Dr San Marino CA 91108-2643 Office Phone: 626-287-1248. E-mail: lilliantomich@aol.com.

**TOMICH, PAUL GEORGE,** obstetrician, director, gynecologist, educator; b. Chgo., June 9, 1947; s. George Charles and Helen M. Tomich; m. Mary Elizabeth Hennessy, June 1, 1974; children: Kevin Paul, Colleen M., Kathleen Elizabeth Benka, BSc, Loyola U., Chgo. 1965—69; MD, Loyola U., Maywood, 1969—73. Lic. obstetrics & gynecology, maternal fetal medicine Am. Bd. Obstetrics & Gynecology, 2005. Prof. obstetrics & gynecology Loyola U. Med. Ctr., Maywood, 1980—; prof., dir. maternal fetal medicine dept. obgyn U. Nebr., Omaha, 2002—. Office: Univ Nebr Med Ctr 983255 Nebraska Medical Ctr Omaha NE 68198-3325 Office Fax: 402-559-7126. Personal E-mail: paultomich@aol.com. Business E-Mail: ptomich@unmc.edu.

**TOMITA, KAZUO (JOE),** automotive executive; m. Sawako Tomita; 4 children. Degree in Tech., Tokyo U., 1969. Staff engr. R&D Ctr. Toyota, Higashifuji, Japan, 1969—72, 1975—87, staff engr. Factory Rep. Office Ann Arbor, Mich., 1972—75, mgr. Toyota City, Japan, 1987, group v.p. Tech. Ctr. Torrance, Calif., 1990—93, with Toyota City, 1993—96, gen. mgr. quality control Kamigo, Japan, 1997—99, project gen. mgr. Higashifuji, 2000—01; group v.p. tech. and regulatory affairs Toyota Motor N.Am., Washington, 2001—.

**TOMIYASU, KIYO,** retired consulting engineer; b. Las Vegas, Nev., Sept. 25, 1919; s. Yonema and Toyono (Kawamura) T.; m. Eiko Nakamizo, Aug. 31, 1947. BS, Calif. Inst. Tech., Pasadena, 1940; MS, Columbia U., 1941; M.E.S., Harvard U., Cambridge, Mass., 1947, PhD, 1948. Instr. Harvard U., 1948-49; head engring. sect. Sperry Gyroscope Co., Gt. Neck, N.Y., 1949-55; with GE, 1955-93; cons. engr. microwave techniques GE Valley Forge Space Ctr., Phila., 1969-93 with Martin Marietta Corp., Phila., 1993-95, Lockheed Martin Corp., Phila., 1995—2005; ret., 2005. Author: The Laser Literature-An Annotated Guide, 1968; articles; patentee in field: Exec. bd. Friendship Hill Civic Assn., Paoli, Pa., 1972-73, pres., 1973. Recipient Steinmetz award Gen. Electric Co., 1977; Mgmt. and Data Systems fellow Martin Marietta Corp., 1993; Lockheed Martin fellow, 2004; established Tomiyasu Meml. ann. scholarship Calif. Inst. Tech., 1977. Fellow IEEE (life, hon. life mem. Microwave Theory and Techniques Soc. 1973, tech. activities bd., awards bd. publs. bd., Disting. Lectr. IV 1985-86, ednl. activities bd. 1987-88, Microwave Career award, 1981, Centennial medal 1984, Millennium medal 2000, established Kiyo Tomiyasu award 2000), Geosci. and Remote Sensing Soc. (hon. life; Geosci. and Remote Sensing Outstanding Svc. award 1986, Microwave Disting. Svc. award 1987); mem. Am. Phys. Soc. Home: Apt 30 890 E Harrison Ave Pomona CA 91767-2075

**TOMKA, PETER,** diplomat, arbitrator, judge, lawyer; b. Banská, Bystrica, Slovakia, June 1, 1956; s. Ján and Kornélia (Plai) T.; m. Zuzana Halgasová, June 30, 1990. Grad., Charles U., Prague, Czechoslovakia, 1979; PhD in Internat. Law, Charles U., 1985. Lectr. Law Sch., Charles U., Prague, 1980-86, assoc. lectr. in internat. law, 1986-91; asst. legal advisor Fed. Ministry of Fgn. Affairs, Czechoslovakia, 1986-90, head pub. internat. law divsn., 1990-91; counsellor, legal advisor Permanent Mission to UN, N.Y.C., 1991-92, amb., dep. permanent rep. of Slovakia, 1993-97, charge d'affaires, 1994-97; legal advisor Ministry Fgn. Affairs, Bratislava, Slovakia, 1997-98, dir. gen. legal and consular affairs, 1998-99; permanent rep. of Slovakia to UN, N.Y.C., 1999—2003; judge Internat. Ct. Justice, The Hague, Netherlands, 2003—; arbitrator Iron Rhine Case, Belgium/Netherlands, 2003—05. Former agt. of Slovakia Internat. Ct. Justice in Gabcikovo-Nagymaros Project Case, Hungary/Slovakia; mem. Permanent Ct. Arbitration, 1994—; chmn. UN Legal Com., 1997; vice chair com. legal advisors Coun. of Europe, 1998—99, chmn. com. legal advisors, 2001—02; mem. UN Internat. Law Commn., 1999—2003, vice chmn., 2000; arbitrator UN Law of the Sea Conv., 2004—; World Bank Internat. Ctr. for Settlement Investment Disputes, 2005—. Office: Internat Ct Justice Peace Palace 2517 KJ The Hague Netherlands Office Phone: (31-70) 3022323.

**TOMKINS, CALVIN,** writer; b. Orange, N.J., Dec. 17, 1925; s. Frederick and Laura (Graves) T.; m. Grace Lloyd Fanning, Sept. 11, 1948; children: Anne Graves, Susan Temple, Spencer; m. Judy Johnston, Nov. 11, 1961 (div. Feb. 1981); m. Susan Cheever, Oct. 1, 1981; 1 child, Sarah Liley Cheever; m. Dodie Kazanjian, May 28, 1988. BA, Princeton U., 1948. Assoc. editor Newsweek mag., N.Y.C., 1955-57, gen. editor, 1957-59; staff writer The New Yorker, N.Y.C., 1960—. Author: The Bride and The Bachelors, 1965, Merchants and Masterpieces, 1970, Living Well Is the Best Revenge, 1971, Off the Wall, 1980, Post- to Neo-, 1988, (with Dodie Kazanjian) Alex: The Life of Alexander Liberman, 1993, Duchamp: A Biography, 1997. Bd. dirs. Cunningham Dance Found., N.Y.C., 1963-90. With USN, 1944-46. Guggenheim fellow, 1978 Mem. Authors League Am. Inc., Pen Am. Ctr. Clubs: Century (N.Y.C.). Home: 145 E 74th St New York NY 10021-3225 Office: New Yorker Mag 4 Times Sq New York NY 10036-6561

**TOMKINS, MARK E.,** manufacturing executive; b. Ill. BS, MBA, Ea. Ill. U. CPA Ill. V.p. fin. and bus. devel. electronic materials divsn. to v.p. fin. and bus. devel. polymers divsn. Allied Signal, 1996—98; sr. v.p., CFO Great Lakes Chem. Co., 1998—2001, Vulcan Materials Co., Birmingham, Ala., 2001—. Office: Vulcan Materials Co 1200 Urban Ctr Dr Birmingham AL 35242

**TOMKOVICZ, JAMES JOSEPH,** law educator; b. L.A., Oct. 10, 1951; s. Anthony Edward and Vivian Marion (Coory) T.; m. Nancy Louise Abboud, June 27, 1987; children: Vivian Rose, Michelle Evelene, Henry James. BA, U. So. Calif., 1973; JD, UCLA, 1976. Bar: Calif. 1976, U.S. Dist. Ct. (so. dist.) Calif., U.S. Ct. Appeals (9th and 10th cirs.), U.S. Supreme Ct. Law clk. to hon. Edward J. Schwartz, San Diego, 1976-77; law clk. to Hon. John M. Ferren Washington, 1977-78; atty. U.S. Dept. Justice, Washington, 1979-80; assoc. prof. law U. Iowa, Iowa City, 1982-86, prof., 1986—. Vis. prof. U. Iowa, Iowa City, 1981, U. Mich., Ann Arbor, 1992, UCLA, 2003, U. San Diego, 2004; adj. prof. UCLA, 1981-82. Author: (casebook) Criminal Procedure, 5th edit. (with W. White), 2004, (book) The Right to the Assistance of Counsel, 2002; (outline) Criminal Procedure, 1997; contrb. articles to profl. jours. Mem. Order of Coif, Phi Beta Kappa. Democrat. Roman Catholic. Avocations: running, softball. Office: U Iowa Coll Law Melrose & Byngton Iowa City IA 52242 E-mail: james-tomkovicz@uiowa.edu.

**TOMLIN, CLAIRE J.,** aeronautical engineer, educator; b. Southampton, Eng., 1969; BASc in Elec. Engring., U. Waterloo, 1992; MSEE, Imperial Coll., London, 1993; PhD in Elec. Engring. and Computer Sci., U. Calif., Berkeley, 1998. Assoc. prof. dept. aeronautics and astronautics Stanford U., Calif. Courtesy assoc. prof. elec. engring Stanford U.; assoc. prof. dept. elec. engring. and computer sci. U. Calif., Berkeley. Contrb. articles to sci. jours., chapters to books; co-editor: Hybrid Systems: Computation and Control, 2002. Named one of Top 100 Innovators, MIT Tech. Rev., 2003; recipient Zonta Amelia Earhart awards for Aeronautics Rsch., 1996—98, Career award, NSF, 2000—03, Donald P. Eckman award, Am. Automatic Control Coun., 2003; MacArthur Fellow, John D. and Catherine T. MacArthur Found., 2006. Office: Stanford U Dept Aeronautics and Astronautics Durand Bldg 496 Lomita Mall Stanford CA 94305-4035 E-mail: tomlin@stanford.edu.*

**TOMLIN, JEANNE BRANNON,** real estate broker, small business owner; b. Carroll, Iowa; d. James Leonard and Mary Agnes (Cavenaugh) Brannon; widowed; children: David, Elizabeth; m. James W. Tomlin; stepchildren: Angela, Julie, Lori, Fran. A in Archtl. Tech., Ind. U. Purdue U., Indpls., 1970, student. Lic. real estate broker. Salesperson F.C. Tucker, Indpls.; mgr. Dan Nichols Builder, Greenwood, Ind.; asst. mgr. Carpenter Better Homes and Gardens, Carmel, Ind., sales broker, 1989-92, Tomlin Realtors, Greenwood, 1992-97, pres., CEO, 1997—. Mem. com. Nat. Handicapped Sports, Indpls., 1986-88; mem tech. task force Met. Indpls. Bd. Realtors, 1993-94, mem. comm. com., 1998—. Mem. Indpls. C. of C., Greenwood C. of C., Golden Key Nat. Honor Soc., Alpha Sigma Lambda. Avocations: scuba diving, skiing. Office: Tomlin Realtors 306 Madison Ave Ste 204 Greenwood IN 46142-3123 Office Phone: 317-882-1044. Personal E-mail: jbtomlin@insightbb.com.

**TOMLIN, LILY,** actress; b. Detroit, Sept. 1, 1939; Student, Wayne State U.; studied mime with Paul Curtis, studied acting with Peggy Feury. Co-founder Lily Tomlin Jane Wagner Cultural Arts Ctr., LA. Appearances in concerts and colls. throughout U.S.; TV appearances include The Music Scene, 1969-70, Laugh In, 1970-73, Lily Tomlin, CBS Spls., 1973, 81, 82; 2 ABC Spls., 1974, 75, Edith Ann Animated Specials, ABC, 1994, The Magic School Bus, 1994 (voice), Murphy Brown, 1996-98, The West Wing, 2002-06; motion picture debut in Nashville, 1975 (N.Y. Film Critics award); also appeared in The Late Show, 1977, Moment by Moment, 1978, The Incredible Shrinking Woman, 1981, Nine to Five, 1980, All of Me, 1984, Big Business, 1987, Shadows and Fog, 1992, The Player, 1992, Short Cuts, 1993, The Beverly Hillbillies, 1993, And the Band Played On, HBO, 1993 (Best Supporting Actress Emmy nominee - Special, 1994, Emmy nominations guest appearance Homicide, 1996), Getting Away with Murder, 1995, The Celluloid Closet, 1995, Blue in the Face, 1995, Flirting With Disaster, 1996, Reno Finds Her Mom, 1997, Get Bruce, 1999, Krippendorf's Tribe, 1998, Tea with Mussolini, 1999, Picking Up the Pieces, 2000, The Kid, 2000, Orange County, 2002, I Heart Huckabees, 2004, A Prairie Home Companion, 2006, (voice) The Ant Bully, 2006; exec. prodr. TV series Citizen Reno, 2001; one-woman Broadway show Appearing Nitely, 1977 (Spl. Tony award), The Search for Signs of Intelligent Life in the Universe, 1985 (Drama Desk award, Outer Critics Circle award, Tony award 1986, Cable Ace award); recs. include This is a Recording, and That's The Truth, Modern Scream, On Stage. Recipient Grammy award 1971, 5 Emmy awards for CBS Spl. 1973, 81, Emmy award for ABC Spl. 1975, Emmy award Magic Sch. Bus, 1995, Peabody award Celluloid Closet, 1997, Peabody Edith Ann's Christmas, 1997, Mark Twain Prize for Am. Humor, Kennedy Center, 2003. Office: Lily Tomlin Jane Wagner Cultural Arts Ctr Village at Ed Gould Plz 1125 N McCadden Pl Los Angeles CA 90038-1212*

**TOMLIN-HOUSTON, LISA,** higher education administrator, director; b. Bklyn., Apr. 6, 1965; d. George L. and Joan J. (Hill) Tomlin; m. Anthony D. Houston, Feb. 2, 1991. BA in Psychology, Oberlin Coll., Ohio, 1987; MEd in Counseling Psychology, Rutgers U., 1990. Career counselor U. Pa., Phila., 1990-93; dir. career svcs. H. John Heinz III Sch. of Public Policy and Mgmt., Carnegie Mellon U., Pitts., 1993-95; mgmt. cons. Ford Found., 1995—97; mgr. undergrad. and MBA recruitment Barclays Capital, 1998—2000; pres. Creative Solutions Strategies, LLC, 2000—02; dir. career svcs. Baldwin-Wallace Coll., Berea, Ohio, 2002—. Mem. Nat. Assn. Coll. and Employers, Pub. Rels. Soc. Am. Soc. Human Resources Profls., Cleve. Soc. Venture Ptnrs. Avocations: reading, travel, woman's issues. Office: Baldwin-Wallace Coll 275 Eastland Rd Berea OH 44017

**TOMLINSON, ALEXANDER COOPER,** investment banker, consultant; b. Haddonfield, N.J., May 13, 1922; s. Alexander Cooper and Mary (Buzby) T.; m. Elizabeth Anne Brierley, Jan. 10, 1953 (div.); children: William Brierley, Deborah T. Marple, Alexander Cooper III; m. Margaret L. Dickey, Nov. 15, 1986. BS, Haverford Coll., 1943; postgrad., London Sch. Econs. and Polit. Sci., 1947-48; MBA, Harvard U., 1950; LLD (hon.), Haverford Coll., 1995. With Morgan Stanley & Co., N.Y.C., 1950-76, prin., 1958-76, mng. dir., 1970-76; dir., pres. Morgan Stanley Can. Ltd. div., Montreal, Que., 1972-97; chmn. exec. com. First Boston, Inc., N.Y.C., 1976-82, dir., 1976-88; pres. Nat. Policy Assn., Washington, 1982-85; exec. dir. Ctr. for Privatization, Washington, 1985-88; pres. Hungarian-Am. Enterprise Fund, Washington, 1990-93; chmn. Fund for Arts and Culture in Ctrl. and Ea. Europe, 1994-97. Mem. U.S. adv. bd. Que. Hydro, 1984-95. Trustee Incorp. Village, Cove Neck, N.Y., 1958-72, 76-82, Cold Spring Harbor Lab., 1976-87, N.Y. Infirmary-Beekman Downtown Hosp., 1968-82, East Woods Sch., Oyster Bay, N.Y., 1962-70, Nature Conservancy, L.I., N.Y., 1970-82, Salisbury Sch., Conn., 1976-87, Carnegie Found. for Advancement Tchg., 1984-90; bd. mgrs. Haverford Coll., 1979-01; bd. dirs. Nat. Bldg. Mus., 1987-94, Nat. Policy Assn., 1982-90, Decatur House Coun., 1990-94; chmn. Am. Friends Can., Inc., 1982-91, Harvard Bus. Sch. Fund, 1981-83. Lt. USNR, 1943-46. Mem. Coun. on Fgn. Rels., Metropolitan Club (Washington), Links (N.Y.). Home: 3314 P St NW Washington DC 20007-2701

**TOMLINSON, J. RICHARD,** retired engineering services company executive; b. Newtown, Pa., Mar. 26, 1930; s. Robert K. and Margaret (Wright) T.; m. Barbara Elizabeth Brazill, Apr. 30, 1955; children: Karin Kathleen Tomlinson Pizzitola, Kimberly Ann Tomlinson Donahue. BA, Swarthmore Coll., 1952; postgrad., George Washington U., 1952-53, U. Mich., 1955-57, Drexel Inst. Tech., 1954-57, Am. U., 1965. Mgmt. analyst Dept. State, Washington, 1952-53; with Old Republic Life Ins. Co., Washington, 1953-54; supr. financial analysis Ford Motor Co., Detroit, 1954-61; cons. McKinsey & Co., Washington, 1961-65; v.p. finance, dir. passenger svcs. Reading Co. Phila., 1965-69; v.p. finance Rollins Internat., Inc., 1969-71; exec. v.p. Amtrak, Washington, 1972-74; ptnr. L.T. Klauder and Assocs., 1974-75, 79-83; exec. v.p. Penn Central Transp. Co., 1975-78; pres. LTK Engring. Svcs., 1984-95. Named Man of Month, Phila. C. of C., 1967 Mem. Union League, Aronimink Golf and Country Club, Phila. Aviation Country Club. Home: 451 Inveraray Rd Villanova PA 19085-1139 E-mail: jrt77@aol.com.

**TOMLINSON, JAMES LAWRENCE,** mechanical engineer; b. Detroit, Sept. 12, 1935; s. James Emmet and Ethel Pearl (Williams) T.; m. Marilyn Joyce Peterson, Aug. 24, 1957; children: James, Mary, Robert, Susan. BSME, Mich. Tech., 1957. Registered profl. engr., Mich. Design engr. Buick Motor div. GMC, Flint, Mich., 1960-61, project engr., 1961-66, sr. project engr., 1966-71; staff analysis engr. GM Corp., Warren, Mich., 1971-82, sr. staff analysis engr., 1983-88; pres. Eastport (Mich.) Engring., 1989—. Mayor City of Grand Blanc, 1985-89, city councilman, 1969-84, police liaison/commr., 1971-82, planning adv. bd., 1978-80, planning commn., 1985-89; nat. coun. mem. Boy Scouts Am., 1979-90, 93—, regional bd. mem., 1995—, coun. commr., 1979-84, coun. v.p., 1984—, nat. camp sch. staff, 1986-88, regional camp inspector/accreditation team, 1988-2004, subcamp chief nat. jamboree, 2001, 05; vice chmn. Genesee County Sml. Cities and Villages Assn., 1986, chmn., 1987; bd. dirs. Three Lakes Assn., Inc., 1997-2003. Capt. USAF, 1958-60. Recipient Silver Beaver Tall Pine coun. Boy Scouts Am., 1980, Silver Antelope Ctrl. region, 1996. Mem. NSPE (treas. Flint chpt. 1968-72, Engr. of the Yr. Flint chpt. 1990), SAE (mem. com. 1992-94, 96-98), ASME (exec. bd. Saginaw Valley chpt. 1968-70), Friends of Torch Lake Twp., Inc. (pres. 1994—). Mem. Congl. Ch. Home: PO Box 25 Eastport MI 49627-0025

**TOMLINSON, JOHN RANDOLPH,** lawyer; b. Seattle, Jan. 11, 1931; s. Charles Lawrence and Irma (Schnauffer) T.; m. Susan Jo Weaver, June 15, 1953; children: John R. Jr., Lynn M., James L., Anne E. BBA, U. Wash., 1953, JD, 1955. Bar: Wash. 1955, U.S. Dist. Ct. (we. and ea. dists.) Wash. 1955, U.S. Ct. Appeals (9th cir.) 1957, U.S. Supreme Ct. 1975. Assoc. Jones, Grey & Bayley, Seattle, 1957-61, ptnr., 1962-78, Lane Powell Spears Lubersky, Seattle, 1979—. Lectr. on continuing legal edn. Editorial bd. U. Wash. Law Rev., 1953. Served to lt. USAFR, 1955-77. Fellow Am. Coll. Trial Lawyers; mem. ABA (chmn. litigation sect. 1986-87, vice chmn. 1984-85, chmn. elect 1985-86), Wash. State Bar Assn., Seattle Bar Assn., Phi Gamma Delta. Lodges: Rotary. Republican. Avocations: golf, skiing, fishing, hunting.

**TOMLINSON, LADAINIAN,** professional football player; b. Rosebud, TX, June 23, 1979; BA general studies, Texas Christian U. Running back San Diego Chargers, 2001—. Founder Tomlinson Touching Lives Foundation. Named to AFC Pro Bowl team, 2002, 2004—05. Achievements include led NFL in rushing touchdowns (17), 2004. Office: c/o San Diego Chargers 4020 Murphy Canyon Rd San Diego CA 92123*

**TOMLINSON, PATRICIA SHORT,** nursing scientist, educator; d. Florence Marie and Aubrey Niles Short; children: Cara Kirsten, Niles Brett. BSN, U. Minn., 1957; MSN, U. Wash., 1973; PhD, Oreg. State U., 1984; PhD (hon.), U. Tampere, Finland, 2005. RN Calif. State Bd. Nursing, 1957, Oreg. State Bd. Nursing, 1971, Minn. State Bd. Nursing, 1985. Assoc. prof. Oreg. Health Scis. U., Portland, 1973—85; prof. U. Minn., Mpls., 1985—2001, prof. emeritus, 2001—; vis. prof. U. Bergen, Norway, 1995—96, Yang Ming U., Taipei, Taiwan, 1997; Fulbright vis. prof. U. Tampere, Finland, 2001. Founder, dir. Family Health Consultants, St. Paul, 2002—. Contrb. articles to profl. jours.; U.S. nat. editor, mem. editl. bd. Scandinavian Jour. Caring Scis., 2000—. Bd. dirs., chair family health sect. Nat. Coun. Family Rels., 1996—99. Recipient Award for Excellence in Clin. Rsch., AACN, 1995; fellow, NIH, 1971—73, Cmty. Mental Health Adminstrn., U. N.C., Chapel Hill, 1972—73; Fulbright Scholar, 2001, Sr. Fulbright Scholar, 2006—. Mem.: Nordic Coll. Caring Sci. (assoc.). Liberal. Avocations: travel, su mei-i painting, writing. Office: Univ Minn 308 Harvard St S E Minneapolis MN 55455-0342 Personal E-mail: ptomli@msn.com. Business E-Mail: tomli001@umn.edu.

**TOMLINSON, WILLIAM HOLMES,** management educator, retired military officer; b. Thornton, Ark., Apr. 12, 1922; s. Hugh Oscar and Lucy Gray (Holmes) T.; m. Dorothy Payne, June 10, 1947 (dec.); children: Jane Axtell, Lucy Gray, William Payne; m. Florence Mood Smith, May 1, 1969 (div.); m. Suzanne Scollard Gill, Mar. 16, 1977. *Since Farrar's Island, VA 1618, the family has been dedicated to duty, honor and country. Ancestral grandparents, Judith Jefferson Farrar (VA), George Gray Sr. (NC), Humphrey Beckett Tomlinson (MD), William Hudson (VA), Samuel Davis (VA), John Timmons (SC) and others served in the Revolution. Great grandfather Jesse Russell (TN) fought under Jackson at New Orleans. Great grandfathers Noah Dortch Holmes (AR), Alexander Mason (AR), and Phillip George Henry (AR) fought for the Confederacy. Father Hugh Oscar Tomlinson (AR) served in the AEF (France) in WWI. Brother Hugh Pat Tomlinson left Byrd HS, Shreveport,LA, to join Navy on his 17th birthday February 2, 1942-April 18, 1997, and fought as amphibious sailor (LST 449) on beacheads from Guadalcanal to Iwo Jima and Okinawa.* After LSU (1950), Regular Army Commission in Field Artillery, Korea, later airborne, Special Forces. Son William, Capt., USAFR, active duty at Headquarters, US Central Command. Student, Centenary Coll., 1938—39; BS, U.S. Mil. Acad., 1943; grad., Field Arty. Sch., 1951, Air Command Staff Coll., 1958; MBA, U. Ala., 1960; MS in Internat. Affairs, George Washington U., 1966; grad., U.S. Army War Coll., 1966, Indsl. Coll. Armed Forces, 1968; PhD in Bus. Adminstrn., Am. U., 1974; grad. Advanced Mgmt. Program, Harvard Bus. Sch., 1968, 69; BAS. U. North Fla., 1988. Commd. 2d lt. U.S. Army, 1943, advanced through grades to Col.; Field Arty., 1966; combat svc. in Leyte and Cebu Philippines 246 Field Arty. Bn. Americal Divsn., 1945; aide de camp to comdg. gen. Robert Eichelberger 8th U.S. Army, Japan, 1945-48; comdr. Btry A, 319th FA Bn and Btry A, 39th FA Bn, 3d Divsn., Ft. Benning, Ga., 1948—50; exec. officer 34 FA Bn, ops. officer 9th Divsn. Arty. Germany and Ft. Carson, Colo., 1954-57; with ODCSPER, 1960—61, Office of Undersec. Army, The Pentagon, Washington, 1961-64; comdr. 2d Bn. 8th Arty. and 7th Divsn. Arty. UN Comd. South Korea, 1964-65; faculty Indsl. Coll. Armed Forces, Ft. McNair,

Washington, 1966-72, U. North Fla., Jacksonville, 1972—2002, prof. mgmt., prof. emeritus, 2002—. Vis. prof. U. Glasgow, Scotland, 1987; vis. lectr. Moscow Linguistics U., Plekhanov Econ. Acad., Ulyanovsk U., Russia, 1993; mem. Nat. Def. Exec. Res., Fed. Emergency Mgmt. Agy., 1976—. Author: Assessment of the National Defense Executive Reserve, 1974; co-author: International Business, Theory and Practice, 1991, Business Policy and Strategy, 2000; contrb. articles to profl. jours. Mem. exec. bd. Jacksonville Campus Ministry, 1991—, pres., 2002–. Decorated Bronze Star, Legion of Merit, Philippine Liberation medal, Japanese Occupation, Asiatic Pacific with Invasion Arrow; recipient Freedom Found. award, 1967-71, Lifetime Sr. Profl. in Human Resources, Tchg. Incentive award Intern Univ. Sys., 1994-95. Mem. SAR, Sons Confederate Vets., Soc. Human Resource Mgmt., Acad. Mgmt., Indsl. Rels. Rsch. Assn., Acad. Internat. Bus., European Internat. Bus. Assn., Internat. Trade and Fin. Assn., Exec. Svc. Corp. Bd., Co. Mil. Historians, Nat. Eagle Scout Assn., N.E. Fla. Employee Svcs. Mgmt. Assn. (charter pres. 1987-89), Stewart Soc. (Edinburgh, regional commr.), West Point Soc. North Fla. (pres. 1976-77), Mil. Order Stars and Bars (comdr. 1980-90), Army Navy Club, Fla. Yacht Club, Masons, Shriners, Rotary, Beta Gamma Sigma (pres. 1988-89), Kappa Alpha. Presbyterian (elder, trustee). Office: 1890 Shadowlawn St Jacksonville FL 32205-9430 Office Phone: 904-388-1148. Personal E-mail: 1shadow@comcast.net.

**TOMLINSON-KEASEY, CAROL ANN,** academic administrator; b. Washington, Oct. 15, 1942; d. Robert Bruce and Geraldine (Howe) Tomlinson; m. Charles Blake Keasey, June 13, 1964; children: Kai Linson, Amber Lynn. BS, Pa. State U., University Park, 1964; MS, Iowa State U., Ames, 1966; PhD, U. Calif., Berkeley, 1970. Lic. psychologist, Calif. Asst. prof. psychology Trenton (NJ) State Coll., 1960-70, Rutgers U., New Brunswick, NJ, 1970-72; prof. U. Nebr., Lincoln, 1972-77, U. Calif., Riverside, 1977-92, acting dean Coll. Humanities and Social Scis., 1986-88, chmn. dept. psychology, 1989-92, vice provost for acad. planning and pers. Davis, 1992-97, vice provost for acad. initiatives, 1997-99, chancellor, 1996—2006. Author: Child's Eye View, 1980, Child Development, 1985, numerous chpts. to books; contrb. articles to profl. jours. Recipient Disting. Tchr. award U. Calif., 1986. Mem. APA, Soc. Rsch. in Child Devel., Riverside Aquatics Assn. (pres.). Office: PO Box 2039 Merced CA 95344 Office Phone: 209-724-4417. E-mail: caroltk@yahoo.com.

**TOMLJANOVICH, ESTHER M.,** retired judge; b. Galt, Iowa, Nov. 1, 1931; d. Chester William and Thelma L. (Brooks) Moellering; m. William S. Tomljanovich, Dec. 26, 1957; 1 child, William Brooks Tomljanovich. AA, Itasca C.C., 1951; BSL, St. Paul Coll. Law, 1953, LLB, 1955. Bar: Minn. 1955, U.S. Dist. Ct. Minn. 1958. Asst. revisor of statutes State of Minn., St. Paul, 1957-66, revisor of statutes, 1974-77, dist. ct. judge Stillwater, 1977-90; assoc. justice Minn. Supreme Ct., St. Paul, 1990—98, ret., 1998. Adv. bd. women offenders Minn. Dept. Corrections, 1999—; leadership com. So. Minn. Legal Svcs. Corp., 1999—. Former mem. North St. Paul Bd. Edn., Maplewood Bd. Edn., Lake Elmo Planning Commn.; trustee William Mitchell Coll. Law, 1995—2004, Legal Rights Ctr., 1995—2004, pres., 1999; bd. dirs. Itasca C.C. Found., 1996—, Medica Health Ins. Co., 2001—, vice chair, 2003—. Recipient Centennial 2000 award William Mitchell Coll., Disting. Alumna award, First Ann. Esther Tomljanovich Lifetime Achievement award, 2005; named one of One Hundred Who Made a Difference William Mitchell Coll. Law. Mem. Minn. State Bar Assn., Bus. and Profl. Women's Assn. St. Paul (former pres.), Minn. Women Lawyers (founding mem.). Office: 8533 Hidden Bay Trail Lake Elmo MN 55042 Office Phone: 612-777-5970.

**TOMMASINI, ANTHONY,** music critic, writer, musician; b. Brooklyn; BA, Yale U., 1970, MusM; DMA, Boston U.; studied with pianists Donald Currier and Leonard Shure. Former critic Boston Globe; chief classical music critic NY Times, NYC. Author: Virgil Thomson's Musical Portraits, 1986, Virgil Thomson: Composer on the Aisle, 1997 (ASCAP-Deems Taylor award, 1998), The New York Times Essential Library: Opera A Critic's Guide to the 100 Most Important Works and the Best Recordings, 2004; pianist: Portraits and Self-Portraits, Mostly About Love: Songs and Vocal Works. Avocation: bicycling. Office: NY Times Culture Desk 229 W 43rd St New York NY 10036 Office Phone: 212-556-4543. Office Fax: 212-556-1516.*

**TOMMEY, CHARLES ELDON,** retired surgeon; b. Nashville, Ark., Jan. 13, 1922; s. William Robert and America Anna (Compton) T.; m. Clara Blair Newman, Aug. 28, 1948; children: Robert, Jean, Phillip, Dale, Scott. Student, Henderson State Tchrs. Coll., 1940-42; BSM, U. Ark. Sch. Medicine, 1944, MD, 1945. Diplomate Am. Bd. Surgery. Intern City Hosp., Columbus, Ga., 1945-46; surg. resident Bapt. Hosp., Little Rock, 1948-49, VA Hosp., Cleve., 1950-54; pvt. practice surgery El Dorado, Ark., 1954-95; ret., 1995. Asst. clin. instr. surgery U. Ark. Coll. Medicine. Capt. U.S. Army Med. Corps, 1943-45, 46-48. Fellow ACS. Baptist. Avocations: golf, photography. Home: 123 Glenridge Pky El Dorado AR 71730-3117

**TOMNITZ, DONALD J.,** construction executive; V.p. RepublicBank, Dallas, Crow Develop. Co.; divsn. v.p. D.R. Horton, Inc., Fort Worth, Tex., 1983, v.p. western region, 1994, pres. home bldg. divsn., 1996, exec. v.p., 1998, vice chmn., CEO, 1998—, pres., 2000—. CEO, U.S. Army. Office: DR Horton Inc Ste 500 301 Commerce St Fort Worth TX 76102*

**TOMOMATSU, HIDEO,** chemist; b. Tokyo, June 8, 1929; arrived in U.S., 1959, naturalized; s. Shinsai Natsu and Suma Tomomatsu; m. Yuko Ito, Nov. 12, 1967; 1 child, Tadao. BSChemE., Waseda U., 1952; MS in Chemistry, U. of the Pacific, 1960; PhD in Chemistry, Ohio State U., 1964. Registered profl. engr., Tex.; cert. U.S. Patent Agt. Chemist Hodogaya Chem. Co., Tokyo, 1952—59, Texaco Chems. Co., Austin, Tex., 1964—72; Quaker fellow Quaker Oats Co., Barrington, Ill., 1972—96; cons. Functional Food Resources, Inc., Escondido, Calif., 1996—. Contrb. articles to profl. jours.; patentee in field. Mem.: Inst. Food Technologists, Am. Assn. Cereal Chemists, Am. Chem. Soc. Home: 2555 Seascape Gln Escondido CA 92026-3862 Personal E-mail: hitomoyuko@earthlink.net.

**TOMPKINS, ALAN W.,** lawyer; b. Ky., 1961; m. Julie R. Tompkins. B in Economics, Ind. State U. (now U. So. Ind.), 1983; MBA, So. Methodist U., 1983; M in Acctg., U. Tex., Dallas, 1990; JD, So. Methodist U., 1993. CPA 1988. Pvt. practice Malouf Lynch Jackson Kessler & Collins, Weil, Gotshal & Manges, Secore & Waller; assoc. gen. counsel Richmont Corp., 1997—2001; pvt. practice Hance, Scarborough, Wright, Ginsberg & Brusilow, 2002—03; v.p., gen. counsel Unity Hunt, 2003—. Adj. prof. bus. law Edwin L. Cox Sch. Bus. Southern Meth. U., 1991—97; lectr. acctg., 1991—97. Bd. dirs. Pegasus Theatre, 1995—2005, USA Film Festival, 1999—2006, For The Love of the Lake Found., 1999—2003; mem City of Dallas Judicial Nominating Commn., 1997—2005. Office: Unity Hunt Inc 1601 Elm St Dallas TX 75201 Office Phone: 214-720-1600. Office Fax: 214-720-1612.*

**TOMPKINS, CHRISTOPHER PAUL,** researcher; b. Providence, Dec. 1, 1955; s. Charles Bryant and Eloise Phylida Tompkins; m. Heather J. Moodie, Aug. 23, 1980; children: Sarah Elizabeth, Matthew Christopher, Caitlin Ruth. BA, Northeastern U., 1979; MM, Brandeis U., 1982, PhD, 1990. Sr. rsch. assoc. Brandeis U., Waltham, Mass., 1990—96, assoc. prof., 1996—. Chair instl. rev. bd. Brandeis U., Waltham, 2004—, chair, privacy bd., 2004—. Office Phone: 781-736-3913. Office Fax: 781-736-3905. Business E-Mail: tompkins@brandeis.edu.

**TOMPKINS, CHRISTOPHER ROBIN,** director, educator; b. Mt. Kisco, N.Y., Apr. 2, 1967; s. John Roger Tompkins, Sr. and Marie Helen Tompkins; m. Katherine Ann Ide Tompkins, July 31, 1993; children: Hannah Elizabeth Ide, Phoebe Neet DeVoe, Christopher Robin Milano. BA, Colby Coll., 1989; MSSc, Syracuse U., 2000. History tchr. Wellington Sch., Columbus, Ohio, 1989—90, Greens Farms Acad., Greens Farms, Conn., 1990—93; tchr., coll. counselor Acad. Cotopax, Quito, Ecuador, 1993—94; dir. admission South Kent Sch., Kent, Conn., 1994—96; dir. admission and fin. aid St. Andrews Sewanee Sch., Sewanee, Tenn., 1996—99; asst. headmaster Canterbury

Episcopal Sch., DeSoto, Tex., 1999—2000; dir. admission and fin. aid Mercersburg Acad., Mercersburg, Pa., 2000—. Chair admission com. Colby Alumni Coun., Waterville, Maine, 1997—2001; bd. dirs. Chambersburg Montessori Sch., Chambersburg, Pa., Cloud Forest Sch. Found., Costa Rica. Author: (novels) Croton Dams and Aqueduct, 2000; contbg. author: Far and Wide: Diversity in Boarding School, 1998. Founding dir. Southeastern Assn. of Boarding Schs., 1997; vice chair bd. dirs. Cloud Forest Sch. Found., 2004—; active St. Johns Episcopal Ch., Hagerstown, Md., 2000—. Mem.: Fountain Head C.C., Yorktown Sportsman's Club. Avocations: model railroading, stamps, golf, cross country skiing, hiking. Home and Office: 300 E Seminary St Mercersburg PA 17236-1550 E-mail: ct3408@hotmail.com.

**TOMPKINS, CURTIS JOHNSTON,** retired academic administrator; b. Roanoke, Va., July 14, 1942; s. Joseph Buford and Rebecca (Johnston) T.; m. Mary Katherine Hasle, Sept. 5, 1964; children: Robert, Joseph, Rebecca. BS, Va. Poly. Inst., 1965, MS, 1967; PhD, Ga. Inst. Tech., 1971. Indsl. engr. E.I. DuPont de Nemours, Richmond, Va., 1965-67; instr. Sch. Indsl. and Systems Engring., Ga. Inst. Tech., Atlanta, 1968-71; assoc. prof. Colgate Darden Grad. Sch. Bus. Adminstrn., U. Va., Charlottesville, 1971-77; prof., chmn. dept. indsl. engring. W.Va. U., Morgantown, 1977-80, dean Coll. Engring., 1980-91; pres. Mich. Technol. U., Houghton, 1991—2004, also bd. dirs., pres. emeritus, univ. prof., 2004—. Mem. engring. accreditation commn. Accreditation Bd. for Engring. and Tech., 1981-86; mem. exec. bd. Engring. Deans Coun., 1985-89, vice chmn., 1987-89; mem. engring. adv. com., chmn. of planning com. NSF, 1988-91, chm. Mich. Univs. pres. coun., 1996-98; Pres. Coun. Assn. Governing bds. 1996-2004, Gov's. Workforce Commn., 1996-2002; mem. engring. adv. bd. U. Cin., 1996-99 Author: (with L.E. Grayson) Management of Public Sector and Nonprofit Organizations, 1983, (with others) Maynard's Industrial Engineering Handbook, 1992; contbr. chpt. to Ency. of Profl. Mgmt, 1978, 83. Co-chmn. W.Va. Gov.'s Coun. on Econ. Devel.; bd. dirs. Pub. Land Corp. W.Va., 1980-89, Mich. C. of C., 1997—, vice chmn., 2002—; mem. faculty Nat. Acad. Voluntarism, United Way Am., 1976-91; mem. Morgantown Water Commn., 1981-87, Morgantown Utility Bd., 1987-91, steering com. W.Va. Conf. on Environ., 1985-89, Coun. on Competitiveness, 1998-2004, Mich. Higher Edn. Assistance Authority, The Mich. Higher Edn. Student Loan Authority, 2002-04; chmn. Monagolia County United Way, 1989-90; campaign chmn. Copper Country United Way, 1995-96. Named to Com. of 100 Va. Tech. Coll., Disting. Alumni Acad. dept. indsl. engring, hon. alumnus Mich. Technol. U., 2004; recipient Frank and Lillian Gilbreth Indsl. Engring. award Inst. Indsl. Engrs., 1998. Fellow Inst. Indsl. Engrs. (life mem., trustee 1983-90, pres. 1988-89), Nat. Soc. Profl. Engrs., Am. Soc. Engring. Edn. (pres. 1990-91), Mich. Soc. Profl. Engrs.; mem. Am. Assn. Engring. Soc. (bd. govs. 1987-90, exec. com. 1987-90, sec.-treas. 1989-90), Jr. Engring. Tech. Soc. (bd. dirs. 1988-91), Nat. Soc. for Sci., Tech. and Society (bd. dirs. 1991-94), Internat. Hall of Fame of Sci. and Engring. (hon. trustee), Ga. Tech. Coll. Engring. Disting. Alumni Acad., Ga. Tech. Sch. Indsl. and Sys. Engring. Disting. Alumni Acad., W.Va. U. Dept. Indsl. Engring. Disting. Alumni Acad. (hon.), Mich. C. of C. (bd. dirs. 1997-2004), Blue Key (hon.), Sigma Xi, Phi Kappa Phi, Tau Beta Pi, Alpha Pi Mu. Internet: Home: 199 Coolidge Ave #111 Watertown MA 02472 Business E-Mail: curt@mtu.edu. E-mail: curtisj42@yahoo.com.

**TOMPKINS, JOSEPH BUFORD, JR.,** lawyer; b. Roanoke, Va., Apr. 4, 1950; s. Joseph Buford and Rebecca Louise (Johnston) T.; children: Edward Graves, Claiborne Forbes. BA in Politics summa cum laude, Washington and Lee U., 1971; M Pub. Policy, JD, Harvard U., 1975. Bar: Va. 1975, U.S. Ct. Appeals (D.C. cir.) 1976, U.S. Ct. Appeals (5th cir.), 1977, U.S. Supreme Ct. 1977, U.S. Dist. Ct. D.C. 1982, U.S. Ct. Appeals (11th cir.) 1982, U.S. Ct. Appeals (3d cir.) 1983, U.S. Ct. Appeals (6th cir.) 1985, U.S. Ct. Appeals (7th cir.) 1991, U.S. Ct. Appeals (4th cir.) 1993, U.S. Ct. Internat. Trade 1996. Assoc. Sidley & Austin (now Sidley Austin LLP), Washington, 1975-79, ptnr., 1982—; assoc. dir. Office Policy and Mgmt. Analysis criminal divsn. U.S. Dept. Justice, Washington, 1979-80, dep. chief fraud sect. criminal divsn., 1980-82. Contbr. articles to profl. jours. Mem. Va. Bd. Health Professions, Richmond, 1984-92, vice chmn., 1984-86, chmn., 1986-88, 90-91. Mem. ABA (white collar crime com. criminal justice sect. 1980—, chmn. task force on computer crime 1982-92), Va. Bar Assn., D.C. Bar Assn., Phi Beta Kappa, Home: 8146 Wellington Rd Alexandria VA 22308-1214 Office: Sidley Austin LLP 1501 K St NW 8th Fl Washington DC 20005 Fax: 202-736-8711. E-mail: jtompkins@sidley.com.

**TOMPKINS, RAYMOND EDGAR,** lawyer; b. Oklahoma City, July 13, 1934; s. Charles Edgar and Eva Mae (Hodges) T.; m. Sue Anne Sharpe, June 10, 1963; children: Matthew Stephen, Christopher T., Katherine Anne. BS, Okla. State U., 1956; JD, U. Okla., 1963. Bar: Okla. 1963, U.S. Dist. Ct. (no. dist.) Okla. 1963, U.S. Dist. Ct. (we. dist.) Okla. 1964, U.S. Ct. Appeals (10th cir.) 1965, U.S. Supreme Ct. 1968, U.S. dist. Ct. (ea. dist.) Okla. 1969, U.S. Ct. Appeals (9th cir.) 1981, U.S. Ct. Appeals (4th cir.) 1986. Adminstrv. asst. U.S. Congress, 1966-68; ptnr. Linn & Helms, Oklahoma City, 1980-90, Daughery, Bradford, Haught & Tompkins, P.C., Oklahoma City, 1990-94; shareholder Conner & Winters, P.C., Oklahoma City, 1994—2003; sole practitioner Oklahoma City, 2003—. Past chmn. bd. trustees Okla. Ann. Methodist Conf., St. Luke's United Meth. Ch.; past chmn. adminstrv. bd.; mem. Okla. Bur. Investigation Commn., past chmn.; past gen. counsel Rep. State com., Interstate Oil Compact. Maj. USAR. Recipient award of Honor Oklahoma City Bi-Centennial Commn., 1976. Fellow Am. Coll. Civil Trial Mediators; master William S. Holliway Am. Inns of Ct. (emeritus, pres.), Robert J. Turner Am. Inn of Ct. (pres.); mem. ABA, Okla. County Bar Assn. (Pres.'s award 1988), Okla. Bar Assn. (chmn. bench and bar com. 1995-97, chmn. ADR sect., Law Day award), Nat. Arbitration Forum, Am. Arbitration Assn. (mediator/arbitrator), NASD (mediator, arbitrator), NYSE (mediator, arbitrator), Am. Judicature Soc., Assn. Atty.-Mediators (past pres. Okla. chpt., nat. dir. and sec., Nat. President's award 2000), Blue Key, Lions (pres. Oklahoma City chpt.). Home: 3148 Birch Bark Ln Oklahoma City OK 73120 Office: 1001 NW 63d St Ste 200 Oklahoma City OK 73116 Office Phone: 405-607-8303. Personal E-mail: raytompkins@coxinet.net.

**TOMPKINS, RONALD GARY,** surgeon, educator, biomedical investigator; b. Many, La., Sept. 24, 1951; s. Horace and Ruby (Warren) T.; m. Denise Marie Clougherty, Mar. 7, 1985; children: Megan Elizabeth, Ryan Coleman, Caitlin Maureen. BS in Chemistry summa cum laude, Tulane U., 1972, MD, 1976; SM in Chem. Engring., MIT, 1983, ScD in Med. and Chem. Engring., 1983. Diplomate Am. Bd. Surgery (bd. dirs. 1994—), Am. Bd. Surg. Critical Care. Intern in surgery Mass. Gen. Hosp., Boston, 1976-77, asst. resident, then resident, 1977-79, 83-85, asst. in surgery, 1985-87, asst. surgeon, 1988-90, assoc. chief trauma and burn svcs., 1987-90, chief, 1990—, assoc. vis. surgeon then vis. surgeon, 1991—; clin. fellow in surgery Harvard Med. Sch., Boston, 1977-79, 92-85, instr., then asst. prof. surgery, 1985-90, assoc. prof., 1990-96, John F. Burke prof. surgery, 1996—. Rsch. assoc. MIT, Cambridge, Mass., 1985-86; asst. in surgery Shriners Burns Inst., Boston, 1987-88, asst. surgeon, 1988-90, chief staff, 1990—; numerous presentations in field at regional, nat. and internat. orgns. Mem. editl. bd. Critical Care Medicine, 1991—, Jour. Tissue Engring., 1994—, Jour. Am. Soc. Artificial Internal Orgns, 1994—; contbr. over 217 articles and revs. to med. jours., chpts. to books; patent for culturing liver cells. DuPont fellow MIT, 1979-80, E.R. Gilliland fellow, 1980-81, William Prince fellow, 1981-83; Edward D. Churchill rsch. fellow Mass. Gen. Hosp., 1981-82, fellow Am. Surg. Assn. Found., 1987-88; grantee Link Found., 1985—, NIH, 1987-91, Whitaker Found., 1988-91, Nat. Inst. Gen. Med. Scis., 1992—, Nat. Inst. Digestive Diseases and Kidney, 1987-94, Shriners Hosps., 1988—. Fellow ACS; mem. AMA, AAAS, AIChE, Assn. for Acad. Surgery, Am. Chem. Soc., Am. Burn Assn., Am. Fedn. for Clin. Rsch., Soc. Critical Care Medicine, Surg. Infection Soc., Am. Soc. for Artificial Internal Organs, Shock Soc., Am. Assn. for Surgery of Trauma, Am. Soc. for Laser Medicine and Surgery, Soc. for Cryobiology, Soc. Univ. Surgeons, Am. Assn. for Study Liver Diseases, Am. Trauma Soc., New Eng. Surg. Soc., Cell Transplant Soc., Phi Beta Kappa, Alpha Omega Alpha, numerous others. Office: GRB1302 Mass Gen Hosp 55 Fruit St Boston MA 02114-2622 Home: 2 Hawthorne Pl Apt 8N Boston MA 02114-2309

**TOMPKINS, RONALD K.,** retired surgeon, educator; b. Malta, Ohio, Oct. 14, 1934; s. Kenneth Steidley and Mildred Lillian (Loomis) T.; m. Suzanne Colbert, June 9, 1956; children: Gregory Alan, Teresa Susan, Geoffrey Stuart. BA, Ohio U., 1956; MD, Johns Hopkins U., 1960; MS, Ohio State U., 1968, DSc (hon.), U. Bordeaux, 1995. Diplomate Am. Bd. Surgery. Intern in surgery Ohio State U., 1960-61, resident in surgery, 1964-68, adminstrv. chief resident in surgery, 1968-69, NIH trainee in acad. surgery, instr. physiol. chemistry, 1966-69; asst. prof. surgery UCLA, 1969-73, assoc. prof., 1973-79, prof., 1979-2001, prof. emeritus, 2001—, chmn. basic surg. trng. program, 1970-79, asst. dean student affairs, 1979-82, chief divsn. gen. surgery, 1982-88, chief gastrointestinal surgery, 1986-97, assoc. dean, 1988-91, dir. surg. edn., 1996—2004; ret. 2004. Cons. VA Hosps. Editor-in-chief World Jour. Surgery, 1993-2004. With M.C. USAF, 1961-64. Recipient Disting Alumni award, Ohio U. Arts & Scis., 2001; fellow, Royal Soc. Medicine Eng., 1976—77; grantee, NIH, 1968—70, John A. Hartford Found., 1970—79. Fellow ACS (So. Calif. chpt. pres. 1987); mem. Am. Surg. Assn., Am. Gastroenterol. Assn., Am. Fedn. Clin. Rsch. Am. Inst. Nutrition, AMA, Assn. Acad. Surgery, Pacific Coast Surg. Assn. (recorder 1986-91, pres. 1995), Japan Surgical Soc. (hon.), Soc. Clin. Surgery, Soc. Surgery Alimentary Tract (sec. 1982-85, pres.-elect 1985, pres. 1986, chmn. bd. trustees 1987), Soc. Univ. Surgeons, Societe Internationale de Chirurgie (U.S. chpt. sec. 1990-94, pres. 1996-98), Internat. Biliary Assn. (pres. 1979-81), Internat. HepatoPancreato-Biliary Assn. (hon.), Bay Surg. Club, LA Surg. Soc. (pres. 1981), Robert M. Zollinger/Ohio State U. Surg. Soc. (pres. 1988-90), Longmire Surg. Soc. (pres. 1997-99), Phi Beta Kappa, Sigma Xi, Alpha Omega Alpha, Delta Tau Delta. Achievements include research numerous publs. in gastrointestinal surgery and gastrointestinal metabolism and biochemistry. Home: 309 20th St Santa Monica CA 90402

**TOMPSON, MARIAN LEONARD,** professional society administrator; b. Chgo., Dec. 5, 1929; d. Charles Clark and Marie Christine (Bernardini) Leonard; m. Clement R. Tompson, May 7, 1949 (dec. 1981); children: Melanie Tompson Kandler, Deborah Tompson Frueh, Allison Tompson Fagerholm, Laurel Tompson Davies, Sheila Tompson Doucet, Brian, Philip. Student public and parochial schs., Chgo. and Franklin Park, Ill. Co-founder La Leche League (Internat.), Franklin Park, 1956, pres., 1956-80, dir., 1956—, pres. emeritus, 1990—; exec. dir. Alternative Birth Crisis Coalition, 1981-85; founder, exec. dir. AnotherLook, Inc., 2001—. Cons. WHO; bd. dirs. N.Am. Soc. Psychosomatic Ob-Gyn, Natural Birth and Natural Parenting, 1981-83; mem. adv. bd. Nat. Assn. Parents and Profls. for Safe Alternatives in Childbirth, Am. Acad. Husband-Coached Childbirth; mem. adv. bd. Fellowship of Christian Midwives; mem. profl. adv. bd. Home Oriented Maternity Experience; guest lectr. Harvard U. Med. Sch., UCLA Sch. Pub. Health, U. Antioquia Med. Sch., Medellín, Columbia, U. Ill. Sch. Medicine, Chgo., U. W.I., Jamaica, U. N.C., Nat. Coll. of Chiropractic, Am. Coll. Nurse Midwives, U. Parma, Italy, Inst. Psychology, Rome, Rockford (Ill.) Sch. Medicine, Northwestern U. Sch. Medicine, NGO Forum/4th World Conf. on Women, Beijing; mem. family com. Ill. Commn. on Status of Women, 1976-85; mem. perinatal adv. com. Ill. Dept. Pub. Health, 1980-83; mem. adv. bd. Internat. Nutrition Comm. Svc., 1980—; bd. cons. We Can, 1984—; exec. adv. bd. United Resources for Family Health and Support, 1985-86; mem. internat. adv. coun. World Alliance of Breast Feeding Action, 1996. Author: (with others) Safe Alternatives in Childbirth, 1976, 21st Century Obstetrics Now!, 1977, The Womanly Art of Breastfeeding, 6th edit., 1997, Five Standards for Safe Childbearing, 1981, But Doctor, About That Shot..., 1988, The Childbirth Activists Handbook, 1983; author prefaces and forwards in 11 books; columnist La Leche League News, 1958-80; columnist People's Doctor Newsletter, 1977-88, mem. adv. bd., cons., 1988-92; assoc. editor Child and Family Quar., 1967—; mem. med. adv. bd. East West Jour., 1980—; also articles. Mem. adv. bd. Shelters for Healthy Environments, 1998—2002, The Beginning Project, 2000. Recipient Gold medal of honor Centro de Rehabilitacao Nossa Senhora da Gloria, 1975, Night of 100 Stars III Achiever award Actors Fund Am., 1990, N.Y. Soc. Ethical Culture Ethical Humanist award, 1999, 100 Women Making a Difference Today's Chgo. Woman. Mem. Nat. Assn. Postpartum Care Svcs. (adv. bd.), Chgo. Cmty. Midwives (adv. bd.), World Alliance for Breast Feeding Action (mem. internat. adv. coun. 1997). Office: 1400 N Meacham Rd Schaumburg IL 60173-4808 Office Phone: 847-869-1278. Personal E-mail: m.tompson@comcast.net. E-mail: mt@anotherlook.org.

**TOMS, KATHLEEN MOORE,** nurse; b. San Francisco, Dec. 31, 1943; d. William Moore and Phyllis Josephine (Barry) Stewart; m. Benjamin Peskoff (dec. Aug. 2002); children from previous marriage: Kathleen Marie Toms Myers, Kelly Terese Toms Shaver. AA, City Coll., San Francisco, 1963; BPS in Nursing Edn., Elizabethtown Coll., Pa., 1973; MS in Edn., Temple U., 1977; MS in Nursing, Gwynedd Mercy Coll., 1988; grad., US Army War Coll., 1999. RN, Calif. Med.-surg. nurse St. Joseph Hosp., Fairbanks, Alaska, 1963-65, emergency rm. nurse Lancaster, Pa., 1965-69, blood, plasma and components nurse, 1969-71; pres. F.E. Barry Co., Lancaster, 1971—; dir. insvc. edn. Lancaster Osteo. Hosp., 1971-75; coord. practical nursing program Vocat. Tech. Sch., Coatesville, Pa., 1976-77; dir. nursing Pocopson Home, West Chester, Pa., 1978-80, Riverside Hosp., Wilmington, Del., 1980-83; assoc. Coatesville VA Hosp., 1983-89, chief nurse, 1984-89; with VA Ctrl. Office; supr. psychiat. nursing Martinez (Calif.) VA Med. Ctr., 1989-94; assoc. chief nursing svc. edn. VA Ho. Calif. Sys. Clinics, Pleasant Hill, 1994—; nurse mgr. VA Ctr. Rehab. and Extended Care, Martinez, 1996—; patient health edn. coord. VA No. Calif. Health Care Sys., Martinez, 2000—. Trainee assoc. chief Nursing Home Care Unit, Washington; mem. Pa. Gov.'s Coun. on Alcoholism and Drug Abuse, 1974-76; mem. Del. Health Coun. Med.-Surg. Task Force, 1981-83; dir. Lancaster Cmty. Health Ctr., 1973-76; lectr. in field. Col. Nurse Corps, USAR. Decorated Army Commendation medals (6), Meritorious Svc. medals (2); recipient Cmty. Svc. award Children United for Better Health, 1971, award Jonuina, Lancaster, 1974, Outstanding Citizen award Sta. WGAL-TV, 1975; U.S. Army Achievement award, 1983. Mem. Elizabethtown U. Alumni Assn., Temple U. Alumni Assn., Pa. Nurses Assn. (bd. dirs. 1972-76), Sigma Theta Tau, Beta Gamma. Achievements include invention of auto-infuser for blood or blood components. Home: 208 Sea Mist Dr Vallejo CA 94591-7748 E-mail: ktoms007@aol.com.

**TOMSON, JON SCOTT,** management consultant; b. Rochester, N.Y., Dec. 13, 1948; s. Peter and Genevieve Helen Tomson; m. Carol Neuman, June 24, 1973; children: Brett Neuman, Christopher William. B of Indsl. Engring., Kettering U., 1971; M of Urban Planning, CUNY, 1974. Asst. dir. N.J. Dept. Higher Edn., Trenton, 1974—77; dir. human resources N.J. Dept. Human Svcs., Trenton, 1977—81; dir. sales and mktg. Getinge Internat., Lakewood, NJ, 1981—90; prin. CUH2A, Inc., Princeton, NJ, 1990—2004, JT Collaborative, 2005—. Trustee Forum Inst. for Pub. Policy, Princeton, 1999—; Internat. Soc. Pharm. Engring. (officer 1995—, chmn. bd. 2002, Mem. of Yr. 1995), Soc. Coll. and Univ. Planning, Soc. Mktg. Profl. Svcs., Am. Inst. Cert. Planners. Avocations: soccer, skiing, scuba diving. Home and Office: JT Collaborative 263 Rt 526 PO Box 74 Cream Ridge NJ 08514-0074 Office Phone: 609-259-1767. Business E-Mail: jon@jtcollaborative.com.

**TOMY, KALAPPARAMBATH PAUL,** radiologist; s. Poulose and Theresa Kalapparambath; m. Annie Chacko, Sept. 5, 1998; children: Matthew K. Paul children: Elizabeth Theresa Paul, Emily Mary Paul. MBBS, Kerala U., India, 1992; DMRE, Gujarat U., India, 1995; postgrad., U. Pa., 2002. Radiologist Little Flower Hosp., Angamaly, India, 1995-97; resident Kingsbrook Jewish Med. Ctr., Bklyn., 1999—2000; resident in nuc. medicine L.I. Jewish Med. Ctr., New Hyde Park, NY, 2000—02; radiologist St. Joseph Mercy Oakland Hosp., Pontiac, Mich., 2003—. Contbr. articles to profl. jours. Mem.: Soc. Nuc. Medicine (assoc.), Radiol. Soc. N.Am. (assoc.). Roman Catholic. Achievements include research in Thyroid scans. Personal E-mail: tomypaulmd@hotmail.com.

**TON, PAUL,** investor, educator; b. Buffalo, Apr. 30, 1926; s. Edward Cornelius Ton and Laura Delia Slotboom; m. Joan Karen Marshall, June 18, 1951; children: Scott, Elizabeth, Robert, John. BS, Union Coll., Schenectady,

N.Y., 1949; MA, Stanford U., Palo Alto, Calif., 1951, U. Denver, 1953, PhD, 1969. Instr. electronics USAF, Denver, 1951—52; tchr. history Denver Pub. Schs., 1952—89; adj. prof. history Metro State Coll., Denver, 1990—2003. Dept. head, Driver Edn. Am. Auto Assn., Denver, 1957—64; dept. chair South H.S., Denver, 1972—77; history cons. Am. Frontier TV series, 1985—87; mng. dir. Westton Prodns., 1995—. Contbg. author (book) The Mining Frontier, 1967, Henry M. Porter, Empire Builder, 1991. Cpl. U.S. Army, 1944—46, PTO. Mem.: Western Hist. Assn., Orgn. of Am. Historians, Am. Hist. Assn. Republican. Presbyterian. Avocation: photography. Home: 390 Lansing St Aurora CO 80010 Personal E-mail: forpton@comcast.net.

**TONCHI, STEFANO,** editor; b. 1959; Classic studies, Liceo Classico Forteguerri, Pistoia, Italy; studied polit. sci., U. Florence, Italy, 1984. Co-founder, editor, art dir. Westuff mag., 1984—87; fashion dir. L'Uomo Vogue, 1987—94; creative dir. Self, 1994—96; creative cons. J. Crew, 1996—98; fashion creative dir. Esquire, 1998—2003; style editor NY Times mag., 2003—; head style dept. T: The NY Times Style mag., 2004—. Co-curator (exhibition) & co-editor (book) Excess: Fashion & the Underground in the 80s, 2004; co-editor: Total Living: Art, Fashion, Design, Architecture, Communication, 2002; co-curator (exhibition) & co-editor (book) Uniform: Order & Disorder, 2001. Office: NY Times 229 W 43rd St New York NY 10036 Office Phone: 212-556-3830, 212-556-7596. Office Fax: 212-556-7618, 212-556-7596. E-mail: tonchi@nytimes.com.*

**TONDEL, LAWRENCE CHAPMAN,** lawyer; b. N.Y.C., Apr. 9, 1946; s. Lyman Mark and Jean (Basch) Tondel; m. Sharyn A. Smith, Aug. 3, 1974; children: Michael Lawrence, Kathryn Chapman. Student, The Lawrenceville Sch., 1964; AB, Wesleyan U., 1968; JD, U. Mich., 1971. Bar: N.Y. 1972. Assoc. Brown & Wood LLP, N.Y.C., 1971-79, ptnr., 1980-97, sr. ptnr., 1997-2001; ptnr. Sidley Austin LLP, N.Y.C., 2001—. Chmn. Internat. Bus. Commn. Ann. Internat. Forum Offshore Funds, 1993—2000. Trustee Elisabeth Morrow Sch., Englewood, NJ, 1988—93; mem. exec. com. parents com. Washington U., St. Louis, 2000—02. Mem.: ABA, Assn. Bar City of N.Y., Am. Bar Found., Am. Law Inst. Republican. Roman Catholic. Office Phone: 212-839-5399. Business E-Mail: ltondel@sidley.com.

**TONDEUR, PHILIPPE MAURICE,** mathematician, educator; b. Zurich, Switzerland, Dec. 7, 1932; came to U.S., 1964, naturalized, 1974; s. Jean and Simone (Lapaire) T.; m. Claire-Lise Ballansat, Dec. 20, 1965. PhD, U. Zurich, 1961. Rsch. fellow U. Paris, 1961-63; lectr. math. U. Zurich, 1963-64, U. Buenos Aires, 1964, Harvard U., Cambridge, Mass., 1964-65, U. Calif. Berkeley, 1965-66; asso. prof. Wesleyan U., Middletown, Conn., 1966-68; assoc. prof. U. Ill., Urbana, 1968-70, prof., 1970—2002, prof. emeritus, 2002—, chair dept. math., 1996-99. Vis. prof. Auckland U., 1968, Eidg. Techn. Hochschule U. Heidelberg, 1973, U. Zurich, 1987, U. Rome, 1984, Ecole Poly., Paris, 1987, U. Santiago de Compostela, Spain, 1987, Max Planck Inst., 1987, U. Leuven (Belgium), 1990, Keio U., Yokohama, Japan, 1993; assoc. mem. Ctr. Advanced Study U. Ill., 1977—78, 1991—92; dir. divsn. math. sci. NSF, 1999—2002. Contbr. articles to profl. jours. Recipient Divsn. Math. Scis. Govtl. Math. award; fellow Swiss Nat. Sci. Found., Harvard U., U. Ill. Mem.: Math. Assn. Am., Soc. Indsl. and Applied Math. (Frederick A. Howes pub. svc. award), Soc. Math. France, Schweiz Math. Gesellschaft, Am. Math. Soc. Office: U Ill Math Dept Urbana IL 61801 E-mail: tondeur@math.uiuc.edu.

**TONEGAWA, SUSUMU,** biology professor; b. Nagoya, Japan, Sept. 5, 1939; arrived in U.S., 1963; s. Tsutoma and Miyoko T. (Masuko) Tonegawa; m. Mayumi Yoshinari, Sept. 28, 1985; children: Hidde, Hanna, Satto. BS, Kyoto U., Japan, 1963; PhD, U. Calif., San Diego, 1968. Rsch. asst. U. Calif., San Diego, 1963—64, teaching asst., 1964—68; mem. Basel (Switzerland) Inst. Immunology, 1971—81; Whitehead prof. biology MIT, Cambridge, 1981—. Investigator Howard Hughes Med. Inst., 1988—; dir. Picower Ctr. for Learning and Memory, 1994—; professorship Amgen, Inc., 1994. Mem. editl. bd. Immunity. Decorated Order of Culture Emperor of Japan; co-recipient Albert Lasker Med. Rsch. award, 1987; named Person with Cultural Merit, Japanese Govt., 1983; recipient Cloetta prize, 1978, Avery Landsteiner prize, Gesselschaft fur Immunologie, 1981, Louisa Gross Horwitz prize, Columbia U., 1982, Gardiner Found. Internat. award, Toronto, Ont., Can., 1983, Robert Koch Found. prize, Bonn, Germany, 1986, Nobel prize in physiology or medicine, 1987. Mem.: NAS (fgn. assoc.), Scandinavian Soc. Immunology (hon.), Am. Assn. Immunologists (hon.). Office: MIT Rm E17-353 77 Massachusetts Ave Cambridge MA 02139-4307 E-mail: tonewaga@mit.edu.*

**TONELLO-STUART, ENRICA MARIA,** political scientist, economist; b. Monza, Italy; d. Alessandro P. and Maddalena M. (Marangoni) Tonello; m. Albert E. Smith; m. Charles L. Stuart. BA in Internat. Affairs, Econs., U. Colo., 1961; MA, Claremont Grad. Sch., 1966, PhD, 1971. Sales mgr. Met. Life Ins. Co., 1974-79; pres., CEO, ETS R&D, Inc., Palos Verdes Peninsula, Calif., 1977—2004; ret. Pub. Editor Tomorrow Outline Jour., 1963—, The Monitor, 1988; pub. World Regionalism-An Ecological Analysis, 1971, A Proposal for the Reorganization of the United Nations, 1966, The Persuasion Technocracy, Its Forms, Techniques and Potentials, 1966, The Role of the Multinationals in the Emerging Globalism, 1978; developed the theory of social ecology and econsociometry. Organizer 1st family assistance program Langley FB Tractical Air Command, 1956-58. Recipient vol. svc. award VA, 1956-58, ARC svc. award, 1950-58. Mem. Corp. Planners Assn. (treas. 1974-79), Investigative Reporters and Editors, World Future Soc. (pres. 1974-75), Soc. Environ. Journalists, Chinese Am. Assn. (life), Palos Verdes C. of C., L.A. Press Club (bd. dirs.), Zonta (chmn. internat. com. South Bay), Pi Sigma Alpha. Avocations: writing, collecting old books and maps, community service, travel. Office Phone: 310-377-7608 Personal E-mail: stuarteeix@netcom.com.

**TONER, MICHAEL F.,** journalist; b. LeMars, Iowa, Mar. 17, 1944; s. Francis F. and Mary Ann (Delaney) Toner; m. Patricia L. Asleson, Aug. 28, 1966; children: Susan Michelle, Sharon Lynn. BA cum laude, U. Iowa, 1966; postgrad., U. Okla., Peru; MS cum laude, Northwestern U., 1967. Reporter UPI, Chgo., 1966—67; bur. chief Miami Herald, Key West, Fla., 1967—68, reporter, 1968—69, asst. city editor, 1970—72; sci./environ. writer Miami (Fla) Herald, 1973—84; sci. editor Atlanta Jour. and Constn., 1984—91; sci. writer, 1991—. Co-author: Florida by Paddle and Pack, 1979; contbr. articles to mags. Recipient Pulitzer Prize for explanatory journalism, 1993, Stanford U. Profl. Journalism fellow, 1973. Avocations: photography, swimming, cooking, stamp collecting/philately. Office: Atlanta Journal and Constn 72 Marietta St NW Atlanta GA 30303-2804

**TONER, STEPHEN J.,** education educator; MA in Edn., Chapman U., Orange, Calif. Math tchr. Apple Valley Unified Sch. Dist., Calif., 1988—2002; coll. prof. Victor Valley Coll., Victorville, Calif., 2001—. Office: Victor Valley Cmty Coll 18422 Bear Valley Rd Victorville CA 92395 Office Phone: 760-245-4271.

**TONEV, THOMAS (TOMA) V.,** mathematics professor; b. Sofia, Bulgaria, Apr. 5, 1932; 2 children. MS, Sofia U., 1969; PhD, Moscow State U., 1974. Adj. prof. Sofia U. - Kliment Ohridski, 1974—88; lectr. Banach Ctr., Warsaw, 1982; sr. rsch. assoc. Inst. Math. and Informatics Bulgarian Acad. Scis., Sofia, 1983—88; vis. mathematician Internat. Ctr. for Theoretical Physics, Trieste, Italy, 1988—89; prof. math. U. Mont., Missoula, 1991; vis. prof. Kent (Ohio) State U., 1999, U. Wash., Seattle, 2000. Senator Faculty Senate, U. Mont., Missoula, 2002. Author: Big Planes, Boundaries and Function Algebras, 1992, (textbooks) Function Algebras and Function Spaces, 1995, Topics in Analysis - Banach Algebras of Continuous Functions, 2005, Shift-Invariant Uniform Algebras on Groups, 2006; co-author (with E. Lyubenova-Toneva): Continued Fractions, 1989; editor: Pliska, Studia mathematica bulgarica, vol. 10, 1990, conf. procs.; contbr. articles to profl. jours. Recipient Rsch. award for Young Mathematicians, Balkan Math. Union, 1975; grantee, NSF, 1992—, IREX, NRC, EPSCOR, Mathematisches Forschungsinstitut, Oberwolfach (Germany), Banach Ctr. (Poland), U. Mont. Fellow: Deutsche Mathematiker-

Vereinigung, Union Scientists in Bulgaria; mem.: Union Bulgarian Mathematicians, European Math. Soc., NY Acad. Scis., Mont. Acad. Scis., Math. Assn. Am., Am. Math. Soc., Phi Kappa Phi, Pi Mu Epsilon. Office: U Mont Dept Math 32 Campus Dr Missoula MT 59812 Office Phone: 406-243-4850. Office Fax: 406-243-2674. Business E-Mail: tonevtv@mso.umt.edu.

**TONEY, ANITA KAREN,** printmaker; b. NYC; d. Anthony and Edna Greenfield Toney. BFA, Syracuse Univ.; MA, San Francisco State Univ. Instr. printmaking City Coll. San Francisco, 1979—. Exhibited in group shows at Nancy Dodds Gallery, Carmel, Calif., Le Celle Gallery, San Anselmo, Calif., Andrea Schwartz Gallery, San Francisco, Images Gallery, Briarcliff, NY, exhibitions include with father, Anthony Toney, Coll. of Marin, 2003. Mem.: Calif. Soc. Printmakers, NAD (academician 1995—). Office: Printmaking City Coll San Francisco 50 Phelan Ave San Francisco CA 94112 Office Phone: 415-239-3000.

**TONG, HING,** mathematician, educator; b. Canton, China, Feb. 16, 1922; s. Shen-Beu and Fung-Kam (Cheng) T.; m. Mary Josephine Powderly, Aug. 19, 1956; children— Christopher Hing, Mary Elizabeth, William Joseph, Jane Frances, James John. AB, U. Pa., 1943; PhD, Columbia, 1947; MA (hon.), Wesleyan U., Middletown, Conn., 1961. NRC postdoctoral fellow Inst. Advanced Study, Princeton, 1947-48; lectr. Canton (China) U., 1949; Cutting travelling fellow Inst. Henri Poincare, Paris, 1950-51; asst. prof. Reed Coll., 1952-53; vis. asst. prof. Barnard Coll., 1953-54; mem. faculty Wesleyan U., 1954-67, prof. math., 1960-67, chmn. dept., 1962-64; prof. math. Fordham U., Bronx, NY, 1966-84, chmn. dept., 1967-74. Mem. U.S. subcom. World Orgn. Gen. Systems and Cybernetics. Contbr. profl. jours. Mem. Phi Beta Kappa, Sigma Xi. Home: 725 Cooper Ave Oradell NJ 07649-2334 Personal E-mail: tong524@optonline.net.

**TONG, KAITY,** anchor; m. Patrick Callahan; 1 child. BA, Bryn Mawr Coll.; MA, Stanford U. Street reporter various West Coast radio/tv networks; anchor KCRA, Sacramento, WABC Eyewitness News, WB-11 News at 10/WPIX-TV, N.Y.C. Recipient Exceptional Achievement award, Disting. Woman award, Star award, Edward R. Murrow award, 3 Emmy awards Acitve United Cerebral Palsy, Children's Mus. of Manhattan, Juvenile Diabetes Found., Friends for Life, League for the Hard of Hearing. Office: WPIX-TV/Tribune Co 220 E 42d St New York NY 10017 Business E-Mail: ktong@tribune.com

**TONG, LOUIS LIK-FU,** information scientist; b. Kowloon, British Hong Kong, June 15, 1962; arrived in U.S., 1980, naturalized, 1994; s. Yu-Tung and Chen (Yao) T. BS, U. Houston, 1985; M Libr. and Info. Sci., U. North Tex., 1992. Info. asst. Houston Acad. Medicine, Tex. Med. Ctr. Libr., Houston, 1990-93; rsch. libr. svc. specialist Internat. Facility Mgmt. Assn., Houston, 1993-98; knowledge and info. mgr. Brown & Root Svc., Houston, 1998-99; web content adminstr. Halliburton Co., Houston, 1999—. Mem.: Tex. Bldg. Energy Inst. (exec. com. 1997—98), Japan-Am. Soc. Houston, Spl. Librs. Assn. (Houston local planning chair 2000—03, sec. Tex. chpt. 2001—03), Med. Libr. Assn. (minority scholar 1992), Internat. Facility Mgmt. Assn. (chmn. codes and regulations com. 1994—98, founding dir. environ., health and safety coun. 1998—2002), Tex. State Rifle Assn. (life), John Birch Soc., NRA (life). Republican. Office: PO Box 230453 Houston TX 77223 E-mail: louis@louistong.com.

**TONG, MEISONG,** electrical engineer, researcher; s. Xiaoyang Tong and Zhaoxiang Zhou; m. Wei Liu, Feb. 19, 1991; 1 child, Zikang. PhD, Ariz. State U., 2004. Lectr. Shanghai U. Fin. and Econ., 1988—90; engr. Shanghai Ship Inst., 1991—2000; tchg./rsch. assoc. Ariz. State U., Tempe, 2000—04; postdoctoral rsch. assoc. U. Ill., Urbana/Champaign, Ill., 2004—. Presenter in field. Contbr. articles to profl. jours. Recipient Best Paper award, 1993, First Level award for rsch., 1995. Mem.: IEEE, ACES. Achievements include design of microwave components; development of wavelet-based numerical method for electromagnetics; Nystrom method for electromagnetics; first to treatment of super-hyper singular integrations related to the Green's function in electromagnetics; development of electromagnetic simulation for a car-roof antenna system. Office Phone: 217-333-7124.

**TONG, QUANSONG,** environmental scientist; PhD, NC State U., Raleigh, 2003. Rsch. assoc. Princeton U., NJ, 2003—06; rsch. scientist Sci. and Tech. Corp., Hampton, Va., 2006—. Office: Stc EPA Mail Drop E243-03 Research Triangle Park NC 27711 Office Phone: 919-541-5150. E-mail: tong.daniel@epa.gov.

**TONG, ROSEMARIE,** humanities educator, philosopher; b. Chgo., July 19, 1947; d. Joseph John and Lillian (Nedued) Behensky; m. Paul Ki-King Tong, Aug. 15, 1971 (dec. Apr. 1988); children: Paul Shih-Mien Tong, John Joseph Tong; m. Jeremiah Putnam, Aug. 1, 1992. BA, Marygrove Coll., 1970; MA, Cath. U., 1971; PhD, Temple U., 1978; LLD (hon.), Marygrove Coll., 1987; LHD (hon.), SUNY, Oneonta, 1993. Asst. and assoc. prof. philosophy Williams Coll., Williamstown, Mass., 1978-88; vis. disting. prof. humanities Davidson (N.C.) Coll., 1988-89, Thatcher Prof. in med. humanities and philosophy, 1989-99; prof. humanities and philosophy U. N.C., Charlotte, 1999—; dir. Ctr. for Profl. and Applied Ethics, Charlotte, 2002—. L. Stacy Davidson vis. chair in liberal arts U. Miss., Oxford, 1998; Louise M. Olmstead vis. prof. philosophy and women's studies, Lafayette Coll., Easton, Pa., 1993; disting. prof. health care ethics U. N.C., Charlotte, 1999—; manuscript reviewer Wadsworth Pub. Co., 1985-92; curriculum reviewer philosophy dept. Carlton and Bowdoin Colls., 1986; honors examiner Hobart and William Smith Colls., 1990; dissertation dir., adj. faculty The Union Inst., 1992-93; cons., judge, panelist, organizer and speaker in field; mem. numerous U. coms. Author: Women, Sex and the Law, 1984, Ethics in Policy Analysis, 1985, Feminist Thought: A Comprehensive Introduction, 1989, Feminist Philosophies: Problems, Theories, and Applications, 1991, Feminine and Feminist Ethics, 1993, Feminist Thought: A More Comprehensive Introduction, 1998, (with Larry Kaplan) Controlling Our Reproductive Destiny, 1994, Feminist Philosophy: Essential Readings in Theory, Reinterpretation and Application, 1994, Feminist Bioethics, 1997, Feminist Thought: A More Comprehensive Ethics, 1998, Globalizing Feminist Bioethics: Crosscultural Perspectives, 2000; editor: (with Anne Donchin and Susan Dodds) Linking Visions: Feminist Bioethics, Human Rights, and the Developing World, 2004; contbr. numerous articles to profl. jours.; mem. various editl. bds. Project reviewer Annenberg/CPB Project, Washington, 1986; policy writer dvsn. health svcs. rsch. and policy U. Minn., 1988, Frank Graham Porter Early Childhood Ctr., U. N.C. Chapel Hill, 1988; mem. Charlotte task force Congl. Task Force Health Care, Congressman Alex McMillan, 1991, standards and ethics com. Hospice N.C., 1991, resource and ethics coms. McMillan-Spratt Task Force Health Care Policy, 1992, pastoral care com. Carolinas Med. Ctr., 1990—, ethics com. Presbyn. Hosp., 1990—, N.E. Regional Hosp., 1991, Nat. Adv. Bd. Ethics in Reproduction, Washington, 1993; active Hastings Ctr. Project Undergrad. Values Edn., Briarcliff Manor, N.Y., 1993, N.C. Found. Humanities and Pub. Policy; mem. bioethics Resource Group, 1992—; mem. feminist approaches to bioethics network, 1996—; dir. med. humanities program Davidson Coll., 1988-98. Named Prof. of Yr., Carnegie Found. and Coun. Advancement and Support of Edn., 1986. Mem. Internat. Assn. for Feminist Approaches to Bioethics Network (coord. 1999—), Internat. Assn. Bioethics (chair 2003—), Am. Assn. for Bioethics and Humanities, Am. Cath. Philos. Assn., Am. Philos. Assn. (ad hoc com. computers, pub. and role of Am. Philos. Assn. 1984, adv. com. to program com. 1986-88, nomination com. 1989-91, nat. com. on status of women 1989-93, 2003—), Am. Legal Studies and Assn., Am. Soc. Pol. and Legal Philosophy, Am. Soc. Law and Medicine, Nat. Coun. Rsch. on Women, Nat. Women Studies Assn., Internat. Assn. Philosophy Law and Social Philosophy, Assn. Practical and Profl. Ethics, Society Christian Ethics, Soc. Women in Philosophy, Soc. Philosophy and Tech., Soc. Philosophy and Pub. Affairs, Soc. Study of Women Philosophers, Network Feminist Approaches to Bioethics, The Hastings Ctr., Triangle Bioethics Group, So. Soc. Philosophy and Psychology. Avocations: aerobics, boating, hiking. Office Phone: 704-687-2850. Business E-Mail: rotong@email.uncc.edu.

**TONG, SIU WING,** computer programmer; b. Hong Kong, May 20, 1950; came to U.S., 1968; BA, U. Calif., Berkeley, 1972; PhD, Harvard U., 1979; MS, U. Lowell, 1984. Rsch. assoc. Brookhaven Nat. Lab., Upton, N.Y., 1979-83; software engr. Honeywell Info. Systems, Billerica, Mass., 1984-85; sr. programmer, analyst Hui Computer Cons., Berkeley, Calif., 1985-88; sr. v.p. devel., chief fin. officer Surgicenter Info. Systems, Inc., Orinda, Calif., 1989-94; sr. sys. specialist Info. Sys. Divsn. Contra Costa County Health Svcs., Martinez, Calif., 1995-97, info. tech. supr. Info. Sys. Divsn., 1997—. Vol. tchr. Boston Chinatown Saturday Adult Edn. Program of Tufts Med. Sch., 1977-79. Muscular Dystrophy Assn. fellow, 1980-82. Mem. AAAS, IEEE, Assn. Computing Machinery, N.Y. Acad. Scis. Home: 17 Beaconsfield Ct Orinda CA 94563-4203 Office: Contra Costa County Health Svcs 595 Center Ave Ste 210 Martinez CA 94553-4634 E-mail: swtong@hsd.cccounty.us.

**TONGE, BRUCE JOHN,** psychiatrist; b. Melborne, Australia, May 9, 1947; s. JOhn Feltham and Joyce (Bates) Tonge; m. Gera Eleanore Degooijer-Tonge, Oct. 12, 1970 (div. June 1996); m. Avril Vaux Brereton, June 10, 1996; children: Jonathan, Rachel, Claire. MB BS, Monash U., Melbourne, 1970; DPM, Royal Coll. Physicians, London, 1974; MD, U. Melbourne, 1985. Cert. child psychiatrist Vic. Child psychiatrist Austin Hosp., Melbourne, 1976—80, dir. dept. child psychiatry, 1980—87; head dept. psychiatry, prof. child psychiatry Royal Alexandra Hosp. for Children, Sydney, N.S.W., 1987—89; med. dir., mental health program So. Health, Melbourne, 1990—, head ctr. for devel. psychiatry and psychology, 1990—; prof. and headdept. psychiatry Monash U., Melbourne, 1989—. Chair child psychiatry and tng. com. RANZCP, Melbourne, 1986—91; bd. dirs. Autism Victoria, Melbourne, 1991—2001; mem. com. on mental health and ID WHO, London, 1997—; bd. dirs. Neurosci. Australia, Melbourne, 2003—. Author: 41 books on child psychiatry; editor: Handbook of Child Psychiatry, 1990; contbr. 52 chpts. to books, articles to profl. jours.; co-author: Developmental Behaviour Checklist; author: Self-Efficacy Questionnaire for Adolescents, Draw a Dream. Flight lt. RAAF, 1961—70. Named Blake Marsh Lectr., Roy Coll. Psychiatrists of Edinburgh, 1989; recipient Rsch. Excellence prize, Monash U., 2001, Nat. Rsch. prize, Australian Soc. for Study of Learning Disabled, 1998, Julian Katz award, RANZCP, 1998. Mem.: Royal Melbourne Tennis Club. Anglican. Office: Ctr for Developmental Psychiatry Monash Medical Ctr 246 Clayton Rd Claton VIC 3168 Ascension Office Fax: 51-3-9594-6937. E-mail: bruce.tonge@med.monash.edu.au.

**TONGLET, JENNIFER PHILIPS,** psychologist; b. New Orleans, Apr. 15, 1968; d. Danny Anthony Philips and Linda Marie Chaix; m. James Edward Tonglet, Mar. 3, 1989; children: Matthew James, Mark Patrick, Joseph Gerard. BSc, U. New Orleans, 1990; MSc, Tulane U., 1996, PhD, 2000. Cert. sch. psychologist La. Sch. psychologist St. Tammany Parish Sch. Bd., Covington, La., 1998—. Trainer, nonviolent crisis intervention Crisis Prevention Inst.; lay min. of ch.; cub scout leader. Mem.: Nat. Assn. Sch. Psychologists, La. Sch. Psychol. Assn. (treas. 2004—). Republican. Roman Catholic.

**TONGUE, PAUL GRAHAM,** financial executive; b. Phila., Dec. 30, 1932; s. George Paul and Florence Amelia (Kogel) T.; m. Marjorie Joan Meyers, May 26, 1954; children: Suzanne Marjorie, Douglas Paul BS in Commerce, Drexel U., 1957; MBA, NYU, 1965. With Chase Manhattan Bank, N.Y.C., 1957-87; chmn. Plus Systems Inc., Denver, 1985; pres. Eppley-Tongue Assocs., Inc., Towson, Md., 1988—; exec. v.p. Veritas Venture Inc., Scotch Plains, NJ, 1990-91. Pres. Our Saviour Luth. Ch., Manhasset, N.Y., 1984; pres. 1st Night of Williamsburg, Inc.; bd. dirs. Ronald Reagan Club, Ford's colony Homeowners' Assn., Williamsburg Area Civic and Cultural Ctr., Inc., Sr. Exec. Resource Corps, Coll. William and Mary. Mem. Ford's Colony Country Club. Avocations: golf, classical music. E-mail: pgtongue@cox.net.

**TONGUE, THOMAS HEALY,** lawyer; b. Portland, Oreg., Nov. 27, 1943; s. Thomas H. and Bernice (Healy) T.; m. Andrea Cibis, July 24, 1971; children: Thomas M., Kathryn Ann. BS, U. Oreg., 1965; JD, U. Wis., 1968. Bar: Oreg. 1968, U.S. Dist. Ct. Oreg. 1970, U.S. Ct. Appeals (9th cir.) 1971, U.S. Supreme Ct. 1973. Assoc. Morrison & Bailey, Portland, 1968-72; ptnr. Dunn Carney Allen Higgins & Tongue, Portland, 1973—. Fellow Am. Bar Found.; Am. Coll. Trial Lawyers (state chair 2000-02 regent 2003—); mem. ABA, Oreg. State Bar (Pres.'s award 1992), Multnomah Bar Assn. (pres. 1976, Professionalism award 1990), Internat. Assn. Def. Counsel, Oreg. Assn. Def. Counsel (bd. dirs. 1993-98, pres. 1998), 9th Cir. Jud. Conf. (lawyer rep. 1992-94) Office: Dunn Carney Allen Higgins and Tongue 851 SW 6th Ave Ste 1500 Portland OR 97204-1357 E-mail: tht@dunn-carney.com.

**TONGUE, WILLIAM WALTER,** economics and business consultant, educator; b. Worcester, Mass., May 24, 1915; s. Walter Ernest and Lena (Brown) T.; m. Beverly Harriet Cohan, Dec. 26, 1936; children— Barbara Tongue Duggan, Kathleen Tongue Alligood. AB, Dartmouth, 1937, M.C.S., 1938; PhD, U. Chgo., 1947. Jr. acct. Price, Waterhouse & Co. (C.P.A.'s), N.Y.C., 1938; instr. Coe Coll., Cedar Rapids, Iowa, 1941-42; spl. com. OSS, 1942; fin. economist Fed. Res. Bank Chgo., 1942-44; economist Jewel Companies, Inc., Chgo., 1944-64; prof. econs. and finance U. Ill. Chgo., 1965-80. Prof. emeritus, 1980—; econ. cons. LaSalle Nat. Bank, Chgo., 1968-91; mem. com. CNA Fin. Separate Fund B., 1997-2003; dir. St. Joseph Light & Power Co., Mo., 1965-86; trustee Signode Employees' Savs. and Profit Sharing Trust Fund, 1980-89. Author articles; contbr.: to books including How We Can Halt Inflation and Still Keep Our Jobs, 1974. Bd. dirs., v.p. rsch. and stats. Chgo. Assn. Commerce and Industry, 1968-69; bd. dirs. Luther Village Owners Corp., v.p., 2002-05 Mem. Nat. Assn. Bus. Economists (pres. 1962-63), Conf. Bus. Economists, Am. Statis. Assn. (pres. Chgo. chpt. 1951-52), Econ. Club Chgo., Investment Analysts Assn. Chgo., Inst. Chartered Fin. Analysts (chartered fin. analyst 1963), Midwest Fin. Assn. (pres. 1972-73). Home and Office: 1220 Village Dr Apt 427 Arlington Heights IL 60004-8123 Office Phone: 847-670-7836. Personal E-mail: williamtongue@yahoo.com.

**TONIETTE, SALLYE JEAN,** physician; b. Sulphur, La., 1929; d. Eugene Augusta and Sallye (Tanner) T. Student, John McNeese Jr. Coll., 1946-47; BS, La. State U., 1949, tchrs. cert., 1950, MD, 1955. Intern Crawford W. Long Meml. Hosp., Emory U., Atlanta, 1955-56, resident in ob-gyn., jr., sr., chief residencies, 1956-59; practice in ob-gyn. Sulphur, La., 1959—. Mem. med. staff West Calcasieu Cameron Hosp., 1959—. Dir. Calcasieu Parish Cancer Soc., 1963-67. Named Woman of Distinction, Calcasieu Parish Police Jurors, also Bus. and Profl. Women's Club of West Calcasieu, 1969; Queen of Krewe of Cosmos, 1963, Mardi Gras. Fellow Am. Coll. Ob-Gyn.; mem. La. Med. Assn., Calcasieu Parish Med. Soc., La. Wildlife Fedn., Am. Quarter Horse Assn., Assn. Am. Physicians and Surgeons, Bayou Oaks Country Club (v.p., bd. dirs. 1974—), Krewe de Bon Coer, Krewe of Cosmos, Alpha Chi Omega, Beta Tau Mu, Iota Sigma Pi, Phi Theta Kappa, Beta Sigma Phi. Republican. Methodist. Home: 4917 La Paix Dr Sulphur LA 70665 Office: 521 Cypress St Sulphur LA 70663-5049 Personal E-mail: sassy29@xspedius.net.

**TONJES, MARIAN JEANNETTE BENTON,** education educator; b. Rockville Center, N.Y., Feb. 16, 1929; d. Millard Warren and Felicia E. (Tyler) Benton; m. Charles F. Tonjes (div. 1965, dec.); children: Jeffrey Charles, Kenneth Warren. BA, U. N.Mex., 1951, cert. 1966, MA, 1969; EdD, U. Miami, 1975. Dir. recreation Stuyvesant Town Housing Project, N.Y.C., 1951—53; tchr. music., phys. edn. Sunset Mesa Day Sch., Albuquerque, 1953—54; tchr. remedial reading Zia Elem. Sch., 1965—67; tchr. secondary devel. reading Rio Grande H.S., 1967—69; rsch. asst. reading Southwestern Coop. Ednl. Lab., 1969—71; assoc. dir., vis. instr. Fla. Ctr. Tchr. Tng. Materials U. Miami, 1971—72; asst. prof. U.S. Internat. U., San Diego, 1972—75; prof. edn. Western Wash. U., Bellingham, 1975—94, prof. emerita, 1994—; dir. summer study at Oriel Coll. Oxford U., England, 1976—93; adj. prof. U. N.Mex., 2005—. Reading supr. Manzanita Ctr., 1968; vis. prof. adult edn. Palomar (Calif.) Jr. Coll., 1974; vis. prof. U. Guam, Mangilao, 1989-90; invited guest Russian Reading Assn., Moscow, 1992; internat. travel adv. Vantage Deluxe Travel, 2002-05; spkr. European Conf. reading, Tallinn, Estonia, 2003, symposium chair World Congress, Manila, 2004; cons. in field. Author: (with Miles V. Zintz) Teaching Reading/Thinking Study Skills in Content Classroom, 3rd edit., Secondary Reading, Writing and Learning, 1991, Integrated Content Literacy, 1999, (with Ray Wolpow) Integrated Content Literacy, 5th edit., 2006. Trustee White Mountain Sch., 2000—; tour dir. In the Footsteps of Dickens, England, 2001; hon. trustee Lomonosov Sch., Moscow; read by three com. Albuquerque Bus. and Edn. Compact, 1999—2002. Tng. Tchr. Trainers grantee, 1975; NDEA fellow Okla. State U., 1969; nominated Profl. Outstanding Alumna McDaniel Coll., 2005. Mem.: Am. Reading Forum, Internat. Reading Assn., PEO (past chpt. pres.), World Congress in Reading Buenos Aires, European Coun. Internat. Schs., European Conf. in Reading, UK Reading Assn., Internat. Reading Assn. (non-print media and reading com. 1980—83, workshop dir. S.W. regional confs. 1982, travel, interchange and study tours com. 1984—86, com. internat. devel. N.Am. 1991—96, Outstanding Tchr. Educator award 1981), Am. Reading Forum (chmn. bd. dirs. 1983—85), Oxonian and Friend of Oriel Coll. (Oxford) (hon.), Circumnavigators, Internat. Soc. Rwy. Travelers, Albuquerque Tennis Club, Delta Delta Delta. Presbyterian. Avocations: miniatures, tennis, bridge, art, travel. E-mail: mtonjes@unm.edu.

**TONKIN, HUMPHREY RICHARD,** academic administrator, educator; b. Truro, Cornwall, Eng., Dec. 2, 1939; arrived in U.S., 1962; s. George Leslie and Lorna Winifred (Sandry) T.; m. Sandra Julie Winberg, Mar. 9, 1968 (div. 1981); m. Jane Spencer Edwards, Oct. 1, 1983; 1 child, Sebastian George. BA, St. John's Coll., Cambridge, Eng., 1962, MA, 1966; AM, PhD, Harvard U., 1966; DLitt (hon.), U. Hartford, 1999. Asst. prof. English U. Pa., Phila., 1966-71, assoc. prof., 1971-80, prof., 1980-83, vice-provost undergrad. studies, 1971-75, coord. internat. programs, 1977-83, master Stouffer Coll. House, 1980-83; pres. State Univ. Coll., Potsdam, NY, 1983-88, U. Hartford, Conn., 1989-98, prof. humanities, pres. emeritus, 1998—; vis. fellow Whitney Humanities Ctr. Yale U., 1998-99. Vis. prof. English Columbia U., N.Y.C., 1980-81; exec. dir. Ctr. Rsch. and Documentation on World Lang. Problems, Rotterdam and Hartford, 1974—. Editor: Language Problems and Language Planning; author: (bibliography) Sir Walter Raleigh, 1971, Esperanto and International Language Problems, 4th edit., 1977, Spenser's Courteous Pastoral, 1972; author: (with Jane Edwards) The World in the Curriculum, 1981, The Faerie Queene, 1989; editor (with Allison Keef): Language in Religion, 1989, Esperanto, Interlinguistics and Planned Language, 1997; editor: (with Timothy Reagan) Language in the 21st Century, 2003; editor: Service Learning Across Cultures, 2004; editor, translator Esperanto: Language, Literature and Community (Pierre Janton), 1993, Maskerado: Dancing Around Death in Nazi Hungary (Tivadar Soros), 2000; contbr. articles to profl. jours. Pres. Pa. Coun. Internat. Edn., 1980-81; bd. dirs. World Affairs Coun. Phila., 1979-83, Zamenhof Found., 1987-94, Hartford Symphony Orch., 1989-98, World Affairs Coun. Conn., 1989-2003, Greater Hartford Arts Coun., 1989-99, Can.-U.S. Found. Ednl. Exchange, 1997-2003, chmn. 1999-2000; bd. dirs. World Learning, 1998—; chmn. Coun. Internat. Exch. Scholars, 1988-94, Esperantic Studies Found., 1991—, Internat. Partnership for Svc.-Learning, 1991-96, v.p., 2001-05; bd. dirs. Am. Forum, 1985—, chmn., 1998-2003. Recipient Lindback award for disting. teaching, 1970; Frank Knox fellow Harvard U., 1962-66; Guggenheim fellow, 1974. Fellow Acad. Esperanto; mem. Universal Esperanto Assn. (pres. 1974-80, 86-89, rep. to UN 1974-83, hon. com. 1995—), Spenser Soc. (pres. 1983-84, former dir.), Internat. Acad. Scis. San Marino, Conn. Acad. Arts and Scis., Cosmos Club. Home: 279 Ridgewood Rd West Hartford CT 06107-3542 Office: U Hartford Mortensen Libr 200 Bloomfield Ave West Hartford CT 06117-1599 Office Phone: 860-768-4448. Business E-Mail: tonkin@hartford.edu.

**TONKIN, LEO SAMPSON,** educational association administrator; b. Suffern, N.Y., Apr. 2, 1937; s. Leo S. and Ann (Petrone) T. AB, Johns Hopkins, 1959; postgrad., Sch. Advanced Internat. Studies, 1962-63; JD, Harvard, 1962; Dr. Pedagogy, SUNY, 1973. Legis. asst. to US Congressman; then Sen. Charles McC. Mathias, Jr., Md., 1962-63; asso. counsel US Ho. of Reps. Select Com. on Govt. Research, 1964; spl. cons. Ho. Spl. Subcom. on Edn., 1965-66; exec. dir. Commrs. Council on Higher Edn., Washington, 1965-66; pres. Leo S. Tonkin Assos., Inc., 1966—; founder, dir., chmn. bd. Washington Workshops Found., 1967—; pres. Travel Seminars, Ltd., 1999—. Mem. White House Conf. on Edn., 1965, White House Conf. on Youth, 1971; spl. asst. to chmn. U.S. Ho. of Reps. Select Com. on Crime, 1972; mem. bd. plebe sponsors U.S. Naval Acad., 1977—; v.p. London Fedn. Boys' Clubs, 1980—; mem. adv. panel Nat. Commn. for Protection of Human Subjects of Biomed. and Behavioral Research, HEW, 1976-77; bd. dirs. Star Scientific, Inc., 1998—; nat. adv. coun. Retinitis Pigmentosa Found., 1999—. Contbr. articles to mags. Bd. dirs. Washington Choral Arts Soc., 1971-73, Nat. Coordinating Council on Drug Edn., 1973, Nat. Student Ednl. Fund, 1974—; chmn. Wall Street Seminar Found., 1978—; chmn. bd. trustees St. Thomas Aquinas Coll., 1966-73, continuing trustee, 1973-78, trustee, chmn. emeritus, 1978—; chmn. bd. trustees City of Phila. Govt. Honors Program; trustee Southeastern U., 1966-73; asso. bd. trustees Immaculata Coll., 1966-73; mem. advisory bd. Pub. Affairs and Govt. Degree Program, Mt. Vernon Coll., 1971-74; bd. dirs. YMCA, Washington, 1969-71. Recipient Americanism award, Valley Forge Freedoms Found, 1973 Mem. Johns Hopkins Alumni Assn. Washington (pres. 1969-72), Harvard Law Sch. Alumni Assn. Washington (exec. com.), Georgetown Club (Washington), City Tavern Club (Washington), Nat. Press Club (Washington), Capitol Hill Club (Washington), Capitol Yacht Club (Washington), Harvard Club (N.Y.C.). Home: 4368 Sunset Ct Warrenton VA 20187-3584 Office: 3222 N St NW Washington DC 20007-2849 Office Phone: 202-965-3434.

**TONKONOGY, JOSEPH MOSES,** physician, neuropsychiatrist, researcher; b. Belaya Tserkov, Kiev, Ukraine, Oct. 22, 1925; came to U.S., 1979, naturalized, 1985; s. Moysey Iosifovich and Beyla (Gdalievna (Schvachkina) T.; married; children: Vitaly, Milla, Bella. MD, Military Med. Acad., Leningrad, USSR, 1947; PhD, All Union Acad. Med. Sci., Moscow, 1956; DSc, 1st Med. Inst., Leningrad, 1966. From asst. to prof. The Bechterev Inst., Leningrad, 1956-66, prof., chmn., 1966-78; assoc. Boston U. Sch. Medicine, 1980-81; physician VA Med. Ctr., Northampton, Mass., 1981-87; assoc. prof. U. Mass. Med. Ctr., Worcester, 1987-95, prof., 1995—. Dir. neuropsychiatry svc. Worcester State Hosp., Mass., 1989—. Author: Introduction to Clinical Neuropsychology, 1973, Vascular Aphasia, 1986, The Brief Neuropsychological Cognitive Examination, 1997; editor: Problems of Contemporary Psychoneurology, 1966, Psychological Experiment in Psychiatry and Neurology, 1969, Mathematical Methods in Psychiatry and Neurology, 1971, Current Problems of Clinical Psychology, 1975; cons. (book) Soviet Military Psychiatry, 1986; contbr. numerous articles to profl. jours. Capt. Med. Corps, Germany, 1947-48. Recipient The Bechterev Prize, All Union Acad. Med. Scis., Moscow, 1974. Fellow: The Royal Soc. Medicine (U.K.); mem.: Internet Psychogeriatric Soc., Soc. Neurosci., Internat. Neuropsychol. Soc., Am. Acad. Neurology, Am. Neuropsychiat. Assn. Jewish. Office: U Mass Med Ctr Dept Psychiatry 55 Lake Ave N Worcester MA 01655-0002

**TONKS, ROBERT STANLEY,** pharmacologist, educator, retired dean; b. Aberystwyth, Wales; emigrated to Can., 1973; s. Robert Patrick Dennis and Prudence Violet (Williams) T.; m. Diana Mary Cownie; children: Pamela Mary, Julia Rosalind, Robert Michael, Sara Katharine. Student, U. Coll. of South Wales, Welsh Coll. Pharmacy; B.Pharm., PhD, Welsh Nat. Sch. Medicine, Cardiff. Organon postdoctoral fellow Med. Sch., Cardiff, Nat. Health Service postdoctoral fellow; Nat. Health Service sr. fellow Cardiff and Nevill Hall Hosp., Abergavenny; lectr. pharmacology U. Wales, Cardiff, 1958-72; vis. fellow Claude Bernard Research Assn., Faculté de Medicine, Paris, 1959; sr. lectr. pharmacology and therapeutics Med. Sch. and U. Wales Hosp., Cardiff, 1972-73; dir. prof. Coll. Pharmacy, Dalhousie U., Halifax, N.S., Canada, 1973-77. dean Faculty of Health Professions, 1977-88, prof. geriatric pharmaco-therapeutics, 1988—, acting head divsn. geriatric medicine, 1991-94. Cons. pharm. industry in U.K., govt. of N.S. Can. Health and Welfare Dept. Can.; advisor health manpower Govt. of N.S.; coordinator N.E. Can./Am. Health Coun. co-chmn., 1974-91; emeritus chmn., mem. Health and Welfare Personnel Career Rev. Com., 1977-91; pharm. scis. grants com.

Med. Rsch. Council Can., chmn.; mem. rev. com. health protection br. fed. govt. div. pharm. chemistry, Can.; chmn. advisory com. N.B. Minister of Health; mem. joint com. on devel. rsch. in nursing Med. Rsch. Coun.-Nat. Health Rsch. Devel. Program; mem. nat. adv. panel on risk/benefit mgmt. of drugs.; adv. com. on restructuring Health Canada's Personnel Career Awards; trustee Lakeridge Health Found., Oshawa, Ont., 2001-02, Lakeridge Health Whitby Found., Ont., 2003-04, coord. drug and med. supplies Ethiopia airlift, 1984. Contbr. articles on pharmacology and pathology to profl. jours. Mem.: Welsh Cultural Soc. (past pres.), Med. Soc. N.S (task force on pharmacare), N.S. Pharm. Soc. (cert. of merit), Can. Geriatrics Soc., Am. Soc. Clin. Pharm. and Therapeutics, Canadian Soc. Clin. Investigation, Brit. Pharmacol. Soc., N.B. Pharm. Soc. (hon.), Can. Soc. Hosp. Pharmacy (hon.). Anglican. Mailing: 6 Tom Edwards Dr Whitby ON Canada L1R 2R4 Office: Dalhousie U Coburg Rd Halifax NS Canada Business E-Mail: bobtonks@dal.ca.

**TONN, ELVERNE MERYL,** pediatric dentist, dental benefits consultant, forensic odontologist; b. Stockton, Calif., Dec. 10, 1929; s. Emanuel M. and Lorna Darlene (Bryant) T.; m. Ann G. Richardson, Oct. 28, 1951; children: James Edward, Susan Elaine Tonn. AA, La Sierra U., Riverside, Calif., 1949; DDS, U. So. Calif., 1955; BS, Excelsior Coll., 1984; grad., Citizens Police Acad., Manteca, 2003. Lic. dentist Calif., 1955, diplomate Am. Bd. Quality Assurance and Utilization Rev. Physicians, Am. Bd. Forensic Dentistry, Am. Bd. Spl. Care Dentistry, Am. Bd. for Cert. in Homeland Security, cert. dental cons., forensic cons. Am. Coll. Forensic Examiners, 2004, med. investigator Am. Coll. Forensic Examiners, 2004; in Homeland Security Am. Bd., 2006. Pediatric dentist, assoc. Walker Dental Group, Long Beach, Calif., 1957-59, Children's Dental Clinic, Sunnyvale, Calif., 1959-61; pediatric dentist in pvt. practice Mountain View, Calif., 1961 72; pediatric dentist, ptnr. Pediatric Dentistry Assocs., Los Altos, Calif., 1972-83; pediatric dentist, ptnr. Valley Oak Dental Group, Manteca, Calif., 1987–2003; from clin. instr. to assoc. prof. Sch. Dentistry, U. Pacific, San Francisco, 1964-84; assoc. prof. Sch. Dentistry, U. Calif., San Francisco, 1984-86. Pediat. dental cons. Delta Dental Plan, San Francisco, 1985–2002; chief dental staff El Camino Hosp., Mountain View, Calif., 1964—65, 1984—85; dental cons. Interplast program Stanford U. Sch. Medicine, 1973; cert. physician adv. Physicians' Review Network, Phoenix, 2004—. Weekly columnist Manteca Bull., 1987-92; producer 2 teaching videos, 1986; contbr. articles to profl. jours. Capt. U.S. Army, 1955—63. Fellow Am. Coll. Dentists, Internat. Coll. Dentists, Am. Acad. Pediatric Dentistry, Royal Soc. Health, Acad. of Dentistry for Handicapped, Pierre Fauchard Acad., Acad. Dental Materials, Am. Soc. Dentistry for Children (mastership award 2001), Am. Acad. Forensic Scis., Am. Coll. Forensic Examiners; mem. ADA, Internat. Assn. Pediatric Dentistry, Internat. Assn. Dental Rsch., Am. Soc. Forensic Odontology, Fedn. Dentaire Internationale, Am. Assn. Dental Cons., Calif. Dental Assn., Calif. Soc. Dentistry for Children (pres. 1968), Calif. Soc. Pediatric Dentistry, NY Acad. Scis., Calif. Acad. Sci., Rotary Internat., Manteca Police Dept. (Badge 2003), Nat. Disaster Med. Svc., Disaster Mortuary Org. Response Team (DMORT region 9), Am. Coll. Med. Quality, Manteca Cert. Emergency Response Team. Republican. Avocations: photography, travel, medieval history, anthropology. Home and Office: Tonn Forensic Consulting Services 374 Laurelwood Cir Manteca CA 95336-7122 Office Phone: 209-815-4824. Personal E-Mail: emtonn@comcast.net.

**TONN, ROBERT JAMES,** retired entomologist; b. Watertown, Wis., June 23, 1927; s. Harry James and Elise (Foogman) Tonn; m. Noemi C. Tonn; children: Sigrid M., Monica E. BS, Colo. State U., 1949, MS, 1950; MPH, Okla. Med. Sch., 1963; PhD, Okla. State U., 1959. Rsch. assoc La. State U., Costa Rica/New Orleans, 1961-63; dir. Taunton (Mass.) Field Sta., 1963-65; chief PMO unit WHO, various locations, 1965-87; ret., 1987. Adj. prof. parasitology U. Tex., El Paso, 1988—; cons. USAID/VBC, 1987—. Contbr. articles to profl. jours. Mem.: Royal Soc. Tropical Medicine and Hygiene, US/Mex. Border Health Assn., Am. Mosquito Control Assn., Soc. Vector Ecology (pres. 1984), Am. Soc. Tropical Medicine, Masons. Congregationalist. Home: 4247 Winchester Rd Las Cruces NM 88011 also: PO Box 772 Cloudcroft NM 88317 Personal E-Mail: tonnapollo@aol.com.

**TONTIRUTTANANON, CHANNARONG,** electrical engineer, researcher; b. Muang, Surin, Thailand, 1971; B in Engring., Chulalongkorn U., Bangkok, 1992; MS, Auburn U., 1997, PhD, 1998. Instr. Assumption U., Bangkok, 1992—95; grad. rsch. asst. Auburn (Ala.) U., 1995—98; postdoctoral rsch. fellow U. Iowa, Iowa City, 1999; sr. mem. sci. staff Nortel Networks Inc., Richardson, Tex., 1999—. Contbr. articles to profl. jours. Mem.: IEEE, Am. Math. Soc., Phi Kappa Phi, Eta Kappa Nu. Achievements include patents for overload control system and method for a telecommunication system. Office Phone: 972-685-4924. E-mail: ctont@nortel.com.

**TONTONOZ, PETER,** molecular biologist, educator; s. David and Susan Tontonoz; m. Keri Gardner, Oct. 30, 2004. BA, Wesleyan U., Middletown, Conn., 1989; MD, Harvard Med. Sch., Boston, 1996; PhD, Harvard U., Cambridge, Mass., 1996. Lic. Med. Bd. Calif. Asst. prof. UCLA, 1999—2002, assoc. prof., 2002—06, prof., 2006—. Author: numerous rsch. articles in jours. Recipient Freedom to Discover award, Bristol-Myers Squibb, 2004, Richard E. Weitzman award, The Endocrine Soc., 2005. Achievements include research in role of nuclear receptors in metabolism and disease. Office: UCLA 675 Charles Young Dr S; MRL 5-748 Los Angeles CA 90095-1662 Office Phone: 310-206-4546.

**TOOHEY, BRIAN FREDERICK,** lawyer; b. Niagara Falls, N.Y., Dec. 14, 1944; s. Matthew and Marilyn (Hoag) T.; m. Mary Elizabeth Monihan; children: Maureen Elizabeth, Matthew Sheridan, Margaret Monihan Mary Catherine, Elizabeth Warner. BS, Niagara U., 1966; JD, Cornell U., 1969. Bar: N.Y. 1969, N.Mex. 1978, Ohio 1980. Ptnr. Jones Day, Cleve., 1981—. Lt. JAG Corps, USNR, 1970-73. Mem. ABA, N.Y. State Bar Assn., State Bar N.Mex., Ohio State Bar Assn., Greater Cleve. Bar Assn., Roman Catholic. Home: 25 Pepper Creek Dr Cleveland OH 44124-5279 Office: Jones Day N Point 901 Lakeside Ave E Cleveland OH 44114-1190 Office Phone: 216-586-7246. E-mail: bftoohey@jonesday.com.

**TOOHEY, JAMES KEVIN,** lawyer; b. Evanston, Ill., July 16, 1944; s. John Joseph and Ruth Regina (Cassidy) T.; m. Julie Marie Crane, Nov. 1, 1969 (div. Aug. 1977); children: Julie Colleen, Jeannne Christine; m. Anne Margaret Boettingheimer, May 28, 1983; children: James Robert, Kevin John, Casey Anne. BBA, U. Notre Dame, 1966; JD, Northwestern U., 1969. BAr: Ill. 1969, U.S. Dist. Ct. (no. dist.) Ill. 1971, U.S. Dist. Ct. (ctrl. dist.) Ill. 1991, U.S. Ct. Appeals (7th cir.) 1973, U.S. Ct. Appeals (8th cir.) 1975, U.S. Supreme Ct. 1988. Assoc. Taylor, Miller, Magner, Sprowl & Hutchings, Chgo., 1970-71; asst. U.S. Atty. Office U.S. Atty., Chgo., 1971-74; assoc. Ross, Hardies, O'Keefe, Babcock & Parsons, Chgo., 1974-77; ptnr. Ross & Hardies, Chgo., 1977—2003, McGuire Woods, LLP, 2003—05, Johnson & Bell, Ltd., 2005—. Mem. St. Mary of the Wood Parish Coun., 1999-2002 Mem. Ill. State Bar Assn., Am. Soc. Trial Lawyers, Assn. Advancement of Automotive Medicine, Ill. Assn. Def. Attys., Trial Lawyers Club Chgo., Edgebrook Sauganash Athletic Assn. (bd. dirs., commr. 1993-96; softball, baseball, and basketball coach), Evanston Golf Club. Office: Johnson & Bell Ltd 33 W Monroe St Chicago IL 60603 Office Phone: 312-984-0280.

**TOOHEY, PHILIP S.,** retired lawyer; b. 1943; BA, Hamilton Coll., 1965; JD, Cornell U., 1968. Bar: N.Y. 1968. Law clk. Hon. Louis B. Greenblatt Appellate Divsn., 1968-69; assoc. Phillips, Lytle, Hitchcock, Blaine & Huber, 1969-74, ptnr., 1975-84; sr. bank counsel Marine Midland Banks, Inc., Buffalo, 1984-88, dep. gen. counsel, 1988-91, gen. counsel, 1991-2000; sr. exec. v.p., gen. counsel, sec. HSBC Bank USA, 2000—04; ret. Mem. N.Y. State Bar Assn. (chmn. bus. law com. of banking, corp. & bus. law sect. 1985-88, sec. bus. law sect. 1988-89, vice chmn., treas. bus. law sect. 1989-90, 1st vice chmn. bus. law sect. 1990-91, chmn. bus. law sect. 1991-92).

---

**TOOKER, GEORGE,** artist; b. Bklyn., Aug. 5, 1920; s. George Clair and Angela Montejo (Roura) Tooker. BA, Harvard U., 1942; student, Art Students League, N.Y.C., 1943-44. Instr. Art Students League, NY, 1965-68. One-man shows include Edwin Hewitt Gallery, 1951, 1955, Robert Isaacson Gallery, 1960, 1962, Durfacher Bros., 1964, 1967, Hopkins Ctr. Dartmouth Coll., 1967, Fine Arts Mus., San Francisco, 1974, Mus. Contemporary Art, Chgo., 1974, Whitney Mus., N.Y.C., 1975, Indpls. Mus. Art, 1975, DC Moore Gallery, 1997, 1998, 2000, exhibited in group shows at Whitney Mus., 1947—50, 1953, 1955—58, 1961, 1964, 1965, 1967, 1975, Venice Biennale, 1956, Art Inst. Chgo., 1951, 1952, 1954, 1959, Inst. Contemporary Arts, London, 1950, Va. Mus., 1964, 1962, Pa. Acad., 1966, Marisa Del Re Gallery, 1985, 1988, 1992, Spoleto Festival, Gibbes Mus. Art, Charleston, S.C., 1987, Robert Hall Fleming Mus., U. Vt., 1987, Marsh Gallery, U. Richmond, Va., 1989, Addison Gallery Art, 1994, Represented in permanent collections Smithsonian Nat. Mus. Am. Art, Smithsonian Hirshorn Mus., Whitney Mus., Dartmouth Coll., Met. Mus., Walker Art Ctr., Mus. Modern Art, S.C. Johnson & Sons, Inc., Art, U.S.A., Sara Roby Fund Collection Am. Art, Addison Gallery, Ariz. State U. Gallery, Bklyn. Mus., Columbus (Ohio) Mus. Recipient Vt. Gov.'s award for Excellence in Arts, 1983, E. Isenberger prize, Nat. Acad., 2005; grantee, Nat. Inst. Arts and Letters, 1960. Mem.: NAD, Acad. Arts and Letters. Address: PO Box 385 Hartland VT 05048-0385 Office: care DC Moore Gallery 724 5th Ave New York NY 10019-4106

**TOOKER, JOHN PHILLIP,** internist, educator, medical association administrator; b. Denver; m. Nancy Tooker; 2 children. MD, U. Colo., 1970; MBA, Temple U. Diplomate Am. Bd. Internal Medicine, Am. Bd. Critical Care Medicine, Am. Bd. Pulmonary Disease. Intern Bellevue Hosp. Ctr., N.Y.C., 1970—71, resident in medicine, 1971—72, U. Colo., 1972—73; fellow Maine Med. Ctr., Portland, 1975—76; fellow internal medicine U. Wash., Seattle, 1976—77; asst. chief dept. internal medicine, program dir. Maine Med. Ctr., Portland; CEO, exec. v.p. ACP, Phila., 2002—. Assoc. prof. medicine U. Vt.; adj. prof. U. Pa. Named one of 50 Most Powerful Physician Execs. in Healthcare, Modern Physician, 2005. Fellow: Coll. Physicians Phila., Am. Coll. Chest Physicians; mem.: AMA, Am. Thoracic Soc., Alpha Omega Alpha. Address: ACP 190 N Independence Mall W Philadelphia PA 19106-1572*

**TOOKEY, ROBERT CLARENCE,** actuary, consultant; b. Santa Monica, Calif., Mar. 21, 1925; s. Clarence Hall and Minerva Maconachie (Anderson) T.; m. Marcia Louise Hickman, Sept. 15, 1956; children: John Hall, Jennifer Louise, Thomas Anderson. BS, Calif. Inst. Tech., 1945; MS, U. Mich., 1947. With Prudential Ins. Co. Am., Newark, 1947-49; assoc. actuary in group Pacific Mut. Life Ins. Co., L.A., 1949-55; asst. v.p. in charge reins. sales and svc. for 17 western states Lincoln Nat. Life Ins. Co., Ft. Wayne, Ind., 1955-61; dir. actuarial svcs. Peat, Marwick, Mitchell & Co., Chgo., 1961-63; mng. prin. So. Calif. office Milliman & Robertson, cons. actuaries, Pasadena, 1963-76; pres. Robert Tookey Assocs., Inc., 1977—. Troop com. mem. Boy Scouts Am., 1969-72. Lt. (j.g.) USNR, 1943-45, 51-52. Fellow Soc. Actuaries, Conf. Consulting Actuaries; mem. Am. Acad. Actuaries, Pacific Ins. Conf., Rotary (Pasadena), Union League Club (Chgo.).

**TOOLE, JAMES FRANCIS,** medical educator; b. Atlanta, Mar. 22, 1925; s. Walter O'Brien and Helen (Whitehurst) T.; m. Patricia Anne Wooldridge, Oct. 25, 1952; children: William, Anne, James, Douglas Sean, Lauren, Robert, Dean, Tyler, Kyle, Kaitlin, Grace. BA, Princeton U., 1947; MD, Cornell U., 1949; LLB, LaSalle Extension U., 1963; Dr. Honoris Causa, U. Targu Mures, Romania, 1998. Intern, then resident internal medicine and neurology U. Pa. Hosp., London, 1949—55, Nat. Hosp., London, 1955—56; mem. faculty U. Pa. Sch. Medicine, 1959—61; prof. neurology, chmn. dept. Sch. Medicine Wake Forest Bapt. Hosp., 1962—83. Vis. prof. neurosis. U. Calif., San Diego, 1969—70; vis. scholar Oxford U., 1989; mem. Nat. Bd. Med. Examiners, 1970—76; mem. task force arteriosclerosis Nat. Heart Lung & Blood Inst., 1970—81; chmn. 6th and 7th Princeton confs. cerebrovascular diseases; cons. epidemiology WHO, Japan, 1972, 73, 93, USSR, 68, Switzerland, 74, Côte d'Ivoire, 77; mem. Lasker Awards com., 1976—77; chmn. neuropharmacologic drugs com. FDA, 1979; chair Commn. on Presdl. Disability, 1994—97; cons. NASA, 1966. Author: Cerebrovascular Diseases, 5th edit., 1999; editor: Current Concepts in Cerebrovascular Disease, 1969—73, Jour. Neurol. Sci., 1990—97; mem. editl. bd. Annals Internal Medicine, 1968—75, Stroke, 1972—74; mem. editl. bd. Jour. AMA, 1975—77; mem. editl. bd. Ann. Neurology, 1980—86, Jour. of Neurology, 1985—89. Pres. N.C. Heart Assn., 1976-77. Served with AUS, 1950-51; flight surgeon USNR, 1951-53. Decorated Bronze Star with V, Combat Med. badge. Master: ACP (licentiate); fellow: AAAS (life), Royal Coll. Physicians; mem.: AMA, Soc. for Neurosci., Hungarian Neurol. Soc., Polish Neurol. Soc., N.C. Stroke Assn. (pres. 1999—2001), Nat. Stroke Assn. (bd. dirs. 1993—), exec. com. 1994—, chmn. Commn. on U.S Presdl. Disability 1994—), Internat. Stroke Soc. (exec. com. 1989—97, program chmn. 1992, pres. 1999—2004), Russian Acad. Neurology (hon.), Austrian Soc. Neurology (hon.), Am. Clin. and Climatol Assn. (life), Assn. Brit. Neurologists (hon.), German Neurol. Soc. (hon.), Irish Neurol. Assn. (hon.), Am. Soc. Neuroimaging (pres. 1992—94), Am. Acad. Neurology, World Fedn. Neurology (sec.-treas. 1982—89, mgmt. com. 1990—98, pres. 1998—2001, chmn. Rsch. and Edn. Found. 1999—2004), Am. Neurol. Assn. (sec.-treas. 1978—82, pres. 1984—85, historian 1988—, archivist 2004), Am. Physiol. Soc., Am. Heart Assn. (chmn. com. ethics 1970—75). Home: 1836 Virginia Rd Winston Salem NC 27104-2316 E-mail: jtoole@wfubmc.edu.

**TOOLE, JAMES GRAY,** political science professor; b. North Hollywood, Calif., Oct. 5, 1964; s. George Gray and Elizabeth Joan Toole; m. Elizabeth Elena Levy, Sept. 20, 1997; children: Phoebe Bliss, Marissa Reed. BA, Haverford Coll., Pa., 1987; PhD, Brandeis U., Waltham Mass., 2000. Fulbright scholar Hungarian Acad. Scis., Budapest, 1996—97; vis. asst. prof. polit. sci. Holy Cross, Worcester, Mass., 2000—02; asst. prof. polit. sci. Ind. U.-Purdue U., Ft. Wayne, Ind., 2002—. Contbr. articles to profl. jours. Mem.: Internat. Studies Assn., Fulbright Assn. Avocations: birding, piano. Office: Ind U-Purdue U Fort Wayne 2101 East Coliseum Blvd Fort Wayne IN 46805 Office Phone: 260-481-6885. Office Fax: 260-481-6985. Business E-Mail: toolej@ipfw.edu.

**TOOLE, JOAN TRIMBLE,** financial consultant; b. Ipswich, Mass., Apr. 3, 1923; d. Dana Newcomb and Barbara (Campbell) T.; m. John R. Marchi, Dec. 28, 1943 (div. Aug. 1959); children: Jon, Jael, Charis, Peter; m. Kenneth Ross Toole, Apr. 22, 1960 (dec. Aug. 1981); children: Dana O'Keefe, David Campbell. BA, Antioch Coll., Yellow Springs, Ohio, 1946; MS in Fin., U. Mont., 1976; MPA, Harvard U., 1985. Rancher J/J and KJ Ranches, 1955-82; Mont. legis. asst., researcher, 1981-83; cons. Mont. Dept. Revenue, 1985-87, U. Mont. Biol. Sta., 1987-89; pvt. practice, 1987—. State coord. Cranston for Pres., 1983-84; lobbyist Office Pub. Interv., 1989-90; tax appeals bd. Ravalli County, 1981-84; active Mont. Bd. Natural Resources and Conservation, 1986-90, LWV, Mont. Environ. Info. Ctr., No. Plains Resource Coun.; bd. dirs. Mont. Conservation Voters, 1992—; mem. Lewis & Clark City/County Health Bd., 1994-98, treas. Montanans for Coal Trust, 1999—, Montanans for Common Sense Mining, 1998-; bd. dirs. Forever Wild Endowment Mem. AARP (vol. income tax preparer 1993—), Harvard Club (bd. dirs. ch. schs. and scholarships), Mont. Dem. Womens Club (regional dir.). Democrat. Episcopalian. Home and Office: 104 S Cooke St Helena MT 59601-5235

**TOOLE, JOHN HARPER,** lawyer; b. Johnson City, N.Y., Apr. 4, 1941; s. Edward Joseph and Anne (Junius) T.; m. Lamar Sparkman, May 30, 1969; children: John Carter, Lucy Bland. BS, U.Va., 1963; JD, Washington Coll. of Law, 1971. Bar: Va. 1971, D.C. 1972. From assoc. to ptnr. Lewis, Mitchell & Moore, Tysons Corner, Va., 1971-77; ptnr. Watt, Tieder, Killian, Toole & Hoffar, Tysons Corner, 1978-82; of counsel, ptnr. McGuire, Woods, Battle & Boothe, Tysons Corner, 1983-90, McLean, Va., 1990-99; ptnr. Cooley Godward LLP, Reston, Va., 2000—. 1st Lt. U.S. Army, 1963—66. Mem. ABA, Va. State Bar, Va. Bar Assn., D.C. Bar Assn. Office: Cooley Godward LLP 11951 Freedom Dr Reston VA 20190-5601 Fax: 703-456-8100. Office Phone: 703-456-8651. E-mail: jtoole@cooley.com.

---

**TOOLSON, KAY,** transportation executive; Exec. positions with two major motor co., 1973—86; pres. Monaco Coach, 1986—2000, chmn., 1993—, CEO. Office: Monaco Coach 91320 Coburg Industrial Way Eugene OR 97408 Office Phone: 541-686-8011. Office Fax: 541-681-8899.

**TOOMAJIAN, WILLIAM MARTIN,** lawyer; b. Troy, N.Y., Sept. 26, 1943; s. Leo R. Tooomajian and Elizabeth (Gundrum) Toomajian; children: Andrew, Philip. AB, Hamilton Coll., 1965; JD, U. Mich., 1968; LLM, NYU, 1975. Bar: N.Y. 1968, Ohio 1978. Mem. firm Cadwalader, Wickersham & Taft, N.Y.C., 1971—77, Baker & Hostetler, Cleve., 1977—. Lt. U.S. Coast Guard, 1968—71. Mem.: ABA, Cleve. Tax Club, Cleve. Bar Assn., Ohio Bar Assn. Home: 3582 Lytle Rd Cleveland OH 44122-4908 Office: Baker & Hostetler 3200 National City Ctr 1900 E 9th St Ste 3200 Cleveland OH 44114-3475 Business E-Mail: wtoomajian@bakerlaw.com.

**TOOMBS, KENNETH ELDRIDGE,** librarian; b. Colonial Heights, Va., Aug. 25, 1928; s. Garnett Eldridge and Susie W. (Bryant) T.; m. Ada Teresa Hornsby, Aug. 29, 1949; children— Susan Elizabeth Shealy, Cheri Lynn Morris, Teresa Ann Heilman. AA, Tenn. Wesleyan Coll., 1950; BS, Tenn. Poly. Inst., 1951; MA, U. Va., 1955; MLS, Rutgers U., 1956; student, La. State U., 1961-63. Reference asst. Alderman Library, U. Va., 1954-55; research asst. Grad. Sch. Library Sci., Rutgers U., 1955-56; mem. staff and faculty La. State U., 1956-63, asst. dir. charge pub. services, 1962-63; dir. libraries, prof. library sci. U. Southwestern La., 1963-67; dir. libraries U.S.C., Columbia, 1967—88; bd. dirs. Southeastern Library Network, 1967-88; disting. dir. of librs. emeritus U. S.C. Columbia, 1988—; vice chmn. Southeastern Library Network, 1973-74, 83-84, chmn., 1974-75, treas., 1984-85. Libr. cons. for bldgs. and adminstrn. for 60 colls. and univs. in past 30 yrs.; chmn. librarians sect. La. Coll. Conf., 1965-67; mem. Bd. La. Libr. Examiners, 1966-67; participant Libr. Mgmt. Inst., U. Wash., Seattle, 1969, Libr. Bldg. Problems Inst., UCLA, 1970; co-founder Southeastern Libr. Network with John Gribbin. Contbr. articles to profl. jours.; editor: Bull. La. Library Assn, 1959-62; mng. editor: SW La. Jour, 1963-67; adv. bd.: Linguistic Atlas Am. Treas. Wesley Found.; v.p. Am. Field Services Internat. Scholarships; bd. dirs. U. S.C. Ednl. Found., 1975-82; Danforth assoc., 1967—; AIA/ALA Bldg. Awards Jury, 1987. Served to 1st lt. AUS, 1946-47, 51-53. Mem. ALA (life), La. Library Assn. (parliamentarian 1962-63, 66-67), Southeastern Library Assn. (Life mem., exec. bd. 1981-85, Rothrock award 1978), Southwestern Library Assn., S.C. Library Assn. (Life mem., pres. 1976, exec. bd. 1981-85), Assn. Southeastern Research Libraries (chmn. 1973-75, adv. com. to OCLC 1979-84), AAUP (sec.), La. Hist. Assn., La. Tchrs. Assn., Soc. Tympanuchus Cupido Pinnatus, South Caroliniana Soc., Nat. Library Bldg. Consultants List (chmn. 1981-84), Tenn. Square (Ky. col.), Assn. of S.C. Retirees (bd. dirs. 1995—), Omicron Delta Epsilon. Clubs: Mason (Shriner), Kiwanis, Torch Club. Methodist. Home: 16 Garden Springs Rd Columbia SC 29209-1716

**TOOMER, AMANI,** professional football player; b. Berkeley, Calif., Sept. 8, 1974; Student, Univ. Mich., 1996. Wide receiver NY Giants, 1996—. Founder The Amani Toomer Found., NYC, 2001. Achievements include holding NY Giants franchise records for yards gained in a single season (1343 in 2002). Office: NY Football Giants Giants Stadium East Rutherford NJ 07073*

**TOOMEY, JEANNE ELIZABETH,** animal activist; b. N.Y.C., Aug. 22, 1921; d. Edward Aloysius and Anna Margaret (O'Grady) Toomey; m. Peter Terranova, Sept. 28, 1951 (dec. 1968); children: Peter Terranova (dec.), Sheila Terranova Beasley. Student, Hofstra U., 1938-40; student law scis., Fordham U., 1940-41; BA, Southampton Coll., 1976; postgrad., Monmouth Coll., 1978-79. Reporter, columnist Bklyn. Daily Eagle, 1943-52; with The Fitzgeralds, NBC Radio, N.Y.C., 1952-53; reporter, writer King Features Syndicate, N.Y.C., 1953-55; reporter, columnist N.Y. Jour.-Am., N.Y.C., 1955-61; newsman AP, N.Y.C., 1963-64; stringer; columnist News Tribune, Woodbridge, NJ, 1976-86; editor Calexico (Calif.) Chronicle, 1987-88; editor community sect. Asbury Park (N.J.) Press, 1988; pres., dir. Last Post Animal Sanctuary, Falls Village, Conn., 1989—. Author: Murder in the Hamptons, 1994, Assignment Homicide, 1998. Chmn. com. to establish Wildlife Preserve Hackensack Meadows, NJ, 1968—69. Named Woman of the Yr. N.Y. Women's Press Club, 1960. Mem. Newswomen's Club of N.Y., Overseas Press Club, N.Y. Press Club, Silurians. Roman Catholic. Address: PO Box 259 Falls Village CT 06031-0259 Office: 95 Belden St Falls Village CT 06031 Office Phone: 860-824-0831. Office Fax: 860-824-5460.

**TOOMEY, PATRICK JOSEPH,** former congressman; b. Providence, R.I., Nov. 17, 1961; m. Kris.; children: Bridget, Patrick. BA cum laude, Harvard U., 1984. Investment banking Chem. Bank N.Y.; v.p., dir. U.S. subsidiary British merchant bank; co-founder internat. fin. svcs. consulting firm; founder Toomey Enterprises, Inc., Allentown, Pa.; mem. U.S. Congress from 15th Pa. dist., 1999—2005. Serves on Banking and Fin. Svcs., Budget and Small Bus. coms. Elected to Allentown Govt. Study Commn., 1994. Elected in 1998 to U.S. Ho. Reps. seat vacated by retiring Rep. Paul McHale. Served an internship with Sen. John Chafee (R-R.I.). Republican. Achievements include Toomey Enterprises, Inc., a family restaurant bus., operates 2 Rookies Restaurants located in Allentown and Lancaster, Pa.

**TOOMEY, RICHARD ANDREW, JR.,** lawyer; b. Portsmouth, NH, Oct. 21, 1944; s. Richard Andrew and Elizabeth Neal (Rylander) T.; m. Jeanne Zurmuhlen; 1 child, Samuel Van Pelt. BA, U. N.H., 1966; JD, NYU, 1969. Bar: N.Y. 1969; Mass. 1989. Atty. VISTA, Mpls., 1969-71; assoc. Carter, Ledyard & Milburn, N.Y.C., 1971-77; v.p., sr. assoc. counsel Chase Manhattan Bank, N.Y.C., 1977-89; gen. coun. Shawmut Bank NA, Boston, 1989-94; dep. gen. coun. Shawmut Nat. Corp., Boston, 1995; group sl. counsel Fleet Fin. Group, Boston, 1996-2000; gen. counsel Fleet Bank NA, Jersey City, 1996—2000; asst. gen. counsel Sovereign Bank, Boston, 2000—05, gen. counsel, 2005—. Mem.: Boston Bar Assn. E-mail: rtoomey@sovereignbank.com.

**TOOMEY, SISTER STEPHANA,** small business owner; b. Wilmington, Del., Nov. 19, 1930; d. Hugh Jeremiah and Ellen (Vahey) Toomey. BS in Art Edn., Moore Coll. Art, 1952; MEd in Art, Temple U., Phila., 1960; cert., Internat. Ctr. Glass-Mosaics, Ravenna, Italy, 1975; postgrad., Paros Sch. Fine Arts, 1975. Lic. lic. liturgical cons. and designer; joined Dominican Order, Roman Cath. Ch., 1956. Tchr. art pub. schs., Camden, NJ, 1952—54, Oak Grove, Del., 1954—56; founder, pres. Efharisto Studio Inc., Balt., 1976—. Cons., mem. liturgical adv. com. Archdiocese of Balt., 1986—91. Contbr. articles and photogs. to various publs.; 5 nat. TV documentaries produced on her work; Represented in permanent collections Nat. Mus. Women in Arts. Mem. New Ventures. Named Top Winner for stained glass in chs., Bene Internat. Competition, San Jose, 2000—01; recipient hon. mention for stained glass in chs., 1991, 1993, 1998. Mem.: Assn. of Liturgical Cons. and Designers, Dominican Order's Internat. Inst. Arts (founder Dominican Inst. Arts 1997, Fra Angelico Lifetime Achievement award 1999), Balt. Writers Alliance, Form Reform, Faith and Form of AIA, Constrn. Specifications Inst., Art Architecture of AIA, Interfaith Forum Religion. Avocations: being with nature, classical music, assisting all religious traditions in design of worship space, liturgical appointments, stained glass. Office: 4 East Rolling Crossroads Ste 303 Catonsville MD 21228 Fax: 410-719-0995. Office Phone: 410-719-1043. E-mail: fharisto@charm.net.

**TOOMRE, ALAR,** applied mathematician, theoretical astronomer; b. Rakvere, Estonia, Feb. 5, 1937; came to US, 1949, naturalized, 1955; s. Elmar and Linda (Aghen) T.; m. Joyce Stetson, June 15, 1958; children: Lars, Erik, Anya. BS in Aero. Engring., BS in Physics, MIT, 1957; PhD in Fluid Mechanics, U. Manchester, Eng., 1960. C.L.E. Moore instr. math. dept. MIT, Cambridge, 1960-62, asst. prof. applied math., 1963-65, assoc. prof., 1965-70, prof., 1970—; fellow Inst. for Advanced Study, Princeton, NJ, 1962-63. Contbr. articles to profl. jours. Guggenheim fellow, 1969-70, MacArthur fellow, 1984-89; Fairchild scholar, 1975, Marshall scholar, 1957-60 Fellow AAAS; mem. Am. Astron. Soc. (Dirk Brouwer award 1993), Internat. Astron.

Union, Am. Acad. Arts and Scis., Nat. Acad. Scis. Office: MIT 77 Massachusetts Ave Rm 2-371 Cambridge MA 02139-4307 Office Phone: 617-253-4326. Business E-Mail: toomre@math.mit.edu.

**TOOMS, ROBERT EDWIN,** retired surgeon; b. Dyersburg, Tenn., Oct. 26, 1933; s. Luke Edwin and Rebecca Carolyn (Farrow) Tooms; m. Geraldine Thornton Ricks, Nov. 8, 1952; children: Robert Cole, Jeffrey Luke, Eva Kristina. Student, Memphis State Coll., Tenn., 1951-52; MD, U. Tenn. Coll. Medicine, Memphis, 1956. Asst. prof. Coll. Engring. U. Tenn., Knoxville, 1975-80, prof. dept. orthop. surgery Memphis, 1964—99, prof. emeritus, 1999—, med. dir. rehab. engring. program, 1974—99; chief staff Campbell Clinic, Memphis, 1987-94, active staff, 1964—99. Chief child amputee clinic Bapt. Hosp., Memphis, 1965—99, med. dir. spinal cord rehab., 1969—99; chief child amputee clinic St. Jude Hosp., Memphis, 1980—99; med. adviser Smith and Nephew Orthopaedics; cons. in field. Co-author: Amputation and Total Knee, Child Amputee, Child and Adult Limb Prostheses, Forearm Injuries; contbr. articles to profl. jours. Pres. Easter Seal Soc., 1968—80; bd. dirs. Memphis Orchestral Soc., 1985—, Trinity Home Health, Memphis Area Command Salvation Army, Bapt. Coll. Health Scis., Trezevant Manor Retirement Home, Campbell Found. Capt. USAF, 1957—59. Recipient Humanitarian award, Memphis Variety Club, 1984, Outstanding Alumnus award, U. Tenn. Coll. Medicine, 2005; grantee, Rehab. Engr. Ctr., Nat. Inst. Handicapped Rsch., 1976—85. Fellow: Rehab. Engring. Soc. N.Am.; mem.: Knee Soc., Am. Med. Assn., Mid-Am. Ortho. Assn., Am. Assn. Hip and Knee Surgeons, Twentieth Centur Orthop. Assn., Assn. Child Prostheses and Orthotic Clinics, Am. Orthop. Assn., Am. Acad. Orthop. Surgeons. Republican. Avocations: reading, music, sports. Personal E-mail: ret@midsouth.rr.com.

**TOON, MALCOLM,** former ambassador; b. Troy, N.Y., July 4, 1916; s. George and Margaret Harcomb (Broadfoot) T.; m. Elizabeth Jane Taylor, Aug. 28, 1943; children: Barbara, Alan, Nancy. AB, Tufts U., 1937, LL.D. (hon.), 1977; MA, Fletcher Sch. Law and Diplomacy, 1938; student, Middlebury Coll., 1950, Harvard U., 1950-51; LL.D. (hon.), Middlebury Coll., 1978, Drexel U., 1980, Am. Coll. Switzerland, 1985, Grove City Coll., 1990. Fgn. service officer, 1946-79; assigned successively Warsaw, Budapest, Moscow, Rome, Berlin, Washington, 1946-60; assigned Am. embassy, London, 1960-63, counselor political affairs Moscow, 1963-67; with Dept. State, Washington, 1967-69; ambassador to Czechoslovakia, 1969-71; to Yugoslavia, 1971-75; to Israel, 1975-76; to USSR, 1976-79. Mem. U.S. del. Nuclear Test Conf., Geneva, 1958-59, Four Power Working Group, Washington, London, Paris, 1959, Fgn. Ministers Conf., Geneva, 1969, Ten Nation Disarmament Com., Geneva, 1960; mem. SALT II del., 1977-79, U.S.-Soviet Summit Conf., Vienna, 1979; Brennen prof. U. N.C., Asheville, 1981; Finch prof. Miami U., Oxford, Ohio, 1982; Allis-Chalmers chair Marquette U., Milw., 1982 Trustee emeritus Tufts U.; bd. overseers Fletcher Sch. Law and Diplomacy, 1992; former chmn. U.S. Delegation to Joint U.S. Russian Commn. on POW's, MIA's. Served from ensign to lt. comdr. USNR, 1942-46. Decorated Bronze Star with combat V; recipient Freedom Leadership award Hillsdale Coll., 1980, Valley Forge Freedom award, 1981, Disting. Honor award Dept. State, 1980, Wallace award, 1984, Gold medal Nat. Inst. of Social Scis., 1987, Degree of Prof., Acad. Natural Scis. of the Russian Fedn., 1996, Silver medal, 1996. Home: 375 Pee Dee Rd Southern Pines NC 28387-2118

**TOOTHE, KAREN LEE,** elementary and secondary school educator; b. Seattle, Dec. 13, 1957; d. Russell Minor and Donna Jean (Drolet) McGraw; m. Edward Frank Toothe, Aug. 6, 1983; 1 child, Kendall Erin. BA in Psychology with high honors, U. Fla., 1977, MEd in Emotional Handicaps and Learning Disabilities, 1979. Cert. behavior analysis Fla. Dept. Profl. Regulation, behavior analyst Nat. Behavior Analyst Bd. Alternative edn. self-contained tchr. grades 2 and 3 Gainesville Acad., Micanopy, Fla., 1979; emotional handicaps self-contained tchr. Ctr. Sch. Alternative Sch., Gainesville, Fla., 1979-80; learning disabilities resource tchr. grades 2 and 3 Galaxy Elem. Sch., Boynton Beach, Fla., 1980-81, learning disabilities self-contained tchr. grades 1-3, 1981, varying exceptionalities self-contained tchr. grades 3-5, 1981-83, chpt. one remedial reading tchr. grades 3 and 4, 1982-83; sec. and visual display unit operator Manpower, London, 1983-84; sci./geography/social studies program Fairley House Sch., London, 1984-86, specific learning difficulties self-contained tchr. ages 8-12, dir. computing program, 1984-89; specific learning difficulties resource tchr. ages 8-16 Dyslexia Inst., Sutton Coldfield, Eng., 1990; behavior specialist, head Exceptional Student Edn. dept. Gateway High Sch., Kissimmee, Fla., 1990, behavior specialist, head ESE dept., 1991, resource compliance specialist, head ESE dept., 1991-93, tchr. summer youth trng. and enrichment program, 1993, Osceola High Sch., Kissimmee, 1992; resource compliance specialist, program specialist for mentally handicapped, physically impaired, occupational and phys. therapy programs St. Cloud (Fla.) Mid. Sch., 1993-96, local augmentative/assistive tech. specialist, 1995—; resource compliance specialist, program specialist physically impaired occupl./phys. therapy programs, local augmentative/assistive tech. specialist Hickory Tree Elem. Sch., 1996-97, program specialist assistive tech., occpl., and phys. therapy, physically impaired programs, 1997-99, program specialist assistive tech., 1999—. Sch. rep. CREATE, Alachua County, Fla., 1979-80, Palm Beach County South Area Tchr. Ctr. Coun., 1980-83, chmn., 1982-83; mem. writing team Title IV-C Ednl. Improvement Grant, Palm Beach County, Fla., 1981; mem. math. curriculum writing team Palm Beach County (Fla.) Schs., 1983; mem., co-dir. Fairley House Rsch. Com., 1984-90; co-founder, dir. Rsch. Database, London, 1984-89; co-chmn. computer and behavior/social aspects writing teams Dyslexia Inst. Math., Staines, Eng., 1990; lectr., course tutor Brit. Dyslexia Assn., Crewe, Eng., 1990; mem. Vocat.-Exceptional Com., 1991-93; mem. Osceola Reading Coun., 1991-98; mem. sch. adv. com. Gateway High Sch., 1991-93, St. Cloud Mid. Sch., 1993-96; mem. sch. adv. com. Hickory Tree Elem. Sch., 1999-2000, Ctr. for Ind. Living Assitance for Tech. Divsn.; presenter in field. Mem. bd. assistive tech. divsns. Ctr. for Ind. Living. Named Mid. Sch. Profl. of Yr. Osceola chpt. Coun. Exceptional Children, 1995, 96, Profl. Recognized Spl. Educator, 1997; winner Disney's Teacherific Spl. Judges award, 1997; recipient Outstanding Svcs. to Coun. for Exceptional Children award, 2002, 2003, Outstanding Related Svcs. Tchr. of Yr., 2003, Outstanding Support Svcs. award, 2003. Mem. CEC (named local chpt. Mid. Sch. Profl. of Yr. 1995, 96, exec. com. 1997-2002, C.A.N. rep. 1997-99, pres.-elect 1999-2000, pres. 2000-01, Outstanding Svcs. to CEC award 2002, 03, Outstanding Related Svcs. Tchr. of Yr. 2003, Outstanding Support Svcs. award 2003), Fla. Soc. for Augmentative and Alt. Comm., Phi Beta Kappa. Avocations: travel, reading, exercise, scuba diving, crafts. Home: 2175 James Dr Saint Cloud FL 34771-8830 Office: Osceola Dist Schs ESE Adminstrv Annex 805 Bill Beck Blvd Kissimmee FL 34744-4492 Office Phone: 407-518-8147. Business E-Mail: toothek@osceola.k12.fl.us.

**TOPEL, DAVID GLEN,** agricultural studies educator; b. Lake Mills, Wis., Oct. 24, 1937; BS, U. Wis., 1960; MS, Kans. State U., 1962; PhD, Mich. State U., 1965; DSc (hon.), Szent Istvan U., Godallo, Hungary, 2002. Assoc. prof. animal sci. and food tech. Iowa State U., Ames, 1967-73, prof. animal sci. and food tech., 1973-79, dean Coll. Agr., 1988-2000, dir. agr. and home econs. experiment sta., 1988-2000; prof., head dept. Auburn U., Ala., 1979—88, M.E. Ensminger endowed chair animal sci., 2000—. Cons., presenter, lectr. in field; mem. Gov. of Iowa's Sci. Adv. Coun., 1990-2000, Gov. of Iowa's Livestock Revitalization Task Force, 1993-98; chair Gov.'s Environ. Agr. Com., 1994; mem. Iowa Corn Promotion Bd.; mem. faculty Royal Vet. and Agrl. U., Denmark, 1971-72; vis. prof. Nat. Taiwan U., 1972. Author: The Pork Industry - Problems and Progress, 1968. Secretariat World Food Prize, Iowa State U., Ames, 1991-96. Fulbright-Hays scholar Royal Vet. and Agrl. U., 1971-72; recipient award of merit Knights of Ak-Sar-Ben, 1973, Commr.'s award Agrl. Commr. Republic of China, 1977, disting. Achievement award Block and Bridle Club, 1979, Ala. Cattlemen's Assn.,1 984, Hon. State Farmer Degree, Ala., 1986, Harry L. Rudnick Educator's award Nat. Assn. Meat Purveyors, 1989, USDA Honor award, 1999, Hon. Prof. award Gyöngyös Coll., Hungary, 2000; named hon. prof. Ukrainian State Agrl. U., 1993. Fellow Am. Soc. Animal Sci. (Disting. Rsch. award in meat sci. 1979, Bouffault Internat. Agr. award 2002); mem. Am. Meat Sci. Assn., Inst. Food

Tech., Iowa Crop Improvement Assn., Extension and Tchg. (pres. North Ctrl. Region 1992), Nat. Assn. State Univs. and Land-Grant Colls. (chair bd. agr. 1993, mem. commn. on food, environ. and renewable resources 1992-99), Ukrainian Acad. Agrl. Scis., Sigma Xi (Outstanding Achievement award Iowa chpt. 1993), Alpha Zeta, Gamma Sigma Delta (Internat. award). Presbyterian. Avocations: fishing, golf. Office: Iowa State U Coll Agriculture 2374 Kildee Hall Ames IA 50011-0001 Home: 4108 Laura Ct Ames IA 50010 Office Phone: 515-294-6304.

**TOPELIUS, KATHLEEN ELLIS,** lawyer; b. July 15, 1948; BA, U. Conn., 1970; postgrad., U. Md., 1971-74; JD, Cath. U. Am., 1978. Bar: D.C. 1978, U.S. Supreme Ct. 1988. Atty. office of gen. counsel Fed. Home Loan Bank Bd., 1978-80; ptnr. Morgan, Lewis & Bockius, Washington, 1985-93, Bryan Cave, Washington, 1993—. Recipient Alpha award Fed. Home Loan Bank Bds., 1979. Office: Bryan Cave 700 13th St NW Fl 7 Washington DC 20005-5921 Office Phone: 202-508-6140. Business E-Mail: ketopelius@bryancave.com.

**TOPINKA, JUDY BAAR,** state official, political organization worker; b. Riverside, Ill., Jan. 16, 1944; d. William Daniel and Lillian Mary (Shuss) Baar; 1 child, Joseph Baar. BS, Northwestern U., 1966. Features editor, reporter, columnist Life Newspapers, Berwyn and LaGrange, Ill., 1966-77; with Forest Park (Ill.) Rev. and Westchester News, 1976-77; coord. spl. events dept. fedn. comm. AMA, 1978-80; rsch. analyst Senator Leonard Becker, 1978-79; mem. Ill. Ho. of Reps., 1981-84, Ill. Senate, 1985-94; treas. State of Ill., Springfield, 1995—; chmn. State Rep. Party, 2002—. Former mem. judiciary com., former chmn. senate health and welfare com.; former mem. fin. instn. com.; former co-chmn. Citizens Coun. on Econ. Devel.; former co-chmn. U.S. Commn. for Preservation of Am.'s Heritage Abroad, serves on legis. ref. bur.; former mem. minority bus. resource ctr. adv. com. U.S. Dept. Transp.; former mem. adv. bd. Nat. Inst. Justice. Founder, pres., bd. dirs. West Suburban Exec. Breakfast Club, from 1976; chmn. Ill. Ethnics for Reagan-Bush, 1984, Bush-Quayle 1988; spokesman Nat. Coun. State Legislatures Health Com.; former mem. nat. adv. coun. health professions edn. HHS; mem., GOP chairwoman Legis. Audit Commn. of Cook County; chmn. Riverside Twp. Regular Republican Orgn., 1994—. Recipient Outstanding Civilian Svc. medal, Molly Pitcher award, Abraham Lincoln award, Silver Eagle award U.S. Army and N.G. Office: Office of Ill State Treasurer 100 W Randolph St Ste 15-600 Chicago IL 60601-3232

**TOPLIN, ROBERT BRENT,** history professor, television producer; b. Phila., Sept. 26, 1940; s. Maurice Cunningham and Janet Rachel (Belsinger) T.; m. Karin Bendel, Dec. 26, 1996; children: Cassandra, Jennifer. BS, Pa. State U., 1962; MA, Rutgers U., 1965, PhD, 1968. Asst. prof. Denison U., Granville, Ohio, 1968-74, assoc. prof., 1976-78; assoc. prof. and program dir. U. Houston-Clear Lake City, 1974-76; assoc. prof. U. N.C. at Wilmington, 1978-80, prof. history, 1980. Vis. prof. U. N.C.-Chapel Hill, 1983; media advisor NEH; lectr. in field. Project dir: A House Divided (TV series) U.S.A.; A Television history, Pres.'s in Crisis, The Am. Frontier; author: The Abolition of Slavery in Brazil, 1972, Unchallenged Violence: An American Ordeal, 1975, Freedom and Prejudice: The Legacy of Slavery in the United States and Brazil, 1982, History By Hollywood: The use and Abuse of the American Past, 1996; author: Reel History: In Defense of Hollywood, 2002, Michael Moore's Fahrenheit 9/11: How One Film Divided a Nation, 2006; editor: Slavery and Race Relations in Latin America, 1974; editor anthology: American History Through Film, 1983, Ken Burns's The Civil War: Historians Respond, 1996, Oliver Stone's USA: Film, History and Controversy, 2000; contbg. editor: Jour. Am. History, 1986—; contbr. articles to hist. jours.; book reviewer various jours.; project dir. Denmark Vesey's Rebellion (PBS TV), 1982, Solomon Northup's Odyssey (PBS TV), 1984; Charlotte Forten's Mission (PBS TV), 1985; (films) The War to End All Wars, 1985, Lincoln and the War Within, 1992; nationwide broadcast appearances on PBS TV, CBS TV, The History Channel, Turner Classic Movie Channel, C-SPAN. Pres. Williston Jr. H.S. PTA; v.p. New Hanover County PTA, New Hanover County Bd. Edn. Grantee or fellow Ford Found., 1967, NEH, 1970, 77-80, 82-89, 90-91, Am. Philos. Soc., 1970m 81, Denison U. Rsch. Found., 1972, Annenberg/Corp. for Pub. Broadcasting, 1983-84; grantee Ill. Humanities Coun., 1991; fellow Am. Coun. Learned Soc., 1991. Mem. Am. Hist. Assn. (tchg. com. 1990-93), Orgn. Am. Historians (mem. com. on radio, TV, film media 1978-80, Erik Barnouw prize 1985, 87-89), Conf. on Latin Am. History (com. on tchg. materials 1978), Erik Barnouw prize com. 1987-88. Democrat. Jewish. Office: U NC at Wilmington Dept History Wilmington NC 28403 Office Phone: 910-962-3307. Business E-Mail: Toplinrb@uncw.edu.

**TOPLITT, GLORIA H.,** music educator, actress, vocalist; b. St. Louis, May 22, 1925; d. Wade Fitzgerald Hathhome and Neyneen Farrell Pires; m. James Parnell, 1942 (div. July 1949); 1 child, Dennis James Parnell; m. Abraham Toplitt, Aug. 19, 1968. Student, Guy Bates Post Acad. Dramatic Arts, L.A., 1941-43. Stage performer, N.Y.C., 1944-59; dir. entertainment Holland Am. Lines, 1959-61; tchr. voice North Hollywood (Calif.) Conservatory, 1965-67; pvt. voice tchr. North Hollywood, 1968-95; music specialist outreach program NASA Space Sci. and Tech., Inc., Springfield, Va., 1997—. Dir. Workshop Theatre Program, North Hollywood, 1968—78; coach for impaired voices, North Hollywood, 1968—. Author, composer: Parade of Planets, 1998, Space Challenge, 1999; actor: (plays, N.Y. stage prodns.) appeared as leading lady Oklahoma, Chocolate Soldier, Lend an Ear, Courtin' Time, Showboat, Take Me Along, Auld Lang Syne, Three Musketeers, Carousel, Oh! Captain, Brigadoon, Guys and Dolls, Hit the Deck, Finian's Rainbow, others; voice rec. Songs of Harriet Ware Meml., Smithsonian Instn. Mem. election bd. Office of Voter Registrar, North Hollywood, 1996—98. Avocations: poetry, travel, theater, elderhostel classes, reading. Home: 4405 Carpenter Ave North Hollywood CA 91607-4110

**TOPOL, ERIC JEFFREY,** academic administrator, cardiologist, educator; b. N.Y.C., June 26, 1954; s. Erwin and Susan (Lepp) T.; m. Susan Leah Merriman, May 5, 1979; children: Sarah, Evan. BA with highest distinction, U. Va., 1975; MD with honors, U. Rochester, 1979. Med. resident U. Calif., San Francisco, 1979-82; fellow Johns Hopkins U. Med. Ctr., Balt., 1982-85; asst. prof. U. Mich. Sch. Medicine, Ann Arbor, 1985-87, assoc. prof., 1987-90, prof., 1990; dir. cardiac catheterization labs. and interventional cardiology U. Mich. Med. Ctr., Ann Arbor, 1986-91; chmn. dept. cardiovasc. medicine Cleve. Clinic Found., dir. Ctr. for Thrombosis and Arterial Biology, 1991—; founder, provost, chief acad. officer Cleve. Clinic Lerner Coll. Medicine, Case Western Reserve Univ., 2002—05, prof. medicine, 2004—06; prof. genetics Case Western Reserve Univ. Sch. Medicine, 2006—. Editor: Acute Coronary Intervention, 1988, Textbook of Interventional Cardiology, 1990, 4th edit., 2002, Textbook of Cardiovascular Medicine, 1st and 2d edits.; mem. editl. bd. Circulation, Circulation Rsch., Am. Jour. Cardiology, Coronary Art Disease, Jour. Am. Coll. Cardiology, Brit. Heart Jour.; mem. editl. bd. of several med. publs.; contbr. articles to profl. jours. Recipient Clin. Rsch. Innovator award, Doris Duke Charitable Found., 2003, Andres Gruentzig award, European Soc. Cardiology, 2004. Fellow ACP, Am. Coll. Cardiology (editor jour., Simon Dack award, 2005), Am. Soc. Clin. Investigation, Am. Heart Assn. (mem. coun. on clin. cardiology, coun. on circulation and thrombosis), European Soc. Cardiology; mem. Cen. Soc. Clin. Rsch., Am. Fedn. for Clin. Rsch. (councilor), Assn. Am. Physicians, AMA (Dr. William Beaumont award in Medicine 2002), IOM, NAS, John Hopkins Soc. Scholars. being one of the first scientists to raise doubts about the safety of Vioxx, and was a key witness in lawsuits against Merck & Co. Office: Case Western Reserve Univ Sch Medicine 10900 Euclid Ave Cleveland OH 44106 Office Phone: 216-445-9490.*

**TOPPELBERG, CLAUDIO O.,** psychiatrist, researcher; MD with honor, U. Buenos Aires, 1982. Diplomate Am. Bd. Psychiatry and Neurology. Rschr. Judge Baker Children's Ctr., Harvard Med. Sch., Boston, 1999—. Chmn. Nat. Psychiat. Residents Conf., Buenos Aires, 1987, 88. Contbr. articles to profl. jours. Recipient Livingston award, Harvard Med. Sch. Dept. Psychiatry, 1996, Travel award, Am. Coll. Neuropsychopharmacology, 1996—97, Eli Lilly Pilot Rsch. award, Am. Acad. Child and Adolescent Psychiatry, 1996, Early Investigator Group award, 2003—04, Children's Studies Harvard Rsch.

award, Harvard Project Schooling and Children, 1998—99, Scientist Devel. award (K01), NIH, 2002—, Nat. Rsch. Svc. award, NIMH, 1996. Fellow: NIMH, Am. Psychiat. Assn. (mentor 2004, Minority Med. Student fellow Harvard med. student 2004). Office: Judge Baker Children's Ctr Harvard Med 53 Parker Hill Ave Boston MA 02120

**TOPPETA, WILLIAM JOHN,** insurance company executive, lawyer; b. NYC, Sept. 18, 1948; s. John Francis and Rita Ann (Carretta) Toppeta. BA, Fordham U., 1970; JD, NYU, 1973, ML, 1977. Bar: NY 1974, US Supreme Ct. 1977. Atty. Met. Life, N.Y.C., 1973-79, asst. v.p., 1979-81, asst. gen. counsel, 1981-82, assoc. gen. counsel, 1982-83, v.p., assoc. gen. counsel, 1983-92; pres., CEO MetLife Can. Ops., 1993-95; sr. v.p. corp. re-engring., 1995-97, exec. v.p., 1995-97; sr. exec. v.p. Met. Life, 1997-99, pres., chief admin. officer, 1999—, pres. internat., 2001—. Adj. prof. Pace U. Law Sch., White Plains, NY, 1984—; mem. Bklyn. Law Sch., 1985—. Mem. ABA (vice-chairperson com. on trial techniques 1986—), NY State Bar Assn., Assn. Bar of City of NY. Democrat. Roman Catholic. Office: MetLife Inc 200 Park Ave New York NY 10166 E-mail: btoppeta@metlife.com.

**TOPPING, AUDREY RONNING,** photojournalist; b. Camrose, Alta., Can., May 21, 1928; arrived in U.S., 1967; d. Chester Alvin and Inga Marie (Horte) Ronning; m. Seymour Topping, Nov. 10, 1949; children: Susan, Karen, Lesley, Robin, Joanna. Student, Augustana Univ., Camrose, 1943-46, Nanking (China) U., 1947-48, Berlin Art Sch., 1956-58, U. B.C., 1949-50; D of Arts (hon.), Rider Coll., N.J., 1983. Freelance journalist N.Y. Times Mag., N.Y.C., 1966—2001; writer, photographer Nat. Geographic, Washington, 1971-79; columnist Earth Times, N.Y.C., 1996—; spl. corr. Houston Chronicle, 1997—2001; photjournalist-at-large Earthuman Mag., 2002—. Advisor U.S.-China Arts Exch., 1997—; commentator, writer Great Wall Across The Yangtze (PBS), Homecoming (Chinese TV), 2002; TV scriptwriter China Mission, 1975. Author: Dawn Wakes In the East, 1972, The Splendors of Tibet, 1981, Charlie's World, 2000; A Day in the Life of Can., 1986, two children's books, N.Y. Times, Nat. Geographic, Readers Digest, Time, Life, Geo, Sci. Digest, Earth Times, others, exhibitions include Royal Ont. Mus., Toronto, 1980, Hallmark Gallery, NYC, 1973, Overseas Press Cub, 1975, Westchester C.C., 1989, 2004, Libby Gallery, Purchase, NY, 2004, Bhutan UN Embassy, NY, 2004, Hammond Mus., North Salem, 2005, CUNY Grad. Ctr. Gallery, 2006. Recipient Alumni award Augustana Univ. Coll., 1989, Medallion award Westchester C.C., 1989, Greenway Winship award Internat. Ctr. Journalists, 2000. Mem.: Coun. of Fgn. Relations, Soc. Woman Geographers, Asia Soc., Fgn. Policy Assn., Fox Meadow Tennis Club, Jr. Fortnightly. Avocations: sculpture, painting, tennis, skiing, exploring. Home and Office: 5 Heathcote Rd Scarsdale NY 10583-4413 E-mail: topaud@aol.com.

**TOPPING, JENNIFER,** Olympic athlete; b. May 30, 1980; Student, U. Wash., 1999; grad., Calif. State. Fullerton, 2003. Mem. U.S. Nat. Team, 2002—, U.S. Women's Softball Team, Athens Olympic Games, 2004. Named Big West Conference Player of the Yr., 2001, 2002, 2003, NFCA First Team All-Am., 2000, 2001, 2002, 2003. Achievements include mem. Gold medal U.S. Nat. Team, Pan Am. Games, 1999, 2003.

**TOPPING, SEYMOUR,** writer; b. N.Y.C., Dec. 11, 1921; s. Joseph and Anna (Seidman) Topolsky; m. Audrey Elaine Ronning, Nov. 10, 1949; children: Susan, Karen, Lesley, Rebecca, Joanna. BJ, U. Mo., 1943; LittD (hon.), Rider Coll., 1983. With I.N.S. (China civil war), Nanking 1946-47; with AP, Nanking, 1948—49, corr. Saigon, 1950—51, London, 1952—56, Berlin, 1956—59; mem. staff N.Y. Times, 1959-93, chief corr. Moscow, Saigon, London, Berlin, 1960-63, chief corr. S.E. Asia, 1963-66, fgn. editor, 1966-69, asst. mng. editor, 1969-76, dep. mng. editor, 1976-77, mng. editor, 1977-86; dir. editl. devel. N.Y. Times Regional Newspapers, 1987-93; chmn. New Directions for News, 1990-91; pres. Am. Soc. Newspaper Editors, 1992—93; prof. Grad. Sch. Journalism Columbia U., N.Y.C., 1993—2002, adminstr. Pulitzer Prizes, 1993—2002, Sanpaolo prof. emeritus of internat. journalism, 2002—, pres. emeritus profs., 2004—. Adviser Internat. Ctr. for Journalists, Found. Am. Comm.; juror Pulitzer Prize com.; lectr. in field. Author: Journey Between Two Chinas, 1972, The Peking Letter, A Novel of the Chinese Civil War, 1999, Fatal Crossroads, A Novel of Vietnam 1945, 2005. Spl. advisor to Sec.-Gen. UN to Earth Summit, Rio de Janeiro, 1992; mem. Nat. Com. U.S.-China Rels.; Served with inf. AUS, 1943-46, PTO. Recipient Greenway-Winship award for contbns. to internat. journalism, 2000, Disting. Svc. award, Mo. Sch. of Journalism, 1968, Disting Alumni award, 1993. Mem. Coun. Fgn. Rels., Asia Soc., Am. Soc. Newspaper Editors, Am. Bd. of Dirs. Internat. Press Inst., Century Assn. Home: 5 Heathcote Rd Scarsdale NY 10583-4413 Personal E-mail: st122@columbia.edu.

**TOPSAKAL, ERDEM,** science educator; b. Istanbul, Turkey, June 27, 1971; arrived in U.S., 1997; s. Mehmet and Imral Topsakal. PhD, Istanbul Tech. U., 1996. Rsch. scientist U. Mich., Ann Arbor, 2001—03; asst. prof. Miss. State U., Mississippi State, 2003—. Recipient Young Scientist award, URSI, 1996, Outstanding Educator award, Miss. State U. Dept. Elec. and Computer Engring., 2005; fellow, NATO, 1997. Mem.: IEEE (sr.), IEEE Antennas and Propagation. Achievements include research in Nanoscale Frequency Selective Surface Design for Near Infrared and Optics; UWB and Multiband Antennas; Design and Analysis; Fast Computational Electromagnetic Tools; Implantable Antennas for Wireless Data Telemetry. Office: Miss State Univ 405 Simrall Hall Hardy St Mississippi State MS 39762 Office Phone: 662-325-3669. Office Fax: 662-325-2298. E-mail: topsakal@ece.msstate.edu.

**TORANZO, NILSA CARIDAD,** special education services professional; b. Bklyn., Sept. 8, 1958; d. Claide and Aurea Esther Toranzo; m. Kenneth Antoine Cherry, Oct. 10, 1999. BSc, Fordham U., 1980; MA, NY U, 1983. Edn. evaluator St. Francis de Sales Sch. for the Deaf, Bklyn., 1983—. Contbr. articles. Mem.: Internat. Reading Assn. Avocations: exercise, reading, travel. Office: St Francis de Sales Sch for the Deaf 260 Eastern Pkwy Brooklyn NY 11225 Office Phone: 718-636-4573. Business E-Mail: ntoranzo@sfdesales.org.

**TORBICA, ZELJKO MARKO,** construction executive, educator; arrived in U.S.A., 92; s. Marko and Nadezda Torbica; m. Maria Jovanov, Oct. 30, 1999; children: Talia, Nada, Dara, Djordje. PhD, U. Fla., 1997—97; diploma, U. of Belgrad, 1986. Cert. quality engr., Am. Soc. Quality; project mgmt. profl. Project Mgmt. Inst. Engr. Energoprojekt, Belgrade, Serbia and Montenegro, 1986—92; asst. prof. Minn. State U., Mankato, 1996—2001; constrn. mgmt. educator Fla. Internat. U., Miami, 2001—04; assoc. prof. Roger Williams U., Bristol, RI, 2004—06; sr. project mgr CAB Developers, Miami, 2006—.

**TORBUSH, DEBORAH NICKELS,** psychology educator; d. John Harvey and Geraldyne (Cornell) Nickels; m. Douglas Bruce Torbush, June 18, 1977; children: C. Ryan, Katherine M. BA, Emory U., 1974; MEd, Ga. State U., 1977, EdS, 1981. Cert. sch. psychologist Ga. Sch. psychologist Griffin (Ga.) CESA, 1977—78, DeKalb County Sch. Sys., Decatur, Ga., 1978—. Pres. Jr. League DeKalb County, Decatur, 1996—97; pres.-elect Alliance of Ga. Dental Assn., 2005—06; trustee DeKalb County Pub. Libr. Bd., Decatur, 2004—; bd. dirs., former chmn. Internat. Women's House, Decatur, 1995—; mem. bd. visitors Grady Hosp., Atlanta, 2000—; mem. spouses' com. Hinman Dental Soc., Ga., 2002—; grad. Leadership DeKalb, 1995—96. Mem.: Nat. Assn. Sch. Psychologists, Ga. Assn. Sch. Psychologists (chmn. profl. stds. 2000—02, publicity chmn. 2002—), Emory U. Alumni Assn. (mem. reunion com.), Smoke Rise Golf and Country Club, Kappa Alpha Theta. Avocations: volunteer work, tennis, travel. Home: 5360 Kanawha Ct Stone Mountain GA 30087 Office: DeKalb Sch Sys EDC Support Svcs 5839 Memorial Dr Stone Mountain GA 30083

**TORBUSH, RODNEY KRISTIAN,** music educator; b. Atlanta, Ga., Mar. 18, 1977; s. Rodney Bruce and Donna Elrod Torbush; m. Rebecca Garcia, July 12, 2002. MusB in Music Edn., Ga. So. U., Statesboro, 2000. Profl. lic. and cert. K-12 music Ohio. Dir. elem. and h.s. orch. Forest Hills Local Sch.

Dist., Cin., 2000—. Recipient Nat. Orch. Festival award, 2006. Mem.: Ohio Music Edn. Assn. (chair S.W. region 2005—06), Am. String Tchr. Assn., Clermont Philharm. Orch. (condr., assoc. concertmaster 2002—05), Cin. Cmty. Orch. (assoc. concertmaster, prin. second violin 2000—06). Office: Anderson H S 7560 Forest Rd Cincinnati OH 45255 Office Phone: 513-232-2772.

**TORCHETTI, JOHN,** former professional hockey coach; Asst. Greensboro Monarchs, 1992—93; head coach, dir. hockey ops. San Antonio Iguanas, 1994—95, asst. gen. mgr., asst. coach, 1996; coach Komets, 1996—98; gen. mgr. Detroit Vipers, 1998—2002; head coach devel. affiliate Fla. Panthers, San Antonio, 2002—03, asst. coach Sunrise, Fla., 2003—04, interim head coach, 2004, LA Kings, 2006. Asst. scouting dir. Tampa Bay Lightning, 2001—02. Named Coach of Yr., CHL, 1995. Office: LA Kings 1111 S Figueroa St, Suite 3100 Los Angeles CA 90015*

**TORELLI, ANTHONY-ALEXANDER,** music educator, conductor, musician; b. Providence, Sept. 15, 1962; s. Alexander Augustino and Marie Barbara Torelli; m. Adriana Maritza Ramos, June 9, 2001. BS, RI Coll., 1986; M, The Hartt Sch. U. Hartford, 1998; D, U. Montreal, 2003; diploma in ARt, The Hartt Sch. U. of Hartford, 2000. Tchg. Cert. RI Dept. of Edn., 2000. Condr. Bel Canto Opera Co., Cranston, RI, 1988—98; assoc. condr. South County Chamber Singers and Orch., Kingston, RI, 1998—; condr. RI Philharm. Youth Orchs., Providence, 2000—05; music dir. and condr. Norton Singers, Mass., 2003—; music dir., condr. German Am. Cultural Soc. Chorus, Pawtucket, RI; music educator North Providence Sch. Dept., North Providence, RI, 2000—. Cons. Pastime Theater Found., Bristol, RI, 2003—. Opera scholar, Bel Canto Opera Scholarship Found., 1993. Mem.: Am. Fedn. of Tchrs. (assoc.), Am. Fedn. of Musicians (assoc.), Conductors Guild (assoc.), Am. Symphony Orch. League (assoc.). Home: 19 Sheridan St Johnston RI 02919 Personal E-mail: anthonyatorelli@yahoo.com.

**TOREN, MARK,** state official, statistician; b. Warsaw, Dec. 7, 1950; s. Jacob Toren and Assia (Hanukayeva) Merson; m. Angela Aleksandrovna, July 12, 1997; children: Alexander Michael, Anna A. Cert., U. Cologne, Fed. Republic Germany, 1974; AA, AAS, SUNY, Suffern, 1972; BA, SUNY, New Paltz, 1975; MA, SUNY, Albany, 1976; MS, Rensselaer Poly. Inst., 1983, PhD, 1992. Sr. statistician Triad Data Scis., Albany, NY, 1980—84; sr. economist NY State Dept. Taxation and Fin., Albany, 1984—85; econometrician NY State Dept. Social Svcs., Albany, 1985—92, NY State Dept. of Health, Albany, 1992—. Faculty bus. mgmt. and econs. SUNY, Empire State Coll., Saratoga Springs, 1994—98; cons. Calay Sys. Inc., Newport Beach, Calif., 1998—2000; rschr. NY State Dept. of Health, Albany, 1999—; part-time faculty Sch. Bus. & Econs. Siena Coll., Loudonville, NY, 2006—. Author: Cost Efficiency in Nursing Homes: A Stochastic Frontier Approach, 1994, Hospital Cost and Efficiency in a Regime of Stringent Regulation, 1996, Economics Macro/Micro, 1996, Economics of Government Regulation and the Market, 1996. With U.S. Army, 1969—71. Mem.: Micro-Computer Users Group, Health Econs. Rsch. Orgn., Am. Statis. Assn., Am. Econ. Assn., Internat. Platform Assn., Omicron Delta Epsilon. Avocations: literature, art, music, photography. Office: NYS Dept of Health 1970 Corning Tower Albany NY 12237-0001 Office Phone: 518-474-5550. E-Mail: mxt10@health.state.ny.us.

**TORG, JOSEPH STEVEN,** orthopaedic surgeon, educator; b. Phila., Oct. 25, 1934; m. Barbara Jane Groenendaal, May 23, 1959; children: Joseph Steven, Elisabeth, Jay Michael. AB, Haverford Coll., 1957; MD, Temple U., 1961. Diplomate: Am. Bd. Orthopaedic Surgeons. Intern San Francisco Gen. Hosp., 1961-62; resident in orthopaedic surgery Temple U. Hosp., Phila., 1964-68, Shriners Hosp. for Crippled Children, Phila., 1966-67; asst. surgeon Episcopal Hosp., Phila., 1968-70; surgeon Shriners Hosp. Crippled Children, 1970-78; mem. staff Temple U. Hosp., 1970-78, instr. orthopaedic surgery, 1968-70, asst. prof., 1970-75, assoc. prof., 1976-78; dir. Center for Sports Medicine and Sci., 1974-78; chief orthopaedic sect. St. Christopher's Hosp. for Children, Phila., 1971-74, mem. staff, 1974—; active staff St. Joseph's Hosp., Phila., 1977—; prof. U. Pa., 1978—, active staff hosp., 1978—; dir. Sports Medicine Center, 1978—; prof. orthopaedic surgery Temple U., 1995. Mem. active staff Children's Hosp., Phila., 1978; med. cons. Pres.'s Council on Phys. Fitness and Sports Mem. editorial bd. Sports Medicine, Yearbook of Sports Medicine, Contemporary Orthopaedics, Jour. Clin. Sport Medicine, Am. Jour. Knee Surgery, Orthopaedic Rev.; contbr. articles to profl. jours. Served with M.C. U.S. Army, 1962-64. Recipient Layman Honor award Pa. State Assn. Health, Phys. Edn. and Recreation, 1970, Grad. Honor award, 1975; Commendation of Merit Phila. Public High Sch. Football Coaches, 1974 Fellow Am. Acad. Orthopaedic Surgeons, Am. Coll. Sports Medicine (trustee 1975-78), Phila. Coll. Physicians; mem. AMA, Eastern Orthopaedic Soc., Am. Orthopaedic Soc., Sports Medicine, Phila. County Med. Soc., Phila. Orthopaedic Soc., Pa. State Med. Soc., Pa. State Orthopaedic Soc. Home: 401 Conestoga Rd Wayne PA 19087-4811 Office: Temple U Hospital 6th Floor 3401 N Broad St Philadelphia PA 19140 Office Phone: 215-707-1321. Personal E-mail: torgmd@aol.com. Business E-Mail: torgjs@tuhs.temple.edu.

**TORGERSEN, PAUL ERNEST,** academic administrator, educator; b. NYC, Oct. 13, 1931; s. Einar and Frances (Hansen) T.; m. Dorothea Hildegarde Zuschlag, Sept. 11, 1954; children: Karen Elizabeth, Janis Elaine, James Einar. BS, Lehigh U., 1953, DEng, 1994; MS, Ohio State U., 1956, PhD, 1959. Grad. tchg. asst. Ohio State U. Columbus, 1957, instr., 1957-59; asst. to assoc. prof. Okla. State U., Stillwater, 1959-66; prof., dept. head, dean Coll. Engring. Va. Tech, Blacksburg, 1967-93, pres., 1993-2000, John W. Hancock chair of engring. Dir. Roanoke (Va.) Electric Steel, 1986-2001, Luna Innovations, 2000—, EDB. Author 5 books. Mem. Gov. Mark Warner's Commn on Bd of Visitor Appts., Richmond, Va., 2002 ; fm Utah Energy Bd., Richmond, 1986-90. Lt. U.S.A.F. 1953-55. Fellow Am. Soc. Engring. Edn. (Lamme medal 1994), Inst. Indsl. Engring (Frank and Lillian Gibreth award 2001); mem. Nat. Acad. Engring. (coun. 1999—). Avocation: tennis. Office: Va Tech 201 Durham Hall Blacksburg VA 24061-0118 Business E-Mail: tennis@vt.edu.

**TORGERSEN, TORWALD HAROLD,** architect, consultant; b. Chgo., Sept. 2, 1929; s. Peder and Hansine Malene (Hansen) T.; m. Dorothy Darlene Peterson, June 22, 1963. BS in Archtl. Engring. with honors, U. Ill., 1951. Lic. architect Ill., D.C.; real estate broker, Ill., interior designer, Ill.; registered architect Nat. Coun. Archtl. Registration Bds. Ptnr. Coyle & Torgersen Architects-Engrs., Washington, Chgo. and Joliet, Ill., 1955—56; coord. project Skidmore, Owings & Merrill, Chgo., 1956—60; corp. architect, dir. architecture, constrn. and interiors Container Corp. Am., Chgo., 1960—86; prin. in charge of orgn. and adminstrn. Jack Train Assocs. Inc., Chgo., 1987—88; cons. Torwald H. Torgersen, AIA, FASID, Chgo., 1988—. Guest lectr. U. Wis. Capt. USNR, 1951-82. Recipient Top Ten Design award Factory mag., 1964 Fellow Am. Soc. Interior Designers; mem. AIA, Naval Res. Assn., Ill. Naval Militia, Am. Arbitration Assn., Am. Soc. Mil. Engrs., Paper Industry Mgmt. Assn. (hon.). Sports Car Club Assn., Nat. Eagle Scout Assn. Clubs: 20 Fathoms. Home and Office: 3750 N Lake Shore Dr Chicago IL 60613-4238

**TORGERSON, KATHERINE P.,** media consultant, corporate communications specialist; Now v.p. human resources and exec. adminstrn. Penton Media, Inc., Cleve., with.

**TORGERSON, LARRY KEITH,** lawyer; b. Albert Lea, Minn., Aug. 25, 1935; s. Fritz G. and Lu (Hillman) Torgerson. BA, Drake U., 1958, MA, 1960, LLB, 1963, JD, 1968; MA, Iowa U., 1962; cert., The Hague Acad. Internat. Law, The Netherlands, 1965, 69; LLM, U. Minn., 1969, Columbia U., 1971, U. Mo., 1976; PMD, Harvard U., 1973; EdM, 1974. Bar: Minn. 1964, U.S. Dist. Ct. Minn. 1964, Wis. 1970, Iowa 1970, U.S. Dist. Ct. (no. dist.) Iowa 1971, U.S. Tax Ct. 1971, U.S. Supreme Ct. 1972, U.S. Dist. Ct. (ea. dist.) Wis. 1981, U.S. Ct. Appeals (8th cir.) 1981. Asst. corp. counsel 1st Bank Stock Corp. (88 Banks), Mpls., 1963-67, 1st Svc. Corp. (27 ins. agys., computer subs.), Mpls., 1965-67; v.p., trust officer Nat. City Bank, Mpls.,

1967-69; sr. mem. Torgerson Law Firm, Northwood, Iowa, 1969-87; trustee, gen. counsel Torgerson Farms, Northwood, 1967—, Redbirch Farms, Kensett, Iowa, 1987—2002, Sunburst Farms, Grafton, Iowa, 1987—, Gold Dust Farms, Bolan, Iowa, 1988—, Torgerson Grain Storage, Bolan, 1988—, Indian Summer Farms, Bolan, 1991—, Sunset Farms, Bolan, 1992—, Sunrise Farms, Grafton, 1994—. CEO, gen. counsel Internat. Investments, Mpls., 1983-96, Transoceanic, Mpls., 1987-96, Torgerson Capital, Northwood, 1996—, Torgerson Investments, Northwood, 1984—, Torgerson Properties, Northwood, 1987—, Torgerson Ranches, Sundance, Wyo., 1998—, Hawaiian Investments Unltd., Maui, Hawaii, 1998—, Internat. Investments Unltd., San Pedro, Belize, 1999—. Recipient All-Am. Journalism award Thomas Arkle Clark Outstanding Achievement award, 1958, Dennis E. Brumfield Outstanding Achievement award, 1958, Johnny B. Guy Outstanding Leadership award, 1958; named to Outstanding Young Men of Am., U.S. Jaycees; Hagen scholar, Honor scholar. Mem. ABA, Am. Judicature Soc., Iowa Bar Assn., Minn. Bar Assn., Wis. Bar Assn., Hennepin County Bar Assn., Mensa, Drake Student-Faculty Coun., Drake Student Alumni Coun. (chmn.), Jaycees, Harvard Bus. Sch. Study (pres., exec. com., univ. editor in chief), Psi Chi, Circle K (pres. local chpt.), Phi Alpha Delta, Omicron Delta Kappa (pres. local chpt.), Pi Kappa Delta (pres. local chpt.), Alpha Tau Omega (pres. local chpt., Silver Bullet Outstanding Leadership award, 1965, 66), Pi Delta Epsilon (founder, chpt. pres.), Alpha Kappa Delta, Alpha Scholastic Hon. (U. editor-in-chief), Harvard Bus. Sch. Exec. Com. (U. editor-in-chief). Lutheran.

**TORGERSON, LINDA BELLE,** music educator; b. Sioux City, Iowa, Dec. 16, 1951; d. Fredric William and Clara Jeanette Wilson; m. Peter Kinsey Torgerson; children: Christopher, Patricia. Diploma, Ctrl. H.S., 1971; MusB Edn., Morningside Coll., 1976; MEd, City U., 1999. Cert. Iowa tchr., tchr. Mont., Washington. Choral dir. First United Meth. Ch., Sioux City, Iowa, 1974—76, First Presbyn. Ch., Kalispell, Mont., 1976—80; pvt. music instr. Self-employed, Kalispell, Mont., 1976—80; music tchr. St. Matthews Sch., Kalispell, Mont., 1976—77; music dir. coord. Flathead County Rural Schools, Kalispell, Mont., 1979—85; music dir. Clarkston Sch. Dist., Clarkston, Wash., 1985—. Treas. Clarkston Edn. Assn., Clarkston, Wash., 1988—90, v.p., 1990—92, Clarkston, 2001—03, pres., 1991—92; sec. Wash. uniserv polit. action com. Wash. Edn. Assn., Olympia, Wash., 1992—93; bldg. rep. Clarkston Edn. Assn., Clarkston, Wash., 1993—94; jazz band dir. Lincoln Mid. Sch., Clarkston, Wash., 1996—; bldg. rep. Clarkston Edn. Assn., Clarkston, Wash., 2000—01, v.p., 2001—03; co-director for asotin county teens against smoking Asotin County Devel. Services, Clarkston, Wash., 2001—02. Singer (composer): (commercial) Flathead County Milk Music Ad for the Radio, 1978; contbr. articles to profl. jours. Mem. U-Pac bd. for SE Wash. Edn. Assn., Kennewick, Wash., 1992—93. Grantee Dist., Clarkston Sch. Dist., 1994, 1995. Mem.: NEA, Clarkston Edn. Assn. (v.p. 2001), Clarkston Edn. Assn. (bldg. rep. 1992—94), Clarkston Edn. Assn. (pres./past pres. 1991—92), Clarkston Edn. Assn. (v.p. 1989—91), Clarkston Edn. Assn. (treas. 1987—89), SE Wash. Music Educators Assn. (pres. 2002—), Wash. Music Educators Assn., Music Educators Nat. Conf. Home: 1505 8th St Clarkston WA 99403 Office: Lincoln Mid Sch 1945 4th Ave Clarkston WA 99403 Office Phone: 509-758-5506 x5245. Personal E-mail: torgersons@cableone.net. Business E-Mail: torgersonl@csdk12.org.

**TORGERSON, WILLIAM T.,** lawyer, electric power industry executive; b. Annapolis, Md., May 29, 1944; s. Theodore A. and Augusta (Melvin) T.; m. Maureen Glynis Reynolds, Apr. 19, 1994; 1 child, John Theodore. AB, Princeton U., 1966; JD with honors, U. Md., 1973. Atty. Hogan & Hartson, Washington, 1973-82; various Potomac Electric Power Co., Washington, 1982-89, v.p., gen. counsel, 1989-94, sr. v.p., gen. counsel, 1994—; vice chmn., gen. counsel Pepco Holdings Inc. (formerly Potomac Electric Power Co.), Washington, 2003—. Bd. dirs. Leadership Md. Lt. USN, 1966-70, Vietnam. Decorated Bronze Star (2). Office: Potomac Electric Power Co 1900 Pennsylvania Ave NW Washington DC 20068-0002

**TORGLER, BENNO,** economist, researcher; b. Zurich, Switzerland, Nov. 30, 1972; s. Jakob and Lisbeth Torgler; m. Manuela Proyer, Oct. 12, 2002; children: Jessica, Vanessa Stephania. PhD, U. Basel, Switzerland, 2003. Rsch. affiliate, lectr. Yale U., New Haven, 2004—; rsch. fellow Ctr. for Rsch. in Econs., Mgmt. and the Arts, Basel, 2004—. Vis. scholar U. Calif., Berkeley, 2006—; mem. editl. bd. various insts. Editor, rschr.: Tax Compliance and Tax Morale: A Theoretical and Empirical Analysis (Amerbachpreis, 2004). Achievements include research in Public Finance, Political Economy and Public Policy, Development Economics, Law and Economics, Non-Market Economics. Home: Apt 2 114 Player Ct Walnut Creek CA 94598 Office: Yale Univ 34 Hillhouse Ave New Haven CT 06520 Office Phone: 203-436-4193. Personal E-mail: benno@torgler.com. Business E-Mail: benno.torgler@yale.edu.

**TORGOW, EUGENE N.,** electrical engineer; b. Bronx, NY, Nov. 26, 1925; s. Frank and Blanche Anita (Revzin) T.; m. Cynthia Silver, Mar. 19, 1950; children: Joan, Martha, Ellen. BSEE, Cooper Union, 1946; MSEE, Poly. Inst. Bklyn., 1949; Engr. in E.E., Poly. Inst N.Y., 1980; postgrad., UCLA, 1983. Rsch. assoc., sect. leader Microwave Rsch. Inst., Poly. Inst. Bklyn., 1947-51, 53-60, instr., 1954-59; mgr. microwave lab. A.B. Dumont Labs, East Patterson, NJ, 1951-53; chief engr., mgr. microwave products Dorne & Magolin, Inc., Westbury, L.I., NY, 1960-64; chief engr., dir. rsch., dir. mktg. Rantec divsn. Emerson Electric, Calabasas, Calif., 1964-68; with Missle Sys. Group, Hughes Aircraft Co., Canoga Park, Calif., 1968-85, assoc. labs. mgr., 1981-85. Cons. various electronics firms, N.Y.C., 1956-59; cons., 1986—; cons. Exec. Svcs. Corps of So. Calif., 1996—; cons. Econ. Adv. Coun., 1999-2000; lectr. Calif. State U., Northridge, 1986-91. Contbr. articles to profl. jours.; patentee in field. Mem. Fair Housing Coun. San Fernando Valley, L.A., 1967—, L.A. Co. Mus. Assn., 1976—2001. With USAAC, 1946—47. Recipient Engr. '85 Merit award San Fernando Valley Engrs, Coun., 1985 Fellow IEEE, Inst. for Advancement Engring., mem. WINCON (bd. dirs. 1984-89, chmn. bd. dirs. 1988-89), Microwave Theory and Techniques Soc. of IEEE (pres. 1966, mem. adminstrn. com. 1962-72, Svc. award 1978), Accreditation Bd. Engring. and Tech. (mem. engring. accreditation com. 1994-99), Amiotropic Lateral Sclerosis Assn. (trustee greater L.A. chpt. 1999-2004, adv. trustee 2004-06), Hughes Mgmt. Club (edn. chmn. 1979-80), Sigma Xi. Democrat. Office: 9531 Donna Ave Northridge CA 91324-1816

**TORKILDSON, RAYMOND MAYNARD,** lawyer; b. Lake City, S.D., Nov. 19, 1917; s. Gustav Adolph and Agnes (Opitz) T.; m. Sharman Elizabeth Vaughn, Sept. 8, 1956; children: Stephen, Thomas. S.B., U. S.D., 1946; JD, Harvard U., 1948. Bar: Calif. 1949, Hawaii 1950. Assoc. James P. Blaisdell, Honolulu, 1949-52; ptnr. Moore, Torkildson & Rice and successors, Honolulu, 1955-64; exec. v.p. Hawaii Employers Council, Honolulu, 1964-67; ptnr. Torkildson, Katz, Fonseca, Jaffe, Moore & Hetherington and predecessors, Honolulu, 1967-72; sr. ptnr., 1972-92; of counsel, 1993—. Mem. mgmt. com. Armed Forces YMCA, Honolulu, 1971; treas. Hawaii Republican Com. 1977-83. Served with U.S.A. Army, 1941-46; lt. col. Res. ret. Mem. ABA, Hawaii Bar Assn. Clubs: Oahu Country, Pacific (Honolulu). Roman Catholic. Personal E-mail: sharman@iopener.net.

**TORN, RIP (ELMORE RUAL TORN JR.),** actor, theater director; b. Temple, Tex., Feb. 6, 1931; s. Elmore and Thelma (Spacek) T.; m. Ann Wedgeworth, Jan. 15, 1955 (div. 1961); 1 child, Danae; m. Geraldine Page, 1963 (div. June 13, 1987); children: Angelica, Anthony, Jonathan; m. Amy Wright. Grad., Tex. A & M U., 1952. Performances include: (stage) Cat on a Hot Tin Roof, 1955, Orpheus Descending, 1958, Chaparral, 1958 (Theatre World award 1959), Sweet Bird of Youth, 1959, on tour, 1960, Daughter of Silence, 1961, Macbeth, 1962, Desire Under the Elms, 1963, Strange Interlude, 1963, Blues for Mr. Charlie, 1964, The Kitchen, 1966, The Country Girl, 1966, The Deer Park, 1967 (Obie award), The Cuban Thing, 1968, The Honest-to-God Schnozzola, 1969, Dream of a Blacklisted Actor, 1969, The Dance of Death, 1970-71, The Marriage Proposal, 1971, Marriage and Money, 1971, Barbary Shore, The Little Foxes, 1974, The Father, 1975, The Glass Menagerie, 1975, Fever for Life, 1975, Creditors, 1977, Night Shift, 1977, Seduced, 1979, Anna Christie, 1992; (motion pictures) Baby Doll, 1956, A Face in the Crowd, 1957, Time Limit, 1957, Pork Chop Hill, 1959,

King of Kings, 1961, Hero's Island, 1962, Sweet Bird of Youth, 1962, Critic's Choice, 1963, The Cincinnati Kid, 1965, One Spy Too Many, 1966, Beach Red, 1967, You're a Big Boy Now, 1967, Beyond the Law, 1968, Sol Madrid, 1968, Coming Apart, 1969, Tropic of Cancer, 1970, Slaughter, 1972, Payday, 1973, Crazy Joe, 1974, Birch Interval, 1976, Maidstone, The Man Who Fell to Earth, 1976, Nasty Habits, 1977, Coma, 1978, The Seduction of Joe Tynan, 1979, First Family, 1980, Heartland, 1980, One Trick Pony, 1980, Jinxed, 1982, Airplane II: The Sequel, 1982, The Beastmaster, 1982, A Stranger is Watching, 1982, Cross Creek, 1983, City Heat, 1984, Misunderstood, 1984, Night Shadows, 1984, Song Writer, 1984, Flashpoint, 1984, Summer Rental, 1985, Beer, 1985, Extreme Prejudice, 1987, Defending Your Life, 1991, Beautiful Dreamers, 1992, Hard Promises, 1992, Robocop 3, 1993, Where the Rivers Flow North, 1994, How to Make an American Quilt, 1995, Down Periscope, 1996, Trial and Error, 1997, Men in Black, 1997, Hercules, 1997, The Mouse, 1997, Senseless, 1998, Wonder Boys, 2000, Men in Black Alien Attack, 2000, Men in Black II, 2002, Rolling Kansas, 2003, Welcome to Mooseport, 2004, Dodgeball: A True Underdog Story, 2004, Eulogy, 2004, Forty Shades of Blue, 2005, Yours, Mine and Ours, 2005, Marie Antoinette, 2006, Zoom, 2006; (TV films and miniseries) Two Plays, 1971, The President's Plane Is Missing, 1973, The FBI Versus the Ku Klux Klan, 1975, Song of Myself, 1976, Betrayal, 1976, The Gift of Love, 1978, Blind Ambition, 1979, A Shining Season, 1979, Sophia Loren: Her Own Story, 1980, Rape and Marriage: The Rideout Case, 1980, The Blue and the Gray, 1982, When She Says No, 1984, Dream West, 1986, April Morning, 1988, Sweet Bird of Youth, 1989, By Dawn's Early Light, 1990, Another Pair of Aces: Three of a Kind, 1991, My Son Johnny, 1991, Death Hits the Jackpot, 1991, T-Bone and Weasel, 1992, Dead Ahead: The Exxon Valdez Disaster, 1992, A Mother's Right: The Elizabeth Morgan Story, 1993, The Almost Perfect Bank Robbery, 1996, Seasons of Love, 1998, Passing Glory, 1999, Balloon Farm, 1999, A Vision of Murder: The Story of Donielle, 2000, Maniac Magee, 2003, The Lyon's Den, 2003; (TV series) The Larry Sanders Show, HBO, 1992-98 (Emmy nominee for best supporting actor 1993, 94, Cable Ace award for best supporting actor 1994), Ghost Stories, 1997 (narrator); dir. plays: The Beard, 1968 (Obie award), Look Away, 1973. Mem. AFTRA, SAG, Actors Equity Assn., Actors' Studio (bd. dirs., prodn. bd., 1st chmn. founding com.), Dirs. Guild Am.*

**TORNABENE, RUSSELL C.,** communications executive; b. Gary, Ind., Sept. 18, 1923; s. Samuel Tornabene and Marion LaVorci Roush; m. Audrey F. Shankey, June 21, 1952; children: Joseph, Leigh, David, Lynn. AA, Gary Jr. Coll., 1941, 46-47; BA, Ind. U., 1949. MA, 1950. Radio, TV newswriter WRC-AM-TV, Washington, 1951-55; network supr. NBC Network News, Washington, 1955-61, network gen. mgr. NYC, 1961-75; v.p. NBC News, NYC, 1975-81; exec. officer Soc. Profl. Journalists, Chgo., 1981-87; Midwest dir. Exec. TV Workshop, Chgo., 1987-96; pres. Russell Communications Cons., 1996—. Bd. dirs. LifeLine Pilots. Contbr. articles on news to mags. and newspapers. Mem. N.Y. Catholic Archdiocese Sch. Bd., N.Y.C., 1972 Recipient Disting. Service award, Sigma Delta Chi, 1949; Ernie Pyle scholar, 1949 Mem. Acad. TV Arts and Scis., Radio TV News Dirs. Assn., Overseas Press Club (former v.p.). Avocation: photography. Office: 626 Sheridan Sq Apt 2 Evanston IL 60202

**TORNELLO, VINCENT JOSEPH,** music educator; b. Bklyn., Feb. 10, 1950; s. Joseph C. and Carmela M. Tornello; m. Nancy Jane Esterline, July 15, 1972; children: Joseph F., Michelle A. Shirey. MusB, Shenandoah Conservatory, 1972; MEd, U. Va., 1976. Asst. band dir. Lane H.S., Charlottesville, Va., 1972—74; saxophone instr. Madison Coll., Charlottesville, Va., 1974—75; dir. of bands Charlottesville H.S., Va., 1974—. Recipient Legion of Honor, Sousa Found., 2005. Mem.: Va. Band. Dir. (pres. 1982—84, Honor Band Hall of Fame 2002), Music Educators Nat. Conf., Va. Music Educators (mem. exec. bd. 1982—84, treas. 1989—, mem. exec. bd. 1989—), Phi Beta Mu. Avocations: volleyball, sports. Office: Charlottesville HS 1400 Melbourne Rd Charlottesville VA 22901 Office Fax: 434-295-8453.

**TORNOW, L. WILLIAM,** musician; b. Devils Lake, ND, Feb. 1, 1949; s. E. Edward and Ellen Naomi Tornow. BMus in Pub. Sch. Music, Concordia Coll., Moorhead, Minn., 1971; MA in Music, Trinity U., San Antonio, 1978; DMA in Piano Performance, U. Minn., Mpls., 1983. Artist in residence Cmty. Music Ctr., Fargo, ND, 1978—79; organist Our Saviour's Evang. Luth. Ch., Cannon Falls, Minn., 1984—85, St. George's Episc. Meml. Ch., Bismarck, ND, 1985—86. Composer: Elegy, 1971, Symphony No. 1 for Chamber Orch., 1989, Overture to Spring on Themes of Beethoven for orchestra, 1998, Symphony No. 2 for Piano and Orch., 2002, Symphony No. 3 on Four Hymn Tunes, 2006. Spl. 4 (E-4) U.S. Army, 1971—74, Germany and Tex. Fellow: Nat. Music Tchrs. Assn.; mem.: Am. Guild of Organists. Avocations: fishing, golf. Home and Studio: 1107 W Capitol Ave Apt 62 Bismarck ND 58501

**TORNQVIST, ERIK GUSTAV MARKUS,** chemical engineer, research scientist, consultant; b. Lund, Sweden, Jan. 13, 1924; came to U.S. 1951; s. Gustav Ivar and Anne Marie (Lassen) T.; m. Linnéa Dagmar Lindborg, June 28, 1969; children: Gunvor, Karin, Carl-Erik. MSChemE, Royal Inst. Tech., Stockholm, 1948; MS in Biochemistry, U. Wis., 1953, PhD in Biochemistry/Organic Chemistry, 1955. Registered engr., Sweden. 1st rsch. asst. divsn. food chemistry Royal Inst. Tech., Stockholm, 1944—51; rsch. asst. dept. biochemistry U. Wis., Madison, 1951—55; rsch. chemist chem. divsn. Esso Rsch. and Engring. Co., Linden, NJ, 1955—58, rsch. assoc., 1958—66, sr. rsch. assoc., 1966—72, Exxon Chem. Co., Tech., Linden, NJ, 1972—86; internat. cons. Watchung, NJ, 1986—90, 2003—; pres. PolymErik, Inc., Watchung, 1990—2003. Vis prof. Royal Inst. Tech., 1987; invited prin. speaker Scandinavian Day, Chautauqua (N.Y.) Instn., 1983, 87; invited speaker, chmn. numerous nat. and internat. meetings. Co-editor: Polymer Chemistry of Synthetic Elastomers, 2 vols., 1969, 69; patentee in field; contbr. articles to profl. jours., chpts. to books. Treas. United Swedish Socs., N.Y.C., 1972-86, Swedish Hist. Assn. N.J., 1988-91; bd. govs. Am. Swedish Hist. Mus., Phila., 1974-89; trustee New Sweden Co., Bridgeton, N.J., 1986-89, Kalmar Nyckel Found., Wilmington, Del., 1987-96, hon. trustee, 1996; bd. dirs. Watchung Hills Soccer Assn., Watchung/Warren, N.J., 1989-95. Recipient award 1st Nat. Inventors Day, 1973, gold Bicentennial medal King of Sweden, 1980, John Hanson award for excellence in pub. svc. Am.-Swedish Cultural Found., Mpls., 1981, citation Swedish Coun. of Am., 1983, cert. of appreciation Swedish New Sweden '88 Com., 1989; grad. fellow Roos' Found., Stockholm, 1949, 51, Govt. of Sweden, 1948, State Coun. for Technol. Rsch., Stockholm, 1949, Adelsköld fellow Royal Acad. Sci., 1951, 53, Univ. fellow Sweden-Am. Found., Stockholm, 1951. Fellow: Swedish Colonial Soc. (gov. 1977—82, hon. gov. Ad Vitam 1982, gov. 1986—89); mem.: John Ericsson Soc., Internat. Union Pure and Applied Chemistry (affiliate), Swedish Assn. Grad. Engrs., Am. Soc. Swedish Engrs. (life; sec. 1965—68, pres. 1968—72, John Ericsson Gold medal 1984), Swedish Am. Soc. Chem. Engrs., Am. Chem. Soc., NY Acad. Scis., Schlaraffia, Wis. Alumni Assn. (life), Svensk I Varlden (life), Am.-Scandinavian Soc., KTH Alumni, Swedish-Am. C of C., Swedish Ski Club (pres. 1972—74), Vasa Order Am. (co-cultural leader NJ Dist. 6, 1997, chmn. Lodge Skandia 2000—05), Sigma Xi, Phi Lambda Upsilon. Lutheran. Achievements include invention and development of numerous catalysts for polymerization of olefins and dienes, especially the catalyst for making most of the isotactic polypropylene over a period of more than 20 years (from about 1958) and still in large-scale use, having resulted in production of billions of dollars worth of polymer, also, elucidation of many aspects of the mode of action of these and other catalysts and the preparation of numerous novel polymers. Home and Office: 38 Mareu Dr Watchung NJ 07069-5025 Personal E-mail: erikgmt@yahoo.com.

**TORNS, DAVID LOREN,** conductor, director, musician; b. San Diego, Oct. 2, 1975; MusB, Vanderbilt U., 1998; MusM, W.Va. U., Morgantown, 2002. Grad. asst. W.Va. U., 1999—2000; asst. condr. Symphony of Mountains, Kingsport, Tenn., 2002—03; music dir. La. Youth Orch., Baton Rouge, 2003—. Recipient Jean Keller Heard prize for Strings, Vanderbilt U., 1998. Mem.: Conductor's Guild. Office: La Youth Orch PO Box 14209 Baton Rouge LA 70898 Office Phone: 225-383-0500. Home Fax: 225-346-1191; Office Fax: 225-346-1191.

**TORNSTROM, ROBERT ERNEST**, lawyer, oil industry executive; b. St. Paul, Jan. 17, 1946; s. Clifford H. and Janet (Hale) T.; m. Betty Jane Hermann, Aug. 5, 1978; children: Carter, Gunnar, Katherine. BA, U. Colo., 1968, JD, 1974; diploma grad. sch. mgmt. exec. program, UCLA, 1990. Bar: Colo. 1974, U.S. Dist. Ct. Colo. 1974, Calif. 1975, U.S. Dist. Ct. (cen. dist.) Calif. 1975. Atty. Union Oil Co. of Calif., L.A., 1974-76, counsel internat. div., 1977-78, regional counsel Singapore, 1976-77; sr. atty. Occidental Internat. Exploration and Prodn. Co., Bakersfield, Calif., 1978-81, mng. counsel, 1981-85, v.p., assoc. gen. counsel, 1985-88, v.p., regional ops. mgr., 1988-91; pres. Occidental Argentina, Buenos Aires, 1991-93, Occidental of Russia, Moscow, 1993-94; dir. comml. negotiations Occidental Internat., 1994-96; chmn. of bd. Sullivan Petroleum Co., 1997—. Bd. dir. and chmn. bd. Parmaneft Joint Venture, Vanyogannef JV, Moscow; bd. dir. Calif. Land and Cattle Co., King City, 602 Operating Corp.; legal cons. Island Creek Coal Co., Lexington, Ky. Exec. bd. Cmty. Ho., Bakersfield; pres. Snowbird Assn., Mammoth Lakes. Capt. U.S. Army, 1968—71, Vietnam. Decorated Bronze Star. Mem. Am. Soc. Internat. Law, Am. Corp. Counsel Assn., Soc. Mayflower Descendants, Moscow Country Club, Stockdale Country Club (bd. dirs.). Republican. Episcopalian. Avocations: skiing, tennis, golf, riding, collecting classic automobiles. Home: 310 Mount Lowe Dr Bakersfield CA 93309-2468 Office: 1508 18th St Ste 222 Bakersfield CA 93301 Office Phone: 661-327-5008.

**TORO, STEPHEN RALPH**, music educator; b. Providence, R.I., Sept. 20, 1952; s. Salvatore and Vincenza Toro. Attended, New Eng. Conservatory Music, 1970—72; MusB, U. R.I., 1975. Tchr. music, dept. head Prout Meml. HS, Wakefield, RI, 1978—83; band dir. Shrine Concert Band, Cranston, RI, 1987—97; tchr. music Notre Dame Sch., West Warwick, RI, 1993, Alperin-Schechter Sch., Providence, 1994—95, Our Lady of Fatima HS, Warren, RI, 1994—95; music dir. Moses Brown Sch., Providence, 1995—. Tchg. sabbatical Tokyo Sch.; founder, music dir., conductor Ocean State Summer Pops Orch.; founding mem. Brass Attack musical group. Past mem., bd. dirs. R.I. Civic Choraler & Orch.; instr. CPR Am. Red Cross, RI. Mem.: R.I. Music Educators Assn. (mem. exec. bd.). Avocations: music, boating. Office: Moses Brown Sch 250 Lloyd Ave Providence RI 02906 Business E-Mail: storo@mosesbrown.org.

**TORO-ALFONSO, JOSE**, psychology professor, researcher; b. Yauco, P.R., May 29, 1952; s. Jorge Toro-Cuberge and Cruz Alfonso-Ramirez; children: Veronica Toro-Ruiz, Adriana Toro-Ruiz. MA, Cath. Univesity P.R., 1974—76; MA in Psychology, Caribbean Ctr. for Advanced Studies, P.R., 1986—88, PhD, 1986—90. Lic. psychology P.R. Licensing Bd., 1990. Exec. dir. P.R. AIDS Found., San Juan, 1988—98; assoc. prof. U. P.R., San Juan, 1998—. Cons. USAID, Santo Domingo, Dominican Republic, 1980—; chair Com. on Psychology and AIDS, Washington, 1999—2000, Com. on Lesbian, Gay, and Bisexual Concerns, Washington, 2003—04; sec. gen. Intermaerican Soc. Psychology, San Juan, PR, 2001—; instl. com. for the protection of humans participants in rsch. U. P.R., San Juan, 2005—. Pres. P.R. Psychol. Assn., San Juan, 2001—02. Mem.: P.R. Psychol. Assn. (assoc.; past pres. 1988—2005). Achievements include research in HIV stigma, same-sex domestic violence, and masculinities. Home: 306 Villamil St Apt 502 San Juan PR 00907 Office: Univ Puerto Rico Dept Psychology PO Box 23345 San Juan PR 00931 Office Fax: 787-763-4599. Personal E-mail: jtoro@uprrp.edu.

**TORQUATI, ALFONSO**, surgeon, educator; s. Giacomo and Maria Torquati; m. Anna Spagnoli, July 30, 1992. MD, U. Rome, 1998; MS in Clin. Investigation, Vanderbilt U., Nashville, 2003. Lic. Am. Bd. of Surgery. Instr. of surgery Vanderbilt U., Nashville, 2001—04, asst. prof. of surgery, 2004—. Dir. foregut and bariatric surgery rsch. Vanderbilt U., Nashville, 2004—. Fellow: ACS (life). Achievements include discovery of RUNX3 role in Barrett's esophagus. Office: Vanderbilt U Medical Center N D5203 Nashville TN 37232 Office Phone: 615-322-7555. Office Fax: 615-343-9485. Business E-Mail: alfonso.torquati@vanderbilt.edu.

**TORQUATO, SALVATORE**, materials scientist, chemistry professor; b. Falerna, Calabria, Italy, Feb. 10, 1954; came to U.S., 1955; s. Vincent and Palma (Vaccaro) T.; m. Kim Tracey Hoberack, Nov. 8, 1975; children: Michelle, Lisa. BSME, Syracuse U., 1975; MSME, SUNY, Stony Brook, 1977, PhD in Mech. Engring., 1980. Rsch. engr. Grumman Aerospace Corp., Bethpage, NY, 1975-78; rsch. asst. dept. mech. engring. SUNY, Stony Brook, 1978-80; asst. prof. dept. mech. engring. GM Inst., Flint, Mich., 1981-82; from asst. to assoc. prof. depts. mech., aerospace & chem. engring., 1991-92; prof. Civil Engring. Princeton (N.J.) U., 1992-99, prof. chemistry, 2000—. Vis. prof. Courant Inst. Math. Scis., N.Y.U., 1990-91; cons. Eastman Kodak, Rochester, N.Y., 1989—; mem. Inst. Advanced Study, 1998-99. Contbr. articles to profl. jours. Grumman Masters fellow, 1975-77; fellow Guggenheim, 1998; recipient Engring. Rsch. Achievement award Alcoa Co., 1987, Disting. Engring. Rsch. award, 1989, Gustus L. Larson Meml. award, 1994. Fellow ASME Am. Phys. Soc.; mem. Am. Inst. Chem. Engrs., Soc. Engring. Sci. (Charles Russ Richards Meml. award, 2002, William Prager medal, 2004), Soc. for Indsl. and Applied Math. Avocations: racquetball, reading, music. Office: Princeton U Princeton Materials Inst Dept Chemistry Princeton NJ 08544-0001

**TORRAS, JOSEPH HILL**, pulp and paper company executive; b. Americus, Ga., Nov. 14, 1924; s. Fernando Joseph and Nell Wilson (Hill) T.; m. Mary Ravenel Robertson, Sept. 20, 1952; children: Mary Martin, Fernanda Maria, Joseph Hill. S.B., Yale U., 1948; MBA, Harvard U., 1950; D in Bus. Administrn., Piedmont Coll., 1997. Asst. to fin. v.p. Seatrian Lines, Inc., 1950—51; with St. Regis Paper Co., 1951—60, sales mgr. printing papers div., 1956—60; exec. v.p. Brown Co., Boston, 1960—64; pres., chmn. bd. Premoid Corp., West Springfield, Mass., 1964—87; pres. Precon, Inc., Ludlow, 1967—87, Astro Tissue Co., Battleboro, Vt., 1968—72; chmn. bd. Whitman Products, Ltd., West Warwick, RI, 1976—89; pres., CEO, Preco Corp., Amherst, Mass., 1976—98; chmn., CEO Lincoln Pulp & Paper Co., Lincoln, Maine, 1968—, Eastern Fine Paper, Inc., Brewer, Maine, 1989—, Eastern Pulp & Paper Corp., 1995—2003. CEO, Shelburne Corp., 1999—; adv. dir. Liberty Mut. Ins. Mem. Mass. Gov.'s Bus. Coun., 1985—89; devel. bd. Yale U.; bd. govs. Mass. Gen. Hosp., 1985—96; bd. dirs. Mass. Taxpayers Assn., 1976—86; trustee Hist. Deerfield, 1990—2004, Piedmont Coll., Ga., 1991—99; dir. Inst. of World Politics, 1990—. Lt. (j.g.) aviator USNR, 1943—46. Mem. Tissue Paper Mfrs. Assn. (dir. 1963-64), Am. Pulp and Paper Mill Supts. Assn., Salesman's Assn. Paper Industry, NAM (dir. 1981-85), Colony Club; assoc. Am. Inst. Ptrs., 1992- Home: 264 Bardwells Ferry Rd Shelburne Falls MA 01370-9744

**TORRE, GARY JEROME**, retired lawyer; b. Oakland, Calif., Oct. 14, 1919; s. Giove M. and Jessie (Garibotto) Torre; m. Carol Desaussiere Goodrich, Dec. 25, 1948; children: Michael Durham, Alicia Hayden, Nicholas Goodrich. BA, U. Calif., 1944, JD, 1948. Bar: Calif. Law clerk Justice William Douglas, Wash., DC, 1948—49; ptnr. Litlick, Gerry, Wheat, Adams and Charles, San Francisco, 1949—81; ret., 1981. Lt. USAF, 1942—45, England. Mem.: Sierra Club (pres., dir. legal defense fund 1968—93). Democrat.

**TORRE, JOE (JOSEPH PAUL TORRE)**, professional baseball team manager; b. Bklyn., July 18, 1940; m. Ali Torre, Aug. 23, 1987; one child, Andrea Rea; children from previous marriages: Michael, Lauren, Tina. HHD (hon.), Rider U., 2006. Profl. baseball player Milw. Braves, 1960-69, St. Louis Cardinals, 1969-74, N.Y. Mets, 1974-77, player-mgr., 1977-82; mgr. Atlanta Braves, 1982-84; TV broadcaster Calif. Angels, 1984-90; mgr. St. Louis Cardinals, 1990-94, N.Y. Yankees, 1995—. Co-founder (with Ali Torre) Joe Torre Safe at Home Found., 2002—. Author: (novels) Chasing the Dream: My Lifelong Journey to the World Series, 1997, Joe Torre's Ground Rules for Winners: 12 Keys to Managing Team Players, Tough Bosses, Setbacks, and Success, 1999; actor: (films) Taking Care of Business, 1990, Analyze That, 2002, (voice) Everyone's Hero, 2006. Named Nat. League's Most Valuable Player, 1971, Player of Yr., Sporting News, 1971, Mgr. of Yr., 1982, 1996, 1998; named to All-Star Team, 1963-67, 70-73, coach 1997, 1999-2002,

2004; recipient Gold Glove award, 1965; hit for cycle, 1973; winner World Series N.Y. Yankees, 1996, 1998, 1999, 2000. over 1,000 career wins, 2006; four world championships. Office: New York Yankees Yankee Stadium E 161 St & River Ave Bronx NY 10451*

**TORRE-AMIONE, GUILLERMO**, cardiologist, researcher; s. Guillermo Torre and Gloria Amione de Torre; m. Maria Eugenia Martinez, Jan. 31, 1986; children: Guillermo Torre, Federico Torre. Degree, Monterrey Tecnologico, 1985. Diplomate Am. Bd. Internal Medicine. Asst. prof. medicine Baylor Coll. Medicine, Houston, 1996—; med. dir. heart transplant program The Meth. Hosp., Houston, 1996—. Office: Baylor College 1709 Dryden Rd Houston TX 77030-2400 Office Phone: 713-441-1100. Business E-Mail: gtorre@tmh.tmc.edu.

**TORRENZANO, RICHARD**, public relations executive; BS, N.Y. Inst. Tech., 1972, LittD (hon.), 1990; postgrad., Stanford Univ., 1986. With NY Stock Exch., 1982—90, sr. v.p., mgmt. and exec. com., chief spokesman; sr. v.p., dir. corp. affairs, mgmt. com. SmithKline Beecham, London, 1990—94; chmn., CEO Torrenzano Group, NYC, 1995—. Coord. Pres. Reagan's Bd. Advisors on Pvt. Sector Initiatives, Washington, 1986—89; pvt. sector adv. com. USIA, Washington, 1983—92; coord. program USSR-USA Conf. on Stock Markets, Moscow, 1990, PRC-USA Conf. on Stock Markets, Beijing, 1986; lectr. in field. Contbr. articles to profl. journals. Trustee, mem. exec. com. NY Inst. Tech., 1985—. Decorated Knight of Malta, knight comdr. Order of Holy Sepulchre, knight ofcl. Order of Sts. Maurice and Lazarus, Royal House of Savoy, knight comdr. jus patronato Sacred Constantinian Order St. George, knight comdr. Constantinian Order of St. George, Royal Order of Francis I, Royal Order of House of Bornone, knight Order of Merit Republic of Italy; recipient Ellis Island Medal of Honor, 1997, Silver anvil, Pub. Rels. Soc. Am. Mem.: Royal Soc. Medicine (London), N.Y. Press Club, Nat. Press Club, Washington, DC. Office: The Torrenzano Group 509 Madison Ave 9th Fl New York NY 10022 Office Phone: 212-681-1700. Office Fax: 212-681-6961. Business E-Mail: richard@torrenzano.com.

**TORRES, CYNTHIA ANN**, marketing professional; b. Glendale, Calif., Sept. 24, 1958; d. Adolph and Ruth Ann (Smith) T.; m. Michael Victor Gisser, Mar. 11, 1989; children: Spencer Williams Gisser, David Westfall Torres Gisser. AB, Harvard U./Radcliffe Coll., 1980; MBA, Harvard U., 1984. Rsch. assoc. Bain & Co., Boston, 1980-82; assoc. Goldman, Sachs & Co., NYC, 1984-88, v.p., 1988, First Interstate Bancorp, LA, 1989—92; dir. Fidelity Investments Mgmt. Ltd., Hong Kong, 1993-96; pres. Integrity Investments Consultants, Ltd., 1996—99; dir. mktg. Diamond Portfolio Advisors LLC, Santa Monica, Calif., 2000—. Mem. fin. oversight com. Santa Monica-Malibu Unified Sch. Dist.; chair site governance coun. Franklin Sch. Santa Monica. Rockefeller Found. scholar, 1976; Harvard U. Ctr. for Internat. Affairs fellow, 1979-80; recipient Leadership award Johnson and Johnson, 1980; by Council for Opportunity in Grad. Mgmt. Edn. fellow, 1982-84. Mem.: Fin. Women's Assn. Hong Kong (past pres.), Asia Soc., Acad. Polit. Sci., Harvard Alumni Assn. (regional dir.), Harvard-Radcliffe Club So. Calif. (pres.). Office: Diamond Portfolio Advisors LLC 10940 Wilshire Blvd Ste 600 Los Angeles CA 90024 Personal E-mail: cynthiatorres@earthlink.net.

**TORRES, DALYS E.**, music educator, consultant; b. Panama, Republic of Panama, Nov. 20, 1948; arrived in U.S., 1970; d. Victor Manuel Torres and Felicidad Bethancourth. Attended, Johnny Colon Sch. Music, 1985—87, studies with Edwina Tyler, 1985—87; BS in Bus. Adminstrn., Boricua Coll., 1986; postgrad. in Bilingual Edn./TESOL (Tchg. English to Students of Other Languages), L.I. U., 1992—94. Eligibility specialist I, translator Spanish/Eng. HRA/Food Stamp Dept. F-14, N.Y.C., 1985—86; eligibility specialist spl. projects HRA/Food Stamp Dept. F-12, N.Y.C., 1986—87; group supr. HRA/Food Stamp Dept. F-16, N.Y.C., 1988—89; classroom bilingual tchr. Bd. Edn. Pub. Sch. 28A Dist. 6, N.Y.C., 1989—92, Bd. Edn. Pub. Sch. 152 Dist. 6, N.Y.C., 1992—95; percussion and creative movement specialist Bd. Edn. Pub. Sch. 27 Dist. 7, Bronx, NY, 1995—98, Bd. Edn. Pub. Sch. 145 Dist. 3, N.Y.C., 2000—; percussion and creative movement instr., cons. and performer, 1992—. Dir. multicultural music activities Pub. Sch. 28A Dist. 6 N.Y.C., 1989—92; percussion specialist N.Y. Pub. Librs., N.Y.C./Bronx, 1993—2000; percussion and creative movement specialist Mich. Internat. Women Music Festival, Grand Rapids, 1998; percussion specialist for HIV Montekiori Hosp./Staten Island Task Force, N.Y.C./Staten Island, 1999; percussion instr. Vision at Selis Manor, N.Y.C., 2002—; marching percussionist Pan-Am. Marching Band, Bklyn., 1999; presenter ann. art edn. conf. Fiorello La Guardia H.S. Arts, 2004. Recipient Cultural Music Contbn. award, UFT/Afro Am. Heritage Com., N.Y.C., 1996, Art Edn. awards, Bravo's 2000 Nat. Awards, N.Y.C., 2000. Roman Catholic. Achievements include design of Percussion and Creative Movement Program for Pub. Sch. at P.S. 27 (Dist. 7); Percussion Program for N.Y. Pub. Libr., 1993-2000; Percussion and Creative Movement for Women, Women with HIV, and Women with Other Diseases, 1999-; Percussion Program for the Blind; Percussion with a Passion at Vision Selis Manor, N.Y.C., 2002-. Avocations: reading, films, rollerskating. Home and Office: 646 9th Ave #5FN New York NY 10036 Office Phone: 212-757-3384. E-mail: panaper81@yahoo.com.

**TORRES, DANIEL**, literature educator; b. Caguas, P.R., Mar. 9, 1961; arrived in U.S., 1984; s. Vicente Torres and Antonia Rodriguez. BA in Comparative Lit., U. P.R., Rio Piedras, 1984; MA in L.Am. Poetry, SUNY, Stony Brook, 1986; PhD in L.Am. Baroque, U. Cin., 1990. Tchg. asst. SUNY, Stony Brook, 1984—86, U. Cin., 1986—88; instr. Ohio State U., Columbus, 1988—90; prof. Ohio U., Athens, 1990—. Author Moriras si da una primavera novel; contbg. editor: Cin. Roman Langs. Rev., 1990—, Chasqui: L.Am. Rev., 2000—, author poetry and criticism. Activist, bd. mem. United Campus Ministry, Athens, Ohio, 1993—2003. Named Book of Yr., Pen Club, P.R., 1990. Mem.: MLA, Internat. Inst. Iberoamerican Lit., L.Am. Studies Assn. Avocations: reading, dance, travel, music, driving. Office: Ohio U Modern Langs 283 Gordy Hall Athens OH 45701 Office Fax: 740-593-0729. Business E-Mail: torres@ohio.edu.

**TORRES, DARA**, Olympic athlete; b. Beverly Hills, Calif., Apr. 15, 1967; Degree in broadcasting, U. Fla. Intern CNN and NBC Sports; commentator TV sports NBC, ESPN, TNT, Fox News, Fox Sports; ret. swimmer TV reporter: Good Morning America, Inside Edition; host Oxygen Sports. Olympic team capt., 1992; spokesperson Tae Bo workout tapes. Host sci. and tech. show Discovery Channel. Recipient Gold medal (2) 4 x 100-meter freestyle, 4 x 100-meter medley (team), Bronze medal (3) 50 and 100-meter freestyle, 100-meter fly Sydney Olympics, 2000, Gold medal 100-meter freestyle, 4 x 100-meter freestyle, 4 x 100-meter relay (team) Pan Pacific Championships, 1987, Gold medal 4 x 100-meter freestyle relay (team) L.A. Games, 1984, Bronze medal 4 x 100-meter freestyle relay (team), Silver medal 4 x 100-meter medley (team), 1988, Gold medal 4 x 100-meter free relay (team) Barcelona Olympics, 1992; 12-time nat. champion; former world-record holder 50-meter freestyle, Am.-record holder 50-meter freestyle and 100-meter fly, 1991 Summer Nationals Kiphuth award, 1991, Summer Nationals Comeback award Achievements include first American female to swim in four Olympics, five time US Open champion, seven time National A team member, two time All Star team. Office: USA Swimming 1 Olympic Plz Colorado Springs CO 80909-5746

**TORRES, ERNEST C.**, federal judge; b. 1941; AB, Dartmouth Coll., 1963; JD, Duke U., 1968. Assoc. Hinckley, Allen, Salisbury & Parsons, 1968-74; ptnr. Saunders & Torres, 1974-80; assoc. justice RI Superior Ct., 1980-85; asst. v.p. Aetna Life and Casualty, 1985-86; ptnr. Tillinghast, Collins & Graham, 1986-87; judge US Dist. Ct. RI, Providence, 1987—99, chief judge, 1999—. Pres. East Greenwich (R.I.) Town Coun., 1972-74; state rep. R.I. Ho. of Reps., 1975-80, dep. minority leader, 1977-80. Recipient Disting. Svc. award Jaycees, 1974; named Man of Yr., Prince Henry Soc. R.I., 1988, Prince Henry Soc. Mass., 1995; Alfred P. Sloan scholar Dartmouth Coll. Mem. ABA, ATLA, FBA, R.I. Bar Assn., Jaycees (Dist. Svc. award 1974), Prince Henry Soc. of R.I., Prince Henry Soc. of Mass. Office: US Dist Ct One Exchange Terrace Providence RI 02903

**TORRES, ESTEBAN EDWARD**, congressman, trade association administrator; b. Miami, Ariz., Jan. 27, 1930; s. Esteban Torres and Rena Baron (Gomez) T.; m. Arcy Sanchez, Jan. 22, 1955; children: Carmen D'Arcy, Rena Denise, Camille Bianca, Selina Andre, Esteban Adrian. Student, East Los Angeles Coll., 1960, Calif. State U., Los Angeles, 1963, U. Md., 1965, Am. U., 1966; PhD (hon.), Nat. U., 1987; DHL (hon.), Whittier Coll., 2001. Chief steward United Auto Workers, local 230, 1954-63, dir. polit. com., 1963; organizer, internat. rep. United Auto Workers (local 230), Washington, 1964; asst. dir. Internat. Affairs Dept., 1975-77; dir. Inter-Am. Bureau for Latin Am., Caribbean, 1965-67; exec. dir. E. Los Angeles Community Union (TELACU), 1967-74; U.S. ambassador to UNESCO, Paris, 1977-79; chmn. Geneva Grp., 1977-78; chmn. U.S. del. Gen. Conf., 1978; spl. asst. to pres. U.S., dir. White House Office Hispanic Affairs, 1979-81; mem. 98th-103rd Congresses from 34th Dist. Calif., 1983-98; mem. appropriations com., subcom. fgn. ops., subcom. transp.; chmn. ho. subcom. coinage; mem. ho. banking com., 1983—; mem. ho. small bus. com. 1983. Campaign coordinator Jerry Brown for Gov., 1974; Hispanic coordinator Los Angeles County campaign Jimmy Carter for Pres., 1976; mem. Sec. of State Adv. Group, 1979-81; v.p. Nat. Congress Community Econ. Devel., 1973-74; pres. Congress Mex.-Am. Unity, 1970-71, Los Angeles Plaza de la Raza Cultural Center, 1974; dir. Nat. Com. on Citizens Broadcasting, 1977; cons. U.S. Congress office of tech. assessment, 1976-77; del to IMF gen. conf., Geneva, 1975, del to U.S. Congress European Parliament meetings, 1984; ofcl. congl. observer Geneva Arms Control Talks; chmn. Congl. Hispanic Caucus, 1987; speaker Wrights Del. to USSR, 1987; Dem. dep. Whip, 1990; chmn. Nat. Latino Media Coun. Contbr. numerous articles to profl. jours. Co-chmn. Nat. Hispanic Dems., 1988—; chmn. Japan-Hispanic Inst. Inc.; bd. visitors Sch. Architecture UCLA, 1971-73; bd. dirs. Los Angeles County Econ. Devel. Com., 1972-75, Internat. Devel. Conf., 1976-78; chmn. Congrl. Hispanic Caucus, 1985-86; pres. Plaza de la Raza Cultural Ctr., 1972-73; trustee Am. Coll. Paris, 1977-79; mem. Calif. Transp. Commn., Sacramento. Served in AUS, 1949-53, ETO. Recipient Congrl. award Nat. Leadership award 1997; sr. fellow UCLA Sch. Pub. Policy, 2000-05. Mem. Americans for Dem. Action (exec. bd. 1975-77), VFW Post 6315, Pico Rivera, Calif., Am. Legion, Smithsonian Inst. (regent emeritus 1999—), Willy C. Velasqez Inst., Calif. Transp. Commn. Democrat. Home: 1104 Montezuma Way West Covina CA 91791 Personal E-mail: etorres_nlmc@hotmail.com.

**TORRES, RICHARD**, literature and language educator; b. Deming, N.Mex., Nov. 17, 1951; s. Esquipula Rascon and Maria Madrid Torres; m. Vicki Lynne Everett, Feb. 16, 1974; children: Victoria Marie, Roxana Michelle. BS in Edn., N.Mex. State U., 1974, MA in Edn. Adminstrn., 1978. Cert. tchr. Tex. Edn. Agy. Tchr., curriculum facilitator Gadsden Ind. Sch. Dist., Anthony, N.Mex., 1974—99; tchr. El Paso Ind. Sch. Dist., 1999—2005, literacy leader, 2005—. Mid. sch. rep. Dist. Edn. Improvement Coun., El Paso, 2000—. Named Tchr. of Month, Santa Teresa Jr. H.S. and Mid. Sch., Gadsden, 1992, 1994, 1999, Tchr. of the Day, El Paso Times, 2000, 2004, Unsung Hero award, El Paso Ind. Sch. Dist. Bd., 2002. Mem.: Assn. Supervision and Curriculum Devel., Phi Delta Kappa. Democrat. Roman Catholic. Office: Lincoln Mid Sch 500 Mulberry Ave El Paso TX 79932 Office Phone: 915-231-2180 x6018.

**TORRES, ROBERT J., JR.**, judge; b. Guam; m. Mary Camacho Torres; 3 children. BBA in Accounting, U. Notre Dame, South Bend, Ind., 1980; JD, Harvard Law Sch. Bar: Guam 1987, Mass. Tax practitioner Lourie and Cutler, Boston, 1985—89; prtnr. Torres Limtiaco Cruz & Sison, 1989—2004; justice Guam Supreme Ct., 2004—. Former chmn. Guam Ninth Circuit Lawyer Representative Coordinating Com.; former mem. Guam Ninth Circuit Jud. Conference Exec. Com.; mem. Guam Jud. Council, 1990—96; chair U.S. Magistrate Judges Merit Selection Panel for Guam. Player, coach, and match commnr. Federation Internationale de Football Assn., Asian Football Confederation. Mem.: ABA, Guam Bar Assn. (past pres.). Office: Guam Supreme Ct Ste 300 Guam Jud Ctr 120 W OBrien Dr Hagatna GU 96910*

**TORRES, RUDY ARNOLD**, artist; b. LA, Dec. 21, 1957; s. Benjamin Tiburcio and Josephine Irene Torres. Student, East Los Angeles Coll., 1981—83, Pacific Inst. Comml. Art, 1984—85, Otis Parsons Sch. Design, 1985—86. Artist, co-owner Echo Park Gallery, L.A., 1989—91. Exhibitions include Alpha Contemporary Exhibits, L.A., 1983—86, Mac Houston Art Gallery, Pasadena, Calif., 1986, Brand Libr. Art Gallery, Glendale, Calif., 1987, Design Ctr. L.A., 1987, L.A. Photography Ctr., 1987, 1989, L.A. Mcpl. Gallery, 1989, L.A. Art Assn., 1989, Echo Park Gallery, L.A., 1990—91, Boathouse Gallery, 1992, Weingart Gallery, 1992, Arthur Coons Gallery, 1992, Galeria Las Americas, 1992—94, 1996, Art & Barbee Art Gallery, Hollywood, Calif., 1993, Hilles Libr. at Harvard U., 1995, Olvera St. Gallery, L.A., 1996, Palette Des Artists, Pasadena, 1996, Galeria Otravez, East Los Angeles, Calif., 1996, 2001, Long Beach (Calif.) Gallery, 1998, Calif. State U. Fullerton grand Ctrl. Art Ctr., Santa Ana, 2001, Guggenheim Gallery, Chapman U., Orange, Calif., 2001, Showcase North Gallery, Santa Ana, 2001—02, Huntington Beach (Calif.) Gallery, 2002, City of Brea (Calif.) Gallery, 2002, one-man shows include Minus Zero Gallery, Torrance, Calif., 1990, Mary Norton Clapp Libr., Occidental Coll., L.A., 2000, Galeria Rustica, Pomona, Calif., 2002, Fullerton (Calif.) Branch Libr., 2002, Aliso Viejo (Calif.) Libr., 2002—03, exhibited in group shows at Latino Art Mus., Pomona, Calif., 2002—03, Huntington Beach (Calif.) Art Ctr., 2003, 2005, Eagle Rock Cmty. Cultural Assn., LA, 2003, Self Help Graphics, East LA, 2003, 2004, Latino Art Mus., Claremont, Calif., 2004, The Green Door Gallery, Santa Ana, Calif., 2004. Recipient cert. of appreciation for mural in Herman Dist., 14th Dist. City of L.A., 1986. Avocations: body building, swimming, jogging, camping, fishing. Home: 700 W La Veta Ave # R5 Orange CA 92868

**TORRESE, DANTE MICHAEL**, prosthodontist, educator; b. Yonkers, N.Y., Feb. 12, 1949; s. Dante Angelo and Matilda (Dal Lago) T.; m. Camille Patricia DiPaola, Aug. 7, 1982. BS in Biology, Manhattan Coll., 1971; DDS, Columbia U., 1975; prosthodontic cert., NYU, 1983. Resident in dentistry Presbyn. Hosp., N.Y.C., 1975-76; clin. instr. dentistry Columbia U., N.Y.C., 1976-78, asst. clin. prof. dentistry, 1978—; pvt. practice dentistry Yonkers, N.Y., 1976—. Attending dentist Presbyn. Hosp., N.Y.C., 1976-86; lectr. in field. Recipient Am. Acad. Oral Pathology Grad. award 1975, Densply Corp. award for removable prosthodontics, 1975, Psi Omega Scholastic Achievement award, 1975. Fellow Am. Coll. of Dentists, Royal Soc. Health; mem. NRA (life), Yonkers Dental Soc., 9th Dist. State Dental Soc., Invested Baker St. Irregular, Sherlock Holmes Wireless Soc., Single Action Shooting Soc. (life), Yonkers Amateur Radio Club, Westchester Astronomy Club, Exch. Club (sec. 1979—), Three Garridebs of Westchester, Priory Scholars of N.Y.C. Club, Montague Street Lodgers of Bklyn. Club, Omicron Kappa Upsilon. Office: 984 N Broadway Ste 503 Yonkers NY 10701-1308 Office Phone: 914-965-4004.

**TORRES FILHO, IVO**, medical educator; b. Belem, Pará, Brazil, Apr. 17, 1958; s. Ivo Pontes and Vilma Torres; m. Luciana Neves, Aug. 27, 2000;; children: Patricia Torres, Rodrigo Torres, Natasha Torres. MD, State U. of Rio de Janeiro, 1981; MSc, Fed. U. of Rio de Janeiro, 1984, PhD, 1988; postgrad., U. Calif.-San Diego, La Jolla, 1994. Lic. physician State U. of Rio de Janeiro, 1981. Instr. State U. of Rio de Janeiro, 1982—84; asst. prof., 1984—88, assoc. prof., 1988—2003, Va. Commonwealth U., Richmond, 2003—. Dir. Microcirculatory Lab. Va. Commonwealth U., Richmond, Va., 2003—. Contbr. over 100 articles and abstracts to profl. jours. Recipient Innovative Instrumentation award, Microcirculatory Soc., Inc, Travel award, Radiation Rsch. Soc., 1993; former Postdoctoral fellow, The PEW Charitable Trusts, Fogarty Internat. Ctr. Mem.: Am. Physiol. Soc. (assoc.), Microcirculatory Soc., Inc (assoc.). Office: Virginia Commonwealth University 1101 East Marshall St Rm B1-012 Richmond VA 23298-0695 Office Phone: 804-828-2066. Office Fax: 804-828-6413. E-mail: itorres@vcu.edu.

**TORRES-GIL, FERNANDO M.**, academic administrator; b. Salinas, Calif., June 24, 1948; BA in Polit. Sci., San Jose State U., 1970; MSW, Brandeis U., 1972, PhD in Social Policy, Planning and Rsch., 1976. Spl. asst. to sec. Dept. Health, Edn. and Welfare, Washington, 1978-79, Dept. Health and Human Svcs., Washington, 1979-80; prof. gerontology and pub. adminstrn. U. So.

Calif., 1981-91, assoc. dir. Nat. Resource Ctr. on Minority Aging Populations, 1988-92, prof. social welfare, 1991-93; assoc. dean Sch. Pub. Policy and Soc. Rsch. UCLA, 1993—, dir., Ctr. for Policy Rsch. on Aging. Staff dir. Select Com. on Aging, U.S. Ho. of Reps., Washington, 1985-87. Contbr. articles to profl. jours. Bd. dirs. Nat. Steinbeck Ctr., Families USA Found., AARP Andrus Found., Calif. Endowment, 2003— White House fellow, 1978-79. Mem. Am. Soc. Aging (pres. 1989-92), Nat. Acad. Social Insurance; fellow Gerontological Soc. of Am., 1985, Nat. Acad. Public Administration, 1995. Office: UCLA Sch Pub Plicy & Social Rsch Box 951656 3250 Public Policy Blvd Los Angeles CA 90095-1656*

**TORRES-ROCA, JAVIER FRANCISCO,** medical educator; b. San Juan, PR, Oct. 14, 1967; s. Francisco Torres and Irma Roca; m. Gisella Monclova; 1 child, Sofia Isabel Torres-Monclova. BS, U. PR, San Juan, 1990; MD, U. PR, 1992. Diplomate Am. Bd. Radiology. Postdoctoral fellow Inst. Pasteur, Paris, 1993—95, Stanford U., Calif., 1995—97; intern U. Calif., Irvine, 1997—98, resident in radiation oncology, 1998—2002; asst. prof. H. Lee Moffitt Cancer & Rsch. Inst., Tampa, Fla., 2002—. Ad hoc reviewer Clin. Cancer Rsch., Tampa, Fla., 2004—, Radiation Rsch., Tampa, 2004—, Internat. Jour. Radiation Oncology*Biology*Physics, Tampa, 2003—, Internat. Jour. Andrology, Tampa, 2004—. Recipient Simon Kramer award for best new investigator, Radiation Therapy Oncology Group, 2005. Mem.: AAAS, Am. Brachytherapy Soc., Am. Assn. Cancer Rsch., Am. Soc. Therapeutic Radiology and Oncology, Am. Coll. Radiology. Achievements include patents pending for CPA7, a novel Stat3 inhibitor radiosensitizes prostate cancer cells; identification of novel targets for radiosensitization using a genomic-based radiation sensitivity classifier. Avocations: opera, piano. Office: H Lee Moffitt Cancer Ctr and Rsch Inst 12902 Magnolia Dr Mod 9 RT Tampa FL 33612 Office Phone: 813-745-8424. Uttice Fax: 813-745-7231. E-mail: torresjf@moffitt.usf.edu.

**TORREY, BARBARA BOYLE,** research council administrator; b. Pensacola, Fla., Nov. 27, 1941; d. Peter F. and Elsie (Hansen) Boyle; m. E. Fuller Torrey, Mar. 23, 1968; children: Michael, Martha. BA, Stanford U., 1963, MS, 1970. Vol. Peace Corps, Tanzania, 1963-65; fiscal economist Office Mgmt. and Budget, Washington, 1970-80; dept. asst. sec. HHS, Washington, 1980-81; dir. Ctr. for Internat. Rsch. Census Bur., Washington, 1984-92; pres. Population Reference Bur., Washington, 1992-93; exec. dir. Commn. on Behavioral and Social Scis. and Edn. NRC, NAS, Washington, 1993—. Bd. dirs. Luxembourg Income Study. Co-editor: The Vulnerable, 1987, Population and Land Use, 1992; contbr. articles to profl. jours. Fellow AAAS; mem. Population Assn. Am. (bd. dirs. 1993—). Office: Population Ref Bur 1875 Connecticut Ave NW Ste 520 Washington DC 20009-5728 Office Phone: 202-939-5455.

**TORREY, DAVID LEONARD,** investment banker; b. Ottawa, Ont., Can., Oct. 6, 1931; s. Arthur Starratt and Josephine Edith (Leonard) T.; divorced; children: Heather Torrey Murphy, John Winthrop, Diana Bruce (dec.), Arthur Bruce, David Molson. BA in Econs., St. Lawrence U., 1953; diploma, Ivey Sch. Bus., U. Western Ont., 1954. With Pitfield Mackay Ross Ltd., Toronto, Ont., Canada, 1954-84, v.p., 1963-73, sr. v.p., 1973-80, vice chmn., 1980-82, pres., 1982-84, also bd. dirs.; vice chmn. Dominion Securities, Inc., 1984-88, RBC Dominion Securities, Inc., 1988-91. Chmn. Montreal Stock Exch., 1971-73, Phillips Cables Ltd., 1991-96; bd. dirs. Can. Stebbins Engring. and Mfg. Co. Ltd.; mem. coun. Montreal Bd. Trade, 1971-72. Chmn. Montreal Downtown YMCA, 1972-74; trustee St. Lawrence U., 1980-92; bd. dirs. Montreal Gen. Hosp. Found. Mem. Investment Bankers Assn. (gov. 1991-73), Securities Industries Assn. (bd. govs. 1972-73), Multiple Sclerosis Can. (past pres., bd. dirs.), Royal Montreal Golf Club, Mt. Royal (Montreal) Club, Toronto Club, Saifish Club Fla. (Palm Beach), Beta Theta Pi. Home: 389 Carlyle Ave Montreal PQ Canada H3R 1T3 Office: PO Box 6001 1 Pl Ville Marie 2E Montreal PQ Canada H3C 3A9 Office Phone: 514-399-9932.

**TORREY, LINDA A.,** art educator; b. Bourne, Mass., Feb. 6, 1951; d. William Ambrose Mozur and Louise Evelyn Christopher; m. Donald E. Torrey, Aug. 28, 1993 (div.); 1 child, Kimberly L. Lopipero. AA, Auburn C.C., 1971; BS in Art Edn., SUNY, Buffalo, 1973. Permanent cert. secondary edn. 1977. Secondary art tchr. Skaneateles (N.Y.) Schs., 1973—. Mem. scholastic art adv. bd. Scholastic Art Awards, Syracuse, NY, 1985—. Exhibited in group shows at Syracuse Pen Women, 2005 (2d Pl. award, 2005), The Vineyard Show (Hon. mention, 2005), O.C.C. Gallery, 2005. Vol. Skaneateles Youth Baseball, 1989; bd. dirs. Skaneateles Hockey Boosters, 1980, 1983—89, 1989; com. mem. Skaneateles Arts Expo, 1990. Recipient Nat. Found. for Advancement in Arts award, 1987—88, Photo/Imaging fellowship, Rochester Inst. Tech., 2005, Kodak Century award for photography edn., 1984, Scholastic Art awards Nat. Citation for Outstanding Educator, 1979, 1980, 1981, 1983, 1984, 1985, 1988, 1989, 2004. Mem.: ASCD, Nat. League Am. Pen Women. Independent. Avocations: golf, kayaking, gardening. Home: 2 Sachem Dr Skaneateles NY 13152 Office: Skaneateles Schs 49 E Elizabeth St Skaneateles NY 13152

**TORREY, RICHARD FRANK,** utilities executive; b. Saratoga Springs, N.Y., Dec. 31, 1926; s. Reginald Frank and Marian (Currey) T.; m. Betty Louise Stetson, July 2, 1949; children: Patricia Ann Torrey Kritsberg, Carol Louise Torrey Kress, Barbara Jean Torrey Friedman. BA cum laude, Syracuse U., 1951. News reporter, Syracuse (N.Y.) Post Standard, 1947-51; pub. rels. account exec. Syracuse, 1951-53; home sec. 35th Congl. Dist., Syracuse, 1952-53; exec. sec. to mayor Syracuse, 1954—57; dir. area devel. Niagara Mohawk Power Corp., Syracuse, 1958-66, comml. v.p. Buffalo, 1966-68, administrv. v.p., 1968-72, v.p., gen. mgr., 1972-76, sr. v.p. Syracuse, 1976-88, ret., 1988; pres. Can. Niagara Power Co. Ltd., Niagara Falls, Ont., Canada, 1968-88, dir., 1968-89. Pres., dir. Caragh Investments Ltd., 1981-85; pres. Opinac Investments Ltd., Toronto, 1982-88, bd. dirs., 1982-89; pres. Opinac Fnergy Ltd., Calgury, Alta., 1983 88, bd. dirs., 1980-89. Pres. Syracuse USO, 1959-61, mem. nat. coun., 1959-62, 68-74; co-chmn. Ctrl. N.Y. Interim Coun. Regional Planning, 1965-66; gen. chmn. Dunbar-Huntington Bldg. Fund, Syracuse, 1963; state campaign chmn. N.Y. Job Devel. Authority, 1961; gen. chmn. United Way of Buffalo and Erie County, 1971; mem. Syracuse U. Corp. Adv. Coun., 1972-76; trustee Elmcrest Children's Ctr., 1962-63, Camp Good Will, Syracuse, 1964-66, Syracuse Area Coun. Chs., 1959-64; bd. dirs. United Way Buffalo and Erie County, 1967-76, Greater Buffalo Devel. Found., Kenmore Mercy Hosp., 1970-76, Crouse Irving Meml. Hosp. Found., 1978-87, Nat. Kidney Found., 1987-89, Bon Secours-Venice (Fla.) Hosp. Found., 1992-98, vice chmn. 1995-96, chmn. 1996-98; bd. dirs. Plantation Cmty. Found., Venice, 1989, pres., 1990-93, pres. emeritus, 1993—; mem. bd. adv. Sisters of St. Joseph, 1967-76; elder Trinity Presbyn. Ch., Venice, 1992-94; assoc. mem. Dewitt Cmty. Ch. Served with Air Corps U.S. Army, 1944-47. Recipient Syracuse Young Man of Yr. award, 1962; Outstanding Citizen award Buffalo Evening News, 1973. Mem. Empire State (v.p., bd. dirs. 1963-80), Buffalo Area (v.p. 1968-72, bd. dirs. 1968-76, pres. 1972-73, chmn. bd. 1973-74, Man of Yr. 1974) C. of C., Associated Industries of N.Y. (bd. dirs. 1978-80), Bus. Coun. N.Y. (bd. dirs. 1980-82), Mfrs. Assn. Cen. N.Y. (bd. dirs. 1977-88), Augusta Villa Assn. (bd. dirs. 1991-73, pres. 1973), Buffalo Club (past 2d v.p., dir.), Syracuse Century Club (gov. 1980-83), Onondaga Golf Club, Automobile Club Western N.Y.(bd. dirs. 1971-73, pres. 1973), N.Y.S. Automobile Assn. (dir. 1975-76). Home and Office: 7333 Scotland Way #2303 Sarasota FL 34238 Personal E-mail: dicktorrey@aol.com.

**TORREZ, CAROLINE HERMINIA,** human resources specialist, director, actress, musician, singer, dancer; d. Philip Hernandez and Lucy Mercedes Rivera; m. Robert Pierre Torrez, June 10, 1995. BA, Calif. State U., Fullerton, 1975. Sec. to exec. dir. Pinto program CSUF, 1972—73, oral history interpreter, 1973—75; asst. Spanish tchr. Cerritos Coll., Calif., 1974—75; export parts specialist export dept. C.B.S. Musical Instruments/Fender, Rogers & Rhodes, Fullerton, 1975—77; bilingual interviewer Orange County Housing Authority, Santa Ana, Calif., 1977—79, field rep., 1979—83, mktg. rep., 1983—87; recreation dir. City of Anaheim (Calif.) Parks and Recreation/Let's Play for Grow program/Joseph P. Kennedy Found., 1983—87; Home Investment Partnership Act coord. Urban County Housing and Cmty. Devel. Orange County, Santa Ana, 1987—99; v.p. internal ops.

CHAMP, Inc., Santa Ana, 2000—06; dir. Champ Steel, Santa Ana, 2006—. Musician (actress): Yorba Linda Symphony Orch.; singer: So. Calif. Chamber Singers. Charter mem. Brea (Calif.) Jaycee Women, 1980; coach Spl. Olympics City of Anaheim, Calif., 1982—87; coord. Hands Across Am., Orange County, 1986; dist. dir. Region 8 Orange County Jaycees, 1987; pres. Fountain Valley (Calif.) Jaycees, 1989; mem. Men-On-A-Missions-Eastside Christian Ch.; mem. bd. dirs. Alliance/Mentally Ill, Orange County, 1988—89. Mem.: SAG, Nat. Assn. Exec. Women, Southern Calif. Chamber Singers. Avocations: acting, viola, dance, singing, opera. Office: CHAMP Inc 633 Young St Santa Ana CA 92705

**TORREZ, MICHELLE MARIE,** artist, educator; b. Denver, Feb. 3, 1956; d. John Thomas and Geri Anne Chestor; children: Gwenevieve Louise, Nicole Michelle. Assocs. Visual Comm. and Advt. Design, Art Inst. Colo., Denver, 1986. Art dir. Mentler and Co., Dallas, 1986—87, Hamilton Sweeney Advt., Denver, 1987—94; owner Studio M, Denver, 1994—98; workshop instr. Art in the Aspens, Colo., 2005—, Taos Painters Workshop, N.Mex., 2005—. Adj. instr. painting Met. State Coll. Denver, 2004—; traveling lectr. U.S. State Dept.-Art in Embassies, Sofia, Bulgaria, 2003; invited participant Coors Invitational We. Art Exhibit, 2002—05. S.W. Art Mag., one-woman shows include Michelle Torrez: One Woman Show, Metaphor - Art in Embassies Calendar, 2003, exhibitions include Colo. Gov.'s Office, 2002—05, Named to Hall of Fame, Art Inst. of Colo., 2004; recipient Colo. ALFIE award for art direction of pub. svc. comml., Denver Advt. Agy., 1991, CLEO award for art direction of pub. svc. TV comml., City of Denver, 1991; Travel grant, Christian Solidarity Internat., 2005. Mem.: Denver Art Students League (assoc.), Denver Art Mus. (assoc.), Nat. Mus. of Women in the Arts (assoc.).

**TORRICELLI, ROBERT G.,** former senator; b. Franklin Lakes, N.J., Aug. 26, 1951; BA, Rutgers U., 1974, JD, 1977; MPA, Harvard U., 1980. Bar: N.J. 1978. Dep. legis. counsel Office Gov. N.J., 1975-77; counsel to V.P. Mondale, Washington, 1978-81; pvt. practice Washington, 1981-82; mem. 98th-104th Congresses from 9th Dist. N.J., Washington, 1983-96, sci., space and tech. com., fgn. affairs com., select com. on intelligence, chmn. Western Hemisphere subcom., 1992-94; U.S. senator from N.J., 1996—2002. Mem. rules, govt. affairs, judiciary and fgn. rels. coms. Bd. govs. Rutgers U., 1977-83. Mem. ABA, N.J. Bar Assn. Democrat. Address: PO Box 229 Rosemont NJ 08556-0229

**TORRUELLA, JUAN R.,** federal judge; b. San Juan, PR, June 7, 1933; BS in Bus. and Fin., U. Pa., 1954; LLB, Boston U., 1957; LLM, U. Va., 1984; MPA, U. P.R., 1984; MSt, Oxford U., 2003; LLD (hon.), St. John's U., 1995, Roger Williams U., 1995. Judge U.S. Dist. Ct. P.R., San Juan, 1974—82, chief judge, 1982—84; judge U.S. Ct. Appeals (1st cir.), San Juan, 1984—, chief judge, 1994—2001. Former mem. jud. conf. com. Adminstrn. Fed. Magistrate Sys.; former mem. jud. conf. exec. com. Adminstrn. Fed. Magistrate Sys.; former mem. jud. conf. com. Internat. Jud. Reform. Mem.: FBA, ABA, P.R. Bar Assn., D.C. Bar Assn., Assn. Labor Rels. Practitioners P.R. and V.I. Office: John J Moakley US Courthouse 1 Courthouse Ste 2500 Boston MA 02210*

**TORSNEY, KATHLEEN M.,** psychologist, educator; d. Jerome and Joan Torsney. BS, Geogetown U., Washington, D.C.; EdM, Columbia U. Tchrs. Coll., N.Y.C., 1989; PhD Psychology, Columbia U., 2000. Cert. psychologist N.J., lic. LPC N.J. Sr. cognitive therapist Headways, Inc., Emerson, NJ, 1992—98; coord. TBI svcs. United Cerebral Palsy Assn., N.Y.C., 1998—99; program dir. Jersey City Med. Ctr., NJ; clin. assoc. Family Counseling Assocs., Kinnelon, NJ, 2001—04; asst. prof. William Paterson U., Wayne, NJ, 2000—. Dir. MA clin. and counseling psychology WPUNJ. Contbr. articles to profl. jours. Mem. DVRT Passaic County, NJ, 2004—; archtl. rev. com. Bloomingdale, NJ, 2000—04. Mem.: APA, Am. Psychol. Soc., N.J. Psychol. Assn. Avocations: art, exercise. Office Phone: 973-720-3395. Business E-Mail: torsneyk@wpunj.edu.

**TORTI, FRANK MICHAEL,** internist, health facility administrator; BA, MA, Johns Hopkins U., 1969; MPH, Harvard U., 1973, MD, 1974. Diplomate in internal medicine and med. oncology Am. Bd. Internal Medicine. Asst. prof. medicine Stanford (Calif.) U., 1979-84, clin. assoc. prof. medicine, 1984-86, assoc. prof. medicine, 1986-93; prof. medicine Wake Forest U. Sch. Medicine, Winston-Salem, NC, 1993—, dir. Comprehensive Cancer Ctr., 1993—, chmn. dept. cancer biology, 1993—. Chair N.C. Gov.'s Commn. on Cancer Coordination and Control, 1993—2003; mem. study sect. Am. Inst. for Cancer Rsch., Bethesda, Md., 1989—. Mem. Am. Assn. for Cancer Rsch., Am. Soc. Clin. Oncology, Am. Soc. Cell Biology, Internat. Soc. Interferon Rsch., Am. Fedn. for Clin. Rsch., Soc. for Biol. Therapy. Office: Wake Forest U Sch Medicine Medical Center Blvd Winston Salem NC 27157-1082 E-mail: ftorti@wfubmc.edu.

**TORTOLANI, ANTHONY JOHN,** surgeon, educator; b. Eastchester, N.Y., Oct. 15, 1943; s. Salvatore Paul and Yolanda (Vecciarelli) Tortolani; m. Beth Callahan, Dec. 15, 1967 (dec. 1993); children: Julia Sue, Paul Justin; m. Katherine Gormley, Sept. 25, 1999. BS, Fordham U., 1965; MD, George Washington Sch. Medicine, 1969. Diplomate Am. Bd. Surgery, Am. Bd. Thoracic Surgery. Chief divsn. cardiovascular & thoracic surgery North Shore U. Hosp., Manhasset, NY, 1978-90, chmn. dept. surgery, 1988-96, chmn. med. bd., 1994-96, chmn. dept. surgery Glen Cove, NY, 1990-96; John D. Mountain chair surgery North Shore U. Hosp.- Cornell U. Med. Coll., Manhasset, 1989-96, program dir. surg. residency program, 1992-96; prof. surgery Cornell U. Med. Coll., N.Y.C., 1993-97, prof. cardiothoracic surgery, 1997-99; mem. staff N.Y. Hosp., N.Y.C., 1993-97; dir., prof. cardiothoracic surgery Jack D. Weiler Hosp./Montefiore Med. Ctr. Albert Einstein Coll. of Medicine, N.Y.C., 1999-2001; prof. clin. cardiothoracic surgery Weill Med. Coll. Cornell U., 2001—. Vice chmn. N.Y. Presbyn. Cornell Cardiothoracic Surgery Network. Active Columbus Citizens Found., N.Y.C. Maj. USAF, 1974-76. Roman Catholic. Avocation: breeding arabian horses. Office: NY Presbyn Hosp 525 E 68th St Rm M-404 New York NY 10021

**TORTORELLA, JOHN,** professional hockey coach; b. Boston, Mass., June 24, 1958; Coach Va. Lancers Atlantic Coast Hockey League, 1986—88; asst. coach Buffalo Sabres, 1989—95; coach Rochester Am. Am. Hockey League, 1995—97; asst. coach Phoenix Coyotes, 1997—99, NY Rangers, 1999—2001; coach Tampa Bay Lightning, 2001—. Named Coach of Yr., Atlantic Coast Hockey League, 1986—87; recipient Jack Adams Award, NHL, 2004. Achievements include coaching Stanley Cup Championship Team, Tampa Bay Lightning, 2004. Office: Tampa Bay Lightning Hockey Club Ice Palace Arena 401 Channelside Dr Tampa FL 33602

**TORTORELLO, NICHOLAS JOHN,** public opinion and market research company executive; b. Maspeth, NY, Dec. 1, 1948; s. John Anthony and Verla Jean (Odel) T.; m. Joan Elizabeth King, Jan. 13, 1973 (div. July 2006); children: Kerry Ann, Jennifer Joan. BS in Polit. Sci. with highest honors, Williams Coll., 1971; M Religious Studies, St. Joseph's Sem., Yonkers, N.Y., 1988. V.p. Louis Harris & Assocs., N.Y.C., 1971-73; sr. v.p., 1973-79; exec. v.p. DMT Inc., N.Y.C., 1979-83; pres. Tortorello Corp., Pearl River, N.Y., 1983-85; pres. Tortorello group Market Facts Inc.-N.Y., N.Y.C., 1985-86; v.p. Total Rsch. Corp., Princeton, N.J., 1986-88; chmn. Rsch. and Forecasts Inc., N.Y.C., 1989-93; sr. v.p. Roper Starch Worldwide Inc., N.Y.C., 1993-98; pres. Guideline Consulting, N.Y.C., 1998—2002; v.p., gen. mgr. Lieberman Rsch. Worldwide Inc., 2003—04; v.p. Internat. Comms. Rsch., N.Y., 2004—06; sr. v.p. The Mktg. Workshop, Inc., 2006—. Editor, author Tortorello Trendline, 1983-85, Rsch. and Forecasts Trendline, 1989-91. Trustee Riverdale (N.Y.) Country Schs., 1982-90, v.p., 1986-89; trustee Marymount Manhattan Coll., N.Y.C., 1986-88; lectr. tchr. religion St. Anthony's Ch., Nanuet, N.Y., 1984-86; mem. CARA Bd. Georgetown U., Washington, 1992-98, rsch. adv. coun., 2000—; mem. Hosp. Chaplaincy Bd., 1991-97; v.p. Class of '71, Williams Coll., 2001. Recipient Am. Legion award for leadership, scholarship, honor and svc., 1967, Disting. Alumnus of Yr. award, Riverdale Country Sch., 1984. Mem. Am. Dirs. Inst. (trustee 1984-87), Coun. Am. Survey Rsch. Orgn. (chmn. bd. dirs. 2001, chmn. publs. com. 1991-94, chmn. pub. rels.

com. 1995-97, chmn. mktg. and comms. com. 1997-99, bd. dirs., chmn. 1999 ann. conf., chmn. bd. dirs. 1999, chmn. bd. trustees 2001, chmn. nominating com. 2002), Am. Assn. Pub. Opinion Rsch.(Counselor-AT Large, 2004-05), Williams Club. Democrat. Avocations: collecting Lionel trains, collecting stereo equipment, golf, collecting american coins. Office: Internat Comms Rsch 60 East 42nd St New York NY 10165 E-mail: njtortorello@yahoo.com.

**TORUÑO-HAENSLY, RHINA M.,** literature educator, researcher, writer; b. San Salvador, El Salvador; came to U.S., 1981; d. Juan Felipe and Juana (Contreras) Toruño; m. Henriquez Trujillo, Nov. 4, 1967 (div.); children: Mario Felipe, José Rodrigo; m. Hector-Neri Castañeda (dec.); m. Paul Haensly, June 25, 2005. Grad., Santa Ines Coll., Nueva San Salvador, El Salvador, 1961; BA in Philosophy, Nat. U. El Salvador, 1971; MA in Philosophy, Cath. U. Louvain, Belgium, 1973, PhD in French Contemporary Philosophy, 1978; MA in Hispanic and Latin Am. Lit., Nat. U. Paris/Sorbonne, 1976; PhD in Latin Am. Lit., Ind. U., Bloomington, 1994. Tchr. asst. Nat. U. El Salvador, San Salvador, 1968-71; prof. philosophy, 1976-81; vis. scholar Sch. Edn. Stanford U., Palo Alto, Calif., 1981-82; vis. asst. prof. Fla. State U., 94-95; asst. prof. U. Tex. of the Permian Basin, Odessa, 1995-97, assoc. prof. 1997-00, prof., 01—, Kathlyn Cosper Dunagan prof. humanities, Spanish area coord., 1997—; grad. head, 2004—. Cons. for edn. com. Mexican-Am. Network of Odessa, 1997—. Author: Time, Destiny and Oppression on the Work of Elena Garro, 1996, 2d edit., 1998, Encounter with Memory: Elena Garro Recounts Her Story, 2004; co-editor: Juan Felipe Toruno in Two Worlds: Critical Analysis of his Works, 2006; assoc. editor Chiricu, 1985-90, Third Woman, 1986-87; contbr. articles to profl. jours. Recipient Ednl. Rscha. award, Pan Am. Round Tablc, Odessa, Tex., 1996, Internat. Prize Emmanuel Mounier, French Assn. of Friends of Emmanuel Mounier, Paris, 1974, Damas de Oro, Odessa, Tex., 2000; grantee U Tex., Odessa, 2000, 02, 03; fellow Internat. Fedn. Univ. Women, Geneva, 1981-83. Mem. Soc. des Amis d'Emmanuel Mounier, Fedn. Internat. des Femmes Deplomées de Univs. Internat., Salvadoran Acad. Scis. (1st female mem.), Salvadoran Acad. Lang. (Royal Acad. of Spain br.), Pan Am. Round Table, Spanish Book Club (pres. 1996—), Hispanic C. of C. Democrat. Roman Catholic. Avocations: reading short stories for children, aerobics, gardening, travel. Office: Univ Tex Permian Basin 4901 E University Blvd Odessa TX 79762-0001 Office Phone: 432-552-2308. Business E-Mail: toruno_r@utpb.edu.

**TORVALDS, LINUS BENEDICT,** application developer; b. Helsinki, Finland, Dec. 28, 1969; s. Nils and Anna Torvalds; m. Tove Torvalds; children: Patricia Miranda, Daniela Yolanda, Celeste Amanda. MS in Computer Sci., Helsinki U., 1996. Developer Transmeta Corp., Santa Clara, Calif., 1997—2003; fellow Open Source Develop. Labs (OSDL), Beaverton, Oreg., 2003—. Co-author (with David Diamond): (autobiography) Just for Fun: The Story of an Accidental Revolutionary, 2001. Named One of the Most Influential People in the World, TIME mag., 2004; recipient Nokia Found. Award, 1997, Lifetime Achievement Award, Uniforum, 1997, Takeda award, 2001. Achievements include invention of Linux operating system. Office: OSDL 12725 SW Millikan Way, Ste 400 Beaverton OR 97005*

**TOSCAN, RICHARD ERIC,** dean, theater educator; b. N.Y.C., July 1, 1941; s. Vincent E. and Stella (Werner) T.; m. Sharon Walker, Dec. 22, 1979. BA, Purdue U., 1963; MA, U. Ill., 1965, PhD, 1970. Postdoctoral teaching resident NEH, 1967-69; dir. Exptl. Coll. Calif. State U., Fresno, 1968-70; asst. chair div. drama U. So. Calif., L.A., 1970-76, assoc. dean sch. performing arts, 1976-79, assoc. prof. div. of drama, 1979-86, assoc. dean ch. of cinema, 1986-90, dean sch. of theatre, 1990-92; dean sch. fine and performing arts Portland (Oreg.) State U., 1992—96; dean sch. arts Va. Commonwealth U.: Sch. of Arts, Richmond, Va., 1996—. Adv. bd. Internat. Contemporary Art Fair, L.A., 1989-91, Tygres Heart Shakespeare Co., Portland, 1992—, Portland Ctr. Performing Arts, 1992—, Image Theatre Mask Ensemble, 1994—; mem. theatre panel Cultural Affairs Dept., L.A., 1990-92; mem. selection com. Javits fellows U.S. Dept. Edn., Washington, 1990-2004. Author numerous stage plays, articles to profl. jours.; producer Radio Drama Series, 1981 (nominee Armstrong award 1982). Woodrow Wilson Found. fellow, 1963-64, U. Ill. fellow, 1964. Internat. Coun. Fine Arts Deans (pres. elect). Office: Virginia Commonwealth University School of Arts 325 North Harrison St Richmond VA 23284 E-mail: rtoscan@vcu.edu.

**TOSCANO, JAMES VINCENT,** medical foundation administrator; b. Passaic, NJ, Aug. 8, 1937; s. William V. and Mary A. (DeNigris) T.; m. Sharon Lee Bowers; children: Shawn Truelson, Lauren Bjorklund, David Brendan, Dania Toscano Miwa. AB summa cum laude, Rutgers U., 1959; MA, Yale U., 1960. Lectr. Wharton Sch., U Pa., 1961-64; chief opinion analyst Pa. Opinion Poll, 1962-64; mng. dir. World Press Inst., St. Paul, 1964-68, exec. dir., 1968-72; dir. devel. Macalester Coll., St. Paul, 1972-74; v.p. resource devel. and pub. affairs Mpls. Soc. Fine Arts, 1974-79; pres. Minn. Mus. Art, 1979-81; exec. v.p. Park Nicollet Inst., 1981—2006; corp. sec. Park Nicollet Clinic, 1983-86; sr. v.p. Am. Med. Ctrs., Inc., 1985-87; pres. Mpls. (Minn.) Heart Inst. Found., 2006—. Adj. prof. sch. of mgmt. U. St. Thomas, 1989-01; co-chair prin. practices nonprofit excellence com. MCN, 1994-98, 2004—05; lectr. Grad. Sch. Mgmt., Hamline U., 2003—. Author: The Chief Elected Official in the Penjerdel Region, 1964; co-author, co-editor: The Integration of Political Communities, 1964. Bd. dirs., exec. sec.-treas. World Press Ins., 1972—; bd. dirs., chmn. Southside Newspaper Mpls., 1975-79; chmn. com. to improve student behavior St. Paul Pub. Schs., 1977-79; bd. dirs. Planned Parenthood St. Paul, 1965-72, Mpls. Action Agy., 1976-79; emeritus dir. Help Enable Alcoholics Receive Treatment; mem. St. Paul Heritage Preservation Commn., 1979-82, vice chmn., 1981; mem. Citizens Adv. Com. on Cable Comm.; bd. dirs. Citizens League, 1980, African-Am. Culture Ctr., 1979 82, Am. Composers Forum, 1981 83, St. Paul Chamber Oren., 1976 80, 83-89, United Theol. Sem., 1985-88; dir. emeritus Minn. Citizens for the Arts; mem. exec. com., chmn. Med. Alley Assn., 1986-96, bd. dirs., 1986-96, task force on tech. assessment Med. Alley, 1992-93; mem. health affairs adv. com. Acad. Health Ctr. U. Minn., 1988-95; bd. dirs. Mother Cabrini House, 1985-92, Minn. Civil Justice Coalition, 1987-91, also chmn.; Minn. Gov.'s Task Force on Health Care Promotion, 1985-86, mem. Gov.'s Com. Promotion Health Care Resources, 1986-87; chmn. bd. Minn. Fin. Counseling Svcs., Inc., 1990-93; mem. task force cost effectiveness Med. Alley, 1994-95; bd. dirs. Meml. Blood Bank, 1995-2001, mem. exec. com., 1996-2001; bd. dirs. Bakken Mus., 1987-2003, Stevens Sq. Cmty. Orgn., 1997-99; bd. dirs. Rainbow Rsch., Inc., 2002—, chmn. bd., 2004—; bd. dirs. Friends of the St. Paul Libr., 2004—; bd. dirs., treas. Pub. Arts St. Paul, 2004—, Minn. Charities Rev. Coun., 2004—; Woodrow Wilson Nat. fellow, 1960. Mem. Minn. Newspaper Found. (bd. dirs. 1987-92), Minn. Coun. Nonprofits (bd. dirs. 1989-95, 97-2003, bd. mem. Vocal Essence 1993-96, alt. Minn. Healthcare Commn., 1993-95, mem. Minn. Healthcare Commn., 1995-97, chair task force on med. edn. and rsch. costs 1994-96; mem. com. on med. rsch. and edn. costs, 1996-2003, chair Minn. Gov.'s Com. on 1993-97; pres. 2000-03, bd. dirs. Summit Ave Residential Preservation Assn., 2000-06, co-chair West Summit Neighborhood Assn. 2004-06), Skylight Club, Informal Club, Mpls. Club. Address: 1982 Summit Ave Saint Paul MN 55105-1460 Office: 920 E 28th St Ste 100 Minneapolis MN 55407 Office Phone: 612-863-3978. Personal E-mail: jvt2@comcast.net. Business E-Mail: jtoscano@mhif.org.

**TOSÉ, MAURICE B.,** communications executive; b. Fort Bragg, NC, 1957; married; 6 children. BS in Ops. Analysis, US Naval Acad., 1978. Commd. ensign advanced to lt. USN; damage control asst. USS Bagley; ops. officer USS Mauna Kea; instr. US Naval Acad.; comdr. Naval Reserves; with US Sec. Def.; ret.; dir., dept. def. programs Techmatics, Inc., Silver Spring, Md.; founder, chmn., CEO, pres. Telecommn. Sys. Inc., Indpls., 1987—. Mem. Wireless Data Forum, AT&T Diversity Roundtable, Internat. Engring. Consortium, Intelligent Network Forum. Mem. Annapolis Jaycees, Annapolis Kiwanis; dir. First Night Annapolis, Ginger Cove Retirement Cmty.; treas., v.p., dir. Arudel on the Bay Homeowners Assn.; mem. Budget & Fin. Coun, Antioch Apostolic Ch., Annapolis Neck Small Area Planning Commn.; co-founder, chmn. bd. US Naval Acad. Samuel P. Massie Edn. Endowment.

Recipient Granville T. Woods award for Outstanding Achievement, Nat. Assn. of Black Telecommunications Profls., AT&T Spectrum award for Innovators. Office: Telecomm Sys Inc 275 West St Annapolis MD 21401

**TOSHACH, CLARICE OVERSBY,** real estate developer, retired computer company executive; b. Firbank, Westmoreland, Eng., Nov. 21, 1928; came to U.S., 1955; d. Oliver and Nora (Brown) Oversby; m. Daniel Wilkie Toshach, July 30, 1965 (dec. Aug. 1992); 1 child, Duncan Oversby Toshach; 1 child from previous marriage, Paul Anthony Beard. Textile designer Storeys of Lancaster, Eng., 1949-55; owner, operator Broadway Lane, Saginaw, Mich., 1956-70; pres., owner Clarissa Jane Inc., Saginaw, 1962-70, Over-Tosh Computers, Inc. dba Computerland, Saginaw and Flint, Mich., 1983-95; mgr., ptnr. Mich. Comml. Devel. L.L.C., Saginaw, 1995—. Trustee Saginaw Gen. Hosp., 1977-83, Home for the Aged, 1978-80; bd. dirs. Vis. Nurse Assn., pres., 1981-83; bd. dirs. Hospice of Saginaw, Inc., v.p., 1981-83; mem. long range planning com. United Way of Saginaw, 1982-83; cmty. advisor Jr. League of Saginaw, 1982-83; pres. Saginaw Gen. Hosp. Aux., 1972-82, pres., 1976-77.

**TOSHCHAKOV, VLADIMIR YUREVICH,** biochemist; b. Kostroma, Russia, June 20, 1960; s. Yuriy Alexandrovich and Getta Fyodorovna (Sidorova) T.; m. Yelena Petrovna Smirnova, June 5, 1981; 1 child, Stepan. Degree, 2d Moscow Med. Inst., 1983; PhD, Inst. Transplantation, Moscow, 1990. Jr. rschr. Inst. Transplantation & Artificial Organs, Moscow, 1983-89, sr. rschr., 1989—. Contbr. chpts. to books; 1994; inventor in field. Grantee Internat. Sci. Found., 1993, Russian Found. Basic Rsch., 1996-98. Home: Ul Shcherbakovskaya 58-A 62 105187 Moscow Russia Office: Inst Transplantation Ul Shchukinskaya 1 123182 Moscow Russia

**TOSKES, PHILLIP PAUL,** gastroenterologist, educator, researcher; b. Balt., Jan. 4, 1940; s. John F. and Mary R. (Vonelli) T.; m. Patricia A. Sponsel, June 3, 1961; children: Tammy Lynn Price, Tracey Lynn, Steven D. BA, Johns Hopkins U., 1961; MD, U. Md., 1965. Diplomate Am. Bd. Internal Medicine (bd. dirs.), Am. Bd. Gastroenterology. Intern, resident U. Md. Hosp., Balt., 1965-68; fellow in gastroenterology Hosp. U. Pa., Phila., 1968-70; asst. prof. medicine U. Fla., Gainesville, 1973-75, assoc. prof. medicine, 1975-78, prof. medicine, 1978—, dir. divsn. gastro, hepatology, 1978-97, prof., chmn. dept. medicine, 1997—2002. Chief gastro sect. Gainesville VA Med. Ctr., 1973-92; chmn. Nat. Digestive Disease Adv. Bd., Washington, 1992-94. Author chpts. to books. Maj. U.S. Army, 1970-73. Recipient Disting. Achievement award Can. Gastroenterol. Assn., 1982. Fellow ACP (Meade Johnson scholar 1966-68); mem. Am. Soc. Clin. Investigation, Am. Fedn. Clin. Rsch., Am. Gastroenterol. Assn. (pres. 1997-98). Avocations: travel, swimming, boating. Home: 202 NW 114th Way Gainesville FL 32607-1122 Office: U Fla Box 100214 1600 SW Archer Rd Gainesville FL 32610-3001 Office Phone: 352-392-2877. Business E-Mail: toskepp@medicine.ufl.edu.

**TOSTE, ANTHONY PAIM,** chemistry educator, researcher; b. Mountain View, Calif., June 26, 1948; BS in Chemistry with honors, Santa Clara (Calif.) U., 1970; PhD in Biochemistry and Chemistry, U. Calif., Berkeley, 1976. Rsch. fellow Cardiovasc. Rsch. Inst., San Francisco, 1977—79; rsch. scientist Battelle Meml. Inst. Pacific N.W. Nat. Lab., Richland, Wash., 1980—88; asst. prof. Mo. State U., Springfield, 1988—94, assoc. prof., 1994—99, prof., 1999—. Cons. Mitsubishi Metal Corp., Tokyo, 1984-87, Dow Chem., Tex., 1994-96; presenter in field. Contbr. articles to jours. in field, cmty. svc. presentations. Bd. dirs. Mid Columbia Arts Coun., Richland, 1987-88, Bot. Soc. S.W. Mo., Springfield, 1997-2002; pres. bd. dirs. Springfield Sister Cities Assn., 1993-96; co-founder, leader Internat. Friendship Dels. to Japan, 1996, 99, 2001, 03, 05. Rsch., equipment grantee NSF, 1990; recipient Diverse Cmty. award Sister Cities Internat., Boston, 1996, STA Rsch. fellow, Japan, 1998 Mem. Am. Chem. Soc. (treas. Ozark sect. 1989-91, chmn.-elect 2000, chmn. 2000-01), Am. Nuc. Soc. (Best Poster award 1987), Assn. Ofcl. Analytical Chemists (program chair 1986, 90), Mo. Acad. Sci. (program chair 1997, 2002). Avocations: picture framing, collecting fine art, woodworking, reading, cinema. Home: 2113 E Woodhaven Pl Springfield MO 65804-6767 Office: Mo State U Dept Chemistry 901 S National Ave Springfield MO 65804 Office Phone: 417-836-5150. Business E-Mail: anthonytoste@issouristate.edu.

**TOSTESON, DANIEL CHARLES,** physiologist, medical school dean emeritus; b. Milw., Feb. 5, 1925; s. Alexis H. and Dilys (Bodycombe) T.; m. Penelope Kinsley, Dec. 17, 1949 (div. 1969); children: Carrie Marias, Heather Tosteson, Tor, Zoe Losada; m. Magdalena Tieffenberg, July 8, 1969; children: Joshua, Ingrid. Student, Harvard U., 1942-44, MD, 1949; DSc (hon.), U. Copenhagen, 1979; Dr. hon. causa, U. Liege, 1983; DSc (hon.), Med. Coll. Wis., 1984, NYU, 1992; DHL (hon.), Johns Hopkins U., 1993; Dr. honoris causa, Cath. U. Louvain, 1996, Duke U., 1996, Emory U., 1996; DMed (hon.), Ludwig Maximilians U., 2002. Fellow physiology Harvard Med. Sch., 1947-48; intern, then asst. resident medicine Presbyn. Hosp., N.Y.C., 1949-51; research fellow medicine Brookhaven Nat. Lab., 1951-53; lab. kidney and electrolyte metabolism Nat. Heart Inst., 1953-55, 57, research fellow biol. isotope research lab. Copenhagen, 1955-56; research fellow Physiol. Lab., Cambridge, Eng., 1956-57; assoc. prof. physiology Washington U. Sch. Medicine, St. Louis, 1958-61; prof., chmn. dept. physiology and pharmacology Duke U. Sch. Medicine, 1961-75, James B. Duke Distinguished prof., 1971-75; dean div. biol. scis., dean Pritzker Sch. Medicine U. Chgo., Lowell T. Coggleshall prof. med. scis., v.p. for Med. Center, 1975-77; dean, Caroline Shields Walker prof. cell biology Harvard Med. Sch., Boston, 1977-97, dean emeritus, Caroline Shields Walker prof., 1997—, pres. Med. Ctr., 1977-97. Mem. molecular biology panel NSF, 1959-62; cons. sci. rev. com. NIH, 1964-67, nat. adv. gen. med. scis. coun., 1982-86; mem. U.S. Office Tech. Assessment, 1976; ethics adv. bd. HEW, 1977-80; nat. adv. gen. med. scis. coun. NIH, 1982—; mem. governing bd. NRC, 1977; mem. sci. com. Found. pour l'Etude du Systeme Nerveux Central et Peripherique, 1982—; nat. adv. com. biomed. scis. PEW Scholars Program, 1984-87. Recipient Harvard medal, 2002. Mem. Inst. Medicine NAS (coun. 1975-78, adv. bd. PEW scholars program 1984-85), AAAS, Acad. Arts and Scis. (pres. 1997-00), Am. Physiol. Soc. (council 1967-75, pres. 1973-74), Soc. Gen. Physiologists (pres. 1968-69), Biophys. Soc. (council 1970-73), Assn. Am. Med. Colls. (chmn. coun. acad. socs. 1970-76, chmn. assembly 1973-74, chmn. physician supply task force 1988-90, Abraham Flexner award 1991), Assn. Am. Physicians, Am. Acad. Arts and Scis. (pres. 1997-2000), Red Cell Club, Soc. Health and Human Values, Danish Royal Soc. (fellow), Alpha Omega Alpha. Achievements include spl. research cellular transport processes, red cell membranes. Office: Harvard Med Sch TMEC Rm 147 260 Longwood Ave Boston MA 02115-5701

**TOSUN, ALI SAMAN,** science educator; s. Asaf and Nebahat Tosun. BS, Bilkent U., Ankara, Turkey, 1991—95; MS, Ohio State U., Columbus, 1997—98, PhD, 1998—2003. Asst. prof. U. Tex., San Antonio, 2003—. Mem.: ACM, IEEE. Office Fax: 210-458-4437. Business E-Mail: tosun@cs.utsa.edu.

**TOTAKURA, SATYANARAYANA RAJU,** secondary school educator; b. Andhra Pradesh, India, Apr. 10, 1937; s. Narasimha Raju and Suramma Totakura; m. Sarada Totakura, June 22, 1961; children: Usharani, Srinivasa Raju, Raghurama Raju. BSc, W.G.B. Coll., 1959; BEd, M.R. Coll., 1961; MSc, Banaras Hindu U., 1969; MEd, Andhra U., 1985; PhD, World U., 1987. Vis. prof. of math. Telugu Assn. of North Am., New York, 1993—98; math tchr. Bd. of Edn., Flushing, NY, 1996—; lectr. in math. DNR Coll., 1979-93. Pres. Inst. of Vedic Math., Detroit, 1993—96, Inst. of Vedic Math. Edn. Found., New York, 1997—. Author: (book) Vedic Mathematics, 1995, Fingers Calculator, 1995, Recreational Mathematics, 1995, Vedaganitam, 1980, Mathematical Shortcuts, 1988, Wonders with Numbers, 1989. Recipient Kannadakoota award, Kannadakoota N.Y., 1996, TLC award, Telugu Lit. and Culture Assn., 1996, TTD grant, Tirumal Tirupati Devastanam, 1987, Tana Excellence in Sci. award. Mem.: Indian Sci. Congress. Achievements include invented and re-invented novel techniques that a student of mathematics may follow without any difficulty to not only learn but also master mathematics;

disseminated his techniques of learning mathematics through TV programs, radio lectures, lectures, seminars and workshops throughout India and U.S.A. Home: 43-32 Kissena Blvd 10-S Flushing NY 11355 Personal E-Mail: srajutotakura@hotmail.com.

**TOTARO, SAMUEL C., JR.,** lawyer; b. Trenton, N.J., July 5, 1947; s. Samuel C. Sr. and Philomena (Marano) T.; m. Andrea Jean Chromchak, Mar. 11, 1978; children: Juliana, Christopher. BS, Ursinus Coll., 1969; JD, U. Memphis, 1974. Bar: Pa. 1975, U.S. Dist. Ct. (ea. dist.) Pa. 1977, U.S. Tax Ct. 1980. Law clk. Hon. Kendall Shoyer, Phila., 1975-79; assoc. Lewis & Sutton, Trevose, Pa., 1979-81; pvt. practice Feasterville, Pa., 1981-84; ptnr. Factor, McCabe, Weisberg & Totaro, Feasterville, 1984-87, Factor, Smolow & Totaro, Trevose, 1987-89, Kellis & Totaro, Bensalem, Pa., 1989—2001, Groen, Lamm, Goldberg & Rubenmstone, LLC, 2001—03, Lamm, Ruben-stine, Totoro & David, LLC, 2003—. Dir. Nat. Coun. for Adoption, Washington, 1990-93. Chmn. 78th Legis. Dist., Bucks County, Pa., 1983; pres. Family of God Luth. Ch., Buckingham, Pa., 1992; advisor Nat. Conf. Commrs. on Uniform State Laws, Chgo., 1990—; candidate for Pa. Senate, 1990. Mem. ABA, Bucks County Bar Assn. (dir. 1990-91), Am. Acad. Adoption Attys. (dir. 1994—, pres. 1996-97), Rotary (pres. 1984-86, 2001-02). Republican. Avocations: reading, bike riding, tennis. Home: 830 Macclesfield Rd Furlong PA 18925-1411 Office: 3600 Horizon Blvd Trevose PA 19053 Office Phone: 215-638-9330. Business E-Mail: stotaro@lrtd.com.

**TOTENBERG, NINA,** journalist; b. NYC, Jan. 14, 1944; d. Roman and Melanie (Shroder) T.; m. Floyd Haskell, Feb. 3, 1979 (dec.); m. H. David Reines, 2000. Student, Boston U.; LLD (hon.), Haverford Coll.; LLD, Mt. Holyoke Coll.; LLD (hon.), Chatham Coll., Gonzaga U., Northeastern U., Mt. Holyoke Coll., St. Mary's, SUNY; LHD, Lebanon Valley Coll.; Westfield State Coll., Pa. State U., Pine Manor Coll., De Paul U., Simmons Coll. Reporter Boston Record Am., 1965, Peabody Times, 1967, Nat. Observer, 1968-71, Newtimes, 1973, Nat. Pub. Radio, Washington, 1974—, Inside Washington, 1992—; reporter Nightline ABC, 1993-98. Contbr. articles to N.Y. Times Mag., Harvard Law Rev., Christian Sci. Monitor, N.Y. Mag., Parade. Recipient Sidney Hillman award, 1983, Alfred I. Dupont award Columbia U., 1988, 91, George Foster Peabody award, 1991, George Polk award, 1991, Joan Barone award, 1991, Silver Gavel award ABA, 1968-98, Woman of Courage award Women in Film, 1991, Athena award, 1994, Presdl. Commendation, Radcliffe Coll., 1998, Ohio U. Carr van Anda award Outstanding Journalists, 2005; named outstanding broadcast journalist of yr. Nat. Press Found., 1999. Mem. Sigma Delta Chi (award 1991). Office: NPR 635 Massachusetts Ave NW Washington DC 20001-3740

**TOTH, BRIAN M.,** social studies educator; s. Joseph S. Toth and Kathy S. Wilkins; m. Kristin M. Toth, Nov. 27, 1999. BA, Mich. State U., East Lansing, 1997; MA, U. Mich., Ann Arbor, 1999. Tchr. East Mid. Sch., Farmington Hills, Mich., 1999—. Coach varsity boys basketball Harrison H.S., Farmington Hills, Mich., 2003—. Mem.: Nat. Coun. Social Studies. Address: 25000 Middlebelt Rd Farmington MI 48336-1345 Office Phone: 248-426-2756.

**TOTH, BRUCE A.,** lawyer; b. Toledo, Feb. 14, 1953; s. Louis W. and Marianne (Tschann) T.; m. Christina Maria Schwarz, Aug. 28, 1976. BS, Ga. Inst. Tech., 1976; MBA, JD, Stanford U., 1980. Bar: Ill., 1981. V.p. Prescott, Ball & Turben, Cleve., 1980-82; assoc. Winston & Strawn, Chgo., 1982-87, ptnr., 1987—; mem. exec. com. Republican. Office: Winston & Strawn 35 W Wacker Dr 45th Fl Chicago IL 60601-1695 Office Fax: 312-558-5700. E-mail: btoth@winston.com.

**TÓTH, PETER PAUL,** physician, researcher; b. Torrington, Conn., May 5, 1959; s. John and Ilona Barbara (Bereczky) T.; m. Karen Faye Ireland, June 3, 1989. AB, Princeton U., 1981; PhD, Mich. State U., 1988; MD, Wayne State U., 1992. Cert. Am. Bd. Family Practice, Am. Bd. of Clin. Lipidology. Resident U. Iowa; dir. preventive cardiology Sterling Rock Falls Clinic, Ltd.; chief of medicine CGH Med. Ctr. Clin. assoc. prof. U. Ill. Coll. Medicine, Peoria, So. Ill. U. Sch. Medicine, Springfield; bd. dirs. Midwest Cardiovascular Rsch. Found. Co-author: (textbooks) Handbook of Family Practice, 1997, Comprehensive Management of High Risk Cardiovascular Patients, 2006, Therapeutic Lipidology, 2007; editor-in-chief: Jour. Applied Rsch. Clin. and Exptl. Therapeutics; co-contbr. articles to Pediatrics Jour., Jour. Pediatrics Surgery, Jour. Biol. Chemistry, Arch. Biochem. Biophysics, Comp. Biochem. Physiol., Methods Enzymol., Nutrition, Circulation, Current Opinion in Cardiology, Am. Jour. Cardiology, Current Opinion in Lipidology, Family Practice Recertification, Clin. Therapeutics; sect. editor: Current Atherosclerosis Reports; mem. editl. bd. Future Lipidology, MosbyGenRx. Recipient Searle-Donald F. Richardson Meml. Prize, Am. Coll. Ob-Gyn. Fellow: Am. Coll. Chest Physicians, Am. Coll. Cardiology, Am. Heart Assn., Internat. Coll. Angiology, Am. Acad. Family Physicians; mem.: AMA, AAAS, Midwest Cardiovascular Rsch. Found. (bd. dirs.), Nat. Lipid Assn. (bd. dirs.), Sigma Xi, Alpha Omega Alpha. Roman Catholic. Achievements include research in mitochondrial respiration, carnitine metabolism, enzymology, spectroscopy, lipidology, heart disease prevention. Home: 17719 Grandview Dr Sterling IL 61081-8564 Office: Sterling Rock Falls Clinic 101 E Miller Rd Sterling IL 61081 Business E-Mail: peter.toth@srfc.com.

**TOTH, ROBERT CHARLES,** retired journalist; b. Blakely, Pa., Dec. 24, 1928; s. John and Tillie (Szuch) T.; m. Paula Goldberg, Apr. 12, 1954; children: Jessica, Jennifer, John. BS in Chem. Engring., Washington U., St. Louis, 1952; MS in Journalism, Columbia U., 1955; postgrad., Harvard U., 1960-61. Started as engr. in Army Ordnance Dept., 1952—54; reporter Providence Jour., 1955—57; sci. reporter N.Y. Herald Tribune, 1957—62, N.Y. Times, 1962—63; mem. staff Los Angeles Times, 1963—93, bur. chief London, 1965—70, diplomatic corr., 1970—71, White House corr. Washington, 1972—74, bur. chief Moscow, 1974—77, nat. security corr. Washington bur., 1977—93; ret. Cons. opinion poll in U.S. and abroad by Times Mirror Ctr. (now Pew Rsch. Ctr.) for People and Press, 1990, sr. assoc., 1993-98. Co-author: The Dimishing Divide, Religion's Changing Role in American Politics, 2000. Served with USMC, 1946-48. Recipient Overseas Press Club award, 1977, Sigma Delta Chi award, 1977, George Polk award in Journalism for fgn. reporting L.I. U., 1978, Columbia U. Alumni award, 1978, Wienthal award Fgn. Service Inst., Georgetown U., 1986, Edwin N. Hood award Nat. Press Club, 1986; Pulitzer Travelling scholar, 1955; Nieman fellow Harvard U., 1960-61 Mem. Coun. on Fgn. Rels. Home: 21 Primrose St Chevy Chase MD 20815-4228 E-mail: tothrc@aol.com.

**TOTLIS, GUST JOHN,** retired title insurance company executive; b. Highwood, Ill., May 15, 1939; s. John Chris and Agape (Galelis) T.; m. Joyce Elaine Edholm, June 5, 1960; children: Kenneth Chris, Charles Gust. BA, Lake Forest Coll., 1962; MBA, U. Chgo., 1964. Fin. planning mgr. Gen. Foods Corp., Battle Creek, Mich., 1964-68; fin. analyst Irving Trust Co., N.Y.C., 1968-69, asst. sec., 1969-71, asst. v.p., 1971-72, v.p. 1972-75; corp. contr. Irving Bank Corp., N.Y.C., 1975-82; exec. v.p., CFO Fidelity Union Bancorp, Newark, 1982-85, Star Banc Corp (formerly First Nat. Cin. Corp.), Cin., 1985-93; sr. v.p., CFO Chgo. Title and Trust Co., 1993-99; sr. ptnr. Dorian Properties, LLC, 2004—. Bd. dirs. Ticor Title Ins. Co., Security Union Title Ins. Co., Chgo. Tech. Corp., Credit Data Reporting Svcs., Inc., Market Intelligence, Inc., Nat. Flood Info. Svcs., Inc.; chmn. gov. bd. Ill. Coun. Econ. Edn., 1997-99. Adv. bd. dirs., treas. Salvation Army, Cin., 1987-93; bd. dirs., pres. Cin. Chamber Orch., 1988-93; pres. May Festival Assn., 1988-93; v.p. Spl. Olympics, 1990-93; vice chmn. United Way, 1991-94; bd. trustees Cin. Inst. Fine Arts, 1991-93. Mem. Fin. Execs. Inst., Univ. club, Kenwood Country Club, Univ. Club Chgo. Presbyterian.

**TOTTEN, GEORGE OAKLEY III,** political science professor; b. Washington, July 21, 1922; s. George Oakley Totten Jr. and Vicken (von Post) Börjesson Totten Barrois; m. Astrid Maria Anderson, June 26, 1948 (dec. Apr. 26, 1975); children: Vicken Yuriko, Linnea Catherine; m. Lilia Huiying Li, July 1, 1976 (dec. Nov. 7, 2004); 1 child, Blanche Maluk Lemes. Cert., U. Mich., 1943; AB, Columbia U., 1946, AM, 1949; MA, Yale U., 1950, PhD,

1954; docentur i japanologi, Stockholm U., 1977. Lectr. Columbia U., N.Y.C., 1954-55; rsch. assoc. Fletcher Sch. Law and Diplomacy Harvard U. and Tufts U., Mass., 1956—58; asst. prof. MIT, Cambridge, 1958-59, Boston U., 1959-61; assoc. prof. U. R.I., Kingston, 1961-64, Mich. State U., 1964—65; assoc. prof. polit. sci. U. So. Calif., L.A., 1965-68, prof., 1968-92, chmn. dept., 1980-86, prof. emeritus, 1992—96, disting. prof. emeritus, 1996—. Dir., founder Calif. Pvt. Univs. and Colls. Yr.-in-Japan program Weseda U., 1967-73; 1st nonlinguistics dir. East Asian Studies Ctr., 1974-77; 1st non-linguistics dir. USC-UCLA Joint East Asian Studies Ctr., 1976-77; 1st affiliated scholar Ctr. for Multiethnic and Transnat. Studies, 1993-98; chair USC Korea Project, 1998—; vis. prof. U. Stockholm, 1977-79, 1st dir. Ctr. Pacific Asia Studies, 1986-89, sr. counselor bd. dirs., 1989—; hon. pres. Huaxiu Pvt. Sch., Anyang City, Henan Province, China, 1999—; vis. prof. Ctr. for Japanese Studies, U. Hawaii, Manoa, 1992-93. Author: The Social Democratic Movement in Prewar Japan, 1966, Chinese edit., 1987, Korean edit., 1997, internet edit., 2005; co-author: Socialist Parties in Postwar Japan, 1966, Japan and the New Ocean Regime, 1984, Japan in the World, the World in Japan, Fifty Years of Japanese Studies at Michigan, 2001; editor: Democracy in Prewar Japan: Groundwork or Facade?, 1965, Helen Foster Snow's Song of Ariran, 1973, Korean edit., 1991, Korean 2d edit., 2005, Chinese edit., 1993, Kim Dae-jung's A New Beginning, 1996, Lee Hee-ho's (Mrs. KimDae-Jung's) Praying for Tomorrow: Letters to My Husband in Prison, 1999; author, co-editor: Developing Nations: Quest for a Model, 1970, Japanese edit., 1975, The Whaling Issue in U.S.-Japan Relations, 1978, China's Economic Reform: Administering the Introduction of the Market Mechanism, 1992, Community in Crisis: The Korean American Community After the Los Angeles Civil Unrest of April 1992, 1994, Korean edit., 2003, Mini Topical Chinese-English Dictionary, 2005, co-trans.: Ch'ien Mu's Traditional Government in Imperial China, 1982, 1st paperback edit., 2000; contbr. Sources of the Japanese Tradition, 1958, Aspects of Social Change in Modern Japan, 1967, Japan in Crisis: Essays on Taishō Democracy, 1974, The Politics of Divided Nations, 1991, Chinese edit., 1995, Japanese edit., 1997, mem. editl. bd. Acta Koreana, 1997—2003. Mem. coun. China Soc. for People's Friendship Studies, Beijing, 1991—; mem. nat. adv. com. Korean Polit. Studies in N.Am., 1992—, v.p., 1996—98; advisor Chinese Am. Alliance for China's Peaceful Reunification, 2002—; mem. nat. adv. com. Japan Am. Student Conf., 1984—2005; v.p. Lilia Li's China Seminar, 1985—2004; mem. U.S.-China People's Friendship Assn., Washington, 1974—, Com. on U.S.-China Rels., N.Y.C., 1975—; chmn. L.A.-Pusan Sister City Assn., L.A., 1976—77; founding mem. L.A.-Guangzhou Sister City Assn., 1981, bd. dirs., 1990—; mem. World Feds., 1982—2004, Citizens for Global Solutions, 2004—; bd. dirs. Assn. for Study of Korean Culture and Identity, 1999—2000. 1st lt. AUS, 1942—46, PTO. Recipient plaque for program on Korean studies, Consulate Gen. of Republic of Korea, 1974, Philippine Liberation medal, 1994; fellow Social Sci. Rch. Coun., 1952—53; grantee Ford Found., 1955—58, NSF, 1979—81, Korea Found., 1993, Rebuild L.A., 1993. Mem.: U. So. Calif. Faculty Ctr., European Assn. Japanese Studies, Japan-Am. Soc. Calif. (bd. dirs. 1990—94), Japanese Polit. Sci. Assn., Internat. Studies Assn., Internat. Polit. Sci. Assn., Asia Soc., Am. Polit. Sci. Assn., Assn. Asian Studies, Swedish Club of L.A., Phi Beta Delta (founding mem. Beta Kappa chpt. 1993—). Episcopalian. Home: 5129 Village Green Ct 17 Los Angeles CA 90016-5205 Office: USC Korea Project Dept Polit Sci VKC 327 Los Angeles CA 90089-0044 Office Phone: 323-296-3963. Business E-Mail: totten@usc.edu.

**TOTTEN, RANDOLPH FOWLER,** lawyer; b. Washington, June 20, 1943; s. Arthur Irving and Margaret Holland (Ross) Totten; m. Virginia Hunton, July 31, 1965; children: Louise, Fitz, Caroline. BA, Yale U., 1965; LLB, U. Va., 1968. Bar: Va. 1968. Law clk. to Hon. Gordon Va. Supreme Ct. Appeals, Richmond, 1968—69; from assoc. to ptnr. Hunton & Williams, Richmond, 1969—. Mem. editl. bd. Va. Law Rev. Chmn. Richmond Cmty. H.S., 1979—81; trustee Westminster-Canterbury Corp., 2003—, Ch. Schs. Episcopal Diocese Va., 1974—86; standing com. Diocese of Va., 1984—87; exec. bd. St. Andrew's Assn., 1981, pres., 1997—; exec. com. Christchurch Schs., 1982—86; exec. bd. Commonwealth Va. Bd. Mental Health, Mental Retardation and Substance Abuse Svcs., 1988—93. Mem.: ABA, Va. Bar Assn., Commonwealth Club, Country Club Va. Office: Hunton & Williams Riverfront Plz PO Box 1535 Richmond VA 23218-1535

**TOTTENHAM, TERRY OLIVER,** lawyer; b. Dallas, June 5, 1944; s. Edwin Pier and Ruth Elizabeth (Paris) T.; m. Carolyn Sue Lewis, July 7, 1967; children: Leslie Jo, Dana Elizabeth, Jessica Leigh. Student, Blinn Jr. Coll., 1962-67; BS in Pharmacy with high honors, U. Tex.-Austin, 1967, JD with honors, 1970; LL.M., George Washington U., 1973. Bar: Tex. 1970, U.S Ct. Mil. Appeals 1971. Assoc. Fulbright, Crooker & Jaworski, Houston, 1970; ptnr. Fulbright & Jaworski LLP, Austin, Tex., 1978—, and head pharmaceutical and med. device litig. group. Mem. faculty South Tex. Coll. Law, U. Houston; vis. prof. med. jurisprudence Baylor U.; vis. prof. health law Tex. Women's U.; adj. prof. law U. Tex. Sch. Law; speaker profl. groups Author: Texas Medical Jurisprudence; editor: Patients Rights Handbook, 1980. Served to capt. USMC, 1971-75. Recipient Gene Cavin award, 1992; named Outstanding Young Lawyer Houston, 1981, Outstanding Young Lawyer Tex., 1981. Fellow Tex. Bar Found. (life, trustee 1986—); mem. Tex. Assn. Def. Counsel, Am. Soc. Law and Medicine, Am. Soc. Pharmacy Law, Tex. Ex-Students Assn. (life), ABA, Nat. Health Lawyers Assn., Am. Acad. Hosp. Attys. (bd. dirs. 1989—), State Bar Tex. (chmn. health law sect., chmn. litigation sect, bd. dirs. 1985-86, chmn. continuing legal edn. com., Cert. of Merit award 1989), Houston Young Lawyers Assn. (dir. 1975-77), Tex. Young Lawyers Assn. (chmn. bd. 1979-80). Democrat. Episcopalian. Office: Fulbright & Jaworski LLP 600 Congress Ave Ste 2400 Austin TX 78701-3271 Office Phone: 512-474-5201. Office Fax: 512-536-4598. Business E-Mail: ttottenham@fulbright.com.

**TOTTON, CARL ALLEN, II,** psychologist; b. L.A., May 10, 1948; s. Carl Allen and Elva T. Student, Calif. State U., 1976, BS in Rehab. Counseling, 1978, MS in Counseling, 1980; PsyD in Clin. Psychology, Pepperdine U., Malibu, Calif., 1998. Cert. sch. psychologist, counselor, Calif.; lic. psychologist, Calif.; ordained Taoist abbot, 1983. Sch. psychologist Alhambra (Calif.) Sch. Dist., L.A., 1990—; dir. Taoist Inst., North Hollywood, Calif., 1981—. Faculty mem. Calif. State U., Northridge, 1993-96, SAMRA U. Oriental Medicine, 1996-98; dir., counselor Rehab. Counseling Assocs., North Hollywood, 1981-83; stress mgmt. cons., hypnotherapist; adj. faculty Phillips Grad. Inst. Clin. Psychology, 2005—; bd. advisors Rancho San Antonio Home for Boys, Chatsworth, Calif., 1996—. Author: Comprehensive Guide to Chinese Medicine and Structural Tui Na, Martial Arts Chi Kung, 1997, Pediatric Tui Na, 1998; editor: Tui Na: Chinese Healing and Acupressure Massage, 1984; author, pub., prodr., The Core System for Martial Arts, Health, and Chi Kung, 2005; contbr. articles to mags. Recipient Presdl. Sports award, 1993, 95, 97; elected to US Martial Arts Hall Fame as Grandmaster, 2002. Mem. APA, Calif. Rehab. Counseling Assn. (pres. 1983-84), Assn. Transpersonal Psychology, Nat. Assn. Sch. Psychologists, Calif. Assn. Sch. Psychologists (bd. dirs., 2001-2003, named Outstanding Sch. Psychologist 2000), Calif. Assn. Lic. Ednl. Psychologists (named Lic. Ednl. Psychologist of Yr. 1999), Calif. Assn. Marriage and Family Therapists. Democrat. Office: Taoist Inst 10630 Burbank Blvd North Hollywood CA 91601-2511 Office Phone: 818-760-4219.

**TOTTON, GAYLE,** professional sports team executive; Owner, CEO Sacramento Sirens (IWFL), Calif. Mailing: Sacramento Sirens 4500 73rd St Sacramento CA 95820 Office Phone: 916-456-8649. E-mail: ceo@sacramentosirens.com

**TOTTORI, DAICHI,** academic administrator, trade association administrator, accountant, lawyer; b. Fukuoka, Japan, Feb. 5, 1980; arrived in US, 2001; s. Takayuki (Stepfather) and Kikuko Tottori (Stepmother), Kazuko Tottori. MBA in Acctg., Americana U., USA, 2002; AS in Fin., Am. Mgmt. and Bus. Adminstrn. Inst. and U., 2003; PhD in Tax Law (hon.), St. Regis U., Liberia, 2003; DBA (hon.), St. Bernard U. Seborga, Italy, 2005; MD, Indian Inst. Alternative Medicine, 2006. CPA Calif.; registered home inspector, Housing Inspection Found., cert. constrn. inspector, Assn. Constrn. Inspectors, constrn.

project mgr., Assn. Constrn. Inspectors; registered property mgmt. dir. Japan, lic. real estate broker Japan, cert. property mgr. Japan; adminstrv. atty., Japan, enrolled agt., IRS; ordained minister Universal Ministries; sr. valuer Internat. Real Estate Inst., environ. inspector Environ. Assessment Assn., testing specialist Environ. Assessment Assn., remediation specialist Environ. Assessment Assn., rev. appraiser Nat. Assn. Rev. Appraisers and Mortgage Underwriters, registered tax preparer Calif. Full prof. St. Regis U., Liberia, 2003—05; pres. St. Bernard U. Seborga, Italy, 2004—; trade attache' Seborga Bus. Ctr., Principality of Seborga, Italy, 2004—; full prof. James Monroe U., Liberia, Liberia, 2004—. Rsch. and study Ctrl. Sch. of Plitics of Liberal Dem. Party, Tokyo, Japan, 2004; bishop Universal Ministries, Japan. Sgt. Japan Def. Force, 2006. Recipient Order of Knight, Ethiopian Order of St.Mary Zion, 2004, Insignia for Social and Cultural Achievement, Principality of Seborga, 2004. Mem.: Internat. Real Estate Inst., Housing Inspection Found., Nat. Assn. of Rev. Appraisers and Mortgage Underwrithers, Environ. Assessment Assn., Assn. of Constrn. Insp., Info. Sys. and Contorol Assn., Assn. of Cert. Fraud Examiners, Ethiopian Royal Order of St.Mary Zion, Order of St.Lazaro (Order of Knight 2004), The Imperial Soc. of St. George of Lalibela, Assn. of Frendship for Seborga, Japan. Achievements include Knight Order from Ethipia Royal Family; Insignia from Principality of Seborga. Personal E-mail: dtottori@hotmail.com.

**TOTTY, TOTTY OKORO,** soccer coach; b. Calabar, Cross River, Nigeria, June 26, 1966; arrived in U.S., 1989; s. Joseph Okoro and Rachael Okoro Totty. BS in Bus. Comm., So. NH U., Manchester, 1993, MS in Internat. Bus., 1995. Camp co-dir. John Rootes Soccer Sch., Manchester, 1990—2000; asst. coach women's soccer So. NH U., Manchester, 1995—97; head coach women's soccer Clayton State U., Morrow, Ga., 1998—; state staff coach Ga. Olympics Devel. Program, Atlanta, 2001—. Mem. adv. com. S.E. region NCAA, Hickory, NC, 2001—04; conf. chair Peach Belt Conf. W. Soc. Coaches, Augusta, Ga., 2001—02; mem. Nigerian Nat. Soccer Team. Mem. Global Citizens Cir., 1990—; active Big Brother/Big Sister, Manchester, 1994. Named Rookie of Yr., New Eng. Conf., 1989; named to Hall of Fame, So. NH U., 2000. Mem.: US Soccer Fedn. (youth soccer referee 1998—), Nat. Soccer Coaches Assn. of Am. (All-Am. Soccer Player 1991—93). Independent. Avocations: music, theater, dance, movies, art. Home: 639 Garden Walk Blvd # 336 College Park GA 30349 Office: Clayton State U 2000 Clayton State Blvd Morrow GA 30260 Office Phone: 678-466-4684. Office Fax: 678-466-4699. Business E-Mail: tottytotty@clayton.edu.

**TOUBY, KATHLEEN ANITA,** lawyer; b. Miami Beach, Feb. 20, 1943; d. Harry and Kathleen Rebecca (Hamper) T.; m. Joseph Thomas Woodward; children: Mark Andrew, Judson David To, by. BS in Nursing, U. Fla., 1965, MRC in Rehab. Counseling, 1967; JD with honors, Nova U., 1977. Bar: Fla. 1978, D.C. 1978. Counselor Jewish Vocat. Svc., Chgo., 1967-68; rehab. counselor Fla. Dept. Vocat. Rehab., Miami, 1968-70; spl. asst., asst. U.S. atty. U.S. Dept. Justice, Miami, 1978-80; assoc. Pyszka & Kessler, P.A., Miami, 1980-83; ptnr. Touby & Smith, P.A., Miami, 1983-89, Touby, Smith, DeMahy & Drake, P.A., Miami, 1989-94, Touby & Woodward, P.A., Miami, 1994—. Chmn. adv. exec. bd. Paralegal Edn. program Barry U., 1986-87; lectr. Food and Drug Law Inst., 1987-89, 91; lectr. environ. law Exec. Enterprises, 1987-88; lectr. trial techniques, Hispanic Nat. Bar Assn., St. Thomas Law Sch.; adj. prof. product liability Can. Govt., U.S. Trade and Mktg. Dept., 1989-95. Co-author: The Environmental Litigation Deskbook, 1989; contbr. chpts. to books, articles to profl. jours. Mem. ABA, Am. Inns of Ct. (pres. 1998-99, pres.-elect St. Thomas Law Sch. chpt. 1997-98, pres. 1998-99), Dade County Bar Assn. (legal aid, pub. svcs. com. 1988), Fed. Bar Assn. (bd. dirs. 1989—, v.p. 1991-92, pres.-elect So. Fla. chpt. 1992-93, pres. 1993-94), Cuban-Am. Bar Assn., Phi Delta Phi (province pres. 1982-85, bd. dirs 1985-87). Roman Catholic. Home: 4150 Bay Point Rd Miami FL 33137-3352 Office: Touby & Woodward PA 2030 Douglas Rd Ste 217 Coral Gables FL 33134 Office Phone: 305-442-2318.

**TOUCHETTE, BRANT WILLIAM,** biologist, researcher; b. Balt., Apr. 3, 1967; s. H. James and Jean C. Touchette; m. Teresa A. Armstrong, June 6, 2000; children: Madeleine, Roman, Sophia. BA in Biology, U. of Del., Newark, 1990; MS in Marine Biology, Nova Southeastern U., Dania, Fla., 1993; PhD in Aquatic Botany, N.C.State U., 1999. Instr. Wilson Tech, Wilson, NC; rsch. assoc. Ctr. for Applied Aquatic Ecology, Raleigh, NC; environ. cons. Coastal Sci. Assocs. Inc., Jacksonville Beach, Fla., 1991—93; asst. prof. of biology Elon U., Elon, NC, 2001—; vis. scientist N.C. State U., Raleigh, NC, 2002—; vis. scholar Duke U., Durham, NC, 2002—04. Contbr. articles to profl. jours. Adv. com. - oil pollution USCG, Miami, Fla., 1992; wetland cons. N.C. Mus. of Life Sci., Durham, NC, 2002—02. Recipient Merit award, Am. Soc. of Plant Physiologist, 1998; fellow NOAA Grad. fellow, NOAA, 1995—99; grantee Rsch. grantee, Water Resources Rsch. Inst., Tarheel Rsch., Ltd., Cape Fear River Assembly. Mem.: NSTA (assoc.), Soc. of Wetland Scientists (assoc.), Aquatic Plant Mgmt. Soc. (assoc.), Am. Soc. of Limnology and Oceanography (assoc.). Achievements include research in Carbon and nitrogen physiology in aquatic plants. Plant oxidative stress physiology. Office: Elon University Department of Biology Campus Box 2625 Elon NC 27244 Business E-mail: btouchette@elon.edu.

**TOUCHY, DEBORAH K.P.,** lawyer, accountant; b. Pasadena, Tex., Dec. 9, 1957; d. Donald Carl and Bobbie Jo (Jackson) Putzka; m. Harry Roy Touchy, Jr., Feb. 23, 1980. BBA, Baylor U., 1979; JD, U. Houston, 1988. Bar: Tex. 1989; CPA, Tex.; cert. in estate planning and probate law Tex. Bd. Legal Specialization. Sr. mgr. tax KMPG Peat Marwick, Houston, 1980-86; assoc. Fizer Beck Webster & Bentley, Houston, 1989-90; pvt. practice law Houston, 1990—; chmn. spl. events Jr. League Houston, 1997-98. Editor Houston Law Rev., 1988-89. Chmn. ticket sales incentives Chi Omega, Houston, 1985; active ticket sales Mus. Fine Arts, Houston, 1984; facilities chmn. Woodland Traila West Civic Orgn., Houston, 1982-83; pres. Women Attys. in Tax & Probate, 1994-95, pres., 2004; bd. dirs. Episcopal Ch. Women at St. John the Divine; active St. John's Sch., 1999-, Lower Sch. Scrapbook Chmn. 2001-02; mem. steering com. Girl Scouts of San Jacinto County Capital Campaign, 2003-. Recipient Outstanding Alumni award, Beta Alpha Psi, 1997. Mem. ABA (estate-probate sect. 1989—, vice chmn. commn. property com. 1994—), AICPA (taxation sect., estate and gift tax com. 1992-95, 98-2000), Tex. Soc. CPAs (bd. dirs. 1995—, chmn. tax inst. com. 1996-97, estate planning com. 1990-94, 96—), Houston Chpt. CPAs (chmn. taxpayer edn. 1985-86, chmn. membership com. 1992-93, v.p. 1993-94, 96-97, chmn. tax forums 1994-95, long range planning com. 1995-96, chmn. leadership devel. 1997-98, treas. 1998-99, chmn. ann. charity event 1999-2000, bd. dirs. 1999-2000, 2002-03, pres. 2001-02), Houston Bar Assn. (estate-probate sect. 1989—), State Bar Tex. (estate-probate sect. 1989—, mem. elder law com. 1991-97), Houston Estate and Fin. Forum, Baylor U. Women's Assn. (treas. 1993-94, chmn. fin. com. 1994-95, parliamentarian 1995-96, sec. 1996-97, pres. 1997-98, chmn. audit com. 1999-2000), Chief Justice-Advocates, Tex. Bd. Legal Specializations (cert. estate planning, probate law 1994), Order of Coif, Omicron Delta Kappa, Phi Delta Phi, Beta Alpha Psi (Outstanding Alumni 1997). Office: PO Box 130122 Houston TX 77219-0122 Personal E-mail: dtouchy@swbell.net.

**TOUFF, MICHAEL,** lawyer; b. 1945; AB, Harvard U.; JD, U. Michigan. Officer, law firm Holmes & Starr, Ireland, Stapleton, Pryor & Pascoe, P.C., 1992-94; v.p., gen. counsel Richmond Amer Homes, 1994—99, sr. v.p., gen. counsel, 1999—. Mem.: ABA. Office: Richmond Amer Homes 6550 Greenwood Plaza Blvd Englewood CO 80111-4934

**TOUHILL, BLANCHE MARIE,** retired academic administrator, historian, educator; b. St. Louis, Mo., July 1, 1931; d. Robert and Margaret (Walsh) Van Dillen; m. Joseph M. Touhill. Aug. 29, 1959. BA in History, St. Louis U., 1953, MA in Geography, 1954, PhD in History, 1962. Prof. history and edn. U. Mo., St. Louis, 1965-73, assoc. dean faculties, 1974-76, assoc. vice chancellor for acad. affairs, 1976-87, vice chancellor, 1987-90, chancellor, 1991—2002, chancellor emeritus, 2002—. Bd. dirs. Peabody Energy, Inc. Author: William Smith O'Brien and His Irish Revolutionary Companions in Penal Exile, 1981, The Emerging University UM-St. Louis, 1963-83, 1985;

editor: Readings in American History, 1970, Varieties of Ireland, 1976. Named Outstanding Educator St. Louis chpt. Urban League, 1976; recipient Leadership award St. Louis YWCA, 1986. Mem. Nat. Assn. State Univs. and Land Grant Colls. (exec. com. 1988—), Am. Com. on Irish Studies (pres. 1991—), Phi Kappa Phi, Alpha Sigma Lambda. E-mail: j_touhill@hotmail.com.

**TOUHILL, C. JOSEPH,** environmental engineer; b. Newark, Aug. 27, 1938; s. Charles J. and Caroline A. T.; m. Helen Elizabeth O'Malley, June 11, 1960; children: Gregory Joseph, Stephen Mark, Christopher Alan, Kathleen Elizabeth. BCE, Rensselaer Poly. Inst., 1960, PhD in Environ. Engring., 1964; SM, MIT, 1961; postgrad., U. Wash., 1970. Diplomate Am. Acad. Environ. Engrs. Mgr. water and land resources dept. Battelle Meml. Inst., Richland, Wash., 1964-71; pres. Baker/TSA Inc., Pitts., 1977-90; group sr. v.p. ICF Kaiser Engrs. Inc., Pitts., 1990-94; exec. v.p. EG&G Environ. Inc., Pitts., 1994-97; pres. Touhill Tech. Mgmt. Corp., Jamison, Pa., 1997-99, 2003—; nat. discipline lead for process and environ. engring. Tetra Tech FW, Inc. (formerly Foster Wheeler Environ. Corp.), Langhorne, Pa., 1999—2003. Co-author: Hazardous Materials Spills Handbook, 1982, Hazardous Waste Management Engineering, 1987; editor: Resource Management in the Great Lakes Basin, 1971; mem. editorial bd. Environ. Progress Jour., 1979-93. Trustee Am. Acad. Environ. Engr., 1971-77, 83-86; bd. dirs. Suburban Gen. Hosp., Pitts., 1986-96; vice chmn. Franklin Park (Pa.) Authority, 1977-96, chmn. adv. com., dept. Environ. and energy Engring., Rensselaer Polytech Inst., 1996-98, mem. adv. bd. dept. civil and environ. engring., 2000-. Recipient fellow award Rensselaer Alumni Assn., 1994; Kappe lectr. AAEE, 1992. Fellow ASCE (life), AIChE (chmn. environ. engring. div. 1977, Inst. fellow 2000), Am. Chem. Soc. (edit. adv. bd. 1975-77), Am. Water Works Assn. (life), Water Environment Fedn. (life). Office: 2269 Sunrise Way Jamison PA 18929 Office Phone: 215-491-5617. Business E-Mail: jtouhill@alum.mit.edu.

**TOULANTIS, MARIE J.,** retail executive; BBA in Mktg., Pace Univ. V.p. The Chase Manhattan Bank, NYC, 1987-96, sr. v.p., 1996-97; exec. v.p. fin. Barnes & Noble Inc., NYC, 1997-99, CFO barnesandnoble.com Inc., 1995—2001, pres., COO, barnesandnoble.com, 2001, now CEO, barnesandnoble.com. Bd. dir. Hershey Foods Corp. Adv. bd. Lubin Sch. Bus., Pace University. Office: Barnes & Noble dot com Barnes & Noble Inc 2nd fl 122 Fifth Ave New York NY 10011

**TOULMIN, PRIESTLEY,** retired geologist; b. Birmingham, Ala., June 5, 1930; s. Priestley and Catharine Augusta (Carey) T.; m. Martha Jane Slason, Aug. 30, 1952; children: Catharine Bosier (Mrs. Robert G. Gibson), Priestley Chewning. AB, Harvard U., 1951, PhD, 1959; MS, U. Colo., 1953. With U.S. Geol. Survey, Washington, 1953-56, 57-89, staff geologist for exptl. geology, 1966, chief br. exptl. geochemistry, 1966-71, geologist geologic div., 1971-89, Reston, Va., 1974-89, ret., 1989; also leader inorganic chemistry team NASA (Viking Project). Adj. prof. Columbia U., 1966; rsch. asso. in geochemistry Calif. Inst. Tech., 1976-77; vis. lectr. Am. Geol. Inst.; dir. petrogenesis and mineral resources program NSF, 1985; bd. dirs., treas. 28th Internat. Geol. Congress, 1985-86 Mng. sci. editor Geochemistry Internat., 1965-68; assoc. editor Am. Mineralogist, 1974-76; contbr. articles to profl. jours. Mem. adv. com. spl. edn., Alexandria, Va., 1977-80. Recipient Exceptional Service medal NASA, 1977; Meritorious Service award U.S. Dept. Interior, 1978 Fellow Geol. Soc. Am., Mineral Soc. Am. (bd. assoc. editors 1974-76), Soc. Econ. Geologists, Explorers Club; mem. AAAS, Geol. Soc. Washington (2d v.p. 1977, councillor 1973-74, 90-91, 1st v.p. 1981, pres. 1982), Am. Geophys. Union, Soc. Mayflower Descs., S.R., SAR, Soc. Colonial Wars (D.C.), Aztec Club of 1847, St. Andrews Soc. (Washington), Cosmos Club (pres. 1993-94, found. trustee 1994—, chmn. 1996-2001), Sigma Xi, Sigma Gamma Epsilon. Home: 418 Summers Dr Alexandria VA 22301-2449 Office: PO Box 183 Alexandria VA 22313-0183

**TOULMIN, STEPHEN EDELSTON,** humanities educator; b. London, Mar. 25, 1922; BA in Math. and Physics, King's Coll., Cambridge, Eng., 1942; PhD, King's Coll., 1948; D Tech. (hon.), Royal Inst. Tech., Stockholm, 1991. Lectr. in philosophy of sci. Oxford U., Eng., 1949-55; prof., chmn. dept. of philosophy U. Leeds, Yorkshire, Eng., 1955-59; dir. unit for history of ideas Nuffield Found., London, 1960-65; prof. history of ideas and philosophy Brandeis U., Waltham, Mass., 1965-69; prof. philosophy Mich. State U., East Lansing, 1969-72; prof. humanities U. Calif., Santa Cruz, 1972-73; prof. com. social thought U. Chgo., 1973-86; Avalon prof. humanities Northwestern U., Evanston, Ill., 1986-92, Avalon prof. emeritus, 1992—; prof. U. So. Calif., L.A., 1993-2001, 2001—. Vis. prof. U. Melbourne, Australia, 1954-55, Stanford U., 1959, Columbia U., N.Y.C., 1960, Hebrew U., Jerusalem, 1964, U. South Fla., 1972, Dartmouth Coll., 1979, SUNY, Plattsburgh, 1980, Colo. Coll., 1980, 82, MacMaster U., 1983, Harvard Project Physics Grad. Sch. Edn., Harvard U., 1965; counselor Smithsonian Inst., Washington, 1977-77; cons., staff mem. Nat. Commn. Protection Human Subjects Biomed. Behavioral Rsch., 1975-78; sr. vis. scholar, fellow Inst. Soc. Ethics and Life Scis., Hastings-on-Hudson, N.Y., 1981-2001; regent's lectr. U. Calif. Med. Sch., Davis, 1985; Mary Flexner lectr. Bryn Mawr Coll., 1977; Reyerson lectr. U. Chgo., 1979, John Nuveen lectr., 1980; Tate-Wilson lectr. So. Meth. U., 1980; Or Emet lectr. Osgoode Hall Law Sch. 1981; McDermott lectr. U. Dallas, 1985; lectr. Sigma Xi, 1965-66, Phi Beta Kappa, 1978-79, Phi Beta Kappa-AAAS, 1984, Thomas Jefferson lectr. NEH, Washington, 1997; Tanner lectr. Clare Hall, Cambridge U., 1998; guest prof. social and human scis. Wolfgang Goethe Universitat, Frankfurt, Germany, 1987; vis. fellow Internationales Forschungszentrum Kulturwissenschaften (IFK), Vienna, 1995. Author: The Place of Reason in Ethics, 1949, The Philosophy of Science: an Introduction, 1953, The Uses of Argument, 1958, Foresight and Understanding, 1961, Human Understanding, vol. 1, 1972, Knowing and Acting, 1976, The Return to Cosmology, 1982, Cosmopolis, 1989; (with J. Goodfield) The Fabric of the Heavens, 1961, The Architecture of Matter, 1963, The Discovery of Time, 1965; (with A. Janik) Wittgenstein's Vienna, 1973; (with R. Rieke and A. Janik) An Introduction to Reasoning, 1978; (with A. Jonsen) The Abuse of Casuistry, 1987; (with B. Gustavsen) Beyond Theory, 1996, Return to Reason, 2001; contbr. numerous scil. articles to profl. jours. Recipient Honor Cross 1st class (Austria), 1991; Getty Ctr. for History of Art and Humanities scholar, 1985-86, First Book of the Year prize Am. Soc. Social Philosophy, 1992; Ctr. for Psychosocial Studies fellow, 1974-76. Fellow Am. Acad. Arts and Scis.

**TOUMANOFF, PETER GEORGE,** educator; b. Calif., May 9, 1950; s. George Irakly and Jane Adams Toumanoff; m. Susanna Cobb Toumanoff, Dec. 27, 1972; children: Nicholas Peter, Andrew Peter. BA, Yale U., New Haven, 1972; PhD, U. Wash., Seattle, 1977. Assoc. prof. Marquette U., Milw., 1979—. Dir. Ctr. for Global and Econ. Studies, Milw., 1997—. Author: (textbook) A Mathematical Approach to Economic Analysis. Recipient John P. Raynor, S.J. award for Tchg. Excellence, Marquette U., 2005; fellow Fulbright Sr. Specialist, Fulbright Assn., 2006; Fulbright Sr. scholar, 2002. Mem.: Am. Econs. Assn. Avocations: master's swimming, sailboat racing. Office: Marquette University PO Box 1881 Milwaukee WI 53072-1881 Office Phone: 414-288-7523.

**TOUMARI, ARMAN,** environmental engineer, chemistry professor; b. Iran, June 7, 1965; s. Mansour Toomari and Molook Simoni. MS in Chem. Engring., CCNY, N.Y., 1996; MCE, The CCNY, N.Y., 1999. Registered profl. engr., Calif., 2001, N.Y., 1999. Environ. engr. N.Y. State Dept. Environ. Conservation, N.Y., 1995—99; engr. water resources control L.A. Water Quality Control Bd., 1999—. Prof. chemistry Santa Monica Coll., Calif., 1993—. Mem.: Am. Acad. Environ. Engrs. (assoc.). Achievements include research in thermal and mechanical properties of asphalt cement when mixed with controlled amounts of polymeric substances. Home: 1115 South Elm Drive Apt 214 Los Angeles CA 90035 Office: Los Angeles Water Quality Control Board 320 West 4th Street Suite 200 Los Angeles CA 90013 Office Phone: 213-576-6758. Home Fax: 213-576-6700; Office Fax: 213-576-6700. Personal E-mail: atoumari@yahoo.com. Business E-Mail: atoumari@waterboards.ca.gov.

**TOUMEY, DONALD JOSEPH,** lawyer; BA, Williams Coll., 1978; JD, Yale U., 1981. Bar: N.Y. 1982, D.C. 1985, U.S. Supreme Ct. 1986. Law clk. to judge U.S. Ct Appeals (2d cir.), N.Y.C., 1981-82; spl. asst. to gen. counsel U.S. Dept. Treasury, Washington, 1982-85; assoc. Sullivan & Cromwell, N.Y.C., 1985-90; ptnr., 1990—. Republican. Office: Sullivan & Cromwell LLP 125 Broad St New York NY 10004-2489 Office Phone: 212-558-4077. Business E-Mail: toumeyd@sullcrom.com.

**TOUPIN, HAROLD OVID,** retired chemical company executive; b. Hibbing, Minn., Jan. 21, 1927; s. Ovid Pascal and Ellen (Holt) T.; m. Edna F. Sallila, Feb. 8, 1948 (div. Feb. 1973); m. Colleen Beverly Lange, Apr. 18, 1981; children: James, Ronald. BS, U. Minn., 1954, MA, 1955, postgrad, 1968; PhD (hon.), Internat. Acad. Color, Las Vegas, Nev., 1982, U. Mont., 1990. Mgr. Firestone Tire Co., East Los Angeles, Calif., 1948-51; dir. vocat. edn. Hopkins (Minn.) Pub. Schs., 1955-75; with research and devel. Power-o-Peat Co., Gilbert, Minn., 1956-67; chief exec. officer, cons. Color Specialties Inc., Mpls., 1976-98; ret., 1999. Pres., founder travel, meeting planners svc. co., 1990; founder internat. office for color specialties, 1994; bd. dirs. Vu-tek Inc., St. Paul, Airport Auto Sales, St. Paul Color Specialties of Nev., Las Vegas, Instant Air Inc., Mpls., Freedom Fin.; cons. Runs Hot Cons. Svc., 1966-75; ptnr. Vermes Jewelry, Mpls., 1956-80. Contbr. articles to profl. jours. Bd. dirs. Hopkins Jaycees, 1958-60. Served with USAAF, 1944-47. Mem. Am. Assn. Mfrs., Internat. Assn. Color, Nat. Ret. Tchrs. Assn., Am. Assn. Self Employeed, Met. Area Dist. Edn. Instrs. Assn. (pres.), Mpls. C. of C. (Super Bowl com. 1992), Am. Legion, VFW, Lions (sec. Hopkins club 1956-76, bd. dirs., 2d v.p. Sun City West Pioneer club 2005—). Democrat. Roman Catholic. Avocations: travel, golf, writing. E-mail: haroldtoupin@peoplepc.com.

**TOURAPIS, ALEXANDROS,** signal processing engineer, researcher; b. Nicosia, Cyprus, Jan. 24, 1973; s. Michael Tourapis and Theodouli Tourapi. Diploma in elec. and computer engring, Nat. Tech. U. Athens, Greece, 1995; PhD, Hong Kong U. Sci.and Tech., 2001. Vis. rschr. Microsoft Rsch. Asia, Beijing; sr. mem. tech. staff Thomson Corp. Rsch., Princeton, NJ, 2003—04; sr. scientist Mobilygen Corp., San Jose, Calif., 2004—04; cons. DoCoMo Labs., USA, San Jose, Calif., 2004—05; sr. staff scientist Dolby Labs., Burbank, Calif., 2005—. Contbr. articles to profl. publs. Recipient Outstanding Reviewer award, IEEE Image Processing Soc., 2006. Mem.: IEEE, SPIE, ACM. Achievements include patents for video compression technologies; patents pending for video compression and signal processing techniques; research in international video coding standards such as MPEG-4 and H.264/AVC. Office: Dolby Lab 3601 W Alameda Blvd Burbank CA 91505 Office Phone: 818-823-2842.

**TOURINO, RALPH GENE,** aerospace transportation executive; b. LA, Mar. 11, 1941; s. John Tourino and Zalia Rose (Perez) Chacon; m. Sherry Lane Tisdail, Sept. 5, 1964; children: Christina Marie, Rebecca Kathleen. BS, UCLA, 1964; MPA, Auburn U., 1973; MBA, U. So. Calif., 1975; postgrad. in nat. security, Harvard U., 1988. Commd. 2d lt. USAF, 1964, advanced through grades to maj. gen., 1992; student Undergrad. Navigator Tng., James Connally AFB, Tex., 1964-65; C-97 navigator AF Western Test Range, Vanderberg AFB. Calif., 1965-66; navigator HQ 7th AF Flight Ops., Tan Son Nhut AB, Vietnam, 1966-67; mem. KC135 Crew, March AFB, Calif., 1967-70; sect. comdr. Squadron Officer Sch., Maxwell AFB, Ala., 1970-73; program control Space Div., L.A. AF Sta., 1975-78; dir. program control NAVSTAR Global Positioning System, L.A. AF Sta., 1978-80; dir. contracts Space Def. Systems Program Office, L.A. AF Sta., 1980-82; systems program dir. Inertial Upper Stage Program, L.A. AF Sta., 1982-85; asst. dep. comdr. for Small ICBM Ballistic Missile Office, Norton AFB, Calif., 1985-87; asst. dep. chief of Staff Systems AF Systems Command, Andrews AFB, Md., 1987-88, insp. gen., 1988-89; comdr. Ballistic Missile Orgn., Norton AFB, 1989-91; program dir. B-2 System Program Office, Wright-Patterson AFB, Ohio, 1991—94; retired as maj. gen. USAF, 1994; v.p. space support systems Lockheed Martin, Santa Maria, Calif. Decorated Legion of Merit, Def. Meritorious Svc. medal, Meritorious Svc. medal, Air medal, Air Force Commendation medal; named one of 50 Most Important Hispanics in Tech. & Bus. Hispanic Engr. & Info. Tech. mag., 2005. Mem. Air Force Assn., AIAA. Republican. Avocation: exercising. Office: Lockheed Martin 6801 Rockledge Dr Bethesda MD 20817*

**TOURKANTONIS, ARTHUR CHARLES,** real estate consultant, lawyer; b. Cambridge, Mass., Sept. 22, 1949; s. Charles Nickolas and Margaret Thresa Tourkantonis; m. Nancy Jane Zolon; children: Arthur, Jason. AS in Criminal Justice, Bunker Hill C.C., Boston, 1982; BS in Philosophy, U. Mass., 1984; JD, New Eng. Sch. Law, 1990. Bar: Mass. 1990. Police officer Woburn Police Dept., Mass., 1971—92; atty. Woburn, 1980—; real estate cons. Keller Williams, Sarasota, Fla., 2004—. With USMC, 1968—69. Mem.: Moose Club, Elks. Roman Catholic. Avocations: motorcycling, tennis, bicycling. Home: 5602 Garden Lakes Majestic Bradenton FL 34203 Office: Keller Williams Realty 6272 Lake Coprey Dr Sarasota FL 34243 Office Phone: 941-556-0550. Office Fax: 941-556-0500. E-mail: turkslaw@aol.com.

**TOURKOW, JOSHUA ISAAC,** lawyer; b. Fort Wayne, Ind., Mar. 5, 1947; s. Frederick Rhinehold and Leah Sarah (Schwartz) T.; m. Donna Susan Dubin, Aug. 30, 1970; children— Illana Joy, Lisa Michelle, Benjamin Ahron. Student Bar Ilan U., Israel, 1968; B.S. in Indsl. Mgmt., Purdue U., 1970; JD, Ind. U., Indpls., 1973. Bar: Ind. 1973, U.S. Dist. Cts. (no. and so. dists.) Ind. 1973, U.S. Ct. Appeals (7th cir.) 1973. Asst. dep. prosecutor Marion County, Indpls., 1972-73; ptnr. Tourkow, Crell, Rosenblatt & Johnston, Ft. Wayne, 1973—. Bd. dirs. Housing & Neighborhood Devel. Services, Inc., Ft. Wayne, 1980-84, Ft. Wayne Redevel. Com., 1983; atty. Ft. Wayne Housing Authority, 1983—87; advisor, atty. Parents Without Partners, Ft. Wayne, 1981-85, Fathers United for Equal Rights, Ft. Wayne, 1980—. Mem. ABA, Ind. Bar Assn. (chair of family law, 1992-99), Allen County Bar Assn. (chair family law sect. 2000-02). Home: 7022 Winchester Rd Fort Wayne IN 46819-1530 Office: Tourkow Crell Rosenblatt & Johnston 814 Anthony Wayne Building Fort Wayne IN 46802 Office Phone: 260-426-0545. Business E-Mail: jtourkow@tcrjlaw.com.

**TOURLENTES, THOMAS THEODORE,** retired psychiatrist; b. Chgo., Dec. 7, 1922; s. Theodore A. and Mary (Xenostathy) T.; m. Mona Belle Land, Sept. 9, 1956; children: Theodore W., Stephen C., Elizabeth A. BS, U. Chgo., 1945, MD, 1947. Diplomate Am. Bd. Psychiatry and Neurology (sr. examiner 1964-88, 90). Intern Cook County Hosp., Chgo., 1947-48; resident psychiatry Downey (Ill.) VA Hosp., 1948-51; practice medicine specializing in psychiatry Chgo., 1952, Camp Atterbury, Ind., 1953, Ft. Carson, Colo., 1954, Galesburg, Ill., 1955-71; staff psychiatrist Chgo. VA Clinic, 1952; clin. instr. psychiatry Med. Sch., Northwestern U., 1952; dir. mental hygiene consultation service Camp Atterbury, 1953-54, Ft. Carson, 1953-54; asst. supt. Galesburg State Research Hosp., 1954-58, supt., 1958-71; dir. Comprehensive Community Mental Health Ctr. Rock Island and Mercer Counties; dir. psychiat. services Franciscan Hosp., 1971-85; chief mental health services VA Outpatient Clinic, Peoria, Ill., 1985-88; clin. prof. psychiatry U. Ill., Chgo. and Peoria, 1955—96; preceptor in hosp. adminstrn. State U. Iowa, Iowa City, 1958-64; ret., 1996. Councilor, del. Ill. Psychiat. Soc.; chmn. liaison com. Am. Hosp. and Psychiat. Assns., 1978-79, chmn. Quality Care Bd., Ill. Dept. Mental Health, 1995-97. Contbr. articles profl. jours. Mem. Gov. Ill. Com. Employment Handicapped, 1962-64; zone dir. Ill. Dept. Mental Health, Peoria, 1964-71; mem. Spl. Survey Joint Commn. Accreditation Hosps.; chmn. Commn. Cert. Psychiat. Adminstrs., 1979-81; pres. Knox-Galesburg Symphony Soc., 1966-68; bd. dirs. Galesburg Civic Music Assn., pres., 1968-70; chair Knox county United Way Campaign, 1989; pres. Civic Art Ctr., 1990-92. Capt. M.C. AUS, 1952-54. Fellow AAAS, AMA, Am. Psychiat. Assn. (chair hosp. and cmty. psychiatry award bd. 1989-90, dist. life fellow 2002), Am. Coll. Psychiatrists, Am. Coll. Mental Health Adminstrs.; mem. Ill. Med. Soc. (chmn. aging com. 1968-71, coun. on mental health and addictions 1987-89), chair mental health substance abuse com. 1987-89), Ill. Psychiat. Soc. (pres. 1969-70), Am. Pub. Health Assn., Soc. Biol. Psychiatry, Ill. Hosp. Assn. (trustee 1968-70), Am. Coll. Hosp. Adminstrs., Assn. for Rsch. Nervous and Mental, Am. Assn. Psychiat. Adminstrs. (pres. 1980), Ctrl. Neuorpsychiat. Assn. (pres. 1988-89). Home and Office: 138 Valley View Rd Galesburg IL  61401-8524  Office  Phone:  309-344-1177.  E-mail: tourlentes@gallatinriver.net. *Feeling useful and needed is the greatest recognition and reward.*

**TOURLITSAS, JOHN CONSTANTINE,** radiologist; b. Cavala, Greece, Oct. 4, 1926; came to U.S. 1956; s. Constantine Nacos and Marica Constantine (Athanasiou) T. MD, U. Athens, Greece, 1955. Diplomate Am. Bd. Radiology. Intern Sioux Valley Hosp., Sioux Falls, SD, 1956-57; resident Midway Hosp., Mpls.-St. Paul, 1957-59, New Eng. Deaconess Hosp./Harvard U., Boston, 1959-60, Mass. Meml. Hosps./Boston U., 1960-61, Toronto (Ont., Can.) Western Hosp.-U. Toronto, 1961-62; rsch. fellow in radiology Postgrad. Rsch. Inst. Hosp for Sick Children, U. Toronto, 1962; resident Sunnybrook VA Hosp.-U. Toronto, 1963, Royal Victoria Hosp., McGill U., Montreal, 1963-65; attending radiologist, vis. radiologist Maimonides Med. Ctr., Coney Island Hosp., Bklyn., 1966-68; attending, cons. radiologist Bronx (N.Y.)-Lebanon Hosp. Ctr.-Albert Einstein Coll. Med., 1968-95; ret. 1995. Instr. radiology Albert Einstein Coll. Medicine, 1972-77. Joslin Clinic fellow, Boston, 1959-60. Fellow Am. Coll. Chest Physicians; mem. AMA, Am. Coll. Radiology, Am. Roentgen Ray Soc., Radiol. Soc. N.Am., N.Y. State Med. Soc. Avocations: reading, walking, travel. Home: 372 Fifth Ave Apt 8C New York NY 10018-8109

**TOURNILLON, NICHOLAS BRADY,** investment company executive; b. New Orleans, Sept. 1, 1933; s. Samuel C. and Anna Mae (Brady) T.; m. Audrey Nicosia, Dec. 15, 1956; children: Brady, Linda, Tracy, Jeffrey, Gregory, Lori. BA, Southeastern La. U., 1958; MBA, La. State U., 1960. Loan officer Export Import Bank U.S., Washington, 1960-66; adminstrv. asst. to exec. officers Atlantic Gulf & Pacific Co. of Manila, 1966-68; asst. treas. GTE Internat., Stamford, Conn., 1968-76, treas., 1976-86, v.p., 1978-86; pres. GTE Fin. Corp., 1984-86; asst. treas. GTE Corp., 1985-86; chmn., chief exec. officer Am. and Internat. Investment Corp., 1986-98; pres., CEO Definco Ltd., 1998—. Bd. dirs. Global Access Corp.; mem. internat. adv. bd. Union Trust Co.; advisor on export fin. to Office of U.S. Pres. (U.S. Trade Rep.). Past chmn. Conn. Dist. Export Council of US Dept. Commerce; mem. monetary com. U.S. Council Internat. Bus.; bd. dirs. Nat. Fgn. Trade Council, Southeastern La. U. Devel. Fund. Served with USNR, 1953-54, Korea. Named Outstanding Alumnus of Yr., Southeastern La. U., 1976 Mem. Soc. Internat. Treasurers, Acad. Internat. Bus., Retired Men's Assn. of Greenwich, Phi Kappa Phi. Home: Midwood Dr Greenwich CT 06831-4400 Office: Definco Ltd 25 Midwood Dr Greenwich CT 06831-4412 *Perseverance is an often mentioned but never overrated quality— the quality that prevents the substitution of expediency for excellence. Throughout life, persevering effort has been responsible for converting ideas and talents into results and recognition.*

**TOURONDEL, LAURENT,** chef; Studied with, Joel Robuchon. Chef Caesar's Palace, Las Vegas, 1998—99, Cello, NYC, 1999, BLT Steak, 2003—, BLT Fish, 2004—. Office: Bistro Laurent Tourondel 21 W 17th St New York NY 10011 Office Phone: 212-691-8888.*

**TOURRE, MARC LOUIS,** music educator; b. Pitts. s. Louis August and Marie Rita Tourre; m. Sandra L. Lawson; children: Thea, Heather, Christopher. B of Music Edn., St. Vincent Coll., 1975; MA, Ind. U. of Pa., 1977. Music tchr. Greater Latrobe Sch. Dist., Pa., 1975—. Mem. Westmoreland Choral Soc., Greensburg, Pa., 2000—. Recipient Excellence in Tchg. award, St. Vincent Coll., 1998—2001, 2005. Mem.: NEA, Pa. Music Educator's Assn., Am. Assn. Choral Dirs. Avocations: winemaking, cooking. Home: Box 70 Darragh PA 15625 Office: Greater Latrobe Sch Dist 410 Main St Latrobe PA 15650 Office Phone: 724-539-4218. Office Fax: 724-539-4295. E-mail: mtourre@wiu.k12.pa.us.

**TOURTELLOTTE, CHARLES DEE,** internist, rheumatologist, educator; b. Kalamazoo, Mich., Aug. 28, 1931; s. Dee and Helen May (Lotz) T.; m. Barbara Richwine, June 25, 1955; children: Daniel DeWitt (dec.), Elizabeth Anne, William Charles, Scott David. AB, Johns Hopkins U., 1953; MS in Biochemistry, MD, Temple U., 1957. Diplomate Am. Bd. Internal Medicine. Intern, resident in medicine U. Mich. Hosp., Ann Arbor, 1957-60; fellow in rheumatology Temple U. Hosp., Phila., 1960-61; fellow in biochemistry Rockefeller U., N.Y.C., 1961-63; faculty Sch. Medicine, Temple U., 1963—; prof. medicine, 1972-97, prof. emeritus, 1997—; chief rheumatology Temple U. Hosp., 1994-97, pres. med. staff, bd. govs., 1984-86. Dir. Greater Delaware Valley Arthritis Control Program, 1974-77; pres. Eastern Pa. chpt. Arthritis Found., 1972-74; mem. active/cons. staff 10 area and regional hosps. Contbr. chpts. to textbooks, articles to profl. jours.; mem. editl. bd.: Arthritis and Rheumatism, 1969-77, 19th-24th Rheumatism Revs, 1969-81. Mem. Haddonfield (N.J.) Bd. Edn., 1968-74, pres., 1974; mem. Borough of Haddonfield Environ. Comm., 1975-87, chmn., 1977-85; mem. Haddonfield Civic Assn., 1963—; South N.J. chmn. Johns Hopkins U. Alumni Schs. Com., 1975-90; trustee Bobby Fulton Meml. Fund, 1979—, 1st Presbyn. Ch. of Haddonfield, 1998-2000. With AUS, 1953-61. Helen Hay Whitney Found. fellow, 1962-63; Arthritis Found. fellow, 1963-66 Fellow ACP, Phila. Coll. Physicians, Am. Coll. Rheumatology (founding fellow); mem. Pa. Med. Soc., Phila. County Med. Soc., Babcock Surg. Soc., Phila. Rheumatism Soc. (pres. 1968-69), Pa. Rheumatology Soc. (founding pres. 1985-86), N.J. Soc. of Pa., Nat. Huguenot Soc. (surgeon gen. 2002-04), Huguenot Soc. Pa., Temple U. Med. Alumni Assn. (pres. 1997-99), Tavistock County Club (N.J.), Little Egg Harbor Yacht Club, Med. Club of Phila. (bd. dirs., pres. 1998-99), Sixty-five Club of Haddonfield (dir. 2004—), Interfaith Caregivers (trustee 2004—), Sigma Xi, Alpha Omega Alpha, Delta Upsilon, Phi Chi. Presbyterian. Home: 6 Lane Of Acres Haddonfield NJ 08033-3505 Office: Temple Univ Hosp Dept Rheumatology Philadelphia PA 19140-5192 Office Phone: 215-707-2000. Personal E-mail: cd_tourte@prodigy.net.

**TOURTELLOTTE, WALLACE WILLIAM,** neurologist, educator; b. Great Falls, Mont., Sept. 13, 1924; s. Nathaniel Mills and Frances Victoria (Charlton) T.; m. Jean Esther Toncray, Feb. 14, 1953; children: Wallace William, George Mills, James Millard, Warren Gerard. PhB, BS, U. Chgo., 1945, PhD, 1948, MD, 1951. Intern Strong Meml. Hosp. U. Rochester Sch. Medicine and Dentistry, NY, 1951-52; resident in neurology U. Mich. Med. Ctr., Ann Arbor, 1954-57, asst. prof. neurology, 1957-59, assoc. prof., 1959-66, prof., 1966-71; prof. dept. neurology UCLA, 1971—, vice chmn. dept. neurology, 1971-98, prof. neurology scale VI, 1991—2000, emeritus vice chmn. dept. neurology, 1998; chief neurology svcs. VA Wadsworth, West LA, Calif., 1971-99, emeritus, 1999—, emeritus dir. tng. program, 1999—; staff neurologist, neuroscientist, 1999—. Vis. assoc. prof. Washington U., St. Louis, 1963-64; hon. mem. med. adv. bd. Nat. Multiple Sclerosis Soc., 1968—, So. Calif. Multiple Sclerosis Socs., 1972—; dir. Multiple Sclerosis Rsch. and Treatment Ctr., Human Brain and Spinal Fluid Resource Ctr., 1961—. Co-editor (with Cedric Raines, Henry McFarland): Multiple Sclerosis, Clinical and Pathogenetic Basis, 1997; mem. editorial bd. Jour. Neurol. Sci., Revue Neurologica, Italian Jour. Neurol. Sci., Multiple Sclerosis Jour.; dedicated The Wallace W. Tourtellotte Clin. and Neurosci. Libr., 1999. Mem. Presdl. Bus. Commn. George W. Bush. Lt. (j.g.) M.C., USNR, 1952-54. Recipient Disting. Alumni Service award U. Chgo., 1982. Fellow Am. Acad. Neurology (S. Weir Mitchell Neurology Reseach award 1959); mem. Am. Neurol. Assn. (counselor 1982—, v.p. 1992), World Fedn. Neurology (founding mem.), Am. Assn. Neuropathologists, Internat. Soc. Neurochemsitry (founding mem.), Soc. Pharmacology and Exptl. Therapeutics, Am. Soc. Neurochemistry (founding mem.), Soc. Neurosci., Confrerie de la Chaine des Rotisseur, Argentier du Baillage de Los Angeles (vice chancellor, comdr.), Ordre Mondial des Gourmets Degustateurs Etats-Unis Chevalier, Pasadena Wine and Food Soc., Physician Wine and Food Soc., Culinary Club French Cuisine LA, Sigma Xi. Republican. Presbyterian. Home: 1140 Tellem Dr Pacific Palisades CA 90272-2244 Fax: 310-454-7650. Office Phone: 310-268-4638. Business Email: wtourtel@ucla.edu.

**TOURTET, CHRISTIANE ANDRÉE,** writer, photojournalist, reporter, advocate; b. Grenoble, France, June 18, 1945; came to U.S.; 1965; d. André and Maria Tourtet. Cert. completion humanistic psychology, Fla. Jr. Coll.,

Jacksonville, 1969; AS with high honors, Fla. Jr. Coll., 1973, AA with high honors, 1974; BA with honors, Jacksonville U., 1975. Hostess interpreter-translator Credit Lyonnais, Grenoble, 1963—65; instr. French Albany Acad. for Girls, NY, 1965—66; instr. French, asst. lang. lab. Coll. of St. Rose, Albany, 1966—67; instr. French Bartram Sch., Jacksonville, 1970; instr. French and modeling Fla. Jr. Coll., 1971—74; prodr.-dir., radio personality ednl. French program Sta. WFAM FM radio, Jacksonville, 1977—79; interpreter, translator French Lang. Bank, Jacksonville, 1980—83. Tutor pvt. and small group classes in French; model for publicity ads, brochures in major mags., newspapers; lectr. in field. Author: Fruits of Life; editor, contbr. New Leaf News, Fla. Flambeau, Back to Sch. Mag., editor, pub., contbr. Environ. Med. and Disability Corner, Tallahassee Area Ch. News, FSView, AARP Newsletter, Tallahassee Alliance with Disabilities Newsletter, pres. Flamingo Studios, Tallahassee, 1986—87; Exhibited in group shows at North Fla. Fair, Tallahassee, 2002 (1st, 2d and 3d pl. photography, 2d pl., 2003, 3 second place awards, 2005, 3 certs. pub. Today's Photographer mag. 2004, three 2d place awards, 2005), paintings exhibited in France, Monte Carlo and U.S., photography exhibited in galleries, pub. in mags. including Today's Photographer; guest appearance Phyllis Fouraker Show, Jacksonville, Fla.; actress on 28 TV commls.:. Pres. Le Cercle Francais, Albany, 1965; founder, pres. Internat. Multiple Chem. Sensitivity Awareness. Named Woman of Yr., Romanian Prince Paltin Sturdza, Princess Cornelia Sturdza and Prince Michael Sturdza, 1995, Internat. Personality of Yr., Ctr. Internat. Biography, 2001; named to Millenium Hall of Fame, Permanent Honor Roll, Internat. Freelance Photographers Orgn., 2004; recipient 1st prize Solfège Artistic Competition, 1957, 1st prize, Accordion Acad. Grenoble, 1958, Bronze medal accordion solo, Cup of France, City of Lyon, 1958, Gold medal Cup of France, 1959, Cup of Europe, 1959, 2d prize in singing, City of Grenoble, 1961, medal of City of Grenoble, 1977, medal of Dauphine County, 1977, medal of Chevalier of Order of Merit, Paris, 1976, medal of Chevalier of French Courtesy, 1977, medal of Nat. Merit, 1976, Silver medal Arts and Scis., 1977, Silver medal honor, Twentieth Century Achievement award, 1993, U.S. flag flown over Capitol in her honor, Washington, 1999—2001, Internat. Woman of Yr., Romanian Prince Paltin Sturdza, Princess Cornelia Sturdza and Prince Michael Sturdza, 1996—97, Lifetime Distinction of Honor for Photographic Achievement, Am. Image Press, 2004, Meritorious Achievement award, Internat. Peace prize, United Cultural Conv. U.S.A., 2005. Mem.: APHA, NAFE, Am. Internat. News Svc. (mem.), Am. Image Press, Freelance Media Svcs., Nat. Assn. Sci. Writers, Am. Med. Writers Assn., Nat. Ctr. Environ. Strategies, Chem. Injury Info. Network (judge arts and talent contest 1999), Environ. Illness Assn. Tallahassee (founder, pres. 1989—), Am. Acad. Environ. Medicine (assoc.), World Nat. Congress (senator 2003—), H.E.A.L. Share, Care, Prayers, Internat. Platform Assn., India Assn. Tallahassee (publicity officer, fashion show judge), Phi Theta Kappa. Address: PO Box 20517 Tallahassee FL 32316-0517 Personal E-mail: tourtet@yahoo.com.

**TOUSLEY, REBECCA PERKINS,** retired librarian; b. Columbus, Miss., Mar. 28, 1926; d. Mosey Miles and Virginia Susan (Shelton) Perkins; m. Jasper Clayton Tousley Jr., Aug. 11, 1946; children: Judith Ann, Roger Clayton, Susan Elizabeth. Student, Trevecca Nazarene Coll., 1947-48; BS in Libr. Sci., Miss. Univ. for Women, 1974, MA in English Lit., 1981. Asst. to serials libr. Fant Libr., Miss. Univ. for Women, Columbus, 1966-74, asst. serials libr., govt. publs. libr., 1974-80, govt. publs. libr., 1980-90, ret., 1990. Treas. Miss. Govt. Documents Roundtable, 1978; libr. Ch. of the Nazarene, Columbus, 1975—. Author: History of the Columbus Mississippi Church of the Nazarene, 1978; co-author Libr. Info. Bull., 1983-84. Mem. AAUW (publicity chmn. 1990-91), Miss. Univ. for Women Alumni Assn., Phi Kappa Phi (sec.-treas. 1980-82, 84-86). Avocations: homemaking, gardening, needlecrafts. Home: 415 Highway 373 Columbus MS 39705-9345

**TOUSSAINT, ALLEN RICHARD,** recording studio executive, composer, pianist; b. New Orleans, Jan. 14, 1938; s. Clarence Matthew and Naomi (Neville) Toussaint; children: Naomi, Clarence, Alison. Student pub. and pvt. schs., New Orleans. Pres. Sea-Saint Rec. Studios, Inc., New Orleans; founder NYNO Music, 1998. Lectr. in field. Pianist for: Shirley & Lee, 1957, U.S. Army Soldiers Choir, 1963—65, recorded albums: Tousan-Wild Sounds of New Orleans, 1958, Life, Love & Faith, 1972, Southern Nights, 1975, Motion, 1978, Connected, 1996, founder, v.p. recorded albums: Sansu Enterprises, Inc., 1965—; composer: (songs) Southern Nights (Country Music Assn. Song of Yr., Broadcast Music, Inc. citation of achievement), The Greatest Love, The Optimism Blues, Viva La Money, Whipped Cream, With You In Mind, Working In A Coal Mine, Yes We Can, Can, All These Things (Broadcast Music, Inc. citation of achievement); performer, dir., choreography: (Broadway plays) The High Rollers Social and Pleasure Club, 1992; performer New Orleans Jazz Festival, annually. With U.S. Army, 1963—65. Named to Rock and Roll Hall of Fame, 1998. Mem.: Contemporary Arts Ctr., Am. Fedn. Musicians, Broadcast Music, Inc.

**TOUSSAINT, ROGER,** labor union administrator; b. Port of Spain, Trinidad, Nov. 7, 1956; m. Donna Toussaint; 4 children. Attended, Brooklyn Coll. Cleaner Met. Transp. Authority (MTA), 1984—85, track maintenance worker, 1985; leader Track Div. Transport Workers Union (TWU) Local 100, NYC, 1994, pres., 2001—. Co-founder On Track newsletter. Office: TWU Local 100 80 West End Ave New York NY 10023 Office Phone: 212-873-6000.

**TOUSSIENG, YOLANDA,** make-up artist; Television work includes: (movies) Fallen Angel, 1981, 1981, Blue de Ville, 1986, (series) Pee-wee's Playhouse, 1986, (mini-series) North and South, Book II, 1986, films include Blue City, 1986, No Man's Land, 1987, Beetlejuice, 1988, Gross Anatomy, 1989, Three Fugitives, 1989, Farewell to the King, 1989, Edward Scissorhands, 1990, Flatliners, 1990, Everybody Wins, 1990, Hoffa, 1992, Batman Returns, 1992, Mrs. Doubtfire, 1993, Rising Sun, 1993, Ed Wood, 1994 (Acad. award for Best Make-up, 1994), Being Human, 1994, Junior, 1994. Office: IATSE Local 706 11519 Chandler Blvd North Hollywood CA 91601-2618

**TOUSTER, SAUL,** law educator; b. Bklyn., Oct. 12, 1925; s. Ben and Bertha (Landau) T.; m. Helen Davidson, Nov. 23, 1954 (div. 1967); children: Natasha Ann, Jonathan Bach; m. Irene Tayler, Jan. 14, 1978. AB magna cum laude, Harvard U., 1944, JD, 1948. Bar: N.Y. 1949. Practiced in, N.Y.C., 1949-55; prof. law SUNY-Buffalo, 1955-69, asst. to pres., 1966-68, mem. adj. faculty in medicine, edn., psychology, 1964-69; prof. law and social scis. State Coll. at Old Westbury, 1969-71; prof., provost, acad. v.p. CCNY, 1971-73; acting pres. Richmond Coll. City U. N.Y., 1973-74; prof. law CUNY Grad. Sch. also John Jay Coll. of Criminal Justice, 1974-80; prof., dir. legal studies, humanities, professions programs Brandeis U., Waltham, Mass., 1980-93, prof. emeritus 1993. Legis. cons. N.Y. State Law Rev. Commn., 1956-61; vis. prof. U. Brussels, summer, 1968, Boston Coll. Law Sch., 1994. Author: Still Lives and Other Lives, 1966, Surrealism and the Art of Samuel Bak, in Between Worlds, 2002; editor, author introduction: A Survivors' Haggadah, 1998, Beyond Words: A Holocaust History in Sixteen Woodcuts done in 1945 by Miklos Adler, A Hungarian Survivor, 2001; contbr. articles to legal periodicals. Served to lt. (j.g.) USNR, 1944-46. NEH fellow, 1978; Am. Bar Found. Legal History fellow, 1977-78 Mem. Internat. Inst. Boston (bd. advisors), Phi Beta Kappa. Home: 180 Beacon St Boston MA 02116-1408 E-mail: stouster@mac.com.

**TOUWAIDE, ALAIN JACQUES ANDRÉ,** science educator, researcher; b. Brussels, Sept. 19, 1953; arrived in Spain, 1993; s. Henry and Simone (Lenelle) T. Degree in classics, Cath. U. Louvain, Belgium, 1975, degree in Oriental studies, 1978, PhD, 1981; Habil, U. Toulouse, 1997. Asst. U. Louvain, 1982-83, sr. rsch. fellow, 1983-85; assoc. prof. U. Nice, France, 1992-93. vis. prof. U. Provence, France, 1989-90, Cen. U., Barcelona, Spain, 1993-94, Consejo Superior de Investigaciones Científicas, 1997-98; prin. in field, 1990—; freelance journalist, 1985—. Author: Farmacopea Araba Medievale, 4 vols., 1992-93, La tossicologia antica a Bisanzio, 1993, Nicandro, Theriaka y Alexipharmaka, 1998, Une histoire du médicament en

Occident (Prix d'Histoire de la Médecine/Acad. Belgium 1996), Therapeutics, an Anthology, 1998. Fellow Linnean Soc. (London); mem. Internat. Acad. History of Pharmacy. E-mail: atouwaide@hotmail.com.

**TOVANI, C. CRISTINE,** literature and language educator; writer; d. Robert J. and Carolyn J. Scavo; m. E. Pete Tovani, Apr. 15, 1989; 1 child, Caroline C. MEd, U. Colo., Boulder, 1986. Tchr. Cherry Creek Schs., Greenwood Village, Colo., 1984—. Author: (writing, international consulting/speak) I Read it, but Don't Get it. Office: Smoky Hill High Sch 16100 E Smoky Hill Rd Aurora CO 80013 Office Phone: 720-886-5643. Personal E-mail: pete_cris_tovani@msn.com. E-mail: ctovani@cherrycreekschools.org.

**TOVAR-MENGIBAR, SALVADOR,** retired government agency administrator; s. Tomás Demetrio Tovar-Centeno and Victoria Dolores Mengíbar-Orellana; m. Grace Salazar, Dec. 19, 1959; children: Enrique Salvador Tovar, Alejandro Tovar. BS, CUNY, Bronx, 1974; MPA, NYU, NYC, 1977; JD, CUNY, Flushing, 1989. Med. lab. technician Montefiore Med. Ctr., Bronx, 1967—89; legal asst. NY State Dept. of Law, NYC, 1990—93; asylum officer US Dept. of Justice, Internat. Rels. Divsn., NYC, 1994—2001; ret. Author: (novels) Florida, mon amour!. E-2 U.S. Army, 1956—58, Fort Dix, NJ. D-Liberal. Avocations: reading, travel, jogging, playing cards. Home: 211-10 18th Ave Bayside NY 11360-1533 Personal E-mail: stmengibar@aol.com.

**TOVI, MURRAY,** futurist, research scientist; b. N.Y.C., Mar. 18, 1937; s. Louis Tovi and Jean Cohen; m. Joan H. Granoff, Oct. 30, 1965; 1 child, Rosanna. BBA, CCNY, 1961. Exec v.p. Tovi and Perris, Inc., N.Y.C., 1969—73; pres. Murray Tovi Designs, Inc., N.Y.C., 1975—78, Concepts in Art and Sci. Inc., Colorado Springs, 1982—89, Transflectors, Inc., Colorado Springs, 1988—90, Theoretical Optics Inc., Colorado Springs, 1988—90, Tovi Scis., Ocala, Fla., 1991—. Cons. Am. Soc. Interior Designers, N.Y.C., 1985—86. Author: Introduction to Neo-Classical Physics, 2001, The Relative Speed of Light Theory, 2003. Achievements include invention of first discreet surveillance system. Office: Tovi Scis PO Box 116 Sparr FL 32192 Office Phone: 352-671-6600. Business E-Mail: ToviSciences@aol.com.

**TOVISH, HAROLD,** sculptor; b. N.Y.C., July 31, 1921; s. Louis Goodman and Anna (Treffman) T.; m. Marianna Pineda (Packard), Jan. 14, 1946 (dec. 1997); children: Margo, Aaron, Nina. Student, WPA Art Project, 1938-40, Columbia U., 1940-43, Ossip Zadkine Sch. Drawing and Sculpture, Paris, France, 1949-50, Acad. De La Grande Chaumiere, Paris, 1950-51. Tchr. sculpture N.Y. State Coll. Ceramics, 1947-49, U. Minn., 1951-54, Sch. of Boston Mus., 1957-66; sculptor in residence Am. Acad. in, Rome, 1966; prof. art Boston U., 1971-85, prof. emeritus, 1986—. Vis. prof. U. Hawaii, 1969-70 Group exhbns. include Met. Mus. of Art, 1943, Toledo Mus. Art, 1948, Galerie 8, 1949, Walker Art Center, 1951, Mpls. Inst. Art, 1953, San Francisco Art Assn., 1953, Whitney Mus. Am. Art, 1954, 58, 60, 64, 80, 28th Venice Biennial, 1956, Mus. Modern Art, 1960, Chgo. Art Inst., 1960, Carnegie Internat, 1960, Am. Fedn. Art, 1964, Decordova Mus., 1964, Internat. Exhbn. of Contemporary Medal, Paris, 1967, Boston Visual Artists Union Gallery, 1975, Boston U., 1975, 78, Colby Coll., 1975, Inst. Contemporary Art, Boston, 1975, 76, Skowhegan Sch., 1975, NYU, 1976, Boston Mus. Fine Arts, 1977, Nat. Mus. Am. Art, 1987, Nat. Acad. Design, 1987, DeCordova Mus., 1987, Howard Yezersky Gallery, 1988; one-man shows include, Walker Art Center, 1953, Swetzoff Gallery, Boston, 1957, 60, 65, Dintenfass Gallery, N.Y.C., 1965, 72, Addison Gallery Am. Art, Andover, Mass., 1965, Alpha Gallery, Boston, 1968, 73, 86, Terry Dintenfass, Inc., N.Y.C., 1980, 85, Boston U., 1980, retrospective exhibit, Wheaton Coll., 1967, Howard Yezerski Gallery, Boston, 1993, 95; survey exhibit, Solomon Guggenheim Meml. Mus., 1968, Fed. Res. Bank, Boston, 1991; retrospective exhbn. Addison Gallery Am. Art, 1988; survey exhibit Muscarelle Mus., Williamsburg, Va., 1990; represented in permanent collections Phila. Mus. Art, Whitney Mus. Am. Art, Walker Art Center, Mpls. Inst. Art, Addison Gallery Am. Art, Chgo. Art Inst., Mus. Modern Art, Boston Mus. Fine Art, Guggenheim Mus., Worcester Mus. Art, Hirshhorn Collection, Sara Roby Found., Colby Coll., Muscarelle Mus. William & Mary Coll., Williamsburg, Va., Nat. Gallery Am. Art, Minn. Gallery Art, Nat. Mus. Am. Art, Boston Pub. Library; (Recipient 1st prize sculpture Boston Arts Festival 1957, 1st prize drawing 1958, award Am. Inst. Arts and Letters 1971, sculpture grantee Am. Inst. Arts and Letters 1960). Guggenheim fellow, 1967; research fellow Center for Advanced Visual Studies, MIT, 1967-68 Mem. NAD (assoc. 1981-90, academician, 1990-)

**TOW, LEONARD,** television executive; b. Bklyn., May 30, 1928; s. Louis and Estelle (Weiss) T.; m. Claire Leona Schneider, Aug. 10, 1952; children: Frank, Andrew, Emily. BA, CUNY, 1950; MA, Columbia U., 1952, PhD, 1960. Instr. Hunter Coll., CUNY, 1952-55, Bklyn. Coll., CUNY, 1955-57; lectr. Coll. Ins., N.Y.C., 1952-57, Columbia U. Sch. Bus., N.Y.C., 1958-60; exec. Venture Capital Projects, N.Y.C., 1960-63; mgmt. cons. Touche Ross & Co., N.Y.C., 1963-64; sr. v.p. Teleprompter Corp., N.Y.C., 1964-73; founder, chmn., CFO, CEO Century Communications Corp., New Canaan, Conn., 1973—90; chmn. bd. dirs., CEO, CFO Citizens Communications Co. (formerly Citizens Utilities Corp.), Stamford, Conn., 1990—, CEO, 1990—2004. Disting. adj. prof. NYU, N.Y.C., 1985-88. Author: Manufacturing Economy of Southern Rhodesia, 1960, also numerous articles to trade publs. Fellow NAS-NRC, Salisbury, So. Rhodesia, 1957-58. Office: Citizens Utilities Co High Ridge Pk PO Box 3801 Stamford CT 06905-0801

**TOWBIN, A(BRAHAM) ROBERT,** investment banker; b. N.Y.C., May 26, 1935; s. Harold Clay and Minna (Berlin) T.; children: Minna Joyce Pinger, Abraham Robert Jr., Zachary Harold. BA, Dartmouth Coll., 1957. With Asiel & Co., N.Y.C., 1958-59; with L.F. Rothschild, Unterberg, Towbin Holdings, Inc. (merged with C.E. Unterberg, Towbin Co. 1977), N.Y.C., 1959-86, vice chmn., 1961-86; mng. dir. Lehman Bros., NY, 1987—94; pres. Russian Am. Enterprise Fund., Moscow and N.Y.C., 1994-95; vice chmn. U.S. Russia Investment Fund, Moscow and N.Y.C., 1995; mng. dir. C.E. Unterberg, Towbin, N.Y.C., 1995—99, co-chmn., 1999—2002; exec. v.p. Stephens, Inc., N.Y.C., 2002—. Bd. dirs. Gerber Sci. Inc., Globecomm Sys. Inc., Northfork Bancorp., Intertrust. Hon. mem. N.Y. State Coun. Arts Mem.: Securities Industry Assn., Nat. Golf Links Am., Century Assn., Chelsea Art Club (London), Antigua Yacht Club, N.Y. Yacht Club (trustee 2004—), Bond Club N.Y. Office: Stephens Inc 65 E 55th St New York NY 10022 Office Phone: 212-891-1720. Business E-Mail: rtowbin@stephens.com.

**TOWE, THOMAS EDWARD,** lawyer; b. Cherokee, Iowa, June 25, 1937; s. Edward and Florence (Tow) T.; m. Ruth James, Aug. 21, 1960; children: James Thomas, Kristofer Edward. Student, U. Paris, 1956; BA, Earlham Coll., 1959; LLB, U. Mont., 1962; LLM, Georgetown U., 1965. Ptnr. Towe, Ball, Enright, Mackey & Sommerfeld, Billings, Mont., 1967—; legislator Mont. House of Rep., Billings, 1971-75, Mont. State Senate, Billings, 1975-87, 91-94. Com. mem. Mont. Senate, 1975—87, 1991—94. Contbr. articles to law revs. Mem. Alternatives, Inc., Halfway House, Billing, 1977-99, pres., 1985-86; mem. adv. com. Mont. Crime Control Bd., 1973-78, Youth Justice Coun., 1981-83; mem. State Dem. Exec. Com., 1969-73; Dem. candidate for Congress, 1976; bd. dirs. Mont. Consumer Affairs Coun., Regl. Cmty. Svcs. for the Devel. Disabled, 1975-77, Rimrock Guidance Found., 1975-80, Vols. of Am., Billings, 1984-89, Youth Dynamics Inc., 1989-96, Zoo Mont., 1985-2001, Inst. for Peace Studies, 1993—, Mont. State Parks Assn., 1993—. Capt. U.S. Army, 1962-65. Named as one of 100 Most Influential Montanans in 20th Century, Missoulian newspaper. Mem. Mont. Bar Assn., Yellowstone County Bar Assn., Billings Cc. of C. Mem. Soc. Of Friends. Avocation: outdoor recreation. Home: 2739 S Gregory Dr Billings MT 59102-0509 Office: Towe Ball Enright Et Al 2525 6th Ave N Billings MT 59101-1358 Office Phone: 406-248-7337. Business E-Mail: t.towe@bresnan.net.

**TOWELL, TIMOTHY LATHROP,** foreign service officer; b. Cleve., Jan. 31, 1934; s. Bernard A. and Eleanor (Assmus) T.; children: Timothy Nichols, Dane Billings. BA, Yale U., 1957; MA, Case-Western Res. U., 1962. Commd. fgn. svc. officer Dept. State; vice consul U.S. Consulate, Valencia, Spain,

1963-65; spl. asst. to ambassador Am. embassy, Madrid, 1965-66; U.S. Consul, Am. embassy, Asuncion, Paraguay, 1966-67; 1st sec. Am. Embassy, La Paz, Bolivia, 1967-68; Bolivian desk officer Dept. State, Washington, 1968-70, Spanish desk officer, 1970-72; U.S. consul U.S. Consulate, Porto Alegre, Brazil, 1972-75; 1st sec. Am. Embassy, Brussels, Belgium, 1975-79; dep. chief of mission, U.S. Mission, Havana, Cuba, 1979-80; congl. liaison officer Europe, Dept. State, Washington, 1980-83; dep. chief of protocol of U.S., Washington, 1983-88; ambassador to Paraguay, 1988-91; regional dir. Africa The Peace Corps, Washington, 1991-92; pres. fgn. policy group, 1992—. Mem. Met. Club (Washington), Tavern Club (Cleve.).

**TOWER, IBROOK,** music educator, conductor, musician; b. Boston, July 21, 1948; s. Osgood and Nancy DuBose (Maxwell) T.; m. Harriet Ellen Darling, July 30, 1982; 1 child, Adams Darling. MusB in Edn., MusB in Clarinet, Peabody Conservatory of Johns Hopkins, 1970; postgrad., Aspen Music Sch., 1971; MusM, Temple U., 1972; diploma fine arts, U. Calgary, 1986; D Mus. Arts, U. Cin., 1994. Cert. tchr., Pa. Tchr. instrumental music Archdiocese of Balt., 1969-70; instr. woodwind Peabody Inst., Balt., 1970-71, Wilmington (Del.) Music Sch., 1969-74; lectr. music, dir. bands Muhlenberg Coll., Allentown, Pa., 1972-74; assoc. instr. music Moravian Coll., Bethlehem, Pa., 1973-74; prin. clarinetist, asst. condr. Altoona (Pa.) Symphony Orch., 1983-96; assoc. prof. music, dir. instrumental music Juniata Coll., Huntingdon, Pa., 1974-94; condr. Ctrl. Pa. Youth Orch., 1989-91; assoc. condr. Cin. Wind Symphony, 1989-90; asst. prof. music, dir. bands Elizabethtown (Pa.) Coll., 1995—98; clarinetist Fasola Orch., Lancaster, Pa., 2002—03, Allegro Chamber Orch., Lancaster, 2003—; mem. faculty Harrisburg Area C.C., 2001—02, Milton Hershey Sch., Hershey, Pa., 1998—, Lebanon Valley Coll., Annville, Pa., 2000—; tchr., arranger Pa. Acad. Music, Lancaster, 1998—. Musician Young Audiences, Inc., Balt., 1968-70, Balt. Actors Theatre, 1968-72; artistic dir. Seven Points Amphitheater, Raystown Lake, Hesston, Pa., 1977-83. Arranger march Our President (S.T. Jones), 1980; contbr. chpts. to books and articles to profl. jours. Bd. dirs. Nittany Valley Symphony Orch., State Coll., Pa., 1978-87, Huntingdon County Arts Coun., 1980-81. Recipient Lindback award for Disting. Teaching, 1980, Thomas prize in instrumental music Peabody Conservatory, 1970; Joseph E. Maddy scholar Peabody Conservatory, 1966-70, univ. grad. scholar Cin. Coll. Conservatory, 1999-90; Settlement Music Sch. fellow Temple U., 1971-72. Mem. NEA, Nat. Assn. Music Edn., Pa. State Edn. Assn., Pa. Music Educators Assn., Coll. Band Dirs. Nat. Assn. (Pa. chmn. 1995—98), Condrs. Guild, Internat. Clarinet Soc., USN Band (hon.). Democrat. Unitarian Universalist. Avocations: sailing, gardening, reading, cooking, computers. Business E-Mail: ibrookitower@jhu.edu.

**TOWER, JOAN PEABODY,** composer, educator; b. New Rochelle, N.Y., Sept. 6, 1938. B.A., Bennington Coll., 1961; M.A., Columbia U., 1964, D.M.A., 1978. Pianist, Da Capo Chamber Players, 1969-84; compositions include: Sequoia (premiered by Am. Composers Orch.), Silver Ladders, 1985 (premiered by St. Louis Symphony, Grawemeyer award, U. Louisville, 1990), Breakfast Rhythms, Black Topaz, Amazon, Wings (solo clarinet), Fantasy (clarinet and piano), Cello Concerto, Piano Concerto, Clarinet Concerto, Flute Concerto, Violin Concerto, "Music for Cello and Orchestra", "Island Prelude" for oboe and strings by Cleveland, Philadelphia, and Seattle Symphony Orchestras and "Fanfare the Uncommon Woman" by more than 200 ensembles; works recorded; Compact Discs have been released on Koch International, Delos, and d'Note Records; commns.: Contemporary Music Soc., Jerome Found., Mass. State Arts Council, Schubert Club St. Paul, Richard Stoltzman, St. Louis Symphony, Pitts. Symphony, Houston Symphony, Elmar Oliveira, N.Y. Philharm., Chgo. Symphony, Sharon Isbin, Carol Wincenc, Fromm Found., NEA, Carnegie Hall, Milw. Ballet, Lincoln Ctr. Chamber Soc., Aspen Festival, Cleve. Muir Quartets, L.A. Chamber Orch.; assoc. prof. Bard Coll., Annandale On Hudson, N.Y., from 1972, currently Asher B. Edelman prof. music (composition); composer-in-residence St. Louis Symphony Orchestra, 1985-88, 1999-2002. Recipient N.Y. State Council for Arts award, 1980, Alfred Dupont award for disting. composers and conductors; Guggenheim fellow, 1976, Nat. Endowment Arts fellow, 1974, 75, 80, 84, Koussevitzky Found. grantee, 1982, Meet the Composer Consortium grantee, 1989, 91, 92, Nat. Endowment Rec. grantee, 1993. Fellow Am. Acad. Arts and Sciences; mem. Am. Acad. of Arts and Letters (award in music Am. Acad. and Inst. Arts and Letters, 1983). Office: Bard Coll Conservatory of Music PO Box 5000 Annandale On Hudson NY 12504-5000 Office Phone: 845-758-7196. Business E-Mail: tower@bard.edu.

**TOWER, MOLLIE GREGORY,** writer, educator, consultant; b. San Antonio, Tex., July 17, 1945; d. Malcolm Russell and Margaret Halm Gregory; children: Debbie Tower Tannert, Sheryl Tower Maklary. MusB, U. Tex., Austin, 1967; MEd, U. Tex., Austin, 1981. Cert. Texas Music K-12 Tex. Edn. Agy., 1967, Texas Supr. Tex. Edn. Agy., 1981. Elem. music tchr., k - 6 Austin Ind. Sch. Dist., Tex., 1967—78, elem. music coord., 1978—92, coord. of choral and gen. music, k-12, 1992—98; author Glencoe/McGraw-Hill, Woodland Hills, Calif., 1995—, Macmillan/McGraw-Hill Pub. Co., N.Y.C., NY, 1982—96, Silver-Burdett Pub. Co., N.Y.C., NY, 2004—; sr. author arts edn. IDEAS Pub. Co., Norwalk, Conn., 1998—. Cons. Various sch. dist., 1975—2006; pres. Tex. Music Educators Conf., Tex., 1993—96, Tex. Music Admintrs. Conf., Tex., 1996—97, Tex. Coalition for Music Edn., Tex., 1992—93. Author: (ann. elem. curriculum program) Music Memory Bulletin, 1981—2005, (textbook) Music Reading Charts, Grade One & Grade Two, 1988, Songs in Spanish, Primary and Intermediate, 1989, Musica para todas, primary and intermediate, 1995, Choral Connections, 1997, Experiencing Choral Music, 2005. V.p., commr. Austin Arts Commn., Austin, Tex., 1985—89. Mem.: Sigma Alpha Iota, Delta Kappa Gamma. Achievements include Am. Host of Riverside Symphony Music Memory Contest, Lincoln Ctr., N.Y.C., 1999-2006; Ann. Host of Kansas State Univ. Music Memory Contest, Manhattan, Kan., 2003-2006. Personal E-mail: mtower@realtime.net.

**TOWERS, JOHN R.,** manufacturing executive, lawyer; b. NYC, 1941; AB in Econs., Princeton U., 1963; LLB, U. Va., Richmond, 1966. V.p. client adminstrn. State Street Bank, Boston, 1969-81; v.p. product devel. Fidelity Investments, Boston, 1981-89; sr. v.p. mutual funds U.S. Trust Co. of N.Y., 1989-90; sr. v.p. securities Bank of Boston, 1990-94; v.p. State St. Bank & Trust, Boston, 1994-97; exec. v.p., gen. counsel State St. Boston Corp., Boston, 1997-2000, vice chmn., chief adminstrv. officer, 2000—. Mem. ABA, Boston Bar Assn., N.Y. State Bar Assn., Mass. Bar Assn., Am. Soc. Corp. Secs. Office: State Street Corp 225 Franklin St Boston MA 02110-2804

**TOWERY, CURTIS KENT,** lawyer; b. Hugoton, Kans., Jan. 29, 1954; s. Clyde D. and Jo June (Curtis) Towery. BA, Trinity U., 1976; JD, U. Okla., 1979; LLM in Taxation, Boston U., 1989. Mem. Curtis & Blanton, Pauls Valley, Okla., 1980-81; lawyer land and legal dept. Trigg Drilling Co., Oklahoma City, 1981-82; adminstrv. law judge Okla. Corp. Commn., Oklahoma City, 1982-85; counsel Curtis & Blanton, Pauls Valley, Okla., 1985-88; adminstrv. law judge Okla. Dept. Mines, Oklahoma City, 1985-88, assoc. gen. counsel, 1989-92; contracts and purchasing adminstr., atty. Okla. Turnpike Authority, Oklahoma City, 1992-93; asst. gen. counsel Okla. Corp. Commn., 1993-97; spl. judge City of Oklahoma City, 1997—2000; adminstrv. law judge Okla. Dept. of Labor, 1998, 2002—04; v.p., trust officer Bank One Trust, Oklahoma City, 1998-2000; mgr. Cherokee Capital Holdings, 2000—. Sr. adminstrv. law judge Okla. Corp. Commn., 2003—04; dept. special trustee Office of Special Trustee, dept. interior, 2004—05; asst. gen. counsel Okla. Dept. Labor, 2006—. Assoc. bd. Mus. Art, 1985—88, Okla. Symphony Orch., 1987—92, Ballet Okla., 1987—92, sec., 1990—91, v.p., 1988—89. Mem.: ABA, Okla. Bar Assn., Tex. Bar Assn., Faculty Ho., Elks, Rotary, Sigma Nu, Phi Alpha Delta. Republican. Presbyterian. Avocations: flying, golf, travel, investment analysis. Home: PO Box 18668 Oklahoma City OK 73154

**TOWERY, JAMES E.,** lawyer; b. Los Alamos, N.Mex., July 12, 1948; s. Lawson E. and Irma (Van Apeldorn) T.; 1 child, Mark J. BA, Princeton U., 1973; JD, Emory U., 1976. Assoc. Morgan Beauzay Hammer, San Jose, Calif., 1977-79; ptnr. Morgan & Towery, San Jose, Calif., 1979-89; assoc.

Hoge Fenton Jones & Appel, San Jose, Calif., 1989-90, ptnr., 1990—. Chmn. bd. trustees Alexian Bros. Hosp., San Jose, Calif., 1995-98. Mem. ABA (ho. of dels. 1989-98, standing com. client protection 1996—2000, chair 1998-00), State Bar Calif. (v.p. and chair discipline com. 1994-95, pres. 1995-96, bd. govs. 1992-96, pres. 1995-96, presiding arbitrator, fee arbitration program 1990-92), Santa Clara County Bar Assn. (counsel 1984-85, treas. 1987, pres. 1989). Office: Hoge Fenton Jones 60 S Market St San Jose CA 95113-2351 Office Phone: 408-947-2432. Business E-Mail: jet@hogefenton.com.

**TOWERY, SARAH CARLISLE,** artist, retired art educator; b. Alexander City, Ala., Oct. 4, 1911; d. Washington Homer Carlisle and Artimisha Motley; children: Carlisle, Misha Sampson, Sarah Wade. Attended, Huntingdon Coll., 1930—32, U. Montevallo, 1940—45, Black Mountain Coll., 1944, Pen State U., 1951. Instr. U. Montevallo, Ala., 1945, So. Union Jr. Coll., Wadley, Ala., 1953—56; docent, team leader pvt. studio, Alexander City, 1948—2000; owner, tchr. pvt. kindergarten sch., Alexander City, 1951—53; organizer, session planner World Art Workshop, San Miguel, Mexico, 1972—94. Tchr. mentor Alexander City Pub. Schs., 1959—61; charter mem. World Art Workshop, San Miguel, 1972—94; found., continuing bd. mem. Sarah Carlisle Towery Art Colony-Lake Martin, Alexander City, 1991—. Wall mural, First Meth. Ch., Alexander City, 1952; executor, designer (wall mural) Town History: Racial Segregation, 1978; wall mural, Alexander City Elem. Sch., 1978; contbr. paintings Operation Downtown, Alexander City, 2001, 2002. Recipient Govs. award, Ala. State Coun. Arts, 1999, Artist Select Exhibit award, Comer Mus. Arts Ctr., 1999. Mem.: Ala. Art League, Birmingham Art Assn., Montgomery Art Guild. Republican. Protestant. Avocation: travel. Home: 273 Glenhaven Dr Alexander City AL 35010

**TOWEY, JIM (H. JAMES TOWEY),** academic administrator, former federal official; b. 1956; m. Mary G. Towey; children: James Marion, Joseph Marius, Maximilian Marian, John Mariano, Marie Therese. BS with high honors, Fla. State U., 1978, JD, 1981. Legis. dir., legal counsel to Senator Mark O. Hatfield US Senate, Washington; cons. Fed. Welfare Reform Fla. State U., to Fla. Gov. Lawton Chiles and US Senator Bob Graham, 1995—96; sec. Fla. Dept. of Health and Rehabilitative Svcs., 1993; dep. asst. to Pres. The White House, Washington, 2002—05, asst. to Pres., 2005—06, dir. Office of Faith-Based and Cmty. Initiatives, 2002—06; pres. Saint Vincent Coll., Latrobe, Pa., 2006—. Author: (document) Five Wishes. Legal cons. Missionaries of Charity, Order of Mother Teresa, 1985—97, full-time vol. in home for people with AIDS, 1990; founder Aging with Dignity, 1996, pres., 1996—2002. Named one of Fifty Most Influential Christians in Am., Church World mag., Power and Influence Top Fifty of 2005, Non-Profit Times mag.; recipient Pro Ecclesia et Pontifice Papal Cross, His Holiness John Paul II, Archbishop John Carroll Award, Archdiocese of Miami. Mem.: KC. Roman Catholic. Office: Saint Vincent Coll Office of Pres 300 Fraser Purchase Rd Latrobe PA 15650-2690*

**TOWLE, ALEXIS CHARLES (LEX TOWLE),** education advocate; b. Newburyport, Mass., Mar. 23, 1946; s. Sidney Norwood and Nancy Lois (Roberts) Towle; m. Maryellen Foote, Oct. 19, 1991; children: Ian, Devon. BA, Oundle Coll., Northants, Eng., 1964, Yale U., New Haven, Conn., 1968. V.p., trust officer Nat. Shawmut Bank, Boston, 1973-78; v.p., fin. cons. Merrill Lynch & Co., Boston, 1979-82, Kidder, Peabody & Co., Boston, 1983-88; v.p., investment banker Boston Bay Capital, Inc., Boston, 1988-93; dir. devel., campaign Boston Renaissance Charter Sch., 1994-95; pres. Apple Tree Inst. Edn. Innovation, Washington, D.C., 1995—2005; dir. Apple Tree Inst. Edn., 2004—; mng. dir. Towle-Magnant Internat., LLC, 2005—. Trustee, trustee Stoneridge Montessori Sch., Beverly Mass., 1994-2003; co-founder, trustee Cesar Chavez Charter Sch., Washington, 1998-99, Washington Math Sci. Charter Sch., 1998-2001, Paul Jr. High Charter Sch., Washington, 1999-2001, Apple Early Literacy Presch., Washington, 2001-. Author (with others) amendments to D.C. School Reform Act of 1995. Lt USMC, 1968—71, Vietnam. Mem.: Nat. Soc. Fundraising Execs. Republican. Episcopalian. Avocations: skiing, ice hockey, gardening. Office Phone: 978-869-2424. Office Fax: 978-768-0130. E-mail: lex@appletreeinstitute.org.

**TOWLE, LELAND HILL,** retired federal agency administrator; b. Boston, Mar. 29, 1931; s. Leland and Bertha May (Hill) T.; m. Carol Peterson, June 5, 1953; children:— Peter Kimball, Gretchen Towle Maynard, Michele. BS, U. N.H., 1952; MS, M.I.T., 1953; Cert. in Bus. and Mgmt, U. Calif., Berkeley, 1962. Nuclear chemist Stanford Research Inst., Menlo Park, Calif., 1956-59, community systems economist, economist, nuclear economist, 1959-68, mgr. health scis. research, 1968-74; asst. dir. Nat. Center for Alcohol Edn., Arlington, Va., 1974-75. Cons. Medicine in the Pub. Interest, Washington, 1975, Internat. Ctr. for Alcohol Policies, 1995-98—; vis. scientist Nat. Inst. on Alcohol Abuse and Alcoholism, Rckville, Md., 1975-76, dep. dir. office of program devel. and analysis, 1976-77, assoc. dir. office of program devel. and analysis, 1977-81, dir. internat. and intergovtl. affairs, 1981-95; dir. LHT Assocs., Inc., 1995-98. Contbr. articles to profl. jours. Bd. dirs. Med. Resources Found., Palo Alto, Calif., 1972-73. Served with USAF, 1952-56. Mem. Am. Pub. Health Assn., Sci. Research Soc. Am., Am. Nuclear Soc., Am. Chem. Soc., Sigma Xi, Phi Kappa Phi.

**TOWLER, EVELYN WHEELER,** retired elementary school educator; b. Northport, Mich., June 29, 1924; d. Lennis H. and Caroline Greiner Wheeler; m. Charles F. Towler (dec.); children: Jacquetta Sue, Charles F. Towler Jr. BA in History, BA in English Bible, Bob Jones U., Greenville, S.C., 1949; postgrad., U. Fla., 1950—54, Fla. So. Coll., Lakeland, 1966—67, U. S. Fla., 1968, Rollins Coll., Winter Park, Fla., 1970, Fla. Technol. U., 1970—75. Cert. elem. tchr., media specialist Fla. Kindergarten tchr., LaBelle, Fla., 1943—44; primary grades tchr. Spring Lake (Fla.) Elem. Sch., 1950—52; youth dir. Presbyn. Ch., Lakeland, Fla., 1952—54; tchg. prin., co-founder Lakeland Christian Sch., 1954—63; asst. to dean of edn Fla So Coll, Lakeland, 1964—67; tchr., lang. arts coord., media specialist Longwood Elem. Sch., Fla., 1967—85; media specialist, libr. Keswick Christian Sch., St. Petersburg, Fla., 1985—91; ret. 1991. Writer Lifepacs Alpha-Omega Pubs., Tempe, Ariz., 1977. Author: (novels) Under Sheltering Wings, 2001, The Road to Home, 2003, Teach Your Child to Write Creatively, 1985, Chronicles of a Hometown Church, 1993, Visitors Guide to Delightful Dunedin, 1995. Vol. Dunedin Hist. Mus.; mem. Dunedin Hist. Soc., Dunedin Friends of the Libr.; camp counselor Children's Bible Mission; bd. dirs. Dunedine Hist. Soc. Named one of Leaders of Am. Bible Coll. Edn., 1971, Outstanding Elem. Tchrs. of Am., 1973; named to Dunedin Sr. Hall of Fame, 2005; recipient HistoryMaker award, Dunedin Hist. Soc., 2000. Republican. Avocation: genealogy.

**TOWLER, KATHERINE,** writer; b. Pontiac, Mich., Sept. 1, 1956; d. Lewis W. Towler and Jane B. Kellogg; m. James A. Sparrell, Sept. 14, 1991. BA in English lit., U. of Mich., Ann Arbor, Michigan, 1974—78; MA in English lit., Middlebury Coll., Middlebury, Vermont, 1980—84; MA in fiction writing, Johns Hopkins U., Baltimore, Maryland, 1981—82. Freelance writer, publications cons. self-employed, Portsmouth, NH, 1987—; mem. faculty MFA Program in Writing, So. NH U., 2006—. Author: (novels) Snow Island, 2002 (Barnes and Noble Discover Great New Writers title, Borders Original Voices title, Booksense selection), Evening Ferry, 2005 (Booksense selection). Fellow George Bennett Fellowship, Phillips Exeter Acad., 1989-1990, Individual Artist Fellowship, NH. State Coun. on the Arts, 2003, Fellowship, Yaddo Artists Colony, 1985, 1983, Va. Ctr. for the Creative Arts, 1987, Working Scholarship, Bread Loaf Writers Conf., 1983. Mem.: Authors Guild, NH Writers Project (assoc.; bd. of trustees 1994—97), PEN New Eng. (assoc.). Avocations: bicycling, gardening, bird watching.

**TOWLES, DONALD BLACKBURN,** retired publishing executive; b. Lawrenceburg, Ky., Sept. 10, 1927; s. Joseph Sterling and Marjorie (Blackburn) Towles; m. Geraldine Gooden, Dec. 20, 1947 (dec. Nov. 1980); children: Sally Blackburn Towles Clark, Rebecca Neale Towles Brown; m. Julia Mason, Dec. 3, 1981. AB in Journalism, U. Ky., 1948. Asst. dir. publicity, editor In Ky. Mag. Commonwealth of Ky., Frankfort, 1948—55; pub. svc. mgr. Courier-Jour. and Louisville Times Co., Louisville, 1956—66, dir. pub. svc. and promotion, 1966—71, v.p., 1974—92, v.p., dir. circulation, 1971—76, v.p., dir. pub. affairs 1976—92; ret., 1993. Author: (book) The

Press of Kentucky 1787-1994; editor: Newspaper Promotion Handbook, 1983. Chmn. Louisville area chpt. ARC, 1987—89; mem. adv. bd. Salvation Army, 1982—97; elder emeritus Disciples of Christ; chmn. program adv. com. Louisville Devel. Program, 1971—80; bd. dirs. Louisville Med. Ctr., 1982—97; pres. Heritage Corp. Louisville, 1982—85; chmn. Thos. D. Clark Found., 2000—04; adv. bd. Christian Ch. Homes Ky., 1992—96; chmn. Sr. Citizens East, 1996—97. With U.S. Army, 1952—54, Korea. Named Outstanding Chpt. Vol., Louisville area ARC, 1993, Outstanding State Vol., 1994; named to Ky. Journalism Hall of Fame, 1992; recipient Cmty. Svc. award, Louisville Devel. Com., 1980. Mem.: Soc. Profl. Journalists (pres.Louisville chpt. 1991—92), Ky. Press Assn. (pres. 1982, Pres.'s Cup Leadership 1982, Disting. Svc. award 1987), Internat. Newspaper Promotion Area (pres. 1980—82, Silver Shovel 1983), Journalism Alumni Assn. U. Ky. (pres. 1979—94, Outstanding Alumnus award 1976, All-Am. Alumni award 1994). Democrat. Home: 4800 Whitekirk Ct Louisville KY 40222

**TOWNE, EDGAR ARTHUR,** theologian, educator; b. Albany, NY, Feb. 27, 1928; s. Arthur Bethuel and Margaret (Shug) T.; m. Sara Jean Wright, June 14, 1952 (div. 1961); children: Mary Michal, Jonathan Wright, Nathan Arthur; m. Marian Kleinsasser, Dec. 18, 1961; 1 child, Stephen Edgar. BA, Coll. Wooster, 1949; BD, Pitts. Theol. Sem., 1952; MA, U. Chgo., 1962, PhD, 1967. Ordained to ministry Presbyn. Ch. (USA), 1952. Assoc. prof. systematic theology Winebrenner Theol. Sem., Findlay, Ohio, 1962-67; prof. philosophy and religion Findlay Coll., 1967-70; min. Hyde Park Union Ch., Chgo., 1971-75; prof. theology Christian Theol. Sem., Indpls., 1975-93, prof. theology emeritus, 1993—. Vis. prof. theology Christian Theol. Sem., Indpls., 1970-71; vis. scholar Grad. Theol. Union, Berkeley, Calif., 1981-82, Pitts. Theol. Sem., 1988-89; co-moderator com. on pub. ministry Synod of Lincoln Trails, Ind., Ill., 1986-88. Author: Two Types of New Theism: Knowledge of God in the Thought of Paul Tillich and Charles Hartshorne, 1997. Ethics com. Meth. Hosp. Ind., Indpls., 1985—90. Recipient Robert Risk award, ACLU of Ind., 2002. Mem. Am. Theol. Soc. (pres. Midwest divsn. 1986-87, 2003-04), Am. Acad. Religion, Ctr. Process Studies, Soc. Christian Ethics, Highlands Inst. for Am. Religious and Philos. Thought. Independent. Home: 5129 N Illinois St Indianapolis IN 46208-2613

**TOWNE, GARY SPAULDING,** music educator; b. Burlington, Vt., June 12, 1950; s. Raymond Duane and Janet Spaulding Towne; m. Page Maurice Towne (dec.); children: Jonathan, Andrew. AB, Yale U., 1971; PhD, U. Calif., Santa Barbara, 1985. From asst. prof. to assoc. prof. U. N.D., Grand Forks, 1988—2002, prof., 2002—, dept. chair, 1999—2006. Vis. asst. prof. Middlebury (Vt.) Coll., 1985—88; organist, choirmaster St. Paul's Episcopal Ch., Grand Forks, 1995—2003; choirmaster United Luth. Ch., Grand Forks, 1988—91; dir. Collegium Musicum U. N.D. 1989—99. Contbr. articles to profl. publs.; editor: (book) Opera Omnia Gasparis de Albertis, vol. 1, 1999. Recipient Fulbright scholarship, USIA, 1994—95, Gladys Krieble Delmas fellowship, 1982—83, 1993, Stanley Krebs Meml. prize, U. Calif.-Santa Barbara, 1980, 1985. Mem.: Hist. Brass Soc., Coll. Music Soc., Am. Musicol. Soc., Internat. Musicol. Soc., Am. Motorcyclists Assn. Episcopalian. Avocation: motorcycling. Office: U ND Music Dept Box 7125 Grand Forks ND 58202 E-mail: gst1630@gra.midco.net.

**TOWNE, JONATHAN BAKER,** vascular surgeon; b. Youngstown, Ohio, Jan. 10, 1942; m. Sandra Green Towne, Aug. 24, 1963; children: Timothy, Heidi, Crista. BS, U. Pitts., 1963; MD, U. Rochester, N.Y., 1967. Intern in surgery U. Mich., Ann Arbor, 1967-68, resident I, 1968-69; resident II, III, IV U. Nebr., Omaha, 1969-72; chief gen. surgery USAF Hosp., Vandenberg AFB, Calif., 1972-74; asst. prof. surgery Med. Coll. Wis., Milw., 1975-79, assoc. prof., 1979-84, prof., 1984—, chair vascular surgery, 1984—. Editor: (book) Complications Vascular Surgery, 1980, Complications Vascular Surgery, II, 1985, Complications Vascular Surgery, III, 1991. Mem.: Wis. Surg. Soc. (pres. 1991—92), Assn. Program Dirs. Vascular Surgery (pres. 1997—98), Ctrl. Surg. Assn. (recorder 1992—97, pres.-elect 2001), Soc. Vascular Surgery (sec. 1994—98, pres.-elect 1999, pres. 2000). Avocation: photography. Office: Med Coll Wis 9200 W Wisconsin Ave Milwaukee WI 53226-3522 Office Phone: 414-805-9160. Business E-Mail: jtowne@mcw.edu.

**TOWNE, SARAH PATTON,** physician; b. Fountain Hill, Pa., Aug. 28, 1953; d. William Frank and Arline Rose (Patton) T. Degree in Nursing, Geisinger Med. Ctr., Danville, Pa., 1973; BS magna cum laude, Kutztown U. Pa., 1988; DO, Phila. Coll. Osteo. Medicine, 1992, MSc in Family Practice, 1995. Diplomate Nat. Bd. Osteo. Med. Examiners. Psychiatric nurse Allentown State Hosp., Pa., 1973-76, NW Inst. Psychiatry, Ft. Washington, Pa., 1976-78; RN, psychotherapist Boulder County Mental Health Ctr., Colo., 1979-85; intern Phila. Coll. Osteo. Medicine, 1992-93, resident in family practice, 1993-95; physician Troup Family Practice, Tex., 1995-97; pvt. practice Denver, 1997—2003. Physician Harleysville Med. Assn., Pa., 1993-95; asst. dean clin. edn., assoc. prof. primary care Touro U. Coll. Osteo. Medicine, Calif., 2003-. Bd. dirs. Boulder County Rape Crisis Team, 1979-81. Faculty Devel. Fellowship, UCSF No. Calif., 2004—05. Mem. Am. Osteo. Assn., Am. Coll. Family Practitioners, Am. Coll. Osteo. Family Practitioners (bd. cert.). Avocations: reading, gardening. Home: 151 Thresher Dr Vallejo CA 94591-7814 Office: Touro U - Calif Coll of Osteo Med 1310 Johnson Ln Mare Island Vallejo CA 94592 Office Phone: 707-638-5200. Business E-Mail: stowne@touro.edu.

**TOWNER, MARK A.,** dean, visual artist; s. Robert Vincent Towner and Nancy Pfeiffer; m. Maria Cusumano; 1 child, Marco Cusumano-Towner. BA, Columbia Coll., 1974—78; MFA, Cranbrook Acad. of Art, 1979—81. Dir. Circlework Visions Ltd, NYC, 1985—87; chief prep. Am. Craft Mus., NYC, 1987—88; asst. dir. Davenport Mus. of Art. Iowa 1989—93, acting dir. 1991—92, dir. of project at U. of Iowa Hospitals and Clinics, 1994—98; asst. dir. NE Document Conservation Ctr., Andover, Mass., 1998—2000; assoc. dean, divsn. of art and design Endicott Coll., Beverly, Mass., 2000—01, dean, sch. of art and design, 2001—. Exhibitions include Cranbrook to Lancaster and Back, New England School of Art and Design, University of Iowa, Merrimack Coll., Essex Art Ctr.; dir.(curator): (exhibition) Art By Healers, Creative Response to 9/11. Activist Merrimack Valley People for Peace, North Andover, Mass., 2004—05. Mem.: Am. Art Therapy Assn., Am. Assn. of Museums, Coll. Art Assn. Office: Endicott Coll 376 Hale St Beverly MA 01915 Office Phone: 978-232-2166. Personal E-mail: mtowner@endicott.edu.

**TOWNES, BOBBY JOE,** travel agency executive; b. Pickens, S.C., Aug. 29, 1932; s. James Harold and Coda Lenora (Nations) T.; m. Addie Elise Ray, May 2, 1956; children: John William, Robert Scott. AA, Mars Hill Jr. Coll., NC, 1952; BA, Furman U., Greenville, SC, 1955; diploma, Rutgers U., 1959. V.p. Peoples Nat. Bank, Greenville, 1954-73; exec. v.p. Community Bank, Greenville, 1973-76; pres. Piedmont Travel, Inc., Greenville, 1976-93, chmn., 1993—; mng. ptnr. Long Beach Properties, 1992—, Pawleys Promise, Pawleys Island, SC, 1998—. Chmn. Greenville World of Travel, 1976-80; pres. Piedco Assocs., Greenville, 1973—; mng. ptnr. Cutter Joint Ventures, Hilton Head, S.C., 1972—; pres. Piedco II, 1992—; chmn. Boutique Ltd., 1971-75; mng. ptnr. Townes Properties, Greenville, 2002, Townes Family Partnership, 2002; instr. Am. Inst. Banking, 1964-70, Charter Life Underwriters, Greenville, 1968; mem. adv. com. KLM Dutch Airlines, Atlanta, 1982, System One Automation, Miami, Fla., 1980, Eastern Airlines, Miami, 1983-87; mem. adv. bd. Mars Plus Data Systems, Miami, 1976-79; bd. dir., Townes Family Charitable Trust Author: Independent Bank Survival, 1968, Townes and Allied Families, 1995. Chmn. United Way, Greenville, 1973; v.p. ARC, Greenville, 1970, Cancer Soc., Greenville, 1966; v.p. Furman U. Alumni Bd., Greenville, 1968-70, Furman U. Paladin Bd., Greenville, 1972-74; mem. Furman U. Com. for Self Study, Greenville, 1976; com. Gov.'s Econ. Coun., Columbia, SC, 1972; mng. mem. founders com. Cmty. Concerts, Greenville, 1976; pres. YMCA Youth Guides, Greenville, 1970; v.p., organizer Centurian Club, 1978; mem. nat. alumni bd. Mars Hill Coll., 1998; Presidents Bd. of Advisors, Mars Hill Coll., 2003; mng. ptnr. Townes Family Charity Trust, 2001; bd. Greenville Little Theatre, 2003, Springwood Found. Recipient Sertoma Internat. Disting. Club Pres. award, 1967, Outstanding Young Mem. of Am. award, 1968, Finalist Ernst & Young Entrepreueur of Yr., 2000. Mem. Am. Inst. Banking (pres. 1964, bd. dirs. 1966), Young Bankers S.C. (bd. dirs. 1965), S.C. Bankers Assn. (bd. dirs. 1969), Greenville Wine Soc. (pres., organzer 1968, 72), S.C. Hist. Soc., Greenville County Hist. Soc., Poinsett Club, Commerce Club, Colonial Club (v.p. 1989, pres. 1991), Sertoma (v.p. 1982, pres. 1968, Gold Honor club 1967), Exec. Sertoma Club (v.p. 1982). Republican. Episcopalian. Avocation: genealogy. Home: 14 Selwyn Dr Greenville SC 29615-1727 Personal E-mail: btownes@bellsouth.net.

**TOWNES, CHARLES HARD,** physics professor; b. Greenville, SC, July 28, 1915; s. Henry Keith and Ellen Sumter (Hard) Townes; m. Frances H. Brown, May 4, 1941; children: Linda Lewis, Ellen Screven, Carla Keith, Holly Robinson. BA, BS, Furman U., 1935; MA, Duke U., 1937; PhD, Calif. Inst. Tech., 1939. Mem. tech. staff Bell Telephone Lab., 1939—47; assoc. prof. physics Columbia U., 1948—50, prof. physics, 1950—61; exec. dir. Columbia Radiation Lab., 1950—52, chmn. physics dept., 1952—55; provost and prof. physics MIT, 1961—66, Inst. prof., 1966—67; v.p., dir. rsch. Inst. Def. Analyses, Washington, 1959—61; prof. physics U. Calif., Berkeley, 1967—86, 1994, prof. physics emeritus, 1986—94, prof. grad. sch., 1994—. Guggenheim fellow, 1955—56; Fulbright lectr. U. Paris, 1955—56, U. Tokyo, 1956; dir. Enrico Fermi Internat. Sch. Physics, 1963; Richtmeyer lectr. Am. Phys. Soc., 1959; Scott lectr. U. Cambridge, 1963; Centennial lectr. U. Toronto, 1967; Lincoln lectr., 1972—73; Halley lectr., 1976; Krishnan lectr., 92; Nishina lectr., 92; Weinberg lectr. Oak Ridge (Tenn.) Nat. Lab., 1997; Rajiv Gandhi lectr., 97; Henry Norris Russell lectr. Am. Astron. Soc., 1989; dir. Gen. Motors Corp., 1973—86; dir. Perkin-Elmer Corp., 1966—69; mem. Pres.'s Sci. Adv. Com., 1966—69, vice chmn., 1967—69; chmn. sci. and tech. adv. com. for manned space flight NASA, 1964—70; mem. Pres.'s Com. on Sci. and Tech., 1976; rschr. on nuc. and molecular structure, quantum electronics, interstellar molecules, radio and infrared astrophysics. Author (with A.J. Schawlow): Microwave Spectroscopy; author: Making Waves, 1996, How the Laser Happened. Adventures of a Scientist, 1999; author, co-editor Quantum Electronics, 1960, Quantum Electronics and Coherent Light, 1964, editl. bd. Rev. Sci. Instruments, 1950—52, Phys. Rev., 1951—53, Jour. Molecular Spectroscopy, 1957—60, Procs. NAS, 1978—84, Can. Jour. Physics, 1995—, contbr. articles to sci. publs., patentee masers and lasers. Mem. corp. Woods Hole Oceanographic Instn.; bd. mem. Calif. Inst. Tech., Carnegie Instn. Washington, Ctr. for Theology and Natural Scis., Mount Wilson Inst. Decorated officier Légion d'Honneur (France); named to Nat. Inventors Hall of Fame, 1976, Engring. and Sci. Hall of Fame, 1983; recipient Nobel prize for Physics, 1964, Stuart Ballantine medal, Franklin Inst., 1962, Thomas Young medal and prize, Inst. Physics and Phys. Soc., Eng., 1963, Disting. Pub. Svc. medal, NASA, 1969, Wilhelm Exner award, Austria, 1970, Niels Bohr Internat. Gold medal, 1979, Nat. medal of Sci., 1982, Berkeley citation, U. Calif., 1986, Common Wealth award, 1993, ADION medal, Obs. Nice, 1995, Henry Norris Russell Lectureship, Am. Astronomical Soc., 1998, Mendel award, Villanova U., 1999, Frank Annunzio award, Christopher Columbus Fellowship Found., 1999, Rabindranath Tagore Birth Centenary plaque, Asiatic Soc., 1999, Karl Schwarzschild medal, Astronomische Gesellschaft, 2002, Drake award, SETI Inst., 2003, Templeton prize, 2005, Vannevar Busch medal, 2006. Fellow: IEEE (life medal of honor 1967), Calif. Acad. Scis., Indian Nat. Sci. Acad., Optical Soc. Am. (Mees medal 1968), Am. Phys. Soc. (pres. 1967, Plyler prize 1977, Frederick Ives medal 1996); mem.: NAE (founders award 2000), NAS (coun. 1968—72, 1978—81, chmn. space sci. bd. 1970—73, Comstock award 1959, Carty medal 1962), N.Y. Acad. Scis., Max-Planck Inst. Physics and Astrophysics (fgn. mem.), Pontifical Acad. Scis., Russian Acad. Scis. (Lomonosov medal 2000, fgn. mem.), Royal Soc. (fgn. mem.), Am. Acad. Arts and Scis., Am. Astron. Soc., Am. Philos. Soc. Office: U Calif Dept Physics 366 Leconte # 7200 Berkeley CA 94720-0001 Business E-Mail: cht@ssl.berkeley.edu.*

**TOWNES, PHILIP LEONARD,** pediatrician, educator; b. Salem, Mass., Feb. 18, 1927; s. Saul and Lillian (Kravetsky) T.; m. Marjorie Joan Greenstone, Aug. 27, 1956; children: Elizabeth Ann, Susan Jane, David Andrew. AB, Harvard, 1948; PhD, U. Rochester, 1952, MD, 1959. Diplomate Am. Bd. Pediat., Am. Bd. Med. Genetics. Intern Strong Meml. Hosp., Rochester, 1959-60, asst. resident, 1963, chief resident pediatrics, 1965; mem. faculty U. Rochester Sch. Medicine, 1952-79, prof. pediatrics, 1969-79; prof. anatomy (genetics), chmn. div. genetics, dir. Genetic Clinic, 1966-79; prof. pediatrics U. Mass. Sch. Medicine, 1979-95, dir. Genetic Clinic, 1979-95, dir. Cytogenetics Lab., 1981-95, prof. pediatrics/ob-gyn. emeritus, 1995—; pediatrician Strong Meml. Hosp. Cons. attending Newark State Hosp., Genesee Hosp.; hon. research asst. Univ. Coll., London, Eng., 1965-66; mem. adv. com. for genetics services Mass. Dept. Pub. Health, 1979-84, chmn. com., 1982-83; mem. steering com. New Eng. Regional Genetics Group, 1981-82. Contbr. articles to med. jours. Mem. com. qualifications cytogenetics N.Y. State Dept. Health, 1968-74; bd. dirs. Monroe County chpt. Nat. Found., 1965-79, chmn. med. adv. com., 1967-79, hon. bd. dirs., 1979—, also cons.; trustee Seven Hills Found., 1996—. USPHS postdoctoral fellow, 1951-52; sr. research fellow, 1960-61; research career devel. award, 1961-66 Mem. Am. Acad. Pediatrics, Am. Assn. Anatomists, Soc. Pediatric Research, Am. Soc. Human Genetics, Am. Pediatric Soc., Teratology Soc., Sigma Xi, Alpha Omega Alpha. Home: 14 Spring Valley Rd Worcester MA 01609-1151 Personal E-mail: pltmdphd@hotmail.com.

**TOWNES, SANDRA L.,** federal judge; BA, Johnson C. Smith, 1966; JD, Syracuse U., 1976. Tchr. English Carver H.S., 1966—67, Dunbar H.S., 1967—70, D.C. Evening Adult Edn. Prog., 1967—70, Corcoran H.S., 1971—73, P.E.A.C.E. Learning Ctr., 1971—73; asst. D.A. County Onondaga, N.Y., 1977—85, sr. asst. D.A., 1983—86, chief asst. D.A., 1986—87; adj. prof. Syracuse U. Coll. Law, 1987—95; judge Syracuse City Ct., 1988—99; adj. prof. Onondaga C.C., 1992—99; justice N.Y. Supreme Ct. (5th jud. dist.), 2000—01; assoc. justice N.Y. Supreme Ct. (Appellate divsn., 2d dept.), 2001—04; judge U.S. Dist. Ct. (ea. dist.) N.Y., 2004—. Mem.: Onondaga County Bar Assn., N.Y. State Women's Bar Assn., N.Y. State Bar Assn. Office: 225 Cadman Plaza E Brooklyn NY 11201 Office Phone: 718-797-7420.

**TOWNLEY, HUGH,** sculptor, educator; b. West Lafayette, Ind., Feb. 6, 1923; s. Hubert Claude and Marguerite (Ozburn) T.; m. Mary Ross, Oct. 3, 1961; 1 child, Hugh Merlyn Zadkine. Student, U. Wis., 1946-48, London County Council Sch. Arts and Crafts, 1949-50; studied with Ossip Zadkine, Paris, 1948-49. Tchr. Layton Sch. Art, Milw., 1951-56, Beloit (Wis.) Coll., 1956-57, Boston U., 1957-61; prof. art Brown U., Providence, 1961—. vis. lectr. U. Calif., Berkeley, 1961, U. Calif. at Santa Barbara, 1968; vis. lectr. Harvard, summer 1967; participant symposium on 20th century sculpture Mus. N. Ariz., 1978 One man shows at, Gallerie Appolnaire, London, 1951, Meml. Union Gallery U. Wis., 1955, Milw. Art Inst., 1957, Swetzoff Gallery, Boston, 1958, 59, Pace Gallery, Boston, 1962, 64, 65, N.Y.C., 1964, Tyler Sch. Art, Phila., 1966, Rigelhaupt Gallery, Boston, 1966, Yale, 1966, DeCordova Dana Mus., Lincoln, Mass., 1969, Bradley Galleries, Milw., 1970, Bell Gallery, Brown U., 1972, Tyler Sch. Arts, Phila., 1972, U. Oreg., 1976, Worcester (Mass.) Art Mus., 1980, Gen. Electric Co., 1983, Providence Art Club, 1988, others; 2 man show, Brockton Mus., 1971, U. Oreg., 1975, Dartmouth Coll., 1975, U. N.H. at Keene, 1976, Inst. Contemporary Art, Boston, 1977; exhibited in group shows at, Chgo. Art Inst., 1953, 54, 64, Mus. Modern Art, 1955, 63, Carnegie Inst. Biennial, 1958, Inst. Contemporary Art, Boston, 1960, 61, 62, 65, 66, U. Ill., 1961-63, New Sch. for Social Research, 1962, Wadsworth Atheneum, Hartford, 1963, Decordova Mus., 1964, 65, Flint Inst. Art, 1966, Nat. Inst. Arts and Letters, 1967, Munson-Williams-Proctor Mus., 1970, Monumenta, Newport, R.I., 1974, Portland (Oreg.) Mus. Art, 1976, Keene (N.H.) State U., 1976, others; represented in permanent collections at, San Francisco Art Mus., Whitney Mus., Milw. Art Inst., Munson-Williams- Proctor Inst., Ithaca, N.Y., Addison Gallery, Andover, Mass., Boston Mus. Fine Arts, De Cordova Mus., Fogg Mus., Williams Coll. Mus., Brown U., Wrexham Found., Mead Corp., First Nat. Bank Boston, others. Served with USAAF, 1942-46. Recipient awards Kalamazoo Art

---

Center Lithographic Workshop, 1964, awards Nat. Inst. Arts and Letters, 1967; Award for Arts, Gov. R.I., 1972; Yaddo Found. fellow, 1964; Tamarind Lithography Workshop fellow, 1969 Mem. Soaring Soc. Am. Office: Dept Art Brown U Providence RI 02912-0001

**TOWNS, EDOLPHUS,** congressman; b. Chadbourn, NC, July 21, 1934; m. Gwendolyn Forbes, 1960; children: Darryl, Deidra. BS in Sociology, NC A&T State U., Greensboro, 1956; MSW, Adelphi U., Garden City, NY, 1973; PhD (hon.), NC A&T State U., Shaw U. Tchr. NYC Pub. Schs., Medgar Evers Coll. Bklyn., Fordham U.; asst. adminstr. Beth Israel Med. Ctr., 1965-71; dep. pres. Borough of Bklyn., 1976-82; mem. US Congress from 11th NY dist., 1983—91, US Congress from 10th NY dist., 1992—, mem. energy and commerce com., mem. govt. reform com., ranking mem. subcommittee on govt. mgmt., fin. and accountability. Mem. adv. council Boy Scouts Am.; active Salvation Army. With U.S. Army, 1956—58. Named Home Care Hero, Nat. Assn. Home Care, Legislator of Yr., Am. Acad. Nurse Practitioners, Am. Acad. Physician Assts., Am. Assn. Cmty. Health Ctrs., Nat. Coalition Poison Control Ctrs., Friend of the Nat. Parks, Nat. Parks and Conservation Assn.; named one of 100 Most Influential Black Americans, Ebony mag., 2006; named to Acad. of Distinction, Adelphi U.; recipient Congl. Leadership award, Am. Coll. Nurse-Midwives, 1999. Mem. NAACP, Nat. Assn. Social Workers, Kiwanis, Phi Beta Sigma. Democrat. Baptist. Office: US Ho Reps 2232 Rayburn Ho Office Bldg Washington DC 20515-0001 Office Phone: 202-225-5936.*

**TOWNSEND, ALAIR ANE,** publishing executive; b. Rochester, N.Y., Feb. 15, 1942; d. Harold Eugene and Dorothy (Sharpe) T.; m. Robert Harris, Dec. 31, 1970 (div. 1994). BS, Elmira Coll., 1962; MS, U. Wis., 1964; postgrad., Columbia U., 1970-71. Assoc. dir. budget priorities Com. on Budget, U.S. Ho. of Reps., Washington, 1975-79, dep. asst. sec. for budget HEW, 1979-80, asst. sec. for mgmt. and budget, 1980-81; dir. Office Mgmt. & Budget NYC, 1981-85, dep. mayor for fin. & econ. devel., 1985-89; pub. Crain's N.Y. Bus., NYC, 1989—2006, v.p., 1993—, pub. dir., 2006—. Bd. overseers Tchrs. Ins. and Annuity Assn.-Coll. Retirement Equities Fund; former mem. adv. bd. Ford Motor Credit Corp.; former bd. mem. Armor Holdings Inc. Former vice-chmn., trustee Elmira Coll.; former mem. Coun. Fgn. Rels.; former bd. govs. Am. Stock Exch.; former chmn. Am. Woman's Econ. Devel. Corp.; former chmn. N.Y.C. Sports Commn.; former chmn. Consol. Corp. Fund of Lincoln Ctr.; bd. dirs. Lincoln Ctr.; vice-chmn. Buffalo Fiscal Stability Auth. Mem. Women's Forum, Partnership for NYC (bd. dirs.), N.Y. State Bus. Coun. (bd. dirs.), Econ. Club N.Y. (bd. dirs.). Office: Crain's NY Bus 711 3d Ave New York NY 10017

**TOWNSEND, BRIAN DOUGLAS,** paralegal; b. Tokyo, Sept. 22, 1961; s. Thomas and Juanita Evora (Sanford) T.; m. Gloria Ann Wigfall, Aug. 23, 1986; children: Brian D. Jr., Brianna A. BA in Criminology, U. Md., 1983. Legal aide Kirkland & Ellis, Washington, 1984-85; legal asst. to mng. clk. Cadwalader, Wickersham & Taft, Washington, 1985-87; paralegal specialist, Office of Chief Counsel U.S. Dept. Transp. Maritime Adminstrn., Washington, 1987-90, U.S. Dept. Treasury, IRS, Washington, 1990-92; litigation support specialist U.S. Dept. Justice, Tax Divsn., Washington, 1992-93; paralegal specialist Resolution Trust Corp., Washington, 1993-95, FDIC, Washington, 1996-98, U.S. Dept. Treasury, OIG, Washington, 1998-99; program specialist FOIA/PA U.S. Dept. Treasury, OFAC, Washington, 1999-2000; mgmt. analyst USDA, Washington, 2000—02; program analyst IRS/OPA, U.S. Dept. Treasury, Washington, 2002—. Avocations: bowling, fishing, swimming, chess, football. Office: US Dept Treasury IRS/OPA 1111 Constitution Ave NW Washington DC 20224-0002 E-mail: briandouglastownsend@yahoo.com, brian.d.townsend@irs.gov.

**TOWNSEND, CARMILLA D.,** history professor, researcher; b. N.Y., Jan. 29, 1965; d. John Kenneth and Carolynn Ericksom Townsend; m. John Graham Nolan, Aug. 29, 1989; children: Loren, Cian. BA, Byrn Mawr Coll., Pa., 1985; PhD in History, Rutgers U., New Brunswick, N.J., 1995. Asst. prof. history Colgate Coll., Hamilton, NY, 1995—2000, assoc. prof. history, 2003—. Grantee Nat. Endowment for Humanities, 2004—05, grant, Am. Philos. Soc., 2005. Democrat. Office: Dept History Rutgers U Van Dyck Hall New Brunswick NJ 08903

**TOWNSEND, CHARLES H.,** publishing executive; m. Joanna E. Townsend. Pres., pub. Family Cir. Mag., 1986—90; pres., CEO N.Y. Times Co. Women's Mag. Group, 1990—94; pub., Glamour Mag. Conde Nast Publs. Inc., NYC, 1994—95, exec. v.p., 1995—2000, COO, 2000—04, pres., CEO, 2004—; COO Advance Mag. Group, NYC, 2001—. Office: Conde Nast Publications Inc 4 Times Sq New York NY 10036-6561*

**TOWNSEND, CHRISTOPHER GORDON,** lawyer; b. New Bedford, Mass., June 9, 1947; s. Christopher Gordon and Rita Mary (Fitzgerald) T.; m. Christine P. Davis, June 17, 1972; children: Christopher IV, Jessica C. BA, Providence Coll., 1969; JD, Georgetown U., 1975. Bar: D.C. 1975. Jud. clk. Supreme Ct. Del., Wilmington, 1975-76; atty. U.S. Dept. Justice, Washington, 1976-77, U.S. SEC, Washington, 1977-82; asst. gen. counsel Marriott Corp., Bethesda, Md., 1982-93; dep. gen. counsel Host Marriott Corp., Bethesda, 1993-96, gen. counsel, 1996-01; ptnr. Patton, Boggs LLP, 2001—. Editor: Am. Criminal Law Rev., 1974-75. Lt. USN, 1969-72. Mem. ABA. Office: Patton Boggs LLP 8484 Westpark Dr Mc Lean VA 22102

**TOWNSEND, COURTNEY M.,** surgeon; b. Lubbock, Tex., 1943; MD, U. Tex., Galveston, 1969. Specialty bd. l Surgery 1975. Intern U. Tex. Med. Br., 1969—70, resident surgery, 1970—74; fellow surg. oncology U. Calif., L.A., 1974—76; staff surgeon, surg. dir. intensive care unit Naval Med. Ctr., Bethesda, 1976—78; assoc. prof. U. Tex. Med. Br., 1978—83, prof., 1983—95, chair, dept. surgery, 1995—. James IV Surg. Traveller U. Tex. Med. Br., 1986; pres. Am. Pancreatic Assn., 1992—93; mem. Tex. Cancer Coun., 1992—; dir. Am. Bd. Surgery, 2000—. Editor-in-chief: Sabiston Textbook of Surgery: The Biological Basis of Modern Surgical Practice, 16th edit., 17th edit. Recipient Rsch. Career Devel. award, NIH, 1982, Asbel Smith Disting. Alumnus, 1986. Fellow: ACS (exec. com. 1999—2003, chmn. bd. govs. 2004—05); mem.: AMA (residency rev. com. 1999—2003), Am. Bd. Surgery (chair 2006—), So. Surg. Assn. (sec. 1999—2003, pres. 2003—04). Office: 301 University Blvd Galveston TX 77555-0527

**TOWNSEND, CRAIG ARTHUR,** chemistry educator; b. Chgo., Aug. 19, 1947; s. Herbert Ward and Thelma Alice (Hayskar) T.; m. S. Darlene Dance, Aug. 7, 1971; children: Reed Lincoln, Andrew Vernon. BA cum laude with honors in Chemistry, Williams Coll., 1969; PhD in Organic Chemistry, Yale U., 1974. Internat. exch. postdoctoral fellow Swiss Fed. Inst. Tech., Zurich, 1974-76; asst. prof. chemistry Johns Hopkins U., Balt., 1976-82, assoc. prof., 1982-85, prof., 1985—, chmn. dept., 1990-94, prof. dept. biology and McCollum-Pratt Inst., 1984—, prof. Thomas C. Jenkins dept. biophysics, 1989—, Alsoph H. Corwin prof. chemistry, 1997—. Vis. prof. chemistry Harvard U., Cambridge, Mass., 1987; disting. lectr. U. Hawaii, 1988; lectr. Robert A. Welch found., 1989; H. Martin Friedman lectr. Rutgers U., 1990; Boehringer-Ingelheim lectr. Yale U., 1992; also numerous others; cons. Lederle Labs., Pearl River, N.Y., 1984-94, ChekTec Corp., Balt., 1993—; Upjohn Co., Kalamazoo, 1995—; mem. adv. panel Office Tech. Assessment, Washington, 1994-95; organizer, co-founder bio-organic chemistry Gordon Rsch. Conf., Kingston, R.I., 1992; Gomberg lectr. U. Mich., 1997; disting. lectr. Colo. State U., 1999. Mem. editl. adv. bd. Jour. Organic Chemistry, 1987-91; contbr. over 120 articles to sci. jours. Recipient award in chemistry Stuart Pharms., 1986; named Md. Chemist of Yr., 1992; NIH postdoctoral fellow Yale U., 1970-73, rsch. fellow Alfred P. Sloan Found., 1982-86; Camille and Henry Dreyfus tchr.-scholar, 1983-88. Mem. Am. Chem. Soc. (Arthur C. Cope scholar award 1995), Royal Soc. Chemistry, others. Research in biosynthesis of natural products; stereochemical and mechanistic studies of enzyme action; application of spectroscopic techniques to the solution of

---

biological problems; molecular biology of secondary metabolism; activation and mechanism of DNA cleavage by calicheamicin. Office: Johns Hopkins U Dept Chemistry 3400 N Charles St Baltimore MD 21218-2680

**TOWNSEND, DAVID W.,** director; s. Philip W. and Martha Fern Townsend; m. Roberta D. Campbell, Aug. 30, 1975; children: Kristy Lynn, Karen Elizabeth. BA, U. Maine, 1974, PhD, 1981; MS, L.I. U., C.W. Post, Greenvale, N.Y., 1977. Rsch. scientist Bigelow Lab. for Ocean Sci., West Boothbay Harbor, Maine, 1981—93; exec. dir. regional marine rsch. program U. Maine, Orono, 1993—97, assoc. rsch. prof. oceanography, 1993—97, assoc. prof. oceanography, 1997—99, prof. oceanography, 1999, dir. Sch. Marine Scis., 2001—. Office: U Maine 5706 Aubert Hall Orono ME 04473 Office Phone: 207-581-4367.

**TOWNSEND, EARL C., JR.,** lawyer, writer; b. Indpls., Nov. 9, 1914; s. Earl Cunningham and Besse (Kuhn) T.; m. Emily Macnab, Apr. 3, 1947 (dec. Mar. 1988); children: Starr, Vicki M., Julia E. (Mrs. Edward Goodrich Dunn Jr.), Earl Cunningham III, Clyde G. Student, De Pauw U., 1932-34; AB, U. Mich., 1936, JD, 1939. Bar: Ind. 1939, Mich. 1973, US Supreme Ct. 1973, US Ct. Appeals (4th, 5th, 6th, 7th cirs.), US Dist. Ct. (no. and so. dists.) Ind., US Dist. Ct. (ea. dist.) Va., US Dist. Ct. (ea. dist.) Mich. Sr. ptnr. Townsend & Townsend, Indpls., 1941-64, 1984—, Townsend, Hovde & Townsend, Indpls., 1964-84. Dep. prosecutor, Marion County, Ind., 1942-44; radio-TV announcer WIRE, WFBM, WFBM-TV, Indpls., 1940-53, 1st TV announcer Indpls. 500 mile race, 1949, 50; Big Ten basketball referee, 1940-47; lectr. trial tactics U. Notre Dame, Ind. U., U. Mich., 1968-79; chmn. faculty seminar on personal injury trials Ind. U. Sch. Law, U. Notre Dame Sch. Law, Valparaiso Sch. Law, 1981; mem. Com. to Revise Ind. Supreme Ct. Pattern Jury Instrns., 1975-83; lectr. Trial Lawyers 30 Yrs. Inst., 1986; counsel atty gen., 1988-92. Author: Birdstones of the North American Indian, 1959; editor: Am. Assn. Trial Lawyers Am. Jour., 1964-88; contbr. articles to legal and archeol. jours.; composer (waltz) Moon of Halloween. Trustee Cathedral High Sch., Indpls., Eiteljorg Mus. Am. Indian and Western Art, Cale J. Holder Scholarship Found. Ind. U. Law Sch.; life trustee, bd. dirs., mem. fin. and bldg. coms. Indpls. Mus. Art; life trustee Ind. State Mus.; founder, dir. Meridian St. Found.; mem. dean's coun. Ind. U.; founder, life fellow Roscoe Pound/Am. Trial Lawyers Found., Harvard U.; fellow Meth. Hosp. Found. Recipient Ind. Univ. Writers Conf. award, 1960, Hanson H. Anderson medal of honor Arsenal Tech. Schs., Indpls., 1971, Lifetime Achievement award, 2002; named to Coun. Sagamores of Wabash, 1969; Rector scholar, 1934, Ind. Basketball Hall of Fame, Newcastle, 1981; hon. chief Black River-Swan Creek Saginaw-Chippewa Indian tribe. Fellow: Ind. Bar Found. (life trustee, disting. fellow award), Internat. Soc. Barristers, Internat. Acad. Trial Lawyers; mem.: ATLA (v.p.), ABA (com. on trial techniques 1964—76, aviation and space 1977—), ASCAP, Mich. Trial Lawyers Assn., Bar Assn. 7th Fed. Cir. (bd. dirs. 1966—68), 34th Jud. Cir. Bar Assn., Roscommon County Bar Assn., State Bar of Mich. (Champion of Justice award 1989), Am. Judicature Soc., Am. Arbitration Assn. (nat. arbitrators panel), Am. Bd. Trial Advocates (diplomate, pres. Ind. chpt. 1980—86), Ind. Trial Lawyers Assn. (pres. 1965, pres. Coll. Fellows 1984—90), Indpls. Bar Found. (disting. charter 1986), Ind. State Bar Assn. (Golden Career award 1989), Genuine Indian Relic Soc. (founder, pres., chmn. frauds com.), Trowel and Brush Soc. (hon.), Marion County/Indpls. Hist. Soc. (bd. dirs.), Ind. Hist. Soc., Soc. Mayflower Descendants (gov. 1947—49), Columbia Club, U. Mich. Pres. Club, Key Biscayne Yacht Club, The Players Club, U. Mich. Victors Club (founder, charter mem.), Shriners, Masons (33 degree), Scottish Rite, Phi Kappa Phi, Delta Kappa Epsilon. Republican. Methodist. Avocations: art, Indian relics. Home: 5008 N Meridian St Indianapolis IN 46208-2624 E-mail: officeect@aol.com

**TOWNSEND, FRAN (FRANCES FRAGOS TOWNSEND),** federal official; b. Mineola, NY, Dec. 28, 1961; m. John M. Townsend; 2 children. BA in Polit. Sci., BS in Psychology, Am. U., 1982; JD, San Diego U., 1984; student, Inst. on Internat. & Comparative Law, London, 1986. Asst. dist. atty., Bklyn., 1985—88; atty., US Atty. Office (so. dist.) NY US Dept. Justice, 1988—91, chief to staff to asst. atty. gen. criminal divsn., 1993—95, dir. internat. affairs criminal divsn., 1995—97, acting dep. asst. atty. gen., 1997—98, counsel Office of Intelligence Policy and Rev., 1998—2001; asst. comdt. for intelligence USCG, US Dept. Homeland Security, 2001—03; dep. asst. to Pres., dep. nat. security advr. for combating terrorism The White House, 2003—04, asst. to Pres for homeland security & counterterrorism, 2004—; chair Homeland Security Coun., 2004—. Office: Eisenhower Exec Office Bldg Rm 313 17th St & Pennsylvania Ave NW Washington DC 20504

**TOWNSEND, GREGORY WILLIAMS,** music educator; b. Saint Louis, Mo., June 3, 1970; s. Frederick Dalton and Joyce Williams Townsend. MusB, So. Ill. U., 1988—93, MA in Music Edn., 1998—. Cert. tchr. Ill. State Bd. Edn., 1996, Mo. State Bd. Edn., 1993. Music dept. chairperson Althoff Cath. H.S., Belleville, Ill., 1995—2000; instrumental music instr. Salem Cmty. H.S., Ill., 2000—02; band dir. Carbondale Cmty. H.S., Ill., 2002—. Composer: (wind band music) The Course, Walking Away. Mem. Salem Theatre Found., Salem, Ill., 2001—01. Recipient Grand Champion Instrumental Ensemble (as Dir.), Music Showcase Festivals, 1999, Who's Who Among America's Teachers, 1998, 2000, 2002; grantee Music Performance Scholarship, So. Ill. U. at Edwardsville, 1988-1993. Mem.: NEA, Ill. Educator's Assn., Music Educator's Nat. Conf., Ill. Music Educator's Assn. (band divsn. co-chairperson/chairperson 2001—03). Avocations: scuba diving - advanced certification, computers, tennis, volleyball. Office: Carbondale Cmty High Sch 1301 E Walnut St Carbondale IL 62902 Office Phone: 618-457-3371 x240. Personal E-mail: gregorytownsend@yahoo.com.

**TOWNSEND, IRENE FOGLEMAN,** accountant, tax specialist; b. Birmingham, Ala., May 29, 1932; d. James Woods and Virginia (Martin) Fogleman; m. Kenneth Ross Townsend, Mar. 18, 1951; children: Marietta Irene, Martha Shapard, Kenneth Ross Jr., Elizabeth Buchanan. BSBA, East Carolina U., 1980. CPA NC, Va. Acct. Norwood P. Whitehurst & Assocs., Greenville, N.C., 1981-86; asst. v.p. Tenet Healthcare Corp., Vienna, Va., 1995—; v.p. NME Psychiatric Hosps., Inc., Vienna, Va., 2001—. Fellow AICPA, N.C. Assn. CPAs, D.C. Inst. CPAs, Va. Soc. CPAs; mem. DAR, N.C. Soc. Daus. of Colonial Wars, Colonial Dames 17th Century. Democrat. Episcopalian (lay reader, chalice bearer). Avocations: bicycling, genealogy. Home: 2521 Paxton St Woodbridge VA 22192-3414 Office: Tenet Healthcare Corp 501 Church St NE Ste 301 Vienna VA 22180-4734 E-mail: irene_townsend@hotmail.com.

**TOWNSEND, JAMES DOUGLAS,** accountant; b. Kokomo, Ind., May 20, 1959; s. Lemon Dale and Diamond Sue (Turner) T.; m. Ariane Antonia Atkins, May 7, 1983 (div. July 1992); 1 child, Bradley Alan; m. Mildred Ann Kurtz, Oct. 18, 1992; children: Heather Marie, Tyler Neil. Student, Ind. U., 1977, Ind. State U., 1977—78; BS Acctg. summa cum laude, Ball State U., 1980. CPA, Ind., Colo.; cert. mgmt. acct. Acctg. intern Chevrolet Motor Divsn. GM, Muncie, Ind., 1979; from staff acct. to sr. mgr. Price Waterhouse, Indpls., 1980—89; from contr. to v.p. fin. Raffensperger, Hughes & Co., Inc., Indpls., 1989—95; sr. v.p., chief adminstrv. officer Nat. City Investments, Inc., Indpls., 1995—99; pres. Fin. Mgmt., Inc., Indpls., 1994—2005; sr. v.p. Madison Ave. Capital Group LLC, 1999—2000; CFO Colo.'s Ocean Journey, 2000—01, exec. v.p., COO, 2001, pres., CEO, 2001—05; v.p., contr. Curian Capital LLC, 2004—, Jackson Nat. Life Distbr., Inc., 2004—. Coord. Seek Program Ind. U. Indpls., 1985-86; cons. project bus. Jr. Achievement, Indpls., 1986; treas., asst. sec. Sagomore Funds Trust, 1991-94; treas. Raffensperger Hughes Capitol Corp., 1991-94, RHGP, Inc., 1993-95. Baseball coach Pike Twp. (Ind.) Youth League, 1986-87; cubmaster Pike Twp. Coun. Boy Scouts Am., 1987-88; mem. Pike Twp. Sch. Bd., 1988-92, v.p., 1989-90, pres., 1990-92; bd. dirs. Project I-Star, 1992-94, Crooked Creek Villages Homeowners Assn., 1998-99; fin. com. Highlands Ranch Cmty. Assn., 2000—02. Fellow Life Mgmt. Inst.; mem. AICPA, Inst. Mgmt. Accts., Ind. CPA Soc. (vice chmn. edn. com. 1988-89, chmn. 1989-90, chmn. govt. rels. com. 1999), Colo. Soc. CPAs, Indpls. C. of C. (SKLA exec. coun. 1992-94), Swallow Hill

Music Assn. Republican. Avocations: boating, golf, guitar, chess, scuba diving. Home: 0052 Hunki Doil Ct Dillon CO 80435 Address: 10586 Parkington Ln B Highlands Ranch CO 80126

**TOWNSEND, JANE KALTENBACH,** biologist, educator; b. Chgo., Dec. 21, 1922; BS, Beloit Coll., 1944; MA, U. Wis., 1946; PhD, U. Iowa, 1950. Asst. in zoology U. Wis., 1944-47, asst., project assoc. in pathology, 1950—53; asst., instr. U. Iowa, 1948-50; rsch. fellow Wenner-Grens Inst. Am. Cancer Soc., Stockholm, 1953—56; asst. prof. zoology Northwestern U., 1956-58; asst. prof. to assoc. prof. zoology Mt. Holyoke Coll., South Hadley, Mass., 1958-70, prof., 1970-93, chmn. biol. scis., 1980-86, prof. emeritus, 1993—; summer investigator Marine Biol. Lab., Woods Hole, Mass., 1993—. Contbr. articles to profl. sci. jours. Fellow AAAS (sec. sect. biol. sci. 1974-78); mem. Am. Assn. Anatomists, Am. Inst. Biol. Scis., Soc. Integrated Comparative Biology, Soc. Exptl. Biology and Medicine, Soc. Devel. Biology, Corp. of Marine Biol. Lab., Sigma Xi, Phi Beta Kappa. Achievements include research in amphibian metamorphosis and immune responses in marine sponges. Office: Mount Holyoke Coll Dept Bio Scis South Hadley MA 01075 Office Phone: 413-538-2124. Business E-Mail: jtownsen@mtholyoke.edu.

**TOWNSEND, JOHN CUNNINGHAM,** optometrist; s. Charles Eby and Marjorie Rhodes Townsend; m. Sheila Frances Anderson, May 26, 1990; children: Alicia, James. BS, U. Fla., 1975; OD, U. Houston, 1979. Lic. optometrist Calif., Fla., Kans., Mo., Okla., Tex., Wash., W.Va. Hosp.-based resident in optometry Kansas City (Mo.) VA Med. Ctr., 1979—80; chief ocular disease So. Calif. Coll. Optometry, Fullerton, 1980—83; optometrist Family Health Plan HMO, Long Beach, Calif., 1984—85; asst. chief optometry svc. West L.A. VA Med. Ctr., 1985 91, chief optometry svc., 1991—96; chief optometry VA Greater L.A. Healthcare, Santa Barbara, Calif., 1996—2000; dir. VHA optometry svc. VA, Washington, 2000—. Instr. So. Calif. Coll. Optometry, 1980—81, asst. prof., 1981—83, 1985—88, assoc. prof., 1988—94, tenured prof., 1994—2000. Author: Visual Fields: Clinical Case Presentations, 1991; mem. editl. bd. Optometry and Vision Sci., 1998—2003, Jour. Rehab. R&D, 2001—; contbr. articles to profl. jours. Mem. therapeutic pharm. agt. adv. com. State of Calif. Dept. Consumer Affairs, Sacramento, 1996—2000; mem. therapeutic pharm. agt. study com. Calif. Optometric Assn., 1997—2000. Named Disting. Optometry Alumnus, U. Houston Coll. Optometry, 2001, Disting. Practitioner Optometry, Nat. Acad. Practice, 2003—; recipient Pres.'s award, Nat. Assn. VA Optometrists, 1993, Optometry award, Amsus, 2005. Fellow: Am. Acad. Optometry; mem.: Am. Optometric Assn. (chair clin. guidelines coordinating com. 2000—05), Armed Forces Optometric Soc. (exec. coun. 2001—), Beta Sigma Kappa, Phi Kappa Phi. Office: VA 103 S Gay St Rm 714 Baltimore MD 21202 Office Phone: 410-779-1576. Business E-Mail: john.townsend@va.gov.

**TOWNSEND, JOHN MICHAEL,** lawyer; b. West Point, N.Y., Mar. 21, 1947; s. John D. and Vera (Nachman) T.; m. Frances M. Fragos, Oct. 8, 1992; children: James E., Patrick K. BA, Yale U., 1968, JD, 1971. Bar: N.Y. 1972, U.S. Dist. Ct. (so. and ea. dists.) N.Y. 1975, U.S. Ct. Appeals (2nd cir.) 1975, U.S. Supreme Ct. 1975, U.S. Ct. Appeals (8th cir.) 1982, U.S. Ct. Appeals (7th and 11th cirs.) 1986, D.C. 1990, U.S. Dist. Ct. D.C. 1990, U.S. Ct. Appeals (D.C. cir.) 1990, U.S. Ct. Appeals (4th cir.) 1991, U.S. Ct. Appeals (fed. cir.) 2000, U.S. Ct. Appeals (11th cir.) 2001, U.S. Ct. Fed. Claims, 2000, U.S. Ct. Appeals 1st cir. 2003. Assoc. Hughes Hubbard & Reed, LLP, N,Y.C., 1971-73, 75-80, ptnr., 1980—; assoc. Hughes Hubbard & Reed, Paris, 1973-74. Bd. dirs., chair exec. com., law com. Am. Arbitration Assn.; trustee U.S. Coun. Internat. Bus. 1st lt. USAR, 1971-75. Mem. ABA, Am. Law Inst., Internat. Bar Assn. (chair mediation com.), Assn. Bar City N.Y., Coll. Comml. Arbitrators, Univ. Club, Yale Club (N.Y.C.). Democrat. Episcopalian. Office: Hughes Hubbard & Reed LLP 1775 I St NW Washington DC 20006-2401 Office Phone: 202-721-4600. Office Fax: 202-721-4646. Business E-Mail: townsend@hugheshubbard.com.

**TOWNSEND, JOHN WILLIAM, JR.,** physicist, retired federal agency administrator; b. Washington, Mar. 19, 1924; s. John William and Elenore (Eby) T.; m. Mary Irene Lewis, Feb. 7, 1948; children: Bruce Alan, Nancy Dewitt, John William III, Megan Lewis; m. JoAnn C. Clayton, Sept. 17, 1996. BA, Williams Coll., 1947, MA, 1949, ScD, 1961. With Naval Research Lab., 1949-55, br. head, 1955-58; with NASA, 1958-68, dep. dir. Goddard Space Flight Ctr., 1965-68; dep. adminstrn. Environ. Sci. Svcs. Adminstrn., 1968-70; asso. adminstr. NOAA, 1970-77; pres. Fairchild Space and Electronics Co., 1977-82; v.p. Fairchild Industries, 1979-85; pres. Fairchild Space Co., 1983-85; sr. v.p. Fairchild Industries, 1985-87; chmn. bd. Am. Satellite Co., 1985, sr. v.p., exec. aerospace group, 1987, exec. v.p., 1987; dir. NASA Goddard Space Flight Ctr., 1987-90; ret., 1990. Mem. U.S. Rocket, Satellite Rsch. Panel, 1950-60; chmn. space applications bd. NRC, 1985-87; bd. dirs., trustee Telos Corp., 1992; mem. adv. bd. Loral Corp., 1990-92; mem. coms. NRC, 1990—; bd. dirs CTA, Inc., 1990-98. Author numerous papers, reports in field. Pres. town council, Forest Heights, Md., 1951-55. Served with USAAF, 1943-46. Recipient Profl. Achievement award Engrs. and Architects Day, 1957; Meritorious Civilian Service award Navy Dept., 1957; Outstanding Leadership medal NASA, 1962; Distinguished Service medal, 1971, 90; recipient Arthur S. Fleming award Fed. Govt., 1963, Edward A. Flinn III award, 1999. Fellow AIAA, AAAS, Am. Meteorol. Soc.; mem. NAE (com. 1990-93), Am. Phys. Soc., Am. Geophys. Union. (fin. com. 1991-98, Edward A. Flinn III award, 1999), Internat. Astronautical Fedn. (mem., tru stee internat., acad. astronautics), Sigma Xi. Home: 6532 79th St Cabin John MD 20818-1201

**TOWNSEND, KATHLEEN KENNEDY,** former lieutenant governor; b. Greenwich, Connecticut, July 4, 1951; d. Robert F. and Ethel S. Kennedy; m. David Townsend; children: Meaghan, Maeve, Kate, and Kerry. BA cum laude, Harvard Univ., 1974; JD, U. N.,Mex., 1978 Instr. Dundalk Cmty. Coll. 1983 86, Essex Cmty. Coll., 1986-87, U. Md. Student Svc. Alliance, State dept of Edn., 1987—93; dep. asst. atty. gen. U.S. Dept. Justice, Washington, 1993-94; lt. gov. State of Md., 1995—2003; pres. Operation Respect, 2003; adj. prof. Georgetown's Sch. of Pub. Policy, 2003. Chair so. region Nat. Conf. Lt. Gov., chair oversight com. Johns Hopkins U., Peabody Inst., 1995-96; nat. adv. bd. Export-Import Bank U.S.; bd. adv. Johns Hopkins U. Sch. Advanced Internat. Studies, Inst. Human Virology U. Md; chair, State House Trust, 1995-2003, Adv. Bd., After-School Opportunity Programs, 1999-, co-chair, Safe Schools Interagency Steering Com., 1999-2003; Delegate, Dem. Party Nat. Conv., 1988, 1996, 2000; chair, Dem. Caucus of Lt. Gov. Editor U. N.Mex. Law Rev.; contbg. articles to profl. jour. and newspapers. Founder Robert F. Kennedy Human Rights Award; chair Cabinet Coun. Criminal and Juvenile Justice, 1995-2003; chair Cabinet Coun. for Bus. and Econ. Devel.; chair Md. del. Pres. Summit Am. Future, 1997; chair State Sys. Reform Task Force for Children and Youth Reform, 1996, Task Force to study increasing availability of substance abuse programs, 1998-2001, Gov.of the Yr. 2000 Pub. Info.; chair adv. bd. After-sch. opportunity programs; co-chair Md. Family Violence Coun.; bd. dir. John F. Kennedy Libr. Found., Nat. Inst. Women's Policy Rsch.; chair external adv. bd. Kennedy Krieger Inst. Early Infant Transition Ctr.; sr. advisor, Appropriations Com., House of Delegates, 1984-85; asst. Atty. Gen., Md., 1985-86; bd. ptnr. Radcliffe Coll. Recipient 4 hon. degrees; Visionary Leadership Award, Healthy Families Am., 2000, Clinton Ctr. Award for Leadership, Dem. Leadership Coun., 2002. mem., Econ. Devel. Commn., Baltimore County, 1987, Gov. Exec. Coun., Gov. Commn. on Svc. and Volunteerism, 1998-. Democrat.

**TOWNSEND, MARJORIE RHODES,** aerospace engineer, engineering executive; b. Washington, Mar. 12, 1930; d. Lewis Boling and Marjorie Olive (Trees) Rhodes; m. Charles Eby Townsend, June 7, 1948; children: Charles Eby Jr., Lewis Rhodes, John Cunningham, Richard Leo. BEE, George Washington U., 1951. Electronic scientist Naval Rsch. Lab., Washington, 1951-59; rsch. engr. to sect. head Goddard Space Flight Ctr.-NASA, Greenbelt, Md., 1959-65, tech. asst. to chief systems divsn., 1965-66, project mgr. small astronomy satellites, 1966-75, project mgr. applications explorer missions, 1975-76, mgr. preliminary systems design group, 1976-80; aero-

space and electronics cons. Washington, 1980-83; v.p. systems devel. Space Am., 1983-84; aerospace cons. Washington, 1984-90; dir. space systems engring. BDM Internat., Inc., Washington, 1990-91; dir. space applications BDM ESC, Washington, 1991-92; sr. prin. staff mem. BDM Fed., Inc., Washington, 1992-93. Aerospace cons., Washington, 1993—. Patentee digital telemetry system. Decorated Knight Italian Republic Order, 1972; recipient Fed. Women's award, 1973, EUR award for Culture, 1974, Engr. Alumni Achievement award George Washington U., 1975, Gen. Alumni Achievement award George Washington U., 1976, Exceptional Svc. medal NASA, 1971, Outstanding Leadership medal NASA, 1980, Eye-of-the-Needle award NASA, 1991. Fellow IEEE (chmn. Washington sect. 1974-75), AIAA (chmn. nat. capitol sect. 1985), AAAS (coun. del. 1985-88), Washington Acad. Sci. (pres. 1980-81); mem. Internat. Acad. Astronautics, Am. Geophys. Union, Soc. Women Engrs., Wing of Aerospace Med. Assn., Inc. (hon.), DAR, Daus. Colonial Wars, Mensa, Sigma Kappa, Sigma Delta Epsilon (hon.). Republican. Episcopalian. Home and Office: 3529 Tilden St NW Washington DC 20008-3122 Office Phone: 202-966-2330. E-mail: mrtownsend@aol.com.

**TOWNSEND, MILES AVERILL,** aerospace and mechanical engineering educator; b. Buffalo, N.Y., Apr. 16, 1935; s. Francis Devere and Sylvia (Wolpa) T.; children: Kathleen Townsend Hastings, Melissa, Stephen, Joel, Philip. BA, Stanford U., 1955; BS MechE, U. Mich., 1958; advanced cert., U. Ill., 1963, MS in Theoretical and Applied Mechanics, 1967; PhD, U. Wis., 1971. Registered profl. engr., Ill., Wis., Tenn., Ont. Project engr. Sundstrand, Rockford, Ill., 1959-63, Twin Disc Inc., Rockford, 1963-65, 67-68; sr. engr. Westinghouse Electric Corp., Sunnyvale, Calif., 1965-67; instr., fellow U. Wis., Madison, 1968-71; assoc. prof. U. Toronto, Ont., Canada, 1971-74; prof. mech. engring. Vanderbilt U., Nashville, 1974-81; Wilson prof. mech. and aerospace engring. U. Va., Charlottesville, 1981—, chmn. dept., 1981-91. Ptnr., v.p. Endev Ltd., Can. and U.S., 1972—; cons. in field. Contbr. numerous articles on dynamics, design dynamical systems, controls and optimization to profl. jours.; 7 patents in field. Recipient numerous research grants and contracts. Fellow ASME, AAAS; mem. N.Y. Acad. Scis., Sigma Xi, Phi Kappa Phi, Pi Tau Sigma. Avocations: running, reading, music. Home: 212 Alderman Rd Charlottesville VA 22903-1704 Office: U Va Dept Mech and Aerospace Engring Thornton Hall Charlottesville VA 22903-2442 Business E-Mail: mat@virginia.edu.

**TOWNSEND, ROBERT I, III,** lawyer; b. NYC, Oct. 6, 1965; AB magna cum laude, Harvard Coll., 1987; JD magna cum laude, Harvard Univ., 1990. Bar: NY 1991. Assoc. Cravath Swaine & Moore, NYC, 1990-98; ptnr., corp., 1998—. Exec. editor Harvard Law Rev. Mem.: ABA, NY State Bar Assn. Office: Cravath Swaine & Moore LLP Worldwide Plz 825 Eighth Ave New York NY 10019-7475 Office Phone: 212-474-1964. Office Fax: 212-474-3700. Business E-Mail: rtownsend@cravath.com.

**TOWNSEND, ROBERT J.,** lawyer; b. Charlotte, Mich., Nov. 11, 1938; s. Robert Wright and Rhea Lucille (Jennings) T.; m. Thea E. Kolb, Aug. 1, 1964; children: Melissa, Bradley, BA, Mich. State U., 1960; LLB, Harvard U., 1963. Bar: Ohio 1964, U.S. Dist. Ct. (so. dist.) Ohio 1964, U.S. Ct. Appeals (6th cir.) 1971, U.S. Supreme Ct. 1992. Assoc. Taft, Stettinus & Hollister, Cin., 1963-72, ptnr., 1972—. With U.S. Army, 1963-64, 68-69. Office: 1800 US Bank Tower 425 Walnut St Cincinnati OH 45202-3923 E-mail: townsend@taftlaw.com.

**TOWNSEND, ROBERT MORRIS,** economics professor, researcher; b. Apr. 23, 1948; BA, Duke U., 1970; PhD, U. Minn., 1975. Rsch. asst. Duke U., Durham, NC, 1970; grad. tchg. asst. microecons. U. Minn., Mpls., 1972—74; asst. prof. econs. Grad. Sch. Indsl. Adminstrn. Carnegie-Mellon U., Pitts., 1975—78, assoc. prof. econs., 1978—80, prof. econs., 1980—85, U. Chgo., 1985—94, dir. admissions, 1992—2000, Charles E. Merriam prof., 1994—98, Charles E. Merriam disting. svc. prof. econs., 1997—. Vis. prof. econs. U. Chgo., 1984—86; Sticerd vis. prof. London Sch. Econs., 1996; disting. vis. prof. CEMFI, Madrid, 1997; vis. prof. MIT, Cambridge, Mass., 2001—; mem. exec. bd. Population Rsch. Ctr., NORC, Chgo.; cons. Inter-Am. Devel. Bank, Washington, IMF, 2001—. The World Bank, Fes. Res. Bank Chgo.; mem. econs. panel NSF, Washington, 1989—91. Author: The Medieval Village Economy, Financial Structure and Economic Organization; editor: Jour. Polit. Economy, 1987—89. Recipient Frisch medal, Econometric Soc., 1998; fellow, Woodrow Wilson Found., Fed. Res. Bank Mpls., 1974—75; scholar, Rsch. Dept., Fed. Res. Bank Mpls., 1978—79. Fellow: Econometric Soc., Am. Acad. Arts and Scis.; mem.: Phi Beta Kappa. Office: University of Chicago 1126 E 59th Street Chicago IL 60637 Office Phone: 772-702-7587.

**TOWNSEND, STEVEN H.,** food products executive; BA, Bryant Univ. Smithfield, RI, 1976, MBA, 1980. V.p. fin., adminstrn. Cornucopia Natural Foods (now United Natural Foods), 1983—95, CFO, 1995—97; real estate developer, 1998—99; bd. dir. United Natural Foods Inc., Dayville, Conn., 2000—, pres., eastern region, 2000—02, pres., 2001—, CEO, 2003—, chmn., 2003—. Recipient Disting. Alumni award, Bryant Univ., 1990. Office: United Natural Foods Inc 260 Lake Rd Dayville CT 06241 Office Phone: 860-779-2800. Office Fax: 860-779-2811.

**TOWNSEND, TERRY,** publishing executive; b. Camden, N.J., Dec. 14, 1920; d. Anthony and Rose DeMarco; m. Paul Brorstrom Townsend, Dec. 8, 1961; 1 child, Kim. BA, Duke U., 1942; LHD (hon.), 1991. Dir. pub. rels. North Shore U. Hosp., Manhasset, NY, 1953—68; pres. Theatre Soc., L.I., 1967—70, Townsend Comm. Bur., L.I., 1970—98; ptnr. L.I. Communicating Svc., Bellport, 1977—. Pub. L.I. Bus. News, 1979-98, pub. emeritus, 1998—; v.p. ParrMeadows Racetrack, Yaphank, N.Y., 1977; mem. Bellport Archtl. Rev. Bd., 1997—. Columnist, writer L.I./Bus., Ronkonkoma, 1970-75. Assoc. trustee North Shore U. Hosp., 1968—; bd. govs. Adelphi U. Friends Fin. Edn., 1970-85; chmn. ann. archtl. awards competition N.Y. Inst. Tech., 1970-83; trustee Dowling Coll., 1984—; trustee L.I. Fine Arts Mus., 1984-85; pub. broadcasting PBS Sta. WLIW TV, Garden City, L.I., N.Y., 1990-93; bd. dirs. Family Svc. Assn. Nassau County, 1982-92; dinner chmn. L.I. 400 Ball, 1987; trustee L.I. Mus. Art, 1994-2003; Recipient Media award 110 Ctr. Bus. and Profl. Women, 1977, Enterprise award Friends of Fin. Edn., 1981, L.I. Loves Bus. Showcase Salute, 1982, Cmty. Svc. award N.Y. Diabetes Assn., 1983, Disting. Long Islander in Comm. award L.I. United Epilepsy Assn., 1984, Spl. award Dowling Coll. Spring Tribute, 1989, Disting. Svc. award Episcopal Health Svcs., 1989, Disting. Citizen award Dowling Coll., 1991, Gilbert Tilles award Nat. Assn. Fundraising Execs., 1994, Hadassah Cmty. Svc. award, 1996, Golden rule award Little Village Sch., 1997, Lifetime Achievement award L.I. Assn., 1998, Promote L.I. Achievement award, 1998, Lifetime Achievement award Advancement for Commerce & Industry, 1999; named 1st Lady of L.I., L.I. Pub. Rels. Assn., 1973, L.I. Woman of Yr. L.I. Assn. Action Com., 1989; Paul and Terry Townsend Sch. of Bus., Dowling Coll., designated in her honor, 2004. Mem.: Bellport Women's Golf Club (pres. 2003—04). Office: LI Communicating Svcs PO Box 915 Bellport NY 11713-0915 E-mail: terytowns@aol.com.

**TOWNSEND, THOMAS PERKINS,** former mining company executive; b. Bryn Mawr, Pa., Mar. 28, 1917; s. John and Mildred (Perkins) T.; m. Laura M. Trench, Sept. 14, 1940; children: Joanne Townsend Taber, Hunter, Elizabeth Robie. BS in Econs., U. Pa., 1939; postgrad., Harvard U., 1944. C.P.A., Pa. Sr. acct. Price Waterhouse & Co., 1945-48; treas., dir. Fox Products Co., 1948-53, Wilcolator Co., 1953-55; staff acct. Tex. Gulf Sulphur Co., N.Y.C., 1955-57, asst. treas., 1958-61, v.p., controller, 1961-62, v.p. treas., 1962-64, v.p. internat. ops., 1964-68; v.p. exec. v.p. Bosco Middle East Oil Corp., Greenwich, Conn., 1968-69; pres. Conn. Real Estate Corp., Greenwich, 1969-70, also bd. dirs., 1972-77; v.p. finance Rosaria Resources Corp., N.Y.C., 1970-81; treas. Unidyne Corp., 1984-85. Cons. AMAX, Inc., 1981-85; bd. dirs. Thermal Exploration Corp., Carlin Gold Co. Trustee Soc. to Advance Retarded, Norwalk, Conn.; mem. New Canaan (Conn.) Bd. Fin., 1985—89; bd. dirs. United Way of Tri-State, Denison Pequotsegos Nature Ctr.; trustee, pres. South Kent Sch. Served to lt. (s.g.) Supply corps USNR, World War II. Mem. Am. Inst. Accts., N.Y. State Soc. CPAs, Fin. Execs. Inst., Mason's Island Yacht Club, Off Soundings Club. Episcopalian (treas.,

vestryman 1960-72, 87-95). *The principal goal in my life has been to be a straight dealer, to be honest in thought, word and deed. It has paid off for me. Crooked dealing may make more money, but it does not lead to a happier life. One must live by his God.*

**TOWNSLEY, LISA GAIL,** mathematics professor; b. Honolulu, June 25, 1960; d. Sidney Joseph and Mary Irmhild (Fuss) Townsley. BS, Santa Clara (Calif.) U., 1981; MS, Northwestern U., 1983, PhD, 1988. Prof. math. Benedictine U., Lisle, Ill., 1987—. Exam. reader, table leader AP/ETS, Clemson, SC, 1991—2005. Author: The DERIVE Calculus Workbook, 1994, Cohomology Rings of Finite Groups, 2003; contbr. articles to profl. jours. Named to Faculty All Stars, Chgo. Tribune, 1994; grantee, NSF, 1993, 2001. Mem. Math. Assn. Am., Assn. for Women in Math., Am. Math. Soc., Phi Beta Kappa, Kappa Mu Epsilon, Alpha Sigma Nu. Democrat. Office: Benedictine U 5700 College Rd Lisle IL 60532

**TOWSLEE, JANET L.,** special education educator; b. Louisville, Apr. 4, 1942; d. James and Juanita (Flowers) T.; m. Donald Collier, Aug. 28, 1964; children: Richard Louis, Rebecca Elizabeth. BS in Russian Studies, Fla. State U., 1963; MA in Spl. Edn., U. Louisville, 1967; EdD in Spl. Edn., Ind. U., 1974. Cert. tchr. spl. edn. Tchr. Jefferson County Schs., Louisville, 1963-69; teaching asst. Ind. U., Bloomington, 1969-72; with dept. spl. edn. Ga. State U., Atlanta, 1972—, assoc. dean, dir. ednl. field svcs. dean's office, 1978-91; faculty dept. spl. edn. Clayton State Coll., 1992—. Instr. edn. U. Louisville, 1966-67, 69; tchr. basic adult edn. Jefferson County Bd. Edn., 1963-69. Author: Future Educator of America Handbook, 1989, 91, 93; editorial cons. Profl. Educator, 1986—; contbr. articles, book revs. to profl. jours. Bd. dirs. Tommy Nobis Tchr., 1987—, also twice pres. Recipient Outstanding Svc. award Tommy Nobis Ctr., 1987; named Disting. Adminstr. of Yr. Mortar Bd. Ga. State U., 1983. Mem. Assn. Tchr. Educators (one of 70 Leaders Tchr. Edn. 1990, pres. 1987-88, Pres. award for Svc. 1983, 86, Honor Roll 1984), Comparative and Internat. Edn. Soc., Nat. Coun. States Insvc. Edn., U.S.-China Tchr. Edn. Consortium, Assn. Spl. Edn. Tech., Coun. Exceptional Children Internat. (divs. mental retardation, tchr. edn., career devel. internat. edn. and svcs.), Am. Assn. Colls. Tchr. Edn. (NCATE exec. bd.), S.E. Regional Assn. Tchr. Educators, Ga. Assn. Tchr. Educators, Ga. Staff Devel. Coun., Ga. Coun. Exceptional Children, Met. Atlanta Tchr. Edn. Group. Home: 1194 W Nancy Creek Dr NE Atlanta GA 30319-1644

**TOWSNER, CYNTHIA MERLE,** academic administrator, educator; b. Washington, Apr. 23, 1939; d. Philip and Edith Towsner; married, 1963; 1 child, Scott David Garrison. BS, U. Md., 1961, postgrad., 1964-65, Am. U. 1987. cert. contracting officer's rep., U.S. Dept. Edn. Tchr. Montgomery County Pub. Schs., Rockville, Md., 1961-66, 72-80; spl. asst. to comm. rehab. svcs. adminstrn. U.S. Dept. Edn., Washington, 1981—85, spl. asst. to the dir. Office Intergovtl. & Interagy. Affairs, 1985—87, acting dir. intergovtl. affairs office, 1987, ednl. program specialist Office Bilingual Edn. & Minority Languages Affairs, 1987—93, edn. program specialist Bilingual Vocat. Tng., 1993—96, nat. coord. health literacy and literacy vols. for adults, 1996—2002, coord lit. vols., 1996—, coord. lit. vols., health literacy, 2005—. Pres. Office Vocat. Adult Edn., U.S. Dept. Edn., Educare Programs, Inc., Chevy Chase, Md., 1988—; cons. R.J. Comer Comm., Inc. Jacksonville, Fla., 1995-97; v.p. Dalmahoy Group Internat., Chevy Chase, 1997-99. Photographer Project Education Reform: Time for Results, vol. 1, 1987. Vol. Holy Cross Hosp., Silver Spring, Md., 1969-74; asst. to pres. for edn. issues, chair nominating com., chair cmty. directory Rock Creek Hills Civic Assn., Kensington, 1968-85; v.p. D.C., Md. and Va. region, chair youth rally, chair radiothon publicity St. Jude's Children's Rsch. Hosp., Aiding Leukemia Stricken Am. Children, Memphis, 1969-81; chair internat. festival Larchmont Elem. Sch. PTA, Montgomery County, MD, 1976-78; bd. dirs., chair Citizens for Edn., Montgomery County, Md., 1977-82; active Renaissance Women, Washington, 1983-87; chair corp. and bus. contbns. Hosp. Relief Fund for the Caribbean, Chevy Chase, 1989-91, annual ball com., 1989-94; vol. tutor Laubach Literacy Action and Literacy Vols. Am., Chevy Chase, 1989-93. Recipient Meritorious Svc. medal Am. Automobile Assn., Washington, Honors award Rock Creek Hills Civic Assn., Kensington, Md., 1979, Pres. award Combined Fed. Campaign, Washington, 1987, Hammer award V.P. of the U.S., Washington, 1996, 1st place ribbon in photography Montgomery County Agrl. Fair, Gaithersburg, Md., 1998, 1st, 2d and 3d place ribbons in photography Montgomery County Agrl. Fair, Gaithersburg, 1999, 1st and 2d place ribbons in photography Md. State Fair, Timonium, 1999, 1st pl. award Md. State Fair, 2000, Achievement in Amateur Photography award, Internat. Libr. Photographs, 2004. Mem. AAUW. Freelance Photographers Orgn. (life, Master Photographer 2002), Assn. for Career and Tech. Edn., Soc. Govt. Meeting Profls., Nat. Trust for Scotland, Nat. Mus. Women in the Arts (founding mem.), Nat. Women's History Mus. (charter mem.). Avocations: photography, reading, travel. Home: 4620 N Park Ave Apt 1404E Chevy Chase MD 20815-4563 Personal E-mail: cindy.towsner@verizon.net.

**TOY, CHARLES DAVID,** lawyer; b. NYC, June 29, 1955; s. Frank H.F. and Louise S.K. (Louie) Toy; m. Sandra Lynn Youla, Mar. 10, 1984; 1 child, Alana May Youla. BA cum laude, Harvard U., 1977, JD, 1980. Bar: NY 1981, DC 2001. Assoc. Milbank, Tweed, Hadley & McCloy, NYC, 1980-84, Kaye, Scholer, Fierman, Hays & Handler, Hong Kong, 1984—88, ptnr., 1989—91, NYC, 1991—93; v.p., gen. counsel Overseas Pvt. Investment Corp., Washington, 1993-2001, v.p., fin., 1995-96, v.p. investment funds, 1998-99; ptnr. Wilmer, Cutler & Pickering, Washington, 2001—02; mem. bd. advisors GMI Capital Corp., Chevy Chase, Md., 2002—04; exec. v.p., 2004; mng. mem., exec. v.p. Pangaea Holdings, LLC, Chevy Chase, 2005—; chief compliance officer, corp. sec. Pangaea Trading Corp., 2005—. Spkr. in field; profile subject Internat. Fin. Law Rev., 1996, Ave. Asia, 1996, 97, ABA 1997-99, 2002, Am. Conf. Inst., 1996, 98, Am. Soc. Internat. Law, 1996-97, Assn. Bar City NY, 2000, World Econ. Devel. Conf., 1996, Corp. Legal Times Roundtable, 1996, Com. of 100, 1996, Asian Am. Bar Assn., 1996, Asian Bus. Assn., 1996, Asian Pacific Am. Bar Assn., 1996, Forbes, 1997, Adam Smith Inst., 1998, Jerome Levy Econs. Inst. Bard Coll., 1998, Asian Pacific Am. Inst. Congl. Studies, 1998, Embassy South Africa, 1998, Harvard Inst. Internat. Devel., 1998, 99, Insight Info., 1998, 99, Nat. Asian Pacific Am. Bar Assn., 1998, U. Fla. Levin Coll. Law, 1999, CNA/Schinnerer Conf., 1999, Case We. Res. U. Sch. Law, 1999, Practising Law Inst., 1999, 2000, U. Iowa Tippie Sch. Mgmt., 2000, Met. Corp. Counsel Interview, 2000, Internat. Project Fin. Assn., 2000, Am. Corp. Counsel Assn., 2000, US Inst. Peace, 2001; interview Legal Times, 2001, Bloomberg, 2002. Contbg. editor Taxes and Investment in Asia and the Pacific, 1985, Tax News Service, 1986—91, Bull. for Internat. Fiscal Documentation, 1986—91; mem. editl. bd. Strategic Alliance Alert, 1994-95. Bd. trustees Lower East Side Tenement Mus., 1994-98. Mem. ABA, NY State Bar Assn., Assn. Bar City of NY, Nat. Asian Pacific Am. Bar Assn., Asian Pacific Am. Bar Assn., Harvard Law Sch. Assn., Am. Club (Hong Kong), Ladies Recreation Club (Hong Kong), Phi Beta Kappa Democrat. Roman Catholic. Home and Office: Pangaea Holdings LLC 4701 Willard Ave Ste 413 Chevy Chase MD 20815-4610 Business E-Mail: toy@pangaeafinance.com.

**TOY, JANET STENMARK,** artist; b. Polo, Ill., June 3, 1926; d. David Alfred and Ellen May (Cockerton) Stenmark; m. William James Lovett, Oct. 12, 1948 (div. 1953); 1 child, Nona Linnea Lovett Stone; m. Bernard Toy, Mar. 17, 1962 Student, Sch. Art Inst. Chgo., Art Students League N.Y., Bklyn. Mus. Art Sch., Santa Ana C.C. Artist-designer Ilse Von Ehrn Christmas Cards, Pittstown, NJ, 1951; comml. artist Le Huray Lithographers, N.Y.C., 1953—56, Package Design, Inc., N.Y.C., 1957—60; package designer Irv Koons Assocs. Inc., N.Y.C., 1960—72; comml. artist Santa Fe Internat. Inc., Orange, Calif., 1974—82, Pix Slide Prodn., Santa Ana, Calif., 1982; artist-designer Antique Glass Works, Inc., Santa Ana, 1982—83; comml. artist Martin Graphics, Fullerton, Calif., 1983—84, Cox Hobbies, Corona, Calif., 1989—92. Mem. Orange County Ctr. for Contemporary Art, Santa Ana, 1983-87, Gallery 318, L.A., 1985-88, Bowers Mus. Galleria Co-op Gallery, Santa Ana, 1985-88, Pahrump (Nev.) Visual and Performing Arts

Coun., 1994-; mgr. (with husband) Court House Gallery, Pahrump, 2000—. Ceramic artist, sculptor, exhibiting in solo and group shows Recipient awards for ceramic sculptures Mem.: Sping Mountain Art Guild. Avocations: music, watercolor painting, quilting.

**TOY, STEPHEN J.,** corporate financial executive; b. Nov. 1972; BS in Bus. Adminstrn., SUNY, 1994. Corp. auditor Kansai Sawayawa; corp. fin. O'Brien Ptnrs., Inc.; mng. dir. WL Ross & Co LLC, N.Y. Office: WL Ross & Co LLC Manhattan Tower 19th Fl 101 East 52d St New York NY 10022

**TOY, TASHA CHANTEY,** academic administrator, educator; b. Augusta, Ga., Oct. 6, 1974; d. Marion and Gloria Davis Toy. BA, N.C. Ctrl. U., 1997, MA in Edn., 2000; postgrad., Seton Hall U., 2001—. Adminstrv. asst. N.C. Ctrl. U., Durham, 1998—2001; grad. programs asst. Seton Hall U., South Orange, NJ, 2001—. Pres. TCT Consulting Firm, South Orange, 2002—. Mem.: AAUW, Am. Edn. Rsch. Assn., Assn. Study Higher Edn., Phi Delta Kappa, Kappa Delta Pi (pres. local chpt. 1999—2000, chpt. advisor 2000—01, pres. local chpt. 2004—05), Alpha Kappa Alpha. Democrat. Baptist. Avocations: travel, reading, volunteer work, white-water rafting. Office: Seton Hall U Coll Edn 400 South Orange Ave South Orange NJ 07079 Office Phone: 973-761-9668. Office Fax: 973-275-2187. Personal E-mail: tashactoy@verizon.net. E-mail: toytasha@shu.edu.

**TOY, VIVIAN,** journalist; Reporter New York Times. Panelist Covering NYC, 1998, Long Island Land Preservation vs. Sprawl, 2005. Author: (articles) Some Immigrants Begin to Lose Food Stamps Over New Law, 1996, Tough Workfare Rules Used as Way to Cut Welfare Rolls, 1998. Office: The New York Times LI Bur 1325 Franklin Ave Garden City NY 11530 Office Fax: 516-746-0930.*

**TOYODA, SHOICHIRO,** automotive executive; b. Nagoya, Japan, Feb. 27, 1925; s. Kiichiro and Hatako Toyoda; m. Hiroko Mitsui, Nov. 30, 1952; children: Atsuko, Akio. B in Engring., Nagoya U., 1947, D in Engring., 1955. Dir. Toyota (Japan) Motor Co., Ltd., 1952-61, mng. dir., 1961-67, sr. mng. dir., 1967-72, exec. v.p., 1972-81; pres. Toyota Motor Sales Co., Ltd., 1981-82, Toyota Motor Corp., 1982-92, chmn., 1992-99, hon. chmn., 1999—. Bd. dirs. Denso Co., Ltd., Nagoya Broadcasting Network; chmn. bd. dirs. Inst. Internat. Econ. Studies; chmn. Japan Assn. for the 2005 World Exposition, 1997—. Chmn. Keidanren, Tokyo, 1994-98; hon. chmn. KDDI, 2000; consul gen. Honorario de Costa Rica, Nagoya, 1984—. Recipient Medal with Dark-Blue Ribbon, Govt. of Japan, 1972, The Deming Prize, 1980, Medal with Blue Ribbon, Govt. of Japan, 1984, FISITA medal, France, Medal of Isabel la Cath., King of Spain, 2000; decorated knight comdr. Most Noble Order of the Crown (Thailand), gran cruz Order Nacional al Merit, Colombia, knight comdr. Brit. Empire, grand cordon Order of the Sacred Treasure (Japan), Order Francisco de Miranda First Class (Venezuela), Ordem Nat. do Cruzeiro do Sul (Brazil), Order of Merit (Turkey), comdr. Legion of Honor (France), Grande Ufficiale, Govt. of Italy, hon. companion Gen. divsn. Order of Australia, grand decoration of honor in gold with star, Austria, comdr.'s cross Order of Merit (Germany), Grand Cordon of the Order of the Rising Sun (Japan). Office: Toyota Motor Corp 1 Toyota-cho Toyota 471-8571 Japan

**TOZER, JEAN FRAME,** gifted and talented educator; d. Thomas Hamiton and Lillian Margaret Frame; children: Michael, Kristen, Scott. BA, Coll. N.J., 1968; Masters Degree, City U., 1998. Health and phys. edn. tchr. Kearny Bd. Edn.; gifted and talented tchr. Brick (N.J.) Twp. Bd. Edn. Bd. dirs. Cape Breton Holding Co., Brick. Mem.: NJGAC. Home: 28 Bretonian Dr Brick NJ 08723

**TOZER, W. JAMES, JR.,** investment company executive; b. Salt Lake City, Feb. 9, 1941; s. W. James and Virginia (Somerville) T.; m. Elizabeth Farran, July 30, 1965; children: Farran Virginia, Katharine Coppins. BA cum laude, Trinity Coll., 1963; MBA, Harvard U., 1965. Investment officer First Nat. City Overseas Investment Corp., N.Y.C., 1965-70; v.p. corp. devel. Citicorp, N.Y.C., 1970-71; sr. v.p. and head Citicorp Subs. Group, 1971-74; sr. v.p., gen. mgr., head Merchant Banking Group, 1974-75, sr. v.p., gen. mgr. N.Y. banking div., 1975-77; sr. exec. v.p., dir. and head investment banking div. Shearson Hayden Stone, Inc., N.Y.C., 1978-79; sr. exec. v.p. Marine Midland Bank and Marine Midland Banks, Inc., 1979-80, sr. exec. v.p. ops., fin. and strategic staff units, 1980-85, mem. office of chmn., sector exec. corp., instl. and internat. banking, 1985-87; chmn. Mountain West Banking Corp., Denver, 1988-89; pres., chief operating officer Prudential-Bache Securities, Inc., N.Y.C., 1989-90; pres., CEO Lincolnshire Mgmt., Inc., N.Y.C., 1993-94; mng. dir. Vectra Mgmt. Group, 1990—. Bd. dirs. LendingTree, Inc., 1998—2003; dir. Alliance Capital; dir., chmn. exec. com. Draper Bancorp; co-founder, dir. Vectra Bank. Trustee Trinity Coll, 2005—, chmn. bd. fellows; trustee, treas. Community Service Soc., 1976-87; trustee, treas. The Sch. for Field Studies, 1995—; trustee Citizens Budget Commn., 1986—; adv. council Atlanta U. Sch. Bus. Adminstrn., 1985-89; bd., v.p. Episcopal Charities, 1999—. Mem. N.Y. State Bankers Assn. (legis. policy com. 1981-87), Assn. Res. City Bankers (govt. rels. com. 1984-87), Am. Bankers Assn. (govt. rels. coun. 1985-87), Economic Club, University Club, Millbrook Club, Mashomack Club, River Club (N.Y.C.), Alta Club (S.L.C.). Home: 550 Park Ave New York NY 10021-7369 Office: 424 W 33St Ste 540 New York NY 10001-2614 Personal E-mail: wjtozer@vectramanagement.com

**TOZER, WILLIAM EVANS,** entomologist, educator; b. Binghamton, N.Y., July 7, 1947; s. William Evans and Gertrude Genevieve (Lewis) T. BS in Natural Sci., Niagara U., 1969; MS in Biology, Ball State U., 1979; PhD in Entomology, U. Calif., Berkeley, 1986. Cert. C.C. biology and zoology tchr. Calif. Jr. H.S. sci. and English tchr. St. Patricks Sch., Corning, NY, 1969-71; tchg. asst. biology Ball State U., Muncie, Ind., 1974-76; pvt. practice biol. environ. cons. Berkeley, Calif., 1976-79, 86-88; rsch. asst. U. Calf., Berkeley, 1979-86; dept. head edn. and tng. USN Disease Vector Ecology and Control Ctr., Poulsbo, Wash., 1988—2004. Mem., acting chmn. San Francisco Bay Area Mosquito Control Coun., Alameda, 1988-96; chmn. com., mem. Armed Forces Pest Mgmt. Bd., Washington, 1994—; bd. dirs. EPA Cert. and Tng. Assessment Group, 2001-05. Editor (field handbook) Navy Environmental Health Center, 1994; contbr. articles to profl. jours. With U.S. Army, 1971-73. Mem. Am. Entomol. Soc., Sigma Xi. Achievements include first to publish evidence for underwater behavioral thermoregulation in adult insects. Office: USN Environ Preventive Medicine Unit 5 3235 Albacore Alley San Diego CA 92136 Office Phone: 619-556-7070. E-mail: wetozer@nepmu5.med.navy.mil.

**TRABER, PETER GEORGE,** dean, educator; b. Johnstown, NY, 1955; m. K. Bobbi Traber; 2 children. Grad., U. Mich., 1977; MD, Wayne State U. Med. Sch., 1981; completed Mgmt. Devel Program for Physician Exec., Wharton Sch. U. Pa. Resident in internal medicine Northwestern U. Med. Sch., Chgo., fellow in gastroenterology, U. Mich. Sch. Medicine, faculty mem. Ann Arbor, 1987—92; chief gastroenterology U. Pa. Sch. Medicine, 1992—97, T. Grier Miller prof. medicine, 1993—97, Frank Wistar Thomas prof. and chair dept. medicine, 1997—2000, interim dean Phila., 2000; interim CEO U. Pa. Health Sys., Phila., 2000; sr. v.p. clinical devel. and med. affairs and chief med. officer GlaxoSmithKline, 2000—03; pres., CEO, prof. medicine Baylor Coll. Medicine, Houston, 2003—. Bd. dir. Tanox Inc., 2004—. Recipient Disting. Alumni award, Wayne State U. Sch. Medicine. Mem.: Assn. Am. Physicians, Am. Soc. Clinical Rsch., Am. Gastroenterologic Assn.*

**TRABITZ, EUGENE LEONARD,** aerospace company executive; b. Cleve., Aug. 13, 1937; s. Emanuel and Anna (Berman) T.; m. Caryl Lee Rine, Dec. 22, 1963 (div. Aug. 24, 1983); children: Claire Marie, Honey Caryl; m. Kathryn Lynn Bates, Sept. 21, 1983; 1 stepchild, Paul Francis Rager. BA, Ohio State U., 1965. Enlisted USAF, 1954, advanced through grades to maj.; served as crew comdr. 91st Strategic Missile Divsn., Minot, SD, 1968-70; intelligence officer Fgn. Tech. Divsn., Dayton, Ohio, 1970-73; dir. external affairs Aero. Systems Divsn., Dayton, 1973-75; program mgr. Air Force

Armament Divsn., Valparaiso, Fla., 1975-80; dir. ship ops. Air Force Ea. Test Range, Satellite Beach, Fla., 1980-83; dep. program mgr. Air Force Satellite Text Ctr., Sunnyvale, Calif., 1983-84; ret., 1984; sr. staff engr. Ultrasystems Inc., 1984-86; pres. TAWD Systems Inc., Palo Alto, Calif., 1986-92, Am. Telenetics Co., San Mateo, Calif., 1992—; pres., CEO Enterprise Def. Inst., Inc., San Mateo, 2002—. Cons. Space Applications Corp., Sunnyvale, 1986-87, Litton Computer Svcs., Mountain View, Calif., 1987-91, Battelle Meml. Inst. Columbus, 1993—. V.p. Bd. County Mental Health Clinic, Ft. Walton Beach, Fla., 1973-75. Decorated Bronze Star. Mem. DAV (life), ASIS Internat., Nat. Def. Indsl. Assn., Armed Forces Comm. and Electronics Assn., Am. Soc. for Indsl. Security Internat., U.S. Space Found. (charter), Air Force Assn. (life), Nat. Sojourners, Masons (32d degree). Avocations: golf, tennis, racketball, sailing, bridge. Home: 425 Anchor Rd Apt 317 San Mateo CA 94404-1058 Office Phone: 650-345-5694. E-mail: gene@amtelenet.com.

**TRACEY, DENNIS HENRY, III,** lawyer; b. NYC, Nov. 8, 1956; s. Dennis Henry Jr. and Mary Catherine (Lunney) T.; m. Marcia Jean Hamelin, July 20, 1985. BA, Cornell U., 1978; JD, NYU, 1981. Bar: N.Y. 1982, U.S. Dist. Ct. (so. and ea. dists.) N.Y. 1982, U.S. Ct. Appeals (4th cir.) 1982. Assoc. Paul, Wells, Rifkind, Wharton & Garrison, N.Y.C., 1981-84; litigation counsel CBS Inc., N.Y.C., 1984; assoc. Davis, Markel & Edwards, N.Y.C., 1984—87, ptnr., 1988—2000, Hogan & Hartson LLP, 2000—, mem. exec. com.; mng. ptnr. N.Y. Office. Co-chmn. Lawyers' Com. for Reelection of Robert Abrams, N.Y.C., 1982. Mem. ABA, N.Y. City Bar Assn. Office: Hogan & Hartson LLP 875 Third Ave New York NY 10022 Office Phone: 212-918-3524. Office Fax: 212-918-3100. Business E-mail: dhtracey@hhlaw.com

**TRACEY, MATTHEW SEAN,** music educator, musician; b. Teaneck, NJ, Feb. 4, 1965; s. Patrick Edward and Kathleen Teresa Tracey; m. Dawn C. Cusimano, Nov. 3, 1990. MusM, Manhattan State U., NJ, 1987—89; MusB, William Paterson U., Wayne, NJ, 1983—87. Cert. K-12 tchr. of music NJ, 1987. Musician Ray Sepulveda Orch., New York, 1993—, Tito Nieves Orch., New York; musical dir. Frankie Negron Orch., New York, 1994—96; k-12 music dept. chairperson Ridgefield Pub. Schools, NJ, 1990—; dir. of bands Ridgefield Meml. HS, 1987—. Hon. lifetime mem. Nat. PTA, NJ; mem. Music Educators Nat. Conf., NJ, 1983—, Internat. Assn. of Jazz Educators, NJ, NEA, NJ. Edn. assoc., Music Educators of Bergen County, NJ. Musician: (studio/ recording musician) commericial jingles, Pop, Jazz, Latin recordings; profesional marching band designer, Drill Designer; composer: (composer/arranger) various works. Recipient World Champion Bushwacker Drum & Bugle Corps, Drum Corps Associates, 1986, 198, 1989, 1990, World Champion-Garfield Cadets, Drum Corps Internat., 1984. Mem.: Nat. PTA (hon. Hon. Lifetime Mem. 2004). Achievements include NJ Governors's Tchr. of the Year. Avocations: music, travel, gastronomy. Office: Ridgefield Memorial High School 555 Walnut street Ridgefield NJ 08657 E-mail: contactus@ridgefieldband.com.

**TRACHSEL, WILLIAM HENRY,** corporate lawyer; b. El Paso, Tex., Apr. 20, 1943; BS in Aerospace Engring., U. Fla., 1965; JD, U. Conn., 1971. Bar: Conn. 1971. V.p., counsel Hamilton Standard, Hartford, Conn., 1978; v.p., counsel automotive div. United Tech. Corp., Hartford, Conn., 1979—83, deputy general counsel, 1983—86, v.p., dep. gen. counsel, 1986—93, v.p., sec. and dep. gen. counsel, 1993-98, sr. v.p., gen. counsel, 1998—, sec., 1998—2004. Mem.: U. Conn. Found. (bd. dir.), U. Conn. Capital Campaign Steering Comm., Am. Bar Assoc., Conn. Bar Assoc., Conn. Bar Found. (bd. dir.), Hartford Hosp. (bd. dir.), MetroHartford Alliance. Office: United Tech Corp Bldg Hartford CT 06101 Business E-mail: william.trachsel@utc.com.

**TRACHTE, GEORGE JOSEPH,** pharmacology educator; b. Pottsville, Pa., Oct. 29, 1953; s. Arthur and Frances Mary (Sharkey) T.; m. Patricia Ann O'Neill, June 30, 1979; children: Gregory Alexander, Samantha Ann. BS, Pa. State U., 1975; Phd, Thomas Jefferson U., Phila., 1979. Postdoctoral fellow U. Va. Med. Sch., Charlottesville, 1979-82; vis. scientist Pharmakologisches Inst., Koln, Germany, 1982; asst. prof. U. Minn. Duluth Sch. Medicine, 1982-88, assoc. prof., 1988-94, prof., rsch. dir. 1994—. Mem. adv. bd. Eicosanoids, Germany, 1990-92. Mem. Am. Physiol. Soc., Am. Soc. Pharm. & Exp. Therapeutics, Sigma Xi (pres. U. Minn. Duluth chpt. 1995-96). Methodist. Office: U Minn Dept Pharm Sch Medicine 10 University Dr Dept Pharm Duluth MN 55812-2403

**TRACHTENBERG, MATTHEW J.,** trust company executive; b. NYC, June 20, 1958; s. Mark Trachtenberg and Joanne Horne. BA magna cum laude, NYU, 1974; JD, Bklyn. Law Sch., 1977; MBA in Fin., Fordham U., 1982. Bar: NY 1979. Mgmt. trainee Mfrs. Hanover Trust Co., NYC, 1977-78, credit analyst, 1978-79, corp. banking rep., 1979-80, asst. sec., 1980-82, asst. v.p., 1982, v.p., 1982-86, v.p., corp. sec., 1987-92; dir. Mfrs. Hanover Found., NYC, 1987-92; v.p., sec. regional bd. Chem. Bank, NYC, 1992-96, v.p., dep. corp. sec., 1992-96, sec. regional bd., 1992-96, v.p., 1992-96, Chem. Banking Corp., NYC, 1992-96; v.p. asst. corp. sec. Chase Manhattan Bank, NYC, 1996—98; sec. Chase Manhattan Regional Bd., NYC, 1996—98; v.p., sr. pvt. banker PNC Bank, NYC, 1999—2000, Fleet Bank, NYC, 2000—02; mng. dir. First Republic Bank, NYC, 2002—04; sr. v.p. US Trust Co., 2004—06. Bd. dirs., chmn., pres., CEO Nat. Orch. Assn.; bd. dirs., past pres. USO Met. NY; bd. dirs., treas., chair fin. com. NY Eye and Ear Infirmary; bd. dirs. Continuum Health Ptnrs. Mem.: NY State Bar Assn., Phi Beta Kappa, Pi Sigma Alpha. Avocations: music, fishing, painting, writing. Office: Nat Orchestral Assn PO Box 7016 New York NY 10150-7016 Office Phone: 212-208-4691. Business E-mail: mtrachtenberg@nationalorchestral.org.

**TRACHTENBERG, STEPHEN JOEL,** academic administrator; b. Bklyn., Dec. 14, 1937; s. Oscar M. and Shoshana G. (Weinstock) Trachtenberg; m. Francine Zorn, June 24, 1971; children: Adam Maccabee, Ben-Lev. BA, Columbia U., 1959; JD, Yale U., 1962; M in Pub. Adminstrn., Harvard U., 1966; LHD (hon.), Trinity Coll., 1986; HHD (hon.), U. Hartford, 1989; LLD (hon.), Hanyang U., Seoul, 1990; DPA (hon.), Kyonggi U., Seoul, 1994; LLD (hon.), Richmond Coll., London, 1995; MD (hon.), Odessa State Med. U., Ukraine, 1996; LLD (hon.), Mount Vernon Coll., 1997; LHD (hon.), Boston U., 1999, Gratz Coll., 1999; LLD (hon.), So. Conn. State U., 2001, U. New Haven, 2002. Bar: N.Y. 1964, U.S. Supreme Ct. 1967. Atty. AEC, 1962—65; legis. asst. to Congressman John Brademas of Ind., Washington, 1965; tutor law Harvard Coll.; tchg. fellow edn. and pub. policy John F. Kennedy Sch. Govt., Harvard U., 1965—66; spl. asst. to U.S. edn. commr. Office of Edn., HEW, Washington, 1966—68; assoc. prof. polit. sci. Boston U., 1969—77, assoc. dean, 1969—70, dean, 1970—74, assoc. v.p., co-counsel, 1974—76, v.p. acad. svcs., 1976—77; pres., prof. pub. adminstrn. U. Hartford, Conn., 1977—88, George Washington U., Washington, 1988—. Mem. joint editl. bd. The Presidency and ACE/Praeger Series on Higher Edn.; mem. Fed. City Coun.; bd. dirs Consortium of Univs. Washington Met. Area, Riggs Bank, Greater Washington Bd. Trade, Nat. Edn. Telecom. Orgn., Washington Rsch. Libr. Consortium, DC Com. to Promote Washington; exec. adv. coun. SCT Edn. Sys. Contbr. articles to profl. jours. Trustee Al-Akhawayn U., Morocco, Com. for Econ. Devel.; active 2001 U.S. Savs. Bonds Vol. Com.; chmn. Md./D.C. Selection Com., 1998—2004, Rhodes Scholarships; mem. Wash-ington Regional Panel for Selection of 2004-05 Class of White House Fellows; chair exec. com. Southeastern Univs. Rsch. Assn.; active D.C. Mayor's Bus. Adv. Coun.; exec. panel Chief Naval Ops.; bd. overseers List Coll. Jewish Theol. Sem. Am.; bd. dirs. D.C. C. of C.; chair, pres. council Atlantic 10 Conf.; bd. dirs. Chiang Chen Indsl. Charity Found. Ltd., Hong Kong. Decorated grand officier du Wissam Al Alaoui King Mohammed VI of Morocco; named Outstanding Young Person, Boston Jr. C. of C., 1970, Alumnus of Yr. James Madison H.S., Bklyn., 1982, Washingtonian of Yr. Washingtonian Mag., 2000; named one of 100 Young Leaders, Acad. Am. Council Learning, 1978. Fifty Outstanding Alumni Problem Solvers, Har-vard's John F. Kennedy Sch. Govt., 1987, The 2002 Forty Forward A, Washington Bus. Forward mag., 2002; recipient Myrtle Wreath award, Hadassah, 1982, Scopus award, Am. Friends of Hebrew U., 1984, Human Rels. award, NCCJ, 1987, NAACP award, 1988, Conn. Bar Assn. citation, 1988, Univ. medal of highest honor, Kyung Hee U., Korea, 1990, Martin Luther King, Jr. Internat. Salute award, 1992, Hannah G. Solomon award, Nat. Coun. Jewish Women, 1992, Father of Yr. award, Washington Urban

League, 1993, Univ. Pres. medal, Kyonggi U., Korea, 1993, Merit award, Am. Czech and Slovak Assn., 1993, John Jay award, Columbia U., 1995, Spirit of Democracy award, Am. Jewish Congress, 1995, Newcomen Soc. award, 1995, Disting. Achievement medal, Greenberg Ctr. for Judaic Studies U. Hartford, 1995, Humanitarian award, B'nai B'rith, 1996, Disting. Pub. Svc. award, U.S. Dept. of State Sec.'s Open Forum, 1997, Tree of Life award, Jewish Nat. Fund, 1999, High Twelve Internat. Founders award, 2000, Key of Life award, Egypt's Internat. Econ. Forum, 2001, medal of merit, U.S. Dept. Treasury, 2001, Father Yr. award, Am. Diabetes Assn., 2002, Humanitarian award, The Albert B. Sabin Vaccine Inst., 2003, Madison Freedom award, 2004, Humanitarian Award, Sabin Vaccine Inst., 2006; Winston Churchill fellow, Eng., 1969, Hon. Wolcott fellow, 1999, Assoc. fellow, Morse Coll. Yale U. Fellow: Am. Acad. Arts and Scis.; mem.: Bus.-Higher Edn. Forum, Ind. Retail Cattleman's Assn. (adv. coun.), Sr. Soc. Sachems, Coun. Fgn. Rels., Newcomen Soc. US (life; former trustee), Am. Coun. Learned Socs. (assoc.), Internat. Assn. Univ. Pres. (N.Am. coun.), N.Y. Acad. Scis., Am. Assn. Univ. Adminstrs. (pres. 1998—2000, Disting. Svc. award 1990), D.C. C. of C. (named Bus. Leader of Yr. 2005), Am. Coun. for the UN U. (vice chair), Hannibal Club (annual award 2004), Nat. Press Club, Cosmos Club, Harvard Club, Tumble Brook Country Club, Univ. Club, George Washington U. Club, Masons (33d degree, Grand Cross pin 2004), Phi Beta Kappa. Office: George Washington U Office of Pres 2121 Eye St N W Rm 802 Washington DC 20052-0001 Office Phone: 202-994-6500. Business E-mail: gwupotu@gwu.edu.

**TRACHUK, ARINA GEORGE,** artist, educator; arrived in U.S., 1986; d. George Alexander and Valentina Alexandra Trachuk. M in Painting, State Acad. Inst. Fine Arts, Moscow, 1982. Instr. painting and drawing Sch. Art, Moscow, 1974—86; restorer of pictorial ensemble of walls and canvas paintings, icons St. Seraphin of Sorin Ch., Nanuet, NY, 1989—95, Sotheby, N.Y.C., N. Roerich Mus., N.Y.C., 1993—95; artist chs. N.Y.C., 1995—. Address: 14945 Ash Ave Flushing NY 11355-1029

**TRACKMAN, PHILIP CHARLES,** biochemist, researcher; b. Montclair, N.J., July 15, 1953; s. John C. and Irene (Boveri) T.; m. Susan Kirkpatrick Troxler, Oct. 24, 1979 (div. 2004); children: Louisa, Eric. BA in chem., Coll. of Wooster, 1975; PhD, Boston Univ., 1980; post doctoral rsch., Brandeis Univ., 1980-83. Staff scientist Novo Labs., Wilton, Conn., 1983-85, team leader, 1985-86; rsch. assist. prof. Boston U., 1987—92; asst. prof. Boston U. Goldman Sch. Dental Medicine, Boston, 1992—2000, assoc. prof., 2000—04, prof., 2004—. Contbr. articles to profl. jours. Recipient First award Nat. Inst. Health, 1994, fellowship Am. Cancer Soc., 1981. Mem. Am. Chem. Soc. (assoc.), Sigma Xi. Protestant. Achievements include first to demonstrate that non-peptidyl amines are substrates for lysyl oxidase and used this to develop a new assay. First to clone lysyl oxidase cDNA; first to study lysyl oxidase regulation by growth factors in osteoblastic cells; and in gingival fibroblasts; first to identify intermediates in a methionine salvage pathway; research in regulation of extracellular matrix biosynthesis in mineralized and non-mineralized tissues in health and disease; discovered mechanism of tumor suppressor function of lysyl oxidase; patentee in field. Office: Boston U Goldman Sch Dental Medicine 700 Albany St # 201 Boston MA 02118-2518 Office Phone: 617-638-4076.

**TRACT, LARRY SCOTT,** construction management consultant; b. Chgo., Apr. 16, 1957; s. Leslie Howard and Barbara Mae Tract; m. Tamra Tract, July 11, 1986; 1 child, Samantha Kathleen. BS, Santa Clara U., Calif., 1979; JD, Thomas Jefferson Law Sch., 1982. Bar: Calif.; cert. tchr. Calif. Law clk., paralegal Escho & Scott, LLP, Esq., Redwood City, Calif., 1984—85; v.p. CCMS, Sacramento, 1986—89, Animal Mech., Inc., Gilroy, Calif., 1989—95, Conservation Documentation Svcs., Santa Clara, Calif., 1986—95; contract adminstr., cons. Lawson Mech., Inc., Sacramento, 1996—99; pres., CEO Larry S. Tract Assocs., Constrn. Mgmt. Svcs., Sacramento, 1999—. Condr. seminars in field; lectr. in field; dispute resolu-tion cons. Bd. dirs. Greater Grandparent Need, 1999 2002, Agewell, 2000; adv. bd. YWCA, 1999—2002, Rep. Congl. Com., 2004—. Named Bus. Mem. of the Yr., RNC Pres.'s Adv. Coun., 2005; recipient Vol. of Yr. award, Greater Grandparent Need, Sacramento Vol. of the Yr., Agewell, 2000, Ronald Reagan Spirit award, Rep. Nat. Com., 2005. Avocations: running, football, sports. Home and Office: Larry S Tract & Associates 8655 Hillmon Ct Sacramento CA 95828

**TRACT, MARC MITCHELL,** lawyer; b. N.Y.C., Sept. 20, 1959; s. Harold Michael and Natalie Ann (Meyerowitz) T.; m. Sharon Beth Widrow; children: Melissa Hope, Harrison Michael, Sarah Michelle. BA in Biology, Ithaca Coll., 1981; JD, Pepperdine U., 1984. Bar: NY 1985, NJ 1985, DC 1986. Assoc. Kroll & Tract, N.Y.C., 1985—90, ptnr., 1990—94, Rosenman & Colin LLP, N.Y.C., 1994—2002, Katten Muchin Rosenman, LLP, N.Y.C., 2002—. Bd. dirs. Rampart Ins. Co., Navigators Group Inc., NYC, MAPFRE Reins. Corp., Florham Park, NJ, AXA Art Ins. Corp., NYC, Maya Assurance Corp., NYC. Bd. dirs. Italian Acad. Found. Decorated Order of Merit of Savoy. Mem. ABA, Assn. Bar City of NY, NY State Bar Assn., NJ State Bar Assn., NY County Lawyers Assn., Am. Coun. Germany, Old Westbury Golf and Country Club, Met. Club, Econ. Club NY. Republican. Office: Katten Muchin Rosenman llp Rm 1106 575 Madison Ave Fl 11 New York NY 10022-2511

**TRACY, ALLEN WAYNE,** management consultant; b. Windsor, Vt., July 25, 1943; s. J. Wayne and Helen (Bernard) T.; m. Karla Noelte, Dec. 14, 1969; children: Tania, Tara. BA, U. Vt., 1965; MBA cum laude, Boston U., 1974. Retail salesman Exxon Corp., Boston, 1965-72; mgr. mfg. Leonard Silver Mfg. Co., Inc., Boston, 1974-78, v.p. ops., 1979-81; pres. OESM Corp., N.Y.C., 1978-81; pres., bd. dirs. Gold Lance Inc., Houston, 1981-91; v.p. ops. Town & Country Corp., 1989-92; sr. v.p. L.G. Balfour Co., 1990-92; asst. to pres. Syratech Corp., Boston, 1993; dir. ops. Goldman-Kolber Co., Inc., Norwood, Mass., 1994; exec. v.p., COO, George H. Fuller & Son Co., Inc., Pawtucket, R.I., 1994-97; COO, BioMatrix Techs., Inc., Lincoln, R.I., 1997-98; mgmt. cons. IPA, Buffalo Grove, Ill., 1998—. Bd. dirs. Verilyte Gold, Inc., L.G. Balfour Co., Inc. Mem. Ashland Bd. Selectmen, 1977-78; chmn. Ashland Study Town Govt. Com., 1976-77; vice chmn. ch. coun. Federated Ch. Ashland, 1979-80, chmn., 1981; bd. dirs. Nottingham Forest Civic Assn., 1886. With U.S. Army, 1965-68. Mem. Nottingham Forest Civic Assn. (bd. dirs. Houston 1986), Beta Gamma Sigma. Home: 118 Lakeview Dr Nokomis FL 34275 Office: IPA 1250 Barclay Blvd Buffalo Grove IL 60089-4500

**TRACY, ANN BLAISDELL,** retired language educator; b. Bangor, Maine, Jan. 2, 1941; d. William Adelbert and Brenna (Blaisdell) T. BA, Colby Coll., 1962; MA, Brown U., 1964; PhD, U. Toronto, 1974. Copywriter J.C. Penney CO, N.Y., 1963-64; Latin tchr. Northampton Sch. Girls, Mass., 1964-65; English tchr. Cushing Acad., Ashburnham, Mass., 1965-67, SUNY, Platts-burgh, 1970—2001; ret. Author: The Gothic Novel 1790-1830, 1981, Higher Ground, 1988, Winter Hunger, 1990, What Do Cowboys Like?, 1995. Episcopalian. Home: 12 Addoms St Plattsburg NY 12901-1420 Office: SUNY Plattsburgh 101 Broad St # CVH102 Plattsburgh NY 12901-2637

**TRACY, CHRISTINA L.,** secondary school educator; b. Marshall, Ill., June 12, 1942; d. Lawrence and Kathryn (Seeler) Gekeler; m. Darrell M. Tracy, Nov. 28, 1964; children: Lawrence, Melissa, Melanie, Megan, Mynda. BS in Edn., Ea. Ill. U., 1964; postgrad., Ill. State U. Cert. secondary chemistry, math., physics, computer edn. tchr., Ill. Chemistry, physics, computer, biology, environ. sci. and math. tchr. Arcola (Ill.) High Sch., 1964-65, Rossville (Ill.)-Alvin High Sch., 1966—2004. State student advisor Ill. Jr. Acad. Sci., 1985-2000. Leader 4-H Club, Rossville, 1966-91; pres. Rossville Jr. Women's Club, 1971; pres., trustee Vermilion County Conservation Dist., Danville, Ill., 1980-89. Recipient Rsch. Sci. Tchr. award Sigma Xi, 1991, Golden Apple award, 1996. Mem. Ill. Beta Clubs (state pres. 1997-99). Office: Rossville-Alvin High Sch 350 N Chicago St Rossville IL 60963-9700

**TRACY, CRAIG ARNOLD,** mathematics educator; b. London, Sept. 9, 1945; s. Robert Craig Tracy and Eileen (Arnold) Isenberg; m. Maureen E. Maloney; children: Ingrid A., Elizabeth M. BS in Physics, U. Mo., 1967; PhD in Physics, SUNY, Stony Brook, 1973. Research assoc. Inst. Fundamental Studies U. Rochester, NY, 1973-75; research assoc. Inst. Theoretical Physics SUNY, Stony Brook, NY, 1975-78; asst. prof. Dept. Math. Dartmouth Coll., 1978—83, assoc. prof., 1983—84; prof. Dept. Math. U. Calif., Davis, 1984—, chmn. Dept. Math., 1994—98, acting dir. Inst. Theoretical Dynamics, 1989, 1992, 2001—02. Vis. rsch. scientist Brookhaven Nat. Lab., 1985; rsch. fellow Inst. Scientific Exch., Torino, Italy, 1986; fall rsch. fellow Rsch. Sch. Physical Sciences Australian Nat. U., 1986; rsch. prof. RIMS Kyoto U., 1991; mem. editl. bd. Mathematical Physics, Analysis and Geometry, Progress in Mathematical Physics, The Annals of Probability, 2006; bd. trustees Mathematical Sciences Rsch. Inst., 1998—2002. Named Disting. Prof., U. Calif. Davis, 2003; Woodrow Wilson fellowship, 1967—68, Japan Soc. for Promotion Sci. fellowship, 1991. Fellow: Am. Acad. Arts and Sciences; mem.: Am. Math. Soc., Am. Physical Soc., Soc. Indsl. and Applied Math. (George Pólya prize 2002). Office: Univ of Calif Dept of Math One Shields Ave Davis CA 95616 Office Phone: 530-754-6769. Office Fax: 530-752-6635. E-mail: tracy@math.ucdavis.edu.*

**TRACY, JAMES DONALD,** historian, educator; b. St. Louis, Feb. 14, 1938; s. Leo W. and Marguerite M. (Meehan) T.; m. Nancy Ann McBride, Sept. 6, 1968 (div. 1993); children: Patrick, Samuel, Mary Ann; m. Suzanne K. Swan, May 2, 1997. BA, St. Louis U., 1959; MA, Johns Hopkins U., 1960, Notre Dame U., 1961; PhD, Princeton U., 1967. Instr. U. Mich., 1964-66; instr. to prof. history U. Minn., Mpls., 1966—, dept. chmn., 1988-91, Union Pacific prof. early modern history, 2001—04. Vis. prof. U. Leiden, Netherlands, 1987, U. Paris IV, 2001, U. Amsterdam, 2004. Author: Erasmus: The Growth of a Mind, 1972, The Politics of Erasmus: A Pacifist Intellectual and His Political Milieu, 1979, True Ocean Found.: Paludanus's Letters on Dutch Voyages to the Kara Sea, 1980, A Financial Revolution in the Habsburg Netherlands: Renten and Renteniers in the County of Holland, 1515-1565, 1985, Holland Under Habsburg Rule: The Formation of a Body Politic, 1506-1566, 1990, Erasmus of the Low Countries, 1996, Europe's Reformations, 1450-1650, 1999, 2d edit., 2006, Emperor Charles V, Impresario of War, 2002, The Low Countries in the Sixteenth Century: Erasmus, Religion and Politics, Trade and Finance, 2005; editor: Luther and the Modern State in Germany, 1986, The Rise of Merchant Empires: Long Distance Trade in the Early Modern Era, 1350-1750, 1990, The Political Economy of Merchant Empires: Long Distance Trade and State Power in the Early Modern World, 1991; editor: (with T.A. Brady and H.A. Oberman) Handbook of European History in the Late Middle Ages, Renaissance and Reformation, Vol. 1, 1994, Vol. 2, 1995, City Walls: The Urban Enceinte in Global Perspective, 2000; editor: (with T.A. Brady, K.G. Brady and S. Karant-Nunn) The Work of Heiko A. Oberman, 2003; editor: (with Marguerite Ragnow) Religion and the Early Modern State: Views from China, Russia and the West, 2004; co-editor: Jour. Early Modern History, 1997—2000; editor, 2000—; mem. editl. bd. Sixteenth Century Jour., 1979—2000. Guggenheim fellow, 1972-73; NEH summer grantee, 1977, 85; Fulbright rsch. grantee, Belgium, 1979, Netherlands, 1980; resident fellow Netherlands Inst. for Advanced Studies, 1993-94. Mem. Am. Cath. Hist. Soc. (pres. 1999-00), Soc. Reformation Rsch. (pres. 1995-97), 16th Century Studies Conf. (pres. 1985-86). Republican. Roman Catholic. Home: 757 Osceola Ave # 2 Saint Paul MN 55105-3327 Office: U Minn History 614 Social Sci Bldg Minneapolis MN 55455 Office Phone: 612-624-0808. Business E-Mail: tracy001@umn.edu.

**TRACY, JAMES JARED, JR.,** retired legal association administrator; b. Cleve., Jan. 17, 1929; s. James Jared and Florence (Comey) T.; m. Elizabeth Jane Bourne, June 30, 1953 (div. 1988); children: Jane Tracy Ahrens, Elizabeth Tracy Jenkins, James Jared IV, Margaret Tracy Rosen; m. Judith Anne Cooper, Feb. 18, 1989. AB, Harvard U., 1950, MBA, 1953. CPA Ohio. Acct., sr. mgr. Price Waterhouse & Co., Cleve., 1953-65; treas., CFO Cleve. Corp., Cleve., 1965-69; from asst. treas. to treas. Republic Steel Corp., Cleve., 1969—75; v.p., treas. Johns-Manville Corp., Denver, 1976-81; v.p., treas., CFO Internat. Techs. Corp., LA, 1981—82; exec. dir. Hufstedler, Miller, Carlson & Beardsley, LA, 1983—84, Shank, Irwin & Conant, Dallas, 1984-85, Pachter, Gold & Schaffer, LA, 1985—86; v.p., sr. cons. Right Assocs., LA, 1987—91; dir. adminstrn. Larson & Burnham, Oakland, Calif., 1991-95; adminstrv. dir. Law Offices of Thomas E. Miller, Newport Beach, Calif., 1996-97; human resources adminstr. Baker & McKenzie, San Francisco, 1997-98; dir. adminstrn. Wartnick, Chaber, Harowitz & Tigerman, San Francisco, 1998-2000, Kasdan, Simonds & Epstein, Irvine, Calif., 2000—03; adj. prof. entrepreneurial bus. planning Santa Ana Coll., 2004. Trustee, v.p. Miss Hall's Sch., Pittsfield, Mass., 1970—78; adv. bd. Arkwright-Boston Ins. Co., 1976—81. Trustee, v.p. Cleve. Soc. for Blind, 1965-76; trustee Western Res. Hist. Soc., Cleve., 1972-76; treas. St. Peters by the Sea Presbyn. Ch., Palos Verdes, Calif., 1981-91; trustee, treas. Literacy Coun. Newport Beach (Calif.) Pub. Libr., 2002—; pres. Harvard Club, Cleve., 1958-59, Harvard Bus. Sch. Club, Cleve., 1959-60, Rocky Mountain Harvard Club, Denver, 1978-79; bd. dirs. Met. YMCA, Cleve., 1972-76, Fedn. for Cmty. Planning, Cleve., 1971-76, v.p. Recipient Alumni award, Harvard U., Denver, 1981. Mem. AICPA, Ohio Soc. CPAs, Assn. Legal Adminstrs., Rotary (pres. Piedmont Montclair chpt. 1995-96), Harvard Radcliffe Club So. Calif., Harvard Bus. Sch. Assn. Orange County (treas. 2004—). Avocations: sailing, golf, gardening. Home: 2204 Fortuna Newport Beach CA 92660 E-mail: jimjudytracy@adelphia.net.

**TRACY, JIM (JAMES EDWARD TRACY),** professional baseball manager; b. Hamilton, OH, Dec. 31, 1955; m. Debra Tracy; children: Brian, Chad, Mark. Attended, Marietta Coll. Bench coach, coord. all on-field activities L.A. Dodgers; mgr. Midwest League Single-A Peoria, Cubs' affiliate, 1987; minor league mgr. Chgo. Cubs, Cin. Reds, Expos, 1987—91, 1993—94; with Reds, 1989—91, minor league field coord., 1992; mgr. Triple-A Ottawa, Montreal's affiliate, 1994; bench coach Felipe Alou, Montreal Expo mgr.; interim mgr. L.A. Dodgers, 2000, mgr., 2000—05, Pitts. Pirates, 2005—. Named The Sporting News' Mgr. of Yr., 1993, Ea. League's Mgr. of Yr., 1993, NCAA Divsn. III All-Am. selection, Marietta Coll., Ohio. Mem.: Marietta Coll. Sports Hall of Fame. Office: Pitts Pirates PNC Pk 115 Federal St Pittsburgh PA 15212*

**TRACY, LYONEL B.,** school system administrator; m. Sharlene Tracy. BA, MA, U. Maine; EdD in Ednl. Adminstrn. and Policy Studies, George Washington U., 1997. Supt. of schs., Maine, Vt., Portsmouth Sch. Bd., NH, 2000; commr. edn. State of NH, 2005—. Adj. faculty mem. U. Sys. of NH, Plymouth State U.; mem. Regional Adv. Com. for N.E. Region, US Dept. of Edn., 2004. Mem.: New England Assn. of Sch. Supts. (pres. 2002—), NH PTA (past chair edn. com.). Office: NH Dept Edn 101 Pleasant St Concord NH 03301-3860 Office Phone: 603-271-3494. Office Fax: 603-271-1953. E-mail: ltracy@ed.state.nh.us.

**TRACY, MICHAEL CAMERON,** choreographer, educator; b. Florence, Italy, Feb. 1, 1952; s. Stanley B. and Elizabeth Lee (McIntosh) T. BA Magna cum laude, Dartmouth Coll., 1973. Adj. faculty Yale U., New Haven, Conn., 1992—. Artistic dir. Pilobolus Dance Theatre, Washington, Conn., 1974—; choreographer Die Zauberflöte, European prodn. with John Eliot Gardiner's Monteverdi Choir and English Baroque Soloists, 1995, Curiouser and Curiouser Nat. Theatre of Deaf, 1996, Sweet Dreams, 2000, Symbiosis, 2001, The Brass Ring (commissioned by Olympic Arts Festival), 2002, My Brother's Keeper, 2003, Warm Heart, 2004, Aquatica, 2005; co-choreographer: Ciona, 1974, Monkshood's Farewell, 1975, Untitled, 1976, Day Two, 1980, Pyramid of the Moon, 1996, Aeros, 1996, Elysian Fields, 1997, Apoplexy, 1998, The Hand That Mocked, The Heart That Fed, 1998, A Selection, 1999. Recipient Berlin Critics award, 1975, New Eng. Theatre Conf. prize, 1977, Brandeis award, 1978, Excellence in Arts award Conn. Commn. on the Arts, 1981, Emmy award 1997, Scripps award, 2002; sr. fellow Dartmouth Coll., 1973. Mem. Dartmouth Players. Office: PO Box 388 Washington Depot CT 06794-0388 Personal E-mail: mtracy@pilobolus.com. Business E-Mail: michael.tracy@yale.edu.

**TRACY, PATRICK F.,** food products executive; Former CEO Dot Foods, Mt. Sterling, Ill., chmn. bd. dir., 2002—. Office: Dot Foods Inc PO Box 192 1 Dot Way Mount Sterling IL 62353*

**TRACY, SAUNDRA J.,** academic administrator; m. Doug Tracy; children: Steve, Elaine. BA in Spanish, Carroll Coll., Waukesha, Wis., 1968; M Ed in Fgn. Lang. Instrn., U. Pitts., 1971; PhD in Edn. Adminstrn., Purdue U., West Lafayette, Ind., 1981. Dir. Greater Cleve. Adminstr. Assessment Ctr., 1968—88; asst. to assoc. prof. edn. Cleve. State U., 1981—88; exec. dir. sch. study coun. Lehigh U., 1989—91, dir. ednl. programs Lee Iacocca Inst., 1990—92, assoc. prof. to prof. edn., 1988—94; dean of coll. of edn. Butler U., 1994—98; v.p. acad. affairs Mt. Union Coll., 1998—2001; pres. Alma Coll., 2001—. Fellow, Am. Coun. of Edn., 1992—93. Office: Alma Coll 614 West Superior St Alma MI 48801-1599 Office Phone: 989-463-7146.

**TRACY, SUSANNE MARY,** nursing researcher, educator; b. Rochester, N.Y., June 9, 1945; d. Edward and Ann (Bihun) Koszalka; m. Daniel A. Tracy, III, June 17, 1967; children: Lisa, Michael, Scott, Erin. BSN, Niagara Univ., 1967; MN, U. S.C., 1975; MA, Rivier Coll., 1992; PhD, U. R.I., 2005. RN N.H., Mass. Instr. nursing Columbus (Ga.) State U., 1975-77; asst. prof. Jefferson C.C., Watertown, NY, 1977-81; asst. head nurse rehab. Penrose Hosp., Colorado Springs, Colo., 1981-82; edn. cons. Penrose & St. Mary Corwin Hosp., Colorado Springs, Pueblo, Colo., 1982-85; asst. prof. Rivier Coll., Nashua, NH, 1985-91, assoc. prof., 1991—2004, Regis Coll., Weston, Mass., 2004—05; asst. prof. U. NH, 2005—. Contbr. articles to profl. jours. Decorated Nat. Svc. medal USN; named Outstanding Young Women Am., Nat. Awards Program, 1977. Mem.: ANA, Nat. League Nursing, Am. Assn. Higher Edn., New Eng. Edn. Assessment Network (bd. dirs. 1995—2006), Fa. Nursing Rsch. Soc., Sigma Theta Tau. Avocations: research, travel, complimentary medicine. Office Phone: 603-862-0554. Personal E-mail: olsldr@aol.com.

**TRACY, THOMAS MILES,** international health organization official; b. Great Barrington, Mass., July 8, 1936; s. Thomas Paul and Marion (Miles) T.; m. June Betts, June 17, 1967; children: Miles Christopher, Keir Thomas John. BA, Colgate U., 1958; MA, Stanford U., 1959; MBA, Columbia U., 1973. Fgn. service officer Dept. State, Washington, 1960-84; counselor Am. Embassy, Moscow, 1975-78, Bonn, Germany, 1978-79; asst. sec. Dept. State, Washington, 1979-83; chief adminstrn. Pan Am./WHO, Washington, 1983-98; mgmt. cons. Dept. State, 2003—. V.p. Pan-Am. Health and Edn. Found., treas. Trustee, vice chmn. Chelsea Sch., 1988-2004. With U.S. Army, 1959-60. Recipient Superior Honor award Dept. State, 1978 Mem.: Am. Fgn. Svc. Protective Found. (sec., treas.), Am. Fgn. Svc. Protective Assn. (dir. 1988—, v.p. 1997—2005, pres. 2005—), Am. Fgn. Svc. Assn. (dir. 1970—72). Home: 5902 Devonshire Dr Bethesda MD 20816-3416

**TRADER, JOSEPH EDGAR,** orthopedic surgeon; b. Milw., Nov. 2, 1946; s. Edgar Joseph and Dorothy Elizabeth (Senzig) T.; m. Janet Louise Burzycki, Sept. 23, 1972 (div. Nov. 1987); children: James, Jonathan, Ann Elizabeth; m. Rhonda Sue Schultz, May 26, 1990. Student, Marquette U., 1964-67; MD, Med. Coll. Wis., 1971. Diplomate Am. Bd. Orthop. Surgery. Physician emergency rm. Columbia, St. Joseph's Hosps., Milw., 1972—76; orthop. surgeon, pres. Orthop. Assn., Manitowoc, Wis., 1979—. Mem. exec. com. Holy Family Meml. Med. Ctr., Manitowoc, 1985-96, chief-of-staff, 1994-96, ethics com., 1995—, chair instnl. rev. com. Former pres., bd. dirs. Holy Innocents Mens Choir; county del. State Med. Soc. Charitable Sci. and Edn. Found.; mem. cobia com. Wisc. Maritime Mus. Fellow ACS, Am. Acad. Orthopaedic Surgeons; mem. AMA, Wis. State Med. Soc., Wis. Orthopaedic Soc., Midwest Orthopaedic Soc., Milw. Orthopaedic Soc., Am. Coll. Sports Medicine, Orthopaedic Assn. Manitowoc (pres.), Crown and Anchor, Wis. Maritime Mus. (cobia com. mem.) Manitowoc Yacht Club,Phi Delta Epsilon, Psi Chi Roman Catholic. Avocations: singing, tennis, skiing, sailing, golf. Home: 1021 Memorial Dr Manitowoc WI 54220-2242 Office: Orthopaedic Assocs 501 N 10th St Manitowoc WI 54220-4039 Office Phone: 920-682-6376. Personal E-mail: jetrader@lakefield.net.

**TRAEGER, CHARLES HENRY, III,** lawyer; b. Bethlehem, Pa., Sept. 30, 1942; s. Charles Henry Jr. and Dorothy Shelly (Weinberger) T.; m. Carole Lynn DeGraff, Feb. 20, 1972; children: Chad, Erin, Seth, Anna, Claire, Ben. AB, Coll. William and Mary, 1964; JD, Stanford U., 1967. Bar: Calif. 1967, N.Y. 1972, Mass. 1976, Ariz. 1980. Assoc. Milbank, Tweed, Hadley & McCloy, N.Y.C., 1967, 71-76; v.p., gen. counsel Shawmut Corp., Boston, 1976-80, Shawmut Bank of Boston, N.A., 1976-80; assoc. Snell & Wilmer, Phoenix, 1980-83, ptnr., 1983-91; v.p., gen. counsel Bank One Ariz. N.A., Phoenix, 1991-95; assoc. gen. counsel Ariz. State U., Tempe, 1996—. Contbr. Stanford Law Rev. Lt. comdr. USNR, 1968-71. Mem. Phi Beta Kappa. Republican. Mem. Lds Ch. Office Phone: 480-965-1418. E-mail: hanktr@asu.edu.

**TRAFFORD, ABIGAIL,** columnist, editor, writer; b. NYC, July 14, 1940; d. William Bradford and Abigail (Sard) T.; children: Abigail Brett Miller, Victoria Brett. BA cum laude, Bryn Mawr Coll., 1962. Researcher Nat. Geog. Soc., Washington, 1964-67; tchr. Hermansberg Mission, Northern Ter., Australia, 1967-68; spl. corr. Time mag., The Washington Post, Houston, 1969-74; writer, asst. mng. editor U.S. News & World Report, Washington, 1975-86; health editor The Washington Post, 1986-00, columnist, 2000—. Author: Crazy Time: Surviving Divorce and Building a New Life, 1982, revised edit., 1992, My Time: Making the Most of the Rest of Your Life, 2004. Journalism fellow Harvard Sch. Pub. Health, 1980, 2000; sr. fellow Civic Ventures. Mem. Washington Press Club Found. (bd. mem. 1989—, pres. 1993-95). Home: 2600 Upton St NW Washington DC 20008-3826 Office Phone: 202-966-3516. Business E-Mail: trafforda@washpost.com.

**TRAFIDLO, JAMES FRANCIS,** marketing communications executive, commercial photographer; b. Boston, Apr. 16, 1953; s. Edward Joseph and Marian Frances (Hennigar) T.; m. Elizabeth Boyd, May 22, 1982 (div. Mar. 1995); m. Sarah Chisholm Lincoln, Oct. 14, 1995; 1 child: Benjamin Lincoln. BA in Psychology, Boston Coll., 1977. Freelance photographer, Boston, 1976—; office mgr., photographers asst. J. Rawle Communications, Bedford, Mass., 1978-80; sr. photographer Liberty Mut. Ins., Boston, 1980-86; owner Trafidlo Communications, Boston, 1986-93; new bus. developer, project mgr. Boston Photo Imaging, Boston, 1994-2000; dir. new bus. devel., project mgr. Multimedia Comm., Natick, 2000—02; new bus. devel., project mgr. Video Transfer, Boston, 2002—, High Speed Video, Southborough, 2002—. Recipient Award of Achievement Soc. for Tech. Communication, 1984, 85. Mem. Am. Soc. Media Photographers, Assn. Multi-Image, Media Comm. Assn. Internat., Boston Advt. Golf Assn., Weston Golf Club, Longwood Covered Cts., Wellesley Tennis Assn., Nahick Raquet Club, The Wellesley Ctr. Avocations: tennis, golf, alpine skiing. Home: 25 Bear Hill Rd Sherborn MA 01770-1135 Office: Video Transfer 580 Harrison Ave Boston MA 02118 also: High Speed Video 150 Cerdaville Rd Southborough MA 01772 Office Phone: 617-247-0100. E-mail: trafcomm@comcast.net.

**TRAFTON, STEPHEN J.,** bank executive; b. Mt. Vernon, Wash., Sept. 17, 1946; m. Diane Trafton; children: John, Roland. BS in Zoology, Wash. State U., 1968. V.p., mgr. dept. money market Seattle-First Nat. Bank, 1968-79; v.p., mgr. bank consulting group Donaldson Lufkin Jennrette, N.Y.C., 1980; exec. v.p., treas. Gibraltar Savings Bank, L.A., 1980-84; banking cons., 1984-86; v.p., treas. Hibernia Bank, San Francisco, 1986-88; sr. v.p., treas. Goldome Bank, Buffalo, N.Y., 1988-90; sr. exec. v.p., CFO Glenfed Inc., 1990-91, vice chmn., CFO, 1991—, pres., 1992—; sr. exec. v.p., CFO Glendale Fed. Bank, 1990-91, vice chmn., CFO, 1991, pres., COO, 1991-92, chmn. bd., pres., CEO, 1992-99, COO, also bd. dirs.; exec. v.p. Golden State Bancorp, 1999—. Mem. Phi Eta Sigma.

**TRAGER, DAVID G.,** federal judge; b. Mt. Vernon, N.Y., Dec. 23, 1937; s. Sol and Clara (Friedman) T.; m. Roberta E. Weisbrod, May 2, 1972; children: Mara Emet, Josiah Samuel, Naomi Gabrielle. BA, Columbia Coll., 1959; LL.B., Harvard U., 1962. Bar: N.Y. Assoc. Berman & Frost, 1963-65, Butler,

Jablow & Geller, 1965-67; asst. corp. counsel Appeals Div. City of N.Y., 1967; law clk. Judge Kenneth B. Keating, N.Y. State Ct. Appeals, 1968-69; asst. U.S. atty. chief, appeals div., 1970-72; U.S. atty. Ea. Dist. N.Y., Bklyn., 1974-78; prof. Bklyn. Law Sch., 1972-94, dean, 1983-94; judge U.S. Dist. Ct. (ea. dist.) N.Y., Bklyn., 1994—; mem. adv. com. on criminal rules Jud. Conf. U.S., 2000—. Chmn. Mayor's Com. on Judiciary, 1982-89, N.Y. State Temp. Commn. on Investigation, 1983-90. Mem. N.Y.C. Charter Rev. Commn., 1986-89. With USAR, 1962-65, USNR, 1965-69. Mem.: Am. Law Inst., Fed. Bar Coun. (pres. 1986—88). Office: US Courthouse 225 Cadman Plz E Brooklyn NY 11201-1818

**TRAGER, MICHAEL DAVID,** lawyer; b. NYC, Feb. 15, 1959; s. Philip and Ina (Shulkin) T.; m. Mariella Gonzalez, Sept. 12, 1987; children: Nicholas, Alexander. BA, Wesleyan U., Middletown, Conn., 1981; JD, Boston U., 1985. Bar: Mass. 1985, Conn. 1986, Fla. 1988, DC 1989. Staff atty. enforcement divsn. SEC, Washington, 1985-87; assoc. Morgan, Lewis & Bockius, Miami, Fla., 1987-88; participating assoc. Fulbright & Jaworski, Washington, 1989-92, of counsel, 1993-94, ptnr., 1995—2004, co-head securities litig. and enforcement, firm chair corp. dept.; ptnr. Arnold & Porter LLP, Washington, 2005—, chmn. securities enforcement practice. Bd. dirs. Jewish Nat. Fund-Mid-Atlantic Region, Wash., 1993-97; officer Horace Mann PTA, Washington, 1997-99. Mem. ABA (bus. law sect. fed. regulation securities com. and civil litig. and SEC enforcement matters subcom., litig. sect. securities litig. com. and SEC enforcement subcom., class action and derivative litig. com. and securities litig. subcom., task force on SEC's insider trading and selective disclosure rules), Assn. SEC Alumni, Securities Industry Assn. (legal and compliance divsn.), DC Bar (corp., fin. and securities law sect. corp. counsel and planning group for broker-dealer programs 1992-94, broker-dealer regulation com., task force on SEC's proposed insider trading and selective disclosure rules), Mass. Bar, Fla. Bar, Conn. Bar, Bond Market Assn. (litig. adv. com.), Wesleyan Univ. Club of Washington (chair 2001-04), Wesleyan U. Alumni Assn. (exec. com. 2001-04), Post-classical Ensemble (adv. bd. 2003—), Children's Law Ctr. (chair Law Firm Sponsors 2004), The Wash. Ballet (bd. dirs. 2004—). Office: Arnold & Porter LLP 555 12th St NW 1153 Washington DC 20004 Office Phone: 202-942-6976. Office Fax: 202-942-5999. Business E-Mail: michael.trager@aporter.com.

**TRAGON, JULIE M.,** music educator; b. Tampa, Fla., Aug. 14, 1979; d. John Michael Tragon, III and Kathleen Elizabeth Tragon. BA in Music and Secondary Edn., U. Tampa, 2003. Cert. in youth ministry studies Ctr. Pastoral Ministry, 2000. Asst. dir. music ministry and lifeteen, dir. confirmation Light of Christ Cath. Ch., Clearwater, Fla., 2000—03; dir. music ministry St. Paschal Baylon Cath. Ch., Highland Heights, Ohio, 2004—. Mem. / vice-president of sponsorship Sertoma Internat., Tampa, Fla., 1997—2003. Scholar, Nat. Lifeteen, 2001—02. Mem.: Nat. Pastoral Musicians, Sertoma Internat. (v.p. sponsorship 1997—2003). Republican. Roman Catholic. Avocations: travel, music, volleyball. Office Phone: 440-442-3410. Personal E-mail: jltragon@sbcglobal.net. Business E-Mail: spbmusiclady@sbcglobal.net.

**TRAGOS, GEORGE EURIPEDES,** lawyer; b. Chgo., July 15, 1949; s. Euripedes G. and Eugene G. (Gatziolis) T.; m. Donna Marie Thalassites, Nov. 18, 1978; children: Louise, Gina, Peter. BA, Fla. State U., 1971, JD, 1974. Bar: Fla., U.S. Dist. Ct. (mid., so. dists.) Fla., U.S. Dist. Ct. (we. dist.) Tenn., U.S. Ct. Appeals (5th, 11th cirs.). Legis. aide Fla. Ho. of Reps., 1972-73; tax analyst tax and fin. com., 1973-74; chief, felony asst. states atty. State of Fla., Clearwater, 1974-78; partner firm Case, Kimpton, Tragos & Burke, P.A., Clearwater Beach, 1978-83; chief criminal dvr. U.S. Atty.'s Office for Middle Dist. Fla., Tampa, 1983-85; lead trial asst. Pres. Organized Crime Drug Enforcement Task Force, Tampa, 1985; sole practice Clearwater, 1985—. Contbr. articles to profl. jours. and frequent lectr. Mem. Clearwater Bar (pres. 1994), Fla. Bar Assn. (chmn. fed. practice com. 1986, chmn. criminal law sect. 2000, chmn. bar evidence com. 1990), Fla. Assn. Criminal Def. Lawyers (pres. 1991), Fla. State U. Alumni Assn. Law Sch. (bd. dirs.), Tampa Bay Fed. Bar Assn. (v.p. 1989), Clearwater Beach Jaycees (pres. 1979), Fla. U. Gold Key Club (pres. 1972), Ahepa. Mem. Greek Orthodox Ch. Avocations: boating, tennis. Office: 600 Cleveland St Ste 700 Clearwater FL 33755-4158 E-mail: greek.law@verizon.net.

**TRAIL, MARGARET ANN,** retired employee benefits company executive, rancher; b. Bryan, Tex., July 17, 1941; d. Louis Milton and Margaret (Stromberg) Thompson; m. Robert A. Rosemier, Aug. 25, 1962 (div. Feb. 1973); 1 child: Gretchen Elisabeth Jolly; m. Newt Shands Trail, Dec. 4, 1989. BSN, U. Iowa, 1963; MS, No. Ill. U., 1971. Instr. Cooley Dickinson Hosp., Northampton, Mass., 1964-65; dir. nursing De Kalb (Ill.) Pub. Hosp., Kishwaukee Cmty. Hosp., 1972—76, Terre Haute (Ind.) Regional Hosp., 1976—78; from mgr. clin. systems to dir. spl. projects Hosp. Corp. Am., Nashville, 1978-86; from dir. med. mgmt. to v.p. Equicor, Nashville, 1986-90; divsn. v.p. The Travelers Ins. Co., Hartford, Conn., 1990-93; asst. v.p. health svcs. quality mgmt. Aetna, Hartford, 1993—2003, ret., 2003. Mem. LWV (pres. DeKalb chpt. 1970-72) Avocations: gardening, beekeeping, genealogy.

**TRAILLE, JOY MYRA,** microbiologist, eldercare service provider; arrived in U.S., 1971; d. Randolph and Leanorah Williams; m. Winston Traille, June 6, 1981; children: Nichola Davis, Kevin. MS, L.I. U., 1981; PhD, Union Inst., Cin., 1991; MBA, Iona, New Rochelle, N.Y., 2002. Cert. Am. Soc. Clin. Pathologist, 1981. Med. technologist Gouverneur Hosp./NYU, N.Y.C., 1978—83; microbiology clin. scientist Kingsbrook Jewish Med. Ctr., Bklyn., 1983—87; microbiologist Mary Immaculate Hosp., Jamaica, NY, 1987—91; adminstrv. dir. Manhattan Eye Ear & Throat Hosp., N.Y.C., 1991—98; dir. Cryobank for Oncology & Reproduction, Middletown, NY, 1998—; owner/pres. Comfort Keepers, Cortlandt Manor, NY, 2003— Infectious disease bd. mem Manhattan Eye Ear & Throat Hosp., N.Y.C., 1991—98; adv. bd. mem. Cryobank for Oncology & Reproduction, Middletown, NY, 1998—. Author, pub.: magazine Caribbean Heritage, 1999—2003; author: (a handbook for caregivers) You Are Not Alone, 2003. Adv. bd. coun. eldercare United Way, Westchester, NY, 2004—05. Mem.: Soc. For Cert. Sr. Advisors, Am. Soc. Microbiology. Avocations: writing, reading, travel, drama/musicals, dance. Office: Comfort Keepers Ste 104B 2127 Crompond Rd Cortlandt Manor NY 10566 Office Phone: 914-734-2616. Business E-Mail: peekskill@comfortkeepers.com.

**TRAIN, HARRY DEPUE, II,** retired naval officer; b. Washington, Nov. 5, 1927; s. Harold Cecil and May (Philipps) T.; m. Catharine Peck Kinnear, July 8, 1950; children: Louise Lucas, Catharine Philipps, Elizabeth Langdon, Cecilia Spencer. BS, US Naval Acad., 1949. Commd. ensign US Navy, 1949, advanced through grades to adm., 1978; comdr. Cruiser-Destroyer Flotilla 8, 1971-72; dir. internat. security affairs East Asia and Pacific Region Office Asst. Sec. Def., 1972-73; dir. Systems Analysis Div., Office Chief Naval Ops., 1973-74; dir. joint staff Orgn. Joint Chiefs of Staff, 1974-76; comdr. U.S. 6th Fleet, 1976-78; comdr.-in-chief U.S. Atlantic Fleet and supreme allied comdr. Atlantic, 1978-82, US Atlantic Command; ret. U.S. Atlantic Fleet and supreme allied comdr. Atlantic, 1982. Mgr. Hampton Rds. Ops. Sci. Applications Internat. Corp., 2006—. Mem. Hart-Rodman Commn. Decorated D.S.M. with 3 gold stars, Def. Disting. Svc. medal, Legion of Merit with 3 gold stars, Meritorious Svc. medal, Joint Svcs. Commendation medal, Navy Commendation medal; comdr. Order Republic of Tunisia; Order Naval Merit Brazil; Pedro Campbell medal Uruguay; Order of Pres. of Republic Chile; decorated Portuguese Mil. Order Christ; Netherlands Order Orange-Nassau; German Order Merit; French Legion of Honor; Colombian Naval Order Admiral Padilla; Mex. Order Spl. Merit; sr. fellow Joint Advanced Warfighting Sch., Joint Forces Staff Coll. Mem. U.S. Naval Inst., Coun. on Fgn. Rels., Columbia Country Club, Town Point Club. Home: 401 College Pl Apt 10 Norfolk VA 23510-1130 E-mail: trainh@cs.com.

**TRAIN, JOHN,** investment advisor, federal official; b. N.Y.C., May 25, 1928; s. Arthur Cheney and Helen (Coster) T.; m. Maria Teresa Cini di Pianzano, 1961 (div. 1976); children: Helen, Nina, Lisa; m. Frances Cheston, July 23, 1977. BA magna cum laude, Harvard U., 1950, MA, 1951. Founder, mng. editor Paris Rev., 1952-54; staff Asst. Sec. Army, Washington, 1954-56;

assoc. de Vegh & Co., 1956-58; chmn. Train, Babcock Advisors (and predecessor firms), N.Y.C., 1958-94, chmn. emeritus, 1995—; co-chmn., then hon. dir. ICAP, S.A., Athens, 1964—; chmn. Montrose Fin. Group, N.Y.C., 1992—; pres. Chateau Malescasse, Lamarque-Margaux, Bordeaux, France, 1970-81; columnist Forbes mag., 1977-83, Harvard mag., 1983-95, Wall St. Jour., 1984—, Worth Mag., Boston, 1991-93, Town and Country mag., 1994-95, Fin. Times, London, 1994—2002, Strategic Rev., 1998—2002, Am. Spectator, 2002—. Bd. dirs. African Devel. Found., Washington, 1988-94; bd. dirs. Bulgarian-Am. Enterprise Fund, Washington, Genesis Funds, London, Internat. Rescue Com., N.Y.C.; chmn. Northcote Parkison Fund, 1988—; bd. govs. East-West Ctr., Hawaii, 1993-96. Author: Dance of the Money Bees, 1973, Remarkable Names, 1977, Even More Remarkable Names, 1979, Remarkable Occurrences, 1978, Remarkable Words, 1980, The Money Masters, 1980, Remarkable Relatives, 1971, Preserving Capital and Making it Grow, 1983, Famous Financial Fiascos, 1984, John Train's Most Remarkable Names, 1985, The Midas Touch, 1987, The New Money Masters, 1989, Valsalva's Maneuver, 1989, John Train's Most Remarkable Occurrences, 1990, Wit, 1991, Love, 1993, The Craft of Investing, 1994, Crazy Quilt, 1996, Oriental Rug Symbols, 1997, Investing and Managing Trusts under the New Prudent Investor Rule, 1999, Money Masters of Our Time, 2001, The Olive: Tree of Civilization, 2004; contbr. articles to profl. publs. Chmn. Italian Emergency Relief Com., 1976-77; pres. Afghanistan Relief Com., 1986-95; trustee Harvard Lampoon, Cambridge, Mass., 1974-90, World Monuments Fund, 1988-92; chmn. Free Elections Project, 1990, Brit. Mus. Nat. Hist. Internat. Trust, 1990—, Northcote Parkinson Fund, 1990—; trustee univ. coun. Am. U. Bulgaria, 1996—. With U.S. Army, 1954-56. Decorated commendatore Ordine del Merito della Repubblica, commendatore Ordine Della Solidarieta, medal Provincia di Udine (Italy); recipient Disting. Grotonian award, 1996, Queen's Birthday honors Order of St. John, 1997. Mem.: Fgn. Policy Assn. (trustee), Internat. Inst. Strategic Studies (London), Coun. on Fgn. Rels., Order Colonial Lords of Manors, Travellers Club (Paris), Beefsteak Club (London), Brook's Club (London), Union Club, Racquet & Tennis Club, Met. Club (Washington), Century Club. Office: 667 Madison Ave New York NY 10021-8029

TRAIN, RUSSELL ERROL, environmentalist; b. Jamestown, R.I., June 4, 1920; s. Charles R. and Errol C. (Brown) T.; m. Aileen Bowdoin, May 27, 1954; children: Nancy, Emily, Bowdoin, Errol. AB, Princeton U., 1941, LL.D. (hon.), 1970; JD, Columbia U., 1948, LL.D. (hon.), 1970, Bates Coll., 1970, Drexel U., 1970; D.E. (hon.), Worcester Poly. Inst., 1970, U. Md., 1975; Sc.D. (hon.), St. Mary's Coll., 1970, Clarkson Coll. Tech., 1973, Salem Coll., 1975, Southwestern U., 1976, Mich. State U., 1976; D.C.L. (hon.), U. of South, 1973; D public svc., Washington Coll., 1996. Bar: D.C. bar 1949. Atty. staff joint com. on internal revenue taxation U.S. Congress, 1948-53; chief counsel Ways and Means Com., U.S. Ho. of Reps., 1953-54, minority adviser, 1955-56; asst. to sec., head legal adv. staff Treasury Dept., 1956-57; judge U.S. Tax Ct., 1957-65; pres. Conservation Found., 1965-69; also trustee; undersec. Dept. Interior, 1969-70; chmn. Council on Environ. Quality, 1970-73; adminstr. EPA, Washington, 1973-77; sr. assoc. Conservation Found., 1977; pres., chief exec. officer World Wildlife Fund, Washington, 1978-85, chmn. bd., 1985-94, chmn. emeritus, 1994—; chmn. bd. Conservation Found., 1985-90; chmn. Nat. Commn. on the Environment, 1991-93; chmn. Nat. Coun. World Wildlife Fund, Washington, chmn. emeritus. Mem. Washington Nat. Monument Assn., Nat. Water Commn., 1968—69; head U.S. del. UN Conf. Human Environment, 1972; rep. Internat. Whaling Commn., 1972, other internat. confs.; mem. Pres.'s adv. com. on trade and trade negotiations, 1991—93. Author: The Bowdoin Family, 2000, The Train Family, 2000, A Memoir, 2000, Politics, Pollution, and Pandas, 2003. Trustee emeritus African Wildlife Found. Decorated Order of the Golden Ark (The Netherlands); recipient Albert Schweitzer medal, Animal Welfare Inst., 1972, Aldo Leopold medal, Wildlife Soc., 1975, Conservationist of Yr. award, Nat. Wildlife Fedn., 1974, 1986, John and Alice Tyler Ecology award, 1978, Freese award, ASCE, 1978, Pub. Welfare award, Nat. Acad. Scis., 1981, Elizabeth Haub prize in internat. environ. law, 1981, Frances K. Hutchinson medal, Garden Club of Am., 1984, Lindbergh award, 1985, Environ. Law Inst. award, 1986, Presdl. Medal of Freedom, 1991, Heinz Chmns. medal, 2001. Fellow: AAAS; mem.: Am. Acad. Arts and Scis., Atlantic Coun., Coun. Fgn. Rels. Office: World Wildlife Fund 1250 24th St NW Fl 6 Washington DC 20037-1193

TRAINA, ALBERT SALVATORE, publishing executive; b. Bklyn., Apr. 30, 1927; s. Salvatore and Guilia (LeBarbara) T.; m. Vail Devereux, June 27, 1957; children: Caroline Vail, Robert Brooks. BS, Seton Hall U., 1950; postgrad., Columbia U., 1950-51; MBA, NYU, 1954. Circulation promotion advt. space salesman Fairchild Publs., N.Y.C., 1951-53; Eastern advt. mgr. Modern Bride mag. Ziff-Davis, N.Y.C., 1953-58; advt. mgr. Bride and Home mag. Hearst Mags., N.Y.C., 1958-60, pub. Bride and Home mag., 1960-64; pub. Sports Afield mag., 1964-65, Town and Country mag., 1965-67, Harpers Bazaar mag., 1967-70; pres., chief exec. officer Bartell Media Corp., 1970-74; pres. Ziff-Davis Mag. Network, 1974-76, group v.p., 1976-78; sr. v.p. Ziff-Davis Pub. Co., 1978-81; pres. Ziff-Davis Consumer Mag., 1981-85; exec. v.p. mags. CBS, N.Y.C., 1985; pres. Trainia Assocs., N.Y.C., 1985—2000. Mem. Scarsdale Bi-Partisan Com., 1975-78; bd. dirs. Crane Berkeley Assn., 1978-88, pres., 1983-84; mem. nat. bd. dirs., chmn. comms. com., treas. Goodwill Industries of Am., 1979-92, chmn. bd., 1988-92; chmn. bd. trustees Chebeague Island Libr., 1997-2001; pres. bd. dirs. Chebeague Recreation Ctr., 1998-2003; bd. dirs. Chebeague Island Hist. Soc., 2000—. With USNR, 1945-46. NY State War Svc. scholar, Columbia U. and NYU, 1950. Mem. NYU Grad. Sch. Bus. Adminstrn. Alumni Assn., NYU Alumni Fedn. (comms. com. 1970-73), Union League Club (N.Y.C.). Home: 11 Springettes Rd Chebeague Island ME 04017-9723 E-mail: sunsethill@earthlink.net.

TRAINER, KARIN A., librarian; BA in English, Rutgers U., 1970; grad. work in English, Bryn Mawr Coll.; MLIS, Drexel U., 1972; M in liberal studies, NYU, 1983. Descriptive cataloguer Libraries of Princeton U., 1972—74, catalogue maintenance libr., 1974—78; dir. tech. and automated services NYU Libraries, 1978—83; assoc. univ. libr. Yale U., 1983—96, fellow and freshman advisor Ezra Stiles Coll.; univ. libr. Princeton U., 1996—. Office: Princeton U Libr One Washington Rd Princeton NJ 08544 Office Phone: 609-258-3170. Business E-Mail: ktrainer@princeton.edu.*

TRAINER, NANCY ROGO, architect, planner; b. Bridgeport, Conn., May 20, 1960; d. Albert and Vilma Rogo; m. Eric John Trainer, Nov. 4, 1959; children: Cameron Jacob, Aidan James. BS in Architecture, Cath. U. Am., 1982; MArch., Pa., 1985. Lic. Pa., 1989, cert. Nat. Coun. Archtl. Registration Bds., 2004; LEED Accredited Professional US Green Bldg. Coun. (USGBC), 2004. Staff arch. Venturi, Scott Brown and Assocs., Inc., Phila., sr. assoc., assoc., 1994—2001, mng. dir. 2001—04, prin., 2004—. Adj. instr. U. Pa., Phila., 1988, Drexel U., 1990—, Temple Univ., 1991—92. Mem. Cntrl. Phila. Devel. Corp., 2001—06; bd. mem. PennDesign Alumni Bd., U. Pa., 2003—. Recipient Paul Philippe Cret medal, U. Pa., 1985; Dales fellow, 1984. Mem.: AIA (N.C. Wyeth Design award 1982), Carpenters' Co. of City and County of Phila., Pa. Planning Assn., Soc. Coll. and U. Planners, Am. Planning Assn. Avocations: travel, cooking, gardening. Office: Venturi Scott Brown and Assocs Inc 4236 Main St Philadelphia PA 19127 Office Phone: 215-487-0400.

TRAINES, ROSE WUNDERBAUM, sculptor, educator; b. Monroeville, Ind., Sept. 13, 1928; d. Louis and Leah (Fogel) Wunderbaum; m. Robert Jacob Traines, June 25, 1949; children: Claudia Denise Traines Lang, Monica Rae Traines Martin Student, Ind. State Tchr.'s Coll., 1946—48, Mich. State U., 1948—49; BS, Ctrl. Mich. U., 1951. Lectr. in field. One person shows include Ctrl. Mich. U., Mt. Pleasant, 1964, Alma Artmobile, Mich., 1972, Ctrl. Mich. Homecoming, Mount Pleasant, 1982, Internat. Inst. Scrap Iron and Steel, Inc., Washington, 1983, Fontainebleau Hotel, Miami Beach, Fla., 1983, Elliott Mus. Art Gallery, Stuart, Fla., 1988, 98, Walt Kuhn Gallery, Cape Neddick, Maine, 1988, Coll. Club Boston, 1990, Brass Latch Gallery, Montpelier, Ind., 1991, 96, 98, Vero Beach Ctr. Arts, Fla., 1992, Maritime and

Yachting Mus., Stuart, 1997, Mid-Mich. Regional Med. Ctr., Healing Arts Gallery, Midland, 1997, Northwood Gallery, Midland, Commerca Bank Art Series, Palm Beach Gardens, 2002, Gallery Five, Tequesta, Fla., 2002, Mich. U. Park Libr. Gallery, 2002, Art Reach Mid. Mich., Mt. Pleasant, 2002, Arthur Glick Jewish Cmty. Ctr., Indpls., 2004, Art Reach Ctr. Mid-Mich., Mt. Pleasant, Elliott Mus. Gallery, Stuart, Fla., 2006; two-person shows include Gallery One, North Palm Beach, 1973, Midland Ctr. Arts, 1976, Springfield Art Mart, Ohio, 1977, Hillel Student Ctr. Gallery-U. Cin., 1993; exhibited in group shows including Saginaw Mus. Art, Mich., 1965, Grand Rapids Mus., Mich., 1966, Kalamazoo Mus.. Mich., 1967, Kellogg/Kresge Art Ctr., Mich. State U., East Lansing, 1967, Art Reach Mid-Mich., 1987, Salmagundi Club, N.Y.C., 1988, 91-92, 96, Copley Soc., Boston, 1990, 95, Allied Artists Am., Inc., N.Y.C., 1995-96, Self Family Arts Ctr., Hilton Head Island, S.C., 1996-97, Palm Beach Gardens Fla. City Hall, 2003, Palm Beach Gardens Cmty. Ctr., 2003, Art Reach Mid Mich., 2006, Elliott Mus., Stuart, Fla., 2006; represented in permanent collections at Dow-Corning Corp. Collection, Midland Ctr. Arts, Elliott Mus., Walt Kuhn Gallery, Coll. Club Boston, Pullen Elem. Sch., Isabella Bank and Trust Co., Ctrl. Mich. U., Blake Libr, Stuart, La Belle Mgmt. Corp., Morey Bandit Industries, Mich., Ctrl. Mich. Cmty. Hosp., Northwood U., Vets. Meml. Libr., Mt. Pleasant, Pub. Libr., Clare, Mich., Brass Latch Gallery, Northville (Mich.) Pub. Libr, Norman Cousins, Carl Gerstacker Found., Fannie Traines, pvt. collections. Tchr. Jewish Sunday Sch., Mt. Pleasant, 1955-70; officer Child and Youth Study Clubs, Mt. Pleasant, 1963-73; mem. City Recreation Commn., Mt. Pleasant, 1963-73, Area Health Planning Coun., Mt. Pleasant, 1974-80; pres. vol. Hosp. Aux. Med. Care, Red Cross Blood Bank, United Fund Cancer Dr., Mt. Pleasant, 1960-80; storyteller pub. libr., Mt. Pleasant, 1957-79 Recipient Northwood U. Artist award, Midland Ctr. for Arts, Mich., 2002. Mem.: Brass Latch Gallery, Art Reach Mid-Mich., Hilton Head Art League S.C. (Lifetime of Creative Excellence award 1998), Copley Soc. Boston (signature), Allied Artists Am. (Merit award 1996, Raymond H. Brumer Meml. award 1999), Nat. Mus. Women in Arts (charter), Salmagundi Club (Philip Isenberg award 1993, Pamela Singleton award 1997, Elliot Liskin Meml. award 1998, Anonymous award 1998, Peters Sculpture Materials award 2001, Alphaeus P. Cole Meml. award 2001, Meml. award 2003). Jewish. Avocations: lecturing, community work, tennis, presenting humorous programs, drums. Home: 1217 North Dr Mount Pleasant MI 48858-3226 Office Phone: 989-773-3873. Personal E-mail: fundametal2@webtv.net.

TRAINOR, BERNARD EDMUND, retired military officer; b. N.Y.C., Sept. 2, 1928; s. Joseph Patrick and Ann Veronica (Whelan) T.; m. Margaret Ann Hamilton, June 13, 1959; children: Kathleen Marie, Theresa Ann, Eileen Cecile, Claire Hamilton. BS, Coll. of Holy Cross, 1951; MA, U. Colo., 1963, postgrad., 1970-73; student, Air War Coll., Montgomery, Ala., 1969-70. Commd. 2nd lt. USMC, 1951, advanced through grades to lt. gen., 1983, inf. comdr. Korea, 1952, assigned to USS Columbus, 1953-55, mem. staff Marine Corps Hdqrs., 1955-58, with exch. office Royal Marine Commandos, 1958-59, inf. comdr. 1st Marine divsn., 1959-61; asst. prof. naval sci. U. Colo., Boulder, 1961-64; assigned to Marine Corps Command and Staff Coll., 1964-65; adv. Republic of Vietnam, 1965-66; instr. Marine Corps Command and Staff Coll., 1966-69; bn. comdr. Vietnam, 1970-71; staff officer Hdqrs. Marine Corps, Washington, 1970-71; dir. First Marine Corps Dist., N.Y.C., 1974-76; asst. depot comdr. Marine Corps Recruit Depot, Parris Island, SC, 1976-78; dir. Edn. Ctr., Quantico, Va., 1978-81; dep. chief of staff for plans, policies and ops. Hdqrs. Marine Corps, 1981-85; ret., 1985; mil. corr. N.Y. Times, 1986-90; dir. nat. security program Kennedy Sch. Govt. Harvard U., Cambridge, Mass., 1990-96, assoc. Ctr. Sci. and Internat. Affairs, 1996—2005; sr. fellow nat. security Coun. on Fgn. Rels., 1999—. Retired USMC, 1985. Author: History of the U.S. Marine Corps, 1968, The Generals' War, 1995; contbg. author: American Defense Annual, 1990, 2d edit., 1996, Defense Beat, 1991, After the Storm, 1992, The Almanac of Seapower, 1993, Newsmen and National Defense, 1991, Perspectives on Warfighting, 1992; mem. editl. adv. bd. Naval War Coll. Rev.; contbr. articles to profl. jours. Mil. analyst NBC News. Decorated D.S.M., Legion of Merit with Combat V and two stars, Bronze Star with Combat V, Navy Commendation medal with Combat V and two gold stars, others; recipient Anderson Meml. award Air War Coll., 1970. Mem. Naval Inst., Marine Corps Assn., Coun. Fgn. Rels., World Affairs Coun. (bd. dirs.). Roman Catholic. Home: 468741 Grissom St Potomac Falls VA 20165 E-mail: mickt51@adelphia.net.

TRAINOR, DEBORA JEAN, school psychologist, consultant; b. Albany, NY., Sept. 21, 1958; d. Thomas Arthur and Marilyn Jean (Quenneville) Trainor; 1 child, Dylan Thomas. MA, U. of Texas-Pan Am., Edinburg, 1998. Lic. specialist in sch. psychology Tex. State Bd. of Examiners of Psychologists. Psychol. cons., intern supr. Diamante Psychol. Svcs., McAllen, 2004—; psychol. examiner Deer Oaks Mental Health Assocs., McAllen, Tex., 2005—; LSSP supr. Diamante Psychol. Svcs., McAllen, 2004—. Actor: (theatrical prodn.) Mother Courage and Her Children. Ordained min. Abundant Grace Cmty. Ch., Edinburg, Tex., 2004—06. Mem.: APA (licentiate). Republican. Avocations: travel, theater. Home: 6104 N 32nd St Mcallen TX 78504 Office: Diamante Psychological Svcs 6104 N 32nd St Mcallen TX 78504 Office Phone: 956-451-3328. Home Fax: 877-823-7557; Office Fax: 877-823-7557. Personal E-mail: traindj@yahoo.com.

TRAINOR, JIM, animator, filmmaker; b. Phila. BA, Columbia U., 1983. Asst. prof.-film, video & new media Sch. Art Inst. Chgo., 2000—. Dir.: (films, screening), Whitney Biennial; (films) From Microbe to Man, 1974, Antrozous, 1976, Torn Up, 1994, The Bat & the Virgin, 1997, The Fetish, 1997, The Bats, 1998, The Ordovicians, The Magic Kingdom, Sun Shames Headhunting Moon: Story of Nazr, Serene Velocity, The Skulls & the Skulls, the Bones & the Bones, The Moschops, 2004, A Net, 2000, Harmony, 2004, Could Be Tropical Fish, 2005, Leafy, Leafy Jungle, 2005, Blood, 2005, New Diagonal Symphony, 2005. Recipient, San Francisco Film Festival, Black Maria Film Festival, NY Underground Film Festival, Cinematexas Film Festival, Big Muddy Film Festival, Ann Arbor Film Festival.

TRAINOR, JOHN FELIX, retired economics professor; b. Mpls., Dec. 1, 1921; s. James Patrick and Myra Catherine (Pauly) T.; m. Margaret Dolores Pudenz, July 3, 1965 (dec. 1977); children: John Anthony, Patrick James. BA cum laude, Coll. St. Thomas, 1943; MA, U. Minn., 1950; PhD, Wash. State U., 1970. Instr. De LaSalle H.S., Mpls., 1946-47, Coll. St. Thomas, 1949-50; v.p. Trainor Candy Co., Mpls., 1949-56; instr., asst. prof. econs. Rockhurst Coll., Kansas City, Mo., 1956-62; instr. Wash. State U., Pullman, 1966-67; asst. prof. Minn. State U., Moorhead, 1967—70, assoc. prof. econs., 1971-87, prof. econs., 1988-89, chmn. dept. econs., 1981-89; prof. emeritus, 1989—. Pres. Minn. Econs. Assn., 1976—77. Author: (with Frank J. Kottke) The Nursing Home Industry in the State of Washington, 1968. Ensign to Lt. (j.g.) USNR, 1943-46, ETO. Mem.: Assn. Social Econs., Omicron Delta Epsilon. Roman Catholic. Avocations: reading, crossword puzzles. Home: 1333 4th Ave S Moorhead MN 56560-2971

TRAISMAN, HOWARD SEVIN, retired pediatrician; b. Chgo., Mar. 18, 1923; s. Alfred Stanley and Sara (Sevin) T.; m. Regina Gallagher, Feb. 29, 1956; children: Barry D. Lifschultz, Edward S., Kenneth N. BS in Chemistry, Northwestern U., 1943, MB, 1946, MD, 1947. Intern Cook County Hosp., Chgo., 1946-47; resident in pediat. Children's Meml. Hosp., Chgo., 1949-51, attending physician divsn. endocrinology, 1951—2002; mem. faculty Med. Sch. Northwestern U., Evanston, Ill., 1951—2002, prof. pediat., 1973—2002, pres., 1999—2002; ret., 2002. Author articles in field, chpts. in books. Capt. M.C. AUS, 1943-46, 47-49. Recipient Northwestern U. Alumni Merit award, 1995, Northwestern U. Alumni medal, 2005. Mem. Am. Diabetes Assn. (Disting. Svc. award 1976), Am. Pediatric Soc., Am. Acad. Pediat., Endocrine Soc., Lawson Wilkins Pediatric Endocrine Soc., AMA, Midwest Soc. Pediatric Rsch., Ill. Med. Soc., Chgo. Pediatric Soc., Chgo. Med. Soc., Inst. Medicine Chgo. Democrat. Jewish. Office: 1325 Howard St Evanston IL 60202-3766

TRAKATELLIS, DEMETRIOS See DEMETRIOS

TRALDI, LORENZO, mathematician, educator; b. Rome, May 22, 1955; arrived in U.S., 1955; s. Giuseppe Alberto Traldi, Ila Dawson Little, Charles Little (Stepfather); m. Sharon Richter; children: Arthur, Matthew, Oliver, Rebecca. BA, CUNY, Flushing, NY, 1976; PhD, Yale U., 1980. Asst. prof. Lafayette Coll., Easton, Pa., 1980—86, assoc. prof., 1986—94, prof. 1994—2001, Marshall R. Metzgar prof. math., 2001—. Contbr. articles and revs. to profl. jours. Grantee, Lafayette Coll., 1983, 1987, 1991, 1996, 1997, 2000, 2001, USAF Office Sci. Rsch., 1991—92, NSF, 1994, 2001, 2003, 2005. Mem.: IEEE, Inst. for Combinatorics and its Applications, Am. Math. Soc. Independent. Home: 725 Coleman St Easton PA 18042 Office: Dept Math Lafayette Coll Easton PA 18042 Office Phone: 610-330-5276. Business E-Mail: traldil@lafayette.edu.

TRAMMEL, KIMBERLY ELISE See ELISE, KIMBERLY

TRAMMELL, ALAN STUART, former professional baseball manager; b. Garden Grove, Calif., Feb. 21, 1958; m. Barbara Leverett, Feb. 21, 1978; children: Lance, Kyle, Jade Lynn. Shortstop Detroit Tigers, 1977—96, asst. to baseball ops., 1996—98, mgr., 2002—05; first base coach San Diego Padres, 2000—02. Named Most Valuable Player, So. League, 1977; winner Gold Glove award, 1980, 81, 83, 84, Silver Slugger award, 1987, 88, 90; mem. Am. League All-Star Team, 1980, 84, 87, 88, 90, World Series Championship Team, 1984; named Most Valuable Player 1984 World Series.

TRAMMELL, BRADLEY ELLIS, lawyer; b. Opelika, Ala., Jan. 11, 1961; s. Herman Bruce and Laura Elizabeth Trammell; m. Katherine Farrell McClintock, Apr. 11, 1992; children: William McClintock, Henry Ellis. BA cum laude, U. of South, Sewanee, Tenn., 1983; JD, U. Ala., Tuscaloosa, 1989. Bar: Tenn. 1989, Ala. 1991. Sr. assoc. exec. Travelers Ins. Co., Plantation, Fla., 1983—86; ptnr. Baker, Donelson, Bearman, Caldwell & Berkowitz, Memphis, 1989—, chair Memphis office recruiting com., 2002—. Campaign chmn. Travelers South Fla. offices United Way, 1984; chmn. ann. ptnrs. campaign Downtown YMCA, Memphis, 1993; jr. warden St. John's Episcopal Ch., Memphis, 2002, vestry mem., 2001—03. Mem.: ABA, Memphis Bar Assn. Young Lawyers (bd. dirs. 1991—93), Memphis Bar Assn., Ala. Bar Assn., Tenn. Bar Assn., Omicron Delta Kappa. Office: Baker Donelson Bearman Caldwell & Berkowitz 165 Madison Ave Ste 2000 Memphis TN 38103 Office Phone: 901-577-2121. Office Fax: 901-557-0781. Business E-Mail: btrammell@bakerdonelson.com.

TRAMMELL, HERBERT EUGENE, retired physicist; b. Laurel, Miss., Apr. 19, 1927; s. Homer Lee and Evie Louisa (Breazeale) T.; m. Jane Walker, Dec. 28, 1948; children— Carmen, Bert, Lisa, Brian. BA in Physics, U. Miss., 1947, MA, 1948. With Nuclear div. Union Carbide, Oak Ridge, 1949-89, mgr. barrier devel. programs, 1967-69, dir. gaseous diffusion devel. div., 1969-77; dir. engring. tech. div. Oak Ridge Nat. Lab., 1977-89, ret., 1989; with Martin Marietta Energy Systems, 1983-89. Bd. dirs. Emory Valley Sch. for Retarded Children, 1962-68, v.p., 1966-68; mem. Tenn. Med. Malpractice Rev. Bd., 1974-80; active PTA. Served with U.S. Navy, 1944-45. Mem.: Rotary (pres. 1980-81). Methodist. Home: 901 Johnson St Key West FL 33040-4745 Personal E-Mail: hjtrammell@aol.com.

TRAMMELL, KENNETH R., automotive executive; married; 2 children. BBA in acctg., U. Houston. Cert. CPA Tex. Sr. mgr. Arthur Andersen LLP; asst. contr. Tenneco Automotive, 1996—97, corp. contr., 1997—99, v.p., contr., 1999—2003, sr. v.p., CFO Lake Forest, Ill., 2003—. Office: Tenneco Automotive 500 N Field Dr Lake Forest IL 60045

TRAMONTE, MICHAEL ROBERT, education educator; AB in Sociology, Boston Coll., 1960; EdM, State Coll. Boston, 1963; Cert. Advanced Edn. Specialization, Boston Coll., 1971; Comprehensive Cert. in Paralegal Studies, Bentley Coll., 1982; EdD in Human Devel. and Edn., Boston U., 1986. Lic. psychologist health svc. provider, ednl. psychologist, cert. social worker, cert. tchr. social studies grades 5-9, grades 9-12, moderate spl. needs tchr., sch. psychologist, supr., guidance counselor, supr., dir., secondary sch. prin. Mass., sch. psychologist N.H., Mass. nat. cert. sch. psychologist. Substitute tchr. Medford (Mass.) Pub. Schs., 1960-61, jr. H.S. tchr. social studies, 1961-68; instr. psychology and edn. Anna Maria Coll., 1968-69; adj. instr. psychology Mass. Bay C.C., 1972, Middlesex C.C., 1977—; sch. psychologist Lowell (Mass.) Pub. Schs., 1970-98; assoc. prof. edn. Rivier Coll., Nashua, NH, 1998—. Adj. prof. edn. Rivier Coll., 1983, 87-98; spkr. in field. Chmn. Medford chpt. Greater Boston Assn. Retarded Children, 1969-70; vol. spkr. support groups Mass. chpt. Nat. Multiple Sclerosis Soc., 1971-88; mem. ARC Disaster Svcs. Human Resources Svcs. Recipient certificate, Medford Mental Health Assn., 1968, Medford chpt. Greater Boston Assn. Retarded Children, 1970, Mass. chpt. Nat. Multiple Sclerosis Soc., 1979, Faculty award for secondary edn., Rivier Coll., 1994, cert. of recognition, ARC of Mass. Bay, 1999, 2000, 2002, 2005. Fellow Am. Acad. Experts in Traumatic Stress. Home: 24 Erie St Woburn MA 01801-4532 Office Phone: 603-897-8487. E-mail: mtramonte@rivier.edu.

TRAMONTO, RICK, chef; b. Rochester, NY; m. Gale Gand. Grill/saute cook The Scotch & Sirloin; chef Strathallen; garde-mgr. chef Tavern on the Green; chef Gotham Bar & Grill, Aurora, Avanzare, Chgo., The Pump Room, Chgo., Scoozi!, Chgo., Charlie Trotter's, Chgo., Stapleford Park Hotel, London; owner, chef Tru, Chgo., 1999—, Brasserie T., Chgo. Appeared on Oprah TV program. Named one of Am.'s rising Star Chefs, Robert Mondavi, 1995; named to Ten Best New Chefs, Food & Wine, 1994. Office: 676 N St Clair St Chicago IL 60611

TRAN, BINH Q., biomedical engineering educator; D in Biomed. Engring., U. Iowa, Iowa City, 1998. Assoc. prof. Cath. U. Am., Washington, 2003—.

TRAN, HENRY AN TIEN, internist; b. McKeesport, Pa., Sept. 6, 1976; s. Huyen Tien Tran and Van Ninh Nguyen. BA, U. Va., Charlottesville, 1998; MS, Georgetown U., Washington, 1999, MD, 2003. Lic. Mephysician NY, 2005. Resident NYU, NYC, 2003—06, sr. chief resident, 2006—. Office Phone: 212-562-6401. E-mail: tranh01@med.nyu.edu.

TRAN, KHANH T., insurance company executive; BA econ., polit. sci., Whittier Coll.; MBA finance and mktg., UCLA. With United Calif. Bank, Flying Tiger Line, Inc.; asst. treas. Vons Cos., Inc.; CFO, Pacific Life Ins., Newport Beach, Calif. Mem.: ACLI (CFO Conf.). Office: Pacific Life Ins Co PO Box 9000 Newport Beach CA 92658-9030

TRAN, LAN P., writer, performer; b. Austin, Tex., June 2, 1973; d. Huy B. and Bay T. Tran. BA, UCLA, 1996; MA, NYU, 1999. Author: Lemongracias, 2002, How To Unravel Your Family, 2003, Lone Stars in Falling Backwards: Stories of Fathers & Daughters, 2004; performer: The American Living Room Festival, 2002, National Literary Caravan, 2002, ONE Festival, 2003, The Quarterly Report, 2004, many others. Finalist Heideman award, 2003; recipient York Prize, 2002;, Hedgebrook, 2002, Ragdale, 2002, Vt. Studio Ctr., 2002, Va. Ctr. for the Creative Arts, 2001.

TRAN, LONG TRIEU, industrial engineer; b. Saigon, Vietnam, Oct. 10, 1956; arrived in US, 1973; s. Nguyen Dinh and Thiet Thi (Nguyen) Tran; m. Khanh Thi-Hong Phan, Aug. 3, 1988. BSME with honors, U. Kans., 1976; MSME, MIT, 1980; MBA with honors, U. Louisville, 1993. Cert. quality engr., mfg. engr., project mgmt. profl. Tchg. asst. U. Kans., 1975-76, U. Calif. Berkeley, 1977, rsch. asst. Lawrence Berkeley Labs., 1977, MIT, 1977-80; libr. staff Harvard U. Med. Sch. Libr., 1977-78; mem. staff New England Deaconess Hosp., Boston, 1978-80; prodn. programming engr. GE, Cleve., 1980-81, advanced mfg. engr. Louisville, 1981-82, quality sys. engr., 1982-84, quality control engr., 1984-86, sr. quality info. equipment engr., 1986-89, sr. quality indsl. engr., 1990-94, sr. supplier tech. assistance engr., 1995-96, sr. advanced supplier quality engr., 1996-98, program mgr. purchased material quality, 1999, combo blackbelt leader supplier quality, 1999-2000, Six Sigma program mgr., 2000—02, sr. purchased material quality engr., 2003—. Exec. advisor Jr. Achievement, Inc., Louisville, 1983—84; monitor/reader Rec. for

Blind, 1994—; fundraiser Dream Factory Inc., 1994—. Vol. NCCJ, 1994—, Clothe-A-Child, 1993—, Dare-To-Care, 1994—, Ronald McDonald House, 1994—. Mem.: ASME, AAAS, Heritage Found., Am. Assn. Individual Investors, Ctr. for Positive Thinking, Cato Inst., Ctr. Positive Thinking, Indsl. Computing Soc. (founding), N.Y. Acad. Scis., Am. Mgmt. Assn., Robotics Internat. (charter), Robot Inst. Am., Am. Prodn. and Inventory Control Soc., Computer and Automated Sys. Assn. (charter), Am. Soc. Quality Control, Instrument Soc. Am. (sr.), Soc. Mfg. Engrs. (sr.), U.S. Libr. Congress Assocs. (founding), Nat. Pks. Conservation Assn. (founding), Assn. Compassion (life), Internat. Platform Assn., PGA Tour Ptnrs. Club, Handyman Club Am. (life), Sigma Xi, Beta Gamma Sigma, Phi Kappa Phi, Tau Beta Pi, Pi Tau Sigma. Republican. Achievements include research in grinding processes and material surface analysis, mfg. project mgmt., supplier quality mgmt. Home: 3642 Windward Way Louisville KY 40220-1818 Office: Gen Electric Co Appliance Park AP2-117 Louisville KY 40225-0001 Office Phone: 502-452-7082. Business E-Mail: long.tran@ge.com.

**TRAN, NANG TRI,** research scientist, electrical engineer; b. Binh Dinh, Vietnam, Jan. 2, 1948; came to the U.S., 1979, naturalized, 1986; s. Cam Tran and Cuu Thi Nguyen; m. Thu-Huong Thi Tong, Oct. 14, 1982; children: Helen, Florence, Irene, Kenneth. BSEE, Kyushu Inst. Tech., Kitakyushu, Japan, 1973, MSEE, 1975; PhD in Materials Sci./Solid State Device, U. Osaka Prefecture, Sakai, Japan, 1979. Rsch. assoc. U. Calif. Irvine, 1979; engr., rsch. scientist Sharp Electronics, Irvine, 1979-80; sr. rsch. scientist Arco Solar Industries, Chatsworth, Calif., 1980-84; sr. rsch. specialist, group leader 3M Co., St. Paul, 1985-96; sr. staff scientist Imation Corp., Oakdale, Minn., 1996—; cons. Khanti Inc. McKnight disting. vis. prof., adj. prof. U. Minn., Mpls.; cons., lectr. Japan industry mgmt.; reviewer NSF. Author: (poetry) My Journey; contbr. articles to profl. jours. Mem. tech. com. various internat. confs. Recipient R&D awards, Photonic Cir. Excellence award; fellow, Govt. South Vietnam, Japan, USAID, Rotary Internat., 1968—79. Mem. IEEE (sr.), Japan Soc. Applied Physics, N.Y. Acad. Scis. Achievements include invention of direct digital x-rays; transparent conducting zinc oxide doped with group III elements; thin film transistors on flexible substrate; structured phosphors thin film solar cells of selenium-based chalcogenides; patents in field; research in amorphous silicon solar cells; image sensors; solid state memory; photoconductors; CD; high density data storage media; diamond like carbon evaporated lubricant; transparent conducting oxide films. Office: Imation Corp Data Storage and Info Mgmt 1 Imation Pl Discovery 1A-03 Oakdale MN 55128-3414 Office Phone: 651-704-4448. Business E-Mail: nttran@imation.com.

**TRAN, SON CAO,** computer science educator; b. Nam Dinh, Vietnam, July 23, 1962; s. Ung Tat Tran and Lang Thi Nguyen; m. Thanh Thi Hong Nguyen; children: Trang Thu, Tra Thanh. PhD in Computer Engring., U. Tex., El Paso, 2000. Postdoctoral rschr. Stanford (Calif.) U., 2000—01; asst. prof. N.Mex State U., Las Cruces, 2001—. Office: NMex State U MSC CS PO Box 30001 Las Cruces NM 88003

**TRAN, VAN THAI,** state legislator; b. Saigon, Vietnam; arrived in US, 1975; m. Cindy Nguyen, 2004. BS in Polit. Sci., U. Calif., Irvine; MS in Public Admin., Hamline U., Saint Paul, Minnesota; JD, Hamline U. Sch. of Law, Saint Paul, Minnesota. Staff aide Congressman Robert K. Dornan, State Sen. Ed Royce; former mng. ptnr. Van Thai Tran & Assoc.; mem. Garden Grove City Council, 2000—02; vice-mayor City of Garden Grove, 2002—03; mem. Calif. State Assembly, 2004—. Mem. Asian-Pacific Congressional Advisory Bd.; mem. bus. and professions com., banking and fin. com., environ. safety and toxic materials com. Calif. State Assembly, mem. select com. on critical issues; mem. Asian Pacific Islander Joint Caucus. Chmn. Vietnamese com. Orange County Republican Party; founder Vietnamese-Am. Voters Coalition, 1990—. Office: Calif Assembly State Capital Rm 4009 Sacramento CA 94249-0068

**TRANGSRUD, ROGER H.,** dean, law educator; BA, Carleton Coll.; JD, U. Chgo. Clerk for Justice Walter Rogosheske Minn. Supreme Ct.; atty. Hogan & Hartson; prof. law George Washington U. Law Sch., 1982—, assoc. dean, 1993—2000, sr. assoc. dean, 2000—04, interim dean, 2000—, Oswald Symister Colclough Rsch. Prof. Law. Contbr. articles to law jours. Office: George Washington U Law Sch 2000 H St NW Washington DC 20052 Office Phone: 202-994-6277. Office Fax: 202-994-5157. E-mail: rtrang@law.gwu.edu.

**TRANI, EUGENE PAUL,** university president, educator; b. Bklyn., Nov. 2, 1939; s. Frank Joseph and Rose Gertrude (Kelly) T.; m. Lois Elizabeth Quigley, June 2, 1962; children: Anne Chapman, Frank. BA in History with honors, U. Notre Dame, 1961; MA, Ind. U., 1963, PhD, 1966. Instr. history Ohio State U., Columbus, 1965-67; asst. prof. So. Ill. U., Carbondale, 1967-71, assoc. prof., 1971-75, prof., 1975-76; asst. v.p. acad. affairs, prof. U. Nebr., 1976-80; prof., vice chancellor acad. affairs U. Mo. Kansas City, 1980-86; prof., v.p. acad. affairs U. Wis. System, 1986-90; pres. Va. Commonwealth U., 1990—; pres. bd. dirs. Va. Biotech Rsch. Park, 1992-97, chmn., 1997—; pres., chmn. VCU Health Sys., 2000—. Vis. asst. prof. U. Wis., Milw., 1969; bd. dirs. Met. Richmond SunTrust Mid-Atlantic Bank, Universal Corp., LandAm. Fin. Group, Inc.; mem. commn. Internat. Edn. Am. Coun. Ed., 1991—; bd. gov. Ctr. Russian Am. Bus., Washington, 1993-98; adv. coun. on Grad. Studies and Rsch., U. Notre Dame, 1994—, NASULGC, 1980—, chair commn. on internat. affairs, 1993-94; vis. prof. Univ. Coll. Dublin, 2002; bd. advisors Inst. for U.S. Studies, U. London, 1993-99; cons. in field. Author, editor: Concerns of a Conservative Democrat, 1968, The Treaty of Portsmouth: An Adventure in American Diplomacy, 1969; (with Donald E. Davis) The First Cold War, 2002; (with David Wilson) The Secretaries of the Department of the Interior 1849-69, 1973; The Presidency of Warren G. Harding, 3d edit., 1989; contbr. articles to profl. jours., newspapers; book reviewer. Permanent mem. Coun. Fgn. Rels., N.Y.C., 1979—; bd. dirs. Richmond Ballet, 1991-96, NCCJ, Richmond, 1991-94, Va. Spl. Olympics, 1991-96, YMCA of Greater Richmond, 1992—, Richmond Renaissance, 1992-96, 2001—, chmn., 2001—; bd. dirs. Met. Bus. Found., 1992-98, Va. Tech. Fund Found., 1993—, Met. Bus. League, 1994—; mem. U.S. Savs. Bond Vol. Com., chmn. higher edn. area, 1992-93; adv. bd. Greater Richmond chpt. ARC, 1992—; mem. Gov.'s Commn. Info. Tech. in Va., 1998-2000; bd. dirs. Collegiate Sch., 1998—; adv. bd. Black History Archives Project, 1992-96; bd. dirs. Va. Ctr. for Innovative Tech., 1990-96, Capital Area Assembly, 1990-93, Richmond Symphony, 1991-94, Richmond Sym-phony Coun., 1995—; mem. coun. advisors Christian Children's Fund, 1992-95; mem. Ctrl. Richmond Assn., 1992-96; bd. trustees Va. Hist. Soc., 1994-96, Theatre Va., 1994-97, Richmond Children's Mus., 1994—, World Affairs Coun. of Greater Richmond, 1999-2003; bd. dirs. Sci. Mus. of Va. Found., 1994—, Va. Tech. Fund Found., 1993—, Met. Bus. Hague, 1994—; mem. Gov.'s Biotech. Initiative Adv. Bd., 2002—; bd. dirs. Qatar Found. for Edn. Sci. Comm. Devel., Va. Tech. Found., 1993—. Fellow Russian and East European Inst., 1964-65, Nat. Hist. Publs. Comm., 1969-70, Woodrow Wilson Internat. Ctr. Scholars, 1972-73, So. Ill. U. Sabbatical Leave, 1975-76, Coun. Internat. Exchange Scholars, 1981, U. Mo. Faculty, 1981; grantee U.S. Dept. Interior Rsch., 1965-66, So. Ill. U. Office Rsch. and Projects, 1967-74, Am. Philos. Soc., 1968, 72, So. Ill U. Summer Rsch. 1970, 72, 75, Lilly Endowment, 1975-76, Sloan Common. Govt. and Higher Edn., 1978, USIA Am. Participants Program, 1984-86, 88, 90; Inst. for U.S. Studies fellow U. London, 1995, fellow commoner St. John's Coll., Cambridge, 1998; recipient Younger Humanist award NEH, 1972-73, Leadership and Achievement award Ctrl. Richmond Assn., 1992, Biotech. Leadership award Va. Biotech. Assn., 1999; recipient Disting. Leadership award, Nat. Assn. Cmty. Leaders, 1994, Richmond Humanitarian award, NCCJ, 1995, Flame Bearer of Edn. award Coll. Fund/UNCF, 1998, Richmond Joint Engrs. Coun. Cmty. Svc. award, 2002; named Style Mag. Richmonder of Yr., 1998, Person of Yr., Fifty Plus Mag., 2004, Crystal Ball Spl. Honoree, Arthritis Fund. Ctrl. Va. Chpt., 2005; Hope Award, Nat. MS Soc., 2003, others. Mem. Internat. Inst. Strategic Studies, Am. Assn. Advancement Slavic Studies, Orgn. Am. Historians, Soc. Historians Am. Fgn. Rels., Greater Richmond C. of C. (bd. dirs. 1991-96,

chmn. 1997-98), Phi Kappa Phi. Roman Catholic. Avocations: reading, travel, basketball, golf. Office: Va Commonwealth U Box 842512 910 W Franklin St Richmond VA 23284-2512 E-mail: etrani@vcu.edu.

**TRANI, JOHN M.,** former consumer products company executive; b. NYC, 1945; B in Aerospace Engring., Bklyn. Poly. Inst., 1966, M in Indsl. Mgmt., Ops. Rsch. With GE, 1978—97; pres., CEO GE Med. Svcs. divsn. GE Co., 1986—97; chmn., CEO Stanley Works, New Britain, Conn., 1997—2003. Home: 30 Stanford Dr Farmington CT 06032 Office Phone: 860-674-3764. E-mail: jmtrani@hotmail.com.

**TRANQUADA, ROBERT ERNEST,** retired internist, educator; b. LA, Aug. 27, 1930; s. Ernest Alvro and Katharine (Jacobus) Tranquada; m. Janet Martin, Aug. 31, 1951; children: John Martin, Katherine Anne, James Robert. BA, Pomona Coll., 1951; MD, Stanford U., 1955; D.Sc. (hon.), Worcester Poly. Inst., 1985. Diplomate Am. Bd. Internal Medicine. Intern in medicine UCLA Med. Center, 1955—56, resident in medicine, 1956—57; resident Los Angeles VA Hosp., 1957—58; fellow in diabetes and metabolic diseases UCLA, 1958—59; fellow in diabetes U. So. Calif., 1959—60, asst. prof. medicine, 1960—63, assoc. prof., 1964—68, chmn. dept. community medi-cine, 1967—70; med. dir. Los Angeles County/U. So. Calif. Med. Center, 1969—74; assoc. dean U. So. Calif. Sch. Medicine, 1974—76; regional dir. Central Region, Los Angeles County Dept. Health Services, 1974—76; assoc. dean Sch. Medicine U. Calif., L.A., 1966—79; chancellor and dean U. Mass. Med. Sch., 1979—86; dean Sch. Medicine U. So. Calif., 1986—91, prof. medicine L.A., 1986—92, Norman Topping/Nat. Med. Enterprises prof. med./pub. policy, 1992—97; prof. emeritus, 1997—. Mem. chair L.A. County Task Force on Health Care Access, 1992—94. Corporator Worcester Art Mus., 1980—86; active Ind. Commn. on L.A. Police Dept., 1991—92; governing bd. LA County Local Initiative Health Authority, 1994—, chmn., 2001—05; bd trustees Pomona Coll., 1969—, vice chmn., 1971—79, chmn., 1991—2000, emeritus trustee chmn., 2000—; bd. fellow Claremont U. Ct., 1971—79, 1991—2000; chmn. bd. overseers Claremont U. Consortium, 2000—06, emeritus chmn. bd. overseers, 2006—; vice-chmn., U. trustees Keck Grad. Inst. Applied Life Scis., 1997—2000, emeritus, 2000—; bd. dirs. Nat. Med. Fellowships, Inc., 1973—2005, chmn., 1980—85; bd. trustees Charles Drew U. Med. and Sci., 1968—79, 1986—95, Orthopaedic Hosp., 1986—91, Barlow Hosp., 1987—89; bd. dirs. Worcester Acad., 1984—86, U. So. Calif. Univ. Hosp., 1988—91, Alliance for Childrens Rights, 1991—95, Cmty. Health Coun., Inc., 1993—, Good Hope Med. Found., 1994—, Ralph M. Parsons Found., 2000—, Huntington Med. Rsch. Inst., 2006—, Congl. Homes, Inc., Mt. San Antonio Gardens, 2006—; mem. coun. pres. Assn. Governing Bodies Colls. and Univs., 2000—03, chair, 2002—03. Fellow Milbank Found., 1967—72. Fellow: AAAS, Am. Antiquarian Soc.; mem.: Inst. Medicine of Nat. Acad. Scis., Calif. Med. Assn., L.A. Acad. Medicine, L.A. County Med. Assn., AMA, Alpha Omega Alpha, Sigma Xi, Phi Beta Kappa.

**TRANSOU, LYNDA LOU,** advertising art administrator; b. Atlanta, Dec. 11, 1949; d. Lewis Cole Transou and Ann Lynette (Taylor) Putnam; m. Lue Gregg Loso, Oct. 25, 1991. BFA cum laude, U. Tex., 1971. Art dir. The Pitluk Group, San Antonio, 1971, Campbell, McQuien & Lawson, Dallas, 1973-74, Bozell & Jacobs, Dallas, 1974-75; art dir., ptnr. The Assocs., Dallas, 1975-77; art dir. Belo Broadcasting, Dallas, 1977-80; creative dir., v.p. Allday & Assocs., Dallas, 1980-85; owner Lynda Transou Advt. & Design, 1986—. Recipient Merit award, N.Y. Art Dirs. Show, 1980, Gold award, Dallas Ad League, 1980, Silver award, 1980, 1981, 1982, 2 Merit awards, Houston Art Dirs. Club, 1978, Dallas Ad League, 1986, Merit award, Broadcast Designers Assn., 1980, Merit awards, Dallas Ad League, 1978, 1987, Silver award, Houston Art Dirs. Show, 1982, Gold award, N.Y. Pub. Rels. Assn., 1985, N.Y. One Show, 1982, Creativity awrd, Art Direction mag., 1986, Print award, Regional Design Annual, 1988, 2 Gold Adrian awards, 1997, Katy award, Dallas Press Club, 2001. Dallas Soc. Visual Comm. (Bronze award 1980, Merit award 1978-86), Delta Gamma (historian 1969-70).

**TRAPP, A.C.,** retired music educator; b. Chase, La., Dec. 1, 1930; parents A. Clayton and Jessie Mae (Stigall) Trapp; m. Beatrice Horn (separated); children: A. Clayton III, Jonathan L. B in Piano Performance and Vocal Suprervision, Northeast Coll.; M, Northwestern State U., 1961. Music supr. Catahoula Parish, 1957; music tchr. DOD, 1959. Judge Nat. Guild of Piano Tchrs. Exhibitions include Delgado Mus., New Orleans, 1956. Mem. Grace Episcopal Ch. Corp. U.S. Army, 1952—54. Named to Hall of Fame, Am. Coll. Musicians, Austin, Tex., 2006. Republican. Episcopalian. Home: 501 S Grand Apt 319 Monroe LA 71201

**TRAPP, PETER JARL RUDOLF,** portfolio manager, farmer; b. Darlington, Eng., Oct. 5, 1945; arrived in U.S., 1971; s. Jarl Rudolph and Olive Lindsay (Fairley) Trapp; m. Regina Antoinette Thomas, Sept. 6, 1969 (div. Dec. 1986); children: Sophia Antoinette, Alexander Rudolf, Olivia Henrietta Elizabeth. Mi-Lic, Fribourg U., Switzerland, 1971; MBA, Columbia U., 1973. V.p. First Boston Corp., N.Y.C., 1973-78, Goldman Sachs & Co., N.Y.C., 1978-81; mgr. dir. Dean Witter Reynolds Inc., N.Y.C., 1982-84; mgr. dir., exec. officer Marine Midland Bank N.A., N.Y.C., 1985-89; sr. v.p. Gerard Klauer Mattison & Co., N.Y.C., 1990-94; mgr. dir. Needham & Co., N.Y.C., 1994—2003; exec. v.p. Needham Investment Mgmt., N.Y.C., 1998—2003; founding ptnr. Bifrost Ptnrs. LLC and Bifrost Fund LP, N.Y.C., 2003—. Cadet sgt. Swedish Army, 1968—69. Mem.: Coral Beach Club (Bermuda), Arma-bel's (London), Leash and Doubles Club (N.Y.). Avocations: skiing, fishing, shooting, farming. Home: Bean Creek Farm 341 Tripp Mcghee Rd Box 948 Pine Plains NY 12567 Office: Bifrost Ptnrs LLC Box 948 Pine Plains NY 12567 Office Phone: 518-398-6810. Business E-Mail: pt@bifrostcapital.com.

**TRASK, THOMAS EDWARD,** religious organization administrator; b. Brainard, Minn., Mar. 23, 1936; m. Shirley Burkhart; children: Kimberly, Bradley, Todd, Tom. BA, North Ctrl. Bible Coll., 1956, DDiv (hon.), 1994. Ordained min. Assemblies of God, 1958. Pastor First Assembly of God, Hibbing, Minn., 1956-60, pastor Vicksburg, Mich., 1960-64; Mich. dist. youth and Sunday sch. dir. Assembly of God, 1964-68; pastor First Assembly of God, Saginaw, Mich., 1968-73, Brightmoor Tabernacle, Southfield, Mich., 1976-88; supt. Mich. Dist. Coun., Dearborn, 1973-76; gen. treas. The Gen. Coun. Assemblies of God, Springfield, Mo., 1988-93, gen. supt., 1993—. Co-author: Back to the Altar: A Call to Spiritual Awakening, 1994, Back to the Word, A Call to Biblical Authority, 1996, The Battle: Defeating the Enemies of Your Soul, 1997, The Blessing: Experiencing the Power of the Holy Spirit Today, 1998, The Choice: Embracing God's Vision in the New Millennium, 1999, The Fruit of the Spirit, 2000, Ministry for a Lifetime, 2001. Mem. Assemblies Of God. Office: Assemblies of God 1445 N Boonville Ave Springfield MO 65802-1894

**TRAUB, J(OSEPH) F(REDERICK),** computer scientist, educator; b. June 24, 1932; m. Pamela Ann McCorduck, Dec. 6, 1969; children: Claudia Renee, Hillary Anne. BS, CCNY, 1954; PhD, Columbia U., 1959; DSc (hon.), U. Cen. Fla., 2001. Computer sci. staff Bell Labs., Murray Hill, NJ, 1959-70; prof. computer sci. and math., head dept. computer sci. Carnegie-Mellon U., Pitts., 1971-79; Edwin Howard Armstrong prof. computer sci., chmn. dept., prof. math. Columbia U., 1979-86; prof. computer sci. Princeton (N.J.) U., 1986-87; pres. John Von Neumann Nat. Supercomputer Ctr., Consortium for Sci. Computing, Princeton, 1986-87; Edwin Howard Armstrong prof., chmn. dept. computer sci., prof. math. Columbia U., N.Y.C., 1987-89, Edwin Howard Armstrong prof. computer sci. and math., 1989—; external prof. Santa Fe Inst., 1995-98, 2004—; fellow Biosgroup, 1998—2003. Dir. N.Y. State Ctr. Computers and Info. Systems, 1982-88; vis. Mackay prof. U. Calif., Berkeley, 1978-79; mem. pres.'s adv. computer sci. Stanford U., 1972-75, chmn., 1976-77; adv. com. Fed. Jud. Ctr.; mem. sci. coun. I.R.I.A. Paris, 1976-80; ctrl. steering com. computing sci. and engring. rsch. study NSF, liaison to panel on theoretical computer sci. and panel on numerical comp., 1977-80; adv. com. Carnegie-Mellon Inst. Research, 1978-79; mem. applied math. divsn. rev. comm. Argonne Nat. Lab., 1973-75; adv. com. math. and computer sci. NSF, 1978-80, mem. com. visitors, 2005; chmn. computer sci. and tech. bd. NRC, 1986-90, computer sci. and telecomms. bd., 1990-92,

Nat. Acads., 2005—; trustee Columbia U. Press, 1983-85; lectr. in field; cons. in field. Author: Iterative Methods for the Solution of Equations, 1964, Russian edit., 1985, (with H. Wozniakowski) A General Theory of Optimal Algorithms, 1980, Russian edit., 1983, (with G. Wasilkowski and H. Wozniakowski) Information, Uncertainty, Complexity, 1983, Information-Based Complexity, 1988, (with A.G. Werschulz) Complexity and Informa-tion, 1998, Chelsea, 1998; editor: Complexity of Sequential and Parallel Numerical Algorithms, 1973, Analytic Computational Complexity, 1976, Algorithms and Complexity: New Directions and Recent Results, 1976, Jour. Assn. Computing Machinery, 1970-76, Transactions on Math. Software, 1974-76, Jour. Computer and Sys. Scis., 1973-86, Internat. Jour. on Comput-ers and Math. with Applications, 1974—, Cohabiting With Computers, 1985, Festschrift, 1993, 2004, (with P. Hut and D. Ruelle) Fundamental Sources of Unpredictability, 1997; founding editor Jour. Complexity, 1985—, Ann. Rev. Computer Sci., 1986-92 Festschrift, 1993, 2004; assoc. editor Complexity, 1995—. Sherman Fairchild Disting. scholar Calif. Inst. Tech., 1991, 92; recipient Award for Disting. Svc. to Computing Rsch. Computer Rsch. Assn., 1992, Lezione Lincee Acad. Nazionale dei Lincei, 1993, Sr. Scientist award Alexander Von Humboldt Found., 1992-98, City of N.Y. Mayor's award for excellence in sci. and tech., 1999. Fellow AAAS (coun. 1971-74), ACM (chmn. award com. 1974-76), N.Y. Acad. Scis.; mem. IEEE (Emanuel R. Piore Gold medal 1991), NAE (membership com. for computer sci., elec. engring. and control 1986-87, membership com. for computer sci. and engring. 1987-91, presdl. search com. 1993-94), Conf. Bd. Math. Scis. (coun. 1971-74), Soc. Indsl. and Applied Math., Am. Math. Soc., Assn. Computing Machinery (founding chair spl. interest group on numerical math. 1965-71). Office: Columbia U Dept Computer Sci 1214 Amsterdam Ave #MC0401 New York NY 10027-7003 Business E-Mail: traub@cs.columbia.edu.

**TRAUB, RICHARD KENNETH,** lawyer; b. Lakewood, NJ, Aug. 4, 1950; s. Harold W. and Muriel N. (Zurlin) T.; m. Barbara Lynn Wright, July 9, 1972; children: Russell S., Melissa L. BBA, U. Miami, Coral Gables, Fla., 1972, JD cum laude, 1975. Bar: Fla. 1975, N.Y. 1976, N.J. 1976, U.S. Dist. Ct. N.J. 1976, U.S. Supreme Ct. 1979, U.S. Dist. Ct. (ea. & so. dists.) N.Y. 1981. Ptnr. Wilson, Elser, Moskowitz, Edelman & Dicker, N.Y.C., 1975-95, Traub Eglin Lieberman Straus LLP, Hawthorne, NY, 1996—. Ptnr. Time for Patty Stables, NJ, 1992—; officer, dir. X-Ray Duplications, Inc., NJ; ptnr., founder Fractured Greetings, NJ; mem., lectr., v.p. Fedn. Def. and Corp. Counsel, 1993—, chair tech. com., mem. admissions com., industry cooperation ins. coverage alt. dispute resolution coms. and tech. sect., v.p., dir., 2004—, dean of curriculum, Litigation Mgmt. Coll., 2006-; lectr. Inst. for Internat. Rsch., Washington, 1988, Engring. News Record Constrn. Claims Conf., 1991. Author: Legal and Professional Aspects of Construction Management, 1990, The Year 2000 and Potential Liabilities and Otherwise, 1999, Litigating Year 2000 Cases, Chapter 8, Insurance Coverage, 1999, Practical Environmental Forensics--Process and Case Histories, 2000; contbr. chpt.: Data Security and Privacy Law-Combatting Cyberthreats, The West Group, 2002; contbr. articles to profl. jours. Mem. ABA (forum com. on constrn. industry 1989, tort and ins. practice sect. 1985—), NY State Bar Assn., NJ Bar Assn., Fla. Bar Assn., Fedn. Def. and Corp. Counsel (spkr. The Millennium Bug ins. coverage sect., vice chair tech. and e-commerce sect., chair tech. com., v.p. 2004—), Def. Rsch. Inst., Assn. Def. Trial Atty. Office: 100 Metroplex Dr Ste 203 Edison NJ 08817 Office Phone: 732-985-1000. Personal E-mail: rtraub@tels.com.

**TRAUGER, ALETA ARTHUR,** judge; BA in English magna cum laude, Cornell Coll., Iowa, 1968; MAT, Vanderbilt U., 1972, JD, 1976. Tchr. Tenn., Eng., 1970-73; assoc., law clk. Barrett, Brandt & Barrett, P.C., Nashville, 1974-77; asst. U.S. atty., first asst., chief of criminal divsn. Mid. Dist. Tenn. 1977-82, No. Dist. Ill., 1979-80; assoc. Hollins, Wagster & Yarbrough, P.C., Nashville, 1983-84; legal counsel Coll. of Charleston, SC, 1984-85; counsel, ptnr. Wyatt, Tarrant, Combs, Gilbert & Milom, Nashville, 1985-91; judge Tenn. Ct. of the Judiciary, 1987-93; chief of staff Mayor's Office, Nashville, 1991-92; bankruptcy judge U.S. Bankruptcy Ct. (mid. dist.) Tenn., Nashville, 1993-98; dist. judge U.S. Dist. Ct. (mid. dist.) Tenn., Nashville, 1998—. Mem. hearing panel bd. profl. responsibility Tenn. Supreme Ct., 1983-84, mem. adv. com. on rules of civil and appellate procedure, 1989-96; lectr. Vanderbilt U. Sch. Law, 1986-88, mem. Law Sch. alumni bd., 1989-92; master of bench Harry Phillips Am. Inn of Ct., 1990-94; mem. Internat. Women's Forum, 1993—, v.p. Tenn. chpt., 1996-97; mem. Nat. Conf. Bankruptcy Judges, 1994-98, chmn. ethics com., 1994-98; trustee Cornell Coll., 1998—. Bd. dirs. Nashville Inst. for Arts, 1992-99, Miriam's Promise (adoption agy.), 1995-98, Renewal House, 1996-98, bd. trustees Cornell Coll, 1998—, mem. Vanderbilt Law Sch. Nat. Coun., 2004—. Fellow: Nashville Bar Found., Tenn. Bar Found. (life), Am. Bar Found. (life); mem.: FBA (v.p. 1983—84, 1985—86), ABA, Fed. Judges Assn., Nat. Assn. Women Judges (liaison to ABA commn. on the status of women in the profession 2000—01), Tenn. Lawyers Assn. for Women (v.p. 1988—89, pres. 1989—90, bd. dirs. 1990—91), Lawyers Assn. for Women (pres. 1982—83, bd. dirs. 1983—84, 1986—88), Nashville Bar Assn. (bd. dirs. 1984, 1989—91). Office: 825 US Courthouse 801 Broadway Nashville TN 37203-3816

**TRAUGER, DONALD BYRON,** nuclear engineer, lab administrator; b. Exeter, Nebr., June 29, 1920; s. Charles C. and Ethel L. (Downey) T.; m. Elaine Causey, Sept. 2, 1945; children: Byron Roscoe, Thomas Charles. AB, Nebr. Wesleyan U., 1942, D.Sc. (hon.), 1974; postgrad., Columbia U., 1942-46, U. Tenn., 1946-49; D.Sc. (hon.), Tenn. Wesleyan Coll., 1977. Supr. test equipment devel. Manhattan Dist. Project, 1942-46; supr. Devel. Lab. Oak Ridge Gaseous Diffusion Plant, 1946-54, with Oak Ridge Nat. Lab., 1954-93, assoc. dir. nuclear and engring. technologies, 1970-84, sr. staff asst. to dir., 1984-93; cons. in energy tech., 1993—. Author: Horse Power to Nuclear Power, 2002; editl. advisor Anns. Nuclear Engring, 1973—; design features editor sect. IV Nuclear Safety Jour., 1989-98. Mem. Oak Ridge Bd. Edn., 1961-67; pres. Oak Ridge PTA Coun., 1969-70, Oak Ridge Parents Adv. Coun., 1958-59; chmn. exec. com., trustee Tenn. Wesleyan Coll., 1976-81, chmn. bd. govs., 1986-90, chmn. bd. trustees, 1990-93. Recipient Alumni Achievement award Nebr. Wesleyan U., 1962 Fellow Am. Nuclear Soc. (chmn. planning com. 1981-83); mem. AAAS, Am. Phys. Soc., Rotary, Sigma Xi (pres. Oak Ridge chpt. 1987-88), Sigma Pi Sigma. Methodist. Office Phone: 865-483-1006. Personal E-mail: dbtrauger@aol.com.

**TRAUGOTT, ELIZABETH CLOSS,** linguist, educator, researcher; b. Bristol, Eng., Apr. 9, 1939; d. August and Hannah M. M. (Priebsch) Closs; m. John L. Traugott, Sept. 26, 1967; 1 child, Isabel. BA in English, Oxford U., Eng., 1960; PhD in English lang., U. Calif., Berkeley, 1964. Asst. prof. English U. Calif., Berkeley, 1964-70; lectr. U. East Africa, Tanzania, 1965-66, U. York, Eng., 1966-67; lectr., then assoc. prof. linguistics and English Stanford (Calif.) U., 1970-77, prof., 1977—2003, chmn. linguistics dept., 1980-85, vice provost, dean grad. studies, 1985-91, mem. grad. record examinations bd., 1989-93, mem. test of English as a fgn. lang. bd., 1990—92, chmn. test of English as a fgn. lang. bd., 1991—92. Mem. higher edn. funding coun. Edn. Assessment Panel, 1996, 2001. Author: (book) A History of English Syntax, 1972; author: (with Mary Pratt) Linguistics for Students of Literature, 1980; author: (with Paul Hopper) Grammaticalization, 1993, rev. edit., 2003; author: (with Richard Dasher) Regularity in Semantic Change, 2002; editor (with ter Meulen, Reilly, Ferguson): On Conditionals, 1986; author (with Laurel J. Brinton): Lexicalization and Language Change, 2005; editor (with Heine): (book) Approaches to Grammaticalization, 2 vols., 1991; series co-editor: Topics in English Linguistics; contbr. articles to profl. jours. Am. Coun. Learned Socs. fellow, 1975—76, Guggenheim fellow, 1983—84, Ctr. Advanced Study Behavioral Scis. fellow, 1983—84. Fellow: AAAS; mem.: AAUW, AAUP, MLA, Internat. Pragmatics Assn. (bd. dirs. 2000—), Internat. Soc. Hist. Linguistic (pres. 1979—81), Linguistic Soc. Am. (pres. 1987, sec.-treas. 1994—98). Office: Stanford Univ Dept Linguistics Bldg 460 Stanford CA 94305-2150 Business E-Mail: traugott@stanford.edu.

**TRAUNER, DIRK,** science educator; b. Linz, Austria, Apr. 17, 1967; s. Dietrich and Helga Trauner. PhD, U. Vienna, Austria. Asst. prof. U. Calif., Berkeley, 2000—06. Fellow, Sloan-Kettering Inst. Cancer Rsch., NYC, 1998—2000. Office: U Calif 602 Latimer Hall Berkeley CA 94720-1460 Office Phone: 510-643-5507. Office Fax: 510-643-9480. E-mail: trauner@berkeley.edu.

**TRAURIG, ROBERT HENRY,** lawyer; b. Waterbury, Conn., June 9, 1925; s. Samuel and Lillian (Rosengarten) T.; m. Jacqueline Block; children: Madeline Traurig Sackel, Wendy Traurig Perlin. Student, U. Fla.; BBA, U. Miami, Fla., 1947, LLB, 1950. Bar: Fla. 1950, U.S. Dist. Ct. Fla. 1950. Co-founder, ptnr., shareholder environ. land devel. Greenberg, Traurig LLP, (formerly Greenberg Traurig, Hoffman, Lipoff, Rosen & Quentel, P.A.), Miami, 1967—. Pres. Greater Miami Opera, 1987-89. Lt. USNR, 1943-46, 51-52. Named one of 100 Most Powerful People in Miami, Miami Bus. mag., 2001; recipient Friend of Israel Humanitarian award, Greater Miami Jewish Fedn., 2003. Mem. Greater Miami C. of C. (chmn.). Democrat. Jewish. Avocation: avid sports spectator. Office: Greenberg Traurig LLP 1221 Brickell Ave Miami FL 33131-3224 Office Phone: 305-579-0500. Office Fax: 305-579-0717. Business E-Mail: traurigr@gtlaw.com.

**TRAUSCH, THOMAS VINCENT,** art educator, artist; b. Chgo., Sept. 4, 1943; s. Joseph Aloyisius and Frances Cecilia Trausch; m. Gale Lynn Gunter; 1 child, Camille Leigh. BFA, U. Ill., 1966. Asst. photographer Hedrich-Blessing, Chgo., 1972—75; profl. fine artist, Algonquin Ill., 1975—. Nat. and internat. workshop instr., 2000—. Co-author (also illustrator): Opera House Sketch Book, 1988. Spec. 5 U.S. Army, 1967—69. Master: Transparent Watercolor Soc. Am. Roman Catholic. Avocations: travel, photography. Studio: 116 E Calhoun St (Rear) Woodstock IL 60098 Office Phone: 815-245-0819. Business E-Mail: thomas@trauschfinearts.com.

**TRAUTH, JOSEPH LOUIS, JR.,** lawyer; b. Cin., Apr. 22, 1945; s. Joseph L. and Margaret (Walter) Trauth; m. Barbara Widmeyer, July 4, 1970; children: Jennifer, Joseph III, Jonathan, Braden, Maria. BS in Econs., Xavier U., 1967; JD, U. Cin., 1973. Bar: Ohio 1973, U.S. Dist. Ct. (so. dist.) Ohio 1973, U.S. Ct. Appeals (6th cir.) 1973, U.S. Supreme Ct. 1988, Ky. 2000. Ptnr. Keating, Muething & Klekamp, PLL, Cin., 1973-80, Keating, Muething & Klekamp, Cin., 1980—. Spkr. real estate law, 1974—. Contbr. articles to profl. jours. Mem. Parish Coun., Cin., 1990. Mem.: Cin. Bar Assn. (mem. grievance com., mem. real estate com., mem. negligence com.). Roman Catholic. Avocations: tennis, reading. Office: Keating Muething & Klekamp 1400 Provident Tower 1 E 4th St Ste 1400 Cincinnati OH 45202-3717 Office Phone: 513-579-6515. E-mail: jtrauth@kmklaw.com.

**TRAUTMAN, DONALD W.,** bishop; b. Buffalo, June 24, 1936; Student, Our Lady Angels Sem., Niagara Falls, NY, Theology Faculty, Innsbruck, Austria, Pontifical Biblical Inst., Rome, Cath. U., St. Thomas Aquinas U., Rome. Ordained priest Roman Cath. Ch., 1962, consecrated bishop Roman Cath. Ch., 1985. Titular bishop of Sassura and aux. bishop Diocese of Buffalo, 1985; bishop, Erie, Pa., 1990—. Past mem. Prolife com. doctrine and migration Nat. Conf. Home: 205 W 9th St Erie PA 16501-1304 Address: 429 E Granview Blvd Erie PA 16514-0397

**TRAUTMAN, MARK ALLEN,** conductor; b. Leonardtown, Md., Mar. 24, 1960; s. Robert and Priscilla Hannen Trautman; 1 child, David. BS, Towson U., 1993; MusM, Westminster Choir Coll., 1995. Dir. music, organist Epiphany Ch., Timonium, Md., 1991—93, Christ Ch., New Brunswick, NJ, 1994—. Adj. prof. music New Brunswick Theological Seminary, New Brunswick, NJ, 1999—. Mason Gross Sch., New Brunswick, NJ, 2003—. Mem.: New Brunswick Arts Coun., Episc. Diocese of NJ Liturgy and Music Comm. (former co-chair), Pi Kappa Lambda. Office: Christ Ch 5 Paterson St New Brunswick NJ 08901 Office Phone: 732-545-6262. Office Fax: 732-545-6264. E-mail: musicatchristchurch@yahoo.com.

**TRAUTMAN, WILLIAM ELLSWORTH,** lawyer; b. San Francisco, Nov. 27, 1940; s. Gerald H. and Doris Joy (Tucker) T.; m. Dorothy (Williamson), June 17, 1962; children: Darcey, Torey. BA, U. Calif., Berkeley, 1962, LLB, 1965. Bar: Calif. 1965, U.S. Supreme Ct., Calif. Dist. Ct., U.S. Ct. Appeals (9th and Fed. Cir.). Assoc. Chickering and Gregory, San Francisco, 1965-71, ptnr., 1972-81, Brobeck, Phleger, and Harrison, San Francisco, 1981—2003, litig. dept. chair, 1984-91, San Francisco mng. ptnr., 1992-96; ptnr. Morgan, Lewis, and Bockius, San Francisco, 2003—05; pvt. practice San Francisco, 2005—. Pres. Oakland, Calif. Mus. Assn., 1981-83; mem. profl. ethics com. State Bar Calif., 1974-77. Fellow: Am. Coll. Trial Lawyers; mem.: Barrister's Club of San Francisco (pres. 1973), Calif. Barristers (bd. dirs., v.p.), Bar Assn. San Francisco (bd. dirs. 1972—73), Legal Aid Soc. (bd. dirs. 1982—93, pres. 1985—88)), U. Calif.-Berkeley Found. (trustee 1998—2000), Boalt Hall Alumni Assn. (bd. dirs. 1993—99, pres. 1997—98). Business E-Mail: trautman17@sbcglobal.net.

**TRAUTMANN, NANCY MORTON,** science educator, writer; b. Rochester, NY, Oct. 10, 1953; d. John Henderson and Ruth Irland Morton; m. Charles Home Trautmann, Jan. 6, 1952; children: Nina Morton, Eric Morton. BA, Hampshire Coll., Amherst, Mass., 1975; MS, Cornell U., Ithaca, NY, 1981, PhD, 2005. Environ. cons. Earth Metrics, Inc., Mountain View, Calif., 1975—76; planner New Eng. River Basins Commn., Boston, 1976—78; water resources specialist NYS Water Resources Inst., Ithaca, NY, 1981—92; dir. environ. inquiry program Cornell U., 1997—, coord. program environ. scis. educators and youth. Dir. Cornell Sci. Inquiry Partnerships, 2000—; vis. scientist Tech. U. Munich, 1987—88; cons. in field. Author: (text books) Decay and Renewal, Assessing Toxic Risk, Composting in the Classroom; co-author: Watershed Dynamics, Invasion Ecology, (sci. textbook) Ecological Roles, Energy and Matter in Ecosystems. Grantee, NSF, 2000—06, 2006—. Mem.: Nat. Sci. Tchrs. Assn., Am. Inst. Biol. Scis., Ecol. Soc. Am. Achievements include design of educational websites that have received multiple awards. Office: Cornell University 100 Rice Hall Ithaca NY 14853 Office Phone: 607-255-9257. Office Fax: 607-255-0349.

**TRAUTMANN, THOMAS ROGER,** history professor, anthropology educator; b. Madison, Wis., May 27, 1940; s. Milton and Esther Florence (Trachte) T.; m. Marcella Hauoliilani Choy, Sept. 25, 1962; children: Theodore William, Robert Arthur. BA, Beloit Coll., 1962; PhD, U. London, 1968. Lectr. in history Sch. Oriental and African Studies, U. London, 1965-68; asst. prof. history U. Mich., Ann Arbor, 1968-71, assoc. prof., 1971-77, prof., 1977—; Richard Hudson rsch. prof., 1979, prof. history and anthropology, 1984—; chmn. dept. history, 1987-90, Steelcase rsch. prof., 1993-94, dir. Interdisciplinary Program, 2001. Author: Kautilya and the Arthasastra, 1971, Dravidian Kinship, 1981, Lewis Henry Morgan and the Invention of Kinship, 1987; author: (edit. with Diane Owen Hughes) Time: Histories and Ethnologies, 1995, Aryans and British India, 1997; author: (edit. with Maurice Godelier and Franklin Tjon Sie Fat) Transformations of Kinship, 1999; editor: Comparative Studies in Society and History, 1997—; contbr. articles on India, kinship and history of anthropology;: The Aryan Debate, 2005. Sr. Humanist fellow NEH, 1984. Mem. Am. Anthrop. Assn., Assn. Asian Studies, Am. Inst. Indian Studies (mem. exec. com. trustee, sr. rsch. fellow in India 1985, 97), Phi Beta Kappa. Office: U Mich Dept History Ann Arbor MI 48109-1003

**TRAUTNER, JOHN JAMES,** real estate executive; b. Simpson, Minn., Dec. 4, 1959; s. John Sylvester and Oridena Francis (Baker) T.; m. Donna L. Jones, June 1960 (div. Dec. 1969); children: Theresa, Carrie, John; m. Carol Lee Rowberry, July 12, 1974 (div. May 1981); 1 child, Lindsey D.; m. Kathy N. Bucy, July 19, 1992; 1 stepchild, Victor. BA, Anchorage C.C., 1968; BBA, U. Alaska, 1970, MBA, 1998. Masters lic. 100 ton U.S. Coast Guard, lic. comml. pilot. Adminstr., pub. affairs RCA Svc. Co., Anchorage, 1965-70; dir. adminstrn. & pub. rels. Alaska Resort, Inc., Girdwood, 1970-71; mgmt. cons. State of Alaska, 1972-73; exec. dir. City of Lost River (Alaska), 1973-74; v.p.,

gen. mgr. C. Bruce Ficke Investments, Girdwood, 1974-76; pres., gen. mgr. Gateway, Inc., Girdwood, 1976-85; CEO Alyeska Mgmt. Svcs., Inc., Girdwood, 1985—. Mem. MD49 Coun. Govs., Fairbanks, Alaska, 1996-97, chmn., 1999-2000; marriage commr. 3d Jud. Dist., Anchorage, 1973-93. Patentee in field. Chmn., mem. Girdwood Bd. Suprs., 1992-95; fire chief Girdwood Fire Dept., 1972-75; chmn. Girdwood Cmty. Coun., 1976-78, Jr.-Inter-Fraternity Coun., Seattle, 1957-58. Sgt. U.S. Army, 1953-64. Melvin Jones fellow, chgo., 1993-94. Mem. N.Am. Nature Photographers Assn., Am. Legion, Lions, Disabled VFW, Alaska Airmens Assn., San Francisco Tennis Club. Republican. Roman Catholic. Avocations: photography, music, art, humanitarianism, flying. Office: Alyeska Mgmt Svcs Inc PO Box 909 Girdwood AK 99587-0909 E-mail: outsidermining@msn.com.

**TRAUTWEIN, GEORGE WILLIAM,** conductor, violinist, educator; b. Chgo., Aug. 5, 1927; s. William Jacob and Hilda (Martin) T.; m. Barbara Wilson, Jan. 20, 1955; children: Paul Martin, Matthew Richard. MusB, Oberlin Conservatory, Ohio, 1951; MusM, Cleve. Inst. Music, 1955; MusD, Ind. U., Bloomington, 1961. Mem. faculty U. Minn., U. Tex., Austin, Armstrong (Ga.) State Coll.; arts cons. Nat. Endowment Arts; dir. internat. study program for Wake Forest U. at Tokai U., Japan, 1995. Violinist Indpls. Symphony Orch., 1946-48, Balt. Symphony Orch., 1951-52, Nat. Symphony Orch., Washington, 1952-53, Cleve. Orch., 1953-57, Chautauqua Symphony Orch., N.Y., 1953-59, Camerata Acad., Salzburg, 1957-58, Mozarteum Orch., Salzburg, 1958 (Fulbright grantee 1958), assoc. condr. Dallas Symphony Orch., 1962-66, Mpls. Symphony, 1966-73; music dir. S.D. Symphony, 1971-75, Internat. Congress Strings, Ohio, 1973-75; music dir., condr. Savannah (Ga.) Symphony Orch., 1974-77; music adv., prin. guest condr. Evansville (Ind.) Philharm., 1979-80; music dir., condr. RIAS Edn. Network, Berlin, 1978, Tucson Symphony Orch., 1977-81; artistic dir., condr. Piedmont Chamber Orch.; prin. condr. Internat. Music program; dir. orchestral programs, N.C. Sch. of Arts, 1981-83; dir. instrumental ensembles, Wake Forest U., 1983-96; dir. Artists Series, 1985-98; guest appearances with orchs., U.S., Germany, Sweden, France, Romania, Jugoslavia, Portugal, Hong Kong, India, P.R., Mex. Adv. bd. Avery Fisher Found.; N.Y.C. Served with USN, 1948-49. Recipient Orpheus award Phi Mu Alpha, 1971, ASCAP award, 1979, 82, World Peace award Ministry of World Harmony, 1983; Fulbright grantee Mozarteum, Salzburg, 1958; Sr. Fulbright lectr., India, 1989-90. Mem. Am. Fedn. Musicians, Chamber Music Soc. Am., Sir Thomas Beecham Soc., Literacy Initiative Assn., Condrs. Guild Am. Avocations: music, art reproduction, poetry, literature. Office: Wake Forest U PO Box 7411 Winston Salem NC 27109-7411 Office Phone: 336-896-1169. Business E-Mail: trautweg@wfu.edu.

**TRAVAGLI, RENATO ALBERTO,** neuroscientist, researcher; b. Milano, Italy, May 7, 1959; s. Cesare Mario Travagli and Zoraide Negrini. PhD, Georgetown U., Washington, 1993; Laurea, Universita' di Ferrara, Italy, 1985. Rsch. scientist Fidia Pharms., Abano Terme, Padova, Italy, 1986—93; postdoctoral fellow Vollum Inst- OHSU, Portland, 1993—95; res. asst prof W. Va. U., Morgantown, 1995—97; asst prof HFHSC, Detroit, 1997—2000; assoc prof U. Mich., Ann Arbor, 2001—04; prof. Pennington Biomed. Rsch. Ctr., Baton Rouge, 2004—. Grantee Rsch. grantee, NIH, 1998—, NSF, 1999—. Mem.: Am. Gastroent. Assn., Soc. for the Neurosci. Office: Pennington Biomedical Research Center- 6400 Perkins Rd Baton Rouge LA 70808 Office Phone: +1-225-763-3042. E-mail: alberto.travagli@pbrc.edu.

**TRAVERS, ANDREW ROBERT,** music educator, musician; b. Norfolk, Va., July 13, 1979; s. Henry Travers and Mary Kay Fausch; m. Maria Louise Denk, Oct. 28, 2006. BSBA, U. of Conn., 2002. Secondary Music Nev., 2006. Sect. cello Las Vegas Philharm., 2002—; cello coach Las Vegas Youth Orchs., Las Vegas, 2004—. Home: 5897 Alcott Ave Las Vegas NV 89142 Office: B Mahlon Brown Jr HS 307 N Cannes St Henderson NV 89015 Office Phone: 702-799-8900. Office Fax: 702-799-3511. Personal E-mail: dracul1@cox.net. E-mail: artravers@interact.ccsd.net.

**TRAVERS, JAMES M.,** application developer; Grad., Pa. State U. Various managerial positions Tex. Instruments, Inc., 1978-94; pres., gen. mgr. Harbinger Corp., Atlanta, 1995-98, pres., chief oper. officer, 1998—. Office: Harbinger Corp 11720 Amberpark Dr Ste 100 Alpharetta GA 30004-2271

**TRAVERS, JASON ERIC,** art educator, artist; MFA, U. Pa., 1998; BA, Moravian Coll., 1994. Prof. Lehigh U., Bethlehem, Pa., 1999—, Kutztown (Pa.) U., 2000—. Exhibitions include Jason Travers: Recent Paintings, one-man shows include Northeast Biennial, 2003 (Best in Show award, 2003), David E. Rodale Gallery, Allentown, Pa., 2005, U. Scranton, Pa., 2005. Mem.: Coll. Art Assn. (assoc.). Office: Lehigh Univ Dept Art and Arch 17 Memorial Dr E Bethlehem PA 18015-3007 Personal E-Mail: jasontravers@earthlink.net.

**TRAVERS, JUDITH LYNNETTE,** human resources executive; b. Buffalo, Feb. 25, 1950; d. Harold Elwin and Dorothy (Helsel) Howes; m. David Jon Travers, Oct. 21, 1972; 1 child, Heather Lynne. BA in Psychology, Barrington Coll., 1972; cert. in paralegal course, St. Mary's Coll., Moraga, Calif., 1983; postgrad., Southland U., 1982-84. Exec. sec. Sherman C. Weeks, P.A., Derry, N.H., 1973-75; legal asst. Mason-McDuffie Co., Berkeley, Calif., 1975-82; paralegal asst. Blum, Kay, Merkle & Kauftheil, Oakland, Calif., 1982-83; CEO, bd. dirs. Dela Pers Svcs. Inc., Concord, Calif., 1983—; pres. All Ages Sitters Agy., Concord, 1986-95; CEO, bd. dirs. Guardian Security Agy., Concord, Calif., 1992—. Sec., bd. dirs. Per Diem Staffing Systems, Inc., Securicorp. Vocalist record album The Loved Ones, 1978. Vol. local Congl. campaign, 1980, Circle of Friends, Children's Hosp. No. Calif., Oakland, 1987—; mem. Alameda County Sheriff's Mounted Posse, 1989, Contra Costa Child Abuse Prevention Coun., 1989; employer adv. coun. Ctrl. Contra Costa County, 1993—; mem. Carondelet/De La Salle H.S. Adult Choir, 1998—. Recipient Outstanding Achievement in Amateur Photography award, Internat. Soc. Photographers, 2004. Mem. NAFE, Am. Assn. Respiratory Therapy, Soc. for Human Resource Mgmt., Am. Mgmt. Assn., Gospel Music Assn., Palomino Horse Breeders Am., DAR, Barrington Oratorio Soc., Commonwealth Club Calif., Nat. Trust Hist. Preservation, Alpha Theta Sigma. Republican. Baptist. Avocations: boating, horses. Home: 3900 Brown Rd Oakley CA 94561-2664 Office: Delta Pers Svcs Inc 1820 Galindo St Ste 3 Concord CA 94520-2447 Office Phone: 925-356-3050. Personal E-mail: jltravers@aol.com.

**TRAVERS, PAUL,** company executive; With Strand Hotels Ltd., Grand Met. Group; fin. dir. Europe Inter-Continental Hotels and Resorts, fin. dir. Forum Hotels, v.p. fin. Middle East and Africa, sr. v.p., group fin. contr., sr. v.p. property mgmt.; CFO REZsolutions, Inc., until 1999; pres. REZsolutions Hospitality Group. Office: Pegasus Solutions 14000 N Pima Rd 100 Scottsdale AZ 85260-3603

**TRAVERSE, LYN D.,** not-for-profit fundraiser, communications executive; b. Kalamazoo, Mich., May 7, 1952; d. Robert Clinton Traverse and Betty Larue Kemp; m. Jonathan G. Tidd (div.); 1 child, Emily. Student, NYU, 1970—74; BA, U. Conn., 1996. Devel. officer NYU, NYC, 1974—80, U. Hartford, Conn., 1980—83; dir. devel. and comms. Forman Sch., Litchfield, Conn., 1983—88, Ethel Walker Sch., Simsbury, Conn., 1988—96, The Nature Conservancy, Middletown, Conn., 1996—2000, Long Wharf Theatre, New Haven, 2000—03, Haskins Labs., New Haven, 2003—06; campaign dir. Friends Sem., NYC, 2006—. Trustee U. Hartford Art, West Hartford, Conn., 1999—; trustee, treas. Endangered Lang. Fund, New Haven, 2004—. Actor: (films) Plainsong, 1983. Mem. patrons bd. New Haven Free Pub. Libr., 2004—; mem. steering com. Simsbury (Conn.) Land Trust, 1999—2002. Mem.: Alpha Sigma Lamda. Office: Friends Seminary 222 E 16th St New York NY 10003

**TRAVI, JASON,** chef; m. Miho Travi. Grad., Culinary Inst. Am., Hyde Park, NY. Cook Granita, Malibu, Calif., Spago Beverly Hills, 2000; chef Opaline; exec. chef La Terza, LA. Named one of LA's Rising Stars, StarChefs.com, 2006.*

**TRAVIS, ALBERT HARTMAN,** retired ancient language educator; b. LA, Dec. 22, 1913; s. Hartman Porter and Adelaide (Ball) Travis; m. Lucile A. Diehl, May 8, 1938; m. Barbara Brown Bettingen, Jan. 25, 1957. BA, U. So. Calif., 1936; MA, Harvard U., 1938; PhD, 1940. Instr. Greek and Latin Harvard and Radcliffe Coll., 1940—42; asst. prof. U. So. Calif., 1946—47; mem. faculty UCLA, 1947—76, prof. classics, 1959—76, prof. emeritus, 1976—, chmn. dept. classics 1954—62, 1965—68, acting chmn., 1975—76. Co-editor: Servianorum in Vergilii Carmina Commentariorum, Vol. III, 1965, U. Calif. Studies in Classical Antiquity, vol. IV, 1971—72, 1972; contbr. articles to profl. jours. Lt. comdr. USNR, 1942—46. Decorated Bronze Star with combat V; recipient Unit citations, Pres. Mem.: Renaissance Conf. So. Calif., Mediaeval Assn. Pacific, Mediaeval Acad. Am., Calif. Classical Assn., Philol. Assn. Pacific Coast, Archaeol. Inst. Am., Am. Philol. Assn., Kappa Alpha, Phi Kappa Phi, Phi Beta Kappa. Home: 1166 Mill Ln San Marino CA 91108

**TRAVIS, FRED THOMAS,** dean, director; b. Binghamton, N.Y., July 5, 1950; s. Arthur James and Nancy Lee Travis; m. Nita Lorraine Travis, May 15, 1976; children: Dariana, Joella, Avery. BSc in Design and Environ. Analysis, Cornell U., 1976; MSc in Psychology, Maharishi U., Fairfield, 1986; PhD in Psychology, Maharishi U., 1988. Postdoctoral rschr. sleep rsch. U. Calif., Davis, Calif., 1988—90; dir. Maharishi U., 1990—, dean grad. sch., 1990—. Chair psychology Maharishi U., 1995—2002, chair, 2002—, sr. rsch. scientist, 2000—. Contbr. scientific papers to profl. jour. Tchr. Maharishi Vedi Edn. Devel., 1973—. Recipient Best Edn. Video, 1999, Best Ednl. Web page, 1999. Mem.: Soc. for psychol. rsch. Office Phone: 641-472-7000.

**TRAVIS, GRANT CARNER,** lawyer; b. Cin., Sept. 24, 1969; BS in Polit. sci., N.Y. Inst. Tech., Old Westbury, 1992; JD, Duquesne U., Pitts., 1995. Bar: Pa. 1995, U.S. Dist. Ct. (we. dist.) Pa. 1995, Erie County, Pa. Ct. of Pleas 1995. Law clk. Conner & Riley, Erie, Pa., 1993—95, atty., 1995—99; pvt. practice The Travis Law Firm, Edinboro and Erie, 1999—. Bd. dirs. Erie County YMCA, Edinboro, 2000—, pres. bd. dirs., 2001—. Mem.: ATLA, Pa. Trial Lawyers Assn. (bd. govs. 2001—), We. Pa. Trial Lawyers Assn. (bd. govs. 1998—), Nat. Assn. Criminal Def. Lawyers, Pa. Assn. Criminal Def. Lawyers, Erie County Bar Assn. (Spkrs. Bur. 1999—), Pa. Bar Assn. Office: The Travis Law Firm Travis Law Bldg 102 Lorna Ln Edinboro PA 16412

**TRAVIS, JEREMY,** academic administrator; b. Worcester, Mass., July 31, 1948; BA in Am. studies cum laude, Yale Coll., 1970; MPA, NYU, 1997, JD cum laude, 1982. Exec. dir. victim/witness assistance project Vera Inst. Justice, 1977—77; exec. dir. NYC Criminal Justice Agy., 1977—79; cons. NYC Bd. Correction, 1979—82; law clk. to Hon. Ruth Bader Ginsburg US Ct. Appeals (DC Cir.), 1982—83; spl. counsel to police commr. NYC Police Dept., 1984—86; spl. counsel to first dep. mayor and asst. dir. law enforcement services, Mayor's Office of Ops. City of NY, 1986, spl. advisor to mayor, 1986—89; chief counsel to subcommittee on criminal justice U.S. Ho. of Reps. Com. on the Judiciary, Washington, 1990; dep. commr. legal matters NYC Police Dept., 1990—94; dir. Nat. Inst. Justice, US Dept. Justice, Washington, 1994—2000; sr. fellow Justice Policy Ctr., The Urban Inst., Washington, 2000—04; pres. John Jay Coll. of Criminal Justice CUNY, 2004—. Vis. lectr. Yale Coll., 1979; adj. prof. Wagner Grad. Sch. Pub. Svc., NYU, 1985-90; adj. assoc. prof., NY Law Sch., 1992-94; vis. prof., George Washington U., 2004; nat. adv. bd., program on State Crime Prevention Initiatives, Nat. Crime Prevention Coun., 2001-, Join Together program, Robert Wood Johnson Found., 2001-, Nat. H.I.R.E. Network, Legal Action Ctr., 2001-, Ctr. for Rsch. on Criminal and Mental Health, Rutgers U., 2002-; nat. adv. com. on Reclaiming Futures, Robert Wood Johnson Found., 2000-; adv. bd., Ctr. for Cmty. Safety, Winston-Salem State U., 2001-; Aspen Inst. Roundtable on Comprehensive Cmty. Initiatives, 1999-. Rockefeller Fellow, Yale Div. Sch., 1970-71; Marden and Marshall Fellow in Criminal Law, NYU Sch. Law, 1983-84; recipient Disting. Alumnus Award, NYU, 1986, Outstanding Pub. Svc. Award, NY County Lawyers Com., 1992, Edmund S. Randolph Award, US Atty. Gen., 2000, August Vollmer Award, Am. Soc. Criminology, 2002, Gerhard O.W. Mueller Award, Internat. Sect., Acad. Criminal Justice Sciences, 2003, Margaret Meade Award, Internat. Cmty. Corrections Assn., 2003. Mem.: NY State Bar. Office: CUNY John Jay Coll Criminal Justice 899 Tenth Ave New York NY 10019

**TRAVIS, LAWRENCE ALLAN,** accountant; b. Bloomington, Ill., Sept. 17, 1942; s. Willard Burns and Florence May (Harvey) T.; m. Katy Quinones, Apr. 16, 1965 (div. Feb. 1978); children: Lawrence Allan Jr., Matthew E.; m. Kathleen Lucas, May 20, 1995. BS in Bus. Edn., Ill. State U., 1968; MA in Pub. Adminstrn., U. Ill., Springfield, 1976. CPA, Ill. Staff acct. Alexander Grant & Co., Chgo., 1969; internal auditor State Farm Ins., Bloomington, 1969-73; dep. dir. Ill. Dept. Ins., Springfield, 1973-74; audit mgr. Ill. Auditor Gen., Springfield, 1974-81; pres. Lawrence Travis & Co., P.C., CPAs, Virden, Normal, Springfield and Jacksonville, Ill., 1979—, also bd. dirs.; registered rep. Terra Securities, 1994—. Pres., bd. dirs. Travco, Inc., Virden; v.p., bd. dirs. Ka-Lar Enterprises, Inc., Springfield, Miller Comm., Inc. Mem. Ill. Common Cause, Springfield. Mem. AICPA, Assn. Govt. Accts., Ill. CPA Soc., Internat. Platform Assn., Nat. Space Soc., Smithsonian Assocs., World Future Soc. Democrat. Roman Catholic. Avocation: sports. Home: 2409 Idlewild Dr Springfield IL 62704-5403 Office: Lawrence Travis & Co PC 1700 S 1st St Springfield IL 62704-3902 E-mail: lawrencetraviscpa@insightbb.com

**TRAVIS, MARTIN BICE,** retired political scientist, educator; b. Iron Mountain, Mich., Sept. 22, 1917; s. Martin Bice and Helen (Carrett) T.; m. Olivia Brewster Taylor, Nov. 29, 1942; children: Elizabeth Nichols (Mrs. Usama Mugharbil), Helen Willard. AB, Amherst Coll., 1939; student, Heidelberg U., Germany, 1937; MA, Fletcher Sch. Law and Diplomacy, 1940; PhD, U. Chgo., 1948. Asst. prof. internat. relations Syracuse U., 1948-49; asst. prof. polit. sci. Duke U., 1949-52; asst. prof., then asso. prof. polit. sci. Stanford U., 1953-61; prof. polit. sci. SUNY-Stony Brook, 1961-92; coordinator SUNY Program Am. U., Beirut, 1972-73; chmn. dept., 1961-68; dir. Inst. Am. Studies SUNY-Stony Brook, 1965-93; ret., 1993. Vis. prof. Sch. Internat. Affairs, Columbia, 1956-57; vis. summer prof. U. Guadalajara, Mex., 1959, 62, U. Wash., 1961; Bd. dirs. State U N.Y. Inst. Am. Studies in France, 1966-77; cons. to industry. Author: (with E.E. Robinson) Powers of the President in Foreign Affairs, 1966; Co-editor, contbr.: (with Philip W. Buck) Control of Foreign Relations in Modern Nations, 1957; bd. editors: Western Polit. Quar. 1956-58; adv. bd.: Almanac of Current World Leaders, 1957—; editorial office for book pubs. Mem. sch. bd., Cold Spring Harbor, N.Y., 1965-71, v.p. 1967-68, pres. 1968-69; trustee Village of Laurel Hollow, 1983-95, police com., 1983-95, mayor, 1985-95; established Martin B. Travis Scholarship fund for pre-law majors at SUNY, Stonybrook, 1995. Grantee Ford Found. 1960-61; recipient Hugh Cleland Meml. Outstanding Prof. award Alumni Assn. SUNY Stony Brook, 2000. Mem. Coun. Fgn. Rels., Phi Delta Theta, Phi Delta Kappa. Home: 533 Cold Spring Rd Syosset NY 11791-1206 Office: Dept Polit Science Suny Stony Brook NY 11794-0001

**TRAVIS, MAUREEN ANN,** elementary school educator; d. Francis Joseph Reust and Mary Jane Toolen; m. James Russell Travis, Apr. 2, 1971; children: Joellyn Marie Bowman, Jessica Louise Powers. BS in Music Edn., Oakland U., Rochester, Mich., 1977; MEd, S.W. Mo. State U., Springfield, 1988. Cert. tchr. Tchr. Richland HS Sch. Mo., 1978—2004, Lebanon R3 Sch., Mo., 2004—. Mem. Fine Arts Task Force, Jefferson City, Mo., 2000—. Grantee, State of Mo., Lebanon Edn. Found., 2006. Mem.: Mo. Choral Dirs. Assn. (state v.p., dist. pres., treas. 1979—), Music Educators Nat. Conf., Mo. Choral Dirs. Assn. (Dir. of the Yr. 5C Dist.), Am. Choral Dirs. Assn., Lebanon Concert Assn.

**TRAVIS, MITCHELL G.,** secondary school educator; s. Morris E. and Mildred M. Travis; m. Marilyn J. Travis, Dec. 22, 1979; children: Nathan J., Laurel M. BA, U. No. Colo., Greeley, 1979; MA, Adams State Coll., Alamosa, Colo., 1983. Cert. tchr. English and drama. Tchr. South Park HS, Fairplay, Colo., 1979—89, Elizabeth HS, Colo., 1989—. Named Outstanding HS Tchr., Elizabeth HS, 2000, Tchr. of Month, 2001. Mem.: Colo. Lang. Arts Assn., Alliance Colo. Theatre (bd. dirs.), Nat. Coun. Tchrs. English. Office: PO Box 660 Elizabeth CO 80107 Business E-Mail: mtravis@esdk12.org.

**TRAVIS, NIGEL,** food service executive; b. Woodford, Essex, Eng. m. Joanna Travis; 2 children. BA with honors in Bus. Studies, Middlesex U., London. With Kraft, Rolls Royce, Massey Ferguson, Parker Hannifin, Grand Met.; sr. v.p. human resources Burger King, Miami, Fla., mng. dir. Europe, Mid. East and Africa, 1991; v.p. Europe to sr. v.p. Europe Blockbuster, 1994—97, pres. internat., 1997—98, pres. worldwide stores divsn., 1998—2001, pres., COO, 2001—05; exec. v.p. Papa John's, 2005, pres., CEO, bd. mem., 2005—. Office: Papa John's Internat Inc 2002 Papa Johns Blvd Louisville KY 40299-2334*

**TRAVIS, RANDALL HOWARD,** retired physiologist, retired endocrinologist; b. Curdsville, Ky., July 11, 1924; s. Charles Spaulding and Celestine Frances Travis; m. Priscilla Beryl Korabeck, June 24, 1949 (div.); m. Ilona Marie Engel, June 14, 1974; children: Randall Howard, Laura Jane. BS, U. Chgo.; MD, Western Res. U., 1948—52. Assoc. prof. Case Western Res. U., Physiology Dept., Cleve., 1968—85; asst. prof. dept. medicine Case Western Res. U., 1963—85; physician dept. medicine Copley Hosp., Morrisville, Vt., 1985—97. Assoc. physician, medicine Cleve. Met. Gen. Hosp., 1974—85. Contbr. articles to biomed. jours. Panel mem., reparations bd. Dept. of Corrections, Waterbury, Vt., 2000—03; adv. RSVP, Morrisville, Vt., 1996—2003, Sr. Companions Program, Barre, Vt., 2000—03. Sgt. USMC, 1943—46. Grantee Established Investigator, Am. Heart Assn., 1956-1959, Rsch. grants, NIH, 1959-1974. Mem.: AAAS, Endocrine Soc., Ctrl. Soc. for Clin. Rsch. (assoc.), Vt. Med. Soc. (life). Liberal. Avocations: boating, skiing, bicycling, hiking. Home: PO Box 553 Waterbury VT 05676 Personal E-mail: randalltravis@attglobal.net.

**TRAVIS, RANDY BRUCE,** musician; b. Monroe, N.C. 1959; married. Musician Country Music U.S.A., 1977-82, Nashville Palace, 1982-85; recording artist, 1986—. Rec. artist Warner Bros. Records, 1985-97, DreamWorks Records, 1997-2000, Inspirational Journey Warner Bros. and Atlantic Christian Music Divsn. (Dove award 2001), Word Records 2002-; albums include debut Storms of Life, 1986 (Album of Yr., Acad. Country Music, 1986, Song of Yr. for On the Other Hand, Acad. Country Music, 1986, Single of Yr. for On the Other Hand, Acad. Country Music, 1986, Single of Yr. for On the Other Hand, Music City News 1987, Album of Decade, BBC Radio Two, 1990), Always & Forever, 1987 (Best Country Record of Yr. for Forever and Ever, Amen, AMOA Jukebox, 1987, Single of Yr. for Forever and Ever, Amen, Acad. Country Music, Song of Yr. for Forever and Ever, Amen, Acad. Country Music, 1987, Album of Yr., Country Music Assn. 1987, Single of Yr. for Forever and Ever, Amen, Country Music Assn., 1987, Best Country Male Vocal Performance, Grammy award, 1987, Album of Yr., Country Music Round Up Internat. Awards, 1987, Single of Yr. for Forever and Ever, Amen, Music City News, 1988, Album of Yr., Music City News, 1988, Favorite Country Album, Am. Music Award, 1988, 89, Favorite Country Single for Forever and Ever, Amen, Am. Music Award, 1988, Favorite Country Video for Forever and Ever, Amen, Am. Music Award, 1988, Favorite Album, Nashville Network Viewers' Choice Awards, 1988, Favorite Video for Forever and Ever, Amen, Nashville Network Viewers' Choice Awards, 1988, Favorite Song for Forever and Ever, Amen, Nashville Network Viewers' Choice Awards, 1988, Favorite Country Album, World Music Award, 1988, Favorite Country Single for I Told You So, Am. Music Award, 1989), Old 8x10, 1988 (Best Male Country Vocal Performance, Grammy award, 1988, Favorite album, Nashville Network Viewers' Choice Awards, 1989, Favorite Country Single for Deeper Than the Holler, Am. Music Award, 1990, Favorite Country Album, 1990), No Holdin' Back, 1989 (Best Selling Country Album, NARM, 1989, award, AMPEX Golden Reel Awards, 1990, Country Record of Yr. for It's Just a Matter of Time, AMOA Jukebox, 1990), An Old Time Christmas, 1989, Heroes and Friends, 1990 (award, AMPEX Golden Reel Awards, 1991), High Lonesome, 1991, Greatest Hits Vol. 1, 1992, Greatest Hits Vol. 2, 1992 (#5 Video of Yr. for Look Heart No Hands, CMT Europe, 1993), Wind in the Wire, 1993, This is Me, 1994, Full Circle, 1996, You And Youa Alone, 1998, A Man Ain't Made of Stone, 1999, Inspirational Journey, 2000 (Bluegrass Album of Yr., Dove Award, 2001), Randy Travis Live, 2001 (Country Recorded Song of Yr. for Baptism, Dove Award, 2001), Anthology, 2002, Rise And Shine, 2002 (Country Album of Yr., Dove Award, 2003, Song of Yr. for Three Wooden Crosses, Christian Country Music Assn., 2003, Best So., Country, Bluegrass, Gospel Album, Grammy award, 2004, Country Recorded Song of Yr. for Three Wooden Crosses, Dove Award, 2004, Song of Yr. for Three Wooden Crosses, Acad. Country Music, 2004), Worship & Faith, 2003 (Country Album of Yr., Dove Award, 2004, Best So., Bluegrass, Gospel Album, Grammy award, 2005), Passing Through, 2004; song collaborator (with Alan Jackson) She's Got the Rhythm (And I Got the Blues), (Top Ten Songs of 1993, Music City News Country Songwriters Award, 1993), Same Old Train (Best Country Vocal Collaboration, Grammy award, 1998); film appearances include: Young Guns, 1988, Frank and Jesse, 1995, Wind in the Wire, 1993, 94, A Holiday to Remember, 1995, Outlaws (The Legend of O.B. Taggart), 1995, Edie & Pen, 1996, Boys Will Be Boys, 1996, The Shooter, 1997, Fire Down Below, 1997, Steel Chariots, 1997, The Rainmaker, 1997, Annabelle's Wish, 1997, T-N-T, 1998, Black Dog, 1998, Baby Geniuses, 1999, Boys Will Be Boys, 1998, Major Reno, 1999, Trial Of Old Drum, 2000, Casper's Haunted Christmas, 2000, The Million Dollar Kid, 2000, Texas Rangers, 2002, White River Kid, 2002, John John In The Sky, 2002, The Long Ride Home, 2003; (documentary series) Fathers of Our Country, 2000, A&E Biography, 2000; (TV Movie) A Holiday to Remember, 1995;(TV mini-series, video release) Texas, 1995; (TV series) Matlock, 1992, 93, Touched by an Angel, 1994, 95, 97, 2001, 03, Sabrina, 1996, Hey Arnold, 1998, King of the Hill, 2000, Blue's Clues, 2002; (TV movie, video) Dead Man's Revenge, 1994, At Risk, 1993; (TV spl.) Down Home, 1990, Happy Trails, 1990, At Risk, 1993. Named Top New Male Vocalist, Acad. Country Music, 1985, New Country Act of Yr., Performance Mag. 1986, Top Male Vocalist, Acad. Country Music, 1986, Male Vocalist, Acad. Country Music, 1987, Male Artist of Yr., Music City News, 1987, 88, Star of Tomorrow, Music City News, 1987, Male Vocalist of Yr., Music City News, 1987, 88, Most Popular Internat. Male Vocalist, Country Music Round Up Internat. Awards, 1987, 89, Favorite Nat. Artist, NECMA, 1987, Entertainer of Yr., Music City News, 1988, 89, Male Artist of Yr., Music City News, 1988, Favorite Entertainer, Nashville Network Viewers' Choice Awards, 1988, 89, Favorite Male Vocalist, Nashville Network Viewers' Choice Awards, 1988, Favorite Country Male Vocalist, Am. Music Award, 1988, 90, Male Vocalist for Country, Playboy Music Poll, 1988, 89, 90, 91, Artist of Yr., AMOA-Jukebox, 1989, Top Internat. Act, British Country Music Assn., 1989, Favorite Country Male Artist, Am. Music Award, 1989, Favorite Male Musical Performer, People's Choice Award, 1989, Best Country Artist, Rolling Stone Ann. Reader's Poll, 1989, 91, Country Act of Yr., Performance Mag., 1989, Favorite Country Artist, World Music Award, 1990, #1 Country Albums Artist, Billboard Music Award, 1990, Top Grossing Country Tour, Amusement Bus., 1990, Country Tour of Yr., Performance Mag., 1990, Favorite Country Music Performer, People's Choice Award, 1990, Internat. Artist, Country Music, People Mag. Internat. Awards, 1992, Mainstream Country Artist of Yr., Christian Country Music Assn., 2003; recipient Horizon award Country Music Assn., 1986, For Excellence in Media, Golden Angel Award, 1990, Star on Hollywood Walk of Fame, Hollywood C. of C., 2004. Mem. Grand Ole Opry. E-mail: traviscorp@home.com.

**TRAVIS, ROBERT M.,** lawyer; b. Lyons, Ga., Dec. 12, 1945; BA, Univ. NC, Chapel Hill, 1968; JD, Univ. Ga., 1972. Bar: Ga. 1972. Ptnr., chmn. Litig. Dept. Powell Goldstein LLP, Atlanta. Editor (assoc.): Ga. Law Rev. Vice chmn. bd., chmn. devel. com. YMCA, Ga.; mem. Episcopal Diocese Atlanta Registrar, 1988—90. Mem.: ABA, State Bar Ga., Def. Rsch. Inst., Ga. Def. Lawyers Assn. (pres.), Atlanta Bar Assn., Lawyers Club Atlanta, Bleckley Inns of Ct. (Master), Assn. Trial Lawyers Am. (assoc.), U. NC Alumni Assn. (life), YMCA (vice chmn. bd. Ga. chpt., chmn. devel. com.), Phi Delta Phi. Office: Powell Goldstein LLP 1 Atlantic Ctr 14th Fl 1201 W Peachtree St NW Atlanta GA 30309-3488 Office Phone: 404-572-6646. Office Fax: 404-572-6999. Business E-Mail: btravis@pogolaw.com.

**TRAVIS, SARAH,** orchestrator; Trained at City U.; trained at Guildhall Sch. Music and Drama, UK. Orchestrator, musical supervisor Mack & Mabel, Pinafore Swing, Fiddler on the Roof, Gondoliers, Ten Cents a Dance, Piaf and Carmen, Sweeney Todd, 2005 (Tony award, best orchestrations, 2006, Drama Desk award, outstanding orchestrations, 2006); composer: Peter Pan, A Star Danced, The Last Fattybottypuss in the World, Tales My Lover Told Me, A Womb With A View; pianist Fascinating Aida, Drop Dead Divas. Office: Eugene O'Neill Theatre 230 W 49th St New York NY 10036*

**TRAVIS, TONI-MICHELLE C.,** political scientist, educator; d. Mark E. and Ada Deans Chapman; m. Theodore W. Travis. BA, Bard Coll., Annandale-on-Hudson, N.Y., 1969; MA, U. Chgo., 1973, PhD, 1983. Asst. prof., govt. George Mason U., Fairfax, Va., 1984—90, asst. dean, Coll. Arts & Scis., 1993—95, host, prodr., Capital Region Roundtable, 1998—2002, assoc. prof., govt., 1990—2004; vis. prof. Simmons Coll., Boston, 1998—2000. Pres. Women's Caucus, Washington, 1994—95. Co-author: The Meaning of Difference, 1996; author: 4th edit., 2005; editor: (book series) Race and Politics, 1995—2002; co-editor: Virginia Almanac of Politics, 2005. Bd. mem. Make Women Count, Richmond, Va., 1998—2000; mem. Higher Edn. Group, Washington, 1997—2003. John Bard Scholar, Bard Coll., 1968, Ford Found Fellowship, U. Chgo., 1969—73. Mem.: Com. on Internat. Polit. Sci., Nat. Capital Area Polit. Sci. Assn. (pres. 1994—95), Am. Polit. Sci. Assn. (coun. mem. 1994—96, mem. com. on internat. polit. sci. 2003—), Fairfax Com. of 100. Avocation: walking. Office: Dept Pub and Internat Affairs George Mason Univ MS 3F4 4400 University Dr Fairfax VA 22030 Business E-Mail: ttravis@gmu.edu.

**TRAVIS, TRACY LEIGH,** emergency physician; b Lynchburg, Va., Aug. 27, 1957, d. Charles C. Jr. and Mildred (Lindsay) T.; m. David Stephens; children: Jennifer Koecke, Travis Stephens. BS in Biology, Lynchburg Coll., 1979; MD, Eastern Va. Med. Sch., 1982. Diplomate Am. Bd. Emergency Medicine. Resident Butterworth Hosp., Grand Rapids, Mich., 1987; emergency physician Mary Washington Hosp., Fredericksburg, Va., 1988-93, ExpressCare, Stafford, Va., 1992-96, Inova Emergency Care, Fairfax, Va., 1996—2002, Inova Fairfax Hosp., 1998—2002; med. dir. DEA Training Acad., Quantico, Va., 2002—. Fellow Am. Coll. Emergency Physicians; mem. Phi Kappa Phi. Home: 10856 Meadow Pond Ln Oakton VA 22124-1446 Office Phone: 703-632-5084. Personal E-mail: tltmd@aol.com.

**TRAVIS, VANCE KENNETH,** petroleum business executive; b. Coriander, Sask., Can., Jan. 30, 1926; s. Roy Hazen and Etta Orilla (Anderson) T.; m. Louise Mary, Nov. 30, 1948 (div. 1979); children: Stuart, Shirley, Gordon, Donald, Marian; m. Mildred Elaine, June 29, 1979; stepchildren: Susan, Nancy, Gordon, Sandra, Karen. Chmn. bd. Turbo Resources Ltd., 1970-83, Challenger Internat., 1977-83, Bankeno Mines Ltd., 1977-83, Queenston Gold Mines Ltd., Toronto, Ont., Canada, 1977-84, Health Risk Mgmt. Inc., Mpls., 1984-86, Triad Internat. Inc., 1985—96; dir. Health Resource Mgmt. Ltd., Edmonton, Alta., Canada, 1990-97. Bd. dirs. Vencap Equities Alta. Ltd., Edmonton, 1981-86, L.K. Resources Ltd., Calgary, 1973-84. Mem. Young Pres.'s Orgn., Calgary, 1964-76, World Pres. Orgn. Recipient Presdl. pin Jr. Achievement, 1963, Best Pitcher award Petroleum Fastball League, 1955. Mem.: Calgary Petroleum Club. E-mail: kentravis@telus.net.

**TRAVOLTA, JOHN,** actor; b. Englewood, N.J., Feb. 18, 1954; s. Salvatore and Helen (Burke) T.; m. Kelly Preston Sept. 12, 1991; children: Jett, Ella Bleu. Appeared in TV series Welcome Back Kotter, 1975-77; TV movies: The Boy in the Plastic Bubble, 1976, Chains of Gold, 1991, Eye of an Angel, 1991; films: Carrie, 1976, Saturday Night Fever, 1977 (Best Actor award Nat. Bd. Rev., 1977, Best Actor Acad. award nominee 1977, Best Actor 1st runner up Nat. Soc. Film Critics 1977, Best Actor 2nd runner up N.Y. Film Critics Circle 1977), Grease, 1978 (Golden Globe World Film Favorite 1978), Moment-By-Moment, 1978, Urban Cowboy, 1980, Blow Out, 1981, Staying Alive, 1983 (Male/Box Office Star of Yr., Nat. Assn. Theatre Owners Show East 1983), Two of a Kind, 1983, Perfect, 1985, The Dumb Waiter, 1987, The Experts, 1989, Look Who's Talking, 1989 (Male/Box Office Star of Yr., Nat. Assn. Theatre Owners ShowEast 1989), Look Who's Talking Too, 1990, The Tender, 1991, Shout, 1991, Look Who's Talking Now, 1993, Pulp Fiction, 1994 (Best Actor Acad. award nominee 1994, Best Actor award nominee Brit. Acad. Film and TV Arts 1994, Golden Globe Best Actor award nominee 1994, Best Actor award nominee SAG 1994, Best Actor award nominee Chgo. Film Critics 1994, Best Actor award nominee Comedy awards 1994, Best Actor award L.A. Film Critics 1994, Best Actor award Stockholm Film Festival 1993, Best Actor award London Film Critics Cir. 1994), Get Shorty, 1995, White Man's Burden, 1995, Broken Arrow, 1996, Phenomenon, 1996, Michael, 1996, Face Off, 1997, Mad City, 1997, She's So Lovely (also exec. prodr.), 1997, Primary Colors, 1998 (Golden Globe nominee), A Civil Action, 1998, General's Daughter, 1999, Battlefield Earth, (also prodr.) 2000, Lucky Numbers, 2000, Swordfish, 2001, Domestic Disturbance, 2001, Basic, 2003, The Punisher, 2004, Ladder 49, 2004, Be Cool, 2005; author: Staying Fit, 1984, Propeller One Way Night Coach; rec. artist album, 1976, 77; author (books) John Travolta Staying Fit, 1984, Propeller One-Way Night Coach: A Fable for All Ages, 1997. Involved with Fight for Kids. Recipient Best Male Vocalist Billboard award, 1976, Best Male Vocalist award Record World and Music Retail mag., 1976, Best Actor Golden Apple award Cue mag., Juno award Can. Acad. Rec. Arts and Scis., 1978, Golden Apple award 1998, Lifetime Achievement award British Acad. Film and TV Assn., 1998, Chgo. Internat. Film Festival, 1998, Palm Springs Internat. Film Festival, 1999, Alan J. Pakula award U.S. Broadcast Film Critics Assn., 1999,; nominated Best New Male Star Women's Press Club, 1976; named Man of Yr., Hasty Pudding Club, Harvard U., 1981. Office: William Morris Agency 151 El Camino Dr Beverly Hills CA 90212

**TRAXLER, WILLIAM BYRD, JR.,** federal judge; b. Greenville, SC, May 1, 1948; s. William Byrd and Bottie (Wooten) Traxler; m. Patricia Alford, Aug. 21, 1972; children: William Byrd III, James McCall. BA, Davidson Coll., 1970; JD, U. S.C., 1973. Assoc. William Byrd Traxler, Greenville, 1973—75; asst. solicitor 13th Jud. Ct., Greenville, 1975—78, dep. solicitor, 1978—81, solicitor, 1981—85, resident cir. judge, 1985—92; U.S. Dist. judge Dist. of S.C., Greenville, 1992—98; judge U.S.Ct. of Appeals (4th cir.), Greenville, 1998—. Recipient Outstanding Svc. award, Solicitors Assn., S.C., 1987, Leadership award, Probation, Parole & Pardon Svcs., S.C., 1990. Office: Fourth Circuit 300 E Washington St Ste 116 Greenville SC 29601-2431*

**TRAYLOR, ANGELIKA,** stained glass artist; b. Munich, Bavaria, Germany, Aug. 24, 1942; Came to U.S., 1959; d. Walther Artur Ferdinand and Berta Kreszentia (Boeck) Klau; m. Lindsay Montgomery Donaldson, June 10, 1959 (div. 1970); 1 child, Cameron Maria Greta; m. Samuel William Traylor III, June 12, 1970. Student, Pvt. Handelsschule Morawetz Jr. Coll., Munich, 1958. Freelance artist, 1960—. Works featured in profl. jours. including the Daylily Jour., 1987, Design Jour., South Korea, 1989, The Traveler's Guide to American Crafts, 1990, Florida Mag., 1991, Florida Today, 1993, Adventures in Art, vol. 3, 1993, Melbourne Times, 1994, The Orbiter, 1996, The Glass Collector's Digest, 1996, (TV) Focus on History, 1993, Focus, 1998, Space Coast Press, 1999, Weekend Decorating Projects-Women's Day, 1999, Pen Women, 1999, Stained Glass for the First Time, 2000, Creative Stained Glass, 2004; represented in permanent collections White House Christmas Ornament Collection, Holmes Regional Med. Ctr., Melbourne, Fla., Williams Childs Hospice House, Palm Bay, Fla., others Recipient Fragile Art award Glass Art mag., 1982, 1st Yr. Exhibitor award Stained Glass Am., 1984, 2d pl. Non-figurative Composition award Vitraux des USA, 1985, Best of Show Stained Glass Assn. Am., 1989, 3d pl., 1989, Merit award George Plimpton All-Star Space Coast Art Open, 1994; named Hist. Woman of Brevard, Brevard Cultural Alliance, 1991, one of 200 Best Am. Craftsmen Early Am. Life mag., 1994-95, 97-98, 2000. Home and Office: 100 Poinciana Dr Indian Harbor Beach FL 32937-4437 Office Phone: 321-773-7640.

**TRAYLOR, CHET D.,** state supreme court justice; b. Columbia, La., Oct. 12, 1945; s. John Hardy and Bernice (Bogan) T.; children: Mary Therese, Leigh Ann, Anna Marie. BA in Govt., N.E. La. State Univ., 1969; JD, Loyola U. Sch. of Law, 1974. Bar: La. Former La. State Trooper; former investigator La. Dept. of Justice Organized Crime & Racketering Unit; former legal advisor La. State Police Narcotics, Detectives & Intelligence Units; asst. dist. atty. Franklin Parish, 1975—76; judge 5th Jud. Dist. Ct., Franklin, Richland and West Carroll Parishes, La., 1985-97; assoc. justice La. Supreme Ct., 1997—. Founding bd. mem. Winnsboro Econ. Devel. Found.; mem. Rocky Mountain Conservation Fund. Military police investigator U.S. Army. Mem. ABA, La. Bar Assn., La. Dist. Judges Assn., NRA (life), Franklin Parish Mental Health Assn. (past bd. dirs.), Winnsboro Lions Club (past bd. dirs.), Greenwings (founder John Adams chpt.). Methodist. Office: La Supreme Ct 400 Royal St New Orleans LA 70130*

**TRAYLOR, ROBERT ARTHUR,** lawyer; b. Syracuse, N.Y., Jan. 15, 1949; s. Robert Arthur and Julia Elizabeth (McNulty) T.; m. Bonita Lynn Schmidt, Nov. 26, 1977. BS, LeMoyne Coll., 1970; JD cum laude, Syracuse U., 1975. Bar: N.Y., U.S. Dist. Ct. (no. dist.) N.Y., U.S. Tax Ct. Assoc. Love, Balducci & Scaccia, Syracuse, N.Y., 1976-77; estate tax atty. IRS, Syracuse, 1977-81; assoc. Scaccia Law Firm, Syracuse, 1981—. Contbr. articles to profl. jours. Mem. coordinating com. Vision 2000 1994—, mem. bd., 1998-2005. With U.S. Army, 1970-72. Mem. ABA, Onondaga County Bar Assn. (vol. lawyer program 1993—, Vol. Lawyer of Month 1994), World Wildlife Fedn. Republican. Roman Catholic. Avocations: motorsports, military history, catholic education. Home: 112 Knowland Dr Liverpool NY 13090-3130 Office: Scaccia Law Firm State Tower Bldg Ste 402 Syracuse NY 13202-1798 Office Phone: 315-422-4000.

**TRAYNHAM, JAMES GIBSON,** chemist, educator; b. Broxton, Ga., Aug. 5, 1925; s. James G. and Eddie Louise (Greer) T.; m. Margaret A. Egert, 1948; children: David F., Peter C.; m. Gresdna A. Doty, 1980. Student, South Ga. Coll., 1942-43; BS, U. N.C., 1946; PhD, Northwestern U., 1950. Instr. Northwestern U., 1949-50; asst. prof. Denison U., 1950-53; mem. faculty La. State U., Baton Rouge, 1953—, prof. chemistry, 1963-88, prof. emeritus, 1988—, chmn. dept. chemistry, 1968-73, vice chancellor for advanced studies and rsch., dean Grad. Sch., 1973-81. Postdoctoral research fellow Ohio State U., 1951-53; oral history cons. Chem. Heritage Found., 1997-2002. Author: Organic Nomenclature: A Programmed Introduction, 1966, 5th edit., 1997; editor: Essays on the History of Organic Chemistry, 1987; contbr. articles to profl. jours. Bd. dirs. Council Grad. Schs. in, U.S., 1981. Recipient Petroleum Research Fund-Am. Chem. Soc. Type D award Eidg. Technische Hochschule, Zurich, Switzerland, 1959-60; Charles E. Coates award Baton Rouge sects. Am. Chem. Soc. and Am. Inst. Chem. Engrs., 1965; NATO sr. fellow in sci. Universität des Saarlandes, Saarbrücken, Fed. Republic Germany, 1972 Mem. Am. Chem. Soc. (past councilor, past chmn. Baton Rouge sect., chmn. divsn. history of chemistry 1988), La. Acad. Sci., Internat. Union Pure and Applied Chemistry (former titular mem. commn. on nomenclature of organic chemistry, sec. 1994-99), Phi Beta Kappa, Sigma Xi, Phi Lambda Upsilon, Phi Kappa Phi (past pres. La. State U. chpt.). Home: 122 Highland Trace Dr Baton Rouge LA 70810-5061 Fax: 225-769-7801. Personal E-mail: jimtraynham@msn.com.

**TRAYNOR, JOHN MICHAEL,** lawyer; b. Oakland, Calif., Oct. 25, 1934; s. Roger J. and Madeleine (Lackmann) Traynor; m. Shirley Williams, Feb. 11, 1956; children: Kathleen Traynor Millard, Elizabeth Traynor Fowler, Thomas. BA, U. Calif., Berkeley, 1955; JD, Harvard U., 1960. Bar: Calif. 1961, U.S. Supreme Ct. 1966. Dep. atty. gen. State of Calif., San Francisco, 1961—63; spl. counsel Calif. Senate Com. on Local Govt., Sacramento, 1963; assoc. firm Cooley Godward, LLP, San Francisco, 1963—69, ptnr., 1969—2004, sr. counsel, 2005—. Adviser 3d Restatement of Unfair Competition, 1988—95, 3d Restatement of Torts, Products Liability, 1992—98, Apportionment, 1994—99, 2d Restatement of Conflict of Laws revs., 1988, 3d Restatement of Restitution and Unjust Enrichment, 1997—; lectr. Boalt Hall Sch. Law U. Calif., 1982—89, 1996—98; chmn. EarthJustice Legal Def. Fund (formerly Sierra Club Legal Def. Fund), 1991—92, trustee, 1974—96. Mem. bd. overseers Inst. for Civil Justice RAND, 1991—97; bd. dirs. Environ. Law Inst., 1991—97, 1999—2005; Sierra Legal Def. Fund. Canada, 1990—96. 1st lt. USMC, 1955—57. Recipient John P. Frank award, 2004. Fellow: Am. Acad. Appellate Lawyers, Am. Acad. Arts and Scis., Calif. Acad. Appellate Lawyers, Am. Bar Found. (life); mem.: Bar Assn. San Francisco (pres. 1973), Am. Law Inst. (coun. 1985—, pres. 2000—). Home: 3131 Eton Ave Berkeley CA 94705-2713 Office: Cooley Godward LLP 101 Calif St 5th Fl San Francisco CA 94111-5800 Office Phone: 415-693-2110. Business E-Mail: mtraynor@cooley.com.

**TREACY, GERALD BERNARD, JR.,** lawyer; b. Newark, July 29, 1951; s. Gerald B. Sr. and Mabel L. (Nesbitt) T.; m. Joyce M. Biazzo, Apr. 6, 1974. BA summa cum laude, Rider Coll., 1973; JD, UCLA, 1981. Bar: Calif. 1981, Wash. 1982, D.C. 1995. Tchr. English Arthur L. Johnson Regional H.S., Clark, NJ, 1973—77; assoc. Gibson, Dunn & Crutcher, L.A., 1981—82; ptnr. Perkins Coie, Bellevue, Wash., 1982—84, McGuire Woods Battle & Boothe, McLean and Bellevue, 1994—96, Egger, Betts, Austin, Treacy, Bellevue, 1996—98; pvt. practice Bellevue and Poulsbo, Wash., 1998—; of counsel Montgomery Purdue Blankinship and Austin, Seattle, 2000—; founder, mgr. Arc Line Cons. LLC, 2006—. Chmn. bd. dirs. estate planning adv. bd. U. Wash., Seattle, 1990-92; presenter TV Seminar, Where There's a Will, PBS affiliate; founder ArcLine Consulting, LLC. Author: Washington Guardianship Law, Administration and Litigation, 1988, supplemented, 1991, 3d edit. supplemented, 2002, Supporting Organizations, 1996, 2d edit., 2002, Community Property, 2005 Endowment fund cons. United Way, Seattle, 1987—89; exec. com. Wash. Planned Giving Coun., 1993—94, 1996—98; bd. dirs., adv. bd. ARC, Seattle, 1985—89, Arthritis Gift, 1987—89, Seattle Symphony, 1992, Seattle U., 1996; bd. dirs. Morning Light Found., Flow Chart Found., Eastside Tyee Theatre, Kitsap Opera, 2003—04; founder, prodr. West Sound Lyric Theater, 2003—. Mem. Kitsap County Estate Planning Coun., Eastside King County Estate Planning Coun., Order of Coif. Avocations: photography, hiking, classical music, poetry. Office: PO Box 710 Keyport WA 98345 Office Phone: 360-697-4142. E-mail: gbtreacy@aol.com.

**TREACY, VINCENT EDWARD,** lawyer; b. Mass., Jan. 30, 1942; m. Judith Anne Mansfield, May 8, 1999. AB, Boston Coll., 1964; JD with honors, George Washington U., 1971. Bar: Va. 1972, D.C. 1973, Md. 1999; U.S. Supreme Ct. 1976. Atty. Fed. Labor Rels. Coun., Washington, 1971-73; legis. atty. Am. law divsn. Congrl. Rsch. Svc., Libr. Congress, Washington, 1973-98; sole practitioner Washington, 1998—. Cons. Romanian Legal Analysis and Legis. Drafting Conf., Senate and Chamber Deputies Romania, Bucharest, 1996. Mem. law rev. staff George Washington Law Rev., 1970. Mem. George Washington Law Alumni Assn. (pres. Capitol Hill chpt. 1986-87), Order of Coif. Office Phone: 202-966-1497. E-mail: vtreacy@msn.com.

**TREACY, WILLIAM JOSEPH,** electrical and environmental engineer; b. NYC, Jan. 16, 1959; s. William Joseph and Angela Bridget (Keane) T.; 1 child, Denise Marie. BSEE, Manhattan Coll., 1981; M in Aero. Sci., Embry-Riddle U., 1987; MBA, Regis U., 2005. Registered profl. engr., N.Y. Commd. 2d lt. USAF, 1981, advanced through grades to capt., project mgr. Victorville, Calif., 1981—84, dept. chief Netherlands GLCM program office Ramstein, Germany, 1984—88, chief engr. Soesterberg, Netherlands, 1988—91, heavy repair supt. Plattsburgh, NY, 1991—92, CFO, 1992—94, chief environ. engr., 1994—95; bldg. sys. supr. Plattsburgh (N.Y.) Airbase Redevelopment Corp., 1995—2004, Plattsburgh (N.Y.) Mcpl. Lighting Dept., 2004—. Computer technician, Plattsburgh, 1992—. Active Red Cross, Plattsburgh, 1992. Decorated Meritorious Svc. medal, Air Force Commendation medal with one oak leaf cluster, others; USAF ROTC Program Acad. scholar, 1978. Mem. IEEE, ASHRAE, Nat. Fire Protection Assn., Internat. Assn. Elec. Insps., Assn. for Facilities Engring., Aircraft Owners and Pilots Assn., Friends of Ft. Ticonderoga, Am. Legion. Republican. Roman Catholic. Avocations: flying, star trek memorabilia, cross country skiing. Home: 60 Leonard Ave Plattsburgh NY 12901-2565 Office: Plattsburgh Mcpl Lighting Dept 32 Green St Plattsburgh NY 12901 Office Phone: 518-563-2200. Business E-Mail: pmld_wjt@westelcom.com.

**TREADWAY, JAMES CRISPIN CURRAN CORBETT,** lawyer, brokerage house executive, investor, federal official; b. Anderson, S.C., May 21, 1943; s. James C. Treadway and Maxine Hall; m. Susan Pepper Davis, Sept. 6, 1969; children: Elizabeth Pepper Hall, Caroline Worrell Harper Corbett. AB summa cum laude, Rollins Coll., 1964; JD summa cum laude, Washington and Lee U., 1967. Bar: Ga. 1967, Mass. 1968, D.C. 1970. Assoc. Candler, Cox, McClain & Andrews, Atlanta, 1967-68, Gadsby & Hannah, Boston and Washington, 1968-72; ptnr. Dickstein, Shapiro & Morin, Washington, 1972-82; commr. SEC, Washington, 1982-85; ptnr. Baker & Botts, Washington, 1985-87; exec. v.p., chmn. mcht. banking dept., mem. exec. com. Paine Webber Group Inc., N.Y.C., 1987—. Commr. Nat. Study Commn., 1985—87; chmn. Nat. Commn. on Fraudulent Fin. Reporting, 1985—87; chmn. bds. dirs. Washington & Lee U. Sch. Law, 1992—94; dir. U. So. Calif., Sch. of Acctg. and Fin. Disclosure, 1985—93; mem. planning com. Garret Securities Law Inst., Northwestern U., 1985—92; dir. nat. study commn., 1985—87; spl. expert adviser, witness various U.S. congl. coms.; lectr. in field; bd. dirs. Parnounblon, Inc., Matchel Hatchens Asset Mgmt. Inc., Pomawufter, Inc., Gradgne Inc.; bd. dirs. Miran Banking Ctr. Boston (Mass.) U. Editor-in-chief Wash. & Lee U. Law reviews, 1966-67. Recipient Wildman Medal Am. Acctg. Assn., 1989. Mem. Mass. Bar Assn., Ga. Bar Assn., D.C. Bar Assn., Chevy Chase (Md.) Club, Bedford (N.Y.) Golf and Tennis Club, City Tavern Club (Washington chpt.), Met. Club (Washington chpt.), Verbank Hunting and Fishing Club (Uniondale N.Y.; dir. 1995—), Order of Coif, Phi Beta Kappa, Omicron Delta Kappa, Omicron Delta Epsilon, Kappa Alpha Order Republican. Roman Cath. Home: Laurel Ledge Farm RD 4 Croton Lake Rd Bedford Corners NY 10549-4227 Office: PaineWebber Group Inc 1285 Ave of Americas New York NY 10019-6028 Home: 1509 Monk Rd Gladwyne PA 19035 Personal E-mail: roundaction@aol.com.

**TREADWAY, SANDRA GIOIA,** library director; b. Jersey City, N.J., Jan. 15, 1950; d. Robert Peter and Essey Grace (Graham) Gioia; m. John David Treadway, Sept. 4, 1976 (div. 2006); 1 child, Robyn Grace. BA in History, Manhattanville Coll., 1971; MA in History, U. Va., 1972, PhD in History, 1978. Instr. history Va. Polytech Inst. & State U., Blacksburg, 1976-78; editor Va. State Libr., Richmond, 1978-91, dir. pubs., 1991-96; deputy dir. Libr. Va., Richmond, 1996—. Author: Women of Mark, 1995; co-author: The Common Wealth: Treasures from the Collections of the Library of Virginia, 1997; co-editor: Dictionary of Virginia Biography, vol. 1, 1999, vol. 2, 2001, vol. 3, 2006. Mdm. bd. St. Mary Sch., Richmond, 1988-96. Mem. Am. Hist. Assn., Orgn. Am. historians, So. Historical Assn., So. Assn. Women Historians (pres. 2002), Va. Hist. Soc., Va. Libr. Assn., Serra Internat. (bd. dirs. 1985—). Roman Catholic. Avocations: reading, travel. Home: 8201 Gaylord Rd Richmond VA 23229-4121 Office: Libr LVa 800 E Broad St Richmond VA 23219-1905 Business E-Mail: streadway@lva.lib.va.us.

**TREADWAY-DILLMON, LINDA LEE,** actress, stuntwoman, dancer, dispatcher; b. Woodbury, NJ, June 4, 1950; d. Leo Elmer and Ona Lee (Wyckoff) Treadway; m. Randall Kenneth Dillmon, June 19, 1982. BS in Health, Phys. Edn. & Recreation, West Chester State Coll., 1972, MS in Health and Phys. Edn., 1975; postgrad., Ctrl. Mich. U., 1978; Police Officer Stds. Tng. cert. complaint dispatcher, Goldenwest Coll., 1982. Cert. EMT Am. Acad. Orthopaedic Surgeons; in safety edn. West Chester State Coll. Grad. asst., instr., asst. athletic trainer West Chester (Pa.) State Coll., 1972-76; asst. prof., program dir., asst. athletic trainer Ctrl. Mich. U., Mt. Pleasant, 1976-80; police dispatcher City of Westminster, Calif., 1980-89; oncology unit sect. Children's Hosp. Orange County, Calif., 1989-96. Stuntwoman, actress United Stunt Artists, SAG, L.A., 1982—; dancer Disneyland, Anaheim, Calif., 1988—; contbr. articles to profl. jours. Athletic trainer U.S. Olympic Women's Track and Field Trials, Frederick, Md., 1972, AAU Jr. World Wrestling Championships, Mt. Pleasant, Mich., 1977, Mich. Spl. Olympics, Mt. Pleasant, 1977, 78, 79. Recipient bronze and gold Spirit of Disneyland Resort awards, 1997; named Outstanding Phys. Educator, Delta Psi Kappa, Ctrl. Mich. U., 1980, Outstanding Young Woman of Am., 1984; named to Disneyland Entertainment Hall of Fame, 1995. Mem. SAG, Nat. Athletic Trainers Assn. (cert., women and athletic tng. ad hoc com. 1974-75, placement com. 1974-79, program dirs. coun. 1976-80, ethics com. 1977-80, visitation team 1978-80, 25 Yr. award 1997). U.S. Field Hockey Assn. (player). Pacific S.W. Field Hockey Assn. (player, Nat. Champion 1980, 81, 82), L.A. Field Hockey Assn. (player), Swing Shift Dance Team (dancer). Presbyterian. Avocations: flying, piano, athletics, stitchery, travel. Home: 18073 Scanlan Ct Fountain Valley CA 92708-5865

**TREADWELL-RUBIN, PAMELA A.,** lawyer; b. Arlington, Tex., Dec. 15, 1960; BA in Polit. sci., U. Ariz., 1982, JD, 1985. Bar: Ariz. 1985. Prosecutor, Tucson City, 1985—87; dep. atty. Pima County, 1987—93; atty. Goering, Roberts, Rubin, Brogna, Enos & Treadwell-Rubin, PC, Tucson. Mem. Ariz. Juvenile Justice Adv. Coun., 1993—96. Fellow: Ariz. Bar Found. (bd. dirs. 1991—94, chair victims' rights pro bono panel 1992—93); mem.: Pima County Bar Assn. (bd. dirs. 1989—90, pres. Young Lawyers divsn. 1989—90, bd. dirs. 1996—2005), Ariz. Women Lawyers Assn., State Bar Ariz. (pres. Young Lawyers divns. 1994—95, cert. specialist worker's compensation 1995—, bd. govs. 1996—2005, pres. 2003—04, Outstanding Young Lawyer 1997). Office: Goering Roberts Rubin Brogna Enos & Treadwell-Rubin PC Ste 200 3320 N Campbell Ave Tucson AZ 85719 Office Phone: 520-577-9300.

**TREANOR, CHARLES EDWARD,** physicist, researcher; b. Buffalo, Oct. 22, 1924; s. William Michael and Margaret Mary (Powers) T.; m. Ruth Ziegelmaier, Jan. 28, 1950; children: Timothy, John, Peter, Michael, Melissa. BA, U. Minn., 1947; PhD, U. Buffalo, 1952-53. Instr. physics U. Buffalo, 1952-53; physicist Cornell Aero Lab., Buffalo, 1954-68, head aerodynamical rsch. dept., 1968-78; v.p. phys. sci. group Calspen Corp., Buffalo, 1978-83, v.p., chief scientist, 1983-90; pres. CTSA, Inc., 1990—2004; ret. Contbr. articles to profl. jours.; patentee in field. Served to 1t. U.S. Army, 1943-46. Recipient C.C. Furnas award SUNY, Buffalo, 1989. Fellow Am. Phys. Soc. (div. chmn. 1977), AIAA (com. chmn. 1975-76, 87-89, Fluid and Plasma Dynamics award 1978); mem. NAE. Home: 535 Seabrook Drive Buffalo NY 14221-1919 Personal E-mail: ctreanor@adelphia.net.

**TREANOR, MARK C.,** lawyer, diversified financial services company executive; b. Proctor, Vt., Dec. 2, 1946; BS, U.S. Naval Acad., Annapolis, 1968; JD with honors, U. Md., 1976. Bar: Md. 1976, U.S. Dist. Ct. Md. 1977, U.S. Ct. Appeals (4th cir.) 1979, U.S. Tax Ct. 1980, U.S. Supreme Ct. 1980, Vt. 1997. Ptnr. Miles & Stockbridge, 1982—85, Treanor, Pope & Hughes, 1987—98; sr. exec. v.p., gen. counsel, sec. Wachovia Corp., Charlotte, NC, 1998—. Mem. Md. Law Rev., 1975—76. Bd. visitors U. Md. Sch. Law; bd. advisors U. N.C. Sch. Law Banking Inst., NC. Capt. USMC, 1968—73. Mem.: ABA, Order of Coif, Md. State Bar Assn., Phi Alpha Delta. Office: Wachovia Corp 1 Wachovia Ctr 301 S College St Charlotte NC 28288-0630

**TREASTER, JOSEPH B. (JOSEPH BLAND TREASTER),** journalist; b. Mt. Union, Pa., May 19, 1941; s. Ellsworth F. and Anna Katherine (Chalupka) T.; m. Barbara A. Gluck, June 6, 1970 (div. Aug. 1976); m. Barbara J. Dill, Feb. 24, 1990; 1 child, Chloe Qiao Xing. BA, U. Miami, 1965; student, Sorbonne, Paris, 1971; San Francisco de Marroquin, Guatemala, 1988; MS, Columbia U., 1996. Reporter Miami (Fla.) Herald, 1963; staff asst. Saigon bur. N.Y. Times, 1965-67; Vietnam corr., 1968-69, 72-74, reporter N.Y.C., 1969-70, chief Conn. bur., 1970-72, investigative reporter N.Y., 1974-75, crime/youth violence writer, 1975-76, rewrite desk and spl. assignments to Washington, L.Am. and Mid. East, 1976-84; chief Caribbean bur., 1984-90, drug policy corr. spl. assignments Latin Am., Mid-East, Europe, Baltic States, 1990-95, fin. writer, 1996—. Freelance corr. Atlantic Monthly, Rolling Stone, The Nation, others; fellow Poynter Inst., St. Petersburg, Fla., 1993, U.S.-Mex. News. Bus. Journalism, 1995; Knight-Bagehot fellow in econs. and bus. Columbia U., 1995-96; Poynter fellow Yale U., 1975; adj. prof. Baruch Coll., Univ. N.Y., 2002. Author (biography): Paul Volcker: The Making of a Financial Legend, 2004; co-author: No Hiding Place: Inside Report on the Hostage Crisis in Iran, 1981; contbg. author: Ency. Brit., Insight Guide to Caribbean, Youth Violence, 1992, Writing About Business, 2000, The New York Times What's Doing Around the World, 2001, The New York Times Almanac, 2006.

Served with U.S. Army, 1963-65, Vietnam. Recipient Page One award N.Y. Newspaper Guild, 1977, 79; Tom Wallace award Inter-Am. Press Assn., 1980, citation and awards Overseas Press Club Am., 1977, 80, 85, News Analysis award Soc. of Silurians, 1993, Casey medal for meritorious journalism U. Md., 1995, others. Avocations: skiing, sport fishing, running, bicycling. Office: NY Times 229 W 43d St New York NY 10036-3959 Office Phone: 212-556-3718. E-mail: treaster@nytimes.com.

**TREBEK, ALEX,** television game show host; b. Sudbury, Ont., Can., July 22, 1940; came to U.S., 1973; s. George Edward and Lucille (Lagace) T.; m. Elaine Callei (div. 1981); m. Jean Currivan, Apr. 30, 1990; 2 children. BA, U. Ottawa, Ont., 1961, PhB. Staff announcer CBC, Toronto, Ont., 1961-73; game show host Wizard of Odds for NBC, Calif., 1973-74, Stars on Ice for Can. TV, 1974-77, High Rollers for NBC, Calif., 1974-79, $128,000 Question for Global TV, Can., 1976-77, Double Dare for CBS, Calif., 1977-78, Battle Stars for NBC, Calif., 1981-82; producer Jeopardy!, Calif., 1984-87, game show host Calif., 1984—, Classic Concentration, Calif., 1987-90, To Tell the Truth, 1991. Owner Creston Vineyards. Film appearances include: Short Cuts, 1993, Spy Hard, 1996, Ellen's Energy Adventure, 1996, Mafia!, 1998, Random Hearts, 1999, The Male Swagger, 1999. Recipient Star on the Walk of Fame, 1999; named Outstanding Game Show Host for Jeopardy!, Daytime Emmy award, Nat. Acad. TV Arts and Sciences, 2006. Mem. Screen Actors Guild, AFTRA, Assn. Can. TV and Radio Artists. Roman Catholic. Avocations: golf, hockey, tennis. Office: Jeopardy! 1020 W Washington Blvd Culver City CA 90232

**TREBING, DAVID MARTIN,** automotive executive; b. Lincoln, Nebr., June 2, 1961; s. Harry Martin and Joyce Alice (Christie) T. BA in Mktg., Mich. State U., 1984; MBA in Fin., Wake Forest U., 1986. Project mgr. mktg.-sales Gilbarco div. Exxon Corp., Greensboro, NC, 1984-86; cash mgmt. analyst Chrysler Fin. Corp., Troy, Mich., 1986-87; sr. corp. fin. specialist Chrysler Corp., Auburn Hills, Mich., 1987-92, mgr. activity-based costing implementation Detroit, 1993-96, mgr. Asia-Pacific Sales Fin., 1996-98; v.p. fin. and adminstn. Daimler Chrysler Taiwan Co. Ltd., 1998—2001; sr. corp. mgr. regional govt. affairs Daimler Chrysler Corp., Auburn Hills, Mich., 2001—. Mem. Internat. Armed Forces Coun., Detroit, 1987-92, St. George's Soc. N.Y., N.Y.C.; trustee Detroit Hist. Soc.; mem. exec. com., bd. dirs. Meadow Brook Theatre and Festival; Chgo. com. Coun. on Fgn. Rels.; mem. Nat. Com. U.S.-China Rels.; bd. dirs. devel. fund Mich. State U.; trustee Hist. Soc. Mich., bd. dirs. Nat. Flag Found. Lt. (j.g.) USNR, 1987-90. Inst. fellow, Inst. Pub. Utilities, 1983. Mem. Econ. Club Detroit, Detroit Com. on Fgn. Rels., Army and Navy Club, Detroit Athletic Club, Grosse Pointe Club, Church Club of N.Y., Vet. Corps Arty. State N.Y., SAR (pres. Detroit chpt. 1987-89), Soc. War 1812, Soc. Colonial Wars (sec. gen., dep. gov. gen. Mich. Soc.), English-Speaking Union, Am. C. of C. in Taipei (bd. supvrs.), Pres. Club Mich. State U., Royal New Zealand Yacht Squadron, Chgo. Yacht Club. Avocations: skiing, tennis, travel, skeet/trap shooting, sailing. Office: Daimler Chrysler Corp CIMS 485-10-95 1000 Chrysler Dr Auburn Hills MI 48326-2766 E-mail: DMT@dcx.com.

**TREBON, THOMAS,** academic administrator; m. Scottie Trebon. B magna cum laude, Seattle U.; M, PhD, U. Denver. Tchr., adminstr. Seattle U.; acad. dean Coll. Arts and Scis. Rockhurst Coll., Kansas City; provost, v.p. acad. affairs Sacred Heart U., Trumbull, Conn.; with St. Norbert Coll., 1995—2001; v.p. acad. affairs, dean Carroll coll., Helena, Mont.; pres. Carroll Coll., 2001—. Office: Carroll College Office of the President 1601 N Benton Ave Helena MT 59625

**TRECARTIN, RYAN,** filmmaker; b. Webster, Tex., 1981; BFA, RI Sch. Design, 2000—04. One-man shows include I Smell Pregnant, QED, LA, Calif., 2006, exhibited in group shows at Sympathetic Magic, 2005, Schindler House, 2006, Whitney Biennial: Day for Night, Whitney Mus. Am. Art, NY, 2006, Reckless Behavior, The Getty Ctr., LA, 2006, Metro Pictures, The Moore Space, Miami, 2006, USA Today, Royal Acad. Arts, Burlington Gardens, 2006, screenings, A Family Finds Entertainment, NY Underground Film Festival, 2006, Chicago Underground Film Festival, 2006, Valentine's Day Girl, Multiplex, Smack Mellon, Bklyn., NY, 2006; performer: Alternative Theatre Endings, 2005, Nothing Wrong With August, 2005. Mailing: c/o Elizabeth Dee Gallery 545 West 20th St New York NY 10011*

**TRECEK, TIMOTHY SCOTT,** lawyer; b. Racine, Wis., Sept. 26, 1968; s. Robert Thomas and Mona Marie Trecek; m. Karyn Marie Kwiatkowski, Aug. 27, 1994; children: Gabrielle Grace, Danielle Terese, Isabella Hope BS in Polit. Sci., Marquette U., 1990, JD, 1993. Bar: Wis. 1993, U.S. Dist. Ct. (ea. dist.) Wis. 1993. Atty. Kasdorf, Lewis & Swietlik, Milw., 1993—95, Habush, Habush & Rottier, S.C., Milw., 1995—. Mem. ABA, Wis. Acad. of Trial Lawyers (com. Office Lawyer Regulation), Wis. State Bar Assn., Assn. of Trial Lawyers of Am. Roman Catholic. Avocation: golf. Office: Habush Habush & Rottier 777 E Wisconsin Ave 2300 Milwaukee WI 53202-5381 Office Phone: 414-271-0900. E-mail: ttrecek@habush.com.

**TRECKELO, RICHARD M.,** lawyer; b. Elkhart, Ind., Oct. 22, 1926; s. Frank J. and Mary T.; m. Anne Kosick, June 25, 1955; children: Marla Treckelo Buck, Mary Treckelo Lucchesi. AB, U. Mich., 1951, JD, 1953. Bar: Ind. 1953, U.S. Dist. Ct. (no. and so. dists.) Ind. Pvt. practice, Elkhart, 1953-70; ptnr. Barnes and Thornburg, Elkhart, South Bend, others, 1971-91, of counsel, 1992—. Sec. Skyline Corp., Elkhart, 1959-94, bd. dirs., 1961-91. Bd. dirs. Elkhart Gen. Hosp. Found.; Elkhart Park Found.; co-chmn. Elkhart Constl. Bicentennial Commn. Served with USAF, 1945-46. Mem. ABA, Elkhart City Bar Assn. (pres. 1975), Ind. Bar Assn., Elkhart County Bar Assn., Pres.'s Club (U. Mich.), Christiana Country Club, Michiana Club (chmn., U. Mich. Elbel Scholarship award), Rotary. Republican. Office: Barnes & Thornburg 121 W Franklin St Ste 200 Elkhart IN 46516-3200 Office Phone: 574-293-0681.

**TRE COOL, (FRANK EDWIN WRIGHT, III),** musician; b. Frankfurt, Germany, Dec. 9, 1972; m. Lisea Lyons, Mar. 1995 (div.); 1 child, Ramona; m. Claudia Tre Cool, 2000 (div. 2003); 1 child, Frankito. Played with the band The Lookouts, 1985—90, Screeching Weasel, Samiam; with the band The Network, 2003—; musician Green Day (formerly Sweet Children), 1990—. Musician, writer (albums) Kerplunk, 1992, musician, writer, singer Dookie, 1994 (Grammy award for Best Alternative Music Performance, 1994); musician: (albums) Insomniac, 1995, Nimrod, 1997, Warning, 2000; musician, writer, singer (albums) American Idiot (Viewers Choice award, MTV Video Music Awards, 2005, Am. Music Awards Favorite Rock Album, 2005); composer: (films) Angus, 1995, Godzilla, 1998, Varsity Blues, 1999, Austin Powers: The Spy Who Shagged Me, 1999; voice (films) Live Freaky Die Freaky, 2003, guest appearances Saturday Night Live, 1994, 2005, Mad TV, 2001, (voice) King of the Hill, 1997, and several others. Recipient Video of Yr., Best Group Video, Best Rock Video, Best Editing in a Video, Best Direction in a Video for Boulevard of Broken Dreams, MTV Video Music Awards, 2005, Pop Group of Yr., Rock Artist of Yr., Modern Rock Artist of Yr., Hot 100 Group of Yr., Billboard 200 Album Group of Yr., Billboard Music Awards, 2005, Rock Song of Yr. for Boulevard of Broken Dreams, 2005, Favorite Group, People's Choice Awards, 2006, Record of Yr. for Boulevard of Broken Dreams, Grammy Awards, 2006.*

**TREE, MICHAEL,** violinist, violist, educator; b. Newark, Feb. 19, 1934; s. Samuel and Sada (Rothman) Applebaum; m. Johanna Kreck, Sept. 8, 1966; children: Konrad Efrem, Anna Louise. Diploma, Curtis Inst. Music, Phila., 1955; DFA (hon.), U. South Fla., 1975, SUNY, Binghamton, 1983. Faculty Harpur Coll., Binghamton, 1965-70, Curtis Inst. Music, 1970—, U. Md., College Park, 1980—; St. Louis Conservatory Music, 1982-88, Rutgers U., 1988—2000, Manhattan Sch. Music, 1996—, Juilliard Sch., NYC, 2002—. Co-artistic dir. Phila. Chamber Orch., 1985-88; Misha Elman chair Manhattan Sch. Music, 1991. Violin recital debut at Carnegie Hall, 1954; soloist with major orchs. and at maj. internat. festivals, 1958—; founding mem. Guarneri String Quartet, 1964—, rec. artist for Philips, RCA, Columbia, Nonesuch,

Vanguard, Sony Classics, Arabesque records. Recipient Seal of Recognition City of N.Y., 1982. Avocations: hiking, tennis. Home: PO Box 193 Marlboro VT 05344-0193 Office: care Herbert Barrett Mgmt Inc 1776 Broadway Ste 1610 New York NY 10019-2002

**TREECE, JAMES LYLE,** retired lawyer; b. Colorado Springs, Colo., Feb. 6, 1925; s. Lee Oren and Ruth Ida (Smith) T.; m. Ruth Julie Treece, Aug. 7, 1949 Idiv. 1984); children: James (dec.), Karen Pelletier, Teryl Wait, Jamilyn Smyser, Carol Crowder. Student, Colo. State U., 1943, Colo. U., 1943, US Naval Acad., 1944—46; BS, Mesa Coll., 1946; JD, U. Colo., 1950; postgrad., U. NC, 1976-77. Bar: Colo. 1952, U.S. Dist. Ct. Colo. 1952, U.S. Ct. Appeals (10th cir.) 1952, U.S. Supreme Ct. 1967. Assoc. Yegge, Hall, Treece & Evans and predecessors, 1951—59, ptnr., 1959—69, v.p. atty. Colo., 1969—77; pres. Treece & Bahr and predecessor firms, Littleton, Colo., 1977—91; mcpl. judge, 1967—68; mem. faculty Nat. Trial Advocacy Inst., 1973—76, Law-Sci. Acad., 1964; ret., 1991. Chmn. Colo. Dept. Pub. Welfare, 1963-68; chmn. Colo. Dept. Social Svcs., 1968-69; active Littleton Bd. Edn., 1977-81. With USNR, 1944-46 Recipient award, Colo. Assn. Sch. Bds., 1981, IRS, 1977, FBI, 1977, DEA, 1977, Fed. Exec. Bd., 1977. Mem. Fed. Bar Assn. (pres. Colo. 1975, award 1975), Colo. Bar Assn. (bd. govs.), Denver Bar Assn. (v.p., trustee). Republican. Episcopalian. Home: 12651 N Pebble Beach Dr Sun City AZ 85351-3327 Personal E-mail: jltreece@juno.com.

**TREFFERT, DAROLD ALLEN,** psychiatrist, writer, hospital administrator; b. Fond du Lac, Wis., Mar. 12, 1933; s. Walter O. and Emma (Leu) T.; m. Dorothy Marie Sorgatz, June 11, 1955; children: Jon, Joni, Jill, Jay. BS, U. Wis., 1955, MD, 1958. Diplomate Am. Bd. Psychiatry and Neurology. Resident in psychiatry U. Wis. Med. Sch., 1959-62, clin. prof. psychiatry, 1965—; chief children's unit Winnebago (Wis.) Mental Health Inst., 1962-64, supt., 1964-79, Ctrl. State Hosp., Waupun, Wis., 1977-78; dir. Dodge County Mental Health Ctr., Juneau, Wis., 1964-74; mem. staff St. Agnes Hosp., Fond du Lac, 1963—; exec. dir. Fond du Lac County Mental Health Ctr., 1979-92. Chmn. Controlled Substances Bd. Wis.; chmn. med. examining bd. State of Wis. Author: Extraordinary People: Understanding Savant Syndrome, 1989, 3d edit., 2006, edits. in U.S., U.K., Italy, Japan, The Netherlands, Sweden; autism cons. (movie) Rainman, 1988. Fellow Am. Coll. Psychiatrists; mem. AMA, Wis. Med. Soc. (pres. 1979-80), Wis. Psychiat. Assn. (pres.), Am. Assn. Psychiat. Adminstrs. (pres.), Alpha Omega Alpha. Home: W 4065 Maplewood Ln Fond Du Lac WI 54935-9562 Office: 430 E Division St Fond Du Lac WI 54935-4560 Office Phone: 920-926-4297. Business E-Mail: daroldt@charter.net. People often spend too much time regretting what they are not and far too little time savoring that which they are.

**TREFNY, JOHN ULRIC,** college president; b. Jan. 28, 1942; s. Ulric John and Mary Elizabeth (Leech) T.; m. Sharon Livingston, 1992; 1 child from previous marriage, Benjamin Robin. BS, Fordham U., 1963; PhD, Rutgers U., 1968. Rsch. assoc. Cornell U., Ithaca, NY, 1967-69; asst. prof. physics Wesleyan U., Middletown, Conn., 1969-77, Colo. Sch. Mines, Golden, 1977-79, assoc. prof., 1979-85, prof., 1985—, assoc. dean rsch., 1988—90, head physics dept., 1990—95, v.p. for acad. affairs, dean faculty, 1995—2000, pres., 2000—. Dir. Amorphous Materials Ctr. Colo. Sch. Mines, 1986-90; cons. Solar Energy Rsch. Inst., Golden, Energy Conversion Devices, Troy, Mich., others. Contbr. articles to profl. jours. Recipient Tchg. award AMOCO Found., 1984, Friend of Sci. Edn. award, 1990. Mem. Colo. Assn. Sci. Tchrs. (bd. dirs. 1986-88), Sigma Xi (N.W. region co-dir. 1994-2000), Sigma Pi Sigma. Avocations: golf, travel. Home: 1722 Illinois St Golden CO 80401-1836

**TREFRY, JOHN H., III,** chemical oceanographer, educator; b. Boston, Sept. 2, 1947; s. John H. Trefry, Jr. and Phyllis Icenogle (Stone) T. m. Susan E. Page, July 20, 1969; 1 child, Caroline Page Kempf; 1 child, John H. IV. BA, Syracuse U., 1969; MS in Chem. Oceanography, Tex. A&M U., 1973, PhD in Chem. Oceanography, 1977. Asst. prof. Fla. Inst. Tech., Melbourne, Fla., 1978—82, assoc. prof., 1982—87, prof., 1987—. Vis. scientist MIT, Cambridge, Mass., 1987—88. Grant, NSF, 1990—94, NOAA, 1977—85, 1995—2000, US Dept. Interior, 1997—. Mem.: Outer Continental Shelf Scientific Com., U.S. Dept. of Interior, Minerals Mgmt. Svc., Fla. Acad. Scis. (pres. 2005—, medalist 2002), Am. Chem. Soc., Am. Geophys. Union. Achievements include first to co-discover deep-sea hydrothermal vents in the Atlantic Ocean. Office: Florida Inst Tech 150 W Univ Blvd Melbourne FL 32901 Office Phone: 321-674-7305. Office Fax: 321-674-7212. Business E-Mail: jtrefry@fit.edu.

**TREFRY, ROBERT J.,** health facility administrator; b. Springfield, Vt., Mar. 29, 1947; married. Bachelors' degree, Ga. Inst. Tech., 1970; Masters' degree, George Washington U., 1974. With Greater Southeast Community Hosp., Washington, 1973, adminstrv. asst., 1973-74, asst. adminstr., 1974-79; sr. v.p. North Kansas City (Mo.) Community Hosp., 1979-83; exec. v.p., chief exec. officer St. Agnes Hosp., White Plains, NY, 1983-88; exec. v.p., chief operating officer Carle Found. Hosp., Urbana, Ill., 1988-91; exec. v.p., chief oper. officer Bridgeport (Conn.) Hosp., 1991-94, pres., CEO, 1994—; exec. v.p. Yale New Haven Health Sys., 1996—. With U.S. mil. 1970-71. Office: Bridgeport Hosp 267 Grant St Bridgeport CT 06610-2870

**TREFTS, JOAN LANDENBERGER,** retired principal; b. Pitts., Jan. 31, 1930; d. Henry III and Eleanore (Campbell) Landenberger; m. Albert Sharpe Trefts Sr., June 20, 1952 (dec.); children: Dorothy, Albert Jr., William, Deborah, Elizabeth. AB, Western Coll. for Women, 1952; M, John Carroll U., 1982, M, 1984. Lic. and cert. home economist, cert. prin., N.Y., Ohio, supr., biol. sci., econs., voact. edn., pre-kindergarten edn. Summer sch. prin. John Adams H.S., Collinwood and South High, Cleve., 1972—95; ret., 1995. Cons. Cleve. Partnership Program. Trustee Chautauqua Literacy and Sci. Cir., Presbyn. Assn. Chautauqua, NY. Named Tchr. of Yr., Cleve., 1994. Mem.: DAR (state officer 2000—), Ohio Vocat. Assn., Am. Vocat. Assn. (nat. com.), Am. Home Econs. Assn., Presbyn. Assn. (trustee), Dames of Ct. of Honor (pres. gen. 2001—), Colonial Daus. of 17th Century (nat. officer), Daus. Am. Colonists (state officer), Nat. Officers Colonial Clergy (nat. officer, chancellor), Colonial Dames Am. (pres. chpt. 18, nat. officer ct. honor), U.S. Daus. of 1912, Colonial Dames of XVII Century, New Eng. Soc. of Western Res. (pres.), Clearwater Country Club, Cleve. Skating Club, Union Club. Republican. Presbyterian. Avocations: curling, rug hooking, needlepoint. Home: 20101 Malvern Rd Shaker Heights OH 44122-2825 Address: 219 Park Cir Dunedin FL 34698 also: PO Box 761 Chautauqua NY 14722

**TREFZGER, RICHARD CHARLES,** surgeon; b. Peoria, Ill., Jan. 27, 1948; s. John Dennis and Marilyn Lestilie (Wilson) Trefzger; m. Nancy Ellen Guy, Dec. 19, 1971; children: Emily Jean, Michael Guy. BS, U. Ill., 1970, MD, 1973. Diplomate Am Bd Surgery. Intern in surgery Med. Coll. Wis., Milw., 1973-74, resident in surgery, 1974-75, Presbyn.-St. Luke's Hosp., Chgo., 1975-78; instr. surgery Rush Med. Coll., Chgo., 1977-78; med. dir. Westminster Village Retirement Ctr., Bloomington, Ill., 1980-84, St. Joseph's Trauma Ctr., Bloomington, 1986-96, BroMenn Regional Trauma Ctr., Normal, Ill., 1994-96; chief surgery Bromenn Regional Med. Ctr., Normal, Ill., 1987-88, 94-96, St. Joseph's Med. Ctr., Bloomington, 1989-91, pres. med. staff, 1991-92. Clin. instr. U. Ill. Coll. Medicine, 1980—2006, clin. asst. prof. surgery, 2006—; chmn. bd. dirs. BroMenn Physician Hosp. Orgn., 1995—96; sec. med. staff BroMenn Regional Med. Ctr., 1998, v.p., 98, bd. dirs. 1999—2002, pres. med. staff, 2000—02. Mem. Ill. State U. Civic Chorale, Normal, 1991—98; bd. dirs. Cmty. Cancer Ctr, Bloomington, 1996—2006, pres., 2000; v.p. ofcl. bd. First Christian Ch., Bloomington, 1981—2006, 1999—2002, 2005—06, elder, 1980—; rector Cursillo Christianity, 2001; bd. dirs. Barton Stone Christian Home, Jacksonville, Ill., 1979—82. Fellow: ACS (councilor Ill. chpt. 1986—88, mem. Ill. chpt. com. trauma 1996—2003); mem.: AMA, Ill. Surg. Soc. (gov. 1990—94, v.p. elect 1997, v.p. elect 1999, pres. 2000, trustee 2001—04), Danvers Cmty. Band-Saxophone, Scottish Rite, Rotary (dir. 1982—85, 1994—99, sec. 1995—96, v.p. 1996—97, pres. 1997—98, band-saxophone, Paul Harris fellow 1989),

Masons, Alpha Omega Alpha. Avocations: music, travel. Home: 41 Pendleton Way Bloomington IL 61704-6243 Office: Surg Assocs 1404 Eastland Dr Bloomington IL 61701-3532 Office Phone: 309-663-4351. Personal E-mail: MENDR2@insightbb.com.

**TREGENZA, NORMAN HUGHSON,** investment banker; b. Morristown, NJ, Feb. 1, 1937; s. Norman J. and Marion Esther (Hughson) T.; m. Alyce Virginia Bruene, Aug. 27, 1966; children: Norman Arthur, Suzanne Carol. BA, St. Lawrence U., 1959; MBA, NYU, 1963. Sr. investment officer Tchrs. Ins. and Annuity Assn., NYC, 1960-71; sr. v.p. Republic Funding Corp., NYC, 1971-82; co-founder Tempo Enterprises, 1975; pres. Convent Capital Corp., 1982—. Bd. dirs. Ameritype Corp., Boulder City, Nev. Chmn. stewardship com. Presbyn. Ch., Morristown, 1978, ruling elder, 1979, pres. bd. trustees, 1982; trustee St. Lawrence U., Canton, N.Y., 1983-95, Gill/St. Bernards Sch. (hon.), 1982-96, The Morris Mus., Morristown, 1983—. Mem. St. Lawrence U. Alumni Assn. N.J. (pres. 1970-72), Nat. Coun. USS Constitution Mus. Clubs: Baltusrol Golf, Park Ave., Indian Mound Golf. Home and Office: PO Box 150 Silver Lake NH 03875-0150 Office Phone: 603-367-8888.

**TREGUBOFF, WILLIAM JACK,** psychologist; b. LA; s. Jack John Treguboff and Sarah Alex Lidgoff; m. Correne Esther Treguboff (dec.); m. Barbara Clara Treguboff, Aug. 30, 1991; children: Lance Steadman, Andrew, Lisa Steadman, Deborah Carr, Edward. BA in Literature, U. Calif., Santa Barbara, 1964; MA in Counseling Psychology, Fresno State U., 1977; PhD in Psychology, Profl. Sch. Psychology, 2006. Lic. marriage and family therapist Calif. Surveyor LA County Rd. Dept., 1951—60; campus min. Intervarsity Christian Fellowship, Davis, Calif., 1965—75; adj. faculty mem. Fresno (Calif.) State U., 1977—82; family therapist Davis Counseling and Therapy, 1982—96; psychiat. emergency clinician Suicide Prevention of Yolo County, Davis, 1997—. Recipient Bell award for Mental Health Team of Yr., 1984. Mem.: APA, Calif. Assn. Marriage and Family Therapists. Avocations: swimming, bicycling. Home: 3413 Cutter Pl Davis CA 95616 Office: Davis Counseling and Therapy 105 E St 2-C Davis CA 95616

**TREGURTHA, PAUL RICHARD,** water transportation executive; b. Orange, NJ, 1935; married. BSME, Cornell U., 1958; MBA, Harvard U., 1963. Contr., v.p. Brown & Sharpe Mfg. Co., 1969-71; v.p. fin. Moore McCormack Resources, Inc., Stamford, Conn., 1971-73, exec. v.p. fin., 1973-78, pres., COO, from 1978, pres., CEO, chmn., 1987-88; chmn., CEO, co-owner Mormac Marine Group, Inc., Stamford, 1988—. Vice chmn., co-owner The Interlake Steamship Co., 1988—; chmn., CEO Moran Transp. Co., 1994—; bd. dirs. FPL Group, Inc. Trustee emeritus Cornell U., Ithaca, NY; trustee Tchrs. Ins. and Annuity Assn. 1st lt. USAF, 1958—61. Named Baker Scholar, Harvard U., 1963. Office: Mormac Marine Group Inc One Landmark Sq Stamford CT 06901-2608 Office Phone: 203-977-8950.

**TREIBLE, KIRK,** retired academic administrator, foundation administrator; b. Newton, N.J., Mar. 29, 1941; s. William Bryan and Grace Almond T.; 1 cons, Todd. BS, W.Va. Wesleyan Coll.; MBA, W.Va. U.; LLD, LaGrange Coll. Bus. mgr. Parkersburg (W.Va.) C.C., 1969-71; devel. officer W.Va. Wesleyan Coll., 1972-75, acting treas., 1975-77; v.p. fin. Southwestern U., Georgetown, Tex., 1977-88; pres. Andrew Coll., Cuthbert, Ga., 1998—2002, now pres. emeritus; ednl. cons., 2002—; exec. dir. United Meth. Found. for Comm., 2003—. Bd. dirs. Citizen Bank, Geogetown, Tex., 1978-88; bd. dirs. Regions Bank, Cuthbert, Ga., 1989-99; cons. Neighbor Meth. ch., 1989—. Mem. So. Assn. Schs. and Colls. Chmn. adminstrv. bd. First United Meth. Ch., 1983-85, univ. senate; mem. W.I.H. and Lula E. Pitts Found., Peed scholarship Trust, United Meth. Ch. Served with USAF, 1966-69. Mem. Assn. Pvt. Colls. and Univs. Ga. (pres. dir.), Nat. Assn. Ch. Bus. Adminstrs. Methodist. Home: 8150 Cleary Blvd Apt 1506 Plantation FL 33324-1375 E-mail: ktreible@aol.com.

**TREICHEL, HELMUTH W.A.,** technology executive; b. Hessberg, Germany, Aug. 26, 1953; s. Otto Treichel, Elise Treichel; m. Ursula M. Fischer; 1 child, Nicola. BSChemE, Acad. Sci. and Tech., Isny, Germany, 1986. Process devel. engr. Siemens AG, Munich, 1986—92; lead engr. Siemens Components, Burlington, Vt., 1992—94; dept. mgr. multilevel metallization, pilot prodn. mgr. Fraunhofer Inst. for Solid State Tech., Munich, 1994—97; sr. engring. mgr. Lam Rsch. Corp., Fremont, Calif., 1997—2000; dir. tech. Novellus Sys., Inc., San Jose, 2000—02. Presenter in field. Contbr. articles to profl. jours. Mem.: Materials Rsch. Soc. Achievements include patents in field. Home: 859 Pheland Ct Milpitas CA 95035 Personal E-mail: treichel@yahoo.com. Business E-Mail: helmuth.treichel@novellus.com.

**TREIGER, IRWIN LOUIS,** lawyer; b. Seattle, Sept. 10, 1934; s. Sam S. and Rose (Steinberg) T.; m. Betty Lou Friedlander, Aug. 18, 1957; children: Louis H., Karen I., Kenneth B. BA, U. Wash., 1955, JD, 1957; LLM in Taxation, NYU, 1958. Bar: Wash. 1958, D.C. 1982, U.S. Dist. Ct. (we. dist.) Wash., U.S. Ct. Appeals (9th cir.), U.S. Supreme Ct. Assoc. Bogle & Gates, Seattle, 1958—63, ptnr., 1964—99, chmn., 1986—94; ptnr. Dorsey & Whitney LLP, Seattle, 1999—. Trustee Am. Tax Policy Inst., 2004—. Pres. Jewish Fedn. Greater Seattle, 1993-95; chmn. Mayor's Symphony Panel, 1986, Corp. Coun. for the Arts, 1987-88; pres. Seattle Symphony Found., 1986—; trustee, co-chmn. Cornish Coll. of the Arts, 1990-96, chair elect 2003—; trustee The Seattle Found., 1992—, vice chair, 1999-2003, chair, 2003-05; trustee., sec. Samis Found., 1989—; chmn. King County Baseball Pk. Commn., 1995 Fellow Am. Coll. Tax Counsel; mem. ABA (chmn. taxation sect. 1988-89, sect. del. 1990-96, bd. govs. 2000-03), Wash. State Bar Assn. (chmn. taxation sect. 1975, co-chmn. nat. conf. lawyers and accts. 1997-2000), Greater Seattle C. of C. (chmn. 1993-94), Seattle Rotary (trustee 1998-2000), Seattle Rotary Svc. Found. (v.p. 1995-96, pres. 1996-97). Jewish. Office: Dorsey & Whitney LLP Ste 3400 1420 5th Ave Seattle WA 98101-4010 Office Phone: 206-903-8705. Business E-Mail: treiger.irwin@dorsey.com.

**TREISTER, GEORGE MARVIN,** lawyer; b. Oxnard, Calif., Sept. 5, 1923; s. Isadore Harry and Augusta Lee (Bloom) T.; m. Jane Goldberg, Jan. 24, 1946; children: Laura, Neil, Adam, Dana. BS, UCLA, 1943; LL.B., Yale U., 1949. Bar: Calif. 1950. Law clk. to chief justice Calif. Supreme Ct., 1949-50; law clk. to Assoc. Justice Hugo L. Black U. S. Supreme Ct., 1950-51; asst. U.S. atty. So. Dist. Calif., 1951-53; dep. atty. gen. Calif., 1953; practiced in Los Angeles, 1953—; mem. Stutman, Treister and Glatt, 1953—; instr. U. So. Calif. Law Sch., 1954-98, Stanford U. Law Sch., 1977-81. Mem., former vice chmn. Nat. Bankruptcy Conf.; former mem. adv. com. on bankruptcy rules Jud. Conf. U.S. Contbr. articles to profl. jours. Served with USNR, 1943-46. Mem. Am. Law Inst. Home: 1201 Neil Creek Rd Ashland OR 97520-9778 Office: 1901 Ave of the Stars 12th fl Los Angeles CA 90067 Office Phone: 800-201-3030.

**TREITEL, DAVID HENRY,** aviation executive; b. Lynn, Mass., Apr. 22, 1954; s. Henry David and Lotte (Elkeses) T.; m. Madelynn Dremmer, Sept. 1982 (div. Oct. 1988); m. Amy Gail Granowitz, Apr. 18, 1990. BA in Econs. with honors, Middlebury Coll., 1976; MBA, Columbia U., 1978. Sr. assoc. Simat Helliesen & Eichner, Inc., NYC, 1980-84, v.p., 1984-88, sr. v.p., 1988-90, exec. v.p., 1990-95; pres. Simat Hellliesen & Eichner, Inc., 1995—, CEO, chmn., 1996—. Bd. dirs. Midwest Airlines, Milw., Aircraft Fin. Trust, Wilmington, Del., Lease Investment Flight Trust, Wilmington, Castle 2003-1 Trust, Wilmington, Castle 2003-2 Trust, Wilmington, 1Stat Found. Contbr. articles to profl. jours. Mem. The Wings Club (bd. dirs.). Republican. Avocations: golf, tennis, tournament bridge, travel. Office: Simat Helliesen & Eichner 90 Park Ave Fl 27 New York NY 10016-1308 Business E-Mail: dtreitel@sh-e.com.

**TREJO, JOANN,** medical researcher; b. Stockton, Calif., Jan. 23, 1964; BS, U. Calif., Davis, 1986; PhD, U. Calif., San Diego, 1992. Postdoctoral fellow Cardiovasc. Rsch. Inst., U. Calif., San Francisco, 1992—2000; asst. prof. pharmacology U. N.C., 2000—. Undergrad. rsch. asst. Lawrence Berkeley Lab. Divsn. Biology and Medicine, 1983—86; tchg. asst. dept. environ. toxicology U. Calif., Davis, 1986, dept. pharmacology, San Diego, 1988—91, dept. biology, 1989. Contbr. articles to profl. jours. Recipient Nat. Hispanic

Scholarship Fund award, 1990—91, Minority Scientist Career Devel. award, Am. Heart Assn., 1995; fellow San Diego and Grad. Opportunity, 1986—88, Dissertation, Nat. Rsch. Coun. Ford Found., 1991—92, Pres.'s Postdoctoral, U. Calif., 1993—95; grantee Ntg., NIH/NHLBI Cardiovasc. Rsch. Inst., 1992—93; scholar Katherine Larcara, 1982, Jack O'Keefe, 1982, Kiwanis Club Undergrad., 1982. Mem.: LWV, AAAS, Am. Soc. Cell Biology, Soc. Advancement of Chicanos and Native Americans in Sci. Home: 303 Lorraine St Carrboro NC 27510-1121 Office: UNC-Sch Medicine Dept Pharmacology 1106 Mary Ellen Jones Bldg Chapel Hill NC 27514

**TREJOS, CHARLOTTE MARIE,** humanities educator, consultant; b. Trout Lake, Mich., July 5, 1920; d. Charles Floyd and Lula May (Force) Draper; m. J. Mario Trejos, Jan. 8, 1961; 1 child, J. Mario Jr. Tchg. credentials, State of Calif., 1989; MA, Hawthorne Coll., 1975; DD, Min. Salvation Ch., 1986. Tchr. English El Colegio Anglo-Am., Cochabamba, Bolivia, 1965-66; tchr. Hawthorne (Calif.) Christian Sch., 1966-75; owner Trejos Literary Cons., Carson, Calif., 1976—. Author: My Carson, Your Carson, 1987, Variegated Verse, 1973, Yesterday Was Sunday, 1994; Artist: Am Legion Post Number 6, Nat. Mus. Women Arts, Mus. Latin Am. Art; contbr. articles to profl. jours. Voter registerer Democrats. With U.S. Army, 1942-43. Named Poet of Yr. Nat. Poetry Pub. Assn., 1974; recipient Golden Poet award World of Poetry, 1993. Mem. Soc. Ibero-Am. Escritores de Los Estados Unidos Am. (pres. 1985—, Cert. Recognition 1986). Avocations: music, tap dancing, art, gardening.

**TREJOS, FRANKLIN ANTHONY,** retired physician assistant; b. Spokane, Wash., July 6, 1955; s. Frank Trejos and Lloydene Louise (Small) Mielbrecht; children: Cerena, Cebrena, Alyssa. Student, We. Coll., 1978; diploma in physician asst., U. Utah, 1984. Advanced EMT Kootenai County Emergency Med. Rescue Svc., Coeur d'alene, Idaho, 1980—82; physician asst. Franklin Park Minor Emergency Ctr., Spokane, 1984—85; physician asst. family practice Cigna Health Plan, Mesa, Ariz., 1985—95; physician asst. gen. surgery, orthop. surgery, neurosurgery Mayo Clinic Scottsdale, Ariz., 1995—97; faculty physician asst. program, physician asst. Midwestern U., Glendale, Ariz., 1997—2001; physician asst. Pain Mgmt. Specialists, Scottsdale, 2000—, Desert Pain Clinic, Scottsdale, 1997—2001, Desert Pain and Rehab. Specialists, Phoenix, 2002—. Adj. faculty Midwestern U. Coll. Osteo. Medicine, Glendale. Fellow: Am. Acad. Physician Assts. Avocations: waterskiing, mountain biking, astronomy, photography, marine life. Personal E-mail: f.trejos@cox.net.

**TRELEASE, ALLEN WILLIAM,** historian, educator; b. Boulder, Colo., Jan. 31, 1928; s. William, Jr. and Helen (Waldo) T.; children: William C. (dec. 1990), Mary E., John A. AB, U. Ill., 1950, MA, 1951; PhD, Harvard U., 1955. Mem. faculty Wells Coll., Aurora, NY, 1955-67, prof. history, 1965-67, chmn. dept. history and govt., 1963-67; prof. history U. NC, Greensboro, 1967-94, head dept., 1984-92, prof. emeritus, 1994—. Author: Indian Affairs in Colonial New York: The Seventeenth Century, 1960, White Terror: The Ku Klux Klan Conspiracy and Southern Reconstruction, 1971, Reconstruction: The Great Experiment, 1971, The North Carolina Railroad, 1849-1871, and the Modernization of North Carolina, 1991, Changing Assignments: A Pictorial History of the U. of N.C. at Greensboro, 1991, Making North Carolina Literate: The University of North Carolina at Greensboro, from Normal School to Metropolitan University, 2003. Mem. Am. So. Hist. assns., Orgn. Am. Historians, Hist. Soc. NC (pres. 1986-87), AAUP, Phi Beta Kappa, Phi Kappa Phi, Phi Eta Sigma, Phi Kappa Psi. Personal E-mail: atrelease@triad.rr.com.

**TRELEWICZ, JENNIFER Q.,** researcher; BS, Carnegie Mellon U., 1988—91; MS, Ariz. State U., 1992—95, MNS, 1996—99, PhD, 1995—2000. Adj. prof. of elec. engring. U. of Colo., 2000—02; instr., computer sci. Scottsdale Coll., Ariz., 2000; cons. self-employed, Phoenix, 1995—98; software engr. Motorola, Scottsdale, Ariz., 1991—95; rsch. staff mgr. IBM Almaden Rsch. Ctr., San Jose, Calif., 2000—05; rsch. relationship mgr., Russia, CIS and Ea. Europe IBM Rsch., San Jose, Calif., 2004—05; lab dir. IBM sys. and tech. lab. Moscow Russian Fedn., 2005—. Editl. bd. mem. IEEE Signal Processing Mag., Piscataway, 2002—; chair IBM Boulder Tech. Vitality Coun. Attraction, Recruitment, and Retention Com., Boulder, Colo., 2002; mem., organizing com. IEEE Signal Processing Soc., ICASSP Conf., Piscataway, 2001—04; chair IEEE Signal Processing Soc., standing com. on industry DSP, Piscataway, 2002—04; mem., steering com. IBM Women's Interest Networking Group, Boulder, Colo., 2001—02; mem. IBM Boulder Tech. Vitality Com., Boulder, Colo., 2001—02; apptd. rep. Ariz. State U. Grad. Student Adv. Coun., Tempe, Ariz., 1998—99; engring. chair Ariz. State U. grad. rsch. support proposal rev. com., Tempe, Ariz., 1997—98. Contbr. scientific papers. Recipient Grad. Student Affairs Coun. Outstanding Mem., Ariz. State U. Grad. Student Affairs Coun., 1998—99, NSF Engring. Edn. Scholars Program fellow, NSF, 1998, Motorola Engring. award for Key Contributions, Motorola, 1994, Motorola Tech. Soc. Membership, 1994, Soc. of Women Engineers Cert. of Academic Excellence, Soc. of Women Engineers, 1989—90; fellow NASA Grad. Student Rschr. Program fellowship, NASA, 1996—99; scholar Pa. Profl. Engring. Soc. Aux. Scholarship, PA Profl. Engring. Soc., 1998, Ariz. Bd. of Regents scholarship, Ariz. Bd. of Regents, 1998—99; Phelps Dodge scholarship, Phelps Dodge, 1999—2000, SPIE scholarship, SPIE (Soc. of Photonic Indsl. Engineers), 1999. Mem.: Inst. of Elec. and Electronic Engineers (mem. at large, bd. of governors 2004—), Am. Math. Soc., Soc. for Indsl. and Applied Math., Phi Kappa Phi (life), Tau Beta Pi (life; treas. 1998—99). Achievements include patents pending for efficient scaling in transform domain; system and method for using hardware assist functions to process multiple arbitrary sized data elements in a register; raster data compression apparatus and method; method and apparatus for electromagnetic drying of printed media; method and apparatus for controlling a spot function for digital halftoning; faster transforms using early abort and precision refinement; faster discrete cosine transforms using scaled terms; method, apparatus and article of manufacture using media roughness as a print parameter; invention of buffer flipper with optional urge unit for continuous form printers; method for secure data in the physical paper medium; patents pending for method and system for scaling a signal sample rate; method and system for providing a high quality halftoned image; method and system for rasterizing and encoding multi-region data; and method and system for minimizing the appearance of image distortion in a high speed inkjet paper printing system. Address: 353 E 10th St Ste E PMB 711 Gilroy CA 95020 Office: IBM EE/A 18 Krasnopresnenskaya NAB 123317 Moscow Russia Office Phone: +1 408 927 2600.

**TRELSTAD, ROBERT LAURENCE,** pathology educator, cell biologist; b. Redding, Calif., June 16, 1940; s. Bertram Laurence and Dorothy (Aust) T.; m. Barbara Stanton Henken, Aug. 27, 1961; children: Derek, Graham, Brian, Jeremy. BA, Columbia U., 1961; MD, Harvard U., 1966. From asst. to assoc. prof. Harvard Med. Sch., Boston, 1972-81; chief pathology Shriners Burns Inst., Boston, 1975-81; staff pathologist Mass. Gen. Hosp., Boston, 1972-81; prof., chair pathology Robert Wood Johnson Med. Sch., Piscataway, New Brunswick, NJ, 1981-98; acting dir. Child Health Inst. of NJ, 1998—2005, Paz chair devel. biology 1999—. Mem. study sect. NIH, Bethesda, Md., 1971-75, 86-90; mem. adv. com. Nat. Inst. Child Health and Human Devel., 1993-97; chmn. health professions adv. com. Princeton U., 2002—. Cofounder, editor-in-chief: Keyboard Pub. Inc., 1990; past mem. editl. bd. various profl. jours. including Jour. Cell Biology, Am. Jour. Pathology, Devel. Biology, Devel. Dynamics. Lt. comdr. USPHS, 1967—69. Helen Hay Whitney Found. fellow, 1969-72; recipient Rsch. Faculty award Am. Cancer Soc., 1972-76, Disting. Tchr. in Basic Scis. award Alpha Omega Alpha and Assn. Am. Med. Colls., 1992. Mem. Am. Soc. Cell Biology (sec. 1982-88), Soc. Devel. Biology (pres. 1983). Home: 35 Westcott Rd Princeton NJ 08540-3038 Office: Robert Wood Johnson Med Sch Pathology and Lab Medicine Piscataway NJ 08854 Office Phone: 732-235-9525. Business E-Mail: trelstad@umdnj.edu.

**TREMAIN, ALAN,** hotel executive; b. Kent, England, Aug. 18, 1935; arrived in U.S., 1966; s. Archibald and Elizabeth (Morris) T.; m. Ingrid K. Olbrich, Dec. 1997; 1 child, Warren. Grad., Westminster Hotel Sch., 1952,

Canterbury Sch. Econs., 1962; LL.B., La Salle Sch., Chgo., 1971. Chef de Partie Grosvenor House, London, 1954-55; food and beverage mgr. Peninsula, Hong Kong, 1956-57; gen. mgr. Warners Hotel, also The Russley, Christchurch, New Zealand, 1958-64, Menzies, Sydney, Australia, 1964-65, Empress Hotel, Vancouver, B.C., Canada, 1966-69; pres. Planned Food Facilities (Internat.) Ltd., Toronto, Canada, 1970-72; resident mgr. Sheraton Boston, 1972; mng. dir. Copley Plaza Hotel, Boston, 1972—. Chmn. Hotels of Distinction, Inc., Boston; dir. The China Fund, Inc., 1992, chmn. 1999—. Author: A Guide to the Fine Art of Living, 1963, A Meal for To-Night, 1965. Decorated officer Order Brit. Empire; recipient Culinary Merit award from Cercle Epicurien Mondel, Paris, 1956. Fellow Hotel and Catering Inst. (U.K.); founding mem. Internat. Soc. Chefs de Cuisine (chmn. 1954), Masons, Montreal Badminton and Squash Club, The Beach Club, Palm Beach Club, Les Ambs. Club, London Club, Rolls Royce Owners Club. E-mail: atremain@aol.com.

**TREMAINE, SCOTT DUNCAN,** astrophysicist; b. Toronto, May 25, 1950; s. Vincent Joseph and Beatrice Delphine (Sharp) T. BSc, McMaster U., Hamilton, Ont., 1971; PhD, Princeton U., 1975. Postdoctoral fellow Calif. Inst. Tech., Pasadena, 1975-77; rsch. assoc. Inst. Astronomy, Cambridge, England, 1977-78; long-term mem. Inst. for Advanced Study, Princeton, NJ, 1978-81; assoc. prof. MIT, Cambridge, 1981-85; prof., dir. Can. Inst. for Theoretical Astrophysics U. Toronto, 1985-96; dir. program in cosmology and gravity Can. Inst. Advanced Rsch., Toronto, 1996—2002; prof. Princeton U., 1997—, chair dept. astrophys. scis., 1998—. Author: Galactic Dynamics, 1987; contbr. articles to profl. jours. E.W.R. Steacie fellow Natural Scis. and Engring. Rsch. Coun., 1988; recipient H.B. Warner prize Am. Astron. Soc., 1983, Steacie prize, 1989, C.S. Beals award Canadian Astron. Soc., 1990, Rutherford medal Royal Soc. Can., 1990, Heinemann prize for Astrophysics, 1997, Brouwer award, 1997. Fellow Royal Soc. London, Royal Soc. Can.; mem. Am. Acad. Arts and Scis. (fgn. hon.), Nat. Acad. Scis. Office: Princeton U Dept Astrophys Sci Peyton Hall Princeton NJ 08544-1001 E-mail: tremaine@astro.princeton.edu.

**TREMAYNE, ERIC FLORY,** lawyer; b. Washington, Nov. 29, 1945; s. Bertram William and Frances (Lewis) Tremayne; m. Barbara Ann Williams, Sept. 18, 1982. BA, Westminster Coll., 1967; JD, Washington U., St. Louis, 1973. Bar: Mo. 1973, U.S. Dist. Ct. (ea. and we. dists.) Mo. 1973, U.S. Tax Ct. 2003. Assoc. Tremayne, Lay, Carr, Bauer, Clayton, Mo., 1973—77, ptnr., 1978—; prosecuting atty. City of Wildwood, Mo., 1996—2000. Dir. Option Computer Corp., St. Louis. Bd. dirs. YMCA of Ozarks; campaign aide Citizens for Kit Bond, St. Louis, 1972. With U.S. Army, 1968—70. Mem.: Bar Assn. Met. St. Louis, St. Louis County Bar Assn. (pres. 1983—84, Outstanding Young Lawyer 1981), Sports Car Club Am. (instr. 1979—), Beta Theta Pi (v.p. 1978—90). Home: 433 Eatherton Valley Rd Wildwood MO 63005-4103 Office: Tremayne Lay & Coleman LLP 7777 Bonhomme Ave Ste 1600 Clayton MO 63105-1911 Office Phone: 314-863-4151. Business E-Mail: etremayne@tremayne.org.

**TREMBLAY, ANDRÉ-MARIE,** physicist; b. Montreal, Que., Can., Jan. 2, 1953; m. Marié à Guylaine Séguin; children: Noémie, Rachel. BSc, U. Montreal, 1974; PhD, MIT, 1978. With Energie Atomique du Can. Limitée, 1973-74, MIT, Boston, 1974-75, Inst. de Recherche de l'Hydro-Que., 1976, Cornell U., Ithaca, NY, 1978-80; prof. physics U. Sherbrooke, Que., 1980—, dir. Rsch. Ctr. Physics of Solids Que., 1991-99. Cons. Cornell U., 1981, Ohio State U., 1982, IBM, 1984; vis. scientist Cornell U., 1986-87, Yale U., 2003; vis. rsch. physicist Inst. for Theoretical Physics, Santa Barbara, Calif., 1989, 96, 2000; vis. scientist Brookhaven (N.Y.) Nat. Lab, 1984; assoc. prof. U. Provence, France, 1982, 83, 97, 99, 2000, 02; Can. Rsch. chair in condensed matter physics, 2000—. Contbr. over 120 articles to profl. publs. Recipient Herzberg medal Can. Assn. Physics, Steacie prize Natural Scis. and Engring. Rsch. Coun., 1987, CAP-CRM prize in Theoretical and Math. Physics, 2001, Urgel-Archaubault prize Assn. francophone pour le savoir, 2003; Killam fellow, 1992-94. Fellow: Royal Soc. Can.; mem.: Can. Inst. Advanced Rsch. Office: Sherbrooke U Dept Physics Sherbrooke PQ Canada J1K 2R1 E-mail: tremblay@physique.usherbrooke.ca.

**TREMBLAY, MARC ADÉLARD,** anthropologist, educator; b. Les Eboulements, Que., Can., Apr. 24, 1922; s. Willie and Laurette (Tremblay) T.; m. Jacqueline Cyr, Dec. 27, 1949; children: Geneviève, Lorraine, Marc, Colette, Dominique, Suzanne. AB, U. Montreal, 1944, L.S.A., 1948; MA, Laval U., 1950; PhD, Cornell U., 1954; PhD (hon.), Ottawa U., 1982, Guelph U., 1983, U. N. B.C., 1994, Carleton U., 1995, U. Ste. Anne, 1997, McGill U., 1998. Research asso. Cornell U., 1953-56; mem. faculty Laval U., 1956-93, prof. anthropology, 1963-68, 81-93, prof. emeritus, 1994, vice dean social scis., 1968-71, dean Grad. Sch., 1971-79, also mem. univ. council.; pres. Quebec Coun. Social Rsch., 1987-91. Dir. Inuit and Circupolar Study Group Laval U., 1991—93; mem. Nunavik Commn., 1999—2001. Author 25 books and monographs in social scis., about 200 articles. Decorated officer Order of Can., gt. officer Order of Que.; recipient Que. Lit. prize, 1965, Innis-Gerin prize Royal Soc. Can., 1979, Molson prize Can. Coun., 1987, Prix Marcel Vincent ACFAS, 1988, Contbn. exceptionnelle Societé de sociologie et d'anthropolotie, 1990, Esdras Minville award Soc. St.-Jean Baptiste, 1991; named to Internat. Order of Merit, Internat. Biog. Inst., Cambridge, Eng., 1990. Mem. Royal Soc. Can. (pres. 1981-84), Acad. des Scis. Morales et Politiques (sec.), Rsch. Inst. Pub. Policy, Am. Anthrop. Assn. (past fellow), Am. Sociology Soc. (past fellow), Can. Soc. Applied Anthropology, Can. Sociology and Anthropology Assn. (founding pres.), Can. Ethnology Soc. (past pres.), Assn. Can. Univs. for Northern Studies (past pres.), Assn. Internat. Sociology, Societe des savants et sci. Can. (v.p., pres. nat. order Quebec 1998-2000). Home: 835 N Orléans St Sainte-Foy PQ Canada G1X 3J4 Fax: 418-653-9865. E mail: matremblay@globetrotter.net.

**TREMBLAY, RAYMOND L.,** ecology and biological conservation educator, researcher; b. Sturgeon Falls, Ont., Can., Mar. 1, 1959; s. Normand Tremblay and Suzanne Lalande; m. Ledith J. Resto-Meléndez; children: Myosotis Andrea Tremblay Resto, Caroline Suzanne Tremblay Resto. BSc with honors, Carleton U., Ottawa, Can., 1991; PhD, U. PR, Rio Piedras, 1996. Assoc. prof. U. PR, Humacao, 1994—2004, prof., 2004—. Chair insitu orchid conservation com. Orchid Specialist Group/ IUCN, Humacao, 2001—. Achievements include research in evolution and conservation of orchids. Home: Brisas del Parque 1 32 Calle Sendero Caguas PR 00791 Office: U PR Dept Biology 100 carr 908 Humacao PR 00791 Office Phone: 787-850-0000 ext 9161. Office Fax: 787-850-9439. E-mail: raymond@hpcf.upr.edu.

**TREMBLAY, RICHARD ERNEST,** psychology educator; b. Nov. 23, 1944; BA, U. Ottawa, Can., 1966; MPsed, U. Montreal, 1970; PhD, U. London, 1976. Asst. prof. U. Montreal, 1976-81, assoc. prof., 1981-86, prof., 1986—, Can. Rsch. chair in child devel., 2001—; dir. Ctr. of Excellence for Early Child Devel., 2001—; clinician St. Charles Psychiatr. Hosp., Joliette, Can., 1966-69, Boscoville, Montreal, Can., 1967-70, Philippe Pinel Psychiat. Inst., Montreal, 1970-73. Chmn. Sch. of Psycho-Edn., Faculty of Arts and Scis., U. Montreal, 1980-90; invited prof. ethology lab. U. Rennes I, 1993-94, dept. psychology U. Jyväskylä, Finland, 1991; invited scientist psychophysiology lab. U. Franche-Com., 1982-83; presenter in field. Author (with others): Face to Face with Giftedness, 1983, Ethologie et Development de l'enfant, 1985, Le Traitement des Adolescents Delinquants, 1985, Les Relations Entre Enfants, 1988, Human Development and Criminal Behavior: New Ways of Advancing Knowledge, 1991, Famille, Inadaption et Intervention, 1991, Les enfants agressifs: Perspective Development Interculturelle, 1991. Preventing Antisocial Behavior from Birth to Adolescency, 1992, Juvenile Crime, Juvenile Justice, 2001, Developmental Origins of Aggression, 2005. Molson fellow Can. Inst. of Advanced Rsch. Fellow Royal Soc. of Can., Can. Psychol. Assn.; mem. AAAS, Internat. Soc. for the Study of Behavioral Devel., (exec. com. 1994—), Internat. Soc. for Rsch. on Agression (coun. mem. 1992-96), Am. Soc. of Criminology, Assn. Canadienne-Française pour l'Avancement des Scis., European Assn. for Psychology and Law, Internat. soc. for Human Ethology, N.Y. Acad. Scis., Soc. for Rsch. in Child Devel. Business E-Mail: grip@umontreal.ca.

**TREMBLAY, WILLIAM ANDREW,** language educator, writer; b. Southbridge, Mass., June 9, 1940; s. Arthur Achille and Irene (Fontaine) T.; m. Cynthia Ann Crooks, Sept. 28, 1962; children: William Crooks, Benjamin Philip, John Fontaine. BA, Clark U., 1962, MA, 1969; MFA in Poetry, U. Mass., 1972. English tchr. Southbridge (Mass.) High Sch., 1962-63, Sutton (Mass.) High Sch., 1963-65, Tantasqua Regional High Sch., Sturbridge, Mass., 1965-67; asst. prof. Leicester (Mass.) Jr. Coll., 1967-70; teaching asst. U. Mass., Amherst, 1970-72; instr. Springfield (Mass.) Coll., 1972-73; prof. English Colo. State U., Fort Collins, 1973—, John F. Stern Disting. prof., 2002, dir. MFA program in creative writing. Fulbright-Hays lectureship, Lisbon, Portugal, 1979, NEH summer program, 1981; mem. program dirs. coun. Associated Writing Programs, 1984-86. Author: The June Rise: The Apocryphal Letters of Antoine Janis, 1994, (poetry) Shooting Script: Door of Fire, 2003 (Colo. Book award 2004), Rainstorm Over the Alphabet, 2001, Duhamel: Ideas of Order in Little Canada, 1986, Second Sun: New and Selected Poems, 1985, Home Front, 1978, The Anarchist Heart, 1977, Crying in the Cheap Seats, 1971; editor-in-chief: Colo. Rev., 1983-91. Nat. Endowment for the Humanities, 1981, Summer writing fellow Corp. of Yaddo, 1989, Creative Writing fellow Nat. Endowment for Arts, 1985; recipient Pushcart prize Pushcart Prize Anthology, 1987, Best Am. Poetry, 2003. Mem.: Puerto del Sol (bd. advisors), Am. Acad. Poetry, Poudre Wilderness Vol. Home: 1917 Kedron Cir Fort Collins CO 80524-2288 Office: Colo State U Dept English Fort Collins CO 80523-0001

**TREMBLY, CRISTY,** television executive; b. Oakland, Md., July 11, 1958; d. Charles Dee and Mary Louise (Cassidy) T.; m. Roman Ziombra. BA in Russian, German and Linguistics cum laude, W.Va. U., 1978, BS in Journalism, 1978, MS in Broadcast Journalism, 1979; advanced cert. travel, West L.A. Coll., 1982; advanced cert. rec. engring., Soundmaster Schs., North Hollywood, Calif., 1985. Engr. videotape Sta. WWVU-TV, Morgantown, W.Va., 1976-78; announcer, engr. Sta. WVVW Radio, Grafton, W.Va., 1979; tech. dir., videotape supr. Sta. KMEX-TV, L.A., 1980—85; broadcast supr. Sta. KADY-TV, Oxnard, Calif., 1988—89; dir. news tech. Sta. KVEA-TV, Glendale, Calif., 1985—89; asst. editor, videotape technician CBS TV Network, Hollywood, Calif., 1989—90; supr. videotape Sta. KCBS-TV, Hollywood, 1990—91; mgr. electronic news gathering ops., 1991—92; studio mgr., engr.-in-charge CBS TV Network, Hollywood, 1992—2001, mgr. transmission and satellite, 1994—, mgr. videotape, 2001, mgr. syndication, 2001, mgr. prodn., 2001—. Radio operator KJ6BX Malibu Disaster Comm., 1987—; coun. mem. L.A. World Affairs 2000—. Prodr. (TV show) The Mountain Scene, 1976-78. Vol. Ch. Coun., L.A. Riot Rebldg., Homeless shelter work, VA Hosps., Mus. docent; sponsor 3 overseas foster children; fundraiser La Mision Orphanage Ensenada Libr. Flying Samaritans, 2000—; L.A. Dist. rep. Calif.-Pacific conf.comm. commn. United Meth. Ch., 2002—; chmn. adminstrv. coun. Malibu United Meth. Ch., 1993—, choir, 1995—, comm. commn. rep., 2002—; sec., mem. adv. com. Tamassee (S.C.) Sch., 1992—; sr. orgn. pres. Children of the Am. Revolution, Malibu, Calif., 1992—; mem. internat. vis. coun. Outstanding Program Resource; mem. L.A. World Affairs Coun., 2000—. Named one of Outstanding Young Women of Am., 1988, Internat. Vis. Coun. Outstanding Pvt. Resource, L.A. County; recipient Asst. editor Emmy award Young and the Restless, 1989-90, Golden Mike award Radio/TV News Assn., 1991, 92, Pub. Svc. commendation, County of L.A., 1999, cert. leadership, USIA, cert. commendation, City of L.A., 1999. Mem.: DAR (state chair motion pictures, radio and TV, Calif. 1988—90, Mex. 1990—, nat. vice-chair units overseas Mex. 1998—, organizing regent Baja Calif. chpt. 1999—, state conf. 2001, state sec. 2001—04, 2001—, nat. vice-chair media awards 2001—, nat. vice-chair chpt. devel. 2004—, state conf. chair 2004—, vice regent Mex. 2004—, Nat. Outstanding Jr. 1993), ATAS (judge local and nat. Emmy awards 1991—, exec. com. on electronic prodn. 1992—, membership com. 1994—96, awards com. 1994—, engring. awards com. 1997—, gov. 2000—, daytime awards com. 2000—, awards com. 2000—, chair tech. com. 2001—, activites com. 2002—, theatre stds. com. 2002—, diversity com. 2004—), Nat. Broadcasting Soc. (conf. spkr. 2001), Women in Comm., Soc. Profl. Journalists, Women in Film Internat. (com. 1999—), Am. Women in Radio and TV (bd. dirs. So. Calif. chpt. 1984—85, 1993—2000, pres. 1996—97), Travelers Century Club (life; program chair 1987—), Mensa (life), Travelers Century Club (life), Beta Sigma Phi. Democrat. Methodist. Avocations: singing, cooking, travel, genealogy, languages. Home: 2901 Searidge St Malibu CA 90265-2969 Office: CBS TV City 7800 Beverly Blvd Los Angeles CA 90036-2188

**TREMBLY, DENNIS MICHAEL,** musician; b. Long Beach, Calif., Apr. 16, 1947; s. Fred Lel and Jewel Fern (Bouldin) T. Student, Juilliard Sch. Music, 1965-68. Adj. asst. prof. U. So. Calif., L.A., 1981—. Bass player, 1959—, with Los Angeles Philharmonic Orch., 1970-73, co-prin. bass, 1973—. Recipient 2d pl. Internat. Solo Bass competition, Isle of Man, 1978 Mem. Internat. Soc. Bassists. Office: L A Philharm Orch 151 S Grand Ave Los Angeles CA 90012

**TREML, VLADIMIR GUY,** economist, educator; b. Kharkov, USSR, Mar. 27, 1929; came to U.S., 1950, naturalized, 1953; s. Guy Alexey and Lydia Vladimir (Timofeev) T.; m. Emma Miro, July 12, 1952; children— Irene Treml Cagney, Tatiana, Alexey. BA in Econs, Bklyn. Coll., 1955; MA in Econs, Columbia U., 1956; PhD in Econs, U. N.C., 1963. Dept. supr. Bache & Co., N.Y.C., 1953-58; research asso. Inst. for Social Scis., U. N.C., Chapel Hill, 1958-61; asso. prof. econs. Franklin and Marshall Coll., 1961-66; research asso. Inst. Study USSR, Munich, Germany, 1966-67; prof. econs. Duke U., 1967—; dir. Ctr. for Slavic Studies U.S. Dept. Edn. of Duke U., 1991—. Cons. in field; expert Dept. Commerce, The World Bank, other fed. agys., 1971—; vis. Ford research prof. U. Calif., Berkeley, 1984-85; vis. research prof. U. Hokkaido, Sapporo, Japan, 1985. Author: (with others) Structure of the Soviet Economy, 1972, Input-Output Analysis and the Soviet Economy, 1975, Western Sovietology in the Soviet Union, 1999; contbr. reports to publs. of Joint Econ. Com., U.S. Congress; contbr. articles to profl. publs.; editor: Soviet Economic Statistics, 1972; editor, contbg. author: Studies in Soviet Input-Output Analysis, 1977, Alcohol in the USSR, 1982; contbg. editor: Soviet Economy Jour. Trustee Nat. Council for Soviet and East European Research, Inc., Washington, 1978-84. Served with USMC, 1951-53. Ford Found. grantee, 1972-81, Dept. Def.-Advanced Rsch. Project Agy. grantee, 1975-76, Dept. State grantee, 1976-77, Dept. Def. grantee, 1985-90, Georgetown U. grantee, 1984-86, Olin Found. grantee, 1989, Internat. Rsch. and Exch. Bd. grantee, 1993-96, Nat. Coun. for Eurasian Rsch. grantee, 1996-98; Fulbright fellow Moscow U., 1992. Mem. So. Econ. Assn., Am. Econ. Assn., Assn. Comparative Econ. Studies (exec. com. 1972-74), Am. Assn. Advancement Slavic Studies, So. Conf. on Slavic Studies. Republican. Eastern Orthodox. Home: 603 Longleaf Dr Chapel Hill NC 27517-3039 Office Phone: 919-660-1800. Business E-Mail: treml@econ.duke.edu.

**TREMPY, JANINE ELYSIA,** microbiologist; b. Kansas City; BS in Microbiology, Kans. State U., Manhattan, 1980; PhD in Microbiology, U. Tex., 1985. Fellow Nat. Cancer Inst. NIH, Bethesda, Md., 1985—90; asst. prof. Oreg. State U., Corvallis, 1990—96, assoc. prof., 1996—2002, assoc. dean undergraduate affairs, 2002—, prof., 2004—. Traveling lectr. fellow Waksman & ASM Found., 2000—02. Author: (textbooks) Fundamental Bacterial Genetics; co-author: Molecular Microbiology Laboratory: A Writing Intensive Course. Named Oreg. Prof. of Yr. award, Carnegie Found. for Advancement of Tchg. & Coun. Advancement & Support Edn., 1996, recipient Horne award for sustained excellence in tchg., U., Oreg. State U., 1999, Faculty Tchg. Excellence award, 2000, Elizabeth P. Ritchie Disting. Prof. award, 2006; fellow, Waksman and ASM Found., 2000—02, Am. Cancer Soc. Mem.: Am. Soc. Microbiology (editor 2001—04). Achievements include patents for methods for detecting bioactive compounds; discovery of a novel cell based biosensor for the detection of food and water borne bacterial pathogens; patents for biopolymer thickener for food and pharmaceutical applications; discovery of a bacterium that produces a safe and useful polymer and the genes coding for this polymer. Avocations: mentoring, writing, exercise, gardening. Office: Oreg State Univ Dept Microbiology Nash Hall 220 Corvallis OR 97331-3804 Office Fax: 541-737-0496. Business E-Mail: trempyj@oregonstate.edu.

**TRENBERTH, KEVIN EDWARD,** atmospheric scientist; b. Christchurch, New Zealand, Nov. 8, 1944; came to U.S., 1977; s. Edward Maurice and Ngaira Ivy (Eyre) T.; m. Gail Neville Thompson, Mar. 21, 1970; children: Annika Gail, Angela Dawn. BSc with honors, U. Canterbury, Christchurch, 1966; ScD, MIT, 1972. Meteorologist New Zealand Meteorol. Service, Wellington, 1966-76, supt. dynamic meteorology, 1976-77; assoc. prof. meteorology U. Ill., Urbana, 1977-82, prof., 1982-84; scientist Nat. Ctr. Atmospheric Research, Boulder, Colo., 1984-86, sr. scientist, 1986—, leader empirical studies group, 1987, head sect. climate analysis, 1987—; dep. dir. climate and global dynamics divsn. Nat. Ctr. Atmospheric Research, Boulder, Colo., 1991-95. Mem. joint sci. com. for world climate rsch. programme, com. climate changes and the ocean Tropical Oceans Global Atmosphere Program Sci. Steering Group, 1990-94; mem. Climate Variability and Predictability Sci. Steering Group, 1995—2004, co-chair, 1996-99; mem. joint sci. com. World Climate Rsch. Program, 1999—, officer 2002—, chair observations and assimilation panel, 2004—. Editor: Climate System Modeling, 1992, Earth Interactions, 1996-98; contbr. Intergovernmental Panel on Climate Change, 1990, 92, lead author, 1995, 2001; contbr. articles to profl. jours. Recipient Disting. Achievement award Nat. Ctr. Atmospheric Rsch., 2003; grantee NSF, NOAA, NASA. Fellow Am. Meteorol. Soc. (editor sci. jour. 1981-86, com. chmn. 1985-87, Editor's award 1989, Jule G. Charney award 2000), AAAS (coun. del. sect. atmosphere and hydrosphere sci. 1993-97), Royal Soc. New Zealand (hon.); mem. NAS (earth scis. com. 1982-85, tropical oceans global atmosphere adv. panel 1984-87, polar rsch. bd. 1986-90, climate rsch. com. 1987-90, global oceans atmosphere land sys. panel 1994-98, panel on reconciling temperature observations, 1999-2000, com. on global change rsch. 1999-02), Meterol. Soc. New Zealand. Home: 5697 Pennsylvania Pl Boulder CO 80303 Office: Nat Ctr Atmospheric Rsch PO Box 3000 Boulder CO 80307-3000 Office Phone: 303-497-1318. Business E-Mail: trenbert@ucar.edu.

**TRENNEPOHL, GARY LEE,** academic administrator, finance educator; b. Detroit, Dec. 6, 1946; s. Leo Donald and Wilma Mae (Tiesnvold) T.; m. Sandra K. Yeager, June 9, 1968; children: Paige E., Adrienne A. BS, U. Tulsa, 1968; MBA, Utah State U., 1971; PhD, Tex. Tech. U., 1976. Asst. prof. aero. studies Tex. Tech. U., Lubbock, 1972-74; asst./assoc. prof. fin. Ariz. State U., Tempe, 1977—82; prof. U. Mo., Columbia, 1982-86, dir. Sch. Bus., 1984-86; prof., head dept. fin. Tex. A&M U., College Station, 1986-91, assoc. dean Coll. Bus., 1991-93, Peters prof. fin., 1992-95, exec. assoc. dean, 1994-95; dean Coll. Bus. Okla. State U., Stillwater, 1995-99; pres. Okla. State U.-Tulsa, 1999—. Mem. faculty options inst. Chgo. Bd. Options Exch., 1987—; bd. dir. Blue Cross/Blue Shield Okla., Okla. Acad. State Goals, Leadership Okla., Tulsa Air and Space Mus. Author: An Introduction to Financial Management, 1984, Investment Management, 1993; assoc. editor Jour. Fin. Rsch., 1983-96; contr. chpts. Encyclopedia of Investments, Options: Essential Concepts; contbr. articles to profl. jours. Capt. USAF, 1968—74. Decorated Commendation medal with oak leaf cluster, Vietnam Svc. medal. Mem. Fin. Mgmt. Assn. (v.p. program 1993, pres. 1993-94). Lutheran. Office: Okla State U Tulsa 700 N Greenwood Ave Tulsa OK 74106-0702 Office Phone: 918-594-8001. Business E-Mail: gary.trennepohl@okstate.edu.

**TRENT, CHARLES H., JR.,** social work educator; b. Abingdon, Va., Sept. 25, 1939; s. Charles Howard Sr. and Sue Sheffey (Coffee) T.; m. Gina Fiering, May 30, 1993. BA, Pace U., 1972; MSW, NYU, 1974; PhD, Fordham U., 1985. Admissions counselor Cooper Union, N.Y.C., 1969-74; supr. II social worker Rapid Intervention Project, N.Y.C., 1974-75; coord. SSI Advocacy Ctr., Hempstead, N.Y., 1975-77; dir. Project Life, N.Y.C., 1977-88; exec. dir. East Harlem Com. on Aging, Inc., N.Y.C., 1977—; asst. prof. Yeshiva U., N.Y.C., 1985-88, assoc. prof., 1985—. Adj. instr., assoc. prof. Fordham U., N.Y.C., 1983—; bd. dirs. Welfare Rsch. Inc., Albany, N.Y. With USAF. Fellow NIMH, 1972-74, Coun. on Social Work Edn. fellow NIMH, 1981-85; Brookdale Inst. scholar, 1981. Mem. NASW, Soc. for Study of Social Problems, Coun. on Social Work Edn., Soc. for Social Work Rsch., Assn. Cmty. Organizers and Social Adminstrs., Fifth Ave. Com. Avocations: writing, reading, computers, sports. Office: Yeshiva U 2495 Amsterdam Ave New York NY 10033-3312 Home: 118 Penn Est East Stroudsburg PA 18301-9029 E-mail: CO925S@aol.com.

**TRENT, DARRELL M.,** ambassador, academic administrator; b. Neosho, Mo., Aug. 2, 1938; s. Clarence Melvin and Edna Ruth T.; children: Darrell Michael, Derek Montgomery, Mercy Ruth. AB, Stanford U., 1961; postgrad., Internat. Law Sch., The Hague, Netherlands, summer 1961, Wharton Grad. Sch. Bus., U. Pa., summer 1962; MBA, Columbia U., 1964. Owner, mgr. Trent Enterprises, Kans. and Mo., 1963-66; pres., CEO N.Am. Carmen, Ltd., Del., 1965-68, Assoc. Stores, Inc., Okla., 1967-69, Plz. Supermarkets, Inc., Kans., 1966-69, Food Svc., Inc., Kans., 1966-69, Supermarkets, Inc., Kans., 1966-69, Acton Devel. Co., Inc., Kans., 1966-81; rsch. writer Nixon for Pres., 1968; staff dir. for pers. Presdl. Transition, 1968-69; commr. Property Mgmt. and Disposal Svc., GSA, 1969; dep. asst. to Pres. U.S., 1969-70; exec. dir. Property Rev. Bd., Exec. Office of Pres., 1969-73; dep. dir. Office Emergency Preparedness, 1970-72, acting dir., 1973; mem. Cost of Living Coun., 1973, Oil Policy Com., 1973; chmn. Joint Bd. Fuel Supply and Fuel Transp., 1973; mem. NSC, 1973; chmn. Pres.'s Adv. Coun. CD, 1973; U.S. mem. NATO Sr. Civil Emergency Planning Com., 1973; sr. rsch. fellow Hoover Inst., Stanford U., 1974-81, 89-94, sr. advisor, 1998—; assoc. dir., 1974-81, bd. overseers, 1985-89; dep. campaign mgr. Citizens for Reagan, 1976; dep. campaign mgr., cons. Reagan for Pres. Com., 1979-80, sr. policy advisor, 1980; dir. Office Policy Coordination, Presdl. Transition, 1980-81; U.S. alt. rep. Nato Com. Challenges of Modern Soc., 1982-83; dep. sec. U.S. Dept. Transp., 1981-82, acting sec., 1982-83; chmn. U.S. del. European Civil Aviation Com., U.S. Amb., 1983-88; chmn. Action Devel. Corp., Inc., 1988—; chmn., CEO Rollins Environ. Svcs., Inc., 1983-88, TEC Systems, Inc., 1990-91, Clean Earth Tech., Inc., 1992-93; amb., sr. adv. Ministry of Transp., Iraq, 2003—04; sr. adv. Sec. Def., 2001—04, Transition on Trans. and Budget, 2000, Iraq Ministry of Trans of Comm., 2003—04; chmn. Trans Adv. Com., Bush Cheney, 2000. Chmn. Fed. Home Loan Bank Pitts., 1983-91; cons. ACDA, 1974-81, HUD, 1974, Dept. Commerce, 1974-76; bd. advisors Chronicle Info. Svcs., Inc., 1984-87. Author: The U.S. and Transnational Terrorism, 1980, Transportation: Policy, Goals, Accomplishments, 1984; co-author: Terrorism: Threat, Reality, Response, 1979; contbr. articles to profl. publs. Bd. regents Pepperdine U., 1985-92; bd. dirs. Found. Teach Econs., 1988-90; dep. chmn. Ronald Reagan Presdl. Found., 1985-88. Mem. Bohemian Club. Republican. Methodist. Office: 1610 S Broadway St Pittsburg KS 66762-5845 E-mail: trent@hoover.stanford.edu.

**TRENT, ELTON ROGER,** educational assessment administrator, writer; b. Manchester, Ohio, Nov. 18, 1942; s. Wallace V. and Jessie Alise Trent; m. Margaret Vivian Lloyd, Aug. 5, 1978; m. Barbara Wilson, Sept. 12, 1964 (div. Mar. 1975); children: Stephanie Trent Flowers, Stacy Trent Dick. BA in Social Studies, The Ohio State U., 1962, BS in Edn., 1962, MA in Mid. Ea. History, 1964, PhD in Psychology, 1974. Cert. edn. admistrv. specialist Ohio. From cons. test devel. to exec. dir. Ohio Dept. Edn., Columbus, 1963—99, exec. dir. sch. standards and assessment, 1999—2000, exec. dir. emeritus, 2001—; v.p., ops. and devel. Am. Testronics, Iowa City, 1984—86; freelance cons. in field Columbus, 2001—. Vis. lectr., stats. The Ohio State U., Columbus, 1978—78. Author: Ohio Survey Tests, 1977, Ohio Interest Survey, 1983, Career Survey, 1984; co-author (with Nancy Cole and Dena Waddell): 3 R's Achievement Test, 1981; co-author: (with Edward Roeber) Contracting For Testing Services in Handbook of Test Development, 2006. Recipient Governor's Employee award, Gov., State of Ohio, 1991, Disting. Svc. award, Ohio Ho. Reps. and Ohio Senate, 2000, Governor's Employee award, Gov., State of Ohio, 1995, Pioneer in Edn. award, Ohio Dept. Edn., 2001. Mem.: Nat. Coun. Measurement in Edn. (mem. editl. bd. 1998—2000), Am. Edn. Rsch. Assn. Presbyn. Avocations: travel, reading, sports. Home: 5301 Hollister Street Columbus OH 43235-7603 Personal E-mail: roger-trent@columbus.rr.com.

**TRENT, HENRY GIBSON, JR.,** insurance company executive, educator; b. Knoxville; s. Henry Gibson Trent and Katherine Cooper Brabson; m. Sophie R. Shadow, May 5, 1956; children: Henry Gibson III, William Shadow. BS in social sci., Tenn. Tech., Cookville, 1949; MA in History, So. Meth. U., Dallas, 1950. Tchr. Putnam Co. Schs., Cookville, Tenn., 1950—52, Baylor Sch., Chattagnooga, 1952—53; ins. claims Crawford and Co., 1953—64; regional claims supt. Great Am. Ins. Co., Atlanta, 1964—69; claims mgr. Home Ins. Co., Atlanta, 1969—81, claims officer; claims cons. Alexander and Alexander, Atlanta, 1981—86, Gay and Taylor, Atlanta, 1987—90; ret. Pres. Atlanta Claims Mgr. Council, 1974—80. Pres. Freinds of the Libr., Athens, Tenn., 1992—96; comm. chem. Athens (Tenn.) Kiwanis Club, 1993—2003; com. mem. United Way, Athens, Tenn., 1992—2006; chmn. Internat. Co-Arbitration Bd., Atlanta, 1969—81; mem. Nat. Auto Theft Bd., Atlanta, 1980—81. Mem.: Sons of the Revolution, Atlanta Claims Assn., So. Loss Assn., MENSA, McMinn Heritage Mus. (life; bd. dirs. 1992—2006). Republican. Episcopalian. Avocations: fishing, gardening, reading, ballroom dancing, hunting. Home: 229 Lynwood Dr Athens TN 57303

**TRENT, JOYCE MILLER,** librarian; b. Dayton, Ohio, Dec. 7, 1946; d. Fielding Leo and Joyce (Henry) Miller; m. Robert Cody Trent, Mar. 17, 1973; children— Michael Frederick Cody, Paul Templeton, Mark Fielding, Harley R. B.A., Stephen F. Austin State U., 1969; M.L.S., U. Tex., Austin, 1975. Pub. service librarian Deer Park Pub. Library, Tex., 1969-73; system interlibrary loan librarian San Antonio Pub. Library, 1975-76; dir. system, county librarian Atascosa County Library System, Jourdanton, Tex., 1976-81; library dir. Leon Valley (Tex.) Pub. Library, 1981—. Biweekly columnist N.W. Leader, 1981. Pres. parish council St. Brigid's Ch., San Antonio, 1980-81; del. Met. Congl. Alliance, San Antonio, from 1982; mem. civic affairs com. Tex. Sesquicentennial Com., Leon Valley, from 1984. Recipient Leon Valley Hometown Hero award; named to San Antonio Women's Hall of Fame. Mem. ALA, Tex. Library Assn. (treas. dist. 10, vice chair-elect, then chair), Leon Valley Bus. and Profl. Assn., San Antonio Geneal. Hist. Soc. (sec. 1977-78). Democrat. Roman Catholic. Home: 5903 Forest Rim St San Antonio TX 78240-3218 Office: Leon Valley Pub Library 6425 Evers Rd San Antonio TX 78238-1453 E-mail: librarian@leonvalley.lib.tx.us.

**TRENT, ROBERT HAROLD,** retired business educator; b. Norfolk, Va., Aug. 3, 1933; s. Floyd Murton and Myrtle Eugenia (White) T.; m. Joanne Bell, Aug. 17, 1951; 1 child, John Thomas. BS, U. Richmond, 1963; PhD, U. N.C., 1968. Asst. prof. U. N.C., Chapel Hill, 1968-69; assoc. prof. commerce McIntire Sch. Commerce U. Va., Charlottesville, 1970-74, prof. commerce, 1975-84, Ralph A. Beeton prof. free enterprise, 1985-91; C. & P. Telephone Co. prof. commerce U. Va., Charlottesville, 1991-98, prof. commerce emeritus, 1998—. Co-author: Marketing Decision Making, 1976, 4th edit., 1988; editor: Developments in Management Information Systems, 1974 Mem.: Omicron Delta Kappa, Beta Gamma Sigma.

**TRENTON, PATRICIA JEAN,** art historian; m. Norman B. Trenton; children: James Davis, Jeffrey Norman. PhD, U. Calif., 1980. Curator of Am. art Denver Art Mus., 1969—74; Editor Am. Personality Drawing Exhibition Catalog, UCLA, 1976; curator of art Union League Club Chgo., 1981; guest curator Western Am. Art, Palm Spring Desert Mus., 1981—82, Bowers Mus., Santa Ana, Calif., 1984, Southwest Mus., Los Angeles, Calif., 1984, Laguna Art Mus., Laguna Beach, Calif., 1987—91, Autry Mus. Western Heritage, Los Angeles, Calif., 1993—97; art curator Los Angeles Athletic Club, 1982—2001; guest curator San Jose Mus. Art, San Jose, Calif., 2003, Irvine Mus., Irvine, Calif., 2005. Lectr. various profl. conf. Contbr. articles various profl. jours.; Crocker Art Mus., Sacramento, Calif., 1990, Laguna Art Mus., Laguna Beach, Calif., 1990, Dixon Gallery and Gardens, Memphis, Tenn., 1991, Montclair Art Mus., Montclair, NJ, 1991, Gene Autry Western Heritage Mus., 1990, Bowers Mus., 1984, Buffalo Bill Hist. Ctr., Wy., 1983, Palm Springs Desert Mus., 1982. Art adv. bd. Yosemite Exhibition, Autry Mus., 2002—. Recipient Susan Koppleman award, 1995, Caroline Bancroft Hist. prize, Indep. Spirits, 1995, Western Heritage Wrangler award, Nat. Cowboy Hall of Fame and Western Heritage Ctr., 1995, Nat. Am. Publisher's award, U. Okla. Press's Publication, 1983; Rockefeller Fellowship award, UCLA, 1977. Mem.: Mus. Western Art (dir, adv. bd. 1985—87), Am. Mus. Assn., Am. Social Studies, Coll. Art Assn., Los Angeles County Mus. of Art, Am. Art Coun. Steering Com., KCET Women's Coun. Home: 10112 Empyrean Way 303 Los Angeles CA 90067 Personal E-mail: pdtrenton@aol.com.

**TREPAGNIER, BARBARA A.,** sociology educator; b. Houston, Tex., Dec. 10, 1940; d. Dell Edward and Virginia Meeske Heasley; children: Patti Money-Coutts, Teresa Day, Renee, Michele. BA in Psychology, U. Houston, 1988, MA in Sociology, 1990; PhD in Sociology, U. Calif., Santa Barbara, 1996. Assoc. prof. Tex. State U. San Marcos, 1996—. Author: (monograph) Silent Racism: How Well-Meaning White People Perpetuate the Racial Divide. Recipient Presdl. award Excellence Tchg., Tex. State U., San Marcos, 2002. Mem.: Am. Sociol. Assn. Democrat. Avocation: gardening. Home: 903 West San Antonio San Marcos TX 78666 Office: Tex State U 601 University Ave ELA 232 San Marcos TX 78666 Office Phone: 512-245-8054. Home Fax: 512-245-8362; Office Fax: 512-245-8326. Business E-Mail: bt03@txstate.edu.

**TREPAKOVA, ELENA S.,** research scientist; BSc in Physiology, Demidov U., Russia, 1987; PhD in Biophysics, Inst. Cell Biophysics, Russian Acad. Scis., 1994. Head quality control, study dir. ChanTest, Inc., Cleve., 2001—04; study dir. Merck & Co., West Point, Pa., 2005—. Contbr. articles to profl. jours. Mgr. Westinghouse Sci. Talent Search, Pushchino, Moscow Region, Russia, 1993—94. Recipient Sci. Excellence award, George Soros Internat. Sci. Found., 1993; Cardiovasc. Basic Sci. Tng. grant, NIH, 1999-2001. Mem.: Biophysical Soc., Safety Pharmacology Soc., N.E. Smooth Muscle Soc., Gen. Physiologists Soc. Office: Merck and Co PO Box 4 WP81-220 770 Sumneytown Pike West Point PA 19486-0004 Office Phone: 215-652-8544.

**TREPPER, MYRON,** lawyer; b. NYC, Mar. 9, 1943; BA, Hunter Coll., 1965; JD, St. Lawrence U., 1968. Bar: NY 1969; US Dist. Ct. (so., ea. dists.) NY 1971; U.S. Ct. Appeals (2nd, 11th cirs.). Co-chmn. Willkie Farr & Gallagher LLP, NYC. Mem. NY County Lawyers Assn., Assn. of Bar of City of NY Office: Wilkie Farr & Gallagher 787 Seventh Ave New York NY 10019-6018 E-mail: mtrepper@willkie.com.

**TREPPLER, IRENE ESTHER,** retired state senator; b. St. Louis County, Mo., Oct. 13, 1921; d. Martin H. and Julia C. (Bender) Hagemann; student Meramec Community Coll., 1972; m. Walter J. Treppler, Aug. 18, 1950; children: John M., Steven A., Diane V. Anderson, Walter W. Payroll chief USAF Aero. Chart Plant, 1943-51; enumerator U.S. Census Bur., St. Louis, 1960, crew leader, 1970; mem. Mo. Ho. of Reps., Jefferson City, 1972-84; mem. Mo. Senate, Jefferson City, 1985-96; chmn. minority caucus, 1991-92. Alt. del. Rep. Nat. Conv., 1976, 84. Recipient Spirit of Enterprise award Mo. C. of C., 1992, appreciation award Mo. Med. Assn., Nat. Otto Nuttli Earthquake Hazard Mitigation award, 1993, Disting. Legislator award Cmty. Colls. Mo., 1995; named Concord Twp. Rep. of Yr., 1992. Mem. Nat. Order Women Legislators (rec. sec. 1981-82, pres. 1985), Nat. Fedn. Rep. Women, Tesson Ferry Twp. Rep. Club. Mem. Evangelical Ch.

**TRESCOTT, SARA LOU,** water resources engineer; b. Frederick, Md., Nov. 17, 1954; d. Norton James and Mabel Elizabeth (Hall) Trescott; m. R. Jeffrey Franklin, Oct. 8, 1983. AA, Catonsville C., Balt., 1974; BA in Biol. Sci., U. Md., Balt., 1980. Sanitarian Md. Dept. Health & Mental Hygiene, Greenbelt, 1982; indsl. hygienist Md. Dept. Licensing & Regualtion, Balt., 1982-85; from water resources engr. to chief dredging divsn. Md. Dept. Natural Resources, Annapolis, 1985-92, chief navigation divsn. Stevensville, 1992-96, chief ops. & maintenance, 1996, dir. maintenance engring. ops., 1996—. Chair adv. bd. EEO, Annapolis, 1990—92; mem. tech. com. Nat. Mgmt. Info. Sys., Balt., 1983. Contbr. articles to profl. jours. Mem.: ASCE, County Engrs. Assn. Md. Democrat. Achievements include research in beneficial uses of dredged materials; development of technology for hydrographic surveying; design of an improved waterway transportation network for Maryland. Home: PO Box 22 Woodbine MD 21797-0022 Office: DNR 580 Taylor Ave Annapolis MD 21401 Office Phone: 410-260-8158.

**TRESKOV, YAKOV MAKS,** engineer; b. St. Petersburg, Russia, May 13, 1936; arrived in U.S., 1994; s. Maks Treskov and Erena Beylenson; m. Zinaida Treskov; children: Erena, Tatiana. Diploma in engring., Inst. Elec. Engring., Leningrad, Russia, 1965. Specialist radar equipment on submarines, Leningrad, 1965—92; P.S. technician Block Sci. Inc., NJ, 1994—2001; ret. Contbr. articles to profl. jours. Achievements include invention of Treskov Magnetometer, Treskov Radiation Receiver, and the Treskov Radiometer. Home: 2329 Hudson Terr Apt B5 Fort Lee NJ 07024 Home Fax: 201-461-4703. E-mail: tresk36@hotmail.com.

**TRESS, NANCY BARSIC,** biologist, educator; b. Frankfurt, Germany, July 13, 1964; d. Alice Joan and Carl Joseph Eck (Stepfather), Joseph John Barsic; m. Gregory John Tress, Mar. 27, 1993; children: Alexandria Rachel, Marcus Logan. BS in Biophysics, Gannon U., Erie, Pa., 1986; PhD in Biochemistry, U. of Pitts., 1994. Postdoctoral fellow Colo. State U., Ft. Collins, 1994—96; instr. of biology Carlow Coll., Pitts., 1996—2000; asst. prof. of biology U. of Pitts. at Titusville, 2000—. Sci. advisor St. Titus Sch., 2000—06. Contbr. textbook; reviewer (textbook) Biology: Concepts and Connections; contbr. articles to profl. jours. Bd. dirs. Titusville Youth Soccer Assn., 2003—06; adv. bd. Titusville Youth Theater, 2005—06; mem. sch. bd. Titusville Sch. Dist., 2001—06. Fellow GAANN fellow, U. of Pitts., 1992—94. Mem.: NAAHP, NSTA. Avocations: reading, coaching youth soccer. Home: 524 West Elm St Titusville PA 16354 Office: University of Pittsburgh at Titusville 504 East Main St Titusville PA 16354 Office Phone: 814-827-4412. E-mail: ntress@pitt.edu.

**TRESSEL, JIM,** college football coach; b. 1954; s. Lee. BS (cum laude) in Edn., Baldwin-Wallace Coll., 1975. Quarterbacks coach Akron Univ., 1975—78, Univ. Miami-Ohio, Syracuse Univ., 1981—83; head coach Youngstown St., 1986—2000; quarterbacks and receivers coach The Ohio St. Univ., 1983—85, head football coach, 2001—. Recipient Chevrolet Nat. Coach Yr., 1993—94, 1997, Am. Football Coaches ASSN. Coach Yr., 1991, 1994, 2002, Eddie Robinson Nat. Coach Yr., 1994, 2002. Achievements include leading Ohio St. Univ. to NCAA Div. I Nat. Championship, 2002l; leading Youngstown Univ. to Div. I-AA Nat. Championship, 1991, 1993, 1994, 1997. Office: Woody Hayes Athletic Ctr 2491 Olentangy River Rd Columbus OH 43210*

**TRESSLER, JAMES F.,** physicist, researcher; b. Lock Haven, Pa., May 2, 1968; s. John F. and Dorothy J. Tressler. BA, Lock Haven U., 1991; BS, Pa. State U., 1991, MS, 1993, PhD, 1997. Postdoctoral fellow Naval Rsch. Lab., Washington, 1997—2000, rsch. physicist, 2000—. Mem.: Pa. State U. Alumni Assn. (Metro Washington chpt. pres. 2004—05). Achievements include patents for Underwater electroacoustic projectors. Office Phone: 202-767-2367.

**TRESTMAN, FRANK D.,** distribution company executive, director; b. Mpls., Sept. 3, 1934; s. Saul and Rose (Hyster) T.; m. Carol Lynn Wasserman, Apr. 3, 1960; children— Lisa Ellen, Jill Susan BBA with high distinction, U. Minn., 1955. Exec. v.p., treas. Napco Industries, Inc., Mpls., 1965-74, pres., dir., 1974-84; chmn, CEO Mass Merchandisers, Inc., Hopkins, Minn., 1984-86; pres. Trestman Enterprises, Golden Valley, Minn., 1987—. Bd. dirs. Best Buy Co., Mpls., Western Container Corp., Mpls.; chmn. Avalon Real Estate Co., Mpls.. Camir Investment Co., Mpls. Mem. bd. govs. Mt. Sinai Hosp., Mpls., 1978-91, Abbott Northwestern Hosp., 1993-2002; chmn. bd. trustees Mpls. Fedn. Endowment Fund; bd. dirs. Harry Kay Fund. With USN, 1957-58. Mem. Oak Ridge Country Club (Mpls.). Office: Trestman Enterprises 5500 Wayzata Blvd Ste 1045 Minneapolis MN 55416-1241 Business E-mail: frank@trestmanenterprises.com.

**TRESTON, SHERRY S.,** lawyer; BA, Dominican U., 1972; MS, Purdue U., 1973; MBA, U. Chgo., 1979; JD with honors, DePaul U., 1983. Bar: Ill. 1983. With planning dept. Fed. Res. Bank, Chgo., 1973—77; with sys. dept. Sears Bank & Trust Co., Chgo., 1977—78; with trust dept. 1st Nat. Bank Chgo., 1978—83; assoc. Sidley Austin LLP, Chgo., 1983—91, ptnr., 1991—. Trustee Dominican U. Office: Sidley Austin LLP 1 S Dearborn Chicago IL 60603-2000 Fax: 312-853-7036.

**TREU, JESSE ISAIAH,** venture capitalist; b. NYC, Apr. 10, 1947; BS, Rensselaer Poly. Inst., 1968; MA, Princeton U., 1971, PhD, 1973. Physicist, liaison sci. components, materials group Gen. Electric Co., Schenectady, N.Y., 1973-77; tech. dir. Technicon Corp., Tarrytown, N.Y., 1977-82; v.p. Channing Weinberg-CW Ventures, N.Y.C., 1982-85; gen. ptnr. Domain Assocs., Princeton, N.J., 1986—. Office: Domain Assocs 1 Palmer Sq Princeton NJ 08542-3718

**TREUMANN, WILLIAM BORGEN,** university dean; b. Grafton, ND, Feb. 26, 1916; s. William King and Dagny Helen (Borgen) T.; m. Mildred Elizabeth Jenkins, Aug. 14, 1948; children— Richard Roy, Robert Evan, Beverly Kay. BS, U. N.D., 1942; MA, U. Ill., 1944, PhD, 1947. Teaching asst. chemistry U. Ill., 1942-45, teaching asst. math., 1945-46, vis. prof., summers 1948-50; from asst. prof. to prof. chemistry N.D. State U., 1946-55; mem. faculty Minn. State U. Moorhead, 1960—, prof. chemistry, 1962—, asso. dean acad. affairs, 1968-70, dean faculty math. and sci., 1970—. Contbr. to profl. jours. Research Corp. Am. grantee, 1954; Minn. U. Bd. grantee, 1967 Fellow Am. Inst. Chemists; mem. Am. Chem. Soc., Am. Assn. U. Profs., Minn. Acad. Sci., Fedn. Am. Scientists, Phi Beta Kappa, Sigma Xi. Home: 1809 11th Ave S Fargo ND 58103 Office: Math Dept Moorhead State U Moorhead MN 56560

**TREUTING, EDNA GANNON,** retired nursing administrator, educator; b. New Orleans, Dec. 16, 1925; d. Alphonse Joseph and Clara Josephine (David) Gannon; m. August Raymond Treuting, Sept. 4, 1948 (dec.); children: Keith Kawu Treuting Stein, Madeline Treuting LeBlanc, Jaime Treuting Gonzales, Jay (dec.). Diploma, Charity Hosp. Sch. Nursing, New Orleans, 1946; BS in Nursing Edn., La. State U., 1953; MPH, Tulane U., 1972, DPH, 1978. RN, La.; cert. family nurse practitioner Tulane U. Head nurse premature nursery Charity Hosp., New Orleans, 1946-47, head nurse pediatrics, 1947-49; instr. pediatrics Charity Hosp. Sch. Nursing, New Orleans, 1949-52, 54, instr. LPN, 1953; pvt. duty Touro, Hotel Dieu, New Orleans, 1957-59; instr. maternal and child health La. State U. Sch. Nursing, New Orleans, 1960, 65, 69-71; from instr. to prof., sec. head Tulane Sch. Pub. Health and Tropical Medicine, New Orleans, 1972-83; dean, prof. Our Lady Holy Cross Coll. Nursing Div., New Orleans, 1983-84; chief nurse Dept. Health and Hosp., New Orleans, 1987-94. Region IV nurse practitioner Baylor U., Health Edn. and Welfare, 1974-76; citizen amb. to South Am. People to People, 1979; presentor U. Hawaii Pub. Health and Nursing, 1977; planner, advisor, reviewer continuing edn. U. Tenn., Memphis, 1990-95. Author, editor: Occupation Health Nursing, 1979; sect. head, prin. investigator Practitioner Programs Family and Pediatric, 1973-83; item writer Nurse Practitioners, Community Health and Occupational Nursing, 1974-80; mem. editl. bd. to sci. jours. and Nurse Practitioner Jour. Pres. Oti-Mrs. Internat., New Orleans, 1955-68; sponsor bd. dirs. Holy Cross H.S. Treuting Scholarship, New Orleans, 1966—; hurricane and disaster nurse ARC, New Orleans, 1966-77; v.p. Pandora Carnival Club, New Orleans, 1968-78; alternate state health dept. Commn. Nursing Supply and Demand by Legislation, 1991-94; planner, presentor La. State Rsch. Day, 1990-92. Named outstanding woman in the mainstream world's fair women of achievement, 1984. Mem. AARP (chpt. 3086 pres. 2000—, sr. mem., chpt. pres. 2001, Mandeville chpt. pres. 2001-, Cmty. Svc. award 2006), New Orleans Dist. Nurses Assn. (First J.B. Hickey Meml. Cmty. award 1985, Great 100 Nurse-First Yr. 1987), La. Pub. Health Assn. (Dr. C.B. White Merritorious Diligent Svc. 1990), La. Nurse Practitioners Assn.(Edna Treuting scholarship named in her honor), Tulane U. Alumni Assn. (past pres.), Tulane Med. Alumni Assn. (past pres.), New Image Club of Mandeville (mem. 1986-2003), Mandeville Rep. Women, Mandeville Srs., New Image Club (chmn. line dance, co-chmn. trips and travel 1995-2004, Young at Heart, New Image Club (chmn. trips and travel, vice chmn.), Delta Omega (nat. and chpt. past pres.), Sigma Theta Tau Republican. Roman Catholic. Avocations: travel, dance, swimming, photography, reading. Home: 1914 Marlin Dr Mandeville LA 70448-1069

**TREVILLIAN, WALLACE DABNEY,** retired economics professor, retired dean; b. Charlottesville, Va., May 1, 1918; s. Robert Carr and Mary Anna (Perry) Trevillian; m. Mary Lou McEachern, Nov. 28, 1963 (dec. Dec. 2001); children: Malcolm McEachern, Edward Dabney. BS, U. Va., 1940, MA, 1947, PhD, 1954; postgrad., U. Calif., 1950-51. Mem. faculty Clemson (S.C.) U., 1947—, from instr. to assoc. prof., 1947-55, prof., head dept. indsl. mgmt., 1955-63, founding dean bus. edn., 1963-80, prof., dean emeritus, 1983—. Mem. Regional Export Expansion Coun., 1965—77; sec. commn. edn. for bus. professions Nat. Assn. State Univs. and Land-Grant Colls., 1975—77; pres. Nat. Coun. Textile Edn., 1978—80. Master sgt. U.S. Army, 1941—45. Vis. scholar, U. Sussex, Eng., 1980—; Econ. in Action fellow, Cast Inst. Tech., 1958. Mem.: Thomas Jefferson Soc. Alumni U. Va., Poinsett Club (Greenville, S.C.), Piedmont Econs. Club, Newcomen Soc., St. Andrews Soc. Upper S.C. Episcopalian. Home: 305 Jones Ave Greenville SC 29605-2862

**TREVINO, GUILLERMO PRIETO,** stock exchange executive; Chmn., CEO Mexican Stock Exch., 2001—. Office: Mexican Stock Exch Paseo de la Reforma No 255 Col Cuauhtemoc 06500 Mexico City Mexico

**TREVINO, JERRY ROSALEZ,** retired secondary school principal; b. Bee County, Tex., July 9, 1943; s. Geronimo R. and Hilaria (Rosalez) T.; m. Juanita Escalante, Jan. 1, 1985; 1 child, John-Michael. BA, U. Houston, 1967, MEd, 1974; PhD, Kennedy-Western U., 1988; postgrad., U. Tex., Permian Basin, 1988-92. Cert. tchr., adminstr., supt., Tex. Tchr. N.E. Houston Sch. Dist., 1966-70, pub. rels. officer, 1970-72, asst. prin., 1972-76; tchr. Harris County Dept. Edn., Houston, 1968-72, Austin (Tex.) Ind. Sch. Dist., 1977-87; asst. prin. Tex. Youth Commn., Pyote, 1987-91, prin., 1991-96, ret., 1996. Chair edn. seminar, 24th Internat. Congress, Oxford (Eng.) U., 1997; reader, U.S. Dept. Edn., 1996-97; mentor Austin Ind. Sch. Dist., 1996-98; Title VII project dir. U.S. Dept. Edn., 1988-96; instr. Austin C.C., 1980-84, chair, Prin. Coun. for Edn. of Lang. Minority Students, S.W. Ednl. Devel. Lab., Austin, 1994-96; rschr. and ednl. cons. Bentiva Edn. Solutions, 2002—. Editor newsletter The Flyer, 1970-72; contbr. articles to profl. pubs. Mem. Cmty. Adv. Coun., Pyote, 1987-96; mem. Tex. Children's Mental Health Plan, Austin, 1991-96; mem. planning com. Permian Basin Quality Work Force, Midland, Tex., 1992-96; mem. Supt.'s Coun., Pyote, 1987-96. Named Outstanding Adminstr. of Permian Basin (Golden Apple award) Permian Basin Private Industry Coun., 1994. Mem. ASCD, Nat. Assn. for Bilingual Edn., Order Internat. Ambs., Tex. Assn. Secondary Sch. Prins., Civil Air Patrol, Soc. Leading Intellectuals of the World, Tex. Coun. Humanities, League United L.Am. Citizens, World Acad Letters, Tex. State Hist. Soc. Presbyterian. Avocations: flying, travel, reading, landscaping. Address: PO Box 299 Paige TX 78659-0299 Office Phone: 512-253-0222. Personal E-mail: juanajet@earthlink.net.

**TREVINO, JESUS SALVADOR,** director; b. El Paso, Tex., Mar. 26, 1946; s. Jesus Victor and Evangelina (Mercado) T.; m. Gayla Lee Beauchamp, June 15, 1968 (div. 1988); m. Barbara Ellen Andrea Murray, Oct. 1, 1989. BA in Philosophy, Occidental Coll., 1968. Producer, writer, journalist KCET-TV, L.A., 1969-74; producer, dir. El Teatro Campesino, San Juan Bautista, Calif., 1974-75; exec. producer Infinity Factory, Edn. Devel. Ctr., Newton, Mass., 1975-76; dir. Conacine Prodns., Mexico City, 1976-77; producer, dir. New Vista Prodns., L.A., 1977-78; exec. producer KLCS-TV, L.A., 1979, KCET-TV, L.A., 1980-81; producer, writer, dir. Interamerican Satellite, Inc., L.A., 1982-85; producer KAET, Phoenix, 1986; freelance writer, dir. L.A., 1987—. Instr. Dept. Am. Studies Occidental Coll., LA, 1979—86; instr. Dept. Comm. and Speech Calif. State U., LA, 1986; vis. lectr. Dept. Media Arts U. Ariz., Tucson, 1986—87. Dir.: (TV series) Mathnet, 1987, Square One TV, 1987, SeaQuest DSV, 1993, NYPD Blue, 1993, Chicago Hope, 1994, The Burning Zone, 1996, The Pretender, 1996, The Practice, 1997, Dawson's Creek, 1998, Star Trek: Voyager, 1997—98, Nash Bridges, 1998, Star Trek: Deep Space Nine, 1997—98, Martial Law, 1998, Babylon 5, 1996, Brimstone, 1999, Crusade, 1999, Resurrection Blvd., 2000, ER, 2002, The Court, 2002, Third Watch, 2002, Revelations, 2002, Miracles, 2003, The O.C., 2003, Crossing Jordan, 2003—05, Prison Break, 2005 (Nat. Coun. La Raza ALMA award (Am. Latin Media Arts) outstanding dir. of TV drama or comedy, 2006), Bones, 2006, Tru Calling, 2006; (TV films) Gangs, 1988, Babylon 5: Thirdspace, 1998, (films) Yo Soy Chicano, 1972; writer and dir. (films) Raíces de sangre, 1979, (TV series) American Playhouse, 1982; author: The Fabulous Sinkhole and Other Short Stories, 1995, Eyewitness - A Filmmaker's Memoir of the Chicano Movement, 2001, The Skyscraper that Flew, 2005. Mem.: Nat. Hispanic Media Coalition, Writers Guild Am., Dirs. Guild Am. (chmn. latino com. 1990).*

**TREVINO, LEE BUCK,** professional golfer; b. Dallas, Dec. 1, 1939; s. Joe and Juanita (Barrett) T.; m. Claudia Bove; children: Richard Lee, Lesley Ann, Tony Lee, Troy Liana, Olivia Leigh, Daniel Lee. Student pub. schs. Head profl. Hardy's Driving Range, Dallas, 1961-65; asst. prof. Horizon Hills Country Club, El Paso, Tex., 1966-67; chmn. bd. Lee Trevino Enterprises, Inc., 1967—; joined PGA Tour, 1967, PGA Sr. Tour, 1989. Hon. chmn. Christmas Seal campaign, 1969-72, sports ambassador, 1971; mem. Pres.'s Conf. on Phys. Fitness and Sports; grand marshal Sun Carnival Parade, 1969-70, 71-72; mem. sports com. Nat. Multiple Sclerosis Soc. Mem. Spl. Svcs. Unit USMC, with USMC Res., 1956—60. Recipient Hickok Belt award, 1971; named Golf Rookie of Yr., 1967, PGA Player of Yr., 1971, Tex. Pro Athlete of Yr., 1970, Gold Tee award, 1971, AP Pro Athlete of Yr., 1971, Player of Yr. Golf Mag., 1971, Sportsman of Yr. Sports Illustrated, 1971, PGA Sr. Tour Players of Yr., 1990, 92, 94, Internat. Sports Personality of Yr. Brit. Broadcasting Assn., 1971, Rookie and Player of Yr., Sr. PGA Tour, 1990; mem. Tex. Hall of Fame, Am. Gulf Hall of Fame, World Golf Hall of Fame. Achievements include Tournament winner Tex. Open, 1965, 66, N.Mex. Open, 1966, U.S. Open, 1968, 71, Amana Open, 1968, 69, Hawaiian Open, 1968, Tucson Open 1969, 70, World Cup, 1968, 71, Nat. Airlinn Cup, 1970, Brit. Open, 1971, 72, Canadian Open 1971, 77, 79, Can. PGA, 1979, Danny Thomas-Memphis Classic, 1971, 72, 80, Tallahassee Open, 1971, Sahara Invitational, 1971, St. Louis Classic, 1972, Hartford Open, 1972, Jackie Gleason Classic, 1973, Doral-Eastern Open, 1973, Mexican Open, 1973, 75, Chrysler Classic, Australia, 1973, PGA Championship, 1974, 84, World Series Golf, 1974, Greater New Orleans Open, 1974, Fla. Citrus Open, 1975, Colonial Nat. Invitational, 1974, 78, Colgate Mixed Team Matches, 1979, Brit. Masters, 1985, U.S. Sr. Open, 1990; King Hassan Moroccan trophy II, 1997; Lancome trophy Benson & Hedges, 1978, 80; 1st golfer to have scored four sub-par rounds in U.S. Open Competition, 1968; leading Money winner, 1970, 2d pl. money winner 1971, 1972; Vardon trophy winner, 1970 1972, 74, 80; Can. PGA, 1983; PGA Seniors Championship, 1994; capt. Ryder Cup Matches, 1985; first golfer to have scored 4 sub-par rounds in PGA competition. Office: Assured Mgmt Co 1901 W 47th Pl Ste 200 Mission KS 66205-1834

**TREVISAN, MAURIZIO,** epidemiologist; b. Naples, Italy, Jan. 31, 1952; came to US, 1979; s. Ilario and Bianca (Bruni) T.; m. Lisa Monagle, Dec. 22, 1983; children: Simona, Alessia, Stefan. MD magna cum laude, U. Naples, Italy, 1977; MS, SUNY, Buffalo, 1989. Cert. in medicine and surgery, Italy, 1977, diabetes and metabolic disease, Italy, 1980. Resident dept. internal medicine Med. Sch. U. Naples, 1977-79; rsch. fellow dept. community health and preventive medicine Med. Sch. Northwestern U., 1979-82; cons. dept. medicine U. Naples, 1983-85; asst. prof. dept. social and preventive medicine SUNY, Buffalo, 1985-88, clinical assoc. prof. dept. family medicine, 1988-89, assoc. prof. dept. social and preventive medicine, 1988-92, clinical assoc. prof. nutrition program, 1989-94, assoc. prof. dept. family medicine, 1990-94, interim chair dept social and preventive medicine, 1991-92, prof. dept. social and preventive medicine, 1993—, prof. dept. family medicine, 1994—, interim dean Sch. Health Related Professions, 2001—03, interim dean Sch. Pub. health and Health Professions, 2003—04, dean Sch. Pub. Health and Health Professions, 2005—; prin. investigator Women's Health Initiative WNY Vanguard Clin. Ctr., 1993—2003, co-investigator Women's Health Initiative, 2003—; chair dept. social and preventive medicine SUNY, 1992—2003. Vis. physician dept. physiology Harvard Med. Sch., 1982; adj. asst. prof. dept. cmty. health and preventive medicine Northwestern U. Med. Sch., 1987-96; adj. prof. nutrition program SUNY, Buffalo, 1994—, dir.,

health in housing, SUNY, Buffalo, 1996—; adj. prof. dept. cmty. health and preventive medicine Northwestern U. Med. Sch., 1996—. Fellow Am. Heart Assn. Coun. on Epidemiology. Recipient Rsch. Career Devel. award NIH, 1989-94. Fellow, Am. Coll. of Epidemiology; mem. Am. Epidemiol. Soc. Achievements include research in population-based epidemiological investigation of risk factors for essential hypertension and coronary heart disease. Office: SUNY Buffalo Sch Pub Health and Health Professions 435 Kimball Tower Buffalo NY 14214-3000 Business E-mail: trevisan@buffalo.edu.

**TREVITHICK, RONALD JAMES,** underwriter; b. Portland, Oreg., Sept. 13, 1944; s. Clifford Vincent and Amy Lois (Turner) T.; m. Delberta Russell, Sept. 11, 1965; children: Pamela, Carmen, Marla, Sheryl. BBA, U. Wash., 1966. CLU, CPA, ChFC, accredited estate planner. Mem. audit staff Ernst & Ernst, Anchorage, 1966, 68-70; pvt. practice acctg. Fairbanks, Alaska, 1970-73; with Touche Ross & Co., Anchorage, 1973-78, audit ptnr., 1976-78. Exec. v.p., treas., bd. dirs. Veco Internat., Inc., 1978-82; pres., bd. dirs. Petroleum Contractors Ltd., 1982-82; bd. dirs. P.S. Contractors A/S, Norcon, Inc., OFC of Alaska, Inc., V.E. Systems Svcs., Inc., Veco Turbo Svcs., Inc., Veco Drilling Inc., Vemar, Inc., 1978-82; with Coopers & Lybrand, Anchorage, 1982-85; field underwriter, registered rep. New York Life Ins., 1985-2000, Princor, 2000—, Prin. Fin. Group, 2000—; instr. acctg. U. Alaska, 1971-72; lectr. acctg. and taxation The Am. Coll., 1972, 97, instr. sr. adv. sales Life Underwriters Tng. Coun., 1988-89; bd. dirs. Ahtna Devel. Corp., 1985-86. Divsn. chmn. United Way, 1975-78, YMCA, 1979; bd. dirs., fin. chmn. Anchorage Arts Coun., 1975-78, Am. Diabetes Assn., Alaska affiliate, 1985-91, chmn. bd. 1988-89, chmn. bd. 1992-96, Am. Heart Assn., Alaska affiliate, 1986-87, Anchorage dist. com., 1994-96, treas. 1996-98, Alaska State Youth Soccer Assn.; mem. Anchorage Estate Planning Coun., 1996-2000, treas., 1998-99, sec. 1999-2000. With U.S. Army, 1967-68. Mem. Fin. Execs. Inst. (pres. Alaska chpt. 1981-83), Soc. Fin. Svcs. Profs. (v.p. Alaska chpt. 1993-94, pres. 1994-96), Alaska Assn. Life Underwriters (sec., treas. 1987-90), Alaska Goldstrikers Soccer Club (pres. 1992-93, youth coach 1985-95, Ina K tournament dir. 1992-98), Petroleum Club (treas. 1996-2000), Beta Alpha Psi. Home: 4421 Huffman Rd Anchorage AK 99516-2211 Office: 1600 A St Ste 110 Anchorage AK 99501-5146 Office Phone: 907-258-5830. E-mail: ron4berta@aol.com.

**TREVITS, MICHAEL ANTHONY,** geologist; b. Colorado Springs, Colo., June 10, 1953; s. Robert Alvin and Elsie (McEuen) T. BS in Geology, U. Pitts., 1975, MBA, 1989. Registered profl. geologist, N.C. Phys. sci. aid U.S. Bur. Mines, Pitts., 1974, phys. sci. technician, 1974-75, geologist, 1975-77, 79-82, geologist supr., 1982—; geologist U.S. Dept. Energy, Pitts., 1977-79. Spl. cons. Am. Pub. Gas Assn., 1979-80. Contbr. articles to profl. jours.; co-patentee for method of enhancing the removal of methane gas and associated fluids from mine boreholes. Recipient Outstanding Paper award Nat. Symposium on Mining, Hydrology, Sedimentology, and Reclamation, 1986. Mem. Nat. Ground Water Assn., Soc. for Mining, Metallurgy and Exploration (bd. dirs. Pitts. chpt. 1991—), ASTM Coal Core Task Force, Fed. Credit Union (bd. dirs. 1994—). Roman Catholic. Avocations: running, reading, music. Office: US Bur of Mines PO Box 18070 Pittsburgh PA 15236-0070

**TREVOR, ALEXANDER BRUEN,** information technology manager, consultant; b. NYC, Apr. 12, 1945; s. John B. Jr. and Evelyn (Bruen) T.; m. Ellen Ruth Armstrong, Sept. 21, 1974; children: Anne Wood, Alexander Jay Bruen. BS, Yale U., 1967; MS, U. Ariz., 1971. Rsch. asst. U. Ariz., Tucson, 1971; systems analyst CompuServe Inc., Columbus, Ohio, 1971-73, dir. systems, 1973-74, v.p., 1974-81, exec. v.p., chief tech. officer, 1981-96, also bd. dirs., 1985-96; pres. Nuvocom, Inc., Columbus, 1996—. Bd. dirs. Applied Innovation, Inc., Dublin, Ohio. Author (software program) CB Simulator, 1980. Trustee Aviation Safety Inst., Worthington, Ohio. 1st lt. Signal Corps, U.S. Army, 1968-70, Vietnam. Decorated Bronze Star. Mem. IEEE, SAR (v.p.), Union Club (N.Y.). Republican. Episcopalian. Home: 1987 My Tern Ct Sanibel FL 33957

**TREVOS, S. TED,** nuclear medicine physician, educator, hospital administrator; BA, Nat. Coll. III, Buenos Aires, 1959; MD, U. Buenos Aires, 1966; MA (hon.), Harvard U., Boston, 1990. Resident in radiology Royal Victoria Hosp., McGill U., Montreal, Canada, 1967—68; clin. fellow in radiology Yale-New Haven Hosp., 1968—70, resident/fellow in nuc. medicine, 1970—71; chief divsn. nuc. medicine Children's Hosp. Boston, 1970—, vice chmn. info. sys., 2000—; exec. dir. nuc. medicine program, dir. joint program nuc. medicine Brigham & Women's Hosp., Boston, 2003—. From asst. prof. to assoc. prof. radiology Harvard Med. Sch., Boston, 1973—87, prof., 1987—. Author, editor: Pediatric Nuclear Medicine, 1985, 3d edit., 2006. Recipient 7th Ann. Holman-Kaplan Meml. lectureship, New Eng. chpt. Soc. Nuc. Medicine, 2004. Office: Childrens Hosp Boston 300 Longwood Ave DV2C12 Boston MA 02115

**TREXLER, EDGAR RAY,** minister, editor; b. Salisbury, N.C., Sept. 17, 1937; s. Edgar Ray and Eula Belle (Farmer) T.; m. Emily Louise Kees, Aug. 21, 1960; children: David Ray, Mark Raymond, Karen Emily. AB, Lenoir-Rhyne Coll., 1959, LittD, 1978; MDiv, Luth. Theol. So. Sem., 1962; MA, Syracuse U., 1964; postgrad., Boston U., 1960, Luth. World Fedn. Study Project, Geneva, 1977, 81; LittD (hon.), Midland Coll.; 1990; DD, Wittenberg U., 1994. Ordained to ministry United Luth. Ch. Am., 1962; pastor St. John's Luth. Ch., Lyons, NY, 1962-65; features editor Luth. Mag., Phila., 1965-72, assoc. editor, 1972-78, editor, 1978-87, Chgo., 1988-99. Sec. Commn. Ch. Papers, Luth. Ch. Am., 1971-72, mem. staff team comm., 1972-78; chmn. Interch. Features, 1971-76; chmn. postal affairs com. Assoc. Ch. Press, 1983-90, Work Group on New Ch. Periodical, 1985-86; Evangelical Luth. Ch. Am. Cabinet of Execs., 1988-99. Author: Ways to Wake Up Your Church 1969, Creative Congregations, 1972, The New Face of Missions, 1975, Mission in a New World, 1977, LWF/6, 1978, Anatomy of a Merger, 1991, High Expectations: Understanding the ELCA's Early Years, 1988-2002, 2003; mem. editl. adv. bd. The New World, Roman Cath. Archdiocese of Chgo., 1994-96. Pres. Lyons Coun. Chs., 1964; trustee Lenoir Rhyne Coll., 1975-84, 97-2006. Luth. Theol. So. Sem., 2003—; vol. Interfaith Assistance Ministries, 2000—. Recipient Disting. Alumnus award Lenoir-Rhyne Coll., 1991, Disting. Svc. award Newberry Coll., 1992, Bachman award for disting. leadership Luth. Theol. So. Sem., 1993, Mauney Leadership Awd., Luth. Theol. So. Seminary (alumni awd.), 1999, award of merit for editls. Assoc. Ch. Press, 1991, 98, award of merit for articles in mission mags. Assoc. Ch. Press, 1974, hon. life mem., Assoc. Ch. Press, 1999. Mem. Nat. Luth. Editors Assn. (pres. 1975-77). Home: 2504 Carriage Falls Ct Hendersonville NC 28791-1816 E-mail: etrexler@bellsouth.net.

**TREYZ, JOSEPH HENRY,** librarian; b. Binghamton, N.Y., Nov. 23, 1926; s. Joseph Henry and Edna Belle (Leonard) T. BA, Oberlin Coll., 1950; postgrad., Harvard U., 1951; M.L.S., Columbia U., 1952. Circulation asst. N.Y. Acad. Medicine Library, 1950-51; cataloger Columbia Libraries, N.Y.C., 1951-53, Stevens Inst. Tech., Hoboken, NJ, 1953-54; adminstry. asst. Yale Library, 1955, asst. head catalogue dept., 1955-61; head new campuses program U. Calif., La Jolla, 1961-65; asst. dir. U. Mich. Library, Ann Arbor, 1965-71; dir. libraries U. Wis., Madison, 1971-83, asst. to chancellor, 1983-85; sec.-treas. L.D. Repos, Inc., 1985-87, pres., 1987—. Univ. rep. Consumer Reaction Project for Catalog Card Reprodn. Study, 1961; condr. survey tech. services Fordham U. Libraries, 1969-69, Brandeis U. Libraries, 1970-71; mem. Wis. Gov.'s Com. on Library Devel., 1973-81, Wis. com. Library Services and Constrn. Act, 1979-81; del. U.S. Mission to China on Libraries, 1979 Author: Books for College Libraries, 1967, also articles. Bd. dirs. Wis. Center for Theatre Research. Served with AUS, 1945-46. Mem. Universal Serials and Book Exchange (v.p. 1976, pres., chmn. bd. dirs. 1977), ALA (councilor 1970-74, 77-81, chmn. various coms. 1964-69, recipient Melvil Dewey medal 1970), Assn. Research Libraries (commn. orgn. materials, dir. 1975-78), Midlnet (v.p. 1978-79, pres. 1979-80), Assn. Coll. and Research Libraries (v.p. chmn. editorial bd. Choice 1968-70), Wis. Library Consortium (pres. 1975-76), Wis. Assn. Acad. Libraries (chmn. 1973-74), Council U. Wis. Librarians (chmn. 1975-76, 79-80, 81-83), Wis. Library Assn. (bd. dirs. 1973-74, mem. White House Conf. com. 1977-78), Madison

Area Library Council (v.p. 1973-74), Mich. Library Assn. (chmn. tech. services sect. 1968-69), N.Y. Tech. Services Librarians (pres. 1959-60). Methodist. Home: 801 N Venetian Dr Miami FL 33139-1031

**TREZZA, ALPHONSE FIORE,** librarian, educator; b. Phila., Dec. 27, 1920; s. Vincent and Amalia (Ferrara) T.; m. Mildred Di Pietro, May 19, 1945; children: Carol Ann Trezza Johnston, Alphonse Fiore. BS, U. Pa., 1948, MS, 1950, postgrad.; LHD (hon.), Rosary Coll., 1997. Cert. libr. Drexel Inst. 1949. Page Free Library, Phila., 1940-41, 45-48, library asst., 1948-49; cataloger, asst. reference librarian Villanova U., 1949-50, instr., 1956-60; head circulation dept. U. Pa. Library, 1950-56; lectr. Drexel Inst. Sch. Library Sci., 1956—60; editor Cath. Library world, 1956-60; exec. sec. Cath. Library Assn., 1956-60; assoc. exec. dir. ALA, exec. sec. library adminstrn. div., 1960-67, assoc. dir. adminstrv. services, 1960—69; dir. Ill. State Library, Springfield, 1969-74; lectr. Grad. Sch. Library and Info. Sci., Cath. U., 1975-82; exec. dir. Nat. Commn. on Libraries and Info. Scis., Washington, 1974-80; dir. intergovt. library Cooperation Project Fed. Library Com./Library of Congress, Washington, 1980-82; assoc. prof. Sch. Library and Info. Studies Fla. State U., Tallahassee, 1982-87, prof., 1987-93, emeritus prof., 1993—. Mem. Ill. Library LSCA TITLE I-II Adv. Commn., 1963-69; mem. network devel. com. Library of Congress, 1977-82; bd. visitors Sch. Library and Info. Sci., U. Pitts., 1977-80; cons. Becker & Hayes, Inc., 1980-84, King Research, Inc., 1981-82; mem. planning com and steering com. Fla. Gov.'s Conf. on Library and Info. Svcs., 1988-91. Nat. chmn. Cath. Book Week, 1954—56; pres. Joliet Diocesan Bd. Edn., 1966—68; auditor Borough of Norwood, Pa., 1958—60; mem. patron's bd. Fla. State U. Sch. Theater, 2000—; bd. mem. Lafayette Oaks Home Assn., 2002—; Dem. committeeman Lombard, Ill., 1961—69; extraordinary min. of Eucharistic Blessed Sacrament Cath. Ch., 1984—, mem. pastoral coun., 2000—. 1st lt. USAF, 1942—45. Decorated Air medal with one cluster; recipient Ofcl. commendation White House Conf. on Libr. and Info. Svc., 1979, citation State Libr. Assn., 1994, Silver award Commn. Libr. Info. Sci., 1996. Mem. ALA (coun. 1973-82, 88-92, mem. exec. bd. 1974-79, chmn. stats. coordinating com. 1970-74, mem. pub. com. 1975-78, 81-83, 87-89, chmn. adv. com. interface, 1979-83, chmn. membership com. 1983-84, chmn. nominating com. 1988-89, mem. legis. com. 1989-91, adv. bd. ALA Yearbook 1976-91, Assn. Specialized and Coop. Library Agys. legis. com., 1987-89, ad hoc com. White House Conf. on Libr. and Info. Svcs. 1989-91, chmn. awards com. 1990-92, Exceptional Achievement award 1981, J.B. Lippincott award 1989), Cath. Library Assn. (life, adv. coun. 1960—), Ill. Library Assn. (chmn. legis.-library devel. com. 1964-69, mem. exec. bd., libr's. citation 1974), Fla. Library Assn. (bd. dirs. 1987-93, pres. 1991-92, intellectual freedom com., chmn. com. on Fla. Librs. publ., editor, publ. com., planning com., 1991, site com.), Continuing Libr. Edn. Network and Exchange (pres. 1982-83), Internat. Fedn. Library Assns. and Institutions (statistics standing com. 1976-85, planning com.), Coun. Nat. Library Assns. (chmn. 1959-61), Assn. Coll. and Research Librarians (pres. Phila. chpt. 1953-55), Drexel Inst. Library Sch. Alumni Assn. (pres. 1955-56, exec. bd. 1956-60, chmn. chief officers State Library Agys. 1973-74), Chgo. Library Club (pres. 1969), Assn. Library and Info. Sci. Edn. (govt. relation com. 1985-87), Drexel U. Alumni Assn. (Outstanding Alumnus award 1963), Kappa Phi Kappa (chpt. pres. 1948), Beta Phi Mu (hon.). Lodges: K.C. Personal E-mail: atrezza@mailer.fsu.edu. *You can't do anything alone. You need support and you need opposition. Opposition provides you with challenge. Challenge brings out the best in you.*

**TRIANDIS, HARRY CHARALAMBOS,** psychologist, educator; b. Patras, Greece, Oct. 16, 1926; s. Christos Charalambos and Louise J. (Nikokavouras) T.; m. Pola Fotitch, Dec. 23, 1966; 1 child, Louisa. B.Engring., McGill U., 1951; M.Commerce, U. Toronto, Ont., Can., 1954; PhD, Cornell U., 1958. Doctorate (hon.), U. Athens, Greece, 1987. Asst. prof. U. Ill., Champaign, 1958-61, assoc. prof., 1961-66, prof. psychology, 1966-97; cons. USIA, 1970-75, NSF, 1968-75; prof. emeritus, 1997—. Author: Attitudes and Attitude Change, 1971, The Analysis of Subjective Culture, 1972, Varieties of Black and White Perception of the Social Environment, 1975, Interpersonal Behavior, 1977, Culture and Social Behavior, 1994, Individualism and Collectivism, 1995; editor: Handbook of Cross-Cultural Psychology, Vol. 1-6, 1980-81, Handbook of Industrial and Organizational Psychology, Vol. 4, 1994; editorial cons.; Jour. Personality and social Psychology, 1963-71, Jour. Applied Psychology, 1970-79, Sociometry, 1971-74, Jour. Cross-Cultural Psychology, 1974—, others. Chmn. fgn. grants com. Am. Psychol. Found., 1968-90. Sr. fellow Ford Found., 1964-65; Guggenheim fellow, 1972-73; grantee USPHS, 1956-60, 62; grantee Office Naval Research, 1960-68, 80-85; grantee Social and Rehab. Service, HEW, 1968-73; grantee Ford Found., 1973-75; recipient award Interam. Soc. Psychology, 1981 Mem. Soc. for Psychol. Study of Social Issues (pres. 1975-76), Internat. Assn. Cross-Cultural Psychology (pres. 1974-76), Interam. Soc. Psychology (pres. 1985-87), Soc. for Exptl. Social Psychology (chmn. 1972-74), Soc. for Personality and Social Psychology (pres. 1976-77), Internat. Assn. Applied Psychology (pres. 1990-94). Home: 1 Lake Park Rd Champaign IL 61822-7101 Office: 603 E Daniel St Champaign IL 61820-6232 Business E-Mail: triandis@uiuc.edu.

**TRIANTAFYLLOU, MICHAEL STEFANOS,** engineering educator; b. Athens, Greece, Oct. 27, 1951; arrived in US, 1974; s. Stefanos M. and Penelopi I. (Koutras) T.; m. Joan I. Kimball, Sept. 22, 1985; children: Stefanos R., Kimon K. MS in Ocean Engring., MIT, 1977, MSME, 1977, ScD, 1979. Rsch. assoc. MIT, Cambridge, Mass., 1978-79, asst. prof., 1979-83, assoc. prof., 1983-86, tenured assoc. prof., 1986-90, prof., dir. ocean engring. testing tank, 1990—; dir. Ctr. Ocean Engring., Cambridge, Mass. Vis. scientist Woods Hole Oceanographic Inst., Mass., 1990—; com. chair MIT/Woods Hole Joint Program in Oceanography. Featured cover Scientific American Science; contbr. articles to profl. jours. Rsch. grantee, Office Naval Rsch., Office Naval Tech., NSF, Doherty Found. Dept. Commerce, 1979—. Mem. Internat. Soc. Offshore and Polar Engrs. (founding mem.), Soc. Naval Architects and Marine Engrs. (papers com., vice chmn. OC-2 com.), Am. Phys. Soc. Office: MIT 77 Massachusetts Ave Rm 5-323 Cambridge MA 02139-4307 Office Phone: 617-253-9614. Business E-Mail: mistetri@mit.edu.

**TRIBBETT, CHARLES,** executive recruiter; b. Alexandria, La., Oct. 25, 1955; m. Lisa Tribbett; children: Jillian, Charlie, Jason. BA magna cum laude, Marquette U.; JD, U. Va. Former corp. securities atty. Skadden, Arps, Slate, Meagher & Flom, N.Y.C.; ptnr. Abraham & Sons; with Russell Reynolds Assoc., Chgo., 1989—; mng. dir., co-head, CEO/bd. services practice Russel Reynolds Assoc., Chgo., 1994—. Bd. trustees Northwestern J.L. Kellogg Bus. Sch.; bd. dirs. Chgo. Children's Mus., AON Pension and Investment Fund, Chgo. Union League. Office: Russell Reynolds Assoc 200 S Wacker Dr Ste 2900 Chicago IL 60606 Business E-Mail: ctribbett@russellreynolds.com.

**TRIBBEY, FERN,** mathematics educator; b. Libertyville, Ill., July 7, 1952; d. Bernard and Beatrice Freda (Weinstock) H. BA in Elem. Edn., Nat. Coll. of Edn., 1974, MEd in Ednl. Therapy, 1977; cert. in ednl. leadership, Nat. Louis U., 1991. Cert. elem. edn., secondary math. and spl. edn., learning disabilities tchr., Ill., Iowa. Tchr. Evanston (Ill.) Sch. Dist. 65, 1974-76; resource tchr. Mason City (Iowa) Alternative Sch., 1977-79, Pleasantdale Sch. Dist., LaGrange, Ill., 1979-90, Wilmette (Ill.) Sch. Dist. 39, 1990—98; math. coord. K-12 Indian Prairie Sch. Dist. 207, Naperville/Aurora, Ill., 1998—2000; chair math. dept., tchr. Fenton H.S. Dist. 100, 2000—01; chair math. dept. Highland Park (Ill.) H.S. Dist. 113, 2001—, co-chair new tchr. induction program, chair long-range planning steering com., math. dept. co-chair, 2001—. Dist. math. coord. Pleasantdale Sch. Dist. 107, 1985-90; math. adv. sec. West 40 Edn. Svc. Ctr., Northlake, Ill., 1988-90; presenter in field. Contbr. articles to profl. jours. Mem. Nat. Coun. Tchrs. of Maths., Met. Math. Club, ASCD, Ill. Computer Educators, Ill. Coun. Tchrs. of Maths., Phi Delta Kappa. Avocation: music. Home: 1015 Whitfield Rd Northbrook IL 60062-3944 Office: Highland Park HS 433 Vine Ave Highland Park IL 60035 Office Phone: 224-765-2221. Business E-Mail: ftribbey@dist113.org.

**TRIBBLE, DENISE HALL,** registrar; b. Cin., Dec. 4, 1953; d. Arthur Lee Hall and Nonie Lee Brandon; m. Dwight Tribble, Sept. 14, 1979 (div. July 21, 2004); children: Dwite V. Tribble Jr., Danielle Joy, Desi Anika. MA, Calif. State U. Dominguez Hills, Carson, 1995. Faculty L.A. City Coll., L.A. 1997—, asst. registrar, 1993—. Contbr. book;, singer Pan African People's Orch. Mem. Sisters Of Jazz, L.A., 1995—2006. Home: 2325 4th Ave Los Angeles CA 90018 Office: Los Angeles City College 855 No Vermont Ave Los Angeles CA 90029 Office Phone: 323-953-4000 2101. Office Fax: 323-953-4013. Personal E-mail: denisetri@msn.com. E-mail: tribbldh@lacitycollege.edu.

**TRIBE, LAURENCE HENRY,** law educator; b. Shanghai, Oct. 10, 1941; s. George Israel and Paulina (Diatlovitsky) Tribe; m. Carolyn Ricarda Kreye, June 20, 1964; children: Mark Alexander, Kerry Katrina. AB summa cum laude in Math., Harvard U., 1962, JD magna cum laude, 1966; LLD (hon.), Gonzaga U., 1980, U. Pacific, 1987, Am. U., 1987, Ill. Inst. Tech., 1988, Colgate U., 1997; LHD (hon.), Hebrew U., 1998. Bar: Calif. 1966, Mass. 1978, US Supreme Ct 1978, US Ct. Appeals DC Cir. 1978, US Ct. Appeals 9th Cir. 1979, US Ct. Appeals 1st Cir. 1980, US Ct. Appeals 2nd Cir. 1982, US Ct. Appeals 3rd Cir. 1991, US Ct. Appeals 4th Cir. 1993, US Ct. Appeals Fed. Cir. 1993. Law clk. to Justice Matthew O. Tobriner Calif. Supreme Ct., 1966-67; law clk. to Justice Potter Stewart US Supreme Ct., 1967-68; exec. dir. tech. assessment panel Nat. Acad. Sciences, Washington, 1968-69; asst. prof. law Harvard Law Sch., Cambridge, Mass., 1968—71, prof., 1972-82, Ralph S. Tyler, Jr. prof. constl. law, 1982—2004, Carl M. Loeb univ. prof., 2004—. Chief appellate counsel Calif. Nuclear Litigation, 1978-83; spl. dep. atty. gen. Hawaii, 1983-84; cons. NSF, Nat. Endowment Humanities, White House, others; cons. Marshall Islands for drafting new constitution, 1978-79; chmn. Marshall Islands Jud. Service Commn. Author: Technology: Processes of Assessment and Choice, 1969, Channeling Technology Through Law, 1973, The American Presidency: Its Constitutional Structure, 1974, American Constitutional Law, 1978, 88, 2000, Constitutional Choices, 1985, God Save this Honorable Court, 1985, Abortion: The Clash of Absolutes, 1990; co-author: Environmental Protection, 1971, The Supreme Ct.: Trends and Development, 1979, 80, 82, 83, 84, On Reading the Constitution, 1991; co-editor: When Values Conflict: Essays on Environmental Analysis, Discourse, and Decision, 1976; contbr. articles to profl. jours. Recipient Beale Prize, 1966, Detur prize, 1969, Coif Triennial Book Award, 1980, Scribe Award, 1980; nat. debate champion, 1961; NSF & Woodrow Wilson Fellow, Harvard U., 1962-63. Fellow Am. Acad. Arts and Sciences; mem. ABA (Silver Gavel Award 1991), ACLU, Phi Beta Kappa. Office: Harvard Law Sch 1563 Massachusetts Ave Cambridge MA 02138 Office Phone: 617-495-4621. Office Fax: 617-495-3383. Business E-Mail: tribe@law.harvard.edu.

**TRIBE, LEE,** sculptor, educator; b. Danbury, Eng., Oct. 3, 1945; arrived in US, 1977; s. Arthur Childs Tribe and Ellenor Marrion (May) Fowler; m. Pamela Liggan (div.); m. Stephanie Laura Franks; 1 child, Lia Xiao Mei Franks. BA in Sculpture with 1st class honors, St. Martins, London, 1974; advanced course cert., St. Martins, 1975; MA in Sculpture, Birmingham (Eng.) Sch. Art, 1977. Tchr. NY Studio Sch., NYC, 1980—2006, Columbia U., NYC, 1980—81; head of sculpture Bennington Coll., Vt., 1985—89; tchr. Pratt Inst., Bklyn., 1998—99; MFA seminar prof. Hunter Coll., CUNY, 2002. Vis. artist, tchr. Manchester (Eng.) U., 1992; tchr. Chautauqua (NY) Summer Program, 1990—2002; vis. artist, tchr. U. NC, Greensboro, 2003; seminar instr. NY Studio Sch., 2003—. One-man shows include Manchester Met. U., 1992, Robert Steel Gallery, NYC, 2002, Muse Etnografico S'Bras de Alporto, Portugal, 2003. Recipient award, Arts Coun. Gt. Britain, 1976; fellow Guggenheim Found., 1987—88, Pollock Krasner Found., 1991; Barnett Newman scholar, NY Studio Sch., 1977—78, Ingram Merrill fellow in sculpture1, 0982—1983. Avocation: collecting African art. Home: 155 Wooster St Apt 7F New York NY 10012 Office: NY Studio Sch 8 W 8th St New York NY 10011 Office Phone: 718-389-8449. E-mail: leetribenyc@aol.com.

**TRIBLE, PAUL SEWARD, JR.,** former United States senator; b. Balt., Dec. 29, 1946; s. Paul Seward and Katherine (Schilpp) T.; m. Rosemary Dunaway; children: Mary Katherine, Paul Seward III. BA, Hampden-Sydney Coll., 1968; JD, Washington and Lee U., Lexington, Va., 1971. Bar: Va. 1971. Law clk. to U.S. dist. judge Albert V. Bryan, Jr., 1971-72; asst. U.S. atty. Office U.S. Atty. Eastern Dist. Va., 1972-74; commonwealth's atty. Essex County, Va., 1974-76; U.S. Congressman 1st Va. Dist., Washington, 1976-82; U.S. Senator from Va., 1982-89; of counsel Shuttleworth, Ruloff & Giordano, Va., 1989—95, Laxalt, Washington, Washington, 1989—91; pres. Jefferson Group, Washington, 1991-95, Christopher Newport U., Newport News, Va., 1996—. Mem.: Washington and Lee Law Rev. Republican. Episcopalian. Office: Christopher Newport Univ Office of President 1 University Pl Newport News VA 23606-2998

**TRIBUS, MYRON,** management consultant, educator; b. San Francisco, Oct. 30, 1921; s. Edward and Marie D. (Kramer) T.; m. Sue Davis, Aug. 30, 1945; children— Louanne, Kamala. BS in Chemistry, U. Calif., Berkeley, 1942; PhD in Engring, U. Calif., LA, 1949; DSc (hon.) (hon.), Rockford Coll., Ill., 1965, Oakland U., Mich., 1971. Registered profl. engr., Mass.; cert. trainer Feuerstein's method, 1996. Instr. to prof. engring. U. Calif. at Los Angeles, 1946-61; dir. aircraft icing research U. Mich., 1951-54; dean engring. Thayer Sch. Engring., Dartmouth Coll., 1961-69; asst. sec. sci. and tech. Dept. Commerce, Washington, 1969-70; sr. v.p. rsch. and engring. info. tech. group Xerox Corp., Rochester, NY, 1970-74; dir. Center for Advanced Engring. Study, Mass. Inst. Tech., Cambridge, 1974-86; cons. in quality mgmt., 1986—; dir. rsch., co-founder Exergy, Inc., Hayward, Calif., 1987-99. Cons. heat transfer Gen. Electric Co., 1950; cons. Fed. Office Saline Water; tech. adv. bd. Dept. Commerce; adviser to NATO, 1953; mem. Nat. Adv. Com. Oceans and Atmosphere, 1971-72. Author: Thermostatics and Thermodynamics, 1961, Rational Descriptions, Decisions and Designs, 1969; Contbr. articles to profl. jours. Bd. govs. Technion, Haifa, Israel, 1973-84. Served to capt. USAAF, 1942-46. Recipient Thurman H. Bane award Inst. Aero. Scis., 1945, Wright Bros. medal Soc. Automotive Engrs., 1945; Alfred Noble prize Engring. Socs., 1952, Robert Fletcher awrd Thayer Sch. Engring., Dartmouth Coll., 1994; named UCLA Alumnus of Yr., 1972. Mem. ASME, IEEE, NSPE. Office Phone: 850-435-7490. Personal E-mail: mtribus@earthlink.net.

**TRICARO, ROBERT COLLET,** biologist, educator, editor, poet; s. Robert and Frances Tricaro. BS cum laude, Adelphi Coll., 1959, MA in Ednl. Philosophy, 1961; MS in Biology, Adelphi U., 1966; Writing Program in Creative Writing, Columbia U., 1998; Writing Program in Poetry, U. Mass., 2001. Asst. prof., then assoc. prof. Miami-Dade C.C., Miami, 1965—80; pres. Med. Data Control, Inc., San Francisco, 1980—95; adj. faculty mem. City Coll. San Francisco, 1981—; co-editor poetry mag. Mother Earth Internat., San Francisco, 2003—; bd. dir. Internat. Poetry Museum Project, 2005—. Cons. in med. mgmt. Author: (book of poetry) Letting Go, 2006; contbr. poetry to lit. jours. Pub. rels. specialist L'Alliance Française, Miami, 1974—78. With U.S. Army, 1954—56. Recipient Svc. award, L'Alliance Française, 1976; biology grantee, NSF, 1963—65. Mem.: Bay Area Poets' Coalition (pub. mem. 2005—, sec. 2005). Independent. Luth. Avocations: opera, sports, poetry. Home: 601 Van Ness Ave Unit 22 San Francisco CA 94102 Office: Internat Poetry Soc 934 Brannan St 2d Fl San Francisco CA 94103

**TRICASE, ELIZABETH,** gymnast; b. Elmhurst, Ill., July 26, 1986; d. Pino and Sheila. Gymnast Ill. Gymnastics Inst./U.S. Natl. Team, 2001—; competed in U.S. Gymnastics Championships, Cleve., 2001, 2002, 2003, Spring Cup, Burlington, Ontario, Canada, 2002, Pacific Alliance Championships, Vancouver, Canada, 2002, U.S. Classic, Pomona, Calif., 2001, Virginia Beach, Va., 2002, San Antonio, 2003, FL Gym Open, Luxembourg City, Luxembourg, 2004, Am. Classic, Ontario, Calif., 2004, Nat. Elite Podium Meet, NYC, 2004. Named U.S. Nat. Vault Champion, 2002; recipient 1st place vault, U.S. Gymnastics Championships, 2002, FL Gym Open, 2004. Avocations: soccer, basketball, running track. Office: 145 Plaza Dr Westmont IL 60559

**TRICE, DAVID A.,** oil industry executive; BA managerial sci., Duke Univ.; JD, Columbia Univ. With Roy M. Huffington, Inc., 1980—89; vice-pres., dir. CFO Newfield Exploration Co., 1989—91; CEO, dir. Huffco Group, Inc., 1991—97; chmn, pres., CEO Newfield Exploration Co., 2000—. Mem. bd. dir. Hornbeck Offshore Services, Inc., Grant Prideco, Inc. and NJ Resources. Mem. bd. trustees Houston Museum Natural Sci. Mem.: Independent Petroleum Assn. Am., Domestic Petroleum Coun. Office: Newfield Exploration Co Ste 2020 363 N Sam Houston Pkwy E Houston TX 77060

**TRICE, WILLIAM HENRY,** paper company executive; b. Geneva, N.Y., Apr. 4, 1933; s. Clyde H. T.; m. Sandra Clayton, July 16, 1955; children: Russell, Amy. BS in Forestry, State U. N.Y., 1955; MS, Inst. Paper Chemistry, Appleton, Wis., 1960, PhD, 1963. With Union Camp Corp., 1963—; tech. dir. bleached div., 1972-74, v.p., corp. tech. dir. research and devel. Wayne, N.J., 1974-79; sr. v.p., 1979-85, exec. v.p., 1985-96. Chmn. bd. dirs. Bush Boake Allen, Inc. Trustee, pres. Western Mich. U.-Paper Tech. Found., Syracuse Pulp and Paper Found. With USAF, 1955-57. Fellow TAPPI (bd. dirs. 1978-81), Inst. Paper Sci. and Tech. (trustee, exec. commn. alumni assn.).

**TRICOLES, GUS PETER,** electrical engineer, physicist, consultant; b. San Francisco, Oct. 18, 1931; s. Constantine Peter and Eugenia (Elias) T.; m. Beverly Mildred Ralsky, Dec. 20, 1953 (dec. Dec. 1974); children: Rosanne, Robin; m. Aileen Irma Arenson, Apr. 1, 1980 (div. June 1980). BA in Physics, UCLA, 1955; MS in Applied Math., San Diego State U., 1958; MS in Applied Physics, U. Calif., San Diego, 1962, PhD in Applied Physics, 1971. Engr. Convair divsn. Gen. Dynamics, San Diego, 1955-59, engr. Electronics divsn., 1962-75, engring. mgr. Electronics divsn., 1975-89, sr. engring. staff specialist, 1989-95, Tracor, 1995-99; engr. Smyth Rsch. Assn., San Diego, 1959-61; rsch. asst. Scripps Instn. Oceanography, La Jolla, Calif., 1961-62; sr. engring. staff specialist G.D.E. Systems, Inc., San Diego, 1992—, BAE Sys., 1999—2000; cons. Sci. Applications Internat. Corp., 2003—04. Engring. staff specialist B&M Sys., 2000-2002; cons. Ga. Inst. Tech., Atlanta, 1972, 79-80, Transco Industries, L.A., 1973, Aero Geo Industries, San Antonio, 1980-82, Vantage Assocs., San Diego, 1988, Sci. Application Internat. Corp., 2004; rsch. reviewer NRC, NAS, Boulder, Colo., 1986-88. Author: (with others) Radome Engineering Handbook, 1970, Antenna Handbook, 1988; contbr. articles to profl. jours.; 19 patents in field. With USN, 1952-53. Fellow IEEE (antenna standards com. 1980—, advancement com. 1988), Optical Soc. Am. (local sect. v.p. 1966); mem. Am. Geophys. Union. Avocations: woodworking, photography. Home: 4633 Euclid Ave San Diego CA 92115-3226

**TRIECE, ANNE GALLAGHER,** magazine publisher; b. Bklyn., July 1, 1955; d. Anthony J. and Mary Ann (Clines) Gallagher; m. David Mark Triece, Nov. 3, 1990; 1 child, Elizabeth Renee. BBA cum laude, CUNY, 1978. Media planner Isidore Lefkowitz Elgort, N.Y.C., 1978-80; sr. media supr. Ted Bates Advt., N.Y.C., 1980-83; account mgr. Prevention mag., N.Y.C., 1983-85; N.Y. mgr. Home mag., N.Y.C., 1985-92; assoc. pub. Met. Home mag., N.Y.C., 1992—. Coord. Arts Program for Homeless, N.Y.C., 1994. Recipient advt. excellence award Knapp Comm., 1985. Mem. Advt. Women N.Y. (commendation 1985). Roman Catholic. Avocations: scuba diving, tennis, skiing. Office Phone: 212-767-5516.

**TRIER, JERRY STEVEN,** gastroenterologist, educator; b. Frankfurt, Germany, Apr. 12, 1933; came to U.S. 1938, naturalized, 1943; s. Kurt J. and Alice L. (Cahn) T.; m. Laurel M. Bryan, June 8, 1957; children: Stanley, Jeryl, Stephen. MD, U. Wash., 1957; MA (hon.), Harvard U., 1973. Diplomate Am. Bd. Internal Medicine. Intern U. Rochester, NY, 1957-58, resident in medicine, 1958-59; clin. assoc. Nat. Cancer Inst., Bethesda, Md., 1959-61; trainee in gastroenterology U. Wash., Seattle, 1961-63; asst. prof. medicine U. Wis., Madison, 1963-67; assoc. prof. U. N.Mex., Albuquerque, 1967-69, Boston U., 1969-73, Harvard U. Med. Sch., Cambridge, Mass., 1973-76, prof., 1976—. Sr. physician Brigham and Women's Hosp.; cons. Dana Farber Cancer Ctr., Nat. Inst. Diabetes and Digestive and Kidney Disease; adv. coun. NIH, 1986-90. Editor: Internal Medicine; mem. editorial bd.: Anatomical Record, 1969-98, Gastroenterology, assoc. editor, 1971-77, mem. editorial bd., 1967-71, 78-83, 93-98, chmn., 1988-93, Am. Jour. Medicine, 1978-87, Current Opinion in Gastroenterology, 1990—; contbr. articles to profl. jours.; contbr. chpts. to books. Served as surgeon USPHS, 1959-61. Recipient Disting. Med. Alumnus award U. Wash., 2004, NIH Merit award, 1988-94; USPHS/NIH grantee, 1963-94. Mem. Am. Soc. Clin. Investigation, Assn. Am. Physicians, Am. Gastroent. Assn. (pres. 1985-86, Julius Friedenwald medal 1999), Am. Soc. Cell Biology, Am. Fedn. Clin. Research. Office: Brigham and Women's Hosp 75 Francis St Boston MA 02115-6110

**TRIFILIO, STEVEN MICHAEL,** pharmacist, educator; b. Chgo., Dec. 20, 1954; m. Sorina Stamate; children: Liliana Aurelia, Steven Peter. Degree in Pharmacy (hon.), U. Ill., Chgo., 1977; graduate studies at large U. Chgo., 1981; degree in Germanic studies, Goethe Inst., Chgo., 1984. Clin. pharmacist Northwestern Meml. Hosp., Chgo., 1978—90, clin. instr., 1990—. Mem. adv. bd. Merck, Chgo., 2000—, Pfizer, Chgo., 2003—. Contbr. articles to profl. jours. Mem. pastoral coun. Immaculate Conception Ch., Chgo., 2005—06. Grantee, Nat. Cancer Inst., 2004—06. Mem.: Am. Soc. Bone Marrow Transplantation (Clin. Rsch. award 2006, 2004), U. Ill. Alumni Assn. (life; sr. class pres. 1976—77, sr. class pres. 1977). Roman Cath. Avocations: golf, jogging, opera, bible studies. Home: 7651 w Myrtle Ave Chicago IL 60631 Office: Northwestern Memorial Hospital 251 E Huron St Chicago IL 60611 Office Phone: 312-926-3383. Business E-Mail: strifili@nmh.org.

**TRIGG, JACK WALDEN, JR.,** retired physician; b. Birmingham, Ala., Apr. 18, 1932; s. Jack Walden Sr. and Florine (Hagood) T.; m. Dorothy Wynne, June 3, 1958; 1 child, James Albert. BS, Va. Mil. Inst., 1953; MD, Med. Coll. of Ala., 1958. Diplomate Am. Bd. Internal Medicine. Intern in medicine Duke U. Hosp., Durham, N.C., 1958-59; resident in medicine Univ. Hosp., Birmingham, 1959-62; physician So. Med. Group, Birmingham, 1964-98. Pres. med. staff St. Vincent's Hosp., 1986. Capt. USAF, 1962-64. Fellow ACP; mem. Birmingham Soc. of Internists, Jefferson County Med. Soc. Republican. Episcopalian. Home: 2006 Garden Pl Birmingham AL 35223-1156 Personal E-mail: jtrig@bellsouth.net.

**TRIGGER, BRUCE GRAHAM,** anthropology educator; b. Cambridge (formerly Preston), Ont., Can., June 18, 1937; s. John Wesley and Gertrude Elizabeth (Graham) T.; m. Barbara Marian Welch, Dec. 7, 1968; children: Isabel Marian, Rosalyn Theodora. BA, U. Toronto, 1959; PhD, Yale U., 1964; DSc (hon.), U. N.B., 2007; LittD (hon.), U. Waterloo, 1990; LLD (hon.), U. Western Ont., 1995, McMaster U., 1999, U. Toronto, 2003. Asst. prof. Northwestern U., 1963-64, McGill U., 1964-67, assoc. prof., 1967-69, prof. anthropology, 1969—, chmn. dept., 1970-75, bd. govs., 1996—2001, James McGill prof., 2001—06, James McGill prof. emeritus, 2006—. Mem. bd. govs. McGill-Queen's U. Press, 1988—; Harry Hawthorn Disting. lectr., 1988; Disting. lectr. in archaeology Am. Anthrop. Assn., 1990; Disting. vis. prof. Am. U. in Cairo, 1992; lectr. context and human soc. Boston U., 1997. Author: History and Settlement in Lower Nubia, 1965, Beyond History, 1968, The Huron: Farmers of the North, 1969, 2d edit., 1990, Gardner's Hochelaga, 1972, Nubia Under the Pharaohs, 1976, The Children of Aataentsic, 1976, Time and Traditions, 1978, Gordon Childe: Revolutions in Archaeology, 1980, Natives and Newcomers, 1985, A History of Archaeological Thought, 1989, 2d edit., 2006, Early Civilizations, 1993, Sociocultural Evolution, 1998, Artifacts and Ideas, 2003, Understanding Early Civilizations, 2003; vol. editor: Handbook of North American Indians, Vol. 15, 1978; editor Native and Northern Series; co-editor: Cambridge History of the Native Peoples of the Americas, North America Volume, 1996. Decorated officer Nat. Order Que., 2001, Order of Can., 2005; recipient Can. Silver Jubilee medal, 1977, Cornplanter medal, 1979, John Porter prize, 1987, Prix Victor-Barbeau Acad. Canadienne-Française, 1991, Prix Léon-Gérin (Prix du Québec), 1991; James R. Wiseman Book award Archaeol. Inst. Am., 1991, 2006, Lifetime Achievement award Soc. for Am. Archaeology, 2006; Woodrow Wilson fellow, 1959-60, Woodrow Wilson dissertation fellow, 1962-63, Can. Coun. Leave fellow, 1968-69, 76-77, Killam rsch. fellow Can. Coun., 1970-71, 90, 91, leave fellow Social Scis. and Humanities Rsch. Coun. of Can., 1983. Fellow

Royal Soc. Can. (Innis-Gerin medal 1985), Soc. Antiquaries of Scotland (hon.); mem. Prehistoric Soc. U.K. (hon.), Huron Great Turtle Clan (adopted), Sigma Xi. Home: Apt 603 3495 rue de la Montagne Montreal PQ Canada H3G 2A5 Office: McGill U Dept Anthropology 855 Sherbrooke St W Montreal PQ Canada H3A 2T7 Office Phone: 514-398-4288. Business E-Mail: bruce.trigger@mcgill.ca.

**TRIGGLE, DAVID JOHN,** dean, pharmacist, consultant; b. U.K., Apr. 5, 1935; came to U.S., 1962; s. William John and Maud F. (Henderson) T.; m. Ann M. Jones, Sept. 22, 1959; children: Andrew B., Jocelyn A. BSc in Chemistry, U. Southampton, Eng., 1956; PhD, U. Hull, Eng., 1959. Sch. fellow U. Ottawa, Ont., Can., 1959-61; rsch. fellow U. London, 1961-62; asst. prof. SUNY Sch. of Pharmacy, Buffalo, 1962-65, assoc. prof., 1965-69, prof., 1985-95, chmn. dept., 1971-85, dean, 1985-95, Disting. prof., 1987—, vice-provost for grad. edn., 1995-2001, dean Grad. Sch., 1995-2001, provost, 2000-01, univ. prof., 2000—; pres. Ctr. for Inquiry, Inst. Buffalo. Cons. to pharm. industry, 1980—. Author: Chemical Aspects of Autonomic Nervous System, 1965, Neurotransmitter-Receptor Interactions, 1971, Chemical Pharmacology of the Synapse, 1976. Recipient Volwiler Rsch. Achievement award Am. Assn. Colls. Pharmacy, 1988, 89, George Koepf award Biomed. Rsch. Med. Found. Buffalo, 1994. Fellow AAAS; mem. Am. Chem. Soc., Am. Soc. Pharmacology and Therapeutics (Otto Krayer award 1995), Soc. Neurosci., Brit. Pharmacology Soc., Am. Pharm. Assn., Rho Chi (Rho Chi award 1998). Office: SUNY Sch Pharmacy 126 Cooke Buffalo NY 14260-0001 Office Phone: 716-645-7315. Business E-Mail: triggle@buffalo.edu.

**TRIGIANO, LUCIEN LEWIS,** physician; b. Easton, Pa., Feb. 9, 1926; s. Nicholas and Angeline (Lewis) T.; children: Lynn Anita, Glenn Larry, Robert Nicholas. Student, Tex. Christian U., 1944-45, Ohio U., 1943-44, 46-47, Milligan Coll., 1944, Northwestern U., 1945, Temple U., 1948-52. Diplomate Am. Bd. Phys. Medicine & Rehab. Intern Meml. Hosp., Johnstown, Pa., 1952-53; resident Lee Hosp., Johnstown, 1953-54; gen. practice Johnstown, 1953-59; med. dir. Pa. Rehab. Ctr., Johnstown, 1959-62, chief phys. medicine & rehab., 1964-70; fellow phys. medicine & rehab. N.Y. Inst. Phys. Medicine & Rehab., 1962—64; dir. rehab. medicine Lee Hosp., 1964-71, Ralph K. Davies Med. Ctr., San Francisco, 1973-75, St. Joseph's Hosp., San Francisco, 1975-78, St. Francis Meml. Hosp., San Francisco, 1978-83, Rehab. Ctr. Nev., Las Vegas, 1998—2000; pvt. practice Las Vegas, 1998—. Asst. prof. phys. medicine and rehab. Temple U. Sch. Medicine; founder Disability Alert; bd. adv. Sch. Medicine Temple U., 2003—, bd. visitors, 2003; adj. prof. Touro U. Sch. Medicine, Las Vegas, 2005—. Served with USNR, 1944-46. Fellow ACP; mem. AMA, Pa. Med. Soc., San Francisco County Med. Soc., Am. Acad. Phys. Medicine and Rehab., Am. Congress Phys. Medicine, Calif. Acad. Phys. Medicine, Nat. Rehab. Assn., Babcock Surg. Soc. Home and Office: 1421 Casa Del Rey Ct Las Vegas NV 89117-1538 Office Phone: 702-242-8402. Personal E-mail: lltmdmd@aol.com.

**TRIGOBOFF, SYBELLE,** artist, educator; b. Bklyn., Feb. 20, 1932; d. Sol and Esther Devorah (Novack) Rosenberg; m. Harold Trigoboff, 1950; children: Norman Jed, Sharon Malva, Hinda Leah. Curator, artist Amontri-gallery, N. Bellmore, NY, 1964-66; lectr., critique Greenbriar Art Workshops, N. Bellmore, NY, 1970—, Drawing From Life Model workshop, N. Bellmore, NY, 1975—. Vis. lectr. B.O.C.E.S. Cultural Arts Ctr., Syosset, NY, 1990-91; Alice Sawyer lectr. Hofstra U., 2005; art adv. com. N. Bellmore Pub. Libr., 1972-77; owner, cons. Atrigart, LI, NY, 1980—; curator Good Deed Link, Nat. Com. Furtherance of Jewish Edn., 1997; lectr. in field. Designer artist 18 ft. menorah commd. by Nat. Com. for Furtherance of Jewish Edn., Nassau County, 1984; contbg. artist: World's Women, 1995-96; contbg. author: Total Immersion, 1995; curated and exhibited: SUNY, Stony Brook, 1999; exhibited: Phoenix Gallery, NYC, 2000, Graphic Eye Gallery, Port Washington, NY, 2003. Pres. LWV, Town of Hempstead, NY, 1965-67; adv., LI rep., Bais Chana Women Internat., 1994—. Spl. Opportunity grant NY Found. Arts and East End Arts Coun., 1997; Sarah Domb Jewish Ed. award NCFJE, NYC, 1999. Avocation: gardening. Home: 1272 Greenbriar Ln North Bellmore NY 11710-2306

**TRIIPAN, MAIVE,** library director; b. Virumaa County, Estonia, Jan. 4, 1942; d. Osvald and Minna (Olesk) Triipan; m. Kalle Dobkevich, Mar. 6, 1971 (div. June 4, 1974); 1 child, Raul. B. of Libr., Tartu U., Tartu, Estonia, 1967. Rsch. mgmt. asst. Libr. of Estonian Acad. Sci., Tallinn, Estonia, 1967-74, asst. dir. rsch. work, 1974-84, dir., 1984—; head PR Astangu Vocat. Rehab. Ctr., Tallinn, 2003. Mem. State Libr. Coun., Tallinn, 1974-87, State Libr. Coun. at Dept. of Culture and Edn., Tallinn, 1989—, Tech. U. Coun., Tallinn, 1993—, Estonian Nat. Libr. Coun., Tallinn, 1994—; fin. mgr. Merelaug, 1998-99; project mgmt. Scis. Dept. Estonian Inst. Pub. Adminstrn.; project mgmt. Style Wear, Tallinn, 2000-01; specialist further edn. Astangu Vocat. Rehab. Ctr., Tallinn, 2000, head dept. IT and staff tng., 2002-, head dept. pub. relationship, 2003. Editl. bd. Estonian Retrospective, 1975; mng. pub. National Bibliography 1525-1940, 1993. Mem. Estonian Librs. Assn. Avocations: literature, music, art. Business E-mail: maive.triipan@astangu.ee.

**TRILLIN, CALVIN,** writer, journalist; b. Kansas City, Mo., Dec. 5, 1935; s. Abe and Edyth T.; m. Alice Stewart, Aug. 13, 1965 (dec.); children: Abigail, Sarah Stewart. BA, Yale U., 1957; DLitt (hon.), Beloit Coll., 1987; LHD (hon.), Albertus Magnus Coll., 1990; LHD hon., U. Mo., 2003; DLitt (hon.), SUNY, 1996, U. N.C., 1998, Susquehanna U., 1999; DLitt. (hon.), Long Island U., 2002. Reporter, writer Time mag., 1960-63; staff writer New Yorker mag., 1963—; columnist Nation mag., 1978-85; syndicated columnist, 1986-95; columnist Time mag., 1996-2001. Trustee N.Y. Pub. Libr. Author: An Education in Georgia, 1964, Barnett Frummer as an Unbloomed Flower, 1969, U.S. Journal, 1971, American Fried, 1974, Runestruck, 1977, Alice, Let's Eat, 1978, Floater, 1980, Uncivil Liberties, 1982, Third Helpings 1983 Killings, 1984, With All Disrespect, 1985, If You Can't Say Something Nice, 1987, Travels With Alice, 1989, Enough's Enough, 1990, American Stories, 1991, Remembering Denny, 1993, Deadline Poet, 1994, Too Soon to Tell, 1995, Messages From My Father, 1996, Family Man, 1998, Tepper Isn't Going Out, 2002, Feeding A Yen, 2003, Obliviously On He Sails, 2004; author, performer one-man show Calvin Trillin's Uncle Sam, Am. Place Theatre, N.Y.C., 1988, Calvin Trillin's Words, No Music, Am. Place Theatre, 1990. Office: care New Yorker 4 Times Sq New York NY 10036-6522 Office Phone: 212-286-5651.

**TRILLING, LEON,** aeronautical engineering educator; b. Bialystok, Poland, July 15, 1924; came to U.S., 1940, naturalized, 1946; s. Oswald and Regina (Zakhejm) T.; m. Edna Yuval, Feb. 17, 1946; children: Alex R., Roger S. BS, Calif. Inst. Tech., 1944, MS, 1946, PhD, 1948. Rsch. fellow Calif. Inst. Tech., 1948- 50; Fulbright scholar U. Paris, 1950-51, vis. prof., 1963-64; mem. faculty MIT, Cambridge, 1951—, prof. aerospace and astronautics, 1962-94, prof. emeritus, 1994—, coun. on primary and secondary edn., 1992—. Mem. Program in Sci. Tech. and Soc., Engring. Edn. Mission to Soviet Union, 1958; vis. prof. Delft Tech. U., 1974-75; vis. prof. Carleton Coll., 1987. Pres. Met. Com. Ednl. Opportunity, 1967-70, Coun. for Understanding of Tech. in Human Affairs, 1984—. Guggenheim fellow, 1963-64. Fellow AAAS. Home: 180 Beacon St Boston MA 02116-1408 Office: MIT 77 Massachusetts Ave Cambridge MA 02139-4307 Business E-Mail: trilling@mit.edu.

**TRIMBLE, GARNET O'CULL,** retired music educator; b. Maysville, Ky., Aug. 18, 1945; d. George and Grace (Thomas) O'Cull; m. Shelby C. Trimble; children: Shelby Scott, Bryant Keith. B in Music Edn., Morehead State U., 1970, MEd, 1974. Tchr. grade 5 May's Lick (Ky.) Elem. Sch., 1965-66; tchr. vocal music K-8 and h.s. chorus Ripley (Ohio)-Union-Lewis Schs., 1966-93; tchr. elem. vocal music Ripley Elem. Sch., 1993—2001; ret., 2001. Part-time prof. music Maysville (Ky.) CC; dist. XVI Rep. Ohio, Music in Our Schs. Month Nat. Educators Conf., 1966—; mem. Best Effort Superior Team Ripley Schs., 1993—94. Contbr. articles to mus. publs. and profl. jours. Leader 4-H Club, Orangeburg, Ky., 1990—94; past mem. Mason-Maysville Arts Commn., 1991—93; chmn. Cmty. Resource Night. Mem.: NEA, Ripley-Union-Lewis Hungtington Edn. Assn. (bldg. rep. 1993—94, v.p. 1995), Ohio

Music Educators, Orangeburg Lioness (sec., past pres. 1993—). Republican. Avocations: quilting, singing, piano. Home: 7421 Mount Carmel Rd Maysville KY 41056-9496 Office: Maysville CC US 68-1855 Maysville KY 41056 E-mail: gstrimble@yahoo.com.

**TRIMBLE, PHILLIP RICHARD,** law educator; b. Springfield, Ohio, Nov. 12, 1937; s. Melvin R. and Dorothy T.; m. Stephanie Gardner, July 20, 1963 (div. 1977); children: John, William; m. Valeria Sislevski, Dec. 21, 2000. BA, Ohio U., 1958; MA, Fletcher U., 1959; JD, Harvard U., 1963. Bar: NY 1964. Legal writing instr. U. Calif., Berkeley, 1963-64; assoc. Cravath, Swaine & Moore, N.Y.C., 1964-70; staff mem. fgn. rels. com. U.S. Senate, Washington, 1971-72; asst. legal adviser Dept. State, Washington, 1973-78; counsel to the mayor N.Y.C., 1978; dep. mayor, 1979; U.S. ambassador Nepal, 1980-81; prof. law UCLA, 1981—2001, vice provost internat. studies, 1999—2000; founding mem. Dalai Lama Found., 2001—. Mem. exec. com. Asia Soc. So. Calif. Ctr., L.A., 1981-94; vis. prof. law Stanford U., 1988-89, U. Mich., 1995-96; U.S. panelist under U.S.-Can. Free Trade Agreement, NAFTA; cons. ACDA, 1989-92. Mem. bd. editors Am. Jour. Internat. Law, 1993-98. Bd. dirs. Milarepa Tibetan Buddhist Ctr., 2001—, Am. Alpine Club, 1978—80, 1982—85. Fellow Explorers Club. Democrat. Avocation: mountain climbing.

**TRIMBLE, PRESTON ALBERT,** retired judge; b. Salina, Okla., Aug. 27, 1930; s. James Albert and Winnie Louella (Walker) T.; m. Patricia Ann Beadle; children: Todd, Beth, Amy. BA, U. Okla., 1956, LL.B., 1960. Bar: Okla. 1960. Practice law, 1960; asst. county atty. Cleveland County, Okla., 1960-62; county atty., 1962-67; dist. atty., 1967-79; dist. judge, 1979-91. Spl. instr. S.W. Center Law Enforcement Edn.; cons. prosecution mgmt. Mem. Jud. Council Okla.; chmn. Okla. Corrections Workshop; mem. planning com. Nat. Inst. Crime and Delinquency; mem. com. on multi-agy. problems in criminal justice Appellate Judges Conf. Bd. dirs. Okla. U. Crisis Ctr., 1970—, ARC, Lakes Murray Conservation Assn.; trustee Nat. Assn. Pretrial Svc. Agys. Resource Ctr., Sarkeys Found., 1994—. With USNR, 1948-52; col. USAFR. Mem. Okla., Cleveland County bar assns., Nat. Dist. Attys. Assn. (past pres.), Okla. Dist. Attys. Assn. (past pres.), Nat. Coll. Dist. Attys. (bd. regents), Am. Legion, Lions, Amateur Field Trial Clubs Am. (trustee 2002—, v.p. 2005—) Democrat. Roman Catholic. Home: 1886 Trailview Dr Norman OK 73072-6655 Office: 231 S Peters Ave Norman OK 73069-6035 Office Phone: 405-321-8272. Personal E-mail: trimble@coxinet.net. *An elected public official must remember that the people own his position and he only holds it in trust for them.*

**TRIMBLE, SANDRA ELLINGSON,** lawyer; b. Buffalo, Wyo., May 10, 1952; d. Andrew C. and Edna E. Ellingson; children: Samuel James, Stephen Joseph. BA with highest distinction, Colo. State U., 1974; MEd, Sul Ross State U., 1977; JD cum laude, Gonzaga U., 1989. Bar: Md. 1989, D.C. 1990. Contract specialist USAF, Pope AFB, N.C., 1979-81; purchasing rep. Damson Oil Corp., Houston, 1982-86; summer assoc. Fried Frank Harris Shriver & Jacobson, Washington, 1988; law clk. Sullivan & Cromwell, Washington, 1988-89; assoc. Cleary Gottlieb Steen & Hamilton, Washington, 1989-97; of counsel Orrick Herrington & Sutcliffe LLP, Washington, 1997—2002; counsel McKee Nelson LLP, 2002—. Assoc. notes editor Georgetown Law Jour., 1988-89. Recipient Disting. Achievement in Advocacy award Internat. Acad. Trial Lawyers, 1989; Nat. Merit scholar, 1970; law fellow Georgetown U. Law Ctr., 1987-88. Mem. ABA, Phi Beta Kappa. Office Phone: 202-327-2110. Business E-Mail: strimble@mckeenelson.com.

**TRIMBLE, STANLEY WAYNE,** hydrologist; b. Columbia, Tenn., Dec. 8, 1940; s. Stanley Drake and Clara Faye (Smith) T.; m. Alice Erle Gunn, Aug. 16, 1964; children: Alicia Anne, Jennifer Lusanne. BS, U. North Ala., 1964; MA, U. Ga., 1970, PhD, 1973. Asst. prof. hydrology and geography U. Wis., Milw., 1972-75; from asst. prof. to prof. UCLA, 1975—. Vis. asst. prof. U. Chgo., 1978, vis. assoc. prof., 1981, vis. prof. environ. geography, 1990—, vis. prof. U. Durham (Eng.), 1998; vis. lectr. U. London, 1985; hydrologist U.S. Geol. Survey, 1974-84; vis. prof. U. Vienna, 1994, 99; Frost lectr. Brit. Geomorphological Rsch. Group, Durham, Eng., 1994; vis. rsch. lectr. Oxford U., 1995; Fulbright scholar in U.K., 1995; vis. fellow Keble Coll., Oxford U., 1995, Hatfield Coll. U. Durham, 1998. Author: Culturally Accelerated Sedimentation on the Middle Georgia Piedmont, 1971, Man-Induced Erosion on the Southern Piedmont, 1700-1970, 1974, Soil Conservation and the Reduction, 1982, Sediment Characteristics of Tennessee Streams, 1984, (with A Ward) Environmental Hydrology, 2004 (ASAE Blue Ribbon award); joint editor-in-chief: Catena, 1995-2006; editor: Dekker Encyclopedia of Water Science, 2003-; contbr. articles to profl. jours. 1st lt. 101 Airborne Divsn. U.S. Army, 1963-65. Grantee U.S. Geol. Survey, Washington, 1974-79, Wis. Dept. Natural Resources, Madison, 1978, 82, 93, 94, 95, NSF, Washington, 1976, Agrl. Rsch. Svc. of USDA, Washington, 1972, Nat. Geographic Soc., 1993. Mem. NAS-NRC (com. on watershed mgmt. 1996-98), Assn. Am. Geographers (Disting. Career award, 2006), Am. Geophys. Union, Soil Conservation Soc. Am., Brit. Geomorphol. Rsch. Group, Sigma Xi. Republican. Avocations: historic houses, documentation and restoration, landscape gardens. Office: UCLA Dept Geography 1255 Bunche Hall Los Angeles CA 90095-1524 Office Phone: 310-825-1071. Business E-Mail: trimble@geog.ucla.edu.

**TRIMBLE, THOMAS JAMES,** retired utilities executive, lawyer; b. Carters Creek, Tenn., Sept. 3, 1931; s. John Elijah and Mittie (Rountree) T.; m. Glenna Kay Jones, Sept. 3, 1957; children: James Jefferson, Julie Kay. BA, David Lipscomb U., 1953; JD, Vanderbilt U., 1956; LLM, NYU, 1959. Bar: Tenn. 1956, Ariz. 1961, U.S. Dist. Ct. Ariz. 1961, U.S. Dist. Ct. D.C. 1963, U.S. Ct. Appeals (10th cir.) 1971, U.S. Supreme Ct. 1972, U.S. Ct. Appeals (9th cir.) 1975. From assoc. to ptnr. Jennings, Strouss & Salmon, Phoenix, 1960 85, mng. ptnr. 1905-97; p. gen. counsel, corp. law. S.W. Gas Corp., Las Vegas, Nev., 1987-96; gen. counsel Primerit Bank, 1987—92, corp. sec., 1990-92; exec. v.p. Energy Ins. (Bermuda) Ltd., 1992-94, bd. dirs., 1992-97, pres., 1994—96. Bd. dirs. Energy Ins. Mut. Ltd., 1988—97, vice chmn., 1992—94, chmn., 1994—96. Mem. editorial bd. Vanderbilt U. Law Rev., 1954-56. Mem. Pepperdine U. Bd. Regents, Malibu, Calif., 1981—, sec., 1982-2000, chmn., 2000-04, mem. exec. com., 1982-89, 95—; bd. visitors Pepperdine Sch. Law, Malibu; trustee Okla. Christian U., Oklahoma City, 1994—; pres. Big Sisters Ariz., Phoenix, 1975, bd. dirs., 1970-76; chmn. Sunnydale Children's Home, Phoenix, 1966-69, bd. dirs., 1965-75; pres. Clearwater Hills Improvement Assn., Phoenix, 1977-79, bd. dirs. Phoenix, 1977-80; trustee Nev. Sch. of Arts, 1988-92, chmn., 1989-90. 1st lt. JAGC, USAF, 1957-60. Fellow Ariz. Bar Found. (editl. bd. Jour. 1975-80), Am. Gas Assn. (legal sect. mng. com. 1987-96), Order of Coif, Southshore Golf Club (Las Vegas), Kiwanis (pres. Phoenix 1972-73), Phi Delta Phi. Republican. Mem. Ch. Christ. Home: 7302 E Berridge Ln Scottsdale AZ 85250 Personal E-mail: ttrimble5@cox.net.

**TRIMBLE, VANCE HENRY,** retired newspaper editor; b. Harrison, Ark., July 6, 1913; s. Guy L. and Josephine (Crump) T.; m. Elzene Miller, Jan. 9, 1932; 1 dau., Carol Ann. Student pub. schs., Wewoka, Okla. Cub reporter Okemah (Okla.) Daily Leader, 1928; worked various newspapers in Okmulgee, Muskogee, Tulsa and Okla.; successively reporter, rewrite man, city editor Houston Press, 1939-50, mng. editor, 1950-55; news editor Scripps-Howard Newspaper Alliance, Washington, 1955-63; editor Ky. Post and Times-Star, Covington, 1963-79. Author: The Uncertain Miracle, 1974, Sam M. Walton, 1990, (biography) E.W. Scripps, 1992, Frederick Smith of Federal Express, 1993, An Empire Undone: Rise and Fall of Chris Whittle, 1995, Alice & J.F.B.-The Hundred Year Saga of Two Seminole Chiefs, 2006; co-author: Happy Chandler Autobiography, 1989; editor: Scripps-Howard Handbook, 1981. Trustee Scripps-Howard Found., 1974-79. Recipient Pulitzer prize for nat. reporting, 1960, Raymond Clapper award, 1960, Sigma Delta Chi award for disting. Washington correspondence, 1960, Frank Luther Mott award for journalism book rsch. U. Mo., 1993; named to Okla. Journalism Hall of Fame, 1974. Mem. Am. Soc. Newspaper Editors, Nat. Press Club (Washington), Press Club (Houston), Wewoka Country Club. Baptist. Home: 25 Oakhurst Rd Wewoka OK 74884-3714 Personal E-mail: vhtrimble@aol.com.

**TRIMBLE, WILLIAM CATTELL, JR.,** retired lawyer; b. Buenos Aires, Feb. 7, 1935; s. William Cattell and Nancy Gordon (Carroll) Trimble; m. Barbara Janney, June 19, 1960; children: William C, Margery M Kennelly. AB, Princeton U., 1958; LLB, U. Md., 1964. Bar: Md 1965. With firm Ober, Grimes & Shriver, Balt., 1965-87, ptnr., 1970-87, mng. ptnr., 1973-77; counsel Semmes, Bowen & Semmes, Balt., 1987—2000; ret., 2000; mem. Gov.'s Commn. to Revise Annotated Code of Md., 1975-83. Hon consul, Netherlands, 1986—2003; pres. bd. trustees Valley Sch., 1968-77; trustee Garrison Forest Sch., 1975—95, Gilman Sch., 1980—84. Lt USNR, 1958—61. Mem. ABA, Md. Bar Assn., Class of 1958 Prinntn U. (pres.), Soc. Cin., Greenspring Valley Hunt Club, Colonial Club (Princeton). Episcopalian. E-mail: williamtrimble@msn.com.

**TRIMMER, JIM,** neuroscientist, educator; BA in Biology, U. Calif., San Diego, 1981; PhD in Marine Biology, U. Calif./Scripps Instn. Oceanography, San Diego, 1987. Prof. med. pharmacology and toxicology Ctr. Neuroscience U. Calif., Davis. Contbr. articles to profl. jours. Recipient Jacob Javits Neuroscience Investigator award, Nat. Inst. Neurol. Disorders and Stroke, 2000—. Mem.: Biophysical Soc., Am. Soc. Cell Biology, Soc. Neuroscience. Office: Ctr Neuroscience U Calif 1544 Newton Ct Davis CA 95616 E-mail: jtrimmer@ucdavis.edu.*

**TRIMMIER, CHARLES STEPHEN, JR.,** lawyer; b. Chgo., June 25, 1943; s. Charles Stephen and Lucille E. (Anderson) T.; m. Rae Wade Trimmier, Aug. 19, 1966; children: Charles Stephen, Hallie Wade. BA, U. Ala., Tuscaloosa, 1965, JD, 1968. Bar: Ala. 1968. From assoc. to ptnr. Rives, Peterson, Pettus and Conway, Birmingham, Ala., 1968-77; pres. TrimmierLaw Firm, Birmingham and Mobile, Ala., Tampa, Fla., 1977—. Gen. counsel Nat. Assn. State Chartered Credit Union Suprs., 1983-2001, Ala. Credit Union League, Fla. Credit Union League, La. Credit Union League. Editor-in-chief: Ala. Law Rev., 1968. Mem. ABA (bus. and banking law sect., credit union com.), Ala. Bar Assn., Birmingham Bar Assn., Comml. Law League, Ala. Law Inst., Shades Valley Rotary, Shades Valley Jaycees (sec. 1973). Episcopalian. Home: 3819 River View Cir Birmingham AL 35243-4801 Office: Trimmier Law Firm PO Box 1885 Birmingham AL 35201-1885 Office Phone: 205-251-3151. Business E-Mail: steve@trimmier.com.

**TRINCHERO, AGNES THERESA,** social services consultant, administrator, educator; b. Niles, Calif. d. Louis Jacob and Theresa Marie (DeMattei) T. BA, San Jose State U.; MSW, U. Calif., Berkeley; DSW, U. So. Calif., L.A. Lic. clin. social worker Calif. Fulbright lectr. U.S. Dept. of State, Italy; pvt. practice Laguna Beach, Calif., 1993—. Bd. dirs. Calif. Social Welfare Archives, LA. Recipient Silver medallion, YWCA of North Orange County, Child Advocacy award, Child Welfare League Am. Mem. NASW (Daniel Koshland Leadership award Calif. chpt.). Democrat. Roman Catholic. Avocations: travel, theater, writing, gardening. Office Phone: 949-494-7156.

**TRINDAL, WESLEY STEELE,** mechanical engineer; b. Superior, Wis., July 21, 1925; s. Glen W. and Mabel Elda Thorp (Steele) T.; m. Mary Elizabeth Steger, Aug. 12, 1949; 1 child, Joseph William. BSME, La. State U., 1956. Test and devel. engr. Ford Motor Co., Chrysler Corp., Detroit, 1956-58; prin. engr. vehicles U.S Army Mobility Equipment Rsch. & Devel. Command, Ft. Belvoir, Va., 1958-82; mech. engr. Radian, Inc., Alexandria, Va., 1982—94. With U.S. Army, 1943—52, ETO. Mem. Soc. Automotive Engrs., Am. Truck Hist. Soc., Nat. Hist. Constrn. Equipment Soc. Avocation: writing. Home: 698 Forest View Rd Edinburg VA 22824-3580 Office Phone: 540-984-8788.

**TRINGALE, ANTHONY ROSARIO,** insurance executive; b. Syracuse, N.Y., Apr. 20, 1942; s. Anthony and Susan Marie Tringale; children: Anthony William, Michael Paul, Mark David, Amber Marie. BSFS, Georgetown U., 1967. CLU. Office mgr. trainee N.Y. Life Ins. Co. No., 1965-66, office mgr. N.Y. Life Ins. Co., N.Y.C., 1966, field underwriter, 1966-68; mgmt. asst. home office N.Y. Life Ins. Co., N.Y.C., 1973, gen mgr. Pitts., 1973-76; gen. mgr. Acacia Mut. Life Ins. Co., Annandale, Va., 1976-83, fin. and ins. planner, mgmt. and mktg. cons., 1983-86; from field rep. to mktg. com. Acacia Mut. Life, Anandale, Va., 1983-86; prin. Benefits-By-Design, Fairfax, Va., 1986—; pres. Acacia Prodn. Clubs, 1984, 86. Mem. steering com. Entrepreneurship Forum, Washington, 1980-; founding bd. mem. Commonwealth Va. DEPA Found., 2003-2005; nat. adv. bd. Entrepreurship Inst., Columbus, Ohio, 1985—; mem. supts. bus. and industry adv. coun. Fairfax County Pub. Schs., 1989-2004, mem. mktg edn. adv. bd., 1980-2004, chmn. 1983-84, 90-91; lectr. in field. Contbr. articles in field of personal and bus. fin. strategies to Md. Bus. Observer, Washington Bus. Jour., NALU's Life Assoc. News; radio host Basically Bus. Sta. WGMS-FM, Washington, 1988-91. Trustee SME-1 Accreditation Inst. U. Memphis, 1990—99, Syracuse U. 1995—99; past liaison rep. Am. Soc. CLUs, Bryn Mawr, Pa., 1988—98; arbitrator Fairfax County Dept. Consumer Affairs; v.p., sec., bd. dir., exec. com. The Jeane Dixon Children to Children Found., 1980—; chmn. VIP panel D.C. and No. Va., 1988—92; pres. VIP panel, D.C. and No. Va., 1992—94, Birch Pond Homeowners Assn., 1998—2000; bd. dir., exec. com., pres. United Cerebral Palsy of D.C. and No. Va., 1985—; pres., adv. bd. Fairfax County Corp. of Salvation Army, 1996—2004; pres. United Cerebral Palsy of D.C. and No. Va., 2002; dir. at large Nat. Christopher Columbus Quincentary Jubilee Adv. Bd., 1995—; active Nat. Italian-Am. Found. Coun. of 1000, 1989—; mem. Italian Am. Leaders Com. Venture Clinic; founding vice chmn. Fairfax Orgn. Christians/Jews United in Svc.; lector, extraordinary minister Basilica Nat. Shrine Immaculate Conception, 1980—2003; bd. dirs., v.p. exec. com., chmn. grants com. No. Va. Cmty. Found., 1979—2004; bd. dir. Summer Opera Theater Co., 1996—98, Nat. Cath. Cmty. Found., 1996—97; adv. bd., grants com. No. Va. Cmty Found., 2004—; adv. bd. Salvation Army, Va., 2005—; Front Royal Warren County Corps., 2005—. Recipient 2000 Crystal award No. Va. Cmty. Found. Mem. No. Va. Soc. CLUs (past pres.), Am. Soc. CLUs, No. Va. Assn. Life Underwriters (treas. 1972, nat. com. 1997-99, Pres.' Cup 1991-92), Assn. Advanced Life Underwriting, Sales and Mktg. Execs. Met. Washington (pres. 1979-80, 95-97, treas. 1989-92, bd. dirs. 1990-2000, sr. v.p. profl. devel. 1993-95, Man of Yr. 2000), Nat. Assn. Life Underwriters (Nat. Mgmt. award Gen. Agts. and Mgrs. Conf. 1976-83, exec. com. 1984-85, life qualifying), No. Va. Estate Planning Coun. (exec. com. 1985-92, pres. 1990-91), Internat. Platform Assn. (trustee, bd. govs. 1990-2002), No. Va. Gen. Agts. and Mgrs. Assn. (pres. 1980-81, dir. 1982-83), Greater Washington Area Health Underwriters, Fairfax County C. of C. (dir. small bus. 1989-90, dir. membership 1993-94, v.p. exec. com. dir. at large 1991-92, Small Bus. Adv. of Yr. award 1990), Million Dollar Round Table (life), John Carroll Soc. Ins. Club Washington (pres. 1997-98) Office Phone: 540-622-2244. Personal E-Mail: icg@direcway.com

**TRINKAUS, ERIK,** paleoanthropologist, educator; b. New Haven, Conn., Dec. 24, 1948; s. John Philip Trinkaus, Galina Ivanovna Gorokhoff; m. Kathryn Maurer Maurer; 1 child, Alexander Yuri. BA, U. Wis., 1970; MA, U. Pa., 1973, PhD, 1975. Asst. to assoc. prof., dept. anthropology Harvard U., Cambridge, Mass., 1975—83; asst., assoc. to full prof., dept. anthropology U. N.Mex., Albuquerque, 1983—96, Regents' prof. anthropology, 1996—97; prof. anthropology St. Louis, 1997—2002, Mary Tileston Hemenway prof. phys. anthropology, 2002—. Author: The Shanidar Neandertals, 1983, The Neanderthals: Changing the Image of Mankind, 1993; contbr. articles to peer-reviewed jours., chapters to books. Mem.: NAS (hon.), Am. Anthropological Assn., Am. Assn. Phys. Anthropologists, Société d' Anthropologie de Paris, Anthropological Soc. Nippon, Paleoanthropological Soc., Acad. Sci. St. Louis (hon.). Office: Dept Anthropology Campus Box 1114 Washington Univ Saint Louis MO 63130 Office Phone: 314-935-5207. Office Fax: 314-935-5207. Business E-Mail: trinkaus@artsci.wustl.edu.*

**TRINKAUS, JOHN WILLIAM,** management educator; b. Mt. Vernon, N.Y., July 17, 1925; s. Bernard and Elsie (Kelly) T.; m. Irene Klimowski, July 31, 1954; children: Joanne Trinkaus Dillon, Robert John, John William. BEE, NYU, 1952, PhD, 1976; MBA, CCNY, 1961. Registered profl. engr., Mass. Engr. Bendix Aviation Corp., Teterboro, NJ, 1947-52, Curtis Wright Corp., Carlstadt, NJ, 1952-53, Sperry Corp., Great Neck, NY, 1953-68; prof. CUNY Baruch Coll., NYC, 1968-81, assoc. dean, 1981-93, prof. emeritus, 1993—,

Engring. cons. Electronic Industries Assoc., Washington, 1960-68, USAF, Washington, 1965-68; mgmt. cons. Ford Found., NYC, 1980-82, Interracial Coun. Bus. Opportunity, NYC, 1983-93; vis. disting. prof. St. John's U., NYC, 1993-96. Chmn., rsch. comm. Am. Acad. Profl. Law Enforcement, Mineola, NY, 1978-79; cons. NYC Vol. Urban Con. Group, 1979-84. Sgt. US Army, 1945-46. Recipient 1st prize paper Nat. Fedn. Ind. Bus., Washington, 1992, (Ig)Nobel award, 2003. Mem.: Assn. Pvt. Enterprise Edn., Acad. Mgmt., Inst. Supply Mgmt. Home: 1 Linden St New Hyde Park NY 11040-2311 Office: Baruch Coll CUNY I Bernard Baruch Way New York NY 10010-5518 Office Phone: 646-312-3693.

**TRINKAUS-RANDALL, GREGOR,** librarian, archivist, preservation administrator; b. Balt., Jan. 10, 1946; s. John Phillip and Galina Ivanovna (Gorokhoff) Trinkaus; m. Vickery Edith Trinkaus-Randall, May 22, 1976; children: Jennifer Alison, Christopher Erik. BA, U. Wis., 1968, MA, 1973, MLS, 1980. Archival asst./accessioner State Hist. Soc. Wis., Madison, 1977—81; libr., limnology dept. U. Wis., Madison, 1977—80; conservation/preservation intern Yale U. Libr., New Haven, 1981; asst. curator USS Constitution Mus., Boston, 1981—82; archivist Computer Mus., Marlborough, Mass., 1982; libr./archivist Peabody Mus., Salem, Mass., 1983—88; preservation specialist Mass. Bd. of Libr. Commrs., Boston, 1988—. Mem. adv. com. Northeast Document Conservation Ctr., 1989—; preservation adv. com. NELINET, 1991—2000; mem. preservation com. New England Hist. Geneal. Soc., 1994—2004; chmn. task force theft and mutilation of libr. and archival materials State of Mass., 1989—90, chmn. task force permanent paper, 1989—90; mem. Mass. Emergency Mgmt. Team, 1996—, Cultural Emergency Mgmt. Team, Mass., 2004—; cons. in field. Author: Protecting Your Collections: A Manual of Archival Security, 1995; contbr. articles to profl. jours. Mem. Nat. Ski Patrol, 1966—, Devil's Head Ski Patrol, Merrimack, Wis., 1976—81, regional tng. advisor, 1978—81, Nashoba Valley Ski Patrol, Westford, Mass., 1981—, tng. advisor, 1982—; instr. outdoor emergency care, 1988—; trainer/evaluator Sr. Outdoor Emergency Care, 1990—, tng. coord., 1999—2002; trainer/evaluator Sr. Ski and Toboggan, 1995—, asst. regional dir. EMARI region, 2005—; tchr. Royal Scottish Country Dance Soc., Boston, 1976—; instr. first aid, CPR ARC, Ward Hill, Mass.; USSF Grade 7 Referee, USSF D coaching license. Fellow: Soc. Am. Archivists, Soc. Antiquaries of Scotland; mem.: Scottish Dance, Cultural and Edn. Assn. (bd. dir. 1987—), New England Archivists (pres. 1995—96), Midwest Archives Conf., Soc. Am. Archivists (host com. chair 2003—04), Phi Kappa Phi. Office: Massachusetts Board Library Commissioners 98 N Washington St Ste 401 Boston MA 02114-1933 Office Phone: 617-725-1860 ext. 236. Business E-Mail: gregor.trinkaus-randall@state.ma.us.

**TRIPATHI, GN R,** research scientist, educator; s. Vishwanath R. and Ramdasi Devi Tripathi; m. Poonam Tewari, June 8, 1962 (dec. Oct. 17, 2004); children: Pratibha, Pradeep R., Amit R. PhD, Gorakhpur U., India. From lectr. to sr. lectr. physics dept. Gorakhpur Univ., 1964—76; sr. commonwealth academic staff fellow dept. physics U. Manchester, Manchester, England, 1976—77; faculty Notre Dame Radiation Lab., Ind., 1978—. Vis. sr. lectr. applied physics UMIST, Manchester, 1976—77. Contbr. sci. papers. Achievements include research in time-resolved Raman spectroscopy of chemical transients in water and nano-metallic interfaces. Office Fax: 574-631-8068. Business E-Mail: tripathi.1@nd.edu.

**TRIPATHI, RAM KISHORE,** physicist, researcher; b. Rae Bareli, India, Jan. 1, 1942; arrived in U.S., 1966; s. Shiva Kumar and Devi Mani Tripathi; m. Pushpa Shukla Tripathi, May 26, 1966; 1 child, Sanjay. BS, U. Lucknow, 1961, MS, 1963; PhD, U. Kans., 1970. Asst. prof. U. Ky., Lexington, 1970—71, prof., 1986—87; scientist Kern Forschungsanlange, Juelich, Germany, 1971—73; sr. faculty fellow U. Sussex, Brighton, England, 1973—76; fellow Tata Inst. Fundamental Rsch., Bombay, 1975—78; assoc. prof. Dept. Energy/Inst. Physics, Bhubaneswar, India, 1978—85; prof. U. Tuebingen, Germany, 1980—82, U. Liege, Belgium, 1985—86; radiation physicist NASA Langley Rsch. Ctr., Hampton, Va., 1987—. Contbr. numerous articles to profl. jours. Pres. internat. cultural activities U. Kans., Lawrence, 1966-68. Fulbright fellow USIA, Washington, 1966-70. Sr. NRC fellow NAS, Washington, 1999; grantee NASA, Dept. of Def., Dept. of Energy, NSF. Fellow AIAA (assoc.). Am. Phys. Soc. (life), AAAS, Am. Nuc. Soc. (life). Avocations: jogging, travel, anthropology. Home: 13 Natalie Dr Hampton VA 23666-5565 Office: NASA Langley Rsch Ctr Ms 188 B Hampton VA 23681-0001

**TRIPATHI, RAMESH CHANDRA,** ophthalmologist, researcher, educator; b. Jamira, India, July 1, 1936; came to U.S., 1977, naturalized, 1983; s. Arjun and G. Tripathi; m. Brenda Jennifer Lane, May 20, 1969; children: Anita, Paul. ISc, Lucknow Christian Coll., 1954; MD, Agra Med. Coll., 1959; M of Surgery in Ophthalmology, Lucknow U., 1963; PhD, U. London, 1970. Ophthalmic resident in surgery and demonstrator Lucknow U. Med. Coll., Kanpur, 1959—63; asst. surgeon, med. officer in charge casualty dept. Rly Hosp., Delhi, 1963; fellow Univ. Eye Clinic, Ghent, Belgium, 1964; ophthalmic registrar Southwest Middlesex Hosp., 1965-68; Hayward fellow, registrar, chief clin. asst. Ophthalmology and Moorfields Eye Hosp., London, 1968-72; lectr. U. London Inst. Ophthalmology, 1968-70; sr. lectr. U. London, 1970-77; cons. ophthalmologist and pathologist Moorfields Eye Hosp., London, 1972-77; prof. ophthalmology U. Chgo., 1977-93, The Coll. prof., 1979-93, sec. dept. ophthalmology, 1977-87, cons. pediatric tumor bd., 1978-80; attending ophthalmologist, attending ocular pathologist, mem. med. staff U. Chgo. Med. Ctr., 1977-93, dir. Eye Pathology Labs., 1977-93; prof. ophthalmology U. S.C., Columbia, 1993—, chmn., 1993—98, endowed chair ophthalmology Columbia, 2000—; dir. ophthalmology edn. Richland Mem. Hosp., SC, 1993—98; prof. The Graduate Sch., 1996—; adj. prof. pathology and microbiology, 2002—. Cons., attending ophthalmologist Oak Forest (Ill.) Hosp., 1986-93, dir. ophthalmology resident program, 1986-89, chmn. instnl. rev. bd., 1988; quality assurance com. U. Chgo. Hosp., 1979-93, med. curriculum com. U. Chgo., 1990-93; cons. Nat. Eye Inst. NIH, 1981—, Fight for Sight Rev. Bd., 1990-91; vis. prof. Yeshiva U., NYC, 1973, U. Wurzberg, Germany, 1974, U. Toronto, 1979, Jefferson U., Phila., 1979, Columbia U., NYC, 1981, U. Oxford, Eng., 1984, 86, 89, Nat. Autonomous U. Mex., Mexico City, 1981, Hotel Dieux de Paris, 1975, U. Tex. Med. Br., Galveston, 1990, Kresge Eye Inst. Wayne State U., Detroit, 1991, NY Eye and Ear Infirmary, NYC, 1991, Boston U. Dept. Ophthalmology, New Eng. Eye Ctr., Tufts U., Boston, 1991, Mayo Clinic Dept. Ophthalmology, Rochester, Minn., 1992, others; preceptor MS and PhD degree candidates in ophthalmology and visual sci., U. Chgo., 1977-93, U. SC, 1993—; mem. coun. Ill. Asian-Am. Adv. Com. to Gov. State of Ill., 1989-93; rep. to AMA & Chgo. Med. Soc. from Oak Forest Hosp./Cook County Hosp. Med. Staff, 1987-93, alt. del. Ill. State Med. Soc., 1991-93; del. Bd. Govs. Southeastern Chgo. Med. Soc. from U. Chgo. Hosp. & Clinics, 1991-93; faculty basic and clin. sci. course Am. Acad. Ophthalmology, 1991-2003; attending ophthalmologist WBJ Dorn VA Hosp., 1993—; vis. prof. Harvard Med. Sch. Eye and Ear Infirmary, Boston, Mass., 1997-; founder Hockwin-Green Meml. Endowment Fund, 2002 Author: Wolff's Anatomy of the Eye and Orbit, 1997; exec. editor Exptl. Eye Rsch., 1973—2000, sect. editor, 1987—99, mem. editl. bd. Ophthalmic Literature, 1974—76, sect. editor, mem. editl. bd. Cornea, 1981—86, assoc. editor Afro-Asian Jour. Ophthalmology, 1993, Drug Devel. Rsch., 1988—92, Lens and Eye Toxicology Rsch., 1989—93, Sci. Rsch. Jour., 1990—; contbr. over 600 articles to profl. jours., over 60 chpts. to books and monographs. Chmn. Med. Coun. Assn. Indians in Am., Chgo., 1983-93, v.p., 1986-88; bd. dirs. Indo-Am. Ophthal. Soc. World Eye Found.; mem. Chgo. Found. for Med. Care, 1977-93; pres. Vision Rsch. Found., 1987—; mem. exec. bd. Assn. Scientists of Indian Origin in Am. Recipient Ophthalmology prize Royal Soc. Medicine London, 1971, Royal Eye London prize Ophthal. Soc. London, 1976, Resolutions Commendation, Ill. State Gen. Assembly, 1987, 88, Outstanding Citizen award, 1984, Internat. prize Alcon Rsch. Inst., 1987; Med. Rsch. Coun. London grantee, 1972-75, Nat. Eye Inst. USPHS grantee, 1977—; named Litchfield endowed lectr. U. Oxford (Eng.), 1986, Ida Mann Gold medal U. Oxford, 1989, Disting. Physician of Am., 1990. Fellow: ACS (diplomate), Am. Acad. Ophthalmology (sect. 2 fundamentals and principles of ophthalmology 1991—2001, chair and past chair, basic and clin. sci. com., Honor award 1984, sr. honor award 1997), Internat. Coll. Surgeons

(diplomate, vice regent U.S. 1984—), Royal Coll. Ophthalmologists London (diplomate), Royal Coll. Pathologists (diplomate), Nat. Acad. Scis. of India (life), Royal Soc. Medicine London (coun. 1973—76); mem.: AAUP, AMA, Ill. Med. Soc. (alternate del.), Internat. Soc. Ocular Toxicology (sec., treas. 1993—97, bd. dirs. 1993—, pres. 1998—2000, founder Hockwin-Green Meml. Endowment Fund 2002), Chgo. Ophthal. Soc., S.C. Ophthal. Soc., Glaucoma Soc., Electron Microscopical Soc. Am., Am. Assn. Ophthalmic Pathologists, Am. Assn. Pathologists, Internat. Acad. Pathologists, Contact Lens Assn. Ophthalmologist, Oxford Ophthal. Soc., Ophthal. Soc. U.S., Assn. for Rsch. Vision and Ophthalmology, Pan-Am. Assn. Ophthalmology, Royal Microscopical Soc., Assn. Eye Rsch. Europe (guest of honor 1974), Indian Med. Assn. U.S.A. (bd. dirs. 1984—85, Disting. Physician award 1987), Chgo. Med. Soc. (v.p. 1993, bd. dirs. Southea. br., pres. 1993), Assn. Indians in Am. (v.p. 1988—90, honor award 1986), Fedn. Am. Soc. Exptl. Biology, Physiol. Soc. London, Royal Coll. Physicians and Surgeons (diplomate, conjoin bd.). Achievements include research in pathophysiology, diagnosis and medical and surgical treatment of various ocular disorders including corneal diseases, glaucoma, cataract, vitreoretinopathy; optic nerve and orbital diseases; pioneer in the field of aqueous humor and cerebrospinal fluid dynamics, growth factors, contact lens spoilage and fibrinolytic therapy of the eye. Avocations: photography, swimming, scientific and technical exhibits, ethnic and civic service. Office: Univ South Carolina Sch Medicine Vision Rsch Lab 6439 Garners Ferry Rd Bldg 28 Columbia SC 29209-3816 Office Phone: 803-733-1508. Office Fax: 803-733-3216. Business E-Mail: tripathi@med.sc.edu.

**TRIPLEHORN, CHARLES A.,** entomologist, educator; b. Bluffton, Ohio, Oct. 27, 1927; s. Murray E. and Alice Irene (Lora) T.; m. Wanda Elaine Neiswander, June 12, 1949 (dec. Nov. 1985); children: Bradley Alyn, Bruce Wayne; m. Linda Sue Parsons, July 11, 1987. B.Sc., Ohio State U., 1949, MS, 1952; PhD, Cornell U., 1957. Asst. prof. entomology U. Del., Newark, 1952-54; teaching asst. entomology Cornell U., Ithaca, NY, 1954-57; asst. prof. entomology Ohio Agrl. Research and Devel. Ctr., Wooster, Ohio, 1957-61, Ohio State U., Columbus, 1961-62, assoc. prof. entomology, 1962-66, prof. entomology, 1966-92, prof. emeritus, 1992—. Econ. entomologist U.S. AID/Brazil, Piracicaba, Sao Paulo, 1964-66; vis. curator Field Mus. Natural History, Chgo., 1974, Can. Nat. Collection, Ottawa, Ont., 1977, Am. Mus. Natural History, N.Y.C., 1982, U. Mich., 1989, U. Ariz., 1989, Nat. Mus. of Natural History, 1998, Cornell U., 1999, Colo. State U., 2000, Brigham Young U., 2000. Co-author: Introduction to the Study of Insects, 7th edit., 2004. Cubmaster Boy Scouts Am., Wooster, Ohio, 1959-60, scoutmaster, Columbus, 1971-72; football coach Upper Arlington Football Assn., Ohio, 1968-71 Grantee Am. Philos. Soc., 1963, NSF, 1979, 85, 92. Mem. Entomol. Soc. Am. (pres. 1985), Coleopterists Soc. (pres. 1976), Royal Entomol. Soc. London, Entomol. Soc. Washington, Sigma Xi, Gamma Sigma Delta Clubs: Wheaton (pres.). Republican. Methodist. Avocations: sports, music, reading, writing. Home: 3943 Medford Sq Hilliard OH 43026-2219 Office: Mus Biol Diversity Div Insects The Ohio State University 1315 Kinnear Rd Columbus OH 43212-1157 Office Phone: 614-292-6839. Personal E-mail: ctriplhrn@aol.com.

**TRIPLETT, ARLENE ANN,** management consultant; b. Portland, Oreg., Jan. 21, 1942; d. Vincent Michael and Lorraine Catherine (Starr) Jakovich; m. William Karrol Triplett, Jan. 27, 1962; children: Stephen Michael, Patricia Ann. BA, U. Calif., Berkeley, 1963. Budgets and reports analyst Cutter Labs., Berkeley, 1963-66; controller Citizens for Reagan, 1975-76; dir. adminstrn. Republican. Nat. Com., 1977-80; asst. sec. Dept. Commerce, Washington, 1981-83; assoc. dir. mgmt. Office Mgmt. and Budget, Exec. Office of Pres., Washington, 1983-85; prin. assoc. McManis Assocs., Inc., 1985-87, v.p., 1987-89, sr. v.p., 1989-93; from v.p. to exec. v.p. Am. Tours Internat., Inc., L.A., 1993-97; prin. McManis Assoc., Manhattan Beach, Calif., 1997-98, IBM, Manhattan Beach, Calif., 1999—2002; fin. mgmt. cons., 2002—. Roman Catholic. Office Phone: 310-650-2822.

**TRIPLETT, E. EUGENE,** editor; b. LaJolla, Calif., Mar. 12, 1949; s. Erbin Eugene Triplett and Marjorie Ann (Aldrich) Heath; m. Vannie Carol Crow, July 19, 1968; 1 child, Aaron Eugene. BA in Journalism, Ctrl. State U., 1975. Reporter, columnist The Okla. Jour., Oklahoma City, 1976-80; entertainment editor The Daily Oklahoman, Oklahoma City, 1981-85, asst. city editor, 1985-89, city editor, 1989-99, sr. feature writer, columnist, 1999—. Bd. dirs. Crime Stoppers Oklahoma City; mem. comm. com. Okla. Heart Assn., 1989-92. With U.S. Army, 1969-71, Vietnam. Recipient 1st pl. Feature Writing award Soc. Profl. Journalists, 1987, 97-98, 2d pl. 1999-2000. Mem. AP/Okla. News Exec. (pres.-elect 1994-95, pres. 1995-96, 2nd pl. Feature Writing award 1988, 1st pl. Feature Writing award, 2002, 1st pl. Rev. Writing award 2003). Democrat. Avocations: collecting recorded music, feature films, vintage tv shows. Home: 8116 NW 118th St Oklahoma City OK 73162-1113 Office: The Daily Oklahoman 9000 Broadway Ext Oklahoma City OK 73114-3799 Office Phone: 405-475-4105. E-mail: etriplett@oklahoman.com, geneoat@cox.net.

**TRIPLETT, GREGORY EDWARD,** educator, researcher; PhD, Ga. Inst. Tech., 2004. Asst. prof. U. Mo., Columbia, 2004—. Recipient, Ga. Inst. Tech., 2004; fellow, Boeing, 1998, Office Naval Rsch., 2001—04; Leslie Wilison Grad. fellow, Fla. State U., 1997. Mem.: IEEE, Am. Soc. Engring. Edn., Sigma Xi. Achievements include research in Compound Semiconductor Device Research. Office: Dept Elec & Computer Engring 219 Engineering Bldg West Columbia MO 65211 Office Phone: 573-882-2781. Office Fax: 573-882-0397. E-mail: triplettg@missouri.edu.

**TRIPLITT, CURTIS LEE,** pharmacist, medical educator, researcher; PharmD, U. Tex., San Antonio. Cert. diebetes educator NCBDE, bd. cert. pharacotherapy specialist BPS. Asst. prof. Butler U., Indpls., 1996—97, UTHSCSA, Dept. of Medicine, Div. of Diabetes, San Antonio. Vice-chair Med. Profs. Adv., Tex. Diabetes Inst., Austin. Office: Tex Diabetes Inst 701 South Zarzamora St San Antonio TX 78207 Office Phone: 210-358-7228. E-mail: curtis.triplitt@uhs-sa.com.

**TRIPODES, JAMES G.,** nuclear safety and environmental regulatory affairs professional; b. San Francisco, Mar. 12, 1954; s. George J. Tripodes and Daisy Natsoulas Pimentel; m. Nham T. Tripodes, Nov. 5, 1983. BS in Environ. Planning and Mgmt., U. Calif., Davis, 1978. Registered hazardous substances profl. Nat. Environ. Health Assn.; registered environ. assessor Calif. EPA. Envir. health/safety technician, cyclotron health physicist U. Calif., Davis, 1972-79, health physics mgr. Irvine, 1979-89, assoc. dir. envir. health/safety for envir. reg. affairs, 1989-2001, interim dir. environ. health and safety, 2001—02; dep. dept. head environ. protection Lawrence Livermore (Calif.) Nat. Lab., 2002—03, scientist, 2003—. Co-founder, oversight chmn. Internat. Conf. on Incineration and Thermal Treatment Techs., 1980-2000; prin. investigator, project mgr. U.S. Dept. Energy and Calif. Dept. Health Svcs., 1982-95. Editor: (book and CD-ROM) Proceedings of International Conferences on Incineration and Thermal Treatment Technologies, 1985-2000; guest editor spl. issue: Health Physics Jour., 1991. Mem. govt. affairs coun. Irvine C. of C., 1995—2002; patron Heritage Found., Washington, 1995—, Commonwealth Club of Calif., 2003—; commr. Southwestern Low-Level Radioactive Waste Commn., 2004-05. Fellow Acad. Polit. Sci.; mem. AAAS, ASME, Health Physics Soc. (Elda E. Anderson award 1994), Am. Soc. for Quality, Ctr. for Study of the Presidency, N.Y. Acad. Scis. Republican. Avocations: fine art and music appreciation, public affairs. Office: Lawrence Livermore Nat Lab PO Box 808 L-309 Livermore CA 94551 Office Phone: 925-424-2875. Business E-Mail: tripodes2@llnl.gov.

**TRIPODI, TONY,** retired social worker, retired dean, editor, writer; b. Sacramento, Nov. 30, 1932; s. Nicola and Christina (Grandinetti); m. Roni Roberts, Oct. 28, 1969 (div. 1986); children: Lee Anna, Anthony, David, Stephen; m. Miriam Potocky-Tripodi, July 25, 1998. AB, U. Calif., Berkeley, 1954, MSW, 1958; D of Social Work, Columbia U., 1964. Rsch. tech. Calif. Dept. Mental Hygiene, Sacramento, 1958-59; rsch. analyst Calif. Youth Authority, Sacramento, 1959-60; from rsch. asst. to asst. prof. Columbia U., NYC, 1962-65; asst. prof. U. Calif., Berkeley, 1965-66; from assoc. prof. to

prof. U. Mich. Sch. Social Work, Ann Arbor, 1966-87; assoc. dean prof. U. Pitts. Sch. Social Work, 1987—92; prof., assoc. dir., head doctoral program Fla. Internat. U., 1992—95; prof. Coll. Social Work Ohio State U., 1995—2005, dean Coll. Social Work, 1995—2005, dean and prof. emeritus, 2005—. Rsch. assoc. Bklyn. Coll., 1963-65; editor in chief Social Work Rsch. and Abstracts, NYC, 1980-84; interim assoc. dean U. Mich. Sch. Social Work, Ann Arbor, 1985, 1986, 1987; rsch. cons. Zancan Found., Padova, Italy, 1974-1992, NIMH, Silver Spring, Md., 1989-, Nat. Rsch. Adv. Com., Clinton, Mich., 1988-95; vis. Zellerbach prof. social welfare U. Calif., Berkeley, 2006, vis. Moses prof. social work Hunter Coll., N.Y.C., 2006—. Author: (with others) Clinical Social Judgement, 1966, Requiem for Torchy, 2003, Tuscan Landscapes, 2005, International Social Work Research, 2006, 21 other books; co-editor: Jour. of Social Work Rsch. and Evaluation: An Internat. Pub., 1998-2005; contbr. articles to profl. jours. Bd. dirs. Parental Stress Ctr., Pitts., 1987-92, Comm, Rsch. Partners, 2000-05, Asian Am. Comm. Svc., 2000-05, Coun. Public Reps. Assoc., NIH, 2003-. With USNR, 1954-56. Doctoral rsch. fellow Sage Found., 1962, NIMH, 1960-63; rsch. grantee NSF, 1965-66; Fulbright Hays scholar U.S. Govt., Italy, 1973-74; invited scholar Tilburg U., the Netherlands, 1977; vis. scholar U. Kent, Canterbury, Eng., 1980. Mem. NASW, Acad. Cert. Social Workers, Coun. Social Work Edn., Soc. Social Work and Rsch. (pres. 1998-2000), Internat. Assoc. Sch. Social Work, WHO (World Health Orgn.), Mensa, Phi Kappa Phi.

**TRIPOLI, MASUMI HIROYASU,** financial consultant; b. Fukuyama, Japan, Apr. 23, 1956; d. Yoshimi and Suzuko Hiroyasu; 1 child, Mona Lisa Tripoli. BA cum laude, U. Wash., 1978; MA, Sophia U., Tokyo, 1981; postgrad., Sydney U., 1982; MBA, Ecole des Hautes Etudes Comml, Jouy-en-Josas, France, 1983. CFP. Corp. planning mgr. Kowa Corp., Osaka, Japan, 1983-85; internat. bond trader Banque Baribas, Tokyo, 1985-86, Westpac Bank, Tokyo, 1987-88; fin. cons. Masumi Tripoli and Assocs., Irvine, Calif., 1989—; anchor newscaster United TV, L.A., 1989-92. Condr. seminars in field. Contbr. articles to profl. jours. CEO Masumi Tripoli and Mona Lisa Tripoli Found. Grantee Sophia U., 1979, H.E.C., 1983. Mem. Internat. Bd. Cert. Fin. Planners. E-mail: masumiusa@hotmail.com.

**TRIPP, AILI MARI,** political scientist, educator; b. Market Harborough, UK, May 24, 1958; came to US, 1974; d. Lloyd William Frederick and Marja-Liisa (Aro) Swantz; m. Warren Earl Tripp, Aug. 28, 1976; children: Lloyd Max, Leila Mari. BA, U. Chgo., 1983, MA, 1985; PhD, Northwestern U., Evanston, Ill., 1990. Prof. dept. polit. sci. and womens studies program U. Wis., Madison, 1992—; dir. Women's Studies Rsch. Ctr., 2000—; assoc. dean Internat. studies Northwestern U, Evanston, Ill., 2003—. Author: Changing the Rules: The Politics of Liberalization and the Urban Informal Economy in Tanzania, 2001, Women and Politics in Uganda, 2001. Am. Coun. of Learned Soc. fellow, 1991; grantee Inst. for the Study of World Politics, 1988, John D. and Catherine T. MacArthur Found., 1993, AAUW, 1993, Social Sci. Rsch. Coun., 1995, UN World Inst. for the Study of Devel. Econ. Rsch., 1987, Am. Scandinavian Found., 1999. Mem. Am. Polit. Sci. Assn. (Victoria Schuck award 2001), African Studies Assn.

**TRIPP, ALAN H.,** educational association administrator, consultant; s. Jasper L. and Sarah Y. Tripp; children: Alexander, Benjamin. AB in Econ. and Internat. Rels., Stanford U., 1985, MBA, 1989. Editor, reporter Wall St. Jour., European edit., Brussels, 1985—86; cons. Boston Consulting Group, San Francisco, 1989—91; founder, CEO, Scoer! Ednl. Crs., San Francisco, 1992—99, InsideTrack Learning, Inc., San Francisco, 1999—. Bd. chair GreatSchools.net, San Francisco, 2001—. Mem.: Phi Beta Kappa. Office: InsideTrack Learning Inc 703 Market St 20th Fl San Francisco CA 94114

**TRIPP, KAREN BRYANT,** lawyer; b. Rocky Mount, NC, Sept. 2, 1955; d. Bryant and Katherine Rebecca (Watkins) Tripp; m. Robert Mark Burleson, June 25, 1977 (div. 1997); 1 child, Hamilton Chase Tripp Barnett. BA, U. NC, 1976; JD, U. Ala., 1981. Bar: Tex. 1981, US Dist. Ct. (so. dist.) Tex. 1982, US, Ct. Appeals (fed. cir.) 1983, US Dist. Ct. (ea. dist.) Tex. 1991, US Dist. Ct. (we. dist.), 2005, US Supreme Ct. 1994, US Dist. Ct. (no. dist.) Tex. 1998, US Ct. Appeals (5th and 9th cirs.) 2000, US Ct. Appeals (3d cir.) 2001. Law clk. Tucker, Gray & Espy, Tuscaloosa, Ala., 1978-81; law clk. to presiding justice Ala. Supreme Ct., Montgomery, Ala., summer 1980; atty. Exxon Prodn. Rsch. Co., Houston, 1981-86, coord. tech. transfer, 1986-87; assoc. Arnold, White and Durkee, Houston, 1988-93, shareholder, 1994-98; shareholder, head intellectual property sect. for Houston office Winstead, Sechrest & Minick, Attys. at Law, Houston, 1998; pres. Blake Barnett & Co., 1996—2003; pvt. practice Houston, 1999—. Creator, program planner, master of ceremonies 1st and 2d intellectual property law confs. for women corp. counsels; adj. prof. of intellectual property law Inst. for Advanced Legal Studies, Houston, 2005—. Editor: Intellectual Property Law Rev., 1995—2006; contbr. articles to profl. jour. Chair U. Houston and Houston intellectual Property Law Assoc. Fall CLE Inst. on Intellectual Property, 2000. Mem. ABA (intellectual property law sect., ethics com. 1992-96), Houston Bar Assn. (interprofl. rels. com. 1988-90), Houston Intellectual Property Law Assn. (outstanding inventor com. 1982-84, chmn. 1994-95, sec. 1987-88, treas. 1991-92, bd. dir. 1992-94, 98-2000, nominations com. 1993, 96, chmn. fall CLE Inst. 2000), Houston Bar Found. (fellow), Tex. Bar Assn. (antitrust law com. 1984-85, chmn. internat. law com. intellectual property law sect. 1987-88, internat. transfer tech. com. 1983-84, planning com. continuing legal edn. conf. on intellectual property 2003), planning comm. for 2003 CLE Inst. on Intellectual property Law, Tex. Exec. Women, Women's Fin. Exch., Am. Intellectual Property Lawyers Assn. (patent law com. 1995), Intellectual Property Owners Assn. (copyright com.), Women in Tech. (founder), Lil Eli's Club (founder), Phi Alpha Delta. Republican. Episcopalian. Office: PO Box 1301 Houston TX 77251-1301 Office Phone: 713-658-9323. Business E-Mail: ktripp@tripplaw.com.

**TRIPP, MARIAN BARLOW LOOFE,** retired public relations executive; b. Lodgepole, Nebr., July 26; d. Lewis Rockwell and Cora Dee (Davis) Barlow; m. James Edward Tripp, Feb. 9, 1957; children: Brendan Michael, Kevin Mark. BS, Iowa State U., 1944. Writer Dairy Record, St. Paul, 1944-45; head product promotion divsn., pub. rels. dept. Swift & Co., Chgo., 1945-55; mgmt. supr. pub. rels. J. Walter Thompson Co., N.Y.C. and Chgo., 1956-76, v.p. consumer affairs Chgo., 1974-76; pres. Marian Tripp Communications Inc., Chgo., 1976-94. Mem. Am. Inst. Wine and Food, Confriere de la Chaine des Rotisseriers (officer Chgo. chpt.), Mayflower Soc., Daughters of the Am. Revolution, Les Dames D'Escoffier. Episcopalian.*

**TRIPP, MICHAEL WINDSOR,** accountant; b. Fall River, Mass. s. Frederick and Elizabeth (Azevedo) T.; m. Ella Charlene Middlebrooks, May 24, 1966; children: Sandra Lee, Wendy Ann. Cert. computer programming with honors, Plus Sch. Bus., Providence, 1971; BSBA in Acctg. cum laude, Bryant Coll., 1975. CPA, R.I.; diplomate Am. Bd. Forensic Acctg. Fin. mgr. trainee I.T.T. Aetna Fin., Pawtucket, R.I., 1969-70; computer programmer B.A. Ballou & Co., Inc., East Providence, R.I., 1970-72; adminstrv. asst. Manasett Corp., Providence, 1972-74; profl. staff Peat, Marwick & Mitchell, Providence, 1974-76; ptnr. Turosz, Maccarone, Keenan & Tripp, East Providence, 1976-88; adminstr. Licht & Semonoff, Providence, 1988-89; pvt. practice East Providence, 1989—. Dir. A New Leaf, Providence, 1988-96; mem. bd. regents LaSalle Acad., Providence, 2005; adj. instr. acctg. Roger Williams Coll., 1979-82. Vice-chmn., clk. Barrington (R.I.) Sch. Com., 1980-88; active Rep. Town Com., Barrington, 1980—; treas. Hampden Meadows PTA, Barrington, 1976-80, Rhode Islanders for Chafee, Providence, 1976. With USMC, 1965-69, Vietnam. Decorated Purple Heart, Air medal, Navy Commendation medal with combat V. Fellow AICPA; mem. R.I. Soc. CPAs, Manny Moniz Meml. Hockey League (treas. 1992—), Barrington Yacht Club (treas. 1992-93), Narragansett Bay Yachting Assn., Am. Coll. Forensic Examiners, Bryant Coll. Alumni Assn. (exec. dir., treas. 1977-80), La Salle Acad. Alumni Assn. (phonathon chmn. 1992-93), Appalachian Mountain Club, U.S. Sailing Assn., VFW (quartermaster Post 9742, 2002—), Barrington United Vets. Coun. (treas. 2005-). Republican. Roman Catholic. Avocations: sailing, hockey, mountain climbing. Home: 40 Lamson Rd Barrington RI 02806-2643 Office: 1481 Wampanoag Trail Ste 2 East Providence RI 02915 Office Phone: 401-434-7200. E-mail: mtripp@mwt-cpa.coxatwork.com.

**TRIPP, SUSAN GERWE,** museum director; b. Balt., Dec. 28, 1945; d. Earl Joseph and Maria Elizabeth (Wise) Gerwe; m. David Enders Tripp, June 9, 1977. BS, U. Md., 1967. Home econs. tchr. Balt. County Pub. Sch. Sys., 1967-74; curator of art Johns Hopkins U., Balt., 1974-76, curator of art, archivist, 1976-78, instr. evening coll., 1978-84, dir. univ. collections, 1979-91; supr., instr. art history Goucher Coll., Notre Dame U., Balt., 1977-86; dir. docent tng. Homewood Mus., Balt., 1987-89; exec. dir. Old Westbury (N.Y.) Gardens, 1992-96; writer Stuyvesant, NY, 1996—. Dir. Homewood Restoration Adv. Com., 1983-92, Evergreen Restoration Adv. Com., 1988-92, Advancement Basilica Hist. Trust, Inc., 2000-2001; lectr. in field. Co-author: The Garrett Collection of Japanese Art, 1993 (NEA Grant 1980), Contbr. articles to profl. jours. Bd. dirs. Columbia County Hist. Soc., 1996-2002, 2003—, pres. bd. dirs., 1997-2002, sec., 2003—; trustee Regional and Cmty. Hist. Preservation Benefit Plan, 2002—; chmn. Vanderpoel house restoration Columbia County Hist. Soc., 2002-03; judge Hist. Hudson Preservation Awards, 2000—; bd. trustees Am. Numismatic Soc., 2003—. Recipient Hist. Preservation award Balt. Heritage, Inc., 1988, 91, Rsch. award Am. Soc. Interior Designers, 1991. Fellow Am. Numismatic Soc. (standing com., libr., trustee 2003—); mem. Oriental Ceramic Soc., Balt. Mus. Art, Furniture History Soc., Columbia County Hist. Soc. (bd. dirs. 2003—, sec. bd. dirs. 2003—), Omicron Nu. Avocations: architecture, archaeology, chinese ceramics, historical restoration. Office: PO Box G Stuyvesant NY 12173-0009

**TRIPP, THOMAS NEAL,** lawyer, political scientist; b. June 19, 1942; s. Gerald Frederick and Kathryn Ann (Siebold) T.; m. Ellen Marie Larrimer, Apr. 16, 1966; children: David Larrimer, Bradford Douglas, Corinne Catherine. BA cum laude, Mich. State U., 1964; JD, George Washington U., 1967. Bar. Ohio 1967, U.S. Ct. Mil. Appeals 1968, U.S. Supreme Ct. 1968, Wyo. 1991. Pvt. practice, Columbus, Ohio, 1969—, Wilson, Wyo., 1991—. Real estate developer, Columbus, 1969—; chmn. bd. Black Sheep Enterprises, Columbus, 1969—; polit. cons. David A. Keene & Assocs., Washington, 1986-96; vice chmn. bd. Sun Valley-Elkhorn Assn. Idaho, 1983-85, chmn. 1986-91; vice chmn. Sawtooth Sports, Ketchum, Idaho, 1983-85; legal counsel Wallace F. Ackley Co., Columbus, 1973—; vice chmn. Triathlon LLC, 1996-2003; presiding judge Ohio Mock Trial Competition, 1986-94; chmn. bd. dirs. White House, 1996; mem. Sawtooth Soc. adv. coun. FCC, 1993-95; dep. sgl. adviser to pres. N.Am. Free Trade Agreement, 1993; polit. columnist. Trustee Americans for Responsible Govt., Washington, GOPAC; mem. Peace Corps Adv. Coun., 1981-85; mem. U.S. Commn. on Trade Policy and Negotiations, 1985-88; campaign mgr., chmn. Charles Rockwell Saxbe, Ohio Ho. of Reps., 1974, 76, 78, 80; campaign mgr. George Bush for Pres., 1980, nat. dep. field dir., nat. dep. polit. dir., 1980; alumni admissions coun. Mich. State U., 1984-2000, George Washington U., 1988-2000; regional co-chmn. Reagan-Bush, 1984, nat. fin. com., 1984; mem. Victory '84 fin. com.; mem. Victory '88 fin. com. Bush-Quayle; co-chmn. Ohio Lawyers for Bush/Quayle, 1988; Rep. candidate 2d U.S. Congl. Dist., Idaho, 1988; candidate U.S. Senate, Wyo., 1996; transition dir. Ohio Sec. of State, 1990-91; bd. trustees Columbus Acad. Pvt. Co-ed Secondary Sch., 1991-94, Prescott (Ariz.) Coll., 1998-2000; chmn. bd. dirs. T.R.E.E. Coalition, 1991—; vice-chmn. Am. Conservative Union Found., 2002-06, sec., 2006—; chmn. FirstPrinciples.US. Pub. Policy Institute, 2003—. 1st lt. U.S. Army, 1967-69. Fellow Pi Sigma Alpha, Vietnam Vet. Am., Phi Delta Phi. Republican. Home: 5420 Clark State Rd Columbus OH 43230-1956

**TRIPP, VICTOR K.,** electrical engineer, researcher; b. Spring Brook, Wis., Apr. 14, 1947; s. Clovis H. and Mildred M. Tripp; m. Carmen V. Couceyro, Mar. 10, 1948; children: Rebecca S. Ziegler, Rachel L. BA in Physics, U. of Chgo., 1970; MSEE, U. of Ill., Urbanna, 1972. Cert. electromagnetic compatability engr., Nat. Assn. of Radio and Telecom. Engrs., 1990. V.p. Wang-Tripp Corp., Marietta, Ga., 1991—95; prin. rsch. engr. Ga. Tech Rsch. Inst., Atlanta, 1991—. Prin. Tripp Tech. Cons., Tucker, Ga., 2002—; editor ElephantJournal.org, Tucker, 2001—; mem. blue ribbon panel of experts on RF com. U.S. Army CECOM, 1996. Contbr. and reviewer (to profl. jours. articles). Elder and deacon various ch. congregations, Tucker, 1979—2000. Recipient Outstanding Performance in Rsch., Ga. Tech Rsch. Inst., ECS Lab, 1988, Commendation for Pioneering New Antenna Technologies, US Air Force, Wright R&D Ctr., Avionics Lab, Electronic Warfare, 1993. Mem.: IEEE (sr.), IEEE Internat. Symposium on Antennas and Propagation (steering com. 1998—98), IEEE Antenna and Propagation Soc. (chmn., atlanta sect. 1987—89), Sigma Xi. Christian. Achievements include 7 patents related to antennas and electromagnetics. Office: Georgia Tech Research Institute 7220 Richardson Rd Smyrna GA 30080 Office Phone: 770-528-7160. Office Fax: 770-528-3187. E-mail: vic.tripp@gtri.gatech.edu.

**TRIPPENSEE, GARY ALAN,** retired aerospace executive; b. Jefferson City, Mo., May 23, 1940; m. Concha Elvira Perez, Aug. 18, 1981; children: Jena, Darin. BSME, U. Mo., Rolla, 1962; AA in Bus., Antelope Valley Coll., Lancaster, Calif., 1974. Lic. airframe and powerplant mechanic, FAA; single/multi-engine comml. aircraft lic. land & sea, Inst.; cert. flight instr., instrument. Aircraft flight test engr. McDonnell Douglas, St. Louis, 1965-79; project mgr. NASA/Dryden Flight Rsch. Ctr., Edwards, Calif., 1979—2001, project mgr. F14, 1983-84, project mgr. F15, 1986-87, project mgr. X-29, 1985-91, project mgr. X-31, 1991-92, internat. test. orgn. dir. X-31, 1993-95, project mgr. X-33, 1996-2000, project mgr. X-37, 2000-01, ret., 2001. Capt. U.S. Army C.E., 1962-65, Vietnam. Recipient Laurels award for aeronautics/propulsion Aviation Week & Space Tech., 1990, 93, Outstanding Alumni award U. Mo.-Rolla, 2000. Mem. EAA, Acad. Mech. Engrs. Avocations: flying, fishing, r/c models. Home: 3410 Callie Dr Grove OK 74344 Office Phone: 918-791-1917. Business E-Mail: gfsbtrip@grandsavingsbank.com.

**TRIPPLEHORN, JEANNE,** actress; b. Tulsa, Okla., June 10, 1963; d. Tommy and Suzanne (Ferguson) T. Student, Juilliard Sch. Appeared in (theatre off-Broadway) The Big Funk, 1990, 'Tis Pity She's A Whore, 1992; (film) Basic Instinct, 1991, The Firm, 1993, The Night We Never Met, 1993, Reality Bites, 1994, Waterworld, 1995, 'Til There Was You, 1996, Sliding Doors, 1997, Office Killer, 1997, Noose, 1997, Very Bad Things, 1998, Talk of the Town, 1998, Mickey Blue-Eyes, 1998, Steal This Movie, 2000, Timecode, 2000, Paranoid, 2000, Relative Values, 2000, Dial 9 for Love, 2001, Swept Away, 2002, The Moguls, 2005; (TV films) Old Man, 1997, My Brother's Keeper, 2002. Office: c/o William Morris Agency One William Morris Pl Beverly Hills CA 90212*

**TRISCO, ROBERT FREDERICK,** church historian, educator; b. Chgo., Nov. 11, 1929; s. Richard E. and Harriet Rose (Hardt) T. BA, St. Mary of Lake Sem., Mundelein, Ill., 1951; STL, Pontifical Gregorian U., Rome, 1955, Hist. Eccl.D., 1962; LHD (hon.), Belmont Abbey Coll., 1992. Ordained priest Roman Catholic Ch., 1954. Faculty Cath. U. Am., Washington, 1959-2000, prof. ch. history, 1975-2000, Kelly-Quinn disting. prof. ch. history, 1999-2000, prof. emeritus ch. history, 2000—. Expert 2d Vatican Coun., 1962-65; pres. Am. subcom. Internat. Commn. Comparative Ch. History, 1978-80, assesseur, 1980—; mem. subcom. Nat. Conf. Cath. Bishops, 1966-76, 87-92; mem. Pontifical Com. Hist. Scis., 1982—; hon. mem. Accademia di San Carlo (Milan), 1986—; hon. prelate (monsignor), 1992; Protonotary Apostolistic Supranumerary, 2005; mem. Internat. Joint Commn. for Theol. Dialogue between Cath. Ch. and Orthodox Ch., 1999-2006; mem. Anglican-Roman Catholic Consultation in U.S., 2002—; mem. adv. com. Assn. Friends of the Archives of Congregation for Doctrine of the Faith (Holy See), 1999—. Author: The Holy See and Nascent Church in the Middle Western U.S., 1826-1850, 1962, Bishops and Their Priests in the United States, 1988; co-author: A Guide to American Catholic History, 2d edit., 1982; editor: Catholics in America, 1976; editor Cath. Hist. Rev., 1963-2005, editor 2005-; co-editor, editor: Studies in Catholic History in Honor of John Tracy Ellis, 1985; contbr. articles to profl. jours. Decorated knight Equestrian Order of the Holy Sepulchre of Jerusalem, 1993, knight comdr., 1998. Mem. Am. Hist. Assn., Am. Soc. Ch. History (exec. coun. 1980-82), Am. Cath. Hist. Assn. (exec. sec. 1961—, sec., treas. 1983-2006), Can. Cath. Hist. Assn. Office: Cath U Am Mullen Library Rm 320 Washington DC 20064-0001 Office Phone: 202-319-5079. Business E-Mail: trisco@cua.edu.

**TRISTANO, ANTONIO GINO,** medical researcher; arrived in U.S., 2003; s. Piero Tristano and Speranza Romano; children: Gianpiero, Fabrizio. MD, Luiz Razetti Sch. Medicine, Caracas, 1991; MS in Biology, Instituto Venezolano de Investigaciones Científicas (IVIC), Caracas, 1997; Specialist in Criminalistics cum laude, U. Inst. Sci. Police, Caracas, 1997; Specialist in Internal Medicine, Luis Razetti Sch. Medicine, Caracas, 2000, Specialist in Rheumatology, 2002. Specialist in Rheumatology Colegio de Medicos del Distrito Metropolitano, 2003, Specialist in Internal Medicine Colegio de Medicos del Distrito Metropolitano, 2001, Medical Assistant Am. Registry of Med. Assistants/Fla., 2004. Rural physician Hosp. de Naiguatá, La Guaira, Vargas, Venezuela; intern Instituto de Clínicas y Urología Tamanaco, Caracas, 1992—93; biology prof. Instituto Universitario de Policía Científica, Caracas, 1996—97; toxicology prof. José Maria Vargas U., Caracas, 1997—97; internal medicine staff in internal medicine program Hosp. Domingo Luciani (U. Hosp.), Caracas, 2002—04; rsch. assoc. NOVA Southeastern U., Ft. Lauderdale, Fla., 2004—. Chief resident internal medicine Internal Medicine Residency Program Domingo Luciani Hosp. (Univrsity Hosp.), Caracas, 1997—98; chief resident rheumatology U. Hosp. of the City of Caracas, 2001—02; mem. soc. interns and residents Domingo Luciani Hosp., Caracas, 1998—2000; presenter in field. Reviewer: So. Med. Jour.; contbr. articles to profl. jours. Vaccination Ministerio de Sanidad y Asistencia Social, Caracas, 1987—87. Scholar, Fundación Gran Mariscal de Ayacucho, 1995—97. Mem.: Venezuelan Assn. Internal Medicine (Spl. Award by thesis 2000), Internat. Reviewers Panel of the Med. Sci. Monitor, Venezuelan Assn. for Pain Studies, Venezuelan Assn. Rheumatology, Internat. Assn. for the Study of Pain, ACP, Am. Soc. Internal Medicine (Award for 1° prize of best paper Pub. 2003). Roman Catholic. Avocations: travel, classical music. Office: NOVA Southeastern University 3200 S University Dr Fort Lauderdale FL 33328 Home: 5274 NW 114th Ave # 204 Miami FL 33178 Office Phone: 954-262-1925. Personal E-mail: mjtristano@cantv.net. E-mail: antoniotristano@bellsouth.net.

**TRITCH, TERESA,** editor, writer; b. LA; BA in German, UCLA, 1984; MA in Journalism, Columbia Univ., 2001. Joined Money Mag., 1988, bur. chief Washington, 1993—97, sr. editor NYC, 1997—2000; contributing editor Gallup Mgmt. Jour., 2001—03, Stanford Social Innovation Rev., 2003; editl. bd. mem. NY Times, 2004—. Co-editor: America at War: The Battle for Iraq in Words, 2003. Knight-Bagehot Fellow in Bus. and Econ. Journalism, Columbia Univ., 2000—01. Office: Editl Bd NY Times 229 W 43rd St New York NY 10036 Office Phone: 212-556-1876. Office Fax: 212-556-3815.*

**TRITLE, LAWRENCE ALAN,** history professor; b. Glendale, Calif., Oct. 13, 1946; s. Robert Charles Jr. and Dorothy (Brown) T.; m. Margaret Burlington, Jan. 31, 1970 (dec. Aug. 24, 2000) BA, UCLA, 1968; MA, U.S. Fla., Tampa, 1972; PhD, U. Chgo., 1978. Prof. Loyola Marymount U., L.A., 1978—, Marie Chilton chair humanities, 1988. Vis. prof. Loyola U. Chgo., 1981-82, 90-91, UCLA, 1992. Author: Phocion the Good, 1988, From Melos to My Lai. War & Survival, 2000, The Peloponnesian War, 2004; editor: The Greek World in the Fourth Century BC, 1997, Balkan Currents, 1998, Text and Tradition: Studies in Greek History & Histiography, 1999, Crossroads of History Age of Alexander, 2003. Lt. U.S. Army, 1968-71, Vietnam. NEH fellow U. Pa., 1979. Mem. Am. Philol. Assn. (chair com. ancient history 1997-99), Am. Hist. Assn., Assn. Ancient Historians, Soc. Mayflower Descendants (So. Calif. chpt.). Democrat. Home: 8301 Fordham Rd Los Angeles CA 90045-2559 Office: Loyola Marymount U 1 LMU Dr Los Angeles CA 90045-2699 Office Phone: 310-338-7385. Business E-Mail: ltritle@lmu.edu.

**TRITTEN, JAMES JOHN,** federal agency administrator, educator; s. James Hanley and Jennie (Szucs) Tritten; m. Kathleen Brattesani (div. 1983); children: Kimberly, James John Jr.; m. Jasmine Clark, Dec. 29, 1990. BA in Internat. Studies, Am. U., 1971; MA in Internat. Affairs, Fla. State U., 1978; AM in Internat. Rels., U. So. Calif., 1982, PhD in Internat. Rels., 1984. Commd. officer USN, 1967, advanced through grades to commdr., 1981; joint strategic plans officer Office Chief Naval Ops., Washington, 1984—85; asst. dir. net assessment Office Sec. Def., Washington, 1985—86; chmn. dept. nat. security affairs Naval Postgrad. Sch., Monterey, Calif., 1986—89; ret. USN, 1989; assoc. prof. nat. security affairs Naval Postgrad. Sch., Monterey, 1989—93; spl. asst. comdr. Naval Doctrine Command, Norfolk, Va., 1993—96; chief policy and plan divsn. US Joint Forces Command, Suffolk, Va., 1996—2001, mem. joint doctrine divsn., 2001—02; chief tng. inspections divsn. Def. Threat Reduction Agy., Albuquerque, 2002—, asst. chief staff, 2002—. Cons. Rand Corp., Santa Monica, Calif., 1982—84; with Nat. Security Rsch., Fairfax, Va., 1992, AmerInd, Alexandria, Va., 1996. Author: (book) Soviet Naval Forces and Nuclear Warfare, 1986, Our New National Security Strategy, 1992 (George Washington Honor medal, 1991), A Doctrine Reader, 1996; contbr. chapters to books, articles to profl. jours. Mem. Adv. Bd. on Alcohol Related Problems, Monterey, 1987—90; bd. dirs., officer Leadership Monterey Peninsula, 1989—92, Carmel Valley (Calif.) Property Owners Assn., 1989—91; commr. Airport Land Use Commn., Monterey County, 1990—93. Decorated Def. Superior Svc. medal Sec. Def., Washington, DC, Meritorious Svc. medal Sec. Navy, Navy Civilian Supr. Svc. medal; recipient Joint Meritorious Civilian Svc. award, Chmn. Joint Chiefs Staff, 1998, Alfred Thayer Mahan award literary achievement, Navy League US, 1986. Mem.: Mil. Ops. Rsch. Soc. (v.p. 1990—91), U.S. Naval Inst. (Silver and Bronze medals), Naval Order U.S., Pi Gamma Mu, Pi Sigma Alpha. Republican. Presbyterian. Avocations: hiking, writing. Office: Def Threat Reduction Agy-CST 1680 Texas St SE Kirtland Afb NM 87117 Office Phone: 505-846-8734. Personal E-mail: jtritten121@comcast.net. Business E-Mail: james.tritten@abq.dtra.mil.

**TRITTER, RICHARD PAUL,** risk management consultant; b. Boston, Sept. 30, 1945; s. Herman Louis and Rose (Greenblatt) T.; children: Melissa Rosanne, Matthew Alexander, Rachel Danielle, Adam Levi. AB, Columbia Coll., N.Y.C., 1967; JD, Northea. U., 1976. Bar: Mass. 1977, U.S. Supreme Ct. 1980. Mktg. mgr./cons. Digital Equipment Corp., Merrimack, NH, 1979-86; pres. Video/Demo Ctrs., Inc., Burlington, Mass., 1986-88; v.p. bus. devel. Info. Resources, Inc., Boston, 1988-91; dir. facilitation consulting svcs. Arthur Andersen LLP, Boston, Chgo., 1991-96; consulting dir. Computer Assocs., Inc., Andover, Mass., 1998—2001; pvt. cons. Israel, 2001—; safety mgr. Nachobonim Storage Base. Panelist MIT Enterprise Forum, Cambridge, 1983-89; ptnr., mng. dir. Horn of Africa Fishing Partnership, 1998. Author: Control Self-Assessment: Experience, Current Thinking and Best Practices, 1996, Control Self Assessment—A Guide to Facilitation-Based Consulting, 2000; creator software application testing svc. in coop. with KPMG Peat Marwick, Compliance Testing and Verification, 1981. UN rep. Jubaland Relief and Rehab. Soc., Somalia; dir. Save Somalia Livestock Campaign, 1993. Recipient Better Govt. award Pioneer Inst. for Pub. Policy Rsch., Yoseftal prize for safest constrn. site in Israel Nachobonim Dry Storage Base. Achievements include facilitating meetings between opposing clans in the Juba region of southern Somalia; initiated lobster export project with cooperation of Gen. Omar Jess, Col. Ahmed Hashi and other Somali leaders. Office: Richard Tritter The Siller Group 76802 Gan Shlomo Israel Home: Kibbutz Givat 60948 Brener Israel E-mail: oleh77@yahoo.com.

**TRITTON, THOMAS RICHARD,** academic administrator, biologist, educator; b. Lakewood, Ohio, Dec. 20, 1947; s. William Frank and Margie Jean (Galbraith) Tritton; m. Louise Meschter Tritton; children: Lara, Christiana. BA, Ohio Wesleyan U., 1969; PhD, Boston U., 1973. Asst. prof. Yale Med. Sch., New Haven, 1975—80; assoc. prof. Yale U., 1980—85; prof. U. Vt., Burlington, 1985—97, vice provost, 1991—97; pres. Haverford Coll., Pa., 1997—. Mem. NIH Exptl. Therapeutics Study Sect., 1988—92; bd. dirs. Fox Chase Cancer Ctr., 1997—. Editor: books; mem. editl. bd.: various profl. jours.; contbr. scientific papers to profl. jours. Mem.: Am. Chem. Soc. Biol. Chemists, Am. Assn. Cancer Rsch. (com. mem.). Mem. Soc. Of Friends. Avocations: music, tennis. Office: Haverford Coll 370 Lancaster Ave Haverford PA 19041-1336 Office Phone: 610-896-1021. Business E-Mail: ttritton@haverford.edu.

**TRIVELPIECE, ALVIN WILLIAM,** physicist, educator, consultant; b. Stockton, Calif., Mar. 15, 1931; s. Alvin Stevens and Mae (Hughes) Trivelpiece; m. Shirley Ann Ross, Mar. 23, 1953; children: Craig Evan, Steve Edward, Keith Eric. BEE, Calif. Poly. Coll., 1953; MEE, Calif. Inst. Tech., 1955, PhD in Elec. Engring. and Physics, 1958. Fulbright scholar Delft (Netherlands), U., 1958—59; asst. prof., then assoc. prof. U. Calif. at Berkeley, 1959—66; prof. physics U. Md., 1966—70; on leave as asst. dir. for research div. controlled thermonuclear research AEC, Washington, 1973—75; v.p. Maxwell Labs. Inc., San Diego, 1976—78; corp. v.p. Sci. Applications, Inc., La Jolla, Calif., 1978—81; dir. Office of Energy Research, U.S. Dept. Energy, Washington, 1981—87; exec. officer AAAS, Washington, 1987—88; dir. Oak Ridge (Tenn.) Nat. Lab., 1989—; v.p. Martin Marietta Energy Systems, 1989—95, Lockheed Martin Energy Systems, 1995; pres. Lockheed Martin Energy Rsch. Corp., 1995—2000; cons. Sandia Nat. Labs., Albuquerque, 2000—. Head del. joint NAS and Soviet Acad. Scis. mtg. and conf. on energy and global ecol. problems USSR, 1989; chmn. math. scis. ednl. bd. NAS, 1990—93; chmn. coordinating coun. for edn. NRC, 1991—93, chmn. com. small innovative firms in Russian nuclear cities, 2001; mem. Commn. on Phys. Scis., Math. and Applications, 1993—96, com. on tech. issues related to the comprehensive test ban treaty NAS, 2000—02, Tenn. Sci. and Tech. Adv. Commn., 1993—96, chmn., 1996—99, adv. com. Fedn. Networking Coun., 1992—96; chmn. and pres. Tenn. Tech. Devel. Corp., 1998—2000; workshop chmn. NAS and Russian Acad. Scis., Yekaterinburg, Russia, 2004; founding bd. mem., sec., treas. Am. Coun. on Global Nuc. Competitiveness, 2006—; bd. dirs. Environ. Literacy Coun., Am. Coun. Global Nuc. Competitiveness. Author: Slow Wave Propagation in Plasma Wave Guides, 1966, Principles of Plasma Physics, 1973; contbr. articles to profl. jours. Named Disting. Alumnus, Calif. Poly. State U., 1978, Calif. Inst. Tech., Pasadena, 1987; recipient U.S. Sec. of Energy's Gold medal for disting. svc., 1986, Disting. Alumni award, 2000, Tenn. Outstanding Svc. commendation, Senate Joint Resolution #530, 2000; fellow Guggenheim, 1966. Fellow: IEEE (Outstanding Engr. award region 3 1995), AAAS, Am. Phys. Soc.; mem.: NAE, AAUP, Am. Assn. Physics Tchrs., Am. Nuc. Soc., Nat. Press Club, Capital Hill Club, Tau Beta Pi, Sigma Xi. Achievements include patents in field. Home and Office: 14 Wade Hampton Trail Henderson NV 89052-6635 Office Phone: 702-492-1602. Personal E-mail: awt511@cox.net.

**TRIVELPIECE, CRAIG EVAN,** computer electronics executive; b. Pasadena, Calif., Apr. 23, 1957; s. Alvin William and Shirley Ann T. Student, Calif. Inst. Tech., 1974-75; BA in Physics, U. Md., 1979. Scientist Maxwell Labs, San Diego, 1979-81; design engr. Rockwell Internat., Costa Mesa, Calif., 1981-83; mgr. engring. Tex. Instruments, Irvine, Calif., 1983-84; owner, pres. CST Engings Inc., Irvine, 1984-91, Circuit Plus, Inc., 1990-2000, 4 Every Wall, Inc., 1990-92, Transnational Telecom Inc., 1995-98; dir. advanced tech. Encryptix, Inc., 2000—01; sr. product mgr. Day Software, Inc., Newport Beach, Calif., 2001—02; v.p. product devel. Questerra, Inc., Aliso Viejo, Calif., 2002—06. Cons. Payview Ltd., Hong Kong, 1985-88, Airmedia, Inc., 1996-98. Co-inventor: Video Scrambling System, 1985, home video product with Smart Card Access, 1992, Interactive Video System, 1997, Interactive Video System, 2002. Republican. Avocations: Karate, running. Home: 848 N Rainbow Blvd #1562 Las Vegas NV 89107 Office Phone: 949-510-4170. E-mail: c_trivelpiece@yahoo.com.

**TRIVISONNO, NICHOLAS LOUIS,** communications company executive, accountant; b. Bklyn., Apr. 10, 1947; BBA in Acctg., St. Francis Coll., Bklyn., 1968. Ptnr. Arthur Andersen & Co., N.Y.C., 1979-85, mng. ptnr. Stamford, Conn., 1985-88; sr. v.p. fin. GTE Corp., Stamford, 1988-95; chmn., CEO, ACNielsen, Stamford, 1996—. Republican. Roman Catholic. Avocation: golf.

**TROCCOLI, MARIANO,** astrophysicist, researcher; b. Bari, Italy, Oct. 13, 1974; s. Vito Troccoli and Anna Tanzella. PhD in Physics, U. Bari, 2001. Post-doctoral mem. tech. staff Bell Labs. Lucent Technologies, Murray Hill, NJ, 2001—03; post doctoral fellow Harvard U., Cambridge, Mass., 2003—. Cons. Agilent Technologies, Palo Alto, Calif., 2004—05. Recipient Premio Civera, 1989, Young Investigator award, European Material Rsch. Soc., 2001. Achievements include patents in field. Office: Harvard University 19 Oxford St Cambridge MA 02138 Office Phone: 617-495-1934. Personal E-mail: mtroccoli@gmail.com. Business E-Mail: troccoli@deas.harvard.edu.

**TROEN, BRUCE ROBERT,** medical educator; s. Philip and Betty Ann Troen; m. Suzanne B. Troen; children: Ben, Eli. AB, Harvard Coll., Cambridge, Mass., 1976; MD, Harvard U., Boston, 1981. Diplomate Am. Bd. of Internal Medicine, Am. Bd. of Internal Medicine and Geriatrics. Assoc. prof. medicine Miami VA Med. Ctr., Miller Sch. Medicine, U. Miami, Fla., 2002—. Office: Miami VA Med Ctr Miller Sch Medicine U Miami 11 GRC 1201 NW 16th St Miami FL 33125 Office Phone: 305-575-3388. Office Fax: 305-575-3365.

**TROFFKIN, HOWARD JULIAN,** lawyer; b. Port Chester, NY, Jan. 30, 1937; s. Irving and Frieda Troffkin; m. Rhea Dorothy, May 12, 1963; children: Stephen, Barbara. BS in Chemistry, St. Lawrence U., 1959; postgrad., Columbia U., 1959-60; JD, Georgetown U., 1970. Bar: Va. 1971, D.C. 1972. Rsch. chemist Am. Cyanamid Co., 1961-66, legal trainee, 1966-67, patent agt., 1967-71; assoc. Pennie, Edmonds, Morton, Taylor & Adams, Washington, 1971-77; patent atty. W.R. Grace & Co., Columbia, Md., 1977-86, sr. patent counsel, 1987-98; pvt. practice, 1998—; sec./counsel Concrete Corrosion Inhibitor Trade Assn. Patentee in chemistry field. Mem. Willerborn Civic Assn., 1971-75. Served with AUS, 1960-61. Mem. ABA, Va. Bar Assn., D.C. Bar Assn., Washington Patent Lawyers Assn., Md. Patent Law Assn. (pres. 1981-83), Am. Intellectual Property Law Assn., Am. Chem. Soc., Concrete Corrosion Inhibitors Assn. (sec./counsel). Jewish. Avocations: woodcrafting, travel. Home and Office: 7808 Ivymont Ter Potomac MD 20854-3218 Personal E-mail: troffkin@aol.com.

**TROFIMOVA, IRINA (IRENE) ALEXEEVNA,** literature and language professor; b. Alma-Ata, Kazakhstan, Sept. 14, 1943; d. Alexei Ivanovich Semyonov and Vitalia Anatolyevna Chirkova. BA in English, Leningrad Tchrs. U., Russia, 1964, MA in English, 1966; PhD in Linguistics, Alma-Ata Tchrs. U., 1974; MA in Western Classical Philosophy, U. Philosophy, Alma-Ata, 1977, MA, 1989. Assoc. prof. English and German langs. U. Nat. Economy, Alma-Ata, Kazakhstan, 1966—72; grad. student Tchrs. Tng. U., Alma-Ata, Kazakhstan, 1972—74; assoc. prof. English Kazakh State U., Alma-Ata, Kazakhstan, 1974—91; prof. langs. and lit. Ouachita Baptist U., Arkadelphia, Ark., 1991—. Cons. Ministry of Fgn. Affairs, Alma-Ata, Kazakhstan, 1979—81; cons. interpreter Ministry of Health, Alma-Ata, Kazakhstan, 1982—83; interpreter Ministry of Higher Edn., Alma-Ata, Kazakhstan, 1989—91. Author: (textbooks) Textbook for Physicists, Part 1, 1987, Textbook for Physicists, Part 2, 1988; contbr. articles to profl. jours. Mem.: Ark. Fgn. Lang. Tchrs. Assn., Ark. Philological Assn., Ctrl. Am. Russian Tchrs. Assn. Baptist. Avocations: interior decorating, reading, writing poetry. Home: 120 Evonshire Dr Arkadelphia AR 71923 Office: Ouachita Baptist Univ 410 Ouachita St PO Box 3692 Arkadelphia AR 71998 Office Phone: 870-245-5344. Business E-Mail: trofimovai@obu.edu.

**TROGAN, ROLAND BERNARD,** composer, educator; b. Saginaw, Mich., Aug. 6, 1933; s. Ricardo Bernardo Trocano and Alicia Archangeli-Trocano; m. Annette Patrice Ellams, Mar. 31, 2001; m. Mona Jane Philpot-Trogan, Feb. 6, 1971 (dec. 2000); m. Barbara Jean Mills-Trogan, July 10, 1955 (div. June 22, 1964); children: Christopher Roland, Timothy Bernard. MusB in Composition, U. Mich., 1954, MusM in Composition, 1955, Dr. of Musical Arts in Composition, 1963. Cert. Am. Fedn. of Musicians Mich., 1948, Broadcast Music Inc. NY, 1966. Performing pianist (live, weekly) WKNX Radio, Saginaw, Mich., 1947—50; assoc. condr., composer-in-residence Saginaw Civic Symphony, 1954—56; fellow English drama U. Mich., Ann Arbor, 1956—59, fellow in music theory, 1956—60; lectr. in music CUNY, 1958—65; dir. music Ecole Francaise, 1967—69, Unitarian Ch., Staten Island, 1967—69; instr. of piano Wagner Coll., Staten Island, NY, 1968; pres. Roland Trogan, Inc. dba Dr. Trogan's Music Sch., Staten Island, 1975—, Patrice Editions, L. L. C., Staten Island, 2003—. Pvt. music instr. to internationally-recognized conductors, soloists, diplomats, and stage and film stars. non-affiliated, NYC, 1963—71; prodr. new music concerts performed by Henry Cowell, Wallingford Riegger, Max Polikoff, Paul Jacobs and Walter Trampler, NYC, 1966—69; featured composer Carnegie Recital Hall pvt. concert, introduced by H. Wiley Hitchcock and sponsored by Sybil Burton, Tom Poston and Harold Rome, NYC, 1968. Composer: (cantata) The Seafarer, 1967, (composition for choir and orch.) Hymn to Spring, 1950, (composition) Sextet for Wind Quintet and Piano, 1951, Elegy for String Quartet and Contralto on poems of Elinor Wiley, 1953, Soliloquey for piano, 1955, Divertimenti for two voices on tone rows, 1955, Incidental music to Bertold Brecht's The Good Woman of Szechuan, 1956, Preludes for Piano, 1957 (pub. in Generation mag., 1951), Sonata for solo violin, 1959, Concerto for Violin and Orchestra, 1963, Fantasy for Piano, 1967, Nocturnes for Piano, 1968, Bagatelles for Piano, 1970, Piano Sonata no 1, 1971, Piano Sonata no 2, 1997, Elegy for piano, 1998, Piano Sonata no 3, 1999, Diptych for piano, 2000, Symphony for Chamber Orchestra, 2001, Two Scenes for Orchestra, 2006 (Louisville Orch. award, 1955), Mas ficciones por Juan Luis Borges, for solo violin, 1951, (performance) Preludes for piano, performed by Don Trusdel at University of Michigan, 1951, Septet for Wind Quintet and Piano, performed by the University of Michigan Wind Quintet and Bruce Wise, pianist, 1953, Elegy for String Quartet and Piano, University of Illinois-Urbana, 1954, The Hat Man, performed in Chicago by the After Dinner Opera Co., and at the Interlochen Music Camp, 1956, Incidental music for Bertold Brecht's The Good Woman of Szechuan, University of Michigan Theatre, 1957, (perfomance) Preludes of Piano, premiered by Paul Jacobs in New York City, 1955, (performance) Divertimenti for two voices on tone rows, University of Michigan, 1959, Sonata for solo violin, premiered by Harold Kohon at Town Hall, New York City, 1955, Two Scenes for Orchestra, performed by Louisville Symphony Orchestra, 1971, Piano Sonata no 1, performed by Richard Woitach at Alice Tully Hall, Lincoln Center, New York City, 1967, The Seafarer, performed by Richard Woitach and William Wiederanders, with a dramatic reading of the text by Jean Sullivan at Carnegie Recital Hall, New York City, 1971, Nocturnes for Piano, performed at Alice Tully Hall, Lincoln Center, New York City, 1971, Bagatelles for piano, performed by Richard Woitach, Alice Tully Hall, Lincoln Center, New York City, 1971, (opera) The Hat Man (Broadcast Music Inc. award, 1954). Rep. Staten Island Mus., 1968. Recipient Fulbright scholarship, Dept. of State, US Govt. (rescinded by Ho. UnAmerican Activities Com. chmn., Eugene McCarthy), 1954, Young Composer award, Broadcast Music Inc., 1954; fellow Music, U. Mich., 1955—56, English, 1955; grantee, AAAL, 1985—87. R-Conservative. Christian. Avocation: travel. Home: 755 Narrows Rd N Apt #914 Staten Island NY 10304-1542 Office: RTrogan Inc /Dr Trogan's Music School 1861 Victory Blvd Staten Island NY 10314-3517 Office Phone: 718-981-5418. Home Fax: 718-370-8008; Office Fax: 718-370-8008. Personal E-mail: mymusicfriend@aol.com.

**TROGOLO, JEFFREY A.,** research scientist; b. 1967; m. Julia Saidenberg, Oct. 16, 2004. BA in Materials Engring., Rensselaer Polytechnic Inst., PhD in Materials Sci. Pres. Niche Microstructural Corp., 1993—96; staff scientist and rsch. dir. for orthopedic device applications Spire Corp., 1996—98; chief tech. officer AgION Technologies, 1998—. Author pub. over 10 papers in various jours. including the Jour. of Materials Sci., Jour. of Electronic Materials. Office: AgION Technologies Corporate Offices 60 Audubon Rd Wakefield MA 01880 Office Phone: 781-224-7100. Office Fax: 781-246-3340. E-mail: sales@agion-tech.com.*

**TROGUS, FRANK J.,** oil industry executive; BS in chem. engring., MS in chem. engring., U. Dayton; PhD in chem. engring., U. Tex. V.p. tech. Westhollow Tech. Ctr. Equilon Enterprises, LLC; now chief info. officer Shell Oil Products US, Motiva Enterprises LLC. Named one of Premier 100 IT Leaders, Computerworld, 2005. Office: Motiva Enterprises LLC 700 Milam St Houston TX 77002 also: Shell Oil Products US 1100 Louisiana Houston TX 77210*

**TROHMAN, JOSEPH MARK,** editor; b. Hollywood, Fla., Sept. 1, 1984; Student, DePaul U. Lead guitarist Fall Out Boy, 2001—. Musician: (albums) Fall Out Boy's Evening Out With Your Girl, 2002, Take This to Your Grave, 2003, From Under the Cork Tree, 2005, (songs) Sugar, We're Going Down, 2003 (MTV2 award, MTV Video Music Awards, 2005, Viewer's Choice award, MTV Video Music Awards, 2006), Dance, Dance, 2005 (Choice Music Single & Choice Rock Track, Teen Choice Awards, 2006). Recipient Choice Music Rock Group award, Teen Choice Awards, 2006. Office: Fall Out Boy Inc Box 219 1187 Wilmette Ave Wilmette IL 60091*

**TROITSKI, IGOR,** laser scientist, researcher; b. Kaluga, Russia, May 2, 1941; arrived in U.S., 1992; s. Nikolai Alekceehich Troitski and Bronislava Gregorevna Lipnitskaya; m. Tateana Viktorovna Gorchikova (div.); 1 child, Maria Igorevna; m. Olga Ivanovna Kharitonova, Sept. 26, 1997; 1 child, Anna Igorevna Kharitonova. BS in Physics, Moscow Physico-Tech. Inst., 1965, MS in Physics, 1970; PhD in Physics, Moscow Physic-Tech. Inst., 1978. Full prof. optical sys. Moscow Physico-Tech. Inst. Rschr., sr. rsch. fellow, gen. rsch. fellow, full prof. optical sys. Moscow Physico-Tech. Inst., 1965—89; sr. rsch. fellow Higher Attestation Commn., Moscow, 1977; IIET Acad. Russia, Moscow, 1989—92; interlink rschr. N.Y.C., 1993—95; rschr. Laser-Tek Design Ltd., Las Vegas, Nev., 1996—98; gen. rsch. fellow Igor Troitski LLC, Las Vegas, Nev., 1999—. Mem.: Internat. Soc. for Optical Engring. Office: 853 Arrowhead Trl Henderson NV 89015

**TROJANOWSKI, JOHN Q.,** medical educator, health facility administrator; b. Bridgeport, Conn., 1946; MD, PhD, Tufts U., 1976. Intern. Mass. Gen. Hosp., Boston, 1977—79, resident, 1977—79, U. Pa. Hosp., Philadelphia, 1979—80; asst. prof. pathology & lab. medicine U. Pa. Sch. Medicine, 1981—90, prof. pathology & lab. medicine, 1990; co-dir. Pa. Ctr. for Neurodegenerative Disease Rsch., 1992—; dir. med. pathology Pa. Inst. on Aging, 1988—2002, interim dir., 2001—02, dir., 2002—; dir. Alzheimer's Disease Ctr. Nat. Inst. Aging, 1991—. Prin. investigator of program project grant on Alzheimers & Parkinson's disease Nat. Inst. Aging, 1990—. Recipient Merit award, NIH, 1986—94, Promising Investigator award for Alzheimer's Disease Rsch., Met. Life Found., 1991, Investigator award, Nat. Alliance for Rsch. on Schizophrenia & Depression, 1994, Pioneer award, Alzheimer's Assn., 1998, Potamkin prize for Rsch. in Pick's, Alzheimer's and Related Diseases, 1998, Stanley N. Cohen Biomed. Rsch. award, 2000. Mem.: Inst. Med., Assn. Am. Physicians, Am. Soc. Clin. Investigation, Am. Assn. Neuropathologists (pres. 1997—98). Office: U Pa Health Sys Dept Pathology and Lab Medicine 3d Fl 36th & Spruce St Philadelphia PA 19104-4283 E-mail: trojanowski@mail.med.upenn.edu.*

**TROLANDER, HARDY WILCOX,** engineering executive, consultant; b. Chgo., June 2, 1921; s. Elmer Wilcox and Freda Marie (Zobel) T.; m. Imogen Davenport, July 3, 1946 (dec.); children: Megan, Patricia. BS in Engring., Antioch Coll., 1947. Instr. Antioch Coll., Yellow Springs, Ohio, 1947-48; co-founder, CEO Yellow Springs Instrument Co., Inc., 1948-86. Dir., co-founder Cook Design Ctr., Dartmouth Coll., Hanover, N.H., 1975-88; bd. dirs. Deban Inc., Yellow Springs, Camax Tool co., Arvada, Colo.; mem. evaluation panel Inst. Basic Stds., Nat. Bur. Stds., 1977-79. Contbr. articles to profl. jours.; patentee in field. Co-founder, trustee Yellow Springs Community Found., 1974-83; trustee Autioch Coll., 1968-74, chmn. bd., 1972-74; trustee Engring. and Sci. Found., Dayton, Engrs. Club Dayton Found., 1994-2005, Engring. and Sci. Hall of Fame, 1994-2002; mem. adv. bd. Coll. Engring. and Computer Sci. Wright State U., 1993-2005; bd. dirs. united Way Greater Dayton Area, 1984-92; small bus. innovative rsch. grant panels Nat. Sci. Found., 1988—. 1st lt. USAF, 1943-46. Named Outstanding Engr., Dayton Affiliate Socs., 1967, 89. Fellow Dayton Engrs. Club, Am. Inst. for Med. and Biol. Engring.; mem. ACLU, Nat. Acad. Engring., Am. Inst. Biol. Scis. (bioinstrumentation adv., coun. 1969-75), Internat. Orgn. of Legal Metrology (tech. advisor, sec. 1975-82), Amnesty Internat. Democrat. Achievements include co-development of melting point of gallium which has become recognized as a primary defining point of the International Temperature Scale. Home and Office: 3 Aspen Ct Yellow Springs OH 45387-1326 Office Phone: 937-767-4551.

**TROLL, KITTY,** actress, writer; b. N.Y.C., Dec. 18, 1950; d. Hans and Lillian Holland (Ellman) T.; m. Douglas Getchell (div.); 1 child, Wyatt Theodore. Student, Cambridge Sch. of Weston; studied with Lee Strasberg, Michael Howard, N.Y.C. Instr. drama Pacific (Calif.) High Sch.; founder Mixed-Media Theatre, Dallas. Appeared in (stage prodns.) A Grape for Seeing, The Night of the Iguana, Blues for Mr. Charlie, A Midsummer Night's Dream, Spoon River Anthology, The Moon is Blue, Day of the Races, Old Wives Tale, Bandits, Survivors, Beggar's Choice, Much Ado About Nothing, (films) Stardust Memories, 1980, The Last to Know, 1981, Sun and Moon, Permanent Wave, 1986, (TV) As the World Turns, All My Children, For Richer, for Poorer, Texas; author (screenplay) Holding the Bag, (teleplay) Malpractice, (book) The Party Book. Mem. Actors' Equity Assn., Screen Actors Guild, AFTRA.

**TROLL, LILLIAN ELLMAN,** psychologist, educator; b. Chgo., Sept. 24, 1915; d. Morris C. and Bertha H. (Holland) Ellman; divorced; children: Kathren, Jeanne, Gregory. BS in Psychology, U. Chgo., 1937, MA in Human Devel., 1966, PhD in Human Devel., 1967. Pers. technician U.S. War Dept., Washington, 1941-45; sch. psychologist Newton (Mass.) Pub. Schs., 1957-63; cons. State Calif., San Francisco 1964-65; sr. rsch. assoc. Merrill-Palmer Inst., Detroit, 1967-70; assoc. prof. psychology Wayne State U., Detroit, 1970-75; prof. Rutgers U., New Brunswick, 1975—87; adj. prof. human devel. and aging, med. anthropology U. Calif., San Francisco, 1986—98; ret. Vis. prof.; lectr. in field 47 convs. and invited talks. Author: Family Issues in Current Gerontology, 1986, Continuations: Development After 20, 1982, Development in Early and Middle Adulthood, 1975, rev. edit., 1985, 32 chpts. in other books; co-author: (with Joan and Kenneth Israel) Looking Ahead: A Woman's Guide to the Problems and Joys of Growing Older, 1977, (with Nancy Schlossberg) Perspectives on Counseling Adults, 1978, (with Sheila Miller and Robert Atchley) Families of Later Life, 1979, (with Barbara Turner) Women Growing Older, 1994; contbr. over 30 articles to profl. jours. Recipient Eminent Women in Psychology award, 1988, Disting. Contbn. Div. Adult Devel. and Aging award APA, 1989, Women's Heritage Inst. award, 1992, Disting. Creative Contbn. to Gerontology award, 1993. Fellow APA (sec.-treas. 1973-76, 84-87, pres. 1986-87); Gerontol. Soc. Am. (sec.-treas. behavioral and soc. scis. sect 1981-87). Home: 1001 Shoreline Dr Apt 302 Alameda CA 94501-5925 E-mail: l.troll@comcast.net.

**TROMBLAY, ERIK JOHN,** social studies educator; b. Beverly, Mass., Sept. 26, 1978; s. Leo Roger and Christine Ethyl Tromblay; m. Sarah Rose Diovon, July 7, 2001. BA History, Gordon Coll., Wehham, Mass., 2000. Staff maintenance House of Seven Gables, Salem, Mass., 1995—2000; tchr. social studies Winthrop H.S., Mass., 2000—01, Charles City County H.S., Va., 2001—. Tchr. Sun. sch. Oak Hall Bapt. Ch., Sandeton, Va., 2005—. Recipient 1st degree Black Belt in Korea Karate, Northshore Karate Acad., Beverly, 1995. Mem.: Nat. Coun. Social Studies. Republican. Avocations: softball, baseball card collecting, travel, guitar. Home: 7176L Erleison Hill Rd Mechanicsville VA 23111

**TROMBLEY, EDWARD FRANCIS, III,** registrar; b. Oneida, NY, Sept. 24, 1964; s. Edward F., Jr. and Sharonlee (Sterling) Trombley. BA, SUNY, Oswego, 1986, MS, 1996. Cert. secondary English tchr. NY. Adj. instr. Bryant & Stratton Bus. Inst., Liverpool, NY, 1993-96, gen. studies dept. coord., 1996, evening and weekend coll. coord., 1996-98, assoc. dean instrn., 1998-2000, dean adminstrn., 2000—01; homebound student tutor North Syracuse Sch. Dist., NY, 1994-96; registrar DeVry U., Arlington, Va., 2001—06, Ft. Wash., Pa., 2006—. Mem. adv. bd. East Syracuse-Minoa Sch. Dist., 1996—97; sch. bus. partnership Cicero-North Syracuse Sch. Dist., 1997; conf. del. Assn. Proprietary Colls., Copperstown, NY, 1997, Saratoga, NY, 98; media cons. Bryant and Stratton Bus. Inst., Liverpool, 1997. Mem.: Va. Assn. Coll. Registrars and Admissions Officers, Am. Assn. Coll. Registrars and Admissions Officers, Trick of the Tail Club (rec. sec. 1995—2001). Office: DeVry U Ft Washington Campus 1140 Virginia Dr Fort Washington PA 19034 Business E-Mail: etrombley@phi.devry.edu.

**TROMETTER, MARY GIONTA,** chef, educator; b. Phila., July 25, 1964; d. Joseph and Rosaire Giunta; m. Jeffrey A. Trometter, Mar. 9, 1986; children: Phillip, Vincent. AAS in Food and Hospitality Mgmt., Williamsport Area CC, Pa., 1984; BS in Hotel & Restaurant Mgmt., Widener U., 1989; MS in Edn., Wilkes U., 1999. Sous chef The Inn at Turkey Hill, Bloomsburg, Pa., 1984—86; asst. chef, supr. Pierre's Continental Catering, Trappe, Pa., 1987—89; environ. protection specialist 1 Bucks County Dept. of Health, Quakertown, Pa., 1989—90; asst. prof. Sch. Hospitality Pa. Coll. Tech., Williamsport, 1990—. Adv. bd. St. Boniface Elem. Sch., Williamsport, 2000; active Bishop Neumann H.S., Williamsport, 2004. Mem.: Nat. Environ. Health Assn., Am. Culinary Fedn. Avocations: catering, gardening. Office: Pennsylvania College Technology One College Ave Williamsport PA 17701

**TRONGALE, NICHOLAS ALBERT,** entrepreneur, researcher; s. Nick and Mary Rose Trongale; m. Mary Kathryn Sullivan, Nov. 30, 1980; children: Daniel Louis, Megan Kathryn. BA, Dominican U., 1978; MA, U.S. Naval Postgraduate Sch., 1986, Stanford U., 1994; EdD, U. San Diego, 2001. Enlisted USN, 1979, advanced through grades to capt., ret., 2001; pres., CEO Pb Solutions, San Diego, 2002—, The Comml. Diving Centre, L.L.C., New Iberia, La., 2003—. Author: (research) Changes in Navy Leadership Theory and Practice: Post-Vietnam, China's Defense Modernization, China's Naval Power, Investment Strategy of Information Operations, Implications of Unmanned Air Vehicles for the Future Shape of the Air Force. Decorated Legion of Merit; named E-2C Hawkeye of Yr., Comdr. Fighter/Airborne Early Warning Wing, Pacific, 1988; recipient Nat. Leadership award, Nat. Rep. Congl. Com., 2003; adm. Arthur S. Moreau scholar, USN, 1992, Fed. Exec. Rsch. fellow, RAND Corp., 1996—97. Mem.: DAV (life), VFW (life), Assn. Gulf Coast Coml. Diving Educators (pres. 2003—), Kappa Delta Pi (life). Achievements include first to commercial diving school specifically tailored to support the Gulf of Mexico oil industry. Office Phone: 858-414-5167. Personal E-mail: trongale@pbsolutions.us.

**TRONTELL, MARIE CELESTINE,** dean; Diploma, Rutgers State U., 1969, MD, 1976. Diplomate Am. Bd. Internal Medicine (chief proctor exam 1988, 89, 90, 91), Am. Bd. Pulmonary Diseases. Intern in internal medicine, resident in internal medicine Coll. Medicine and Dentistry of N.J.-Rutgers Med. Sch. Hosp., 1976-79, med. chief resident, 1978-79, fellow in pulmonary disease Piscataway, 1979-81; asst. chief medicine for tng. Robert Wood Johnson Univ. Hosp., New Brunswick, 1980-96, dir. resident tng., 1982-96, chief inpatient svcs., 1987-96; asst. prof. medicine UMDNJ-Robert Wood Johnson Med. Sch., New Brunswick, 1981-87, program dir. internal medicine residency, 1983-96, acting chief divsn. gen. internal medicine, 1986-87, assoc. prof. medicine, 1987-96, assoc. chmn. dept. medicine, 1991—, prof. clin. medicine, 1996—, assoc. dean acad. affairs Piscataway, 1996—. Mem. editl. adv. bd. Info Trends: Medicine, Law, and Ethics; contbr. articles to profl. jours.; spkr. in field. Fellow ACP (mem. grad. med. edn. com. N.J., mem. career change task force 1994), Am. Coll. Chest Physicians; mem. Am. Thoracic Soc., Assn. Behavioral Scis. and Med. Edn., Assn. Program Dirs. in Internal Medicine (nat. coun. mem., mem. membership svcs. com., mem. program planning com.), N.J. Thoracic Soc., Soc. Gen. Internal Medicine., Phi Beta Kappa, Alpha Omega Alpha. Home: 1111 S Branch Dr Whitehouse Station NJ 08889-3234 Office: 675 Hoes Ln # R-102 Piscataway NJ 08854-5627 also: UMDNJ Robert Wood Johnson Med Sch Dept Acad Affairs 675 Hoes Ln Piscataway NJ 08854-5627

**TROOBOFF, PETER DENNIS,** lawyer; b. Balt., June 22, 1942; s. Benjamin M. and Rebecca (Cohen) Trooboff; m. Rhoda Morss, Aug. 10, 1969; children: Hannah, Abigail. BA cum laude, Columbia U., 1964; LLB cum laude, Harvard U., 1967; LLM, London Sch. Econs., 1968; diploma cum laude, Hague Acad. Internat. Law, Netherlands, 1968. Bar: N.Y. 1968, D.C. 1970. Rsch. assoc. Harvard U. Law Sch., Cambridge, Mass., 1968—69; asst. to exec. editor for The Advocates Sta. WGBH-TV, Boston, 1969; assoc. Covington & Burling, Washington, 1969—75, ptnr., 1975—. Lectr., dir. seminars The Hague Acad. Internat. Law, 1972, 82, lectr., 86, mem. curatorium, 1991—; lectr. The Hague Acad. External Program, Beijing, 1987,

Harare, 93; lectr. internat. orgns. U. Va. Sch. Law, 1973; head US del. 3d Inter-Am. Specialized Conf. Pvt. Internat. Law, La Paz, Bolivia, 1984; mem. US del. Hague Conf. pvt. internat. law, 1993, 96, 1997—, expert US del., 2003—04; arbitrator Internat. Ctr. Settlement Investment Disputes. Contbr. chapters to books, articles to profl. publs.; editor: Law and Responsibility in Warfare-The Vietnam Experience, 1975. Frank Knox Meml. fellow. Mem.: Washington Inst. Fgn. Affairs, Internat. Law Assn., Am. Soc. Internat. Law (bd. editors Am. Jour. Internat. Law 1980—92, pres. 1990—92, bd. editors Am. Jour. Internat. Law 1994—2003), Am. Law Inst., Coun. Fgn. Rels., City Club (Washington), Cosmos Club. Office: Covington & Burling 1201 Pennsylvania Ave NW Washington DC 20004 Office Phone: 202-662-5512. E-mail: ptrooboff@cov.com.

**TROOP, PAUL MELVIN,** public relations executive, journalist; b. Jersey City, N.J., May 13, 1942; s. Bernard Lazarus and Ruth (Weiss) T.; m. Maxine Rubin, Dec. 6, 1970; 1 child, Wendy. BA, U. State of N.Y., 1980. Reporter L.I. Press, Jamaica, NY, 1965-66; political editor Suffolk Sun, Deer Park, NY, 1966-67; asst. news dir. L.I. Network News, Freeport, NY, 1967; asst. editor Am. Sch. & U., N.Y.C., 1967-68; acct. exec. Ruder & Finn, N.Y.C., 1969-70; mng. editor L.I. Comml. Rev., Syosset, NY, 1970; bus. writer Atlanta Jour.-Constn., 1970-78; pres. Fin. Comm. Co., Atlanta, 1978—. Cpl. NJNG, 1965-71. Newspaper Fund scholar, 1961, Banking Sch. of the South fellow, 1975.

**TROOSKIN, STANLEY Z.,** surgeon; b. Linden, N.J., July 24, 1949; s. Martin and Irene Trooskin; m. Estelle Kost Trooskin; children: Stacey, Gerri, Amy. BA, Rutgers U., 1971; MD, U. Pitts., 1975. Diplomate Am. Bd. Surgery, Am. Bd. Surgery, lic. physician Pa., N.J., N.Y. Asst. prof. surgery U. Medicine and Dentistry N.J., Piscataway, 1980—85, assoc. prof. surgery, 1985—89, clin. assoc. prof., 1988—89; prof. surgery SUNY, Bklyn., 1989—92, Med. Coll. Pa., 1993—94, Hahnemann U. Sch. Medicine, 1994, MCP Hahnemann U. Sch. Medicine, 1995—2002, UMDNJ-Robert Wood Johnson Med. Sch., New Brunswick, 2002—; adj. prof. surgery Drexel U. Sch. Medicine, New Brunswick, NJ, 2003—. Mem. editl. bd.: Trauma Quar., 1989—2002, Trauma Chronicle, 1990—91. Mem.: Ea. Assn. for Surgery of Trauma, Am. Coll. Surgeons. Achievements include patents in field. Office: Robert Wood Johnson Med Sch 1 RWJ Pl CN 19 MEB 443 New Brunswick NJ 08903 Office Phone: 732-235-7920. Business E-Mail: trooskz@umdnj.edu.

**TROOST, BRADLEY TODD,** neurologist, educator; b. Mankato, Minn., July 5, 1937; s. Henry Bradley and Elizabeth (Todd) T.; m. Elizabeth Gail Godet, Apr. 17, 1976; children: Elizabeth Claire, Laurie Anne. BS with honors in Biophysics, Yale U., 1959; MD, Harvard U., 1963. Diplomate Am. Bd. Psychiatry and Neurology. Intern, Colo. Gen. Hosp., Denver, 1963-64; resident in neurology U. Colo., Denver, 1966-69; NIH fellow in neuro-ophthalmology U. Calif.-San Francisco, 1969-70; asst. prof. U. Miami (Fla.), 1970-76; assoc. prof. U. Pitts., 1976-80; prof. Case Western Res. U., Cleve., 1980-83; prof., chmn. dept. neurology Wake Forest U. Sch. Medicine, Winston-Salem, N.C., 1983—; chief dept. neurology VA med. ctrs., Pitts., Cleve. Bd. dirs. Greater Miami Epilepsy Found., 1973-76. Served to capt. U.S. Army, 1964-66. Fellow Am. Acad. Neurology; mem. Am. Neurol. Assn., Am. Assn. Univ. Profs. Neurology (pres.-elect), Barany Soc. Republican. Episcopalian. Contbr. numerous articles to profl. publs.

**TROP, SANDRA,** museum director; b. Bklyn. BS, NYU; cert. in arts adminstrn., Harvard U. Dir. Everson Mus. Art, Syracuse, NY, 1995—. Advt. copy writer; adj. prof. Syracuse U. Mem. founding bd. dirs. Lowe Art Ctr., Syracuse U., Salt City Playhouse, Folk Art Gallery, Syracuse Landmark Theatre; mem. Internat. Com. for Museums and Collections of Modern Art; mem. Literacy Vols. Am.; appointed to Mayor's Commn. on Fin. Planning for City of Syracuse. Mem. Am. Arts Alliance, Am. Assn. Museums, N.E. Regional Mus. Conf. Office: Everson Museum Art 401 Harrison St Syracuse NY 13202-3091

**TROPEZ-SIMS, SUSANNE,** pediatrician, educator; b. New Orleans, Apr. 13, 1949; d. Maxwell Stanley and Ethel (Ross) Tropez; m. James Carnell White, Apr. 10, 1971 (div. 1992); children: Lisa, Janifer, James Carnell; m. Michael Milroy Sims, Feb. 18, 1995. BS, Bennett Coll., 1971; MD, U. N.C., 1975, MPH, 1982. Diplomate Am. Bd. Pediatrics. Resident pediat. N.C. Meml. Hosp., Chapel Hill, 1975—76, 1977—79; pediatrician Darnell Army Hosp., Ft. Hood, Tex., 1976—77; acting dir. pediat. day clinic Wake County Med. Ctr., Raleigh, NC, 1979—82; dir. pediat. day clinic, asst. prof. U. N.C., Chapel Hill, 1982—88; assoc. prof. pediat. La. State U. Med. Ctr., New Orleans, 1988—97; dir. divsn. pediat. emergency rm. La. State U., New Orleans, 1988—89, chief divsn. ambulatory care, 1989—97; chmn. and prof. dept. pediat. Meharry Med. Coll., Nashville, 1997—2005; chair Meharry Med. Svc. Found., Nashville, 2000—02; chair curriculum com. Meharry Med. Coll., Nashville, 2003—, assoc. dean acad. support, 2005—. Clin. dir. maternal and child health units New Orleans Health Dept., 1992-97, chief divsn. cmty. pediat. and adolescent medicine, 1992-97; pediatrician Shelly Child Devel. Ctr., Raleigh, 1981-88, child med. examiner program, 1979-88; chair sch. health com. local chpt. AAP, 1993-96; mem. Nat. Com. Sch. Health, 1992-99; chair health info. network bd. Nat. Edn. Assn., 2000-02. Contbr. articles to profl. jour. Chair adminstrv. bd. Cornerstone U.M.C., 1993-96, chair edn. com., 1991-92; mem. United Meth. Women, Walnut Terr. Child Devel. Ctr., Raleigh, 1981-83, chmn., 1982-83; chmn. pastor parish com. Longview Ch., Raleigh, 1982-84, 87-88, chmn. membership care com.; chair bd. NEA-Health Info. Network, 2000-02; chair bd. trustees Clark Meml. United Meth. Ch., 2002—. Fellow preventive medicine, 1979-82, Faculty Devel. fellow U. NC Sch. Medicine, 1985-87. Fellow Am. Acad. Pediatrics (mem. sch. health com.); mem. N.C. Pediatric Soc. (com. child abuse and neglect, adolescent pregnancy), La. Pediatric Soc., Ambulatory Pediatric Assn., Adolescent Pregnancy Coalition United Way, Bennett Coll. Alumnae Assn. Democrat. Office Phone: 615-327-6332. Business E-Mail: stsims@mmc.edu.

**TROPIN, KENNETH G.,** fund management executive; b. N.Y.C., Aug. 17, 1953; s. Leonard and Ruth (Safron) Tropin; m. Kathleen Tropin, Aug. 6, 1986; children: Nicholas, Kelly. BA, Goddard Coll., 1974. Fin. cons. Shearson, N.Y.C., 1980-82; v.p. Dean Witter Reynolds, N.Y.C., 1982-89; pres., chief exec. officer John W. Henry & Co., Inc., Westport, Conn., 1989—93; founder, chmn. Graham Capital Mgmt., Rowayton, Conn., 1994—. Mem.: Managed Futures Assn. (chmn. 1991). Avocations: golf, skiing, tennis, sculpture. Office: Graham Capital Mgmt Rockledge Financial Ctr Norwalk CT 06853 Office Phone: 203-899-3400.

**TROSINO, VINCENT JOSEPH, SR.,** insurance company executive; b. Upland, Pa., Nov. 19, 1940; s. Sylvester N. and Stella Trosino; m. Patricia Ann Gibney, June 18, 1960; children: Laura, Valerie, Vincent Jr. BS in Psychology, Villanova U., 1962; MS in Psychology, Ill. State U., 1973. Ops. supr. State Farm Mut. Auto Ins. Co., Springfield, Pa., 1962-70, personnel mgr. Bloomington, Ill., 1970-72, dir. personnel, 1972-74, corp. v.p., 1986-87, exec. v.p., 1987—, pres., vice-chmn. bd., COO, 1998—, vice-chmn. bd. dirs. Costa Mesa, Calif., 1995, dep. regional v.p., 1976-80, regional v.p. Wayne, NJ, 1981-85. Bd. dirs. State Farm Fire & Casualty Co., State Farm Life Ins. Co., State Farm Internat. Services, State Farm Investment Mgmt. Corp., all Bloomington; dir. Vulcan Materials Co., Ala., 2003-. Bd. dirs. Chilton Hosp., Pompton Lakes, N.J., 1982-85, Jr. Achievement, McLean County, Ill., 1971, McLean County Law and Justice Com., 1970, McLean County Alcohol and Drug Assistance Corp. 1970-74, The Brookings Inst., Washington, 1996. Recipient Disting. Alumni award, Villanova U., 2000, Humanitarian award, Joseph Cardinal Bernardin, 2001, Disting. Arts and Sci. Alumni award, Ill. State U., 2006. Mem. N.J. Ins. News Svc. (pres. 1984-85, bd. dirs.), N.J. Joint Underwriting Assn. (bd. dirs. 1982-85), Jud. Inquiry Bd. State of Ill. (apptd. by Gov. Edgar, 1992—), Nat. Italian Am. Found. (bd. mem.). Avocations: trout fishing, tennis, golf. Office: State Farm Ins Cos 1 State Farm Plz Bloomington IL 61710-0001

**TROST, BARRY MARTIN,** chemist, educator; b. Phila., June 13, 1941; s. Joseph and Esther T.; m. Susan Paula Shapiro, Nov. 25, 1967; children: Aaron David, Carey Daniel. BA cum laude, U. Pa., 1962; PhD, MIT, 1965; D (hon.), U. Claude Bernard, Lyons, France, 1994; Technion, Israel, 1997. Mem. faculty U. Wis., Madison, 1965—, prof., chemistry, 1969—, Evan P. and Marion Helfaer prof. chemistry, from 1976, Vilas rsch. prof. chemistry; prof. chemistry Stanford U., 1987—, Tamaki prof. humanities and scis., 1990, chmn. dept., 1996—2002; Lord Todd vis. prof. Cambridge U., England, 2002—. Cons. Merck, Sharp & Dohme, E.I. duPont de Nemours.; Chem. Soc. centenary lectr., 1982 Author: Problems in Spectroscopy, 1967, Sulfur Ylides, 1975; editor-in-chief Comprehensive Organic Synthesis, 1991—; ChemTracts/Organic Chemistry, 1993—; editor: Structure and Reactivity Concepts in Organic Chemistry series, 1972—; assoc. editor Jour. Am. Chem. Soc., 1974-80; mem. editl. bd. Organic Reactions Series, 1971—, Chemistry A European Jour., 1995—, Sci. of Synthesis, Houben-Weyl Methods of Molecular Transformations, 1995—; contbr. numerous articles to profl. jours. Named Chem. Pioneer, Am. Inst. Chemists, 1983; recipient Dreyfus Found. Tech.-Scholar award, 1970, 1977, Creative Work in Synthetic Organic Chemistry award, 1981, Baekland medal, 1981, Alexander von Humboldt award, 1984, Guenther award, 1990, Janssen prize, 1990, Roger Adams award, Am. Chem. Soc., 1995, Presdl. Green Univ. Challenge award, 1998, Nicholas medal, 2000, Yamada prize, 2001, Yamada Prize, 2001, ACS Nobel Laureate Signature award, Graduate Ed. Chemistry, 2002, John Scott award, City of Phila., 2004; fellow, NSF, 1963—65, Sloan Found., 1967—69, Am. Swiss Found., 1975—, Zencca, 1997; scholar Cope scholar, 1989. Mem.: NAS, AAAS, Chem. Soc. London, Am. Acad. Arts and Scis., Am. Chem. Soc. (award in pure chemistry 1977, Roger Adams award 1995, Herbert C. Brown award for creative rsch. in synthetic methods 1999, Nobel Laureate Signature award for grad. edn. in chemistry 2002, Arthur C. Cope award 2004). Office: Stanford U Dept Chemistry Stanford CA 94305

**TROST, CARLISLE ALBERT HERMAN,** retired naval officer; b. Valmeyer, Ill., Apr. 24, 1930; s. Elmer Herman and Luella Caroline (Hoffman) T.; m. Pauline Louise Haley, May 1, 1954; children— Carl, Laura Lee, Steven, Kathleen. Student, Washington U., St. Louis, 1948-49; BS, U.S. Naval Acad., 1953; Olmsted scholar, U. Freiburg, W. Ger., 1960-62. Commd. ensign U.S. Navy, 1953, advanced through grades to adm., 1985; exec. officer U.S.S. Scorpion, 1962-63, U.S.S. Von Steuben, 1963-65; mil. asst. to Dep. Sec. Def., 1965-68; commdg. officer U.S.S. Sam Rayburn, 1968-69; staff Comdr. Sub Force Atlantic, 1969-70; exec. asst. to Sec. Navy, 1970-73; comdr. Submarine Group Five, 1973-74; asst. chief Bur. Naval Personnel, 1974-76; dir. systems analysis div. Office Chief Naval Ops., Washington, 1976-78; dep. comdr.-in-chief U.S. Pacific Fleet, 1978-80; comdr. U.S. Seventh Fleet, 1980-81; dir. Navy program planning Office Chief Naval Ops., 1981-85; comdr.-in-chief U.S. Atlantic Fleet, 1985-86, chief naval ops., 1986-90. Bd. dirs. Lockheed Martin Corp., Gen. Pub. Utility Corp., GPU Nuclear Corp., Bird-Johnson Co., Gen. Dynamics Corp., Precision Components Corp.; chmn. Olmsted Fedn. Trustee U.S. Naval Acad. Found. Decorated Def. D.S.M. with cluster, Navy D.S.M. with 2 clusters, Army D.S.M., Air Force D.S.M., Legion of Merit with 2 oak leaf clusters, Navy Achievement medal; named Outstanding Young Man of Am. Nat. Jr. C. of C., 1964 Mem. U.S. Naval Inst., U.S. Naval Acad. Alumni Assn. (chmn.). Episcopalian. Home: 11 Compromise St Annapolis MD 21401-1806

**TROST, EILEEN BANNON,** lawyer; b. Teaneck, N.J., Jan. 9, 1951; d. William Eugene and Marie Thelma (Finlayson) Bannon; m. Lawrence Peter Trost Jr., Aug. 27, 1977; children: Lawrence Peter III, William Patrick, Timothy Alexander. BA with great distinction, Shimer Coll., 1972; JD cum laude, U. Minn., 1976. Bar: Ill. 1976, U.S. Dist. Ct. (no. dist.) Ill. 1976, Minn. 1978, U.S. Tax Ct. 1978, U.S. Supreme Ct. 1981. Assoc. McDermott, Will & Emery, Chgo., 1976-82, ptnr., 1982-93; v.p. No. Trust Bank Ariz. N.A., Phoenix, 1993-95; ptnr. Sonnenschein Nath & Rosenthal, Chgo., 1995—. Mem. Am. Coll. Trust and Estate Coun., Minn. Bar Assn., Internat. Acad. Estate and Trust Law, Chgo. Estate Planning Coun. Roman Catholic. Office: Sonnenschein Nath & Rosenthal 7800 Sears Tower Chicago IL 60606 Office Phone: 312-876-8149. E-mail: etrost@sonnenschein.com.

**TROST, GLENN W.,** lawyer; b. Boston, Mar. 27, 1956; BS, MIT; JD cum laude, Southwestern Univ., 1984. Bar: Calif. 1984, US Dist. Ct. (no. & ctrl. Calif.), US Ct. Appeals (9th & Fed. cir.), Supreme Ct. Calif., Supreme Ct. Colo., US Supreme Ct. 2000. Ptnr. mng. partner LA office Coudert Bros. LLP, LA. Adj. prof. Southwestern Univ. Sch. Law, 1986—91. Office: Coudert Brothers Llp 555 S Flower St Los Angeles CA 90071-2300 Office Phone: 213-229-2900. Office Fax: 213-229-2999. Business E-Mail: gtrost@coudert.com.

**TROST, LOUIS FREDERICK, JR.,** banker, financial planner; b. Kansas City, Mo., Dec. 11, 1926; s. Louis Frederick and Roberta Ford (Broadus) T.; m. Ann Horner Tillma, Mar. 23, 1951 (div. Oct. 1978); children: Louis Frederick III, Scott Tillma; m. Charlotte Granville Graham, Nov. 15, 1984. BBA, U. Okla., 1951; postgrad., Northwestern U., 1960, grad. Bell Sys. Execs. program, 1960; grad., Sch. Banking of South, Baton Rouge, 1968, Coll. Fin. Planning, Denver, 1989. Divsn. mgr. South Western Bell Tel. Co., Oklahoma City, 1951—64; sr. v.p. Liberty Nat. Bank & Trust Co., Oklahoma City, 1964—91; pres., CEO Lincoln Nat. Bank, Oklahoma City, 1991—95, vice chmn., 1995—2003, CEO, 2002—03. Advisor Bapt. Found. Okla., Oklahoma City, 1995-2005, hon. dir. emeritus, 2006—; bd. rep., exec. com. Coun. Fed. Home Loan Banks, Washington, 1998-2001; dir., chmn. housing com. Fed. Home Loan Bank Topeka, 1995-2001; mem. gov.'s Cmty. Devel. Capital Formation Task Force, 1998-2003; cert. fin. planner, 1989-2004; bd. dirs. Great Expectations Found, 2004—; bd.dirs. Educator's Leadership Acad., 2004—05; bd. dirs. Okla. State Capitol Preservation Commn., 2005—. Pres., bd. dirs. Travelers Aid, Oklahoma City, 1962; treas., bd. dirs. Okla. Symphony Orch., 1983—87; pres., bd. dirs. Mental Health Assn., Oklahoma City, 1996; mem. Cmty. Devel. Adv. Coun. of Fed. Res. Bank of Kansas City, 2002—03. Master sgt. U.S. Army 1945 46, PTO. Named Outstanding Young Man in Oklahoma City, Oklahoma City, 1960; named Ky. Col., Gov. of Ky., 1970; recipient letter of commendation Mental Health Assn., 1996. Mem. Ind. Bankers Assn. Am., Okla. Bankers Assn. (sr. mgmt. com. 1995-2003), Oklahoma City Golf and Country Club (bd. dirs. 1989-91), Petroleum Club Oklahoma City (v.p., treas., bd. dirs. 1979-81), The Assocs. (U. Okla.), Faculty Club (bd. dirs.,1968-1970), Masons, Scottish Rite, Shriners, Kiwanis (past pres. Oklahoma City), Assn. U.S. Army, Phi Gamma Delta (treas., bd. dirs. Ednl. Found. 1989-97, Wall of Fame award 1997, Disting. Fiji award 2004, trustee emeritus 2004). Baptist. Avocations: gardening, reading, travel. Home and Office: 1601 Queenstown Rd Nichols Hills OK 73116-5522 Business E-Mail: ltrost@cox.net.

**TROTT, MENA,** application developer; b. 1977; m. Ben Trott. Co-founder, pres. Six Apart, Inc., 2004—. Named one of Top 100 Young Innovators, MIT Tech. Review, 2004. Achievements include creator of TypePad and Moveable Type, software tools for publishing weblogs. Office: Six Apart 548 4th St San Francisco CA 94107-1621

**TROTT, NANCY ROBERTS,** editor; b. New Britain, Conn., 1968; BA, U. NH. Supervising editor AP, Concord, NH, 1993—96; with Seattle Post-Intelligencer, 1996, ABC News, Seattle, 1997—99; news editor AP, Seattle, 1999—2002, regional news editor Washington, 2002—03, Wash. & Idaho bur. chief Seattle, 2003—06, regional news dir. Western burs., 2006—. Office: AP Seattle Bur Ste 750 3131 Elliot Ave Seattle WA 98121 Office Fax: 206-682-1812. Office Fax: 206-621-1948. E-mail: ntrott@ap.org.*

**TROTT, SABERT SCOTT, II,** marketing professional, consultant; b. Concord, N.C., Nov. 21, 1941; s. Sabert Scott and Mary Welker (Crooks) T.; m. Brenda Lee Bost, Nov. 27, 1964; children— Sabert Scott III, David Lee BS in Textile Tech., N.C. State U., 1964; MBA, U. N.C., 1969. Mgr. trainee Cannon Mills Co., Kannapolis, NC 1969-70, mktg. mgr., 1970-75, v.p mktg., 1975-82, sr. v.p. mktg., 1982-86, dir. telemktg. and premium sales, 1987-89; mgr. spl. markets, mktg. & sales Fieldcrest Cannon Inc., mktg. mgr., telemarketing sales mgr., 1989-92; v.p. mktg. and sales Spencer's Inc., Mt.

Airy, NC, 1992-93; v.p. mktg. Carpenter Co., Richmond, Va., 1994—. Chmn. Cabarrus-Rowan Parks and Recreation Commn., N.C., 1982-86; mem. Cabarrus County Parks and Recreation Commn., N.C., 1980-88; Rep. candidate County Commr., Cabarrus County, 1990; bd. dirs. Cabarrus Meml. Hosp., 1992, N.C. Ctr. for Applied Textile Tech.; vestryman local Episcopal ch., 1988-93. Capt. U.S. Army, 1965-70. Decorated Commendation medal (2) Mem.: Rotary. Republican. Avocations: canoeing, rafting, golf, basketball, racquetball. Office: Carpenter Co 5016 Monument Ave Richmond VA 23230-3620 Home: 1208 Belair Ave Kannapolis NC 28083 Office Phone: 804-897-5557. Personal E-mail: sbtrott@aol.com. Business E-Mail: scott.trott@carpenter.com.

**TROTT, STEPHEN SPANGLER,** federal judge; b. Glen Ridge, NJ, Dec. 12, 1939; s. David Herman and Virginia (Spangler) Trott; m. Carol C. Trott; children: Christina, Shelley. BA, Wesleyan U., 1962; LLB, Harvard U., 1965; LLD (hon.), Santa Clara U., 1992; LLD (hon.), U. Idaho, 2001. Bar: Calif. 1966, U.S. Dist. Ct. (cen. dist.) Calif. 1966, U.S. Ct. Appeals (9th cir.) 1983, U.S. Supreme Ct. 1984. Guitarist, mem. The Highwaymen, 1958—; dep. dist. atty. L.A. County Dist. Atty.'s Office, L.A., 1966—75, chief dep. dist. atty., 1975—79; US dist. atty. Central Dist. Calif., L.A., 1981—83; asst. atty. gen. criminal divsn. US Dept. Justice, Washington, 1983—86; faculty Nat. Coll. Dist. Attys., Houston, 1973—80; chmn. central dist. Calif. Law Enforcement Coord. Com., Houston, 1981—83; coord. L.A.-Nev. Drug Enforcement Task Force, 1982—83; assoc. atty. gen. US Dept. Justice, Washington, 1986—88; chmn. U.S. Interpol, 1986—88; judge US Ct. Appeals (9th Cir.), Boise, Idaho, 1988—2004, sr. judge, 2004—. Trustee Wesleyan U., 1984—87; adv. council Big Brothers, Big Sisters S.W. Idaho, 2001—03; ofcl. photographer World Cup Wrestling Championship, 2003—; bd. dirs., pres. Children's Home Soc., Idaho, 1990—2004. Recipient Gold record as singer-guitarist for Michael Row the Boat Ashore, 1961, Disting. Faculty award, Nat. Coll. Dist. Attys., 1977. Mem.: Am. Coll. Trial Lawyers, Boise (Idaho) Philharm. Assn. (bd. dirs. 1995—, v.p. 1997—99, pre-concert lectr. 1997—, pres. 1999—2003), Idaho Classic Guitar Soc. (founder, pres. 1989—2004), Internat. Brotherhood Magicians, Idaho Racing Pigeon Assn., Magic Castle, Brentwood Racing Pigeon Club (pres. 1977—82), Wilderness Fly Fishers Club (pres. 1975—77). Republican. Office: US Ct Appeals 9th Cir 666 US Courthouse 550 W Fort St Boise ID 83724-0040*

**TROTT, THOMAS G.,** lawyer; b. Delavan, Wis., Jan. 2, 1946; s. John Jerome and Louise Trott; m. Cynthia Wood, Feb. 13, 1994; children: Owen, Nicholas, Thomas. BA, U. Ill., 1968, MBA, 1977, JD, 1978. Bar: Tex. 1978, U.S. Ct. Appeals (5th cir.) 1978, U.S. Dist. Ct. (so. dist.) Tex. 1978, Pa. 1985; oil, gas and mineral law Bd. Legal Specialization, 1990. Atty. Exxon Co. USA, Houston, 1978—83; v.p. legal Mitchell Energy Corp., The Woodlands, Tex., 1983—2001; assoc. gen. counsel Devon Energy Corp., Houston, 2001—. Mem. dist. adv. group Civil Justice Reform Act, Houston, 1992—93; mem. adv. bd. Ctr. for Am. and Internat. Law, Plano, Tex., 2001—. Mem. allocation com. United Way, Houston, 1985—90; trustee United Way Ctr., Houston, 1985—95. Lt. (j.g.) USN, 1969—74. Office: Devon Energy Corp 1200 Louisana St Houston TX 77002 Office Phone: 713-495-7145. Business E-Mail: tom.trott@dvn.com.

**TROTTA, RIC CHARLES,** aerospace transportation executive, consultant; b. N.Y.C., Mar. 7, 1942; s. Sigmund Robert and Anita Dolores (La Penna) T.; m. Carolyn Carey Bealle Trotta, May 29, 1965; children: Bradley Charles, Ric Charles Jr., Lauren Carey. Student in elec. engring., U. Va., 1959-62; BA in Physics, NYU, 1966; MBA in Mktg., Hofstra U., 1977; postgrad., Carnegie Mellon U., 1987. Engr. Grumman Aerospace Corp., Bethpage, NY, 1966-68, asst. to v.p., 1968-70, advanced programs mgr., 1970-78, mgr. technology planning, 1978-81, asst. dir. advanced systems, 1981-83; dir. corp. ind., rsch. and devel. Grumman Corp., 1983-86, dir. corp. devel. and resources, 1986-94; pres. Trotta Assoc., Cons. to Govt. and Industry, Centerport, 1994—. Sr. player global war games U.S. Naval War Coll., Newport, RI, 1985—; mem. resources working group Fed. Emergency Mgmt. Agcy., Washington, 1991—; vice-chair nat. adv. coun. Fed. Lab. Consortium, 1999—, vice chmn., 2000, chmn., 01; mem. nomination and award selection com. L.I. Tech. Hall of Fame, 2003—; bd. dirs. Beachcomber Ltd., Montauk, NY, pres. bd. dirs., 2005. Author: Industry Independent Rsch. and Devel. Study, 1996, Assessing the Impact of Regulatory and Legislative Changes to the DOD Independent Research and Developement Program, 1997, Maritime Industry Definition and Structure- A Workbook for Assessing Organization Capabilities Versus Industry Needs, 1997; Contbg. author: Public Control of Medical Care, 1978, National Security Assessment of the U.S. Maritime Industry Surveys: Building and Repairing of Ships, Boats and other Marine Platforms, Maritime Research Development and Education, 2000, Nat. Security Assessment of Shipbldg. and Repair Ind., 2001, Assessment of Industry Attitudes on Collaborating with U.S. Department of Defense in Research and Developement and Technology Sharing, 2003. Mem. com. on sch. utilization Harborfield Sch. Dist., Greenlawn, 1984; bd. dir. Community Sch., Centerport, NY, 1985. Recipient Community Svc. award, Town of Huntington, N.Y., 1985, Merit award, Chief Naval Rsch., 2000, Outstanding Svc. Award, Fed. Lab. Consortium for Tech. Transfer, 2005. Mem. Nat. Security Indsl. Assn., Electronic Industries Assn., Mine Warfare Assn. (bd. dirs. 1997), Assn. Nat. Def. and Emergency Resources, Sigma Nu (historian 1961). Avocations: fishing, tennis, sailing, cooking. Home and Office: 21 Little Bull Ct Centerport NY 11721-1450 Office Phone: 631-424-3700. Personal E-Mail: RicTrotta@aol.com. Business E-Mail: RTrotta@TrottaAssociates.com.

**TROTTER, BETTY LOU,** retired secondary school educator; b. Junction City, Kans., Mar. 20, 1925; d. Claude Frank and Mertie (Ware) Short; m. James Brown Trotter, June 4, 1946; children: James B., Jay M., Mark R., Lee R.F. AA, Stephens Coll., l945; BA cum laude, U. N.Mex., l948; MA, U. Mo., Kansas City, l972. Cert. music and secondary English tchr., Mo. Substitute tchr. Denver Pub. Schs., 1960—63; tchr. English Consol. Sch. Dist. 2, Raytown, Mo., 1967—83, ret., 1985, sales assoc. Jones Store Co., Kansas City, 1987—91. Neighborhood Coun., 1985-89, councilwoman (Mo.) Neighborhood Coun., 1985-89, 91-92; Dem. supr. Kansas City Election Bd. Recipient outstanding svc. award Nat. Coun. Tchrs. English, 1979. Mem. AAUW (pres. Raytown l980-82), Raytown Arts Coun. (sec.), Mortar Bd., Phi Kappa Phi, Pi Lambda Theta, Sigma Alpha Iota (pres. Denver l960-62). Democrat. Mem. Ch. of Christ. Avocations: reading, embroidery, crocheting, travel, quilting. Home: 11833 E 47th Ter Kansas City MO 64133-2487 Personal E-mail: bettyltrotter@aol.com.

**TROTTER, CHARLIE,** chef; Degree in polit. sci., U. Wis. 1982. Owner, chef Charlie Trotter's, Chgo. Author: Charlie Trotter's, Charlie Trotter's Vegetables, Charlie Trotter's Seafood, Charlie Trotter's Desserts, Charlie Trotter's Meat and Game, Kitchen Sessions with Charlie Trotter, Gourmet Cooking for Dummies; host: (tv series) Kitchen Sessions with Charlie Trotter. Recipient Grand award, Wine Spectator, Best Restaurant in U.S., 2000. Office: 816 W Armitage Ave Chicago IL 60614

**TROTTER, CORTEZ,** city official, former fire commissioner; b. Chgo. First dep. fire commr. Chgo. Fire Dept., fire commr., 2001—; exec. dir. Office of Emergency Mgmt. and Comm. (formerly Office of Emergency Comm.), 2006—. Apptd. to bd. dirs. Emergency Comm. (911) Bd., 1990—. Recipient Martin Luther King Jr. Excellence in Leadership award, Suburban Human Rels. Com. Office: City Hall 121 N La Salle Chicago IL 60602*

**TROTTER, F(REDERICK) THOMAS,** retired academic administrator; b. LA, Apr. 17, 1926; s. Fred B. and Hazel (Thomas) T.; m. Gania Demaree, June 27, 1953; children— Ruth Elizabeth, Paula Anne (dec.), Tania, Mary. AB, Occidental Coll., 1950, DD, 1968; STB, Boston U., 1953, PhD, 1968; LHD, Ill. Wesleyan U., 1974, Cornell Coll., 1985, Westmar Coll., 1987; LLD, U. Pacific, 1978, Wesleyan Coll., 1981; EdD, Columbia Coll., 1984; LittD, Alaska Pacific U., 1987; DD, Emory U., 1989. Exec. sec. Boston U. Student Christian Assn., 1951-54; ordained elder Calif.-Pacific, Methodist Ch., 1953; pastor Montclair (Calif.) Meth. Ch., 1956-59; lectr. Sch. Theology at Claremont, 1959—73; gen. sec. Bd. Higher Edn. and Ministry United Meth. Ch., 1973—87; pres. Alaska Pacific U., Anchorage, 1988-95; ret., 1995.

Author: Jesus and the Historian, 1968, Loving God with One's Mind, 1987, God Is with Us, 1997, Politics, Morality, and Higher Education, 1997, weekly column local newspapers; editor-at-large: Christian Century, 1969-84. Trustee Dillard U. Served with USAAF, 1944-46. Kent fellow Soc. for Values in Higher Edn., 1954; Dempster fellow Meth. Ch., 1954 Mem. Rotary Internat. (Anchorage Downtown), Commonwealth North. Home: 900 E Harrison Ave Pomona CA 91767-2075

**TROTTER, HERMAN EAGER, JR., (HERMAN TROTTER),** retired music critic; b. Providence, Sept. 25, 1925; s. Herman Eager, Sr. and Shelley Fern (Jones) T.; m. Johanne Marguerite Haberstro, Sept. 22, 1956 (div. Apr. 1996); children: Kim Avery. Holly Anne. Joy Caroline; m. Rosa Spillane Whetzle, July 22, 1996. BA, Yale U., 1947. Sales engr., mgr. Mut. Life Ins. Co., Springfield, 1947-51; sales engr., mgr. Buffalo office B-I-F Industries, Providence, 1951-56; asst. sec. Buffalo Batt and Felt Co, Depew, NY, 1956-68; account exec. Harold Warner Advt., Buffalo, 1968-77; freelance music critic Buffalo News, 1968-77, staff music critic, 1977—2001, music critic emeritus, 2002. Contbr. articles to profl. and popular jours., and to New Grove Dictionary of Music. Program annotator Buffalo Philharm., 1964-70. Lt. (j.g.) USN, 1943-46, PTO. Mem.: Music Critics Assn. (v.p. 1988—93, sec. 1999—2003). Avocations: travel, record collecting. Home: 107 Oakland Pl Buffalo NY 14222-2047 E-mail: herros72296@aol.com.

**TROTTER, JEREMIAH,** professional football player; b. Texarkana, Tex., Jan. 20, 1977; s. Myra; m. Tammi Trotter; children: TreMil, Jeremiah Jr. Student, Stephen F Austin Univ. Linebacker Phila. Eagles, 1998—2001, 2004—, Wash. Redskins, 2002—03. Co-founder, co-owner Trott-Spot Carwash, 2003—. Vol. United Way; founder Jeremiah Trotter Found. Named to Pro Bowl, NFL, 2002—04. Address: Phila Eagles 1621 Franklin Mills Cir Philadelphia PA 19154 Office: Trott-Spot Carwash 1000 Haddonfield Rd Cherry Hill NJ 08002*

**TROTTER, JOE WILLIAM, JR.,** history professor, writer; b. Vallscreek, W.Va., June 18, 1945; s. Joe William and Thelma Odell Trotter; m. H. LaRue Mack, May 19, 1972. AA, Kendall Coll., 1967; BA, Carthage Coll., 1969; MA, U. Minn., 1978, PhD, 1980. Social studies tchr. Tremper Sr. HS, Kenosha, Wis., 1969—75; adult edn. instr. Gateway Tech. Inst., Kenosha, Wis., 1970—73; instr. dept. history U. Minn., 1977—79, vis. prof. dept. history, 1993; asst. prof. dept. history U. Calif.-Davis, 1981—84, assoc. prof. dept. history, 1984—85, Carnegie Mellon U., Pitts., 1985—89, prof. dept. history, 1990—96, Mellon prof. history, 1996—, head dept. history, 2001—; dir. Ctr. for Africanamerican Urban Studies and the Economy, Pitts., 1995—. Editl. bd. mem. Jour. Urban History, Thousand Oaks, Calif., 1997—, Labor History, London, 1991—2003, Jour. Am. Ethnic History, Piscataway, NJ, 1991—, Pa. History, Middletown, 1987—, Labor, Durham, NC, 2003—, Ohio Valley History, 2002—, Jour. of Am. History, Bloomington, Ind., 1992—95, Pa. History, Middletown, Pa., 1987—. Author: (book) Black Milwaukee: The Making of an Industrial Proletariat, 1915-45, 1985, Coal, Class, and Color: Blacks in Southern West Virginia, 1915-32, 1990, African Americans in Depression and War, 1929-1945, 1995, River Jordan: African American Urban Life in the Ohio Valley, 1998, The African American Experience, 2001; editor: (edited volume) The Great Migration in Historical Perspective: New Dimensions of Race, Class, and Gender, 1991; co-editor: Blacks in the Industrial Age: A Documentary History, 1915-1945, 1996, African Americans in Pennsylvania: Shifting Historical Perspectives, 1997, (book) African American Urban Studies: Perspectives From the Colonial Era to the Present, 2004. Spkr. NAACP, Arlington, Va., 1992, 19th dist., Homewood Brushton, Pitts., 1999; keynote spkr. Lemington Elder Care Svcs/, Pitts., 2002; pres. Kenosha Black Caucus, 1972—74; spkr. Friendship Bapt. Ch., Massillon, Ohio, 2001. Recipient Outstanding Svc. award, Pa. chpt. Nat. Assn. Real Estate Brokers, 1991, Gambrinus award, Milw. Hist. Soc., 1985; grantee, U.S. Dept. Edn. Grant, 2002-05, Ford Found., 1997-99, 2001-2002. Mem.: Labor and Working Class History Assn., Am. Studies Assn., So. Hist. Assn., Pa. Hist. Assn., Pitts. Ctr. for Social History, Urban History Assn., Assn. for the Study of Afro-American Life and History, Am. Hist. Assn., Orgn. Am. Historians. Office: Carnegie Mellon Univ Dept of History 5000 Forbes Ave Pittsburgh PA 15213 Office Phone: 412-268-2875. Office Fax: 412-268-1019. Business E-Mail: trotter@andrew.cmu.edu.

**TROTTER, LESLIE EARL,** operations research specialist, educator; b. Muskogee, Okla., Nov. 17, 1943; s. Leslie Earl and Sylvia Helene (Freeze) T.; m. Jomi Tuggle, July 19, 1968 (div. Dec. 1995); children: Colleen Nicole, Eamonn Scott; m. Jeannine Rouch, July 7, 2000. AB in Math., Princeton U., 1965; MS in Indsl. and Systems Engring., Ga. Inst. Tech., 1971; PhD in Ops. Rsch., Cornell U., 1973. Sci. computer programmer Lockheed-Ga. Co., Marietta, 1965-68; computer applications analyst Control Data Corp., Atlanta, 1968-70; postdoctoral rsch. assoc. Math. Rsch. Ctr., U. Wis., Madison, 1973; asst. prof. Yale U. Sch. Orgn. and Mgmt., New Haven, 1974-75; assoc. prof. Cornell U. Sch. Ops. Rsch. and Indsl. Engring., Ithaca, NY, 1975-84, dir. of Sch., 1983—87, 1998—99, prof., 1984—; dir. Advanced Computational Optimization Lab. Cornell Theory Ctr., 1995—2001. Vis. prof. Bonn (Germany) U., 1977-79, math. dept. E.P.F.L., Lausanne, Switzerland, 1984-85, 91-92, 2000, Math. Inst., Augsburg (Germany) U., 1987-88; ind. eng. lab. E.C.-Paris, 2006—; vis. cons. Bell Labs., Holmdel, N.J., 1981. Editor optimization area Jour. Ops. Rsch., 1982-87; contbr. numerous articles to profl. jours. Recipient tchg. excellence awards Cornell U., 1977, 81, 93, 94, 98, sr. U.S. scientist award Alexander von Humboldt Found., Germany, 1988; numerous rsch. grants NSF, 1974—, including High Performance Computing and Comms. Grand Challenge award, 1995—01. Mem. Inst for Ops Rsch and Mgmt. Sci., Math. Programming Soc. (treas. 1988-94), Soc. for Indsl. and Applied Math. Avocations: exercise, hiking, music. Office: Cornell U Sch Ops Rsch Engring Rhodes Hall Ithaca NY 14853 Office Phone: 607-255-5360. Business E-Mail: ltrotter@cs.cornell.edu.

**TROTTER, LLOYD G.,** electric power industry executive; b. Cleveland, Apr. 9, 1945; m. Teri Trotter; 3 children. BBA, Cleve. State U., 1972, PhD (hon.) in Bus. Adminstrn., 2001. Field svc. engr. GE Lighting, 1970; various positions GE, 1970-90; v.p., gen. mgr. mfg. ED&C, 1990-98; sr. v.p. GE, 1998-99; pres., CEO GE Indsl. Sys., 1999—; CEO, consumer & indsl. divsn. GE, 2004—06; pres., CEO GE Indsl., 2006—; vice chmn. GE, 2006—. Started GE African-Am. forum, 1990. Rep. for GE America's Promise. Named 50 Most Important African-Am. in Tech., USBE&IT and Blackmoney.com, 2004. Avocation: collector of Harlem Renaissance Period art and wine. Office: GE 3135 Easton Tpke Fairfield CT 06431-0002*

**TROTTER, THOMAS ROBERT,** lawyer; b. Akron, Ohio, Apr. 11, 1949; s. Fred and Josephine (Daley) Trotter; m. Martha Kaltenbach, 2003. BA, Ohio U., 1971; JD, Tulane U., 1975. Bar: Ohio 1975, D.C. 2000, U.S. Dist. Ct. (no. dist.) Ohio 1975. Assoc. Squire, Sanders & Dempsey, Cleve., 1975-80; shareholder Buckingham, Doolittle & Burroughs, Akron, 1980—. Trustee Cascade Capital Corp., 2006—; nat. chair, taxation and legis. com. Greater Akron C. of C., 1988-95; trustee Akron-Summit Solid Waste Mgmt. Authority, 1994-97 Trustee Akron Symphony Orch., 1984-93, trustee Weathervane Cmty. Playhouse, 1996-2003, pres., 1999-2001. Mem. ABA, Ohio Bar Assn. (chair local govt. law com.), Akron Bar Assn., Nat. Assn. Bond Lawyers, Sigma Alpha Epsilon. Democrat. Home: 180 W Fairlawn Blvd Akron OH 44313 Office: Buckingham Doolittle & Burroughs LLP PO Box 1500 50 S Main St Akron OH 44309-1500 Office Phone: 330-258-6488. E-mail: ttrotter@bdblaw.com.

**TROTTER, TIMOTHY HOWARD,** thoracic and cardiovascular surgeon, medical educator; b. Oklahoma City, Okla., Sept. 3, 1960; s. Lanny Floyd and Patsy Ann Trotter; m. Jennifer Jean Jones (div.); m. Mary Catherine Nicoloff, Nov. 30, 1991; children: Nicole Melissa, Nathaniel Powell. Student, Duke U., 1981; MD, U. Okla., 1985. Commd. ens. USN, 1983, advanced through grades to capt.; assoc. prof. U. Okla., Oklahoma City, 2000—. Fellow: ACS, Am. Coll. Chest Physicians. Republican. Methodist. Avocations: Aikido, Judo. Office: U Okla 920 Stanten L Young Blvd WP-2230 Oklahoma City OK 73190

**TROTTIER, BRYAN JOHN,** professional sports team executive, former professional hockey player and coach; b. Val Marie, Sask., Can., July 17, 1956; s. Eldon J. and Mary (Gardner) Trottier; m. Laura Lynn Theis, July 14, 1976; children: Bryan John, Lindsay Ann. Profl. hockey player NY Islanders, 1975—90, Pitts. Penguins, 1990—92, 1993—94, asst. coach, 1993—97; head coach Portland Pirates (Am. Hockey League), 1997—98; asst. coach Colo. Avalanche, 1998—2002; head coach NY Rangers, 2002—03; exec. dir. player devel. NY Islanders, 2006—. Hockey cons. Right Guard Corp., Phila.; spokesman 1980 Winter Olympics, Lake Placid, NY; former pres. NHL Player's Assn.; owner, operator Bryan Trottier Skating Acad., Port Washington, NY. Recipient Calder Meml. Trophy, 1976, Hart Meml. Trophy, 1979, Art Ross Trophy, 1979, Conn Smythe Trophy, 1980, King Clancy Meml. Trophy, 1989. Achievements include mem. Stanley Cup Champion, NY Islanders, 1980, 1981, 1982, 1983; mem. Stanley Cup Champions, Pitts. Penguins, 1991, 1992; inducted into Hockey Hall of Fame, 1997. Office: NY Islanders Nassau Veterans Meml Coliseum 1255 Hempstead Turnpike Uniondale NY 11553*

**TROTZ, BARRY,** professional hockey coach; Asst. coach U. Manitoba, 1984; head coach, gen. mgr. Dauphin Kings Jr. Hockey Club, 1985-87; head coach U. Manitoba, 1987; chief western scout Washington Capitals, 1988, asst. coach, 1991, head coach, 1992-95, US Team at Am. Hockey League All Star Game, 1996, Nashville Predators, 1997—. Office: Nashville Predators 501 Broadway Nashville TN 37203-3932*

**TROUILLE, MARY SEIDMAN,** foreign language educator; b. Chgo., Feb. 23, 1951; d. Nathaniel and Virginia (Crosley) Seidman; m. Guy Andre Nodot, Apr. 5, 1971 (div. Sept. 1977); 1 child, Jennifer Lynn; m. Bruno Jean-Louis Trouille, Apr. 15, 1978; children: David Alexander, Laura Elizabeth. BA in French, Loyola U., 1972; MA in French, Northwestern U., 1974, PhD in French, 1988. Editor Scott, Foresman Publs., Glenview, Ill., 1976-83; grad. teaching asst. Northwestern U., Evanston, Ill., 1983-88, lectr. French, 1988-89; lectr. humanities & French U. Chgo., 1990-93; asst. prof. French Ill. State U., Normal, 1993-96, assoc. prof. French, 1996—2002, prof. French, 2002—. Presenter in field. Author: Sexual Politics in the Enlightenment: Women Writers Read Rousseau, 1997; mem. editl. bd. Studies in 18th-Century Culture, 2000-2003; Translator: The Writing of Melancholy: Modes of Opposition in Early French Modernism, 1993, Les Lieux de Mémoire, vol. 1, 1998; contbr. chpts. to books and articles to profl. jours. Travel grantee Am. Coun. Learned Socs., 1995; Sch. Criticism & Theory fellow, 1985, Internat. Summer Inst. Semiotic and Structural Studies fellow, 1986. Mem. Am. Soc. Eighteenth-Century Studies (co-chair women's caucus 1995-98, mem. editl. bd. Studies in 18th-Century Culture 2000-03, chair tchg. prize selection com. 2002-03), Clifford Prize Com. (chair 2004-2005), Internat. Soc. Eighteenth-Century Studies. Office: Ill State U Dept Fgn Langs PO Box 4300 Normal IL 61790-0001 Office Phone: 309-438-7983.

**TROUNSTINE, PHILIP JOHN,** communications consultant, academic administrator; b. Cin., July 30, 1949; s. Henry P. and Amy May (Joseph) Trounstine; children: Jessica, David; m. Deborah Williams, May 1, 1993; children: Amy, Ryan, Patrick Wilkes. Student, U. Vt., 1967-68, Stanford U., 1968-70; BA in Journalism, San Jose State U., 1975. Graphic artist Eric Printing, San Jose, Calif., 1972-75; reporter Indpls. Star, Ind., 1975-78, San Jose Mercury News, Calif., 1978-83; editl. writer Calif., 1983-86, polit. editor Calif., 1986-99; ednl. cons. Teen Recovery Strategies, 1995-99; comms. dir. Gov. Gray Davis, Calif., 1999-2001, comm. cons. Calif., 2001—; dir. Survey and Policy Rsch. Inst. at San Jose State U., 2001—. Co-author: Movers & Shakers: The Study of Community Power, 1981. Creator, writer SPJ Gridiron Show, San Jose, 1981-91. Pulliam fellow, 1975, Duke U., 1991, J.S. Knight fellow Stanford U., 1993-94. Mem. Soc. Profl. Journalists (nat. ethics com. 1993-96), Am. Assn. Pub. Opinion Rsch., Seascape Golf Club. Jewish. Avocations: golf, fishing. Home: 620 Middlefield Dr Aptos CA 95003-3560 Office Phone: 408-924-6993.

**TROUP, ELLIOTT V., JR.,** psychologist; b. Nashville, Tenn., July 15, 1961; s. Elliott Vanbrugh and Linda Elizabeth Troup; m. Rasa Troup, June 28, 2005. BA in Psychology, U. Wis., 1983; M in Edn., Howard U., 1990. Lic. Psychologist Minn. Bd. of Psychology, 1994. Tchr., therapist Ada S. McKinley Therapeutic Ctr., Chgo., 1985—86, Lawrence Hall Sch. for Boys, Chgo., 1987—88; multicultural counselor George Wash. U., Washington, 1990; therapist Family and Children Svc., Mpls., 1990—92; lic. psychologist United Behavioral Systems, Brooklyn Center, Minn., 1992—95; psychologist Behavioral Health Svc. Inc., Golden Valley, Minn., 1995—2005, Pvt. Practice, Mpls., 1998—. Mem: APA (assoc.). Office: Elliott V Troup Jr MEd LP 431 S 7th St #2402 Minneapolis MN 55415 Office Phone: 612-708-4242.

**TROUP, GORDON A.,** health facility administrator; With Am. Hosp. Supply Corp., Cardinal Distbn., 1991—99, exec. v.p. field ops., 1999—2000; pres. pharm. distbn. and splty distbn. bus. Cardinal Health, Inc., 2000—03, exec. v.p., 2003—, pres. nuclear pharmacy svcs., 2003—. Office: Cardinal Health Inc 7000 Cardinal Pl Dublin OH 43017

**TROUPE, WILLIAM HAROLD,** lawyer; b. Quincy, Mass., Aug. 7, 1945; s. George Harold and Elizabeth (Harvey) T.; m. Linda M. Corbett, July 19, 1970; children: Allyson Leigh, Adam Jeremy. BBA, U. Mass., 1967; JD, Suffolk U., 1972. Bar: Mass. 1972, U.S. Dist. Ct. Mass. 1975, U.S. Ct. Appeals (1st cir.) 1975, U.S. Supreme Ct., 1991. New Eng. claims mgr. Greater N.Y. Ins. Co., Boston, 1972-73; ptnr. Lawrence Locke & Assocs., Boston, 1973-84, Wynn & Wynn PC, Boston, 1984-89, Hislop Carney & Troupe, Boston, 1990-98; founding ptnr. Carney & Troupe, Boston, 1998—. Spkr. continuing legal edn. programs. Contbr. numerous articles on worker's compensation to legal jours. Mem. Mass. Bar Assn. (chmn. worker's compensaton com.), Boston Bar Assn. Office: Carney & Troupe 5th Fl 10 High St Fl 5 Boston MA 02110-1605 Office Phone: 617-426-9797. Personal E-mail: willtrou@aol.com.

**TROUSDALE, STEPHEN RICHARD,** newspaper editor; b. LA, May 29, 1963; s. Richard Gardner Trousdale and Geraldine Barbara Wisdom. AB, Stanford U., 1985. News editor L.A. Daily Commerce, 1986—87; edit. page editor L.A. Daily Jour., 1987—89; mng. editor, 1989—96; bus. editor Copley L.A. Newspapers, 1996—97; dep. bus. editor Contra Costa Times, 1997—2000, bus. editor, 2000—. Mem. Soc. Profl. Journalists (past pres. L.A. chpt.), AP Mng. Editors, Calif. Soc. Newspaper Editors, So. Am. Bus. Editors and Writers. Avocations: skiing, karate. Office: Contra Costa Newspapers 2640 Shadelands Dr Walnut Creek CA 94598-2513 Home: 2335 Valley St Berkeley CA 94702-2133 Office Phone: 925-943-8099. Business E-Mail: strousdale@cctimes.com.

**TROUSIL, HANS KURT,** mayor; b. Rodheim v.d.Hohe, Hessen, Germany, Jan. 11, 1953; s. Otto K. and Wilfriede E. Trousil; m. Deb E. Moss, Aug. 12, 1972; children: Andrea C., Brian M., Brandon J. City coun. mem. City of West Burlington, 1986—, mayor, 1994—. Exec. bd. S.E. Iowa Regional Planning Commn., Burlington, Iowa, 2004—. Bd. mem. Emergency Mgmt. Commn., West Burlington, 1994—2006. Named Firefighter of Yr., West Burlington Fire Dept., 1984, Govt. Ofcl. of Yr., Burlington/West Burlington C. of C., 2004; recipient Iowa H.S. Vol. award, Iowa H.S. Athletic Union, 2006. D-Conservative. Roman Catholic. Avocations: boating, travel, reading, sports. Office: City of West Burlington 122 Broadway West Burlington IA 52655 Office Phone: 319-752-5451. E-mail: trousilh@westburlington.org.

**TROUT, CHARLES HATHAWAY,** historian, educator; b. Seattle, Nov. 3, 1935; s. Charles Whyron and Elizabeth (Hathaway) T.; m. Margot Shaws, Dec. 30, 1961 (div. 1983); children: Nicholas H., Benjamin C.; m. Katherine Taylor Griffiths, Oct. 6, 1984. BA, Amherst Coll., 1957; MA, Columbia U., 1961, PhD, 1972. History instr. Hill Sch., Pottstown, Pa., 1958-59, Philips Exeter Acad., (N.H.), 1960-69; prof. history Mt. Holyoke Coll., South Hadley, Mass., 1969-80; provost, dean faculty Colgate U., Hamilton, N.Y., 1980-90; pres. Washington Coll., Chestertown, Md., 1990-95; tchr. Tchr. for Africa, Korongoi, Litein, Kenya, 1996-97. Vis. prof. U. Mass. Labor Rels. and Rsch.

Ctr., 1974-80; interim pres., Harcum Coll., Bryn Mawr, Pa., 2002-03, pres., 2003—. Author: Boston, The Great Depression, and the New Deal. Chmn. bd. World Edn. Inc.; trustee Sultana Projects, Inc. Columbia U. Pres.'s scholar, 1959-60; NEH rsch. fellow, 1975-76; Charles Warren fellow Harvard U., 1978-79. Democrat. Episcopalian. Home: 211 N Queen St Chestertown MD 21620-1627 Office: Harcum Coll Office of President Bryn Mawr PA 19010 Business E-Mail: ctrout@harcum.edu.

**TROUT, GWENN LOUISE,** minister; b. Gettysburg, Pa., July 5, 1958; d. Thomas Arthur and Nancy Ruth (Shanebrook) Trout. BA in Speech Comms. and, Theatre, Mansfield U. Pa., 1980; MDiv Luth. Theol. Sem. at Gettysburg, 1997. Ordained to min. of Word and Sacrament Evangel. Luth. Ch. in Am., 1997. Mng. dir. Profl. Summer Theatre, Harrisburg Area C.C., Harrisburg, Pa., 1980; asst. to the dir. Pa. Coun. on the Arts, Harrisburg, Pa., 1980—86; publs. design cons. Pa. Dept. of Gen. Svcs., Harrisburg, 1986—93; student helper, pub. rels. and devel. Gettysburg Luth. Sem., Gettysburg, 1993—97; vicar Trinity Luth. Ch., Taneytown, Md., 1996—97; pastor St. James Luth. Ch., Columbia, Pa., 1997—2003, Zion Luth. Ch., Enola, Pa., 2003—. Mem. synod coun. Lower Susquehanna Synod, 2001—. Mem.: Greater Harrisburg Sweet Adelines Internat. Lutheran. Avocation: singing, photography, travel, theatre. Office: Zion Luth Church 265 Enola Dr Enola PA 17025 Home: 2460 Brookwood St Harrisburg PA 17104-2111 Office Phone: 717-732-9652. E-mail: revbass@juno.com.

**TROUT, LINDA COPPLE,** state supreme court justice; b. Tokyo, Sept. 1, 1951; BA, U. Idaho, 1973, JD, 1977; LLD (hon.), Albertson Coll. Idaho, 1999. Bar: Idaho 1977. Atty. Blake, Feeney & Clark, 1978—83; judge magistrate divsn. Idaho Dist. Ct. (2d jud. divsn.), 1983-90, dist. judge Lewiston, 1991-92, acting trial ct. adminstr., 1987-91; justice Idaho Supreme Ct., 1992—, chief justice, 1997—2004. Instr. coll. law U. Idaho, 1983, 88; chair Idaho State Supreme Ct. Judicial Education Com. Mem. bd. directors Lewiston City Library, Northwest Children's Home, Idaho Women's YWCA. Mem. Idaho State Bar Assn., Clearwater Bar Assn. (pres. 1980-81). Office: Idaho Supreme Court PO Box 83720 Boise ID 83720-3720*

**TROUT, MAURICE ELMORE,** diplomat; b. Clifton Hill, Mo., Sept. 17, 1917; s. David McCamel and Charlotte Temple (Woods) T.; m. Margie Marie Mueller, Aug. 24, 1943; children— Richard Willis, Babette Yvonne. BA, Hillsdale Coll., 1939; MA in Pub. Adminstrn, St. Louis U., 1948, PhD in Polit. Sci. 1950. Joined U.S. Fgn. Service, 1950; assigned Paris, 1950-52, Vienna, 1952-55, London, 1955-59, Vientiane, Laos, 1959-61; with Office Exec. Dir. Bur. Far Eastern Affairs, Dept. State, Washington, 1961-65; Am. consulate gen. Munich, 1965-69; 1st sec., consul Am. embassy, Bangkok, 1969—72; dep. office dir. Bur. Politico-Mil. Affairs, Dept. State, Washington, 1972-75; Dept. State advisor Armed Forces Staff Coll., Norfolk, Va., 1975-77. Bd. dirs. Internat. Sch., Bangkok, 1970-72. Served with USCG, 1939-45; capt. USAFR, 1951-55. Recipient Achievement award, Hillsdale Coll., 1962. Mem. Am. Fgn. Service Assn., Diplomatic and Consular Officers Ret., Delta Tau Delta, Delta Theta Phi, Pi Gamma Mu. Home: 6203 Hardy Dr Mc Lean VA 22101-3114

**TROUT, MONROE EUGENE,** health facility administrator; b. Harrisburg, Pa., Apr. 5, 1931; s. David Michael and Florence Margaret (Kashner) T.; m. Sandra Louise Lemke, June 11, 1960; children: Monroe Eugene, Timothy William. AB, U. Pa., 1953, MD, 1957; LLB, Dickinson Sch. of Law, 1964, JD, 1969; LLD (hon.), Dickinson Sch. Law, 1996, Bloomfield Coll., 1994, Cumberland Coll., 2003. Intern Great Lakes (Ill.) Naval Hosp., 1957-58; resident in internal medicine Portsmouth (Va.) Naval Hosp., 1959-61; chief med. dept. Harrisburg State Hosp., 1961-64; dir. drug regulatory affairs Pfizer, Inc., N.Y.C., 1964-68; v.p., med. dir. Winthrop Labs., N.Y.C., 1968-70; med. dir. Sterling Drug Inc., N.Y.C., 1970-74, v.p., dir. med. affairs, 1974-78, sr. v.p., dir. med. affairs, bd. dirs., mem. exec. com., 1978-86; pres., CEO Am. Healthcare Sys., Inc., 1986-95, chmn., 1987-95; also bd. dirs. Am. Healthcare Systems, Inc.; chmn. emeritus Am. Healthcare Sys., Inc., 1995—; interim CEO Cytran Inc., 1996. Chmn. bd. dirs. Cytyc Inc., 1998—2002, Ineed MD, Inc., Am. Excess Ins. Ltd., 1990—95; adj. assoc. prof. Bklyn. Coll. Pharmacy; spl. lectr. legal medicine, trustee Dickinson Sch. Law, 1970—93; trustee Ariz. State U. Sch. Health Adminstrn., 1988—91; mem. rsch. bd. Sterling Winthrop, 1977—86; mem. Joint Commn. Prescription Drug Use, 1976—80; sec. Commn. on Med. Malpractice, HEW, 1971—73, cons., 1974; co-chmn. San Diego County Health Commn., 1992—94. Mem. editl. bd. Hosp. Formulary Mgmt., 1969-79, Forensic Sci., 1971—, Jour. Legal Medicine, 1973-79, Reg. Tox. and Pharmac, 1981-87, Med. Malpractice Prevention, 1985—; editl. reviewer Annals of Internal Medicine; contbr. articles to profl. jours. Exec. com. White House Mini Conf. on Aging, 1980; mem. Nat. Health Adv. Bd. AAA; chmn. bd. Am. Coll. Legal Medicine Found., 1983—87; mem. N.Y. State Commn. Substance Abuse, 1978—80, Town Coun., New Canaan, 1978—86, vice chmn., 1985—86; trustee Cleve. Clinic, 1971—87, Albany Med. Coll., 1977—86, St. Vincent DePaul Ctr. for the Homeless, 1987—90, U. Calif.-San Diego Thornton Hosp. and Med. Ctr., 1990—97, San Diego Mus. Art, 1996—98, Bapt. Health Sys. Found., Knoxville, 1999—; trustee, vice chmn. Morehouse Med. Sch., 1980—89; assoc. trustee U. Calif. San Diego Found., 1994—97; vice chmn. Med. Commn. for Food and Shelter, Inc.; chmn. Internat. B'nai B'rith Dinner, 1989, 1994; Rep. dist. leader New Canaan, 1966—68; bd. dirs. New Canaan Interchurch Svc. Com., 1965—69, Athletes Kidney Found., Cir. in the Sq. Theatre Inc., 1984—86, Knoxville Symphony Soc., 2001—04, Knoxville Opera Co., 2001—04, East Tenn. Hist. Soc., 2003—04. Recipient Alumni award of merit U. Pa., 1953, Disting. Alumni award Dickinson Sch. Law, 1989, Nat. Healthcare award Internat. B'nai B'rith, 1991, Entrepreneur of Yr. award San Diego, 1994, Horatio Alger award, 1995, Salvation Army Tradition of Caring award, 1996, Cívis Universitatus award U. Calif. San Diego, 1997, Gold Medal award, Am. Coll. Legal Medicine, 1999, Bapt. Health Sys. Visionary award, 2002, Knoxville Philanthropist of Yr., 2004, Cumberland Coll. Caring Servant award, 2005. Fellow Am. Coll. Legal Medicine (v.p., pres., bd. govs.); mem. AMA (Physician's Recognition awards 1969, 72, 76, 82, 85, 88, 92), Med. Execs. (pres. 1975-76), Delta Tau Delta (Alumni Achievement award 1996, Named to 100 Most Influential Delts of Twentieth Century 2000). Lutheran. Office: 2110 Cove View Way Knoxville TN 37919

**TROUTMAN, HOLMES RUSSELL,** lawyer; b. Beckley, W.Va., July 27, 1933; s. Holmes Fielding and Florence Lillo (Wallett) T.; m. Patricia Lee Bullion, Nov. 12, 1954; children: Holmes Russell, Richard Byron, Teresa Lee. AB, Marshall U., 1955; postgrad., Stetson Law Sch., 1955-56; LLB, U. Miami, 1958. Bar: Fla. 1958. Assoc., ptnr. firm Akerman, Turnbull, Senterfitt & Eidson, Orlando, Fla., 1958-62; ptnr. firm Fishback, Davis, Dominick & Troutman, Orlando, Fla., 1962-69, Troutman, Williams, Irvin, Green & Helms, P.A., Winter Park, Fla., 1969—. Spl. city prosecutor, City of Winter Park, 1965, city atty., 1968-72, acting county solicitor, 1967-69; spl. counsel Fla. Turnpike Authority, 1968-70, Fla. Pub. Svc. Commn., 1978-79; mem. Fla. Supreme Ct. Nominating Commn., 1978-82, chmn., 1981-82; chmn. bd. trustees Fla. Supreme Ct. Historical Soc., 2000—. Contbr. articles to profl. jours. Host, prodr. Discussion programs Sta. WFTV, 1968-85. Pres. Friends of Orlando Pub. Libr., 1971-73, Fla. Supreme Ct. Hist. Soc., 1997-99; mem. Orange County Charter Study Commn., 1973-74; chmn. Winter Park Charter Study Commn., 1982-83; chmn. bd. advisors Rollins Coll. Hamilton Holt Sch., 1996-98, chmn. emeritus Hamilton Holt Sch. Bd. Rollins Coll.; pres. Fla. Supreme Ct. Hist. Soc., 1997-99; commencement spkr. Rollins Coll. 1999. Recipient Orlando Jr. C. of C. Good Govt. award, 1969, Marshall U. Alumnus Civic Contbrn. award, 1979, Winter Park C. of C. Good Govt. award, 1985. Mem. ABA (mem. ho. of dels. 1978-80), Am. Acad. Trial Lawyers, Fla. Acad. Trial Lawyers, Fla. Bar (mem. bd. govs. 1972-78, pres. 1977-78), Orange County Bar Assn. (mem. exec. coun. 1966-68, pres. 1968-69, co-founder Legal Aid Soc. 1969), Orlando Tiger Bay Club (pres. 1988-89). Home: 1600 Barcelona Way Winter Park FL 32789-5615 Office: Troutman Williams Irvin Green & Helms PA 311 W Fairbanks Ave Winter Park FL 32789-5094 Office Phone: 407-647-2277. Business E-Mail: btroutman@troutmanwilliams.com.

**TROUTNER, JOANNE JOHNSON,** director, consultant, secondary school educator; b. Muncie, Ind., Sept. 9, 1952; d. Donal Russel and Lois Vivian (Hicks) Johnson; m. Lary William Troutner, May 17, 1975. BA in Media and English, Purdue U., 1974; MS in Edn., 1976. Media spls. Lafayette (Ind.) Sch. Corp., 1974-77, 81-83, computer resource tchr., 1983-84; media splst. Tippecanoe Sch. Corp., Lafayette, 1984-85, ednl. support, 1985-87, coord. instrl. support, 1988-94, dir. tech. and media, 1994—; tchr. English Minot (N.D.) Pub. Schs., 1978-79, media specialist, 1979-81; instr. freshman honors seminar Purdue U., Coll. Tech., 2006—. Vis. prof. continuing edn. U. S.C., Columbia, 1983, U. N.D.; instr. Purdue U., West Lafayette; software selector Elem. Sch. Libr. Collection. Author: The Media Specialist, The Microcomputer and the Curriculum, 1983, World Desk-Classroom Internet Guide, 1998, The Internet: A Curriculum Oriented Guide, 1998, 2005, Using the Internet and Technology to Strengthen Learning in English/Language Arts and Social Studies, 1999, Integrating Technology and the Internet into English and Social Studies Classroom, 2002, 2006, Strengthen Your Classroom with Technology, 2004; materials rev. columnist: Sch. Libr. Media Quar., computer literacy columnist: Jour. Computers Math. and Sci. Tchg., computer software columnist: Tchr. Libr., 1989—, internet columnist, 1995—; editor: Ind. Computer Educators newsletter. Active Greater Lafayette Leadership Acad. Alumni Group, 1983—; bd. dirs. Lafayette Family Svc. Agy., 1987—89; treas. Greater Lafayette Mortar Bd. Alumni Group, 2006—; bd. dirs. Tippecanoe County Pub. Libr., trustee, 1990—2000, pres. 1994—95; mem. dean's adv. coun. Sch. Edn. Purdue U., 2003—. Recipient Disting. Alumni award, Purdue U. Sch. Edn., 2003. Mem.: ASCD, ALA, Internat. Soc. Tech. Educators, Ind. Computer Educators (bd. dirs. 1986—92, pres. 1990—91), Internat. Coun. Computers in Edn. (interactive video spl. interest group newsletter editor 1986—87), Am. Assn. Sch. Libros. (sec. 1983—84, 2d v.p. 1985—86), Ind. Assn. Media Educators (chmn. computer divns. 1982—84), Phi Beta Kappa, Phi Delta Kappa (v.p. programs 1987—88, v.p. memberships 1988—89, pres. 1989—90), Kappa Delta Gamma. Home: 4001 Penny Packers Mill Rd Lafayette IN 47909-3557 Office: Tippecanoe Sch Corp 21 Elston Rd Lafayette IN 47909-2899 Office Phone: 765-474-2481. Personal E-mail: troutner@mindspring.com.

**TROUTT, KENNY,** communications executive; b. Mt. Vernon, Ill., Jan. 8, 1948; s. Nadine Adams; m. Lisa Troutt; 3 children. BS, Southern Ill. U. Founder Excel Comm., 1988, CEO, chmn., vice chmn.; co-owner WinStar Farms, Ky.; dir. Mt. Vernon Investments, Inc. Vice chmn. Teleglobe, bd. dirs.; trustee Thoroughbred Owners & Breeders Assn.; bd. dirs. Breeders' Cup. Coach boys' basketball. Named one of Forbes' Richest Americans, 2006. Christian. Mailing: WinStar Farms 3001 Pisgah Pike Versailles KY 40383 Office Phone: 859-873-1717. Office Fax: 859-873-1612.*

**TROUTT, WILLIAM EARL,** academic administrator; b. Bolivar, Tenn., June 13, 1949; s. Jack and Earline (Shearin) Troutt; m. Carole Pearson, Nov. 26, 1970; children: Carole Anne, Jack. BA, Union U., Jackson, Tenn., 1971; MA, U. Louisville, 1972; PhD, Vanderbilt U., 1978. Admissions counselor Union U., 1973—75; asst. dir. Tenn. Higher Edn. Commn., Nashville, 1975—78; sr. assoc. McManis Assocs. Inc., Washington, 1978—80; exec. v.p. Belmont Coll., Nashville, 1981—82, pres., 1982—99, Rhodes Coll., Memphis, 1999—. Chmn. Am. Coun. on Edn. Chmn. Jacob Javits Fellowship Bd., Nat. Assn. Ind. Colls. & Univs., Nat. Commn. Cost Higher Edn. Named one of Nation's Most Effective Coll. Pres., Exxon Found. Study, 1986. Mem.: So. Assn. Colls. and Schs. (commnr. commn. colls. 1986—), Tenn. Ind. Colls. Fund (sec.-treas. 1986—), Tenn. Coun. Pvt. Colls. (chmn.), Nashville Area C. of C. (bd. dirs. 1985—), Rotary. Office: Office of the Pres 2000 N Pkwy Memphis TN 38112-1690

**TROUTWINE, GAYLE LEONE,** lawyer; b. Kansas City, Mo., Feb. 26, 1952; BS, N.W. Mo. U., 1973; JD with honors, U. Mo., 1978, postgrad., 2003—. Bar: Mo. 1978, Oreg. 1983, U.S. Dist. Ct. (we. dist) Mo., Wash. 1984, U.S. Ct. Appeals (9th cir.) 1984, U.S. Dist. Ct. (we. dist.) Wash., U.S. Supreme Ct., Hawaii 1995. Ptnr. Williams & Troutwine, P.C., Portland, Oreg., 1986—99, Troutwine Law Offices, Maui, Columbia, Osage Beach, Mo., 1999—; pres., CEO Hula Moons Farm, Maui, Hawaii, 1999—2002, Apricot Rose, Kahului, Hawaii, 1999—2003; CEO Aloha Enterprises, 2004—. Spkr. in field; mem. Maui Bd. Realtors. Contbr. articles to profl. jours. Mem. Jud. Steering Com., 1994, Made in Hawaii Coun., 2000—02, pres., 2004—; bd. mem. Portland Area Women's Polit. Caucus, 1992—95, Oreg. Women's Polit. Caucus, 1996—99; candidate Columbia City Coun., 2005; steering com. mem. Breast Implant Litig., 1992—, Tobacco Litig. Named Queen of Torts, Wall St. Jour., 1996. Mem.: ATLA (bd. govs.), Cmty. Assn. Inst., Maui Bd. Realtors, Western Trial Lawyers Assn. (bd. govs. 1992—), Greater Kansas City (sec. 1981—82), Women Lawyers Assn., Wash. Trial Lawyers Assn., Hawaii Trial Lawyers Assn., Calif. Trial Lawyers Assn., Oreg. Trial Lawyers Assn. (bd. govs. 1987—91), Wash. State Bar, Oreg. State Bar (exec. bd. litig. sect. 1984—88, chmn. 1987—88, procedure and practice com. 1985—88, bd. govs. 1990—93), Mo. Bar, Hawaii State Bar. Democrat. Office: 1218 Hwy KK Osage Beach MO 65065 Office Phone: 573-348-2434. Office Fax: 573-348-4204. Business E-Mail: gtroutwine@troutwinelaw.com.

**TROWBRIDGE, JOHN PARKS,** physician; b. Dinuba, Calif., Mar. 24, 1947; s. John Parks and Claire Dovie (Noroian) Trowbridge; children: Sharla Tyann, Lyndi Kendyll. AB in Biol. Scis., Stanford U., 1970; MD, Case Western Res. U., 1976; postgrad., Fla. Inst. Tech., 1983-85. Diplomate in Preventive Medicine, Am. Bd. Clin. Metal Toxicology (examiner for bd. 1987—, protocol coun. 1996-98), Am. Bd. Biologic Reconstructive Therapy (examiner for bd. 1994-97), Am. Bd. Anti-Aging Medicine, 1998, Nat. Bd. Med. Examiners. Intern in gen. surgery Mt. Zion Hosp. & Med. Ctr., San Francisco, 1976-77; resident in urol. surgery U. Tex. Health Sci. Ctr., Houston, 1977-78; pvt. med. practice (health recovery unit, pain relief unit, life long health unit) Life Celebrating Health Assn., Humble, Tex., 1978—. Chief corp. med. cons. Tex. Internat. Airlines, Houston, 1981-83; immunology rsch. asst. Stanford U. Med. Ctr., Stanford, Calif., 1967-70; night lab. supr. Kaiser Found. Hosp., Redwood City, Calif., 1971-72; advisor to bd. dirs. Am. Inst. Med. Preventics, Laguna Hills, Calif., 1988-90; sr. aviation med. examiner FAA, 1983-96; invited guest lectr. Taipei Med. U., Taiwan, 2005; lectr., cons. in field. Co-author: The Yeast Syndrome, 1986, Chelation Therapy, 1985, 2d edit., 1990, Yeast Related Illnesses, 1987, Do What You Want to Do, 1996, The Rumble in Humble: Heart Surgery and All That Jazz, 1997, Living Well Past 50: Rejuvenate Your Heart and Arteries, 1998; contbr. Challenging Orthodoxy: America's Top Medical Preventives Speak Out, 1991; weekly radio show host (KBME-AM): Feeling Better...Naturally, with Dr. John Trowbridge, Houston, 2003-2004; contbr. articles to profl. jours. Adv. bd. Tex. Chamber Orchestra, Houston, 1979-80; med. dir. Humble unit Am. Cancer Soc., 1980-81; med. cons. personal fitness program Lake Houston YMCA, 1981-83. Nat. Merit scholar, 1965-69, Calif. State scholar, 1967-69; recipient Resolution of Commendation house of dels., 1974 Am. Podiatry Assn., Spl. Profl. Svc. Citation bd. trustees, 1976, Am. Podiatry Students Assn. Fellow: Am. Coll. Advancement in Medicine (v.p. 1987—89, pres.-elect 1990—91), Am. Soc. for Laser Medicine and Surgery; mem.: AMA, Am. Bd. Clin. Metal Toxicology (bd. dirs. 2006—), Neuro Cranial Restructuring Drs. Assn., Neuro Cranial Reconstruction Rsch. Inst. (pres. 2003-) (pres. 2002—03, rsch. instr. pres. 2003—), Am. Soc. Life Ext. Physicians (founding), Am. Assn. Nutritional Cons., Am. Acad. Thermology, Nat. Health Fedn. (chmn. bd. govs. 1989), Am. Soc. Gen. Laser Surgery, Am. Acad. Environ. Medicine, Laser and Edn. Found. Am. Preventive Med. Assn. (bd. dirs. 1996—99, charter), Am. Coll. Preventive Medicine, Internat. Coll. Integrative Medicine (editor newsletter 2000—01, bd. dirs. 2000—, sec. 2002—), N.Am. Cervicogenic Headache Soc., Royal Soc. Medicine (London, sect. orthop.), Soc. for Orthomolecular Medicine, Great Lakes Coll. Clin. Medicine (bd. dirs. 1991—95, med. rsch. instnl. rev. bd., v.p. 1993—94, pres. 1994—95, program chair Advanced Tng. Seminar in Heavy Metal Toxicology 1996—98, bd. dirs. 1999—2000), Huxley Inst. for Biosocial Rsch., Inst. Health Freedom (bd. dirs. 1991—2001), Arthritis Trust Am. (med. adv. bd. 1995—), Internat. Acad. Bariatric Medicine, N.Y. Acad. Scis., Aerospace Med. Assn., Houston Acad. Medicine, Harris County Med. Soc., Tex. Med. Assn., Am. Acad. Anti-Aging Medicine, Assn. Am. Physicians and Surgeons. Avocations:

private piloting, computer applications. Office: Life Celebrating Health Assn 9816 Memorial Blvd Ste 205 Humble TX 77338-4206 Office Phone: 281-540-2329. Personal E-mail: jptlch@earthlink.net. Business E-mail: info@healthchoicesnow.com.

**TROWBRIDGE, THOMAS, JR.,** mortgage company executive; b. Troy, NY, June 28, 1938; s. of Thomas and Elberta (Wood) T.; m. Delinda Bryan, July 3, 1965; children: Elisabeth Tacy, Wendy Bryan. BA, Yale U., 1960; MBA, Harvard U., 1965. V.p. James W. Rouse & Co., Balt., 1965-66, Washington, 1966-68, San Francisco, 1968-73, 76-78; pres. Rouse Investing Co., Columbia, Md., 1973-76, Trowbridge, Kieselhorst & Co., San Francisco, 1978-97, CEO, chmn., 1997-2000; ret., 2000. Bd. dirs. Columbia Assn., 1975-76; trustee, treas. The Head-Royce Sch., Oakland, Calif., 1980-84; trustee, pres. Gen. Alumni Assn. Phillips Exeter Acad., 1984-90. Lt. USNR, 1960-63. Mem. Urban Land Inst., Calif. Mortgage Bankers Assn. (bd. dirs. 1991-98, pres. 1996-97), Mortgage Bankers Assn. Am. (bd. govs. 1993-2000), Naval War Coll. Found., 2000-, Olympic Club, Pacific Union Club, Lambda Alpha Internat. Republican. Presbyterian. Avocation: golf. Home: 4 Ridge Ln Orinda CA 94563-1318

**TROXEL, DAVID B.,** pathologist; b. Elgin, Ill., 1936; MD, Northwestern U., 1962. Intern Chgo. Wesley Meml. Hosp., 1962—63; residency Mayo Clinic Found., Rochester, 1963—64, Presbyn. Hosp., Denver, 1966—68; clinical prof. Divsn. of Health & Med. Sci., U. Calif., Berkeley. Cons., govr. Doctors Ins. Com. Contbr. articles to jours. Mem.: Calif. Soc. of Pathologists (former pres.), Am. Bd. of Pathology (former pres.). Office: U Calif Berkeley 570 Univ Hall Berkeley CA 94720

**TROXELL, LUCY DAVIS,** management consultant; b. Cambridge, Mass., Apr. 25, 1932; d. Ellsworth and Mildred (Enneking) Davis; m. Charles DeGroat Bader, June 13, 1952 (div. Aug. 1974); children: Christie P. Walker, Mary Bader Montgomery, Charles D. Bader Jr., David Bradford Bader; m. Victor Daniel Shirer Troxell, Aug. 1974. BA, Smith Coll., Northampton, Mass., 1952; grad., Inst. Paralegal Training, Phila. Cert. employee benefit specialist, assoc. in risk mgmt. Paralegal O'Melveny & Myers, L.A., 1976-77; asst. exec. Olanie Hurst & Hemrich, L.A., 1977-78; asst. to trustee Oxford Ins. Mgmt., L.A., 1978-80; dir. corp. svcs., asst. corp. sec. Consolidated Elec. Distbrs., Inc., Westlake Village, Calif., 1980-93; pres. MONMAK LDT, Westlake Village, 1993—. Vol. Friends of the Westlake Village Libr., 2000—, ARC; bd.dirs. Friends of the West Lake Village, 2004—, v.p., 2006; clk. St. Mathew's Parish Vestry, Pacific Palisades, Calif., 1988, sr. warden, 1989—90; lic. lay eucharistic min. Episcopal Ch.; sustaining bd. dirs. Jr. League, Hartford, Conn., 1952—58, L.A., 1952—60; bd. dirs. Smith Coll. Club, Hartford, 1952—58, Nat. Charity League, L.A., 1964—68, Theater Palisades, 1960—74; bd. dirs., treas. HOA Lakeshore Cmty. Assn., 1999—2002, v.p., 2005—. Sophia Smith scholar. Fellow: Risk and Ins. Mgmt. Soc. (program chmn. L.A. chpt. 1985—86), Internat. Soc. Cert. Employee Benefit Specialists (bd. dirs., sec., treas. 1988—89, pres. 1989—90, edn. chmn. L.A. chpt. 1986—88). Republican. Avocations: finance, acting, music, art. Home: 450 Puerto Del Mar Pacific Palisades CA 90272-4233 Office: MONMAK LDT 32001 Viewlake Ln Westlake Village CA 91361

**TROXLER, WILLIE THOMASENE,** retired elementary school educator; b. Raleigh, N.C., Sept. 3, 1925; d. Charles Gilmer Cates and Addie Gaye Long; m. Roger Vernon Troxler, Mar. 18, 1950; children: Bonnie Lynn, Teri. BA, St. Mary's Jr. Coll., Raleigh, 1945; BA Journalism, U. N.C., Chapil Hill, 1947; MA Lang. Arts, U. Charlotte, N.C., 1976. Reporter State Advt. Divsn., NC, 1947—48; assoc. editor Carolina Road Builders Trade Mag., NC, 1948—50; tchr. elem. sch. Salisbury City Schs., NC, 1961—78. Exhibited in group shows at Page Walker Arts and History Ctr., Cary, NC, 1999, Rowan Regional Hosp., Salisbury, 1999, Davidson County Mus. Art, Lexington, NC, 1999, one-woman shows include Depot Visual Arts Ctr., Mooresville, NC, 1997, Rowan Pub. Libr., Salisbury, 1982, Chatham County Hosp., Asheboro, NC, 1982, Salisbury Pub. Sch. Supplementary Ctr. Art Gallery, 1982. Active Salisbury Symphony Guild; 2d v.p. Rep. Women, Salisbury. Recipient 1st pl. Collage, Rowan County Silver Arts, 2005, 2d pl., Rowan County Art Group, 2005, 1st Pl. Mem. Choice award, Rowan County Art Show, 2005. Mem.: Stanley County Art Guild, Davidson County Art Guild (Judges Commendation 1986, Pres. Choice Stuffer Myer's Meml. award 1995, Third pl. 1998, First pl. 2002), Mooresville Art Guild, Waterworks Visual Art Works, Watercolor Soc. N.C. (Fifth pl. Fall Show 1997, Merit award Spring Show 1999), Carolina Artist (past pres.). Home: 131 Richmond Rd Salisbury NC 28144-2847 E-mail: ttroxler@salisbury.net.

**TROY, ANTHONY FRANCIS,** lawyer; b. Hartford, Conn., Apr. 16, 1941; children: Anthony John, Francis Gerard II. BA in Govt., St. Michael's Coll., Vt., 1963; LLB, U. Richmond, Richmond, Va., 1966. Bar: Va. 1966, D.C. 1972, U.S. Dist. Ct. (ea. dist.) Va. 1966, U.S. Dist. Ct. (we. dist.) Va. 1967, U.S. Ct. Appeals (4th cir.) 1967, U.S. Supreme Ct. 1969. Asst. atty. gen. Commonwealth of Va., Richmond, 1966-72, atty. gen., 1977-78; assoc. Colson & Shapiro, Washington, 1972-74; ptnr., govtl. law, spl. investigations Troutman, Sanders LLP, Richmond, 1978—, and mem., exec. com. Conard Mattox Dining. adj. prof. chair law U. Richmond Law Sch. Contbr. articles to profl. jours. Trustee Sci. Mus. Va. Fellow Am. Law Found., Va. Law Found. Office: Troutman Sanders LLP 1001 Haxall Point Richmond VA 23219 Office Phone: 804-697-1318. Office Fax: 804-698-5162. E-mail: tony.troy@troutmansanders.com.

**TROY, CAROL MARIE,** neuroscientist; b. N.Y.C., Sept. 18, 1955; d. Edward James Troy and Marie Patricia (Pennington) O'Donnell; m. Allan J. Brot, Oct. 13, 1995; children: Samantha Juliette, Esther Jordan. AB, Brandeis U., 1977; MS, NYU, 1980, PhD, NYU, 1984. Med. intern Bellevue Hosp./NYU Med. Ctr., N.Y.C., 1984-85; neurology resident Columbia U. Coll. of Physicians and Surgeons, N.Y.C., 1985-88, postdoctoral fellow neuropathology, 1988-89; instr. exptl. neuropathology Columbia U. Coll. Phys. and Surgeons, N.Y.C., 1989-92, from asst. to assoc. prof. pathology and neurology, 1992—; physician dept. neurology Memory Disorders Clinic Columbia Presbyn. Med. Ctr., N.Y.C., 1988—93. Contbr. articles to profl. jours., chpt. to book in field, 1990. NIH med. scientist tng. fellow, 1977-84, clin. neurosci. fellow NINDS, 1987-88, individual postdoctoral rsch. fellow NIH, 1988-89, clin. investigator award NIH, 1989-94, MDA grantee, 1995—. Mem. AAAS, Am. Soc. Cell Biology, N.Y. Acad. Scis. Avocations: cooking, reading, gardening. Office: Columbia Univ Coll Physicians & Surgeons 630 W 168th St New York NY 10032-3795

**TROY, FREDERIC ARTHUR, II,** medical biochemistry professor; b. Evanston, Ill., Feb. 16, 1937; s. Charles McGregor and Virginia Lane (Minto) T.; m. Linda Ann Price, Mar. 23, 1959; children: Karen M., Janet R. BS, Washington U., St. Louis, 1961; PhD, Purdue U., 1966; postdoctoral, Johns Hopkins U., Balt., 1968. Asst. prof. U. Calif. Sch. Medicine, Davis, 1968-74, assoc. prof., 1974-80, prof., 1980—2006, chmn., 1991-94, 2006—, prof. emeritus, 2006—; co-founder SianGen Therapeutics, Inc., Davis, Calif., 2003—, pres., 2003—, CEO, 2003—. Cons. NIH, Bethesda, Md., 1974—. NSF, Washington, 1975—, Damon Runyon Cancer Found., NYC, 1980-81, VA, Washington, 1984-88, US Army Breast Cancer Study Sect., 1999—; vis. prof. Karolinska Inst. Med. Sch., Stockholm, Sweden, 1976-77. Mem. editl. bd. Jour. Biol. Chem. (Glycobiol.), 1990—; contbr. articles to profl. jours. Recipient Research Cancer Devel. award Nat. Cancer Inst., 1975-80; Eleanor Roosevelt Internat. Cancer fellow Am. Cancer Soc., 1976-77. Mem. AAAS, Am. Soc. Biol. Chemistry and Molecular Biology, Am. Assn. Cancer Rsch., Am. Chem. Soc., Am. Soc. Microbiologists, Biochemistry Soc., Biophysics Soc., Am. Fedn. for Clin. Rsch., N.Y. Acad. Scis., Soc. for Glycobiol. (pres. 1991-92), Am. Med. and Grad. Sch. Dept. Biochem. (pres.-elect 1995—), Sigma Xi. Office: Sch Medicine Dept Biochem and Molecular Medicine U Calif Davis CA 95616 Business E-mail: fatroy@ucdavis.edu.

**TROY, NANCY J.,** art history educator; BA in Art, magna cum laude with honors, Wesleyan U., 1974; MA, Yale U., 1976, PhD, 1979. Gallery asst. Waddington Galleries, London, 1973; rsch. asst. Soc. Anonyme Collection, Yale U., New Haven, 1975, tchg. asst. history of art dept., 1975-76; asst. prof. dept. history of art Johns Hopkins U., Balt., 1979-83; asst. prof. dept. art history Northwestern U., Evanston, Ill., 1983-85, assoc. prof., 1985-92, prof., 1992-93, chmn. dept., 1990-92; vis. prof. UCLA, 1994; vis. prof. art history U. So. Calif., 1994-95, prof., 1995—, chmn. dept., 1997—. Scholar-in-residence Getty Rsch. Inst. for History Art and Humanities, L.A., 1993-96, organizer Work in Progress lecture series, 1993-98; series co-editor Histories, Culturs, Contexts, Reaktion Book, London; curatorial coord., spl. cons. to Ilya Bolotowsky Retrospective, Solomon R. Guggenheim Mus., N.Y.C., summers 1972-74; asst. to curator French paintings Nat. Gallery Art, Washington, summer 1975, bd. advisors Ctr. for Advanced Study in VisualArts, 1999-2002; guest curator Yale U. Art Gallery, 1979; mem. fine arts accessions com. and com. on collections Balt. Mus. Art, 1979-82; cons. De Stijl: 1917-1931, Visions of Utopia exhbn. Walker Art Ctr., Mpls., Washington, The Netherlands, 1982; cons. amplifying art program Art Inst. Chgo., 1984-85; mem. vis. com. Harvard U. Art Mus., Cambridge, Mass., 1992-98; lectr., chmn. moderator numerous symposia, 1980—; numerous invited lectures, 1975—, including U. Brighton, Eng., U. London, Middlexex U., London, Royal Coll. Art, London, U. Toronto, Mt. Holyoke Coll., Barnard Coll., Columbia U., Newcomb Coll., Tulane U., Los Angeles County Mus. Art, Art Inst. Chgo., Terra Mus. Art, Chgo., N.C. Mus. Art, Raleigh, McGill U., Montreal, Vassar Coll; mus. projects peer rev. panelist NEH, 1991; peer reviewer Woodrow Wilson Ctr., Washington, 1994, 96; external reviewer dept. art history U. Mich., 1987; bd. dirs. Nat. Com. for History Art, 1998—; peer reviewer for promotion and tenure Boston U., Lake Forest Coll., Middlesex U., Occidental Coll., U. Mo., Columbia U. Va., 1996-98. Author: The De Stijl Environment, 1983, Modernism and the Decorative Arts in France: Art Nouveau to Le Corbusier, 1991, (exhbn. catalog) Mondrian and Neo-Plasticism in America, 1979; editor-in-chief The Art Bull., 1994-97; editor: (with Eve Blau) Architecture and Cubism, 1997; series co-editor Histories, Cultures, Contexts; mem. editl. bd. Art Bull., 1993—, Grey Room, 1998—; contbr. articles and book revs. to profl. jours., including Decorative Arts Soc. Jour., Design Issues, Art Bull., October, Archithese, Arts mag., Portfolio, Design Book Rev., chpts. to books. Mem. Md. Coun. on Arts, 1981-82; trustee Wesleyan U., 1994-97. Recipient Disting. Alumna award Wesleyan U., 1991, postdoctoral tchg. award Lilly Endowment, 1985, Andrew W. Mellon professorship for advanced study in the visual arts Nat. Gallery Art (declined), 2000-02; Fulbright-Hays grantee, The Netherlands, 1977-78, travel grantee Kress Found., summer 1976, spring 1977, grantee Am. Coun. Learned Soc., summers 1981, 91, 98-99; grantee Graham Found. for Advanced Studies in Fine Arts, 1982, publ. grantee, 1989; grantee NEH, 1982-83, Am. Philos. Soc., 1986, Inst. for Advanced Study Sch. Hist. Studies, 1987, Getty Rsch. Inst. for History Art and Humanities, 1989-90, Zumberge Faculty Rsch. and Innovation Fund, U. So. Calif., 1998-99, Guggenheim Found., 1998-99; AT&T rsch. fellow Northwestern U., 1992-93. Mem. Coll. Art Assn. Am. (nominating com. 1990, bd. dirs. 1992-97, ann. meeting local host com. L.A. 1998-99), Soc. Archtl. Historian (sec. Chgo. chpt. 1984-85, peer reviewer Jour. 1996), Nat. Com. for the History of Art (bd. dirs.), Sterling and Francine Clark Art Inst. (mem. fellowship com.). Office: U So Calif Dept Art History University Park 104 Watt MC 0293 Los Angeles CA 90089-0001

**TROY, RICHARD HERSHEY,** lawyer; b. Boston, Sept. 24, 1937; married. AB, Georgetown U., 1959; postgrad., U. Munich, Fed. Republic Germany, 1959-60; LLB, Harvard U., 1963. Bar: Mass. 1963, N.Y. 1965, U.S. Dist. Ct. (so. and ea. dists.) N.Y. 1965, U.S. Ct. Appeals (2d cir.) 1968, U.S. Supreme Ct. 1969, Conn. 1985. Law clk. to presiding justice U.S. Dist. Ct. N.H., Concord, 1963-64; assoc. Shearman & Sterling, N.Y.C., 1964-73; asst. gen. counsel, asst. sec. Combustion Engring., Inc., Stamford, Conn., 1974-81, v.p., assoc. gen. counsel, 1982-85, v.p., dep. gen. counsel, 1985-90, Asea Brown Boveri, Inc., Stamford, 1990; v.p., assoc. gen. counsel UST, Inc., Greenwich, Conn., 1990-92; v.p. fin., law and adminstrn. Cell Pathways, Inc., Denver and Tucson, 1992-97, sr. v.p. corp. devel., gen. counsel and sec. Horsham, Pa., 1997—2003; v.p., gen. counsel, sec. Aerogel Composite, Inc., Bloomfield, Conn., 2006—. Speaker in field. Contbr. articles to profl. publs. Mem. Am. Soc. Corp. Secs. (bd. dirs. 1988-91, chmn. securities law com. 1984-89, chmn. proxy system com. 1990-93), Conn. Bar Assn. (mem. exec. com. corp. sect. 1986—), Westchester Fairfield Corp. Counsel Assn. (bd. dirs. 1978-83, pres. 1982). Office: 428 Laurel Rd New Canaan CT 06840 Office Phone: 203-594-9626. Business E-Mail: rhtroy@troylegal.com.

**TROY, ROBERT SWEENEY, SR.,** lawyer; b. Quincy, Mass., Aug. 13, 1949; s. Robert F. and Winifred (Sweeney) T.; m. Sabina Greene, Oct. 12, 1985; children: Robert Sweeney Jr., Michael Francis, Matthew Thomas. AB, Georgetown U., 1971; JD, Boston Coll., 1974. Bar: Mass. 1974, Fla. 1976, U.S. Dist. Ct. Mass. 1976, U.S. Ct. Appeals 1977, U.S. Ct. Mil. Appeals 1982, U.S. Supreme Ct. 1990. Asst. dist. atty. Cape and Islands, Mass., 1974-76; counsel Town of Bourne, Mass., 1978—. Counsel Town of Duxbury, Mass., 1986—, Barnstable County, 1992—. Mem. Mass. Bar Assn. (bd. dels. 1977-80), Barnstable County Bar Assn., Plymouth County Bar Assn., Town Counsel Assn. Home: 150 Nichols Rd Cohasset MA 02025 Office: 90 Route 6A Sandwich MA 02563-5301 Office Phone: 508-888-5700.

**TROYANSKAYA, OLGA,** biomedical researcher, computer scientist; BS in biology and computer sci. summa cum laude, Richmond U., 1999; PhD in biomedical informatics, Stanford U. Asst. prof. dept. computer sci. Princeton U. Contbr. articles to profl. jour. Named one of Top 100 Young Innovators, MIT Tech. Review, 2004; Predoctoral Fellow, Howard Hughes Med. Inst., 1999. Office: Princeton U Dept Computer Sci 35 Olden St Princeton NJ 08544 Business E-mail: ogt@cs.princeton.edu.

**TROYER, ALVAH FORREST,** agricultural products executive, horticulturist; b. LaFontaine, Ind., May 30, 1929; s. Alvah Forrest and Lottie (Wagoner) T.; m. Joyce Ann Wigner, Sept. 22, 1950; children: Anne, Barbara, Catherine, Daniel (dec.). BS, Purdue U., 1954; MS, U. Ill., 1956; PhD, U. Minn., 1964. Rsch. assoc. U. Ill., Urbana, 1955-56; rsch. fellow U. Minn., St. Paul, 1956-58; rsch. sta. mgr. Pioneer Hi-Bred Internat., Inc., Mankato, Minn., 1958-65, rsch. coord., 1965-77; dir. R & D, Pfizer Genetics, St. Louis, 1977-81, v.p. and dir. R & D, 1981-82; v.p. R&D, DEKALB Plant Genetics, 1982-93; cons. Hybrid Seed divsn. Cargill, Mpls., 1993-98; adj. prof. crop sci. dept. U. Ill., 1998—. Rschr. corn breeding, econ. botany, crop physiology, increasing genetic diversity, recent corn evolution. Contbr. articles to numerous publs.; developer of popular corn inbred lines and hybrids. Master sgt. U.S. Army, 1951-53, Korea. Recipient Nat. Coun. Comml. Plant Breeders Genetics and Plant Breeding award, 1992, Outstanding Achievement award U. Minn., 1998, nat. award for agrl. excellence Nat. Agrl. Mktg. Assn., 1999. Fellow AAAS, Am. Soc. Agronomy, Crop Sci. Soc. Am.; mem. Am. Genetic Assn., Genetic Soc. Am., N.Y. Acad. Scis., CAST, VFW, Masons, Sigma Xi, Gamma Sigma Delta (Award of Merit 1996), Alpha Zeta, Lambda Chi Alpha, Gamma Alpha. Methodist. Home: 611 Joanne Ln Dekalb IL 60115 Business E-Mail: atroyer@uiuc.edu.

**TROYER, DAN N.,** music educator; b. Winchester, Ind., Apr. 26, 1977; s. George Marian and Mary Ann Troyer; m. Heidi Lynn Wickard. BS in Music, BS in Edn., Ind. Wesleyan U., 2000, MEd, 2005. Interim band dir. Marion (Ind.) Sch. Corp., 2000; dir. bands Ea. Pulaski Sch. Corp., Winomas, Ind., 2000—03, Frankfort (Ind.) HS, 2003—. Recipient Crystal Apple award, 2002—03. Mem.: NEA, Music Educators Nat. Conf., Ind. Music Educators Assn., Ind. State Tchrs. Assn. Republican. Avocations: softball, music. Office Phone: 765-654-8545. Office Fax: 765-654-9224. E-mail: troyerd@frankfort.k12.in.us.

**TROYER, LEROY SETH,** architect; b. Middlebury, Ind., Nov. 23, 1937; s. Seth and Nancy (Miller) T.; m. Phyllis Eigsti, May 24, 1958; children: Terry, Ronald, Donald. BArch, U. Notre Dame, 1971. Founder, pres. LeRoy Troyer and Assocs., South Bend, Ind., 1971; chmn. Troyer Group, Inc. (formerly LeRoy Troyer and Assocs.), Mishawaka, Ind., 1988—; pres. Southfield, Inc.,

1988—. Pres. Lead Devel., Inc. Author numerous documents; contbr. numerous papers and articles to publs. Past pres., chair Environc Found. Internat., Inc.; bd. dirs. Habitat for Humanity Internat. Americus, Ga., 1987-93, global leadership coun., 2003—; bd. dirs. Coun. of Christian Colls. and Univs. 1991-96, Habitat for Humanity St. Joseph County, Ind., 1992-99, 2001-, Bethel Coll. 1988-97, 2001-, bd. chair 2005-, Evangelicals for Social Action, Wynnewood, Pa., 1997-2003, Mishawaka, CONNECT, HHS, South Bend, 1999-2003; bd. dirs., exec. com., trustee Fourth Freedom Forum Internat., 1996-2004; chmn. Miracle of Nazareth Internat. Found., 2000-03, trustee 2000-. Recipient numerous local, state and nat. awards and honors. Fellow AIA (practice mgmt. com., chmn. 1983-84), Ind. Soc. Archs., Mennonite Econ. Devel. Assn. Internat. (chmn. bd., 1987-91). Avocations: photography, travel, reading, art, woodworking. Home: 1442 Deerfield Ct South Bend IN 46614-6429 Office: The Troyer Group Inc 550 Union St Mishawaka IN 46544-2346 Office Phone: 574-259-9976. Business E-Mail: leroy@troyergroup.com.

**TROYER, THOMAS ALFRED,** lawyer; b. Omaha, Aug. 15, 1933; s. Robert Raymond and Dorothy (Darlow) T.; m. Sally Jean Brown, June 28, 1958; children: Kenneth D., Robert C., Virginia D., Thomas C. BA, Harvard U., 1955; JD, U. Mich., 1958. Bar: Colo. 1958, U.S. Ct. Appeals (D.C. cir.) 1967. Assoc. Holme, Roberts, Moore & Owen, Denver, 1958—61; USAF, Denver, 1961-62; trial atty. U.S. Dept. Justice, Washington, 1962-64; legal staff Asst. Sec. Treasury for Tax Policy, Washington, 1964-66; assoc. tax legis. counsel U.S. Dept. Treasury, Washington, 1966-67; mem. Caplin & Drysdale, Washington, 1967—. Pres. Stern Fund, N.Y.C., 1985—86; bd. dirs. Children's Def. Fund, Washington, 1977—, Animal Policy Ctr., Washington, 1988—2002; trustee Natural Resources Def. Coun., N.Y.C., 1977—, Carnegie Corp., N.Y.C., 1983—91, Cmty. Found. Nat. Capital Region, 1992—2000; chair Ctr. for Lobbying in Pub. Interest, Washington. Contbr. numerous articles to profl. jours. Bd. dirs. Common Cause, Washington, 1980-83; mem. Treasury Adv. Commn. on Pvt. Philanthropy and Pub. Needs, Washington, 1976-77; mem. adv. group to Commr. Internal Rev., Washington, 1978-80; mem. com. of visitors U. Mich. Law Sch., Ann Arbor, 1982—; mem. IRS Commr.'s Exempt Orgn. Adv. Group, Washington, 1987-90. Fellow Am. Bar Found., Am. Coll. Tax Counsel; mem. ABA (vice chmn. govt. rels. tax sect. 1989-91, commn. on homelessness and poverty 1992-94), Coun. for Excellence in Govt., Am. Law Inst. Democrat. Home: 5514 Cedar Pkwy Chevy Chase MD 20815-3444 Office: Caplin & Drysdale Chartered 1 Thomas Cir NW Ste 1100 Washington DC 20005-5894 Office Phone: 202-862-5025. Business E-Mail: tat@capdale.com.

**TROZZOLO, ANTHONY MARION,** chemistry professor; b. Chgo., Jan. 11, 1930; s. Pasquale and Francesca (Vercillo) T.; m. Doris C. Stoffregen, Oct. 8, 1955; children: Thomas, Susan, Patricia, Michael, Lisa, Laura. BS, Ill. Inst. Tech., 1950; MS, U. Chgo., 1957, PhD, 1960. Rsch. chemist Chgo. Midway Labs., 1952-53; assoc. chemist Armour Rsch. Found., Chgo., 1953-56; tech. staff Bell Labs., Murray Hill, NJ, 1959-75; Charles L. Huisking prof. chemistry U. Notre Dame, 1975-92, Charles L. Huisking prof. emeritus, 1992—; asst. dean U. Notre Dame Coll. Sci., 1993-98; P.C. Reilly lectr. U. Notre Dame, 1972, Hesburgh Alumni lectr., 1986, Disting. lectr. sci., 1986. Vis. prof. Columbia U., N.Y.C., 1971, U. Colo., 1981, Katholieke U. Leuven, Belgium, 1983, Max Planck Inst. für Strahlenchemie, Mülheim/Ruhr, Fed. Republic Germany, 1990; vis. lectr. Academia Sinica, 1984, 85; Phillips lectr. U. Okla., 1971; C.L. Brown lectr. Rutgers U., 1975; Sigma Xi lectr. Bowling Green U., 1976, Abbott Labs., 1978; M. Faraday lectr. No. Ill. U., 1976; F.O. Butler lectr. S.D. State U., 1978; Chevron lectr. U. Nev., Reno, 1983; J. Crano lectr. U. Akron, 2000; plenary lectr. various internat. confs.; founder, chmn. Gordon Conf. on Organic Photochemistry, 1964; trustee Gordon Rsch. Confs., 1988-92; cons. in field. Assoc. editor Jour. Am. Chem. Soc., 1975-76; editor Chem. Revs., 1977-84; editorial adv. bd. Accounts of Chem. Rsch., 1977-85; cons. editor Encyclopedia of Science and Technology, 1982-92; contbr. articles to profl. jours.; patentee in field. Fellow AEC, 1951, NSF, 1957-59; named Hon. Citizen of Castrolibero, Italy, 1997; recipient Pietro Bucci prize U. Calabria/Italian Chem. Soc., 1997. Fellow: AAAS (life), Inter-Am. Photochem. Soc., N.Y. Acad. Scis. (chmn. chem. scis. sect. 1969—70, Halpern award in photochemistry 1980), Am. Inst. Chemists (Student award 1950); mem.: Am. Chem. Soc. (lectr., Tex. sect. 1975, Disting. Svc. award St. Joseph Valley sect. 1979, Coronado lectr. 1980, Pacific Coast lectr. 1981, Coronado lectr. 1993, N.Y. State lectr. 1993, Hoosier lectr. 1995, Ozark lectr. 1995, Coronado lectr. 1998, Osage lectr. 1998, Rocky Mountain lectr. 1996, 2002), Sigma Xi. Roman Catholic. Home: 53419 Hansel Ln South Bend IN 46637-5248 Office: U Notre Dame Dept Chemistry-Biochemistry Notre Dame IN 46556-5670 Office Phone: 574-631-5768. Business E-Mail: trozzolo.4@nd.edu.

**TRPIS, MILAN,** vector biologist, educator; b. Mojsova Lucka, Slovakia, Dec. 20, 1930; came to U.S., 1971, naturalized, 1977; s. Gaspar and Anna (Sevcikova) T.; m. Ludmila Tonkovic, Dec. 15, 1956; children: Martin, Peter, Katarina. MS, Comenius U., Bratislava, 1956; PhD, Charles U., Prague, 1960. Research asst. Slovak Acad. Sci., Bratislava, 1953-56, sci. asst., 1956-60, scientist, 1960-62, inst. scientist, 1962-69; ecologist-entomologist East Africa-Aedes Rsch. Unit WHO, Dar es Salaam, Tanzania, 1969-71; asst. faculty fellow dept. biology U. Notre Dame, 1971-73, visit. faculty fellow, 1973-74; assoc. prof. med. entomology Johns Hopkins U. Sch. Hygiene and Pub. Health, 1974-78, prof., 1978—, dir. labs. med. entomology, rsch. assoc. U. Ill., Urbana, 1966-67, Coun. Dept. Agr., Lethbridge, Alta., 1967-68; dir. Biol. Rsch. Inst. Am., 1971-79; external dir. rsch. Liberian Inst. Biomed. Rsch., 1981-89; dir. AID project on transmission of river blindness in areas of Liberia, Sierra Leone, and Cote d'Ivoire; dir. WHO rsch. grant; tech. adv. com. AID Vector Biology and Control Project, 1986-91; dir. Johns Hopkins U./Fed. U. Tech. Akure Onchocerciasis Project in Nigeria, 1991-94, John Hopkins U./Orgn. Coordination et de Cooperation pour la Lutte les Grandes Endemies-Pierre Richet Inst. Onchocerciasis Project, Bouaké, Ivory Coast, 1993-96; dir. Johns Hopkins U./Pierre Richet Inst./ORSTOM onchocerciasis project in Ivory Coast, 1993-96; prof.,advisor doctoral students, USA, Can., Africa, Asia, Cen. Am., 1979—. Editor: Jour. Biologia, 1956-71, Jour. Entomol. Problems, 1956-72; zool. sect.: Jour. Biol. Works, 1960-71; contbr. articles to profl. jours. Dir. WHO project on prophylactic drugs for river blindness, Liberia, 1985-87. Recipient Slovak Acad. Sci., 1st prize for research project. Mem. AAUP, AAAS, Am. Inst. Biol. Soci., Am. Mosquito Control Assn., Am. Soc. Parasitologists, Helminthol. Soc. Washington, Am. Soc. Tropical Medicine and Hygiene, Entomol. Soc. Am., Am. Genetic Assn., Soc. of Vector Ecology, N.Y. Acad. Scis., Johns Hopkins U. Tropical Medicine Club, Smithsonian Assocs., Royal Soc. Tropical Medicine and Hygiene, Royal Entomol. Soc. of London, Sigma Xi, Delta Omega (Alpha chpt.). Home: 1504 Ivy Hill Rd Cockeysville MD 21030-1418 Office: Johns Hopkins U 615 N Wolfe St Baltimore MD 21205-2103 Office Phone: 410-955-3475. E-mail: mtrpis@jhsph.edu.

**TRUAX, DENNIS DALE,** civil engineer, educator, consultant; b. Hagerstown, Md., July 25, 1953; s. Bernard James and Dorothy Hilda Truax; m. Jeanie Ann Knable, Aug. 20, 1977. BSCE, Va. Poly. Inst. and State U., 1976; MS, Miss. State U., 1978, PhD, 1986. Registered profl. engr., Miss.; diplomate Environ. Engring. Asst. dep. constrn. mgr. Fairfax County, Va., 1972-74; design engr. Washington County, Md., 1976; instr. Miss. State U., Starkville, 1980-86, asst. prof. civil and environ. engring., 1986-91, assoc. prof., 1991-96, prof., 1996—2006, James T. White chair, dept. head, prof., 2006—, Bagley Coll. Engring. fellow, 2006—. Prin. corp. pres. ASD, LLC, 1997-2000; prin., v.p. engring. ATi, Inc., 2000—; environ. engring. cons. Mem. editl. bd. ASCE/NSPE Profl. Issues Jour., 1999—. Lay leader Aldersgate United Meth. Ch., Starkville, 1983-2001; chmn. pastor/parish rels., 1985-86, chmn. coun. on ministries, 1986-90, chmn. adminstrv. bd., 1990-92, chmn. fin. com. 1992-94, 2001-2003, chmn. bd. trustees, 1996-97; adviser Triangle Fraternity, Starkville, Alumni Bd. Dirs. treas., 1998-99; cert. Miss. Conf. United Meth. Ch., also vice chmn. com. on higher edn.; active Starkville dist. lay coun. Miss. State Herrin-Hess prof., 1993-94, 94-95, 95-96. Recipient Golden Key Outstanding Faculty award Golden Key Nat.

Honor Soc., 1994, Miss. Outstanding Civil Engr. of Yr., ASCE Miss. sect., 1995; named Outstanding Young Man Am., U.S. Jaycees, 1983. Fellow ASCE (chair student svcs. com. 1995-96, vice chair 1996-97, adv. Miss. State student chpt. 1981—, chair career guidance com. 1991-92, sec. 1990-91, Miss. sect. pres. 1991-92, chmn. student svc. com. 1995-96, scholarship com. 1998—, chair scholarship com. 2000-01, No. Miss. br. pres. 2000-01, 2014 coun. dir. 2001-04, fin. com., com. on diversity and women in civil engring., Outstanding Faculty Advisor 2001-03, 05-06); mem. NSPE, Am. Water Works Assn. (Ala.-Miss. chpt. scholarship bd. dirs. 1994—, bd. sec.-treas. 1998—), Miss. Engring. Soc. (pres., pres.-elect region 3 v.p., bd. dirs., Tombigbee chpt. pres., chpt. pres.-elect, Engring. educator 1995, Educator of the Yr. award 1995), Water Environ. Fedn. (rsch. com.), Sigma Xi (sec., pres.-elect, pres. Miss. State chpt.), Tau Beta Pi, Chi Epsilon. Democrat. Home: 1054 Southgate Dr Starkville MS 39759-8810 Office: Miss State Univ PO Box 9546 Mississippi State MS 39762-9546 Office Phone: 662-325-7187. Personal E-mail: djcktruax@aol.com, dtruax@aeration101.com. Business E-Mail: truax@ciee.msstate.edu.

**TRUBEE, R. ELDON,** minister, writer; b. Wauseon, Ohio, Mar. 16, 1944; s. Franklin L. and Viola Harbaugh Trubee; m. Bonnie Mae Cox, June 26, 1971; children: Kenton James, Heather Sue. BA, Coll. of Wooster, Ohio, 1966; MDiv, Pitts. Theol. Seminary, 1969, DDiv, 1994. Ordained pastor Presbyn. Ch., 1969. Pastor First Presbyn. Ch., Hanoverton, Ohio, 1969—75; assoc. pastor John Knox Presbyn. Ch., Canton, Ohio, 1975—77; pastor Columbian-Union Presbyn. Ch., Columbia, Ky., 1977—80; staff mem. Louisville Union Presbyn., 1977—80; pastor Covington (Ohio) Presbyn. Ch., 1980—84, First Presbyn. Ch., Millersburg, Ohio, 1984—, Clark (Ohio) Cmty. Presbyn. Ch., 1984—. Chaplain Jackson Twp. Fire Dept., Canton, Ohio, 1975—78; mem. med. ethics bd. Pomerene Hosp., Millersburg, Ohio, 1999—, Castle Nursing Home, Millersburg, Ohio, 2003—. Author: (book) Like As A Fire, 1986, (newspaper column) Farm & Dairy, 1987—. Mem. Habitat for Humanity, Homes County, Ohio, 1993—, Holmes County Vol. Guardianship Bd., Millersburg, Ohio, 2004—, Holmes Dem. Party, Millersburg, Ohio, 2000—; chaplain Millersburg (Ohio) Police Aux., 1991—; co-founder Assn. of Town and Rural Congregations of the Synod of the Convenant Presbyn. Ch. Mem.: MENSA, Honorable Order of Ky. Colonels, Royal Arch, Scottish Rite, Freemason, Rotary Internat. (pres. 1992). Democrat. Presbyterian. Avocations: old cars, old radio programs, golf, history. Home: 291 N Monroe St Millersburg OH 44654 Office: First Presbyn Ch 90 S Clay St Millersburg OH 44654 Personal E-mail: mbgpres@valkyrie.net.

**TRUBETSKOY, OLGA V.,** medical researcher, educator; b. Egorievsk, Russia, Mar. 4, 1958; d. Vasily T. Merzlikin and Volna F. Kruglova; m. Vladimir S. Trubetskoy, Feb. 9, 1984; children: Sergey V., Vasily V., Ivan V. MSc, Moscow State U., 1975—80. Rsch. scientist Nat. Ctr. of Cardiology, Moscow, 1980—90, OsteoArthritis Sciences, Cambridge, Mass., 1994—95; assoc. scientist BioTransplant, Charlestown, Mass., 1996—97; sr. scientist Panvera Corp., Madison, Wis., 1997—2004; rsch. fellow Quintessence Biosci., Madison, 2004—. Faculty and a mem. of planning com. for intro. into drug metabolism for pharmaceutiacl scientists UW, Dept of Pharmacy, Madison, Wis. Mem.: Am. Assn. Pharm. Scientists, Internat. Soc. for Study Xenobiotics (ISSX), Chaos and Complexity Seminar. Orthodox Christian. Achievements include patents in field; research in human drug metabolism, cardiovascular diseases and arthritis. Office: Quintessence Biocis 505 S Rosa Rd Madison WI 53719 Office Phone: 608-441-2953. Business E-Mail: olgat@quintbio.com.

**TRUBEY, LILLIAN PRISCILLA,** retired secondary school educator; b. Hastings, Mich., Jan. 18, 1917; d. Leon George and Ethel Ada (Harlem) Tolhurst; m. Stanley Roger Trubey, Aug. 12, 1940 (dec. May 1965); children: Roger, Cornelia. BA, U. Mich., 1938, MA, 1942; MEd, Fla. Atlantic Univ., 1967; PhD, Fla. State U., 1972. Tchr. River Rouge (Mich.) H.S., 1938-41, South Broward H.S., Hollywood, Fla., 1951-69; tchr., head Eng. dept. Hollywood Hills H.S., 1969-84; tax preparer H&R Block, Ft. Lauderdale, 1985-92. Tchr. Fla. State U., Tallahassee, 1970-71, Miami Dade Jr. Coll., Miami, Fla. 1971-72. Sec. Women's Rep. Club, Broward Co., 1947-49, v.p., 1950-51; sec. Victoria Park Civic Assn., Ft. Lauderdale, 1975-78; vol. VITA, 1993-2005; pres. Fla. Speech Assn., 1968-69. Mem. Geneal. Soc. Broward County (sec. 1991-93, pres. 1993-95, 99, editor IMPRINTS 1993-2004), Ret. Educators Broward County (Pioneer of Broward County, 2005), Ft. Lauderdale Hist. Assn, Stranahan House, Ft. Lauderdale Bridge Club (dir. 1995, 97-99), Guild Miniature Artisans, Delta Kappa Gamma. Episcopalian. Avocations: duplicate bridge, miniatures, genealogy. Home: 1415 NE 4th Pl Fort Lauderdale FL 33301-1371

**TRUBO, RICHARD M.,** writer; b. LA, Calif., Apr. 2, 1946; s. William Trubo, Ida Trubo; m. Donna R. Grodin; children: Melissa, Michael. BA, UCLA, 1967, MS, 1968. Co-host ("Confrontation"), writer KOST-FM, LA, 1968—71; bur. chief, contbg. editor Med. World News HEI Pub. / Miller Freeman Pub., San Francisco, 1983—88, Houston; med. editor, writer, cons. Feeling Fine Co., LA, 1989—2000. Cons. documentary film Am. Acad. of Pediat., 2002—03. Author: (book) An Act of Mercy, 1975, From Victim to Victor, 1987, The H.A.R.T. Program, 1992, Flying Through Hollywood by the Seat of My Pants, 1992, The Mental Edge, 1999, Tapping the Healer Within, 2001, Courage, 2001, Stairway to Heaven, 2002, 12 addtional books; prodr.: (Website) WebMD, 2002—05; (films) Children of the State, 1977; contbr. articles to profl. jours. Recipient Journalism award of Excellence, Am. Acad. Facial Plastic and Reconstructive Surgery, 1990, Blakeslee award, Am. Heart Assn., 1991. Mem.: Am. Soc. Journalists & Authors, Nat. Assn. Med. Communicators, Am. Med. Writers Assn., Nat. Assn. Sci. Writers.

**TRUBY, BETSY KIRBY,** artist, illustrator, photographer; b. Winchester, Va., Nov. 8, 1926; d. Thomas Gomery and Nellie Gray Kirby; m. Frank Keeler Truby, Sept. 4, 1948; children: Thomas Lee, Scott R., Susan Alida. Student, Hiram Coll., 1946—48, Cleve. Sch. Art, 1949, N.Mex. Tech., 1951—54, U. N.Mex., 1960. Asst. dir. Yucca Art Gallery, Old Town Albuquerque, 1970—71. Exhibitions include N.Mex. State Mus., 1964—68, Nat. Art Show, Lawton, Okla., 1974, commd. by Congressman Albert G Simms, 1964, Christmas card, Easter Seal Soc., 1969, Cystic Fibrosis Found., N.Mex., 1976—77, one-woman shows include Hiram Coll., 1987, exhibitions include Bardean Gallery, N.Mex., 2004 (2d pl., 2004), PBS TV show, The Creative Process, 1983. Mem.: Pastel Soc. N.Mex. (charter mem.), Nat. League Am. Pen Women (v.p. Yucca br. 1978—79, photographer Yucca br. 1992—2005, 1st pl. painting 1974, Best of Show 2003, 1st pl. 2003, 2d pl. in pastel State Show, Socorro, N.Mex. 2005), Yucca Art Gallery (charter mem.). Presbyterian. Avocations: boating, swimming. Home: 6609 Loftus Ave NE Albuquerque NM 87109 Office Phone: 505-884-8459.

**TRUCANO, MICHAEL,** lawyer; b. Washington, May 28, 1945; s. Peter Joseph and Fern Margaret (Bauer) T.; m. Doreen E. Struck, 1969; children: Michael, David. BA, Carleton Coll., 1967; JD, NYU, 1970. Assoc. Dorsey & Whitney, Mpls., 1970-75, ptnr., 1976—2004, head office, 2000—03, of counsel, 2005—. Office: Dorsey & Whitney LLP Ste 1500 50 S 6th St Minneapolis MN 55402-1498 Office Phone: 612-340-2673. Business E-Mail: trucano.mike@dorsey.com.

**TRUCKENBRODT, YOLANDA BERNABE,** retired air force officer, consultant; b. Manila, June 17, 1952; d. Nestor Leynes and Zenaida Bernabe Javier; m. Edmund Phillip Truckenbrodt, July 27, 1972. BA, Far Ea. U., Manila, 1971; AAS, C.C. of Air Force, 1979; MBA, Angelo State U., 1980; MPA, U. West Fla., 1987; D of Pub. Adminstrn., Nova Southeastern U., 2000; diploma, Air Command and Staff Coll., 1995. Cert. Dept. of Def.'s Acquisition Profl. in Program Mgmt., USAF Software Quality Assurance. Enlisted USAF, 1974, advanced through grades to maj., 1992, ret., 1998; program mgr. KC-135 Reengine Dep. for Airlift and Trainer Sys., Wright-Patterson AFB, Ohio, 1980—84; mgr. electronic warfare program Tactical Sys. Divsn., Eglin AFB, Fla., 1985—89; program mgr. Airborne Warning and Control Sys. Elec. Sys. Ctr., Hanscom AFB, Mass., 1989—92; program analyst ballistic missile def. hdqs. Air Force Materiel Command, Wright-Patterson AFB, 1992—94; congl. liaison staff officer Plans and Programs Divsn., Wright-Patterson AFB,

1995—98. Flight comdr. detachment 847 Res. Officers Tng. Corps, San Angelo, Tex., 1978—80; chairperson Asian-Am. Pacific Islander Heritage Com., Eglin AFB, 1986—87; officer-in-charge Air Force Assn. Nat. Acquisition Symposium, Wright-Patterson AFB, 1993—94; student-in-residence Def. Sys. Mgmt. Coll., Ft. Belvoir, Va., 1994; staff officer Directorate of Plans and Programs, Wright-Patterson AFB, 1995—98; guest spkr. Nat. Bus. and Profl. Assn., San Angelo, 1993. Contbr. articles to profl. jours. Pres. Filipino-Am. Assn., Fort Walton Beach, Fla., 1987; vol. Air Force Mus., Dayton, Ohio, 1995—96; vol. reading tutor Ohio Reads Program, 2002—; vol. Nightingale Ho., Wright-Patterson AFB, 1996—98; vol. income tax preparer Ret. Officers Assn., Wright-Patterson AFB, 1999—; vol. social worker United Way, Dayton, 1982—84; bd. dirs. Filipino-Am. Assn., Ft. Walton Beach, Fla., 1987, Filipino-Am. Coun. N.W. Fla. Nominee Lt. Robert Sullivan Meml. award, Eglin AFB, 1985; named Airman of the Quarter, Air Weather Svc. Comm. Squadron, 1975, Career Woman of Yr., Gayfers Career Club of Okaloosa County, Fla., 1987, Jr. Officer of the Quarter, Airlift and Trainer Sys., Wright-Patterson AFB, 1983, Airborne Warning and Control Systems, Hanscom AFB, 1991, winner, State of Ohio Summer Biathlon Series Championship Cup, 2002, 2d Pl. Overall winner for half-marathon, 4th Internat. Marathon on Great Wall, China, 1999, winner numerous race awards in track and field and Summer Biathlons; named one of Outstanding Young Women of Am., 1983, 20 Outstanding Filipino-Ams. in U.S. and Can., 2004; recipient Appreciation and Recognition award, Dyess AFB Human Rels. Coun., 1976, 1977, Air Force Res. Tng. Corps (ROTC) Leadership award, 1979, Arnold Air Soc. Outstanding Pledge award, 1979, Drill Commandant of Yr. award, 1978; Robert G. Carr scholar, Detachment 847 ROTC, Angelo State U., 1978, 1980. Mem. Women in Mil. Svc. Am. Meml. (charter), Air Force Women Officers Assoc., Air Force Meml. Found. (charter), Angelo State U. Alumni Assn. (Disting. ROTC Alumnae of Yr. 2002), Air Force Meml. Found. (charter), Ohio River Rd. Runners Club, Sigma Beta Delta. Avocations: travel, arts and music, summer biathlons, marathons, photography.

**TRUCKER, ALBERT,** retired plastic surgeon; b. St. Joseph, Mich., Aug. 5, 1924; s. Albert and Louise (Goebel) T. BA, Johns Hopkins U., 1951; MD, U. Md., 1956. Diplomate Am. Bd. Plastic Surgery. Intern in gen. surgery U. Calif., San Francisco, 1956-59; resident in plastic surgery Mayo Clinic, Rochester, Minn., 1959-62; pvt. practice Santa Rosa, Calif., 1962—2004; ret., 2004. Mem. Am. Soc. Plastic Surgery, Calif. Soc. Plastic Surgery. Mailing: PO Box 5799 Santa Rosa CA 95402-5799

**TRUCKSIS, THERESA A.,** retired library director; b. Hubbard, Ohio, Sept. 1, 1924; d. Peter and Carmella (DiSilverio) Pagliasotti; m. Robert C. Trucksis, May 29, 1948 (dec. May 1980); children: M. Laura, Anne, Michele, Patricia, David, Robert, Claire, Peter; m. Philip P. Hickey, Oct. 19, 1985 (dec. May 1993). BS in Edn., Youngstown Coll., 1945; postgrad., Youngstown State U., 1968-71; MLS, Kent State U., 1972. Psychometrist Youngstown (Ohio) Coll., 1946-49; instr. ltd. svc. Youngstown State U., 1968-71; libr. Pub. Libr. Youngstown & Mahoning County, Youngstown, 1972-73, asst. dept. head, 1973-74, asst. dir., 1985-89, dir., 1989-97, NOLA Regional Libr. System, Youngstown, 1974-85. Contbr. articles to profl. jours. Mem. bd. Hubbard Sch. Dist., 1980-85. Mem. ALA, Ohio Libr. Assn. (bd. dirs. 1979-81), Pub. Libr. Assn. Address: 133 Viola Ave Hubbard OH 44425-2062

**TRUDEAU, GARRETSON BEEKMAN (GARRY TRUDEAU),** cartoonist; b. N.Y.C., July 21, 1948; m. Jane Pauley, June 14, 1980; children: Ross and Rachel (twins), Thomas. BA, Yale U., 1970, MFA, 1973, DHL, 1976. Syndicated cartoonist, writer. Creator: comic strip Doonesbury; syndicated nationwide comic strip; author: Still a Few Bugs in the System, 1972, The President is a Lot Smarter Than You Think, 1973, But This War Had Such Promise, 1973, Call Me When You Find America, 1973, Guilty, Guilty, Guilty, 1974, Joanie, 1974, The Doonesbury Chronicles, 1975, What Do We Have for the Witnesses, Johnnie?, 1975, Dare to be Great, Ms. Caucus, 1975, Wouldn't a Gremlin Have Been More Sensible?, 1975, We'll Take it From Here, Sarge, 1975, Speaking of Inalienable Rights, Amy..., 1976, You're Never Too Old for Nuts and Berries, 1976, An Especially Tricky People, 1977, As the Kid Goes For Broke, 1977, Stalking the Perfect Tan, 1978, Any Grooming Hints for Your Fans, Rollie?, 1978, Doonesbury's Greatest Hits, 1978, But The Pension Fund was Just Sitting There, 1979, We're Not Out of the Woods Yet, 1979, A Tad Overweight, but Violet Eyes to Die For, 1980, And That's My Final Offer!, 1980, The People's Doonesbury, 1981, He's Never Heard of You, Either, 1981, In Search of Reagan's Brain, 1981, Ask for May, Settle for June, 1982, Unfortunately, She Was Also Wired for Sound, 1982, Adjectives Will Cost You Extra, 1982, Gotta Run, My Government is Collapsing, 1982, The Wreck of the Rusty Nail, 1983, You Give Great Meeting, Sid, 1983, Guess Who Fish Face, 1983, It's Supposed to be Yellow Pinhead: Selected Cartoons From Ask For May, Settle For June, Vol. I, 1983, Do All Birders Have Bedrooms, 1983, Farewell to Arms, 1984, Doonesbury Dossier: The Reagan Years, 1984, Doonesbury: A Musical Comedy, 1984, Check Your Egos at the Door, 1985, That's Doctor Sinatra, You Little Bimbo, 1986, Death of a Party Animal, 1986, Doonesbury Deluxe: Selected Glances Askance, 1987, Downtown Doonesbury, 1987, Calling Dr. Whoopee, 1987, The Doonesbury Desk Diary 1988, 1987, Talking Bout My G-G-Generation, 1988, We're Eating More Beets, 1988, Read My Lips, Make My Day, Eat Quiche & Die! A Doonesbury Collection, 1989, Small Collection, 1989, The Doonesbury Stamp Album, 1990, 1990, Recycled Doonesbury: Second Thoughts on a Gilded Age, 1990, You're Smokin' Now, Mr. Butts! A Doonesbury Book, 1990, Welcome to Club Scud: A Doonesbury Book, 1991, Action Figure: The Life and Times of Doonesbury's Uncle Duke, 1992, The Portable Doonesbury, 1993, In Search of Cigarette Holder Man: A Doonesbury Book, 1994, Doonesbury Nation, 1995, Flashbacks: Twenty-five Years of Doonesbury, 1995, The Bundled Doonesbury: A Pre-Millennial Anthology, 1998, Peace Out, Dawg! Tales from Ground Zero, 2002, Got War?, 2003, The Long Road Home: One Step at a Time, 2005; co-author: Tales From the Margaret Mead Taproom, 1979; plays include: Doonesbury, 1983, Rapmaster Ronnie, A Partisan Review (with Elizabeth Swados), 1984 Pulitzer Prize for Editorial Cartooning, 1975, Commander's Award for Pub. Svc., US Dept. Army, 2006.

**TRUDEL, MARC J.,** botanist, educator; PhD, Cornell U. Prof. plant physiology and horticulture Laval U., 1969—2003, prof. emeritus, 2005—; former dean sch. agrl. and food scis., 1983-91, former dir. gen. continuing edn., 1992-97, v.p. devel., 1997—2003. Office: 19 Rue de Liege Saint Jean Sur Richelieu PQ Canada J3B 8N4 E-mail: marc.trudel@plg.ulaval.ca.

**TRUDNAK, STEPHEN JOSEPH,** landscape architect; b. Nanticoke, Pa., Feb. 25, 1947; s. Stephen Adam and Marcella (Levulis) T.; m. Arden Batchelder Well, Sept. 6, 1980. BS in Landscape Arch., Pa. State U., 1970. Jr. landscape arch. Klingpartnership, Phila., 1970-72; mem. landscape arch. firm Keith French Assocs., Washington, 1972-73; head dept. landscape arch. Linganore Ctr. Design, Frederick, Md., 1973-74, Toups and Loiederman, Rockville, Md., 1974-76; project landscape arch. Kaiser Transit Group, So. Calif. Rapid Transit Dist.; Dade County Transit Improvement Program, Metro Rail Transit Cons.; v.p. Harry Weese & Assocs., Chgo., Miami, Fla., 1976-84; v.p. landscape arch. Canin Assocs., Orlando, Fla., 1984-87; dir. planning and design Bonita Bay Properties, Inc., Bonita Springs, Fla., 1987-91; prin. Stephen J. Trudnak, P.A. Landscape Arch. and Land Planning, 1991—. Bd. dirs., v.p. Koreshan State Hist. Site, 1991; mem. "not for profit" com. Bonita Springs Cmty. Redevel. Agy., 1994—97; v.p. Bonita Springs Mainstreet Program, 1996, 2000, pres., 1997—98; bd. dirs. Bonita Springs YMCA, 1999—, mem. exec. com., 2000—03, chair facilities design task force, 2000—04; del. for Congressman Porter Goss Congl. Small Bus. Summit, 1998, 2000; del. representing Fla. state rep. Carol Green Fla. Small Bus. Summit, 1999. Recipient Alumni Achievement award, Pa. State U., Dept. Landscape Architecture, 2003. Fellow Am. Soc. Landscape Archs. (pres. Fla. chpt. 1983, chpt. adv. bd. 1984-85, elections task force 1986, publs. task force 1987, trustee 1987-89, membership task force, chmn. 1989-91, nat. v.p. chpt. and mem. svcs. 1992-94, non-dues revenue task force 1994-95, ASLA On-Line com. 1997-2005, chair 1999, specifications task force 1998-99), Nat. Xeriscape Coun. (Fla. steering com.), Nat. Speleol. Soc. SCARAB; mem.

Bonita Springs C. of C. (chair beautification com. 1991-92, 94-95, chair awards task force 2000, bd. dirs. 1995-2000, v.p. edn. divsn. 1996-98, vice chmn. cmty. devel. divsn. 1998-99, chmn. tech. com. 2003-04, Affiliate of Yr. 1997, Citizen of Yr. 1999, Charter Class Leadership Bonita Grad. 2000). Office: 4259 Bonita Beach Rd Bonita Springs FL 34134 Office Phone: 239-495-6464. E-mail: strudnak@trudnak.com.

**TRUE, JEAN DURLAND,** entrepreneur, oil industry executive, gas industry executive; b. Nov. 27, 1915; d. Clyde Earl and Harriet Louise (Brayton) Durland; m. Henry Alfonso True Jr., Mar. 20, 1938; children: Tamma Jean (Mrs. Donald G. Hatten), Henry Alfonso III, Diemer Durland, David Lanmon. Student, Mont. State U., 1935-36. Ptnr. True Drilling Co., Casper, Wyo., 1951—94, True Oil Co., Casper, 1951-94, Eighty-Eight Oil LLC, 1955-94, True Geothermal Energy Co., 1980—, True Ranches, 1981-94. Officer, dir. White Stallion Ranch, Inc., Tucson, Smokey Oil Co., Casper. Mem. steering com. YMCA, Casper, 1954-55, bd. dirs., 1956-68; mem. bd. dirs. Gottsche Rehab. Ctr., Thermopolis, Wyo., 1966-93, mem. exec. bd., 1966-93, v.p., 1983-90; mem. adv. bd. for adult edn. U. Wyo., 1966-68; mem. Ft. Casper Commn., Casper, 1973-79; bd. dirs. Mus. of Rockies, Bozeman, Mont., 1983-87, mem. Nat. Adv. Bd., 1997-2000; bd. dirs. Nicolaysen Art Mus., 1988-93, Nat. Cowboy and We. Heritage Mus., 1997-2002, dir. emeritus, 2002--; mem. Nat. Fedn. Rep. Women's Clubs; dep. Rep. Nat. Conv., 1972; trustee Trooper Found., 1995—. Mem.: Casper Area C. of C., Casper Country Club, Petroleum Club, Alpha Gamma Delta. Episcopalian. Office: PO Box 2360 Casper WY 82602-2360

**TRUE, MICHELLE AILENE,** editor, writer; Author: (poetry) True Reflections, 2004, True Emotions, 2005, True Identities, 2006, (non-fiction) The Poet's Manual: How to Go From Aspiring Writer to Published Author and Beyond, 2006; editor (contbr.): An Anthology of Poetry by Poetic License Writers Group, 2005, In Katrina's Wake, An Anthology of Inspirational Poetry, 2005; contbr. Website editor Congregation Beth Judea, Long Grove, Ill., 1999—2006. Recipient Vol. Appreciation Cert., Indian Trails Pub. Libr. Dist., 2004—05. Mem.: Chgo. Writers Assn., Ill. State Poetry Soc., Soc. Midwest Authors. Democrat. Jewish. Office: Michelle Ailene True Writer PO Box 7387 Buffalo Grove IL 60089-7387

**TRUE, RAYMOND STEPHEN,** editor, writer; b. Lowell, Mass., June 29, 1934; s. Sylvester Raymond and Madeline Rose (Farrell) T.; m. Doreen Therese Jambrosek. BA, U. Chgo., 1961, MBA, 1968, postgrad., 1968—69. Commd. 2nd lt. USAF, 1953, advanced through grades to col., 1980; master navigator USAFR, Chgo., 1957—77, dir. ops. Milw., 1977—80, base civil engr., 1980—87, chief planning analyst, 1987—89; regional cons. U.S. Bur. Census, 1970—71; owner Classic Comics Libr., 1990—. Fire marshall Milwaukee County, 1980-87, chmn. membership Res. Officers Assn., Wash. 1975-78. Editor Classics Newsletter, 1971-75; pub. The Platform Rep. Newsmag., 2004—. Precinct committeeman, Libertyville, Ill., 2000—; pres. ROA chpt. 61, 2000-02; chmn. Rep. Assembly Lake County, 2001-; mem. steering com. Ill. Ctr. Rights Coalition, 2004-05; mem. Ill. Rep. State Platform Com., 2004. Mem. Air Force Assn., Grad. Sch. Bus. Exec. Coun. U. Chgo. Roman Catholic. Avocations: stamp collecting/philately, antique books, videophile. Address: 839 Terre Dr Libertyville IL 60048-1649 Office Phone: 847-367-5231. E-mail: raymon8844@aol.com.

**TRUE, ROY JOE,** lawyer; b. Shreveport, La., Feb. 20, 1938; s. Collins B. and Lula Mae (Cady) T.; m. Patsy Jean Hudsmith, Aug. 29, 1959; children: Andrea Alane, Alyssa Anne, Ashley Alisbeth. Student, Centenary Coll., 1957; BS, Tex. Christian U., 1961; LLB, So. Meth. U., 1963, postgrad., 1968—69. Bar: Tex. 1963. Pvt. practice, Dallas, 1963—; pres. Invesco Internat. Corp., 1969-70. True & Shackelford and predecessors, 1975—2002; of counsel Shackelford, Melton & McKinley, 2002—. Bus. adviser, counselor Mickey Mantle, 1969-95; dir. The Mickey Mantle Found., 1995-98. Mem. editl. bd. Southwestern Law Jour., 1962-63. With AUS, 1956. Mem. ABA, Dallas Bar Assn., Tex. Assn. Bank Counsel, Phi Alpha Delta. Home: 5837 St Marks Circle Dallas TX 75230 Office: 3333 Lee Pkwy 10th Fl Dallas TX 75219 Office Phone: 214-780-1400. Business E-Mail: rtrue@shacklaw.net.

**TRUE, WILLIAM L. (BILL TRUE),** retired real estate company executive; b. Apr. 1954; s. Cecil True. m. Ruth True. Chmn., CEO Gull Industries, Inc., Seattle. Co-founder Western Bridge Gallery, Seattle; mem. adv. bd. Seattle Arts & Lectures; bd. dirs. Pike Place Market Found., Seattle; mem. Betty Bowen com. Seattle Art Mus., 2004. Named one of Top 200 Collectors, ARTnews mag., 2003—06. Avocation: Collector of Contemporary art. Home: 832 37th Ave E Seattle WA 98112-4326

**TRUEB, MARTIN R.,** toy company executive; Asst. treas. Amway Corp., 1995—97; sr. v.p., treas. Hasbro Inc., 1997—. Adv. bd. The NeuGroup Inc. Office: Hasbro Inc 1027 Newport Ave Pawtucket RI 02862

**TRUEBLOOD, HARRY ALBERT, JR.,** oil industry executive; b. Wichita Falls, Tex., Aug. 28, 1925; s. Harry A. and Marguerite (Barnhart) T.; m. Lucile Bernard, Jan. 22, 1953; children: Katherine T. Astin, John B. Student, Tex. A&M Coll., 1942-43; BS in Petroleum Engring., U. Tex., 1948. Petroleum engr. Cal. Co., 1948-51; chief engr. McDermott & Barnhart Co., Colo., Tex., 1951-52; cons. petroleum and geol. engr. Denver, 1952-55; pres. Colo. Western Exploration Inc., Denver, 1955-58, Consol. Oil & Gas., Inc. 1958-88, chmn. bd., CEO, 1969-88, Princeville Devel. Corp., 1979-87, pres., 1984-86; chmn. bd., CEO Columbus Energy Corp., 1983-2000; pres., mng. mem. HAT Resources LLC, 2001—. Chmn. bd., CEO, Princeville Airways, Inc., 1979-87; chmn. bd. dirs., pres. CEC Resources, Ltd., 1984-99; bd. dirs. NYTIS Exploration Co. With USNR, 1944-46, ensign, 1949-55. Mem. Soc. Petroleum Engrs., Am. Petroleum Inst., World Pres. Orgn., Chief Execs. Orgn. (bd. dirs.), Ind. Petroleum Assn. Am. (exec. com.), Natural Gas Supply Assn. (exec. com.), Cherry Hills Country Club, One Hundred Club. Roman Catholic. Home: 2800 S University Blvd Apt 82 Denver CO 80210-6056 Office: 1720 S Bellaire St Ste 912 Denver CO 80222-4334 Office Phone: 303-300-6792. E-mail: hajtrueblood@yahoo.com.

**TRUEHEART, HARRY PARKER, III,** lawyer; b. Rochester, NY, Mar. 27, 1944; s. Harry Parker and Bertha (Hendryx) T.; m. Karen Ellingson, June 26, 1965; children: Eric Parker, Kathryn Marie. BA, JD, Harvard U. Bar: NY 1970, Fla. 1975. Assoc. Nixon, Hargrave, Devans & Doyle LLP, Rochester, 1969-77, ptnr., 1977—99, spkr. fed. ct. practice, 1979-83, mng. ptnr., 1995—99, Nixon Peabody LLP, Rochester, 1999—. Arbitrator, mediator Ctr. Pub. Resources, Inst. Dispute Resolution, Am. Arbitration Assn.; bd. dirs. Rochester Bus. Alliance, Inc. Co-author: Federal Civil Practice; contbr. chpt. to book; contbr. articles on fed. ct. litigation, microfilm records, profl. liability in connection with use of computers to profl. jours. Fellow NY Bar Found., The Chartered Inst. Arbitrators, The Coll. Law Practice Mgmt., Coll. Comml. Arbitrators; mem. ABA, NY State Bar Assn. (chair comml. and fed. litig. sect. 1992-93, house of del.), Monroe County Bar Assn., Fed. Bar Coun. (v.p.), Am. Arbitration Assn., CPR Inst. for Dispute Resolution. Office: Nixon Peabody LLP 1300 Clinton Sq Rochester NY 14604 also: Nixon Peabody LLP 437 Madison Ave New York NY 10022-7001 Office Phone: 212-940-3027. Business E-Mail: htrueheart@nixonpeabody.com.

**TRUEHILL, MARSHALL, JR.,** minister; b. New Orleans, Sept. 5, 1948; s. Marshall Truehill and Inez Gray Williams; adopted s. Elizabeth (May) T.; m. Mary Ola Williams, Dec. 20, 1969 (div. 1972); m. Valli Maria Dobard, July 22, 1972 (div. 1999); children: Briana Traci, Marshall III, Jessica, Quentin; m. Miranda Sally Farr, Dec. 28, 1999. B in Music Edn., Xavier U., 1973; BTh, Christian Bible Coll., 1979; MDiv, Orleans Bapt. Theol. Sem., 1986; D Ministry, New Orleans Bapt. Theol. Seminary, 1990; postgrad., U. New Orleans; ThD, A.P. Clay Christian Theol. Coll., 2004. Ordained to ministry Bapt. Ch., 1980; cert. tchr., La. Tchr. Orleans Parish Sch. Bd., New Orleans, 1973-78, Delgado Community Coll., 1975-78; pastor Faith in Action Bapt. Ch., 1982—95; founder, pastor First United Bapt. Ch., 1995—. Founder, dir. Faith in Action Evangel. Team, New Orleans, 1977—; lectr. Nat. Bapt. Conv. on Congl. Evangelism, New Orleans, 1977-79; cons. So. Bapt. Conv. Home

Mission Bd., La., 1986-1997; CEO TradeWins Ptnrs. LLC, 2001. Bd. dirs. Project New Orleans, 1983-99, New Orleans Jobs Initiatives, vice chmn., 1997-2002; apptd. by mayor to New Orleans City Planning Commn., 1998-2007. Democrat. Avocations: computers, aquariums, interior decorating, aerobics. Personal E-mail: mtruejr@aol.com. *The greatest investment one can make in this life is an investment in the life of another person. That is the only investment with eternal value.*

**TRUEMAN, WILLIAM PETER MAIN,** broadcaster, columnist; b. Sackville, N.B., Can., Dec. 25, 1934; s. Albert William and Jean Alberta (Miller) T.; m. Eleanor Joy Wark, Dec. 22, 1956; children: Anne, Mark, Victoria. Student, U. N.B., 1951-54. UN corr. Montreal Star, 1957-62, Washington corr., 1962-65; parliamentary corr. Toronto Star, Ottawa, Ont., 1965-67; nat. dir. UN Assn. in Can., 1967-68; nat. news writer CBC, Toronto, 1968-69, exec. producer news, head network news, 1969-72; freelance reporter, 1972-73; anchor Global TV News, Don Mills, Canada, 1974—88; free lance broadcaster, 1988-2000; media critic Toronto Star's Starweek mag., 1988-96; Kingston Whig-Std., 1989-96. Host, mng.editor Canadian Discovery Channel TV series Great Canadian Parks, 1995-2000. Decorated officer Order of Can.; recipient Bowater award for journalism, 1962, Sam Ross award, 1983, Queen's Golden Jubilee Medal, 2002; Paul Harris fellow, Rotary, Kingston, 2005. Personal E-mail: peter.trueman@sympatico.ca.

**TRUEMPER, JOHN JAMES, JR.,** retired architect; b. Helena, Ark., June 18, 1924; s. John James and Mary Ann (Jacob) T.; m. Julia Clare Wood, Nov. 21, 1956; children: Zachary Wood, John James III, Ann Truemper Penick. BS in Arch., U. Ill., 1950; DHL (hon.), Lyon Coll., 1995. With archtl. firm Cromwell, Truemper, Levy, Thompson, Woodsmall Inc. (and predecessors), Little Rock, 1950-94, v.p., 1972-74, pres., 1974-81, chmn. bd., 1980-89; ret., 1994. Mem. Ark. Bd. Architects, 1974-82, pres., 1980 Prin. works include Ark. system for edn. and tng. mentally retarded, 1956-78, Winrock Farm, Morrilton, Ark., 1953-58, Ark. State Parks, 1955-75, Ark. Power & Light Co., 1961-89, Lyon Coll., Batesville, 1983-94; author: A Century of Service, 1885-1985, 1985. Pres. Ark. Arts Ctr., 1979, chmn. bd., 1980; mem. Little Rock Bldg. Code Bd. Appeals, 1961-86, chmn., 1971-86; mem. Ark. Hist. Preservtion Rev. Bd., 1987-99; bd. dirs. Little Rock Met. YMCA, 1975-84; pres.Ctrl. YMCA; mem. Friends of Libr. Bd., U. Ark., Little Rock, 1989-99, pres. 1995-97; bd. dirs. Greater Little Rock C. of C., 1986-88. With USAAF, 1943-46. Recipient Winthrop Rockefeller Meml. award Ark. Arts Center, 1980 Fellow: AIA (pres. Ark. chpt. 1968); mem.: Sigma Chi. Roman Catholic. Home: 6502 Cantrell Rd Little Rock AR 72207-4219

**TRUESDALE, JOHN CUSHMAN,** federal agency administrator, lawyer; b. Grand Rapids, Mich., July 17, 1921; s. John Cushman and Hazel (Christianson) T.; m. Karin A. Nelson, Feb. 10, 1957; children— John Cushman, Charles N., Margaret E., Andrew C. AB, Grinnell Coll., 1942; MS, Cornell U., 1948; JD, Georgetown U., 1972. Bar: Md. bar 1972, D.C. bar 1973. Field examiner NLRB, Buffalo and New Orleans, 1948-52, adminstrv. analyst Washington, 1952-57, assoc. exec. sec., 1963-68, dep. exec. sec., 1968-72, exec. sec., 1972-77, 81-94, mem., 1977-81, 94, 95, chmn., 1998-2001, labor arbitrator, 1994—98, 2001—; mem. Fgn. Svc. Grievance Bd., 1997—2003. Dir. info., dir. World Data Center/Rockets and Satellites, IGY, Nat. Acad. Scis., Washington, 1957-63 Editor-in-chief: How to Take a Case Before the NLRB, 1997-98, 2002--. With USCG, 1943—46. Recipient Presdl. award Pres. of U.S., 1988. Mem. ABA, Nat. Acad. Arbitrators, D.C. Bar Assn., Assn. Labor Rels. Agys. (pres. 1992-93). Democrat. Congregationalist. Personal E-mail: jctrue@aol.com.

**TRUESDELL, TIMOTHY L.,** private investor; b. Niles, Mich., Oct. 8, 1951; s. Patrick Daniel and LaVonne Marie (Fries) T. BA, U. Notre Dame, 1974. Asst. to exec. dir. Notre Dame U. Alumni Assn., 1974-77, asst. dir., 1977-79; alumni editor Notre Dame mag., 1979-83; v.p. Truesdell Real Estate Investment, Sacramento, 1983-85; dir. devel. rsch. U. Notre Dame, 1985-99; portfolio mgr. Kamm Partnership, South Bend, Ind., 1999—2005; pres. Timothy Truesdell Investments, Kalamazoo, 2005—, Marco Island, Fla., 2005—. Devel. cons. Am. Acad. Neurology, 1991-92, Harvest Devel., Ponte Vedra, Fla., 1999-2003, Hospice of St.-Joseph County, South Bend, Ind., 1992-93, St. Thomas, Mpls., Xavier U., Cin., 1993-94, Niles Comty. Libr. 1993-97, St. Joseph Mishawaka (Ind.) Health Svcs., 1995-96, Berrien County ARC, 1996, Advancement Ptnrs., Inc., Columbus, 1996-2003, Little Flower Cath. Ch., South Bend, Ind., 1997-98, No. Ind. Ctr. for History, South Bend, 1998-2000; bd. dirs. Women's Care Ctr., Mishawaka, Ind., 1999-2000. Councilman City of Niles, 1983-91; pres. St. Mary's Sch Bd. Edn., Niles, 1981-82; chmn. S.W. Mich. Comty. Ambulance, Niles, 1985-89; mem. Rep. Nat. Com.; pres. Fernwood Bot. Garden, Niles, 1997-98. Mem. Am. Assn. Individual Investors, Optimists (sec. 1983-84), Knights of Malta, Notre Dame Club of Kalamazoo. Republican. Roman Catholic. Avocations: golf, antiques. Office: Ste 41 5380 Holiday Terr Kalamazoo MI 49009 Office Phone: 269-353-3800. Personal E-mail: timothytruesdell@verizon.net.

**TRUETT, HAROLD JOSEPH, III, (TIM TRUETT),** lawyer; b. Alameda, Calif., Feb. 13, 1946; s. Harold Joseph and Lois Lucille (Mellin) T.; 1 child, Harold Joseph IV; m. Anna V. Billante, Oct. 1, 1983 (dec. June 2000); 1 child, James S. Carstensen; m. Patricia Maynord, Mar. 5, 2002. BA, U. San Francisco, 1968, JD, 1975. Bar: Calif. 1976, Hawaii 1987, U.S. Dist. Ct. (ea., so., no., and cen. dists.) Calif. 1976, Hawaii 1987, U.S. Ct. Appeals (9th cir.) 1980, U.S. Supreme Ct. 1988, U.S. Ct. Fed. Claims, 1995. Assoc. Hoberg, Finger et al, San Francisco, 1975-78, Bledsoe, Smith et al, San Francisco, 1979-80, Abramson & Bianco, San Francisco, 1980-83; mem. Ingram & Truett, San Rafael, 1983-90; prin. Winchell & Truett, San Francisco, 1991— Lectr. trial practice Am. Coll. Legal Medicine, 1993-94, 2003, Calif. Continuing Edn. of the Bar. Bd. dirs. Shining Star Found. 1991—, pres., 2001—, Marin County, Calif.; mem. Marin Dem. Coun., San Rafael, 1983-90, 2002. Lt. aviator USN, 1967-74. Mem. ABA, Hawaii Bar Assn., Calif. Bar Assn. (com. for adminstrn. of justice, conf. of dels.), San Francisco Bar Assn., San Francisco Trial Lawyers Assn., Lawyers Pilots Assn. Roman Catholic. Home: 48 Valley Rd San Anselmo CA 94960 Office Phone: 415-989-9001. E-mail: tim@truettlaw.com.

**TRUEX, DOROTHY ADINE,** retired university administrator; b. Sedalia, Mo., Oct. 6, 1915; d. Chester Morrison and Madge (Nicholson) T AB, William Jewell Coll., 1936; MA, U. Mo., 1937; EdD, Columbia U., 1956. Asst. dean women N.W. Mo. State U., Maryville, 1939-43, dean women, 1943-45, Mercer U., Macon, Ga., 1945-47, U. Okla., Norman, 1947-69, assoc. prof., .1969-72, dir. rsch. and program devel., 1969-74, prof. edn., 1972-74, dir. grad. program in student pers. svcs., 1969-74; vice chancellor for student affairs U. Ark., Little Rock, 1974-83, alumni specialist, 1983-84, acad. adviser, 1984-87. Exec. bd. N. Cen. Assn. Schs. and Colls., 1977—83. Author: Rich Choices, 1994, A Visit to Spitesville, 1999, The 13th Bridesmaid, 1999, Carved in Stone, 2000, Full Circle, 2002, The Twenty Million Dollar Giveaway, 2001, A Left Handed Chord, 2003, Life with Cheryl, 2005. Mem. Nat. Assn. Women Deans, Adminstrs. and Counselors (pres. 1973-74), So. Coll. Pers. Assn. (pres. 1970), Okla. Coll. Pers. Assn. (pres. 1972-73), William Jewell Coll. Alumni Assn. (pres. 1970-73), Woman's City Club (pres. 2000-2001), Pi Beta Phi, Alpha Lambda Delta, Mortar Bd., Sigma Tau Delta, Cardinal Key, Gamma Alpha Chi, Kappa Delta Pi, Pi Lambda Theta, Alpha Psi Omega, Pi Gamma Mu, Delta Kappa Gamma, Phi Delta Kappa, Phi Kappa Phi. (nat. v.p. 1986-89) Avocations: writing, aerobics. Home: 14300 Chenal Pkwy Apt 7422 Little Rock AR 72211-5819

**TRUHLAR, DONALD GENE,** chemist, educator; b. Chgo., Feb. 27, 1944; s. John Joseph and Lucille Marie (Vancura) T.; m. Jane Teresa Gust, Aug. 28, 1965; children: Sara Elizabeth, Stephanie Marie. BA in Chemistry summa cum laude, St. Mary's Coll., Winona, Minn., 1965; PhD in Chemistry, Calif. Inst. Tech. 1970. Asst. prof. chemistry and chem. physics U. Minn., Mpls., 1969—72, assoc. prof., 1972—76, prof., 1976—93, Inst. of Tech. prof., 1993—98, Inst. of Tech. disting. prof., 1998—, Lloyd H. Reyerson prof., 2002—. Cons. Los Alamos Sci. Lab.; vis. fellow Joint Inst. for Lab. Astrophysics, 1975-76; sci. dir. Minn. Supercomputer Inst., 1987-88, dir., 1988—. Editor Theoretical Chemistry Accounts (Theoretica Chemica Acta),

1985—2001, Computer Physics Comms., 1986—, Topics Phys. Chemistry, 1992—99, Understanding Chem. Reactivity, 1990—92, mem. editl. bd. Jour. Chem. Physics, 1978—80, Chem. Physics Letters, 1982—, Jour. Phys. Chemistry, 1985—87, Understanding Chem. Reactivity, 1993—, Advances in Chem. Physics, 1993—, Internat. Jour. Modern Physics C., 1994—, IEEE Computational Sci. and Engring., 1994—98, Internat. Jour. Quantum Chemistry, 1996—2000, Computing in Sci. and Engring., 1999—, Jour. Chemical Theory and Computation, 2004—, Chemical Physics, 2005, chief adv. editor Theoretical Chemistry Accounts, 2002—. Recipient Minn. award, 2003, NAS award for Sci. Reviewing, 2004, award for sci. computing, NAS, 2004; fellow, Alfred P. Sloan Found., 1973—77; grantee, NSF, 1971—, NASA, 1987—95, US Dept. Energy, 1979—, NIST, 1995—98, Dept. of Def., 2001—; scholar, Ruhland Walzer Meml. scholar, 1961—62; John Stauffer fellow, 1965—66, NDEA fellow, 1966—68. Fellow AAAS, Am. Phys. Soc.; mem. Am. Chem. Soc. (sec.-treas. theoretical chemistry subdivsn. 1980-89, councilor 1985-87, assoc. editor jour. 1984—, Award for computers in chem. and pharm. rsch. 2000, Peter Debye award in phys. chemistry 2006). Achievements include research, numerous publications in field. Home: 5033 Thomas Ave S Minneapolis MN 55410-2240 Office: U Minn 207 Pleasant St SE Minneapolis MN 55455-0431 Office Phone: 612-624-7555. Business E-mail: truhlar@umn.edu.

**TRUHLAR, ROBERT J.,** lawyer; b. Chgo., Apr. 11, 1948; BA, St. Mary's Coll., 1970; JD, U. Denver, 1981. Bar: Colo. 1981, U.S. Dist. Ct. Colo. 1981, U.S. Ct. Appeals (10th cir.) 1981, U.S. Supreme Ct. 1981. Ptnr. Truhlar and Truhlar, LLP, Littleton, Colo. Part-time faculty master program in human resource mgmt. Chapman U., 1990—96; adj. prof. U. Denver Coll. Law, 1992—93. Bus. editor. Denver Law Jour., 1979—80; contbr. chapters to books. Mem.: Coll. Labor and Employment Lawyers, Arapahoe County Bar Assn. (bd. dirs. 1991—93, 1994—2001, officer 1996—2000, pres. 1999—2000), Colo. Bar Assn. (mem. legal fee arbitration com. 1982—83, 1984—, labor law com. 1988—, co-chmn. 1989—92, v.p. 1997—98, bd. govs. 1997—2001, pres.-elect 2002—, bd. govs. 2002—, pres. 2003). Office: Colo Bar Assn Ste 900 1900 Grant St Denver CO 80203 also: Truhlar Truhlar Llp 7340 E Caley Ave Ste 310 Centennial CO 80111-6710

**TRUINI PALOMBA, MARIA GIUSEPPINA,** supreme court lawyer, judge; b. Borbona, Ri-Latium, Italy, Aug. 25, 1935; d. Costanzo and Ezia (Giorgi) Truini; m. Emilio Palomba, Jan. 11, 1964; children: Francesco Maria, Giovanna Palomba. Degree in Law, State U. Rome, 1960. Tchr. State High Sch., Rieti, Italy, 1955-84; local magistrate Rieti, Italy, 1974-86; judge Fiscal Commn., Rieti, Italy, 1974—, Fiscal Commn. Reg. Rome v.p., 1996—. Author: La Cucina Sabina, 1991; contbr. articles to profl. jours. Mem. drug Prevention Assn., L'Aquila, 1979—; hon. guard Nat. Inst. Royal Tombs of Pantheon, Rome, 1980—. Decorated Cavalier of the Merit of the Italian Rep., 1984, Lady of the Order of Chivalry of the Holy Sepulchre of Jerusalem, Grand Master Cardinal, 1990, Lady of the Sovereign and Military Order of the Temple of Jerusalem, 1998; mem. Italian Red cross, 1986—, patroness, 1978; vol. UNICEF. Mem. Nat. Civil Lawyers Union (dist. pres. Rieti, nat. councillor 1990—), Italian Women Jurists Assn. (dist. pres. Rieti and nat. councillor 1990—), Internat. Assn. of Lawyers, Eurojuris Internat. Geie, Italian Acad. Cooking (nat. cons. 1974, dist. del.), Italian Women's Nat. Assn., Italian Women's Nat. Coun., Amnesty Internat. Lawyers, Aeroclub (pres. 1992-93), Rotary (councillor 1994-95, pres., 1996-97, 2006-), v.p. FILDIS-IFUW, Rome, 2000—. Avocations: travel, cinema, theater, cooking, volleyball. Home and Office: A Gherardi 70 02100 Rieti Italy Office Phone: +39-746-203077. E-mail: studiolegale@palombatruini.it.

**TRUITT, GORDON EDWARD,** editor, writer; b. Balt., Dec. 30, 1944; s. Gordon Edward and Mary Angela Truitt; m. MaryCarole Smith, Mar. 16, 1985; children: Jaime Carole Rice, Brendan John, Kevin James. MA, MST, Cath. U. Am., Washington, 1970, DST, 1978. Assoc. pastor Archdiocese of Balt., 1970—74, asst. dir. liturgy, 1974—76, dir. liturgy, 1976—82, assoc. pastor, 1982—84; asst. editor The Liturgical Conf., Washington, 1985—88; editor Nat. Assn. Pastoral Musicians, Silver Spring, Md., 1988—. Chair bd. dir. Fedn. of Diocesan Liturgical Commns., Washington, 1978. Editor: (journal) Pastoral Music; author: A Pastoral Musician's Book of Days, 2000; co-author: Minstries in Sung Worship, 2005. Mem.: North Am. Acad. Liturgy. Roman Catholic. Office: Nat Assn Pastoral Musicians Suite 210 962 Wayne Ave Silver Spring MD 20912-4461 Office Phone: 240-247-3000.

**TRUITT, RICHARD BYRON,** landscape architect; b. El Paso, Tex., Dec. 25, 1937; s. Charles Lee and Elenia May Truitt; m. Doris Iva House, Feb. 23, 1963; 1 child, Bonnie Leona. Cert. in Hort. and Landscape, Dayton Beach (Fla.) C.C., 1956. Cert. law and ornamental pest control; registered landscape architect, Fla. Pvt. practice, Ormond Beach, Fla., 1956—. Contbr. articles to profl. jours. Pres. Civitan Club, Ormond Beach; vice chair Devel. Rev. Bd., Ormond Beach, 1995-98; chair Beautification Bd., Ormond Beach, 1978-95; bd. dirs., trustee Louitte Manor retirement Ctr., Daytona Beach, 1984-97; charter mem. Bot. Gardens of Volusia County; bd. dirs. Episc. Ch., Diocese of Ctrl. Fla., Orlando, 1979-81; Eucharistic minister Episc. Ch. With Army N.G., 1956-66. Recipient Spl. award City of Ormond Beach for outstanding svcs. as chair and mem. of beautification Bd., 1995. Mem. Ormond Beach C. of C. (pres. 1990, Spl. Award for contbn. and dedication to beautification 1989), Holly Hill C. o C. (pres. 1989), Fla. Nurseryman and growers Assn. (pres. Ctrl. East Coast chpt. 1977). Republican. Episcopalian. Home and Office: 115 Country Club Dr Ormond Beach FL 32176-5415

**TRUITT, RODGERS PAUL,** educator; b. Edinburg, Tex., June 13, 1975; s. Paul Truitt and Patricia Bader; m. Kathryn Koch, Dec. 18, 1999; children: Kathryn Lynne, Kaden Paul. MA, St. Mary's U., San Antonio, Tex., 1999. Prof. South Tex. Coll., McAllen, 1999—2006. Office: South Tex Coll 3201 W Pecan Blvd McAllen TX 78501 Office Phone: 956 872 2606.

**TRUJILLO, J. ROBERTO,** virologist; b. Mexico City, July 14, 1963; s. Maria Guadalupe Martinez and Roberto Trujillo; m. Elaine B. Barbella, Nov. 19, 1988; children: Daniel Robert, Jacquelyn Elizabeth. BS summa cum laude, Inst. Art and Scis., Mex., 1988; MD summa cum laude, U. Autonomous State of Mex., 1988; PhD, Harvard U., Boston, 1995. Lic. surgeon Faculty of Medicine, State of Mex., Mex., 1988. Rsch. fellow Harvard U., Boston, 1989—95, rsch. assoc., 1996—98, rsch. assoc. in neurovirology 1998—2002; sr. scientist Internat. Nat. Inst. of Neurol. Disorders and Stroke, Bethesda, Md., 2002—05; chief lab. of neurovirology Inst. of Human Virology, UMBI, U. Md., Balt., 2005—; asst. prof. Baltimore, 2005—; adj. prof. U. Autonomous of Nuevo Leon, Monterrey, Mexico, 2002—. Pres., founder Pan-Am. Soc. for NeuroVirology, Boston, 2000—; NIH reviewer Nat. Inst. of Allergy and Infectious Diseases, Bethesda, Md., 2005; dir. rsch. virology and neuroscience Inst. of Human Virology, UMBI, U. Md., Baltimore, 2005—; com. mem. of faculty and administrs. Harvard Sch. of Pub. Health, Boston, 2003—; instr. Harvard Coll., Cambridge, Mass., 1997—99; supr. Harvard Sch. of Pub. Health, Boston, 1997—2002; sci. advisor U. Autonomous of Nuevo Leon, Monterrey, Mexico, 1998—; prof. advisor biomed. sci. careers program, minority faculty devel. program Harvard Med. Sch., Boston, 2004—; internat. editl. bd. Revista Mexicana de Neurociencia, Mexico City, 2004; reviewer Office of AIDS Rsch., NIH, Bethesda, Md., 2002. Prodr.: (Pan.-Am. symposium programs) Scientific & Graphic Design; contbr. articles to profl. jours. Pres. Pan-Am. Soc. for NeuroVirology, Boston, 2000; mem. Faculty of Medicine, UANL, Monterrey, Nuevo Leon, Mexico, 2000—04; dir. Inst. of Human Virology of Mex., Monterrey, Nuevo Leon, 2005. Recipient A-H Robins of Mex. award, Med. Sch., State of Mex., 1981-83, Outstanding Young Presenter, Govt. of Mex. State, 1987, T32 Tng. award, NIH, 1989-1992, Helena Rubinstein award, Harvard Sch. of Pub. Health, 1996-1999, Key of the City, Acapulco, Mex., 1997, 2000, Group Merit award, Nat. Inst. of Neurol. Disorders and Stroke, 2004, Internat. Prof. award, U. Complutense, Spain, 2005, Key of the City, Chihuahua, Mex., 2005; grantee, NIH, 1999-2002, 2000; Med. scholarship, Med. Sch., State of Mex., 1983-1985, Internat. fellowship, Govt. of Mex. State, 1996-1987. Mem.: AAAS (assoc.), Internat. AIDS Soc., Pan-Am. Soc. Ft. NeuroVirology (pres. 2000), Mexican Acad. of Neurology (assoc.). Achievements include first to Molecular Mimicry in NeuroAIDS; Field of NeuroVirology; research

in Mannose Receptor and AIDS Vaccine; design of HIV-1 Neurotropism Movie; development of Latin American Program of Virology; Pan-American Program of NeuroVirology. Avocations: black belt in martial arts, poetry, soccer player. Home: 2308 McCormick Rd Rockville MD 20850 Office: Inst of Human Virology UMBI U Md 725 West Lombard St Baltimore MD 21201 Office Phone: 410-706-7443. Home Fax: 410-706-7453; Office Fax: 410-706-1952. Business E-Mail: trujillo@umbi.umd.edu.

**TRUJILLO, ROBERT,** musician; b. Santa Monica, Calif., Oct. 23, 1964; Former band mem. Suicidal Tendencies, Infectious Grooves, Ozzy Osbourne; band mem. Metallica, 2003—. Musician (bassist, also prodr.): (albums) (with Infectious Grooves) Plague That Makes Your Booty Move, 1991, Sarsippius' Ark, 1993; musician: (bassist) Groove Family Cyco, 1994, Mas Borracho, 2000, (with Suicidal Tendencies) Art of Rebellion, 1992, Suicidal for Life, 1994, (with Ozzy Osbourne) Down to Earth, 2001, Live at Budokan, 2002, Ozzman Cometh: Greatest Hits, 2002, (with Metallica) St. Anger, 2003 (Grammy award for Best Metal Performance, 2003), (others) Poder Latino, A.N.I.M.A.L., 1998; musician: (bassist, vocals, prodr., engr., mastering) Twelve Piece Band, Project Tru, 1999; musician: (bassist) Christmas That Almost Wasn't, Various Artists, 2001, Metallic Assault: A Tribute to Metallica, Various Artists, 2001, Problem Child, Cyco Mike, 2001, Revolution, Insolence, 2001, 1919 Eternal, Zakk Wylde's Black Label Society, 2001, Degradation Trip, Jerry Cantrell, Vol. 1 & Vol. 2, 2002, Different Shade of Green: Tribute to Green Day, Various Artists, 2003, Prison Cell, Wirebox, 2003, Immaculate Deception: A Tribute to the Music of Madon, 2004, Stairway to Rock (Not Just) A Led Zepplin Tribute, Various Artists, 2004; performer: (TV soundtrack) Osbourne Family Album, 2002. Office: Elextra Entertainment Group 75 Rockefeller Plaza New York NY 10019-7284

**TRUJILLO-CUTHRELL, LORETTA MARIE,** chemical engineer; b. Santa Fe, N.Mex., May 22, 1959; d. Jose E.F. and Irene D. (Fernandez) Trujillo; m. Robert Blair Cuthrell, May 16, 1987. BSChemE, U. N.Mex., 1988. Process engr. Kerr McGee Chem., Trona, Calif., 1989-91; chem. engr. N.Am. Chem. Co., Trona, 1991-98, quality coord., 1992-98, IMC Chem., Trona, Calif., 1998-2000; lab. supr. GTC, Albuquerque, 2000—01; chemist State of N.Mex. Health Dept. Mem. AIChE (vice chmn. 1995—), Women in Mining.

**TRULEAR, HAROLD DEAN,** minister, theological educator, social researcher; b. Phila., Oct. 4, 1954; s. Harold Holland and Elizabeth C. (Dean) T.; m. Vickie Lynette Butler, June 27, 1981; children: Harold Butler, Jared Morgan, Frances Elizabeth. BA, Morehouse Coll., 1975; MPhil, Drew U., 1979, PhD, 1983. Club dir. Youth for Christ, Paterson, NJ, 1977-83; assoc. prof. ch. and society Drew U., Madison, NJ, 1978-87; dir. black ch. studies Ea. Bapt. Theol. Sem., Phila., 1987-90; dean 1st profl. programs N.Y. Theol. Sem., N.Y.C., 1990-96, prof. ch. and society, 1990-98; v.p. Pub./Pvt. Ventures, Phila., 1998—. Assoc. pastor Cmty. Bapt. Ch., Paterson, 1981-87, 91-97; pastor Mt. Zion Bapt. Ch., Phila., 1987-90; assoc. min. Zion Bapt. Ch., Ardmore, Pa.; clergy assoc. St. Mary's Episcopal Ch., Ardmore; cons. Christian Coll. Consortium, 1990, Vanderbilt U. Div. Sch., Nashville, 1995; mem. adv. bd. Phila. Project for Youth Ministry, 1995-97; bd. dirs. N.Y. Christian Higher Edn. Consortium, N.Y.C. Guest editor The Pastor Scholar, 1997; contbr. chpts. to books. Bd. dirs. Paterson Clergy Assn., 1977-83, Opportunities Industrialization Ctr., Paterson, 1981-87, Inter Varsity Christian Fellowship, Madison, Wis., 1995—, Indwelling, World Impact, Chester, Pa. Grantee N.J. Hist. Commn., 1984, Assn. Theol. Schs., 1984, Ford Found., 1994-95. Fellow Partnership for Rsch. on Religion and At Risk Youth; mem. Am. Acad. Religion, Soc. for the Study Black Religion, Soc. for Pentecostal Studies, Bapt. Mins. Conf., Am. Bapt. Chs. N.J. (mins. coun.), Phi Beta Kappa. Republican. Achievements include research on youth, young adults, religion and public policy. Home: 912 Church Ln Yeadon PA 19050-3717 Office: Pub Pvt Ventures 2005 Market St Ste 900 Philadelphia PA 19103-7060

**TRULY, RICHARD H.,** academic administrator, retired pilot, retired federal agency administrator; b. Fayette, Miss., Nov. 12, 1937; s. James B. Truly; m. Coleen Hanner; children: Richard Michael, Daniel Bennett, Lee Margaret. B in Aero. Engring., Ga. Inst. Tech., 1959; D in Sci. (hon.), Millsaps Coll., Duquesne U.; D in Engring. (hon.), Colo. Sch. Mines, Stevens Inst. Tech. Commd. ensign USN, 1959; advanced through grades to vice adm.; assigned Fighter Squadron 33; served in U.S.S. Enterprise; served in U.S.S. Enterprise; astronaut Manned Orbiting Lab. Program USAF, 1965—69, NASA, 1969—, comdr. Columbia Flight 2, 1981, Challenger Flight 3, 1983; dir. Space Shuttle program, 1986—89; adminstr. NASA, 1989—92; v.p., dir. Georgia Tech Rsch. Inst., Atlanta, 1992—97; dir. Nat. Renewable Energy Lab., Golden, Colo., 1997—2004; ret., 2004. Recipient Robert H. Goddard Astronautics award, AIAA, 1990, Presdl. Citizen's Medal, 1989. Mem.: NAE. Office: Nat Renewable Energy Lab 1617 Cole Blvd Golden CO 80401-3305

**TRUMAN, BRIDGET MARY,** psychologist; b. Albuquerque, N.Mex., Oct. 27, 1965; d. Gary Duane and Joan Truman; m. A. Pitt Beam, Sept. 5, 1997. BA, Northeastern State U., 1987, MS, 1989; PhD, U. Memphis, 1996. Counselor Frayer-Millington, Memphis, 1989—92, program dir. victims asst., 1992, part time counselor, 1992—95; psychologist U. Tenn. Regional Med. Ctr., 1997—2003; assoc. dir. counseling Rhodes Coll., Memphis, 1999—2006; psychologist VA Med. Ctr., Memphis, 2006—. Race coord. Celebrate Everybody 5K, Memphis, 2005. Mem.: APA, Mempis Area Psychol. Assn. (pres. 2000—02), Tenn. Psychol. Assn. (West Tenn.v.p. 2003). Cath. Avocations: gardening, hiking, quilting. Home: 4133 Hedge Hills Ave Memphis TN 38117 Office: VA Med Ctr 1030 Jefferson Ave Memphis TN 38104

**TRUMAN, MARGARET,** writer; b. Independence, Mo., Feb. 17, 1924; d. Harry S (32nd Pres. U.S.) and Bess (Wallace) T.; m. E. Clifton Daniel Jr., Apr. 21, 1956; children: Clifton T., William, Harrison, Thomas. LHD, Wake Forest U., 1972; HHD, Rockhurst Coll., 1976. Concert singer, 1947-54, actress, broadcaster, author, 1954—; author: Souvenir, 1956, White House Pets, 1969, Harry S. Truman, 1973, Women of Courage, 1976, Murder in the White House, 1980, Murder on Capitol Hill, 1981, Letters from Father, 1981, Murder in the Supreme Court, 1982, Murder in the Smithsonian, 1983, Murder on Embassy Row, 1985, Murder at the FBI, 1985, Murder in Georgetown, 1986, Bess W. Truman, 1986, Murder in the CIA, 1987, Murder in the National Gallery, 1996, Murder in the House, 1997, Murder at the Kennedy Center, 1989, Murder in the National Cathedral, 1990, Murder at the Pentagon, 1992, Murder on the Potomac, 1994, First Ladies, 1995, Murder in the Watergate, 1998, Murder in the Library of Congress, 1999, Murder at Foggy Bottom, 2000, Murder in Havana, 2001, Murder at Ford's Theatre, 2002, The President's House, 2003, Murder at Union Station, 2004, Murder at the Washington Tribune, 2005; editor: Where the Buck Stops: The Personal and Private Writings of Harry S. Truman, 1989. Trustee and v.p. Harry S. Truman Inst.; sec. bd. trustees Harry S. Truman Found.

**TRUMBULL, DAVID LEWIS KITCHEN,** trade association executive; b. Highland Park, Mich. s. Ben Gordon and Lois Virginia (Wilson) Kitchen; m. Mary N. DiZazzo, Sept. 29, 2003. AB, U. Mich., 1991. Rsch. asst. U. Mass., Boston, 1992-93; programmer Commonwealth of Mass., Boston, 1993-94; dir. mem. svcs. Nat. Textile Assn., Boston, 1994—; exec. dir. Am. Flock Assn., Boston, 1994-2001. Chmn. Cambridge (Mass.) Rep. City Com., 1994-2002; asst. sec. Nat. Textile Assn., 1994—; v.p. 1996-98; chmn. Ward 3, Boston Rep. Com., 2003—. Mem. Textile Club (exec. com. 1996—, treas. 1998—). Roman Catholic. Home: 130 Bowdoin St # 1110 Boston MA 02108 Office: Nat Textile Assn 6 Beacon St # 1125 Boston MA 02108 E-mail: trumbulld@earthlink.net.

**TRUMBULL, STEPHEN MICHAEL,** entrepreneur, musician; b. Columbus, Ohio, Sept. 18, 1954; s. Clyde Austin and Patricia Ann (Ranck) T. MusB in Voice Performance and Choral Edn., DePauw U., Greencastle, Ind., 1977; postgrad., Ohio State U., 1982-85, Trinity Luth. Sem., 2005—. Cert. profl. music educator, Ohio; cert. broker/dealer. Dir. vocal music Columbus City Schs., 1978-87; pres., owner Columbus Music Studios, 1984—; pres. The

Trumbull Pub. Co., Washington, 1986—, Stephen M. Trumbull, Inc., Columbus, 1986—, Goldmark Securities Corp., Columbus, 1987-90; exec. v.p. Hamilton Capital Corp., Columbus, 1988-90, also bd. dirs., corp. v.p., sec., bd. dirs., 1987-90; v.p. Hamilton Mktg. Corp., Columbus, 1988-90, Kaiser Enterprises, Columbus, 1988-90; pres. Shelter One Group Corp., Columbus, 1988-90, also bd. dirs.; chmn. bd., chief exec. officer Ascona Communications, Inc., L.A., 1990-92; chief exec. officer Recording Industry Sourcebook, L.A., 1990-92; mng. ptnr. SRS Pub. Co., 1991-95; pres., CEO Music Bus. Registry, Inc., L.A., 1995—. Soloist First Cmty. Ch., Columbus, 1982—90, Bay Shore Cmty. Ch., Long Beach, 1999—2001; dir. music First Bapt. Ch., Granville, Ohio, 2003—; mktg. cons. Beckenhorst Press, Inc., Columbus, 1986—87; exec. prodr. Wake Up and Dream, L.A., 1990—92; cons. The Source Group, Toronto, Canada, 1986—, Events Can., Toronto, 1999—. Adviser Lambda Chi Alpha, Ohio State U., chmn. alumni adv. bd., 1982-87; pres. Friends of Neoteric Dance Theatre, Columbus, 1986-88; coord. nat. competition Jr. Achievement Nat. Conf., Bloomington, Ind., 1973-95; bd. dirs. Neoteric Dance Theatre, 1986-88, Susan Van Pelt Dance Ensemble, 1989-92, Reach for the Stars, Inc., L.A., 1990-92, The Awareness Found., L.A., 1992-93; bus.-mktg. com. Jr. Achievement Ctrl. Ohio, Inc., 1987-92; cons. Nat. Hockey League Awards, Toronto, 1990-99; chair Granville (Ohio) Arts Commn., 2004—. Named Outstanding Alumni, Lambda Chi Alpha, 1984. Mem. Columbus Edn. Assn. Lodges: Optimist. Avocations: swimming, travel, sailing. Home: PO Box 411 Granville OH 43023-0411 Office: 7510 W Sunset Blvd # 1041 Los Angeles CA 90046-3400 Office Phone: 617-314-6221. E-mail: steve@musicregistry.com.

**TRUMP, BLAINE (MARTHA LINDLEY BLAINE BEARD TRUMP),** philanthropist; m. Robert Trump, 1984; 1 child, Christopher. Student, U. Tokyo. Clothing line creator Am. Classics by Blaine Trump, QVC, 1999. Fundraiser Am. Ballet Theatre, Meml. Sloan-Kettering Cancer Ctr.; vice-chair God's Love We Deliver. Named one of 50 Most Beautiful People World, People mag., 1998; recipient Marietta Tree award for pub. svc., Citizen's Com. for NYC, 1998. Achievements include all proceeds from clothing line Am. Classics by Blaine Trump go to God's Love We Deliver. Office: God's Love We Deliver 166 Ave of the Americas New York NY 10013

**TRUMP, DONALD JOHN,** real estate developer; b. N.Y.C., 1946; s. Fred C. and Mary Trump; m. Ivana Zelnicek, Apr. 9, 1977 (div. 1991); children: Donald, Jr., Ivanka, Eric; m. Marla Maples, Dec. 30, 1993 (div. June 8, 1999); 1 child, Tiffany Ariana; m. Melania Knauss, Jan. 22, 2005; 1 child, Barron William. BS Economics, U. Pa., Wharton Sch. Fin., 1968. Pres. Trump Orgn., N.Y.C.: owner Trump Tower, Trump Parc, Trump Palace, Trump Bldg. at 40 Wall St., N.Y.C., Trump Internat. Hotel and Tower, N.Y.C., Chgo., Trump Plz. Hotel and Casino, Trump Marina, Trump Taj Mahal, Atlantic City, Trump Casino Riverboat, Buffington Harbor, Ind., Trump 29 Casino, Palm Springs, Calif., W. Side Rail Yards devel. as Trump Pl., N.Y.C., Mansion at Seven Springs, Bedford, NY, Mar-a-Lago Club, Palm Beach, Fla.; ptnr.-owner 610 Park Ave. and Trump World Tower, N.Y.C., Trump Park Ave. (formerly Delmonico Hotel), Trump Grande Ocean Resort and Residences, Miami Beach, Fla., Trump Internat. Hotel and Twr., Chgo.; chmn., pres. Trump Org., N.Y.C.; chmn. Trump Entertainment Resorts, Inc., 2005—. Owner Trump Internat. Golf Club, Palm Beach, Trump Nat. Golf Club, Briarcliff Manor, NY, Ocean Trails Golf Course, Palos Verde, Calif., Trump Nat., Bedminster, NJ, Trump Mgmt. Group develop/Talent Agy.; pres. Trump Pageants LP, includes Miss Universe, Miss USA and Miss Teen USA.; launched line of men's suits, 2004; launched signature fragrance, Donald Trump The Fragrance, 04; announced launching of Trump University will consist of online courses, CD-ROMS, blogs, consulting services and Learning Annex-type seminars, 05. Author (with Tony Schwartz): The Art of the Deal, 1988; author: (with Charles Leerhsen) Surviving at the Top, 1990, The Art of Survival, 1991; author: (with Kate Bohner) The Art of the Comeback, 1997; author: (with Dave Shiflett) The America We Deserve, 2000; author: (with Meredith McIver) How To Get Rich, 2004, Think Like a Billionaire: Everything You Need to Know About Success, Real Estate, and Life, 2004; author: The Way to the Top: The Best Business Advice I Ever Received, 2004; host, exec. prodr. (TV series) The Apprentice, 2004—, launched Trump World mag., 2004, host on syndicated radio program Trumped!, Premiere Radio Networks, 2004. Com. mem., Celebration of Nations Commemorating 50th Anniversary UN and UNICEF; Co-chmn. N.Y. Vietnam Vets. Meml. Fund; founding mem. constrn. com. Cathedral of St. John the Divine; mem. N.Y. Citizens Tax Coun., Fifth Ave Assn., Realty Found. of N.Y., Met. Mus. of Art's Real Estate Coun.; mem. adv. bd. Lenox Hill Hosp., United Cerebral Palsy; spl. advisor to Pres.'s Coun. on Phys. Fitness and Sports; mem. N.Y. Sportsplex Commn.; chmn. N.Y. citizens com. 78th Ann. NAACP Conv., 1987; grand marshall Nation's Parade, 1995; bd. dirs. Police Athletic League; bd. overseers Wharton Sch.; founding mem. adv. bd. Wharton Real Estate Ctr.; bd. dirs. Fred C. Trump Found.; chmn. Donald J. Trump Found. Named Developer of Yr., Constrn. Mgmt Assn. Am., 1999, Hotel and Real Estate Visionary of the Century, UTA Fedn., 2000; named one of Forbes' Richest Americans, 2006; named to Wharton Hall of Fame, Benefactors bd. dirs. Hist. Soc. Palm Beach County, 2003; recipient Entrepreneur of Yr. award, Wharton Entrepreneurial Club, 1984, Ellis Island Medal of Honor, 1986. Achievements include the three-month rebuilding of Wollman Skating Rink in Central Park.

**TRUMP, IVANKA (IVANA MARIE TRUMP),** model, real estate company executive; b. NYC, Oct. 30, 1981; d. Donald and Ivana Trump. B. in economics, UPenn. Wharton Sch. Bus., 2004. Model, 1997—; v.p. real estate devel. Trump Orgn., NYC. Appears in (documentaries) Born Rich, 2003, (TV series) The Apprentice, 2006—. Office: Trump Orgn 725 5th Ave New York NY 10022

**TRUMP, STEPHANIE,** music educator; m. Mark Trump; children: Hana, Nicklaus. MusB in Music Edn., Augsburg Coll., 1991, MusB in Voice Performance, 1991; MusM in Edn., U. Hawaii, 2006. Dir. choral Tech. and Lang. Campu, Robbinsdale, Minn., 1992—97, Armstrong H.S., Plymouth, Minn., 1996—. Mem.: Am. Choral Dirs. Assn., Music Educators Nat. Conf. Office: Armstrong High School 10635 36th Ave N Plymouth MN 55441 Office Phone: 763-504-8857. Business E-Mail: stephanie_trump@rdale.k12.mn.us.

**TRUMPBOUR, JOHN,** historian, researcher, director; b. Greensboro, NC, Feb. 23, 1959; s. Robert and Virginia Trumpbour. BA, History, Stanford U., Palo Alto, Calif., 1977—82; PhD, History, Harvard U., Cambridge, Mass., 1982—96. Rsch. dir. Harvard Trade Union Program, 1999—, Labor & Worklife Program at Harvard Law Sch., 2002—. Cons. and rschr. African Am. Labor Leaders' Econ. Summit, Cambridge, Mass., 1997—; rschr. and fellowships com. Sci. & Engring. Workforce Project at Nat. Bur. of Econ. Rsch., Cambridge, Mass., 2001—; editl. bd. Labor History, London, 2004—. Author: (book) Selling Hollywood to the World: U.S. and European Struggles for Mastery of the Global Film Industry, 1920-1950, 2002 (Allan Nevins prize for Lit. Excellence.); editor: How Harvard Rules, 1989, The Dividing Rhine: Politics and Society in Contemporary France and Germany, 1989. Bd. of directors Boston Moblzn., 1999—2001; co-chair Samia Tenants Orgn., Boston, 1996—2000; fellowships com., Rhodes and Marshall scholarships Leverett Ho., Harvard U., 1987—. Recipient Best Essay prize, NAAA Found., 1984, James Birdsall Weter award, Stanford U., Dept. History, 1982; fellow Sawyer fellow, Mellon Found., 1996-97, Belgian Am. Edn. Found. Fellow, Brussels, Belgium, 1989-1990; grantee, Sloan Found., 2002. Mem.: Labor and Working-Class History Assn., Soc. for Historians of Am. Fgn. Rels. Home: 60 Woodstock Avenue #14 Brighton MA 02135 Office: Harvard Law Sch Labor and Worklife Program 125 Mt Auburn St 3d Fl Cambridge MA 02138 Office Phone: 617-495-9265. Personal E-mail: john_trumpbour@harvard.edu.

**TRUNDLE, W(INFIELD) SCOTT,** publishing executive newspaper, lawyer; b. Maryville, Tenn., Mar. 24, 1939; s. Winfield Scott and Alice (Smith) T.; m. Elizabeth Latshaw, Oct. 14, 1989; children: Stephen, Allison. BA, Vanderbilt U., 1961, JD, 1967. Bar: Tenn. 1967. Spl. agt. U.S. Secret Service, 1963-66; asso. to partner firm Hunter, Smith, Davis & Norris, Kingsport,

Tenn., 1967-72; pub. Kingsport (Tenn.) Times-News, 1972-78; pres. Greensboro (N.C.) Daily News, 1978-80; exec. v.p. Jefferson Pilot Publs., Inc., Greensboro and Clearwater, Fla., 1980-82; v.p., bus. mgr. Tampa Tribune (Fla.), 1982-91; sr. v.p. Hillsborough C.C., 1991-93; publisher Ogden (Utah) Standard Examiner, 1993—2005. Assoc. prof. East Tenn. State U., 1973-77; v.p. spl. projects Sandusky Newspapers, Inc., 2005—; bd. dirs., vice chmn. Container Recycling Inst., Washington. Trustee Eccles Dinosaur Park and Mus. Found., Ogden, Utah. Mem.: Tenn. Bar Assn. Methodist. Home: 2380 Park Forest Blvd Mount Dora FL 32757 Office Phone: 801-625-4501. E-mail: strundle@aol.com.

**TRUNK, JAMES FRANCIS,** secondary school educator; b. Cleve., Feb. 23, 1943; s. Frank A. and Dorothy A. (McCann) T.; m. Catalina Delgado, Oct. 30, 1965; children: Maria, Sean. BA, St. Edward U., 1965; MA, U. Mid-Fla., 1973. Cert. secondary sch. English tchr., N.Mex. 7th grade tchr. St. Mary Sch., Chardon, Ohio, 1965-66; 9th-12th grade English tchr. St. Frederick H.S., Monroe, La., 1966-67; 5th and 6th grade English and reading tchr. St. John Vianney Sch., Orlando, Fla., 1974-75, St. Andrew Sch., Orlando, 1975-98, Robinswood Mid. Sch., Orlando, 1998-2000, Annunciation Sch., Albuquerque, 2000—. Part-time English grammar tchr. Orlando Cath. Coll., 1975-84. Mem. Nat. Coun. Tchrs. English, Assn. Tchrs. in Cath. Schs. in Orlando Diocese (founder). Avocation: photography. Home: 1804 Dartmouth Dr NE Albuquerque NM 87106-1744

**TRUOG, WILLIAM EDWARD, III,** pediatrician, educator, researcher; b. Kansas City, Mo., Feb. 5, 1947; s. William E. and Virginia (Sylvester) Truog; m. Jill D. Jacobson, July 11, 1992. BA cum laude, Carleton Coll., 1969; MD, U. Chgo., 1973. Intern, resident pediat., chief resident Children's Orthop. Hosp.-U. Wash., Seattle, 1973—76, rsch. fellow neonatology, 1976—78; asst. prof., assoc. prof., prof. pediat. U. Wash., Seattle, 1978—93; prof. pediat. Sch. Medicine U. Mo. Kansas City, 1993—. Med. dir. infant ICU Children's Orthop. Hosp., Seattle, 1982—91. Author: Critical Care of the Newborn, 1983, 1988; contbr. articles to profl. jours. Named First Physician Scientist, Children's Mercy Hosp., 1993; named to Best Doctors in Am., 2005; recipient Sosland Endowed Chair Neonatal Rsch., 2001; grantee, NIH, 1981, 1984, 1997, 2002. Mem.: Perinatal Rsch. Soc., We. Soc. Pediat. Rsch., Soc. Pediat. Rsch., Am. Pediat. Soc., Am. Thoracic Soc. (grantee 1978). Episcopalian. Office: Children's Mercy Hosp 2401 Gillham Rd Kansas City MO 64108-4619

**TRUONG, D. HIEP,** lawyer; b. Saigon, Vietnam, May 16, 1972; BBA, U. Calif., Berkeley; JD, Santa Clara U., 1999. Bar: Calif. Law clk. intern Office of US Atty., Ea. Dist., Sacramento, 1998, Office of US Atty., No. Dist., San Jose, Calif., 1999; cert. law clk. LA County Dist. Atty.'s Office, 1999—2000; assoc. Grancell, Lebovitz et al., San Jose, Calif., 2000—01, Manning & Marder et al. LLP, San Francisco, 2001—. Moot ct. judge Stanford (Calif.) U., 2002. Contbr. articles to profl. jours. Incentives and awards scholarship selection com. U. Calif., Berkeley, 2000—. Recipient Am. Jurisprudence Bancroft-Whitney award, 1999; scholar Chancellor's, Regents scholar, U. Calif.; B.T. Collins scholar. Mem.: ABA. Home: 2504 Stonebrook Dr Modesto CA 95355 Office Phone: 415-537-6990 226. Personal E-mail: hiep_9@yahoo.com. Business E-Mail: dht@mmker.com.

**TRUONG, DOTHANG,** information scientist, educator; b. Hanoi, Vietnam, Jan. 22, 1973; s. Tin D. Truong and Thinh T. Le; m. Van T. Nguyen; 1 child, My D. BS with hons. in Engring., Hanoi (Vietnam) U. Tech., 1994; MBA, Asian Inst. Tech., 1997; PhD in Mfg. Mgmt., The U. Toledo, 2004. Instr. Hanoi (Vietnam) U. Tech., 1997—2000; tchg. asst. The U. Toledo, 2000—03; instr. Fayetteville (N.C.) State U., 2003—04, asst. prof., 2004—. Project coord. Vietnam Coal Corp., Hanoi, 1997—98; instr. Vietnam Mgmt. Devel. Program Swiss AIT, Hanoi, 1998—99. Contbr. articles to profl. jours. Recipient Nguyen Truong To awards, VINAHELP and Hanoi U. Tech., 1992—94, Outstanding Tchg. awards, Hanoi (Vietnam) U. Tech., 1998—99, 2004 Student Pacemaker of Yr. award, The U. Toledo, 2004; grantee, Hanoi U. of Tech., 1989—94, Fayetteville State U., 2004; scholar, Swiss-AIT-Vietnam Mgmt. Devel. Program, 1995—97, 1999, The U. Toledo, 2000—03. Mem.: Mid West Bus. Administrn. Assn., Decision Sci. Inst. (Hon. Mention award 2005), Instn. Supply Mgmt. (scholar 2005), Grad. Alumni, Asian Inst. Tech., Info. Sys. Soc. (corr.), Grad. Alumni The U. Toledo, Sigma Iota Epsilon (life). Buddhist. Achievements include research in impacts of radio frequency identification on the supply chain management; e-marketplace usage from the buyer perspective; e-marketplaces and supply chain integration. Office: Fayetteville State University 1200 Murchison Rd Fayetteville NC 28301 Office Phone: 910-672-1020.

**TRUPP, MICHAEL SARON,** psychiatrist; b. Balt., Oct. 26, 1933; s. Irvin Israel and Frances (Marcus) T.; m. Irma Judith Davidow, Sept. 1959; children: David, Stephen, Claudia. BA, Western Md. Coll., 1953; MD, U. Md., 1957. Diplomate Am. Bd. Psychiatry. Pvt. practice, N.Y.C. and Scarsdale, NY, 1965—; psychiatrist Jennie Clarkson, Valhalla, NY, 1988—; med. dir. Daytop, Hartsdale, NY, 1997—2000; assoc. attending psychiatry N.Y. Hosp., Westchester, NY, 1997—2000. Author: On Freud, 2000; contbr. articles to profl. jours. Capt. USAF, 1961-63. Mem. Am. Psychiat. Assn. (life), Am. Psychoanalytic Inst. (life), Am. Psychoanalytic Assn. Office: 969 Park Ave New York NY 10028-0322 Office Phone: 212-744-1222. Office Fax: 914-949-0130.

**TRURAN, JAMES WELLINGTON, JR.,** astrophysicist, educator; b. Brewster, NY, July 12, 1940; s. James Wellington and Suzanne (Foglesong) T.; m. Carol Kay Dell'Acy, June 26, 1965; children— Elaina Michelle, Diana Lee, Anastasia Elizabeth. BA in Physics, Cornell U., 1961; MS in Physics, Yale U., 1963, PhD in Physics, 1966. Postdoctoral rsch. assoc. NAS-NRC Goddard Inst. Space Studies, NASA, N.Y.C., 1965-67; asst. prof. physics Belfer Grad. Sch. Sci., Yeshiva U., 1967-70; rsch. fellow in physics Calif. Inst. Tech., 1968-69; assoc. prof. Belfer Grad. Sch. Sci., Yeshiva U., 1970-72, prof., 1972-73; prof. astronomy U. Ill., Urbana, 1973-91; sr. vis. fellow, Guggenheim Meml. Found. fellow Inst. Astronomy, U. Cambridge, Eng., 1979-80; trustee Aspen Ctr. Physics, 1979-85, 91-93, 96-99, v.p., 1985-88; assoc. U. Ill. Ctr. for Advanced Study, 1979-80, 86-87; prof. astronomy astrophysics U. Chgo., 1991—; sr. physicist Argonne Nat. Lab., 2000—. Alexander von Humboldt-Stiftung sr. scientist Max-Plank Inst., Munich, Germany, 1986-87, 94; Beatrice Tinsley vis. prof. U. Tex., Austin, 1999; Biermann lectr. in astrophysics, Max-Planck Inst., Munich, 2001. Contbr. articles to profl. jours.; co-editor: Nucleosynthesis, 1968, Nucleosynthesis—Challenges and New Developments, 1985, Nuclear Astrophysics, 1987, Type Ia Supernovae: Theory and Cosmology, 2000, Cosmic Chemical Evolution, 2002; editor: Physics Letters B, 1974-80. Co-recipient Yale Sci. and Engring. Assn. annual award for advancement basic or applied sci., 1980 Fellow AAAS, Am. Phys. Soc.; mem. Am. Astron. Soc., Am. Phys. Soc., Internat. Astron. Union. Home: 210 Wysteria Dr Olympia Fields IL 60461-1202 Office: U Chgo Dept Astronomy Astrophysics 5640 S Ellis Ave Chicago IL 60637-1433 Business E-Mail: truran@nova.uchicago.edu.

**TRURAN, WILLIAM RICHARD,** electrical engineer; b. Franklin, NJ, Feb. 14, 1951; s. Wilfred Hardy and Stella Eva (Hall) Truran; m. Virginia Lynn Johnson, Aug. 18, 1979; children: Michael, Wendy. BSEE, U. Tenn., 1972; MBA, Fairleigh Dickinson U., 1981; MS in Indsl. Engring., Columbia U., 1994; PhD in Tech. Mgmt., Stevens Inst. Tech., 2000. Registered prof engr, NJ, NY, Pa, Calif; prof planner, NJ; cert. project mgmt. profl. Design engr. Gordos Corp., Bloomfield, NJ, 1973-82; project engr. Edwards Engring., Pompton Plains, NJ, 1973-78; sr. engr. Apollo Tech., Whippany, NJ, 1978-81; elec. product mgr. Dodge-Newark, Fairfield, NJ, 1981-96; pres. Trupower Engring., Sparta, NJ, 1984—. Pres TEC Corp NJ, Sparta, 1988—; adj prof Stevens Inst Technology; adj. prof. Seton Hall U.; consult in field. Author: Images of America: Franklin, Hamburg, Oodensburg, Hardyston, 2004, Sparta, N.J.: Head of the Wallkill, 2005, Minding for America, 2006; contbr. articles to profl jours. Active foster child orgn Christian Children's Fund; bd. mgrs. Columbia Engring. Sch. Alumni; v.p bd. mgrs. Columbia Engring. Sch. Alumni Assn., v.p. student rels.; commr. Sussex County Mcpl. Utilities Authority; bd. dirs. Franklin (N.J.) Mineral Mus., Sparta (N.J.) Hist. Soc.

Mem.: NSPE (legis action network, minuteman), Acad. of Mgmt., Nta. Assn. Environ. Profls., Sierra Club, Nature Conservancy. Episcopalian. Avocations: skiing, water-skiing, triathalons and marathons. Home and Office: 37 Rainbow Trl Sparta NJ 07871-1724 Office Phone: 973-729-1471. Business E-Mail: wrt1@columbia.edu.

**TRUS, BENES LOUIS,** structural chemist; b. Tyler, Tex., May 9, 1946; s. Joseph N. and Ruthie Trus; m. Susan Evans, Apr. 23, 1972; children: Aaron Baram, Anthony Phillip. BS cum laude with honors, Tulane U., 1968; PhD, Calif. Inst. Tech., 1972. Rsch. chemist NIH, Bethesda, Md., 1980—93, chief imaging processing rsch. sect., 1993—2002, chief imaging scis. lab., 2002—, dep. dir. divsn. computational biosci., 2003—. Mem. steering com. NIH wide image processing group, 1984— (NIH Dirs. award, 1987, 94, Group Merit award 1998). Contbr. articles to profl. jours., chpt. to books. Mem. NIH Marathon Team, 1986-88, 1st pl. Marine Corps Marathon, Govt. Team Competition, 1986, 3d pl., 1987, 88, 2d pl. Masters Team, 1993. Jane Coffin Childs postdoctoral fellow Calif. Inst. Tech., Pasadena, 1972-75, Rsch. fellow NIH, Bethesda, Md., 1975-77, Sr. Rsch. fellow, 1977-80; Tulane U. scholar and fellow, 1965-68. Mem. Chesapeake Soc. for Microscopy, Microscope Soc. Am., Reston Road Runner Club, Phi Beta Kappa, Sigma Xi. Avocations: music, running, carpentry. Office: NIH Bldg 12A Rm 2033 Bethesda MD 20892-5624

**TRUSCOTT, CARL J.,** federal agency administrator; b. Augusta, Ga., 1957; married; 1 child. BS in Criminal Justice, U. Del., 1979. U.S. Secret Svc. agent, 1981—2004; spl. agent in charge Presdl. Protective Divsn., 2001—03; asst. dir. Office Protective Rsch., U.S. Dept. Homeland Security, 2003—04; dir. Bur. Alcohol, Tobacco, Firearms and Explosives, U.S. Dept. Justice, Washington, 2004—. Recipient Dirs. Life Saving award, 1986, Sr. Exec. Svc. Performance award, 2001, 2002, Spl. award for disting. svc. to the Exec. Office of the Pres., 2002, Presdl. Rank award as Meritorious Exec., 2003. Office: Bur Alcohol Tobacco Firearms and Explosives 650 Massachusetts Ave NW Washington DC 20226

**TRUSDELL, MARY LOUISE CANTRELL,** retired state educational administrator; b. Chandler, Okla., Oct. 24, 1921; d. George Herbert and Lois Elizabeth (Bruce) Cantrell; m. Robert William Trusdell, Jan. 7, 1943; children— Timothy Lee, Laurence Michael. BA, Ga. So. Coll., 1965; MEd, U. Va., 1974. Dir. specific learning disabilities program Savannah Country Day Sch., Ga., 1960-65; learning disabilities tchr. Richmond pub. schs., Va., 1966-73; dir. New Community Sch., Richmond, 1974-75; dir. Fed. Learning Disabilities Project, Dept HEW, Mid. Peninsula, Va., 1975-76; supr. programs for learning disabled Va. Dept. Edn., Richmond, 1976-86; bd. dirs. Learning Disabilities Council, Richmond, Very Spl. Arts- Va., 1986-91; mem. adv. com. Learning Disabilities Research and Devel. Project, Woodrow Wilson Rehab. Ctr., Fisherville, Va., 1983. Co-editor: Understanding Learning Disabilities: A Parent Guide and Workbook, 1989, 3d edit., 2002. Bd. dirs. Savannah Assn. Retarded Children, 1957-60, Meml. Guidance Clinic, Richmond, 1966-69. Named Tchr. of Yr., Learning Disabilities Ctr., Richmond, 1972. Mem. Orton Dyslexia Soc. (pres. capital area br. 1968-70, nat. bd. dirs. 1970-72, Va. br. 1986-91), Alliance for the Mentally Ill. Cen. Va. (pres. 1991-93). Presbyterian. Avocations: travel, theater, reading.

**TRUSKOWSKI, JOHN BUDD,** lawyer; b. Chgo., Dec. 3, 1945; s. Casimer T. and Jewell S. (Kirk) T.; m. Karen Lee Sloss, Mar. 21, 1970; children: Philip K., Jennifer B. BS, U. Ill., 1967; JD, U. Chgo., 1970. Bar: Ill. 1970, U.S. Dist. Ct. (no. dist.) Ill. 1970, U.S. Tax Ct. 1977. Assoc. Keck, Mahin & Cate, Chgo., 1970-71, 74-78, ptnr., 1978-97, Lord, Bissell & Brook, Chgo., 1997—. Author, editor Callaghan's Federal Tax Guide, 1987. Lt., USNR, 1971-74. Mem. ABA, Ill. State Bar Assn., Chgo. Bar Assn. Republican. Unitarian. Avocations: model railroading, stamp collecting/philately. Home: 251 Kimberly Ln Lake Forest IL 60045-3862 Office: Lord Bissell & Brook Harris Bank Bldg 115 S Lasalle St Chicago IL 60603-3801 Office Phone: 312-443-0257.

**TRUSSELL, CHARLES TAIT,** columnist; b. Balt., May 9, 1925; s. Charles Prescott and Beatrice (Tait) T.; m. Woodley Grizzard, Dec. 27, 1953 (div. 1990); children: Galen Tait, Thomas Marshall; m. Nancy Rathbun Billington, Dec. 19, 1990. BA in Journalism, Washington and Lee U., Lexington, Va., 1949. Reporter St. Petersburg (Fla.) Times, also; writer Congl. Quar. News Features, 1951-54; reporter Wall St. Jour., 1954-56, Washington Evening Star, 1956; asso. editor Nation's Business mag., 1956-64, mng. editor, 1964-69; sr. editor Congressional Quar., Inc., 1969-70; dir. pub. relations and advt. Investment Co. Inst., Washington, 1970-72; free-lance writer, real estate investor, 1972-74; v.p. Am. Forest Inst., Washington, 1974-79, sr. v.p., 1980-81; v.p. Am. Enterprise Inst., 1981-86; dir. comms. Constitution Bicentennial Commn., 1986-88; freelance writer, columnist, 1988—. Nat. corr. Clear Mountain Comms. Producer: documentary record album The Best of Washington Humor, 1963; author: Beating the Competition, 1992; editor: Successful Management, 1964, (with Paul Hencke) Dear NASA Please Send Me a Rocket, 1964, Timeless Truths for Kids, 2002, Washington Doctor: A Parable on Love & Death. Served with USNR, 1944-46. Recipient Loeb Spl. Achievement award for mags. U. Conn., 1961, Benjamin Fine Journalism award, 1992. Mem. Washington Assembly (exec. com. 1961-65, chmn. 1965), Beta Theta Pi. Home: 2467 Cherry Rd Manistee MI 49660- E-mail: ttrussell@chartermi.net.

**TRUSSELL, JAMES,** economist, educator, dean; b. Columbus, Ga., Oct. 17, 1949; BS summa cum laude in Maths., Davidson Coll., 1971; BPhil, Oxford U., 1973; PhD in Econs., Princeton U., 1975. Econ. mat. prof. econs. to prof., dean Princeton (N.J.) U., 1975—. Co-author: The Loving Book, 1972, Contraceptive Technology, 18th edit., 2004; contbr. articles to profl. jours. Mem. Am. Statis. Assn., Am. Pub. Health Assn., Population Assn. Am., Australia Population Assn., Phi Beta Kappa., Assn. Reproductive Health Profls., Internat. Union for the Scientific Study of Population. Office: Princeton U Office of Population Rsch Wallace Hall Princeton NJ 08544-2007 Office Phone: 609-258-4946. Business E-Mail: trussell@princeton.edu.

**TRUTOR, GENEVIEVE WILLIAMSON,** museum director; b. Benson, Vt., Aug. 26, 1923; d. Clayton John and Caroline Aileen (Walker) Williamson; m. John Trutor, May 4, 1946 (dec.); children: Barry, John W., Elizabeth, William C. Diploma, Rutland Bus. Coll., 1942. Sec. War Prodn. Bd., Washington, 1942—45, Soc. Am. Foresters, Washington, 1945—47; adminstrv. asst. Benson Village Sch., Benson, Vt., 1971—89; dir. Benson Lumbar Yard Inc., Benson, 1963—2002; founder, curator Benson Mus., Benson, 1980—. Lib. commr. Town of Benson, 1959—61; dir. Lower Champlain Housing Corp., 1977—82; mem. Benson's Cmty. Hall Restoration project, 1975—80; chmn. Nat. Bicentennial Celebration, Benson, Vt., 1976, State Bicentennial Celebration, Vt., 1977, Benson Bicentennial Celebration, 1980; sec., treas. Benson Health Com., 1961—70; trustee Pub. Funds, 1981—87, 1996—, Bertha R. Franke Scholarship Fund, 1971—79. Republican.

**TRUTTER, JOHN THOMAS,** telecommunications industry executive, educator, writer; b. Springfield, Ill., Apr. 18, 1920; s. Frank Louis and Frances (Mischler) T.; m. Edith English Woods II, June 17, 1950 (dec.); children: Edith English II, Jonathan Woods. BA, U. Ill., 1942; postgrad., Northwestern U., 1947-50, U. Chgo., 1947-50; LHD (hon.), Lincoln Coll., 1986. Various positions Ill. Bell, Chgo., 1946-58, gen. traffic mgr. from asst. v.p. pub. rels. to gen. mgr., 1958-69, v.p. pub. rels., 1969-71, v.p. operator svcs., 1971-80, v.p. community affairs, 1980-85; mem. hdqrs. staff AT&T, N.Y.C., 1955-57; pres. John T. Trutter Co., Inc., Chgo., 1985—; pres., CEO Chgo. Conv. and Visitors Bur., 1985-88; pres. Chgo. Tourism Coun., 1988-90; v.p. Profl. Impressions Media Group, Inc., 1998-2000, prof. emeritus, 2001. Mem. adv. bd. The Alford Group, Chgo., 1999—, Bozell-Worldwide, Chgo., 1994-96; chancellor Lincoln Acad. of Ill., 1985-2001. Co-author: Handling Barriers in Communication, 1957, The Governor Takes a Bride, 1977 Past chmn., life trustee Jane Addams Hull House Assn.; chmn. United Cerebral Palsy Assn. Greater Chgo., 1967-95, hon. chmn., 1995—, chmn. Canal Corridor Assn., 1991-99; bd. dirs. Chgo. Crime Commn., Abraham Lincoln Assn., Lyric

Opera Chgo.; v.p. English Speaking Union, 1989-91, bd. govs., 1980—; chmn. bd. City Colls. Chgo. Found., 1987-91; past chmn. Children's Home and Aid Soc. Ill.; v.p. City Club Chgo.; treas. Chgo. United, 1970-85; mem. Ill. Econ. Devel. Commn., 1985; past presiding co-chmn. NCCJ; numerous others; bd. govs. Northwestern U. Libr. Coun., 1984—; trustee Lincoln (Ill.) Coll., 1987-90, Mundelein Coll., 1988-91; mem. sch. problems coun. State Ill. Assembly, 1985-91, spl. commn. on adminstrn. of justice in Cook County, 1986-92; founding chmn. adv. coun. Evanston Hist. Soc., 1995-98. Lt. col. U.S. Army, 1945. Decorated Legion of Merit; recipient Laureate award State of Ill., 1980, Outstanding Exec. Leader award Am. Soc. Fundraisers, Humanitarian of Yr. award, Jane Addams award The Hull House Assn., 1991, Nat. Infinitec award for individual leadership in assistive technology for disabled people, 1997, Jack Brickhouse award for outstanding svcs., 2000. Mem. Pub. Rels. Soc. Am., Sangamon County Hist. Soc. (founder, past pres.), Ill. State Hist. Soc. (pres. 1985-87), Coun. on Ill. History (chmn. 1991—), U. Ill. Alumni Assn. (bd. dirs. 1990-94), Tavern Club, Econ. Club, Mid-Am. Club, Alpha Sigma Phi (Nat. Merit Achievement award 1994), Phi Delta Phi. Office Phone: 847-446-4267. Office Fax: 847-441-0582.

**TRUWIT, MITCHELL,** Internet company executive; b. 1969; BS in Polit. Sci., Vassar College, Poughkeepsie, NY; MBA, Harvard Univ., 1997. Dir. bus. devel. Oxford Health Plans, Conn., 1997; COO Priceline.com, Conn.; CEO, global online consumer travel Cendant Corp., Chgo. Spkr. in field. Named one of 40 Under Forty, Crain's Bus. Chgo., 2005. Office: Orbitz Inc Ste 1900 200 S Wacker Dr Chicago IL 60606 Office Fax: 312-894-5001.*

**TRYBAN, ESTHER ELIZABETH,** lawyer; b. Chgo., Aug. 14, 1958; d. Chester Joseph and Lottie Elizabeth (Napora) Tryban. AAS with honors, Elgin (Ill.) C.C., 1977, AS with honors, 1982; BS with honors, Roosevelt U., Chgo., 1986; JD, U. Chgo., 1989. Bar: Ill. 1989, U.S. Dist. Ct. (no. dist.) Ill. 1989, U.S. Ct. Appeals (7th cir.) 1990, U.S. Supreme Ct., 1996. Supr. adminstrv. svcs. law dept. Motorola, Inc., Schaumburg, Ill., 1977-86; staff law clk. U.S. Bankruptcy Ct. No. Dist. Ill., Chgo., 1989-90; sr. counsel City of Chgo., 1990—. Mem. ABA, Nat. Lawyers Guild, Assn. Former Bankruptcy Law Clks, Ill. State Bar Assn., Chgo. Bar Assn. (chair govt. svc. com. 1996-97), Advocates Soc. (2d v.p. Chgo. chpt. 2006—). Roman Catholic. Avocations: reading, football, travel. Office: City Chgo Dept Law 30 N Lasalle St Ste 900 Chicago IL 60602-2503 Office Phone: 312-744-1846. Business E-Mail: lw00026@cityofchicago.org.

**TRYGSTAD, LAWRENCE BENSON,** lawyer; b. Holton, Mich., Mar. 22, 1937; BA, U. Mich., 1959; JD, U. So. Calif., 1967. Bar: Calif. 1968, U.S. Supreme Ct. 1974. Legal counsel Calif. Tchrs. Assn., Calif. Tchrs. L.A., L.A., 1968-71; ptnr. Trygstad & Odell, L.A., 1971-80; pres. Trygstad Law Corp., L.A., 2004—; ptnr. Trygstad, Schwab & Trygstad, L.A., 2004—. Instr., tchr. negotiation U. Calif.-Northridge; panelist TV shows Law and the Teacher. Bd. dirs. George Washington Carver Found., L.A. Mem. ABA, Calif. Bar Assn., Consumer Attys. Calif., L.A. County Bar Assn., Calif. Trial Lawyers Assn., Nat. Orgn. Lawyers for Edn. Assns., Am. Trial Lawyers Assn., Consumer Attys. L.A., Phi Alpha Delta. Home: 4209 Aleman Dr Tarzana CA 91356-5405 Office: 1880 Century Park E Ste 1104 Los Angeles CA 90067-1609 Office Phone: 310-552-0500. Business E-Mail: ltrygstad@trygstadlawoffice.com.

**TRYLOFF, ROBIN S.,** food products executive; BS, U. Mich.; MS, U. Chgo. Exec. dir., cmty. rels. Sara Lee Corp.; exec. dir. Sara Lee Found., pres., 2002—. Chair, bd. dirs. Donors Forum of Chgo., 2004. Office: Sara Lee Found 3 First Nat Plz Chicago IL 60602-4260

**TRYON, MARGARET A.,** director, school psychologist; b. Billings, Mont., July 22, 1950; d. Roy N. and Bunny Morrison; 1 child, Tiffany Nicole. BA, U. Mont., 1972; MS, Ea. Mont. Coll., 1977. Cert. sch. psychologist. Spl. edn. tchr. Plains Pub. Schs., Mont., 1975—77, Ronan Pub. Schs., Mont., 1977—92; spl. edn. dir., sch. psychologist Miles City Pub. Schs., Mont., 1992—. Mem.: NASP, Mont. Coun. Adminstrs. (pres. Disting. Svc. award 2000), Coun. for Exceptional Children (Spl. Educator award 1999). Office Phone: 406-834-3812.

**TRYTEK, DAVID DOUGLAS,** insurance company executive; b. Cleve., Jan. 18, 1955; s. Edmund Trytek and Mary Elaine Salzwedel Blech; m. Lorie Ann Stone, Apr. 10, 1982; children: Dane, Douglas. BS in BA, Bowling Green (Ohio) State U., 1977. Claims adjuster Liberty Mus. Ins. Co., Toledo, 1977-80, claims supr. Milw., 1980-85, spl. claims examiner Boston, 1986-89, claims mgr. Green Bay, Wis., 1989-93; tech. svcs. mgr. Liberty Mut. Ins. Co., Milw., 1993-95; regional field investigations mgr. Liberty Mutual Ins. Co., Milw., 1996—, Wausau Ins. Co., Milw., 2001—. Arbitrator Inter-Co. Arbitration Com., Milw., 1984-85. Coach Toledo Optimists Youth Hockey Assn., 1979-80, Wauwatosa (Wis.) Recreation Dept., 1980-85, YMCA Youth Baseball, 1994; alt. Worker's Compensation divsn. Ins. Adv. Com., Madison, Wis., 1994 youth football coach, Sussex, Wis., 1994-99, youth baseball coach, 1994-99, 2002-03. Mem. Exptl. Aircraft Assn., Warbirds of Am., USA Hockey Inc., Internat. Assn. of Spl. Investigation Units, Wis. Street Rod Assn. (bd. dirs. 1999-2002). Avocations: camping, ice hockey, golf, military aircraft. Office: Liberty Mut Ins Co 11800 W Park Pl Milwaukee WI 53224-3009 Business E-Mail: david.trytek@libertymutual.com.

**TRYTHALL, HARRY GILBERT,** music educator, composer; b. Knoxville, Tenn., Oct. 28, 1930; s. Harry Gilbert and Clara Hannah (Akre) T.; m. Jean Marie Slater, Dec. 28, 1951 (div. 1976); children: Linda Marie, Karen Elizabeth; m. Carol King, Sept. 19, 1985. BA, U. Tenn., 1951; MusM, Northwestern U., 1952; DMA, Cornell U., 1960. Asst. prof. music Knox Coll., Galesburg, Ill., 1960-64; prof. music theory and composition George Peabody Coll. Tchrs., Nashville, 1964-75; dean Creative Arts Ctr., 1975-81; prof. music W.Va. U., Morgantown, 1975-96; ret., 1997. Vis. prof. U. Federal do Espirito Santo, Vitoria, Brazil, 1999—. Author: Principles and Practice of Electronic Music, 1974, Eighteenth Century Counterpoint, 1993, Sixteenth Century Counterpoint, 1994; past mem. editorial bd. Music Educators Jour.; composer orchestral music, chamber and electronic music. With USAF, 1953-57. Office Phone: 972-407-1081. Personal E-mail: htrythal@yahoo.com.

**TRYTTEN, DEBORAH ANNE,** computer scientist, educator; b. Ann Arbor, Mich., Apr. 14, 1960; d. Richard Wesley and Marilyn McCall Trytten. MS in Applied Math., Mich. State U., 1984, MS in Computer Sci., 1988, PhD in Computer Sci., 1992. Asst. prof. U. Okla., Norman, 1992—98, assoc. prof., 1998—; pres., founder, chief tech. officer Beyond Paper, Inc., Norman, 2001—02. Achievements include patents pending for electronic textbook format. Office: U Okla 200 Felgar Rm 108 Norman OK 73019

**TRZASKA, JOYCE ANNE,** publishing executive; b. Great Falls, Mont., Jan. 4, 1950; d. Wendell Babe and Valerie Hurst; m. Gregory Warren Trzaska, June 27, 1970; children: James Warren, Gena Anne McKinnon, Lori Lynn. Student, Taft Coll., 1968—69. Pub. A Snow Man with Feelings, The Giraffe That Wore A Necklace, Mister Giraffe: Bow Tie & Long Gold Chain!. Mem.: Port Ludlow Yacht Club. Home: 45 Jackson Ln Port Ludlow WA 98365 Personal E-mail: gtrz100160@aol.com.

**TRZASKO, JOSEPH ANTHONY,** psychologist, educator; b. Jamaica, N.Y., June 4, 1946; s. Joseph Anthony and Lottie Marion (Nadraus) T.; m. Ann Elizabeth Kidd, June 26, 1971; 1 son, Joshua Damon. BA cum laude, U. N.H., 1967; MA, U. Vt., 1969, PhD, 1972. Cert. behavioral therapy, 1976, psychologist 1977; diplomate Am. Bd. Psychol. Specialties, 1997, Am. Bd. Forensic Examiners, 1998; cert. profl. qualification in psychology Assn. State and Provincial Psychology Bds. Prof. dep. psychology Mercy Coll., Dobbs Ferry, N.Y., 1969—; postdoctoral internship Ridge State Home and Tng. Sch., Colo. Dept. Insts., 1980; staff psychologist St. Dominic's Intermediate Care Facility for Devel. Disabled, Blauvelt, N.Y., 1980—; cons. psychologist Jewish Guild for Blind, N.Y.C., 1983—2002, Orange County A.H.R.C., Newburgh, N.Y., 1985—; Opengate Inc., Somers, NY, 2006—; pvt. practice

clin. psychology. Chair ednl. psychology test devel. Ednl. Testing Svc., 2000—04; neuro-forensic psychologist Supervised Life Styles Behavioral Health Clinic, 2002—. Contbg. author: Working with Visually Impaired Young Children: A Curriculum Guide for Birth -3 Year Olds, 1992; contbg. author: Working with Visually Impaired Young Students: A Curriculum Guide for 3 to 5 Year Olds, 1998. NDEA fellow U. Vt., 1967-69; NSF faculty rsch. participation grantee Ednl. Commn. States/Nat. Assessment Ednl. Progress, 1976. Mem. AAUP, Am. Psychol. Assn., Am. Coll. Forensic Examiners. Roman Catholic. Home and Office: 30 Lake Dr Somers NY 10589-2420 Office Phone: 914-277-1743. Personal E-mail: jatphd@optonline.net. Business E-Mail: jtrzasko@mercy.edu.

**TRZYNA, CHRIS,** physical education educator; b. Chgo. d. Edward and Helen Trzyna. BS, No. Ill. U., 1976, MS, 1983, C.A.S. in Adminstrn. and Supervision, 1991. Cert. tchr. Ill. Tchr., asst. athletic dir. Libertyville HS, 1976—; girls volleyball coach Libertyville HS, 1987—2005. Recipient Volleyball Coach of Yr., Libertyville H.S., 2000, 2005. Mem.: AAHPERD, Ill. Athletic Dirs. Assn., Ill. High Sch. Assn. (soccer adv. com.), Ill. Assn. Health, Phys. Edn. Recreation and Dance, Delta Psi Kappa (v.p. 1975—76). Office: Libertyville High School 708 W Park Ave Libertyville IL 60048-2604 Business E-Mail: chris.trzyna@district128.org.

**TSACOUMIS, STEPHANIE,** lawyer; b. Aug. 31, 1956; BA magna cum laude, Coll. of William & Mary, 1978; JD, Univ. Va., 1981. Bar: DC 1981, Md. 1982. Of counsel Morrison & Foerster, Washington, 1988—91, ptnr., 1991—96; of counsel, corp. fin. Gibson Dunn & Crutcher LLP, Washington, 1996—2000, ptnr. corp. transactions and securities, 2000—, and co-ptnr.-in-charge DC office. Adj. faculty Georgetown Univ. Law Ctr., 2001—. Sr. editor Va. Jour. of Internat. Law, contributing author Corporate Communications and the Federal Antifraud Rules, 1992, Securities in the Electronic Age, 2001. Mem.: ABA, Md. State Bar Assn., DC Bar, Phi Beta Kappa. Office: Gibson Dunn & Crutcher LLP 1050 Connecticut Ave NW Washington DC 20036 Office Phone: 202-955-8277. Office Fax: 202-530-9613. Business E-Mail: stsacoumis@gibsondunn.com.

**TSAI, CHRISTINA W.,** civil engineer, educator; arrived in U.S., 1995; d. Jin-Yi Tsai and Jau-Jr Chen; m. Shih-Ping Ho, Jan. 4, 2001; 1 child, Julianne Y. BS in Civil Engring., Nat. Taiwan U., Taipei, 1995; MS in Civil Engring., U. Ill., Urbana, 1997, MS in Applied Math., 2000, PhD in Civil Engring., 2001. Rsch. scientist Ill. State Water Survey, Champaign, Ill., 2000—01; asst. prof. SUNY, Buffalo, 2002—. Contbr. articles to profl. jours. Recipient Stout Water Resources Rsch. award, U. of Ill. at Champaign-Urbana, 2000, award, NSF, 2005; grantee SUNY at Buffalo Interdisciplinary Rsch. and Creative Activities Fund, 2002, Environ. Sci. Inst. SUNY at Buffalo, 2003. Mem.: ASCE (assoc. ExCEED tchg. fellow 2003), Am. Soc. of Engring. Edn., Internat. Assn. of Hydraulic Rsch., Internat. Water Resources Assn., Am. Geophys. Union, Am. Soc. of Women Engineers, Phi Kappa Phi. Avocations: reading, travel. Office: SUNY at Buffalo 233 Jarvis Hall Buffalo NY 14260 Office Phone: 716-645-2114 2414. E-mail: ctsai4@eng.buffalo.edu.

**TSAI, FRANK TSUNG-CHEN,** engineering educator, researcher; m. Shwu-Huey Lee; children: Brian, Emma. BS, Nat. Chung-Hsing U., Taiwan, 1993; PhD, UCLA, 2002. Postdoctoral fellow UCLA, 2002—03; asst. prof. La. State U., Baton Rouge, 2003—. Office: La State Univ CEE 3507 CEBA Bldg Baton Rouge LA 70803 Office Phone: 225-578-4246. Business E-Mail: ftsai@lsu.edu.

**TSAI, JAMES C.,** ophthalmologist, researcher; BA in Neurosci., Amherst Coll., 1985; MD, Stanford U., 1989; MBA, Vanderbilt U., 1998. Diplomate Am. Bd. Ophthalmology, Nat. Bd. Med. Examiners. Intern Cedars-Sinai Med. Ctr., LA, 1989—90; resident in ophthalmology U. So. Calif./Doheny Eye Inst., LA, 1990—93; fellow Bascom Palmer Eye Inst., Miami, Fla., 1993—94, Moorfields Eye Hosp., London, 1994—95; asst. prof. ophthalmology and visual scis. Vanderbilt U. Sch. Medicine, Nashville, 1995—2001; dir. glaucoma divsn., assoc. prof. ophthalmology Harkness Eye Inst., Columbia U. Coll. Physicians and Surgeons, N.Y.C., 2001—06; Robert Young prof., chair dept. ophthalmology and visual sci. Yale U. Sch. Medicine, New Haven, 2006—. Homer McK. Rees Glaucoma scholar, Columbia U., 2001—04. Fellow: ACS, Am. Acad. Ophthalmology (Achievement award). Office: Yale Eye Ctr PO Box 208061 New Haven CT 06520-8061 Office Phone: 646-422-0200, 203-785-2020. Office Fax: 203-785-7694. Business E-Mail: jct2002@columbia.edu, james.tsai@yale.edu.

**TSAI, JINGPHA (JEFFREY TSAI),** computer scientist, educator; b. Cha-I, Taiwan; m. Fuh-Te Tsai; children: Edward, Christina. MS, Northwestern U., 1983, PhD, 1985. Prof. U. Ill., 1997—. Author 9 books; co-editor-in-chief Artificial Intelligence Tools, 1994; contbr. more than 200 articles to profl. jours. and confs. Recipient Univ. scholar award U. Ill., Tech. Achievement award IEEE Computer Soc. Fellow IEEE, AAAS, Soc. for Design and Process Sci. Office: MCI 154 EECS Dept 851 S Morgan St Chicago IL 60607-7042

**TSAI, JOHN JENGSHYONG,** publishing executive; b. Taiwan, Sept. 9, 1942; BS in Physics and Chem., Nat. Taiwan Normal U., 1965; MS in Physics, Coll. of William and Mary, Va., 1970; PhD in Ocean Physics, U. Miami, 1977; MBA, Fla. Internat. U., 1987. Rsch. physicist, ocean acoustics div. Atlantic Oceanographic and Meteorological Lab., 1977—2001; founder, pres. Integrated Tech. Internat., Inc., 1986—90; publisher, chief editor Overseas Chinese News, 1990—. Bd. mem. Atlantic Inst. of Oriental Medicine, Ft. Lauderdale, Fla. Mem. Chinese Federation of Fla., exec. sec., 1994—95, v.p., 1996—97, pres., 1998—99. Mem.: Chinese Am. Press Inst. (pres.), Asian Am. Journalists Assn., Am. Geophysical Union, Acoustical Soc. of Am. Office: Overseas Chinese News 8100 SW 92 Ct Miami FL 33173

**TSAI, MING,** chef; b. Dayton, OH; m. Polly Tsai. ME, Yale U.; attended, Le Cordon Bleu cooking school, Paris; M in Hotel Adminstrn. and Hospitality Mktg., Cornell U. Co-owner, exec. chef Blue Ginger, Boston, 1998—. Founding mem. Chefs For Humanity, 2005—; ptnr. Blue Ginger line, Target, 2000—. Host East Meets West, Food Network, 1998 (Emmy award, 1998), Ming's Quest, Fine Living Network, host, exec. prodr. Simply Ming, Pub. TV celebrity judge Cooking Under Fire, PBS, 2005—; author: Blue Ginger: East Meets West Cooking with Ming Tsai (Named One of 25 Best Cookbooks, Food and Wine Mag., 1999), Simply Ming, 2003, Ming's Master Recipes, 2004. Recipient Chef of Yr., Esquire Mag., 1998, Best Chef Northeast, James Beard Found., 2002, Restaurateur of Yr., Mass. Restaurant Assoc., 2005. Office: Blue Ginger 583 Wasington St Wellesley MA 02482*

**TSAI, TOM CHUNGHU,** chemical engineer; b. Kaohsiung, Taiwan, Oct. 24, 1948; arrived in U.S., 1971, naturalized, 1984; s. Shu and Kwei (Kao) T.; m. Joyce Chionhwa Pai, Dec. 17, 1974; children: Wayne, Jimmy Payne. BS in Chem. Engring., Nat. Taiwan U., Taipei, 1970; MS in Chem. Engring., Purdue U., 1973, PhD in Chem. Engring., 1975. Reappointed prof. engr., Tex. Sr. process engr. CE-Lummus Co., Bloomfield, NJ, 1975-80; sr. engr. Bechtel Petroleum Inc., Houston, 1980-83; cons. engr. TDS Assocs., Houston, 1983-88; process engring. assoc. Dow Chem. Co., Freeport, Tex., 1988—. Internat. adv. bd. Ency. Chem. Processing and Design, 1995—. Co-author, contbr.: Ethylene-Keystone to the Petrochemical Industry, 1980, Kirk-Othmer Encyclopedia of Chemical Technology, 1980, Pyrolysis: Theory and Industrial Practice, 1983, Refining & Petrochemical Tech. Yearbook, 1987, Encyclopedia of Chemical Processing and Design, 1990, 94-96, 2005, Unit Operations Handbook, 1992; contbr. articles to profl. jours. Bd. dirs. H.S. for Performing and Visual Arts PTO, Houston, 1995-99. 2d lt. Republic of China Army, 1970-71. Mem.: AIChE, Assn. Chinese Orgns. (Houston) (pres. 2003), Assn. Chinese Am. Profls. (divsn. chmn. 1988—89, v.p. 2000—01, pres.-elect 2001—02, pres. 2002—03), Taiwan Chorus of Houston (pres. 2005—06). Achievements include patents in field. Home: 1503 Ashford Hollow Ln Houston TX 77077-3903 Office: The Dow Chem Co 400 W Sam Houston Pkwy S Houston TX 77042-1299 Office Phone: 713-978-2324. E-mail: tomctsai@dow.com.

**TSAI, VICTOR CHEN,** geophysicist; b. Mass., Mar. 19, 1982; BS, Calif. Inst. Tech., Pasadena, 2004. Geophysicist Harvard U., Cambridge, Mass., 2004—. NSF Grad. fellow, 2005—. Mem.: Am. Geophys. Union (Outstanding Student Paper award 2005). Democrat. Achievements include research in characterization of glacial earthquakes. Avocations: music, puzzles, bridge. Office Phone: 617-495-9604.

**TSAI, WEN-YING,** sculptor, painter, engineer; b. Xiamen, Fujian, China, Oct. 13, 1928; came to U.S., 1950, naturalized, 1962; s. Chen-Dak and Ching-Miau (Chen) T.; m. Pei-De Chang, Aug. 7, 1968; children: Lun-Yi and Ming Yi (twins). Student, Ta Tung U., 1947-49; BSME, U. Mich., 1953; postgrad., Art Students League N.Y., 1953-57, Faculty Polit. and Social Sci., New Sch., 1956-58. Cons. engr., 1953-63; project mgr. Cosentini Assocs., 1962-63; project engr. Guy B. Panero, Engrs., 1956-60. Creator cybernetic sculpture based on prin. harmonic motion, stroboscopic effects; one-man shows include, Ruth Sherman Gallery, N.Y.C., 1961, Amel Gallery, N.Y.C., 1964, 65, Howard Wise Gallery, N.Y.C., 1968, Kaiser Wilhelm Mus. Haus Lange, Krefeld, Germany, 1970, Hayden Gallery of MIT, Cambridge, Ont. Sci. Centre, Toronto, Can., 1971, Corcoran Gallery Art, 1972, Denise René Gallery, 1972, 73, Musée d'Art Contemporain, Montreal, 1973, Museo de Arte Contemporáneo, Caracas, 1975, Wildenstein Art Center, Houston, 1978, Museo de Bellas Artes, Caracas, 1978, Hong Kong Mus. Art, 1979, Isetan Mus. Art, Tokyo, 1980, Galerie Denise René, Paris, 1983, Nat. Mus. History, Taipei, Taiwan, 1989, Taiwan Mus. of Art, Taichung, 1990, China Nat. Mus. Fine Arts, Beijing, 1997, Centre Georges Pompidou, 2001; one man show: Galerie Denise René, Paris, 2000, Shanghai Art Mus., 2002; represented maj. internat. exhbns., also numerous group exhbns., in permanent collections, Centre Georges Pompidou, Paris; Tate Gallery, London, Albright-Knox Gallery, Buffalo Mus., Addison Gallery Am. Art, Andover, Mass., Museo de Arte Contemporáneo, Caracas, Museo de Bellas Artes, Caracas, Whitney Mus., Chrysler Art Mus., Orlando Sci. Ctr., MIT, Hayden Gallery, Kaiser Wilhelm Mus., Mus. Modern Art, Israel Mus., Jerusalem, Artware, Kunst und Elektronik, Honnover-Messe, Great Exploration-The Hands on Mus., Taiwan Mus. Art, Saibu Gas Mus., Nagoya City Mus., Mus. fü Holographie, Kanagawa Sci. Pk., Hong Kong Sci. Mus., others; commd. works include: fountain at Land Mark, Hong Kong, 1980,, water sculpture at Shell Tower, Singapore, 1982, cybernetic upward falling fountains (2), Paris; creator spatial dynamic hydro-cybernetic systems for 42d Internat. Exhbn. Art-La Biennale di Venezia, 1986, Digital Visions-Computers and Art, Everson Mus. of Art, 1987, Contemporary Arts Ctr. Cin., 1987, IBM Gallery of Sci. and Art, N.Y.C., 1988, Phenomena Art Expo, Fukuoka, Japan, 1989, Wonderland of Sci.-Art Kanagawa Internat. Art Sci. Exhbn., Kawasaki, Japan, 1989, Vienna Messe-Wiener Festwochen, 1989, Kanagawa Internat. Art & Sci. Exhbn., Kawasaki, Japan, 1989, Artec 91, Internat. Biennale in Nagoya, Japan, 1991 (Artec Grand Prix winner), Homage à Denise Reńe-Cybernetic Arts, Musée Nat. d'art Modern Ctr. Georges Pompidon, 2001, Shanghai Internat. Biennale for Contemporary Arts, Shanghai Art Mus., 2004; developed concept "5 elements," proposal for new modern sculpture park for Oriental Plz., Beijing, 1996-98; creator first CD-ROM version of cybernetic sculpture, 1995, Info-Art Kwang Ju Internat. Biennale Korea, Osaka Triennale, 1995—, Internet Graphics Gallery, 1995; featured: Art for Tomorrow-The 21st Century, CBS-TV, 1969, Video Variation, WGBH-TV, 1971, Science and Art, Japan TV Man Union, 1982, Art and Sci.-Innovation, Sta. WNET-TV, 1988, The World of Wen-Ying Tsai, Taiwan Pub. TV, 1991. Recipient Soc. Merit award U. Mich., 2001; John Hay Whitney fellow, 1963, MacDowell fellow, 1965, fellow Center Advanced Visual Studies, MIT, 1969, 70. Inventor upward falling fountain, computer mural, multiple light computer array, utilizing environ. feedback control system.

**TSAKALIS, KONSTANTINOS,** electrical engineer, educator; PhD, U. So. Calif., L.A., Calif., 1988. From asst. prof. to rof. Ariz. State U., Tempe, Ariz., 1988—2003, prof., 2003—. Author: Linear Time-Varying Systems: Control and Adaptation; contbr. articles to profl. jours. Mem.: IEEE. Achievements include patents for temperature control system for a thermal reactor and run-to-run controllers for applications in semiconductor manufacturing. Office: Arizona State University PO Box 875706 Tempe AZ 85287-5706 Office Phone: 480-965-1467. Personal E-mail: tsakalis@asu.edu. Business E-Mail: tsakalis@asu.eddu.

**TSALIKIAN, EVA,** physician, educator; b. Piraeus, Greece, June 22, 1949; came to U.S., 1974; d. Vartan and Arousiak (Kasparian) T.; m. Arthur Bonfield, Apr. 8, 2000. MD, U. Athens, 1973. Rsch. fellow U. Calif., San Francisco, 1974-76; resident in pediatrics Children's Hosp., Pitts., 1976-78, fellow in endocrinology, 1978-80; rsch. fellow Mayo Clinic, Rochester, Minn., 1980-83; from asst. prof. to prof. pediats. U. Iowa, 1983—2004, prof. pediats., 2004—; dir. pediat. endocrinology hosps. and clinics, 1988—, vice chmn. clin. affairs Dept. Pediats., 2005—, chief staff hosp., 2006—. Recipient Young Physician award, AMA, 1977; fellow, Juvenile Diabetes Found., 1978—80, Heinz Nutrition Found., 1980—81. Mem. Am. Diabetes Assn. (bd. dirs. Mid-Am. sect.), Endocrine Soc., Soc. Pediat. Rsch., Am. Pediat. Soc., Lawson Wilkins Soc. for Pediat. Endocrinology, Internat. Soc. Pediat. and Adolescent Diabetes Home: 206 Mahaska Dr Iowa City IA 52246-1606 Office: U Iowa Dept Pediatrics 2856 JPP Iowa City IA 52242

**TSANG, RAYMOND,** electronics executive; Mng. dir. and strategic bus. dir. for China Nat. Semiconductor Asia, 1987—94; mng. dir. Sunrise Tech. Ltd., 1995—97; v.p. gen. mgr. Pericom Tech. Inc., 1998—2000; CEO Sunrise Tech., Ltd., 2000—01; v.p. and regional dir. Avnet Elec. Mktg. Hong Kong and China Ops., Avent, Inc., 2001—02; v.p. Avnet, Inc., 2002—. pres. Avnet Elec. Mktg. Asia, Avent, Inc., 2002—. Office: Avnet Inc 2211 S 47th St Phoenix AZ 85034

**TSAO, GUS,** information technology executive; b. Chongqing, China; arrived in U.S., 1968, naturalized, 1989; Mem. staff City of Columbus; head R&D Dept. DennisonTRG Sys.; founder Daybreak Technologies Inc., Evermore Software, Monterey Pk., Calif., 1995—, pres., 1999—, CEO, 1999—. Office: Evermore Software 1101 Northridge Place Monterey Park CA 91754

**TSAO, HENSIN,** dermatologist, researcher; BA, Brown U., Providence, 1986; MD, Coll. Physicians and Surgeons Columbia U., N.Y.C., 1993; PhD, Grad. Sch. Arts and Scis. Columbia U., N.Y.C., 1993. Diplomate Am. Bd. Dermatology, 1997, lic. Mass., 1997. Dir. melanoma genetics program Mass. Gen. Hosp. Cancer Ctr., Boston, 2001—; dir. melanoma and pigmented lesion ctr. Mass. Gen. Hosp., 2005—. Med. adv. bd. Mass. Melanoma Found., 2000—; Samuel Bluefarb invited lectr. U. Chgo. Recipient Physician-Scientist Clin. Career Devel. award, Dermatology Found., Clin. Career Devel. award, Dermatology Found. and Am. Acad. Dermatology, Alfred Steiner Rsch. award, Columbia U., Titus Munson Coan Rsch. prize, Young Investigator's award, Am. Acad. Dermatology, Deborah Shalita Marmour Clin. Career award, Dermatology Found.; D.M. Carter scholar, Am. Skin Assn. Fellow: Am. Acad. Dermatology; mem.: Alpha Omega Alpha, Phi Beta Kappa. Office: Mass Gen Hosp Dept Dermatology 48 Blossom St Boston MA 02114 Office Phone: 617-726-9569. Office Fax: 617-726-1206.

**TSAO, JENNIE CHING-I,** research scientist, educator; d. Jean Huang and James Chih-Ming Tsao; m. Aram Dobalian, June 2, 2002. BA, UCLA, 1981, PhD, 1999; BS, City U., London, Eng., 1994. Cert. clin. psychology Fla. Rsch. asst. City U., London, 1994—94; grad. therapist UCLA Psychology Clinic, 1995—96; project collaborator UCLA Anxiety Disorders Behavioral Program, 1995—97; sr. therapist and assessor, 1996—98, project dir., 1996—99; supr. Cmty. Outreach Prevention and Edn. Svc., UCLA Sch. of Medicine, 1997—98; post-doctoral rsch. coord. UCLA Pediatric Pain Program, Sch. of Medicine, 1999—2000, asst. rsch. psychologist, 2000—01; rsch. asst. prof. NIMH Ctr. for the Study of Emotion and Attention, U.Fla., Gainesville, 2001—03, Nat. Rural Behavioral Health Ctr., U. Fla., Gainesville, 2002—04; rsch. scientist UCLA Pediatric Pain Program, Sch. Medicine, L.A., 2004—. Clin. supr. Fanning Springs Primary Care Clinic, Nat. Rural Behavioral Health Program, U. Fla., 2002—04; Nat. Rural Behavioral Health Program, Gainesville, 2002—04, Fear & Anxiety Disorders Clinic, U. Fla., Gainesville, 2001—04; peer reviewer Jour. Abnormal Psychology, 2000—,

Health Psychology, 2000—01, Jour. of Pediatric Psychology, 2000—, Psychosomatic Medicine, 2000—, Behavior Rsch. and Therapy, 2000—, Jour. of Pain and Symptom Mgmt., 2000—, Jour. Cons. and Clin. Psychol., 2004—. Sr. sect. editor: Cognitive and Behavioral Practice, 2004—, assoc. editor: Jour. Pediatric Psychology, Spl. Issue: Pain, 2004—; contbr. chapters to books, articles to profl. jours. Recipient Social Sci. prize, KPMG, 1993, Young Investigators Travel award, Am. Pain Soc., 2001, 2003—04; fellow, UCLA Dept. Psychology, 1994—95; grantee, 1995, 1995—97. Nat. Insts. Mental Health, 1996—98, UCLA Dept. Psychology, 1997, Health Resources and Svcs. Adminstrn., 2003—04, Aty. Healthcare Rsch. and Quality, 2003—, Nat. Inst. Drug Abuse, 2004—; Regents scholar, UCLA Coll. Letters and Sci. 1978—81. Mem.: Anxiety Disorders Assn. Am. (Career Devel. Travel award 2003), Am. Pain Soc., Am. Assn. for the Advancement of Behavior Therapy, Phi Beta Kappa. Achievements include Professional Appearance on ABC's 20/20 segment entitled, Don't Panic; Professional Appearance on NBC's Dateline segment entitled, Butterflies are Free; Professional Appearance on Canadian Broadcasting Corporation program The Nature of Things. Office: UCLA Pediatric Pain Rsch Program 10940 Wilshire Blvd Ste 1450 Los Angeles CA 90024 Office Phone: 310-824-7667. Business E-Mail: jtsao@mednet.ucla.edu.

**TSAO, VIVIAN J.,** artist, educator; arrived in US, 1974, naturalized; d. Sheng Fen and Wendy (Hsiung) Tsao; m. Raymond Clyde Coreil, June 5, 1976. BA, Nat. Taiwan Normal U., 1973; MFA Painting, Carnegie Mellon U., Pitts., 1976. Art instr. Nat. Taipei Tchrs. Coll., 1972—74; corr. in US Hsiung Shih Art Monthly, Taiwan, 1980—96; artist Ceres Gallery, N.Y.C., 1984—; artist in residence Asian Am. Arts Ctr., N.Y.C., 1985—86; adj. asst. prof. fine arts Pace U., N.Y.C., 1990—; artist Biddington's Internet Gallery, N.Y.C., 2000—; art commentator in US United Daily News (Chinese), Taiwan, 2003—. Artist presenter on panel China Inst. Gallery, N.Y.C., 1989; program auditor (art reviewer) N. Y. State Coun. Arts, N.Y.C., 1990—96, mem. jury panel, 1996—99. Author: (Chinese) The Mark of Time: Dialogues with Vivian Tsao on Art in New York, 2003; exhibitions include Pastel Soc. Am., Butler Inst. Am. Art, Ohio, 2003, Nat Arts Club, NYC, 2003, Am. Acad. Arts and Letters, Bklyn. Mus., Butler Inst. Am. Art, Ohio, Ceres Gallery, NYC, 2005, more than 61 solo and group exhbns. Sponsor student presentations Dyson Coll., Soc. Fellows, Pace U., 1994, 1995, 2000; interpreter internat. symposium Met. Mus. Art, N.Y.C., 1985; judge Employees Art Show N.Y. State Supreme Ct., 1995. Scholarship grantee, Carnegie Mellon U., Pitts., 1975, artist in residence grantee, N.Y. State Coun. Arts Asian Am. Arts Ctr. 1985—86. Fellow: Soc. Fellows Dyson Coll., Pace U.; mem.: Coll. Art Assn. Am., Pastel Soc. Am. (Cert. Merit 1981). Avocations: films, music, seashell collecting. Home: 17 Fuller Pl Brooklyn NY 11215-6006 Office: Pace U Dept Fine Arts 41 Park Row New York NY 10038 Personal E-mail: viviantsao@earthlink.net.

**TSCHERNISCH, SERGEI P.,** academic administrator; BA, San Francisco State U.; MFA in Theatre, Stanford U.; student, San Francisco Actors' Workshop, Stanford Repertory Theatre. Founding mem. Calif. Inst. of Arts, 1969, mem. faculty, assoc. dean Sch. Theatre, dir., 1969-80; prof. dept. theatre U. Md., College Park, 1980-82; dir. divsn. performing and visual arts Northeastern U., Boston, 1982-92; dean Coll. of Comm. and Fine Arts Loyola Marymount U., L.A., 1992-94; pres. Cornish Coll. of Arts, Seattle, 1994—. Advisor NEA; mem. com. USIA; cons. to many festivals. Office: Cornish College of the Arts 1000 Lenora St Seattle WA 98121-2718

**TSCHERNY, GEORGE,** graphics designer; b. Budapest, Hungary, July 12, 1924; s. Mendel and Bella (Heimann) T.; m. Sonia Katz, July 7, 1950; children— Nadia, Carla Student, Pratt Inst., Bklyn., 1947-50. Staff designer Donald Deskey & Assocs., N.Y.C., 1950-53; designer, assoc. George Nelson & Assocs., N.Y.C., 1953-55; pres. George Tscherny, Inc., N.Y.C., 1955—. Instr. Pratt Inst., Bklyn., 1956, bd. advisors, 1979; instr. Sch. Visual Arts, N.Y.C., 1955-64; curriculum cons. Phila. Coll. Art, 1967; Mellon vis. prof. Cooper Union, N.Y., 1978 Retrospective exhbn. Visual Art Mus., N.Y.C., 1992; exhibited in group shows, Germany, 1962-67, Italy, 1974, U.S., 1975; represented in permanent collections Mus. Modern Art, N.Y.C., Cooper Hewitt Mus., N.Y.C., Libr. of Congress, Washington, Bibliotheque nationale de France, Paris, Kunstgewerbeschule der Stadt Zurich; monograph of work George Tscherny, Minimum Means, Maximum Meaning, 2004; author: Changing Faces, 2004. Contbr. design svcs. to UN Council, Sta. WNET Pub. TV, Am. Lung Assn., Peace Corps, Cystic Fibrosis Found., L.I. State Park Commn. With U.S. Army, 1943-46, ETO. Recipient numerous awards, Am. Inst. Graphic Arts medal, 1988, Art Dirs. Club N.Y. (hall of fame 1997), N.Y. Type Dirs. Club, Silver medal Warsaw Biennale, 1976; inducted into Art Dirs. Club Hall of Fame, 1997. Mem. Am. Inst. Graphic Arts (pres. 1968), Alliance Graphique Internationale. Office: 238 E 72nd St New York NY 10021-4503 Office Phone: 212-734-3277. Personal E-mail: gtscherny@aol.com.

**TSCHETTER, LOIS JEAN,** retired elementary education educator; b. Algona, Iowa, Nov. 21, 1936; d. Clifford Wayne and Floy Faye (Eckstein) Riebhoff; m. Calvin Joe Tschetter, June 13, 1956; children: Scott, Susan Tschetter Grandgeorge. BS in Elem. Edn., U. No. Iowa, 1978; MS in Elem. Adminstrn., Drake U., 1991. Kindergarten tchr. Kalona schs., Iowa, 1956-58; title I tchr. Eagle Grove Cmty. Schs., 1967-69, 2d grade tchr., 1969-85, chair for curriculum coms., 1980—95, 1st grade tchr., 1985-95, co-facilitator of sch. improvement team, 1994-95, curriculum dir., at-risk coord., 1995—99. Cert. tchr., trainer for Growing Healthy Nat. Ctr. for Health Edn., San Bruno, CAlif., 1981—. Mem. NEA, Iowa State Edn. Assn., Internat. Reading Assn., Iowa Reading Assn., Iowa Coun. Tchrs. of Math., Alpha Delta Kappa (treas. 1992—), Iowa Ret. Sch. Pers. Assn., Beta Sigma Phi (pres. 1987-88). Republican. Meth. Avocations: bridge, fishing, boating, music.

**TSCHUMI, BERNARD,** architect; b. Lausanne, Switzerland, Jan. 25, 1944; MArch, Fed. Inst. Tech., Zurich, Switzerland, 1969. Tchr. Archtl. Assn., London, 1970—80, Inst. Architecture and Urban Studies, N.Y.C., 1976, Princeton U. Sch. Architecture, 1980—81, Cooper Union, 1980—83; dean Columbia U. Grad. Sch. Architecture, Planning & Preservation, N.Y.C., 1988—2003; head firm Bernard Tschumi Architects, Paris, 1983—, NYC, 1988—. Davenport vis. prof. arch. Contbr. The Manhattan Transcripts, 1981, Architecture and Disjunction, 1994, Event Cities, 1994, Bernard Tschumi: Architecture and Event, 1994. Decorated Legion d'Honneur, Ordre des Arts et Lettres; recipient 1st prize for design of Parc de la Villette, Paris, 1983, award for design of New Acropolis Mus., Athens, 2001, Grand Prix National d'Architecture, 1996. Mem.: College Internat. de Philosophie. Office: Bernard Tschumi Architects 227 W 17th St 2nd Fl New York NY 10011 Office Phone: 212-807-6340. Office Fax: 212-242-3693. E-mail: nyc@tschumi.com.

**TSE, CHARLES YUNG CHANG,** pharmaceutical executive, lawyer; b. Shanghai, Mar. 22, 1926; s. Kung Chao and Say Ying (Chen) T.; m. Vivian Chang, Apr. 25, 1955; 1 dau., Roberta. BA in Econs, St. John's U., Shanghai, 1949; MS in Acctg, U. Ill., 1950; JD, N.Y. Law Sch., 1990. Asst. to controller Am. Internat. Group, N.Y.C., 1950-54, asst. mgr. Singapore-Malaysia, 1955-57; with Warner-Lambert Co., Morris Plains, NJ, 1957-86, area mgr. S.E. Asia, 1966-68, regional dir. S.E. Asia, 1968-69, v.p. Australasia, 1970-71, pres. Western Hemisphere Group, 1971-72, pres. Pan Am. Mgmt. Center, 1972-76, pres. European Mgmt. Center, 1976-78, pres. Internat. Group, 1979-86, sr. v.p. corp., 1980-83, exec. v.p. corp., 1984-85, vice chmn., 1985-86. Dir. Foster Wheeler Corp., Livingston, N.J., 1984-98, Superior Telecom., Inc., 1996—, Com. of 100; mem. faculty bus. adminstrn. dept. Fairleigh Dickinson U., 1961-64; pres. Cancer Rsch. Inst., Inc., N.Y.C., 1991-92, bd. dirs., chmn. bd. dirs. CCNY, 1974-78; trustee Morristown Meml. Hosp. (N.J.), 1982-86; bd. dirs. Bus. Council for Internat. Understanding, 1984-87. Mem. NAM (dir. 1984-86), Assn. of the Bar of the City of N.Y. (mem. Asian affairs com. 1991-2001). Office: 300 Park Ave Fl 17 New York NY 10022-7402

**TSE, EDMUND SZE-WING,** insurance company executive; b. Hong Kong, Jan. 2, 1938; m. Peggy Pik-Kin Wai, Dec. 18, 1965; children: Ada Koon-Hang, Elaine Koon-Ming. BA in Math., U. Hong Kong, 1960, DSS (hon.),

2002; diploma mktg. mgmt. program, Stanford U., 1980. Dep. gen. mgr. Nan Shan Life Ins. Co., Ltd., Taipei, Taiwan, 1970—74, pres., mng. dir., 1975—, chmn., 1990, hon. chmn., 2003—; various positions Am. Internat. Assurance Co., Ltd., Hong Kong, 1961—70, dir., 1983, chmn., CEO, 2000—; dir. Am. Internat. Group, Inc., 1996—, sr. vice chmn., 2001—. Mng. dir. Nan Shan Life Ins. Co. Ltd., 1975, chmn., 2004; nat. and area chmn. Pacific Ins. Conf. Hong Kong, ', 1985—; dir. Am. Internat. Assurance Co. (Hong Kong), Ltd., 1983, chmn., CEO, 2000; dir. UGC Holdings Ltd., British Virgin Islands, 1994, Shanghai Jin Jiang-Universal Devel. Co. Ltd., China, 1994, Am. Internat. Group, Inc., 1996, sr. vice chmn., 2001; dir. Am. Internat. Assurance Co. (Australia) Ltd., 1985, chmn., 97; dir. AIG Global Investment Corp. (Asia) Ltd., Bermuda, 1996, AIG Global Investment Corp. (Hong Kong) Ltd., 1999, Underwriters Adjustment Co., Inc., Panama, 1997, Project Hope Hong Kong Found. Ltd., 2000—, Am. Internat. Assurance Co. (Bermuda) Ltd., 1983, pres., 92; dir., pres. AIA Found., Hong Kong, 1995—, Tri Star Enterprises Ltd., Bermuda, 2002; dir., chmn. AIA Fin. Svcs. Ltd. (formerly known as Superannuation Co.) Ltd., Australia, 1986—97; dir., chmn. bd. Am. Internat. Assurance Co. (Vietnam) Ltd., 2000; dir., vice-chmn. Philippine Am. Life and Gen. Ins. Co., 1991, Am. Life Ins. Co., Wilmington, Del., United States, 1992; non-exec. dir. PICC Property and Casualty Co. Ltd., China, 2004; pres. Komisaris P.T. Asuransi AIA Indonesia, 1997; chmn. bd. suprs. Dana Pensuin Lembaga Keuangan AIA Indonesia, 1997; v.p. commr. P.T. AIG Life (formerly known as P.T. Asuransi AIG Lippo Life), Indonesia, 1999. Gov.'s advisor Internat. Consultative Conf. on the Future Econ. Devel. of Guandong Province, 2005; chmn. stats. and info. subcom. Ins. Coun. Hong Kong, 1988—88; nat. and area chmn. Hong Kong Pacific Ins. Conf., 1985—; dep. chmn. Gen. Ins. Coun., 1988—89, chmn., 1989—90; mem. Hong Kong Govt.'s Ins. Adv. Com., 1988—96, Working Com. on Reinsurance and Captive Ins., 1996—98, Hong Kong Ins. Industry Coalition, 1996—98, Hong Kong Forum, 1998—; Internat. Consultative Forum Mayor of Tianjin, China, 2006—; mem. election sub-com. Hong Kong Fedn. Insurers, 1990—92, trustee ednl. trust, 1990—93, dep. chmn., 1991—92, chmn., 1992—93; exec. com. mem. Bus. and Profls. Fedn. Hong Kong, Hong Kong, 1994—; mem. bd. dirs. Life Ins. Mktg. and Rsch. Assn. (LIMRA), 1994—97; mem. selection com. election of HKSAR Chief Exec. and Provisional Legislature, 1996; mem. election com. HKSAR Legis. Coun. election, 1998, 2000; mem. adv. bd. Mandatory Provident Fund, 1996—98; mem. adv. bd. BSc in Actuarial Sci. program. Dept. Stats. and Actuarial Sci. U. Hong Kong, 1998—2006, hon. v.p. alumni assn., 2003—06; mem. exec. com. China Overseas Friendship Assn., 1997—; chmn. Asia adv. bd. Project HOPE, USA, 1997—99; mem. Hong Kong com. Pacific Basin Econ. Coun., 1998—; mem. career devel. bd. Chinese U. Hong Kong, 1998—2000, 2000—02, 2002—06; founding mem. Hong Kong chpt. World Presidents' Orgn., 2002—; mem. bd. trustees Fudan U., China, 2003—07, mem. coun. edn. devel. found., 2004; patron Soc. Registered Fin. Planners Ltd., 2003—; mem. adv. coun. Asia Soc. Hong Kong Ctr., 2004; gov.'s econ. advisor Internat. Consultative Conf. Future Econ. Devel. Guangdong Province, 2005. Named to Ins. Hall of Fame, 2003; recipient Disting. Businessman Yr., Taiwan, 1997, Gold Bauhinia Star (GBS), Hong Kong Spl. Adminstrv. Region, 2001; Hon. fellow, U. Hong Kong, 1998. Home: 10C Headland Rd Repulse Bay Hong Kong Office: 35/F AIG Tower 1 Connaught Rd Ctrl Hong Kong Hong Kong Office Fax: 852-2572-4695.

**TSE, MARIAN A.,** lawyer; AB, Vassar Coll., 1976; JD, Columbia Univ., 1979. Bar: Mass. 1979. Ptnr., chair, ERISA/employment benefits practice Goodwin Procter LLP, Boston, mem., diversity com. Bd. dir. Greater Boston Legal Services. Mem.: ABA, Asian Am. Lawyers Assn., New England Employee Benefits Coun., Boston Bar Assn. Office: Goodwin Procter LLP Exchange Pl 53 State St Boston MA 02109 Office Phone: 617-570-1169. Office Fax: 617-523-1231. Business E-Mail: mtse@goodwinprocter.com.

**TSELEV, ALEXANDER,** physicist, researcher; s. Yevgeniy Tselev and Ludmila Tseleva. BS in Radiophysics and Electronics, MS in Radiophysics and Electronics, Wizhny Novgorod State U., Russia; PhD in Materials Sci., U. Tech. Dresden, Germany, 2000. Rsch. assoc. Georgetown U., Washington, 2003—06, Duke U., Durahm, NC, 2006—. Mem.: Am. Physics Soc. Achievements include research in development of crossed-beam pulsed laser deposition; establishment of dielectric properties of Ca-Cu-Ti-oxide thin films. Office: Duke U Dept Chemistry Box 90349 Durham NC 27708-0349 Office Phone: 919-660-1624. Business E-Mail: a.tselev@duke.edu.

**TSENG, HOWARD SHIH CHANG,** business educator, investment company executive, economics professor; b. Tainan, Taiwan, Jan. 14, 1935; came to U.S., 1963; s. Picheng and Chaoliu (Wang) T.; m. Evelina M. Young, Dec. 25, 1965; 1 child, Elaine Evelina. BA, Nat. Taiwan U., Taipei, 1957, MA, 1963; PhD, U. Okla., 1972. Chief economist Cooperative Bank Taiwan, Taipei, 1959-61; dir. tax services Bur. Taxation, Govt. Taiwan, Republic China, Taipei 1961-63; instr. U. Okla., Norman, 1968; asst. prof. Ga. So. U., Statesboro, 1968-71; prof. bus. and econs. Catawba Coll., Salisbury, 1971—2001; adj. prof. San Francisco State U., 2002—, 2002—. Pres. Am. Prudential Investments, Salisbury, 1981-89; pres. Tsengs Investments, 1990—. Author: Investments, 1982; contbr. articles to profl. jours. Coordinator, supporter study mathematically precocious youth Johns Hopkins U., Balt., 1982—; ptnr. World Vision, Calif., 1986-92. Academic research grantee Academia Sinica, Taipei, 1962; Ford Found. fellow, Taipei, 1963. Mem. AAUP, Ea. Econ. Assn., Am. Econ. Assn., Am. Assn. Individual Investors, Taiwan Investment (organizer 1986—), Taiwanese-Am. Assn. Greater Charlotte (pres. 1994-96), Nat. Travel Club. Avocations: antiques, travel, reading. Office: Catawba Coll W Innes St Salisbury NC 28144 Fax: 704-637-5724. E-mail: tsengstrading@yahoo.com.

**TSENG, ROSE,** academic administrator; BS, Kansas State U.; MS, U. Calif., Berkeley, PhD Nutrition. Registered dietician. Prof., chair, dir., assoc. dean San Jose State U., 1970—86, dean Coll. Applied Scis. and Arts, 1986—93; chancellor, CEO West Valley-Mission C.C., Calif., 1993—98; chancellor U. Hawaii-Hilo, 1998—. Office: U Hawaii-Hilo 200 W Kawili Hilo HI 96720-4091

**TSIEN, CHRISTINA,** radiologist, oncologist; d. Thomas Tsien and Ida Hsu; m. Stephen Mullen, Aug. 24, 1995; children: Lawrence Mullen, Nigel Mullen. MD, McGill U., Montreal, Quebec Can., 1995. Bd.-cert. Radiation Oncologist Am. Bd. of Radiology, 2003. Fellowship U. Mich., 2000—01, asst. prof. Ann Arbor, Mich., 2003—. Recipient Career Devel. Award, ASCO, 2005, Jr. Mem. Clin./Basic Sci. Award, ASTRO, 2001; scholar McLaughlin Scholarship, McGill U., 1995. Fellow: Royal Coll. of Physicians and Surgeons; mem.: Soc. Neuro-Oncology (assoc.), Am. Soc. Clin. Oncology (assoc.), Am. Soc. Radiation Oncology (assoc.). D-Conservative. Lds. Achievements include research in Imaging biomarkers of tumor response. Office: U Mich 1500 E Med Ctr Dr Ann Arbor MI 48109 Office Phone: 734-936-4300. Office Fax: 734-763-7370.

**TSIEN, RICHARD WINYU,** biology professor; b. Tating, Kweichow, People's Republic China, Mar. 3, 1945; s. Hsue-Chu and Yi-Ying (Li) T.; m. Julia Shiang Aug. 29, 1971; children: Sara Shiang-Ming, Gregory Shiang-An, Alexa Tsien-Shiang. BS, MIT, 1965, MS, 1966; DPhil, Oxford U., Eng., 1970. Rsch. student Eaton Peabody Lab. Auditory, Physiology, Mass. Eye and Ear Infirmary, 1966; asst. prof. dept. physiology, Yale U. Sch. Medicine, New Haven, 1970-74, assoc. prof., 1974-79, prof., 1979-88; George D. Smith prof. molecular and cellular physiology Stanford (Calif.) U., 1988—, chmn. dept., 1988-94. Established investigator Am. Heart Assn., 1974-79. Author: Electric Current Flow in Excitable Cells, 1975. Recipient Otsuka award Internat. Am. Heart Assn., 1985; Rhodes Scholar, 1966; Weir Rsch. fellow, 1966-70 Univ. Coll., Oxford, 1966-70, lecturing fellow Balliol Coll., Oxford, 1969-70 Mem. Soc. Gen. Physiologists (pres. 1988), Biophys. Soc. (Kenneth S. Cole award 1985), Soc. for Neurosci. Democrat. Home: 866 Tolman Dr Palo Alto CA 94305-1026 Office: Stanford U Dept Molecular & Cellular Physiology 300 Pasteur Dr Palo Alto CA 94304-2203

**TSIEN, ROGER YONCHIEN,** chemist, cell biologist; b. NYC, Feb. 1, 1952; s. Hsue Chu and Yi Ying (Li) T.; m. Wendy M. Globe, July 30, 1982. AB in Chemistry and Physics summa cum laude, Harvard Coll., 1972; PhD in Physiology, U. Cambridge, 1977; PhD (hon.), Cath. U., Leuven, Belgium, 1995. Rsch. asst. U. Cambridge, Eng., 1975-78; asst. prof. Dept. Physiology-Anatomy U. Calif., Berkeley, 1981-85, assoc. prof., 1985-87, prof., 1987-89, prof. pharmacology, chemistry and biochemistry San Diego, 1989—; biological investigator Howard Hughes Med. Inst. Rsch. Lab, Calif., 1989—; co-found. Aurora Bioscis. Corp., 1994, Senomyx, Inc., 1998. T.Y. Shen vis. prof. Medicinal Chem., MIT, 1991, Todd vis. prof. Chem., U. Cambridge, 2003. Contbr. chpts. to books, articles to profl. jours. Recipient Herbert Sober Lectureship, Am. Soc. Biochemistry and Molecular Biology, 2000, Pearse Prize, Royal Microscopical Soc., 2000, Am. Chem. Soc. award for Creative Invention, 2002, Anfinsen award, Protein Soc., 2002, Dr. H.P. Heineken Prize for Biochemistry and Biophysics, 2002, Lamport prize NY Acad. Scis., 1986, Javits Neurosci. Investigator award Nat. Inst. Neurol. Disorders and Stroke, 1989, Young Scientist award Passano Found., 1991, W. Alden Spencer Neurobiology award Columbia U., 1991, Bowditch lectureship Am. Physiol. Soc., 1992, Gairdner Found. Internat. award, 1995, Artois-Baillet-Latour Health prize (Belgium), 1995, Basic Rsch. prize Am. Heart Assn., 1995, Faculty Rsch. lectureship U. Calif., San Diego, 1997, Faculty Rsch. Lectureship, Univ. Calif., San Diego, Acad. Senate, 1997, EG&G Wallac award for Innovation in High Throughput Screening Soc. for Biomolecular Screening, 1998, Max Delbrück medal, Max Delbrück Centrum für Molekulare Medizin, Berlin, 2002, Wolf prize in Medicine, Israel, 2004, Keio Med. Sci. Prize, 2004 Keio U., 2004, Assn. Biomolecular Resource Facilities award, 2006; Comyns Berkeley Rsch. fellow Gonville & Caius Coll., 1977-81; Marshall scholar British Govt., 1972-75, Searle scholar, 1983-86; Hugh Davson Disting. Lecturer, Am. Physiological Soc., 2003, Konrad Bloch Lectureship, Harvard U., 2003, Keith Porter Lectureship, Am. Soc. Cell Biology, 2003. Mem. Amer. Acad. Arts & Sciences, NAS, IOM, Phi Beta Kappa. Achievements: development and extensive biological application of molecules to measure and/or manipulate intracellular calcium, sodium, and hydrogen ions, cyclic adenosine-3', 5'-monophosphate, nitric oxide, inositol phosphates, membrane potential, protein trafficking, protein-protein interaction, and gene expression; developed biochemistry and redesign of green fluorescent protein; elucidation fo signal transduction mechanisms in calcium oscillations and synaptic plasticity; inventor new methods for microscopic imaging and pharmaceutical high-throughput screening. Office: Tsien Lab HHMI - UCSD CMM West 310 9500 Gilman Dr La Jolla CA 92093-0647 Office Phone: 858-534-4891. Fax: 858-534-5270. E-mail: rtsien@ucsd.edu.*

**TSIGELNY, IGOR,** research scientist; m. Valentina Kouznetsova. PhD, Inst. Physics and Mechanics, Acad. Sci. Ukraine, 1972—78. Asst. scientist U. Calif., San Diego, 1994—99, assoc. scientist, 2000—. Author: Molecular Cybernetics, 1990; editor: Protein Structure Prediction: Bioinformatic Approach, 2002; contbr. over 180 articles to profl. jours. Mem.: Biophysical Soc., US Fencing Assn. Achievements include 11 Patents. Business E-Mail: itsigeln@ucsd.edu.

**TSIKLAURI, GEORGI VICTOR,** physicist, researcher; b. Rovenki, Ukraine, Nov. 7, 1935; s. Victor Abram and Ekaterina Paul Tsiklauri; m. Marina Alexander Serednitskaia, Aug. 30, 1937; 1 child, Mikhail Georgi. PhD, Moscow Energy Inst., 1964. DSc, High Certification Com., Moscow, 1975. Dir. dept. Energy Inst. (ENIN), Moscow, 1985—91; lab. fellow Battelle, Pacific NW Nat. Lab., Richland, Wash., 1991—. Author: Two-Phase Cooling and Corrosion in Nuclear Power Plants. Fellow, Internat. Ctr. For Heat and Mass Transfer, 1978. Mem.: Am. Nuc. Soc., US Tennis Assn. Achievements include patents for nuclear power plants. Home: 361 Westmoreland Dr Richland WA 99354 Office: Battelle Pacific Northwest National Lab 902 Battelle Blvd Richland WA 99352 Office Phone: 509-373-4081.

**TSIMBERIDOU, APOSTOLIA MARIA,** medical educator; d. Velissarios Tsimberidis and Kalliopi Tsimberidou. MD, Aristotelian U., 1991; PhD, Kapodistrian U. Athens, 2001. Instr. MD Anderson Cancer Ctr., Houston, 2001—04, asst. prof., 2004—. Cons. ACP, Phila., 2003—. Contbr. chapters to books. Mem.: Arkaglathos Gouttas Hematology (Merit award), Am. Soc. Clin. Oncology (Merit award), Am. Soc. Hematology (Travel award). Office: MD Anderson Cancer Ctr 1400 Holcombe Blvd Unit 428 Houston TX 77030 Office Phone: 713-792-4259. Personal E-Mail: atsimber@mdanderson.org.

**TSIRCOU, KYRIACOS STAVROU,** lawyer; s. Steve and Antigoni Tsircou; m. Marika Krissman Tsircou, Nov. 13, 2004. BS in Astronautical Engring., USAF Acad., Colorado Springs, Colo., 1992; JD, Loyola U., L.A., 2000. Registered: patent atty. US Patent and Trademark Office. Patent atty. Sheppard, Mullin, Richter, & Hampton LLP, L.A., 2000—06, Tsircou Intellectual Property Law, L.A., 2006—. Mem. Young Profls. Group benefiting Good Shepherd Ctr. for Homeless Women, L.A., 2000—06, Para Los Ninos, L.A., 2005—06. Capt. USAF, 1993—99. Decorated Air Force Commendation medal (2). Mem.: ABA, LA County Bar Assn., Am. Intellectual Property Law Assn. Greek Orthodox. Avocations: travel, skiing, golf. Office: Tsircou Intellectual Property Law 4470 W Sunset Blvd #410 Los Angeles CA 90027 Office Phone: 323-660-9916. Office Fax: 323-660-9917. Business E-Mail: kyri@tsircoulaw.com.

**TSIROS, MICHAEL,** science educator, researcher; BS, St. John's U., N.Y., 1990, MBA, 1992; PhD, Temple U., Phila., 1997. Asst. prof. Washington U., St. Louis, 1997—99; assoc. prof. U. of Miami, Coral Gables, Fla., 1999—. Vis. assoc. prof. Athens U. of Bus. Adminstrn., Greece, 2003—, Dartmouth Coll., Hanover, NH, 2005, London Bus. Sch., 2006. Office Phone: 305-284-5935. E-mail: tsiros@miami.edu.

**TSIRPANLIS, CONSTANTINE N.,** theology, philosophy, classics and history educator; b. Kos, Greece, Mar. 18, 1935; came to U.S., 1957; m. Sophia Kappas, July 12, 1967; children: Kalliope-Chrysoula, Nike. BA, STM, lic. in theology magna cum laude, Halke Theol. Sem., Istanbul, Turkey, 1957; ThM, Harvard U., 1962; ThD, Union Theol. Sem., 1963; MA, Columbia U., 1966, PhD, 1970, Fordham U., 1973; DLitt (hon.), World Acad. Arts and Culture, 1993. Instr., organizer Greek-Am. cmtys., 1958-63; founder, chmn., prof. modern Greek studies NYU, 1963-70; prof. world history NY Inst. Tech. NYC and Delaware County Coll., Media, Pa., 1967-75; disting. prof. theology, sociology, history, ecumenism, Greek studies Union Theol. Sem., Barrytown, NY, 1976-97; chmn., prof. scriptures, patristics, Greek lang. St. Sophia Ukraine Orthodox Theol. Sem. Am., Somerset, NJ, 1999—. Chmn., prof. classics Collegiate Sch., NYC, 1967-69; prof. modern Greek lang. and lit. New Sch. for Social Rsch., NYC, 1968-70; prof. classical mythology Hunter Coll. CUNY, 1968-70. Author numerous books including A Short History of the Greek Language, 1966, rev. edit., 1970, rev. augmented edit., 2004, A Modern Greek Reader for Americans, 1967, rev. edit., 1968, A Modern Greek Idiom and Phrase Book, 1978, Mark Eugenicus, 1979, N. Cabasilas, 1979, Greek Patristic Theology, 23 vols.; founder, editor The Patristic and Byzantine Rev., 1981—; pub., editor-in-chief Hellenism In Am., 1969—; contbr. articles to profl. jours. Decorated Medal of Nat. Rebirth 1821 (Greece), medals of Byzantine nobility, including count, baron, G. chevalier, Gt. Prior of N.Am., medal of Accademia Ferdinandea, medals of Diethnes Hetereia Hellenon Logotechnon, also hon. pres. Mem. Am. Soc. Neohellenic Studies (founder, v.p.), Pan Dodecanisian Fedn. US, Pan-European Inst. and U. Ecumenical Hellenism (founder, pres.), Am. Hist. Assn., Am. Philog. Assn., Am. Acad. Medieval Studies, Internat. Assn. Byzantine Studies, Am. Philos. Assn., N.Am. Patristic Soc., Hellenic Philog. Assn., Am. Soc. Papyrologists, Am. Inst. Patristic-Byzantine Studies (pres., founder), Justinianum Oikoumenikon R.C. (pres., founder), World Acad. Arts and Culture (hon.), PIVNE (pres., founder), POEL (pres., founder). Home and Office: 12 Minuet Ln Kingston NY 12401-6955 Office Phone: 845-336-8797. Home Fax: 845-336-8797.

**TSITVERBLIT, NAFTALI ANATOL,** physicist, fluid mechanics engineer, researcher; b. Kiev, Ukraine, Oct. 29, 1963; arrived in Israel, 1987; s. Isaac Avraham and Zoya (Beletsky) T. MSc, Kiev Poly. Inst., 1981-87; PhD, Tel-Aviv U., 1995. Engr. Scientific Rsch. Inst. Robotics, Kiev, 1985-87;

postdoc. fellow Lamont-Doherty Earth Obs. Columbia U., Palisades, NY, 1995-97. Tchg. asst., instr. mech. engring. Tel-Aviv U., 1988-94, vis., 1997—; vis. scientist Cornell U., 1994. Co-author: (chpt.) Nonlinear Instability of Nonparallel Flows, 1994; contbr. papers to profl. jours. Woods Hole Oceanographic Inst. fellow, 1996. Mem. AAAS, N.Y. Acad. Sci., Am. Phys. Soc., Am. Geophys. Union. Achievements include discovery of two new mechanisms for convection in double-component fluid systems, resulting from different boundary conditions; mechanism for three-dimensionality of instability disturbances; finite-amplitude steady flows arising from one such a convective mechanism that are disconnected from the conduction state; research in multiplicity of the equilibrium states in laterally heated stably stratified fluid systems and its role in explaining diversity of previous observations in such systems; clarification of nature of the oscillatory instability in confined vortex flows with vortex breakdown and formulation of general method for identification of nature of complex instability mechanisms; identifying mechanisms and their role in various fluid mechanical configurations. Home: 1 Yanosh Korchak St Apt 6 Netanya 42495 Israel Business E-Mail: naftali@eng.tau.ac.il.

TSIVIDIS, YANNIS P., electrical engineering educator; b. Piraeus, Greece, Dec. 22, 1946; came to U.S., 1970; s. Pelopidas I. and Maria (Filippa) T. BS, U. Minn., 1972; MS, U. Calif., Berkeley, 1973, PhD, 1976. Asst. prof. elec. engring. Columbia U., N.Y.C., 1976-81, assoc. prof., 1981-84, prof., 1984—. Nat. Tech. U., Athens, Greece, 1992-95; Charles Batchelor chair prof. Columbia U., N.Y.C., 1998—. Cons. AT&T Bell Labs., Murray Hill, N.J., 1977-88. Author: Operation and Modeling of the MOS Transistor, 1987, 2d edit., 1999, Mixed Analog-Digital VLSI Devices and Technology, 1996; co-editor: Design of Mos VLSI Circuits for Telecommunications, 1985, Integrated Continuous-Time Filters, 1993, Design of Analog-Digital VLSI Circuits for Telecommunications and Signal Processing, 1994; contbr. over 100 articles to profl. jours.; patentee in field. Recipient best paper award European Solid State Cirs. Conf., 1986, Great Tchr. award Columbia U., 1991, Disting. Faculty Tchg. award Columbia Engring. Sch. Alumni Assn., 1998, Presdl. award for outstanding tchg. Columbia U., 2003. Fellow: IEEE (Baker best paper award 1984, Darlington award 1987, Guillemin-Cauer award 1998, Circuits and Sys. Golden Jubilee 2000, co-recipient L. Winner Outstanding Paper award 2003, Undergrad. Tchg. award 2005). Office: Columbia Univ Dept Elec Engring New York NY 10027

TSO, TIEN CHIOH, federal agency administrator, researcher, agronomist; b. Hupeh, China, July 25, 1917; came to U.S., 1947, naturalized, 1961; s. Ya Fu and Suhwa (Wang) T.; m. Margaret Lu, Aug. 28, 1949; children: Elizabeth, Paul. BS, Nanking U., China, 1941, MS, 1944; PhD, Pa. State U., 1950; postgrad., Oak Ridge Inst. Nuclear Studies. Supt. exptl. farm Ministry Social Affairs, China, 1944-46; exec. sec. Tobacco Improvement Bur., 1946-47; rsch. chemist Gen. Cigar Rsch. Lab., 1950-51; with USDA, 1952—; prin. plant physiologist crop research div. Agrl. Rsch. Svc./USDA, Beltsville, Md., 1964-66, leader tobacco quality investigations, tobacco and sugar crops research br., 1966-71, chief tobacco lab., 1972-83, sr. exec. service, 1974-83, collaborator, 1984—; exec. dir. Internat. Devel. and Edn. in Agr. and Life Scis., 1984-96, chmn. bd., 1997-2001, hon. chmn. bd., 2001—. Cons. World Bank, Nat. Cancer Inst., Ky. Tobacco Health Rsch. Inst., China Nat. Tobacco Corp., Philippine Tobacco Rsch. Ctr., Philip Morris Tobacco Corp. Author: Physiology and Biochemistry of Tobacco Plants, 1972, Production, Physiology and Biochemistry of Tobacco Plants, 1991, Agriculture in China: 1949-2030, 1998; contbg. author: Ann. Rev. Plant Physiology, Vol. 9, 1958, The Chemistry of Tobacco and Tobacco Smoke, 1972, Toward Less Harmful Cigarettes, 1968, 71, 75, 80; editor: Structural and Functional Aspects of Phytochemistry, 1972, Recent Advances in Tobacco Science, vol. 1, 1975, Agriculture in China: 1949-2030, 1998, Dare to Dream: Vision of 2050 Agriculture in China, 2004, Comfort Ye, My People in My Journey in Science and Life, 2006. Fellow AAAS, Am. Soc. Agronomy (chmn. colloquium on agr. and life scis. in China 1983, 84, 85, 86, 87, 88-89), Am. Inst. Chemists; mem. Am. Chem. Soc., Am. Soc. Plant Physiologists, Phytochem. Soc. N.Am. (pres. 1971, life mem.), Tobacco Chemists Rsch. Conf. (symposium chmn. 1965, 79, chmn. 1975, 83), World Conf. Smoking and Health (sect. chmn. 1967, 71, 75), Tobacco Workers Conf., N.Y. Acad. Scis., Interagy. Smoking and Health Forum (chmn. 1979-83), Nat. Coordinating Com. on Tobacco-Related Rsch., Sigma Xi, Gamma Sigma Delta. Achievements include research in loci of alkaloid formation, biosynthetic pathway, interconversion and fate of alkaloids in tobacco plants, chem. composition as affected by macro and micro elements, homogenized leaf curing, healthrelated factors including two mycotoxins and phenolics, potential for agricultural self-sufficiency in China in the next century. Home: 3152 Gracefield Rd # 216 Silver Spring MD 20904 Office: Beltsville Agr Rsch Ctr Bldg 005 10300 Baltimore Ave Beltsville MD 20705 Office Phone: 301-504-5422. E-mail: tsot@ba.ars.usda.gov. *We are thankful to those fools who dare to dream of something new and seemingly impossible.*

TSOI, EDWARD TZE MING, architect, urban planner, interior designer; b. New Orleans, Aug. 7, 1943; s. Edward Mong Yok and Ruby Liu Wei (Hsia) T.; m. Louise Smoyer, June 15, 1968; children: Laura Li Ling, Alison Li Mei. BArch, MIT, 1966; MArch, U. Pa., 1968, M in City Planning, 1968, cert. in urban design, 1969. Registered architect, Mass., La. Assoc. Sert/Jackson & Assocs., Cambridge, Mass., 1969-76; assoc. prin. Skidmore Owings & Merrill, Boston, 1976-83; prin. Tsoi/Kobus & Assocs., Inc., Cambridge, 1983—, pres., 1985-89, 93—. Instr. Sch. Design, Harvard U., Cambridge, 1980-84. Designer Marine Resource Ctr., 1994. Chmn. Arlington (Mass.) Redevel. Bd., 1972—; chmn. 1st parish Unitarian Universalist Ch., Arlington, 1990; pres. bd. dirs. Cambridge Salvation Army, 1990—; mem. Boston Civic Design Commn., 1993—. Recipient Best New Med. Facility award Symposium on Healthcare, 1993, Grand Honor award Assn. Gen. Contractors, 1993, award Lotus Devel. Corp. landscape award Urban Design, 1991, nat. award for innovation Ford Model T plant Urban Land Inst., 1995. Fellow AIA, mem. Boston Soc. Architects (pres. 1993-94). Democrat. Associations: windsurfing, boating, woodworking, carpentry. Home: 16 Devereaux St Arlington MA 02476-8114 Office: Tsoi/Kobus & Assocs Inc PO Box 9114 Cambridge MA 02238-9114 Office Phone: 617-475-4000. Business E-Mail: etsoi@tka-architects.com.

TSONTAKIS, GEORGE, composer, conductor; b. Astoria, NY, Oct. 24, 1951; Student, Juilliard Sch. Tchr. composition Aspen Music Sch., 1976—; conductor, Aspen Music Festival Contemporary Ensemble; dir. Met. Greek Chorale, NY, Riverside Orchestra; founding dir. Aspen Contemporary Ensemble, 1991—98. Composer: String Quartet No. 4, 1989 (Kennedy Ctr. award, 1989), Perpetual Angelus, 1992 (Kennedy Ctr. award, 1992), Ghost Variations, October, Violin Concerto No. 2, 2005 (Grawemeyer award for musical composition, U. Louisville, 2005). Recipient Lifetime Achievement award, AAAL, 1995; Vilar fellow, Am. Acad. Berlin, 2002. Office: Aspen Music Festival and Sch 2 Music School Rd Aspen CO 81611*

TSOU, MING-HSIANG, geographer, educator; b. Tao-yuan, Taiwan, Nov. 20, 1969; s. Feng-Shing Tsou and Nancy Lee; m. Chun-Yi Eva Chen, Jan. 8, 1995; children: Shu-An Sophie, Kaiwen, Kailing. BS, Nat. Taiwan U., Taipei, 1991; MA, SUNY, Buffalo, 1996; PhD, U. Colo., Boulder, 2000. Asst. prof. geography dept. San Diego State U., 2000—05, assoc. prof., 2005—. Co-chmn. earth sci. enterprise data sys. working group, std. process group NASA, 2004—; mem. sci. bd. GIS Planet, U.K. GIS Conf., 2005—; mem. web-based geoinfo. and svcs. tech. commn. U.K. Soc. Photogrammetry and Remote Sensing, 2005—. Co-author: Internet GIS: Distributed Geographic Information Services for the Internet and Wireless Networks.; website creator: Web-based Mapping Services for San Diego Wildfires, 2003, The Gateway of Geospatial Information Technology. Recipient Outstanding Faculty award, San Diego State U., 2004; grantee, NASA, 2003—, City of San Diego, 2004—06, South Coast Resource Conservation Devel. Coun., 2004—06, NSF, 2005—. Mem. Assn. Am. Geographers (vice chmn. cartography specialty group 2006—). Achievements include research in advanced web-based cartographic mapping tools; mobile GIS and wireless communication integration; web-based geospatial information technology; web-based GIS education and tool development; web GIS for homeland security and

disaster management. Office: San Diego State U Geography Dept 5500 Campanile Dr San Diego CA 92182-4493 Office Phone: 619-594-0205. Home Fax: 619-594-4938; Office Fax: 619-594-4938. Business E-Mail: mtsou@mail.sdsu.edu.

TSOU, YU-MIN, science administrator, chemistry researcher; b. Ping-Dong, Taiwan, Aug. 28, 1953; arrived in US, 1979; s. Shung-Chu Tsou and Ping-Wen Chen; m. Yah-Lih Chao, Apr. 26, 1980; children: Amy Meng Shuan, Benjamin Jiann. BS in Chemistry, Nat. Tsing-Hua U., Taiwan, 1975; MS in Chemistry, Nat. Taiwan U., 1979; PhD in Chemistry, Calif. Inst. Tech., Pasadena, 1985. Sci. rsch. assoc. U. of Tex., Austin, 1985—86; sr. rsch. chemist Dow Chem. Co., Freeport, Tex., 1986—88, project leader, 1989—93, rsch. leader, 1994—2000; R&D mgr. E-Tek divsn. De Nora Northamerica, Inc, Somerset, NJ, 2001—04; tech. dir. E-TEK divsn. PEMEAS USA, Somerset, 2005—. Chief tech. officer for Dept. of Energy program E-TEK divsn. De Nora Northamerica, Inc., Somerset, 2002—05; leading scientist of De Nora for Aqueous Hydrochloric Acid Electrolysis project De Nora NA/Bayer Joint Venture, Somerset, 2001—03; head mfr. and devel. PEMEAS USA, Inc., Somerset, 2006—. Author: The Key to Understand Lau-Tze Philosophy and Its Practice in Chinese History, (philosophy/history writings) Chinese/Western Philosophy Comparisons; contbr. articles to profl. jours. Fund raiser Calif. Inst. Tech. Alumni Assn., Freeport, 1998. Recipient Electrochem. Soc. New Tech. award, E-TEK, 2005, Dow Chem. Tech. Excellence award, 1990, 1992, 1996. Mem.: Electrochem. Soc. (assoc.). Achievements include patents and publications on electrolysis, fuel cells, electro-catalysts, gas diffusion electrodes, porous electrode structure; invention of anode and cathode coating technology; first to invent mass production of membranc-cell-assembly with electrode-membrane approach in fuel cell industry; invention of highest performing Pt alloy methanol oxidation anode and Pt oxygen reduction cathode catalysts and supply to customers; poisoning-resistant hydrogen cathode cathode on thin substrates and implemented in zero-gap membrane chlorine cells; first to consistent method to manufacture rhodium catalyst and the rhodium electrode for converting waste hydrochloric acid to chlorine; catalysts/gas diffusion electrodes for the pioneering PEMEAS over 160 C high temperature MEA; invention of novel electrode structure for realizing Pt alloy advantage. Home: 533 Mercer Rd Princeton NJ 08540 Office: PEMEAS USA Inc E-TEK Divsn 39 Veronica Ave Somerset NJ 08873 Office Phone: 732-545-5100 145. Office Fax: 732-545-5170. Personal E-Mail: tsou4507@yahoo.com. E-mail: ym.tsou@etek-inc.com.

TSOUCALAS, NICHOLAS, federal judge; b. NYC, Aug. 24, 1926; s. George Michael and Maria (Monogenis) T.; m. Catherine Aravantinos, Nov. 21, 1954; children: Stephanie, Georgia. BSBA, Kent State U., 1949; LLB, N.Y. Law Sch., 1951. Bar: N.Y. 1953. Sole practice, N.Y.C., 1953-55, 59-68; asst. U.S. atty. (So. dist.) N.Y. US Dept. Justice, 1955-59; judge Criminal Ct., City of N.Y., 1968-86; acting supreme ct. judge State of N.Y., N.Y.C., 1975-82; judge U.S. Ct. Internat. Trade, N.Y.C., 1986—, now sr. judge. Dist. leader Republican Party N.Y. County, N.Y.C., 1961-68; mem. Rep. Exec. Com., N.Y.C., 1961-68. Served with USN, 1944-46, 51-52. Recipient Proficiency in Constl. Law award N.Y. Law Sch., N.Y.C., 1951, Man of Yr. award St. Paul Soc., N.Y.C., 1971. Mem. ABA, N.Y. County Lawyers Assn., Fed. Bar Assn., Greek Am. Lawyers Assn., Am. Hellenic Ednl. Prog. Assn. Lodges: Parthenon, Masons. Republican. Greek Orthodox. Avocations: basketball, racquetball, stamp collecting/philately, walking, dance. Office: US Ct Internat Trade 1 Federal Plz New York NY 10278-0001

TSOUKAS, MARIA MAGDALENE, dermatologist, educator; arrived in U.S., 1992; d. Ioannis Athanassios and Danai Kalliroi Tsoukas; m. Dimitrios Christos Nikas, June 13, 1999; children: Christos Nikas, Ioannis Nikas, Odysseas Nikas. MD, U. Athens, Greece, 1992, PhD, 2002. Diplomate Am. Bd. Dermatology. Rsch. fellow dermatology Harvard Med. Sch, Boston, 1992—95; intern in medicine Tufts Med. Sch., Boston, 1997; resident in dermatology Roger Williams Med. Ctr., Boston U., Boston, 1998—2000; chief resident in dermatology Dartmouth Med. Sch., Hanover, NH, 2000—01, clin. fellow in cosmetic and surg. dermatology, 2001—02; asst. prof. dermatology U. Chgo., 2005—. Fellow: Am. Acad. Dermatology; mem.: Am. Soc. for Photobiology, Am. Soc. for Laser Medicine and Surgery. E-mail: mtsoukas@med.une.bsd.uchicago.edu.

TSU, I-FEI, materials engineer; s. Jung-Chang Tsu and Chiou-Kuei Chang; m. Han-Fang Ying, Jan. 11, 1969. PhD, U. Wis. Madison, 1996. Post doctoral rsch. assoc. Argonne Nat. Lab., Argonne, Ill., 1996—97; sr. staff engr. Seagate Tech., Bloomington, Minn., 1998—. Mem. Materials Rsch. Soc., Pittsburgh, Pa., 1996—. Author: (scientific research) Transmission Electron Microscopy study of Grain Boundary structure of YBCO Bi-Crystals (Outstanding scholar, Am. Soc. of Microscopy, 1996). Mem.: Materials Rsch. Soc. Achievements include patents for increasing the read-back amplitude in magnetic recording heads by adding a nonmagnetic metallic layer in the reader gap. Office: Seagate Tech 7801 Computer Ave Bloomington MN 55435 Office Phone: 952-402-8359. E-mail: itsu@seagate.com.

TSUANG, MING TSO, psychiatrist, educator; b. Tainan, Taiwan, Nov. 16, 1931; came to U.S., 1971; s. Ping Tang and Chhun Kuei (Lin) T.; m. Snow Huei S. Ko; children— John, Debby, Grace. MD, Nat. Taiwan U., Taipei, 1957; PhD in Psychiatry, 1965, PhD (Sino-Brit. Fellowship Trust scholar); certs. in epidemiology and stats., population genetics, psychiat. genetics, U. London, 1965; D.Sc. in Psychiat. Genetics and Epidemiology, Faculty of Sci., U. London, 2001. Intern Nat. Taiwan U. Hosp., 1956-57, resident in psychiatry, 1957-61, assoc. prof. psychiatry, staff psychiatrist, 1968-71; collaborating investigator Internat. Pilot Study of Schizophrenia, WHO, 1966-71; vis. assoc. prof. psychiatry Washington U. Sch. Medicine, St. Louis, 1971-72; assoc. prof. staff psychiatrist U. Iowa Coll. Medicine, Iowa City, 1972-75, prof. psychiatry, 1975-82, prof. psychiat. epidemiology, 1978-82; clin. tchr., lectr. to residents, med. students; cons. psychiatrist VA Hosp., Iowa City, 1972-82; prof., vice chmn. sect. of psychiatry and human behavior Brown U., Providence, 1982-85; assoc. med. dir. Butler Hosp., Providence, 1982-85, dir. psychiat. epidemiology research unit, 1982-85; prof. psychiatry Harvard Inst. Psychiat. Epid. and Genetics Harvard U. Med. Sch. and Harvard Sch. Pub. Health; dir. psychiat. epidemiology and genetics Mass. Mental Health Ctr., Boston; chief psychiatry, chmn. Ctr. for Mental Health Brockton-West Roxbury VA Med. Ctr., 1985-94; head and supt. dept. psychiatry Harvard U. at Mass. Mental Health Ctr., 1992—; Stanley Cobb prof. Psychiatry Harvard U., 1993—; dir. Harvard Inst. Psychiat. Epedemiology and Genetics, 1994—; Univ. prof. dept. psychiatry, dir. Ctr. Behavioral Genomics U. Calif., San Diego, 2003—. Mem. epidemiol. studies rev. com. NIMH, 1976-79, mem., chmn. rsch. scientist devel. rev. com. NIMH, 1982-86, chmn. epidemiologic studies rev. com., 1989-90; mem. extramural sci. adv. bd. NIMH, 1990—; mem. mental health. svc. planning coun. Vets. Health Svcs. and Rsch. Adminstrn., VA Cen. Office, 1990—; vis. prof. psychiatry (Josiah Macy faculty scholar award) Oxford U., Eng., Warneford Hosp., 1979-80; chmn. mental health policy working group, div. health and policy research and edn. Harvard U., 1986— Author: (with R. Vandermey) Genes and The Mind: Inheritance of Mental Illness, 1980, Schizophrenia: The Facts, 2d edit., 1997, (with S.V. Faraone) The Genetics of Mood Disorders, 1990; co-editor: Schizoaffective Psychoses, 1986, Handbook of Schizophrenia, vol. 3, 1988, Affective and Schizoaffective Disorders, Similarities and Differences, 1990, (with S.V. Faraone and D. Tsuang) Genetics of Mental Disorders: A Guide for Students, Clinicians and Researchers, 1999, (with M. Tohen) A Textbook on Psychiatric Epidemiology, 2d edit., 2002, (with W.S. Stone and S.V. Faraone) Early Clinical Intervention and Prevention in Schizophrenia, 2004, also monographs.; contbr. chpts. to books, numerous articles to profl. jours. Recipient Clin. Rsch. award Am. Acad. Clin. Psychiatrists, 1983, Rema Lapous award APHA, 1984, Stanley Dean award for rsch. on schizophrenia Am. Coll. Psychiatrists, 1989, Lifetime Achievement award Internat. Soc. Psychiat. Genetics, 1995, Taiwanese-Am. award for Achievement in Sci. and Engring., 1995, Gold Medal award Soc. Biol. Psychiatry, 2000, award for rsch. in psychiatry Am. Psychiat. Assn., 2003. Mem. Am. Psychopathol. Assn. (pres. 2005), Internat. Soc. Psychiat. Genetics (pres. 2005—, Lifetime Achievement award 1995), Inst. of Medicine/NAAS,

Academia Sinica Taiwan, Sigma Xi. Office: U Calif San Diego Dept Psychiatry Med Tchg FAcility Rm 453 9500 Gilman Dr Mail Code 0603 La Jolla CA 92093-0603 Office Phone: 858-822-2464. Business E-Mail: mtsuang@ucsd.edu. *My constant goal is to do the best work I can, to eschew anxiety about the result, to learn from failure, and to build upon success, not for personal honor but for the good of mankind, as God's servant within a serving profession. Helping others is not possible without self-discipline, self-sufficience, and self-sacrifice; at the same time, helping others strengthens the self for its tasks.*

TSUBAKI, ANDREW TAKAHISA, theater director, educator; b. Chiyoda-ku, Tokyo, Japan, Nov. 29, 1931; s. Ken and Yasu (Oyama) T.; m. Lilly Yuri, Aug. 3, 1963; children: Arthur Yuichi, Philip Takeshi. BA in English, Tokyo Gakugei U., Tokyo, Japan, 1954; postgrad. in Drama, U. Saskatchewan, Saskatoon, Canada, 1958-59; MFA in Theatre Arts, Tex. Christian U., 1961; PhD in Speech & Drama, U. Ill., 1967. Tchr. Bunkyo-ku 4th Jr. High Sch., Tokyo, 1954—58; instr., scene designer Bowling Green (Ohio) State U., 1964—68; asst. prof. speech & drama U. Kans., Lawrence, 1968—73, assoc. prof., 1973—79; vis. assoc. prof. Carleton Coll., Northfield, Minn., 1974; lectr. Tsuda U., Tokyo, 1975; vis. assoc. prof. theatre Tel-Aviv (Israel) U., 1975—76; vis. prof. theatre Mo. Repertory Theatre, Kansas City, Mo., 1976, Nat. Sch. Drama, New Delhi, 1983; prof. theatre, film, east Asian Languages and Cultures U. Kans., Lawrence, 1979—2000, prof. emeritus, 2000—. Dir. Internat. Theatre Studies Ctr., U. Kans., Lawrence, 1971-2000, Operation Internat. Classical Theatre, 1988—; Benedict disting. vis. prof. Asian studies Carleton Coll., 1993; area editor Asian Theatre Jour., U. Hawaii, Honolulu, 1982-94; chmn. East Asian Langs. and Cultures, U. Kans., Lawrence, 1983-90; mem. editl. bd. Studies in Am. Drama, Oxford, Miss., 1985-88. Dir. plays Kanjincho, 1973, Rashomon, 1976, 96, King Lear, 1985, Fujito and Shimizu, 1985, Hippolytus, 1990, Busu and the Missing Lamb (Japan) 1992, Suehirogari and Sumidagawa, 1992, 93, Tea, 1995; choreographed Antigone (Greece), 1987, Hamlet (Germany); 1989, The Resistible Rise of Arturo Ui, 1991, Man and the Masses (Germany), 1993, The Children of Fate (Hungary), 1994, The Great Theatre of the World (Germany); editor Theatre Companies of the World, 1986; contbg. author to Indian Theatre: Traditions of Performance, 1990; contbr. 7 entries in Japanese Traditional plays to the Internat. Dictionary of Theatre, vol. 1, 1992, vol. 2, 1994. Recipient citation, Min. Fgn. Affairs Japan, 2003, Statement of Appreciation, chmn., bd. dirs. Hiratsuka Internat. Exch. Assn., 2004; World Univ. Svc. scholar, U. Saskatchewan, 1958—59, University fellow, U. Ill., 1961—62, Rsch. fellow, The Japan Found., 1974—75, 1990, Rsch. Fulbright grantee, 1983. Fellow Coll. Am. Theatre (elected 2002); mem. Am. Theatre Assn., Asian Theatre Program (chair 1976-79), Assn. for Asian Studies, Assn. Kans. Theatres., Assn. Kans. Theatres U/C Div. (chmn. 1980-82), Assn. for Theatre in Higher Edn., Assn. for Asian Performance. Democrat. Buddhist. Avocations: ki-aikido (4th dan), photography, travel. Home: 924 Holiday Dr Lawrence KS 66049-3005

TSUBOUCHI, DAVID H., Canadian provincial official; BA in English, York U., 1972; LLB, Osgoode Hall Law Sch., 1975; LLD (hon.), Assumption U., Windsor, 2006. Ward 5 councillor Town of Markham, 1988-94; sr. ptnr. Tsubouchi & Nichols & Assocs., 1994-95; progressive conservative mem. Legis. Assembly Ont., 1995—2003; Min. Cmty. and Social Svcs. Ont. Progressive Conservative Govt., 1995-99. Min. Consumer & Comml. Affairs Can., 1996—99, chair cabinet legis. and regulations com., 1996, re-elected mem. Provincial Parliament for Markham, 1999; registrar gen. Province of Ont., 1996, solicitor gen., 1999—2001, chair health and social svcs. policy com., chair mgmt. bd. cabinet, 2001—03, min. culture, 2002—03, min. consumer and comml. relations; cons., coun. Fraser, Milner Casgrain LLP, Toronto, Canada, 2004—. Chmn. planning and devel. com., econ. alliance com., indsl. and corp. devel. com. Markham Hist. Mus.; bd. dir. Teranet Inc.; trustee Terenet Operating Trust. Contbr. articles to Law Gazette. Assoc. dir. Japanese Canadian Cultural Centre; dir. Rouge Valley Adv. Com., Unionville Home Soc. Seniors' Found.; bd. gov., also audit com. and student issues roundtable York U., 2004—. Named Optimist of Yr., 1985-86; recipient Air Can. Heart of Gold award, 1988; granted Coat of Arms, Gov. Gen.'s Office, 1993, award of appreciation, First Nations Chiefs of Police, Ontario Soc. for the Prevention of Cruelty to Animals, Bruce Bryden award for Leadership, York U., 2003, The Queen's Golden Jubilee award, Canadian Horse Racing Industry award of Recognition, Ont. Grape Growers award of Merit, Hon. Patron of the Gardiner Mus. Ceramics, Japanese Cultural Centre award for Leadership. Mem.: Optimist Club of Markham, Markham Lions Club. Office: Fraser Milner Casgrain LLP 1 First Canadian Pl 39th Fl 100 King Street West Toronto ON M5X 1B2 Canada*

TSUI, DANIEL C., electrical engineer, physicist; b. Henan, China, 1939; Diploma, Augustana Coll., 1961; PhD in Physics, U. Chgo., 1967. Rsch. assoc. U. Chgo., 1967—68; mem. technical staff Bell Labs., Murray Hill, NJ, 1968—82; Arthur LeGrand Doty prof. dept. elec. engring. Princeton U., NJ, 1982—. Contbr. articles to profl. jours. Recipient Buckley prize for Condensed Matter Physics, 1984, Benjamin Franklin medal in Physics, 1998, Nobel prize in Physics, 1998. Fellow: AAAS; mem.: NAE, NAS, Materials Research Soc., Am. Physical Soc., IEEE, Acad. Sinica. Office: Princeton U Dept Elec Engring Rm B 426 PO Box 5263 Princeton NJ 08544-0001 Fax: 609-258-6279. E-mail: tsui@ee.princeton.edu.*

TSUI, LAP-CHEE, academic administrator, molecular genetics educator; b. Shanghai, Dec. 21, 1950; arrived in Can., 1981; s. Jing Lue Hsue and Hui Ching Wang; m. Ellen Lan Fong, Feb. 11, 1977; children: Eugene, Felix. BS, Chinese U. Hong Kong, 1972, MPhil, 1974; PhD, U. Pitts., 1979; DSc (hon.), Chinese U. Hong Kong, 1991; DCL (hon.), U. King's Coll., Halifax, N.S., Can., 1991; DSc (hon.), U. N.B., Can., 1991; DLL (hon.), U. St. Francis Xavier, Antigonish, N.S., Can., 1994; DSc (hon.) York U., Can. 2001. Postdoctoral Investigator Oak Ridge Nat. Lab., Tenn., 1979—80; postdoctoral fellow Hosp. for Sick Children, Toronto, Ont., Canada, 1981—83, geneticist-in-chief, 1996—2002; asst. prof. depts. genetics and med. genetics U. Toronto, Ont., Canada, 1983—88, assoc. prof. Ont., 1988—90, prof. Ont., 1990—, univ. prof. Ont., 1994—; H.E. Sellers chair in cystic fibrosis, 1998—; head genetics and genomic biology program, 1998—2002. Chmn. chromosome 7 subcom. Human Gene Mapping Workshop, 1986-97; mem. mammalian genetics study sect. NIH, Bethesda, Md., 1988-93; dir. Cystic Fibrosis Rsch. Ctr., Hosp. for Sick Children Sci. Rsch. Ctr., 1994-2002; scientist Med. Rsch. Coun. Can., 1989-2002; advisor European Jour. Human Genetics, 1992—, Molecular Medicine Today, 1995—; adj. prof. U. New Brunswick, 2000-2002; vice-chancellor U. Hong Kong, 2002—. Editor Cytogenetics and Cell Genetics, 1988-92, Internat. Jour. Genome Rsch., 1990—; assoc. editor Am. Jour. Human Genetics, 1990-93, Genomics, 1994—; mem. editl. bd. Mammalian Genome, 1990, Clin. Genetics, 1991—, Human Molecular Genetics, 1991-99; communicating editor Human Mutation, 1995—, Molec. Medicine Today, sr. editor: Physiological Genomics, 2000-01; internat. adv. The Chinese Jour. of Medical Genetics, 2000—; editor Biochimica et Biophysica Acta, 2002—; contbr. over 300 articles to sci. jours.; co-discoverer cystic fibrosis gene, 1989. Trustee Edn. Found., Fedn. Chinese Canadian Profls., Toronto, 1987—. Recipient Paul di Sant Agnese Disting. Achievement award Cystic Fibrosis Found., 1989, Zellers SR. Scientist award, 2001, Gold medal of honor Pharm. Mfrs. Assn. Can., 1989, award of excellence Genetics Soc. Can., 1990, Gairdner Internat. award 1990, Cresson medal Franklin Inst., 1992, E. Mead Johnson award, 1992, Disting. Scientist award The Canadian Soc. Clin. Investigation, 1992, Canadian Conf. medal 1992, Sarstedt Rsch. prize, 1993, Sanremo Internat. award for Genetic Rsch., 1993, J.P. Lecocq prize Inst. de France, 1994, Henry Friesen award The Canadian Soc. for Clin. Investigation and the Royal Coll. of Physicians and Surgeons of Can., 1995, Can. Med. Assn. award of honour, 1996, Jonas Salk award Ontario March of Dimes, 1997, Initiative Cmty. Svc. award Toronto Biotech., 1998, Disting. Scientist award Med. Rsch. Coun., 2000, Killam prize Can. Coun., 2002; named scholar Can. Cystic Fibrosis Found., 1984-86. Fellow Royal Soc. Can., Royal Soc. London, Academia Sinica, Royal Coll. Physicians U.K. (hon.); mem. Human Genome Orgn., Am. Soc. Human Genetics, NAS (fgn. assoc.). Office: Vice-Chancellor's Office U Hong Kong Pokfulam Rd Hong Kong Hong Kong Office Phone: (852) 2859 2100. Office Fax: (852) 2858 9435. Business E-Mail: tsuilc@hkucc.hku.hk.

**TSUI, STEPHEN ALAN,** researcher; b. Houston, Aug. 16, 1980; s. Steve and Annie Lim Tsui. BS in Physics, U. Houston, 2002, MS in Physics, 2004. Undergrad. rsch. asst. Tex. Ctr. Superconductivity, U. Houston, 1999—2000, rsch. asst., 2002—; undergrad. rsch. asst. U. Houston Medium Energy Physics Group, 2000—02; tchg. asst. dept. physics U. Houston, 2002—03. Lit. anthology, Aquilae Stilus: Klein Forest's Literary and Art Anthology; contbr. poetry to anthologies (Internat. Libr. of Poetry Bronze medal, 2000). Ednl. outreach lectr. Tex. Ctr. for Superconductivity, U. of Houston, 2002—06. Recipient merit scholarship, Houston Livestock Show and Rodeo, 1998—2002, 2d Pl. award Student Challenge Undergrad. Divsn., U. of Houston Coll. of Natural Scis. and Math., 2002, 3d Pl. award, Student Challenge Grad. Divsn., 2003, 3d Pl., Tex. Ctr. for Superconductivity and Advanced Materials, 2003, 1st pl., Tex. Ctr. for Superconductivity Student Symposium, 2006. Mem.: Am. Phys. Soc. (pres. chpt. of Soc. Physics Students 2001—02), U. of Houston (pres. 2001—02), U. of Houston Alumni Orgn., Golden Key, Alpha Lambda Delta-Phi Eta Sigma, Sigma Pi Sigma, Nat. Art Honor Soc. (sec. Klein Forest chpt. 1997—98), Phi Kappa Phi (life). Achievements include development of Prototype straw particle tracker for project MECO at the University of Houston; research in Static negative dielectric constant in a nano-colloid; Resistive switching in metal-oxide interfaces. Avocations: jogging, poetry, cooking. Office: U Houston Tex Ctr for Superconductivity Houston TX 77204

**TSUJI, FREDERICK ICHIRO,** biochemist, molecular biologist; b. Honolulu, Aug. 23, 1923; s. Kijiro Tsuji and Sadako Moriyama; m. Masako Koga, Mar. 31, 1991. BA, Cornell U., Ithaca, NY, 1946, M in Nutritional Sci., 1948, PhD, 1950. Asst. prof. Duquesne U., Pitts., 1950—52; rsch. asst. Princeton (NJ) U., 1952—55; rsch. biochemist, head basic sci. rsch. VA Hosp., Pitts., 1955—72; rsch. prof. U. So. Calif., L.A., 1972—76; dir. biochemistry program NSF, Washington, 1976—78; rsch. biochemist, prof. U. Calif., San Diego, La Jolla, 1978—. Vis. prof. dept. protein crystallography Osaka (Japan) U., 1998—99. Administr. grant applications and awards for rsch. in biochemistry NSF, Washington, 1976—78. Grantee, NSF, 1970—2000. Achievements include research in chemistry of light production by animals and plants. Avocations: classical music, history of modern physics, literature, art. Office: University California San Diego 9500 Gilman Dr La Jolla CA 92093 Office Phone: 858-534-3197. Office Fax: 858-534-7313. Business E-Mail: ftsuji@ucsd.edu.

**TSUJI, TAKAKO,** financial analyst; BA summa cum laude, SUNY, Albany, 1996; M of Internat. Affairs, Columbia U. Rsch. verifier Brookings Instn., Washington, 1998—2000; grad. intern Fed. Res. Bank NY, NYC, 1997; assoc. analyst Congl. Budget Office, Washington, 2000—01; budget analyst Ho. Budget Com., Washington, 2001—. Office: House Budget Com 309 Cannon House Office Bldg Washington DC 20515

**TSUJI, TOSHIZO,** hospital administrator, educator; b. Kyoto, Jan. 2, 1932; s. Yasujiro and Yuki (Nakamura) T.; m. Yoshiko Taniguchi, Mar. 21, 1977; children: Mari, Toshifumi. MD, Kyoto Prefectural U. Medicine, 1957, DSc, 1964. Intern Kyoto 1st Red Cross Hosp., 1957-58; clin. fellow Kyoto Prefectural U. Medicine, 1959-60, asst. prof., 1971-74, assoc. prof., 1974-97; clin. fellow U. Ala. Med. Ctr., Birmingham, 1964-67, instr. medicine, 1967-68; postdoctoral fellow in molecular biology U. Edinburgh, Scotland, 1968-70; v.p. Kyoto Prefectural Yosanoumi Hosp., Iwataki, 1983—; pres. Kyoto Prefectural Yosanoumi Blood Ctr., Iwataki, 1974-83; prin. Kyoto Prefectural Nursing Sch., Iwataki, 1988-94; pres., med. juridical person Ohtha Found. Ohta Hosp., Kyoto, 1997—2006; pres., med. juridical person Miyazu Kosei Found., Miyazu Takeda Hosp., Kyoto, 2006—. Mem. WHO, Kyoto, Japan, 1983—. Contbr. articles to profl. jours. Recipient med. diploma Japanese Ministry Health and Welfare, 1958; fellow NIH, 1965, European Molecular Biology Orgn., 1968. Fellow Japanese Soc. Internal Medicine, Japanese Soc. Gastroenterology, Japanese Soc. Hepatology; mem. AAAS, NY Acad. Scis. Avocations: golf, tennis, stamp collecting/philately, gardening, music. Home: 988 Uoya Kyoto 626-0015 Japan Office Phone: 0772-22-2157.

**TSUKAMOTO, DANIEL,** piano instructor, church organist; b. Encarnación, Itapúa, Paraguay, Apr. 18, 1970; s. Minoru and Yoko Tsukamoto; m. Sarah K. Klusendorf, July 12, 2003. BA, Asbury Coll., 1994; MusM, U. SD, Vermillion, 1995. Electronic organist Free Meth. Ch., Encarnación, Itapúa, Paraguay, 1982—86; instr. HS orch. Rapid City Ctrl. HS, SD, 1986—88; instr. HS orch. (double bass/cello player) Watertown Sr. HS, SD, 1988—89; instr. coll. orch. (double bass player/cello player) Asbury Coll., Wilmore, Ky., 1989—94; instr. U. orch. (double bass/cello player) U. SD, Vermillion, 1994—95, piano grad. asst., 1994—95; instr. U. orch. (double bass player) SD State U., Brookings, 1996—99; ch. organist Romeo United Meth. Ch., Romeo, Mich., 2000—, piano lesson tchr., 2002—. Double bass player Rapid City Symphony Orch., SD, 1987—88; all-state orch. SD Pub. Schs., Aberdeen, 1988—88, all-state honor's orch., Brookings, 1989—89, all-state band, Huron, 1989—89; double bass player Pit Orch., Wilmore, Ky., 1989—89; piano accompanist, musical singer (tenor) Romeo United Meth. Ch., Romeo, Mich., 2002—03; ch. organist for weddings, Mich., 2003—. Bell ringer Salvation Army, Watertown, SD. Named to Nat. Honor Soc., Rapid City Ctrl. HS, 1987; recipient Faculty Award, Watertown Sr. High, 1988—89, Nat. HS Orchestra award, 1989. Mem.: Am. Guild Organists (assoc.). Home: 42221 Toddmark Ln Apt 124 Clinton Township MI 48038 Office: Romeo United Meth Ch 298 N Main St Romeo MI 48065 Home Fax: 586-412-9015. Personal E-Mail: z5aj@sbcglobal.net.

**TSUNG, CHRISTINE CHAI-YI,** financial executive, treasurer; b. Nanking, China, Mar. 23, 1948; came to U.S., 1970; d. Chi-Huang Tsung and Siao-Tuan Huang. BBA, Nat. Taiwan U., Taipei, 1970; postgrad., Washington U., St. Louis, 1970-71; MBA, U. Mo., 1973. Acct. Capital Land Co., St. Louis, 1972-74; chief acct. Servis Equipment Co., Inc., Dallas, 1974-75; acctg. supr. Calif. Microwave, Sunnyale, 1975-76; budget and sales mgr. Columbia Pictures TV Internat., Burbank, Calif., 1976-77; acctg. mgr. Husquarna, San Diego, 1977-82; sr. acct. City of Poway, Calif., 1982-88, fin. mgr. Calif., 1988-95; pres., CEO China Airlines 2000—. Pres., treas. Jade Poly Investment, Beverly Hills, Calif., 1989—; cons. assoc. Metro Properties, San Diego, 1989—; cons. Kaohsiung City, Taiwan, 2000—. Tchr. San Diego North County Chinese Sch., 1985-86; v.p. San Diego Chinese Culture Assn. 1982-86, bd. dirs., 1988-90, 93-94. Mem. Asian Pacific Airlines, Pacific Asia Travel Assn. (exec. bd.), Govt. Fin. Officers Assn. (Cert. of Achievement 1988-94), Calif. Soc. Mcpl. Fin. Officers (standing com. membership devel., Cert. of Award 1988-94), Mcpl. Treas. Assn. U.S. and Can., Taiwanese C. of C. of N.Am. (bd. dirs. 1994-95). Avocations: travel, swimming, tennis, golf, reading. Office: China Airlines 2F 131 Sec 3 Nanking E Rd Taipei Taiwan Office Phone: 882-2-2514-5799. Business E-Mail: c_tsung@china.airlines.com.

**TSUTAKAWA, EDWARD MASAO,** management consultant; b. Seattle, May 15, 1921; s. Jin and Michiko (Oka) T.; m. Hide Kunugi, Aug. 11, 1949; children: Nancy Joyce, Margaret Ann Langston, Mark Edward. Student, U. Wash., 1941, Wash. State U., 1949. Free-lance comml. artist, Spokane, 1943-47; artist Maag & Porter Comml. Printers, Spokane, 1947-54; organizer Litho Art Printers, Inc., Spokane, 1954—, gen. mgr., pres., 1965-80. Charter organizer, dir. Am. Comml. Bank, 1965-80; prin. E.M. Tsutakawa Co., bus. cons. U.S., Japan Trade Negotiator, 1980-89; v.p. operation officer, dir. Mukogawa Ft. Wright Inst.; exec. in residence Whitworth Coll. Grad. Sch., 1999; hon. prof. edn. dept. Wash. State U., 2000. Pres. emeritus Spokane-Nishinomiya Sister City Soc., Sister Cities Assn. of Spokane; mem. Eastern Wash. State Hist. Soc.; bd. dirs. Spokane Regional Internat. Trade Alliance, Leadership Spokane. Recipient Disting. Svc. medal Boy Scouts of Japan, 1967, Cultural medal in Edn., Japan, 1985, Disting. Svc. award City of Nishinomiya, 1971, Disting. Svc. to Expo '74 State of Wash., 1974, Book of Golden Deeds award Exch. Club, 1978, Disting. Cmty. Svc. award UN Assn., 1979, Whitworth Coll., 1987, Svc. to Youth award Spokane YMCA, 1988, Silver Hawk medal Boy Scouts Japan, 1997, Internat. Rels. and Trade Pioneer Recognition, Spokane Area C. of C., 1998; decorated Order of Sacred

Treasure medal Govt. of Japan, 1984. Mem. Japanese Am. Citizens League, Japan Am. Soc. Wash. State (pres.'s award 1991), Kiwanis (Spokane). Methodist. Home: 4116 S Madelia St Spokane WA 99203-4229 E-mail: etsutakawa@mfwi.org.

**TSUTSUMI, TSUYOSHI,** musician, educator; b. Tokyo; arrived in U.S., 1984; s. Kiyoshi and Mineko Tsutsumi; m. Harue Saji, May 14, 1978; children: Seizo, Mie. Diploma, Ind. U., 1965. Artist-in-resident Ind. U., Bloomington, 1966—68, prof. music, 1988—; from artist-in-resident to assoc. prof. U. Western Ont., London, Canada, 1968—84; prof. music U. Ill., Urbana, 1984—88; pres. Toho Gakuen Sch. Music, Tokyo, 2004. Author: My Illinois Diary, 1990, LIfe with the Cello, 2002. Bd. dirs., pres. Suntory Music Found., Tokyo, 1989. Recipient Music prize, Suntory Music Found., 1971, Acad. of Arts prize, Govt. of Japan, 1993, Chevalier du Violon-celle, Ind. U., 2003. Mem.: Japan Cello Soc. (pres.). Avocations: reading, trains. Home: 2715 Bluff Ct Bloomington IN 47401 Office: Ind U Sch Music 1201 E 3d St Bloomington IN 47405 Office Phone: 812-855-1552. Business E-Mail: tsutsum@indiana.edu.

**TSVANKIN, ILYA DANIEL,** geophysics educator; b. Moscow, Apr. 6, 1956; came to U.S., 1990; s. Daniel and Maya (Slonimskaya) T.; m. Olga Dashevskaya, July 27, 1985; children: Edward, Daniel. MS in Geophys. Exploration, Moscow State U., 1978, PhD in Geophysics, 1982. Rsch. scientist Inst. Physics of Earth, Moscow, 1978-86, dep. chief lab., 1986-89; cons. Rsch. Ctr., Amoco Prodn. Co., Tulsa, 1990-92; assoc. prof. geophysics Colo. Sch. Mines, Golden, 1992-99, prof., 1999—. Dir. rsch. project Ctr. for Wave Phenomena Contbr. articles to profl. publs.; patentee in field. Recipient Gold medal in Geophysics for Young Scientists, Soviet Acad. Scis., 1988. Mem. Am. Geophys. Union, Denver Geophys. Soc., Soc. Exploration Geophysicists (transl. com. 1990—, rsch. com. 1997—, Virgil Kauffman gold medal award 1996), European Assn. Geoscientists and Engrs. Avocations: classical music, soccer, ice hockey, skiing. E-mail: ilya@dix.mines.edu.

**TSYBAKOV, BORIS SOLOMON,** information theory and communication networks researcher, educator; b. Moscow, May 14, 1934; s. Solomon Mark and Evdokia Tikhon (Tsybakova) Pinsker; m. Lidia Sergey Tsybakova, Oct. 14, 1956; 1 child, Alexander. D of Sci. in Engring., Moscow Inst. of Physics/Tech. Jr. rschr. Inst. for Radio and Electronic Engring., Moscow, 1958—63, sr. rschr., 1963—77; head of lab. Inst. for Info. Transmission Problems, Moscow, 1977—2000; prin. engr. Qualcomm, Inc., San Diego, 1999—2006; vis. scholar Calitz U. Calif., San Diego, 2006—. Prof. Moscow Inst. of Physics and Tech., 1965—93; supr. Post-grads. in Info. Theory. Mem. editl. bd. Problems of Info. Transmission Jour., 1965—; editor Wireless Personal Comms., An Internat. Jour., 1992—, Jour. Comms. and Networks, 1999—; mem. internat. adv. com. Advanced Electronic Comm. Rsch. & Edn. Jour.; contbr. articles to profl. publ. and lecture courses on info. theory and commn. sys. Recipient full prof. title diploma, 1979, Prominent Comm. Profl. of Russia award Pres. of Russia, 1996, Paper award INFOCOM'95 on Math. Analysis of the Self-Similar Traffic, 1995. Mem.: IEEE (Info. Theory Soc. paper award on Invention of the Stable Multiple-Access Algorithm 1981), Russian Acad. Sci. Club. Avocation: lawn tennis. Office: Unit 256 10292 Wateridge Cir San Diego CA 92121 Personal E-mail: btsybakov@yahoo.com.

**TSYGAN, LEONID IOSIFOVICH,** civil engineer, writer; b. Kiev, Ukraine, Dec. 22, 1938; arrived in U.S., 1979; s. Iosif Haim-Garshevech and Bluma Leybovna Tsygan; m. Emmilia Igorevna Shustova, 1971 (div. 1984); 1 child, Russell; m. Zhanna Iosifovna Polonskaya, 1997; 1 child, Joshua 1 stepchild, Lana Polonskaya. BSCE, Kiev Inst. Hwy. Engring., 1968; computer programmer, Syrit Computer Sch. Sys., N.Y.C., 1983. Sr. engr. State Design Inst. Hwys., Kiev, 1968—78; draftsman King and Gavaris Cons. Engrs. Inc., N.Y.C., 1979—81; designer, draftsman Berger, Lehman Assocs. P.C., Rye, NY, 1982—84; bridge designer E. Pavlo Consulting Engr., N.Y.C., 1984—89; engr. Anuman & Whitney Cons. Engr., N.Y.C., 1990—91; asst. civil engr. N.Y.C. Dept. Transp., N.Y.C., 1992—. Contbr. poetry to anthologies. Alt. del. N.Y.C. Dept. Transp. local 375, chpt. 37, DC 37 AFSCME, AFL-CIO, N.Y.C., 2000—. Co-recipient medal for design of Moscow cable-stay bridge, State Design Inst. Hwys., 1976; named to Poetry's Elite: The Best Poets of 2000. Achievements include test track for road pavement and bridge structure with test material in Willowbrook Park, Staten Island.

**TU, CHING-I,** humanities educator, researcher; b. Nanking, China, May 13, 1935; s. Show-mei and I-fang Tu; m. Sabrina S. Wang, June 14, 1970; children: Stephen Shih-chung, Sylvia Shih-yun. PhD, U. Wash., Seattle, 1967; BA, Nat. Taiwan U., 1958. Prof., chair Rutgers U., New Brunswick, NJ, 1975—, asst. and assoc. prof., 1966—75. Chair, adv. bd. Asian Studies Rutgers U., New Brunswick, NJ, 1998—; vis. prof. Nat. Taiwan U., Taipei, 1974—75; vis. assoc. prof. U. Hawaii, Honolulu, 1971—72. Author: Poetic Remarks in the Human World, 1970, Anthology of Chinese Literature, 1972, Readings in Chinese Classical Literature, 1981; editor: Tradition and Creativity: Essays on East Asian Civilizations, 1986, Classics and Interpretations: The Hermeneutic Traditions in Chinese Culture, 2000. Grantee Grant for Developing Chinese Studies at Rutgers U., Chiang Ching-kuo Found. for Internat. Scholarly Exch., 1993-1994, Grant for Developing Korean Studies at Rutgers U., The Korea Found., 1995-1998, Grant for Developing Japanese Studies at Rutgers U., The Japan Found., 1993-1995, Grant for Developing Korean Studies at Rutgers U., The Korea Found., 2001-2004. Mem.: Assn. Asian Studies, Am. Assn. for Chinese Studies, Assn. for Fgn. Lang. Dept. Chairs. Avocations: travel, reading, exercise. Office: Asian Studies Rutgers University College Ave New Brunswick NJ 08901-1164

**TU, FANG,** research scientist; b. Nanchang, Jiangxi, China, Oct. 15, 1974; d. Xiaohui Zhang and Jinhai Tu; m. Feili Yu, Sept. 22, 1972; 1 child, Felix H. Yu. BS, Zhejiang U., Hangzhou, China, 1994, MS, 1998; PhD, U. Conn., Storrs, 2003. Sr. rsch. scientist Qualtech Systems, Inc., Wethersfield, Conn., 2003—. Contbr. articles to profl. jours. Mem.: Sigma Xi. Office Phone: 860-257-8014. Personal E-mail: fangtu@ieee.org.

**TU, HOANG HUY,** lawyer; b. Saigon, Vietnam, May 22, 1963; arrived in U.S., 1975; s. Thanh Van Tu and Ky Tu Nguyen; m. Hang Thuy Chau Tran, Sept. 7, 1995; children: Huy Hoang, Dai Long. AA, El Camino Coll., 1984; BS, UCLA, 1992; JD, Western States Sch. Law, 1999. Bar: Calif., U.S. Dist. Ct. (ctrl. dist.) Calif., U.S. Dist. Ct. (so. dist.) Calif. Pres., CEO IBF Enterprise, L.A., 1990—96; pres. Escrow Divsn. Group, 1992—96; ptnr. Hoang Huy Tu Attys., Fountain Valley, 1999—. Mem.: Vietnamese Am. Bar Assn. (bd. dirs. 1999—), Consumer Atty. Calif., Orange County Bar Assn., Am. Immigration Lawyers Assn. Avocations: tennis, golf, Kung Fu, movies. E-mail: hoangtu@usaluat.com

**TU, JIUFENG J.,** physics professor; b. Nanjing, Jiangsu Province, China, Nov. 26, 1968; s. Shude Tu and Lizhen Tang; m. Qing R. Fan, Mar. 2, 1971. AB, AM, Harvard U., Cambridge, Mass., 1993; PhD, Cornell U., Ithaca, N.Y., 2000. Rsch. assoc. Brookhaven Nat. Lab., Upton, NY, 2000—03; prof. of physics CCNY, N.Y.C., 2003—. Exec. prodr.: Recipient rsch. grants, NSF, 2004—09. Mem.: Am. Phys. Soc. (assoc.). Achievements include patents pending for Room temperature manufacturing of ultra-thin films. Office: CCNY J-330A Dept of Physics 160 Convent Ave New York NY 10031 Office Phone: 212-650-5558. Office Fax: 212-650-6940. Business E-Mail: jtu@sci.ccny.cuny.edu.

**TU, SUSAN,** retired librarian; b. Taipei, Taiwan, June 10, 1923; arrived in U.S., 1961, naturalized, 1976; d. Tsungming Tu and Sonsui Lin; children: Helene Lin, Andy Lin, Jean Lin, Charlyn Lin. Student, Surugadai Girl's Jr. Coll., Tokyo, 1942, Taihoku Imperial U., Taiwan, 1944, U. Calif., Berkeley, 1961; BA, Utah State U., 1965; MA, U. Utah, 1971; MSLS, La. State U., 1973, cert. of med. librarianship, 1975, MEd, 1977, postgrad., 1976-77. Tchr. Taipei (Taiwan) Mcpl. Girls' High Sch., 1958-61; chief libr. Saints Coll., Lexington, Miss., 1974-76; hosp. libr. U.S. Army, Ft. Polk, La., 1977-79; dist. libr. Rock Island (Ill.) dist. U.S. Army Corps Engrs., 1979-83, div. libr. North Atlantic div. N.Y.C., 1984-88; dist. libr. N.Y. Dist., N.Y.C., 1988-90. From

TIU to NTU- The Reminiscences of Miss Susan Tu, 2002; co-prodr.: (videos, slide prodns., TV program). Mem. adv. bd. The Formosa Chamber Music Soc., Inc. Mem. Spl. Librs. Assn., Chinese-Am. Librs. Assn., Photographic Soc. Am. Avocations: photography, travel, beauty appreciation, literature, music.

**TUAN, KAILIN,** management consultant, educator; b. Hefei, China, Sept. 9, 1925; m. Liau G. Tuan; 1 child, Wayne. BS, Chiao Tung U., Shanghai, 1948; MBA, U. Pa., 1952; PhD, New Sch. for Social Rsch., N.Y.C., 1966. Asst./assoc. prof. Upsala Coll., East Orange, NJ, 1959—74; prof. U. Balt., 1974—77, Temple U., Phila., 1977—93, prof. emeritus 1993—. Prof., dir. Internat. Ins. Inst., Nankai U., Tianyin, China, 1987—97; hon. prof. various Chinese univs.; lectr. in field; econ. adviser to Taiwan and the Philippines, 1970—73; adviser Ministry of Fin., Taiwan, 1970—90; Far Ea. rep. Internat. Coop. Alliance, 1970; cons. to several maj. U.S. and Brit. ins. and bus. cos., 1970—80. Contbr. articles more than 100 numerous articles to profl. jour. publ. in profl. and academic jour. and bus./ins. mag. USA, UK, Japan, China, Taiwan and other Asian countries; author: Modern Insurance Theory and Edn./Ins. Inst. for Asia and the Pacific, 1972—75, Essays in Risk Management, 1988, The Risk Management Movement, 1999, Studies in the Theory of Risk and Insurance, 1995. Recipient Internat. Friendship award, Chinese Govt., 2000, FLMI Ins. Edn. award, Life Office Mgmt. Assn., 2001, Pres.'s award, Ins. Acctg. and Sys. Assn., 2002. Mem.: U.S. Am.-China C. of C. (founder, bd. dirs.), Am. Risk and Ins. Assn., Internat. Ins. Soc. Avocations: gardening, Go. Office: Temple Univ Dept Risk Mgmt and Ins Philadelphia PA 19122

**TUBB, BETTY FREEZE,** music educator; b. Oklahoma City, Oct. 6, 1932; d. Eugene Woodrow Freeze and Otha Merle Perkins; m. Boyd Junior Bryce, Aug. 6, 1948 (dec. June 1965); children: Donna Bryce Lacquement, DiAnn Bryce Neff; m. Curtis O'Connor Tubb, Dec. 30, 1969; 1 child, Tara Elizabeth Tubb Foster. BMus in Piano, Oklahoma City U., 1966. Cert. piano tchr. Ala. Pvt. music tchr., Oklahoma City, 1960—70; faculty Tonsmeire Sch. Music, Mobile, Ala., 1970—71, Mobile Christian Sch., 1971—73; pvt. music tchr. Cross City, Fla., 1980—85; faculty Wrights Girls Sch., Mobile, 1986—87; pvt. music tchr., ind. piano tchr. Mobile, 1988—. Adjudicator Nat. Guild Piano Tchrs., 1962—91. Mem.: Music Tchrs. Nat. Assn., Ala. Music Tchrs. Assn., Nat. Guild Piano Tchrs. (adjudicator 1962—99, treas., chair scholarship com.), Mobile Music Tchr. Assn. (pres. 1972—74, treas. 2001—02, scholarship chmn.), Sigma Alpha Iota. Republican. Mem. Church Of Christ. Avocation: heritage. E-mail: bettyt10063@cs.com.

**TUBB, JAMES CLARENCE,** lawyer; b. Corsicana, Tex. s. Cullen Louis and Sarah Elmore (Chapman) T.; m. Suzanne Alice Smith, Nov. 25, 1954; children: James Richard, Sara Elizabeth, Daniel Chapman. BA, So. Meth. U., 1951, JD, 1954. Bar: Tex. 1954, U.S. Dist. Ct. (no. dist.) Tex. 1955, U.S. Ct. Appeals (5th cir.) 1959, U.S. Supreme Ct. 1978; cert. comml. real estate specialist, 1983; lic. Tex. real estate broker; cert. mediator Dallas Bar Assn. With legal dept. Schlumberger Well Surveying Corp., Houston, 1954-55; claims atty. Franklin Am. Ins. Co., Dallas, 1957-58; ptnr. Vial, Hamilton, Koch, Tubb & Knox and predecessor firm Akin, Vial, Hamilton, Koch & Tubb, Dallas, 1958-84; dir., ptnr. Winstead, McGuire, Sechrest & Minick, Dallas, 1984-90; pvt. practice Dallas, 1990—. Guest lectr. on real estate broker liability Real Estate Ctr., Tex. A&M U., 1987. Mem. bd. deacons Highland Park Presbyn. Ch., Dallas, 1972—78, ruling elder, 1978—84, 1988—91; mem. permanent jud. commn. Grace Presbytery, 1984—90; bd. dirs. Christian Concern Found., 1965—71, Dallas County affiliate Am. Diabetes Assn., 1991—95. With Tex. Air N.G., 1949—51, 1st lt. JAGC, SAC USAF, 1955—57, 1st lt. USAF, ret. Recipient Outstanding Student award Student Bar Assn., 1954. Fellow Tex. Bar Found.; mem. ABA (chmn. comml. law com. gen. practice sect. 1982-84, real estate probate and trust law sect.), Tex. Bus. Law Found., Tex. Bar Assn., Am. Arbitration Assn. (sec. comml. arbitration panelist), Dallas Country Club, Dallas County Rep. Men's Club (sec. 1978-79). Home and Office: 3407 Haynie Ave Dallas TX 75205-1842 Office Phone: 214-232-8964.

**TUBBS, DAVID EUGENE,** mechanical engineer, marketing professional; b. Springfield, Ill., Jan. 12, 1948; s. Eugene Lewellyn and Jacqueline Flo (Jones) T.; m. Linda Alyson Smith, Aug. 2, 1970; children: Corbin David, Cavan Scott. BSME, Ill. Inst. Tech., 1970; postgrad., Okla. State U., 1992. Registered profl. engr., Ill., Okla. Project engr. Sargent & Lundy, Chgo., 1970-82, bus. devel. mgr., 1982-83; mgr. power sales Yuba Heat Transfer Corp., Tulsa, 1983-85; with press products mktg. Nordam, Tulsa, 1985-86; dir. mktg. Brooks Aero. Svc. div. Nordam, Tulsa, 1986-91; mech. dept. mgr. The Benham Group, Tulsa, 1991-93; chief mech. engr. EDECO Engrs./Cons., Tulsa, 1993-94; mktg. support mgr. AGC Tech. Svcs. Inc., Tulsa, 1994-97; lead piping engr. Black & Veatch Pritchard, Overland Park, Kans., 1998—. Mem. ASME, Am. Welding Soc., Ill. Inst. Tech. Alumni Assn. (bd. dirs 1977-80), Delta Tau Delta, Pi Tau Sigma. Clubs: Toastmasters. Republican. Avocations: bridge, racquetball, ussf soccer referee. Office: Black & Veatch Pritchard Inc 10905 Grandview St Overland Park KS 66210-1504

**TUBBS, EDWARD LANE,** banker; b. Delmar, Iowa, Apr. 17, 1920; s. Clifton Marvin and Mary Ellen (Lane) T.; m. Grace Barbara Dyer, Nov. 27, 1941 (dec.); children: Steven, Alan, William; m. Elaine Marshall, Mar. 11, 2000. BS, Iowa State U., 1941; postgrad., U. Wis. Grad. Sch. Banking. With Iowa State U. Agrl. Ext. Svc., Newton, 1942; instr. vets. on-farm DeWitt (Iowa) Schs., 1957-58; v.p., dir. Jackson State Bank, Maquoketa State Bank, 1959-66, chmn. Mem.—. Pres., dir. Ohnward Bancshares, Inc.; chmn., dir. 1st Ctrl. State Bank, DeWitt; dir. Tri-County Bank & Trust; pres., dir. Mabsco Agrl. Svcs., Inc.; 1982-87; supt. banking State of Iowa, 1987-89; bd. dirs. Iowa Bus. Growth Corp.; lectr. banking schs.; exeh. del. USSR, 1959, 85; banking industry del. Baltic Countries, 1993; state dir. Conf. State Bank Supts., 1988-89. Contbr. articles to profl. jours. Pres. Elwood (Iowa) Sch. Bd., 1956-62; treas. City of Maquoketa, 1975-81; mem. People to People; trustee Sharar Found., Clinton Coll., 1983-86; v.p., bd. dirs. Timber City Indsl. Devel. Corp., Jackson County Sr. Ctr.; treas. Maquoketa Cmty. Svcs., 1967-80; trustee Iowa 4-H Found., 1987-91, Hoover Presdtl. Libr. Assn. Inc., truatee, 1987—; gov. Iowa State U. Found., 1989—; trustee CCFA Found., 1990-94; coach Little League; elder, moderator United Ch. of Christ; mem. awards com. Pearson Found. With AUS, 1942-43. Recipient 4-H Club Alumni award, 1962, 2001, Century Farm award Iowa Dept. Agr., 1976, Disting. Pub. Svcs. award Jackson County, 1990, Gold Clover award Iowa 4-H Club, Heart of Gold award, 1996, Iowa Agrl. Ext. Assn. award, 1982, Floyd Andre award, 1985, Cmty. Svc. award Mt. St. Clare Coll., 2002; named Jaycee Boss of Yr., 1970; named to Iowa Agrl. Hall of Fame, 1985, Clinton Fair Hall of Fame, 1999. Mem. Bank Adminstrn. Inst., Am. Bankers Assn. (dir., coun. 1984-86, Ag Bruning award 2000, award for lifetime contbn. to agrl. banking 2000), Iowa Bankers Assn. (treas. 1978-79, pres. 1980-81, James Leach Lifetime Contribution to Banking award 2002), Am. Legion, Isaac Walton League, Iowa State U. Alumni Assn. (dir. 1980-86), Maquoketa C. of C. (dir. 1966-69), Order of Knoll (founders club Iowa State U.), Iowa Friends of Agr. (exec. com. 1987—95), Rotary (Paul Harris fellow), Gamma Sigma Delta (Alumni Achievement award 1989), Alpha Zeta. Home: 1804 Swagosa Dr Maquoketa IA 52060 Office: 203 N Main St Maquoketa IA 52060-2204

**TUBBS, MARY S.,** curriculum coordinator; m. Ronald James Tubbs, Jr., Mar. 25, 2000. AA in Humanities with honors, Chabot Coll., 1975; BA in Psychology, U. Calif-Berkeley, 1978; MEd with honors, San Francisco State U., 1982. Cert. K-8 tchr., Calif.; Hawaii. Head tchr. Jack & Jill Nursery Kindergarten, San Francisco, 1979—80; kindergarten tchr. St. James Early Childhood Devel. Ctr., San Francisco, 1980—81; substitute tchr. San Francisco Unified Sch. Dist., 1981—82; clin. psychol. asst. State Hawaii, 1982; owner Amaaia Tutoring, Kailua, Hawaii, 1988—89; psychol. examiner State Hawaii, Dept. Edn., Windward Oahu, 1983—88, spl. edn. tchr. Waianae, 1989—90, Title I reading coord., 1999—2001, tchr. Kailua, 2001—02, curriculum and standards coord., 2003: dist. resource, diagnostic prescriptive tchr. State Hawaii, Dept. Edn. Spl. Svcs., Honolulu, 1991—99, title I math. coord., 2005—. Chair Windward Oahu Dist. Sch. Climate Task Force, Kailua, 1986—88; facilitator Tchr. Assistance Team, Nanaikapono E., Hawaii, 1989—90. Recipient Summer Tchg. Trning. scholarship, Whittier Coll., 1971, Am. Bus. Women's scholarship, Alameda Bus. Women, 1978. Mem.: NEA, Hawaii State Tchr. Assn. (dist. rep. 1998), Nat. Assn. Sch. Psychologists, Hawaii Humane Soc., Susan G. Komen Breast Cancer Assn. (sec. 2003—), Reading Club (program creator, facilitator 1995—96, grant 1995). Avocations: reading, German shepherds, remodeling. Office: Mokapu Elem Sch 1193 Mokapu Rd Kailua HI 96734 Home (Summer): PO Box 1434 Kailua HI 96734-1434 Office Phone: 808-254-7964.

**TUBBS, RAYMOND ROY,** pathologist; b. Roy Leonard and Naomi Fern Tubbs; m. Mary Kirkham, Aug. 8, 1969; children: Alisa Marie, Matthew Ray. DO, Kirksville Coll. Osteo. Medicine, 1973. Diplomate Am. Bd. Pathology, Am. Bd. Hematopathology, Am. Bd. Molecular Genetic Pathology. Sect. head molecular genetic pathology Cleve. Clinic Found., 1993—2006, chmn. dept. clin. pathology, 2007—; prof. pathology Cleve. Clinic Lerner Coll. Medicine Case Western Res. U., Cleve., 2003—. Contbr. articles to websites. Mem.: Internat. Soc. Analytical and Molecular Morphology (pres. 2003—06). Office: Cleve Clinic and Lerner Coll Medicine 9500 Euclid L11 Cleveland OH 44195 Office Phone: 216-444-2844. Office Fax: 216-444-4414. Business E-Mail: tubbsr@ccf.org.

**TUBERVILLE, TOMMY,** college football coach; b. Sept. 18, 1954; m. Suzanne Fette; children: Thomas Tucker, Troy Allen. BS in Phys. Edn., So. Ark. Univ., 1976. Defensive coach Ark. State, 1980—85, Univ. Miami, 1986—93, defensive coord., 1993, Texas A&M, 1994—95; head football coach Ole Miss, 1998—99, Auburn Univ., 1999—. Office: Auburn Athletics PO Box 351 Auburn AL 36831-0351*

**TUBESING, RICHARD LEE,** library director; b. Kansas City, Mo., Nov. 25, 1937; s. Clarence and Letha (Thacker) T. BA, Yale U., 1959; MA, U. Chgo., 1969; MSL, Western Mich. U., 1972. Asst. to dir. U. Louisville, 1972-73; reference libr. Ga. Tech. Libr., Atlanta, 1973-76; head bus. and sci. Atlanta Pub. Libr., 1976-79; libr. dir. Lewis U., Romeoville, Ill., 1979-81; collection devel. coord. U. Toledo Libr., 1981-86; libr. dir. Coll. of the Southwest, Hobbs, N.Mex., 1986-89; libr. dir., dir. libr. sci. program Glenville (W.Va.) State Coll., 1989-99; ret., 1999. Part-time libr. Gilmer Pub. Lib., Glenville, W.Va. Author: Architectural Preservation, 1978, Architectural Preservation and Urban Renovation, 1982. Program coord. Lea County Archaeol. Soc., Hobbs, 1987-89. Lt. j.g. USNR, 1960-63. Mem. W.Va. Libr. Assn., Lea County Libr. Assn. (v.p. 1987-88, pres. 1988-89). Avocation: collecting primitive and peasant art. Home: 351 E Valley Dr Glenville WV 26351-9416 E-mail: ricktubesing@lycos.com.

**TUBMAN, WILLIAM CHARLES,** lawyer; b. N.Y.C., Mar. 16, 1932; s. William Thomas and Ellen Veronica Griffin; m. Dorothy Rita Krug, Aug. 15, 1964; children: William Charles Jr., Thomas Davison, Matthew Griffin. BS, Fordham U., 1953, JD, 1960; postdoctoral, NYU Sch. Law, 1960-61. Bar: N.Y. 1960, U.S. Ct. Appeals (2d cir.) 1966, U.S. Supreme Ct. 1967, U.S. Ct. Customs and Patent Appeals 1971. Auditor Peat, Marwick Mitchell & Co., NYC, 1956-60; sr. counsel Kennecott Corp., NYC, 1960-82, Phelps Dodge Corp., NYC, 1982-85, sec., 1985-95, v.p., 1987-95; pres. Phelps Dodge Found., Phoenix, 1988-95. Author: Legal Status of Minerals Beyond the Continental Shelf, 1966. Scholarship adv. U. Ariz., 1990-92; active Big Bros., Inc., N.Y.C., 1963-73; trustee Phoenix Art Mus., 1989-94; bd. dirs. St. Joseph Hosp. Found., 1994-2003, emeritus, 2003—, chmn. 1994-95; bd. dirs. The Phoenix Symphony, 1994-95. Recipient Disting. Svc. cert. Big Brothers Inc., 1968. Mem.: ABA, N.Y. State Bar Assn. Democrat. Roman Catholic. Home: 8008 N 66th St Paradise Valley AZ 85253-2612

**TUBUTIS, TODD J.,** anthropologist; b. John P. and Barbara J. Tubutis. BA, Beloit Coll., Beloit, Wis., 1988—92; MA, U. B.C., Vancouver, Can., 1996—98. Conversational english tchr. Váci Mihály Gimnázium, Encs, Hungary, 1993—94; pub. programs asst. The Newberry Libr., Chgo., 1994—95; vis. lectr. cultural anthropology U. Miskolc, Hungary, 1998—99; seminars mgr. The Newberry Libr., Chgo., 1999—2001; sr. project mgr., exhibitions The Field Mus., Chgo., 2001—. Author: (encyclopedia entry) The Encyclopedia of Chgo.; photographer (book) Pepper in Our Eyes: The APEC Affair; contbr. papers to profl. jours. and pubs. Mem. Chgo. Pub. Radio Cmty. Adv. Coun., 2004—. Recipient Departmental Honors, Anthropology, Beloit Coll., 1992; grantee James E. Lockwood Anthropology scholarship, 1991—92, R. Howard Webster fellowship, U. B.C., 1997—98. Mem.: Am. Assn. Museums (Diversity fellowship 2005), Phi Beta Kappa.

**TUCCI, GERALD FRANK,** manufacturing executive; b. NYC, Sept. 9, 1926; s. Frank and Mary (Fattizzi) T.; m. Eva G. Gyllander, May 14, 1968; children: Francis Henrik, Michael Fredrik, Amy Christina. Student, Dartmouth Coll., 1944; BSc in Naval Sci., Brown U., 1946, BSME, 1948; MBA with distinction, Harvard U., 1950. Mfg. trainee Am. Can Co., Jersey City, 1950—51; asst. v.p., plant mgr. Artcraft Hosiery Mills, Inc., Darby, Pa., 1951—53; v.p. Leach & Garner, Co., Attleboro, Mass., 1953-63, Gen. Findings, Inc., Attleboro, 1953-63; chmn. Micro Contacts, Inc., Hicksville, NY, 1963—; pres. Micro Pneumatic Logic, Inc., Ft. Lauderdale, Fla., 1973—. Chmn. Micro Group, 2004—. Lt. (s.g.) USNR, 1944-47. Mem. ASME, Am. Soc. Mfrs., North Hempstead Country Club, Met. Club (NY), Harvard Bus. Sch. Club, Beta Theta Pi. Republican. Roman Catholic. Office: 62 Alpha Plz Hicksville NY 11801-2618 Office Phone: 516-433-4830. E-mail: gerrytucci@aol.com.

**TUCCI, JOSEPH M.,** computer software and services executive; b. Bklyn., 1947; m. Maureen Tucci. BA, Manhattan Coll., 1968; MBA, Columbia U., 1984. With RCA Corp., 1970—86; pres. U.S. ops. Unisys Corp., 1986-90; exec. v.p. ops. Wang Labs., Inc., 1990-93, pres., chmn., CEO Lowell, Mass., 1993—99; dep. CEO Getronics NV, 1999; pres., COO EMC Corp., Hopkinton, Mass., 2000—01; pres., CEO, 2001—, chmn., 2006—. Bd. dirs. Paychex, 2000—, EMC Corp., 2001—. Office: EMC Corp 176 South St Hopkinton MA 01748*

**TUCCI, JOSEPH RALPH,** endocrinologist, educator; s. Ralph and Brigida Tucci; m. Marjorie Jane Puffer, Sept. 24, 1960; children: Elizabeth Anne, Paula Marie. AB cum laude, BrownU., 1951; MD, Boston U., 1959. Diplomate Nat. Bd. Med. Examiners, lic. R.I., Am. Bd. Internal Medicine. Rotating intern St. Elizabeth's Hosp., Boston, 1959—60, resident in medicine, 1960—62; clin. fellow in nephrology, metabolism, and endocrinology Georgetown Univ. Hosp., Washington, 1962—63, fellow in endocrinology and metabolism, 1963—64; sr. 3d-yr. resident in medicine (endocrinology) VA Hosp., Washington, 1964—65; rsch. fellow in medicine Harvard Med. Sch. and Peter Bent Brigham Hosp., Boston, 1965—67; asst. prof. medicine Brown U., Providence, 1969—74, program dir. fellowship program in endocrinology and metabolism, 1969—84, head subsect. endocrinology, 1974—84, assoc. prof. medicine, 1997—98, Boston U. Sch. Medicine, 1998—; active med. staff Roger Williams Med. Ctr., Providence, 1969—, dir. endocrinology and metabolism dept. medicine, 1969—84, dir. bone and mineral unit, 1984—. Adj. prof. medicine Brown U. Sch. Medicine, Providence, 1998—; cons. in endocrinology; mem. endocrine study sect. NIH, Bethesda, Md., 1968—69; physician, cons. Neighborhood Health Ctr., 1970—99; mem. profl. adv. com. Providence Health Ctrs., 1974—99; cons. diabetes program R.I. Dept. Health, 1978; mem. corp. Blue Cross and Blue Shield of R.I., 1979—, cons., 1984—; chmn. New Eng. Osteoporosis Bd., 2003—. Assoc. editor Endo Trends, 2002—; reviewer: profl. jours.; contbr. articles to profl. jours. mem. Comdr. USNR, 1968—69. Fellow: ACP, Am. Coll. Endocrinology; mem.: R.I. Med. Soc., Soc. for Clin. Densitometry, Am. Assn. Clin. Endocrinology, Am. Soc. for Bone and Mineral Rsch., Clin. Diabetes Assn. R.I., Endocrine Soc. Avocations: tennis, swimming, reading. Office: Roger Williams Med Ctr 825 Chalkstone Ave Providence RI 02908

**TUCCI, STANLEY,** actor; b. Peekskill, NY, Nov. 11, 1960; m. Kate Tucci, 1995; 3 children. BFA, SUNY, Purchase, 1982. Appeared in films Fear Anxiety and Depression, 1990, Men of Respect, 1991, In The Soup, 1992,

Beethoven, 1992, Prelude to A Kiss, 1992, Undercover Blues, 1993, The Pelican Brief, 1993, Somebody to Love, 1994, It Could Happen to You, 1994, Mrs. Parker and the Vicious Circle, 1994, Jury Duty, 1995, Kiss of Death, 1995, A Modern Affair, 1995, Captive, 1995, The Daytrippers, 1996, Montana, 1997, Life During Wartime, 1997, The Eighteenth Angel, 1997, Deconstructing Harry, 1997, A Life Less Ordinary, 1997, The Imposters, 1998, A Midsummer Night's Dream, 1999, Joe Gould's Secret, 1999, In Too Deep, 1999, The Whole Shebang, 2000, Bull, 2000, Sidewalks of New York, 2001, America's Sweethearts, 2001, Big Trouble, 2002, Road to Perdition, 2002, Maid in Manhattan, 2002, The Core, 2003, The Life and Death of Peter Sellers, 2004, The Terminal, 2004, Lucky Number Slevin, 2006, The Devil Wears Prada, 2006; (TV series) Murder One, 1995, Winchell, 1998 (Emmy award 1998), (TV film) Conspiracy, 2001 (Golden Globe award 2001); actor, co-dir., co-prodr. (film) Big Night, 1996 (Ind. Spirit award for best 1st screenplay 1996). Office: William Morris Agy c/o David Yocum 151 S El Camino Dr Beverly Hills CA 90212-2775*

**TUCH, HOWARD STANLEY,** long-term care administrator, geriatrics services professional; b. Boston, Mass., Mar. 14, 1952; MD, U. NC Sch. Medicine, 1984. Cert. Internal Medicine, Geriatric Medicine, med. dir. in long-term care, in hospice and palliative medicine. Resident, internal medicine Francis Scott Key Med. Ctr., Balt., 1985—88; fellow, geriatrics John Hopkins Sch. Medicine, Balt., 1988—90; former dir., pain mgmt. and palliative care services Genesis Eldercare; med. dir. Tidewell Hospice and Palliative Care, Sarasota, Fla. Served on Nat. Hospice and Palliative Care Organization's Task Force on Palliative Care in the Nursing Home; served on numerous state comm. to improve end-of-life care in Fla.; asst. prof. U. South Fla. Sch. Medicine. Recipient Robert Wood Johnson Health Policy fellow, IOM, 2006. Office: Tidewell Hospice and Palliative Care 5955 Rand Blvd Sarasota FL 34238 Office Fax: 941-923-5822.*

**TUCHMAN, AVRAHAM (AVI),** physicist, researcher; b. NYC, July 1, 1935; s. Max and Rebecca (Brick) T.; m. Sylvia Crystal, Dec. 26, 1957; children: Davida, Ari, Sima, Pnina. BA, Yeshiva U., 1956; PhD, MIT, 1963. Scientist, group leader to sect. chief Avco Rsch. and Advanced Devel., Wilmington, Mass., 1963; prin. scientist, staff scientist to prin. staff scientist Avco Systems Div., Wilmington; chief scientist Textron Def. Systems, Wilmington, 1988-93; owner, pres., CEO Added Value Innovations, Brookline, Mass., 1994—. Vis. prof. Weizmann Inst. Sci., Rehovot, Israel, 1974, 78, 82. Contbr. numerous articles to profl. jours. Founder, pres. Kehilla Day Camp of Jewish Community Ctrs., Westwood, Mass., 1975-86; chmn. Brookline (Mass.) Traffic Commn., 1975-81; pres. Mikvah Rescue Svc., Brighton, Mass., 1969-77; pres. Temple Beth Avraham, Brookline, 1969—. Recipient award for outstanding cantorial artistry Am. Soc. Forktwangers, Detroit, 1970. Fellow AIAA (sr.). Avocations: computers, gardening, homecraft, snowboarding, downhill racing.

**TUCHMAN, PHYLLIS,** critic; b. Passaic, NJ, Jan. 4, 1947; d. Jack and Evelyn (Sugarman) T. BA in Fine Arts with distinction, Boston U., 1968; MA, NYU, 1973. Ind. critic, N.Y.C., 1968—. Inst. art hist., Sch. Visual Arts, NY, 1972-75; adj. lectr. art history Hunter Coll., CUNY, NYC, 1976-79; vis. prof. art Williams Coll., Williamstown, Mass., 1981-83; curator Six in Bronze, Williams Coll. Mus. Art and tour, 1985, Big Little Sculpture, Williams Coll. Mus. Art and tour, 1988, Venezuela: The Next Generation, Baruch Coll. Gallery, 1990, Drawing Redux, San Jose Mus. Art and tour, 1992, Norte del Sur: Venezuelan Art Today, Philbrook Art Mus., 1997. Author: George Segal, 1983; contbr. articles to profl. jours., popular mags. Art Critics grantee NEA, 1978-79; vis. fellow Princeton U., NEH, 1980. Mem. Internat. Assn. Art Critics (Am. sect. pres. 1986-90, v.p. internat. parent body, 89-91); Art Table (bd. dirs. 1984-87, v.p. 1987-88), AICA (v.p. Am. sect. 2004—) Home: 340 E 80th St New York NY 10021-0927

**TUCHMANN, ERIC P.,** lawyer; m. Cheri Fancsali; children: Isabel, Amelia. BS, U. Wis., Madison, 1988; JD, NY Law Sch., 1994. With Am. Arbitration Assn., 1994—, dir. comml. dept. NY, dir. Internat. Ctr. Dispute Resolution, assoc. gen. counsel, gen. counsel, 2004—. Office: Am Arbitration Assn 335 Madison Ave 10th Fl New York NY 10017-4605 Office Phone: 212-716-5800.

**TUCHMANN, ROBERT,** lawyer; b. N.Y.C., July 7, 1946; s. Frederick C. and Hildegard (Jung) Tuchmann; m. Naomi R. Walfish, June 1, 1969; children: David, Paul. AB, Oberlin Coll., 1967; JD, Harvard U., 1971. Bar: Mass. 1971, U.S. Dist. Ct. Mass. 1971. Assoc. Hale and Dorr, Boston, 1971-76, jr. ptnr., 1976-80, sr. ptnr., 1980—2004, Wilmer, Cutler, Pickering, Hale and Dorr, Boston, 2004—. Lectr. Mass. Continuing Legal Edn., 1976—99. Pres. Project Bread-The Walk for Hunger, Boston, 1990—98; chair Ctrl. Artery Environ. Oversight Com., 1992—; mem. New Fed. Courthouse Task Force, 1993—99; bd. overseers Rogerson Cmtys., 1995—; co-chair Mayor's Ctrl. Artery Completion Task Force, 2001—; mem. com. Oberlin Coll., 1990. Mem.: Real Estate Bar, Boston Soc. Archs. (bd. dirs. 2004—), Downtown Boston Transp. Mgmt. Assn. (chmn. 1996—), Boston Bar Assn. (com. chmn. 1977—81), Island Alliance (trustee 1997—2000), Abstract Club. Office: Wilmer Cutler Pickering Hale and Dorr LLP 60 State St Boston MA 02109-1816 Office Phone: 617-526-6920. Business E-Mail: robert.tuchmann@wilmerhale.com

**TUCHO, ADMASU ETAFA,** education educator; s. Etafa Tucho and Etatu Fogi; m. Tizita Erkissa Mengesha, Feb. 21, 1996; children: Aangoo Admasu, Soortuu Admasu. EdD, Temple U., 2000. Cert. edn. Pa., 2000. Secondary sch. history tchr. Ministry Edn., Addis Ababa, Ethiopia, 1982—88; instr. C.C. Phila., 1991—2005; asst. prof., grad. programs coord. Lincoln U. Pa., Phila., 2004—. Pres., sec. Oromo Evang. Ch. Phila., 1994—2003. Recipient Service award, U.C. Phila. Mem.: ALRA (board's). Home: 152 Melrose Ave East Lansdowne PA 19050 Office: Lincoln University Graduate Programs 3020 Market St Philadelphia PA 19104 Office Phone: 215-590-8223. Office Fax: 215-387-3834. Business E-Mail: atucho@lincoln.edu.

**TUCK, AMY,** lieutenant governor; b. Starkville, Miss., July 8, 1963; d. Grady William and Mary (Boykin) Tuck. BA in Polit. Sci., Miss. State U., Starkville, 1985; postgrad., Miss. State U., Miss. State U., Starkville, 1992—; JD, Miss. Coll., 1989. Legal asst. Ben. F. Hilburn Jr., Atty. at Law, Starkville, Miss., 1984-85; grad. asst. dept. polit. sci. Miss. State U., Starkville, 1986-87; law clk. Minor Buchanan, Jackson, Miss., 1987-88, Deposit Guaranty Nat. Bank, Jackson, 1988-89; state senator dist. 15 State of Miss., Jackson, 1990-99, lt. gov., 2000—. Adj. prof. Wood Jr. Coll., Mathiston, Miss., 1990-95. Mem. Oktibbeha County Voter Re-Registration Com., Oktibbeha County Fedn. Dem. Women; bd. dirs. Oktibbeha County Am. Cancer Soc., 1991-92; mem. local rels. com. Children and Family Svcs.; mem. Nat. Mus. Women in the Arts, 1992-93. Mem. NAFE, Am. Legis. Exch. Com., Am. Soc. Pub. Adminstrs., Nat. Conf. State Legislature, Nat. Order Women Legislators, Miss. State U. Alumni Assn., Starkville Area Bus. and Profl. Women's Club, Oktibbeha County C. of C., Gamma Beta Phi, Pi Sigma Alpha, Omicron Delta Kappa, Phi Delta Phi (vice-magister 1988, historian 1988-89). Democrat. Methodist. Office: Office of the Lt Gov PO Box 1018 Jackson MS 39215-1018 Office Phone: 601-359-3200. Office Fax: 601-359-4054. E-mail: ltgov@mail.senate.state.ms.us.*

**TUCK, GRAYSON EDWIN,** real estate agent, gas industry executive; b. Richmond, Va., May 11, 1927; s. Bernard Okly and Erma (Wiltshire) T.; m. Rosalie Scroggs, June 6, 1947; children - Janice Lorrain, Kenneth Edwin, Carol Lynn BS, U. Richmond, 1950. Payroll clk., cost clk. Gen. Baking Co., Richmond, 1948-51; jr. accountant Commonwealth Natural Gas Corp., Richmond, 1951-55, sr. accountant, 1956-57, accounting supr., 1957-58, asst. treas., 1959-62, asst. sec., asst. treas., 1963-64, treas., asst. sec., 1965-77; treas. Commonwealth Natural Resources, Inc., 1977-81, CNG Transmission Co. subs., 1977-79; sec.-treas. Air Pollution Control Products, Inc., Richmond, 1970-73; asst. treas., asst. sec. Commonwealth Gas Distbn. Corp., Richmond, 1969-79; mgr. taxes and cash mgmt. Commonwealth Gas Pipeline Corp., subs. Columbia Gas System Inc., 1981-86; investor, realtor Bill Eudailey & Co., 1986—. Active Boy Scouts Am., 1965—69; bd. dirs.

Henrico Area Mental Health Retardation Svcs., 1983—85; active Elpis Christian Ch., 2001—; deacon Presbyn. Ch., 1958—86, elder, 1986—2001, treas., 1968—70. With USNR, 1945—46. Mem.: Nat. Assn. Accts. (assoc. dir. 1963—64). Home: 2923 Oakland Ave Richmond VA 23228-5827 Office: 6401 Mallory Dr Richmond VA 23226-2911 Office Phone: 804-282-7678. E-mail: realtortuck1@comcast.net.

**TUCK, LILY,** writer; b. Paris, 1938; Author: Interviewing Matisse; Or the Women Who Died Standing Up, 1991, The Women who Walked on Water, 1996, Siam; Or the Women Who Shot a Man, 1999 (nominated PEN/Faulkner Award, 2000), The News from Paraguay, 2004 (Nat. Book Award for Fiction, 2004), (collection) Limbo: And Other Places I Have Lived, 2002. Address: c/o Georges Borchardt 136 E 57th St New York NY 10022

**TUCK, RUSSELL R., JR.,** college president emeritus; b. June 9, 1934; m. Marjorie Gay Tuck; children: Russell R. III, Catherine Elizabeth. BS in Chemistry, Union U., 1956; MS in Biology, George Peabody Coll. Vanderbilt U., 1957, PhD in Curriculum and Instrn., 1971; studied, Wash. U., 1960—61, Instr. biology, asst. coordinator Korean Tchr. Edn. Program George Peabody Coll. Vanderbilt U., Nashville, 1957-59; tchr. biology, chmn. sci. dept. University City (Mo.) Sr. High Sch., 1960-63, from asst. prin. to prin., 1963-70; prin. Parkway North Sr. High Sch., St. Louis County, Mo., 1971-78; asst. supt. Parkway Sch. Dist., St. Louis County, 1979-81, assoc. supt., 1981-84; pres. Calif. Bapt. U., Riverside, 1984-94, pres. emeritus, 1994—. Contbr. articles to profl. jours. Bd. dirs. Opera Assn.; pres. Riverside County chpt. ARC, 1989-90; active Bapt. Ch., ch. elder, local hosp. assn. bd., local edn. com.; World Affairs Coun. Mem. Calif. Bapt. Hist. Soc. (bd. dirs.), Calif. Bapt. Devel. Found. (bd. dirs.), Am. Assn. Sch. Adminstrs., Inland Empire Higher Edn. Coun. (pres. 1987-88), Rotary, Kappa Delta Pi, Phi Delta Kappa. Lodges: Rotary. Home: 14000 Chelmsford Dr Gainesville VA 20155

**TUCKER, ALAN CURTISS,** mathematics professor; b. Princeton, NJ, July 6, 1943; s. Albert William and Alice Judson (Curtiss) T.; m. Amanda Almira Zeisler, Aug. 31, 1968 (div. 1997); children: Lisa, Kathryn, Edward, James; m. Ann K. Hong, Feb. 16, 1997. BA, Harvard U., 1965; MS, Stanford U., 1967, PhD, 1969. Asst. prof. applied math. SUNY, Stony Brook, 1970-73, assoc. prof. applied math., 1973-78, prof. applied math., chmn., 1978-89, SUNY Disting. Teaching prof., 1989—. Vis. asst. prof. math. U. Wis., Madison, 1969-70; vis. assoc. prof. computer sci. U. Calif., San Diego, 1976-77; vis. prof. ops. research Stanford U., 1983-84; cons. Sloan Found., 1981-85; acad. cons. 40 colls. and univs. Author: Applied Combinatorics, 1980, Unified Introduction to Linear Algebra, 1987, Linear Algebra, 1993; assoc. editor Math. Monthly, 1996-2001, Applied Maths. Letters, 1986—; contbr. 45 rsch. articles to profl. jours. Ga. U. Consortium Disting. Visitor, 1982; NSF grantee, 1972-86. Mem. Math. Assn. Am. (chmn. publs. 1982-86, editor Studies in Math. series 1979-86, v.p. 1988-90, chmn. ednl. coun. 1990-96, Disting. Tchr. award 1994, Trevor Evans award 1996, Meritorious Svc. award 2005), U.S. Commn. Math. Instrn., Am. Math. Soc., Ops. Rsch. Soc. Am., Soc. Indsl. Applied Maths., Sigma Xi (chpt. pres. 1987—). Home: 19 Crosby Place Cold Spring Harbor NY 11724-2404 Office: SUNY At Stony Brook Dept Of Applied Math Stony Brook NY 11794-3600 Office Phone: 631-632-8365. Business E-Mail: atucker@notes.sunysb.edu.

**TUCKER, ALAN DAVID,** publisher; b. Erie, Pa., Mar. 9, 1936; s. Meredith LaDue and Monica (Klocko) Tucker; m. Kiyoko Iizuka, Feb. 8, 1963; 1 child, Kumi. AB, Princeton U., 1957. Lic. real estate salesperson N.Y. Assoc. editor Hawthorn Books, N.Y.C., 1964-66; editor John Day Co., Inc., N.Y.C., 1966-72; mng. editor David McKay Co., Inc., N.Y.C., 1972-75, v.p., 1975-78, exec. v.p., editl. dir., 1978-84; editl. dir. Fodor's Travel Guides, Inc., N.Y.C. 1978-84; founder, prodr. Penguin Travel Guides and other publs., N.Y.C., 1984-91; gen. editor Berlitz Travellers Guides, N.Y.C., 1991-95; consulting sr. analyst Genesis Group Assocs., Montclair, NJ, 1995—2001; v.p. mktg. strategy Oxygen Advt., Inc., N.Y.C., 1996—; consulting sr. analyst Adis Bus. Intelligence, Langhorne, Pa., 2002. Real estate sales assoc. Halstead Property Co., N.Y.C., 1999—. Author: Capitation and Risk Sharing, 1995, Integrated Health Information Systems, 1997, Provider-Sponsored Managed Care, 1998, Convergence in Coordinated Care, 1998; co-author: The Electronic Superhighway 1997-2010: Opportunities for the Healthcare Industry, 1996, Diabetes Disease Management, 1995, 2d edit., 1998, Asthma Disease Management, 1997, 2d edit., 1999, Hypertension Management, 1999, Management of Congestive Heart Failure, 1999, Intelligence Report: Depression, 1999, Intelligence Report: Lung Cancer, 2000, Strategic Audit: Alzheimer's and Parkinson's Diesease, 2000, Strategic Audit: Stroke and Multiple Sclerosis, 2000, Asthma Forum, 2001, Osteoporosis Forum, 2001, Psoriasis Forum, 2001, Congestive Heart Failure Forum, 2001, Obesity Forum, 2002, Allergic Rhinitis Forum, 2002, Pain Management Forum, 2002, Handbook of Healthcare Marketing, 2003. With USNR, 1957—60. Mem.: Real Estate Bd. N.Y., Am. Coll. Healthcare Execs. (regent's adv. coun. N.Y.C. region), N.Y. Travel Writers Assn. (past pres.), Soc. Am. Travel Writers. Office: 186 Riverside Dr New York NY 10024-1007 also: 34 Still Meadow Rd Sharon CT 06069-2133

**TUCKER, ALVIN LEROY,** retired government official; b. Bklyn., Sept. 7, 1938; s. Alvin Leroy Jr. and Alveria (Klune) T.; m. Jacqueline Twiggs, Aug. 27, 1966; children: Hazel, Pluma, Jacqueline, Alvin. BS, U. Md., 1965. CPA, Md.; cert. internal auditor; cert. govt. fin. mgr.; cert. def. fin. mgr. Auditor Dept. Army, Washington, 1965-67; dep. insp. gen. HUD, Washington, 1986-89; auditor Dept. Def., Washington, 1967-72, budget analyst, 1972-79, dir. tng. and edn., 1979-83, dep. asst. insp. gen., 1983-86, dep. comptr., 1989-94, dep. CFO, 1991-97, chmn. concessions com., 1989-97; sr. mgr. Grant Thornton LLP, Alexandria, Va., 1997—2006, dir., 2006—. Mem. steering com. Joint Fin. Mgmt. Improvement Program, 1990-93; mem. CFO's Coun., 1989-97, chmn. fin. sys. com., 1989-97; mem. Fed. Acctg. Stds. Adv. Bd., 1991-97, chmn. Cert. Del. Fin. Mgt. Commn., 2000—. With U.S. Army, 1958-61. Recipient Def. medal for disting. civilian svc. with Bronze Palm, 1997, meritorious sr. exec. medal, 1985, 92. Mem. AICPA, Am. Soc. Mil. Comptrs., Assn. Govt. Accts. (nat. exec. com. 1993-94), Kiwanis (club pres. 1981-82, 86-87). Avocation: genealogy. Office: Grant Thornton 333 John Carlyle St Ste 500 Alexandria VA 22314 Office Phone: 703-837-4464.

**TUCKER, ANITA LYNN,** science educator; b. New Haven, Conn., July 16, 1968; d. Paul Willis and Audrey Elaine Carson; m. Jeffrey Alan Tucker, June 12, 1993; children: Maegan, Audrey. BSc, U. of Mass., Amherst, 1990; MSc, Purdue U., West Lafayette, Ind., 1992; DBA, Harvard U., Cambridge, Mass., 2003. Asst. prof. U. of Pa., Phila., 2003—. Author: (dissertation) Organizational Learning from Operational Failures (Acad. Health Dissertation award, 2004); contbr. articles to sci. jours. (Accenture award Calif. Mgmt. Rev., 2004). Recipient Sloan Industry Studies fellowship, Alfred P. Sloan Found., 2006. Office: U Pa 551 Huntsman Hall 3730 Walnut St Philadelphia PA 19104-6340 Office Phone: 215-573-8742. Office Fax: 215-898-3664. Business E-Mail: tuckera@wharton.upenn.edu.

**TUCKER, ANNE WILKES,** curator, historian, photographer, critic; b. Baton Rouge, Oct. 18, 1945; BA in Art History, Randolph-Macon Women's Coll., Lynchburg, Va., 1967; AAS in Photographic Illustration, Rochester Inst. Tech., 1968; MFA in Photographic History, SUNY-Buffalo, 1972. Rsch. asst. Internat. Mus. Photography at the George Eastman House, Rochester, NY, 1968—70; rsch. assoc. Gernsheim Collection U. Tex., Austin, 1969, 1979; curatorial intern dept. photography Mus. Modern Art, N.Y.C., 1970—71; photography cons. Creative Artists Pub. Svc. Program, N.Y.C., 1971—72; vis. lectr. New Sch. for Social Rsch., 1973; dir. photography lecture series Cooper Unionm Forum, N.Y.C., 1972—75; lectr. Cooper Union for Advancement of Arts and Sci., 1972—75; vis. lectr. Phila. Coll. Art, 1973—75; affiliate artist U. Houston, 1976—80; curator photography Mus. Fine Arts, Houston, 1976—; Gus and Lyndall Wortham cur., photographic historian and critic, lectr., 1984—. Trustee Visual Studies Workshop, 1980—2000, Houston Ctr. Photography, 1991—96, Houston Foto Fest, 1988—; visual arts panel The Houston Festival, 1981—83; adv. bd. Randolph-Macon Woman's Coll. Art Gallery, 1982—84; dir. numerous exhbns. and workshops; lectr. in field; mem. numerous juries and panels. Author: (books and catalogues) The Woman's Eye, 1973; author: (with William C. Agee) The Target Collection of

American Photography, 1977; author: Target II: 5 American Photographers, 1981, Target III: In Sequence, 1982; author: (with Philip Brookman) Robert Frank: New York to Nova Scotia, 1986; author: (with Maggie Olvey) The Sonia and Kaye Marvins Portrait Collection, 1986; author: Photo Notes and Filmfront, 1977; author: (with other curators) The Museum of Fine Arts, Houston: A Guide to the Collection, 1981; author: Unknown Territory: Photography by Ray K. Metzker, 1957-83, 1984, Fifth Annual International Fine Art Photography Exposition, 1984; author: (with Andy Grundberg) American Prospects: The Photographs of Joel Slernfeld, 1987, 1994; author: (with William Morris) American Classroom: The Photographs of Catherine Wagner, 1988; author: (with Pamela Allara) Crosscurrents/Crosscountry, 1988; author: (with other authors) Money Matters: A Critical Look at Bank Architecture, 1990; author: The Blue Moon: Photographs by Keith Carter, 1990; author: (with Pete Daniel) Carry Me Home: Photographs by Debbie Fleming Caffery, 1990; author: George Krauze, 1991, Tradition and the Unpredictable: The Allan Chasanoff Photographic Collection, 1994, Quest for the Moon and other stories: Three Decades of Astronauts in Space, 1994, TGoshio Shibata: Landscape, 1996, Crimes and Splendors: The Desert Cantos of Richard Misrach, 1996 (Golden Light award, 1996), Charles Schorre, 1997, Myths, Dreams and Realities: Contemporary Argentine Photographs, 1997, Irving Penn, 1999, Mario Carvo Neto, 1999, Amy Blakemore, 1999, Heart and Soul: The Photographs of Ray Carrington III 1993-2002, 2002, Joe Mills: Inner City, 2003, History of Japanese Photography 1853-2003, 2003 (Golden Light award), First Down Houston, Birth of An NFL Franchise, 2003, La Oscura Piel De La Luz; La Obra Fotografica De Mario Cravo Neto, 2003, American Prospects: The Photographs of Joel Sternfeld, 1987, 2003, David Carol: 40 Miles of Bad Road, 2004, Alec Soth: Sleeping by the Mississippi, 2004, Documenting Poetry Contemporary Latin American Photography, 2005, Icons of Photography, 2005, On Assignment, 2005, Mark Cohen: Grim Street, 2005, David Maisel: Terminal Mirage, 2005, (exhbns. and catalogues) A Fotografia Na Arte Contemporanea, 1995;: The Sonia and Kaye Marvins Portrait Collection, 1995, Keith Carter: Reinventing the World, 1995, Illuminations: Women writing on Photography from the 1850's to the present, 1996, Brassai: Eye of Paris, 1999, Louis Faurer, 2002, History of Japanese Photography, 2003; co-prodr. (video) Fire in the East: The Portrait of Robert Frank, 1986; editor: (books and catalogues) The Anthony G. Cronin Memorial Collection, 1979, (manual) Susanne Bloom and Ed Hill, 1980, (exhbns. and catalogues) Reframings, New American Feminist Photographies, 1995, The Photo League, 1987, Czech Modernism 1900-1945, 1990, Paul Strand: Essays on His Life and Work, 1991, George Krause, 1992, singer (photographer): Caught in Act: Lou Stoumen Vintage Photographs, 1995; contbr. articles to profl. jours. and mags., esays to books. Recipient Third Ann. Publ. award, Internat. Ctr. Photography, 1987, John Simon Guggenheim Meml. Alumna Achievement award, Randolph-Macon Woman's Coll., 1993, Alumnae Achievement award, 1993, Lifetime Achievement award, Griffin Mus., 2006; fellow Found. fellow, 1983—84; grantee Nat. Endowment Arts grantee, 1976, 1986, 1989. Mem.: Houston Ctr. for Photography, Art Table, Inc., Coll. Art Assn., Soc. Photographic Edn. (nat. bd. dirs. 1976—80, sec. 1977—79). Office: Mus Fine Arts PO Box 6826 Houston TX 77265 Office Phone: 713-639-7347. Business E-Mail: atucker@mfah.org.

**TUCKER, BETTY J.,** literature and language educator; b. Martins Ferry, Ohio, Feb. 12, 1946; d. Jess F. and Grace I. Pugh; m. Robert P. Tucker, May 27, 1966; 1 child, Robert E. BS in Elem. Edn., Ohio U., 1970; MS in Ednl. Adminstrn., U. Dayton, 1980. Tchr. 1st grade St. John's Sch., Bellaire, Ohio, 1967—68, St. Mary's Sch., St. Clairsville, 1968—69; tchr. 5th grade Bellaire Sdh. Dist., 1969—70; tchr. 3d grade St. Mary's Sch., 1970—73; tchr. reading, English Union Local Sch. Dist., Morristown, 1973—. Praxis assessor Ohio Dept. Edn., Columbus, 2000—05. Aide Cub Scouts, Barnesville, Ohio, 1989—92; swim ofcl. YMCA, Wheeling, W.Va., 1994—2000, SCCA, 1998—2000; treas. Union Local ACT. Martha Holden Jennings scholar, Athens, Ohio, 1985—86. Mem.: Ohio Edn. Assn. Methodist. Avocations: reading, walking. Home: 37350 Barnesville-Bethesda Rd Barnesville OH 43713 Office: Union Local Sch Dist 201 W Cross St Morristown OH 43759

**TUCKER, BEVERLY SOWERS,** library and information scientist; b. Trenton, N.J., Dec. 1, 1936; d. Eldon Jones and Verbeda Eleanor (Roberts) Sowers; m. Harvey Richard Tucker, Dec. 27, 1958 (div. Nov. 1983); children: Randall Richard, Brian Alan. BS in Chemistry with distinction, Purdue U., 1958; MS in Geology, No. Ill. U., 1985; MA in Library and Info. Sci., Rosary Coll., 1989. Asst. rsch. librarian CPC Internat., Argo, Ill., 1958-62; chem. patent searcher Chgo., 1962-66; info. specialist C. Berger & Co., Wheaton, Ill., 1986, Amoco Corp., Naperville, Ill., 1987-99; faculty Coll. Du Page, Glen Ellyn, Ill., 1989—; libr. cons. Baxter Healthcare, Round Lake, Ill., 1999—2003; libr. Seyfarth and Shaw, Chgo., 2005—. Mem. Spl. Libraries Assn., Ill. Fedn. Women's Club (treas. 5th dist. 1979-81, Outstanding Jr. Clubwoman award 1979-80), Garden Club Council Wheaton (pres. 1981-82), Wheaton Jr. Woman's Club (pres. 1977-78, Single Parent scholar 1984), Gardens Etc. Club (pres. 1978-79), Alpha Lambda Delta, Delta Rho Kappa, Theta Sigma Phi, Alpha Chi Omega (grantee 1985). Republican. Presbyterian. Avocations: bridge, needlecrafts, gourmet cooking. Home: 1507 Paula Ave Wheaton IL 60187-6135

**TUCKER, BOWEN HAYWARD,** lawyer; b. Providence, Apr. 13, 1938; s. Stuart Hayward and Ardelle Chase (Drabble) T.; m. Jan Louise Brown, Aug. 26, 1961; children: Stefan Kendric Slade, Catherine Kendra Gordon. AB in Math., Brown U., 1959; JD, U. Mich., 1962. Bar: R.I. 1963, Ill. 1967, U.S. Supreme Ct. 1970. Assoc. Hinckley & Allen, Providence, 1962-66; sr. atty. Caterpillar, Inc., Peoria, Ill., 1966-72; counsel FMC Corp., Chgo., 1972-82, sr. litigation counsel, 1982-95, assoc. gen. counsel, 1995-2000; v.p. eLaw Forum, Washington, 2000—01; owner Strategic Litigation Mgmt., Arlington Heights, Ill., 2000—. Chmn. legal process task force Chgo. Residential Sch. Study Com., 1973-74, mem. Commn. on Children 1983-85, Ill. Com. on Rights of Minors, 1974-77, Com. on Youth and the Law, 1977-79; mem. White House Conf. on Children, ednl. svcs. subcom., 1979-80; chairperson Youth Employment Task Force 1982-83; mem. citizens com. on Juvenile Ct. (Cook County), 1978-94, chmn. detention subcom., 1982-92; mem. econ. effects adv. com. Rand Inst. Civil Justice, 1990-92; bd. dirs. Voices Ill. Children, 1998—. 1st lt. U.S. Army, 1962-69. Mem. ABA, Am. Law Inst., Ill. State Bar Assn., R.I. Bar Assn., Chgo. (chmn. com. on juvenile law, 1976-77), Chgo. Lincoln Inn of Ct. (sec., treas. 1996-98), Constrn. Industry Mfrs. Assn. (exec. com. of Lawyers' Coun. 1972, 75-79, vice chmn. 1977, chmn. 1978-79), Mfrs. Alliance (products liability coun. 1974-95, vice chmn. 1981-83, chmn. 1983-85), Product Liability Adv. Coun. (bd. dirs. 1986-2000, exec. com. 1990-97, vice chmn. 1991-93, chmn. 1993-95), ACLU (bd. dirs. Ill. divsn. 1970-79, exec. com. 1973-79, sec. 1975-77), Am. Arbitration Assn. (mem. panel of arbitrators 1985-96), Phi Alpha Delta, Brown Univ. of Chgo. Club (Brown alumni schs. com. 1973-85, 2000—, v.p. 1980-81, pres. 1981-86), Lawyers Club of Chgo. Home: 107 W Noyes St Arlington Heights IL 60005-3747 Office Phone: 312-861-5940.

**TUCKER, BRENDA BRUNETTE,** elementary school educator; b. Corinth, Miss., Nov. 1, 1958; d. Willie Bishop and Maggie Belle Graham; m. Ralph O. Tucker, Dec. 24, 1980; children: Orion, Jonathan, Cameron. BS, Kust Coll., 1980; MEd, We. Ky. U., 1993, cert. in Prin. Supr., 2002. Lic. tchr. Ky. Dept. Profl. Bds. Tchr. spl. edn. Corinth (Miss.) H.S., 1981; instr. Dept. Def., Wurzburg, Germany, 1981—87; tchr. Hardin County Schs., Radcliff, Ky., 1987—98, Ft. Knox (Ky.) Schs., 1998—, guidance counselor, 1999—. Prof. McKendree Coll., Radcliff, 2000—. Chmn. publicity NAACP, Radcliff, 2004. Mem.: Counselors Assn., Optimist Club Radcliff (pres. 1998, chmn. programs 1998—99, named Optimist Educator of Yr.), Delta Sigma Theta (pres. 1995, chaplain 1997—2003). Avocations: reading, g. community service, walking, watching sunrise and sunsets. Office: Kingsolver Elementary Sch 1488 3rd Ave Fort Knox KY 40121-2287

**TUCKER, CYNTHIA ANNE,** journalist; b. Monroeville, Ala., Mar. 13, 1955; d. John Abney and Mary Louise (Marshall) Tucker; m. Michael Pierce, Dec. 26, 1987 (div. 1989). BA, Auburn U., 1976. Reporter The Atlanta Jour., 1976-80, editorial writer, columnist, 1983-86; reporter The Phila. Inquirer,

1980-82; assoc. editorial page editor The Atlanta Constitution, 1986-91, editorial page editor, 1992—. Bd. dirs. ARC, 1989-93, Families First, 1988—, Internat. Women's Media Found., 1994—. Nieman fellow Harvard U., 1988-89; Pulitzer Prize finalist for commentary, 2004. Mem.: Coun. Fgn. Rels., Nat. Assn. Minority Media Execs., Nat. Assn. Black Journalists, Am. Soc. Newspaper Editors (Disting. Writing award 2000). Mem. United Ch. Christ. Office: Atlanta Constitution 72 Marietta St NW Atlanta GA 30303-2804

**TUCKER, DON EUGENE,** retired lawyer; b. Rockbridge, Ohio, Feb. 3, 1928; s. Beryl Hollis and Ruth (Primmer) T.; m. Elizabeth Jane Parke, Aug. 2, 1950; children: Janet Elizabeth, Kerry Jane, Richard Parke. BA, Aurora Coll., 1951; LL.B., Yale, 1956. Bar: Ohio 1956. Since practiced in, Youngstown, Ohio; asso. Manchester, Bennett, Powers & Ullman, 1956-62, ptnr., 1962-73, of counsel, 1973-87; gen. counsel Comml. Intertech Corp., Youngstown, 1973-75, v.p., gen. counsel, 1975-83, also dir., sr. v.p., gen. counsel, 1983-87, sr. v.p., 1987-93; ret., 1993. Solicitor Village of Poland, Ohio, 1961-63; former chmn. bd., pres., trustee United Cerebral Palsy Assn.; former trustee, pres. Indsl. Info. Inst.; former pres., trustee Ea. Ohio Lung Assn.; trustee, former chmn. Cmty. Corp.; trustee, former pres. Butler Inst. Am. Art. With USMCR, 1946-48, 51-53. Mem. Ohio Bar Assn., Mahoning County Bar Assn. (pres. 1972, trustee 1970-73), Youngstown Area C. of C. (chmn. bd. dirs. 1979). Methodist. Home: 6005 Martins Point Rd Kitty Hawk NC 27949-3819

**TUCKER, EDWIN WALLACE,** law educator; b. NYC, Feb. 25, 1927; s. Benjamin and May Tucker; m. Gladys Lipschutz, Sept. 14, 1952; children: Sherwin M., Pamela A. BA, NYU, 1948; LLB, Harvard U., 1951; LLM, N.Y. Law Sch., 1963, JSD, 1964; MA, Trinity Coll., Hartford, Conn., 1967. Bar: N.Y. 1955, U.S. Dist. Ct. (ea. and so. dists.) N.Y. 1958, U.S. Ct. Appeals (2d cir.) 1958, U.S. Supreme Ct. 1960. Pvt. practice, N.Y.C., 1955-63; Disting. Alumni prof. and prof. emeritus bus. law U. Conn., Storrs, 1963—, mem. bd. editors occasional paper and monograph series, 1966-70. Author: Adjudication of Social Issues, 1971, 2d edit., 1977, Legal Regulation of the Environment, 1972, Administrative Agencies, Regulation of Enterprise, and Individual Liberties, 1975, CPA Law Review, 1985; co-author: The Legal and Ethical Environment of Business, 1992; book rev. editor Am. Bus. Law Jour., 1964-65, adv. editor, 1974—99; co-editor Am. Bus. Jour., 1965-73; editor Jour. Legal Studies Edn., 1983-85, editor-in-chief, 1985-87, adv. editor, 1987—99; mem. editl. bd. Am. Jour. Small Bus., 1979-86, North Atlantic Regional Bus. Law Rev., 1984—2004. With USAF, 1951-55. Recipient medal of excellence, Am. Bus. Law Assn., 1979. Mem. Acad. Legal Studies in Bus., North Atlantic Regional Bus. Law Assn. Home: 11 Eastwood Rd Storrs Mansfield CT 06268-2401

**TUCKER, FRANK HAMMOND,** history professor; b. Millville, NJ, Dec. 29, 1923; s. Frank Edmund and Evalyn Godfrey Tucker; m. Kathryn Churchill Libby (dec. Dec. 1994), Aug. 23, 1947; children: Elizabeth T. Gould, Sarah T. Owens, Margaret T. Mitchell. BS, Johns Hopkins U., 1948; MA, Georgetown U., 1950, PhD, 1954. Bassoonist Balt. Symphony Orch., 1941—43; commd. ensign USN, 1943, advanced through grades to lt. comdr., 1954, ret., 1963; lectr. history extension divsn. U. Md., Yokohama, Japan, 1956-57, lectr. history College Park, 1959-63; prof. history Colo. Coll., Colorado Springs, 1963-89, prof. emeritus, 1989—. Author: The White Conscience, 1969, The Frontier Spirit and Progress, 1979, Knights of the Mountain Trails, 2003; contbr. over 35 articles, 40 revs. to profl. jours. Bassoonist Balt. Symphony Orch., 1941-43; bd. mem., Charter Assn., Colorado Springs, 1964-67; pres. Landmarks Preservation Coun., Pike's Peak Region, 1969-73, mem. exec. bd. ARC, 1965-71, head Pike's Peak region Westerners Internat., 1991-92, gov. Pike Bicentennial com., 2004. Fellow Am. Coun. Learned Socs.; mem. Am. Hist. Assn., Rocky Mountain Social Sci. Assn. (bd. mem. 1966-69), Maine Hist. Soc., Gloucester County Hist. Soc., Cumberland County Hist. Soc., Atlantic County Hist. Soc., Rotary (exec. bd. 1971-73). Episcopalian. Avocation: hiking. Home and Office: 1525 Alamo Ave Colorado Springs CO 80907

**TUCKER, GARY ALLAN,** information scientist, educator, minister; b. Aurora, Colo., July 17, 1963; s. Belva Rozella and Julian Glenwood Tucker; m. Mary Louise Hubbard, July 29, 1989; children: Caroline Lenora, Rosemary Louise, Anna Elizabeth. BS, Averett Coll., 1985; PhD, Duke U., 1993. Assoc. prof. Averett U., Danville, Va., 1991—, dir. inf. tech., 1995—99; interim pastor Keen St. Bapt. Ch., Danville, Va., 2003—05. Sec. So. Piedmont Tech. Coun., Danville, Va., 2003—06. Independent. Baptist. Office: Averett Univ 420 W Main St Danville VA 24541 Business E-Mail: gary.tucker@averett.edu.

**TUCKER, GARY JAY,** psychiatrist, educator; b. Cleve., Mar. 6, 1934; s. Isadore Martin and Blanche Hanna (Luftig) T.; m. Sharon Ruth Pobby, June 10, 1956; children: Adam, Clare. AB, Oberlin Coll., 1956; MD, Case Western Res. U., 1960; postdoctoral fellow, Yale U., 1961-64; MA (hon.), Dartmouth Coll., 1977. Diplomate Am. Bd. Psychiatry and Neurology. Asst. prof. psychiatry Sch. Medicine Yale U., New Haven, 1967-70, assoc. prof. psychiatry, 1970-71; with Dartmouth Med. Sch., Hanover, N.H., 1971-85, prof. psychiatry, 1974-85, chmn. dept., 1978-85; chmn. psychiatry and behavioral scis. Sch. Med. U. Wash., Seattle, 1985-98; prof. psychiatry U. Wash., Seattle, 1985—99, prof. emeritus, 1999—. Bd. dirs. Am. Bd. Psychiatry and Neurology. Co-author: Rational Hospital Psychiatry, 1974, Behavioral Neurology, 1985; editor: Seminars in Clinical Neuropsychiatry, Journl. Watch Psychiatry; contbr. articles to profl. jours. Lt. Commdr. USN, 1964-67. Fellow Am. Psychiat. Assn.; mem. W. Coast Coll. Biol. Psychiatry, Sigma Xi, Alpha Omega Alpha. Democrat. Jewish. Avocations: photography, motorcycling.

**TUCKER, H. RICHARD,** oil industry executive; b. Streator, Ill., Oct. 2, 1936; s. H. L. and Dorothy A. Tucker; m. Cheryl L. Kirk, Jan. 14, 1984; children from previous marriage: Randall R., Brian A. BS in Chem. Engring., Purdue U., 1958; MBA, Northwestern U., 1962. Project engr. crude oil supply Amoco Corp., Chgo., 1958-64, specialist product supply, 1965-66, coord. fgn. crude oil supply, 1967-68; coord. orgn. planning Amoco Internat. Corp., Chgo., 1969-70, Amoco Corp., Chgo., 1970-72, mgr. adminstrv. svcs., 1972-84, mgr. real estate svcs., 1984-86, coord. spl. studies, 1986-89, dir. quality mgmt., 1989-92; mgr. cost mgmt., 1992-94. V.p. Amoco Realty Co., 1984-91, Amoco Devel. Co., 1984-91. Mem. adv. com. Sch. Bd. Wheaton, Ill., 1966; mem. Citizen's Nominating Com., Wheaton, 1972; leader Boy Scouts Am., Wheaton, 1979-82; dir. Oak Brook Colony Condominium Assn., 1992-94. Mem. Wheaton Home Owners Assn. (pres. 1966-57), Phi Eta Sigma, Omega Chi Epsilon, Beta Gamma Sigma, Tau Beta Pi. Avocations: tennis, bridge, hiking.

**TUCKER, HELEN WELCH,** writer; b. Raleigh, NC, Nov. 1, 1926; d. William Blair and Helen (Welch) Tucker; m. William T. Beckwith, Jan. 9, 1971. BA, Wake Forest Coll., 1946; postgrad., Columbia U., N.Y.C., 1957—58. Reporter Burlington Times-News, NC, 1946—47, Times-News, Twin Falls, Idaho, 1948—49, Idaho Statesman, Boise, 1950—51; copy writer Sta. KDYL, Salt Lake City, 1952—53; copy writer Sta. WPTF, Raleigh, NC, 1953—55; reporter Raleigh Times, NC, 1955—57; editl. asst. Columbia U. Press, N.Y.C., 1959—60; dir. publicity and publs. N.C. Mus. Art, Raleigh, NC, 1967—70. Author: The Sound of Summer Voices, 1969, The Guilt of August Fielding, 1971, No Need of Glory, 1972, The Virgin of Lontano, 1973, A Strange and Ill-Starred Marriage, 1978, A Reason for Rivalry, 1979, A Mistress to the Regent, 1980, An Infamous Attachment, 1980, The Halverton Scandal, 1980, A Wedding Day Deception, 1981, The Double Dealers, 1982, Season of Dishonor, 1982, Ardent Vows, 1983, Bound by Honor, 1984, The Lady's Fancy, 1985, Bold Impostor, 1991; contbr. (to nat. mags. short stories). Named Artist of Yr., Arts Coun. Frankling Co. (N.C.), 1992; recipient Disting. Alumni Award in Journalism, Wake Forest U., 1971. Anglican. Home: 2930 Hostetler St Raleigh NC 27609-7702

**TUCKER, HOWARD MCKELDIN,** investment banker, consultant; b. Washington, Apr. 1, 1930; s. Howard Newell and Bessie Draper (McKeldin) T.; m. Julia Spencer Merrell, Feb. 1, 1952 (div. 1975); children: Deborah, Mark, Alexander, H. David; m. Megan Evans, Aug. 17, 1979. BA, U. Va., 1954; postgrad., NYU, 1956. CFA. With J.P. Morgan & Co., 1954—61, Mackall & Coe, Washington, 1962—69, Legg Mason Wood Walker & Co., Washington, 1969—79, Govt. Rsch. Corp./Nat. Jour., 1979—82, Potomac Asset Mgmt., 1982—91; ptnr., mng. dir. Capital Insights Group, Washington, 1992—2001; with Skillsmith, LLC, 2002—05. Mem. task force balance-of-payments U.S.Treasury Dept., 1967-72; cons. County Natwest (Washinton Analysis Corp.), 1985-90; bd. dirs. Monarch Enterprises, Inc., Uniflight, Inc., Sci. Mgmt. Assocs., Inc., Jeffrey Bigelow Assocs. Author: Literature in Medicine, In Memoriam, Michael Halberstam, M.D., 1984; book reviewer Washington Post; contbr. articles to profl. jours. Dir. Washington Area Coun. Chs., 1973; vestryman Christ Episcopal Ch., Georgetown, 1962-65; mem. chpt. Washington Nat. Cathedral, 1966-72; del. Va. Republican Conv., 1968; trustee Nat. Cathedral Sch. for Girls, 1977; chmn. Missionary Devel. Fund Episcopal Diocese D.C., 1974; co-dir. Andover-Exeter Washington Intern Program, 1976-86; co-organizer U.S.-German Parliamentary Exchange, 1980-82; observer OECD, 1980-82; spl. overseas visitor Australian Govt., 1982; patron West Europe program Woodrow Wilson Ctr., 1985-86; bd. dirs. Am. Hort. Soc., 1998--. With USNR, 1950-56. Mem.: Fin. Analysts Fedn., Washington Soc. Investment Analysts, Nat. Economists Club, Dumplings, Cogswell Soc., Hist. Alexandria Found., Alexandria Seaport Found., Saints and Sinners Club, Naval and Mil. Club London, Nat. Press Club, Georgetown Visitation Tennis Club, Beta Theta Pi. Home: 4 Potomac Ct Alexandria VA 22314-3821 Office Phone: 703-683-4413.

**TUCKER, J. WALTER, JR.,** manufacturing executive; Vice chmn. Keystone Consolidated Industries, Inc., Dallas, chmn., 1987—. Office: 3 Lincoln Ctr 5430 LBJ Fwy Ste 1740 Dallas TX 75240-2697 Fax: 972-458-8108.

**TUCKER, JACK WILLIAM ANDREW,** writer, film editor, film producer; b. Portland, Oreg., May 1, 1944; s. Admyrl Foster and Aileen Eloise (McDaniels) T. BA in English, Portland State U., 1964. Film editor MGM TV, Culver City, Calif., 1984-86, Cannon Film Group, Beverly Hills, Calif., 1988, Columbia TV, Burbank, Calif., 1988, Paramount Pictures, Hollywood, Calif., 1990—. Editor: (TV) Winds of War, 1982 (Emmy award nominee 1983), The Fifth Missile, 1986, 240-Robert, 1979, Flatbed Annie and Sweetpie, 1979, (films) Shogun, 1980, Salsa, 1988, They're Playing With Fire, 1983, Viper, 1988, Nightmare on Elm Street IV, 1988, Distortions, 1987, Diplomatic Immunity, 1991, Illusions, 1992, Double-O-Kid, 1993, A Million to Juan, 1994, To the Ends of Time, 1996, Cotton Mary, 1999; prodr.: The Magazine, 1997, Earth Minus Zero, 1998. Sgt. USAF, 1964-68, Vietnam. Mem. NATAS, Am. Cinema Editors (treas. 1993—, editor CINEMEDITOR mag. 1994—).

**TUCKER, JAMES L., Jr.,** art educator, artist; b. New Eagle, Pa., Mar. 28, 1944; s. James Louis Tucker Sr. and Gueraldine Esther (Johnson) Sawyer. MA, Temple U., 1967, BFA, 1966; postgrad., George Washington U., 1977—79, postgrad., 1982—86. Art instr. continuing edn. Germantown H.S., Phila., 1968—69; chmn. art dept. Woodrow Wilson H.S., Washington, 1969—70; art specialist Gallaudet Coll., Washington, 1970—77; from specialist in the arts to chief arts and humanities program Md. State Dept. Edn., Balt., 1979—2003, coord. fine arts, 2003—. Art instr. Pastorius Elem. Sch., Phila., 1966—69, Emlen Elem. Sch., Phila., 1966—69; steering com. Art Edn. in Md. Schs. Alliance, 1992—; adj. instr. Md. Inst. Coll. Art, George Washington U.; team leader Brazilian curriculum project Ptnrs. of the Americas, 1984—86; arts assessment standing com. Nat. Assessment Ednl. Progress, 1996—97; cons., presenter in field. Editor: Better Fine Arts Edn., 4 vols., 2004. Co-dir. Kenya-Tanzania project Fulbright-Hays Group Projects Abroad, 1989, co-dir. Ghana-Senegal project, 1993, co-dir.Namibia project, 1995; edn. com. Balt. Symphony Orch., 1995—2000; adv. Ctr. for VSA Arts Md., Balt., 1980—2002, bd. dirs., 2002—, Md. Alliance for Arts Edn., Balt., 1980—2002, exec. sec.-treas., 1980—86; bd. dirs. Md. Artist Equity Found., Balt., 1992—2004, v.p., 2002—04. Named Md. State Adminstr. of Yr., State Employees Assn., 1986; recipient State of Md. Performance award, Md. State Employee's Conf., 1986, Outstanding Svc. award, Md. Coun. for Dance, 2002, Cert. Achievement, Md. State Bd. Edn., 2003. Fellow: Nat. Art Edn. Assn. (review panel Art Edn. 1995—97, chmn. nat. conv. Miami Beach 2002, convention task force 2002, Eastern Region Art Educator of Yr. 1995, J. Eugene Grigsby award 1984, Disting. Svc. award 2003, Nat. Supervision/adminstrn. Art Educator of Yr. 1997, Ea. Supervision/adminstrn. Art Educator of Yr. 1994, Md. Art Educator award 1987); mem.: Music Educators Nat. Conf., Nat. Assn. State Dirs. Art Edn. (pres.), Nat. Coun. State Arts Edn. Cons. (founding mem., pres. 1995—97), Md. Music Educators Assn. (exec. bd. dirs., Corwin Taylor award 1997), Md. Art Edn. Assn. (dept. edn. rep. 1980—82, dir. supervision/adminstrn. divsn. 1982—86, v.p. programs 1986—88, pres.-elect 1990—92, pres. 1992—94, awards coord. 1994—96, parliamentarian 1996—2000, historian 2000—, officer). Avocations: painting, reading, cooking, travel. Office: Md State Dept Edn 200 W Balt St Baltimore MD 21201-2595 Office Phone: 410-767-0352. Business E-Mail: jtucker@msde.state.md.us.

**TUCKER, JAMES RAYMOND,** primary school educator; b. Pueblo, Colo., Apr. 18, 1944; s. James George and Pauline F. (Sena) T.; m. Kathie Owens; 1 child, Brittany. BA, U. So. Colo., 1966; MA, U. No. Colo., 1990, postgrad., 1991. Tchr. Sinclair Mid. Sch., Englewood, Colo., 1971-93, Denver Pub. Schs., 1993—. Co-dir. Nick Bolleteri Tennis Acad., Boulder, Colo., 1986; head tennis coach Englewood High Sch., 1971—. Sgt. U.S. Army, 1967-70. Finalist Coach of Yr., Nat. H.S. Coaches Assn., 2001, 2004. Mem. NEA, US Profl. Tennis Assn., US Profl. Tennis Registry, Internat. Platform Assn., Colo. Edn. Assn., Meadow Creek Tennis and Fitness, Colo. HS Coaches Assn. (co-founder, Achievement award 1989, 92, Tchr. of Yr. 1973, 78, 86, Coach of Yr. 1986-87, 90, 96-97, Franklin award 1988, 89, Nat. Asst. Coach of Yr., 2002, H.S. Hero of Week). Home: 8801 W Belleview Ave Unit A207 Littleton CO 80123

**TUCKER, JEFFREY ALLEN,** education educator; b. Kans. City, Kans., Dec. 2, 1966; s. Gwen Tucker; m. Belinda Sharon Redden, Aug. 1, 1998; 1 child, Elizabeth Sophia Redden. AB, U. Mo., Columbia, 1988; MA, U. Mo., 1990; PhD, Princeton U., NJ, 1997. Asst. prof. Ohio U., Athens, 1997—99; assoc. prof. U. of Rochester, NY, 1999—. Author: (book of literary criticism) A Sense of Wonder: Samuel R. Delany, Race, Identity, & Difference. Summer stipend, Nat. Endowment for the Humanities, 2000, DuBois-Mandela-Rodney Post-Doctoral fellowship, U. of Mich. Ctr. for African and African-American Studies, 2000—01. Mem.: MLA. Achievements include research in africanamerican science fiction. Office: Univ of Rochester-Dept of English 500 Wilson Blvd-404 Morey Hall Rochester NY 14627-0451 Office Phone: 585-275-2064. Office Fax: 585-442-5769. E-mail: jat@mail.rochester.edu.

**TUCKER, JOHN MARK,** librarian, educator; s. Paul Marlin and Edith Tucker; m. Barbara Ann Wilson, Mar. 22, 1968. BA, David Lipscomb Coll., 1967; MLS, George Peabody Coll. Tchrs., 1968, specialist in edn., 1972; PhD, U. Ill., 1983. Head libr. Freed-Hardeman Coll., Henderson, Tenn., 1968-71; reference libr. Wabash Coll., Crawfordsville, Ind., 1973-79, Purdue U., West Lafayette, Ind., 1979-82, asst. prof. libr. sci., 1979-85, assoc. prof. libr. sci., 1985-89, sr. reference libr. Humanities, Social Sci. and Edn. Libr., 1982-90, prof. libr. sci., 1989—2003, libr. Humanities, Social Sci. and Edn. Libr. 1990—2003, prof. emeritus library sci., 2003—; dean libr., info. resources Abilene Christian U., 2003—. Mem. grantee com. instl. coop. NEH, 1991—94. Co-editor: Reference Services and Library Education, 1983, User Instruction in Academic Libraries, 1986, American Library History, 1989, Reading for Moral Progress, 1997; editor: Untold Stories: Civil Rights, Libraries and Black Librarianship, 1998; mem. editl. bd. Dictionary of American Library Biography, 2002; mem. editl. bd.: Librs. and Culture: Libr. Issues; contbr. articles to profl. jours. Thomas S. Wilmeth grantee, 1988, Frederick B. Artz Rsch. grantee, Oberlin Coll. Archives, 1991, Rsch. fellow, Coun. Libr. Resources, 1990. Mem.: SCV, ALA (chair libr. history round table 1993—94), Disciples of Christ Hist. Soc., Assn. Coll. and Rsch. Librs., Beta

Phi Mu, Phi Kappa Phi. Democrat. Mem. Ch. Of Christ. Home: 1687 Bent Tree Dr Abilene TX 79602 Office: Brown Libr Abilene Christian U Box 29208 Abilene TX 79699-9208 Office Phone: 325-674-2387. Business E-Mail: mark.tucker@acu.edu.

**TUCKER, JONATHAN BRIN,** political scientist; b. Boston, Aug. 2, 1954; s. Leonard Walter and Deborah Alice (Brin) T.; m. Karen Fern Fifer, Aug. 27, 1980 (div.). BS in Biology, Yale U., New Haven, Conn., 1975; MA in Internat. Rels., U. Pa., 1982; PhD in Polit. Sci., MIT, Cambridge, 1990. Mem. bd. editors Scientific Am. mag., NYC, 1976-79; freelance sci. writer Phila., 1979-83; sr. editor High Tech. mag., Boston, 1983-85; arms control fellow U.S. Dept. of State, Washington, 1989-90; def. policy analyst U.S. Congress Office of Tech. Assessment, Washington, 1990-93; fgn. affairs splst. U.S. Arms Control and Disarmament Agy., Washington, 1993-95; sr. policy analyst Presdl. Adv. Com. on Gulf War Vets. Ilnesses, Washington, 1995; dir. chem., biol weapons nonproliferation program Ctr. for Nonproliferation Studies Monterey Inst. Internat. Studies, Calif., 1996—. Vis. fellow Hoover Instn. Stanford (Calif.) U., 1999-2000, U.S. Inst. Peace, Washington, 2002-03, Am. Acad. in Berlin, 2006. Author: Ellie: A Child's Fight Against Leukemia, 1982; editor: Toxic Terror: Assessing Terrorist Use of Chemical and Biological Weapons, 2000, Scourge: The Once and Future Threat of Smallpox, 2001, War of Nerves: Chemical Warfare from World War I to Al-Qaeda, 2006; govt. reports; contbr. articles to profl. jours. Mem. Arms Control Assn., Coun. Fgn. Rels., Robert Bosch Found. Fellowship Alumni Assn. Democrat. Avocations: ballroom dancing, walking. Office: Ctr for Nonproliferation Studies/MIIS Fl 12 1111 Nineteenth St NW Washington DC 20036-2623

**TUCKER, KEITH A.,** investment company executive; b. 1945; BBA, U. Tex., 1967, JD, 1970. With KPMG Peat Marwick, Dallas, 1970-85, Stephens, Inc., Little Rock, 1985-87, Trivest Inc., Miami, Fla., 1987-91; dir. Waddell & Reed Inc., Shawnee Mission, Kans., 1989—, vice chmn., 1991—, chmn. Home: 3831 Turtle Creek Blvd Apt 6h Dallas TX 75219-4412

**TUCKER, KIMBERLY JOAN,** music educator; b. Racine, Wis., May 4, 1977; d. Joan Marie and Robert Edward Griswold (Stepfather), Joseph Zoltan and Lilac Kriston (Stepmother); m. Christopher Michael Tucker, Aug. 14, 2004. B Music Edn., U. North Tex., 2000; postgrad., Tex. A&M U., Commerce, 2005—. asst. band dir. DeSoto West Jr. H.S. and Amber Ter. Intermediate Sch., Tex., 2000—02; dir. bands, 2002—05; band rep. Rockwall ISD, 2005—. Sch. rep. DeSoto Dist. Advocacy Com., 2000—02. Recipient Sweepstakes award, U. Interscholastic League Region 20, 2002—04, Beach Within Reach Contest, 2002—04, Sandy Lake Music Festival, 2002—04. Fellow: Alpha Lambda Delta (life); mem.: Nat. Flute Assn. (corr.), Internat. Clarinet Assn. (corr.), Music Educators Nat. Conf. (corr.), Tex. Bandmasters Assn. (corr.), Tex. Music Educators Assn. (corr.), Sigma Alpha Iota (life; rec. sec. 1998—2000, Sword of Honor 1999). Roman Catholic. Avocations: practicing instruments, singing, sketching. Home: 684 Danielle Ct Rockwall TX 75087 Office Phone: 972-768-4784. Office Fax: 214-771-0026. Personal E-Mail: kimberkris1@aol.com.

**TUCKER, LAUREY DAN,** lawyer; s. Floyd A. and Harriet Kathleen (Graves) T.; m. Katherine Washburn, June 21, 1958; children: Laurie Tucker Diaz, Dana Tucker Kleine. BSChemE, U. Okla., 1959, LLB, 1962. Bar: Okla. 1962, Tex. 1972. Patent atty. Phillps Petroleum Co., Bartlesville, Okla., 1964—67, Monsanto Co., St. Louis, 1967—70, patent mgr. Texas City, Tex., 1970—74; ptnr. Hubbard, Tucker & Harris, Dallas, 1974—94, Harris, Tucker & Hardin, Dallas, 1994—97, Locke Purnell Rain Harrell, Dallas, 1997—98, Locke Liddell & Sapp LLP, Dallas, 1999—2006. Past pres. Dallas-Ft. Worth Patent Assn. Capt. USAR, 1959—69, 1st lt. U.S. Army, 1962—64. Mem.: Internat. Trademark Assn., Dallas Bar Assn., State Bar Tex. (past officer Intellectual Property Law Section), Okla. Bar Assn. Republican. Episcopalian. Avocations: fishing, hunting, travel. Office Phone: 214-740-8000. Business E-Mail: ldtucker@lockeliddell.com.

**TUCKER, LOUIS LEONARD,** retired historical society administrator; b. Rockville, Conn., Dec. 6, 1927; s. Joseph and Dora (Conn) T.; m. Beverley Jones, Mar. 27, 1953; children: Mark T, Lance K.; m. Carolyn woollen, Sept. 14, 1996. BA, U. Wash., 1952, MA, 1954, PhD, 1957. Instr. history U. Calif., Davis, 1958; fellow Inst. Early Am. History and Culture, Williamsburg, Va., 1958-60; instr. history Coll. William and Mary, 1958-60; dir. Cin. Hist. Soc., 1960-66; asst. commr., state historian of NY, N.Y State Edn. Dept., 1966-76; also dir. N.Y. State Bicentennial Commn., 1969-76; dir. Mass. Hist. Soc., Boston, 1977-97. Author: Puritan Protagonist, 1962, Cincinnati During Civil War, 1962, Cincinnati's Citizen Crusaders, 1967, Our Travels, 1968, Cincinnati: Students Guide to Local History, 1969, James Allen, Jr.: From Elkins to Washington, 1969, Connecticut's Seminary of Sedition, Yale College, 1974, Clio's Consort: Jeremy Belknap and the Founding of the Massachusetts Historical Society, 1990, The Massachusetts Historical Society: A Bicentennial History, 1791-1971, 1996, Worthington Chauncey Ford: Scholar and Adventurer, 2001. Dir. Shaker Mus., 1967-74; Am. Heritage Co., 1973-75, Ft. Ticonderoga Assn., 1990-97. Served with AUS, 1946-47. Winston Churchill fellow, 1969 Mem. Am. Assn. State and Local History (pres. 1972-74) Home: 328 Harvard St Cambridge MA 02139-2002

**TUCKER, MARC STEPHEN,** education policy analyst, author; b. Boston, Nov. 15, 1939; s. David Jones and Natalie (Croman) T.; m. Linda Beth Hepler, Sept. 27, 1964 (div. 1973); children: Matthew, Joshua; foster child, Julie Beers. AB, Brown U., 1961; MSS, George Washington U., 1982. Lighting dir., camera Sta. WGBH-TV, Boston, 1962-64, asst. dir. edn. div., 1964-66; asst. to pres. Edn. Devel. Ctr., Newton, Mass., 1966-71; asst. dir. NWREL, Portland, Oreg., 1971-72, assoc. dir. Nat. Inst. Edn., Washington, 1972-81; dir. Project on Info. Tech. and Edn., Washington, 1981-84; exec. dir. Carnegie Forum on Edn. and the Econ., Washington, 1985-87; pres. Nat. Ctr. on Edn. and the Economy, Rochester, NY, 1988—; prof. edn. U. Rochester, 1988— Staff dir., prin. author Carnegie report-A Nation Prepared: Teachers forthe 21st Century, 1986. Chmn., pres. Brace Chamber Music Soc., Annapolis, Md., 1980-81; mem. bd. advisors Apple Edn. Found., 1984-85, bd. visitors Wake Forest U., 1987—, bd. visitors U. Pitts. Sch. of Edn., 1987—, bd. advisors Bank St. Coll. Edn. Ctr. for Children and Tech., 1987— Democrat. Office: Natl Ctr On Educ And The Economy 555 13th St NW Ste 500w Washington DC 20004-1109

**TUCKER, MELVIN JAY,** education educator, researcher; s. Earle Homer and Florence Gertrude Tucker; m. N. Evelyn Rapalus, June 27, 1953; children: Ann Evelyn Jobson, Ellen Marie Tucker-Cohen, Michael Jay. BA, U. Mass., Amherst, Mass., 1953, MA, 1954; PhD, Northwestern U., Evanston, Il., 1962. Instr. Colby Coll., Waterville, Maine, 1959—60, MIT, Cambridge, Mass., 1960—63; assoc. prof. U. Buffalo, Buffalo, 1963—. Dir. grad. studies, history Univ. Buffalo, 1979—85; fellow Medieval Ctr., SUNY, Binghampton, 1970—77. Author: The Life of Thoms Howard, Earl of Surrey and Second Duke of Norfolk, 1443-1524; co-author: Centering: A Guide to Inner Growth, 2nd ed.; contbr. chapters to books; contbg. editor: History of Childhood Quarterly, 1973—76, Journal of Psycho History, 1976—84. 1st lt. USAF, 1954—56, Japan. Recipient Fulbright Award, Fulbright Commn., 1958-1959, Cert. of Merit, Buffalo & Erie County Hist. Soc., 1974, Cert. of Recognition, Career Planning, U. Buffalo, 2002. Mem.: Assn. for the Bibliography of History (exec. mem. 1982—92), Am. Hist. Assn., North Am. Conf. of Brit. Studies. Roman Catholic. Avocations: walking, movies. Office: History Dept Univ Buffalo 580 Pk Hall Buffalo NY 14260 Business E-Mail: mjtucker@acsu.buffalo.edu.

**TUCKER, PAUL THOMAS,** computer company executive; b. Evanston, Ill., Apr. 9, 1948; s. Charles E. Jr. and Francine G. Tucker; m. Carolyn K. Montgomery, 1967 (div. 1981); 1 child, Sean P.; m. Patricia M. Merlie, 1984 (div. 1995). BEE, U. Ill., 1970, MEE, 1971, PhD in elec. engring., 1975. Founder, ptnr., primary design engr. HAL Devices, 1968-71; pres., dir. engring., and chmn. bd. HAL Communications Corp., 1971-83; sr. rsch. engr., assoc. prof. U. Ill. Grad. Coll., 1971-83, 1983-87; sr. v.p. Commodity News Svcs., Inc., subs. Knight-Ridder, Inc., 1983-88; sr. v.p. Bus. Info. Svcs. div.

Knight-Ridder, Inc., 1985-90; COO Knight-Ridder Fin., Inc., N.Y.C., 1990-91, pres., CEO, 1991-96; v.p., corp. develop. Computer Sciences Corp., El Segundo, Calif., 1996—. Cons. Magnavox Corp., 1974-78, Control Data Corp., 1978, TDK Corp., Tokyo, Japan, 1976-82, Commodity News Svcs., Inc., 1980-82; tchr. Parkland Jr. Coll., 1980-81; mem. U. Ill. President's Coun., 1978—. Patentee (3) in field. Strategic tech. planning bd. Mercy Hosp. Found., 1978-82; bd. dirs. Urbana C. of C., 1980-82. Office: Computer Sciences Corp 2100 East Grand Ave El Segundo CA 90245 E-mail: ptucker@csc.com.

**TUCKER, RHONDA RENEÉ,** music educator; b. Gallapolis, Ohio, Apr. 11, 1959; d. Jimmy Gene and Margaret June Tucker. BME, Birmingham-So. Coll., 1981; MusM in Edn., Samford U., 1990. Cert. tchr. Ala., nat. bd. cert. tchr. Music tchr. Southside Baptist Ch. Early Childhood Ctr., Birmingham, Ala., 1981—82, Shades Cahaba Elem. Sch., Homewood, Ala., 1982—. Author: Words to Play By, 2001. Nominee Disting. Tchr., Birmingham Post Herald, 1998—99. Mem.: NEA, Ala. Music Educator's Assn. (pres. elect 2001—03, pres. 2003—05), Am. Orff-Schulwerk Assn. (pres. 1993—95). Republican. Methodist. Avocations: musical theatre, singing, playing piano, playing flute, tap dancing. Office: Shades Cahaba Elementary School 3001 Montgomery Hwy Homewood AL 35209

**TUCKER, RICHARD LEE,** civil engineer, educator; b. Wichita Falls, Tex., July 19, 1935; s. Floyd Alfred and Zula Florence (Morris) T.; m. Shirley Sue Tucker, Sept. 1, 1956; children: Bryan Alfred, Karen Leigh. BCE, U. Tex., 1958, MCE, 1960, PhDCE, 1963. Registered profl. engr., Tex Instr. civil engring. U. Tex., 1960-62, from asst. prof. to prof. Arlington, 1962-74, assoc. dean engring., 1963-74; v.p Luther Hill & Assoc., Inc., Dallas, 1974-76; Joe C. Walter chair in engring. U. Tex., Austin, 1976—, dir. Constrn. Industry Inst., 1983-98, dir. Ctr. Constrn. Industry Studies, 1998—2003. Pres. Tucker and Tucker Cons., Inc., Austin, 1976—. Contbr. numerous articles and papers to profl. jours. Recipient Erwin C. Perry award, Coll. Engring., U. Tex., 1978, Faculty Excellence award, 1986, Joe J. King Profl. Engring. Achievement award, 1990, Hocott Rsch. Award, 2000, Disting. Engring. Grad., 1994; Ronald Reagan award for Individual Initiative, Constrn. Industry Inst., 1991; named Outstanding Young Engr., Tex. Soc. Profl. Engrs., 1965, Outstanding Young Man, City of Arlington, 1967; fellow Inst. for Constructive Capitalism, 1990-91. Fellow ASCE (R.L. Peurifoy award 1986, Thomas Fitch Rowland prize 1987, Tex. sect. award of honor 1990); mem. NSPE (Constrn. Engr. Educator award 1993, Engr. of Yr. 2001), NAE (Engr. of Year, 2003), Soc. Am. Mil. Engrs., The Moles (hon.), Acad. Engring. Sci. Baptist. Office: Univ Tex Coll Engring Constrn Industry Inst ECJ5 2 Austin TX 78712

**TUCKER, ROBERT DENNARD,** health care products executive; b. Tifton, Ga., July 18, 1933; s. Robert Buck and Ethel Margaret (Dennard) T.; m. Peggy Angelyn Smith, June 23, 1957; children: Robert Barron, Jennifer Lee. BBA, Ga. State U., 1958. With sales and sales mgmt. Johnson & Johnson Inc., New Brunswick, NJ, 1958-68; v.p. gen. mgr. ASR Med. Industries, N.Y.C., 1968-72, Howmedica Suture div. Pfizer Inc., N.Y.C., 1972-75; exec. v.p., chief operating officer R. P. Scherer Corp., Detroit, 1976-79; pres., chief operating officer Scherer Sci. Inc., Atlanta, 1980-95, also bd. dirs; chmn., chief exec. officer Scherer Health Care Inc., Atlanta, 1980-95, also bd. dirs. Bd. dirs., pres., CEO Splty. Surgictrs., Inc., Atlanta, 1997—2002; bd. dirs., chmn., CEO Maximum Benefits Co., Atlanta; chmn., CEO Throwleigh Techs., LLC, 1995—; bd. dirs., mem. exec. com. Horizon Med. Products, 2002—. Pub: Tuckers of Devon, 1983; author, pub.: Descendants of William Tucker of Throwleigh, Devon. Chmn. bd. Health Industries Mfrs. Assn. polit. action com., Washington, 1983-85; trustee, past pres. Ga. Horse Found.; Atlanta; trustee Brenau Coll., Gainesville, Ga., 1985—. Served with USN, 1951-54, Korea. Decorated Knight of Malta, Imperial Russian Order of St. John; recipient Disting. Service award Brenau Coll., 1987. Mem. Nat. Assn. Mfrs., Health Industries Mfrs. Assn. (bd. dirs. 1979-86, disting. service recognition 1981, 86), Pharm. Mfrs. Assn., Thoroughbred Owners and Breeders Assn. Ky. and Ga. (Man of Yr. 1984). Clubs: Cherokee (Atlanta); Big Canoe (Ga.). Republican. Methodist. Avocations: scuba diving, tennis, genealogy. Home: 405 Townsend Pl NW Atlanta GA 30327-3037 Office: Throwleigh Techs PO Box 220 Ball Ground GA 30107

**TUCKER, ROY W.,** lawyer; b. Buffalo, Aug. 31, 1952; BA in Polit. Sci. & English, with dist. in Polit. Sci., magna cum laude, Kenyon Coll., 1974; JD, SUNY Buffalo, 1979. Bar: NY 1980, Oreg. 1985. Law clk. to Hon. Reid S. Moule Appellate Divsn., NY State Supreme Ct., 1979—80; with Davis Polk & Wardwell, NY, 1980—84; ptnr., mem. mgmt. com. Perkins Coie LLP, Portland, Oreg. Assoc. editor Buffalo Law Rev., 1977—78, sr. editor, 1978—79. Mem.: Phi Beta Kappa. Office: Perkins Coie LLP 1120 NW Couch St Floor 10 Portland OR 97209-4128 Office Phone: 503-727-2044. Office Fax: 503-727-2222. Business E-Mail: rtucker@perkinscoie.com

**TUCKER, SHIRLEY LOIS COTTER,** botanist, educator; b. St. Paul, Apr. 4, 1927; d. Ralph U. and Myra C. (Knutson) Cotter; m. Kenneth W. Tucker, Aug. 22, 1953. BA, U. Minn., 1949, MS, 1951; PhD, U. Calif., Davis, 1956. Asst. prof. botany La. State U., Baton Rouge, 1967-71, assoc. prof., 1971-76, prof., 1976-82, Boyd prof., 1982-95, prof. emerita, 1995—. Adj. prof. dept. biology U. Calif., Santa Barbara, 1995—. Co-editor: Aspects of Floral Development, 1988, Advances in Legume Systematics, Vol. 6, 1994; contbr. numerous articles on plant devel. to profl. jours. Recipient, Outstanding Alumni Achievement award U. Minn., 1999; fellow Linnean Soc., London, 1975—, Fulbright fellow Eng., 1952-53. Mem. Bot. Soc. Am. (v.p. 1979, program chmn. 1975-78, pres.-elect 1986-87, pres. 1987-88, Merit award 1989), Am. Bryological and Lichenological Soc., Brit. Lichenological Soc., Am. Inst. Biol. Scis., Am Soc Plant Taxonomists (pres.-elect 1994-95, pres. 1995-96), Phi Beta Kappa, Sigma Xi. Home: 5987 Primavera Rd Santa Barbara CA 93110-1467 Office: U Calif Dept Biology EEMB Santa Barbara CA 93106 Business E-Mail: tucker@lifesci.ucsb.edu.

**TUCKER, SUSAN,** mathematics professor; BA, Smith Coll., Northampton, Mass., 1974; PhD, U. Mich., Ann Arbor, 1980. Prof. biostatistics and applied math. U. Tex. MD Anderson Cancer Ctr., Houston, 1980—. Contbr. articles to profl. jours. Office: UT MD Anderson Cancer Center Unit 237 1515 Holcombe Blvd Houston TX 77030 Office Phone: 713-792-2613. Business E-Mail: sltucker@mdanderson.org

**TUCKER, SUSAN COBB,** design executive, chemist; b. Poughkeepsie, NY, May 31, 1962; d. Stuart Gordon Tucker and Sandra Wooten Legler. BA in Chemistry, Colgate U., Hamilton, NY, 1984; PhD in Chemistry, U. Minn., Mpls., 1989. Prof. chemistry U. Calif., Davis, 1991—2005; design assoc. Lehrman Cameron Studio, Seattle, 2005—. Chair, chair-elect, vice chair theoretical subdivsn. Am. Chem. Soc., 1999—2001; awards panelist divsn. phys. chemistry NSF, Washington, 2003. Contbr. articles to profl. jours.; adv. editor Theoretical Chem. Accounts, 1999—2001. Recipient Young Investigator award, NSF, 1994—99, Camille Dreyfus Tchr.-Scholar award, Dreyfus Found., 1998—2001, Sejour Sci. de Haut Niveau, 2001, Disting. Tchg. award, U. Calif., Davis, 2003; fellow, French Ministry Rsch.; grad. fellow, NSF, 1984—87. Mem.: Am. Assn. Museums, Phi Beta Kappa. Avocation: Aikido. E-mail: sctucker@ucdavis.edu.

**TUCKER, TANYA DENISE,** singer; b. Seminole, Tex., Oct. 10, 1958; d. Beau and Juanita Tucker; children: Presley Tanita, Beau Grayson, Layla LaCosta. Singer Tanya Tucker Inc., 1959—. Regular on Lew King Show; rec. artist formerly with Columbia Records, MCA Records, Capital Records; albums include The Sound of Tanya Tucker, 1972, Tear Me Apart, Chagnes, Delta Dawn, 1972, What's Your Mamma's Name, 1973. Would You Lay With Me (In a Field of Stone), 1974, Girls Like Me, Tanya Tucker's Greatest Hits, 1975, Greatest Hits, 1975, Tanya Tucker, 1975, Greatest Hits Encore, 1976, Here's Some Love, 1976, Lovin' and Learnin', 1976, You Are So Beautiful, 1977, Greatest Hits, 1978, T.N.T., 1978, Ridin' Rainbows, 1979, Tear Me Apart, 1979, Should I Do It, 1981, Dream Lovers, 1981, Live, 1982, The Best of Tanya Tucker, 1982, Changes, 1983, Love Me Like You Used To, 1987, Strong Enough to Bend, 1988, Greatest Hits, 1989, Tennessee Women, 1990,

Ridin Rainbows/Here's Some Love, 1990, Lovin' and Learnin'/Tanya Tucker, 1990, Greatest Country Hits, 1991, What Do I Do With Me, 1991, Collection, 1992, The Best of Tanya Tucker, 1992, (with Delbert McClinton) Can't Run From Youself, 1992, Greatest Hits, 1992, Lizzie & the Rain Man, 1993, Greatest Hits (CEMA), 1993, Greatest Hits (Capitol), 1993, Country Queen, 1993, Greatest Hits 1990-1992, 1993, Soon, 1993, Girls Like Me, 1994, Fire to Fire, 1995, (with T. Graham Brown, Delbert McClinton) Tanya, 1995, Christmas with Tanya Tucker and Suzy Bogguss, 1995, The Best of My Love, 1995, Love Songs, 1996, Complicated, 1997, Little Things, 1997, Super Hits, 1998, What's Your Mama's Name/Would You Lay With Me (In a Field of Stone), 1999, Best of My Love, 2000, Sisters: An Anthology, 2000, Country Classics, Vol. 2, 2000, 20 Greatest Hits, 2000, 20th Century Masters-The Millennium Collection: The Best of Tanya Tucker, 2000, The Dresden Dolls, 2001, Tanya Tucker Country Classics, 2001, Tanya, 2002, The Upper 48 Hits 1972-1997, 2002, Country Classics, 2002, Very Best Of, 2004, Country Greatest: EMI Years, 2004, Live at Billy Bob's Texas, 2005; TV appearances include A Country Christmas, 1979, The Georgia Peaches, 1980, The Love Boat, 1982, Delta, 1992; actress: (mini-series) The Rebels, 1979, (film) Jeremiah Johnson, 1972, Amateur Night At the Dixie Bar & Grill, 1978, When I Was A Girl, 2003, (TV series) Tuckerville, 2005-; published (autobiography) Nickel Dreams, 1997; author: 100 Ways to Beat the Blues, 2005. Nat. amb. Nat. Multiple Sclerosis Soc.; philanthropist March of Dimes, St. Jude's Children's Hosp., Doris Kupferle Breast Centers, Coors Literacy Project, Recording Artists Against Drunk Driving, Planet Hope, Boys and Girls Clubs, charitable events for T.J. Martell Found. Named Top New Female Vocalist, Acad. Country Music, 1972, Most Promising Female Artist of Yr., Music City News Country, 1973, Female Vocalist of Yr., Country Music Assn., 1991, Female Video Artist of Yr., Country Music TV, 1993, Showcase Artist of Month, Country Music TV, 1997; recipient Music Video of Yr., Country Music Assn., 1992, Video of Yr. for Two Sparrows in a Hurricane, Acad. Country Music, 1993; nominee for two Grammy awards, 1994. Avocations: avid competitor in cutting horse contests, motorcycling. Office: Tanya Tucker Inc c/o Curtis & Co Plc 109 Westpark Dr Ste 400 Brentwood TN 37027-5032*

**TUCKER, THOMAS JAMES,** retired investment company executive; b. Atlanta, Sept. 5, 1929; s. Thomas Tudor and Carol (Govan) T.; m. Margaret Guerard. BA, U. of the South, 1952. With CIT Corp, N.Y.C., 1957—72; pres., CEO AmSouth Fin. Corp., Birmingham, Ala., 1972—82, chmn. bd., 1982, also dir., 1972—93; exec. v.p AmSouth Bank N.A., Birmingham, 1982—93, chief credit officer, 1992; prin. Tucker Investments, Birmingham, 1993—2003; ret., 2003. Exec. v.p. AmSouth Bancorp, Birmingham, 1982-93; bd. dirs. Alabanc Properties Corp., Birmingham, chmn., 1991-93; bd. dirs. Birmingham Broadway Series Inc., treas., 1996-97, pres., 1997-99, chmn., 1999-2001; co-founder Garland-Govan Scholarship Fund, Sewanee-U. of the South. Contbr. articles on credit and leasing to trade jours.; photographer gen. interest mags., 1970—. Bd. dirs. Birmingham Cmty. Devel. Corp.; chmn. bd., 1990-93. 1st lt. USAF, 1952-56. Mem. Vulcan Trail Assn., Birmingham Art Mus. Assn., Birmingham Bot. Soc., Friends of Emmt O'Neal Libr., Birmingham Canoe Club (bd. dirs. 1990-96), Photography Guild, Cahaba River Soc. (adv. bd. 1991-92, bd. dirs. 1993-98, v.p. orgnl. devel. 1995-98), Ala. Growth Strategies Task Force, Regional Open Space and Trails Alliance, Manigault Soc., Sewanee Devel. Coun., Order of Purple/Sewanee-U. of the South, Never Failing Succession of Benefactors/Sewanee-U. of the South, The Club, Jefferson Club, Silhouettes Club Episcopalian. Avocations: photography, high altitude hiking, white water canoeing. Office: 6 Office Park Cir Ste 308 Birmingham AL 35223 Home: 415 Club Pl Birmingham AL 35223

**TUCKER, THOMAS WILLIAM,** mathematics professor; b. Princeton, NJ, July 15, 1945; s. Albert William Tucker and Alice Judson (Curtiss) Beckenbach; m. Mollie Dalton; children: Thomas John, Emily McDonnell. AB magna cum laude, Harvard U., 1967; PhD, Dartmouth Coll., 1971. Instr. Princeton U., 1971-73; from asst. prof. to prof. math. Colgate U., Hamilton, NY, 1973-83, prof., 1983—, Charles G. Hetherington prof. math., 1994—; chmn. math. dept., 1982-86, acting dean coll., 1991-92, dir. divsn nat. sci., 1993-96. Vis. assoc. prof. Dartmouth Coll., Hanover, NH, 1978-79; cons. Ednl. Testing Svc., 1973—, Inst. for Def. Analyses, Princeton, 1974-75, 78-79, 84-85; chmn. advanced placement calculus com. Coll. Bd., NYC, 1983-87; pres. Calculus Consortium for Higher Edn., Inc., 1998-2005. Co-author: Topological Graph Theory, 1987; editor: Priming the Calculus Pump, 1990; contbr. numerous articles to profl. jours. NSF grantee, 1976-77, 80-82, 86-88, 89, 90-97. Mem. Math. Assn. Am. (mem., chmn. many coms., v.p. 1990-92), Am. Math. Soc. Home: 21 Hamilton St Hamilton NY 13346-1329 Office: Colgate U Dept Math Hamilton NY 13346 Business E-Mail: ttucker@mail.colgate.edu.

**TUCKER, WATSON BILLOPP,** lawyer; b. Dobbs Ferry, NY, Nov. 16, 1940; s. Watson Billopp and Mary (Prema) T.; children: Robin, Craig, Christopher, Alexander, John. BS, Northwestern U., Evanston, Ill., 1962; JD magna cum laude, Northwestern U., 1965. Bar: Ill. 1965, U.S. Dist. Ct. (no. dist.) Ill. 1966, U.S. Supreme Ct. 1971, U.S. Dist. Ct. (no. dist.) N.Y. 1976, U.S. Ct. Appeals (2d, 3d, 5th, 6th, 7th, and 9th cirs.). Ptnr. Mayer, Brown, Rowe & Maw, Chgo., 1972-99, Smith & Tucker, Sycamore, Ill., 1999—. Fellow Am. Coll. Trial Lawyers. Office: Smith & Tucker 1958 Aberdeen Ct Sycamore IL 60178 Office Phone: 815-787-7033. Business E-Mail: wbtucker@smithtucker.com.

**TUCKER, WILLIAM EDWARD,** academic administrator, minister; b. Charlotte, NC, June 22, 1932; s. Cecil Edward and Ethel Elizabeth (Godley) T.; m. Ruby Jean Jones, Apr. 8, 1955; children: Janet Sue, William Edward, Gordon Vance. BA, Barton Coll., Wilson, N.C., 1953, LLD (hon.), 1978; BD, Tex Christian U Ft Worth, 1956; MA, Yale U., New Haven, Conn., 1958, PhD, 1960; LHD (hon.), Chapman U., Orange, Calif., 1981, LHD (hon.), Bethany Coll., 1982; DD (hon.), Austin Coll., Sherman, Tex., 1985; LHD (hon.), Ky. Wesleyan Coll., Owensboro, 1989. Ordained to ministry Disciples of Christ Ch., 1956; prof. Barton Coll., 1959-66, chmn. dept. religion and philosophy, 1961-66; mem. faculty Brite Div. Sch., Tex. Christian U., 1966-76, prof. ch. history, 1969-76, dean, 1971-76, chancellor, 1979-98, chancellor emeritus, 1998—. Pres. Bethany (W.Va.) Coll., 1976-79; dir. RadioShack Corp., 1985-2003, Brown and Lupton Found.; mem. gen. bd. Christian Ch. (Disciples of Christ), 1971-74, 75-87, adminstrv. com., 1975-81, chmn. theol. edn. commn., 1972-73, mem. exec. com., chmn. bd. higher edn., 1975-77; dir. Christian Ch. Found., 1980-83; moderator Christian Ch. (Disciples of Christ), 1983-85 Author: J.H. Garrison and Disciples of Christ, 1964, (with others) Journey in Faith: A History of the Christian Church (Disciples of Christ), 1975; also articles. Bd. dirs. Van Cliburn Found., 1981—, Ft. Worth Symphony Orch.; bd. trustee Amon Carter Mus. Mem. Exch. Club, Phi Beta Kappa. Home: 2337 Colonial Pkwy Fort Worth TX 76109-1030 Office: 777 Taylor St Ste P2-J Fort Worth TX 76102 Office Phone: 817-347-3220. Business E-Mail: w.tucker@tcu.edu.

**TUCKER, WILLIAM P.,** lawyer, writer; b. Kingston, N.Y., Jan. 26, 1932; s. Philip and Mary (McGowan) T.; m. Dolores F. Beaudoin, June 10, 1961; children: Andrew M., Thomas B., Mary A. BA, Hunter Coll., 1958; JD, St. John's U., 1962. Bar: NY 1962, Fla. 1980, U.S. Dist. Ct. (ea. dist.) N.Y. 1963, U.S. Dist. Ct. (ea. dist.) N.Y., 1963, U.S. Cir. Ct. (2d cir.) Ill. Assoc. Mendes & Mount, N.Y.C., 1962-63; ptnr. Cullen and Dykman, Bklyn. and Garden City, N.Y., Washington, Newark, Hauppauge, 1963-98, Golden, Wexler & Sarnese, Garden City/Purchase/S.I., 1998-2001; pvt. practice, 2001—. Former gen. counsel Broadway Nat. Bank, Wartburg Luth. Svcs., Luth. Ctr. for the Aging, Martin Luther Ter. Apts., Inc., Interfaith Med. Ctr., Roosevelt Savs. Bank, Olympian Bank, GreenPoint Bank, Ridgewood Savs. Bank, Atlantic Liberty Savs., F.A., Brehtage Fed. Credit Union, Mcpl. Credit Union, Lincoln Savs. Bank, Bklyn. Savs. Bank, Met. Savs. Bank, Crossland Savs. Bank, Bushwick Savs. Bank, Anchor Savs. Bank, Episc. Diocese L.I., St. John's Episc. Hosp., Bklyn., Rockaway, Smithtown; former spl. counsel OCI Mortgage Corp., Bklyn C. of C., Downtown Bklyn. Bus. Assn., Bank of N.Y., Chase Manhattan Bank, Fleet Bank, Kraft Credit Union, Apple Bank for Savs., Barclays Bank of N.Y.; chmn. bd. dirs. Broadway Nat. Bank; co-owner Salem Keizer Volcanoes N.W. League baseball team; former owner Norwich

Navigators Ea. League baseball beam; former v.p., N.W. Profl. Baseball League; bd. dirs. Bklyn. Sportsplex, Inc.; mem. WWII vets. history com. Libr. of Congress; rschr. U.S. Assassination Archives. Author: DP-or Billy and Jerry in the Promised Land, 1996, Moving Home Plate, 1999, (novels) Excalibur, 2001, With Justice for All, 2003, Kingsway 37, 2004; contbr. articles to profl. jours. Past mem. Selective Svc. Bd. 33; past pres. St. Vincent Ferrer Home Sch. Assn.; del. Diocesan Union Holy Name Socs.; mem. coun. St. John's U.; mem. coun. of regents St. Francis Coll., Bklyn.; bd. dirs. Faith Home Found., St. Joseph's Coll. Served U.S. Army, Korean War. Mem. Am. Coll. Real Estate Lawyers, N.Y. State Bar Assn., Fla. Bar Assn., Savs. Bank Lawyers Assn. Bklyn. (pres.), Suffolk County Bar Assn., Savs. Bank Assn. N.Y. State (law com.), Bklyn. Mcpl. Club (pres.), Knight of Malta. Home: 23 Bunker Hill Dr Huntington NY 11743-5705 Office: 145 East Main St Huntington NY 11743 Office Phone: 631-351-1112. E-mail: wptucker@optonline.net.

**TUCKSON, REED V.,** academic administrator; Grad., Howard U.; PhD, Georgetown U. Commr. pub. health, Washington, 1986—90; sr v.p. progs. March of Dimes Birth Defects Found., 1990—91; pres. Charles R. Drew U., LA, 1991—97; sr. v.p. profl. stds. AMA, Chgo., 1998—2000; sr. v.p. consumer health and med. care advancement UnitedHealth Grp., 2000—. Office: UnitedHealth Grp PO Box 1459 Minneapolis MN 55440

**TUDMAN, CATHI GRAVES,** elementary school educator; b. Fresno, Calif., June 24, 1953; d. Robert Eugene and Bettyelou (Seagraves) Graves; divorced; children: Colleen Melissa, Andrew James. BA in Music cum laude, Calif. State U., Fresno, 1978, MA in Communication, 1991. Gen. elem., English, music and gen. sci. teaching credentials, Calif. Founder, coord. Lake Sequoia Symphonic Music Camp, Miramonte, Calif., 1985—; asst. lectr. communications speech dept. Calif. State U., 1988-91, instr. reading ednl. opportunity program summer bridge, 1990, instr. writing ednl. opportunity program summer bridge, 1991, coach, judge Peach Blossom Festival, 1988-91; band dir. Yosemite Mid. Sch., 1991—2004, Mayfair Elem. Sch., 1991—2000, Hidalgo Elem. Sch., 1991-92, 94-96, Balderas Elem., 1992-93, Turner Elem., 1993-96, Burroughs Annex Elem. Sch., 1993-95; art dir. Yosemite Mid. Sch., 2000—04, Ft. Miller Med. Careers Magnet Sch., SC, 2004—; physical sci. instr. Ft. Miller Med. Careers Ctr., 2004—. Instr. comms. dynamics Phillips Coll., Fresno, 1989-90; rsch. assoc. Renshaw Assocs., Fresno, 1989-91; flutist, piccoloist Fresno Philharm. Orch., 1981—, libr., 1985, pers. mgr., 1984-85; flute clinician Selmer Corp., Ind., 1988-93; festivals chmn. cen. sect. Calif. Music Educators, 1972-82, publicity chmn., 1992-93; pvt. tutor in math., music and social studies; chmn. Fresno Unified Showcase Mid. Sch. Massed Band, 1991, 93. Flute clinician Fresno County Schs., 1980—; founder San Joaquin Valley Instrument Fund, 1984; bd. dirs. Community Concert Series, Fresno County, 1986-88; liaison com. bd. dirs. Fresno Philharm. Orch., 1992-94; mem. bd., 2002-04, mem. comm., 2003-05; asst. chair FMCMEA info. Band, 1992-93; bd. dirs. Cen. Valley YMCA, 1994-95; music chair Fresno Met. Mus., 1996-97; mem. Yosemite Mid. Sch. Site Coun. 2000-2003, pres., sec., by-laws chair Fresno Arts Coun., bd. dirs. 2002-04, Tree Fresno-Rails to Trails Project, 2000; Great TV auction vol. Valley Pub. TV, 2005. Rsch. grantee Calif. State U., 1991, Cmty. Enrichment grant, 1999-2002; recipient Outstanding Teaching award Internat. Communication Assn., 1991. Mem. Western States Communication Assn., Fresno-Madera Music Educators Assn., Fresno Tchrs. Assn. (dir.-at-large, 2002-05), Calif. Tchrs. Assn. (rep. coun. 2000-2005), Fresno Mus. Club (social chmn. 1992-95) Calif. Music Educators (festival chmn. cen. sect. 1972-82), Sci. & Math. Educators Consortium, Calif. State U.-Fresno Alumnae Assn. (sec. 1982-83, nat. friendship chmn. 1979-81), Blue Key (Tokalon alumni 1978), Phi Kappa Phi, Mu Phi Epsilon (pres., v.p. Phi Chi chpt.). Avocations: quilting, kite making, church musician. Home: 5467 E Saginaw Way Fresno CA 93727-7536 Office: Fort Miller Mid Sch 1302 E Dakota Fresno CA 93704 Office Phone: 559-248-7100. E-mail: cgtudman@att.net.

**TUDOR, BRENDA S.,** retail company executive; CPA. Acct. Strand, Skees, Jones & Co., Asheville, N.C.; gen. acctg. mgr. Ingles Markets, Inc., Black Mountain, N.C., 1984-88; controller, sec., 1988-98; v.p., CFO, 1998—; also bd. dirs.

**TUELL, JACK MARVIN,** superintendent, retired bishop; b. Tacoma, Nov. 14, 1923; s. Frank Harry and Anne Helen (Bertelson) T.; m. Marjorie Ida Beadles, June 17, 1946; children— Jacqueline, Cynthia, James. BS, U. Wash., 1947, LL.B., 1948; S.T.B., Boston U., 1955; MA, U. Puget Sound, 1961, DHS, 1990; D.D., Pacific Sch. Religion, 1966; LLD, Alaska Pacific U., 1980. Bar: Wash. 1948; ordained to ministry Meth. Ch., 1955. Practice law with firm Holte & Tuell, Edmonds, Wash., 1948-50; pastor Grace Meth. Ch., Everett, Wash., 1950-52, South Tewksbury Meth. Ch., Tewksbury, Mass., 1952-55, Lakewood Meth. Ch., Tacoma, 1955-61; dist. supt. Puget Sound dist. Meth. Ch., Everett, 1961-67; pastor 1st United Meth. Ch., Vancouver, Wash., 1967-72; bishop United Meth. Ch., Portland, Oreg., 1972-80, Calif.-Pacific Conf., United Meth. Ch., LA, 1980-92, ret., 1992; interim sr. pastor First United Meth. Ch., Boise, Idaho, 1995; interim supt. Seattle Tacoma Dist., 2004—05. Mem. gen. conf. United Meth. Ch., 1964, 66, 68, 70, 72; pres. coun. of Bishops United Meth. Ch., 1989-90. Author: The Organization of the United Methodist Church, 1970, 10th edit. 2005, (autobiography) From Law to Grace, 2004. Pres. Tacoma U.S.O., 1959-61, Vancouver YMCA, 1968; v.p. Ft. Vancouver Seamens Ctr., 1969-72; vice chmn. Vancouver Human Rels. Commn., 1970-72; pres. Oreg. Coun. Alcohol Problems, 1972-76; trustee U. Puget Sound, 1961-73, Vancouver Meml. Hosp., 1967-72, Alaska Meth. U., Anchorage, 1972-80, Willamette U., Salem, Oreg., 1972-80, Willamette View Manor, Portland, 1972-80, Rogue Valley Manor, Medford, Oreg., 1972-76, Sch. Theology at Claremont, Calif., 1980-92, Methodist Hosp., Arcadia, Calif., 1983-92; pres. nat. div. bd. global ministries United Meth. Ch., 1972-76, pres. ecumenical and interreligious concerns div., 1976-80, Commn. on Christian Unity and interreligious concerns, 1980-84, Gen. Bd. of Pensions,1984-92, Calif. Coun. Alcohol Problems, 1985-88. Jacob Sleeper fellow, 1955. Methodist. Home and Office: 816 S 216th St 637 Des Moines WA 98198-6331

**TUEPKER, MAX C.,** lawyer; b. Oklahoma City, Oct. 21, 1953; s. Gilbert H. and Mildred E. (Boatright) T.; children: Tara Leigh, Kye Trenton. BS in Edn., Ctrl. State U., Edmond, Okla., 1976; JD, U. Tulsa, 1980. Bar: Okla. 1980, Colo. 1981, U.S. Dist. Ct. (we., ea. and no. dists.) Okla., Colo., U.S. Ct. Appeals (10th cir.) 1982, U.S. Supreme Ct. 2004. Law clk. Honorable H. Dale Cook U.S. Dist. Ct. (no. dist.) Okla., Tulsa, 1980-81; assoc. Roath & Brega, Denver, 1981-82, Mock & Schwabe, Oklahoma City, 1982-87; ptnr., prin. Max C. Tuepker, P.C., Oklahoma City, 1987—, Instr., lectr. Ctrl. State U., Edmond, Okla., 1982-83. Trustee Cen. State U. Found., Edmond, 1988—. Mem. ABA, Okla. Bar Assn., Oklahoma County Bar Assn. Avocations: skiing, softball, running. Office: City Place Bldg 25th FL 204 N Robinson Ave Oklahoma City OK 73102-6803 Office Phone: 405-235-1700. Personal E-mail: mtuepker@swbell.net.

**TUERK, WILLIAM F.,** federal agency administrator, lawyer; AB, Univ. Notre Dame, 1971; JD, George Washington Univ., 1978. Bar: D.C. 1978. Legis. analyst US Dept. Treasury, 1974—76; atty. pvt. practice, 1978—86, US Dept. Vet. Affairs, 1986—91; minority gen. counsel Com. Vet. Affairs, U.S. Senate, 1991—95, gen counsel, 1995—99, chief counsel & staff dir., 1999—2005; under sec. memorial affairs US Dept. Vet. Affairs, Washington, 2005—. Mil. policeman U.S. Army, 1971—73. Office: US Dept Vets Affairs 810 Vermont Ave NW Rm 400 Washington DC 20420*

**TUETING, SARAH,** professional hockey player; b. Winnetka, Ill., Apr. 26, 1976; Student, Dartmouth Coll., 1994—96. Goaltender U.S. Nat. Women's Hockey Team, 1996—. Recipient ice hockey Gold medal Olympic Games, Nagano, Japan, 1998. Avocations: soccer, tennis, playing piano and cello. Office: c/o USA Hockey 1775 Bob Johnson Dr Colorado Springs CO 80906

**TUFANO, CHARLES C.,** paper company executive; b. Rochester, NY, Sept. 29, 1944; BS in Indsl. Engring., Tex. A&M U., 1966. From sales staff to sales mgr. St. Regis, Cleve., 1967—82; gen. mgr. to dir. Packaging, Buffalo, 1982—95; from dir. printing papers to sr. v.p. Paper Distbn., 1995—2001; pres. Unisource, Norcross, Ga., 1999—. Office: Unisource 600 Govewrnors Lake Pkwy Norcross GA 30071

**TUFANO, PAUL J.,** computer company executive; Degree in Econs., St. John's U.; MBA in Fin., Acctg., Internat. Bus., Columbia U. With IBM, 1984—2001; CFO Maxtor Corp., 1996—2001, exec. v.p., COO, 2001—03, pres., CEO, 2003—04; CFO Solectron Corp., Milpitas, Calif., 2006—. Bd. dir. Terradyne Corp. Office: Solectron Corp 847 Gibraltar Dr Milpitas CA 95035-6332*

**TUFT, MARY ANN,** executive search firm executive; b. Easton, Pa., Oct. 11, 1934; d. Ben and Elizabeth (Reibman) T. BS, West Chester State Coll., Pa., 1956; MA, Lehigh U., 1960. Cert. assn. exec. Nat. trainer Girl Scouts U.S.A., N.Y.C., 1965-68; cons. Nat. League for Nursing, N.Y.C., 1968-69; exec. dir. Nat. Student Nurses Assn., N.Y.C., 1970-85; mem. Commn. on Dietetic Registration, Am. Dietetic Assn., 1981-85; pres. Specialized Cons. Ltd., 1983-85; exec. dir. Radiol. Soc. N.Am., Oak Brook, Ill., 1985-88; pres. Tuft & Assocs., Inc., 1989—. Trustee, Found. of the Nat. Student Nurses Assn. 2001—; adv. bd. Cognitive Neurology and Alzheimer's Disease Ctr. of Northwestern Univ./Feinberg Sch. of Medicine; mem. pres.'s adv. coun. Sch. Nursing, Saint Xavier U., 2006—. Bd. dirs. Nurses House, Inc., 1981-85, nat. bd. Am. Friends of Hebrew U., 2000-06; mem. exec. com. Chgo. Sinai Cong., 1987-91, v.p., 1988. Recipient Disting. Alumnus award West Chester State Coll., 1979; Mary Ann Tuft Scholarship Fund named in her honor Found. Nat. Student Nurses Assn.; Kepner-Tregoe scholar, 1966. Mem. ALA (pub. mem. com. on accreditation 1993-95), Am. Soc. Assn. Execs. (bd. dirs. 1980-83, trustee for cert. 1980-83, vice chmn. 1983-84), N.Y. Soc. Assn. Execs. (pres. 1978-79, bd. dirs. 1975-78, 1st Outstanding Exec. award 1982), Continuing Care Accreditation Assn. (bd. dirs. 1983-85), Specialized Cons. in Nursing (faculty), Am. Dietetic Assn. (pub. mem. commn. on accreditation for dietetics edn.), Sigma Theta Tau. Office Phone: 312-642-8889. Business E-Mail: matuft@tuftassoc.com.

**TUFT, THOMAS E.,** diversified financial services company executive; m. Diane Tuft. Inst. salesman Goldman Sachs, vice chmn., mng. ptnr. NYC. Trustee Whitney Mus. Am. Art, NYC; bd. dir. Boys & Girls Harbor. Office: Goldman Sachs 85 Broad St New York NY 10004 Office Phone: 212-902-1000. Office Fax: 212-902-3000.

**TUFTE, EDWARD ROLF,** statistician, educator; b. Kansas City, Mo., Mar. 14, 1942; s. Edward E. and Virginia (James) T.; m. Inge Druckrey BS, Stanford U., 1963, MS, 1964; PhD, Yale U., 1968 HHD (hon.), Cooper Union, 1992, Conn. Coll., 1995, St. Joseph's Coll., 1997, Md. Art Inst., 1999, Mpls. Coll. Art, 2000, Williams Coll., 2000; HHD hon., Univ. of the Arts, 2003. Asst. prof. pub. policy Princeton U., 1967-71, assoc. prof., 1971-74, prof., 1974-77; prof. polit. sci., stats., computer sci. Yale U., New Haven, 1977-99; pres. Graphics Press, Cheshire, 1983—. Author: Quantitative Analysis of Social Problems, 1970, Size and Democracy, 1973, Data Analysis, 1974, Political Control of the Economy, 1978 (Kammerer award 1979, Citation Classic 1989), The Visual Display of Quantitative Information, 1983 (Citation Classic 1992), 2d edit., 2001, Envisioning Information, 1990, Visual Explanations, 1997, Beautiful Evidence, 2006 Pres. Cheshire Neighborhood Assn., 1984-87. Recipient Best Graphic Design award Internat. Design, 1990, Wittenborn award, 1991, Best Book Design award Assn. Ind. Publs., Computer Press Assn. award, 1991, Sci. award Phi Beta Kappa, 1991, AIGA book show, 1998, book award AIGA, 1998, book award STC, 1998, book award Internat. Design, 1998, book award Am. Ctr. for Design, 1998; Ctr. for Advanced Study in Behavioral Scis. fellow, 1973-74; Guggenheim fellow, 1977. Fellow Am. Acad. Arts and Scis., Am. Statis. Assn. Office: Graphics Press PO Box 430 Cheshire CT 06410

**TUGEND, ALINA NURIT,** journalist; b. L.A., Sept. 23, 1959; d. Thomas and Rachel Tugend; m. Mark Andrew Steven; children: Benjamin Tugendstein, Gabriel Tugendstein. BA, U. Calif., Berkeley, 1981; MS in Law, Yale U., 1987. Staff writer UPI, Providence, 1982—83, Education Week, Washington, 1985—86, L.A. Herald Examiner, 1987—89; environ. writer Orange County Register, Santa Ana, Calif., 1989—94; London corrs. Chronicle Higher Edn., London, 1994—2000; freelance writer NY, 2000—; columnist NY Times, 2005—. Jewish.

**TUGGLE, CLYDE CEBRON,** beverage company executive; b. Atlanta, Apr. 9, 1962; s. Arthur Coleman and Nelle (Martin) T. Student, Ludwig-Maxillian U., Munich, 1982-83; completed exec. program, U. VA. Darden Sch. Bus.; BA in German studies and Econ., Hamilton Coll., Clinton, N.Y., 1984; MDiv, Yale U., 1988. Market analyst Scott, Fitton & Co., New Haven, 1987-88; editor, corp. issues comm. dept. The Coca-Cola Co., Atlanta, 1989—92, mng. editor, 1992, exec. asst. to chmn. and CEO, 1992—98, dir. ops. devel., dep. to div. pres., region mgr. Vienna, 1998—2000, exec. asst. for chmn. and CEO to v.p. Atlanta, 2000—03, dir., Worldwide Comm., 2001—02, sr. v.p., Worldwide Public Affairs and Comm., 2002—, mem., exec. com., 2003. Bd. dirs. Sledco, Inc., Ga. Rsch. Alliance. Bd. dirs. So. Ctr. Internat. Studies, Yale U. Divinity Sch., Atlanta Symphony Orch., East Lake Cmty. Found., High Mus. Arts, Metro Atlanta C. of C.; trustee Agnes Scott Coll.; bd. vis. Emory U. Mem.: US Austrian C. of C., Coun. on Foreign Relations. Episcopalian. Office: The Coca-Cola Co PO Box 1734 Atlanta GA 30301-1734

**TUGGLE, FRANCIS DOUGLAS,** entrepreneur, consultant, management educator, scientist; b. Portsmouth, Va., Jan. 19, 1943; s. Francis Joyner and Florence Eleanor (Dahlgren) T.; m. Mary Ann Tredway, June 3, 1967; children: Wendy Elizabeth, Laura Michelle. SB, MIT, 1964; MS, Carnegie-Mellon U., 1967, PhD, 1971. Prof. bus. adminstrn. and computer sci. U. Kans., Lawrence, 1968-78; Jesse H. Jones prof. mgmt. Rice U., Houston, 1978-90; dean Kogod Coll. Bus. Adminstrn., Am. U., Washington, 1990-96, prof. info. systems and strategic planning, 1996—2002; Robert J. & Carolyn A. Waltos Jr. dean Argyros Sch. Bus. Econs. Chapman U., Orange, Calif., 2002—06, prof., 2006—; founder Family Health Info. Svcs., Inc., Yorba-Linda, Calif., 2006—. Bd. dirs. Equus II, Inc., Houston, Internat. Expert Sys. Inc., Houston, v.p. mktg. devel.; dir.-at-large Inst. for Ops. Rsch. and Mgmt. Scis., 1995; cons. in field. Author: How to Program a Computer, 1975, Organizational Processes, 1978. Com. chmn. United Way Tex. Gulf Coast, Houston, 1985-88. Fellow, Ford Found., 1966. Mem. Inst. for Ops. Rsch. and Mgmt. Scis. (bd. dirs. 1995, v.p. 1992-94), Am. Artificial Intelligence, Assn. for Computing Machinery, Acad. of Mgmt., Sigma Xi, Beta Gamma Sigma, Alpha Kappa Psi. Episcopalian. Avocations: golf, bicycling, jogging, painting, drawing. Home: 20465 Via Torralba Yorba Linda CA 92887 Office: Argyros Sch Bus Econs Chapman U 1 University Dr Orange CA 92866 Office Phone: 714-997-6537. Business E-Mail: tuggle@chapman.edu.

**TUGGLE, MARLA L.,** science educator; d. Ruth King, Bonnie King (Stepmother); m. Jeff Tuggle, July 2, 1988; children: Nicole Brady, Adam Brady, Thomas. BS in Zoology, Ea. Ill. U., Charleston, 1987; MS in Biology, Western Ill. U., Macomb, 1997. Cert. master tchr. in sci. NBPTS. Horticulture tng. supr. Springhill Nurseries and Brecks Bulbs of Holland, Peoria, Ill., 1988—89; sci. tchr. Richwoods H.S., Peoria, 1989—. Curriculum devel. Peoria Pub. Schs., 1998—2000, coord. of summer biology field trip, 2001, coord. for h.s. marine biology inst. field trip, 1996. Com. chair Boys Scout Troop, Edwards, Ill., 2004—06; Boy Scout merit badge counselor Heartland/WD Boyce Boy Scouts Am., Peoria, 2002—06. Named Inspirational Tchr., Western Ill. U., 1997, 1999; recipient Teacher's Rsch. fellowship, USDA, 1991. Avocations: scuba diving, stained glass. Office: Richwoods H S 6301 N University St Peoria IL 61614 Office Phone: 309-693-4400.

**TUITE, GERALD FRANCIS,** lawyer, commercial real estate manager; b. Rockford, Ill., Nov. 15, 1928; s. John Christopher and Mildred Tuite; m. Francine Lynn Williams, Aug. 2, 1980; children: Gregory, Gerald F., Michael, Tracy. Degree, Georgetown U., 1955; JD, Chgo. Kent Coll. Law, 1958. Bar: Ill. 1958. Sr. ptnr. Gerald Tuite & Assocs. Law Firm, Rockford, Ill., 1958—; asst. atty. gen. Ill., 1961—68. Spkr. in field. Vice chmn. Dem. Party, Ill., 1961—64, precinct committeeman; candidate State Atty., 1960. Cpl. U.S. Army, 1950—52, Korea. Recipient Svc. to Youth award, City and County Officials Rockford, Ill., 1960, Svc. award, Am. Legion, 1961, AFL-CIO Unions, 1980, 1986. Mem.: ATLA, ABA, Ill. Trial Assn., Ill. Bar Assn. Democrat. Roman Catholic. Avocations: travel, boating, swimming, golf, tennis. Office: Greg Tuite & Assocs 119 North Church St Rockford IL 61101 Home: Embassy Club #604 1717 Gulf Shore Blvd N Naples FL 34102

**TUITELE, LUI,** school system administrator; b. Leone Village; BS in Biology, Truman State U., Mo.; MEd in Secondary Edn., Brigham Young U., EdD in Ednl. Leadership. Classroom tchr., Am. Samoa; high school principal Am. Samoa; asst. dir. edn. Am. Samoa Dept. Edn., dir. edn., 2003—. Program dir. Goals 2000, Teacher Cert.; dep. dir. Instrnl. Services. Mem.: Am. Samoa Humanities Coun. (chmn.), Bd. Higher Edn., Territorial Planning Commn., Coun. Chief State Sch. Officers. Office: Am Samoa Dept Edn Education Bldg PO Box 186 Pago Pago AS 96799 Office Phone: 684-683-5237. Office Fax: 684-633-4340. E-mail: luituitele@doe.as.

**TUKE, ROBERT DUDLEY,** lawyer, educator; b. Rochester, NY, Dec. 5, 1947; s. Theodore Robert and Doris Jean (Smith) T.; m. Susan Devereux Cummins, June 21, 1969; children: Andrew, Sarah. BA with distinction, U. Va., 1969; JD, Vanderbilt U., 1976. Bar: Tenn. 1976, U.S. Dist. Ct. (mid. dist.) Tenn. 1976, U.S. Ct. Appeals (6th cir.) 1976, U.S. Ct. Appeals (4th cir.) 1978, U.S. Ct. Appeals (fed. cir.) 1993, U.S. Supreme Ct. 1986, U.S. Ct. Internat. Trade 1993. Assoc. Farris, Warfield & Kanaday, Nashville, 1976—79, ptnr., 1980—94, Tuke Yopp & Sweeney, Nashville, 1994—99, Trauger, Ney & Tuke, Nashville, 2000—05, Trauger & Tuke, Nashville, 2006—. Adj. prof. law Vanderbilt U. Law Sch., Nashville; faculty PLI, 1995—. Author: (with others) Tennessee Practice, 1992—; editor-in-chief Vanderbilt Law Rev.; contbr. articles to profl. jours. Mem. Tenn. Adoption Law Study Commn., 1993-96, Metro CATV Com.; chmn. Tenn. Dem. Party, 2005-. Capt. USMC, 1969-73. Decorated Cross of Gallantry; Patrick Wilson Merit scholar. Mem. ABA, Am. Health Law Assn., Nat. Assn. Bond Lawyers, Am. Acad. Adoption Attys. (past pres.), Tenn. Bar Assn., Nashville Bar Assn., Order of Coif. Democrat. Episcopalian. Avocations: rowing, running, bicycling, hiking, travel. Office: 222 4th Ave N Nashville TN 37219-2115 Office Phone: 615-327-9779. Business E-Mail: tuke@tndp.org.

**TULAFONO, TOGIOLA T.A.,** governor; b. Aunu'u Island, American Samoa, Feb. 28, 1947; s. Aitu and Silika (Vaatu'itu'i) T.; m. Maryann Taufaasau Mauga, Sept. 17, 1984; children: Puataunofo, Olita, Chelianne, Emema, Timoteo, Rosie. Grad., Honolulu Police Acad., 1967; BA, Chadron State Coll., 1970; JD, Washburn U., 1975. Bar: Kans., Am. Samoa. Police instr. Am. Samoa Police Dept., Pago Pago, 1967; adminstrv. asst. Sec. of Samoan Affairs, Pago Pago, 1970-71; legal asst. Atty. Gen., Pago Pago, 1971-72; assoc. Law Offices of George A. Wray, Pago Pago, 1975-77; v.p. South Pacific Island Airways, Pago Pago, 1977-79; judge Dist. Ct. of Am. Samoa, Pago Pago, 1979-80; chmn. bd. dirs. Am. Samoa Power Authority, Pago Pago, 1978-80; mem. Am. Samoa Senate, Pago Pago, 1981-85, 89—; pres. Nayram Samoa, Ltd., Pago Pago, 1985-88; lt. gov. Am. Samoa Pago Pago, 1997—2003; gov. Am. Samoa, 2003—. Chmn. Senate Investigation Com., 1993—. Chmn. Bd. Higher Edn., Am. Samoa, 1993—; bd. dirs. Am. Samoa Jr. Golfers' Assn.; deacon Sailele Congrl. Ch. Mem. ATLA, Am. Samoa Bar Assn., Kans. Bar Assn., Samoa Profl. Golfer's Assn. (pres. 1985-87), Am. Samoa Golf Assn. (pres.). Democrat. Congregationalist. Office: Office of the Gov Ter of American Samoa Pago Pago AS 96799 Office Phone: 684-633-4116. Office Fax: 684-633-2269.*

**TULAIMAT, AIMAN,** physician; MD, Damascus U., 1994. Bd. cert. in internal medicine ABIM, 1999, bd. cert. in pulmonary disease ABIM, 2002, bd. cert. in critical care medicine ABIM, 2003, cert. in sleep medicine ABSM, 2003. Sr. physician John H Stroger Hosp. Cook County, Chgo., 2002—. Dir. Turath, Chgo., 2005—06. Mem.: ATS. Office Phone: 312-864-7372.

**TULCHIN, DAVID BRUCE,** lawyer; b. NYC, Dec. 2, 1947; s. Philip Tulchin and Mary (Weiner) Black; m. Nora Barrett, Aug. 20, 1972; children: Rachel, Daniel, Laura. BA, U. Rochester, 1970; JD, Harvard U., 1973. Bar: N.Y. 1974, U.S. Dist. Ct. (so. & ea. dists.) N.Y. 1975, U.S. Ct. Appeals (2d cir.) 1975, U.S. Supreme Ct. 1977, U.S. Ct. Appeals (5th cir.) 1978, U.S. Ct. Appeals (1st & 6th cirs.) 1984, U.S. Dist. Ct. (no. dist.) Ohio 1984, U.S. Ct. Appeals (3d, 4th & Fed. cirs.) 1988, U.S. Ct. Appeals (7th cir.) 1991, U.S. Dist. Ct. (we. dist.) N.Y., 1996. Law clk. to judge Frederick V.P. Bryan U.S. Dist. Ct. So. Dist. N.Y., N.Y.C., 1973-75; assoc. Sullivan & Cromwell, N.Y.C., 1975-82, ptnr., 1982—. Fellow Am. Coll. Trial Lawyers; mem. ABA, Assn. Bar City N.Y., Fed. Bar Coun., N.Y. State Bar Assn., Fed. Cir. Bar Assn. Office: Sullivan & Cromwell 125 Broad St Fl 28 New York NY 10004-2489

**TULL, C. THOMAS,** investment advisor; b. Dayton, Ohio, Sept. 5, 1946; s. James Theron and Emma Louise (Geppinger) T.; m. Carole Lynn Thoryk, June 20, 1970; children: Christopher James, Matthew Thomas. BS, Ohio State U., 1971; MBA, Xavier U., 1975. Chartered fin. analyst. Asst. trust investment officer Nat. City Bank, Cleve., 1973-75; dir. investments Cleve.-Cliffs Iron Co., 1975-83; v.p. Western Res. Capital Mgmt., Inc., Cleve., 1983-87, Dallas, 1987-90, 1984-87; dir. employee benefit fund investments LTV Corp., Dallas, 1987-90; pres. Tull, Doud, Marsh & Triltsch, Inc., Dallas, 1990—2001; founding ptnr., mng. dir. Gulfstream Global Investors, Ltd., Dallas, 1990—2001; founding ptnr Tull Global Investors, L.P., 2002—. Vis. lectr. Cleve. State U., 1980-83. Sgt. U.S. Army, 1964-67. Mem. CFA Inst., Dallas Soc. Fin. Analysts, Inst. Chartered Fin. Analysts. Avocations: reading, travel, investing. Personal E-mail: ttull4@aol.com.

**TULL, THERESA ANNE,** retired diplomat; b. Runnemede, N.J., Oct. 2, 1936; d. John James and Anna Cecelia (Pauli) T. BA, U. Md., 1972; MA, U. Mich., 1973; postgrad., Nat. War Coll., Washington, 1980. Fgn. svc. officer Dept. State, Washington, 1963, Brussels, 1965-67, Saigon, 1968-70; dep. prin. officer Am. Consulate General, Danang, Vietnam, 1973-75; prin. officer Cebu, Philippines, 1977-79; dir. office human rights, 1980-83; charge d'affaires Am. Embassy, Vientiane, Laos, 1983-86; Dept. State Senior Seminar, 1986-87; ambassador to Guyana, 1987-90; diplomat-in-residence Lincoln U., Pa., 1990-91; dir. office regional affairs, bur. East Asian & Pacific affairs Dept. State, Washington, 1991-93; amb. to Brunei Bandar Seri Begawan, 1993-96. Recipient Civilian Service award Dept. of State, 1970, Superior Honor award, 1977 Mem. Am. Fgn. Svc. Assn., Women's Civic Club. Address: 3500 Boardwalk Apt 726N Sea Isle City NJ 08243

**TULL, WILLIS CLAYTON, JR.,** retired librarian; b. Crisfield, Md., Feb. 22, 1931; s. Willis Clayton and Agnes Virginia (Milbourne) T.; m. Taeko Itoi, Dec. 18, 1952. Student U. Balt., 1948, Johns Hopkins U., 1956; BS, Towson State Coll., Md., 1957; MLS, Rutgers U., 1962; postgrad., Miami U., Oxford, Ohio, 1979. Editl. clk. 500th Mil. Intelligence Svc. Group, 1952-53; tchr. Hereford Jr.-Sr. H.S., Parkton, Md., 1957-59; aide Enoch Pratt Free Libr., Balt., 1959-61, profl. asst., 1962-64; coord. adult svcs. Washington County Free Libr., Hagerstown, Md., 1964-67; asst. regional libr. Eastern Shore Regional Libr., Salisbury, Md., 1967; br. libr. Balt. County Pub. Libr., Pikesville, Md., 1968-71, asst. area br. libr. Essex, Md., 1971-72, sr. info. specialist Catonsville, Md., 1972-87, on-line sevr. Towson, Md., 1988-89, sr. info. specialist Reisterstown, Md., 1989-90; exec. dir. Milbourne and Tull Rsch. Ctr., 1991—2002; ret. Contbr. to profl. and geneal. jours. Mem. Rep. Ctrl. Com. Baltimore County, 1971-72. With U.S. Army, 1944-52. Fellow Nat. Congress Patriotic Orgns.; mem. Freedom To Read Found., Md. Libr. Assn. (chmn. intellectual freedom com. 1969-70), Friends Johns Hopkins U. Librs., Md. Assn. for Adult Edn. (coord. Western Md. region 1965-67), Am. Coun. Trustees and Alumni, Am. Acad. Religion, Ctr. for Theology and the

Natural Scis., Metaphys. Soc. Am., Nat. Assn. Scholars, Woodrow Wilson Internat. Ctr. for Scholars, Assn. for Asian Studies, World Future Soc., Freedom House, Internat. Rescue Com., Nature Conservancy, Unitarian Universalist Hist. Soc, Unitarian and Universalist Geneal. Soc. (founder, bd. dirs. 1971-87), Md. Geneal. Soc., Royal Soc. St. George, Sons and Daus. Pilgrims, Descs. Early Quakers, SAR, Soc. War of 1812, Ancient and Hon. Mech. Co. Balt., Rutgers Club, Kappa Delta Pi. Home: 800 Southerly Rd Apt 414 Towson MD 21286-8407 Business E-Mail: wctulljr@bcpl.net.

**TULLER, HARRY LOUIS,** materials scientist; BS, Columbia U., 1966, MS, 1967, DSc in Engring., 1973. Rsch. assoc. physics Technion, Haifa, Israel, 1974-75; from asst. to assoc. prof. materials sci. and engring. MIT, Cambridge, 1975-81, prof. materials sci. and engring., 1981—; dir. Crystal Physics and Electroceramics Lab., Cambridge, 1985—. Vis. prof. U. Pierre et Marie Curie, Paris, 1990; faculty chair Sumitomo Electric Industries, 1992-98, co-founder Boston Micro Sys., Woburn, Mass, organized Internat. Conf. on Electroceramics, 2003. Co-editor: High Temperature Superconductors, 1988, Electroceramics and Solid State Ionics, 1988, Science and Technology of Fast Ion Conductors, 1989, Sold State Ionics, 1992, Interfacially Controlled Functional Materials: Electrical and Chemical Properties, 2000, Oxygen Ion and Mixed Conductors and Their Technological Applications, 2000; series editor: Electronic Materials: Science and Technology; editor-in-chief Jour. Electroceramics. Fulbright travel grantee, 1990, Alexander von Humboldt fellow, 1997; F.H. Norton award, 2005. Fellow Am. Ceramic Soc. (N.E. chair 1983); mem. IEEE, Electrochem. Soc. (co-organizer 1st, 2d and 3d internat. symposium ionic and mixed conducting ceramics 1991, 94, 97, co-organizer 1997 NATO/ASI Oxygen Ion & Mixed Conductors Summer Sch.), Materials Rsch. Soc. Avocations: photography, gardening. Office: MIT 77 Massachusetts Ave Rm 13-3126 Cambridge MA 02139-4307 Business E-Mail: tuller@mit.edu.

**TULLIS, EDWARD LEWIS,** retired bishop; b. Cin., Mar. 9, 1917; s. Ashar Spence and Priscilla (Daugherty) T.; m. Mary Jane Talley, Sept. 25, 1937; children: Frank Loyd, Jane Allen (Mrs. William Nelson Offutt IV); m. Katharine Crum Irwin, Sept. 4, 1997. AB, Ky. Wesleyan Coll., 1939, LHD, 1975; BD, Louisville Presbyn. Theol. Sem., 1947; DD, Union Coll., Barbourville, Ky., 1954, Wofford Coll., 1976; LHD, Claflin Coll., 1976, Lambuth Coll., 1984. Ordained to ministry Methodist Ch., 1941; service in chs. Frenchburg, Ky., 1937-39, Lawrenceburg, Ky., 1939-44; asso. pastor 4th Ave. Meth. Ch., Louisville, 1944-47, Irvine, Ky., 1947-49; asso. sec. ch. extension sect. Bd. Missions, Meth. Ch., Louisville, 1949-52; pastor First Meth. Ch., Frankfort, Ky., 1952-61, Ashland, Ky., 1961-72; resident bishop United Meth. Ch., Columbia, SC, 1972-80, Nashville area, 1980-84, ret., 1984. Instr. Bible Ky. Wesleyan Coll., 1947-48; instr. Louisville Presbyn. Theol. Sem., 1949-52; mem. Meth. Gen. Conf., 1956, 60, 64, 66, 68, 70, 72, Southeastern Jurisdictional Conf., 1952, 56, 60, 64, 68, 72, bd. mgrs. Bd. Missions, 1962-72, mem. bd. discipleship, 1972-80, v.p. Gen. Coun. on Fin. and Adminstrn., 1980-84; Chaplain Ky. Gen. Assembly, 1952-61; chmn. Frankfort Com. Human Rights, 1956-61, Mayor's Adv. Com. Human Rels., Ashland, 1968-72. Author: Shaping the Church from the Mind of Christ, 1984, The Birth of the Book: A Study in the Origin and Growth of the Bible, 1998. Contbr. articles to religious jours. Sec., bd. dirs. Magee Christian Edn. Found.; trustee Emory U., 1973-80, Alaska Meth. U., 1965-70, Ky. Wesleyan Coll., Martin Coll., Lambuth Coll., McKendree Manor, Meth. Hosps., Memphis, Lake Junaluska Assembly, 1966-88; chair adv. bd. Found. for Evangelism, United Meth. Ch., 1991—. Recipient Outstanding Citizen award Frankfort VFW, 1961, Mayor's award for outstanding svc. Ashland, 1971, Heroes, Sts. and Legends award, Wesley Meth. Village Ky., 1997, Chief Junaluska award Lake Junaluska Assembly, 1998, Outstanding Alumnus award Ky. Wesleyan Coll., 2000, Disting. Alumnus award Louisville Presbyn. Sem., 2002; named to Ky. Wesleyan Coll. Hall of Fame, 2004. Mem.: Kiwanis. Methodist. Home: 510 Crum Dr Lake Junaluska NC 28745 E-mail: etullis1@mindspring.com.

**TULLMAN, GLEN,** management consultant; BA in Economics and Psychology, Bucknell U., 1981; Masters in Social Anthrop., Oxford U., Eng. With CCC Info. Svcs. Group, 1983—94; CEO Enterprise Sys., Inc., 1994—97, Allscripts Healthcare Solutions Inc., Libertyville, Ill., 1997—, chmn., 2001—. Capital campaign chmn. Juvenile Diabetes Rsch. Found. Ill. Chap. Office: Allscripts Healthcare Solutions Inc 2401 Commerce Ave Libertyville IL 60048

**TULLY, CATHERINE T.,** lawyer; b. N.Y., Aug. 22, 1953; d. Charles S. and Julia T. Tully; m. Jack Dierks, June 21, 1975; children: Erin Tully Dierks, Stephen Tully Dierks, Caitlin Tully Dierks. BA, Valparaiso U., Valparaiso, Ind., 1975; JD, Marquette U. Law Sch., Milw., Wis., 1978. Atty. Riordan, Crivello & Carlson, Milw., 1978—83; atty./shareholder Habush Habush & Rottier, Milw., 1983—. Sch. coun. Elm Creative Arts Sch., Milw., 1991—97, Roosevelt Mid. Sch. for the Arts, Milw., 1996—2000; jr. class parents/parents assoc/athletic assoc/fine arts assoc Divine Savior Holy Angels HS, Milw., 1997—2006; parents assoc Marquette U. HS, Milw., 2000—04; mgr. Milw. Kickers Soccer, Milw., 1991—99, Little League, Milw., 1995—2000; trinity booster club Trinity Acad. of Irish Dance, Milw., 1996—2005; core team coord. Milw. Inner City Congregations Allied for Hope, Milw., 1986—93; social concerns com. Holy Angels Congreation, Milw., 1985—93, All Saints Congregation, Milw., 1993—2006. Mem.: ABA, Am. Assn. of Trial Lawyers, Wis. Assoc of Trial Lawyers, Milw. Bar Assn., Wis. Bar Assn. Avocation: quilting. Office: Habush Habush & Rottier SC 777 E Wis Ave Ste 2300 Milwaukee WI 53202 Office Phone: 414-271-0900. Business E-Mail: ctully@habush.com.

**TULLY, DARROW,** newspaper publisher; b. Charleston, W.Va., Feb. 27, 1932; s. William Albert and Dora (McCann) T.; m. Victoria Lynn Werner; children: Bonnie Tully Paul Michael Andrew. Student, Purdue U., 1951, BA in Journalism, St. Joseph's Coll., 1972; PhD in Journalism (hon.), Calumet Coll., Ind., 1975. V.p., gen. mgr. Stus. WDSM-AM-FM and WDSM-TV, Duluth, Minn., 1956-59; bus. mgr. Duluth Herald & News Tribune, 1960-62; gen. mgr. Duluth Paul Dispatch & Pioneer Press, 1962-66; pub. Gary (Ind.) Post-Tribune, 1966-73; v.p., pub. Wichita (Kans.) Eagle & Beacon, 1973-75; pres. San Francisco Newspaper Agy., 1975-78; exec. v.p., pub. Arizona Republic & Phoenix Gazette, 1978-85; editor, pub., chief exec. officer Ojai (Calif.) Valley News, 1987-90; pres., pub., CEO Beacon Comms., Acton, Mass., 1990-92; asst. to pres. newspaper divsn. Chronicle Pub. Co., 1992-94. Author: Minority Representation in the Media, 1968. Trustee Calumet Coll. Recipient Disting. Achievement award Ariz. State U., 1982, Disting. Journalist award No. Ariz. U./AP, 1983, 1st Pl. Editorial Writing award Ariz. Planned Parenthood, 1983. Mem. Am. Soc. Newspaper Editors, Soc. Profl. Journalists. Office: 9862 Bridgeton Dr Tampa FL 33626-1802 Office Phone: 813-926-9709. Personal E-mail: dtully1@tampabay.rr.com.

**TULLY, HERBERT BULLARD,** chemical manufacturing executive; b. Glen Ridge, NJ, Sept. 3, 1943; s. Richard Golfe and Marie Foster (Towne) T.; m. Nancy Dee Zook, Dec. 22, 1967; children: Kimberly, Christine, Gregory. BS, U. Calif., Berkeley, 1967. Mem. fin. mgmt. staff Gen. Electric Co., San Jose, Calif., 1967-70, mem. corp. audit staff Schenectady, N.J., 1970-73, mgr. acct. dept. San Leandro, Calif., 1973-75; mgr. audit dept. Am. Express Co., Fireman's Fund, San Francisco, 1975-77; asst. controller Fireman's Fund Ins. Co., San Francisco, 1977-81; controller Wilbur-Ellis Co., San Francisco, 1981-86, asst. treas., 1986-89, vp treas., 1989—2000, CEO, pres., 2000—. Bd. dirs. Overseas Cos., San Francisco. Roman Catholic. Office: Wilbur Ellis 345 California Street Flr 27 San Francisco CA 94104

**TULLY, JOHN CHARLES,** research chemical physicist; b. NYC, May 17, 1942; s. Harry V. and Pauline (Fischer) T.; m. Mary Ellen Thomsen, Jan. 23, 1971; children: John Thomsen, Elizabeth Anne, Stephen Thomsen. BS, Yale U., 1964; PhD, U. Chgo., 1968. NSF postdoctoral fellow U. Colo. and Yale U., 1968-70; mem. tech. staff AT&T Bell Labs., Murray Hill, NJ, 1970-82, disting. mem. tech. staff, 1982-85, head physics chemistry rsch. dept., 1985-90, head materials chem. rsch. dept., 1990-96; Kemp prof. dept. chemistry, physics and applied physics Yale U., New Haven, 1996—. Vis. prof.

Princeton (N.J.) U., 1981-82, Harvard U., Cambridge, Mass., 1991. Contbr. articles to sci. jours.; author, prodr. movie Dynamics of Gas-Surface Interactions, 1979. NSF predoctoral fellow, 1965-68. Fellow AAAS, Am. Phys. Soc. (chem. physics exec. com. 1983-86), Am. Acad. Arts & Scis.; mem. Am. Chem. Soc. (chmn. theoretical chemistry subdiv. 1991-92, phys. chemistry divsn. 1993-94, Peter Debye award 1995, Madison Marshall award 1999, Theoretical Chemistry award 2004), NAS, Internat. Acad. Quantum Molecular Scis., Conn. Acad. Sci. and Engring., Sigma Xi. Achievements include patent on Method and Apparatus for Surface Characterization Utilizing Radiation from Desorbed Particles; fundamental theoretical contributions towards atomic level understanding of chemical reaction dynamics. Office: Yale Univ Dept Chemistry PO Box 208107 New Haven CT 06520-8107

**TULLY, ROBERT GERARD,** lawyer; b. Dubuque, Iowa, Sept. 7, 1955; s. Thomas Alois and Marjorie May (Fosselman) T. BA, U. Notre Dame, 1977; postgrad., U. Notre Dame, London, summer 1979; JD, Drake U., 1981. Bar: Iowa 1981, U.S. Dist. Ct (no. and so. dists.) Iowa 1981, U.S. Ct. Appeals (8th cir.) 1981, U.S. Supreme Ct. 1986. Assoc. Verne Lawyer & Assocs., Des Moines, 1981-93, Michael J. Galligan Law Firm; ptnr. Galligan, Tully, Doyle & Reid P.C., 1993, Anderson & Tully. Bd. dirs. Dubuque Lumber Co., sec., treas., 1984-87; lectr. Nat. Collegiate Mock Trial Drake U., Des Moines, 1984-93, atty., coach, 1985-93; bd. counselors Drake U. Law Sch., 1986-92, chmn. alumni rels. com. Contbr. articles to profl. jours. Com. mem. Dubuque County Dem. party, 1976-78, Polk County Dem. party, 1982-83, 87-89, 92—, del. state convs., 1988, chmn. IA Dem. Party. 1999—; bd. dirs. nat. Coun. Alcoholism and Other Drug Dependencies for Des Moines Area, pres. 1985-92; mem. nat. commn. on future of Drake U.; Dem. candidate for U.S. Congress 2d Dist., 1998; chmn. Iowa Dem., 1999-2001. Fellow Iowa Acad. Trial Lawyers (compiler various profl. pubs.); mem. ABA, ATLA (state del. 1991—, bd. govs. 1993—, mem. key peron com.), Iowa Bar Assn. (Uniform Jury Instructions rules com., young lawyers sect., com. legal svcs. for elderly chmn. fed. practice com., law related edn. com.), Assn. Trial Lawyers Iowa (pres. 1992-93, pres.-elect 1993-94, v.p. legis. 1988-91, bd. govs. 1985—, Outstanding Key Person 1983-84, 91-92, chmn. key person com. 1985-88), Polk County Bar Assn. (bd. dirs. 1993—, grievance com.), Iowa Citizens Action Network (bd. dirs. 1989-98), Blackstone Inn of Ct., Notre Dame Club of Des Moines (pres. 1981-83), Drake Student Bar Assn. (pres. 1980-81), Phi Alpha Delta. Roman Catholic. Home: 4315 Greenwood Dr Des Moines IA 50312 Office: Anderson and Tully 700 W Towers 1200 Valley West Dr West Des Moines IA 50266-1908 E-mail: tully@andersontullylaw.com.*

**TULLY, SUSAN BALSLEY,** pediatrician, educator; b. San Francisco, July 12, 1941; d. Gerard E. Balsley Sr. and Norma Lilla (Hand) Carey; m. William P. Tully, June 19, 1965; children: Michael William, Stephen Gerard. BA in Premed. Studies, UCLA, 1963, MD, 1966. Diplomate Am. Bd. Pediat. with subsplty. in pediatric emergency medicine. Intern L.A. County-U. So. Calif. Med. Ctr., 1966-67, jr. resident pediat., 1967-68; staff pediatrician, part-time Permanente Med. Group, Oakland, Calif., 1968; sr. resident pediat. Kaiser Found. Hosp., Oakland, 1968-69, Bernalillo County Med. Ctr., Albuquerque, 1969-70, chief resident pediatric outpatient dept., 1970; instr. pediat., asst. dir. outpatient dept. U. N.Mex. Sch. Medicine, Albuquerque, 1971-72; asst. prof. pediat., dir. ambulatory pediat. U. Calif., Irvine, 1972-76, asst. prof. clin. pediat., vice chair med. edn., 1977-79; staff pediatrician Ross-Loos Med. Group, Buena Park, Calif., 1976-77; assoc. prof. clin. pediat. and emergency medicine U. So. Calif. Sch. Medicine, 1979-86; dir. pediatric emergency dept. L.A. County/U. So. Calif. Med. Ctr., 1979-87; prof. clin. pediat. and emergency medicine U. So. Calif. Sch. Medicine, 1986-89; dir. ambulatory pediat. L.A. County/U. So. Calif. Med. Ctr., 1987-89; clin. prof. pediat. UCLA, 1989-93, vice chair pediat., 1996-97, prof. clin. pediat., 1993-97, prof. emeritus, 1997—; dir. ambulatory pediat. Olive View-UCLA Med. Ctr., 1989-96, chief pediat., 1996-97, cons. pediatrician, 1997—. Mem. survey team pediatric emergency svcs. L.A. Pediatric Soc., 1984—86; mem. adv. bd. preventive health project univ. affiliated program Children's Hosp. L.A., 1981—83; lectr. nursing pediat. nurse practitioner program Calif. State U., L.A., 1997—; pediat. toxicology cons. L.A. County Regional Poison Control Ctr. Med. Adv. Bd., 1981—97; clin. faculty rep. pediatric advancement and promotion com. UCLA Sch. Medicine, 1992—93; pediatric liaison dept. emergency medicine Olive View/UCLA Med. Ctr., 1989—96, dir. lead poisoning clinic, 1993—99; mem. quality assurance com. Los Angeles County Cmty. Health Plan, 1986—89. Author: (with K.E. Zenk) Pediatric Nurse Practitioner Formulary, 1979; (book chpt. with W.A. Wingert) Pediatric Emergency Medicine: Concepts and Clinical Practice, 1992, 2d edit., 1997; (with others) Educational Guidelines for Ambulatory/General Pediatrics Fellowship Training, 1992, Physician's Resource Guide for Water Safety Education, 1994; reviewer Pediatrics, 1985-89; editl. cons. Advanced Pediatric Life Support Course and Manual, 1988-89, Archives of Pediatrics and Adolescent Medicine, 1996-2001; dept. editor Pediatric Pearls Jour. Am. Acad. Physician Assts., 1989-94; tech. cons., reviewer Healthlink TV Am. Acad. Pediatrics, 1991; reviewer Pediatric Emergency Care, 1992—; question writer sub-bd. pediatric emergency medicine Am. Bd. Pediatrics, 1993-98; assoc. editor: Curriculum for the Training of General Pediatricians, 1996; cons. to lay media NBC Nightly News, Woman's Day, Sesame Street Parents, Parenting, Los Angeles Times; author numerous abstracts; contbr. articles to profl. jours. Cons. spl. edn. programs Orange County Bd. Edn., 1972-79; mem. Orange County Health Planning Coun., 1973-79; co-chairperson Orange County Child Health and Disability Prevention Program Bd., 1975-76; mem. Orange County Child Abuse Consultation Team, 1977-79; mem. project adv. bd. Family Focussed "Buckle Up" Project, Safety Belt Safe, U.S.A., 1989-96. Fellow Am. Acad. Pediat. (life, active numerous sects. and coms., active Calif. chpt.); mem. Ambulatory Pediatric Assn., L.A. Pediatric Soc. (life). Democrat. Avocations: art needlework, reading. Office: Olive View UCLA Med Ctr Pediatrics 3A108 14445 Olive View Dr Sylmar CA 91342-1495 Personal E-mail: SBTully@aol.com.

**TULLY, THOMAS ALOIS,** building materials executive, consultant, educator; b. Dubuque, Iowa, Nov. 11, 1940; s. Thomas Aloysius and Marjorie Mae (Fosselman) T.; m. Joan Vonnetta Dubay, Nov. 30, 1963; children: Thomas Paul, Maureen Elizabeth. BA, Loras Coll., 1962; postgrad., Georgetown U., 1963-66; MPA, Harvard U., 1968. Mgmt. trainee Office of Sec. Def., Washington, 1962-63, fgn. affairs officer, 1963-70; v.p. Dubuque Lumber Co., 1970-84, pres., 1984-91, Tully's, 1991-92, LBM Mktg. Assocs., Inc., 1992—; gen. mgr. Kane How Appraisor Svcs., 2006—. Adj. instr. Divine Word Coll., 1971, Loras Coll., 1972; adj. instr. Clarke Coll., 1987-89, instr., 1989-91, asst. prof., 1992-97, chmn. dept. acctg. and bus., 1993-97, dir. small bus. inst., 1994-97; dir. MBA program U. Dubuque, 1997-2000; founder, exec. dir. Dubuque Area Com. on Fgn. Rels., 2001—, pres., 2002—; pres. Hills and Dales Child Devel. Ctr., Inc., 1992-96; trustee Alverno Apts., 1995-2001, pres., 1999-2001. Mem. Dubuque Human Rights Commn., 1974—75, chmn., 1975, Iowa State Com. for Employer Support of Guard and Res. Forces, 1988—, area chmn., 2000—05, Iowa state coord., 2004—; city councilman Dubuque, 1975—79; bd. dirs. League Iowa Municipalities, 1977—79; mayor City of Dubuque, 1978; vice chmn. Iowa Temporary State Land Preservation Policy Com., 1978—79; pres. N.E. Iowa Regional Coordinating Coun., 1985—93, East Ctrl. Intergovtl. Assn. Bus. Growth Inc., 1987—2002, chmn., 1993—2002; bd. dirs. Pvt. Industry Coun. of Dubuque and Delaware Counties, Inc., 1983—86; trustee Divine Word Coll., 1989—97; pres. Barn Cmty. Theatre, 1988—89; chmn. bd. trustees United Way Svcs. of Dubuque, 1990, campaign chmn., 1991, bd. mem., 1980—94; trustee Carnegie-Stout Pub. Libr., 2001—, pres., 2003—04. Recipient Meritorious Civilian Svc. award Sec. of Def., 1970, Gov.'s Vol. award, 1989. Mem. Nat. Lumber and Bldg. Material Dealers Assn. (exec. com. 1988-90), Iowa Lumbermen's Assn. (pres. 1984, chmn. legis. com. 1985-90), Northwestern Lumbermen's Assn. (bd. dirs. 1984-87, 2d v.p 1988, 1st v.p. 1989-90, pres. 1990-91). Democrat. Roman Catholic. Home: 838 Stone Ridge Pl Dubuque IA 52001-1362 Office: LBM Mktg Assocs 838 Stone Ridge Pl Dubuque IA 52001 Office Phone: 563-590-6565. E-mail: tully.thomas@alumni.ksg.harvard.edu.

**TULLYS, MARILYN STEEN,** retired elementary school educator; b. Alliance, Ohio, Feb. 28, 1938; d. Paul Clair and Edna Meryl (Malott) Steen; m. Joseph Preston Tullys (div. 1977); children: Steven Lawrence, Julie Ann

Tullys Kempthorne. BS, Kent State U., 1966, MA, 1969; postgrad., U. Akron, 1975—89; splty. degree in learning disability, Walsh U., 1979. Tchr. West Branch Dist., Alliance, 1958—66; asst. prof. Kent (Ohio) State U., 1969—77; tchr. coord. Alliance H.S., 1972—74; founding dir. Campus Child Care, Canton, Ohio, 1976—77; tchr. Canton City Schs., 1978—94. Cons. State of Ohio Dept. Edn., Columbus, 1974, Wonder World, Canton, 1990; missionary Interfaith Campus Ministry, Canton, 1976—77; designer, instr. Memoir Cir., Massillon, Ohio, 1977—2005. Author: (poems) Sabbatical, 1996 (Norma award Greater Canton Writers Guild, 2000), Between the Hours, 2001 (Shakespeare award Canton Poetry Soc., 2003), After School. Chair Unifying Ohio for Peace, Stark County, 1988—89; founder Malott Toy Librs., Stark County, 1991; benefactor Steen Gazebo at Silver Park, Alliance, 1991; campaign coord., mem. adv. bd. Stark County Regional Transit, 1997—2006; mem. Stark County Children's Advocacy and Adv. Bd., 1997; pres. Ohio Poetry Day, 1994—2006; trustee YWCA of Canton, 2000—06; past pres. Stark County Ret. Tchrs. Recipient commendation, Ohio Ho. of Reps., 1992, Gov.'s Leadership award, State of Ohio, 1992, award, State of Ohio Dept. Edn., 1993; scholar Soc. Vis. Scholars, Cambridge U., Eng., 1995. Mem.: AAUW (pres. Canton br. 2000—06), Mayor's Literacy Commn., Phi Delta Kappa, Kappa Delta Pi, Delta Kappa Gamma. Avocations: photography, Scrabble, contra dancing. Home: 3392 Brunnerdale NW Canton OH 44708

**TULSIANI, DAULATRAM P.,** biologist, researcher; s. Pridhandas D. and Bhagwani D. Tulsiani; m. Geneva K. Tulsiani, Dec. 28, 1946; 1 child, Ashok K. PhD, Allahabad U., India, 1968. Assoc. prof. Vanderbilt U., Nashville, 1989—95, prof., 1996—. Dir. glycoprotein core Vanderbilt U., Nashville, 1990—95. Editor: Introduction to Mammalian Reproduction. Grantee, NIH, 1989—. Mem.: Soc. Study Reproduction (life). Hindu. Home: 2131 Hartland Rd Franklin TN 37069 Office: Vanderbilt Univ 1161 21st Ave S Nashville TN 37232 Office Phone: 615-343-1993. Home Fax: 615-343-8806. Business E-Mail: daulat.tulsiani@vanderbilt.edu.

**TUMA, MYM,** sculptor, painter, educator; b. Berwyn, Ill., Sept. 23, 1940; d. William Anthony Thuma and Mabel Otradovec Thuma. BS, Northwestern U., 1959—62; MA in painting and philosophy, Stanford U., 1963—64; postgraduate study under Esteban Vicente, NYU, 1964—65. Cert. art tchr. NY, 1993. Tchr. State of Ill., 1972—73, The Clearing, Ellison Bay, Wis., 1978. Guest lectr. O'Keeffe Centennial Celebration Columbia Coll., SC, 1987, Bklyn. Mus., 1993. Exhibitions include Canyon Road Art Gallery, Sante Fe, 1971, Clayton-Liberatore Gallery, Bridgehampton, NY, 1992, Merchants Bank, So. Hero, Vt., 2005; artist (one-woman shows) Art League, La Grange, Ill., 1987, Edens Gallery, Columbia Coll., 1987, (prin. works) Pastel Drawings and Abstract Sculptured Paintings, (permanent collections) Hirshhorn Mus., Wash., Stanford Mus., Palo Alto, Calif.; author: Awakening the Spirit, 2001, The Shell Theory of the Sculptured Paintings, 2002, The Blue Planets, 2003, O'Keeffe & Me: Abstracts of Our Letters, 2004, Radiant Energy, 2005; exhibitions include Madelle H. Semerjian Gallery, Rogers Meml. Libr., 2006. Harley J. Earl scholar, art and arch. dept. Stanford U., 1963—64. Mem.: Nat. Mus. Women in Arts (charter mem.), Coll. Art Assn. Home: PO Box 549 Southampton NY 11969 Personal E-mail: okeeffeand-me.com.

**TUMA, STANISLAV JOSEF,** radiologist; b. Mělník, Czech Republic, Mar. 30, 1934; s. Josef and Marta (Panochová) T.; m. Vanda Langrová, May 10, 1954 (div. 1966); children: Zuzana, Ondřej, Magdalena; m. Jitka Fabichová, Nov. 2, 1990. MD, Charles U., Prague, Czech Republic, 1958, cert. pediat. I, 1962, cert. radiology I, 1964, CSc, 1970, cert. radiology II, 1971. Med. registrar Dist. Hosp., Šumperk, Czech Republic, 1958-60, Clinic of Pediat., Prague, 1960-64, X-Ray Dept., Prague, 1964-70; rsch.fellow Pediat. Cardiocenter, Prague, 1970-90; head Clinic Imaging Methods, Prague, 1990-99; head dept. rsch. and edn. Ministry Health Czech Republic, 2000—02. Prof. South Bohemian U., Ceske Budejovice, 2003. Editor: Congenital Anomalies, 1995, Dextrocardia, 1999; contbr. articles to profl. jours. Office: Clinic for Imaging Methods U Hosp Motol V Uvalu 84 CZ 150 06 Prague 5 Czech Republic Office Phone: 4202 244 38 101. E-mail: sttuma@volny.cz.

**TUMAS, MICHAEL B.,** lawyer; b. South Bend, Ind., Apr. 25, 1959; BA in Econs., SUNY, Binghamton, 1981; JD, U. Pa., 1984. Ptnr. Potter Anderson & Corroon LLP, Wilmington, Del. Office: Potter Anderson & Corroon LLP 1313 N Market St Wilmington DE 19801 Office Phone: 302-984-6029. Office Fax: 302-778-6029. E-mail: mtumas@potteranderson.com.

**TUMAY, MEHMET TANER,** geotechnical engineering educator, researcher; b. Feb. 2, 1937; came to U.S., 1959; s. Bedrettin and Muhteren (Uybadin) T.; m. Karen Nuttycombe, June 15, 1962; children: Peri, Suna. BSCE, Robert Coll. Sch. Engring., Istanbul, Turkey, 1959; MSCE, U. Va., 1961; postgrad., UCLA, 1963—64; PhD, Tech. U. Istanbul, 1971. Lic. civil engr. La., Ga., SC, Turkish Chamber of Civil Engring. Instr. civil engring. U. Va., Charlottesville, 1961-62; asst. prof. civil engring. U. Louisville, 1962-63; tchg. fellow UCLA, 1963-64; asst. prof. civil engring. Robert Coll. Sch. Engring., Istanbul, 1966-71; assoc. prof. dept. civil engring. Bogazici U., Istanbul, 1971-75; Ga. Gulf disting. prof. La. State U., Baton Rouge, 1976—; Fugro-Cesco postdoctoral rsch. fellow U. Fla., Gainesville, 1975-76. Adv. prof. U. Vicosa, Minas Gerais, Brazil, 1991—, Tongji U., Shanghai, 1991—; dir. geomechanics program NSF, Washington, 1990-94; dir. rsch. La. Transp. Rsch. Ctr., Baton Rouge, 1994-97; assoc. dean rsch. and grad. studies Coll. Engring., La. State U., 1997-2004; maitre de conferences Ecole Nationale des Ponts et Chaussees, Paris, 1980-94; geotech. cons. Sauti, Spa, Cons. Engrs., Italy, 1969-72, SOFRETU-RATP, Paris, 1972-73, D.E.A., Cons. Engrs., Istanbul, 1974-75, BOTEK, Ltd., Istanbul, 1973-76. Cons.-Engrs., Louisville, 1979-90, Fugro Gulf-Geogulf, Houston, 1980-83; cons. in field. Contbr. articles to profl. jours. AID scholar, 1975-76, French Military External Rels. scholar, 1982. Fellow: ASCE; mem.: ASTM, Transp. Rsch. Bd. of the Nat. Acads. (emeritus), Internat. Soc. Soil Mechanics and Found. Engring., Turkish Chamber Civil Engrs., Turkish Soil Mechanics Group, La. Engring. Soc., Am. Soc. Engring. Edn., Tau Beta Pi, Chi Epsilon, Sigma Xi. Home: 2217 Dove Hollow Dr Baton Rouge LA 70809-1275 Office: La State U Coll Engring Baton Rouge LA 70803-0001 Office Phone: 225-578-9165. Business E-Mail: mtumay@eng.lsu.edu.

**TUMBARELLO, PHILLIP A.,** lawyer; b. Bklyn., May 22, 1952; BA cum laude, SUNY, New Paltz, 1974; JD cum laude, St. John's U., 1979. Bar: NY 1980, US Dist. Ct. So., Ea., No. & We. Districts NY. Ptnr. Wilson, Elser, Moskowitz, Edelman & Dicker LLP, White Plains, NYC. Mem.: Indsl. Truck Assn. (lawyers com.), NY State Bar Assn. (com. on ins. negligence & compensation law). Office: Wilson Elser Moskowitz Edelman & Dicker LLP 3 Gannett Dr White Plains NY 10604 Office Phone: 914-323-7000 ext. 4343. Office Fax: 914-323-7001. Business E-Mail: tumbarellop@wemed.com.

**TUMEY, RITA MARIE,** retired middle school educator; b. Jackson, Mich., Nov. 2, 1947; d. Robert George and Felicia Marie (Dziesupek) Carlson; m. John Henry Tumey, Nov. 27, 1970; 1 child, Patrick Jacob. AD, Jackson Community Coll., 1967; BA, Mich. State U., 1969. Cert. elem. and secondary tchr. Tchr. 6th-8th grade social studies St. Mary Star of the Sea, Jackson, 1970-71; tchr. 5th and 6th grade math. and sci. St. Phillip Sch., Battle Creek, Mich., 1971-73; tchr. 5th-8th grade social studies and math. St. Stanislaus Kostka Sch., Jackson, 1973-75; tchr. 7th and 8th grade lang. arts Jackson Cath. Middle Sch., 1976-2004; ret.; pharmacy technician Foote Hosp., Jackson, Mich., 2006—. Roman Catholic. Avocations: reading, boating.

**TUMOLO, MICHAEL L.,** corporate lawyer; V.p., counsel Toys 'R' Us, Paramus, N.J., 1981—. Office: Toys R Us Inc One Geoffrey Way Wayne NJ 07470-2035 Office Phone: 973-617-5739. E-mail: tumolom@toysrus.com.

**TUNE, BRUCE MALCOLM,** pediatrics educator, renal toxicologist; b. NYC, Aug. 26, 1939; s. Buford M. and Sylvia Tune; m. Nancy Carter Doolittle, Sept. 13, 1969; children: Sara E., Steven M. AB, Stanford U., 1963, MD, 1965. Diplomate Am. Bd. Pediat., Am. Bd. Pediatric Nephrology, Nat. Bd. Med. Examiners. Intern in medicine and pediatrics Strong Meml. Hosp.,

Rochester, NY, 1965—66; rsch. assoc. Lab. Kidney and Electrolyte Metabolism, Nat. Heart Inst., NIH, Bethesda, Md., 1967—69, clin. assoc., 1968—69; resident in pediat. Stanford (Calif.) U. Sch. Medicine, 1966—67, chief resident, 1969—70, fellow in pediatric renal and metabolic disease, 1970—71, asst. prof. pediat., 1971—77, assoc. prof., 1977—83, prof., 1983—, acting chmn. dept., 1991—93, dir. pediatric nephrology, 1971—97, prof. pediat. divsn. pediatric nephrology, 1998—, now emeritus prof. pediat. divsn. pediatric nephrology. Attending physician, chief pediatric renal svcs. Stanford U. Hosp., Palo Alto, Calif., 1971—76, Children's Hosp. at Stanford, Palo Alto, 1971—91; cons. physician Santa Clara Valley Med. Ctr., San Jose, Calif., 1973—; attending physician, chief pediatric renal svcs. Lucile Salter Packard Children's Hosp. at Stanford, 1991—98, acting chief pediatric medicine, 1991—93, attending physician, 1997; mem. rev. panel internat. study kidney diseases in children N.Y.C. NIH, 1973—74; polycystic kidney disease study group, Albuquerque, 1984; mem. spl. study sect. on genetics and kidney maturation, Bethesda, Md., 92; cons. Lilly Rsch. Labs., Indpls., 1980, Merck Sharp and Dohme Labs., Rahway, NJ, 1980, Bristol Labs., Syracuse, NY, 1982, ICI Pharms., Cheshire, England, 1992, Gilead Scis., Foster City, Calif., 1993, Zeneca Pharms., Mereside, England, 1994—; organizing mem., chmn. session on antibiotics NIH and EPA Conf. on Nephrotoxicity of Drugs and Environ. Toxicants, Pinehurst, NC, 1981; co-dir. Coop. Study Therapy of Steroid-Resistant Focal Glomerulosclerosis in Children, 1988—; mem. rsch. grant rev. panel Ont. (Can.) Ministry Health, 1992—, Wellcome Trust, London, 1994—; reviewer bd. environ. studies and toxicology NRC, 1994. Editl. bd. Am. Jour. Kidney Diseases, 1981—94, guest editor Contemporary Issues in Nephrology, 1984, Jour. Am. Soc. Nephrology, 1991; contbr. articles to med. jours. Grantee NIH, 1974—77, 1979—83, 1985—89, 1990—95. Mem.: Am. Soc. Pharmacology and Exptl. Therapeutics, Am. Heart Assn. (coun. on kidney diseases, grantee 1985—88, 1989—92), Western Soc. for Pediatric Rsch., Internat. Pediatric Nephrology Assn., Am. Soc. Pediatric Nephrology (coun. 1978—82, rsch. subcom. 1993—), Internat. Soc. Nephrology, Am. Soc. Nephrology, Alpha Omega Alpha, Phi Beta Kappa. Office: Stanford U Sch Medicine Dept Pediatrics 300 Pasteur Dr Rm G306 Palo Alto CA 94304-2203

**TUNE, JAMES FULCHER,** lawyer; b. Danville, Va., May 13, 1942; s. William Orrin and Susan Agnes (Fulcher) T.; m. Katherine Del Mickey, Aug. 2, 1969; children: Katherine Winslow, Jeffrey Bricker. BA, U. Va., 1964; MA, Stanford U., 1970, JD, 1974. Bar: Wash. 1974, U.S. Dist. Ct. (we. dist.) Wash. 1974. Assoc. Bogle & Gates, Seattle, 1974-79, ptnr., 1980-99, head comml./banking dept., 1985-93, mng. ptnr., 1986-93, chmn., 1994-99; ptnr. Dorsey & Whitney LLP, Seattle, 1999-2001, Stoel Rives LLP, Seattle, 2001—05, Seattle mng. ptnr., 2002—05; pres., CEO ArtsFund, Seattle, 2006—. Bd. dirs. Keynetics Inc., Boise, Idaho, Click Sales Inc., Boise, Coloc8 Inc., Boise, Pay-Track Inc., Boise, Puget Sound Bank; chmn. Seattle-King City Econ. Devel. Coun., 1992. Chmn. Seattle Repertory Theatre, 1995, Corp. Coun. for the Arts, 2001—02, United Way King County, 2004. Lt. USN, 1964—69, Vietnam. Woodrow Wilson fellow, 1964, Danforth Found. fellow, 1964. Mem. ABA, Wash. State Bar Assn. (lectr. CLE 1976, 78, 84, 99, 02), Seattle C. of C. (vice chmn. City Budget Task Force 1980-82), Greater Seattle C. of C. (trustee 2006—), Ranier Club (trustee 2006—), Seattle Tennis Club, Phi Beta Kappa. Presbyterian. Office: ArtsFund PO Box 19780 10 Harrison St Ste 200 Seattle WA 98109 Office Phone: 206-386-7565, 206-281-9050. Business E-Mail: jimtune@artsfund.org. E-mail: jftune@stoel.com.

**TUNG, KO-YUNG,** lawyer; b. Peking, China, Feb. 20, 1947; came to U.S., 1964; s. Hung-Fang T. and Koichiro Tanaka; m. Alison Heydt, Feb. 2, 1975; children: Vanessa, Adrian, Cameron, Gregory. BA, Harvard U., 1970; JD, U. Tokyo, 1972. Bar: NY, 1972. Assoc. Debevoise & Plimpton, N.Y.C., 1973—76; ptnr. Tung, Drabkin & Boynton, N.Y.C., 1976—84, O'Melveny & Myers, N.Y.C., 1985—99; v.p., gen. counsel The World Bank, Washington, 1999—2003; sec.-gen. Internat. Ctr. Settlement Investment Disputes, Washington, 2000—03; sr. counsellor Morrison & Foerster, N.Y.C., 2003—. Adj. assoc. prof. sch. law NYU, 1974—88; vis. lectr. Yale Law Sch., 2003—. Mem. Coun. on Fgn. Rels., N.Y.C., 1986—, The Brookings Inst., 1999, Overseas Devel. Coun., Washington, 1999, The Japan Soc., 1990, Asia Soc., 1994-99, Presl. Commn. U.S. Pacific Trade Investment Policy, 1996-97, Trilateral Commn., N.Y.C., 1990-97; bd. govs. East West Ctr., Honolulu, 1990-99, 2003—, chmn., 1997-99; U.S. Nat. Commn. for Pacific Econ. Cooperation, 1991—; bd. dirs. Asian Am. Legal Def. and Edn. Fund, 1990-99, 2003—; vice chmn. adv. coun. Human Rights Watch/Asia, 1997-99, Am. Law Inst., 1997—. Fellow Harvard Law Sch., 1973. Mem. Am. Law Inst., Am. Arbitration Assn., Internat. Panel Arbitrators, Phi Beta Kappa. Office: Morrison & Foerster 1290 Avenue of the Americas New York NY 10104 Office Phone: 212-468-8055. Business E-Mail: Ktung@mofo.com.

**TUNG, PRABHAS,** plastic surgeon; b. Ubol, Thailand, Apr. 3, 1944; s. Sathee and Seng (Ngium) T.; m. Patarin C. Sinjin; children: Tony, Tommy. MD, Mahidol U., Bangkok, 1968. Diplomate Am. Bd. Plastic Surgery. Plastic surgeon pvt. practice, Flint, Mich., 1980-82, Sacramento, Calif., 1982—. Office: 2801 K St Ste 200 Sacramento CA 95816-5118

**TUNHEIM, JERALD ARDEN,** academic administrator, physicist, educator; b. Claremont, S.D., Sept. 3, 1940; s. Johannes and Annie Tunheim; children: Jon, Angie, Alec. BS in Engring. Physics, S.D. State U., 1962, MS in Physics, 1964; PhD in Physics, Okla. State U., 1968. Vis. scientist Sandia Corp., Albuquerque, 1970-71, Ames (Iowa) AEC Labs., 1972; asst. prof. S.D. State U., Brookings, 1968-73; assoc. prof., 1973-78, prof., 1978-80, prof., head physics dept., 1980-85; dean Ea. Wash. U., Cheney, 1985-87; pres. Dakota State U., Madison, S.D., 1987—. Bd. dirs. Nat. Skill Stds. Bd., 1998—. Co-author: Elementary Particles and Unitary Symmetry, 1966, Quantum Field Theory, 1966; contbr. articles to profl.jours. Bd. dirs. Lake Area Improvement Corp. Grantee USDA, 1987-88, S.D. Govt. Office Edn. Devel., 1988-89, U.S. Dept. Edn., Eisenhower Program, 1985-86, 87-90, 92-93, 95-96, U.S. Dept. Edn. Math. and Sci. Program, 1989-92; named Tchr. of Yr. S.D. State U., 1972. Mem. NSPE, Am. Phys. Soc., Am. Assn. Physics Tchrs., Madison C. of C. (bd. dirs. 1990—), Rotary. Republican. Lutheran. E-mail: Jerald.Tunheim@dsu.edu.

**TUNICK, MICHAEL HOWARD,** chemist; b. Phila., Dec. 18, 1954; s. Allan Charles and Bernice Marilyn (Gordon) T.; m. Gail Eileen Seltzer, Mar. 24, 1985; children: Daniel, Susan. BS, Drexel U., 1977; PhD, Temple U., 1985. Chemist USDA, Phila., 1977-85, rsch. chemist, 1985—. Evening faculty instr. St. Joseph's U., Phila., 1986-88. Recipient award for individual tech. accomplishment Phila. Fed. Exec. Bd., 1990, gold medal for group tech. accomplishment, 1994; Tech. Transfer award Agrl. Rsch. Svc., 1995. Mem. Thermal Analysis Forum of Delaware Valley (councilor 1992-96, v.p. 1997, pres. 1998), Am. Chem. Soc. (chmn. food and nutritional biochemistry subdivsn. agr. and food chem. divsn. 1996, chmn. agr. and food chem. divsn. 2001, sec. agr. and food chem. divsn. 2003—) Office Phone: 215-233-6454. Business E-Mail: michael.tunick@errc.ars.usda.gov.

**TUNNICLIFF, DAVID GEORGE,** civil engineer, consultant; b. Ord, Nebr., Sept. 18, 1931; s. George Thomas and Ada Ellen (Ward) Tunnicliff; m. Elaine Jean Interrante, Oct. 17, 1959 (div.); children: Martha Allison Tunnicliff Loeb, Vivian Jean; m. Joan Elizabeth Duchesneau, Oct. 25, 1975. BS, U. Nebr.-Lincoln, 1954; MS, Cornell U., Ithaca, NY, 1958; PhD, U. Mich., Ann Arbor, 1972. Registered profl. engr., Nebr., Mass. Engr. Nebr. Dept. Rds., Lincoln, 1954-60; from asst. prof. to assoc. prof. Wayne State U., Detroit, 1960-67; chief tech. svcs. Warren Bros. Co., Cambridge, Mass., 1967-79; prin., cons. engr. D.G. Tunnicliff, Cons. Engr., Omaha, 1979—. Contbr. articles to profl. jours. Rep. precinct del., Detroit, 1965—66. With U.S. Army, 1955—56. Mem.: ASCE, ASTM, Transp. Rsch. Bd. (com. chair 1983—89), Assn. Asphalt Paving Tech. (bd. dirs. 1976—78). Mem. Evangel. Covenant Ch. Home and Office: DG Tunnicliff Cons Engr 9624 Larimore Ave Omaha NE 68134-3038 Office Phone: 402-572-8955. Personal E-mail: dgtnnclff@aol.com.

**TUNUGUNTLA, HARI SIVA GURUNADHA RAO,** urologist; s. Arjuna Rao and Sundara Suseela Tunuguntla; m. Renuka Tunuguntla. B of Medicine & B of Surgery, Guntur Med. Coll., Andhra Pradesh, India, 1984; MS in Gen. Surgery, All India Inst. of Med. Scis., New Delhi, 1987; M Chirurgie in Urology, Postgraduate Inst. of Med. Edn. And Rsch., Chandigarh, India, 1995. Lic. Andhra Pradesh Med. Coun., Hyderabad, India, 1984, Tamil Nadu Med. Coun., Chennai (previously, Madras), India, 1993, cert. Ednl. Commn. for Fgn. Med. Grads., 1996, indefinite cert. Ednl. Commn. for Fgn. Med. Grads., 2002, application status letter Med. Bd. of Calif., 2002, temporary lic. for resident tng. program Commonwealth of Va., Bd. of Medicine, 2002, tng. lic. Fla. Bd. Medicine, 2003. Rotating intern Govt. Gen. Hosp. and Guntur Med. Coll., Andhra Pradesh, India, 1982—83; jr. resident in gen. surgery All India Inst. of Med. Scis., New Delhi, 1984—87; sr. resident and tchg. fellow, dept. of surgery, gastrointestinal surgery and liver transplantation All India Inst. Of Med. Scis., New Delhi, 1987—89; registrar, divsn. of surgery Kugler's Hosp., Guntur, Andhra Pradesh, India, 1990—92; registrar, dept. of urology and renal transplantation Christian Med. Coll. and Christian Med. Coll. Hosp., Vellore, Tamil Nadu, India, 1993; sr. resident, dept. of urology Postgraduate Inst. of Med. Edn. and Rsch., Chandigarh, India, 1993—95; sr. resident, tchg. fellow dept. of urology and renal transplantation SRI Venkateswara Inst. of Med. Scis., Tirupati, Andhra Pradesh, India, 1995—96, asst. prof., dept. urology and renal transplantation, 1997, Sanjay Gandhi Postgrad. Inst. of Med. Scis., Lucknow, Uttar Pradesh, India, 1997—99; rsch. fellow North Fla. Rsch. Inst., Gainesville, 2000—01; clin. fellow dept. of urology U. of Calif., Davis Sch. of Medicine, Sacramento, 2001—02; clin. fellow dept. urology U. Miami, Sch. Medicine, Fla., 2003—. Mem. editl. asst. Indian Jour. of Urology; reviewer: Indian Jour. Med. Scis., 2003; mem. working com. Nat. Med. Jour. of India, mem. internat. reviewers panel Med. Sci. Monitor;. co-author chpts. in 10 textbooks; contbr. articles to profl. jours. Mem., hosp. computerization com. Sanjay Gandhi Postgraduate Inst. of Med. Scis., Lucknow, Uttar Pradesh, India, 1997—99, mem., hosp. mortality com., 1999. Grantee Chakroborti Fellowship in Urology, U. of Calif., 1999; scholar In Urology, PFIZER, 2002; Intramural Rsch. Grant, Sanjay Gandhi Postgraduate Inst. of Med. Scis., India, Hargoving Meml. Traveling Fellowship, Urological Soc. of India, 1993. Mem.: AMA, Am. Urol. Surgeons, Soc. Internat. Urology, European Assn. Of Urology, Am. Urol. Assn. (corr.), North Zone Chpt. Of The Urol. Soc. Of India (life), Indian Soc. Of Organ Transplantation (life), Urolithiasis Soc. Of India (life Young Sci. Medallion award 1993), Urol. Soc. Of India (life), Alumni Assn. Of Guntur Med. Coll., India. Achievements include development of endoscopic injection sclerotherapy for radiation-induced hemorrhagic cystitis; research in clinicopathologic and molecular correlations in prostate cancer; etiopathogenesis of recurrent calcium oxalate urolithiasis; clinical management of upper gastrointestinal hemorrhage in a tropical country; the role of ultrasound vs. lithoclast (pneumolithotripsy) in ureteroscopic lithotripsy for ureteral calculi; the role of holmium laser in management of calcified ureteral stents; urodynamic evaluation of patients with chronic non-bacterial prostatitis; determination of optimal frequency of self-calibration of urethra to prevent recurrence of urethral strictures in men; long-term outcomes following open pyeloplasty for congenital ureteropelvic junction obstruction; metabolic and urodynamic evaluation of bowel segments incorporated in the urinary tract; metabolic abnormalities in patients with congenital ureteropelvic junction obstruction and ipsilateral renal calculi; duplex dopper ultrasonography vs. Mag-3 diuretic renogram vs. whitaker test in evaluation of equivocal ureteropelvic junction and ureterovesical junction obstruction; experimental induction and study of portal hypertension in rabbits; immunoglobulin abnormalities in oral cancer; kidney stones, a study of pattern of citrate excretion in normal healthy controls and calcium stone patients and the effect of potassium citrate treatment; interstim sacral neuromodulation for lower urinary tract dysfunction; sling surgery for female urinary incontinence; urethroplasty for male urethral strictures; urolithiasas urodynamics; urinary diversions. Home: 753 Classon Ave Apt 9K Brooklyn NY 11238-4698

**TUOHEY, CONRAD GRAVIER,** lawyer; b. Bklyn., Dec. 27, 1933; s. James L. and Rose Gravier Tuohey; m. Judith Octavia Jeeves, July 7, 1956; children: Octavia Jeeves, Heather Gravier, Meighan Judith, Caragh Rose. BA, George Washington U., 1957; JD, U. Mich., 1960. Bar: Calif. 1962, N.Y. 1980, D.C. 1980. Dir. Fed. Home Loan Bank, San Francisco, 1980—83; legal cons., counsel Calif. State Senate, 1981—87; counsel Senate Select com. Pacific Rim, 1986—87. Mem. Citizens adv. bd. Orange County Transit com., 1966—68; pres. Friends of Calif. State U., Fullerton, 1969—71, Calif. Alliance Ptnrs. Progress, 1969—72; mem. InterAm. bd. Ptnrs. Alliance Progress, 1969—72; mem. nat. bd. dirs., 1970—72. Contbr. articles to profl. jours. With U.S. Army, 1951—54, leader rifle squad. Decorated Combat Infantryman's badge, Korean Svc. medal with 3 battle stars. Mem.: N.Y. Bar Assn., D.C. Bar Assn., State Bar Calif., Phi Sigma Kappa, Phi Delta Phi. Home and Office: 23391 Rockrose Mission Viejo CA 92692-1686 E-mail: tuohey@lawyer.com.

**TUOHEY, MARK HENRY, III,** lawyer; b. Rochester, NY, Sept. 27, 1946; s. Mark Henry Tuohey; m. Martha Tuohey; children: Brendan, Sean, Devin. BA in History, St. Bonaventure U., 1968; JD, Fordham U., 1973. Bar: D.C. 1973, U.S. Supreme Ct. 1980, U.S. Ct. Appeals (D.C. cir.) 1974, U.S. Dist. Ct. D.C. 1974, N.Y. 1984. Asst. U.S. atty. U.S. Atty.'s Office, Washington, 1973-77; spl. trial counsel U.S. Dept. Justice, Washington, 1977-79; spl. counsel to U.S. Atty. Gen. Washington, 1979; co-adminstrv. ptnr. Washington office Vinson & Elkins, Washington; dep. ind. counsel Whitewater Investigation, 1994-95; spl. counsel D.C. City Coun. Investigation of Met. Police Dept., 1998. Trustee Cath. U. Am., 2002—, Washington Jesuit Acad., 1999—, Gonzaga Coll. H.S., 1993—2003. Served to 1st lt. U.S. Army, 1970—71. Master: Wm. Bryant Inn of Ct.; fellow: Am. Bar Found. (bd. dir. 1980—85), Am. Law Inst., Am. Coll. Trial Lawyers; mem.: ABA (chair standing com. on continuing edn. bar 1980—85, litig. sect. coun. 1980—90, mem. Am. Law Inst./ABA com. continuing profl. edn. 1983—), Bar Assn. D.C. (Lawyer of the Yr. 2001), Jud. Conf. US Ct. Appeals (DC cir.), DC Bar Found. (chair 1998—), DC Bar (bd. govs. 1988—94, pres. 1993—94), DC Sports and Entertainment Commission (chair 2003—). Home: 1655 Kalmia Rd NW Washington DC 20012-1125 Office: Vinson & Elkins The Willard Office Bldg 1455 Pennsylvania Ave NW Fl 7 Washington DC 20004-1013 Office Phone: 202-639-6660. Business E-Mail: mtuohey@velaw.com.

**TUPPER, LEON F.,** manufacturing executive; BS in Indsl. Psychology, Wayne State U.; MS in Indsl. Psychology, U. Mich.; postgrad., Dartmouth U. Tng. mgr. Am. Motors Corp., Detroit, 1972-77, buyer/procurement specialist, 1977-83, sr. buyer interior trim group, 1983-86, purchasing mgr. interior trim group, 1986-88; sales mgr. steering divsn. Sheller-Globe Corp., Toledo, Ohio, 1984-88; dir. sales and engring. Gilreath Mfg., Inc., Howell, Mich., 1988-91, pres., CEO, owner, 1991—. Trustee Cleary Coll., Ypsilanti, Mich.; treas., trustee High/Scope Edn. Rsch. Found.; bd. trustees Rehab. Inst. of Mich., Detroit Med. Ctr.; bus. sch. bd. exec. advisors Wayne State U.; mem. friends of the Detroit Area Pre-Coll. Engring. Program, Nat. Conf. for Cmty. Justice, 100 Black Men of Detroit. Address: PO Box 408 Howell MI 48844-0408 Fax: 248-728-1753.

**TURANO, DAVID A.,** lawyer; b. Ashtabula, Ohio, Sept. 9, 1946; s. Egidio A. and Mary Agnes (Bartko) T.; m. Karen J. Emmel, Aug. 29, 1970; children: Aaron, Thad, Bethen, Kyle. BS, Kent State U., 1968; JD, Ohio State U., 1971. Bar: Ohio 1971. Staff atty. The Pub. Utilities Commn. Ohio, Columbus, 1971-72; assoc., then ptnr. George, Greek, King, McMahon and McConnaughey, Columbus, 1972-79; ptnr. Baker & Hostetler, Columbus, 1979-96, Harris, Carter, Mahota, Turano & Mazza, Columbus, 1996-97, Harris, Turano & Mazza, Columbus, 1997—2003; of counsel Shoemaker, Howarth & Taylor, LLP, Columbus, 2003—. Mem. ABA, Ohio State Bar Assn., Columbus Bar Assn., Transp. Lawyers Assn. Roman Catholic. Office: Shoemaker Howarth & Taylor LLP 471 E Broad St Ste 2001 Columbus OH 43215 Office Phone: 614-232-0426. Business E-Mail: dturano@midohiolaw.com.

**TURBIDY, JOHN BERRY,** investor, management consultant; b. Rome, Ga., Oct. 18, 1928; s. Joseph Leo and Louyse (Berry) T.; m. Joan Marsales, Dec. 19, 1958 (dec.); children: John Berry, Trevor Martin; m. Jaquelin Lamond

Schulter, June 8, 1996 Grad., Darlington Sch., 1945; BA, Duke U., 1950; postgrad., NYU, 1952, Emory U., 1954-56. Various positions Lockheed Aircraft, Marietta, Ga., 1951-56; gen. mgmt. cons. McKinsey & Co., NYC and London, 1956—62; v.p. adminstrn. ITT Europe, Inc., Brussels, 1963, v.p., group exec. European consumer products, 1963—65, v.p., group exec. for No. Europe, 1965-67; corp. v.p. adminstrn. Celanese Corp., N.Y.C., 1967-68; pres., mng. dir. SIACE, S.P.A. subs., Milan, 1968-69; chmn. bd., pres. Vecta Group, Kalamazoo, 1970-74; sr. v.p. corp. devel. IU Internat. Corp., Phila., 1974-78, exec. v.p., 1978-83; pres., chief exec. officer Pitcairn Fin. Mgmt. Group, Jenkintown, Pa., 1984-90; chmn. Office John Turbidy, 1990-95; mng. dir. Friedman, Turbidy & Co., Inc., N.Y.C., 1995—2000. Bd. dirs. Statute of Liberty Ellis Island Found., chmn. 2004—. Served with USNR, 1952 Mem. Sea Island Club, Sea Bright Beach Club. Address: 113 Biltmore Saint Simons Island GA 31522 Personal E-mail: jbturb@hotmail.com.

**TURBIN, RICHARD,** lawyer; b. NYC, Dec. 25, 1944; s. William and Ruth (Fiedler) T.; m. Rai Saint Chu-Turbin, June 12, 1976; children: Laurel Mei, Derek Andrew. BA magna cum laude, Cornell U., 1966; JD, Harvard U., 1969. Bar: Hawaii 1971, U.S. Dist. Ct. Hawaii 1971. Asst. atty. gen., Western Samoa, Apia, 1969-70; dep. pub. defender Pub. Defender's Office, Honolulu, 1970-74; dir. Legal Aid Soc. Hawaii, Kaneohe, 1974-75; sr. atty., pres. Law Offices Richard Turbin, Honolulu, 1975—. Legal counsel Hawaii Crime Commn., 1980-81. Co-author: Pacific; author: Medical Malpractice, Handling Emergency Medical Cases, 1991; editor Harvard Civil Rights-Civil Liberties Law Rev., 1969. Legal counsel Dem. Party, Honolulu County, 1981-82; elected Neighborhood Bd., 1985, elected chair, 1990-97; bd. dirs. Hawaii chpt. ACLU, 1974-78, East-West Ctr. grantee, 1971, 72; commn. State of Hawaii Civil Rights com., 2002-05. Recipient Traphagen Disting. Alumnus award, Harvard Law Sch. Mem. ATLA, ABA (chair internat. torts and ins. practice section 1999-2000, governing coun., chair tort and ins. practice sect. 1999-2000), Hawaii Bar Assn. (pres. 2005), Hawaii Trial Lawyers Assn. (pres. 2002), Hawaii Jaycees (legal counsel 1981-82), Chinese Jaycees Honolulu (legal counsel 1980-81), Honolulu Tennis League (undefeated player 1983), Hawaii Harlequin Rugby Club (sec., legal counsel 1978-82), Pacific Club, Outrigger Canoe Club. Jewish. Home: 4817 Kahala Ave Honolulu HI 96816-5231 Office Phone: 808-528-4000. Personal E-mail: richturbin@aol.com.

**TURBOW, DAVID JOSEPH,** education educator, musician; b. Anaheim, Calif., July 2, 1969; s. Bernard A. and Phyllis Y. Turbow. BA, U. Calif. at Santa Barbara, 1991; MS, Calif. State U. at Fullerton, 1994; PhD, U. Calif. at Irvine, 2005. Sr. scientist Eisenberg Olivieri and Assoc., Oakland, Calif., 2003; asst. prof. health sci. Touro U. Internat., 2004—. Founder Onset Records, 1994. Contbr. articles to profl. jours. Adv. Surfrider Found., 1992—. Recipient Outstanding Mentor award, Irvine Sch. Ecology, 2002. Mem.: Nat. Gov. Health Assn. Jewish. Avocations: surfing, music. Home: 7426 Upper Bay Dr Huntington Beach CA 92648 Office: Touro U Internat 5665 Plaza Dr Cypress CA 90630

**TURCO, ALFRED, JR.,** language educator; b. Providence, 1940; s. Alfred and Delia Maria Turco; m. Elizabeth Nora Davis, 1969 (div. 1981); children— Ellen, Jeffrey AB, Brown U., 1962; A.M., Harvard U., 1963, PhD, 1969; MA ad eundem gradum (hon.), Wesleyan U., 1981. Instr. English Wesleyan U., Middletown, Conn., 1967-69, asst. prof., 1969-74, assoc. prof., 1974-80, prof., 1980—; vis. assoc. prof. Cornell U., Ithaca, N.Y., 1980. Cons. Cornell U. Press, U. Toronto Press, Hartford Stage Co., Hackett Pub. Co.; mem. adv. coun. Internat. Shaw Soc., 2003—. Author: Shaw's Moral Vision, 1976; guest editor: Shaw's Neglected Plays (Shaw: Vol. 7), 1987; contbr. articles on Scandinavian lit. to profl. jours.; mem. editorial bd. Ann. of Bernard Shaw Studies, 1985—. Danforth Found. fellow, 1963-67; Woodrow Wilson Found. hon. fellow, 1963 Mem. Phi Beta Kappa Avocation: gourmet cooking. Home: 58 Prospect St Portland CT 06480-1131 Office: Wesleyan U Middletown CT 06459 Office Phone: 860-685-3599. E-mail: aturco@wesleyan.edu.

**TURCO, LEWIS PUTNAM,** language educator; b. Buffalo, May 2, 1934; s. Luigi and May Laura (Putnam) T.; m. Jean Cate Houdlette, May 29, 1934; children: Melora Ann, Christopher Cameron. BA, U. Conn., 1959; MA, U. Iowa, 1962; LHD (hon.), Ashland U., 2000. Instr. Cleve. State U., 1960-64; asst. prof. Hillsdale (Mich.) Coll., 1964-65; asst. prof. to full prof. SUNY, Oswego, 1965-96, poet-in-residence, 1995, prof. emeritus, 1996. Grad. asst. English, U. Conn., 1959; editorial asst. Writer's Workshop, U. Iowa, 1959-60; vis. prof. SUNY, Potsdam, 1968-69; Bingham Poet in Residence, U. Louisville, 1982; Writer in Residence, Ashland U., 1991; founding dir. Cleve. State U. Poetry Ctr., 1962, program in writing arts, SUNY Oswego, 1968. Author: First Poems, 1960, Awaken, Bells Falling: Poems 1959-67, 1968, The Inhabitant, 1970, Pocoangelini: A Fantography and Other Poems, 1971, American Still Lifes, 1981, numerous other poetry books including The Shifting Web: New and Selected Poems, 1989, The Green Maces of Autumn, Voices in an Old Maine House, 2002, The Collected Lyrics of Lewis Turco/Wesli Court, 2004; author numerous non-fiction books including The Book of Forms: A Handbook of Poetics, 1968, 3d edit., 2000, Visions and Revisions of American Poetry, 1986, Emily Dickinson, Woman of Letters, 1993, The Book of Literary Terms, 1999, The Book of Dialogue, 2004, A Sheaf of Leaves: Literary Memoirs, 2004, Fantorseers, A Book of Memories, 2005, others; editor: The Life and Poetry of Manoah Bodman, 1999; contbr. articles to profl. jours. Sec. City of Oswego Charter Revision Commn., 1990-91; active Oswego Opera Theater Chorus, Oswego Festival Chorus, 1986—. With USN, 1952-56. Recipient scholarship Meriden Record-Jour. Pub. Co., U. Conn., 1957-58, 58-59, Disting. Alumnus award, 1992, Melville Cane award Poetry Soc. Am., 1986, Bordighera Bilingual Poetry prize Sonia Raiziss-Giop Charitable Found., 1997, John Ciardi Award for lifetime achievement in poetry Italian-Am., Found., 1999, others; resident fellowships Yaddo Found., 1959, 77, Faculty fellowships Rsch. Found. of SUNY, 1966-67, 69, 71, 73, 78; grant-in-aid, 1969; inducted into Meriden Hall of Fame, 1993. Home: PO Box 161 Dresden ME 04342-0161 Office Phone: 207-737-4512. E-mail: mathom@gwi.net.

**TURCOT, MARGUERITE HOGAN,** medical researcher; b. White Plains, N.Y., May 19, 1934; d. Joseph William (dec.) and Marguerite Alice (dec.) Barrett) Hogan; children: Michael J., Susan A. Turcot, William R. Student, Syracuse U., 1951-54; BSN, U. Bridgeport, 1968. RN, Conn., N.C. Nurse Park City Hosp., Bridgeport, Conn., 1968-69, Meml. Mission Hosp., Asheville, N.C., 1969-70; instr. St. Joseph's Hosp., Asheville, 1970-71, oper. rm. nurse, 1973-77, charge nurse urology-cystoscopy, 1977-85; tchr. Asheville-Buncombe Tech. Coll., Asheville, 1971-72, Buncombe County Child Devel., Asheville, 1972-73; rschr. VA Med. Ctr., Asheville, 1988—; owner Reed House Bed & Breakfast, Asheville, 1985—2001. Bd. dirs. RiverLink, Quality Foreward. Charter mem. French Broad River Planning Com., Asheville, 1987—, Biltmore Village Hist. Mus.; mem. Asheville Bicentennial Commn., 1990-93; exec. dir. Preservation Soc. Asheville and Buncombe County. Recipient Griffin award, 1994, Friend of the River award, Land of Sky Regional Coun., 1995, Sondley award, Hist. Resources Commn. Asheville and Buncombe County, 1996, Vol. of Yr. award, RiverLink, 2001, Critical Link award, 2003, grantee U. Bridgeport, 1967—68; scholar Syracuse U. Faculty, 1951—54. Mem. Am. Urology Assn. (presenter VA urology workshop Asheville chpt. 1981, nat. meeting allied), Am. Bd. Urologic Allied Health Profls., Nat. Trust for Hist. Preservation, Preservation Found. N.C., Blue Ridge Pkwy. Assn., Preservation Soc. Asheville and Buncombe County (bd. dirs., past pres.), Asheville Newcomers Club (founder, 1st pres.), Earthwatch, Friends of Blue Ridge Pkwy. Inc. Republican. Roman Catholic. Avocations: preservation, history, architecture, sewing, hiking. Office: Preservation Soc Asheville & Buncombe County PO Box 2806 Asheville NC 28802

**TURCOTTE, DONALD LAWSON,** geophysical sciences educator; b. Bellingham, Wash., Apr. 22, 1932; s. Lawson Phillip and Eva (Pearson) Turcotte; m. Joan Meredith Luecke, May 17, 1957; children: Phillip Lawson, Stephen Bradford. BS, Calif. Inst. Tech., 1954, PhD, 1958; M in Aero. Engring., Cornell U., 1955; PhD (hon.), U. Paris, 2005. Asst. prof. aero.

engring. U.S. Naval Postgrad. Sch., Monterey, Calif., 1958-59; asst. prof. aero. engring. Cornell U., Ithaca, NY, 1959-63, assoc. prof., 1963-67, prof., 1967-73, prof. geol. scis., 1973-85, Maxwell Upson prof., 1985—2002, chmn., 1981-90; disting. prof. geology U. Calif. Davis, 2003—. Author (with others): Statistical Thermodynamics, 1963, Space Propulsion, 1965, Geodynamics, 1982, Fractals and Chaos in Geology and Geophysics, 1992, Mantle Convection, 2001. Trustee U. Space Rsch. Assn., 1975—79. Recipient Wegener medal, European Union Geosci., 1991, Disting. Alumni award, Calif. Inst. Tech., 1999; sr. postdoctoral rsch. fellow, NSF, 1965—66, Guggenheim fellow, 1972—73. Mem.: NAS, Am. Acad. Arts and Scis., Seismol. Soc. Am., Geol. Soc. Am. (Day medal 1982), Am. Geophys. Union (Charles A. Whitten medal 1995, William Bowie Medal 2003), El Macero Country Club. Home: 27104 Middle Golf Dr El Macero CA 95618 Office: Univ Calif Dept Geology Davis CA 95616 Office Phone: 530-572-6808. Business E-Mail: turcotte@geology.ucdavis.edu.

**TURCOTTE, JEAN-CLAUDE CARDINAL,** archbishop; b. Montreal, Que., Can., June 26, 1936; s. Paul-Émile and Rita (Gravel) Turcotte. Student, U. Cath., Lille, France; DD (hon.), McGill U.; lic. theology, Grand Seminaire Montreal. Ordained priest Roman Catholic Ch., 1959, consecrated bishop. Aux. bishop Diocese of Montreal, Que., Canada, 1982—90, archbishop, 1990—. Mem.: Coun. of Social Commn., Congregation of Causes of Saints. Roman Catholic. Office: 2000 Sherbrooke Ouest Montreal PQ Canada H3H 1G4

**TURCOTTE, MARGARET JANE,** retired nurse; b. Stow, Ohio, May 17, 1927; d. Edward Carlton and Florence Margaret (Hanson) McCauley; m Rene George Joseph, Nov. 24, 1961 (div. June 1967); 1 child, Michael Lawrence. RN, Ohio. Nurse St. Thomas Hosp., 1949-50; pvt. duty nurse, 1950-57; polio nurse Akron Children's Hosp., 1953-54; mem. nursing staff Robinson Meml. Hosp., Ravenna, Ohio, 1958-67, head ctrl. svc., 1963-67; supr. ctrl. svc. Brentwood Hosp., Warrensville Heights, Ohio, 1967-93, infections control nurse, 1982-91; emergency med. technician. Mem. aux. Robinson Meml. Hosp.; vol. Portage County Vis. Nurse Svc. and Hospice; active RSVP, Cozy Kitchen Quilters. Mem.: St. Thomas Hosp. Alumni Assn., Cozy Christian Quilters. Presbyterian. Mem. Christian Ch. (Disciples Of Christ). Home: 714 Woodgate Blvd Apt 201 Ravenna OH 44266-2548

**TURCOTTE, MATHIEU,** Olympic athlete; b. Sherbrooke, Que., Can., Feb. 8, 1977; Profl. speed skater, Canada, 1998—. Recipient Gold medal, World Team Championships, 1998, 2000, 2001, 2003, Gold medal 5000m short track men's relay, 2002 Olympic Games, Bronze medal 1000m. Avocation: movies. Office: Speed Skating Can 2781 Lancaster Rd Ste 402 Ottawa ON K1B 1A7 Canada

**TUREK, SONIA FAY,** journalist; b. NYC, Aug. 2, 1949; d. Louis and Julia (Liebson) Turek; m. Gilbert Curtis, June 18, 1995. BA in English, CCNY, 1970; MSLS, Drexel U., 1972; MS in Journalism, Boston U., 1979. Children's libr. Wissahickon Valley Pub. Libr., Ambler, Pa., 1973; supr. children's svcs. Somerville Pub. Libr., Somerville, Mass., 1973-78; stringer The Watertown (Mass.) Sun, 1979, The Bedford (Mass.) Minuteman, 1979; reporter The Middlesex News, Framingham, Mass., 1979-83, The Boston Herald, 1983, asst. city editor, city editor, 1983-86, asst. mng. editor features, 1986-89, asst. mng. editor Sunday, 1989-93, dep. mng. editor, arts and features, 1993-99, wine columnist, 1984—. Tchr. Cambridge (Mass.) Ctr. for Adult Edn., 1982, 83; adj. prof. Boston U., 1986; travel writer The Boston Herald, 1984-2003. Avocations: wine and food, travel, sailing. Personal E-mail: sfturek@aol.com.

**TURETKEN, OZGUR,** information scientist, educator; b. Ankara, Turkey, June 2, 1972; s. Naif and Serife Turetken; m. Jessica Brooke Evans, Oct. 27, 2002; 1 child, Sean Mert. BS, Mid. East Tech. U., Ankara, Turkey, 1994, MBA, 1999; PhD, Okla. State U., Stillwater, 2001. Asst. prof. mgmt. info. sci. Temple U., Phila., 2000—. Contbr. conf. proceedings, articles to profl. jours. Mem.: ACM, Inst. Ops. Rsch. and Mgmt. Scis., Assn. Info. Sci. Office: Temple Univ 1810 N 13th Philadelphia PA 19122 Office Phone: 215-204-3058. E-mail: turetken@temple.edu.

**TURI, LOUIS,** publishing executive; b. Pont Saint Esprit, French Riviera, France (incl. Monaco), Feb. 26, 1950; s. Marie Angela Di-Rollo, Joseph DiCaprio Turi. CEP - FPA, College de Pont St Esprit, Pont Saint Esprit, 1956—73. Cert. FPA -ASME section 9 welding 1973. Recording artist Phillips -Phonogram, Paris, 1975—83; pres. Startheme Pubs. LTD, Phoenix, 1991—. Lectr. in field. Author: Astropsychologist -Futuristic Stock Market. Recipient Distinction Cup Musicianship, Royal Sch. of Music, 1976, Writer's Digest award for 3 books, 2001. Mem.: Am. Assn. of Astrologers (Phoenix 1998—2002, AFA Conv. Fla. 1998). Republican. Christian. Avocation: travel. Home and Office: Startheme Publications Inc 4411 N 23rd St Phoenix AZ 85016-5515 E-mail: dr.turi@cox.net.

**TURIN, LARS,** secondary school educator, artist; b. Albany, NY, Mar. 29, 1949; s. Poul and Grete Turin; m. Patricia Luttrell, June 29, 1980; children: Daniel, Brian, Ethan, Kyle. BFA in Ceramics, SUNY, New Paltz, 1972. Elem. art tchr. Leroy (N.Y.) Ctrl. Schs., 1972, Guilderland (N.Y.) Ctrl. Schs., 1972—76, middle sch. art tchr., 1976—84; owner, mgr. retail Danco Scandinavian Furniture, Clifton Park, NY, 1984—87; H.S. art tchr. Mohonasen Ctrl. Sch., Schenectady, NY, 1987—. H.S. art tchr. fellow, Skidmore Coll., 2005. Mem.: Am. Craftsman Assn., N.Y. State United Tchrs., N.Y. State Art Tchr. Assn., Mohonasen Tchrs. Assn., Mohonasen Art Club. Avocations: sports, sculpting, ceramics, performing arts. Office: Mohonasen Cntl Schs 2072 Curry Rd Schenectady NY 12303

**TURINO, GERARD MICHAEL,** internist, educator; b. N.Y.C., May 16, 1924; s. Michael and Lucy (Arciero) T.; m. Dorothy Estes, Aug. 25, 1951; children: Peter, Phillip, James. AB, Princeton U., 1945; MD, Columbia U., 1948. Diplomate: Am. Bd. Internal Medicine. Intern Columbia U., Bellevue Hosp., 1948-49; asst. resident in medicine, 1949-50; resident in medicine New Haven Hosp., 1950-51; chief resident in medicine Columbia U. div. Bellevue Hosp., 1953-54; sr. fellow N.Y. Heart Assn., 1956-60; career investigator Health Research Council City of N.Y., 1961-71; asst. prof. medicine Columbia U., 1960-67, assoc. prof., 1967-72, prof. medicine, 1973-83, John H. Keating prof. medicine, 1983—; mem. staff Presbyn. Hosp., N.Y.C., 1960—; attending physician 1983—; dir. med. svcs. St. Lukes-Roosevelt Hosp., N.Y.C., 1983-92; dir. St. Lukes-Roosevelt Hosp. James P. Mara Ctr. 1997. Cons. on sci. affairs Am. Thoracic Soc., 1992—; mem. sci. adv. com. Nat. Heart, Lung, and Blood Inst., Am. Lung Assn., Am. Heart Assn., N.Y. Lung Assn., N.Y. Heart Assn., Alpha, Antitrypsin Found.; mem. staff divsn. med. sci. Nat. Rsch. Coun., Washington; cons. VA Hosp., East Orange, N.J., 1962-67; cons. in medicine Englewood (N.J.) Hosp., Hackensack (N.J.) Hosp.; pres.-elect Am. Bur. Med. Advancement in China, 1994, pres., 1994-2001, chmn., 2001-; chmn. bd. dirs. Chronic Obstructive Pulmonary Disease Found., 2004 Contbr. articles to med. jours. Mem. Bd. Edn., Alpine, N.J., 1960-67; chmn. Chronic Obstructive Pulmonary Disease Found., 2004. Served to capt. USAF, 1951-53. Recipient Joseph Mather Smith prize Columbia U., 1965, Alumni medal, 1983, Silver medal Alumni Assn. Coll. Physicians and Surgeons Columbia U., 1979, gold medal, 1986, Edward Livingston Trudeau medal Am. Lung Assn., 2003, Fellow AAAS; mem. Assn. Am. Physicians, Am. Soc. Clin. Investigation, Harvey Soc., Am. Thoracic Soc. (pres. 1987-88, Edward Livingston Trudeau prize 2003), Am. Fedn. Clin. Rsch., Am. Physiol. Soc. (chmn. steering com. respiration sect.), Am. Heart Assn. (award of merit 1980, Disting. Achievement award 1989, bd. dirs.), N.Y. Heart Assn. (pres. 1981-83, dir.), N.Y. Lung Assn. (dir.), N.Y. Med.-Surg. Soc. (pres. 1995), N.Y. Clin. Soc., Princeton Club (N.Y.C.), Maidstone Club, Devon Yacht Club, Century Assn. Club. Home: 66 E 79th St New York NY 10021-0244 Office: St Lukes Roosevelt Hosp 1000 10th Ave New York NY 10019-1192 Business E-mail: GMT1@Columbia.edu.

**TURINSKY, PAUL JOSEF,** nuclear engineer, educator; b. Hoboken, N.J., Oct. 20, 1944; s. Paul J. and Wilma A. (Budig) T.; m. Karen Ann DeLuca, Aug. 29, 1966; children: Grant Dean, Beth Noelle. BS, U. R.I., 1966; MSE, U. Mich., 1967, PhD, 1970; MBA, U. Pitts., 1979. Asst. prof. Rensselaer Poly. Inst., Troy, NY, 1971-73; engr., mgr. nuclear design Westinghouse Elec. Corp., Pitts., 1973-78, mgr. core devel.. 1978-80; head dept. nuclear engring. NC State U., Raleigh, 1980-88, 99—, prof., 1980—, dir. Electric Power Rsch. Ctr., 1989—2006; pres. Nuclear Fuel Mgmt. Assocs., 1994—. Bd. dirs. Quantum Rsch. Svcs.; cons. Electric Power Rsch. Inst., Palo Alto, Calif., 1980-98, Sci. Applications Internat. Corp., 1990-92, US Dept. Energy, 1993; tech. specialist Internat. Atomic Energy Agy., Vienna, Austria, 1982—; mem. nuc. safety rev. bd. Duke Power Co., Charlotte, NC, 1986-2001; cons. Can. Nuc. Safety Commn., 2000-, Western Svcs. Corp., 2006-; mem. CEA nuc. sci. advisory bd., France, 2006-. Author: (with others) CRC Handbook of Nuclear Reactor Calculations, 1986; contbr. more than 100 articles to tech. jours. Recipient Outstanding Tchr. award, N.C. State U., 1985, Supercomputer award, IBM, 1991, Alcoa Disting. Rschr. award, 1993, E.O. Lawrence award in nuc. tech., U.S. Dept. Energy, 2002, Merit award, Alumni Soc. U. Mich., 2003. Fellow: Am. Nuc. Soc. (chmn. reactor physics divsn. 1987—88, chmn. math. and computer divsn. 1995—96, bd. dirs. 1990—93, Mark Mills award 1971, Eugene E. Wigner Reactor Physics award 2003, Arthur Holly Compton award 2004); mem.: AAAS (math. com.), Soc. Indsl. and Applied Math., Edison Electric Inst. (Power Engring. Educator award 1992), Am. Soc. Engring. Educators (mem. nuc. engring. divsn. 1984—85, Glenn Murphy award 1990). Office: NC State U Dept Nuclear Engring PO Box 7909 Raleigh NC 27695-7909 Business E-Mail: turinsky@ncsu.edu.

**TURITS, RICHARD LEE,** history professor; b. Passaic, N.J., Oct. 11, 1960; s. Philip Daniel Turits and Nancy Barnett Morse; m. Hannah Rosen, July 22, 1963. BA, Brown U., 1983; MA, Yale U., 1986; PhD, U. Chgo., 1997. Asst. prof. history Princeton U., NJ, 1997—2003; assoc. prof. history and Afro-Am. and African studies U. Mich., Ann Arbor, 2003—. Author: Foundations of Despotism: Peasants, the Trujillo Regime, and Modernity in Dominican History, 2003. Recipient Outstanding Acad. Book award, Choice Mag., 2003, James Alexander Robertson Meml. prize, Conf. Latin Am. History, 2003, Bolton-Johnson prize, 2005, John Edwin Fagg prize, Am. Hist. Assn., 2004; scholar, Harvard Acad. Internat. and Area Studies, 1996—97, 1998—99. Home: 702 N 5th Ave Ann Arbor MI 48104-1058 Office: Univ Mich Dept History 1029 Tisch Ann Arbor MI 48109-1003 Office Phone: 734-647-4873.

**TURITZIN, JOHN N.,** lawyer; b. Manhasset, NY; m. Barbara Turitzin; children: Allison, David, Emily. Grad., Earlham Coll., 1976; M in Pub. Affairs, Princeton U., 1981; JD, NYU, 1981. Assoc. Cahill Gordon & Reindel, NY, 1981—84; ptnr. Battle Fowler LLP, Stamford, Conn., 1985—2000, Paul, Hastings, Janofsky & Walker LLP, 2000—04; exec. v.p., gen. counsel Marvel Entertainment Inc., NYC, 2004—. Office: Marvel Entertainment Inc 417 Fifth Ave 11th Fl New York NY 10016 Office Phone: 212-576-4000. Office Fax: 212-576-8517.*

**TURK, AUSTIN THEODORE,** social studies educator; b. Gainesville, Ga., May 28, 1934; s. Hollis Theodore and Ruth (Vandiver) T.; m. Janet Stuart Irving, Oct. 4, 1957 (div. 1977); children: Catherine, Jennifer; m. Ruth-Ellen Marie Grimes, July 27, 1985. BA cum laude, U. Ga., 1956; MA, U. Ky., 1959; PhD, U. Wis., 1962. Acting instr. sociology U. Wis., Madison, 1961-62; from instr. to prof. sociology Ind. U., Bloomington, 1962-74; prof. U. Toronto, Can., 1974-88, U. Calif., Riverside, 1988—, chmn. dept. sociology, 1989-94; interim dir. Robert B. Presley Ctr. for Crime and Justice Studies, 1994-95. Author: Criminality and Legal Order, 1969, Political Criminality, 1982; gen. editor crime and justice series SUNY Press, Albany, 1990—; contbr. articles to jours. in field. Mem. Calif. Mus. Photography, 1988—, Citizens Univ. Com., 1990—. Recipient Paul Tappan award Western Soc. Criminology, 1989. Fellow Am. Soc. Criminology (pres. 1984-85); mem. Am. Sociol. Assn. (chair criminology sect. 1975-76), Law and Soc. Assn. (trustee 1982-85), Acad. Criminal Justice Scis. Democrat. Avocations: gardening, reading, swimming, tennis. Office: Dept Sociology U Calif Riverside Riverside CA 92521-0001 E-mail: austin.turk@ucr.edu.

**TURK, ELIZABETH ANN,** music educator; b. N.Y.C., July 10, 1957; d. William Robert Turk, Elizabeth Ann Brittingham. BA in Music and History, Dowling Coll.; MA in German Lang. and Lit., Hofstra U.; MA in European History, SUNY Stony Brook; MA in Music Libr. Sci., Columbia U. Tchg. asst SUNY, Stony Brook, 1986—88; lectr. music Dowling Coll., Oakdale, NY, 1988—91; choral tchr. music Amityville (NY) Pub. Schs., 1991—; dir. theater arts, dir. choral music Miller Pl. HS; theater dir. Amityville HS; music dir. theater prodns. Commack HS South, Carriage House Players, Kids for Kids Theater, Inc.; music dir. theater Syosset Mid. Sch., Conn.; Jericho H.S. Tchr. vocal music Miller Place Middle Sch., Miller Place, NY, Hewlett Woodmere HS, NY; pvt. tchr. and vocal coach, Massapequa, NY. Singer (soloist): (lead rolls) Rome Opera Festival, 1989, 1990; performer: Tchaikovsky Competition, 1978, 1982, 1986, Minn. Opera, 1979, 1980, 1981, L.I. Youth Orch. Summer Tours; dir.: Sleeping Beauty, Sound of Music, Fiddler on the Roof, Little Shop of Horrors, Cinderella, Oliver, numerous others; choreographer Fiddler on the Roof, Sound of Music, Little Shop of Horrors, Oliver, Grease; dir.: 42nd Street, West Side Story, Guys & Dolls, Mikado, HMS Pinafore & Pirates of Penzance, King and I, Best of Broadway. Recipient award for further study, Met. Opera, 1981—90, Herald award for choreography and music dir. Mem.: Suffolk County Music Educators Assn., Music Educators Nat. Assn., Suffolk County Wrestling Assn. (tournament dir. league V 1974—, numerous awards), White Star Triangle (Beloved Queen 1973—74), Order Ea. Star (various offices, assoc. condr.). Home: 90 Clock Blvd Massapequa NY 11758

**TURK, JAMES CLINTON,** federal judge; b. Roanoke, Va., May 3, 1923; s. James Alexander and Geneva (Richardson) T.; m. Barbara Duncan, Aug. 21, 1954; children— Ramona Leah, James Clinton, Robert Malcolm Duncan, Mary Elizabeth, David Michael. AB, Roanoke Coll., 1949; L.L.B., Washington and Lee U., 1952. Bar: Va. 1952. Assoc. Dalton & Poff, Radford, Va., 1952-53; ptnr. Dalton, Poff & Turk, Radford, 1953-72; state senator from Va., 1959-72; judge U.S. Dist. Ct. (we. dist.) Va., Roanoke, 1972-73, chief judge, 1973—. Dir. 1st & Mchts. Nat. Bank of Radford Mem. Va. Senate, from 1959, minority leader.; Trustee Radford Community Hosp., 1959—. Served with AUS, 1943-46. Mem.: Order of Coif, Omicron Delta Kappa, Phi Beta Kappa. Baptist (deacon). Home: 1002 Walker Dr Radford VA 24141-3018 Office: US Dist Ct 246 Franklin Rd SW # 220 Roanoke VA 24011-2214 Office Phone: 540-857-5122. Office Fax: 540-857-5123. Business E-Mail: jamest@vawd.uscourts.gov.

**TURK, JAMES CLINTON, JR.,** lawyer; b. Radford, Va., Oct. 27, 1956; s. James Clinton and Barbara (Duncan) T.; m. Allison Blanding, Oct. 16, 1993; children: Lindsey Leigh, Katherine Alexandra, Alana Rae. BA in Econs., Roanoke Coll., 1979; JD, Samford U., 1984. Bar: Va. 1984, U.S. Dist. Ct. (ea. and we. dists.) Va. 1984, U.S. Bankruptcy Ct. 1985, U.S. Ct. Appeals (4th cir.) 1985, U.S. Supreme Ct. 1989. Cert. specialist in civil and criminal trial advocacy Nat. Bd. Trial Advocacy; cert. players agt. Nat. Basketball Players Assn. Ptnr. Harrison & Turk, Radford, 1985—. Adj. prof. criminal justice dept. Radford U.; bd. dirs. New River Bus. SunTrust Bank, Va. Tech. Found. Sec. Radford Rep. Com., 1984—; fundraising chmn. Am. Heart Assn., Radford, 1986—; bd. dir. New River Valley Workshop, Inc., v.p., 1990-92, pres., 1992-93; bd. dirs. new River C.C. Ednl. Found.; apptd. chmn. and dir. Va. Student Assistance Authorities by Gov. George Allen, 1994—; escheator City of Radford and Pulaski County; rep. western dist. CJA Panel Atty., Va.; mem. 4th Cir. Jud. Conf., 2000-01; bd. dirs. Va. Tech. Athletic Found. Named a Va. Super Lawyer, 2006; recipient Bill Geimer Capital Defender award, Va. Capital Case Clearinghouse, 2000—01. Mem. ATLA (sustaining, fellow Coll. of Advocacy), Ted Dalton Am. Inn Courts (barrister), ABA, Am. Bd. Trial Adv., Am. Coll. Barristers, Va. Bar Assn. (civil litig. sect. coun. 1991—, criminal litig. sect. coun. 1994—), Nat. Assn. Criminal Def. Lawyers (life; death penalty com. and indigent def. com.), Va. Trial Lawyers Assn., Inn of Cts., Jaycees, Am. Inn of Ct., Rotary. Republican. Roman Catholic. Avoca-

tions: weightlifting, golf, travel, flying, scuba diving. Home: 460 Quailwood Dr Blacksburg VA 24060-6724 Office: Stone Harrison Turk PC PO Box 2968 Radford VA 24143-2968 Office Phone: 540-639-9056. Personal E-mail: jimturk@aol.com.

**TURK, JOHN COBB,** architect, educator; b. Buffalo, Oct. 16, 1930; s. Roswell Lester and Alice Knoche (Cobb) Turk; m. Joanna D. Paulat, 1959 (dec. Apr. 1966); 1 child, Christine Paulat; m. Sandra Miriam Baruch, Mar. 18, 1967 (dec. June 1986); m. Mary Jean Raftery, June 25, 1988. BA, Colgate U., 1952. Registered arch., S.C. Apprentice Frank Lloyd Wright's Taliesin Fellowship, Spring Green, Wis., Scottsdale, Ariz., 1955—57; archtl. draftsman various archs., Buffalo, 1959-72; instr. archtl. engring. tech. Midlands Tech. Coll., Columbia, SC, 1972-77, head dept. archtl. engring. tech., 1977-79, head constrn. tech. dept., 1979-84; arch. Carlisle Assocs., Columbia, 1984-87; arch., dir. engring. and housing Ft. Jackson, Columbia, 1987-88; arch., head design and estimating dept. Facilities Mgmt. Office U. S.C., Columbia, 1988-2000, arch., 2001—04, ret., 2004; owner Architecture Light, Columbia, 2004—. Dir. Lake Murray assn., 2001—02. With C.E. U.S. Army, 1953—55. Mem.: Am. Legion, Constrn. Specifications Inst. (bd. dirs. Columbia chpt. 1996—98, v.p. 1998—99, pres.-elect 1999—2000, pres. 2000—01, dir. 2001—, constrn. documents technician), Intertel, Mensa (v.p. Columbia chpt. 1978, sec. 1998—2001, v.p. 2005—), Am. Legion. Republican. Unitarian Universalist. Avocation: boating. Home and Office: 112 Schooner Ln Columbia SC 29212-8032 Personal E-mail: johncturk@att.net.

**TURK, RICHARD ERRINGTON,** retired psychiatrist; b. Staten Island, NY, Oct. 6, 1925, s. Richard Jason and Marian (Errington) T.; m. Dec. 30, 1948 (widowed Dec. 23, 1978); children: Stephanie, Jeffrey, Alan. BA, Dartmouth Coll., 1945; MD, Johns Hopkins Med. Sch., 1948. Diplomate Am. Bd. Psychiatry. Intern Highland-Alameda County Hosp., Oakland, Calif., 1948-49; resident Herrick Meml. Hosp., Berkeley, Calif., 1949-50; fellow psychiatry Med. Sch. Harvard U., Boston, 1950-51, 53-54; clin. instr. Med. Sch. U. Calif., San Francisco, 1954—70; pvt. practice psychiatry Berkeley, 1954-85. Pvt. practice, Walnut Creek, Calif., 1972-88; staff Herrick Meml. Hosp., 1954-85, Walnut Creek Hosp., 1972-88, John Muir Meml. Hosp., Walnut Creek, 1972-88. Capt. USAF Res., 1951—53, Korea. Mem. AMA, Am. Psychiat. Assn., No. Calif. Psychiat. Assn., Calif. Med. Assn., Alameda-Contra Costa County Med. Assn. Avocations: travel, bicycling, boating, car camping.

**TURK, THOMAS LIEBIG,** cultural organization administrator; b. Indpls., July 4, 1936; s. Laurel Herbert and Esther Lucille (Liebig) T.; m. Judith Ann Prochnow, July 26, 1969; children: Martisha Emily, Benjamin Edward. AB, DePauw U., 1958; MA, Mich. State U., 1960; cert., Harvard U., 1973. Promotion and publicity dir. Sta. WMSB-TV Mich. State U., East Lansing, 1961, asst. editor news bur., 1962-63, fine arts assoc. producer Sta. WKAR-TV, 1963-68, fine arts producer Sta. WKAR-TV, 1969-81; acting dir. publicity DePauw U., Greencastle, Ind., 1961-62; exec. dir. Cultural Activities Ctr., Temple, Tex., 1981-91, Met. Nashville Arts Commn., 1993—2003, Tennesseans for the Arts, 2003—06; mng. dir. Texarkana (Tex.) Regional Arts & Humanities Coun., 1991-93. Pres. Met. Lansing (Mich.) Fine Arts Coun., 1975-77, Mich. Assn. Comm. Arts Agys., East Lansing, 1979-81; Gov. apptd. mem. Mich. Coun. for Arts, 1979-81; chmn. Mich. Arts Forum, 1980-81; pres. U.S. Urban Arts Fedn., 1999-00; mem. State Arts Action Network Coun., 2005-06. Producer, co-producer: 400 programs for local, nat. and internat. distbn. on pub. TV, 1963-81. With USAF, 1960. Mem.: Tennesseans for Arts (bd. dirs. 2000—03), Nat. Assembly Local Arts Agys. (bd. dirs. 1979—85), Rotary, Sigma Chi. Episcopalian. Home and Office: 643 Harpeth Trace Dr Nashville TN 37221-3147 Personal E-mail: turktj@comcast.net.

**TURKEL, STANLEY,** hotel executive, management consultant; s. Nathan and Mollie (Kurtzman) Turkeltaub; m. Barbara Bell (div. Apr. 1971); children: Marc Alexander, Allison Lee; m. Rima Sokoloff; stepchildren: Joshua Bernard Forrest, Benay Debra Forrest. BS, NYU, 1957. Laundry cons. Victor Kramer Co. Inc., N.Y.C., 1957—62; with spl. hotel svcs. Loews Hotel Corp., N.Y.C., 1962-63; res. mgr. Americana Hotel, N.Y.C., 1963-64; gen. mgr. Drake Hotel, N.Y.C., 1964-66, Summit Hotel, N.Y.C., 1966-67; product line mgr. hotels ITT, N.Y.C., 1968—75; owner Stanley Turkel Co., Hotel Cons., Kew Gardens Hills, NY, 1976—. Mem. faculty NYU Ctr. Hospitality, Tourism and Sports Mgmt. Author: Heroes of the American Reconstruction, 2005; contbr. articles to N.Y. Times, Wall St. Jour., N.Y. Newsday, Washington Post, N.Y. Post, N.Y. Daily News, Hotel and Motel Mgmt., Cornell Quar., Lodging Hospitality, The Bottomline, Nat. Real Estate Investor, Hotel Interactive, Hotel Online. Mem. ACLU. Mem.: Internat. Soc. Hospitality Cons. (cert.), Am. Hotel and Lodging Assn. (MHS cert.), City Club NY (trustee 1964—97, chmn. 1977—88). Avocations: Reconstruction period of America, autograph collecting. Office Phone: 917-628-8549. Personal E-mail: stanturkel@aol.com. *As a lifelong civic activist, I cherish the godless constitution and especially the first amendment which provides protection for unpopular speech and creates a wall of separation between church and state.*

**TURKIEWICZ, ANTHONY MICHAEL,** rheumatologist; b. Birmingham, Ala., Mar. 27, 1973; s. Witold Wladyslaw and Sarah Marie Rose Turkiewicz; m. Eleanor Mathews Carroll, Dec. 15, 2001; 1 child, Andrew Michael. BS, Georgetown U., 1995, MD, 1999. Intern in internal medicine Georgetown U. Med. Ctr., Washington, 1999—2000, resident in internal medicine, 2000—02, fellow in rheumatology, 2002—04; asst. prof. medicine Divsn. Rheumatology U. Ala., Birmingham, 2004—. Scholar, So. Med. Assn., 1998. Mem.: ACP, AMA, Am. Coll. Rheumatology, Sigma Xi. Roman Catholic.

**TURKNETT, JAMES C.,** minister; b. Dallas, May 8, 1967; s. Jerry Claid and Frances Ann Turknett; m. Katy Frances Turknett, July 31, 1992. Student, Cameron U., 1986, Central Tex. Coll., 1990; DMin, Tex. Christian Bible Inst., Fort Worth, 1996. Master driver U.S. Army, Republic of Korea, 1987—91, equal opportunity officer Okla., 1988—94, drill sgt. Okla., 1992—94; ins. agt. Atlanta Life Ins., Tex., 1995—96; fin. svc. regional mgr. Primerica/So. Security, Tex., 1996—98; minister Faith and Power Ministry Ch., Tex., 1994—; CEO Life Changers Enterprise, Tex., 2003—. Author: (books) How To Be a Paymaster, 2003, How To On Radio, 2003, How To Start a Business, 2003. Mem. Dallas C. of C., 2002—. Decorated 7 Achievement Medals U.S. Army. Democrat. Avocations: basketball, football, soccer, track, ping pong/table tennis. Office: Faith and Power Ministry Ch 2120 N St Augustine #126 Dallas TX 75227 Office Phone: 972-329-1358. Business E-Mail: takingthecity@sbcglobal.net.

**TURKOT, DOROTHY REGESTER FELTON,** writer, illustrator; b. Knoxville, Jan. 31, 1927; d. John William and Dorothy Ester (Regester) Felton; divorced; children: Lynda Anne, Karl Wayne, Terry Nolan, Paul Allison. Student, Chgo. Inst. Fine Arts, 1945. Art tchr. Haddonfield (N.J.) Friends, 1962-86; builder Progress Photos, Haddonfield, 1972; model, actress Phila. and N.Y.C., 1985—. Author, illustrator: (children's books) Mother Cat, 1989, Greta Goose, 1990, (cookbook) Star-lit Kitchens, 1996; designer toy Study Buddy, 1995; paintings exhibited in shows in N.J., Pa. (awards); solo shows include Beach Haven Yacht Club, 1984, High Bar Harbor Yacht Club, 1985; group shows include Phila. Bank, 1986-96, Pine Shore Art Assn., Massahawkin, N.J., 1988-96, Old New Castle, Del., 1991—. Palacio Dio Negro Mus., Brazil, 1999; appeared in various stage prodns., including Arsenic and Old Lace, Fort Carats, Dear Me, The Sky is Falling, Second Time Around, The Man, The Children's Hour, Guys 'N Dolls, also various indsl. films and commls. Recipient award Nat. Libr. of Poetry, 1994. Mem. Long Beach Island Hist. Assn., Ship Bottom Civic Assn., N.Y. Theater Guild, Friends of Surf-light Theater. Avocations: biking, swimming, boating, boat refurbishing, travel. Home: 312 E Bay Ave Apt 209 Manahawkin NJ 08050-3353

**TURKOVÁ, HELGA,** librarian; b. Prague, Czech. Apr. 20, 1942; d. Johann Turek and Anna (Kusbachová) Turková. Grad., Charles U., Prague, Czech, 1964, PhD, 1969. Diploma in librarianship. Libr. Czechoslovak Acad. of Scis., Prague, 1964—65, Prague Info. Svc., 1965—65; ind. specialist. libr. Nat. Mus. Libr., Prague, 1967—90, dir., 1990—2005; dir. dept. hist. Castles

Libr., Prague, 2005—. Co-author: (book) Rilke and Kraus and Vrchotovy J., 1985, (catalogue) Catalog incunabula in Castle Libraries, 1992, 2001; editor: Sborník Národního muzea-rada C-literární historie, 1990—. Mem coun Friends Old Prague, 1963—, Soc R M Rilke, 1992—. Mem.: Literary Sci Soc Sci Acad Czech Republic, Spolecnost Národního muzea, Asn Librarians. Roman Catholic. Avocations: history, history, art. Office: Knihovna Národni muzeum Václavské náměstí 68 115 79 Prague 1 Czech Republic Office Phone: 00420-224-497-368. Business E-Mail: helga_turkova@nm.cz.

**TURKS, HILDEGARD MARIA (HILDEGARD MARIA CHRONIS),** retired security investigator, writer; b. Bruckander Mur, Austria, Nov. 10, 1949; arrived in U.S., 1962; d. Karl Franz Ignaz Popetschnigg and Margarete Galfuss; m. Ray Turks Jr., Apr. 16, 1970 (div. Apr. 20, 1971); 1 child, Joana Margarete Lee; m. James Chronis, Dec. 6, 1975 (dec. Aug. 6, 1994). Various civilian duties USAF, Baumholder and Zweibrucken, Germany, 1964—71; restaurant mgr. Jackson Heights, NY, 1976—84; bartender N.Y.C., 1976—84; undercover investigator, security pers., 1978—85. Author: Little Snapple, 1992. Recipient Golden Globe award, World of Poetry, 1987—89, Editor's Choice award, Internat. Libr. Poetry, 2001—03. Avocations: art, writing, walking, travel, helping others. Home: 4700 S Virginia St Apt 330 Amarillo TX 79109-6076

**TURLEY, JAMES S.,** corporate financial executive; m. Lynn Turley; 1 child, Jay. BS in economics and managerial studies, Rice U., 1977, MS in acctg., 1978. With Ernst & Young, Houston, 1977—79, St. Louis, 1979—87, US nat. dir. client services and bus. devel. NYC, 1987—90, coord. ptnr. St. Louis, 1991—93, area dir. entrepreneurial svcs., 1993—94, mng. ptnr. upper midwest area, 1994—98, mer. NY area mng. ptnr. NYC, 1998—2000; dep. global chair Ernst & Young Internat. NYC, 2000—01, global chair, 2001—, global CEO, 2003—. Mem. Bus. Roundtable, Com. to Encourage Corp. Philanthropy, Transatlantic Bus. Dialog. Bd. dirs. Boy Scouts of Am., Catalyst; v.p. bd. dirs. Nat. Corp. Theater Fund; mem. nat. leadership coun. Character Edn. Partnership. Office: Ernst & Young 5 Times Sq New York NY 10036*

**TURLEY, MICHAEL ROY,** lawyer; b. St. Louis, Mar. 7, 1945; s. W. Richard and Mary Jeanne (Ogle) T.; m. Patricia Ederle, Aug. 21, 1968; children: James, Alisyn. AB, Princeton U., 1967; JD, Mo. U., 1970. Bar: Mo. 1970, U.S. Dist. Ct. (ea. dist.) Mo. 1975. Assoc. Lewis, Rice & Fingersh (formerly Lewis & Rice), St. Louis, 1970-71, 74-80, ptnr., 1980—. Mem. Jefferson County Planning and Zoning Commn., 1987—2000; bd. dirs., sec.-treas. Ctr. for Emerging Techs. Mem. ABA, Mo. Bar Assn., St. Louis Met. Bar Assn., Princeton Club. Episcopalian. Office: Lewis Rice & Fingersh 500 N Broadway Ste 2000 Saint Louis MO 63102-2147 E-mail: mturley@lewisrice.com.

**TURLEY, STEWART,** retired retail company executive; b. Mt. Sterling, Ky., July 20, 1934; s. R. Joe and Mavis S. Turley; children from previous marriage: Carol Cohen, Karen Shockley; m. Linda A. Mulholland; stepchildren: Kathleen Smiley, Kristine Johnson. Student, Rollins Coll., 1952-53, U. Ky., 1953-55. Plant mgr. Crown Cork & Seal Co., Orlando (Fla.), Phila., 1955-66; mgr. non-drug ops., dir. corporate employee rels. and spl. svcs. Eckerd Corp. (formerly Jack Eckerd Corp.), Clearwater, Fla., 1966-68; v.p. Eckerd Corp., Clearwater, Fla., 1968-71, sr. v.p., 1971-74, dir., 1971-97, pres., chief exec. officer, 1974-96, chmn. bd., 1975-97. Bd. dirs. WCI Cmtys., Inc. Past chmn. U.S. Ski Team Found.; bd. dirs. Vilar Ctr. Found., Vail Valley Found., Steadman-Hawkins Sports Medicine Found., Eckerd Youth Alternatives, Inc. Mem. Nat. Assn. Chain Drug Stores (bd. dirs., chmn. bd. 1978-79, 88-89), Fla. Coun. 100 (past chmn.), Chief Execs. Orgn., Carlouel Yacht Club, Belleair Country Club, Eagle Springs Golf Club, Kappa Alpha. Office: 1465 S Fort Harrison Ave Clearwater FL 33756-2505

**TURLEY, SUSAN LYNN WELKER,** military officer; d. Dudley Struan and Marilyn Post Welker; m. Ernest Carl Turley, Aug. 24, 1984; children: Jared Carl, Robert Carl, Cody Carl. AA in Journalism, Ea. Ariz. Coll., 1980; BA in Journalism, U. Ariz., 1983; JD, U. Tex. Sch. of Law, 1995; LLM, Judge Adv. General's Sch. of the Army, 2002. Admitted to Practice: U.S. Supreme Ct. 2002, US Ct. of Appeals for the Armed Forces 1995, Supreme Ct. of Tex. 1995. Missile launch officer 351st Strategic Missile Wing, Whiteman Air Force Base, Mo., 1988—92; polit. reporter, bus. editor Cox Ariz. Publs., Mesa, Ariz., 1983—85; nat. editor Latter-Day Sentinel, Phoenix, 1985—87; chief, civil law and adverse actions 30th Space Wing Staff Judge Advocate's Office, Vandenberg Air Force Base, Calif., 1995—97; area def. counsel Air Force Legal Svcs. Agy., Western Circuit, Vandenberg Air Force Base, 1997—99; dep. staff judge adv. 36th Air Base Wing Staff Judge Advocate's Office, Andersen Air Force Base, 1999—2001; acquisition atty. Air Force Materiel Command Law Office, Wright-Patterson Air Force Base, Ohio, 2002—03; staff judge adv. Hdqs. Ops. and Sustainment Systems Group, Maxwell-Gunter Air Force Base, Ala., 2004—. Acting pub. affairs officer Hdqs. Ops. and Sustainment Systems Group, Maxwell-Gunter Air Force Base, Ala., 2004—05. Author: (book review) Military Law Review; associate editor (journal) Texas Law Review. Merit badge advisor, instr. Boy Scouts of Am., Montgomery, Ala., 2004—06; media rels. asst. Ch. of Jesus Christ of Latter-day Saints, Montgomery, Ala., 2005—06, edn. counselor, women's group Prattville, Ala., 2005—06. Lt. col. Air Force, 1988—2006, United States. Decorated Crew Mem. Excellence award Eighth Air Force, Disting. Grad. U.S. Air Force Officer Tng. Sch.; recipient Outstanding Career Armed Services Atty. award, Judge Advocates Assn., 2005, Disting. Honor Grad., Judge Adv. General's Sch. of the Army, 2002, Award for Profl. Merit, ABA, 2002, Achievement award, Bus. Associations, Real Estate Transactions, U. of Tex. Sch. of Law, 1994. Mem. J.r. Mgmt. Assn. (chair, bd. of sr. advs. 2004—06), Montgomery Chpt. (exec. com. mem. 2004—06). Ch. Of Jesus Christ Of Latter-Day Saints. Home: 5351 Jane Rd Millbrook AL 36054 Office: Staff Judge Advocate's Office 490 E Moore Dr Ste 280 Montgomery AL 36114 Office Phone: 334-416-3385.

**TURLINGTON, CHRISTY,** model; b. Walnut Creek, Calif., Jan. 2, 1969; d. Dwain and Elizabeth Turlington; m. Ed Burns, June 7, 2003; 1 child. BA in Comparative Religion and Eastern Philosophy, NYU, 1999. With Ford Models, Inc., 1985; model Calvin Klein, 1986, Calvin Klein's Eternity Fragrance, 1988; with Maybelline Cosmetics, 1992; co-creator, skin care line Sundari, 2000—; co-creator, clothing line Nuala. Beauty spread with Vogue, 1987; has worked with Herb Ritts, Patrick Demarchelier, Steven Meisel; has worked for Anne Klein, Michael Kors, Chanel, Perry Ellis; appeared in George Michael's "Freedom" video. Author: Living Yoga. Spokesperson for anti-smoking CDC. Office: United Talent Agy 9560 Wilshire Blvd Ste 500 Beverly Hills CA 90212-2427 also: 344 E 59th St New York NY 10022-1513*

**TURLINGTON, PATRICIA RENFREW,** artist, educator; b. Washington, Sept. 14, 1939; d. Henry Wilson and Anne Ruth (Bright) Renfrew; m. William Troy Turlington III, June 3, 1963 (div. Oct. 1971); children: William Troy IV, David Yelverton; m. William Archie Dees, Jr., June 4, 1994. Student, Meredith Coll., 1957, Washburn U., 1965-66, N.C. State UY., 1969-72. Comml. artist Adlers Inc. & McJoseph's, Raleigh, N.C., 1959-62; exec. dir. Goldsboro (N.C.) Art Ctr., 1973-78; elem. art tchr. Wayne County Day Sch., Goldsboro, 1979-86; art prof. Wayne C.C., Goldsboro, 1986—2005. Artist-in-residence Edward Laredo Inst. of the Humanities, Cochabamba, Bolivia, summer 1988; vis. artist Va. Western C.C., Roanoke, Va., 1986, Wake Forest U., Winston Salem, 1987, Catawba Valley C.C., Hickory, N.C., 1989, Salem Coll., Winston Salem, N.C., 1992. Works represented in permanent colections Blue Cross-Blue Shield, Durham, N.C., Duke Med. Ctr., Mint Mus., Charlotte, U. N.C., Chapel Hill, Wachovia Bank and Trust Co., Winston-Salem; corp. and pub. brick sculpture commissions Brick Assn. N.C., Greensboro, Cohn Enterprises, Lenoir, N.C., Cordova Elem. Sch., Rockingham, N.C., Wilkes C.C., Wilkesboro, N.C., Hocker Bros. Brick and Tile Co., Inc., Green Bay, Wis., Kincaid Brick Co., Tampa, Fla., Koontz Masonry, Lexington, N.C., McDonald's Restaurants, Knoxville, Tenn., Jonesville, N.C., Cary, N.C., Gastonia, N.C., Knightdale, N.C., Fayetteville, N.C, N.Y.C. Transit Authority, N.Y.C., North Dr. Elem. Sch., Goldsboro, N.C., Rowan

Meml. Hosp., Salisbury, N.C. Atlantic Ctr. for the Arts fellow, New Smyrna Beach, Fla., 1986; Pntrs. of the Ams. grantee, U.S. Info. Agy., Washington, 1988. Home: 709 Park Ave Goldsboro NC 27530-3834 Office Phone: 919-734-3459. E-mail: turlingtondees@nc.rr.com.

**TURNAGE, FRED DOUGLAS,** retired lawyer; b. Ayden, N.C., Sept. 24, 1920; s. Fred C. and Lou (Johnson) T.; m. Margaret Futrell, Aug. 21, 1943 (div. Nov. 1980); children: Betty Lou Griffith, Douglas C.; m. Elizabeth Louisa Turnage, Jan. 23, 1981. Grad. Naval Sch. on Far Eastern Civil Affairs, Princeton U., 1945; LLB, Wake Forest U., 1948, LLD, 1970. Bar: N.C. 1948, U.S. Supreme Ct. 1953, US Dist. Ct. D.C. 1965, U.S. Ct. Appeals (D.C. cir.) 1967, U.S. Ct. Appeals (4th and 7th cirs.) 1979. Trial atty. antitrust div. U.S. Dept. Justice, Kansas City, Mo., 1948-51, sr. trial atty. antitrust div. Washington, 1951-65, spl. asst. to atty. gen., 1965; sr. ptnr. Cleary, Gottlieb, Steen & Hamilton, Washington, 1968—, counsel, 1990—2004, ret., 2004. Lectr. continuing legal edn. courses, 1973-77. Contbr. articles to profl. jours. Bd. Visitors Wake Forest U. Sch. Law, Winston-Salem, N.C., 1980—. Served to 1st lt. AUS, 1942-46. Recipient Disting. Service in Law citation Wake Forest U., 1990. Mem. ABA (antitrust and litigation sects.), Fed. Bar Assn., Adv. Bd. Antitrust Bulletin, Wake Forest U. Alumni Assn. (pres. 1977), Nat. Lawyers Clubs. Methodist. Avocations: fishing, golf, writing. Office: 2 Fifth Ave Southern Shores NC 27949

**TURNAGE, JEAN ALLEN,** retired state supreme court chief justice; b. St. Ignatius, Mont., Mar. 10, 1926; JD, Mont. State U., 1951; D of Laws and Letters (hon.), U. Mont., 1995. Bar: Mont. 1951, US Supreme Ct. 1963. Former ptnr. Turnage, McNeil & Mercer, Polson, Mont.; former Mont. State senator from 13th Dist.; pres. Mont. State Senate, 1981—85; chief justice Supreme Ct. Mont., 1985-2001. Mem. Mont. State Bar Assn., Nat. Conf. Chief Justices (past pres.), Nat. Ctr. State Courts (past chair). Office: Turnage & Mercer PO Box 460 Polson MT 59860 Office Phone: 406-883-5367. Personal E-mail: jeanturnage@centurytel.net.

**TURNBAUGH, WILLIAM ARTHUR,** archaeologist, educator; b. Williamsport, Pa., June 1, 1948; s. William Hugh and Louise Elizabeth (Muller) Turnbaugh; m. Sarah Ropes Peabody, Oct. 12, 1974. BA in History summa cum laude, Lycoming Coll., 1970, LHD (hon.), 2006; PhD in Anthropology, Harvard U., 1973. Accredited mem. Register Profl. Archaeologists. Curator of archaeology Lycoming County Mus., Williamsport, 1968-70; tchg. fellow, dept. anthropology Harvard U., Cambridge, Mass., 1971-72, asst. to dir. Peabody Mus., 1973-74; asst. prof. anthropology U. R.I., Kingston, 1974-78, assoc. prof. anthropology, 1978-83, prof. anthropology, 1983—2006, prof. emeritus, 2006—. Ind. contracting archaeologist ea. U.S. and Can., 1968—74; dir. U. R.I. Mus., 1975—77; adv. bd. Inst. Conservation Archaeology, Cambridge, 1976—83. Author: Man, Land and Time, 1975, Material Culture of RI-1000, 1984; co-author: Indian Baskets, 1986, rev. edit., 2004, R.F.D. Country!, 1988, Indian Jewelry of the American Southwest, 1988, rev. edit., 2006, Basket Tales of the Grandmothers, 1999, Understanding Physical Anthropology & Archaeology, 1981, 8th edit., 2002; assoc. editor: Historical Archaeology, 1986—; contbr. articles to profl. jours., chapters to books. V.p., acting pres. Lycoming County Hist. Soc., Williamsport, 1968—70; designed ofcl. flag Lycoming County, Pa., 1970. Recipient Archie award, Soc. Pa. Archaeology, 1967, J. Alden Mason award, 1988; fellow NSF, 1970—73, Woodrow Wilson Found., 1970—71. Fellow: Explorers Club; mem.: Soc. Hist. Archaeology, Soc. Am. Archaeology, Sigma Xi, Phi Alpha Theta, Phi Kappa Phi. Unitarian Universalist. Avocations: travel, geology, American history. Office: Univ RI Dept Sociol and Anthropol Kingston RI 02881 Business E-Mail: wtu4496u@postoffice.uri.edu.

**TURNBULL, ANN PATTERSON,** special education educator, consultant, research director; b. Tuscaloosa, Ala., Oct. 19, 1947; d. H. F. and Mary (Boone) Patterson; m. H. Rutherford Turnbull III, Mar. 23, 1974; children: Jay, Amy, Kate. BS in Edn., U. Ga., 1968; MEd, Auburn U., 1971; EdD, U. Ala., 1972. Asst. prof. U. N.C., Chapel Hill, 1972-80; prof., co-dir. Beach Ctr. U. Kans., Lawrence, 1980—. Author: Free Appropriate Public Education, 2000, Exceptional Lives: Special Education in Today's Schools, 2004, Families, Professionals and Exceptionality, 2006. Recipient Rose Kennedy Internat. Leadership award, Kennedy Found., 1990, 20th Century award in Mental Retardation, 1999; Joseph P. Kennedy Jr. Found. fellow, 1987-88. Mem.: The Arc-U.S. (named Educator of Yr. 1982), Am. Assn. on Mental Retardation (bd. dirs. 1986—88, v.p. 2001, pres.-elect 2002, pres. 2003—04, Rsch. award 2004). Democrat. Avocations: travel, exercise. Office: Univ Kans Beach Ctr 3136 1200 Sunnyside Dr Lawrence KS 66045-7534 Home: 730 New Hampshire St Ste 3K Lawrence KS 66044 Office Phone: 785-864-7608. E-mail: turnbull@ku.edu.

**TURNBULL, CHARLES WESLEY,** governor; b. St. Thomas, V.I., Feb. 5, 1935; BS, Hampton U., 1958, MS, 1959; PhD, U. Minn., 1976, Elem., sec. sch. tchr., asst. prin. various pub. schs.; prin. Charlotte Amalie H.S.; asst. commr. to commr. Dept. Edn.; prof. history U. V.I.; gov. V.I. St. Thomas, 1999—. Chair V.I. Bd. Edn.; bd. dirs. U. V.I., Roy Lester Schneider Hosp.; chmn., Public Fin. Authority. Democrat. Methodist. Office: Office of the Governor Government House 21-22 Kongens Gade St Thomas VI 00802 Office Fax: 340-693-4374.*

**TURNBULL, H. RUTHERFORD, III,** lawyer, educator; b. NYC, Sept. 22, 1937; s. Henry R. and Ruth (White) T.; m. Mary M. Slingluff, Apr. 4, 1964 (div. 1972); m. Ann Patterson, Mar. 23, 1974; children: Jay, Amy, Katherine. Grad., Kent (Conn.) Sch., 1955; BA, Johns Hopkins U., 1959; LLB with honors, U. Md., 1964; LLM, Harvard U., 1969. Bar: Md., N.C. Law clk. to Hon. Emory H. Niles Supreme Bench Balt. City, 1959-60; law clk. to Hon. Roszel C. Thomsen U.S. Dist. Ct. Md., 1962-63; assoc. Piper & Marbury (now Piper Rudnick), Balt., 1964-67; prof. Sch. Govt. U. N.C., Chapel Hill, 1969—80, U. Kans., Lawrence, 1980—. Prof. spl. edn., courtesy prof. law U. Kans. Editor-in-chief Md. Law Rev. Cons.; author, lectr., co-founder, co-dir. Beach Ctr. on Disability, U. Kans.; pres. Full Citizenship Inc., Lawrence, 1987-93; spl. staff-fellow U.S. Senate subcom. on disability policy, Washington, 1987-88; bd. dirs. Camphill Assn. N.Am., Inc., 1985-87; trustee Judge David L. Bazelon Ctr. Mental Health Law, 1993—, chmn., 2000-05. With US Army, 1960-65. Recipient Nat. Leadership award Nat. Assn. Pvt. Residential Resources, 1988, Internat. Coun. for Exceptional Children, 1996, Am. Assn. on Mental Retardation, 1997, Century award Nat. Trust for Hist. Preservation in Mental Retardation, 1999, Nat. Adv. award Am. Music Therapy Assn., 2002, Leadership award Camphill Assn. N.Am., 2004, Leadership award The Arc of the US, 2004, U. Kans. Gene A. Budig Disting. Tchg. Professorship award, 2005, Nat. award advocacy positive supports Assn. Persons with Severe Handicaps, 2005, Kans.U. Sch. of Edn. Disting. Leadership award, 2005, Burton Blatt award Coun. Exceptional Children, 2006; named Nat. Educator of Yr., The Arc of the U.S., 1982; Pub. Policy fellow Joseph P. Kennedy, Jr. Found., 1987-88. Fellow Am. Assn. on Mental Retardation (pres. 1985-86, bd. dirs. 1986—88); mem. ABA (chmn. disability law comm. 1991-95), U.S.A. Assn. for Retarded Citizens (sec. and dir. 1981-83), Assn. for Persons with Severe Handicaps (treas. 1988, bd. dirs. 1987-90), Nat. Assn. Rehab. Rsch. and Tng. Ctrs. (chair govt. affairs com. 1990-93), Internat. Assn. Sci. Study of Mental Deficiency, Internat. League of Assns. for Persons with Mental Handicaps, Johns Hopkins U. Alumni Assn. (pres. N.C. chpt. 1977-79). Democrat. Episcopalian. Office: U Kans 3111 Haworth Hall 1200 Sunnyside Ave Lawrence KS 66045-7534 Office Phone: 785-864-7600. Business E-Mail: Rud@ku.edu.

**TURNBULL, JOHN CAMERON,** retired pharmacist, consultant; b. Regina, Sask., Can., Sept. 5, 1923; s. Cameron Joseph and Lillian Irene (Pentz) T.; m. Hazel Evelyn Rockwell, July 31, 1948; children— Lillian Elizabeth, John Rockwell, Jocelyn Hazel. BS in Pharmacy, U. Sask., 1949. Pharmacist with village and city pharmacies, 1945-50; supr. pharm. services Dept. Pub. Health, Sask., Regina, 1950-52; ops. mgr. Nat. Drugs Ltd., Winnipeg, and Saskatoon, 1953; exec. dir. Can. Pharm. Assn., Toronto, Ont., 1953-78; ret. Sec.-treas., mng. dir. Canadian Pharm. Realty Co. Ltd.; mem. provisional bd. Pharmacare Ltd.; registrar-treas. Pharmacy Examining Bd. of Can., 1963-68, mem. bd., 1963-78; pharmacy cons., dir. drug service Ministry of Health,

Barbados, 1979-84; staff assoc. Mgmt. Scis. for Health, Boston, 1984-85; cons. logistics and pharms. USAID, East Caribbean, PanAm. Health Orgn./WHO (Belize, Cen. Am.), 1985—. Chmn. Govt.'s Spl. Com. on Acetylsalicylic Poisonings, 1967; mem. Emergency Health Svcs. Adv. Com.; gen. chmn. Allied Air Forces Reunion, 1995, 96. Served to squadron leader RCAF, 1941-45. Decorated D.F.C., 1944, Order of Can., 1975; recipient Can. Centennial medal, 1967, Queen's Jubilee medal, 1977, Can. 125th Anniversary medal, 1992, John C. Turnbull rsch. ann. award in socio-econs. pharmacy established in his honor Can. Pharm. Assn., 1990. Mem. Fedn. Internationale Pharmaceutique (v.p.), Inst. of Assn. Execs. (hon. life), Conf. of Pharmacy Registrars of Can. (sec.), Commonwealth Pharm. Assn. (coun. 1969-78); hon. mem. Am., Canadian, Saskatchewan, B.C., Alta., Ont., Man., N.S. Pharm. Assns., Sask. Pharm. Assns., Ont. Pharmacists Assn., Canadian Soc. Hosp. Pharmacists, Rho Pi Phi. Mem. United Ch. of Canada. Club: Bayview Country (past dir.). Office: John and Hazel Turnbull 303-15 Barberry Pl Toronto ON Ontario Canada M2K 1G9 Office Phone: 416-222-4086.

**TURNBULL, MARJORIE REITZ,** foundation executive, retired state legislator; b. Madison, Wis., July 4, 1940; d. J. Wayne and Frances H. (Millikan) R.; m. Augustus Bacon Turnbull, Nov. 26, 1965 (dec. Nov. 1991). Student, Agnes Scott Coll., 1958-60; BA, U. Fla., 1962; MA, U. Ga., 1968. Legis. analyst Fla. Ho. of Reps., Tallahassee, 1973-85, staff dir. com. on health and rehab. svcs., 1975-78, exec. asst. to speaker, 1978-80; asst. dir. Devel. Svc. Program Office, Tallahassee, 1980-82; dep. asst. sec. Health Planning State Fla., 1982-84; ind. cons. legis. mgmt. and planning, Tallahassee, 1984-95, state rep., 1994-2000; exec. dir. Tallahassee C.C. Found., 1995—. County commr. Leon County, Tallahassee, 1988-94; bd. dirs. Fla. Assn. Counties, Tallahassee, 1993-94, Tallahassee Symphony Orch., 1992—, Apalachee coun. Girl Scouts U.S., Tallahassee, 1988—. Recipient Outstanding Svc. in Govt. award Delta Kappa Omega, Tallahassee, 1996; named Woman of Yr., AAUW, Tallahassee, 1991, County Champion in the Legislature, Fla. Assn. Counties, 1995, Legislator of Yr., Fla. Assn. Sch. Supts., 1999; recipient Girl Scout Woman of Distinction award, 1999, Disting. Svc. award Fla. Student Assn., 2000, Disting. Citizens award Boy Scout Coun., 2000, Meritorious Achievement award Fla. A&M U., 2000, Legis. Advocacy award Fla. Coalition Against Domestic Violence, 2000, Freedom from Violence Leadership awrd, 2000, Model of Achievement award Tallahassee C.C., 2001. Mem. Rotary (program com. 1992—), Zonta Internat., Fla. Blue Key. Democrat. Presbyterian. Avocations: scuba diving, travel, cultural activities. Home: 3221 E Lakeshore Dr Tallahassee FL 32312-2062 Office: Tallahassee C C 444 Appleyard Dr Tallahassee FL 32304 E-mail: turnbulm@tcc.fl.edu.

**TURNBULL, MARY REGINA,** secondary school educator; b. Phila., Aug. 27, 1935; d. Thomas Lawrence and Mary Catherine (Shaughnessy) T. BA in Humanities, Villanova U., 1965; MA in Theology/Adolescent Psychology, LaSalle U., Phila., 1969. Cert. tchr., Pa. Tchr. elem. sch., suburban Phila., 1953-64, secondary sch., Warminster, Pa., 1964-69; supr. State Farm Ins., Springfield, Pa., 1969-73; optometric asst. Dr. Ellis S. Edelman, Newtowne Square, Pa., 1973-76; tchr. vocal h.s., Phila., 1976-80, secondary sch., Drexel Hill, Pa., 1980—2005. Tutor special need young adults; vol. Surry Svcs. for Srs.; instr., catechist St. Pius X. Roman Catholic. Office: Msgr Bonner HS 263 Lansdowne Ave Drexel Hill PA 19026 E-mail: jeant19008@msn.com.

**TURNBULL, THOMAS LEIGH,** social studies educator, secondary school educator; b. Bronxville, N.Y., Mar. 2, 1951; s. Kenneth Hamilton and Carolyn Mays Turnbull; 1 child, Sarah McCurrach. BA, U. Calif., Berkeley, Calif., 1983; MA, San Francisco State U., Calif., 1987. Tchr. San Ramon Valley H.S., Danville, Calif., 1986—87, Ygnacio Valley H.S., Concord, Calif., 1993—94, Acalanes H.S., Lafayette, Calif., 1995, Clayton Valley H.S., Concord, 1996—. Home: 10 Park Ave Walnut Creek CA 94595 Office: Clayton Valley High Sch 1101 Alberta Way Concord CA 94521-3799 Office Phone: 925-682-7474.

**TURNBULL, VERNONA HARMSEN,** retired education educator, counseling administrator; b. Teeds Grove, Iowa, Dec. 6, 1916; d. Henry Ferdinand and Ida Amelia (Dohrmann) Harmsen; m. Alexander Turnbull, Oct. 12, 1961. BA, Cornell Coll., Mt. Vernon, Iowa, 1939; MEd, U. Colo., Boulder, 1947, profl. cert. edn., 1955. Cert. secondary and h.s. tchr. Tchr. English, Latin and phys. edn. Winslow (Ill.) H.S., 1939-45; dir. women's activities, instr. Trinidad (Colo.) State Jr. Coll., 1947-53; counselor women, assoc. prof. edn. Western State Coll., Gunnison, Colo., 1953-54; instr., residence counselor Stephens Coll., Columbia, Mo., 1955-61; ret., 1961. Active Salvation Army Aux. Mem. AAUW, AARP (corr. sec. 1986-87), Kena Kampers Camping Club. Avocations: photography, camping, art, dance, baking.

**TURNDORF, HERMAN,** anesthesiologist, educator; b. Paterson, N.J., Dec. 22, 1930; s. Charles R. and Ruth (Blumberg) T.; m. Sietske Huisman, Nov. 24, 1957; children: David, Michael Pieter. AB, Oberlin Coll., 1952; MD, U. Pa., 1956. Diplomate Am. Bd. Anesthesiology. Instr. anesthesiology U. Pa. Hosp., 1957-59; asst. anesthetist med. sch. Harvard U., Mass. Gen. Hosp., Boston, 1961-63; assoc. attending anesthesiologist, asst. dir. dept. anesthesiology Mt. Sinai Hosp., N.Y.C., 1963-70, clin. prof. anesthesiology, 1966-70; prof., chmn. dept. anesthesiology W.Va. U. Sch. Medicine and Med. Ctr., Morgantown, 1970-74, NYU Sch. Medicine, 1974—2000; dir. anesthesiology NYU Tisch Hosp., Bellevue Hosp. Ctr., 1974—2000; pres. med. bd., med. dir. Bellevue Hosp. Med. Ctr., 1990—91, 1997; ret., 2000. Co-author: Anesthesia and Neurosurgery, 2nd edit., 1986, Trauma, Anesthesia and Intensive Care, 1990; contbr. over 200 articles to profl. jours. Lt. M.C., USNR, 1959-61. Fellow Am. Coll. Chest Physicians, Am. Coll. Anesthesiologists (mem. bd. govs. 1977-85, chmn. bd. govs. 1984), N.Y. Acad. Medicine; mem. AMA, Am. Soc. Anesthesiologists, Assn. Univ. Anestheists, Internat. Soc. Study of Pain, Soc. Acad. Anesthesia Chairmen, Soc. Critical Care Medicine, Soc. Neurosurg. Anesthesia and Neurologic Supportive Care, N.Y. Acad. Scis., N.Y. State Soc. Anesthesiologists. Personal E-mail: hermanturndorf@bellsouth.net.

**TURNER, ALICE KENNEDY,** editor; b. Mukden, Manchuria; d. William Taylor and Florence Bell (Green) T. BA, Bryn Mawr Coll., 1962. Sr. editor Holiday mag., N.Y.C., 1969-70; assoc. editor Publishers Weekly, N.Y.C., 1972-74; sr. editor Ballantine Books, N.Y.C., 1974-76, New York mag., N.Y.C., 1976-80; fiction editor Playboy mag., Chgo., N.Y.C., 1980—2001. Author: Yoga for Beginners, 1973, The History of Hell, 1993; co-author: The New York Woman's Guide, 1975; editor: Playboy Stories, 1993, The Playboy Book of Science Fiction, 1996; contbg. editor: Playboy Mag., 2001—; co-editor: Snake's-hands: The Fiction of John Crowley, 2002. Home: 2 Charlton St New York NY 10014-4909 Personal E-Mail: aktnyc@gmail.com.

**TURNER, ALMON RICHARD,** retired art historian, educator; b. New Bedford, Mass., July 28, 1932; s. Louis Alexander and Margaret (Mather) T.; m. Jane Beebe; children: Louis Hamilton, David Alexander. AB, Princeton U., 1955, MFA, 1958, PhD, 1959. Instr. in fine arts U. Mich., Ann Arbor, Mich., 1959-60; from instr. to prof. art and archaeology Princeton U., NJ, 1960-68; prof. fine arts Middlebury Coll., Vt., 1970-74; dean faculty Vt., 1970-74; prof. fine arts, pres. Grinnell Coll., Iowa, 1975-79; prof., dir. Inst. Fine Arts NYU, NYC, 1979-82, dean faculty arts and scis., 1982-85, prof. dept. fine arts, 1985-2000, dir. N.Y. Inst. Humanities, 1986-93, Paulette Goddard prof. in arts and humanities, 1994—2000, prof. emeritus, 2000—. Author: Vision of Landscape in Renaissance Italy, 1966, 73, (With G. Andres and J. Hunisak) Art of Florence (L'Art de Florence), 1988 (prix 1989), Inventing Leonardo, 1993, Renaissance Florence: The Invention of a New Art, 1997, La Pietra: Florence, a Family, and a Villa, 2002 Mem. Coll. Art Assn., Century Assn., NJ Audubon Soc. (1st v.p. 1990-93, pres. 1993-96), Phi Beta Kappa. Democrat. Unitarian Universalist. Avocations: birding, photography. Home: PO Box 2322 Cape May NJ 08204-7322

**TURNER, AMY,** music educator; s. Michael Dawes and Emmie Manning Turner. BMusEd, Wheaton Coll. Conservatory of Music, Ill., 2002; MusM, Ohio State U., Columbus, 2004. Chorus dir. and camp counselor Blue Lake

Fine Arts Camp, Twin Lakes, Mich., 2002; children's choir dir. and organist Winnetka Bible Ch., Ill., 2002—03; chorus and music tchr. Abbott Mid. Sch., Waukegan, 2003; choir dir. Meadowcreek H.S., Norcross, Ga., 2004—. Honors condr. Wheaton Coll. Concert Choir, Ill., 2001—02; pvt. piano tchr., 2003—; mem. Atlanta Sacred Chorale, 2004—; accompanist Ohio State U. Women's Glee Club, Ohio State U. Chorale, Ohio State U. Mastersingers, Ga. Music Educators Assn. Dist. 13 Honors Chorus. Mem. choir Peachtree Corners Bapt. Ch., Norcross, Ga., 2004—. Named to Wheaton Coll. Honor Soc., 2003; fellow, Ohio State U. Grad. Sch. 2003—04. Mem.: Music Educators Nat. Conf., Am. Choral Dir. Assn., Phi Kappa Lambda. Avocations: hiking, reading.

**TURNER, ANDREW L.,** healthcare management company executive; BA, Ohio State Univ. Adminstr skilled nursing facility, Springfield, Ohio, 1970-75; mgr. regional nursing home chain; sr. v.p. ops. Hillhaven Corp.; co-founder Horizon Healthcare Corp., 1986-89; founder, chmn.,CEO Sun Healthcare Group, Albuquerque, 1989—2000; chmn. Ballantrae Healthcare, 2000—; founder, chmn. Endura Care, 2000—; Code Blue Staffing Solutions, 2001—; mem. bd. of directors Sports Clubs/L.A., Watson Pharmaceuticals.

**TURNER, BRACHA,** painter; b. Jerusalem; Exhbns. include 55 solo exhbns. and numerous juried exhbns.: J.F. Kennedy Art Gallery, Montreal, New Eng. Fine Arts Inst., Boston, Internat. Women in the Arts Conf., Beijing, Galerie Everarts, Paris; permanent display of paintings include Hadassah Hdqrs., N.Y., ZOA House, Tel-Aviv, Nat. Coun. of Jewish Women, N.Y., Ichilov Hosp., Tel-Aviv, Office of the Mayor of Jerusalem, Israel, The Bible Mus. Tel Aviv, Office of the Mayor N.Y.C., Rambam Hosp., Haifa, Israel, others; painting reproduced on cards by Hadassah; conthr drawings to Sara's Daughters Sing, 1989.

**TURNER, CRAIG,** editor, journalist; b. Pasadena, Calif., May 24, 1949; s. Donald Leslie and Dorothy A. (Kupseck) T.; m. Ellen Bevier, Oct. 10, 1973 (div. Dec. 1983); m. Joyce Huyett, Sept. 10, 1988. BS in Journalism, San Jose State U., 1971. Reporter LA Times, Orange County, Calif., 1971-79, asst. city editor San Diego, 1979-83, asst. met. editor, 1983-89, met. editor, 1989-93, fgn. corr. Toronto, Ont., Canada, 1994-95; bur. chief UN, 1997-99; editor Nat. Edit., LA Times, 1999—2001, weekend editor, 2001—. Co-recipient Pulitzer Prize for journalism, 1993, George Polk award Long Island U., 1993, Korn Ferry award, 1998. Mem. Soc. Profl. Journalists. Episcopalian. Avocations: outdoor activities, travel, theater. Office: Los Angeles Times 202 W 1st St Los Angeles CA 90012 E-mail: craig.turner@latimes.com.

**TURNER, DALLAS G., JR.,** physics professor; s. Dallas G. and Georgia L. Turner; m. Wendy J. Watson, Aug. 13, 1994. BS, Eureka Coll., Ill., 1992. Cert. secondary edn. Ill., 1992. Physics tchr. Rockford Pk. (Ill.) H.S., 1992—94; sci. tchr. Harvard (Ill.) H.S., 1994—95; interim pastor United Brethren in Christ Ch., Urbandale, 1996—97; physics tchr. Jefferson H.S., Rockford, Ill., 1997—. Mem.: Am. Assn. Physics Tchrs. (assoc.), Nat. Assn. Rocketry (assoc.). Avocations: theology, rockets, softball. Office: Jefferson High Sch 4145 Samuelson Rd Rockford IL 61109 Office Phone: 815-397-7853. Business E-Mail: dallas.turner@rps205.com.

**TURNER, DAVID REUBEN,** publisher, author; b. N.Y.C., Dec. 9, 1915; s. Charles and Eva (Turner) Turner; m. Ann Louise Perkins, Apr. 29, 1946 (div. 1976); children— Eve (Mrs. William Watters), Ruth. BS, Coll. City N.Y., 1936, MS in Edn. 1937. Co-founder Arco Pub. Co., N.Y.C., 1937, pub. dir., 1937-78; v.p. parent co. Prentice-Hall, Inc., 1979-80; pres. Turner Pub., 1980-92. Pub. cons. under Ford Found. contract Burma Translation Soc., Rangoon, 1955—60. Author: more than 300 books on tests and testing, including High School Equivalency Diploma Tests, 1951, 75, How to Win a Scholarship, 1955, Scoring High On College Entrance Tests, 1969, 71, Food Service Supervisor, 1968, Bank Examiner, 1968, Accountant-Auditor, 1960, 77, Officer Candidate Tests, 1978, Professional-Administrative Career Exams, 1979, English Grammar and Usage for Test-Takers, 1976, College Level Examination Program, 1979. Advisor bd. publs. Union Am. Hebrew Congregations. Home and Office: 13 Glengary Rd Croton On Hudson NY 10520-2139

**TURNER, DEL L.,** social studies educator; b. Maywood, Calif., June 2, 1950; s. Dwight and Mary Turner; m. Kathryn Collins-Turner, Dec. 25, 1978; children: Patrick, Rochel. BA in Sociology, Whittier Coll., Calif., 1972. Cert. tchr. Wyo. Tchr. ESL U.S. Peace Corps, Iran, 1973—75; constrn. foreman Fluor Corp., Valdez, Alaska, 1975—77; tchr. social studies Chinle H.S., Ariz., 1978—81; tchr. history and govt. Lyman Mid. and H.S., Wyo., 1982—. Baseball coach Chinie H.S., 1979—81; football coach Lyman H.S., Wyo., 1986—88, 1996—99, Lyman Mid. Sch., 1982—85, 2000—05, wrestling coach, Wyo., 1982—85, 1990—93. Recipient Paul Willie award, Lyman H.S., 1997. Avocation: gardening. Office: Lyman HS PO Box 1090 Lyman WY 82937-1090

**TURNER, E. DEANE,** lawyer; b. Auburn, NY, Aug. 4, 1928; s. Alfred Edward and Bertha (Deane) T. AB summa cum laude, Princeton U., 1950; LLB cum laude, Harvard U., 1953. Bar: NY 1953. Assoc. Dewey Ballantine LLP and predecessor firms, N.Y.C., 1953-63, ptnr., 1963—, of counsel, 1991—. Treas. Harvard Law Sch. Assn., N.Y.C., 1964-83; elder, trustee Brick Presbyn. Ch., N.Y.C., 1976—; pres. bd. trustees, 1988-90; trustee Presbytery N.Y.C., 1993-98, pres. bd. trustees, 1995-98; com. to adminstr. James N. Jarvie Endowment, 1993-2000. Fellow Am. Coll. Investment Counsel (emeritus); mem. Soc. Mayflower Descendants, Soc. Colonial Wars, Union Club, John's Island Club, Phi Beta Kappa. Republican. Home: 1120 5th Ave New York NY 10128-0144 also: 381 Llwyds Ln Johns Island Vero Beach FL 32963 Office: Dewey Ballantine LLP 1301 Avenue Of The Americas New York NY 10019-6022

**TURNER, ELAINE S.,** allergist, immunologist; b. Glen Cove, N.Y., 1947; MD, Med. Coll. Pa., 1974. Diplomate Am. Bd. Allergy & Immunology, Am. Bd. Internal Medicine. Intern Michael Reese Hosp., Chgo., 1974-75; resident in internal medicine Cleve. Clinic, 1976-78; fellow in allergy & immunology Northwestern U., Chgo., 1978-80; with St. Mary's Hosp., Va., Henrico Drs. Hosp., Va. Mem. ACP, Am. Acad. Allergy, Asthma and Immunology, Va. Allergy Soc., Richmond Acad. Medicine. Office: Va Adult & Pediat Allergy & Allergy Ste 103 7605 Forest Ave Richmond VA 23229-4936

**TURNER, ELIZABETH ADAMS NOBLE (BETTY TURNER),** real estate company executive; b. Yonkers, NY, May 18, 1931; d. James Kendrick and Orrel (Baldwin) Noble; m. Jack Rice Turner, July 11, 1953; children: Jay Kendrick, Randall Ray. BA, Vassar Coll., 1953; MA, Tex. A&U U., 1964. Ednl. cons., Tex. sales mgr. Noble & Noble Pub. Co., N.Y.C., 1956-67; psychometrist Corpus Christi Guidance Ctr., 1967-70; psychologist Corpus Christi State Sch., 1970-72, dir. programs asst. supt., 1972, dir. devel. and vol. svc., 1972-76, dir. rsch. and tng., 1977-79; psychologist Tex. Mental Health and Mental Retardation, 1970-79, program cons., 1979-85; pres. Turner Co., 1975-82; mayor pro tem Corpus Christi, 1981-85; mayor, 1987-91; CEO, pres. Corpus Christi C. of C., 1991-94; pres. Betty Turner Real Estate, 1999—. V.p. bus. and govt. rels. ctrl. and south Tex. divsns. Columbia Healthcare Corp., 1994—99. Author: The Noble Legacy. Dir. alumni Corpus Christi State U., 1976-77; coord. vols. Summer Head Start Program, Corpus Christi, 1967; chmn. spl. gifts com. United Way, Corpus Christi, 1970; mem. Corpus Christi City Coun., 1979-91; family co-founded Barnes and Noble, N.Y.C.; founder Com. of 100 and Goals for Corpus Christi; pres. USO; bd. dirs. Coastal Bend Coun. Govts., Corpus Christi Mus., Harbor Playhouse, Cmtys. in Schs., YWCA, Y-Teen Sponsor, Del Mar Coll. Found., Tex. A&M at Corpus Christi Pres.' Coun., Food Bank, Hispanic C. of C., TAMACC Corp. Ptnrs., Salvation Army, Jr. League, Coun. Deaf Silent Found.; bd. Southside Cmty. Hosp., 1987-93, Gulfway Nat. Bank, 1985-92, bd. dirs.; strategic planning com. Meml. Hosp., 1992, Tex. Capital Network Bd., 1992-95, Humana Hosp., Physician Relocation and Condo Sales, Rehab. Hosp., dir. of vols., South Tex., Admiral Tex. Navy; bd. dirs. Pacific Southwest Bank, 1997-2000, St. David's/Austin and Medth. Healthcare Sys.,

San Antonio, 1997-99; apptd. Gov.'s Commn. for Women, 1984-85, Leadership Tex. Class I, Corpus Christi, Class II; founder Goals for Corpus Christi, Bay Area Sports Assn., Assn. Coastal Bend Mayor's Alliance; founder Mayor's Commn. on the Disabled, Mayor's Task Force on the Homeless; active Port Aransas Cmty. Ch., U. Tex. Sch. Nursing Adv. Coun., 1998-99; bd. dirs. Del Mar Coll. Found., 1988-89. Mem. Am. Heart Assn., 1999-2000, Bethune Day Care Nursery, 1999-2004, Jr. League Cmty. Adv. Coun., 1999-2000, Strategic Planning Com., 2000—, Silent Found., 2001—, 21st Century Charter Sch., 2001-02, Boys and Girls Club of Corpus Christi, 2002-05, Nat. AARP, 2002-04; pres. Food Bank, 2004-05; elder Cmty. Presbyn. Ch. Named Corpus Christi Newsmaker of Yr., 1987; recipient Love award, YWCA, 1970, Y's Women and Men in Careers award, 1988, Recognition award, Rotary, 1991, Comdr.'s award for pub. svc., U.S. Army, Scroll of Honor award, Navy League, award, Tex. Hwy Dept., Road Hand award, Tex. Hwy. Commn., Women of Distinction award, Girl Scouts Tex. Mem. NAACP (life), Tex. Psychol. Assn. (pres., mem. exec. bd.), Psychol. Assn. (pres., founder), Tex. Mcpl. League (bd. dirs.), Jr. League Corpus Christi, Tex. Bookman's Assn., Tex. Assn. Realtors, Corpus Christi Town Club, Corpus Christi Yacht Club, Jr. Cotillion Club, hon. Delta Kappa Gamma, Kappa Kappa Gamma. Home: 403 Blue Heron Dr Port Aransas TX 78373 Office Phone: 361-749-5712. Business E-Mail: bettyturner@centurytel.net.

**TURNER, ELVIN L.,** retired school system administrator; b. Springfield, Ohio, Jan. 9, 1938; s. Willie and Jinada (Lawson) T.; m. Betty Jo Breckinridge, June 11, 1966 (div. Jan. 1972); 1 child, Anthony; m. Carrie Johnson, Aug. 3, 1972; 1 child, Brenetta Bell. BS in Biology and Chemistry, Knoxville Coll., Tenn., 1962; MEd, U. Cin., 1968; postgrad., Nova U., Ft. Lauderdale, Fla., 1973, Kensington U., Glendale, Calif., 1993—. Cert. secondary prin., tchr., Ohio. Spl. edn. tchr. Cin. Pub. Schs., 1965-69, coord. spl. edn., 1969-72, asst. prin., 1972-78, prin., 1978-90, asst. prin., 1990-93. Part-time adj. prof. Mt. St. Joseph Coll., Ohio, 1987—88; mem. adv. com. Millcreek Psychiat. Ctr. for Children, Cin., 1988—89; bus driver Bristol Village Retirement Cmty., 1997—99; ombudsman Pro-Srs., Cin., 1993—96, Waverly, Ohio, 1997—2005; vol. ombudsman rep. Area Agy. on Aging Dist. Seven, Inc., Portsmouth, Ohio; sec. Bristol Village Residents Assn., 1997. Author: numerous poems. Vol. Ohio Dept Aging, Columbus, 2002—; asst. feeding program Visiting The Sick Ministries; master of ceremonies Black History Month Soul Food Luncheon; elected sec. exec. adv. coun. Bristol Village Nat. Ch. Residencies, Waverly, 1997; bd. deacons New Hope Bapt. Ch., Hamilton, Ohio, 1993; Sunday sch. tchr. Bethel AME Ch., Lebanon, Ohio, 1996; chmn. sick com. Usher Bd.; Bible study course instr. Asbury North United Meth. Ch., Columbus, 2000—01, instr. Vacation Bible Sch., 2000; bd. dirs. Big Bros./Big Sisters, Cin., 1973. Recipient plaque for statewide outstanding sr. vol. radio, TV and newspaper coverage, Independence, Ohio, 2001. Mem. Nat. Assn. for Secondary Sch. Prins., Ohio Assn. Secondary Sch. Adminstrs., So. Law Poverty Ctr. (named to Wall of Tolerance 2004), Knoxville Coll. Alumni Assn., Phi Delta Kappa, Alpha Phi Alpha. Avocations: bowling, golf, reading, travel, writing. Home: PO Box 13617 Columbus OH 43213-0617

**TURNER, EUGENE ANDREW,** manufacturing executive; b. Bridgeton, N.J., Aug. 7, 1928; s. Benjamin Homer and Pearl Irene (Wolbert) T.; m. Paula Ann Webb, 1987; children: Mary Ann, John-Reed. BA, Rutgers U., 1956; student, Columbia U., 1980. With Owens Ill., 1950-73, regional mgr. West Coast, 1970-73; v.p. adminstrn. Midland Glass Co., Cliffwood, NJ, 1973-76, pres., chief operating officer, 1981-82, also bd. dirs.; v.p., gen. mgr. Anchor Hocking Corp., Lancaster, Ohio, 1976-81; dir. ops. Theo Chem. Labs., Tampa, Fla., 1988-90, Profit Counselors Inc, Sarasota, Fla., 1990-94; pres. Profit Sys. Inc., Oklahoma City, 1994—. Mng. cons. 1987-88; trustee Glass Packaging Inst. Mem. Harbor Island Club, Seaview Country Club, Navesink Country Club. Home: 1103 Tedford Way Oklahoma City OK 73116-6006 Office Phone: 405-209-1103. Personal E-mail: gene227@juno.com. *Take time to learn the chosen business then develop credibility by doing what you say you will do.*

**TURNER, FLORENCE FRANCES,** ceramist; b. Detroit, Mar. 9, 1926; d. Paul Pokrywka and Catherine Gagal; m. Dwight Robert Turner, Oct. 23, 1948; children: Thomas Michael, Nancy Louise, Richard Scott, Garry Robert. Student, Oakland C.C., Royal Oak, Mich., 1975-85, U. Ariz., Yuma, 1985, U. Las Vegas, 1989—. Pres., founder Nev. Clay Guild, Henderson, 1990-94, mem. adv. bd., 1994-2000, v.p., 2000—02. Workshop leader Greenfield Village, Dearborn, Mich., 1977-78, Plymouth (Mich.) Hist. Soc., 1979, Las Vegas Sch. System, 1989-90, Detroit Met. area, 1977-85. Bd. dirs. Las Vegas Art Mus., 1987-91; corr. sec. So. Nev. Creative Art Ctr., Las Vegas, 1990-94. Mem.: Nev. Camera Club, Las Vegas Gem Club, Phi Kappa Phi. Avocations: photography, collecting gems, travel.

**TURNER, FRANK MILLER,** historian, educator; b. Springfield, Ohio, Oct. 31, 1944; s. Ronald O. and Mary Elizabeth (Miller) T.; m. Margaret Good, Aug. 26, 1967 (div. 1981); m. Nancy Rash, July 29, 1984 (dec. Mar. 1995); m. Ellen L. Tillotson, Aug. 7, 1999. BA, Coll. of William and Mary, 1966; MPhil, Yale U., 1970, PhD, 1971; LHD (hon.), Coll. William and Mary, 1991. Asst. prof. Yale U., New Haven, 1972-77, assoc. prof., 1977-82, prof., 1982—, provost, 1988-92, John Hay Whitney prof. history, 1992—, dir. Beinecke Rare Book and Manuscript Libr. Author: Between Science and Religion, 1974, The Greek Heritage in Victorian Britain, 1981, Contesting Cultural Authority: Essays in Victorian Intellectual Life, 1993, Reflections on the Revolution in France, 2003; co-author: The Western Heritage, 1979, 83, 87, 91, 94, 97, 2000, 2003, Heritage of World Civilizations, 1985, 90, 93, 96, 99; editor: John Henry Newman, The Idea of a University, 1996.; contbr. articles to profl. jours. Trustee Conn. Coll., New London, 1996—. Guggenheim fellowship, 1983; recipient Brit. Coun. prize Conf. on Brit. Studies, 1982, Yale Press Gov.'s award, 1983. Office: Yale U History Dept PO Box 208324 New Haven CT 06520-8324 Office Phone: 203-432-1367, E-mail: frank turner@yale.edu.

**TURNER, FRED L.,** retired fast food company executive; b. 1933; married. BS, Drake U., 1954. With McDonald's Corp., Oak Brook, Ill., 1956—2004, exec. v.p., 1967—68, pres., chief adminstrv. officer, 1968—73, CEO, 1973—87, chmn., 1977—90, sr. chmn., 1990—2004, hon. chmn. With U.S. Army, 1954-56. Office: McDonald's Corp One Kroc Dr Oak Brook IL 60523

**TURNER, GEORGE MASON,** lawyer; b. Butte, Mont., Sept. 2, 1935; s. William Dale and Bernice (Ownby) T.; m. Angela Gloria Aparicio, Oct. 14, 1995; children: Esther, Lesley, Allyson, Aarin, Alexander. BS in Polit. Sci., Brigham Young U., Provo, Utah, 1959, MS in Polit. Sci., 1960; JD, UCLA, 1968. Bar: Calif. 1969, U.S. Dist. Ct. Calif. 1969, U.S. Supreme Ct. 1976, U.S. Ct. Claims 1981, U.S. Tax Ct. 1981. Assoc. Munns & Kofford, Pasadena, Calif., 1969-72; ptnr. Turner & Smart, Pasadena, 1985—; pvt. practice, 1972—. Instr. estate tax law Am. Coll. Bryn Mawr, Pa., 1976; monitor Continuing Edn. of Bar, Calif., 1985. Author: Revocable Trusts, 5th edit., 2003, Irrevocable Trusts, 3d edit., 1997, Revocable Trusts-The Centerpiece of Estate Planning, 2d edit., 2005, Practical Approaches to Estate Planning, 2005. V.p. San Gabriel Valley Boy Scouts Am., Pasadena, 1976-78; pres. San Gabriel Valley Estate Planning Co., Pasadena, 1979-80; bd. dirs., chmn. bd. Calif. Family Study Ctr., North Hollywood, 1975-92, Ettie Lee Homes, Los Angeles, 1984-90. Recipient Silver Beaver award Boy Scout Am., 1979. Mem. ABA, Calif. Bar Assn., Los Angeles Bar Assn., Pi Sigma Alpha. Republican. Mem. Lds Ch. Avocation: photography. Office Phone: 626-795-8491. E-mail: gmt9235@yahoo.com.

**TURNER, HARRY SPENCER,** preventive medicine physician, educator; b. Dayton, Ohio, Sept. 25, 1938; s. Eli and Daphne (Cunagin) T.; m. Jan (Fairley) T.; children: Michael, Mary, Daniel. BA, Manchester Coll., North Manchester, Ind., 1960; MD summa cum laude, Ohio State U., 1963, MS in Preventive Medicine, 1968. Diplomate Am. Bd. Preventive Medicine. Resident in preventive (aerospace) medicine Ohio State U., Columbus, 1966-69, chief resident, 1968-69, clin. asst. prof. dept. preventive medicine, 1969-80, dir. Univ. Health Svc., 1970-80; pvt. practice Dayton 1980-90; dir. Univ. Health Svc., head team physician U. Ky., Lexington, 1991—2003, prof. preventive medicine and environ. health, 1991—2003, prof. emeritus, 2003, dir. emeri-

tus, 2003; med. dir. Sutton Pl. Behavioral Health, 2003—. Editor: (textbook) History and Practice of College Health, 2002; contbr. articles and papers to profl. jours. and meetings. Bd. dirs. Blue Shield, 1981-86; mem. Cin. Internat. Chorale, 1989-94; mem. Lexington Singers, 1992—2003. Capt. U.S. Army, 1964-66. Fellow Am. Coll. Preventive Medicine, Am. Coll. Health Assn. (pres. 1980, Ruth Boynton award 1982, Edw. Hitchcock award 1996, Lifetime Achievement award 2003), Alpha Omega Alpha Avocation: music. E-mail: hturner904@comcast.net.

**TURNER, HARRY WOODRUFF,** lawyer; b. Blairsville, Pa., May 2, 1939; s. James McKinnie and Dorothy Elizabeth (Tittle) Turner; m. Mary Elizabeth Phelan, Dec. 30, 1972; children: James William, David Woodruff. AB, U. Pitts., 1961; JD, Harvard U., 1964. Bar: Pa. 1965, U.S. Supreme Ct. 1979. Assoc. Kirkpatrick & Lockhart, Nicholson, Graham LLP, Pitts., 1964-71; ptnr. Kirkpatrick & Lockhart, Nicholson, Graham, Pitts., 1971—. Bd. vis. Coll. Arts & Scis. U. Pitts., 1988—2003, chmn. bd. vis. Sch. Info. Scis., 1994—2002, trustee, 1995—2003, bd. vis. Med. Sch., 1995—2002; mem. Fed. Jud. Selection Commn., Pa., 1995—, chmn., 1997—. Trustee Pitts. Opera, 1993—, pres., 2001—04; trustee, v.p. Torrance (Pa.) State Hosp., 1969—73; chair distbn. com. William L. Benz Found., 1985—; bd. dirs. Am. Heart Assn., Pitts., 1993—2002; alt. del. Rep. Nat. Conv., Miami, 1968, Houston, 1992, Phila., 2000, Rep. State Com., 1994—; trustee U. Pitts., 1995—2003, Wilson Coll., Chambersburg, Pa., 1978—89, Pitts. Cultural Trust, 2002—04. Mem.: SAR (pres. 1995—96), ABA, Allegheny County Acad. Trial Lawyers, Allegheny County Bar Assn., Internat. Acad. Trial Lawyers, Am. Law Inst., Pa. Bar Assn., Hist. Soc. Western Pa. (trustee 1993—2006, vice chmn. 1999—2003), U. Pitts. Alumni Assn. (pres. 1991 92), Duquesne Club, Fox Chapel Golf Club. Presbyterian. Office: Kirkpatrick & Lockhart Henry W Oliver Bldg 535 Smithfield St Ste 535 Pittsburgh PA 15222 Office Phone: 412-355-6478. E-mail: wturner@klng.com.

**TURNER, HENRY BROWN,** finance company executive, director; b. NYC, Sept. 3, 1936; s. Henry Brown III and Gertrude (Adams) T.; m. Sarah Jean Thomas, June 7, 1958 (div.); children: Laura Eleanor, Steven Bristow, Nancy Carolyn. AB, Duke U., 1958; MBA, Harvard U., 1962. Controller Fin. Corp. of Ariz., Phoenix, 1962-64; treas., dir. corporate planning Star-Kist Foods, Terminal Island, Calif., 1964-67; dir., 1st v.p. Mitchum, Jones & Templeton, Los Angeles, 1967-73; asst. sec. Dept. Commerce, Washington, 1973-74; v.p. fin. N-Ren Corp., Cin., 1975-76; v.p. Oppenheimer & Co., N.Y.C., 1976-78; exec. v.p., mng. dir. corporate fin. Shearson Hayden Stone Inc., N.Y.C., 1978-79; sr. mng. dir. Ardshiel Inc., 1980-81, pres., 1981-93, chmn. emeritus, 1994—. Vis. lectr. U. Va. Sch. of Bus.; bd. dirs. MacDonald & Co., Pembrook Mgmt., Inc., Golden State Vitners, Inc., Cellu-Tissue Corp., Wrangler Four Peaks Ranch, Rio Verde, Ariz. Sponsor Jr. Achievement, 1964-67. Served to lt. USNR, 1958-60. Coll. Men's Club scholar Westfield, N.J., 1954-55 Mem. Fed. Govt. Accountants Assn. (hon.), Duke Washington Club, Omicron Delta Kappa.

**TURNER, HUGH JOSEPH, JR.,** lawyer; b. Paterson, NJ, Oct. 5, 1945; s. Hugh Joseph and Louise (Sullivan) T.; m. Charlene Chiappetta, Feb. 11, 1983. BS, Boston U., 1967; JD, U. Miami, Coral Gables, Fla., 1975. Bar: Fla. 1975, U.S. Dist. Ct. (so. and mid. dists.) Fla. 1975, U.S. Ct. Appeals (11th cir.) 1981, U.S. Supreme Ct. 1984. Tchr. Browne & Nichols, Cambridge, Mass., 1968-72; ptnr. Smathers & Thompson, Miami, Fla., 1981-87, Kelley Drye & Warren, Miami, 1987-93, English, McCaughan & O'Bryan, Ft. Lauderdale, 1993—2001, Redgrave & Turner LLP, Boca Raton, Fla., 2001—03, Akerman Senterfitt, Ft. Lauderdale, 2003—. Chmn. Fla. Bar internat. law sect., 1988-89. Contbg. author book on internat. dispute resolution Fla. Bar, 1989; contbr. articles to profl. jours. Bd. dirs. Japan Soc. South Fla., Miami, 1989-97; mem. Sea Ranch Lakes Village Coun., 1997-2000; mayor Sea Ranch Lakes, 2000-02. Mem.: ABA, Def. Rsch. Inst. Avocation: running. Office: Akerman Senterfitt Ste 1600 350 E Las Olas Blvd Fort Lauderdale FL 33301-2229 Office Phone: 954-463-2700. Business E-Mail: hugh.turner@akerman.com.

**TURNER, JAMES A.,** architecture educator; BS, U. Mich., 1971, MArch, 1973. Tchg. asst. U. Mich. Sch. Arch., Ann Arbor, 1971—73, instr., 1976—79, asst. prof., 1979—85, assoc. prof., 1985—92; prof. arch. U. Mich. Taubman Coll. Arch. and Urban Planning, Ann Arbor, 1992—, assoc. chair arch., 1992—; assoc. rsch. scientist U. Mich. Sch. Arch., Ann Arbor, 1985—92; mem. computer policy com. U. Mich. Coll. Arch. and Urban Planning. Author: Architectural Acoustic Teaching Software, 1997. Mem.: Assn. Computer-Aided Design in Arch. Office: Univ Mich Taubman Coll Arch and Urban Planning 2000 Bonisteel Blvd Ann Arbor MI 48109-2069

**TURNER, JAMES LEE,** utilities executive, lawyer; b. Muncie, Ind., Aug. 20, 1959; s. Jack Edwin and Nancy Kathleen (Marvin) T.; m. Leah Wakeland, Dec. 26, 1981; 3 children. BS, Ball State U., 1981; JD cum laude, Ind. U., 1984. Bar: Ind. 1984, U.S. Dist. Ct. (so. dist.) Ind. 1984. Assoc. Bingham, Summers, Welsh & Spilman, Indpls., 1984—90, ptnr., 1990—91; Utility Consumer Counselor State of Indiana, 1991—93; principal Lewis & Kappes, Indpls., 1993—95; with Cinergy Corp., Cin., 1995—, v.p. cust svc., 1999—2000, pres. energy delivery bus. unit, 2000—01, CEO regulated bus. unit, 2001—04, exec. v.p., CFO, 2004—05, pres., 2005—. Mem. exec. com. Nat. Assn. State Utility Consumer Advocates, 1992; bd. dir. NAM. Mem. Ohio State Bd. of Edn., 2000—04; bd. mem. Cin. Mus. Ctr., Boys & Girls Clubs Greater Cin. Mem. ABA, (environ. law com., Tort & Ins. Practice Sect.), Ind. State Bar Assn., Indpls. Bar Assn. Def. Research Inst. Clubs: Sierra (Hoosier chtp. Indpls.). Democrat. Office: Cinergy Corp 139 E 4th St Cincinnati OH 45202 Mailing: Cinergy Corp PO Box 960 Cincinnati OH 45201-0960*

**TURNER, JAMES THOMAS,** judge; b. Clifton Forge, Va., Mar. 12, 1938; s. James Thomas and Ruth (Greene) T.; m. Patricia Sue Renfrow, July 8, 1962; 1 child, James Thomas A. Wake Forest Coll., 1960; JD, U. Va., 1965. Bar: Va. 1965, U.S. Ct. Appeals (4th and fed. cirs.), U.S. Supreme Ct. Assoc. Williams, Worrell, Kelly & Greer, Norfolk, Va., 1965, ptrn., 1971-79; U.S. magistrate U.S. Dist. Ct. (ea. dist.) Va., Norfolk, 1979-87; judge U.S. Ct. Fed. Claims, 1987—. Mem. ABA, Fed. Bar Assn., Va. Bar Assn., Norfolk and Portsmouth Bar Assn. (sec. 1975-79). Office: 717 Madison Pl NW Washington DC 20439-0002

**TURNER, JANET SULLIVAN,** painter, sculptor; b. Gardiner, Maine, Nov. 15, 1935; d. Clayton Jefferson and Frances (Leighton) Sullivan; m. Terry Turner, Oct. 6, 1956; children: Lisa Turner Reid, Michael Ross, Jonathan Brett. BA cum laude, Mich. State U., 1956. Rep. Am. Women in Art, UN World Conf. on Women, Nairobi, Kenya, 1985. One-woman shows include San Diego Art Inst., 1971, St. Joseph U., Phila., 1981, Villanova (Pa.) U. Gallery, 1982, Pa. State U., Middletown (Pa.), 1985, Temple U. (Pa.), 1986, Widener U. Art Mus., Chester, Pa., 1987, 94, Rosemont Coll., Pa., 1995, Sande Webster Gallery, Phila., 1998, 2000, retrospective Widener U. Art Gallery, 2005; exhibited in group shows at Del. Art Mus., Wilmington, 1978, Woodmere Art Mus., Phila., 1980, 2000, Port of History Mus., Phila., 1984, Allentown Art Mus., 1984, Trenton (NJ) City Mus. Ellarslie Open VIII, 1989, Ammo Gallery, Bklyn., 1989, Pa. State Mus., Harrisburg, 1990-94, Galeria Mesa, Ariz., 1991, Del. Ctr. for Contemporary Arts, Wilmington, 1992, Holter Mus., Helena, Mont., 1992, S.W. Tex. State U., San Marcos, 1993, Fla. State U. Mus., Tallahassee, 1993, Newark Mus., 1993, U. Del., 1994, 1st St. Gallery, NYC, 1994, Noyes Mus., NJ, 1995, Sande Webster Gallery, Phila. 1995-2006, Phila. Art Mus., 1997, Krasdale Gallery, White Plains, NY, 2001, Moore Coll. of Art, Phila. Sculptors, Phila. Pa., 2002, Philips Mus. Franklin Marshall Coll., 2004, Widener U. Art Gallery, 2005, Retrospective Sumner Sch. Art Mus., Washington, otheres; represented in permanent collections Nat. Mus. Women in Arts, "American Album", Wash. D.C., Avocat Art Mus., East Lansing, Mich, ARA Svc. Inc., Phila., Blue Cross/Blue Shield, Phila., Am. Nat. Bank and Trust Co., Rockford, Ill., Burroughs Corp., Lisle, Ill., State Mus. Pa., Harrisburg, Bryn Mawr (Pa.) Coll., Rosemont Coll., Villanova (Pa.) Coll., LaSalle U. Art Mus., Phila., Noyes Mus., NJ, Nat. Liberty Mus., Phila., Kimmel Ctr., Phila. Bd. dirs. Rittenhouse Sq. Fine Arts Ann., Phila.,

1984—86. Recipient 2d pl. award San Diego Art Inst. 19th Ann. Exhbn., 1971, award of merit Pavilion Gallery, Mt. Holly, N.J., 1991, 3d pl. Katonah Mus. of Art, N.Y., 1992, purchase award State Mus. of Pa., Harrisburg, 1992. Mem. Artists Equity (pres. 1987-88), Nat. League of Am. Pen Woman, Phila Watercolor Club, Delta Phi Delta. Republican. Roman Catholic. Home: 88 Cambridge Dr Glen Mills PA 19342-1545 Office Phone: 610-358-2094.

**TURNER, JIM (JAMES W. TURNER),** lawyer, former congressman; b. Ft. Lewis, Wash., Feb. 6, 1946; m. Ginny; 2 children. BBA, U. Tex., 1968, MBA, JD, U. Tex., 1971. Lawyer; mayor City of Crockett, Tex., 1989—91; mem. Tex. Ho. Reps., 1981—84, Tex. State Senate, 1991—96, 105-108th Congresses from 2nd Tex. dist., 1997—2005; mem. govt. oversight com.; former mem. nat. security com.; ranking mem. House Select Com. on Homeland Security; ptnr. Arnold & Porter LLP, Washington, 2005—. Mem. Econ. Growth, Natural Resources, and Regulatory Affairs subcom., Nat. Security, Internat. Affairs, and Criminal Justice subcom. House Govt. Reform and Oversight Com., Mil. Rsch. and Devel. subcom., Mil. Procurement subcom. House Nat. Security Com. Served in U.S. Army, 1970—78. Democrat. Baptist. Office: Arnold & Porter LLP 555 Twelfth St NW Washington DC 20004

**TURNER, JOHN ANDREW,** economist; b. Chgo., July 9, 1949; s. Henry Andrew and Mary Margaret (Tilton) T.; m. Kathleen King Peery, June 21, 1975; 1 child, Sarah. BA, Pomona Coll., Claremont, Calif., 1971; MA, Stanford U., 1972; PhD, U. Chgo., 1977. Rsch. econ. SSA, Washington, 1976-80, U.S. Dept. Labor, Washington, 1980-96, ILO, Geneva, 1996-98; rsch. econ. Office of Sec. U.S. Dept. Labor, 1999-2000, Pub. Policy Inst., AARP, 2000—. Cons. OECD, Paris, 1989, IMF, 1995, AFL-CIO, 1996; chmn. Internat. Pension Conf., U.S. Dept. Labor, Washington, 1990; adj. prof. George Washington U., 1994-96. Author: Pension Policy for a Mobile Labor Force, 1993, Individual Accounts for Social Security Reform, 2006; editor: Trends in Pensions, 1989 (transl. into Japanese 1991), Pension Policy: An International Perspective, 1991, Trends in Health Benefits, 1993, Private Pension Policies in Industrialized Countries, 1995, Securing Employer-Based Pensions, 1996, Social Security: Development and Reform, 2000. Fulbright scholar Institut de Recherches Economiques et Sociales, France, 1994. Mem. Am. Econ. Assn., Nat. Acad. Social Ins. Methodist. Avocation: tennis. Home: 3713 Chesapeake St NW Washington DC 20016-1813 Office: AARP 601 E St NW Washington DC 20049 Personal E-mail: turnerjilo@aol.com, jturner47@verizon.net. Business E-Mail: jturner@aarp.org.

**TURNER, JOHN FREELAND,** former federal agency administrator, retired state legislator; b. Jackson, Wyo., Mar. 3, 1942; s. John Charles and Mary Louise (Mapes) T.; m. Mary Kay Brady, 1969; children: John Francis, Kathy Mapes, Mark Freeland. BS in Biology, U. Notre Dame, 1964; postgrad., U. Innsbruck, 1964-65, U. Utah, 1965-66; MS in Ecology, U. Mich., 1968. Rancher, outfitter Triangle X Ranch, Moose, Wyo.; chmn. bd. dirs. Bank of Jackson Hole, 1985-89; photo-journalist; mem. Wyo. Ho. of Reps., 1970-74, Wyo. Senate, 1974-89, pres., 1987-89; dir. Fish and Wildlife Svc. US Dept. Interior, Washington, 1989-93; pres. Conservation Fund, Arlington, Va., 1993—2001; asst. sec. for oceans, internat. environ., & scientific affairs US Dept. State, Washington, 2001—05. Exec. adv. Hancock Timber Resource Group, 1993—2001; chmn. rev. com. Argonne Nat. Lab.-West, U. Chgo., 1999—2001; vice-chmn. Land Trust Alliance, bd. dirs., 1994—2000, N.E. Utilities, 1995—2001, Internat. Paper Co., Stamford, Conn., 2005—; chmn. bd. dirs. Inst. Environ. and Natural Resources, U. Wyo., Laramie, 2001—; mem. Nat. Coal Coun., 1995—, Teton Sci. Sch. Bd., Nat. Wetland Forum, 1983, 87; mem. exec. com. Coun. of State Govts.; chmn. Pride in Jackson Hole Campaign, 1986; chmn. steering com. UN Conv. on Wetlands of Internat. Importance, 1990—93; head U.S. delegation Conv. on Internat. Trade Endangered Species. Author: The Magnificent Bald Eagle: Our National Bird, 1971. Named Citizen of Yr. County of Teton, 1984; recipient Nat. Conservation Achievement award Nat. Wildlife Fedn., 1984, Sheldon Coleman Great Outdoors award, 1990, Pres.'s Pub. Svc. award The Nature Conservatory, 1990, Stewardship award Audubon Soc., 1992, Nat. Wetland Achievement award Ducks Unlimited, 1993, Chevron/Times-Mirror Nat. Conservation Leadership award, 1995. Mem. Nat. Wildlife Refuge Assn. (bd. dirs.), Boone and Crockett Club (profl. mem.). Republican. Roman Catholic.

**TURNER, JOHN GOSNEY,** insurance company executive, director; b. Springfield, Mass., Oct. 3, 1939; s. John William and Clarence Oma (Gosney) T.; m. Leslie Corrigan, June 23, 1962; children: John Fredric, Mary Leslie, James Gosney, Andrew William. BA, Amherst Coll., 1961; student, Advanced Mgmt. Program, Harvard U., 1980. Assoc. actuary Monarch Life Ins. Co., Springfield, Mass., 1961-67; group actuary Northwestern Nat. Life Ins. Co., Mpls., 1967-75, sr. v.p. group, 1975-79, sr. v.p., chief actuary, 1979-81, exec. v.p., chief actuary, 1981-83, pres., chief operating officer, 1983—; chmn., CEO Northwestern Nat. Life Ins. Co. (now ReliaStar Fin. Corp.), Mpls., 1993—. Dir. NWNL Reins. Co., NWNL Gen. No. Life, North Atlantic Life Ins. Co. N.Y. Trustee Abbott-Northwestern Hosps., Evans Sch. Found.; chmn. Minn. Trustees of the Evans Scholars Found. Fellow Soc. Actuaries; mem. Am. Acad. Actuaries, Western Golf Assn. (dir.), Minn. Golf Assn. Clubs: Minikahda (Mpls.). Home: 301 Kenwood Pkwy Apt 502 Minneapolis MN 55403-1165

**TURNER, JOHN NAPIER,** former prime minister of Canada, legislator; b. Richmond, Eng., June 7, 1929; s. Leonard and Phyllis (Gregory) T.; m. Geills McCrae Kilgour, May 11, 1963; children: Elizabeth, Michael, David, Andrew. BA with honors in Polit. Sci., U. B.C., Can., 1949; BA, Oxford U., Eng., 1951, BCL, 1952; MA, Oxford U., 1957; postgrad., U. Paris, 1952-53; LLD (hon.), U.N.B., 1968, York U., Toronto, 1969, U.B.C., 1986, U. Toronto, 1996, Assumption U., Windsor, 2002; D of Civil Law (hon.), Mt. Allison U., N.B., 1980. Bar: Eng. 1953, Que. 1954, Ont. 1968, B.C. 1969, Y.T. 1969, N.W.T. 1969, Barbados 1969, Trinidad 1969. With Stikeman, Elliot, Tamaki, Mercier and Turner, Montreal, Que., 1953-65, McMillan Binch, Toronto, 1976-84; M.P. for St. Lawrence-St. George Montreal, 1962-68, Ottawa-Carleton, 1968-76; parliamentary sec. to Minister of Northern Affairs and Nat. Resources, 1963-65; minister without portfolio, 1965-67; registrar-gen. Govt. of Can., 1967-68, minister of consumer and corp. affairs, 1968, solicitor-gen., 1968, minister of justice and atty.-gen. of Can., 1968-72, minister of fin., 1972-75, prime minister of Can., 1984; leader Liberal Party Can., 1984-90; mem. parliament Vancouver Quadra, 1984-93; with Miller Thomson, Toronto, 1990—. Created Queen's Counsel, Ontario and Quebec, 1968. Author: Senate of Canada, 1961, Politics of Purpose, 1968. Can. Track Field Champion, 1948; mem. English Track and Field Team, 1950-51. Appointed Companion of Order of Can., 1995. Mem. Eng. Bar Assn., Grey's Inn London, Bar. Assns. of Ont., Que., B.C., Barbados, Trinidad, Mt. Royal Club, Montreal Racquet Club, York Club, The Vancouver Club, Nat. Club. Liberal. Roman Catholic. Avocations: tennis, canoeing, skiing. Home: 59 Oriole Rd Toronto ON Canada M4V 2E9 Office: Miller Thomson LLP 2500 20 Queen St W Toronto ON Canada M5H 3S1 Office Phone: 416-595-8607. Business E-Mail: jturner@millerthomson.ca.

**TURNER, JOHN SIDNEY, JR.,** retired otolaryngologist, educator; b. Bainbridge, Ga., July 25, 1930; s. John Sidney and Rose Lee (Rogers) T.; m. Betty Jane Tigner, June 5, 1955 (dec.); children: Elizabeth, Rebecca, Jan Marie; m. Nina Jones, June 16, 1999. BS, Emory U., 1952, MD, 1955. Diplomate Am. Bd. Otolaryngology. Intern U. Va. Hosp., 1955-56; resident in otolaryngology Duke U. Med. Ctr., 1958-61; prof. otolaryngology Emory U., Atlanta, 1961-95, chmn. divsn., 1961—95; ret. Ear specialist, chief otolaryngology Emory Clinic, 1961-95; area cons. in field U.S. 3d Army, 1962-69; assoc. dir. heart disease control program Fla. Bd. Health, 1956-58; Ga. state chmn. Deafness Rsch. Found., 1968-95; v.p. Clifton Casualty Ins. Co., Atlanta, 1975-95. Mem. internat. editl. bd. Drugs Jour., 1982-2004, Ethicals in Med. Progress, 1982—, Dialogue Jour., 1988-95; mem. editl. bd. Otolaryngolog—Head and Neck Surgery, 1991; contbr. chpts. to books, articles to profl. jours. With USPHS, 1956-58. Recipient Appreciation award Children of Fulton County and Fulton County Health Dept., 1975, Citation for Disting. Svc., Fla. divsn. Am. Cancer Soc., 1957, Lester A. Brown award Ga. Soc. Otolaryngology*Head and Neck Surgery, 1995. Mem. AMA, So.

Med. Assn. (chmn. otolaryngology sect. 1974, cert. of appreciation 1974), Am. Acad. Otolaryngology--Head and Neck Surgery (Honor award 1994), Triological Soc. (v.p., chmn. so. sect. 1991—), Am. Acad. Otolaryngic Allergy, Ga. Soc. Otolaryngology (pres. 1973), Med. Assn. Ga., Med. Assn. Atlanta, Assn. Acad. Depts. Otolaryngology, Optimists (pres. Atlanta 1975), Alpha Omega Alpha. Democrat. Methodist.

**TURNER, KATHLEEN,** actress; b. Springfield, Mo., June 19, 1954; m. David Guc, 1977 (div. 1982); m. Jay Weiss, 1984; 1 child, Rachel Ann. Student, Cen. Sch. of Speech and Drama, London, Southwest Mo. State U.; BFA, U. Md., 1977. Various theater roles, Broadway debut: Gemini, 1978, Cat on a Hot Tin Roof, 1990, Indiscretions, 1995, Who's Afraid of Virginia Woolf?, 2005; appeared in TV series The Doctors, 1977, Style and Substance, 1996; TV movies inlcude Friends At Last, 1995, Moonlight and Valentino, 1995; films include Body Heat, 1981, A Breed Apart, 1982, The Man With Two Brains, 1983, Crimes of Passion, 1984, Romancing the Stone, 1984, Prizzi's Honor (Golden Globe award for best actress), 1985, The Jewel of the Nile, 1985, Peggy Sue Got Married, (D.W. Griffith award for best actress, Oscar nomination for best actress) 1986, Julia and Julia, 1988, Switching Channels, 1988, Who Framed Roger Rabbit, 1988, Accidental Tourist, 1988, The War of the Roses, 1989. V.I. Warshawski, 1991, Undercover Blues, 1993, House of Cards, 1993, Serial Mom, 1994, Naked in New York, 1994, A Simple Wish, 1997, The Real Blonde, 1998, Baby Geniuses, 1999, The Virgin Suicides, 1999, Prince of Central Park, 2000, Beautiful, 2000, Without Love, 2004, (voice) Monster House, 2006, (TV films) Love in the Ancient World, 1997, Legalese, 1998, Cinderella, 2000; dir. (Showtime cable movie) Leslie's Folly, 1994; also performed in radio shows with the BBC, 1992, 93; voice: Bad Baby, 1997, Beautiful, 2000. Office: ICM care Chris Andrews 8942 Wilshire Blvd Beverly Hills CA 90211-1934*

**TURNER, KATHY ANN,** special education educator; b. Cinn., May 16, 1962; d. James Robert and Alice Louise Taylor; m. Michael Arcia Turner, Jr., June 1, 1985; children: Joseph Paul, Christopher James, Sarah Alyse. AA, Riverside C.C., 1998; BS in Edn., Lewis Clark State Coll., 2002. Spl. edn. asst. Corona-Norco Unified Sch. Dist., Norco, Calif., 1996—98; direct care provider devel. disabilities Inclusion North, Inc., Grangeville, Idaho, 1998—2000; tech. for tchrs. asst. Lewis Clark State Coll., Lewiston, Idaho, 2000—01; sub. tchr. Prairie Sch., Idaho, 2001—03; psychol. social rehab. provider Frontier Journeys, Grangeville, Idaho, 2002—05; specialist devel. disabilities Opportunities Unltd., Inc., 2003—05; psycho social rehab provider Camas Profl. Counseling, 2005—06; spl. edn. tchr. lower Kuskokwim sch. dist. Bethel Regional HS, Ark., 2006—. Counselor Hope Pregnancy Ctr., Grangeville, 2003—06. Portrait, Liz (2nd pl. award Idaho County Art Competition, 1998). Daffodil days chmn. Am. Cancer Soc., Corona, Calif., 1995—98; com. mem. Relay for Life, 2005. Named Life Woman of the Yr., Norco C. of C., 1995. Mem.: Coun. for Exceptional Children, Grangeville Elks, Kappa Delta Pi (pres. 2001—03). R-Consevative. Avocations: baking, canning, fishing, card playing. Home: PO Box 1901 Bethel AK 99559 Office Phone: 907-543-3957. Personal E-mail: imspcl2002@yahoo.com.

**TURNER, KERRI E.,** music educator, musician; b. Midland, Tex., May 26, 1973; d. Don Edward and Delores June Griffitts; m. John Christopher Turner, May 15, 1999; 1 child, Andrew Christopher. MusB, Tex. A&M U., 1996; MusM, Ark. State U., 1998. Instr. of music Ark. State U., Jonesboro, 1998—2003; instr. of piano Pensacola (Fla.) Jr. Coll., 2003—04; music ministry asst. Olive Bapt. Ch., Pensacola, 2004—05; ind. piano instr. Milton, Fla., 2006—. Piano accompanist, 1999—; ch. accompanist/pianist 1st Christian Ch., Kingsville, Tex., 1995—96, 1st United Meth. Ch., Jonesboro, 1997—2002. Musician piano masterclass; pianist (faculty recital). Missionary, Kazakhstan. Mem.: Nat. Guild of Piano Tchrs. (assoc.), Music Tchrs. Nat. Assn. (assoc.). Republican. Avocations: travel, caring for two lhasa apsos, movies, scrapbooks, exercise.

**TURNER, KEVIN (B. KEVIN TURNER),** information technology executive; m. Shelly Turner; 3 children. BS, E. Ctrl. U., 1987. Cashier Wal-Mart Stores, Inc., Ada, Okla., 1985—88, with internal audit dept., 1988—89, bus. analyst info. sys. div., strategy mgr. info. sys. div., dir. info. sys. div., v.p. and asst. chief info. officer info. sys. div., chief info. officer info. sys. div., 2000—03, exec. v.p., 2000, pres. and CEO Sam's Club div., 2002—05; COO Microsoft Corp., Redmond, Wash., 2005—. Office: Microsoft Corp 1 Microsoft Way Redmond WA 98052-6399

**TURNER, LEE,** travel company executive; b. 1952; BS, Worcester Polytechnic Inst., 1974; MBA, Dartmouth, 1976. With Baxter Healthcare, Deerfield, Ill., 1976-79, 82-87, Southeastern Pub. Svc. Co., Miami Beach, Fla., 1979-82; exec. v.p. BTI Ams., Inc., Northbrook, Ill., 1987-98; CFO WorldTravel Ptnrs., Northbrook, 1998—. Office: World Travel Ptnrs 2700 Patriot Blvd Ste 200 Glenview IL 60025-8064

**TURNER, LETITIA RHODES,** artist; b. Media, Pa., Aug. 17, 1923; d. Samuel Noblit and Letitia (Eves) Rhodes; m. Ellwood Jackson Turner Jr., Aug. 1, 1942; children: Rue Baronsky, Letitia Mayo, Elizabeth Rorke. Diploma, Cowanova Sch. Dancing, 1941. Dance instr. Cowanova Sch. Dancing, 1939—41; sec., treas. Rose Tree Realty Inc., Media, Pa., 1961-81. Dance tchr., 1939, 40, 41. Portrait painter (Portrait of Mary 3d pl. 1990, Portrait of Brett 2d pl. 1987); painter portrait commns., 1977-95. Mem. Optimisses 1956-1958, pres Am. Legion Aux., Media, 1991-2002, photographer, 1992, sec., 1993—; sec. Del. County Am. Legion Aux., 1994, historian, 1995; 1st v.p. Woman's Aux. Media Presbyn. Ch., Media, 1963; mem. D.A.R.E., Media, 1983-91, 92, 93—. Mem. Artist Guild Delaware County, Art League Delaware County, Artist Guild of Riddle Village, Am. Legion Aux. (sec. Del. County 1993, historian 1994). Republican. Avocation: needlepoint. Home and Office: Riddle Village L-302 Media PA 19063

**TURNER, LISA PHILLIPS,** human resources executive; b. Waltham, Mass., Apr. 10, 1951; d. James Sinclair and Virginia Turner. BA in Edn. and Philosophy magna cum laude, Washington Coll., Chestertown, Md., 1974; AS in Electronics Tech., AA in Engring., Palm Beach Jr. Coll., 1982; MBA, Nova U., 1986, DSc, 1989; PhD, Kennedy Western U., 1990. Cert. sr. profl. in human resources; cert. quality engr.; lic. USCG capt.; lic. pvt. pilot FAA, IFAA lic. airframe and powerplant mechanic, 2004. Founder, pres. Turner's Bicycle Svc., Inc., Delray Beach, Fla., 1975-80; electronics engr., quality engr. Audio Engring. and Video Arts, Boca Raton, Fla., 1980-81; tech. writing instr. Palm Beach Jr. Coll., Lake Worth, Fla., 1981-82; administr. tng. and devel. Mitel Inc., Boca Raton, 1982-88; mgr. comm. and employee rels. Modular Computer Systems, Inc., Ft. Lauderdale, Fla., 1988-89; U.S. mktg. project mgr. Mitel, Inc., Boca Raton, 1990-91; v.p. human resources Connectronics, Inc., Ft. Lauderdale, 1991-93; sr. mgr. human resources Sensormatic Electronics Corp., Boca Raton, 1993-98, dir. human resources 1998—2001; chief tng. officer and dir. human resources Tyco Fire and Security Svcs., Inc., Boca Raton, 2001—05, Six Sigma black belt, 2005—. Contbg. author Kitplanes Mag. With USCG Aux. Recipient Human Resources Profl. Excellence award, Soc. Human Resource Mgmt., 1999. Mem. Soc. for Human Resource Mgmt., Internat. Assn. Quality Cirs., Am. Soc. Quality Control, Fla. Employment Mgmt. Assn., Am. Acad. Mgmt., Employment Assn. Fla., Am. Capts. Assn., Citizens Police Acad., Aircraft Owners and Pilot's Assn., Exptl. Aircraft Assn., Fla. Aero. Club. Achievements include being the first female to construct, complete and fly a pulsar XP aircraft. Home: 1358 Fairfax Cir E Boynton Beach FL 33436-8612 Office: Tyco 1 Town Center Rd Boca Raton FL 33436-1010 Office Phone: 561-989-7979. Personal E-mail: lisaturner@prodigy.net. Business E-Mail: lisaturner@tycoint.com.

**TURNER, LOUISE (LEE) KREHER,** retired dance educator; b. New Orleans, July 30, 1914; d. Charles William Kreher and Hazel Hilliary Brennan; m. Frank Allen Turner, Sept. 5, 1954. BA, Southwestern La. Inst., 1933; MA, La. State U., 1936; MS, La State U., 1937; PhD, NYU, 1970; Assoc. Prof. Emerita (hon.), Auburn U., 1975. Dance instr. La. State Normal Coll., Natchitoches, 1934; tchg. fellow La. State U., Baton Rouge, 1935—37;

dance instr. Stuart Hall, Staunton, Va., 1937; assoc. prof. Auburn U., Ala., 1938—76. Playground and teenage ctr. dir. City of St. Petersburg, Fla., 1948—49; recreation dir. City of Opelika, Ala., 1950; recreation broadcaster Sta. WJHO, Auburn, 1952; in-sch. ednl. telecaster PBS Channel 7, Auburn, 1953; dir./coord. Forest Ecology Preserve, Sch. of Forestry, Auburn U., 1997—2000. (choreography) Choreography; author: (genealogy/historical novel) Margaretha's Trunk. Recipient Assoc. Health, Phys. Edn. and Recreation award, State of Ala., 1956, Auburn Citizen of Yr., Auburn Civitan Club, 1954, 2000, Outstanding Alumnus, U. of SW La., 1979, W. Kelly Mosley Environ. award, Auburn U., 2000, Martha Wayles Jefferson Cmty. Svc. award, DAR, 2004, Environ. Awareness award, 2004. Mem.: Am. Assn. Health Phys. Edn. Recreation and Dance, Delta Zeta, Delta Kappa Gamma. Achievements include donated land and established Forest Ecology Preserve, Auburn University, 1993; established F. Allen and Louise K. Turner Charitable Foundation, 2000; development of cultural exchange program with Guatemala, Partners in America with Auburn, 1974; historic preservation of Pre-Civil War dwelling, 1980-1985. Home: P O Box 1407 Auburn AL 36831 Personal E-mail: turnelo@mindspring.com.

**TURNER, LYNDA E.,** science educator; b. Atlanta, Ga., Feb. 19, 1955; d. John David and Jean Yarbrough English; m. Kenneth G. Turner, Jr., June 25, 1977; children: Mindy Lynne, Jacob Scott, Jeffrey Kyle. BS in Elem. Edn., Ga. State U., Atlanta, 1977, MEd i n Mid. Grades Sci., 1984. Cert. educator Ga. Tchr. elem. edn. Fulton County Bd. Edn., Atlanta, 1977—81, Fayette County Bd. Edn., Brooks, Ga., 1985—94, tchr. mid. sch., 1994—. Cheerleading coach Whitewater Middle Sch., Fayetteville, Ga., 1993—2002, Fayette County H.S., Fayetteville, 1993—2002, Rising Starr Mid. Sch., Fayetteville, 1993—2002. Mem.: NEA, Ga. Edn. Assn., Ga. Sci. Tchrs. Assn., Nat. Sci. Tchrs. Assn. Avocation: music. Home: 209 Tiverton Trl Peachtree City GA 30869

**TURNER, MARGUERITE ROSE COWLES,** retired library director; b. June 21, 1941; d. John Clinton and Marguerite Eileen (Slaybaugh) Cowles; 1 son, Jeffrey Jason. BA, U. New Orleans, 1963; MLS, La. State U., 1966; MA in History, U. So. Miss., 1970. Reference libr. U. So. Miss., 1966—76, Pascagoula Jr. H.S., Miss., 1970-71, Irwin County HS, Ocilla, Ga., 1971-72; dir. Fitzgerald Carnegie Libr., Ga., 1974-80, Jacob S. Mauney Meml. Libr., Kings Mountain, NC, 1983—2004; administrv. libr. Assumption Parish Libr., Napoleonville, La., 1980-83; ret., 2004. Author poems, short stories; writer weekly column Kings Mountain Herald, Shelby Star: contbr. articles to profl. jours. Sunday sch. tchr., First Baptist Ch., libr., 1975—, Fitzgerald, 1978-80, Napoleonville, 1980-83. Mem. ALA, NC Libr. Assn., Broad River Libr. Assn. Republican. Avocations: gardening, sewing, quilting, reading, writing.

**TURNER, MICHAEL R.,** congressman; b. Dayton, Ohio, Jan. 11, 1960; s. Ray and Vivian Turner; m. Lori Turner; 2 children. BS in Polit. Sci., Ohio No. U., Ada, 1982; JD, Case Western Res. U. Sch. Law, 1985; MBA, U. Dayton, Ohio, 1992. Bar: Ohio 1985. Corp. counsel Modern Technologies Corp., Dayton, Ohio; pres. JMD Devel.; mayor Ohio, 1994—2002; mem. US Congress from 3rd Ohio dist., 2003—. Mem. armed svcs. com. US Congress, 2003—, mem. govt. reform com., 2003—, chmn. federalism and the census subcommittee, 2005—, mem. vets. affairs com., 2005—. Recipient Nat. Legis. Leadership award, US Conf. Mayors, 2005, Restore Am. Hero award, Nat. Trust Hist. Preservation and HGTV, 2005. Mem.: Am. Corp. Counsel Assn., Ohio Bar Assn., Dayton Bar Assn., ABA. Republican. Office: US Ho Reps 1740 Longworth Ho Office Bldg Washington DC 20515 Office Phone: 202-225-6465.*

**TURNER, MICHAEL STANLEY,** astrophysics professor, researcher; b. LA, July 29, 1949; s. Paul Joseph and Janet Mary (Lindholm) T.; m. Terri Lee Shields, Aug. 1978 (div. Sept. 1980); m. Barbara Lynn Ahlberg, Sept. 10, 1988; children: Rachel Mary, Joseph Lucien. BS in Physics, Calif. Inst. Tech., 1971; MS in Physics, Stanford U., 1973, PhD in Physics, 1978; DSc (hon.), Mich. State U., 2005. Enrico Fermi fellow U. Chgo., 1978-80, from asst. to assoc. prof. physics and astronomy and astrophysics, 1980-85, prof., 1985—, chmn. dept. astronomy and astrophysics, 1997—2003, Bruce V. and Diana M. Rauner Disting. Svc. prof., 1998—; scientist Fermi Nat. Accelerator Lab., Batavia, Ill., 1983—2003, 2006—; dir. U.S. NSF, 2003—06. Trustee Aspen (Colo.) Ctr. Physics, 1984—97, pres., 1989—93, hon. trustee, 2002—; Halley lectr. Oxford U., 1994; Klopsteg lectr. Am. Assn. Physics Tchrs., 1999; Neils Bohr lectr. Copenhagen U., 2001; Marker lectr. Pa. State U., 2002; W. Paul fellow Bonn U., 2000; Houston lectr. Rice U., 2003; Herzfield lectr. Cath. U., 2004; Buhl lectr. Carnegie Mellon U., 2004; Heinrich Hertz lectr. DESY-Germany, 2004; Kaczmarczk lectr. Dexel U., 2004; Buhl lectr. Carnegie Melon, 2004; Fisher lectr. Brandeis U., 2005; Centennial lectr. Purdue U., 2005; Shaw lectr. So. Ill. U., 2005. Author: (with E.W. Kolb) The Early Universe, 1990; contbr. over 200 articles to profl. jours. Bd. trustees Ill. Math. Sci. Acad., 1998-2003, Project Exploration, Ill., 2002-03. Sloan fellow A.P. Sloan Found., 1983-88; recipient Disting. Alumni award Caltech, 2006. Fellow AAAS (chair physics sect. 2003), Am. Acad. Arts and Scis., Am. Phys. Soc. (mem. exec. bd. 1992-94, chmn. publ. oversight com. 1993-94, chmn. nominating com. 1999-2000, Lilienfeld prize 1997, Primakoff lectr., 2003), Phi Beta Kappa (nat. lectr. 2002-2003); mem. NAS (NRC astronomy astrophysics survey com. 1998-2000, chair NRC com. Physics of Universe, 2000-02), Am. Astron. Soc. (Helen B. Warner prize 1984), Internat. Astron. Union, Sigma Xi. Office: U Chgo Astron & Astrophysics Ctr 5640 S Ellis Ave Chicago IL 60637-1433 Office Phone: 773-702-7974. Business E-Mail: mturner@uchicago.edu.

**TURNER, NANCY K.,** archivist, librarian; b. Muncie, Ind., May 5, 1930; d. Mike and Dorothy (Landers) Marvin; m. Jack E. Turner, June 17, 1948; children: Jack Jr., Luann, Joe, Kathy, Jeff, Jim, Jane, Jay. BS in history, Ball State Univ., Muncie, IN, 1982, MLS (Libr. Sci.), 1984, MA in history, 1988. MLS, profl. libr. Bibliographic searcher Ball State Univ., Muncie, IN, 1976-83, archives technician, 1983-87, univ. archivist, 1987-90, head archives and spl. collections, 1990-98, archivist emeritus, 1998—. Mem. bd. trustees Pub. Employees Retirement Fund, Ind., 1992—2003; archival cons. Ind. Hist. Soc. Author: Having Fun With It, The Man Haters Project (booklet, video proj. dir.), 1915. Libr. bd., Muncie Public Libr., 1992—; apptd. to Ind. Oversight Com. on Pub. Records by Gov. Joe Kernan, 2003--. Recipient Sagamore of the Wabash, Gov. Indiana, 1998, emeritus mem., Midwest Archives Conf., Chgo., 1999, Disting. Alumni, History Dept., Ball State Univ., 1994, Advancing Status of Women, Soroptomists Internat., 1999. Mem.: AAUW (pres. 1989—90), Midwest Archives Conf. (chair). Democrat. Roman Catholic. Avocations: gardening, dance, swimming, reading. Home: 3009 W Riverside Ave Muncie IN 47304-3856 Personal E-mail: pickle1930@aol.com.

**TURNER, NATALIE A.,** retired consultant; b. Vancouver, B.C., Can. d. Walter P. and Jenny (Ferley) Koohtow; m. George M. Turner, Jr. BS, McGill U., 1949. Rsch. assist. in neurophysiology Allen Meml. Inst., Montreal, 1949—51; rsch. asst. Harvard Med. Sch., Boston, 1951—54; prem. program mgr. in r&d, tech. svc. mgr. to Internat. Ops., clearance officer for Latin-Am. and Asia-Pacific comapnies Gillette Co., Boston, 1954—88; ret., 1989. Technician Red Cross Blood Transfusion Svc., Montreal, 1949; tech. cons. Damon Biotech, Boston, 1988-89, rsch. asst., Harvard Sch. of Pub. Health Co-author rsch. publs. in field. Bd. dirs. Children's Mus. in Easton, Mass., 1989—. Mem. NAFE, Internat. Congress Physiology, Am. Chem. Soc., Soc. Cosmetic Chemists (life, pres. New Eng. chpt., dir. US Nat. Bd., US rep. to Internat. Fedn. Exec. Bd.), New Eng. Women Bus. Owners, Kappa Alpha Theta (life). Avocations: sewing, golf, portraits in fabric and oils.

**TURNER, NORV (NORVAL EUGENE TURNER),** professional football coach; b. LeJeune, NC, May 17, 1952; m. Nancy Turner; children: Scott, Stephanie, Drew. Asst. coach U. So. Calif., 1976—84; receivers coach LA Rams, 1985—90; offensive coord. Dallas Cowboys, 1991—93, San Diego Chargers, 2001, Miami Dolphins, 2002—03; head coach Washington Redskins, 1994—2000, Oakland Raiders, 2004—06; offensive coord. San Francisco 49ers, 2006—. Office: c/o San Francisco 49ers 4949 Centennial Blvd Santa Clara CA 95054*

**TURNER, PATRICK NOEL WADDINGTON,** portfolio manager; b. Burnham, Eng., Mar. 31, 1960; came to U.S., 1981; s. Noel Walter and Shirley (Vaughn) T.; m. Hilary Jennifer Cosell, Sept. 18, 1982 (div. Dec. 1989); 1 child, Payton; m. Amber Lea Bohmfalk, Feb. 2, 1991; children: Benton, Lily. BA with honours, Oxford (Eng.) U., 1981, MA with honours, 1982; MBA in Fin., NYU, 1988. Asst. treas. Bankers Trust Co., NYC, 1981-84; v.p. Marine Midland Bank, NYC, 1984-89; dir Barclays Bank PLC, NYC, 1989-95; mng. ptnr. Canterbury Mezzanine Capital LP, NYC, 1985—; mng. dir. TCW/Crescent Mezzanine, NYC, 2005—. Trustee Manhattan Sch. Music, NYC, 1998-. Mem. Racquet and Tennis Club, Creek Club, Field Club. Episcopalian. Avocations: music, golf, skiing, tennis, charities. Office: TCW/Mezzanine Crescent 200 Park Ave Ste 2200 New York NY 10166 E-mail: patrick.turner@tcw.com.

**TURNER, PHILIP MICHAEL,** academic administrator, writer; b. West Acton, Mass., Nov. 26, 1948; s. William Albert and Evelyn Olena (Peterson) T.; m. Lis Jane VanderBeke, Aug. 16, 1969; children: Gabrielle, Adrienne. BS in Edn., Boston State Coll., 1970; MS, U. Wis. at La Crosse, 1972; MSLS, EdD, East Tex. State U., 1977. Tchr. math. Edgewood Jr. High Sch., Merritt Island, Fla., 1969-71; ptnr. Video Guide Prodn. Co., Denver, 1973; libr. media specialist Edison Jr. High Sch., Green Bay, Wis., 1973-76; prof. libr. sci. U. Ala., Tuscaloosa, 1977-88; dean Sch. Libr. and Info. Studies U. North Tex., Denton, 1996—2004; asst. vice chancellor acad. affairs U. Ala. System, 1991-96; assoc. v.p. for acad. affairs for distance edn. U. North Tex., Denton, 1996—. Author: Handbook for In-School Media Personnel, 1980, Helping Teachers Teach, 1985, 3d edit., 2003. Vol. Meals on Wheels, Tuscaloosa, 1987-96. Recipient Outstanding Commitment To Teaching award U. Ala. Alumni Assn., 1979, Outstanding Svc. award Ala. Libr. and Media Prodrs., 1987, publ. award Div. Sch. Libr. Media Specialist, 1987, award for menng. info. tech., 1994, Ala. Sch. Assn. Disting. Svc. award, 1996; named Libr. of Yr., Beta Phi Mu, 1991. Mem. ALA (mem. accreditation com. 2000—), Assn. Sch. Librs. (chair rsch. com. 1987-90, bd. dirs. 1990-94). Unitarian Universalist. Office: U North Tex PO Box 310889 Denton TX 76203-0889 Office Phone: 940-565-4462. Business E-Mail: pturner@unt.edu.

**TURNER, RALPH HERBERT,** sociologist, educator; b. Effingham, Ill., Dec. 15, 1919; s. Herbert Turner and Hilda Pearl (Bohn) T.; m. Christine Elizabeth Hanks, Nov. 2, 1943; children: Lowell Ralph, Cheryl Christine. BA, U So. Calif., 1941, MA, 1942; postgrad., U. Wis., 1942-43; PhD, U. Chgo., 1948. Rsch. assoc. Am. Coun. Race Relations, 1947-48; faculty UCLA, 1948—, prof. sociology and anthropology, 1959-90, prof. emeritus, 1990—, chmn. dept. sociology, 1963-68; chmn. Acad. Senate U. Calif. System, 1983-84. Vis. summer prof. U. Wash., 1960, U. Hawaii, 1962; vis. scholar Australian Nat. U., 1972; vis. prof. U. Ga., 1975, Ben Gurion U., Israel, 1983; vis. fellow Nuffield Coll. Oxford U., 1980; disting. vis. prof. Am. U., Cairo, Egypt, 1983; adj. prof. China Acad. Social Scis., Beijing, People's Republic China, 1986. Author: (with L. Killian) Collective Behavior, 1957, 2d edit., 1972, 3d edit., 1987, The Social Context of Ambition, 1964, Robert Park on Social Control and Collective Behavior, 1967, Family Interaction, 1970, Earthquake Prediction and Public Policy, 1975, (with J. Nigg, D. Paz, B. Young) Community Response to Earthquake Threat in So. Calif., 1980, (with J. Nigg and D. Paz) Waiting for Disaster, 1986; editl. cons., 1959-62; editor: Sociometry, 1962-64; acting editor: Am. Rev. of Sociology, 1977-78; assoc. editor, 1978-79, editor, 1980-86; adv. editor: Am. Jour. Sociology, 1954-56, Sociology and Social Rsch., 1961-74; editl. staff: Am. Sociol. Rev., 1955-56; assoc. editor: Social Problems, 1959-62, 67-69; cons. editor: Sociol. Inquiry, 1968-73, Western Sociol. Rev., 1975-79; mem. editl. bd. Mass Emergencies, 1975-79, Internat. Jour. Crit. Sociology, 1974-76, Symbolic Interaction, 1977-90, 95—, Mobilization, 1996—. Mem. behavioral scis. study sect. NIH, 1961-66, chmn., 1963-64; dir.-at-large Social Sci. Rsch. Coun., 1965-66; chmn. panel on pub. policy implications of earthquake predictions Nat. Acad. Scis., 1974-75, also mem. earthquake study del. to Peoples Republic of China, 1976; mem. policy adv. bd. So. Calif. Earthquake Preparedness program, 1987-92, mem. com. social edn. and action L.A. Presbytery, 1954-56. Served to lt. (j.g.) USNR, 1943-46. Recipient Faculty prize Coll. Letters and Scis. UCLA, 1985; Faculty Rsch. fellow Social Sci. Rsch. Coun., 1953-56; Sr. Fulbright scholar U.K., 1956-57; Guggenheim fellow, U.K., 1964-65; Faculty Rsch. lectr. UCLA, 1987, UCLA Emeritus of Yr., 1997. Mem. AAAS (exch. del. to China 1988), AAUP, Am. Sociol. Assn. (coun. 1959-64, chmn. social psychology sect. 1960-61, pres. 1968-69, chmn. sect. theoretical sociology 1973-74, chmn. collective behavior and social movements sect. 1983-84, Cooley-Mead award 1987), Pacific Sociol. Assn. (pres. 1957), Internat. Sociol. Assn. (coun. 1974-82, v.p. 1978-82), Soc. Study Social Problems (exec. com. 1962-63), Soc. for Study Symbolic Interaction (pres. 1982-83, Charles Horton Cooley award 1978, George Herbert Mead award 1990), Sociol. Rsch. Assn. (pres. 1989-90), Am. Coun. of Learned Soc. (exec. com. of coun. 1990-93), UCLA Emeriti Assn. (coun., pres. 1992-93), U. of Calif. Emeriti Assns. (chair-elect 1996-97, chair 1997-98, Panunzio award 2002). Home: 1126 Chautauqua Blvd Pacific Palisades CA 90272-3808 Office: UCLA 405 Hilgard Ave Los Angeles CA 90095-9000

**TURNER, REGINALD MAURICE, JR.,** lawyer; b. Detroit, Feb. 25, 1960; s. Reginald and Anne Laura (Mims) T.; m. Marcia Holland, June 10, 1989. BS in indsl. Psychology, Wayne State U., 1982; JD, U. Mich., 1987. Bar: Mich. With UPS, Livonia, Mich., 1977-83, Profl. Pers. Svc. div. B.P.A. Enterprises, Detroit, 1983-84; summer assoc. Office of the Gen. Counsel GM Corp., Detroit, 1985, 86; law clk. Sachs, Nunn, Kates, Kadushin, O'Hare, Helveston & Waldman, Detroit, 1987; jud. law clk. to Hon. Dennis W. Archer Mich. Supreme Ct., Detroit, 1987-89; ptnr. Sachs, Waldman PC, Detroit, 1989—2000; atty. Clark Hill PLC, Detroit, 2000—. Vice chair Detroit Police Found.; active Mich. State Bd. Edn., 2003—, Detroit Bd. edn., 2000-2003. White House fellow, 1996-97; recipient Irving Stenn Jr. award U. Mich. Law Sch., 1987; named Barrister of the Yr., Outstanding Young Lawyer State Bar Mich., 1999, named one of Most Influential Black Americans, Ebony mag., 2006. Mem. ABA (pres. 2005-06), ACLU, NAACP, Fed. Bar Assn., Nat. Bar Assn. (pres. 2005—), State Bar Mich. (commr., pres. 2002-03), Wolverine Bar Assn. (past pres., Damon J. Keith award 2004), Detroit Bar Assn., Alpha Phi Alpha. Office: Clark Hill PLC 500 Woodward Ave Ste 3500 Detroit MI 48226-3435 E-mail: rturner@clarkhill.com.

**TURNER, ROBERT COMRIE,** composer; b. Montreal, Que., Can., June 6, 1920; s. William Thomson and Myrtle Wellsteed (Snowdon) T.; m. Sara Nan Scott, June 30, 1949; children: Alden, Martin, Carolyn. BM, McGill U., 1943, MusD, 1953; postgrad., Royal Coll. Music, London, 1947—48; MusM, Vanderbilt U., 1950. Sr. music producer Canadian Broadcasting Corp., Vancouver, B.C., 1952—68; lectr. music U. B.C., Vancouver, 1955—57; prof. composition U. Manitoba, Winnipeg, 1969—85, prof. emeritus, 1985—. Composer-in-residence MacDowell Colony, Peterborough, N.H., 1987. Composer: Opening Night: A Theatre Overture, 1955, The Third Day (Easter Cantata), 1962, Symphony for Strings, 1960, Capriccio Concertante, 1975, 3 String Quartet, 1944, 1954, 1975, opera The Brideship, 1967, Trio (transition) for Violin Cello and Piano, 1969, The Phoenix and the Turtle, 1964, Concerto for Two Pianos and Orchestra, 1971, Johann's Gift to Christmas, 1972, Eidolons, 1972, Variations on The Prairie Settler's Song, 1974, From a Different Country, 1976, Lament for Linos, 1978, Amoroso Canto, 1978, Shadow Pieces (after Joseph Cornell), 1981, opera Vile Shadows, 1983, Symphony in One Movement, 1983, Encounters I-IX, 1984, Time for Three, 1985, Playhouse Music, 1986, Concerto for Viola and Orchestra, 1987, Shades of Autumn, 1987, Manitoba Memoir, 1989, Third Symphony, 1990, a Group of Seven, 1991, The River of Time, 1994, House of Shadows, 1994, Four "Last Songs", 1995, Festival Dance, 1997, Diverti-Memento for Chamber Orch., 1997, Premiere of House of Shadows by Winnipeg Symphony, 2006; All-Turner concert, 1989, Canada House, London, All-Turner concert, Victoria, 2003, All Turner concert, Winnipeg, 2005; composer (recordings): Portrait, Robert Turner, 2005, Ovation IV, Robert Turner, 2005; adjudicator Met. and San Francisco Opera auditions; Bramwell Tovey and The Winnipeg Symphony Orch. premiered The River of Time for SATB chorus and orch. in celebration of Robert Turner's 75th yr., 1996. Bd. dirs. Vancouver Internat. Festival. Recipient Commemorative medal for 125th Anniversary of Confedn. Can., 1993, Queen's Golden Jubilee medal, 2003,

Order of Can., 2003, Outstanding Classical Composition award Western Can. Music Alliance, 2004; nominee Juno award Can. Acad. Recording Arts and Scis., 2004. Mem.: Can. League Composers, Authors and Music Pubrs. of Can., Soc. Composers, Can. Music Ctr. Home: One Evergreen Pl #2602 Winnipeg MB Canada R3L 0E9

**TURNER, ROBERT EDWARD,** psychiatrist, educator; b. Hamilton, Ont., Can., June 8, 1926; s. Robert William and Alice May T.; m. Gene Anne Stewart, Sept. 27, 1952; children: Margaret, John, Robert, Richard. BA with honors in Zoology and Chemistry, McMaster U., 1948; MD, U. Toronto, 1952. Intern Hamilton Gen. Hosp., 1952-53; resident Bristol (Eng.) Mental Hosps. Group, 1953-55; practice medicine specializing in psychiatry Toronto, Ont.; dir. Forensic Clinic Toronto Psychiat. Hosp., 1958-66; sr. psychiatrist forensic service Clarke Inst. Psychiatry, Toronto, 1966, chief forensic service, 1967-69, med. dir., 1969-76; asst. prof. dept. psychiatry U. Toronto, 1964-68, prof., 1973-77, prof. emeritus, 1991—. Cons. in psychiatry Law Reform Commn. Can., 1972-85; staff psychiatrist, 1987—; dir. Met. Toronto Forensic Service, 1977-87; hon. cons. Clarke Inst. Psychiatry, 1991—. Author: Pedophilia and Exhibitionism, 1964; contbr. articles on psychiatry and law to profl. jours. Pres. Kenneth G. Gray Found., 1971-2006; mem. legal task force Com. on Mental Health Svcs. for Ont., 2003. Recipient Queen's Commemorative Jubilee medal, 2002. Fellow Royal Coll. Physicians and Surgeons Can., Am. Psychiat. Assn. (disting. life fellow), Can. Psychiat. Assn. (life, bd. dirs. 1974-77), Ont. Psychiat. Assn. (life, pres 1975-76), Can. Med. Assn., Am. Med. Assn., Med.-Legal Soc. Toronto (coun. 1979-82). Home: 301 1387 Bayview Ave Toronto ON Canada M4G 3A5 Office: Clarke Inst Psychiatry 250 College St Toronto ON Canada M5T 1R8 Office Phone: 416-979-6831. Business E-Mail: dr_turner@rogers.com.

**TURNER, ROBERT FOSTER,** law educator, writer; b. Atlanta, Feb. 14, 1944; s. Edwin Witcher and Martha Frances (Williams) T. AB, Ind. U., Bloomington, 1968; postgrad., Stanford U., 1972-73; JD, U. Va., 1981, SJD, 1996. Bar: Va. 1982, U.S. Supreme Ct. 1986. Rsch. assoc., pub. affairs fellow Hoover Instn. on War, Revolution and Peace, Stanford U., 1971-74; spl. asst., legis. asst. U.S. Sen. Robert P. Griffin, 1974-79; co-founder, assoc. dir. Ctr. for Nat. Security Law U. Va., Charlottesville, 1981, 87—; sr. fellow, 1985-86; spl. asst. undersec. for policy Dept. Def., 1981-82; counsel Pres.'s Intelligence Oversight Bd., White House, 1982-84; prin. dep. asst. sec. for legis. and intergovtl. affairs Dept. State, 1984-85; pres. U.S. Inst. Peace, Washington, 1986-87; lectr. in law and in govt. and fgn. affairs U. Va., Charlottesville, 1988-93, assoc. prof., 1993-97, prof., 1997—; Charles H. Stockton prof. internat. law Naval War Coll., 1994-95. Disting. lectr. U.S. Mil. Acad., West Point, 1995. Author: Myths of the Vietnam War: The Pentagon Papers Reconsidered, 1972, Vietnamese Communism: Its Origins and Development, 1975, The War Powers Resolution: Its Implementation in Theory and Practice, 1983, Nicaragua v. United States: A Look at the Facts, 1987, Repealing the War Powers Resolution: Restoring the Rule of Law in U.S. Foreign Policy, 1991, The ABM Treaty and the Senate: Issues of International and Constitutional Law, 1999, The Real Lessons of the Vietnam War, 2002, (with John Norton Moore) The Legal Structure of Defense Organization, 1986, International Law and the Brezhnev Doctrine, 1987, Readings on International Law, 1995, National Security Law, 2d edit., 2005, (with John Norton Moore and Guy B. Roberts) National Security Law Documents, 1995, 2d edit., 2006, (with John Norton Moore and Ross Fisher) To Oppose Any Foe, 2006; contbr. articles to profl. jours. and newspapers. Pres. Endowment of U.S. Inst. Peace, 1986-87; trustee Intercollegiate Studies Inst., 1986-92; bd. dirs. Thomas Jefferson Inst. for Pub. Policy, 1997—; chmn. scholars commn. on Jefferson-Hemings matter Thomas Jefferson Heritage Soc., 2000-01. Grantee Hoover Press, 1972, Earhart Found., 1980, 1989-90, Inst. Ednl. Affairs, 1980, Carthage Found., 1980. Mem. ABA (chmn. com. on exec.-congl. rels., sec. internat. law and practice 1983-86, adv. com. on law and nat. security 1984-86, standing com. on law and nat. security 1986-92, chmn. 1989-92, editor ABA Nat. Security Law Report 1992-99), Federalist Soc. (chmn. subcom. on nat. security law 1998—), Com. on the Present Danger, 2005-, Bd. Rsch. Cons., Inst. Fgn. Policy Analysis, Mensa, Am. Soc. Internat. Law, Nat. Eagle Scout Assn., Coun. on Fgn. Rels., Acad. of Polit. Sci. Office: Univ Va Sch of Law Ctr for Nat Security Law 580 Massie Rd Charlottesville VA 22903-1738 Office Phone: 434-924-4083. Business E-Mail: bobturner@virginia.edu.

**TURNER, ROBERT GERALD,** academic administrator; b. Atlanta, Tex., Nov. 25, 1945; s. Robert B. and Oreta Lois (Porter) T.; m. Gail Oliver, Dec. 21, 1968; children: Angela Jan, Jessica Diane AA, Lubbock Christian Coll., 1966, LLD (hon.), 1985, Pepperdine U., 1989; BS, Abilene Christian U., 1968; MA, U. Tex., 1970, PhD, 1975. Tchr. Weatherford High Sch., Tex., 1968-69; tchr. Lanier High Sch., Austin, Tex., 1969-70; instr. psychology San Antonio Coll., 1970-72; instr. Prairie View A & M U., Tex., 1973-75; asst. prof. psychology Pepperdine U., Malibu, Calif., 1975-78, assoc. prof. psychology, 1978-79, dir. testing, 1975-76, chmn. social sci. div., 1976-78, assoc. v.p. univ. affairs, 1979; assoc. prof. psychology U. Okla., Norman, 1979-84, exec. asst. to pres., 1979-81, acting provost, 1982, v.p. exec. affairs, 1981-84; chancellor U. Miss., University, 1984-95; pres. So. Meth. U., Dallas, 1995—. Pres. Southeastern Conf., 1985-87; trustee Pepperdine U., 1994-95; mem. Pres.'s Commn., NCAA, 1989-92, chmn., 1991-92; mem. Knight Commn. on Intercollegiate Athletics, 1991—; chmn. pres. coun. Miss. Assn. Colls., 1985-86; mem. def. adv. com. Svc. Acad. Athletic Programs, 1992—; bd. dirs. J.C. Penney, Am. Beacon Funds. Author: (with L. Willerman) Readings About Individual and Group Differences, 1979. Contbr. articles to profl. jours. Recipient Outstanding Alumni award Abilene Christian U., 1989; named to New Boston HS Athletic Hall of Fame, 1993. Mem. Young Pres. Orgn., Sigma Xi, Beta Alpha Psi, Phi Theta Kappa, Alpha Chi, Phi Kappa Phi. Mem. Ch. of Christ. Avocations: reading, tennis, golf, travel. Office: So Meth Univ Office Of The Pres Dallas TX 75275-0001

**TURNER, ROBERT LLOYD,** state legislator; b. Columbus, Miss., Sept. 14, 1947; s. Roosevelt and Beatrice (Hargrove) T.; m. Gloria Harrell; children: Roosevelt, Robert, Ryan. BS, U. Wis., Racine, 1976. Mgr. French Quarter Restaurant, Racine, 1989; legislator Wis. State Assembly, Madison, 1990—, mem. transp. com. bldg. commn., mem. ways and means com., labor com., fin. institutions com., minority vice chmn. caucus, highway com., chmn. Dem. Caucus. Br. sales mgr. ETG Temporaries, Inc., Racine, 1989—; pub. Communicator News, Racine, 1989—; v.p. Racine Raider Football Team. State chmn. Dem. Black Polit. Caucus, Madison; pres. Bd. Health, Racine; chmn. Wis. State Elections Bd., Madison, 1990; alderman Racine City Coun., 1976—; chair Econ. Devel. Com., Racine; regional dir. Badger State Games, Racine; active Pvt. Industry Coun. Southeastern Wis., 1988-89, bd. dirs. Racine County Youth Sports Assn.; active Racine Juneteenth Day Com., bd. advisors Big Bros./Big Sisters. Sgt. USAF, 1967-71, Vietnam. Decorated Commendation medal; named Man of Yr. 2d Missionary Bapt. Ch., 1983. Mem. Dem. Caucus (chmn. 2003, 05), Urban League (pres. bd. dirs.), NAACP (2d v.p.), VFW, Vietnam Vets. Am. (life mem.), Am. Legion, Masons (supreme coun. 33rd degree), Shriners. Democrat. Home: 36 Mckinley Ave Racine WI 53404-3414 Office: Wis Assembly PO Box 8953 Madison WI 53708-8953

**TURNER, ROGER D.,** lawyer; b. Madison Ind., Feb. 3, 1952; BS with highest honors, Purdue Univ., 1973; JD, Univ. Chgo., 1976. Bar: NY 1977. Assoc. Cravath Swaine & Moore LLP, NYC, 1976—83, ptnr., 1983—, head corp. real estate. Mem. Chgo. Law Rev. Mem.: Assn. Bar City NY. Office: Cravath Swaine & Moore LLP Worldwide Plz 825 Eighth Ave New York NY 10019-7475 Office Phone: 212-474-1668. Office Fax: 212-474-3700. Business E-Mail: rturner@cravath.com.

**TURNER, RONALD L.,** information services executive; BS in Aeorspace Engring., U. Tenn.; MS in Engring., U. Fla.; MS in Mgmt., MIT. Sys. command USAF, 1968—73; sys. mgr. through v.p. Martin Marietta,

1973—87; pres., CEO GEC Marconi Electronic Sys., 1987—93; pres., CEO computing devices internat. Ceridian Corp., Mpls., 1993—97, exec. v.p. ops., 1997—98, pres., COO, 1998—2000, chmn., pres., CEO, 2000—06, pres., CEO, 2006. Bd. dir. Ceridian Corp., Brink's Co.; mem. bd. gov. Electronic Industries Alliance. Bd. dir. Danny Thompson Meml., Minn. Bus. Partnership; mem. Bus. Roundtable. Office: Ceridian Corp 3311 E Old Shakopee Rd Minneapolis MN 55425-1640*

**TURNER, ROSS JAMES,** investment company executive; b. Winnipeg, Man., Can., May 1, 1930; permanent U.S. resident, 1980; s. James Valentine and Gretta H. (Ross) T.; children: Ralph, Rick, Tracy., U. Man. Extension, 1951, Banff Sch. Advanced Mgmt., 1956. Chmn./pres., CEO Genstar Corp., San Francisco, 1976-86, also bd. dirs.; chmn. Genstar Investment Corp., San Francisco, 1987—. Fellow Soc. Mgmt. Accts. Can.; mem. Pacific Union Club, Rancho Santa Fe Golf Club, Peninsula Golf and Country Club. Office: Genstar Investment Corp Four Embarcadero Ctr Ste 1900 San Francisco CA 94111-4191 E-mail: dcordell@gencap.com.

**TURNER, SCOTT MACNEELY,** lawyer; b. Clinton, N.Y., Nov. 8, 1948; s. Frederick George and Ruth Alys (Thomas) T.; children: Katherine, Benjamin, Robert; m. Mary A. Worboys, June 15, 2002. AB with honors, Colgate U., 1970; JD magna cum laude, Washington and Lee U., 1973. Bar: N.Y. 1974, D.C. 1996, U.S. Dist. Ct. (we. dist.) N.Y. 1974, U.S. Ct. Appeals (2d cir.) N.Y. 1987, (3d cir.) N.Y. 1988. Assoc. Nixon Hargrave Devans & Doyle, Rochester, NY, 1973-80; ptnr. Nixon Peabody LLP (formerly Nixon Hargrave Devans & Doyle), Rochester, NY, 1981—; chmn. environ. practice group Nixon Hargrave Devans & Doyle, 1984-97, Rochester mng. ptnr., 2006—. Chmn. legis. regulatory affairs com. Internat. Gas Turbine Inst. Atlanta, 1993-95; chair coll. coun. SUNY Coll. at Brockport, 2004—. Editor: N.Y. Environmental Law Handbook, 1999. Bd. dirs. Unity Health Sys., Rochester, N.Y., 1992—, Park Ridge Found., Rochester, 1987-92, Rochester Hist. Soc., 2004—; town leader Ogden Rep. Party, Spencerport, N.Y., 1981-86. Capt. USAR, 1972-73. Mem. Air and Waste Mgmt. Assn. (chmn. legal com. 1984-88), N.Y. State Bar Assn. (environ. sect., co-chmn. solid and hazardous waste com. 1982-94), Genesee Valley Club, Order of Coif. Republican. Home: 408 Dewey St Churchville NY 14428-9103 Office: Nixon Peabody LLP Clinton Sq PO Box 31051 Ste 1300 Rochester NY 14603-1051 E-mail: sturner@nixonpeabody.com.

**TURNER, SHARON LOU WILLSON,** elementary and gifted education educator; b. St. Louis, June 17, 1946; d. Louis Willis and Marjorie May (Stephens) Willson; m. James Richard Turner, Dec. 27, 1968; children: Kimberly Beth, Douglas Ryan. BS in Elem. Edn., So. Ill. U., Carbondale, 1968; MS in Reading, Western Ill. U., 1981; gifted edn. cert., Sangamon State U., Springfield, Ill., 1983. Cert. elem. tchr., remedial reading, Ill. Elem. tchr. Springfield Pub. Schs., 1967—2002, tchr. gifted edn., 1983—2002, staff devel. trainer dist. 186, 1988-90; computer facilitator, 1988—2002; ret. Del. Internat. Reading. Conv., Chgo., 1984, Ill. Gifted Conf., Chgo., 1987-90. Com. chmn. Jr. League Springfield, 1986—; mem. Hist. Sites Commn., Springfield, 1987-92; deacon Westminster Presbyn. Ch., 1990-92, elder 1992—. Scholar Ill. Scholarship Commn., 1964-67. Mem. NEA (bldg. rep. 1968—), AAUW (edn. chmn. Springfield 1988-89, community chmn. 1989-90, pres.-elect 1990-91, pres. 1991, membership director editor 1993, Ednl. Found. scholarship named in her honor 1987], Ill. Edn. Assn., Vachel Lindsay Assn. (bd. dirs. Springfield 1987-90). Avocations: reading, computers, travel. Home: 1809 S Noble Ave Springfield IL 62704-3457 Office: Jane Addams Sch 10 Babiak Ln Springfield IL 62702-3594

**TURNER, SHARON P.,** dean, dentist, educator; b. Charleston, W.Va., Aug. 8, 1950; d. George Brock and Anna Hopkins Pullen; m. Aubrey Williams Turner, Jr., Feb. 26, 1972; children: Brock Leslie Turner, Martin Gresham Turner, Karen Anna Turner. BA in Biology, Winthrop U., 1971; DDS, U. N.C., 1979; JD, N.C. Ctrl U., 1995. Lic.: N.C. (atty.); dentist N.C., Oreg., Ky., diplomate Am. Acad. Pain Mgmt. Pvt. dental practitioner Dengler & Turner, Raleigh, NC, 1985-86; asst. prof. of diagnostic scis. U. N.C. Sch. of Dentistry, Chapel Hill, 1986-94, assoc. prof. of diagnostic scis., 1994-98, dir. patient admissions and emergency svcs., 1986-94, dir. dental faculty practice, 1989-98, assoc. dean for adminstrn. planning, 1994-98; dean, prof. dentistry Oreg. Health and Sci. U. Sch. Dentistry, Portland, 1998—2003; dean U. Ky. Coll. Dentistry, Lexington, 2003—. Cons. Va Hosp., Durham, N.C., 1999. Contbg. author: Oral Surgery, 1999. Youth group leader Eno River Unitarian Universalist, Durham, 1996-97, Sunday Sch. tchr., 1997-98; girl scout leader Pines of Carolina Coun., Girl Scouts U.S., Durham, N.C., 1990-94. Named one of Top 25 Visionary Leaders in Dentistry, Am. Student Dental Assn., 1999. Fellow Internat. Coll. Dentists, Am. Coll. Dentists, Am. Coll. Legal Medicine, Piere Fourchard Acad.; mem. ADA, Am. Dental Edn. Assn., Am. Acad. Pain Mgmt., Internat. Assn. Dental Rsch., Intenat. Assn. for Study of Pain, Soc. for Exec. Leadership in Academic Medicine (v.p. 1999-2000, pres. 2000-01), Acad. General Dentistry. Avocations: swimming, hiking, singing, reading. Office: U Ky Coll Dentistry Chandler Med Ctr D136 800 Rose St Lexington KY 40536-9707 Office Phone: 859-323-5786. Business E-Mail: turnersp@uky.edu.

**TURNER, STANSFIELD,** former CIA director, retired military officer; b. Chgo., Dec. 1, 1923; s. Oliver Stansfield and Wilhelmina Josephine (Wagner) T.; m. Eli Karin Gilbert, Mar. 16, 1985 (dec. Jan. 2000); m. Marion Weiss Turner, Sept., 2003. Student, Amherst Coll., 1941-43, DCL, 1975; BS, U.S. Naval Acad., 1946; MA (Rhodes scholar), Oxford U., 1950; LHD, Sierra Nev. Coll., 1984; HumD, Roger Williams Coll., 1975; DSc in Edn, Bryant Coll., 1977; LLD, Salve Regina Coll., 1977, The Citadel, 1980, Pace U., 1980. Ensign USN, 1946, advanced through grades to adm., 1975, ret., 1979; served primarily in destroyers; commd. U.S.S. Horne, guided missile cruiser, 1967 68? aide to Sec. Navy; commd. carrier task group 6th Fleet, 1970 71; dir. systems analysis div. Office Chief Naval Ops., Navy Dept., Washington, 1971-72; pres. Naval War Coll., Newport, RI, 1972-74; comdr. U.S. Second Fleet, 1974-75; comdr.-in-chief Allied Forces So. Europe, NATO, 1975-77; dir. CIA, Washington, 1977-81; John M. Olin Disting. prof. nat. security U.S. Mil. Acad., West Point, 1989-90; prof. U. Md. Grad. Sch. Pub. Policy, College Park, 1991—; Raymond H. Spruance Disting. Fellow Naval War Coll., Newport, RI, 2000—. Sr. rsch. fellow Norwegian Nobel Inst., Oslo, Norway, 1995-96; bd. dirs., Chase Investment Counsel Corp., Internat. Spy Mus.; bd. visitors U.S. Naval Acad., 1996—. Author: Secrecy and Democracy, 1985, Terrorism and Democracy, 1991, Caging the Nuclear Genie: An American Challenge to Global Security, 1997, Caging the Genies: A Workable Plan for Chemical, Biological and Nuclear Weapons, 1999, Spy Stories, 2003, Burn Before Reading: Presidents, CIA Directors, and Secret Intelligence, 2005. Decorated Legion of Merit, Bronze Star; Recipient Nat. Security medal, 1981, Fgn. Policy Assn. medal, 1998. Office: 488 River Bend Rd Great Falls VA 22066 Office Phone: 703-438-8408. Personal E-Mail: admturner@aol.com.

**TURNER, STEVEN JAY,** director; b. Memphis, May 23, 1974; s. Franklin Delano and Bessie May Turner. B of Music Edn., U. Mo., Kansas City, 2002. Cert. music tchr. La. Asst. dir. performing arts dept. Blue Valley North HS, Kansas City, 1999—2003; fine arts dept. chair, dir. bands Southwood HS, Shreveport, La., 2003—04; dir. bands Elm Grove (La.) Mid. Sch., 2004—. Mem.: Phi Mu Alpha (life). Republican. Mem. Ch. Of Christ. Avocations: trumpet, bodybuilding, travel, cartooning. Office: Elm Grove Mid Sch 1541 Old Hwy 71 Elm Grove LA 71051 Office Phone: 318-549-6553. Office Fax: 318-549-6513. Business E-Mail: steven.turner@bossierschools.com.

**TURNER, TED (ROBERT EDWARD TURNER),** retired broadcast company executive, philanthropist; b. Cin., Nov. 19, 1938; s. Robert Edward and Florence (Rooney) Turner; m. Judy Nye (div.); children: Laura Lee, Robert Edward IV; m. Jane Shirley Smith, June 1965 (div. 1988); children: Beau, Rhett, Jennie; m. Jane Fonda, Dec. 21, 1991 (div. 2001). Grad. in classics, Brown U.; DSc in Commerce (hon.), Drexel U., 1982; LLD (hon.), Samford U., 1982, Atlanta U., 1984; D Entrepreneurial Sci. (hon.), Cen. New Eng. Coll. Tech., 1983; D in Pub. Adminstrn. (hon.), Mass. Maritime Acad., 1984; D in Bus. Adminstrn. (hon.), U. Charleston, 1985. Account exec. Turner Advt. Co., Atlanta, 1961—63, pres., COO, 1963—70; pres., chmn. bd. Turner

Broadcasting Sys., Inc. (TBS), Atlanta, 1970—96; vice chmn. Time Warner Inc. (merger Turner Broadcasting Sys.), 1996—2000; vice chmn., sr. advisor AOL Time Warner (merger of Time Warner Inc. and AOL, Inc.), 2001—03; chmn. Turner Enterprises, Inc., 2003—; owner Atlanta Braves, 1976—. Bd. dirs. Time Warner, 1996—2001, Time Warner Inc. (formerly AOL/Time Warner), 2001—06. Co-founder, co-chair Nuclear Threat Initiative, Washington, 2001—; bd. dirs. Martin Luther King Ctr., Atlanta; donations to a number of non-profit foundations, including Turner Found., Inc., Endangered Species Fund, UN Found. and the Nuclear Threat Initiative. Named Yachtsman of Yr. 4 times; named one of 50 Most Generous Philanthropists, Fortune Mag., 2005, Forbes Richest Americans, 2006; named to Hall of Fame, Promotion and Mktg. Assn., 1980, Nat. Assn. for Sport and Phys. Edn. Hall of Fame, 1986; recipient Outstanding Entrepreneur of Yr. award, Sales Mktg. and Mgmt. Mag., 1979, Salesman of Yr. award, Sales and Mktg. Execs., 1980, Pvt. Enterprise Exemplar medal, Freedoms Found. at Valley Forge, 1980, Communicator of Yr. award, Pub. Rels. Soc. Am., 1981, N.Y. Broadcasters, 1981, Internat. Communicator of Yr. award, Sales and Mktg. Execs., 1981, Nat. News Media award, VFW, 1981, Disting. Svc. in Telecomm. award, Ohio U. Coll. Communication, 1982, Carr Van Anda award, Ohio Sch. Journalism, 1982, Spl. award, Edinburgh Internat. TV Festival, Scotland, 1982, Media Awareness award, United Vietnam Vets. Orgn., 1983, Bd. Govs. award, Atlanta chpt. NATAS, 1982, Spl. Olympics award, Spl. Olympics Com., 1983, Dinner of Champions award, Ga. chpt. Multiple Sclerosis Soc., 1983, Praca Spl. Merit award, N.Y. Puerto Rican Assn. for Cmty. Affairs, 1983, World Telecomm. Pioneer award, N.Y. State Broadcasters Assn., 1984, Golden Plate award, Am. Acad. Achievement, 1984, Outstanding Supporter Boy Scouting award, Nat. Boy Scout Coun., 1984, Silver Satellite award, Am. Women in Radio and TV, Lifetime Achievement award, N.Y. Internat. Film and TV Festival, 1984, Corp. Star of Yr. award, Nat. Leukemia Soc., 1985, Disting. Achievement award, U. Ga., 1985, Tree of Life award, Jewish Nat. Fund, 1985, Bus. Exec. of Yr. award, Ga. Security Dealers Assn., 1985, Life Achievement award, Popular Culture Assn., 1986, George Washington Disting. Patriot award, SAR, 1986, Mo. Honor medal, Sch. Journalism, U. Mo., 1987, Golden Ace award, Nat. Cable TV Acad., 1987, Sol Taishoff award, Nat. Press Found., 1988, Citizen Diplomat award, Ctr. for Soviet-Am. Dialogue, 1988, Chmn.'s award, Cable Advt. Bur., 1988, Directorate award, NATAS, 1989, Paul White award, Radio and TV News Dirs. Assn., 1989, Bus. Marketer of Yr. award, Am. Mktg. Assn., 1989, Disting. Svc. award, Simon Wiesenthal Ctr., 1990, Glasnost award, Vols. Am. and Soviet Life mag., 1990, Time Mag. Man of the Year, 1991, Cable & Broadcasting's Man of the Century, 1999, Carnegie Medal of Philanthropy, 2001, Bower award for Bus. Leadership, Franklin Inst., 2006, numerous others; won America's Cup in his yacht Courageous, 1977. Mem.: NAACP (life; bd. dirs. Atlanta chpt.), Nat. Cable TV Assn. (Pres.'s award 1979, 1989, Regional Employer of Yr. award 1976), Cousteau Soc., Nat. Audubon Soc., Bay Area Cable Club (hon.). Avocations: sailing, fishing. Office: Nuclear Threat Initiative 1747 Pennsylvania Ave NW 7th Flr Washington DC 20006*

TURNER, THOMAS MARSHALL, telecommunications executive, consultant; b. Cumberland, Md., Aug. 17, 1951; s. James Richard and Laura Roselie (Durst) T. BS in Indsl. Tech. and Mgmt., U. Md., 1973, MA in Indsl. Tech. and Mgmt., 1980. Grad. asst U. Md., College Park, 1975-76; sales assoc., gen. mgr. Equity Trades Reality, Riverdale, Md., 1976-83; account exec. RCA Corp., Greenbelt, Md., 1983; sr. telecomm. cons. CMC, Inc., Washington, 1984-86, ORS Assoc., McLean, Va., 1986-87; owner, pres. T-1 Comm., Boca Raton, Fla., 1987—; Optimum Reconciliation Svc., Inc., Pompano Beach, Fla., 1996—. Cons. Marriott Corp., Bethesda, Md., 1990-99, Group Health, Inc., N.Y.C., 1991-92, Colgate-Palmolive Co., 1993-94, State of Md., 1993, Trump Corp., 1993, Martin-Marietta, 1994, Matsushita, 1994, Montgomery Wards, 1994, Nabisco Foods, 1994, Harris Corp., 1995-99, Urban League, 1995-99, EDS, 1995-99, Chem. Bank, 1996-99, Chase Manhattan Bank, 1997-99, Arnold & Porter, 2001, Bechtel, 2001—, Booz, Allen & Hamilton, 2002, Comsat, 2001—, Fairchild, 2001—, GEICO, 2001—, Howard Hughes Med. Inst., 2001—, IBM, 2001—, State Farm Ins., 2001—, Swales Aerospace, 2002—, Wells Fargo, 2001—; grad. asst. instr. Dale Carnegie Inst., 1992. Contbr. articles to profl. jours. Vol. ARC, Riverdale, Md., 1977-80; instr. Jr. Achievement Bus. Co-op, Rockville, Md., 1979-82. Recipient Highest Achievment award Dale Carnegie Inst., 1989. Mem. ASTD, Telecomm. Mgrs. Assn. of Capital Area, Toastmasters, Sigma Alpha Epsilon Alumni Assn.

TURNER, TINA (ANNA MAE BULLOCK), singer; b. Brownsville, Tenn., Nov. 26, 1939; m. Ike Turner, 1956 (div. 1978); children: Craig, Ike Jr., Michael, Ronald. Singer (with): Ike Turner Kings of Rhythm, and Ike and Tina Turner Revue; appeared in (films) Gimme Shelter, 1970, Soul to Soul, 1971, Tommy, 1975, Sgt. Pepper's Lonely Hearts Club Band, 1978, Mad Max Beyond Thunderdome, 1985, Break Every Rule, 1986, Last Action Hero, 1993, concert tours of Europe, 1966, Japan and Africa, 1971, Showtime TV concert Wildest Dreams, albums with Ike Turner Hunter, 1970, Ike and Tina Show II, Ike and Tina Show, 1966, Ike and Tina Turner, Bad Dreams, 1973, Ike and Tina Turner Greatest Hits, vol. 1.2 and 3, 1989, Greatest Hits, 1990, Proud Mary, 1991, The Ike and Tina Turner Collection, 1991, solo albums Let Me Touch Your Mind, 1972, Tina Turns the Country On, 1974, Acid Queen, 1975, Love Explosion, 1977, Rough, 1978, Airwaves, 1979, Private Dancer, 1984, Break Every Rule, 1986, Tina Live In Europe, 1988, Foreign Affair, 1989, Simply the Best, 1991, What's Love Got to Do With It? (soundtrack), 1993, All the Best, 2005, recordings Sixties to Nineties, with others, 1994, Wildest Dreams, 1996, Twenty Four Seven, 2000; performer (with USA): for Africa on song We are The World, 1985; author: (autobiography) I, Tina, 1985; (film of autobiography) What's Love Got To Do With It?, 1993. Nominee Grammy (Best Pop Female Vocal) for "I Don't Wanna Fight", 1994; named to Rock and Roll Hall of Fame, 1991; recipient Grammy award, 1972, 1985, 1986, Kennedy Ctr. Honor, John F. Kennedy Ctr. for Performing Arts, 2005.*

TURNER, TOM, writer, editor; b. Oakland, Calif., 1942; m. Mary Jorgensen; children: Bret and Kathryn (twins). BA in Polit. Sci., U. Calif., 1965. Vol. Peace Corps, Turkey, 1965-67; grant analyst Head Start, 1968; editor, adminstrv. asst. Sierra Club, 1968-69; various positions including exec. dir. Friends of the Earth, 1969-86, also editor Not Man Apart; staff writer, dir. publs., sr. editor Earthjustice, 1986—. Author: Wild By Law: the Sierra Club Legal Defense Fund and the Places It Has Saved, 1990, Sierra Club: 100 Years of Protecting Nature, 1991, Justice on Earth, Earthjustice and the People It Has Served, 2002; contbr. to The Ency. of the Environment, 1994, also chpts. to books; contbr. articles to Sierra, Defenders, Wilderness, San Francisco Chronicle, San Francisco Examiner, L.A. Times, Oakland Tribune, Washington Post, Mother Earth News, Outside, others. Office: Earthjustice 426 17th St 6th Fl Oakland CA 94612 Office Phone: 510-550-6715. Business E-Mail: tturner@earthjustice.org

TURNER, VICKY JO, music educator; b. Kans. City, Mo., Mar. 17, 1968; d. James Phillip and Virginia Joan Turner. BS in Music Edn., N.W. Mo. State U., 1992. Lic. tchr. Mo., 1993. Music tchr. Linn County Sch. Dist., Purdin, Mo., 1994—96, McDonald County Sch. Dist., Jane and Rocky Comfort, Mo., 1999—2002, Kennett Sch. Dist., Mo., 2002—06, Adrian R-III Sch. Dist. 2006—. Mem. first bapt. choir First Bapt. Ch., Kennett, 2002, Sunday sch. sec. 1st and 2d grade students, 2003. Recipient Cert. of Appreciation, Am. Legion, 1999. Mem.: Mo. Band Dir.'s Assn. (licentiate), Am. Choral Dir.'s Assn. (licentiate), Music Educator's Nat. Conf. (licentiate), Mo. State Tchr.'s Assn. (licentiate). Baptist. Avocations: creative singing, birdwatching, hiking, music. Office: Adrian R III Sch Dist Butler MO 64730 Office Phone: 816-287-2158. Office Fax: 816-297-2980.

TURNER, WARREN AUSTIN, state legislator; b. Berkeley, Calif., Dec. 21, 1926; s. Warren Mortimer and Rebecca Oline (Noer) T.; m. Beverly Daune Mackay, Mar. 29, 1952; children: Daune Scott, Warren Adair, Alan Corey. BA, U. Calif., Berkeley, 1950, BS, 1952, MPH, 1958. Pub. acct. Price Waterhouse, San Francisco, 1951-52, AW Blackman, Las Vegas, Nev., 1952-56; asst. administr. Marin Gen. Hosp., San Rafael, Calif., 1958-60; assoc. dir. UCLA Hosp., 1960-68; founding administr. Walter O. Boswell

---

Meml. Hosp., Sun City, Ariz., 1968-81; pres. Sun Health Corp., 1981-89; mem. Ariz. Senate, Phoenix, 1993-97, chmn. rules com., vice chair health com., mem. appropriations, family svcs. and transp. com., 1995-97. Chmn. appropriation subcom., K-12, C.C.'s and natural resources. With USN, 1944—46. Mem.: Ariz. Acad. Republican. Avocations: breeding and showing siamese cats, fishing, mining. Home: 18432 W Glendale Ave Waddell AZ 85355-9737

TURNER, WESLEY R., publishing executive; m. Shirley Turner; children: Sara, Leslie. Grad., U. Tex. With Ft. Worth Press, 1973-75; from advtsg. sales rep. to v.p. advtsg. Ft. Worth Star-Telegram, 1975-86, pres., publ., 1997—; exec. v.p., gen. mgr. Kansas City Star, 1990-97; pres. Sutton Industries, 1987-90. Bd. visitors Coll. Mass Communication Middle Tenn. State U. Recipient John S. Knight Gold Medal, 2002, Pat Taggart award for Tex. Newspaper Leader of Yr., Tex. Daily Newspaper Assn., 2005. Office: Fort Worth Star-Telegram 400 W 7th St Fort Worth TX 76102-4701*

TURNER, WILLARD CRAIG, academic administrator; b. Mobile, Ala., Jan. 7, 1947; s. A. C. and Sybil Willard Turner; m. Annette Louise Enloe, Dec. 20, 1969; children: Scott Craig, Shannon Leigh Hays. BA, Baylor U., 1969, MA, 1971; PhD, Tulane U., 1977. Asst., assoc. prof. English Tex. A&M U., Coll. Station, Tex., 1976—85; prof., chair English Miss. Coll., Clinton, 1985—92; exec. v.p., chief academic officer Hardin-Simmons U., Abilene, Tex., 1996—2001, pres., 2001—. Mem., distance edn. adv. com. Tex. Higher Edn. Coordinating Bd., Austin, Tex., 1999—2001; bd. dirs. Ind. Coll., Univ. Tex., 2001—, Assn. Tex. Coll., Univ., 2004—. Editor: Critical Essays on Eudora Welty, Critical Essays on American Humor, The Poet Robert Browning and His Kinsfolk, by His Cousin, Cyrus Mason. Bd. dirs. Abilene (Tex.) C. of C., 2001, United Way of Abilene, 2000—05, Serenity Found. of Tex., Abilene, 2003, Consortium for Global Edn., Atlanta, 2005; bd. govs. Abilene Philharm., 2002—05. Avocations: fishing, reading, motion pictures. Office: Hardin-Simmons U Box 16000 Abilene TX 79698 Office Phone: 325-670-1227. Business E-Mail: cturner@hsutx.edu.

TURNER, WILLIAM COCHRANE, international management consultant; b. Red Oak, Iowa, May 27, 1929; s. James Lyman and Josephine (Cochrane) T.; m. Cynthia Dunbar, July 16, 1955; children: Scott Christopher, Craig Dunbar, Douglas Gordon. BS, Northwestern U., 1952; LLD (hon.), Thunderbird Am. Grad. Sch. Internat. Mgmt., 1993. Pres., chmn. bd. dirs. Western Mgmt. Cons., Inc., Phoenix, 1955-74, Western Mgmt. Cons. Europe, S.A., Brussels, 1968-74; U.S. amb., permanent rep. OECD, Paris, 1974-77, vice chmn. exec. com., 1976-77, U.S. rep. Energy Policy Com., 1976-77, mem. U.S. dels. internat. meetings, 1974-77; chmn., CEO Argyle Atlantic Corp., Phoenix, 1977—. Mem. western internat. trade group U.S. Dept. Commerce, 1972-74; U.S. Rep. Consultative Group parent orgn. Coord. Com. (COCOM) Multilateral Export Controls Communist Nations, Paris, 1974-77; chmn. European adv. coun., 1981-88, Asia Pacific adv. coun. AT&T Internat., 1981-88; mem. U.S.-Japan Bus. Coun., Washington, 1987-93, European adv. coun. IBM World Trade Europe/Mid. East/Africa Corp., 1977-80; Asia Pacific adv. coun. Am. Can Co., Greenwich, Conn., 1981-85, GE of Brazil adv. coun. GE Co., Coral Gables, Fla., 1979-81, Caterpillar of Brazil adv. coun. Caterpillar Tractor Co., Peoria, Ill., 1979-84, Caterpillar Asia Pacific Adv. Coun., 1984-90, U.S. adv. com. Trade Negotiations, 1982-84; chmn., dir. WorldWideTalk, Inc., Melbourne, Fla., 1999—; founding mem. Pacific Coun. Internat. Policy, L.A., 1995—; chmn. internat. adv. coun. Avon Products, Inc., N.Y.C., 1985-98; adv. coun. Spencer Stuart and Assocs., N.Y.C., 1984-90; chmn., internat. adv. coun. Advanced Semiconductor Materials Internat. NV, Bilthoven, The Netherlands, 1985-88; co-chmn. internat. adv. bd. Univ. of Nations, Lausanne, Switzerland and Kona, Hawaii, 1985—; bd. govs. Joseph H. Lauder Inst. Mgmt. and Internat. Studies, U. Pa., 1983-2001; trustee Heard Mus., Phoenix, 1983-86, nat. adv. bd., 1986-93; chmn. adv. bd. One Touch, Encinitas, Calif., 2002—; Significant Ventures, Inc., Solano Beach, Calif., 2002—. Bd. dirs. Rural Metro Corp., Phoenix, 1993—; mem. vestry Am. Cathedral, Paris, 1976—77; nat. trustee Phoenix Country Day Sch., 1971—74; bd. govs. Atlantic Inst. Internat. Affairs, Paris, 1977—88; dir. Atlantic Inst. Found., Inc., N.Y.C., 1984—90; active European vestry.-U.S. Businessmen's Coun., 1978—79; nat. trustee Nat. Symphony Orch. Assn., Washington, 1973—83, Am. Sch., Paris, 1976—77, Orme Sch., Mayer, Ariz., 1970—74; nat. coun. Salk Inst., 1978—82; mem. U.S. Adv. Com. Internat. Edn. and Cultural Affairs, 1969—74; nat. rev. bd. Ctr. Cultural and Tech. Interchange Between East and West, 1970—74; trustee and environ. com. Nat. Adv. Coun. for Environ. Policy and Tech.-U.S. EPA, Washington, 1991—95; chmn. Internat. Adv. Coun. Plasma Tech., Inc., Santa Fe, 1992—97; trustee Thunderbird Am. Grad Sch. Internat. Mgmt., 1972—, chmn. bd. trustees, 1987—89; adv. bd. Ctr. Strategic and Internat. Studies, Georgetown U., 1977—81; bd. govs. Am. Hosp. of Paris, 1974—77; pres., bd. dirs. Phoenix Symphony Assn., 1969—70; chmn. Ariz. Joint Econ. Devel. Com., 1967—68; exec. com. & bd. dirs. Ariz. Crippled Children's Svcs., 1964—65; treas. Ariz. Rep. Com., 1956—57; chmn. Ariz. Young Rep. League, 1955—56; founding chmn. bd. Mercy Ships Internat., Inc., Lindale, Tex., 1985—2000, bd. dirs. 2000—; dir. exec. com. internat. com. Ariz. Econ. Coun., Phoenix, 1989—93; dir. exec. com. Orgn. for Free Trade and Devel., Phoenix, 1991—93; bd. dirs. World Wildlife Fund/US, 1983—85, World Wildlife Fund/The Conservation Found., 1985—89, Nat. Coun., 1989—2002. Recipient East-West Ctr. Disting. Svc. award, 1977. Mem. U.S. Coun. Internat. Bus. (trustee, exec. com.), Coun. Fgn. Rels., Coun. Am. Ambs. (vice chmn. bd.), Nat. Adv. Coun. on Bus. Edn., Met. Club (N.Y.C.), Paradise Valley (Ariz.) Country Club, Bohemian Club (San Francisco), Metropolitan Club, NYC. Fax: 480-948-4674. Office Phone: 480-998-1890. E-mail: wct-aac@cox.net.

TURNER-RICHARD, LANA R., musician, director, composer; b. Wood River, Ill., Oct. 14, 1952; d. George A. and Grace E. (Brake) Turner; m. Robert Richard, Oct. 27, 1984. MusB in Edn. and Piano Performance, So. Ill. Univ., Edwardsville, Ill., 1974, M in Piano, 1977; doctoral studies in piano, Washington Univ., 1984. Instr. various C.C., St. Louis, 1985—95; accompanist St. Louis (Mo.) Children's Choir; music dir. Summer Playhouse Prodns., Crestwood, 1989—, St. Lucas U.C.C., St. Louis, 1996—. Chmn. auditions Piano Guild, Ill., Mo., 1974—90; judge variuos music festivals U.S., 1971—. Worker habitat for Humanity, St. Louis, 2006. Mem.: U.S. humane Soc., Pi Kappa Lambda. Office: St Lucas UCC 11735 Denny Rd Saint Louis MO 63126

TURNER VANLYDEGRAF, CLAUDIA BETH, writer, researcher; b. Salinas, Calif., Mar. 19, 1945; d. Prentiss Dixon Hill and Barbara Clayborne, Leonard Francis Balch (Stepfather); m. Robert Michael Turner, May 21, 1966 (div. Aug. 14, 1972); children: David Michael Reinhardt, Jeffrey Warren Gregory, Amber Beth Turner. Student, El Camino Coll., 1969—72. Cert. Nev. State Ins. Bd., 1990; Nev. Real Estate Divsn., 1979. Cost, manpower budget analyst Hughes Aircraft Co., Culver City, Calif., 1972—77; auditor No. Nev. Health & Welfare & Pension Plans Adminstrv. Office, Reno, 1980—81; co-owner TV Signal Corp, Cold Springs, Nev., 1981—86; flagger, laborer Laborers Local 169, Reno, 1989—94; jewelry sales assoc. SuperPawn/Camco, Reno, 1994—96; sales, loan assoc. Pioneer Jewelry and Loan, Reno, 1996—97; owner document rsch. firm Coyote Svcs., Cold Springs, 1998—; pub./owner Coyote News, Cold Springs, 1998—2002. Author: Notes from Nobody, 2001. Citizens adv. bd. Washoe County Commn., Cold Springs, 1999—2001; adv. - reporter Cold Springs Cmty. Assoc, 1998—2003; lobbyist Nev. Mem.: UnNamed Writers Group, Ea. Star. Independent. Avocations: genealogy, gemology, antiques, history, art. Home: 17890 Fantail Circle Cold Springs NV 89506 Office: Coyote Services 17890 Fantail Circle Cold Springs NV 89506 Office Phone: 775-972-6530. E-mail: cltvcoyote@aol.com.

TURNEY, RICHARD KENNETH, display designer, artist; s. Marcellus Reuter Turney and Jennie Elvira Erickson; m. Dorothy Smith, Jan. 1, 1940; children: Pamela A., Marda Jan. Attended, Carnegie Inst., Pitts., 1929, U. Pitts., 1933. Display dir. C. Livingston & Sons, Youngstown, Ohio, 1950—75, G.M. Mckelvey Co., Youngstown, Ohio, 1976—77; owner Ken T. Sailboats, Boardman, Ohio, 1973—79; artist Fort Meyers, Fla., 1970—. Set

---

designer Amateur Theatricals, Greensburg, Pa.; fashion shows set designer, Youngstown, Ohio. One-man shows include Fort Myers Beach Art Assn., 1986, 1987, 1988, 1989, 1990, Lee County Alliance of Arts, 1987, exhibitions include Cape Coral Art Studio, 1985, Merrick Free Art Gallery, New Brighton, Pa., 1988. Pres. Art Coun. S.W. Fla., 1983—84. With USN, 1943—45. Mem.: Fla. Watercolor Soc., B.I.G. Arts, Lee County Alliance of Arts (mem. Gallery Shop), Naples Art Assn., Sanibel-Captiva Art League, Fort Myers Beach Art Assn. (treas. 1982—83, bd. mem. 1982—84, dir.). Democrat. Avocation: sailing. Office Phone: 239-466-1247.

TURNEY, SHARON JESTER, retail executive; b. 1958; BA in Bus. Edn., U. Okla. With Foley's, 1979—88, Neiman Marcus, 1989—2000, sr. v.p. gen., mgr. gen. merchandise, 1997—98, exec. v.p. merchandising, creative prodn., advt. and pub. rels., 1998; pres., CEO Neiman Marcus Direct, 1999—2000; CEO, pres. Victoria's Secret Catalogue, 2000—. Office: Victorias Secret Direct LLC 3425 Morse Crossing Columbus OH 43219

TURNG, LIH-SHENG, education educator; b. Taiwan, Sept. 21, 1959; MS, Cornell U., Ithaca, N.Y., 1984, PhD, 1990. Task leader C-MOLD, Ithaca, 1990—2000; prof. U. Wis., Madison, Wis., 2000—. Co-dir. Polymer Enging. Ctr., Madison, Wis., 2001—. Dir., prin. investigator (engring. rsch.) Microcellular Nanocomposites (3M Non-Tenured awards, 2002, 2003). Bd. mem., chair edn. com. Soc.Plastics Engrs., Injection Molding Divsn., Brookfield, Conn., 2002—06. Grantee, NSF, 2001. Mem.: ASME. Achievements include research in computer simulation for injection molding and lightweight, high-performance polymer composites. Office: Univ Wis 1513 University Ave Madison WI 53706 Office Phone: 608-262-0586. Business E-Mail: turng@engr.wisc.edu.

TURNIPSEED, BARNWELL RHETT, III, journalist, public relations consultant; b. Apr. 6, 1929; s. Barnwell Rhett and L. (Rogers) T.; m. Jane Whitley, June 12, 1982. BA in Journalism, U. Ga., 1950, MA in Journalism, 1960. With Sta. WGGA, Gainesville, Ga., 1943-46; prodn. mgr. Sta WGGA, Gainesville, Ga., 1958-60; with Sta. WRFC, Athens, Ga., 1947-50; program dir. Sta. WKYW, Louisville, 1953, Sta. WGBA, Columbus, Ga., 1953-55; sr. corr., sci. editor Voice of Am. Worldwide English, 1960-72; coord. radio-TV pub. affairs HEW, 1972-73; mem. staff Ga. Congressman Phil Landrum, 1974-75; dir. solar energy tech. info. Dept. Energy, Washington, 1975-77, spl. asst., 1977-81; pvt. practice, 1981-88, 94—; instr. West Ga. Coll., Carrollton, 1988-89, 90-94; asst. prof. Brenau Coll., Gainesville, Ga., 1989-90; mgr. WBCX-FM, Gainesville, Ga., 1989—90, WWGC-FM, Carrollton, Ga., 1990-94. Dir. Ga. Broadcasters Annual Awards, 1998—2005. Author: History of Georgia Broadcasting, 1972; prin. corr. Voice of Am. (Peabody award winning space exploration broadcasts, 1969). Symphony Guild rep. Louisville, Columbus, Ga. Jaycees; active symphony and arts devel. Sgt. U.S. Army, 1950-52. Named to Ga. Broadcasters Hall of Fame, 2003; recipient Two Meritorious Svc. awards, USIA. Mem. Nat. Acad. Sci. Writers (life), Aircraft Owners and Pilots Assn., Sigma Delta Chi. Democrat. Methodist. Home and Office: 295 Greenfield Cir Fayetteville GA 30215-2622

TURNLEY, DAVID CARL, photojournalist; b. Fort Wayne, Ind., June 22, 1955; s. William Loyd and Elizabeth Ann (Protsman) Turnley; m. Karin Nicolette, Apr. 15, 1989. BA in French, U. Mich., 1977; student, Sorbonne, Paris, 1975; DMus (hon.), Keele (Eng.) U., 1991. Staff photographer Sliger Home Newspapers, Northville, Mich., 1978—80, Detroit Free Press, 1980—99; European based photographic corr. Detroit Free Press/Black Star Paris, 1988—99; Neiman fellow Harvard U., Boston, 1997—98; internat. exec. prodr. Corbis Sygma, N.Y.C., 1999—. Author: Why Are They Weeping? South Africans under Apartheid, 1988, Beijing Spring, 1989, Moments of Revolution: Eastern Europe, 1990; London Decca Records. Recipient Canon essay award for S. African coverage, 1985, World Press Picture of Yr. award for Earthquake in Armenia, 1988, Robert Capa Gold medal for China, Romania coverage, 1990, Pulitzer Prize for China, E. Europe coverage, 1990.

TURNLUND, JUDITH RAE, nutritionist; b. St. Paul, Sept. 28, 1936; d. Victor Emanuel and Vida Mae (Priddy) Hanson; m. Richard Wayne Turnlund, Nov. 9, 1957; children: Michael Wayne, Mark Richard, Todd Hanson. BS in Chemistry and Psychology, Gustavus Adolphus Coll., 1958; PhD in Nutrition, U. Calif., Berkeley, 1978. Registered dietitian. Postdoctoral fellow U. Calif., Berkeley, 1978-80, lectr., 1984-92, adj. assoc. prof., 1989-97; rsch. nutrition scientist Western Regional Rsch. Ctr./Western Human Nutrition Ctr., USDA, San Francisco, Albany, and Davis, Calif., 1980—; rsch. leader Western Human Nutrition Ctr. USDA, San Francisco, 1993-96; adj. prof. nutrition U. Calif., Davis, 2000—. Vis. asst. prof. Am. U. Beirut, Lebanon, 1979, 80. Editor: Stable Isotopes in Nutrition, 1984; contbr. articles to profl. jours. Recipient Cert. of Merit, USDA/ARS, 1984, 93, 98, Disting. Alumni citation Gustavus Adolphus Coll., 1988, Am. Inst. Nutrition's Lederle award in Human Nutrition, 1996; USDA grantee, Nat. Dairy Coun. grantee. Fellow Am. Soc. Nutritional Scis.; mem. Am. Soc. Clin. Nutrition, Am. Dietetic Assn. Home: 2276 Great Hwy San Francisco CA 94116-1555 Office: U Calif USDA/ARS Western Human Nutrition Rsch One Shields Ave Davis CA 95616 E-mail: jturnlun@whnrc.usda.gov.

TURNOVSKY, STEPHEN JOHN, economics professor; b. Wellington, New Zealand, Apr. 5, 1941; came to U.S., 1981; s. Frederick and Liselotte Felicitas (Wodak) T.; m. Michelle Henriette Louise Roos, Jan. 21, 1967; children: Geoffrey George, Jacqueline Liselotte. BA, Victoria U., Wellington, 1962, MA with honors, 1963; PhD, Harvard U., 1968. Asst. prof. econs. U. Pa., Phila., 1968-71; assoc. prof. U. Toronto, Ont., Canada, 1971-72; prof. Australian Nat. U., Canberra, 1972-82; IBE disting. prof. econs. U. Ill., Champaign, 1982-87; prof. econs. U. Wash., Seattle, 1987—, chmn. dept., 1990-95; Castor prof., 1993—. Rsch. assoc. Nat. Bur. Econ. Rsch., Cambridge, Mass., 1983-93. Author: Macroeconomic Analysis and Stabilization Policy, 1977, International Macroeconomic Stabilization Policy, 1990, Methods of Macroeconomic Dynamics, 1995, 2d edit., 2000, International Macroeconomic Dynamics, 1997; mem. editl. bd. several jours.; contbr. articles to profl. jours. Fellow Econometric Soc., Acad. Social Scis. in Australia; mem. Soc. Econ. Dynamics and Control (pres. 1982-84, editor Jour. Econ. Dynamics and Control 1981-87, 95-2001), Soc. Computational Econs. (pres. 2004-05). Avocations: skiing, hiking, music. Home: 6053 NE Kelden Pl Seattle WA 98105-2045 Office: Dept Econs U Wash Box 353330 Seattle WA 98195-3330 Office Phone: 206-685-8028. E-mail: sturn@u.washington.edu.

TURNQUIST, JERRY L., communications educator, journalist; b. Elgin, Ill., Mar. 5, 1949; s. Ralph C. and Frances B. T.; m. Kathleen A. Turnquist, Dec. 29, 1984; adopted children: Dennis, Eric. AA, Elgin C.C., 1969; BS, No. Ill. U., 1971, MS, 1979. Tchr. history and sci. Sch. Dist. U. - 46, Elgin, Ill., 1972—; tax preparer H&R Block Premium, Elgin, 1977—. Columnist Daily Herald, Elgin, 1995—; co-host: (local radio show) Elgin 100 Years Ago, Sta. WRMN, 1995—. Trustee Gail Borden Pub. Libr., Elgin, 1999-2005; bd. dirs. Ill. State Hist. Soc., Elgin, Springfield, 1998-2000; chmn. Elgin Heritage Commn., 1986-91, others. Named Disting. Alumnus Elgin C.C., 1989, Keyman of the Yr., Elgin Jaycees, 1981; recipient Outstanding Svc. award Elgin Heritage Commn., 1995. Mem. Elgin Area Hist. Soc. (bd. dirs. 1986-98). Home: 619 Canyon Ln Elgin IL 60123-2523 Personal E-mail: ibemrt@aol.com.

TUROCK, BETTY JANE, library and information science professor; b. Scranton, Pa., June 12; d. David and Ruth Carolyn (Sweetser) Argust; m. Frank M. Turock, June 16, 1956; children: David L., B. Drew. BA magna cum laude (Charles Wesin scholar), Syracuse U., 1955; postgrad. (scholar), U. Pa., 1956, MLS, Rutgers U., 1970, PhD, 1981. Library and materials coordinator Holmdel (N.J.) Public Schs., 1963—65; story-teller Wheaton (Ill.) Public Library, 1965—67; ednl. media specialist Alhambra Public Sch., Phoenix, 1967—70; br. librarian, area librarian, head extension service Forsyth County Public Library System, Winston-Salem, NC, 1970—73; asst. dir., dir. Montclair (N.J.) Public Library, 1973—76; asst. dir. Monroe County Library System, Rochester, NY, 1978—81; asst. prof. Rutgers U. Sch. Comms., Info. and Libr. Studies, 1981—87, assoc. prof., 1987—93, prof.,

1994—, dept. chair, 1989—95, 2002—03, dir. MLS program, 1990—95, 2002—03, assoc. dean, 2002—04, Rutgers U. Sch. Comm. Info and Libr. Studies, 2004—06; prof. emeritus, assoc. dean emeritus; pres. Rock Info. Assocs., 2004—. Vis. prof. Rutgers U. Grad. Sch. Library and Info. Studies, 1980-81; adviser U.S. Dept. Edn. Office of Libr. Programs, 1988-89. Author: Serving Older Adults, 1983, Creating a Financial Plan, 1992; editor: The Bottom Line, 1984-90; contbr. articles to profl. jours. Trustee Raritan Twp. (N.J.) Pub. Libr., 1961—62, Keystone Coll., 1991—, Freedom to Read Found., 1994—97, Libr. for the Future, 1994—97, Fund for Am.'s Librs., 1995, Trejo Found., 1995—, Bd. Am. Libr., Paris, 1999—; mem. Bd. Edn. Raritan Twp., 1962—66; ALA coord. Task Force on Women, 1978—80; mem. action coun.; treas. Social Responsibilities Round Table, 1978—82; mem. bd. visitors Johns Hopkins Sch. Medicine, 2005—. Charles Weston scholar Syracuse U., 1955; recipient N.J. Libr. Leadership award, 1994; named Woman of Yr. Raritan-Holmdel Woman's Club, 1975. Mem. AAUP, Am. Soc. Info. Sci., Assn. Libr. and Info. Sci Edn., ALA (pres. 1995-96, pres.-elect 1994-95, exec. bd. 1991-97, coun. 1988-97, Equality award 1998, Lippincott award 2006), Rutgers U. Grad. Sch. Library and Info. Studies Alumni Assn. (pres. 1977-78, Disting. Alumni award 1994), Phi Theta Kappa, Psi Chi, Beta Phi Mu, Pi Beta Phi. Unitarian Universalist. Office: Rutgers Univ 4 Huntington St New Brunswick NJ 08901-1071 Home: The Colony House 1050 George St 12-D E New Brunswick NJ 08901 Business E-Mail: bturock@scils.rutgers.edu.

**TUROK, PAUL HARRIS,** composer, commentator, music critic; b. N.Y.C., Dec. 3, 1929; s. Joseph and Esther (Pashman) T.; m. Susan Kay Frucht, Mar. 24, 1967. BA, Queens Coll., N.Y.C., 1950; MA, U. Calif., Berkeley, 1951; MS, Baruch Coll., 1986. Music dir. Sta. KPFA, Berkeley, 1955-56; lectr. CCNY, 1959-63, vis. prof. Williams Coll., Williamstown, Mass., 1963-64; music critic New York Herald-Tribune, 1964-65; critic, columnist Music Jour., New York, 1964-79, Ovation mag., New York, 1980—; critic, contbr. New York Times, 1984—, Sta. WQXR, First Hearing, New York, 1985—. Pub. Turok's Choice, 1990—. Composer musical compositions, premiered Indpls. Symphony, 1971, Louisville Orch., 1973, Cleve. Orch., 1973, Phila Orch., 1976; opera Richard III, 1975, Sousa Overture, 1976, Lanier Songs, 1978, English Horn Quintet, 1982, Cello Sonata, 1984, Organ Toccata, 1984, Tourist Music, 1985, String Quartet No. 4, 1986, Rhapsody for Band, 1987, Piano Dance, 1988, Violin Sonata, 1989, From Sholem Aleichem, 1990, Abac for trumpet and organ, 1990, Partita for three winds, 1991, Concerto for two violins and orchestra, 1991, Piano Trio, 1992, C.C. 6 for bassoon and orchestra, 1992, Fantasy for 4 flutes and piano, 4 hands, 1994, Clap, Cluck, Count: Three Interactive Proverbs for Chidren and Orchestra, 1995, Sonata No. 2 for Cello and Piano, 1996, Concerto for Piano and Orch., 1997, Canzone Concertante No. 7 for viola, percussion and strings, 1998, Reeling in the Y2K, 1999, Flute Sonata, 2000, Behold, Thou Art Fair, 2001, Sextet for piano and winds, Partita No.3 for English horn, 2002, Variations on a theme by Grieg for 8 trombones, Elegy in Memory of Nathan Schwartz, 2002, C.C. No. 8 for Violin and Orch., String Quartet No. 5, 2003, C.C. No. 9 for Trumpet and Strings, 2003, C.C. No. 10 for Piano and Strings, 2006, Caprice d'Octobre for 3 violins, 2004, Brass Quintet No. 2, 2004, Fanfare for Brass Ensemble, 2005, Sonata for Piano, 2006, Barbershop Variations for Five Horns, 2006. Served with U.S. Army, 1953-55. Hertz travelling scholar, U. Calif., 1956-58; Grammy nominee 1992, 93. Jewish. Avocations: world travel, computing. E-mail: paulhtk@verizon.net.

**TURÓN, MERCEDES,** emeritus language professor; b. Madrid, Aug. 12, 1930; d. Vicente Turón-Bonello and Mercedes Castells Cabezón. PhD, Mich. State U., 1970. Vice dir. Instituto de Cultura Hispánica, Brasilia, Brazil, 1972-77; prof. U. Montevallo, Ala., 1984-95, prof. emeritus, Ala., 1995—. Lectr. in field. Contbr. articles to profl. publs.; contbr. poetry to jours Home: 630 Riverchase Pkwy W Birmingham AL 35244-1128

**TUROW, SCOTT F.,** writer, lawyer; b. Chgo., Apr. 12, 1949; s. David D. and Rita (Pastron) Turow; m. Annette Weisberg, Apr. 4, 1971; 3 children. BA magna cum laude, Amherst Coll., 1970; MA, Stanford U., 1974; JD cum laude, Harvard U., 1978. Bar: Ill. 1978. U.S. atty. U.S. Dist. Ct. (no. dist.) Ill. 1978, U.S. Ct. Appeals (7th cir.) 1979. Asst. U.S. atty. U.S. Ct. Appeals (7th dist.), Chgo., 1978—86; ptnr. Sonnenschein Nath & Rosenthal, Chgo., 1986—. E.H. Jones lectr. Stanford U., 1972—75. Author: One L.: An Inside Account of Life in the First Year at Harvard Law School, 1977, Presumed Innocent, 1987, The Burden of Proof, 1990, Pleading Guilty, 1993, The Laws of Our Fathers, 1996, Personal Injuries, 1999, Reversible Errors, 2002, Ultimate Punishment: A Lawyer's Reflections on Dealing With the Death Penalty, 2003 (Robert F. Kennedy Book award, 2004), Ordinary Heroes, 2005; contbr. articles to profl. jours. Mem.: Chgo. Coun. Lawyers, Chgo. Bar Assn. Office: Sonnenschein Nath Rosenthal 233 S Wacker Dr Ste 8000 Chicago IL 60606-6491

**TURPEN, MICHAEL CRAIG,** lawyer; b. Tulsa, Nov. 10, 1949; s. Wallace Kendall and Marjorie Allyce (Kinkaid) T.; m. Susan Lynn Haugen; children: Sean Michael, Patrick Michael, Sarah Allyce. BS in History Edn., U. Tulsa, 1972, JD, 1974. Bar: Okla. 1975. Legal adviser Muskogee Police Dept., Okla., 1975-76; asst. dist. atty. City of Muskogee, 1976, dist. atty., 1977-82; atty. gen. State of Okla., 1983-87; ptnr. Riggs, Abney, Neal & Turpen, Oklahoma City, 1987—. Conf. speaker; mem. Okla. Spl. Legis. Com. on Criminal Justice System, 1978-79; adj. prof. bus. law N.E. Okla. State U.-Tahlequah, 1977; adj. prof. criminal law Connors State Coll., 1977-79. Author: Police-Prosecutor Training Manual, 1975; contbr. articles to profl. jours. Mem. Gov.'s Alts. to Incarceration Com., 1980-81; bd. dirs. Call Rape, Inc., Okla. Acad. State Goals; apptd. by Pres. Clinton JFK Performing Arts Ctr. Adv. Bd.; vice chmn. Okla. Crime Commn., 1980-81; commr. Okla. State Bur. Investigation, 1978-79; bd. dirs., coach Muskogee Green Country Girls Softball Assn.; mem. Muskogee H.S. Booster Club; mem. coach Muskogee Knothole League Boys Baseball Assn.; mem. Muskogee County Human Soc., Muskogee County Women's Den. Club, hon. mbr. Okla. Hwy. Patrol, 1980, co-chmn. Clinton/Gore Okla., 1992, 96, Al Gore for Pres., 1988; chmn. State Dem. Party Okla., 1992-94; active Westminster Presbyn. Ch., Okla. Recipient Maurice Merrill Golden Quill award Okla. Bar Jour., 1981, Donald Santarelli award Nat. Com. Victim Assistance, Toronto, 1981, Mayor's commendation City of Muskogee, 1976, Mayor's commendation City of Owasso, 1975, $10,000 Cash award Found. for Improvement Justice, Inc., Achievement award Found. for Improvement Justice, Inc., 1986; named Outstanding Young Oklahoman, Okla. Jaycees, 1979, Outstanding Young Lawyer, Okla. Bar Assn., 1975, Outstanding Young Man, Muskogee Jaycees, 1979, One of Ten Outstanding Nat. Leaders in field of victim rights, Nat. Orgn. for Victim Assistance, 1986, One of Men and Women Under 40 Who are Changing Nation, Esquire Mag., 1985. Mem. ABA, Okla. Bar Assn., Muskogee County Bar Assn. (past sec.), Okla. Dist. Attys. Assn. (pres. 1980-81, bd. dirs.), Tulsa U. Alumni Assn., Rotary, Tulsa U. Hurricane Club, Fraternal Order of Police. Office: Riggs Abney Neal & Turpen The Paragon Bldg 5801 Broadway Ext Ste 101 Oklahoma City OK 73118-7484 also: 502 W 6th St Tulsa OK 74119-1016 Office Phone: 405-843-9909. E-mail: mturpen@riggsabney.com

**TURPENING, PATRICIA EILEEN KELLER,** retired law librarian; b. Columbus, Ohio, Mar. 1, 1952; d. William Waite and Eileen Catherine (Miller) Keller; m. Richard Whitley Denham, Oct. 10, 1981 (div. Mar. 1986); 1 child, Michael Richard; m. Glen Thomas Turpening, Apr. 16, 1997. BS, Findlay Coll., 1974; MSLS, U. Ky., 1978. Cert. in preservation mgmt. Sch. Communication, Info. and Libr. Studies, Rutgers U., 1999. Acquisitions libr. Supreme Ct. Ohio Law Libr., Columbus, 1974-76, Robert S. Marx Law Libr., U. Cin., 1978-88, head preservation and archives, 1988—2006, sr. libr., 2003—06; ret., 2006. Libr. Rendigs, Fry, Kiely & Dennis, Cin., 1979-85. Editor Tech. Svcs. Law Libr., 1990-94, The Abbey Newsletter: Preservation of Library and Archival Materials, 2003; contbr. articles to profl. jours. Mem. ALA, LWV, AAUW, NOW, AAUP, Am. Assn. Law Librs. (travel grantee 1984, preservation cons., coord. of library programs, Renee D. Chapman Meml. award for Outstanding Contbns. in Tech. Svcs. Law Librarianship 2004), Ohio Preservation Coun., Ohio Regional Assn. Law Librs. Episcopalian. Business E-Mail: pat.turpening@uc.edu. E-mail: bookloverconsulting@yahoo.com.

**TURPIN, DAVID HOWARD,** biologist, educator, academic administrator; b. Duncan, BC, Can., July 14, 1956; s. George Howard and Marilyn Elizabeth (Jones) T.; children: Chantal, Joshua. BSc in Biology, U. BC, 1977, PhD in Botany and Oceanography, 1980. Postdoctoral rsch. fellow Natural Scis. Engring. Rsch. Coun., 1980—81; rsch. assoc. Simon Fraser U., 1980; v.p. Sigma Resource Cons., Vancouver, BC, 1980—81; from asst. prof. to assoc. prof. Queen's U., Kingston, Ont., Canada, 1981—90, prof. biology, 1990—91, dean arts and sci., 1993—95, vice prin. acad., 1995—2000; prof., head botany U. BC, 1991—93; pres., vice-chancellor U. Victoria, BC, 2000—. Invited spkr. profl. meetings univs. worldwide. Co-editor: Plant Physiology, Biochemistry and Molecular Biology, 1990, 2d edit., 1996; mem. editl. bd. Jour. Phycology, 1992-96, Plant Physiology, 1988-92, Plant Cell and Environ., 1994-96, Jour. Exptl. Botany, 1995-98; contbr. chpts. in books; author numerous articles, conf. procs. V.p. Great Lakes Tomorrow, 1986-90; mem. program com. Great Lakes Course-Ont. Sci. Ctr., 1988; Kingston City rep. Cataraqui Regional Conservation Authority, 1984-86; hon. adv. mem. Soong Ching Ling Found. Ltd., 2001-. Recipient Excellence in Tchg. Alumni award Queen's U., 1989, Outstanding Alumni award U. B.C., 1990, Darbaker prize in phycology Am. Bot. Assn., 1991; Natural Scis. and Engring. Rsch. Coun. E.W.R. Stacie Meml. fellow, 1989-90, Royal Soc. Can. fellow, 1998-; Capt. T.S. Byrne Meml. scholar U. B.C., 1980; postgrad. scholar Natural Scis. and Engring. Rsch. Coun., 1979-81, Edith Ashton Meml. scholar U. B.C., 1979, NRC scholar, 1978-79; Natural Scis. and Engring. Rsch. Coun. grantee, 1982—. Mem. Phycological Soc. Am., Am. Soc. Limnology and Oceanography, Can. Soc. Plant Physiologists (C.D. Nelson award 1989), Am. Soc. Plant Physiologists (cert. recognition 1992), Minister Nat. Defence Edn. Adv. Bd., Discovery Found. Bd., Assn. Univs. and Colls. Can. (mem. bd. dirs 2002-). Office: Office of the Pres U Victoria Bus and Econ Bldg Rm 454 Victoria BC Canada V8W 2Y2 Business E-Mail: pres@uvic.ca

**TURPIN, MICHAEL HUNTER,** academic administrator; s. Irving Hunter Turpin and Mary Ruth Piercy; m. Terry Swann, July 26, 1980; children: Zachary Hunter, Philip Hamilton. BS in Music, Lamar U., Beaumont, Tex., 1979; MusM in Edn., U. S.C., Columbia, 1981; PhD, Tex. A&M U., College Station, 2003. Lic. tchr. Tex. State Bd. Edn., 1979, profl. counselor Tex. State Bd. Edn., 1993. Tchg. asst. U. S.C., Columbia, SC, 1980—81; instr. music Kilgore (Tex.) Coll., 1984—, dir. self-study, 1995—99, coord. counseling and advising, 1997—, dean instl. planning, 2002—; instr. music Gladewater (Tex.) Mid. and H.S., 1981—84. Musician: Longview (Tex.) Cmty. Theatre, 1998—2005. Music asst., tchr. bible study First Bapt. Ch., Longview, 1981—2005; music dir. Woodland Christian Ch., Longview, 1997—2000. Named Outstanding Adminstr., Kilgore Coll., 1999; recipient Bingman Outstanding Svc. and Leadership award, Lamar U., 1979, Plummer Outstanding Acadmic Achievement award, 1979. Mem.: Jr. Cmty. Coll. Student Pers. Assn. Tex. (Darrell Truitt Rsch. award 2003), Tex. C.C. Tchrs. Assn., Tex. Assn. Instl. Rsch., Piney Woods Counseling Assn., Nat. Academic Advising Assn. (scholar 2002), Phi Eta Sigma, Pi Kappa Lambda, Blue Key, Phi Kappa Phi. Achievements include research in assessment of writing skills; validity of writing assessment; student preferences for advisor personality types. Avocations: reading, travel, gardening. Home: 1913 Buckner St Longview TX 75604 Office: Kilgore College 1100 Broadway Kilgore TX 75662 Office Fax: 903-983-8214. E-mail: mturpin@kilgore.edu.

**TURQUETTE, ATWELL RUFUS,** logician; b. Texarkana, Tex., July 14, 1914; s. Rufus Watson and Dale Cook (Warmack) Turquette; m. Lucille Case Le Roy, June 2, 1937 (dec. Feb. 1956); m. Maxine Harriot Kennedy, Apr. 2, 1958 (dec. Aug. 1992); m. Frances D. Bond, Dec. 27, 1998. BA, U. Ark., 1936; MA, Duke U., 1937; PhD, Cornell U., 1943. Assoc. prof. Fla. So. Coll., Lakeland, 1937-38; fellow U. Chgo., 1938-39; assoc. prof. Fla. So. Coll., Lakeland, 1939-40; assistantship, fellow Cornell U., Ithaca, N.Y., 1940-43, instr., 1943-45; asst. prof. U. Ill., Champaign-Urbana, 1945-48, assoc. prof., 1948-52, prof., 1952-75, prof. emeritus, 1975—. Co-author: Many-valued Logics, 1952; contbg. author: Les 265 communications, Congrès International des Mathématiciens, Nice, 1970; editor: Jour. of Symbolic Logic, 1950-68; patentee in field. Duke U. scholar, 1936; U. Chgo. fellow, 1938; grantee NSF, 1968-70, Rockefeller Gen. Edn. Bd., 1954. Mem. Am. Math. Soc., Soc. Indsl. and Appl. Math., Symbolic Logic Assn., London Math. Soc., Calcutta Math. Soc., AAAS, N.Y. Acad. Scis., Am Phil. Assn. Achievements include design for multi-valued circuits, functional completeness and incompleteness results for many-valued logics; minimal axiomatizations for many-valued logics; relating Pascal triangles to Post sets; deciphering Peirce's triadic logic. Home: 914 W Clark St Champaign IL 61821-3328 Personal E-mail: turquette@sbcglobal.net.

**TURQUETTE, FRANCES BOND,** editor; b. Atlanta, Sept. 25, 1931; d. Sewell Hinton and Lavonia DeLay Dixon; m. Charles Eugene Bond, Sept. 12, 1952 (div. Jan. 1969); children: Turner D., Laura S., L. Irene, Cynthia D., Nelson K.; m. Atwell Rufus Turquette, Dec. 27, 1998. Student, Wesleyan Coll., 1948—50; BA in Journalism, U. Ga., 1952; MA in Art History, U. Ill., 1971. Editl. asst. Meth. Pub. Ho., Nashville, 1952-53, Rsch. Press, Champaign, Ill., 1972-73; editing supr. McGraw-Hill Book Co., N.Y.C., 1974-80; publs. editor pub. affairs U. Ill., Urbana, 1974, 80-88; editor Nat. Ctr. for Supercomputing Applications, Champaign, 1988-96. Vis. faculty, editor Coll. of Commerce, U. Ill. Urbana, 1972-74; ref. com., Editorial and Composition Standards McGraw Hill Book Co., N.Y.C., 1975-77; editor, writer access, 1988-96. Mem. program chair, liaison, bd. govs. Channing Murray Found., Urbana, 1982-92; mem. adv. bd. to freeze nuclear weapons 15th Congrl. Dist., 1982-87; co-pres. SANE/Freeze, Champaign County, 1992-94. Mem. Nat. Assn. Sci. Writers, Art Inst. Chgo. (family mem.), Lyric Opera Chgo., Oriental Inst., U. Chgo., Champaign-Urbana League Women Voters, Channing-Murray Found., Am. Assn. U. Women, Theta Sigma Phi. Unitarian Universalist. Avocations: travel, writing, gardening, photography. Home: 914 W Clark St Champaign IL 61821-3328 Personal E-mail: turquette@sbcglobal.net.

**TURRELL, JAMES ARCHIE,** sculptor; b. Los Angeles, May 6, 1943; s. Archibald Milton and Margaret (Hodges) T.; children: Shana Sequoia, Jennifer Lynn, Anya Regina. BA, Pomona Coll., Claremont, Calif., 1965; MA in Art, Claremont Grad. Sch., 1974; ArtsD, Chgo. Art Inst., 1999; Doctorate (hon.), Claremont Grad. Sch., 2001, Royal Acad. Art, London, Eng., 2002. Vis. artist, Pomona Coll., 1971-73, Claremont Grad. Sch., 1972-73; artist-in-residence Mus. No. Ariz., Flagstaff, 1979—; exhbns. include: Pasadena (Calif.) Art Mus., 1967, Main and Hill Studio, Santa Monica, Calif., 1968-70, Stedelijk Mus., Amsterdam, Netherlands, 1976, ARCO Center Visual Arts, Los Angeles, 1976, Whitney Mus., N.Y.C., 1980, Castelli Gallery, 1980, Ctr. Contemporary Art, Seattle, 1982, Israel Mus., Jerusalem, 1983, Flow Ace Gallery, Los Angeles, 1983, Hayden Gallery, MIT, Boston, 1983, Portside Gallery, Yokohama, Japan, 1995, Whitney Mus. of Am. Art, NY, 1999 & 2000, Angles Gallery, Santa Monica, Calif., 2000, Scottsdale Mus. of Contemporary Art, Scottsdale, Ariz., 2001, Mus. Modern Art N.Y., 2001, National Gallery of Art, Washington D.C., 2002, Galerie Henry Art, Seattle, Wash., 2003, Pace Wildenstein Gallery, N.Y., 2004 and several others; commns. include, Villa Panza, Varese, Italy, 1974, Villa Schiebler, Milan, Italy, 1979, Roden Crater (Ariz.) project, 1975—. Conscientious objector 1966. Recipient Louman award, 1981, Bessie award, 1985, Chevalier des Arts et des Lettres, France, 1991, Friedrich Prize, Frankfurt, Germany, 1992, Skowhegan Award for Sculpture, 1997 Governor's Arts Award, Artist of the Year, Ariz., 1994, Wolf prize in arts (sculpture), Wolf Found., Israel, 1998, Grande Médailles d'argent, Arts Plastiques, Fondation Académie d'Architecture, Paris, France 2000, Jefferson medal in Architecture, U. Va., 2002, Distinguished Alumnus award, Claremont Grad. U., Calif., 2003; named Artist of the Year, Scottsdale Cultural Arts Coun., 2000; grantee Nat. Endowment Arts, 1968, 75, 80; Dia Art Found., 1975-79; Guggenfellow fellow, 1974, Katherine T. and John D. MacArthur Found. fellowship, 1984; Ariz. Commn. for the Arts and Humanities, visual arts fellowship, 1980 Fellow: Am. Acad. Arts and Sciences.*

**TURRELL, RICHARD HORTON, SR.,** banker; b. Kingston, Pa., Apr. 9, 1925; s. George Henry and Margaret (Clark) T.; m. Sally Wolfe, May 28, 1955; children: Richard H. Jr., David C., Douglas W. (dec.). Student, Cornell

U., 1943; BS in Commerce, Washington and Lee U., 1949. Rep. sales Del. Lackawanna and Western Coal Co., Phila., 1949-51; asst. to pres. N.Y.C. 1951-58; broker Auchincloss Parker & Redpath, N.Y.C., 1958-61; mgr. investments Fiduciary Trust Co. Internat., N.Y.C., 1961-94, v.p., 1965-94, sr. v.p., 1968-94, sec., 1971-84. Asst. sec. Blue Coal Corp., N.Y.C., 1953-58; v.p., bd. dirs. Pine Raleigh (N.C.) Corp., 1966-93. Trustee, overseer Simon's Rock of Bard Coll., Gt. Barrington, Mass., 1968-93; trustee Monmouth Univ., West Long Branch, N.J., 1980—, chmn. bd. trustees, 1989-92; chmn. Millburn-Short Hills (N.J.) Rep. Com., 1973-78; trustee Children's Specialized Hosp. Found., Mountainside, N.J., 1989-95; bd. dirs. ARC Martin County, Fla., 2000. With Signal Corps, U.S. Army, 1943-46, PTO. Named Disting. Alumnus, Washington and Lee U., 1986. Mem. Baltusrol Golf Club (Springfield, N.J., gov. 1977), Capitol Hill Club (Washington), Turtle Creek Club (Tequesta, Fla.), Masons, Irem Temple Aaonms, Phi Beta Kappa, Phi Eta Sigma, Alpha Kappa Psi, Omicron Delta Kappa (hon.), Beta Gamma Sigma, Phi Delta Theta. Presbyterian. Avocations: golf, history, education. Home: 114 Turtle Creek Dr Tequesta FL 33469-1547

**TURRENTINE, HOWARD BOYD,** federal judge; b. Escondido, Calif., Jan. 22, 1914; s. Howard and Veda Lillian (Maxfield) T.; children: Howard Robert, Terry Beverly; m. Marlene Lipsey, Nov. 1, 1991. AB, San Diego State Coll., 1936; LLB, U. So. Calif., 1939. Bar: Calif. 1939. Practiced in, San Diego, 1939-68; judge Superior Ct. County of San Diego, 1968-70, U.S. Dist. Ct. (so. dist.) Calif., Calif., sr. judge San Diego, 1970—. Served with USNR, 1941-45. Mem. ABA, Fed. Bar Assn., Am. Judicature Soc. Office: US Dist Ct 940 Front St San Diego CA 92101-8994 Office Phone: 619-557-6630.

**TURRI, JOSEPH A.,** lawyer; b. Seneca Falls, N.Y., July 24, 1943; s. Louis Arthur and Assunta (Faiola) T.; m. Susan Ruth Testa, Dec. 29, 1975 (dec.); 1 child, Michael James. BA, SUNY, Buffalo, 1965; JD, Cornell U., 1970. Bar: N.Y. 1971, U.S. Dist Ct. (we. dist.) N.Y. 1971, U.S. Supreme Ct. 1974, U.S. Dist. Ct. (so. dist.) N.Y. 1996, U.S. Ct. Appeals (2d cir.) 1990. Mem. Harris Beach PLLC, Rochester, NY, 1970—, chmn. constrn. law dept., 1992-98, 2002—, chmn. pres., 1999—2002. Bd. dirs. Thousand Island Park Corp., N.Y., O'Connell Electric Co.; v.p. Castle Bay Ltd., Rochester, N.Y.; arbitrator Am. Arbitration Assn., Syracuse, 1985—. Bd. dirs. Rochester Downtown Devel. Corp., 1992-97. Mem. N.Y. State Bar Assn., Monroe County Bar Assn., Assn. Gen. Contractors, Met. Forum (trustee). Avocations: horseback riding, antique wooden boats. Home: 21 Evergreen Ln Rochester NY 14618-4719 Office: Harris Beach PLLC 99 Garnsey Rd Pittsford NY 14534 Office Phone: 585-419-8644.

**TURRO, NICHOLAS JOHN,** chemistry professor; b. Middletown, Conn., May 18, 1938; s. Nicholas John and Philomena (Russo) T.; m. Sandra Jean Misenti, Aug. 6, 1960; children: Cynthia Suzanne, Claire Melinda. BA, Wesleyan U., 1960, DSc (hon.), 1984; PhD, Calif. Inst. Tech., 1963; doctorate (hon.), U. Fribourg, Switzerland, 2004. Instr. chemistry Columbia U., N.Y.C., 1964-65, asst. prof., 1965-67, assoc. prof., 1967-69, prof. chemistry, 1969—; William P. Schweitzer prof. chemistry, 1982—, chmn. chemistry dept., 1981-84, co-chmn. dept. chem. engring. and applied chemistry, 1997-2000, prof. earth and environ. engring., 1998—. Author: Molecular Photochemistry, 1965; author: (with A.A. Lamola) Energy Transfer and Organic Photochemistry, 1971; author: Modern Molecular Photochemistry, 1978; mem. editl. bd.: Jour. Reactive Intermediates, Langmuir and Proceedings of Nat. Acad. Scis., 2004. Recipient Eastman Kodak award for excellence in grad. rsch. pure chemistry, 1973, award, E.O. Lawrence U.S. Dept. Energy, 1983, Porter medal, European Photochem. Soc., Inter-Am. Photochem. Soc., 1994, Havinga medal, Leiden, The Netherlands, 1994, Disting. Alumnus award, Calif. Inst. Tech., 1996, Strahlenchemie preis, Max-Planck-Inst., Mülheim, Germany, 1998, Dir's. award for Tchr.-Scholar, NSF, 2002, Mayor's award for Excellence in Sci. and Tech., N.Y.C., 2004; fellow NSF, Alfred P. Sloan Found., Guggenheim fellow, Oxford U., 1985. Mem.: AAAS, NAS (editl. bd. Procs. NAS 2002—), European Photo-Chem. Assn. (Porter medal), Inter-Am. Photochemistry Soc. (award 1991, 1994), N.Y. Acad. Scis. (Freda and Gregory Halpern award in photochemistry 1977), Am. Chem. Soc. (mem. editl. bd. jour. 1984—87, Fresenius award 1973, award for pure chemistry 1974, Harrison Howe award Rochester, N.Y. sect. 1986, Arthur C. Cope award 1986, James Flack Norris award 1987, award in colloid and surface chemistry 1999, Gibbs medal award Chgo. sect. 2000, George C. Pimentel award 2004), Sigma Xi, Phi Beta Kappa. Office: Columbia U 3000 Broadway New York NY 10027-6941 Business E-Mail: njt3@columbia.edu.

**TURSO, VITO ANTHONY,** government agency administrator, public information officer; b. N.Y., Jan. 3, 1948; s. Vito Anthony and Helen (Smanko) T.; m. MaryAnn Ponzo, July 12, 1980; children: Lisa Lynn, Laura Mae, Nicole Vita. Student, Queens Coll., Flushing, N.Y., 1965-69. Reporter L.I. Press, Jamaica, N.Y., 1966-77; asst. Metro editor The Trib, N.Y.C., 1977-78; dir. pub. affairs N.Y.C. Dept. Sanitation, 1978-90; dep. commr. for pub. affairs N.Y.C. Dept. Correction, 1990-94; dep. commr. for pub. affairs and community svcs. N.Y.C. Dept. of Environ. Protection, 1994-95; exec. v.p. Dan Klores Comms. Pub. Rels., 1995—2002; dep. commr. pub. info and cmty. affairs N.Y.C. Dept. Sanitation, 2002—. Guest lectr. New Sch. for Social Rsch., NYC, 1988, Pace U., 1990, NYU, 1998, St. John's U., 2004-05. Host pub. affairs shows on TV and radio, 1981, 88, 2004, 2005; contbr. articles to pop. mags. Bd. dirs. Ozone Tudor Civic Assn., Ozone Park, N.Y., 1982-90. Recipient Bronze medal Internat. Film and TV Festival N.Y., 1985, Page One award N.Y. Newspaper Guild, 1976. Mem. Pub. Rels. Officers Soc. N.Y. (pres. 1983-85), Pub. Rels. Soc. Am. (bd. dirs. 1987-88), Am. Diabetes Assn. (bd. dirs. N.Y. chpt. 1989-91), Bklyn. Tech. H.S. Alumni Assn. (bd. dirs. 1984—90), N.Y. Press Club, Inc. (bd. dirs. 1978, journalism award judge 1996-). Roman Catholic. Avocations: golf, music. Office: 133-33 84th St Ozone Park NY 11417 1919 Office: 125 Worth St Rm 1 New York NY 10013 Office Phone: 646-885-5020. E-mail: vturso@dsny.nyc.gov.

**TURTELL, NEAL TIMOTHY,** librarian; b. NYC, Nov. 1, 1949; s. Richard Roland and Ann Grace (Glover) T. AB, Fordham U., 1971; MLS, Pratt Inst., 1975. Cataloger-libr. Ford Found., N.Y.C., 1972-75, U.S. Dept. Transp., Washington, 1975-77; spl. projects libr. Smithsonian Instn., Washington, 1977-81, chief catalogue records, 1981-82; asst. dir. tech. svcs. U. Wis. Oshkosh, 1982-83, asst. prof. libr. sci., 1982-83; asst. chief libr. Nat. Gallery of Art, Washington, 1983-87, exec. libr., 1987—. Contbr. to book revs. Libr. Jour., 1972-75; exhbn. catalogue. Bd. trustees Pyramid Atlantic Ctr. for Printmaking and the Art of the Book, Riverdale, Md., 1988—, v.p. bd. trustees, 1991—. Mem. Art Librs. Soc. N.Am., Rsch. Librs. Group (steering com. for art and architecture 1988-89), Assn. Internat. de Bibliophilie, Grolier Club. Home: 1631-B S Hayes St Arlington VA 22202-2713 Office: Nat Gallery of Art 4th & Constitution Ave NW Washington DC 20565-0001

**TURTIL, LAWRENCE CHARLES,** psychiatrist; b. N.Y.C., Dec. 30, 1951; s. Joseph Fredric and Estelle Rebecca Turtil. BA cum laude, U. Pa., 1972; MD, Georgetown U., 1977. Diplomate Am. Bd. Psychiatry and Neurology, Am. Bd. Internal Medicine, Am. Bd. Adolscent Psychiatry. Resident in internal medicine Lenox Hill Hosp., N.Y.C., 1977-80, attending physician emergency svc., 1980-81, attending physician dept. psychiatry, 1989-90, asst. chief inpatient psychiatry unit, 1990-94; resident in psychiatry Cornell N.Y. Hosp., White Plains, 1981-84; attending physician N.Y. Hosp., Westchester div., 1984-85; med. dir. Four Winds Hosp., Katonah, N.Y., 1985-89; pvt. practice N.Y.C. & Katonah, N.Y.; attending psychiatrist Manhattan Psychiatric Ctr., N.Y.C., 1994; med. dir. Four Winds Hosp., Katonah, N.Y., 1994-97; med. dir. Psych Sys. Manhattan partial hospitalization Gracie Square Hosp., N.Y.C., 1997—2001; psychiatric cons. Counseling Ctr. Student Health Svcs. Fashion Inst. Tech., 1999—2001, Children's Aid Soc. PINS Diversion Program, 2001—04. Mem. Am. Psychiat. Assn. Office: 40 E 83d St Ste 1E New York NY 10028 Office Phone: 212-734-5482.

**TURTURRO, AIDA,** actress; b. NYC, Sept. 25, 1962; Grad., State U. NY, New Paltz, 1984. Actor: (films) Life with Mikey, 1993, Money Train, 1995, Sleepers, 1996, Fallen, 1998, Celebrity, 1998, Deep Blue Sea, 1999, Mickey Blue Eyes, 1999, Bringing Out the Dead, 1999, Play It to the Bone, 1999,

Crocodile Dundee in Los Angeles, 2001; (TV series) As the World Turns, 1998, The Soprano's, 2000—; (Broadway plays) A Streetcar Named Desire, 1992, (guest appearance): (TV series) Law and Order, 1990.

**TURTURRO, JOHN,** actor; b. Brooklyn, Feb. 28, 1957; s. Nicholas and Katherine Turturro; m. Katherine Borowitz; children: Amedeo, Diego. Grad., SUNY (New Paltz), 1978; student, Yale Drama Sch. Worked in regional theater and off-Broadway prodns.: Danny and the Deep Blue Sea; Men Without Dates; Tooth of the Crime; La Puta Vida; Chaos and Hard Times; The Bald Soprano; Of Mice and Men; The Resistable Rise of Arturo Ui, 1991; Waiting for Godot; appeared in Broadway prodn.: Death of a Salesman, 1984; appeared in films: Raging Bull, 1980; The Flamingo Kid, 1984; To Live and Die in L.A., 1985; Desperately Seeking Susan, 1985; Hannah and Her Sisters, 1986; Gung Ho, 1986; Offbeat, 1986; The Color of Money, 1986; The Sicilian, 1987; Five Corners, 1988; Do the Right Thing, 1989; Miller's Crossing, 1990; Men of Respect, 1990; Jungle Fever, 1991; Barton Fink, 1991; Backtrack, 1991; Brain Donors, 1992; Fearless, 1993; Festival, 1991; Being Human, 1994; Quiz Show, 1994; Grace of My Heart, 1994; Search and Destroy, 1995; Unstrung Heroes, 1995; Clockers, 1995; Box of Moonlight, 1996; Girl 6, 1996; The Big Lebowski, 1997; Animals, 1997; The Truce, 1998; Lesser Prophets, 1998; Rounders, 1998; He Got Game, 1998; The Source, 1999; The Cradle Will Rock, 1999; Company Man, 1999; Two Thousand and None, 1999; Oh Brother, Where Art Thou?, 1999; The Man Who Cried, 1999; The Luzhin Defense, 1999; Anger Management, 2003; appeared in films Collateral Damage, 2000, Mr. Deeds, 2002, Secret Passage, 2002, Secret Window, 2004; actor: (TV films) Monday Night Mayhem, 2002; dir.: (films, debut) Mac; (films) Illuminata, 1998, Thirteen Conversations About One Thing, 2000. also: 16 N Oak St 2 A Ventura CA 93001-5620

**TURTURRO, NICHOLAS,** actor; b. Queens, NY, Jan. 29, 1962; m. Jamie Biunno, 1984 (div. 1985) 1 child; m. Lissa Espinosa, 1986; 1 child. Actor films including: Mo' Better Blues, 1990, Men of Respect, 1991, Jungle Fever, 1991, Mac, 1992, Malcolm X, 1992, Men Lie, 1994, Cosmic Slop, 1994, Federal Hill, 1995, The Search for One-eye Jimmy, 1996, Shadow Conspiracy, 1997, Excess Baggage, 1997, Recess: School's Out, 2001, The Shipment, 2001, Purgatory Flats, 2002, The Biz, 2002, The Hollow, 2004, The Hillside Strangler, 2004, The Longest Yard, 2005, (TV series) NYPD Blue, 1993-2000, (TV movies) Dead and Alive: The Race for Gus Farace, 1991, Cosmic Slop, 1994, In the Line of Duty: Hunt for Justice, 1995, Falling from the Sky: Flight 174, 1995, Mercenary II: Thick & Thin, 1997, Witness to the Mob, 1998, Monday Night Mayhem, 2002, Big Shot: Confessions of a Campus Bookie, 2002; TV guest appearances include: Law & Order, 1992, L.A. Law, 1993, Drew Carey Show, 1997, The District, 2001, Touched by an Angel, 2002, The Twilight Zone, 2002, Third Watch, 2003, 04. Office: United Talent Agy 9560 Wilshire Blvd Ste 500 Beverly Hills CA 90212-2427

**TUSCHMAN, JAMES MARSHALL,** lawyer; b. Nov. 28, 1941; s. Chester and Harriet (Harris) T.; m. Ina S. Cheloff, Sept. 2, 1967; children: Chad Michael, Jon Stephen, Sari Anne. BS in Bus., Miami U., Oxford, Ohio, 1963; JD, Ohio State U., 1966. Bar: Ohio 1966, U.S. Ct. Appeals (6th and 7th cirs.), U.S. Supreme Ct. Assoc. Shumaker, Loop & Kendrick, Toledo, 1966—84, ptnr., 1970—84; co-founder, chmn. ops. com. Jacobson Maynard Tuschman & Kalur, Toledo, 1985—97; COO Ohio Ferrous Group Omnisource Corp., Toledo, 1998—99, dir. bus. devel. No. Ohio group, 1999—2001; of counsel Barkan & Robon Ltd., Maumee, Ohio, 2002—. Chmn. bd., sec. Tuschman Steel Co., Toledo, 1969-76, Toledo Steel Supply Co., 1969-86; vice-chmn. bd. Kripke Tuschman Industries, Inc., 1977-85; ptnr. Starr Ave. Co., Toledo, 1969-86. Past trustee, chmn. bd. trustees U. Toledo; past trustee, chmn. fin. com., past treas. Maumee Valley Country Day Sch.; past trustee, v.p., treas. Temple B'nai Israel, 1984-88; mem. nat. alumni coun. Ohio State U. Coll. Law; mem., co-chmn. subcom. on structure, governance and fin. Gov.'s Commn. on Higher Edn. and Economy; mem Ohio Bd. Regents. Fellow Internat. Soc. Barristers; mem. ATLA, Am. Bd. Trial Advocates, Ohio Bar Assn., Toledo Bar Assn., Ohio Trial Lawyers Assn., Million Dollar Advocates Forum, Toledo Club, Inverness Country Club, Zeta Beta Tau, Phi Delta Phi. Home: 2579 Olde Brookside Rd Toledo OH 43615-2233 Office: Barkan & Robon Ltd 1701 Woodlands Dr Maumee OH 43537-4092 Office Phone: 419-897-6500. Business E-Mail: jmt.bar-rob@buckeye-express.com.

**TUSHLA, RICHARD JAMES,** physician; b. Auburn, Nebr., Jan. 24, 1941; s. Francis Michael and Ruth Jeanette (Shelly) T.; m. Connie Rose Bernard, Aug. 6, 1966; children: Todd, Jennifer. BS, U. Notre Dame, 1963; MD, U. Nebr., 1967. Diplomate Am. Bd. Family Medicine. Intern Santa Clara County Hosp., San Jose, Calif., 1968; resident Ventura (Calif.) County Hosp., 1970; pvt. practice, 1973—. Clin. prof. medicine U. Calif., Davis, 1976-77; asst. clin. prof. of medicine UCLA, 1977—; physician Santa Paula (Calif.) Meml. Hosp., Ventura Gen. Hosp., Community Meml. Hosp., Ventura, St. John's Regional Med. Ctr., Oxnard, Calif. Mem. editorial bd. Patient Care mag. Maj. U.S. Army, 1970-73. Fellow Am. Acad. Family Practice; mem. AMA (Physician Recognition award 1977, 82, 87, 92), Calif. Med. Assn. (alt. del. 1978, 79, 80, del. 1981-98), Ventura County Med. Soc. (bd. govs. 1980-86, sec. 1981-83, pres. 1985). Roman Catholic. Home: 400 E Santa Barbara St Santa Paula CA 93060-2675 Business E-Mail: drt@westfp.com.

**TUSIANI, JOSEPH,** foreign language educator, author; b. Foggia, Italy, Jan. 14, 1924; came to U.S., 1947, naturalized, 1956; s. Michael and Maria (Pisone) T. Dottore in Lettere summa cum laude, U. Naples, 1947, LittD, 1971; Dottore (hon.), U. Foggia, 2004. Lectr. in Italian lit. Hunter Coll., 1950-62; chmn. Italian dept. Coll. Mt. St. Vincent, 1948-71. Vis. assoc. prof. NYU, 1956-64, CUNY, 1971-83; prof. Herbert H. Lehman Coll., 1971-83; NDEA vis. prof. Italian Conn. State Coll., 1962. Author: Dante in Licenza, 1952, Two Critical Essays on Emily Dickinson, 1952, Poesia Missionaria in Inghilterra ed America, 1953, Sonettisti Americani, 1954, Melos Cordis: Poems in Latin, 1955, Lo Speco Celeste, 1956, Odi Sacre; poems, 1958, The Complete Poems of Michelangelo, 1960, Rind and All, 1962, Lust and Liberty (The Poems of Machiavelli), 1963, The Fifth Season, 1963, (novels) Envoy from Heaven, 1965, Tasso's Jerusalem Delivered, 1970, Boccaccio's Nymphs of Fiesole, 1971, Gente Mia and Other Poems, 1978, (poems in Latin) In Exilio Rerum, 1985, (autobiography) La Parola Difficile, vol. I, 1988, (poems in Latin) Confinia Lucis et Umbrae: La Parola Nuova, vol. II, 1991, La Parola Antica, vol. III, 1992, (poems in Italian) Il Ritorno, 1992, Bronx America, 1992, Annemale Parlante, 1994, Carmina Latina, 1994, La Poceide, 1996, Carmina Latina, vol. 11, 1998, Li Quatte Staggione, 1998, Lu Deddú, 1999, Maste Peppe Cantarine, 2000, Lu Ponte de Sóla, 2001, In Quattro Lingue, 2001, Dante's Divine Comedy (As told for young people), 2001, L'ore de Gesu Bambine (a Christmas play in verse), 2001, La Prima Cumpagnia, 2002, (in Apulian dialect) La Tomba de Patre Pí, 2003, (plays) (in verse) La Cunte de Pasqua, 2003, La Padula (in Apulian dialect, 2004, Lu Scazzamuredde, 2005, Storie dal Gargano, 1955-2005, 2006; translator: Pulci's Morgante, 1998. Recipient Greenwood prize for poetry in England, 1956, Outstanding Tchr. award, 1969, cavaliere ufficiale Italian Republic, 1973, Leonardo Covello's educator award, 1980, Leone di San Marco award, 1982, Avis award, 1983, Joseph Tusiani scholarship fund established in his honor at Lehman Coll., 1983, Congl. medal merit, 1984, Progresso medal liberty, 1986, Gold plaque City Hall San Marco, 1986, Outstanding tchr. award Am. Assn. Tchrs. Italian, 1986, Renoir literary award, 1988, Joseph Tusiani, Poet, Translator, Humanist (An Internat. Homage), 1995, Enrico Fermi award, 1995, Fiorello La Guardia award, 1998; Melvin Jones fellow, 1995, Gov.'s award for excellence, 1999, Apulia prize of Regione Puglia, 1999, Gold medal at Rome's Capitol, 2004, Gold medal Gov. of Regione Puglia, 2004, prize Italiani nel Mondo, 2004; Joseph Tusiani Found. established at U. Lecce, 1998, NEH, 1998. Mem. Poetry Soc. Am. (v.p.), Cath. Poetry Soc. Am. (dir. 1958, Spirit gold medal 1968) Home: 308 E 72nd St New York NY 10021-4727 *Strange how this continually re-edited Who's Who forces one to work and achieve.*

**TUSKA, JON,** writer, publishing executive; b. South Milwaukee, Wis., Apr. 30, 1942; s. Andrew and Florence Catherine (Tommet) T.; m. Vicki Piekarski, May 24, 1980; 1 child, Jennifer Lee. BA, Marquette U., 1965. Owner Pers. Cons., Milw., 1969-74; editor, pub. Views & Revs. mag., 1969-75; freelance writer, 1975–91; co-owner, agt. Golden West Literary Agy., Portland, Oreg., 1992—. Adj. faculty MA and tchg. program and undergrads. Lewis and Clark Coll., 1979-88' staff music critic Ovation mag., 1987-89, Fanfare mag., 1989-95; spl. film. cons. Images of Indians, PBS, 1980, Images of Appalachia, PBS, 1984, Mommy, Who's Winning Now? The Cold War in America, Turner, 1986, Say It with Music: Irving Berlin's America, PBS, 1986, Broadway's Eternal Romantics: Lerner and Loewe, PBS, 1988, John Wayne: Standing Tall, PBS, 1989, Big Guns Talk, Turner, 1997; prodr. classical music programs, art and news features and interviews with musicians and motion picture personalities, and film revs. for radio stas. Oreg. Pub. Broadcasting. Author: Philo Vance: The Life and Times of S.S. Van Dine, 1973, The Films of Mae West, 1973, The Filming of the West, 1976, The Detective in Hollywood, 1978, The Vanishing Legion: A History of Mascot Pictures 1927-35, 1982, 2d edit., 1986, Billy the Kid: A Bio/Bibliography, 1983, Dark Cinema: American Film Noir in Cultural Perspective, 1984, The American West in Film: Critical Approaches to the Western, 1985, In Manors and Alleys: A Case-Book on the American Detective Film, 1988, A Variable Harvest: Essays and Reviews in Literature and Film, 1989, Encounters with Filmmakers: Eight Career Studies, 1991, The Complete Films of Mae West, 1992, Billy the Kid: His Life and Legend, 1994, (with Vicki Piekarski) The Frontier Experience: A Reader's Guide to the Life and Literature of the American West, 1984; editor-in-chief (with Piekarski) Ency. of Frontier and Western Fiction, 1983; editor: The Western Story: A Chronological Treasury 1894-1994, 1994, Shadow of the Lariat, 1995, Star Western: Twenty-Two Western Stories from the Golden Age, 1995, The Big Book of Western Action Stories, 1995, (with Piekarski) The Morrow Anthology of Great Western Short Stories, 1997, The First Five Star Western Corral, 2000, Five Star Westerns, 2000, Stories of the Golden West, Book One, 2000, Book Two, 2001, Book Three, 2002, Book Four, 2003, Book Five, 2004, Book Six, 2005, Odyssey to the North: Northwestern Stories, 2003. Avocations: reading, classical music, film history, book collecting. Home and Office: 2327 SE Salmon St Portland OR 97214-3943 Office Phone: 503-232-0238. Personal E-mail: jtuska@qwest.net.

**TUSKEY, LAURA JEANNE,** music educator, pharmacologist; b. Virginia Beach, Va., May 7, 1966; d. Cromer Lee Ishmael and Annabell E. Eschbach; m. John Phillip Tuskey, June 26, 1998. Student, Old Dominion U., Norfolk, Va., 1984—86. Cert. pharmacy technician Pharmacy Technician Certification Bd., 2003. Pianist Cath. Ch. of St. Mark, Virginia Beach, Va., 1991—; office mgr. CompuGeek, L.L.C., Chesapeake, Va., 2002—03; pharmacy technician Farm Fresh, Inc., Virginia Beach, Va., 2002—, Phar Mor, Inc., Norfolk and Virginia Beach, Va., 1991—98; music therapist Our Lady of Perpetual Health, Virginia Beach, Va., 1999—2000. Aromatherapy educator, Hampton Roads, Va., 2000—. Contbr. articles to profl. jours. Mem.: Alzheimer's Assn. (chm. memory walk com. 2001), Nat. Pastoral Musicians Assn. R-Liberal. Roman Catholic. Avocations: aromatherapy, musical scenes, reading, travel. Office: Catholic Church of St Mark 1505 Kempsville Rd Virginia Beach VA 23464

**TUTASHINDA, KWELI (BRIAN P. ALTHEIMER),** chiropractic physician, educator; b. Wynne, Ark., May 14, 1956; s. Joe Porché and Lura Ella (Darden) Altheimer; divorced; 1 child, Chinyere R.; m. Leonor Quiñonez, June 13, 1987; children Xihuanel, Rukiya, Jomoké. BA in Philosophy summa cum laude, U. Ark., 1978; D of Chiropractic cum laude, Life Chiropractic Coll. West, San Lorenzo, Calif., 1989. Tchr. English Oakland (Calif.) Pub. Schs., 1984-86; instr. phys. diagnosis and chiropractic tech. Life Chiropractic Coll. West, Haywood, Calif., 1989—99; pvt. practice Berkeley, 1989—; owner Imhotep Chiropractic & Wellness Clinic; dir. Imhotep Wellness Workshops & Seminars. Tchr. spl. programs U. Calif., Berkeley, Calif., 1984—92, 1994—95, 1998—2000, 2005; lectr. in field. Editor, pub. Foresight Mag., 1982-84; author, pub. Toward a Holistic Worldview, 1985, Therapeutic Exercises for the Spine, 1999, Seven Steps To Health, 2006; contbr. articles to Chiropractic History. Recipient 1st degree Black Belt Tae Kwon Do, 1976. Mem. Sufi Order of the West, Naqshbandi Sufi Order. Islam. Avocations: yoga, martial arts, writing, reading, walking. Office: 3358 Adeline St Berkeley CA 94703-2737 Business E-Mail: tutateam@sbcglobal.net.

**TUTHILL, JAY DEAN, II,** investment executive; b. Wilmington, Del., Dec. 10, 1953; s. Jay Dean Tuthill and Annabelle (Carney) Kressman; m. Laura Ann Behr, Nov. 23, 1972 (div. May 1981); 1 child, Elizabeth; m. Assunta Sera, Oct. 10, 1991; children: Lori, Michael, Mark. BSChemE, U. Del., 1981; MBA with honors, U. Mich., 1988. Engr. Exxon, Detroit, 1981-86; mgr. bus. planning Am. Cyanamid, Wayne, NJ, 1988-94; portfolio mgr. Am. Express, Paramus, NJ, 1994-95; pres. Buckingham Fin., Ridgewood, NJ, 1995—; CFO Prismatic Corp., Newburgh, NY, 1997—; mng. dir. Tuthill & Merker LLC, Ridgewood, NJ, 1999—. Mem. Assn. Investment Mgmt. and Rsch., N.Y. Soc. Security Analysts (vice chair comms. and mktg. com. 1994—, Vol. of Yr. award 1995), Inst. Chartered Fin. Analysts (chartered CFA), Ridgewood C. of C. (profl. com. 1996), Beta Gamma Sigma, Tau Beta Pi. Republican. Roman Catholic. Avocations: golf, piano. Home: 530 Valley Rd Apt 3T Montclair NJ 07043-2714 Office: Tuthill & Merker LLC 999 Riverview Dr Ste 304 Totowa NJ 07512-1165

**TUTHILL, OLIVER W., JR.,** psychologist, consultant; b. Orange, N.J., Aug. 8, 1945; s. Oliver W. and Virginia Tuthill. BA in Sociology, Olivet Coll., 1968, BA in Psychology, 1968; MA in Psychology, Antioch U., 2002. Singer, songwriter, Chgo., 1955—72; actor Columbia, Hollywood, Calif., 1972—84, Universal, Hollywood, 1973—84; pres., profl. spkr. Autumn Tree Prodns., Seattle, 1999—2005; pres. Blue Pony Trail Music, Seattle, 2005—. Pres. 140th St Promotions, Seattle, 1986—88, Blue Wood Films LLC, Seattle, 2003—05; cons. Jr. Achievement, Seattle, 1996—2000; advisor, com. mem. Gov. Blue Ribbon Commn., Seattle, 2000—02. Dir.: (films) Understanding 6 Forms of Emotional, 1999 (Bronze Telly award, 2000, 2003), Dysphoria, 2001 (Best Feature Film, 2001), Children's Rights: Why America Says No, 2004 (4 Bronze Telly awards, 2004); prodr.: (albums) Acoustic Concerto, 2005; prodr.(dir.): (films) Willatuk: The Legend of Seattle's Sea Serpent, featuring Graham Greene, 2006; prodr. (dir.): (films) Child Abuse; prodr.(dir.): (films) Wounded Heart: Pine Ridge Run and The Sioux Featuring Russell Means, 2005 (Bronze Telly award, 2005, Grand Goldie Film award, 2005). Recipient Media award, Gov. Wash. State, 2002, Horace Mann award, Antioch U., 2003, Silver Plaque, Music Intercom Video Competition, 2001, Silver Telly award, 2006. Mem.: APA (assoc.), Assn. Ind. Film and Video, NW Screenwriters Guild, NW Film Forum, Internat. Documentary Assn., Screen Actors Guild, Broadcast Music Inc. Avocations: sports, swimming, singing, reading, politics. Office: Blue Wood Films 17171 Bothell Way NE PMB 108 Seattle WA 98155 Home: 17111 Bothell Way Ne Bothell WA 98011-1926 Office Phone: 206-364-9202. Personal E-mail: owtuth@earthlink.net.

**TUTHILL, WALTER WARREN,** accountant, management consultant; b. Madison, NJ, Nov. 28, 1941; s. Walter Warren and Elizabeth Emma (Kniskern) T.; m. Barbara Ann Stephens, Apr. 22, 1967. BSBA, U. N.C., 1964. CPA N.Y., N.J., N.C.; cert. info. systems auditor. Sr. mgr. Price Waterhouse, N.Y.C., 1964-77; dir. internal audit Carter Hawley Hale Stores Inc., L.A., 1977-82, gen. auditor, 1982-85, v.p., 1985-93; sr. v.p. retail control Broadway Stores, Inc., L.A., 1993-96; v.p. retail control Federated Dept. Stores, Inc., L.A., 1996-97; COO Gelhand, Rennert & Feldman divsn. PricewaterhouseCoopers LLP, L.A., 1997-2001; dir. comprehensive bus. svcs. WongHolland LLP, CPAs, Woodland Hills, Calif., 2001—. Lectr. in field. Contbr. articles to profl. jours. Mem. AICPA, N.Y. Soc. CPAs, Am. Acctg. Assn., Nat. Retail Fedn. (chmn. bd. internal audit group 1982-84, bd. dirs.), Info. Sys. Audit and Control Assn. Avocations: international travel, computers, classical music, photography, philanthropy. Office: WongHolland LLP CPAs and Cons 4919 Topanga Canyon Blvd Woodland Hills CA 91364-3113 Office Phone: 818-999-5273. Personal E-mail: wwtuthill@earthlink.net. *Life is what happens when we're planning something else.*

**TUTINS, ANTONS,** electronics and audio engineer; b. Ludza, Latvia, May 2, 1933; s. Francis and Veronika (Seipulniks) Tutins; came to U.S., 1950, naturalized, 1963; student U. Minn., 1951-55; BS in Elec. Engring., Ill. Inst. Tech.; 1970; MBA, U. Chgo., 1974; m. Raita Snebergs, July 8, 1961; 1 child, Robert. With Motorola Communications div., Chgo., 1964-73; product engring. mgr. Knowles Electronics, Inc., Franklin Park, Ill., 1973-81; dir. quality assurance and mfg. engring. Perma Power Electronics Inc., Chgo., 1982-95; pres. AT Systems, Des Plaines, Ill., 1995—; tech. cons. Accord, Inc., Westchester, Ill., 1995—. Bd. dirs. Spl. Interest Group of Object Oriented Tech., 1995—. With USN, 1955-57. Mem. IEEE, Acoustical Soc. Am., Chgo. Acoustical and Audio Group (pres. 1977-78), Audio Engring. Soc., Midwest Acoustics Conf. (exec. com., pres. 1980), Latvian Cath. Student Assn. Dzintars (pres. 1979-81), Am. Latvian Cath. Assn. (registered agt. 1978—, v.p. 1985), Baltic Info. Exch. (v.p. 1991—), Motorola Engring. Club (pres. 1970-71). Roman Catholic. Home: 1338 Briar Ct Des Plaines IL 60018-2146 Office: 10301 W Roosevelt Rd Westchester IL 60154-2575

**TUTOR, RONALD N.,** construction company executive; b. Oct. 13, 1940; BS in Finance, U. So. Calif., 1963. Pres., CEO Tutor-Saliba Corp.; bd. dir. Perini Corp., 1997—, COO, 1997—2000, vice chmn., 1998—99, chmn., 1999—, CEO, 2000—. Bd. dirs. Southdown Corp.; mem. adv. com. U. So. Calif. Sch. Engring. Recipient L.A. Conservancy Preservation award, 1994, Greater L.A. African-Am. C. of C. Contractor of yr. award, 1994, U.S. Army C.E. L.A. Dist. Contractor of Yr. award, 1994, NCCJ Real Estate and Constrn. Industry Humanitarian award, 1992. Mem. Am. Concrete Inst.*

**TUTTLE, ANNE PALMER,** artist, education educator; b. Phila., Pa., May 28, 1922; d. Edward Lionel and Anna Margaret Palmer; m. Herbert Robert Pfister, Dec. 11, 1976 (dec.); m. Bruce Nelson Tuttle (div.); children: William, Patricia, David, Stephen, Amy. Ba, Long Isl. Univ. N.Y., 1944; MA, SUNY, Stony Brook, N.Y., 1977; student, Madison Art Sch., 1966—73, Pratt Graphics Ctr., N.Y., 1975. Tng. supr. Fredrick Loeser & Co., Bklyn., 1944—46; proprietor Anne Tuttle Studios, Setauket, NY, 1973—; printmaker Bermond Art Ltd., Lake Success, NY, 1975—86; instr. Empire State Coll., Old Westaury, NY, 1980—2004; master instr. Islip Art Mus., East Islip, NY, 1982—. Vis. artist Pima County Cultural, Tucson, 1994; judge art exhibits, Long Island, NY, 1978—; lectr. in field, Long Island, NY, 1980—. Prin. works include portrait Arthur Tuttle v.p. treas. RCA, 1976, pres. Patricia Designs, 1980, pres. Elec. workers union, 1981, prin. works include in numerous galleries, U.S., Can., Eng., France, Germany, Holland, South Africa. Pro bono mentor to artists, Long Island, NY. Recipient 1st prize portraits, Awixa Art League, 1969, Felician Art League, 1973, 2nd prize etching, Krishna Reddy, 1978. Republican. Avocations: reading, sailing, camping. Home: 239 Sheep Pasture Rd PO Box 142 East Setauket NY 11733 Office: Ann Tuttle Studios 239 Sheep Pasture Rd PO Box 142 East Setauket NY 11733-0142 Office Phone: 631-751-0111. Personal E-mail: annetuttle@hotmail.com.

**TUTTLE, EDWARD X.,** architect, lawyer; b. Ann Arbor, Mich., June 28, 1927; s. Edward X. and Betty F. Tuttle; m. Eunice Scott Tuttle, July 2, 1948; children: Nora, Nancy, Roy. BS in Engring., Brown U., R.I., 1947; B in Arch., U. Mich., 1954; JD, Detroit Coll. Law, 1977. Lic. Mich.; bar: Mich. Engring. draftsman Giffells & Vallett, Detroit, 1948—49; architect Mich., 1953—58, self-employed, Mich., 1958—17; lawyer Garan Lucow, Detroit, 1977—78, Denenberg Tuffley, Southfield, Mich., 1978—91; cons. forensic arch. self-employed, 1977—. Author: (book) With Benefit of Architect, 1967. Comdr. USNR. Home: 29242 Wildbrook Dr Southfield MI 48034 Personal E-mail: tedwardx@yahoo.com.

**TUTTLE, JEREMY BALLOU,** neuroscientist; s. John Bauman and Charlotte Marion (Root) T.; m. Sara Jane Stasko, Mar. 23, 1971. AB, U. Rochester, 1969; PhD, Johns Hopkins U., 1977. Postdoctoral fellow U. Conn., Storrs, 1976-79, vis. asst. prof., 1980, asst. prof. in residence, 1981-84; asst. prof. physiology U. Va., Charlottesville, 1984-87, asst. prof. neuroscience, 1987-90, rsch. asst. prof., 1990-93, assoc. prof. urology neuroscience, 1993-98, prof., 1999—. Contbr. articles to Devel. Biology, Science, Jour. Neuroscience, others; mem. editl. bd. Investigative Urology, Jour. Urology. Chmn. mem. Common Area Planning Commn., 1984-87; pres. bd. Earlysville Forest Homeowner's Assn., 1986-89, Earlysville, Va.; chmn. urology spl. emphasis panel NIH, 1996-2001; chmn. spl. emphasis panel on female pelvic floor disorders Nat. Inst. Child Health and Human Devel., 1999; mem. promotion and tenure com. U. Va., 2004—. U. Rochester Hon. scholar, 1965-69, Regent's scholar for Medicine, 1969, NIH predoctoral fellow, 1971-75, Nat. Rsch. Svc. fellow, 1976-79, Nat. Spinal Cord Injury Found. rsch. fellow, 1979-80; recipient Rsch. Career Devel. award Nat. Inst. Neurol. Disease/NIH, Muscular Dystrophy Assn. Rsch. award, 1990—; Am. Heart Assn. grantee, 1987-89, 90—, fellowship, Fogarty Internat. Ctr. for Rsch. NIH, Japan, 1997. Mem.: AAAS, Am. Soc. Cell Biology, Biophys. Soc., Soc. Neuroscience, Sigma Xi. Achievements include research on NGF dynamics in hypertrophic disease, carbon dioxide transport and chemosensitivity, molecular mechanisms of quantal synaptic transmission, nerve growth factor synthesis by vascular smooth muscle, trophic regulation of motor neurons, neurodegenerative diseases. Office: U Va Med Sch PO Box 801392 Charlottesville VA 22908-1392 Office Phone: 434-924-5634. Business E-Mail: tuttle@virginia.edu.

**TUTTLE, JERRY OWEN,** retired military officer, information technology executive; b. Hatfield, Ind., Dec. 18, 1934; s. Charles Merritt and Wenonah Hathaway (Parker) T.; m. Barbara Ann Bonifay, Dec. 31, 1956; children: Michael Charles, Vicky Ann, Mark Jerreld, Stephen Scott, Monique Therese. Grad., Devry Tech. Inst., 1954; BS, Naval Postgrad. Sch., 1962; MA in Internat. Relations, George Washington U., 1969; postgrad., Naval War Coll., 1968-69. Enlisted U.S. Navy, 1955, commd. ensign, 1956, advanced through grades to vice adm., 1987; aide and flag lt. to comdr-in-chief Pacific Fleet, 1969-70; exec. officer Attack Squadron 174, 1970-71, Attack Squadron 81, comdg. officer, 1971-73; mem. staff comdr. U.S. Naval Air Forces, Atlantic Fleet, 1973-74; comdr. Attack Carrier Air Win 3, 1974-75; comdg. officer USS Kalamazoo, 1975-76, comnavairlant, 1976-77; comdg. officer USS John F. Kennedy, 1977-78, 78-79; spl. asst. to chief of naval ops. Def. Intelligence Agy., Washington, 1979; dir. for plans and policy div., 1979-81; comdr. Carrier Group 8, Norfolk, Va., 1981-83, Carrier Group 2/Battle Force 6th Fleet, Naples, Italy, 1983-84; naval insp. gen. Washington, 1984-85; dep., chief of staff U.S. Atlantic Fleet/Chief of Staff, U.S. Atlantic Command, 1985-86; dir. for command, control, communication systems Office of Joint Chiefs of Staff, 1987-89, dir. space & electronic warfare, 1989-93; ret. USN, 1993; v.p. bus. devel. Oracle Corp., 1994-96; pres. ManTech Sys. Engring. Corp., 1996-2000, SAVANTAGE (formerly Reltek Sys. and Design, Inc.), 2000—02; pres., CEO J.O.T. Enterprises, LLC, 2002—. Decorated Def. Superior Svc. medal, Legion of Merit (4), Meritorious Svc. medal (2), D.F.C. (3), Air medal (23), Def. Disting. Svc. medal, Disting. Svc. medal; comdr. Nat. Order of Merit (France); recipient John Paul Jones awd for inspirational leadership Navy League, 1978; listed in Fed. Computer Week's 1991, 92 Federal 100 for his impact on govt. computer systems. Mem. AIAA (Control, Com. and Intelligence award for contbn. to overall effectiveness of C3I Systems 1991), AFCEA (contbn. award 1989, Jon Boyce award 1992), Assn. Naval Aviators (Gold Eagle). Office Phone: 703-385-7522. Office Fax: 703-385-7733. Business E-Mail: jt@sseusa.com. *Drive yourself to lead others; to think only of the best; to work only for the best and expect only the best; to be just as enthusiastic about the success of others as you are about your own.*

**TUTTLE, KENNETH LEWIS,** retired engineering educator, consultant, researcher; b. Toledo, Oreg., Apr. 4, 1944; s. Martin Lewis and Norma Corinne (Nichols) T.; m. Susanna Anna Maria Woodworth, June 24, 1967; children: Stephanie, Meghan, Lewis. BS, U.S. Naval Acad., 1967; MS, Oreg. State U., 1974, PhD, 1978. Registered profl. engr., Oreg. (environ. branch added in 1995). Commd. ensign USN, 1967, advanced through grades to lt., 1971, line officer Norfolk, Va., 1967-69, intelligence officer Tan An, Vietnam, 1970-71; grad. asst. Oreg. State U., Corvallis, 1972-76; rsch. engr. Weyerhaeuser Co., Tacoma, 1977-81; pvt. practice Federal Way, Wash., 1982-83;

assoc. prof. mech. engring. US Naval Acad., Annapolis, Md., 1983—2004, dir. marine propulsion labs., 1984—90, ret., 2004; rschr. and cons. solid fuel rsch. Tuttle Engring. Dir. Ocean and Marine Engring. Divsn., Am. Soc. for Engring. Edn., Washington, 1989-91; mem. com. on shipboard pollution control, Nat. Rsch. Coun., Washington, 1994-96; chmn. environ. panel Soc. Naval Arch. and Marine Engrs., Jersey City, 1993-2000; prin. cons. Solid Fuel Rsch., Annapolis, 1984—. Author: Combustion Mechanisms in Wood Fired Boilers, 1978, Review of Biomass Gasification in Progress in Biomass Conversion, 1984, Thermodynamics: A Computer-Based Approach, 2001, 2003; contbr. articles to profl. jours. Mem. Combustion Inst., George C. Marshall Inst. Achievements include development of a prototype for new high-compression ratio vane-in-rotor compressor; pulverized wood burner and fixed-bed wood gasifier; discovery of the effect of underfire air on emissions; patents in field. Home: 25609 Dog Creek Rd John Day OR 97845 also: 405 Widgeon Way Chester MD 21619 Office Phone: 410-490-9534. Personal E-mail: tklewis@my180.net. E-mail: KenTuttle@1967.usna.com.

**TUTTLE, MARCIA,** retired elementary school educator, music educator; b. Spirit Lake, Iowa, Dec. 30, 1945; d. Frank Ewing and Ann Parsons Tuttle; 1 child, Amy Beth Gould. BA in English, Elem. Edn., U. Iowa, 1969, MA in Reading Disabilities, 1975; BA in Piano Pedagogy summa cum laude, Mt. Mercy Coll., 1985. Cert. tchr. Iowa. Elem. tchr. Cedar Rapids (Iowa) Cmty. Schs., 1969—2001; piano tchr. Cedar Rapids, 1981—2001, Salmon Creek Piano Studio, Vancouver, Wash., 2002—. Composer, performer Iowa Composers Concerts, Cedar Rapids, 1983—85; adjudicator Pvt. Music Teachers Assn. Competition, Cedar Rapids, 1994—95, Kalina Piano Studio Competition, Cedar Rapids, 1996—2000. Composer: Tempus Suite, Sibelius Publication. Coord. Cedar Rapids Cmty. Sch. Dist. Music Contest, 1987—92; big sister Big Bros./Big Sisters Assn., Cedar Rapids, 1986—; vol. HOSTS Reading Readiness, Vancouver, Wash., 2002—; music dir., pianist Living Branch Luth. Ch., Woodland, Wash., 2002—. Named honoree, Belin-Blank Ctr. for Gifted Edn., U. Iowa, 1996, 1998; recipient Outstanding Music Grad. award, Mt. Mercy Coll., 1985, Hero award, Big Bros./Big Sisters, Cedar Rapids, 2000. Mem.: Music Tchrs. Nat. Assn., Wash. Music Tchrs. Assn., Clark County Music Tchrs. Assn. (2d v.p. 2003—), S.W. Wash. Watercolor Soc., Beethoven Club. Avocations: watercolor painting, music, travel. Home: 2202 NW 143d Cir Vancouver WA 98685

**TUTTLE, MARTHA BENEDICT,** artist; b. Cin., Feb. 4, 1916; d. Harris Miller and Florence Stevens (McCrea) Benedict; m. Richard Salway Tuttle, June 3, 1939; children: Richard, Jr., McCrea Benedict (dec.), Martha (dec.), Elisabeth Hall. Grad. high sch., Cin.; student, Art Acad. Cin., 1934-38. V.p. Barq Bottling Co., Inc., Cin., 1948-80. One-woman shows include KKAE Gallery, 1963, Univ. Club, 1967, Miller Gallery, 1971, St. Clements, N.Y., 1973, Livingston Lodge, 1974, Holly Hill Antiques, 1979, Peterson Gallery, 1983, Art Acad. Cin., 1984, Closson Gallery, 1986, Camargo Gallery, 1992; represented in permanent collection Cin. Art Mus. Tchr. Sunday sch. Grace Episcopal Ch. and Indian Hill Ch., Cin., 1953-75; shareholder Cin. Art Mus.; founder partnership to save the William and Phebe Betts House; donor with partnership to The Nat. Soc. Colonial Dames of Am. the William and Phebe Betts House for establishing a Rsch. Ctr. Mem. Soc. Colonial Dames Am. (bd. dirs. 1976-89), Camargo Club, Univ. Club. Republican.

**TUTTLE, MARV,** finance association executive; b. 1955; BA in journalism, Drake U. CEO Fin. Planning Assn., 2004—, assoc. exec. dir., pub., editor Jour. Fin. Planning. Mem.: Am. Soc. Assn. Exec. (ASAE) (cert. assn. exec. (CAE) 1996, Most Improved Mag./Jour. for Jour. Fin. Planning), Colo. Soc. Assn. Exec. (pres.).

**TUTTLE, RICHARD,** artist; b. Rahway, N.J., 1941; BA, Trinity Coll., 1963. One-man shows at Betty Parsons Gallery, N.Y.C., 1965, 67, 68, 70, 72, 74, 78, 82, Galerie Schmela, Dusseldorf, Fed. Republic Germany, 1968, 78, 84, 85, Nicholas Wilder Gallery, N.Y.C., 1969, Albright-Knox Gallery, Buffalo, 1970, Dallas Mus. Fine Arts, 1971, The Helman Gallery, St. Louis, 1971, Mus. Modern Art, N.Y.C., 1972, Galerie Rudolf Zwirner, Cologne, Fed. Republic Germany, 1972, Galerie Yvon Lambert, Paris, 1972, 74, 76, 78, 81, 84, 85, 87, The Clocktower Inst. for Art and Urban Resources, N.Y.C., 1973, Kunstraum Munchen, Munich, 1973, 77, Daniel Weinberg Gallery, San Francisco, 1973, 78, Los Angeles, 1984, Francoise Lambert, Milan, 1973, 78, Galerie Heiner Friedrich, Munich, 1973, 77, Galleria Toselli, Milan, 1974, 85, Galleria Marilena Bonomo, Bari, Italy, 1974, 79, 85, Annemarie Verna Galerie, Zurich, 1974, 79, 81, 84, 87, Barbra Cusack Gallery, Houston, 1974, 75, Nigel Greenwood Inc. Ltd., London, 1974, 77, 82, Wadsworth Atheneum, Hartford, Conn., 1975, Whitney Mus. Am. Art, N.Y.C., 1975, Parsons-Truman Gallery, N.Y.C., 1975, Brooke Alexander Inc., N.Y.C., 1976, Fine Arts Bldg. Gallery, N.Y.C., 1976, Graeme Murray Gallery, Edinburgh, 1976, McIntosh Gallery U. Western Ont., London, Can., 1976, Galleria Ugo Ferranti, Rome, 1977, 78, 79, 81, 82, 83, 84, Kunsthalle Basel, 1977, Young Hoffman Gallery, Chgo., 1978, Bell Gallery Brown U., Providence, 1978, Mus. van Hedendaagse Kunst, Gent, Belgium, 1978, Stedelijk Mus., Amsterdam, 1979, Truman Gallery, N.Y.C., 1979, Centre d'Arts Plastiques Contemporains de Bordeaux, 1979, Centre d'Art Contemporain, Geneva, 1980, Ga. State U. Art Gallery, Atlanta, 1980, Baxter Art Gallery Calif. Inst. Tech., Pasadena, 1980, Baronian-Lambert, Gent, 1981, Mus. de Calais, 1982, Taidemaalariliiton Galleria 4, Helsinki, 1983, Blum Helman Gallery, N.Y.C., 1983, 84, 86, Galerie Hubert Winter, Vienna, 1983, 87, Studio La Citta, Verona, 1984, Galleriet, Lund, Sweden, 1984, Portland (Oreg.) Ctr. for Visual Arts, 1984, Stadtisches Mus. Abteiberg, 1985, Inst. Contemporary Arts, London, 1985, Victoria Miro Gallery, London, 1986, Reinhard Onnasch Galerie, Berlin, 1986, CAPC Mus. d'Art Contemporain, Bordeaux, 1986, Neue Galerie Am Landesmuseum Joanneum, Graz, Austria, 1987, Galerie des Arènes, Nîmes, France, 1987, Andere Tornberg Gallery, Lund, 1987, various others; exhibited in group shows at San Francisco Mus. Art, 1965, 73, Byron Gallery, N.Y.C., 1965, Ralph Wilson Gallery Lehigh U., Bethlehem, Pa., 1965, 66, Penthouse Gallery Mus. Modern Art, N.Y.C., 1966, 70, 74, 76, 80, Bykert Gallery, N.Y.C., 1968, 71, Austin Art Ctr. Trinity Coll., Hartford, 1968, 70, Pitts. Plan for Art, 1968, 80, Brainerd Art Gallery SUNY at Potsdam, 1968, 82, Corcoran Gallery Art, Washington, 1969, Whitney Mus. Am. Art, N.Y.C. and Fairfield, Conn., 1969, 73, 77, 78, 81, 83, 84, 85, Detroit Inst. Arts, 1969, 76, 79, Paula Cooper Gallery, N.Y.C., 1971, U. N.C., Greensboro, 1969, 75, Galerie Schmela, Dusseldorf, 1972, 82, 85, Galerie Yvon Lambert, 1970, 72, Yale U. Art Gallery, New Haven, 1973, 75, 82, Art Inst. Chgo., 1975, 82, Stedelijk Mus., Amsterdam, 1978, 82, 84, Brooke Alexander Inc., N.Y.C., 1974, 78, 80, 85, Betty Parsons Gallery, N.Y.C., 1979, 83, Centre Nat. d'Art et de Culture Georges Pompidou, Paris, 1981, Daniel Weinberg Gallery, Los Angeles, 1983, N.Y.C., 1984, Kent Gallery, N.Y.C., 1987, Blum Helman Gallery, 1982, 84, 86, 87, Kunsthalle, Bielefeld, 1987, Galerie Harald Behm, Hamburg, Fed. Republic Germany, 1987, Holly Solomon Gallery, N.Y.C., 1987, Damon Brandt Gallery, N.Y.C., 1986, 87, Galería Juana de Aizpuru, Madrid, Spain, 1986, 87, Genovese Graphics, Boston, 1987, Madison Art Ctr., 1987, numerous others; represented in permanent collections Fogg Art Mus., Cambridge, Mass., Kaiser Wilhelm Mus., Kreefeld, Fed. Republic Germany, Kunsthaus, Zurich, La. Mus. Modern Art, Humleback, Denmark, Ludwig Mus., Cologne, Fed. Republic Germany, Met. Mus. Art, N.Y.C., Mus. Nat. d'Arte Moderne, Paris, Staatliche Kunstsammlungen, Kassel, Fed. Republic Germany, Stedelijk Mus., Whitney Mus. Am. Art; subject of retrospective tour The Art of Richard Tuttle, San Francisco Mus. Modern Art, Whitney Mus., etc. Mailing: c/o Sperone Westwater 415 W 13th St #2 New York NY 10014-1104*

**TUTTLE, ROBERT HOLMES,** ambassador, former federal official; b. Calif., 1944; m. Maria Hummer; children: Tiffany, Alexandra. BA, Stanford U., 1965; MBA, U. So. Calif., 1968. Asst. to U.S. Pres. Office of Presdl. Personnel, Washington, 1982-85, dir., 1985—89; bd. dir. Woodrow Wilson Internat. Ctr. Scholars, Washington, 1989—; former mng. ptnr. Tuttle-Click Automotive Group, Irvine, Calif.; US amb. to UK US Dept. State, London, 2005—. Mem. bd. Ronald Reagan Pres. Lib., USC Sch. Comm., LA Mus. Contemporary Art, chmn. bd., 2001—04. Co-chmn. Calif. Rep. Presdl. Campaign, 1980. Office: American Embassy London England UK PSC 801 Box 3 FPO AE 09498-4040*

**TUTTLE, TIMOTHY JOSEPH,** secondary school educator; b. San Juan, PR, Oct. 26, 1948; s. John William and Kathline Mary Tuttle; m. Michele Louise Harthcock, Sept. 20, 1969; children: Stephanie Louise Tuttle-Kamon, Amy Nicole. BA in History, U. LaVerne, Calif., 1977; MEd, Calif. State Poly. U., Pomona, 1982; constl. scholar, UCLA, 1990. Ryan Life Tchg. Credential in history Calif., Ryan Life Tchg. Credential in social studies Calif. Tchr. social studies Pomona Cath. Girls HS, 1977—84; adult evening instr. psychiat. facilities Pomona Unified Sch. Dist., 1980—89; tchr. social studies Corona Norco (Calif.) Unified Sch. Dist., 1984—, home and sch. instr. for traumatically brain injured student, 1998—2000; tchr. h.s. traumatic brain injury program Casa Colina Hosp. for Rehab. Medicine, Pomona, 1985—87; instr. continuing edn. U. LaVerne, 1993. Guest lectr. U. of Calif., Riverside, 1990—90; presenter in field. Pre-marriage counselor Sacred Heart Cath. Ch., Alta Loma, Calif., 1990—99. Recipient Golden Bell award, Calif. Sch. Bd. Assn., 1986, A+ award for excellence in edn., NEA, 1988, Found. in Excellence in Edn. award, 2002, Program of Excellence award, Calif. Coun. Social Studies, 1988, Unsung Hero in Edn. award, No. Life Ins., 1998; grantee, Calif. State Dept. of Edn., 1988, grantee and awardee, Constl. Rights Found. Mem.: Nat. Coun. Social Studies (Nat. Tchr. of Yr. 2001), Corona Norco Tchr. Assn., Calif. Tchr. Assn. Office: Corona Norco Unified Sch Dist 2820 Clark Ave Norco CA 92860-1903 Office Phone: 951-739-5600. Office Fax: 951-739-5639. E-mail: ttuttle@cnusd.k12.ca.us.

**TUTTLE, WILLIAM MCCULLOUGH, JR.,** history professor; b. Detroit, Oct. 7, 1937; s. William McCullough and Geneva (Duvall) T.; m. Linda Lee Stumpp, Dec. 12, 1959 (div.); children: William McCullough III, Catharine T., Andrew S.; m. Kathryn Nemeth, May 6, 1995. BA, Denison U., 1959; MA, U. Wis., 1964, PhD, 1967. From mem. faculty to prof. history U. Kans., Lawrence, 1967—2000, prof. Am. studies, 2000—. Vis. scholar Radcliffe Coll., 1993—94; Charles Warren fellow Harvard U., Cambridge, Mass., 1972—73; sr. fellow Johns Hopkins U., 1969—70; vis. prof. U. S.C., Columbia, 1980; fellow Humanities Ctr. Stanford U., 1983—84; rsch. assoc. U. Calif., Berkeley, Calif., 1986—88. Author: Race Riot: Chicago in the Red Summer of 1919, 1970, 2d edit., 1996, W.E.B. Du Bois, 1973, (with David M. Katzman) Plain Folk, 1982, (with others) A People and A Nation, 1982, 7th edit., 2005, Daddy's Gone to War: The Second World War in the Lives of America's Children, 1993; contbr. chpts. to books, articles to profl. jours. Dem. precinct committeeman, Lawrence, 1980-90. Lt. USAF, 1959-62. Recipient Merit award Am. Assn. for State and Local History, 1972, Balfour S. Jeffrey Rsch. Achievement award Humanities and Social Scis., 2004, Chancellors Club Career Tchg. award, 2004; Younger Humanist fellow NEH, 1972-73, Guggenheim fellow, 1975-76, NEH fellow, 1983-84, rsch. fellow Hall Ctr., 1990, Kemper fellow for tchg. excellence, 1998; Evans grantee, 1975-76, Beveridge grantee, 1982; NEH grantee, 1986-89. Mem. Soc. Am. Historians (elected), Am. Hist. Assn., Orgn. Am. Historians, Am. Studies Assn., Assn. for Study of African Am. Life and History, Lawrence Trout Club, Golden Key (hon.), Omicron Delta Kappa, Phi Beta Delta, Phi Gamma Delta. Home: 713 Louisiana St Lawrence KS 66044-2339 Office: U Kans Dept Am Studies Lawrence KS 66045-0001 Office Phone: 785-864-9476. Business E-Mail: tuttle@ku.edu.

**TUTU, DESMOND MPILO,** retired archbishop; b. Klerksdorp, Republic of South Africa, Oct. 7, 1931; m. Leah Nomalizo Shenxane; children: Trevor Thamsanqa, Theresa Thandeka, Naomi Nontombi, Mpho Andrea. Diploma in teaching, Pretoria Bantu Normal Coll., South Africa, 1953; BA, U. South Africa, 1954; licentiate in theology, St. Peter's Theol. Coll., South Africa, 1960; postgrad, King's Coll., U. London; DD (hon.), Gen. Theol. Sem., NY, 1978, Aberdeen U., Scotland, 1984, Trinity Luth. Sem., 1985, Trinity Coll., Hartford, Conn., 1986, Chgo. Theol. Sem., 1986, U. West Indies, Trinidad and Tobago, 1986, Oberlin Coll., 1986, U. South, 1988, Emory U., 1988, Wesleyan U., 1990, Lincoln U., Pa., 1990, Oxford U., Eng., 1990; DCL (hon.), Kent U., Eng., 1978; LLD (hon.), Harvard U., 1979, Claremont Grad. Sch., 1984, Temple U., 1985, 86, Mt. Allison U., Can., 1988, Northeastern U., 1988; ThD (hon.), Ruhr U., 1981; STD (hon.), Columbia U., 1982, Dickinson Coll., 1984; LHD (hon.), St. Paul's Coll., 1984, Howard U., 1984, Morehouse Coll., 1986, Cen. U., 1986, CUNY, 1986; HHD (hon.), Wilberforce U., 1985; PhD (hon.), U. Rio, Rio de Janeiro, 1986; doctorate (hon.), U. Strasbourg, France, 1988, Wesleyan U., 1990, Lincoln U., 1990, U. Mo., 1990, U. New Rochelle, 1990, 1990, Brown U., 1990, Seton Hall U., 1990, U. PR, 1990. Ordained priest Anglican Ch., 1961. Schoolmaster, 1954-57; parish priest, 1960—; lectr. Fed. Theol. Sem., 1967-69, UBLS Roma, Lesotho, 1970-72; assoc. dir. theol. edn. fund World Coun. Chs., Bromley, Kent, England, 1972-75; dean of Johannesburg South Africa, 1975-76; bishop of Lesotho, 1976-78; bishop of Johannesburg, 1985-86; archbishop of Cape Town South Africa, 1986-96; archbishop emeritus City of Capetown, 1996—; chairperson Truth and Reconciliation Commn., 1996—; vis. prof. The Episcopal Div. Sch., Cambridge, 2002. Sec.-gen. South African Council Chs., 1978-85; vis. prof. Anglican Studies, N.Y. Gen. Theol. Sem., 1984; pres. All Africa Conf. of Chs., 1987-97; chancellor U. Western Cape, Republic of South Africa, 1988—. Author: (collections of sermons and addresses) Crying in the Wilderness, 1982, Hope and Suffering, 1983, The Rainbow People of God: The Making of a Peaceful Revolution, 1994, An African Prayer Book, 1995, No Future Without Forgiveness, 1999, God has a Dream, 2004. Vice chmn. Internat. Alert, 1986; mem. disbursements adv. com. Fund for Edn. in South Africa, N.Y.C., 1988; mem. com. of honor for meml. to Imre Nagy and companions Hungarian Human Rights League, 1988; mem. hon. com. Spl. Fund for Health in Africa, 1990. Recipient Prix d'Athene Onassis Found., 1980, Family of Man gold medallion, 1983, Martin Luther King Jr. Humanitarian award Ann. Black Am. Hero and Heroines Day, 1984; Nobel prize for peace, 1984, Martin Luther King Jr. Peace award, 1986, Internat. Integrity award John-Roger Found., 1986, Pres. award Glassboro State Coll., 1986, World Pub. Forum award City of San Rafael, Calif., 1986, Order of So. Cross Govt. of Brazil, 1987, Order of Merit Govt. of Brazil, 1987, Pacem in Terris award Quad Cities, 1987, Albert Schweitzer Humanitarian award Emmanuel Coll., 1988, Freedom of the City Florence, Italy, 1985, Methyr Tydfil, U.K., 1986, Durham, Eng., 1987, Hull, Eng., 1988, Disting. Peace Leadership award Nuclear Age Peace Found., 1990, Pres.'s medal Claremont Grad. Sch., U.S., 1990, Freedom of the Borough of Lewisham, U.K., 1990, Freedom of the City of Kinshasa, 1990, Grand Officier de la Légion d'Honneur, Pres. Chirac of France, 1998, Lifetime Achievement award CARE USA, 1999, Vision 2000 award Cath. Charities USA, 1999, award Ho. of Commons, Can., 1999, The Wilberforce medallion Lord Mayor and City Coun. Kingston upon Hull, 1999, Pres. meda. Georgetown U., Washington, 2001, Humanitarian award N.Y.C. Office Comptr., 2002; co-recipient Third World prize, 1989; King's Coll. fellow, 1978. Mem. NAACP (life), World Council Global Co-operation. Anglican. Office: PO Box 1092 Milnerton 7435 Cape Town South Africa

**TUTUC, EMANUEL,** research scientist; b. Slatina, Romania, Oct. 14, 1974; s. Dumitru and Stela Tutuc; m. Livia Roxana Dogaru, Nov. 1, 2000; 1 child, Andrew Daniel. PhD, Princeton (N.J.) U., 2004. Postdoctoral rsch. assoc. Princeton U., 2004; rsch. scientist IBM T.J. Watson Rsch. Ctr., Yorktown Heights, NY, 2004—. Contbr. articles to sci. jours. Recipient Charlotte E. Procter fellowship, Princeton U., 2003, Bronze medal, 24th Internat. Physics Olympiad, 1993. Mem. Am. Phys. Soc. Office: IBM TJ Watson Rsch Ctr 1101 Kitchawan Rd Rte 134 Yorktown Heights NY 10598 Office Phone: 914-945-1909. Office Fax: 914-945-2141. E-mail: etutuc@us.ibm.com.

**TUUL, JOHANNES,** physics professor, researcher; b. Tarvastu, Viljandi, Estonia, May 23, 1922; came to U.S., 1956, naturalized, 1962; s. Johan and Emilie (Tulf) T.; m. Marjatta Murtoniemi, July 14, 1957 (div. Aug. 1971); children: Melinda, Melissa; m. Sonia Esmeralda Manosalva, Sept. 15, 1976; 1 child, Johannes. Elem. Tchg. Credential, Tartu Normal Sch., Estonia, 1941; diploma in Elec. Engring., Stockholm Tech. Inst., 1947; BS, U. Stockholm, 1955, MA, 1956; ScM, Brown U., 1957, PhD, 1960. Tchr. Valuste Elem. Sch., 1941-43; escaped to Finland December, 1943; after Finland surrendered to Russia escaped to Sweden, 1944; instr. Stockholm Tech. Inst., 1947-49; lab. engr. Electrical Prospecting Co., Stockholm, 1949-53; elec. engr. LM Ericsson Telephone Co., Stockholm, 1954-55; rsch. physicist Am. Cyanamid Co., Stamford, Conn., 1960-62; sr. rsch. physicist Bell & Howell Rsch. Ctr.,

Pasadena, Calif., 1962-65; from asst. to assoc. prof. Calif. State Poly. U., Pomona, 1965-68, chmn. physics and earth scis. dept., 1971-75, prof. physics 1975-91; prof. emeritus, 1992—. Vis. prof. Pahlavi U., Shiraz, Iran, 1968-70; cons. Bell & Howell Rsch. Ctr., Pasadena, Calif., 1965, Teledyne Co., Pasadena, Calif., 1968; guest researcher Naval Weapons Ctr., China Lake, Calif., 1967, 72; resident dir. Calif. State U. Internat. Programs in Sweden and Denmark, 1977-78. Author: Physics Made Easy, 1974; contbr. articles to profl. jours. Pres. Group Against Smoking Pollution, Pomona Valley, Calif., 1976; foster parent Foster Parents Plan, Inc., Warwick, R.I., 1964-2003; block capt. Neighborhood Watch, West Covina, Calif., 1982-84; citizen amb. People to People Internat., 1990—; mem. Physics Edn. Del. to Peoples Rep. China, 1990; mem. Baltic Assist Delegation, 1992; mem. Industry and Sci. Initiative 1 Delegation to Cuba, 2000; mem. Mission in Understanding to Iceland and Greenland, 2002; mem. Global Peace Initiative to Egypt, 2003. Fellow Brown U., 1957-58; rsch. grantee U. Namur (Belgium), 1978, Ctr. Nat. Recherche Scientifique, France, 1979; recipient Humanitarian Fellowship award Save the Children Fedn., 1968, spl. award Travelers' Century Club, 1998. Mem. AAAS (life), N.Y. Acad. Scis., Am. Phys. Soc. Republican. Roman Catholic. Achievements include research in energy conservation and new energy technologies. Personal E-mail: tuuljohannes@hotmail.com.

**TUZLA, KEMAL,** mechanical engineer, researcher; b. Adapazari, Sakarya, Turkey, Feb. 23, 1943; came to U.S., 1974; s. Hayrettin and Muberra (Horozlu) T.; m. Asuman Fatma Cokmez. MME, Istanbul (Turkey) Tech. U., 1966, PhD in Mech. Engring., 1972. Instr. Istanbul Tech. U., 1966-72, asst. prof., 1974, assoc. prof., 1978-81; instr. Air Force Coll., Istanbul, 1973-74; rsch. asst. prof. U. Wash., Seattle, 1974-78; sr. rsch. scientist Lehigh U., Bethlehem, Pa., 1981—2002, assoc. chair, chem. engring., 2003. Mem. organizing com. 2d Thermal Sci. Conf., Istanbul, 1979, 3d Conf., Trabzon, Turkey, 1981; cons. Goodyear Tire & Rubber Co., Akron, Ohio, 1984-86, Exxon Nuclear, Richland, Wash., 1985-88. Editor Proc. 2d Thermal Sci. Conf., 1979; contbr. articles in area of thermal scis. to profl. jours. Co-founder Turkish Am. Cultural Assn., Seattle, 1977. Grantee rsch. grantee, Los Alamos (N.Mex.) Nat. Lab., 1989—91, Ben Franklin Tech. Ctr., Bethlehem, 1989—2001, Gas Rsch. Inst., 1987—91, Elec. Power Rsch. Inst., 1991—94; Goodyear Tire & Rubber Co., 1985—86. Mem. ASHRAE, AIChE, Sigma Xi. Achievements include research in heat transfer in two-phase flows, boiling, fluidized beds, electronic components and nuclear safety. Office: Lehigh U Chem Engring Iacocca Hall 111 Research Dr Bethlehem PA 18015-4732 Home: 968 N 33rd St Allentown PA 18104-3404

**TÜZÜN, ERDEM,** neurologist, consultant; b. Istanbul, Marmara, Turkey, Nov. 11, 1971; s. Neriman and Muhsin Burhanettin T. MD, Istanbul Med. Faculty, 1995. Specialist in neurology; med. diplomate. Intern U. Istanbul, 1994-95, resident in neurology, 1995-2000, specialist in neurology, 2000—01; postdoctoral fellow U. Tex. Med. Br., Galveston, Tex., 2002—05; sr. rsch. investigator U. Pa., Phila., 2006—. Sec. Archives of Neuropsychiatry, 1998—2000. Commando Mil. doctor Commando Mil. Hosp., 2000. Recipient 1st degree award, project prize Brain Rsch. Orgn., 1999. Mem. European Neurol. Soc. Achievements include research in measurements of intracavernosal endothelin levels of impotent men, providing evidence for use nitric oxide (antagonist of endothelin) agonist drugs in male erectile dysfunction; detection of ganglioside levels of salivary glands; treatment of congenital penile deformity by a new surgical method; demonstration of the presence of antibodies against voltage-gated potassium channels in patients with limbic encephalitis; identification of the autoimmune etiology of neuromyotonia and demonstration of the role of autoantibodies against thalamic structures as a casual factor for Morvan's syndrome; identification of cytokines and complements as important contributors of pathogenesis in myasthenia gravis. Home: 2529 Webster St Philadelphia PA 19146 Office: Hosp Univ Pa Neuro-Oncology 3 West Gates 3400 Spruce St Philadelphia PA 19104 Office Phone: 215-746-2824. E-mail: drerdem@yahoo.com.

**TVERDOVSKY, OLEG,** professional hockey player; b. Donetsk, Ukraine, May 18, 1976; Defenseman Anaheim Mighty Ducks, 1994—95, 1999—2002, Winnipeg Jets, 1995—96, Phoenix Coyotes, 1996—99, NJ Devils, 2002—03, Avangard Omsk, Russia, 2003—05, Carolina Hurricanes, 2005—. Named to All-Star team, 1997. Achievements include being a member of Stanley Cup Champion NJ Devils, 2003, Carolina Hurricanes, 2006. Office: Carolina Hurricanes RBC Ctr 1400 Edwards Mill Rd Raleigh NC 27607-3624*

**TVILDIANI, DIMITRY,** cardiologist; b. Tbilisi, Georgia, June 30, 1956; s. David Tvildiani and Juliana Zubiashvili; m. Khatuna Chkheidze; children: Tamar, Gegi, Michael. MD, State Med. U., Tbilisi, 1978; PhD, State Inst. Transplantology, Moscow, 1980. Chief scientist diagnostic dept. State Inst. Cardiology, Tbilisi, 1980—89; dean AIETI Med. Sch., Tbilisi, 1989—99; gen. mgr. Dimas Radiology, N.Y.C., 1999. Achievements include patents for noninvasive index of cardiac contractility; noninvasive method of renal blood flow assesmnet. Office: Image Pro LLC 101-18 Queens Blvd Forest Hills NY 11375 Personal E-mail: tvildianid@aol.com.

**TWAGILIMANA, AIMABLE,** language educator, writer; b. Muyira, Butare, Rwanda, Dec. 4, 1961; arrived in U.S., 1992; s. Louis Mudugu and Belancila Nyiragakinga; m. Marie-Rose Nkundimfura, Dec. 26, 1987; children: Leandre Munyana, Raissa Umwari. BA in English, Nat. U. of Rwanda, Butare, 1984, MA in English, 1986; MA in Applied Linguistics, U. of Reading, Berkshire, Eng., 1989; PhD in English, SUNY, Buffalo, 1995. Cert. tchr. h.s. Nat. U. of Rwanda. Lectr. Nat. U. of Rwanda, Ruhengeri, 1986—92; asst. prof. SUNY, Buffalo, 1995—2000, assoc. prof. English, 2000—04, prof., 2004—. Dir. of studies faculty of letters Nat. U. of Rwanda, Ruhengeri, 1991—92. Author: (novel) Manifold Annihilation, 1996, (book) Race and Gender in the Making of an African American Literary Tradition, 1997, In Their Own Voices: Rwandan Refugees Speak Out, 1997, Hutu and Tutsi (The Heritage Library of African People series), 1998, The Debris of Ham: Ethnicity, Regionalism and the 1994 Rwandan Genocide, 2003. Fellow, NEH, 1999, 2003; scholar, Fulbright Found., 1992—95, Brit. Coun., 1988—89. Mem.: MLA, Assn. of Am. Transls., Nat. Coun. of Tchrs. of English, Nat. Assn. of Lit. Critics. Roman Catholic. Home: 68 Fairchild Pl Buffalo NY 14216 Office: SUNY 1300 Elmwood Avenue Buffalo NY 14222 Office Phone: 716-878-5407. Personal E-mail: twagila12@hotmail.com. E-mail: twagila@bscmail.buffalostate.edu.

**TWAIN, SHANIA (EILEEN REGINA EDWARDS),** musician; b. Windsor, Ontario, Can., Aug. 28, 1965; d. Sharon and Jerry Twain (Stepfather), Clarence Edwards; m. Robert John Lange, Dec. 28, 1993; 1 child, Eja. Recs. Beginnings, 1989—90, 1999, Shania Twain, 1993, The Woman in Me, 1995 (Acad. Country Music Assn. Award for Album of Yr., 1995, ABC Radio Networks Country Music Award for Female Video Artist of Yr., 1995, Billboard Music Award for Country Album of Yr., 1996, Grammy award for Best Country Album, 1996), These Blues are Mine, 1996, Come on Over, 1997, Star Profile, 1999, Maximum Shania, 2000, Complete Limelight Sessions, 2001, Up!, 2002 (Can. Country Music Assn. Award for Album of Yr., 2003, Billboard Music Award for Country Album of Yr., 2003), Greatest Hits, 2004. Recipient Country Music TV (Europe) Rising Star award, 1993, Am. Music Award for Favorite New Country Artist, 1995, Can. Country Music Assn. Award for female vocalist of yr., 1995, Acad. of Country Music Award for Top New Female Vocalist, 1995, Best Country Album Grammy award, 1995, Blockbuster Entertainment Award for Favorite New Country Artist, 1996, Country Music TV (Europe) award for Female Artist of Yr., 1996, Juno Award for Country Female Vocalist of Yr., 1996, Juno Award for Entertainer of Yr., 1996, World Music Award for World's Best Selling Country Artist, 1996, Favorite New Artist award, Am. Music Awards, 1996, Am. Music Award for Best Female Country Artist, 1997, Juno Award for Country Female Vocalist of Yr., 1997, Juno Award for Internat. Achievement, 1997, Am. Music Award for Favorite Female Country Artist, 1998, Billboard Music Award for Female Artist of Yr., 1998, Country Music Assn. Award for Entertainer of Yr., 1999, 1999, Acad. Country Music Award for Entertainer of Yr., 1999, Am. Music Award for Favorite Female Country Artist, 1999, Am. Music Award for Favorite Female Pop/Rock Artist, 1999, Blockbuster Entertainment Award for Favorite Overall Single, 1999, Juno Award for

Country Female Vocalist of Yr., 1999, Grammy Award for Best Female Country Vocal Performance (You're Still The One), 1999, Grammy Award for Best Country Song (You're Still The One), 1999, Juno Award for Best Songwriter, 2000, Juno Award for Best Country Female Artist, 2000, Grammy Award for Best Female Vocal Country Performance (Man!I Feel Like A Woman), 2000, Grammy Award for Best Country Song (Come On Over), 2000, Acad. Country Music Award for Entertainer of Yr., 2000, Billboard Music Award for Top County Artist of Yr., 2003, Billboard Music Award for Country Album Artist of Yr., 2003, Juno Fan Choice Award, 2003, Juno Award for Artist of Yr., 2003, Juno Award for Country Rec. Yr. (I'm Gonna Getcha Good), 2003, Can. Country Music Assn. Award for Video of Yr. (I'm Gonna Getcha Good), 2003, Can. Country Music Assn. Award for Female Artist of Yr., 2003, Order of Canada, 2005. Office: Mercury Records 66 Music Sq W Nashville TN 37203-4315 Address: Shore Fire Media c/o Georgette Pascale 32 Court St Fl 16 Brooklyn NY 11201-4404 Office: c/o Q Prime 131 S 11th St Nashville TN 37206

**TWARDY, STANLEY ALBERT, JR.**, lawyer; b. Trenton, NJ, Sept. 13, 1951; s. Stanley Albert Twardy and Dorothy M. Stonaker. BS with honors, Trinity Coll., 1973; JD, U. Va., 1976; LLM, Georgetown U., 1980. Bar: Conn. 1976, D.C. 1978, U.S. Supreme Ct. 1979, U.S. Ct. Appeals (2d cir.) 1984. Assoc. Whitman & Ransom, Greenwich, Conn., 1976-77; counsel com. on small bus. U.S. Senate, 1977-79, counsel to Senator Lowell Weicker Jr., 1979-80; ptnr. Silver, Golub & Sandak, Stamford, Conn., 1980-85; U.S. atty. Dist. of Conn., 1985-91; chief of staff Office of Gov. Lowell Weicker, Conn., 1991-93; ptnr. Day, Berry & Howard LLP, Stamford, Conn., 1993—. Mem. nat. alumni exec. com. Trinity Coll., 1985—90, mem. athletic adv. com., 1992—97, bd. dirs., 1996—2002; chmn. City of Stamford Police Chief Selection Panel, 1993—94; mem. area adv. com. U. Conn. Stamford, 1993—96; mem. strategic planning mgmt. com. U. Conn., 1993—95; bd. dirs. Drugs Don't Work!, 1989—93, 1994—2000, chmn. program com. 1989—91; bd. dirs. Rehab. Ctr., 1995—2002, Stamford Health Found., 1995—, NCCJ Fairfield County Region, 1996—2004. Mem.: ABA, Conn. Bar Assn., Phi Beta Kappa. Office Phone: 203-977-7300. E-mail: satwardy@dbh.com.

**TWEARDY, DAVID JOHN**, physician, educator; b. Monessen, Pa., Feb. 12, 1952; s. John Tweardy Sr. and Helen Kotch Tweardy; m. Ruth Falik, Jan. 21, 1982; children: Samuel David, Benjamin John, Daniel James. AB in Chemistry, Princeton U., 1974; MD, Harvard U., 1978. Diplomate Am. Bd. Internal Medicine, 1983, Am. Bd. Infectious Diseases, 1984. Asst. prof. medicine U. Pitts. Sch. Medicine, 1987—93, assoc. prof. medicine, 1993—99; prof. medicine Baylor Coll. Medicine, Houston, 1999—, chief sect. infectious diseases, 1999—. Grantee, NIH, 1997—2005, 2002—, 2004—. Mem.: Am. Clin. and Climatological Assn., Assn. Am. Physicians. Home: 3769 Nottingham St Houston TX 77005 Office Phone: 713-798-8918. E-mail: dtweardy@bcm.edu.

**TWEDELL, TERRI DANNI**, writer, educator, artist; b. Modesto, Calif., Oct. 28, 1955; d. Nyle Arnon Reed and Dolores Mae Thornton; children: Errol, Michael, Jacob; m. Dean Michael Shalhoup, May 25, 2002. BS in Elem. Edn., SUNY, New Paltz, 1986, MS in Spl. Edn., 1989, postgrad., 1990-91. Cert. spl. edr., N.H.; pupil personnel. Tchr. spl. edn. Sullivan Diagnostic Treatment Ctr., Harris, N.Y., 1986-89; dir. Head Start, Kingston, N.Y., 1989-91, edn. coord. Manchester, N.H., 1994-95; presch. spl. edn. cons. Nashua (N.H.) Sch. Dist., 1995-98; freelance artist, writer Nashua, 1998—; prin., owner Tara's Edn. & Art for the Soul, Nashua, NH, 2000—; dir., spl. edn. tchr. Happenings Art Program, Nashua, NH, 2005—06. Cons., spkr, mem. N.H. Dept. Edn. Interagy. Forum, Concord, N.H., 1994-98; mem. ADaPT, Concord, 1995-98; adj. faculty spl. edn. subjects Notre Dame Coll., Manchester, N.H., 1994-95. Contbg. author: Women Living with MS, 1998; featured artist Nashua Telegraph, 1999, Hunt Bldg. Gallery, Nashua, N.H., 2006; represented in exhbn. Nashua Art Walk, 2005-06. Mem. N.H. Dept. Edn. Homeless Commn., 1995-96, Area Agy-Interagy. Commn., 1995-98. Preschool Improvement grant N.H. Dept. Edn., 1995, 96, 97, Summer Inst. grant, 1996, 97. Mem.: Soc. Children's Book Writers and Illustrators, New Hampshire's Own, Nashua Area Artists Assn. Avocations: rock collecting, gemology, Native Am. arts and crafts, archaeology, ancient history. Home: 14 Skyline Dr Nashua NH 03062-3516 Office: 14 Skyline Dr Nashua NH 03062-3516 Office Phone: 603-595-0958. E-mail: TerrDT2@aol.com.

**TWEEN, DOUGLAS M.**, lawyer, former prosecutor; b. 1962; BA, Columbia Univ., 1984; JD cum laude, Northwestern Univ., 1989. Bar: NY, Conn. Law clk. Judge William Timbers, US Ct. Appeals 2d Cir.; trial atty. Antitrust Div., U.S. Dept. Justice, 1990—2005; ptnr., Global Antitrust & Global Litigation practices Baker & McKenzie LLP, NYC, 2005—. Moderator Prog. on Cartel Enforcement So. African Competition Com., 2004. Recipient Antitrust Div. Award of Distinction, U.S. Dept. Justice, 2000, Attorney Gen. Disting. Svc. award, 2003. Mem.: Bar of City of N.Y., NY State Bar Assn., ABA. Office: Baker & McKenzie LLP 1114 Ave of the Americas New York NY 10036 Office Fax: 212-310-1655. Business E-Mail: douglas.tween@bakenet.com.

**TWENGE, JEAN M.**, psychology professor, writer; b. Winona, Minn., Aug. 24, 1971; BA, U. Chgo., 1993, 93, MA, 1992—93; Ph.D., U. Mich., Ann Arbor, 1993—98. Asst. prof. San Diego State U., 2001—05, assoc. prof., 2005—. Author: (nonfiction book) Generation Me: Why Today's Young Americans Are More Confident, Assertive, Entitled and More Miserable Than Ever Before. Office: San Diego State Univ 5500 Campanile Dr San Diego CA 92182-4611

**TWICHELL, CHASE**, poet; b. New Haven, Conn., Aug. 20, 1950; d. Charles P. and Ann (Chase) T. BA, Trinity Coll., Hartford, 1973; MFA, U. Iowa, 1976. Asst. editor Pennyroyal Pr., W. Hatfield, Mass., 1976-84; assoc. prof. English U. Ala., 1984-88; mem. MFA Program in Creative Writing, Warren Wilson Coll., 1999—; editor Ausable Press, 1999—. Asst. prof. Hampshire Coll., 1983-84; co-editor Alabama Poetry Series, 1984-88; lectr. Princeton U., 1990-98; faculty MFA program in creative writing Goddard Coll., 1997-99. Author: (poetry) Northern Spy, 1981, The Odds, 1986, Perdido, 1991, The Ghost of Eden, 1995, (book) Dog Language, 2005; editor: The Practice of Poetry, 1992, The Snow Watcher, 1998, Ausable Press, 1999—; translator The Lover of God, 2003. Recipient Acad. award in lit. Am. Acad. Arts and Letters, 1994; Nat. Endowment for Arts fellow, 1987, 93, Guggenheim fellow, 1990.

**TWIGGS, DENNIS GLENN**, psychologist, writer; b. Marion, N.C., Feb. 5, 1946; s. James Glenn and Velra Ledford Twiggs; m. Tamara Jean Hatley, July 13, 1969; 1 child, Jason Scott. BS, Appalachian State U., 1965—69, Masters, 1972—73; PhD, Tulane U., 1973—77. Lic. psychologist NC, 1979, Tex., 1978. Counselor US Army Green Beret, Fort Bragg, NC, 1972; therapist Mt. Vernon Clinic, Wilmington, NC, 1972; tchg. asst. Tulane U., New Orleans, 1974—77; staff psychologist Mexia State Sch., Mexia, Tex., 1978; dir. adjunctive therapy San Antonio State Sch., 1978; lic. psychologist pvt. practice, Winston Salem, NC, 1979—. Cons. Cardiac Rehab., NC, 1980—85; bd. psychologists Vocat. Rehab., NC, 1980—2000; adj. faculty High Pt. U., Winston Salem, NC, 1983—90. Author: (book) Psychological and Spiritual Health, 1995, Integrational Psychology, 1996, Psyche, Soul, and Spirit, 1998. Co-founder Soc. Reform Mental Health, 2002, bd., 2002, Assn. Mentally Handicapped, Winston Salem, 1981, pres., 1982; bd. Piedmont Handicapped Assn., Winston Salem, 1983. 1st lt. Army Green Beret USAR, 1969—72, various. Recipient Nat. Hon. Rsch. Soc., Sigma Xi, 1978, Disting. Svc. Award, NC Rehab. Assn., 1982; grantee Grant for Delayed Stress, Veterans Admin., 1982. Achievements include discovery of integrational psychology. Avocations: book reviewer lib. journ and others, classical guitar, reading, study of physics and cosmology, hiking. Home: 3664 Heathrow Dr Winston Salem NC 27127 Office: Pvt Practice PO Box 25881 Winston Salem NC 27114 E-mail: twiggsmanny@aol.com.

**TWIGG-SMITH, THURSTON**, newspaper publisher; b. Honolulu, Aug. 17, 1921; s. William and Margaret Carter (Thurston) Twigg-S.; m. Bessie Bell, June 9, 1942 (div. Feb. 1983); children: Elizabeth, Thurston, William, Margaret, Evelyn; m. Laila Roster, Feb. 22, 1983 (div. Dec. 1994); m. Sharon Smith, Feb. 28, 1996. B.Engring., Yale U., 1942. With Honolulu Advertiser, 1946-2000, mng. editor, 1954-60, asst. bus. mgr., 1960-61, pub., 1961-86; pres., dir., chief exec. officer Honolulu Advertiser, Inc., 1962-93, chmn. 1993-2000. Chmn., dir., CEO Persis Corp., 1962-2002, chmn. Twigg-Smith Group LLC, 2002—. Trustee Honolulu Acad. Arts, The Contemporary Mus., Hawaii, The Skowhegan Sch., Maine, Yale Art Gallery, New Haven. Maj. AUS, 1942-46. Mem. Waialae Country Club, Pacific Club, Oahu Country Club, Outrigger Canoe Club. Personal E-mail: ttwiggsmith@aol.com.

**TWINAME, JOHN DEAN**, minister, human services administrator; b. Mt. Kisco, N.Y., Dec. 27, 1931; s. C. G. and Constance Jean (Ulmer) Twiname; m. Carolyn Anderson, Aug. 6, 1955; children: Karen, Jeanne, Julia. AB, Cornell U., 1953; MBA, Harvard U., 1957; MDiv, Union Theol. Sem., 1983. Ordained to ministry Presbyn. Ch., 1983. Sales rep. Am. Hosp. Supply Corp., Evanston, Ill., 1957-60, dir. product research, 1961, sales mgr., 1962, asst. to div. pres., 1963, product mgr., 1964, mktg. mgr., 1965-67, mktg. v.p., 1968-69; dep. adminstr. Social and Rehab. Svc., HEW, Washington, 1969-70, adminstr., 1970-73; adminstr. Office Health Cost of Living Coun., 1973-74; pvt. cons. Mott-McDonald Assocs., Inc., Washington, 1974-76, pres., 1976-78; exec. v.p. Am. Health Found., N.Y.C., 1978-81; co-pres. HealthCare Chaplaincy, Inc., N.Y.C., 1983-93, co-chair exec. com., 1993-94, life trustee, 1995—, exec. v.p., 1999—2000. Cons. exec. Coll. Chaplains, 1997; acting sr. min. Green's Farms Congl. Ch., Westport, Conn., 2001—03, pastoral assoc., 2003—. Treas. U.S. com. Internat. Coun. Social Welfare, 1977—80; mem. pres. coun. United Hosp. Fund, 1991—99; voting mem. Empire Blue Cross/Blue Shield, 1994; chmn. bd. dirs. Bauman Bible Telecasts, Inc., 1976—80; sec. bd. dirs. U.S. Coun. Internat. Yr. of Disabled Persons, 1979—81; founding bd. dirs. Am. Paralysis Assn. (formerly Paralysis Cure Rsch.), 1976—85; bd. dirs. Epilepsy Found. Am., 1978—85; chmn. bd. dirs. Chgo. Bus.-Indsl. Project, 1967—68, People to People Com. for Handicapped, 1976—78; bd. dirs. N.Y. Regional Transplant Program, 1988—92, Beck Mack & Oliver Ptnrs. Fund, 2000—05. 1st lt. AUS, 1953—55. Recipient Disting. Svc. award, Coll. Chaplains, 1992, Wholeness of Life award, The Health Care Chaplaincy, Inc., 2003, Disting. Alumnus award, Union Theol. Sem., 2004; Baker scholar, Bus. Sch. Harvard U. Home: 60 East End Ave New York NY 10028 Office: 163 Harbor Rd Southport CT 06890 Office Phone: 203-254-1506.

**TWISDALE, HAROLD WINFRED**, dentist; b. Roanoke Rapids, N.C., Apr. 28, 1933; s. James Robert and Elma (Smith) T.; m. Barbara Ann Edmonds, Aug. 2, 1958 (div. Apr. 1974); children: Harold Winfred, Leigh Ann.; m. Frances Jean Winstead, July 1983. BS in Dentistry, U. N.C., 1955, D.D.S., 1958. Individual practice dentistry, Charlotte, NC, 1961—; head, dept. dental prosthetics Meml. Hosp., 1964-66; lectr. dental subjects.; pres., gen. mgr. WCTU-TV, Charlotte Telecasters, Inc., 1967-69, WATU-TV, Augusta, Ga., Augusta Telecasters, Inc., 1968-69, Television Presentations, Inc., Charlotte, 1967-69; partner Twisdale and Steel Assocs., Charlotte, 1965-70; propr. Twisdale Enterprises, Charlotte, 1965-70. Pres. Memphis Telecasters, Inc., 1966-76, Va. Telecasters, Inc., Richmond, 1966—, Durham-Raleigh Telecasters, Inc., Durham, N.C., 1966-70, Gentil Elite, Inc., 1979— Transp. chmn. Miss N.C. Pageant, 1965; v.p. N.C. Jaycees, 1963-64; Trustee Boys Home, Lake Waccomaw, N.C., 1966-67. Served to capt. USAF, 1958-60. Recipient various awards Charlotte Jaycees, 1962-66. Fellow Acad. Dentistry Internat.; mem. ADA, N.C. Dental Found., N.C. Dental Soc., Charlotte Dental Soc. (chmn. various coms. 1961—), Am. Analgesia Soc., Internat. Analgesic Soc. (dir. 1980-85), N.C. Dental Soc. Anesthesiology (v.p. 1983-84), Charlotte Analgesia Study Club (co-founder 1970), N.C. 2d Dist. Dental Soc., Metrolina Dental Soc. (founder 1994, pres. 1994-95), U. N.C. Dental Alumni Assn., Southeastern Analgesia Soc. (founder 1972, pres. 1972-74), Lambda Chi Alpha, Delta Sigma Delta. Republican. Methodist. Home: 2221 Streatley Ln Matthews NC 28105-6648 Office: 6623 Executive Circle #110 PO Box 25528 Charlotte NC 28229-5528 Office Phone: 704-537-5224. *I must give the full credit for any achievement I might have accomplished in life to my mother and father. They not only provided me the means and direction one needs to make even the slightest accomplishment in our mortal life, but most of all, they gave me love, understanding, and a sense of values. These values have never deserted me, nor have they been compromised, even in the darkest hours of depression or during the brightest times of accomplishment. They have been my steady companions.*

**TWITCHELL, THEODORE GRANT**, music educator, composer; b. Melrose, Kans., Jan. 26, 1928; s. Curtis and Sarah Frances (Lane) T.; m. Rebecca Janis Goldsmith, Nov. 18, 1989; stepchildren: Ralph Norman, Russell Norman, Dawn Jiricek. AA in Music, L.A. City Coll., 1949; BA in Social Studies, Calif. State U., L.A., 1951, MA in Secondary Edn., 1955; EdD in Secondary and Higher Edn., U. So. Calif., L.A., 1964. Tchr. Barstow (Calif.) Union High Sch., 1952, Burbank (Calif.) Unified Sch. Dist., 1954-66; dean instrn., dir. evening divsn., dir. summer sessions, 1966-69; pres. Palo Verde Coll., Blythe, Calif., 1969-70; adult tchr. L.A. Unified Sch. Dist., 1977-78; faculty Columbia West U., L.A., 1993—. Pvt. English tutor, 1979—. Composer: The Gettysburg Address, Tidewater, The Pride of Monticello, Labor Day March, Valley Forge, Normandy Prayer, Christmas in L.A., Overture to Tidewater, The Lord Is My Shepherd, The Joy of Snow, Walt Whitman and Friends, over 90 others; contbr. articles to profl. jours.; author: Dear Mr. President, 1982, Courage, Conflict and Love, 1988, The Magnificent Odyssey of Michael Young, 1992; author of poems. With U.S. Army, 1952-53. Recipient Coll. Faculty Senate Award for Achievements for the coll., Palo Verde Coll. Student Body award. Mem. Internat. Poetry Hall Fame, Cmty. Coll. Pres.'s Assn., Am. Assn. Composers, Authors and Pubs., Calif. PTA (hon. life mem.), Rho Delta Chi. Republican. Methodist. Avocations: music, writing, travel, hiking, photography.

**TWITTY, SUSAN KAY**, music educator; b. Peoria, Ill., Sept. 9, 1950; d. William Paul Evans and Alberta Eugenie Gebhardt; m. Lillard Bates Twitty, Jr., Aug. 22, 1970; children: Regina Lynne Leffers, Anne Elizabeth Degenhart. AA, Ill. Ctrl. Coll., 1970. Cert. piano tchr. Pvt. practice piano tchr., Peoria, 1982—; tchr. music Montessori Children's Ho., Peoria, 1991—2002. Editor (columnist): Pamta Notes, 1999—. Mem.: Nat. Guild Piano Tchrs., Ill. State Music Tchrs. Assn., Music Tchrs. Nat. Assn., Peoria Area Music Tchrs. Assn. (sec. 1990—92, v.p. 1996—98, pres. 2001—03, Mem. of Yr. 2001). Independent. Roman Catholic. Avocations: reading, gardening, swimming. Home: 604 Fondulac Dr East Peoria IL 61611

**TWOMBLY, CY (EDWIN PARKER TWOMBLY JR.)**, artist; b. Lexington, Va., Apr. 25, 1928; Student, Boston Mus. Sch. Fine Arts, 1948-49, Washington and Lee U., 1950, Art Students League, 1951; studied with, Frank Kline and Robert Motherwell, Black Mountain Coll., 1952. Head dept. art So. Sem. and Jr. Coll., Buena Vista, Va., 1955-56; opening of Cy Twombly Gallery at the Menil Collection, Houston, 2005. One man shows include: Milw., 1968, Nicholas Wilder Gallery, 1969, Herron Inst. Art, Indpls., 1969, Guggenheim Mus., N.Y.C., 1976, Mus. Modern Art, N.Y.C., 1976, Vancouver Art Gallery, 1982, Mus. Hans Lange, Krefeld, W.Ger., 1982, Santa Barbara Contemporary Arts Forum, 1984, New York, Elkon Gallery, 1996, Whitney Mus. Am. Art, 1996, Cheim & Reed, 1997, Gagosian Gallery Madison, 2003, Brussels, Xavier Hufkins, 1997, Colonge, Galerie Karsten Greve, 1997, Los Angeles, Gagosian Gallery, 1998, County Mus. Art, 2001, Hannover, Sprengel Mus., 2000, Munich, Pinakothek der Moderne, 2002, Fifty Years of Works On Paper, St. Petersburg, State Hermitage Mus. travelled to Munich, Paris, London, 2003, Paris, Centre Pompidou, 2004, London, Serpentine Gallery, 2004; retrospective exhbn. Whitney Mus. Art, N.Y.C., 1979; group exhbns. include N.Y.U., 1967, Whitney Mus. Am. Art Annual, 1967, Royal Acad. Arts, 1981, Larry Gagosian Gallery, Los Angeles, 1982, Young Hoffman Gallery, Chgo., 1982, Blum Gallery, N.Y.C., 1982, Talking Pieces, Leverkusen, Mus. Morsbroich, 2003, Jasper Johns to Jeff Koons, Bilbao, Guggenheim Mus., 2003, Graz, Neue Galerie, Phantom der Lust-Visionen des Masochismus in der Kunst, 2003, Graz, Neue Galerie, SUPPORT 1- Die

Neue Galerie als Sammlung, 2003, Mori Art Mus., Happiness- A Survival Guide for Art and Life, Tokyo, 2003, London, Gagosian Gallery Heddon, Drawings, 2004, Berlin, Neue Nationalgalerie, Das Mus. Modern Art in Berlin, 2004; large-scale masterworks include: The Age of Alexander, 1959—60, Triumph of Galatea, 1961, Untitled (Say Goodbye Catallus, to the Shores of Asia Minor), 1994; represented in permanent collections R.I. Sch. Design, Whitney Mus. Am. Art, Mus. Modern Art, N.Y.C., Ludwig Collection, Aachen, Thomas Segal Gallery, Tavelli Gallery, Adler Gallery, also pvt. collections N.Y.C., Chgo., Washington and Europe. Va. Mus. Fine Arts fellow 1952-53; recipient Leone d'Oro for Contemporary Art, Venice Biennale, 2001. Fellow Am. Acad. Arts and Letters. Office: Cy Twombly Gallery 1511 Branard Houston TX 77006 Office Phone: 212-744-2313.

**TWOMBLY, STEPHEN DOANE**, magazine publisher; b. Summit, NJ, July 26, 1953; s. Doane and Betty (Bowers) T.; m. Jean Sawyer. BA summa cum laude, Drew U., 1976. Dist. mgr. McGraw-Hill Pubs. Co., N.Y.C., 1978-83; dir. advt. IDG Communications, Peterborough, N.H., 1983-84, pub. RUN, 1984-87, pub. AmigaWorld, 1985—; group pub. Consumer/Home Mag., Special Products, 1987-88; v.p. IDG Communications/Peterborough, 1988-89, exec. v.p., 1989—90; pub. dir. PC Resource, 1988; exec. v.p., pub. dir. PCResource IDG Communications/Peterborough, 1989—90, Cahners Pubs. Co., Newton, Mass., 1990—97; nat. sales mgr. Datamation, 1990—92, assoc. pub., 1993—94; pub. Digital News & Rev., 1994—95, Reseller Mgmt., 1995—97; v.p. sales IDG Channel Svcs. Corp., Framingham, Mass., 1997—98; v.p., pub. New Age Jour & Body & Soul, 1998—2001; pub. dir. Weider Pubs. Natural Health mag., 2001—03; group pub. Advanstar Comm. Sensors & Frontline Solutions, 2003—04; pub. CMO mag. Internat. Data Group, 2004—. Spkr. in field. Mem. Sigma Phi. Avocations: composing, painting, outdoor sports. Home: PO Box 1365 New London NH 03257 Office: CXOMedia Inc 492 Connecticut Path Rd Framingham MA 01701 Office Phone: 508-987-7962, 617-929-2706. Personal E-mail: stwombly@globe.com. Business E-Mail: stwombly@cxo.com.

**TWOMEY, KEVIN**, pharmaceutical executive; BA in econ. and acctg., St. John's U. Various positions Deloitte & Touche, 1972—89, Fleming Companies, Inc., 1989—2000, sr. v.p., fin. and contr., 1999—2000, dir., planning and analysis, promoted to ops. contr., then, v.p. and contr., 1995—99; sr. v.p., chief acctg. officer Rite Aid Corp., 2000—05, CFO, exec. v.p., 2005—. Office: Rite Aid Corp 30 Hunter Lane Camp Hill PA 17011*

**TWOMEY, THOMAS A., JR.**, lawyer, educator; b. N.Y.C., Dec. 8, 1945; s. Thomas A. and Mary (Maloney) T.; m. Judith Hope Twomey, Dec. 15, 1979; stepchildren: Erling Hope, Nisse Hope. BA, Manhattan Coll., 1967; postgrad., U.Va., 1967-68; JD, Columbia U., 1970. Bar: N.Y. 1972, U.S. Tax Ct. 1974. Asst. town atty. Town of Southampton N.Y., 1973-74; spl. asst. dist. atty. Suffolk County, NY, 1973-74; pvt. practice law Riverhead, NY, 1974-75; ptnr. Hubbard & Twomey, Riverhead, 1976-79, Twomey, Latham, Shea & Kelley, Riverhead, 1980—. Chair N.Y. State East End Econ. and Environ. Task Force, 1993; mem. deans coun. Stonybrook Sch. Medicine, 1991—; adj. prof. environ. law Southampton Coll., 1977-78. Bd. dirs. East End Arts Coun., Riverhead, 1983, Guild Hall East Hampton, 1993—; bd. dirs. East Hampton Libr., 1994—, pres., 1998—; trustee L.I. Power Authority, 1989-94; town historian, Town of East Hampton, 1999, vice chair East Hampton Town 350th Anniversary com., 1998, editor East Hampton Histor. Collection; historian N.Y. State Dem. Com., 2000-01; chair East Hampton 350th lecture series, 1998. Recipient Environ. award, U.S. EPA, 1980, Citizen of Yr. award L.I. Farm Bur., 2002. Mem. ABA, Suffolk County Bar Assn., State Energy Coun., N.Y. State Fresh Water Wetlands Appeals Bd. Democrat. Home: #9 Two Holes of Water Rd East Hampton NY 11937 Office Phone: 631-727-2180.

**TWOMEY, TIMOTHY**, architect; Grad., U. So. Calif.; MArch, Harvard U.; JD, UCLA. Prin. Shelpley Bulfinch Richardson & Abbott, Boston, 1993, prin. chief adminstrv. officer, in-house counsel, 1993—. Past mem. bldg. design and constrn. faculty Northeastern U.; lectr. in field; constrn. dispute mediator, arbitrator, ct. apptd. master. Contbr. articles to profl. jours. Chair local cmty. planning commn. and sch. com. Mem.: AIA, Boston Soc. Archs. Office: Shepley Bulfinch Richardson & Abbott 40 Broad St Boston MA 02109-4306

**TYACK, THOMAS MICHAEL**, lawyer; b. Columbus, Ohio, June 20, 1940; s. George E. and E. Naomi (Ballard) T.; m. Patricia J. Clark, Sept. 7, 1969; children: Jonathan, Jeffrey, James, Justin. BA cum laude, Ohio State U., Columbus, 1962, Jd, 1965. Bar: Ohio 1965, U.S. Ct. Appeals (6th cir.) 1970, U.S. Supreme Ct. 1970, U.S. Dist. Ct. (so. dist.) Ohio 1972. Ptnr. Tyack, Scott & Colley, Columbus, 1965-79, Tyack Scott & Wiseman, Columbus, 1979-81; prin. Thomas M. Tyack Assocs. Co., L.P.A., Columbus, 1981-90; ptnr. Tyack & Blackmore Co., L.P.A., Columbus, 1991-94; pres. Tyack, Blackmore & Liston Co. LPA, Columbus, 1994—. Bar examiner Ohio Supreme Ct., 1975-80; lectr., legal asst. program Capital U., Ohio, 1977-90. Fellow Am. Coll. Trial Lawyers; mem. ABA, Ohio Bar Assn., Columbus Bar Assn., Franklin Ct. and Trial Lawyers, Assn. Trial Lawyers Am., Ohio Acad. Trial Lawyers, Ohio Acad. Trial Lawyers, Ohio Acad. Criminal Def. Lawyers, NDCDL. Republican. Methodist. Office: 536 S High St Columbus OH 43215-5605 Office Phone: 614-221-1341.

**TYAGARAJAN, KRISHNA CARTHIK**, investment banker; b. Udyogamandal, India, July 20, 1973; s. Sadasivam and Usha Kumari Tyagarajan; m. Madhavy Raj, Dec. 15, 2004. BA in Econs., Lawrence U., 1996; MBA in Fin., U. Pa., 2002. Cert. broker N.Y., 2002. Assoc. cons. Deloitte Consulting, Mpls., 1996—2000; assoc. investment banking CIBC World Markets, N.Y., 2002—. Co-author: The Value Enterprise. Recipient Academic All Conf. award, Lawrence U., 1994; scholar, 1992—96, Kholer Co., 1995. Mem.: Lamda Sigma. Avocations: tennis, cricket, golf, aeromodeling. Office Phone: 212-885-4753.

**TYAGI, MAYANK**, research scientist; s. Uttam Chand and Satya Tyagi; m. Arti Singh, June 23, 2004. PhD, La. State U., Baton Rouge, 2003. Rsch. assoc. Ctr. Computation and Tech., La. State U., Baton Rouge, 2003—06, rsch. scientist, 2006—. Mem.: AIAA, ASME. Office: Ctr Computation and Tech La State U 318 Johnston Hall Baton Rouge LA 70803 Office Phone: 225-578-8929. Personal E-mail: mtyagi@lsu.edu. E-mail: mtyagi@cct.lsu.edu.

**TYBOUT, RICHARD ALTON**, economics professor; b. Phila., Sept. 28, 1920; s. Richard Raymond and Lillian (Alton) T.; m. Rita Holloway, Sept. 7, 1946; children: Alice Marie, James Richard, Robert Maxwell. BChemE, U. Del., 1943; MSChemE, U. Mich., 1946, MA in Econs., 1947, PhD in Econs., 1952. Instr. U. Mich., Ann Arbor, 1952-54; asst. prof. Ohio State U., Columbus, 1954-57, assoc. prof., 1957-62, prof., 1962-88, prof. emeritus, 1988—. Editor: Economics of Research and Development, 1965, Environmental Quality and Society, 1975; author: Government Contracting in Atomic Energy, 1956, The Reactor Supply Industry, 1960, Atomic Power and Energy Resource Planning, 1958; co-author: The Columbus Area Economy, 1966. Named Ford Faculty Study Fellow, Ford Foun., 1959-60, Phoenix Predoctoral Fellow, U. Mich., 1949-51. Mem. Am. Econ. Assn., Sierra Club (chmn. econs. com. 1975-85), Toastmasters Internat. (pres. Worthington chpt., 2002-03), Tau Beta Pi, Phi Kappa Phi, Beta Gamma Sigma. Avocations: construction, swimming, sailing. Home: 324 Pingree Dr Columbus OH 43085-3158 Office: Ohio State U Dept Econs 1945 N High St Columbus OH 43210-1120

**TYBURSKI, JAMES GERARD**, surgeon; b. Chester and Elizabeth Tyburski; m. Julie Tyburski, May 5, 1990. BS, SUNY, Binghamton, 1983; MD, Upstate Med. Ctr., Syracuse, NY, 1987. Cert. Am. Bd. Surgery, 1993, critical care Am. Bd. Surgery, 1993. Resident surgery Wayne State U. Detroit Med. Ctr., 1987—92, trauma fellow, 1992—94; asst. prof. surgery Wayne State U. Sch. Medicine, Detroit, 1994—2001, assoc. prof. surgery, 2001—; program dir. Wayne State Dept. Surgery, Detroit, 1997—; chief surgery Detroit Receiving Hosp., 2004—. Recipient Wayne State Faculty Tchg. award, Wayne State U. Sch. Medicine, 2003, 2005. Mem.: Western Surg. Assn.,

Midwest Surg. Assn., Eastern Assn. for the Surgery of Trauma, Am. Assn. for the Surgery of Trauma, ACS, Alpha Omega Alpha Honor Med. Soc. (life). Office: Detroit Receiving Hosp 4201 St Antoine Ste 4S-13 Detroit MI 48201 Office Phone: 313-745-3487.

**TYCZYNSKI, JERZY EDWARD,** epidemiologist; b. Radom, Poland, Jan. 16, 1959; s. Zdzislaw Tyczynski and Aleksandra Tyczynska; m. Elzbieta Jakubiak, June 29, 2001. MSc, U. of Warsaw, 1977—83; PhD, Nat. Cancer Ctr. Scientist Nat. Cancer Ctr., Warsaw, 1985—2001, Internat. Agy. for Rsch. on Cancer, Lyon, Rhone-Alp, France (incl. Monaco), 2001—04; rsch. scientist Cancer Prevention Inst., Dayton, Ohio, 2004—05; assoc. prof. Wright State U., Dayton, Ohio, 2004—05; with Bristol-Myers Squibb, Wallingford, Conn., 2005—. Dir. Health Promotion Found., Warsaw, 1992—2000; pres. Assn. of Cancer Registries in Poland, Warsaw, 1999—2001; exec. sci. officer European Network of Cancer Registries, Lyon. IARC Sci., Internat. Agy. for Rsch. on Cancer, 1991—92. Mem.: Am. Assn. for Cancer Rsch., Am. Coll. of Epidemiology. Home: 9 Bret Dr Meriden CT 06450-2506 Office: Bristol-Myers Squibb 5 Research Pkwy Wallingford CT 06492 Office Phone: 203-677-3709. E-mail: jerzytyczynski@bms.com.

**TYDINGCO-GATEWOOD, FRANCES MARIE,** judge; b. Oahu, Hawaii, Jan. 21, 1958; d. Daniel J. and Francesca S. Tydingco; m. Robert Gatewood; children: Daniel Gatewood, Michael Gatewood, Stephen Gatewood. BA in Polit. Sci., Marquette U., 1980; JD, U. Mo., Kansas City, 1983. Law clk. to Hon. Forest W. Hanna Jackson County Cir. Ct., Kansas City, 1983—84; asst. atty. gen. Govt. of Guam, 1984—88, chief prosecutor, 1990—94; asst. prosecutor Jackson County Prosecutor's Office, Mo., 1988—90; trial judge Superior Ct. Guam, 1994—2002; assoc. judge Supreme Ct. Guam, 2002—. Profl. Tech. scholar, Govt. of Guam. Office: Supreme Ct Guam Guam Jud Ctr Ste 300 120 W O'Brien Dr Hagatna GU 96910 Home: 222 Chalan Santo Papa Ste 222 Hagatna GU 96910 Business E-mail: ftgate@guamsupremecourt.com.*

**TYER, TRAVIS EARL,** librarian, consultant; b. Lorenzo, Tex., Oct. 23, 1930; s. Charlie Earl and Juanita (Travis) T.; m. Alma Lois Davis, Nov. 6, 1951; children: Alan Ross, Juanita Linn. BS, Abilene Christian U., 1952; BLS, U. North Tex., 1959; AdM in LS, Fla. State U., 1969, postgrad., 1969-71. Librarian, tchr. pub. schs., Gail, Lubbock, and Seminole, Tex., 1952-61; with Dallas Pub. Library, 1961-66, coordinator young adult services, 1962-66; library dir. Lubbock Pub. Library, 1966, Lubbock City-County Libraries, 1967-88; grad. library sch. faculty-state personnel coordinator Emporia (Kans.) State U., 1971-72; sr. cons. profl. devel. Ill. State Library, Springfield, 1972-80; exec. dir. Great River Libr. Sys., Quincy, Ill., 1980-94; cons. pub. rels. and comm. Alliance Libr. Sys., Quincy, 1994-97; ind. libr. cons., 1997—. Lectr. summer workshops Tex. Woman's U., U. Okla., U. Utah, Fla. State U. U. North Tex.; adj. faculty U. Mo., 1986-89; cons. in field; mem. adv. com. Ill. State Libr., 1984-87, 93-96; pres. Resource Sharing Alliance West Ctrl. Ill., Inc., 1981-94, sec., 1994-97; pres. Ill. Libr. System Dirs. Orgn., 1992-94. Contbr. articles to library jours. Inductee U. North Tex. Libr. and Info. Sci. Hall of Fame, 1990. Mem. ALA, Ill. Libr. Assn., Ill. Ctr. for the Book, Friends of Librs. U.S.A., U. North Tex. Sch. Libr. and Info. Sci. (life), Friends Lubbock City-County Librs. (life), Ill. Sch. Libr. MEdia Assn. Democrat. Mem. Ch. of Christ. Home and Office: 2008 S Arrowood Ct Quincy IL 62305-8961 Office Phone: 217-223-5024.

**TYGRETT, HOWARD VOLNEY, JR.,** judge, lawyer; b. Lake Charles, La., Jan. 12, 1941; s. Howard Volney and Hazel (Wheeler) T.; m. Linda Lee; children: Carroll Diane, Howard V. III. BA, Williams Coll., 1961; LLB, So. Methodist U., 1964. Bar: Tex. 1964. Gen. atty. SEC, 1964-65; law clk. to chief judge U.S. Dist. Ct. No. Dist. Tex., 1965-67; ptnr. Tygrett & Walker and predecessors, Dallas, 1968-98; state dist. judge, 86th dist. Kaufman County, Tex., 2003—. Bd. dirs. Routh St. Center, 1976-83, Theatre Three, 1974-75, Shakespeare Festival, 1978-81, Suicide and Crisis Ctr., 1983-88, Kaufman County Civic Theatre, 2005-, Terrell Christian Acad., 2005-; chmn. Terrell Hist. Preservation Commn., 2000-03. Mem. Tex. Bar Assn., Civitan (lt. gov. Tex. dist. 1976-77, gov. 1979-80), Terrell Heritage Soc. (v.p. 1992-95), Delta Phi, Delta Theta Phi. Episcopalian. Home: 505 Pacific Ave Terrell TX 75160-2073 Office: Kaufman County Courthouse 100 W Mulberry Kaufman TX 75142

**TYKESON, DONALD ERWIN,** broadcast executive; b. Portland, Oreg., Apr. 11, 1927; s. O. Ansel and Hillie Martha (Haveman) T.; m. Rilda Margaret Steigleder, July 1, 1950; children: Ellen, Amy, Eric. BS, U. Oreg., 1951. V.p. dir. Liberty Comm., Inc., Eugene, Oreg., 1963-67, pres., CEO, dir., 1967-83; mng. ptnr. Tykeson/Assocs. Enterprises, 1983—; chmn. bd. Bend Cable Comm., LLC, 1983—2002, vice chmn., 2002—; chmn. bd. Ctrl. Oreg. Cable Advt., LLC, 1992—. Mem. coun. pub. reps. NIH, 2002-05, NIH Pub. Access Working Group Bd of Regents Nat. Libr. Medicine, 2005-; trustee. Tykeson Family Charitable Trust, 1995—; mem. Hoover Instn. bd. overseers Stanford U., 2002-. Vice-chmn. we. area Nat. Multiple Sclerosis Soc., 1983—2002, bd. dirs., 1987—2003, life bd. dirs., 2004—; bd. dirs. Nat. Coalition Rsch. in Neurol. and Communicative Disorders, 1984—89, Sacred Heart Med. Ctr. Found., 1995—2004; chmn. pub. and gov. info. com. Nat. Coaltion in Rsch., C-SPAN, 1980—89; trustee U. Oreg. Found., 1996—, Eugene Art Found., 1980—85, Oreg. Health Scis. U. Found., 1988—91; trustee emeritus Sacred Heart Med. Ctr. Found., 2004—; mem. bus. adv. coun. U. Oreg. Coll. Bus. Adminstrn., 1973—, mem. steering coun., 1997—2001, dean search com., 1998—; mem. Oreg. Investment Coun. State of Oreg., vice chmn., 1988—92. Recipient 1st citation honoree, Eugene C. of C., 2006. Mem. Nat. Assn. Broadcasters, Nat. Cable TV Assn. (dir. 1976-83), Chief Execs. Orgn., Vintage Club (bd. dirs. 1996-99, chmn. fin. com., treas. 1996-99, pres. Custom Lot Assn. 1992-97), Country Club Eugene (dir. 1975-77, sec. 1976, v.p. 1977), Multnomah Athletic Club, Arlington Club, Rotary, Alexis de Tocqueville Soc., Confrérie Chevaliers du Tastevin Sous Commanderie de Coachella Valley. Home: 447 Spyglass Dr Eugene OR 97401-2091 Office: Tykeson Assocs Enterprises PO Box 70006 Eugene OR 97401-0101 Office Phone: 541-683-4511.

**TYL, NOEL JAN,** retired vocalist, astrologer, writer; b. West Chester, Pa., Dec. 31, 1936; BA, Harvard U. 1958. Bus. mgr. Houston Grand Opera Assn., 1958-60; account exec. Ruder and Finn Pub. Rels., N.Y.C., 1960-62; profl. astrologer, 1970—; editor Astrology Now mag., 1974-79. Pres. Tyl Assocs., Inc. pub. rels. and advt., 1980-89; media spokesman; internat. lectr., locations including U.S., Moscow, London, Oslo, Copenhagen, Berlin, Amsterdam, The Netherlands, Toronto, Ont., Tel Aviv, Bologna. Winner Am. Opera Auditions, 1964; opera singer U.S. and Europe, 1964-80; Wagner specialist; appearances include Vienna State Opera, Düsseldorf, Rome, Milan, Barcelona, N.Y.C. Opera; also throughout U.S.; author: Principles and Practice of Astrology, 12 vols., 1973-75, Teaching and Study Guide, 1976, The Horoscope as Identity, 1974, Holistic Astrology, 1980, Prediction in Astrology, 1991, Synthesis and Counseling in Astrology, 1994, Astrology of the Famed, 1995, Predictions for a New Millennium, 1996, Astrological Timing of Critical Illness, 1998, Creative Astrologer, 1999, Solar Arcs, 2001, Intimacy, Sexuality, and Relationship, 2002, Vocations, 2005. Mem. Astrology's World Orgn./AFAN (presiding officer 1982-98). Home: 16800 E El Lago Blvd Unit 2083 Fountain Hills AZ 85268-4778 Office Phone: 480-816-0000. Personal E-mail: njt@mindspring.com.

**TYLE, CRAIG S.,** lawyer, investment company executive; b. Syracuse, NY, 1960; BA with high honors, Swarthmore Coll., 1982; JD magna cum laude, Harvard Univ., 1985. Bar: NY 1988, DC 2004. Assoc Sullivan & Cromwell, NYC, 1982—88; atty. Investment Company Inst., Washington, 1988—97, gen. counsel, 1997—2004; ptnr., asset mgmt. group Shearman & Sterling LLP, Washington, 2004—05; named sr. v.p. & gen. counsel elect Franklin Resources Inc. (Franklin Templeton Investments), San Mateo, Calif., 2005. Mem. NASDAQ Quality of Markets com., 1997—2003, co-chmn., 2003. Contbr. articles to profl. jours. Mem.: ABA, Assn. Bar City of NY. Office: Shearman & Sterling Ste 900 801 Pennsylvania Ave NW Washington DC

20004-2604 also: Franklin Resources Inc 1 Franklin Pkwy San Mateo CA 94403-1906 Office Phone: 202-508-8016. Office Fax: 202-508-8100. Business E-Mail: craig.tyle@shearman.com.

**TYLER, ANNE (MRS. TAGHI M. MODARRESSI),** writer; b. Mpls., Oct. 25, 1941; d. Lloyd Parry and Phyllis (Mahon) T.; m. Taghi M. Modarressi, May 3, 1963 (dec. Apr. 1997); children: Tezh, Mitra. BA, Duke U., 1961; postgrad., Columbia U., 1962. Author: If Morning Ever Comes, 1964, The Tin Can Tree, 1965, A Slipping-Down Life, 1970, The Clock Winder, 1972, Celestial Navigation, 1974, Searching for Caleb, 1976, Earthly Possessions, 1977, Morgan's Passing, 1980, Dinner at the Homesick Restaurant, 1982, The Accidental Tourist, 1985, Breathing Lessons, 1988 (Pulitzer Prize for fiction 1989), Saint Maybe, 1991, (juvenile) Tumble Tower, 1993, Ladder of Years, 1995, A Patchwork Planet, 1998, Back When We Were Grownups, 2001, The Amateur Marriage, 2004, (juvenile) Timothy Tugbohom Says No, 2005, Digging to America, 2006; contbr. short stories to nat. mags. Home: 222 Tunbridge Rd Baltimore MD 21212-3422

**TYLER, ASHLEY SUZANNE,** music educator; d. Jerry Duane and Linda Elaine Tyler. MusB in Edn., Auburn U., Ala., 2005. Cert. tchr. Ala. Band dir. Auburn U. Bands, 2002—05, Homewood (Ala.) City Schs., 2005—. Mem.: Nat. Band Assn., Music Educators Nat. Conf., Sigma Alpha Iota (life; charter mem.). Office: Homewood Mid Sch 395 Mecca Ave Birmingham AL 35209 Office Phone: 205-877-4567. E-mail: atyler@homewood.k12.al.us.

**TYLER, CHRISTOPHER WILLIAM,** scientist, director; b. Leicester, Eng., Dec. 16, 1943; s. David William Tyler; m. Lorraine Komisarjevsky, Dec. 21, 1968 (div. 1978); m. Rebecca Anne Turner, Feb. 14, 1985; 1 child, Austin David. BA, Leicester U., 1966; MSc, Aston U., 1967; PhD, Keele U., 1970, DSc, 2004. Rsch. fellow Northeastern U., 1970—72, Bristol U., 1972—73, Bell Labs, 1974—75; rsch. assoc. The Smith-Kettlewell Eye Rsch. Inst., 1976—80; assoc. scientist SK Brain Imaging Ctr., 1976—80, scientist, 1980—82, sr. scientist, 1982—, head, 2002—. Adj. asst. prof. U. Calif., Santa Barbara, 1971, Northeastern U., 1973—74, UCLA, 1973; hon. rsch. assoc. Inst. Ophthalmology, 1978—82; vis. prof. Jules Stein Inst., 1985—88; adj. prof. U. Calif., Berkeley, 1988. Editor: Human Symmetry Perception and Its Computational Analysis, 1996; contbr. over 200 articles to profl. jours., chapters to books; assoc. editor Perception and Psychophysics, 1985—93, feature editor Spatial Vision, 1994—95, distbn. editor Perception, 1998—, action editor Vision Research, 2001—. Fellow Bellagio fellow, Rockefeller Found., 2005; grantee Rsch. grantee, Found. Fund Rsch. Psychiatry, Nat. Eye Inst., Nat. Inst. Mental Health, NSF, Wellcome Found., Retinitis Pigmentosa Found. Mem.: ECVP, SPIE, VSS, Optical Soc. Am. Office: Smith-Kettlewell Eye Research Inst Rm 401 2318 Fillmore St San Francisco CA 94115

**TYLER, DANA,** anchor; b. Columbus, Ohio; BA in Mktg. and Broadcast Journalism, Boston U. Intern WBNS-TV, Columbus, gen. assignment reporter, 1981—83, co-anchor weekday newscasts, 1983—90; weekend co-anchor/corr. WCBS-TV, N.Y.C., 1990—. Lectr. in field. Vol. N.Y.C. Sch. Vol. Programs. Honored by Harlem YMCA, Y of Greater N.Y.; recipient Emmy award for outstanding anchor, 1987, Emmy award for outstanding newscast, 1996, Emmy award for coverage of NYC Blackout, 2004. Office: WCBS-TV/CBS Corp 524 W 57th St New York NY 10019-2924

**TYLER, DAVID EARL,** retired veterinary medical educator; b. Carlisle, Iowa, July 12, 1928; s. Guy Earl and Beatrice Virginia (Slack) T.; m. Alice LaVon Smith, Sept. 6, 1952; children: John William, Anne Elizabeth. BS, Iowa State U., 1953, D.V.M., 1957, PhD, 1963; MS, Purdue U., 1960. Instr. dept. vet. sci. Purdue U., 1957-60; asst. prof. dept. pathology Coll. Vet. Medicine, Iowa State U., 1960-63, asso. prof., 1963-66; prof., head dept. pathology and parasitology Coll. Vet. Medicine, U. Ga., 1966-71, head dept. pathology, 1971-79, prof., 1971-91, prof. emeritus, 1991—; ret., 1991. Co-founder internat. net. pathology slide bank, 1984, co-dir., 1984-98; apptd. discussant Charles L. Davis Found. for Advancement Vet. Pathology, 1977-91. Cub Scout master, 1967-69, scout com. chmn., 1970-72; elder Disciples of Christ Ch., 1968—, chmn. ch. bd., 1973-74, 92-94; mem. citizens com. to County Bd. Edn., 1968-70; bd. dirs. Christian Coll., Ga., 1974-77. With AUS, 1946-48. Recipient Borden award Gail Borden Co., 1956, Norden Disting. Teaching award Norden Labs., 1964, 69, 81, 85, 91, Prof. of Yr. award Coll. Vet. Medicine, Iowa State U., 1965, Outstanding Prof. award Coll. Vet. Medicine, U. Ga., 1970, 76, 80-81, 83, 86, 87-88, 90, Joshia Meigs Teaching award, 1985, Stange award Coll. Vet. Med., Iowa State U., 1987, Phi Zeta Teaching award, 1985, N.Am. Outstanding Tchr. award, 1991, Omicron Delta Kappa Outstanding Prof. award U. Ga., 1981, Harold W. Casey award C.L. Davis Found., 1995. Mem. AVMA, Farm House, Am. Coll. Vet. Pathologists (mem. council 1975-77, exam. com. 1982-85), Am. Assn. Vet. Med. Colls. (chmn. com. teaching materials 1975-77), Nat. Program for Instructional Devel. in Vet. Pathology (adv. com. 1977), Aghon, Sigma Xi, Phi Eta Sigma, Alpha Zeta, Gamma Sigma Delta, Phi Kappa Phi, Phi Zeta (chpt. sec.-treas. 1982-84), Omega Tau Sigma. Home: 160 Sunny Brook Dr Athens GA 30605-3348

**TYLER, DIANE LAZZELLE,** elementary school educator; b. Morgantown, W.Va., Feb. 5, 1941; d. Frank Glen DeVille and Mary Jeanne Lazzelle; m. Karl A. Henry, July 23, 1962 (div. Apr. 1987); 1 child, Karoline Louise Henry; m. James L. Tyler, Apr. 10, 1992. BS in Elem. Edn., W.Va. U., 1962; MS in Elem. Edn., SUNY, Fredonia, 1987. Elem. tchr. Pitts. Pub. Schs., 1962—63, Rochester (N.Y.) City Schs., 1963—67, Hamburg (N.Y.) Cen., 1967—98, mentor, 1994, social studies coord., 1995—96, N.Y. state stds. coord., 1996—98; adj. prof, Canisius Coll. 1997—2002 Coop learning trainer South Town Tchrs. Ctr., Hamburg, NY, 1990—98; bd. rep. Erie County Mental Health, Buffalo, 1984—87. Pres. Sweet Adelines, Hamburg, 1971—73; co-chmn. Hamburgh Holidays, Hamburg, 1973—75. Recipient Tchr. of Excellence, Western N.Y. Women Adminstrs., 1997. Mem.: Writers by the Sea (leader 1999—2002), Newcomers at Beaches (bd. dirs. 2001—02), Young Reps. Club (pres. 1972—74), Phi Delta Kappa. Republican. Episcopalian. Home: 315 S Ocean Grande Dr PH-1 Ponte Vedra Beach FL 32082 E-mail: songster41@aol.com.

**TYLER, ERIC OWEN,** pediatrician; b. Columbia, Tenn., Oct. 18, 1955; s. Harry Everett and Elizabeth (Lawrence) T.; m. Fran Till Tyler, July 29, 1978; children: Emily, Mallory, Mollie. BS, Harding U., 1977; MD, U. Tenn., 1981. Intern, resident U. Ala., Birmingham, 1984; pediatrician Pediat. Assocs. Alexander City, Ala., 1985—. Bd. dirs. ARC, Tallapoosa County, 1998—. Fellow: Am. Acad. Pediats., Am. Coll. Pediats.; mem.: Am. Coll. Physician Execs. Avocations: reading, gardening. Office: Pediat Assocs of Alex City PO Box 1269 1962 Cherokee Rd Alexander City AL 35010-3437

**TYLER, H. RICHARD,** physician; b. Bklyn., Oct. 16, 1927; s. Max M. and Beatrice F. T.; m. Joyce Colby, June 17, 1951; children— Kenneth, Karen, Douglas, Lori. AB, Syracuse U., 1947; BS in Medicine, Washington U., 1951, MD, 1951; MA (hon.), Harvard U., 1989. Diplomate Am. Bd. Neurology and Psychiatry. Intern Peter Bent Brigham Hosp., Boston, 1951-52; resident in neurology Boston City Hosp., 1952-54; public health fellow Neurol. Inst., Queen's Sq., London, Salpêtrière, Paris, 1954-55; asst. in pediatrics and neurology Johns Hopkins Hosp., Balt., 1955-56; neurologist Peter Bent Brigham Hosp., Boston, 1956-74; asst. in neurology Harvard Med. Sch., Boston, 1956-59, assoc. in neurology, 1959-61, from instr. to prof., 1961—98, prof. emeritus, 1998—; ret., 1999. Sr. physician Brigham and Women's Hosp., Boston, 1974—; dir. neurol. svc., 1979-88. Co-editor: Current Neurology I and II, 1979, 80; mem. editorial bd.: Jour. Neurology, 1979-84, Classics on Neurology and Neurosurgery Libr., 1983—; contbr. articles to profl. jours. Trustee Brookline Pub. Libr., 1970-2001, chmn. bd. trustees, 1985-86, 90-91. Served with U.S. Army, 1946-47. Mem. Am. Neurol. Assn., Am. Acad. Neurology (hon.). Mass. Med. Soc. Office: 1 Brookline Pl Ste 503 Brookline MA 02445-7224 Office Phone: 617-738-1554. E-mail: HTyler1798@aol.com.

**TYLER, JEAN M.,** special education services professional; b. Erie, Pa., June 18, 1951; d. Betty Miller; m. Len A. Tyler, Oct. 15, 1977. Cert. advanced study in spl. edn., Syracuse U., N.Y., 1996. Tchr. New Berlin Ctrl. Sch., 1974—76; spl. edn. tchr., coach Sherburne-Earlville Ctrl. Sch., NY, 1978—96; dir. spl. edn. Unadilla Valley Ctrl. Sch., New Berlin, NY, 1996—, dir. spl. edn., athletic dir., 2000—06. Coach varsity girls basketball, girls volleyball, modified field hockey, basketball, softball, track and field, soccer. Achievements include coaching varisty girls basketball to Tri-Valley West and overall Tri-Valley League Championships. Home: 1222 County Rd 28 New Berlin NY 13411 Office: Unadilla Valley Ctrll Sch PO Box F 4238 State Hwy 8 New Berlin NY 13411 Office Phone: 607-847-7500. Personal E-mail: jtyler@uvstorm.org.

**TYLER, JOHN DUKE,** psychologist, educator; b. Nashville, Nov. 30, 1943; s. John Duke and Eleanora (Hammond) Tyler; m. Shirley Kay Montgomery; 1 child, Wade McLeod. BA, Vanderbilt U., 1965; PhD, U. Tex., Austin, 1970. Bd. cert. diplomate Am. Bd. Profl. Psychology. Prof. psychology U. N.D., Grand Forks, 1970—2006; dir. Family Inst., Grand Forks, 1980—2006. Dir. Psychol. Svcs. Ctr. U. ND, Grand Forks, 1979—98. Contbr. articles to profl. jours. Fellow: Acad. Clin. Psychology; mem.: APA, N.D. Psychol. Assn. (pres. 1982—83). Office: Family Inst Grand Forks ND 58201 Personal E-mail: jdtyl@mfire.com.

**TYLER, JOHN EDWARD, III,** lawyer; b. Kansas City, Mo. BA, U. Notre Dame, 1986, JD, 1989. Bar: Mo. 1989, Kans. 1990. From assoc. to ptnr. Lathrop & Gage L.C., Kansas City, 1989-99; gen. counsel, sec. Ewing Marion Kauffman Found., Kansas City, 1999—, chief ethics officer, 1999—. Adj. prof. Rockhurst U., Kansas City, 2000—; bd. advisors Nat. Ctr. Philanthropy and Law, NYU, 2003-06; sec. Kauffman Scholars, Inc., Kansas City, 2003—, UEP Gulf Coast, Inc., Kansas City, 2006—; chair Kauffman Innovation Network, Inc., Kansas City, 2006—. Contbr. articles to profl. jours. Pres. Genesis Sch., Kansas City, 1995-97; pres. Archbishop O'Hara H.S., Kansas City, 1994-97, bd. dirs.; pres. Sch. Bd. Diocese of Kansas City-St. Joseph, 2002-2004; chmn. tax increment fin. commn. city of Raytown, Mo., 1997-99; bd. dirs. Ctr. for Mgmt. Assistance, Kansas City, pres., 1999-2001. Recipient Bernie Hoffman award Cmty. Svc. Awards Found., 1997; named Man of Yr. Leukemia Soc., Kansas City, 1998, Best of the Bar, Kansas City Bus. Jour., 2004. Mem. ABA, Mo. Bar Assn. (Thomas D. Cochran award for cmty. svc. 1995), Kans. Bar Assn., Kansas City Met. Bar Assn. (Young Lawyer of Yr. 1998). Home: 2420 SW Wintercreek Ct Lees Summit MO 64081-4085 Office: Ewing Marion Kauffman Found 4801 Rockhill Rd Kansas City MO 64110-2046 Office Phone: 816-932-1293.

**TYLER, LIV,** actress; b. Portland, Maine, Jan. 7, 1977; d. Steven Tyler (lead singer: Aerosmith) and Bebe Buell; m. Royston Langdon, Mar. 25, 2003; 1 child. Motion picture actress and print model. Actress (films): Silent Fall, 1994, Heavy, 1995, Empire Records, 1995, Stealing Beauty, 1996, That Thing You Do!, 1996, Inventing the Abbotts, 1997, U-Turn, 1997, Armageddon, 1998, Onegin, 1999, The Little Black Book, 1999, Cookie's Fortune, 1999, Plunkett & MaCleane, 1999, Dr. T & the Women, 2001, One Night at McCool's, 2001, Lord of the Rings: The Fellowship of the Ring, 2001, The Lord of the Rings: The Two Towers, 2002, The Lord of the Rings: The Return of the King, 2003, Jersey Girl, 2004.; appeared in Aerosmith's music video, Crazy, 1994. Office: c/o Creative Artists Agy 9830 Wilshire Blvd Beverly Hills CA 90212-1804*

**TYLER, LLOYD JOHN,** retired lawyer; b. Aurora, Ill., May 28, 1924; s. Lloyd J. and Dorothy M. (Curtis) T.; m. Inez Chappell Busener, Feb. 25, 1970; children by previous marriage: Barbara Tyler Miller, John R., Benjamin C., Robert B. Amy C. Tomas. BA, Beloit Coll., 1948; JD, U. Mich., 1951. Bar: Ill. 1951, Mich. 1951. Mem. firm Sears, Streit, Tyler and Dreyer and (predecessors), Aurora, Ill., 1951-62, Tyler and Hughes (P.A.), Aurora, 1962-99; ret. Lectr., spkr. on profl. subjects, 1964—. Contbr. chpts. to profl. books, articles to profl. jours. Democratic precinct committeeman, 1954-59; mem. Batavia (Ill.) Sch. Bd., 1959-62. Served with USAAF, 1943-46. Fellow Am. Bar Found.; mem. Am. Bar Assn. (Ho. of Dels. 1975-79), Ill. Bar Assn. (gov. 1970-78, pres. 1978-79, chmn. legislative com. 1980, task force on alternative forms of legal service 1981-82, long range planning com. 1982-88, fed. judiciary appointment com. 1984-90, spl. com. on merit selection 1987—), Ill. Bar Found. (pres. 1972-75), Ill. Inst. Continuing Legal Edn. (dir. 1971-75, 77-79), Ill. Lawyers Polit. Action Com. (trustee 1982—, chmn. 1987-88), Soc. Trial Lawyers Ill., Appellate Lawyers Assn., Phi Beta Kappa, Omicron Delta Kappa. Presbyterian. Home: 701 Fargo Blvd Geneva IL 60134-3227

**TYLER, MICHAEL ROBERT,** lawyer; b. Hollywood, Calif., May 20, 1956; m. Christine D. von Wrangel. BA in history, UCLA, 1979, MA in history, 1980; JD, Loyola Law Sch., LA, 1983; LLM in comparative law, Fitzwilliam Coll., Cambridge U., 1986. Bar: Calif. 1984. Law clk. to the Hon. Arthur Alcaron US Ct. Appeals (9th Cir.), San Francisco, 1987—88; assoc. Heller Ehrman White & McAuliffe, LA, 1991—95; sr. corp. counsel internat. Northrop Grumman Corp., LA, 1995—2000; v.p., group counsel for Europe, Middle East, and Africa ops. Gateway Inc., London, 2000—02, v.p. law for procurement activities Irvine, Calif., 2002—03, v.p., asst. gen. counsel, 2003—04, sr. v.p., gen. counsel, sec., 2004—05, sr. v.p., chief legal & adminstrv. officer, 2005—. Mem.: State Bar Calif. (exec. com. internat. law sect. 1999), ABA (editor-in-chief European Law Bulletin 1989—91, chair European law com. of internat. law and practice sect. 1998). Office: Gateway Inc 7565 Irvine Ctr Dr Irvine CA 92618*

**TYLER, PEGGY LYNNE BAILEY,** lawyer; b. Seattle, Oct. 15, 1948; d. John Thomas and Doris Mae (Lindgren) Bailey; m. Tom Kenneth Newton, May 25, 1975 (div. 1980); m. Allan Gregory Lambert, Aug. 3, 1980 (div. May 1996); m. Charles Kevin Tyler, Sept. 12, 1997; children: Eli Raven, Joshua Alec. BA in Psychology, Beloit Coll., 1970; MS in Counseling Psychology, Ill. Inst. Tech., 1973; JD, Syracuse U., NY, 1978. Bar: D.C. 1983. Mental health specialist Ill. Dept. Mental Health, Chgo., 1971-72; mem. rsch. faculty Cornell U., Ithaca, N.Y., 1973-75; assoc. O'Connor, Sovocool, Pfann and Greenburg, Ithaca, 1978, Dacy, Rivkin & Meyers, Silver Springs, Md., 1979-81; ins. adminstr. Nat. Assn. Broadcasters, Washington, 1981-86, dir. ins. programs, 1986-90; assoc. gen. counsel Architect of the Capitol, Washington, 1990—. Co-author, editor: Broadcaster's Property and Liability Insurance Buying Guide, 1989. Bd. dirs. Hartford-Thayer Condominium Assn., 2004-2006, pres., 1995-96, sec., 1999-2000, treas., 2000-05. Mem. D.C. Bar Assn. (mem. steering com. of arts entertainment, sports law sect. 1989-90, sect. editor newsletter 1989-90). Independent. Jewish. Avocations: antiques, gourmet cooking, ballet. Office: Architect of the Capitol Office General Counsel Rm H2-265A Ford House Office Bldg Washington DC 20515-0001 Office Phone: 202-225-1210. Business E-Mail: ptyler@aoc.gov.

**TYLER, RICHARD,** fashion designer; b. Sunshine, Australia, Sept. 22, 1950; m. Doris Taylor (div.); 1 child, Sheridan; m. Lisa Trafficante, 1989; 1 child, Edward Charles. Design dir. owner Richard Tyler Fashions, Melbourne, Australia, 1968-80, Tyler-Trafficante, L.A., 1988—; design dir. Anne Klein Collection, N.Y.C., 1993-94, 99; fashion dir. owner Tyler Trafficante, Inc., 1999—. Designer Richard Tyler Couture introduced for Women, 1989, Richard Tyler Collection debut for Men, April 1997, Richard Tyler Shoes for Women, 1996, Richard Tyler Collection for Women, 1997, Richard Tyler Shoes for Men, 1997. Recipient New Fashion Talent Perry Ellis award Coun. Fashion Designers Am., 1993, Womenswear Designer of Yr. award, 1994, Perry Ellis award for new fashion talent in menswear, 1995.*

**TYLER, RICHARD JAMES,** personal and professional development educator; b. Warwick, R.I., June 16, 1957; s. Virginia (Campanella) Tyler. Gen. mgr. Gem Exch., Charlotte, NC, 1977; mgr. nat. sales So. Merchandising, Charlotte, 1978; pres. Direct Import Distributing, New Orleans, 1981; dir. nat. territory TV Fanfare Pub., 1982; v.p. ARC Pub., New Orleans, 1983; exec. v.p., gen. mgr. Superior Bedrooms, Inc., 1984; CEO Richard Tyler Internat., Inc., Houston, Internat. Bus. Inst., Inc., Houston, Tyler Internat. Rsch. Inst.,

Inc., Houston, Shopportunities, Houston, Richard Tyler Investments Ltd., 2000. Mem. adv. bd. Sales and Mktg. Mag., N.Y.C., 1991—; founder Leadership of Tomorrow program; profl. speaker, cons. in field. Author: Creating Excellence in Quality and Service, 1991, The Science and Art of Excellent Selling, 1993, Richard Tyler's Guide to Entrepreneurial Excellence, 1993, Richard Tyler's Smart Business Strategies: The Guide to Small Business Marketing Excellence, 1996, The Power of Professional Selling Program, 2002; co-author: Conversations on Faith, 2004, Conversations on Customer Service and Sales, 2005, Conversations on Health and Wellness, 2004, Conversations on Success, 2004, Marketing Magic, 2005, Real World Service Strategies That Work, 2004, Real World Teambuilding Strategies That Work, 2004, Real World Human Resource Strategies That Work, 2004, Leadership Defined, 2005; pub.: (newsletter) Richard Tyler's Excellence Edge, 1992, Entrepreneur Cover Story, 1999; contbr. articles to profl. publs. Mem. Rep.-Senatorial Inner Cir., Washington, 1991, presdl. victory team Rep. Nat. Com.-2002, Tex. rep. pres. club, 2002, Be An Angel Fund Charity. Mem. ASTD, Soc. Human Resource Mgmt., Nat. Speakers Assn., Internat. Platform Assn., Internat. Assn. Entrepreneurs. Avocations: sports, theater, deep sea fishing, amateur wrestling. E-mail: richardtyler@richardtyler.com.

**TYLER, ROBERT R.,** psychologist, consultant; s. Roy E. and Betty J. Tyler; m. Carol J. Albrecht, Mar. 8, 1968; children: Robert R. Tyler, Jr., M. Suzanne McGann. BS in Bus., Chaminade Coll., 1974; MS in Safety, U. So. Calif., 1981; PhD in Psychology, U. Ctrl. Fla., 1997. Cert. comml. pilot FAA, 1970, modeling and simulation profl. Nat. Tng. Systems Assn., Arlington, VA, 2002. Commd. 2d lt. USMC, 1967, advanced through grades to col., 1993; exec. officer, ops. officer Marine Wing Support Group 17, Marine Corps Base Camp Butler, Okinawa, Japan, 1986—87; commdg. officer Marine Aerial Refueling Transport Tng. Squadron 253, Marine Corps Air Station, Cherry Point, NC, 1987—89; dir. aviation safety Hdqs., USMC, Washington, 1990—93; dir. marine corps programs Naval Tng. Systems Ctr., Orlando, 1993—97; ret. USMC, 1997; chief adminstr., nat. aviation & transp. ctr. Dowling Coll., Oakdale, Long Island, NY, 1998—98; human factors advisor to the faa Advancia Corp., Washington, 1998—99; chief scientist Crown Consulting, Inc., 1999—2001; prin. human factors advisor Trios Associates, 2001—02; divsn. dir., simulation tech. svcs. MTS Technologies, Arlington, Va., 2002—05; rsch. scientist Evidence Based Rsch., Inc., Vienna, Va., 2005—. Co-chmn. Internat. / Industry Tng. Simulation and Edn. Conf., Orlando, 1993—97; assoc. editor Marine Corps Gazette, Marine Corps Base Quantico, Va., 1990—93; adj. prof. Embry-Riddle Aero. U., Andrews AFB, 1999—. Co-pres. Potomac H.S. Crew Booster Club, Dumfries, Va., 1984—86; congl. pres. Holy Trinity Luth. Ch., Falls Church, 2000—02; congregational pres. St. Timothy Luth. Ch., Havelock, NC, 1989—99. Decorated 32 Strike Flight Air Medals, Meritorious Svc. medal,, Legion of Merit. Mem.: APA, Marine Corps Aviation Assn., Human Factors and Ergonomic Soc., Aircraft Owners and Pilots Assn., Phi Kappa Phi. Home: 9322 Branchside Lane Fairfax VA 22031-6017 Office: Evidence Based Rsch Inc Ste 250 1595 Spring Hill Rd Vienna VA 22182-2216 Office Phone: 703-287-0382. Personal E-mail: robttyler@msn.com. Business E-Mail: tyler@ebrinc.com.

**TYLER, RONNIE CURTIS,** museum director, art historian; b. Temple, Tex., Dec. 29, 1941; s. Jasper J. and Melba Curtis (James) T.; m. Paula Eyrich, Aug. 24, 1974. BSE, Abilene Christian Coll., TEx., 1964; MA, Tex. Christian U., 1966, PhD (Univ. fellow), 1968; DHL, Austin Coll., 1986. Instr. history Austin Coll., Sherman, Tex., 1967-68, asst. prof., 1968-69; curator history Amon Carter Mus., Ft. Worth, 1969, dir. publications, asst. dir. history and publications, asst. dir. collections and programs, 1984—86, dir., 2006—; prof. history U. Tex., Austin, 1986—2006. Adj. prof. history Tex. Christian U., 1971-72; cons. visual materials Western. Am. art. Author: Santiago Vidaurri and the Confederacy, 1973, The Big Bend: The Last Texas Frontier, 1975, The Image of America in Caricature and Cartoon, 1975, The Cowboy, 1975, The Mexican War: A Lithographic Record, 1974, The Rodeo Photographs of John Addison Stryker, 1978, Visions of America: Pioneer Artists in a New Land, 1983, Views of Texas: The Watercolors of Sarah Ann Hardinge, 1852-56, 1988, Nature's Classics: John James Audubon's Birds and Animals, 1992, Audubon's Great National Work: The Royal Octavo Edition of the Birds of America, 1993, Prints of the West, 1994, Alfred Jacob Miller: Artist as Explorer, 1999; (with Paula Eyrich Tyler) Texas Museums: A Guidebook, 1983; editor: (with Lawrence R. Murphy) The Slave Narratives of Texas, 1974, Posada's Mexico, 1979, Alfred Jacob Miller: Artist on the Oregon Trail, 1982, Wanderings in the Southwest in 1855 (J.D.B. Stillman), 1990, Prints and Printmakers of Texas, 1997. Pres. Tarrant County (Tex.) Hist. Soc., 1975-77; dir. Tex. State Hist. Soc., 1986-2005. Good Neighbor Commn. scholar Instituto Tecnologico Monterrey, Mex., 1967; Am. Philos. Soc. grantee, 1970-71; recipient H. Bailey Carroll award, 1974; Coral H. Tullis award, 1976, Alonso de León medal Sociedad Nuevoleonsa História Geografía y Estadística, 2002. Mem. Am. Antiquarian Soc., Tex. Inst. Letters (Friends of Dallas Pub. Libr. award), Philos. Soc. Tex. (sec. 1990), Phi Beta Kappa. Office: Amon Carter Museum 3501 Camp Bowie Blvd Fort Worth TX 76107-2695 Office Phone: 512-232-2179, 817-989-5095. Business E-Mail: ron.tyler@cartermuseum.org. E-mail: rtyler@mail.utexas.edu.

**TYLER, STEVEN,** singer; b. Yonkers, N.Y., Mar. 26, 1948; children: Liv, Mia. Lead singer Aerosmith, 1970—. Albums Aerosmith, 1973, Get Your Wings, 1974, Toys in the Attic, 1975, Rocks, Pure Gold, 1976, Draw the Line, 1977, Live Bootleg, 1978, A Night in the Ruts, 1979, Greatest Hits, 1980, Rock in a Hard Place, 1982, Done with Mirrors, Classics Live, 1986, Permanent Vacation, 1987, Gems, Pump, 1989, Pandora's Box, 1991, Get a Grip, 1993, Big Ones, Box of Fire, 1994, Nine Lives, 1997, (songs) Honkin' On Bobo, 2004, (from Armageddon soundtrack songs) I Don't Want To Miss A Thing, 1999 (Nominated Oscar Best Song, 1999). Recipient w/Aerosmith: MTV Video of the Year for "Cryin", 1994, Grammy award Best Rock Group.

**TYLER, W(ILLIAM) ED,** finance company executive; b. Cleve. Nov. 3, 1952; s. Ralph Tyler and Edith (Green) Kauer; m. Vickie Sue Boggs, Feb. 7, 1976; children: Stacia Leigh, Adam William. BSEE, Ind. Inst. Tech., 1974; MBA, Ind. U., 1977; postgrad., Harvard U., 1981, Baruch U., 1988. From electronic engr. to exec. v.p. R.R. Donnelley & Sons Co., Warsaw, Ind., 1974—95, exec. v.p. & chief info. officer, 1995—98; CEO, pres. Moore Corp. Ltd., 1998—2001, Willoughby Capitol, Lake Forest, Ill., 2001; CEO Ideapoint Ventures, 2002—. Office Phone: 847-567-7111. Personal E-mail: edtyler1@aol.com.

**TYLER, WILLIAM HOWARD, JR.,** advertising executive, educator; b. Elizabethton, Tenn., May 21, 1932; s. William Howard and Ethel Margaret (Schueler) T.; m. Margery Moss, Aug. 31, 1957; children: William James, Daniel Moss. Student, Iowa State U., 1950-52, U. Iowa, 1952; AB in Lit., BJ in Advt., U. Mo., 1958, MA in Journalism, 1966. Advt. mgr. Rolla (Mo.) Daily News, 1958-59; instr. sch. journalism U. Mo., Columbia, 1959-61; copy writer, then v.p. copy dir. D'Arcy Advt. Agy., St. Louis, 1961-67; writer, producer, creative supr. Gardner Advt. Co., St. Louis, 1967-69; sr. v.p., creative dir. D'Arcy, McManus, Masius, St. Louis, 1969-77; exec. v.p., creative dir. Larson Bateman Advt. Agy., Santa Barbara, Calif., 1977-80; v.p. advt. Pizza Hut, Inc., Wichita, Kans., 1980-82; v.p., creative dir. Frye-Sills/Y&R, Denver, 1980; exec. v.p., creative dir. Gardner Advt. Co., St. Louis, 1982-88; exec. v.p., ptnr., creative dir. Parker Group, St. Louis, 1988-91; pres. Tylertoo Prodns., St. Louis, 1991—. Assoc. prof. St. Louis U., 1993-2003, prof., 2003—. Mng. editor St. Louis Advt. Mag., 1992-95. Trustee Blackburn Coll., Carlinville, Ill., 1983—84; bd. advisors U. Mo. Journalism Sch., 1986—91. Named AAF 9th Dist. Educator of Yr., 1998. Mem. U. Mo. Alumni Assn. (dirs. 1969-70), Advt. Club Greater St. Louis, Golden Key (hon.), Mensa, Kappa Tau Alpha (hon.). Episcopalian. Office: Saint Louis U Dept Comm Xavier 300 3733 W Pine Blvd Saint Louis MO 63108-3305 Office Phone: 314-977-3190. Business E-Mail: tylerwh@slu.edu.

**TYLER GUIDRY, CAROLYN E.,** bishop; b. Jackson, Miss., Aug. 25, 1937; m. Don Guidry; 6 children. Assoc., J.P Campbell Coll., Jackson, Miss.; masters theology, Fuller Theological Seminary, 2004. Women's voter registration chair NAACP; with Security Pacific Bank; pastor AME Church, Indio, Calif., Cane Memorial AME church, Bakersfield, Calif., 1983—89, Walker

Temple AME Church, LA, 1989—94; bishop AME, 2004. Sec. bd. John F. Kennedy Hospital, Indio, Calif.; with Riverside Co. Bd. Mental Health. Office: AME Church 4710 University Blvd N Jacksonville FL 32277 Office Phone: 904-744-0933.

**TYLEVICH, ALEXANDER V.,** sculptor, architect; b. Minsk, Belarus, Sept. 12, 1947; arrived in U.S., 1989; s. Wulf Tylevich and Asia Klebanova; m. Poline M. Dvorkin, Jan. 22, 1981; children: Alexei, Katherine. BA in Arch., Minsk Archtl. Inst., 1965; MA in Arch., Byelorussian Poly. Inst., Minsk, 1971. Prin., sc arch. Minskprojekt, 1971-84; artist, arch. Fine Arts Found., Minsk, 1984-89; sculptor-arch. Tylevich Studio Inc., St. Paul, 1989—. Prin. works include Vincentian Letter, DePaul U., Chgo., Letterdance, Minn. State U., Mankato, River of Memory, La. State Mus., Baton Rouge, Midtown Exchange Sculpture, Mpls., St. Francis de Sales, Morgantown, W.Va., Thomas More Chapel, U. St. Thomas, Mpls., Suspended Cross, Church of St. Peter, Mendota, Minn., St. Victoria Ch., Victoria, Minn., Processional Cross, Cathedral of Christ the King, Superior, Wis., Blue Springs.Net, Blue Springs, Mo., Letters of Creation, Wayzata, Minn., Montessori's Vision: Through the Eyes of a Child, Lake Country Sch., Mpls., Tree of Life, U. Minn., Mpls., Sculpture Anoka Ramsey C.C., Coon Rapids, Minn., Resurrection, Ch. of St. Stephen, Anoka, Minn., Madonna and Child, The Ch. of St. Mary, Alexandria, Minn., Gateway to Belief/Point of Belief, St. Mary's U., Winona, Minn., Thomas Becket, Cath. Cmty. of Thomas Becket, Eagan, Minn., Tribute to Erich Mendelsohn, FORECAST Pub. Artwork, St. Paul, Zenon Possis, North Meml. Hosp., Mpls., Winona Tech. Coll. Aviation Facility, North Shore Synagogue, Syosset, N.Y., Mt. Zion Temple, St. Paul, St. Paul Sem., St. Joseph Abbey, St. Benedict, La., Mepkin Abbey, S.C., Immaculate Conception Cath. Ch., Durham, N.C., Ctr. of Minsk, Minsk City Govt. Bldg., Subway Sta., pvt. collections, exhibited in group shows at Monumental Art of Byelorussia, Minsk, 1989, Nat. Jewish Mus., Washington, 1993, Harvard U. Grad. Sch. Design New Eng., 1993, St. John's U., Collegeville, Minn. Grantee Minn. Met. Regional Arts Coun., 1991, Howard B. Brin Arts Endowment, 1991, FORECAST Pub. Artworks, 1993. Fellow Archtl. Assn. USSR. Home: 1937 Highland Pkwy Saint Paul MN 55116-1350 Personal E-mail: tyleart@aol.com.

**TYLKA, GREGORY L.,** plant pathologist, educator; BS in Biology, California U. Pa., 1983, MS in Biology, 1985; PhD in Plant Pathology, U. Ga., 1990. Asst. prof. dept. plant pathology Iowa State U., Ames, 1990-95, assoc. prof. dept. plant pathology, 1995—. Recipient Prodn. Rsch. award United Soybean Bd., 1998. Mem. Agronomy Soc. Am., Am. Phytopathol. Soc. (Excellence in Ext. award 1999), Am. Soybean Assn., Iowa Soybean Assn., Helminthological Soc. Washington, Soc. Nematologists, Soil Sci. Soc. Am., Sigma Xi, Beta Beta Beta (Outstanding Alumnus award 1992), Gamma Sigma Delta. Achievements include research on the effects of cultural practices and soybean resistance and tolerance on soybean cyst nematode population densities and soybean yields. Office: Iowa State U Dept Plant Pathology 321 Bessey Hall Ames IA 50011 Fax: 515-294-3851. E-mail: gltylka@iastate.edu.

**TYLLIA, FRANK MICHAEL,** academic administrator, educator; b. Rossland, B.C., Can., Dec. 1, 1942; arrived in US, 1942; s. Alex J. and Lenora M. (Janni) T.; m. Kathryn A. McWalter, Mar. 21, 1970. BBA, Gonzaga U., 1965, BA in Edn., 1967; MA in Edn., Seattle U., 1972. Tchr. pub. schs., Seattle, 1967-72, prin., 1972-78, Edmonds Sch. Dist., Lynnwood, Wash., 1978-97; field supr. M Tchg. City U., Bellevue, Wash., 1997—, field supr. edn. leadership, 1999—. Adj. prof. Seattle Pacific U., 1990—, Mont. State U., 1999—. Active alumni mentoring program Gonzaga U., Seattle, 1993—; mem. Kirkland Cmty. Accountability Bd.; active King County Juvenile Justice, 1997—; mem. King County Diversion Adv. Bd., 1998—. Mem. ASCD, Assn. Wash. Sch. Prins. (various coms.), Washington Athletic Club, Phi Delta Kappa. Home and Office: 4527 103d Ln NE Kirkland WA 98033-7639

**TYMAS-JONES, RAYMOND,** dean; s. Raymond Jones, Sr. and Burnetta Tymas Jones; m. Shirley Diane Romeo, June 22, 1968 (div. Sept. 19, 1982); children: Chrishaun Jones, Raymond Jones. MusB, Howard U., 1977; MusM, Wash. U., 1979; PhD, Wash. U., St. Louis, 1988. Assoc. prof. music Buffalo State Coll., 1983—93, assoc. dean, asst. to dean, 1990—93; assoc. prof. music U. No. Iowa, Cedar Falls, 1993—97, dir. of the sch. of music, 1993—98, prof. of music, 1997; prof. music Ohio U., Athens, 1998—, dean, coll. fine arts, 1998—. Music dir. World Student Games, Buffalo, 1991; music director, chorus director Univ. Games, Buffalo, 1993; panelist Ohio Arts Coun., Columbus, Ohio, 2001—; Guber nat. appointment Ohio Arts Coun. Bd., 2004. Bd. dirs. Southwestern Ohio Cultural Arts Ctr., Athens 2000; ex-officio bd. dirs. Ohio Valley Summer Theatre, Athens, 2000; v.p. Athena Cinemas Co/Athena Cinema Theater, Athens, Ohio, 2000. Grantee Rsch. Multiculturalism Music Edn., SUNY, 1991, Cmty. Enrichment, Rouse Corp., 1994, Ohio Arts Coun., 2002, Ohio U., 2002. Mem.: Coun. Coll. Arts Sci. (assoc.; presenter 2001), Ohio Arts Coun. (assoc.; support panel 2001), Internat. Coun. Fine Arts Deans (assoc.; bd. dirs. 1999). Avocations: wine, reading, cooking. Office: College of Fine Arts Ohio University 54 E Union St Jennings House Athens OH 45701 Office Phone: 740-593-1809. Personal E-mail: tymas-jo@ohio.edu, rtymasjones2@msn.com.

**TYMES, NATHANIEL, JR.,** statistician, educator; b. Montgomery, Ala., Feb. 10, 1959; s. Nathaniel Tymes, Sr. and Annie Jean Tymes. BS, U. Ala., Tuscaloosa, 1981; MDiv, United Theol. Sem., Dayton, Ohio, 1985; MS, Air Force Inst. Tech., Dayton, 1987; MA, U. NMex, 1995, PhD, 2002. Commd. 2d lt. USAF, 1981, advanced through grades to maj., 1994; space systems performance analyst Nat. Aerospace Intelligence Ctr., Wright-Patterson AFB, Ohio, 1981—85; air-to-air vulnerability analyst Aero. Sys. Divsn., Eglin, AFB, Fla., 1987—91; operational effectivenss test mgr. HQ Air Force Operational Test and Evaluation Ctr., Kirtland AFB, N.Mex., 1991—94; sr. weapon systems analyst Office Aerospace Studies, Kirtland AFB, N.Mex., 1994—97; ret. USAF, 1997; asst. prof. stats. Ferris State U., Big Rapids, Mich., 2002—. Part time instr. Okaloosa-Walton C.C., Niceville, Fla., 1988—91; adj. instr. math and religion St. Leo Coll., Hurlburt FLD, Fla., 1989—91; instr. math and quantitative methods Troy State U. - Fla. Region, Hurlburt FLD, Fla., 1990—91; part-time instr. math. Albuquerque Tech.-Vocat. Inst., 1996—2002; tchg. asst. U. N.Mex, Albuquerque, 1997—2002. Tutor Wesley Cmty. Ctr., Dayton, Ohio, 1982—87; vol. mentor Partness In Success, Dayton, 1983—2000; mem. Ferris State Univ. Academic Senate, 2002—; mem. applied stats. team COB Rep. Ferris Faculty Assn. Exec. Book, 2002—; asst. to pastor Home Ave First Ch. of God, Dayton, 1983—87. Named Vol. of the Yr., Wesley Cmty. Ctr., 1983, Partners In Success, 1984—85. Mem.: Soc. for Indsl. and Applied Math., Interface Found. N.Am., Inst. Ops. Rsch. and Mgmt. Sci., Am. Stats. Assn., Am. Math. Soc., Kappa Mu Epsilon. Libertarian. Achievements include research in attrition at the Air Force Academy; use of multiwavelets in signal denoising. Home: 18912 Serenity Dr Big Rapids MI 49307 Office: Ferris State Univ 119 South St Big Rapids MI 49307 Office Phone: 231-591-2767. Personal E-mail: ntymes@charter.net. E-mail: tymesn@ferris.edu.

**TYMKOVICH, TIMOTHY MICHAEL,** federal judge; b. Denver, Nov. 2, 1956; married; 2 children. BA, Co. Coll., 1979; JD, U. Colo. Sch. Law, 1982. Clk. Co. Supreme Ct., 1982—83; assoc. Davis, Graham & Stubbs, 1983—89; of counsel Bradley Campbel Carney & Madsen, 1990—91; solicitor gen. Office of Co. Atty. Gen., 1991—96; ptnr. Hale Hackstaff Tymkovich & ErkenBrack, 1996—2003; judge US Ct. of Appeals (10th cir), 2003—. Mem.: ABA, Internat. Soc. Barristers, Colo. Bar Found., Am. Law Inst. Office: Byron White US Courthouse 1823 Stout St Denver CO 80257*

**TYMOCZKO, JULIANNA SOPHIA,** mathematics professor; b. Northampton, Mass., Aug. 10, 1975; d. Thomas and Maria Tymoczko. BA, Harvard U., Cambridge, Mass., 1997; MA, Princeton U., NJ, 2003. Habdarsh asst. prof. U. Mich., Ann Arbor, 2003—. Contbr. articles to profl. jours. Nat. Def. Sci. and Engring. grad. fellow, Dept. of Def., 1999—2002, Postdoctoral Rsch. fellow, NSF, 2004—.

**TYNDALL, DAVID GORDON,** business educator; b. Bangalore, India, Nov. 19, 1919; s. Joseph and Annie E. (Parsons) T.; m. Margaret Patricia Davies, Apr. 4, 1942; children: Caroline Lee, David Gordon, Benjamin. BComm, U. Toronto, 1940, MA, 1941; PhD, U. Calif., 1948. Asst. prof. bus. adminstrn. Cornell U., Ithaca, N.Y., 1947-49; assoc. prof. Carnegie-Mellon U., Pitts., 1949-53; assoc. prof., dir. analytical studies U. Calif., Berkeley, 1955-67. V.p. fin. and adminstrn., investment officer U. Alta., Edmonton, 1967-74; prof. fin., 1974-79; lectr. U. Calif. Berkeley, 1979-82; investment adv. Berkeley, 1979-96. With Royal Can. Air Force and Army, 1942—45. Fulbright fellow, 1952 Unitarian-Buddhist. Home: 88 Clarewood Ln Oakland CA 94618-2243 E-mail: gordonty@pacbell.net.

**TYNE, MICHAEL D.,** architectural firm executive; Founding mem. Ross Planning Assocs., 1968—77; joined Karlsberger Cos., Columbus, Ohio, 1977, COO, exec. v.p., pres., CEO, 1987—, chmn., 1994—. Former pres. Simon Kenton Coun., Ohio. Office: Karlsberger Cos 99 E Main St Columbus OH 43215-5189

**TYNER, LEE REICHELDERFER,** lawyer; b. Annapolis, Md., Mar. 12, 1946; d. Thomas Elmer and Eleanor Frances (Leland) Reichelderfer; m. Carl Frederick Tyner, Aug. 31, 1968; children: Michael Frederick, Rachel Christine, Elizabeth Frances. BA, St. John's Coll., 1968; MS, U. Wash., 1970; JD, George Washington U., 1975. Bar: D.C., U.S. Dist. Ct. (D.C.), U.S. Ct. Appeals (4th cir., 1st cir., 9th cir., D.C. cir., 5th cir., 8th cir., 11th cir., 10th cir.), U.S. Ct. Claims, U.S. Supreme Ct. Profl. staff U.S. Senate Commerce Com., Washington, 1970-72; trial atty. Land and Natural Resources div. U.S. Dept. Justice, Washington, 1975-85; atty. Office of Gen. Counsel U.S. EPA, Washington, 1985—. Bd. dirs. Grace Episcopal Day Sch., Silver Spring, Md., 1987-89, vestry Grace Episcopal Ch., 1997-2003, 2004—; den leader, cubmaster Boy Scouts Am., Silver Spring, 1987-91. Recipient Bronze medals, U.S. EPA, 1988, 1992, 2002, 2003. Mem.: Order of the Coif. Episcopalian. Home: 1401 Geranium St NW Washington DC 20012-1401 Office: US EPA 2366A 1200 Pennsylvania Ave NW Washington DC 20460 Personal E-mail: skildpadde@aol.com. Business E-Mail: tyner.lee@epa.gov.

**TYNER, NEAL EDWARD,** retired insurance company executive; b. Grand Island, Nebr., Jan. 30, 1930; s. Edward Raymond and Lydia Dorothea (Kruse) T.; children: Karen Tyner Redrow, Morgan. BBA, U. Nebr., 1956. Jr. analyst Bankers Life Nebr., Lincoln, 1956-62, asst. v.p. securities, 1962-67, v.p. securities, treas., 1967-69, fin. v.p., treas., 1970-72, sr. v.p. fin., treas., 1972-83, pres., chief exec. officer, 1983-87, chmn., pres., chief exec. officer, 1987-88, chmn., CEO, 1988-95; pres. Net Cons., Paradise Valley, Ariz., 1995—. Bd. dirs. Union Bank & Trust Co. Trustee U. Nebr. Found., Lincoln Found. Capt. USMC, 1950-54, Korea. Fellow: CFAs. Lutheran. Avocations: tennis, computers. Office: 8225 N Golf Dr Paradise Valley AZ 85253-2716

**TYNER, WALLACE EDWARD,** agricultural economics educator; b. Orange, Tex., Mar. 21, 1945; s. Richard D. and Jeanne (Gullahorn) T.; m. Jean M. Young, May 2, 1970; children: Davis, Jeffrey. BS in Chemistry, Tex. Christian U., 1966; MA in Econs., U. Md., 1972, PhD in Econs., 1977. Vol. Peace Corps., India, 1966-68, math, sci., ednl. skill desk chief Washington, 1968-70; grad. teacher asst. U. Md., Balt., 1971-73; assoc. scientist Earth Satellite Corp., Washington, 1973-74; rsch. assoc. Cornell U., Ithaca, NY, 1974-77; asst. prof., assoc. prof. natural resource econs. and internat. devel. policy Purdue U., West Lafayette, Ind., 1977-84, prof., asst. dept. head, 1983-88, dept. head, 1989—2002. Cons. UN Food and Agrl. Orgn., Rome, Office Tech. Assessment, Washington, U.S. Dept. Interior, Washington, OECD, Paris, World Bank, Washington, USDA, Washington. Author: Energy Resources and Economic Development in India, 1978, A Perspective on U.S. Farm Problems and Agricultural Policy, 1987. Recipient Disting. Policy Contbn. award, AAEA, 2005. Mem. Am. Agrl. Economists, Am. Econs. Assn., Internat. Assn. Agrl. Economists, Internat. Soc. Xi, Gamma Sigma Delta. Home: 116 Arrowhead Dr West Lafayette IN 47906-2105 Office: Purdue U Krannert Bldg West Lafayette IN 47907-1145 Office Phone: 765-494-0199. Business E-Mail: wtyner@purdue.edu.

**TYNES, ROBERT DICK,** artist, educator; b. Chgo., Jan. 7, 1953; s. Marion F. and Faye Tynes Dick; m. Bette L. Bates, June 13, 1981; children: Alison Hayley, Robin Elizabeth. BA with hons. in Art, Rhodes Coll., Memphis, Tenn., 1975; MFA in Painting, East Carolina U., Greenville, NC, 1981. Lectr. art East Carolina U., 1981—82, Humboldt State U., Arcata, Calif., 1982—84; vis. asst. prof. art U. Hawaii Manoa, Honolulu, 1986—87; artist-in-residence U. NC, Asheville, 1987—91, from asst. prof. to prof. art, 1991—2004, prof. art, 2004—. Dir. U. Gallery U. NC, 1994—. Over 20 one-man exhbns., over 95 group shows, exhibitions include Fay Gold Gallery, Atlanta, Ga., 2001, Lee Hansley Gallery, Raleigh, NC, 2004, Weizenblatt Gallery, Mars Hill Coll., 2005, Blue Spiral, Asheville, NC, 2006, Represented in permanent collections Charlotte Pub. Arts Commn., IBM Corp., Field Engring. Ctr., Atlanta, Ga. Chair Black Mountain Coll. Mus. and Art Ctr., Asheville, NC, 1993—95; dir. Asheville Area Arts Coun., 1994—2002, sec., 2000—02; dir. Black Mountain Ctr. Arts, NC, 2003—04, sec., 2004. Recipient We. NC Regional Juried Exhbn. 1st prize, Asheville Art Mus., 1993; fellow, Roswell Mus. and Art Ctr., Roswell, N.Mex., 1985, 1991, Ucross Found. Residency Program, Wyo., 1986. Democrat. Unitarian Universalist. Achievements include development of original style of painting juxtaposing abstract brush marks with hyperrealistic trompe l'oeil illusionism; original style of cutout paintings. Avocations: hiking, tennis. Office: Dept of Art Univ of NC Asheville One University Heights Asheville NC 28804 Office Phone: 828-251-6880. Business E-Mail: rtynes@unca.edu.

**TYNG, ANNE GRISWOLD,** architect; b. Kuling, Kiangsi, China, July 14, 1920; d. Walworth and Ethel Atkinson (Arens) T.; 1 child, Alexandra Stevens. AB, Radcliffe Coll., 1942; M of Architecture, Harvard U., 1944; PhD, U. Pa., 1975. Assoc. Stonorov & Kahn, Architects, 1945-47; assoc. Louis I. Kahn Architect, 1947-73; pvt. practice architecture Phila., 1973—; adj. assoc. prof. architecture U. Pa. Grad. Sch. Fine Arts, 1968-96. Assoc. cons. architect Phila. Planning Commn. and Phila. Redevel. Plan, 1954; vis. disting. prof. Pratt Inst., 1979-81, vis. critic architecture, 1969; vis. critic architecture Rensselaer Poly. Inst., 1969, 78, Carnegie Mellon U., 1970, Drexel U., 1972-73, Cooper Union, 1974-75, U. Tex., Austin, 1976; lectr. Archtl. Assn., London, Xian U., China, Bath U., Eng., Mexico City, Hong Kong U., 1989, Baltic Summer Sch., Architecture and Planning, Tallinn, Estonia, Parnu, Estonia, 1993, Alicante U., Spain, 1997, Barcelona U., Spain, 1997; panel spkr. Nat. Conv. Am. Inst. Architects, N.Y.C., 1988, also numerous univs., throughout U.S. and Can.; asst. leader People to People Archtl. del. to China, 1983; vis. artist Am. Acad., Rome, 1995. Subject of films Anne G. Tyng at Parsons Sch. of Design, 1972, Anne G. Tyng at U. of Minn., 1974, Connecting, 1976, Forming the Future, 1977; interview by Robert Kirkbride, Form is Number and Number is Form, 2005; work included in Smithsonian Travelling Exhbn., 1979-81, 82, Louis I. Kahn: In the Realm of Architecture, 1990-94, Mus. Contemporary Art Travelling Exhbn., L.A., 1998—; author, editor: Louis Kahn to Anne Tyng, The Rome Letters 1953-1954, 1997; contbr. articles to profl. publs.; prin. works include Walworth Tyng Farmhouse (Hon. mention award Phila. chpt. AIA 1953); builder (with G. Yanchenko) Probability Pyramid, 1984. Fellow, Graham Found. for Advanced Study in Fine Arts, 1965, 1979—81. Fellow AIA (Brunner grantee N.Y. chpt. 1964, 83, dir. mem. exec. bd. dirs. Phila. chpt. 1976-78, John Harbeson Disting. Svc. award Phila. chpt. 1991); mem. Nat. Acad. Design (nat. academician), C.G. Jung Ctr. Phila. (planning com. 1979-97), Form Forum (co-founder, planning com. 1978-85). Democrat. Episcopalian. Office Phone: 415-464-1424.

**TYRANGIEL, JOSH,** editor; MA in Am. Studies, Yale U. News prodr. MTV; with Rolling Stone, Vibe; music critic Time mag., NYC, 2001—06; editor Time.com, NYC, 2006—. Office: Time & Life Bldg Rockefeller Ctr 1271 Ave of the Americas New York NY 10020-1393 Office Phone: 212-522-9883. Office Fax: 212-522-0003. E-mail: josh_tyrangiel@timemagazine.com.*

**TYRBERG, BJÖRN,** cell biologist; b. Lund, Skåne, Sweden, Sept. 18, 1970; s. Pär and Elisabeth Tyrberg; m. Ulrika Bergström, July 15, 2006. MS in Pharmacy, Uppsala U., Sweden, 1995, PhD, 1999. Fellow Uppsala U., Sweden, 1995—99, post doctoral fellow, 2000—05; scientist Burnham Inst. Med. Rsch., La Jolla, Calif., 2006—. Contbr. articles to profl. jours. 2d lt. Swedish Army, 1999—2000. Fellow, Swedish Acad. Pharm. Scis., 2000—01, Swedish Soc. Medicine, 2000—01, U. Calif., La Jolla, 2000—05, Larry L. Hillblom Found., 2002—05, Calif. Inst. Regenerative Medicine, 2006; grantee, Novo Nordisk Found., 2005, Royal Physiographic Soc., 2005. Mem.: Swedish Acad. Pharm. Scis. (bd. mem. Uppland sect. 1994—95), European Assn. Study Diabetes, Internat. Soc. Stem Cell Rsch. (assoc.). Lutheran. Achievements include research in growth and differentiation of pancreatic insulin producing beta-cells, as well as destruction of beta-cells in diabetes. Office: Burnham Institute for Medical Research 10901 N Torrey Pines Rd La Jolla CA 92037 Office Phone: 1-858-822-4178. Office Fax: 1-858-795-6298.

**TYREE, ALAN DEAN,** clergyman; b. Kansas City, Mo., Dec. 14, 1929; s. Clarence Tillman and Avis Ora (Gross) T.; m. Gladys Louise Omohundro, Nov. 23, 1951; children: Lawrence Wayne, Jonathan Tama, Sharon Avis. BA, U. Iowa, 1950; postgrad., U. Mo.-Columbia, 1956-58, U. Mo.-Kansas City, 1961-62. Ordained to ministry Cmty. of Christ, 1947. Appointee min., Lawrence, Kans., 1950-52; mission administr. (Mission Sanito), French Polynesia, 1953-64; regional adminstr. Denver, 1964-66; mem. Council Twelve Apostles, Independence, Mo., 1966-82, sec., 1980-82, mem. First Presidency, 1982-92; ret. First Presidency, 1992; pastor East 39th Street Congregation Cmty. of Christ, Independence, 2000—02. Mem. Joint Coun. and Bd. Appropriations, 1966-92; originator music appreciation broadcasts Radio Tahiti, 1962-64, Mission Sanito Radio Ministry, 1960-64; instr. Music/Arts Inst., 1992-2005, Met. C.C.'s, 1994-2005. Editor: Cantiques des Saints French-Tahitian hymnal, 1965, Exploring the Faith: A Study of Basic Christian Beliefs, 1987; mem. editing com.: Hymns of the Saints, 1981; author: The Gospel Graced by a People: A Biography of Persons in Tahiti, 1993, From Enry: Proclaimer of Good News, 1995, Priesthood: For Other's Sake, 1996, God: Getting to Know the Unknown, 1998. Bd. dirs. Outreach Internat. Found., 1979-82, mem. corp. body, 1982-92; mem. corp. body Independence Regional Health Ctr., 1982-92, v.p., 1983-92, bd. dirs., 1984-93; mem. bd. pupils. Herald House, 1984-92; mem. corp. body Restoration Trail Found., 1982-92; chmn. Temple Art Com., 1988-94; bd. dirs. Independence Symphony Orch., 1992-96, pres., 1995-96; mem. human rels. commn. city of Independence, 1995-97, chmn., 1996-97. Recipient Elbert A. Smith Meml. award for publ. articles, 1968, 72 Mem. Phi Beta Kappa, Phi Eta Sigma. Home and Office: 3408 S Trail Ridge Dr Independence MO 64055 Office Phone: 816-373-8151. E-mail: tyree@mail.com.

**TYREE, JAMES C.,** insurance company executive; b. 1957; m. Eve Tyree; 3 children. BS in Finance, Ill. State U., 1978, MBA, 1980. With Mesirow Ins. Svcs. Inc., Chgo., 1980—, chmn., CEO, 1994—. Mem. Juv. Diabetes Rsch. Found. Internat.; bd trustee Roosevelt Univ.; bd. dirs. Illinois State U. Found., Saint Xavier U., Marist High Sch.; chmn. bd. City Colleges of Chgo. Named Person of the Year, Juv. Diabetes Rsch. Found., 2004; recipient E. Burton Mercier Service award, Illinois State U., 2000, Coll. of Business Alumni Hall of Fame, 2003, Disting. Alumni award, 2005. Mem.: Exec. Club, Econ. Club. Office: Mesirow Ins Svcs Inc 350 N Clark St Chicago IL 60610-4712

**TYRITY, KATHY MILICA,** reporter, editor; b. Akron, Ohio, Dec. 19, 1953; d. Zirovko Chirich and Ada Fay Tyrity; m. Robert Laird Brockruoy, Oct. 12, 1974 (div. Dec. 19, 1977); 1 child, Sara Bays. BS, Butler U., Indianapolis, IN; Diploma (hon.), Silva. Reporter Sarasota (Fla.) Herald Tribune, 1978—83; city editor Sarasota Times, 1983—89; corr. reporter Akron Beacon Jour., Akron, Ohio, 1991—94; city editor Coshocton Tribune, Coshocton, Ohio, 1994—95; sec. Estate of Don Quist, Hudson, Ohio, 1995—2000; corr. reporter Sun Newspaper, Medina, Ohio, 1999—2002; asst. tchr. Akron(Ohio) Pub. Schools, 2001—02. Author: three books. Active Republicans of Sarasota Club, Sarasota, Fla., 1977—89; psychic Akron Psychic Fairs, Cleveland, Akron, Canton, Ohio; healer Akron Theosophy Soc., Akron, Ohio. Recipient Second Pl., Nat. Associated Collegiate Press, 1976, Mark Distinciton as Photo Editor, 1976, Most Coop., Journalism Award, Kenmore H.S., 1971. Mem.: Grand Cross, Rainbow Order (advisor 1970—74), Internat. Theosophy Club, Sigma Delta Chi (hon.; journalist 1976—). Achievements include research in Notable findings in medical research on psychics. Avocations: drawing, sketching, painting, doing healings, giving readings.

**TYRL, PAUL,** mathematics professor, researcher; b. Prague, Czech Rep., Dec. 24, 1951; came to U.S., 1970, naturalized, 1978; s. Vladimir Tyrl and Marta Kocian. BA with honors, N.J. City U., 1977, MA, 1980; EdD, Rutgers U., 1987. Cert. tchr. secondary edn., higher edn. N.J. quality contr. Agfa-Perutz, Munich, 1969—70; technician AT&T, Kearny, NJ, 1970—73; acquisition libr. N.J. City U., 1973—74, supr. post office, 1974—76, dir. math. lab., instr. math., 1976—80; instr. math. Hudson County C.C., NJ, 1980—82, assoc. prof., coord. math., 1982—84; prof., chmn. math., acad. coord., curriculum dir. Sch. New Resources-New Rochelle Coll., N.Y.C., 1984—. Rschr. Rutgers U., New Brunswick, N.J., 1980—; cons. Jersey City Bd. Edn., N.J., 1982—. Contbr. articles to profl. jours. Recipient Commemorative medal of honor, 1986. Mem. AAAS, ASCD, Nat. Coun. Tchrs. Math. (reviewer and referee), N.Y. Acad. Scis., Am. Ednl. Rsch. Assn., Math. Assn. Am., Am. Math. Assn. 2-Yr. Colls., Am. Math. Soc., Am. Mus. Natural History, Nat. Geog. Soc., Nat. Wildlife Fedn., Smithsonian Instn. Roman Catholic. Achievements include research in math. anxiety and math. problem solving.

**TYRRELL, D. LORNE J.,** university dean; Dean U. Alberta Faculty Medicine and Dentistry, Edmonton, Canada, 1994—; dir. Glaxo Heritage Research Institute. Officer of the Order of Canada Govt. of Canada, 2002. Recipient ASTech award for innovation and science, Kaplan award for excellence in research, Prix Galien Canada medal for research, Gold medal, The Canadian Liver Foundation, 2000, Alberta Order of Excellence, Province of Alberta, 2000. Office: Dept Medical Microbiology & Immunology Univ Alberta 606 Heritage Medical Rsch Ctr Edmonton AB T6G 2S2 Canada

**TYRRELL, GERALD GETTYS,** banker; b. Canton, China, Dec. 27, 1938; came to U.S., 1940. s. Gerald Fraser and Virginia Lee (Gettys) T.; m. Jane Haldeman, June 1961 (div. Aug. 1975); children: Gerald F., Jane N., Robert M.; m. Elizabeth Ann Drautman, Mar. 31, 1978. BA, Yale U., 1960; MA, Rutgers U., 1971. Cert. real estate financier. With 1st Nat. Bank of Louisville, 1961—89, sr. v.p., 1975—81, exec. v.p., 1981—89; pres., chmn. Churchill Mortgage Corp., 1975—77; chief fin. cons. City of Louisville Office of Downtown Devel., 1989—2000; exec. v.p. Univ Group, Consultants for Bus., Prospect, 2000—. Vice chmn. bd. dirs. Porcelain Metals Corp., 2001—06. Author: A Positive Approach to Financing Black Business, 1972 Trustee, treas. Patton Mus., Ft. Knox, Ky., 1970—96; treas. Soc. Colonial Wars in Commonwealth of Ky., 1970—89, sec., 1996—99, gov., 2000—05; treas. gen. Gen. Soc. Colonial Wars, 2004—; mem. exec. bd. Boy Scouts Am., 1983—; bd. dirs. The Louisville Orch., 1984—90, Crane Ho., The Asia Inst., 1988—, pres. 1995—97; bd. dirs., chmn. fin. com. Glassworks Found., Inc., 2001—03; bd. dirs. Thomas Merton Found., 2003—05. Served to capt. U.S. Army, 1960—68. Recipient Disting. Service Ribbon Ky. Nat. Guard, 1966 Mem. Robert Morris Assocs., Nat. Soc. Real Estate Fin. (bd. govs), Louisville Country Club, Pendennis Club. Democrat. Avocations: fine wines, tennis. Personal E-mail: betsyandgerald@aol.com.

**TYRRELL, JOSEPH MORTEN,** retired history professor; b. Kirkland Lake, Ontario, Can., Sept. 19, 1927; s. George Carey and Dora Madeline Joslin Tyrell; m. Margaret Bell Smith, Dec. 17, 1955; children: Anne Katherine Mary Tyrell, Joseph Douglas George Tyrell, Diana J.B. Tyrell Suchla. BA, U. Toronto, Can., 1950; diplome in French, U. Rennes, France, 1951; MA, U. Toronto, Can., 1955; PhD, Emory U., Atlanta, 1961. Acting asst. prof. Coll. Charleston, SC, 1958—59; asst. prof. Old Dominion U., Norfolk, Va., 1959—79, prof. emeritus of history, 1984—. Author: A History

of the Estates of Poitou, 1968, Louis XI (#82 in Twayne World Leaders Series), 1980; contbr. articles to encys., to profl. jours. Mem.: Mediaeval Acad. of Am., Am. Hist. Assn. Episcopalian.

**TYRRELL, ROBERT EMMETT, JR.,** editor-in-chief, writer; b. Chgo., Dec. 14, 1943; s. R. Emmett and Patricia (Rogers) T.; m. Judy Mathews Tyrrell, Feb. 12, 1972 (div. Dec. 1989); children: Patrick, Kathryn, Anne; m. Jeanne Hauch Tyrrell, May 23, 1998. BA, Ind. U., 1965, MA, 1967. Founder, editor-in-chief The Am. Spectator, Arlington, Va., 1967—. Chmn. Am. Alternative Found., Inc., Arlington, Va., 1967—; adj. fellow Hudson Inst. Author: Public Nuisances, 1979, The Liberal Crack-Up, 1984, The Conservative Crack-up, 1992, Boy Clinton: The Political Biography, 1996, (with anonymous author) The Impeachment of William Jefferson Clinton, 1997, Madame Hillary: The Dark Road to the White House, 2004; editor: Network News Treatment of the 1972 Democratic Presidential Candidates, 1972, The Future That Doesn't Work, 1977, Orthodoxy, 1987; writer nationally syndicated polit. column; contbg. editor: The New York Sun. Recipient Am. Eagle award Invest in Am. Coun., 1977; named Greatest Pub. Svc. Performed by an American 35 Years or Under award Am. Inst. for Pub. Svc., 1977, Ten Most Outstanding Young Men in Am., Jaycees, 1978. Roman Catholic. Avocations: handball, fishing, listening to classical music, reading. Office: The American Spectator 1611 N Kent St Arlington VA 22201

**TYSON, CICELY,** actress; b. NYC, Dec. 19, 1933; d. William and Theodosia Tyson; m. Miles Davis, 1981 (div. 1988). Student, NYU, Actors Studio; doctorate (hon.), Atlanta U., Loyola U., Lincoln U. Former sec., model. Co-founder Dance Theatre of Harlem; bd. dirs. Urban Gateways Actor: (off-Broadway plays) The Blacks, 1961-63, Moon on a Rainbow Shawl, 1962-63, Tiger, Tiger, Burning Bright, Broadway; (films) Odds Against Tomorrow, 1959, The Last Angry Man, 1959, A Man Called Adam, 1966, The Comedians, 1967, The Heart is a Lonely Hunter, 1968, Sounder, 1972 (Best Actress, Atlanta Film Festival, Nat. Soc. Film Critics, Acad. award nominee, Best Actress, Emmy award, Best Actress in a spl., 1973), The Blue Bird, 1976, The River Niger, 1976, A Hero Ain't Nothin' but a Sandwich, 1978, The Concorde-Airport 79, 1979, Bustin' Loose, 1981, Fried Green Tomatoes, 1991, Hoodlum, 1997, Because of Winn-Dixie, 2005, Diary of a Mad Black Woman, 2005 (Outstanding Supporting Actress in a Motion Picture, NAACP Image award, 2006), Madea's Family Reunion, 2006, Fat Rose and Squeaky, 2006, Idlewild, 2006; (TV series) East Side, West Side, 1963-64, The Guiding Light, 1966, Sweet Justice, 1994-95; (TV films) Marriage: Year One, 1971, The Autobiography of Miss Pittman, 1974 (Emmy award Actress of the Year, 1974, Emmy award Best Lead Actress in a Drama, 1974), Just an Old Sweet Song, 1976, Wilma, 1977, A Woman Called Moses, 1978, The Marva Collins Story, 1981, Benny's Place, 1982, Playing With Fire, 1985, Samaritan: The Mitch Snyder Story, 1986, Acceptable Risks, 1986, Intimate Encounters, 1986, The Women of Brewster Place, 1989, Heat Wave, 1990 (Cable Ace award 1991), The Kid Who Loved Christmas, 1990, When No One Would Listen, 1992, Duplicates, 1992, House of Secrets, 1993, Oldest Living Confederate Widow Tells All, 1994 (Emmy award Best Supporting Actress), Road to Galveston, 1996, Bridge of Time, 1997, The Prince of Heaven, 1997, Riot, 1997, Ms. Scrooge, 1997, Mama's Flora Family, 1998 (Image award 1999), Always Outnumbered, 1998, A Lesson Before Dying, 1999, Aftershock: Earthquake in NY, 1999, Jewel, 2001, The Rosa Parks Story, 2002; (TV miniseries) Roots, 1977, King, 1978,; TV appearances include: Frontiers of Faith, 1961, The Nurses, 1962, Naked City, 1963, I Spy, 1965, 66, Cowboy in Africa, 1967, The FBI, 1968, 69, Here Comes the Brides, 1970, Mission Impossible, 1970, Gunsmoke, 1970, Emergency!, 1972, B.L. Stryker, 1990, Touched by an Angel, 2000, The Outer Limits, 2000. Trustee Human Family Inst.; trustee Am. Film Inst. Recipient Vernon Price award, 1962; also awards NAACP Nat. Council Negro Women; Capitol Press award. Mem.: Delta Sigma Theta (hon.).*

**TYSON, CYNTHIA HALDENBY,** academic administrator; b. Scunthorpe, Lincolnshire, Eng., July 2, 1937; came to U.S., 1959; d. Frederick and Florence Edna (Stacey) Haldenby; children: Marcus James, Alexandra Elizabeth. BA, U. Leeds, Eng., 1958, MA, 1959, PhD, 1971; DHL (hon.), Mary Baldwin Coll., 2003, Queens U., Charlotte, 2006. Lectr. Brit. Council, Leeds, 1959; faculty U. Tenn., Knoxville, 1959-60, Seton Hall U., South Orange, NJ, 1963-69; faculty, v.p. Queens Coll., Charlotte, NC, 1969-85; pres. Mary Baldwin Coll., Staunton, Va., 1985—2003, pres. emerita, 2003—; pres. Robert Haywood Morrison Found., 2002—. Pres. adv. cir. Queens U., Charlotte, NC, 2005—; WDAV radio adv. bd. Davidson (NC) Coll., 2005—. Contbr. articles to profl. jours. Mem. Va. Internat. Trade Commn., Richmond, 1987; trustee Am. Frontier Culture Mus., Va.; mem. Va. Lottery Bd., 1987-94; chair selection com. State of Va. Rhodes Scholarship Competition, 1993-97; bd. dirs. Cmty. Found. Staunton, Augusta County and Waynesboro, 1993-98; mem. adv. bd. WDAV Radio of Davidson Coll., 2005—; mem. pres.'s adv. cir. Queens U. of Charlotte, 2005—. Fulbright scholar, 1959; Ford Found. grantee Harvard U., 1981; Shell Oil scholar Harvard U., 1982. Mem.: Assn. Presbyn. Colls. and Univs. (bd. dirs. 1998), So. Assn. Colls. and Schs. (vice chair 1984, pres.-elect 2001, pres. 2002), Assn. Va. Colls. and Univs. (pres. 1997—98), So. Assn. Colls. for Women (pres. 1980—81), Mary Baldwin Coll. (hon.), Phi Beta Kappa. Republican. Office: Robert Haywood Morrison Found 1373 East Morehead St Ste 2 Charlotte NC 28204-2979

**TYSON, DANIEL S.,** chemist, researcher; s. Dennis G. Tyson; m. Molly J. Wilde, July 11, 1998; 1 child, Mackenzie R.; 1 child, Benjamin B. BS, U. Pitts., 1998; MS, Bowling Green State U., 2000, PhD, 2002. Stockroom asst. U. Pitts., Bradford, Pa., 1995—98; chemist Dept. Environ. Protection, Harrisburg, Pa., 1997, Nat. Starch and Chem. Co., Bridgewater, NJ, 1998; grad. rschr. Bowling Green State U., 1998—2002, 1998—2002; vis. asst. prof. chemistry U. Toledo, 2002—03; sr. rsch. assoc. Ohio Aerospace Inst., Brook Park, 2003—. Contbr. articles to profl. jours. Sci. fair judge NE Ohio Sci. and Engring. Fair, Cleve., 2004—06, Dist. 5, Akron, Ohio, 2004—06, Horizon Sci. Acad., Cleve., 2004—06; alt. counsilor, isotopics editor, younger chemists comm. co-chair, nat. chemistry week com. Am. Chem. Soc., Cleve. Sect., 2004—06. Recipient Phys. Sci. award, Sigma Xi, 2000, Charles E. Shanklin award, Bowling Green State U., 2000, Performance award, Ohio Aerospace Inst., 2004—06; grantee, NASA Glenn Rsch. Ctr., 2003—06; scholar, U. Pitts., 1998; Hammond fellow, Bowling Green State U., Ctr. Photochem. Scis., 2000—02. Mem.: Am. Chem. Soc. (alt. counsilor 2004—06), Alpha Lambda Delta. Office: Ohio Aerospace Inst and NASA Glenn 21000 Brookpark Rd Cleveland OH 44135 Office Phone: 216-433-3187.

**TYSON, DAVID RICHARD,** lawyer, political party official; BA in Polit. Sci., W.Va. U., 1975, MA, 1976; JD, Calif. Western Sch. Law, 1980. Bar: W.Va. 1980, U.S. Dist. Ct. (so. dist.) W.Va. 1980. Mng. ptnr. Tyson & Tyson, Huntington, W.Va., 1980-95; pvt. practice, 1980—. Counsel W.Va. Dept. Agr., 1987-93; mcpl. judge Village of Barboursville, W.Va., 1987-88; hearing examienr Workers Compensation Commn., 1987-91; spl. dep. atty. gen. State of W.Va., 1987-88; acting mcpl. judge City of Huntington, 1981-82; ex-officio mem. W.Va. Bd. Regents, 1978-80; adj. prof. law Marshall U., Huntington, 1981-89, adj. prof. dept. polit. sci., 1986-87, 92-94. Dir. paralegal program Cabell County Jail, Huntington, 1984—; dep. mental hygiene commr., Wayne County, W.Va.; mem. Republican State Exec. Com. of W.Va., 1980—, state chmn., 1997-2001; del.-at-large Rep. Nat. Conv., 1976, 84, 88, 92, 96; state sec. W.Va. Legal Svcs., 1982-84; mem. St. Joseph H.S. Bd., 1986—, v.p., 1989—; mem. Cabell County Com. on Crime and Delinquency, 1982; former mem. bd. dirs. YMCA, sec., 1996; bd. dirs. Guyandotte Med. Ctr., 1982-84; mem. adv. com. on arts, John F. Kennedy Center, 2002-. Mem. ABA (vice chair profl. competency com. 1986), W.Va. State Bar, W.Va. Bar Assn., Cabell County Bar Assn., Rotary Club of Huntington. bd. dirs. 1994—, pres. 1997-98).

**TYSON, H. MICHAEL,** retired bank executive; b. Houston, Aug. 16, 1938; s. Howard Ellis and Myrle (Daunoy) m. Judith O. Gilbert, June 24, 1960; children: H. Michael II, Michelle Lee. BBA cum laude, U. Tex., 1962; postgrad., Rutgers U., 1974. Personnel mgr. Foods div. Anderson Clayton Co., Dallas, 1962-70; exec. v.p. adminstrn. Tex. Commerce Bancshares,

Houston, 1970-79; v.p. fin. and adminstrn., chief fin. officer, dir. Houston Chronicle Pub. Co., 1979-87; vice chmn., dir. Tex. Commerce Bank-Houston; exec. v.p., exec. trust officer Tex. Commerce Bancshares, 1987-95. Dir. Paranet Inc., Assoc. Bldg. Svcs., MCG/Dulworth Inc. Bd. dirs. Sam Houston coun. Boy Scouts Am.; Houston Livestock Show & Rodeo, Houston Festival Found.; trustee McCullough Found., W.A. Smith Found.; chmn. The Houston Parks Bd. Served with USMCR, 1961-67. Mem. Houston C. of C. (com. chmn.), Pers. Round Table, Am. Newspaper Pub. Assn., Houston Indsl. Rels. Group, Fin. Execs. Inst. (bd. dirs.), Internat. Newspaper Fin. Execs., Houston Club (dir., pres.), River Oaks Country Club (dir.), Houston Yacht Club (dir.). Methodist. E-mail: hmtyson@sbcglobal.net.

**TYSON, JOHN H.,** food products executive; b. Springdale, Ark., Sept. 5, 1953; s. Don and Jean Tyson; m. Kimberly McCoy; children: John Randal, Olivia Laine. BBA, So. Meth. U., 1975. Complex mgr. N.C. area Tyson Foods, Inc., Springdale, Ark., v.p. mktg. corp. accounts, purchasing mgr., retail sales mgr. N.E. states, pres. beef and pork divsn.; pres., chmn. Tyson Foods Inc., Springdale, 1998-00, pres., chmn., CEO, 2000—01, chmn., CEO, 2001—06, chmn., 2006—. Polit. liaison to Washington and Little Rock Tyson Foods, Inc. Bd. dirs. Area United Way; supporter Farm Aid; vol. activities for well-being and edn. of Ark. children. Named Man of Yr., Ark. Poultry Industry, 1994. Mem.: Ark. Poultry Fedn. (past pres.), Am. Meat Inst., Nat. Assn. Mfrs. Avocations: deep sea fishing, music, golf. Office: Tyson Foods Inc 2210 W Oaklawn Dr Springdale AR 72762-6999*

**TYSON, JOSEPH B., JR.,** lawyer; b. Roanoke Rapids, N.C., Feb. 19, 1949; AB, U. N.C., 1971; JD, U. Va., 1977. Bar: N.Y. 1978, Wis. 1979. Ptnr. Foley & Lardner LLP, Milw., chmn. bus. law dept. Mem. ABA, State Bar Wis., Phi Beta Kappa, U. Club (officer & dir.). Office: Foley & Lardner LLP Firstar Ctr 777 E Wisconsin Ave Ste 3800 Milwaukee WI 53202-5367 Office Phone: 414-297-5631. Office Fax: 414-297-4900. Business E-Mail: jtyson@foley.com.

**TYSON, KATHLEEN HAYHURST,** educational association administrator; b. Oakland, Calif., Mar. 6, 1947; d. Amos Ira and Marie Gertrude (Sanchez) Hayhurst; 1 child, Kathryn Elena. BA, San Jose State U., Calif., 1971; Std. Elem. Credential, Calif. State U., Hayward, 1972; Learning Handicapped Credential, St. Mary's Coll., Moraga, Calif., 1981, MA, 1995; Resource Specialist Credentials, San Francisco State U., 1983; Cert. Addiction Studies, John F. Kennedy U., Orinda, Calif., 1990. Tchr. elem. Richmond Sch. Dist., Calif., 1972—79; tchr. learning handicapped Richmond Elem. Sch. Dist., Calif., 1979—81; resource specialist West Contra Costa Sch. Dist., Pinole and Hercules, Calif., 1992—. Software designer Beck Tech., Berkeley, Calif., 1991—92; coord. At Risk Program Dept. Drug and Alcohol, Hercules, Calif., 1994—97; dir. Reading Intervention Program Elem. Schs., Hercules; instr. lang. arts Calif. State, Hayward San Pablo; ednl. cons., intervention tutor self employed, Orinda; supr. student tchrs. San Francisco State U., Hercules, 2005. Author: (Intervention Program) Star Trak, 1989—92 (1st pl., 1989); author: (, dir.) (Reading Intervention program) Firebear, 1995—2003; editor: (book) Habitats, 1998 (1st pl.c.c. reading). Organizer, fund raiser Tsunami Toy Drive Orinda Sch., Hercules, 2005; facilitator, instr. Parent Workshop for At Risk Students, Hercules, 1996—97; literacy trainer staff training workshops Hercules, 1998—99; min. Unity Ch., 1999—; spiritual mentor, 1997—99; amb. People to People, Spokane, Wash., 2000. Recipient You Make a Difference award, Contra Costa County, 1991, Cert. Excellence in Svc., Contra Cost. County, 1992. Mem.: Calif. Reading Assn., Coun. for Exceptional Children, Calif. Tchrs. Assn. Avocations: gardening, reading, travel, tennis. Office: West Contra Costa Sch Dist 1616 Pheasant Dr Hercules CA 94563

**TYSON, KENNETH ROBERT THOMAS,** surgeon, educator; b. Houston, July 30, 1936; s. Howard Ellis and Myrle Henrietta (Daunoy) T.; m. Sue Ann Delahoussaye, Nov. 20, 1971; children: Deborah, Kenneth, Michael, Jill. BA, U. Tex., 1956; MD, U. Tex. Med. Br., 1960. Diplomate: Am. Bd. Surgery, Am. Bd. Thoracic Surgery. Intern Ind. U. Med. Ctr., Indpls., 1960-61; resident in gen. and thoracic surgery Ind. U. Med. Center, 1961-66; resident in pediatric surgery Children's Hosp. Med. Center, Boston, 1966-67; chief pediatric gen., thoracic surgery U. Tex. Med. Br., Galveston, 1967-80, asst. prof. surgery, 1967-71, asso. prof., 1971-75, prof., 1975-80; surgeon-in-chief Child Health Center, 1974-80; clin. prof. surgery U. Calif., Davis, 1980-91, U. Tex. Med. Br., Galveston, 1991—. Contbr. articles to profl. jours. Fellow A.C.S., Am. Acad. Pediatrics, Am. Coll. Cardiology; mem. Am. Assn. Thoracic Surgery, Soc. Surgery Alimentary Tract, So. Thoracic Surg. Assn., Am. Pediatric Surg. Assn., Soc. Univ. Surgeons, So. Surg. Assn., Pacific Coast Surg. Assn., Sigma Xi, Alpha Omega Alpha, Delta Kappa Epsilon, Alpha Kappa Kappa. Episcopalian. Home: 7126 Las Ventanas Dr Austin TX 78731-1814 Office: U Tex Med Br Dept Pediatric Surgery Galveston TX 77550

**TYSON, KIRK W. M.,** management consultant; b. Jackson, Mich., July 2, 1952; s. George Carlton and Wilma Marion (Barnes) Tyson; m. Terri Lynn Long, Mar. 25, 2000; 1 child, Gabriel 1 stepchild, Robert. BBA, Western Mich. U., 1974; MBA, DePaul U., Chgo., 1982. CPA, Ill.; cert. mgmt. cons. Bus. cons. Arthur Andersen & Co., Chgo., 1974-84; v.p. cons. First Chgo. Corp., 1984; chmn. Kirk Tyson Internat., 1984-2000; pres. The Perpetual Strategist, Chgo., 2001—. Author: Business Planning, 1982, Business Intelligence: Putting It All Together, 1986, Competitor Intelligence: Manual and Guide, 1990, Competition in the 21st Century, 1996, The Complete Guide to Competitive Intelligence, 1998, 4th rev. edit. 2006, The Perpetual Strategist, 2006. Pres., Chgo. Jr. Assn. Commerce and Industry Found., 1977-79; active Easter Seals Soc., 1977, Am. Blind Skiing Found., 1977-78, Jr. Achievement, 1976-77, United Way Met. Chgo., 1979-80, Urban Gateways, 1975; Rep. precinct committeeman Downers Grove Twp., 1985-89, treas. St. Charles H.S. Football Booster Club, 1994-95. Fellow Soc. Competitive Intelligence Profls. (Meritorious award, 2005); mem. Rotary Club of Springboro (asst. dist. gov., 2005-), Alpha Kappa Psi (Disting. Alumni Svc. award 1974-86, named Alumnus of Yr. 2003). Office: The Perpetual Strategist 30 S Wacker Dr Ste 2200 Chicago IL 60606-7456 Business E-Mail: kirk.tyson@perpetualstrategist.com. E-mail: kirk.tyson@kirktyson.com.

**TYSON, LAURA D'ANDREA,** dean, finance educator; b. Bayonne, NJ, June 28, 1947; BA, Smith Coll., 1969; PhD, MIT, 1974. Prof. econ. and bus. adminstrn. U. Calif., Berkeley, 1978-98, BankAmerica dean Haas Sch. Bus., 1998—2001; chmn. Coun. Econ. Advisors Exec. Office of the Pres., Washington, 1993-95; nat. econ. advisor to Pres. U.S. Nat. Econ. Coun., Washington, 1995-96; dean London Sch. Bus., 2002—. Bd. dirs. S&C Comm., Inc., Eastman Kodak Co., Morgan Stanley, BRUEGEL, Brookings Instn., Coun. Fgn. Rels. Editor: (with John Zysman) American Industry in International Competition, 1983, (with Ellen Comisso) Power, Purpose and Collective Choice: Economic Strategy in Socialist States, 1986, (with William Dickens and John Zysman) The Dynamics of Trade and Employment, 1988, (with Chalmers Johnson and John Zysman) Politics and Productivity: The Real Story of How Japan Works, 1989, Who's Bashing Whom? Trade Conflict in High Technology Industries, 1992; econ. viewpoint columnist: Bus. Week mag. Mem. Nat. Bipartisan Commn. Future Medicare, 1997—99. Office: London Business Sch Regent's Park London NW1 4SA England Office Phone: 020 7262 5050. Office Fax: 020 7724 7875.

**TYSON, LUCILLE R.,** health facility administrator, geriatrics nurse; b. North Wales, Pa., Feb. 14, 1939; d. Edwin Shelly and Marion (Wenhold) Rosenberger; m. Ronald Saylor Tyson, June 29, 1963; children: Bryan, Bruce. AS, Middlesex County Coll.; BA, Wheaton Coll.; MSW, Rutgers U. Cert. gerontol. nurse; lic. social worker; RN. Dir. N.J. Parkinson Info. & Referral Ctr. Robert Wood Johnson U. Hosp., New Brunswick, NJ; human svcs. planner Middlesex County Dept. Human Svcs., New Brunswick; dir., right to know regulations Roosevelt Hosp., Edison, NJ; dir., quality assurance Cen. N.J. Jewish Home for Aged, Somerset, NJ; mem. Piscataway (N.J.) Twp. Coun., 1990—; mem. rev./appeals com. Middlesex County Dept. Human Svcs., 1992—; bd. dirs. Metlar Ho. Found.; mcpl. dir. Piscataway Rep. Orgn., 1995—; county committeewoman Middlesex County Rep. Orgn.,

1995—2001; rep. exec. committeewoman Greenville County, SC, 2001-. Mem. ANA, NASW, Nat. Soc. DAR, N.J. Nurses Assn., Assn. Quality Assurance Profls. N.J., Geriatric Inst. N.J., Rep. Exec. Comm.

**TYSON, MIKE G.,** boxer; b. N.Y.C., June 30, 1966; s. John Kilpatrick and Lorna Tyson; m. Robin Givens, Feb. 7, 1988 (div. Feb. 1989). Defeated Trevor Berbick to win World Boxing Coun. Heavyweight Title, Nov. 1986; defeated James Smith to win World Boxing Assn. Heavyweight Title, 1987; defeated Tony Tucker to win Internat. Boxing Fedn. Heavyweight Title, Aug. 1987; defeated Michael Spinks to win Internat. Boxing Fedn. Heavyweight Title, June 1988; undisputed heavyweight champion 1988-90 (defeated by James "Buster" Douglas); defeated Frank Bruno to win WBC Heavyweight Title, 1996; defeated by Evander Holyfield, 1996; won over Frans Botha, 1998. Commentator for Showtime. Hon. sports chmn. Cystic Fibrosis Assn. N.Y., 1987—, Young Adult Inst., N.Y.C., 1987—. Achievements include being the youngest heavyweight champion in history.

**TYSON, NEIL DEGRASSE,** astrophysicist, museum director; BA in Physics, Harvard U., 1980; MA in Astronomy, U. Tex., Austin, 1983; PhD in Astrophysics, Columbia U., 1991; DS (hon.), CUNY, 1997, Ramapo Coll., 2000, Dominican Coll., 2000, U. Richmond, 2001, Bloomfield Coll., 2002. Postdoctoral rsch. assoc. dept. astrophysics Princeton U., 1991—94; staff scientist Am. Mus.-Hayden Planetarium, NYC, 1994—95, acting dir., 1995—96; chair dept. astrophysics Am. Mus. Natural Hist., NYC, 1997—99, Frederick P. Rose dir. Hayden Planetarium, 1999—. Contbr. articles to profl. jours., chapters to books; author: Merlin's Tour of the Universe, 1989, Universe Down to Earth, 1994, Just Vis. This Planet, 1998, The Sky is not The Limit: Adventures of an Urban Astrophysicist, 2000; co-author: One Universe: At Home in the Cosmos, 2000 (Sci. Writing award, Am. Inst. Physics, 2001), Origins: Fourteen Billion Years of Cosmic Hist., 2004; co-editor: Cosmic Frontiers: Astronomy at the Cutting Edge, 2001. Named Sexiest Astrophysicist Alive, People Mag., 2000; named one of 40 under 40, Craines Mag., 1996; recipient Medal of Honor, Columbia U., 2001. Fellow: NY Acad. Scis.; mem.: Nat. Soc. Black Physicists, Internat. Planetarium Soc., Astron. Soc. Pacific, Am. Phys. Soc., Am. Astron. Soc. Office: Dept Astrophysics Am Mus Natural Hist Central Park W at 79th St New York NY 10024 E-mail: tyson@amnh.org.

**TYSZKOWSKI, ROBERT,** investigating services executive; b. Boston, May 25, 1961; s. Walter and Nora Francis (Lange) T.; m. Patricia Anne McArdle, Dec. 30, 1995. Sci. diploma, Riverside Mil. Acad., 1979; grad., U.S. Army ROTC Program, 1979; BA, U. Mass., 1983; BS, U. N.H., 1985; postgrad., Harvard U., 1985-87, 90-93. Lic. cons. Mass. Dept. Pub. Health; cert. instr. Mass. State Police. Rsch. asst. Ritzman Rsch. Lab., Durham, NH, 1984-85; clin. pathology intern Brigham & Women's Hosp., Harvard Med. Sch., Boston, 1985-87; clin. rsch., cell biologist Mass. Gen. Hosp., Harvard Med. Sch., Boston, 1987—; CEO Lange Internat., Boston, 1987—; dir. ops. Renal Rsch. Unit, Boston, 1989—, radiation safety officer, 1990-96; exec. dir. Radiation Safety Svcs., Inc., Boston, 1996—; sr. ptnr. P.M.T. Assoc., Inc., Boston, 1996—; sr. v.p. Evidant Investigations, Inc., N.Y.C., 1997-99, CFO, 1999—; sr. ptnr. Back Bay Assocs., Boston, 2001—. Vice-chmn. bd. Evidant Investigations, Inc., Boston, 1997—; chmn. bd. Ea. Equine Assocs., Inc., Hamilton, Mass., 1985—, Lange Internat., Boston, 1987—, Radiation Safety Svcs., Inc., Boston, 1996—; Armser Corp., 1999—; mem. adv. com. U.S. Combined Tng. Assn., 1986-90, Ptnrs. Healthcare Sys., 1997—; mem. adv. bd. P.M.T. Assocs. Inc., Boston, 1996—, Middlesex County Dep. Sheriff's Assn., 2000—, Mass. Assn. Italian-Am. Police Officers, 2000—. Author: Why Children Fail, 1982, Battle in the North Georgia Hills, 1983, The Judges, Part I and II, 1987, Brief History of the Union Club of Boston, 1997, Biography of Pastor G.B. Dangers, 2000; editor, contbg. author The Constables rion, 2000—, The Guardian, 2000—; contbr. numerous articles to profl. jours. Co-chmn. organizing com. Harvard-Yale Benefit Polo, Hamilton, 1990, U. N.H. Fund Raising Event, Boston, 1991; mem. organizing com. U. N.H. Equestrian Events, 1983-85, Ledyard Three-day Event, Wenham, Mass., 1987-88, 90, U. Mass. Fund Raising Drive, Amherst, 1980-81. Dana fellow, 1981-82, fellow Harvard U., 1987-89. Mem. AAAS, Am. Coll. Forensic Examiners, Am. Nuc. Soc., Admiral Nimitz Found., N.Y. Acad. Scis., Am. Soc. Notaries, Assn. of Offcl. Analytical Chemists Internat., Boston Athenaeum (life), Health Physics Soc., Inst. of Early Am. History and Culture (inst. assoc.), New Eng. Hist. Geneal. Soc., Nat. Assn. Investigative Specialists, Mus. Fine Arts/Boston, Redwood Libr. and Athenaeum, Nimitz Mus. Pacific War, Tex. State Archives, Manhattan C. of C., U.S. Ct. Tennis Assn., U.S. Golf Assn., U.S. Polo Assn., Faculty Club, Nat. Tennis Club (Newport, R.I.), Myopia Polo Club, Tennis and Racquet Club, Union Club, Univ. Club. Republican. Episcopalian. Avocations: equestrian sports, royal tennis. Office: Lange Internat PO Box 5669 Boston MA 02114-0011 also: Armser Corp 100 Park Ave Fl 16 New York NY 10017 also: Evidaunt Investigations Inc 60 State St Ste 700 Boston MA 02109-1803 E-mail: armser@aol.com.

**TYTELL, JOHN,** literature educator, writer; b. Antwerp, Belgium, May 17, 1939; arrived in U.S., 1941; s. Charles and Lena (Gano) T.; m. Mellon Gregori, May 28, 1967. BA, CCNY, 1961; MA, NYU, 1963, PhD, 1968. Grad. reader NYU, 1963-67; lectr. Queens Coll., N.Y.C., 1963-68, assoc. prof., 1968-73, 1973-76, prof. English, 1977—; exec. editor Am. Book Rev., 1979—; vis. prof. Rutgers U., 1980, U. Paris, 1983; cons. Nat. Humanities Faculty, Ga., 1978—. Author: The American Experience, 1970, Naked Angels, 1976, 3d edit., 2006, Ezra Pound: The Solitary Volcano, 1987, 2d edit., 2004, Passionate Lives, 1991, The Living Theatre: Art, Exile and Outrage, 1995, Paradise Outlaws: Remembering the Beats, 1999, Reading New York,, 2003; contbr. articles to mags. including Am. Scholar, Partisan Rev., Vanity Fair, Fame. Fellow, NEH, 1974. Home: 69 Perry St New York NY 10014-3297 Office: Queens Coll Flushing NY 11367 Office Phone: 718-997-4654.

**TYTLER, LINDA JEAN,** science administrator, retired state legislator; b. Rochester, NY, Aug. 31, 1947; d. Frederick Easton and Marian Elizabeth (Allen) Tytler; m. George Stephen Dragnich, May 2, 1970 (div. July 1976); m. James Douglas Fisher, Oct. 7, 1994. AS, So. Va. Coll., Buena Vista, Va., 1967. Spl. asst. to Congressman John Buchanan, Washington, 1971-75; legis. analyst US Senator Robert Griffin, Washington, 1975-77; ops. supr. Pres. Ford Com., Washington, 1976; office mgr. US Senator Pete Domenici Re-election, Albuquerque, 1977; pub. info. officer S.W. Cmty. Health Svc., Albuquerque, 1978-83; cons. pub. rels. and mktg. Albuquerque, 1983-84; account exec. Rick Johnson & Co., Inc., Albuquerque, 1983-84; dir. mktg. and comm. St. Joseph Healthcare Corp., 1984-88; mktg. and bus. devel. cons., 1987-90; dir. comm. and pub. affairs Def. Avionics Systems Honeywell Inc., 1990-2000, dir. comms., 2000—01; dep. dir. pub. affairs Los Alamos Nat. Lab., 2001—05, group leader emergency response instl. svcs., 2006—. Capt. N.Mex. Mounted Patrol, 1998—2002; bd. dirs. Jobs for N.Mex., N.Mex chpt. ARC, Albuquerque, 1984; chmn. legis. campaign com. Rep. Com.; co-chair del. to China Am. Coun. Young Polit. Leaders, 1988; mem. N.Mex. Ho. of Reps., Santa Fe, 1983—95, vice chmn. appropriations and fin. com., 1985—86, chmn. Rep. Caucus, 1985—88. Recipient award, N.Mex. Advt. Fedn., Albuquerque, 1981, 1982, 1985, 1986, 1987, Honeywell Cmty. Svc. award, 1997. Mem.: N.Mex. Assn. Commerce and Industry (bd. dirs., exec. com. 1996—2002), Am. Mktg. Assn., Soc. Hosp. Planning and Mktg., Nat. Advt. Fedn., Am. Soc. Hosp. Pub. Rels. (cert.). Republican.

**TYURIN, MIKHAIL,** cosmonaut; b. Kolomna, Russia, Mar. 2, 1960; m. Tatiana Anatolevyna; 1 child, Alexandra. Grad. with a degree in engring. and specialization in creating math. models related to mechanical flight, Moscow Aviation Inst., 1984. Engr. Energia Corp.; began cosmonaut tng., 1993; started tng. as flight engr. for Expedition-3 crew, 1998. Served as back-up crew mem. for the first Internat. Space Station (ISS) mission STS-105 Discovery, 2001; will serve as Soyuz comdr., flight engr. on the Expedition-14 mission to the Internat. Space Station set to launch in September, 2006. Avocation: sailing.*

**TZAKIS, ANDREAS GERASIMOS,** surgeon, educator, research scientist; MD, U. Athens, Greece, 1974; PhD, Nat. U. Athens, 1999. Intern Mt. Sinai Hosp., N.Y.C., 1977—78, resident surgery, 1978—79, SUNY at Stony Brook, Long Island, NY, 1979—82, chief resident surgery, 1982—83; fellow in transplantation surgery U. Pitts., 1983—85; asst. prof. surgery U. Pitts. Sch. Medicine, 1985—89, assoc. prof. surgery, 1989—94, prof. surgery, 1994, U. Miami (Fla.) Sch. Medicine, 1994. Mem. adv. bd. Archives of Gastroenterohepatology, 1997; presenter, panelist, lectr. in field. Mem. editl. bd.: Clin. Tranplantation, 1993, Transplantation, 1994, Pediat. Transplantation, 1997, Jour. Investigative Surgery, 1997, Graft, 1998, Annals Gastroenterology, 1999, Liver Transplantation, 1999; contbr. numerous articles to profl. jours. 2nd lt. Med. Corp Greek Air Force, 1974—77. Mem.: ACS, AMA, Internat. Pediat. Transplant Assn., Inc., Xenotransplantation Assn., Am. Surg. Assn., Am. Assn. for the Study of Liver Diseases, Internat. Coll. Surgeons, Am. Coll. Angiology, Internat. Pancreas and Islet Transplant Assn., Hellenic Tranplantation Soc., Soc. Internat. Surgery, Soc. U. Surgeons, Assn. for Acad. Surgery, Acad. Surg. Rsch., The Transplantation Soc., Am. Soc. Transplant Surgeons. Office: 1801 NW 9th Ave Ste 511 Miami FL 33136 E-mail: atzakis@med.miami.edu.

**TZEKOVA, KRASSIMIRA KRUSTEVA,** resident director; d. Svetlinka Tzekova and Tzeko Tzekov. BA in Polit. Sci., U. NH, Durham, 2001; MBA, Franklin Pierce Coll., Rindge, NH, 2005. Legal asst. Swartz and Swartz Law Office, Portland, Maine, 1995—2000; asst. resident dir. U. NH, Durham, 2000—01; resident dir. Colby-Sawyer Coll., New London, NH, 2001—, office of citizenship edn., 2001—. Advisor coll. jud. hearing bd. Colby-Sawyer Coll., 2001—. Named Advisor of Yr., Colby-Sawyer Coll., 2005; recipient Maine's Leadership Award, 1997, New Hampshire's Movers and Shakers, U. NH, 2000. Mem.: Assn. for Student Jud. Affairs, N.E. Assn. Coll. and Univ. Housing Officers, Am. Coll. Pers. Assn., N.E. Assn. Colls. Residence Life Assn. of the Granite State (assoc.; plannnig bd. 2004—05). Business E-Mail: ktzekova@colby-sawyer.edu.

**TZIMAS, NICHOLAS ACHILLES,** orthopedic surgeon, educator; b. Greece, Apr. 18, 1928; arrived in U.S.A., 1955, naturalized, 1960. s. Archilles Nicholas and Evanthia B. (Exarchou) T.; m. Helen J. (Papastylopoulos), Apr. 22, 1958; children: Yvonne and Christina. MD, U. Athens, Greece, 1952. Intern St. Mary's Hosp., Hoboken, NJ, 1955—86; resident in gen. surgery Misericordia Hosp., N.Y.C.; resident in orthopedic surgery Bellevue Hosp., N.Y.C., NY, 1957—60; instr. orthopedic surgery N.Y. U. Sch. Medicine, 1961—63, asst. clin. prof., 1963—65, asso. clin. prof.; 1965—71, clin. prof., 1971—. Mem. staff Univ. and Bellevue Hosp.; chief children's orthopedics, 1966; orthopedic cons. Inst. Rehab. Medicine, N.Y. U., 1966, St. Agnes Hosp., White Plains, N.Y., 1972; advisory com. Bur. Handicapped Children, N.Y.C., 1975; spl. invitations for tchg., Osaka, Japan, 1970, Jerusalem, 1974, São Paolo, Brazil, 1976, Taranto, Italy, 1977, Bari, Italy, 1978, Barquisimeto, Venezuela, 1979, Bogotá, Colombia, 1983, Buenos Aires, Argentina, 1983. Author of articles on spina bifida child mgmt. Served with M.C. Greek Army, 1952-55. Named Ofcl. Knight of Italian Republic, 1979 Fellow Am., Internat. Coll. Surgeons; mem. N.Y. Acad. Medicine, N.Y. State, N.Y. County Med. Soc., Am. Acad. Orthopedic Surgeons, Am. Congress Rehab. Medicine, Am. Acad. Cerebral Palsy. Mem. Greek Orthodox Ch.; Archon of the Ecumenical Patriarchate of Constantinople. Home: 33 Edgewood St Tenafly NJ 07670-2909 Office: 530 1st Ave New York NY 10016-6402 Office Phone: 212-263-7278. Personal E-mail: ntzimas@aol.com. Business E-Mail: nicholasotzimas@med.nyu.edu.

**TZITSIKAS, HELENE,** retired literature educator; b. Athens, Greece, Apr. 2, 1926; came to U.S., 1944; d. Christos Jean and Evangelia (Chouases) T. BA, Lake Forest (Ill.) Coll., 1952; MA, Northwestern U., 1954, PhD, 1963. Instr. Rockford (Ill.) Coll., 1962-63, asst. prof., 1963-65; assoc. prof. Hispanic lit. Mich. State U., East Lansing, 1965-71, prof., 1971-91, prof. emerita, 1991—. Author: Santiago Ramón y Cajal-Obra Literaria, 1965, El Pensamiento Español 1898-1899, 1967, Fernando Santiván - Humanista y Literato, 1971, 2d edit., 1985, Dos Revistas Chilenas: Los Diez y Artes y Letras, 1973, El sentimiento Ecológico, 1977, La supervivencia existencial de la mujer, 1982, El Quijotismo y la raza en la Generacion de 1898, 1988, Los exiliados argentinos en Montevideo durante la óoca de Rosas, 1991. Recipient Diana award YWCA, Lansing, Mich., 1988, cert. of employee recognition, 1988. Mem. MLA, AAUP, MLA Am., Am. Assn. Tchrs. Spanish and Portuguese, Univ. Club Mich. State U., Daus. Penelope. Greek Orthodox. Avocations: theater, music, painting, gardening. Office: Mich State U Dept Romance and Classical Langs East Lansing MI 48824

**UBELL, ROBERT NEIL,** editor, educator, publishing executive, consultant; b. Bklyn., Sept. 14, 1938; s. Charles and Hilda (Kramer) U.; m. Rosalyn Deutsche, Sept. 24, 1976; children: Jennifer Hayslett-Ubell, Elizabeth Miller. BA, Bklyn. Coll., 1961; postgrad., Acad. Fine Arts, Rome, Italy, 1959-60, CUNY, 1961-62, Pratt Graphic Arts Workshop, N.Y.C., 1972-73. Assoc. editor Nuclear Industry, Atomic Indsl. Forum, 1962-64; from editor to sr. editor Plenum Pub. Corp., N.Y.C., 1965-70, v.p., editor in chief, 1970-76; editor The Sciences, N.Y. Acad. Scis., N.Y.C., 1976-79; Am. pub. Nature, N.Y.C., 1979-83; founding pub. Nature Biotechnology, 1983; pres., CEO Robert Ubell Assocs., N.Y.C., 1983—97; pres. BioMedNet, Ltd., 1996-97; exec. v.p. Marcel Dekker, Inc., N.Y.C., 1997-99; dir. web-based distance learning Stevens Inst. Tech., Hoboken, NJ, 1999—2001, dean online learning, 2001—03, dean sch. profl. edn., 2004—. Instr. MIT, 1987, Columbia U. Coll. Physicians and Surgeons, 1987; mem. editl. com. The Scientist, 1987-90; mem. Book Industry Study Group, Inc., 1992; vis. com. Nat. Acad. Press, NRC, NAS, 1986; books subcom. Am. Inst. Physics, 1985-91; awards com. Am. Inst. Physics-U.S. Steel Sci. Writing Awards, 1983-82; publs. com. Am. Inst. Biol. Scis., 1994, N.Y. Acad. Scis., 1976-97; cons. Lotus Devel. Corp., 1987-89, Coalition for Networked Info., 1995-98, Am. Soc. Addiction Medicine, 2003-04; pub. info. com. Nat. Acad. Engring., 1989-02; program com. Soc. Scholarly Pub., 1989-91; rev. panel NSF, 2000, 03, Nat. Sci., Math. and Tech. Edn. Digital Libr., 2000, Internat. Opportunities Scientists and Engrs., 2003, Reform Undergrad. Engring. Edn., 2003; distance learning observer Middle States Commn. on Higher Edn., 2000-04; chair Sloan Found. Greater N.Y.C. ALN Conf., N.Y.C., 2002; mem. planning com. Breakthrough Thinking in Online Bus. Edn., 2002-03; mem. adv. panel Nat. Rsch Inst. on Wireless Tech. in Edn. and Industry, 2002; mem. adv. coun. Alliance Expanded Tchr. Preparation Cmty. Colls.; co-host Stevens Views Radio, 2002—; adv. bd. comm. industry network N.J. Tech. Coun., 2002—, Sloan Found. Corp. e-Learning, 2003—, Sloan Found. Program Com., Sloan C-Conf., 2005—; prin. investigator Sloan Greater N.Y.C. Online Learning Ctr., 2000-03; co-chair Sloan Workshop Corp.-Acad. Online Learning, 2004; mem. adv. task force Nat. Hwy. Inst. Distant Learning Program; cons. in field. Author: (with Marvin Leiner) Children Are the Revolution, 1974; (with Mark Tesoriero) Negotiating Networked Licensing Agreements, 1995, Cost Centers and Measures in the Networked Information Value Chain, 1997, The R&D Economics in the Digital Environment, 1998; editor Nature Directory of Biologicals, 1981, Physics Today Buyer's Guide, 1984-89; exec. editor: Linguistics: The Cambridge Survey, 1987-88, Pre-Med Handbook, 1986, International Encyclopedia of the Social Sciences, Vol. 19, 1991, Encyclopedia of Astronomy and Astrophysics, 1991, Sci. Am. Triumph of Discovery, 1995, Oxford Encyclopedia of Climate and Weather, 1996; cons. editor ISI Press, 1985-87, Am. Inst. of Physics Book Program, 1986-96; Am. Chem. Soc. Book Program, 1989; cons. pub. Computers in Physics, 1987-91; series editor Masters of Modern Physics, 1991-96, Creators of Modern Chemistry, 1994-95, Sci. Am. Focus, 1995-96; mem. editl. bd. ISI Press, 1986-90, Grants Mag., 1981-85, Nonprofit Mgmt. and Fin., 1980-85; editl. dir. Nutrition Advisor, 1998-99; mem. editl. bd. Innovations in End of Life Care, 1999-2003; editl. advisor Cancer Practice, Am. Cancer Soc., 1997-98; contbr. articles to profl. jours. Chmn. bd. Woodword Sch., 1971-74; adv. com. Children's TV Workshop, 1980, Interpol, Inc., 2006-; v.p., bd. dirs. Parkinson's Walk Found., 2001—, Hekate, 2003-04, Lianyungang Universal Vehicle Mfg. Co., Ltd. Mem. AAAS, ASTD, NY Acad. Scis. (mem. publs. com. 1976-97), Nat. Assn. Sci. Writers. Office: Stevens Inst Tech WebCampus Stevens Castle Point Hudson Hoboken NJ 07030

**UBERALL, HERBERT MICHAEL STEFAN,** physicist, researcher; b. Neunkirchen, Austria, Oct. 14, 1931; arrived in U.S., 1953, naturalized, 1963; s. Michael and Stefanie U.; m. Reyna Tosta, 1981; children by previous marriage: Bernadette Chauvallon, Bertrand. PhD, U. Vienna, Austria, 1953, Cornell U., 1956; PhD (honoris causa), U. Le Havre, France, 1987. Staff mem. Signal Corps Labs., Ft. Monmouth, NJ, 1953-54; research asst. Cornell U., 1954-56; research fellow Nuclear Physics Research Lab., U. Liverpool, Eng., 1956-57; Ford Found. fellow CERN, Geneva, 1957-58; research physicist Carnegie Inst. Tech., Pitts., 1958-60; asst. prof. U. Mich., Ann Arbor, 1960-64; assoc. prof. Cath. U. Am., Washington, 1964-65, prof. physics, 1965-94, prof. emeritus, 1994—. Vis. prof. U. Paris VII Jussieu, 1984-85, U. Le Havre, 1990, 92, 94, 96, U. Bordeaux, 1993, 95, U. Aix-Marseille II and Lab. Mech. Acoustics, 1995, Ecole Centrale de Lille, 1997, Tech. U. Denmark, 1998; cons. Naval Rsch. Lab., Washington, 1966-92. Author: Electron Scattering from Complex Nuclei, 1971; co-author: Giant Resonance Phenomena, 1980, Nuclear Pion Photoproduction, 1991; editor: Acoustic Resonance Scattering, 1992; co-editor: Long Distance Neutrino Detection, 1979, Classical and Quantum Dynamics, 1991, Coherent Radiation Sources, 1985, Coherent Radiation Processes in Strong Fields, 1991, Radar Target Imaging, 1994; contbr. 300 articles to profl. jours. Recipient Fgn. medal French Soc. Acoustics, 1996. Fellow (life) IEEE, (life) Am. Phys. Soc., Acoustical Soc. Am., Washington Acad. Scis. (Achievement award 1984); mem. AAUP, Am. Acad. Mech., Electromagnetics Acad., Internat. Union Radio Sci. Office: Catholic U Dept Physics Washington DC 20064-0001 E-mail: uberallh@msn.com.

**UBEROI, MAHINDER SINGH,** aerospace engineer, researcher; b. Delhi, India, Mar. 13, 1924; arrived in U.S., 1945, naturalized, 1960; s. Kirpal Singh and Sulaksha (Kochar) Uberoi. BS, Punjab U., Lahore, India, 1944; MS, Calif. Inst. Tech., 1946; DEng, Johns Hopkins U., 1952. Registered profl. engr. Mem. faculty U. Mich., Ann Arbor, 1953-63, prof. aerospace engring., 1959-63, vis. prof., 1963—64; prof. U. Colo., Boulder, 1963—2000, chmn. dept. aerospace engring., 1963-75; fellow F. Joint Inst. Lab. Astrophysics, Boulder, 1963-74; rschr., 2004—. Exch. scientist Soviet Acad. Scis., 1966, U.S. Nat. Acad. Scis.; invited prof. U. Que., Canada, 1972—74; vis. scientist Max Planck Inst. Astrophysics, Munich, 1974; hon. rsch. fellow Harvard U., 1975—76. Contbr. articles to profl. jours.; editor: Cosmic Gas Dynamics, 1974. Coun. mem. Ednl. TV Channel 6, Inc., Denver, 1963—66. Guggenheim fellow, Royal Inst. Tech., Sweden, 1958. Mem.: Am. Phys. Soc., Tau Beta Pi. Home: 819 6th St Boulder CO 80302-7418

**UBINGER, JOHN WALTER, JR.,** lawyer; b. Pitts., Jan. 31, 1949; BBA cum laude, Ohio U., 1970; JD, U. Notre Dame, 1973. Bar: Pa. 1973. Ptnr. Jones Day, Pitts. Instr. environ. dispute resolution Duquesne U. Bd. dirs. Pa. Environ. Coun., Regional Environ. Edn. Ctr.; bd. dirs. Allegheny Land Trust; adv. com. Allegheny County Dept. Air Pollution Control, 1992-95, Allegheny County Contaminated Sites Redevel. Study, 1994-95 Fellow: Air and Waste Mgmt. Assn. (chmn. Western Pa. sect. 1989—90); mem.: ABA (natural resources, energy, environ. law and alternative dispute resolution sects.), Assn. Conflict Resolution (practitioner/educator/rschr. membership), Allegheny County Bar Assn. (chmn. environ. law sect. 1991), Environ. Law Inst. (assoc.), Pa. Bar Assn. (chmn. environ., mineral and natural resources law sect. 1990—91). Office: Jones Day 1 Mellon Ctr 500 Grant St Pittsburgh PA 15219-2502 Office Phone: 412-394-7908. Business E-Mail: jwubinger@jonesday.com.

**UBOGU, EROBOGHENE EKAMERENO,** physician; s. Roland and Rebecca Ubogu; m. Anisa Seana Namirimo Ssengoba, Aug. 10, 2002; children: Orezimena Nanyanzi children: Oghenekome Kaddu. MBBS with honors, Imperial Coll. Sch. Medicine, U. London, 1998. Diplomate in neurology and in clin. neurophysiology Am. Bd. Psychiatry and Neurology, bd. cert. Am. Bd. Electrodiagnostic Medicine. Adult neurology resident, chief resident Case Western Res. U., Univ. Hosps. of Cleve., 2000—03; clin. neurophysiology fellow Emory U. Sch. Medicine, Atlanta, 2003—04; asst. prof. neurology Case Western Res. U. Sch. Medicine, Cleve., 2004—; staff neurologist Louis Stokes Cleve. Vets. Affairs Med. Ctr., Cleve., 2004—. Fellow: Am Assn. for Neuromuscular and Electrodiagnostic Medicine; mem.: NY Acad. Scis., Am. Acad. Neurology. Achievements include research in role of chemokines in neuroinflammation, electrodiagnostic criteria for carpal tunnel syndrome in axonal polyneuropathies; asymptomatic middle cerebral artery stenosis diagnosed by magnetic resonance angiography; the preferential involvement of extraocular muscles in myasthenia gravis; acute motor sensory axonal neuropathy associated with systemic lupus erythematosus; amaurosis fugax and phencyclidine inhalation; vertebrobasilar dolichoectasia diagnosed by magnetic resonance angiography and risk of stroke and death; transverse myelitis associated with acinetobacter baumanii intrathecal pump catheter-related infection; mirtazapine-induced serotonin syndrome; ketamine in refractory status epilepticus and neurotoxicity; rectus sheath hematoma complicating percutaneous endoscopic gastrostomy; recurrent transient ischemic attacks and type A aortic dissections; otalgia as the sole presenting manifestation of subdural hematoma; cervicomedullary junction compression and vertebral artery dolichoectasia. Office: Neurology Svc Louis Stokes Cleve Vets Affairs Med Ctr 10701 E Blvd Cleveland OH 44106 Office Phone: 216-421-3040, 216-791-3800 x 5230. Business E-Mail: Erobophene.Ubogu@med.va.gov. Business E-Mail: eroboghene.ubogu@case.edu.

**UBUKA, TOSHIHIKO,** biochemist, educator, academic administrator; b. Kagaminocho, Okayama, Japan, Jan. 31, 1934; s. Yoshio and Shigeko (Hashimoto) U.; m. Satoko Iwamiya, Oct. 18, 1960; children: Takayoshi, Hiromi, Atsue. MD, Okayama U., 1959, PhD, 1964. Rsch. assoc. Med. Coll. Cornell U., NYC, 1968—71; with Okayama U., 1964-73, asst. prof., 1973-80, assoc. prof. Med. Sch., 1980-81, prof. Med. Sch., 1981-99, dean Med. Sch., 1997-99, prof. emeritus, 1999—; prof., dean Kawasaki U. of Med. Welfare, 1999—2001, v.p., 2001—05, prof., dean, v.p., 2005—. Co-author: Methods in Enzymology, vol. 143, 1987; editor Acta Med. Okayama, 1980-99, Physiol. Chem. Phys. and Med. NMR, 1982—, Amino Acids, 1991—; chief editor Acta Med. Okayama, 1987-90. Fellow Japanese Biochem. Soc., Japanese Soc. Nutrition and Food Sci.; mem. AAAS, Am. Chem. Soc., NY Acad. Scis., Internat. Soc. Amino Acid Rsch., Soc. Study Inborn Errors Metabolism, The Protein Soc. Achievements include research in sulfur biochemistry, sulfur nutrition, cysteine metabolism in mammals, protein modification with mixed disulfides; inborn errors of cysteine metabolism, analysis of sulfur compounds. Avocation: Kendo (Japanese fencing). Home: 527-1 Nishikarakawa Okayama 701-1213 Japan Office: Kawasaki U Med Welfare De Clin Nutrition 288 Matsushima Kurashiki Okayama 701-0193 Japan

**UCCIARDO, FRANK JOSEPH,** journalist, reporter; b. N.Y.C. s. Joseph J. and Jeanne Barraca Ucciardo. BFA in Comms., MA in Comms., N.Y. Inst. Tech. UN corr. Mut. Radio Network, N.Y.C.; corr. Newsday, Melville, N.Y., CNN Cable News Network, N.Y.C.; anchorman Fin. News Network, N.Y.C.; corr. NBC Radio Network, N.Y.C.; bur. chief UPI Radio, N.Y.C.; reporter NEWS 12, L.I., N.Y.; TV journalist, investigative reporter Sta. WPIX-TV, N.Y.C.; film cameraman, editor Channel 67, Action News, Long Island, N.Y.; dir., prodr. All Points Broadcasting, N.Y.C.; reporter Sta. WOR-Radio 710, N.Y.C.; corr., anchorman Sta. WLIW-TV PBS, Garden City, N.Y.; anchor, reporter Sta. WATR-TV, Channel 20, Waterbury, Conn.; reporter Sta. WNEW Radio, N.Y.C.; TV journalist, investigative reporter UPN 9 News, Secaucus, N.J., 2000—. Writer, dir., prodr.: (documentary) The Berlin Candy Bomber, 1998 (Deadline Club News Feature award Soc. Profl. Journalists 1999). Folio award for investigative reporting L.I. Coalition for Fair Broadcasting, 1996, (2), 2000, award for investigative journalism Silaurian Soc. N.Y.; RIAS fellow in econs. and politics. Mem. UN Corrs. Assn. (broadcasting chmn. UN hdqs. 1996), Soc. Profl. Journalists (treas. Deadline club, Deadline Club News Feature award 1999), Am. Fedn. Radio & TV Artists, NATAS (N.Y. chpt., Emmy award N.Y. chpt. 2007), N.Y. Press Club (emeritus mem.), Drama Desk of N.Y., Press Club L.I. Avocations: travel, cinema, dance, boating, theater. E-mail: unca42@usa.net.

**UCHIDA, KINYA,** consumer products company executive; Joined Canon, Inc., 1963, with camera export divsn. Japan; joined Canan L.Am., Panama, 1969; pres. Canon, Inc., Brazil, Canon, Inc., L.Am., Inc., 1979, Canon, Inc., Singapore, 1986, Canon France S.A., 1995; pres., CEO Canon USA, Inc., Lake Success, NY, 1999—, also bd. dirs., sr. mng. dir. bd. dirs., 2004. Office: Canon USA Inc One Canon Plaza Lake Success NY 11042

**UCHIDA, MITSUKO,** pianist; b. Dec. 20, 1948; d. Fujio and Yasuko Uchida. Student, Hochschule für Musik, Vienna, Austria. Artist-in-residence Cleve. Orch., 2001—. Performer: performs with Berlin Philharm., Vienna Philharm., Cleve. Orch., LA Philharm., Chgo. Symphony Orch., London Symphony, NY Philharm., others, recs. include complete piano sonatas and concertos of Mozart, Beethoven's piano concertos, Debussy's Etudes, Schubert Sonatas and Impromptus, Schoenberg Piano Concerto, Carnegie Hall recital series Mitsuko Uchida: Vienna Revisited, 2002—. Recipient Gramophone award, 2001, Instrumental Award, Royal Philharm. Soc., 2004. Avocation: music. Address: Victoria Rowsell Artist Mgmt Ltd 34 Addington Sq London SE5 7LB England E-mail: management@victoriarowsell.co.uk.

**UCHIDA, RICHARD Y.,** lawyer; b. Mars, Pa., Sept. 18, 1957; s. Henry S. and Sachiko (Sakaguchi) U. BA, Colby Coll., 1979; JD, Franklin Pierce Law Ctr., 1984. Bar: N.H. 1984, U.S. Dist. Ct. N.H. 1984. Reporter, editor Lake Charles (La.) Am. Press., 1979-81; assoc. Rinden Profl. Assn., Concord, NH, 1984-86, Law Offices Raymond P. D'Amante, Concord, 1986—92; ptnr. Hebert & Uchida, Concord, NH, 1992—. Lectr. Franklin Pierce Law Ctr., Concord, 1985—, N.H. Liquor Commn., Concord, 1986—. Mem. Assn. Trial Lawyers Am., N.H. Trial Lawyers, N.H. Bar Assn. (chmn. pub. info. com 1987-90, continuing legal edn. com. 1990, ethics com. 1990, pres. 2005). Republican. Avocations: golf, hiking, volleyball. Office: Hebert & Uchida PLLC Ste 3 244 N Main St Concord NH 03301

**UCHIN, ROBERT ALLEN,** dean, endodontist; b. Phila., Apr. 19, 1933; s. Harry and Doris (Goodman) U.; m. Marlene Florence Neiman; children: Andrew, Richard, Carol. Student, Franklin and Marshall Coll., 1951-53; DDS, Temple U., 1957. Diplomate Am. Bd. Endodontics. Fellow research teaching. dept. endodontics Temple U., Phila., 1959-60, instr. Sch. of Dentistry, 1960-69; co-chmn. endodontic sect. Dade County (Fla.) Dental Research Clinic, 1961-75; founding v.p., chmn. Endodontic sect. Broward County (Fla.) Dental Research Clinic 1974-79; clin. assoc. Sch. of Dentistry U. Fla., Gainsville, 1970; practice dentistry specializing in endodontics Ft. Lauderdale, Fla., 1960—2000; assoc. dean, dir. extramural programs Coll. Dental Medicine, Nova Southeastern U., Ft. Lauderdale, Fla., 1996—2000, dean, 2000—. Chmn. Endodontic sect. Atlantic Coast Research Clinic, 1971-75; vis. lectr. Emory U., 1965, U.N.C., 1970, 72, U. Wash., 1972, U. Pitts., 1974, U. Pa., 1973-89; cons. VA Hosp., Miami, 1968-86, Cen. Office, 1972-84, dir. endodontic residency, 1972-79; bd. dirs., founding chmn. Gold Coast Savs. and Loan Assn. of Fla., 1984-90, Commonwealth Savs. and Loan of Fla., Ft. Lauderdale, 1979-84; adv. dir. Landmark First Nat. Bank, Ft. Lauderdale, 1974-81; vice chmn. Fla. Dental Assn. Services, Inc. Assoc. editor Jour. Endodontics and Traumatology, 1981-89; contbr. numerous articles to profl. jours. Pres., Temple Emanu-El Reform Congregation, Ft. Lauderdale, 1967-69; trustee, Vanguard Sch., Haverford, Pa., 1971-77; bd. dirs., Vanguard Sch., Ft. Lauderdale, 1970-73, Performing Arts Found., Broward County, Fla., 1986-90. Served to capt. USAF, 1957-59. Fellow: Am. Assn. Endodontists (pres. 1976), Internat. Coll. of Dentists, Am. Coll. of Dentists; mem.: Broward County Dental Assn. (pres. 1982), Fla. Dental Assn. (past pres.), Am. Dental Assn. Holding Co. (past pres.), Fla. Assoc. of Endodontics, So. Endodontic Study Group, Am. Dental Assn., Rotary (pres. Ft. Lauderdale 1969—70). Republican. Jewish. Avocations: fly fishing, stamp collecting/philately, orchids. Office: Coll Dental Medicine Nova Southeastern U 3200 S Univ Dr Fort Lauderdale FL 33328 Office Phone: 954-262-7312. Office Fax: 954-262-1782. Business E-Mail: ruchin@nova.edu.

**UCHITELLE, LOUIS,** journalist; b. NYC, Mar. 21, 1932; s. Abraham and Alice Lee (Cronbach) Uchitelle; m. Joan Eva Shapiro, Oct. 7, 1966; children: Isabel Anne, Jennifer Emily. BA, U. Mich., 1954. Reporter Mt. Vernon Daily Argus, 1955-57; with AP, 1957-80, fgn. corr. and bur. chief San Juan, PR, 1964-67, Buenos Aires, 1967-73; supervising editor AP Newsfeatures, NYC, 1974-76; bus. news editor AP, 1977-80; asst. bus. and fin. editor NY Times, 1980-87, economics reporter, 1987—. Instr. journalism Sch. Gen. Studies Columbia U., 1976—89. Author: The Disposable American: Layoffs and Their Consequences, 2006. Office: NY Times 229 W 43rd St New York NY 10036-3959 Office Phone: 212-556-1705. Office Fax: 212-556-8762. Business E-Mail: louisu@nytimes.com.

**UCHIYAMA, CRAIG LYONS,** neuropsychologist; s. John Keyomara Uchiyama and Mary Louise Lyons. BA in Psychology, U. Minn., Mpls., 1986; PhD, U. Minn., 1990; postgrad., UCLA, 1993. Cert. clin. neuropsychology Am. Bd. Profl. Psychology. Asst. clin. prof. U. Calif., San Francisco, 1993—95; neuropsychologist Tolwin Psychiat. Med. Group, LA, 1995—2001, LA County Dept. Mental Health, LA, 2001—. Asst. clin. prof. UCLA, 1997—2001. Contbr. articles to profl. jours. Grad. Minority Student fellow, U. Minn., 1986, Psychology Departmental Grad. Student fellow, 1987, Psychology Departmental fellow, 1988. Mem.: APA, Am. Acad. Clin. Neuropsychology, Psi Chi. Achievements include co-development of the Color Trails Test. Business E-Mail: cuchiyama@lacdmh.org.

**UCHUPI, ELAZAR,** geologist, researcher; b. NYC, Oct. 31, 1928; parents Alfonso and Carmen (Urbizu) U. BS, CCNY, 1952; MS, U. So. Calif., 1954, PhD, 1962. Rsch. assist. U. So. Calif., L.A., 1955-62, Woods Hole (Mass.) Oceanographic Inst, 1962-64, assoc. scientist, 1964 79, sr. scientist Woods Hole (Mass.) Oceanog. Inst., 1979-93, sr. scientist emeritus, 1993—, J. Seward Johnson chmn. oceanography, 1989-93. Mem. Gulf of Mexico panel Joint Oceanog. Instns. Deep Earth Sampling, 1972-74; sci. com. Oceanic Rsch. Working Group 41, 1973-74; steering com. US Oceanog. Office Relief Map Worlds' Oceans; site survey panel Joint Oceanog. Instns., 1978-85; compiler geol. maps on ocean margin drilling; adj. rschr. Inst. Exploration, Mystic, Conn., 1997—. mem. editl. staff Offshore Mag., 1972-74, Marine Geology, 1971-75; co-author 4 books North Atlantic, geology of Atlantic Ocean, and morphology of rocky mems. of Solar Sys. Recipient cert. of recognition Nat. Assn. Geology Tchrs., Inc., and its Crustal evolution Edn. project, 1979, medal editl. adv. bd. Offshore Mag., 1974, Frances P. Shepard award, 1991. Mem. Am. Geophys. Union, Archeol. Inst. Am., Sociedad Geologica de España. Achievements include research in seismic reflection, magnetic and gravity profiles of the eastern Atlantic continental margin and adjacent deep seafloor, Caribbean, Bahamas, Iberian Margins, New England margin, Branefield Trough, South Scotia Ridge, Canary Islands, Red Sea, Persian Gulf, Gulf of Oman, Black Sea, Egyptian Margin, Western Mediterranean, East Pacific Rise, Mohns Ridge, suspended matter and other properties of surface waters of the northeastern Atlantic Ocean, the continental margin off western Africa: Angola to Sierra Leone, Senegal to Portugal, sediments of 3 bays of Baja, Calif.; Sebastian Viscaino, San Cristobal and Todos Santos, characteristics of sediments of the mainland shelf of southern Calif., submarine geology of the Santa Rosa-Cortes Ridge, sediments on the continental margin off eastern U.S., the continental slope between San Francisco and Cedrow Island, Mex., sediments of the Palos Verdes shelf and topography of Kane Basin, statistical parameters of Cape Cod Beach and eolian sands, basins of Gulf of Mex., structure of Georges Bank, and the continental margin of the Atlantic coast of the U.S. and off west Africa, topography and structure of Northeast Channel, Gulf of Mex., and Cashes Ledge, Gulf of Maine, distribution and geologic structure of Triassic rocks in the Bay of Fundy and the northeastern part of the Gulf of Maine, microrelief of the continental margin south off Cape Lookout, N.C., shallow structure of the Straits of Fla., sub-surface morphology of L.I., Block Island, Rhode Island sounds, and Buzzards Bay, bathymetry of the Gulf of Mex., slumping on the continental margin southeast of L.I., N.Y., woody debris on the mainland shelf off Ventura, southern Calif., the continental margin south of Cape Hatteras, N.C., the Atlantic continental shelf and slope off the U.S.,

geological structure of the continental margin off Gulf Coast of the U.S., continental margin of West Africa, the Caribbean Canary Islands, margin off northwest Spain. Office: Woods Hole Oceanographic Inst Dept Geology Geophysic Woods Hole MA 02543

**UCKO, BARBARA CLARK,** writer; b. Cambridge, Mass., Mar. 27, 1945; d. Hugh Kidder and Marie (Folsom) Clark; m. David Alan Ucko, Aug. 13, 1972; 1 child, Aaron Mark. BA in Art History, Oberlin Coll., 1967; MA in English, U. Mo., Kansas City, 1992. Copywriter Bantam Books, N.Y.C., 1974—76; promotion dir. Pocket Books, N.Y.C., 1976—77, Antioch Bookplate, Yellow Springs, Ohio, 1977; instr. composition Sch. of Chgo. Art Inst., Chgo., 1986; mgr. corp. comm. Sprint, Westwood, Kans., 1992—98; pvt. piano tchr. Kansas City, Mo., 1998—2001. Author: (novels) Family Trappings, 1985, Scarlett Greene, 1987, (short stories) Laurel Review, Nit and Wit, Open, Artful Dodge and Chatelaine. Various libr. bds., sch. vol. and hosp. bds. Calif., Mo., Washington D.C. Recipient 1st pl. award, Barbara Storck Short Fiction Competion, U. Mo., 1991, 2d pl., 1992. Mem.: Soc. Midland Authors. Democrat. Avocations: crafts, crossword puzzles, piano, walking, reading. E-mail: Barbara.Ucko@verizon.net.

**UCKO, DAVID ALAN,** science foundation official; b. N.Y.C., July 9, 1948; s. Lawrence L. and Helen H. Ucko; m. Barbara Alice Clark, Aug. 13, 1972; 1 child, Aaron. BA, Columbia Coll., N.Y.C., 1969; PhD, MIT, 1972. Asst. prof. chemistry Hostos C.C., CUNY, Bronx, 1972-76, Antioch Coll., Yellow Springs, Ohio, 1976-79, assoc. prof. chemistry, 1979; rsch. coord. Mus. Sci. and Industry, Chgo., 1979-80, dir. sci., 1981-87, v.p., 1986-87; dep. dir. Calif. Mus. Sci. and Industry, L.A., 1987-90; prcs. Kansas City (Mo.) Mus., 1990-2000, Sci. City at Union Sta., 1999-2000; exec. dir. Koshland Sci. Mus. and Sci. Outreach, NAS, Washington, 2001—02; pres. Mus. + More LLC, 2002—, head sci literacy section, 2004—; program dir. Informal Sci. Edn. NSF, 2003—; guest faculty mus. mgmt. program U. Colo., Boulder, Colo., 2001. Rsch. assoc. and assoc. prof. dept. edn. U. Chgo., 1982—87; adj. staff scientist C. F. Kettering Rsch. Lab., Yellow Springs, Ohio, 1977—79; mem. pub. engagement working group, nanoscale sci. edn. and tech. subcom. Nat. Sci. and Tech. Coun., 2005—. Author: (book) Basics for Chemistry, 1982, Living Chemistry, 2d edit., 1986; contbr. articles to profl. jours.; host, prodr. (radio program) Science Alive!, 1983—87, developer numerous mus. exhibits. Apptd. Nat. Mus. Svcs. Bd., 1996—2003; trustee Mus. Without Walls, 1996—2000, Sci. Pioneers, 2000. Recipient Up and Comers award, Jr. Achievement Mid.-Am., 1992; fellow Woodrow Wilson, 1969, NIH postdoctoral, 1972; grantee, NSF, NEH, U.S. Dept. Edn., Ill. Humanities Coun., 1976—88. Fellow: AAAS (at large sect. Y 1987—93); mem.: Am. Assn. Museums (mus. assessment program adv. com. 2000—03), Assn. Sci. Tech. Ctrs. (publs. com. 1984—94, chmn. 1988—94, ethics com. 1994—95, legis. com., chmn. 1996—2000), Phi Lambda Upsilon, Sigma Xi, Alpha Sigma Nu (hon.). Home: 2528 Queen Anne's Ln NW Washington DC 20037-2148 Office Phone: 703-292-5126. Personal E-mail: d.ucko@verizon.net.

**UDALL, MARK,** congressman; b. Tucson, July 18, 1950; m. Maggie Fox; children: Jed, Tess. B.Am. Civilization, Williams Coll., 1972. Course dir., educator Colo. Outward Bound Sch., 1975-85, exec. dir., 1985-95; mem. dist. 13 Colo. Ho. of Reps., 1997-99; mem. U.S. Congress from 2d Colo. dist., Washington, 1999—; Dem. dep. regional whip for western U.S.; mem. armed svcs. com., resources com., sci. com. Democrat. Avocation: mountain climbing. Office: US Ho Reps 240 Cannon Ho Office Bldg Washington DC 20515-0602 also: Ste 206 8601 Turnpike Dr Westminster CO 80031-7044

**UDALL, THOMAS S. (TOM UDALL),** congressman; b. Tucson, May 18, 1948; s. Stewart and Lee Udall; m. Jill Z. Cooper; 1 child, Amanda Cooper. BA in Govt. and Polit. Sci., Prescott Coll., Ariz., 1970; LLB in Internat. Law, Cambridge U., Eng., 1975; JD, U. N.Mex. Sch. Law, 1977. Bar: N.Mex. 1978. Legis. asst. Staff of US Senator Joseph R. Biden of Del., 1973; law clk. to Chief Justice Oliver Seth US 10th Cir. Ct. Appeals, Santa Fe, 1977-78; asst. US atty. criminal divsn. US Atty.'s Office, 1978-81; atty. pvt. practice, Santa Fe, 1981-83; chief counsel N.Mex. Health and Environ. Dept., 1983-84; atty. to ptnr. Miller, Stratvert, Togerson and Schlenker, P.A., Albuquerque, 1985-90; atty. gen., 1991—99; mem. US Congress from 3rd N.Mex. dist., 1999—, co-vice chair Native Am. caucus, mem. small bus. com., mem. vets. affairs com., mem. resources com., ranking minority mem. forests and forest health subcommittee. Pres. Rio Chama Preservation Trust; mem. N.Mex. Environ. Improvement Bd., 1986—87; bd. dirs. La Compania de Teatro de Albuquerque, Santa Fe Chamber Music Festival, Law Fund, 1991—98. Recipient Leadership award, Nat. Commn. Against Drunk Driving, Legal Impact award, N.Mex. Bar Prosecution Sect., Pub. Svc. award, Nat. Highway Traffic Safety Adminstrn. Mem. Nat. Assn. Attys. gen. (pres. 1996), Kiwanis. Democrat. Office: US Ho Reps 1414 Longworth Ho Office Bldg Washington DC 20515-3103 Office Phone: 202-225-6190.*

**UDALL, VESTA HAMMOND,** special education educator; b. Jacksonville, Fla., Dec. 8, 1942; d. Vesta Shields and Gladys Wilcox Hammond; m. John Scriven Udall, July 18, 1964 (div. Feb. 27, 1973); children: Adrien Evelyn, Peter John. BA, Winthrop U., 1964; MEd, U. Phoenix, 1997; postgrad., U. Fla., No. Ariz. U., Ariz. State U. Cert. tchr. Ariz. Various elem. and H.S. tchg. positions Duval County Schs., Jacksonville, 1964—68; tchr. Flagstaff (Ariz.) Jr. H.S., 1974—76, Fickett Jr. H.S., Tucson, 1976—78, Devereux Schs., Scottsdale, Ariz., 1978—80, East Valley H.S., Maricopa County Regional Sch. Dist., Phoenix, 1989—97, Madison Jail and Maricopa County Sheriff's Office, Phoenix, 1997—2000; prof. Phoenix Coll., 1998—; spl. edn. tchr. Westwood H.S., Mesa (Ariz.) Sch. Dist., 2000—. Presenter in field; developer spl. edn. programs. Precinct committeeman Rep. Party, Mesa, 1985—. Named Educator of Yr., Phoenix Sun, 1995. Mem.: Nat. Edn. Assn., Mesa Edn. Assn. Ariz. Republican. Mem. Lds Ch. Avocations: hiking, river running, birdwatching, biking. Home: 2264 E Fairfield St Mesa AZ 85213 Office: Phoenix Coll 1100 W Thomas Rd Phoenix AZ 85013 Personal E-mail: vhudall@aol.com.

**UDELL, HOWARD R.,** pharmaceutical executive; Grad., CUNY; LLB, NYU. Bar: N.Y., Conn., U.S. Supreme Ct. Former ptnr. Millard, Greene & Udell, Stamford, Conn.; gen. counsel Purdue Pharma, Stamford, Conn., 1977—89, group v.p., gen. counsel, 1989—99, exec. v.p., gen. counsel, 1999—2003, exec. v.p., chief legal officer, 2003—. Office: Purdue Pharma 1 Stamford Forum Stamford CT 06901

**UDELL, RICHARD,** lawyer; b. Bklyn., Dec. 27, 1932; s. Alvin and Gertrude (Langsam) U.; m. Marguerite Hartshorne, July 3, 1955; m. children: Benjamin Alan, Edward H. BA, Reed Coll., 1955; LLB, U. Pa., 1958. Bar: N.Y. 1958. Fla. 1984. Pvt. practice, N.Y.C., 1959-65; counsel RCA Records, N.Y.C., 1965-69; assoc. firm Machat & Kronfeld, N.Y.C., 1969-71; counsel Famous Music Corp., N.Y.C., 1971-72, Random House, Inc. subs. RCA, N.Y.C., 1972-75; gen. counsel Simon & Schuster, Inc. subs. Gulf & Western Industries, Inc., N.Y.C., 1975-77; adminstrv. v.p., chief counsel Harcourt Brace Jovanovich, Inc., N.Y.C., 1977-92; v.p., gen. counsel The McGraw Hill Sch. Pub. Co. unit McGraw-Hill Cos., Inc., 1992—. Mem. Bar Assn. City N.Y., Orange County Bar Assn., Fla. Bar Assn. Jewish. Office: McGraw-Hill Sch Pub Co 2 Penn Plz New York NY 10121-0101

**UDEN, DAVID ELLIOTT,** cardiologist, educator; b. Montreal, Sept. 7, 1936; s. Reginald and Elsie Ada (Elliott) U.; children: Thomas Elliott, Linda Ann, Christopher Elliott. BSc, McGill U., 1958; MD, McGill U., Quebec, Can., 1962. Diplomate Am. Bd. Internal Medicine; cert. cardiovascular disease, cert. interventional cardiology. Attending cardiologist Toronto We. Hosp., 1972—93, Wellesley Hosp. Toronto, 1990—93; asst. prof. medicine U. Toronto, 1975—93; chief cardiology Oconee Meml. Hosp., Seneca, SC, 1993—97, chief medicine, 1994—96, 2000—02; elected mem. S.C. Med. Discipline Commn., 1996—98, 2000—04; apptd. Discipline Commn., 2000—04. Contbr. articles to profl. jours. with RCAf, 1963-66. Fellow Am.

Coll. Cardiology, Am. Heart Assn. Coun. on Clin. Cardiology, Soc. for Cardiac Angiography and Intervention. Avocations: travel, photography. Office: Oconee Cardiology Assocs 704 N Pine St Seneca SC 29678 Office Phone: 864-882-0847.

**UDESHI, TUSHAR JAIRAJ,** application developer, consultant; arrived in US, 1997; s. Jairaj D. and Kalpana J. Udeshi; m. Manjula T. Udeshi; 1 child, Anushka T. BEngring. in Cmputer Sci. with honors, Birla Inst. Tech. and Sci., 1997, MSc in Physics with honors, 1997; MS, U. Utah, 1999. With Argonne (Ill.) Nat. Lab., 1997—99; sr. software engr. Zyvex Corp., Richardson, Tex., 2000—. Reviewer Jour. Computing and Info.Sci. Engring.; contbr. articles to profl. jours. Mem.: Assn. Computing Machinery (mem. spl. interest group graphics and interactive techniques). Achievements include patents for system and method for robust and efficient resizing of simple polygons. Office: Zyvex Corporation 1321 North Plano Rd Richardson TX 75081 Office Phone: 972-235-7881. Office Fax: 972-235-7882.

**UDEVITZ, NORMAN,** publishing executive; b. Cheyenne, Wyo., Jan. 22, 1929; s. Jay and Edith (Stienberg) U.; m. Marsha Rae Dinner, Dec. 17, 1960; children: Jane, Kathryn, Andrew. Student, U. Colo., 1946-49. With Cheyenne Newspapers Inc. Cheyenne, 1949-54; editor-pub. Wyo. Buffalo, Cheyenne, 1954-63; account supr. Tilds & Cantz Advt. Agy., L.A., 1963-66; exec. v.p. Fitzgerald, Maahs & Miller, L.A., 1966-71; staff writer The Denver Post, 1971-88; dir. pubs. Am. Water Works Assn., Denver, 1988-97; ret., 1997. Sgt. USNG, 1950-53. Named Colo.'s Outstanding Journalist, U. Colo., 1977; recipient Pulitzer Prize Gold medal Columbia U., 1986. Mem. Investigative Reporters and Editors Inc., (bd. dirs. 19/8-80, 81-83), The Newspaper Guild (McWilliams award 1976, 77). Jewish. Home: 4677 E Euclid Ave Littleton CO 80121-3224

**UDEY, MARK C.,** dermatologist, researcher; B in chemistry, U. Wis., Madison; MD, PhD, Washington U., St. Louis. Med. intern Barnes Hosp., St. Louis, dermatology resident; now chief Dermatology Br. Ctr. Cancer Rsch., Nat. Cancer Inst. Office: Dermatology Br Ctr Cancer Rsch 10 Center Dr Bldg 10 Rm 12N238 Bethesda MD 20892-1908 Office Phone: 301-496-1741. Office Fax: 301-496-5370. E-mail: udey@helix.nih.gov.

**UDLER, RUBIN YAKOVLEVICH,** linguist; b. Braila, Muntenia, Romania, Sept. 27, 1925; came to U.S., 1992; s. Yakov Aronovich and Dina Vladimirovna (Gleizer) U.; m. Malka Il'inichna Alexenberg, July 8, 1956; children: Arthur, Angela. B in Philol. Sci., U. Chernovtsy, Ukraine, 1951; M in Philol. Sci., USSR Acad. Scis., Moscow, 1961; D in Philol. Sci., USSR Acad. Scis., Leningrad, 1974. Dep. chmn. fgn. langs. dept. Chernovtsy State Pedagogical Inst., 1951-56; jr. sci. rschr. dialectology sect. Moldavian br. USSR Acad. Scis., Kishinev, Moldova, 1956-61; chief dialectology and exptl. phonetics sect. Moldavian Acad. Scis., 1961-80, chief dialectology and history of lang. sect., 1980-86, chief dialectology and linguistic geography dept., 1986-92, dep. of academician-sec. of social studies dept., 1989-92; ctr. assoc. U. Ctr. for Internat. Studies U. Pitts., 1994—. Translator Soviet Bucovina newspaper, Chernovtsy, 1951-52; mem. editl. bd. Moldavian Lang. and Lit., 1961-91, Jour. Linguistics and Study of Lit., 1991-92; sr. sci. rschr. All-Union Cert. Com., Moscow, 1963; presenter at cong., confs., and symposiums. Author: Moldavian Dialects of the Chernovtsy Area Consonantism, 1964, Dialectological Division of the Moldavian Language, Parts 1 and 2, 1976, The Cursed Years, 2003, Russian edit., 2005, English edit., 2005; co-author: The Moldavian Linguistic Atlas, 4 parts, 1968-73, Dialectological Dictionary, 5 vols., 1985-86, Dialectological Texts, 6 parts, 1969-87, The Historical Grammar of the Moldavian Language, 1964, Notes on Modern Moldavian Literary Language, 1967, Moldavian Dialectology, 1976, The Carpathian Dialectological Atlas, 7 vols., 1987-2005, The Romanian Linguistic Atlas by Regions, 1993-2003; author more than 250 pub. works with total volume of more than 475 editl. sheets; mng. editor, co-editor approximately 60 monographs, dictionaries, atlases, collection of dialectological texts, collections of articles, theses, brochures with total volume of more than 1275 editl. sheets. Corr. mem. Moldavian Acad. Scis. Presidium of Moldavian Acad. Scis.; mem. Holocaust Ctr. United Jewish Fedn. Greater Pitts. Jewish. Avocations: collecting old books, coin collecting/numismatics, travel. Home: 1535 Shady Ave Pittsburgh PA 15217-1455 Office: Univ Ctr Internat Studies U Pitts 41 G40 Forbes Quadrangle Pittsburgh PA 15260 Personal E-mail: artriu@hotmail.com.

**UDOFF, ERIC JOEL,** diagnostic radiologist; b. Balt., Oct. 8, 1948; s. Melvin Jerome and Esther (Fisher) U.; m. Ronni Ann Chapin, June 7, 1980; children: Brian Evan, Jonathan Andrew. AB, Washington U., 1969; MD, U. Rochester, 1973. Intern, resident in diagnostic radiology U. Chgo., 1973-77; instr. in cardiovasc. diagnostic Johns Hopkins U., Balt., 1977-79; radiologist Sinai Hosp., Balt., 1979-86, Mt. Sinai Med. Ctr., Milw., 1986-88, Sinai Hosp., Balt., 1988-90; asst. prof. radiology Johns Hopkins U. Hosp. 1990-91; radiologist North Fulton Regional Hosp., Roswell, Ga., 1991-97; instr. thoracoabdominal imaging U. Va., 1997-98, Radiologist, Diagnostic Imaging Specialists, Atlanta, 1998—. Mem. AMA, Am. Roentgen Ray Soc., Am. Coll. Radiology, Radiol. Soc. N.Am., Ga. Radiol. Soc., Phi Beta Kappa. Avocations: reading, tennis. Office: 6000 Lake Forrest Dr Ste 475 Atlanta GA 30328 Office Phone: 404-459-8440. Personal E-mail: ejurad@yahoo.com.

**UDOLF, BRUCE LEE,** lawyer; s. Roy Joseph and Marcelle Udolf; m. Sheryl Singer Udolf, Oct. 24, 1992; 1 child, Hayley. BA, Hofstra U., 1973; JD, Emory U. Sch. Law, 1979. Bar: Ga. 1979, US Dist. Ct. (no. dist.) Ga. 1979, US Ct. Appeals (11th cir.) 1982, Fla. 1991, US Dist. Ct. (so. dist.) Fla. 1998, US Dist. Ct. (mid. dist.) Fla. 1999. Atty. Mishan, Sloto, Greenberg, Hollinger & Udolf, P.A., Miami, Fla., 1998—2000, Eckert, Seamans, Cherin and Mellott, LLC, Ft. Lauderdale, 2000—01, Ruden McClosky, P.A., 2001—06, Berger Singerman, Ft. Lauderdale, 2006—; law clerk to Hon. Arthur W. Fudger Talhapoosa Jud. Cir. Ga., 1979—80; asst. dist. atty. Northeastern Jud. Cir. Ga., 1980—83, dist. atty., 1983—87; asst. US atty. appellate divsn. US Atty.'s Office, US Dist. Ct. (so. dist.) Fla., 1987—98; major crimes sect. US Dept. Justice, 1987—88, narcotics sect., 1988, pub. corruption sect., 1988—97, chief pub. corruption sect., 1992—97, assoc. ind. counsel Office Ind. Counsel Washington, 1997—98. Tchr. Law Edn. Inst., Steamboat Springs, Colo., 2002, US Dept. Treasury, Office Tech. Assistance, US Dept. Justice, Office Profl. Devel. and Tng. Corruption and Organized Crime Symposium, St. Petersburg, Russia, Fla. Internat. U., Ctr. Adminstrn. Justice Pub. Corruption Seminars, La Paz, Caracas, Venezuela, Tegucigalpa, Honduras, Atty. Gen.'s Advocacy Inst., Washington, Nat. Inst. Trial Advocacy, Trial Techs. Program, Emory U. Sch. Law, Atlanta, Fla. Bar CLE. Recipient commendation, Bur. Alcohol, Tobacco and Firearms, 1989, Dirs., FBI, 1991, 1994, Drug Enforcement Adminstrn., Office Profl. Responsibility, 1994, US Customs Svc., Office Internal Affairs, 1997. Mem.: Fla. Bar (criminal law sect. edn., ethics subcom.), Fla. Bar Criminal Procedure Rules com. (chair subcom. I, fast track subcom., chair joint appellate, civil, criminal rules subcom.), Palm Beach County Bar Assn., Broward County Bar Assn., Dade County Bar Assn. (chair meetings com., vice chair fed. practice com.), ABA, Fla. Assn. Criminal Def. Lawyers, Nat. Assn. Criminal Def. Attys., Eugene Spellman Am. Inns of Ct., Fed. Bar Assn. (pres., v.p., dir. Broward County chpt., asst.), US Atty.'s Assn. (past pres.). Office: Berger Singerman 350 E Las Olas Blvd Ste 1000 Fort Lauderdale FL 33301 Office Phone: 954-527-2486. Office Fax: 954-333-4086. Business E-Mail: bruce.udolf@ruden.com.

**UDOLF, ROY,** psychology professor, lawyer; b. N.Y.C., Aug. 7, 1926; s. Barney and Esther (Iadis) U.; m. Marcelle Temkin, July 1, 1950; children: Bruce Lee, Penny Jill, Brad Robert, David William. B.E.E., NYU, 1950; JD cum laude, Bklyn. Law Sch., 1954; MA, Hofstra Coll., 1963; PhD, Adelphi U., 1971. Bar: N.Y. 1954, U.S. Dist. Ct. (so. and ea. dists.) N.Y., 1954, U.S. Supreme Ct. 1958. Electronic engr. Arma Corp., Garden City, N.Y., 1956-63; asst. dept. head Gyrodyne Co., St. James, N.Y., 1963-67; prof. psychology New Coll. of Hofstra U., Hempstead, NY, 1967—2004. Author: Criminal

Justice System and its Psychology, 1979; Handbook of Hypnosis, 1981; Forensic Hypnosis, 1983. Served with USMC, 1944-46, PTO. Home: 2777 Granz Ct East Meadow NY 11554-4302 Office: Roosevelt Hall New Coll of Hofstra U Hempstead NY 11550

**UDRYS, ALMIS GERARDAS,** health policy consultant; s. Arunas Teodoras Udrys and Virginia Ruta Ruzgas; m. Claudia Orsi, Feb. 28, 2002. BA in Internat. Bus., Hillsdale Coll., 1999; M Pub. Policy, Pepperdine U., 2001. Auditor evaluator Bur. State Audits, Sacramento, 2001—03, sr. auditor evaluator, 2003—05; policy cons. Calif. Assembly Rep. Caucus, Sacramento, 2005—. Named Rookie of Yr., Bur. State Audits, 2002. Republican. Roman Catholic. Avocations: travel, reading, basketball, hiking.

**UDVAR-HAZY, STEVEN F.,** leasing company financial executive; b. Budapest, Hungary, Feb. 23, 1946; came to U.S., 1958. m. Christine L. Henneman, June 7, 1980; 3 children. BA, UCLA, 1968; HHD (hon.), U. Utah, 1990; D (hon.), Emory Riddle Aero. U., 2000. Cert. airline transp. jet pilot. Chmn., CEO Internat. Lease Fin. Corp., Beverly Hills, Calif., 1973—. Bd. dirs. Sky West Inc., St. George, Utah; chmn. bd. dirs. Ocean Equities, Inc. Active Smithsonian's Udvar-Hazy Nat. Air & Spave Mus. Named one of Forbes' Richest Americans, 2006. Mem. Wings Club (Achievement to Aviation award 1989). Office: Internat Lease Fin Corp 10250 Cconstallation Blvd 35th Fl Los Angeles CA 90067 Office Phone: 310-788-1999.

**UDWADIA, FIRDAUS ERACH,** engineering educator, consultant; b. Bombay, Aug. 28, 1947; arrived in U.S., 1968; s. Erach Rustam and Perin P. (Lentin) Udwadia; m. Farida Gagrat, Jan. 6, 1977; children: Shanaira, Zubin. BS, Indian Inst. Tech., Bombay, 1968; MS, Calif. Inst. Tech., 1969, PhD, 1972; MBA, U. So. Calif., 1985. Mem. faculty Calif. Inst. Tech., Pasadena, 1972-74; asst. prof. engring. U. So. Calif., LA, 1974-77, assoc. prof. mech., civil, and aerospace engring. and bus. adminstrn., 1977-83, prof., 1983-86, bd. dirs. Structural Identification Computing Facility, prof. engring. bus. adminstrn., maths., 1986—2005, prof. civil engring., aerospace mech. engring., math., info. ops., mgmt., and sys. architecture engring., 2005—. Cons. Jet Propulsion Lab., Pasadena, 1978—, Argonne Nat. Lab., 1982—83, Air Force Rocket Lab., Edwards AFB, Calif., 1984—, Air Force Rsch. Lab., 1990—; vis. prof. applied mechanics and mech. engring. Calif. Inst. Tech., Pasadena, 1993. Author: Analytical Dynamics, A New Approach, 1996; assoc. editor: Applied Math. and Computation, Discrete Dynamics Nature and Soc., Jour. Optimization Theory and Applications, Jour. Franklin Inst., Jour. Differential Equations and Dynamical Sys., Nonlinear Studies, Jour. Math. Analysis and Applications, Jour. Math. Problems in Engring.; editor: Jour. Aerospace Engring., Advances in Dynamics and Control, 2000; co-editor: Dynamics and Control, 1999; chief editor Dynamical Systems and Control, 2004, mem. adv. bd. Jour. Tech. Forecasting and Social Change; contbr. articles to profl. jours. Bd. dirs. Crisis Mgmt. Ctr. U. So. Calif., LA. Recipient Golden Poet award, 1990; NSF grantee, 1976—. Fellow: ASME; mem.: ASCE (Outstanding Tech. Achievement in Aerospace Engring. 2005), AIAA, Seismol. Soc. Am., Soc. Indsl. and Applied Math., Am. Acad. Mechanics, Sigma Xi (mem. Earthquake Engring. Rsch. Inst. 1971, 1974, 1984). Achievements include patents in field; patents for control of nonlinear systems, 2002. Avocations: poetry, piano, chess. Home: 2100 S Santa Anita Ave Arcadia CA 91006-4611 Office: U So Calif 430K Olin Hall University Park Los Angeles CA 90007 Office Phone: 213-740-0495. Business E-Mail: fudwadia@usc.edu.

**UDY, RAE,** columnist, writer; b. Ogden, Utah, Mar. 24, 1950; d. Verl Nish Udy and Elizabeth Jones White; m. Steven James Weese, Apr. 9, 1971; children: Nation Verl Weese, Luke Ray Weese. Student, Weber State U., 1968. Columnist Longview News-Jour., Longview, Tex., 1989—; lifestyle editor Marshall News Messenger, Marshall, Tex., 1999—2000. Mem. and past v.p. East Tex. Writers Assn., 1987—; former contbr. Idaho Enterprise, Harleton Happenings. Author: (book) Countdown Cooking, 1993. Mem.: Ladies Aux. of Frat. of Eagles. Democrat. Christian. Avocations: gardening, travel, camping. Office: PO Box 5965 Longview TX 75608 Office Phone: 903-777-2723. Personal E-mail: raeudy@gmail.com.

**UEBERROTH, PETER VICTOR,** former baseball commissioner; b. Evanston, Ill., Sept. 2, 1937; s. Victor and Laura (Larson) U.; m. Virginia Nicolaus, Sept. 1959; children— Vicky, Heidi, Keri, Joe BS in Bus., San Jose State Coll., 1959. Ops. mgr. then v.p. Trans Internat., 1959-62; founder, chmn. Transp. Cons. Internat., 1963-79; pres., mng. dir. Los Angeles Olympic Organizing Com., 1979-84; commr., chief exec. officer of major league baseball N.Y.C., 1984-89; mng. dir. Contrarian Group, 1990—; co-chmn. Doubletree Hotels Corp., Phoenix, 1993—; co-owner, co-chmn. Pebble Beach Co., 1999—; chmn. U.S. Olympic Comm., 2004—; dir. McLeodUSA, 2001—. Former chmn. Ask Mr. Foster Travel Service; chmn. Colony Hotels, Intercontinental Tours, Inc., First Travel Corp; mem. bd. dirs. California Angels. Ambassadors Internat., Coca-Cola Co., Hilton Hotels Corp. Author: Made in America, 1985 Named Man of Yr., Time Mag. and Sporting News, 1984; recipient Scopus award Am. Friends of Hebrew U., Jerusalem, 1985 Fellow: Am. Acad. Arts and Scis. Office: Ambassadors Intl Inc 110 S Ferrall St Spokane WA 99202

**UECKER, BOB,** actor, radio announcer, former baseball player, television personality; b. Milw., Jan. 26, 1935; m. Judy Uecker, 1976 (div. 2001); 4 children. Major league baseball player Milw. Braves, Nat. League, 1962, 63; major league baseball player St. Louis Cardinals, 1964, 65, Phila. Phillies, 1966-67, Atlanta Braves, 1967; commentator ABC Monday Night Baseball, 1976-82; commentator playoff and world series NBC Baseball, 1994-98; radio-TV baseball announcer Milw. Brewers, 1971—. Host War of the Start, Bob Ueckers Wacky World of Sports, Saturday Night Live; guest Tim Conway show, Who's the Boss, Peter Marshall Show; appeared in Fatal Instinct. Co-star TV series Mr. Belvedere, ABC-TV, 1985-1990; guest TV appearances include Late Night with David Letterman, The Tonight Show, Midnight Special, LateLine, 1998; also numerous commls.; author: Catcher in the Wry, 1985; films include: Major League, 1989, Major League 2, 1994, (voice over) Homeward Bound II: Lost in San Francisco, 1996, Major League: Back to the Minors, 1998, Andre the Giant: Larger Than Life, 1999. Recipient Big B.A.T. award Baseball Assistance Team, 1995; inducted Wis. Performing Artists Hall of Fame, 1993, Wis. Broadcasters Assn. Hall of Fame, 1994, Wis. Sports Hall of Fame, 1998. Office: Milw Brewers Baseball Club Milw County Stadium 1 Brewers Way Milwaukee WI 53214-3651*

**UECKER, GRANT GORDON,** financial consultant; b. Tripp, S.D., July 27, 1947; m. Pamela Kay Brodeen, June 28, 1968; children: Gregg Garrison, Melissa Dawn Sears. Grad., Dakota Wesleyan U., Mitchell, S.D., 1970. Asst. bus. mgr. Dakota Wesleyan U., Mitchell, SD, 1973—79; fin. aid coord. Mitchell Tech. Inst., SD, 1979—. Pres. S.D. Assn. of Fin. Aid Adminstrs., 1985—86. Pres. Jaycees, Mitchell, SD, 1975—76. Mem.: Mitchell Exch. Club (bd. mem. 1995—96). Home: 1315 Roland Ln Mitchell SD 57301 Office: Mitchell Tech Inst 821 N Capital St Mitchell SD 57301 Office Phone: 605-995-3025. Office Fax: 605-996-3299. E-mail: GUecker@hotmail.com.

**UEDA, REED TAKASHI,** historian, educator; b. Honolulu, Sept. 14, 1949; s. Goro and Mildred (Yoshimoto) Ueda; m. Peggy Lynn Rubin; children: Katya, Alyona. BA, UCLA, 1970; MA, U. Chgo., 1973, Harvard U., 1976, PhD, 1981. Rsch. editor Harvard Ency. Am. Ethnic Groups, Cambridge, Mass., 1977-79; instr. Harvard U., Cambridge, 1980-81, assoc. Ctr. Am. Polit. Studies, 2001—; prof. Tufts U., Medford, Mass., 1981—. Vis. prof. Brandeis U., Waltham, Mass., 1986, Harvard U., 1987—89, 1996; steering group com. on internat. migration MIT, 1996—; assoc. New Global History Initiative. Author: Avenues to Adulthood, 1987, Postwar Immigrant America, 1994; editor: The Companion to Immigration, 2006; adv. editor: New Dictionary of the History of Ideas, 2005; co-editor: Faces of Community, 2003; assoc. editor: Jour. Interdisciplinary History, 1996—; mem. editl. bd. Harvard Edn. Rev., 1977—78, Am. Quar., 1993, Mass. Hist. Rev. —. Mem. Gov.'s Edn. Reform Rev. Commn., 1994—2002; mem. coun. fgn. rels. Boston Working Group Nat. Interest, 1995; mem. coun. for basic edn. Review Panel

for Nat. Standards in History, 1995; mem. US Dept. Edn. Nat. Assessment of Ednl. Progress, 1991—92, Nat. Adv. Planning Com. for U.S. Hist. Framework, 1992—94, Nat. Standards in Civics and Govt., 1994—95, Nat. Standards in Profl. Tchg. Fellow, Am. Coun. Learned Soc., Woodrow Wilson Internat. Ctr., NEH, Charles Warren Ctr. Fellow: Mass. Hist. Soc. (mem. planning com. immigration and urban history sem. 1999—); mem.: Immigration and Ethnic Hist. Soc. (exec. bd. 2001—04). Office: Tufts U Dept History Medford MA 02155 Office Phone: 617-627-3520. Business E-Mail: reed.ueda@tufts.edu.

**UEHLEIN, EDWARD CARL, JR.,** lawyer; b. Boston, May 7, 1941; s. Edward Carl and Elizabeth (Thatcher) U.; m. Judith Taylor, June 16, 1962; children: Christine, Sara. Student, Bowdoin Coll., Brunswick, Maine, 1958-59; BA, Swarthmore Coll., 1962; LLB, Boston Coll., 1965. Bar: Mass. 1965, D.C. 1968. Atty. Nat. Labor Relations Bd., Atlanta, 1965-68; assoc. Morgan, Lewis & Bockius, Washington, 1968-71; exec. asst. to sec. U.S. Dept. Labor, Washington, 1971-73; ptnr. Morgan Lewis & Bockius, Washington, 1973—2001, counsel, 2001—. Sec.-treas. Carlou Corp., Wilmington, Del., 1969-71. Fellow, Ford Found., 1961. Mem. ABA, FBA, D.C. Bar Assn., Belle Haven Country Club, Ballybunion Golf Club, Royal Dornoch Golf Club. Avocations: travel, golf, reading. Office: Morgan Lewis & Bockius 1111 Pennsylvania Ave Washington DC 20004 Office Phone: 202-739-5075. Business E-Mail: ecuehlein@morganlewis.com.

**UEHLING, GORDON ALEXANDER, JR.,** investment company executive; b. Providence, Sept. 1, 1939; s. Gordon Alexander and Alice Bishop (Tomb) U.; m. Victoria M. Eckert, Dec. 30, 1967 (div. Oct. 1975); 1 child, Gordon A. III; m. Mary Elizabeth Shields, Sept. 15, 2002. BS, U.S. Naval Acad., 1961; postgrad., Columbia U., 1968. Mktg. mgr. Communitype Corp., N.Y.C., 1968-70; asst. treas. Mfrs. Hanover Trust Co., N.Y.C., 1970-73; v.p. The Manhattan Savs. Bank, N.Y.C., 1973-87; pres. Turnstone, Inc., Cresskill, NJ, 1988—2000; gen. ptnr. Palisades Ptnrs., L.P., Cresskill, 1988—. Lt. USN, 1961-67, Vietnam. Recipient Air medal (14 awards), USN, 1967. Mem. Naval Inst., Naval Acad. Alumni Assn., Army Navy County Club, Gipsy Trail Club. Republican. Avocations: flying, playing tennis, skiing. Home: 222 Ruckman Rd Closter NJ 07624 Office: Palisades Ptnrs LP 100 Union Ave Cresskill NJ 07626-2137 Office Phone: 201-871-2200. E-mail: duehling@alpineassociates.com.

**UEKI, TARO,** nuclear engineer; b. Koganei, Tokyo, Japan, June 18, 1962; s. Shunji and Tomiko Ueki. BS in Nuclear Engring., Nagoya U., Aichi, Japan, 1987; PhD in Nuclear Engring., U. Mich., 1998. Entry level rsch. engr. Hitachi, Ltd., Hitachi Works and Energy Rsch. Lab., Hiatchi, Ibaraki, Japan, 1987—92; postdoctoral staff Delft U. of Tech., Netherlands, 1998—2000; postdoctoral assoc. Los Alamos (N.Mex.) Nat. Lab., 2001—. Contbr. articles to sci. jours. Recipient Rackham predoctoral fellowship, Rackham Grad. Sch. at U. of Mich., 1996—97. Mem.: Inst. of Math. Stats., Am. Nuclear Soc. Achievements include patents for fuels of boiling water nuclear reactor.

**UELTSCHI, ALBERT LEE,** air transportation executive; b. Ky., May 15, 1917; s. Robert and Lena Ueltschi; m. Eileen Ueltschi (dec.); 4 children. Pilot Pan Am, 1941—68; founder FlightSafety Internat., Flushing, NY, 1951, pres., 1951—2003, now chmn. Chmn. Orbis Internat. Named one of Forbes' Richest Americans, 2006; named to Nat. Aviation Hall of Fame, 2001; recipient Nat. Bus. Aircraft Assn. Award, 1991, Award for Extraordinary Svc., FAA, 1991, Disting. Achievement Award, The Wings Club, 2006. Office: Teterboro Airport 100 Moonachie Ave Moonachie NJ 07074*

**UFFELMAN, MALCOLM RUCJ,** electronics executive; b. Clarksville, Tenn., Oct. 22, 1935; s. Malcolm C. and Margaret Lillian (Davidson) U.; m. Sarah White Barksdale, June 11, 1957; children: Malcolm Rucj Jr., Katharina White, Davidson Barksdale, Jefferson Churchill. BS, Vanderbilt U., 1957; MS, George Washington U., 1963. Engr. Melpar, Inc., Falls Church, Va., 1957-60; v.p. Scope, Inc., Reston, Va., 1960-73; sr. cons. MRI, Inc., McLean, Va., 1973-78; v.p. Racal Communications Inc., Rockville, Md., 1978-80; sr. cons. MRJ, Inc., Fairfax, Va., 1980-82; v.p., gen. mgr., Ctr. Advanced Planning and Analysis E-Systems Inc., Fairfax, 1982-96; v.p. Constellation Comm., Inc., Fairfax, 1996-99; patent agt., 1999—2000; exec. v.p. Contact Corp., 2000—. Contbr. numerous articles to profl. jours.; holder 7 patents in field. Scoutmaster Troop 183 Boy Scouts Am., Oakton, Va., 1973-79; bd. dirs. Camco Fund, 2002—. Capt. USAR, 1957-69. Fellow IEEE; mem. Cosmos Club (Washington), Internat. Brotherhood Magicians. Episcopalian. Avocations: sailing, reading, travel, magic, fly fishing. Personal E-mail: rucj@ieee.org.

**UFFELMAN, MINOA D.,** history professor; b. Clarksville, Tenn., Oct. 2, 1959; d. Osman Samuel Uffelman and Helen Ann McCreary; m. Joel H. Evans. BS, Austin Peay State U., Clarksville, Tenn., 1981; MA, Austin Peay State U., 1983; PhD, U. Miss., Oxford, 2003. Assoc. prof. dept. history Austin Peay State U., Clarksville. Author: Plessey vs. Ferguson, 2006, Mississippi Farm Women, 2006; contbr. articles to encys. Mem. history and preservation com. First Presbyn. Ch., Clarksville, 2006; mem. HCHS Heather Uffelman Meml. Scholarship Com., Erin, Tenn., 1994—2000; peacemaking com. First Presbyn. Ch., Clarksville, 2004—06. Fellow Grad. fellow, U. Miss., 1996—2000; grantee Horace Samuel and Marion Galbraith Merrill Travel grantee, Orgn. Am. Historians, 2000. Mem.: Tenn. Hist. Assn., Orgn. Am. Historians, Am. Assn. Historians. Democrat. Presbyterian. Avocations: reading, walking. Home: 230 Longwood Ln Clarksville TN 37043 Office Phone: 931-221-7704.

**UFFNER, MICHAEL S.,** automotive executive; b. Phila., July 18, 1945; s. Ray and Shirley A. (Block) Uffner; m. Marilyn A. Ursomarso; 1 child, Lauran R. BA, MA, U. Pa., 1971. V.p. Union Park Pontiac, BMW, Honda, Wilmington, Del., 1972-82; pres. Del. Motor Sales Inc., Auto Team Del., Wilmington, 1982—. Mem. manpower tng. adv. com. GM, pres. dealer adv. coun., 1985, mem. dealer policy bd., 1990—91; trustee Christiana Health Care Sys., 2002—. Mem. Wilmington Police Bus. Adv. Coun., 1991—; bd. dirs., mem. exec. com. BBB Del., 1992—, chmn., 1998—2000; mem. New Castle County Small Bus. Commn., 1993—. Recipient Quality Dealer award, Time Mag., 1997, numerous other awards. Mem.: Del. Automobile and Truck Dealers Assn. (bd. dirs., v.p. 1992—93, pres. 1994—95), Am. Econ. Assn., Cadillac Motor Car Divsn. Nat. Dealers Coun. (vice chmn. 1989—90, chmn. 1990—91, chmn. DeVille brand com. 1995—97), Tavistock Civic Assn. (pres. 1976—77), U.S. C. of C. (bd. dirs. 1998—2004, chmn. pub. affairs com. 2001—04), Del. C. of C. (chmn. small bus. com. 1991—95, bd. dirs. 1993—, chmn. small bus. alliance 1995—96, mem. exec. com. 1995—, vice chmn. bd. dirs. 1996—99, chmn. bd. dirs. 2000—02), Am. Heart Assn. (bd. dirs. Del. chpt. 1981—98, pres. 1985—86, chmn. 1986—87, v.p., bd. dirs. Nat. Ctr. 1987—90), U. Pa. Alumni Assn. (v.p. Del. chpt. 1978—80, pres. 1980—81), Univ. Whist Club, Ocean City Yacht Club, Hidden Creek Golf Club, Fieldstone Golf Club. Office: 1606 Pennsylvania Ave Wilmington DE 19806-4018

**UFFORD, CHARLES WILBUR, JR.,** lawyer; b. Princeton, N.J., July 8, 1931; m. Isabel Letitia Wheeler, May 20, 1961; children: Eleanor Morris Ufford Léger, Catherine Latourette Ufford-Chase, Alison Wistar Ufford Salem. BA cum laude (Francis H. Burr scholar), Harvard U., 1953, LLB, 1959; postgrad. (Lionel de Jersey Harvard studentship), Cambridge U., Eng., 1953-54. Bar: N.Y. 1961, U.S. Tax Ct. 1963. Assoc. Riggs, Ferris & Geer, N.Y.C., 1959-61; from assoc. to ptnr. Jackson, Nash, Brophy, Barringer & Brooks, 1961-78; ptnr. Skadden, Arps, Slate, Meagher & Flom, N.Y.C. 1978-92, of counsel, 1993-96. Contbr. articles to legal jours. Trustee Nat. Squash Racquets Ednl. Found., N.Y.C., 1972-81; mem. Princeton Monthly Meeting, Soc. of Friends, clk., 1986-88, 99; mem. exec. com. Friends Com. on Nat. Legislation, 1997-98; bd. dirs. Pennswood Village, 1998—, Friends Fiduciary Corp., 1999—. Nat. Intercollegiate Squash Racquets champion, 1952-53; mem. NCAA All-Am. Soccer title team, 1952. Fellow Am. Coll. Trust and Estate Counsel (transfer tax study com. 1990-93); mem. ABA, N.Y. Bar Assn. (chmn. trusts and estates law sect. 1984), Assn. Bar City N.Y., N.Y.

State Office of Ct. Adminstrn. (Surrogates Ct. Adv. Com., 1994-96), U.S. Squash Racquets Assn. (hon. life; trustee endowment fund 1984-96), Internat. Lawn Tennis Club U.S.A. (dir. 1982-2005). Office: 150 Mercer St Princeton NJ 08540-6827 Office Phone: 609-921-8085. E-mail: cuffordl@aol.com. *Integrity, perseverance, compassion and humor are all very well--but the key is to be blessed by a Divine Improvidence.*

**UFIMTSEV, PYOTR YAKOVLEVICH,** physicist, electrical engineer, educator; b. Ust'-Charyshskaya Pristan', Altai Region, Russia, July 8, 1931; s. Yakov Fedorovich and Vasilisa Vasil'evna (Toropchina) U.; m. Tatiana Vladimirovna Sinelschikova; children: Galina, Ivan, Vladimir. Grad., Odessa State U., Ukraine, 1954; PhD, Ctrl. Rsch. Inst. Radio Industry, 1959; DSc, St. Petersburg State U., Russia, 1970. Engr., sr. engr., sr. scientist Ctrl. Rsch. Inst. of Radio Industry, Moscow, 1954-73; sr. scientist, head scientist Inst. Radio Engring. & Electronics Acad. Scis., Moscow, 1973-90; prin. engr. Northrop Grumman Corp., 1995—2000; prof. U. Calif., Irvine, 2003—04. Vis. prof., adj. prof. UCLA, 1990—2003; mem. sci. bd. radio waves Acad. Scis., Moscow, 1960—90. Author: Method of Edge Waves in the Physical Theory of Diffraction, 1962, Theory of Edge Diffraction in Electromagnetics, 2003; contbr. articles to profl. jours. Recipient USSR State Prize, Moscow, 1990, Leroy Randle Grumman medal for outstanding sci. achievement, N.Y.C., 1991, 20th Century Achievement medal, Cambridge, 1996, Hall of Fame medal, Cambridge, 1996. Fellow IEEE; assoc. fellow AIAA; mem. Electromagnetics Acad. (U.S.), A.S. Popov Sci. Tech. Soc. Radio Engring., Electronics & Telecommunication (Russia). Achievements include origination of the Physical Theory of Diffraction, used for design of American stealth aircrafts and ships; for radar-cross-section calculation, and antenna design.

**UGGAMS, LESLIE,** entertainer; b. N.Y.C., May 25, 1943; d. Harolde Coyden and Juanita Ernestine (Smith) Uggams; m. Grahame John Kelvin-Pratt, Oct. 16, 1965; children: Danielle Nicole Pratt, Justice Harolde John Kelvin-Pratt. Student, Juillard Sch. Music, 1961-63; degree (hon.), Jarvis Coll., Tyler, Tex., Wilberforce U., Ohio. Appeared on (TV series) Beulah, 1949, featured on Sing Along with Mitch, 1961—64, starred in (Broadway plays) Hallelujah Baby, 1967 (Tony award, 1968), Her First Roman Broadway Musical, 1968, On Golden Pond, 2005 (nominated Helen Hayes award for best actress, 2005), star of (weekly TV variety show) The Leslie Uggams Show, 1969, appearances in nightclubs top TV mus. variety shows, appeared in films Two Weeks in Another Town, Black Girl, 1962, Skyjacked, 1972, Poor Pretty Eddie, 1973, appeared in (TV miniseries) Roots, ABC-TV, 1977 (Critics Choice award as best supporting actress, 1977), (TV films) Sizzle, 1981, Harlem, 1993, star (Broadway musicals) Blues in the Night, 1982, (Broadway musical) Jerry's Girls, 1985, Anything Goes, 1987, (off-Broadway) The Old Settler, 1999 (Audelco award as best actress), (dramatic play), 1999; appeared in: Thoroughly Modern Millie, 2004; star (musical play) King Hedley II, 2001 (nominated Tony award best actress, 2001), Thunder Knocking on the Door, 2002 (Audelco award best actress, 2002), (TV miniseries) Backstairs at the White House, 1979, co-host (TV series) Fantasy TV, 1982—83 (Emmy award 1983, 1983); author: The Leslie Uggams Beauty Book, 1966. Founding mem. BRAVO chpt. City of Hope, Los Angeles, 1969, treas., 1969—79. Named best singer on TV, 1962—63; recipient Drama Critics award, Newspaper and TV critics, 1968, Tony award, 1968, Emmy award, 1993. Mem.: SAG, NARAS, AFTRA, Actors' Equity Assn. Democrat. Presbyterian. Avocations: needlepoint, knitting, tennis, squash, exercising. Office: The Gage Group Inc care Phillip Adelman 315 W 57th St Frnt 4H New York NY 10019-3158 Business E-Mail: leslie@leslieuggams.com

**UGHETTA, JAMES C.,** lawyer; BA, Denison U., 1977; JD, St. John's U., 1981. Bar: NY 1982, NJ 1982, US Dist. Ct. Dist. NJ, US Dist. Ct. Ea. Dist. NY, US Dist. Ct. So. Dist. NY, US Dist. Ct. No. Dist. NY, US Supreme Ct. Ptnr. Wilson, Elser, Moskowitz, Edelman & Dicker LLP, White Plains, NYC. Mem.: Soc. Automotive Engineers (product liability adv. coun.), Assn. for the Advancement of Automotive Medicine, Def. Rsch. Inst. Office: Wilson Elser Moskowitz Edelman & Dicker LLP 3 Gannett Dr White Plains NY 10604 Office Phone: 914-323-7000 ext. 4248. Office Fax: 914-323-7001. Business E-Mail: ughettaj@wemed.com.

**UGHETTA, WILLIAM CASPER,** lawyer, manufacturing executive, director; b. N.Y.C., Feb. 8, 1933; s. Casper and Frieda (Bohland) U.; m. Mary L. Lusk, Aug. 10, 1957; children: William C., Robert L., Edward F., Mark R. AB, Princeton U., 1954; LLB, Harvard U., 1959. Bar: N.Y. 1959. Assoc. Shearman & Sterling, N.Y.C., 1959-67; asst. sec. Corning Glass Works, NY, 1968-70, sec., counsel NY, 1971-72, v.p., gen. counsel NY, 1972-82, sr. v.p., gen. counsel NY, 1983-98. Bd. dirs. Covance Inc. Bd. dirs. Steuben Area coun. Boy Scouts Am. Lt. (j.g.) USN, 1954-56. Mem. Assn. of Bar of City of N.Y., ABA, N.Y. State Bar Assn., Am. Corp. Counsel Assn. (trustee 1982-85), Princeton Club (N.Y.C.), Univ. Club (N.Y.C.), Corning Country Club. Home: 10519 North Rd Corning NY 14830-3235

**UHDE, THOMAS WHITLEY,** medical educator; b. Louisville, Jan. 6, 1948; s. George Irwin and Maurine U.; m. Marlene Ann Kraus, Oct. 22, 1977; children: Miles August, Katherine Kraus. BS, Duke U., 1971; MD, U. Louisville, 1975. Postdoctoral fellow Yale U., New Haven, 1975-79, chief resident clin. rsch. unit, 1979; rsch. fellow NIMH, 1977-81; pvt. practice in psychiatry Bethesda, Md., 1979-93; clin. adminstr. sect. psychobiology BPB, NIMH, ADAMHA, Bethesda, Md., 1979-80, chief unit on anxiety and affective disorders, 1982-89, chief 3-West clin. rsch. unit, 1980-90, chief sect. on anxiety and affective disorders, 1989-93; asst. clin. prof. Uniformed Svcs. U. Health Scis., Bethesda, Md., 1982-89, assoc. clin. prof. uniformed svcs., 1985-91; attending staff Clin. Ctr. NIH, Bethesda, Md., 1982-93; chmn. dept. psychiatry Detroit Receiving Hosp. and Harper Hosp., 1994-98; psychiatrist in chief Detroit Med. Ctr., 1993—2001; clin. prof. Uniformed Svcs. U. Health Scis. Sch. Medicine, Bethesda, 1991—; chmn. dept. psychiatry and behavorial neurosci. Wayne State U. Sch. Medicine, Detroit, 1993—2001; prof. dept. pharmacology Wayne State U. Sch. of Medicine, Detroit, 1993—2003; prof., chair dept. psychiatry Penn State Coll., Hershey, Pa., 2004—, dir. ctrl. Pa. Psychiatric Inst., 2004—, dir. neurosci. rsch. inst., 2004—. Prof., psychiatry and behavioral neuroscis. dept., Wayne State U. Sch. Medicine, 1993-2003, assoc. dean rsch. and grad. programs, 1999-2001; asst. dean neuroscis., 2001-03; mem. sci. adv. com. Bethesda, Md., 1990; cons. Rsch. Scientist Devel. Rev. Com., HHS, ADAMHA, 1983, Career Devel. Program Awards Com., VA, Washington, 1986, Primary Care Rsch. Program, AD-AMHA, 1988; exec. bd. Anxiety Disorders Assn. Am., 1991-93, 99-, chair sci. adv. bd. Anxiety Disorders Assn. Am., 1991-93, 99-, chair sci. adv. bd. Rockville, Md., 1991-93. Editor-in-chief (jour.) Anxiety; editor-in-chief Depression and Anxiety; mem. editl. bd. Actualities Medicales Internationales en Psychiatrie, 1983, Jour. Affective Disorders, 1986, Jour. Anxiety Disorders, 1987-95, Biol. Psychiatry, 1998—2001; contbr. more than 300 sci. articles to profl. jours. Capt. USPHS, 1979-93. Recipient The Ackerly award, 1975, Nat. Rsch. Svc. award, 1979, A.E. Bennet Neuropsychiat. Rsch. Found. award, Brain, Body & Mind award USPHS, Recognition award ADAA; Am. Coll. Neuropsychopharmacology travel fellow. Mem. Am. Coll. Neuropsychopharmacolgy, Am. Coll. Psychiatry, Am. Soc. of Clin. Psychopharmacology, Internat. Brain Rsch. Orgn., Sleep Rsch. Soc. Officer: Penn State Coll Medicine Dept Psychiatry PO Box 850 500 University Dr Hershey PA 17033-0850 Office Phone: 717-531-8515. E-mail: tuhde@psu.edu.

**UHL, HENRY STEPHEN MAGRAW,** internist, educator; b. Wilkes-Barre, Pa., July 23, 1921; s. John Hamilton and Rebecca Ursula (Magraw) Uhl; m. Louise Powell Butler, Nov. 30, 1946 (div. 1979); 1 child, Meredith Louise Conley; m. Nancy Hyde Easley, Feb. 16, 1980 (dec. Jan. 29, 1998); m. Bernice Mallard Everett, June 25, 1999. AB, Princeton U., 1943; MD, Harvard U., 1947; MA adeundem hon., Brown U., 1967. Diplomate: Am. Bd. Internal Medicine. Intern in pathology John Hopkins Hosp., Balt., 1947-48; asst. resident Johns Hopkins Hosp., Balt., 1948, asst. dept. medicine, 1949; asst. in pathology Johns Hopkins Med. Sch., 1947-48, instr. anatomy and pathology, 1948-49; intern med. service Henry Ford Hosp., Detroit, 1949-50; Mich. Heart Assn. research fellow Wayne State U. Coll. Medicine and Detroit Receiving Hosp., 1950-51, sr. asst. resident med. service and asst. in medicine, 1951-52, instr. medicine rsch and research assoc., 1952-53; dir. med. edn. Worcester City Hosp. (Mass.) and Bay State Med. Ctr., Springfield,

Mass., 1953-60; mem. faculty, adminstrn. Albany Med. Coll., NY, 1960-66; prof. med. sci. Brown U, Providence, 1966-71; dir., prof. medicine U. NC, Mountain Area Health Edn. Ctr., 1973-78; prof. medicine Creighton U., Omaha, 1978-86, Bowman Gray Sch Medicine, Wake Forest U., Winston-Salem, NC, 1986—; cons. NIH, also hosps., 1960-78. Contbr. articles to profl. jours. Served to ensign M.C. USNR, 1942-45. Recipient Disting. Service award Mountain Area Health Edn. Found., Asheville, NC, 1978 Mem. ACP, Alliance Continuing Med. Edn., Am. Soc. Internal Medicine, Assn. Hosp. Med. Edn. (pres. 1958-60, John C. Leonard Meml. award 1984), Soc. Health and Human Values Clubs: Princeton (NYC); Press (Omaha); Fontenelle Hills Country (Bellevue, Nebr.), Pine Brook Country Club. Achievements include research in Uhl's anomaly.

**UHL, KATHLEEN,** federal agency administrator; b. May 12, 1962; BA in Chemistry, Temple U.; MD, Med. Coll. Pa. Intern, resident Fort Benning, Ga.; fellow Uniformed Svcs. U. Health Scis.; physician Walter Reed Army Med. Ctr., Washington, until 1998—, reviewer office clin. pharmacology and biopharmaceutics, dep. divsn. dir. office post-mktg. drug risk assesment, acting divsn. dir., supervisory med. officer ctr. drug eval. and rsch., dir. Office Women's Health, 2005—. Capt. USPHS. Contbr. articles to profl. jours. Recipient Meritorious Svc. Medal. Office: FDA 5600 Fishers Ln Rockville MD 20857

**UHL, PHILIP EDWARD,** artist, photographer, cinematographer; b. Toledo, Aug. 19, 1949; s. Philip Edward and Betty Jean U. Student, Dayton Art Inst., 1967-68, Art Students League, 1974. Creative dir. Ctr. for Civic Initiative, Milw., 1969-71; VISTA vol. Office Econ. Opportunity, 1969-71; artist, photographer Assn. Honolulu Artists, 1974-77; pres. U Hl Enterprises div. Makai Photography, Honolulu, 1977—; Videoscapes div. Channel Sea TV Honolulu, 1977—. Cons. Pan Am. Airways, N.Y.C., Honolulu, 1979-84, ITTC Travel Ctr., Honolulu, 1982-83, Royal Hawaiian Ocean Racing Club, Honolulu, 1984—, Sail Am.-Am's Cup Challenge, Honolulu, 1985-86, Am. 3 Found., Am. Cup Def., San Diego, 1991-92, Am. 3 Found. Womens Team, 1994-95, UHL Studios, Hawaii, 2000—. Co-prodr. video documentary White on Water, 1984 (Emmy 1984), Racing the Winds of Paradise (Golden Monitor award Internat. TV Assn. 1989); prodr.: Joy of Life (Golden Monitor award Internat. TV Assn. 1988), Sailors on the Sea, 1990, Teamwork, Talent, Technology (Tele award 1993); cameraman, prodr.: Pan Am. Clipper Cup 1980, 82, 84, Kenwood Cup, 1986, 88, 90, 92, 94, 96, 98, 2000 (2 Tele awards 1994), ESPN Kenwood Cup, 1990, 92, 94, ESPN Am.'s Cup, 1991-92, 94-95, Transpac, 1991, 93, 95, 97, 99, 2001, 05, (video documentary) Rocking the Boat, 1994-95, Dateline NBC Setting Sail 1994-95, numerous spls., reports on ABC-TV, NBC-TV, CBS-TV, PBS, NHK, BBC, TFI, F1, TVNZ and numerous other major worldwide broadcast networks; prodr. At the Helm, America' Cup 2000 TVNZ; photographer, dir. graphic design/photography (video documentary) Transpac 100 years across the Pacific, 2001: (book) Nautical Quar. (Soc. Pub. Designer award 1984); contbr. numerous articles, photos to yachting publs., numerous exhbns. fine/digital art; exhibited in group shows in Honolulu, Tokyo, Hong Kong, Syndey, Paris, Boston, Palm Beach, Isle of Wight, Las Vegas, N.V., San Diego, San Francisco, L.A., N.Y.C., Osterville, Mass.; represented in permanent collections City and County of Honolulu, Hawaii Maritime Mus., UCLA Med. Ctr., others. Mem. Am. Print Alliance, Am. Soc. Marine Artists, Soc. Internat. Nautical Scribes, Internat. Yacht Restoration Sch., Honolulu Printmakers, Digital Art Soc. Hawaii, Assn. Hawaii Artists, U.S. Sailing Assn., Royal Hawaiian Ocean Racing Club, Tutukaka South Pacific Yacht Club, Waikiki Yacht Club. Office: UHL Enterprises 1750 Kalakaua Ave Ste 3-757 Honolulu HI 96826-3766 E-mail: uhl@aol.com.

**UHL, SCOTT MARK,** state agency administrator; b. Balt., July 6, 1950; s. Edward George and Maurine Barbara (Keleher) Uhl; m. Charlene Hughins, Feb. 29, 1988. BA, Lehigh U., 1972. Cmty. systems developer Md. Mental Hygiene Adminstrn., Balt., 1979-82, chief, housing and cmty. support, 1982-89; adminstr., cmty. programs, dep. secretariat pub. health Md. Health and Mental Hygiene, Balt., 1989-95; dep. dir. Md. Devel. Disabilities Adminstrn., Balt., 1995—. Pres. Waterfields Press, Inc., 1994—2004; mem. CARE adv. bd. Md. Dept. Human Resources, Balt., 1987—94; prin. staff Md. Gov.'s Task Force Long Term Fin. Planning for Individuals with Disabilities, 1991—92. Mem. State Adv. Coun. Adminstrv. Hearings, 1993—97. Recipient Gov's Citation, 1992. Republican. Home: 2004 Sleepy Hollow Dr Woodbine MD 21797 Office: Md Health & Mental Hygiene 201 W Preston St Baltimore MD 21201-2323

**UHLENHUTH, EBERHARD HENRY,** psychiatrist, educator; b. Balt., Sept. 15, 1927; s. Eduard Carl Adolph and Elisabeth (Baier) Uhlenhuth; m. Helen Virginia Lyman, June 20, 1952; children: Kim Lyman, Karen Jane, Eric Rolf. BS in Chemistry, Yale U., 1947; MD, Johns Hopkins U., 1951. Intern Harborview Hosp., Seattle, 1951-52; resident in psychiatry Johns Hopkins Hosp., Balt., 1952-56, asst. psychiatrist in charge outpatient dept., 1956-61, psychiatrist in charge, 1961-62; chief adult psychiatry clinic U. Chgo. Hosps. Clinics, 1968-76; instr. psychiatry Johns Hopkins U., 1956-59, asst. prof., 1959-67, assoc. prof., 1967-68, U. Chgo., 1968-73, prof., 1973-85, acting chmn., 1983-85; prof. psychiatry U. N.Mex., Albuquerque, 1985-97, prof. emeritus, 1997—, Disting. Univ. prof., 2005—, vice chmn. for edn., 1991-94. Cons. in field; clin. psychopharmacology rsch. rev. com. NIMH, 1968-72, mem. treatment devel. and assessment rsch. rev. com., 1987-88; mem. psychopharmacology adv. com. FDA, 1974-78; adv. group to Treatment of Depression Collaborative Rsch. Program, NIMH, 1978-82; study rev. com. Xanax discontinuation program Upjohn Co., 1988-92, Nat. Adv. Coun. on Drug Abuse, NIDA, 1989-92, Coop. Studies Evaluation Com., VA, 1989-92. Mem. editl. bd. Jour. Affective Disorders, 1978—, Psychiatry Rsch, 1979-96, Behavioral Medicine, 1982—, Neuropsychopharmacology, 1992-95, Exptl. and Clin. Psychopharmacology, 1992-99, Depression and Anxiety 1992—; contbr. articles to profl. jours. Recipient Rsch. Career Devel. award USPHS, 1962-68, Rsch. Scientist award, 1976-81. Fellow: Collegium Internat. Neuro-Psychopharmacologicum, Am. Psychopath. Assn., Am. Psychiat. Assn., Am. Coll. Neuropsychopharmacology; mem. Psychiat. Rsch. Soc., Balt.-Washington Soc. Psychoanalysis. Office: U NMex Dept Psychiatry MSC05 030 1 Univ New Mex Albuquerque NM 87131-0001 Office Phone: 505-272-8876. Business E-Mail: uhli@unm.edu.

**UHLER, KATHRYN L.,** music educator; b. Easton, Pa., Dec. 22, 1975; d. Ronald Thomas Uhler and Jamie Ann Abel. BS in Music Edn., Millersville U., 1998. Cert. profl. instrrn. Pa. Music instr., music mgr. Michael's Music Studio and Store, Sinking Spring, Pa., 1999—2002; music tchr., acad. coord. Cmty. Sch. Music and the Arts, Reading, Pa., 2003—; pvt. music tchr. Composer (duet for clarinet and cello) Willow, 1998 (Leo Ascher award, 1998). Mem.: Nat. Piano Guild. Avocations: singing, song writing. Office: Cmty Sch Music and the Arts Rm 556 Goggleworks 201 Washington St Reading PA 19601 Office Phone: 610-374-7167.

**UHLER, WALTER CHARLES,** government official, writer; b. Lebanon, Pa., Feb. 23, 1948; s. Victor Cornelius and Barbara Jean (Malin) U.; m. Judy Ann Sherk, Aug. 7, 1967 (div. 1984); children: Terry Allen, Matthew David. Life partner: Carol A. DePrisco. BA in Polit. Sci. cum laude, Pa. State U., 1973, BA in Russian cum laude, 1973, cert. Russian area, 1973, MPA, 1992. Tchg. asst. Pa. State U., University Park, 1975-76; procurement agt. Naval Aviation Supply Office, Phila., 1976-80; contracts adminstr. GSA, Phila., 1980-81; contracting officer Def. Logistics Agy., Phila., 1981-86, corp. contracting officer, 1986-94; chief fin. svcs., 1993—2001; chief of ops. Def. Contract Mgmt. Agy., Lockheed Martin Delaware Valley, 2001—; regional cons. Def. Logistics Agy., L.A., 1985-86, nat. cons. Cameron Station, Va., 1989-90, leader Testing Labs. Privatization Assessment Team Ft. Belvoir, Va., 1997-98. Participant Air Force Intelligence Conf. on Soviet Affairs, Arlington, Va., 1988, Venona Conf., Washington, 1996, Ballistic Missile Def. Conf., Washington, 1998, AP/Harriman Inst. Conf., N.Y.C., 1999, State of the World Forum, N.Y.C., 2000; testified against nat. missile def., Vt. Ho. of Reps., 2002; gave radio interviews on nat. missile def., Vt., Calif., Wis., Radio Free Europe/Radio Liberty, 2002; presenter, 11th ann. Russia-Am. Conf., St. Petersburg, Russia, 2002; spkr. on contracts DOD Conf., Cleve., 1988, on

restructuring costs, Memphis, 1994; chmn. Ann. Nat. Conf. Contracting Officers and Auditors, 1987-93; mem. Citizen Amb. Archivists' Del. to Russia and Poland, 1995, Citizen Amb. Del. to China, 1996, Russia and Finland, 1998; prodr., interviewer (with George Enteen) Sergei Vasilievich Utechin's Oral Reminiscences, 1997—; pres. Russian-American Internat. Studies Assn. 2004-. Contbr. articles to profl. jours. Baseball coach Valley Athletic Assn., Bensalem, Pa., 1979-88, basketball coach, 1980-85, coord., 1981; tutor Ctr. for Literacy, Phila., 1991-93, Project GIVE, Phila., 1995-98. Recipient Comdrs. Excellence award Defense Contract Mgmt. Area Ops., 1993. Mem. Am. Assn. for Advancement of Slavic Studies, Soc. for Mil. History, Acad. Polit. Sci., Nat. Book Critics Cir., Am. Acad. of Polit. and Social Scis., Friends of the Free Libr. of Phila., Am. Hist. Assn. Democrat. Avocations: history, literature, Pennsylvania State University football. Office: DCMA LMDV L-3 Bldg 1 Federal St Camden NJ 08102 E-mail: waltuhler@aol.com.

**UHLIR, ARTHUR, JR.,** electrical engineer, academic administrator; b. Chgo., Feb. 2, 1926; s. Arthur and Helene (Houghteling) U.; m. Ingeborg Williams, July 24, 1954; children: Steven, Donald, David. BS, Ill. Inst. Tech., 1945, MSChemE, 1948; SM in Physics, U. Chgo., 1950, PhD in Physics, 1952. Process analyst Douglas Aircraft, Chgo., 1945; asst. engr. Armour Rsch. Found., Chgo., 1945-48; tech. staff Bell Telephone Labs., Murray Hill, NJ, 1951-58; dir. semi- condr. research and devel., mgr. semicondr. div., group v.p. engring. Microwave Assos., Inc., Burlington, Mass., 1958-69; dir. rsch. Computer Metrics, Rochelle Park, NJ, 1969-73; prof. elec. engring. Tufts U., Medford, Mass., 1970-94, chmn. dept. elec. engring., 1970-75, dean of engring., 1973-80. Fellow, AEC, 1949—51. Fellow: AAAS, IEEE; mem.: Am. Phys. Soc., Sigma Xi. Home: 45 Kendal Common Rd Weston MA 02493-2159 Office: Tufts Univ Dept Elec Engring & Computer Sci Medford MA 02155 Personal E-mail: auhlir@mailaps.org

**UHLMANN, ELENORE ARLENE,** interior designer, writer; b. Ada., Mich., July 18, 1922; d. Arthur Benjamin and Arla Mary (Kriedler) Hale; m. Robert Carl Uhlmann, Jan. 14, 1939 (dec. Jan. 5, 1995); children: J. Louise Uhlmann Zielke, Nancy Jean Uhlmann. Student, U. Mich., 1939, 68, Kendall Sch. Design, 1940, Heaneys Bus. Coll., 1941. Designer, sales rep. Mfr.'s Showroom, Grand Rapids, Mich., 1966-71; designer, decorator Regent Interiors, Clearwater, Fla., 1971, Chandlers, Dunedin, Fla., 1972-76, Square Yard, Dunedin, Fla., 1976-80; instr. Palm Harbor (Fla.) Libr., 1997-98. Presentor at numerous workshops and clubs. Contbr. articles and essays to mags. Mem. Jr. League, 1972-83. Avocations: writing, painting, travel. Home: 16623 N West Point Pkwy Apt 114 Surprise AZ 85374-6009 also: 16623 N West Point Pkwy Apt 114 Surprise AZ 85374-6009

**UHLMANN, FREDERICK GODFREY,** securities trader; b. Chgo, Dec. 31, 1929; s. Richard F. and Rosamond G. (Goldman) U.; m. Virginia Lee Strauss, July 24, 1951; children: Richard, Thomas, Virginia, Karen, Elizabeth. BA, Washington and Lee U., 1951. Ptnr. Uhlmann Grain Co., Chgo., 1951-61; v.p. Uhlmann & Co., Inc., Chgo., 1961-65; sr. v.p. H. Hentz & Co., Chgo., 1965-73, Drexel Burnham Lambert Inc., Chgo., 1973-84; exec. v.p., dir. bus. futures Dean Witter Reynolds Inc., Chgo., 1984-85; sr. v.p., mgr. commodity dept. Bear, Stearns & Co., Inc., Chgo., 1985-88; exec. v.p. Rodman & Renshaw, Inc., 1988-95; sr. v.p. LIT-Divsn. of First Options Inc., Chgo., 1995-98; chmn. Chgo Bd. Trade, Ill., 1973-74; sr. v.p., exec. dir. MAN Financial, 1998—. Ptnr. Uhlmann Price Securities LLC. Bd. dir. Dist. 113 H.S. Found., 1990—, Mt. Sanai Hosp. Inst., Chgo., 1999—. Mem. Nat. Futures Assoc. (dir. 1981-2000, vice chair 1998-2000), Futures Industry Assn. (bd. dir., chmn. 1975-76), Futures Industry Inst. (bd. dir.). Home: 783 Whiteoaks Ln Highland Park IL 60035-3656 Office Phone: 847-444-1104. E-mail: fgu73@aol.com.

**UHR, JONATHAN WILLIAM,** immunologist, educator, researcher; b. N.Y.C., Sept. 8, 1927; s. Jacques Stanley Uhr and Mary Wetsman; m. Roberta Joy Klibanoff (div.); children: Jacqueline, Sarita. AB, Cornell U., 1948; MD, NYU, 1952. Diplomate Am. Bd. Internal Medicine. Dazian fellow dept. microbiology NYU Med. Ctr., 1955-56; chief resident in medicine Mt. Sinai Hosp., N.Y.C., 1956-57; instr. dept. microbiology NYU Sch. Medicine, 1957-58, asst. prof. medicine, 1958-62, assoc. prof., 1962-68, prof., 1968-72; prof. dept. microbiology and internal medicine U. Tex. Southwestern Med. Ctr. & Cancer Immunobiology Ctr., Dallas, 1972—; chair dept. microbiology U. Tex. Southwestern Med. Ctr., Dallas, 1972-97. Dir. Irvington House Inst. for Rheumatic Fever and Allied Diseases, N.Y.C., 1962-72; vis. prof. microbiology Yale U., 1970-72; assoc. attending physician Univ. Hosp., N.Y.C., 1963-72; assoc. vis. physician Bellevue Hosp., N.Y.C., 1959-72; cons. internal medicine Manhattan Vet.'s Hosp., 1964-74. Contbr. articles to profl. publs. WWII, 1945-46. Recipient Newcomb Cleveland prize AAAS, 1963, Squibb award Infectious Diseases Soc. Am., 1971, NAS award, 1984, Faculty medal Med. Sch. Montpellier, France, 1984, Abbott-ASM Lifetime Achievement award, 1999; Commonwealth fellow Walter and Eliza Hall Inst. Med. Rsch., 1961-62. Mem. Am. Assn. Immunologists (pres. 1989—), Am. Assn. Pathologists, Am. Soc. Clin. Investigation, Transplantation Soc., Assn. Am. Physicians. Office: U Tex Southwestern Med Ctr Dept Cancer Immunobiology 5323 Harry Hines Blvd Dallas TX 75390-8576 E-mail: jonathan.uhr@utsouthwestern.edu.

**UHRICH, KEVIN PATRICK,** editor; Contbg. writer LA Reader, 1986—96, LA Weekly, 1996—99, Pasadena Weekly, 1996—99; staff writer Simi Valley Enterprise, 1986—90, Pasadena Star-News, 1990—94; contbg./freelance writer LA Times, 1994—95; overnight editor City News Svc., 1995—96; editor Pasadena Weekly, 1999—; sr. editor LA City Beat/Valley Beat, 2003—; Recipient award for Outstanding Dedication, Greater LA Press Club, 1992, First Place in Newswriting, 1997, First Place in Investigative Reporting, 1999, John Anson Ford award for outstanding svc. in furthering racial understanding, LA County Human Rels. Commn., 1999, First Place Group Reporting, Pasadena Weekly, 1999, Cmty. Svc. award for outstanding svc. following Sept. 11, 2002, Third Place Investigative Reporting, 2004. Home: 615 N Kenwood St #10 Glendale CA 91206

**UHRIG, ROBERT EUGENE,** nuclear engineer, educator; b. Raymond, Ill., Aug. 6, 1928; s. John Matthew and Anna LaDonna (Fireman) U.; m. Paula Margaret Schnepf, Nov. 27, 1954; children: Robert John, Joseph Charles, Mary Catherine, Charles William, Jean Marie, Thomas Paul, Fredrick James. BS with honors, U. Ill., 1948; MS, Iowa State U., 1950, PhD, 1954; grad. Advanced Mgmt. Program, Harvard U., 1976. Registered profl. engr., Iowa, Fla. Instr. engring. mechanics Iowa State U., 1948-51; assoc. engr., rsch. asst. Inst. Atomic Rsch. (at univ.), 1951-54, assoc. prof. engring. mechanics and nuc. engring., also group leader, 1956-60; prof. nuc. engring., chmn. dept. U. Fla., Gainesville, 1960-68, on leave, 1967-68, dean Coll. Engring., 1968-73, dean emeritus, 1989—; dep. asst. dir. rsch. Dept. Def., Washington, 1967-68; dir. nuc. affairs Fla. Power & Light Co., Miami, 1973-74, v.p. for nuc. affairs, 1974-75, v.p. nuc. and gen. engring., 1976-78, v.p. advanced systems and tech., 1978-86; disting. prof. engring. emeritus, 2003—; disting. scientist Oak Ridge Nat. Lab., 1986—2002, disting. scientist emeritus, 2003—. Instr. engring mechanics U.S. Mil. Acad., 1954-56; rep. Dept. Def. to com. on acad. sci. and engring. Fed. Coun. Sci. and Tech., 1967; chmn. engring. edn. adv. com. NSF, 1972-73; bd. dirs. Engring. Coun. Profl. Devel., 1968-72; mem. commn. edn. for engring. profession Nat. Assn. State Univs. and Land Grant Colls., 1969-72; apptd. mem. adv. com. on reactor safeguards U.S. Nuc. Regulatory Commn., 1997-2001. Author: Random Noise Techniques in Nuclear Reactor Systems, 1970, trans. into Russian, 1974; co-author: (with Lefteri H. Tsoukalas) Fuzzy and Neural Approaches in Engineering, 1997—. Served to 1st lt. USAF. Recipient Svc. of Def. Civilian Svc. award, 1968, Outstanding Alumni award U. Ill. Coll. Engring., 1970, Alumni Profl. Achievement award Iowa State U., 1972, President's medallion U. Fla., 1973; Disting. Achievement citation Iowa State U. Alumni Assn., 1980, Glenn Murphy award Am. Soc. for Engring. Edn., 1992; Named to Hall Disting. Alumni, Aerospace Dept., Iowa State U., 2005. Fellow ASME (life, Richards Meml. award 1969, ASME medal, 2005), AAAS, Am. Nuc. Soc. life, chmn. edn. com. 1962-64, chmn. tech. group for edn. 1964-66, bd. dirs. 1965-68, exec. com. bd. 1966-68); mem. Am. Soc. Engring. Edn. (pres. S.E. sect. 1972-73, chmn. nuc.

engring. divsn. 1966-67, 88-89, rsch. award S.E. sect. 1962), John Henry Newman Honor Soc., Sigma Xi, Tau Beta Pi, Phi Mu Epsilon, Pi Tau Sigma, Phi Kappa Phi (Disting. Mem. award 1997). Home: 5221 NW 44th Pl Gainesville FL 32606-4328 Office: U Tenn Pasqua Nuc Engring Bldg Knoxville TN 37996-2300 Business E-Mail: ruhrig@utk.edu.

**UICKER, JOSEPH BERNARD,** retired engineering company executive; b. Mar. 29, 1940; s. John Joseph and Elizabeth Josephine (Flint) U.; m. Mary Catherine Howze, June 5, 1965 (div. Oct. 1971); children: Patricia, Suzzane; m. Janet Ann Ballman, Sept. 22, 1973. BSME, U. Detroit 1963, MS, 1965. Registered profl. engr., Mich. Engr. Smith Hinchman & Grylls, Detroit, 1964-72, chief mech. engr. health facilities, 1972-73, asst. dir. health facilities, 1973-75, v.p., dir. mech. engring., 1975-82, v.p., dir. profl. staff, 1983-2000; also bd. dirs.; ret., 2000. Dir. Smith Group, Detroit, 1984-2000. Capt. U.S. Army, 1966—67. Mem. NSPE, ASME, ASHRAE, Soc. Am. Mil. Engrs., Engring. Soc., Athletic Club. Avocations: golf, photography, gardening. Home: 15250 Knolson St Livonia MI 48154-4736 E-mail: juicker@ameritech.net.

**UILKEMA, JOHN K.,** lawyer; BSE in Mech. Engring., U. Mich., 1957; JD, George Washington U., 1961. Bar: D.C. 1962, Calif. 1963, U.S. Patent and Trademark Office, U.S. Dist. Ct. (all dists.) Calif., U.S. Ct. Appeals (Calif.), U.S. Dist. Ct. (all dists.) D.C., U.S. Ct. Appeals (D.C.), U.S. Ct. Appeals (fed. cir.), U.S. Supreme Ct. Ptnr. Thelen Reid & Priest LLP, San Francisco. Mem.: ABA (bd. govs. sect. intellectual property 2002—05, ho. dels. 1992—2005, property law sect. 1987—88). Office: Thelen Reid & Priest LLP Ste 1800 101 Second St San Francisco CA 94105 Office Phone: 415-369-7641, 415-371-1200. Business E-Mail: juilkema@thelenreid.com.

**UKE, ALAN KURT,** finance company executive; b. L.A., Nov. 24, 1952; s. Mustafa Tugrul Uke and Gladys Jean Hunnicott; m. Lisa Joyce Katter, 1975 (div.); 1 child, Gregory; m. Diane Christiansen, Jan. 12, 1985; children: Leslie, John. Student, Dartmouth Coll., 1971, Univ. Calif., San Diego, 1975. Prin., owner Underwater Kinetics, Powag, Calif., 1971—; pres. UK Corp., Del Mar, Calif., 1980—. Patentee, inventor in field. Pres. San Diego Aircraft Carrier Mus., 1993—, San Diego Taxpayers Assn. Found., 1996-98, North County Coun. Aging, Vista, Calif., 1998-2000; chmn. learning for life divsn. Boy Scouts Am., 1999-2000. Recipient Entrepreneur of Yr. award San Diego County, 1997, Headliner of Yr. award San Diego Press Club, 1997. Mem.: World Pres.'s Assn. Republican. Lutheran. Avocations: travel, reading, astronomy. Office: Underwater Kinetics 13400 Danielson St Poway CA 92064 E-mail: auke@uwkinetics.com.

**UKPOLO, VICTOR,** economics educator; b. Lagos, Nigeria, Mar. 23, 1950; came to U.S., 1972; s. Samuel Obuje and Gladys (Arugbo (Olotewo) U.; m. Pamela Davies, June 19, 1977 (div.); 1 child, Victor; m. Fawn Teresa Coffey, Dec. 30, 1989; children: Mercy, Oghenekewe. BA in Econs., U. Md., 1975; MA in Econs., Am. U., 1977, PhD in Econs., 1985. Asst. prof. Ahmadu Bello U., Zana, Nigeria, 1986-87, Austin Peay State U. Clarksville, Tenn., 1988-92, assoc. prof.; interim assoc. vice chancellor academic affairs, spl. asst. to chancellor for academic rsch. Tenn. Bd. Regents; assoc. v.p. academic affairs Calif. State U., LA; sys. v.p. academic and student affairs So. U. New Orleans (SUNO), 2003—05, chancellor, 2005—06, pres., 2006—. Adj. lectr. Am. U., Washington, 1984-85, U. Washington, 1985-86; adj. assoc. prof. Lagos (Nigeria) State U., 1993—. Contbr. articles to profl. publs. Bd. dirs. United Meth. Urban Ministry, Clarksville, 1991—. Mem. Rotary (sec. 1992-93), Phi Kappa Phi, Omicron Delta Kappa. Avocations: tennis, running. Office: So Univ at New Orleans 6801 Press Dr New Orleans LA 70126*

**UKROPINA, JAMES R.,** lawyer; b. Fresno, Calif., Sept. 10, 1937; s. Robert J. and Persida (Angelich) Ukropina. AB, Stanford U., 1959, MBA, 1961; LL.B., U. So. Calif., 1965. Bar: Calif. 1966. Assoc. firm O'Melveny & Myers, Los Angeles, 1965-72, ptnr., 1972—80, 1992—2000, of counsel Los Angeles, 2001—; exec. v.p., gen. counsel Santa Fe Internat. Corp., Alhambra, Calif., 1980-84, dir., 1981-86; exec. v.p., gen. counsel Pacific Enterprises, Los Angeles, 1984-86, pres. and dir., 1986-89, chmn. bd. and chief exec. officer, 1989-91; chmn., CEO Directions, LLC, 2002—. Bd. dir. Lockheed Martin Corp., Pacific Life Ins. Co., Trust Co. of the West, Ctrl. Natural Resources, Keck Found. Editor in chief So. Calif. Law Rev, 1964-65. Trustee Stanford U., 1991-2000 Mem. ABA, Calif. Bar Assn., Los Angeles County Bar Assn., Annandale Golf Club, Calif. Club, Beta Theta Pi. Office: O'Melveny & Myers 400 S Hope St Los Angeles CA 90071-2899

**ULAKOVICH, RONALD STEPHEN,** real estate developer; b. Youngstown, Ohio, Nov. 17, 1942; s. Stephen G. and Anna (Petretich) Ulakovich. BS, Indsl. Engring. Coll., 1967; MS Method Engring., Ill. Inst. Tech., 1969. Methods engr. Supreme Products, Chgo., 1964—66; pres. Contract Chair, 1966—70; v.p. sales Amrep Corp., Rosemont, Ill., 1970—73; pres. Condo Assoc., Ltd., Arlington Heights, Ill., 1973—. Pres. Am. Resorts Internat. Ltd., 1983. Named Employee of Yr., 1965, Ky. Col., State of Ky., 1982; recipient Grand award, Nat. Home Builders, 1977, Million Dollar Cir. award, Chgo. Tribune, 1978, Recognition Cert. award, Congl. Com., 1982, Merit Cert. award, Pres. Reagan's Task Force, 1984. Mem.: Am. Resort and Residential Devel. Assn., Real Estate Soc. Syndicators and Investors, Am. Assn. Investors, Apt. Owners Assn. Avocations: golf, auto racing. Home: 510 Van Buren Dundee IL 60118 Office Phone: 224-558-3910. E-mail: RSGU@cometlink.com.

**ULANOFF, STANLEY M.,** communications executive; b. Bklyn., May 30, 1922; s. Samuel H. and Minnie (Druss) U.; m. Bernice Mayer, June 13, 1947; children: Roger, Amy Ulanoff Christie, Lisa M. Ulanoff, Dory Ulanoff Kennedy. BA in Journalism, U. Iowa, 1943; MBA in Mktg., Hofstra U., 1955; PhD in Comm., NYU, 1968. Copywriter promotions dept. N.Y. Times, 1946—49; asst. to pres. SUNY, Stony Brook, 1962—86; prof. mktg., head advt., sales promotion & pub. rels. divsn. Baruch Coll. (CUNY), NY, 1964—86; pres. Viewmark Prodns. Inc. d.b.a. Advisions, 1986—. Cons. U.S. Dept. Def., Grosset & Dunlap pubs., Siebel/Mohr, U.S. Postal Svc.; cons. asst. to pres. Compton Advt.; arbitrator N.Y. Stock Exch., Nat. Assn. Securities Dealers; cons. Hasbro Toys. Author or editor 34 books including Handbook of Sales Promotion; also mags., newspaper articles, rsch. papers; prodr. over 200 video documentaries. From 2d lt. to brig. gen. U.S. Army, 1942-84. Decorated chevalier Ordre des Palmes Academique, Republic of France, Legion of Merit, Meritorious Svc. medal, Army Commendation medal, Army Achievement medal, U.S. Army, Silver Conspicuous Svc. Cross, Merit medal State of N.Y., 1st prize award Am. Assn. Advt. Agys.; named VIP (Very Important Prof.) Splty. Adv. Assn. Internat. (2); Am. Assn. Advt. Agys. fellow, Eastman-Kodak fellow in film prodn.; Lewis Kleid Direct Mail Advt. scholar. Mem. Mil. Intelligence Res. Soc., Res. Officers Assn. (pres.); disting. alumnus. Hofstra Univ. Office: 17 The Serpentine Roslyn NY 11576-1736 Fax: 516-801-2501. Office Phone: 516-621-1603.

**ULE, GUY MAXWELL, JR.,** stockbroker; b. Chgo., Jan. 2, 1940; s. Guy Maxwell and Margaret (Karahuta) U.; m. Angela Joanne Genelli, Nov. 17, 1975. BA, Harvard U., 1961, MBA, 1967. Analyst, phys. distbn. specialist TWA, N.Y.C. and Phila., 1967—69, supr. commd. passenger sales N.Y.C., 1969—71; pvt. practice cons. N.Y.C., 1971—72; mgr. sales mktg. Source Equities, N.Y.C., 1972; ptnr., N.Y.C. office mgr. Daley, Coolidge & Co., 1973—77; v.p. divsn. mgr. Rosenkrantz, Ehrenkrantz, Lyon & Ross Inc., 1977—85, Ingham Becker & Co., Inc., 1985—87; v.p. asst. sec. Meyers, Pollock, Robbins Inc., 1987—89; v.p.; Max Ule divsn. Herzog Heine Geduld Inc., 1989—2000; v.p. investments Shields & Co., Inc., 2000—. Pres. Max Ule & Co., Inc., N.Y.C., 1977-2004, Max Ule Advt. & Mktg., Inc., N.Y.C., 1980—; brokerage info. cons. Internet World Wide Web, 1995 Creator first discount brokerage sys. on computer, 1980. Chmn., pres. Assn. in Manhattan for Autistic Children, 1985-86. Lt. USN, 1962-65 Mem.: Racquet Club Phila., Knickerbocker Club, Racquet and Tennis Club. Republican. Episcopalian. Avocations: photography, tennis, travel. Home: 8 Gramercy Park S Apt 5B

New York NY 10003-1721 Office: Shields and Co 140 Broadway 44th Fl New York NY 10005 Office Phone: 800-809-1160. Personal E-mail: maxule@aol.com. Business E-Mail: maxule@shieldsandco.com.

**ULETT, GEORGE ANDREW,** psychiatrist; b. Needham, Mass., Jan. 10, 1918; s. George Andrew and Mabel Elizabeth (Caswell) U.; m. Pearl Carolyn Lawrence; children: Richard Carlton, Judith Anne, Carol Lynn. BA in Psychology, Stanford U., 1940; MS in Anatomy, U. Oreg., 1943, PhD in Anatomy, 1944, MD, 1944. Diplomate Am. Bd. Psychiatry and Neurology. Asst. psychiatrist Barnes Hosp., St. Louis, 1950-64; med. dir. Malcolm Bliss Hosp., St. Louis, 1951-61; dir. Mo. Dept. Mental Health, Jefferson City, Mo., 1962-72; prof., chair Mo. Inst. Psychiatry, St. Louis, 1964-73; dir. psychiatry Deaconess Hosp., St. Louis, 1973-94; interim dir. Mo. Inst. of Mental Health, St. Louis, 1990-91, assoc. dir. for policy and ethics, 1991-94; clin. prof. dept. family and cmty. medicine St. Louis U. Sch. Medicine, 1995-98. Mem. adv. coun. Mental Health Assn. St. Louis, 1965-66, 69-70, mem. profl. adv. com., 1965; chair health and hosp. com. Health & Welfare Coun. St. Louis, 1960; mem. alcohol rev. com., psychopharmacology study sect., alcoholism study sect., 1993, grants rev. com. for alternative medicine NIMH, Rockville, Md.; prof. psychiatry Washington U. Sch. Medicine, St. Louis, 1956-61; clin. prof. psychiatry St. Louis U. Sch. Medicine, 1981-89, U. Mo. Sch. Medicine, 1990—. Author 12 books, including The Biology of Acupuncture, 2001, Sleight of Mind, 2006; contbr. over 270 articles to profl jours. Capt. U.S. Air Force, 1946-47. Recipient Ann. award Mo. Assn. for Mental Health, 1966, Recognition award, 1970, AMA Honorable Mention award Foster Com. Exhibit, 1974, Pax Mundi Fellowship award for profl. excellence, 1989, Silver Key award Mental Health Assn. Greater St. Louis, 2005; named hon. mem. Turkish Coll. Neuropharmacology, 1969. Fellow Am. Psychiat. Assn.; mem. Am. Soc. Acupuncture (past pres.), Am. Soc. of Med. Psychiatry (past pres.), Mo. Acad. Psychiatry (past pres.). Office: Mo Inst Mental Health 5400 Arsenal St Saint Louis MO 63139-1400 Office Phone: 314-877-6480. E-mail: george.ulett@mien.edu.

**ULEVICH, NEAL HIRSH,** photojournalist; b. Milw., June 18, 1946; s. Ben and Lea Jean (Klitsner) U.; m. Maureen Ann Vaughan, Sept. 25, 1974; children: Jacob Vaughan, Sarah Beatrice. BA in Journalism, U. Wis., 1968. Reporter A.P., 1968-69; photographer, photo editor, 1971-78, Asia photo editor, 1978-83. Freelance writer, Vietnam, Hong Kong, 1969-71; fellow in journalism U. Wis.-Madison, 1971-72 Recipient Pulitzer prize for news photography, 1977. Jewish. Home: Apt E101 8135 S Poplar Way Centennial CO 80112

**ULIN, DAVID LAWRENCE,** writer, editor, educator; b. NYC, Aug. 21, 1961; s. Richard Irwin and Susan Dana (Borkow) U.; m. Rae Dubow, Aug. 27, 1988; children: Noah Dubow, Sophie Dubow. BA, U. Pa., 1984. Contbr. LA Times, 1991—; book editor LA Reader, 1993-96; instr. UCLA Extension, 1993—; contbr. Newsday, Melville, NY, 1994—, LA Weekly, 1996—, Chgo. Tribune, 1997—; editor LA Times Book Rev., 2005—. Author: Cape Cod Blues, 1992, Myth of Solid Ground, 2004 (Best Book of 2004, Chgo. Tribune and San Francisco Chronicle), Clash's London Calling (33 1/3), 2005; (editor) Another City: Writing from Los Angeles, 2001, Writing Los Angeles: A Literary Anthology, 2002. Trustee Beyond Baroque Literary Arts Ctr., Venice, Calif., 1995. Mem. PEN West (treas. 1995—), Nat. Book Critics Cir. (bd. dirs. 1994-2002).

**ULIN, RICHARD IRWIN,** pediatric orthopedist, educator; b. N.Y.C., May 26, 1936; s. Albert Jay and Ruth Charlotte (Newman) Ulin; m. Susan Dana Borkow; children: David, John. BS, Franklin and Marshall Coll., 1958; MD, Columbia U., 1962. Diplomate Am. Bd. Orthopedic Surgery. Chief pediatric orthopedics Mt. Sinai Med. Ctr., N.Y.C., 1975—2005, acting chair dept orthopedics, 1994—96, clin. prof. orthopedics, 1995—. Oral examiner Am. Bd. Orthopedic Surgeons, 1975—. Cpt. U.S. Coast Guard, 1964—70. Fellow: Scoliosis Rsch. Soc., Pediat. Orthopedic Soc. Am., Am. Orthopedic Assn. Avocations: photography, reading, writing. Office: 1095 Pk Ave New York NY 10128 Office Phone: 212-860-0905.

**ULLBERG, KENT JEAN,** sculptor; b. Gothenburg, Sweden, July 15, 1945; arrived in US, 1974; s. Jean Wilgot and Kerstin Alva (Axelson) U.; m. Veerle Rufina Vermeir, May 5, 1978; children: Robert, Gerald. Diploma in sculpture, Swedish State Sch., 1966. Cert. conservator German Assn. Museology. Curator Nat. Mus. and Art Gallery, Botswana, Africa, 1971-74; curator III Mus. Natural History, Denver, 1974-75. Prin. works include Lincoln Ctr. Eagle, Dallas, 1981, Wind in the Sails, Corpus Christi, Tex., 1983, Genesee Eagle, Mumford, N.Y., 1984, Deinonychus Dinosaurs, Phila., 1987, Whooping Cranes Fountain, Washington, 1989, Christ Monument, Corpus Christi, 1993, Swordfish Monument, IGFA Hdqs., Dania, Fla., 1999, Broward Conv. Ctr., Fountain, Ft. Lauderdale, Fla., Rudor Monument, Stockholm, 1991, Monumental Triptych Art Mus. South Tex., 1993, Bird Mountain Telecom. Hdqs., Stockholm, 1994, Christ Monument, Corpus Christi, 1995, Grizzly Bear Monument, Nat. Mus. Wildlife Art, Jackson, Wyo., 1994, King Penguin Monument, Mystic Marine Life Aquarium, Conn., 1997, R.T. Peterson Meml., Mystic Sealife Aquarium, Conn., 1997, Cougar Monument San Antonio Zoo, 1998, Otters Monument St. Louis Zoo, 1998, Tex. State Aquarium, 1998, Swordfish Monument, Dania Beach, Fla., 1998, Spanish Bull Monument, Johnson C. Smith U., Charlotte, N.C., 1999, Ram Monum, U. N.C., Chapel Hill, 2001, First Nat. Bank Omaha Can. Geese Monument, 2002, Eagle Monument, Fed. Res. Bank, Houston, 2005, Danzamar, Performing Arts Ctr., Tex. A&M, Corpus Christi, 2005. Recipient Gold medal Tex. Rangers Hall of Fame, 1980, Rungius award Nat. Mus. Wildlife Art, 1996, Prix de West award Nat. Cowboy Hall of Fame, 1998, award for wildlife Autry Nat. Ctr., 2004; named Master Wildlife Artist, 1987. Fellow: NAD (academician 1990, Barnett prize 1995, Speyer prize 1995), Am. Soc. Marine Artists, Nat. Acad. Western Art (gold medal 1981, 1982, 1988, 1995, 1999), Nat. Sculpture Soc. (Percival Dietsch award 1979, gold medal 1983, Hering award 1993, Silver medal and John Cavanaugh Meml. prize 2002); mem.: Soc. for Wildlife Art of Nations, Allied Artists of Am. (N.Y. Silver medal 1989), Soc. Animal Artists (medal merit 1979, 1980, 1982, 1987, 1996, 2001, E. Haller award 2001, Sponsor award 2002), Explorers Club N.Y.C. Office Phone: 361-851-1600. Personal E-mail: ullberg@sbcglobal.net.

**ULLESTAD, MERWIN ALLAN,** tax specialist, director; b. Hampton, Iowa, June 29, 1949; s. Allan L. and Georgia E. (Simms) Ullestad; m. Crystal R. Kleppinger, Sept. 17, 1977. BS, Iowa State U., 1971. CPA; PFS Iowa, Tenn., lic. capt. inland waters USCG. Ptnr. Coopers and Lybrand, Des Moines, 1971-83; ptnr. in charge, tax svcs. Touche Ross and Co., Nashville, 1983-89; ptnr. tax svcs. Deloitte & Touche, LLP, Nashville, 1989—2002; mem.-in-charge tax svcs., mgmt. com. Kraft CPAs LLC, Nashville, 2002—. Adj. tax prof. Simpson Coll., 1981—82; sprk. profl. acct. seminar Lipscomb U., 1990—2004; mem. mgmt. com. Kraft CPAs LLC, Nashville, 2002— Editor: Abingdon Clergy Income Tax Guide, 1989—98. Sustaining membership capt. Mid. Tenn. coun. Boy Scouts Am., 1985—88; ednl. adv. com. Nashville Health Care Coun., 1998—2002; bd. dirs., exec. com., treas. United Way Mid. Tenn., 1990—96, mem. allocations panel, 1983—89; bd. dirs., mem. exec. com. Am. Cancer Soc., Des Moines, 1977—83, Nashville City Ballet, 1983—85; bd. dirs., chmn. fin. com. Watkins Coll. Art and Design, 1996—2001; bd. dirs. Gilda's Club, Nashville, treas., 1996—2002; trustee, program chmn., sec., pres. Tenn. Fed. Tax Inst., 2001—; bd. dirs., treas. Tenn. chpt. Arthritis Found., 2003—. Mem.: AICPA (cert. pers. fin. specialist), Nashville Estate Planning Coun. (pres. 1996—97, bd. dirs.), Internat. Assn. Fin. Planning (pres., bd. dirs. Nashville chpt. 1987—90), Iowa Soc. CPAs, Tenn. Soc. CPAs, Nashville C. of C. (mem. econ. devel. com. 1988—90, mem. employment coun. 1999—2002, editor HR notes 2000—01), Seven Seas Cruising Assn., Nlue Yacht Club, Commonwealth Yacht Club, Nashville City Club, Old Hickory Country Club. Avocations: sailing, hiking, music. Office: 555 Great Circle Rd #200 Nashville TN 37228-1310 Office Phone: 615-242-7351. E-mail: mullestad@kraftcpas.com.

**ULLMAN, EDWIN FISHER,** biotechnologist, consultant; b. Chgo., July 19, 1930; s. Harold P. and Jane F. Ullman; m. Elizabeth J. Finlay, June 26, 1954; children: Becky L., Linda J. BA, Reed Coll., 1952; MA, Harvard U., 1954, PhD, 1956. Research chemist Lederle Labs., Am. Cyanamid, Pearl River, NY, 1955-60; group leader central research div. Am. Cyanamid, Stamford, Conn., 1960-66; sci. dir. Synvar Research Inst., Palo Alto, Calif., 1966-70; v.p. dir. research Syva Co., Palo Alto, 1970-95; v.p., dir. rsch. Behring Diagnostics Inc., San Jose, Calif., 1995-97; scientific cons., 1997—; chief sci. officer Thau MDx, LLC, Santa Barbara, Calif., 2001—02, Adv. DiscovrRx, Corp., Fremont, Calif., 2002—06. Mem. various sci. adv. bds.; mem. adv. bd. San Francisco State U. Coll. of Sci. and Engring., 1994-96. Mem. editl. bd. Jour. Organic Chemistry, 1969-74, Jour. Immunoassay, 1979—, Jour. Clin. Lab., Analysis, 1986-87, Jour. Clin. Ligand Assay Soc., 1999—; contbr. articles to sci. jours.; patentee in field. NSF predoctoral fellow, 1952-53; U.S. Rubber Co. fellow, 1954-55. Recipient Clin. Ligand Assay Soc. Mallinckrodt award, 1981, Can. Soc. Clin. Chemists Health Group award, 1982, Inventor of Yr. award Peninsula Patent Law Assn., 1987. Fellow AAAS; mem. Am. Chem. Soc., Am. Assn. Clin. Chemistry (Van Slyke award N.Y. sect. 1984, No. Calif. sect. award 1991, Outstanding Contbns. to Clin. Chemistry in Selected Area of Rsch. award 1997, Ann. Edwin F. Ullman award established 1998), Phi Beta Kappa.

**ULLMAN, GERALD LEE,** transportation engineer; b. Grand Junction, Colo., Feb. 15, 1961; s. Sylvester Lawrence and Bernice Maxine Ullman; m. Brooke Rae Durkop, Nov. 3, 2001; children: Brandon Lee, Nicholas John. BS, U. Nebr., 1983, MS, 1984; PhD, Tex. A&M U., 1995. Registered profl. engr., Tex., 1989. Engring. tech. assoc. Tex. Transp. Inst., College Station, 1985—90, asst. rsch. engr., 1990—95, assoc. rsch. engr., 1995—99, program mgr., 1999—2002, rsch. engr., 2002—. Contbr. articles to profl. jours. Tchr. religious edn. St. Joseph's Cath. Ch., Bryan, Tex., 1993—2006. Recipient TTI/Trinity Rschr. award, Tex. Transp. Inst., 1999. Mem.: Transp. Rsch. Bd. (mem. work zone traffic control tech. com., Fred Burgraff award 1994), Inst. Transp. Engrs. Roman Catholic. Avocations: scuba diving, golf. Office: Texas Transportation Institute 3135 Tamu College Station TX 77843-3135 Office Phone: 979-845-9908. Office Fax: 979-845-6006. Business E-Mail: g-ullman@tamu.edu.

**ULLMAN, JEFFREY DAVID,** computer scientist, educator; b. NYC, Nov. 22, 1942; s. Seymour and Nedra L. (Hart) Ullman; m. Holly E. Ullman, Nov. 19, 1967; children: Peter, Scott. BS, Columbia U., 1963; PhD, Princeton U., 1966. Mem. tech. staff Bell Labs., Murray Hill, NJ, 1966-69, cons., 1969-89; prof. elec. engring., computer sci. Princeton (N.J.) U., 1969-79; prof. computer sci. Stanford (Calif.) U., 1979—2003, prof. emeritus, 2003—; CEO Gradiance Corp., 2003—. Mem. computer sci. adv. panel NSF, 1974—77, mem. info., robotics and intelligent sys. adv. panel, 1986—88; mem. exam. com. computer sci. grad. record exam. Endl. Testing Svc., 1978—86; chmn. doctoral rating com. computer sci. N.Y. State Regents, 1989—93, 1998—99; mem. tech. adv. bd. Google, 1998—, Viquity, 1999—2002, Surromed, 1999—, Whizbang Labs, 1999—2002, Quiq, 1999—2002; adv. bd. World Wide Web Consortium, 1998—99; bd. dirs. Junglee, 1996—98, Kirusa, 2001—03, Enosys software, 2000—01, 2002—03; mem. internat. sci. advisory group Nat. Info. & Comms. Tech., Australia, 2003—. Author: (book) Principles of Database and Knowledge-Base Systems, 1988, 1989; author: (with A. V. Aho and J. E. Hopcroft) Data Structures and Algorithms, 1983; author: (with A. V. Aho and R. Sethi) Compilers: Principles, Techniques and Tools, 1986; author: (with A. V. Aho) Foundations of Computer Science, 1992, Elements of ML Programming, 1994, 1998; author: (with J. Widom) A First Course in Database Systems, 1997, 2002; author: (with J. E. Hopcroft and R. Motwani) Intro. to Automata, Languages, and Computation, 2001; author: (with H. Garcia-Molina and J. Widom) The Complete Book of Database Systems, 2002. Guggenheim fellow, 1989. Fellow: Assn. Computing Machinery (coun. 1978—80, Spl. Interest Group Mgmt. Data Contbns. award 1996, Outstanding Educator award 1998, Knuth prize 2000); mem.: NAE, Spl. Interest Group Mgmt. Data (vice chmn. 1983—95), Computing Rsch. Assn. (bd. dirs. 1994—2001), Spl. Interest Group Automata and Computability Theory (sec.-treas. 1973—75). Home: 1023 Cathcart Way Palo Alto CA 94305-1048 Office: Stanford U Dept Computer Sci 433 Gates Hall 4A-Wing Stanford CA 94305-9040 E-mail: ullman@gmail.com.

**ULLMAN, LEO SOLOMON,** lawyer; b. Amsterdam, The Netherlands, July 14, 1939; s. Frank Leo and Emily (Konijn) U.; m. Katharine Laura Marbut, Aug. 27, 1960; chldren: Laura, Susan, Valerie, Frank. AB, Harvard U., 1961; JD, MBA, Columbia U., 1964. Bar: N.Y. 1966, U.S. Ct. Claims 1966, U.S. Tax Ct. 1969, U.S. Customs Ct. 1970. Assoc. Sullivan & Cromwell, N.Y.C., 1965-68; pres., mem. Ullman, Miller & Wrubel and predecessors, N.Y.C., 1970-81; mem. Reid & Priest, 1984-91; of counsel, 1991-92, Schnader, Harrison, Segal & Lewis, N.Y.C., 1993-99; chmn., CEO Cedar Shopping Ctrs., Inc. (NYSE). Adj. prof. internat. bus. NYU, 1972-77; lectr., panelist profl. organs. programs. Co-author: Investeringen in Onroerend Goed in de Verenigde Staten, 1982; editor: European Taxation, Internat. Bur. Documentation, Amsterdam, 1964-65; founding editor: Taxation of Private Investment Income in Europe; contbr. articles to profl. publs. Mem. Port Washington (N.Y.) Bd. Edn., 1970-73, pres., 1972-73; bd. dirs. Found. for Jewish Hist. Mus. in Amsterdam, Inc.; bd. dirs. Anne Frank Ctr., U.S.A., chmn., 1994-2000; bd. dirs. Cmty. Chest of Port Washington. Served with USMCR, 1959-65. Co-recipient Cmty. Svc. award, Port Washington, 1981, Citizen of Yr. award, Cmty. Chest, Port Washington, 2003, Entrepreneur of Yr. award in greater NY area Ernst & Young, 2005; Harlan Fiske Stone scholar Columbia Law Sch., 1963. Mem. ABA (tax sect. com. U.S. taxation of fgn. persons), N.Y. State Bar Assn. (tax sect. com. internat. trade and investment), Harvard Club, Netherlands Club. Home: Seacoast Ln Sands Point NY 11050-1230 Office: 44 S Bayles Ave Port Washington NY 11050 E-mail: leoullman@aol.com.

**ULLMAN, MICHAEL THOMAS,** science educator; s. Fred and Rose-Marie Ullman; m. Paola Scalabrin, Oct. 13, 1996; children: Adrian Taylor, Clementina. BA, Harvard U., 1984; PhD, MIT, 1993. Prof. Georgetown U., Washington, 1996—. Office: Dept Neuroscience Georgetown Univ 3970 Reservoir Rd NW Washington DC 20057 Office Phone: 202-687-6064.

**ULLMAN, MYRON EDWARD, III, (MIKE ULLMAN),** retail executive; b. Youngstown, Ohio, Nov. 26, 1946; s. Myron Edward Jr. and June (Cunningham) U.; m. Cathy Emmons, June 20, 1969; children: Myron Cayce, Denver Tryan, Peter Brynt, Benjamin Kyrk, Kathryn Kwynn, Madylin Ming Yan. BS in Indsl. Mgmt., U. Cin., 1969; postgrad. Inst. Ednl. Mgmt., Harvard U., 1977. Internat. account mgr. IBM Corp., Cin., 1969-76; v.p. bus. affairs U. Cin., 1976-81; White House fellow The White House, Washington, 1981-82; exec. v.p. Sanger Harris div. Federated Stores, Dallas, 1982-86; mgr. dir., chief oper. officer Wharf Holdings Ltd., Hong Kong, 1986-88; chmn., CEO, dir. R.H. Macy & Co. Inc., NYC, 1988-95; dir., deputy chmn. Federated Dept. Stores, Inc.; chmn., CEO DFS Group Ltd., San Francisco, 1995-98, group chmn., 1999-2000; also bd. dirs.; dir. gen., group mng. dir. LVMH, Louis Vuitton Moet Hennessy, Paris, 1999—2002; chmn. DeBeers-LV, 2000—02; dir., chmn., CEO J.C. Penney Co. Inc., 2004—. Mng. dir. Lane Crawford Ltd., Hong Kong, 1986-88; bd. advisors St. Traditions Corp., Cin.; chmn. Omni Hotels, Hampton, N.H., 1988; co-chmn. Global Crossing, Ltd., 2002-04; chmn. bd. dirs. Mercy Ships Internat., 1992-; bd. dirs. Starbuck's Coffee Co., Polo Ralph Lauren, Taubman Ctrs., 2002-04, Kendall Jackson Wine Estates, 2001-04, Lucille Packard Found. Children's Health, 2001-04, Segway LLC, 2003-05. Internat. v.p. U. Cin. Alumni Assn., 1980—; bd. dirs. Nat. Multiple Sclerosis Soc., NYC; bd. dirs. Brunswick Sch., Greenwich, Conn., U. Cin. Found., Lincoln Ctr. Devel., Deafness Rsch. Found., 1997-01, Stanford U. Children's Med. Ctr., 2004-04; chmn. exec. coun. U. Calif. Med. Ctr. Found., San Francisco, 2002-; bd. dirs., 1998—. Mem. White House Fellow Alumni Assn., Econ. Club N.Y.C. (bd. dirs., exec. com.), Nat. Retail Fedn. (vice chmn., bd. dirs., exec. com.). Republican. Office: c/o Jackson Hole Group Ste 935 100 Spear St San Francisco CA 94105 also: JC Penney Dir Inc 6501 Legacy Dr Plano TX 75024-3698 Business E-Mail: mike@meullman.com.

**ULLMAN, TRACEY,** actress, singer; b. Slough, Eng., Dec. 30, 1959; m. Allan McKeown, 1983; children: Mabel Ellen, John Albert Victor. Student, Itaia Conti Stage Sch., London. Appeared in plays Gigi, Elvis, Grease, The Rocky Horror Show, Four in a Million, 1981 (London Theatre Critics award), The Taming of the Shrew, 1990, The Big Love, (one-woman stage show) 1991; films include Give My Regards to Broad Street, 1984, Plenty, 1985, Jumpin' Jack Flash, 1986, I Love You To Death, 1990, Household Saints, 1993, Robin Hood: Men in Tights, 1993, I'll Do Anything, 1994, Bullets over Broadway, 1994, Ready to Wear (Prêt-à-Porter), 1994, Everybody Says I Love You, 1996, Panic, 2000, Small Time Crooks, 2000, A Dirty Shame, 2004, (voice) Corpse Bride, 2005, (TV films) Women of the Night IV, 1995, Once Upon a Mattress, 2004; Brit. TV shows include Three of a Kind, A Kick Up the Eighties, Girls on Top; actress TV series: The Tracey Ullman Show, from 1987-90 (Emmy award Best Performance, Outstanding Writing, 1990, Golden Globe award Best Actress, 1987), Tracey Takes On, 1996—99 (four Emmys including Outstanding Music, Comedy and Variety Show 1997, Cable Ace award for best comedy variety series 1996), Visible Panty Lines, 2001-; albums You Broke My Heart in Seventeen Places (Gold album), You Caught Me Out, 1984, Takes on the Hits, 2002. Recipient Brit. Acad. award, 1983, Am. Comedy award, 1988, 90, 91, Emmy award for Best Performance in a Variety/Music Series for "Tracey Ullman Takes on New York", 1994. Office: IFA Talent Agy 8730 W Sunset Blvd Ste 490 Los Angeles CA 90069-2248

**ULLMANN, OWEN,** journalist; b. Neptune, NJ, Nov. 16, 1947; s. Marcel Andre Ullmann and Jane Horowitz; m. Lois M. Kietur, Aug. 6, 1977; children: Cara L., Daniel E. BA, Rutgers U., 1969; MA, U. Wis., 1973. Reporter Daily Jour., Elizabeth, NJ, 1969—71, State Jour., Madison, Wis., 1972; automotive reporter AP, Detroit, 1973—77, labor, econs. reporter Washington, 1977—83; econs., White House, State Dept. reporter Knight-Ridder Newspapers, Washington, 1983—93; econs. corr., news editor Bus. Week, Washington, 1993—99; reporter, editor USA Today, 1999—. Author: (biography) Stockman: The Man, The Myth, The Future, 1986; exec. editor Internat. Economy, 2000—; contbg. editor: Washingtonian, 1987—. Recipient Merriman Smith award, White House Corrs. Assn., 1988, Aldo Beckman award, 1989, Disting. Journalist award, U. Wis. Journalism Sch., Madison, 1999. Office: USA Today 7950 Jones Branch Dr Mc Lean VA 22102

**ULLOA, MAURICIO,** geneticist, researcher; MS, N.Mex State U., Las Cruces, 1990, PhD, 1993. Rsch. assoc. dept. agronomy & horticulture U. N.Mex State U., Las Cruces, 1996—98; rsch. geneticist USDA-ARS, Genetic and Crop Rsch. Unit, Stoneville, Miss., 1998—2001; rsch. geneticist USDA-ARS, WIICS, Rsch. Unit, Shafter, Calif., 2001—. Rsch. assoc. Dept. Agronomy & Hoticulture, Las Cruces, 1996—98. Promote recruitment minorities in workforce, Calif. Office: USDA-ARS 17053 N Shafter Ave Shafter CA 93263 Office Phone: 661-746-8009. Home Fax: 661-746-1619; Office Fax: 661-746-1619. Business E-Mail: mulloa@pw.ars.usda.gov.

**ULLRICH, DIETER CLAUS,** archivist; b. Bradford, Pa., Jan. 20, 1964; s. Claus Dieter Ullrich and Kathleen Patricia O'Brien. BA, Met. State Coll., Denver, 1987; MA, Ind. U. Penn., 1991; MS, U. Ky., 1992. Lic.: Colo. (Paralegal) 1989. Spl. collections libr., archivist SUNY, Oswego, 1992—95, U. Tenn., 1995—99, Millersville (Pa.) U., 1999—2002; archivist Auburn (Ala.) U., 2002—04, Ctrl. Wash. U., Ellensburg, Wash., 2004—06. Author: (articles) Chattanooga Regional Hist. Jour., Jackson Purchase Hist. Soc. Jour., (book) The Civil War Diaries of Van Buren Oldham: Company G, Ninth Tennessee Volunteer Infantry, C.S.A. Sec., bd. mem. Safe Haven (Jewish Refugees to U.S.), Oswego, NY, 1993—95; mem. Oswego (N.Y.) County Hist. Preservation Consortium, 1993—95; bd. mem. State Bicentennial Com. of Weakley County, Dresden, Tenn., 1995—97, Carroll County Hist. Soc., McKenzie, Tenn., 1997—2000; mem. Lancaster (Pa.) County Hist. Soc., 1999—2002, Wash. Civil War Assn., Wash., 2004—06, Kittitas County Hist. Soc., Ellensburg, Wash., 2004—06. Specialist U.S. Army, 1987—89, Ft. Myer, Arlington, Va. Grantee Funding for microfilm project, Wash. Preservation Initiative, 2005. Mem.: Soc. of Tenn. Archivists (assoc.), Mid-Atlantic Regional Archives Conf. (assoc.), Del. Valley Chpt., Assn. of Coll. and Rsch. Libraries (assoc.; archivist 2000—02), Ctrl. Pa. Archivists (assoc.), Soc. Ala. Archivists (assoc.), NW Archivists (assoc.), Soc. Am. Archivists (assoc.), West Tenn. Hist. Soc. (assoc.), Phi Alpha Theta (life). Democrat. Roman Catholic. Achievements include U.S. Military Academy ROTC Military History Fellowship. Avocations: soccer, reading, bicycling, hiking. Home: 2518 North Ellington St Ellensburg WA 98926 Office: Ctrl Washington Univ 400 East University Way Ellensburg WA 98926-7548 Office Phone: 509-963-1717. Office Fax: 509-963-3684. Personal E-mail: dullrich@kvalley.com. Business E-Mail: ullrichd@cwu.edu.

**ULLRICH, POLLY,** art critic; BA in Journalism, MA in Journalism, U. Wis., Madison; MA in Art History, Theory and Criticism, Sch. Art Inst. Chgo. Lectr. in field; served on panels and juried and curated exhbns. Independent art critic, freelance journalist for New York Times, Newsweek, Chicago Magazine, Chicago Sun-Times and the Milwaukee Journal, written analyses and reviews on contemporary art for Sculpture Magazine, frieze, American Craft, KeramikMagazin, Bridge, Metalsmith, Surface Design Journal, New Art Examiner, Ceramics Art and Perception. Mem.: Chgo. Art Critics Assn. Address: 852 W Wolfram St Chicago IL 60657 E-mail: PUllr1234@aol.com.

**ULLRICH, ROBERT ALBERT,** academic administrator; b. Port Jefferson, N.Y., Mar. 25, 1939; s. Albert Herman and Marie Kathryn (Miller) U.; m. Portia M. Little; children: Karl Albert, Eleanor Marie. BS, U.S. Mcht. Marine Acad., 1960; MBA, Tulane U., 1964; D in Bus. Adminstrn., Washington U., 1968. Marine engr. Lykes Bros. Steamship Co., New Orleans, 1960-62; trainee IBM Corp., New Orleans, 1964-65; sr. rsch. officer London Sch. Econs., 1968-69; prof. Vanderbilt U., Nashville, 1969-88; dean Clark U., Worcester, Mass., 1988-96, prof., 1996-98; dean Ithaca (N.Y.) Coll., 1998—2004. Author: Motivation Methods, 1981, Robotics Primer, 1983; co-author: Organization Theory and Design, 1980; editor: The American Work Force, 1984. Lt. j.g. USNR, 1960-66. Mem. Beta Gamma Sigma. Office: 33 Friendship St Jamestown RI 02835 E-mail: rullrich1@msn.com.

**ULMER, EVONNE GAIL,** health science association administrator; b. Bagley, Minn., Sept. 12, 1947; d. John Ferdinand and Elsie Mabel (McCollum) Lundmark; m. G. Bryan Ulmer, Jan. 11, 1969; 1 child, G. Bryan. Diploma, St. Luke's Hosp., Duluth, Minn., 1968; BS, St. Joseph's Coll., N. Windam, Maine, 1981; MHA, U. Minn., 1984; JD, T.M. Cooley Law Sch., Lansing, Mich., 1997. Bar: Mich. 1997. Staff nurse Baton Rouge Gen., 1969—70, St. Luke's Hosp., Duluth, Minn., 1968—69, 1971—72; asst. adminstr. Hickory Heights Care Ctr., Metarie, La., 1972—73; asst. head nurse Eisenhower Hosp., Colorado Springs, Colo., 1973—74; dir. patient care svcs. St. Vincent's Gen. Hosp., Leadville, Colo., 1974—78; dir. insvc., quality assurance Watsatch Hosp., Heber City, Utah, 1979; adminstr. Prospect Park Living Ctr., Estes Park, Colo., 1982—84; asst. adminstr. Estes Park Med. Ctr., 1979—84; CEO Weston County Hosp. and Manor, Newcastle, Wyo., 1984—92, Ionia County Meml. Hosp., Mich., 1992—; pres. Ionia County Health Sys., 1995—, Ulmer Law Firm Evonne G. Ulmer, PLC, 2006—. Mem. Am. Hosp. Assn. Chgo. (trustee 1998-01, past tech. small and rural governing coun., past del. region and policy bd., past chair small and rural governing com., leadership coun.), Am. Soc. Healthcare Risk Mgmt. (editl. adv. bd.), Medicare Geog. Reclassification Rev. Bd., Mich. Health and Hosp. Assn. (past bd. dirs., vice-chair smaller hops. coun.). Republican. Lutheran. Home: 536 Skyview Dr Ionia MI 48846-9776 Office Phone: 616-523-1000. Personal E-mail: evonneulmer@hotmail.com. Business E-Mail: eulmer@ioniahospital.org.

**ULMER, FRANCES ANN,** retired state official; b. Madison, Wis., Feb. 1, 1947; m. Bill Council; children: Amy, Louis. BA in Econs. and Polit. Sci., U. Wis.; JD with honors, Wis. Sch. Law. Polit. advisor Gov. Jay Hammond, Alaska, 1975-81; former mayor City of Juneau, Alaska; mem. Alaska Ho. of Reps., 1986-94, minority leader, 1992-94; lt. gov. State of Alaska,

1995—2002; U.S. rep. to North Pacific Anadramous Fish Commn., 1994—; disting. prof. U. Alaska, Anchorage, 2003—; dir. Inst. Social and Econ. Rsch., 2004—. Office Phone: 907-786-7710. E-mail: fran.ulmer@uaa.alaska.edu.

**ULMER, JEANNE WILDE,** judge; b. Nanticoke, Pa., Sept. 17, 1925; d. Charles Gordon and Ethel M. (Jones) Wilde; m. Herbert T. Ulmer Jr., Oct. 26, 1945; children: Carol, H. Thomas III, Joanne, Deborah. Student, Hood Coll., 1944. Bar: SC (municipal judge). Woman's page editor Times and Democrat, Orangeburg, SC, 1954—58; spl. corr. News and Courier, Charleston, SC, 1958—59; dir. Calhoun County Mus., St. Matthews, SC, 1959—83; mcpl. judge Cameron Mcpl. Ct., SC, 1989—95. Pres. Calhoun County Health and TB Assn., St. Matthews, SC, 1963; mem. SC Tricentennial Comm., SC, 1968—70. Author: The Ulmers of South Carolina, Billets-Doux, 2000, (poetry) The Rebuttal and Rebound Thoughts, 2000. Chmn. March of Dimes, 1950—60; leader, coun. chmn. Girl Scouts USA, 1954—65; chmn. Cameron Election Comm., Cameron, 1984—88. Recipient Prof. Svc. award, SC Confederation of Mus., 1993. Mem.: Calhoun County Friends of Mus., Nat. Jud. Coll. Alumni Chpt. of SC, Nat. Welsh - Am. Found., Welsh Soc. of Phila. Home and Office: 106 Old Orangeburg Rd Cameron SC 29030-9518

**ULMER, MELVILLE PAUL,** physics and astronomy educator; b. Washington, Mar. 12, 1943; s. Melville Jack and Naomi Louise (Zinkin) U.; m. Patricia Elifson, Dec. 28, 1968; children: Andrew Todd, Jeremy John, Rachel Ann. BA, Johns Hopkins U., 1965; PhD, U. Wis., 1970. Asst. research U. Calif., San Diego, 1970-74; astrophysicist Harvard Smithsonian Ctr. for Astrophysics, Cambridge, Mass., 1974-76; dir. Lindheimer and Dearborn Obs. Northwestern U., 1982—; asst. prof. Dept. Physics and Astoronomy, Northwestern U., Evanston, Ill., 1976-82, assoc. prof., 1982-87, dir. astro physics program, 1982—, prof., 1987—, chmn. Co-investigator on Gamma Ray Ob. experiment and Orbiting Solar Ob. 7. Contbr. articles to profl. jours. Fellow Am. Phys. Soc.; mem. Am. Astron. Soc., Soc. Photo-optical Instrumentation Engrs., Internat. Astron. Union. Office: Northwestern U Dearborn Obs 2131 Tech Dr Evanston IL 60208-2900 Office Fax: 847-491-3135. E-mail: m-ulmer2@northwestern.edu.

**ULRICH, LARS,** drummer; b. Gentofte, Denmark, Dec. 26, 1963; Drummer Metallica, 1981—. Albums include Kill 'em All, 1983, Ride the Lightning, 1984, Master of Puppets, 1986, ...And Justice for All, 1988, Metallica, 1991, Live Sh*t: Binge and Purge, 1993, Kill 'Em All, 1995, Load, 1996, Reload, 1997, Garage Inc., 1998 (Grammy award), S & M, 1999, St. Anger, 2003 (Grammy award best metal performance, 2003); played on compilation albums including Metal Massacre, 1982, The Good, The Bad and The Live, 1990, Rubaiyant: Elektra's 30th Anniversary, 1990, For Those About To Rock: Moscow, 1992, Woodstock '94, 1994, Spawn: The Album, 1997, Woodstock '99, 2000, WCW: Mayhem The Music, 1999, M:I-2, 2000, NASCAR: Full Throttle, 2001, Swizz Beatz Presents G.H.E.T.T.O. Stories, 2002, Biker Boyz Soundtrack, 2003, We're A Happy Family: Tribute to the Ramones, 2003, I've Always Been Crazy: Tribute to Waylon Jennings, 2003. Office: care Metallica Elektra Records 75 Rockefeller Plz New York NY 10019-6908

**ULRICH, LAUREL THATCHER,** historian, educator; b. Sugar City, Idaho, July 11, 1938; d. John Kenneth and Alice (Siddoway) Thatcher; m. Gael Dennis Ulrich, Sept. 22, 1958; children: Karl, Melinda, Nathan, Thatcher, Amy. BA in English, U. Utah, 1960; MA in English, Simmons Coll., 1971; PhD in History, U. N.H., 1980. Asst. prof. humanities U. N.H., Durham, 1980-84, asst. prof. history, 1985-88, assoc. prof., 1988-91, prof., 1991-95; prof. history and women's studies Harvard U., Cambridge, Mass., 1995—; James Duncan Phillips prof. early Am. history, 1997—, dir. Charles Warren Ctr., 1997—. Audiocourse cons. Annenberg Found.; cons., participating humanist numerous exhibits, pub. programs, other projects; project humanist Warner (N.H.) Women's Oral History Project; bd. editors William & Mary Quar., 1989-91, Winterthur Portfolio, 1991—. Author: Good Wives: Image and Reality in the Lives of Women in Northern New England, 1650-1750, 1982, A Midwife's Tale: The Life of Martha Ballard Based on Her Diary, 1785-1812, 1990 (Pulitzer Prize for history 1991), The Age of Homespun: Objects and Stories in the creation of an American Myth, 2001; contbr. articles, abstracts, essays and revs. to profl. publs. Coun. mem. Inst. Early Am. History and Culture, 1989-91; trustee Strawberry Banke Mus., 1987-93. NEH fellow, 1982, 84-85, MacArthur Fellowship award, 1992-97, John Simon Guggenheim fellow, 1991-92; women's studies rsch. grantee Woodrow Wilson Fellowship Found., 1979; co-recipient Best Book award Berkshire Conf. Women's Historians, 1990; recipient Best Book award Soc. for History of Early Republic, 1990, John S. Dunning prize and Joan Kelly Meml. prize Am. Hist. Assn., 1990, Bancroft Prize for Am. History, 1991. Mem. Orgn. Am. Historians (nominating com. 1992—, ABC-Clio award com. 1989), Am. Hist. Assn. (rsch. coun. 1993-96). Office: Harvard U Charles Warren Ctr Emerson Hall 4th Fl Cambridge MA 02138

**ULRICH, PAUL GRAHAM,** lawyer, writer, editor; b. Spokane, Wash., Nov. 29, 1938; s. Donald Gunn and Kathryn (Vandercook) U.; m. Kathleen Nelson Smith, July 30, 1982; children: Kathleen Elizabeth Pennington, Marike Rae McCracken, Michael Graham Ulrich. BA with high honors, U. Mont., 1961; JD, Stanford U., 1964. Bar: Calif. 1965, Ariz. 1966, U.S. Ct. Appeals (9th cir.) 1965, U.S. Supreme Ct. 1969. Law clk. judge U.S. Ct. Appeals, 9th Circuit, San Francisco, 1964-65; assoc. Lewis and Roca, Phoenix, 1965-70, ptnr., 1970-85; pres. Paul G. Ulrich P.C., Phoenix, 1985-92, Ulrich, Thompson & Kessler, P.C., Phoenix, 1992-94, Ulrich & Kessler, P.C., Phoenix, 1994-95, Ulrich, Kessler & Anger, P.C., Phoenix, 1995-2000, Ulrich & Anger, P.C., Phoenix, 2000—03, Paul G. Ulrich P.C., 2003—; owner Pathway Enterprises, 1985-91. Judge pro tem divsn. 1, Ariz. Ct. Appeals, Phoenix, 1986; instr. Thunderbird Grad. Sch. Internat. Mgmt., 1968-69. Ariz. State U. Coll. Law, 1970-73, 78, Scottsdale C.C., 1975-77, also continuing legal edn. seminars Author and pub.: Applying Management and Motivation Concepts to Law Offices, 1985; co-author: Arizona Appellate Handbook, 1978-, co-editor, 1978-2000; Working With Legal Assistants, 1980, 81; editor, co-author Future Directions for Law Office Management, 1982, People in the Law Office, 1985-86; co-author, pub.: Arizona Healthcare Professional Liability Handbook, 1992, supplement, 1994, Arizona Healthcare Professional Liability Defense Manual, 1995, Arizona Healthcare Professional Liability Update Newsletter, 1992-99; co-author, editor: Federal Appellate Practice: Ninth Circuit, 1994, 2d edit., 1999, supplement, 2006; contbg. editor Law Office Econs. and Mgmt., 1984-97, Life, Law and the Pursuit of Balance, 1996, 2d edit., 1997. Mem. Ariz. Supreme Ct. Task Force on Ct. Orgn. and Adminstrn., 1988-89; mem. com. on appellate cts. Ariz. Supreme Ct., 1990-91; bd. visitors Stanford U. Law Sch., 1974-77; adv. com. legal assisting program Phoenix Coll., 1985-95; atty. rep. 9th Cir. Jud. Conf., 1997-2000. With U.S. Army, 1956. Recipient continuing legal edn. award State Bar Ariz., 1978, 86, 90, Harrison Tweed spl. merit award Am. Law Inst./ABA, 1987. Fellow Ariz. Bar Found. (founding 1985—); mem. ABA (chmn. selection and utilization of staff pers. com., econs. of law sect. 1979-81, mem. standing com. legal assts. 1982-86, co-chmn. joint project on appellate handbooks 1983-85, co-chmn. fed. appellate handbook project 1985-88, chmn. com. on liaison with non-lawyers orgns. Econs. of Law Practice sect. 1985-86), Am. Acad. Appellate Lawyers, Am. Law Inst. (life), Am. Judicature Soc. (Spl. Merit citation 1987), Ariz. Bar Assn. (chmn. econs. of law practice com. 1980-81, co-chmn. lower ct. improvement com. 1982-85, co-chmn. Ariz. appellate handbook project 1976-2000), Coll. Law Practice Mgmt., Maricopa County Bar Assn. (bd. dirs. 1994-96), Calif. Bar Assn., Phi Kappa Phi, Phi Alpha Delta, Sigma Phi Epsilon. Democrat. Home and Office: 131 E El Caminito Dr Phoenix AZ 85020-3503 Office Phone: 602-248-9465. Personal E-mail: ulrichpc@aol.com.

**ULRICH, ROBERT J.,** retail executive; b. 1944; Grad., U. Minn., 1967, Stanford U., 1978. Chmn., chief exec. officer, dir. Dayton Hudson Corp.; with Dayton Hudson Corp. (now Target Corp.), Mpls., 1967—, exec. v.p. dept. stores divsn., 1981-84, pres. dept. stores divsn., 1984-87, chmn., CEO Target stores divsn., 1987-93, dir., 1993—; chmn, CEO Target Corp. (formerly Dayton Hudson Corp.), Mpls., 1994—. Bd. dirs. Yum Brands!, Inc. Office: Target Corp 1000 Nicollet Mall Minneapolis MN 55403-2467*

**ULRICH, THEODORE ALBERT,** lawyer; b. Spokane, Wash., Jan. 1, 1943; s. Herbert Roy and Martha (Hoffman) Ulrich; m. Nancy Allison, May 30, 1966; children: Donald Wayne, Frederick Albert. BS cum laude, U.S. Mcht. Marine Acad., 1965; JD cum laude, Fordham U., 1970; LLM, NYU, 1974. Bar: NY 1971, U.S. Ct. Appeals (2d cir.) 1971, U.S. Supreme Ct. 1974, U.S. Ct. Claims 1977, U.S. Customs Ct. 1978, U.S. Ct. Internat. Trade 1981, U.S. Ct. Appeals (5th cir.) 1988, U.S. Ct. Appeals (DC cir.) 1992, Colo. 1993, U.S. Ct. Appeals (10th cir.) 1994. Mng. clk. U.S. Dept. Justice, NYC, 1968-69, law clk. to fed. dist. judge, 1969-70; assoc. Cadwalader, Wickersham & Taft, NYC, 1970—94, ptnr., 1980-94. Popham, Haik, Schnobrich & Kaufman, Ltd., Denver, 1994-96; pvt. practice law Denver, 1996—. Author: Arbitration of Construction Contracts, V, 1991; co-author: Encyclopedia of International Commercial Litigation, 1991; contbg. author: Marine Engineering Economics and Cost Analysis, 1995; author, editor Fordham Law Rev., 1969. Leader Boy Scouts Am., Nassau County, NY, 1984-94, Denver, 1994—. Capt. USCGR, 1965-86. Mem. ABA, Colo. Bar, Denver Bar, Maritime Law Assn., Am. Soc. Internat. Law, Soc. Naval Archs. and Marine Engrs., U.S. Naval Inst., Am. Arbitration Assn. Home and Office: 4300 E 6th Ave Denver CO 80220-4940 E-mail: tnulrich@gte.net.

**ULRICH, WERNER,** patent lawyer; b. Munich, Mar. 12, 1931; came to U.S., 1940, naturalized, 1945; s. Karl Justus and Grete (Rosenthal) U.; m. Ursula Wolff, June 28, 1959; children— Greta, Kenneth. BS, Columbia U., 1952, MS (NSF fellow 1952-53), 1953, Dr.Engring. Sci., 1957; MBA, U. Chgo., 1975; JD, Loyola U., Chgo, 1985. Bar: Ill., 1985. With AT&T Bell Labs, Naperville, Ill., 1953-95; head electronic switching dept. AT&T Bell Labs., Naperville, Ill., 1964-68; dir. Advanced Switching Tech., Naperville, 1968-77, head maintenance architecture dept., 1977-81; sr. atty. Intellectural Property Law Orgn., Naperville, 1981-95; pvt. practice Glen Ellyn, Ill., 1995—. Vis. lectr. U. Calif., Berkeley, 1966-67 Inventor of over 20 telecommunications inventions; patentee electronic switching systems. Fellow IEEE; mem. ABA, Ill. State Bar Assn., Am. Intellectual Property Law Assn., Tau Beta Pi, Beta Gamma Sigma. Office: 434 Maple St Glen Ellyn IL 60137-3826

**ULRICKSON, VIRGINIA GAYLE,** elementary school educator, librarian; b. Conrad, Mont., Jan. 16, 1951; d. L. Dwane and Grace Lucille Hewitt; m. Jack Ulrickson (dec.); children: Rachel, Paul. BS in Elem. Edn., Mont. State U., 1974. Tchr. North Harlem Hutterite Coun., Mont., 1976—77, Dodson Pub. Schs., 1977—78; tchr., libr. Frontier Elem. Sch., Wolf Point, 1978—2005, Wolf Point Pub. Sch. Dist. # 45, Mont., 2005—. Co-dir. region 10 Make It Yourself with Wool Contest, 1998—; project leader Frontier 4-H Club, 1988—95; co-dir. RCIA program Immaculate Conception Ch., Wolf Point, 2000—05, mem. parish coun., 1999—2005. Mem.: Mont. Edn. Assn., Alpha Delta Kappa. Roman Catholic. Avocations: crafts, reading. Home: 723 1st Ave N Wolf Point MT 59201 Office: Northside Elem Sch 4th Ave N Wolf Point MT 59201 Office Phone: 406-653-1653.

**ULSENHEIMER, DEAN,** language educator; b. Cleve., Dec. 20, 1941; s. Lon Sherwood and Mary Dorothy (Kupstas) U.; m. Sharon Lee Williams, Dec. 27, 1963 (div. June 1980); children: Cathi, Chris, Shelley, Scott.; m. Monica Joan Rigo, Aug. 10, 1984. BS in Edn., Ohio U., Athens, 1964; postgrad., John Carroll U., 1969—70, postgrad., 2006, Kent State U., 1979. Cert. secondary sch. tchr. Tchr. English South Amherst (Ohio) Schs., 1964-66; project engr. Otto Konigslow Mfg. Co., Cleve., 1966-67; tchr. English Cardinal Schs., Middlefield, Ohio, 1967-80, Shaw High Sch., East Cleveland, Ohio, 1980-92; instr. English Cuyahoga C.C., Cleve., 1980—, Lakeland C.C., Mentor, Ohio, 1984—. Owner, cons. DU Power Reading, 2000, Power Writing; spkr. Lakeland C.C. Spkrs. Bur., Mentor, 1988—; hon. poetry intern NEH, Hiram Coll., 1977; cons. in field. Author: Easy Writing, 1977, Sentence Analysis, 1977, Communication Problems, 1978, Short Story Starters, 1980. Mem. NEA, Am. Cons. League, Ohio Edn. Assn., Greater Cleve. Growth Assn., Coun. Smaller Bus. Ent. Roman Catholic. Avocations: tennis, golf, phys. fitness. Home and Office: 6691 Morley Rd Concord OH 44077-5924

**ULSH, GORDON A.,** battery manufacturing company executive; BA, Butler Univ. With Ford Motor Corp., 1968—84; v.p. Cooper Industries, 1984—97, exec. v.p., 1997—98; exec. v.p. worldwide aftermarket div. Federal-Mogul Corp., 1998, pres., COO, 1999; ptnr. Ripplewood Equity Partners, 1999—2001; chmn., pres., CEO Fleetpride Inc., 2001—05; pres., CEO, dir. Exide Technologies, Lawrenceville, NJ, 2005—. Mem.: Soc. Mfg. Engineers, Soc. Automotive Engineers. Office: Exide Technologies Crossroads Corp Ctr Ste 230 3150 Brunswick Pike Trenton NJ 08648

**ULSTROM, ROBERT A.,** retired pediatrician; b. Mpls., Feb. 23, 1923; m. Mary Janet McGrath, 1946 (dec. 1981); 3 children; m. Betty Bernard, 1982 (div. 1985). BS, U. Minn., 1944, MD, 1946; postgrad., Strong Meml. Hosp. Lic. physician, Minn., Calif.; diplomate Am. Bd. Pediatrics with subsplty. in endocrinology (bd. dirs. 1980-86, v.p. 1985, chmn. rsch. and devel. com. 1980-86, tech. adv. com. for devel. of computerized exams. 1983-86), Am. Bd. Emergency Medicine (bd. dirs. 1982-86). Intern, resident in pediats. U. Rochester, 1946-48; instr., asst. prof. U. Minn., Mpls., 1950-53, assoc. prof., 1956-61, prof. pediatrics, 1961-64, 66-90, prof. emeritus, 1990—, mem. Ctr. for German and European Studies, Inst. for Global Studies, 2004—, acting head dept. pediats., 1961—62, assoc. dean Coll. Med. Scis., 1967-70; asst. prof. UCLA, 1953-56, prof., 1964-67, chmn. dept. pediatrics, 1964-67; vis. prof. medicine U. So. Calif., 1982-83, ret. Chief pediats. 97th Gen. Hosp., 1949-50; cons. in pediats. Harbor Gen. Hosp., L.A., 1953-56, 64-67, Mpls. Gen. Hosp., 1956-64, Hennepin County Gen. Hosp., 1967-90, hon. staff, 1990—; Well Child Clinic cons. City of L.A., 1953-56; track physician Donneybrooke Racetrack, Brainerd, Minn., 1968-73; dir. Reg. Ctr. for Metabolic Defects, 1975-79; cons. Ellwood & Assocs., 1986-87; med. legal cons. various plaintiff, 1985 95; mem. med. adv. bd. Group Health, Inc. 1967-90, Diabetes Detection and Edn. Ctr., 1969-71; mem. grants review com. Human Growth Inc., 1974-78; mem. tech. adv. com. on human genetics Minn. State Bd. Health, 1976-90; mem. pers. selection com. NIH, 1979, mem. gen. medicine study sect. NIH, 1964-68; mem. divsn. med. scis. NRC, 1961-64; oral examiner Am. Bd. Pediats., 1970-89; expert witness for prosecution U.S. Fed. Dist. Ct., Mpls., 1994-95; instr. computer course for beginners Elder Learning Inst., Coll. Continuing Edn., U. Minn., 1995—, bd. dirs., 1996-2000, webmaster, author, 1997-2002, v.p., 1998-99, mentor undergrad. students Coll. Liberal Arts, 1992—2004. Mem. editl. bd. Jour. Pediats., 1962-65; contbr. articles to profl. jours. Sec.-treas. Minn. Med. Found., 1967-68. With M.C., U.S. Army, 1948-50. Markle scholar in med. scis., 1954-59; Pew Found. fellow, 1985-86; recipient Wyeth award for med. rsch., 1963. Mem. AAAS, Am. Pediat. Soc., Am. Soc. Clin. Investigation, Ctrl. Soc. for Clin. Rsch., Endocrine Soc., Lawson-Wilkins Pediat. Endocrine Soc. (founding mem., membership com. 1971-75, chmn. 1975), Midwestern Pediat. rsch. Soc. (coun. 1961-64), Soc. for Pediat. Rsch. (NRC rep. 1961-64), Western Soc. for Clin. rsch., Western Soc. for Pediat. Rsch., Ctr. for German and European Studies at U. Minn., Alpha Omega Alpha, Phi Rho Sigma. Home: 4616 Sunset Rdg Minneapolis MN 55416-3335 Personal E-mail: ulstr001@tc.umn.edu.

**ULTAN, LLOYD,** historian, educator; b. Bronx, NY, Feb. 16, 1938; s. Louis and Sophie U. BA cum laude, Hunter Coll., 1959; MA, Columbia U., 1960. Assoc. Edward Williams Coll., Fairleigh Dickinson U., Hackensack, NJ, 1964-74, asst. prof. history, 1974-75, assoc. prof. history, 1975-83, prof., 1983-. Adj. prof. history H. Lehman Coll. CUNY, 2004-; cons. in field. Editor Bronx County Hist. Soc. Jour., 1964—, Bronx County Hist. Soc. Press, 1981—; author: The Beautiful Bronx, 1920-50, 1979, Legacy of the Revolution: The Valentine-Varian House, 1983, The Bronx in the Innocent Years, 1890-1925, 1985, The Presidents of the United States, 1989, The Bronx in the Frontier Era: From the Beginning to 1696, 1993, The Bronx: It Was Only Yesterday, 1935-65, 1993, Roots of the Republic, Vol. VI, 1996, The Bronx Cookbook, 1997, Bronx Accent: A Literary and Pictorial History of the Borough, 2000, The Birth of The Bronx, 1609-1900, 2000; contbr. Ency. N.Y. City, 1995. Gen. sec. Bronx Civic League, 1964—67; v.p. bd. trustees Bronx County Hist. Soc., 1965—67, 1977—84, curator, 1968—71, pres., 1971—76, historian, 1986—; founding mem., bd. dirs. Bronx Coun. on Arts, 1968—71;

chmn. Bronx County Bicentennial Commn., 1973—76, Bronx Borough Pres.'s Bicentennial Adv. Com., 1974—76; vice chmn. Commn. Celebrating 350 Yrs. of the Bronx, 1989; mem. program guidelines com. N.Y.C. Dept. Cultural Affairs, 1976—77; mem. N.Y.C. Com. on Cultural Concerns, 1982—88, N.Y.C. Mayor's Task Force on Spontaneous Memls., 2002; bd. sponsors Historic Preservation com. St. Ann's Ch. Morrisania, 1987—; ofcl. historian Bronx Borough, NY, 1996—; bd. dirs. Nat. Shrine Bill of Rights, Mt. Vernon, NY, 1983—, 91 Van Cortlandt Owners Corp., 1986—. Recipient Fairleigh Dickinson U. 15-Yr. award, 1979, 20-Yr. award, 1984, 25-Yr. award, 1989, 30-Yr. award, 1994, 35-Yr. award, 1999, Outstanding Tchr. of Yr. award, 1994, 40-Yr. award, 2004; named N.Y.C. Centennial Historian, 1999, NYC Book award for borough history NY Soc. Libr. 2001; named to Hunter Coll. Alumni Hall of Fame, 1974; NY State Regents Coll. tchg. fellow, 1959. Mem.: AAUP (v.p. Teaneck chpt. 1992—93, sec. coun. of FDU chpts. 1992—93), N.Y. Hist. Soc., Am. Hist. Assn., Sigma Lambda, Alpha Chi Alpha, Phi Alpha Theta. Home and Office: 91 Van Cortlandt Ave W Bronx NY 10463-2712 *Transmitting the heritage of the past to the youth and to the mature adult, either through the spoken or written word, not only ensures that the civilization we inherited will be passed on, it will also warn people about earlier mistakes that should now be shunned and will, hopefully, inspire them to add their own positive contribution. I believe I am continuing to perform this service.*

**ULUDAG, UMUT,** electrical engineer, researcher; b. Izmir, Turkey, Feb. 11, 1977; s. Mehmet and Fahriye Uludag. BS, Bogazici U., Istanbul, Turkey, 1995—99, MS, 1999—2001. Rschr. Marmara Rsch. Ctr., Kocaeli, Turkey, 1999—2001; rsch. asst. Mich. State U., East Lansing, 2001—. Contbr. articles to profl. jours. Mem.: IEEE, The Computer Soc. Avocation: classical guitar. Office: Mich State Univ 3115 Engineering Bldg East Lansing MI 48824 Office Phone: 517-355-9319. Office Fax: 517-432-1061. E-mail: uludagum@cse.msu.edu.

**UM, KI SUNG,** research scientist; b. Gongju, Choongnam, Republic of Korea, Apr. 13, 1961; s. Dong Seop Um and Kyung Sook Lee; m. Soon Yi Yang, Apr. 16, 1988; children: Jung Yong, Se Yong. MPH, Yonsei Grad. Sch. Health Sci. and Mgmt., Seoul, 1989; PhD, Kyungpook Nat. U., Daegu, Republic of Korea, 2004. Cert. info. process engr. Human Resources Devel. Svc. Korea. Rschr. NIH, Rockville, Md., 2005—. Maj. Republic of Korea Air Force, 1985—2001. Recipient Sci. award for best paper of yr., Korean Soc. Med. Informatics, 2003; Postdoctoral fellow, Korea Rsch. Found., 2004—05. Mem.: Health Level Seven Inc. (cert. specialist). Achievements include patents for linear streaming algorithm as an HL7 parsing method. Office: NIH 6116 Executive Blvd Suite 705 Rockville MD 20852 Office Phone: 301-451-6364. Office Fax: 301-480-4222. Personal E-mail: vangelis@paran.com. Business E-mail: umkis@mail.nih.gov.

**UMANOFF, DAN F.,** medical association administrator; MD, Med. Coll. Va., Richmond, 1977. CEO, founder Nat. Assn. Advancement and Advocacy Addicts, Sarasota, Fla., 2000—, pres., 2000—06. Author: Hypoic's Handbook. Achievements include discovery of Hypoism - The Neurobiological Cause of Addictions. Home and Office: 8779 Misty Creek Dr Sarasota FL 34241 Personal E-mail: umanoff@comcast.net.

**UMANS, ALVIN ROBERT,** manufacturing executive; b. N.Y.C., Mar. 11, 1927; s. Louis and Ethel (Banner) U.; m. Nancy Jo Zadek, June 28, 1953 (div.); children: Kathi Lee Umans Lind, Craig Joseph; m. Madeleine Sayer, Sept. 21, 1985; 1 child, Valentine Brett. Student, U. Rochester, N.Y., 1945. Sales mgr. Textile Mills Co., Chgo., 1954-56; regional sales mgr. Reflector Hardware Corp., Melrose Park, Ill., 1956-58, nat. sales mgr., 1959-62, v.p., 1962-65, pres., treas., dir., 1965-92; pres., CEO RHC/Spacemaster Corp., Melrose Park, 1992-97, chmn., CEO, 1997—2003, Commerce Nat. Group, Chgo., 2004—. Past chmn., bd. dirs. Goer Mfg. Co., Inc., Charleston, SC, Morgan Marshall Industries, Inc., Ill., Capitol Hardware, Inc., Ill., Spartan Showcase Inc., Mo.; v.p., dir. Adams Comm., Chgo.; bd. dirs. Monroe Comm., Chgo.; trustee Driehaus Mut. Funds, 1996—, chmn. bd., 2005—; mem. adv. bd. Capsonic Group, Elgin, Ill. Trustee Mt. Sinai Hosp. Med. Ctr., Chgo., 1970—, chmn. bd.; 1987-89; trustee Schwab Rehab. Hosp., Chgo., 1987—, chmn. bd.; 1987-89; trustee Sinai Health Sys., Chgo., 1993—, chmn., 1995-97; mem. Cook County Bur. Adv. Com., 1994—; bd. dirs. Milton & Rose Zadek Fund, 1965-78; governing bd. mem. Cinema/Chgo., 1988-89. Served with AUS, 1945-46. Mem. Nat. Assn. Store Fixture Mfrs. (dir. 1969-70), Industry Res.'s Orgn., Chgo. Pres.'s Orgn. Clubs: Standard (Chgo.). Home: 132 E Delaware Pl Chicago IL 60611-1445 Office: Commerce Nat Group 194 E Delaware Pl Chicago IL 60611 Office Phone: 312-654-9150. Fax: 312-654-9180. E-mail: arumans@gmail.com.

**UMANSKY, DIANE,** editor-in-chief; B in journalism, U. RI. Corr. Bergen Record; writer various teen publs. including Scholastic; mng. editor Nickelodeon; sr. editor First for Women; editor-in-chief MediZine Guidebook, 1995—. Freelance writer First for Women, SELF, Family Circle, American, Harper's Bazaar, Working Mother, Good Housekeeping, Weight Watchers. Office: Medizine Inc Fl 2 298 5th Ave New York NY 10110-0002 Office Phone: 212-695-2223.*

**UMBAYEMAKE, LINDA,** library director; b. Cleve., Feb. 19, 1953; d. Charles Morgan and Helen Loretta (Ballard) McDonald; m. Thomas L. Hayes; children: Manu, Kumar, Bari, Mayi, Thurayya, GlennChinua. AA, Cuyahoga C.C., Cleve., 1980; BA, Kent State U., 1984; MLS, Tex. Woman's U., 1989; MRC, U. Ky., 1998. Dir. African Am. Ctr. Toledo-Lucas County Pub. Libr., Toledo, 1989; libr. young adult, correctional and homebound Cuyahoga County Pub. Libr., Warrensville, Ohio, 1989-90; libr. supr. Western N.Mex. Correctional Facility, Grants, 1990, instr. and libr. supr. Santa Fe C.C., 1990; libr. supr. Ga. Dept. Corrections, Buford, 1991; instr. Ky. State U., Frankfort, Ky., 1992—96, head circulation, 1992—93, inter libr. loan and reference libr., 1993—96; pub. svcs. asst. libr. Owensboro C.C., 1996; substitute tchr. Franklin County Pub. Schs., Frankfort, 1997—98; offender rehab. counselor, substance abuse program Luther Luckett Correctional Ctr., 1998—99; collection devel. specialist Book Wholesalers Inc., 1999-2000; STAR program coord. U. Akron, Ohio, 2001—02; br. mgr. East Cleve. Pub. Libr. Caledonia Br., 2001—. Founder Lumbay, 1997—; mem. Kent Ohio Cable Commn., 2003—. Apptd. to Ky. Foster Care Rev. Bd., 1999—2000; child support, visitation com. Franklin County Family Ct., Ohio, 1999—2000; mem. Bd. Elections Franklin County. Mem.: NAMI, Nat. Rehab. Assn., Black Caucus of ALA (chair new mem. orientation com. 1994—96, membership com. 1989—96, ALA Shirley Olofson com. 1993—96, mem. minority recruitment com. 1993—96), Chi Sigma Iota. E-mail: lumbay2000@yahoo.com.

**UMBERG, THOMAS JOHN,** lawyer; b. Cin., Sept. 25, 1955; s. John H. and Joan (Jansen) U.; m. Robin Bailey; children: Erin, Brett, Tommy. BA cum laude, UCLA, 1977; JD, U. Calif., San Francisco, 1980. Bar: Calif. 1980, U.S. Dist. Ct. (ctr. dist.) Calif. 1981, U.S. Dist. Ct. (so. dist.) Calif. 1986, U.S. Ct. Appeals (9th cir.) 1988. Asst. U.S. atty. Ctrl. Dist. Calif., criminal div., L.A., 1987—90; mem. Calif. Assembly, Sacramento, 1990—94, 2004—; ptnr. Morrison & Foerster LLP, Irvine, Calif., 1995—97; dep. dir. White House Office Nat. Drug Control Policy, 1997—2000; mng. ptnr.-Orange County Office Morrison & Foerster LLP, Irvine, Calif., 2000—. Adj. prof. law Southwestern U., 1995—97. Military Prosecutor, U.S. Army, Korea, Italy 1980-1985; col. USAR. Mem.: Calif. Coun. Criminal Justice (mem. 1991—95). Roman Catholic. Office: Morrison & Foerster LLP 19900 MacArthur Blvd Irvine CA 92612-2445 Office Phone: 949-251-7500. Office Fax: 949-251-0900. Business E-Mail: tumberg@mofo.com.

**UMBERSON, MARILYN KAY,** music educator; d. Lester V. Zobac and Agnes M. Drahos Zobac; m. George E. Umberson, Oct. 22, 1933; children: Brad D. Smith, James A. Smith, Rhonda Murray, Janna Hosmer, Alicia Kassenbrock. BA, Clarke Coll., 1968, BA in Music, 1968; MusM in Edn., No. Ariz. U., 1986. Cert. tchr. basic elem. and music Ariz., 1975, tchr. Am. Orff Schulwerk Assn., 1983, Kodaly, 2000, educator early child/mid. child music

Nat. Bd. Profl. Tchg. Standards, 2002. Tchr. music and classroom St. Thomas the Apostle Sch., Phoenix, 1976—79; educator music and strings Creighton Sch. Dist., Phoenix, 1980—84; tchr. music Kyrene Sch. Dist., Tempe, Ariz., 1985—. Presenter in field. Contbr. articles to mags.; performer: USO, 1964—65. People to people ambassador, Russia, 2004. Recipient A. Sullivan Music award, Clarke Coll., 1968. Mem.; Ariz. Music Educators Assn., Am. Orff Schulwerk Assn. (tchr. tnr. 1993—99), Music Educators Nat. Conf. Roman Catholic. Avocations: golf, skiing, brain and music research, composing, travel.

**UMBREIT, WAYNE WILLIAM,** bacteriologist, educator; b. Markesan, Wis., May 1, 1913; s. William Traugott and Augusta (Abendroth) U.; m. Doris McQuade, July 31, 1937; children: Dorayne Loreda, Jay Nicholas, Thomas Hayden. BA, U. Wis., 1934, MS, 1936, PhD, 1939. Instr. soil microbiology Rutgers U., 1937-38; faculty U. Wis., Madison, 1938-44, asst. prof. bacteriology and chemistry, 1941-44; faculty Cornell U., 1944-47, prof. bacteriology, 1946-47; head dept. enzyme chemistry Merck Inst., Rahway, NJ, 1947-58; asso. dir., 1958; chmn. dept. bacteriology Rutgers U., New Brunswick, NJ, 1958-75, prof. microbiology, dir. grad. programs, 1969-83, prof. emeritus microbiology, 1983—; dir. labs. So. Br. Watershed Assn. 1983-89. Author: (with Burris, Stauffer) Manometric Techniques, 1945, 5th edit., 1972, (with Oginsky) An Introduction to Bacterial Physiology, 1954, Metabolic Maps, 1960, Modern Microbiology, 1962, Essentials of Bacterial Physiology, 1976; Editor: Advances in Applied Microbiology, vols. 1-10, 1959-68; Contbr. articles to profl. jours. Recipient Biochem. Congress Symposium medal Paris, France, 1952 Fellow Am. Acad. Microbiology, NY Acad. Sci., AAAS; mem. Am. Soc. for Microbiology (Eli Lilly award 1947, Carski Found. award 1968), Soc. Biol. Chemists, Am. Chem. Soc., Theobald Smith Soc. (Waksman award 1957, past pres.), AAUP, Sigma Xi. Home: c/o TH Umbreit PO Box 5352 Rockville MD 20848 Personal E-mail: wumbreit@comcast.net.

**UMELO, ANTHONY N.,** science educator; arrived in U.S., 1967; s. Ogaraku and Nuena Umelo; m. Elaine M.W. Umelo, June 10, 1980; children: Adaku Alexius, Chukaulmeka. BS, DC Tchrs. Coll., 1977; MA, George Washington U., Washington, 1979; PhD, Am. U., Washington, 1982. Sci. tchr. DC Pub. Schs., Washington, 1982—. Fellow Rsch. Tng. Program-Rsch. Experience for Tchrs., Smithsonian Instn./Johns Hopkins U., 2002, Advanced Placement Sci. Follow-On Inst., Carnegie Instn. Washington, 2003, Advanced Placement Environ. Sci., Howard U., 2003, Advanced Placement Chemistry, Montgomery Coll., 2004. Mem.: Nat. Sci. Tchr. Assn., Nat. Assn. Biology Tchrs., Smithsonian. Roman Catholic. Avocation: star gazing. Office: DC Pub Schs/Anacostia 1601 R St SE Washington DC 20020

**UMENYIORA, OSI,** professional football player; b. Nov. 16, 1980; Graduate, Troy State U. Defensive end NY Giants, 2003—. Named to NFC Pro-Bowl Team, 2005, NFL All-Pro Team, 2005. Office: New York Football Giants Giants Stadium East Rutherford NJ 07073*

**UMETSU, DALE T.,** pediatrics educator, physician; b. Bowling Green, Ohio, Aug. 30, 1951; BA, Columbia U., 1973; MD, NYU, 1979. Intern, jr. then sr. resident Harvard Med. Sch. and Children's Hosp., Boston, 1979-82; instr. Harvard U., 1984-86; asst. prof. pediatrics Stanford U., 1986—. Contbr. articles to profl. jours. Recipient Hyde Watson award Asthma and Allergy Found., 1986-91; rsch. grantee Soc. for Pediatric Rsch., 1986-88, Basil O'Connor grantee March of Dimes, 1986-90, Am. Lung Assn. grantee, 1989-90, ROI grantee NIH, 1989—. Fellow Am. Acad. Allergy/Immunology, Am. Acad. Pediatrics; mem. Am. Fedn. for Clin. Rsch., Calif. Thoracic Soc. Office: Stanford U Med Ctr Dept Pediatrics Rm S217 Stanford CA 94305

**UMHOEFER, AURAL M.,** retired dean, educational consultant; b. Wausau, Wis., May 11, 1942; d. Mark John Vladick, Alice Marion Vladick; m. Paul Anthony Umhoefer. MS, U. Wis., 1965; BA in French, Rosary Coll., 1964—64; degree (hon.), U. Wis., Baraboo, 2006. Head libr. Green Bay ctr. U. Wis., 1965—68, dir. learning resource ctr. Baraboo, 1968—80, dean, campus exec. officer Baraboo/Sauk county campus, 1980—2002, ret., 2002; cons. U. Wis. Sys., 2003—05. Bd. dirs. Wells Fargo, Baraboo; bd. dirs. Hist. Sites Found. Circus World Mus., Baraboo, 1984—90. Bd. dirs. Al Ringling Theatre, Friends of Campus, Inc., Boy Scouts Am., Madison, Wis., 1985—97; devel. coun. St. Clare Hosp., Baraboo 1993—97. Named Outstanding Young Women of Am., 1975, Aural M. Umhoefer bldg. in her honor, U. Wis.-Baraboo, 2002; recipient Outstanding Alumni award, Newman H.S.- Wausau, Wis., 1992, Citation from Senate, State of Wis., 1991, 2002, Pub. Svc. award, Fed. Bur. Prisons, 1991, 2002, Appreciation award, Circus World Mus., 1986, Citation from Govt., State of Wis., 2002. Mem.: AAUW (corp. rep. 1985—97, Wis. Women Leaders in Edn. award 1986, 1989), Wis. Correctional Edn. Assn. (v.p., pres. 1994—98), U. Wis. Alumni Assn. (pres. 1984—86, Spark Plug award 1992), Rotary Internat. (vocat. chair. bd.dirs.) Avocations: cooking, reading, travel, gardening. Home: 700 Effinger Rd Baraboo WI 53913 Office: University of Wisconsin 1006 Connie Rd Baraboo WI 53913 Personal E-mail: pauralum@julmet.com. Business E-Mail: aumhoefe@uwc.edu.

**UMHOLTZ, CLYDE ALLAN,** financial analyst; b. Du Quoin, Ill., Dec. 20, 1947; s. Frederick Louis and Opal Kathleen (Beard) U. BS, U. Ill., 1969; MS, U. Miss., 1972; MBA, Memphis State U., 1983, PhD, 1986; Dr of Higher Learning (hon.), London Sch. Econs., 2002. CFA; cert. systems profl., tax practitioner; registered profl. engr.; cert. data processor. Supr. quality control Champion Internat. Corp., Oxford, Miss., 1971-72; mgr. divsn. quality control Cook Industries, Memphis, 1973; engring. planner Northwest Industries and subs., Memphis, 1974-75; long range planning and analysis W.R. Grace and Co. and subs., Memphis, 1975-78; mgr. planning and analysis Ctr. Nuc. Studies Memphis State U., 1979-83; data processing mgr. Shelby County (Tenn.) Govt., 1983-87, dep. adminstr., 1987—2005, spl. asst. to county exec., 1989—2005, vice chancellor higher edn. commn., 2005—. Adj. prof. U. Tenn., Memphis, 1985—; ptnr. Custom Data Systems Inc., Memphis, 1987—, Western Techs. Inc., Memphis, 1988—; bd. dir. Am. Tech. Inst., Memphis, Am. Info. Cons., Atlanta, Eastgate Corp., Anaheim, Calif., CIPCO Corp., Chgo., Sanford Cons. Group, London, Paris; bd. underwriters Lloyd's of London; diplomate editl. adv. bd. Brent's Peerage, London, Memphis-Amsterdam Gateway Com., Holland, 1997; Ukrainian Trade Alliance, Kiev, 1997—; Asian Econ. Recovery Coun., Tokyo, 1998—; elected to U.S. China Bd. of Trade, 2002; adv. bd. Fed. Res. Bank, Memphis, 1998—; mem. Am.-Japanese Tire Safety Adv. Bd., 2000, Tenn. Commn. on Homeland Security, 2002—; diplomate Multi-Country Healthcare Exch., 2003, Medicare Nat. Study Com., 2003; oversight com. Internat. Energy Prodn. Alliance, 2003, 06; adv. com. OPEC Price Stblzn. Coop., 2004, 06; mem. Internat. Symposium Strategic Energy Resources, 2005, 06, Congressional Com. Social Security Reform, 2005, 06, Citizens' Congl. Ethics Coun., 2006, Emergency Mgmt. Comms. Coordinating Com., 2006, Accreditation Com., Internat. Baccalaureate Edn. Program, 2006, Mid-East Stabilization Planning Conf., 2006; cons. in field. Author: Prototyping of Computerized Financial Systems, 3rd edit., 1997, Context Analysis in System Design, 2nd edit., 1999, The Family Partnership-An Estate Planning Model, 3rd edit., 2000, The Use of Chemical Molecules as Computer Switches, 2002; contbr. articles to profl. jours.; inventor angle trisector. Active presdl. election campaigns, 1968-72, 80-2004; del. Rep. Nat. Conv., 1996-2004; mem. Rep. Nat. Com., 2002—; active mayoral campaign Memphis, 1975, 83, 87, 91, Shelby County, 1990, 94, sheriff's campaign Shelby County, 1990, 94, Mid-South Billy Graham Crusade, 1978; del. So. Govs.' Conf., 1992-93; gov. staff State of Tenn., 1993-94; mem. Mayor's Adv. Com., Memphis, 1991; steering com. Future Memphis, 1992, Arena Football League, Memphis, 1994; mem. Houston Oilers Relocation Com., 1996; adv. coun. Kordes' Gardens, Hamburg, Germany; study com. Nat. Electoral Coll., 2001; co-chmn. 27th Ann. Pres.'s Dinner, 2002; oversight com. Fin. Acctg. Stds. Bd., 2002—; reg. dir. west Tenn. Cmty. Found., 2006—. Recipient Oratorical award Optimist Club, 1963, Leadership and Human Rels. award Blue Carnegie Inst., 1977, Disting. Svc. award State of Tenn., 1991; NSF fellow, 1970-72. Fellow NAS, Australian Acad. Scis., NY Acad. Scis., Am. Acad. Info. Tech.; mem. AAAS, AIChE, Am. Mgmt. Assn., Fin. Execs. Inst., Am.

Chem. Soc., Assn. MBA Execs., Data Processing Mgmt. Assn., Planning Execs. Inst., Am. Assn. Investment Advisors, U. Ill. Alumni Assn., U. Miss. Alumni Assn., Memphis State U. Alumni Assn., Am. Rose Soc. (accredited life rose judge 1990), Am. Iris Soc., Am. Hemerocallis Soc., Elvis Presley Meml. Soc., Am. Hort. Soc., Internat. Platform Assn., Gt. Am. Pyramid Boosters Memphis, Mensa, Admirals Club, Oxford Club, London Club, Exec. Club Memphis, Petroleum Club Memphis, Olympic Soc. Atlanta, Order of De Molay, Phi Beta Kappa Baptist. Home: 3580 Hanna Dr Memphis TN 38128-3451 Office: 100 N Main St Memphis TN 38103-5011 Office Phone: 901-388-3997. Business E-Mail: cau@memphis.gov. E-mail: cau@hannamem.gov.

**UMLAUF, JON,** physician, director; b. Akron, Ohio, Jan. 26, 1959; s. Robert Charles Umlauf and Anne Stoddar Adams; m. Atu Asako Miyakoshi, June 12, 2002. BS, Pa. State U., 1985; MPH, George Washington U., 2000; MD, Pa. State U., 1989. Bd. cert. family medicine Am. Acad. Family Physicians, bd. cert. aerospace medicine ABPM. Gen. med. officer USS Seattle, Earle, NJ, 1990—92; squadron med. officer Combat Logistics Squadron 2, Earle, 1992—93; head dept. family medicine Naval Hosp. Yokosuka, Japan, 1995—97, team leader primary care, 1997—98; sr. med. officer USS George Washington, Norfolk, Va., 2001—03; head clin. ops. Naval Ambulatory Care Ctr., Groton, Conn., 2003; sr. med. officer Naval Health Care New Eng., Groton, 2004—. Commdr. USN, 2001—. Home: 368 Meridian St Groton CT 06340 Office: Naval Ambulatory Care Ctr Groton 1 Wahoo Ave NLON Groton CT 06349

**UMMER, JAMES WALTER,** lawyer; b. Pitts., July 16, 1945; s. Walter B. and Rose P. (Gerhardt) U.; m. Janet Sue Young, Dec. 21, 1968; children: James Bradley, Benjamin F. BA, Thiel Coll., 1967; JD, Duke U., 1972. Bar: Pa. 1972. Trust officer Pitts. Nat. Bank, 1972-75; tax atty., shareholder Buchanan Ingersoll P.C., Pitts., 1975-92; prin. Hirtle, Callaghan & Co., Pitts., 1992-93; shareholder Babst, Calland, Clements and Zomnir, Pitts., 1993-99; ptnr. Reed, Smith, Shaw & McClay, Pitts., 2000—03, Rothman Gordon, P.C., Pitts., 2003—. Golf course cons., Orlando, Fla. Trustee Thiel Coll., Greenville, Pa., 1984—, The Childrens' Inst., Pitts., 1984—; mem. bd. visitors Duke U. Div. Sch., 1999—. Fellow Am. Coll. Probate Counsel, Am. Coll. Trust and Estate Counsel; mem. Estate Planning Coun. Western Pa. (pres. 1986-87), Tax Club (Pitts.), Duquesne Club, Rolling Rock Club, Oakmont Country Club. Republican. Presbyterian. Home: 200 Woodland Farms Rd Pittsburgh PA 15238-2024 Office: Rothman Gordon PC 3d Fl Grant Bldg 310 Grant St Pittsburgh PA 15219 Office Phone: 412-338-1105. E-mail: jwummer@rothmangordon.com.

**UMMINGER, BRUCE LYNN,** government agency administrator, research scientist, educator, consultant; b. Dayton, Ohio, Apr. 10, 1941; s. Frederick William and Elnora Mae Umminger; m. Judith Lackey Bryant, Dec. 17, 1966; children: Alison Grace, April Lynn. BS in Biology magna cum laude with honors, Yale U., 1963, MS, 1966, MPhil, 1968, PhD, 1969; postgrad., U. Calif., Berkeley, 1963—64; cert. univ. adminstrv./mgmt. tng. program, U. Cin., 1975; cert., Fed. Exec. Inst., 1984. Asst. prof. dept. biol. scis. U. Cin., 1969-73, assoc. prof. dept. biol. scis., 1973-75, acting head dept. biol. scis., 1973-75, prof. dept. biol. scis., 1975-81, dir. grad. affairs, 1978-79; program dir. regulatory biology program NSF, Washington, 1979-84, dept. dir. cellular bioscis., 1984-89, mem. sr. exec. svc., 1984—, acting divsn. dir., 1985-87, 88-89, divsn. dir. cellular bioscis. divsn., 1989-91, divsn. dir. integrative biology and neurosci., 1991—99, sr. scientist office integrative activities, office of dir., 1999—2006, cons., 2006—, expert, 2006—; sr. advisor on health policy Office of Internat. Health Policy Dept. State, Washington, 1988; sr. advisor on biodiversity Smithsonian Instn., Washington, 1993-94. Exec. sec. Nat. Sci. Bd. Com. on Ctrs. and Individual Investigator Awards, 1986-88; rev. panel exptl. program to stimulate competitive rsch. NSF, 1989, Rsch. Improvement in Minority Instns., 1986-87, US-India Coop. Sci. Program, 1981-82, U.S.-India Exch. of Scholars Program, 1979-81; vice chmn. biotech. rsch. subcom. Fed. Coord. Coun. on Sci. Engring. and Tech., Office Sci. and Tech. Policy, 1991-94; exec. sec. subcom. biodiversity and ecosystem dynamics, com. on environment and natural resources Nat. Sci. and Tech. Coun., 1994, interagy. working group on rsch. misconduct policy implementation, 2000-06; group nat. experts on safety in biotech. OECD, 1988-89; sr. exec. panel Exec. Potential Program, Office Pers. Mgmt., 1988-89; space shuttle proposal rev. panel in life scis. NASA, 1978, rsch. assocs. in space biology award com., 1985-91, chmn. cell and devel. biology discipline working group, space biology program, 1990-91, chmn. gravitational biology panel, NASA Specialized Ctrs. Rsch. and Tng., 1990, chmn. specialized ctrs. rsch. and tng. peer rev. panel NASA 1995, exec. steering com. in life scis., 1991, gravitational biology facility sci. working group, 1992-95, space sta. biol. rsch. project sci. working group, 1995-96, neurolab. steering com., 1993; panel study biol. diversity, Bd. Sci. and Tech. Internat. Devel. NRC, 1989; exec. sec. adv. planning bd. Nat. Biodiversity Info. Ctr., Smithsonian Instn., 1993-94; adv. screening com. in life scis. Coun. for Internat. Exch. of Scholars, 1978-81; liaison rep. nat. heart, lung and blood adv. coun. NIH, 1979-87, nat. adv. child health and human devel. coun., 1990-99; recombinant DNA adv. com., 1988; liaison rep. agrl. biotech. Rsch. Adv. com., USDA, 1989-94; animal com. Interagy. Rsch., 1984-88; Interagy. working group on Internat. Biotech., 1988-94; chmn. proposal panel in biology Sci. Found. Ireland, 2002, Human Proteomics Site Visit, 2003. Author book chpts. and contbr. articles to profl. jours.; assoc. editor Jour. Exptl. Zoology, 1977-79; editl. adv. bd. Gen. and Comparative Endocrinology, 1982. World mission com. Ch. of the Redeemer, New Haven, 1967-68; Sunday Sch. steering com. Calvary Episcopal Ch., Cin., 1972-73, sr. acolyte, 1972-77, adult edn. com., 1975-76; deacon Faith Presbyn. Ch., Springfield, Va., 1996-99; adv. com. Wakefield H.S., 1991-92, PTA exec. bd., 1991-92; sci. adv. com. Arlington Pub. Schs., 1987-92, adv. coun. on instrn., 1991-92; adv. bd. Campbell Comml. Coll., Cin., 1977-79. Recipient George Rieveschl, Jr. Rsch. award U. Cin., 1973, Presdl. Rank Meritorious Exec. award NSF, 1992; U. Cin. Grad. Sch. fellow 1977—, NSF fellow 1964; rsch. grantee NSF 1971-79. Fellow AAAS (coun. 1980-83, 89-90, program com. for 1989 ann. meeting 1988, chmn.-elect sect. G-Biol. Scis. 1987-88, chair 1988-89, ret. 1989-90); mem. Assn. of Yale Alumni (dir. 1990-93), Mory's Assn., Sigma Xi (Disting. Rsch. award U. Cin. chpt. 1973, pres. U. Cin. chpt. 1977-79), Mensa. Home: 205 Helmsdale Dr Chapel Hill NC 27517 Personal E-mail: bruce.u@hotmail.com.

**UMPAICHITRA, VATCHARAPAN,** pediatrician, endocrinologist; Pediatric endocrinologist The Brookdale Univ Hosp. and Med. Ctr., Bklyn., 2002—. Office: The Brookdale Univ Hosp & Med Ctr 1 brookdale Plaza room 300 CHC Brooklyn NY 11212 Office Phone: 718-240-5233. Office Fax: 718-240-6515. Personal E-mail: umpaiv07@yahoo.com. Business E-Mail: vumpaich@brookdale.edu.

**UMPENHOUR, KEN EUGENE,** protective services official; b. Dayton, Ohio, Sept. 14, 1928; s. Richard George and Ruby Ann Umpenhour; m. Astrid Helen Byttner (dec.); children: Kathy, Kurt, Kent, Kristopher; m. Janet Elaine Gaffney, July 7, 1997. AS, Sinclair C.C., Edison C.C. Border patrol agt. US Border Patrol, Brownsville, Tex., 1952—53; dep. sheriff Montgomery County, Dayton, Ohio, 1958—68, chief of detectives, 1956—68; auto racer Lotus and Jaguar Autos, Dayton, 1969—74, Can-Am Championship Races, 1970—74; owner Boston Stroker Tobacco Shop, Naples, 1975—86; state corrections officer Fla. Dept of Corrections, Naples, Fla., 1995. Dep. sheriff Polk County Sheriff's Office, Bartow, Fla., 1995—97; state trooper Fla. Hwy. Patrol, Lakeland, Fla., 2000—. 1st lt., pilot USAAF, 1945—49. Decorated DFC, Air medals. Mem.: Fraternal Order of Police, Sports Car Club of Am. Avocations: flying, motorcycling, boating. Home Fax: 868-956-3154. E-mail: srgtump@tampabay.rr.com.

**UNAKAR, NALIN JAYANTILAL,** biological sciences educator; b. Karachi, Sindh, Pakistan, Mar. 26, 1935; came to U.S., 1961; s. Jayantilal Virshankar and Malati Jaswantrai (Buch) U.; m. Nita Shantilal Mankad; children: Rita, Rupa. BS, Gujerat U., Bhavnagar, India, 1955; MSc, Bombay U., 1961; PhD, Brown U., 1965. Research asst. Indian Cancer Research Ctr., Bombay, 1955-61; USPHS trainee in biology Brown U., Providence, 1961-

65; research assoc. in pathology U. Toronto, Ont., Canada, 1965-66; asst. prof. biology Oakland U., Rochester, Mich., 1966-69, assoc. prof., 1969-74, prof., chmn. biology dept., 1974-87, prof., 1974-2000, prof. emeritus, 2000—, adj. prof. biomed. scis., 1984—. Mem. coop. cataract research group Nat. Eye Inst., Bethesda, Md., 1977—; mem. visual scis. study sect. NIH, Bethesda, 1982-86, mem. cataract panel, 1980—. Mem. vis. bd. Lehigh U., Bethlehem, Pa., 1986-89. Grantee Nat. Cancer Inst., NIH, 1967-70, Nat. Eye Inst., NIH, 1976-97. Mem. AAAS, Am. Soc. Cell Biology, Assn. Rsch. in Vision and Ophthalmology, Sigma Xi. Home: 2822 Rhineberry Rd Rochester Hills MI 48309-1912

**UNAN, GEORGE VINCENT,** adult education educator; b. Bell Island, Newfoundland, Can., July 19, 1920; arrived in U.S., 1958; s. Samuel S. Unan and Ellen A. Kennedy-Unan; m. Myra Lanza Unan, Apr. 3, 1948 (div. July 1974); children: Veronica Gonzalez, Vivien Irving, Valerie Kitto, Venessa Mangione, Vernon A.; m. Gahyle Rich Unan, July 26, 1975; 1 child, Diane Baer. BS, Calif. State U., Long Beach, 1965, MBA, 1967. Cost estimator Hydro Electric Power Commn., Toronto, Ont., Canada, 1950—58; chief acct. Darco Industries, El Segundo, Calif., 1959—62; contr. sec./dir. State Industries, L.A., Calif., 1962—68; contr. Direct Energy Corp., Monterey Park, Calif., 1968—70, Harrington Indsl. Plastics, L.A., 1970—83; CFO Long Beach Conv. Ctr., 1984—86; educator Anaheim (Calif.) Adult H.S. Dist., 1997—. Seminar instr. in field; educator, exploratory seminars U. Sydney, Australia, 1987—96, Nat. U. Buenos Aires, Argentina, 1993, Charles U., Prague, Czech Republic, 1996. Author: Anecdotes and Quintessences From The Holy Bible, 1999. Adv. bd. Orange County, Santa Ana, Calif., 1984—97; mem. oversight com. Orange County Transp. Authority, Santa Ana, 1997—99; chmn., mem. Citizens Adv. Commn., Cypress, Calif., 1985—96. Home: 6424 Anguilla Ave Cypress CA 90630-5308 Office: Anaheim Adult High Sch Dist 1800 Ball Rd Anaheim CA 92804 Office Phone: 714-999-5616.

**UNANUE, JOSEPH A.,** retired food products executive; b. NYC, Mar. 14, 1925; s. Prudencio and Carolina (Casal) Unanue; m. Carmen Ana Casal, 1956; 6 children. BSME, Cath. U Am., 1950; LHD (hon.), Seton Hall U. 2004. Chmn., pres., CEO Goya Foods, Inc., Secaucus, NJ, 1976—2004. Served U.S. Army, WWII. Named Man of Yr., Nat. Conf. Christians and Jews; named to Sovereign Order of the Knights of Malta; recipient Nat. Hispanic Achievement Award, Hispanic Mag., 1991, leadership award, Nat. Minority Suppliers Assn.*

**UNANUE, ROBERT I.,** food products executive; s. Anthony Unanue. Pres. Goya Foods of Fla., 1999—2004, Goya Foods, Inc., Secaucus, NJ, 2004—. Office: Goya Foods Inc 100 Seaview Dr Secaucus NJ 07096*

**UNCAPHER, MARK ELSON,** lawyer, trade association administrator; b. Buffalo, Aug. 4, 1953; s. Mark Elson Uncapher Jr. and Joan (Willard) Gruen; m. Robin Nixon, Aug. 27, 1977; children: Peter McLane, Elizabeth Cameron. BA, George Washington U., 1975; JD, N.Y. Law Sch., 1978. Bar: N.Y., 1979, D.C. 1998. Asst. counsel Comptr. State of N.Y., N.Y.C., 1978-83; sales exec. Sta. WZFM-FM, Pleasantville, N.Y., 1983-86; sales exec. Sta. WPAT Park Comm., Inc., N.Y.C., 1986-94; nat. pres. The Ripon Soc., Washington, 1987-90; co-owner Sta. WWCO, Waterbury, Conn., 1994-97; dir. audit svcs. N.Y.C. Dept. Homeless Svcs., 1994-95; counsel House Subcom. on Govt. Mgmt., Info. and Tech., 1995-98; v.p. and counsel divsn. internet commerce and comm. Info. Tech. Assn. Am., Arlington, Va., 1998—2002, sr. v.p. and counsel, 2002—. Chmn. Ripon Edn. Fund, 1982-89, bd. dirs., 1982-97; mng. dir. Signal Properties, Brooklyn Heights, N.Y., 1987-95; ptnr. McLane Farms, LaPorte, Inc., 1980-95; U.S. chmn. 5th Transatlantic Conf., London and Cambridge, Eng., 1988. Contbr. articles to profl. jours. including Broadcast Fin. Jour., Ripon Forum. Chmn. Mark O. Hatfield Scholarship Com., Washington, 1985-97; del. candidate for George Bush 14th Congl. Dist., Bklyn., 1980; fin. chmn. Kings County Rep. Com., 1993-94, Montgomery County (Md.) Rep. Com., 2000, 05—; mem. Pres.-elect Bush's Transition Team for the FCC, 2000-01. Mem. ABA, Fed. Comm. Bar Assn., Computer Law Assn., Capitol Hill Club (Washington), Men's Rep. Club of Montgomery County. Republican. Congregationalist. Home: 6210 Greentree Rd Bethesda MD 20817-3362 Office: Info Tech Assn Am 1401 Wilson Blvd Ste 1100 Arlington VA 22209-3101 E-mail: muncapher@ITAA.Org.

**UNDAR, AKIF,** research scientist, biomedical engineer, educator; b. Istanbul, Turkey, Aug. 3, 1963; arrived in U.S., 1987; s. Fikret and H. Neriman Undar; m. F. Pinar Albayrak; children: Damla, Akifcan. BS, Yildiz U., Istanbul, 1986; MS, S.W. Tex. State U., 1992; MSE, U. Tex., 1994, PhD, 1996. Asst. instr., dir. surg. rsch. U. Tex. Health Sci. Ctr., San Antonio, 1996—97; instr. Baylor Coll. Medicine, Houston, 1997—99, asst. prof. surgery, 1999—2002, assoc. prof., 2002—03; assoc. prof. pediat., surgery and bioengring. Pa. State Coll. Medicine, Hershey, 2003—. Tchg. asst. U. Tex., Austin, 1994—96; dir. perfusion rsch. Tex. Children's Hosp., Houston, 1997—2001, dir. rsch., 2001—03; presenter, lectr. in field. Mem. editl. bd. Artificial Organ, 2003—, ASAIO Jour., 2004—; contbr. articles to profl. jours. Rsch. grantee, AHA Tex. affiliate, 1998-2000, Tanox, Inc., 1999-2001, NIH, 2000, NHLBI, 2005—, Pa. Health Dept., 2004—. Mem.: ASAIO, AHA (cert. 2000), Internat. Soc. Rotary Blood Pumps, Biomedical Engring. Soc., Internat. Soc. Artificial Organs. Office: Pa State Milton S Hershey Med Ctr Pa State Children's Hosp Dept Pediat 500 University Dr P Box 850 Hershey PA 17033 Office Phone: 717-531-6706. Business E-Mail: aundar@psu.edu.

**UNDERBERG, MARK ALAN,** lawyer; b. Niagara Falls, N.Y., July 9, 1955; s. Alan Jack and Joyce Love (Wisbaum) U.; m. Diane Englander, Mar. 22, 1986; children: Andrew Englander, James Englander. BA, Cornell U., 1977, JD, 1981. Bar: N.Y. 1981. Law clk. to chief judge U.S. Ct. Appeals (3d cir.), Wilmington, Del., 1981-82; assoc. Debevoise & Plimpton, N.Y.C., 1982-87; mng. dir., dep. gen. counsel Henley Group, Inc., N.Y.C., 1987-90, mng. dir. gen. counsel, 1990-92; v.p., gen. counsel Abex Inc., Hampton, NH, 1992-95. V.p., gen. counsel Fisher Sci. Internat. Inc., Hampton, N.H., 1991-97, cons. 1997-98; counsel Paul, Weiss, Rifkind, Wharton & Garrison, N.Y.C., 1998-99, ptnr., 2000—. Editor-in-chief Cornell Law Rev., 1980-81. Mem. ABA, Assn. of Bar of City of N.Y., Genesee Valley Club, University Club. Office: Paul Weiss Rifkind Wharton & Garrison 1285 Avenue Of The Americas New York NY 10019-6065 Office Phone: 212-373-3368. Business E-Mail: munderberg@paulweiss.com.

**UNDERDOWN, DAVID EDWARD,** historian, educator; b. Wells, Eng., Aug. 19, 1925; s. John Percival and Ethel Mary (Gell) U. BA, U. Oxford, 1950, MA, 1951, Yale U., 1952; B.Litt., U. Oxford, 1953; D.Litt. hon., U. of South, 1981. Asst. prof. U. of South, Sewanee, Tenn., 1953-58, assoc. prof., 1958-62; then assoc. prof. U. Va., Charlottesville, 1962-68; prof. Brown U., Providence, 1968-85, Munro-Goodwin Wilkinson prof., 1978-85; vis. prof. Yale U., New Haven, 1979, prof., 1986-94, George Burton Adams prof., 1994-96, emeritus, 1996—. Dir. Yale Ctr. Parliamentary History, 1985-96; vis. Mellon prof. Inst. for Advanced Study, 1988-89; vis. fellow All Souls Coll., Oxford, 1992; Ford's lectr. Oxford U., 1992. Author: Royalist Conspiracy in England, 1960, Pride's Purge, 1971, Somerset in the Civil War and Interregnum, 1973, Revel, Riot and Rebellion, 1985, Fire from Heaven, 1992, A Freeborn People, 1996, Start of Play, 2000. Guggenheim fellow, 1964-65, 91-92, fellow Am. Coun. Learned Socs., 1973-74, NEH fellow, 1980-81. Fellow Royal Hist. Soc., Brit. Acad. (corr.); mem. Am. Hist. Assn. (award for scholarly distinction 2005), Conf. Brit. Studies. Office: Yale U Dept History New Haven CT 06520 Business E-Mail: david.underdown@yale.edu.

**UNDERHILL, JACOB BERRY, III,** retired insurance company executive; b. NYC, Oct. 25, 1926; s. Jacob Berry, Jr. and Dorothy Louise (Quinn) U.; m. Cynthia Jane Lovejoy, Sept. 9, 1950 (div. Sept. 1962); children: David Lovejoy, Kate Howell Underhill Kerwin, Benedict Quinn; m. Lois Beachy, Nov. 2, 1963 (div. July 1987); m. Betsy F. Ashton, Oct. 17, 1987. Grad. Phillips Exeter Acad., 1944; AB, Princeton U., 1950. Editor Courier & Freeman, Potsdam, NY, 1950-53; reporter Democrat & Chronicle, Rochester, NY, 1953-56; chief editorial writer St. Petersburg (Fla.) Times, 1956-59; asso. editor McGraw Hill Publ. Co., N.Y.C., 1959-61, Newsweek, N.Y.C., 1961-63;

asst. press sec. to Gov. N.Y., 1963-67; dep. supt., 1st dep. supt. State N.Y. Ins. Dept., 1967-72; v.p., sr. v.p., exec. v.p., dir., vice chmn. bd., pres. N.Y. Life Ins. Co., N.Y.C., 1972-86. Hon. chmn. bd. dirs. Manhattan Eye, Ear and Throat Hosp.; trustee emeritus Nat. Trust for Hist. Preservation. With USNR, 1944-46. Mem. Players Club, Links Club, Piping Rock Club (Locust Valley, N.Y.).

**UNDERWEISER, IRWIN PHILIP,** mining executive, lawyer; b. NYC, Jan. 3, 1929; s. Harry and Edith (Gladstein) U.; m. Beatrice J. Kortchmar, Aug. 17, 1959; children: Rosanne, Marian, Jeffrey. BA, CCNY, 1950; LL.D., Fordham U., 1954; LL.M., NYU, 1961. Bar: N.Y. 1954. With firm Scribner & Miller, N.Y.C., 1951-54, 56-62; partner firm Feuerstein & Underweiser, 1962-73, Underweiser & Fuchs, 1973-77, Underweiser & Underweiser, 1977—. V.p. sec. Sunshine Mining Co., Kellogg, Idaho, 1965-70, chmn. bd., 1970-78, pres., 1971-74, 77, v.p., 1977-83; vice chmn., dir. Underwriters Bank and Trust Co., N.Y.C., 1969-73; sec., dir. Bus. Consortium Fund, 1994—, Triad Capital Corp. N.Y., 1994—; dir. Anchor Post Products, Inc. Bd. dirs. Silver Inst. Inc., vice chmn., 1998-2001; bd. dirs. Bronx Mus. of the Arts, 1993-2001, Sheltering the Homeless is Our Responsibility, 1993-2001, 02—; gen. counsel, mem. bus. council Friends City Center Music and Drama, N.Y.C., 1966-67; pres. W. Quaker Ridge Assn., 1969-70; treas. Scarsdale Neighborhood Assn. Presidents, 1970-71. Served with AUS, 1954-56. Mem. Am., N.Y. State bar assns., Bar Assn. City N.Y., Phi Beta Kappa, Phi Alpha Theta. Home: 7 Rural Dr Scarsdale NY 10583-7701 Office: 1 Water St White Plains NY 10601

**UNDERWOOD, ANTHONY PAUL,** lawyer; b. Atlanta, June 25, 1955; s. Paul L. and Charlene B. (Snider) U.; children: Andrew Ryan, Elizabeth Kaitlin, Caroline MacKenzie. BA, U. North Ala., 1977; MA, JD, Samford U., 1980; MS, Johns Hopkins U., 1983; LLM, Judge Adv. Gen.'s Sch., 1994. Bar: Ala. 1980, U.S. Ct. Mil. Appeals 1981, U.S. Supreme Ct. 1983. Trial atty. U.S. Army, various locations, 1980-87; sr. assoc. Doke & Riley, Dallas, 1987-89; legal counsel, dir. contracts Hughes Aircraft Co., Torrence, Calif., 1989-93; mgr., contracts Hughes Missile Systems Co., Tucson, 1993-95; dir., licensing and regulatory affairs Lockheed Martin Internat. Launch Svcs., San Diego, 1995—2000; prof. bus. Piedmont Coll., Demorest, Ga., 2000—01; chief bus. counsel U.S. Army Space Command, Colorado Springs, Colo., 2001—02; dir. contracts and export compliance Ball Aerospace and Tech Corp., Boulder, Colo., 2002—. Author: A Progressive History of the Young Men's Business Club of Birmingham, Ala.: 1946-70, 1980. Lt. col. USAR, 1980-2002 Mem. ABA (vice chair various coms., pub. contract law sect). Republican. Avocations: church, travel, reading, skiing. Office: Ball Aerospace & Tech Corp 1600 Commerce St Boulder CO 80306 Office Phone: 303-939-4222. Business E-mail: aunderwo@ball.com.

**UNDERWOOD, BLAIR,** actor, television producer; b. Tacoma, Aug. 25, 1964; s. Frank and Marilyn Underwood; m. Desiree Da Costa, Sept. 17, 1994; 3 children. Student, Carnegie-Mellon U. TV debut The Cosby Show, 1985; actor, prodr.: (films) Straight Out of Compton 2, 2005; actor (films) Krush Groove, 1985, The Second Coming, 1992, Posse, 1993, Just Cause, 1995, Set It Off, 1996, Gattaca, 1997, Deep Impact, 1998, Asunder, 1998, The Wishing Tree, 1999, Rules of Engagement, 2000 (NAACP Image award for sup. actor, 2001), G, 2002, Full Frontal, 2002, Malibu's Most Wanted, 2003, Fronterz, 2004, How Did it Feel, 2004, Do Geese See God?, 2004, Something New, 2006, Madea's Family Reunion, 2006; (TV series) One Life to Live, 1985-86, Downtown, 1986, LA Law, 1987-94, High Incident, 1996, City of Angels, 2000 (NAACP Image award for lead actor, 2001), Fatherhood, 2004-, LAX, 2004-05, (TV movies) The Cover Girl and the Cop, 1989, Murder in Mississippi, 1990, Heat Wave, 1990, Father and Son: Dangerous Relations, 1993, Soul of the Game, 1996, Mistrial, 1996, Mama Flora's Family, 1998; theater credits include Measure for Measure, 1993, El Negro en Peru, The Game of Love and Chance, and Love Letters, Purlie, 2005. Co-founder Artists for a New South Africa, 1989. Named Artist of the Year, Harvard Found., Harvard U., 2002; recipient Humanitarian Award, Muscular Dystrophy Assoc., LA, 1993. Office: William Morris Agency 151 El Camino Dr Beverly Hills CA 90212*

**UNDERWOOD, CARRIE MARIE,** singer; b. Muskogee, Okla., Mar. 10, 1983; d. Stephen and Carol Underwood. BA magna cum laude, Northeastern State U., 2006. Recording artist RCA Music Group, NYC, 2005—. Singer: (albums) Some Hearts, 2005, (songs) Inside Your Heaven, 2005, Jesus, Take the Wheel, 2005 (Single Record of Yr., Acad. Country Music, 2006), Some Hearts, 2005. Named Country Single Sales Artist of Yr., Billboard Music Awards, 2005, New Female Vocalist, Acad. Country Music award, 2006; recipient Top-Selling Hot 100 Song of Yr. for song Inside Your Heaven/Independence Day, Billboard Music Awards, 2005, Top-Selling Country Single of Yr., 2005, Female Video of Yr. and Breakthrough Video of Yr. for Jesus Take the Wheel, CMT Awards (Country Music TV), 2006. Baptist. Achievements include winning the fourth season of American Idol on May 25, 2005. Avocations: guitar, piano. Office: RCA Music Group 1540 Broadway New York NY 10036*

**UNDERWOOD, CECIL HARLAND,** retired governor, diversified financial services company executive; b. Josephs Mills, W.Va., Nov. 5, 1922; s. Silas and Della (Forrester) U.; m. Hovah Hall, July 25, 1948 (dec.); children: Cecilia A., Craig Hall, Sharon. AB, Salem Coll., W.Va., 1943; AM, W.Va. U., 1952; rsch. fellow, Amelia Earhart Found., Ann Arbor, Mich., 1954-56; LLD (hon.), Marietta Coll., Ohio, 1957, Bethany Coll., 1957, W.Va. U., 1957, W.Va. Inst. Tech., 1957; doctorate of Humanics (hon.), Salem Coll., 1957; degree in pub. administrn. (hon.), W.Va. Wesleyan Coll., 1958; LLD (hon.), Concord Coll., 1960, W.Va. State Coll., 1961; LHD (hon.), Shepherd Coll., 1964; LittD (hon.), Western New Eng. Coll., 1969; LHD (hon.), Marshall U., 1997; degree in pub. svc. (hon.), Alderson Broaddus Coll., 1997; DSc (hon.), W. Va. Sch. Osteopathic Med., 1998; degree (hon.), Davis and Elkins Coll., 1998, Fairmont State Coll., 1999. Tchr. high sch., 1943-46; staff Marietta Coll., 1946-50; v.p. Salem Coll., 1950-56; gov. State of W.Va., 1957—61, 1997—2001; v.p. Island Creek Coal Co., 1961-64; dir. civic affairs Monsanto Co., 1965-67, v.p., 1967; pres. Cecil H. Underwood Assocs., 1965-80, Franswood Corp., 1968-75, Bethany (W.Va.) Coll., 1972-75, Princess Coals, Inc., Huntington, 1978-81, Morgantown (W.Va.) Indsl. Park, Inc., 1983-96, Software Valley, 1989-92, Mon View Heights of W.Va., 1993-96; field underwriter N.Y. Life Ins. Co., 1976-78; chmn. bd. Princess Coals, Inc., Huntington, 1981-83. Sec. bd. dirs. Huntington Fed. Savs. and Loan Assn., 1961-96; pres. Huntington Found.; chair Cecil H. Underwood Inst. Mem. W.Va. Ho. Dels., 1944-56, minority floor leader, 1949, 51, 53, 55; Mem. exec. com. Gov's Conf., 1959; chmn. So. Regional Edn. Bd., 1959-60, 1999-2000; Pres. Young Republican League of W.Va., 1946-50; parliamentarian Young Rep. Nat. Conv., Boston, 1951; del.-at-large Rep. Nat. Conv., 1960, 64, 72, 76, 80, 84, 88, 2000, temporary chmn., 1960; Chmn. bd. dirs. W.Va. Found. Ind. Colls., Appalachian Regional Hosps.; chmn. bd. dirs. W.Va. div. Am. Cancer Soc., nat. bd. dirs., chmn. nat. crusade com., 1976-77, chmn. com. on legacies and planned giving, 1979; chmn. bd. dirs. Salem Coll., 1978-89, Salem Internat. U., 1989—; bd. dirs. Higher Edn. Loan Program of W.Va., 1980-94; chair W.Va. Com. on Vocat. Edn., 1982-96, W.Va. State Coll. System, 1991, Nat. Edn. Goals Panel, 1998-99; regional vice chmn. Boy Scouts Am., 1961-67; dir. Fed. Home Loan Bank of Pitts. Mem. Nat. Assn. State Coun. Vocat. Edn. (pres. 1994-96), Masons, Shriners, Elks, Rotary, Sigma Phi Epsilon, Pi Kappa Delta. Republican. Methodist. Office Phone: 304-746-1989. Personal E-mail: underwood@marshall.edu.

**UNDERWOOD, DEANNA KAY,** librarian; b. Medicine Lodge, Kans., Oct. 2, 1962; d. Kenneth Edward and Janet Sue (Hammond) Winters; m. Roger Alan Underwood, Aug. 2, 1986; children: Lane Lindsey Kay. BS in Elem. Edn., Sterling (Kans.) Coll., 1984. Tchr. 4th grade White Rock Elem. Sch., Burr Oak, Kans., 1984-86, tchr. kindergarten Esbon, Kans., 1986-87; libr. aide mid. and high schs. White Rock Schs., Esbon and Burr Oak, 1987-91, K-12 libr., 1992—. Chmn. reading com., mem. ednl. leadership team com. Unified Sch. Dist. 104, Esbon and Burr Oak, 1993—. Chmn. administrv. coun. United Meth. Ch., Esbon, 1989—, trustee coun., 1993—

Mem.: Kans. Assn. Sch. Librs. Republican. Avocations: reading, cooking, cross-stitch. Home: RR 1 Box 14 Esbon KS 66941-9703 Office: White Rock HS PO Box 345 633 Main St Burr Oak KS 66936-9738 Business E-Mail: dunderwood@usd.104.com.

**UNDERWOOD, ELAINE M.,** elementary school educator; b. Steubenville, OH, Sept. 24, 1947; d. Joseph P. and Mary D. Hruschak; m. Robin R. Underwood, Mar. 17, 1978; 1 child, Annette J. BA, West Liberty State Coll., 1968; MA, W.Va. U., 1977. Tchr. Cove Sch., Weirton, W.Va., 1968—69, 1974—84, Weirton Heights Elem., 1969—71, reading tchr., 1984—; tchr. Washington Sch., Wheeling, W.Va., 1971—74. Mem.: NEA, Internat. Reading Assn. Democrat. Roman Catholic. Avocations: gardening, swimming, walking. Home: 207 Arena Dr Weirton WV 26062 Office: Hancock County Schs Court St New Cumberland WV 26062

**UNDERWOOD, JANE HAINLINE HAMMONS,** anthropologist, educator; b. Ft. Bliss, Tex., Oct. 30, 1931; d. Frank and Lydia (Williams) Hammons; m. Van K. Hainline, Oct. 20, 1947 (div. 1966); children: Michael K., Susan J.; m. John W. Underwood, July 4, 1968; 1 dau., Anne K. AA, Imperial Valley Coll., 1957; BA, U. Calif., Riverside, 1960; MA, UCLA, 1962, PhD, 1964. Asst. prof. U. Calif., Riverside, 1963-68; research anthropology Yap Islands, 1964, 65-66; prof. anthropology U. Ariz., Tucson, 1968-99, prof. emeritus, 1999—, assoc. dean Grad. Coll., 1979-80, asst. provost for grad. studies, 1980-82, acting dir. Sch. Health Related Professions, 1980-82, asst. v.p. research, assoc. dean Grad. Coll., 1982-87; assoc. Micronesian Area Rsch. Ctr., 1987—. Contbr. articles to profl. jours. Woodrow Wilson fellow, 1960-61; UCR Jr. Faculty fellow, 1968 Fellow AAAS; mem. Am. Asns. Phys. Anthropologists (v.p. 1980-82), Assn. Study Human Biology, Pacific Sci. Assn. (life), Assn. for Study Social Biology (bd. dirs. 1996-99), Sigma Xi (pres. U. Ariz. chpt. 1991-92). Home: 2228 E 4th St Tucson AZ 85719-5118 E-mail: kammagar@prodigy.net.

**UNDERWOOD, JULIE K.,** dean, former law educator; b. 1954; d. Kenneth and Shirley Underwood; m. William Young, July 4, 1991; children: David, Chris, Kate, Maggie. BA in Polit. Sci. and Sociology, DePauw U., 1976; JD, Ind. U., 1979; PhD, U. Fla., 1984. Clk. Ind. Ct. Appeals, 1979-81; instr. sch. law U. Fla., Gainesville, 1981-82; rsch. assoc. Inst. Ednl. Fin., 1981-82; asst. prof. ednl. adminstrn. U. N.D., 1982-85, assoc. prof., 1982-86, asst. dean Ctr. Teaching and Learning, 1986; asst. prof. dept. ednl. adminstrn. U. Wis., Madison, 1986-89, prof., edn. adminstrn., 1990-93, chair, dept. edn. adminstrn., 1993—94, assoc. prof. sch. law, 1992—95, dean, Sch. Edn., 2005—; interim counsel Wis. Dept. Pub. Instrn., Madison, 1990; dean, Sch. Edn. & Allied Professions Miami Univ., Ohio, 1995—98; assoc. exec. dir, gen. counsel Coun. Sch. Attys, Nat. Sch. Bds. Assn., Alexandria, Va., 1998—2005. 2d level spl. edn. reviewing officer State Wis., 1988; hearing officer Wis. Tchr. Cert., 1993. Author: Legal Aspects of Special Education and Pupil Services, 1994; editor: (with D. Monk) Microlevel School Finance: Issues and Implications for Policy, 1988, (with W. Camp and M. Connelly) Principals' Handbook: Current Issues in School law, 1989, (with D. Verstegen) The Impact of Litigation and Legislation on Public School Finance, 1989, (with W. Camp, M. Connelly and K. Lane) The Principal's Legal Handbook, 1993; asst. editor Jour. Edn. Fin., 1981-83, legis. editor, 1985-88, legal editor, 1988—; mem. author's com. Edn. Law Reporter, 1982—; editor The Sch. and the Cts.; contbr. articles to profl. jours., chpts. to books. Grantee U. Wis., 1988, 89, 90-93. Mem. Am. Edn. Fin. Assn. (bd. dirs. 1984-88, chair Outstanding Svc. award 1987-88), Nat. Org. Legal Problems of Edn. (chair membership com. 1987-88, bd. dirs. 1987-91, chair ann. conf. program com. 1988-89, chair publs. com. 1989-91, constl. review com. 1990-92). Office: Dean Sch Edn 123 Edn Bld Univ Wisconsin 1000 Bascom Mall Madison WI 53706-1398 Office Phone: 608-262-6137.

**UNDERWOOD, KIRSTEN FEDJE,** musician, educator; MusB, Willamette U., 1978; MusM, Boston U., 1981; postgrad., U. Okla., 1998—. Cellist Okla. City Philharm., 1990—96; asst. prof. Cameron U., Lawton, Okla., 1997—. Founder Lawton Cello Club, Okla. Mem.: AAUW, Am. String Tchrs. Assn., Am. Fedn. Musicians, Hardanger Fiddle Assn. Am., Lawton Bus. & Profl. Women, Gamma Beta Phi, Phi Kappa Phi, Mu Phi Epsilon, Pi Kappa Lambda (pres., Theta Sigma chpt. 1999—2004). Office: Cameron Univ Dept of Music & Theatre 2800 W Gore Blvd Lawton OK 73507 Office Phone: 580-581-2445. E-mail: kirstenu@cameron.edu.

**UNDERWOOD, LORAINE BALLARD,** literature and language educator; b. Opelousas, La., Feb. 6, 1940; d. Lawrence James and Vertna Estelle Ballard; m. Albert McThomas Underwood, Jan. 7, 1976 (dec. Aug. 12, 2004); children: Kirk Albert, Antonio McVhea; m. Charles James Taylor (dec.); children: Christopher Charles, Jennifer Vertna. BA in Polit. Sci., U., Baton Rouge, 1963; MEd, U. La., 1987. Cert. tchr. Chgo. State U., 1966. Sec. Kraft Foods Divsn., Nat. Dairy Products Corp., Chgo., 1964—65; tchr. Chgo. Bd. Edn., 1965—80, St. Landry Parish Sch. Bd., Opelousas, 1980—2000, Lafayette Parish Sch. Sys., La., 2002—. Fellow mem. The Nature Conservancy, Arlington, Va., 2002—, So. Poverty Law Ctr., 2004—, Nat. Com. to Preserve Social Security, Washington, 2004—, NAACP, Balt., 2004—; organizer, coord. com. to erect a commemorative marker for St. Landry Parish Tng. Sch., 2004—; fellow mem. Dem. Nat. Com., Washington, 2004—; recording sec. Seventh Dist. Bapt. Assn. Women's Aux. and Missionary Soc.; deaconess Little Zion Bapt. Ch. Mem.: La. Fedn. Tchrs./AFT Profl. Educators Group (membership chair 1989—95), La. Ret. Tchrs. Assn. (life). Democrat. Baptist. Avocations: sewing, Bible reading, singing. Home: 1508 Laurent St Opelousas LA 70570

**UNDERWOOD, MARK FOREST,** lawyer; b. Ft. Campbell, Ky., Feb. 14, 1964; s. Harry Wayne and Alicia Elkins Underwood; m. Cynthia Jean Walker, Sept. 13, 2003. BBA, Marshall U., 1986; JD, Pepperdine U., 1989; grad., Nat. Inst. Trial Advocacy, 1992, Am. Trial Lawyers Ultimate Advocacy Coll., 2002; diplomate, Gerry Spence Trial Lawyers Coll., 2002. Bar: Calif. 89, W.Va. 96, D.C. 97, U.S. Ct. Appeals (4th cir.) 99. Assoc. Hagenbaugh & Murphy, L.A., 1989—92, Crosby, Healey, Roach & May, L.A., 1992—94; ptnr. Fredeking & Fredeking, Huntington, W.Va., 1994—96; pvt. practice Underwood Law Offices, Huntington, 1997—. Mem. W.Va. State Legis., 1997—98. Recipient Frasure Singleton Legis. fellowship, W.Va. Legislature, 1985. Mem.: ATLA, Nat. Coll. DUI Defense. Democrat. Presbyterian. Home and Office: Underwood Law Offices 910 Fourth Ave Ste 1111 Huntington WV 25701 Office Phone: 304-522-0508. Business E-Mail: markunderwood@markunderwood.com.

**UNDERWOOD, PAUL BENJAMIN,** gynecologist, oncologist, educator; b. Greer, S.C., Aug. 8, 1934; s. Paul Benjamin and Gladys (Guest) Underwood; m. Peggy Joyce Outen, July 7, 1957; children: Paul Benjamin III, Mary Barton. MD, Med. U. S.C., 1959. Diplomate Am. Bd. Ob-gyn., Am. Bd. Gynecol. Oncology. Intern Med. U. S.C., Charleston, 1959—60, resident, 1960—64; fellow M.D. Anderson Hosp. and Tumor Inst., Houston, 1966—67; asst. prof. Med. U. S.C., Charleston, 1967—70, assoc. prof., 1970—74, prof., 1974—99, staff, dir. gynecology, assoc. dean admissions Med. Sch., 1999—, dir. divsn. gynecol. oncology, 2002; dept. ob-gyn. U.Va. Sch. Medicine, Charlottesville, 1979-99. Contbr. articles to profl. jours. With USN, 1964—66. Recipient Alumni of Yr. award, Med. U. S.C., 1989. Mem.: Thegos Soc., S.C. Ob-Gyn. Soc., Charlottesville Med. Soc. So. Med. Soc., Felix Rutledge Soc. (pres. 1977), Am. Assn. Ob-Gyn. (sec. 1992—95, pres. 1999—), Soc. Gynecol. Oncologists (mem. coun. 1972—75, v.p. 1977—78, pres. 1983), Am. Coll. Ob-Gyn., Am. Gynecol. Club (pres. 1996), Alpha Omega Alpha. Office: 171 Ashley Ave Charleston SC 29425-0001 Office Phone: 843-792-4026. Business E-Mail: underwp@musc.edu.

**UNDERWOOD, PAUL LESTER,** cardiologist; b. Knoxville, Tenn., Mar. 23, 1960; MD, Mayo Med. Sch., 1984. Diplomate Am. Bd. Cardiovascular Disease. Intern Henry Ford Hosp., Detroit, 1984-85; resident in internal medicine Mayo Grad. Sch. Medicine, Rochester, Minn., 1985-87; fellow in cardiology Cleve. Clinic, 1990-93; fellow in interventional cardiology Iowa Heart Ctr., Des Moines, 1993; dir. emergency medicine, dir. ICU St. Croix

Hosp., U.S. V.I., 1987-90; staff North Phoenix (Ariz.) Heart Ctr., 2001—. Mem. AMA, Nat. Med. Assn., Assn. Black Cardiologists (pres.), Am. Coll. Cardiology (councilor), Am. Heart Assn. (bd. dirs. Ariz. affiliate), Soc. for Cardiac Angiography and Interventions. Office: North Phoenix Heart Ctr 9100 N 2d St Ste 321 Phoenix AZ 85020 Personal E-mail: drundrwd@aol.com.

**UNDERWOOD, PAULA KAY,** military officer; d. Agnes Josephine Underwood; m. Juan Guillermo Jaramillo Angel, June 11, 1987; 1 child, Paula Alicia Jaramillo-Underwood. BS, U. of Denver, 1973; S.R.N. (State RN), Gloucestershire Royal Sch. of Nursing, Gloucester, Eng., 1977; S.C.M. (State Cert. Midwife); Simpson Meml. Maternity Pavilion, Edinburgh, Scotland, U.K., 1978—79; MD, U. of Colo., Denver, 1984; MPH, Harvard U., Boston, 1987; MHA, U.S. Army-Baylor U. Program, San Antonio, Tex., 2001. Cert. healthcare exec. Am. Coll. of Healthcare Execs., 2001. Stewardess Pan Am. Airways, Boston, 1973—74; staff nurse Dilke Hosp., Chepstow, Gloucestershire, England, 1977—78; intern Tripler Army Med. Ctr., Honolulu, 1984—85; gen. med. officer Irwin Army Cmty. Hosp., Ft. Riley, Kans., 1985—86; resident in preventive medicine Walter Reed Army Inst. of Rsch., Washington, D.C., 1987—88; gen. med. officer Irwin Army Cmty. Hosp., Ft. Riley, Kans., 1985—86; chief of preventive medicine 98th Gen. Hosp., Nuernberg, Bavaria, Germany, 1988—89; preventive medicine officer 1st Armored Divsn., Southeast Asia-Gulf War, Iraq, 1990—91; chief of preventive medicine 3rd Combat Support Hosp., Nuernberg, Bavaria, Germany, 1991—93, Evans Army Cmty. Hosp., Ft. Carson, Colo., 1993—96; dep. comdr. for clin. svcs. (chief of the med. staff) Winn Army Cmty. Hosp., Ft. Stewart, Ga., 2001—03; comdr. U.S. Army Med. Rsch. Unit, Rio de Janeiro, Rio de Janeiro, 1997—99; preventive medicine staff officer Office of The Army Surgeon Gen., Falls Church, Va., 2003—04, dep. functional proponent for preventive medicine, 2004—. Residency adv. bd. mem. Walter Reed Army Inst. of Rsch., Washinton, 2004—; chair Joint Preventive Medicine Policy Group, Washington, 2004—; army preventive medicine rep. Armed Forces Epidemiology Bd., Washington, 2003—04. Col. U.S. Army, 1984. Decorated Bronze Star, Meritorious Svc. medal Winn Army Cmty. Hosp., Walter Reed Army Inst. of Rsch., Evans Army Cmty. Hosp., 3rd Combat Support Hosp., Army Commendation Medal; recipient Alumni Assn. award, U.S. Army Baylor U. Alumni Club, 2001, Peter Shaul Peer award, 2001; scholar Acad. scholar, U. of Denver, 1969—73. Fellow: Am. Coll. of Preventive Medicine (cert.); mem.: U.S. Army Baylor U. Alumni Club, U. of Colo. Alumni Assn. (life), Assn. of the U.S. Army (life), VFW (life), Desert Storm Vets. Assn.; The Army Hist. Found. (life), Mil. Officers Assn. of Am. (life). Avocations: running, travel, reading. Office: Office of The Army Surgeon General 5111 Leesburg Pike Falls Church VA 22041 Office Phone: 703-681-3130. E-mail: paula.underwood@otsg.amedd.army.mil.

**UNDERWOOD, RAY STUART,** music educator; b. Perryville, Ky., Oct. 23, 1951; s. Eugene and Helen Underwood; m. Sheila Kester Underwood, Aug. 11, 1972. BS in Music, Campbellsville U., 1974; postgrad., Ea. Ky. U., 1982. Min. of music Perryville Bapt. Ch., 1970—72, First Bapt. Ch., Shepherdsville, Ky., 1972—74; choral dir. Lincoln County H.S., Stanford, Ky., 1974—; min. of music Stanford Bapt. Ch., Ky., 1995—. Com. mem. Lincoln County Jr. Miss, Stanford, 1984—; sec. Ky. Jr. Miss, Lexington, 1995—2002. Named H.S. Tchr. of Yr., Ky. Music Educators Assn., 1992; recipient Big Apple award, Lincoln County C. of C. Mem.: NEA, Am. Choral Dirs. Assn., Music Educators Nat. Conf. Democrat. Baptist. Home: 535 Springview Dr Stanford KY 40484 Office Phone: 606-365-9111. Office Fax: 606-365-1750.

**UNDERWOOD, ROBERT LEIGH,** venture capitalist; b. Paducah, Ky., Dec. 31, 1944; s. Robert Humphreys and Nancy Wells (Jessup) Underwood; m. Susan Lynn Doscher, May 22, 1976; children: Elizabeth Leigh, Diana Whitney, George Gregory. BS with great distinction, Stanford U., 1965, MS, 1966, PhD, 1968; MBA, Santa Clara U., 1970. Rsch. scientist, project leader Lockheed Missiles & Space Co., Sunnyvale, Calif., 1967—71; spl. asst. for engring. scis. Office Sec., Dept. Transp., Washington, 1971—73; sr. mgmt. assoc. Office Mgmt. and Budget, Exec. Office Pres., 1973; with TRW Inc., L.A., 1973—79, dir. retail nat. accts., 1977—78, dir. product planning and devel., 1978—79; pres., CEO OMEX, Santa Clara, Calif., 1980—82; v.p. Heizer Corp., Chgo., 1979—85; pres. No. Capital Corp., Chgo., 1985—86; mng. ptnr. ISSS Ventures, 1986—88; founding ptnr. N.Am. Bus. Devel. Co., Chgo., 1988—; pres., CEO Polymer Corp., Rockland, Mass., 2003—. Trustee Burridge Mut. Funds, 1996—98; bd. dirs. Summa Industries. Contbr. articles to profl. jours. Mem. sch. bd. Avoca Dist. 37, 1990—99, v.p., 1996—99; mem. adv. bd. Leavy Sch. Bus. and Adminstrn. Santa Clara U., 1995—; mem. adv. com. on indsl. innovation NSF, 1982—96; trustee Kenilworth Union Ch., 2003—; elder Presbyn. Ch., 1978—79. Fellow, NASA, NSF; scholar, Alcoa. Mem.: IEEE, Farmington Country Club (Charlottesville, Va.), Indian Hill Club (Winnetka, Ill.), Union League Chgo., Chgo. Club, Beta Gamma Sigma, Tau Beta Pi, Phi Beta Kappa, Sigma Xi. Home: 59 Woodley Rd Winnetka IL 60093-3748 Office: 135 S La Salle St Chicago IL 60603-4159

**UNDERWOOD, RONALD BRIAN,** director, producer; b. Glendale, Calif., Nov. 6, 1953; s. Laurence Joseph and Ella Julia (Green) U.; m. Sandra Joyce Archer, June 8, 1974; children: Larissa, Lana, Lauren. BA in Cinema, U. So. Calif., 1974. Dir. (films) Deer in the Works, 1980, The Mouse and the Motorcycle, 1986, Runaway Ralph, 1988, Tremors, 1990 (also writer), City Slickers, 1991, Heart and Souls, 1993, Speechless, 1994, Mighty Joe Young, 1998, The Adventures of Pluto Nash, 2002, Stealing Sinatra, 2003, In the Mix, 2005, (TV films) The Mouse and the Motorcycle, 1986, Runaway Ralph, 1988, Back When We Grownups 2004; assoc. prodr. (films) Crawlspace, 1986. Recipient Peabody award, 1986; Am. Film Inst. fellow, 1975. Office: United Talent Agy 9560 Wilshire Blvd Fl 5 Beverly Hills CA 90212 2400

**UNDERWOOD, STEVEN CLARK,** publishing executive; b. Arlington Heights, Ill., Dec. 1, 1960; s. Donald William and Mary Frances (Clark) U.; m. Gloria Jean Dec, Sept. 8, 1999. BBA, U. Tex., 1982, MBA, 1987; JD, So. Meth. U., 1985. Cert. mgmt. accountant, 2000; bar: Tex. 1985. Sr. fin. analyst CBS, Inc., NYC, 1987—89; assoc. bus. mgr. Supplementary Edn. Group Simon & Schuster, Englewood Cliffs, NJ, 1989—90, bus. mgr. Fearon/Janus/Quercus divsn. Belmont, Calif., 1990—91, pres. Fearon/Janus/Quercus divsn., 1991—92; pres. Globe Fearon Divsn. Upper Saddle River, NJ, 1993—96; v.p. bus. devel. Simon & Schuster, NYC, 1997—98; v.p. dir. bus. devel. Secondary Edn. Group, Upper Saddle River, 1996—97; v.p. sch. markets Troll Comms., Mahwah, NJ, 1998—2001; v.p., contr. Current Med. Directions Divsn., WWP Group, NYC, 2002—. Mem. ABA, Am. Mgmt. Assn. (pres.'s assn.), Assn. Am. Pubs., Inst. Mgmt. Accts., Nat. Eagle Scout Assn., Coll. Bus. Adminstrn. Found., Tex. Bar Assn., Tex. Alumni assn., U. Tex. Century Club, Alpha Phi Omega, Beta Gamma Sigma, Phi Kappa Phi, Phi Eta Sigma, Golden Key. Republican. Methodist. Avocations: sailing, camping. Home: 902 Somerset Ct Ramsey NJ 07446-2919

**UNGAR, ERIC EDWARD,** mechanical engineer; b. Vienna, Nov. 12, 1926; arrived in U.S., 1939; s. Irwin Isidor and Sabina (Schlesinger) U.; m. Goldie Edna Becker, July 1, 1951; children: Judith Fishman, Susan Green, Ellen Borgenicht, Sharon Ungar Lane. BSME, Washington U., St. Louis, 1951; MS, U. N.Mex., 1954; D.Eng.Sc., NYU, 1957. Aero-ordnance engr. Sandia Corp., Albuquerque, 1951-53; rsch. scientist, asst. prof. NYU, 1953-58; chief cons. engr. Bolt Beranek & Newman, Inc., Cambridge, Mass., 1958-96. Chief engring. scientist Acentech Inc., Cambridge, 1993—. Co-author: Structure-Borne Sound, 1973, 2nd edit. 1988; contbr. articles to profl. jours., chpts. to books. 1st lt. U.S. Army, 1945—48, ETO. Recipient Lifetime Achievement award, Shock and Vibration Info. Analysis Ctr., 2004. Fellow ASME (life; chmn. design engring. divsn. 1978-80, Centennial medallion 1981, Per Bruel Gold medal for noise control and acoustics 1994), AIAA (assoc.), Acoustical Soc. Am. (pres. 1991-92, Trent-Crede Silver medal 1983); mem. Inst. for Noise Control and Engring. (bd. cert., pres. 1985, Disting. Noise Control Engr. award 2004). Home: 15 Considine Rd Newton MA 02459-3603 Office: Acentech Inc 33 Moulton St Cambridge MA 02138-1118 Office Phone: 617-499-8022. E-mail: eungar@acentech.com.

**UNGAR, IRWIN ALLAN,** botany educator; b. N.Y.C., Jan. 21, 1934; s. Isidore and Gertrude (Fageles) U.; m. Ana Celia Del Cid, Aug. 10, 1959; children: Steven, Sandra, Sharon. BS, CCNY, 1955; MA, U. Kans., Lawrence, 1957; PhD, 1961. Instr. U. R.I., Kingston, 1961-62; asst. prof. Quincy Coll., Ill., 1961-66, Ohio U., Athens, 1966-69, assoc. prof., 1969-74, prof. botany, 1974—, chmn. dept. botany, 1984-89. Dir. Dysart Woods Lab., 1985—99, Environ. Studies Program, 1991—95; vis. prof. dept. plant scis. and vis. fellow Wolfson Coll., Oxford (Eng.) U., 1990—91; panelist Nat. Sea Grant Program, 1984; grant proposal reviewer NSF, 1980—2002. Contbr. articles to profl. jours.; manuscript reviewer Am. Jour. Botany, Internat. Jour. Plant Scis. NSF grantee, 1974-76, 76-78, 80-83, 94-95, 98-2001; rsch. grantee Petroleum Environ. Rsch. Forum, 1992-96. Fellow Ohio Acad. Sci.; mem. AAAS, Am. Inst. Biol. Scis., Bot. Soc. Am., Ecol. Soc. Am., Sigma Xi. Home: 44 Walker St Athens OH 45701-2252 Office: Ohio Univ Dept Of Botany Athens OH 45701 E-mail: ungar@ohio.edu.

**UNGARETTI, RICHARD ANTHONY,** lawyer; b. Chgo., May 25, 1942; s. Dino Carl and Antoinette (Calvetti) U.; children: Joy A., Paul R. BS, DePaul U., 1964, JD, 1970. Bar: Ill. 1970, U.S. Dist. Ct. (no. dist.) Ill. 1970, U.S. Supreme Ct. 1980. Assoc. Kirkland & Ellis, Chgo., 1970-74; ptnr. Ungaretti & Harris, Chgo., 1974—. Mem. adv. coun. DePaul Coll. Law, Chgo., 1988. Mem. ABA, Chgo. Bar Assn., Ill. State Bar Assn., Internat. Coun. Shopping Ctrs., Am. Coll. Real Estate Lawyers, Justinian Soc., Urban Land Inst. (assoc.), Lamda Alpha Avocations: golf, fishing, hunting. Office: Ungaretti & Harris 3500 Three First Nat Plz Chicago IL 60602 Office Phone: 312-977-4430. Business E-mail: raungaretti@uhlaw.com.

**UNGARO, JOSEPH MICHAEL,** newspaper publishing executive, consultant; b. Providence, Nov. 4, 1930; s. Rocco and Lucy (Motta) U.; m. Evelyn Short, Apr. 15, 1961; children: Elizabeth Anne, Joseph Michael, Ellen Lucia. BA, Providence Coll., 1952; MS in Journalism, Columbia, 1953. With Providence Jour.-Bull., 1951-73, mng. editor Evening Bull., 1967-72; mng. editor Eve. Bull., also dir. planning and devel. Providence Jour. and Bull., 1972-73; mng. editor Westchester-Rockland Newspapers, White Plains, NY, 1974-75, v.p., exec. editor, 1975-84, pres., gen. mgr., 1984-86, pres., publisher, 1986-90; pres., chief exec. officer Detroit Newspaper Agcy., 1990-91; cons., 1991—. Mem. Am. Newspaper Pubs. Assn. (past chmn. research inst., conv. program com.), Am. Soc. Newspaper Editors, AP Mng. Editors Assn. (past pres.) Home: 379 Pond Shore Dr Charlestown RI 02813-2007 Office Phone: 401-364-6032. Personal E-mail: joeungaro@aol.com.

**UNGARO, MARIO,** pathologist, educator; s. Fabricio Ungaro and Enriquetta Zevallos. MB, Nat. U. San Marcos, Peru, 1954, MD. Diplomate in pathology. Intern Marymount Hosp., Cleve., 1954-55; resident St. Vincent Charity Hosp., Cleve., 1955-57; resident in pathology New Britain Gen. Hosp., 1958-59, Roswell Park Meml. Inst., Buffalo, 1959-60; fellow forensic pathology Frank E. Bunts Ed. Inst., Cleve., 1957-58; asst. pathologist Mercy Hosp., Buffalo, 1960-61; prof. pathology Nat. U. Trujillo, Peru, 1961—87; chmn. pathology Hosp. Regional Tchg. Hosp., Trujillo, Peru, 1980—87; prof. emeritus Nat. U. Trujillo, 1992. Mem. Peruvian Assn. Pathology, Peruvian Med. Assn., Nat. Club, Golf Country Club. Avocation: swimming. Office: Hosp Regional Tchg Hosp Trujillo Peru

**UNGARO, SUSAN KELLIHER,** foundation administrator, former magazine editor; married; 3 children. BA, MA, William Patterson Coll., Wayne, NJ. From editl. asst. to editor-in-chief Family Circle mag., NYC, 1976—94, editor-in-chief, 1994—2005; pres. James Beard Found., NYC, 2006—. Bd. dirs. Brazelton Found., Nat. Marrow Found., H.E.L.P. (Housing Enterprise for the Less Privileged). Named named Top Businessperson of Yr., Irish America magazine; recipient President's Award, New Jersey Press Women's Assn., 1995, William Paterson University Legacy Award, 1998, Muriel Fox communications award for professional excellence and commitment to advocacy journalism, NOW Legal Defense Fund, 1998. Mem.: Am. Soc. Mag. Editors (bd. dir. 1998—, pres. 2003—). Office: James Beard Foundation 167 West 12th St New York NY 10011 Office Phone: 212-499-1986, 212-675-4984.*

**UNGARO-BENAGES, URSULA MANCUSI,** federal judge; b. Miami Beach, Fla., Jan. 29, 1951; d. Ludivico Mancusi-Ungaro and Ursula Berliner; m. Michael A. Benages, Mar., 1988. Student, Smith Coll., 1968-70; BA in English Lit., U. Miami, 1973; JD, U. Fla., 1975. Bar: Fla. 1975. Assoc. Frates, Floyd, Pearson et al, Miami, 1976-78, Blackwell, Walker, Gray et al, Miami, 1978-80, Finley, Kumble, Heine et al, Miami, 1980-85, Sparber, Shevin, Shapo et al, Miami, 1985-87; cir. judge State of Fla., Miami, 1987-92; U.S. dist. judge U.S. Dist. Ct., Miami, 1992—. Mem. Fla. Supreme Ct. Race & Ethnic & Racial Bias Study Commn., Fla., 1989-92, St. Thomas U. Inns of Ct., Miami, 1991-92; mem. Jud. Resources Com. Jud. Conf. U.S.; chmn. Ct. Svcs. Com. So. Dist. Fla., chmn. Magistrate Judge Com.; mem. personnel com. 11th Cir. Jud. Coun. U.S. Bd. Govs. United Family & Children's Svcs., Miami, 1981-82; mem. City of Miami Task Force, 1991-92. Mem. ABA, Fed. Judges Assn., Fla. Assn. Women Lawyers, Dade County Bar Assn., Eugene Spellman Inns of Ct. U. Miami. Office: US Dist Ct 301 N Miami Ave Fl 11 Miami FL 33128-7702 Office Phone: 305-523-5550.

**UNGER, BARBARA,** poet, retired educator; b. NYC, Oct. 2, 1932; d. David and Florence (Schuchalter) Frankel; m. Bernard Unger, 1954 (div. 1976); m. Theodore Sakano, 1987; children: Deborah, Suzanne. BA, CCNY, 1955, MA, 1957; advanced cert., NYU, 1970. Grad. asst. Yeshiva U., 1962-63; edn. editor County Citizen, Rockland County, NY, 1960-63; tchr. English N.Y.C. Pub. Schs., 1955-58, Nayack (N.Y.) H.S., 1963-67; guidance counselor Ardsley (N.Y.) H.S., 1967-69; prof. English Rockland C.C., Suffern, NY, 1969—95, ret., 1995. Adj. prof. Rockland C.C., 1995-2003, Rockland Sr. Citizen Coll., 2001-2003; poetry fellow Squaw Valley Cmty. of Writers, 1980; writer-in-residence Rockland Ctr. for Arts, 1986. Author: (poetry) Basement, 1975, Learning to Fox Trot, 1989, The Man Who Burned Money, 1980, Inside the Wind, 1986, Blue Depression Glass in Troika One, 1991, (fiction) Dying for Uncle Ray, 1990; co-author (with Lloyd Ultan): (non-fiction) Bronx Accent: A Literary and Pictorial History of the Borough, 2001 (N.Y. Soc. Libr. Book award, 2001, J.M. Kaplan Furthermore grantee, Hermalyn Family Urban History award, 05); contbr. Anthology Mag. Verse, Yearbook Am. Poetry, 1984, Anthology Mag. Verse, Yearbook Am. Poetry, 1989, poetry and fiction to more than 75 lit. mags. Ragdale Found. fellow, 1985, 86, 89, SUNY Creative Writing fellow, 1981-82, Edna St. Vincent Millay Colony fellow, 1984, Djerassi Found. fellow, 1991, Hambidge Ctr. for Creative Arts and Scis. fellow, 1988, Dorset Colony fellow, 2005; NEH grantee, 1975; recipient Goodman Poetry award, 1989, Anna Davidson Rosenberg award Judah Magnes Mus., 1989, Roberts Writing award, 1990, New Letters Lit. awards, 1990; finalist Am. Fiction Competition, 1982, John Williams Narrative Poetry Competition, 1992; honorable mention Chester Jones Nat. Poetry Contest. Mem.: PEN, Assn. Writers and Writing Programs, Poets and Writers.

**UNGER, DAVID C.,** journalist; b. Bklyn. AB, Cornell U., 1967; postgrad., U. Wis., Madison, 1967—68; PhD, U. Tex., Austin, 1979. Elem. sch. tchr., Staten Island, Bklyn.; joined NY Times, 1977, now sr. editl. writer, fgn. affairs, mem. editl. bd. Office: Editl Bd NY Times 229 W 43rd St New York NY 10036 Office Phone: 212-556-7159. Office Fax: 212-556-3815. Business E-Mail: editorial@nytimes.com.

**UNGER, GARY ALLEN,** recording industry singer, lyricist; b. Clinton, Iowa, Aug. 14, 1947; s. Charles Elmer Unger and Lois Grace Haack. Grad. high sch., Ill., 1967. Mgr., pres. Narrowroad Music, Clinton, 1965—96; internat. import-export mgr. G & U Enterprises, Clinton, 1968—; mgr., pres. Groove Song Music, Clinton, 1968—; ECI Internat. Records, Clinton, 1980-96, GTM, Clinton, 1973, Nashville, 1979—; pres. Sugarvine Music (BMI). On Art Bell Radio Talk Show, Radio Network, 1996-97. Lyricist: songs I Will Always Love You Part I and II, I Like It, I Love It, Thinkin About You, Give Them All to Jesus, My White Rabbit, 1995, My Coloring Book, 1955, In My Life, 1954, I Knew You When, 1958, A Stranger In My House, 1959, Birthday, 1959, God Bless the Service, Lyricist (with D. Swanson):

songs Please! Don't Tell Me No More Lies, Lyricist: songs The Wink, Lord I Lift Your Name on High, 1961, Jesus Oh! Jesus, Oh!, The Shake, 1961, You and Me, 1961, The Closer You Get, 1961, Home, 1961, You Light Up My Life, 1968, Don't Tell Me No Lies, 1963, Check Yes or No, Country Sunshine, 1965, Tennessee River, 1965, Blue, 1965, One Day At a Time, 1965, Dancin Shaggin on the Boulevard, 1965, Careing Your Love With Me, 1965, If Your Not In It for Love I'm Out of Here, 1966, Lyricist (with G. Russen): songs The Love in Her Soul, Lyricist: songs Heart to Heart, 1968, Fool for Your Love, God Bless You Jesus Parts I, II and III, 1967, No Doubt, I've Never Been to England, Real Love, Hey June and Darline, I Got Jesus on My Mind, Heaven O Sweet Angel, Please Remember Me, Oh! Country Doll, Oh! Baby Doll, You Win My Love, Lyricist (with G.A. Unger and J. Ward): songs Oh! Sweet Honey, 1997, Lyricist: songs Girl, I Love You, Love is Like a Butterfly, Let Us Pray Together, Lost in the 50's Tonight, Kentucky Rain, Blue I'm So Blue, All I Want, On the 4th of July, Boot Scootin Boogie, Love Is, Lyricist (with Joan Brothers): songs Almost Like a Song, Lyricist: songs Why Can't Every Day Be Like Christmas, Moody Blues, Third Rock From the Sun, Maybe You Can Drive My Car, Oh, My, My, Those Rock N Years, My Achin Breakin Heart, Born to Love You, We Were Meant for Each Other, Jesus OH! Jesus I Love You, Don't Worry Be Happy Like Happy, Lyricist: songs Please Don't Bump the Jukebox, Lyricist: songs Hey It's a Small Town, God Bless the U.S.A. (Born in the USA), 1967, The Happiest Guy in the Whole USA, God Writes the Songs, When You Walked In, You Better Think Twice Again, Independence Day, Together With Our Heartfelt Love, She's Gone Country, You Light Up My Life, Give Them All to Jesus, Chasing That Neon Rainbow, 1963, Touched By a Holy Angel?, Almost Everywhere, Praise the Lord, On American Bandstand, If Tomorrow Never Comes, In My Life, The Long and Winding Roads, Please! Remember Me, Hello-Good-Buy, Oh! Country Doll, Creator of the Stars, Our Heart Felt Love, 1997, Lyricist (with Joan Brothers): songs Sweet Country Girl, 2001, Lyricist (with G.A. Unger and W. Cochran): songs God Bless the American Veterans, 2001, Lyricist: songs Tennessee Love In America, lyricist: songs The Power of His Love, God Bless the U.S.A. and Those Who Were Born in the U.S.A., Shout to the World, You Are My Song. Mem. RIAA, GNACMAI, Nat. Assn. Songwriters Internat., Nat. Music Found. Fax: 563-243-1334. Office Phone: 563-242-0718.

**UNGER, HOWARD ALBERT,** artist, photographer, educator; b. Mt. Vernon, N.Y., Oct. 13, 1944; s. Howard Albert and Florence A. (Peterson) U.; m. Anrita Abelow, Aug. 25, 1972; son, Christopher Howard. Student, Art Students League, N.Y.C., 1960-61, Sch. Visual Arts, 1975-76, N.Y. Inst. Holography, 1976; BFA, Kent State U., 1966, MA, 1968; MEd, Columbia U., 1972, EdD, 1975; MA, N.Y. Inst. Tech., 1994. Cert. open water diver, 1988, advanced scuba diver, 1989. Grad. tchg. fellow in photo-journalism Kent State U., 1966-67, instr. in art, 1966-67, grad. teaching fellow in art, 1967-68; head program in art, tchr. at Kew-Forest Prep. Sch., Kew Gardens, NY, 1968-69; technician TV sta. Tchrs. Coll., Columbia U., 1971-72, instr. art and edn., 1972-75, instr. curriculum and tchg., 1976-82, instr. dept. comm., computing and tech. in edn., 1982—; asst. prof. visual comm. tech. dept. humanities Ocean County Coll., 1972-78, assoc. prof., 1979-82, prof., 1982—, gallery coord. Fine Arts Ctr., 1972—. Part-time grad. instr. comm. arts N.Y. Inst. Tech., N.Y.C., 1994-95; instr. comm. and edn. Sch. Edn. NYU, 1973-74; design and photograph coord. RCA Records, N.Y.C., 1969-70; freelance designer, 1965—. Exhibitor photography in one-man shows, Photographis Societas Photographis, Columbia U., 1971, Ziegefeld Gallery, N.Y.C., 1972; group shows, Kent State U., 1965-68, Ocean County Coll., 1973-83, 14 Sculptor Gallery, N.Y.C., 1995; permanent collections, Internat. Ctr. Photography, N.Y.C., Mus. Holography, N.Y.C., Kent State U., Ocean County Coll., Tchrs. Coll., Columbia U., pvt. collections; lectr. in photography; co-author: (with William Maxwell) photog. illustrator Printmaking: A Beginner's Handbook, 1977; photog. illustrator The Fourth R. Stewart Kranz, 1971; contbg. author: A Tour Through The Realm of Science Plus Art, 1974; photography critic: Village Voice, 1976-77; photography columnist Soho Weekly News, 1977-78. Recipient 1st place award Am. Greeting Card Competition, 1966; recipient honararium dept. curriculum and teaching Tchrs. Coll., Columbia U., 1973 Mem. Soc. Photography Educators, NEA, Mus. Modern Art, N.J. Edn. Assn., Met. Mus. Art, Am. Mus. Natural History, Profl. Assn. Diving Instrs. (lic. advanced scuba diver), Nat. Assn. Underwater Instrs. (lic. advanced scuba diver). Republican. Home: 515 E 79th St New York NY 10021-0705 Office: Ocean County Coll College Dr Toms River NJ 08754-2001 Office Phone: 732-255-0400.

**UNGER, IRWIN,** historian, educator; b. Bklyn., May 2, 1927; s. Elias C. and Mary (Roth) U.; m. Bernate Myra Spaet, Feb. 1956 (div.); children: Brooke David, Miles Jeremy, Paul Joshua; m. Debi Irene Weisstein, May 11, 1970; stepchildren: Anthony Allen, Elizabeth Sarah. B in Social Scis., CCNY, 1948; MA, Columbia U., 1949, PhD, 1958; student, U. Wash., 1949—51. Instr. Columbia U., 1956-58; asst. prof. Long Beach (Calif.) State Coll., 1959-62; assoc. prof. U. Calif., Davis, 1962-66; prof. history NYU, NYC, 1966—2000, prof. emeritus, 2000—. Vis. lectr. U. PR, 1958—59. Author: The Greenback Era: A Social and Political History of American Finance: 1865-1879, 1964 (Pulitzer prize for History, 1965), The Movement: A History of the American New Left 1959-1972, 1974, These United States: Questions of Our Past, 1978, The Best of Intentions: The Triumph and Failure of the Great Society Under Kennedy, Johnson and Nixon, 1996; (with Debi Unger) The Vulnerable Years: The United States, 1896-1917, 1978, Turning Point: 1968, 1988, LBJ: A Life, 1999, The Guggenheims: A Family History, 2005. Served with AUS, 1952-54. Guggenheim fellow, 1972-73, 1987-88; Rockefeller humanities fellow, 1980-81. Home: 507 Evergreen Ave Bradley Beach NJ 07720 Personal E-mail: ungerclio@aol.com.

**UNGER, KAREN VIRGINIA,** director; d. Gunnar Fredrick Unger and Florence Mae Tawyea; m. John Anton Geisen, Aug. 23, 1964 (div.); 1 child, Rebecca Lynn Geisen. MEd, Calif. State Poly. U., 1969; M in Counseling Psychology, Chapman Coll., 1974; MSW, Ariz. State U., 1976; EdD, Boston U., 1987. Dir. Phoenix Alternative H.S., Westwood, Mass., 1978—81; dir. supported edn. svcs. Ctr. Psychiat. Rehab., Boston U., Boston, 1981—93; dir. rsch. and tng. Vinfen Corp., 1993—94; rsch. assoc. prof. U. Ariz., Tucson, 1995—98; pres. Rehab. Through Edn., Portland, 1995—. Vice chmn. Outside In, Portland, 1998—2001; bd. sec. Garlington, 1997—99; mental health adv. bd. Dept. Mental Health, Salem, Oreg., 1999—2002. Author: Handbook of Supported Education: Providing Services for People With Psychiatric Disabilities; contbg. author: Readings in Psychiatric Rehabilitation, Psychiatric Rehabilitation: Putting Theory into Practice; co-author: New Directions for Mental Health Services Sourcebook; editor (guest editor): Spl. Edit. Supported Edn., Jour.Psychiatric Rehab., Spl. Edit. Supported Edn. The Jour. Calif. Alliance Mentally Ill; contbr. articles to profl. jours.; (video) It Can Happen Here. Recipient Mertious Svc. award, Mass. Alliance Mentally Ill, 1987, Nat. Recognition award, Assn. Higher Edn. and Disability, 1997; fellow, NIMH, 1976—77; grantee, Dept. Edn., 1988—91, U.S. Dept. Edn., 1995—98; scholar, Sears and Roebucks, 1960, N.D. State U., 1960, Boston U., 1976. Democrat. Achievements include development of Supported Education, Exemplary Practice in Psychiatric Rehabilitation. Avocations: yoga, reading. Office: Rehabilitaion Through Education PO Box 82176 Portland OR 97282 Business E-mail: dvungeror@comcast.net.

**UNGER, LAURA SIMONE,** lawyer, commissioner; b. NYC, Jan. 8, 1961; d. Raymond and Susan Marie (Vopata) Simone; m. Peter Van Buren Unger, June 29, 1991. BA in Rhetoric, U. Calif., Berkeley, 1983; JD, N.Y. Law Sch., 1987. Bar: Conn. 1987, N.Y. 1988. Staff atty. divsn. enforcement SEC, 1988-90; legis. counsel to Sen. Alfonse M. D'Amato, 1990-91; minority counsel Senate com. banking, housing and urban affairs, 1991-95, counsel, 1995-97; commr. U.S. SEC, Washington, 1997—, acting chmn., 2001. Bd. dirs. MBNA Corp., 2004—. Recipient Performance award SEC, N.Y., 1988, D.C., 1989. Mem. ABA (subcom. on civil litigation and SEC enforcement matters and subcom. on SEC adminstrn., budget and legislation of the ABA bus. law sect. com. on federal regulation of securities), Fed. Bar Assn., Jr. League Washington, Decade Soc., Women in Housing and Fin. Roman Catholic. Avocations: tennis, jogging, movies, concerts, music. Office: US SEC 450 5th St NW Ms 6/8 Washington DC 20549-0001

**UNGER, PAUL WALTER,** retired soil scientist; b. Winchester, Tex., Sept. 10, 1931; s. Edwin Herman and Elsie Anna U.; m. Barbara Charlene Dutton Steelman, Sept. 13, 1960; children: Gary Robert, Paula Dianne. BS, Tex. A&M U., 1961; MS, Colo. State U., 1963, PhD, 1966. Soil scientist USDA Agrl. Rsch. Svc., Bushland, Tex., 1965-81; soil scientist/rsch. leader, 1981-87, supervisory soil scientist/rsch. leader, 1987-93, soil scientist, 1993-2000; ret., 2000. Cons. Food and Agrl. Orgn. UN, Rome, 1986. Author or co-author bulls. and articles; co-editor conf. proc.; editor book. With U.S. Army, 1952-55. Recipient Disting. Svc. award Great Plains Agrl. Coun., 1984; named Scientist of Yr., USDA-Agrl. Rsch. Svc., So. Plains Area, 1987. Fellow Am. Soc. Agronomy (emeritus, selection com. 1988-89), Soil Sci. Soc. Am. (emeritus, assoc. editor 1977-82, divsn. chmn. 1986, mem. selection com. 1994-95, Applied Rsch. award 1991), Soil and Water Conservation Soc. (various local and state offices, photography awards 1990-92); mem. Internat. Soil Tillage Rsch. Orgn., World Assn. Soil and Water Conservation. Lutheran. Avocations: photography, gardening, woodworking. E-mail: pwunger@cox.net.

**UNGER, PETER KENNETH,** philosophy educator; b. N.Y.C., Apr. 25, 1942; s. Sidney and Naomi (Fein) U.; m. Susan Gill, June 2, 1977; 1 child, Andrew. BA, Swarthmore Coll., 1962 DPhil, Oxford U., Eng., 1966. Instr. U. Wis., Madison, 1965-66, asst. prof., 1966-70, assoc. prof., 1970-72; assoc. prof. NYU, N.Y.C., 1972-75, prof., 1975—. Author: Ignorance, 1975, 2d edit., 2002, Philosophical Relativity, 1984, 2d edition, 2002, Identity, Consciousness and Value, 1990, Living High and Letting Die, 1996, All the Power in the World, 2006; contbr. articles to profl. jours. Guggenheim fellow, 1974, NEH fellow, 1993. Mem. Am. Philos. Assn. Democrat. Home: 100 Bleecker St New York NY 10012-2202 Office: Dept Philosophy NYU 503 Main Bldg Washington Sq New York NY 10003 Office Phone: 212-998-8321. E-mail: peter.unger@nyu.edu.

**UNGER, RICHARD WATSON,** history professor; b. Huntington, W.Va., Dec. 23, 1942; s. Abraham I. and Marion Patterson U.; 1 child, Emily Patterson. BA, Haverford Coll., Pa., 1963; AM, U. Chgo., 1965; MA, Yale U., 1967, MPhil, 1969, PhD, 1971. Prof. dept. history U. B.C., Vancouver, Canada, 1969—. Author: Dutch Shipbuilding Before 1800, 1978, The Ship in the Medieval Economy, 600-1600, 1980, The Art of Medieval Technology: The Image of Noah the Shipbuilder, 1991, Ships and Shipping in the North Sea and Atlantic, 1400-1600, 1997, A History of Brewing in Holland, 900-1900, Economy, Technology and the State, 2001, Beer in the Middle Ages and the Renaissance, 2004; editor: Cogs, Caravels and Galleons, 1994; co-editor: War at Sea in the Middle Ages and the Renaissance, 2003, Studies in Medieval and Renaissance History, 1978-95; contbr. articles to profl. jours. Trustee Vancouver Maritime Mus., 1979-83, 97-98. Mem. Medieval Assn. Pacific (pres. 1994-96), Econ. History Soc., Soc. Nautical Rsch., Soc. Hist. Tech. Office: U BC Dept History 1297-1873 East Mall Vancouver BC Canada V6T 1Z1 E-mail: richard.unger@ubc.ca.

**UNGER, ROGER HAROLD,** physician, research scientist; b. NYC, Mar. 7, 1924; s. Lester and Beatrice (Raphael) Unger. BS, Yale U., 1944; MD, Columbia U., 1947; MD (hon.), U. Geneva, 1976, U. Liège, Belgium, 1980. Diplomate Am. Bd. Internal Medicine. Asst. prof. internal medicine U. Tex. Med. Sch., Dallas, 1959—64, assoc. prof., 1964—69, prof., 1969—; dir. Ctr. for Diabetes Rsch., U. Tex. Health Sci. Ctr., Dallas, 1985—, Touchstone/West Disting. chair diabetes rsch., 1989—. Sr. med. investigator VA Med. Ctr., Dallas, 1979—99; mem. Nat. Diabetes Adv. Bd., Bethesda, Md., 1985—; mem. adv. coun. Nat. Inst. Diabetes, Digestive and Kidney Diseases, 1990—94. Editor: Glucagon, 1972, Glucagon Physiology etc., 1981; assoc. editor Diabetes, 1979—84, mem. editl. bd., 1975—79, Endocrinology, 1976—81; contbr. articles to profl. jours., chapters to books. With U.S. Army, 1946—48, with USPHS, 1950—52. Recipient Lilly award, Am. Diabetes Assn., 1964, Banting medal, 1975, David Rumbough award, Juvenile Diabetes Assn., 1975, Joslin medal, Harvard U., 1979, Claude Bernard award, European Assn. for Study of Diabetes, 1979, Fred Conrad Koch award, Endocrine Soc., 1983, Maurice Derot prize, Jour. Diabetique, Paris. Mem.: Am. Soc. for Clin. Investigation (emeritus), Assn. Am. Physicians, Am. Acad. Arts and Scis., NAS.

**UNGER, SUSAN J.,** automotive executive; b. Detroit, Apr. 8, 1950; BA in Economics, Mich. State U., 1972; MBA in Fin., Wayne State U., 1976. Fin. analyst, sales and mktg. DaimlerChrysler AG, 1972, various financial positions, fin. dir. product devel. and Jeep/Truck Ops., exec. dir. mgmt. info. sys., 1993, sr. v.p., 1998—, chief info. officer, 1998—. Mem. past pres., Eli Broad Bd. Coll. Bus. Mich. State U.; bd. dir. Cyberstate.org; nat. adv. com. Coll. of Engring. U. Mich.; adv. tech. bd. Oakland U. Named 100 Leading Women in N.Am. Auto Industry, Automotive News, 2002, CIO of Yr., Automation Alley, 2002, Salomon Smith Barney, 2002, Disting. Alumnus of Yr., Wayne State U. Sch. Bus. Adminstrn., 2002; named one of Detroit's Most Influential Women, Crain's Detroit Bus., 2002; recipient Top Am. Woman award, Assn. Woman in Computing, 2003, Pioneer award, Phoenix Hill Women's Mus., 2004, Disting. Svc. Citation, Automotive Hall of Fame, 2006. Mem.: Automotive Womens Alliance, Kleiner Perkins CIO Strategy Exch. Forum. Office: Daimler-Chrysler Corp 1000 Chrysler Dr Auburn Hills MI 48326-2766

**UNGER, SYDNEY ELLIOTT,** lawyer; b. 1947; BA, U. Chgo., 1968; MBA with distinction, NYU, 1970, JD cum laude, 1974, LLM in Taxation, 1979. Bar: NY 1975, US Tax Ct. 1975, US Ct. Claims 1975, US Dist. Ct. (so. and ea. dists.) NY 1975, US Ct. Appeals (2d cir.) 1975, US Ct. Appeals (fed. cir.) 1982, US Supreme Ct. 1995. Ptnr., chair Tax Dept. Kaye, Scholer LLP, NYC; adj. prof. NY Law Sch., 2005—. Lectr. in field. Editor, bus. mgr. Am. Survey Am. Law, 1973-74; articles editor The Tax Lawyer, 1981-84, mng. editor, 1984-87; contbr. articles to profl. jours. Mem. ABA (publications com., chmn. Tax Lawyer subcom., sect. on taxation 1984-87), NY State Bar Assn., Assn. of Bar of City of NY (tax com. 1988-89, taxation of corporations com. 1990-99). Office: Kaye Scholer LLP 425 Park Ave New York NY 10022-3506 E-mail: sunger@kayescholer.com.

**UNGLESBY, LEWIS O.,** lawyer; b. New Orleans, July 6, 1949; s. Lewis Huber and Mary Jane (Holloway) U.; m. Gail Hoy, Aug. 15, 1970; children: Lewis, Lance, Blake. BS, U. Miss., 1971; JD, U. Miss., 1974. Bar: La. 1974, U.S. Dist. Ct. (ea., mid., and we dists.) La. 1974, U.S. Ct. Appeals (5th cir.) 1974, U.S. Supreme Ct. 1980; bd. cert. criminal and civil trial adv. Nat. Bd. Trial Advocacy. With Unglesby & Marrineaux Law Firm; mem. judge's benchbook com. La. Supreme Ct., 1982—. Spl. counsel La. State Senate, 1991-98, Gov. La., 1996-98; lectr. La. Assn. Criminal Def. Lawyers, 1987-91. Editor criminal law sect. La. Trial Lawyers Brief, 1988—. Fellow Am. Bd. Criminal Lawyers; mem. ABA, La. Bar Assn. (no. of dels. 1979-87, lectr.), NACDL, ATLA (criminal law com. 1989-90, Best Lawyer Am. 1987-2006), La. Trial Lawyers Assn. (chmn. criminal law sect. 1983-85, bd. govs. 1983-94, exec. com. 1991-2005, lectr.) Home: 14415 Highland Rd Baton Rouge LA 70810-5312 Office: 246 Napoleon St Baton Rouge LA 70802-5937 Office Phone: 225-387-0120. Business E-Mail: 1westmoland@bellsouth.net.

**UNGVARSKI, PETER J.,** nursing administrator; Diploma in Nursing, Bellevue-Mills Schs., N.Y., 1964; BA in Psychology, Marymount Manhattan Coll., 1974; BSN, SUNY, Albany, 1985; MSN, Hunter Coll., 1989. RN: N.Y., N.J. Staff nurse critical care NYU Med. Ctr., 1964-65; head nurse prison ward Bellevue Hosp. Ctr., NY, 1965-66; charge nurse amputee svc. U.S. Naval Hosp., Phila., 1966-67; charge nurse aeromedical evac. unit U.S. Naval Hosp. Guam, Marianas Islands, 1967-68; supr. critical care Cabrini Med. Ctr., NY, 1968-70; head nurse drug addiction svc. Beth Israel Med. Ctr., NY, 1970-71; clin. instr. critical care Bellevue Hosp. Ctr., NY, 1971-73, asst. dir. nursing-prison health NY, 1973-76; staff nurse burn unit Cornell U., NY, 1976-77; clin. instr. emergency svcs. Cabrini Med. Ctr., NY, 1977-79, supr. emergency svcs. NY, 1981-82, critical care instr. NY, 1982-85, AIDS rsch. nurse NY, 1985-86; dir. AIDS program Vis. Nurse Svc. of NY, 1986-87, clin. nurse specialist HIV infection, 1987—. Mem. faculty Inst. for Emergency Care, St. Vincent's Hosp., N.Y., 1983—, Hunter-Bellevue Sch. Nursing, CUNY, 1989—, Sch. Nursing Columbia U., 1993—; clin. nurse specialist HIV

Infection Vis. Nurse Svc. of N.Y., 1987—; clin. dir. HIV/AIDS Svcs., 1994—; mem. clin. nursing adv. com. Health Resources and Svcs. Adminstrn., Rockeville, Md., 1993—; mem. editl. bd. Home Healthcare Nurse, 1993—; Nursing Leadership Forum, 1994—, The Jour. of Care Mgmt., 1994—, Am. Jour. Nursing, 1995—; adv. Office of Technology Assessment U.S. Congress, Washington, D.C., 1994—; lectr. Sch. of Social Svc. Fordham U., 1994—, Sch. Nursing Doctoral Program NYU, 1994—; mem. disting. bd. adv. in pub. health Springer Pub. Co., 1994—. With U.S. Navy Nurse Corps, 1966-68. Recipient Disting. Svc. award N.Y. Counties Reg. Nurses Assn., 1987, Nursing Excellence in Long Term Cmty. Care award Nat. League for Nursing/Ross Labs., 1989, Leadership award Assn. Nurses in AIDS Care, 1991; named to Hunter Coll. Alumni Hall of Fame, 1990. Fellow Am. Acad. Nursing; mem. ANA (Hon. Nursing Practice award 1994), APHA, Am. Assembly of Men in Nursing (Luther Christman award 1993), N.Y. State Nurses Assn. (adv. nursing practice and ethics coms. 1989—, Nursing Practice award 1988, Excellence in Writing award 1991), N.Y. Counties Reg. Assn. (Disting. Svc. award 1987, Lavina Dock award for nursing practice, 1988), Assn. Nurses in AIDS Care (bd. dirs. 1993—), Sigma Theta Tau. Alpha Phi. Office: Vis Nurse Svc NY 1250 Broadway New York NY 10001-3701

**UNHJEM, MICHAEL BRUCE,** lawyer; b. Fargo, ND, Aug. 22, 1953; s. Kalmer Joseph and Lorelei Mae (Myhra) U.; m. Mary Ruth Burges, June 19, 1976; children: Kaia Mary, David Burges, Kirsten Elizabeth. BA magna cum laude, Jamestown Coll., 1975; JD with distinction, U. N.D., 1978. Bar: N.D. 1978. Pvt. practice, Jamestown, ND, 1978-86; compliance officer Norwest Bank, Jamestown, ND, 1981-84; planned giving officer Jamestown Coll., Anne Carlsen Sch., Jamestown, 1984-86; asst. to pres., gen. counsel Blue Cross Blue Shield of N.D., Fargo, 1986-91, pres., chief exec. officer, 1991—; Pioneer Mutual Life Ins. Co., Fargo, 1997—99. Mem. bd. dirs. Lincoln Mut. Life & Casualty Ins. Co., Fargo, Noridian Adminstr. Svc., LLC, Fargo, Noridian Ins. Svc., Inc., Fargo; chmn. TriWest HC All, Western Conf. Prepaid Health Plans; bd. dirs. Prime Ther, Jamestown Coll., Cass Clay United Way, Blue Cross Blue Shield Assn. State rep. N.D. Legis. Assembly, Bismarck, 1974-86; mem. Nat. Conf. Commrs. on Uniform State Laws, Chgo., 1981—, chmn., Bismarck, 1982-86; co-chmn. Bush for Pres. Com., 1980, 88, 92; presdl. appointee Nat. Coun. on Disability, Washington, 1990. Named Outstanding Young North Dakotan, N.D. Jaycees, 1983; recipient Nat. Excellence in Leadership award State of N.D., 1988, Disting. Leadership award N.D. Psychol. Assn., 1988, Spl. Presdl. Commendation award Am. Psychiatric Assn., 1989, Toastmaster Internat. Comm. and Leadership award, 1992. Mem. ABA, N.D. Bar Assn., Cass County Bar Assn., Kiwanis, Elks, Masons, Shriners. Republican. Lutheran. Office: Blue Cross Blue Shield 4510 13th Ave S Fargo ND 58121-0002

**UNIATOWSKI, JOANNE M.,** singer, educator; b. Garfield Heights, Ohio, Oct. 29, 1963; d. Joseph J. and Joan T. Uniatowski. DMA, Cleve. Inst. of Music, 1997. Mem. voice faculty Ashland (Ohio) U., 1996—2000, Baldwin-Wallace Coll., Berea, Ohio, 2000—; exec. dir. Art Song Festival, Berea, 2001—. Cantor Cathedral of St. John the Evangelist, Cleve., 1993—. Mem.: Nat. Assn. Tchrs. of Singing. Roman Catholic. Avocations: travel, reading. Office: Baldwin-Wallace Coll 275 Eastland Rd Berea OH 44017-2088 Office Phone: 440-826-8086. Office Fax: 440-826-3239. Business E-Mail: juniatow@bw.edu.

**UNIKEL, EVA TAYLOR,** interior designer; b. Hungary; arrived in Can., 1956; came to U.S., 1967; d. Istvan Domolky and Lea Maria (Koszegi) Coan; m. Alan L. Unikel; 1 child, Renee Christine; m. June 26, 1993. BS, So. Ill. U., 1972. Dir. mktg. Lococo Design, St. Louis, 1982-83; project mgr., nat. dir. mktg. hosp. div. Hotel Restaurant Planners div. Profl. Interiors, St. Louis, 1983-87; founder Interior Solutions Inc., Hinsdale, Ill., 1987—. Mem. AIA (assoc.), Nat. Assn. Women Bus. Owners, Am. Soc. Interior Design (chairperson 1984-86), Nat. Assn. Indsl. Office Pks., Bldg. Owners and Mgrs. Assn., Internat. Interior Design Assn. Roman Catholic. Office: 500 E Ravine Rd Hinsdale IL 60521-2449 Office Phone: 630-986-0166.

**UNIS, RICHARD L.,** judge; b. Portland, Oreg., June 11, 1928; BS, JD, U. Oreg. Bar: Oreg. 1954, U.S. Dist. Ct. Oreg. 1957, U.S. Ct. Appeals (9th cir.) 1960, U.S. Supreme Ct. 1965. Judge Portland Mcpl. Ct., 1968-71, Multnomah County Dist. Ct., 1972-76, presiding judge, 1972-74; former judge Oreg. Cir. Ct. 4th Judicial Dist., 1977-90; former sr. dep. city atty. City of Portland; assoc. justice Oreg. Supreme Ct., Portland, 1990-96; spl. master US Dist. Ct. House, Portland, 1996—2005. Adj. prof. of local govt. law and evidence Lewis & Clark Coll. Northwestern Sch. Law, 1969-76, 77-96; spl. master supr. La.-Pacific Inner-Seal Siding nationwide class action litig.; faculty mem. The Nat. Judicial Coll., 1971-2000; former faculty mem. Am. Acad. Judicial Edn. Author: Procedure and Instructions in Traffic Court Cases, 1970, 101 Questions and Answers on Preliminary Hearings, 1974. Bd. dirs. Oreg. Free from Drug Abuse; mem. Oreg. Adv. Com. on Evidence Law Revision, chmn. subcom., 1974-79. Maj. USAFR, JAGC, ret. Recipient Meritorious Svc. award U. Oregon sch. Law, 1988; named Legal Citizen of Yr. Oreg. Law Related Edn., 1987; inducted into The Nat. Judicial Coll. Hall of Honor, 1988. Mem. Am. Judicature Soc. (bd. dirs. 1975, Herbert Harley Nat. award 1999), Am. Judges Assn.; Multnomah Bar Found., Oregon Judicial Conf. (chmn. Oreg. Judicial Coll. 1973-80, legis. com. 1976—, exec. com. of judicial edn. com., judicial conduct com.), N.Am. Judges Assn. (tenure, selection and compensation judges com.), Dist. Ct. Judges of Oreg. (v.p., chmn. edn. com.), Nat. Conf. Spl. Ct. Judges (exec. com.), Oreg. State Bar (judicial adminstrn. com., sec. local govt. com., com. on continuing certification, uniform jury instrn. com., exec. com. criminal law sect., trial practice sect. standards and certification com., past chmn., among others), Oreg. Trial Lawyers Assn. (named Judge of Yr. 1984). Office: 28338 Hist Colum Riv Hwy Troutdale OR 97060-9372 Office Phone: 503-669-7286. Personal E-mail: rlugg@comcast.net.

**UNISON-PACE, WENDY JANE,** nursing professor; b. Mar. 20, 1964; d. Harvey Charles and Bette Adele (Aimone) U. BS, No. Ill. U., 1988; BSN, Concordia U. and West Suburban Coll. Nursing, 1995; MS in Nursing Adminstrn., Va. Commonwealth U., 2002. Bd. cert. in traumatic stress. Mem. faculty Coll. at W.Va., 1996-97; emergency rm./trauma ctr. nurse, clin. nurse Charleston Area Med. Ctr., Charleston, W.Va., 1997-98; emergency rm./trauma ctr. nurse, clin. nurse, quality assurance coord., newsletter editor Med. Coll. Va. Hosps./Va. Commonwealth U. Health Sys., Richmond, 1998—2002; asst. Office of Health Policy, dir. nursing emergency svcs. Va. Commonwealth U. Health Sys., Richmond, 2002—03; mgr. emergency and trauma svcs. and pediat. ctr. Suburban Hosp., Bethesda, Md., 2004; assoc. prof. nursing No. Va. C.C. Med. Edn. Campus, 2004—; adminstrv. supr. VA Hosp. Ctr., 2004—05; RNII Joint Replacement Ctr. India Healthcare Sys. Mount Vernon Hosp., 2005. Instr. ARC, Lombard, Ill., 1986-98. Recipient 1st pl. Award of Hon., Addison Cultural Arts Devel. Commn., 1982, Vol. Educator Excellence awards ARC, 1984-87; 1994, Cmty. Health Edn. & Safety Svcs. award, ARC, 1988, Cert. Appreciation, 1992, Dr. Alma J. Labuski Leadership award Student Nurses Assn. Ill., 1994, Pres. Svc. award West Suburban Coll. of Nursing, 1995, Nursing Spectrum Excellence award tchg., 2005. Mem.: ANA, Nat. League Nursing, Student Nurses Assn. Ill. (hon.), v.p. 1994—95, programs com. chair 1994—95), Phi Theta Kappa, Sigma Theta Tau, Sigma Lambda Sigma (v.p. 1985—86, pres. 1986—87). Home: 206 American Dr Ruther Glen VA 22546 Office Phone: 703-822-6648. Business E-Mail: wunisonpace@nucc.edu.

**UNITHAN, DOLLY,** visual artist; b. Kelantan, Malaysia; arrived in US, 1976; Postgrad., Brit. Coun. Fine Arts Exch., 1974, Ecole Nationale des Beaux Arts de Nancy, France, 1974; BFA, Hornsey Coll. Art, 1975; MFA, Pratt Inst., 1978. Summer intern Guggenheim Mus, NYC, 1976; panelist, artist in residence Asian Am. Arts Ctr., 1993; lectr. in field. One-woman shows include Internat. Art Ctr., London, 1975, Am. Assn. State Colls., Univ. Orlando, Fla., 1977, Sloan Gallery, Lock Haven State Coll., Pa., 1978, Permanent Mission Malaysia, UN, NYC, 1987, Kerr Gallery, 1987, Lyman Allyn Art Mus., New London, Conn., 1990, UN Secretariat, NYC, 1991, Gracie Mansion, 1994, Angel Orensanz Found., 1995, Cathedral of St. John the Divine, St. Boniface Chapel Gallery, 1996, exhibited in group shows at

Palace of Westminster, Hos. of Parliament, London, 1978, City Mus. Art Gallery, Gloucester, Eng., 1978, Contemporary Gallery, Warsaw, Poland, 1978, BWA Gallery, Wroclaw, Poland, 1978, Szczecin, Poland, 1978, Arts Coun. Gallery, Belfast, No. Ireland, 1978, Parrish Art Mus., Southampton, NY, 1979, Modern Art Ctr., Guadalajara, Mex., 1979, Alternative Mus., NYC, 1981, Nat. Mus. Fine Arts, Havana, Cuba, 1986, Hillwood Art Mus., Brookville, NY, 1988, PS 1 Mus., NYC, 1990, Nat. Art Gallery, Kuala Lumpur, 1991—92, League of Nations Archives, Palais des Nations, Geneva, 1993, Jewish Mus., Vienna, Austria, 1993, Peace Mus., Remagen, Germany, Westbeth Galleries, NYC, Tweed Courthouse Gallery, 1994, China Art Mus., Beijing, 1995, Raiffeisenkasse, Ulrich bei Steyr, Peace parish, Austria, 1996, Ctrl. Children's & Youth Arts Palace, Samarkand, Uzbekistan, 1997, Palais des Nations, UN Office, Geneva, 1998, Firehouse, NYC, 1999, Cathedral of St. John the Divine Synod Hall, 2002, Asian Am. Arts Ctr., 2002, Represented in permanent collections Lock Haven State Coll., Pa., Am. Assn. State Colls., Univ., Washington, Permanent Mission of Malaysia to UN, Wilfredo Lam Ctr., Havana, Malaysian Embassy, Washington, Spirit Found., NYC, Asian Am. Arts Ctr., World Bank, Washington, Lib. Congress, artwork included in jours., Multicultural Edn., 1994, Artspiral, 1994, books, Imagine Strawberry Fields, Sculpture, Technique, Form, Content. Named grad. scholar, Mara, Malaysia, 1976—78, Archives of Contemporary Arts, Venice Biennale, 1990; recipient Artist award, Rainbow Art Found., NYC, 1985, Art award ArtQuest '88, Internat. Art Competition, Calif., 1988; grantee, Lee Found., Singapore, 1972, 1976, Pollock-Krasner Found., 1991—92. Avocation: collecting antiques. Office Phone: 212-583-1946. Personal E-mail: dollyunithan@yahoo.com.

**UNKOVIC, JOHN CLARK,** lawyer; b. Pitts., Oct. 2, 1943; s. Nicholas and Mary (Clark) Unkovic; m. Mary L. Marks, Mar. 15, 1980; 1 child, Rachel. BA in history, Harvard U., 1965; diploma in economics, St. Edmund Hall, Oxford, Eng., 1966; JD, U. Mich., 1970. Bar: Pa., 1971, US Supreme Ct., US Ct. Appeals 3rd Cir., 1973, US Ct. Appeals 5th Cir., 1981, US Ct. Appeals 11th Cir., 1981, US Ct. Appeals 6th Cir., 1986, US Ct. Appeals Fed. Cir., 1984, US Ct. Appeals 7th Cir., 1989. Atty. Reed Smith LLP (formerly Reed Smith Shaw & McClay), Pitts., 1971—, now ptnr., gen. counsel. Adj. prof. law Duquesne U., Pitts., 1978-89; bd. mem. Mine Safety Appliances Co., 2002-. Contbr. articles to profl. journals. Chair Pitts. Pub. Schools Found.; bd. mem. Manchester Bidwell Corp. Fulbright Fellow, 1970-71. Mem. ABA, Pa. Bar Assn., Allegheny County Bar Assn., Am. Law Inst. Office: Reed Smith LLP 435 Sixth Ave Pittsburgh PA 15219 Office Phone: 412-288-3294. Office Fax: 412-288-3063. Business E-Mail: junkovic@reedsmith.com.

**UNKOVIC, NICHOLAS C.,** lawyer; b. Pitts., 1951; AB magna cum laude, Harvard U., 1973; JD with honors, U. Mich., 1976. Bar: Calif. 1976. Mng. ptnr.-Palo Alto Office Squire, Sanders & Dempsey LLP, mem. mgmt. com. Dir. British Am. Coun. No. Calif., Redem Corp. Named a No. Calif. Super Lawyers, Law & Politics Mag., 2004; named one of Silicon Valley's top corp. lawyers, San Jose Mag. Mem.: ABA (Bus. Law Sect.), State Bar Calif. Fluent in French. Office: Squire Sanders & Dempsey LLP 600 Hansen Way Palo Alto CA 94304-1043 Office Phone: 650-843-3238. Office Fax: 650-843-8777. Business E-Mail: nunkovic@ssd.com.

**UNPINGCO, JOHN WALTER SABLAN,** chief federal judge; b. 1950; BA, St. Louis U., 1972; MBA, JD, NYU, 1976; LLM, Georgetown U., 1983. Bar: Guam 1977, D.C. 1983, Calif. 1992. Atty. Ferenz, Bramhall, Williams & Gruskin, Guam, 1976-77; atty. Office Staff Judge Advocate USAF, 1977-85, civilian atty., Office Staff Judge Advocate, 1985-87; counsel US Naval Air Warfare Ctr., China Lake, Calif., 1987-92; judge US Dist. Ct. (Guam dist.), 1992—, now chief judge. Part-time instr. U. Md. Far East divsn., Yokota Air Base, Tokyo, 1983-87, European divsn., RAF Mildenhall, Suffolk, U.K., 1979-82, U. Guam, 1994-99. Pres. Guam Swim League, 2000; pres. parish coun. Our Lady of Hope Parish, 2000-. Mem. ABA, State Bar Calif., Guam Bar Assn., Internat. Legal Soc. Japan, D.C. Bar Assn., NWC Community Fed. Credit Union (bd. dirs. 1991-92). Office: US Dist Ct 4th Fl US Courthouse 520 W Soledad Ave Hagatna GU 96910

**UNRAU, JACK,** application developer; b. Washington, Apr. 19, 1977; BS in Math. and Computer Scis., Colo. Sch. Mines, Golden, Colo., 1999. Systems analyst Tri-State Generation and Transmission Assn., Inc., Westminster, 1999—2000; software engr. Gateway, Inc., Lakewood, 2000—05, Computer and Comm. Technologies, Inc., Englewood, 2005—. Mem. Ken Caryl Bapt. Ch., Littleton, Colo., 1990. Mem.: ACM, Mensa. Personal E-mail: jack@unraunet.com. E-mail: jack.unrau@cctus.com.

**UNRUH, ERIC W.,** academic administrator, music educator; s. Cecil A. and Maurine Unruh; m. Gayle A. Christenson, Aug. 23, 1980; children: D. Alexander, Michael, Christopher. BA, Bethany Coll., 1979; MusM, Northwestern U., Evanston, Ill., 1981, Mus D, 1989. Chmn. dept. music Casper Coll., Wyo., 1991—2006, chmn. divsn. fine arts, 2006—; music min. Anglican Ch., Casper, 2005—. Commr. cmty./jr. coll. accreditation Nat. Assn. Schs. Music, Reston, Va., 1998—2002, chair commn. cmty./jr. coll. accreditation, 2003—. Composer: (music composition) Magnificat, 2000, Te Deum, 2004, Lyrical Burns, 2006. Named Educator of Yr., Wyo. Music Educators Assn., 2002—; recipient Rosenthal Outstanding Educator award, 1998; grantee, Wyo. Cmty. Found., 1999, 2004. Mem.: Music Tchrs. Nat. Assn., Music Educators Nat. Conf. Home: 4440 S David Casper WY 82601 Office: Casper Coll 125 College Dr Casper WY 82601 Office Phone: 307-268-2537. Business E-Mail: unruh@caspercollege.edu.

**UNRUH, GARY LEE,** retired music educator; b. Reedley, Calif., July 7, 1941; s. Vera E. Unruh; 1 child, Holly Elizabeth. MusD, U. Ill., 1973. Prof. emeritus Calif. State U., Fresno, Colo., 1999—. Dir. performance tours Kingsway Internat., Colo. Springs, Colo., 1997—. Dir. hundreds of performances and tours. V.p. Santa Barbara (Calif.) Vocal Jazz Found., 2005. Named Educator of Yr., Fresno Arts Coun., 1976; recipient, 1979, 1984, 2001, award, Calif. State Senate Resolutions, 1998. Mem.: Am. Choral Dirs. Assn. (life; pres. we. divsn. 1989—91). Office Phone: 805-962-8832. Personal E-mail: glunruh@verizon.net.

**UNRUH, HOWARD K., JR.,** military officer, university administrator; b. Balt. m. Diane R. Caslow; three children: Meredith, Allison, H. Kirk III. AB, Princeton U., 1970; MEd, Harvard U., 1971; MA in Am. Studies, U. Hawaii. Commd. ensign U.S. Navy, 1970, advanced through ranks to rear adm.; various assignments to Dep. Comdr. Naval Surface Force, U.S. Atlantic Fleet, 1995—; comdr. Readiness Command Midwest. Dir. devel. rels., rec. sec. Princeton U.; trustee or bd. dirs. several civic orgns. Decorated Legion of Merit (2), Meritorious Svc. medal (2), Navy Commendation medal (4), Nat. Def. medal with Bronze Star, Republic of Vietnam Svc. medal with Bronze Star, others. Mem. Naval Res. Assn., Surface Navy Assn., Univ. Cottage Club, Princeton Club N.Y.C. Office: Princeton Univ Recording Sec 330 Alexander St Princeton NJ 08540-7123

**UNRUH, JAMES ARLEN,** bank executive; b. Goodrich, N.D., Mar. 22, 1941; m. Candice Leigh Voight, Apr. 28, 1984. BSBA, Jamestown Coll., 1963; MBA, U. Denver, 1964. Dir. corp. planning and analysis Fairchild Camera & Instrument, Calif., 1974-76, v.p. treasury and corp. devel. Calif., 1976-79, v.p. fin. Calif., 1979-80, Memorex Corp., Santa Clara, Calif., 1980-82, Burroughs Corp. (now known as Unisys Corp.), Detroit, 1982-84, sr. v.p. fin., 1984-86, exec. v.p. fin., 1986, exec. v.p., 1986-89, pres., COO, 1989-90, pres., CEO, 1990-91, chmn. bd. dirs., CEO, 1991-97; founding prin. Alerion Capital Group L.L.C., Scottsdale, Ariz., 1998—. Bd. dirs. Prudential Fin. Corp., Qwest Comm. Internat. Inc., Tenet Healthcare Corp., CSG Sys. Internat., Inc., Apex Microtech. Corp., LumenIQ Corp., BioVigilant Corp., Steton Tech. Group, Inc., Worldlink, Inc. Trustee Jamestown Coll., N.D. Home: 5426 E Morrison Ln Paradise Valley AZ 85253 Office Phone: 480-367-0900. E-mail: jimunruh@alerion.com.

**UNSAL-TUNAY, NURAN,** geological engineer, researcher; b. Igdir, Turkey, Dec. 26, 1956; came to U.S., 1995; d. Kamil and Feride (Gunay) Tunay; m. Ilhan Unsal, Oct. 28, 1979; 1 child, Volkan. Diploma in Geol. Engring., Earth Sci. Geol. Engring. Turkey, 1982; cert. in Civil Engring., Min. Pub. Works Turkey, 1985. Geol. engr. Gen. Directorate of Bank of Provinces, Konya-Ankara, Turkey, 1982—84, Gen. Directorate of Hwy., Kayseri-Ankara, Turkey, 1984—89, Adminstrn. Pub. Works, Manisa, Turkey, 1989—95. Cons. Pub. Works, Manisa, Turkey, 1989-95; adv. bds. Pub. Works, Municipality, Civil Cts., Manisa, Turkey, 1992-95. Inventor: Adaptation of Stabilized Hydrated Lime, Publication of the Chamber of Geol. Engring. of Turkey, 1993. Recipient of presentations 46th Congress of Geology of Turkey, Ankara, 1993. Fellow Geol. Assn. Can.; mem. Geol. Soc. Am., Chamber of Geol. Engrs. of Turkey. Achievements include the soil improvement with hydrated lime stabilization; applied in the area of Manisa Teachers House Buildings, was one of the first applications in Turkey. Home: 23-13 28th Ave Apt 2F Astoria NY 11102 Personal E-mail: nuranunsal@hotmail.com.

**UNSWORTH, MICHAEL EDWARD,** university librarian; b. Indpls., July 10, 1950; s. Cecil Walker and Dorothy Louise (Wolf) U.; m. Lynn Maria Kaczor, Feb. 12, 1977 (div. Sept. 1981). BA, Ind. U.-Purdue U., Indpls., 1973; MLS, Ind. U., Bloomington, 1974; MA, U. Notre Dame, 1978. Libr. U. Notre Dame, Ind., 1974-79, Colo. State U., Ft. Collins, 1979-84, Mich. State U., East Lansing, 1984—. Cons. Chadwyk-Healey, Inc., Alexandria, Va., 1988-95; intern Inst. for Editing of Hist. Documents, Madison, Wis., 1993; asst. dir. Can. Studies Ctr. Mich. State U., 1999—. Co-author: Future War Novels, 1984; editor: Military Periodicals, 1990; mem. editl. bd. Mich. State U. Press, 1994-2000; contbr. articles to profl. publs. Mem. faculty coun. U. Notre Dame, 1978; mem. Mich. Freedom of Info. Com.; bd. dirs. Greater Lansing Hist. Soc., 1991-93. Recipient Faculty Rsch. grant Can. Embassy, 1997. Mem. Assn. for Bibliography of History, Soc. for Mil. History, Hist. Soc. Mich., Mich. Oral History Soc. Avocations: hiking, backpacking, cross country skiing, bicycling. Home: PO Box 6253 East Lansing MI 48826-6253 Office: Mich State Univ Libraries East Lansing MI 48824 Office Phone: 517-432-6123 125.

**UNSWORTH, RICHARD PRESTON,** minister, educator, director; b. Vineland, N.J., Feb. 7, 1927; s. Joseph Lewis and Laura (MacMillan) U.; m. Joy Merritt, Aug. 20, 1949; children: Sarah, John, Mary, Lucy. BA, Princeton U., 1948; BD, Yale U., 1954; ThM, Harvard U., 1963; STD, Dickinson Coll., 1971; LHD, Washington and Jefferson Coll., 1971; LLD, Smith Coll., 1992. Ordained to ministry Presbyn. Ch., 1953. Tchr. Bible and English Mt. Hermon Sch., 1948-50; asst. chaplain Yale U., New Haven, 1950-54; chaplain, assoc. prof. Smith Coll., Northampton, Mass., 1954-64, chaplain, prof. religion, 1967-80; dean William Jewett Tucker Found. and prof. religion Dartmouth (N.H.) Coll., 1963-67; headmaster Northfield (Mass.) Mt. Hermon Sch., 1980-88, pres., 1989-91, headmaster emeritus, 1991—; headmaster Berkshire Sch., Sheffield, Mass., 1991-96; dean of the chapel Smith Coll., 1996-98, lectr. religion, 1996—99, sr. fellow Kahn Inst., 1998—. Pres. Critical Langs. and Area Studies Consortium, 1987-97; cons. Ednl. Assocs., Inc., 1967-69, U.S. Office Edn., 1969-77. Author: Sexuality and the Human Community, 1970, Dignity and Exploitation: Christian Reflections on Images of Sex in the 1970s, 1974, A Century of Religion at Smith College, 1975; (with Arnold Kenseth) Prayers for Worship Leaders, 1978; editor: Rethinking Childhood, 2004; contbg author: The Dispossessed, 2005; contbr. chpts. to books. Leader Operation Crossroads Africa unit, Nigeria, 1961, mem. adv. bd., 1961-66; mem. adminstrv. com. Student Christian Movement New Eng., 1964; mem. Mass. unit So. Christian Leadership conf., 1968; trustee Conf. on Religion in Ind. Schs., 1961-63; pres. Am. Friends of Coll. Cevenol, France, 1957-63, 90-94, Am. rep., 1958-82; trustee Mt. Holyoke Coll., 1982-89, chair, 1984-89, chmn. emeritus, 1989—, Am. Sch. Tangier, Morocco, 1982-87, Eaglebrook Sch., 1992-98, Acad. Music, Northampton, 1998-99, Mus. Sci., Boston, 1993-95; bd. dirs. Family Planning Coun. Western Mass., 1972-81; bd. dirs. Ind. Schs. Assn. Mass., 1992-96. Mem. AAUP, Nat. Assn. Coll. and Univ. Chaplains, Am. Acad. Religion, Assn. Ind. Schs. New Eng. (pres. 1993-96), Headmasters Assn. Nat. Commn. on Asia in Schs., Asia Soc. N.Y.C., U. Club.

**UNTERBECK, AXEL JOACHIM,** pharmaceutical executive, director; b. Leipzig, Germany, Nov. 10, 1953; came to U.S., 1986; s. Joachim and Brigitte (Noack) U.; m. Anett Maria Sartor-Unterbeck, Aug. 29, 1987. Abitur, Gymnasium, Bergneustadt, Germany, 1973; MS in molecular biology, U. Bonn., Germany, 1982; PhD, U. Cologne, Germany, 1986. Rsch. assoc. U. Cologne, 1982-86; sr. rsch. scientist Bayer AG, West Haven, Conn., 1986-89, assoc. dir. Wuppertal, Germany, 1989-92; dir. Bayer Corp., West Haven, 1992—97; pres., chief science officer Memory Pharm. Corp., 1998—. Cons. Software House, Cologne, 1978-86; adv. bd. Dahlem Confs., Berlin, 1990-91; rev. com. mem. NIH, Bethesda, Md., 1988-92. Author: Molecular Biology of Aging, 1989; inventor in field. Mem. trainer Life Rescue, Germany, 1973-75; trainer German Air Force, 1973-75. Sgt. German Air Force, 1973-75. Mem. N.Y. Acad. Scis., Swimming Club, Yacht Club. Avocations: photography, sailing, travel, swimming, music. Office: Memory Pharmaceuticals Corp 100 Philips Pkwy Montvale NJ 07645

**UNTERBERGER, BETTY MILLER,** history professor, writer; b. Glasgow, Scotland, Dec. 27, 1923; d. Joseph C. and Leah Miller; m. Robert Ruppe, July 29, 1944; children: Glen, Gail, Gregg. BA, Syracuse U., N.Y., 1943; MA, Harvard U., 1946; PhD, Duke U., 1950. Asst. prof. E. Carolina U., Greenville, 1948-50; assoc. prof., dir. liberal arts ctr. Whittier Coll., Calif., 1954-61; assoc. prof. Calif. State U.-Fullerton, 1961-65, prof., chmn. grad. studies, 1965-68; prof. history Tex. A&M U., College Station, 1968—. Vis. prof. U. Hawaii, Honolulu, summer 1967, Peking U., Beijing, 1988; vis. disting. prof. U. Calif., Irvine, 1987, Patricia and Bookman Peters prof. history, 1991—2005; vis. prof. Charles U., Prague, Czechoslovakia, summer 1992. Regents prof., 2000—; mem. adv. com. fgn. rels. U.S. Dept. State, 1977-81, chair, 1981; mem. hist. adv. com. U.S. Dept. Army, 1980-82, USN, 1991—; mem. Nat. Hist. Publs. and Records Commn., 1980-84; mem. history rev. panel to Dir. of CIA, 1999—. Author: America's Siberian Expedition 1918-1920: A Study of National Policy, 1956, 69 (Pacific Coast award Am. Hist. Assn. 1956); editor: American Intervention in the Russian Civil War, 1969, Intervention Against Communism: Did the U.S. Try to Overthrow the Soviet Government, 1918-20, 1986, The United States, Revolutionary Russia and the Rise of Czechoslovakia, 1989, paperback edit. with a 2000 yr. perspective, 2000; contbr.: Woodrow Wilson and Revolutionary World, 1982, The Liberal Persuasion, 1997, The United States and the Russian Civil War, microfilm edit., 25 reels, 2001; mem. editl. adv. bd. The Papers of Woodrow Wilson, Princeton U., 1982-92, Internt. History, 1999—; bd. editors: Diplomatic History, 1981-84, Red River Valley Hist. Rev., 1975-84. Trustee Am. Inst. Pakistan Studies, Villanova U., Pa., 1981—, sec., 1989-92; mem. League of Women Voters. Woodrow Wilson Found. fellow, 1979; recipient Disting. Univ. Tchr. award State of Calif. Legislature, 1966; Betty Miller Unterberger dissertation prize, Soc. Historians Am. Fgn. Rels., 2004. Mem. LWV, NOW, AAUW, Am. Hist. Assn. (chair 1982-83, nominating com. 1980-83), Orgn. Am. Historians (govt. relations com.), Soc. Historians of Am. Fgn. Relations (exec. council 1978-81, 86-89, govt. relations com. 1982-84, v.p. 1985, pres. 1986, co-winner Myrna F. Bernath prize 1991), Am. Soc. for Advancement Slavic Studies, Coordinating Com. on Women in Hist. Profession, Rocky Mountain Assn. Slavic Studies (program chair 1973, v.p. 1973-74), So. Hist. Assn., Asian Studies Assn., Assn. Third World Studies, Czechoslovak Soc. Arts and Scis., Czechoslovak History Conf., Women in Nat. Security, Women's Fgn. Policy Coun., Beyond War, Peace History Soc., Sierra Club, Phi Beta Kappa, Phi Beta Delta. Office: Tex A&M U Dept History College Station TX 77843-0001 Business E-Mail: bettymu@tamu.edu.

**UNTERMAN, THOMAS,** venture capitalist, lawyer; b. Newport, RI, Oct. 23, 1944; s. Martin D. and Ruth (Marcus) U.; m. Janet M. Mead, Sept. 27, 1980; children: Rebecca, Amy. AB, Princeton U., 1966; JD, U. Chgo., 1969. Bar: Calif. 1970. Assoc. Orrick, Herrington & Sutcliffe, San Francisco, 1969-75, ptnr., 1975-86, Morrison & Foerster, San Francisco, 1986-92; sr. v.p., gen. counsel The Times Mirror Co., L.A., 1992-95, sr. v.p., CFO,

1995—, exec. v.p., CFO, 1998-99; mng. ptnr. Rustic Canyon Ventures, Santa Monica, Calif., 2000—. Democrat. Jewish. Office: Rustic Canyon Ventures 2425 Olympic Blvd Ste 6050W Santa Monica CA 90404-4030

**UNTERMEYER, CHARLES GRAVES (CHASE UNTERMEYER),** ambassador, diplomat; b. Long Branch, N.J., Mar. 7, 1946; s. Dewitt Edward and Marguerite Alonza (Graves) U.; m. Diana Cumming Kendrick, Oct. 6, 1990; 1 child, Ellyson Chase. AB, Harvard Coll., 1968. Polit. reporter Houston Chronicle, 1971-74; exec. asst. County Judge of Harris County, Houston, 1974-76; state rep. Tex. Ho. of Reps., Austin, 1977-81; exec. asst. V.P. George H.W. Bush, Washington, 1981-83; dep. asst. sec. installations & facilities Navy Dept., Washington, 1983—84, asst. sec. manpower & reserve affairs, 1984—88; asst. to the pres. White House, Washington, 1989-91; dir. Voice of Am., Washington, 1991-93; dir. govt. affairs Compaq Computer Corp., Houston, 1993—2002; v.p. prof. pub. policy U. Tex. Health Sci. Ctr., Houston, 2002—04; U.S. amb. to Qatar US Dept. State, 2004—. Bd. visitors U.S. Naval Acad., Annapolis, Md., 1993-96, chmn., 1995; mem. Tex. State Bd. Edn., 1999-2003, chmn., 1999-2001. Author: Houston Survival Handbook, 1980. Commnr. Port of Houston, 1995-98; bd. dirs. Nat. Pub. Radio, 1996-98. Lt. USNR, 1968-70. Inst. Politics fellow Harvard U., 1980; recipient George Washington Honor medal Freedoms Found., 1969. Republican. Episcopalian. Home and Office: Am Embassy Arcent-QA Box 520 APO AE 09898 Office Phone: 974-488-4101 ext. 6055. E-mail: untermeyercg@state.gov.

**UNWIN, STEPHEN FORMAN,** advertising executive, educator; b. Higham, Leicestershire, Eng., Aug. 7, 1927; s. Philip Henry and Decima (Forman) Unwin; m. Pamela Susan Brett, June 6, 1953; children: Philip, Tessa, Sam. *Son, Sam, is a commercial advisor for development economics of oil and gas exploration worldwide at Exxon/Mobil. Son, Philip, provides restaurant and limousine services for Colorado resorts. Mr. Unwin and his family are direct descendents of Rev. John Wheelwright, the founder of Exeter, New Hampshire, (1638) and Nathaniel Sylvester, the proprietor of Shelter Island, New York (1660).* BA with honors, Oxford U., 1952, MA, 1968. Account exec. London Press Exch., 1951-66; dir. London Press Exch. Orgn. Ltd., 1966-67; assoc. dir. LPE Ltd., London, 1967-69; vis. lectr. U. Ill., Urbana, 1969-70, asst. prof., 1970-74; assoc. prof. U. Ala., Tuscaloosa, 1974-79, Wash. State U., Pullman, 1979-81, U. Oreg., Eugene, 1981-85; pres. Bus. Dynamics, Kingwood, Tex., 1985—. Cons. advt. Ill. Bell, Chgo., 1974—75, J. Walter Thompson, San Francisco, 1983; dir. Forest Industries Comm. Inst., Atlanta, 1975—76; publicist Brit. Tourist Authority, London, 1978—81; vis. prof. Am. Assn. Advt. Agys., Chgo., 1971, Am. Ad Fedn., San Francisco, 1983; instr. Lifelong Learning, Kingwood, 2005—. *Mr. Unwin executed a communication program for the launch of the world's first synthetic penicillin by Beecham Pharmaceuticals (now Smith/Kline Glaxo). He was a speaker and panel member for the Alzheimer's Association from 2002-2004. Since 1974, he has published numerous articles on his theory of the industrial life cycle and on the service economy in the marketing media of the United States, the United Kingdom, and Singapore.* Author: How Nations Grow Rich, 1992; co-author: The Future of Advertising, 2003; contbr. articles to profl. jours. Mem. Nat. Com. Advt. Edn., N.Y.C., 1983—84; bicentennial judge Advt. Age mag., Chgo., 1976; mem. Future Journalism Edn., Eugene, Oreg., 1982—84, Internat. Advt. Edn. Com., Chgo., 1982, Wheelwright Mus., Santa Fe, Worcester Coll., Oxford U. 2d lt. Brit. Army, 1946—48. Libr. fellow, Mass. Hist. Soc., 1990—95. Mem.: Am. Sci. Affiliation, Am. Acad. Advt. Episcopalian. Avocations: travel, genealogy. Office Phone: 281-360-0393.

**UPADHIAYA, UMESH CHANDRA,** engineer, consultant; b. Dabha, India, July 11, 1927; arrived in US, 1977; s. Bhagwati Prashad and Shri (Devi) Upadhiaya; m. Susila Devi, Nov. 7, 1954; children: Anita, Amit. Diploma in Elec. and Mech. Engring., Tech. Coll., Dayalbagh, India, 1948; MSME, Fla. Internat. U., 1991. Registered profl. engr., Fla. Asst. engr. Hindusthan Sugar, Gola, India, 1954—60; mech. engr. Bagpat Sugar, India, 1960—61; erection engr. Dhampur Sugar, India, 1961—62; cons. Mehta Group, Uganda, 1962—73; project mgr. KCP Ltd., Madras, India, 1973—74; design engr. Joint Sugar Project Unit, Surabaya, Indonesia, 1974—77; cons. engr. Tate & Lyle Enterprises Inc., Miami, Fla., 1977—85, ATV Projects, Bombay, 1990—93; ind. cons. Davie, Fla., 1993—. Contbr. articles to profl. jours. Home: 6510 Sedgewyck Cir W Davie FL 33331-3455 Office Phone: 954-434-5265. Personal E-mail: ravaY2K@bellsouth.net.

**UPADHYAY, YOGENDRA NATH,** physician, educator; b. Gorakhpur, India, Dec. 21, 1938; arrived in U.S., 1963; s. Murlidhar and Vansraji (Pande) U.; m. Cecile R. Yonish; children: Asha, Sameer, Sanjay. MB, BS, All India Inst. Med. Scis., New Delhi, 1962. Diplomate Am. Bd. Psychiatry and Neurology, Am. Bd. Psychiatry and Child and Adolescent Psychiatry. Instr. in pediatrics Johns Hopkins U. Sch. Medicine, Balt., 1969-71; fellow in child psychiatry Johns Hopkins Hosp./Johns Hopkins U., Balt., 1971-72; resident, then sr. resident in psychiatry Albert Einstein Coll. Medicine/Bronx Mcpl. Hosp. Ctr., 1972-74, fellow in child psychiatry, 1974-75; chief, partial hosp. program for children, dept. psychiatry Brookdale Hosp., Bklyn., 1976-77; med. dir. West Nassau Mental Health Ctr., Franklin Sq., NY, 1977-80; asst. prof. clin. psychiatry SUNY, Stony Brook, 1977-82; dir. child and adolescent psychiatry Nassau County Med. Ctr., East Meadow, NY, 1980-92; sr. psychiatrist South Oaks Hosp., Amityville, NY, 1992—, pres. med. staff, 1995-97, svc. med. dir. child and adolescent psychiatry, 1995-97, med. dir., 1997—; sr. v.p., Medical Affairs South Oak Hosp. and Broadlawn Nursing Home, 2001—. Sr. v.p. med. affairs LI Home, Amityville, NY, 2001—. Fellow Am. Psychiat. Assn. (cons. task force treatments psychiat. disorders 1989—), Am. Acad. Child and Adolescent Psychiatry, Allmsonians of Am. (founding pres. 1982-86). Office: S Oaks Hosp 400 Sunrise Hwy Amityville NY 11701-2508 Office Phone: 631-608-5227. Business E-Mail: yupadhyay@south-oaks.org.

**UPADHYAYA, KRIPA SHANKAR,** academic administrator, educator; b. Mirzapur, India, Oct. 7, 1948; s. Tej Bahadur and Indrawati Upadhyaya; m. Jarawati Upadhyaya; children: Usha, Rakesh Kumar, Sanjeev Kumar. BSc, Banaras Hindu U., Varanasi, India, 1968, MSc, 1970, PhD, 1973. Head physics dept. K. N. Govt. P. G. Coll., Gyanpur, India, 1998—2005; prin. Govt. P. G. Coll. Lalganj, Mizzapur, India, 2006—. Participant nat. and internat. confs.; mem. acad. coun. VBS Purranchal U., Jaunpur, India, 2004—; mem. R.B.R., A.B.I., 2000—. Contbr. scientific papers to rsch. publs.; referee Indian Jour. Pure and Applied Physics, 2006—. Recipient rsch. grants medal. Mem.: Indian Physics Assn., U.P. Govt. Acad. Soc. (life), Purvanchal Acad. Scis. (life), Indian Physics Assn. (life; chmn. Gyanpur chpt. 1990—). Achievements include research in theoretical solid state physics; lattice dynamics, high pressure physics, nanomaterials. Home: 4/56 Narain Colony Gyanpur Bhadohi 221304 India Office: Govt P G Coll Lalganj Mirzapur 231211 India

**UPATNIEKS, JURIS,** retired optical engineer; b. Riga, Latvia, May 7, 1936; arrived in U.S., 1951; s. Karlis and Eleonora (Jegers) Upatnieks; m. Ilze Induss, July 13, 1968; children: Ivars, Ansis. BSEE, U. Akron, Ohio, 1960; MSEE, U. Mich., 1965. Rsch. asst., then rsch. assoc. Willow Run Labs. U. Mich., Ann Arbor, 1960-69; rsch. engr. Inst. Sci. and Tech., U. Mich., Ann Arbor, 1969-72, Environ. Rsch. Inst. Mich., Ann Arbor, 1973-93; sr. engr. Applied Optics, Ann Arbor, 1993—2001; ret., 2001. Lectr. elec. engring. dept. U. Mich., 1971—73, adj. assoc. prof. elec. engring. and computer sci. dept., 1974—2001, adj. rsch. scientist dept. mech. engring. and applied mechanics, 1996—2001. Contbr. articles to profl. jours. 2d lt. U.S. Army, 1961—62. Recipient Holley medal, ASME, 1976, Inventor of the Yr. award, Assn. Advancement Invention and Innovation, 1976. Fellow: Latvian Acad. Sci. (Grand medal 1994), Acad. Soc. Austrums, Soc. Photographic Instrumentation Engrs. (Robert Gordon award 1965), Optical Soc. Am. (R. W. Wood prize 1975), Am. Latvian Assn. Achievements include patents in field. Avocations: camping, gardening, hiking. Personal E-mail: upatnks@ic.net.

**UPBIN, HAL J.,** consumer products company executive; b. Bronx, N.Y., Jan. 15, 1939; s. David and Evelyn (Sloan) U.; m. Shari Kiesler, May 29, 1960; children: Edward, Elyse, Danielle. BBA, Pace Coll., 1961. CPA, N.Y. Tax sr. Peat, Marwick, Mitchell & Co., N.Y.C., 1961-65; tax mgr. Price Waterhouse & Co., N.Y.C., 1965-71; dir. taxes Wheelabrator-Frye Inc., N.Y.C., 1971-72, treas., 1972-74; pres. Wheelabrator Fin. Corp., N.Y.C., 1974-75; v.p., chief fin. officer Chase Manhattan Mortgage and Realty Trust (became Triton Group Ltd. 1980), N.Y.C., 1975-76, pres., 1976-78, pres., chmn., 1978-83, also dir.; chmn., pres., dir. Isomedics, 1983-85; chmn., pres. Fifth Ave. Cards, Inc., Fifth Retail Corp., Ashley's Stores, Ashley's Outlet Stores, 1984-88; bd. dirs. Stacy Industries, 1984-88; vice chmn. Am. Recreation Products, St. Louis, 1985-88, vice chmn., pres., 1988—, chmn., 1992—; v.p. corp. devel., chmn. acquistion com. Kellwood Co., Chesterfield, Mo., 1990—, exec. v.p. corp. devel., chmn. acquisition com., 1992—, pres., COO, 1994—, pres., COO, dir., 1995-97, pres., CEO, 1997—2005, chmn., 1999—, also bd. dirs. Bd. dirs. First Banks, Inc., Regional Bus. Coun., Coun. Nat. Trustees, Nat. Jewish Med. and Rsch. Ctr., Nat. Coun. Wash. U. Olin Sch. Bus., Brown Shoe Co.; trustee Pace U. Past pres. Jewish Temple. Mem. AICPA, N.Y. State Soc. CPA's, Franklin Jaycees (v.p.). Home: 3740 S Ocean Blvd Apt 801 Highland Beach FL 33487-3403 Business E-Mail: HJU@kellwood.com.

**UPBIN, SHARI,** agent; b. NYC; children: Edward, Elyse, Danielle. Master tap instr. Talent mgr. Goldstar Talent Mgmt., Inc., N.Y.C., 1989-91. Faculty Nat. Shakespeare Conservatory, N.Y. Asst. dir.: (plays, 1st Black-Hispanic Shakespeare prodn.) Julius Ceasar, 1979; dir.(choreographer): (plays) Matter of Opinion, 1980, Side by Side, 1981; prodr.(dir.): Vincent, The Passions of Van Gogh, 1981,: (Broadway plays) Bojangles, The Life of Bill Robinson, 1984; dir.: Captain America, 1996; dir., choreographer (plays) Fiddler of the Roof, Cabaret, Life with Father, Roar of the Grease Paint, 1979—82; dir.: (plays) Feminist Movements, 1997, Danny Kaye and Sylvia, 2005; co-prodr.: One Mo' Time; prodr., dir.: Flypaper, 1991—92; Women on Their Own, Things My Mother Never Told Me; How Could Cupid Be So Stupid!, 1999; Timeless Divas, 2003, 2005; prodr.: Vintage 2001, Timeless Divas! Salute to Women in Cabaret, Broadway Over 40, Timeless Divas! Musical Stars of The Silver Screen, 2004. Founder Queens Playhouse, N.Y., Children's Theatre, Flushing, N.Y.; mem. Willy Mays' Found. Drug Abused Children. Recipient Jaycees Svc. award Jr. Miss Pageants Franklin Twp., N.J., 1976. Mem. League Profl. Theatre Women (past pres.), Soc. Stage Dirs. and Choreographers, Coalition of Women in Arts & Media (bd. dirs.), Actors Equity Assn., Villagers Barn Theatre (1st woman pres.), N.Y. Womens Agenda (bd. dirs.). Personal E-mail: sharivpbin@aol.com.

**UPCHURCH, LESLIE PURCELL,** music educator; b. Pitts., Sept. 22, 1953; d. John (Jack) Edward and Jeanne Jolliffe Purcell; 1 child, Alicia Nicole. BFA, Carnegie Mellon U., 1976; MusM, U. Wis., Madison, 1980. Elem. cert. in Dalcroze Eurhythmics Carnegie-Mellon U./Jaques-Dalcroze Inst., 1976, cert. in Dalcroze Eurhythmics Ithaca Coll./Jaques-Dalcroze Inst., 1981, lic. Carnegie-Mellon U./Jaques-Dalcroze Inst., 1982. Music tchr. and vocal accompanist Muskingum Coll., New Concord, Ohio, 1981—83; dalcroze eurhythmics tchr. trainer - outreach program The Westchester Conservatory of Music, White Plains, NY, 1987—89; music tchr. Horace Mann Sch. for Nursery Years, New York, NY, 1989—92; piano and dalcroze eurhythmics tchr. Sonatina Sch. of Music and Sonatina Internat. Piano Camp/Sonata Programs, Bennington, Vt., 1992—97; organist and choir dir. St. James Episcopal Ch., Arlington, Vt., 1994—99; music dept. dir. and founding tchr. Maple St. Sch., Manchester Center, Vt., 1998—2005; piano improvisation and pedagogy tchr. Dalcroze Tng. Program Carnegie Mellon U., Pittsburgh, Pa., 2003—; dir. of dalcroze eurhythmics program J.C.C. on the Palisades/Thurnauer Sch. of Music, Tenafly, NJ, 2004—; tchr. music Mustard Seed Sch., Hoboken, NJ, 2005—, dir. chorus, 2005—. Adv. bd. mem. Manchester Music Festival, Manchester, Vt., 1998—2001; bd. dirs. Vt. MIDI Project, Essex Junction, 2003—, sec., 2003—05. Prodr., host (TV series) Music and The Young Child, 1994—96, asst. music dir., musician Arlington Lions Variety Shows, 1999—2005; musician, choir master children's chorus: opera Hansel and Gretel with Opera Theater of Weston, 2001, Help! Help! The Globolinks!, 2003; musician, music dir. Dorset Players holiday prodns., 2002, 2004. Vol. Manchester Sch. Fund, 1999—2000; bd. dirs. GNAT-TV, Manchester, Vt., 1994—96. Grantee, Mockingbird Found., 2005. Mem.: Dalcroze Soc. Am. (treas. tri-state chpt. 1983—85, treas. nat. assn. 1984—88, tri-state Chpt., Elsa Findlay scholar 1991). Achievements include invention of double adjusting piano seat that adjusts for seat and feet. Avocations: cross country skiing, hiking, gardening, home decorating, meditating and Buddhist studies, travel. Home and Office: 6305 JFK Blvd E Apt A6 West New York NJ 07093 Office: Mustard Seed School 422 Willow Ave Hoboken NJ 07030 Personal E-mail: upchurch_leslie@yahoo.com.

**UPDEGRAFF, STEVEN PHILLIP,** music educator; b. Williamsport, Pa., July 3, 1973; s. Steven Leigh Updegraff and Helen Louise Peterson; m. Jessica Michelle Santibanez, July 31, 2004. B in Music Edn., Westminster Choir Coll., 1995. Music tchr. North Hunterdon H.S., Annandale, NJ, 1996—99; choir dir. Old Bridge H.S., Matawan, NJ, 1999—. Profl. singer Opera Festival N.J., Princeton, NJ, 1996—2003. Youth group leader Martinsville (N.J.) United Meth. Ch., 2002. Mem.: MENC. Democrat-Npl. Avocations: Broadway shows, comic book collecting. Office: Old Bridge High Sch 4209 Rte 516 Matawan NJ 07747 Office Phone: 732-290-3947. Personal E-mail: s.updegraff@att.net.

**UPDIKE, HELEN HILL,** financial advisor; b. NYC, Mar. 27, 1941; d. Benjamin Harvey and Helene (Gray) Hill; m. Charles Bruce Updike, Sept. 7, 1963 (div. 1989); m. Asa Rountree, Oct. 10, 1998. BA, Hood Coll., 1962; PhD, SUNY, Stony Brook, 1978; postgrad., Harvard U., 1986. Lectr. SUNY, Stony Brook, 1969-75; asst. prof. U. Mass., Boston, 1975-77, Hofstra U., Hempstead, NY, 1978-85, assoc. prof., 1985-90, chmn. dept. econs. and geography, 1981-84, assoc. dean Hofstra Coll., 1984-87; pres. Interfid Capital Corp., 1987—2001; prin. Bridgewater Advisors, N.Y.C., 2001—. Cons. econ. policy, 1973—; vis. asst. prof. SUNY, Stony Brook, 1977—78; commentator WNYC Radio, 1997—; bd. dirs. Faberge, McCrory Corp. Author: (book) The National Banks and American Economic Development, 1870-1900, 1985. Trustee Madeira Sch., Greenway, Va., 1984—88, Literacy, Inc., 1998—2001; mem. nat. adv. bd. Outward Bound, 1986—92; trustee, v.p. L.I. Forum Tech., 1979—85; trustee NY Outward Bound, 1988—97. Mem.: AAAS. Office: Bridgewater Advisors 489 Fifth Ave New York NY 10017

**UPDIKE, JOHN HOYER,** writer; b. Shillington, Pa., Mar. 18, 1932; s. Wesley R. and Linda G. (Hoyer) U.; m. Mary E. Pennington, June 26, 1953 (div. 1976); children: Elizabeth, David, Michael, Miranda; m. Martha Bernhard, Sept. 30, 1977. AB, Harvard U., 1954; student, Ruskin Sch. Drawing and Fine Art, 1954-55. With New Yorker mag., N.Y.C., 1955-57. Author: (novels) The Poorhouse Fair, 1959 (Richard and Hinda Rosenthal Found. award Am. Acad. and Nat. Inst. Arts and Letters 1960), The Same Door, 1959, Rabbit, Run, 1960, Pigeon Feathers, 1962, The Centaur, 1963 (Nat. Book award for fiction 1963, Prix Medicis Etranger 1966), Olinger Stories, 1964, Of the Farm, 1965, The Music School, 1966, Couples, 1968, Bech: A Book, 1970, Rabbit Redux, 1971, Museums and Women, 1972, Warm Wine, 1973, A Month of Sundays, 1975, Marry Me, 1976, Couples, 1976, The Coup, 1978, From the Journal of a Leper, 1978, Problems, 1979, Too Far to Go: The Maples Stories, 1979 (Am. Book award nomination 1980), Three Illuminations in the Life of an American Author, 1979, Your Lover Just Called: Stories of Joan and Richard Maple, 1980, The Chaste Planet, 1980, Rabbit Is Rich, 1981 (Pulitzer prize for fiction 1982, Nat. Book Critics Circle award 1982, Am. Book award 1982), Invasion of the Book Envelopes, 1981, Bech Is Back, 1982, The Beloved, 1982, The Witches of Eastwick, 1984, Confessions of a Wild Bore, 1984, Roger's Version, 1986 (Nat. Book Critics Circle award nomination 1986), Trust Me, 1987, More Stately Mansions, 1987, S., 1988, Rabbit at Rest, 1990 (Pulitzer prize for fiction 1991, Nat. Book Critics Circle award 1991), Memories of the Ford Administration, 1992, Brazil, 1994, The Afterlife, 1994, In the Beauty of the Lilies, 1996, Toward the End of Time, 1997, Bech at Bay, 1998, Gertrude and Claudius, 2000, Licks of Love: Short Stories and a Sequel, Rabbit Remembered, 2000, The Complete Henry Bech, 2001, Seek My Face, 2002, The

Early Stories 1953-75, 2003 (PEN/Faulkner award 2004), Villages, 2004, Terrorist, 2006; (non-fiction) Assorted Prose, 1965, On Meeting Authors, 1968, A Good Place, 1973, Picked-Up Pieces, 1975, Hub Fans Bid Kid Adieu, 1977, Talk from the Fifties, 1979, Ego and Art in Walt Whitman, 1980, Hawthorne's Creed, 1981, Hugging the Shore, 1983 (Nat. Book Critics Circle award 1984), Emersonianism, 1984, Just Looking, 1989, Self-Consciousness, 1989, Odd Jobs, 1991, Golf Dreams, 1996, More Matter, 1999, On Literary Biography, 1999, Still Looking: Essays on American Art, 2005 (poetry) The Carpentered Hen and Other Tame Creatures, 1958, Telephone Poles, 1963, A Child's Calendar, 1965, The Angels, 1968, Bath after Sailing, 1968, Midpoint, 1969, Seventy Poems, 1972, Six Poems, 1973, Tossing and Turning, 1977, Sixteen Sonnets, 1979, Five Poems, 1980, Spring Trio, 1982, Jester's Dozen, 1984, Facing Nature, 1985, Collected Poems 1953-1993, 1993, A Helpful Alphabet of Friendly Objects, 1995, In the Cemetery High Above Shillington, 1996, Radiators, 1998, Americana, 2001, Not Cancelled Yet, 2003; adapter: (librettos) The Magic Flute, 1962, The Ring, 1964; (plays) Bottom's Dream, 1969, Three Texts from Early Ipswich, 1968, Buchanan Dying, 1974; author words and music: (with Gunther Schuller) The Fisherman and His Wife, 1970; editor: Pens and Needles, 1970, (with S. Ravenel) The Best American Short Stories 1984, 1984, A Century of Arts and Letters, 1998, (with K. Kenison) The Best Am. Short Stories of the Century, 1999, Karl Shapiro: Selected Poems, 2003. Recipient O. Henry First Short Story award, 1966, 91, MacDowell medal for literature, 1981, Medal of Honor for literature Nat. Arts Club, 1984, PEN/Malamud Meml. prize PEN/Faulker award Found., 1988, Nat. Medal of Arts, 1989, Harvard Arts medal, 1998, Nat. Book Found. award Lifetime Achievement, 1998, Nat. Humanities medal, 2003; Guggenheim fellow, 1959. Mem. AAAL, Am. Acad. Arts. and Scis. Democrat. Episcopalian.

**UPFAL, ELIEZER (ELI UPFAL),** computer scientist, educator; b. Haifa, Israel, July 29, 1954; s. Moshe and Miriam Upfal; m. Liane L. Live, Sept. 3, 1994; children: Tamara L., Ilan M.L. BSc in Math. and Stats., Hebrew U., Jerusalem, 1980; MSc in Computer Sci., Weizmann Inst. Sci., Rehovot, Israel, 1980; PhD, Hebrew U., Jerusalem, 1983. Rsch. staff mem. and project mgr. IBM Rsch. Divsn., San Jose, Calif., 1985—97; prof. computer sci. Brown U., Providence, 1998—, chair computer sci., 2002—. Author: Probability and Computing, 2005. Recipient Outstanding Innovation Award, IBM, 1993, Levinson Prize in Math. Scis., The Weizmann Inst., 1994, IBM Rsch. Divsn. award, IBM, 1997. Fellow: IEEE (hon.), Assn. for Computing Machinery (hon.). Achievements include patents in field. Office: Brown University Dept Computer Sci 115 Water St Providence RI 02906 Office Phone: 401-863-7600. Office Fax: 401-863-7657. Business E-Mail: eli@cs.brown.edu.

**UPGREN, ARTHUR REINHOLD, JR.,** astronomer, educator, writer; b. Mpls., Feb. 21, 1933; s. Arthur Reinhold and Marion (Andrews) U.; m. Joan Koswoski, Jan. 7, 1967; 1 child, Amy Joan. BA, U. Minn., 1955; MS, U. Mich., 1958; PhD, Case Western Res. U., 1961. Research assoc. Swarthmore Coll., Pa., 1961-63; astronomer U.S. Naval Obs., Washington, 1963-66; asst. prof. Wesleyan U., Middletown, Conn., 1966-73, assoc. prof., 1973-81, dir. Van Vleck Obs., 1973-93, John Monroe Van Vleck prof., 1981—, chmn. dept. astronomy, 1968-86, 90-93; v.p. Fund Astrophys. Research, N.Y.C., 1973—, chmn. grants com., 1985—2005. Vis. lectr. U. Md., 1964-66, George Washington U., 1965-66, Thames Sci. Ctr., New London, Conn., 1990, 92; vis. prof. Yale U., 1979-80, sr. rsch. scientist, 1997—; adj. prof. U. Fla., 1984-99; outdoor lighting cons. Wesleyan U., 1991—, Vt. State Agy. Natural Resources, 1993-94; reviewer books in astronomy, meteorology, classical music and urban demographics. Author: Night Has a Thousand Eyes: A Naked-Eye Guide to the Sky, its Science and Lore, 1998; co-author (with Jurgen Stock): Weather: How it Works and Why It Matters, 2000, The Turtle and The Stars: Observations of an Earthbound Astronomer, 2002, Many Skies: Alternative Histories of the Sun, Moon, Planets, and Stars, 2004; editor: The Nearby Stars and the Stellar Luminosity Function, 1983, Mapping the Sky-Past Heritage and Future Directions, 1988, Star Catalogues: A Centennial Tribute to A.N. Vyssotsky, 1989, Fundamentals of Astronomy, 1990, Precision Photometry: Astrophysics of the Galaxy, 1991, Objective Prism and Other Surveys, 1991, Databases for Galactic Structure, 1993, Hot Stars in the Halo, 1994, New Developments in Array Technology and Applications, 1995, Anni Mirables: A Symposium Celebrating the 90th Birthday of Dorrit Hoffleit, 1997. Conn. state chair New Eng. Light Pollution Adv. Group, 1994—. Grantee NSF, 1967-99; fellow Wesleyan Ctr. for Humanities, 1996. Fellow Royal Astron. Soc.; mem. Internat. Astron. Union (commn. v.p. 1982-85, pres. commnn. 24 1985-88), Am. Astron. Soc. (Harlow Shapley lectr. 1977—, vice-chmn. dynamical astronomy div. 1988-89, chmn. 1989-90, chmn. AAS com. on light pollution 2000-04), Astron. Soc. Pacific, Internat. Dark Sky Assn. (bd. dirs. 1997—). Business E-Mail: aupgren@wesleyan.edu

**UPHAM, FRANK K.,** law educator; b. 1945; AB, Princeton U., 1967; JD, Harvard U., 1974. Bar: Mass. 1974. Asst. atty. gen. Mass. Atty. Gen.'s Office, Boston, 1975—77; Japan Fedn. Fellow Doshisha U. Faculty Law, Kyoto, 1977—78; asst. prof. Ohio State U. Coll. Law, 1978—81; vis. prof. Harvard Law Sch., 1981—82, Boston Coll. Law Sch., 1982—83, assoc. prof. to prof., 1983—94; vis. prof. NYU Sch. Law, 1993, prof., 1994—, dir. Global Law Sch. Program, 1997—2002, now Wilf Family prof. property law. Author: Law and Social Change in Postwar Japan, 1987. Office: NYU Sch Law Vanderbilt Hall Rm 502 40 Washington Sq S New York NY 10012-1099 Office Phone: 212-998-6243. E-mail: frank.upham@nyu.edu.

**UPHAM, STEADMAN,** academic administrator, anthropologist, educator; b. Denver, Apr. 4, 1949; s. Albert Tyler and Jane Catherine (Steadman) U; m. Margaret Anne Cooper, Aug. 21, 1971; children: Erin Cooper, Nathan Steadman. BA in English Lit and Spanish, U. Redlands, Calif., 1971; MA in Anthropology, Ariz. State U., 1977, PhD in Anthropology, 1980. Dist. sales mgr. Ind. News Co. Inc., Los Angeles, 1971-72; regional sales mgr. Petersen Pub. Co, Los Angeles, 1972-74; archeologist, researcher Bur. Land Mgmt., Phoenix, 1979; research asst. Ariz. State U., Tempe, 1979-80; chief archeologist Soil Sytems Inc., Phoenix, 1980-81, N.Mex. State U., Las Cruces, N.Mex., 1981-85, asst. prof. to assoc. prof., 1982-87, assoc. dean, 1987-90; prof. anthropology, vice provost for rsch., grad. dean U. Oreg., Eugene, 1990—98; pres. Claremont Graduate Univ., Calif., 1998—2004; chancellor U. of Tulsa, Okla., 2004—. Interim dir. Cultural Resources Mgmt. divsn. N.Mex. State U., Las Cruces, 1988; mem. exec. com. Assn. Grad. Schs., 1994—2004; bd. dirs. Coun. Grad. Schs., 1995—2004. Author: Politics and Power, 1982, A Hopi Social History, 1992; editor: Computer Graphics in Archaeology, 1979, Mogollon Variability, 1986, The Sociopolitical Structure of Prehistoric Southwest Societies, 1989, The Evolution of Political Systems, 1990; also articles. Advanced seminar grantee Sch. of Am. Rsch., 1987, research grantee NSF, 1979, 1984-85, Hist. Preservation grantee State of N.Mex., 1982-84, 1991, 92, Ford Found. 1991-92, U.S. Dept. Edn. 1991-93. Fellow Am. Anthropol. Assn.; mem. Nat. Phys. Sci. Consortium (pres. 1992-95), We. Assn. Grad. Schs. (pres. 1994-95), Assn. Grad. Schs. (exec. com. 1995—), Coun. Grad. Schs. (bd. dirs. 1995—). Office: Off of Pres Univ of Tulsa 600 S College Ave Tulsa OK 74104 Office Phone: 918-631-2305. E-mail: steadman-upham@utulsa.edu.*

**UPMACIS, RITA KARINA,** chemist; d. Janis and Herta Paulina Upmacis; m. Gerard Parkin, July 30, 1993; children: Lia Aleksandra Parkin, Catherine Emma Parkin. BS in Chemistry, U. Nottingham, England, 1983, PhD in Inorganic Chemistry, 1986. Postdoctoral fellow Calif. Inst. Tech., 1986—88; sr. rsch. chemist Rohm and Haas Co., Spring House, Pa., 1988—94; rsch. assoc. biochemistry Weill Med. Coll. Cornell U., NYC, 1994—97, instr. biochemistry, 1997—99, asst. prof. pathology and lab. medicine, 1999—. Contbr. articles to profl. jours. Named Gertrude Cropper scholar, U. Nottingham, 1985; recipient Coop. award Sci. and Engring., ICI New Sci. Group, 1983—86, Sam Tallucci Quality award, Rohm and Haas Chem. Co., 1994; fellow, Weill Med. Coll. Cornell U., 1996—98, Calif. Inst. Tech., Pasadena, 1986—88; grantee Scientist Devel. award, Am. Heart Assn., 1997—2000, The Atorvastatin award, Parke-Davis and Pfizer, 1999—2001, External Rsch. Program award, Philip Morris USA Inc. and Philip Morris Internat., 2005—; Postdoctoral Fellowship award, Norman and Rosita Winston Found. Mem.:

Am. Soc. Investigative Pathology, North Am. Vascular Biology Orgn., Am. Chem. Soc., Royal Soc. Chemistry. Achievements include patents for processes for the preparation, purification and stabilization of acrylic acid. Office: Weill Medical College of Cornell Univ 1300 York Avenue New York NY 10021 Office Phone: 212-746-6469. Business E-Mail: rupmacis@med.cornell.edu.

**UPRETY, KRISHNA K.,** physicist, materials scientist; s. Chiranjibi and Ishwara Uprety; m. Susmita Mainaly; children: Kusal, Kritika. PhD, U. of Wollongong, NSW, Australia, 2003. Scientist, NSW. Rsch. assoc. U. of Wollongong, 2002—03; postdoctoral rsch. assoc. Argonne (Ill.) Nat. Lab. 2003—. Recipient JSPS postdoctoral fellowship, Japan, 2003, postdoctoral rsch. fellowship, Argonne Nat. Lab., 2003, Excellent Rsch. Merit award, U. of Wollongong, 2002, overseas postgrad. rsch. scholarship, 1999. Achievements include patents pending for use of SRO for the development of HTS YBCO coated conductor by ISD technique. Office: Argonne Nat Lab Bldg 212 G225 9700 S Cass Ave Argonne IL 60439 Office Phone: 630-252-3823. Office Fax: 630-252-3604. Business E-Mail: uprety@anl.gov.

**UPRIGHT, DIANE WARNER,** art dealer; b. Cleve. d. Rodney Upright and Shirley (Warner) Lavine. Student, Wellesley Coll., 1965-67; BA, U. Pitts., 1969; MA, U. Mich., 1973, PhD, 1976. Asst. prof. U. Va., Charlottesville, 1976-78; assoc. prof. Harvard U., Cambridge, Mass., 1978-83; sr. curator Ft. Worth Art Mus., 1984-86; dir. Jan Krugier Gallery, N.Y.C., 1986-90; sr. v.p., head contemporary art dept. Christie's, N.Y.C., 1990-95; pres. Diane Upright Fine Arts, N.Y.C., 1995—. Author: Morris Louis: The Complete Paintings, 1979, Ellsworth Kelly: Works on Paper, 1987, various exhbn. catalogues; contbr. articles to art jours. Mem.: Art Table, Inc. Office: Diane Upright Fine Arts 188 E 76th St New York NY 10021-2826

**UPSHAW, GENE (EUGENE UPSHAW),** sports association executive; b. Robstown, Tex., Aug. 15, 1945; s. Eugene and Cora (Riley) U.; 1 son, Eugene; m. Teresa Buich, 1986; children: Justin, Daniel. BS, Tex. A&I U., 1968; postgrad., Calif. State U., 1969, Golden Gate U., 1980. Player Oakland Raiders, 1967-82; player rep.-alt. NFL Players Assn., Oakland, Calif., 1970-76, mem. exec. com., 1976-80, pres., 1980-83, exec. dir., 1983—; ptnr. Gene Upshaw & Assocs., Mgmt. Cons. Firm, Oakland, Calif., 1970-78. Chmn. bd. NFL Players Inc., or Players Inc. Mem. Calif. Gov.'s Council Wellness and Phys. Fitness; mem. Calif. Bd. Govs. for Community Colls.; former planning commr. Alameda County, Calif., coordinator voter registration and fund raising. Served with U.S. Army, 1967-73. Named Offensive Lineman of Yr., Am. Football Conf., 1973, 74, 77, Lineman of Yr., NFL, 1977, Pro Bowl selection 6 times, All Pro selection Sporting News, 1967-77, All Pro selection UPI, 1967-77, All Pro selection AP, 1967-77, All Pro selection TV Guide, 1967-77, All Pro selection Profl. Football Writers, 1967-77; mem. NFL Championship Team, 1976, 1980; recipient Byron (Whizzer) White Humanitarian award NFL Players Assn., 1980, A. Philip Randolph A. Philip Randolph Inst., 1982; listed 13th in Top 100 Most Powerful People in Sports, Sporting News, 1993; Named one of Most Influential Black Americans, Ebony mag., 2006. Mem. Alpha Phi Alpha. Democrat. Baptist. Office: NFL Players Assn 2021 L St NW Fl 6 Washington DC 20036-4909*

**UPSHAW, HARRY STEPHAN,** psychologist, educator; b. Birmingham, Ala., July 10, 1926; s. N.H. and Florence (Arnold) U.; m. Paula Binyon, June 18, 1950; children: Alan Binyon, Phyllis, David Arnold, Stephan Lipner. Student, U. Ala., 1946-47; AB, U. Chgo., 1949; MA, Northwestern U., 1951; PhD, U. N.C., 1956. Asst prof. psychology U. Ala., 1954-57; spl. instr. psychology Simmons Coll., Boston, 1957-58; research asso. Edn1. Research Corp., Cambridge, Mass., 1957-58; asst. prof., then assoc. prof. pub. health U. N.C., 1958-61, lectr., assoc. prof. psychology, 1958-64, rsch. prof. psychology, 1991-97; assoc. prof. Bryn Mawr (Pa.) Coll., 1964-65; assoc. prof., then prof. emeritus psychology U. Ill., Chgo., 1965-91, prof. emeritus, 1991—, dept. head, 1968-72; assoc. dir. Office of Social Sci. Rsch., 1981-87. Guest prof. U. Mannheim, Germany, 1975, Fulbright scholar Technische U., Berlin, 1978-79; vis. scholar Inst. for Rsch. in social Sci., U. N.C., 1972; del. to South Africa, People to People Amb. Program, 2004. Editorial cons., Jour. Exptl. Social Psychology, Research in Personality, Jour. Applied Social Psychology, Jour. Personality Social Psychology; Contbr. articles to profl. jours. Served with AUS, 1944-46. Fellow Am. Psychol. Assn., Soc. Exptl. Social Psychol. Home: 155 N Harbor Dr Apt 1303 Chicago IL 60601-7397 Office Phone: 312-819-0408. Personal E-Mail: hupshaw@uic.edu.

**UPSHAW, JANE THOMAS,** mathematician, educator, academic administrator; b. Valley, Ala., Oct. 31, 1946; d. Roy Holton Burgess and Julia Wyla Branch; m. G. Thomas Upshaw, July 19, 1980; children: Elizabeth Anna, Mark Holton Thomas, Madison Thomas. BS, Auburn U., 1969, MS, 1971; PhD, U. S.C., 1993. Cons. So. Engring. Co. Ga., Atlanta, 1977—79; sr. applications engr. Sangamo Weston, Norcross, Ga., 1979—80; econ. analyst Ga. Power Co., Atlanta, 1980—81; sr. math. tchr. May River Acad., Bluffton, SC, 1981—86; math. prof. U. S.C. Beaufort, 1986—98, dean 1999—2002, chancellor, 2002—; v.p. of strategy Mid-Atlantic/Carolinas Region of AMA, Bluffton, SC, 1998—99. Exec. com. mem. Auburn Alumni Assn., 2003; chair Hilton Head Island (S.C.) Bluffton C. of C., 2002; mem. Hilton Head Health Svcs., 2003, Heart and Stroke Found., Hilton Head Island, 1998; pres. Literacy Vols. of the Lwocountry, Hilton Head Island, 1990—94. Named Hilton Head Rotary Master Tchr., Rotary Club, 1984. Mem.: Nat. Coun. Tchrs. Math. (editl. rev. com. 1995—96), Math. Assn. Am. (instl. liaison 1990—97), U.S.C. Alumni Assn. (life), Auburn Alumni Assn. (life; bd. dirs. 2003, exec. com. 2005, chair strategic planning com. 2005). Presbyterian. Avocations: reading, bridge, travel. Office: Univ SC Beaufort One University Blvd Bluffton SC 29909 Office Phone: 843-208-8242. Business E-Mail: jupshaw@uscb.edu.

**UPSON, DONALD V.,** retired corporate financial executive; b. Hutchinson, Kans., Feb. 8, 1934; s. William Ernest and Luella Beatrice (Hutchison) U.; m. Janis Carol Anderson, Sept. 16, 1956; children: Mark Steven, Brent William. BS, Kans. State U., 1956. C.P.A. With Peat, Marwick, Mitchell & Co., 1956, 60-81, ptnr., 1974-81; exec. v.p., dir. internal audit Del E. Webb Corp., Phoenix, 1981-85; mgr. info. systems Tiernay Turbines Inc., Phoenix, 1986; chief fin. officer Schomac Corp., Tucson, 1986-88; administr. U. Ariz., Tucson, 1988-90; pres., chief exec. officer Ariz. Commerce Bank, Tucson, 1990-91; chief fin. officer O'Connor, Cavanagh, Anderson, Westover, Killingsworth & Beshears, P.A., Phoenix, 1991-94; fin. cons., 1995-97; ret., 1997. Pres. Community Orgn. for Drug Abuse, Alcohol and Mental Health Services, Inc., 1977-78; bd. dis Phoenix council Boy Scouts Am., elder Presbyterian Ch. Served to lt. USAF, 1956-59. Mem. Am. Inst. C.P.A.s, Ariz. Soc. C.P.A.s, Beta Theta Pi (pres. 1955-56) Republican. Home: 1313 E Sheena Dr Phoenix AZ 85022-4485 Personal E-Mail: DVUPSON@aol.com.

**UPSON, STUART BARNARD,** advertising agency executive; b. Cin., Apr. 14, 1925; s. Mark and Alice (Barnard) U.; m. Barbara Jensen, Nov. 2, 1946; children: Marguerite Nichols, Anne Marcus, Stuart Barnard. BS, Yale U., 1945. With Dancer, Fitzgerald, Sample, Inc., N.Y.C., 1946-86, sr. v.p., 1963-66, exec. v.p., 1966-67, pres., 1967-74, chmn., 1974-86, DFS-Dorland, N.Y.C., 1986-87; dir. Saatchi & Saatchi Inc., N.Y.C., 1987—. Bd. dirs. Fresh Air Fund, N.Y., 1943-46. Mem. St. Elmo Soc. Clubs: Wee Burn Country (Darien); Sky (N.Y.C.); Blind Brook, Pine Valley Golf, Ocean Forest Golf. Home: 16 Wrenfield Ln Darien CT 06820-2201 Office: Saatchi & Saatchi Inc 375 Hudson St New York NY 10014-3658

**UPSON, THOMAS FISHER,** judge, retired state senator, lawyer; b. Waterbury, Conn., Sept. 30, 1941; s. J. Warren and Grace (Fisher) U.; m. Barbara Secor (div. Jan. 1979); children: Secor, Chauncey Julius; m. Katherine Wolff, June 1, 1996. BA in History, Washington and Jefferson Coll., 1963; LLB, U. Conn., 1968; postgrad., Trinity Coll., 1969—72, Georgetown U., 1971—72. Bar: Conn. 1969, U.S. Dist. Ct. (2d dist.) 1969, U.S. Supreme Ct. 1973. Lawyer Upson & Secor, Waterbury, 1969—70, 1974—76; lawyer, spl. asst. U.S. Dept. Commerce, Washington, 1970—72; lawyer, spl. asst. to

adminstr. GSA, Washington, 1973—74; dir. admissions St. Margaret's McTernan Sch., Waterbury, 1977—78; with divsn. spl. revenue State of Conn., Hartford, 1978—82; assoc. Moynahan & Ruskin, Waterbury, 1979—81; ptnr. Upson & Daly, Waterbury, 1981—2001; mem. Conn. Senate, Hartford, 1985—2001, chmn. gen. law com., vice-chmn. jud. com., majority whip, 1985—86, asst. minority leader, 1987-88, 89-90, minority leader protempore, 1991-92, dep. minority leader, 1993-94, dep. majority leader, chmn. jud. com., 1995-96, dep., then asst. minority leader, ranking mem. jud. com., 1997-2000; judge Superior Ct. State of Conn., Hartford, 2001—. Moderator 1st Congl. Ch., Waterbury, 1986-91; bd. dirs. Easter Seals-United Way, Waterbury, 1984-88; Rep. candidate for Congress, 6th Dist. Conn., 1976; mem. Conn. Rep. Ctrl. com., 1983-91; mem. Waterbury Rep. Town Com., 1980-85; dir. Mattatuck Mus., 1993-2003; former dir. Waterbury Symphony Orch.; former sec. and dir. First Ch. Housing, Inc.; pres. Naugatuck Valley Devel. Corp., 1975-76. Mem. ABA, Conn. Bar Assn., Waterbury Bar Assn., SAR, Soc. Colonial Wars, Soc. of the Founders of the Hartford, Phi Gamma Delta, Univ. Club (Waterbury). Lodges: Kiwanis (former pres., lt. gov. SW New Eng. dist.), Elks. Republican. Congregationalist. Avocations: hiking, music, history. Home: 210 Southwest Rd Waterbury CT 06708-3214 Office: Waterbury Jud Dist 400 Grand St Waterbury CT 06702

**UPTIGROVE, KENNETH R.,** library administrator; b. Flint, Mich., Oct. 6, 1943; s. Kenneth R. and Ilah L. (Horton) U.; m. Suzanne C. Glass, Apr. 6, 1968; children: Chad K., Kathy S. BA, U. Mich., 1967, MLS, 1969. Br. rsch. libr. Genesee County Libr., Flint, 1963-69; sch. libr. Kearsley Community Schs., Flint, 1969-70; dir. Owosso (Mich.) Pub. Libr., 1970—94, Shiawassee Dist. Libr., Owosso, 1994—. Contbr. articles to mags. Mcm. ALA, Mich. Library Assn. (Pub. library div. sec.-treas. 1981-82, chmn. coop. caucus 1986-87, mgmt. and adminstrn. caucus, sec.-treas. 1988-89), Flint Area Library Assn. (pres. 1970), Ruffed Grouse Soc. (pres. Lansing chpt. 1979-81, treas. Mich. coun. 1983-89, pres. 1989—), Owosso Circulators (pres. 1987-88), Kiwanis (Chmn. coms. 1980—, pres. 1999-2000, sec. 2001-02). Congregationalist. Office: Shiawassee Dist Libr 502 W Main St Owosso MI 48867-2687

**UPTON, ARTHUR CANFIELD,** experimental pathologist, educator; b. Ann Arbor, Mich., Feb. 27, 1923; s. Herbert Hawkes and Ellen (Canfield) Upton; m. Elizabeth Bache Perry, Mar. 1, 1946; children: Rebecca A., Melissa P., Bradley C. Grad., Phillips Acad., Andover, Mass., 1941; BA, U. Mich., 1944, MD, 1946. Intern Univ. Hosp., Ann Arbor, 1947, resident, 1948—49; instr. pathology U. Mich. Med. Sch., 1950—51; pathologist Oak Ridge (Tenn.) Nat. Lab., 1951—54, chief pathology-physiology sect., 1954—69; prof. pathology SUNY Med. Sch. at Stony Brook, 1969—77, chmn. dept. pathology, 1969—70, dean Sch. Basic Health Scis., 1970—75; dir. Nat. Cancer Inst., Bethesda, Md., 1977—79; prof., chmn. dept. environ. medicine NYU Med. Sch., N.Y.C., 1980—92, prof. emeritus, 1993—; clin. prof. radiology U. N.Mex. Sch. Medicine, 1993—95, clin. prof. pathology, 1992—95; clin. prof. environ. and cmty. medicine U. Medicine and Dentistry N.J.-Robert Wood Johnson Med. Sch., 1995—. Attending pathologist Brookhaven Nat. Lab., 1969—77; dir. Inst. Environ. Medicine, Med. Sch., NYU, 1980—92; mem. various coms. nat. and internat. orgns.; lectr. in field; mem. adv. bd. GM Cancer Rsch. Found. Assoc. editor Cancer Rsch., mem. editl. bd. Internat. Union Against Cancer. With U.S. Army, 1943—46. Named nat. lectr., Sigma Xi, 1989—91; recipient Ernest Orlando Lawrence award for atomic field, 1965, Claude M. Fuess award, 1980, Sarah L. Poilley award for pub. health, 1983, CHUMS Physician of Yr. award, 1985, Basic Cell Rsch. in Cytology Lectureship award, 1985, Fred W. Stewart award, 1986, Ramazzini award, 1986, Lovelace Med. Found. award, 1993. Fellow: N.Y. Acad. Sci., Soc. Risk Analysis (Outstanding Achievement award 1997); mem.: AAAS, Ramazzini Inst. (pres. 1992—2003), Assn. Univ. Environ. Health Sci. Ctrs. (pres. 1982—90), Internat. Assn. Radiation Rsch., N.Y. State Health Rsch. Coun. (chmn. 1982—90), Soc. Exptl. Biology and Medicine, Sci. Rsch. Soc. Am., Gerontol. Soc., Peruvian Oncology Soc. (hon.), Japan Cancer Assn. (hon.), Am. Soc. Exptl. Pathology (pres. 1967—68), Am. Assn. Cancer Rsch. (pres. 1963—64), Internat. Assn. Radiation Rsch. (pres. 1983—87, 1983—87), Radiation Rsch. Soc. (councilor 1963—64, pres. 1965—66), Inst. Medicine of NAS (Comfort-Crookshank award for cancer rsch. 1979), Internat. Acad. Pathology, Am. Assn. Pathologists and Bacteriologists, Sigma Xi, Nu Sigma Nu, Alpha Omega Alpha, Phi Gamma Delta, Phi Beta Kappa. Achievements include research in pathology of radiation injury and endocrine glands, on cancer, on carcinogenesis, on experimental leukemia on aging. Office: Robert Wood Johnson Med Sch Rm N-112 675 Hoe's Ln Piscataway NJ 08854 Home (Winter): 250 E Alameda Apt 636 Santa Fe NM 87501 Home (Summer): 780 West End Ave Apt 20 New York NY 10025 Office Phone: 732-235-3460. Business E-Mail: acupton@cresp.org.

**UPTON, BARBARA M.,** music director; b. James David and Peggy Marie Lawler; m. Wayne S. Upton, June 10, 1972; children: Zachary Michael, Elizabeth Lawler, Zebediah George. BS, Regis U., 1972. Area coord. leaders La Leche League Colo., Aurora, 1983—85; assoc. dir. music leader applicants La Leche League Internat., Schaumburg, Ill., 1984—86; dir. music St. Stephen Ch., Trumbull, Conn., 1985—; exec. dir. Greater Bridgeport Youth Orchs., Fairfield, Conn., 1999—, Fanfare Concerts, Ltd. Inc., Monroe, Conn., 2000—. Dir. musician (musicals) Guys and Dolls, The Fantastiks. Ex-officio Greater Bridgeport Youth Orchs., Fairfield, 1992—2005. Mem.: Chamber Music Am., Nat. Pastoral Musicians. Avocations: gourmet cooking, reading, volunteer work. Office: Greater Bridgport Youth Orchs PO Box 645 Fairfield CT 06824-0645 Personal E-Mail: bupton2@aol.com.

**UPTON, FREDERICK STEPHEN,** congressman; b. St. Joseph, Mich., Apr. 23, 1953; s. Stephen E. and Elizabeth Brooks (Vial) U.; m. Amey Richmond Rulon-Miller, Nov. 5, 1983; 2 children BA in Journalism, U. Mich., 1975. Staff asst. to Congressman David A. Stockman, Washington, 1976-81; legis. asst. Office Mgmt. and Budget, Washington, 1981-83, dep. dir. legis. affairs, 1983-84, dir. legis. affairs, 1984-85; mem. US Congress from 6th Mich. dist., Washington, 1987—; mem. energy and commerce com. Field mgr. Stockman for Congress, St. Joseph, 1975; campaign mgr. Globensky for Congress, St. Joseph, 1981. Recipient Spirit Enterprise award, US C. of C., 1988—93, Legis. of Yr., Am. Ambulance Assn., 2000. Mem.: Emil Verban Soc. Republican. Congregationalist. Office: US House of Reps 2183 Rayburn House Office Bldg Washington DC 20515-2206 also: District Office 157 S Kalamazoo Mall Ste 180 Kalamazoo MI 49006 also: District Office Ste 106 800 Ship Street Saint Joseph MI 49085-2182 Office Phone: 202-225-3761, 269-385-0039, 269-982-1986. Office Fax: 269-982-0237, 202-225-4986.*

**UPTON, HOWARD B., JR.,** writer, lawyer; b. Tahlequah, Okla., May 17, 1922; s. Howard B. and Marjorie (Ross) U.; m. Jean Devereaux, June 14, 1945; children—Pamela, Barbara, Martha, Brian BA, U. Okla., 1943, LLB, 1948. Cert. assn. exec. Dir. indsl. relations Western Petroleum Refiners Assn., Tulsa, 1948-51; exec. v.p. Petroleum Equipment Inst., Tulsa, 1951-87; dir. Telex Corp., Tulsa, 1972-88; mgmt. columnist Inflight Mag. of Southwest Airlines, 1988-93. Lectr. dept. engring. devel. U. Wis., 1988-97, U. Alaska, Fairbanks, 1991-93. Frequent contbr. to Wall St. Jour.; columnist Petroleum Equipment and Tech. Mag.; book rev. Tulsa World, 1999—. Dir. Tulsa Zoo Friends, Inc., 1993-97. Mem. Am. Soc. Assn. Execs. (bd. dirs. 1964-68, Gold Circle award 1977, 82), Okla. Bar Assn. Democrat. Home: 5133 E 25th Ct Tulsa OK 74114-3749

**UPTON, MIKE E.,** producer, director; b. Syracuse, N.Y., Dec. 7, 1965; m. Kelly Kingston. BS, U. Tex., 1988. Head, studio ops. Concorde/New Horizons, Venice, Calif., 1992-96; independant prodr. The Source, L.A., 1996—. Prodr.: (films) Where Evil Lies, 1995, Caged Heat 3000, 1995, Hot Ticket, 1996, Alien Terminator, 1996, The Coroner, 1999, Madea's Family Reunion, 2006; line prodr.: (films) Attraction, 2000, Undiscovered, 2005, (TV films) Casper: A Spirited Beginning, 1997, The Cowboy and the Movie Star, 1998, Men in White, 1998, Casper Meets Wendy, 1998, Dangerous Waters, 1999, Au Pair, 1999, Au Pair II, 2001; co-prodr.: (films) Not Like Us, 1995, The Crazysitter, 1995, (TV films) The Wasp Woman, 1995, Sawbones, 1995; actor, dir.; editor: (films) Raven's Ridge, 1997.*

**UPTON, RICHARD THOMAS,** artist; b. Hartford, Conn., May 27, 1931; s. Ray Granville and Helen Marie (Colla) U.; 1 son, Richard Thomas, II. BFA, U. Conn., 1960; MFA; Ind. U., 1963. Artist-in-residence Artists for the Environ., Del. Water Gap, 1972, UGA Program Abroad, Cortona, Italy, 1982-85. Numerous exhibns. including most recently, exhibitions include Condeso/Lawler Gallery, N.Y.C., 1995, Nat. Acad. of Design, 1996, The Language of Landscape, 1997, Sordoni Art Gallery, 1997, The Drawings of Richard Upton: Ireland & Italy, List Art Gallery, Swarthmore, Ben Shahn Art Galleries, 1998, Landscape and Memory: The Paintings and Drawings of Richard Upton, 1982-1999, Houghton Gallery, The Cooper Union for the Advancement of Sci. and Art, N.Y.C., 1999, Represented in permanent collections Zimmerli Art Mus., Nat. Mus. of Am. Art, Smithsonian Instn., Mus. Modern Art, N.Y.C., Victoria and Albert Mus., London, Bibliot Nat., Paris, Montreal Mus. Fine Arts, Rose Art Mus. Brandeis, Mus. Fine Art, Houston, Nat. Acad. Design, N.Y.C., Met. Mus. Art, The Tang Tchg. Mus. and Art Gallery, Skidmore Coll.; artist (commns. include) Eros Thanatos Suite (German poem and woodcuts), Interlaken Corp., Providence, 1967, Salamovka Poster, Okla. Art Ctr., 1974, artist (with poems by Stanley Kunitz) River Road Suite, 1976, suite of drawing Robert Lowell at 66, 1977, suite of drawings Salmagundi mag. for humanities, The Anxious Landscape, paintings, drawings Bellarmine Coll., Louisville, 1989. With USNR, 1950-54. Recipient designer award Interlaken Gallery, 1967; subject of monographs: Richard Upton and the Rhetoric of Landscape, Paul Hayes Tucker, U. Mass., U. Wash. Press, 1991, The Tuscan Landscapes of Richard Upton, Stanley C. Grand, Sordoni Art Gallery & Fred Licht, curator, Collezione Peggy Guggenheim, Venice, Wilkes U., 1997, The Drawings of Richard Upton, David Shapiro, Salmagundi, Skidmore Coll., 1997, Landscape & Memory: The Paintings & Drawings of Richard Upton, 1982-98, The Irwin S. Chanin Sch. Architecture of Cooper Union, 1999, A Table of Green Fields: Richard Upton's Cortona Landscapes, Richard Howard, 1999, List Gallery, Ben Shahn Galleries About Painting; Tang Teaching Mus. Art Gallery, 2004; fellow Fulbright Found., 1964, Ballinglen Arts Found., Ireland, 1994; grantee Nat. Endowment for Arts/Artists for Environ., 1972, Richard Florsheim Fund, 1992; elected to Nat. Acad. of Design, 1995, Tang Teaching Mus. and Art Gallery, 2004. Home: 1 North Ln Saratoga Springs NY 12866-4369

**UPTON, WADE,** energy executive; Mem. staff to sr. v.p. transp. svcs. Valero Energy Corpn., San Antonio, 1984—. State fuel coord., Tex. Bd. dirs. Waterways Coun., Inc. Office: Valero Energy Corpn 1 Valero Way San Antonio TX 78292-0500 Office Phone: 210-345-2555. E-mail: wade.upton@valero.com.*

**URABE, TOHSUKE,** mathematics professor, researcher; b. Tokyo, Aug. 3, 1953; s. Syun-ichi and Mariko (Namikawa) U.; m. Yasuko Ichikawa, May 25, 1986; 1 child, Mika. BA, Kyoto (Japan) U., 1978, MA, 1980, PhD in Math. 1984. Sci. worker Max-Planck Inst. for Math., Bonn, Germany, 1987-89, 98-99; assoc. prof. math. Tokyo Met. U., 1981-87, 89-98; prof. math. Ibaraki (Japan) U., 1999—. Author: (with Heisuke Hironaka) Introduction to Analytic Spaces, 1981; Dynkin Graphs and Quadrilateral Singularities, 1993. Avocations: mountain climbing, personal computers. Office: Ibaraki U Dept Math Scis Mito Ibaraki 310-8512 Japan

**URAM, GERALD ROBERT,** lawyer; b. Newark, July 11, 1941; s. Arthur George and Mildred (Stein) U.; m. Melissa Gordon, May 27, 1995; children: Michael, Alison, Carolyn Gordon Lewis. BA, Dartmouth Coll., 1963; LLB, Yale U., 1967. Bar: NY 1967. Assoc. Paul, Weiss, Rifkind, Wharton & Garrison, NYC, 1967-74; v.p., corp. counsel Prudential Bldg. Maintenance Corp., NYC, 1974; ptnr. Davis & Gilbert, NYC, 1974—. Lectr. NY Law Sch. Contbr. to profl. publs. Bd. dirs. Francis Friends of Poor, Inc. Mem. ABA, NY State Bar Assn., Assn. Bar City of NY. Office: 1740 Broadway Fl 3 New York NY 10019-4315 Office Phone: 212-468-4815. Business E-Mail: guram@dglaw.com.

**URANGA, JEAN R.,** lawyer; b. West Point, N.Y., Sept. 30, 1949; BA, Western Wash. U., 1971; JD, Willamette U., 1975. Bar: Idaho 1975, U.S. Dist. Ct. Idaho 1975, U.S. Ct. Appeals (9th cir.) 1980. Atty. Uranga & Uranga, Boise, Idaho. Mem.: Idaho State Bar (discipline hearing com. 1983—86, continuing legal edn. com. 1987—90, Supreme Ct. com. on child custody mediation 1989—, bar commr. 1990—93, pres. 1992, bankruptcy and family law sects., pres. 1993). Office: Uranga and Uranga PO Box 1678 714 N Fifth St Boise ID 83701-1678

**URBACH, ADAM ROBERT,** chemistry professor; s. Michael Urbach and Rose Marie Mauzy; m. Dana Michelle Norwood, June 11, 2000. BS in Chemistry, U. Tex., Austin, 1996; PhD in Chemistry, Calif. Inst. Tech., Pasadena, 2002. Postdoctoral rsch. fellow Harvard U., Cambridge, Mass., 2002—04; asst. prof. of chemistry Trinity U., San Antonio, Tex., 2004—. Faculty adviser Am. Chem. Soc. Student Affiliates, Trinity U., San Antonio, 2004—. Contbr. articles to sci. jours. Judge Jr. Acad. of Sci., San Antonio, 2006. Recipient Cottrell Coll. Sci. award, Rsch. Corp., 2006—08, Type G grant, Am. Chem. Soc. Petroleum Rsch. Fund, 2005—07, Nat. Rsch. Svc. award, NIH, 2003—04, NSF grad. fellowship, 1996—99, Dean's Honored Grad. award, Coll. of Natural Sci., U. Tex., Austin, 1996, Summer Undergrad. Fellowship in Synthetic Organic Chemistry, Pfizer Inc., 1995. Mem.: Project Kaleidoscope, Coun. on Undergrad. Rsch., Am. Chem. Soc. (Outstanding Sr. award cen. Tex. divsn. 1996, student affiliate scholarship 1995), Phi Beta Kappa. Achievements include research in artificial receptors and sensors for proteins. Office: Trinity Univ Dept Chemistry One Trinity Pl San Antonio TX 78212 Office Phone: 210-999-7660. Business E-Mail: aurbach@trinity.edu.

**URBACH, DAVID ROBERT,** surgeon, educator; b. Toronto, Ont., Can., June 2, 1968; MD, U. of Toronto, Can., 1993. Lic. gen. surgery Ont. Assoc. prof. dept. medicine U. of Toronto, Toronto, 2005—. Achievements include research in Surgical Health Services Research. Office: Toronto Gen Hosp 200 Elizabeth St Ontario Toronto Canada M5G 2C4 Office Phone: (416) 340 4284. Office Fax: (416) 340 4211.

**URBAN, AMANDA (BINKY URBAN),** literary agent; m. Ken Auletta, 1977; 1 child. BA in English, Wheaton Coll., Mass. Gen. mgr. N.Y. mag.; editl. mgr. Esquire mag.; literary agent Internat. Creative Mgmt., N.Y.C., v.p., co-dir. lit. dept., 1988—98, co-head, 1999—. Office: Internat Creative Mgmt 40 W 57th St New York NY 10019 E-mail: aurban@icmtalent.com.*

**URBAN, DIANE,** psychologist, educator; b. Queens, N.Y., June 27, 1954; d. Jerome and Carmela Chiappise; m. Walter Urban, Dec. 29, 1979; children: Nicholas, Amanda. BA, Queens Coll., 1976; MA, St. John's U., Queens, N.Y., 1979; PhD, New Sch. U., N.Y.C. Lic. psychologist N.Y. Asst. prof. Westchester C.C., Valhalla, NY, 1980—; instr. Manhattan Coll., Riverdale, NY, 2004—. Active Westchester Emergency Vol. Res., Med. Res. Corps. Mem.: APA. Home: 106 Eastview Dr Valhalla NY 10595

**URBAN, HENRY ZELLER,** publishing executive; b. Buffalo, July 11, 1920; s. George Pennock and Florence Lenhard (Zeller) U.; m. Ruth deMoss Wickwire, Apr. 28, 1948; children: Ruth Robinson Urban Smith, Florence de Moss Urban Hunn, Henry Zeller, Ward Wickwire. Grad., Hotchkiss Sch., 1939; BS, Yale U., 1943. Treas. George Urban Milling Co., 1946-53; with Buffalo Eve. News, 1953—asst. mng. 1957-62, bus. mgr., 1962-71, treas., dir., 1971-74, pres., pub. 1974-83. Dir. Travelers Aid Soc. 1953-59, Buffalo Fine Arts Acad., 1960-63, 73-76, 82-89, YMCA, 1955-58, trustee Elmwood-Franklin Sch., 1967-70; trustee Canisius Coll., 1977-83, bd. regents, 1972-78; adv. bd. Medaille Coll., 1968-83; chmn. parents council Hamilton Coll., 1977. Lt. USNR, 1942-46. Mem. Buffalo C. of C., N.Y. State Pubs. Assn. (dir. 1970-73, 76-79) Clubs: Mid-day (Buffalo), Tennis and Squash (Buffalo), Buffalo (Buffalo), Buffalo Country (Buffalo), Saturn (Buffalo), Pack (Buffalo); Sankaty Head (Nantucket); Nantucket Yacht. Home: 57 Tudor Pl Buffalo NY 14222-1615 Office: 1 News Plz Buffalo NY 14203-2930

**URBAN, JOSEPH JAROSLAV,** engineer, consultant; b. Chocen, Czechoslovakia, Mar. 11, 1922; came to U.S., 1955; s. Josef and Ludmila (Moravcova) U.; children: H.U. Heinicke, R. Bruce. Diploma in engring., U. Prague, Czechoslovakia, 1948; postgrad., U. Toronto, 1952-55. Registered profl. engr. Mgr. Urban Mfg., Chocen, 1942-48; prof. Masaryk U., Nuernberg, Fed. Republic Germany, 1950; designer C.A. Meadows Cons. Engrs., Toronto, 1952-55, Rondo Devel. Corp., Stamford, Conn., 1955-58; designer, chief engr., v.p. Huck Co. Inc. Engrs., Montvale, NJ, 1958-72, also bd. dirs.; pvt. practive cons. engr. Pleasantville, NY, 1972—. Exec. cons. Crown Cork and Seal Co. Inc., Phila., 1972=94. Designer various types of machines for U.S. govt. and U.S. industries-printing presses, book binding and can mfg. equipment, pinsetter, computers, glass machines; writer tech. books; patentee in field. Recipient World War II decoration Field Marshall Alexander, 1945. Outstanding Person 20th Century Internat. Biographical Ctr., Eng, named one of top 100 scientists, 2005. Mem. Acad. Art and Sci., Moose, K.C. (worthy sir knight). Roman Catholic. Avocations: naturalist, painting, classical music, fine art collector. Home and Office: 71 Bacon Hill Rd Pleasantville NY 10570-3501

**URBAN, KEITH,** country singer, songwriter; b. New Zealand, Oct. 26, 1967; m. Nicole Kidman, June 25, 2006. Former band mem. (with Peter Clarke) The Ranch, Nashville, 1997; signed record deal with Capital Nashville, 1997; signed mgmt. contract with I.R.S., Tenn., 1997. Singer: (albums) Keith Urban "1991", 1997, Ranch, 1997, Keith Urban, 1999, Golden Road, 2002, In the Ranch, 2004, Be Here, 2004 (Album of Yr., Acad. Country Music Awards, 2005), Days Go By, 2005, (singles) Raining on Sunday, 2003; singer, prodr.: singles "Somebody Like You", How To Lose A Guy In 10 Days (Original Soundtrack), 2003; singer: (songs) Days Go By (Video of Yr., Country Music Television Music award, 2005), You'll Think of Me (Grammy award, Best Male Country Vocal Performance, 2006). Named Top New Male Vocalist, Acad. Country Music, 2001, 2005, Top Male Vocalist, 2006, Male Vocalist of Yr., Country Music Assn., 2004, 2005, Entertainer of Yr., 2005, Country Artist Yr., Radio Music Awards, 2005; recipient Grammy award nomination for best country instrumental performance for "Rollercoaster", ARIA award for outstanding achievement, Australian Record Industry Assn., 2001, Horizon award, Country Music Assn., 2001, Video of Yr for Better Life, CMT award (Country Music TV), 2006. Mailing: Capital Records 3322 W End Ave Nashville TN 37203 Office Phone: 615-269-2000.*

**URBANC, BRIGITA,** physicist, researcher; d. Jozef Urbanc and Mihaela Sustersic; m. Luis Rafael Cruz, Apr. 17, 1999; children: Marguerita Malina Cruz-Urbanc, Francisco Julian Cruz-Urbanc. PhD, U. Ljubljana, 1993. Rsch. assoc. Jozef Stefan Inst., Ljubljana, Slovenia, 1994—99; vis. scientist Boston U., 1994—96, rsch. scientist, 1999—. Fellow Adler Found. Fellowship, 1997—2000; grantee R21 rsch. grant, NIH, 2005—, NIA-R03 rsch. grant, Nat. Inst. of Aging, 2004—. Achievements include research in Predictions of Amyloid Beta Oligomer Structure. Office: Boston Univ 590 Commonwealth Ave Boston MA 02215 Office Phone: 617-353-3411. Business E-Mail: brigita@bu.edu.

**URBANETTI, JOHN SUTHERLAND,** internist, consultant; b. Mineola, N.Y., Aug. 14, 1943; s. Anthony Joseph and Mildred S. U.; children: Andrew, Alexis. AB, Johns Hopkins U., 1964, MD, 1967. Diplomate Am. Bd. Internal Medicine and Pulmonary Diseases. Internal medicine intern Johns Hopkins Hosp., Balt., 1967-68, internal medicine resident, 1968-69; fellow in pulmonary cardiology McGill U., Montreal, Can., 1971-74; asst. prof. medicine and dir. pulmonary lab. Tufts New Eng. Med. Ctr. Hosp., Boston, 1974-80; asst. prof. clin. medicine and pulmonary diseases Yale U., New Haven, Conn., 1980—. Cons. toxic inhalation US Surgeon Gen., U.S. Army, USN, USAF, 1974—; cons. biochem. terrorism Dept. of Def., Dept. Justice, 1974—, Dept. State, 1999—. Author: Carbon Monoxide Poisoning, 1980, Pulmonary Management of Surgical Patients, 1982, Battlefield Chemical Inhalation, 1988, Chemical and Biological Warfare, 1997; contbr. articles to profl. jours. Capt. USAF, 1969-71. Recipient Commdr's award for pub. svc. U.S. Army, 1990. Fellow Royal Coll. Physicians and Surgeons (Can.), Am. Coll. Physicians, Am. Coll. Chest Physicians; mem. Am. Thoracic Soc., Aerospace Medicine Soc. Avocation: swimming. Office: Southeastern Pulmonary Assocs 155 Montauk Ave New London CT 06320-4842 Office Phone: 860-444-2223. Business E-Mail: jsu@jhu.edu.

**URBANIK, THOMAS, II,** civil engineering educator, researcher; b. Oceanside, N.Y., Feb. 15, 1946; s. John George and Helen Rita (Waterhouse) U.; m. Cynthia Ellen Myers, Feb. 23, 1948; children: Michael T., Steven J. BS, N.Y. State Coll. Forestry, 1968; BSCE, Syracuse U., 1969; MSCE, Purdue U., 1971; PhD, Tex. A&M U., 1982. Registered profl. engr., Mich., Tex., Tenn. Traffic engr. City of Ann Arbor (Mich.), 1971-76; rsch. engr. Tex. A&M U., College Station, 1977—2001; prof., Goodrich chair of excellence in transp. U. Tenn., Knoxville, 2001—. Cons. Battelle Pacific N.W. Labs., Richland, Wash., Fed. Hwy. Adminstrn., Washington, Kittelson and Assocs., Portland, Oreg., Entergy, Buchanan, NY. Mem. ASCE, Inst. Transp. Engrs., Transp. Rsch. Bd. (assoc.). Republican. Lutheran. Office Phone: 865-974-7709. Business E-Mail: turbanik@utk.edu.

**URBANO, JUAN ANTONIO,** broadcast executive, television producer, television director; b. Havana, Cuba, Jan. 5, 1968; s. Antonio and Nereyda (Perez) Urbano; m. Veronica Delgado; children: Christian Michael children: John Anthony. AS in Film Prodn., Miami Dade C.C. Creative svcs. editor WSVN Channel 7, Miami Beach, Fla., 1988—94; prodr. editor Visionline, Inc., Miami, Fla., 1994—2005; sr. prodr., sr. editor MGM Networks L.Am. LLC, Miami, Fla., 1999—, promotions mgr., 2002—03, promotions and opers. mgr., 2003—04; prodr., editor MTV Networks Latin Am., 2004—. Recipient Suncoast Regional Emmy, NATAS, 1997, 1998. Mem.: Nat. Acad. of Arts and Scis. Roman Catholic. Avocations: scuba diving, camping, travel. Office Phone: 308-934-2740. Personal E-mail: urbanob@bellsouth.net. E-mail: juanurbano@bellsouth.net.

**URBANOWICZ, E. PETER (EUGENE PETER URBANOWICZ JR.),** lawyer; b. NYC, Jan. 26, 1964; BA in Eng. and polit. sci., Tulane U., 1985, JD, 1989. Bar: La. 1989, US Dist. Ct. Ea., Mid., We. Dists. of La. 1989, US Supreme Ct. 2003. Ptnr. Monroe & Lemann, New Orleans, 1987—98, Liskow & Lewis, New Orleans, 1998—2000, Locke Liddell & Sapp, New Orleans, 2000—01; dep. gen. counsel USHHS, 2001—03; gen. counsel Tenet Healthcare Corp., Dallas, 2003—. Mem. ABA, Am. Law Inst., La. Bar Assn., Am. Health Lawyers Assn., Supreme Ct. Hist. Soc., Delta Tau Delta, Omicron Delta Kappa. Republican. Episcopalian. Office: Tenet Healthcare 13737 Noel Rd Ste 100 Dallas TX 75240

**URBANOWSKI, JOHN RICHARD,** lighting systems company official; b. Jamaica, N.Y., May 31, 1947; s. John Casimir and Alfreda (Dabrowski) U.; m. Linda Holmes, Dec. 17, 1967 (div. June 1973); 1 child, Richard. BA, U. South Fla., 1968. Cert. lighting profl. Nat. Coun. Qualifications for Lighting Professions. Ptnr. Freeman Assocs., Ft. Lauderdale, Fla., 1972-76; sales engr. Holophane Lighting Co., Portland, Oreg., 1977—. Author computer program Microlux, 1984. With USN, 1969-72. Mem. Illuminating Engring. Soc. (bd. dirs. 1981-86, 96-98, pres. 1983-84, Cert. Tech. Knowledge 1996, lighting cert. 1998), Holophane Lighting Co. Dir.'s Club, Founder's Club, Quarter Century Club. Unitarian Universalist. Avocations: writing, aviation. Office: Holophane Lighting Co 3015 NE Couch St Portland OR 97232 E-mail: jurbanowski@comcast.net.

**URBANOWSKI, MELENA HASKOVEC,** elementary school educator; b. Waukon, Iowa, May 10, 1976; d. Melvin William and Edna Lena Haskovec. BA in Elem. and Early Childhood Edn., U. No. Iowa, 1998, MS in Literacy Edn., 2003. Lic. tchr. Iowa, 1998. Tchr. Gladbrook Elem. Sch., Gladbrook, Iowa, 1998—2004, Van Buren Elem. Sch., Cedar Rapids, Iowa, 2004—. Asst. camp dir. Girl Scouts, Dorchester, Iowa, 2002. Girl scout trainer Conestoga Coun. of Girl Scouts, Waterloo, Iowa, 1997—2006. Grantee, McElroy Excellence in Edn. Enrichment grantee, 2002—03; scholar Purple and Gold Merit scholar, U. of No. Iowa, 1998. Mem.: Internat. Reading Assn.

Avocations: camping, hiking, travel, canoeing, crafts. Office: Van Buren Elementary 2525 29th St Cedar Rapids IA 52404 Office Phone: 319-558-3799. Personal E-mail: murbanowski@cr.k12.ia.us.

**URBANSKI, JANE F.,** retired microbiologist; b. Buffalo, N.Y., Aug. 21, 1943; d. Francis C. and Jane J. Urbanski. BS in Med. Tech. cum laude, Rosary Hill Coll., 1965. Registered med. tech. Am. Soc. Clin. Pathology. Med. tech. Millard Fillmore Hosp., Buffalo, 1965—68, microbiology supr., 1968—72; lab. supr. Physician's Diagnostic Lab., Buffalo, 1972—73; microbiology supr. Sister's of Charity Hosp., Buffalo, 1973—74; chief bacteriologist Erie County Pub. Health Lab. Health Dept., Buffalo, 1974—2002; ret., 2002. Clin. instr. SUNY, Buffalo, 1975—2002. Vol. Haven House, Buffalo, 1985, City Mission, Buffalo, 2004. Mem.: Am. Soc. for Clin. Lab. Sci. (ret.), Empire State Assn. for Med. Tech. (ret.), Am. Soc. Clin. Pathologists (ret.), English First, Am. Immigration Control, Second Amendment Found., Mensa. Conservative. Roman Catholic. Avocations: travel, growing orchids, reading, logic puzzles. Home: 185 Bridle Path Orchard Park NY 14127

**URBANSKI, JOSEPH V.,** mathematics educator; b. Balt., Feb. 14, 1942; s. Barney Joseph and Lottie (Chiborowski) U.; m. Mary Margaret Lewis, Nov. 4, 1967 (div. Oct. 1996); children: Deborah, Christopher, Mary Kathrine. BS in Phys. Sci. Edn., Bloomsburg (Pa.) State U., 1963; MMath., W.Va. State U., 1969; PhD in Math. Edn., N.C. State U., 1981. Cert. secondary phys. sci. and math. tchr., Pa. Tchr. math. Annapolis (Md.) High Sch., 1963-68; asst. prof. edn. West Tex. State U., Canyon, 1981-82; instr., adj. asst. prof. Pa. State U., State College, 1983-89; asst. prof. math. W.Va. Inst. Tech., Montgomery, 1969-80, assoc. prof., 1990—2001, chmn. dept. math., 1992—2001, prof. math., 2001—. U. S.C. scholar, 1990-91 (ath. math. grantee, 1977. Mem. Math. Assn. Am., Nat. Coun. Tchrs. Math., Phi Delta Kappa.

**URBIK, JEROME ANTHONY,** financial consultant; b. Chgo., Oct. 30, 1929; s. Anthony Frank and Sophie Elizabeth Urbik; m. Barbara Jean Chamernik, Sept. 1956; children: Laura M. Kern, Michael A., Anthony J., Mary King Gil, John T., Maria T. BA in Philosophy, St. Mary's Coll., Techny, Ill., 1953; CLU degree, Am. Coll., 1970, ChFC degree, 1979. Chartered fin. cons. Field underwriter MONY Fin. Svcs., Chgo., 1955-59, merchandising specialist N.Y.C., 1959; pvt. practice brokerage cons. Northfield, Ill., 1960-64; CEO Hinsdale (Ill.) Assocs. Fin. Svcs. Corp., 1964-90, CEO emeritus, 1990—. V.p. Interstate Coll. Personology, San Diego, 1982-87; pres. Gen. Agts. Mgrs. Conf., 1967-68. Mem. publ. com. Crisis mag., Washington 1989—; contbr. articles on industry to profl. jours.; mem. editl. bd. Leaders mag., 1981-90. Mem. adv. coun. Congressman Henry Hyde, Nat. Rep. Com., Washington; mem. Small Bus. Devel. Ctr. exec. bd. advisors Lewis U., Lockport, Ill., 1987-90; exec. coord. Legatus of Chgo., 1990-91 (Cath. CEO); bd. dirs. United Rep. Fund, 1987-92; bd. advisors Am. Life League, Washington, 1990-98, Cath. Ciizens Ill., 1997—; bd. dirs. Nat. Rep. Coalition for Life, 1990—. Named Small Bus. Acct. of Yr. for State of Ill. SBA, 1987. Mem. Am. Soc. CLUs, Chgo. Orchestral Assn., Chgo. Lyric Opera, Latin Liturgy Assn. (v.p. Chgo. chpt. 1997—). Roman Catholic. Avocations: reading, writing, power boating, classical music. Home: 474 South St Elmhurst IL 60126-4120 Office: Hinsdale Assoc Fin Svc Corp 15 Spinning Wheel Rd Ste 414 Hinsdale IL 60521-2987 Office Phone: 630-325-7100. E-mail: jaurbik@comcast.net.

**URBINA, FEBE GLORIA,** elementary school principal; b. Nuevo Laredo, Tamaulipas, Mexico, Aug. 25, 1942; came to U.S., 1947; d. Manuel Urbina and Irene Salce de Urbina. BA, Howard Payne Coll., 1965; MEd, U. Houston, 1975. Cert. tchr., adminstr., biling. educator, spcl. edn., mid mgmt., ednl. diagnostician, Tex. Cashier Weingarten Grocery, Houston, 1960-64; social worker Neighborhood Ctrs. Assn., Houston, 1965-68; elem. sch. tchr. Houston Ind. Sch. Dist., 1968-70, curriculum coord., 1970-2000, prin., 1973—. Adj. instr. Adult Edn. Houston C.C., 1965-71; mem. Legal United L.Am. Citizens Ednl. Adv. Bd., Houston, 1975-76; adj. English tchr. Harris County C.C., Pasadena, Tex., 1986-88; mem. supt.'s adv. bd. Houston Ind. Sch. Dist., 1990-97; presenter Conv. of Excellence, 1988, 90, 95, 98, Conv. Sch. External Funds, 1998, Lightspan Conv., 1998. Co-author: (book) Strategies for Bilingual/ESL Teachers, 1968. Sunday Sch. Tchr. Southmain Bapt. Ch., Houston, 1970-76; ch. pianist Heights Bapt. Temple, Houston, 1976-86; mem. Meadowbrook Civic Club, Houston, 1987-98. Recipient Mary Hill Davis award Home Mission Bd., Atlanta, 1961; named Hispanic Principal of Yr., Houston Ind. Sch. Dist. 1975, Principal of Yr. 1994. Mem. ASCD, Houston Assn. for Sch. Adminstrs. Avocations: travel, music, mission trips, translating, reading. Home: 899 Old Genoa Red Bluff Rd Houston TX 77034-4010

**URBOM, WARREN KEITH,** federal judge; b. Atlanta, Nebr., Dec. 17, 1925; s. Clarence Andrew and Anna Myrl (Irelan) U.; m. Joyce Marie Crawford, Aug. 19, 1951; children: Kim Marie, Randall Crawford, Allison Lee, Joy Renee. AB with highest distinction, Nebr. Wesleyan U., 1950, LLD (hon.), 1984; JD with distinction, U. Mich., 1953. Bar: Nebr. 1953. Mem. firm Baylor, Evnen, Baylor, Urbom, & Curtiss, Lincoln, Nebr., 1953—70; judge U.S. Dist. Ct. Nebr., 1970—; chief judge U.S. Dist. Ct. Dist. Nebr., 1972—86, sr. judge, 1991—. Mem. com. on practice and procedure Nebr. Supreme Ct., 1965-95; mem. subcom. on fed. jurisdiction Jud. Conf. U.S., 1975-83; adj. instr. trial advocacy U. Nebr. Coll. Law, 1979-90; bd. dirs Fed. Jud. Ctr., 1982-86; chmn. com. on orientation newly apptd. dist. judges Fed. Jud. Ctr., 1986-89; mem. 8th Cir. Com. on Model Criminal and Civil Jury Instrns., 1983—; mem. adv. com. on alternative sentences U.S. Sentencing Com., 1989-91. Contbr. articles to profl. jours. Trustee St. Paul Sch. Theology, Kansas City, Mo., 1986-89; active United Methodist Ch. (bd. mgrs., bd. global ministries 1972-76, gen. com. on status and role of women 1988-96, gen. conf. 1972, 76, 80, 88, 92, 96, 2000); pres. Lincoln YMCA, 1965-67; bd. govs. Nebr. Wesleyan U., chmn. 1975-80. With AUS, 1944-46. Recipient Medal of Honor, Nebr. Wesleyan U. Alumni Assn., 1983. Fellow Am. Coll. Trial Lawyers; mem. ABA, Nebr. Bar Assn. (ho. of dels. 1966-70, Outstanding Legal Educator award 1990), Lincoln Bar Assn. (Liberty Bell award 1993, pres. 1968-69), Kiwanis (Disting. Svc. award 1993), Masons (33 deg., Grand Master's Humanitarian award 2003), Am. Inns of Ct. (Lewis F. Powell Jr. award for Professionalism and Ethics 1995), Robert Van Pelt Am. Inn of Ct. (Lifetime Mentor award, 2002). Methodist. Home: 4421 Ridgeview Dr Lincoln NE 68516-1516 Office: US Dist Ct 586 Fed Bldg 100 Centennial Mall N Lincoln NE 68508-3859 Office Phone: 402-437-5231. Personal E-mail: urbom1@alltel.com. Business E-Mail: urbom1@neb.rr.com.

**URCHAK, JILL DANIELLE,** commentator; b. Chgo., Feb. 19, 1971; d. Woodrow John and Frances Mary Urchak; BA radio and TV comms., Columbia U., Chgo., 1994. Traffic reporter Shadow Traffic, Chgo., 1994—96; disc jockey Dundee, 1995—96; hostess morning show WBNQ/CBS, Bloomington, Ill., 1996—97; traffic reporter Chicago, 1997—; hostess TV show Casino TV, on-air traffic reporter Chgo., 2002; disc jockey Sta. WRXQ, Joliet, Ill., 2004—. Contbr. Best Poems and Poets, Stories in Life. Vol. Breast Cancer Fund Drive, Chgo., 2001; bd. dirs. Make A Wish, Chgo., 2002. Roman Catholic. Avocations: antiques, jewelry recycling, music, reading. Personal E-mail: jillurchak@hotmail.com, jillikens@aol.com.

**URCIOLO, JOHN RAPHAEL, II,** real estate developer, real estate educator, finance educator; b. Washington, June 29, 1947; s. Joseph John and Phillie Marie (Petrone) U.; m. Jean Marie Manning, Jan. 2, 1972 (div. Jan. 1990); m. Andrea Zedalis, Mar. 9, 2002. BBA, Am. U., 1969, MS in real estate, 1971. Cert. real estate broker, appraiser. Rschr. Homer Hoyt Inst., Washington, 1967-69; econ. Nat. Assn. Home Builders, Washington, 1971-75; lectr., assoc. prof. Montgomery Coll., Rockville, Md., 1971-72; assoc. prof. U. Md., College Park, 1972-79; property mgr. Urciolo Realty Co., Washington, 1976-79; comml. broker Urciolo & Urciolo, Washington, 1980-82; real estate developer Urciolo Properties, LLC, Takoma Park, Md., 1982—. Cons. Nat. Ski Area Assn., Hartford, 1978-79, Montgomery County Govt., Rockville, 1980-81; adj. prof. Am. U., Washington, 1980-91; court expert Superior Ct. for D.C., Civil and Criminal divsns.; lectr. to various orgns. Author: Real Estate Manual, 1976; co-author: The White Book of Ski Areas (U.S. and Can.), 1977-79, Industry Edition-The White Book, 1978, The Housing Fact Book, 1976, Housing Component Costs, 1975, 2d edit., 1976, Material Usage in Housing, 1970; co-editor: Labor Wage Rate Bulletin, 1976. Co-chair bd. dirs. Liz Lerman Dance Exch., Takoma Park, Md., 1997—; chmn. facade adv. bd. and Econ. Devel. Com., City of Takoma Park; chmn. bd. Lido Civic Club of Washington. Fellow Urban Mass Transp. Assn., 1969, Am. U., 1970; Soc. Real Estate Appraisers scholar, 1968. Mem. Cert. Real Estate Appraisers, Am. Planning Assn., Am. Univ. Real Estate Assn. (charter, v.p. edn., v.p. award 1983), Rho Epsilon (editor newsletter 1969). Republican. Roman Catholic. Avocations: skiing, golf. Office: Urciolo Properties LLC 6935 Laurel Ave Ste 100 Takoma Park MD 20912-4413 Office Phone: 301-270-4442. Personal E-mail: jurciolo@comcast.net.

**URCIUOLI, J. ARTHUR,** brokerage house executive; b. Syracuse, NY, Nov. 13, 1937; s. Joseph R. and Nicoletta Anne (Phillips) U.; m. Margaret Jane Forelli, Aug. 13, 1966; children: Caryn Sloan Jacoby, Christian J.A. BS, St. Lawrence U., 1959; JD, Georgetown U., 1966; grad. Advanced Mgmt. Program, Harvard Bus. Sch., 1982. Bar: N.Y. 1966. Attn. Brown, Wood, Fuller, Caldwell & Ivey, N.Y.C., 1966-69; internat. investment banker, dir. internat. fin. Merrill Lynch, N.Y.C., Paris, 1970-78; pres. Merrill Lynch Internat., 1978-82; chmn. Merrill Lynch Internat. Bank, London; dir. banking div. Merrill Lynch Capital Markets, 1980-84; dir. Merrill Lynch Bus. Fin. Services, Merrill Lynch Co., 1984-93; dir. mktg. group Merrill Lynch Pvt. Client, 1993-97, chmn. Internat. Pvt. Client Group N.Y.C., 1997-99, ret., 1999; chmn. Archer Group, 1999—. Bd. dirs. Kroll Inc., 1999—2004, Family Capital Growth Ptnrs., L.P. Contbr. articles to profl. jours. Trustee St. Lawrence U., 1976-89, Bruce Mus., Greenwich, Conn., 1990-94; bd. dirs. United Way, Greenwich, 1978-81. Capt. USMC, 1959-65. Mem. Securities Assn. (chmn. sales and mktg. com. 1987-89), Forum Investor Advice (chmn. 1996-98), River Club (NYC), Riverside (Conn.) Yacht Club, The Oaks Club (Sarasota, Fla.). Republican. Congregationalist. Office Phone: 941-966-4941. E-mail: archie22@comcast.net.

**URDANG, LAURENCE,** editor, publishing executive; b. N.Y.C., Mar. 21, 1927; s. Harry Rudman and Annabel (Schafran) U.; m. Irena B. Ehrlich vel Sluszny, May 23, 1952 (div.); children: Nicole Severyn, Alexandra Stefanie. BS, Columbia U., 1954, postgrad., 1954-58. Lectr. gen. linguistics NYU, 1956-61; assoc. editor dictionary dept. Funk & Wagnalls, Inc., N.Y.C., 1957; reference editor Random House, Inc., N.Y.C., 1957-61, dir. reference dept., 1962-69; pres. Laurence Urdang, Inc., Old Lyme, Conn. and Aylesbury, Eng., 1969—; chmn. bd. Laurence Urdang Assocs., Ltd., Aylesbury, 1969-78; editor Verbatim Books, Old Lyme and Aylesbury, 1974—. Compiler, editor, author numerous books; mng. editor: Random House Unabridged Dictionary, 1966; editor in chief: Random House College Dictionary, 1968, Random House Dictionary of Synonyms and Antonyms, 1960, N.Y. Times Everyday Reader's Dictionary of Misunderstood, Misused, Mispronounced Words, 1972, 2d edit., 1985, Editor, Verbatim, The Language Quar., 1974-97, Dictionary of Advertising Terms, 1977, Official Associated Press Almanac, 1976, Hammond Almanac, 1977, Picturesque Expressions, 1980, 2d edit., 1985, Illustrated Children's Dictionary, 1979, Basic Dictionary of Synonyms and Antonyms, 1979, 2d edit., 1986, The Synonym Finder, 1979, Collins English Dictionary, 1979, Verbatim: Vols. I, II, 1978, Vols. III, IV, V, VI and Index, 1981, -Ologies & -Isms, 1978, 81, 86, Twentieth Century American Nicknames, 1979, A Treasury of Biblical Quotations, 1980, The Timetables of American History, 1981, 3d edit., 2001, Mosby's Medical and Nursing Dictionary, 1983, Allusions, 1982, 86, Modifiers, 1982, Suffixes, 1982, Prefixes, 1984, Holidays and Anniversaries, 1985, Slogans, 1985, Mottoes, 1986, Numerical Allusions, 1986, Names and Nicknames of Places and Things, 1987, Loanwords Dictionary, 1987, The Whole Ball of Wax, 1988, The Dictionary of Confusable Words, 1988, A Fine Kettle of Fish, 1990, The Oxford Thesaurus, 1992, 2nd edit., 1997, The Oxford Desk Dictionary, 1995, The Oxford Desk Thesaurus, 1995, The New Century Dictionary, 1996, The New Century Thesaurus, 1996, The Compact Oxford Thesaurus, 1997. Served with USNR, 1944-45. Fellow Dictionary Soc. N.Am. (hon.); mem. Linguistic Soc. Am. (hon.), Soc. Nautical Rsch., Nat. Maritime Mus. (bd. dir.), N.B. White Libr., Mystic Mus., Am. Name Soc., Am. Dialect Soc., Soc. Indexers, Euralex. Office Phone: 860-434-2104. Personal E-mail: urdang@sbcglobal.com.

**URE, COLIN,** research scientist; Scientist Procter & Gamble Co., Cin. Co-recipient Nat. Inventor of Yr. award, Intellectual Property Owners Edn. Found., 2006. Achievements include development of PuR Purifier of Water Sachets, which can purify 10 liters of non-drinkable water by pulling out contaminants; patents in field. Office: Health Scis Inst Procter & Gamble Co 1 P&G Plaza Cincinnati OH 45202*

**U'REN, MARIE RITA,** retired travel company executive, pre-school educator; b. Ft. Monmouth, NJ, Jan. 12, 1940; d. Paul Robert and Ray Rita Tyler; m. William Francis Henry U'Ren, Jr., Jan. 31, 1959; children: William Tyler, Christine Marie. Tchr. Calvary Luth. Nursery Sch., Millbrae, Calif., 1967—82; group sales Bulanti Travel, Redwood City, Calif., 1980—82; ptnr., dir. of group sales Custom Travel Consultants, Woodside, Calif., 1982—94. Prodr.: The Gin Game, 2005, Cmty. Alliance, Performing Arts. Chair numerous coms. PTAs, Belmont, Calif., 1972—84; Christmas wreath co-chmn. Main St. Easton, 1995—2004; co-chmn. Olde Tyme Holiday Parade, Easton, Md., 1995—; vol. duck stamp booth Waterfowl Festival, Easton, Md., 1996—; house tour co-chmn. Festival of Trees, Easton, Md., 1999—2003, fashion show co-chmn., 2000—01; shut down the town day steering com. Easton Bus. Mgmt. Assn./Main St. Easton, Easton, Md., 2000—01; chmn. promotions com. Easton Main St., Inc., Easton, Md., 2000—05; treas. charity antiques show Mental Health Assn. in Talbot County, Easton, Md., 2004—; bd. dirs. First Night Talbot, 1997—; treas. Talbot County Am. Heart Assn., Easton, Md., 1998—2002; grant writer Cmty. Alliance for the Performing Arts, Easton, Md., 2000—06, mem. agy. rev. com., 2000—03, sec., 2003—06; Welcome Ctr. liaison gala fundraising com. The Avalon Found., Easton, Md., 2001—04, sec., bd. dirs., 2006, Dance Harrison St., Easton, Md., 2002—05; registrar, reunion com. 1st Bn. 7th Marines Vietnam, Washington, 2000—02, Las Vegas, 2004; pres. Bay Area Aux., Myasthenia Gravis Found., San Mateo, Calif., 1976—78; costume com. Habitat for Humanity Follies, Easton, Md., 1996—99; chmn. or co-chairman. Talbot county antiques show and sale Talbot County Am. Heart Assn., Easton, Md., 1997—2001; costumer Cricket Theatre, Easton, Md., 2000—; treas. Benjamin Fox Elem. Sch. PTA, 1977, Silver Hon. Svc. award, Ralson Mid. Sch. PTA, 1980, Hon. Svc. award, Carlmont H.S. PTSA, 1984, Vol. of the Yr., Dickens of a Christmas and Easton Bus. Mgmt. Authority, 1995, Cert. of Appreciation, Talbot County Am. Heart Assn., 1996, Vol. Excellence, First Night Talbot, 1997, Cert. of Appreciation, Talbot County Am. Heart Assn., 1997, Vol. Recognition award, Easton Bus. Mgmt. Authority, 2000, Talbot County and State of Md., 2002. Mem.: Friends Hospice (sec. 2001—02, bd. dirs.), Hist. Soc. Talbot County (vol. asst. mgr. Tharpe Antiques 1996—, chmn. Heritage award com. 2002—05, auditorium com. 2001—, prin. com. 2002—), Mental Health Assn. Talbot County (chmn. parenttalk 1998—2001, co-chmn. antiques show preview party 2003, bd. dirs. 2003—, treas. charity antiques show 2004—), Acad. Art Mus. (co-chmn. arts marketplace 1998—2001, chmn. preview party 2002, sec., bd. dirs. 2004—05, chmn. libr. com. 2002—, co-chmn. arts marketplace 2005, chmn. arts marketplace 2006). Home: 127 S Harrison St Easton MD 21601 Personal E-mail: muren@bluecrab.org.

**UREÑA, ALEX,** chef; Garde mgr., dishwasher River Café, Brooklyn; chef Bouley, NYC; apprentice chef El Bulli, Spain; chef Restaurant Martin Berasategui, Jo Jo, NYC, Le Cote Basque, NYC, La Caravelle, NYC; chef de cuisine, co-owner Blue Hill, NYC, 2000—01; exec. chef Marseille, NYC, 2001—03; consulting chef Suba, NYC, 2004—; owner, chef Ureña, NYC, 2006—. Named one of NYC's Rising Stars, StarChefs.com, 2006. Office: Urena 37 E 28th St New York NY 10016 Office Phone: 212-213-2328.*

**URGESSA, GIRUM SOLOMON,** structural engineer, researcher; s. Tigist Taffesse Haile and Solomon Urgessa Dadi. BS, Addis Ababa U., Ethiopia, 1996—2000; MS, U. N.Mex, Albuquerque, 2001—02, PhD, 2003—06. Lic. Engring. Intern, N.Mex State Bd. Licensure for Profl. Engrs., 2004. Rsch.

asst. U. N.Mex, 2001—02, 2003—06; structural engr. Dekker/Perich/Sabatini Ltd., Albuquerque, 2002—03; engr./analyst Weidlinger Assoc. Inc., Albuquerque, 2005—06. Grantee N.Mex Grad. Scholars award, U. N.Mex, 2001—03. Fellow: N.Mex Alliance Grad. Edn. and the Professorate (fellowship 2004); mem.: Structural Engrs. Assn. of N.Mex, Am. Concrete Inst., Chi Epsilon (marshall 2003—04). Home: PO Box 92632 Albuquerque NM 87199 Office: Univ N Mex Dept Civil Engring Albuquerque NM 87131 Office Phone: 505-277-7349. Personal E-Mail: girumsol@gmail.com. Business E-Mail: girum@unm.edu.

**URI, GEORGE WOLFSOHN,** accountant; b. San Francisco, Dec. 8, 1920; s. George Washington and Ruby Uri; m. Pamela O'Keefe, May 15, 1961. AB, Stanford U., 1941, IA, 1943, MBA, 1946; postgrad., U. Leeds, Eng., 1945. CPA, Calif.; CFP. CMA, ChFC; Accredited Estate Planner. Mem. acctg., econs. and stats. depts. Shell Oil Co., Inc., San Francisco, 1946—48; ptnr., ret. Irelan, Uri, Mayer & Sheppie; pres. F. Uri & Co., Inc. Instr. acctg. and econs. Golden Gate U., 1949-50. Contbr. articles to profl. jours. Chmn. San Rafael Redevel. Adv. Com., 1977-78, mem., 1978-91, mem. emeritus, 1991—; bd. dirs. San Francisco Planning and Urban Renewal Assn., 1958-60. Served with AUS, 1942-46, to col. Aus. (ret.). Recipient Meritorious Service medal, Sec. of Army, 1978. Mem. AICPA (hon., personal fin. specialist), Calif. Soc. CPA (hon.; sec.-treas. San Francisco chpt. 1956-57, dir. 1961-63, state dir. 1964-66, Forbes medal com. 1968-69, chmn. 1969-71), San Francisco Estate Planning Coun. (dir. 1965-68, Am. Soc. Mil. Comptr., Execs. Assn. San Francisco (pres. 1965-66), Soc. Fin. Profls., Fin. Planning Assn., World Trade Club (San Francisco), Commonwealth Club (quar. chmn. 1971), Stanford Alumni Assn. (San Francisco; dir. 1990-99), Army and Navy Club Washington Office: 1209 Tennessee St San Francisco CA 94107 Personal E-mail: georgeuri@aol.com.

**URIE, ALAN T,** bank executive; b. Ogden, Utah, Sept. 25, 1957; s. Hurschell G. Urie and E. Mary Petersen; m. M. Mae Christensen, July 26, 1980; children: Marcus Timothy, Kristi Mae Harvey, Scott Alan, Catherine Elizabeth, Teresa Janette, Mary Elizabeth. BS, Brigham Young U., 1982; MBA, U. Utah, 1984. National Compliance School Graduate Am. Bankers Assn., 1991. Assoc. dept. mgr. Zions Coop. Merc. Inst., Orem, Utah, 1979—83; officer First Security Bank of Utah, N.A., Salt Lake City, 1983—91, asst. v.p., 1991—94, v.p., sr. compliance officer, 1994—2000; v.p. First Security Corp., Salt Lake City, 1996—2000; sr. v.p. Wells Fargo Bank NW, N.A., 2000—, Wells Fargo Bank, N.A., 2004—. Planning cons. City of South Salt Lake, Utah, 1996. Chmn. City Housing Rehab. Loan Com., South Salt Lake, Utah, 2002—06, Gen. Plan Com., South Salt Lake, 1992—96; commr., chair South Salt Lake Planning Commn., 1988—90; chmn. Cmty. Affairs Com., South Salt Lake, 1988—90; budget adv. bd. mem. Ogden City, Utah, 1986—88; unit com. mem., leader Boys Scouts Am., South Salt Lake, 1985—2006; bishop Ch. of Jesus Christ of Latter-day Saints, South Salt Lake, 2003—04, stake presidency mem., 2004—06; exec., governance com. Girl Scouts of Utah, 2002—; exec. com. Utah Microenterprise Loan Fund, Inc., 2000—; bd. mem., incorporator South Salt Lake Works, Inc., 2004—; com. mem. Utah Bankers Assn., 1990—2006. Recipient Eagle Scout, Boy Scouts of Am., 1973; Sterling scholar (music), Ogden H.S., 1976, President's scholarship, Brigham Young U., 1976, 1979. Mem.: Robert Morris Assoc. (assoc.). Church Of Jesus Christ Of Latter-Day Saints. Office: Wells Fargo 299 South Main St Salt Lake City UT 84111-2263

**URIE, JOHN JAMES,** retired lawyer, former Canadian federal judge; b. Guelph, Ont., Can., Jan. 2, 1920; s. G. Norman and Anna A. U.; m. Dorothy Elizabeth James.; children: David, Janet, Alison. B.Commerce, Queen's U.; LL.B., Osgoode Hall Law Sch. Bar: Ont. 1948. Ptnr. firm Burke-Robertson, Urie, Weller & Chadwick, Ottawa, Ont., 1948-73; judge Fed. Ct. Can., Ottawa, 1973-90; counsel Scott and Aylen, Ottawa, 1991-2000, Borden, Ladner, Gervais, Ottawa, 2000—. Gen. counsel to Joint Com. of Senate and House of Commons on Consumer Credit; chmn. planning com. First Nat. Conf. on Law, Ottawa, 1972; judge Ct. Martial Appeal Ct., 1973-90. Past pres. County of Carleton Law Assn.; past v.p. Children's Aid Soc.; past pres. Eastern Profl. Hockey League. Served with Cameron Highlanders of Ottawa Can. Army, 1942-45. Mem. Royal Can. Mil. Inst., Phi Delta Phi. Mem. United Ch. of Canada. Clubs: Cameron Highlanders of Ottawa Assoc. (Ottawa), Ottawa Hunt and Golf (Ottawa), Rideau (Ottawa). Office: Borden Ladner Gervais 100 Queen St Ottawa ON Canada K1P1J9 Office Phone: 613-237-5160.

**URKOWITZ, MICHAEL,** banker; b. Bronx, N.Y., June 18, 1943; s. David and Esther (Levy) U.; m. Eleanor Naomi Dreazen, July 2, 1966; children: Brian, Denise. B.Engring., CCNY, 1965, M.M.E., 1967. Project engr. Lunar Module program Grumman Corp., Bethpage, NY, 1964-72; asst. to dep. commr. for housing code compliance, project mgr. City of N.Y., 1972-74; 2d v.p. Chase Manhattan Bank, N.Y.C., 1974-77, v.p. group exec. ops. dept., 1977-80, sr. v.p., 1980-85, exec. v.p., corp. ops. and sys. exec., 1985-87; sector exec. Chase InfoServ Internat., N.Y.C., 1987-95, exec. consumer products integration and tech., 1995-96, Chase credit card bus. exec., 1996-2000, ret., 2000; sr. adv. Deloitte Cons., N.Y.C.; prin. Michael Urkowitz, LLC, 2005—. Bd. dirs. Bank Leumi, U.S.; lectr. CCNY, 1967—68. Contbg. author: Thermal Control and Radiation, 1972. Mem. adv. bd. N.Y.C. chpt. Salvation Army, 1989—2001. Mem. Tau Beta Pi, Pi Tau Sigma. Personal E-mail: murkowitz@aol.com. *Working against my own standards as opposed to the standards set by others, provides the greater challenge but yields greater satisfaction.*

**URLACHER, BRIAN,** professional football player; b. Pasco, Wash., May 25, 1978; children: Pamela, Riley. Attended, U. New Mex. Linebacker Chgo. Bears, 2000—. Vol. United Way. Vol. Spl. Olympics, Ill., N.Mex. Named NFL Defensive Rookie of the Year, AP, 2000, NFL Defensive Player of Yr., 2005; named to Pro Bowl, NFL, 2001—04, NFL All-Pro Team, 2005. Office: Halas Hall 1000 Football Dr Lake Forest IL 60045*

**URMAN, JEFFREY DAVID,** physician, educator; b. N.Y.C., May 23, 1944; s. Julius and Rose Claire Urman; m. Marian K. Kleinfeld, June 28, 1970; children: Jamie David, Daniel Jay. BS, U. Conn., 1967; MD, Cornell U., 1972. Diplomate Am. Bd. Internal Medicine and Rheumatology. Int. Wash. Hosp. Ctr., Wash., D.C., 1972-73, res., 1973-75; fellshp. in rheumatology Univ. Conn. Health Ctr., Farmington, CT, 1975-77; physician Redwood Med. Clinic, Redwood City, Calif., 1977-90; clin. prof. medicine Stanford (Calif.) U. Med. Ctr., 1977—; physician Permanente Med. Group, Mountain View, Calif., 1990—, physician-in-charge, 1995—. Contbr. articles to profl. jours. Fellow: ACP, Am. Coll. Rheumatology. Office: 555 Castro St Mountain View CA 94041-2060

**URMY, NORMAN B.,** hospital administrator; b. Ft. Smith, Ark., June 26, 1944; married. BA, Williams Coll., 1966; MA, U. Chgo., 1969. Various positions Mass. Gen. Hosp., Boston, 1966-67; administr. resident NYU Med. Ctr., 1968, administrv. asst., 1969-70, asst. administr., 1970-76, assoc. administr., 1976-79, administr., v.p. ops., 1979-82; exec. dir. Vanderbilt Univ. Hosp. & Clinic, Nashville, 1985-98; exec. v.p. clin. affairs Vanderbilt Univ. Med. Ctr., Nashville, 1998—; exec. dir. and CEO Vanderbilt U. Hosp. and Clinic, 2002—05. Mem. ACHE. Office: D-3300 MCN Vanderbilt U 1161 21st Ave Nashville TN 37232-2104*

**UROWSKY, RICHARD J.,** lawyer; b. NYC, June 28, 1946; s. Jacob and Anne (Granick) Urowsky. BA, Yale U., 1967, JD, 1972; BPhil, Oxford U., Eng., 1970. Bar: N.Y. 1973, U.S. Dist. Ct. (so. dist.) N.Y. 1973, U.S. Ct. Appeals (2d cir.) 1973, U.S. Supreme Ct. 1977. Law clk. to Justice Reed U.S. Supreme Ct., Washington, 1972—73; assoc. Sullivan & Cromwell LLP, N.Y.C., 1973—83, ptnr., 1980—. Mem. ABA, Assn. of the Bar of the City of N.Y., Fed. Bar Coun., N.Y. County Lawyers Club, Yale Club, Links Club, India House Club, Lyford Cay Club. Office: Sullivan & Cromwell LLP 125 Broad St New York NY 10004-2498 Business E-Mail: urowskyr@sullcrom.com.

**URQUHART, JOHN,** medical researcher, educator; b. Pitts., Apr. 24, 1934; s. John and Wilma Nelda (Martin) U.; m. Joan Cooley, Dec. 28, 1957; children: Elizabeth Urquhart Vdovjak, John Christopher (dec. 1965), Robert Malcolm, Thomas Jubal. BA with honors, Rice U., 1955; MD with honors, Harvard U., 1959; D honoris causa, U. Utrecht, 1997. Lic. physician, Calif. Walter B. Cannon fellow in physiology Harvard Med. Sch., Boston, 1956, Josiah Macy, Jr. fellow, 1956-58, 59-61; intern in surgery Mass. Gen. Hosp., 1959-60, asst. resident, 1960-61; investigator Nat. Heart Inst., NIH, Bethesda, Md., 1961-63; asst. prof. physiology U. Pitts. Sch. Medicine, 1963-66, assoc. prof., 1966-68, prof., 1968-70; prof. biomed. engring. U. So. Calif., LA, 1970-71; prin. scientist ALZA Corp., Palo Alto, Calif., 1970-86, dir. biol. scis., 1971-74, pres. rsch. divsn., 1974-78, dir., 1976-78, chief scientist, 1978-82, sr. v.p., 1978-85. Co-founder APREX Corp., Fremont, Calif., pres., 1986-88, dir., 1986-95, chmn., 1988-91, chief scientist, 1988-95; co-founder, chief scientist AARDEX Ltd., Zug, Switzerland, 1995-; vis. prof. pharmacology U. Limburg Sch. Medicine (now Maastricht U.), Maastricht, Netherlands, 1984-85, vis. prof. pharmacoepidemiology, 1986-91, prof. pharmacoepidemiology, 1991-2004, prof. emeritus, 2004—; adj. prof. biopharm. scis. U. Calif.-San Francisco, 1984-; mem. dir.'s adv. com. NIH, 1986-88; Boerhaave lectr. U. Leiden, Netherlands, 1991, 94, 95, 97; bd. dirs. HBM BioVentures Ltd., Cayman Islands. Co-author: Risk Watch, 1984; contbr. numerous articles to sci. jours.; patentee therapeutic systems for controlled drug delivery and regimen compliance monitoring (43). Trustee Kettering U. (formerly GMI Engring. and Mgmt. Inst.), Flint, Mich., 1983-. Served with USPHS, 1961-63. Recipient Disting. Alumni award, Rice U., 2002; NIH grantee, 1963-70. Fellow AAAS, Royal Coll. Physicians of Edinburgh, Royal Soc. Edinburgh (corr.), Internat Soc. for Pharmacoepidemiology, Biomed. Engring. Soc. (pres. 1976, Disting. Svc. award 2005); mem. Boyleston Med. Soc., Internat. Soc. Pharmaco-epidemiology, Am. Soc. Clin. Pharmacology and Therapeutics, Soc. for Clin. Trials, Endocrine Soc., Saturday Morning Club Palo Alto, Am. Physiol. Soc. (Bowditch lectr. 1969), Soc. Risk Analysis, Calif. Acad. Medicine, Illuminati Edinburgh. Home and Office: 975 Hamilton Ave Palo Alto CA 94301-2213 E-mail: urquhart@ix.netcom.com.

**URQUHART, TONY,** artist, educator; b. Niagara Falls, Ont., Can., Apr. 9, 1934; s. Archer Marsh and Maryon Louise (Morse) U.; m. Madeline Mary Jennings, July 1958 (div. 1976); children: Allyson, Robin, Marsh, Aidan; m. Mary Jane Carter Keele, May 1976; 1 dau., Emily. B.F.A., U. Buffalo, 1958. Artist-in-residence U. Western Ont., London, 1960-63, 64-65, asst. prof. fine arts, 1967-70, assoc. prof., 1970-72; lectr. McMaster U., Hamilton, Ont., 1966—67; prof. fine art U. Waterloo, Ont., 1972—79, chmn. dept. Ont., 1977-79, 82-85, Ont., 94-96, ret. Ont., 1999. One-man shows Winnipeg Art Gallery, 1959, Walker Art Gallery, Mpls., 1960, Richard Demarco Gallery, Edinburgh, Scotland, 1975, Power of Invention: Drawings from seven decades, Nat. Gallery Can., 2003; group shows, Pitts. Biennial, 1958, Guggenheim Internat., N.Y.C., 1958, Art of the Ams. and Spain, Madrid, Barcelona, Rome, Paris, 1964, Nat. Gallery Can.: Toronto, 1972, Mus. Modern Art, Paris, 1976, Mus. Modern Art, N.Y.C., 2006; represented permanent collections, Nat. Gallery Can., Art Gallery, Ont., Fed. Art Bank of Ottawa, Montreal Mus., Vancouver Art Gallery, Mus. Modern Art, Victoria and Albert Mus., London, Museo Civico, Lugano, Switzerland, Hirshhorn Mus., Washington, Bibliotec Nat. Paris; chmn., Jack Chambers Meml. Found., 1978-85, 2004—; artist in residence Kitchener-Waterloo Art Gallery, Kitchener, Ont., 1981-83, City of Kitchener, 2005; illustrator: The Broken Ark: A Book of Beasts, 1969, I Am Walking in the Garden of His Imaginary Palace by Jane Urquhart, 1982, False Shuffles by Jane Urquhart, 1982, (50 drawings) Ourselves of Ourselves (text G.M. Dault), 1989, Memories of a Governor General's Daughter, 1990, Warbrain: poems by Stuart MacKinnon, 1994, Walking to the Saints, by Anne McPherson, 2000. Artist in residence City of Kitchener, 2005. Decorated Order of Can.; recipient Edits, I Arts Coun., Ont., 1974, Kilchener Waterloo Visual Arts award, 1994; winner Nat. Outdoor Sculpture Competition MacDonald Stewart Art Ctr., 1987, Outdoor Sculpture competition, Rim Park, Waterloo, 2002; grantee Can. Coun. award, 1963, 79, travel grantee, 1967, 69, 70, 74, 75, 76, 88, 91, project cost grantee, 1981, 82, short-term grantee, 1991, All Can. Coun. Mem. Can. Artists Representation (1 of 3 founding mem.'s, sec. 1968-71, life 1999), Nat. Gallery of Can. (life), Art Gallery of Ont. (life), London Reginal Art Gallery (life), MacDonald Stewart Art Centre Gallery Stratford (life). Office: Dept Fine Arts U Waterloo Waterloo ON Canada N2L 3G1

**URREA, LUIS ALBERTO,** writer; b. Tijuana, Mex., Aug. 20, 1955; s. Alberto and Phyllis U.; m. Cinderella Urrea; 3 children. BA, Univ. Calif., San Diego, 1977; MA, Univ. Colo., Boulder, 1997. Tchr., expository writing, fiction Harvard Univ., 1982—87; assoc. prof., asst. to pres. for spl. projects Mass. Bay Cmty. Coll., 1987—90; freelance writer, editor, workshop leader, 1990—96; writer in residence, assoc. prof. Univ. SW La., Lafayette, 1996—99; assoc. prof., English, creative writing Univ. Ill., Chgo., 1999—. Author: (non-fiction) Across the Wire, 0199 (Christopher award, 1993, NY Times Notable Book, 1994), By the Lake of Sleeping Children, 1996, Nobody's Son, 1998 (Am. Book award), Wandering Time, 1999, The Devil's Highway, 2004, (poetry) The Fever of Being, 1994 (Western States Book award, 1994, Colo. Ctr. for the Book award, 1994), Ghost Sickness, 1996 (Best Am. Poetry Selection); author: (photos by Jose Galvez) Vatos, 2000; author: (short stories) Six Kinds of Sky, 2002 (Book of Yr. Foreword Mag., 2002), (novels) In Search of Snow, 1994, The Hummingbird's Daughter, 2005; adv. bd. El Andar Mag., 2000—, adv. coun. Paso al Norte Immigration Mus., Univ. Tex.-El Paso, 2001—. Named to Latino Literary Hall of Fame, 2001; recipient Lannan Found Lit. award for non-fiction, 2004, Premio Fronterizo award, 2004. Address: c/o Carolyn Sawyer Little Brown & Co 1271 Ave Of Americas New York NY 10020 Office: 2027 University Hall Univ Ill 601 S Morgan St Chicago IL 60607-7120 E-mail: luisurrea@luisurrea.com, lurrea@uic.edu.

**URROZ-RAPOLD, PATRICIA JULIA S.,** retired diplomat, writer; b. Key West, Fla., Feb. 16, 1949; children: Jean Sebastien Bodin Rapold, Nicolas Richard Rapold. BA in Polit. Sci., Boston U., 1971. Consul ad-honorem Nicaragua Boston Ministerio de Relaciones Exteriores, Managua, Nicaragua, 1969—74; social security disability examiner Mass. Rehab. Commn., Boston, 1971—72. Author, pub., poet: Seasonal Living In The Catskills Windham High Peak And Finds, 1994 (Internat. Poet Of Merit award, 1996). Hospitality coord. for fgn. visitors Internat. Ctr., N.Y.C., 1991—93. Recipient Appreciation award for vols., Internat. Ctr., N.Y.C., 1993. Mem.: AAUW (member). Roman Catholic. Avocations: hiking, swimming, reading, collecting. Office: Worldstar Corp 245 E 93d St Apt 29 C New York New York Home: PO Box 1870 New York NY 10021-0048 Personal E-mail: Rapold@aol.com. Business E-Mail: LordSeb@aol.com.

**URSANO, ROBERT JOSEPH,** psychiatrist; b. Heidelberg, Ger., May 26, 1947; s. James Joseph and Neoma Faye (Summers) U.; m. Diane T. Ursano; children: Amy, Anna. BS magna cum laude, U. Notre Dame, 1969; MD, Yale U., 1973; grad., Washington Psychoanalytic Ins, 1986. Diplomate Nat. Bd. Med. Examiners, Am. Bd. Psychiatry and Neurology; lic. physician N.Y., Tex., Md. Resident in psychiatry Wilford Hall USAF Med. Ctr., 1973-75; postdoctoral fellow in psychiatry Yale U/Yale Psychiat. Inst., 1975-77; staff psychiatrist USAF Sch. Aerospace Medicine, Brooks AFB, Tex., 1977-79; clin. asst. prof. U. Tex. Health Sci. Ctr., San Antonio, 1977-79; asst. prof. and dir. third yr. clerkships dept. psychiatry Uniformed Svcs. U. Health Scis., Bethesda, Md., 1979-81, assoc prof and dir. 3rd yr. clerkships, 1981-83, assoc. prof. and assoc. chmn. dept. psychiatry, 1983-86, prof. and assoc. chmn. dept. psychiatry, 1987-92, prof., chair dept. psychiatry, dir.Ctr. for the Study of Traumatic Stress Bethesda, Md., 1992—. Examiner Am. Bd. Psychiatry and Neurology, 1984—; asst. prof. Nat. Naval Med. Ctr Dept. Psychiatry, Georgetown U. Sch. Medicine, Washington, 1980-84, assoc. prof., 1984-88, prof., 1988—; mem. grant rev. study sect. for trauma and disaster, NIMH, 1990—, chmn. various study sects. Author: Concise Guide to Psychodynamic Psychotherapy, 1990, Concise Guide to Principles and Practice of Psychodynamic Psychotherapy in the Era of Managed Care, 1998; editor: Individual and Community Responses to Trauma and Disaster: The Structure of Human Chaos, 1994, Emotional Aftermath of The Persian Gulf War: Veterans, Families, Communities and Nations, 1996, Acute and Chronic

PTSD, 1997, Trauma and Disaster: Responses and Management, 2003, Terrorism and Disaster: Individual and Community Mental Health Interventions, 2004, Bioterrorism: Indivduals and the Public's Health, 2004, Principles of Psychodynamics Psychotherapy: Brief, Intermittent and Long-Term, 2004; reviewer Am. Jour. Psychiatry, Jour. Nervous and Mental Disease, Psychosomatics, Psychiatry, Jour. Applied Social Psychology, Archives of Gen. Psychiatry, Hosp. and Community Psychiatry, all 1986—, Jour. Neuropsychiatry and Clin. Neurosci., 1988—, Jour. Traumatic Stress, 1989—; editor-in-chief Psychiatry, 1999—; mem. editl. bd. Mil. Medicine; contbr. articles to profl. jours., chpts. to books. Decorated Air Force Commendation medal; recipient Dept. Def. Humanitarian Svc. medal, Dept. Def. Superior Svc. award, William C. Porter award Assn. Mil. Surgeons of U.S.; recipient Disting. Tchg. award Am. Soc. Psychoanalyst Physicians, Life Time Achievement award Internat. Soc. Traumatic Stress Studies. Fellow Am. Psychiat. Assn. (disting.), Am. Coll. Psychiatrists, Am. Coll. Psychoanalysts; mem. Am. Psychoanalytic Assn., Psychosomatic Soc., Washington Psychiat. Soc., Washington Psychoanalytic Soc., Acad. Medicine Washington DC, Soc. USAF Psychiatrists (v.p. 1981-82), Assn. for Acad. Psychiatry, Washington DC Academy Medicine, Alpha Epsilon Delta, Phi Beta Kappa. Home: 3900 Cleveland St Kensington MD 20895-3804 Office: Uniformed Svcs U Health Sci 4301 Jones Bridge Rd Bethesda MD 20814-4712

**URSERY, FREDERICK STANLEY,** lawyer; b. Pine Bluff, Ark., Mar. 5, 1942; s. William Stanley and Mary Charles (Lee) U.; m. Sharon Lee Davidson, Jan. 30, 1971; children: Stephen, Catherine. BA, Vanderbilt U., 1964; LLB, Columbia U., 1967. Bar: Ark. 1967, U.S. Dist. Ct. (ea. and we. dists.) Ark. 1970, U.S. Ct. Appeals (8th cir.) 1970. Atty. Friday, Eldredge & Clark, Little Rock, 1969—. Chmn. Pulaski County Red Cross, Little Rock, 1989-90; bd. dirs. Ouachita Girl Scout Coun., Little Rock, 1987-93. With U.S. Army, 1967-69. Vietnam. Fellow Am. Coll. Trial Lawyers, Am. Bar Found.; mem. State Bd. Law Examiners 1979-82, Am. Bd. Trial Advocates, Ark. Bar Assn. (exec. coun. chmn. 1989-90, pres. 2004, Outstanding Lawyer award 1996), Pulaski County Bar Assn. (pres. 1987-88), Downtown Kiwanis Club (pres. 1991-92), William R. Overton Inn of Ct. (pres. 1990-91). Democrat. Methodist. Home: 2804 N Taylor St Little Rock AR 72207-2837 Office: Friday Eldredge & Clark 2000 Regions Ctr 400 W Capitol Ave Little Rock AR 72201-3436 Office Phone: 501-370-1555. Business E-Mail: ursery@fec.net.

**URSO, IDA,** psychologist; arrived in U.S., 1954; BA, Kent State U., 1969; MA, UCLA, 1974, PhD, 1983; cert., N.Y. Open Ctr., 1997. Sr. staff assoc. Ctr. for Human Interdependence, Orange, Calif., 1986—90; lectr. Chapman Coll., Orange, 1984—90; dir. World Goodwill, N.Y.C., 1990—96; integrative spiritual psychologist Chaitanya, Hoboken, NJ, 1997—; pres., founder Aquarian Age Cmty., Jersey City, 1998—. Elem. sch. cons. St. Pedro St. Sch., L.A., 1976—77; bd. mem. Calif. Coun. for UN U., L.A., 1982—84; lectr. Immaculate Heart Coll. Ctr., L.A., 1985, L.A., 98. Writer, editor: newsletter Diamond Light, 1997—; contbr. chapters to books. Bd. mem. Orange County chpt. UN Assn./USA, 1986—90; edin. chairperson Orange County, 1989—90; UN Dept. Publ. Info., Non Govtl. Orgn. World Goodwill, N.Y.C., 1990—96, Children of Earth Lifebridge, N.Y.C., 1998—2000, Aquarian Age Cmty., N.Y.C., 2003—. Mem.: Nicholas Roerich Mus., Am. Mus. Natural History. Avocations: community service, reading, music, meditation. Office: Aquarian Age Cmty 233 Bay St #206 Jersey City NJ 07302 Office Phone: 201-659-3060 ext. 145. Business E-Mail: ur@aquaac.org.

**URSO, JULIE ANN,** secondary school educator; b. Cin., Nov. 21, 1974; d. Neil Allen and JoAnn Helen Rush; m. Benjamin Joseph Urso, June 5, 2004. BS in Edn., U. Dayton, Ohio, 1997; MA in Tchg. Biology, Miami U., Oxford, Ohio, 2001. Biology tchr. McAuley HS, Cin., 1997—. Office: McAuley High Sch 6000 Oakwood Ave Cincinnati OH 45224-2398 Office Phone: 513-681-1800. E-mail: ursoj@mcauleyhs.net.

**URSTADT, CHARLES J.,** real estate company officer; b. Oct. 27, 1928; s. Charles G. and Claire (Jordan) U.; m. Elinor McClure Funk, Mar. 23, 1957; children: Charles Deane, Catherine Urstadt Biddle. BA, Dartmouth Coll., 1949, MBA, 1951; LLB, Cornell U., 1953; LLD with honors, Pace U., 1990. Bar: N.Y. Assoc. Nevius Brett & Kellogg, N.Y.C., 1953-58; asst. sec. Webb & Knapp, Inc., N.Y.C., 1958-63; v.p., sec. counsel Alcoa Residences, Inc., N.Y.C., 1963-67; commr. N.Y. State Divsn. Housing and comty. Renewal, N.Y.C., 1967-73; chmn. Battery Park City Authority, N.Y.C., 1968-78, Urstadt Property Co. Inc., 1979—. Chmn. Urstadt Biddle Properties, 1986—; trustee Tchrs. Ins. and Annuity Corp., 1985-97; N.Y; mem. NY Stocke Exchange, 2004—. Trustee Pace U., 1973— Hist. Hudson Valley, 1997—; mem. fin. com. N.Y. Rep. State Com., 1981—, del. Rep. Nat. Conv., 1988; mem. Gov.'s Task Force on N.Y. Housing, 1988-90; bd. dirs. N.Y.C. Partnership, Inc., 1984-93; chmn. Realty Found. of N.Y., 1989—, N.Y. State Statue of Liberty Celebration Found., 1983-84, N.Y. State Housing Fin. Agy., 1969, Tri-State Regional Planning Commn., 1969-70; vice-chmn. Battery Park City Authority, 1997—; mem. Pres.'s Commn. on Housing, 1981-82, others. Lt. USNR, 1954-56. Office: Urstadt Biddle Properties 321 Railroad Ave Greenwich CT 06830-6306

**URUSHADZE, LEVAN Z.,** political scientist, human rights activist; b. Tbilisi, Republic of Georgia, Feb. 7, 1964; parents: Zurab D. and Guranda E. (Gvaladze) U. Diploma, Tbilisi State U., Tbilisi, 1986; Dr., Inst. of History of the Georgian Acad. of Scis., Tbilisi, 1990. Rsch. fellow Inst. History of Georgian Acad. Scis., Tbilisi, 1986—95; sr. rsch. worker Inst. History of the Georgian Acad. Scis., Tbilisi, 1990-95; co-founder, mem. editl. bd. Independent Newspaper Tavisupali Sakartvelo (Free Georgia), Tbilisi, 1991-95; editor in chief Independent Newspaper Adamianis Uplebebi (Human Rights), Tbilisi, 1995—; pres. Natl. Sect. of Georgia of the Interatl. Soc. for Human Rights, Tbilisi, 1997—2000; chmn. Georgian Natl. Sect. of Eurosci, Tbilisi, 1998—. Author (monograph), Bolshevism-Menshevism and the Democratic Republic of Georgia, 1991, The Problems of the History of Georgia in the 20th Century Turkish Historiography, 1994, (scientific work) The Role of Russia in Ethnic Conflicts in the Caucasus, Caucasus War and Peace, Aus der Gesichte der Georgisch-Schweizerischen Verbindungen Mitteilungsblatt der Vereinigung der Freunde Georgiens in der Schweiz, Nr. 1. Grant, Westminster Found. for Democracy, U.K., 1997. Fellow Internat. Acad. Intercultural Rsch.; mem. World Peace Acad. Office: G Tsabadze Street 3-32 380012 Tbilisi Georgia

**URWITZ, JAY P.,** lawyer; b. 1949; BA cum laude, Harpur Coll., SUNY, Binghamton, 1970; MPP, Harvard Univ., 1974, JD cum laude, 1974. Bar: DC 1976. Law clk. Judge Irving L. Goldberg, US Ct. Appeals (5th cir.), 1974—75; former legis. asst. for domestic policy U.S. Senator Edward M. Kennedy, Washington; ptnr. Wilmer Cutler Pickering Hale & Dorr, Washington, 1985—, co-chmn. Def., Nat. Security & Govt. Contracts dept. Mem. & chmn. Software Com. Govt.-Industry Technical Data Com.; mem. Presdl. Rank Rev. Bd., Washington, 1995. Editor (sr.): Harvard Law Rev.; contbr. articles to newspapers & profl. jours. Office: Wilmer Cutler Pickering Hale & Dorr 1801 Pennsylvania Ave NW Washington DC 20006 Mailing: Wilmer Cutler Pickering Hale & Dorr Willard Office Bldg 1455 Pennsylvania Ave NW Washington DC 20004 Office Phone: 202-663-6084 Office Fax: 202-663-6363. Business E-Mail: jay.urwitz@wilmerhale.com.

**URY, FREDERIC STEPHEN,** lawyer; b. Zanesville, Ohio, Sept. 11, 1952; s. Perry S. and Lorraine (Greenstein) U.; m. Debby Hagopian, June 6, 1976; children: Jennifer, Robert. BS, Babson Coll., 1974; JD, Suffolk U., 1977. Bar: Conn. 1977, U.S. Dist. Ct. Conn. 1978, U.S. Supreme Ct. 1982. Assoc., ptnr. Sherwood, Garlick & Cowell, Westport, Conn., 1977-84; ptnr. Rubenstein & Ury, Westport, Conn., 1984; now ptnr. Ury & Moskow, Fairfield, Conn. Instr. Fairfield (Conn.) U., 1979-86; mem. exec. com. Nat. Conf. Bar Pres., 2005—. Pres. Cmty. Coun., Westport, 1983-85; bd. dirs. Westport-Weston United Way, 1985—, exec. v.p., 1988—; corp. mem., trustee Babson Coll., Wellesley, Mass., 1974-84, pres. Congregation For Humanistic Judaism 1997-2000; founder Charity Treks, Inc. Mem. ABA, Conn. Bar Assn. (exec. com. civil justice, pres. 2005), Assn. Trial Lawyers Am., Westport Bar Assn.,

Kiwanis. Democrat. Jewish. Avocations: hiking, skiing, long distance cycling. Office: Ury & Moskow LLC 883 Black Rock Tpk Fairfield CT 06825 Office Phone: 203-610-6393. Business E-Mail: fred@urymoskow.com.

**USCINSKI, RONALD HENRY,** medical educator; b. NYC, Apr. 3, 1943; s. Henry John and Marie Antionette Uscinski; m. Donna Lyn Cutsail, May 25, 1975; children: Benjamin Joseph, David Michael, Daniel Eric, Jessica Lyn. BS, Fordham U., NYC, 1964; MD, Georgetown U., Washington, 1968. Clin. prof. neurol. surgery & pediat. Georgetown U., Washington, 1980—; clin. prof. neurol. surgery George Wash. U., 1995— Lt USN, 1969—71. Scholar, Potomac Inst. Policy Studies, Arlington, Va., 2004—. Fellow: ACS (life); mem.: Congress Neurosurgeons (licentiate), Am. Assn. Neurol. Surgeons (licentiate), Polish Acad. Neurosurg. (corr.), Potomac Boat Club. Roman Catholic. Avocations: rowing, music, writing. Office: 18111 Prince Philip Dr Olney MD 20832 Office Phone: 301-260-0535. Business E-Mail: ruscinski@potomacinstitute.org.

**USDIN, GENE LEONARD,** psychiatrist; b. N.Y.C., Jan. 31, 1922; s. I. L. and Eva (Miller) U.; m. Cecile Weil, Nov. 8, 1947; children: Cecile Catherine Burka, Linda Ann, Steven William, Thomas Michael. Student, U. N.C., 1939—40, U. Fla., 1940—41; BS, Tulane U., 1943, MD, 1946. Diplomate Am. Bd. Psychiatry and Neurology (asst. examiner, 1956-80), Am. Bd. Legal Medicine. Intern Touro Infirmary, New Orleans, 1946—47; resident psychiatry Cin. Gen. Hosp., 1949—51; fellow psychiatry Tulane Sch. Medicine, 1951—52; pvt. practice psychiatry New Orleans, 1952—86; pvt practice psychiatry, 1996—; asst. prof. clin. psychiatry Tulane U., 1959—62, assoc. clin. prof., 1962—67, La. State U., 1967—96 clin. prof., 1971—96, clin. prof. emeritus, 1996—; sr. psychiatrist Ochsner Clinic, 1986-96, sr. psychiatrist emeritus, 1996—; prof. Notre Dame Sem., 1969-75; chief divsn. neurology and psychiatry Touro Infirmary, New Orleans, 1962—66, dir. psychiat. svcs., 1966—71. McLaughlin-Gallie vis. prof. Royal Coll. Physicians and Surgeons of Can., 1983; Robert O. Jones lectr. Atlantic Maritime Provinces Psychiat. Assn. (Can.), 1976; sr. psychiatrist DePaul and Charity Hosps.; sr. psychiat. cons. Ochsner Med. Found., New Orleans, 1980-85, Timberlawn Psychiat. Hosp., Dallas, 1979-93; chmn. psychiat. cons. com. Am. Bar Found., 1970-73; mem. nat. psychiat. adv. bd. Achievement and Guidance Ctrs. Am., Inc., 1991-92. Editor-in-chief Psychiatry Digest, 1964—71, 1975—79, ACP-Psychiat. Update, 1980—94, Psychiatry Digest (Europe), 1981—92, ACP-Psychiat. Update, 1995—96, 2000—04, co-editor, 1994—95; editor: Psychoneurosis and Schizophrenia, 1966, Practical Lectures in Psychiatry for the Medical Practitioner, 1966, Adolescence: Care and Counseling, 1967; editor: (with Peter A. Martin and A.W. Swipe) A Physician in the General Practice of Psychiatry, 1970; editor: Perspectives on Violence, 1972, The Psychiatric Forum, 1973, Psychiatry: Education and Image, 1973, Sleep Research and Clinical Practice, 1973, Overview of the Psychotherapies, 1975, Psychiatric Medicine, 1977, Depression: Clinical, Biological and Psychological Perspectives, 1977, Schizophrenia: Biological and Psychological Perspective, 1978; editor: (with Charles K. Hofling) Aging: The Process and the People, 1978; editor: (with Jerry M. Lewis II) Psychiatry in General Medical Practice, 1979; editor: (with David R. Hawkins) The Office Guide to Sleep Disorders, 1980; editor: Medilex Digest of Psychiatry, 1980—92; editor: (with Jerry M. Lewis) Treatment Planning in Psychiatry, 1982; mem. editl. bd. Clin. Medicine, 1965—71, 1975—88, Med. Digest, 1965—71, Mental Hygiene, 1969—76, Jour. Hosp. and Cmty. Psychiatry, 1975, chmn., 1980—81, mem. editl. bd. Jour. Psychiat. Edn., 1975—89, Psychiatry Bookshelf, 1976—78, Jour. Ottawa Med. Sch., 1976—90, Am. Jour. Family Therapy, 1978—92, Am. Jour. Social Psychiatry, 1981—87, Swiss Med. Digest, Psychiatry, 1981—92, Extracta Medica Practica Psychiatrie, 1981—92, Behavioral Scis. and the Law, 1982—92, Dynamic Psychotherapy, 1982—90, Psychiatric Medicine, 1982—88, 1982—88, Women's Psychiat. Health, 1982—94, Advances in Therapy, 1983—96, Clin. Psychiatric News, 1983—92, Contemporary Psychiatry, 1984—93, The Psychiat. Times, 1985—, book rev. editor, 1988—2002, Health Disease, 1986—93, Clin. Advances in Treatment of Psychiat. Disorders, 1987—93, Acad. Psychosomatic Medicine (mem. exec. coun. 1974-76), New Orleans Soc. Psychiatry and the Law, 1988, Outstanding Contbrn. to Social Psychiatry award Am. Assn. for Social Psychiatry, 1993, Lifetime Achievement awards Tulane Med. Alumni Assn., 1996, Fla. Hosp. Ctr. for Psychiatry, 1996, La. State U. Sch. Medicine Dept. Psychiatry Chmn.'s award, 1998-99, Champion of Pub. Health award Tulane U. Sch. Pub. Health and Tropical Medicine, 2001, Outstanding Contributions award Tulane Univ. Med. Sch., 2005; named Psychiatrist of Yr., La. Psychiat. Med. Assn., 1994, Psychiat. Times, 1997. Fellow Am. Psychiat. Assn. (chmn. com. on psychiatry and law 1964-68, mem. com. on ethics 1970-74, com. on membership 1970-74, com. on evaluation svcs. bd. 1974-77, com. on pub. affairs 1976-78, chmn. ad hoc com. on election procedures, 1980-81, trustee at large 1978-81, coun. on internat. affairs 1986-91, sec. gen. Interamerican Coun. of Psychiat. Orgns. 1988-91, recipient 3d ann. Certificate of Recognition for Excellence in Med. Student Edn. 1993, Warren Williams award, 1995, Spl. Presdl. commendation 1998), So. Psychiat. Assn. (bd. regents 1969-72, chmn. 1971-72, pres. 1973-74), La. Psychiat. Assn. (past pres.), Am. Coll. Psychiatrists (bd. regents 1967-70, pres. 1978-79, E.B. Bowis award for Outstanding Contbns. 1973, Disting. Svc. award for Oustanding Contbns. in Am. Psychiatry 1980), Acad. Psychosomatic Medicine (mem. exec. coun. 1974-76), New Orleans Soc. Psychiatry and Neurology (past pres.), Group Advancement Psychiatry (bd. dirs. 1970-77, treas. 1973-77), Am. Assn. Social Psychiatry (pres. 1986-88), World Assn. for Social Psychiatry (exec. coun. 1988-90); mem. La. Med. Soc. (chmn. com. on mental health 1966-70), Orleans Parish Med. Soc., Nat. Assn. Mental Health (mem. profl. adv. coun. 1968-75), Inst. of Mental Hygiene (pres. 1978-79). Home and Office: 3 Newcomb Blvd New Orleans LA 70118-5527 Office Phone: 504-866-5405. Personal E-mail: GUsdin3333@aol.com.

**USELTON, BILL W.,** secondary school educator; b. Oklahoma City, Dec. 14, 1959; s. Jerry Max and Minnie Jewel Uselton; m. Cathy Sue Uselton, Oct. 16, 1982; children: Kelly Irene, Jennifer Elaine. A in Fine Arts, Oscar Rose Jr. Coll., Midwest City, Okla., 1980; BFA, Ctrl. State U., Edmund, Okla., 1982. Cert. secondary sch. tchr. Constract substitute Choctaw (Okla.) Pub. Schs., 1982-84; tchr. Choctaw Jr. H.S., 1984-86, Choctaw H.S., 1986—. Author: Triad of Evil, 1993. Mem. World Jewish Congress; tour guide S.W. Radio Ch., Oklahoma City, 1982; chmn. Confederate Meml., Choctaw, 1996—. Republican. Baptist. Home: 1024 S Anderson Rd Choctaw OK 73020 Office Phone: 405-390-8899.

**USERA, VINCENT L.,** state agency administrator; b. Buenos Aires, 1942; BS, Coll. Holy Cross, 1964; BA in Philosophy, cum laude, George Washington U., 1978; JD, Catholic U., 1981. Bar: Alaska 1985, admitted to practice: US Fed. Ct. 1985, US Ct. Appeals (9th Cir.) 1985, US Dist. Ct. (Alaska) 1986. Asst. atty. gen. Alaska Dept. Law, Comml. Sec., 1991—99; acting dir. Dept. Cmty. and Econ. Devel., 1999—. Office: Dimond Courthouse PO Box 110300 123 4th St Juneau AK 99811-0300 Office Phone: 907-562-0440. Office Fax: 907-452-2520.

**USHAKOV, YURY VIKTOROVICH,** ambassador; b. Moscow, Mar. 13, 1947; married; 1 daughter. Grad., Moscow State Inst. Internat. Relations, 1970; PhD in History, Diplomatic Acad. With Soviet Embassy in Denmark Ministry Fgn. Affairs of the USSR, 1970-75, with 1975-86; dep. chief mission, min.-counsellor Embassy of the USSR/Russian Fedn., Denmark, 1986-92; dir. Dept. of All-European Coop. Ministry Fgn. Affairs Russian Fedn., 1992—96; amb., permanent rep. Russian Fedn. to the Orgn. Security and Coop. Europe, Vienna, 1996-98; dep. min. fgn. affairs Govt. Russian Fedn., 1998-99, amb. to the U.S. Washington, 1999—. Office: Embassy of the Russian Fedn 2650 Wisconsin Ave NW Washington DC 20007-4600 Fax: 202-298-5749. Office Phone: 202-298-5701. E-mail: russianembassy@mindspring.com.

**USHER, THOMAS JAMES,** metal products executive; b. Reading, Pa., Sept. 11, 1942; s. Paul T. and Mary (Leonard) Usher; m. Sandra L. Mort, Aug. 14, 1965; children: Leanne, Jimmy, Lauren. BS in Indsl. Engring., U. Pitts., 1964, MS in Ops. and Rsch., 1965, PhD in Systems Engring., 1971. Indsl. engr. U. S. Steel Corp., Pitts., 1966—76, asst. gen. supt., 1975—78, asst. div. supt. Gary, Ind., 1978—81, asst. to pres., mng. dir. facility planning and engring. Pitts., 1982—83, v.p. engring., 1982—83, pres., 1991, U.S. Steel Mining Co., Inc., Pitts., 1983—84, v.p. engring. steel, 1984—, sr. v.p. steel ops., 1984—, exec. v.p. heavy products steel divsn., 1986—89, pres. steel divsn., 1990; pres., COO USX Corp., Pitts., 1994—95, chmn., CEO, 1995—2001; chmn. US Steel Corp., Pitts., 2001—06. Bd. dir. PNC Fin. Svcs.; bd. dirs. PPG Industries, H.J. Heinz Co.; bd. dir. non-exec. chmn. Marathon Oil Corp. Mem. Leadership Pitts., 1984; trustee Multiple Sclerosis, Pitts., 1985; chmn. Allegheny Trails coun. Boy Scouts Am., Pitts, 1985, United Way, Pitts., 1985, U.S.-Korea Bus. Coun., 1993—; U.S.-Japan Bus. Coun.; trustee U. Pitts., 1994—, The Bus. Roundtable Nat. Found., 1995; vice chmn. Internat. Iron and Steel Inst. Bus. Coun., 1997. Mem. Am. Iron and Steel Engrs. (bd. dirs. 1984—85), Dinamo/Ovia (bd. dirs. 1985), Am. Iron and Steel Inst., The Club at Nevillewood, Augusta Nat. Golf Club, Duquesne Tree Club, Oakmont Club, Dougle Eagle Club, Laurel Valley Club, Duquesne Club, Rolling Rock Club. Avocations: golf, tennis, racquetball, scuba diving, swimming. Mailing: Marathon Oil Corp Bd Directors 5555 San Felipe Rd Houston TX 77056-2723*

**USHER, See RAYMOND, USHER IV**

**USIP, EBENGE ETEFIA,** economics professor; b. Ikot Obiokoi, Akwa Ibom, Nigeria, Oct. 22, 1948; arrived in USA, 1970, permanent resident, 1987; s. Etefia Essiet and Mary Unwaedo Usip; m. Sharon Elaine Lord, May 27, 1984; children: Nsikan, Ebenge Jr., Kufre, Unyime. BS, SUNY, Albany, NY, 1974, MA, 1976; PhD, U of Conn., Storrs, Conn., 1984. Asst. prof. Youngstown State U, Youngstown, Ohio, 1985—89, assoc. prof., 1990—98, prof., 1999—. Author: (Teaching Home Page) The Ctr. for Web-Based Ed. in Quantitative Econ., 1996 (creativity on Intergrating New Tech. in the tchg. of Undergrad. Econ., 1998), (jour. publication) Coll. Student Jour., 1998, Soc. Sci. Computer Rev., 1998, The Ohio Jour. of Econ. and Politics, 1998, Jour. of Econ. Ed. (JEE), 1999, (book) Learning Econ. and Bus. Stats. with SPSS/win, 4th edit., 2003. Recipient Perseverance in Application of External Funding, The Graduate School/OH, 2002; grantee CCLI-Ed. Material Develop. NSF Grant #0127362, Nat. Sci. Found. (NSF)/DC, 2001. Mem.: Ea. Econ. Assoc. (assoc.), Am. Statis. Assoc. (assoc.), Am. Econ. Assoc. (assoc.). Methodist. Avocations: soccer, tennis, photography, video games, travel. Home: 1202 Will-O-Wood Dr Hubbard OH 44425 Office: Youngstown State Univ 1 University Plaza Youngstown OH 44555

**USISKIN, ZALMAN PHILIP,** mathematics educator; b. Chgo., Jan. 1, 1943; s. Nathan and Esther (Chukerman) U.; m. Karen Hesse, Sept. 2, 1979; children: Robert, Laura. BS in Math., U. Ill., 1963, BS in Edn., 1963; MA in Teaching of Math., Harvard U., 1964; PhD in Edn., U. Mich., 1969. Tchr. math. Niles Twp. High Sch.-West, Skokie, Ill., 1964-66; asst. prof. U. Chgo., 1969-74, assoc. prof., 1974-82, prof. edn., 1982—. Vis. prof. U. Ga., Athens, 1980; mem. nat. adv. bd. Children's TV Workshop, Square One TV, N.Y.C., 1986-92; dir. U. Chgo. Sch. Math. Project, 1987—; mem. math. scis. edn. bd. NRC, Washington, 1988-91; mem. U.S. Nat. Commn. on Math. Instrn., 1995-97, chmn., 1998—2001. Co-author: Geometry-A Transformation Approach, 1971, UCSMP Geometry, 1990, 2nd edit., 1996; author: Advanced Algebra with Transformations and Applications, 1975, Algebra Through Applications, 1976, UCSMP Transition Mathematics, 1989, 2nd edit., 1995; mem. editl. bd. Am. Jour. Edn., 1983—2003; contbr. articles to profl. jours. Recipient Max Beberman award Ill. Coun. Tchrs. Math., 1981, Glenn Gilbert award Nat. Coun. Suprs. Math., 1994; named Disting. speaker ASCD, 1991; grantee. Mem. Nat. Assessment Ednl. Progress (mem. math. adv. com. 1995—), Nat. Coun. Tchrs. Math. (bd. dirs. 1995-98, Lifetime Achievement award 2001), Math. Assn. Am., Nat. Coun. Suprs. Math. (1st v.p. 1982-83), Met. Math. Club Chgo. (bd. dirs. 1970-73), Phi Beta Kappa, Phi Delta Kappa. Office: U Chgo 6030 S Ellis Chicago IL 60637

**USTIAN, DANIEL C.,** trucking executive; With Navistar Internat. Corp., 1973—, group v.p., gen. mgr. engine group, 1990—99, pres., 1999—, COO 2002—03, CEO, 2003—, chmn., 2004—. Office: Navistar International Corp PO Box 1488 4201 Winfield Rd Warrenville IL 60555 Office Phone: 630-753-5000.*

**USUI, LESLIE RAYMOND,** apparel executive; b. Wahiawa, Hawaii, Feb. 2, 1946; s. Raymond Isao and Joyce Mitsuyo (Muramoto) U.; m. Annie On Nor Hom, Oct. 23, 1980; 1 child, Atisha. BA in Zool., U. Hawaii, 1969, MA in Edn., 1972. Cert. tchr. Hawaii. Flight steward United Airlines, Honolulu, 1970; spl. tutor Dept. Edn., 1971-73; v.p. Satyuga, Inc., Honolulu, 1974-80, pres., 1980-97; also bd. dir.; pres. Masktique LLC, 2006—. Cons. Hawaii Fashion Guild, 1978-79. Composer: Song to Chenrayzee, Song to Karmapa: author: The Early History of Tibetan Buddhism in Hawaii, 2005. Co-founder, Kagyu Thegchen Ling Meditation Ctr., 1974-03; bd. dir. Maitreya Inst., 1983-86, Palpung Found., 1984-2006; mem. US Senatorial Bus. Adv. Bd., Wash., 1988; charter mem. Citizens Against Govt. Waste, 1988—, Citizens for Sound Economy, 1987-91, Nat. Tax Limitation Com., 1988-89. Mem. Am. Biog. Inst. (life, bd. govs. 1990), Internat. Biog. Centre (life), World Inst. Achievement (life), Cousteau Soc., Nature Conservancy, Waikiki Aquarium. Republican. Buddhist. Avocations: oriental gardening, music. Home: PO Box 161257 Honolulu HI 96816-0926 Office: Satyuga Inc PO Box 161257 Honolulu HI 96816-0926

**USWATTE, GITENDRA,** psychology professor; s. G. and M. Uswatte-Aratchi; m. Dilhani Donna Jayamanne Uswatte, July 15, 2000; 1 child, Suman Anthony. PhD, U. Ala., 2001. Cert. psychologist Ala. Bd. Examiners in Psychology, 2004. Asst. prof. dept. psychology U. Ala., Birmingham, 2001—. Contbr. articles to profl. jours. Mem.: Am. Congress Rehab. Medicine, Am. Psychology Assn. Buddhist. Achievements include development of method for objectively measuring how much rehabilitation patients use their arm during their daily activities. Office: Dept Psychology UAB 1530 3rd Ave S CH415 Birmingham AL 35294

**UTHMANN, RICHARD W.,** retired music educator; b. Chanute, Kans., Mar. 18, 1938; s. Walter Henry and Susie Elizabeth Uthmann; m. Edith L. Uthmann, June 29, 1963; 1 child, James Richard. BA in Music Edn., Wash. State U., 1960; MA in Music Edn., Wash. Music Edn., 1971. Tchr. band Garfield Pub. Schs., Wash., 1961—63, Mukilteo Pub. Schs., 1963—67; tchr. music Granger Pub. Schs., 1967—68, Billings Pub. Schs., 1971—73; tchr. band Kelso Pub. Schs., Wash., 1973—88, Wahkia Kun Pub. Schs., Cathlamet, 1988—97, Cornerstone Christian Sch., Kelso, 1997—2006; with Winds Woodwing Quintet, 2004—. Dir. theatre orch. Performing Arts Ctr., Longview, Wash., 1976—; bd. dirs. Mt. Solo Homeowners Assn., 1997—. Capt. U.S. Army, 1968—69, Vietnam. Mem.: Wash. Music Educators Assn. (Hall of Fame 2002), Southwest Wash. Symphony (bd. dirs. 1980—), Southwest Wash. Youth Symphony (sect. chair). Methodist. Avocations: gardening, woodworking, music. Home: 120 Ridgecrest Ln Longview WA 98632 Office Phone: 360-430-7283. Personal E-mail: duthmann@peoplepc.com.

**UTKU, SENOL,** civil engineer, computer science educator; b. Suruc, Turkey, Nov. 23, 1931; s. Sukru and Sukufe (Gumus) U.; m. Bisulay Bereket, May 9, 1964; children: Ayda, Sinan. Diploma in engring., Istanbul Tech. U., 1954; MS, MIT, 1959, ScD, 1960. Civil engr., Istanbul, Turkey. Rsch. engr. IBM, 1959-60; asst. prof. structural engring MIT, 1960-62; assoc. prof. Middle East Tech. U., Ankara, Turkey, 1962-63; exec. dir., head of founding com. Computation Ctr., Istanbul Tech. U., 1963-65; tech. staff Jet Propulsion Lab., Pasadena, Calif., 1965-70, tech. cons., 1975—91; assoc. prof. civil engring Duke U., Durham, N.C., 1970-72, prof., 1972-79, prof. civil engring., prof. computer sci., 1979—2001, dir. undergrad. studies, 1980-87, dir. grad. studies, 1987-89, prof. emeritus civil engring. and computer sci., 2002—; prof. emeritus engring. scis. Istanbul Tech. U., 1994—. Sr. Fulbright lectr.,

Turkey, 1998. Author: ELAS Software, 1968, Elementary Structural Analysis, 4th edit., 1991, Linear Analysis of Discrete Structures, 1991, Theory of Adaptive Structures, 1998; co-author: Dynamics of Offshore Structures, 1984, Finite Element Handbook, 1987, Parallel Processing in Computational Mechanics, 1992, Intelligent Structural Systems, 1992; contbr. articles to profl. jours. Fulbright scholar, Turkey, 1957, Fulbright lectr. Turkey, 1998; recipient Pres.'s Fund award Calif. Inst. Tech., 1981, NASA award, 1969, 71, 77, 84, 86-87, Internat. Joint Rsch. award NSF, 1991-92. Fellow ASCE; mem. AAUP, Am. Acad. Mechanics, Fulbright Assn., Am. Soc. for Engring. Edn., Structural Engring. Inst. (charter), Sigma Xi, Chi Epsilon. Office: Duke U 121 Hudson Hall Durham NC 27708-0287 E-mail: bsutku@ttnet.net.tr, senol.utku@duke.edu.

**UTLEY, CHASE,** professional baseball player; b. Dec. 17, 1978; Garduated, UCLA. Second basemen Phila. Phillies, 2003—. Mem. Team USA, World Baseball Classic, 2006. Named to NL All-Star Team, MLB, 2006. Office: Citizens Bank Park One Citizens Bank Way Philadelphia PA 19148*

**UTLEY, F. KNOWLTON,** library director, educator; b. Northampton, Mass., May 4, 1935; s. Frederick K. and Florence E. (Moore) Utley; m. Faith E. Green, July 2, 1960; children: Richard F., Stephen R., David E. BS, Castleton State Coll., 1960; MA, U. Conn., 1967; EdD, Boston U., 1979; MLS, U. Ala., 1983. Tchr. indsl. arts Montpelier (Vt.) High Sch., 1960-61, Southwick (Mass.) H.S., 1961-63; tchr., drafting instr. Putnam (Conn.) H.S., 1963-68; media specialist Ctrl. Conn. State U., New Britain, 1968-69, dir. media svcs., 1969-72; doctoral tchg. fellow Boston U., 1972-73; dir. libr., media svcs. Manchester (Mass.) Pub. Schs., 1973-79; assoc. prof. libr. scis. U. Maine, Farmington, 1979—80; dir. grad. program libr. media Livingston (Ala.) U., 1980—83; dir. libr. media svcs. Am. Internat. Coll., Springfield, Mass., 1983—. Pres. C/W Mars-Ctrl. and We. Mass. Auto Res., 1987—88; chmn. bd. dirs. Cooperating Librs. of Great Springfield, 1988—89, We. Mass. Media Coun., 1991—93; founder, headmaster Hampshire Christian Acad., South Hadley, Mass., 1996—2002. Active Belchertown (Mass.) Housing Authority, 2000—, Belchertown Hist. Commn., 2004—; trustee Clapp Meml. Libr., Belchertown, 2003—. Mem.: ALA, Mass. Libr. Assn., New Eng. Libr. Assn., Assn. Edn. Comm. and Tech., Am. Christian Schs. Internat., Phi Delta Kappa. Home: 11 Canal Dr Belchertown MA 01007-9224 Office: Am Internat Coll 1000 State St Springfield MA 01109-3151 Office Phone: 413-205-3225. Business E-Mail: kutley@cwmars.org.

**UTLEY, JON BASIL,** think-tank executive, journalist; b. Moscow, Mar. 10, 1934; came to U.S., 1939, naturalized, 1952; s. Arcadi and Freda (Utley) Berdichevsky; m. Ana Maria Hijar, 1968. Student, U. Munich, 1952, Alliance Française, Paris, 1956; BS, Georgetown U., 1956. Mgr. Am. Internat. Underwriters, Cali, Colombia, 1959-60; editor, pub. Bogotá Bull., 1960-61; v.p. Universal Investors Svcs., Nassau, 1962-67; real estate developer Washington, 1968—; mng. gen. ptnr. Kimwill Oil Assocs., Warren, Pa., 1978-86; pres. Ocean McLean Corp., 1989-97, Needle in a Haystack, Washington, 1990-98, Needle Express, 1993-98; fgn. corr. Jour. Commerce, Internat. Reports, S. Am., 1969-74; columnist Times of the Ams., 1974-92, assoc. editor, 1981-92; columnist Washington Inquirer, 1981-90, Washington Times, 1981-82; contbg. editor Conservative Digest, 1984-89; mem. editl. adv. bd. Internat. Reports, 1981-91. Lectr. Accuracy in Media, treas., Ukraine, 1997, Cyprus, 99, Freedoms Found. Valley Forge; commentator Voice of Am., 1985—2003; Jamestown Found. observer Russian elections, 2000. Assoc. pub. The Am. Conservative, 2005—; contbr. articles to Washington Post, Harvard Bus. Rev., Nat. Rev., Human Events, Miami Herald, Lincoln Rev., N.Y.C. Tribune, Am. Legion mag., El Salvador Gazette, The World and I, Antiwar.com, Lima Times, others. Observer Guatemalan elections George-town U. Ctr. Strategic Studies, 1985, Romanian elections, 1990; trustee Ctr. Internat. Rels., adv. com. Solidarity Endowment; co-founder Com. to Avert a Mideast Holocaust, 1990-94; pres. Fred Utley Found., 2002—. Assoc. scholar Competitive Enterprise Inst., 1995-98; Robert A. Taft fellow Ludwig Von Mises Inst., 1998—. Fellow: Atlas Econ. Rsch. Found. (sr.; dir. Russian projects 2000—); mem.: Coun. Nat. Policy, Ams. Against Bombing/Ams. Against World Empire (chmn. 1998—), Hispanic Am. Ctr. Econ. Rsch. (bd. dirs. 1997—), World English Lang. Newspaper Assn. (pres. 1996), United Srs. Assn. (bd. dirs. 1993—2001, v.p. Amcham Cuba 2003—), Coun. Inter-Am. Security (bd. dirs. 1988—93), Phila. Soc. Nat. Press Club. Office: 910 17th St NW Ste 422 Washington DC 20006-2605 Personal E-mail: Jutly@aol.com, jbutley@earthlink.net.

**UTLEY, NANCY,** film company executive; Exec. v.p. mktg., media, and rsch. 20th Century Fox, Beverly Hills, Calif.; pres. mktg. Fox Searchlight Pictures. Office: 20th Century Fox PO Box 900 Beverly Hills CA 90213-0900*

**UTT, GLENN S., JR.,** retired medical products executive; b. Neodesha, Kans., Aug. 7, 1926; s. Glenn S. and Reba Pauline (White) U.; m. Mary Lou Ford, Aug. 8, 1948; 1 child, Jan A. BSEE, BSBA, Kans. State U., 1949; MBA, Harvard U., 1951. Salesman Drexel Furniture Co., NC, 1951-55; v.p. Booz Allen & Hamilton, Chgo. and Zurich, Switzerland, 1955-62; exec. v.p. Abbott Labs., North Chicago, Ill., 1962-83, also dir., ret., 1983. Chmn. bd. U.P. Hotel Group Inc., Houghton, Mich.; ret. dir. Synergen, Selectide and Sugen biotech cos. Co-author: Lalique Perfume Bottles, 1990. Alderman City of Lake Forest, Ill., 1972-76, chmn. recreational bd., 1975-78; mem. exec. com. Lake County Republican Fedn., Waukegan, Ill., 1974-83. With USN, 1944-46, USAF (res.), 1948-53. Mem.: Beta Theta Pi. Avocations: antiques, objects of art. Home: PO Box 810 Houghton MI 49931 Personal E-mail: mlbud@webtv.net.

**UTTAL, WILLIAM R(EICHENSTEIN),** psychology and engineering educator, research scientist; b. Mineola, NY, Mar. 24, 1931; s. Joseph and Claire (Reichenstein) U.; m. Michiye Nishimura, Dec. 20, 1954; children: Taneil, Lynet, Lisa. Student, Miami U. Oxford, Ohio, 1947-48; BS in Physics, U. Cin., 1951; PhD in Exptl. Psychology and Biophysics, Ohio State U., 1957. Staff Psychologist, mgr. behavioral sci. group IBM Rsch. Ctr., Yorktown Heights, NY, 1957-63; assoc. prof. U. Mich., Ann Arbor, 1963-68, prof. psychology, 1968-86, rsch. scientist, 1963-86; prof. emeritus, 1986—; grad. affiliate faculty dept. psychology U. Hawaii, 1986-88; rsch. scientist Naval Ocean Systems Ctr.-Hawaii Lab., Kailua, 1985-88; chmn. dept. psychology Ariz. State U., Tempe, 1988—90, prof. dept. indsl. engring., 1992—99, affiliated prof., Dept. of Computer Sci. and Engring., 1993-98, prof. emeritus, 1999—. Vis. prof. Kyoto (Japan) Prefectural Med. U., 1965-66, Sensory Sci. Lab., U. Hawaii, 1968, 73, 03-06, U. Western Australia, 1970-71, U. Hawaii, 1978-79, 80-81, U. Auckland, 1996, U. Freiburg, 1997, U. Sydney, 1999; pres. Nat. Conf. on On-Line Uses Computers in Psychology, 1974. Author: Real Time Computers: Techniques and Applications in the Psychological Sciences, 1968, Generative Computer Assisted Instruction in Analytic Geometry, 1972, The Psychobiology of Sensory Coding, 1973, Cellular Neurophysiology and Integration: An Interpretive Introduction, 1975, An Autocorrelation Theory of Visual Form Detection, 1975, The Psychobiology of Mind, 1978, A Taxonomy of Visual Processes, 1981, Visual Form Detection in Three Dimensional Space, 1983, Principles of Psychobiology, 1983, The Detection of Nonplanar Surfaces in Visual Space, 1985, The Perception of Dotted Forms, 1987, On Seeing Forms, 1988, The Swimmer: A Computational Model of a Perceptual Motor System, 1992, Toward a New Behaviorism: The Case Against Perceptual Reductionism, 1998, A Computational Model of Vision: The Role of Combination, 1999, The War Between Mentalism and Behaviorism, 2000, The New Phrenology: Limits on the Localization of Cognitive Processes in the Brain, 2001, A Behaviorist Looks at Form Recognition, 2002, Psychomythics, 2003, Dualism, 2004, Neural Theories of Mind, 2005, Human Factory in the Courtroom, 2006; editor: Readings in Sensory Coding, 1972; assoc. editor Readings in Sensory Coding, 1972, Behavioral Rsch. Method and Instrn., 1968—90, Computing: Archives for Electronic Computing, 1963—75, Jour. Exptl. Psychology, Perception and Performance, 1974—79, cons. editor Jour. Exptl. Psychology: Applied, 1994—97; contbr. articles to profl. jours. Served to 2d lt. USAF, 1951-53. USPHS spl. postdoctoral fellow, 1965-66; NIMH research scientist award, 1971-76 Fellow AAAS, APA, Am. Psychol. Soc.

(charter), Soc. Exptl. Psychologists (chmn. 1994-95); founding fellow Ariz. Acad. Sci., Arts & Tech.; mem. Psychonomics Soc. Achievements include patents in field. Office: Ariz State U Dept Indsl Engring Tempe AZ 85287-1104 Business E-Mail: aowru@asu.edu.

**UTTER, BRENDA LU**, adult education educator; b. Rochester, Ind., July 21, 1961; d. Richard Leroy and Juanita Joan Utter. BA, Ball State U., 1984; lic. tchr., Ind. U., 1994, MS in Edn., 2005. With R.R. Donnelley & Sons Co., Warsaw, Ind., 1979—95; Spanish tchr. Tippecanoe Valley Schs., Montone, Ind., 1996—97; profl. devel. coord., intake coord., tchr. Warsaw Cmty. Schs/Warsaw Adult Edn., 1997—; program coord., 2000—. Spkr. in field. Author: Brain Based Lesson Planning, 2005. Lay leader, fin. officer, adult Sunday sch. tchr. Talma (Ind.) United Meth. Ch. Mem.: ASCD, Ind. Assn. Adult and Continuing Edn., Emmaus Soc. Republican. Avocations: reading, gardening. Home: 213 S Main St Etna Green IN 46524 Office: Warsaw Cmty Schs/Warsaw Adult Edn 850 E Smith St Warsaw IN 46580 Office Phone: 574-371-5019 ext 4010. Office Fax: 574-371-5033. E-mail: butter@warsaw.k12.in.us.

**UTTER, DONALD L.**, music educator; b. Poughkeepsie, N.Y., Apr. 18, 1951; s. Clarence and Marion (Cobb) U. BS, Susquehanna U., 1974; MusM, Ind. U., 1979. Cert. tchr. music K-12 N.Y. Music educator Webutuck Ctrl. Sch., Amenia, NY, 1979-84, Pawling (N.Y.) High Sch., 1984—. Rep. N.Y. State Sch. Music, Pawling, 1995-98; solo festival judge N.Y., 1990—; past v.p. Tchrs. Assn., 1993-94. Bd. dirs. Pawling (N.Y.) Concert Series, 1988—, County Farm Bur., Millbrook, N.Y., 1991-95; bd. dirs. Rep. Party, Pawling, 1993, chmn., 2000-03; varsity golf coach Pawling H.S; chmn. Pawling Rep. Com., 2002-05. Named Coach of the Yr., Pawling High Sch., 1994. Mem. Dutchess County Music Educators (chmn. All-County Music Festival 1993-95), Music Educators Nat. Conf., Am. Fedn. Musicians Local 85. Republican. Methodist. Avocations: golf, skiing, reading. Home: 93 Harmony Rd Pawling NY 12564-0089 Office: Pawling HS Reservoir Rd Pawling NY 12564

**UTTER, ROBERT FRENCH**, dean, retired judge; b. Seattle, June 19, 1930; s. John and Besse (French) Utter; m. Elizabeth J. Stevenson, Dec. 28, 1953; children: Kimberly, Kirk, John. BS, U. Wash., 1952; LLB, 1954. Bar: Wash. 1954. Pros. atty., King County, Wash., 1955-57; individual practice law Seattle, 1957-59; ct. commr. King County Superior Ct., 1959-64, judge, 1964-69, Wash. State Ct. Appeals, 1969-71, Wash. State Supreme Ct., 1971-95, chief justice, 1979-81; ret., 1995; dean of faculty Ctrl. and Eastern European Legal Inst., Prague, Czech Republic, 2001—04, faculty, 2005—. Lectr. in field; leader comparative law tours; adj. prof. constl. law U. Puget Sound, 1987—94; cons. CEELI, 1991, 1993—, USIA, 1992; vis. scholar Kyrgystan Judiciary, Kazakhstan, 1993—96, Mongolia, 1997; commentator on Moldovan constitution, 2003. Editor: books on real property and appellate practice; author: books on state constl. law. Pres., founder Big Brother Assn., Seattle, 1955—67, Job Therapy Inc., 1963—71; mem. exec. com. Conf. Chief Justices, 1979—80, 1981—86; pres. Thurston County Big Bros./Big Sisters, 1984; lectr Soviet Acad. Moscow, 1991; USIA visitor to comment on jud. sys. Latvia, 1992, Kazakhstan, 1993—94; trustee Linfield Coll. Named Alumnus of the Yr., Linfield Coll., 1973, Judge of the Yr., Wash. State Trial Lawyers, 1989, Outstanding Judge, Wash. State Bar Assn., 1990, Seattle-King County Bar Assn., 1992, Outstanding Jurist, 2005, Conder-Faulkner lectr., U. Wash. Sch. Law, 1995, Disting. Alumnus, Sch. Law U. Wash., 1995; recipient Henry Jackson Disting. Pub. Svc. award, Nat. Wash. Sch. Law, 2000, Warren E. Burger award, Nat. Ctr. for State Cts., 2003, Vol. award, ABA-CEELI Program, 2003; Disting. Jud. scholar, U. Ind., 1987. Fellow: Chartered Inst. Arbitrators; mem.: ABA (commentator on proposed constns. of Albania, Bulgaria, Romania, Russia, Lithuania, Azerbaijan, Uzbekistan, Byelarus, Kazakhstan, and Ukraine), Am. Judicature Soc. (sec. 1987—, chmn. bd. dirs., mem. exec. com., Herbert Harley award 1983, Justice award 1998), Order of Coif. Baptist. Personal E-mail: rutter4804@aol.com.

**UTZ, SARAH WINIFRED**, nursing educator; b. San Diego; d. Frederick R. and Margaret M. (Gibbons) U.; BS, U. Portland, 1943, EdM, 1958; MS, UCLA, 1970; PhD, U. So. Calif., 1979. Clin. instr. Providence Sch. Nursing, Portland, Oreg., 1946-50, edn. dir., 1950-62; edn. dir. Sacred Heart Sch. Nursing, Eugene, Oreg., 1963-67; asst. prof. nursing Calif. State U., L.A., 1969-74, assoc. prof., 1974-81, prof., 1981—, assoc. chmn. dept. nursing, 1982—; cons. in nursing curriculum, 1978—; healthcare cons., 1991—; past chmn. ednl. adminstrs., cons., tchrs. sect. Oreg. Nurses Assn., past pres. Oreg. State Bd. Nursing; mem. rsch. program Western Interstate Commn. on Higher Edn. in Nursing; chmn. liaison com. nursing edn. Articulation Coun. Calif. Author articles and lab manuals. Served with Nurse Corps, USN, 1944-46. HEW grantee, 1970-74, Kellogg Found. grantee, 1974-76, USDHHS grantee, 1987—; R.N., Calif., Oreg. Mem. Am. Nurses Assn., Calif. Nurses Assn. (edn. commr. region 6 1987—, chair edn. interest group region 6, 1987—), Am. Ednl. Rsch. Assn., AAUP, Phi Delta Kappa, Sigma Theta Tau. Formerly editor Oreg. Nurse; reviewer Western Jour. Nursing Rsch. Home: 1409 Midvale Ave Los Angeles CA 90024-5454 Office: 5151 State University Dr Los Angeles CA 90032-4226

**UVENA, FRANK JOHN**, retired printing company executive, lawyer; b. Ernest, Pa., Feb. 2, 1934; AB, Ohio U., Athens, 1959; LLB, Ohio State U., Columbus, 1963. Bar: Ill. 1963. Assoc. firm McDermott, Will & Emery, Chgo., 1963-68; atty. R.R. Donnelley & Sons, Chgo., 1968-75, v.p., gen. counsel, 1975-84, sr. v.p. law and corp. staffs, 1984-95. Bd. dirs. Am. Liver Found., Ill., 1996, national, 2001, Parents/Friends Elizabeth Ludeman Devel. Ctr., 1986. With AUS, 1954-56. Mem.: Chgo. Bar Assn., Ill. Bar Assn.

**UVERSKY, VLADIMIR NIKOLAEVICH**, biophysicist, researcher; b. Borovichi, Novgorod, USSR, Apr. 20, 1963; s. Nikolay Valentinovich and Galina Alexeevna (Ivanova) U.; m. Elena Borisovna Shubina, Apr. 11, 1987; children: Alexey, Sergey. Bachelor's degree, Leningrad State U., USSR, 1986; Candidate of Scis., Inst. Protein Rsch., Pushchino, Russia, 1991. Cert. physicist. Probationer Inst. Protein Rsch., Pushchino, 1986-88, jr. scientist, 1991-93, scientist, 1993—; tchr. Moscow State U., Pushchino, 1991-93; asst. prof. Pushchino State U., 1994—. Contbr. to sci. jours. Mem. trade-union com. Inst. Protein Rsch., Pushchino, 1987-93. Recipient premium for Young Russian Scientists, European Acad., 1992; grantee Human Frontier Sci. Program, 1993-96, Russian Found. for Fundamental Rschs., 1993-96. Fellow Biochem. Soc.; mem. Russian Biochem. Soc. Avocations: books, wood and natural materials crafts, fishing, cooking. Office: Inst Protein Rsch Russian Acad Scis 142292 Pushchino Russia

**UYEHARA, OTTO ARTHUR**, mechanical engineering educator emeritus, consultant; b. Hanford, Calif., Sept. 9, 1916; s. Rikichi and Umi (Nakayama) U.; m. Chisako Suda, Aug. 12, 1945; children: Otto Kenneth, Susan Joy Uyehara Schultheiss, Emi Ryu Uyehara-Stewart. BS, U. Wis., 1942, MS, 1943, PhD, 1946. Postdoctoral fellow U. Wis., Madison, 1945-46, rsch. assoc., 1946-47, asst. prof., then assoc. prof., 1949-57, prof., 1957-82, prof. emeritus, 1982—; pvt. practice cons. Anaheim, Calif., 1985—. Mem. sci. adv. com. Echlin Corp., Branford, Conn., 1980—. Recipient Sci. Achievement award Japan Soc. Automotive Engrs, Internal Combustion Engine award ASME, 1994. FEllow Soc. Automotive Engrs.; mem. ASME (internal combustion divsn., Internal Combustion award 1994), Japan Soc. Mech. Engrs. (hon.). Home: 824 Ashbury St San Francisco CA 94117-4464

**UYGUR, MUSTAFA ETI**, engineering educator; b. Kayseri, Turkey, Jan. 22, 1941; s. Ali and Mumine (Oktay) U.; m. Selime Kobakci, Dec. 16, 1971; children: Ayse, Esra, Zeynep, Ali. BSME, Mid. East Tech. U., Ankara, Turkey, 1963, MSc in Mech. Engring., 1964; MSc in Engring., Purdue U., 1967; PhD in Materials Sci. and Engring., Mid. East Tech. U., Ankara, Turkey, 1971. Rsch. assoc. Am. Oil Co. Rsch. Labs., Whiting, Ind., 1967; instr. Mid. East Tech. U., Ankara, Turkey, 1964-71, asst. prof., 1971-77, assoc. prof., 1977-84; prof. Gazi U., Ankara, Turkey, 1984-90; engring. sci. cons. King Saud U., Riyadh, Saudi Arabia, 1990—2003; pvt. practice cons. Fairfax, Va., 2003—. Asst. chmn. materials sci. and engring. dept. Mid. East Tech. U., Ankara, 1977-80; dep. dean faculty tech. edn. Gazi U., Ankara, 1984-86, univ. coll.

coun., grad. coll. coun., univ. senate, 1984-90; tech. & sci. advisor to dep. Min. of Nat. Def., Def. Industries Devel. Adminstrn., Ankara, 1987-90. Author: Dynamic NDT of Materials, 1976, 83, Glossary of Powder Metallurgy Terms, 1982, X-Ray Crystallography, 1983, Materials Science and Engineering, 1997, 2d edit., 2002, Laboratory Manual for Materials Science and Engineering, 1997, 2d edit., 2002, CD-Materials Sci & Engring., 1997, 4th edit., 2002, CD-Laboratory for Materials Science and Engineering, 1998, 3d edit., 2002, (4 CDs) Database for Color Micrographs, 2003; editor-in-chief: Science-Research-Technology Five-Year Main Plan, 1988; contbr. over 100 articles to profl. jours.; supr. for devel. of many ednl. computer programs. Specialization com. on nonferrous materials State Planning Orgn., Ankara, 1982, chmn. specialization com. on transfer of high tech. and employment, 1987-88, specialization com. on sci. rsch., tech., 1987-88, chmn. editl. com. on sci., rsch., tech., 1988. Lt. (engr.) Turkish Army Tech. Svc.-Weapons Dept., 1973-74. Scholar Turkish Iron-Steel Works, 1963-64; rsch. grantee Turkish Sci. Rsch. Coun., 1971-73. Mem. Internat. Plansee Soc. Powder Metallurgy, Internat. Soc. Crystallographers, Am. Powder Metallurgy Inst. Internat., Am. Soc. for Metals Internat., Am. Soc. for Metals Internat.-Metall. Soc., Materials Rsch. Soc., Turkish Assn. for Powder Metallurgy (founder). Avocations: reading, music, computers, swimming, bowling. Home: 6926 Emma Ct Warrenton VA 20187 Personal E-mail: mustafauygur@hotmail.com.

**UYS, JURGEN PETER BRINKER**, securities analyst; came to U.S., 1955; s. Johannes Marthinus and Reinette McKay (Weidemann) U. BS, U. Pa., 1974; MBA, Columbia U., 1977. CFA. Securities analyst Equibank, N.A., Pitts., 1974-76; fin. analyst Amax Inc., Greenwich, Conn., 1978-80; v.p. Equitable Investment Mgmt., N.Y.C., 1980-85; securities analyst Swiss Am. Securities, N.Y.C., 1986-91; gen. ptnr. Peter Uys Partnership, Ltd., N.Y.C., 1991—. Mem. Huguenot Soc. Am. (treas. 1991-92), CFA Inst. Episcopalian. E-mail: jpbu@msn.com.

**UZMAN, BETTY BEN GEREN**, retired pathologist; b. Fort Smith, Ark., Nov. 17, 1922; d. Benton Asbury and Myra Estelle (Petty) Geren; m. L. Lahut Uzman, Dec. 17, 1955 (dec.); 1 dau., Betty Tuba. Student, Ft. Smith Jr. Coll., 1939—40; BS, U. Ark., 1942; MD, Washington U., 1945; postgrad., MIT, 1948—50; MA (hon.), Harvard U., 1968. Intern Childrens Hosp., Boston, 1945—46; resident pathology Barnes Hosp., St. Louis, 1946—48; Am. Cancer Soc. rsrch. fellow MIT, Cambridge, 1948—50; chief biol. ultra structure and exptl. pathology Children's Cancer Rsch. Found., Boston, 1950—71; instr. Harvard Med. Sch., Boston, 1949—53, assoc., 1953—56, rsch. assoc., 1956—67, assoc. prof., 1967—71, 1971-72; head rsch. dept. Sparks Regional Med. Ctr., Ft. Smith 1972—74; prof. pathology La. State U., Shreveport, 1974—77, U. Tenn., Memphis, 1978—89, ret., 1989. Assoc. chief staff rsch. VA, Shreveport, 1974-77; staff pathologist VA, Memphis, 1978-89, chief lab. svc., 1986-87; chief field ops., spl. asst. to dir. VA Ctrl. Office, Washington, 1978-79, dir. med. rsch. svcs., 1979-80; chmn. pathology A Study sect. NIH, 1973-76; cons. to sci. dir. Children's Cancer Rsch. Found., Boston, 1971-73; mem. adv. com. on prevention, diagnosis and treatment Am. Cancer Soc., 1970-73, 77-80; mem. adv. bd. Office Regeneration Rsch., VA, 1985-89; disting. vis. investigator Inst. Venezolano Investigation Cientificas, Caracas, 1972-74 Decorated Order Andres Bello 1st class Venezuela; recipient Weinstein award United Cerebral Palsy, 1964 Mem. AAAS, Am. Soc. Cell Biology (emerita), Microscopy Soc. Am. (emerita, Diatome poster award 1985), Internat. Acad. Pathology (emerita), Am. Assn. Neuropathology (emerita, assoc.), Soc. Neurosci. (emerita), Am. Assn. Cancer Rsch. (emerita). Home and Office: Geren Farm 16048 E State Hwy 197 Scranton AR 72863-0048 Personal E-mail: bettyguzman@wildblue.net. E-mail: bguzman@aol.com.

**UZZELL-BAGGETT, KARON LYNETTE**, career officer; b. Goldsboro, NC, Apr. 28, 1964; d. Jesse Lee and Ernestine Smith Uzzell; m. Ronald Walter Baggett, July 26, 1990; 1 child, Kathleen; stepchildren: Christina, Brian, Adam. BS, U. N.C., Chapel Hill, 1986; postgrad., U. Md., College Park, 1993—96. Commd. 2nd lt. USAF, 1986, advanced through grades to lt. col., 1990, exec. officer 6ACCS Langley AFB, Va., 1986—88, ops. tng. officer 7393MUNSS Murted AFD, Turkey, 1988—89, command and control officer 52FW Spangdahlem AB, Germany, 1989—92, SENEX mission dir. 89AW Andrews AFB, Md., 1995—95, dep. chief classified control Office Sec. Def., 1995—97, chief classified control Office Sec. Def., 1998—99, flight comdr., dir. ops. 82TRSS Sheppard AFB, Tex., 1999—2001; detachment comdr. USAFE MSS, Vicenza, Italy, 2001—02; comdr. 78MSS, Robins AFB, Ga., 2002—04, 416EMSS, Karshi-Khanabad, Uzbekistan, 2003—04; dir. pers. OSC-A, Kabul, Afghanistan, 2005, plans officer, 2005; dir. pers. Air U., Maxwell AFB, Ala., 2004—. Emergency med. technician Orange County Rescue Squad, Hillsborough, N.C., 1985-86; treas. Melwood PTA, Upper Marlboro, Md., 1994-97; meml. vol. Women in Mil. Svc., Washington, 1993—; entitlements vol. Whitman Walker Clinic, Washington, 1993-98. Mem. So. Poverty Law Ctr. Democrat. Baptist. Avocations: running, weight-lifting, sewing, cross stitching, gardening. Home: 2319 Walbash Dr Montgomery AL 36116

**VACANO, JOST**, cinematographer; Cinematographer The Skouras Agy., Santa Monica, Calif., 1977—. Cinematographer: (films) Soldier of Orange, 1977, Spetters, 1980, Das Boot, 1981, The Neverending Story, 1984, 52 Pick-up, 1986, Robocop, 1987, Rocket Gibraltar, 1988, Total Recall, 1990, Untamed Heart, 1993, Showgirls, 1995, Starship Troopers, 1997, The Hollow Man, 1999.

**VACANTI, JOSEPH PHILIP**, pediatric and transplant surgeon; b. Omaha, Oct. 31, 1948; BS summa cum laude, Creighton U., 1970; MD with high distinction, U. Nebr., 1974. Diplomate in gen. surgery and pediatric surgery Am. Bd. Surgery. Clin. fellow in surgery Harvard Med, Sch. Boston, 1979-93, attd. In surgery Children's Hosp., Boston, 1983-90, sr. assoc. in surgery, 1990-98, dir. organ transplant, 1990-98, dir. lab. for transplant and tissue engring., 1990—; asst. prof. surgery Harvard Med. Sch., Boston, 1983-90, assoc. prof., 1990-97, prof., 1997—; John Homans prof. surgery Harvard Med. Sch./Mass. Gen. Hosp., 1998—; dir. Tissue Engring. and Organ Fabrication Mass. Gen. Hosp., 1998—, dir. Pediat. Transplant, 1998—, chief Dept. Pediat. Surgery, 2003—; surgeon-in-chief Mass. Gen. Hosp. Children, 2003—. Rsch. affiliate MIT, Cambridge, 1988—. Author some 30 book chpts. and more than 150 sci. articles; co-founder, sr. editor Tissue Engring.; mem. editl. bd. Cell Transplantation; mem. editl. adv. bd. Tissue Engring. Intelligence Unit, R.G. Landes. Recipient Sidney Farber award Children's Hosp., 1983, Spl. Recognition award Am. Liver Found., 1987. Fellow ACS; mem. Tissue Engring. Soc. (co-founder, pres.), Am. Soc. Transplant Surgeons, Transplantation Soc., Am. Pediat. Surg. Assn., Soc. Univ. Surgeons, Inst. Medicine. Office: Mass Gen Hosp 55 Fruit St Boston MA 02114-2696 Office Phone: 617-724-1725. Business E-Mail: jvacanti@partners.org.

**VACANTI, MARY PARISI**, director, consultant; b. Buffalo, Oct. 28, 1947; d. Joseph Anthony and Marjorie Ronan Parisi; children: Michael Charles, David Joseph. BS Edn., SUNY Buffalo, 1969, MSEd, 1972. Cert. sch. adminstr. NY. Reading specialist Tonawanda Bd. Edn., NY, 1987—2004; dir. Tonawanda/Grand Island Tchr. Ctr., 2001—. Instr. Canisius Coll., Buffalo, 2000—01. Recipient Outstanding Achievement award, Regional Reading Conf., 1989; Spl. Legis. grantee, NY State Legislature, 2001—05. Mem.: Assn. Supervision Curriculum and Devel., Niagara Frontier Reading Coun. (bd. dirs. 1987—98, Outstanding Achievement 1989), Phi Delta Kappa (assoc.). Avocations: travel, reading, piano. Home: 450 Berryman Dr Amherst NY 14226 Office: Tonawanda/Grand Island Tchr Ctr 80 Clinton St Tonawanda NY 14150 Office Phone: 716-695-6172. Office Fax: 716-694-7394. Personal E-mail: mvacanti@localnet.com.

**VACCARIELLO, LIZ**, editor-in-chief; b. 1968; m. Steve Vaccariello; 2 children. BA, U. Mich. Editor-in-chief, v.p. editorial Cleve. mag.; articles editor, dep. editor Fitness mag., 1999, exec. editor, 2000—06; editor-in-chief Prevention mag., 2006—. Office: Rodale Inc 33 E Minor St Emmaus PA 18098-0099 Office Phone: 610-967-5171. Office Fax: 610-967-7726.*

**VACCARO, BRENDA**, actress; b. Bklyn., Nov. 18, 1939; d. Mario and Christine (Pavia) V. Student, Neighborhood Playhouse, 1958-60. Appeared in Broadway plays: Everybody Loves Opal, 1961, The Affair, 1962, Tunnel of Love, 1962, Children from Their Games, 1963, Cactus Flower, 1965 (Tony award best supporting actress), The Natural Look, 1967, How Now Dow Jones, 1968 (Tony nomination best actress in mus. comedy), The Goodbye People, 1968 (Tony nomination for best actress in drama): Father's Day, 1971, California Suite with Neil Simon, The Odd Couple, 1985 with Sally Struthers, Jake's Women, 1992 with Alan Alda-A Neil Simon Play, Full Gallop (one woman show), 1998; motion pictures include: House by the Lake, 1977, Midnite Cowboy, 1969, Where It's At, 1969, I Love My Wife, 1970, Summer Tree, 1971, Going Home, 1971, Once Is Not Enough, 1975, Airport '77, 1977, Fast Charlie, 1977, Capricorn One, 1978, First Deadly Sin, 1980, Zorro, The Gay Blade, Supergirl, 1984, Water, 1986, Heart of Midnight, 1988, Cookie, 1988, Ten Little Indians, 1988, Masque of the Red Death, 1989, Love Affair, 1994, The Mirror Has Two Faces, 1996, Sonny, 2002, The Boyton Beach Bereavement Club, 2005; TV appearances in The Greatest Show on Earth, 1963, Fugitive, 1963, Defenders, 1965, Doctors and Nurses, 1965, Coronet Blue, 1967, Naked City, The FBI, 1969, The Psychiatrist, 1971, Name of the Game, 1971, Marcus Welby, M.D, 1972, Banacek, 1972, McCloud, 1972, McCoy, Streets of San Francisco, Sara, 1976 (Emmy nomination for best dramatic actress), Paper Dolls, Dear Detective, 1979, The Pride of Jesse Hallam, 1980, A Long Way Home, 1981, Star Maker, 1981, The Love Boat, 1984, Deceptions, 1985, St. Elsewhere, Murder She Wrote, 1990, Trials of Rosie O'Neil, 1991, Civil Wars, 1991, Flesh and Blood, 1991, Friends, 1995, The King of Queens, 1998, Ally McBeal, 1998, Becker, 2001, American Dad!, 2005, The War at Home, 2006; TV movie appearances in Travis Logan, D.A, 1971, What's A Nice Girl Like You, 1971, Honor Thy Father, 1973, Sunshine, 1973, The Big Ripoff, 1975, Julius and Ethel Rosenberg, 1978, Guyana Tragedy: The Story of Jim Jones, 1980, Paper Dolls, Dear Detective, 1989, Stolen: One Husband, Columbo, 1990, Once Is Not Enough (Academy award, Golden Globe award, People's Choice award), The Shape of Things (Emmy award for supporting actress), Golden Girls Ebbs Tide Revenge (Emmy award 1991), Red Shoe Diaries, 1991, Following Her Heart, 1994, Sing Me the Blues Lena, 1995, Touched by an Angel, 1996, Stolen One Husband, 1997, Johnny Bravo Show (voice over series animation), 1993-2000, When Husbands Cheat, 1998, Fat Girl (voice over series animation), 2001, Just A Walk in the Park, 2002, Just Desserts, 2004; TV Series (voice) Spawn, 1997. Recipient Theatre World award, 1961-62, 3 Tony nominations, 2 Hollywood Fgn. Press Assn. nominations.*

**VACCHELLI, ROBERT FRANCIS**, lawyer; b. Hartford, Conn., Jan. 29, 1951; s. Frank P. and Helen (DeRobertis) V.; m. Cathy Kinnane; 1 child. AB, Coll. of the Holy Cross, Worcester, Mass., 1973; JD, Suffolk U., 1977. Bar: Conn. 1977, U.S. Dist. Ct. Conn. 1978, U.S. Ct. Appeals 1979, U.S. Supreme Ct. 1981, Calif. 1983. Assoc. Stoner, Gross & Chorches, Hartford, 1977-78; asst. atty. gen. Conn. Atty. Gen.'s Office, Hartford, 1978—. Tutor Sch. Law U. Conn., 1997-98; contbr. seminar U.S. Bur. Alcohol, Tobacco & Firearms, 1984; spkr. various seminars, 1986—; argued before U.S. Supreme Ct., 1989; advisor Conn. Gen. Assembly Law Revision Commn., 1992; state coord. Internat. Extraditions, 1998—. Author: Liquor Licensing in Connecticut, 1987. Commr. Glastonbury, Conn. Pub. Bldg. commn., 1986, Glastonbury Wetlands Authority, 1987; mem. Dem. Town Com., Glastonbury, 1986-91; vice chmn. bd. dirs. Glastonbury ABC, 1989-94; elected mem. Glastonbury Conn. Bd. Assessment Appeals, 2003—. Recipient Am. Jurisprudence Book prize Lawyer's Co-op. Publ. Co., 1976, proclamation Glastonbury Conservation Commn., 1988, Merit award State of Conn., 1986, 91, 92, 95, 97, 98, 2004, 06. Mem. ABA, ATLA, Conn. Bar Assn. (chmn. adminstrv. law exec. com., specialization certification subcom. 1982-89, mcpl. law com. 1982-87), U.S. Supreme Ct. Hist. Soc., Conn. Bot. Soc., Wadsworth Atheneum. Avocation: astronomy. Office: Office of the Atty Gen Mackenzie Hall 110 Sherman St Hartford CT 06105-2267

**VACCO, DENNIS C.**, lawyer; b. Buffalo, Aug. 16, 1952; s. Carmen A. and Mildred V.; m. Kelly McIlroy; children: Alex, Connor. BA, Colgate U., 1974; JD, SUNY, Buffalo, 1978. Bar: N.Y. 1978, Fed. Ct. 1978, 82. Asst. dist. atty. Office of Erie County Dist. Atty., Buffalo, 1978-82, chief G.J. bureau, 1982-88; U.S. Atty. We. Dist. N.Y. Buffalo, 1988-93; atty. gen. State of New York, Albany, 1993-98; v.p. for govtl. affairs Waste Mgmt. Inc., 1998-99; pres. Waste Mgmt. N.Y. LLC, 1999—2003; pvt. practice atty. Boston, 2003—; ptnr. Carne & Vacco LLC, 2004—. Chmn. Atty. Gen.'s Environ. Subcom., Atty. Gen.'s Subcom. on Organized Crime and Violent Crime; mem. Nat. Environ. Enforcement Coun. Co-chair Erie County Community Commn. on Alcohol and Substance Abuse; bd. dirs. United Way of Erie County. Recipient Environ. Enforcement Leadership award Atty. Gen. Dept. of Justice, Washington, 1991. Mem. N.Y. State Bar Assn., Erie County Bar Assn., Nat. Dist. Attys. Assn., N.Y. State Dist. Attys. Assn., NCCJ, Hamburg Devel. Corp., 100 Club of Buffalo, U. Buffalo Law Alumni Assn. (bd. dirs.). Republican. Roman Catholic. Avocations: travel, sports. Office Phone: 518-426-0606.

**VACEK, JAMES**, cardiologist; b. Omaha, July 13, 1951; BS in Math., Creighton U., Omaha, 1977, MD, 1977. Cons. cardiology Mid Am. Cardiology, Kansas City, Mo., 1989—2001, U. Kans. Hosp., Kansas City, 2001—, dir. rsch. Contbr. articles to profl. jours. Maj. United State Air Force USAF, 1982—86. Achievements include patents for catheter design. Office: Mid Am Cardiology KU Hosp 3901 Rainbos Blvd Kansas City KS 66061 Office Phone: 913-588-9600. E-mail: jlvacek@mac.md.

**VACHHER, PREHLAD SINGH**, psychiatrist; b. Rawalpindi, Punjab, Pakistan, Nov. 30, 1933; came to U.S., 1960; s. Thakar Singh and Harbans Kaur (Ghai) V.; m. Margaret Mary Begley, Oct. 9, 1963; children: Paul, Sheila, Mary Ann, Fileen Mari Ghai, Khallut Coll., India, 1950, MD, Panjab U., Amritsar, India, 1956. Diplomate Am. Bd. Psychiatry. Staff N.J. State Hosp., Trenton, 1965-66, Wayne County Gen. Hosp., Eloise, Mich., 1966-68; pvt. practice Livonia, Mich., 1966-75, Woodstock, Va., 1991-96; pres. Vachher Psychiat. Ctr., P.C., Livonia, 1975-91. Dir. community psychiatry Northville (Mich.) State Hosp., 1968-71; cons. staff Kingswood Hosp., Ferndale, Mich., 1967-72, Annapolis Hosp., Wayne, 1967-88, St. Joseph Mercy Hosp., Ann Arbor, 1970-89; westland staff Margaret Montgomery Hosp., 1988-91; bd. dirs. Oakland Rental Housing Assn., 1990-91; med. dir. mental health unit Shenandoan County Meml. Hosp., Woodstock, Va., 1991-94. Mem. Am. Psychiat. Assn., Va. Psychiat. Soc., Sikh Physicians in Mich. (bd. dirs. 1987), Canton C. of C. (pres. 1975), Sikh Bus. Profl. Coun. (pres. 1988—), Rotary (Canton and Plymouth, Mich., Woodstock).

**VACHIO, VINCENT J.**, consumer products company executive; Dir. e-business Newell Rubbermaid Inc. Named one of Premier 100 IT Leaders, Computerworld, 2005. Office: Newell Rubbermaid Inc Ste 600 10B Glenlake Pkwy Atlanta GA 30328 Office Phone: 770-407-3800.*

**VACHON, REGINALD IRENEE**, mechanical engineer; b. Norfolk, Va., Jan. 29, 1937; s. Rene Albert Vachon and Regina (Galvin) Radcliffe; m. Mary Eleanor Grigg, Jan. 16, 1960; children: Reginald Irenee, Eleanor Marie. Student, U.S. Naval Acad. 1954-55; BME, Auburn U., 1958, MS, 1960; PhD, Okla. State U., 1963; LLB, Jones Law Sch., 1969. Registered profl. engr.; Ala., Ga., Miss., La., Wis., Tex., chartered engr., U.K., cert. d'Ingenieur Mecanicien, France, lic. engr., European Fedn. Nat. Engring. Assns.; bar: Ala. 1971. Engr. Hayes Internat., 1958; instr., rsch. asst. Auburn U., 1958-60, rsch. assoc., 1961, assoc. prof., 1963-78; R&D engr. E.I. DuPont, 1960; aerospace engr., technologist NASA Marshall Space Flight Ctr., summers, 1964, 65; pres. Vachon Nix & Assoc., 1977—, VNA Sys. Inc., 1982—; COO Thacker Constrn. Co., Thacker Orgn., Inc., 1981—90, United Info. Techs., Inc., Global Interated Techs. Inc.; pres., CEO Compris Tech., Inc., 1991—92; chmn. Global Risk Mgr., Inc., 1992—; Direct Measurements, Inc., 2002—; prin. Gipco Holdings Internat., Ltd., 1994—; mem. sci. tech. adv. com. U.S. Dept. Homeland Security. Contbr. articles to profl. jours. With U.S. Army, 1960—61. Fellow: AIAA (assoc.), Singapore Instn. Engrs., Hong Kong Instn. Engrs., Instn. Mech. Engrs. U.K.; mem.: NSPE, ABA, ASME (hon.; pres. 2003—04), Soc. Frances des Mecaniciens, Ala. Bar Assn., Pan Am. Acad.

Engring., Phoenix Soc. Atlanta, Peachtree Racket Club, N.Y. Yacht Club, Cosmos Club. Roman Catholic. Achievements include patents in field. Home: 1414 Epping Forest Dr NE Atlanta GA 30319-2539 Office: PO Box 190093 Atlanta GA 31119-0093 Office Phone: 404-388-6588. E-mail: vachonr@asme.org.

**VACKETTA, CARL LEE,** lawyer, educator; b. Danville, Ill., Aug. 3, 1941; s. Peter G. and Julia M. (Columbus) V. BS with honors, U. Ill., Urbana-Champaign, 1963, JD, 1965. Bar: Ill. 1965, DC 1968, US Dist. Ct. DC 1968, US Ct. Fed. Claims 1968, US Supreme Ct. 1970. Tax lawyer GM, Detroit, 1965; ptnr. Sellers, Conner & Cuneo, Washington, 1968—74, Pettit & Martin, 1974—95, Piper & Marbury, 1995—99, Piper Rudnick LLP, 1999—2004; ptnr., former chmn. Govt. Contracts practice group DLA Piper Rudnick Gray Cary, Washington, 2005—06, DLA Piper LLP, 2006—. Adj. prof. law Georgetown U., 1971—. Co-author: Government Contract Default Termination, 1991, 93, 95, 97, 99; co-editor Extraordinary Contractual Relief Reporter, 1974-2002; editor in chief, pub. contract law sect., Pub. Contract Law Jour., 1994-2006; mem. adv. bd. The Government Contractor. Past pres. Bd. vis., U. Ill. Coll. Law Capt. Judge Advocate Corps U.S. Army, 1966—68. Fellow ABA (sec. pub. contract law sect. 1978-79, coun. 1979-82, Nat. Contract Mgmt. Assn.; mem. Fed. Bar Assn., DC Bar Assn., Ill. State bar Assn., Nat. Assn. Purchasing Mgrs., University Club (Washington). Roman Catholic. Office: DLA Piper LLP 1200 19th St NW Washington DC 20036-2412 Office Phone: 202-861-6460. Office Fax: 202-223-2085. Business E-Mail: carl.vacketta@dlapiper.com.

**VADAPARTY, KUMAR VENKATA,** finance company executive, director; b. Visakhapatnam, Andhra Pradesh, India, June 1, 1961; s. Jagannadha Rao and Bhavani Vadaparty; m. Dawn Cohen. Degree in electronics engring., Andhra U.; M Computer Sci., Indian Inst. Tech., Kanpur; PhD, Rutgers U., 1992. Cert. java architect Microsoft, 1999. Asst. prof. Case Western Res. U., Cleve., 1992—96; sr. rschr. Bell Comm. Rsch., Morristown, NJ, 1995—96; dir. mgmt. dept. Merrill Lynch. Cons. Bell Comm. Rsch., 1987—95. Translator: A Modern View of Telugu Prosody, 2001. Recipient Gold Medal award, Andhra U., 1983, Young Investigator award, NSF, 1993; fellow, Elai Lilly Pharm. Co., 1993. Mem.: Internat. Exec. Guild (life). Achievements include first to architected a major system that enables Merrill Lynch accept customer orders at substantially lower cost of ownership. E-mail: kumar_vadaparty@ml.com, vadaparty@yahoo.com.

**VADDI, KRISHNA,** pharmaceutical executive; s. Subba Rao Venkata and Swarajya Lakshmi Vaddi; m. Lakshmi Ayalasomayajula, Dec. 4, 1994; children: Tej, Neel. In Vet. Sci. and Animal Husbandy, Andhra Pradesh Agrl. U., Tirupati, India, 1986; PhD, U. Fla., Gainesville, 1992. Postdoctoral fellow DuPont Merck Pharm. Co., Wilmington, Del., 1992—94; sr. scientist ProScript, Inc, Cambridge, Mass., 1994—95; sr. rsch. scientist Genzyme Corp., Framingham, Mass., 1995—98; dir. inflammatory diseases rsch. DuPont Pharmaceuticals Co., Wilmington, 1998—2001; v.p. preclinical biology Incyte Corp., Wilmington, 2002—. Author: (book) Chemokine Facts Book; contbr. articles to profl. jours. Bd. dirs. Sci., Math and Tech. Alliance, Wilmington, 1999—2002. Doctoral fellow, U. Fla., 1989—92. Mem.: AAAS, Soc. for Leukocyte Biology, Am. Assn. Immunology, Am. Assn. Cancer Rsch. Achievements include patents for method to monitor proteasome activity following Velcade administration in multiple myeloma; discovery of molecules that inhibit a key mediator of inflammation; molecules that inhibit a receptor on inflammatory cells; role of a chemokine receptor in mediating insulin resistance; patents for use of sheddase inhibitors to treat cancer. Home: 108 Forest Dr Kennett Square PA 19348 Office: Incyte Corporation Henry Clay Rd Wilmington DE 19880 Office Phone: 302-498-6733. Business E-Mail: kvaddi@incyte.com.

**VADEN, SANDRA DRAKE,** academic administrator; d. William Jay and Agnes Marie Drake; m. Robert Grayson Vaden, Oct. 1, 1977; children: Amanda Elizabeth, Kelly Lynn. BA in English, U. Vt., Burlington, 1968; MA in English, SUNY, Binghamton, 1971; EdS in Higher Edn. Adminstrn., George Washington U., Washington, 1977, EdD in Higher Edn. Adminstrn., 1989. English tchr. Beacont Ctrl. Sch., NY, 1971—72, Hamburg Ctrl. Sch., NY, 1974—75; assoc. prof. English Broome Cmty. Coll., Binghamton, 1975—76; rsch. assoc. Am. Assn. CCs, Washington, 1976—77; dir. planning and rsch. Cumberland County Coll., Vineland, NJ, 1980—. Editor: National Director of Community and Junior Colleges, 1975, 3d edit., 1977. Founding mem. Nat. Coun. Rsch. and Planning. Recipient Pres. award, Cumberland CC; fellow, US Dept. Edn., Washington, 1975. Mem.: NJ CC Assn. Rsch. and Planning, Assn. Instnl. Rsch. Avocation: travel. Office: Cumberland County Coll 3322 College Dr Vineland NJ 08362

**VADUS, GLORIA A.,** scientific document examiner; b. Forrestville, Pa. Diploma, Cole Sch. Graphology, Calif., 1978; BA in Psychology Counseling, Columbia Pacific U., 1981, MA in Psychology, 1982; diploma handwriting expert, Edith Eisenberg, Bethesda, Md., 1991. Diplomate Am. Bd. Forensic Examiners (founding mem.); cert. Am. Acad. Graphology, Washington, 1978, ct. qualified sci. document examiner, registered graphologist 1978, cert. behavioral profiling and cert. questioned documents Am. Bd. Forensic Examiners, CHS Am. Bd. Homeland Security, 2004, cert. Am. Handwriting Analysis Found. Pres., owner Graphinc, Inc., 1985—. Accredited instr. graphology Montgomery County Schs., Md., 1978—79; cert. instr. Psychogram Centre, 1978—85; instr. Coun. Graphol. Socs., 1980; testifier superior and probate cts.; pub. forum panelist, lectr., rschr., script therapist pers. selection specialist; writer in field; cons. graphologist; developed Trilogy base for rsch. Am. Handwriting Analysis Found. Author: numerous studies and papers in field, also environ. papers. Chmn. Letter of Hope for POWs; vol. Montgomery County, 1985—87; bd. dirs. East Gate I Civic Assn., Potomac, Md., 1985—87, cmty. affairs chair, 1985—87; sovereign amb. Order Am. Ambs. USA, 2006. Named Outstanding Women of the 20th Century, 2000; named to Am. Hall of Fame U.S.A. for outstanding commitment, dedication and inspirational leadership, 2005; recipient Spl. award, US Japan Marine Facilities Panel Valuable Contbr. Japanese Panel UJNR, MFP, 1978—94, Gold Nib Analyst of Yr. award, Am. Handwriting Analysis Found., 1982, Dancing Fan award, Marine Tech. Soc., Tokyo chpt., 1991, Profound Contbr. to Soc. to the Yr., 2000, Am. Bronze Medal of Hon., 2001, Internat. Peace prize, United Cultural Conv. of USA, 2003, Legion of Honor Gold medal, United Cultural Conf., 2005, Lifetime Achievement award, World Congress of Arts, Scis. and Comm., 2005, World Freedom medal, United Cultural Ctr., 2006. Fellow: Am. Coll. Forensic Examiners Internat. (life; awards chair 1993—94, Meritorious award 1994, Outstanding Contbn. cert.); mem.: Coun. Graphical Socs. (bd. dirs. 1982—84), Soc. Francaise de Graphologie for Am. Handwriting Analysis Found., Nat. Assn Document Examiners (bd. dirs. 1985—92, ethics hearing bd. 1986, chmn. nominations com. 1987—88, elections chmn. 1988, parliamentarian 1988—92), Nat. Forensic Ctr., Am. Handwriting Analysis Found. (life; chmn. rsch. com., chmn. adv. bd. 1981—87, bd. dirs. 1981—91, pres. 1982—84, chmn. nominations com 1985—86, officiator 1986, policy planning and ethics com. 1986—91, ethics chmn. 1989—91, chmn., past pres. adv. bd. 1989—91, hon. profl. women's adv. bd. 1999, cert.), Nature Conservancy, Charles F. Menninger Soc., IEEE-Distaff (internat. chmn. bd. dirs. 1969—72, fashion show chair 1969—72), Internat. Platform Assn., Nat. Wildlife Fedn., Nat. Capitol Jaguar Owners Club (judge 1975—78), Sierra Club, Henry Hicks Garden Club of the Westburys, N.Y. (v.p. pres. elect, judge, chair flower shows, bd. dirs. 1967—71), Soroptomist Internat. (internat. chair, regional del., v.p. chpt., bd. dirs. 1967—71), 92, regional dir. 1987—92), Nat. Writers Club. Home: 8500 Timber Hill Ln Potomac MD 20854-4237 Office Phone: 301-299-5477. Personal E-mail: jvadus@ieee.org.

**VAGNINI, LIVIO LEE,** chemist, consultant, forensic specialist; b. North Bergen, N.J., Apr. 26, 1917; s. Frank S. and Margaret (Avondo) V.; m. Daniele Hogge, Sept. 29, 1949; children: Frank, Stephen, Eric. BS in Chemistry, Fordham U., 1938; postgrad., U. Md. Med. Sch., 1938—39. Diplomate Am. Bd. Forensic Examiners. Chemist H.A. Wilson Co. div. Englehard Industries, Inc., 1940—42; chief chemist U.S. Army Graves Registration, Liege, Belgium, 1946—48; chief forensic chemist U.S. Army Criminal Investigation

Lab., Frankfurt, Germany, 1948—60; sr. chemist FDA, Washington, 1960—62, CIA, Washington, 1963—73; project engr. Mitre Corp., McLean, Va., 1973—75; staff scientist Planning Research Corp., McLean, 1975—77; program dir. L. Miranda Assocs., Washington, 1978—81; forensic cons. Carmel, Calif., 1981—. Contbr. articles to profl. publs. Active Ft. Ord (Calif.) Retiree Coun., 1989—; treas. Alliance Francaise Monterey Peninsula; adv. commn. Monterey County Commn. Vets. Svcs., 1990-92; Assn. Former Intelligence Officers, 1973—. With U.S. Army, 1942-46, lt. col. ret., 1975. Decorated Bronze Star; named Vet. of Yr. in Monterey County, 2000. Fellow Am. Inst. Chemists, Am. Acad. Forensic Scis., Am. Chem. Soc.; mem. Nat. Assn. for Uniformd Svcs. (Monterey chpt.)Internat. Soc. Blood Transfusion, Internat. Soc. Forensic Toxicology, Ret. Officers Assn. (pres. Monterey County chpt. 1985), Sons in Retirement (pres. Pebble Beach br. 1986), Am.-Scandinavian Soc. (pres. 1989, program dir. Monterey County 1989) Internat. Assn. of Forensic Sci., Am. Coll. of Forensic Examiners (diplomate). Roman Catholic. Home: 26069 Mesa Dr Carmel CA 93923-8952 Personal E-mail: liviaki@aol.com.

**VAGT, ROBERT F.,** academic administrator; m. Ruth Anne Vagt, 1968; children: Ashley, Lindsey. BA in Psychology, Davidson Coll., 1969; MDiv, Duke U. Ordained to ministry Presbyn. Ch. Dir. clin. programs N.W. Ala. Mental Health Ctr.; exec. dir. Mcpl. Assistance Corp., N.Y.C., 1979—80; chmn., pres., COO Seagull Energy Corp.; pres. Davidson Coll., 1997—. Bd. dirs. Cornell Cos., Inc. Bd. vis. Davidson Coll., 1992—, mem. Ultra Soc., nat. leader Ann. Fund, 1993—95. Recipient Alumni Svc. award, Davidson Coll., 1996. Office: Pres's Office Davidson Coll PO Box 1719 Davidson NC 28036-1719 Office Phone: 704-889-2000. E-mail: bovagt@davidson.edu.*

**VAGTS, DETLEV FREDERICK,** law educator; b. Washington, Feb. 13, 1929; s. Alfred and Miriam (Beard) Vagts; m. Dorothy Larkin, Dec. 11, 1954; children: Karen, Lydia. Grad., Taft Sch., 1945; AB, Harvard U., 1948, LLB, 1951. Bar: Mass. 1961. Assoc. Cahill, Gordon, Reindel & Ohl, N.Y.C., 1951-53, 56-59; asst. prof. law Harvard U. Law Sch., Cambridge, Mass., 1959-62, prof., 1962—, Eli Goldston prof., 1981-84, Bemis prof. internat. law, 1984—2005, prof. emeritus, 2005—, dir. internat. tax program, 1998-2000. Counselor internat. law Dept. of State, 1976—77. Author (with others): Transnational Legal Problems, 1968, 4th edit., 1994, Basic Corporation Law, 1973, 3d edit., 1989, Transnational Business Problems, 3d edit., 2003; editor: Secured Transactions Under the Uniform Commercial Code, 1963—64; assoc. reporter (with others): Restatement of Foreign Relations Law, book rev. editor: Am. Jour. Internat. Law, 1986—93, co-editor-in-chief; 1993—98. 1st lt. USAF, 1953—56. Recipient Max Planck Rsch. award, 1991. Mem.: ABA, Coun. Fgn. Rels., Am. Soc. Internat. Law, Phi Beta Kappa. Home: 29 Follen St Cambridge MA 02138-3502 Office: Sch Law Harvard U Cambridge MA 02138 Business E-Mail: vagts@law.harvard.edu.

**VAHAVIOLOS, SOTIRIOS JOHN,** electrical engineer, researcher, engineering executive; b. Mistra, Greece, Apr. 16, 1946; s. John Apostolos and Athanasia (Pavlakos) Vahaviolos; m. Aspasia Felice Nessas, June 1, 1969; children: Athanasia, Athena, Kristy. BSEE, Fairleigh Dickinson U., 1970; MSEE, Columbia U., 1972, M in Philosophy, 1975, PhDEE, 1976. Mem. tech. staff Bell Tel. Labs., Princeton, NJ, 1970-75, supr., 1975-76, dept. head, 1976-78; founder, pres., CEO Phys. Acoustics Corp., Princeton, 1978—, MISTRAS Holdings Corp., Princeton, 1984-94, chmn. quality svcs. labs., 2000—. Adviser General Ministry Def., Athens, 1986—88; bd. dirs. Orthosonics, Inc., N.Y.C.; chmn. policy com., life fellow Internat. Com. Nondestructive Testing, life mem. bd. dirs., 2004—. Contbr. scientific papers to profl. publs. Chmn. Princeton sect. United Fund, 1976—78; adv. bd. Trenton State Coll., 1983—; chmn. Greek Independence Parade, NYC, 2002—03; v.p. Fedn. Greek Soc. in Greater N.Y.; bd. dirs. Holy Cross Greek Orthodox Sch. Theology, Boston, 1989—; pres. bd. trustees St. George Greek Orthodox Cmty., Trenton, NJ; elector archon Order of St. Andrew the Apostle of the Holy Ecumenical Patriarchate of Constantinople, 2004. Recipient Spartan Merit award, Spartan World Soc., 1987, Entrepreneur of the Yr. award, Arthur Young/Inc. Mag., 1989. Fellow: IEEE (Centennial Medal award 1984, Mittleman Achievement award 1993), Acoustic Emission Working Group (Gold medal 2005), Am. Soc. Nondestructive Testing (bus. and fin. com. 1984—87, 1988—, bd. dirs. 1985, sec. 1989, treas. 1990, v.p. 1991, pres. 1992, chmn. bd. 1993, chmn. internat. com. nondestructive testing 1994—, editor handbook on acoustic emission 1988, Lester Honor award 1998, Gold medal 2001); mem.: ASTM, Fairleigh Dickinson U., Coll. of Sci. and Math. Adv. Coun., Montclair State U., Internat. Fund Advancement Nondestructive Testing (v.p.), N.Y. Acad. Scis., IEEE Indsl. Electronics Soc. (sr. mem. adminstv. com. 1988, founder, v.p. conf. 1974—78, editor Trans. on Indsl. Electronics 1976—82, 2d prize Student Paper Constest 1970, Outstanding Young Engr. award 1984). Greek Orthodox. Achievements include patents in field. Avocations: bird hunting, soccer, technical writing, gardening. Home: 7 Ridgeview Rd Princeton NJ 08540-7601 Office: Mistras Holdings Group 195 Clarksville Rd Princeton Junction NJ 08550 Personal E-mail: sotirios@pacnett.com.

**VAIDHYANATHAN, SIVA,** journalist, educator; b. Buffalo, June 16, 1966; s. Vishnampet S. and Virginia Ann (Evans) V. BA, U. Tex., 1992, PhD in Am. Studies, 1999. Reporter Dallas Morning News, 1988, Austin (Tex.) Am. Statesman, 1989-91, Ft. Worth Star-Telegram, Tex., 1992; freelance journalist, 1992—; history lectr. Concordia U., Austin, 1996; instr. Am. studies U. Tex., 1997, Wesleyan U., U. Wis., Madison; asst. prof. culture and comm. NYU. Author: Copyrights and Copywrongs: The Rise of Intellectual Property and How It Threatens Creativity, 2001, The Anarchist in the Library: How the Clash Between Freedom and Control is Hacking the Real World and Crashing the System, 2004. Election judge Travis County (Tex.), 1984. Mem. MLA (exec. com. 1996), Am. Studies Assn. of Tex. (students com. 1995-97). Hindu. Office: NYU E Bldg. 239 Greene St 707 New York NY 10003-4746 Office Phone: 212-992-9494. Office Fax: 212-995-4046. E-mail: sv24@nyu.edu.

**VAIDYA, JAIDEEP SHRIKANT,** engineering educator; b. Mumbai, Maharashtra, India, Oct. 15, 1977; s. Shrikant Madhusudan and Sushma Shrikant Vaidya; m. Bhakti Tulpule, Apr. 13, 2005; 1 child, Vivek Jaideep. BS in Engring., U. Mumbai, India, 1995—99; PhD, Purdue U., W. Lafayette, Ind., 1999—2004. asst. prof. Rutgers U., Newark, 2004—. Contbr. articles to profl. jours. Finalist Best Paper award, Acm Sigkdd, 2003. Mem.: IEEE (Best Paper award 2005), ACM, Upsilon Pi Epsilon. Hindu. Achievements include research in privacy-preserving data mining. Office: Rutgers University 180 University Avenue Newark NJ 07102 Office Fax: 973-353-5003. Personal E-mail: jsvaidya@yahoo.com. Business E-Mail: jsvaidya@rbs.rutgers.edu.

**VAIDYANATHAN, GANESH,** information technology executive, educator; b. India; s. Vaidyanathan Thiagarajan and Subbu Vaidyanathan; m. Meena Nathan; children: Kavya Nathan, Gautham Nathan. PhD, Tulane U., New Orleans, 1985—89. Chief info. officer eReliable Commerce, Chgo., 1999—2002. Contbr. papers to profl. jours. and pubs. Recipient CEO award, Honeywell Inc., 1985. Achievements include patents for 4 Patents in Management Information Systems. Business E-Mail: gvaidyan@iusb.edu.

**VAIL, CHARLES DANIEL,** veterinarian, consultant; b. Denver, June 11, 1936; s. Allan Paden and Katherine Marie (Phillips) V.; m. Jean Williams Ebsen, June 15, 1963; children: Ellen Marie, David Elston. BS, Colorado A&M, 1958; DVM, Colo. State U., 1960. Asst. veterinarian Colo. Racing Commn., Littleton, 1958-60; equine practitioner Littleton Large Animal Clinic, 1960—; track veterinarian Centennial Race Track, Littleton, 1962-63. Editor in chief Equine Practice, 1986-2000; contbr. articles to profl. jours. Mem. selection com. Outstanding Biology Tchr. award Colo., 1978-80. 88—; Arapahoe Fair Assn., Littleton, 1965-84, gallery disting. grads. Colo. State U. Coll. Vet. Medicine, 1989; chmn. Littleton Rotary Western Heritage Art Fair; bd. dirs. Animal Assistance Found. Denver, 1991-2004, v.p., 1995-96, pres., 1996-97, Western Vet. Conf., 1997-2000, v.p., 2001, pres. elect, 2002, pres., 2003, Friends Littleton Pub. Libr./Mus., 2000-04, Rocky Mountain Stroke Assn., Araphoe C.C. Found., 2004—; mem. devel. coun. Colo. State U., 2002—. Recipient Honor Alumni award Coll. Vet. Medicine, Colo. State U., 1991. Mem. AVMA (publs. com. 1981-87), Am. Assn. Equine Practitioners

(pres. 1985), Colo. Vet. Medicine Assn. (pres. 1980, Veterinarian of Yr. award 1987), Denver Area Vet. Medicine Soc. (pres. 1975), Arapahoe Town and Gown Soc. (v.p. 1999, pres. 2000), Colo. State U. Alumni Assn. (pres. 2001-02), Nottingham Club, Rotary (pres. Littleton 1992-93), Sigma Alpha Epsilon, Omicron Delta Kappa. Home: 5921 S Cherrywood Cir Littleton CO 80121-2465 Office: Littleton Large Animal Clinic 8025 S Santa Fe Dr Littleton CO 80120-4305 Office Phone: 303-794-6359. Office Fax: 303-794-9466. E-mail: cdvm1@yahoo.com.

**VAIL, IRIS JENNINGS,** civic worker; b. NYC, July 2, 1928; d. Lawrence K. and Beatrice (Black) Jennings; grad. Miss Porters Sch., Farmington, Conn.; m. Thomas V.H. Vail, Sept. 15, 1951; children: Siri J., Thomas V.H. Jr., Lawrence J.W. Mem. exec. com. Garden Club Cleve., 1962—83; mem. women's coun. Western Res. Hist. Soc., 1960—, Cleve. Mus. Art, 1953—. Chmn. Childrens Garden Fair, 1966-75, Public Square Dinner, 1975; bd. dirs. Garden Center Greater Cleve., 1963-77; trustee Cleve. Zool. Soc., 1971-98, life trustee 1998—; mem. Ohio Arts Coun., 1974-76, pub. sq. com. Greater Cleve. Growth Assn., 1976-93, pub. sq. preservation and maintenance com. Cleve. Found., 1989-93, chmn. pub. sq. planting com., 1993. Hon. trustee Cleve. Bot. Garden, 2001. Recipient Amy Angell Collier Montague medal Garden Club Am., 1976, Ohio Gov.'s award, 1977. Mem. Chagrin Valley Hunt Club, Cypress Point Club, Kirtland Country Club, Colony Club, Women's City of Cleve. Club (Margaret A. Ireland award). Home: 14950 County Line Rd Chagrin Falls OH 44022-6800 Office Phone: 216-360-0505.

**VAIL, NANCY L. SCOTT,** retired elementary school educator, artist; d. Mitchell Clark and Mollie Lee (Turner) Savage; m. Jackie C. Scott (dec. 1999); 1 child, Jeff Michael Scott; m. Joseph L. Vail, Sr., Nov. 4, 2000; stepchildren: Joseph L. Vail, Jr., Chris, Jennifer Allison. BE with summa cum laude, Abilene Christian Coll., Tex., 1962, MEd with summa cum laude, 1965. Cert. in Tchg. Tex., 1962, Tex., 1985. Tchr. Jane Long Elem., Abilene, Tex., 1962—65, Canyon Creek Elem., Richardson, Tex., 1965—71, Prestonwood Elem., Richardson, 1971—78, Rountree Elem., Allen, Tex., 1978—89, Vaughan Elem., Allen, 1989—98; ret., 1998. Display, Anthurium Gallery, McKinney, Tex. Nominee Tchr. of Yr., Allen Ind. Sch. Dist., 1988, 1989. Mem.: Rountree Retirees Assn., Women's Mus. Art, Scarlet O'Hatters, Richardson Civic Art (Ribbon award 2000, 2001), Allen Retired Educators Assn. (officer, com. chmn. 2001—, Outstanding Vol. of Yr. 2003, 2004, 2006), Alpha Delta Kappa Internat. Honorary Educators Sorority (pres., v.p., historian, corresponding sec., Silver Sister award 2003). Republican. Ch. Of Christ. Achievements include starting the Epsilon Lambda Chpt. of Alpha Delta Kappa in Allen, Texas. Avocations: piano, reading, exercise, travel, painting.

**VAIL, THOMAS PARKER,** orthopaedic surgeon; m. Lisa Ann Giannetto. MD, Loyola U., 1985. Diplomate Am. Bd. Orthopaedic Surgery. Prof. orthopaedic surgery Duke U. Med. Ctr., Durham, NC, 1992—. Dir. adult reconstructive surgery Duke U. Med. Ctr., Durham. Office Phone: 919-684-6166.

**VAIL, THOMAS VAN HUSEN,** retired publishing executive; b. Cleve., June 23, 1926; s. Herman Lansing and Delia (White) V.; m. Iris W. Jennings, Sept. 15, 1951; children: Siri Jennings Burki, Thomas Van Husen, Jr. AB in Politics cum laude, Princeton U., 1948; HHD (hon.), Wilberforce U., 1964; LHD, Kenyon Coll., 1969, Cleve. State U., 1973. Reporter Cleve. News, 1949-53, polit. editor, 1953-57; with Cleve. Plain Dealer, 1957-91, v.p. 1961-63, pub., editor, 1963-91, pres., 1970-91; dir. AP, 1968-74; ret., 1991. Bd. dirs. Greater Cleve. Growth Assn.; bd. dirs., past pres. Cleve. Conv. and Visitors Bur.; mem. Nat. Adv. Commn. on Health Manpower; presdl. apptd. to U.S. Adv. Commn. on Info., Pres.'s Commn. for Observance 25th Anniversary UN; trustee No. Ohio region NCCJ, Nat. Brotherhood Week chmn., 1969; trustee Cleve. Coun. World Affairs; fellow Cleve. Clinic Found.; former mem. Downtown Cleve. Corp.; former mem. distbn. com. Cleve. Found.; chmn.; founder New Cleve. Campaign; trustee, founder Cleve. Tomorrow; former trustee Cleve. Econ. Devel.; former mem. Pres.'s Adv. Coun. on Pvt. Sector Initiatives. With USNR, 1944-46, lt. (j.g.), 1950. Recipient Nat. Human Rels. award, 1970, Cleve. Man of Year award Sales and Mktg. Execs. Cleve., 1976, Ohio Gov.'s award, 1982, Downtown Bus. Coun. recognition award Greater Cleve. Growth Assn., 1983, award NCCJ, 1970, award Mt. Vernon Adv. Com., 1994. Mem. Nat. Assn. Profl. Journalists (Lifetime Hall of Fame), Am. Newspaper Pubs. Assn., Am. Soc. Newspaper Editors, Soc. Profl. Journalists, Kirtland Country Club (Willoughby, Ohio), Sand Ridge Golf Club (Chardon, Ohio), Cypress Point Club (Pebble Beach, Calif.), Bohemian Club (San Francisco), Chagrin Valley Hunt Club (Gates Mills, Ohio), Links Club (NYC). Episcopalian. Home: L'Ecurie 14950 County Line Rd Hunting Valley Chagrin Falls OH 44022 Office: 29225 Chagrin Blvd Ste 200 Pepper Pike OH 44122-4632

**VAIL, VAN HORN,** German language educator; b. Buffalo, Dec. 23, 1934; s. Curtis Churchill and Faith Newbrook (Ely) V.; m. Michele Juliette Edelstein, May 5, 1969; 1 son, Mark Curtis. BA, U. Wash., 1956; MA, Princeton U., 1961, PhD, 1964. Instr. Princeton U., 1962-65, asst. prof., 1965-66; asst. prof. German Middlebury (Vt.) Coll., 1966-69, assoc. prof., 1969-75, prof., 1975—; chmn. dept. Middlebury Coll., Vt., 1970-73, 87-88, dir. studies Middlebury Sch. in Germany, 1967-68, 70-71, 74-75, 85-86, 88-89, 92-93, 95-96. Mem. nat. screening com. Fulbright Scholarships, 1979-81. Author in Review, 1967, 4th edit., 2004, Der Weg zum Lesen, 1967, 3d edit., 1986, Modern German, 1971, 3d edit., 1992, Tonio Kröger als Weg zur Literatur, 1974, Workbook for Modern German, 1992, Student Manual for 3d edit. of German in Review, 2000, Classroom Manual for 4th Edit. of German in Review, 2004. Served to 1st lt. M.I., U.S. Army, 1956-58. Fulbright scholar U. Heidelberg, 1958-59 Mem. MLA Home: 352 Cider Mill Rd Middlebury VT 05753-9407 Office: Middlebury Coll Middlebury VT 05753 E-mail: vail@middlebury.edu.

**VAILLANCOURT, JEAN-GUY,** sociology educator, researcher; b. Chelmsford, Ont., Can., May 24, 1937; s. Royal A. and Marie (Lavallée) V.; m. Pauline Hansen, June 6, 1966 (div. 1983); 1 child, Véronique. BA magna cum laude, Laurentian U., Sudbury, Ont., 1957; licenciate in Philosophy, Faculté des Jésuites, Montreal, Que., Can., 1961; licentiate in Sociology, Gregorian U., Rome, 1964; PhD in Sociology, U. Calif., Berkeley, 1975. Lectr. St. Boniface (Man.) Coll., Canada, 1964-65; asst. prof. U. Montréal, Que., Canada, 1969-76, assoc. prof., 1976-83, prof. sociology, 1983—, chmn. dept., 1984-87. Adminstr., 1998; mem. consultative com. Can. amb. for disarmament, Ottawa, Ont., 1984-91, consultative com. on environ. Hydro-Que., 1984-90. Author: Papal Power, 1980, Essais d'écosociologie, 1982; co-editor: Le processus électoral au Québec, 1976, Roots of Peace, 1986, Environnement et développement Problèmes socio-politiques, 1991, Gestion de l'environnement, éthique et société, 1992, Instituer le développement durable, 1994, Aspects sociaux des précipitations acides au Québec, 1994, La recherche sociale en environnement, Nouveaux paradigmes, 1996, L'énergie au Québec, Quels sont nos choix? Montréal, Ecosocieté, 1996, Les sciences sociales de l'environnement, 1999, La gestion écologique des déchets, 2000, Développement durable et participation publique, 2003, Mouvements Sociaux et Changements Institutionnels, 2005; editor-in-chief Sociologie et Sociétés, 1978-87. Mem. coun. City of Dunham, Que., 1976-80; bd. dirs. Oxfam-Que., 1976-79, Can. Inst. Internat. Peace and Security, Ottawa, Ont., 1986-89, European Univ. Ctr. for Peace Studies, Burg Schlaining, Burgenland, Austria, 1989-93, Groupement forestier du Haut-Yamaska, 1993—; Club 2/3, 1995-2005. Grantee Conseil de Recherche en sci. sociale du Canada, 1982, FCAR, 1989-95, 96—, Social Sci. Rsch. Coun., 1983-86, 90—, Can. Inst. Internat. Peace and Security, 1985, 91; fellow Can. Coun., 1965-68. Mem. Internat. Sociol. Assn., Assn. Can. des sociologues et anthropologues de langue française, Sci. for Peace, Pugwash, Group 78. Roman Catholic. Avocations: tree farming, travel. Home: 953 Cherrier Apt 3 Montreal PQ Canada H2L 1J2 Office: U Montréal Dept Sociology Montreal PQ Canada H3C 3J7 Office Phone: 514-343-5959. Business E-Mail: jean.guy.vaillancourt@umontreal.ca.

**VAIRA, PETER FRANCIS,** lawyer; b. McKeesport, Pa., Mar. 5, 1937; s. Peter Francis and Mary Louise (Bedogne) V.; m. Mary Hohler, 1981. BA, Duquesne U., 1959, JD, 1962. Bar: Pa. 1963, D.C. 1968, Ill. 1984, U.S. Dist. Ct. (no. dist.) Ill., U.S. Dist. Ct. (ea. dist.) Pa., Ill. Supreme Ct. 1984. Atty. Chgo. Strike Force, Justice Dept., 1968-72; atty. in charge Phila. Strike Force, 1972-73, Chgo. Strike Force on Organized Crime, 1973-78; U.S. atty. Ea. Dist. Pa., Phila., 1978—83; ptnr. Lord Bissel & Brook, Chgo., 1983-86, Fox, Rothschild, O'Brien & Frankel, Phila., 1986-90, Buchanan Ingersoll, Phila., 1990-92, Vaira & Assocs., Phila., 1992-93, Vaira & Riley, Phila., 1993—. Exec. dir. Pres.'s Commn. on Organized Crime, 1983; ind. hearing officer Laborers Internat. Union N.Am., 1995—; panelist, seminar, controlling internat. organized crime, Rome, Sorrento, Italy, June 1994; panelist, Internat. Conf. on Trial by Jury, Buenos Aires, Oct. 1996. Author: Eastern District Practice Rules Annotated, 2006, Corporate Responses to Grand Jury Investigations, 2004; contbr. articles to profl. jours. Mem. Mayor's Search Com. Police Commr., Phila., 1992; corruption task force Phila. Police, 1997; press officer women's amateur championship U.S. Golf Assn., 2003. Lt. USNR, 1963-68. Recipient Spl. Commendation award Justice Dept., 1976, Disting. Alumni award Duquesne U. Law Sch., 2005; named a Pa. Super Lawyer, Phila. Mag., 2006. Fellow Am. Coll. Trial Lawyers (chmn. criminal procedure com. 1995-98, comms. com.), Chartered Inst. Arbitrators; mem. ABA (criminal justice coun. 1986), Am. Law Inst. (mem. editl. bd. Legal Intelligencer, Phila. Lawyer), Union League (Chgo.), Phila. Country Club, Com. of 70. Office: Vaira & Riley 1600 Market St Ste 2650 Philadelphia PA 19103-7226 Office Phone: 215-751-2700. Personal E-mail: p.vaira@vairariley.com.

**VAIRO, ROBERT JOHN,** insurance company executive; b. Bklyn., Sept. 27, 1930; s. John and Antonietta (DeRose) V.; m. Carol P. Andross, Apr. 8, 1951 (div. Feb. 1979); children: Robert J., Gregory J.; m. Inge R. Buhlbecker, Feb. 20, 1979. Student, Coll. Ins., N.Y.C., 1953-62; Exec. Program in Bus. Adminstrn., Columbia U., 1973. CPCU. Under asst. mgr. Atlantic Cos., N.Y.C., 1952-62; underwriter mgr., v.p. Fireman's Fund Ins. Co., N.Y.C., 1962-75; v.p., sr. v.p. underwriting C & F Ins. Cos., Morristown, NJ, 1975-79; exec. v.p., pres. U.S. Ins. Group, Morristown, NJ, 1979-82; chmn., chief exec. officer C & F Underwriters Group and The North River Ins. Co., Morristown, NJ, 1982-86; pres., chief oper. officer Crum and Forster, Inc., Morristown, 1987-88, pres., chief exec. officer, 1988-90, chmn., pres., chief exec. officer, 1990-92, also bd. dirs. Chmn. Ins. Services Office, N.Y.C., 1983, Am. Ins. Assn., Washington, 1990. Pres. Lincoln Park City Council, N.J., 1971-76. Served with USMC, 1951-53. Mem. Soc. CPCUs, Am. Inst. for Chartered Property Casualty Underwriters (dir., chmn. 1991-92), Desert Highlands Golf Club (pres. 1997-99), Coalition Pinnacle Peak, Inc. (pres. 1998—). Roman Catholic. Home: # 451 10040 E Happy Valley Rd Scottsdale AZ 85255-2388 E-mail: sonoran@aol.com.

**VAISEY, DAVID GEORGE,** librarian, archivist; b. Tetbury, Eng., Mar. 15, 1935; s. William Thomas and Minnie (Pamphlet) V.; m. Maureen Anne Mansell, Aug. 7, 1965; children: Katharine, Elizabeth. BA, Oxford U., Eng., 1959, MA, 1962. Archivist Staffordshire County Council, Stafford, Eng., 1960-63; from asst. librarian to sr. asst. librarian Bodleian Library, Oxford, Eng., 1963-75, keeper of western manuscripts, 1975-86, Bodley's librarian, 1986-96, Bodley's librarian emeritus, 1997—. Dep. keeper Oxford U. Archives, 1966-75, keeper, 1995-2000; vis. dept. library studies UCLA, 1985; commr. Royal Commn. Hist. Manuscripts, 1987-98; founding chmn. Nat. Coun. Archives, 1988-91. Served to 2d lt. Brit. Army, 1954-56. Decorated encomienda Order of Isabel la Catolica (Spain), comdr. Order Brit. Empire; fellow Exeter Coll., Oxford, 1975, emeritus fellow, 2000; hon. rsch. fellow, Univ. Coll., London, 1987, hon. fellow Kellogg Coll., Oxford, 1996. Fellow: Soc. Antiquaries, Royal Hist. Soc.; mem.: Soc. Archivists (pres. 1999—2002), Brit. Records Assn. (v.p. 1998—2006). Office: Bodleian Libr Broad St Oxford OX1 3BG England E-mail: david.vaisey@bodley.ox.ac.uk.

**VAITUKAITIS, JUDITH LOUISE,** medical researcher; b. Hartford, Conn., Aug. 29, 1940; d. Albert George and Julia Joan (Vaznikaitis) V. BS, Tufts U., 1962; MD, Boston U., 1966. Investigator, med. officer reproductive rsch. Nat. Inst. Child Health and Human Devel., NIH, Bethesda, Md., 1971-74; assoc. dir. clin. rsch. Nat. Rsch. Resources NIH, 1986-91, dir. gen. clin. rsch. ctr., 1986-91, dep. dir. extramural rsch., 1991, acting dir., 1991-92, dir., 1993—2005; sr. advisor on sci. infrastructure and resources to dir. of NIH, 2005—; from assoc. prof. to prof. medicine Sch. Medicine Boston U., 1974-86, assoc. prof. physiology, 1975-80, assoc. prof. ob-gyn., 1977-80, program. dir. gen. clin. rsch. ctr., 1977-86, prof. physiology, 1980-86; head sect. endocrinology and metabolism Boston City Hosp., 1974-86. Mem. internat. sci. adv. bd. Wellcome Trust-UIC. Author: Clinical Reproductive Neuroendocrinology, 1982; mem. editl. bd. Jour. Clin. Endocrin. and Metabolism, 1973-80, Proc. Soc. Exptl. Biol. and Medicine, 1978-87, Endocrine Rsch., 1984-88; contbr. articles to profl. jours. Chair rev. com. Nat. Space Biomedical Rsch. Inst. Strategic Rsch. Plan Office of Biol. and Phys. Rsch., NASA, Washington, 2002; mem. NIH Stem Cell Task Force, 2002; bd. trustees Tufts U., 1998—. Recipient Disting. Alumna award Sch. Medicine, Boston U., 1983, Mallincrodt award for Inv. Rsch. Clin. Radiossay Soc., 1980, Alumni award Boston U., 2003; named to Nat. Inst. for Child Health and Human Devel. Hall of Honor, 2003. Mem. Am. Fedn. Clin. Rsch., Endocrine Soc., Am. Soc. Clin. Rsch., Inst. Medicine-NAS. Office: Sr Advisor Sci Infrastructure & Resources NIH Dir Elias A Zerhouni MD Bldg 1 Rm 25 1 Center Dr MSC 0162 Bethesda MD 20892-0162 Office Phone: 301-435-6721, 301-435-6721. Personal E-mail: vaitukai@verizon.net. Business E-Mail: vaitukai@mail.nih.gov.

**VAJDA, JUDITH PARSONS,** psychology professor; b. Norfolk, Va., July 16, 1945; d. Harry Vernon Parsons and Carrie Elizabeth Petty; m. Frank Stephen Vajda, June 7, 1983. AS, No. Va. C.C., Annandale, 1986; BA in Psychology, George Washington U., 1990, MA in Psychology, 1995. Adj. instr. No. Va. Women. Coll. for Women, Washington, 1995—98, No. Va. C.C., Annandale, 1995—, George Washington U., Washington, 1999—. Vol. Neighborhood Watch, Annandale, 1989-2006. Mem.: APA, Va. Psychol. Assn., Am. Psychol. Soc. Achievements include research in psychology of violent criminal offenders. Office: George Washington University 2125 G Street NW Washington DC 20052 Office Phone: 202-994-6323. Business E-Mail: jvajda@gwu.edu.

**VAJK, HUGO,** manufacturing executive; b. Ljubljana, Slovenia, Mar. 26, 1928; emigrated to Can., 1947, naturalized, 1953; s. Hugo and Magda (Slatnar) V.; m. Barbara Luis Hallin, June 13, 1953; children: Tanja Astrid, Hugo Anthony, Madeleine Louise, Anita Marie, Nicolette Cecile, Moira Suzanne. Student, Inst. Poly., Grenoble, France, 1947; B.Eng. with honors, McGill U., Montreal, Que., Can., 1951; MS, Carnegie Mellon U., 1953. With Standard Iron and Steel Works Ltd., Toronto, Canada, 1953—56; product mgr. Joy Mfg. Co., Buffalo, 1957-59, dir. gen. Paris, 1960-63; with Massey-Ferguson Ltd., 1964-78; pres. Moteurs Perkins S.A., Paris, 1964-65, Massey-Ferguson Ltd., Paris, 1966-69, v.p. logistics parent co. Toronto, 1970-72, exec. v.p., 1973-78; dir. GEC Inc., subs. Gen. Electric Co., Eng., 1979; chmn. English Electric Corp., Elmsford, N.Y., 1979; with Garrett Corp. divsn. Signal Cos., 1980-84; v.p. Garrett Automotive Products; pres. Garrett Automotive Group; Allied-Signal, Inc., 1985—90; chmn. Inovatek Advisors, Inc., New Port Richey, Fla., 1988—; pres. ATM Communications Internat., Inc., Wilmington, Del., 1991—. Mem.: ASME, Assn. Profls. Engrs. Ont., Yacht Club de France (Paris), Royal Can. Yacht Club (Toronto), Univ. Club of Toronto. Home and Office: PO Box 1115 New Port Richey FL 34656-1115 Personal E-mail: hugovajk@aol.com. Business E-Mail: atmcomm@cardpay.com.

**VAKANAS, GEORGE P.,** process engineer, research scientist, consultant, entrepreneur; s. Petros and Maria (Loizou) Vakanas. BS in Physics, U. Ariz., 1990, BSME, 1990; MS, Stanford U., 1995; PhD, Ariz. State U., 2002. Rsch. engr. Cyprus Neuroscience & Tech. Inst., Nicosia, Cyprus, 1990—93; prodn. mgr. The Multimedia Factory, Nicosia, Cyprus, 1993—95; curriculum engr. and cons. Cybernet Institutes, Nicosia, Cyprus, 1995—98; sr. equipment devel. engr. Intel Corp., Santa Clara, Calif., 2001—. Author: (digital materials and curriculum) Multi-lingual Computer Curriculum for Children (INPEX'95 Silver Medal in Ednl. Tech., 1995). Mem.: US-EU Initiative for Gender Ednl. Infrastructure (co-founder 1999—2000), Stanford Alumni Assn. (life). Achievements include patents pending for Laser Fabrication Method for Subsurface Microstructures; A Repair Capability for thermofluidic Microelectromechanical Systems (MEMS). Office: Assembly Tech Capital Equipment Devel CH3-111 Intel Corp 5000 W Chandler Blvd Chandler AZ 85226 Personal E-mail: vakanas@stanfordalumni.org. E-mail: george.p.vakanas@intel.com.

**VAKERICS, THOMAS VINCENT,** lawyer; b. Lorain, Ohio, Mar. 26, 1944; s. Paul Peter and Margaret Theresa (Dobos) V.; m. Kathryn Ida Rogers, Aug. 7,1965; children: Meredith Vakerics Ehler, Mitchell Thomas. BA, Bowling Green State U., 1965; JD with honors, George Washington U., 1968. Bar: U.S. Dist. Ct. D.C. 1968, U.S. Ct. Appeals (D.C. cir.) 1969, U.S. Supreme Ct. 1974, U.S. Ct. Internat. Trade 1982, U.S. Ct. Appeals (Fed. cir.) 1982. Antitrust trial atty. FTC, Washington, 1969—73; assoc. Gore, Cladouhos & Brashares, Washington, 1973—75; ptnr. O'Connor & Hannan, Washington, 1975—84, Bayh, Tabbert & Capehart, Washington, 1984—86, Morgan, Lewis & Bockius, Washington, 1986—88, Winthrop, Stimson, Putnam & Roberts, Washington, 1988—94, Perkins Coie, 1994—2004, Sandler, Travis & Rosenberg, P.A., Washington, 2004—. Vis. prof. Nihon U., Tokyo, 1981-88. Author: Antitrust Basics, 1985, Antidumping, Countervailing Duty and Other Trade Actions, 1987; contbr. articles to profl. jours. Mem. ABA (vice chmn. internat. antitrust law com. sect. internat. law and practice 1992-95), Internat. Bar Assn., D.C. Bar Assn., Solar Energy Rsch. Inst. (editl. adv. bd. Solar Energy Law Reporter 1979-82), Order of Coif, Phi Delta Phi, Pi Sigma Alpha, Phi Alpha Delta, Sigma Chi. Democrat. Roman Catholic. Office: Sandler Travis & Rosenberg PA 1300 Pennsylvania Ave NW Ste 400 Washington DC 20004 Office Phone: 202-216-9307. Office Fax: 202-842-2247. Business E-Mail: tvakerics@strtade.com.

**VAKHSHOORI, DARYOOSH,** chemicals executive; BS, U. California, Irvine; PhD in Quantum Electronics, U. California, Berkeley. Rsch. scientist Bell Laboratories; co-founder CoreTek, Inc.; founder, v.p. bus. devel., v.p. engring., chief tech. officer, CEO Ahura Inc. Achievements include patents for 28 filed or pending. Office: Ahura Corp 46 Jonspin Rd Wilmington MA 01887 Office Phone: +1 978 657 5555. Office Fax: +1 978 657 5921. E-mail: info@ahuracorp.com.*

**VAKILI, BAHMAN FAKHIMI,** urologist; b. Soossangard, Khoozes, Iran, Jan. 22, 1936; arrived in U.S., 1962; s. Mehdi Fakhimi Vakili and Noah Jalali; m. Sarah Ann Lovejoy, June 4, 1967 (div. 2002); children: Susan Elizabeth Vakili Ballenway, David Andrew, Daniel Edward. MD, Tehran U., Iran, 1962. Diplomate Am. Bd. Urology, 1974. Intern Worcester City Hosp., Mass., 1962—63; resident gen. surgery Beth Israel Hosp., N.Y.C., 1963—64; resident Urology Boston U. Med. Ctr., 1964—67; fellow Urology and Nuc. Medicine Roger Williams Gen. Hosp., Providence, 1967—68; urologist VA, Newington, Conn., 1968—69; fellow Pediat. Urology Babies Hosp. Columbia-Presbyn. Med. Ctr., N.Y.C., 1971—72; urologist A.O. Fox Meml. Hosp., Oneonta, NY, 1972—86, VA Hosp., Beckly, W.Va., 1986—87, Bath, NY, 1987—89, Lebanon, Pa., 1990—2000; ret., 2000. Assoc. clin. prof. Urology Pa. State Med. Sch., Hershey, 1990—98; cons. Urology Margarettvill Meml. Hosp., NY, 1972—86, Stamford Cmty. Hosp., NY, 1974—86. Contbr. articles to profl. jours. Maj. Med. Corps U.S. Army, 1969—71. Fellow: ACS; mem.: AMA, Am. Urol. Assn. Republican. Unitarian Universalists. Avocations: carpentry, gardening, bicycling, writing, poetry.

**VAKULENKO, SERGEI BORISOVICH,** medical researcher, educator; b. Stavropol, Russia, Oct. 31, 1952; s. Boris Vladimirovich and Valentina Michailovna Vakulenko; m. Marta Toth. MD, Sch. Medicine, St. Petersburg, Russia, 1976; PhD, Nat. Ctr. for Antibiotics, Moscow, 1981, DSc, 1991. Rsch. assoc. Nat. Ctr. for Antibiotics, Moscow, 1981—86, asst. prof., 1986—91, assoc. prof., 1991—93; rsch. assoc. Sch. Medicine Wayne State U., Detroit, 1993—98, rsch. asst. prof. Sch. Medicine, 1998—2003; rsch. asst. prof. dept. chemistry and biochemistry U. Notre Dame, Ind., 2003—06, rsch. assoc. prof., 2006—. Mem.: Am. Soc. for Microbiology. Office: Univ Notre Dame 417 Nieuwland Sci Hall Notre Dame IN 46556-5670 Office Phone: 574-631-2935. E-mail: svakulen@nd.edu.

**VALA, MARTIN THORVALD,** chemistry professor, researcher; b. Bklyn., Mar. 28, 1938; s. Martin Thorvald and Norun (Nilson) V.; m. Vibeke Wilken-Jensen, June 23, 1966; children: Lars, Carsten, Steffen. BA, St. Olaf Coll., Northfield, Minn., 1960; MS, U. Chgo., 1962, PhD, 1964. NSF postdoctoral fellow U. Copenhagen, 1965-66; NSF U.S.-Japan coop. sci. postdoctoral fellow Nagoya (Japan) U., 1966-67; asst. prof. chemistry U. Fla., Gainesville, 1967-72, assoc. prof., 1972-78, prof., 1978—, Fla. Blue Key disting. prof., 2005. Contbr. articles to phys. chemistry jours. Fellow Merck Found., 1970-71, NATO, Paris, 1973, sr. Fulbright fellow, Paris, 1974. Fellow Am. Inst. Chemists; mem. Am. Chem. Soc., Am. Phys. Soc., Interam. Photochem. Soc., Phi Beta Kappa. Democrat. Lutheran. Office: U Fla Dept Chemistry Gainesville FL 32611 Office Phone: 352-392-0529. Business E-Mail: mvala@chem.ufl.edu.

**VALACHOVIC, RICHARD W.,** medical association administrator; Former assoc. prof. oral medicine Harvard U., former chief of dentistry, Health Svcs.; exec. dir. Am. Assn. Dental Schs., Washington, 1997; now exec. dir. Am. Dental Edn. Assn., Washington. Fellow: Am. Coll. Dentists, Am. Acad. Pediat. Dentistry. Office: Am Dental Edn Assn Ste 1100 1400 K St NW Washington DC 20005 Office Phone: 202-289-7201. Business E-Mail: Valachovich@ade.org *

**VALADE, ALAN MICHAEL,** lawyer; b. Berwyn, Ill., Jan. 26, 1952; s. Merle F. and Vera M. Valade; m. June 17, 1978. Attended, Oakland C.C., 1970—72; BA, U. Mich., 1974; JD, Wayne State U., 1977; LLM in Taxation, NYU, 1978. Bar: Mich. 1978, Fla. 1987. Assoc. Kemp, Klein, Endelman & Beer, Southfield, Mich., 1978-79; shareholder Valade, MacKinnon & Higgins, P.C., Detroit, 1979-84, Schwendener & Valade, P.C., Mason, Mich., 1985-91; ptnr. Honigman Miller Schwartz and Cohn LLP, Detroit, 1991—, chmn. tax dept., 2002—06. Co-author: The Michigan Single Business Tax, 1991; contbr. articles to profl. jours. Fellow Mich. State Bar Found.; mem. ABA, State Bar Mich. (chmn. state and local tax com. 1991, tax. coun. 1989-92), State Bar Fla. Office: Honigman Miller Schwartz and Cohn LLP 2290 First National Bldg 660 Woodward Ave Detroit MI 48226-3506 Office Phone: 313-465-7636. Business E-Mail: avalade@honigman.com.

**VALADEZ, RUDOLPH ANTONIO,** security firm executive, consultant, writer, artist; b. Elmertownship, Mich., July 30, 1942; s. Aldofo Valadez and Catalina Gamez; m. Jo Ann Gomez; children: John L. children: Rudolph A., Monique M., Emilio Alejandro. BS, Am. U., 1971; postgrad., St. Thomas U., 1990, Pacific West Coll., 1995. Spl. agt.-mgr., chief Soviet CounterIntelligence, Chief of Counter Internat. Terrorism FBI, Washington, 1967—92; adminstr.-commr. Western Regional U.S. Immigration & Naturalization Svc., Laguna Niguel, Calif., 1992—93; TV and radio commentator Spanish Channel 52, KTNQ, L.A., 1993—95; security cons. Valadez Assocs. Internat., Inc., L.A., 1994—. Author: (Book) Uncommon Common Sense: The Anatomy of Peril, 2001, Instant Philosopher, 2002, Emilio Kosterlitzky, 2002; exhibitions include Global Art Gallery, Seattle, 2002, Cambria (Calif.) Art Gallery, 2002. Bd. dirs. Basic Adult Spanish Edn. for Spanish Illiteracy, L.A., 1986—90. Recipient Pub. Svc. Recognition, Calif. State Senate, 1992, Outstanding Pub. Svc. award, L.A. County Bd. Suprs., 1992, Cold War Svc. Recognition award, U.S. Dept. Def., 2001. Mem.: Am. Soc. Indsl. Security. Roman Catholic. Achievements include patents for handcuff holster; self recharging battery; automobile third rear light to indicate driver activity and pending action. Avocations: painting, flying, woodworking, travel. Home: 12582 Navel Ct Riverside CA 92503-7056 Personal E-mail: r.valadez@attworldnet.com. Business E-Mail: r.valadez@mai_assoc.com.

**VALANCE, MARSHA JEANNE,** library director, storyteller; b. Evanston, Ill., Aug. 2, 1946; Children's libr. trainee N.Y. Pub. Libr., N.Y.C., 1968-69; ref. libr. Acton (Mass.) Meml. Pub. Libr., 1969-70; mgr. The Footnote, Cedar Rapids, Iowa, 1976-78; assoc. editor William C. Brown, Dubuque, Iowa, 1978-79; dir. Dubuque County Libr., 1979-81, G.B. Dedrick Pub. Libr., Geneseo, Ill., 1981-84, Grand Rapids (Minn.) pub. Libr., 1984-89; mgmt. libr. Wis. Regional Libr. for Blind and Physically Handicapped, 1989—. Workshop coord., participant, sect. chmn. profl. confs.; LSCA grant reviewer Dept. Edn., 1989-95. Author: (with others) Mystery, Value and Awareness, 1979, Pluralism, Similarities and Contrast, 1979; contbr. articles and book revs. to publs. Troop leader Miss. Valley Coun. Girl Scouts USA, Cedar Rapids, 1976-78; mem. liturgy com. St. Malachy's Roman Cath. Ch., Geneseo, 1983; com. judging clinic 4-H, Moline, Ill., 1984; trustee KAXE No. Cmty. Radio, 1986-89, ICTV, 1988-90; sec. Grand Rapids Cmty. Svcs. Coun., 1986; coach Itasca County 4-H Horse Bowl Team, 1987; dir. Grand Rapids Storyfest, 1987-89; program chmn. Spotlight on Books Conf., 1989; bd. dirs., trustee Vols. in Svc. to the Visually Handicapped, 1989—; audio describer Artreach, Milw., 1991-98. Nat. merit scholar, 1964-68; recipient Weavers award Telephone Pioneers, 1992, outstanding svc. award Badger Assn., 1999; grantee Iowa Humanities Bd. 1981, Minn. Libr. Found., 1985, 86, 87, Blandin Found., 1986, Arrowhead Regional Arts Coun., 1987, 89, Ms. Soc., 1989, Sunrise Found., 2000. Mem. ALA, Wis. Libr. Assn., Iowa Librs. Medium Size (sec. 1981), Northlands Storytelling Network (bd. dirs. 1988-94, v.p. 1989, pres. 1990, editor Grapevine 1991-94), Nat. Storytelling Assn., Alliance Info. and Referral Svcs., DAR (constn. chmn. 1983-84), Miss. Valley Morgan Horse Club, Wis. Morgan Horse Club (newsletter editor 1994-95, sec. 1995), Western Working Family Morgan Horse Club, Am. Morgan Horse Assn., Geneseo Jr. Women's Club (internat. chmn. 1983-84), UCLA Club Wis. (pres. 1990-91), Alpha Gamma Delta. Home: 343 N 62d St Milwaukee WI 53213-4130 Office: Wis Regional Libr Blind & Physically Handicapped 813 W Wells St Milwaukee WI 53233-1436 Office Phone: 414-286-3010. Business E-Mail: mvalan@mpl.org.

**VALASQUEZ, JOSEPH LOUIS,** industrial engineer; b. Balt., Apr. 15, 1955; s. Jose Louis and Edith Rosabel (Saunders) V.; m. Nicole Diane Feldser, Sept. 4, 1983; children: Alexandra Nicole, Joseph Jr. AA, Essex Coll., 1977; BS in Indsl. Engring., U. Ariz., 1982; MBA in Fin., So. Ill. U., 1985. Registered profl. engr., Fla.; cert. quality engr.; cert. quality auditor; cert. quality mgr.; cert. project mgmt. profl.; cert. integrated resource mgmt.; pvt. pilots license. Machinist Bausch & Lomb, Balt., 1974-77; indsl. engr. IBM Corp., Tucson, 1980-81; sr. indsl. engr. Gen. Dynamics, San Diego, 1981-83; supr. engring. Avco Corp., Nashville, 1983-84; mgr. engring. Burroughs Corp., Coral Springs, Fla., 1984-85; dir. total quality mgmt. Lambda Novatronics, Inc., Pompano Beach, Fla., 1984-94; champoint of continuous improvement Allied Signal, 1994-97, Sensormatic Corp., 1997-98; v.p. corp. quality Sunbeam Corp., Delray Beach, Fla., 1998-2001; quality/productivity exec. Bank Am., Charlotte, NC, 2001—. Computer cons., Margate, Fla., 1987; founder, owner E.P.I. Cons., Pompano Beach. Mem. Am. Inst. Indsl. Engrs., Fla. Engring. Soc. Republican. Roman Catholic. Avocations: real estate management, computer programming, mountain climbing, canoeing, private pilot. Home: PO Box 49616 Charlotte NC 28277-0082 Personal E-Mail: jlvalasquez@yahoo.com. Business E-Mail: joe.l.valasquez@bankofamerica.com.

**VALAUSKAS, EDWARD JUSTIN,** librarian, editor, Internet consultant; b. Chgo., Oct. 3, 1950; s. Edward Anthony and Madeline (Markovich) V.; m. Nancy R. John, May 3, 1980. BA, U. Ill., Chgo., 1980; MA, U. Chgo., 1982. Asst. dir. libr. Charles E. Merriam Ctr. for Pub. Adminstrn., Chgo., 1985-91; head pub. svcs., libr. and info. svcs. Superconducting Super Collider Libr., Dallas, 1991-93; prin., founder Internet Mechanics, Chgo., 1993—; mgr. hort. resource ctr. Chgo. Bot. Garden, Glencoe, Ill., 1998—2004, curator rare books libr., 2004—. Guest lectr. Emporia (Kans.) State U. Sch. Libr. and Info. Mgmt., 1995—98, Dominican U. Sch. Libr. and Info. Sci., River Forest, Ill., 1995-2003, sr. fellow, 2003-04, Follett chair, 2004—; mem. adv. bd. Internat. Ctr. for Info. Mgmt. Systems and Svcs., Copernicus U., Torun, Poland. Co-author: Internet Troubleshooter, 1994; contbr. articles to profl. jours.; co-editor: Macintoshed Libraries, 6 edits., 1987-94, Internet Initiative, 1995, Internet for Teachers and School Media Specialists, 1996; chief editor First Monday, Jour. of the Internet, Denmark, 1996—. Named Apple Tchg. fellow Apple Cons. Educator, 1993; Summer Student fellow Woods Hole Oceanog. Instn., 1973; Shinner scholar Field Mus. Natural History, 1969. Mem. ALA (Libr. fellow 1995-96), Spl. Librs. Assn. (Pub. Rels. award 1997), Internat. Fedn. Libr. Assns. (profl. bd. 1995—99), Grolier Club, Caxton Club, Assn. Librs. in Romanian Pub. Librs. (hon.), Palaeontol. Assn., Palaeontol. Soc. Office: Grad Sch Libr and Info Sci Dominican Univ 7900 W Division St River Forest IL 60305 Business E-Mail: ejv@dom.edu.

**VALBUENA, VIVIAN,** brokerage house executive; b. Wilmington, Del., Sept. 29, 1965; d. Julian Valbuena-Briones and Barbara Hobart Valbuena; m. David Wiliam Buxbaum, Nov. 22, 1996. BA, U. Del., 1988. Sr. editor Banco Santander, N.Y.C., 1996—99; mng. editor, emerging mkts. BNP Paribas, N.Y.C., 1999—2001; assoc. dir., fixed income Barclays Capital, N.Y.C., 2001—. Contbr. articles to profl. jours. Budget com. Episc. Diocese of NY, N.Y.C., 2000—03; bd. dirs. China Barrett Assn., Carmel, NY, 2003. Mem.: Soc. Profl. Journalists. Achievements include speak English, Spanish, French. Avocations: tennis, travel, food, theater, mysteries. Office: Barclays Capital 200 Park Ave New York NY 10016 Office Phone: 212-412-1339. Office Fax: 212-412-7335. Personal E-mail: vivian.valbuena@mindspring.com.

**VALBUENA-BRIONES, ANGEL JULIAN,** retired language educator, author; b. Madrid, Jan. 11, 1928; naturalized, 1963; s. Angel Valbuena-Prat and Francisca Briones; m. Barbara Northrup Hobart, Nov. 9, 1957; children: Teresa, Vivian Teresa. Lido summa cum laude, Murcia U., Spain, 1949; PhD with honors, Madrid U., 1952. Prof. Ayudante Murcia U., 1949-51; lectr. Oxford (Eng.) U., 1953-55; prof. Ayudante Madrid U., 1955-56; vis. lectr. U. Wis., 1956-58; asst. prof. Yale U., 1958-60; Elias Ahuja prof. Spanish lit. U. Del., 1960-2000, Elias Ahuja prof. emeritus, 1999—. Lecture tour, S.Am., 1957; vis. prof. NYU, 1960, 61, U. Madrid, 1970-71, 1965, 77, U. Mex. at Aragon, 1979, Inst. Caro y Cuervo, Bogota, Colombia, 1980; mem. Fulbright-Hays nat. screening com., 1981-83, 89-90; mem. editl. com. for CD-ROM edit. Spanish Golden Age Theatre, Chadwyck-Healey/Spain, 1995-98; bd. dirs. publs. U. Barcelona, Spain, Bull. Comediantes, U. Calif., Riverside, Hispanic Jour., Pa., Juan de la Cuesta Edits., Del.; profl. cons. NEH. Author: Nueva Poesia de Puerto Rico, 1952, Comedias de Capa y Espada de Calderon, 1954, Dramas de Honor de Calderon, 2 vols., 1956, Obras Completas de Calderon, vol. I, 1959, 3d reprinting, 1991, vol. II, 1956, 6th edit. 2 vols., 1988, Literatura Hispanoamericana, 1962, revised and enlarged, 1969, Perspectiva critica de los dramas de Calderon, 1965, Ideas y Palabras, 1968, El alcalde de Zalamea de Calderon, 1971, rev. 13th edit., 1995, Primera Parte de Comedias de Pedro Calderon de la Barca, Vol. 1, 1974, Vol. 2, 1981, La Dama Duende de Calderon, 1976, 8th printing, 1986, Calderon y la comedia nueva, 1977, La vida es sueno. Antes que todo es mi dama. Pedro Calderon de la Barca, 1988, El mayor monstruo del mundo. de Calderon, 1995; author (cd-rom) Teatro Espanol de Siglo de oro, 1998, Historia y Creación Literaria en Don Pedro Calderón de la Barca, 2002. Founder, pres. Valbuena Inst. Spanish Lit., Inc., 1996-99. Consejo Superior de Investigaciones Científicas fellw, 1951, 70-71, Instituto de Cultura Hispánica fellow, 1951-52; recipient Excellence in Teaching award U. Del., 1988, Outstanding Scholar award U. Del. Coll. Arts and Sci., 1996. Mem. MLA, AAUP, Am. Assn. Tchrs. Spanish and Portuguese, Inst. Iberoam. Lit., Internat. Fedn. Modern Langs. and Lits., Assn. Am. Lit. Scholars and Critics, Internat. Assn. Hispanists, Am. Comparative Lit. Assn., Assn. for Hispanic Classic Theatre, Old Bohemia Hist. Soc., Sigma Delta Pi (hon., Order of Don Quijote, 1999), Phi Kappa Phi. Home: 726 Loveville Rd Cottage 6 Hockessin DE 19707-1504

**VALDES, ARLENE H.,** assistant principal; b. NYC, Dec. 31, 1965; d. Israel and Magaly Hernandez; m. Bert Valdes, Sept. 3, 1988; children: Kevin Andrew, Brianna Nicole. PhD, Nova Southeastern U., 2002. Cert. Microsoft NT adminstr., Windows security, tech. specialist; tchr. Fla. Asst. prin.

Archbishop McCarthy H.S., Fort Lauderdale, Fla., 1998—; dual enrollment liaison St. Thomas U., Miami, Fla., 1999—. Spkr., presenter in field. Outstanding support of law enforcement ops. Metro Dade Police Dept., Miami, 1993—93. Recipient cert. of appreciation, Future Bus. Leaders, 1998. Mem.: Fla. ASCD (assoc.). Office: Archbishop Edward McCarthy HS 5451 South Flamingo Rd Fort Lauderdale FL 33330 Office Phone: 954-434-8820. Office Fax: 954-680-4835.

**VALDES, GINA,** writer; b. LA, June 6, 1943; 1 child, Rosalia Hayakawa. MA, U. Calif., San Diego, 1981. Vis. lectr. U. Calif. Davis, 1987-89, 90, Colo. Coll., Colorado Springs, 1990, U. Wash., Seattle, 1990-91, UCLA, 1992-93, U. Calif., San Diego, 1994, 96, 98-2001, 03-05. Author: (bilingual poetry) Eating Fire, 1986, Bridges and Borders, 1996.

**VALDÉS, KAREN W.,** art gallery director, educator; b. L.A., May 25, 1945; d. Richard Victor and Eleanor M. (Tomte) V.; m. Thomas E. Schwarz, Oct. 14, 1989. BFA, U. Calif., Irvine, 1968; MFA, Fla. State U., 1974. Dir. cultural events Fla. State U., Tallahassee, 1973-75; curator exhbn. Art Mus. So. Tex., Corpus Christi, 1975-76; assoc. prof., dir. gallery Miami (Fla.)-Dade Community Coll., 1976-84; dir. Gloria Luria Gallery, Miami, 1985; curator exhbn. Mus. Art, Ft. Lauderdale, Fla., 1985-89; assoc. prof., dir. univ. galleries U. Fla., Gainesville, 1989-95; gallery curator Arts Ctr. Galleries, Okaloosa-Walton C.C., Niceville, Fla., 1995—. Panelist NEA, Ft. Lauderdale, 1978-80, Dade County Art in Pub. Places, Miami, 1980-83, GSA Commn., 1982, Arts in State Bldgs., Gainesville, 1989—. Mem. Am. Assn. Mus., Coll. Art Assn., U. Fla. Hispanic Faculty Assn. Democrat. Avocation: sailing. Office: Arts Ctr Galleries Okaloosa-Walton CC 100 College Blvd E Niceville FL 32578-1347

**VALDÉS-PÉREZ, RAUL E.,** computer scientist, researcher; b. Havana, Cuba, Oct. 13, 1956; came to U.S., 1961; s. Thomas Valdes and Hilda (Perez) Booth; m. Carmen B. Arenas, Apr. 9, 1988; children: Tomas, Daniela. BSE, U. Ill., Chgo., 1980, MS, 1982; PhD, Carnegie Mellon U., Pitts., 1991. Engr. Itaú Tecnologia, São Paulo, Brazil, 1982-84; rsch. scientist MIT AI Lab., Cambridge, Mass., 1984-86; adj. rsch. computer scientist Carnegie Mellon U., Pitts., 1991—; co-founder, pres., chmn. Vivisimo Inc., Pitts., 2000—. Vis. lectr. Hefei Poly. U., China, 1987, Nat. U. Cordoba, Argentina, 1994. Contbr. articles to profl. jours. including Artificial Intelligence, Machine Learning, Catalysis Letters, Jour. Computational Chemistry, Jour. Phys. Chemistry, Jour. Theoretical Biology, Computer Physics Comms. USAF grad. fellow, 1987-91; named one of 50 Most Important Hispanics in Tech. & Bus. Hispanic Engr. & Info. Tech. mag., 2005. Mem. AAAS, ACM, Am. Assn. Artificial Intelligence. Achievements include various machine discoveries in natural science. Office: Vivisimo Inc Ste 300 1710 Murray Ave Pittsburgh PA 15217 Office Phone: 415-422-2499. Office Fax: 415-422-2495.*

**VALDES-RODRIGUEZ, ALISA,** writer; b. Albuquerque, N.Mex., 1969; married; 1 child. BA, Berklee Coll. Music, Boston; MA in journalism, Columbia Univ. Staff writer & reporter Boston Globe, 1994—99, LA Times, 1999—2001. Co-founder Dirty Girls Productions, 2005. Author: The Dirty Girls Social Club, 2003, Playing with Boys, 2004. Named one of 25 Most Influential Hispanics, Time Mag., 2005. Mailing: Joy Harris Literary Agency Ste 617 156 Fifth Ave New York NY 10010-7002

**VALDEZ, DENISE,** newscaster; BA in TV broadcasting, Pepperdine U. Reporter KMIR-TV, Palm Springs, 1992; weekend anchor, reporter KCCN-TV, Monterey, Calif., 1992—93; co-anchor, reporter KSAT-TV, San Antonio, 1994—2001; weekend anchor, reporter KXAS-TV (NBC), Dallas/Ft. Worth, 2001—02; co-anchor, Channel 4 News with Furnell Chatman NBC4, Los Angeles, 2002—05; noon and 4pm anchor KLAS-TV, Las Vegas, Nev., 2005—. Mem.: Nat. Assn. of Hispanic Journalists. Address: PO Box 921295 Sylmar CA 91392

**VALDEZ, JOSE CARBAJAL, JR.,** poet, lyricist; b. Solano, Nueva Vizcaya, Philippines, Jan. 8, 1932; arrived in U.S., 1969; s. Jose Abella Valdez, Sr. and Laureana Cabato (Carbajal) Valdez; m. Clavel Garduque Corrales-Valdez, July 26, 1956; children: Fred, Icena, Jose III, Walter, Meha. AA, Luna Cells., Tayug, Pangasinan, The Philippines, 1952; BS in Edn., Adventist-U. of the Philippines, Cavite, Silang, 1954. Cert. sr. tchr. civil svc. eligibility Civil Svc. Commn. Tchr. Polillo Acad., Quezon, Philippines, 1955—56, Namuac Acad., Sanchez Mira, Cagayan, Philippines, 1960—67, Thoburn Meml. Acad., Sanchez Mira, Cagayan, Philippines, 1967—69, San Diego City Schs., 1977—78; med. technician Paradise Valley Hosp., National City, Calif., 1990—95; writer Internat. Soc. Poets, Owings Mills, Mo., 1997—; lyricist Hilltop Records, Hollywood, Calif., 2000—. Author: (book) Golden Treasures, 1999. Recipient Editor's award, Internat. Libr. Poetry, 2000, Merit award, Internat. Soc. Poets, 2000, 2002. Republican. Seventh-Day Adventist. Achievements include experimentation and research on plant propagation: hybridization or cross-breeding of plants (fruit trees); produced the most-grafted lemon tree with 40 varieties in one tree; cross-bred guava from Thailand and Philippine guavas. Avocations: gardening, reading, painting, fishing, walking. Home: 1440 Lorenz Ave San Diego CA 92114 E-mail: josclavelvaldez@aol.com.

**VALDEZ, JOSH,** health insurance company executive; Assoc. degree, Cmty. Coll. of Air Force; BS, Nat. U. Sacramento; MBA, Golden State U.; D in Bus. Adminstrn., So. Calif. U. Vp. managed care AltaMed Health Svcs., Calif.; CFO, exec. dir. West Covina Med. Clinic, Eastland Med. Group, Combined Mgmt. Svcs.; regional dir. Fed. Dept. Health and Human Svcs., 2001—04; sr. v.p. Blue Cross Blue Shield, 2004—. Health care adminstr. USAF. Named Man of Yr., Hollenbeck Youth Ctr./Inner-City Games LA, 2005; named one of Top 10 Latinos in Healthcare, LatinoLeaders mag., 2004. Office: Blue Cross Calif 1 WellPoint Way Thousand Oaks CA 91362-5035*

**VALDMAN, BERTRAND A.,** utilities executive; BA, Northwestern U.; MA, PhD., Stanford U. With JP Morgan Securities, Inc., 1987—2003, former mng. dir. natural resources group; sr. v.p., CFO Puget Sound Energy, Bellevue, Wash., 2004—. Office: Puget Sound Energy 10885 NE 4th St PO Box 97034 Bellevue WA 98009

**VALDRINI, RITA,** prosecutor; Bar: Pa. 1988. Acting US atty. (no. dist.) W. Va. US Dept. Justice, Wheeling, W.Va., 2006—. Del. Nat. Assn. Assist. US Attorneys. Office: US Attys Office PO Box 591 Wheeling WV 26003-0011*

**VALENCIA, MARGARITA,** Spanish language educator; b. Bogotá, Colombia, Nov. 28, 1952; arrived in U.S., 1973; BA, U. Calif., Santa Barbara, MA in Polit. Sci. Profl. clear single subject tchg. credential in Spanish; cert. eligibility for Calif. prelim. adminstrv. svcs. credential. Tchr. Spanish Manual Arts H.S. L.A. Unified Sch. Dist., 1994—. Mem.: Acad. Polit. Sci. N.Y., L.A. World Affairs Coun., Sierra Club. Personal E-mail: mvalenciab@aol.com.

**VALENCIA LAVAO, JESUS M.,** electrical engineer, consultant; b. Bogota, Distrito Capital, Colombia, Sept. 19, 1965; s. Jesus Maria Valencia Tapiero and Maria Elena Lavao de Valencia; m. Zoraya Ines Contecha Carrillo, Jan. 6, 1996 (div. May 15, 2002); m. Isabel Cristina Patino Devia, Feb. 20, 2005; children: Angel Gabriel Valencia Patino children: Nicolas Andres Valencia Contecha, Daniela Valencia Contecha. Degree in mgmt., Servicio Nacional De Aprendizaje, Bogota, 1988; degree in electrical engring., Distrital U., Bogota, 1994; MSEE, Los Andes U., Bogota, 2004. Lic. Consejo Nacional de Ingenierias, 1998. Radiofrequency engr. SKYTEL, Bogota, 1994—97; sr. engr. Avantel Motorola, Bogota, 1997—2001, Galaxy Engring. Svcs., Alpharetta, Ga., 2001—03, Incode Wireless, St. Louis, 2003—. Math and physics tchr. Grancolombiano H.S., Bogota, 1992—93; info. tech. and computer engr. cons. Microlink, Bogota, 1993—94; internat. telecom. cons. Skytel Mobile Telecomm. Techs. Corp., Bogota, 1995—97; assoc. prof. San Buenaventura U., Bogota, 1998—2001. Author: (drama) Once in the heavens; composer: (song) While the Sun Rises. Mem.: Profl. Assn. Diving Instrs. Diving Soc. (assoc.), IEEE (assoc.), Consejo Profesional Nacional de Ingenieria (life; electronic engr. 1998—). Achievements include invention of electronic circuit to generate chaotic signals for use in broadband telecom-

munications. Avocations: scuba diving, snowboarding, mountain biking, travel. Office: 115 S 84th St Ste 101 Milwaukee WI 53214 Home: 3640 S Riverside Dr Unit 5 Greenfield WI 53228 Personal E-mail: eldurissimo@yahoo.com. Business E-mail: jvalencia@incodewireless.com.

**VALENSTEIN, ARTHUR F.,** psychiatrist, educator; b. NYC, Jan. 15, 1914; s. Abraham and Jennie (Friedman) Valenstein; m. Katrina Ely Burlingham, Dec. 29, 1958; 1 child, David Arthur. BA, Cornell U., 1934, MD, 1938. Diplomate Am. Bd. Psychiatry and Neurology. Intern Cin. Gen. Hosp., 1938-39; resident in psychiatry Boston Psychopathic Hosp. (now The Mass. Mental Health Ctr.), 1939—40, sr. physician N.Y.C., 1941-42; resident in neurology Bellevue Hosp., N.Y.C., 1940—43; from instr. to clin. prof. psychiatry Harvard U. Med. Sch., Boston, 1948-84; clin. prof. emeritus Med. Sch. Harvard U., Boston, 1984—; asst. chief psychiatry Mental Health Clinic VA Med. Ctr., Boston, 1946-49; from assoc. psychiatrist to hon. psychiatrist Beth Israel Hosp., Boston, 1949—; from assoc. in psychiatry to physician Brigham and Women's Hosp. (formerly Peter Bent Brigham Hosp.), Boston, 1949—; pvt. practice Cambridge, Mass., 1949—. Cons. child psychiatrist Mt. Auburn Hosp., Cambridge, 1975—, McLean Hosp., Belmont, Mass., Mass. Gen. Hosp., Boston. Contbr. articles to profl. jours., chapters to books. Maj. M.C. USAAF, 1942—46, PTO. Recipient Sigourney award for contbn. to psychoanalysis, 2000. Fellow: Am. Psychiat. Assn. (life; disting., Disting. fellow); mem.: Boston Psychoanalytic Soc. and Inst. (pres. 1974—75), Pyschoanalytic Inst. New Eng. E. (tng. and supervising analyst 1975—), Internat. Psychoanalytic Assn. (v.p. 1971—77), Am. Psychoanalytic Assn. (mem. com. 1963—81). Office: 140A Foster St Cambridge MA 02138-4746 Business E-Mail: arthur_valenstein@hms.harvard.edu.

**VALENTE, GIORGIO,** finance educator; b. Rome, Oct. 9, 1973; s. Antonio Valente and Rita Leonino; m. Vicky Poon, July 10, 2002. Laurea in Economics, La Sapienza U. Rome, 1998; MA in Econ. and Econometrics, Centre for Econ. Rsch., U. Tilburg, The Netherlands, 2000; PhD in Fin., Warwick Bus. Sch., U. Warwick, Coventry, UK, 2003. Assoc. prof. fin. U. Warwick, Coventry, England, 2003—05, Chinese U. of Hong Kong, 2005—. Recipient Oddone Fantini award, Istituto per lo Studio dei Problemi del Credito, Rome, 1998, Angelo Costa award, Rivista di Politica Economica, Rome, 1998; grantee, ESRC, London, UK, 2000, 2003. Office: Finance Dept Faculty Business Admin Chinese Univ Hong Kong Shatin NT Hong Kong Office Phone: (852) 2609 7443. Business E-Mail: giorgio.valente@cuhk.edu.hk.

**VALENTE, LOUIS PATRICK (DAN VALENTE),** financial planner, director; b. Somerville, Mass., July 26, 1930; s. Luigi and Mary Constance (Fedele) V.; m. Jeanne Barbara Peters, Oct. 3, 1992; children: Louis, Marianne, Steven, Diane, Richard, Carol, Susan. CPA, Bentley Coll., Boston, 1955. Cost acct. Cambridge Corp., Lowell, Mass., 1953-55; sr. acct. Flaherty, Bliss & Co., CPAs, Boston, 1956-61; fin. analyst Sanders Assocs., Nashua, NH, 1961-62; contract audit adminstr. Dept. Def. Audit Agy., Boston, 1962-66, DOE, Las Vegas, 1966-68; asst. controller EG&G, Inc., Wellesley, Mass., 1968-71, asst. v.p., treas., 1971-74, dir. fin., 1974-79, officer, corp. treas., 1979-83, v.p. bus. devel., 1985-91, sr. v.p. mergers, acquisitons and investments, 1991-95; bus. and fin. cons., 1995-97; chmn., CEO Palomar Med. Tech., Inc., Burlington, Mass., 1997—. Bd. dirs. Meditech Inc., Westwood, Mass., Patient Care Tech., Atlanta, MKS Instruments, Inc., Andover, Mass., Palomar Med. Tech. Inc., Burlington, SurgiLight, Inc., Orlando, Fla. Selectman Town of Burlington, 1970-73, 76-79, chmn., 1972-79; trustee, mem. fin. com. Choate-Symmes Hosp., Woburn, Mass., 1972-80; pres.'s adv. coun. Bentley Coll. With USAF, 1951-53. Mem. AICPA, Fin. Execs. Inst., Mass. Soc. CPAs, Bentley Coll. Alumni Assn., New Eng. Coun., KC Lodge. Roman Catholic. Home: 44 Concord Rd Weston MA 02493-1223 Business E-Mail: dvalente@palmed.com.

**VALENTE, PETER CHARLES,** lawyer; b. NYC, July 3, 1940; s. Francis Louis and Aurelia Emily (Cella) V.; m. Judith Kay Nemeroff, Feb. 19, 1966; children: Susan Lynn, David Marc. BA, Bowdoin Coll., 1962; LLB, Columbia U., 1966; LLM, NYU, 1971. Bar: N.Y. 1967. Assoc. Blank Rome LLP (formerly Tenzer Greenblatt LLP), N.Y.C., 1967-73, ptnr., 1973—, practice group leader pvt. client practice group, 2003—. Co-author column on wills, estates and surrogates's practice N.Y. Law Jour. Fellow Am. Coll. Trust and Estate Counsel; mem. ABA, N.Y. State Bar Assn. (lectr. on wills, trusts and estates), Assn. of Bar of City of N.Y., N.Y. County Lawyers' Assn. (former bd. dirs. and chmn. com. on surrogates' ct., lectr. on wills, trusts and estates), Phi Beta Kappa. Office: Blank Rome 405 Lexington Ave New York NY 10174-0002 Office Phone: 212-885-5320. Office Fax: 917-332-3717. Business E-Mail: pvalente@blankrome.com.

**VALENTI, ELIZABETH JEANNE,** environmental services administrator; b. Toledo, June 1, 1978; d. Richard Philip and Virginia Helen Slawinski; m. Benjamin Michael Valenti, Apr. 13, 1976. BS in Environ. Health, Bowling Green State U., 2000. Registered environ. health specialist Nat. Environ. Health Assn., 2003. Environ. health specialist USCG/USPHS, Norfolk, Va., 2001—03; tng. staff program mgmt. officer Office of Force Readiness and Deployment/Office of the Surgeon Gen./USPHS, Rockville, Md., 2003—06; coord. program mgmt. FDA/USPHS, 2006—. Lt. USPHS, 2001—. Mem.: Commd. Officer Assn. of USPHS, Nat. Environ. Health Assn. (sec./treas. uniformed svcs. affiliate 2005—). Achievements include John C. Eason Rising Star award. Office: 1401 Rockville Pike MS HFM-481 Rockville MD 20852 Office Phone: 240-453-6095, 301-827-3070. Office Fax: 240-453-6110. Personal E-mail: betsyvalenti@hotmail.com. Business E-Mail: evalenti@osophs.dhhs.gov, elizabeth.valenti@fda.hhs.gov.

**VALENTI, JACK JOSEPH,** former motion picture executive; b. Houston, Sept. 5, 1921; m. Mary Margaret Wiley, June 1, 1962; children: Courtenay Lynda, John Lyndon, Alexandra Alice. BA, U. Houston, 1946; MBA, Harvard U., 1948. Co-founder, formerly exec. v.p. Weekley and Valenti, Inc. (advt.), 1952-63; spl. asst. to Pres. Lyndon Johnson The White House, 1963-66; chmn., CEO Motion Picture Assn. Am., Inc., 1966—2004. Adj. prof. govt. and pub. adminstrn. Am. U., 1977; bd. dirs. Riggs Nat. Corp. Washington. Author: Bitter Taste of Glory, 1971, A Very Human President, 1976, Speak Up With Confidence: How To Prepare, Learn and Deliver an Effective Speech, 1982, Protect and Defend, 1992, Speak Up With Confidence, 2002; contbr. articles to mags. Trustee, bd. dirs. Am. Film Inst. Served with USAAF, 1942-45. Decorated D.F.C., Air medal with five oak leaf clusters, Disting. Unit Citation with cluster, European Theater Ribbon with 4 battle stars, Chevalier de la Legion d'honneur (France).

**VALENTIN, JOAN MARIE,** secondary school educator; b. Gettysburg, Pa., Aug. 14, 1960; d. Joseph Leroy Hess and Anna Jane (Wetzel) Hess Bucher; m. Javier Valentin, Oct. 17, 1987; children: Andrea Leigh, Samuel Brady. BS in Math. Edn., Shippensburg U., 1981, MA, 1987. Cert. secondary sch. tchr., Pa.; cert. math supr. Math. tchr. Downingtown (Pa.) Sr. High Sch., 1982—. Mem. Nat. Coun. Tchrs. of Math., Pa. Coun. Tchrs. Math., Ctrl. Pa. Assn. Tchrs. Math. Republican. Roman Catholic. Avocations: reading, crafts. Home: 142 Carriage House Dr Willow Street PA 17584-9025 Office: Downingtown High Sch West 445 Manor Ave Downingtown PA 19335-1725 Office Phone: 610-269-4400. E-mail: jvalentin@dasd.org.

**VALENTINE, ALAN DARRELL,** performing company executive, conductor; b. San Antonio, July 18, 1958; s. Lonnie Darrell Jr. and Marjorie (Childs) V.; m. Jari Ann Ruhl, Aug. 10, 1979 (div. 1987); children: Brandon Darrell, Chelsea Michelle; m. Karen Kay Bingham, Oct. 21, 1989 (div. 2001); 1 child, Nathan Lee; m. Connie Linsler, July 21, 2002. MusB, U. Houston, 1981. Orch. mgr. U. Houston Symphony, 1977-81; gen. mgr. Mid-Columbia Symphony Soc., Richland, Wash., 1981-83, Greensboro (N.C.) Symphony Soc., 1983-85; orch. mgr. Symphony Soc. San Antonio, 1985-87; mng. dir. Chattanooga Symphony and Opera, 1987-88; exec. dir. Okla. Philharm. Soc., Oklahoma City, 1988-98, Nashville Symphony, 1998—. Mem. adj. faculty Arts Administrn., Oklahoma City U., 1992—. Recs. include Best of Greensboro Symphony Orchestra Silver Season, 1983, A Christmas Festival-San

Antonio Symphony, 1986, A Time of Healing-Oklahoma City Philharmonic, 1995; (CD) Howard Hanson The Nashville Symphony, 2000, Charles Ives The Nashville Symphony, 2000, George Whitefield Chadwick-Nashville Symphony, 2002, Bertnein's West Side Story, Nashville Symphonyh, 2002, Amy Beach Gaelic Symphony, Nashville Symphony, 2003, Beethoven's Missa Solemnis, 2004, Elliott Carter: Piano Concerto, 2004; TV prodns. include Music of the Americas-Placido Domingo with San Antonio Symphony, 1986, Perry Como Christmas Special-San Antonio Symphony, 1986, Sagebrush Symphony-Oklahoma City Philharmonic with Michael Martin Murphey, 1996, Kathie Lee: Just In Time for Christmas-Okla. City Philharmonic & Guests, 1996, Martina McBride Christmas Special Nashville, Symphony and Guests, 1998. Bd. dirs. Classen Sch. for Artistically and Academically Gifted, 1995-98, Arts Festival Okla., 1991-. Mem. NARAS (bd. dirs. 2002-), Am. Symphony Orch. League (bd. dirs. Cmty. and Urban Symphony Orch. divsn. 1981-83, policy com. A 1995-98, chmn. group III mgrs. 1996-98, vice chmn. group III mgr. 2003), Rotary, Phi Mu Alpha. Presbyterian. Avocations: computers, racquetball, travel. Office: Nashville Symphony 2000 Glen Echo Ste 204 Nashville TN 37215 Personal E-mail: alandv@aol.com. Business E-Mail: alandv@nashvillesymphony.org.

**VALENTINE, BOBBY (ROBERT JOHN VALENTINE),** professional baseball manager; b. Stamford, CT, May 13, 1950; m. Mary Branca, Jan. 8, 1977; 1 child, Robert John Jr. Student, U. Southern California, Arizona State U. Player Pioneer League, Ogdon, 1968, Pacific Coast League, Spokane, Wash., 1969-71, Los Angeles Dodgers, Los Angeles, Calif., 1971-72, California Angels, Calif., 1973-75, International League, Charleston, W.Va., 1975, Pacific Coast League, Salt Lake City, 1975, Hawaii, Hawaii, 1976, San Diego Padres, San Diego, 1975-77, New York Mets, NY, 1977-78, Seattle Mariners, Seattle, W.Va., 1979; scout, infield instr. San Diego Padres, San Diego, 1981; minor league infield instr. New York Mets, 1982, third base coach, 1983-85; mgr. Texas Rangers, Arlington, Tex., 1985-96, N.Y. Mets, 1996—2002, Chiba Lotte Marines, Japan, 2004—; commentator, Baseball Tonight ESPN, 2003. Owner Bobby Valentine's Sports Gallery Cafe, Conn., Tex., and R.I. Named Am. League Mgr. of Yr. UPI, 1986; recipient William A. Shea Disting. Little League Grad. award, 1987; inductee Italian Am. Sports Hall Fame, 1990. mgr., Japan Series Champions, 2005. Office: Bobby Valentine's Sports Gallery Cafe 225 Main St Stamford CT 06903*

**VALENTINE, BRIAN,** information technology executive; BS in Computer Sci., Ea. Washington U. Software engr. Intel Corp.; with Microsoft Corp., Redmond, Wash. 1987—; gen. mgr., server application div., 1998, v.p., Windows group, 1998—99, v.p., bus. and enterprise, 1999, sr. v.p. Windows core operating systems divsn., 1999—. Office: One Microsoft Way Redmond WA 98052-6399*

**VALENTINE, DEAN,** film producer; AB, U. Chicago, 1976. Pres. Walt Disney TV/Touchstone TV; pres., CEO United Paramount Network, Los Angeles, 1997—2002; with Europlay Capital Advisors, LLC, 2002—03; pres. First Family Entertainment, Beverly Hills, 2004. Named one of Top 200 Collectors, ARTnews Mag., 2004, 2006. Avocation: Collector of Comtemporary Art. Office: Dean Valentine First Family Entertainm 11601 Wilshire Blvd Ste 750 Los Angeles CA 90025-1743*

**VALENTINE, DEBRA A.,** lawyer; b. Cleve., Apr. 16, 1953; AB magna cum laude in History, Princeton U., 1976; JD, Yale U. Law School, 1980. Bar: D.C., U.S. Dist. Ct. D.C., U.S. Ct. Appeals (D.C. Cir., 11th Cir.), U.S. Supreme Ct. Law clk. Judge Arlin M. Adams, U.S. Ct. Appeals, 3d Cir., Phila., 1980-81; atty/advisor Office of Legal Counsel, Dept. of Justice, Washington, 1981-85; assoc. O'Melveny & Myers, Washington, 1985-91, ptnr., 1991-95; dep. dir. policy planning FTC, Washington, 1995-96, asst. dir. for internat. antitrust, 1996-97, gen. counsel, 1997-2001; ptnr., co-chair antitrust practice group O'Melveny & Myers, Washington, 2001—04; v.p., sec., assoc. gen. counsel United Technologies Corp., 2004—. Cons. Sec. of State's Adv. Com. South Africa. Bd. editors BNA Antitrust & Trade Regulation Reporter; contbr. articles to profl. jours. Bd. dirs. The Hartford Symphony; bd. electors Wadsworth Athenaeum. Fulbright scholar, 1976-77. Mem. ABA, Internat. Bar Assn., Am. Law Inst., D.C. Bar, Coun. on Fgn. Rels., Phi Beta Kappa. Office: United Technologies Corp United Technologies Bldg Hartford CT 06101

**VALENTINE, FOY DAN,** clergyman; b. Edgewood, Tex., July 3, 1923; s. John Hardy and Josie (Johnson) V.; m. Mary Louise Valentine, May 6, 1947; children: Mary Jean, Carol Elizabeth, Susan Foy. BA, Baylor U., 1944, LLD (hon.), 1979; ThM, Southwestern Baptist Theol. Sem., 1947, ThD, 1949; DD, William Jewell Coll., 1966, Louisiana Coll., 1989. Ordained to ministry Bapt. Ch., 1942. Dir. Bapt. student activities colls. in Houston, 1949-50; pastor First Bapt. Ch., Gonzales, Tex., 1950-53; dir. Christian life commn. Bapt. Gen. Conv. Tex., 1953-60; exec. dir., Christian life commn. So. Bapt. Conv., 1960-87, exec. officer for devel., 1987-88; chmn. So. Bapt. inter-agy. council, 1965-67. Willson lectr. applied Christianity Wayland Bapt. Coll., 1963; Christian ethics lectr. Bapt. Theol. Sem., Ruschlikon-Zurich, Switzerland, 1966; Layne lectr. New Orleans Bapt. Theol. Sem., 1974; Jones lectr. Union U., 1976; Staley Disting. Christian scholar/lectr. La. Coll., 1981; Simpson lectr. Acadia Divinity Coll., Nova Scotia, 1982; H.I. Hester lectr. on preaching Midwestern Bapt. Theol. Sem., 1984; Belote lectr. Christian ethics Hong Kong Bapt. Theol. Sem., 1990; co-chmn. commn. religious liberty and human rights Bapt. World Alliance, 1966-75, chmn. commn. Christian ethics, 1976-80, mem. gen. coun., 1976-80; mem. Nashville Met. Human Rels. Commn., 1966-78, Pres.'s Commn. for Nat. Agenda for the Eighties, 1980; guest columnist USA Today; lectr. on Christian ethics Bible Inst. for Evangelism and Missions, St. Petersburg, USSR, 1991; co-chmn. Baylor U. Heritage Club, 2000-01. Author: Believe and Behave, 1964, Citizenship for Christians, 1965, The Cross in the Marketplace, 1966, Where the Action Is, 1969, A Historical Study of Southern Baptists and Race Relations 1917-1947, 1980, What Do You Do After You Say Amen?, 1980, Hebrews, James, 1 and 2 Peter: Layman's Bible Book Commentary, 1981, Whatsoever Things Are Lovely, 2004; editor: Christian Faith in Action, 1956, Peace, Peace, 1967, Christian Ethics Today, 1995-2000; contbr. to numerous anthologies, articles to profl. jours. Pres. Ctr. for Christian Ethics, 1990-2000; trustee Interfaith Alliance, 1994—; Ams. United for Separation of Ch. and State, 1960-93, pres., 1989-93; bd. dirs. Bapt. Joint Com. Pub. Affairs, 1960-87, Chs. Ctr. Theology and Pub. Policy, 1976-87, T.B. Maston Found., Texans Against Gambling; mem. bd. fellows Interpreter's House, 1967-78, Ctr. for Dialogue and Devel., 1987-96. Recipient Disting. Alumnus award Southwestern Bapt. Theol. Sem., 1970, Brooks Hays Meml. Christian Citizenship award, 1983, Disting. Alumni award Baylor U., 1987. Mem. Am. Soc. Christian Ethics. Democrat. Home and Office: 12527 Matisse Ln Dallas TX 75230-1741

**VALENTINE, GARY (GARY LACHMAN),** musician; Bassist with Blondie, 1975—77. Author: New York Rocker: My Life in the Blank Generation with Blondie, Iggy Pop and Others, 2002; musician: (albums) Tomorrow Belongs to You, 2003, (with Blondie) Blondie, 1976, Plastic Letters, 1977; composer: (songs) I'm Always Touched by Your Presence Dear, I Like Girls, Kung Fu Girls, Scenery, The First One, Tomorrow Belongs to You, X Offender, You Wanted Me to Hang Around. Named to Rock and Roll Hall of Fame, 2006. Office: Overground Records PO Box 1NW Newcastle-Upon-Tyne NE99 1NW England*

**VALENTINE, GENE C.,** securities dealer; b. Washington, Pa., June 19, 1950; s. John N. and Jane S. Valentine. BS in Psychology, Bethany Coll., 1972; student, U. Vienna, Austria, 1971-72. Commd. ensign USN, 1972, advanced through grades to lt., 1987, hon. discharged, 1978; owner Horizon Realty, San Francisco, 1978-82; dir. land acquisitions Windfarms Ltd. subs. Chevron, U.S.A., San Francisco, 1980-82; v.p. mktg. Christopher Weil & Co., Sherman Oaks, Calif., 1982-85; chmn., CEO Pacific Asset Group Inc. (name now Fin. West Group, Inc.), Westlake Village, Calif., 1985—. Bd. dirs. Fin. West Group, Inc., Paradox Holdings; founder, chmn., dir. Second Byte Found.; founder, chmn. Peace Point Farms Equestrian Facility, LLC and Found., Bethany, W.Va. Mem. Rep. Party, L.A. Mem. NASD, Internat. Assn.

Fin. Planning (bd. dirs. L.A. chpt. 1982-87). Episcopalian. Avocations: equestrian, sailing, tennis, golf, running. Office Phone: 304-829-4800. Personal E-mail: qcvalentine@yahoo.com.

**VALENTINE, H. JEFFREY,** legal association executive; b. Phila., Sept. 28, 1945; s. Joshua Morton and Olga W. (Wilson) V.; 1 child, Karyn. BS, St. Louis U., 1964, postgrad., 1966-68. Programmer, systems analyst Honeywell Electronic Data Processing, Wellesley Hills, Mass., 1964-66; account sales exec., Mid-Atlantic regional mgr. Electronic Instrumentation Co., 1968-70; pres. Free Lance Photographers Assn., Doylestown, Pa., 1970-89; pres., dir. Towne Print & Copy Ctrs. Inc.; v.p., exec. dir. Nat. Paralegal Assn., 1982—; pres. Paralegal Assocs., Inc., 1982—; chief operating officer Doylestown Parking Corp., 1977-88. Bd. dirs. Law Enforcement Supply Co., Solebury, Valtronics Supply Co., Towne Print & Copy Centers Inc., Solebury, Doylestown Stationery and Office Supply, Energy Mktg. Assocs., Inc., Solebury, Paralegal Placement Network; pres. Paralegal Pub. Corp., 1983-90; pub. Paralegal Jour.; pres. Valco Enterprises Inc., 1986—, Paralegal Employment Sys., Inc., 1988, Solebury Press, Inc., 1989—; ptnr. J&S Gen. Contractors, 1993—, J&S Landscaping Tree Svc., 1993—, J&S Estate and Property Mgmt., 2001—; owner Specialized Computer Consulting, 1992—. Author: Photographers Bookkeeping System, 1973, rev. edit., 1978, Photographers Pricing Guides, 1971, 72, 74, 75, Available Markets Director's - 4 Vols., 1973-77, National Model Sources Directory, Nat. Paralegal Salary and Employment Survey, 1985-86, 88, 90-92, 93-94; also articles, bulls. and pamphlets. Exec. sec. Doylestown Bus. Assn., 1972-78, pres., 1979, 83, v.p., 1981. Recipient Internat. Men of Achievement award, 1988; named Personalities of the Am., 1988. Mem. London Coll. Applied Scis., Nat. Fedn. Paralegal Assns., Photog. Industry Coun., Nat. Assn. Legal Assts., Am. Soc. Assn. Execs., Assn. Assn. Mgrs., Nat. Fedn. Ind. Business (mem. action coun. com.), Nat. Parking Assn., Nat. Office Products Assn., Graphic Arts Assn. Delaware Valley, Nat. Assn. Federally Licensed Firearms Dealers, Nat. Compostition Assn., Internat. Platform Assn. Office: PO Box 406 Solebury PA 18963-0406

**VALENTINE, JAMES BURGON,** musician; b. Lincoln, Nebr., Oct. 5, 1978; Guitarist Maroon 5, LA, 2001—. Musician: (albums) Songs About Jane, 2002, 1.22.03.Acoustic, 2004, Live Friday the 13th, 2005, (songs) Harder to Breathe, 2003, This Love, 2004 (MTV Video Music award for Best New Group, 2004, Grammy award for Best Group Pop Performance, 2006), She Will Be Loved, 2004, (with Maroon 5, also to Spider-Man 2 soundtrack, 2004. Recipient World Music award for Best New Group, 2004, MTV Europe award for Best New Act, 2004, Grammy award for Best New Artist (with Maroon 5), 2005. Address: Maroon 5 PO Box 884564 San Francisco CA 94188 Office: Octone Records Rm 500 560 Broadway New York NY 10012 Office Phone: 646-613-0200. E-mail: maroon5@maroon5.com.*

**VALENTINE, JAMES WILLIAM,** paleontologist, educator, writer; b. LA, Nov. 10, 1926; s. Adelbert Cuthbert and Isabel (Davis) V.; m. Grace Evelyn Whysner, Dec. 21, 1957 (div. 1972); children: Anita, Ian; m. Cathryn Alice Campbell, Sept. 10, 1978 (div. 1986); 1 child, Geoffrey; m. Diane Mondragon, Mar. 16, 1987. BA, Phillips U., 1951; MA, UCLA, 1954, PhD, 1958. From asst. prof. to assoc. prof. U. Mo., Columbia, 1958-64; from assoc. prof. to prof. U. Calif., Davis, 1964-77, prof. geol. scis. Santa Barbara, 1977-90, prof. integrative biology Berkeley, 1990-93, prof. emeritus, 1993—. Author: Evolutionary Paleoecology of the Marine Biosphere, 1973, On the Origin of Phyla, 2004; editor: Phanerozoic Diversity, 1985; co-author: Evolution, 1977, Evolving, 1979; contbr. articles to profl. jours. Served with USNR, 1944-46, PTO. Recipient Lapworth medal Palaeontological Assn., 2004; Fulbright rsch. scholar, Australia, 1962-63; Guggenheim fellow Yale U., Oxford U., Eng., 1968-69; Rockefeller Found. scholar in residence, Bellagio, Italy, summer 1974; grantee NSF, NASA. Fellow: AAAS, Geol. Soc. Am., Am. Acad. Arts and Scis.; mem.: NAS, Paleontol. Soc. (medal 1996). Avocation: collecting works of Charles Darwin. Home: 1351 Glendale Ave Berkeley CA 94708-2025 Office: U Calif Dept Integrative Biology Berkeley CA 94720-0001 Business E-Mail: jwvsossi@socrates.berkeley.edu.

**VALENTINE, JEAN,** poet, educator, writer; b. Chgo., 1934; BA, Radcliffe Coll. Poetry workshop tchr. Swarthmore Coll., 1968—70, Hunter Coll., 1970—75, Sarah Lawrence Coll., NYU, Grad. Writing Prog., Columbia U., 92nd St Y, New York, NY. Author: Dream Barker, 1965, Pilgrims, 1969, Ordinary Things, 1974, The Messenger, 1979, Home Deep Blue: New and Selected Poems, 1989, The River at Wolf, 1992, The Under Voice: Selected Poems, 1995, Growing Darkness, Growing Light, 1997, The Cradle of the Real Life, 2000, Door in the Mountain: New and Collected Poems 1965-2003, 2004 (Nat. Book Award for Poetry, 2004). Recipient awards, NEA, Bunting Inst., Rockefeller Found., NY Coun. for Arts, NY Found. for Arts, Maurice English Prize, Teasdale Poetry Prize, Shelley Mem. Prize, Poetry Soc. Am., 2000; grantee Guggenheim Fellowship.

**VALENTINE, JOHN LESTER,** state legislator, lawyer; b. Fullerton, Calif., Apr. 26, 1949; s. Robert Lester and Pauline C. V.; m. Karen Marie Thorpe, June 1, 1972; children: John Robert, Jeremy Reid, Staci Marie, Jeffrey Mark., David Emerson, Patricia Ann. BS in Acctg. and Econs., Brigham Young U., 1973, JD, 1976. Bar: Utah 1976, U.S. Dist. Ct. Utah, U.S. Ct. Appeals (10th cir.), U.S. Tax Ct., U.S. Supreme Ct. 2002; CPA, Utah. Howard, Lewis & Petersen, Provo, Utah, 1976—; mem. Utah Ho. Reps., 1988-98, Utah Senate, Dist. 14, Salt Lake City, 1999—, pres. of Senate, 2004—. Instr. probate and estates Utah Valley State Coll.; instr. fin. planning, adj. prof. law Brigham Young U.; chmn. revenue and taxation com. Utah Senate, 1999-2000, vice chmn. exec. appropriations com., judiciary com., pub. edn. subcom., majority whip 2001—; mem. exec offices, cts., corrections and legis. appropriations subcom., Utah Ho. of Reps., 1988-90, capital facilities subcom., 1988-90, retirement com., 1988-90, judiciary com., 1988-92, strategic planning steering com., 1988-90, interim appropriations com., 1988-94, tax. review commn., 1989-98, ethics com., 1990-92, human svcs. and health appropriations subcom., 1990-92, revenue and taxation com., 1988-98, vice chmn. 1990-92; vice chmn. exec. appropriations., 1990-92; chmn. exec. appropriations com., 1992-94, chmn. rules com., 1994-96, higher edn. appropriations com. 1994-96, asst. majority whip, 1996-98; apptd. to state senate, 1998, elected, 2000, majority whip, 2000-04, pres., 2004—. Mem. adv. bd. Internat. Sr. Games, 1988—; active Blue Ribbon Task Force on Local Govt. Funding, Utah League Cities and Towns, 1990-94, Criminal Sentencing Guidelines Task Force, Utah Judicial Coun., 1990-92, Access to Health Care Task Force, 1990-92, Utah County Sheriff Search and Rescue, Orem Met. Water Bd., Alpine Sch. Dist. Boundary Line Com., 1986-90, Boy Scouts Am.; bd. regents Legis. Adv. Coun. UVCC.; mem. exec. bd. Utah Nat. Parks Coun.; mem. adv. coun. Orchard Elem. Sch., Mountainlands Com. an Aging; bd. trustees Utah Opera Co.; judge nat. and local competitions Moot Ct.; voting dist. chmn.; state, county del.; lt. incident command sys. Utah County Sheriff. Recipient Silver Beaver award Boy Scouts Am., Taxpayer Advocate award Utah Taxpayer Assn. Mem. ABA (tax sect.), Utah State Bar, CPA Com., Tax Sect. Specialization Com., Bicentennial Com. Republican. Mem. Lds Ch. Avocation: mountain climbing. Office: Howard Lewis & Petersen 120 E 300 N Provo UT 84606-2907

**VALENTINE, MARK CONRAD,** dermatologist; b. Parkersburg, W.Va., Sept. 26, 1948; s. Sestel and Margaret Elaine (Sabolo) V.; m. Elizabeth Michelle Monezis, Apr. 21, 1975; children: Perry Martin, Owen Mark. BA, W.Va. U., 1970; MD, Johns Hopkins U., 1974. Intern, resident U. Hosps. Cleve., 1974-76, resident, 1976-79; dermatologist pvt. practice, Everett, Wash., 1979—. Clin. prof. U. Wash., Seattle, 1979—; active med. staff Providence Everett Gen. Med. Ctr., 1979—. Editl. bd. Jour. of Am. Acad. Dermatology, 1998—2005. Bd. dirs., sec. City Libr. Bd., Mukilteo, Wash., 1994-99; bd. dirs., v.p. Everett Symphony Bd., 1982-85, 2001—2006; bd. dirs. Book Arts Guild, Seattle, 1988-90. Nat. Merit scholar, 1966. Mem. AMA, Am. Acad. Dermatology (adv. coun. 1983-86), Wash. State Dermatol. Assn. (pres.-elect 1996, pres. 1996-97), Seattle Dermatology Soc. (pres. 1985-86), Snohomish County Med. Soc. (bd. dirs. 2001—, pres. 2006),

Rotary (Everett), Phi Beta Kappa. Avocations: book collecting, book binding, guitar, piano. Office: 3327 Colby Ave Everett WA 98201-6403 Office Phone: 425-258-6767. Personal E-mail: mark1105@aol.com.

**VALENTINE, PHYLLIS LOUISE,** counseling administrator; d. Harold Gray and Velma Eura Long; m. Samuel L. Valentine, Dec. 30, 1995. BA, St. Augustine's Coll., 1970; MEd, Bowie State Univ., 1992; student, Trinity Coll., 1974—77, Georgetown U., 1989, U. D.C., 1974—88. Cert. sch. counselor K-12, reading tchr. K-12. Evening reading reacher Loton Reformatory Youth Ctr. II PSI Assocs., Washington, 1984—86; chpt. 1 reading/math. lab tchr. D.C. Pub. Schs., 1986—92, chpt. 1 resource asst., 1992—93; chpt. 1 CAI lab tchr./team coord. C.W. Harris Elem. Sch., Washington, 1992—95; sch. counselor J.C. Nalle Elem. Sch., Washington, 1995—. Mem. tchr. adv. bd. Ctr. for Artistry in Tchg., Washington, 1999—; dir., presenter J.C. Nalle Sch. Extended Day, 1998. V.p. Brandywine Sta. Townhouse Assn., Upper Marlboro, Md., 1990—97. Recipient Letter of Commendation, Exec. Dir. Chpt. 1 program, 1987, AIMs Pilot, Bryan Elem. Sch., 1984, HOST Corp., 1994, DCPS Parent Ctr. Incentive, 1997. Mem.: D.C. Sch. Counseling Assn. (newsletter editor 2004—05, corr. sec.); Am. Sch. Counseling Assn., Am. Counseling Assn., Tots & Teens Inc. (pres. 1985—93, corr. sec. 1985—93, youth leader 1987—91, D.C. chpt., award 1990—91), D.C. Counseling Assn. (pres.-elect 2001—02, pres. 2002, dedicated svc. plaque 1993), Phi Delta Kappa (mem. Beta chpt., grammateus 2003—), Nat. Sorority Phi Delta Kappa (Beta chpt.), Sigma Gamma Rho (recording sec., anti-basilus 1971—78). Avocations: gardening, listening to jazz music, dance. Business E-Mail: phyllis.valentine@k12.us.

**VALENTINE, RALPH SCHUYLER,** chemical engineer, director; b. Seattle, Nov. 3, 1932; s. John Campbell and Elizabeth Florence (Patterson) V.; m. Jeanne Marie Belanger, June 15, 1957; children: Elizabeth Anne, Jacqueline Leigh, John Campbell. BSChemE, U. Wash., 1955, PhDChemE, 1963; MSChemE, U. Ill., 1956. Registered profl. engr., Calif., Va., Wash. Rsch. engr. Chevron Rsch. Corp., Richmond, Calif., 1956-61; instr. U. Wash., Seattle, 1961-63; mgr. fluid dynamics Aerojet-Gen., Sacramento, 1963-69; mgr. chem. tech. Atlantic Rsch. Corp., Alexandria, Va., 1969-79; mgr. rsch. United Techs. Chem. Systems, San Jose, Calif., 1979-91; gen. mgr. Greater Pocatello Sr. Citizens, Inc., 2001—. Lectr. U.S. Naval Postgrad. Sch., Monterrey, Calif., 1968, UCLA Modern Devels. in Propulsion, L.A., 1967-68, USAF Astronautics Labs., Lancaster, Calif., 1967, U.S. Army R & D Unit, Sacramento, 1966. Contbr. 23 tech. articles to profl. jours.; patentee in field. Recipient NASA commendation for Apollo work, Houston, 1969, 1st prize Ceramographic Exhbn. Am. Ceramics Soc., 1974, Andrus award AARP, 2005. Mem. AIChE (life). Republican. Home: 1515 Satterfield Dr Pocatello ID 83201-8002 E-mail: ralph_s_valentine@yahoo.com.

**VALENTINE, RAWSON JAMES,** surgeon, educator; b. Pensacola, Fla., July 15, 1954; s. Andrew Jackson and Marjorie Ann (Parks) V.; m. Tracy Williams, Oct. 2, 1982; children: Elizabeth Atlee, John Randol. BA cum laude, Vanderbilt U., 1976; MD cum laude, Emory U., 1980. Diplomate in surgery and gen. vascular surgery Am. Bd. Surgery. Resident in surgery U. Tex. Southwestern Med. Sch., Dallas, 1980-85, vascular fellow, 1985-86, asst. prof. surgery, 1990-93, assoc. prof. surgery, 1993—99, prof. surgery, 1999—, dir. grad. med. edn., dept. surgery, 1996—, vice chmn. dept. surgery, 2001—, Frank Kidd MD disting. prof. surgery, 2002. Asst. prof. surgery Uniformed Svcs. U. Health Scis., Bethesda, Md., 1986-90; head divsn. vascular surgery dept. surgery Naval Hosp., Bethesda, 1986-90; chief vascular surgery sect. VA Med. Ctr., Dallas, 90-97; mem. attending staff dept. surgery Parkland Meml. Hosp., Dallas, Zale Lipshy U. Hosp., Dallas, St. Paul Med. Ctr., Dallas; assoc. dir. Ctr. Vascular Disease, 1997—, lectr. in field. Author: (with G.G. Wind) Anatomic Exposures in Vascular Surgery, 1991, 2d edit., 2003; contbr. articles to profl. jours., chpts. to books. Lt. M.C., USNR, 1980-86, lt. comdr. 1986-90, comdr., 1990-93. Traveling fellow Royal Coll. Surgeons, 1992, R&D grantee USN, 1989-90, Instl. Rsch. grantee, 1990-91, AHA grantee, 1991-93, 93-95, VA grantee, 1994-96. Fellow ACS (sec.-treas. North Tex. chpt. 1995-98, pres. 1999, gov. 2000-06); mem. AMA (stroke coun.), Am. Surg. Assn., Western Surg. Assn., Assn. Program Dirs. in Surgery (sec. 2002-05, pres. 2006), Internat. Soc. Cardiovascular Surgery, Soc. for Vascular Surgery, So. Assn. Vascular Surgery (budget com. 1993-95, program com. 1997—2001, pres. 2006, Pres.'s award 1994), Assn. Acad. Surgeons, Soc. Univ. Surgeons, Dallas County Med. Soc. (program chair 1994), Parkland Surg. Soc. (program chmn. 1993, 94, pres. 2002), Peripheral Vascular Surg. Soc. Episcopalian. Office: U Tex Southwestern Med Ctr Dept Surgery 5323 Harry Hines Blvd Dallas TX 75390-9031

**VALENTINE, STEVEN RICHARDS,** lawyer; b. Memphis, Jan. 30, 1956; s. William Robert and Lenita Joanne (Nelms) V.; m. Susan Marie Burke, Jan. 14, 1984; children: Christina Michele, William Robert II, Steven Richards Jr., Thomas Burke, Diana Elizabeth. Grad., Capitol Page Sch., Washington, 1974; student, Earlham Coll., 1974-77; B of Gen. Studies with distinction, Ind. U., 1979, JD, 1982. Bar: Ill. 1983, D.C. 1985, U.S. Ct. Appeals (D.C. cir.) 1986, U.S. Supreme Ct. 1986, U.S. Ct. Appeals (9th cir.) 1989. Chief investigator consumer protection divsn. Office Atty. Gen., Chgo., 1980-82; exec. dir. Ams. United for Life Legal Def. Fund, Chgo., 1982-83; chief counsel subcom. on separation of powers U.S. Senate, Washington, 1983-85, chief counsel subcom. on cts., 1985; adminstrv. asst. U.S. Senator John P. East, Washington, 1985-86; dir. Office of Policy Devel. and Comm. Legal Svcs. Corp., Washington, 1986-87; counselor to asst. atty. gen. civil divsn. U.S. Dept. Justice, Washington, 1987-88; dep. asst. atty. gen. civil divsn. U.S. Justice Dept., Washington, 1988-93, gen. counsel to U.S. Senator Robert C. Smith, 1993-99; legis. dir. to U.S. Senator Robert C. Smith, 1996-99; of counsel Preston Gates Ellis & Rouvelas Meeds LLP, Washington, 1999—2002, ptnr., 2002—. Mem. exec. com., bd. dirs. Deluxe West Inc.; bd. dirs. The Preston Project, Inc.; sr. fellow John C. Stennis Ctr. for Pub. Svc.; bd. visitors Ind. U. Sch. Law, Indpls., 2006—. Author: Each Time A Man, 1978, All Shall Live, 1980; co-author: Abortion and the Constitution, 1987, Principle Over Politics, 2004; contbr. articles to profl. jours. Recipient spl. commendation U.S. Atty. Gen., 1993; John C. Stennis Congl. staff fellow, 1995-96. Mem.: SAR, Rep. Nat. Lawyers Assn., Federalist Soc., Capitol Hill Club. Republican. Roman Catholic. Avocations: history, baseball. Home: 6487 Warwick Cir Alexandria VA 22315-5045 Office: 1735 New York Ave NW Ste 500 Washington DC 20006-5209 Office Phone: 202-661-3802. Personal E-mail: rick.valentine@cox.net. Business E-mail: rickv@prestongates.com.

**VALENTINE, WILLIAM NEWTON,** retired physician, educator; b. Kansas City, Mo., Sept. 29, 1917; s. Herbert S. and Mabel W. Valentine; m. Martha Hickman Winfree; children: William, James, Edward. Student, U. Mich., 1934—36, U. Mo., Columbia, 1936—37; MD, Tulane U., 1942. Diplomate Am. Bd. Internal Medicine. Intern Strong Meml. Hosp., Rochester, NY, 1942—43, asst. resident in medicine, 1943, chief resident in medicine, 1943—44; specialist, attending physician in internal medicine Wadsworth Hosp., L.A., 1949—88, VA Ctr., L.A., 1949—88; specialist, attending physician in internal medicine Ctr. Health Scis. UCLA, 1949—, prof. medicine, 1957—88, chmn. dept., 1963—71; prof. emeritus medicine, 1988—. Contbr. articles to profl. jours. Capt. MC AUS, 1944—47. Recipient Mayo Soley award for excellence in rsch., Western Soc. Clin. Rsch., 1978, 53d Annual UCLA faculty rsch. lectr., 1978. Master: ACP (John Phillips Meml. award for disting. achievements in internal medicine 1979); fellow: Am. Soc. Hematology (Henry Stratton lectr. 1978), Internat. Soc. Hematology (v.p. U.S. 1976—80); mem.: NAS, Am. Acad. Arts and Scis., We. Soc. Clin. Rsch., We. Assn. Physicians (pres. 1969—70), Assn. Am. Physicians, Am. Soc. Clin. Investigation (v.p. 1962), Am. Bd. Internal Medicine. Republican.

**VALENTINER, DAVID PETER,** psychologist, educator; b. Bklyn., N.Y., Feb. 24, 1962; s. Paul Terry Valentiner and Sue Lee; m. Nina S. Mounts, June 4, 1961; children: Caleb Ethan Weiss, Adam Micah Weiss, Leah Danielle. PhD, of Tex., Austin. Assoc. prof. No. Ill. U., DeKalb. Clin. cons. Linden Oaks Hosp., Naperville. Mem.: APA, Anxiety Disorders Assn. of Am., Obsessive Compulsive Found., Assn. for Behavioral and Cognitive Psycho-

therapies, Am. Psychol. Soc. Avocation: bee keeping. Office: No Ill U Dept of Psychology Dekalb IL 60115 Office Phone: 815-753-7086. Home Fax: 815-753-8088; Office Fax: 815-753-8088. Personal E-mail: dvalentiner@niu.edu.

**VALENTINO, (VALENTINO GARAVANI),** fashion designer; b. Voghera, Italy, May 11, 1932; Student, Academia Dell'Arte, Paris, Ecole des Beaux-Arts. Asst. designer Fashion Ho. of Jean Dessès, 1950-55, Fashion Ho. of Guy Laroche, 1956-58; opened House of Valentino, Rome, 1959, began partnership with Giancarlo Giammetti, 1960; internat. debut Florence, Italy, 1962; launched women's & men's ready-to-wear collections, 1972; opened boutiques in Rome and Milan, 1972; developer Valentino Più, 1973; launched Valentino perfume in Paris, 1978; established boutiques in US & Japan, 1980. Designer Italian athletes' uniforms Olympic Games, Los Angeles, Calif., 1984. Exhibited at Victoria and Albert Mus., London, 1971, La Jolla Mus. Art, Calif., 1982; costume designer (films) Wild and Wonderful, 1964, Hello-Goodbye, 1970; designer and prodr. exhibition: Atelier of Illusion, 1985, Accademia, 1991. Founder (with Giancarlo Giamcarlo) L.I.F.E., 1990—. Recipient Neiman-Marcus award, 1967, Grand'Ufficiale dell'Ordine al Merito, Italian Ministry of Industry, 1985, Lifetime Achievement award, American Designer awards, NY, 2000; named Cavaliere di gran Croce, Italy, 1986, Cavaliere del Lavoro, 1996. Office: Piazza Mignanelli 22 00187 Rome Italy also: 11 W 42nd St New York NY 10036*

**VALENZUELA, HERALDO MUÑOZ See MUÑOZ, HERALDO**

**VALENZUELA, JULIO SAMUEL,** sociologist, educator; b. Concepción, Chile, Mar. 30, 1948; came to U.S., 1970; s. Raimundo Arms and Dorothy Dueul (Bowie) V.; m. Erika Fresia Maza, Mar. 22, 1969. Licenciatura, Universidad de Concepcion, 1970; PhD, Columbia U., 1979. Asst. prof. Yale U., New Haven, 1977-80, Harvard U., Cambridge, Mass., 1980-85, assoc. prof., 1986, U. Notre Dame, Ind., 1987-89, prof., dept. chairperson Ind., 1989-92, fellow Kellogg Inst. 1987—. Sr. assoc. fellow St. Antony's Coll., Oxford U., 1992-93, 96—; campaign adv. presidl. election, Chile, 1999; cons. labor policy Chilean Govt., 2000, 01. Author: Democratizacion via Reforma, 1986; co-author: Chile, A Country Study; co-editor: Chile: Politics And Society, 1976, Military Rule In Chile, 1986, Issues In Democratic Consolidation, 1992, El Eslabon Perdido Familia Modernizacion y Bienestar en Chile, 2006; contbr. chpts. to books, articles to profl. jours. Fellow NEH ind. scholarship rsch. 1983-84, conf. grant 1987; John Simon Guggenheim fellow, 1996. Mem. Am. Sociol. Assn., Internat. Sociol. Assn. (v.p. rsch. com. #44 1990—), Latin Am. Studies Assn. (nominating com. 1987-88), Am. Polit. Sci. Assn., Soc. for the Advancement of Socio-econs., New Eng. Coun. Latin Am. Studies (pres. 1984-85). Methodist. Office: U Notre Dame Kellogg Inst Notre Dame IN 46556 Business E-Mail: valenzuela.1@nd.edu.

**VALERI, TONY,** Canadian government official, small business owner; m. Terri Boswell; 2 children. Degree in econs., McMaster U. M.P. for Hamilton East-Stoney Creek House of Commons, 1993—, parliamentary sec. to Min. Fin. Paul Martin, 1997—99, mem. standing com. on fin., vice chair standing com. on industry, chair standing com. on govt. ops., leader govt. Parliament Hill, 2005—; min. transport Govt. of Canada, Ottawa, 2003—04. Chair Nat. Liberal Caucus Task Force on Jobs and Small Bus. Mem. Ind. Ins. Brokers Assn. Can. (bd. dirs.), Hamilton and Dist. Sub-Contractors Assn. (v.p.). Office: Parliament Hill Centre Block Rm 209 S Ottawa ON Canada K1A 0A6

**VALERIANI, NICHOLAS J.,** health products executive; b. Newark; married; 2 children. BS in Indsl. Engring., Rutgers U., MBA. With engring. divsn. Ethicon, Inc. Johnson & Johnson, 1978, v.p. profl. edn. Ethicon Endo-Surgery, Inc., 1991, mem. mgmt. bd. Ethicon Endo-Surgery, Inc., 1991, gen. mgr. Indigo Med., Inc., 1996—97, pres. Ethicon Endo-Surgery, Inc., 1997, co. grp. chmn., 2001, worldwide chmn. DePuy, 2002, corp. v.p. human resources, mem. exec. com., 2003, worldwide chmn. diagnostics, 2004—05, worldwide chmn. cardiovasc. devices and diagnostics grp., mem. exec. com., 2005—. Bd. dirs. Action for Healthy Kids; bd. visitors U. NC Kenan-Flagler Bus. Sch. Office: Johnson & Johnson 1 Johnson & Johnson Plz New Brunswick NJ 08933*

**VALERIO, JOSEPH MASTRO,** architectural firm executive, educator; b. Dec. 26, 1947; m. Linda A. Searl; children: Joseph Jr., Anthony, BArch., U. Mich., 1970; MArch, UCLA, 1972. Registered architect, Wis., Ill., Ind., Mo., Calif., Tex., Ariz., Minn., Ala., Iowa, Ind., Md., Mich., Okla., Ga., Mass., N.J., N.Y., N.C., Va., Utah, D.C., Wash., Oreg.; cert. Nat. Coun. Archtl. Registration Bds. Pres. Chrysalis Corp. Architects, 1970-85; assoc. prof. U. Wis., 1973-86; design dir. Swanke Hayden Connell Architects, 1985-86; v.p. architecture A. Epstein and Sons, Inc., 1986-88; pres. Valerio-Assocs. Inc., 1988-94; prin. Valerio Dewalt Train Assocs., Inc., Chgo., 1994—. Mem. nat. bd. peer reviewers GSA; spkr. Ariz. State U., UCLA, U. Ariz., U. Cin., others; cons. USG Interiors, Formica Corp., AAAS, NAS, NEA: vis. critic and lectr. in field. Prin. works include corp., high-tech. indsl., retail, instl. and residential bldgs.; author: Movie Palaces, 1983; (monograph) Joe Valerio 1999; editor: Architectural Fabric Structures, 1985; featured in Inside Architecture, Domestic Interiors, 1997, New Am. Apt., 1997, Internat. Interiors, 1997, Lofts/Living and Working Spaces, 1999. Mem. exec. bd. men's coun. Mus. Contemporary Art, 1989-91; mem. exec. bd. Contemporary Arts Coun., 1994-96 (pres. 1999). Recipient Honor awards Wis. Soc. Architects, 1975, 81, 84, 85, Gov.'s Award for Design Excellence, State of Mich., 1979, Gold medal Inst. Bus. Designers, 1988, Design award Progressive Architecture, 1991, Architectural Record Interiors award 1993, 95, 96, Disting. Interior award Inst. Bus. Designers, Chgo., 1993; honored by Emerging Voices series Archtl. League N.Y., 1984, Met. Home mag., Interiors mag. Fellow AIA (programs chmn. Chgo. chpt. 1990, long range planning com. 1992, chair nat. com. on interiors 1997, Nat. Honor award 1981, 93, Interiors award Chgo. chpt. 1988, 90, 92, 95-97, 99-2002, 04, Disting. Bldg. award 1991, 93, 2004, Nat. Interior Honor award 1993, 96, 2003, Divine Detail award 1999, 2001), Chgo. Architecture Club (pres. 1994), Lambda Alpha. Office: Valerio Dewalt Train Assocs 500 N Dearborn St Fl 9 Chicago IL 60610-4900 Office Phone: 312-332-0363. Business E-mail: jvalerio@buildordie.com.

**VALERIO, MATTHEW F.,** lawyer; b. Lawrence, Mass., Sept. 28, 1963; s. Fred Ernest Jr. Valerio and Carole Elaine (Closson) Mimeault; m. Joanne F. Stockton, Aug. 6, 1988. BA, St. Michael's Coll., 1985; JD, Western New Eng. Coll., 1988. Bar: Mass. 1989, Vt. 1989, U.S. Dist. Ct. Mass. 1989, U.S. Dist. Ct. Vt. 1989, U.S. Ct. Appeals (2d cir.) 1998. Pvt. practice, Springfield, Mass., 1989; assoc. Abatiell & Wysolmerski, Rutland, Vt., 1989-94; ptnr. Abatiell & Valerio, Rutland, Vt., 1994—2001; defender gen. State of Vt., 2001—. Adj. prof. Coll. St. Joseph, Rutland, 1993-99. Fin. chmn. Rutland County Rep. Com., 1991-93. Mem. ABA (young lawyers divsn. dist. rep. Vt., Maine 1994-96, Vt. state membership chair 1995—), New Eng. Bar Assn. (bd. dirs. 1997—, pres. 1999-2000, 05-06), Vt. Trial Lawyers Assn., Vt. Bar Assn. (treas., exec. com. young lawyers sect. 1990-92, chmn. exec. com. 1993-94, bd. bar mgr. 1992-2003, pres. 2001-02, bd. bar mgr. 2005—, treas. 2005—), Vt. Criminal Def. Lawyers Assn. (bd. dirs. 1993-96), Assn. Trial Lawyers Am., Kiwanis (bd. dirs. Rutland chpt. 1996-99, v.p. 1991-92, pres. 1993-94, pres. Rutland area mentor program 1994-96, disting. svc. award 1989-92, N.E. dis disting. pres. award 1993-94). Avocations: baseball, wrestling, blues. Office: Office Defender Gen 14-16 Baldwin St Montpelier VT 05633-3301 Office Phone: 802-828-3168.

**VALERIO, MICHAEL ANTHONY,** diversified financial services company executive; b. Detroit, Sept. 20, 1953; s. Anthony Rudolph and Virginia (Popoff) V.; m. Barbara Ann Nabozny, Oct. 8, 1983. BA, U. Mich., Dearborn, 1975. CPA, Mich. Jr. acct. Carabell, Bocknek CPA's, Southfield, Mich., 1975-76; sr. acct. Purdy, Donovan & Beal, CPA's, Detroit, 1976-77; mgr. Buctynck & Co., CPA's, Southfield, 1978-79; contr. Transcontinental Travel, Harper Woods, Mich., 1979—80; exec. v.p. Holland Cons., Inc. Detroit, 1980-85; contr., CFO SLC Recycling Industries, Inc., Warren, Mich., 1985—98; owner Pinnacle Fin. Consulting, PLLC, Livonia, Mich., 1994—.

Owner Pinnacle Fin. Svcs., LLC, 2002—; rep. Wealth and Wisdom, Inc.; fin. cons. Am. Group Retirement Strategy Ctrs. Mem. AICPA, Mich. Soc. CPAs. Roman Catholic. Office: Pinnacle Fin Consulting PLLC 33300 Five Mile Rd Ste 102 Livonia MI 48154-3074

**VALERO, MARIA TERESA,** photographer, art educator; b. Venezuela; BFA in graphic design & art history, U. Kans., M art history. Dir. Sch. Art, U. Tulsa, prof., Gallery Dir., Alexandre Hogue Gallery; founder & dir. Third Floor Designs (a student run design studio). Exhibitions include, Kans., Mo., Okla., Ariz., Tex., Ark., Venezuela, Beauty of the Levant (Images of Lebanon & Syria Through Western Eyes), Syria. Recipient Graphex Award, Tulsa Addy, Creativity Today Award. Office: University of Tulsa Phillips Hall 104 600 South College Ave Tulsa OK 74104 Office Phone: 918-631-2740. Office Fax: 918-631-3423. E-mail: maria-valero@utulsa.com.

**VALERO, RENÉ ARNOLD,** clergyman; b. N.Y.C., Aug. 15, 1930; s. Caesar J. and Maria Luisa (Cordova) Valero; B.A. in Liberal Arts, Immaculate Conception-Cathedral Coll., 1952; M.S.W., Fordham U., 1962. Ordained to ministry Roman Cath. Ch., 1956; asso. pastor St. Michael-St. Edward, Bklyn., 1956-57, St. Agatha, Bklyn., 1957-60; dir. Bklyn. Cath. Charities Family Service, 1960-69; dir. Bklyn. Diocesan Office for Aging, 1969-74; coordinator Bklyn. Diocesan Hispanic Apostolate, 1974-79; pastor Blessed Sacrament, Jackson Heights, N.Y., 1979-82; aux. bishop Diocese of Bklyn., 1980—; vicar for immigrants and refugees Diocese of Bklyn., 1983-90; regional bishop Queens, 1990-94, Queens North, 1994—. Home: 34-43 93rd St Jackson Heights NY 11372-3743 Office: Immaculate Conception Ctr 7200 Douglaston Pky Douglaston NY 11362-1941 Office Phone: 718-229-8001 x710.

**VALETTE, JEAN PAUL,** writer; b. Paris, Oct. 21, 1937; s. Jean and Monique (Lavie) V.; m. Rebecca M. Valette, Aug. 6, 1959; children: Jean-Michel, Nathalie, Pierre. Baccalaureat, U. Poitiers, France, 1954; Diplome, Hautes Etudes Commls. de Paris, 1959; PhD, U. Colo., 1962. Acct. Arthur Andersen, 1964-66; rsch. economist Charles River Assocs., 1966-69. Author: Lisons, 1968, The Role of Transportation in Regional Economic Development, 1971, France, A Cultural Review Grammar, 1973, C'est comme ça, 1978, 1986, Spanish for Mastery, 1980, 1984, 1988, 1996, French for Mastery, 1975, 1981, 1986, 1989, 1990, Contacts: langue et culture françaises, 1976, 1982, 1985, 1989, 1994, 1997, 2001, French for Fluency, 1985, Rencontres, 1985, Situaciones, 1988, 1994, Discovering French Nouveau, 1993, 5th edit., 2000, Discover French, 2004, Discovering French Interactive, 1994, A votre tour, 1995, Ventanas, 1998, Europak, 2000, Weaving the Dance, Navajo Yeibichai Textiles (1910-1950), 2000. Decorated officer Palmes Académiques (France). Mem. Am. Assn. Tchrs. French, Am. Coun. on Tchg. of Langs. Address: 16 Mount Alvernia Rd Chestnut Hill MA 02467-1019

**VALETTE, REBECCA MARIANNE,** Romance languages educator; b. N.Y.C., Dec. 21, 1938; d. Gerhard and Ruth Adelgunde (Bischoff) Loose; m. Jean-Paul Valette, Aug. 6, 1959; children: Jean-Michel, Nathalie, Pierre. BA, Mt. Holyoke Coll., 1959, LHD (hon.), 1974; PhD, U. Colo., 1963. Instr., examiner in French and German U. So. Fla., 1961-63; instr. NATO Def. Coll., Paris, 1963-64; Wellesley Coll., 1964-65; asst. prof. Romance Langs. Boston Coll., 1965-68, assoc., 1968-73, prof., 1973—2003, prof. emeritus, 2003—. Lectr., cons. fgn. lang. pedagogy; Fulbright sr. lectr., Germany, 1974; Am. Coun. on Edn. fellow in acad. adminstrn., 1976-77. Author: Modern Language Testing, 1967, rev. edit., 1977, French for Mastery, 1975, rev. edit., 1988, Contacts, 1976, rev. edit., 1993, 97, 2001, C'est Comme Ça, 1978, rev. edit., 1986, Spanish for Mastery, 1980, rev. edit., 1989, 94, Album: Cuentos del Mundo Hispanico, 1984, 3d edit., 2005, French for Fluency, 1985, Situaciones, 1988, rev. edit., 1994, Discovering French, 1994, 97, 2001, A votre tour, 1995, Ventanas Uno, 1998, Images 1, 2, 3, 1999, Reflections on the Connolly Book of Hours, 1999, Weaving the Dance, 2000, Discovering French Nouveau, 2004, 2d edit., 2007, Federation of Alliances Francaises USA Edn. Handbook, 2005; contbr. articles to fgn. lang. pedagogy and Native Am. art publs. Decorated comdr. Palmes Académiques, chevalier Ordre Nat. du Mérite (France). Mem. MLA (chmn. divsn. on tchg. of lang. 1980-81), Am. Coun. on Tchg. Fgn. Langs., Am. Assn. Tchrs. French (v.p. 1980-86, pres. 1992-94), Alliance Francaise of Boston and Cambridge (pres. 2002—), Fedn. Alliances Francaises USA (v.p. 2003—06), Phi Beta Kappa, Alpha Sigma Nu, Pi Delta Phi. Home: 16 Mount Alvernia Rd Chestnut Hill MA 02467-1019 Office: Boston Coll Lyons 304 Chestnut Hill MA 02467-3804 Business E-Mail: valette@bc.edu.

**VALGEMAE, MARDI,** language educator; b. Viljandi, Estonia, Nov. 10, 1935; came to U.S., 1949; s. Parfeni and Ella (Peterson) V.; m. Mare M. Kivijarv, Dec. 28, 1957; children: Monika L., Sven M. BA, Rutgers U., 1957; PhD, UCLA, 1964. Asst. prof. English UCLA, L.A., 1964-68; assoc. prof. English Lehman Coll., CUNY, Bronx, 1968-74; prof. English Lehman Coll. CUNY, Bronx, 1975—; dir. city and humanities program Lehman Coll., CUNY, 1984-88, chmn. English dept., 1988-97. Vis. assoc. profl. lectr. George Washington U., Washington, 1968. Author: Accelerated Grimace, 1972, Ikka Teatrist Moteldes, 1990, Linn ja Teater, 1995, Kaugekone, 1999, Eelarvamusi, 2003; co-editor: Baltic Literature and Linguistics, 1973. 1st lt. U.S. Army. 1958-60. ACLS European Travel grantee, 1970, 81; Woodrow Wilson fellow, 1960. Mem. Modern Lang. Assn. Am., Assn. Advancement Baltic Studies, PEN. Office: CUNY Lehman Coll Dept English Bronx NY 10468 Office Phone: 718-960-8372. Personal E-Mail: mardival@mindspring.com.

**VALIA, HARDARSHAN S.,** research scientist; b. Khurda, Orisa, India, June 15, 1945; arrived in U.S., 1969; s. Santokh Singh and Harbans Kaur; m. Bhupinder Kaur Valia, Jan. 10, 1982; children: Vikram Singh, Anu Kaur. MS, Nagpur U., India, 1968; MA, Bryn Mawr Coll., 1971; PhD, Boston U., 1976. Asst. prof. Case Western U., Cleve., 1978, Oberlin (Ohio) Coll., 1978—79; staff scientist Inland Steel, East Chicago, Ind., 1979—. Mem. tech. com. Am. Iron and Steel Inst., Washington, 1995—2001. Contbg. author Kirk-Othmer Encyclopedia, 1993, Making, Shaping, and Treating of Steel, 1999, (website) Am. Iron and Steel Inst. Recipient J.B.T. gold medal, Nagpur U., 1965, medal, Am. Iron and Steel Inst., 1989. Mem.: Soc. for Organic Petrology, Iron and Steel Soc. (program com. 1995—, chmn. J. Becker award 2001—, Joseph Becker award 1999). Office: Ispat Inland Steel 3001 E Columbus Dr East Chicago IN 46312

**VALIANT, LESLIE GABRIEL,** computer scientist, educator; b. Mar. 28, 1949; s. Leslie and Eva Julia (Ujlaki) V.; m. Gayle Lynne Dyckoff, 1977; children: Paul A., Gregory J. BA, Kings Coll., Cambridge, U.K., 1970; DIC, Imperial Coll., London, 1973; PhD, U. Warwick, U.K., 1974. Vis. asst. prof. Carnegie-Mellon U., Pitts., 1973-74; lectr. U. Leeds, Eng., 1974-76; lectr., reader U. Edinburgh, Scotland, 1977-82; vis. prof. Harvard U., 1982, Gordon McKay prof. computer sci. and applied math., 1982-2001, T. Jefferson Coolidge prof. computer sci. and applied math., 2001—. Guggenheim fellow, 1985-86; recipient Nevanlinna prize Internat. Math. Union, 1986, Knuth prize, 1997. Fellow Royal Soc., Am. Acad. for Artificial Intelligence; mem. NAS. Office: Harvard U 33 Oxford St Cambridge MA 02138-1903

**VALIANTI, DEBORAH L.,** playwright; b. Marlboro, Mass., May 10, 1952; d. Frank J. and Kathlyn V. Valianti; m. Henry J. Klim; children: Genevieve Marie Klim, Delia Goodness Klim. MAET, Lesley Coll., Cambridge, Mass., 1992; MA, Boston U., 1987; BA, Goddard Coll., Plainfield, Vt., 1977. Dir. Mission-in-Action Players, Mission Hill, Mass., 2000—04, All-bad Teen Theater Co., Brighton, Mass., 1993—98; educator expressive therapies Lesley Coll., Cambridge, Mass., 1992—98; dir. City Hall Smoking Cessation Project, Boston Against Drugs, Boston, 1995; dir. and co-founder Uppity Productions, Boston Playwright Theater, Boston, 1985—90; tchg. fellow Creative Writing Program, Boston U., Boston, 1985—87; Celtic cantor All Saints Parish, Brookline, Mass., 2003—. Author: (plays) 39 Witherbees St., 1977, Starcrossed, 1987, The Friendship of Her Thighs, 1992, Too Many

Willies, 2002, Why Can't We Share, 2003, (screenplays) Europe, 1988, Build to Suit, 2002, numerous poems. Democrat. Roman Catholic. Avocations: singing, tap dance, liturgical dance, travel, skiing. Home: 8 Oak Square Avenue Brighton MA 02135-2517

**VALLABHAJOSYULA, RAVISHANKAR RAO,** application developer; b. Anakapalle, Andhra Pradesh, India, Jan. 14, 1969; s. Balakrishna and Lalitha Vallabhajosyula; m. Ruchitha Kalimata Vittala, Dec. 27, 2002. B of Tech in Mech. Engring., Indian Inst. Tech., Chennai, 1990, MS in Applied Mechanics, 1992; MSME, Rice U., Houston, 1994, PhD in Mech. Engring., 2000. Rsch. asst. mech. engring. Rice U., 1992—95; project engr. Wright Logue & Assocs., 1998—2000, Energy Solutions Internat. 2000—04; sr. software engr. Indus Valley Cons., 2004—04; postdoctoral fellow Keck Grad. Inst., Claremont, Calif., 2004—. Indsl. cons. Indian Inst. Tech., Tamilnadu, 1990—92; internat. office liaison, coord. Wright Logue & Assocs., Houston, 1998—99; project engr. Energy Solutions Internat., 2000—04. Founding pres., Houston Chpt. India Bus. Tech. Consortium, Rice U., 1998—99. Achievements include research in development of a robust algorithm based on Householder QR metho for accurate computation of conserved moieties in large biochemical networks; first to create a website called the Indian Corporate Gateway. Home: 1334 West Foothill Blvd Apt 21-H Upland CA 91786 Office: Keck Graduate Institute 535 Watson Drive Claremont CA 91711 Office Phone: 909-607-0112. Personal E-mail: ravi@alumni.rice.edu. Business E-Mail: rrao@kgi.edu.

**VALLADARES-BARBUSH, LISETTE MARIE,** mathematics educator; d. Jorge Luis Valladares, Jr. and Violeta Gutierrez Valladares; m. J. Otto Barbush; children: Alec, Noah. BS in Math., UCLA, 1992, MA in Math., 1994; secondary tchg. credential, Nat. U., L.A., 2004. Computer programmer Hughes Aircraft Co., L.A., 1994—96; math. tchr., math. dept. chair Archer Sch. for Girls, L.A., Calif., 1996—2001; math. tchr. Milken Cmty. H.S., L.A., 2001—. Mem.: Nat. Coun. Tchr. Math. Home: 5325 Royer Ave Woodland Hills CA 91367

**VALLANCE, JEFFREY,** sculptor, painter; b. Torrance, Calif., 1955; BA, Calif. State U., Northridge, 1979; MFA, Parsons Sch. Design, 1981. Instr. UCLA, 1984—85, vis. prof. art; instr. L.A. Pierce Coll., Woodland Hills, Calif., 1987, Parsons Sch. Design, 1987—92, CC of So. Nev., Las Vegas, 1996, U. Nev., 1995—98; prof. internat. contemporary art Umea U., Sweden, 1999—2002; vis. artist Chgo. Art Inst., 1999, Cranbrook Acad. of Art, Detroit, 2001; artist-in-residence Majestic Ranch, U. Tex., San Antonio, 2002, U. Tasmania, Australia, 2002. One-man shows include The US Senate: A Survey on the Arts, Washington Project for Arts, 1978, Machines and Other Articles, Rosamund Felsen Gallery, 1981, Icelandic Women and the King of Tonga, 1987, The Throne Room: Icelandic Women and the King of Tonga Part II, 1998, The Nixon Mus., Galerie Praz-Delavallade, Paris, 1994, Clown Stains, U. Tex., 2002, The Shape of Texas, Majestic Ranch, Boerne, Tex., 2002, Relics from LBJ's 1966 Visit to Australia, Tasmanian Mus. and Art Gallery, 2002, Saami and Aboriginal Flags, Black Kettle Mus., 2002, exhibited in group shows at Faith, Dynamite Gallery, 2000, Off the Grid, Lehmann Maupin, 2002, Five by Seven by X, The Jones Ctr. for Contemporary Art, 2002, A Thousand Clowns, Robert Berman Gallery, 2002, To Whom it May Concern, Logan Galleries, Calif. Coll. Arts and Crafts, 2002. Grantee Guggenheim Meml. Found., 2004. Office: UCLA Dept Art 11000 Kinross Ave, Ste 245 Los Angeles CA 90095

**VALLBONA, CARLOS,** physician; b. Granollers, Barcelona, Spain, July 29, 1927; came to U.S., 1953, naturalized, 1967; s. José and Dolores (Calbó) V.; m. Rima Gretel Rothe, Dec. 26, 1956; children— Rima Nuria, Carlos Fernando, María Teresa, Marisa. BA, BS, U. de Barcelona, 1944, MD, 1950. Diplomate Am. Bd. Pediatrics. Child health physician Escuela de Puericultura, Barcelona, 1952, Stagier Etranger Hôpital des Enfants Malades, Paris, 1952-53; intern, resident U. Louisville, 1953-55; resident Baylor Coll. Medicine, Houston, 1955-56, prof. rehab. medicine, 1967—, assoc. prof. physiology and pediatrics, 1962-69, prof., chmn. dept. community medicine, 1969-95, prof. family medicine, 1980-95, Disting. Svc. prof. family and cmty. medicine, 1995—. Adj. prof. U. Tex. Sch. Pub. Health, U. Tex. Health Sci. Ctr., Houston; chief community medicine service Harris County Hosp. Dist.; staff gen. med. service Tex. Children's Hosp.; staff The Inst. Rehab. and Research; staff St. Luke's Episcopal Hosp., con. staff VA Med. Ctr., Houston; Fulbright vis. prof., 1967; cons. WHO, NIH, Nat. Center Health Stats. Pan Am. Health Orgn., Nat. Center Health Service Research; advisor Conseller Sanitat, Catalunya. Author numerous articles in field; editorial bd. several Sci. jours. French Ministry of Edn. fellow, 1952; Children's Internat. Center fellow, 1953; co-recipient Gold medal 6th Internat. Congress Phys. Medicine, 1972; Public Citizen of Yr. San Jacinto chpt. Nat. Assn. Social Workers, 1974; Outstanding Tchr. award Baylor Coll. Medicine Class of 1980, 83, 85, 87, 88; decorated officer Order of Civil Merit (Spain), Medalla Narcis Monturiol (Catalunya). Mem. Am. Acad. Family Physicians, Am. Coll. Med. Informatics (founding mem. 1984), Nat. Acad. Practice (disting. practitioner 1984), Soc. Pediatric Research (emeritus), AMA, Tex. Med. Assn., Am. Coll. Chest Physicians, Am. Pub. Health Assn. (chmn. elect med. care sect. 1989-90), Am. Coll. Preventive Medicine, U.S.-Mex. Border Health Assn., AAAS, Am. Congress Rehab. Medicine, Catalan Soc. Pediatrics (hon.), Argentinian Soc. Internal Medicine (hon. 1986), Argentinian Med. Soc. (hon. 1986), Spanish Acad. Pediatrics (ambulatory pediatrics sect. hon. 1987), Assn. Tchrs. Preventive Medicine, Spanish Profls. Am. (pres. 1988), Soc. Catalana Hipertensio (hon.), Sigma Xi, Alpha Omega Alpha. Roman Catholic. Home: 2001 Holcombe Blvd Houston TX 77030-4222 Office: Baylor Coll Medicine One Baylor Plz Rm 650E Houston TX 77030-3404

**VALLBONA, RIMA-GRETEL ROTHE,** retired foreign language educator, writer; b. San Jose, Costa Rica, Mar. 15, 1931; arrived in U.S., 1956, naturalized, 1997; d. Ferdinand Hermann and Emilia (Strassburger) Rothe; m. Carlos Vallbona, Dec. 26, 1956; children: Rima-Nuri, Carlos-Fernando, Maria-Teresa, Maria-Luisa. BA/BS, Colegio Superior de Senoritas, San Jose, Costa Rica, 1948; diploma, U. Paris, 1953; diploma in Spanish Philology, U. Salamanca, Spain, 1954; MA, U. Costa Rica, 1962; D in Modern Langs., Middlebury Coll., 1981. Tchr. Liceo J.J. Vargas Calvo, Costa Rica, 1955—56; faculty U. St. Thomas, Houston, 1964—95, prof. Spanish, 1978—95, Cullen Found. prof. Spanish, 1989, head Spanish dept., 1966—71, chmn. dept. modern fgn. lang., 1978—80, prof. emeritus, 1995—. Vis. prof. U. Houston, 1975—76, Rice U., 1974, 1980—83, 1995, U. St. Thomas, Argentina, 1972, U. St. Thomas, Merida program, 1975—97. Author: Noche en Vela, 1968, Yolanda Oreamuno, 1972, La Obra en Prosa de Eunice Odio, 1981, Baraja de Soledades, Las Sombras que Perseguimos, 1983, Polvo del Camino, 1972, La Salamandra Rosada, 1979, Mujeres y Agonias, 1982, Cosecha de Pecadores, 1988, El arcangel del perdon, 1990, Mundo, demonio y mujer, 1991, Los infiernos de la mujer y algo mas, 1992, (crit. edit.) Vida i sucesos de la Monja Alferez, 1992, Flowering Inferno-Tales of Sinking Hearts, 1994, La narrativa de Yolanda Oreamuno, 1996, Tormy, la Prodigiosa Gata de Donaldito, 1997, Tejedoras de sueños versus realidad, 2003; mem. (editl. bd.) Letras Femeninas, 1984—98, Alba de America, U.S., sec. (culture) Inst. Literario i Cultural Hispanico; co-dir.: Foro Literario, 1987—89; contbg. editor: The Americas Rev., 1989—99; contbr. numerous articles and short stories to lit. mags. Mem. scholarship com. Inst. Hispanic Culture, 1978, 1979, 1988, 1991, chmn. 1979, bd. dirs., 1974—76, 1988—89, 1991—92, chmn. cultural activities, 1979, 1980, 1985, 1988—89; bd. dirs. Houston Pub. Libr., 1984—86, Cultural Arts Coun. Houston, 1991—92. Recipient Aquileo J. Echeverria Novel prize, 1968, Jorge Luis Borges Short Story prize, Argentina, 1977, Agripina Montes del Valle Novel prize, 1978, Constantin Found. grant for rsch., U. St. Thomas, 1981, Lit. award, S.W. Conf. Latin Am. Studies, 1982, Ancora Lit. award, Costa Rica, 1984, Civil Merit award, King Juan Carlos I of Spain, 1989, Children's Book award, Bay Area Writers League, 2003. Mem.: Soc. Children's Book Writers and Illustrators, Nat. Writers Assn., Inst. Lit. y Cultural Hispanico, Casa Argentina de Houston, Inst. Hispanic Culture Houston, Latin Am. Writers Assn. Costa Rica, Inst. Internat. de Lit. Iberoam., Latin Am. Studies Assn., Academia Norteamericana de la Lengua Espanola (elected), S.W. Conf. Orgn. Latin Am Studies, South Ctrl. MLA, Houston

Area Tchrs. Fgn. Lang., Houston Area Tchrs. Spanish and Portuguese, Am. Assn. Tchrs. Spanish and Portuguese, Sigma Delta Pi, Phi Sigma Iota. Roman Catholic. Home: 3706 Lake St Houston TX 77098-5522 E-mail: rvallbona@aol.com.

**VALLEE, JUDITH DELANEY,** environmentalist, writer, not-for-profit fundraiser; b. N.Y.C., Mar. 14, 1948; d. Victor and Sally Hammer; m. John Delaney, Apr. 9, 1974 (div. 1978); m. Henry Richard Vallee, May 15, 1987. BA, CUNY, 1976. Exec. dir. Save the Manatee Club, Maitland, Fla., 1985—. Apptd. U.S. Manatee Recovery Plan Team, Jacksonville, Fla., 1988-97, Fla. Manatee Tech. Adv. Coun., Tallahassee, 1989-2002, Save the Manatee Com., Orlando, Fla., 1985-92, World Conservation Union/Sirenia Specialist Group, Switzerland, 1996; advisor Save the Wildlife Inc., Chuluota, Fla., 1992-93; bd. dirs. Environ. Fund for Fla. Lobbyist Save the Manatee Club, 1989; vol. Broward County Audubon Soc., Ft. Lauderdale, 1983-84, Wild Bird Care Ctr., Ft. Lauderdale, 1984. Recipient Refuge Support award Chassahowitzka Nat. Wildlife Refuge, 1989. Democrat. Avocations: creative writing, antiques, wildlife observation, canoeing. Office: Save the Manatee Club Inc 500 N Maitland Ave Ste 210 Maitland FL 32751-4458 Office Phone: 407-539-0990. E-mail: jvallee100@aol.com.

**VALLEE, ROY A.,** electronics executive; b. Southbridge, Mass. married; 2 children. AS in electronics tech., Don Bosco Tech. Inst., 1971. Electronics tech. radio products Don Bosco Tech. Inst., 1971; field sales rep. Avnet, Inc., Great Neck, NY, 1977—92, from sys. bus. mgr., gen. sales mgr. to vice-chmn., pres., COO, 1992—98, chmn., CEO, Phoenix, 1998—, bd. dirs., 1991—. Bd. dirs. Teradyne, Synopsys, Inc.; exec. com. Global Tech. Distbn. Coun. Mem. Govs. Coun. of Innovation and Tech. Named to Hot 25 Execs., Electronic Buyer's News, 1997, 1999, 2000. Office: Avnet Inc 2211 S 47th St Phoenix AZ 85034-6403*

**VALLEE-RETTKE, JOAN E.,** chemistry educator, science education consultant; b. Welsh, La., Apr. 16, 1944; children: Susan, Anne Connella; m. Bob Rettke, May 24, 2003. BS in Biol. Scis., McNeese State U., 1965; MA in Biol. Scis., U. New Orleans, 1969; 2d in sci. edn., McNeese State U., 1974. Tchr. chemistry, physics, biochemistry Barbe H.S., Lake Charles, La., 1969—86; asst. prof. chemistry McNeese State U., Lake Charles, La., 1986—; dir. McNeese Honors Coll., Lake Charles, La., 1999—. Recipient multimedia grant L.A. Edn. Quality Support Fund, 1996, Celebration of Tchg. award Geraldine R. Dodge 1980, 94. Mem. Nat. State Tchrs. of Yr. (exec. dir. 1990-93, also v.p., sec.; pres. La. chpt. 1987-93; La. Tchr. of Yr. 1985), Phi Delta Kappa (pres., v.p., sec.). Roman Catholic. Office Phone: 337-475-5780. E-mail: jvalle@mcneese.edu.

**VALLERAND, PHILIPPE GEORGES,** sales executive; b. Montreal, Que., Can., June 12, 1954; arrived in U.S., 1982; s. Louis Philippe and Beatrice (Goupil) V.; m. Laura Jean Frombach, Sept. 25, 1979; children: Harmonie May, Jeremy Thomas, Emilie Rose. Cert. mktg. and sales Internat. Orgn. for Standardization, 2002. Dir. resort Club Mediterranee Inc., Bahamas, Switzerland, Africa, Guadaloupe, West Indies, 1978—80; v.p. Franglo/Sunsaver Inc., London and Hyeres, France, 1980-82; v.p. sales Source Northwest, Inc., Woodinville, Wash., 1982—93; pres., CEO The PGV Group, Inc. Sr. comdr. Royal Rangers Boys Club, Monroe, Wash., 1988-96; bd. dirs. Christian Faith Ctr., Monroe, 1988-94; mem. Rep. Nat. Com.; co-chmn. Rep. Bus. Adv. Coun.; bd. dirs. Northwest U., 2005; pres. leadership coun., Trinity Western U.; bd. dirs. Northwest U. Recipient Disting. Sales & Mktg. Exec. award Internat. Orgn. Sales & Mktg. Execs., 1993, 96. Avocations: skiing, travel. Personal E-mail: phil.vallerand@verizon.net.

**VALLES, JAMES M., JR.,** physics professor; BA magna cum laude in Physics, Dartmouth Coll., 1981; PhD in Physics, U. Mass., 1988. Tchg. asst. U. Mass., 1981—82, rsch. asst., 1982—87; postdoctoral assoc. AT&T Bell Labs., 1987—89; asst. prof. physics U. Oreg., 1989—92; asst. prof. Brown U., 1992—96, assoc. prof., 1996—2002, prof., 2002—. Exec. officer dept. physics Brown U., 1999—2002. Contbr. articles to profl. jours. Grantee Alfred P. Sloan Found. fellowship, 1990—92. Mem.: Am. Phys. Soc., Sigma Xi. Office: Dept Physics Brown U Box 1843 Providence RI 02912 E-mail: valles@physics.brown.edu.*

**VALLETTA, AMBER,** actress, model; b. Phoenix, Feb. 9, 1974; m. Herve Le Bhihan, 1994 (div. 1996); m. Christian McCaw, Sept. 2003; 1 child. Auden. With Boss Models, N.Y.C.; Elite Models, N.Y.C., 1996—. Exec. prodr.: (films) Ticks, 1999; actor: Drop Back Ten, 2000, What Lies Beneath, 2000, The Family Man, 2000, Perfume, 2001, Max Keeble's Big Move, 2001, Duplex, 2003, Raising Helen, 2004, Hitch, 2005, Transporter 2, 2005; (TV films) Hysteria: The Def Leppard Story, 2001. Office: Fl 2 300 Park Ave S New York NY 10010-5313

**VALLI, FRANKIE (FRANCIS CASTELLUCCIO),** singer; b. Newark, May 3, 1937; Student pub. schs., Newark. With vocal group Four Lovers, 1956—61, The Four Seasons, 1962—77, albums (with The Four Seasons) Sherry, Greetings, Big Girls Don't Cry, Ain't That A Shame, 1963, Stay, Golden Hits, We Love Girls, Live On Stage, Dawn, Born To Wander, Rag Doll, 1964, Sing Big Hits, Entertain You, Gold Vault Hits, Working My Way Back To You, 1965, Christmas Album, Genuine Imitation, Life Gazette, Seasoned Hits, 1968, Edizione D'oro, 1969, Big Ones, 1971, Chameleon, 1972, Gold, Our Day Will Come, Close To You, Fallen Angel, Who Loves You, Helicon, 1975, The Four Seasons Story, 1976, Reunited, 1981, Hope and Glory, 1992, (as solo artist) Solo, 1967, Timeless, 1968, Inside You, Closeup, Our Day Will Come, 1975, Valli, 1977, Frankie Valli Is The Word, 1978, Grease (original soundtrack), 1978, The Very Best of Frankie Valli, 1979, Heaven Above Me, 1980, Frankie Valli: Hits from the 60's, 1983; actor: (films) Beach Ball, 1965, All This and World War II, Ebony, Ivory and Jade, 1976, Grease, Sergeant Pepper's Lonely Hearts Club Band, 1978, Dirty Laundry, 1987, Eternity, 1989, Modern Love, 1990, Opposite Corners, 1995; (TV films) Witness to the Mob, 1998; (TV series) The Sopranos, 2004—. Named to Rock 'n' Roll Hall of Fame (with The Four Seasons), 1990.

**VALLIÈRES, ERIC,** thoracic surgeon; b. Detroit, Apr. 28, 1959; s. André Vallières and Huguette Poulin; life ptnr. Christine Ann Lee; children: Frédérique Paule, Charles-Antoine, Thomas Eric. MD, U. Laval, Quebec, Can., 1982. Asst. prof. surgery U. Alta., Edmonton, Canada, 1991—94, U. Ottawa, Ontario, Canada, 1994—96; assoc. prof. surgery U. Wash. Med. Sch., Seattle, 1996—2004; surg. dir. lung cancer program Swedish Cancer Inst., Seattle, 2004—. Chair S.W. Oncology Group Thoracic Surg. Com., 1998—. Recipient John K. Stevenson awardfor Tchg. Excellence, U. Wash., 1996-7, Outstanding Faculty in Continuing Med. Edn. award, U. Wash. Sch. of Medicine, 1999. Fellow: Royal Coll. of Surgeons Can. (Walter C. Mackenzie-Ethicon fellowship 1991). Office: Swedish Cancer Inst 1221 Madison Ste 400 Seattle WA 98104 Office Phone: 206-215-6800. Office Fax: 206-215-6801.

**VALLNER, JOSEPH J.,** medical products executive; BS in Pharmacy, U. Wis., MS in Phys. Chemistry, PhD in Pharmaceutics. Former assoc. prof. pharmaceutics U. Ga.; formerly with G.D. Searle and Co., Syntex Corp., Sequus Pharms.; exec. v.p., COO Cell Genesys, Inc., Foster City, Calif., 1999—2001, pres., COO, 2001—.

**VALOIS, ROBERT ARTHUR,** lawyer; b. N.Y.C., May 13, 1938; s. Frank Jacob and Harriet Frances (LaCroix) V.; m. Ruth Emilie Skacil, Dec. 23, 1961; children: Marguerite Jeannette, Robert Arthur Jr. BBA, U. Miami, 1962; JD, Wake Forest U., 1972. Bar: N.C. 1972, Fla. 1972, U.S. Ct. Appeals (4th cir.) 1973, U.S. Dist. Ct. (ea. and mid. dists.) 1973, U.S. Supreme Ct. 1975, U.S. Ct. Appeals (6th cir.) 1986. Field examiner NLRB, Winston-Salem, NC, 1962-70; from assoc. to ptnr. Maupin, Taylor & Ellis, P.A., Raleigh, NC, 1972—, chmn. labor and employment sect., 1972-97, chmn. bd. dirs., pres., 1997—2002. Vice chmn. Legal Svcs. Corp., Washington, 1984-

90, bd. dirs. Served with USN, 1956-59. Mem. Greater Raleigh C. of C. (chmn. fed. govt. com. 1991—). Democrat. Presbyterian. Home: 3952 Bentley Bridge Rd Raleigh NC 27612 Office Phone: 919-981-4000. E-mail: rvalois@maupintaylor.com.

**VALUKAS, ANTON RONALD,** lawyer, former prosecutor; b. Chgo., June 21, 1943; s. Anton J. and Mary Ann (Giusto) Valukas; m. Janice C. Valukas (div.); children: Amy Paige, Beth Catherine; m. Maria Finitzo; children: Catherine Sara, Paul Alexander. BA in Polit. Sci., Art History, Lawrence U., 1965; JD, Northwestern U., 1968. Bar: Ill. 1968, U.S. Dist. Ct. (no. dist.) Ill. 1968, U.S. Ct. Appeals (7th cir.) 1969, U.S. Ct. Appeals (10th cir.) 1977, U.S. Ct. Appeals (3d cir.) 1982. Sr. dir. Nat. Defender Project, Chgo., 1968-70; asst. U.S. atty. (No. dist.) Ill. US Dept. Justice, Chgo., 1970—74, chief spl. prosecutions divsn. (No. dist.) Ill., 1974, first asst. US atty (No. dist.) Ill., 1975—76, U.S. atty. (No. dist.) Ill. Chgo., 1985-89; ptnr. Jenner & Block LLP, Chgo., 1976—85, 1989—. Instr. John Marshal Law Sch., 1972—76; adj. prof. law Northwester U. Sch. Law, 1980—82; dir., treas. Met. Fair and Exposition Authority, Chgo., 1985; spl. counsel to investigate report health care sys. City of Chgo., 1991. Bd. dirs. Boys Scouts Am., Bus. and Profl. People for Pub. Interest, 1998—, Smithsonian Inst. Librs., 2004—; mem. several commns. and coms. Evanston Housing Commn., Ill.; chmn. Ill. Task Force Crime and Corrections, 1992—93; mem. vis. com. Northwestern U. Sch. Law, 1992—95. Named one of Ten Outstanding Young Citizens of Chgo., Jr. C. of C., 1976; recipient Spl. Commendation award, U.S. Dept. Justice, Chgo., 1975, Disting. Grad. award, Palatine HS, Ill., 1984, Freedom award, John Marshall Sch. Law, 1985, Citizen of the Yr. award, Constn. Rights Found., 1987, Civillian of the Yr. award, Armed Forces Coun. Chgo., 1988, Man of the Yr. award, WBBM Radio, 1988, Disting. Pub. Svc. award, Anti-Defamation League B'nai B'rith, 1990, Disting. Achievement award, Lawrence U., 1990, Disting. Svc. award, Chgo. C. of C. and Industry, 1990, Alumni Merit award, Northwestern U. Alumni Assn., 1995, Richard N. Rovner award, Epilepsy Found. Greater Chgo., 2004, Judge Learned Hand award, 2005. Fellow: Am. Coll. Trial Lawyers; mem.: ABA, Chgo. Inn Ct. (pres. 2000—01), Ill. State Bar Assn., Chgo. Bar Assn., Chicagoland C. of C. (bd. dirs. 1999—), Law of Chgo. Club, Exec. Club Chgo. (bd. dirs. 1996—), Econ. Club. Chgo. (bd. dirs. 1990—). Office: Jenner & Block LLP 1 IBM Plz Chicago IL 60611-7603 Office Phone: 312-923-2903. Business E-Mail: avalukas@jenner.com.

**VALVERDE, PALOMA,** biochemist, educator; b. Murcia, Murcia, Spain, Jan. 15, 1968; d. Gregorio Valverde and Paz de los Angeles Hernandez; m. David Irwin Sherris, Nov. 2, 1997; children: Gregory Alexander Sherris children: Michael Gregory Sherris. BSc, U. Murcia, Spain, 1990, MSc, 1991, PhD, 1994. Scientist Human Nutrition Rsch. Ctr. of Aging, Tufts U., Boston, 2002—04; asst. prof. Sch. Dental Medicine, Tufts U., Boston, 2004—. Contbr. articles to profl. jours. John W. Hein Rsch. fellow, Forsyth Inst., Boston, 1999—2002. Mem.: Internat. Assn. for Biomed. Rsch. (v.p. 2004—). Achievements include discovery of first mutations in human melanocortin receptor 1; gene called WW45 or Salvador; first to use of scorpion venom to treat periodontal disease; development of first antibody to recognize WW45/Salvador gene; discovery of axl receptor tyrosine kinase is ubiquitinated by its ligand Gas6; RANKL and BSP induce bone loss synergistically. Avocations: painting, writing. Home: 37 Neillian Crescent Jamaica Plain MA 02130 Office: Tufts Univ DHS Bldg Rm 633 One Kneeland St Boston MA 02111 Office Phone: 617-636-0341. Business E-Mail: paloma.valverde@tufts.edu.

**VALVERDE, ROLDAN ARTURO,** education educator, researcher; s. Claudio Valverde and Arabela Espinoza; m. Leonilde Nonita Villalba, Jan. 15, 1993; children: Raquel A., Eric M. PhD, Tex. A&M U., College Station, 1996. Field coord. green sea turtle program tortuguero Caribbean Conservation Corp., Gainesville, 1996; postdoctoral fellow biology U. Mich., Ann Arbor, 1997—2001; asst. prof. biology Xavier U. of La., New Orleans, 2001—04, Southeastern La. U., Hammond, 2004—; field rsch. asst. Universidad Nacional, Heredia, Costa Rica. Rev. panelist NSF, Arlington, Va., 2005. Author: (rsch. article) Jour. of Endocrinology. Grant, U.S. EPA, 2005—, U.S. Fish and Wildlife Svc., Internat. Sea Turtle Conservation Program, 2006—, La. Bd. of Regents, 2006—. Mem.: Am. Soc. of Icthyologists and Herpetologists (assoc.). Office: Southeastern La Univ 808 N Pine St extension Hammond LA 70402 Office Phone: 985-549-3029. Office Fax: 985-549-3851.

**VALVO, BARBARA-ANN,** lawyer, surgeon; b. Elizabeth, NJ, June 7, 1949; d. Richard and Vera (Kovach) V. BA in Biology, Hofsta U., 1971; MD, Pa. State U., 1975; JD, Loyola Sch. Law, 1993. Bar: La. 1993; diplomate Am. Bd. Surgery. Surg. intern Nassau County Med. Ctr., East Meadow, NY, 1975-76; resident gen. surgery Allentown-Sacred Heart Med. Ctr., Pa., 1976-80; asst. chief surgery USPHS, New Orleans, 1980-81; pvt. practice gen. surgery New Orleans, 1981-89; pvt. practice med. malpractice law, 1995—. Upjohn scholar, 1975. Fellow ACS; mem. ABA, Fed. Bar Assn., La. Bar Assn., La. Trial Lawyers Assn. Republican. Avocations: computers, raising animals. Office: 41 Harley Pl Willow Spring NC 27592 Personal E-mail: bavalvo@nc.rr.com.

**VALYI-NAGY, TIBOR G.,** neuropathologist, virologist; b. Debrecen, Hungary, Jan. 7, 1958; arrived in U.S., 1988; s. Tibor Valyi-Nagy and Ilona Gonczol; m. Klara Peto, Sept. 11, 1982; children: Tibor, Zsofia. MD, Debrecen U., 1982; PhD, Hungarian Acad. Scis., Budapest, 1994. Cert. anatomic and neuropathology Am. Bd. Pathology, 2003, med. microbiology Hungarian Bd. Med. Microbiology, 1988. Rsch. assoc. Nat. Inst. Dermatology, Budapest, 1982—88; rsch. fellow U. Tex. Med. Br., Galveston, 1984—86; rsch. assoc. The Wistar Inst., Phila., 1988—95; resident physician in anatomic and neuropathology Vanderbilt U. Med. Ctr., Nashville, 1995—2000, instr. and attending neuropathologist Vanderbilt U. Sch. Medicine, Nashville, 2000—02; dir. neuropathology, asst. prof. U. Ill. Chgo., 2002—. Home: 597 Glen Ellyn Pl Glen Ellyn IL 60137 Office: U Ill at Chgo 840 S Wood St Rm 130 Chicago IL 60612-4325 Office Phone: 312-996-1772. Personal E-mail: valyint@aol.com. E-mail: tiborv@uic.edu.

**VAMVAKIDIS, ATHANASIOS,** economist; b. Thessaloniki, Greece, Sept. 23, 1970; s. Charalambos and Despina Vamvakidis; m. Konstantia Mamada, Aug. 28, 2004. PhD, Harvard U., Cambridge, Mass., 1997. Sr. economist Internat. Monetary Fund, Washington, 1997—. Contbr. articles to profl. jours. Office: International Monetary Fund 700 19th Street NW Washington DC 20431 Office Phone: 202-623-5405. Business E-Mail: avamvakidis@imf.org.

**VAN, FRITZ See VAN DUYSE, FRANCIS**

**VANAGAS, RIMANTAS (RAY) ANDRIUS (RAY VANAGAS),** entrepreneur, real estate developer, real estate company executive; b. Chgo., Jan. 10, 1958; s. Liudas and Birute A. (Bielskis) Vanagas. Student, Northwestern U., 1980-81; BA in Physics, Econs. and Polit. Sci., Lake Forest Coll., Ill., 1982. Prof. basketball player European divsn., Munich, 1982; ski instr., capt. race team Breckenridge (Colo.) Ski Sch., 1979-80; chmn. bd. dirs. Vancher Corp., Wheeling, Ill., 1980-84; sales exec. Chgo. HMO, 1984-85; exec. dir. Physique, Inc., Highland Park, Ill., 1985; pres., CEO Sports Life, Inc., Highland Park, 1985-88; sr. v.p. JPC Consulting, Chgo., 1988-91; pres., CEO Printing Advisors, Inc., Naperville, Ill., 1990-94, Cafe Alexander, Naperville, 1995—2002; sr. exec. George S. May Internat. Consulting Co., Park Ridge, Ill., 1994-95; pres. Movie Magic Workshops, 2002—; founder, real estate investor and devel. RBML Real Estate Inc., 2002—; pres. and CEO Pinemeadow Corp. DBA Park Shore Marina, 2004—, Vanagas Investment Group, LLC, 2005—. Cons. Nautilus Exercise Ctrs., Inc., Wheeling, 1979—83, G. Ross Comm., Lake Bluff, Ill., 1986; mng. dir. Ford Model Mgmt., Chgo., 2000—; pres., CEO Alexander Talent Mgmt., 2001—. Actor:, 1981—; (films) Shut-Eye, 2001; prodr.:, 1981—, numerous music videos, commls., inds. and corp. films. Leader Lithuanian Air Scouts, 1976—80; campaign asst. Ronald Reagan Re-Election Campaign, Ill., 1983; active Baltic Nations Athletic Olympiad; vol. coach basketball, baseball, 1984—87.

Mem.: Mensa. Roman Catholic. Avocations: collecting coins and stamps, travel, skiing, golf, tennis. Home: 1684 Greene Ridge Dr Naperville IL 60565-6753 Office Phone: 269-445-3100. E-mail: rayvanagas@aol.com.

**VAN AKEN, JOHN HENRY,** retired marine surveyor, engineer, consultant; b. Haarlem, Netherlands, Sept. 26, 1922; arrived in U.S., 1952; s. Antony and Maria Petronella (Renzen) van Aken; m. Hendrika A. Bonneur, Sept. 25, 1947 (div. Feb. 1960); 1 child, Antony Laurens; m. Helen Jemison Waterman, July 17, 1962 (dec. Feb. 1978); m. Marilyn McDaniel, July 13, 1980 (dec. Sept. 2001). Marine Engr., Acad. Tech. Sci. and Arts of Design, 1940. Asst. mgr. repair dept. Wilton-Feyenoord Dockyards, Schiedam, Netherlands, 1945—52; supt. machinery Ala. Dry Dock & Shipbldg. Co., Mobile, 1958—60; mgr. project Kerr-McGee Oil Industries, Oklahoma City, 1954—58, 1960—63; insp. George Sharp Co., Naval Architects, Newport News, Va., 1960; pres. John H. van Aken Co. Inc., Marine Surveyors and Cons. Inc., Mobile, 1963—99; ret., 2002. Non-exclusive surveyor Panama Bur. Shipping, Internat. Cargo Gear Bur., Registr. Italiano Navale, Lloyd's Register of Shipping; Named hon. consul gen. Republic South Africa, 2002-06. Decorated comdr. Order Good Hope, South Africa; Paul Harris fellow Rotary. Mem. Soc. Naval Architects and Marine Engrs., Nat. Assn. Marine Surveyors, Netherlands Soc. Marine Technologists, Rotary Home: 500 Spanish Ft Blvd #52 Spanish Fort AL 36527-5004 Personal E-mail: jhvanaken@wvsf.org.

**VAN AKEN, NORMAN,** chef; Chef, owner Norman's Restaurant, Coral Gables, Fla., Orlando, Fla., LA. Chef's coun. Chefs for Humanity. Author: Feast of Sunlight, 1988, The Exotic Fruit Book, 1995, Norman Van Aken's New World Cuisine, 1997, New World Kitchen, 2003. Named Best Chef in the Southeast, James Beard Found.; recipient Robert Mondavi Culinary Award of Excellence, Food Arts Silver Spoon Lifetime Achievement award. Office: Normans 12328 SW 117th Ct Miami FL 33186-3919*

**VAN ALFEN, NEAL K.,** plant pathologist; b. Ogden, Utah, July 17, 1943; s. Gerrit Johan and Marguerite (Noorda) Van A. BS, Brigham Young U., 1968, MS, 1969; PhD, U. Calif., Davis, 1972. Asst. plant pathologist Conn. Agr. Exp. Sta., New Haven, Conn., 1972-75; asst. prof. biology Utah State U., Logan, 1975-78, extension plant pathologist, 1975-78, assoc. prof. of biology, 1978-82, prof. of biology and molecular biology/biochem., 1982-90; prof. and head/dept. of plant pathology/microbiology Tex. A&M U., College Station, Tex., 1990-99; dean agrl. and environ. scis. U. Calif., Davis, 1999—. Fellow AAAS, Am. Phytopathol. Soc.; mem. Am. Phytopathol. Soc. (councilor-at-large 1994-97, v.p., pres. 1997-99). Mem.: Am. Soc. for Microbiology. Office: U Calif-Davis Coll Agrl and Environ Scis 1 Shields Ave Davis CA 95616-5270 Office Phone: 530-752-1605, 530-661-2298. Business E-Mail: nkvanalfen@ucdavis.edu.

**VAN ALLEN, VERONICA ELAINE,** marketing and public relations professional; b. Jamaica, NY, May 6, 1936; d. William James and Florence Veronica (Lester) Van Allen; children: Veronica E. Davis, Valerie E. Boyd; m. Ian Helsby, July 4, 1998. BEd, U. Miami, 1963. Cert. tchr. Fla. English, phys. edn. tchr. Dade County Sch. Sys., Miami, Fla., 1963-67; founder, coach girls' track team Acad. of the Holy Names, Tampa, Fla., 1972—74; exec. dir. Royal Palm Festival Inc., West Palm Beach, Fla., 1978-82; exec. v.p. No. Palm Beaches C. of C., Palm Beach Gardens, Fla., 1982-88; dir. mktg., pub. rels. Operation Explore, Palm Beach Gardens, Fla., 1993—. Exec. dir. World Trade Coun., 1983-86. Editor (newspaper supplement) Royal Palm Festival, 1978-82 (Advt. Club aw and 1980), video pub., 1981 (Internat. Festival Assn. award 1981); editor (ann. chamber mag.) Guide to No. Palm Beaches, 1984-88, Air Show mag., 1987. Vice chmn. Tourist Devel. Coun. Palm Beach County, 1987, mem., 1983—88; vice chmn. Leadership Palm Beach County, 1985—86, bd. dirs., 1984—89; mem. mil. acad. screening com. Congressman Tom Lewis, Palm Beach Gardens, 1986—94; bd. dirs. Sun Fest, 1982—84; mem. Internat. Coun. Air Shows, 1981—86, Alumni Assn.LPBC, 1987—; coord. religious instrn. St. Paul of the Cross, North Palm Beach, Fla., 1977—80. Mem. U. Miami Alumni Assn., Internat. Festival Assn., Am. C. of C. Execs. Republican. Roman Catholic. Avocations: reading, yoga, theater, tennis, aerobics. Home: 170 Esperanza Way Palm Beach Gardens FL 33418 Office Phone: 561-951-4389, 561-694-0822. Personal E-mail: ronnieandian@adelphia.net.

**VAN ALLEN, WILLIAM KENT,** lawyer; b. Albion, N.Y., July 30, 1914; s. Everett Kent and Georgia (Roberts) Van A.; m. Sally Schall, Nov. 11, 1944; children: William Kent, Jr., George Humphrey, Peter Cushing. AB, Hamilton Coll., 1935; LL.B., Harvard U., 1938. Bar: N.Y. 1938, D.C. 1939, N.C. 1951, U.S. Dist. Ct. (we. dist.) N.C. 1951, U.S. Dist. Ct. (mid. dist.) N.C. 1953, U.S. Ct. Appeals (4th cir.) 1951, U.S. Ct. Claims 1946, U.S. Tax Ct. 1940, FCC 1939, ICC 1940, U.S. Supreme Ct. 1946. With Hanson, Lovett & Dale, Washington, 1938-41, 46-50; ptnr. Lassiter, Moore and Van Allen and Moore and Van Allen, Charlotte, NC, 1951-87; of counsel Moore & Van Allen, Charlotte, 1988—. Permanent mem. Jud. Conf. 4th Jud. Circuit. Vestryman Episc. Ch., 1957-60, 66-69; mem. Mecklenburg County Bd. Public Welfare, 1954-59, chmn. 1957-59; bd. dirs. N.C. Found. Commerce and Industry, 1965-73, Found. U. N.C. at Charlotte, 1979-89, Charlotte Symphony Orch., 1981-82, Mercy Health Svcs., 1983-88; chmn. Charlotte Area adv. coun. Am. Arbitration Assn., 1967-76; bd. dirs. United Community Svcs., 1972-77, v.p., 1972; bd. mgrs. Charlotte Country Day Sch., 1956-61, chmn., 1959-61, bd. visitors, 1978-2004, chmn., 1987-88; bd. advisers U. N.C.-Charlotte, 1983-84; trustee Spastics Hosp., 1951-60, Mint Mus. Art, 1976-79, Surtman Found., 1955-90, Mercy Hosp. Found., 1979-84; bd. visitors Johnson C. Smith U., 1978-89; pres. Charlotte Symphony League, 1980-81, Friends of U. N.C. at Charlotte, 1990-91. Served with USNR, 1941-45, commdg. officer destroyer escort ATO and PTO; released to inactive duty as lt. comdr. Mem. ABA, Charlotte C. of C. (bd. dirs. 1971-75, v.p. 1972-75). Mil. Order of Carabao, Holland Soc. N.Y., Charlotte Country Club, Charlotte City Club, Chevy Chase Club (Md.), Mullett Lake Country Club (Mich.), Mill Reef Club, Phi Beta Kappa, Chi Psi. Office: Moore & Van Allen Ste 4700 100 N Tryon St Charlotte NC 28202-4003 Office Phone: 704-331-1021.

**VAN ALLSBURG, CHRIS,** writer, artist; b. Grand Rapids, Mich., June 18, 1949; s. Richard Allen and Doris Marie (Christiansen) Van A.; m. Lisa Carol Morrison, Aug. 17, 1976. BFA, U. Mich., 1972; MFA, R.I. Sch. Design, 1975. Tchr. R.I. Sch. Design, Providence. Author, illustrator: The Garden of Abdul Gasazi, 1979 (Caldecott Honor Book 1980, Irma Simonton Black award Bank St. Coll. Edn. 1980, Boston Globe/Horn Book award 1980), Jumanji, 1981 (Caldecott medal 1982, Boston Globe/Horn Book award 1982, Children's Choice award Internat. Reading Assn. 1982, Am. Book award, 1982, Ky. Bluegrass award No. Ky. U. 1983, Buckeye Children's Book award Ohio State Libr. 1983, Wash. Children's Choice Picture Book award Wash. Libr. Media Assn. 1984, W. Va. Children's Book award 1985), Ben's Dream, 1982 (Parents Choice award for illustration Parents' Choice Found. 1982), Wreck of the Zephyr, 1983 (Silver medal Soc. Illustrators 1983), The Mysteries of Harris Burdick, 1984 (Parents Choice award for illustration Parents' Choice Found. 1984, Irma Simonton Black award Bank St. Coll. Edn. 1985, Boston Globe/Horn Book award 1985, World Fantasy award 1985), The Polar Express, 1985 (Parents Choice award for illustration Parents' Choice Found. 1985, Caldecott medal 1986, Boston Globe/Horn Book award 1986, Ky. Bluegrass award No. Ky. U. 1987), The Stranger, 1986 (Parents Choice award for illustration Parents' Choice Found. 1986), The Z Was Zapped: A Play in Twenty-Six Acts, 1987, Two Bad Ants, 1988, Just A Dream, 1990, The Wretched Stone, 1991, The Widow's Broom, 1992, The Sweetest Fig, 1993, The Two Figs, 1993, Bad Day at River Bend, 1995, Zathura, 2002; illustrator: Swan Lake, 1989; exhibited works at Whitney Mus. Art, N.Y.C., Mus. Modern Art, N.Y.C., Alan Stone Gallery, N.Y.C., Grand Rapids (Mich.) Art Mus., Port Washington (N.Y.) Pub. Libr.; permanent collections include Kerlan Collection at U. Minn. Recipient Hans Christian Andersen award nomination, 1985. Jewish. Office: Houghton Mifflin Co 222 Berkeley St Boston MA 02116-3748

**VANALSTINE, RICK G.,** secondary school educator; b. Beaver Dam, Wis., Feb. 22, 1951; s. Betty Krenz VanAlstine; m. Debra Kay White, Apr. 1, 1973. BAS, Western N.Mex. U., Silver City, 1990. Patrolman N.Mex. State U., Las Cruces, 1971—72; detective Las Cruces Police Dept., 1972—76; detective, dep. Otero Sheriff's Dept., Alamogordo, N.Mex., 1978—79; chief of police Western N.Mex. U., Silver City, 1981—89; Am. history tchr. Gallup McKinnley Pub. Schs., N.Mex., 1989—96, Truth or Consequences Pub. Schs., N.Mex., 1996—99; tchr. econs. and govt. Alamagordo Pub. Schs., 1999—. Mem.: NEA, Am. Fedn. Tchrs., Nat. Assn. Social Studies Educators. Avocations: camping, travel. Address: PO Box 2333 Alamogordo NM 88311-2333

**VAN ALSTYNE, VANCE BROWNELL,** management consultant; b. Rochester, N.Y., Feb. 3, 1924; s. Guy and Jessie Van Alstyne; m. Jane Van Alstyne, Aug. 12, 1950; children: Cary B., Stacey E. BA, U. Rochester, 1948; LLB, Blackstone Coll. Law, 1964. Rsch. asst. indsl. rels. Gilbert Assoc, Inc., NYC, 1950-56; corp. sec., v.p., dir. R.C. Simpson & Staff Inc., Newark and Ridgewood, NJ, 1956-74; pres., dir. R.C. Simpson & Staff Inc., Newark and Ridgewood, NJ, 1975—91, Charlotte, NC, 1991—. 2d lt., navigator 12th Air Force USAF, 1942—45. Mem.: Indsl. Rels. Rsch. Assn., Am. Arbitration Assn., Atlantic Salmon Fedn. Republican. Office: RC Simpson Inc 5950 Fairview Rd Ste 604 Charlotte NC 28210-3178 Office Phone: 704-553-0716. E-mail: van.fsh@att.net.

**VAN ALSTYNE, W. SCOTT, JR.,** lawyer, educator; b. East Syracuse, N.Y., Sept. 21, 1922; s. Walter Scott and Cecil Edna (Folmsbee) Van A.; m. Margaret Reed Hudson, June 23, 1949 (div.); children: Gretchen Anne, Hunter Scott; m. Marion Graham Walker, May 3, 1980. BA, U. Buffalo, 1948; MA, U. Wis., 1950, LL.B., 1953, S.JD, 1954. Bar: Wis. 1953. Assoc. Shea & Hoyt, Milw., 1954-56; asst. prof. law U. Nebr., 1956-58; pvt. practice Madison, Wis., 1958-72; prof. law U. Fla., 1973-90, prof. emeritus, 1990—; lectr. law U. Wis., 1958-72; lectr. Cambridge-Warsaw Trade Program Cambridge U. (Eng.), 1976. Vis. prof. law Cornell U., 1977, U. Leiden, The Netherlands, 1988, 91; spl. lectr. U. Utrecht, The Netherlands, 1991; vis. prof. Wake Forest U., 1997; spl. counsel Gov. of Wis., 1966-70; bd. dirs. non-resident divsn. State Bar Wis., 1981-96, pres., 1988-90, bd. govs. 1988-90. Prin. author: Goals and Missions of Law Schools, 1990; contbr. articles to profl. jours. Mem. Gov.'s Commn. on Edn., Wis., 1969-71; cons. Wis. Commn. on Legal Edn., 1995-96. Served with AUS, 1942-45, 61-62; col. Res., ret. Decorated Legion of Merit. Fellow: Wis. Bar Found. (life); mem.: Holland Soc., S.R. (N.Y.), Netherland Club (N.Y.C.), Madison (Wis.) Club, Ft. Rensselaer Club (N.Y.), Phi Beta Kappa, Order of Coif, Phi Delta Phi, Omicron Delta Kappa. Republican. Presbyterian. Office: U Fla Holland Law Ctr Gainesville FL 32611

**VAN ANDEL, STEVE ALAN,** consumer products company executive; b. Ada, Mich., Oct. 9, 1955; BLS in Econs. and Bus., Hillsdale Coll., 1978; MBA in MKtg., Miami U., Oxford, Ohio, 1979. V.p. mktg. Amway Corp., Worldwide, chmn. exec. com. policy bd. Ada; vice chmn. Amway Japan Ltd.; chmn. Amway Asia Pacific Ltd., Amway Corp., 1995—, CEO, 1995—. Dir. Met Found., Operation Enterprise-AMA; bd. dirs. Met. Hosp. Found., Mich. Nat. Bank Corp., Ctr. for Internat. Pvt. Enterprises, Gerald Ford Found., Std. Fed. Bank, Grand Rapids John Ball Zoo Soc., Borgess Metro Health Alliance, Met. Health Corp.; mem. dean's adv. bd. Seidman Sch. of Bus.; co-CEO, Alticor Inc. Bd. dirs. Grand Rapids John Ball Soc., Amway Environmental Found. Mem. U.S. C. of C. (chmn. 2002). Office: Amway Corp 7575 Fulton St E Ada MI 49355-0001*

**VAN ANTWERPEN, FRANKLIN STUART,** federal judge; s. Franklin John and Dorothy Van Antwerpen; m. Kathleen Veronica O'Brien, Sept. 12, 1970; children: Joy, Franklin W., Virginia. BS in Engring. Physics, U. Maine, 1964; JD, Temple U., 1967; postgrad., Nat. Jud. Coll., 1980. Bar: Pa. 1969, U.S. Dist. Ct. (ea. dist.) Pa. 1971, U.S. Ct. Appeals (3d cir.) 1971, U.S. Supreme Ct. 1972. Corp. counsel Hazeltine, Corp., N.Y.C., 1967-70; chief counsel Northampton County Legal Aid Soc., Easton, Pa., 1970-71; assoc. Hemstreet & Smith, Easton, 1971-73; ptnr. Hemstreet & VanAntwerpen, Easton, 1973-79; judge Ct. Common Pleas of Northampton County, Pa., 1979-87, U.S. Dist. Ct. (ea. dist.) Pa., Phila., 1987—2004, U.S.Ct. Appeals (3rd. cir.), 2004—. Apptd. to US Sentencing Commn. Jud. Working Group, 1992-93; apptd. to US Jud. Conf. Com. on Defender Svcs., 1997, chmn. subcom. on fed. defender funding, 2000-01; trial judge US vs. Scarfo, 1988-89; adj. prof. Northampton County Area CC, 1976-81; solicitor Palmer Twp., 1971-79; gen. counsel Fairview Savs. and Loan Assn., Easton, 1973-79; lectr. on law of evidence Pa. Bar Inst., 1985-92. Contbr. articles to Cardozo Law Rev., 1967. Recipient Booster award Bus. Indsl. and Profl. Assn., 1979, George Palmer award Palmer Twp., 1980, Citizen of Yr. award, 1981, Law Enforcement Commendation medal Nat. Nat. SAR, 1990, Disting. Alumni Achievement award Newark Acad., 2001. Law Day award Temple Law Sch. Alumni Assn., 2004; named an Alumnus Who Has Made a Difference in the World, U. Maine, 1991. Mem. ABA (com. on jud. edn.), Fed. Bar Assn. (hon.), Fed. Cir. Bar Assn., Pa. Bar Assn., Northampton County Bar Assn., Am. Judicature Soc., Fed. Judges Assn., Pomfret Club, Union League Club, Pa. Soc. Club, Sigma Pi Sigma. Office: 4th Fl Holmes Bldg 101 Larry HOlmes Dr Easton PA 18042-7722*

**VAN ARSDALEN, KEITH NORMAN,** urologist; b. Plainfield, N.J., Sept. 26, 1951; s. Norman Charles and Thelma Marie Svendsen Van Arsdalen; children: Bryce, Leigh, Jill, Kyle. BS, Muhlenberg Coll., 1973; MMS, CMDNJ, 1975; MD, Med. Coll. Va., 1977. Intern, resident U.Md., Balt., 1977-79; resident Med. Coll. Va., Richmond, 1979-82; asst. prof. surgery, urology U. Pa., Phila., 1983-89, asst. prof. surgery, urology, radiology, 1989-97, prof. surgery, urology, radiology, 1997—. Dir. male fertility sect, U. Pa. Sch. Medicine Divsn. Urology, 1983—; dir. shock wave lithotripsy svcs., 1985—; attending urologist Children's Hosp. Phila., 1989—; chief urology sect. Phila. V.A. Med. Ctr., 1990—2001; expert adv. panel U.S. Pharm. Conv., Rockville, Md., 1990—95; mem. scientific bd. Nat. Kidney Found., N.Y.C., 1992—98. Asst. editor Jour. Endourology, 1987-2003; contbr. articles to profl. jours., chpts. to books. Recipient Paul Rodin Leberman Teaching award Urology Residents, Phila, 1993, 98, Alumni Star award Va. Commonwealth U., 1993, John Morgan Soc. award, 1998; U. Pa. NKF-AUA rsch. fellow, 1982-83. Fellow: ACS (program com. 1992); mem.: AAAS, Urodynamics Soc., Soc. Univ. Urologists, Soc. Study Male Reproduction, Soc. Study Impotence, Soc. Reproductive Surgeons, Soc. Minimally Invasive Therapy, Soc. Laparoendoscopic Surgeons, Soc. Basic Urologic Rsch., Internat. Soc. Urology, Phila. Urol. Soc. (sec.-treas. 1992—98, pres.-elect 1998—99, pres. 1999—2000), Urol. Assn. Pa., Assn. Acad. Surgery, Am. Soc. Reproductive Medicine, Am. Soc. Andrology, Am. Assn. Clin. Urologists, Am. Urol. Assn., Coll. Physicians Phila. (mid-Atlantic sect. com. 1989—90, rsch. com. rep. 1990—94, local arrangements com. 1991—94, chmn. 1992—93, program com. 1996—97, rsch. com. rep. 1999—2002). Avocations: fishing, skiing, swimming, reading, house restoration. Office: Urology 9 Penn Tower 3400 Spruce St Philadelphia PA 19104-4206 Office Phone: 215-662-6790.

**VAN ARSDALL, ROBERT ARMES,** engineer, retired military officer; b. Omaha, Oct. 5, 1925; s. Samuel Peter and Althea (Armes) Van A.; m. Margaret Cooper Kiersted, June 9, 1948; children—Robert Armes, Janet Althea, Susan DeBaun, Kathryn Ann. BS, U.S. Mil. Acad., 1948; postgrad., U. Colo., spring 1961; MS, George Washington U., 1968. Commd. 2d lt. USAF, 1948, advanced through grades to col., 1968; grad. Randolph AFB, Tex., 1949; assigned 5th Air Rescue Group, Westover AFB, Mass., 1949-51; student USAF Squadron Officer Sch., Maxwell AFB, Ala., 1950; pilot, ops. officer 9th Air Rescue Group, Burton-Wood, Manston and Bushy Park, England, 1951-55; ops. officer Hdqrs. Air Rescue Service, Orlando AFB, Fla., 1955-57; plans officer Hdqrs. Air R & D Command, Balt., also Andrews AFB, Md., 1957-60; grad. USAF jet capitol course, Randolph AFB, 1959; tng.-with-industry Air Force Inst. Tech., Martin Co., Denver, 1960-61; chief plans div. Hdqrs. Space Systems Div., L.A., 1961-63; exec. officer Office Space Systems, Office Sec. Air Force, 1963-67; assoc. Air War Coll. program, Washington, 1964-66; student Naval War Coll., 1967-68; dep. dir. Dept. Def. Manned Space Flight Support Office, Patrick AFB, Fla., 1968-69; dir. range engring., 1969-70; dir. range ops. Air Force Eastern Test Range, 1970-72; comdr. USAF Satellite Test Ctr., Sunnyvale, Calif., 1972-73; vice comdr. USAF Satellite Control Facility, L.A., 1973-74, comdr., 1974-76; staff engr. Pan Am. World Airways, Cocoa Beach, Fla., 1976-78, project dir., 1978-79, program mgr., 1980-85, dir. internat. projects, 1985-88; program dir. Diego Garcia, 1989, ret., 1989. Decorated Air Force Commendation medal with two oak leaf clusters, Legion of Merit with oak leaf cluster. Life mem. Assn. Grads. U.S. Mil. Acad.; charter mem. Nat. Soujourners, USAF Acad. Athletic Assn. Clubs: Mason, Burtonwood Air Force (gov.), Bushy Park Air Force (gov.), Orlando Air Force (gov.), Andrews Air Force (gov.), Space Systems Division Air Force (gov.). Republican. Methodist. Home: 660 Cinnamon Ct Satellite Beach FL 32937-4301 Personal E-mail: ravanarsdall@earthlink.net.

**VANARSDALL, ROBERT LEE, JR.,** orthodontist, educator; b. Crewe, Va., Feb. 7, 1940; s. Robert Lee Sr. and Margie Mae (Jenkins) V.; m. Sandra E. Hoffman, Aug. 11, 1962; children: Robert Lee III, Lesley, Ashley. BA in Econs., Coll. William and Mary, 1962; DDS, Med. Coll. Va., 1970; cert. Orthodontics and Periodontics, U. Pa., 1973. Diplomate Am. Acad. Periodontology, Am. Bd. Orthodontics. Staff Children's Hosp., Phila., 1973—; prof. orthodontics, chmn. dept. orthodontics U. Pa., Phila., 1981—; prof. dentistry, chmn. Med. Coll. Pa., Phila., 1989—. K.G. prof. orthodontics U. Sydney, Australia, 2001; bd. dir. Nat. Dental Ins. Co., Denver. Editor: Internat. Jour. Adult Orthodontics and Orthognathic Surgery, 1986-2003, Orthodontics: Current Principles and Techniques, 2d edit., 1994, 4th edit., 2005, Applications of Orthodontic Mini-Implants, 2006; editl. bd. profl. jours.; contbr. articles to profl. jours. Bd. dirs. Phila. Soc. William and Mary Alumni Assn. Lt. USNR, 1962-65. Fellow Coll. Physicians of Phila. 1978, Am. Coll. Dentistry 1980. Mem. ADA, Am. Assn. Orthodontists, Stomatological Club Phila., Angle Soc. Orthodontists (v.p. ea. component, pres. 2004-2005), Phila. Soc. Orthodontists (pres. 1989, chmn. sci. affairs coun. 1990—), Internat. Coll. of Dentists. Roman Catholic. Avocations: antiques, architecture. Home: 208 Ashwood Rd Villanova PA 19085-1504 Office: Penn Dental 34th and Market St Philadelphia PA 19104 Office Fax: 215-898-0998. Business E-Mail: rlv@pobox.upenn.edu.

**VANARSDEL, ROSEMARY THORSTENSON,** English studies educator; b. Seattle, Sept. 1, 1926; d. Odin and Helen Catherine (McGregor) Thorstenson; m. Paul P. VanArsdel Jr., July 7, 1950 (dec. Jan. 1994); children: Mary M., Andrew P. BA, U. Wash., 1947, MA, 1948; PhD, Columbia U., 1961. Grad. tchg. asst. Columbia U., N.Y.C., 1944—50; acting instr. U. Wash., Seattle, 1961—63; asst. prof. U. Puget Sound, Tacoma, 1967—69, assoc. prof., 1970—77, prof. English, 1977—87, chair dept. English, 1970—75, dir. Writing Inst., 1976—86, dir. semester abroad, 1977, dir. Legal English program Sch. Law, 1973—77, disting. prof. emeritus, 1987—. Vis. prof. Gonzaga U., Pacific Luth. U., Whitman Coll., Willamette U., 1977. Author: Victorian Periodicals: A Guide to Research, Vol. I, 1978, Vol. II, 1989, George Eliot: A Centenary Tribute, 1982, Victorian Periodicals and Victorian Society, 1994, Periodicals of Queen Victoria's Empire, An Exploration, 1996, Florence Fenwick Miller: Victorian Feminist, Journalist, Educator, 2001, Victorian Periodicals, Aids to Research: A Selected Bibliography on the Internet (updated annually); mem. edit. bd. Wellesley Index to Victorian Periodicals, 1824-1900, 1968-88, A Union List of Victorian Serials, 1979-85, Victorian Rev., 1990—; contbr. articles to profl. jours. Recipient Doris Bronson Morrill award Kappa Kappa Gamma, 1982, Disting. Alumnae award Broadway H.S., Seattle, 1991. Fellow Royal Soc. Lit.; mem. MLA, Oxford Bibliog. Soc., Nat. Coun. Tchrs. English (Achievement awards, dir. 1974-77), Rsch. Soc. for Victorian Periodicals (pres. 1981-83). Home: 5051 50th Ave NE Apt 48 Seattle WA 98105-2863

**VANASEK, JAMES GEORGE,** commercial banker; b. Chgo., Jan. 20, 1944; s. James Harold and Virginia Edna (Von Asch) V.; m. Deborah Ann Zaccagnini, Nov. 28, 1975. AB, Ind. U., 1966; MBA, Penn State U., 1968. Sr. v.p. Pitts. Nat. Bank, 1968-79, Banc Ohio Nat. Bank, Columbus, 1979-84; exec. v.p. First Interstate Bank of Ariz., Phoenix; chief credit officer Norwest Bank; sr. v.p., chief credit risk officer Washington Mutual Inc., 1999—2001, exec. v.p., chief enterprise risk officer, 2001—04, chief enterprise risk officer, 2004—. Bd. dirs. Robert Morris Assocs., Phoenix, Assn. for Corporate Growth, Phoenix. Sgt. U.S. Army Res., 1968-74. Mem. Phi Beta Kappa. Republican. Home: 20547 NE 27th Pl Redmond WA 98074-4351 Office: Washington Mutual Inc 1201 3rd Ave Seattle WA 98101

**VANASKIE, THOMAS IGNATIUS,** federal judge; b. Shamokin, Pa., Nov. 11, 1953; s. John Anthony and Delores (Wesoloski) V.; m. Dorothy Grace Williams, Aug. 12, 1978; children: Diane, Laura, Thomas. BA magna cum laude, Lycoming Coll., 1975; JD cum laude, Dickinson U., 1978. Bar: Pa. 1978, U.S. Dist. (mid. dist.) Pa. 1980, U.S. Ct. Appeals (3d cir.) 1982, U.S. Supreme Ct. 1983. Law clk. to chief judge U.S. Dist. Ct. (mid. dist.) Pa., Scranton, 1978—80; assoc. Dilworth, Paxson, Kalish & Kauffman, Scranton, 1980—85, ptnr., 1986—92; prin. Elliott, Vanaskie & Riley, 1992—94; dist. judge U.S. Dist. Ct. (mid. dist.) Pa., 1994—99, chief judge, 1999—. Counsel Gov. Robert P. Casey Com., Harrisburg, Pa., 1987-92; chair Jud. Conf. Com. Info. Tech.; mem. Third Cir. Jud. Coun.; chair automation and tech. com. U.S. Cir. Ct. 3d cir., 2004, co-chair 3d cir. task force on info. resources, 1998—; lectr. in field. Contbr. articles to profl. jour. Mem. Scranton Waste Mgmt. Com., 1989; trustee Scranton Prep. Sch., 1997—. Recipient James A. Finnegan award, Finnegan Found. Mem. Judicature, Pa. Bar Assn., Fed. Judges Assn. (bd. dirs. 1998). Democrat. Avocations: golf, reading. Office: William J Nealon Fed Bldg & US Courthouse PO Box 913 235 N Washington Ave Scranton PA 18501

**VANATTA, BOB,** athletic administrator; b. Columbia, Mo., July 7, 1918; s. Claude W. and Viola (Toler) V.; m. Lois A. Williams; children: Robert, Thomas, Timothy. BA, Cent. Meth. Coll., 1942; MEd, U. Mo., 1949. Tchr., coach Boonville (Mo.) High Sch., 1942-43, Kemper Mil. Sch., Boonville, 1943-44, Springfield (Mo.) High Sch., 1944-47; tchr., dir. athletics, coach Ctrl. Meth. Coll., Fayette, Mo., 1947-50, S.W. Mo. State U. Springfield, 1950-53; coach U.S. Mil. Acad., West Point, NY, 1953-54; dir. athletics, coach Bardley U., Peoria, Ill., 1954-56; tchr., coach Memphis State U., 1956-62, U. Mo., Columbia, 1962-68; bank mktg. officer Empire Bank, Springfield, 1968-71; profl. basketball exec. dir. Memphis Pros, 1971-72; tchr., coach Delta State U., Cleve., 1972-73; dir. athletics Oral Roberts U., Tulsa, 1973-77; commr. Ohio Valley Athletic Conf., Nashville, 1977-80, Trans Am. Athletic Conf., Shreveport, La., 1980-83; dir. athletics La. Tech. U., Rustin, 1983-86; commr. Sunshine State Athletic Conf., Jupiter, Fla., 1986-94. Assoc. dir athletics Fla. Atlantic U. Author: Coaching Pattern Play Basketball, 1959; contbr. articles to profl. jours. Chpt. mem. Nat. Football Found. Named to Ctrl. Meth. Coll. Hall of Fame, S.W. Mo. State U. Hall of Fame, Nat. Athletic Intercollegiate Assn. Hall of Fame, Greater Springfield Hall of Fame, John Q. Hammons Mo. Sports Hall of Fame, U. Memphis Hall of Fame, Nat. Assn. Collegiate Dir. of Athletics, Nat. Assn. Collegiate Dir. of Athletics Hall of Fame, 1997; recipient Lifetime Achievement award in football All-Am. Football Found., 1997, NCAA Divsn. II Commrs. award Merit, 1999, Champions of Character award NAIA, 2002. Mem. Nat. Assn. Basketball Coaches, Nat. Football Coaches Assn., Nat. Assn. Collegiate Dirs. Athletics, All Am. Football Found. (Bud Dudley Outstanding Exec. award in Football, 2000, Asa Bushnell Commr. award 2001). Office: Apt 103 301 Ocean Bluffs Blvd Jupiter FL 33477-7329

**VANATTA, CHESTER B.,** management consultant, educator; b. Bartlesville, Oklahoma, Sept. 3, 1935; s. Benjamin Franklin and Iona Ruth (Hayes) V.; m. Patsy Lou (Straub), May 29, 1958; children: Tracy Ann, Christopher B., John Scott BS in Mktg., U. Kans., Lawrence, 1959, MS in Acctg., 1962; Advanced Mgmt. Program, Harvard U., Cambridge, Mass., 1972. Mem. staff Arthur Young and Co., Kansas City, Mo., 1962—69, regional dir. Dallas, 1969—72, ptnr., 1969—85, mng. ptnr. Chgo., 1972—76, dir., 1973—85, mng. ptnr., vice chmn. ops. N.Y.C., 1976—81, mng. ptnr., vice chmn. S.W. Region Dallas, 1981—85; exec. in residence, Paul J. Adam Disting. lectr. U. Kans. Sch. Bus., Lawrence, Mo., 1985—90; pres. Exec. Coms Group, Lawrence, Kans., 1985—96. Bd. dir. Atlantis Plastics, Inc., Miami., Fla. Trustee Kans. U. Endowment Fund, 1983-2005; bd. dir. Kans. Alumni Assn.

1984-91, pres., 1986-87. Mem. AICPA, Shangri La Country Club. Democrat. Avocations: golf, seminary, travel, auctioneering, photography. Home: 29990 S 567 Rd Monkey Island OK 74331-8180 Personal E-mail: chet@aboutvanatta.com.

**VAN ATTA, DAVID MURRAY,** lawyer; b. Berkeley, Calif., Oct. 20, 1944; s. Chester Murray and Rosalind (Eisenstein) Van A.; m. Jo Ann Masaoka; 1 child, Lauren Rachel. BA, U. Calif., Berkeley, 1966; JD, U. Calif., Hastings, 1969. Bar: Calif. 1970. Asst. gen. counsel Boise Cascade Corp., Palo Alto, Calif., 1970-73; ptnr. Miller, Starr & Regalia, San Francisco, 1973-87, Graham & James, San Francisco, 1987-93, Hanna & Van Atta, Palo Alto, 1993—. Instr. Golden Gate U., San Francisco, 1984-85; U. Calif., Berkeley, 1976-84. Author: (with Hanna) California Common Interest Developments Law and Practice, 1999. Mem. ABA, Am. Coll. Real Estate Lawyers (bd. govs., sec.), Calif. Bar Assn. (vice chmn. exec. com. real property law sect. 1982-85, chmn. condominium and subdivsn. com. real property law sect. 1981-83), Cmty. Assn. Inst., Urban Land Inst., Anglo-Am. Real Property Inst.(treas.), Rotary Club Palo Alto, Lambda Alpha Internat. Soc. Avocations: skiing, tennis, painting. Office: Hanna & Van Atta 525 University Ave Ste 705 Palo Alto CA 94301-1921

**VAN AUKEN, STUART,** marketing educator; b. Sherman, Tex., July 19, 1941; s. Frank Monroe and Sally (McCormick) Van A.; m. Linda Lou Nance, June 1, 1963 (div. Jan. 1980); children: Paige, Steve, Stacie. BBA, U. North Tex., 1964, PhD, 1970; MBA, So. Meth. U., 1966. Asst. prof. mktg. Tex. Tech U., Lubbock, 1969-72; disting. prof. mktg., chair dept. mktg. and bus. stats. U. Louisville, 1972-86; prof. mktg. Calif. State U., Chico, 1986—, dean Coll. Bus., 1986-90. Contbr. articles to profl. jours. Mem. Am. Mktg. Assn., Assn. for Consumer Rsch., Am. Acad. Advt. Republican. Presbyterian. Avocations: reading, jogging, weightlifting, bowling, sailing. Office: Calif State U Chico Dept Fin And Mktg Chico CA 95929-0001

**VAN BAALEN, DONNA GALE,** artist, retired pharmacist; b. Sterling, Colo., Jan. 29, 1930; d. Felix Thomas and Edna (Burgess) Ems; m. Chase Van Baalen, June 20, 1954 (dec. Jan. 1988); children: Patricia, Aaron, Julie. BS in Pharmacy, U. Tex., Austin, 1954. Mem.: South Tex. Miniature Art Soc., Corpus Christi Art Guild, Art Ctr. Corpus Christi, World Fedn. Miniaturists, Hilliard Soc. Miniaturists, Miniature Art Soc. Fla., Miniature Artists Am. Home: 116 N 11 PO Box 417 Port Aransas TX 78373 Personal E-mail: dvanbd@netscape.net.

**VAN BEEK, ALLEN LESTER,** plastic surgeon; b. Westfield, N.D., Jan. 21, 1943; m. Sharon Van Beek; children: Gregory, Troy, Jeremy. MD, U. Minn., 1968. Cert. Am. Bd. Plastic Surgery, 1979. Intern Brooke Army Gen. Hosp., San Antonio, 1968—69; resident, gen. surgery Ind. U. Sch. Medicine, Indpls., 1971—75; resident, plastic surgery So. Ill. U., Springfield, 1976—78; fellow U. Louisville, 1975; clin. assoc. prof., dept. surgery U. Minn. Med. Sch., Mpls.; pres. Plastic Surgery Ednl. Found., 2003—. Flight surgeon U.S. Army, 1969—71, Vietnam. Mem.: Am. Soc. Plastic Surgeons, Am. Cleft Palate-Craniofacial Assn., Am. Coll. Surgeons, Am. Assn. Hand Surgery. Office: 7373 France Ave S Ste 510 Edina MN 55435

**VAN BEEM, JANNY,** geneticist, researcher; d. Gilbert van Beem and Graciela Sanchez de van Beem; m. Fred Harwood, Jan. 4, 1990; children: Maya Harwood, Alani Harwood. PhD, Cornell U., NY, 1990—95. Scientist CIMMYT, Internat., Mexico City, 1996—2002. Contbr. articles to profl. jours. Rsch. grant for wheat breeding program, German Govt., 1998—2002. Home: 5007 Riverside Oaks Dr Kingwood TX 77345 Personal E-mail: jvanbeem@kingwoodcable.net.

**VANBEMMELEN, PAUL S.,** surgeon, educator; b. The Hague, Netherlands, Sept. 13, 1956; s. Anthonius M. and Estera StruickvanBemmelen; m. Daphne G. Geiringer, June 10, 1979; children: Lauren Rebecca, Jeremy Daniel, Joel Noah, Jonah Gabriel. MD, Rijksuniversiteit Leiden, 1972, PhD, 1978. Cert. Surgeon European Cmty., 1988, Vascular Surgeon Netherlands Bd. of Surgeons, 1991. Assoc. prof. surgery SUNY, Stony Brook, 1998—2003; chief vascular surgery VA Med. Ctr., Northport, NY, 1998—2003; assoc. prof. surgery Temple U., Phila., 2004—. Author: (jours. vascular surgery/tech.) Venous valve incompetence (Young Investigator Award -Soc. Vascular Tech., 1990). Lt. Royal Dutch Navy, 1980—81. Fellow: Soc. Vascular Surgery (disting.). Achievements include patents for Arterial Assist Device: ArtAssist. Avocation: classic sportscars. Office: Temple Univ Dept Surgery 3401 N Broad St Philadelphia PA 19140 Office Phone: 215-707-3622.

**VAN BOGAERT, CYNTHIA A.,** lawyer; BS in Math., U. Wis., 1980, JD, 1982; postgrad., U. Chgo., 1990-93. Bar: Wis. 1983, Ill. 1988. Atty. U.S. Steel Corp., Pitts. and Dallas, Peoples Gas, Chgo., Inland Steel Industries, Inc., Chgo., Adminstrv. Mgmt. Group, Arlington Heights, Ill., 1994-96, Boardman, Suhr, Curry & Field LLP, Madison, Wis., 1996—. Co-author: 401(k) Plans, 2000—. Mem. State of Wis. Employee Trust Funds Bd., 1998—2006. Mem. WEB (pres. Madison, Wis. chpt. 1998-99, nat. dir.-at-large 1998-2000, nat. pres. 2000-02, past pres. 2002-04), ABA, Wis. Bar Assn., Dane County Bar Assn., Chgo. Bar Assn., Legal Assn. Women. Office Phone: 608-283-7543. Business E-Mail: cvanbog@boardmanlawfirm.com.

**VAN BOKKELEN, JOSEPH SCOTT,** prosecutor; b. Chgo., June 7, 1943; s. Robert W. and W. Louise (Reynolds) Van B.; m. Sally Wardall Huey, Aug. 14, 1971; children— Brian, Kate. B.A., U. Ind., 1966, J.D., 1969. Bar: Ind. 1969, US Dist. Ct. (so. dist.) Ind. 1969, US Dist. Ct. (no. dist.) Ind. 1973, US Ct. Appeals (7th cir.) 1973, US Supreme Ct. 1973. Dep. atty. gen. State of Ind., Indpls., 1969-71, asst. atty. gen., 1971-72; asst. US atty. (no. dist.) Ind., Hammond, 1972-75; ptnr. Goldsmith, Goodman, Ball & Van Bokkelen, Highland, Ind., 1975—2001; US atty. (no. dist.) Ind., 2001—. Recipient Outstanding Asst. US Atty. award US Dept. Justice, 1974. Mem. ABA, Fed. Bar Assn., Ind. Bar Assn., Criminal Def. Lawyers Assn. Home: 1744 Poplar Ln Munster IN 46321-3849 Office: US Attys Office 5400 Federal Plz Hammond IN 46320*

**VAN BORM, JULIEN LUDOVICUS ADELIA,** library director; b. Lippelo, Antwerpen, Belgium, Feb. 16, 1942; s. Albert and Clothilde (Van Aken) Van B.; m. Anny El. Peers, Dec. 15, 1972; children: Johan, Wim, Toon. Licentiat in History, U. Leuven, Belgium, 1965. Dep. curator KU-Leuven Ctrl. Libr., 1967-70, UCL-Ctrl. Libr., Louvain, Belgium, 1971-72; dep. dir. U. Antwerp (Belgium) Uia-Libr., 1972-88; dir. U. Antwerp (Belgium) Via-Libr., 1989—, pres. bd. libr. automation network 1989—. CEC expert European Commn., Brussels, 1992—; pres Flemish Pub. Librs. Coun., 2000—. Contbr. articles to profl. jours. Mem. Conf. U. Librs., Belgian Nat. Focal Point CEC-Librs. Program, CEC Nat. Focal Points Conf. Avocations: reading, gardening, walking. Home: Fort VI Straat 150 B 2610 Antwerp Belgium Office: U Antwerp Uia Libr PO Box 13 B 2610 Antwerp Belgium

**VAN BOSSE, HAROLD J.P.,** orthopedic surgeon; MD, U. Ill., 1984—89. Cert. Orthopedic Surgery, 1997. Residence orthopedics U. Ill., Chgo.; fellow Hosp. for Sick Children, Toronto, 1994—95; surgeon Schneider Children's Hosp. Long Island Jewish Med. Ctr.; pediatric orthopedic surgeon NYU Hosp. for Joint Diseases, 1998—; asst. prof. orthopaedic surgery N YU Med. Ctr. Founder A Leg to Stand On, India, 2003; vol. surgeon Silver Service Children's program, Colombia. Named one of Medical Marvels, New York Mag., 2006. Mailing: Hosp for Joint Diseases 301 East 17 St New York NY 10003 Office Phone: 212-598-2310. Office Fax: 212-598-2311.*

**VAN BRUGGEN, COOSJE,** artist, writer; b. Groningen, The Netherlands, June 6, 1942; came to U.S., 1978, naturalized, 1993; d. J.A.R. Van Bruggen and A.M. Andriessen; m. Claes Oldenburg, July 22, 1977. MS in Art History, Rijks U. of Groningen, 1967; DFA (hon.), Calif. Coll. Art and Craft, 1996; DLitt (hon.), U. Teesside, Middlesbrough, Eng., 1999; DFA, Nova Scotia Coll. Art and Design, Halifax, 2005. Asst. curator Stedelijk Mus., Amsterdam, The Netherlands, 1967-71; prof. Acad. Fine Arts, Enschede, The Netherlands, 1971-76; sr. critic dept. sculpture Yale U., New Haven, 1996-97. Co-editor

Catalogue Sonsbeek, 1971; mem. selection com. Documenta 7, Kassel, Germany, 1982; curator (with Dieter Koepplin) Bruce Nauman: Drawings, 1965-1986, Basel, Switzerland, 1986-88. Author: Bruce Nauman, 1989, John Baldessari, 1990, Frank O. Gehry: Guggenheim Museum Bilbao, 1997; co-author (with Claes Oldenburg): Claes Oldenburg: Sketches and Blottings Toward the European Desk Top, 1990, Large-Scale Projects, 1994, Claes Oldenburg Coosje van Bruggen, 1999, Down Liquidambar Lane: Sculpture in the Park, 2001; co-author: (with Claes Oldenburg and Frank O. Gehry) Il Corso del Coltello, 1985; two-person shows (with Claes Oldenburg) No. Ctr. Contemporary Art, Sunderland, 1988, Leeds City Art Gallery, 1988, Palais des Beaux-Arts, Brussels, 1988, IVAM Ctr. Julio González, Valencia, 1988, Galleria Christian Stein, Milan, 1990, Leo Castelli Gallery, N.Y.C., 1990, Pace Gallery, 1994, Venice Biennale, 1997, Museo Correr, Venice, 1999, Museu Serralves, Porto, 2001, Metropolitan Mus. Art, N.Y.C., 2002, PaceWildenstein, 2003, Frederik Meijer Gardens and Sculpture Park, Grand Rapids, Mich., 2002; Paula Cooper Gallery, 2004, Pace Wildenstein Gallery, 2005, exhibited in group shows at Guggenheim Mus., N.Y.C., 1993, Nat. Gallery, London, 2000, others; contbr. Artforum, 1983—88, sculptor numerous pub. sculptures, including Nollen Plz. Civic Ctr., Des Moines, Mpls. Sculpture Garden, Walker Art Ctr., Mpls., Parc de la Villette, Paris, Ctrl. Gardens, Middlesborough, Eng., Guggenheim Found., others. Recipient Distinction in Sculpture, Sculpture Ctr., N.Y.C., 1984, Nathaniel S. Saltonstall award, ICA, Boston, 1996, Nat. Medal award, Sch. of Mus. Fine Arts, Boston, 2004.

**VAN BRUNT, ARTHUR HOFFMAN (PETER),** economist, educator; b. Orange, Nj, May 27, 1942; s. Arthur Hoffman Van Brunt, Jr. and Mary Harrison Van Brunt; m. Debi Sue Stec, Oct. 10, 1999; children: Justin, Kristina Elena. BA in Econs., Tufts Univ., 1965; MBA, Wharton Sch., 1967. Coop. vol. Peace Corps, Barquisimito, Venezuela, 1967—69; tng. ctr. dir. BASICO, Inc., San Jose, Costa Rica, 1970—75; asst. v.p Manufacturer's Hanover Trust Co., NYC, 1976—80; dir. strategic planning Save the Children Fedn., Westport, Conn., 1980—84; regional manager-latin am. CARE, Inc., NYC, 1984—89; prof. SUNY, Delhi, 1990—2005. Cons. CARE, Inc., NYC, 1991, Save the Children Fedn., Westport, 1992—93, Lawyers in Delaware County, NY, 1991—. Contbr. articles to profl. jours. Treas., v.p., pres., adv. bd. mem. Habitat for Humanity, Delaware County, NY, 1990; treas., v.p., exec. bd. United U. Professors of Delhi, Delhi, 2000. Mem.: Nat. Bus. Edn. Assn., Tchrs. of Acctg. at Two Yr. Colls. Avocations: reading, bicycling, chess, tennis. Office: SUNY Sanford Hall Delhi NY 13753 Home: 527 SW Sundance Trl Port Saint Lucie FL 34953-8223 E-mail: vanbruap@delhi.edu.

**VAN BRUNT, EDMUND EWING,** physician; b. Oakland, Calif., Apr. 28, 1926; s. Adrian W. and Kathryn Anne (Shattuck) Van B.; m. Claire Monod, Feb. 28, 1949; children: Karin, Deryk, Jahn. BA in Biophysics, U. Calif., Berkeley, 1952; MD, U. Calif., San Francisco, 1959; ScD (hon.), U. Toulouse, France, 1978. Postdoctoral fellow NIH, 1961-63; rsch. assoc. U. Calif., San Francisco, 1963-67; staff physician Kaiser Permanente Med. Ctr., San Francisco, 1964-91; dir. div. rsch. Kaiser Permanente Med. Program, Oakland, Calif., 1979-91; assoc. dir. Kaiser Found. Rsch. Inst., Oakland, 1985-91, sr. cons., 1991—; Kaiser Permanente Med. Program No. Calif. region. Adj. prof. U. Calif., San Francisco, 1975-92; chmn. instnl. rev. bd. Kaiser Permanente No. Calif. region, 1986-. Contbr. articles to profl. books and jours. Mem. bd. dirs Alameda County Meals on Wheels, 2004—; pres. bd. trustees French Found. Med. Res. & Edn., San Francisco, 1994-98. With U.S. Army, 1944—46. Fellow ACP, Am. Coll. Med. Informatics; mem. Calif. Med. Assn., U. Calif. San Francisco Emeritus Faculty Assn. Avocations: flying, photography, swimming. Office Phone: 510-625-3431. Personal E-mail: e.vanbrunt@comcast.net.

**VAN BRUNT, GARY T.,** tire dealer company executive; Asst mgr. to mgr., 2d Phoenix store Discount Tire Co. Inc., Scottsdale, Ariz., 1970—77, asst. v.p. Ariz. region, 1977—80, v.p. purchasing. We. region, 1980—85, sr. v.p. purchasing, all regions, 1985—97, exec. v.p. co. ops., 1997—99, CEO, 1999—2004, vice chmn., 2004—. Office: Discount Tire Co Inc 20225 N Scottsdale Rd Scottsdale AZ 85255*

**VAN BRUNT, WILLIAM A.,** lawyer; m. Gail Van Brunt; 3 children. BS with honors, Pa. State U.; grad., MIT; JD, Boston U.; grad., Harvard U. Rschr. AVCO Rsch. and Develop.; sr. v.p., gen. counsel Carlson Cos., Minnetonka, Minn., 2000—. Office: Carlson Cos 701 Carlson Pkwy Minnetonka MN 55305 E-mail: bvanbrunt@carlson.com.

**VANBRUNT-KRAMER, KAREN,** business administration educator; b. Milw., May 1, 1934; D. Roy Charles and Viola Marguerita (Yerges) VanBrunt; m. Allen Lloyd Weitermann (div. 1963); 1 child, Tera Lee Johnson; m. Keith Kramer (div. 1979); children: Holden Jon, Stafford James. BS, U. Wis., 1956; MA, NYU, 1976; PhD, Ohio State U., 1992. Owner Design By Karen Lee, Larchmont, NY, 1975—82; interior designer Maurice Vallency Design, N.Y.C., 1976—79; grad. rsch. assoc. Ctr. on Edn. and Tng. for Employment, Columbus, Ohio, 1987—92; assoc. prof. bus. adminstrn. St. Joseph Coll., West Hartford, Conn., 1992—99. Lectr. and curriculum developer entrepreneurship state vocat. schs., high schs., colls., and univs. throughout U.S. and Ea. Europe, 1987-92; instr. Berkeley Sch., White Plains, N.Y., 1968-82; adj. instr. N.Y.C. C.C., 1979-83, Milw. Area Tech. Coll., 1983-85, Columbus State C.C., 1986-90, Capital U., Columbus, 1998, U. Wis. Milw., Mt. Mary Coll., Milw.; participant Women in Soc. Citizen Amb. Program to China, 1997, leader Women in Exec. Mgmt. Bus., 1998; mem. Inst. World Affairs, U. Wis., Milw., 1999—. Mem. Wadsworth Atheneum, Hartford, 1992—99, West Hartford Art League, 1993—99; vol. U. Conn. Health Ctr., Farmington, Little Sisters of the Poor, St. Joseph Residence, Enfield, Conn., 1989—92, Milw. Art Mus.; docent Columbus Symphony Orch., 1986—92; mem. women's guild First Cmty. Ch., Columbus, 1985—92. Mem.: NAFE, AAUW (past social chair Wis. br.), AAUP (membership chair 1993—97), Svc. Corp. of Ret. Exec., Omicron Tau Theta, World Federalist Assn., Nat. Edn. Ctr. for Women in Bus. (Milw. sec./treas. 2001—03), Am. Mgmt. Assn., Am. Mktg. Assn., Coalition for Effective Orgns., Ohio Vocat. Assn., Am. Vocat. Assn., World Affairs Coun., Mil. Intercity Congregations Allied for Hope (bd. dirs. 2005—), Peace Seekers (Peace Action and Steering com.) 2004—), Citizens for Global Solutions (treas. 2004—), Delta Pi Epsilon, Phi Delta Kappa, Phi Lambda Theta, Phi Kappa Phi, Phi Beta Kappa. Avocations: theater, art, music, photography, ice dancing. Home: 125 N University Dr Unit 322S West Bend WI 53095-2954

**VAN BULCK, HENDRIKUS EUGENIUS,** accountant; b. Beek en Donk, The Netherlands, Dec. 13, 1950; came to U.S., 1972; s. Marcellus Maria and Josephina Theodora (Koelman) Van B.; m. Margaret West, Aug. 7, 1976; children: Marcel Allen, Sydney Josette. Grad., Nijenrode, The Netherlands, 1972; MBA, U. Ga., 1974, PhD in Bus. Adminstrn., 1979. CPA, S.C. Cert. Int. U. S.C., Sumter, 1975-77; asst. prof. Clemson (S.C.) U., 1977-80; chmn. dept., assoc. prof. St. Andrew's Presbyn. Coll., Laurinburg, NC, 1980-83; staff acct. L. Allen West, CPA, Sumter, 1983-84; ptnr. West & Van Bulck, CPAs, Sumter, 1984-88, Van Bulck & Co., Sumter, 1989—. Part time instr. U. S.C., Sumter, 1983-85; cons. med. practice mgmt./bus. valuations. Contbr. articles to profl. jours. Chmn. Make-a-Wish Found., Midlands, S.C., 1983-90; asst. scout master and dist. com. chmn. Boy Scouts Am.; treas. YMCA, Sumter, S.C.; mem. exec. com., fin. com. Pee Dee Area Coun. Recipient Mktg. award Netherlands Ctr. of Dirs., 1972. Mem. AICPA (accredited in bus. valuation 1999), S.C. Assn. CPAs, Ga. Soc. CPAs, Physicians Viewpoint Network, Kiwanis (pres. Sumter chpt. 1996-97), Med. Group Mgmt. Assn., Beta Gamma Sigma. Presbyterian. Avocations: sailing, photography. Home: 234 Haynsworth PO Box 1327 Sumter SC 29151-1327 Office: Van Bulck & Co CPAs 15 Broad St Sumter SC 29150-4224 Office Phone: 803-775-3600. Business E-Mail: hennie@vanbulckCPAs.com.

**VAN BUREN, ABIGAIL (JEANNE PHILLIPS),** columnist, educator; b. Mpls., Apr. 10, 1942; d. Morton and Pauline (Friedman) Phillips, (the founder of the Dear Abby advice column in 1956). Student, U. Colo., 1960—62. Writer Dear Abby Radio Show, CBS, 1965—71; columnist Dear Abby, 1987—. Bd. mem. Planned Parenthood of Los Angeles, 1989—90; life-time cons. Group for Advancement of Psychiatry, 1995—; bd. adv. Alzheimers Assn. of Los Angeles, 1996—; bd. mem. Rose and Jay Phillips Found., 1991—, ACLU of So. Calif. Found., 1998—; adv. bd. L.A. Internat. Women's Media Found. Courage in Journalism, 2000—; bd. adv. UCLA Med. Ctr., Ctr. for Rsch. and Training in Humane and Ethical Med. Care (CHEC), 2000—. Bd. advs. Planned Parenthood Fedn. Am., 2004; bd. judges Talbot's Charitable Found. Women's Scholarship Fund, 2006—; mem. White House Commn. Rememberance; bd. dirs. Planned Parenthood of LA, 1989—90, MADD, 2003—, Children's Rights Coun., 2003—; mem. Leadership Coun. Aids Project, LA, 2004; bd. dirs. Nat. Kidney Found., 2004. Recipient Generations of Choice award, Planned Parenthood of L.A., 1999, Minority Organ/Tissue Transplant Edn. Program (MOTTEP) Key of Life award, Howard U., Wash. D.C., 2000, Award of Appreciation, U.S. Gen. Svcs. Adminstrn. Fed. Consumer Info. Ctr., 2000, Star on Hollywood Walk of Fame for Dear Abby Radio Show, 2001, Recognition by the Office of Nat. Drug Control Policy (ONDCP), award from the White House and Substance Abuse and Mental Health Svcs. Adminstrn. for help in launching Nat. Inhalants and Poisons Awareness Week, 2001, Erasing the Stigma Leadership award, Didi Hirsch Mental Health Ctr., 2001, MOTTEP Award of Excellence, 2001, Commendation for Operation Dear Abby and OperationDearAbby.net, Dept. Navy and USMC, 2002, Appreciation for support of the military svc. mems. of the U.S. for Operation Dear Abby and OperationDearAbby.net, Space and Naval Warfare Sys. Ctr. (SPAWAR), 2002, Alzheimer's Assn. Maureen Reagan Advocacy Award, 2003, Appreciation award, Overeaters Anonymous, 2003, Advocacy award, Alzheimer's Assn. L.A., 2003, award of Appreciation, U.S. GSA Fed. Citizen Info. Ctr., 2004. Mem.: Nat. Adv. Coun. of Alzheimers Assn. Syndicated in the U.S., Brazil, Mex., Japan, Philippines, Fed. Republic Germany, India, Holland, Denmark, Can., Korea, Thailand, Italy, Hong Kong, Taiwan, Ireland, Saudi Arabia, Greece, France, Dominican Republic, P.R., Costa Rica, U.S. Virgin Islands, Bermuda, China, Kuwait and Guam; published on the Internet at DearAbby.com and OperationDearAbby.net for messages to the military. Office: Philips-Van Buren Inc Ste 2710 1900 Ave of the Stars Los Angeles CA 90067

**VANBUREN, CAROLYN JEAN,** special education educator; d. Joseph A. and Hannah Caroline Meyers; m. Robert Mathew Simons, Sept. 1, 2001; children: Garrick Rhett, Kari Jane. BS magna cum laude, Bemidji State U., 1972; MS with honors in Edn., U. Wis., 1987. Cert. mentally retarded tchr. Wis. Dept. Pub. Instrn., 1978, early childhood-exceptional needs tchr. Wis. Dept. Pub. Instrn., 1978, 1st-8th grade tchr. Wis. Dept. Pub. Instrn., 1978. Spl. edn. tchr. Anoka Sch. Dist., Minn., 1972—74, Rice Lake Sch. Dist., Wis., 1980—; spl. edn. cons. Coop. Ednl. Svc. Agy., Cumberland, 1975—76; exceptional edn. early childhood tchr. Turtle Lake Sch. Dist., 1976—78. Ednl. cons. Countryway Group Home, Cameron, Wis., 1984—87; home health care worker Gemini, Richfield, Wis., 2004, Indianhead, Barron, Wis., 2000—00; group home house parent Ag-Ri-Cove, Cameron, 2000—. Vol. Spl. Olympics, Barron County, 2000—01; pub. rels. rep. First Luth. Ch., Barron, 2001—05. Mem.: NEA (assoc.), Wis. Edn. Assn. (assoc.). Democrat-Npl. Lutheran. Avocations: travel, interior design, walking, yoga, gardening. Personal E-mail: carolyn@rmsimons.com.

**VANBUREN, DENISE DORING,** corporate communications executive; b. Troy, N.Y., May 15, 1961; d. James L. and Eunice A. (Myers) Doring; m. Steven Paul VanBuren, Apr. 1, 1989; children: Schuyler Paul, Troy James Doring, Brett Steven VanBuren. BA in Mass Comm. magna cum laude, St. Bonaventure U., 1983; MBA, Mount St. Mary Coll., 1997. Reporter, news anchor Sta. WGNY-AM-FM, Newburgh, NY, 1982—; news dir., anchor NewsCtr. 6, Dutchess County, NY, 1985-90; dir. media rels. Ctrl. Hudson Gas & Electric, Poughkeepsie, NY, 1993—, mgr. corp. comms., 1998-99, asst. v.p. corp. comm., 1999-2000, v.p. corp. comm. and cmty. rels., 2000—. Adj. prof. Marist Coll., Poughkeepsie, NY. Co-author: Historic Beacon, 1998, Beacon Revisited, 2003. Councilwoman City of Beacon, 1992-93, chmn. 85th anniversary celebration; pres. Beacon Hist. Soc., 1989-94; bd. dirs. Locust Grove Hist. Site, Stony Kill Found., Inc.; chmn. Dutchess County United Way Campaign, 2005. Recipient Salute to Women in Bus. & Industry award D.C. YWCA, 1990, 97, Outstanding Chpt. Regent award N.Y. State orgn. DAR, 1999, Dutchess award, Dutchess County Hist. Soc., 2005; named Vol. of Yr. award, City of Beacon, 1999. Mem.: DAR (vice regent Melzingah chpt. 1990—98, regent 1998—2001, chmn. state historian com. NY state 1998—2001, nat. chmn. PR 1999—2004, editor-in-chief, Am. Spirit mag.). Greater So. Dutchess C.C. (bd. dirs.), Nat. Soc. Daus. of Union Vets. of the Civil War, Exch. Club of So. Dutchess (bd. dirs.). Republican. Roman Catholic. Avocations: genealogy, needlecrafts. Office: CH Energy Group Inc 284 South Ave Poughkeepsie NY 12601-4838

**VAN BUREN, WILLIAM BENJAMIN, III,** retired pharmaceutical executive; b. Bklyn., Mar. 25, 1922; s. William Benjamin and Dorothy Marjorie (Way) Van B.; m. Joan Cottrell Whitford, Sept. 11, 1948 (dec. June 1997); children— Susan (dec.), Patricia, William S., Richard W.; m. Norma A. Sutton, Mar. 6, 1990. BA, Washington and Lee U., 1944; LLB, Yale U., 1949. Bar: N.Y. 1950. V.p., sec. Merck & Co., Inc., 1976-86; pres. Merck & Co. Found., 1982-86. Served with USNR, 1943-46. Mem. Phi Beta Kappa. Home: 1035C Long Beach Blvd Beach Haven NJ 08008-5620

**VAN BUSKIRK, RONALD E.,** lawyer; b. Santa Fe, N. Mex., Oct. 19, 1946; BA, Stanford Univ., 1968; JD, Univ. Mich., 1974. Bar: Calif. 1975, US Dist Ct. (ea., no., ctrl., so. dist. Calif.), US Ct. Claims, US Ct. Appeals (9th cir.). Assoc. to ptnr. Pillsbury Winthrop Shaw Pittman, San Francisco, 1975—, gen. counsel, chmn. Profl. Responsibility com. Founding mem. Law Firm Gen. Counsel Roundtable; bd. dir. Pacific Legal Found., 1994—, MPC Insurance Ltd., 1995—. Served U.S. Army, 1968—71. Office: Pillsbury Winthrop Shaw Pittman 50 Fremont St San Francisco CA 94105 Office Phone: 415-983-1496. Office Fax: 415-983-1200. Business E-Mail: ronald.vanbuskirk@pillsburylaw.com

**VAN BUSKIRK, WILLIAM CHARLES,** engineering educator; b. Mayfield, Utah, Mar. 11, 1942; s. Ellis Cornelius Van Buskirk and Edith Whitlock; m. Joyous Ann Moore, June 4, 1964; children: William Charles Van Buskirk, Jr., Christopher Todd. BS, U.S. Mil. Acad., West Point, N.Y., 1964; MS, Stanford U., Calif., 1966; PhD, Stanford U., 1970. Registered profl. engr. La., 1972. Prof. and head of biomed. engring. Tulane U., New Orleans, 1977—91, dean of engring., 1991—98; provost N.J. Inst. of Tech., Newark, 1998—2004, disting. prof., 2004—. Fellow: Biomedical Engring. Soc., Am. Inst. of Med. and Biol. Engring., ASME. Home: 94 Washington Ave Carteret NJ 07008 Office: New Jersey Institute of Technology Department of Biomedical Engineering Newark NJ 07102 Office Phone: 973-596-8380. Personal E-mail: vanb@comcast.net. E-mail: vanbuskirk@njit.edu.

**VANBUTSEL, MICHAEL R.,** real estate broker, construction executive; b. Alma, Nebr., Dec. 7, 1952; s. Julius and Margaret (McCorkle) VanB.; m. Susan Parsons; children: Jamie, Krysta, Alexis. BArch, U. Nebr., 1975. Lic. real estate broker Fla. V.p. devel. J.C. Nichols Co. Real Estate, St. Petersburg, Fla., 1987-96; pres. North Star Devel., St. Petersburg, 1996—; real estate mgr., designated broker Danka Office Imaging, 1998-99; v.p., project exec. Beers Skanska USA Bldg. Co., Tampa, Fla., 1999—2004; project mgr. Tower divsn. Taylor Woodrow Cmtys., 2004—06; v.p. The Beach Residences Condominiums The Ritz Carlton Beach Club, 2004—06; sr. project mgr. tower divsn. WCI Cmtys. Inc., Palm Beach Gardens, Fla., 2006—. Chair Environ. Devel. Commn., St. Petersburg, 2003-04; chair cmty. advancement coun. U. So. Fla., St. Petersburg, 1998—2004. Housing commr. City of Phoenix; mem. Paradise Valley Planning Com.; bd. dirs. Am. Stage Theater, Cmty. Water Leadership Program; chmn. facilities and strategic planning com. U. South Fla., St. Petersburg, 1999—2002, chmn. acad. planning com.; bd. dirs. Pinellas Econ. Devel. Coun.; vice-chair environ. adv. com. S.W. Fla. Water Mgmt. Dist., 2002—; Pinellas adv. bd. ARC; allocations com. United Way, 1998—2000; mem. Real Estate Investment Coun., St. Petersburg USA and Russia Birthday Commemoration, 2002—03, Pinellas County Transp. Task Force, Pinellas Redevel. Task Force; mem. CEO search com. U. South Fla., St. Petersburg; chair legis. affairs com. devel. coun. All Children's Hosp.; pres. Mariners for Sen. John McCain, Ariz.; surrogate spkr. for

Congressman Eldon Rudd; mem. Senate roundtable Sen. Connie Mack, Fla.; Westside campaign chair Rick Baker for Mayor, 2001; mem. Ivory Club Pinellas County Rep. Party, 2001—05, Pinellas County Assembly, 2002; bd. dirs. Gran Prix St. Petersburg 2003 Found. Mem. Fla. Gulfcoast Comml. Assn. Realtors, Pinellas Leadership (mem. selection com. 2003), Leadership Tampa Bay, St. Petersburg C. of C. (chair environ. com., chair transp. com.), Valley Leadership (Phoenix). Republican. Avocations: gourmet cooking, geo-political books, tai chi. Office: WCI Cmtys Inc 11601 Kew Gardens Ave Palm Beach Gardens FL 33410 Office Phone: 727-563-9882, 561-340-1100. Personal E-mail: michaelvb4@yahoo.com. Business E-Mail: michael.vanbutsel@us.taylorwoodrow.com, michaelvanbutsel@wcicommunities.com.

**VANCAMP, ALOHA,** education educator; d. Henry Jerome Ruddy and Aloha Keywood; 1 child, Christine. BA, Wayne State U., Detroit, PhD, 2003. Co-chair, assoc. prof. U. Detroit Mercy, dean Weekend Coll. Bd. Cmtys. in Schs., Detroit. Business E-Mail: vancampa@ud.mercy.edu.

**VAN CAMP, BRIAN RALPH,** judge; b. Halstead, Kans., Aug. 23, 1940; s. Ralph A. and Mary Margaret (Bragg) Van C.; m. Diane D. Miller, 1992; children: M. Megan, Laurie E. AB, U. Calif., Berkeley, 1962, LLB, 1965. Bar: Calif. 1966. Dep. atty. gen., Calif., 1965-67; agy. atty. Redevel. Agy., City of Sacramento, 1967-70; asst./acting sec. Bus. and Trans. Agy., State of Calif., 1970-71; commr. of corps. State of Calif., Sacramento, 1971-74; partner firm Diepenbrock, Wulff, Plant & Hannegan, Sacramento, 1975-77, Van Camp & Johnson, Sacramento, 1978-90; sr. ptnr. Downey, Brand, Seymour & Rohwer, 1990-97; judge Superior Ct. Calif., Sacramento County, 1997—. Lectr. Continuing Edn. Bar, Practicing Law Inst., Calif. CPA Soc., Calif. Ctr. for Jud. Edn. and Rsch. Contbr. articles to profl. jours. Mem. Rep. State Ctrl. Com. Calif., 1974-78; mem. electoral coll. Presdl. Elector for State of Calif., 1976; mem. Calif. Health Facilities Fin. Authority, 1985-89; mem. Capital Area Devel. Authority, 1989-97, chmn., 1990-97; mem. Calif. Jud. Coun. Task Force on Quality of Justice, 1998-99, Jud. Coun. Adv. Com. on Civil and Small Claims Law, 2002—, chair subcom. uniform rules, 2004-; bd. dirs. Sacramento Symphony Assn., 1973-85, Sacramento Symphony Found., 1993-2003, Sacramento Area Commerce and Trade Orgn., pres. 1986-87, Sacramento Valley Venture Capital Forum, 1986-90, League to Save Lake Tahoe, 1988-95, Valley Vision, Inc., 1993-97; elder Fremont Presbyn. Ch., 1967-. Recipient Sumner-Mering Meml. award Sacramento U. Calif. Alumni Assn., 1962, Thos. Jefferson award Am. Inst. Pub. Svc., 1994, Excellence in Achievement award Calif. Alumni Assn., 1997; named Outstanding Young Man of Yr., Sacramento Jaycees, 1970, Internat. Young Man of Yr., Active 20-30 Club Internat., 1973, Judge of Yr., Capitol City Trial Lawyers Assn., 2003. Mem. Boalt Hall Alumni Assn. (bd. dirs. 1991-94), Lincoln Club Sacramento Valley (bd. dirs. 1975-90, pres. 1984-86), U. Calif Men's Club (pres. 1968), Sutter Club, Kanadhar Ski Club, Rotary Club Sacramento (pres. 1993-94, Paul Harris Fellow award 1995), Comstock Club (pres. 1976-77). Republican. Presbyterian. Office: 720 9th St Sacramento CA 95814-1302 Office Phone: 916-874-8030. Business E-Mail: vancamp@saccourt.com.

**VAN CAMPEN, STEPHEN BERNARD,** executive recruiter, consultant; b. East Stroudsburg, Pa., Oct. 1, 1941; s. Bernard Allen and Marion (Van Whye) Van C.; m. Ellen Baars, July 22, 1989; children: Brendon, Regan, Meghan, Taylor, Hannah. BS in Sci. and Pre-Veterinary Med., Pa. State U., 1959-64; postgrad. in indsl. rels., George Washington U. Grad. Sch., 1965-68; law student, U. Balt., 1966-68. With FDA, Balt., Washington, 1964-66; indsl. rels. officer Joseph E. Seagrams & Sons, Balt., N.Y.C., San Francisco, 1966-72; worldwide dir. exec. staffing RCA/Hertz Corp., N.Y.C., 1972-74; dir. internat. indsl. rels. Revlon Internat., N.Y.C., 1974; pres., owner, cons. Gilbert & Van Campen Exec. Search, Internat. (subs.: J.B. Gilbert Assocs., Inc., Amtrade Assocs., Internat., GVC Fin. Svcs.), N.Y.C., 1974—; past owner, pres. Lillagaard Hotel Corp., Ocean Grove, NJ, 1992—; owner N.J. Profl. Meeting Planners Group; chmn. No. Shore Region Convention and Vis. Bur., Encore Svcs., Hackettstown, NJ, 1999—; pres. spl. investigations and verificatiuons divsn. Van Campen Assoc. Internat., 2003—. Appointed to N.J. Gov.'s Commn. on Internat. Trade, 1992; Bush White House nominee to Nat. Parks Adv. Commn., Dept. Interior; chmn. internat. trade subcom. ad hoc N.J. Assembly Small Bus. Adv. Coun.; bd. dirs. N.J. SBDC, N.J. Shore Region Tourism Coun.; named to Commerce and Econ. Devel. Transition Team for Gov.-elect Christine Todd Whitman; chmn. Econ. Devel. Task Force, Warren County, N.J., 1994; participant in meetings with Pres. Castro 1st U.S.-Cuba Bus. Summit, Havanna, 1998. Rep. fundraiser; active N.J. Rep. Gov.'s Club, N.J. State Fin. Com.; appointed to Congressman Zimmer's Warren County N.J. Fed. Adv. Com., Warren County Econ. Adv. Coun., N.J. Gov.'s appointee 1988— and chmn. fed. enacted Del. Water Gap Nat. Recreation Area citizens adv. com., Gov.-elect Christie Todd Whitman Transition Team-Commerce and Econ. Devel. and Tourism; elected to Warren County Rep. Com.; chmn. adv. bd. Warren Presdl. Correctional Facility; chmn. Calno Cemetery Assn.; chmn. Warner County Econ. Devel. Blue Ribbon Task Force; vice chmn. bd. trustees Warren County C.C., 1983—, chmn. found. bd., presdl. search com. 2003, ops. com. 2003, ambassador N.Y. Coun. Cmty. Colls.; exec. bd. Tri-County Washington coun. and George Washington coun. Boy Scouts Am.; bd. dirs. N.J. Shore Regional Tourism Coun., N.Y. dir. SBDC, N.J. Juvenile Justice Adv. Bd.; mem. 1st N.J. Trade Del. Soviet Union; mem. commerce and econ. devel. transition team Gov.-elect Christie Whitman, N.J., 1994; chmn. N.J. assembly bus. retention com. of Task Force for Bus. Rentention, Attraction, Expansion and Internat. Trade; chmn. N.J. Gov.'s Conf. Travel and Tourism, Atlantic City, 1994; mem. N.J. No. Shore Region CUB Allaire Airport Conv. Ctr.; pres.-elect Warren County Econ. Partnership. Recipient Medal of Honor, Ellis Island, 1994, Disting. Citizen award Boy Scouts Am., 1992. Mem. ASTD, Am. Mgmt. Assns., Am. Coun. on Germany, U.S.C. of C., Nat. Fgn. Trade Coun., World Trade Inst., U.S.-USSR Trade and Econ Coun., N.Y. C. of C. and Industry, N.J. C. of C., Commerce and Industry Assn., N.J., Am. C. of C.s and U.S. Bus. Couns. Abroad, Soc. Human Resource Mgmt., Nat. Assn. Corp. and Profl. Recruiters, Employment Mgmt. Assn., N.J. Hotel/Motel Assn. (bd. dirs., mem. exec. bd.), N.J. Travel Industry Assn. (bd. dirs., v.p. exec. bd.), N.Y. Pers. Mgmt. Assn., Soc. Plastics Engrs., Soc. Cosmetic Chemists, Small Bus. Adv. Coun., Ocean Grove C. of C. (vice chmn.). Republican. Methodist. Home: 37 Petersburg Rd Hackettstown NJ 07840-4903 Personal E-mail: stevevancampen@goes.com.

**VANCE, DAVID A.,** information systems educator; b. Anchorage, 1948; s. Alvin V. and Mary Vance; m. Nancy Niemann; children: John, Emily, Ryan. AA, Grossmont Coll., 1976; BBA, Nat. U., 1982, MBA, 1984, postgrad. 1985; PhD, So. Ill. U., 2000; postgrad., Trinity Sem., Ind., 2004—. Ordained to ministry United Christian Faith Ministries, 2002. Tech. supr. USN, San Diego, 1970-74; engr., project mgr. Wavetek Data Communications, San Diego, 1975-79; v.p. ops. Specialized Systems, Inc., San Diego, 1979-81; prin. Sunhill R&D, San Diego, 1981-84; exec. dir. Brunswick Inst. Tech., San Diego, 1985; tech. staff mem. Veda, Inc., Orlando, Fla. and San Diego, 1985-88; tng. analyst Eagle Tech., Inc., Winter Park, Fla., 1988-89; prof. mgmt. Fla. So. Coll., Orlando, 1988-94; tchr., student mgmt. doctoral program So. Ill. U., Carbondale, 1994-99; asst. prof. Miss. State U., 1999—2000, prof., 2000—. Prin. DA Vance & Assocs., Winter Park, 1986-94; adj. prof. mgmt. Webster U., 1991-94, Fla. So. Coll., 1988-94; vis. asst. prof. So. Ill. U., 1991-94; lectr. in field. Rep. precinct committeeman, Orange County, Fla., 1988, del. state conv., 1988; chmn. svc. com. CSO, Inc., 1991. Recipient Achievement award ACCESS, San Diego, 1980; Worthy scholar Woodrow Wilson Found., 1966, Leadership scholar Nat. U., San Diego, 1984. Mem.: Info. Resources Mgmt. Assn., Computer Profls. for Social Responsibility, Am. MENSA, Ltd. Avocations: outdoor sports, music. Office: Miss State U Dept Mgmt and IS PO Box 9581 Mississippi State MS 39762-9581

**VANCE, PATRICIA H.,** state senator; b. Williamsport, Pa., Mar. 19, 1936; RN, Harrisburg Hosp. Sch. Nursing; 1957. Former mem. Pa. Ho. of Reps., Harrisburg, 1990—2004; mem. Pa. Senate, Harrisburg, 2004—. Home: 3806 Market St Camp Hill PA 17011-4327 Office: Pa Senate Rm 187 Main Capitol PO Box 203031 Harrisburg PA 17120-3031

**VANCE, ROBERT PATRICK,** lawyer; b. Feb. 12, 1948; s. James Robert and Lucy Juanita (McMath) V.; m. Sarah Elizabeth Savoia, June 11, 1971; 1 child, Robert Patrick, Jr. BA with honors, La. State U., 1970, JD, 1975. Bar: La. 1975, U.S. Dist. Ct. (ea. dist.) La. 1975, U.S. Dist. Ct. (mid. dist.) La. 1978, U.S. Dist. Ct. (we. dist.) La. 1979, U.S. Ct. Appeals (5th cir.) 1975, U.S. Ct. Appeals (11th cir.) 1981, U.S. Supreme Ct. 1981. Assoc. Jones, Walker, Waechter, Poitevent, Carrere & Denegre, New Orleans, 1975-80, ptnr., 1980—, exec. com., 1991—95, 1997—2002, 2004—, mng. ptnr., 1994—95, 1999—2000, 2004, chmn. litigation, 2003—. Contbr. articles to profl. jours. Fellow Am. Coll. Bankruptcy, Nat. Bankruptcy Conf. (mem. exec. com.); mem. ABA (past chair bankruptcy litigation com.), Am. Law Inst., La. State Bar Assn. (past chair consumer and bankruptcy law sect., chmn. continuing legal edn. com.), New Orleans Bar Assn., La. Bankers Assn. (chmn. bank counsel com. 1992-93), Pi Sigma Alpha, Phi Beta Kappa (Faculty Group award), Phi Kappa Phi. Democrat. Roman Catholic. Office: Jones Walker Waechter Poitevent Carrere & Denegre 201 Saint Charles Ave Ste 5200 New Orleans LA 70170-5100 Office Phone: 504-582-8194. Business E-Mail: pvance@joneswalker.com.

**VANCE, VERNE WIDNEY, JR.,** retired lawyer; b. Omaha, Mar. 10, 1932; s. Verne Widney and June Caroline (Henckler) V.; m. Anita Paine, June 27, 1970; children: Lisa J. Castleton, Charles Hebard Paine, Virginia Caroline. AB, Harvard U., 1954, JD, 1957. Bar: D.C. 1957, Mass. 1964. Law clk. U.S. Dist. Judge, Mass., 1957-58; assoc. Covington & Burling, Washington, 1958-60; atty. adv. Devel. Loan Fund, Washington, 1960-61; legal counsel US AID, Washington, 1961-63; assoc. Foley, Hoag & Eliot LLP, Boston, 1963-67, ptnr., 1967-2000; ret., 2001. Lectr. law Boston U., 1964-66; corp. clk. S.S. Pierce Co., 1971-72. Pres. UN Assn. Greater Boston, 1964-66, 77-78, treas., 1974-77; mem. Mass. Adv. Council on Edn., 1969-75, chmn., 1975; mem. Dem. City Com., Newton, Mass., 1972—, Gov.'s Local Govt. Adv. Commn., 1986-90; alderman City of Newton, 1982-91, 2004—; pres. Newton Bd. of Aldermen, 1988-91; mem. Newton Sch. Com., 1994-2001, chair 2000-01; trustee Judge Baker Children's Ctr., 1994—, clk., 2002--; trustee Mass. Bay C.C., 1987-98, vice chmn., 1989-91, chmn. 1991-97; pres. Mass. C.C. Assn., 1996-97. Mem. Boston Bar Assn. (bd. editors bar jour. 1986-90), Longwood Cricket Club. Home: 101 Old Orchard Rd Chestnut Hill MA 02467-1202 Office: Foley Hoag LLP 155 Seaport Blvd Boston MA 02109-2106 E-mail: vvance@rcn.com.

**VAN CLEAVE, MICHELLE KIM,** former federal official; b. 1953; BA, MA, JD, U. So. Calif. Assoc. Horvitz and Greines, LA; asst. for def. and foreign policy to Congressman Jack Kemp, 1981—87; nat. security asst. Ho. Rep. Conf., 1981—87; staff mem. Ho. Appropriations subcom. on Fgn. Ops., 1981—87; gen. counsel, asst. dir. nat. security affairs White House Office of Sci. and Tech. Policy, 1987—93; minority counsel to com. on sci., space, and tech., 1989; of counsel Feith & Zell, P.C., 1993—97; co-founder, pres. Nat. Security Concepts, Inc., 1997—2001; spl. asst. to under sec. for policy, sr. advisor for homeland def. US Dept. Def., Washington, 2001—03; nat. counterintelligence exec. Office Nat. Counterintelligence Exec., Washington, 2003—05. Mem.: DC Bar Assn., Calif. Bar Assn.

**VAN CLEVE, ROBERT BALDWIN,** cardiologist; b. St. Louis, Dec. 1, 1931; s. William T. and Catherine Cornelia (Moore) Van C.; m. Sarah Agnes Towers, July 9, 1955; children: Sarah Elizabeth Weldon, Catherine Moore Bauman, Mary Agnes Miller, Robert B. Jr. AB, Princeton U., 1954; MD, Columbia U., 1958. Diplomate Am. Bd. Internal Medicine, Am. Bd. Cardiovasc. Disease. Intern, resident U. of Va. Hosp., Charlottesville, 1958-61; ward resident Barnes Hosp., St. Louis, 1962; Harvard Med. Sch. fellow Mass. Gen. Hosp., 1965; cardiologist Riverside Clinic, Jacksonville, Fla., 1965-98, Jacksonville Cardiology Clinic, 1998—2004, Diagnostic Cardiology, 2004—. Cardiology cons. USN Hosp., Jacksonville, 1965-72; clin. prof. medicine U. Fla., 1977-88; chief of staff Riverside Hosp., Jacksonville, 1983-84, chief cardiology, 1985-90; chmn. hosp. authority U. Hosp.; v.p. attending staff Found. Duval County Interns and Residents. Contbr. articles to profl. jours., including Circulation, Jour. Am. Med Assn., Jour. Fla. Med. Assn. Chmn. recreation adv. bd. City of Jacksonville; elder 1st Presbyn. Ch.; bd. dirs. Salvation Army, Jacksonville. Lt. comdr. USN, 1962—64. Fellow: ACP, Am. Coll. Cardiology. Republican. Avocations: tennis, scuba diving, golf, gardening. Home: 3500 Richmond St Jacksonville FL 32205-9422 Office: 1801 Barrs St Ste 500 Jacksonville FL 32204 Office Phone: 904-388-1820.

**VAN CLEVE, RUTH GILL,** retired lawyer; b. Mpls., July 28, 1925; d. Raymond S. and Ruth (Sevon) Gill; m. Harry R. Van Cleve, Jr., May 16, 1952 (dec. Oct. 2001); children: John Gill, Elizabeth Webster, David Hamilton Livingston. Student, U. Minn., 1943; AB magna cum laude, Mt. Holyoke Coll., 1946, LLD, 1976; LLB, Yale U., 1950. Bar: D.C. 1950, Minn. 1950. Intern Nat. Inst. Pub. Affairs, 1946-47; atty. Dept. Interior, 1950-54, asst. solicitor, 1954-64; dir. Office Territorial Affairs, 1964-69, 1977-80, dep. asst. sec., 1980-81, acting asst. sec., 1993; atty. Solicitor's Office, 1981-93, FPC, 1969-75, asst. gen. counsel, 1975-77. Author: The Office of Territorial Affairs, 1974, The Application of Federal Laws to the Territories, 1993. Mem. Guam War Claims Rev. Commn., 2003—04. Recipient Fed. Woman's award, 1966, Disting. Svc. award Dept. Interior, 1968, Presdl. Rank award, Pres. U.S., 1989. Mem.: Phi Beta Kappa. Unitarian. Home: 3440 S Jefferson St Apt 1015 Falls Church VA 22041

**VANCO, JOHN L.,** art museum director; b. Erie, Pa., Aug. 21, 1945; s. John Jr. and Alice (Crozier) V.; m. Kathleen Merski, 1971; children: John H., Jesse L. BA, Allegheny Coll., 1967. Dir. Erie (Pa.) Art Mus., 1968—. Mem. adv. panels Pa. Coun. on the Arts, Harrisburg, 1974—, Mid Atlantic Arts Found., Balt., 1992, 2002, Nat. Endowment for Arts, 2000; curator Contemporary Music Series, 1982—, Erie Art Mus. Blues and Jazz Festival, 1992—. Photographic and numerous exhibit., curator miscellaneous exhibs. including A Peculiar Vision: The Work of George Ohr, The Mad Potter of Biloxi, From Mickey to the Grinch: Art of the Animated Film, Poems in Clay: Arthur Osborne's Plastic Sketches for the Low Art Tile Works, Teco: Art Pottery of the Prairie Sch., In Harmony with the Earth; author: A Roycroft Desktop: Musings on Elbert Hubbard and the Roycroft Shops, 1994, Loud & Clear: Resonator Guitars and the Dopyera Brothers' Legacy to American Music, 1998, Structured Color: Kiyokatsu Matsymiya, 2003. Chief adminstrv. officer Discovery Square, Erie, 1991-92; bd. dirs. Pa. Humanities Coun., 2001—. Office: Erie Art Mus 411 State St Erie PA 16501-1106 Office Phone: 814-459-5477. E-mail: jvanco@erieartmuseum.com.

**VAN CURA, JOYCE BENNETT,** librarian; b. Madison, Wis., Mar. 25, 1944; d. Ralph Eugene and Florence Marie (Cramer) Bennett; m. E. Jay Van Cura, July 5, 1986. BA in Liberal Arts (scholar), Bradley U., Peoria, Ill., 1966; MLS, U. Ill., Champaign-Urbana, 1971. Libr. asst. Rsch. Libr. Caterpillar Tractor Co., Peoria, Ill., 1966-67; ref. libr., instr. libr. tech. Ill. Ctrl. Coll., East Peoria, Ill., 1967-73; asst. prof. Sangamon State U. (U. Ill.-Springfield), Springfield, Ill., 1973-80, assoc. prof., 1980-86; head libr. ref. and info. svcs. dept. Ill. Inst. Tech., 1987-90; dir. Learning Resources Ctr. Morton Coll., 1990—2003. Reviewer Libr. Jour., Am. Ref. Books Ann.; convenor Coun. II, Ill. Clearinghouse for Acad. Libr. Instrn., 1978; presentor 7th Ann. Conf. Acad. Libr. Instrn., 1977, Nat. Women's Studies Assn., 1983, others; participant Gt. Lakes Women's Studies Summer Inst., 1981, Nat. Inst. Leadership Devel. seminar, 1995. Contbr. articles to profl. jours. Pres. Springfield chpt. NOW, 1978—79; invited Susan B. Anthony luncheon, 1978, 1979; mem. adv. bd. Suburban Libr. Sys. 1992—94. Nat. Commn. Learning Resources; v.p. membership Riverside chpt. Lyric Opera Chgo., 1994—96, 1999—, exec. bd., 2006—; active Riverside Arts Ctr.; Dem. precinct Committeewoman, 1982—85; vice-moderator Fourth Presbyn. Women, 1989—90; elder Riverside (Ill.) Presbyn. Ch., 1992—, mem. session, 1993—96, 2000—01, mem. adminstrn. com., 1993—2003, chmn. adminstrn. com., 1993—96, 1999, 2000—01; mem. endowment com., 1996—98, treas. bd. trustees, 2004—; bd. trustees, 2005—, sec. bd. trustees, 2005—; bd. dirs. Berwyn-Cicero Coun. on Aging, 2000—03. Ill. state scholar, 1962-66; recipient Citizenship award Am. Legion, 1962, Cert. of Recognition Ill. Bicentennial Commn., 1974. Mem.: AAUW (bd. dirs. Riverside br. 1992—94, 1997—99, chmn. standing com. on women Springfield br., com.

on women Ill. state divsns.), ALA, Ill. Libr. Assn. (presenter 1984), Nat. Assn. Women in C.C., Springfield Art Assn., No. Ill. Learning Resources Consortium (del. 1990—2000), steering com. West Suburban postsecondary consortium 1996—2000), Nat. Women's Studies Assn. (presenter 1983, 1984, 1995), Women in Mgmt., Am. Mgmt. Assn., No. Ill. Learning Resources Consortium Bd. (del. 2006—), Spl. Librs. Assn., Ill. Assn. Coll. and Rsch. Librs. (bibliog. instrn. com.), Libr. Info. and Tech. Assn., Libr. Adminstr. and Mgmt. Assn. (ref. and adult svcs. divsn.), Assn. Coll. and Rsch. Librs., Riverside Presbyn. Ch. Women, Nat. Trust Hist. Preservation, Am. Opera Soc., Riverside Dancing Club, Riverside Garden Club, Musicians Club of Women Chgo., Beta Phi Mu. Home: 181 Scottswood Rd Riverside IL 60546-2221

**VAN DAM, HEIMAN,** psychoanalyst; b. Leiden, Netherlands; s. Machiel and Rika van D.; m. Barbara C. Strona, Oct. 6, 1945; children: Machiel, Claire Ilena, Rika Rosemary. AB, U. So. Calif., 1942, MD, 1945. Fellow in child psychiatry Pasadena (Calif.) Child Guidance Clinic, 1950; gen. practice psychiatry and psychoanalysis L.A., 1951—; instr. L.A. Psychoanalytic Inst., LA, 1959—2000, co-chmn. com. on child psychoanalysis, 1960-67, tng. and supervising psychoanalyst, 1972—; supr. child and adolescent psychoanalysis So. Calif. Psychoanalytic Inst., 1986—. Cons. Reiss Davis Child Study Center, 1955-76, Neighborhood Youth Assn., LA, 1964-69; assoc. clin. prof. psychiatry and pediats. UCLA Sch. Medicine, 1960-96, clin. prof. psychiatry and pediats., 1996—; vis. supr. child psychoanalysis San Francisco Psychoanalytic Inst., 1969-79, 2002—, Denver Psychoanalytic Inst., 1972-74; adv. bd. Western State U. Coll. Law, Fullerton, Calif., 1965-83. Corr. editor Arbeits Hefte Kinderanalyse, 1985—2005; contbr. articles to profl. jours. Trustee, edn. com. Center for Early Edn., 1964-92, v.p., 1978-79; bd. dirs. Child Devel. and Psychotherapy Tng. Program, LA, 1975-80, pres., 1975-77; bd. dirs. LA Child Devel. Center, 1977-86, treas., 1978-80; mem. cult clinic Jewish Family Service, L.A., 1978-86; bd. dirs. Lake Arrowhead Crest Estates, 1990-99. Capt. M.C. AUS, 1946-48. Mem. Am. Psychoanalytic Assn. (com. on ethics 1987), Assn. Child Psychoanalysis (councillor 1966-69, sec. 1972-74, nominating com. 1978-84, membership com. 1988—2005, Marianne Kris lectr. 1995), Internat. Assn. Infant Psychiatry (co-chmn. program com. 1980-83), Internat. Soc. Adolescent Psychiatry (sci. adv. com. 1988-2004), Phi Beta Kappa. Office: 2864 McConnell Dr Los Angeles CA 90064-4658 Office Phone: 310-559-4947.

**VANDAME, JEAN-MARIE RICHARD,** diversified financial services company executive; b. Gien, France, Oct. 30, 1960; s. Marc and Antoinette (Dumouchel de Premare) V.; m. Chantal Marie de Blocquel de Croix de Wismes, Sept. 3, 1983; children: Thomas, Camille, Clemence, Alix. MS, Inst. Super. Electronique, Paris, 1982; MBA, Inst. Administrn. Entreprises, Paris, 1984. Product mktg. engr. Tex Instruments, Paris, 1983-84, field sales engr. Rennes, France, 1984-86; sr. mgr. Ernst & Young, Paris, 1986—92, assoc. ptnr., 1995—96, internat. ptnr., 1996—2000; pres. KnowledgeWare, Brussels, 1992—95; v.p. CG Ernst & Young, Chgo., 2000—03; ptnr. Ernst & Young, Paris, 2004—. Home: 24 Avenue Theophile Gautier 75016 Paris France Office Phone: +33 146 93 44 03. E-mail: jean-marie.vandame@fr.ey.com.

**VANDAMENT, WILLIAM EUGENE,** retired academic administrator; b. Hannibal, Mo., Sept. 6, 1931; s. Alva F. and Ruth Alice (Mahood) V.; m. Margery Vandament, Feb. 2, 1952; children: Anne Louise, Lisa Ann. BA, Quincy Coll., 1952; MS, So. Ill. U., 1953; MS in Psychology, U. Mass., 1963, PhD, 1964; LittD, No. Mich. U., 1997. Psychologist Bacon Clinic, Racine, Wis., 1954-61; NDEA fellow U. Mass., Amherst, 1961-64; asst. prof. SUNY, Binghamton, 1964-69, univ. examiner and dir. instl. research, 1969-73, asst. v.p. planning, instl. research, 1972-76; exec. asst. to pres., dir. budget and resources Ohio State U., Columbus, 1976-79, v.p. fin. and planning, 1979-81; sr. v.p. adminstrn. NYU, N.Y.C., 1981-83; provost, vice chancellor acad. affairs Calif. State U. System, Long Beach, 1983-87; Trustees prof. Calif. State U., Fullerton, 1987-92; pres. No. Mich. U., 1991-97, ret., 1997. Contbr. articles to psychol. jours. and books on higher edn. Office: 2662 E 20th St Apt 310 Signal Hill CA 90755 E-mail: vandament@aol.com.

**VAN DE BOGART, DEBRA SCHERWERTS,** medical/surgical nurse, researcher; b. Claremont, N.H., Aug. 6, 1954; d. William Earl and Barbara Louise (Hadley White) Scherwerts. RN, Sacred Heart Sch. Nursing, Manchester, NH, 1975; student, Cypress Coll., 1976, U. Calif., Riverside, 1978. RN Calif., 1975, cert. home health nurse, Calif., 1997. Charge nurse, med.-surg. pediat. West Anaheim Cmty. Hosp., Anaheim, Calif., 1975—84; charge nurse, med.-surg. geriat. Humana West Anaheim, Anaheim, Calif., 1984—87; home health nurse, obstet. Physician's Care, Brea, Calif., 1988—90, Am. Home Health, Santa Ana, Calif., 1988—92; staff nurse, rsch. clin. studies ctr. Harbor-UCLA Med. Ctr., Torrance, Calif., 1993—94; nurse rschr. various profit and non-profit orgns., Anaheim, Calif., 1994—, RN coord., cons., 1994—. Contbr. workshop Focus on Health, 1982; mem. citizens adv. com., health Calif. State Assembly, 1982—; cons., home care for MD's Am. Home Health We. Med. Ctr., Santa Ana, 1991—; RN clin. advisor, staff devel. Cmty. Svcs. Projects, Orange and LA Counties, 2000—. Recipient cert. of recognition, Calif. State Legis., 1982. Mem.: ANA, Assn. Am. Acad. Bereavement, Sigma Theta Tau. Democrat. Roman Catholic. Avocations: violin, travel.

**VAN DE BOVENKAMP, HANS,** artist; b. Holland, June 1, 1938; Degree, U. Mich., 1961. Exhibited sculpture in numerous one-man and group shows including most recently Tiffany's, N.Y., 1981, Michener Mus., Doylestown, Pa., 1996, Louis K. Meisel Gallery, N.Y.C., 2002, 04, 05, Neiman Marcus, Dallas, Tex., 2003, Sculpture Site Gallery, San Francisco, N.Y., 2004, 05, Camino Real Gallery, Boca Raton, Fla., 2004, Ground for Sculpture Mus., Trenton, NJ, 2005, Grounds for Sculpture, Hamilton, N.J., 2005-06, Danubiana Mus., Bratislava, Slovakia, 2006—; represented in numerous pub. collections including Boca Raton (Fla.) Mus. Fine Art, U. Mo., Columbia, Stony Brook (N.Y.) U., Estate of Nelson Rockefeller, Youngstown (Ohio) Mus., Lowe Mus., Coral Gables, Fla. Recipient Emily Lowe award, 1964, award Am. Inst. Arts & Letters, 1976, award Nebr. Bicentennial Competition, 1976. Home and Office: 93 Merchants Path PO Box 1300 Sagaponack NY 11962

**VAN DE BOVENKAMP, SUE ERPF,** charitable organization executive; b. N.Y.C.; d. George Norton and Bettina Lions (Hearst) Mortimore; student Gardner Sch., Art Students League, Cooper Union; m. Armand Grover Erpf, 1965 (dec.); children: Cornelia Aurelia, Armand Bartholomew; m. Gerrit Pieter Van de Bovenkamp, Aug. 11, 1973 (div.). Pres. Armand G. Erpf Fund, N.Y.C., 1971—; founder, hon. chmn. Erpf Catskill Cultural Ctr., 1972—. Bd. advisors, founder N.Y. Zool. Soc., 1971—, 1001 Nature Trust, 1973, William Beebe fellow, 1983—; fellow in perpetuity Met. Mus. Art, 1977; life fellow Pierpont Morgan Libr., 1974—; mem. coun. of friends Whitney Mus. Am. Art, 1971-77; mem. Whitney Circle, 1978-93; bd. dirs. Catskill Ctr. for Conservation and Devel., 1983-86; mem. adv. coun., dept. art history and archaeology Columbia U., 1972—, established univ. seminar on uses of oceans, 1977, mem. adv. coun. Translation Ctr., 1986; life conservator N.Y. Pub. Libr., 1980; fellow Frick Collection; 1971—, Whitney fellow, 2994—; mem. coun. Agribus. Coun., Inc., 1979-87; founder, life mem. World Wildlife Fund, 1973—, bd. dirs., 1984-89; mem. pres.'s coun. Columbia U., 1973-78; life mem. Mus. City N.Y., 1972—, mem. pres.'s coun., 1971—. Mem. N.Y. Acad. Scis., The Planetary Soc., Mus. Natural History (life), Asia Soc. (pres.'s coun.), Wildlife Fedn. (adv.), African Wildlife Found. (pres.'s cir.). mem. Mus. of Natural Hist. press., coun. of the Asia Soc. Office: The Armand G Erpf Fund 640 Park Ave New York NY 10021-6126

**VANDEBROEK, SOPHIE VERDONCKT,** printing company executive; b. Leuven, Belgium, Feb. 17, 1962; came to U.S.; 1986; d. Norbert and Jeanine (Ringoir) V.; m. Bart Vandebroek, Aug. 2, 1986 (dec. Aug. 1996); children: Elena, Arno, Jonas. B in Engring. magna cum laude, Katholieke U., 1982, MS in Electro-Mech. Engring. magna cum laude, 1985; PhDEE in Microelectronics, Cornell U., 1990. Devel. staff mem. IBM T.J. Watson Rsch. Ctr., Yorktown Heights, NY, 1990-92; competency leader J.C. Wilson Ctr. for Rsch. and Tech., Xerox, Webster, NY, 1992-95, lab. mgr., 1995-96; platform

mgr. Ink-Jet Supplies Bus. Unit Xerox Corp., Webster, 1996-97, mgr. document systems coherence program, 1997-98, tech. advisor Office of the Chmn., 1998-99, chief engineer Stamford, Conn., 2002—06, chief tech. officer, 2006—, corp. v.p., 2006—; v.p. Xerox Rsch. Ctr. Can., 1999—2000, Xerox Engring. Ctr., 2002—06; pres. Xerox Innovation Group, 2006—; chief tech. officer Carrier Corp., 2000—02. Contbr. articles to profl. jours. Fulbright fellow, 1986; hon. grad. fellowship Belgian-Am. Ednl. Found., 1986; internat. travel grant Belgium Nat. Sci. Found., 1986-87; recipient Monsanto award 1986, Kieckhefer Adirondack award 1986. Mem. IEEE (sr. mem.), IEEE Electron Devices Soc. (adminstrv. com. 1995-97, internat. electron device meeting 1994-98, tech. program com. 1994-95, chair solid state devices com. 1996, publicity chair 1998, chair Rochester chpt. IEEE/EDS 1994, disting. lectr. 1994). Avocations: reading, skiing, kayaking, rollerblading. Office: Xerox Corp 800 Long Ridge Rd Stamford CT 06904*

**VANDE HEY, JAMES MICHAEL,** retired air force officer; b. Maribel, Wis., Mar. 15, 1916; s. William Henry and Anna (Zimmerman) VandeH.; m. Jean Margretta Schilleman, June 23, 1944; children: James Todd, Dale Michael, Dean Clark. Student, U. Wis., 1947-49; BA, U. Philippines, 1955; postgrad., Air War Coll., Maxwell AFB, Montgomery, Ala., 1956-57. Commd. 2d lt. USAAF, 1941; advanced through grades to brig. gen. USAF, 1967; fighter pilot PTO, 1941-45; including Hawaii, Dec. 7, 1941; duty in command and USAF level including duty in Europe (NATO) and Philippines, 1945-69; dep. chief of staff Hdqrs. USMACV, Saigon, Vietnam, 1969-71; assigned Hdqrs. Tactical Air Command, 1971—; mem. faculty Air War Coll., 1957-59, dep. for acads., dean of faculty, 1959-61; ret., 1971; pres. Vanson Inc., 1971—, Vande Hey Inc., 1976—. Decorated D.S.M., Legion of Merit with two oak leaf clusters, D.F.C. with two oak leaf clusters, Bronze Star, Air medal with 7 oak leaf clusters, decorations from Philippine, Vietnamese and Korean govts. Mem. USAF Hist. Found., Air Force Assn., Pearl Harbor Survivors Assn., Iwo Jima Survivors Assn. Roman Catholic. Home: 3374 S El Dorado Austin TX 78734-5232

**VAN DE KAMP, JOHN KALAR,** lawyer; b. Pasadena, Calif., Feb. 7, 1936; s. Harry and Georgie (Kalar) Van de K.; m. Andrea Fisher, Mar. 11, 1978; 1 child, Diana. BA, Dartmouth Coll., 1956; JD, Stanford U., 1959. Bar: Calif. 1960. Asst. U.S. atty., L.A., 1960—66; U.S. atty., 1966—67; dep. dir. Exec. Office for U.S. Attys., Washington, 1967—68, dir., 1968—69; spl. asst. Pres.'s Commn. on Campus Unrest, 1970; fed. pub. defender L.A., 1971—75; dist. atty. Los Angeles County, 1975—83; atty. gen. State of Calif., 1983—91; ptnr. Dewey Ballantine, L.A., 1991—96, of counsel, 1996—; pres. Thoroughbred Owners, Calif., 1996—2004. Mem. Calif. Dist. Attys. Assn. (pres. 1975-83), Nat. Dist. Attys. Assn. (v.p. 1975-83), Peace Officers Assn. L.A. County (past pres.), Nat. Assn. Attys. Gen. (exec. com. 1983-91), Conf. Western Attys. Gen. (pres. 1986), State Bar Calif. (bd. govs. 2001-04, pres. 2004-05), Calif. Commn. Fair Adminstrn. of Justice (chair 2006-). Office: Dewey Ballantine LLP 333 So Grand Ave Ste 2600 Los Angeles CA 90071-1530 Office Phone: 213-621-6511. Business E-Mail: jvandekamp@deweyballantine.com.

**VANDELICHT, ROY DEAN,** music educator; b. Indpls., July 3, 1955; s. Roy Dean and Barbara Anne Vandelicht; m. Melody Rochelle Estill, Nov. 10, 1979; children: Adrian Elise Newell, Matthew Trent. MusB in Edn., Ctrl. Meth. Coll., 1977; MEd, U. Mo., 1985. Dir. bands Fayette (Mo.) R-III Sch. Dist., 1977—. Music adjudicator Mo. State H.S. Activities Assn., Columbia, Mo., 1995—; adj. dir. marching bands Ctrl. Meth. Coll., Fayette, 1983—95. Bd. dirs. Fayette (Mo.) Music Boosters, 1977—2005. Named Music Tchr. of Yr. award, Mo. Fedn. of Women's Clubs, 1982; recipient Outstanding Young Alumni award, Ctrl. Meth. Coll., 1990, Orpheus award, Phi Mu Alpha Sinfonia, 1991, Laureate Legion of Honor award, John Philip Sousa Found., 2004. Mem.: Mo. State Tchrs. Assn. (chmn., regional nominating com. 2000—05), Fayette Cmty. Tchrs. Assn. (pres. 2001—03), Mo. Music Educators Assn., Mo. Bandmasters Assn. (pres. 1994—96), Phi Beta Mu. Office: Fayette High School 510 N Cleveland Fayette MO 65248 Office Phone: 660-248-2124. Business E-Mail: svandeli@mail.fayette.k12.mo.us.

**VANDELL, KERRY DEAN,** real estate consultant, educator, director, finance educator; b. Biloxi, Miss., Jan. 8, 1947; s. Benedict Sandy and Eleanor Ruby (Lenhart) V.; m. Deborah Ann Lowe, May 16, 1970; children: Colin Buckner, Ashley Elizabeth. BA, MME, Rice U., 1970; M City Planning, Harvard U., 1973; PhD, MIT, 1977. Assoc. engr. Exxon Co., USA, Houston, 1970-71; asst. prof. So. Meth. U., Dallas, 1976-80, assoc. prof., 1980-86, prof., chmn. dept., 1986-89; prof. real estate and urban land econs., chm. dept. U. Wis., Madison, 1989-93, dir. Ctr. for Urban Land Econs. Rsch., 1991—2004, Tiefenthaler chair holder, 1996—2006; exec. dir. Bolz Ctr. Arts Adminstrn., Madison 2000—05; prof. fin., dir. Ctr. Real Estate Paul Merage Sch. Bus. U. Calif.-Irvine, 2006—. Vis. assoc. prof. Harvard U., Cambridge, Mass., 1985-86; vis. prof. U. Calif., Berkeley, 1988-89, U. Hong Kong, 1997; bd. dirs. Chrisken Realty Trust. Mem. editl. bd. Jour. Real Estate Fin. and Econs., 1989—, Land Econs., 1989—, Jour. Property Rsch., 1989-94, Real Estate Econs., 1980—, Internat. Real Estate Rev., 2002—; contbr. numerous articles on mortgage default risk, real estate liquidity, housing market behavior, econs. of architecture, and appraisal theory to profl. jours. Fellow Homer Hoyt Advanced Studies Inst. (faculty 1989—); mem. Urban Land Inst., Am. Real Estate and Urban Econs. Assn. (2nd v.p. 1989, 1st v.p. 1990, pres. 1991, co-editor jour. 1991-96), Asian Real Estate Soc. (bd. dirs. 2002—), Am. Real Estate Soc. Episcopalian. Office: U Calif Irvine Paul Merage Sch Bus Irvine CA 92697 Home: 2658 Victoria Dr Laguna Beach CA 92651 Office Phone: 949-824-2985. Business E-Mail: kvandell@bus.wisc.edu, kvandell@uci.edu.

**VANDEMARK, MICHELLE VOLIN,** critical care, neuroscience nurse; b. Sioux Falls, S.D., Feb. 14, 1962; d. Verlynne V. and Suzanne (Cronin) Volin; m. Richard E. VanDemark, June 5, 1982; children: Andrew Porter, Hannah Elizabeth. BA in Biology, Lake Forest (Ill.) Coll., 1984; BSN, Northwestern U., Chgo., 1986; MS in Nursing, Loyola U., Chgo., 1990. RN, Ill., S.D.; cert. neurosci. nursing, CNRN, CMSN. Staff nurse neurosci. unit Evanston Hosp., Ill., 1986-90, staff nurse intensive care unit Ill., 1990-93; neurosci. clin. nurse specialist Sioux Valley Hosp., Sioux Falls, S.D., 1995—. Mem. Am. Assn. Neurosci. Nurses (pres. Gt. Plains chpt. 1995-96, bd. dirs. 2000-03), Sigma Theta Tau, Alpha Sigma Nu. Home: 321 E 27th St Sioux Falls SD 57105-3032

**VANDEMARK, ROBERT GOODYEAR,** retired retail executive; b. Youngstown, Ohio, Sept. 1, 1921; s. Arthur Glenn and Lola (Goodyear) V.; m. Jean Chapman, Sept. 19, 1943; children: Ann (Mrs. William K. Butler), Peggy Lynn (Mrs. Michael Murray). BSc, Ohio U., 1943. Dept. mgr. F. & R. Lazarus, Columbus, Ohio, 1947-54; asst. controller Boston Store, Milw., 1954-57; v.p., treas. Cleland Simpson Co., Scranton, Pa., 1957-65; asst. to exec. v.p. Bergdorf Goodman, N.Y.C., 1965-68; treas. Garfinckel, Brooks Bros., Miller & Rhoads, Inc., Washington, 1968-69, v.p., 1969-73, exec. v.p., 1973-79, vice chmn., 1979-83; chmn., chief exec. officer Garfinckel's, 1983-87. Head dept. and specialty stores div. United Fund, Scranton, Pa., 1960-65; bd. dirs. Goodwill Industries, 1964-65; treas. Washington Nat. Cathedral. Served to 1st lt. AUS, 1943-46; col. Res. Decorated Bronze Star with V and cluster, Mil. Order of Wilheim. Mem. Fin. Execs. Inst., Nat. Retail Mchts. Assn. (sec., treas., 1st v.p., pres., dir., mem. exec. com. fin. exec. divsn.), Delta Tau Delta, City Club Washington, Washington Golf and Country Club, Army-Navy Club, Burning Tree Golf Club, Laurel Oak Country Club (Fla.) Masons (32d degree), Kiwanis (Fla.), Tower Club. Home: 933 Woburn St Mc Lean VA 22102-2132 also: 3362 Charles MacDonald Dr Sarasota FL 34240

**VANDENBERG, JOKA MARIA,** physicist, researcher; b. Heemstede, The Netherlands, Jan. 24, 1938; came to the U.S., 1968; d Antonius Vandenberg and Maria Elisabeth Van Ameronger; m. Rudolf Johannes Voorhoeve, May 11, 1968 (div. Aug. 1975); children: Lucy, Niels; m. James Charles Philips, Mar. 1, 1996. B in Physics, State U., Leiden, The Netherlands, 1959, M in Phys. Chemistry, 1962, PhD in Solid State Physics, 1964. Tchg. asst. Lab. Inorganic Chemistry, Leiden, 1959-60; rsch. asst. Lab. Crystallography,

Amsterdam, 1962-64; rschr. Royal Dutch Shell Lab., Amsterdam, The Netherlands, 1964-68; postdoctoral staff Bell Labs., Murray Hill, N.J., 1968-69, cons., 1972; mem. tech. staff Lucent Techs., Murray Hill, 1973-2001. Mem. affirmative action com. Bell Labs., Murray Hill, 1990-91. Mem. Am. Phys. Soc., Royal Dutch Acad. Scis. (corr.). Achievements include patent for super conducting films. Home: 204 Springfield Ave Summit NJ 07901 Personal E-mail: joka_berg@comcast.net.

**VAN DEN BERG, SARA JANE,** language educator; b. St. Paul, May 19, 1942; d. Henry John and Edith Ann (Hutchins) Streich; m. Kent Talbot van den Berg, June 11, 1976; 1 child, David Talbot. BA summa cum laude, U. Minn., 1964; MA, Yale U., 1965, PhD, 1969. Instr. Fordham U., N.Y.C., 1968-70; asst. prof. Fairfield (Conn.) U., 1970-73, Occidental Coll., L.A., 1973-76, Ohio State U., Columbus, 1976-80, U. Wash., Seattle, 1980-87, assoc. prof. English, 1987—2000, chmn. curricular policy bd., 1996-98; prof. English St. Louis U., 2000—, chmn. English dept., 2000—, Dorothy McBride Orthwein prof., 2004—05. Mem. editl. bd. Modern Lang. Quar., 1995-2000, The Ben Jonson Jour., 1995—, Psyart: The Jour., 1997—, Conversations, 2004—, Explorations in Media Ecology, 2005—; author: The Action of Ben Jonson's Poetry, 1987. Huntington Libr. fellow, 1987, NEH fellow, summer 1987, 2003. Mem. MLA (divsn. lit. and psychology 1990-94, chmn. 1992-93), Renaissance Soc. Am., Milton Soc. Am., Pacific Ancient and Modern Lang. Assn. (exec. com. 1997-99). Office: St Louis U Dept English 3800 Lindell Blvd Saint Louis MO 63108 Office Phone: 314-977-3010. Business E-Mail: vandens@slu.edu.

**VAN DEN BERGH, SIDNEY,** astronomer; b. Wassenaar, Netherlands, May 20, 1929; emigrated to U.S.; 1948; s. Sidney J. and Mieke (van den Berg) vandenB.; m. Paulette Brown; children by previous marriage: Peter, Mieke, Sabine. Student, Leiden U., The Netherlands, 1947-48; AB, Princeton U., 1950; M.Sc., Ohio State U., 1952; Dr. rer. nat., Goettingen U., 1956, DSc (honoris causa), 1995, DSc (honoris causa), 2001. Asst. prof. Perkins Obs., Ohio State U., Columbus, 1956-58; research assoc. Mt. Wilson Obs., Palomar Obs., Pasadena, Calif., 1968-69; prof. astronomy David Dunlap Obs., U. Toronto, Ont., Canada, 1958-77; dir. Dominion Astrophys. Obs., Victoria, B.C., 1977-86; prin. rsch. officer NRC Can., 1977-98, rschr. emeritus, 1998—. Adj. prof. U. Victoria, 1977—. Decorated officer Order of Can. Fellow Royal Soc. London; mem. Am., Royal Astron. Soc. (assoc.), Canadian Astronomy Soc. (sr. v.p. 1988-90, pres. 1990-92). Home: 418 Lands End Rd Sidney BC Canada V8L 5L9 Office Phone: 250-363-0006. Business E-Mail: sidney.vandenbergh@nrc.ca.

**VANDENBERGHE, JAMES H.,** financial executive; With Lear Siegler, Inc., 1973—, v.p. fin. plastics divsn., v.p. ops. gen. seating divsn.; sr. v.p. fin., CFO, sec. Leasing Seating Corp., 1988-93, exec. v.p., 1993-97, pres., COO N.Am. ops., 1997-98, also bd. dirs.; vice-chmn. Lear Corp., Southfield, Mich., 1998—. Office: Lear Corp 21557 Telegraph Rd Southfield MI 48034-4248*

**VAN DEN BERGHE, PIERRE LOUIS,** sociologist; b. Lubumbashi, Congo, Jan. 30, 1933; s. Louis and Denise (Caullery) van den B.; m. Irmgard C. Niehuis, Jan. 21, 1956; children: Eric, Oliver, Marc. BA, Stanford U., 1952, MA, 1953; PhD, Harvard U., 1960. Asst. prof. sociology Wesleyan U., Middletown, Conn., 1962-63; asso. prof. sociology SUNY, Buffalo, 1963-65; prof. sociology and anthropology U. Wash., Seattle, 1965-98, prof. emeritus, 1998—. Vis. prof. U. Natal, South Africa, 1960-61, Sorbonne, Paris, 1962, U. Nairobi, Kenya, 1967-68, U. Ibadan, Nigeria, 1968-69, U. Haifa, Israel, 1976, U. New South Wales, Australia, 1982, U. Strasbourg, France, 1985, U. Tuebingen, Germany, 1986, Tel Aviv U., 1988, U. Cape Town, South Africa, 1989, U. Ljubljana, Slovenia, 2005; fellow Advanced Study in Behavioral Scis., Stanford, Calif., 1984-85. Author: 22 books including South Africa, A Study in Conflict, 1965, Race and Racism, 1967, Academic Gamesmanship, 1970, Man in Society, 1978, Human Family Systems, 1979, The Ethnic Phenomenon, 1981, Stranger in Their Midst, 1989, State Violence and Ethnicity, 1990, The Quest for the Other, 1994. Served with M.C. U.S. Army, 1954-56. Mem. Am. Sociol. Assn., Am. Anthrop. Assn., Sociol. Rsch. Assn., Human Behavior and Evolution Soc. Home: 2006 19th Ave E Seattle WA 98112-2902 Office: U Wash Dept Sociology 353340 Seattle WA 98195-3340 Office Phone: 206-543-2051. Business E-Mail: plvdb@u.washington.edu.

**VAN DEN BOSCH, MARGARETA,** apparel company executive; Grad., Beckman's Sch. Design; educated as a profl. tailor, St. Göran's Sch. Stockholm. Designer, Italy, 1976—88; head of design H&M Hennes & Mauritz AB, 1988—. Head of design complete off-stage wardrobe for Team Madonna on Confessions World Tour, 2006. Named one of 25 Masters of Innovation, BusinessWeek. Office: H&M Hennes & Mauritz AB Regeringsgatan 48 SE-106 38 Stockholm Sweden

**VANDEN BOUT, PAUL ADRIAN,** astronomer, physicist, educator; b. Grand Rapids, Mich., June 16, 1939; s. Adrian and Cornelia (Peterson) Vanden B.; m. Rachel Ann Eggebeen, Sept. 1, 1961; children: Thomas Adrian, David Anton AB, Calvin Coll., 1961; PhD, U. Calif.-Berkeley, 1966. Postdoctoral fellow U. Calif., Berkeley, 1966-67, Columbia U., N.Y.C., 1967-68, instr., 1968-69, asst. prof., 1969-70, U. Tex., Austin, 1970-74, assoc. prof., 1974-79, prof., 1979-84; dir. Nat. Radio Astronomy Obs., Charlottesville, Va., 1985—2002, sr. sci., 2003—; dir. Atacama Large Millimeter Array, Charlottesville, Va., 2002—03. Cons. NSF, NASA, NRC. Fellow Fulbright Found., Heidelberg, Fed. Republic Germany, 1961-62, Leiden, Netherlands, 1977 Fellow AAAS, Am. Phys. Soc.; mem. Am. Astron. Soc., Internat. Astron. Union, Internat. Radio Sci. Union. Office: Nat Radio Astronomy Obs 520 Edgemont Rd Charlottesville VA 22903-2454 Office Phone: 434-296-0231. Business E-Mail: pvandenb@nrao.edu.

**VAN DEN BRANDE, RENE ALBERT,** retired accountant; b. Antwerp, Belgium, Aug. 14, 1916; arrived in Can., 1925; s. Henry Van den Brande and Maria Josephine Christ; m. Lily Pearson, July 7, 1947 (dec.). Cert. in pub. adminstrn., Queen's U., Ont., Can., 1963. Chartered acct., Can. Instr. Leamington Bus. Coll., Ont., 1938—40; asst. dept. head Dept. Nat. Revenue, Toronto, 1948—51; pvt. practice acct. Oakville, Ont., 1951—54; office mgr. Erb Lumber Co., Royal Oak, Mich., 1954—57; mgr. Sullivan Homes Inc., Dunedin, Fla., 1957—80; county adminstr. County of Essex, Ont., 1980—81; cons. Fed. Bank Can., Windsor, Ont., 1981—83; town adminstr. Town of South Palm Beach, Fla., 1983—88; ret. Flying officer Royal Can. Air Force, 1940—45, Camp Borden. Avocations: woodworking, reading. Address: 1792 Trappers Ave N8P1T1 Windsor Canada Personal E-mail: van814@email.com.

**VAN DEN DAELE, LELAND DOUGLAS,** psychology professor, psychological measurement company executive; s. Leopold Francis van den Daele and Dorothy Catherine Krolik; m. Lee Ling Tham, June 9, 2000; children: Alphonse Francis children: Leopold Augustine. BA in Psychology, U. of San Francisco 1962; MS, Purdue U., 1964, PhD, 1967. Lic. psychoanalysis Am. Inst. of Psychoanalysis, psychologist Bd. of Psychology, Calif., doctorate clin. psychology Am. Bd. of Profl. Psychology, Washington, cert. stress mgmt. Inst. for Personality and Ability Testing, lic. psychologist SUNY, N.J.; cert. Yoga instr. Internat. Sivananda Yoga Vendanta Ctr. Asst. prof. of psychology U. of Ill., Urbana, Ill., 1969—72; vis. assoc. prof. Tchrs. Coll., Columbia U., N.Y.C., 1973—75; lectr. in psychology Rutgers U., New Brunswick, NJ, 1976—81; faculty Am. Inst. of Psychoanalysis, N.Y.C., 1979—85, supervising psychoanalyst, 1983—85; assoc. prof. Calif. Sch. of Profl. Psychology, San Diego, 1985—94; prof. of psychology Calif. Inst. of Integral Studies, San Francisco 1994—; divsn. dir. of psychology, 1996—97, dean of profl. studies, 1999—2002; pres. faculty senate Calif. Inst. Integral Studies, San Francisco, 1996—97; CEO Psychodiagnostics Inc., Las Vegas, 2005—. Dir. of psychol. rsch. Oceana, Ltd., San Francisco 1994—96; cons. Ctr. for Moral Judgment, Harvard U., Cambridge, Mass., 1976—87; rsch. cons. Inst. for Pedagogical Studies, Tchrs. Coll., Columbia U., N.Y.C., 1970—74; head bio-psychological investigation, internat. biol. program Milton Olive Found., Brown County, Miss., 1968—72; statistician Inst. for

Rsch. on Exceptional Children, U. of Ill., Urbana, 1968—70; editl. bd. Am. Jour. of Psychoanalysis, N.Y.C., 1978—. Author: (monograph) A Developmental Study of the Ego Ideal; editor: (spl. jour. issue) Symposium on Narcissism: Differing Psychoanalytic Perspectives; author: (chpt.) Lifespan Developmental Psychology: Normative Life Crises, Organization and Transformation, Dialectical Psychology, Procedings of the First International Conference on Jung's Psychology and Chinese Culture; contbr. articles to profl. jours. Pres. Assn. for Psychoanalytic Edn. and Tng., La Jolla, Calif., 1987—89; chair pro tem Princeton Soc. for Psychology and Psychoanalysis, Princeton, 1981—82. Named Lawra Hansen Meml. Lectr., Iowa State U., 1970; recipient David Ross fellowship, Purdue U., 1965—66, Sr. postdoctoral fellowship, NIMH, 1970—72, postdoctoral fellowship, Internat. Inst. for Humanistic Studies, 1978. Fellow: Am. Acad. of Clin. Psychology; mem.: APA, Internat. Soc. for the Study of Neuropsychoanalysis, Am. Assn. for Advancement of Psychoanalysis (counselor, mem. exec. com. 1982—85). Green Party. Buddhist Anglican. Achievements include development of Music Apperception Test; Life Span Theory of Preference; first to Direct Interpretation of Dreams; New Program in Preschool Education; Contributions to Neuro-Psychoanalysis. Avocations: nutrition and food preparation, mountain climbing, meditation, art collection, bicycling. Office: Calif Inst Integral Sudies 1453 Mission St San Francisco CA 94103 Home: 10 Mohave Ct Corte Madera CA 94925 Business E-Mail: lvandendaele@ciis.edu.

**VAN DEN HENDE, FRED J(OSEPH),** human resources executive; b. Chgo., Sept. 28, 1953; s. Maurice Everett and Alice Helen (Davey) Van Den H.; m. Sharon Joyce Kucharski, Oct. 4, 1975; children: John Michael, Karen Michelle. BA, DePaul U., 1975; grad., U. Wash. Sch. Exec. Dev., 1981; MS, Nat. Louis U., 1998. Cert. sr. profl. human resources. Asst. v.p. human resources Land of Lincoln Savs. and Loan, Berwyn, Ill., 1977-84; v.p. human resources Uptown Fed. Bank FSB, Niles, Ill., 1984-88; dir. human resources Archdiocese of Chgo., 1988—. Mem. Savs. Assn. Pers. Adminstrn., Berwyn, 1977-84; part-time instr. Inst. Fin. Edn., Chgo., 1984-90; Moraine Valley C.C., Palos Hills, Ill., 1984-90; adj. prof. Coll. Mgmt. and Bus., nat. Louis U., 1998- Sch. bd. treas. St. Rene Sch., Chgo., 1981; sch. bd. mem. St. Daniel the Prophet Sch., Chgo., 1986-88, 93-95, sch. bd. chmn., 1988-89; boy scout leader St. Daniel Parish, Chgo., 1987-94. Recipient Oustanding Achievement in the Field of Athletics award St. Rita H.S. Alumni Assn., Chgo., 1991; Athletic scholar DePaul U., Chgo., 1971-75. Mem. Nat. Assn. Ch. Pers. Adminstrs., Soc. for Human Resource Mgmt. (mem. sch.-to-work com. 1998-2000), Ill. State C. of C. (human resources com. 1979-2003, healthcare com. 1998-2003), Inst. Internat. Human Resources, Am. Mgmt. Assn. (Chicago Area Tng. Coun. 2001—), Soc. for Human Resource Profls. (edn. adv. com. 2002—), KC (4th degree). Roman Catholic. Avocations: camping, fishing, coaching youth sports teams, horseback riding. Home: 5130 S Mulligan Ave Chicago IL 60638-1316 Office: Archdiocese of Chgo 155 E Superior St Chicago IL 60611-2911 Office Phone: 312-751-5352. E-mail: fvandenhende@archchicago.org.

**VANDEN HEUVEL, KATRINA,** publishing executive; b. NYC, Oct. 7, 1959; d. William Jacobus and Jean Babette (Stein) Vanden H.; m. Stephen F. Cohen, Dec. 4, 1988; 1 child, Nicola Anna. BA summa cum laude in Politics, Princeton U., 1982. Prodn. assoc. ABC Closeup Documentaries, 1982-83; asst. editor The Nation, N.Y.C., 1984-89, editor-at-large, 1989-93, acting editor-in-chief, 1994-95, editor-in-chief, 1995—, and pub., gen. ptnr., 2005—. Vis. journalist Moscow News, 1989; Moscow coord. Conf. Investigative Journalism After the Cold War, 1992; co-founder, co-editor Viy i Myi, 1990—. Editor: The Nation, 1865-1990; The Best of the Nation, 1990-2000: Selections from the Independent Magazine of Politics and Culture, 2001, A Just Response: The Nation on Terrorism, Democracy and September 11, 2001, 2002, The Dictionary of Republicanisms, 2005; co-editor: Voices of Glasnost: Interviews with Gorbachev's Reformers, 1989, Taking Back America-And Taking Down the Radical Right, 2004; contbr. articles to newspapers. Recipient Maggie award Planned Parenthood Fedn. Am., 1994. Mem. Correctional Assn. N.Y. (dir.), Inst. for Women's Policy Rsch. (bd. dirs.), Coun. Fgn. Rels., Inst. Policy Studies (trustee), Network of East-West Women (ad. advisors), Franklin and Eleanor Roosevelt Inst. (trustee), Moscow Ctr. for Gender Studies (mem. adv. com.). Office: The Nation 33 Irving Pl Fl 8 New York NY 10003-2332 Personal E-Mail: kat@thenation.com.

**VAN-DEN-NOORT, STANLEY,** neurologist, educator; b. Lynn, Mass., Sept. 8, 1930; s. Judokus and Hazel G. (Van Blarcom) van den N.; m. June Le Clere, Apr. 17, 1954; children: Susanne, Eric, Peter, Katherine, Elizabeth. AB, Dartmouth, 1951; MD, Harvard, 1954. Intern then resident Boston City Hosp., 1954-56, resident neurology, 1958-60; rsch. fellow neurochemistry Harvard U., 1960—62; instr. medicine Case Western Res. U., Cleve., 1962-66, asst. prof., 1966-69, assoc. prof., 1969-70; prof. neurology U. Calif., Irvine, 1970—, chief dept. neurology, 1970—72, chair dept. neurology, 1986—98, assoc. dean Coll. Medicine, 1972-73, dean, 1973-85. Mem. cons. staff U. Calif., Irvine (Calif.) Med. Ctr., Long Beach (Calif.) VA Hosp.; mem. revision com. U.S. Pharmacopoeial Conv., 1990-95. Mem. med. adv. bds., Nat. Multiple Sciersois Soc./Myasthenia Gravis Edn., 1971—, Orange County chpt. Nat. Multiple Sclerosis Soc., 1971—, Orange County Health Planning Coun., 1971-85, Nat. Com. Rsch. in Neurol. Disease, 1982-87. Lt. M.C. USNR, 1956-58. Fellow ACP, Am. Acad. Neurol.; mem. AMA, Am. Neurol. Assn., Nat. Multiple Sclerosis Soc. (chief med. officer 1997-2002), Orange County Med. Assn., Calif. Med. Assn. Home: 17592 Orange Tree Ln Tustin CA 92780-2353 Office: Gottschalk Med Plaza 1 Medical Plaza Dr Irvine CA 92697 Office Phone: 949-824-6486. Business E-Mail: svandenn@uci.edu.

**VANDEPUTTE, DIXIE DIANNE,** psychologist, educator; b. Little River, Kans., Oct. 16, 1942; d. William Dean and Charlotte Juanita Wright m Gregory Charles Vandeputte, Aug. 21, 1959; children: Holly Ann Bell, Gregory Jr., Kerry Lynn Doll. BA summa cum laude in English and Psychology, U. Colo., 1990, MA in Psychology, 1992; PhD in Clin. Psychology, U. Kans., 1997. Lic. clin. psychologist Colo. Program mgr., lead clinician Pikes Peak Mental Health, Colo. Springs, Colo., 1997—2002; dir. Rocky Mountain Brain Injury Rehabilitation Day Clinic, Colo. Springs, 2002—03; dir. Counseling and Testing Ctr. U. Colo., Colo. Springs, 2003—. Instr. U. Colo., 2003—; presenter in field. Contbr. articles to profl. jours. Sec. bd. dirs. Suicide Prevention Partnership, Colo. Springs, 2001—; sec. bd. Nat. Alliance for the Mentally Ill-CS, Colo. Springs, 2002—; mem. steering com. KP Women's Endowment, Colo. Springs, 2003—; bd. dirs. Suicide Prevention Edn. and Advocacy Coalition, Colo. Springs, 2004—. Recipient Outstanding Undergrad. Social Sci. award, U. Colo., 1990. Republican. Avocations: reading, hunting, crafts. Office: Univ Colo Colo Springs 1420 Austin Bluffs Pky Colorado Springs CO 80918 Office Phone: 719-262-3257. Business E-Mail: dvandepu@uccs.edu.

**VAN DE PUTTE, LETICIA,** pharmacist, state senator; b. Tacoma, Dec. 6, 1954; d. Daniel and Isabel (Aguilar) San Miguel; m. Henry P. Van de Putte, Jr., Oct. 223, 1977; children: Nichole, Vanessa, Henry, Gregory, Isabella, Paul. Student, St. Mary's U., San Antonio, 1973-74, U. Houston, 1975, 76-77, U. Tex., 1979; cert. JFK sch. exec. program, Harvard U., 1993. Registered pharmacist, Tex. Pharmacist in charge Botica Guadalupana, San Antonio, 1982-85; owner Loma Park Pharmacy; State Senator Dist. 26, Tex., 1999—. Mem. Tex. State Hispanic Caucus, vice-chair, 2000—01, chair, 2001—03; mem. Veteran Affairs and Military Installations Com., chair, 2003—; mem. Adminstrn. Com., 2003, Bus. & Commerce Com., 2003, Edn. Sub-com. on Higher Edn., 2003; pres. Nat. Hispanic Caucus State Legislatures, 2003—; vice-pres. Nat. Conf. State Legislatures, 2004—. Bd. mem. Santa Rosa Children's Hosp. Found., 2003—; steering com. Milbank Mem. Fund. Recipient Legis. Excellence Award, ACLU, 2001, Session Player 77th Legis. Session, Tex. Monthly Mag., 2001, Best of 77th Legis., Hispanic Jour. Mag., 2001, Pub. Policy Award, Am. Lung Assn., Tex., 2001, Champion for Diabetes Recognition Award, Am. Diabetes Assn., 2003, Pub. Servant of Yr., Am. with Disabilities Act, 2003, Women of Yr., Mex. Am. Bus. Profl. Women, 2003, Legis. Champion Award, Tex. Dept. Pub. Safety Officer's Assn., 2004, Children's Championship Award, United Way of San Antonio,

2004, Appreciation Award, SAISD-Fine Arts Edn. Coalition, San Antonio, 2004. Democrat. Office: Senator Leticia Van De Putte 700 N Saint Marys St Ste 1725 San Antonio TX 78205-3546 E-mail: leticia.vandeputte@senate.state.tx.us.

**VANDER ARK, TOM,** foundation administrator; s. Gary; m. Karen Vander Ark. B in mineral engring., Colo. Sch. Mines; MBA, U. Denver. Sr. exec. Pace Membership Warehouse, Inc.; dir. mktg. devel. Cap Gemini Am.; supt. Federal Way Pub. Schools, Wash., 1994—99; exec. dir. edn. Bill & Melinda Gates Found., Seattle, 1999—. Office: Bill & Melinda Gates Found PO Box 2350 Seattle WA 98102 Office Phone: 206-709-3100.*

**VANDERBEEK, JEFFREY,** professional sports team executive; b. July 19, 1957; m. Deborah Vanderbeek; 2 children. BS, Bloomfield Coll. With Donaldson Lufkin & Jenrette; mng. dir., COO, fixed income ctrl. funding dept. Lehman Brothers Holdings Inc., 1984—93, COO, fixed income govt. dept., 1993—96, COO, fixed income derivative dept., 1993—96, head, global fixed income divsn., 1996—2000, head, capital markets divsn., 2000—02, head, global risk mgmt., pvt. equity and strategy, 2002—04; prin. owner, chmn. NJ Devils, East Rutherford, NJ, 2004—. Vice chmn., bd. mem. Dorothy Rodbell Cohen Found.; mem. exec. com. Boston Coll. Wall St. Coun. Office: NJ Devils Continental Airlines Arena PO Box 504 East Rutherford NJ 07073 also: Nat Newark Bldg 744 Broad St Newark NJ 07102

**VANDERBEKE, PATRICIA K.,** architect; b. Detroit, Apr. 3, 1963; d. B. H. and Dolores I. VanderBeke. BS in Architecture, U. Mich., 1985, MArch, 1987. Registered arch., Ill. Archtl. intern Hobbs & Black, Assocs., Ann Arbor, Mich., 1984-86, Fry Assocs., Ann Arbor, 1988; arch. Decker & Kemp Architecture/Urban Design, Chgo., 1989-92; prin., founder P. K. VanderBeke, Arch., Chgo., 1992—. Mem. adv. com. dept. arch., Triton Coll. Contbr. photographs and articles to Inland Arch. mag.; contbr. photographs to AIA calendar. Chair recycling com. Lake Point Tower Condo. Assn., Chgo., 1990-05, chair. ops. com., 1993; mem. benefit com. The Renaissance Soc., U. Chgo., Redmoon Theater, Chgo. George S. Booth travelling fellow, 1992. Mem. AIA (participant 1st ann. leadership inst. 1997, 1st place nat. photog. contest award 1992, hon. mention 1994, Chog. chpt. membership com., bd. dirs. 2006—), Chgo. Archl. Club, hon. mention 2000 Burnham Prize Competition, The Cliff Dwellers (mem. arts com.). Office: 155 W Burton Pl Apt 16 Chicago IL 60610-1326

**VANDERBILT, ARTHUR T., II,** lawyer; b. Summit, NJ, Feb. 20, 1950; s. William Runyon and Jean (White) V. BA, Wesleyan U., Middletown, Conn., 1972; JD, U. Va., 1975. Bar: NJ 1975. U.S. Dist. Ct. N.J. 1975, U.S. Supreme Ct. 1978. Jud. clk. to presiding justice N.J. Superior Ct., 1975-76, dep. atty. gen., 1976-78, asst. counsel to gov., 1978-79; ptnr. Carella, Byrne, Bain & Gilfillan, Roseland, NJ, 1979—. Chmn. Supreme Ct. Ethics Com.; mem. Supreme Ct. Adv. Com. Profl. Ethics. Author: Changing Law 1976, Jersey Justice, 1978, Law School, 1981, Treasure Wreck, 1986, Fortune's Children 1989 (Book of the Month Club, Readers Digest and fgn. edits.), New Jersey's Judicial Revolution, 1997, Golden Days, 1998 (fgn. edits.), Jersey Jurists, 1998, The Making of a Bestseller, 1999, Gardening in Eden, 2003. Trustee Elizabeth Presbytery, Summit Free Pub. Libr.; Manley-Winser Found., Land of PureGold Found., Greenwood Gardens. Named to N.J. Literary Hall of Fame. Fellow: ABA Found.; mem.: ABA (Scribes award 1976), Nat. Writers Union, The Authors Guild, Inc., Nat. Assn. Bond Lawyers, Am. Judicature Soc., N.J. Bar Assn., Baltusrol Golf Club, Capitol Hill Club, Hyannis Yacht Club. Republican. Presbyterian. Avocation: writing. Office: Carella Byrne Bain & Gilfillan 5 Becker Farm Rd Roseland NJ 07068-1735 Office Phone: 973-994-1700. Business E-Mail: avanderbilt@carellabyrne.com.

**VANDERBILT, GLORIA MORGAN,** artist, actress, fashion designer; b. NYC, Feb. 20, 1924; d. Reginald Claypoole and Gloria (Morgan) V.; m. Pasquale di Cicco (div.); m. Leopold Stokowski, 1945 (div. 1955); children-Stanislaus, Christopher; m. Sidney Lumet, 1956 (div.); m. Wyatt Emory Cooper, 1963; children—Carter V. (dec.), Anderson H. Attended, Mary C. Wheeler, Miss Porter's schs.; studied acting with, dir. Sanford Meisner, beginning 1955. Exhibited in one-man shows at Rabun Studio, N.Y.C., 1948, Bertha Shaeffer Gallery, N.Y.C., 1954, Juster Gallery, N.Y.C., 1956, Hammer Gallery, N.Y.C., 1966, 68, Cord Gallery, N.Y.C., 1966, Washington Gallery Art, 1968, Neiman-Marcus, Dallas, 1968, Vestart Gallery, N.Y.C., 1969, Parish Museum, Southampton, N.Y., also in Nantucket, Mass., Houston, Reading, Pa., Monterey, Calif., Nashville; exhibited in group shows, Washington Gallery Art, 1967, Hoover Gallery, San Francisco, 1971, stage career; acted in summer stock prodn. The Swan; made Broadway debut in The Time of Your Life, 1955; other stage appearances include Picnic, 1955, The Spa, 1956, Peter Pan, 1958, The Green Hat; made TV debut in Tonight At 8:30; other TV appearances include Colgate Comedy Hour, 1955, Flint and Fire on U.S. Steel Hour, 1958, Family Happiness on U.S. Steel Hour, 1959, Very Important People; appeared in film Johnny Concho, 1955; dir. design film, Riegel Textile Corp., N.Y.C., from 1970; designer stationary and greeting cards, Hallmark Co., fabrics, Bloomcraft Co., bed linens, Martex Co., table linens, Peacock Co., Gloria Vanderbilt jeans; also china, glassware, scarves. Recipient Sylvania award 1959, Fashion award Neiman-Marcus 1969. Author: Love Poems, 1955, (with Alfred Allen Lewis) Gloria Vanderbilt Book of Collage, 1970, Woman to Woman, 1979, Once Upon a Time: A True Story, 1985, novel Never Say Good-Bye, 1989, The Memory Book of Starr Faithfull, 1994; author: (with Alfred Allen Lewis) play Three by Two, early 1960's, Black White, White Knight, 1987; poems and short stories. Mem. Actors Equity, Screen Actors Guild, AFTRA, Authors League Am., Am. Fedn. Arts.*

**VANDERBILT, KERMIT,** language educator; b. Decorah, Iowa, Sept. 1, 1925; s. Lester and Ella (Qualley) V.; m. Vivian Osmundson, Nov. 15, 1947; 1 dau., Karen Paige. BA, Luther Coll., Decorah, 1947, Litt. D. (hon.), 1977; MA, U. Minn., 1949, PhD, 1956. Instr. English U. Minn., 1954-57; instr. U. Wash., 1958-60, asst. prof. English, 1960-62; asst. prof. San Diego State U., 1962-65, assoc. prof., 1965-68, prof., 1968-90, prof. emeritus, 1990—. Vis. prof. Am. lit. U. B.C., Can., Vancouver, summer 1963; vis. prof. U. Oreg., summer 1968 Author: Charles Eliot Norton: Apostle of Culture in a Democracy, 1959, The Achievement of William Dean Howells: A Reinterpretation, 1968, Kurt Vonnegut in The Utopian Vision, 1983, American Literature and the Academy: The Roots, Growth and Maturity of a Profession 1986 (Choice award for outstanding acad. books), Theodore Roethke in A Literary History of the American West, 1987; editor: (with others) American Social Thought, 1972, April Hopes (W.D. Howells), 1975, The Rise of Silas Lapham, 1983, spl. issue Am. Literary Realism, winter 1989, La Litterature Americaine, 1991, 3d edit., 1997, The Beautiful and Damned (F. Scott Fitzgerald), 1998; mem. edit. bd. U. Wash. Press, 1960-62, Twentieth Century Lit., 1969-2002; contbr. numerous articles to profl. jours. Served with USNR, 1943-46. Outstanding Prof. San Diego State U., 1976; Guggenheim fellow, 1978-79; Huntington Library fellow, 1980; Am. Philos. Soc. grantee, 1964, Am. Council Learned Socs. grantee, 1972, Nat. Endowment for Humanities grantee, 1986. Mem. Am. Studies Assn. (exec. council 1968-69), So. Calif. Am. Studies Assn. (pres. 1968-69), Philol. Assn. Pacific Coast (chmn. sect. Am. lit. 1968), MLA, Internat. Mark Twain Soc. (hon.), United Profs. of Calif. (Disting. prof. 1978) Home: 6937 Coleshill Dr San Diego CA 92119-1920

**VANDERBURG, PAUL STACEY,** insurance executive, consultant; b. Detroit, Apr. 13, 1941; s. Harold Stacey and Alice Bertha (Lyle) V. Cert. in plastics tech., Oakland U., 1966; AS in Bus., C.S. Mott C.C., 1971; Casualty Claims Law Assoc., Am. Ednl. Inst., 1986; BA in Bus. Adminstrn. and Mgmt., Columbia Pacific U., 1990; cert. in human resource devel., U. South Fla., 1992; fraud claims law assoc., Am. Ednl. Inst., 1995; grad., FBI Citizens Acad., Tampa, 2003. Lic. ins. adjuster Mich., Fla.; cert. cir. civil mediator U. South Fla. Mediation Inst., 2001, cert. county court mediator State Fla. Supreme Ct., 2002. Ins. field claims adjuster Underwriters Adjusting Co., Pontiac, Mich., 1972-76; pres., CEO Sun Cycle, Inc., Drayton Plains, Mich., 1975-77; sr. ins. claims adjuster Kemper Ins. Group, Tampa, Fla., 1979-80;

ins. field claims adjuster Auto-Owners Ins. Co., Lakeland, Fla., 1981-82; sr. recovery specialist CIGNA Corp., Tampa, 1984-85; ins. field claims adjuster Seaboard Adjustment Bur., Lakeland, 1985-87; sr. field claims ins. adjuster Hallmark Ins. Adjusters, Clearwater, Fla., 1987-88; pvt. practice Tampa, 1988—. Author: Insurance Subrogation Management, 1991. Apptd. law enforcement rep. Hillsborough County (Fla.) Human Rels. Bd., 1999—. Staff sgt. U.S. Army, 1963-69. Mem.: Am. Property and Casualty Claims Profls., Soc. of Claims Law Assocs., assn. of Workers' Compensation Claims Profls., Fla. Acad. Profl. Mediators, Ctr. for Internat. Security Studies, Fla. Sheriffs Assn., Am. Security Coun. (nat. adv. bd.), FBI Citizens Acad. Alumni Assn. (bd. dirs.), Am. Legion. Republican. Avocations: boating, fishing, photography. Home and Office: 5448 Circle Dr (WWG) Spring Hill FL 34607-1407 Office Phone: 813-886-9669. Office Fax: 352-592-2191. Personal E-mail: A_Van0123@bellsouth.net.

**VANDERBURG, TIMOTHY WARREN,** history professor; b. Concord, NC, Aug. 10, 1959; s. Warren Howard and Elizabeth Henley Vanderburg; m. Marsha Shyrl Turner, Aug. 28, 1981; 1 child, Zachary Howard. BA, Gardner-Webb Coll., Boiling Springs, NC, 1977—81; MA, U. NC, Charlotte, 1991—94; PhD, Miss. State U., Starkville, 1995—2000. History tchr. First Assembly Christian Sch., Concord, NC, 1981—89, asst. prin., athletic dir., 1989—93; history instr. U. NC, Charlotte, 1994—95; grad. tchg. asst. Miss. State U., Starkville, 1996—2000, instr. coll. ind. study courses, 1998—2000; asst. prof. history Gardner-Webb U., 2000—. Adv. com. mem. NC Hwy. Hist. Marker Adv. Com., Raleigh, 2005—. Contbr. articles to profl. jours. Mem.: So. Hist. Assn. (assoc.), Alpha Theta Chi, Phi Alpha Theta. Home: 1810 Clary Rd Shelby NC 28152 Office: Gardner-Webb Univ PO Box 7343 Boiling Springs NC 28017 Business E-Mail: tvanderburg@gardner-webb.edu.

**VANDERHOEF, LARRY NEIL,** academic administrator; b. Perham, Minn., Mar. 20, 1941; s. Wilmar James and Ida Lucille (Wothe) Vanderhoef; m. Rosalie Suzanne Slifka, Aug. 31, 1963; children: Susan Marie, Jonathan Lee. BS, U. Wis., Milw., 1964, MS, 1965; PhD, Purdue U., 1969, Doctorate (hon.), 2000, Inje U. Korea, 2002. Postdoctorate U. Wis., Madison, 1969—70; asst. prof. biology U. Ill., Urbana, 1970-74, assoc. prof., 1974—77, prof., 1977—80, head dept. plant biology, 1977—80; provost Agrl. and Life Scis., U. Md., College Park, 1980—84; exec. vice chancellor U. Calif., Davis, 1984—91, exec. vice chancellor, provost, 1991—94; chancellor, 1994—. Rsch. assoc. U. Wis., 1970—72; vis. investigator Carnegie Inst., 1976—77, Edinburgh (Scotland) U., 1978; cons. in field. Fellow, NRC, 1969—70, Eisenhower fellow, 1987; grantee Dimond Travel grantee, 1975, NSF, 1972, 1974, 1976—79, NATO, 1980. Mem.: AAAS, Nat. Assn. State Univ. and Land Grant Colls. (exec. com. 2000—), Am. Soc. Plant Physiology (bd. editors 1977—82, trustee, exec. com., treas. 1982—88, chmn. bd. trustees 1994—97). Home: 16 College Park Davis CA 95616-3607 Office: U Calif Davis Office Chancellor Davis CA 95616

**VAN DER HOEK, SHERRY A.,** counselor; b. Chgo., July 20, 1956; d. John Albert and Stella Rose (dec.) Troike; m. Herman Vanderhoek (dec.); stepchildren: Michiel, Martin. AAS, Prairie State Coll., 1992; BA, Govs. State U., 1994, MA, 1997. Lic. profl. counselor, Ill.; cert. counselor Nat. Bd. Cert. Counselors. Counselor South Suburban Coun. on Alcoholism, East Hazel Crest, Ill., 1990-93, South Suburban Family Shelter, Hazel Crest, Ill., 1996-97; facilitator Aunt Martha's Youth Svcs. Ctr., Inc., Park Forest, Ill., 1991-92; grad. asst. Govs. State U. University Park, Ill., 1995-97; pvt. practice counselor Matteson, Ill., 1998—. Mem.: ACA, Aunt Martha's Youth Svcs. Ctr. (founding mem. 1972), Ill. Alcoholism and Drug Dependence Assn., Assn. Counselor Edn. and Supervision (Outstanding Grad. Student Scholarship award 1997), Internat. Assn. Addiction and Offender Counseling, Ill. Counselor Educators and Suprs. (Outstanding Grad. Student award 1996), Ill. Alcohol and Other Drug Profl. Cert. Assn., Ill. Counseling Assn. (founder Govs. State Chpt., pres. 1996, regional gov. 1997—2000), Chi Sigma Iota (chpt. sec. 1995), Psi Chi (chpt. founder, pres. 1997). Avocations: stained glass, cross-stitch, cooking. Home and Office: 3761 W 216th Pl Matteson IL 60443

**VAN DER HORST, BRIAN CHRISTOPHER,** communications consultant, author, educator; b. NYC, Sept. 11, 1944; s. Louis Ferdinand von Pritzelwitz Van der Horst and Emilia (Jennewein) Triggs; children: Nicholas Christopher, Lorelei Eloise. Student, Duke U., 1960-62, New Sch. for Social Rsch., 1962-64, NLP Ctr. for Advanced Studies, Larkspur, Calif., 1981-83. Promotion mgr. Loew's Theatres, N.Y.C., 1965-66; publicist Metro-Goldwyn-Mayer, N.Y.C., 1966-67; publicity mgr. 20th Century-Fox, N.Y.C., 1967-70; v.p. Cannon Group, N.Y.C., 1970-71; dir. publicity and advt. Atlantic Recording Corp., N.Y.C., 1971-73; dir. Neuro-Linguistic Programming Ctr. for Advanced Studies, 1986—90, Repere: Centre Internat. des Etudes Advancees NLP, Paris, 1985—2003, Dirigeants et Partenaires, Paris. Chief facilitator Integral Inst. Europe, Paris, 2000—; columnist, staff writer Village Voice, N.Y.C., 1973-77; columnist Playboy mag., N.Y.C., 1975-77; editor J.P. Tarcher, Inc., San Francisco, 1979-82; cons. SRI Internat., Menlo Park, Calif., 1980-81. Author: Folk Music in America, 1970, Rock Music, 1971, The Outcome Strategy, 2006; author more than 1000 articles on sci., music, and psychology; contbr. articles to Playboy, Omni, Practical Psychology, Penthouse, Cosmopolitan, others. Named Toastmaster of Yr. Paris Toastmasters, 1989. Fellow Nat. Assn. NLP, Internat. Coaching Confederation (founder), Internat. Coaching Fedn.; mem. Assn. for Humanistic Psychology, Toastmasters Am., French Assn. NLP (founding fellow). Avocations: guitar, scuba diving, painting, skiing, gardening, cooking. Personal E-Mail: brianvanderhorst@compuserve.com.

**VANDERHORST, MONICA S.,** physical education educator; b. Bluffton, Ohio, July 4, 1966; d. John Leslie and Judith Kay Badertscher; m. Gerald Keith VanderHorst, Dec. 19, 1987; 1 child, Ryan John. BA, Bluffton Coll., Ohio, 1988; M, Wright State U., Fairborn, Ohio, 1998. Instr. health and phys. edn. Hardin Houston Schs., Ohio, 1989—96, St. Marys City Schs., 1996—. Recipient Martha Harding Jennings award. Mem.: NEA, Ohio H.S. Volleyball Coaches Assn. Home: 10305 State Rte 66 Saint Marys OH 45885 Office: Meml HS 10 W South St Saint Marys OH 45885-2599

**VANDERJAGT, KATHLEEN SUE,** parochial school educator; b. Grand Rapids, Mich., Feb. 12, 1971; d. Kenneth and Grace Ann Vander Jagt. BA, Grand Valley State U., Allendale, Mich., 1993, MA, 2002. Tchr. Covenant Christian Sch., Abilene, Tex., 1993—94, Reformed Heritage Christian Sch., Kalamazoo, 1994—96, Lamont Christian Sch., Coopersville, Mich., 1996—2003, Zion Christian Sch., Byron Center, Mich., 2003—. Vol. Pregnancy Resource Ctr., Grand Rapids, 2006. United Reformed. Avocations: reading, piano, bicycling, travel. Home: 641 Saint Clair NW Grand Rapids MI 49534 Office: Zion Christian Sch 7555 Byron Center Ave Byron Center MI 49315

**VANDERJAGT, MIKE,** professional football player; b. Oakville, Ontario, Canada, Mar. 24, 1970; Student, Mich. State U.; grad., W.Va.U., 1993. Kicker punter Saskatchewan Roughriders (CFL), 1993, Minn. Fighting Pike (AFL), 1996, Toronto Argonauts (CFL), 1996—98; kicker Indpls. Colts, 1998—2006, Dallas Cowboys, 2006—. Named to NFL Pro-Bowl, 2003. Achievements include being a member of Grey Cup Champion Toronto Argonauts, 1996, 1997; being the only kicker in NFL history to go a full season (including playoffs) without missing a field-goal or point-after attempt, 2003. Office: Dallas Cowboys 1 Cowboys Pkwy Irving TX 75063*

**VANDERKOLK, MARY DEDECKER,** nursing educator; b. Highland Park, Mich., Feb. 7, 1951; d. Frank Joseph and Jean Marie (Halmich) DeDecker; m. Michael Homer VanderKolk, June 18, 1977; children: Lauren, Christopher, Nicole, Allison. BS in Psychology, Mich. State U., 1972, BSN, 1975; MSN, Wayne State U., 1980, postgrad., 1989—; MBA, Lake Superior State U., 1993. Nurse externe E.W. Sparrow Hosp., Lansing, Mich., 1974-75, charge nurse gen. surgery unit, 1975-76, staff nurse ICU, 1976-77; staff nurse SICU Catherine McCauley Health Ctr., Ann Arbor, Mich., 1977-81, summer 1982; asst. prof. Ea. Mich. U., Ypsilanti, 1981-84; mem. contingency staff

ICU Munson Med. Ctr., Traverse City, Mich., 1984-85; lead instr. advanced med./surg. nursing Northwestern Mich. Coll., Traverse City, 1985-87, dept. head nursing, 1987-98, nursing prof., 1998—. Defendant nurse expert witness, 1989-94, 96, 97-98; mem. adj. fculty MSN program Grand Valley State U., Grand Rapids, Mich., 1991; com. mem. devel. coun. Munson Med. Ctr., 1992-93; sec./treas. Rural Emergency Med. Edn. Consortium, Traverse City, 1993-95, bd. dirs., 1993-99; bd. dirs., sec. Twin Bays Skating Club, 2000—. Co-author: Adoption Without Fear, 1989; co-author, co-prodr. (video) Tracheostomy Care and Suctioning Techniques, 1984. Coord. health edn. team Immaculate Conception Ch., Traverse City, 1994-95, mem. adv. com. health ministry, 1994—; mem. course devel. team Nursing Virtual C.C. Collaborative of Mich., 2000-01. Recipient Excellence in Teaching award Nat. Inst. Staff & Orgnl. Devel., 1993. Mem. ANA, Nat. League Nursing, Mich. Nurses Assn. (mem. cabinet administrn. and edn., rep. at large bd. dirs. 1987-89, 89-91, rec. sec. 1988-89), Mich. Coun. Nursing Edn. Administrs. (corr. sec. bd. dirs. 1988-89, 89-90, v.p./pres. elect 1990-91, pres. 1991-92, immediate past pres. 1992-93), Mich. League Nursing (dir. area V 1994-96), King. Internat. Nursing Soc. (founding mem. 1996—), County Med. Soc. Aux., Sigma Theta Tau. Avocations: travel, water sports, downhill skiing, figure skating. Office: Northwestern Mich Coll 1701 E Front St Traverse City MI 49686-3016

**VANDER LAAN, MARK ALAN,** lawyer; b. Akron, Ohio, Sept. 14, 1948; s. Robert H. and Isabel R. (Bishop) Vander L.; m. Barbara Ann Ryzenga, Aug. 25, 1970; children: Aaron, Matthew. AB, Hope Coll., Holland, Mich., 1970; JD, U. Mich., 1972. Bar: Ohio 1973, U.S. Dist. Ct. (so. dist.) Ohio 1973, U.S. Ct. Appeals (6th cir.) 1978, U.S. Supreme Ct. 1981. Assoc. Dinsmore, Shohl, Coates & Deupree, Cin., 1972-79; ptnr. Dinsmore & Shohl, Cin., 1979—. Chair litig. dept., 2001—, spl. counsel Ohio Atty. Gen.'s Office, 1983—; spl. prosecutor State of Ohio, 1985-94; city solicitor City of Blue Ash, Ohio, 1987—, City of Silverton, Ohio, 1999-2005; trustee Cin. So. Railway, 1994—, pres., 1999—. Mem. Cin. Human Rels. Commn., 1980-86; mem. Leadership Cin. Class XIII, 1989-90; trustee Legal Aid Soc. of Cin., 1981-94, pres., 1988-90; trustee Volunteer Lawyers for the Poor Found., pres., 2003-06. Mem. ABA, Ohio Bar Assn., Cin. Bar Assn. (ethics com. 1983—), Sixth Cir. Jud. Conf. (life), Potter Stewart Am. Inn of Ct. (master), Queen City Club. Office: Dinsmore & Shohl 1900 Chemed Ct 255 E 5th St Cincinnati OH 45202-4700 Office Phone: 513-977-8000. Business E-Mail: mark.vanderlaan@dinslaw.com.

**VANDERLINDEN, CAMILLA DENICE DUNN,** telecommunications industry executive; b. Dayton, July 21, 1950; d. Joseph Stanley and Virginia Danley (Martin) Dunn; m. David Henry VanderLinden; Oct. 10, 1980; 1 child, Michael Christopher. Student, U. de Valencia, Spain, 1969; BA in Spanish and Secondary Edn. cum laude, U. Utah, 1972, MS in Human Resource Econs., 1985. Asst. dir. Davis County Community Action Program, Farmington, Utah, 1973-76; dir. South County Community Action, Midvale, Utah, 1976-79; supr. customer service Ideal Nat. Life Ins. Co., Salt Lake City, 1979-80; mgr. customer service Utah Farm Bur. Mutual Ins., Salt Lake City, 1980-82; quality assurance analyst Am. Express Co., Salt Lake City, 1983-86, quality assurance and human resource specialist, 1986-88, mgr. quality assurance and engring. Denver, 1988-91; mgr. customer svc. Tel. Express Co., Colorado Springs, Colo., 1991-97; dir. Call Ctr. United Membership Mktg. Group, Lakewood, Colo., 1997-98; televscs. industry mgr. Piton Found., Denver, 1998—; customer care and mktg. dir. SafeRent, 2000—; dir. quality assurance Tele-Servicing Innovations, 2000—02; ops. mgr. Bayaud Industries, 2002—05. Adj. faculty Westminster Coll., Salt Lake City, 1987-88. adj. faculty, quality adv. bd. Red Rocks C.C., 1990-91; cons. in field. Vol. translator Latin Am. community; vol. naturalist Roxborough State Park; internat. exch. coord. EF Fgn. Exch. Program. Mem. Internat. Customer Svc. Orgn. (officer call ctr. chpt.), Colo. Springs Customer Svc. Assn. (officer). Christian. Avocation: swimming. Home: 44 Lake Lea Rd Rochester NY 14617 Personal E-mail: camillavan@usa.net.

**VAN DER LINDEN, FRANK MORRIS,** historian; b. Hendersonville, N.C., Mar. 8, 1919; s. William Harrison and Floride Bowden (Morris) van der L.; m. Georgia Kathlyn Huddle, Feb. 11, 1951; children: Frank Robert, Margaret Lyn, Anne Morris. AB, Lenoir-Rhyne Coll., 1939. Reporter, editl. writer Hickory N.C. Daily Record, 1939-42; mng. editor Hickory Daily Record, 1942-45; reporter Cottrell News Bur., Washington, 1945-52; Washington bur. chief Nashville Tenn. Banner, 1952-86; White House corr. Sacramento Calif. Union, 1979-89; columnist United Feature Syndicate, N.Y., 1971-76. Guest panelist NBC-TV Meet the Press, 1956-75. Author: Dark Horse, 1944, The Turning Point: Jefferson's Battle for the Presidency, 1962, Nixon's Quest for Peace, 1972, The Real Reagan, 1981, Lincoln: The Road to War, 1998, The Dark Intrigue: Democrats and Confederates Combine Against Lincoln, 2006. Mem. The Lincoln Commn., Washington, 1989-98. Mem. U.S. Capitol Hist. Soc. (oral history program dir. 1976-94), The Cosmos Club (editl. bd. 1988—). Presbyterian. Avocation: historical research. Home and Office: 5301 Westbard Cir Apt 247 Bethesda MD 20816-1430

**VANDERLIP, ELIN BREKKE,** professional society administrator, volunteer; b. Oslo, June 7, 1919; came to the U.S., 1934; m. Kelvin Cox, Nov., 1946 (dec. 1956); children: Kelvin Jr., Narcissa, Henrik and Katrina (twins). With Norwegian Embassy, Washington, Norwegian Fgn. Ministry, London, 1941-44, Red Cross, Calcutta, India; pres. Friends of French Art, Portuguese Bend, Calif. Sponsor of charity art conservation fundraising events Friends of French Art; tour leader Ile de France, Anjou, Bordelais, Provence-Cote d'Azur, Alsace, Dordogne, Lyonnais-Isere, Brittany, Burgundy, Normandy, Languedoc, Loire, Gascony, Le Nord, Charente, Champagne, Eure et Loir, 1978-96, Route de Berry, Auvergne and Toulouse. Decorated Comdr. Order of Arts and Letters (France) Chevalier of the Legion of Honor. Home and Office: Villa Narcissa 100 Vanderlip Dr Rancho Palos Verdes CA 90275-5920 Fax: (310) 377-4584. E-mail: VillaCissa@aol.com.

**VAN DER MARCK, JAN,** art historian; b. Roermond, The Netherlands, Aug. 19, 1929; arrived in U.S., 1957; s. Everard and Anny (Finken) van der Marck; m. Ingeborg Lachmann, Apr. 27, 1961 (dec. 1988); m. Sheila Stamell, May 24, 1990. BA, U. Nijmegen, The Netherlands, 1952, MA, 1954, PhD in Art History, 1956; postgrad., U. Utrecht, The Netherlands, 1956-57, Columbia U., 1957-59. Curator Gemeentemuseum, Arnhem, Netherlands, 1959-61; asst. dir. fine arts Seattle World's Fair, 1961-62; curator Walker Art Center, Mpls., 1963-67; dir. Mus. Contemporary Art, Chgo., 1967-70; assoc. prof. art history U. Wash., Seattle, 1972-74; dir. Dartmouth Coll. Mus. and Galleries, 1974-80, Center for Fine Arts, Miami, 1980-85; curator 20th century art, chief curator Detroit Inst. Arts, 1986-95. Author: (book) Romantische Boekillustratie in Belgie, 1956, George Segal, 1975, Arman, 1984, Bernar Venet, 1988, The Art of Contemporary Bookbinding, 1997, Art and the American Experience, 1998, Lucio Pozzi, 2001; contbr. articles to art jours., essays to catalogues. Decorated officer Order Arts and Letters, knight Order of Orange Nassau; fellow Netherlands Orgn. Pure Rsch., 1954—55, Rockefeller Found., 1957—59, Aspen Inst., 1974, 1994, Ctr. Advanced Study in Visual Arts, Nat. Gallery, Washington, 1986. Fellow: Pierpont Morgan Libr.; mem.: Les Amis de la Reliure Originale, Internat. Art Critics Assn.

**VANDERMEER, JOHN H.,** ecologist, educator; Sloan Found. postdoctoral fellow U. Chgo., 1969; coord., mem. full-time faculty, vis. scientist Orgn. Tropical Studies, 1969—99; asst. prof. biology SUNY, Stony Brook, 1969—70; asst. prof. zoology U. Mich., 1970—74, assoc. prof. biology, 1974—81, prof., 1981—, Margaret Davis Collegiate prof. ecology and evolutionary biology, 2002—. Vis. scholar Princeton U., 1969; vis. scientist Nat. Inst. Rsch. Amazon, Manaus, Brazil, 1974; vis. lectr. Superior Sch. Tropical Agr., Tabasco, Mexico, 1978; vis. prof. Autonomous U. Nicaragua, 1984, Southeastern Ctr. Ecol. Investigations, Chiapas, Mexico, 1991, U. C.Am., Managua, Nicaragua, 1994, Fed. U. Minas Gerais, Belo Horizonte, Brazil, 2004; chair dept. ecology and evolutionary biology U. Mich., 1985—86, faculty assoc. prog. in Latin Am. and Caribbean Studies, 1993—, faculty assoc. prog. in Am. culture, 1994—, Alfred Thurnau Disting. prof., 1994—97, Sokal scholar, 1996—97, faculty assoc. Ctr. Study of Complex Systems, 2000—, faculty assoc. Mich. Consortium on Theoretical Physics,

2001—; vis. prof. agroecology Superior Inst. Farming Scis., 1986—87, Fulbright scholar, Nicaragua, 1986—87; Fulbright scholar dept. ecol. agr. Wageningen Agrl. U., Netherlands, 1996—97. Contbr. articles to sci. jours., chapters to books; co-editor: Biology as a Social Weapon, 1977, Nicaraguan Reader: Documents of a Revolution Under Fire, 1983, Nicaragua: Unfinished Revolution, 1986, Agroecology, 1990; author: Elem. Math. Ecology, 1981, The Ecology of Intercropping Systems, 1989, Reconstructing Biology: Genetics and Ecology in the New World Order, 1996; co-author: A Breakfast of Biodiversity: The True Causes of Rain Forest Destruction, 1995, Population Ecology: First Principles, 2003, Elem. Population Ecology, 2003; editor: Tropical Agroecosystems, 2002. Office: Dept Ecology and Evolutionary Biology U Mich Ann Arbor MI 48109 E-mail: jvander@umich.edu.*

**VAN DER MEULEN, JOSEPH PIERRE,** neurologist; b. Boston, Aug. 22, 1929; s. Edward Lawrence and Sarah Jane (Robertson) Van Der Meulen; m. Ann Irene Yadeno, June 18, 1960; children: Elisabeth, Suzanne, Janet. AB, Boston Coll., 1950; MD, Boston U., 1954. Diplomate Am. Bd. Psychiatry and Neurology. Intern Cornell Med. div. Bellevue Hosp., N.Y.C., 1954-55, resident, 1955-56, Harvard U., Boston City Hosp., 1958-60, instr., fellow, 1962-66; assoc. Case Western Res. U., Cleve., 1966-67, asst. prof., 1967-69, assoc. prof. neurology and biomed. engring., 1969-71; prof. neurology U. So. Calif., L.A., 1971—; also dir. dept. neurology Los Angeles County/U. So. Calif. Med. Center; chmn. dept. U. So. Calif., 1971-78, v.p. for health affairs, 1977—2005, dean Sch. Medicine, 1985-86, 95-97, vice dean med. affairs, 1995-97; dir. Ind. Health Professions, L.A., 1991—2005. Vis. prof. Autonomous U., Guadalajara, Mexico, 1974; pres. Norris Cancer Hosp. and Rsch. Inst., 1983—98, chmn., 2002—; pres. Scott Newman Ctr., 1987—89. Contbr. articles to profl. jours. Mem. med. adv. bd. Calif. chpt. Myasthenia Gravis Found., 1971—75, chmn., 1974—75, 1977—78; mem. adv. bd. Amyotrophic Lateral Sclerosis Found., Calif., 1973—75, chmn. Calif., 1974—75; mem. Com. to Combat Huntington's Disease, 1973—; bd. dirs. Calif. Hosp. Med. Ctr., Good Hope Med. Found., LA Hosp. Good Samaritan, Barlow Respiratory Hosp., U. So. Calif. Univ. Hosp., chmn., 1991—2004; bd. dirs. Assn. Acad. Health Ctrs., chmn. Served to lt. M.C. USMC, 1956—58. Nobel Inst. fellow, Karolinska Inst., Stockholm, 1960—62, NIH grantee, 1968—71. Mem.: AMA, L.A. Acad. Medicine, Calif. Med. Soc., L.A. Med. Assn., L.A. Soc. Neurology and Psychiatry (pres. 1977—78), Am. Acad. Neurology, Am. Neurol. Assn., Phi Kappa Phi, Alpha Omega Alpha (councillor 1992—). Roman Catholic. Home: 39 Club View Ln Palos Verdes Peninsula CA 90274-4208 Business E-mail: vanderme@usc.edu.

**VANDER MOLEN, THOMAS DALE,** lawyer; b. Ann Arbor, Mich., Oct. 30, 1950; s. John and Eleanor Ruth (Driesens) Vander M.; m. Judith P. Wrahlstad, June 16, 2001; children from previous marriage: Laura, David, Eric. BA, Calvin Coll., 1972; JD magna cum laude, Harvard U., 1975. Bar: Minn. 1976, U.S. Dist. Ct. Minn. 1981, U.S. Claims Ct. 1983, U.S. Tax Ct. 1977, U.S. Ct. Appeals Fed. Cir., 1988. Law clk. to judge U.S. Ct. Appeals-First Cir., Boston, 1975-76; assoc. Dorsey & Whitney, Mpls., 1976-81; ptnr. Dorsey & Whitney LLP, Mpls., 1982—, gen. counsel, 1993—2001. Mem. editorial bd. Harvard Law Rev., 1973-75. Presbyterian. Office: Dorsey & Whitney LLP 50 South 6th St Minneapolis MN 55402-1498 Office Phone: 612-340-2934. Business E-Mail: vander.molen.tom@dorsey.com.

**VAN DER PAARDT, TAMARA ANN,** music educator; d. Glenn Elmer and Darlene Margaret Schultz; m. Peter van der Paardt, June 27, 1987; children: Nicole Marie, Melissa Krystine, Andrew Scott. BA in Music Edn., Calif. State U., Fresno, 1985. Cert. clear credential music edn. Calif., 1987. Profl. musician Fresno Philharm. Orch., Calif., 1979—; music tchr. Clovis Unified Sch. Dist., 1987—. Dir. Winter Drumline Ensemble, Jazz Ensemble. Named Outstanding Jazz Ensemble, Downbeat Internat. Music Awards, 1995, Class A World Champions, WGI Drumline Competition, 2003. Mem.: CBDA (assoc.), FMCMEA (assoc.), IAJE (assoc.), Internat. Assn. Jazz Educators, Calif. Band Dirs. Assn., Fresno-Madera (Calif.) County Music Educators Assn., Music Educators Nat. Conf. (assoc.), Calif. Music Edn. Assn. (assoc.; pres. ctrl. Calif. sect. 2003—), Winter Guard Internat. Avocations: travel, gardening, softball. Home: 1692 Richert Ave Clovis CA 93611 Office: Reyburn Intermediate Sch 4300 N DeWolf Clovis CA 93611 Office Phone: 559-327-4731.

**VANDERPAN, NORMA,** retired elementary school educator; b. Starkweather, N.D. m. Leslie Vanderpan; 7 children. BA, Concordia Coll.; MA, U. S.D. Mem. negotiation team West Lyon Tchr. Assn., Inwood, Iowa, 1967—69, Brookings Edn. Assn., 1973—74; organizer, rep. Ea. S.D. Uniserv, Sioux Falls, SD, 1974—75. Named Brookings Tchr. of Yr., Brookings Pub. Schs., 1976; Nat. Def. Edn. grant, U. S.D., 1965. Mem.: PEO (chapt. Chpt. P 2004—05), BARTA, Saturday Literary Club (pres. 2005—), Phi Delta Kappa, Alpha Delta Kappa (Eta chpt. sec., Eta chpt. treas., state treas. 1976—78, state chaplain 1990—92, Fidelis Gamma chpt. pres. 1992—94, Fidelis Gamma chpt. chaplain 1995—2005). Republican. Lutheran. Avocations: reading, writing, quilting, antiques, needlepoint. Home: 2009 Derdall Dr Brookings SD 57006

**VANDERPLOEG, JAMES M.,** preventive medicine physician; b. Upland, Calif., Nov. 22, 1950; BA, U. Iowa, 1975. Cert. Aerospace Medicine and Occupational Medicine. Intern U. Hosp./U. Calif., San Diego, 1975-76; resident in otolaryngoloty U. Iowa Hosps., Iowa City, 1978-79; resident in occupational medicine U. Tex. Sch. Pub. Health, Houston, 1980-82, assoc. prof. occupational health; mem. staff St. John Hosp., Nassau Bay, Tex.; pres., partner Ctr. Aerospace & Occupl. Medicine, Houston. Bd. mem. Am. Bd. Preventive Medicine, Schiller Park, Ill., 1993—98, exec. dir., 1998—. Mem. Am. Coll. Occupational Medicine, ACPrM-AerosMA. Office: Ctr for Aerospace & Occupl Medicine 700 Gemini St Ste 110 Houston TX 77058-2735*

**VANDERRYN, JACK,** environmental services administrator; b. Groningen, The Netherlands, Apr. 14, 1930; came to U.S., 1939; s. Herman Gabriel and Henrietta S.E. (Hartog) V.; m. Margrit Wolfes, Mar. 18, 1956; children: David, Judith, Amy, Daniel. BA, Lehigh U., 1951, MS, 1952, PhD, 1955. Rsch. and grad. teaching asst. Lehigh U., Bethlehem, Pa., 1952-55; asst. prof. chemistry Va. Poly. Inst., Blacksburg, 1955-58; rsch. participant Oak Ridge (Tenn.) Nat. Labs., 1957; chemist AEC, Oak Ridge, 1958-62, tech. adviser to asst. gen. mgr. R & D, Washington, 1962-67, asst. to gen. mgr., 1971-72, tech. asst. to dir. div. applied tech., 1972-73, chief energy tech. br., div. applied tech., 1973-75; acting dir. div. energy storage Energy Rsch. and Devel. Adminstrn., Washington, 1975, dir. Office Internat. R & D Programs, 1975-77; dir. Office Internat. Programs Dept. Energy, Washington, 1977-82; dir. energy and natural resources AID, Washington, 1982-91; program dir. environment Moriah Fund, Washington, 1991—2003; sr. fellow, environ. and devel. Moriah Fund., 2003—06. Sr. sci. adviser U.S. Mission to Internat. Atomic Energy Agy., Dept. State, Vienna, Austria, 1967-71; lectr. Brookings Instn., 1965-66. Mem., dep. pres., exec. bd. Am. Internat. Sch., Vienna, 1968-71; v.p. Oak Ridge Civic Music Assn., 1959-60; pres. Washington Print Club, 1986-91; pres. Consultative Group on Biodiversity, 1997-2000; bd. dirs. Ctr. for Internat. Environ. Law, 2004—; Forest Stewardship Coun. U.S., 2004—, Inst. for Conservation Leadership, 2003—, Endangered Species Coalition, 2003—. Home: 8112 Whittier Blvd Bethesda MD 20817-3123 Office Phone: 202-783-8488. E-mail: jackvanderryn@msn.com.

**VANDERSLICE, ELLEN,** information technology manager, composer; b. Ann Arbor, Mich., Oct. 8, 1953; d. Ralph L. Vanderslice, Carolyn G. Vanderslice; married. MArch Coll. Architecture and Urban Planning, U. Mich., 1983, BS, 1981. Lic. Architect, Oreg., 1996. Project mgr. Office of Transp., City of Portland, 1994—99, 2003—; project designer David Giulietti and Assocs., Portland, 1990—94; pres. America Walks, Portland, Oreg., 1996—2003. Pres. Willamette Pedestrian Coalition, Portland, 2001—03; mem. com. on pedestrians Transp. Rsch. Bd., Washington, 2001—04; mem. adv. com. Pub. Rights-of-Way Access, Washington, 1999—; co-treas. Portland chpt. Women's Transp. Seminar, 1997—98; prin. Ellen Vanderslice AIA, Portland, 1999—2003. Composer (CD): Once in a Blue Moon, 2000, The Standard Vanderslice, 2001, Don't Look Before You Sing, 2003. Sec.

Northwest Dist. Assn., Portland, 1986—88. Recipient Pl. Planning award for Portland Pedestrian Master Plan and Pedestrian Design Guide, Environ. Design and Rsch. Assn., 2000, Exemplary Svc. to Pedestrian Transp. Program and Unwavering Commitment to Advocacy of Walking award, Portland Office of Transp. Engring. and Devel., 1999, Outstanding Project award for Portland Pedestrian Design Guide, Inst. Transp. Engrs. Oreg. Sect., 1999, Reclaiming Our Streets All-Star award, City Commr. Earl Blumenauer, 1991, Northwest Traffic Circulation Project Leadership award, Neighbor Newspaper, 1987, 1st prize jazz, USA Songwriting Competition, 2002, Golden Sole award, Willamette Pedestrian Coalition, 2005. Mem.: AIA (sec. Portland chpt. 1998—99, Nehemiah Housing Project award of excellence Portland chpt. 1993), Assn. Pedestrian and Bicycle Profls., Women's Transp. Seminar (co-treas. Portland chpt. 1997, Woman of Yr. Portland chpt. 2000), Nat. Assn. Watch and Clock Collectors, Jazz Soc. Oreg., Portland Songwriters Assn. (1st pl. Blues/Jazz/R&B Category 1999, 2000, 2001, 2003). Avocations: restoring eight-day clocks, canoeing, hiking. Office: 1120 SW 5th Ave Rm 800 Portland OR 97204 Office Phone: 503-823-4638. Business E-Mail: ellen.vanderslice@pdxtrans.org.

**VANDERSLICE, THOMAS AQUINAS,** electronics executive; b. Phila., Jan. 8, 1932; s. Joseph R. and Mae (Daly) V.; m. Margaret Hurley, June 9, 1956; children: Thomas Aquinas, Paul Thomas Aquinas, John Thomas Aquinas, Peter Thomas Aquinas. BS in Chemistry and Philosophy, Boston Coll., 1953; PhD in Chemistry and Physics, Cath. U. Am., 1956. With GE, Fairfield, Conn., from 1956, gen. mgr. electronic components bus. div., 1970-72, v.p., 1970, group exec. spl. systems and products group, 1972-77, sr. v.p., sector exec. Power System Sector, 1977-79, exec. v.p., sector exec. Power System Sector, 1979-84; pres., chief oper. officer, dir. Gen. Tel. & Electronics Corp., Stamford, Conn., 1979-83; chmn., CEO, Apollo Computer, Inc., Chelmsford, Mass., 1984-89, M/A COM, Inc., Lowell, Mass., 1989-95. Bd. dirs. Texaco, Inc. Patentee low pressure gas measurements and analysis, gas surface interactions and elec. discharges; co-author: Ultra High Vacuum and Its Applications, 1963; reviser: Scientific Foundations of Vacuum Technique, 1960; contbr. to profl. jours. Trustee Boston Coll., past chmn., past trustee Comm. Econ. Devel. Recipient Bicentennial medal Boston Coll., 1976; Fulbright scholar, 1953-56. Mem. NAE, ASTM, Am. Vacuum Soc., Am. Chem. Soc., Am. Inst. Physics, Royal Poinciana Golf Club (Naples, Fla.), Oyster Harbors Club, Sigma Xi, Tau Beta Pi, Alpha Sigma Nu, Sigma Pi Sigma. Office: LeRivage Unit 10N 4351 Gulf Shore Blvd N Naples FL 34103-2697

**VAN DER SPIEGEL, JAN,** engineering educator; b. Aalst, Belgium, Apr. 12, 1951; arrived in U.S., 1980; BSEE, U. Leuven, 1971, MSEE, 1974, PhD in Elec. Engring., 1979; M of Arts and Sci., U. Pa., 1988. 2d lt. Belgian Air Force, 1979—80; asst. prof. elec. engring. U. Pa., Phila., 1981-87, assoc. prof., 1987-95, prof. elec. engring., 1995—, dir. Sensor Tech., 1989-98, chmn. dep. elec. engring., 1998—2002, interim chmn. dept. elec. and sys. engring., 2002—04. Patentee integ. ambient sensing, radiation sens. retina sens., gen prupost neural comp., novel ferroelectric sensors, background calibration for pipelined analog-digital converters; editor Sensors and Actuators, 1986-2004. Postdoctoral fellow U. Pa., 1980-81; named Presdl. Young Investigator The White House, 1984. Fellow IEEE; mem. Tau Beta Pi.

**VANDERSTAPPEN, HARRIE ALBERT,** art educator; b. Heesch, The Netherlands, Jan. 21, 1921; arrived in US, 1959; s. Johannes and Johanna (van de Poel) V. Student, Theol. Sch., Helvoirt and Teteringen, The Netherlands, 1939-45, Chinese Lang. Sch., Peking, People's Republic of China, 1946-48; PhD in Far Eastern Art, U. Chgo., 1955. Ordained priest Roman Cath. Ch., 1945. Student lang., also instr., writer, Tokyo, 1955-57; tchr. Nanzan U., Nagoya, Japan, 1957-59; prof. Far Eastern art U. Chgo., 1959-92, chmn. dept. art, 1964-69, prof. emeritus dept. art, 1991—. Author: The T.L. Yuan Bibliography of Chinese Art and Archaeology, 1975; author, editor: Ritual and Reverence, 1989; assoc. editor Monumenta Serica, 1955—; contbr. articles to profl. jours. Recipient Teaching of Art History award Nat. Coll. Art Assn. Am., 1985; Harrie A. Vanderstappen Disting. Chair established at U. Chgo., 1995. Mem. Asia Soc., Assn. Asian Arts Home: 1901 Waukegan Rd Techny IL 60082-6000 Personal E-mail: hvanderstappen@aol.com.

**VAN DER VEEN, STEVEN ROGER,** manufacturing executive; b. N.Y.C., Oct. 20, 1947; s. Herre and Marie (Van Gulik) V.; m. Dianne C. Shields, Dec. 12, 1969; children: Timothy J., Michael T., Elizabeth K., William S., Kristen K. AB in Physics, NYU, 1969, MS in Oceanography, 1972; MBA, Harvard Bus. Sch., 1974. Physicist U.S. Navy Underwater Systems Ctr., New London, Conn., 1969-72; dir. corp. strategy Kennecott Corp., Stamford, Conn., 1974-80; sr. bus. analyst Cabot Corp., Boston, 1980-83; v.p. bus. devel. Heizer Corp., Chgo., 1983-85; prin. S.R. Van der Veen & Co., Norwich, Conn., 1985-86; v.p. planning Connell Ltd. Partnership, Boston, 1986-91; prin. SRV Assocs., Duxbury, Mass., 1991—. Mem. Am. Soc. Materials, Assn. Corp. Growth. Episcopalian. Home: 35 Mt Hope Cir Duxbury MA 02332-3237 Office: SRV Assocs 35 Mount Hope Cir Duxbury MA 02332-3237 Office Phone: 617-934-9700.

**VANDER VELDE, WALLACE EARL,** aeronautical and astronautical engineering educator; b. Jamestown, Mich., June 4, 1929; s. Peter Nelson and Janet (Keizer) Vander V.; m. Winifred Helen Bunai, Aug. 29, 1954; children: Susan Jane, Peter Russell. BS in Aero Engring, Purdue U., 1951; Sc.D, Mass. Inst. Tech., 1956. Dir. applications engring. GPS Instrument Co., Inc., Newton, Mass., 1956-57; mem. faculty Mass. Inst. Tech., 1957—, prof. aero. and astronautics, 1965—. Cons. to industry, 1958— Author: Flight Vehicle Control Systems, Part VII of Space Navigation, Guidance and Control, 1966, (with Arthur Gelb) Multiple-Input Describing Functions, 1968; also papers. Served to 1st lt. USAF, 1951-53. Recipient Edn. award Am. Automatic Control Coun., 1988. Fellow AIAA; mem. IEEE. Home: 50 High St Winchester MA 01890-3314 Office: MIT Rm 9-335 Dept Aero and Astronautics Cambridge MA 02139

**VANDERVER, TIMOTHY ARTHUR, JR.,** lawyer; b. Birmingham, Ala., Jan. 25, 1944; s. Timothy Arthur and Jeannette (Grimes) V.; m. Virginia Cassandra Nye, Oct. 1, 1966 (dec. July 2001); m. Susan Elliotte McVay, Mar. 20, 2003; children: Timothy A. III, Glenn Bruce, Benjamin Richard. BA, Washington and Lee U., 1965; BA in Law, Oxford (Eng.) U., 1967, MA, 1983; JD, Harvard U., 1969. Bar: D.C., U.S. Ct. Appeals (D.C. cir.) 1969, U.S. Ct. Appeals (5th cir.) 1984, U.S. Ct. Appeals (3d and 11th cirs.) 1989, U.S. Supreme Ct. 1978. Assoc. Covington & Burling, Washington, 1969—72, Dept. of Interior, Washington, 1972—73, Dept. Housing and Urban Devel., Washington, 1973—76; ptnr. Patton Boggs L.L.P., Washington, 1976—. Editor: Clean Air Law and Regulation, 1992, Environmental Law Handbook, 1994. Capt. U.S. Army, 1970-71. Presbyterian. Home: 9000 Congressional Ct Potomac MD 20854-4608 Office: Patton Boggs LLP 2550 M St NW Ste 500 Washington DC 20037-1350 Office Phone: 202-457-6074. Business E-Mail: tvanderver@pattonboggs.com

**VAN DER VOO, ROB,** geophysicist; b. Zeist, The Netherlands, Aug. 4, 1940; arrived in U.S., 1970; s. Maximiliaan and Johanna Hendrika (Baggerman) Van der V.; m. Tatiana M. C. Graafland, Mar. 26, 1966; children: Serge Nicolas, Bjorn Alexander. BS, U. Utrecht, Netherlands, 1961, MS, 1965, PhD, 1969. Rsch. assoc. U. Utrecht, 1964-65, rsch. assoc., 1965-69, sr. rsch. assoc., 1969-70; vis. asst. prof. U. Mich., Ann Arbor, 1970-72, asst. prof., 1972-75, assoc. prof., 1975-79, prof. geophysics, 1979—, chmn., 1981-88, 91-95, Arthur F. Thurnau prof., 1994-97, dir. honors program Coll. Lit., Sci. and the Arts, 1998—2003. Guest prof. ETH, Zurich, Switzerland, 1978, Kuwait U., 1979, Utrecht U. and Delft U. Tech., 1997-98. Author: Paleomagnetism of the Atlantic, Tethys and Iapetus Oceans, 1993; contbr. articles to profl. jours. Recipient Russell award, U. Mich., 1976, Disting. Faculty Achievement award, 1990, Benjamin Franklin medal in Earth Scis., 2001. Mem. Geol. Soc. Am. (pres. 2004), Am. Geophys. Union, Geologische Vereinigung (Germany), Royal Acad. Scis. (Netherlands), Royal Norwegian

Soc. Scis. and Letters, Sigma Xi, Phi Kappa Phi. Home: 2305 Devonshire Rd Ann Arbor MI 48104-2703 Office: U Mich 4534 CC Little Bldg Ann Arbor MI 48109-1005 Office Phone: 734-764-8322. Business E-Mail: voo@umich.edu.

**VANDERWALKER, DIANE MARY,** materials scientist; b. Springfield, Mass., Nov. 1, 1955; BS, Boston Coll., 1977; PhD, MIT, 1981. NATO fellow U. Oxford, Eng., 1981-82; asst. prof. SUNY, Stony Brook, 1983-85; materials rsch. engr. Army Rsch. Lab. (formerly U.S. Army Materials Tech. Lab.), Watertown, Mass., 1986-94. Cons. IBM, Yorktown Heights, N.Y. Contbr. articles to profl. publs. Mem. N.Y. Acad. Scis. Roman Catholic.

**VANDER WEG, PHILLIP DALE,** art educator, academic administrator, sculptor; b. Benton Harbor, Mich., Aug. 16, 1943; s. Sam Dirk and Trena (Poort) Vander W.; m. Judith Greville, Dec. 15, 1966; 1 child, Kara Sue. BS in Design, U. Mich., 1965, MFA, 1968. Art instr., prof. art Mid. Tenn. State U., Murfreesboro, 1968-89, acting head Mufreesboro, 1983-85, 88-89; chair dept. art, prof. art We. Mich. U., Kalamazoo, 1989-97, 00—, prof. art, 1998—, dir. sch. art, 1999—. Cons., editl. reviewer Prentice-Hall Pubs., Englewood Cliffs, N.J., 1978-90; mem. region 5 adv. panel Mich. Artist Program, Detroit Inst. Art, 1990-92; mem. rev. panel Tenn. Art Commn. Visual Arts, Nashville, 1986-89. Prin. works include Columbia State U., 1979, Vanderbilt U., Nashville, 1987, Tenn. Arts Commn., 1988. Mem. Kalamazoo Pub. Art Commn., 1992—. Mem. Nat. Assn. Schs. of Art and Design, Nat. Coun. Art Adminstrs., Founds. in Art Theory and Edn. (founder, bd. dirs. 1976-84). Home: 6791 Penny Ln Kalamazoo MI 49009-8539 Office: Western Mich U Dept Art Oliver St Kalamazoo MI 49008 Office Phone: 616-387-2436. Business E-Mail: vanderweg@wmich.edu.

**VANDER WOUDE, RICHARD JOHN,** lawyer; b. Longview, Tex., Nov. 11, 1954; s. Jack Clarence and Jeanette Helen (Uddenberg) Vander W.; m. Jane Kay Robertson, June 7, 1975; children: Jeffrey Chad, Michael Craig, Kevin Clay. BBA, So. Meth. U., 1975, JD, 1978. Bar: Tex. 1978, U.S. Dist. Ct. (we. dist.) Tex. 1981, U.S. Ct. Appeals (5th cir.) 1982, U.S. Dist. Ct. (no. dist.) Tex. 1985, U.S. Dist. Ct. (ea. dist.) Tex. 1987. Assoc. Sheehy, Lovelace & Mayfield P.C., Waco, Tex., 1978-83, ptnr., 1983—. Bd. dirs. Heart of Tex. Legal Svcs., Inc., Waco, also pres. 1986-89. Bd. dirs. Heart of Tex. Council on Alcoholism and Drug Abuse, Waco, 1983-88, sec., 1985, v.p., 1986; adv. bd. Waco Rape Crisis Ctr., 1983-84; mem. City of Woodway Planning and Zoning Commn., 1986—. Mem. ABA (various sects), Tex. Bar Assn. (various sects.), Waco-McLennan County Bar Assn., Cen. Tex. Bankruptcy Bar Assn., Waco-McLennan County Young Lawyers Assn., Tex. Assn. of Bank Counsel, Waco Jaycees (bd. dirs. 1979-84, sec. 1983). Methodist. Avocations: running, tennis. Home: 609 Ivy Ann Dr Waco TX 76712-3550 Office: Sheehy Lovelace & Mayfield PC 1200 American Amicable Buil Waco TX 76701

**VAN DER WYST, GEON,** dancer; b. Melbourne, Australia; Student, Australian Ballet Sch., 1989—90, St. Francis Xavier's Coll., 1987—88. Mem. Australian Ballet, 1991—95, soloist, 1995—96, sr. artist, 1996—2001; prin. dancer Nat. Ballet Can., Toronto, Canada, 2001—. Dancer (ballets) The Sleeping Beauty, Romeo and Juliet, Cinderella, Onegin, Manon, Apollo, The Competition, Madam Butterfly, Anna Karenina, The Merry Widow, Don Quixote, Songs of a Wayfarer, Theme and Variations, The Taming of the Shrew, Etudes, In the Night, Divergence, Jardi Tancat, Gemini, Three of Us, Fall River Legend, Por vos Muero, Rites, Equus. Office: Walter Carsen Ctr Nat Ballet Can 470 Queens Quay West Toronto ON Canada M5V 3K4 Home: 155 Dalhousie St # 1048 Toronto ON Canada M5B 2P7

**VANDE STEEG, NICKOLAS W.,** manufacturing executive; m. Jeanne Vande Steeg; 3 children. BS, Univ. Calif., Irvine, 1968; MBA, Pepperdine Univ., 1985. With Parker Hannifin Corp., Cleve., 1971—; pres. seal group, 1987—2002, v.p., 1995—2002, corp. v.p., 2002, sr. v.p., 2002—03, exec. v.p., COO, 2003—04, pres., COO, bd. dir., 2004—. Bd. dir. Trimble Navigation Ltd. Bd. dir. Azusa Pacific Univ. Office: Parker Hannifin Corp 6035 Parkland Blvd Cleveland OH 44124-4141*

**VAN DEUSEN, LOIS M.,** lawyer; married. BA summa cum laude, Cedar Crest Coll., 1961; JD, Rutgers Univ., Newark, 1977. Bar: NJ, US Dist. Ct. NJ. Assoc. McCarter & English, Newark, 1977—86, ptnr. real estate law, 1986—2002, mem. exec. com., 1991—, mng. ptnr., 2002—. Twp. atty., Livingston, NJ, 1989—2002; bd. dir. CIT Group Inc., 2003—; lectr. NYU Sch. Law. Bd. mem. Habitat for Humanity Newark. Named one of NJ Women of Influence, NJBiz mag., 2002, 10 Most Powerful Women in NJ Bus., Star-Ledger, 2006; recipient Woman of Substance award, Seton Hall Law Sch., 2003, Lifetime Achievement award, Ctr. for Italian & Italian-Am. Culture, 2002, Disting. Alumna award, Rutgers Newark Law Sch., 2004. Mem.: ABA, NJ Bar Assn. Office: McCarter & English 4 Gateway Ctr 100 Mulberry St Newark NJ 07102 Office Phone: 973-639-2017. Office Fax: 973-624-7070. Business E-Mail: lvandeusen@mccarter.com.*

**VAN DEVENDER, J. PACE,** research scientist, science administrator; b. Jackson, Miss., Sept. 12, 1947; m. Nancy Jane Manning, 1971; 3 children. BA in Physics, Vanderbilt U., 1969; MA in Physics, Dartmouth Coll., 1971; PhD in Physics, U. London, 1974. Physicist diagnostics devel. Lawrence Livermore Lab., 1969; mem. tech. staff pulsed power rsch. and devel. Sandia Nat. Labs., Albuquerque, 1974-78, divsn. supr. pulsed power rsch. divsn., 1978-82, dept. mgr. fusion rsch., 1982-84, dir. pulsed power scis., 1984-93, dir. corp. comm., 1993, dir. Nat. Indsl. Alliances Ctr., 1993-95; pres. Prosperity Inst., 1995-98; dir. strategic rsch. ctr. Sandia Nat. Labs., Albuquerque, 1998—, chief info. officer, 1998—2002, dir. exec. staff, 2002—03, v.p. sci. tech and partnerships, chief tech. officer, 2003—. Mem. bd. trust Vanderbilt U., 1969-73. With U.S. Army, 1969-71. Recipient Ernest Orlando Lawrence Meml. award US Dept. Energy, 1991; named one of 100 Most Promising Scientists Under 40, Sci. Digest, 1984; Marshal scholar U. London, 1971-74. Fellow Am. Phys. Soc.; Phi Beta Kappa, Omicron Delta Kappa, Sigma Xi. Office: Sandia Nat Labs MS 0103 PO Box 5800 Albuquerque NM 87185-0103 Office Phone: 505-844-5148. E-mail: jpvande@sandia.gov.

**VANDEVER, WILLIAM DIRK,** lawyer; b. Chgo., Aug. 1, 1949; s. Lester J. and Elizabeth J. V.; m. Kathi J. Zellmer, Aug. 26, 1983; children: Barton Dirk, Brooke Shelby. BS, U. Mo., Kansas City, 1971, JD with distinction, 1974. Bar: Mo. 1975, U.S. Dist. Ct. (we. dist.) Mo. 1975, Kans. 2005. Dir. Popham Law Firm, Kansas City, Mo., 1975—. Lectr. in field, Kansas City Mo., 1979—. Issue editor U. Mo.-Kansas City Law Rev., 1974. Bd. govs. IOLTA, 1989—91. Fellow Am. Bd. Trial Advs. (treas. 2004-05, pres.-elect 2006, Best Lawyers in Am.-tort law); mem. ABA, ATLA, Mo. Assn. Trial Attys., Kansas City Met. Bar Assn. (treas., sec., pres., elected to 16th Jud. Commn. 1989-94), Kansas City Bar Found. (treas. 1992, sec. 1994, pres. 1996-98, pres. award domestic violence 1999), Interest on Lawyer Trust Accts. of Mo. (bd. govs.), Kansas City Mem. Svcs. (pres. 1988—, commr. 16th jud. cir. selection com.), U. Mo. Kansas City Found. (fin. com. 1998), Phi Delta Phi, Beta Theta Pi. Avocations: tennis, skiing, running, reading. Home: 11380 W 121st Ter Shawnee Mission KS 66213-1978

**VAN DE WALLE, CHRIS GILBERT,** physicist; b. Gent, Belgium, May 10, 1959; came to U.S., 1982; s. Gaston Eduard and Louise Armanda (De Moor) Van de W. Engr., Rijks U. Gent, 1982; MSEE, Stanford U., 1983, PhD, 1986. Vis. scientist IBM Watson Rsch. Ctr., Yorktown Heights, N.Y., 1986-88; sr. mem. rsch. staff Philips Labs., Briarcliff Manor, N.Y., 1988-91; mem. rsch. staff Xerox Palo Alto (Calif.) Rsch. Ctr., 1991—. Adj. prof. Columbia U., N.Y.C., 1991; chmn. Trieste (Italy) Semicondr. Symposium, 1992, Conf. on Physics and Chemistry of Semicondr. Interfaces, 1996, others. Editor: Wide-Band-Gap Semiconductors, 1993; contbr. chpts. to books, numerous articles to profl. jours. Recipient Isabella Van Portugal prize U. Gent, 1982, prize City of Gent, 1982; Belgian-Am. Ednl. Found. fellow, 1982-83. Fellow Am. Phys. Soc.; mem. Materials Rsch. Soc. Office: Xerox PARC 3333 Coyote Hill Rd Palo Alto CA 94304-1314

**VANDEWALLE, GERALD WAYNE,** state supreme court chief justice; b. Noonan, N.D., Aug. 15, 1933; s. Jules C. and Blanche Marie (Gits) VandeW. BSc, U. N.D., 1955, JD, 1958. Bar: N.D., U.S. Dist. Ct. N.D. 1959. Spl. asst. atty. gen. State of ND, Bismarck, 1958-75, 1st asst. atty. gen., 1975-78; justice ND Supreme Ct., 1978-92, chief justice, 1993—. Mem. faculty Bismarck Jr. Coll., 1972-76; mem. Nat. Ctr. for State Cts. Rsch. adv. coun.; mem. fed.-state jurisdiction com. Jud. Conf. of the U.S. Editor-in-chief N.D. Law Rev, 1957-58. Active Bismarck Meals on Wheels Recipient Sioux award U. N.D., 1992, Ednl. Law award N.D. Coun. Sch. Attys., 1987, Love Without Fear award Abused Adult Resource Ctr., 1995, N. Dakota State Bar Assoc. Dist. Service award, 1998. Mem. ABA (co-chmn. bar admissions com. 1991-99, mem. coun. sect. legal edn. and admissions, chmn. coun. sect. legal edn. and admissions), State Bar Assn. N.D., Burleigh County Bar Assn., Conf. of Chief Justices (past pres., bd. dirs. 1996-98, chmn. fed.-state tribal rels. com.), Am. Contract Bridge League, Order of Coif, N.D. Jud. Conf. (exec. com.), Elks, KC, Phi Eta Sigma, Beta Alpha Psi (Outstanding Alumnus award Zeta chpt. 1995), Beta Gamma Sigma, Phi Alpha Delta. Roman Catholic. Office: ND Supreme Ct State Capitol 600 E Boulevard Ave Bismarck ND 58505-0530 Office Phone: 701-328-2221. Business E-Mail: gvandewalle@ndcourts.com.*

**VAN DE WATER, MARK E.,** investment company executive; b. Dec. 17, 1963; BA in Polit. Sci. and Econs., St. Lawrence U., 1986; MA in Internat. Devel., George Washington U., 1998. Legis. asst. Congressman Les AuCoin; ptnr. VanFleet, Metzner & Meredith; profl. staff mem. Senate Com. on Appropriations, 1991-94, dep. staff del., 1994-96; v.p. investment devel. dept. Overseas Pvt. Investment Corp., 1996—; now sr. v.p. bus. devel. Intellibridge, Washington, 1996-2000. Presdl. scholar; John C. Stennis fellow John C. Stennis Ctr. for Pub. Svc., 1995. Office: NW #100B 1101 30TH St Washington DC 20007-3706

**VAN DE WATER, READ,** federal official; b. Charlotte, NC; m. Mark Van de Water; 3 children. Degree, U. South, 1986; M, George Washington U.; JD, Georgetown U. Appropriations assoc., legis. asst. Congressman Tom DeLay, Tex., 1987—91; legis. coun., dir. govt. affairs Northwest Airlines, 1991—97; legis. coun. internat. trade and investment Bus. Roundtable, 1997—99; founder Carson King Cons., 2000; asst. sec. aviation & internat. affairs U.S. Dept. Transp., Washington, 2001—03. Mem. Nat. Mediation Bd., Washington, 2003—, chmn., 2005—. Republican. Office: Nat Mediation Bd 1301 K St NW Ste 250 E Washington DC 20005-7011 E-mail: vandewater@nmb.gov.

**VANDE WOUDE, GEORGE FRANKLIN,** molecular biologist, cancer researcher; b. Brooklyn, N.Y., Dec. 25, 1935; s. George Franklin Sr. and Alice Beatrice (Leudesdorff) V.W.; m. Dorothy Helen Stapel, Apr. 5, 1959; children: Susan Joan, Gail Louise, Cynthia Irene, Alice Helene. Student, Hope Coll., 1953-54; BA, Hofstra U., 1959; MS, Rutgers U., 1962, PhD, 1964. Postdoctoral rsch. assoc. USDA Plum Island, Greenport, N.Y., 1964-65, rsch. scientist, 1965-72; chief virus tumor biochemistry Nat. Cancer Inst. NIH, Bethesda, Md., 1972-81, chief lab. molecular oncology, 1981-83; dir. basic rsch. program Nat. Cancer Inst.-Frederick (Md.) Cancer R & D Ctr., 1983—98; dir. disting. scientific investigator Van Andel Rsch. Inst., Grand Rapids, Mich., 1999—. Contbr. over 100 articles and sci. papers to profl. publs., 35 book chpts. Recipient Robert J. and Claire Pasarow Found. award, 1989. Mem. AAAS, Am. Soc. for Microbiology, Am. Assn. for Cancer Rsch.; fellow Am. Acad. Arts & Sciences Achievements include research in fields of biology and cancer. Office: Van Andel Inst 201 Monroe Ave NW Grand Rapids MI 49503*

**VAN DE ZILVER, PETER A.L.,** economist, financial analyst; b. June 26, 1949; MA in Econs., U. So. Calif., 1979. CFA, Calif. MIS mgr. Sunnyglen Corp., Newport Beach, Calif., 1984-92; v.p., quatitative analyst PIMCO, Newport Beach, 1992—. E-mail: zilver@pimco.com.

**VAN DIJK, FRITS,** food products executive; b. Jakarta, Indonesia, Oct. 6, 1947; married; 2 children. B in Econs., U. Rotterdam, The Netherlands; grad. program for exec. devel., Internat. Inst. Mgmt. Devel., Lausanne, Switzerland. Sales rep. Nestlé U.K., 1970—71; asst. to mng. dir. Nestlé India, 1972—74; product mgr. (milks) Nestlé Philippines, 1975—78, mktg. dir., 1985—86; mktg. beverage divsn. Nestlé, Vevey, Switzerland, 1979—81; mktg. mgr. Nestlé Sri Lanka, 1982—84; COO Nestlé Malaysia, 1987—88, market head, 1988—94, Nestlé Japan, 1995—99; chmn., CEO Nestlé Waters, 2000—; dep. exec. v.p. Nestlé S.A., 2002, exec. v.p., 2003—. Office: Nestle Waters NAm Holdings Inc 777 W Putnam Ave Greenwich CT 06830

**VAN DINE, ALAN CHARLES,** advertising agency executive, writer; b. Ford City, Pa., Jan. 12, 1933; s. Albert and Helen (Remaley) Van D.; m. Joan Anne Hodges, Jan. 29, 1955 (div. Jan. 1971); children: Lynn, Mark, Barbara, Michael; m. Holly Long Shefler, Apr. 23, 1977. BA, Duquesne U., 1955; postgrad., U. Pitts., 1968—71. Editor Mt. Lebanon News, Pa., 1956-58; editorial dir. Pitts. Suburban Newspapers, 1958-61; writer and assoc. creative dir. Batten, Barton, Durstine & Osborne, Pitts., 1961-70; pres., creative dir. Van Dine, Horton, McNamara, Manges, Inc., Pitts., 1970-89; chmn. Van Dine, Humphrey, Inc., Pitts., 1989-95; cons. in field, 1996—. Mem. adv. coun. Internat. Poetry Forum, Pitts., 1969-80. Author: Can You Imagine?, 1967, Unconventional Builders, 1977, revised edit., 2001, (humor) The Encyclopedia of Advertising, 1987, Clyde Hare's Pittsburgh, 1994, Light Verse for a Heavy Universe, 2004; columnist Pitts. mag., 1977-78, Pa. Illustrated, 1979-81; contbr. articles, essays, short stories, and poems to mags. 1st lt. USAF, 1956. Recipient numerous awards Art Dirs. Club NY, 1964—, Bus. and Profl. Advt. Assn., 1964—, Am. Advt. Fedn., 1999. Mem.: Chartiers Country Club. Avocations: golf, tennis, darkroom photography, cartooning, computer programming. E-mail: AVDZZZ@bellatlantic.net.

**VAN DINE, HAROLD FORSTER, JR.,** architect, artist; b. New Haven, Aug. 28, 1930; s. Harold Forster and Marguerite Anna (Eichstedt) Van D.; m. Maureen Kallick, Mar. 1, 1983; children by previous marriage: Rebecca Van Dine, Stephanie Van Dine Natale, Gretchen Van Dine Natale. BA, Yale Coll., 1952; MArch, Yale Sch. Arch., 1958. Registered architect. Designer Minoru Yamasaki & Assocs., Detroit, 1958-60; chief designer Gunnar Birkerts & Assocs., Detroit, 1960-67; prin. Straub, Van Dine & Assocs., Troy, Mich., 1967-80; chief architecture and design officer Harley Ellis, Southfield, Mich., 1980-95; archtl. cons. Birmingham, Mich., 1995—, San Miguel de Allende, Mexico, 1995—. V.p. Fields, Devereaux, HEPY, L.A., 1984-95. Prin. works include Mcpl. Libr., Troy, Mich., campuses for Oakland CC, Mich., North Hills Ch., Troy, First Ctr. Office Plaza, chemistry bldgs at. U. Mich. and Ind. U., G.M.F. Robotics Hdqrs., Flint Ink Rsch. and Devel. Ctr., Comerica Bank Ops. Ctr., Christ the King Mausoleum, Chgo., Resurrection Mausoleum, Staten Island, Mich. Biotech Inst., Ford Sci. Rsch. Labs, Fetzer Inst. Hdqrs. and Retreat Ctr., Cen. Mich. U. Music Sch., Oakland U. Sci. Techs. Bldg., Corning Credit Union, NY. Bd. dirs. Cultural Coun. Birmingham/Bloomfield, 1990-99. Served to lt. (j.g.) USN, 1952-55 Recipient Book award AIA, 1958, Excellence in Architecture Silver medal AIA, 1958, Gold medal Detroit chpt. AIA, 1987, Mich. Soc. of Architects gold medal, 1991, over 50 major design awards; William Wirt Winchester travelling fellowship Yale U. Sch. Architecture, 1958; elect. to AIA Coll. Fellows, 1979. Mem.: Pewabic Soc. (bd. dirs. 1983—2002). Personal E-mail: mvandhv@aol.com. E-mail: artwork@harryvandine.com.

**VAN DINE, VANCE,** investment banker; b. San Francisco, July 2, 1925; s. Melvin Everett and Grace Winifred (Harris) Van D.; m. Isabel Erskine Brewster, Sept. 8, 1956 (dec.); 1 dau., Rose M. (dec.). BA. Yale U., 1949; LLB, NYU, 1955. Assoc. Morgan Stanley & Co., NYC, 1953-59, 61-63, ptnr., 1963-75; mng. dir. Morgan Stanley & Co., Inc., NYC, 1970-83; adv. dir. Morgan Stanley & Co., NYC, 1983—. Cons. Internat. Bank for Reconstn. and Devel., 1959-61; chmn. Doane Western Co. Author: The Role of the Investment Banker in International Transactions, 1970, The US Market After Controls, 1974. Bd. dirs. Yale U. Alumni Fund, Combined Health Appeal of Greater NY, Rec. for Blind, Inc., NYC, 1979-89; trustee Cancer Rsch. Inst., NYC, Nassau County Art Mus., LI U., 1979-91; gov. dir. Fgn. Policy Assn. 1980-89. With USN, 1943-46. Recipient Yale Class of 1949 Disting. Service

award, 1983. Mem. The Pilgrims of the US, Union Club, Piping Rock Club, NY Yacht Club, Seawanhaka Corinthian Yacht Club, Church Club, Yale Club (NYC), Met. Opera Club. Republican. Episcopalian. Office: Morgan Stanley & Co Ste C2E 1221 Avenue Of The Americas New York NY 10020-1008 Home: 525 E 72nd St Apt 251 New York NY 10021-9608 Office Phone: 212-762-8849, 212-634-1220. Business E-Mail: vancevandine@ms.com.

**VANDIVER, RENEE LILLIAN AUBRY,** interior designer, architectural preserver; b. New Iberia, La., Nov. 7, 1929; d. Harold George and Josephine Fortier (Brown) Aubry; m. Arthur Roderick Carmody, Jr., Jan. 1952 (div. 1979); children: Helen Bragg Carmody Stroud, Renee Josephine Carmody Mathews, Arthur Roderick III, Patrick Gerard, Timothy H.A., Mary Joellyn, Virginia Caroline, Joseph Barry; m. Frank Everson Vandiver, Mar. 21, 1980. BFA, Sophie Newcomb Coll. Tulane U., 1951; postgrad., U. Paris, 1951-52, Centinary Coll., 1966-68, La. State U., Shreveport, 1978. Designer, supt. art New Iberia Parish Elementary Schs., 1951; archtl. drafter and designer Perry L. Brown, Inc., Baton Rouge, 1950-52; tchr. art St. Joseph's Elem. Sch., Shreveport, 1960-69; designer, illustrator, saleswoman Stierwalt Interiors, Shreveport, 1974-78; design cons. for president's homes and gardens North Tex. State U., Tex. A&M U., Denton, College Station, 1980-88; design cons., planner, saleswoman, pres. Renee Aubry Vandiver Interiors, College Station, Tex., 1980—; design cons. Am. U. in Cairo, 1997—; proofreader, editor, rschr., asst. Office of Frank E. Vandiver, College Station, 1998—. Interior design and house constrn. cons. Heritage Antiques and Interiors, New Iberia, 1972—; interior design cons., Tenn., La., S.C., 1980—; invited student Middle Eastern master painter Sabri Raghab; involved with consultations and contruction large new campus, pres.'s home grounds Am. U., Cairo. Editl. and illustrations collaborator works on gen. mil. history with Frank E. Vandiver, 1990—; works include design constrn. of new Pres.'s Home on campus of Am. U. of Cairo, 2004. Mem. NAFE, DAR, Constrn. Specifications Inst., Dallas Market Ctr., Houston Market Ctcr., Jr. League, Textile Mus., Mus. Women in Arts, Tex. A&M U. Women's Club (hon. pres. 1981—), Fedn. Tex. A&M U. Mother's Club. Avocations: painting, playing piano, gardening, travel, reading. Home: PO Box 10600 College Station TX 77842-0600

**VANDIVER, SARA ELIZABETH SHARP RANKIN,** retired postmaster; d. James Earl and Celeste Heskett Sharp; m. William Doyle Vandiver, Aug. 18, 1978 (dec. Feb. 27, 1997); m. James Dorothy Rankin, Sr., Aug. 25, 1934 (dec. Aug. 3, 1971); children: James Dorothy Rankin Jr., William Earl Rankin, Carolyn Vandiver Pollan. Postmaster US Postal Svc., Driver, Ark., 1954—80; ret. Sec. St. Louis Region Postmaster Tng. Conf., 1962—73; v.p. Ark. Chpt., Nat. Assn. Postmasters, 1976—78; columnist Ark. Postmaster. Charter mem. Nat. Mus. Women in the Arts, Washington, 1990—2006; contbg. mem. Smithsonian Instn., Washington, 2000—06; pres. Wilson PTA, Ark., 1950—52, Wilson Co-Operative Club, 1952—54, Gen. Fedn. of Women's Clubs Prog. Club, Osceola, 1985—90; organizer Adopt-a-Teacher Program, Osceola Pub. Schs., 1985, Kids and Kindness Program, Osceola Pub. Schs., 1985, Gt. Am. Family Recognition and Awards Program, Osceola, Ark., 1987; pres., state advisor Gen. Fedn. Women's Clubs, Dist. II, Ark., 1990—92, state chmn. cmty. improvement program, 1994—96; mem. Miss. County Geneal. and Hist. Soc., 1993—2006; bd. mem. Interfaith Neighbors, Osceola, 1996—2006; leader Miss. County Explorers Bible Study, Ark., 1983—96; pres. Wilson Women's Missionary Union, 1953—55; Sunday sch. tchr., 1963—. Mem.: Riverlawn Country Club.

**VANDIVER, THOMAS K.,** lawyer; b. Leonard, Mo., Mar. 1, 1951; BA cum laude, DePauw U., 1973; JD, Wash. U., 1977. Bar: Mo. 1977, Ill. 1978, DC 1983. Named ptnr. Armstrong, Teasdale, Kramer & Vaughan, St. Louis, 1984; now ptnr. Sonnenschein Nath & Rosenthal LLP, St. Louis. Mem.: ABA, Am. Health Lawyers Assn., Nat. Assn. Bond Attorneys, DC Bar Assn., Ill. Bar Assn., Mo. Bar Assn. Office: Sonnenschein Nath & Rosenthal LLP Ste 3000 One Met Sq Saint Louis MO 63102 Office Phone: 314-259-5829. Office Fax: 314-259-5959. Business E-Mail: tvandiver@sonnenschein.com.

**VAN DOMELEN, JOHN FRANCIS,** academic administrator; b. Havana, Cuba, Oct. 19, 1942; s. Floyd and Sara (Molina) Van D.; m. Naomi Ruth Kittlesen. BS in Applied Physics, Mich. Tech. U., 1964; MS in Water Res. Mgmt., U. Wis., Madison, 1972; PhD in Civil Engring., U. Wis., 1974. Commd. 2nd lt. USAF, 1964, advanced through grades to col., 1988; mgr. engring. Charmin Paper Products Co., Green Bay, Wis., 1969-70; asst. prof. Norwich U., Northfield, Vt., 1974-79, head engring. and tech. dept., 1979-83, head engring. and tech. div., 1983-85, v.p. acad. affairs, dean of faculty, 1985-90; pres. Wentworth Inst. Tech., Boston, 1990—. Mem. Engring. Workforce Commn. Contbr. articles to profl. jours. Trustee New Eng. Assn. Schs. and Colls., 2003—. Decorated Cross of Gallantry (Vietnam); recipient Centennial medal IEEE, 1984. Mem. ASCE, Am. Soc. Engring. Edn., Sci. Rsch. Soc. N.Am. Avocations: golf, science fiction. Office: Wentworth Inst Tech 550 Huntington Ave Boston MA 02115-5998 Business E-Mail: vandomelenj@wit.edu.

**VAN DOVER, JAMES KENNETH,** education educator; b. St. Louis, Mo., Jan. 1, 1950; s. James Kenneth and Virginia Van Dover; m. Sarala Abreu, June 9, 1979; children: Lara Kiran, Andrew Siddharth. BA, Lafayette Coll., Easton, Pa., 1968—72; MA, Bryn Mawr Coll., Pa., 1972—74, PhD, 1974—78. Prof. Lincoln U., Pa., 1978—. author: (literary criticism) Defoe's World Mapp'd, Murder in the Millions, You Know My Method, We Must Have Certainty, At Wolfe's Door, Polemical Pulps; editor: Critical Responses to Raymond Chandler; author: Isn't Justice Always Unfair, Centurions, Knights, and Other Cops, Understanding William Kennedy. Recipient Fulbright Prof., Fulbright Commn., Germany 80, 88; China 00; Austria 07, Lindback award for Tchg. Excellence, Lincoln U., 1986; fellow Whiting Dissertation, Whiting Found., 1976—77. Independent. Protestant. Office: English Dept Lincoln Univ Lincoln University PA 19352 Office Phone: 610-932-8300. Office Fax: 610-932-1256. Business E-Mail: vandover@lincoln.edu.

**VAN DRESER, MERTON LAWRENCE,** ceramics engineer; b. Des Moines, June 5, 1929; s. Joseph Jerome and Victoria (Love) Van D.; m. Evelyn Lenore Manny, July 12, 1952; children: Peter, Jennifer Sue. BS in Ceramic Engring., Iowa State U., 1951. Tech. supt. Owens-Corning Fiberglas Corp., Kansas City, Mo., 1954-57; rsch. engr. Kaiser Aluminum & Chem. Corp., Milpitas, Calif., 1957-60, rsch. head, 1960-63, lab. mgr., 1963-65, assoc. dir., 1965-69, dir. refractories rsch. Pleasanton, Calif., 1969-72, dir. non-metallic materials rsch., 1972-83, v.p., dir. rsch. Indsl. Chem. div. and Harshaw/Filtrol Partnership Cleve., 1983-85, dir. bus. devel. Pleasanton, 1985-88, cons., 1988—2003. Mem. adv. bd. dept. ceramic engring. U. Ill., 1974-78; intern. tech. adv. com. Refractories Inst., 1980-84; mem. nat. materials adv. bd. Nat. Acad. Sci.; mem. Indsl. Rsch. Inst. Contbr. articles to sci. jours.; patentee in field. Sustaining membership chmn. local dist. Boy Scouts Am., 1980; pres. PTA, 1967-68; vol. exec. Pakistan Internat. Exec. Svc. Corps, 1990-91. Aviator C.E., U.S. Army, 1951-54. Recipient Profl. Achievement citation Iowa State U., 1978; named to Lambda Chi Alpha hall of fame, 1996. Fellow: Am. Ceramic Soc. (v.p. 1973—74); mem.: AIME, ASTM (hon.), Metall. Soc., Nat. Inst. Ceramic Engrs., Brit. Ceramic Soc., Masons, Rotary (pres. Pleasanton Club 2002—03, pres. Club Found. 2003—04, Paul Harris fellow), Keramos (pres. 1976—78, herald 1980—84, Greaves Walker Roll of Honor award). Avocation: flying. Home and Office: 40 Castledown Rd Pleasanton CA 94566-9749

**VAN DUSEN, ALBERT CLARENCE,** academic administrator; b. Tampa, Fla., Aug. 30, 1915; s. Charles H. and Maude E. (Green) Van D.; m. Margaret Davis, Jan. 3, 1943; children: Margaret Van Dusen Pysh, Jane Katherine, Sara Elizabeth (Mrs. Frank J. Matyskiela). BS, U. Fla., 1937, AM, 1938; PhD, Northwestern, 1942; LittD, U. Tampa, 1959; L.H.D., Duquesne U., 1967. Instr., assoc. prof. dept. psychology U. Fla., 1938-41; assoc. prof. psychology Northwestern U., 1946, dir. summer session, 1948-52, v.p. pub. relations, 1952-56; prof. psychology, bus. adminstrn. and edn. U. Pitts., 1956-85, asst. chancellor for planning and devel., 1956-59, vice chancellor the professions, 1959-67, vice chancellor program devel. and pub. affairs, 1967-71, vice chancellor, sec. univ., 1971-80, vice chancellor emeritus, spl. asst. for pub.

affairs, 1980-85, vice chancellor emeritus, prof. emeritus psychology, bus. adminstrn. and edn., 1985—, ctr. assoc. univ. ctr. for internat. studies, 1986—. Editor: Proc. Am. Coll. Personnel Assn; contrb. articles to profl. jours. Bd. govs. Pinchot Inst. Conservation Studies; vice chmn. bd. dirs. The Buhl Found., World Affairs Coun. Pitts., vice chmn. bd. dirs. Duquesne U., acting chmn., 1987-88; bd. dirs. Pitts. YMCA, ACTION Housing, Inc., Assn. Am.'s Pub. TV Stas., QED Communications Inc., chmn. 1981-88; bd. dirs Japan-Am. Soc. Pa.; mem. Pa. Pub. TV Network Commn.; chmn., bd. trustees Pitts. History and Landmarks Found.; pres. bd. trustees H.C. Frick Ednl. Commn., United Way Pa.; dir. South Hills Child Guidance Ctr.; chmn. selfcare study Health Edn. Ctr., Pitts., 1979-80; mem. Walter Reed Hovey Fellowship com. Pitts. Found. Lt. USNR, 1942-46. Fulbright sr. scholar Australian-Am. Ednl. Found., 1980 Fellow Am. Psychol. Assn., Am. Psychol. Soc., Pa. Psychol. Assn., Internat. Found. Social Econ. Deve.; mem. Internat. Assn. Schs. Insts. Adminstrn., C. of C. (dir. 1953-55), Am. Coll. Pub. Rels. Assn. (v.p. 1956-58), Assn. Deans and Dirs. Summer Sessions (sec. 1950-51), Profl. Schs. and World Affairs Com. (chmn. edn. and world affairs 1965-67), Am. Pers. and Guidance Assn., Midwest Psychol. Assn., Ea. Psychol. Assn., Pitts. Psychol. Assn., Internat. Assn. Applied Psychology, Western Pa. Coun. Econ. Edn., Internat. Assn. Schs. and Insts. Adminstrn., Friends of Art for Pitts. Schs. (charter mem.), Phi Beta Kappa, Sigma Xi, Beta Theta Pi, Beta Gamma Sigma. Clubs: Univ. (Pitts.), Duquesne (Pitts.), St. Clair Country (Pitts.). Home: 1290 Boyce Rd Apt C333 Pittsburgh PA 15241-3958

VAN DUYNE, RICHARD PALMER, analytical chemistry educator, chemical physics educator; b. Orange, N.J., Oct. 28, 1945; s. John Palmer and Lorraine Montgomery (Stoller) Van D.; m. Jerilyn Elise Miripol BA, Rensselaer Poly. Inst., 1967; PhD, U. N.C., 1971. Asst. prof. analytical chemistry and chem. physics Northwestern U., Evanston, Ill., 1971-76, assoc. prof., 1976-79, prof., 1979-87, Charles E. and Emma H. Morrison prof. chemistry, 1987—. Cons. Beckman Instrument Co., Fullerton, Calif., 1982-90, Eastman Kodak Co., Rochester, N.Y., 1978-91; disting. vis. prof. U. Tex., Austin, 1979; chmn. Vibrational Spectroscopy Gordon Conf., 1982; Camille and Henry Dreyfus lectr. U. Colo., Boulder, 1981; Kilpatrick lectr. Ill. Inst. Tech., 1982; O.K. Rice lectr. U. N.C., 1984; Henry Werner lectr. U. Kans., 1986; Arthur A. Vernon lectr. Northeastern U., 1992. Mem. advc. bd. Jour. Phys. Chemistry, 1983-88; contrb. chpts. to books, articles to profl. jours. Recipient Coblentz award, 1980, Fresenius award, 1981, Excellence in Surface Sci. award, 1996, Pitts. Spectroscopy award, 1991. Fellow AAAS, Am. Phys. Soc. (recipient Earle K. Plyler prize, 2004), Am. Acad. Arts & Sci.; mem. Am. Chem. Soc. Home: 1520 Washington Ave Wilmette IL 60091-2417 Office: Northwestern Univ 2145 Sheridan Rd Evanston IL 60208-0834

VAN DUYSE, FRANCIS DONALD (FRITZ VAN), publisher; b. Sturgeon Bay, Wis., May 2, 1926; s. Francis Lewis and Gertrude (Simon) Van D.; m. Dorothy Marie Walden, May 15, 1953 (div. Feb. 1978); children: Susan, Rebecca, Francis Roy, Sarah. BBA, Spencerian Coll., 1949. Baseball announcer Albany Cardinals, Ga.; 1953—54, Waycross Bears, Ga., 1955, Valdosta Tigers, Ga., 1956; pub., editor Wis. All-Sports, Green Bay, 1958—68, Wis. Playground, Green Bay, 1958—68, Pro Football Exclusive, 1969—72; dir. sports WLUK-TV, Channel 11, Green Bay, 1962—63; CEO announcer Gemini Broadcasting Co., Appleton, Wis., 1980—82; pres., CEO MegaPrint Internat., Sturgeon Bay, Wis., 1986—2000; pub., editor Fritz Van Newsletter, 2002—05, Pro Mag., 2005—; pub. Mega Press Internat., Wis., 2004—. Freelance sports announcer, 2003—. Author: History of the Green Bay Packers, 1965; pub., editor (yearbooks) Salute to the Packers 1961-68. With USN, 1944—46. Avocations: chess, writing. Home: 1811 Michigan St Apt 1E Sturgeon Bay WI 54235-3704

VAN DYCK, PETER CUYLER, federal agency administrator; b. Dec. 9, 1939; married; 3 children. BA in Physiology, U. Ill., 1962; MS in Physiology, U. Ill., Chgo., 1966, MD, 1966; MPH in Maternal and Child Health, U. Calif., Berkeley, 1973. Diplomate Nat. Bd. Med. Examiners. Intern then resident in pediatrics Children's Meml. Hosp., Chgo., 1966-68, chief resident, 1968-89; instr. Med. Sch. Northwestern U., Chgo., 1968-69; chief pediatrics Health Clinic U.S. Army, Frankfurt, Germany, 1969-71, primary nursery physician 97th Gen. Hosp., 1971-72; pediatric cons. Internat. Red Cross, Amman, Jordan, 1973; dir. maternal and child health Utah State Divsn. Health, Salt Lake City, 1973-74, dir. divsn. family health services, 1974-92, acting exec. dir., 1984-85, acting dir. divsn. health care financing (Medicaid), 1986-87; asst. prof. Med. Ctr. U. Utah, Salt Lake City, 1976-82, prof. Med. Ctr.; sr. med. advisor to the directors of Maternal and Child Health Bur. and Health Resources and Services Adminstrn., HHS, 1992—95; dir. Office of State and Cmty. Health Maternal and Child Health Bur., Health Resources and Services Adminstrn., US HHS, 1995—98, acting assoc. adminstr., 1998—99, assoc. adminstr., 1999—. Adj. assoc. prof. health Univ. Utah, Salt Lake City, 1975—, adj. asst. prof. Coll. Nursing, 1976—; mem. adv. com. U. Utah Coll. Nursing, 1976-80, Albert Einstein Coll. Medicine, Ctr. for Disease Control, 1983-86, John F. Kennedy Child Devel. Ctr., Denver, 1979-82; faculty coord. Crippled Children's Svcs. Advanced Inst., Children's Hosp., Columbus, Ohio, 1983—; mem. maternal and child health/Medicaid tech. assistance group Health Care Financing Adminstrn., 1987-93; mem. planning com., faculty Surgeon Gens. Conf., 1987; mem. various coms. and task forces; presenter, cons., reviewer in field; cons. Interagy. Efforts Children Spl. Health Needs Federated States Micronesia, 1991, Third Pacific Basin Interagy. Conf. Individuals Spl. Health Care Needs No. Marianas Islands, 1992; faculty mem. Med. Ctr. Georgetown U., Washington, 1993; chief party U.S. Del. Third Regional Follow-up Meeting World Summit Children, Antigua, Guatemala, 1995. Contbr. articles to profl. jours. Co-chmn. sch. health com. Utah State Bd. Edn., Utah Dept. Health, 1974-92, statewide immunization action com. Awareness Com., 1977-78; project dir. Sudden Infant Death Syndrome Regional Ctr., Utah, 1975-80; chmn. Govs. Adv. Coun. for Developmentally Disabled Children, 1976-78; mem. task force on svcs. to presch. handicapped children Utah State Legis., 1984, tech. adv. coun. Utah Children, 1985-88, adv. bd. Jr. League, 1985-88; bd. dirs. Exceptional Child Ctr., Utah, 1975-80. Recipient Nat. Leadership award Dept. Health and Human Svcs., 1989, Nat. Achievement award Healthy Mothers, Healthy Babies, 1991; named one of 500 Most Influential Healty Policymakers Health Care 500, 1992; grantee U.S. Dept. Health and Human Svcs., Ctrs. for Disease Control., Devel. Diabetes Coun., Bur. Edn. for the Handicapped, Bur. Community Health Svcs.; WHO fellow, 1995. Mem. APHA (mem. various coms., chmn. maternal and child health sect. 1988—, Ross award 1977), Nat. Acad. for State Health Policy (mem. steering com. 1987-95), Nat. Found. March of Dimes (chmn. med. adv. bd. 1975-93, Plaque for Outstanding Svc. 1977-78), Nat. Early Childhood Tech. Assistance System (mem. nat. adv. com. 1988-90), Am. Acad. Pediatrics (mem. various coms.), Nat. Assn. of State Bds. Edn. (mem. task force on adolescent pregnancy 1979-80), Nat. Assn. State and Territorial Maternal and Child Health and Crippled Children Dirs. (pres. 1978-80), March of Dimes Birth Defect Found. (mem. nat. chpt. grants rev. com. 1988-92), Intermountain Pediatrics Soc. (mem. legis. and child abuse coms. 1974-76), Utah Pub. Health Assn. (mem. various coms., pres. 1984-86, mem. editorial bd. 1976-77, Beaty award 1985). Office: Maternal & Child Health Bur Parklawn Bldg Rm 18-05 5600 Fishers Ln Rockville MD 20857 Office Phone: 301-443-2170.*

VAN DYCK, WENDY, dancer; b. Tokyo; Student, San Francisco Ballet Sch.; BA in performing Arts, St. Mary's Coll., 2003. With San Francisco Ballet, 1979—96, prin. dancer, 1987—96, instr., tchr. 1996; co-dir. Lawrence Pech Dance, San Francisco, 1996—. Performances include Forgotten Land, The Sons of Horus, The Seawander Fantasy, Romeo and Juliet, The Sleeping Beauty, Swan Lake, Concerto in d: Poulenc, Handel-a-Celebration, Menuetto, Intimate Voices, Hamlet and Ophelia pas de deux, Connotations, Sunset, Rodin, In the Night, The Dream: pas de deux, La Sylphide, Beauty and the Beast, Variations de Ballet, Nutcracker, The Comfort Zone, Dreams of Harmony, Rodeo, Duo Concertant, Who Cares; performed at Reykjavik Arts Festival, Iceland, 1990, The 88th Conf. of the Internat. Olympic Com., LA, 1984, with Kozlov and Co. Concord Pavilion; guest artist performing role

Swan Lake (Act II), San Antonio Ballet, 1985, Giselle, Shreveport (La.) Met. Ballet, 1994; featured in the TV broadcast of Suite by Smuin. Mailing: PO Box 29190 San Francisco CA 94129 Office Phone: 415-308-5881. E-mail: wvandyck7@earthlink.net.

VAN DYK, FREDERICK THEODORE, political scientist, writer; b. Bellingham, Wash., Oct. 6, 1934; s. Ted and June Ellen (Williams) Van Dyk; m. Julia Jean Covacevich, Nov. 22, 1957 (dec. 1996); children: Theodore, Robert, Terry Jean, Sue Ellen. BA, U. Wash., Seattle, 1955; MS, Columbia U., N.Y.C., 1956. Reporter, editor Seattle Times, 1956-57; advt. public relations exec. Boston and N.Y.C., 1958-62; acting dir. European Community Info. Service, Washington, 1962-64; asst. to Hubert Humphrey, Vice Pres. of U.S., 1964-68; v.p. Columbia U., N.Y.C., 1968-69; pres. Van Dyk Assocs., Washington, 1969-76; asst. adminstr. AID, Washington, 1977; v.p. Weyerhaeuser Co., Tacoma, 1978—80; pres. Center for Nat. Policy, Washington, 1981-85, Van Dyk Assocs., 1985-98; exec. v.p. Milken Inst., Santa Monica, Calif., 1998-99; vis. scholar Claremont (Calif.) Grad. U., 1999-2000; sr. fellow UCLA Sch. Pub. Policy and Social Rsch., 1999-2000; columnist Seattle Post-Intelligencer, 2001—. Contbr. articles to newspapers incl. the Wall St. Jour., NY Times, Wash. Post, L.A. Times. Mem. Coun. Fgn. Rels., Presdl. Commn. Fgn. Assistance, Pacific Coun. Internat. Policy; bd. dirs. Com. Study Am. Electorate, Franklin and Eleanor Roosevelt Inst., Jean Monnet Coun., Humphrey Inst. With M.I. U.S. Army, 1957, with M.I. U.S. Army, 1961—62. Mem.: Rainier Club (Seattle), Delta Upsilon. Personal E-mail: t_van_dyk@hotmail.com.

VAN DYKE, CLIFFORD CRAIG, retired bank executive; b. Ft. Madison, Iowa, June 23, 1929; s. Charles Clifford and Frances Mary (Butterwick) Van D.; m. Edith Ellicott Powers, Aug. 4, 1951 (dec. Oct. 1980); children: Carol Elizabeth, Deborah Ellicott, Jill Anne, Lisa Ellicott. BA, Knox Coll., 1951; MBA, Harvard U., 1955. Asst. v.p. Nat. Bank of Detroit, 1962-65, v.p., 1965-76; pres. Peoples Nat. Bank & Trust Co. of Bay City, Mich., 1976-78, chmn. bd., pres. Mich.; 1979-86; chmn. bd., pres., chief exec. officer New Ctr. Bank Corp., Bay City, Mich., 1986; chmn. First of Am. Bank-Bay City, N.A., 1987-89; sr. v.p. First of Am. Bank-Mid Mich. N.A., 1990-94; ret., 1994. Trustee Kantzler Found., Bay City, 1979—; chmn. bd., pres. Bay County Growth Alliance, 1987—. 1st lt. U.S. Army, 1951-53, Korea. Mem. Bay City Country Club, Saginaw Valley Torch Club, Rotary. Independent. Unitarian Universalist. Office: Bay County Growth Alliance PO Box 369 Bay City MI 48707-0369 Office Phone: 989-893-5596.

VAN DYKE, CRAIG, psychiatrist, director; b. Detroit, Oct. 4, 1941; married; two children. BS, U. Wash., 1963, MD, 1967. Asst. prof. psychiatry Yale U., New Haven, Conn., 1974-78; from assoc. to prof. psychiatry U. Calif., San Francisco, 1979-86, prof., chmn. dept. psychiatry, 1994—. Mem. Am. Psychosom. Soc., Internat. Coll. Psychosom. Medicine, Soc. Neurosci., Internat. Neuropsychol. Soc. Office: U Cal San Francisco Langley Porter Psychiatric Inst 401 Parnassus Ave San Francisco CA 94143-0984 E-mail: cvd@lppi.ucsf.edu.

VAN DYKE, DANIEL L., geneticist; b. Paterson, N.J., Mar. 1, 1947; PhD, Ind. U., 1976. Cert. med. genetics and clin. cytogenetics Am. Bd. Med. Genetics. Divsn. head genetics labs. Henry Ford Hosp., Detroit, 1975—; faculty U. Mich. Med. Sch., Detroit, 1978-94, Case Western Res. U., Cleve., 1994—. Mem.: Am. Bd. Med. Genetics (pres. 1998—2000, chair dept. med. genetics 1999—). Office: Mayo Clinic 200 1st St SW Rochester MN 55902 Office Phone: 507-284-6776.

VAN DYKE, DICK, actor, comedian; b. West Plains, Mo., Dec. 13, 1925; m. Marjorie Willett, Feb. 12, 1948 (div. May 1984); children: Christian, Barry, Stacey, Carrie Beth. With Wayne Williams, founded advt. agy., Danville, Ill., 1946. Chmn. Nick at Nite, 1992—. Appeared with Philip Erickson in pantomine act The Merry Mutes, Eric and Van, 1947-53; TV master ceremonies The Music Shop, Atlanta, Morning Show, CBS, 1955, Cartoon Show, 1956; TV variety show Dick Van Dyke Show, New Orleans; guest appearances TV shows, 1958, Golden Girls, 1985 (Emmy nominee), Jake and the Fatman, 1987, Coach, 1989, Sabrina the Teenage Witch, 1996, Becker, 1998; TV host Flair, ABC, 1960; Broadway debut in The Girls Against the Boys, 1959, Van Dyke and Company, 1976, The Van Dyke Show, CBS, 1988; performed in Broadway musical Bye Bye Birdie, 1960-61 (also motion picture version); (TV) Dick Van Dyke Show, CBS, 1961-66, New Dick Van Dyke Show, 1971-74; performer weekly comedy program Carol Burnett Show; (TV series) Diagnosis Murder, 1993-2002; (TV movies) Daughters of Privilege, 1991, The House on Sycamore Street, 1992, Diagnosis of Murder, 1992, A Twist of the Knife, 1993, The Dick Van Dyke Show Remembered, 1994; star, exec. prodr. Without Warning, 2002, A Town Without Pity, 2002, Murder 101, 2006; performed in motion pictures including What a Way To Go, 1964, Mary Poppins, 1965, Divorce American Style, 1967, Chitty, Chitty, Bang, Bang, 1968, The Comic, 1969, Some Kind of Nut, 1969, Cold Turkey, 1971, The Morning After, 1974, The Runner Stumbles, 1979, Drop-Out Father, 1982, Found Money, 1983, Dick Tracy, 1990, Buitenspel, 2005, (voice) Curious George, 2006; Author: Faith, Hope, and Hilarity, 1970. With USAAC, World War II. Recipient Theater World award 1960, Antoinette Perry award for best mus. comedy actor 1961, Emmy award for comedy NATAS, 1962, 64, 65, 77, Life Career award Acad. Sci. Fiction, Fantasy and Horror Films, 2000, Lifetime Achievement award in comedy, 1999. Office: William Morris Agy Inc care Sol Leon 151 S El Camino Dr Beverly Hills CA 90212-2775*

VAN DYKE, GENE, oil industry executive; b. Normal, Ill., Nov. 5, 1926; BS in Geol. Engring., U. Okla., 1950. Geologist Kerr-McGee, Oklahoma City, 1950; chief geologist S.D. Johnson Co., Wichita Falls, Tex., 1950-51; ind. geologist, oil operator, 1951-58; ptnr. Van Dyke and Mejlaender, Houston, 1958-62; founder, owner, chmn. Van Dyke Oil Co. (now Vanco Energy Co.), Houston, 1962—, also bd. dir. Bd. dirs. Van Dyke Netherlands, Inc. Compiler index of geol. articles to South La. With AC US Army, 1945. Named Living Legend in Wildcatting, Houston Geol. Soc., 2000; named to Hall of Fame, Dutch Am. Heritage Soc., 2001. Mem.: Am. Assn. Petroleum Geologists, Ind. Petroleum Assn., Houstonian Club, Houston Petroleum Club, Houston Club. Republican. Episcopalian. Vanco Energy Company is active in deepwater west Africa and is currently the largest license holder with over 20 million acres in depths between 1,000 and 10,000 feet; Vanco has been awarded the Prykerchenska Block in southeast Ukraine Black Sea, being 3.2 million acres and its water depth ranges from 150 meters to 2,200 meters. Office: Vanco Energy Corp 3 Greenway Plz 12th Fl Houston TX 77046 Office Phone: 713-877-8544. Office Fax: 713-877-8476. Business E-mail: info@vancoenergy.com, gvandyke@vancoenergy.com.

VAN DYKE, MICHELLE, bank executive; BA in Bus. Econ., Calvin Coll., 1985. Joined Old Kent Bank, 1985; former sr. v.p., regional mgr. of Ill. mortgage region Old Kent Mortgage Co., pres., central region, 1997—98; exec. v.p., mgr. of retail distribution for Mich.; Ind. and Ill. Old Kent Bank, 1998—2004, pres., Ill. div., 2000—04; pres., CEO, western Mich. Fifth Third Bank, Grand Rapids, Mich., 2004—. Bd. dirs ICCF, Porter Hills Retirement Village. Named one of 25 Women to Watch, US Banker mag., 2005. Office: Fifth Third Bank 3785 Plainfield Ave NE Grand Rapids MI 49525*

VAN DYKE, MILTON DENMAN, aeronautical engineering educator; b. Chgo., Aug. 1, 1922; s. James Richard and Ruth (Barr) Van D.; m. Sylvia Jean Agard Adams, June 16, 1962; children: Russell B., Eric J., Nina A., Brooke A. and Byron J. and Christopher M. (triplets). BS, Harvard U., 1943; MS, Calif. Inst. Tech., 1947, PhD, 1949. Research engr. NACA, 1943-46, 50-54, 55-58; vis. prof. U. Paris, France, 1958- 59; prof. aero. Stanford, 1959—; prof. emeritus, 1992—. Pres. Parabolic Press. Author: Perturbation Methods in Fluid Mechanics, 1964, An Album of Fluid Motion, 1982; editor: Ann. Rev. Fluid Mechanics, 1969-99. Trustee Soc. For Promotion of Sci. and Scholarship, Inc. Served with USNR, 1944-46. Guggenheim and Fulbright fellow,

1954-55 Mem. Am. Acad. Arts and Scis., Nat. Acad. Engring., Am. Phys. Soc., Phi Beta Kappa, Sigma Xi, Sierra Club. Office: Stanford U Div Mechs & Computation Stanford CA 94305-4040

VAN DYKE, THOMAS WESLEY, lawyer; b. Kansas City, Mo., May 12, 1938; s. Harold Thomas and Elizabeth Louise (Barritt) Van D.; m. Sharon Edgar, Jan. 30, 1960; children: Jennifer Van Dyke Winters, Jeffrey. BA, U. Kans., 1960; JD, U. Mich., 1963. Bar: Mo. 1963, Kans. 1983. Atty. SEC, Washington, 1963-64; legal asst. to commr. Hamer E. Budge, Washington, 1964-65; from assoc. to ptnr. Linde Thomson Langworthy Kohn & Van Dyke, P.C., Overland Park, Kans., 1965-91. Co-chmn. ALI-ABA Tax and Bus. Planning Seminar, 1987-96, 2005; mem. securities adv. panel Sec. of State of Mo., 1984-89. Mem. ABA (fed. regulation securities com. bus. law sect. 1982-2005, negotiated acquisitions com. 1989-2005), Kans. Bar Assn., Mo. Bar Assn. (corp. banking and bus. law com., chmn. full com. 1983-84, past chmn. securities law subcom.), Carriage Club (bd. dirs. 1986-89). Republican. Avocations: tennis, golf, reading. Office: Bryan Cave LLP 3500 One Kansas City Pl 1200 Main St Kansas City MO 64105 Office Phone: 816-374-3201. Business E-Mail: twvandyke@bryancave.com.

VAN DYKE, WILLIAM GRANT, manufacturing executive; b. Mpls., June 30, 1945; s. Russell Lawrence and Carolyn (Grant) Van D.; m. Karin Van Dyke; children: Carolyn Julie, Colin Grant, Alexander Grant, Stephanie Joyce. BA in Econs., U. Minn., 1967, MBA, 1972. V.p., CFO Northland Aluminum Co., Mpls., 1977-78; controller Donaldson Co., Inc., Mpls., 1978-80, v.p controller, 1980-82, v.p., CFO, 1982-84, v.p., gen. mgr. indsl. group, 1984-94, pres., COO, 1994-96, pres. CEO, 1996—2004, chmn., 1996—, also bd. dirs. Graco Inc., Alliant Techsystems. Lt. U.S. Army, 1968-70, Vietnam. Mem. Kappa Sigma Alumni Assn. Avocations: running, bicycling. Office: Donaldson Co Inc 1400 W 94th St Minneapolis MN 55431-2370

VAN DYKEN, AMY, Olympic athlete; b. Englewood, Colo., Feb. 15, 1973; d. Don and Becky Van Dyken; m. Alan McDaniel, Oct. 1995. Student, Colo. State U. Swimmer U.S. Nat. Resident Team, Colorado Springs, Colo., 1994, U.S. Olympic Team, Atlanta, 1996, Sydney, 2000; ret. Named Female NCAA Swimmer of Yr., 1994, Assoc. Press Female Athlete of the Yr., 1996, USOC Sports Woman of the Yr., 1996, Woman's Sports Found. Woman of the Yr., 1996, USA Swimming Swimmer of the Yr., 1996, Phillips Performance of the Yr. award 1996, Female Athlete of Yr. AP, 1996; named one of Glamour's Top Ten Women of the Yr., 1996; recipient Bronze medal, World Championships, 1994, Triple Gold medals, Pan Am. Games, 1995, Silver medal, 1995, Gold medal 50 meter freestyle, Atlanta Olympic Games, 1996, Gold medal 100 meter butterfly, 1996, Gold medal 4x400 meter freestyle relay, 1996, Gold medal 4x100 meter medley relay, 1996, Gold medal 4x400 freestyle, Sydney Olympic Games, 2000, ESPY award, best female athlete, 1997. Achievements include 1st American women to win 4 gold medals in any event during a single Olympic game.

VANE, DENNIS, physician; BA, Cornell U., 1970; MS, U. Brussels, 1974, MD, 1978; MBA, U. Vt., 2000. Intern in surgery Ind. u. Med. Ctr., Indianapolis, 1978-79, resident in surgery 1979—82; physician Riley Hosp. for Children, 1981; chief resident surgery Ind. U. Med. Ctr., 1982-83; resident ped. surgery Columbus Children's Hosp. Ohio State U., 1983-84, chief resident ped. surgery, 1984-85; chmn. divsn. pediat. surgery U. Vt., Burlington, 1990—, prof. pediats, surgery, 1996—, vice chmn. clin. affairs dept. surgery, 1996—; attending in surgery Fletcher Allen Health Care, Burlington, 1990—, Southwestern Vt. Med. Ctr., Bennington, 1993—; surgeon-in-chief Vt. Children's Hosp. at Fletcher Allen Health Care, Burlington, 2002—. Contbr. articles to profl. jours. Med. dir. Charlotte (Vt.) Rescue Squad, 1997—. Office: U Vt Coll Medicine Dept Surgery Fletcher 460 111 Colchester Ave Burlington VT 05401-1473 Business E-Mail: dennis.vane@vtmednet.org.

VANE, SYLVIA BRAKKE, anthropologist, writer; b. Fillmore County, Minn., Feb. 28, 1918; d. John T. and Hulda Christina Brakke.; m. Arthur Bayard Vane, May 17, 1942; children: Ronald Arthur, Linda, Laura Vane Ames. AA, Rochester Jr. Coll., 1937; BS with distinction, U. Minn., Mpls., 1939; postgrad, Radcliffe Coll., Cambridge, Mass., 1944; MA, Calif. State U., Hayward, 1975. Med. technologist Dr. Frost and Hodapp, Willmar, Minn., 1939-41; head labs. Corvallis (Oreg.) Gen. Hosp., 1941-42; dir. lab. Cambridge (Mass.) Gen. Hosp., 1942-43; staff Peninsula Clinic, Redwood City, Calif., 1947-49; v.p. Cultural Systems Rsch. Inc., Menlo Park, Calif., 1978—; pres. Ballena Press, 1981—2005. Cons. cultural resource mgmt. So. Calif. Edison Co., Rosemead, 1978-81, San Diego Gas and Elec. Co., 1980-83, Pacific Gas and Elec. Co., San Francisco, 1982-83, Wender, Murase & White, Washington, 1983-87, Yosemite Indians, Mariposa, Calif., 1982-91, San Luis Rey Band of Mission Indians, Escondido, Calif., 1986-89, U.S. Ecology, Newport Beach, Calif., 1986-89, Riverside County Flood Control and Water Conservation Dist., 1985-95, Infotec, Inc., 1989-91, Alexander & Karshmer, Berkeley, Calif., 1989-92, Desert Water Agy., Palm Springs, Calif., 1989-90, Met. Water Dist., 1992-2001, Nat. Park Svc., 1992-2001, Applied Earthworks, Inc., 1997-2001, N.W Econ. Assocs., 2002-2004, County of Riverside, 2002-03, Aqua Caliente Cultural Mus., 2005—; bd. dirs. XEl Scientific. Author: (with L.J. Bean), California Indians, Primary Resources, 1977, rev. edit., 1990, The Cahuilla and the Santa Rosa Mountains, 1981, The Cahuilla Landscape, 1991, Ethnology of the Alta California Indians, vol. I Pre Contact, vol. II POst Contact, 1992, Spanish Borderlands Sourcebooks, vols. 3, 4; contbr. chpts. to several books. Bd. dir. Sequoia Area coun. Girl Scouts U.S., 1954-61; bd. dirs.-v.p., pres. LWV, South San Mateo County, Calif., 1960-65. Fellow Soc. Applied Anthropology, Am. Anthropology Assn.; mem. Southwestern Anthropology Assn. (prog. chmn. 1976-78, newsletter editor 1976-79), Soc. for Am. Archaeology, Soc. Calif. Archaeology (Martin A. Baumhoff Spl. Achievement award 1998, Lifetime Achievement award 2005). Mem. United Ch. of Christ. Office: 823 Valparaiso Ave Menlo Park CA 94025-4206 Office Phone: 605-323-9261.

VANE, TERENCE G., JR., finance company executive, lawyer; b. Elgin, Ill., Jan. 17, 1942; s. Terence Gregory and Velma Mary (Mersman) V.; m. Patricia Bryant, Aug. 29, 1964; children: Terence Gregory III, Lourdene DeLynne, Christopher Theodore. BA, Ind. U., 1964, JD, 1967. Bar: Ind. 1967, Tex. 1977, N.C. 1992, Fla. 2002. Staff atty. Assocs. Discount Corp., South Bend, Ind., 1967-69; asst. gen. counsel Assocs. Mgmt. Corp., South Bend, 1969-74, Assocs. Comml. Corp., South Bend, 1974-76, Assocs. Ins. Group, Inc., Dallas, 1976-77; gen. counsel, v.p. ins. ops. Assocs. Corp. N.Am., Dallas, 1977-80, gen. counsel, sr. v.p. ins. ops., 1981-82, gen. counsel, sr. v.p consumer fin. and ins. ops., 1982-86, gen. counsel, sr. v.p. diversified consumer fin. svcs. and credit card ops., 1986-88; exec. v.p., gen. counsel, sec., dir. Barclays Am. Corp., Charlotte, NC, 1988-91; pres. Vector Fin. Svcs., Inc., Charlotte, 1991-95, dir. sr. v.p., assoc. gen. counsel EquiCredit Corp., Jacksonville, Fla., 1996-97; sr. v.p., gen. counsel, sec. First Street Mortgage Corp., Jacksonville, 1997-98, Home Alliance Mortgage Co., Jacksonville, 1998-2000, Alliance Capital Ptnrs. Group, Jacksonville, 2000—02, Slott & Barker, Jacksonville, 2002—04; pvt. practice Jacksonville, 2005—. Chmn. bd. dirs., sec. Youth Concert Found. for Promotion Creative Arts, 1981—; bd. dirs. N.C. Bus. Com. Edn., 1988-91. Mem. ABA (com. on consumer fin. svcs. law), Fla. Bar Assn., Ind. Bar Assn., Tex. Bar Assn., N.C. Bar Assn., Nat. Assn. Ind. Insurers (laws com. 1978-86), Consumer Credit Ins. Assn. (chmn. property ins. legis. com. 1979-85), Am. Fin. Svcs. Assn. (law com., chmn. environ. law subcom.), Conf. Consumer Fin. Law (governing com.), Nat. Home Equity Mortgage Assn., Lawyers Round Table, Safari Club Internat. (pres., dir. North Fla. chpt.). Conservative. Episcopalian. Home: 13802 Fiddlers Point Dr Jacksonville FL 32225-5427 Office: Terence G Vane Jr PA 233 E Bay St Ste 620 Jacksonville FL 32202-3447

VANEK, JAROSLAV, economist, educator; b. Prague, Czechoslovakia, Apr. 20, 1930; came to U.S., 1955, naturalized, 1960; s. Josef and Jaroslava (Tucek) V.; m. Wilda M. Marraffino, Dec. 26, 1959; children: Joseph, Francis, Rosemarie, Steven, Teresa. Degree in stats., Sorbonne, Paris, 1951; license in econ., U. Geneva, 1954; PhD, MIT, 1957. Instr., then asst. prof. Harvard U.,

1957-63; adviser AID, 1964; mem. faculty Cornell U., 1964-96, prof. econs., 1966-96, Carl Marks prof. internat. studies, 1969-96, dir. program comparative econ. devel., 1968-73, dir. program participation and labor-managed systems, 1969-96, prof. emeritus, 1996—. Mem. nat. adv. bd. econs. NSF, 1969-70; founder, pres. S.T.E.V.E.N. Found. (Solar Tech. and Energy for Vital Econ. Needs), 1985—. Author: International Trade: Theory and Economic Policy, 1962, The Balance of Payments, Level of Economic Activity and the Value of Currency, 1962, The Natural Resource Content of United States Foreign Trade, 1870-1955, 1963, General Equilibrium of International Discrimination, 1965, Estimating Foreign Resource Needs for Economic Development, 1966, Maximal Economic Growth, 1968, The General Theory of Labor-Managed Market Economies, 1970, The Participatory Economy, 1971, Self-Management: Economic Liberation of Man, 1975, The Labor-Managed Economy, 1977, Crisis and Reform: East and West: Essays in Social Economy, 1989, Toward Full Democracy, Political and Economic, In Russia, 1993, Unified Theory of Social Systems: A Radical Christian Analysis, 2000; also manuscripts on solar tech.; contbr. to Advances in the Economic Analysis of Participatory and Labor-Managed Firms, Vol. 2, 1987, Vol. 7, 2003, Destructive International Trade from Justice for Labour to Global Strategy, 1998, inventor several solar tech. designs, including solar steam engines, pumps, refrigerators, cookers, holder 1 patent. Roman Catholic. Home: 414 Triphammer Rd Ithaca NY 14850-2521 Business E-Mail: jv19@cornell.edu.

**VANEMAN, CHRISTOPHER M.,** music educator, musician; b. Detroit, Feb. 12, 1970; s. Gerald Leroy and Karen Haslanger Vaneman; m. Kelly Aileen McElrath, Feb. 18, 1995; 1 child, Taliesin Ruth. MusB, Eastman Sch. Music, 1991; MusM, Yale U., 1994, M of Mus. Arts, 1995, DMA, 2002. Flutist Echo, N.Y.C., 1993—2003; lectr. Presbyn. Coll., Clinton, SC, 1998—2002; flutist Ensemble Kdicuse, Spartanburg, SC, 1998—; asst. prof. Converse Coll., Spartanburg, 2002—. Adj. instr. Anderson (S.C.) Coll., 1998—2000; freelance writer, Spartanburg, 1996—. Rec. artist: CD Inbox, 2004. Recipient artist grant, Arts Spartanburg, 2003, rsch. grant, Converse Coll., 2002, scholar fellowship, Belgian Am. Ednl. Found., 1995. Mem.: Nat. Flute Assn., Waxing Gibbous (1st Tiger 2004—), Pi Kappa Lambda (sec. Rho chpt. 2004—). Liberal. Episcopalian. Avocations: basketball, archery, puppeteering. Home: 412 E Park Dr Spartanburg SC 29302 Office: Converse Coll Petrie Sch Music 580 E Main Spartanburg SC 29302

**VAN ETTEN, PETER WALBRIDGE,** foundation executive; b. Boston, May 10, 1946; s. Royal Cornelius Van Etten and Peggy June (Walbridge) Hutchins; m. Mary Peters French, Sept. 5, 1968; children: Molly, Clarissa, Ellen. BA, Columbia U., 1968; MBA, Harvard U., 1973. Br. mgr. BayBanks, Brookline, Mass., 1968-71; loan officer Bank of Boston, 1973-76; CFO Univ. Hosp., Boston, 1976-79; exec. v.p., CFO New Eng. Med. Ctr., Boston, 1979-89; pres., CEO Transition Systems, Boston, 1986-89; dep. chancellor U. Mass. Med. Ctr., Worcester, 1989-91; CFO Stanford U., Calif., 1991-94; pres., CEO Stanford Univ. Hosp., 1994-97; CEO UCSF Stanford Health Care, 1997-99; exec. com. U. Healthsystem Consortium, 1997-99, vice chmn., 1998-99; dir. Calif. Healthcare Assn., 1998-99, IDX Sys., Inc., 1999-2001; pres., CEO Juvenile Diabetes Found. Internat., NYC, 2000—06. Dir. Transition Sys., Inc., 1996—98, Duke U. Health Sys., 2003—, Rsch. Am., 2005—06. Chair campaign United Way San Francisco, 1998. Business E-Mail: pvanetten1@yahoo.com.

**VAN EXEL, NICKEY MAXWELL,** professional basketball player; b. Kenosha, Wis., Nov. 27, 1971; s. Nickey Maxwell and Joyce Van Exel; 1 child, Nickey Maxwell III. Attended, Trinity Valley C.C., 1989-91; BA in Sociology, U. Cin., 1993. Guard L.A. Lakers, 1993-98, Denver Nuggets, 1998—2002, Dallas Mavericks, 2002—03, Golden State Warriors, 2003—04, Portland Trailblazers, 2004—. With Nat. Benevolent Assn., Christian Ch. Named to NBA All-Rookie Team, 1994, NBA All-Star Game, 1998; recipient Victor Award for Comeback Player of the Yr., 1998, Chopper Travaglini award. Avocation: collecting baseball cards, hats, books. Office: c/o Portland Trailblazers 1 Cneter Court ste 200 Portland OR 97227

**VAN FAASEN, WILLIAM C.,** health insurance company executive; Past sr. v.p. operational svcs. Blue Cross/Blue Shield Mich.; exec. v.p., COO Blue Cross/Blue Shield Mass., Boston, 1990-92, pres., CEO, 1992—2002, chmn., pres., CEO, 2002—04, chmn., CEO, 2004—05, chmn., 2005—. Bd. dirs. IMS Health, Inc., Liberty Mut. Group, NSTAR, PolyMedica Corp. Office: Blue Cross/Blue Shield MA Landmark Ctr 401 Park Dr Boston MA 02215-5000

**VAN FLANDERN, GEOFFREY JAMES,** orthopedist, surgeon; b. Cin., Ohio, July 26, 1963; s. James Brian and Aileen Marguerite Van Flandern; m. Linette Marie Kammermeier, Aug. 14, 1993; children: Elizabeth Mary, Erin Marie, Claire Marie, Michael Charles. BS, U. Notre Dame, Ind., 1985; MD, Northwestern U., Chgo., 1989. Cert. orthop. surgery bd. Am. Acad. of Orthop. Surgeons, 1998. Asst. clin. prof. Tufts U. Sch. Medicine, Boston, 1998—; attending surgeon New Eng. Bapt. Bone and Joint Inst., 1998—. Home: 18 Appian Dr Wellesley MA 02481 Office: Longwood Orthop Assocs 830 Boylston St #106 Chestnut Hill MA 02467 Office Phone: 617-277-1205. Office Fax: 617-232-6528. E-mail: gvanflan@caregroup.harvard.edu.

**VAN FLEET, DAVID DOMINIC,** management educator; b. Binghamton, N.Y., Nov. 27, 1940; s. Walter Anthony van Fleet, Sr. and Katherine Elizabeth Van Fleet; m. Ella Webb, Aug. 27, 1966; children: Marijke, Dirk. BS, U. Tenn., 1962, PhD, 1969. Instr. U. Tenn., Knoxville, 1963—67, Kingsport Grad. Study Program, Kingsport, Tenn., 1967—70; asst. prof. U. Akron, Akron, 1970—73; from asst. prof. to prof. Tex. A&M U., College Station, 1973—89; prof. Ariz. State U.W., Phoenix, 1989—, MBA dir., 1999—2004. Prin. lectr. A. Frank Smith Jr. Lectureship series Southwestern U., 2000. Author: (book) Military Leadership: An Organizational Behavior Perspective, 1986, Organizational Behavior: A Managerial Viewpoint, 1983, Contemporary Management (3rd. edition), 1994, Contemporary Management (2nd edition), 1991, Contemporary Management (1st edition), 1991, Behavior in Organizations, 1991; contbr. numerous articles to profl. jours., chpts. to books; editor: N-File Newsletter, 1976—78, Acad. of Mgmt. Newsletter, 1979—82, Jour. of Mgmt., 1987—89. Recipient Faculty Achievement award in Rsch., Scholarship, and Creative Activity, Ariz. State U. West Campus, 2001, Faculty Achievement award in Svc., 2005, Outstanding Svc. award, Coll. Bus. Adminstrn., Tex. A&M U., 1985. Fellow: Acad. Mgmt. (chmn. mgmt. history divsn. 1980—81, dep. dean 1996—99), So. Mgmt. Assn. (pres. 1995, Sustained Outstanding Svc. award 2005); mem.: Southwestern Fedn. of Adminstry. Disciplines (bd. dirs. 1985—87), Allied So. Bus. Assn. (pres. 1995), S.W. Acad. of Mgmt. (pres. 1986—87). Home: 4849 E Altadena Ave Scottsdale AZ 85254 Office: Arizona State University West PO Box 37100 Phoenix AZ 85069-7100 Personal E-mail: ddvf@asu.edu.

**VAN FLEET, GEORGE ALLAN,** lawyer; b. Monterey, Calif., Jan. 20, 1953; s. George Lawson and Wilma Ruth (Williams) Van F.; m. Laurie Elise Koch, July 20, 1975; children: Katia Elaine, Alexander Lawson. BA summa cum laude, Rice U., 1976; JD summa cum laude, Columbia U., 1979. Bar: Tex. 1978, U.S. Dist. Ct. (so. dist.) Tex. 1978, U.S. Dist. Ct. (we. dist.) Tex. 1987, U.S. Dist. Ct. (no. dist.) Tex, 1988, U.S. Dist. Ct. (ea. dist.) Tex. 1991, U.S. Tax Ct., 1984, U.S. Ct. Appeals (5th cir.) 1978, U.S. Ct. Appeals (11th cir.) 1981, U.S. Ct. Appeals (D.C. cir.) 1982, U.S. Ct. Appeals (fed. cir.) 1993, U.S. Supreme Ct. 1981. Law clk. U.S. Ct. Appeals (2d cir.), N.Y.C., 1977; assoc. Vinson & Elkins, Houston, 1977-84, ptnr., 1984—2006; shareholder Greenberg Traurig, LLP, 2006—. Co-chmn. Antitrust Practice Group. Co-author: Federal Civil Procedure Before Trial–Firth Circuit, 1997, The Competition Laws of NAFTA, Canada, Mexico and the United States, 1997, Business and Commercial Litigation in Federal Courts, 1998, supplement, 2005; editor: Annual Review of Antitrust Law Developments, 2000; co-author: Am. Legal Ethics Libr., 2002, Doing Business in Texas, 2003, State Antitrust Practice and Statutes, 2004, Inside the Minds: Leading Lawyers on Unfair Competition, Trade Regulation and Litig., 2003; contbr. articles to profl. jour. Mem. bd. visitors Columbia U., 1992—; mem. City of Houston Ethics Com., 1992—98, chmn., 1995—98; bd. dirs. Nat. Appleseed Found., 2002—, Tex. Appleseed Ctr., 1998—, vice chmn., 1999—2002, chmn., 2002—04. Recipient Ordroneaux prize Columbia U., 1977, W. Frank Newton

award for outstanding contbns. in provision of access to legal svcs. to the poor State Bar Tex., 2002; James Kent scholar Columbia U., 1974-77. Fellow: Am. Bar Found., Tex. Bar Found.; mem.: ABA (com. chmn. 1987—95, coun. 1996—99, com. chmn. 2000—02, sect. officer 2002, ho. dels. 2002—05, nominating com. 2003—05), Latin Am. Law Initiative (coun. 2005—), Tex.-Mex. Bar Assn. (pres. 1998—2000), Houston Bar Assn. (sect. chair 1991—93), Tex. Commn. on Access to Justice, State Bar Tex. (coun. 2000—04, dir. 2005—), Phi Beta Kappa. Democrat. Home: 3430 S Parkwood Dr Houston TX 77021-1238 Office: Greenberg Traurig LLP 1000 Louisiana Ste 1800 Houston TX 77002 Office Phone: 713-374-3555. Business E-Mail: vanfleet@gtlaw.com.

**VANFLEET, HOWARD BAY,** physicist, educator; b. Salt Lake City, June 5, 1931; S. Willard P. and Celia May (Bay) V.; m. Helen Haacke, Sept. 9, 1954; children: Pamela (dec.), Vennette, Leslie Howard, James Parker, May Lyn, David C., Richard R. BS, Brigham Young U., Provo, Utah, 1955; PhD, U. Utah, Salt Lake City, 1961. Nuclear engr. Gen. Dynamics, Ft. Worth, 1955-57; sr. scientist Ft. Monmouth, Eatontown, N.J., 1966-67; vis. prof. Am. U., Cairo, 1973-74; prof., chmn. physics dept. Brigham Young U., Provo, 1960—. Contbr. articles to profl. jours. Served with U.S. Army, 1952-54. Grantee USAF Office of Sci. Rsch., 1962-66, NSF, 1969-77. Mem. Am. Assn. Physics Tchrs., Am. Phys. Soc., Sigma Xi, Sigma Pi Sigma. Mem. Lds Ch. Home: 1722 N 1500 E Provo UT 84604-5751 E-mail: hbv@sisna.com.

**VAN FLEET, LISA A.,** lawyer; BSW, Valparaiso U., 1982, JD, 1985. Bar: Ind. 1985, US Tax Ct. 1987, US Claims Ct. 1988, Mo. 1989, Ill. 1990. Ptnr., group leader Employee Benifits Bryan Cave LLP, St. Louis. Office: Bryan Cave LLP One Metropolitan Square 211 N Broadway, Ste 3600 Saint Louis MO 63102 Office Phone: 314-259-2326. E-mail: lavanfleet@bryancave.com.

**VANFOSSEN, PHILLIP J.,** academic administrator; b. East Lansing, Mich., Jan. 18, 1964; s. Gerald James VanFossen, Jr. and Margaret Joyce VanFossen; m. Bethany Hutchings, June 27, 1987; children: Madsion Tayler, Liliana Grace. BS in Ed., Miami U., Oxford, Ohio, 1986, MEd, 1990; PhD, Ohio State U., Columbus, 1993. Dir. Ackerman Ctr. for Dem. Citizenship Purdue U., West Lafayette, Ind., 2000—, James F. Ackerman prof. of social studies edn. Coll. Edn., 2004—. Assoc. dir. Purdue U. Ctr. for Econ. Edn., West Lafayette, 1997—. Author: (textbook) Using Internet Primary Sources to Teach Critical Thinking Skills in Government, Economics, and Contemporary World Problems, Focus: Institutions and Markets, Learning, Earning and Investing, Focus: Globalization. Mem. Purdue U. Ctr. for Econ. Edn., West Lafayette, 1997—2006. Named Outstanding U. Prof., Kappa Delta Pi, 2002, 2000; recipient univ. scholarship, Purdue U., 2002—07, Outstanding Tchg. award, Coll. of Edn., Purdue U., 2001. Mem.: Nat. Coun. for the Social Studies, Nat. Coun. on Econ. Edn. (chair tech. com. 2002—05). United Methodist. Avocations: golf, home repair, weightlifting, reading. Office: Ackerman Ctr for Dem Citizensh Purdue Univ 100 N University St West Lafayette IN 47907-2098 Office Phone: 765-494-2367. Business E-Mail: vanfoss@purdue.edu.

**VAN GALDER, VALERIE,** broadcast executive; Head mktg. Fox Searchlight Pictures; exec. v.p. mktg. Sony Screen Gems; pres. TriStar Pictures, 2004—05; pres. domestic mktg. Columbia TriStar Motion Picture Group, 2005—. Internat. adv. bd. Bermuda Internat. Film Festival, 2005—. Mailing: Sony Pres TriStar Pictures 9050 West Washington Blvd Culver City CA 90232*

**VANGATES, DESS,** retired military officer; b. Monticello, Fla., June 1, 1942; s. Fred and Rachel Etta Vangates. Contbr. articles to profl. jours. Sgt. U.S. Army, 1975—81, Korea. Mem.: Vet. Foreign Wars of U.S. (life). Democrat. Achievements include research in global warming. Avocations: poker, reading, singing. Home: 2145 NW 152nd Terrace Miami Gardens FL 33054 Office Phone: 305-687-9671.

**VAN GELDER, LYDIA M.,** artist, educator; d. Henry Harrison and Lydia Ester McClain; m. Homer Whitney Van Gelder, July 6, 1936 (dec.); children: Peter, Dirk, Roger. Student, Calif. Sch. Fine Art, 1930—32. Instr. Santa Rosa (Calif.) Jr. Coll., 1969—85. Instr. Christ Ch., Italy. Author: IKAT, 1980, IKAT II, 1992; Represented in permanent collections Smithsonian, N.Y.C. Named Textile Legend, Textile Soc., 2004. Mem.: Sacramento Weavers and Spinners Guild (founding pres.), Spindles and Dyers Guild (hon.), Redwood Empire Hand-weavers and Spinners Guild (hon.). Republican. Episcopalian. Avocations: spinning, weaving, knitting.

**VAN GELDER, MARC CHRISTIAAN,** retail executive; b. Amsterdam, The Netherlands, May 21, 1961; s. Bob Frits and Maria Johanna (Van Teeseling) Van G.; m. Karah L. Henry, July 7, 1990; children: Alexander F., Robert H. M of Econs., Erasmus U., Rotterdam, The Netherlands, 1986; MBA, Wharton Sch., U. Pa., 1990. Asst. v.p. Drexel-Burnham Lambert, N.Y.C., 1986-88; sr. mgr. McKinsey & Co., Amsterdam, 1990-96; dir. bus. devel. Ahold, Netherlands, 1996—98; v.p. supply chain mgmt. The Stop & Shop Supermarket Company, 1998—99, sr. v.p., logistics & supply chain mgmt., 1999-2000; pres. & CEO Peapod Inc., Skokie, IL, 2000—. Author: Venture Capital Market, 1985. Mem. Wharton Alumni Club The Netherlands (pres. 1991-98), Netherlands Am. C. of C. (bd. dirs.). Avocations: skiing, horseback riding, arts.

**VANGER, MILTON ISADORE,** historian, educator; b. N.Y.C., Apr. 11, 1925; s. Max Manuel and Rose (Rothstein) V.; m. Elsa M. Oribe, Sept. 10, 1956; children: John, Mark, Rachel. AB, Princeton U., 1948; MA, Harvard U., 1950, PhD, 1958. Teaching fellow history Harvard U., 1952-56; instr. Okla. State U., 1956-58; asst. prof. history Sacramento State Coll., 1958-62; mem. faculty Brandeis U., Waltham, Mass., 1962—, prof. history, 1973-84, prof. emeritus, 1984—. Chmn. com. Latin Am. studies, 1971-81; invited lectr. 50th anniversary conf. commemorating death of Batlle y Ordoñez of Uruguay, 1979; invitee to inauguration of pres. Sanguinetti, Uruguay, 1985; Barnette Miller vis. prof. history, Wellesley Coll., 1990. Author: José Batlle y Ordoñez of Uruguay: The Creator of His Times, 1902-1907, 1963, 2d edit., 1980, Spanish transl., 1968, 2d edit., 1992, The Model Country: José Batlle y Ordoñez of Uruguay, 1907-1915, 1980, Spanish transl., 1983, 2d edit., 1991, Reforma o Revolución La Polémica Batlle-Mibelli, 1917, 1989; outside reviewer NEH, Radcliffe Inst.; contbr. articles to profl. jours. Juror for Lindahl Prize, Inst. Latin Am. Studies, Stockholm. With AUS, 1943-45. Doherty Found. fellow, 1950-52; grantee Am. Philos. Soc., 1966; recipient Hermes prize for best history pub. in Uruguay, 1983. Mem. New Eng. Council Latin Am. Studies (sec.-treas. 1970-72), Am. Hist. Assn., Conf. on Latin Am. History, Amnesty Internat., Phi Beta Kappa. Democrat. Jewish. Address: 931 Massachusetts Ave Ste 503 Cambridge MA 02139

**VAN GESTEL, ALLAN,** judge; b. Boston, Dec. 3, 1935; BA, Colby Coll., 1957; LLB, Boston U., 1961; MA (hon.), Colby Coll., 1999. Bar: Mass. 1961, U.S. Dist. Ct. Mass. 1963, U.S. Ct. Appeals (1st cir.) 1969, U.S. Supreme Ct. 1972, U.S. Ct. Claims 1979, U.S. Ct. Appeals (2d cir.) 1980, U.S. Dist. Ct. (no. dist.) N.Y. 1980, U.S. Dist. Ct. (we. dist.) N.Y. 1993, U.S. Ct. Appeals (3d cir.) 1993, U.S. Ct. Appeals (5th cir.) 1995. Assoc. firm Goodwin, Procter & Hoar, Boston, 1961-70, ptnr., 1970-96; assoc. justice Superior Ct. Mass., 1996—2006, recalled, 2006—; presiding justice Superior Ct. Bus. Litigation Session, 2000—. Spl. counsel Boston Fin. Commn., 1974; spl. counsel to Mass. Commn. on Jud. Conduct, 1986; mem. Scituate (Mass.) Bd. Zoning Appeals, 1970, Scituate Planning Bd., 1972; spl. counsel Gov. of N.Y. on Indian Land Claims, 1985-96; spl. counsel to Gov. and Atty. Gen. of Vt. on Indian Claims, 1987-90; chmn. standing adv. com. Mass. Rules Civil Procedure, 1986-93; overseer Colby Coll., 1990-99, trustee, 1999—2005. Contbr. numerous articles on Eastern Indian land claims, ct. administrn., capital punishment to profl. jours. Fellow Am. Coll. Trial Lawyers; mem. ABA, Mass. Bar Assn., Boston Bar Assn. (chmn., task force on drugs and the cts.), Supreme Jud. Ct. Hist. Soc. (chmn. bd. overseers 1993-96), Mass. Hist. Soc.

**VAN GILDER, JOHN CORLEY,** neurosurgeon, educator; b. Huntington, W.Va., Aug. 14, 1935; s. John Ray and Sarah Pool (Corley) Van G.; m. Kerstin Margareta Olesson, Mar., 1965; children: Sarah, John, Rachel, David. BA, W.Va. U., 1957, BS, 1959; MD, U. Pitts., 1961. Diplomate Am. Bd. Neurol. Surgery (examiner 1976, 79, 84). Intern Pa. Hosp., Phila., 1961, asst. resident in surgery, 1964-65, Wilkes-Barre Hosp., Pa., 1962; asst. resident neurosurgery Barnes Hosp., St. Louis, 1966-68, sr. resident, 1968-69; instr. neurosurgery Yale U. Sch. Medicine, New Haven, 1970, asst. prof., 1970-73, assoc. prof., 1973-76; prof. neurosurgery U. Iowa, Iowa City, 1976—, chmn. divsn. neurosurgery, 1976—, exec. com. dept. surgery 1978-81. Fellow neurosurgery Washington U. Sch. Medicine, St. Louis, 1965 -66, instr., 1966; attending neurosurgeon VA Hosp., New Haven, 1970-73, cons. 1973-76; assoc. to attending neurosurgeon Yale-New Haven Med. Ctr., 1970-76; cons. VA Hosp., Iowa City, 1976—; neurol. surg. cons. Vets. Affairs Hdqrs., Washington; mem. clin. coordinating com. U. Iowa Cancer Ctr., 1979—; vis. prof. U. Tenn., 1984, Tufts U. Med. Ctr., Boston, 1986, U. Tex., San Antonio, 1987, U. Mich., Ann Arbor, 1988, People's Republic China at Hunan Med. Coll., Beijing Neurol. Inst., Tianjin Med. Coll. Hosp., Tiantan Xili, Xian Gen. Hosp., 2d Mil. Coll., Shanghai, Suzhou Med. Coll. Shanghai, 1985, USSR at Burdenk Inst., Kiev Neurol. Inst., Leningrad Neurol. Soc., 1989, Western Res. U., Cleve., 1993, Yale U., 1994, U. Wash., Seattle, 1997, Mayo Clinic, 1998, U. Calif., San Francisco, 1998, Ind. U., 1999; mem. ad. hoc rev. bd. Surg. Neurology, 2001—, Spine, 2000—, Army-Navy, Bethesda-Walter Reed, 2005; presenter in field. Author: (with others): Principles of Surgery, 2d edit., 1973, Brief Textbook of Surgery, 1976, Aneurysmal Subarachnoid Hemorrhage, 1981, Operative Meurosucgical Techniques, Indications, Methods, and Results, 1982, Sports Medicine, 1982, Neurosurgery, 1982, Clinical Neurosurgery, 1982, Operative Neurosurgical Technique, Vol. II, 1982, 88, Vol. III, 1995, Current Therapy in Neurosurgical Surgery, 1985, 2d edit., 1987, Craniovertebral Junction Abnormalities, 1987, Decision Making in Neurological Surgery, 1987, Neurological Surgery, 3d edit., 1988, Anterior Cervical Spine Surgery, 1993, Brain Surgery: Complication Avoidance and Management, 1993, Neurosurgical Emergencies, 1994, Techniques of Spinal Fusion and Instrumentation, 1995, Somatic Gene Therapy, 1995, Infections in Neurological Surgery, 1999; contbr. numerous articles and abstracts to profl. jours.; co-author teaching films; mem. editorial bd. Neurosurgery jour., 1978-84. Capt. USAF, 1962-64. Grantee NIH, 1973-78, Nat. Cancer Inst., 1980-88. Fellow: ACS (membership com. Iowa dist. #1 1983—); mem.: AMA, Am. Bd. Neurol. Surgery (dir. 1992—98, chmn. 1997—98, residency rev. com.-neurol. surgery 1995—2001, neurosurgery chmn. 1999—2001), Am. Acad. Neurol. Surgery (v.p. 1995—), Midwest Surg. Assn., Soc. Neurol. Surgeons (chmn. membership com. 1986—87, treas. 1991—, pres 1997—98, treas. 1991—96, pres. 1997, Disting. Svc. award 2004), Iowa-Midwest Neurosurg. Soc. (pres. 1978—79), Johnson County Med. Soc. (program com. 1984—88, chmn. 1985—86), Iowa Med. Soc., Neurol. Soc. Am. (long range planning com. 1984—, v.p. 1985, pres. 1998—99), Rsch. Soc. Neurol. Surgeons, Am. Assn. Neurol. Surgeons (awards com. 1986—87, bd. dirs. 1986—90, chmn. 1987—88, Disting. Svc. award 2005), Congress Neurol. Surgeons (resident placement com. 1970), Am. Physiol. Soc., Ga. Neurosurg. Soc. (hon.), Sigma Xi. Home: 330 S Summit St Iowa City IA 52240-3220 Office: U Iowa Hosps & Clinics Dept Neurosurgery 200 Hawkins Dr Iowa City IA 52242-1009 Office Phone: 319-356-2772. Business E-Mail: john-vangilder@uiowa.edu.

**VAN GINKEL, BLANCHE LEMCO,** architect, educator; b. London, 1923; d. Myer and Claire Lemco; m. H. P. Daniel van Ginkel, 1956; children: Brenda, Marc. B.Arch., McGill U., 1945; M.C.P., Harvard U., 1950; Doctorate (hon.), U. Aix-Marseille, France, 2005. Tech. asst. Nat. Film Bd. Can., 1943-44; mgr. City Planning Office, Regina, Sask., Canada, 1946; architect Atelier Le Corbusier, Paris, 1948; asst. prof. architecture U. Pa., 1951-57; ptnr. van Ginkel Assocs., Montreal, Que., Canada, also Toronto, Ont., Canada, 1957—; prof. architecture U. Toronto, 1977—92, dir. Sch. Architecture, 1977-80, dean faculty architecture and landscape architecture, 1980-82. Vis. critic Harvard U., 1958, 70; adj. prof. U. Montreal, McGill U., others; curator exhbns. RCA, U. Toronto, others. Contbr. articles to profl. jours. Mem. Nat. Capital Planning Com., Ottawa, Art Adv. Com., Ottawa; mem. adv. com. Nat. Mus.'s Corp.; mem. Que. Provincial Planning Commn.; founder, v.p. Corp. of Urbanists of Que., 1963-65; bd. dirs. Montreal Internat. Film Festival, 1961-66. Decorated Order of Can., 2000; recipient Internat. Fedn. Housing and Planning Grand Prix award, 1956, Massey medal for arch., 1962, Mademoiselle Mag. award, 1957, Queen's Silver Jubilee medal, 1977, Citizenship citation Can. Govt., 1991, Queen's Golden Jubilee medal, 2002, award Order of Urbanists of Que., 2003. Fellow AIA (hon.), Royal Archtl. Inst. Can. (exec. com. 1971-74), Toronto Soc. Arch.; mem. Can. Inst. Planners (bd. dirs. 1961-64), Assoc. Collegiate Schs. Architecture (bd. dirs. 1981-84, v.p. 1985-86, pres. 1986-87, Disting. Prof. award 1989), Royal Can. Acad. Art (bd. dirs. 1992—2000), Internat. Archive of Women Architects (bd. dirs. 1985-2001), Ont. Assn. Arch. (life), Order of Can. Office: 38 Summerhill Gardens Toronto ON Canada M4T 1B4

**VAN GOOR, ANTHONY JAY,** military officer; b. Yankton, SD, Feb. 16, 1953; s. Marjorie L Van Goor; m. Marilyn Judy Staehli, Oct. 27, 1990; children: Brittany Marie, Michael Joseph. MD, U. of SD, 1978—82; M in med. mgmt., Tulane U., 2004—05. Board Certification in Internal Medicine Am. Bd. of Internal Medicine, 1990, Board Certification in Medical Management Certifying Commn. in Med. Mgmt., 2004. Chief med. staff 21st Med. Group, Peterson Air Force Base, Colo., 1994—97; comdr. 77th Med. Ops. Squadron, McClellan/Mather Air Force Base, Calif., 1997—2000, 347th Med. Group, Moody Air Force Base, Ga., 2000—02, 42nd Med. Group, Maxwell Air Force Base, Ala., 2002—04; assoc. chief, med. staff Keesler Med. Ctr., Keesler Air Force Base, Miss., 2004—. Pres. parish coun. Maxwell/Gunter Cath. Parish, Maxwell Air Force Base, Ala., 2002—03. Col. USAF, 1978—2005, Keesler Air Force Base, MS. Decorated 5 Meritorious Svc. medals USAF, Air Force Commendation Medal. Mem.: AMA, ACP, Am. Coll. Healthcare Execs., Am. Coll. Physician Execs. Catholic. Avocations: vocal performance, travel, physical conditioning, skiing. Office: Keesler USAF Med Ctr 301 Fisher St Keesler Afb MS 39534 Office Phone: 228-377-6512.

**VAN GORDER, JAN REID,** lawyer, insurance company executive; b. Endicott, N.Y., Dec. 28, 1947; s. George Austin and Elizabeth Anne Van G.; m. Linda Susan Massarelli, July 31, 1976; children: Austin Reid, Lewis Evan, Thomas Drew, Elizabeth Marie. BA, U. Pa., 1970; JD, Temple U., 1975. Assoc. gen. counsel Phila. Life Ins. Co., 1975-78, Harleysville (Pa.) Ins. Co., 1978-81; v.p., sec., gen. counsel Erie (Pa.) Ins. Group, 1981-82, sr. v.p., sec., gen. counsel, 1983-90, exec. v.p., sec., gen. counsel, 1990—. Bd. dirs. Pa. Assigned Claims Plan, Ins. Fedn. Pa., Pa. Profl. Liability Joint Underwriting Assn. Bd. dirs. Pennsylvanians for Effective Govt. Mem. ABA, Pa. Bar Assn., Erie County Bar Assn., Nat. Assn. Ind. Insurers (legis. com.), Newcomen Soc. U.S., Kahkwa Club, Erie Club. Republican. Episcopalian. Avocations: hunting, fishing, skiing, golf. Office: Erie Ins Group 100 Erie Insurance Pl Erie PA 16530-0001

**VAN GORDER, JOHN FREDERIC,** lawyer; b. Jacksonville, Fla., Mar. 22, 1943; s. Harold Burton and Charlotte Louise Van G.; m. Sandra Joan Hagen, June 4, 1977 (div. June 1995); children: Alyssa Jane, Kathryn Ann; m. Ann Michele Brancato, Oct. 7, 1995. Grad., Dover Coll., Eng., 1961; AB, Dartmouth Coll., 1965; postgrad., Air Force Inst. Tech., 1967-68; MS in Adminstrn., George Washington U., 1973; postgrad., U. Va., Coll. William and Mary, Cath. U. Am., Northeastern U., Babson Coll., U. South; JD, Fordham U., 1981. Bar: N.J. 1981, U.S. Dist. Ct. N.J. 1981, N.Y. 1983, U.S. Supreme Ct. 1989. Commd. 2d lt. USAF, 1965, advanced through grades to capt., 1968; weapons contr. Aerospace Def. Command., Ft. Lee, Va., 1965-67; buyer electronics sys. devel. Air Force Sys. Commd., Bedford, Mass., 1968-69; project mgr. rsch. and devel. Hdqrs. USAF, Washington, 1969-73, br. chief pers., 1973-74; presdl. social aide The White House, Washington, 1971-74; assoc. Louis C. Kramp & Assocs., Washington, 1975; program officer J.M. Found., N.Y.C., 1975-81; assoc. Winne, Banta & Rizzi Esqs., Hackensack, N.J., 1981-83; asst. v.p., program administr. Glenmede Trust Co., Phila., 1983—86; exec. dir., asst. sec. Leon Lowenstein Found., 1986—. Atty. Rent Leveling Bd., Borough of Bergenfield, N.J., 1983; pres. Vanguard Corp.,

Massapequa, N.Y., 1996-2001; adj. prof. Grad. Sch. Edn., Fordham U., N.Y.C., 1997—, mem. adv. com. N.Y.C. Pub. Schs. Supts.' Network, 1998—, judge Nat. Sch. Change awards, 2001—, mem. program devel. adv. com. Grad. Sch. Edn., 2000—. Chmn. N.Y.C. steering com. Nat. Congress on Volunteerism and Citizenship, 1976; mem. exec. com. Mayor's Vol. Action Coun., 1977-78; bd. govs. N.Y. Jaycees Found., 1978-79; bd. govs., 4th v.p. First Assembly Dist. Rep. Club, 1977-82; vestryman All Saints Episc. Ch., Bergenfeld, 1982-83; mem. Tabernacle Twp. Planning Bd., 1985-88, Tabernacle Bd. Edn., 1988-91, Tabernacle Rep. Club, 1983-93; jr. warden, 1987-88, sr. warden, 1989-90, vestryman, lay reader St. Peter's Episc. Ch., Medford, N.J., 1985-93; program adv. com. Toshiba Am. Found., 1993-99; trustee, dir. Support Ctr. of N.Y., N.Y.C., 1995-97, Robert A. Taft Inst. Govt., N.Y.C., 1994-97; bd. dirs. N.Y.C. Pub./Pvt. Initiatives, Inc., 1996-2000, bd. dirs. NY Regional Assn. Grantmakers, 1998—; bd. trustees Calvin K. Kazanjian Econs. Found., 2002—; mem. adv. com. Ctr. for Advancement of Children's Mental Health, Columbia U., N.Y.C., 2003-05; serving brother, Priory in U.S.A., Order of St. John, 2003-; bd. dirs. USO Met. NY, 2005—. Col. USAFR, ret. Named Outstanding Young Man of VA., 1975, USAF Res. Officer of Yr., 1985. Mem. Internat. (senator; v.p. 1975; rep. to UN 1976), U.S. (nat. v.p. 1973-74), D.C. (pres. 1972-73), N.Y.C. (bd. govs. 1978-79) Jaycees, SAR, Soc. Mayflower Descs., ABA, N.Y. Bar Assn., Student Bar Assn. (class pres. 1978-81), Toastmasters (local pres. 1969-70, area gov. 1970-71), Lions (pres. Medford Twp. club 1985-86, co-chmn. Charity Ball 1987), Masons, Alpha Delta Phi. Republican. Episcopalian. Address: 7 E Bayview St Massapequa NY 11758-7602 Office Phone: 212-319-0670.

**VAN GORP, GARY WAYNE,** clergyman; b. Reasnor, Iowa, July 16, 1953; s. Laverne Leroy Sr. and Emma Jean (Meyers) Van G.; m. Marietta Louise Burns, Dec. 29, 1972; children: Caleb Aaron, Kari Beth, Micah Alan, Faith Elise, Melinda Amy, Joy Annette, Kristina Nicole. Diploma in Pastoral Studies, Bible and Doctrine, Berean Coll., 1975; BS in Pastoral Studies, Religious Edn., North Cen. Bible Coll., Mpls., 1978; Diploma in profl. office mgmt., Alexandria (Minn.) Tech. Sch., 1984; various positions, ADIA Employment, 1993. Ordained to ministry Assembly of God Ch., 1981. Pastor Verndale (Minn.) Assembly of God Ch., 1979—82; asst. mgr., caretaker Lake Geneva Bible Camp, Alexandria, 1982—83; Christian edn. and outreach pastor Alexandria Assembly of God Ch., 1983—84; pastor, adminstrv. asst. Allison Park (Pa.) Assembly of God Ch., 1984—90; interim pastor Assembly God Ch., Bklyn. Ctr. and Winona, Minn., 1991; mem. maintenance pers. staff South Ridge Mall, 1991—92; farmhand J&V Van Gorp, Inc., 1992; developer ministry program Berean Assembly of God Ch., Des Moines, 1992; founder, owner GW Enterprize, 1993—; with ADIA The Employment People, Temp. Svc., 1992—94; pastor Lighthouse Assembly of God, Glencoe, Minn., 1994—99; security officer Roland Security, 1995—99; office mgr. Spruce Ridge Resource Mgmt., 1999—2000; adminstrv. asst. Koobi LLC, 2000—; sr. pastor Two Rivers Fellowship, Greeley, Colo., 2001—. Chmn. Glencoe Ministerium, 1995-96; vice prin. Faith Acad. Christian Sch., 1980-82; mgr. book store Gospel Supply Ctr., Minn., 1981-82; pastor Elbow Lake (Minn.) Assembly of God, 1983-84; sec. pastoral care adv. com. No. Colo. Nat. Ctr., 2006—; mem. adv. com. Will Rothman Family Chaplaincy, 2006-. Bd. dir., treas., mem. adv. bd. The DoorWay, Inc., Pitts., 1988-92; mem. adv. bd. Glory Home Sch. Corp., Des Moines, 1994; coord. West League Jr. Bible Quiz State of Minn., 1995-2001; coach Rocky Mountain Dist. Coun., 2004—; chmn. Faith Cmty. Svc. Fund, Greeley, Colo., 2005—; coach team Rocky Mtn. Dist. Coun., 2002—; vol. night chaplain No. Colo. Med. Ctr., 2006—; sec. pastoral care adv. com. No. Colo. Med. Ctr., 2006—; mem. Bldg. Strayer Marriages Weld County, Colo., 2005—; Housing Emergency Svcs. Network, United Way Weld County, 2005—. Named to, Outstanding Young Men Am. Mem. Nat. Assn. Ch. Bus. Adminstrs. (pres. Pitts. chpt. 1987-90). Home and Office: 3915 W 21st St Greeley CO 80634 Office Phone: 970-351-6622. E-mail: vangorp53@msn.com.

**VAN GRAAFEILAND, GARY P.,** lawyer; b. 1946; s. Ellsworth A. Van Graafeiland; married, 1977; 2 children. BA in Eng., Union Coll., 1968; JD, Cornell U., 1972. Bar: NY 1973. Atty. Harter, Secrest & Emery, Rochester, NY; mem. corp. legal staff Eastman Kodak Co., Rochester, NY, 1979—89, asst. gen. counsel, head corp. legal staff, 1989—92, sec., 1990—95, sr. v.p. gen. counsel, 1992—, chief compliance officer. Bd. dirs. ESL Fed. Credit Union; bd. trustees US-China Legal Cooperation Fund. Bd. dirs., former chmn. Rochester Sch. of the Holy Childhood. Mem.: Monroe County Bar Assn., NY State Bar Assn., ABA, Civil Justice Reform Group, Assn. of Gen. Counsel (v.p.), Am. Corp. Counsel Assn.

**VAN GRACK, STEVEN,** lawyer; b. Memphis, Oct. 6, 1948; s. Irving and Edna (Schwartz) Van Grack; m. Gail Beverly Lang, Nov. 18, 1972 (div.); children: Adam, Ryan, Brandon, Allison; m. Susan M Freeland, May 21, 1993. BA, U. Md., 1970, JD, 1974. Bar: 1974 (Md), DC 1976, US Dist Ct Md 1976, US Dist Ct DC 1976, US Ct Appeals (4th cir) 1977, US Supreme Ct 1978. Law clk. to presiding justice Montgomery County Cir. Ct., Rockville, Md., 1974-75; assoc. Joseph Roesser Law Offices, Silver Springs, Md., 1975-78; ptnr. Ebert & Bowytz, Washington, 1978-80; mng. ptnr. Van Grack, Axelson & Williamowsky, Rockville, 1980—. Instr, lectr Montgomery Col, Germantown, Md., 1983—85. Cubmaster packs 1343 and 1449 Boy Scouts of Am.; coach Rockville Baseball Assn.; trustee Shady Grove Adventist Hosp. Found.; co-chmn. Montgomery County March of Dimes WalkAmerica Com., 1998—2003; pres. Md. Inst. for Continuing Profl. Edn. of Lawyers, 2003—; chmn. Md. Real Estate Commn., 2001—; gen. counsel Montgomery County Dem. Ctrl. Com., Kensington, Md., 1978—82; campaign mgr. Com. to Elect the Sitting Judges, Rockville, Md., 1982; mayor City of Rockville, Md., 1985—87; Dem. candidate 8th Congl. Dist. Md., 1994; bd. dirs. Washington Met. Coun. Govts. With USAR, 1970—71. Named one of Oustanding Young Men Am, Jaycees, 1978, 1981; recipient Fifth Ann Pro Bono Serv Award, Montgomery County Bar Found, 1998, Extraordinary Commitment to the Delivery of Legal Servs Award, 1999, Nancy Dworkin Award, Montgomery County Comn Children and Youth, 2001, Pro Bono Svc. award, Women's Bar Assn. Md., 2003, The Daily Record Leadership in Law award, 2004. Fellow: Md Bar Found (Profl. Legal Excellence award 2002); mem.: ATLA, ABA, Rockville CofC (bd dirs), Montgomery County Bar Asn (Outstanding Comt Chair of the Yr Award 1981), Md Trial Lawyers Asn, Md Bar Asn. Jewish. Avocations: running, swimming, exercising, coin collecting/numismatics, political button collecting. Home: 808 Fordham St Rockville MD 20850-1018 Office: Van Grack Axelson & Williamowsky 401 N Washington St Rockville MD 20850-2223 Office Phone: 301-738-7671. E-mail: sug@vawlaw.com.

**VAN GUNDY, GREGORY FRANK,** retired lawyer; b. Columbus, Ohio, Oct. 24, 1945; s. Paul Arden and Edna Marie (Sanders) Van G.; m. Lisa Tamara Langer. BA, Ohio State U., Columbus, 1966, JD, 1969. Bar: NY 1971. Assoc. atty. firm Willkie Farr & Gallagher, N.Y.C., 1970-74; v.p. legal, sec. Marsh & McLennan Cos., Inc., N.Y.C., 1974-79, v.p., sec., gen. counsel, 1979-2000, sec., 2000—03, retired, 2003. Mem. Phi Beta Kappa. Roman Catholic. Home: 232 Fox Meadow Rd Scarsdale NY 10583-1640 Personal E-mail: vgfam@aol.com.

**VAN GUNDY, JEFF,** professional basketball coach; b. Hemet, Calif., Jan. 19, 1962; married. Graduate cum laude, Nazareth Coll. Head coach McQuaid Jesuit H.S., Rochester, N.Y., 1985-86; grad. asst., asst coach Providence Coll., 1986-88; asst. coach Rutgers U., N.J., 1988-89, N.Y. Knicks, N.Y.C., 1989-96, head coach, 1996—2001, Houston Rockets, 2003—. Office: Houston Rockets 1510 Polk St Houston TX 77002-7130

**VAN GUNDY, SEYMOUR DEAN,** plant pathologist, educator; b. Feb. 24, 1931; s. Robert C. and Margaret (Holloway) Van G.; m. Wilma C. Fanning, June 12, 1954; children: Sue Ann, Richard L. BA, Bowling Green State U., 1953; PhD, U. Wis. 1957. Asst. nematologist U. Calif., Riverside, 1957-63, assoc. prof., 1963-68, prof. nematology and plant pathology, 1968-73, assoc. dean rsch., 1968-70, vice chancellor rsch., 1970-72, chmn. dept. nematology, 1972-84; prof. nematology and plant pathology, assoc. dean rsch. Natural and Agrl. Scis., 1985-88, acting dean, 1986, interim dean, 1988-90, dean, 1990-93, emeritus dean, prof., 1993—. Former mem. editl. bd. Rev. de Nematologie, Jour. Nematology and Plant Disease; contbr. numerous articles

to profl. jours. Grantee, Rockefeller Found., Cancer Rsch., NSF, USDA; NSF fellow, Australia, 1965—66. Fellow AAAS, Am. Phytopathol. Soc., Soc. Nematologists (editor-in-chief 1968-72, v.p. 1972-73, pres. 1973-74, hon. mem. 1997, hon. mem. Acad. Scis. Moldova 2006). Home: 1188 Pastern Rd Riverside CA 92506-5619 Office: U Calif Dept Nematology Riverside CA 92521-0001 Personal E-mail: vangundy@hotmail.com.

**VAN HALEN, EDDIE (EDWARD LODEWIJK VAN HALEN),** musician; b. Nijmegan, The Netherlands, Jan. 26, 1957; arrived in U.S., 1967; s. Jan and Eugenia Van Halen; m. Valerie Bertinelli, Apr. 11, 1981 (separated); 1 child, Wolfgang William. Student, Pasadena City Coll.; studied piano. Formed group with brother Alex: Broken Combs (name changed later to Mammoth); founder, lead guitarist Van Halen, 1974—; musician: (albums) Van Halen, 1978 (named one of The 500 Greatest Albums of All Time, Rolling Stone, 2003), Van Halen II, 1979, Women and Children First, 1980, Fair Warning, 1981, Diver Down, 1982, Nineteen Eighty-Four, 1984, 5150, 1986, OU812, 1988, For Unlawful Carnal Knowledge, 1991 (Am. Music Awards Favorite Hard Rock Album, 1992), Van Halen Live: Right Here Right Now, 1993, Balance, 1995, Best of Van Halen, Vol. 1, 1996, Van Halen III, 1998, The Best of Both Worlds, 2004, (songs) Runnin' With the Devil, 1978 (Rock & Roll Hall of Fame's 500 Songs that Shaped Rock & Roll, 1997), Jump, 1984 (MTV: 100 Greatest Videos Ever Made, 1999, VH1: 100 Greatest Rock Songs, 2000, Rolling Stone & MTV: 100 Greatest Pop Songs, 2000, VH1: 100 Greatest Videos, 2001, VH1: 100 Best Songs of the Past 25 Yrs., 2003, Rock & Roll Hall of Fame's 500 Songs that Shaped Rock & Roll, 1997), Hot for Teacher, 1984 (Rolling Stone: 100 Top Music Videos, 1993, VH1: 100 Greatest Videos, 2001), Right Now, 1991 (3 MTV Video Music awards, 1992, #6 on Rolling Stone: The 100 Top Music Videos, 1993, MTV: 100 Greatest Videos Ever Made, 1999). Named one of Greatest Artists of Rock & Roll, VH1, 1998, 100 Greatest Artists of Hard Rock, 2000; recipient Grammy Award, Best Hard Rock Performance, 1992. Office: Warner Bros Records 75 Rockefeller Plz New York NY 10019-6908*

**VAN HANDEL, MICHAEL J.,** staffing company executive; BS magna cum laude, Marquette Univ.; MBA, Univ. Wis. Dir., internal audit Manpower, Inc., Milw., 1989—93, v.p., internat. acctg.. 1993—95, chief acctg. officer, treas., 1995—98, sr. v.p., 1998—2002, CFO, 1999—, exec. v.p., 2002—. Office: Manpower Inc 5301 N Ironwood Rd Milwaukee WI 53217 Mailing: Manpower Inc PO Box 2053 Milwaukee WI 53201*

**VANHARN, GORDON LEE,** academic administrator; b. Grand Rapids, Mich., Dec. 30, 1935; s. Henry and Edna (Riemersma) VanH.; m. Mary Kool, June 12, 1958; children: Pamela L., Mark L., Barbara A. BA, Calvin Coll., 1957; MS, U. Ill., 1959, PhD, 1961. Asst. prof. biology Calvin Coll., Grand Rapids, 1961-68, prof., 1970-82, acad. dean, 1982-85, provost, 1985-94, sr. v.p./ provost, 1994-96, prof. interdisciplinary studies, 1996-99, prof. emeritus, 1999—; dir. Van Andel Edn. Inst., 2002—. Assoc. prof. biology Oberlin Coll., Ohio, 1968-70; assoc. physiologist Blodgett Meml. Med. Ctr., Grand Rapids, 1970-76; rsch. assoc. U. Va., Charlotteville, 1975-76. Contbr. articles to profl. jours. Mem. sci. adv. com. Gerald R. Ford, 1972-73; mem. rsch. and rev. com. Blodget Hosp., 1978-84; pres. bd. Grand Rapids Christian Sch. Assn., 1982-85; v.p. Christian Schs. Internat., 1987-93; mem Grand Rapids Pub. Sch. Bd., 1996-2002; bd. dirs. Pine Rest Found., 1997—; trustee Van Andel Edn. Inst., 2000—, dir., 2001—; exec com. Grand Rapids Edn. Reform Initiative, 2000—, Grand Rapids Student Advancement Found., 2003-2004; coord. Assn. Reformed Instns. of Higher Edn., 2001-2003. Grass Found. fellow, 1969. Mem. Phi Kappa Phi. Mem. Christian Reformed Ch. Home and Office: 1403 Cornell Dr SE Grand Rapids MI 49506

**VAN HECKE, GERALD RAYMOND,** chemist, educator; b. Evanston, Ill., Nov. 1, 1939; s. Joseph Michael and Sylvia Alina (Brygarri) Van H. BS, Harvey Mudd Coll., Claremont, Calif., 1961; MA, Princeton U., 1963, PhD, 1966. Chemist Shell Devel. Co., Emeryville, Calif., 1966-70; prof. chemistry Harvey Mudd Coll., 1970—, Donald A. Strauss prof. chemistry, 2001—, assoc. dean adminstrn., 2006—. Bd. govs. Harvey Mudd Coll., pres., 1986-89, 68, v.p., 1967, sec., 1972. Contbr. articles to Jour. Chem. Edn., Liquid Crystals in a Jour., Jour. Phys. Chemistry, Liquid Crystals and Ordered Fluids, Inorganic Chemistry, Jour. Am. Chem. Soc., and others. ARCS scholar Harvey Mudd Coll.; LeRoy Wiley McKay fellow Princeton U., NSF fellow, NASA Sci. Faculty fellow; Outstanding Alumnus of Yr. Harvey Mudd Coll., 2001 Fellow Am. Inst. Chemists; mem. AAAS, Am. Chem. Soc. (chair San Gorgonio chpt. 1987-88), Royal Chem. Soc., Sigma Xi. Achievements include research in thermodynamics and statistical thermodynamics of liquids, particularly liquid crystals, preparation of new liquid crystalline materials, light-scattering methods for determination of thermodynamic properties. Office: Harvey Mudd Coll 301 Platt Blvd Claremont CA 91711-5901 Office Phone: 909-607-3935.

**VAN HEERTUM, RONALD LANNY,** physician; b. Englewood, N.J., Nov. 23, 1940; s. Arnold and Irene Gladys (Ostheimer) V.; children: Richard Jonathan, Beth Jennifer, Jonathan Jason, Kristin Ashley; m. Elyse Ann Murphy, Apr. 3, 2004. BA, Gettysburg Coll., 1962; MD, N.J. Med. Sch., 1966. Diplomate Nat. Bd. Med. Examiners, 1967, Am. Bd. Radiology, 1971, Am. Bd. Nuclear Medicine, 1973. Intern Hackensack Hosp., NJ, 1966-67; resident in radiology St. Vincent's Hosp. & Med. Ctr. NY, 1967—70, fellow in radiology and nuclear medicine, 1970-71, clin. asst. dept radiology, 1971, asst. chief nuclear medicine sect., asst. attending radiologist, 1975-76, chief nuclear medicine sect., 1977-91, assoc. attending physician depts. radiology and medicine, 1977-78, attending physician depts. radiology and medicine, 1978-91, dir. Nuclear Radiology Residency Tng. Program, 1980-88, 80-91, asst. dir. dept. radiology, 1981-91, med. dir. Sch. Nuclear Medicine Tech., 1982-91; asst. chief nuclear medicine svc. Tripler Army Med. Ctr., Honolulu, 1972, chief nuclear medicine svc., 1972-74; adj. prof. Sch. Pharmacy U. Pacific, Stockton, Calif., 1973-74; fellow in nuclear medicine SUNY, 1974-75; clin. asst. prof. of radiology Sch. Medicine NYU, 1977-83; assoc. prof. clin. radiology NY Med. Coll., Valhalla, 1983-88, prof. clin. radiology, 1988-91; dir. mini-fellowship program St. Vincent's Hosp. Cerebral SPECT Learning Ctr., 1991—2001; prof. clin. radiology Coll. Physicians & Surgeons of Columbia U., NY, 1991—2001; attending physician dept. radiology Columbia-Prsbyn. Med. Ctr., 1991—, dir. nuclear medicine residency tng. program, 1980—88, 1991—; attending physician dept brain imaging NY Psychiatric Inst., 1993—, attending physician Dept. Neurosci., 1996—; vice chmn. dept. radiology Coll. Physicians and Surgeons Columbia U., 1993—, prof. radiology, 2002—. Cons. nuclear medicine Catholic Med. Ctr. of Bklyn. and Queens, 1979-88, The Long Island Coll. Hosp., 1980-88, dept. radiology St. Vincent's Hosp. and Med. Ctr. of NY, 1991-92, biol. studies unit NY Psychiat. Inst., 1993—, The Oxford Project to Investigate Memory and Aging, The John Radcliffe Infirmary and Dept. of Clin. Pharmacology Oxford U., 1993—; alt. del. Am. Coll. Nuclear Physics, 1980-82; core mem. DOE Sponsored Consensus Panel Brain SPECT Perfusion Imaging: Optimizing Image Aquisition and Processing, 1991; vis. prof. Brooke Army Med. Ctr., San Antonio, 1978, Howard U. Med. Coll., Washington, 1980, South Hills Health Systems, Pitts., 1981, St. Barnabas Med. Ctr., Livingston, NJ, 1989, Eastern Va. Med. Sch. Norfolk Gen. Hosp., 1990, U. PR Med. Ctr., VA Med. Ctr., 1993, U. Wash. Med. Ctr., Seattle, 1994, Washington U., St. Louis, 1998, Robert Wood Johnson Med. Sch., 1999, Stonybrook HSC, 2005, U. Puerto Rico, 2005; mem. Am. Bd. Nuc. Medicine, 1995—, vice chair, 1999-2000, chair, 2000-02; dir. Columbia Kreitchman PET Ctr., 1993-. Contbr. articles to profl. jours. Major USAR, 1971-74. Recipient Physician Recognition award AMA, 1974-93; numerous rsch. grants in field. Fellow Am. Coll. Radiology (commn on nuc. medicine 1994-2000, chmn. nuc. medicine accreditation com. 2000-06, chair accreditation program chiefs com., 2002-06, vice chmn. 2002-06), NY Acad. Medicine (sec. nuclear medicine sect. 1993—); mem Am. Roentgen Ray Soc., Radiological Soc. N. Am., NY Roentgen Soc., Soc. Nuclear Medicine (mem. bd. govs. greater NY chpt. 1982-84, 86-89, mem. acad. coun. 1988, mem. brain imaging coun 1988—, sub-chmn. gastroenterology sci. program com 1989-90, pres. elect brain imaging coun. 1990-92, pres. 1992-94, sub.-chmn. psychiatry-clin. sci. program com 1993-94), Soc. Thoracic Radiology (sr. mem.). Presbyterian. Business E-Mail: rvhs@columbia.edu.

**VAN HELDEN, PETE,** food products executive; Sr. v.p. of oper., Jewel-Osco (subs. of Albertson's Inc.), Melrose Park, Ill.; pres. Midwest Div. Albertson's Inc., Melrose Park, Ill., 1999—, pres. & CEO, Calif. Food Div., 2004—. Office: Albertsons Inc 250 Parkcenter Blvd Boise ID 83706 Office Phone: 208-395-6200. Office Fax: 208-395-6349.

**VAN HENGEL, MAARTEN,** banker; b. Amsterdam, The Netherlands, Mar. 29, 1927; came to U.S., 1950, naturalized, 1957; s. Adrianus J. and Helena (Gips) van H.; m. Drusilla Drake Riley, Dec. 1, 1951; children: Maarten, Virginia, Hugh, Drusilla. Student, Kennemer Lyceum, Bloemendaal, Holland, 1939-45. With tng. programs of Amsterdamsche Bank, N.V., Amsterdam, Lazard Bros. & Co. Ltd., London and Canadian Bank of Commerce, Montreal, Que., Canada, 1945-49; with Brown Bros. Harriman & Co., 1950—, ptnr., 1968—. Bd. dirs. Netherlands-Am. Found. Served with AUS, 1951-53. Mem.: India House, Netherland (N.Y.C.); Fishers Island Country, Hay Harbor (Fishers Island); Sleepy Hollow Country (Scarborough, N.Y.). Home: 350 River Rd Briarcliff Manor NY 10510-2418 Office: Brown Bros Harriman & Co 140 Broadway New York NY 10005

**VAN HOFTEN, JAMES DOUGAL ADRIANUS,** former astronaut, transportation executive; b. Fresno, Calif., June 11, 1944; s. Adriaan and Beverly (McCurdy) van H.; m. Vallarie Davis, May 31, 1975; children: Jennifer Lyn, Jamie Juliana, Victoria Jane. BS, U. Calif.-Berkeley, 1966; MS, Colo. State U., 1968, PhD, 1976. Asst. prof. U. Houston, 1976-78; astronaut NASA, Houston, 1978-86; sr. v.p., mgr. advanced systems line Bechtel Nat., Inc., San Francisco, 1986-93; project mgr. Hong Kong New Airport projects, 1993-96; sr. v.p., mgr. N.E. Asia, gen. mgr. Bechtel Civil Co., Hong Kong, 1996-98; sr. v.p., mgr. N.Am. projects Bechtel Infrastructure, San Francisco, 1998-99; program mgr. New Scottish Air Traffic Control Ctr., London, 1999-2000; dir. programmes Nat. Air Traffic Svcs., 2000—02; mng. dir. aviation Bechtel Corp., 2002—. Served with USN, 1969-74; lt. col. Air N.G. 1984-88. Recipient Disting. Service award Colo. State U., 1984; Disting. Citizen award Fresno Council Boy Scouts Am., 1984; Disting. Achievement award Pi Kappa Alpha, 1984 Fellow AIAA; mem. ASCE (Aerospace Sci. and Tech. Application award 1984). Republican. Home: 2C Thorney Ct Palace Gate London W8 5NJ England

**VAN HOLDE, KENSAL EDWARD,** biochemistry educator; b. Eau Claire, Wis., May 14, 1928; s. Leonard John and Nettie (Hart) Van H.; m. Barbara Jean Watson, Apr. 11, 1950; children: Patricia, Mary, Stephen, David. BS, U. Wis., 1949, PhD, 1952. Research chemist E.I. du Pont de Nemours & Co., 1952-55; research assoc. U. Wis., 1955-56; asst. prof. U. Wis. at Milw., 1956-57; mem. faculty U. Ill., Urbana, 1957-67; prof. dept. biochemistry and biophysics Oreg. State U., Corvallis, 1967; Am. Cancer Soc. rsch. prof., 1977-93; disting. prof., 1988-93; disting. prof. emeritus, 1993—; instr.-in-charge physiology course Marine Biol. Lab., Woods Hole, Mass., 1977-80; mem. research staff Centre des Recherches sur les Macromolecules, Strasbourg, France, 1964-65; mem. study sect. USPHS, 1966-69, 91—; staff Weizmann Inst., Israel, 1981, Lab. Léon Brillouin, Saclay, France, 1989-90. Author: Physical Biochemistry, 1971, Chromatin, 1988; (with C. Mathews) Biochemistry, 1989, 2d edit., 1995, 3d edit, 2000, Principles of Physical Biochemistry, 1998, 2d edit., 2006; editor: Biochmica Biophysica Acta, 1966-68; mem. editl. bd. jours. Biol. Chemistry, 1968-75, 81-87, 91-92, assoc. editor, 1992—, Biochemistry, 1973-76. 82-89; contbr. profl. jours. Trustee Marine Biol. Lab., Woods Hole, 1979—82, 1984—92. NSF sr. postdoctoral fellow, 1964-65; Guggenheim fellow, 1973-74; European Molecular Biology Orgn. fellow, 1975; Humbolt fellow, 2000-01. Fellow AAAS; mem. NAS, Am. Soc. Biochemistry and Molecular Biology, Biophys. Soc., Am. Acad. Arts and Scis. Home: 229 NW 32nd St Corvallis OR 97330-5020 Office: Oreg State U Dept Biochemistry Corvallis OR 97331

**VANHOLE, WILLIAM REMI,** lawyer; b. Denver, June 25, 1948; s. Joseph and Mildred VanHole; m. Gemma VanHole. BS, Colo. State U., 1970; JD, U. Idaho, 1976. Bar: Idaho 1976, U.S. Dist. Ct. Idaho 1976, U.S. Dist. Ct. (ea. dist.) Wis. 1998, U.S. Ct. Appeals (9th cir.) 1983, U.S. Supreme Ct., 2003. Law clk. to judge U.S. Dist. Ct. Idaho, Boise, 1976-78; assoc. Quane, Smith, Howard & Hull, Boise. 1978-81, Langroise, Sullivan & Smylie, Boise, 1981-83; asst. U.S. atty. U.S. Dept. of Justice, Boise, 1983-87; U.S. atty. Dist. of Idaho, 1984-85; assoc. gen. counsel Boise Cascade Corp., 1987—2004, OfficeMax Inc., 2004—. Served with U.S. Army, 1970-72 Mem. Fed. Bar Assn., Idaho Bar Assn., Idaho Assn. Def. Counsel, Def. Rsch. Inst. Republican. Avocations: skiing, fishing, golf. Office: OfficeMax Inc PO Box 50 Boise ID 83728-0050

**VAN HOLLEN, CHRISTOPHER, JR.,** congressman; b. Karachi, Pakistan, Jan. 10, 1959; s. Christopher and Eliza (Farnsworth) Van H.; m. Katherine A. Wilkens; children: Anna, Nicholas, Alexander. BA, Swarthmore Coll., 1982; MPP, Harvard U., 1985; JD cum laude, Georgetown U., 1989. Legis. asst. for def. and fgn. policy Office of Senator Charles McC. Mathias, Md., 1985-87; profl. staff mem. US Senate Fgn. Rels. Com., Washington, 1987-89; sr. legis. advisor Washington office Md. Gov. William D. Schaefer, 1989-91; assoc. Arent, Fox, Kintner, Plotkin & Kahn, Washington, 1991—; mem. Md. Ho. Dels., Annapolis, 1991-94; mem. dist. 18 Md. Senate, Annapolis, 1995—2001; mem. US Congress from 7th Md. dist. (formerly 8th), Washington, 2003—. Mem. Ho. Judiciary com., chair Health./Human Svcs. subcom., 2000—. Councillor Atlantic Coun. US; mem. Kensington Citizens Assn. Recipient Resolution of Excellence, US Senate Fgn. Rels. Com. Democrat. Office: US Ho Reps 2235 Rayburn HoOffice Bldg Washington DC 20515-2007*

**VAN HOLLEN, JOHN BYRON,** former prosecutor, lawyer; b. 1966; Grad., St. Olaf's Coll., U. Wis. Asst. U.S. atty. (we. dist.) Wis. US Dept. Justice, 1991—93; dist. atty. Ashland County, Wis., 1993—99, Bayfield County, Wis., 1999—2002; U.S. atty. (we. dist.) Wis. US Dept. Justice, 2002—05.

**VANHOOK, TRACIE LYNNETTE,** small business owner; b. Oakland, Calif., May 17, 1965; d. Herman Curtis Gray and Ritchie Lee Ross; children: Titus Alexander, Lawrence Emanuel. Assoc. in Sci., Merritt Coll., 1999; BS, San Francisco State U., 2002; MS, Calif. U. Pa., 2005. Cert. health and fitness instr. Am. Coll. Sports Medicine, performance enhancement specialist, personal trainer Nat. Acad. Sports Medicine, in enhanced sports nutrition HK Academic Online Edn. Ctr. Cons.; presenter E.C. Reems Women's Internat. Ministries Nat. Conf., Oakland, 1997—2000; fitness supr. Sports Club LA-San Francisco, 2003—05; therapy and rehab asst. Body Focus Health Ctr., San Francisco, 2003—04; fitness mgr./master trainer Axis Performance Ctr., Menlo Park, Calif., 2005—06; owner Fit to the Core Personal Tng., Menlo Park, 2006—. Dancer/actor (play) Navigators. Avocations: youth dance choreography, hiking. Office: Axis Performance Ctr 550 Ravenswood Ave Menlo Park CA 94025 Office Phone: 650-463-1920. Office Fax: 650-463-1926. Business E-Mail: tracie@fittothecorept.com.

**VAN HOOMISSEN, GEORGE ALBERT,** state supreme court justice; b. Portland, Oreg., Mar. 7, 1930; s. Fred J. and Helen F. (Flanagan) Van H.; m. Ruth Madeleine Niedermeyer, June 4, 1960; children: Geroge T., Ruth Anne, Madeleine, Matthew. BBA, U. Portland, 1951; JD, Georgetown U., 1955, LLM in Labor Law, 1957; LLM in Jud. Adminstrn., U. Va., 1986. Bar: D.C. 1955, Oreg. 1956, Tex. 1971, U.S. Dist. Ct. Oreg. 1956, U.S. Ct. Mil. Appeals 1955, U.S. Ct. Customs and Patent Appeals 1955, U.S. Ct. Claims 1955, U.S. Ct. Appeals (9th cir.) 1956, U.S. Ct. Appeals (D.C. cir.) 1955, U.S. Supreme Ct. 1960. Law clk. for Chief Justice Harold J. Warner Oreg. Supreme Ct., 1955-56; Keigwin teaching fellow Georgetown Law Sch., 1956-57; dep. dist. atty. Multnomah County, Portland, 1957-59; pvt. practice Portland, 1959-62; dist. atty. Multnomah County, 1962-71; dean nat. coll. dist. attys., prof. law U. Houston, 1971-73; judge Cir. Ct., Portland, 1973-81, Oreg. Ct. Appeals, Salem, 1981-88; justice Oreg. Supreme Ct., Salem 1988—2001. Adj. prof. Northwestern Sch. Law, Portland, Williamette U. Sch. Law, Portland State U; mem. faculty Am. Acad. Judicial Edn., Nat. Judicial Coll.; Keigwin Teaching fellow Georgetown U. Law Sch. Mem. Oreg. Ho. of Reps., Salem, 1959-62, chmn. house jud. com. With USMC, 1951-53; col. USMCR (ret.). Recipient

Disting. Alumnus award U. Portland, 1972. Master Owen M. Panner Am. Inn of Ct.; mem. ABA, Oreg. State Bar, Tex. Bar Assn., Oreg. Law Inst. (bd. dirs.), Arlington Club, Multnomah Athletic Club, Univ. Club. Roman Catholic. Office: Oreg Supreme Ct 2105 SW Elm St Portland OR 97201 Office Phone: 503-221-2202. Personal E-mail: gavanhoomissen@msn.com.

**VAN HOOSER, PATRICIA LOU SCOTT,** art educator; b. Springfield, Mo., Oct. 4, 1934; d. Arthur Irving and Isoline Elizabeth (Jones) Scott; m. Buckley Blaine Van Hooser, Mar. 28, 1956 (div.); children: Buckley Blaine II, Craig Alan. BA, Drury U., 1956; MS in Art, Pittsburg State U., Kans., 1968. Society writer Springfield News & Leader & Press, 1955—56; hostess radio program Sta. KSEK, Pittsburg, Kans., 1962—63; tchr. art and home econs. Hurley (Mo.) HS, 1956—57; art supr. elem. sch. Mountain Grove, Mo., 1960; tchr. art Hickory Hills Sch., Springfield, 1960—61; tchr art and English jr. and sr. schs., Baxter Springs, Kans., 1965—75; art coord. Joplin (Mo.) Elem. Sch. Dist., 1975—. Lectr. in field; chmn. for S.W. Mo., Nat. Youth Art Month. Bd. dirs. Spiva Art Ctr.; sec. Parents without Ptnrs., CV & FE Credit Union; bd. recorder S.W. Mo. Credit Unions. Mem.: ASCD, NEA, AAUW (2d v.p. Joplin br.), Epsilon Sigma Alpha, Pittsburg State U. Alumni Assn. (sec., pres. Joplin br.), Joplin Cmty. Concert Assn., S.W. Mo. Mus. Assn., Mo. Edn. Assn., S.W. Mo. Dist. Art Tchrs., Mo. Art Edn. Assn., Nat. Art Edn. Assn., Assn. Childhood Edn. Internat. (pres. Joplin br., pres. Mo. state), Writers of Six Bulls, Joplin Writer's Guild, Cafe au Lait Club. Methodist. E-mail: Pvanhooser6@cs.com.

**VANHORN, BRADLEY KENT,** musician; b. Mason City, Iowa, Sept. 26, 1970; s. Myron John and Lyla Pearl VanHorn; m. Brenda Diane Baily, July 9, 1994; children: Melanie, Jonah. BA in Music Edn., Ctrl. Coll., Pella, Iowa, 1993. Vocal instr., band instr. Spring Grove (Minn.) Pub. Schs., 1993—96; 7-12 grade vocal mus instr. Hampton (Iowa)-Dumont Pub. Schs., 1996—99; music dir., organist Trinity Luth. Ch., Mason City, Iowa, 1999—. Recipient Thirty Under Forty award, Globe Gazette, Mason City, 2005. Avocations: singing, golf, farming. Home: 2110 Hwy 65 Sheffield IA 50475

**VAN HORN, CHARLES E.,** lawyer; b. Phila., Jan. 30, 1942; BSChemE, Lehigh U., 1963; JD, Am. U., 1968; MBA, George Washington U., 1973. Bar: Va. 1968, DC 1998, US Patent & Trademark Office. Ptnr. Finnegan, Henderson, Farabow, Garrett & Dunner LLP, Washington, mem. mgmt. com., leader, Prosecution Sect. Mem.: Patent & Trademark Soc., Intellectual Property Owners Assn., Am. Intellectual Property Law Assn. Office: Finnegan Henderson Farabow Garrett & Dunner LLP 901 New York Ave NW Washington DC 20001-3315 Office Phone: 202-408-4000. Office Fax: 202-408-4400. Business E-Mail: charles.vanhorn@finnegan.com.

**VAN HORN, HUGH M.,** physicist, astronomer, educator; b. Williamsport, Pa., Mar. 5, 1938; s. Robert Dix and Virginia Elizabeth (Moody) Van H.; m. Mary Susan Boon, Sept. 17, 1960; children: Kathleen Susan, Mary Margaret, Michael Hugh George. BSc, Case Inst. Tech., 1960; PhD, Cornell U., 1965. NASA predoctoral trainee Cornell U., Ithaca, 1963-65; rsch. assoc. U. Rochester, 1965-67, asst. prof., 1967-73, assoc. prof., 1973-77, prof., 1977-96, chmn. dept. physics and astronomy, 1980-86, acting assoc. dean Coll. Arts and Scis., 1987-89, acting chmn. dept. physics and astronomy, 1992-93, adj. prof., 1996—2005, prof. emeritus, 2005—; Shapley lectr. Am. Astron. Soc., 1981-95; dir. divsn. astron. sci. NSF, Arlington, Va., 1993-2000, sr. sci. advisor Directorate Math. Phys. Sci., 2000—02, dir. nat. facilities divsn. materials rsch., 2002—04. Vis. fellow Joint Inst. Lab. Astrophysics, 1973—74; sr. scientist Lab. Laser Energetics, 1985—96; vis. prof. U. Tex., 1987; vis. investigator dept. terr. magnetism Carnegie Inst. Washington, 2000—02; prin. investigator NASA and NSF grants. Editor: (with V. Weidemann) White Dwarfs and Variable Degenerate Stars, 1979, (with S. Ichimaru) Strongly Coupled Plasma Physics, 1993; contbr. articles on white dwarfs, neutron stars and dense matter to profl. jours. Fellow AAAS; mem. Internat. Astron. Union. E-mail: vanhorns@frontiernet.net.

**VAN HORN, KEITH,** professional basketball player; b. Oct. 23, 1975; m. Amy Van Horn; children: Sabrina, Nicholas. Grad., U. Utah, 1997. Basketball player N.J. Nets, East Rutherford, NJ, 1997—2001, Phila. 76ers, 2002—03, New York Knicks, 2003—04, Milwaukee Bucks, 2004—05, Dallas Mavericks, 2005—. Named first team All-Am., U. Utah, 1997. Achievements include being the top scorer U. Utah and Western Athletic conf. hist; 3 time Western Athletic Conf. Player of Yr. 1995-97. Office: 2909 Taylor St Dallas TX 75226

**VAN HORN, O. FRANK,** retired counselor, consultant; b. Grand Junction, Colo., Apr. 16, 1926; s. Oertel F. and Alta Maude (Lynch) Van H.; m. Dixie Jeanne MacGregor, Feb. 1, 1947 (dec. Nov. 1994); m. Evelyn Anne Carroll, Mar. 22,1998; children: Evelyn (dec.), Dorothy. AA, Mesa Coll., 1961; BA, Western State Colo., 1963; MEd, Oreg. State U., 1969. Counselor, mgr. State of Oreg.-Employment, Portland and St. Helens, 1964-88; pvt. practice counselor and cons. St. Helens, 1988-96. Chair Task Force on Aging, Columbia County, 1977-79; advisor Western Interstate Commn. on Higher Edn., Portland, 1971, Concentrated Employment and Tng., St. Helens, 1977, County Planning Bd., Columbia County, Oreg., 1977-80, City Planning Bd., St. Helens, 1978, Youth Employment Coun., St. Helens, 1978, Task Force on Disadvantaged Youth, St. Helens, 1980; counselor Career Mgmt. Specialists Internat.; instr. Portland C.C. Mem. ACA, Oreg. Counseling Assn., Internat. Assn. Pers. in Employment Svc. (Outstanding Achievement award 1975), Nat. Employment Counselors Assn. Democrat. Home: 464 Leelo Ct Florence OR 97439-8909

**VAN HORN, RICHARD LINLEY,** academic administrator; b. Chgo., Nov. 2, 1932; s. Richard Linley and Mildred Dorothy (Wright) Van H.; m. Susan Householder, May 29, 1954 (dec.); children: Susan Elizabeth, Patricia Suzanne, Lynda Sue; m. Betty Pfefferbaum, May 29, 1988. BS with highest honors, Yale U., 1954; MS, MIT, 1956; PhD, Carnegie-Mellon U., 1976; D of Bus. (hon.), Reitsumeikan U., Kyoto, Japan, 1991. Asst. dir. Army EDP Project, MIT, Cambridge, 1956-57; research staff Rand Corp., Santa Monica, Calif., 1957-60, head mgmt. systems group, 1960-61; dir., prof. mgmt. systems European Inst. Advanced Studies in Mgmt., Brussels, 1971-73; assoc. dean Grad. Sch. Indsl. Adminstrn., Carnegie-Mellon U., Pitts., 1967-71, dir. budget and planning, 1973-74, v.p. for bus. affairs, 1974-77, v.p. for mgmt., 1977-80, provost and prof. mgmt., 1980-83; chancellor U. Houston, 1983-86, pres., 1986-89, U. Okla., 1989-94; pres. emeritus and regent's prof. Coll. of Bus. U. Okla., Norman, 1994—; Clarence E. Page prof. aviation U. Okla., Norman, 1995—; dir. mgmt. info. sys. divsn. Coll. Bus. U Okla., 1997—2000. Author: (with Robert H. Gregory) Automatic Data Processing Systems, 1960, 2nd edit. 1963, (with R.H. Gregory) Business Data Processing and Programming, 1963, (with C.H. Kriebel and J.T. Heames) Management Information Systems: Progress and Perspectives, 1971, (with A. Schwarzkopf and R. Leou Price) Information System Solutions: a Project Approach, 2006; contbr. articles to profl. jours.; asso. editor: Jour. Inst. Mgmt. Scis, 1964-78 Mem. Inst. Mgmt. Sci. (nat. council mem. 1963-65, sec.-treas. 1964), Assn. for Computing Machinery (nat. lectr. 1969-70), Council on Govt. Relations (bd. dirs. 1981-83) Avocation: commercial pilot. Office: U Okla Coll Of Bus Norman OK 73019-0001 Home: 3900 N Harvey Pkwy Oklahoma City OK 73118 Office Phone: 405-325-0900. E-mail: rvanhorn@ou.edu.

**VAN HORNE, JAMES CARTER,** economist, educator; b. South Bend, Ind., Aug. 6, 1935; s. Ralph and Helen (McCarter) Van H.; m. Mary A. Roth, Aug. 27, 1960; children: Drew, Stuart, Stephen. AB, De Pauw U., 1957, DSc (hon.), 1986; MBA, Northwestern U., 1961, PhD, 1964. Comml. lending rep. Continental Ill. Nat. Bank, Chgo., 1958-62; prof. fin. Stanford U. Grad. Sch. Bus., 1965-75, A.P. Giannini prof. fin., 1976—, assoc. dean, 1973-75, 76-80; dep. asst. sec. Dept. Treasury, 1975-76. Bd. dirs. Montgomery St. Income Securities, 2d Synnex Corp.; commr. workers compensation Rate Making Study Commn., State of Calif., 1990-92. Author: Function and Analysis of Capital Market Rates, 1970, Financial Market Rates and Flows, 2001, Financial Management and Policy, 2002; co-author: Fundamentals of Financial Management, 2005; assoc. editor Jour. Fin. and Quantitative Analysis,

1969—85, Jour. Fin., 1971—73, Jour. Fixed Income, 1990—. Mem. bd. trustees DePauw U., 1989-96. With AUS, 1957. Mem. Am. Fin. Assn. (past pres., dir.), Western Fin. Assn. (past pres., dir.), Fin. Mgmt. Assn. Home: 2000 Webster St Palo Alto CA 94301-4049 Office: Stanford U Grad Sch Bus Stanford CA 94305

**VAN HOUSE, ROBERT ARTHUR,** small business owner, contractor; b. Evanston, Ill., Sept. 12, 1945; s. Eldon Russell and Lorraine Ellen Huff; m. Sharon Lynn Leonard, Apr. 10, 1999; children: Michael, Jackie. Commd. USN, 1962, advanced through grades to radioman chief petty officer, ret., 1986; comms. sys. analyst Validity Corp., Clinton, Md., 1989—96; with Arlington Annex Comms. Ctr. HQ Marine Corps., Washington, 1989—90; with Naval Electromagnetic Spectrum Ctr. USN, Alexandria, Va., 1990—97; with Integrated Sys. Control., Inc., San Diego, 1997—99; with Space and Missile Sys. Ctr. Spectrum Mgmt. Office, L.A., 1999—2001; coord. naval frequency We. U.S. Dept. Def., Magu, Calif., 2001—04, ret, 2004. Recipient Outstanding Svc. award, USN, 1986. Mem.: IEEE (sr.), Nat. Defense Internat. Assn. Democrat. Lutheran. Avocations: history, classical music, reading. Home and Office: Van House RF Spectrum Consulting 1456 Barca St Camarillo CA 93010 Office Phone: 805-484-5145.

**VAN HOUSEN, THOMAS CORWIN, III,** retired architect; b. Oak Park, Ill., Jan. 2, 1927; s. Thomas Corwin and Dorothea (Saunders) Van H.; children: Deborah, Victoria, Constance. BA, Lawrence U., 1951; BArch, U. Minn., Mpls., 1954; MArch in Urban Design, Harvard U., 1962. Registered architect, Minn., Wis. With Ellerbe Assocs., Inc., St. Paul, 1951-61; architect, prin. Progressive Design Assocs., Inc., St. Paul, 1961-71, architect, developer, v.p. Landmark Devel. Corp./Appletree Enterprises, Inc., Bloomington, Minn., 1971-85; architect, developer Mortenson Devel. Co., Mpls., 1985-88; architect, design, bldg. dir. D&B Collaborative, Inc., Mpls., 1989—99; mktg. cons. Horty, Elving & Assoc., Mpls., 1999—2005. Bldg. official City of North Oaks, Minn., 1964-78; mem. Minn. League of Municipalities-Metro, St. Paul, 1970-72, Gov.'s Open Space Adv. Com., St. Paul, 1972-74. With U.S. Air Force, 1945-47, ETO. Recipient Outstanding House award St. Paul Jaycees, 1958, 62; named finalist (team mem.) Archtl. competition Boston City Hall, 1962. Fellow AIA (nat. bd. dirs. 1985-88, v.p., pres.-elect Minn. chpt. 1994-95, pres. 1995, spl. award 1981, Presdl. citation 1988, 90, 2000); mem. N.W. YMCA. Republican. Lutheran. Avocations: tennis, swimming, music, reading. Office Phone: 612-332-4422.

**VAN HOUTEN, FRANKLYN BOSWORTH,** geologist, educator; b. N.Y.C., July 14, 1914; s. Charles Nicholas and Hessie Osborne (Bosworth) Van H.; m. Jean Oliver Sholes, Feb. 18, 1943 (dec. Sept. 23, 1997); children: Jean S., F. Bosworth, David Gordon. BS, Rutgers U., 1936; PhD, Princeton U., 1941. Instr. dept. geology Williams Coll., 1939-42; asst. prof. Princeton U., 1946-51, assoc. prof., 1951-55, prof., 1955-85, prof. emeritus, 1985—; vis. prof. geology UCLA, 1964, State U. N.Y. at Binghamton, 1971; geologist U.S. Geol. Survey, 1948-67. Temporary geologist Geol. Survey Can., 1953, Yukon Expdn., geol. expdns. to Morocco, Tunisia, Libya, Egypt, Madagascar Author reports and articles on geology. Served as lt. USN, 1942-46. Fellow Geol. Soc. Am.; mem. Am. Assn. Petroleum Geologists, Soc. Econ. Paleontologists and Mineralogists (hon. mem., Twenhofel medal), Internat. Assn. Sedimentologists, Colombia Geol. Soc. (hon.), Delta Upsilon. Home: 168 Fitzrandolph Rd Princeton NJ 08540-7224

**VAN HOUTEN, G. DAVID, JR.,** beverage company executive; b. Waco, Tex. m. Carol Van Houten; children: Tara, Brant, Blaine. Mgmt. degree, Tex. A&M U. Various positions Coca-Cola Bottling Bus., 1972—86; pres., gen. mgr. Coca-Cola Bottling Co. of N. Tex., 1986-96; sr. v.p., pres., Ctrl. N.Am. Group Coca-Cola Enterprises Inc., Atlanta, 1996—2000, sr. v.p., pres., Western N.Am. Group, 2000—01, pres. N.Am. Group, 2001—, exec. v.p., 2001—, COO, 2004—. Office: Coca-Cola Enterprises Inc 2500 Windy Ridge Pkwy Atlanta GA 30339

**VAN HOUTEN, JAMES FORESTER,** former insurance company chief executive, educator, consultant; b. Fullerton, Calif., Jan. 13, 1942; s. James Forester and Lois Evangeline (Trout) V.H.; m. Mary Ann Nelson; children: Kimberly Evangeline, Lori Lynn. BA in Econs., State U. St. Mary's U.; MBA, Ill. State U. CPCU, CLU. Sales mgr. for Can. Motors Ins. Corp. divsn. GM, Detroit, 1963-74; v.p. sales Volkswagen Group St. Louis, 1974-78; v.p. personal lines mktg. Wausau Ins. Cos., St. Louis, 1978-80, v.p., chief mktg. officer life and health, 1980-84; v.p. chief mktg. and strategic planning officer Country Cos., Bloomington, Ill., 1984-89; pres., CEO Mut. Svc. Ins. Cos., St. Paul, 1989—2002. Prof. strategic mgmt. Carlson Sch. Mgmt. and Humphrey Inst., U. Minn., 1990—, Vienna U. Econs., 2006, Metro State U., 2002-2004; bd. dirs. Strategic Mgmt. Rsch. Ctr., U. Minn., EMPO Corp., J.J. Hill Bus. Ref. Libr; pres. Minn. Assn. of Scholars; pres. Tocquelville Ctr.; vis. prof. Vienna U. Econ. Program leader Youth Black Achievers, St. Paul; exec. bd. Arrowhead coun. Boy Scouts Am.; lead planning cons. Sissketon Wahpeton Sioux Tribe, 2004 active Minn. Acad. Stds. Com., Minn. Acad. Excellence Found-Friends; trustee Minn. State Coll. and U. Sys. Fellow: ASCA; mem. Ins. Fedn. Minn. (past chmn. bd.), Minn. Assn. Mutual Ins. Cos. (past pres.), Nat. Coop. Bus. Assn. (bd. dirs. and exec. com., chair fin. com.), Minn. Bus. Partnership (bd. dirs., Minn. K-12 edn. com.), Minn. Assn. Scholars (pres., chair), Ctr. Am. Experiment Think Tank (bd. dirs., ex com., chair fin. and audit com.), Milestone Growth Fund (chair devel. com.). Office Phone: 612-836-0120. Personal E-mail: jvanhouten01@msn.com.

**VAN HOY, PHILIP MARSHALL,** lawyer; b. Washington, Nov. 8, 1947; s. Joe Milton and Helen Virginia (Spangler) V.; m. Sylvia Kathryn Smith, Dec. 30, 1972; children: Marshall, Travis. AB, Duke U., 1970; JD, U. N.C., 1973. Bar: N.C. 1973, U.S. Dist. Ct (w. and mid. dists.) N.C. 1974, U.S. Ct. Appeals (4th cir.) 1974, U.S. Supreme Ct. 1978. Labor counsel Duke Power Co., Charlotte, NC, 1973—80; assoc. Siegel, O'Connor & Kainen, Charlotte, 1980—83; ptnr. Mullins & Van Hoy, Charlotte, 1983—89, Van Hoy, Rentlinger, Adams & Dunn, Charlotte, 1989—. Mem. N.C. OSHA Rev. Bd., 1985-92, Mecklenburg County, N.C. Personnel Commn., 1985-92, N.C. Leadership Coun. Co-state chmn. Gardner for Lt. Gov., 1988, alt. del. Rep. Nat. Conv., Detroit, 1980; chmn. Mecklenburg County Young Rep. Com., 1979, vice chmn., 1980-83; Duke U. Athletics Coun., 1999-02. 1st lt. U.S. Army, 1973-81. Named top employment lawyer N.C., Bus. N.C. Mag., 2002; named to Best Lawyers in Am., 2001—, Outstanding Lawyers of Am., 2003; recipient Salute to Am.'s Best Lawyers, Forbes Mag. and Am. Airlines Sky Radio, 2005. Mem. N.C. Bar Assn. (councillor labor and employment law sect. 1985-88, chmn. EEOC cmte. 1983-92), N.C. State Bar, 4th Cir. Jud. Conf., Rotary, Charlotte Cotillion Club (pres. 1979-80), City Club, Myers Park Country Club (dir. 1994-96, 2000-03). Republican. Methodist. Home: 2615 Hampton Ave Charlotte NC 28207-2521 Office: Van Hoy Reutlinger Adams & Dunn 737 East Blvd Charlotte NC 28203-5113 Office Phone: 704-375-6022.

**VANIER, JACQUES,** physicist; s. Henri and Emma Vanier; m. Lucie Beaudet, 1961; children: Lyne, Pierre. BA, U. Montreal, 1955, BSc, 1958; MSc, McGill U., 1960, PhD, 1963. Lectr. U. Montreal, 1961-63, McGill U., 1960-63; physicist Varian Assocs., Beverly, Mass., 1963-67, Hewlett Packard Co., Beverly, 1967; prof. elec. engring. U. Laval, Que., 1967-83; physicist Nat. Rsch. Coun., Ottawa, 1983-94, head elec. and time standards, 1984-86, dir. Lab. Basic Standards, 1986-90, dir. gen. Inst. for Nat. Measurement Standards, 1990-93; prof. physique U. Montreal, 1995—. Cons. Comm. Components Corp., Costa Mesa, Calif., 1974-76, EGG Co., Salem, Mass., 1979-82, Kernco, Danvers, Mass., 1995—; chmn. com. A URSI, 1990-93; chmn. exec. com. CPEM, 1990-94; mem. Internat. Com. Weights and Measures, 1992-96; guest worker IEN, Torino, Italy, 1996-97. Author: Basic Theory of Lasers and Masers, 1971, (with C. Audoin) The Quantum Physics of Atomic Frequency Standards, 1989; contbr. articles to profl. jours.; patentee (1) in field. Recipient Disting. Precision Time & Time Interval Svc. award PTTI Organizing Com., 1998. Fellow IEEE (Centennial medal 1984, I.I. Rabi award 1994, Instrument & Measurement Soc. award 1999), Royal Soc. Can., Am. Phys. Soc. Business E-Mail: jac.vanier@sympatico.ca.

**VAN INWAGEN, PETER JAN,** philosophy educator; b. Rochester, N.Y., Sept. 21, 1942; s. George Butler and Mildred Gloria (Knudson) van I; m. Margery Bedford Naylor, Mar. 31, 1967 (div. Apr. 1988); 1 child, Elizabeth Core; m. Elisabeth Marie Bolduc, June 3, 1989. BS, Rensselaer Poly. Inst., 1965; PhD, U. Rochester, 1969. Vis. asst. prof. U. Rochester, NY, 1971-72; asst. prof. Syracuse U., NY, 1972-74, assoc. prof. NY, 1974-80, prof. philosophy NY, 1980-95; John Cardinal O'Hara prof. of philosophy U. Notre Dame, South Bend, Ind., 1995—. Vis. prof. U. Ariz., Tucson, 1981; lectr. U. of St. Andrews, 2003, Oxford U., 2000, U. London, 1998. Author: An Essay on Free Will, 1983, Material Beings, 1990, Metaphysics, 1993, God, Knowledge and Mystery, 1995, The Possibility of Resurrection, 1997, Ontology, Identity, and Modality, 2001, The Problem of Evil, 2006; editor: Time and Cause, 1980, Alvin Plantinga, 1985, Metaphysics: The Big Questions, 1998, Christian Faith and The Problem of Evil, 2004; mem. editl. bd. Jour. Faith and Philosophy, Philos. Perspectives, Nous, Philos. Studies, Jour. of Ethics, Philosophy and Phenomenological Rsch.; contbr. articles to profl. jours. Served to capt. U.S. Army, 1969-71 NEH grantee, 1983-84, 89-90. Mem. Am. Acad. Arts and Scis., Am. Philos. Assn., Soc. Christian Philosophers. Democrat. Episcopalian. Home: 52145 Farmington Square Rd Granger IN 46530-6403 Office: U Notre Dame Dept Philosophy South Bend IN 46556-4619 Office Phone: 574-631-5910. E-mail: peter.vaninwagen.1@nd.edu.

**VAN KALDEKERKEN, ROLF,** retail executive; With Inmac; country mgr. Viking, 1994—98, v.p., country mgr. Germany, Benelux and Austria, 1998—2000, exec. v.p. European ops., 2000; pres. European ops. Office Depot, Inc., Delray Beach, Fla., 2000 . Office: Office Depot Inc 2200 Old Germantown Rd Delray Beach FL 33445

**VAN KIRK, JOHN ELLSWORTH,** retired cardiologist; b. Dayton, Ohio, Jan. 13, 1942; s. Herman Corwin and Dorothy Louise (Shafer) Van K.; m. Patricia L. Davis, June 19, 1966 (div. Dec. 1982); 1 child, Linnea Enya. BA cum laude, DePauw U., Greencastle, Ind., 1963; BS, Northwestern U., Chgo., 1964, MD with distinction, 1967. Diplomate Am. Bd. Internal Medicine, Am. Bd. Internal Medicine subspecialty in cardiovasc. disease; cert. Nat. Bd. Med. Examiners. Intern Evanston (Ill.) Hosp., 1967-68; staff assoc. Nat. Inst. of Allergy & Infectious Diseases., Bethesda, Md., 1968-70; resident internal medicine U. Mich. Med. Ctr., Ann Arbor, 1970-72, fellow in cardiology, 1972-74, instr. internal medicine, 1973-74; staff cardiologist Mills Meml. Hosp., San Mateo, Calif., 1974—2001, vice-chief medicine, 1977-78, dir. critical care, 1978-96, critical care utilizaton rev., 1988-99, dir. pacemaker clinic, 1976-99; staff cardiologist Mills-Peninsula Hosp., Burlingame, Calif., 1996-99; ret., 1999. Dir. transitional care, 1996—99; mem. courtesy staff Sequoia Hosp., 1984—2001, ret., 1999. Contbr. rsch. articles to profl. jours. Recipient 1st prize in landscaping Residential Estates, State of Calif., 1977. Fellow Am. Coll. Cardiology; mem. AMA (Physician's Recognition award 1968, 72, 75, 77, 80, 82, 85, 87, 89, 93, 97, 2000), Calif. Med. Assn., San Mateo County Med. Soc., Am. Heart Assn., San Mateo County Heart Assn. (bd. dirs. 1975-78, mem. Bay area rsch. com. 1975-76, mem. edn. com. 1975-77, pres.-elect 1976-77, pres. 1977-79), Alpha Omega Alpha. Republican. Mem. United Brethren Ch. Avocations: gardening, computer science, tennis, woodworking, electronics, amateur radio. Home: 235 Amherst Ave San Mateo CA 94402-2201 Personal E-mail: John_VanKirk@msn.com.

**VAN KIRK, ROBERT JOHN,** nursing case manager, educator; b. Jersey City, Sept. 18, 1944; s. Robert and Doris Van Kirk; m. Marjorie Ann Carroll, Mar. 23, 1968 (div. Nov. 1993); children: Walter, Michael, Robert Jr., Peggy; m. Nancy A. Fix, Aug. 31, 1996. BA cum laude, U. Conn., 1974; MEd, Kent State U., 1983; D of Nursing, Case Western Res. U., 1986. RN Ohio, cert. diabetes educator (CDE). Sales mgr. Nutmeg Home Protection, Middlebury, Conn., 1972-74; theater mgr. SBC Mgmt. Corp., Boston, 1974; dist. supr. Selected Theatres Mgmt. Corp., Lyndhurst, Ohio, 1974-86; nat. sales mgr. ZBS Video, Inc., Lyndhurst, 1981-82; staff nurse Cleve. Clinic Found., 1986-87, clin. instr., 1987-88, head nurse, 1988-93, case mgr., 1993—, diabetes educator, 2002—; asst. clin. prof. Case Western Res. U., Frances Payne Bolton Sch. Nursing, Cleve., 1990—; case mgr. Cleve. Clin. Home Care, 1993—2002; CEO Lifelong Learning, Inc., Chagrin Falls, Ohio, 2002—. Health officer Lake County (Ohio) Bd. Alcohol, Drug Addiction and Mental Health Svcs., 1991—; co-chmn. United Way, Cleve., 1991-93. Staff sgt. U.S. Army, 1964—71, Vietnam. Recipient Achievement award, Greater Cleve. Nurses Assn., 1986. Mem. AACN, Am. Assn. Tchrs. German, Am. Assn. Tchrs. Portuguese and Spanish, Assn. Specialists in Aging, Frances Payne Bolton Sch. Nursing Alumni Assn. (pres. 1992-93), Kappa Delta Pi, Sigma Theta Tau. Avocations: pocket billards, furniture making. Home: 495 Bell Rd Chagrin Falls OH 44022-4160 Office: Cleve Clinic Found 6801 Brecksville Rd Ste 10 Independence OH 44131 also: Lifelong Learning Inc 495 Bell Rd Chagrin Falls OH 44022 E-mail: drbobvankirk@adelphia.net.

**VAN KIRK, THOMAS L.,** lawyer; b. Pa., June 25, 1945; s. Theodore and Mary Jane (Young) Van K.; children: Thomas Jr., Christopher. BA, Bucknell U., 1967; JD cum laude, Dickinson U., 1970. Bar: Pa., U.S. Dist. Ct. (we. and ea. dists.) Pa. 1971, U.S. Ct. Appeals (3d cir.) 1972, U.S. Supreme Ct. 1976. Clk. Pa. Superior Ct., 1970-71; assoc. Buchanan Ingersoll PC, Pitts., 1971-78, ptnr., 1978—, COO, 1985—2003; CEO, chmn. Buchanan Ingersoll & Rooney PC, Pitts., 2006—. Bd. dirs. Buchanan Ingersoll P.C.; exec. com. bd. mem. State Pa. Economy League; bd. dirs. Western Pa. Economy League, chair. Chmn. emeritus Pitts. Downtown Partnership; bd. dirs., exec. com. mem. Pitts. Cultural Trust, Catalyst Connection, U. Pitts. Cancer Inst., Doyle Ctr. for Mfg. Tech., Allegheny Conf., chair PEG. Mem.: ABA, Allegheny County Bar Assn., The Club at Nevillewood, Rivers Club, Duquesne Club. Democrat. Lutheran. Home: 1010 Osage Rd Pittsburgh PA 15243-1014 Office: Buchanan Ingersoll Rooney One Oxford Ctr 301 Grant St Fl 20 Pittsburgh PA 15219-1410 Office Phone: 412-562-8875. Business E-Mail: vankirktl@bipc.com.

**VANLANDINGHAM, MARK JENNINGS,** sociologist, educator; b. Riverdale, Md., Apr. 24, 1958; s. Frances (Henson) and Don VanLandingham; m. Rebecca Mowbray, Mar. 23, 2002. BA, Mercer U., 1980; MPH, U. Mich., 1987; PhD, Princeton U., 1993. Vol. U.S. Peace Corps, Chiang Rai, Thailand, 1980—82; tchr. sci. and math Fairmount H.S., Ga., 1983—85; NIH postdoctoral rsch. fellow CSDE U. Wash., Seattle, 1993—96; asst. prof. U. Tex., Galveston, 1996—99; assoc. prof. Tulane U., New Orleans, 1999—2005, prof., 2005—. Mem. NIH Population Scis. Subcom., Bethesda, Md., 2003—. Bd. mem. Planned Parenthood of La. and Miss. Delta, New Orleans, 2001—05. Mem.: Population Assn. Am. (internat. outreach committtee 2004—). Office: Tulane University 1440 Canal St Ste 2200 New Orleans LA 70112

**VAN LARE, WENDELL JOHN,** lawyer, director; b. Newark, N.Y., Mar. 1, 1945; s. Julian J. and Doris Elizabeth (Lacknor) Van L.; m. Sheila Gilbert, Aug. 20, 1967 (div. Apr. 1987); children: Jonathan S., Allison R.; m. L. Karen Stack, May 7, 1987. BS, SUNY, New Paltz, 1967; JD, Union U., 1972. Bar: N.Y. 1973, U.S. Supreme Ct., 1980; cert. corp. counsel VA, 2004. Assoc. Harter, Secrest & Emery, Rochester, NY, 1972-77; asst. dir. labor rels. Gannett Co., Inc., Rochester, 1977-80, dir. labor rels. Rochester and Arlington, NY, 1980-93, v.p., labor counsel Arlington, 1993-94, v.p., sr. labor counsel, 1994—2006, v.p. labor rels., 2006—. Comments editor Albany Law Rev., 1971-72. Pres. Opera Theatre of Rochester, N.Y., 1983-85; trustee SUNY New Paltz Found. Lt. (j.g.) USNR, 1968-70. Mem. ABA, N.Y. Bar Assn., Va. Bar Assn., River Bend Golf and Country Club. Avocation: genealogy. Office: Gannett Co Inc 7950 Jones Branch Dr Mc Lean VA 22102

**VAN LEEUWEN, JEAN See GAVRIL, JEAN**

**VAN LIEROP, JOHN HENRY, JR.,** music educator; b. St. Louis, Oct. 3, 1947; s. John Henry and Mary Frances Van Lierop. BA in Music Edn., Seattle Pacific U., 1969; postgrad., U. Wash., 1976—78. Cert. tchr. Wash. 6th grade tchr. Seattle Christian Sch., Seattle, 1969—74; 3d grade tchr. Clark County Christian Sch., Vancouver, Wash., 1974—75; 2d grade tchr. Mountlake

Christian Sch., Mountlake Terrace, Wash., 1975—76; pvt. piano instr. West Seattle Piano Studio, Seattle, 1976—. Organist, pianist Mount Baker Park Presbyn. Ch., Seattle, 1976—80, Tibbetts United Meth. Ch., Seattle, 1981—; piano adjudicator Am. Coll. Musicians, Austin, Tex., 1987—, Nat. Fedn. Music Clubs, Indpls., 1988—. Contbr. articles to profl. publs. Named Tchr. of Yr., Western Assn. Christian Schs., 1976; named to Hall of Fame, Am. Coll. Musicians, 1992. Mem.: Seattle Music Tchrs. (pres. 1984—86), Nat. Guild Piano Tchrs., Nat. Fedn. Music Clubs (treas. 1988—). Republican. Methodist. Avocations: hiking, trains, cats. Home and Office: 6552 40th Ave SW Seattle WA 98136 E-mail: musicman@nwlink.com.

**VAN LINT, VICTOR ANTON JACOBUS,** physicist; b. Samarinda, Indonesia, May 10, 1928; came to U.S., 1937; s. Victor J. and Margaret (DeJager) Van L.; m. M. June Woolhouse, June 10, 1950; children: Lawrence, Kenneth, Linda, Karen. BS, Calif. Inst. Tech., Pasadena, 1950, PhD, 1954. Instr. Princeton (N.J.) U., 1954-55; staff mem. Gen. Atomic, San Diego, 1957-74; physics cons. San Diego, 1974-75; staff mem. Mission Research Corp., San Diego, 1975-82, 83-91; cons., 1991—; spl. asst. to dep. dir. on sci. and tech. Def. Nuclear Agy., Washington, 1982-83. Author, editor: Radiation Effects in Electronic Materials, 1976; contbr. articles to profl. jours. Served with U.S. Army, 1955-57. Recipient Pub. Service award NASA, 1981. Fellow IEEE. Republican. Mem. United Ch. of Christ. Home and Office: 1032 Skylark Dr La Jolla CA 92037-7733

**VAN LOUCKS, MARK LOUIS,** venture capitalist, financial planner; b. Tampa, Fla., June 19, 1946; s. Charles Perry and Lenn (Bragg) Van L.; children: Brandon, Charlie; m. Lee Ann Rose, Oct. 1, 1998. BA in Comm. and Pub. Policy, U. Calif., Berkeley, 1969. Sr. v.p. mktg., programming and corp. devel. United Cable TV Corp., Denver, 1970-81, advisor, 1983-89; sr. v.p., office of chmn. Rockefeller Ctr. TV Corp., N.Y.C., 1981-83; advisor United Artists Commun. Corp., Englewood, 1989-91; investor, business advisor in pvt. practice Englewood, 1983—; founder, prin. owner Glory Hole Saloon & Gaming Hall, Central City, Colo., 1990—, The Canyon Casino, Black Hawk, Colo., 1990—; chmn., CEO Bask Internat., Englewood, 1990—. Bd. dirs. Wild West Devel. Corp., Denver; sr. v.p., bd. dirs. GSI Cable TV Assocs., Inc., San Francisco, 1984-90; guest lectr. on cable TV bus., 1985-91; cons. Telecommunications, Inc., Denver, 1989-93. Producer HBO spl. Green Chili Showdown, 1985; producer TV spl. 3 Days for Earth, 1987; producer, commd. artist nuclear war armament pieces; contbr. articles to profl. jours. Chmn. Cops in Crisis, Denver, 1990—; bd. dirs. The NOAH Found., Denver, 1976—; founding dir. Project for Responsible Advt., Denver, 1991-92; chmn. mayor's mktg. adv. bd., Central City, Colo. Named hon. capt. Denver Police Dept., 1991—, fin. advisor L. Rose Co., 1995—. Mem. Casino Owners Assn. (founding dir. 1989—), Colo. Gaming Assn. (dir. 1990—), recipient S'nnael Evol award, 1995), Glenmoor Country Club, The Village Club. Republican. Jewish. Avocations: music, woodworking, philanthropy, classic cars. Office: MLVL Inc 1515 E Tufts Ave Cherry Hills Village CO 80113 Office Phone: 303-781-0827.

**VANMANY, SENG DAO,** microbiologist; b. Vientiane, Laos, Feb. 25, 1977; arrived in U.S. 2005 BS in Biological Sci., So. Ill. U., Carbondale. Former prof. So. Ill. U. at Carbondale; former microbiologist Lourdes Hosp., Ky.; dir. hematology/oncology tissue bank U. Ill. Sch. of Med., Chicago, 2003—05. Former prof. bio. Paducah Community Coll.; recruiter US Air Force. Served in USAF.

**VANMARCKE, ERIK HECTOR,** civil engineer, educator; b. Menen, Belgium, Aug. 6, 1941; arrived in U.S., 1965, naturalized, 1976; s. Louis Eugene and Rachel Louisa (van Hollebeke) Vanmarcke; m. Margaret Marie Delesie, May 25, 1965 (div. Feb. 22, 1999); children: Lieven Vanmarcke, Ann Vanmarcke Forzani, Kristien Vanmarcke Webber; m. Marilyn Durkee, July 14, 2001. BS, U. Leuven, Belgium, 1965; MS, U. Del., 1967; PhD in Civil Engring, MIT, 1970. From instr. to prof. civil engring. MIT, Cambridge, 1969-85, Gilbert W. Winslow Career Devel. prof., 1974-77, dir. civil engring. sys. group, 1976-80; prof. civil engring. and ops. rsch. Princeton (N.J.) U., 1985—, affiliated faculty mem. Bendheim Ctr. Fin., 1998—, dir. grad. studies civil engring. and ops. rsch., 1990—94. Cons. Office Sci. and Tech. Policy, 1978—80, Nat. Inst. Stds. and Tech., 2003, various govt. agys. and engring. firms; vis. scholar in engring. Harvard U., 1984—85; Shimizu Corp. vis. prof. Stanford U., 1991; mem. exec. com. Princeton (N.J.) Materials Inst., 1991—93; mem. Princeton (N.J.) Environ. Inst., 1996—; mem. com. vulnerability critical infrastructure Nat. Res. Coun., 1999—2001; mem. com. program on robotics and intelligent sys. Princeton (N.J.) U., 1999—. Author: Random Fields: Analysis and Synthesis, 1983, revised and expanded edit., 2005, Quantum Origins of Cosmic Structure, 1997; editor: Internat. Jour. Structural Safety, 1981—91. Named Disting. Probabilistic Methods Educator, Soc. Automotive Engrs., 2002; recipient Sr. Scientist award, Japan Soc. Promotion Sci., 1991, Disting. Engring. Alumnus award, U. Del., 1994. Mem.: ASCE (chair com. risk assessment and mgmt. Geo-Inst. 1996—2000, chair com. risk and vulnerability Coun. Natural Disaster Reduction 1998—2003, chair exec. com. coun. disaster risk mgmt. 2003—, chair internat. roundtable disaster risk mgmt. 2005, Raymond C. Reese Rsch. award 1975, Walter L. Huber Rsch. prize 1984), Royal Acad. Arts and Sci. Belgium (fgn.), Internat. Soc. Soil Mechanics and Geotech. Engring. (chair com. TC32 risk assessment and mgmt. 1998—2001), Seismol. Soc. Am., Am. Geophys. Union. Home: 44 Lake Ln Princeton NJ 08540-7212 Office Phone: 609-258-5896. Business E-Mail: evm@princeton.edu.

**VANMEER, MARY ANN,** publishing executive, writer, webmaster; b. Mt. Clemens, Mich., Nov. 22, 1947; d. Leo Harold and Rose Emma (Gulden) VanM. Student, Micha. State U., 1965-66, 67-68, U. Sorbonne, Paris, summer 1968; BA in Edn., U. Fla., 1968-70. Pres. VanMeer Tutoring and Translating, N.Y.C., 1970-72; freelance writer, 1973-79; pres. VanMeer Publs., Inc., Clearwater, Fla., 1980-88, VanMeer Media Advt., Inc., Clearwater, 1987-88; exec. dir., founder Nat. Ctrs. for Health and Med. Info., Inc., Palm Beach, Fla., 1990-93; pres., CEO ThriftyTraveling.com, Inc. (formerly Traveling Free Pubs.,) 1993—. Author: Traveling with Your Dog, U.S.A., 1976, How to Set Up a Home Typing Business, 1978, Freelance Photographer's Handbook, 1979, See America Free, 1981, Free Campgrounds, U.S.A., 1982, Free Attractions, U.S.A., 1982, VanMeer's Guide to Free Attractions U.S.A., 1984, VanMeer's Guide to Free Campgrounds, 1984, The How to Get Publicity for Your Business Handbook, 1987, Asthma: The Ultimate Treatment Guide, 1991, Allergies: The Ultimate Treatment Guide, 1992, Thrifty Traveling, 1995, 2d edit., 1996; pub. Nat. Health and Med. Trends Mag., 1986-88, ThriftyTraveling.com Newsletter and website, 1993—, online and hard-copy edits., 1999—, Over 50 Thrifty Traveler Newsletter, 1997-98, Net News for the Thrifty Traveler Newsletter, 1997-98, LuxuryTraveling.com Newsletter and website, 2001—; webmaster ThriftyTraveling.com, ThriftyTravelPortal.com, 2003—, LuxuryTraveling.com and VanMeer.com websites. Pub. info. chairperson, bd. dirs. Pinellas County chpt. Am. Cancer Soc.; Clearwater, 1983-84, 86-88; mem. fin. devel. com. ARC, Palm Beach County, 1990-92. Mem. Am. Booksellers Assn., Soc. Am. Travel Writers. Office: ThriftyTraveling.com Inc PO Box 8168 Clearwater FL 33758-8168 E-mail: editor@thriftytraveling.com.

**VAN METER, ABRAM DEBOIS,** lawyer, retired banker; b. Springfield, Ill., May 16, 1922; s. A.D. and Edith (Graham) Van M.; m. Margaret Schlipf, Dec. 1, 1956; children: Andy, Alice, Ann. BS, Kings Point Coll., 1946; JD, Northwestern U., 1948. Bar: Ill. 1949. Ptnr. Van Meter, Oxtoby & Funk, Springfield, 1949—2001; adminstrv. asst. to treas. State of Ill., Springfield, 1963; v.p. Ill. Nat. Bank, Springfield, 1964-65, pres., 1965-88, chmn. bd. dirs., 1988-90, also bd. dirs.; chmn. bd. dirs. Nat. City, Springfield, 1990-93, dir. emeritus, 1993—. Chmn. bd. dirs. Ill. Housing Devel. Authority, 1977-2003; chmn. bd. trustees So. Ill. U., 1989-2001; past bd. dirs., exec. com. Meml. Med. Ctr. Mem. ABA, Ill. Bar Assn., Sangamon Bar Assn., Chgo. Club, Chgo. Athletic Club, Sangamo Club, Island Bay Yacht Club Home: 6 Fair Oaks St Springfield IL 62704-3222 Office: Nat City 1 N Old State Capitol Plz Springfield IL 62701-1323 Personal E-mail: omvideo@aol.com.

**VAN METER, LEROY RAY,** music educator; b. Moline, Ill., Oct. 18, 1965; s. Elwyn Lee Van Meter and Ruth Anabelle Lingner; m. Sherry Lynn LaPayne, May 23, 1987; children: Nicholas David, Alexander Lucas. BA in Music Edn. magna cum laude, Western Ill. U., Macomb, 1987; MA in Sch. Improvement Leadership, Olivet Nazarene U., Bourbonnais, Ill., 2006. Cert. tchr. Ill., ednl. adminstr. Dir. music Greenfield Schs., Ill., 1987—90; dir. bands Alwood Schs., Woodhull, 1990—95, Herscher H.S., 1995—. Marching, jazz, concert adjudicator, clinician numerous schs., Ill., 1990—. Designer: marching band drills, arranger: various musical pieces. Vol. firefighter Galva (Ill.) Fire Dept., 1991—95, Herscher Fire Dept., 1995—2001. Mem.: Music Educators Nat. Conf., Phi Mu Alpha Sinfonia, Kappa Delta Pi, Phi Kappa Phi. Avocations: history, cars, flying, travel, golf. Office: 501 N Main Herscher IL 60941

**VANMETER, VANDELIA L.,** retired library director; b. Seibert, Colo., July 17, 1934; d. G.W. and A. Pearl Klockenteger; m. Victor M. VanMeter, Jan. 21, 1954; children: Allison C., Kristopher C. BA, Kansas Wesleyan U., 1957; MLS, Emporia State U., 1970; PhD, Tex. Woman's U., 1986. Cert. libr. media specialist. Tchr. Ottawa County Rural Sch., Kans., 1954-55; social scis. tchr. McClave (Colo.) High Sch., 1957-58, Ellsworth (Kans.) Jr. High Sch., 1959-68; libr., media specialist Ellsworth (Kans.) High Sch., 1968-84; asst. prof. libr. sci. U. So. Miss., Hattiesburg, 1986-90; chair dept. libr./info. sci. Spalding U., Louisville, 1990-96, libr. dir., 1991-99, prof., 1991—99. Cons. to sch., pub. and spl. librs., Kans., Miss., Ky., 1970-99; mem. Ky. NCATE Bd. Examiners. Author: American History for Children and Young Adults, 1990, World History for Children and Young Adults, 1992, America in Historical Fiction, 1997; editor: Mississippi Library Media Specialist Staff Development Modules, 1988, Library Lane Newsletter, 1991-99; contbr. chpts. to books; contbr. articles to profl. jours. Active City Coun., Ellsworth, Kans., 1975-79, Park Bd., Ellsworth, 1975-79; bd. dirs. Robbins Meml. Libr., 1977-79. Grantee Kans. Demonstration Sch. Libr., 1970-72, Miss. Power Found., 1989, Project Technology Enhances Curriculur Instrn., 1996-97; named Women of Yr. Bus. and Profl. Women of Ellsworth, Kans., 1976. Mem. ALA, Assn. Coll. and Rsch. Librs., Ky. Libr. Assn., Assn. for Libr. and Info. Sci. Educators.

**VAN METRE, MARGARET CHERYL,** performing company executive, dancer, educator; b. Maryville, Tenn., Nov. 24, 1938; d. Robert Fillers and Margaret Elizabeth (Goddard) Raulston; m. Mitchell Robert Van Metre II, Aug. 25, 1956; 1 child, Mitchell Robert. Elem., intermediate and advanced tchg. certs. Dir. Van Metre Sch. of Dance, Maryville, 1958-96; artistic dir. Appalachian Ballet Co., Maryville Coll., 1972-96; founding dir. Appalachian Ballet Co., 1972; dir. Van Metre Arts Mgmt., SC, 1996—. Chmn. dance panel Tenn. Arts Commn., 1973-74; chmn. Bicentennial Ballet Project, Tenn., 1975-76; mem. Nat. Bd. Regional Dance Am., 1997—; owner Van Metre Arts Mgmt., Edisto Island, S.C., 1996—. Choreographer ballets: Delusion, 1965, Hill Heritage Suite, 1972, Dancing Princesses, 1983. Mem. Tenn. Assn. of Dance (pres. 1972), Southeast Regional Ballet Assn. (pres. 1996, 97, 98, 99, 2003—). Democrat. Episcopalian. Home: 2103 Myrtle St Edisto Island SC 29438-3437

**VAN MIDDLESWORTH, LESTER,** physiology, biophysics and medicine educator, internist; b. Washington, Jan. 13, 1919; s. Lester and Hazel Lucile (Brandt) VanM.; m. Nellie Rue Franklin, June 29, 1948; children: Linda V. Anderson, Jane V. Norman, Frank L., Paul E. BS in Chemistry, U. Va., 1940, MS in Chemistry, 1942, MS in Physiology, 1944; PhD in Physiology, U. Calif., Berkeley, 1946; MD, U. Tenn., 1951. Teaching asst. dept. physiology U. Va., 1944, U. Calif., Berkeley, 1944—45; instr. U. Tenn. Med. Units, Memphis, 1946—52, instr. in medicine, 1953—57, asst. prof. physiology, 1952—54, assoc. prof., 1954—59, prof., 1959—89, prof. emeritus physiology and biophysics, 1989—, asst. prof. medicine, 1957—61, assoc. prof., 1961—72, prof. medicine, 1972—89, prof. medicine emeritus, 1989, Disting. prof. physiology and medicine, 1986—. Rotating intern City of Memphis Hosps., 1951-52; cons. chief chemist Piedmont Apple Products Corp., Charlottesville, Va., 1940-46, Crocker Radiation Lab., U. Calif., Berkeley, 1946-47, Oak Ridge Inst. Nuclear Studies, 1950-54; guest co-investigator Endocrine Labs. Tufts Med. Coll., Boston, summers 1954, 55, 56, 59, 61, 64, 66, 69, Scripps Clinic and Rsch. Found., La Jolla, Calif., 1957; guest investigator in endocrinology Harbor Gen. Hosp., UCLA, 1971, Frederick Joliot Hosp., Orsay, France, 1972, Lawrence Livermore Radiation Lab. U. Calif., 1970; staff mem. clinic for med. thyroid disease patients, City of Memphis and U. Tenn., 1951—; mem. internat. com., 1990-2002. Author 145 publs. in profl. jours., 186 abstracts and oral presentations; work on permanent display Smithsonian Nat. Mus. Am. History, Washington, D.C. Recipient Disting. Svc. award, 1985, Disting. Alumnus award, U. Tenn. Coll. Medicine, 1989, USPHS career rsch. grantee, 1962-89. Mem. Am. Chem. Soc., Am. Physiol. Soc., AAAS, Soc. Exptl. Biology and Medicine, Am. Soc. Clin. Investigation, So. Soc. Clin. Investigation, Health Physics Soc., Endocrine Soc., Am. Thyroid Assn. (Disting. Svc. award 1988), Sigma Xi (rsch. award 1944, 86, nat. lectr. 1989-91), Alpha Chi Sigma. Achievements include research in audiogenic seizures and worldwide radioiodine fallout, and radium in normal human thyroid glands. Home: 1950 Lyndale Ave Memphis TN 38107-5109 Office: U Tenn Health Sci Ctr 894 Union Ave Memphis TN 38163-3514 Office Phone: 901-448-5837. Business E-Mail: lvanmid@physio1.utmem.edu.

**VAN MOL, LOUIS JOHN, JR.,** public relations executive; b. Knoxville, Tenn., Oct. 7, 1943; s. Louis John and Evelyn (Ramsay) Van M.; m. Deborah Ruth Boyd, Nov. 1, 1969; children: Derek, Millicent. BS, U. Tenn., 1966. Staff writer, editor AP, Knoxville and Nashville, 1963-66, 69; account exec. to exec. v.p. Holder, Kennedy & Co., Nashville, 1970-74, exec. v.p., 1978-79; dir. info. TVA, Knoxville, 1974-78; co-founder, ptnr. Dye, Van Mol & Lawrence, Nashville, 1980—. Bd. dirs. East Tenn. Children's Hosp., Knoxville, 1977-78, Martha O'Bryan Ctr., Nashville, 1985-87, United Way Comm. Com., 1987-91, Am. Heart Assn. Mid. Tenn., Nashville, 1991-92, Leadership Nashville 1992-93, Crime Stoppers Nashville, 1986-92, Alcohol and Drug Coun. Mid. Tenn., Nashville, 1991-93, Martha O'Bryan Found., 1998-2000, Pencil Found., 2003—, Nashville Songwriters Found., 2004—, Tenn. Chamber Commerce and Industry, 2005—; chmn. bd. dirs. Nashville Downtown Partnership, 1999-2000; bd. govs., exec. com. Nashville C. of C., 1999-2000; chmn. Goodwill Industries Mid. Tenn., 1996-97, mem. exec. com., 1996-. Lt. U.S. Army, 1966-68. Decorated Bronze Star. Mem. Richland Country Club (bd. dirs. 1997-99, pres. 1999), Sigma Delta Chi Presbyterian. Home: 2836 Wellesley Trace Nashville TN 37215-1049 Office: Dye Van Mol & Lawrence Pub Rels 209 7th Ave N Nashville TN 37219-1802

**VAN MOLS, BRIAN,** publishing executive; b. LA, July 1, 1931; s. Pierre Matthias and Frieda Carthyll (MacArthur) M.; m. Barbara Jane Rose, Oct. 1, 1953 (dec. 1968); children: Cynthia Lee, Matthew Howard, Brian; m. Nancy Joan Martell, June 11, 1977; children— Thomas Bentley, Cynthia Bentley, Kristi AB in English, Miami U., Oxford, Ohio, 1953. Media supr. McCann-Erickson Inc., 1955-58; salesman Kelly Smith Co., 1959; with sales Million Market Newspaper Inc., 1959-63; sales mgr. Autoproducts Mag., 1964; sr. salesman True Mag., 1965-68, Look Mag., 1969-70; regional advt. dir. Petersen Pub. Co., Los Angeles, 1971-74; pub. Motor Trend, 1982-84; nat. automotive mktg. mgr. Playboy Enterprises, Inc., N.Y.C., 1984-85, nat. sales mgr., 1985—; western advt. dir. Playboy mag., 1985-86; assoc. pub., advt. dir. Cycle World CBS, Inc., Newport Beach, Calif., 1974-81, pub., 1981; v.p., advt. dir. Four Wheeler Mag., Canoga Pk., Calif., 1986-88; v.p., dir. advt. western div. Gen. Media, Inc., 1988-91; v.p., dir. new bus. devel. Paisano Pub., Inc., Agoura Hills, Calif., 1991-92; dir. mktg. Crown Publs., 1993-94; exec. v.p. Voice Mktg. Inc., Thousand Oaks, Calif., 1994, DMR The Reis Co., Tustin, Calif., 1995-96; COO Mesa Exhaust Products, Inc., Costa Mesa, Calif., 1996-97. Mktg. dir. McMullen Argus Pub., Inc., Anaheim, Calif. 1998-2001. Served with U.S. Army, 1953-55 Mem. Los Angeles Advt. Club, Adcraft Club Detroit. Advt. Sportsmen of N.Y. Republican. Home: 57 St Andrews Cir Durango CO 81301 E-mail: bvanmols@frontier.net.

**VANN, JOHN DANIEL, III,** library consultant, historian; b. Raleigh, NC, June 14, 1935; s. John Daniel Jr. and Sybil Dean (Wilson) V.; m. Ellen Jane Rogers, June 21, 1969; children: John Daniel IV, Justin Fitz Patrick. BA with honors, U. N.C., 1957; MA, Yale U., 1959, PhD, 1965; M in Librarianship, Emory U., 1971; postgrad., Columbia U., 1962-63, Stanford U., 1977-78. Ordained deacon, elder Presbyn. Ch., commd. temporary supply preacher Northumberland Presbytery. Assoc. prof. history Campbell Coll., Buie's Creek, N.C., 1961-63; bibliographer European history and lit. Newberry Libr., Chgo., 1963-65, asst. reference librarian, 1963-65; prof. history Calif. Bapt. Coll., Riverside, 1965-66; dir. libr., prof. history Bapt. Coll. at Charleston, S.C., 1966-69; libr. Keuka Coll., Keuka Park, N.Y., 1969-71; chief libr., prof. libr., chmn. libr. dept. S.I. Community Coll. CUNY, 1971-76; prof. libr. Coll. S.I. CUNY, 1976-79; head libr. Lockwood Libr./SUNY, Buffalo, 1979-80; asst. dir. for planning, univ. librs. SUNY, Buffalo, 1980-81; exec. dir. librs. and learning resources, prof. U. Wis., Oshkosh, 1981-87; libr. svcs. Bloomsburg U. Pa., 1987-89, dean libr. svcs., 1989-98; spl. asst. to vice chancellor for info. technology Pa. State Sys. Higher Edn., 1999; prin. J. Daniel Vann Consulting, 2000—. Interim dir., vis. prof. bibliography Union Theol. Sem. and Presbyn. Sch. Christian Edn., 2003-04; resident planner, cons. on libr. bldgs. and collection devel.; sec-treas. Susquehanna Libr. Coop., 1993-95. Mem. internat. editl. bd. Libr. Times Internat., 1984—; contbr. chpts. to books, articles to profl. jours. Trustee Maplewood (N.J.) Meml. Libr., 1977-79, v.p., 1979; bd. dir. Coun. Wis. Librs., 1983-86, Midwest Rotary Multi-Dist. Short Term Internat. Youth Exch., 1987, Oshkosh (Wis.) Symphony Assn., 1986-87, Protestant campus ministry Bloomsburg U., 1999—2002, United Cerebral Palsy of Winnebagoland, Oshkosh, 1986-87; active coms. Winnebago Presbytery, Presbyn. Ch., 1984-87; com. on min. Northumberland Prsbytery, Presbyn. Ch., 1992-96, com. on preparation for ministry, 1996—2002, coun., 1999—2002; commr. Synod of Trinity Presbyn. Ch. (USA), 1999—2003, exec. com., 2002—2003. Paul Harris fellow Rotary Internat.; Acad. Libr. Mgmt. intern Coun. on Libr. Resources Stanford U., 1977-78. Mem. ALA (com. mem.), Am. Hist. Assn., Archons of Colophon, Assn. for Libr. Collections and Tech. Svcs., Assn. Coll. and Rsch. Librs. (com. chmn., sec. chmn. 1977-78, editl. bd., bd. dirs. 1976-78), Bibliog. Soc. Am., Libr. Adminstrn. and Mgmt. Assn. (com. mem.), Libr. and Info. Tech. Assn., Reference and User Svcs. Assn., Medieval Acad. Am., Beta Phi Mu, Phi Alpha Theta. Republican. Home: 1216 Rennie Ave Richmond VA 23227-4723 Home and Studio: 1 Clear Vista Dr Asheville NC 28805 Business E-Mail: vann@aya.yale.edu.

**VANN, LILLIE MAE,** retired nurse; b. Harriman, Tenn., July 15, 1924; d. Robert Hebert Miller and Winnie Lillie Johnson; 1 child, Connie Vann Colboth. RN, Bapt. Meml., Memphis, 1947. RN Tenn. Nurse Harriman City Hosp., Harriman, Tenn., St. Elizabeth Hosp., Dayton, Ohio, H. Stratton Jones, MD, Harriman, Tenn., Oak Ridge Pub. Health, Tenn., Roane County Pub. Health, Kingston, Tenn., State Area Vocat. Sch., Harriman, Tenn. Cadet Nurse Corps, 1944—47. Republican. Baptist. Avocations: sewing, quilting, reading. Home: 248 Spencer Dr Harriman TN 37748

**VAN NAGELL, JOHN RENSSELAER,** oncologist, gynecologist; b. N.Y.C., Sept. 16, 1939; s. John Rensselaer and Rosamond Musgrave Van Nagell; m. Elizabeth Gay, June 10, 1977; children: John R Van Nagell III, Elizabeth Knox Pfister, Lucy Tepper. MD, U. Pa., 1967. Diplomate Am. Bd. Ob/Gyn. Prof., dir. divsn. gynecol. oncology U. Ky. Med. Ctr., Lexington, 1973—, Am. Cancer Soc prof. clin. oncology. Cons. NCI - PLCO Trial, Bethesda, Md., 1992—2003. Author: Modern Concepts of Gynecologic Oncology. Lt. USN, 1971—77. Named one of Top Doctors for Women, Ladies Home Jour., 2001—05, Ams. Top Doctors, Castle Connolly, 2002—05. Mem.: Masters of Foxhounds Assn. (bd.dirs. 2005), Soc. Gynecol. Oncologists (pres. 1994—95). Avocations: horseback riding, fox hunting. E-mail: jrvannagell@aol.com.

**VANNATTA-GAIL, MARY LOUISE,** public relations executive; b. Harrisburg, Pa., Aug. 15, 1964; d. Frederick William and Mariel Dawn (Fahlstrom) VanN. BA, Willamette U., 1986—. Asst. librarian Statesman-Jour. Newspaper, Salem, 1981-86; features editor Willamette U. Collegian Newspaper, Salem, 1985-86; translator Spanish lang. Employment Div., Workers Compensation Dept., Salem, 1986—; prin., owner VanNatta Pub. Rels., Inc., 1987—. Exec. dir. Assn. Engring. Employees, Salem, 1986—, editor, 1988—; staff writer Salem-Keizer Bus. Jour., 1989—; media cons. Conf. Entrepreneurship, Salem, 1989. Author: Association of Engineering Employees: Working Together for 40 Years, 1988 (award 1989). Campaign asst. Com. to Reelect Senator L.B. Day, Salem, 1986; mem. support staff Salem/Simferopol Sister City Orgn., 1987; mem. steering com. Friends of Vic Gillium, Salem, 1988. Mary L. Collins scholar Willamette U., 1985, Rotary Internat. scholar, 1982. Mem. UN Assn (dir. 1986—), AAUW (bd. dirs. 1987-88), Capitol Area Media and Pub. Rels. Orgn., Capitol Club, Phi Sigma Iota, Omicron Delta Kappa. Republican. Lutheran. Avocations: writing, travel.

**VANNATTER, DAVID ALAN,** history educator, coach; b. Kalamazoo, Mich., July 26, 1952; s. Donald and Susan J. Vannatter; m. Barbara J. Stockamp, June 21, 1975; children: Eric, Kyle. BA in Edn., Ctrl. Wash. U., Ellensburg, 1976; MA in Edn., Heritage U., Toppewish, Wash., 1991. Substitute tchr. West Valley Sch. Dist., Spokane, Wash., 1976—78, Cheney Sch. Dist., Wash., 1976—78, Spokane Sch. Dist., Wash., 1976—78, White River Sch. Dist., Buckley, Wash., 1978—79, Eneumelaw Sch. Dist., Wash., 1978—79, alternative sch. tchr. Wash., 1978—79; tchr. social studies grades 7-12 Mabton Jr./Sr. H.S., Wash., 1979—. Grantee Tchg. Our Past for the Future, Tchg. Am. History Grant, 2005—06. Mem.: NEA, Mabton Edn. Assn. Avocations: travel, hiking, coaching. Office: Mabton Sch Dist 500 E B St Mabton WA 98935 Personal E-mail: v3dblitz@yahoo.com.

**VAN NESS, JAMES EDWARD,** electrical engineering educator; b. Omaha, June 24, 1926; s. Hubert James and Jean (Woodruff) Van N.; m. Mary Ellen Dolvin, Dec. 28, 1948; children: Rebecca Ellen, Barbara Jean, Margaret Ann, Julie Lynn. BS, Iowa State U., 1949; MS, Northwestern U., 1951, PhD, 1954. Faculty elec. engring. dept. Northwestern U., 1952—, prof. emeritus, chmn. dept., 1969-72; dir. Computer Center, 1962-65; vis. assoc. prof. U. Calif., Berkeley, 1958-59. Vis. prof. MIT, 1973-74, Ariz. State U., winter 1984 Contbr. articles to profl. jours. Served with USNR, 1944-46. Fellow: IEEE; mem.: NAE (elected). Home: 2333 Central St Unit 404 Evanston IL 60201 E-mail: vanness@northwestern.edu.

**VAN NESS, LOTTYE GRAY,** writer, genealogist; b. Clarksville, Tenn., Nov. 14, 1925; d. Charles Robert and Willie (Murphy) Gray; m. Robert Parmelee Van Ness, Jan. 3, 1947; 1 child, Marc Robert. Student, Austin Peay State U., 1946, Murray State U., 1963. Civilian sec. U.S. Army, 1944—48; mgr. Associated Underwriters, Inc., Louisville, 1948—51; exec. sec. to the pricing dir. Reynolds Metals Co., Louisville, 1951—53. Instr. classes on genealogy, Paducah, Ky., 1962-64, Louisville, 1970. Author: The Van Ness Heritage and Allied Genealogies, 1960, The Cookie Connection, 13th rev. edition, 1992; newspaper poetry columnist, 1947-48. Cookbook judge various orgns., Louisville, 1986. Named to hon. Ky. Col., 1978. Mem. Nat. Soc. So. Dames of Am., Northfield Garden Club (v.p. 1976-77, various chairmanships), Filson Hist. Club, United Daus. of Confederacy, Beta Sigma Phi. Republican. Episcopalian. Avocations: cooking, restoring antiques, travel, gardening. Home: 6644 Foxdale Cir Colorado Springs CO 80919-1778

**VAN NESTE, KAREN LANE,** librarian, editor; b. Washington, Oct. 18, 1951; d. Wilbur Lane and Phyllis Worthington Van Neste; m. Howard Wayne Owen, Aug. 18, 1973. BA, U. Va., 1973; MS in Libr. Sci., U. N.C., 1976. Libr. divsn. disorders devel. and learning U. N.C., Chapel Hill, 1976—77; libr. Fla. State U., Tallahassee, 1977—78; libr., rschr. Media Gen., Inc., Richmond, Va., 1979—88; libr. Richmond (Va.) Times-Dispatch, 1988—98; restaurant critic Richmond Times-Dispatch, Richmond, Va., 2003—04; libr., 2004—; pub. Van Neste Books, Midlothian, Va., 1996—2001. Copy editor Richmond Times-Dispatch, 1999—2002; freelance editor, Richmond 2001—. Author: The Question Finder, 1986; editor: Littlejohn, 1992, Fat Lightning, 1994, Answers to Lucky, 1996, The Measured Man, 1997, Styll in Love, 1998, One August Day, 1998, The Edge of Things, 1999, Floating in a Most Peculiar Way, 1999, Lumen, 1999, Survivors, 2000, A Better Man, 2000, Steal My Heart, 2000 (Peace Corps Fiction award, 2001), Harry and Ruth, 2000, Divisible by One, 2001, Liar Moon, 2001, The Rail, 2002, Turn Signal, 2004,

Rock of Ages, 2006. Mem. Edgehill Condominium Assn., Richmond, Va., 1981—83; contbr. James River Writers Festival, Richmond, 2002—06; editor, writer newsletter The Prestwould Condominium Assn., Richmond, 2001—06. Mem.: Am. Biographical Inst., Va. Mus. Fine Arts, Spl. Libraries Assn., Profl. Women's Adv. Bd., U. Va. Alumni Assn. (life), 2300 Club (house rules com. 2006, mem. house rules com.). D-Liberal. Avocations: travel, interior decorating, cooking. Home: 612 West Franklin St Apt 6-B Richmond VA 23220 Office: Richmond Times-Dispatch 300 E Franklin St Richmond VA 23219 Office Phone: 804-649-6074. Business E-Mail: kowen@timesdispatch.com.

**VANNIASINGHAM, SAMUEL KANAGASABAPATHY,** accountant; b. Singapore, Oct. 16, 1950; arrived in U.K., 1974; s. Nathan Kesagar and Mabel Gnanaratnam (Subramaniam) V.; m. Heather Christine Clark, August 5, 1981; children: Daniel James, David Joseph. Diploma in Acctg., Stamford Ctr., Singapore, 1972; degree Profl. Acctg., Chartered Assn. Cert. Accts., London, 1979. Articled clk. Peat, Marwick, Mitchell, Singapore, 1974-75; part-time tchr. Adult Edn. Bd., Singapore, 1972-75; mgmt. trainee E. Russell Ltd., London, 1977-79, accounts mgr., 1980-85; mgmt. acct. MAT Transport Internat. Ltd., London, 1985-86, group mgmt. acct., 1986-87, group acct., 1988; group fin. contr. and co. sec. C & S Group, 1989; mgr. fin. acct. Channel Four TV, London, 1989-92; pvt. practice Sam Vann & Co., Chartered Cert. Accts., London, 1992. Staff sgt. in nat. svc. Police dept., Singapore, 1968-75. Recipient Bravery commendation medal Police Force, Singapore, 1974. Fellow Chartered Assn. Cert. Accts.; mem. Brit. Inst. Mgmt., Singapore Cricket Assn. (test cricketer 1971-75), North London Enterprise Club (dir. 1994-2001), North London C. of C. (co-opted dir. 1999-2001), Hazelwood Squash Club (North London). Methodist. Avocations: squash, cricket. Office: Sam Vann & Co Lee Valley Technopark London N14 5HN England

**VANNICE, M. ALBERT,** chemical engineering professor, researcher; b. Broken Bow, Nebr., Jan. 11, 1943; s. Duane M. and Eugenia R. (Farmer) Vannice; m. Bette Ann Clark, Jan. 2, 1971. BSChemE, Mich. State Univ., 1964; MS, Stanford Univ., 1966, PhD, 1970. Engr. Dow Chem. Co., Midland, Mich., 1966, Sun Oil Co., Marcus Hook, Pa., 1970; sr. rsch. engr. Esso Rsch. & Engr. Co., Linden, NJ, 1971—76; assoc. prof. Pa. State Univ., State College, 1976—80, prof., 1980—, disting. prof., 1991—2002, M.R. Fenske prof. chem. engring., 1996—2002, W.H. Joyce chair in chem. engring., 2002—05, emeritus, 2005—. Cons. Eastman Chem. Co., Kingsport, Tenn., 1980—2000; mem. adv. bd. Absorption Sci. and Tech., 1982—95. Mem. editl. bd. Jour. of Catalysis, 1988—94, assoc. editor, 1994—2001; contbr. articles to profl. jours. Recipient award, N.Y. Catalysis Soc., 1985, P.H. Emmett award, 1987, award, Pa.-Cleve. Catalysis Soc., 1988, Humboldt Rsch. award, 1990, Fulbright award, 1996. Mem.: AIChE (profl. Progress award 1986), N.Am. Catalysis Soc. (pres. 1997—2001), Am. Chem. Soc. Achievements include patents in field; research in effects of strong metal-support interactions on catalytic behavior; studies of CO hydrogenation; studies NOx reduction; catalyst characterization. Office: Pa State Univ 107 Fenske Lab University Park PA 16802-4400 Office Phone: 814-863-4803. Business E-Mail: mavche@engr.psu.edu.

**VAN NOORD, DIANE C.,** artist, educator; b. Muskegon, Mich., Dec. 12, 1950; d. Ernest Raymond and Judith Ann Olsen; m. Calvin G. Van Noord, Sept. 26, 1981; children: Tawn Star, Brian Calvin, Timothy John. BA, Hope Coll., 1991; MA, We. Mich. U., 1994. Artist, Holland, Mich.; tchr. pvt. and group art, 2000—. Guest lectr. Counterpart Assn., Grand Haven, Mich., 1997, Lakeland Painters, Grand Haven, 1997, Traverse City (Mich.) Art Assn., 1997, Holland Christian Schs., 1998, 99, 2000. Exhbns. include Neville Pub. Mus., Green Bay, Wis., 1994, Carillon Gallery, Ft. Worth, 1995, 97, Sedona (Ariz.) Arts Ctr., 1995, 96, 99, Holland Area Arts Coun., 1995, Pitts. Ctr. for the Arts, 1995, Miss. Mus. Art, Jackson, 1995, Unitarian Universalist Ch., Phoenix, 1996, Lakeland Painters, Grand Haven, Mich., 1996, Sun Cities Mus. Art, Sun City, Ariz., 1997, Art Inst. Phoenix, 1998, Hill Country Arts Found., Ingram, Tex., 1998, Mus. Tex. Tech. U., Lubbock, 1998, Dunton Gallery, Arlington Heights, Ill., 2000, Internat. Mus. Art, El Paso, 2000; one-woman shows include Gallery Upstairs, Grand Haven, 1996, Moynihan Gallery, Holland, 1997, Trinity Presbyn. Ch., Denton, 1997, Show Sabbatical, 1998, 99, Freedom Village, Holland, 2000, Acad. Artists Assn., Springfield, Mass., 2001, Hilton Head Art League, 2001, Oil Painters Am., Chgo., 2002, Audubon Artists N.Y., 2002, Magnum Opus XIV, Sacramento, 2002, Am. Artists Profl. League, N.Y.C., 2002, Celebration of Western Art, San Francisco, 2002, Hilton Head Art League, 2003, 2004, Oil Painters Am., Taos, N.Mex., 2003, Scottsdale Artists Sch, 2004, Nat. Watercolor Soc., 2004, Rocky Mountain Plein Air Painters, 2004, Allied Artists, Inc., N.Y.C., Biennale Internazionale Dell'Arte Contemporanea, Florence, Italy, 2005—, Catharine Lorillard Wolfe Art Club, 2006; Group Shows include: Gallery Uptown, 2006, el Presido Gallery, Ariz., 2006; permanent collections in Fla., Ariz., Mich., Nebr., Ind.; contbng. author: How Did You Paint That? 100 Ways to Paint the Landscape, 2004, How Did You Paint That? 100 Ways to Paint Flowers and Gardens, 2004, Art Still on the Easel, Am. Art Collector Mag., 2006; contbr. articles to profl. jours. Recipient Mcht.'s award Lakeland Painters, 1996, No. Ariz. Watercolor Soc., Sedona Arts Ctr., 1999, Diane Parssinen Meml. award No. Ariz. Watercolor Soc., 2001, 2d prize Internat. Artist Mag., 2002, Honorable Mention, Artists Mag., 2002, 2004. Mem. Ariz. Watercolor Assn., No. Ariz. Watercolor Assn., Oil Painters Am. (assoc.), Nat. Watercolor Soc. (assoc.), Allied Artists (assoc.), Tucson Plein Air Painters Soc., Great Lakes Pleun Air Painters. Republican. Home: 6418 Oakridge Dr Holland MI 49423-8999 Personal E-Mail: dvn@dianevannoord.com.

**VAN NOSTRAND, RICHARD CHARLES,** lawyer; b. Johnstown, N.Y., Sept. 20, 1955; s. Charles F. and Delores M. (Trajlinek) Van N.; m. Deborah A. Genovese, Aug. 6, 1977; children: Emily Kate, Kelsey Lynn. BA in History, Binghamton, 1977; JD, Duke U., 1980. Bar: Mass. 1980, U.S. Dist. Ct. Mass. 1981, U.S. Ct. Appeals (1st cir.) 1983, U.S. Ct. Claims 1983, U.S. Supreme Ct. 2003. Assoc. Bloom and Schwartz, Westborough, Mass., 1980-83, Bloom and Van Nostrand, Westborough, 1983-84; pvt. practice Westborough, 1984—; assoc. Mirick, O'Connell, DeMallie and Lougee, Worcester, Mass., 1984-87, ptnr., 1988—. Legal counsel Mass. Jaycees, 1985—86; bd. dirs. Legal Assistance Corp. of Cen. Mass., treas., 1996—99; chmn. Northborough Pers. Bd., 1994—97; trustee Mass. Legal Assistance Corp., 2001—; mem. Joint Bar on Judicial Appointments, 2001—, chair, 2001—02. Bd. dirs. United Way of Cen. Mass., 1991—99, chmn. allocations divsn., 1991—93. Named Outstanding Young Leader of Worcester, 1995. Mem.: ABA (nat. conf. bar pres. 1995—96, del. 2003—04), New England Bar Assn. (v.p. 2003—04, pres. 2004—), Mass. Continuing Legal Edn., Inc. (trustee 1997—2004), Worcester County Bar Assn. (chmn. trial practice sect. 1988—90, chmn. Superior Ct. com. 1990—91, exec. com. 1991—97, pres. 1995—96, Pres. award 1996, 1997), Mass. Bar Assn. (bd. dels. 1995—96, budget and fin. com. 1997—2004, v.p. 2001—02, pres.-elect 2002—03, pres. 2003—04), Worcester County Bar Found. (life; pres. 1996—97), Worcester Jaycees (pres. 1984—85). Democrat. Lutheran. Home: 109 Madison Rd Northborough MA 01532-2280 Office: Mirick OConnell 100 Front St Worcester MA 01608-1477 Office Phone: 508-791-8500. Business E-Mail: rvannostrand@modl.com.

**VANORA, JEROME PATRICK,** lawyer; b. Dec. 18, 1941; s. Jerome Anthony and Mary (Fitzpatrick) V.; m. Marianne Elizabeth Hartmann, Oct. 12, 1968; children: Judith, Kimberly. BA, Queens Coll., 1963; JD, St. John's U., 1966. Bar: N.Y. 1967. Atty. N.Y. Dept. of State Corp. Bur., Albany, 1967-70; sr. atty. divsn. human rights N.Y.C., 1970-81; assoc. atty. divsn. housing cmty. renewal, 1981—2002. Dir. hearings unit (chief adminstrv. law judge) office of rent adminstrn., divsn. housing and cmty. renewal, N.Y.C., 1984—99; asst. counsel Nassau County Rent Guidelines Bd., 1982—86; lectr. (twice yearly) L.I. U., Greenvale, NY, 1984—85; per diem administrv. law judge N.Y. State Divsn. Human Rights, 2002—. Contbr. articles to profl. jours. Mem.: N.Y. State Bar Assn., Nat. Assn. Adminstrv. Law Judges, Phi Beta Kappa. Republican. Roman Catholic. Home: 1100 Delmar Ave Franklin Square NY 11010-2703

**VAN ORDEN, PHYLLIS JEANNE,** librarian, educator; b. Adrian, Mich., July 7, 1932; d. Warren Philip and Mabel A. Nancy (Russell) Van O. BS, Ea. Mich. U., 0954; AMLS, U. Mich., 1958; EdD, Wayne State U., 1970. Sch. librarian East Detroit (Mich.) Pub. Schs., 1954-57; librarian San Diego Pub. Library, 1958-60; media specialist Royal Oak (Mich.) Pub. Schs., 1960-64; librarian Oakland U., Rochester, Mich., 1964-66; instr. Wayne State U., Detroit, 1966-70; asst. prof. Rutgers U., New Brunswick, NJ, 1970-76; prof. library science Fla. State U., Tallahassee, 1977-91, assoc. dean for instrn., 1988-91; prof. libr. sci. program Wayne State U., Detroit, 1991-93; dir. Grad. Sch. of Libr. and Info. Sci. U. Wash., Seattle, 1993-96; cons. in field, 1996—. Author: Collection Program in Schools, 2001, Library Service to Children, 2005, Selecting Books for the Elementary School Library Media Center, 2000; editor: Elementary School Library Collection, 1974—77. Fla. State Libr. grantee, 1984, 86, 88; Lillian Bradshaw scholar Tex. Woman's U., 1993. Mem.: ALA (libr. resources and tech. svcs. divsn., Blackwell/N.Am. scholarship award 1983), Assn. for Libr. and Info. Sci. Edn. (pres. 1990, Svc. award 1997), Assn. Libr. Svc. to Children (past pres., Dist. Svc. award 2002), Pi Lambda Theta. Avocations: music, knitting, physical fitness, cooking, travel. E-mail: vanordp@u.washington.edu.

**VAN OSS, STEPHEN A.,** electronics executive; CPA. Auditor Price Waterhouse; with acctg., investor rels., ops. Reliance Electric; dir. info. sys. WESCO, Pitts., 1997—2000, v.p., CFO, 2000—. Office: WESCO Four Station Sq Commerce Ct Ste 700 Pittsburgh PA 15219

**VAN OST, LYNN,** physical therapist, Olympic team official; b. Englewood, N.J., Sept. 7, 1960; d. William Carlisle and Marijane Dorward Van Ost. BSN, West Chester State Coll., Pa., 1982; MEd, Temple U., Phila., 1987; BS Phys. Therapy, Temple U., 1988. RN Pa, 1982; cert. athletic trainer Nat. Athletic Trainer's Assn., 1984. Staff nurse Abington Meml. Hosp., Pa., 1982—84; nurse/ athletic trainer U.S. Sports Acad., Mobile, Ala., 1984—85; coord. sports medicine Providence Hosp., Mobile, 1985—86, Del. County Meml. Hosp., Drexel Hill, Pa., 1988—90; staff phys. therapist Hunterdon Phys. and Sports Therapy, Flemington, NJ, 1990—91, Sports Phys. Therapy, Somerset, NJ, 1991—92; clin. specialist sports medicine Thomas Jefferson U. Hosp., Phila., 1992—98; asst. dir. Sports Phys. Therapy Inst., Princeton, NJ, 1998—2000, dir. Flemington, 2000—02; clin. specialist, sports phys. therapy Hunterdon Med. Ctr., Flemington, 2002—. Vol. athletic trainer U.S. Olympic Com., Colorado Springs, 1989—96, U.S. Field Hockey, Colorado Springs, 1993—96, U.S. Short Track Speed Skating, Lake Placid, NY, 1994—99. Author: (study guide) Athletic Training Student Guide to Success, 2003, 3d edit., 2006, (cd rom) Goniometry, 1999. Scholar Athletic Tng., Temple U., 1982—84. Mem.: Nat. Athletic Trainer's Assn., Abbes' Soc., Panhellenic (pres. 1981—82), Alpha Phi (panhellenic rep. 1980—81). Achievements include patents for Athletic Tng. Jacket. Avocations: golf, travel. Home: 2 Riverview Drive West Trenton NJ 08628 Office: Hunterdon Med Ctr 2100 Wescott Drive Flemington NJ 08822-4604 Office Phone: 908-782-1095. Personal E-mail: kmanfre@comcast.net.

**VAN OTTEREN, JULIET,** photographer; d. Wilbur van Otteren; m. Iain McGarvie-Munn. Student, Santa Monica City Coll., Calif., 1968—69, UCLA, 1968, student, 1970. Photography book, Heart of the Horse, Represented in permanent collections Bibliothèque Nat., Paris. Mus. City of N.Y., N.Y.C., Nat. Portrait Gallery, London, Santa Barbara Mus. Art, Calif., Nat. Arts Club, N.Y.C., Nat. Portrait Gallery, Canberra, Australia, Nat. Mus. Women in Arts, Washington, Bklyn. Mus. Art, High Mus. Art, Atlanta, Internat. Ctr. Photography, N.Y.C., Musée d'Art Moderne et d'Art Contemporain, Nice, France. Personal E-mail: mail@jvop.com.

**VAN OVERBEKE, DEBBIE ANN,** education educator; m. Gary Van Overbeke; children: Troy, Jeffrey, Brittany. BS in Elem. Edn., S.W. Minn. State U., Marshall, 1989, MS in Elem. Leadership, 2000; EdD in Adult and Higher Edn., U. S.D. 2003. Tchr. 4th grade Canby (Minn.) Parochial Sch., 1989—94; tchr. 6th grade Holy Redeemer Sch., Marshall, Minn., 1994—98, tchr. mid. sch., 1998—2003; asst. prof. undergrad. and grad. edn. S.W. Minn. State U., Marshall, 2003—. Bd. dirs. ARC, Lincoln/Lyon County, 2003—05. Mem.: ASCD, Internat. Reading Assn., Minn. Coun. Tchrs. Math., Nat. Coun. Tchrs. Math. Home: 2582 State Hwy 19 Ivanhoe MN 56142 Office: SW Minn State U 1510 State St Marshall MN 56258 Office Phone: 507-537-7120. E-mail: vanoverbeke@southwestmsu.edu.

**VAN PATTEN, BILL,** foreign language educator; BA, U. Santa Clara; MA, PhD, U. Tex. Asst. prof. of Spanish Mich. State Univ., Univ. Ill., Urbana-Champaign, 1985-89, assoc. prof., 1989—95, prof. Spanish and Second Lang. Acquisition Chgo., 1995—. Mem. adv. com. for Studies in Second Lang. Aquisition; dir. Grad. Studies in Spanish, Italian and Portuguese. Chief designer of PBS series: Destinos: An Introduction to Spanish, 1992. Recipient Nelson Brooks award Excellence in the Teaching of Culture, Tchr. Scholar award. Office: Univ Ill at Chgo 601 S Morgan MC 315 Chicago IL 60667-7117*

**VAN PATTEN, JAMES JEFFERS,** education educator; b. North Rose, N.Y., Sept. 8, 1925; s. Earl F. and Dorothy (Jeffers) Van P.; married. BA, Syracuse U., 1949; ME, Tex. Western Coll., 1959; PhD, U. Tex., Austin, 1962. Asst. prof. philosophy and edn. Central Mo. State U., Warrensburg, 1962-64, assoc. prof., 1964-69; assoc. prof. fis. overseas U. Okla., Norman, 1969-71; prof. edn. U. Ark., Fayetteville, 1971-99, prof. emeritus, 1999—. Visiting scholar, U. Mich., 1981, UCLA, 1987, U. Tex., Austin 1987; vis. prof./scholar U. Fla., Gainesville, 1994; adj. Fla. Atlantic U., 2000-05. Editor: Conflict, Permanency and Change in Education, 1976, Philosophy, Social Science and Education, 1989, College Teaching and Higher Education Leadership, 1990, Social-Cultural Foundations of Educational Policy in the U.S., 1991, Watersheds in Higher Education, 1997, Challenges and Opportunities For a New Millennium, 1998, Higher Education Culture, Case Studies For A New Century, 2000, A New Century In Retrospect and Prospect, 2000; Author: Academic Profiles in Higher Education, 1992, The Many Faces of the Culture of Higher Education, 1993, The Culture of Higher Education: A Case Study Approach, 1996, What's Really Happening in Education: A Case Study Approach, 1997; Co-author: (with G. Chen and George Davidson) Individual and Collective Contributions to Humaneness In Our Time, 1997, (with John Pulliam) History of Education in America, 8th edit., 2003, (with Timothy J. Bergen) A Case Study Approach to a Multi-Cultural Mosaic for Education, 2003; contbr. articles to profl. jours. including Futures Rsch. Quar.; founder Jour. of Thought, Educational Systems for the 21st Century, Futures Rsch. Quarterly, summer 2000. Served with inf. U.S. Army, 1944-45. Decorated Purple Heart, Bronze Star. Mem. Am. Ednl. Studies Assn., Southern Future Soc., World Future Soc., Am. Philosophy Assn., Southwestern Philosophy of Edn. Soc. (pres. 1970), Am. Ednl. Rsch. Assn., Edn. Law Assn. Legal Assts., Kiwanis, Phi Delta Kappa (pres. chpt. U. Ark. 1976-77). E-mail: jvanpatt@aol.com.

**VAN PELT, ROBERT IRVING,** retired firefighter; b. Chgo., May 4, 1931; s. Irving Henry and Lillian Christene (Balder) Van P.; m. Donna Arlene Bengtson, Feb. 3, 1962; children: Robert Scott, Barbara Gail, James Arthur. Grad. H.S., Chgo. Fire dept. capt. Chgo. Fire Dept., 1954—89; ret., 1989. Dir. Edgebrook Cmty. Assn., Chgo., 1974-95, U. Ill. Dad's Assn., 1988-92; dist. vice-chmn. programs Chgo. Area coun. Boy Scouts Am., 1985-93; scouting coord. Edgebrook Luth. Ch., Chgo., 1971—; active PTA Edgebrook Sch., Taft H.S. With U.S. Naval Air Res., 1949-65. Decorated Combat Air Crew Wings, 1951, Armed Svcs. medal; recipient Merit award Boy Scouts Am., 1982, Silver Beaver award, 1987, Svc. award VFW, 1987, Lamb award Luth. Ch., 2000; named to Chgo. Sr. Citizen Hall of Fame, 2000; PTA scholar, 1956. Mem. Naval Air Mus. (founding life), Exptl. Aviation Assn., War Birds Am., E.A.A. War Bird Squadron 4, Am. Legion, Order of Arrow, Liberator (San Diego), U.S. Navy Meml. Washington (plank), Patrol Bomber Y Consolidated MFG (PBY) Catalina Assn. (life). Avocations: photography, woodworking, model making. Home: 6317 N Hiawatha Ave Chicago IL 60646-4219

**VAN PILSUM, JOHN FRANKLIN,** biochemist, educator; b. Prairie City, Iowa, Jan. 28, 1922; s. John Peter and Vera Elisabeth (Moore) Van P.; m. Shirley Elaine Newsom, Oct. 14, 1958; children: John Robert, Patricia Mona, Barbara Joyce, Mary Ann, Elizabeth Joan, William Franklin. BS State U. Iowa, 1943, PhD, 1949. Instr. L.I. Coll. Medicine, Bklyn., 1949-51; asst. prof. coll. medicine U. Utah, Salt Lake City, 1951-54; asst. prof. biochemistry U. Minn., Mpls., 1954-63, assoc. prof. biochemistry, 1963-71, prof. biochemistry, 1971—92, prof. biochemistry emeritus, 1992—. Contbr. articles to profl. jours. Lt. USN, 1944-46. Recipient numerous grants NIH. Mem. Am. Soc. Biochemistry and Molecular Biology, Am. Inst. Nutrition, Histochem. Soc. Achievements include work with Guanidinium compound metabolism. Home: 4356 Leander Ln Columbia Heights MN 55421-3067 Office: U Minn Dept Biochem Molecular Biolog & Biophysics 1395 Gortner Ave Saint Paul MN 55108 Office Phone: 612-624-1542.

**VAN PRAAG, HERMAN MEIR,** psychiatrist, educator, researcher; b. Schiedam, The Netherlands, Oct. 17, 1929; s. Marinus Maurits and Charlotte Frederique (Leverpoll) V.P.; m. Cornelia Eikens; children: Marinus, Gido, Charlotte, Bart. MD, Leiden U., The Netherlands, 1956; PhD in Neurobiology, U. Utrecht, The Netherlands, 1962. Chief of staff dept. psychiatry Dijkzigt Hosp., Rotterdam, The Netherlands, 1963-66; founder, prof., head dept. biol. psychiatry Psychiat. Univ. Clinic State U., Groningen, Netherlands, 1966-77; prof., head dept. psychiatry Acad. Hosp. State U., Utrecht, 1977-82, Albert Einstein Coll. Medicine, Bronx, NY, 1982—92; prof., head dept. psychiatry and neuropsychology Acad. Hosp. U. Maastricht, Netherlands, 1992—99, sci. advisor dept. psychiatry and neuropsychology, 1999—. Emeritus prof. Albert Einstein Coll. Medicine, 1992—; psychiatrist-in-chief Montefiore Med. Ctr., Bronx, 1982—92; Lady Davis vis. prof. Hebrew U. Hadassah U. Hosp., Jerusalem, 1976—77; head WHO Nat. Ref. Ctr. for Study of Psychotropic Drugs, 1969, WHO Collaborating Ctr. for Rsch. and Tng. in Biol. Psychiatry, 1974; founder Interdisciplinary Soc. Biol. Psychiatry, 1966, Found. for Psychiatry and Religion, 1998; guest lectr. numerous univs. around the world. Editor: Psychiatria Neurologia Neurochirurgia, 1968-70, Advances in Biological Psychiatry, 1978—; editor-in-chief Psychiatria Neurologia Neurochirurgia, 1971-74, Biology of Behavior, 1975-82, Handbook of Biological Psychiatry, 1975-81, Einstein Monograph Series in Experimental and Clinical Psychiatry, 1988—; European chief-editor Progress in Neuro-Psychopharmacology, 1993—; mem. editl. bd. numerous publs. in field; reviewer Am. Jour. Psychiatry, Archives of Gen. Psychiatry, Jour. Nervous and Mental Disease; mem. internat. scientific commn. Jour. Brazilian Psychiat. Assn. Decorated knight Order of the Dutch Lion, Queen Beatrix of The Netherlands; recipient numerous awards and honors. Fellow Am. Coll. Neuropsychopharmacology, Am. Psychiat. Assn.; mem. Royal Acad. Scis. of The Netherlands, Soc. Biol. Psychiatry, Collegium Internationale Neuro-Psychopharmacologicum, Assn. for Advancement of Psychotherapy, Internat. Group for Study of Affective Disorders, Internat. Soc. Psychoneuroendocrinology, European Brain and Behavior Soc., Internat. Assn. for Suicide Prevention, Brit. Pharmacol. Soc., European Soc. for Clin. Investigation, Bataafsch Genootschap der Proefondervindelijke Wijsbegeerte, Am. Coll. Neuropharmacology, Deutsche Gesellschaft fur Psychiatrie und Nervenheilkunde, Israel Med. Assn., Psychiat. Rsch. Soc., NY Acad. Medicine, Am. Psychopathol. Assn., Internat. Coll. Neurobiology, Biol. Psychiatry and Psychopharmacology, Serotonin Club, Internat. Soc. for Rsch. on Emotion, Internat. Soc. Psychoneuroendocrinology, Arbeitsgemeinschaft fur Neuropsychpharmakologie und Pharmakopsychiatrie, World Psychiat. Assn. (chmn. religion, spirituality and psychiatry sect.). Office: Acad Hosp Maastricht PO Box 5800 6202 AZ Maastricht Netherlands Office Phone: 31-55-5760795. Personal E-mail: h.m.van.praag@vanpraag.com.

**VAN RHYN, JACQUELINE J.,** curator; b. Greenwich, Conn., May 29, 1970; d. Richard and Stephanie van Rhyn; m. James J. Hoisington, July 30, 2005. Bachelor, NYU, 1992; Masters, Williams Coll., 1997. Asst. curator Mass MoCA, North Adams, Mass., 1996—97; Werner and Maren Otto curatorial intern Busch-Reisinger Mus., Cambridge, Mass., 1997—98; curatorial asst. Fogg Art Mus., Cambridge, 1998—2000; curator prints and photographs The Print Ctr., Phila., 2000—. Chair exhbns. and adv. com. Art in City Hall Adv. Coun., Phila., 2002—06; guest curator Allentown (Pa.) Art Mus., 2003; mem. programming com. Philagrafika, Phila. Print Collaborative, 2004—. Author: (exhibition catalog) IMPRINT: A Public Art Project. Mem.: Am. Assn. Museums, Coll. Art Assn. Office: The Print Ctr 1614 Latimer St Philadelphia PA 19103 Office Phone: 215-735-6090. Office Fax: 215-735-5511. Business E-Mail: jvanrhyn@printcenter.org.

**VAN RIPER, PAUL PRITCHARD,** political science professor; b. Laporte, Ind., July 29, 1916; s. Paul and Margaret (Pritchard) Van R.; m. Dorothy Ann Dodd Samuelson, May 11, 1964; 1 child, Michael Scott Samuelson. AB, DePauw U., 1938; PhD, U. Chgo., 1947. Instr. Northwestern U., 1947-49, asst. prof. polit. sci., 1949-51; mgmt. analyst Office Comptroller Dept. Army, 1951-52; mem. faculty Cornell U., 1952-70, prof., 1957-70; chmn. gov. bd., exec. com. Cornell Social Sci. Research Center, 1956-58; prof., head dept. polit. sci. Tex. A&M U., 1970-77, prof., 1977-81, prof. emeritus, 1981—, coordinator M.P.A. program, 1979-81, named prof. Bush Sch. Govt. and Pub. Svc., 1997—. Vis. prof. U. Chgo., 1958, Ind. U., 1961, U. Strathclyde, Scotland, 1964, U. Mich., 1965, U. Okla., 1969-97, U. Utah, 1979. Author: History of the United States Civil Service, 1958, Some Educational and Social Aspects of Fraternity Life, 1961, (with others) The American Federal Executive, 1963, Handbook of Practical Politics, 3d edit., 1967; editor and co-author: the Wilson Influence on Public Administration, 1990. Mem. exec. com. Civil Svc. Reform Assn., 1963, 1964-66, hist. adv. com. NASA, 1964-66; bd. dirs. Brazos Valley Cmty. Action Agy., 1975-79, Brazos County Hist. Commn. 1981, Brazos Indian Heritage Pgn. 1977-79, Maj. AUS, 1942-46; lt. col. USAR ret. Decorated Croix de Guerre (France). Mem. Am. Polit. Sci. Assn., So. Polit. Sci. Assn., S.W. Polit. Sci. Assn. (exec.com. 1975-77), Am. Soc. Pub. Adminstrn. (nat adv. com. 1957-60, Dimock award 1984, Waldo award 1990, Van Riper award created in his honor 2002), Internat. Personnel Mgmt. Assn., Rotary (pres. Bryan club 1991-92), Phi Beta Kappa, Beta Theta Pi (v.p. 1962, gen. sec. 1963-65), Pi Alpha Alpha, Pi Sigma Alpha, Phi Kappa Phi, Sigma Delta Chi. Republican. Baptist. Home: 713 E 30th St Bryan TX 77803-4789 Office: Tex A and M Univ Dept Polit Sci College Station TX 77843-4348 Office Phone: 979-845-2511.

**VAN RIPER, ROBERT AUSTIN,** writer, retired public relations executive; b. Mt. Vernon, N.Y., June 18, 1921; s. Austin Millard and Gladys Brownell Van R.; m. Barbara Jean Jacobs, Dec. 2, 1944; children: Alexandra, Tracy. BA, Oberlin Coll., 1943. Acct. exec. Edward L. Bernays Pub. Rels., N.Y.C., 1946-50, N.W. Ayer & Son, Inc., N.Y.C., 1950-54, acct. supr. Phila., 1954-61, v.p. N.Y.C., 1961-67, sr. v.p., 1967-73; pub. rels. counsel Fin. Acctg. Standards Bd., Norwalk, Conn., 1973-91, ret., 1991. Author: (novels) A Really Sincere Guy, 1958, The Governor, 1970, (nonfiction) Setting Standards for Financial Reporting: FASB and the Struggle for Control of a Critical Process, 1994, A Life Divided: George Peabody, Pivotal Figure in Anglo-American Finance, Philanthropy and Diplomacy, 2007; contbr. articles to profl. jours. Bd. dir. exec. com. United Fund, Phila., 1956-61; trustee Lawrence Hosp., Westchester County, 1966-73, v.p., 1971-73. Lt. (j.g.) USN, 1943-46. Mem. Pub. Rels. Soc. Am. (pres. Phila. chpt. 1960-61), Fairfield County Pub. Rels. Assn. (bd. dir. 1987-89), Holland Soc., Bronxville Field Club (N.Y.). Presbyterian. Avocations: tennis, music. Home: 4100 N Charles St Apt 810 Baltimore MD 21218

**VAN ROEKEL, DENNIS,** educational association administrator; b. LeMars, Iowa; m. Julie Van Roekel; children: Brian, Chad. BA, Iowa; MA, No. Ariz. U. Pres. Paradise Valley Edn. Assn., Ariz. Edn. Assn.; sec., treas. NEA, Washington, DC, 1991—2002, v.p., 2002—; chair Interactive and Adv. Com. on Membership. Mem. Nat. Commn. on Math. and Sci. Tchg. for 21st Century, 1999; math tchr. Paradise Valley HS, Phoenix. Office: NEA 1201 16th St, NW Washington DC 20036-3290 Office Phone: 202-833-4000. Office Fax: 202-822-7974.

**VAN RYN, MICHELLE,** healthcare educator; children: Nick, Zoe. BS, Regents Coll., Albany, N.Y., 1981; MPH, U. Mich., Ann Arbor, 1985, PhD, 1990. Sr. rsch. assoc. Mich. Prevention Rsch. Ctr., Ann Arbor, 1990—91; from asst. to assoc. prof. Sch. Pub. Health, U. Albany, NY, 1991—2000, dir. social behavior and cmty. health Sch. Pub. Health, 1997—2000; assoc. dir. Ctr. for Chronic Disease Outcomes Rsch., VA Med. Ctr., Mpls., 2000—03; dir. Colorectal Cancer Quality Enhancement Rsch. Initiative, Mpls., 2001—04; assoc. prof. Sch. Pub. Health, U. Minn., Mpls., 2000—; assoc. prof. dept. family medicine and cmty. health U. Minn. Med. Sch., Mpls., 2004—. Dir. Van Ryn Evaluation Rsch., Albany, NY, 1990—2000. Contbr. articles to profl. jours. Co-chair Cancer Care and Outcomes Rsch. and Surveillance Consortium, Washington; exec. com. Colorectal Cancer Quality Enhancement Rsch. Initiative, Mpls.; participant Robert Wood Johnson Found. Conf. on Disparities. Recipient Lena Rowland award for best preventive intervention, Nat. Mental Health Assn., 1990, Nuala McAnn Drescher Profl. Devel. award, United Univ. Professions, 1995. Mem.: Soc. for Pub. Health Edn., Assn. for Health Svcs. Rsch., APHA. Office: Dept Family Medicine and Cmty Health Rm 225 925 Delaware SE Minneapolis MN 55414 Office Fax: 612-624-3037. E-mail: vanry001@umn.edu.

**VAN SAMBEEK, JEROME WILLIAM,** physiologist, educator; b. Milbank, S.D., Aug. 1, 1947; s. Henry Lambert and Janet Marie Van Sambeek; m. Carol Marie Crandall, Dec. 30, 1972; children: Rachel Virginia, Jeffrey Crandall, Melissa Janet Van Sambeek Ambler, William Glenn, Lindsey Marie. BS, S.D. State U., 1969; PhD, Washington U., St. Louis, Mo., 1975. Postdoctoral rsch. fellow U. of Mo., Columbia, 1975; rsch. plant physiologist biochemist USDA Forest Svc., So. Forest Experiment Sta., Pineville, La., 1976—79; rsch. plant physiologist USDA Forest Svc., No. Ctrl. Forest Experiment Sta., Carbondale, Ill., 1980—88, project leader, physiologist, 1989—97; rsch. plant physiologist USDA Forest Svc., North Ctrl. Rsch. Sta., Columbia, Mo., 1998—. Editor: (procs.) Knowledge for the Future of Black Walnut (Black Walnut Achievement award, 1989); contbr. articles to profl. jours. and conf. procs. Recipient Gen. Motors Acad. scholarship, S.D. State U., 1966—69, Sta. Tech. Transfer award, USDA Forest Svc., North Cen. Res. Stn., 2000. Mem.: Soc. of Am. Foresters, No. Nut Growers Assn., Walnut Coun., Internat. bd. dirs. 1981—, Black Walnut Achievement award 1989). Achievements include research in Procedures for white ash micropropagation. Avocation: gardening. Office: USDA Forest Svc Northern Res Stn 202 Natural Resource Building UMC Columbia MO 65211-7260 Office Phone: 573-875-5341 233. Office Fax: 573-882-1977. E-mail: jvansambeek@fs.fed.us.

**VAN SCHENKHOF, CAROL DOUGHERTY (CAROL DOVAN),** soprano, music educator; b. Reading, Pa., Apr. 20, 1942; d. Harry Hammond Dougherty and Magdalen Mary Doviak; m. Mark Anton van Schenkhof, Feb. 18, 1995; m. John William Heierman, Sept. 4, 1965 (div. July 6, 1986). BA, Chatham Coll., 1964; student, Julliard Sch., N.Y.C., 1964—65, Julliard Sch., 1970; MA Ethno-musicology, Hunter Coll., 1970, student, 1971, Mannes Coll., 1980, Westminster Choir Coll., Princeton, N.J., 1992, Westminster Choir Coll., 1996, Oberlin Conservatory, 2000, student, 2002, Westminster Choir Coll. Conservatory, 2004. Tchr. voice Sch. Music Lab. Chatham Coll., Pitts., 1964; resource profl. Lincoln Ctr., N.Y.C., 1972; vis. artist, lectr. Ewha U., Seoul, 1975, Emissora Nacional de Radioifusao, Lisbon, Portugal, 1976, Conservatorio Nacional, Lisbon, 1976; lectr. opera C.W. Post Coll., L.I. U., Greenvale, NY, 1982—83; profl. coord. Port Washington Libr.-Music Adv. Coun., NY, 1985—87; tchr. voice Stony Brook U., NY, 1998—99, Carol Dovan-van Schenkhof Studios, Port Washington, 1980—. Singer: Rhodesia TV Ltd., 1974, Rhodesia Orgn., 1974, South African Broadcasting, 1974, Emissora Nacional de Radiodifusão, 1976, (soloist) Met. Opera Studio, 1971—72, Alice Tully Hall, 1983, recitals with composer Jeanne Singer, 1983—87, Nat. Grand Opera, 1983, (Operas) Best of Opera, Carnegie Hall, 1982, La Boheme, 1981, Ninth Symphony of Beethoven- Reading Sympony Orch., 1983, others. Recipient 1st Pl. award, Competition Pitts. Musicians Club, 1962, Pitts. Concert Soc. Youth Auditions, 1962, Pitts. Concert Soc. Major Auditions, 1963; scholar, Chautauqua (NY) Inst. Music, 1962—63, Aspen (Colo.) Music Festival, 1964. Mem.: N.Y. Singing Tchrs., Am. Guild Musical Artists, Nat. Assn. for Music Edn., Nat. Assn. Tchrs. Singing (adjudicator, Ea. Region auditions), Associated Music Tchrs. League (exec. bd. 1994—). Episcopalian. Avocations: gardening, sailing. Home and Studio: 6 Hillview Ave Port Washington NY 11050 Office Phone: 516-944-5140. E-mail: caroldov@optonline.net.

**VAN SCHILFGAARDE, JAN,** retired agricultural engineer, federal agency administrator; b. The Hague, Netherlands, Feb. 7, 1929; came to US, 1946, naturalized, 1957; married; 3 children. BS, Iowa State Coll., 1949, MS, 1950, PhD in Agrl. Engring. and Soil Physics, 1954. Instr., assoc. agrl. engr. Iowa State Coll., 1949-54; asst. prof. agrl. engring. NC State Coll., 1954-57, assoc. prof., 1957-62, prof., 1962-64; drainage engr. Agrl. Rsch. Svc. USDA, Raleigh, NC, 1954-64, from chief water mgmt. engr. soil/water conservation rsch. divsn. to dir. Beltsville, Md., 1964—72, dir. Salinity Lab. Riverside, Calif., 1972-84, dir. Mountain States Area Agrl. Rsch. Svc. Ft. Collins, Colo., 1984-86, assoc. dir. no. plains area Agrl. Rsch. Svc., 1986-91, assoc. dep. adminstr. for natural resources Agrl. Rsch. Svc. Beltsville, Md., 1991-96, dir. Pacific West area, 1996-97; ret., 1997. Vis. prof. Ohio State U., 1962 Mem. ASCE, NAE, Am. Soc. Agrl. Engrs., Soil Sci. Soc., Soil Conservation Soc. Am. E-mail: j.-r.vanschilfgaarde@worldnet.att.net, j_rvs@msn.com.

**VAN SCHOIK, D. RICK,** think-tank executive; BS in Oceanography and Engring., U.S. Naval Acad.; MS in Biology, San Diego State U.; postgrad., Harvard U., Tufts U., Natural Resources Leadership Inst., N.C. Environ. fellow Surdna Found., N.Y.C.; environ. cons. S.W. Rsch. Assocs., Inc., calif; aquatic conservation biologist The Natural Conservancy, NY, Naval Ocean Sys. Ctr., Calif.; CEO Partnership for the Sounds, NC; mng. dir. S.W. Ctr. for Environ. Rsch. and Policy, San Diego, 1998—. Adj. prof. U. Calif., San Diego, U. Redlands, Palomar C.C., Nassau County Coll. Co-chair Binational Environ. Edn. Coun. of the Californias, City of Encinitas Blue Ribbon Environment Com. With USN. Office: SW Ctr for Environ Rsch and Policy 5250 Campanile Dr San Diego CA 92182-1913 Office Phone: 619-594-0568.

**VAN SCHOONENBERG, ROBERT G.,** lawyer; b. Madison, Wis., Aug. 18, 1946; s. John W. and Ione (Henning) Schoonenberg. BA, Marquette U., 1968; MBA, U. Wis., 1972; JD, U. Mich., 1974. Bar: Calif. 1975, Fla. 1976. Atty. Gulf Oil Corp., Pitts., 1974-81; v.p., gen. counsel to sr. v.p., gen. counsel, sec. Avery Dennison Corp., Pasadena, Calif., 1981—2004, exec. v.p., gen. counsel, sec., 2004—. Judge pro tem Pasadena Mcpl. Ct., 1987-89. Dir., v.p. fin. adminstrn. Am. Cancer Soc., San Gabriel Vally Unit, 1987—; v.p., treas., dir., v.p. investments Pasadena Symphony Assn.; bd. dirs. Pasadena Recreation and Parks Found., 1983-84; mem. Pasadena Citizens Task Force on Crime Control, 1983-84; dir. Boy Scouts, San Gabriel Valley Coun., dir. public coun.; bd. dirs. Verugo Hills Hosp. Found.; trustee Southwestern U. Sch. Law. Mem.: Am. Soc. Corp. Secs. (pres., so. Calif. chpt.), Am. Corp. Counsel Assn. (dir.), L.A. County Bar Assn. (past chmn., corp. law dept. sect.). Office: Avery Dennison Corp 150 N Orange Grove Blvd Pasadena CA 91103-3534

**VANSELOW, NEAL ARTHUR,** retired academic administrator, retired internist; b. Milw., Mar. 18, 1932; s. Arthur Frederick and Mildred (Hoffmann) Vanselow; m. Mary Ellen McKenzie, June 20, 1958; children: Julie Ann, Richard Arthur. AB, U. Mich., 1954, MD, 1958, MS, 1963. Diplomate Am. Bd. Internal Medicine, Am. Bd. Allergy and Immunology. Intern Mich. Gen. Hosp., 1958—59; resident Univ. Hosp. Ann Arbor, Mich., 1959—63; instr. medicine U. Mich., 1963—64, asst. prof., 1964—68, assoc. prof., 1968—72, prof., chmn. dept. postgrad. medicine and health professions edn., 1972—74; dean Coll. Medicine U. Ariz., Tucson, 1974—77; chancellor med. ctr. U. Nebr., Omaha, 1977—82, v.p., 1977—82; v.p. health scis. U. Minn., 1982—89, prof. internal medicine, 1982—89; chancellor Tulane U. Med. Ctr., New Orleans, 1989—94, chancellor emeritus, 1997—; prof. internal medicine Tulane U., New Orleans, 1989—97, prof. internal medicine emeritus, 1997—. Adj. prof. health sys. mgmt. Tulane U., New Orleans, 1993—99, prof. emeritus, 1999—; chmn. Joint Bd. Osteo. and Med.

Examiners Ariz., 1974—77; chmn. coun. on Grad. Med. Edn. Dept. Health and Human Svcs., 1986—91; mem. com. on educating dentists for future Inst. Medicine NAS, 1993—95, chairperson com. on future of primary care, 1994—96, co-chairperson com. on U.S. physician supply, 1995—96, scholar in residence, 1994—95, mem. com. to assess occupl. health and safety tng. needs, 1999—2000, chmn. com. on introducing social and behavioral sci. into med. sch. curriculum, 2002—04; chairperson continuing eval. panel Am. Internat. Health Alliance, 2000—01; mem. adv. com. Medschool.com, 2000—01; adj. prof. Sch. Health Adminstrn. and Policy Ariz. State U., 2000—05; mem. spl. emphasis panel NIH, 2005. Panel on interdisciplinary health profl. edn. Nat. League Nursing, 1996—97; exec. com. United Way Midlands, 1980—82, vice-chmn. 1981 campaign; mem. Commn. on Health Professions Pew Charitable Trusts, 1990—92, 1997—99, Commn. on the Future of Med. Edn. U. Calif., 1996—97; mktg. mgmt. governing coun. U. Hosp. Consortium, 1993—95; trustee Meharry Med. Coll., 1996—, chair presdl. search com., 2006; pres., chmn. bd. Am. Friends London Sch. Hygiene and Tropical Medicine, 1998—2002; com. on relationships between medicine and nursing Josiah Macy Jr. Found., 1999—2000; mem. Gov.'s Pan Am. Commn., La., 1991—92; bd. dirs. Devel. Authority for Tucson's Economy, 1975—77, Minn. High Tech. Coun., 1983—86, Minn. Coalition for Health Care Costs, 1983—87, La. Health Care Authority, 1989—90, United Way Greater New Orleans Area, 1992—97; bd. dirs., exec. com. Health Planning Coun. Midlands, Omaha, 1978—82, v.p., 1981—82. Fellow: ACP (workgroup on physician workforce and financing med. edn. 1996), Ariz. Acad. Arts, Sci. and Tech. (bd. govs. 2005—, 2005—, founding mem.), Am. Coll. Physician Execs., Am. Acad. Allergy; mem.: Inst. Med. NAS, Soc. Med. Adminstrs., Assn. Acad. Health Ctrs. (bd. dirs. 1983—89, chmn. bd. dirs. 1988), Rio Verde (Ariz.) Cmty. Assn. (bd. dirs. 2000—04), Phi Beta Kappa, Nu Sigma Nu, Beta Theta Pi, Alpha Omega Alpha, Sigma Xi. Office: 18942 E Mountainaire Dr Rio Verde AZ 85263-7093

**VAN SETERS, JOHN,** retired biblical literature educator; b. Hamilton, Ont., Can., May 2, 1935; s. Hugo and Anne (Hubert) Van S.; m. Elizabeth Marie Malmberg, June 11, 1960; children: Peter John, Deborah Elizabeth. BA, U. Toronto, 1958; MA, Yale U., 1959, PhD, 1965; BD, Princeton Theol. Sem., 1962; ThD (hon.), U. Lausanne, Switzerland, 1999. Asst. prof. dept. Near Eastern studies Waterloo Luth. U., 1965-67; assoc. prof. Old Testament Andover Newton Theol. Sch., 1967-70; assoc. prof. dept. Near Eastern studies U. Toronto, 1970-76, prof., 1976-77; James A. Gray prof. Bibl. lit., dept. religion U. N.C., Chapel Hill, 1977-2000, chmn. dept. religious studies, 1980-88, 93-95, prof. emeritus, 2000—. Adj. prof. dept. religion and culture Wilfrid Laurier U., 2000—. Author: The Hyksos: A New Investigation, 1966, Abraham in History and Tradition, 1975, In Search of History, 1983, Der Jahwist als Historiker, 1987, Prologue to History, 1992, The Life of Moses, 1994, The Pentateuch, 1999, A Law Book for the Diaspora, 2003, The Edited Bible, 2006. Recipient James Henry Breasted prize Am. Hist. Assn., 1985, Book award Am. Acad. Religion, 1986, R.B.Y. Scott Book award Can. Soc. Bibl. Studies, 2004; Woodrow Wilson fellow, 1958; J.J. Obermann fellow, 1962-64; Guggenheim fellow, 1979-80; NEH fellow, 1985-86, Am. Coun. Learned Socs. fellow, 1991-92, sr. rsch. fellow Cath. U. Leuven, Belgium, 1998, Fgn. Rsch. fellow Nat. Rsch. Fund S.Africa, 2002. Mem. Soc. Bibl. Lit., Am. Schs. Oriental Rsch., Soc. Study of Egyptian Antiquities, Am. Oriental Soc., Cath. Bibl. Assn., Can. Soc. Bibl. Studies (pres. 1999-2000), Old Testament Soc. South Africa (hon.). Home: 70-139 Father David Bauer Dr Waterloo ON Canada N2L 6L1 E-mail: john.vanseters@sympatico.ca.

**VAN SICE, JAMES,** career military officer, academic administrator; b. Wilmington, Del. m. Clarke Hutchinson; 2 children. BS, USCG Academy, 1974; MS in Engring., Purdue Univ.; MA in Bus., Webster Coll. Commd. ensign USCG, 1974, advanced through grades to rear adm.; comdr. Coast Guard Air Station, Borinquen, PR; chief of ops. & chief of staff Eighth Coast Guard Dist., New Orleans; dep. dir. U.S. No. Command, Peterson AFB, Colo.; dir. reserve & training USCG, 2004—05; supt. USCG Academy, New London, Conn., 2005—. Decorated Def. Superior Svc medal, Meritorious Svc medal (3 awards), Coast Guard Commendation medal, Coast Guard Achievement medal, Commandant's Letter of Commendation Ribbon with disting. device. Office: US Coast Guard Academy 31 Mohegan Ave New London CT 06320-8103

**VAN SICKLE, FREDERICK L.,** federal judge; b. 1943; m. Jane Bloomquist. BS, U. Wis., 1965; JD, U. Wash., 1968. Ptnr. Clark & Van Sickle, 1970-75; prosecuting atty. Douglas County, Waterville, Wash., 1971-75; judge State of Wash. Superior Ct., Grant and Douglas counties, 1975-79, Cheland and Douglas Counties, Wash., 1979-91, U.S Dist. Ct. (ea. dist.) Wash., Spokane, 1991—, chief judge, 2000—. Co-chair rural ct. com. Nat. Conf. State Trial Judges, 1987-91. 1st lt. U.S. Army, 1968-70. Mem. Am. Adjudicature Soc., Wash. State Bar Assn., Masons (pres. Badger mountain lodge 1982-83), Scottish Rite, Spokane Rotary, Shriners. Office: US Dist Cts US Courthouse 920 W Riverside Ave Rm 840 PO Box 2209 Spokane WA 99201

**VANSKA, OSMO,** music director; m. Pirkko Vanska. D (hon.), U. Glasgow. Prin. chair Turku Philharm., 1971—76; co-prin. chair Helsinki Philharm., 1977—82; music dir. Lahti Symphony Orch., 1988—96; chief condr. BBC Scottish Symphony Orch. of Glasgow, 1996—2002; music dir. Minn. Orch., 2002—. Guest condr. Boston Symphony Orch., 2002. Condr. numerous recordings with the Lahti Symphony Orch. (Gramophone award, 1996, Cannes Classical award, 2002), (recording) The Tempest (1993 Prix Academic Charles Cros.). Nominee Grammy award for Best Orchestral Performance for a recording with the BBC Scottish Symphony; named Conductor of Yr., Musical Am. Internat. Dir. Performing Arts, 2005; recipient First prize, Besancon Internat. Young Conductor's Competition, Royal Philharm. Soc. award, 2002. Achievements include led Lahti Ensemble on US tour, includign performance at Avery Fisher hall, NYC. Avocations: sports, motorcycling. Office: Minnesota Orchestra Orchestra Hall 1111 Nicollet mall Minneapolis MN 55403*

**VAN SLOOTEN, RONALD HENRY JOSEPH,** dentist; b. Paterson, NJ, July 12, 1937; s. Henry and Edythe (De Marco) Van S.; m. Joyce Elenor Mandel, 1962 (div. 1969); children: Ronald Henry Jr., Timothy Jay, Lauren; m. Barbara Rose Durante, July 1, 1979; children: Jonathan Henry, Brian Joseph. DDS, Fairleigh Dickinson U., Teaneck, N.J., 1962. Dentist pvt. practice, Paterson, 1965-76, Ridgewood, NJ, 1969-78, Ho Ho Kus, NJ, 1978—; staff mem. Bainert Meml. Hosp., Paterson, 1965-75, Ridgewood Valley Hosp., 1975—2004; assoc. prof. Fairleigh Dickinson Dental Sch., Hackensack, NJ, 1973-90; pres. Van Slooten Harbour Marina Inc., Port Henry, NY, 1989—. Cons. NJ Mfrs. Ins. Co., Trenton, 1966-2003. Pres. Fairleigh Dickinson Sch. Dentistry Alumni Assn., 1976-77. Lt. comdr. USN, 1962-65. Fellow Acad. Gen. Dentistry, Acad. Dentistry Internat.; mem. ADA, Internat. Dental Health Found., NJ Dental Soc., Bergen County Dental Soc. (chmn. Nat. Dental Health Week citation 1970), Moriah C. of C., Ho-Ho-Kus C. of C. Republican. Roman Catholic. Avocations: racquetball, fishing, boating. Office: Ho Ho Kus Profl Bldg 110 Warren Ave Ho Ho Kus NJ 07423-1561 Office Phone: 201-447-1116.

**VAN STEENWYK, JOHN JOSEPH,** healthcare plan consultant; b. Mpls., July 25, 1931; s. Elmer Arnold and Marion Ione (Thompson) van S.; m. Janice Kevin Sharp, July 11, 1959; children: Jennifer Lee, Edward Arnold, Julie Anne AB, Oberlin Coll., 1953; MBA, U. Pa., 1955. V.p., cons. The Segal Co., N.Y.C., 1957—81; pres. Health Econs., Inc., Spring House, Pa., 1982—. Clin. asst. prof. cmty. and preventive medicine N.Y. Med. Coll., Valhalla, NY, 1980—2002. With USN, 1955-57. Sr. scholar, Dept. Health Policy, Jefferson U., 2005—. Mem.: APHA, Am. Health Ins. Plans, Acad. Health (formerly Assn. Health Svs. Rsch.). Episcopalian. Avocation: gardening. Home: 921 Tennis Ave Ambler PA 19002-2312 Office: Health Economics Inc 768 N Bethlehem Pike PO Box 710 Spring House PA 19477 Office Phone: 215-628-3838.

**VAN STONE, WILLIAM WEBB,** psychiatrist; b. Denver, Mar. 14, 1929; s. Wilfred Douglas and Cora Coleman (Kampf) Van S.; m. Joan Kay Kinnear, Nov. 27, 1958 (dec. Dec. 2004); children: Lisa Kay, Kathryn Louise, David William. BA, Swarthmore Coll., 1951; MD, Cornell U., 1955. Intern Mary Hitchcock Meml. Hosp., Hanover, N.H., 1955-56; resident Menninger Sch. Psychiatry, Topeka, 1958-61; unit chief Topeka VA Hosp., 1963-67; asst. chief of staff Palo Alto (Calif.) VA Med. Ctr., 1967-89, chief treatment svcs., 1989-2000; assoc. chief for psychiatry VA Central Office, Washington, 2001—. Clin. assoc. prof. psychiatry emeritus Stanford (Calif.) U. Med. Sch., 1968—; mem. faculty Menninger Sch. Psychiatry, 1963-67. Contbr. 30 articles to profl. jours., chpts. to books. Chmn. bd. Miramonte Mental Health Assn., Palo Alto, 1976; pres. No. Calif. Psychiat. Soc., San Francisco, 1986-87, bd. dirs. Cmty. Sch. Music and Arts, Mountain View, Calif., 1969-75, Parents Family and Friends of Lesbians and Gays, 1996-2003. Capt. USNR, 1956-79. Postdoctoral fellow C.F. Menninger Meml. Hosp., 1961-63. Fellow Am. Psychiat. Assn. (disting. life); mem. Washington Psychiat. Assn. E-mail: wvsdc@aol.com.

**VAN SUSTEREN, GRETA CONWAY,** newscaster, lawyer; b. Appleton, Wis., June 11, 1954; d. Urban Peter and Margery (Conway) Van Susteren; m. John Purcell Coale, Oct. 12, 1987. BA in Geology. U. Wis., 1976; JD, Georgetown U., 1979, LLM, 1982; LLD (hon.), Stetson Law Sch. Bar: D.C. 1979, U.S. Supreme Ct. 1982, Md. 1985, Wis. 1987, U.S. Ct. Appeals (D.C., 2d and 4th cirs.). Ptnr. Milliken, VanSusteren & Canan, Washington, 1982—; with CNN, 1991—2002, host The Point with Greta Van Susteren, co-host Burden of Proof, legal cons. The World Today; host On the Record With Greta Van Susteren Fox News Channel, 2002—. Adj. prof. Georgetown Law Ctr., Washington, 1984—99; lectr., panelist Jud. Conf., Washington, 1986. Co-author: My Turn at the Bullypulpit: Straight Talk About the Things That Drive Me Nuts. Bd. dirs. Stuart Stiller Found., Washington, 1982—. Named one of 100 Most Powerful Women, Forbes; recipient Sandra Day O'Conner Medal of Honor, Seton Hall Univ., 2000—01, 1st Place, "Attack on America", Nat. Headliners award, 2002; Stiller fellow, Georgetown Law Ctr., 1980. Mem.: ATLA (lectr. conf. 1986—), ABA (Presdl. award for Excellence in Journalism 2001), D.C. Bar Assn. Office: FOX News Channel 1211 Avenue of the Americas New York NY 10036

**VAN SYOC, CLIFFORD LEE,** lawyer; b. Des Moines, Apr. 2, 1954; s. Willard Baird and Mary Ellen Van Syoc; m. Lorraine Augusta Hill, Dec. 20, 1974 (div.); children: Rhett Alexander, Scarlett Amantha. BBA cum laude, U. Miami, 1976, BA cum laude, 1977; JD, U. Wash., 1979; postgrad., U. Pa., 1978-79. Bar: Fla. 1979, N.J. 1980, U.S. Dist. Ct. N.J. 1980, U.S. Ct. Appeals (3d cir.) 1982. Law clk., gen. counsel IRS, Washington, 1978; assoc. Tomer, Parks, Seliger, Simonoff & Adourian, Haddonfield, NJ, 1979-84; pvt. practice Cherry Hill, NJ, 1984—. Nat. Merit Scholar, Ford Found., 1972. Mem. ABA, Am. Trial Lawyers Assn. Republican. Avocations: hiking, reading. Home: 77 S Chew Rd Hammonton NJ 08037-3305 Office: 535 Rte 38 Ste 501 Cherry Hill NJ 08002-2962*

**VAN TASSEL, JAMES HENRY,** retired electronics executive; b. LaCrosse, Wis., Feb. 15, 1929; s. John Henry and Agnes Cecilia (Anderson) Van T.; m. Mary Louise Carman, Dec. 23, 1961; children: John Peter, James George. BS, U. Wis.-LaCrosse, 1951; MS, Tex. Tech. Coll., 1957, PhD, 1959. Postdoctoral fellow Princeton U., NJ, 1959-60; mem. tech. staff, mgr. Tex. Instruments Co., Dallas, 1960-80; v.p. microelectronics div. NCR Corp., Dayton, Ohio, 1980-91; ret., 1991. Cons. in field; mem. adv. group on electron devices DOD, 1992-97; bd. dirs. Chartered Semiconductor, Singapore, 1994—. Contbr. articles to profl. jours.; patentee in field; co-inventor of hand-held caculator. Bd. dirs. Dayton Philharm. Orch., 1983-89, Miamisburg (Ohio) Mound Cmty. Improvement Corp., 1993—. Recipient Florilege d'Or Am Ecia, Paris, 1976, Disting. Alumnus award U. Wis.-LaCrosse, 1979, Holley medal ASME, 1989. Episcopalian.

**VAN TASSEL, LOWELL THOMAS,** mathematics professor; b. Mpls., Jan. 31, 1932; s. Evan Thomas Van Tassel and Sophia Anna Huebner; m. Diane Laura Diedrich, June 14, 1953; children: Thomas, Laurie, Karin. BS, U. Minn., 1952, MA, 1962. Cert. secondary tchr. Calif. Rsch. asst. U. Minn., Mpls., 1954-56; math. tchr. San Diego Unified Sch. Dist., 1956-65; prof. math. San Diego C.C. Dist., 1965-92, prof. emeritus of math., 1992—. Dept. chmn. math. dept. San Diego City Coll., 1971-72, 74-75; math/physics instr. Naval Tgn. Ctr., San Diego, 1962-65; proctor profl. engring. exams State of Calif. License Bd., Sacramento, 1957-65. Contbr. articles to profl. jours. V.p. Am. Fedn. of Tchrs., San Diego, 1971-72; faculty advisor Ind. Dems. for Action San Diego City Coll., 1967-71; mem. Clairemont Dem. Club, San Diego, 1966-76; juror, criminal trial Superior Ct., San Diego, 1990; elder Holy Cross Luth. Ch., San Diego, 1972-74, 92-94. With USMC, 1951-54; USMCR, 1954-71, maj., 1966-71. Mem. Math. Assn. Am., Calif. Retired Tchrs. Assn., Marine Corps Mus., U. Minn. Alumni Assn. (life), Nat. Coun. of Tchrs. of Math., Am. Fedn. of Tchrs. (retiree mem.), Phi Delta Kappa, Psi Chi. Lutheran. Avocations: travel, reading, word puzzles, games, bridge. Home: 5550 Lodi St San Diego CA 92117-1138 Personal E-mail: lowellv@webtv.net.

**VAN TASSEL, MICHAEL L.,** music educator; b. Grand Forks, N.D., Jan. 31, 1962; MusB, U. Mich., 1985, MusM, 1986. Cert. tchr. State of Mich. Dir. of bands and coord. of instrumental music Van Buren Pub. Schs., Belleville, Mich., chair dept. music and tchr. mentor. Named Dist. 12 Tchr. of Yr., mich. Sch. Band and orch. Assn., 2005; recipient Citation of Excellence, Nat. Band Assn., 1999, 2002, Exemplary Svc. award, Van Buren Pub. Schs., 1992, Golden Apple award, Wayne County RESA, 1992. Mem.: Music Educators Nat. Conf., Mich. Sch. Band and Orch. Assn. (v.p., dist. 12 1991—94), Pi Kappa Lambda (life). Home: 2709 Lillian Ann Arbor MI 48104 Office: Belleville High School 501 West Columbia Belleville MI 48111 Office Phone: 734-697-9133. Personal E-mail: mvantass@vanburenschools.net.

**VAN TATENHOVE, GREGORY F.,** federal judge, former prosecutor; JD, U. Ky. Aide to Senator Mitch McConnell US Senate, Ky.; law clerk US Dist. Ct., Ky.; trial atty. US Dept. Justice, Ky.; U.S. atty. (ea. dist.) Ky, 2001—06; chief of staff, legal counsel to Congressman Ron Lewis US Congress; judge US District Ct. (ea. dist.) Ky, 2006—. Office: US Dist Ct 110 Main St Ste 210 -H Pikeville KY 41501

**VAN TINE, KIRK KELSO,** lawyer, former federal agency administrator; b. Syracuse, N.Y., Aug. 30, 1948; s. George Kelso and Hariot (Van Alst) V.; m. Barbara Ann Byers, Aug. 14, 1971; children: Lindsay, Meredith. BS in Fgn. Affairs, U.S. Naval Acad., 1970; JD, U. Va., 1978. Bar: D.C. 1978, U.S. Ct. Appeals (D.C. crct.) 1979, U.S. Ct. Appeals (5th crct.) 1980, U.S. Ct. Appeals (8th crct.) 1992, U.S. Ct. Appeals (9th crct.) 1992, U.S. Ct. Appeals (10th crct.) 1993, U.S. Supreme Ct., 1982, U.S. Dist. Ct. D.C. 1979. Commd. ensign USN, 1970, advanced through grades to lt., 1974, resigned, 1975; assoc. Baker & Botts LLP, Washington, 1978-86, ptnr., 1986—2001, sr. ptnr., 2005—; gen. counsel U.S. Dept. Transp., Washington, 2001-03, acting dep. sec., 2003—04, dep. counsel. 2004. Mem.: Order of Coif, D.C. Bar Assn. (co-chair litig. and lawyer practice mgmt. sect., chair election bd.). Office: Baker Botts LLP 1299 Pennsylvania Ave NW Washington DC 20004 Office Phone: 202-639-7741. Business E-mail: kirk.vantine@bakerbotts.com.

**VAN TRAN, TAM,** painter; b. Kontum, Vietnam, 1966; arrived in Denver, 1975; BFA in Painting, Pratt Film Inst., 1990; grad. Film & TV Program, UCLA, 1996. One-man shows include Turkey Beaul, Dirt Gallery, LA, 1999, Cold Frost, Irvine Fine Arts Ctr., Calif., 2000, Susanne Vielmetter LA Projects, 2000, 2001, Beetle Manifesto, 2002, Project Room: Lover of Air, Cohan Leslie & Browne, NY, 2002, Vegetarian Summer, 2003, Cord of Hot Butter, Anthony Meier Fine Arts, San Francisco, 2003, Knoxville Mus. Art, Tenn., 2005, exhibited in group shows at Kassel Documenta Archiv, Ludwig Mus., Cologne, 1990, House of Styles, Tri Gallery, LA, 1995, Asian Am. Art Ctr., NY, 2000, Other Paintings, Huntington Beach Art Ctr., Calif., 1999, Pierogi 2000: Flat Files, Yerba Buena Ctr. Arts, San Francisco, 2000, Luminous, Ikon Fine Art, Santa Monica, Calif., 2000, Radar Love, Gallery

Marabini, Italy, 2000, Car Pooling from LA, Asian Am. Art Ctr., NY, 2000, New Work: LA Painting, Hosfelt Gallery, San Francisco, 2001, Black Dragon Soc., LA, 2001, Panorama, Room Interior Products, 2002, Cohan Leslie & Browne, NY, 2002, Drawing Biennial, Weatherspoon Art Gallery, NC, 2002, In the Making: Drawings from a Pvt. Collection, U. Mass. Amherst, 2003, Internat. Paper, UCLA Hammer Mus., 2003, Whitney Biennial, Whitney Mus. Am. Art, NY, 2004, Around About Abstraction, Weatherspoon Art Gallery, NC, 2005. Recipient Joan Mitchell Found. Award, 2001; Creative Fellowship Visual Arts, Colo. Coun. Arts & Humanities, 1991, Ucross Artists Residency, Ucross, Wyo., 1993, Pollock Krasner Fellowship, 2000. Mailing: c/o Cohan Leslie & Browne 138 Tenth Ave New York NY 10011

**VAN TYNE, ARTHUR MORRIS,** geologist; b. Syracuse, NY, Aug. 12, 1925; s. Roy Hanford and Isabelle Marguerite (Hoag) Van T.; m. Patricia Wilson Boyd, July 13, 1946; children: Judith, Cynthia, Mark, Peter. AB, Syracuse U., 1951, MS, 1958. Cert. petroleum geologist; lic. geologist, Pa., 1994. Field asst. Syracuse U. Rsch. Inst., 1951-53; geologist Shell Oil Co. Rockies, Gulf Coast, 1953-57; sr. geologist-in-charge NY State Geol. Survey-Oil and Gas Rsch. Office, Wellsville and Alfred, NY, 1958-81; geol. cons. Van Tyne Cons., Wellsville, NY, 1981—. Gov. appointee mem. NY State Oil, Gas, and Solution Mining Adv. Bd., 1996. Contbr. articles to profl. jours. Dep. mayor Village of Wellsville, 1992—2004; mem. Allegany County Econ. Devel. Com.; committeeman Rep. Party, 1962—77, 1998—2000; bd. dir. Jones Meml. Hosp., Wellsville, 1973—2001, bd. chmn., 1986—95; bd. dir. Wellsville United Way, 1968—80, pres., 1974—75; bd. mem. Drake Well Found. Recipient Cert. of Appreciation Am. Petroleum Inst., 1975, 80, Award of Merit Internat. Oil Scouts Assn. and Appalachian Sect., 1961, 66, 88. Mem.: Syracuse U. Geol. Devel. Coun., Geol. Soc. Am., No. Appalachian Geol. Soc. (pres. 1966—68), Ind. Oil and gas Assn. NY (pres. 1985—88), N.Y. State Oil Prodrs. Assn. (exec. com. 1980—, dir., Svc. award 1981, Oilman of Yr. award 2001), Russian Assn. Oil and Gas Geologists, Am. Assn. Petroleum Geologists (sec., dir. 1989—91, nat. and ea. sect. hon. mem., Nat. and Ea. Disting. Svc. award 1987, 1994, John T. Galey Meml. award ea. sect. 1997, Ho. of Dels. long svc. award 2001), N.Y. Acad. Sci., Rotary (pres. Wellsville 1979—80, Paul Harris fellow). Achievements include discovery of gas production from Queenston formation in NY; Bass Islands thrust structure, a major oil and gas producer in N.Y. and Pa.; contributed for N.Y. State to Appalachian Gas Atlas. Home: 24 Oak St Wellsville NY 14895-1026 Office: Van Tyne Cons PO Box 326 159 1/2 N Main St Wellsville NY 14895-0326 Office Phone: 585-593-6650. Personal E-mail: avantyne@yahoo.com.

**VAN UMMERSEN, CLAIRE A(NN),** academic administrator, biologist, educator; b. Chelsea, Mass., July 28, 1935; d. George and Catherine (Courtovich); m. Frank Van Ummersen, June 7, 1958; children: Lynn, Scott. BS, Tufts U., 1957, MS, 1960, PhD, 1963; DSc (hon.), U. Mass., 1988, U. Maine, 1991; LHD (hon.), U. New Eng., 2005. Rsch. assoc. Tufts U., 1957-60, 60-67, grad. asst. in embryology, 1962, postdoctoral tchg. asst., 1963-66, lectr. in biology, 1967-68; asst. prof. biology U. Mass., Boston, 1968-74, assoc. prof., 1974—86, assoc. dean acad. affairs, 1975-76, assoc. vice chancellor acad. affairs, 1976-78, chancellor, 1978-79, dir. Environ. Sci. Ctr., 1980-82; assoc. vice chancellor acad. affairs Mass. Bd. Regents for Higher Edn., 1982-85, vice chancellor for mgmt. systems and telecom., 1985-86; chancellor Univ. System NH, Durham, 1986-92; sr. fellow New Eng. Bd. Higher Edn., 1992-93; sr. fellow New Eng. Resource Ctr. Higher Edn. U. Mass., 1992-93; pres. Cleve. State U. 1993—2001, pres. emerita, 2004—; v.p., dir. Office of Women Am. Coun. Edn., Wash., DC, 2001—05, v.p. Ctr. for Effective Leadership, 2005—. Cons. Mass. Bd. Regents, 1981-82, AGB, 1992—, Kuwait U., 1992-93; asst. Lancaster Course in Ophthalmology, Mass. Eye. and Ear Infirmary, 1962-69, lectr., 1970-93, also coord.; reviewer HEW; mem. rsch. team which established safety stds. for exposure to microwave radiation, 1958-65; participant Leadership Am. program, 1992-93; bd. dirs. Nat. Coun. Sci. Environment, 1998—, mem. subcom. for future and fin. Active NH Ct. Systems Rev. Task Force, 1989-90, Leadership Cleve. Class '95, Ohio Gov.'s Coun. on Sci. and Tech., 1996-98, Strategy Coun. Cleve. Pub. Schs., 1996-98, Cleve. Sports Commn., 1996-2001, Cleve. Mcpl. Sch. Dist. Bd., 1999-2001; New Eng. Bd. Higher Edn., 1986-92, exec. com., 1989-92, NH adv. coun., 1990-92; chair Rhodes Scholarship Selection Com., 1986-91; bd. dirs. NH Bus. and Industry Assn., 1987-93; governing bd. NH Math. Coalition, 1991-92; exec. com. 21st Century Learning Cmty., 1992-93; state panelist NH Women in Higher Edn., 1986-93; bd. dirs. Urban League Greater Cleve., 1993-2001, strategic planning com., chair edn. com., 1996-99, sec., exec. com., 1997-99; bd. dirs. Great Lakes Sci. and Tech. Ctr., 1993-2001, edn. com., 1995-2001; bd. dirs. Greater Cleve. Growth Assn. 1994-2001, Civic Vision 2000 and Beyond, Cleve., 1997-98; bd. dirs., exec. com. Sci. and Tech. Coun. Cleve. Tomorrow, 1998-99; rep. NE Ohio Tech. Coalition, 1999-2001; trustee Ohio Aerospace Inst., 1993-2001, exec. com., 1996-2001; strategic planning com. United Way, 1996-2000, chair environ. scan subcom. 1996-2001; leadership devel. com. ACE, 1995-98, women's commn., 1999-2001; bd. dirs. United Way, 1995-2001; co-chair Pub. Sector Campaign, 1997-98; bd. dirs. NCAA, divsn. 1, exec. com., 1999-2001; mem. AGB Ctr. for Pub. Higher Edn. Trusteeship and Governance, 2001-03, Assn. Liaison Officers Adv. Com., 1998-2001. Recipient Disting. Svc. medal U. Mass., 1979, Woman of the Yr. Achievement award YWCA, 1998; Am. Cancer Soc. grantee Tufts U., 1960. Mem. Am. Coun. on Edn. (com. on self-regulation 1987-91), Nat. Conf. Cmty. and Justice (program com. 1996-2001), Nat. Coun. for Sci. and the Environment (bd. dirs. 1999-, fin. and futures coms.), State Higher Edn. Exec. Officers (fed. rels. com., 1986-92, cost accountability task force, exec. com. 1990-92), ACE (com. leadership devel.), Nat. Assn. Sys. Heads (exec. com. 1990-92), Nat. Ctr. for Edn. Stats. (network adv. com. 1989-92) New Eng. Assn. Schs. and Colls. (commn. on higher edn. 1990-93), North Ctrl. Assn. Schs. and Colls. (evaluation 1993-2001, chair accreditation teams 1986-90), Greater Cleve. Round Table (bd. dirs. 1993-2001, exec. com. 1995-2001), Cleve. Playhouse (trustee 1994-2001), Nat. Assn. State Univs. and Land Grant Colls. (exec. com. on urban agenda, mem. commn. tech. transfer), Am. Assn. State Colls. and Univs. (state rep. 1994-96, commn. on urban agenda 1996-2001, bd. dirs. 1996-99, mem. emerging issues task force 1996-98), Phi Beta Kappa, Sigma Xi. Office: American Coun on Edn One DuPont Cir NW Washington DC 20036-1193 Office Phone: 202-939-9376. Business E-Mail: claire_van_ummersen@ace.nche.edu.

**VAN VALER, JOE NED,** lawyer, real estate developer; b. Gas City, Ind., Mar. 13, 1935; s. Richard Carl and Wilma Amy (Kelly) Van V.; m. Constance Joy Richardson, June 25, 1960; children: Kimberly Joy, Kelli June, Lynn Louise, Joseph Jeffrey. AB, Franklin Coll., 1959; LLB, Ind. U., 1963. Bar: Ind. 1963, U.S. Dist. Ct. (so. dist.) Ind. 1963. Assoc. Van Valer Law Firm and predecessor firms, 1963-65, ptnr., 1965-75, sr. ptnr., 1975—. Pres. Home Owners Warranty Corp. of Central Ind., Indpls., 1984-91, chmn. bd. dirs. 1991-95; cons. bd. Nat. City Bank Greenwood; chmn. adv. group Home Owners Warranty Corp., Washington, 1989-90, 92-94 also bd. dirs.; pres. atty. 8th Jud. Dist., Franklin, Ind., 1967-74; chmn. Johnson County, Ind., Contractors' Listing Bd.; chmn. bd. Bldg. Industry Svc. Corp., 1995-2000. With AUS, 1957-58. Recipient Alumnus Citation award Franklin Coll., 1996. Mem. ABA, Indpls. Bar Assn., 8th Jud. Cir. Bar Assn., Nat. Assn. Home Builders (bd. dirs.), Ind. Home Builders Assn., Builders Assn. Greater Indpls. (dir.), Indpls. Soc. Republican Methodist. Office: Van Valer Law Firm 299 W Main St Greenwood IN 46142-3129 Office Phone: 317-881-7575. Business E-Mail: joe@vanvalerlaw.com.

**VAN VALKENBURG, EDGAR WALTER,** lawyer; b. Seattle, Jan. 8, 1953; s. Edgar Walter and Margaret Catherine (McKenna) Van V.; m. Turid L. Owren, Sept. 29, 1990; children: Ingrid Catherine, Andrew Owren. BA, U. Wash., 1975; JD summa cum laude, Willamette Coll. of Law, 1978; LLM, Columbia U., 1984. Bar: Oreg. 1978, U.S. Dist. Ct. Oreg. 1979, U.S. Ct. Appeals (9th cir.) 1980. Law clk. to assoc. justice Oreg. Supreme Ct., Salem, 1978-79; assoc. Stoel, Rives, Boley, Fraser & Wyse, Portland, Oreg., 1979-82, 84-86; ptnr. Stoel Rives LLP, Portland, Oreg., 1986—; instr. Columbia U., N.Y.C., 1983-84. Bd. dirs. Oreg. Sports Authority; chair Oreg. Econ. and Cmty. Devel. Commn., 2003—. Editor-in-chief: Williamette Law

Jour. 1977-78. Bd. dirs., chmn. Multnomah County Legal Aid, 1997-98; bd. dirs. Portland Ctr. Stage, 2004—. Mem. ACLU (pres. Oreg. chpt. 1991-93), Oreg. State Bar (chmn. antitrust sect. 1989-90, mem. Ho. of Dels. 1996-98). Office: Stoel Rives LLP 900 SW 5th Ave Ste 2300 Portland OR 97204-1229 E-mail: wvanvalkenburg@stoel.com.

**VAN VLEET, WILLIAM BENJAMIN,** lawyer, retired insurance company executive; b. Milw., Dec. 4, 1924; s. William Benjamin and Irene (Peppey) Van V.; m. Marilyn Nilles, Dec. 26, 1946; children: Terese Van Vleet Svetich, Susan Van Vleet Waldo, William Benjamin III, Monica Van Vleet McCarthy, Mark. Student, Marquette U., 1942-43, Lawrence Coll., Appleton, Wis., 1943-44; LLB, JD, Marquette U., 1948. Bar: Wis. 1948, Ill. 1950. Gen. counsel George Rogers Clark Mut. Casualty Co., Rockford, Ill., 1948-59, Pioneer Life Ins. Co. Ill., Rockford, 1950-68, 81-94, v.p., 1959-91, gen. counsel, 1968-91, exec. v.p., 1981-95, also bd. dirs.; exec. v.p., gen. counsel Pioneer Fin. Svcs., Inc., Rockford, 1993-95, gen. counsel emeritus, dir., 1995-97; pres. Nat. Group Life Ins. Co., Rockford, 1992-93, exec. v.p., gen. counsel, 1993-94, also bd. dirs. Pres. Western Life Ins. Co. Am., Rockford, 1981-82, Health & Life Ins. Co. Am., Rockford, 1984-92, exec. v.p., gen. counsel, 1993-94; pres. Manhattan Nat. Life Ins. Co., Cin., 1990-92, exec. v.p., gen. counsel, 1993-94, also bd. dirs.; exec. v.p., gen. counsel Continental Life and Accident Co., Boise, Idano, 1993-94, also bd. dirs.; bd. dirs. Nat. Health Svcs. Milw. Mem. adminstrn. Boylan Cath. Cath. H.S., Rockford, 1965-72; pres. Diocesan Bd. Edn., Rockford, 1970-78; v.p., pres. Nat. Assn. Bds. Edn., 1972-78; mem. bd. advisors Marion Coll., 1976-79; mem. adv. bd. St. Anthony's Hosp., Rockford, 1978-91; bd. dirs. Crimestoppers, Rockford, 1982-90; co-chmn. United Cerebral Palsy Telethon, Rockford, 1985-95. Mem. Ill. Bar Assn., Winnebago County Bar Assn.

**VAN VLIET, CAROLYN MARINA,** physicist, researcher; b. Dordrecht, Netherlands, Dec. 27, 1929; arrived in U.S., 1960, naturalized, 1967; d. Marinus and Jacoba (de Lange) Van V.; m. A.J. Cappon, Dec. 29, 1953 (div. 1983); children: Elsa Marianne, Mark Edward, Cynthia Joyce, Renata Annette Carolina. BS, Free U. Amsterdam, Netherlands, 1949, MA, 1953, PhD in Physics, 1956. Rsch. fellow Free U. Amsterdam, 1950-54, rsch. assoc., 1954-56, asst. dir., 1958-60; postdoctoral fellow U. Minn., Mpls., 1956-57, faculty, 1957-58, 60-70, prof. elec. engring. and physics, 1965-70; prof. theoretical physics U. Montreal, Que., Can., 1969-95, sr. rschr. math. rsch. ctr. Que., 1969-2000, prof. emerita, 1998—. Vis. prof. U. Fla., 1974, 78-88; prof. elec. and computer engring. Fla. Internat. U., 1992-2000; adj. prof. physics U. Miami, 2001—. Contbg. author: Fluctuation Phenomena in Solids, 1965; contbr. articles to profl. jours. Rsch. grantee, NSF, Air Force OSR, Nat. Sci. and Engring. Rsch. Coun., Ottawa. Fellow IEEE (life); mem. Am. Phys. Soc., NY Acad. Scis. Office: U Miami James L Knight Physics Bldg 1320 Campo Sano Dr Coral Gables FL 33146 Office Phone: 305-284-2325. Business E-Mail: vanvliet@physics.miami.edu. *The purpose of life is to honor God and to serve mankind.*

**VAN VLIET, CLAIRE,** artist; b. Ottawa, Ont., Can., Aug. 9, 1933; d. Wilbur Dennison and Audrey Ilene (Wallace) Van Vliet. AB, San Diego State Coll., 1952; MFA, Claremont Grad. Sch., 1954; DFA (hon.), U. of the Arts, Phila., 1993, San Diego State U., 2002. Instr. printmaking Phila. Coll. Art, 1959-65; owner The Janus Press, 1954—; vis. lectr. printmaking U. Wis.-Madison, 1965-66. Mem. bd. advisors Hand Papermaking. One-man exhbns. include Print Club Phila., 1963, 66, 73, 77, Wiggin Gallery, Boston Pub. Libr., 1977, Rutgers U. Art Gallery, 1978, AAA Gallery, Phila., 1980, Dolan/Maxwell Gallery, Phila., 1984, 91, Mary Ryan Gallery, NYC, 1986, Mills Coll., 1986, U. of the Arts, Phila., 1989, Victoria and Albert Mus., London, 1994, Ottawa Sch. of Art Gallery, Can., 1994, Bates Coll. Mus. of Art, Lewiston, Maine, 1994, 99, ND Mus. Art, 1999, Rosenwald Wolf Gallery U. Arts. Phila, 2001, Grolier Club, NY, 2006, Nat. Gallery Art Libr., 2006, Humanities Gallery, Scripps Coll., 2006; group exhbns. include Bklyn. Nat., Phila. Arts Festival, Kunst zu Kafka, Germany, Paper as Medium, Smithsonian Instn., Washington, Paper Now, Cleve. Mus. Art, 1986, Boyle Arts Festival, Ireland, 1993, Libr. Congress, 1997—, ND Mus. Art, 1999; represented in permanent collections Nat. Gallery Art, Phila. Mus. Art, Boston Pub. Libr., Libr. of Congress, Cleve. Mus. Art, Montreal Mus. Fine Arts, Victoria and Albert Mus. London, Tate Gallery, London, US Dept. of State, Nat. Libr. Canada, British Libr. Grantee, Ingram-Merrill Found., 1989; NEA grantee, 1976—80, MacArthur fellow, 1989—94. Mem.: Nat. Acad., Soc. Printers Boston, Vt. Arts and Scis. Home and Office: 101 Schoolhouse Rd West Burke VT 05871-9773 Office Phone: 802-467-3335.

**VAN VOORST, CAROL,** ambassador; BA, Hope Coll.; MA, Nat. War Coll. 1998; MA, PhD, Princeton U. Tchr. City U. NY; spl. asst. to dep. sec. US Dept. State, 1984—85, Norway/Denmark desk officer, 1989—91, spl. asst. to under sec. polit. affairs, 1991—92, assigned to Panama, 1992—95, dir. Office Nordic & Baltic Affairs, 1995—97, chief polit. dept. to dep. high rep. office of high rep. Sarajevo, 1998—99; dep. chief of mission Am. Embassy, Helsinki, 1999—2002; dir. Austrian, German, Swiss affairs, Bur. European and Eurasian Affairs US Dept. State, 2002—04, US. amb. to Iceland Reykjavik, 2005—. Office: Am Embassy 5640 Reykjavik Pl Washington DC 20521*

**VAN VOORST, ROBERT E.,** theology educator, minister; b. Holland, Mich, June 5, 1952; s. Robert Eugene and Donna Mae (Boeve) Van V.; m. Mary Lind Bos, June 15, 1974; children: Richard William, Nicholas John. BA, Hope Coll., 1974; MDiv, Western Sem., 1977; PhD, Union Sem., N.Y., 1988. Ordained to ministry Classis of Holland Reformed Ch. in Am., 1977. Pastor Rochester Reformed Ch., Accord, NY, 1977-89; prof. religion Lycoming Coll., Williamsport, Pa., 1989-99, dept. chair, 1997-99; prof. New Testament Western Theol. 9em., Holland, Mich., 1999 . Adj. prof. Susquehanna U., Selinsgrove, Pa., 1991, Bucknell U., Lewisburg, Pa., 1993; vis. prof. Westminster Coll., Oxford, Eng., 1997; N.T. seminar lectr. Oxford U., 2000; interim pastor Lycoming Presbyn. Ch., Williamsport, 1997-99. Author: Ascents of James, 1989; Building New Testament Vocabulary, 1990, 3d edit., 2001, Anthology of World Scriptures, 1994, 5th edit., 2005, Readings in Christianity, 1996, 2d edit., 2000, Anthology of Asian Scriptures, 1999, Jesus Outside the New Testament, 2000, Italian edit., 2004, Reading the New Testament Today, 2004, Anthology of World Scriptures: Eastern Religions, 2006, Anthology of World Scriptures: Western Religions, 2006; co-author: Death of Jesus in Early Christianity, 1998, Pastor's Bible Study, 2006; editor Reformed Rev., 2000—; contbr. articles Eerdmans Dictionary of the Bible, 2001, Ency. of Jesus in History, Culture and Thought, 2003, Eerdmans Bible Commentary, 2003, Pastors Bible Study, vol. 3, 2006; contbr. articles to profl. jours. Mem. Phi Beta Kappa, Phi Kappa Phi, Phi Sigma Iota. Avocations: golf, cooking. Home: 1114 Post Ave Holland MI 49424-2550 Office: Western Theol Sem 101 E 13th St Holland MI 49423-3622 Business E-Mail: bob.vanvoorst@westernsem.edu.

**VAN VUGT, ERIC J.,** lawyer; b. Grand Rapids, Mich., Sept. 17, 1951; s. Ernest and Phyllis N. (Van Someren) Van Vugt; m. Wendy S. Yonker, June 3, 1972; children: Erin L., Heather J., Timothy D. BA, Calvin Coll., 1973; JD, Marquette Univ., 1976. Bar: Wis. 1976, U.S. Dist. Ct. (ea. and we. dist. Wis., ea. & we. dist. Mich., Ariz., no. dist. Ill.). Fed. Trial Bar, U.S. Ct. Appeals (3d, 6th, 7th, 9th, Fed. cir.), U.S. Supreme Ct. 1994. Assoc. Kluwin, Dunphy & Hankin, Milw., 1976-80; ptnr. Kluwin, Dunphy, Hankin & McNulty, Milw., 1980-85, Minahan & Peterson, Milw., 1985-91; ptnr., litig. practice Quarles & Brady, Milw., 1991—. Fellow Am. Coll. Trial Lawyers; mem. ABA, State Bar Wis., Milw. Bar Assn. Avocations: aviation, golf. Office: Quarles & Brady Ste 2040 411 E Wisconsin Ave Milwaukee WI 53202-4497 Office Phone: 414-277-5625. Office Fax: 414-978-8625. Business E-Mail: ejv@quarles.com.

**VAN WACHEM, LODEWIJK CHRISTIAAN,** petroleum company executive; b. Pangkalan Brandan, Indonesia, July 31, 1931; m. Elisabeth G. Cristofoli, June 10, 1958; 3 children. Degree Mech. Engring., Delft U., Delft, The Netherlands, 1953. With Bataafsche Petroleum Maatschappij, The Hague, The Netherlands, 1953; pres. Royal Dutch Petroleum Co., The Hague, The Netherlands, 1982-92; chmn. com., mng. dir. Royal Dutch/Shell Group,

The Hague, Netherlands, 1985—92; chmn. supr. bd. Royal Dutch Petroleum Co., The Hague, Netherlands, 1992—2002, with Rotterdam, Netherlands, 2002—. Chmn. bd. dirs. Zurich Fin. Svcs., 2002—05, Global Crossing Ltd.; supervisory bd. De Nederlandsche Bank N.V., 1987—92, AKZO Nobel n.v., Arnhem, 1992—2002, BMW A.G., Munich, 1994—2002, Bayer A.G., Leverkusen, 1997—2002; non. exec. dir. IBM Corp., Armonk, 1992—2002, AAB Area Brown Boveri Ltd, Zurich, 1996—99; chmn. supervisory bd. Philips Electronics n.v., Amsterdam, 1993—2005; bd. dirs. Atco Ltd., Calgary. Decorated comdr. Brit. Empire, knight Brit. Empire (Eng.), comdr. Order of Oranje Nassau, knight Order Netherlands Lion (Netherlands). Office: Nedlloyd Holding BV PO Box 487 NL-3000 AL Rotterdam Netherlands Office Phone: +31 10 4006810.

**VAN WAGENEN, PAUL G.,** gas industry executive; BA, Brigham Young Univ., 1970; JD, Univ. Washington, 1973. With Exxon Corp.; mgmt. positions with Pogo Producing, 1979—90, pres., 1990—91, chmn., pres., CEO, 1991—. Dir. Domestic Petroleum Council; mem. exec. com. U.S. Oil & Gas Assn. Mem. Greater Houston Round Table, Greater Houston Partnership; mem. exec. com. Greater Houston YMCA. Mem.: Ctr. Strategic and Internat. Studies-Houston Roundtable, Royalty Owners Assn., Texas Independent Producers, Nat. Ocean Industries Assn. (exec. com., bd. dir.), Nat. Petroleum Coun., All-American Wildcatters. Office: Po Box 2504 Ste 2700 5 Greenway Plz Houston TX 77252-2504 Office Phone: 713-297-5000.*

**VAN WIE, PAUL DAVID,** secondary school educator, historian; b. Manhasset, N.Y., Sept. 29, 1956; s. Joseph Paul and Florence Elizabeth (Wagner) van W.; m. Ellen Mary van Wie, June 25, 1983; children: Mary Ellen, Elisabeth, Paul David, Joseph. BA, C.W. Post Coll., 1978, MA, 1987; PhD, CUNY, 1989. Cert. secondary edn. Tchr. Spackenkill High Sch., Poughkeepsie, N.Y., 1981-82, Schreiber High Sch., Port Washington, N.Y., 1982-84, Wheatley Sch., Old Westbury, N.Y., 1984—; adj. prof. N.Y. Inst. Tech., Old Westbury, 1987-92, Hofstra U., Hempstead, N.Y., 1992—. Mem. dean's adv. com. L.I. U., Old Brookville, N.Y., 1992-96. Author: The Way it Was, 1994, Image, History and Politics, 1998. Historian Village of Franklin Square, N.Y., 1979—, libr. trustee, 1989—; landmarks commr. Town of Hempstead, 1989—; pres. Franklin Square Hist. Soc.; v.p. Franklin Square Cmty. League, 1990-96. Nat. Humanities fellow U.S. Govt., 1988, Fulbright scholar U.S. Govt., 1990, Coun. Basic Edn. fellow, 1996; recipient Leadership award Nat. Soc. Daughters of Am. Revolution, 1982, N.Y. State Tchr. of Yr. award N.Y. Dept. Edn., 1992. Mem. Am. Hist. Assn., L.I. Coun. Social Studies, Franklin Square Hist. Soc. (pres.). Office: The Wheatley Sch 11 Bacon Rd Old Westbury NY 11568-1502

**VAN WINKLE, DANNY L.,** lawyer; b. Houston, Feb. 20, 1947; BC, Rice U., 1969; JD with honors, U. Tex., 1972. Bar: Tex. 1972. Ptnr. Vinson & Elkins, L.L.P., Houston; of counsel Tekell, Book, Matthews & Limmer, LLP, Houston, 1995—. Mem.: Am. Bd. Trial Advocates, Fed. Bar Assn., State Bar Tex., Phi Delta Phi. Office: Tekell Book Matthews & Limmer LLP 1 Houston Ctr 1221 McKinney Ste 4300 Houston TX 77010-2015 Office Phone: 713-222-9542. Office Fax: 713-655-7727.

**VAN WINKLE, EDGAR WALLING,** retired electrical engineer; b. Rutherford, NJ, Oct. 12, 1913; s. Winant and Jessie Walcott (Mucklow) Van W.; m. Jessie Stetler, Apr. 23, 1938 (dec. July 1992); children: Barbara Van Winkle Clifton (dec. Mar. 2000), Catrina Van Winkle Poindexter, Cornelia Van Winkle Schloss; m. Martha Polyé, May 22, 1993. BEE, Rutgers U., 1936; MS in Indsl. Engring., Columbia U., 1943, PE in Indsl. Engring., 1966. Registered profl. engr., N.J. Elec. engr. A.B. Dumont Labs., Passaic, NJ, 1943-48; chief engr. Facsimile Electronics, 1948-52; cons. Bur. Ships, Washington, 1952; asst. sr. staff scientist Bendix Corp., Teterboro, NJ, 1952-67; sr. staff scientist Conrac Corp., West Caldwell, 1967-78; pres. Empac, Inc., Rutherford, 1979-2001; ret., 2001. Contbr. articles to profl. jours.; patentee in field. Ruling elder Presbyterian Ch. Rutherford, 1984-91, chmn. endowment com., 1984—. Mem. IEEE (life, treas. artificial intelligence sect. North N.J. Chpt. 1982-84), Bendix Mgmt. Club (life), North N.J. Automatic Control Group (chmn. 1967-68), Met. Engring. Mgmt. (chmn. 1966-67), Mensa, Holland Soc., Green Pond Yacht Club (past commodore), Upper Montclair Country Club, Delta Phi. Republican. Achievements include research in artificial intelligence, mathematical software. Home (Summer): 154 Lake End Rd Newfoundland NJ 07435-1207 Personal E-mail: empacem@aol.com.

**VAN WINKLE, HANS A.,** military officer; m. Debra Van Winkle; 4 children. BS, U.S. Mil. Acad., 1971; MS in Pub. Policy, U. Calif., Berkeley, 1976. Registered profl. engr., Va., 1980. Commd. C.E. U.S. Army, 1971, advanced through grades to maj. gen., 1999; comdr. Co. A, 10th Combat Engr. Bn., 3d Inf. Divsn. U.S. Army Europe, Germany, 1977—79, comdr. 10th Combat Engr. Bn., 3d Inf. Divsn.; asst. prof. econs. U.S. Mil. Acad., West Point, NY, 1979—82; exchange officer Royal Sch. Mil. Engring., England, 1983—85; exec. officer 82d Engr. Bn. U.S. Army Europe, Germany, 1985—87, ops. officer 7th Engr. Brigade, 1987—89; comdr. 8th Engr. Bn.; 1st Cavalry Divsn. U.S. Army, Ft. Hood, Tex., 1989—91, comdr. Divsn. Engr. Brigade, 4th Inf. Divsn. Ft. Carson, Colo., 1992—94; dir. eng. U.S. Army Engr. Sch., Ft. Leonard Wood, Mo., 1994—95; dep. chief of staff, engr. U.S. Army Europe and 7th Army, Heidelberg, Germany, 1995—97; comdr., divsn. engr. Great Lakes and Ohio River Divsn. U.S. Army C.E., Cin. and Chgo., 1997—99, dep. commanding gen. Washington, 1999—2003. Decorated Legion of Merit, Bronze Star medal, Army Commendation medal (3), Meritorious Svc. medal (3), many others.

**VANWOERKOM, JACK A.,** lawyer, retail executive; m. Barbara L. Moore; 1 child, Carolyn. BS, MIT, 1975; JD cum laude, Boston U., 1978. Atty. Hale and Door LLP, Boston, 1978—85; with Winthrop Fin. Associates, Boston, 1985—94, gen. counsel, COO, vice chmn., mng. dir. Asian ops., 1993—94; chief legal counsel, v.p. devel., mng. dir. Europe A.W. Chesterton Co., 1994—97; gen. counsel Teradyne, Inc., 1998—99; sr. v.p., gen. counsel, sec. Staples, Inc., Framingham, Mass., 1999—2003, exec. v.p., gen. counsel, sec., 2003—. Office: Staples Inc 500 Staples Dr Framingham MA 01702

**VAN WYCK, GEORGE RICHARD,** insurance company executive; b. Wilmington, Vt., Feb. 6, 1928; s. Harold Wait Van Wyck and Ruth Anna Learnard; m. Jeanne Mildred Anderson, Apr. 17, 1948; children: Diana Lee Van Wyck Jenkins, Beryl Jeanne. BS in Math. cum laude, St. Lawrence U., 1953. Actuarial clk. Aetna Life Ins. Co., Hartford, Conn., 1953-55; with Am. Bankers Ins. Group, Miami, Fla., 1955-91, sec., bd. dirs., 1983-89, ret., 1991. Bd. dirs. Jr. Achievement of Greater Miami, 1966-83, pres., 1975-76; bd. dirs. Epworth Village Retirement Complex, Miami, 1966-2000, v.p., 1998-99, chmn. investment com. 1995-99; founding dir., pres. Brickel Children's Ctr., Miami, 1980-82; mem. pers. adv. bd., vice chmn. Dade County, Miami, 1987-89. With USAF, 1946-49. Fellow Life Office Mgmt. Inst.; mem. 1st United Meth. Ch. So. Miami, Phi Beta Kappa. Democrat. Methodist. Avocations: photography, golf, bridge, writing. Home: 8455 SW 44th St Miami FL 33155-4126 Personal E-mail: gvanwyck@cs.com.

**VAN WYLEN, GORDON JOHN,** former college president; b. Grant, Mich., Feb. 6, 1920; s. John and Effa (Bierema) Van W.; m. Margaret E. DeWitt, Dec. 29, 1951; children— Elizabeth Ann Van Wylen Rudenga, Stephen John, Ruth Margaret Van Wylen Jasperse, David Gordon, Emily Jane Van Wylen Overway. AB, Calvin Coll., 1942; BSE., U. Mich., 1942, MS, 1947; Sc.D., MIT, 1951. Indsl. engr. duPont Co., 1942-43; instr. mech. engring. Pa. State U., 1946-48; asst. prof. mech. engring. U. Mich., 1951-55, assoc. prof., 1955-57, prof., 1957-72, chmn. dept., 1958-65, dean Coll. Engring., 1965-72; pres. Hope Coll., Holland, Mich., 1972-87, pres. emeritus, 1987—. Author: Thermodynamics, 1959; author (with R.E. Sonntag) Fundamentals of Classical Thermodynamics, 1965; author: 6th edit., 2003, Fundamentals of Statistical Thermodynamics, 1966, Introduction to Thermodynamics, 1971, 3d edit., 1991, Encounter at Sea, 1994; contbr. articles to profl. jours. Trustee

Van Andel Edn. Inst. Lt. USNR, 1943-46. Fellow ASME, AAAS; mem. Phi Beta Kappa (hon.), Sigma Xi, Tau Beta Pi, Phi Kappa Phi. Mem. Reform Ch. Am. Home: Apt 600 145 Columbia Ave Holland MI 49423-2980

**VANYO, BRUCE GORDON,** lawyer; b. Cleve., Dec. 4, 1945; BS summa cum laude, Miami U., 1967; JD, Columbia U., 1972. Bar: Calif. 1974. Law clk. to Hon. William Timbers US Ct. Appeals (2nd cir.), 1972-73; ptnr. McCutcheon, Doyle, Brown & Enersen, 1979—84, Wilson, Sonsini, Goodrich & Rosati, Palo Alto, Calif., 1984—2006, co-chair litigation group, 1984—96; ptnr. Kirkland & Ellis LLP, LA, 2006, Katten Muchin Rosenman LLP, LA, 2006—, co-chair securities litig. practice. Prof. securities regulation Hastings Coll. Law, 1983-86; chmn. recent devels. in securities litigation, PLI, 1984-85; chmn. securities litigation prosecution and def. strategies, PLI, 1985, 86, 87; panelist ALI-ABA patent litigation avoidance and successful resolution, 1986. Mng. editor Columbia Law Rev., 1971-72. Mem. ABA (litigation sect., securities litigation com., corp. counsel com. 1981—), State Bar Calif. (chair administrn. of justice com. 1985-86), Bar Assn. San Francisco, Order of Coif. Office: Katten Muchin Rosenman LLP 2029 Century Pk E Ste 2600 Los Angeles CA 90067 E-mail: bruce.vanyo@kattenlaw.com.*

**VAN ZANDT, DAVID E.,** dean, law educator; b. Princeton, NJ, Feb. 17, 1953; m. Lisa A. Huestis; children: Caroline, Nicholas. AB summa cum laude, Princeton U., 1975; JD, Yale U., 1981; PhD in Sociology, U. London, 1985. Bar: Ill. Clk. to Hon. Pierre N. Leval U.S. Dist. Ct. (so. dist.) N.Y., 1981-82; clk. to Hon. Harry A. Blackmun U.S. Supreme Ct., Washington, 1982-83; atty. Davis, Polk & Wardwell, 1984-85; mem. faculty Northwestern U. Law Sch., Chgo., 1985—, dean, 1995—. Mem. planning com. Northwestern U. Corporate Counsel Inst., Northwestern U. Corp. Counsel Ctr. Author: Living in the Children of God, 1991; mng. editor Yale Law Jour., 1980-81; contbr. articles to profl. jours. Named Calif. Educator of Yr. Calif. State Dept. of Edn./Milken Found., 1989, Blue Ribbon Sch., U.S. Dept. of Edn., 1994; recipient Educator's award Freedom's Found., 1990. Mem. Nat. Assn. Elem. Sch. Prins. (bd. dirs., state leader, Disting. Prin. award 1988), Calif. Alliance for Edn. (coord.), Assn. Calif. Sch. Administrs. (chair elem. adminstrn.), Poway Assn. Sch. Mgrs. (pres. 1982), San Diego/Imperial County Adminstrs. (pres. 1993-94), Delta Kappa Gamma (pres. 1990-92). Baptist. Home: 16204 Quail Rock Rd Ramona CA 92065-7214 E-mail: suvanzant@aol.com.

**VAN ZANDT, STEVEN,** actor, musician, radio personality; b. Winthrop, Mass., Nov. 22, 1950; m. Maureen Santoro. Guitarist E-Street Band, 1975—84, 1999—; host/D.J. Little Steven's Underground Garage, Syndicated Radio, 2002—. Actor: (TV series) The Soprano's, 1999—; musician, composer: albums Men Without Women, 1982, Voices of America, 1984, Sun City, 1985, Freedom - No Compromise, 1987, Revolution, 1989, Born Again Savage, 1999. Office: c/o The Endeavor Agy 10th Fl 9601 Wilshire Blvd Beverly Hills CA 90212

**VAN ZANT, SUSAN LUCILLE,** principal; b. Torrance, Calif., Apr. 29, 1942; d. Paul McHenry and Lucille Eileen (McQuarrie) Mansfield; m. Jerry Brian Van Zant, Oct. 27, 1960; children: Steven Brian, Karen Daphne Van Zant Hosaka. BA in History and Social Sci., Calif. State U., Long Beach, 1966; MA in Curriculum, No. Ariz. U., 1974; EdD in Adminstrn., U.S. Internat. U., 1982. Cert. elem. tchr., kindergarten and secondary sch. adminstr., Calif. Tchr. Borrego Springs (Calif.) Unified Sch., 1967-69, Poway (Calif.) Unified Sch. Dist., 1969-76, prin., 1976—. Instr. community rels., sch. adminstr. law and fin. Nat. U., San Diego, 1987-92; prof. ednl. leadership Aliant U. Author: (with others) The Principal as Chief Executive, 1991; contbr. articles to profl. jours. Named Calif. Educator of Yr. Calif. State Dept. of Edn./Milken Found., 1989, Blue Ribbon Sch., U.S. Dept. of Edn., 1994; recipient Educator's award Freedom's Found., 1990. Mem. Nat. Assn. Elem. Sch. Prins. (bd. dirs., state leader, Disting. Prin. award 1988), Calif. Alliance for Edn. (coord.), Assn. Calif. Sch. Administrs. (chair elem. adminstrn.), Poway Assn. Sch. Mgrs. (pres. 1982), San Diego/Imperial County Adminstrs. (pres. 1993-94), Delta Kappa Gamma (pres. 1990-92). Baptist. Home: 16204 Quail Rock Rd Ramona CA 92065-7214 E-mail: suvanzant@aol.com.

**VAN ZANTE, SHIRLEY M(AE),** magazine editor; b. Elma, Iowa; d. Vernon E. and Georgene (Woodmansee) Borland; m. Dirk C. Van Zante. AA, Grandview Coll., 1950; BA, Drake U., 1952. Assoc. editor Mchts. Trade Jour., Des Moines, 1952-55; copywriter Meredith Pub. Co., Des Moines, 1955-60, book editor, 1960-67; home furnishings editor Better Homes and Gardens Spl. Interest Publs., Meredith Corp., 1967-74; home furnishing and design editor Better Homes and Gardens mag., 1974-89; writer, editl. cons., 1989-98. Named Advt. Woman of Yr. in Des Moines, 1961; recipient Dorothy Dawe award, 1971, 73, 75, 76, 77, Dallas Market Ctr. award, 1983, So. Furniture Market Writer's award, 1984. Mem. Alpha Xi Delta. Address: 1905 74th St Des Moines IA 50322-5701

**VAN ZANTEN, DAVID THEODORE,** humanities educator; b. Aug. 31, 1943; BA, Princeton U., 1965; MA, Harvard U., 1966, PhD, 1970. Asst. prof. McGill U., Montreal, 1970-71; from asst. to assoc. prof. U. Pa., Phila., 1971-79; from assoc. prof. to prof. Northwestern U., Evanston, Ill., 1979—. Office: Northwestern Univ 3-400 Kresge Hall Evanston IL 60208-2208 Office Phone: 847-491-8024. Business E-Mail: d-van@northwestern.edu.

**VAN ZANTEN, FRANK VELDHUYZEN,** library director; b. Heemstede, The Netherlands, Oct. 21, 1932; came to U.S., 1946, naturalized, 1953; s. Adrian V. and Cornelia (Van Eesteren) Van Z.; m. Lois Ruth Holkeboer, June 17, 1961; children— Kiki Maria, Lili Roxanne, Amy Suzanne. AB, Calvin Coll., Mich., 1959; postgrad., U. Wash., 1960; MA in L.S., U. Mich., 1961. Cataloger, extension project asst. Mich. State Library, Lansing, 1961-62; dir. Dickinson County (Mich.) Library, 1962-65, Mid-Peninsula Library Fedn., Iron Mountain, Mich., 1963-65, St. Clair County (Mich.) Library, 1965-68, Tucson Pub. Library, 1968-73; library cons. Ill. State Library, Springfield, 1973-75, asso. dir. for library devel., 1975-78; dir. Mid-Hudson Library System, Poughkeepsie, N.Y., 1978-95; ret., 1995. Home: Served with AUS, 1953-55. Mem. ALA, N.Y. Libr. Assn. Home: 138 Wilbur Blvd Poughkeepsie NY 12603-4635 Personal E-mail: FVZcolors@aol.com.

**VAN ZELST, THEODORE WILLIAM,** civil engineer, engineering company executive; b. Chgo., May 11, 1923; s. Theodore Walter and Wilhelmina (Oomens) Van Z.; m. Luann Hurter, Dec. 29, 1951; children: Anne, Jean, David. BS, U. Calif., Berkeley, 1944; BS in Naval Sci., Northwestern U., 1944, BAS., 1945, MS in Civil Engrng., 1948. Registered profl. engr., Ill. Pres., Soil Testing Services, Inc., Chgo., 1948-52; pres. Soiltest, Inc., Chgo., 1948-78, chmn. bd., 1978-80; sec., dir. Exploration Data Cons., Inc., 1980-82; exec. v.p. Cenco Inc., Chgo., 1962-77, vice chmn., 1975-77, also dir., 1962-77. Bd. dirs. Minann, Inc., Testing Sci., Inc., Van Zelst, Inc., chmn. bd. dirs. Envirotech Svcs., Inc., 1983-85; sec., bd. dirs. Van Zelst, Inc. Wadsworth, Ill., 1983—; pres. Geneva-Pacific Corp., 1969-83, Geneva Resources, Inc., 1983-91. Treas. Internat. Road Fedn., 1961-64, sec., 1964-79, dir., 1973-88, vice chmn., 1980-87; pres. Internat. Road Edn. Found., 1978-80, 87-88, hon. life bd. dirs., 1988—; bd. dirs. Chgo. Acad. Scis., 1983-86, v.p., 1985-86, hon. dir., 1986—; bd. dirs. Pres.'s Assn. Chgo., 1985-86, Friends of Mitchell Mus., 2003-2004; Asian art coun. Art Inst. Chgo., 2004—. Lt. j.g. USNR, 1944—46. Recipient Service award Northwestern U., 1970, Merit award, 1974, Alumni medal, 1989, Svc. award U. Wis., 1971, La Sallian award, 1975; named Disting. Engring. Alumnus, U. Calif., Berkeley, 2002. Mem. ASCE (Chgo. Civil Engr. of Yr., 1988), Nat. Soc. Profl. Engrs., Western Soc. Engrs., Evanston C. of C. (v.p. 1969-73), Ovid Esbach Soc. (pres. 1968-80), Northwestern U. Alumni Assn., Tau Beta Pi, Sigma Xi. Clubs: Economic, North Shore. Achievements include invention of engring. testing equipment for soil, rock, concrete and asphalt; co-invention of Swing-wing for supersonic aircraft. Home: 1213 Wagner Rd Glenview IL 60025-3297 Office: PO Box 582 Glenview IL 60025-0582 Personal E-mail: tvz@earthlink.net.

**VANZURA, LIZ (ELIZABETH K. VANZURA),** automotive executive; b. May 1964; m. Rick Vanzura; children: Danielle, Jacqueline. BS, GMI Engring. and Mgmt. Inst.; MBA, Harvard U. With GM Corp., 1994—96, global dir. mktg. Hummer, 2001—06, mktg. dir. Cadillac, 2006—; dir. mktg. Volkswagen of Am., 1995—2000. Exec. bd. mem. Internat. Automotive Advt. Awards. Named Marketer of Yr., Advertising Age, 1998; named one of Top

100 Mktg. Profls., 1999; recipient Top Women to Watch Award, 2001, All Star award, Automotive News, 1999, 2000. Office: GM 300 Renaissance Ctr Detroit MI 48265-3000 Office Phone: 313-556-5000. Office Fax: 313-556-5108.*

**VAPIWALA, NEHA,** radiation oncologist; BA, Johns Hopkins U., Balt. 1996; MD, U. Pa., Phila., 1997—2001. Chief resident dept. radiation oncology U. Pa., Phila., 2004—06, asst. prof., 2006—, asst. tng. program dir., 2006—. Sr. editor OncoLink Abramson Cancer Ctr. U. Pa., Phila., 2005—. Recipient Pharmacology award, U. Pa., 2001; Twenty-First Century scholar, U. Pa. Sch. Medicine, 1997—2001. Mem.: Am. Coll. Radiology, Am. Soc. Therapeutic Radiology and Oncology, Am. Soc. Clin. Oncology, Phi Beta Kappa, Alpha Omega Alpha. Office Phone: 215-662-2428.

**VAPORCIYAN, ARA ASADUR,** thoracic surgeon, educator; b. Detroit, Aug. 12, 1964; s. Harry and Nadya Vaporciyan; m. Phillipa Sheffer, July 6, 2002; children: Alexander, Madison Sheffer, Ashton. BS, MD, U. Mich., Ann Arbor. Lic. Tex., 1989. Asst. prof. surgery U. T. M. D. Anderson Cancer Ctr., Houston, 1998—2004, assoc. prof. surgery, 2004—. Rsch. grant, Thoracic Surgery Found. Rsch. & Edn., 2005—. Fellow: ACS; mem.: Soc. U. Surgeons, Am. Assn. Thoracic Surgery, Soc. Thoracic Surgeons. Office: Univ Tex MD Anderson 1400 Holcombe Blvd Ste 92004 Houston TX 77030-4009

**VARADARAJAN, SRINIDHI,** computer scientist; PhD in computer sci., SUNY, Stony Brook, 2000. Dir. Terascale Computing Facility Va. Polytechnic Inst. and State U., asst. prof. computer sci. Named one of Top 100 Young Innovators, MIT Tech. Review, 2004. Achievements include architect of System X, the third fastest supercomputer in the world. Office: Terascale Computing Facility Va Polytechnic Inst and State U Blacksburg VA 24061 Business E-Mail: srinidhi@cd.vt.edu.

**VARAIYA, PRAVIN P.,** electrical engineer; Mem. tech. staff Bell Labs., 1962-63; instr. MIT, Fed. U. Rio de Janeiro; prof. econ. U. Calif., Berkeley, 1975-92, James Fife prof. elec. engring. and computer scis., Nortel Networks disting. prof. elec. engring./computer sci. Dir. Calif. PATH. Mem. editl. bd. Transp. Rsch. Part C, Discrete Event Dynamical Sys: Theory and Applications, Jour. Econ. Dynamics and Control, (Birkhauser series) Progress in Sys. and Control Theory; contbr. numerous articles to profl. jours. Guggenheim fellow; Miller Rsch. prof. Fellow IEEE, Am. Acad. Arts & Sciences; mem. NAE Office: Dept Elec Engring U Calif 271M Cory Hall Berkeley CA 94720 Office Phone: 510-642-5270. Office Fax: 510-642-7815. Business E-Mail: varaiya@eecs.berkeley.edu.*

**VARANASI, KRIPA KIRAN,** research scientist; b. Bhimavaram, Andhra Pradesh, India, Jan. 2, 1977; s. Jagan Mohan Rao Varanasi and Suryakantham Kompella; m. Manasa Kambhampati, Dec. 13, 2004. B in Tech., Indian Inst. Tech., Madras, Chennai, India, 1998; MS in Mech. Engring., MIT, Cambridge, 2002, MS in Elec. Engring. and Computer Sci., 2002, PhD in Mech. Engring., 2004. Grad. rschr. MIT, Cambridge, 1998—2004; rsch. scientist Gen. Electric Global Rsch. Ctr., Nanotechnology Advanced Tech. Program, Energy and Propulsion Technologies, Niskayuna, NY, 2004—. Summer intern Bajaj Auto Ltd., Pune, Maharastra, India, 1996—96; student rschr. Machine Dynamics Lab, Indian Inst. Tech., Madras, Chennai, 1997—98, Thermodynamics Lab, Indian Inst. Tech., Madras, Chennai, 1997—98, Machine Elements Lab, Indian Inst. Tech., Madras, Chennai, 1997—98; cons. Indian Space Rsch. Orgn., 1997; cons. Precision Engring. Rsch. Group MIT, Cambridge, 1998—2004, cons. Rapid Autonomous Machining Lab, 2002; cons. New Way Air Bearings, Aston, Pa., 1999, Optikos Inc., Cambridge, 2000, Laser Interferometer Gravity Wave Obs. (LIGO), MIT/Caltech, Cambridge, 2003—04; vis. rschr., cons. Silicon Valley Group Inc., Ridgefield, Conn., 2000—01. Contbr. articles to profl. jours. Vol., blood donor Red Cross, 1994—98. Named Best Tech. Project of Yr., GE Rsch. Ctr., 2005; recipient Best Sci. Project award, Dept. Edn., A.P., India, 1988—92, Math. Olympiad award, Assn. Math. Tchrs., India, 1993, Inventor award, GE, 2005, GE Mgmt. award for rsch. in nanotechnology, GE Rsch. Ctr., 2005; scholar, Eveready Welfare Svcs., 1994—98, H.E.H. Nizam Trust, India, 1998; Merit scholar, Dept. Telecom., India, 1989—94, Govt. Andhra Pradesh, India, 1989—94, Nat. Merit scholar, Govt. India, 1994—98, Excel scholar, Excel Industries India, Ltd. 1998. Mem.: ASME (mem. nanomanufacturing com. Nanotechnology Inst.), Internat. Soc. for Optical Engring., Am. Soc. Precision Engring., Materials Rsch. Soc., Sigma Xi. Achievements include patents pending for method and apparatus for damping vibrations using low-wave-speed media; area of nanotechnology; area of energy at GE Research; research in Low-Wave-Speed Materials at MIT; nanotextured superhydrophobic and superhydrophilic surfaces at GE Research. Avocations: music, reading, sports, documentaries, movies, cooking. Home: 27 Squire Ln Clifton Park NY 12065 Office: General Electric Global Research Center One Research Circle Niskayuna NY 12309 Office Phone: 518-387-6732. Office Fax: 518-387-7292. Personal E-mail: kripa@alum.mit.edu. Business E-Mail: varanasi@research.ge.com.

**VARAT, JONATHAN D.,** law educator, dean; b. 1945; BA, U. Pa., Phila., 1967, JD, 1972. Law clk. to judge Walter Mansfield U.S. Ct. Appeals (2d cir.), N.Y.C., 1972-73; law clk. to justice Byron White U.S. Supreme Ct., Washington, 1973-74; assoc. O'Melveny & Myers, Los Angeles, 1974-76; acting prof. UCLA Sch. Law, 1976-81, prof., 1981—, assoc. dean, 1982-83, 91-92, dean, 1998—2003. Co-author: Constitutional Law: Cases and Materials, 2001. Office: UCLA Sch Law PO Box 951476 Los Angeles CA 90095-1476

**VARCHMIN, THOMAS EDWARD,** public health service officer; b. Chgo., Dec. 5, 1947; s. Arthur William and Laurie Eileen (Allen) V.; m. Beth Virginia Plank, Dec. 16, 1972; children: Jeffrey Thomas, Brian Arthur, Jennifer Beth, Matthew James. BA, St. Mary's Coll., Winona, Minn., 1969; MS, Western Ill. U., Macomb, 1977. Registered sanitarian Wis., lic. envirin. health practitioner Ill. Virologist, microbiologist Chgo. Dept. Health, 1974-78; environ. health and safety mgr. Great Atlantic & Pacific Tea Co., Chgo., 1978-79; adminstr. occupational safety and environ. health Nat. Safety Council, Chgo., 1979-80; mgr. environ. health Lake County Health Dept., Waukegan, Ill., 1980-84, mgr. environ. health and pub. relations, 1984-87; mgr. environ. health Cook County Dept. Pub. Health, Oak Park, Ill., 1987-89, asst. dir. environ. health, mgr. intergovtl. rels., 1989-98, dir. environ. health, 1998—. Co-chmn. West Nile Virus Com. Cook County, Ill., 2001—03; environ. health cons. Author: Final Report of West Nile Virus Committee for Cook County, 2002—03; editor: Food and Beverage Newsletter, Hospital and Health Care Newsletter, Trades and Services Newsletter, 1979—80; contbr. articles to profl. jours. NSF grantee, 1968-69 Mem.: Am. Soc. Microbiology, Nat. Safety Coun., Ill. Environ. Health Assn., Nat. Environ. Health Assn., Delta Epsilon Sigma, Phi Mu Alpha. Achievements include research on autumn food habits of game fish, behavioral and phys. devel. of barred owl nestlings in Ill. Office: Cook County Dept Pub Health 1010 Lake St Ste 300 Oak Park IL 60301-1133

**VARDALOS, NIA,** actress, screenwriter; b. Winnipeg, Can., Sept. 24, 1962; d. Constantine and Doreen Vardalos; m. Ian Gomez, 1993. Attended, Ryerson U. Actor: (films) No Experience Necessary, 1996, Men Seeking Women, 1997, Short Cinema, 1998, Meet Prince Charming, 1999, (also writer) My Big Fat Greek Wedding, 2002, (also writer, exec. prodr.) Connie and Carla, 2004, (voice): (TV series) Team Knight Rider, 1997, (guest appearance): High Incident, 1996, Common Law, 1996, The Drew Carey Show, 1997, Boy Meets World, 1998, It's Like, You Know, 1999, Two Guys, a Girl and a Pizza Place, 1999, Curb Your Enthusiasm, 2000. Office: c/o Brillstein Grey Mgmt 9150 Wilshire Blvd Ste 350 Beverly Hills CA 90212

**VARDAMIS, ALEX A.,** foundation administrator, retired military officer; b. Bangor, Maine, Sept. 10, 1934; s. Alex and Pauline Vardamis; m. Frances Diem, June 29, 1957; children: Sharon, Daniel. BS, US Mil. Acad., West Point, 1957; MA, Columbia U., 1967, PhD, 1970. Commd. 2d lt. US Army, 1957, advanced through grades to col., 1979, ret., 1986; from asst. to assoc. prof. Dickinson State U., ND, 1986—88; adj. prof. English U. Vt.,

Burlington, 1988—98; pres., CEO, trustee Robinson Jeffers Tor House Found., Carmel, Calif., 2000—. Author: (non-fiction) The Critical Reputation of Robinson Jeffers, 1972, (novel) Dingus Dreaming, 2003; contbr. articles to newspapers and periodicals. Fellow, Ctr. Sci. and Internat. Affairs, Harvard U., Cambridge, Mass., 1978; Fulbright fellow, Norway, 1996. Home: PO Box 5323 Carmel CA 93921 Office: Robinson Jeffers Tor House Found PO Box 2713 Carmel CA 93921

**VARDAVAS, STEPHANIE J.,** lawyer; b. Balt., Aug. 3, 1956; d. John and Elaine V. BA, Yale U., 1979; JD, Fordham U., 1985. Bar: NY 1986. Exec. trainee Maj. League Baseball Office of Commr., N.Y.C., 1979-80, asst. counsel, 1986—89; mgr. waivers and player records Am. League of Profl. Baseball Clubs, N.Y.C., 1980-85; v.p. legal and bus. affairs ProServ, Inc. (SFX Sports), 1989—97; atty. endorsement and league affairs Nike, Inc., N.Y.C., 1997—. Vol. D'Amours for U.S. Senate, N.H., 1984, Kanjorski for U.S. Ho. of Reps., Pa., 1986, Mark Green for U.S. Senate, N.Y., 1986, Dukakis for Pres., N.Y., 1988, Clinton-Gore, 1992-96, Gore-Lieberman, 2000, Howard Dean for Pres., 2004; pres. Friends of the Multnomah County Libr. Mem.: ABA (forum com. on the entertainment and sports law industries), Sports Lawyers Assn. (bd. dirs. and co-chair tech. com.). Democrat. Greek Orthodox. Avocations: reading, writing, photography, travel. Office: Nike World Headquarters One Bowerman Dr Beaverton OR 97005-6453

**VARDELL, JAMES C., III,** lawyer; b. Columbia, SC, Dec. 18, 1954; BA, Washington & Lee Univ., 1977; JD, Yale Univ., 1980. Bar: NY 1981. Assoc. Cravath Swaine & Moore LLP, NYC, 1980—87, ptnr., corp. dept., 1987—. Office: Cravath Swaine & Moore LLP Worldwide Plz 825 Eighth Ave New York NY 10019-7475 Office Phone: 212-474-1900. Office Fax: 212-474-3700. Business E-Mail: jvardell@cravath.com.

**VARDIN, PATRICIA ANNE,** education educator; b. Chgo. d. William and Catherine Vardin; m. Thomas W. Vris; 1 child, Elizabeth Vardin Newman. BS, U. Wis.; Doctorate, M. Columbia U. Tchr's. Coll., 1984. Adj. assoc. prof. Columbia U. Tchr's Coll., NYC, 1983—84; assoc. prof. St Francis Coll., Dept Edn., Bklyn. Heights, NY, 1992—99, Manhattanville Coll., Purchase, NY, 2002—, chmn. early childhood edn., 2002—. Editor: Children's Rights: Contemporary Perspectives, 1979; author: Internat. Encyclopedia of Education, 1984, Montessori Life, 2003. Founder, bd chair New Amsterdam Sympony Orchestra, NYC, 1976—80; bd. chair New Amsterdam Symphony Orchestra, NYC, 2004—; mem. Norwalk Hosp., Norwalk, Conn., 2001—; ednl. coord. Armstrong Chamber Concerts Music Enrichment Program; co-chair MEP Gala. Mem.: Westchester Assn. for the Edn. of Young Children (bd. dirs.), Nat. Assn. Edn. of Young Children. Episcopal. Avocations: swimming, sailing, violin, cmty. vol. Office: Manhattanville Coll 2900 Purchase St Purchase NY 10577 E-mail: vardinvrisp@mville.edn.

**VARELA, ALAN MARK,** government agency administrator, lawyer; b. Santa Fe, NMex, 1962; BA in Government and Psychology, Univ. NMex., JD, 1987; graduate Leadership for 21st Century, Harvard JFK Sch. Govt. Prin. Varela Law Office, Albuquerque; engring. dept. Qwest Comm.; policy, law dept. US West Comm.; now exec. dir. State Workers' Compensation Adminstrn., Albuquerque, 2004—. Mem.: NMex Hispanic Bar Assn. (past pres.), Hispanic Nat. Bar Assn. (pres. 2004—05, regional pres., NMex, Utah, v.p., pres.-elect). Office: Workers' Compensation Adminstrn 2410 Centre Ave SE PO Box 27198 Albuquerque NM 87106 Office Phone: 505-841-6007. Office Fax: 505-841-6009. Business E-Mail: a.varela@state.nm.us.

**VARELLA, HAZEL L.,** historian, educator; b. Beverly, Mass., Dec. 17, 1932; d. John Luke and Olivia McDonald Luke; m. M David Varella, June 24, 1961; children: John David, James Robert. BS, Bridgewater State Coll., 1954, MEd, 1956; MA, Boston U., 1962. Chmn. social studies Easton (Mass.) Sch. Sys., 1956—97; adj. faculty Bridgewater State Coll., Mass., 1998—; sr. lectr. Curry Coll., Milton, Mass., 1988—. Adv. placement cons. Coll. Bd., Princeton, 1988—. Author: (book) History of Easton V II, 1972, (pamphlets) Growing Up at Sheep Pasture, 1976. Trustee North Easton Savings Bank, 1996—; dir. Ames Free Libr., Easton, 1989—. Recipient Hon. Grand Marshall, Town of Easton, Mass., 2000, Ind. Study Scholar, NEH, Washington, DC, 1984, Outstanding Svc. award, Easton Lions Club, 1997, Disting. Svc. award, Curry Coll., 2004. Mem.: Easton Hist. Soc. (sec., pres. 1969—71, 1990—94). Episcopalian. Avocations: reading, travel. Home: 121 Center St North Easton MA 02356 E-mail: mdhvarella@comcast.net.

**VARELLAS, SANDRA MOTTE,** judge; b. Anderson, S.C., Oct. 17, 1946; d. James E. and Helen Lucille (Gilliam) Motte; m. James John Varellas, July 3, 1971; children: James John III, David Todd. BA, Winthrop U., 1968; MA, U. Ky., 1970, JD, 1975. Bar: Ky. 1975, Fla. 1976, U.S. Dist. Ct. (ea. dist.) Ky. 1975, U.S. Ct. Appeals (6th cir.) 1976, U.S. Supreme Ct. 1978. Instr. Midway Coll., Ky., 1970-72; adj. prof. U. Ky. Coll. Law, Lexington, 1976-78; instr. dept. bus. adminstrn. U. Ky., Lexington, 1976-78; ptnr. Varellas, Pratt & Cooley, Lexington, 1975-93, Varellas & Pratt, Lexington, 1993-97, Varellas & Varellas, Lexington, 1998—. Fayette County judge exec., Ky., 1980—; hearing officer Ky. Natural Resources and Environ. Protection Cabinet, Frankfort, 1984-88; bd. trustees Lexington Network 1994-98, 2002-2004, sec., 1994-98. Committeewoman Ky. Young Dems., Frankfort, 1977-80; pres. Fayette County Young Dems., Lexington, 1977; bd. dirs. Ky. Dem. Women's Club, Frankfort, 1980-84, bd. dirs., Bluegrass Estate Planning Coun., 1995-98; grad. Leadership Lexington, 1981; chairwoman Profl. Women's Forum, Lexington, Ky., 1985-86, bd. dirs., 1984-87, Kequum award com., 1989-92; mem. devel. coun. Midway Coll., 1990-92; co-chair Gift Club Com., 1992; mem. pub. svc. section com. United Way of Bluegrass, 2004. Named Outstanding Young Dem. Woman, Ky. Young Dems., Frankfort, 1977, Outstanding Former Young Dem., Ky. Young Dems., 1983. Mem. Ky. Bar Assn. (treas. young lawyers divsn. 1978-79, long range planning com. 1988-89), Fla. Bar, Fayette County Bar Assn. (pres. 1977-78, bd. govs. 1978-80), LWV (nominating com. 1984-85), Greater Lexington C. of C. (legis. affairs com. 1994-95, bd.d irs. coun. smaller enterprises 1992-95), The Lexington Forum (bd. dirs. 1996-99), Lexington Philharm. Guild (bd. dirs. 1979-81, 86—), Nat. Assn. Women Bus. Owners (chmn. cmty. liaison/govtl. affairs com. 1992-93). Office: Varellas & Varellas 167 W Main St Ste 1310 Lexington KY 40507-1398

**VARESE, FEDERICO,** sociology professor; b. Italy, Nov. 12, 1965; m. Galia Kravtchenko. Laurea, Bologna (Italy) U., 1990; PhM, Cambridge (Eng.) U., 1991; PhD, Oxford (Eng.) U., 1997. Rsch. fellow Oxford U., 1996-2000; William H. Orrick asst. vis. prof. Yale U., New Haven, 2000—02; asst. prof. Williams Coll., Williamstown, 2002—03; sr. lectr. in criminology Ctr. for Criminological Rsch. U. Oxford, England, 2003—06, prof. criminology Law Faculty, 2006—. Author: The Russian Mafia, 2001. Cpl. maj. paratrooper Italian armed forces, 1992-93. Grantee Internat. Consortium for Polit. and Social Rsch., 1997; Nuffield Coll. studentship, 1991; Lester B. Pearson scholar Ministry of Fgn. Affairs, 1982; receipient Ed. A. Hewett Book Prize, Am. Assoc. for the Advancement of Slavic Studies, in conj. with Nat. Coun. for Eurasian and East European Rsch., 2002. Mem. Am. Polit. Sci. Assn., Am. Sociol. Assn. Office: Linacre Coll Univ Oxford St Cross Rd Oxford OX1 3JA England Office Phone: 44-1865-281150. Business E-Mail: federico.varese@linacre.ox.ac.uk.

**VARET, MICHAEL A.,** lawyer; b. NYC, Mar. 9, 1942; s. Guster V. and Frances B. (Goldberg) V.; m. Elizabeth R. Varet, June 3, 1973; 3 children. BS in Econs., U. Pa., 1962; LLB, Yale U., 1965. Bar: N.Y. 1966, U.S. Supreme Ct. 1975, U.S. Dist. Ct. (ea. and so. dists.) N.Y. 1975, U.S. Tax Ct. 1975, U.S. Claims Ct. 1975, U.S. Ct. Appeals (2d cir.) 1975. Mem., chmn. Varet & Fink PC (formerly Milgrim Thomajan & Lee PC), NYC, 1982—95; mem. DLA Piper Rudnick Gray Cary US LLP (formerly Piper Rudnick LLP), NYC, 1995—. Bd. dir., exec. com. chmn audit com. compensation com., Salisbury Bank and Trust Co., Lakeville, Conn., Salisbury Bancorp, Inc., Lakeville. Trustee Montefiore Med. Ctr., Bronx, NY, 1980-92, mem. exec. com., 1985-92; bd. dirs. Sem. Libr. Corp. Jewish Theol. Sem., NYC, 1983-87, United Jewish Appeal-Fedn. Jewish Philanthropies of Greater NY, Inc.,

1979-86, coun. of overseers, 1986-95, bd. overseers, 2005—; bd. dirs. Moshou Preservation Corp., Bronx, 1982-88, Yale Law Sch. Fund, 2000—; bd. overseers Jewish Theol. Sem., 1982-90, Jewish Publ. Soc. Am., 1986-96, exec. com., 1989-96; exec. com. Yale Law Sch. Assn., 1990-93; bd. dirs. B. de Rothschild Found. for Advancement Sci. in Israel, 1986—, Piatigorsky Found., 1990—, Scenic Hudson, Inc., 2003—; v.p., sec., bd. dirs. Am. Found. for Basic Rsch. in Israel, 1990—; dir. Plz. Jewish Cmty. Chapel, 2001—; bd. dirs. Am. and Internat. Friends of Victoria and Albert Mus., Inc., 1997-99, treas., 1997-99. Mem. ABA, N.Y. State Bar Assn., Assn. of Bar of City of N.Y. (bd. dirs., exec. com. 1971-75), Internat. Fiscal Assn., Internat. Tax Planning Assn., Yale Club of N.Y.C., Lotos Club. Democrat. Office: DLA Piper US LLP 1251 Ave of Americas New York NY 10020-1104 Office Phone: 212-835-6250. Business E-Mail: mavaret@varet.com, michael.varet@dlapiper.com.

**VARGA, PAUL C.,** beverage products executive; b. Louisville, Ky., 1964; m. Melissa Varga; 2 children. BA business administration, finance, U Ky.; MBA, Purdue U. Various marketing positions Brown-Forman Corp., 1987—96, sr. v.p., 1996—2003; CEO, bd. dir. Brown-Forman Beverages Co., 2003—; pres., CEO Brown-Forman Corp., 2005—. Office: c/o Brown-Forman PO Box 1080 Louisville KY 40201

**VARGA, RICHARD STEVEN,** retired mathematics professor; b. Cleve., Oct. 9, 1928; s. Steven and Ella (Krejcs) V.; m. Esther Marie Pfister, Sept. 22, 1951; 1 dau., Gretchen Marie. BS, Case Inst. Tech., 1950; AM, Harvard U. 1951, PhD, 1954; doctorate (hon.), U. Karlsruhe, 1991, U. Lille, 1993. With Bettis Atomic Power Lab., Westinghouse Electric Co., 1954-60, adv. mathematician, 1959-60; full prof. math. Case Inst. Tech. (now Case We. Res. U.), 1960-69; Univ. Prof. math. Kent State U., Ohio, 1969—2006, dir. rsch. Inst. for Computational Math.; ret., 2006. Cons. to govt. and industry. Author: Matrix Iterative Analysis, 1962, Functional Analysis and Approximation Theory in Numerical Analysis, 1971, Topics in Polynomial and Rational Interpolation and Approximation, 1982, Zeros of Sections of Power Series, 1983, Scientific Computation on Mathematical Problems and Conjectures, 1990, Matrix Iterative Analysis, 2d revised and expanded edit., 2000, Gersgorin and his Circles, 2004; editor: Numerical Solution of Field Problems in Continuum Physics, 1970, Padé and Rational Approximations: Theory and Applications, 1977, Rational Approximations and Interpolation, 1984, Computational Methods and Function Theory, 1990, Numerical Linear Algebra, 1993; editor-in-chief. Numerische Math., 1988-2002, Electronic Transactions Numerical Analysis; mem. editl. bd. Linear Algebra and Applications, Constructive Approximation, Computational Mathematics (China), Numerical Algorithms, Analysis, Electronic Jour. Linear Algebra, Comms. in Applied Analysis. Recipient Rsch. award Sigma Xi, 1965, von Humboldt prize, 1982, Pres.' medal Kent State U., 1981, Hans Schneider prize, 2005; Guggenheim fellow, 1963; Fairchild scholar, 1974. Home: 7065 Arcadia Dr Cleveland OH 44129-6065 Office: Kent State U Inst Computational Mat Kent OH 44242-0001 Business E-Mail: varga@math.kent.edu.

**VARGAS, ELIZABETH,** newscaster; b. Paterson, NJ, Sept. 6, 1962; m. Marc Cohn, July 20, 2002; children: Zachary Raphael, Samuel Wyatt; 2 stepchildren. BA in Journalism, U. Mo., Columbia. Reporter/anchor KOMU-TV, Columbia, Mo.; reporter KTVN-TV, Reno; lead reporter KTVK-TV, Phoenix, 1986—89; reporter/anchor WBBM-TV, Chgo., 1989—93; corr./anchor NBC News, NYC, 1993—97; corr. Dateline, NBC, NYC, 1993—96; news anchor, substitute co-host Good Morning Am., NBC, NYC, 1996—97; corr. ABC News, NYC, 1997—2005, co-anchor, 20/20 newsmagazine, 2004—; interim anchor ABC World News Tonight, NYC, 2005, co-anchor, 2006. Recipient Emmy award for Outstanding Instant Coverage of News Story (Elian Gonzales case), 2000. Office: ABC News Press Rels Fl 2 47 W 66th St New York NY 10023-6201*

**VARGAS, TERESA MARIE BRADLEY,** elementary school educator; b. Blackfoot, Idaho, June 3, 1958; d. Dal Gene and Helen Marie (Walton) Bradley; m. Leonardo Almira Vargas, 1987; 3 children. AA, Ricks Coll., Rexburg, Idaho, 1978; BA, Idaho State U., Pocatello, 1985; MEd in Ednl. Leadership, U. Idaho, Moscow, 2000. First grade tchr. Minidoka County Sch. Dist 331, Heyburn, Idaho. Mem.: NEA, Idaho Edn. Assn., Phi Kappa Phi. Home: 1559 Malta Ave Burley ID 83318-1945 E-mail: isha@pmt.org.

**VARGAS-BARON, EMILY,** educational development specialist; d. Anibal Alejandro Vargas-Baron and Ingeborg Raven de Vargas-Baron; children: Ninfa Santiago, Ingeborg Charlotte Adams Pizarro, Allan Wilfred Adams, III. BA magna cum laude, U. of Wash., 1962, MA, 1964, Stanford U., Palo Alto, Calif., 1965; PhD, Stanford U., 1968. Asst. prof. U. of Wash. Seattle, 1967—68; program specialist UNESCO, Paris, 1969—72; program advisor in edn. The Ford Found., Bogota, Distrito Federal, Colombia, 1972—78; vis. lectr. in anthropology and edn. U. of Tex., Austin; exec. dir. and founder CEDEN Family Resource Ctr., Austin, Tex., 1979—94; dep. asst. adminstr. and dir., ctr. for human capacity devel. U.S. AID, Washington, 1994—2001; exec. dir. Inst. for Reconstruction and Internat. Security through Edn. (The RISE Inst.), Washington, 2001—. Cons. UNICEF, UNESCO, World Bank, Inter-Am. Devel. Bank, Assn. for the Devel. of Edn. in Africa, others, 1979—; mem., adv. bd. Down Home Ranch for Children with Disabilities, Elgin, Tex., 1990—; many internat. working groups and bd. directorships; adj. prof., advisor Early Childhood Devel. Virtual U., Victoria, Canada, 2004—05. Author: From Bullets to Blackboards: Education for Peace in Latin America and Asia, Planning Policies for Early Childhood Development; Guidelines for Action, Non-Formal Education in Lesotho: A National Study for Policy Planning and Program Development, Non-Formal Education: Assessment at the National Level, La educacion no-formal en Colombia: hacia un diagnostico de su realidad; co-author: Strategic Foreign Assistance; Civil Society in International Security; contbr. articles and poetry to profl. jours. Advisor and vol. The Austin Project, Austin, Tex., 1990—94. Named Masoner Lectr., U. of Pitts., 1996; recipient Meritorious Honor award, U.S. AID, 2001, Award for Outstanding Leadership, Svc. and Achievements as a Presdl. Appointee, Minority Leadership Orgn., 2000, Hammer Award for Achievement in Reinventing Govt. to Increase Productivity and Efficiency, V.P. of the US, 1999, Woman 2000 award, City of Austin, 1992; fellow Sr. Specialist fellow, Fulbright Commn., 2003, Ford Pregrad. assistantship, U. of Wash. and The Ford Found., 1961—62, Fulbright and Fulbright Hays fellow, Fulbright Commn., 1962—63; grantee, 1966—67. Mem.: World Orgn. for Early Childhood Edn., Consultative Group for Early Childhood Care and Devel., Coun. on Anthropology and Edn., Conf. on Latin Am. History, Comparative and Internat. Edn. Soc., Am. Ednl. Rsch. Assn., Am. Anthrop. Assn., Americans for UNESCO (v.p., chair edn. com. 2003—06), The Cosmos Club (life), Phi Alpha Theta, Phi Beta Kappa. Avocations: travel, languages and literature, painting, poetry. Office: The RISE Institute 3012 Porter St NW Washington DC 20008 Office Phone: 202-686-7044. Office Fax: 202-537-7473. E-mail: vargasbaron@hotmail.com.

**VARGAS LEGASPI, JUAN,** manufacturing executive; b. Aguascalientes, Mex., Feb. 25, 1953; s. Juan Medina and Maria Legaspi De La Luz; m. Martha Perez Carreño; children: Juan, Abraham, Christopher. Bookkeeper, UNAM, Mexico City, 1974-78; diploma in taxes and fin., U. of Specialization, Mexico City, 1987; diploma human resources, U. Iberoam., Mexico City, 1979; diploma in fin. analysis, Dun & Bradstreet Inc., 1980; diploma in Econs., Inst. Integration Ibero Am., Mexico City; MBA in Mgmt., Grad. Coll., Mexico City, 1992. Dir. Guantes Vargas, S.Am., 1977—. Owner Bd. Colegio de Graduados en Alta Direccion, 1995-2000, Centro de Investigaciones sobre la Libre Empresa, A.C., 1990-2000; CEO Grupo Banacci, 1996-2000; fin. cons. in field. Contbr. articles to profl. publs. Cesar Gaviria's bus. assessor Am. States Orgn., 1994-98. Roman Catholic. Avocations: writing, speaking, Karate, soccer. Home: Col Indsl Calz de Guadalupe 392 07800 Mexico City Mexico Office: Guantes Vargas SAm Calzada de Guadalupe 392 Col Industrial 07800 Mexico City Mexico

**VARGAS-WILLIAMS, TRACI JUNELLE,** special education educator; b. Wichita, Kans., Mar. 30, 1964; d. Judith Ann and James Dwayne Hilliard (Stepfather); m. Vance Allen Williams; children: Steven Dwayne, Christopher

Jordan. BS, Northeastern State U., 1997, BEd, 2005. Emotional disturbance Okla. State Dept. Edn., learning disability Okla. State Dept. Edn., other health impairment Okla. State Dept. Edn., autism Okla. State Dept. Edn. Spl. educator Claremore Pub. Schs., Okla., 1997—2006; spl. educator Cherry Tree Elem. Sch. Carmel-Clay Sch. Dist., 2006—. Trainer Crisis Prevention and Intervention, Claremore, 2006—; presenter Diffusing Volatile Situations in Classrooms Okla. Edn. Assn. Conv.; candidate Nat. Bd. Profl. Tchg. Standards, 2005. Named Tchr. of Yr., 1990, 2004. Mem.: NEA (corr.), CEC (corr.), Okla. Edn. Assn. (corr.), Union H.S. Key Club (assoc.; pres. 1981—82), Future Tchrs. of Am. (assoc.; treas. 1993—94). Democrat. Avocations: gardening, reading. Home: 203 E 36th St Anderson IN 46013 Office: Cherry Tree Elem Sch 13989 Hazel Dell Pl Carmel IN 46033 Office Phone: 317-846-3086. E-mail: vanceandtraci@sbcglobal.net.

**VARGHESE, OOMMAN KULATHINTHEKKETHIL,** materials scientist, researcher; s. Varghese Kochumman Geevarghese and Marykutty Varghese; m. Maggie Paulose, Jan. 19, 1998; 1 child, Tushar Varghese Oomman. BSc, Mahatma Gandhi U., Kerala, India., 1989; MSc, Mahatma Gandhi U., 1991; PhD, Indian Inst. of Tech., Delhi, 2001. Rsch. fellow Mahatma Gandhi U., Kottayam, Kerala, India, 1992—94, Indian Inst. of Tech., New Delhi, 1994—98, project scientist, 1998—2000; postdoctoral fellow U. of Ky., Lexington, 2000—01; postdoctoral scholar Pa. State U., University Park, 2001—06, rsch. assoc., 2006—. Mem. editl. bd.: Sensor Letters, 2003—, mem. internat. adv. bd.: Ency. of Sensors, 2004—, peer reviewer: IEEE Electron Device Letters, 2004—, Jour. Applied Physics, 2004—, Nanotech. Jour., 2005—, Jour. Phys. Chemistry, 2005—, Semiconductor Sci. and Tech., Advanced Functional Materials, 2006—; contbr. more than 60 articles to profl. jours. Fellow Jr. Rsch. fellow, Indian Inst. of Tech., Delhi, India, 1994—97, Sr. Rsch. fellow, Coun. of Sci. and Indsl. Rsch. (CSIR), India, 1997—98. Mem.: Am. Phys. Soc., Materials Rsch. Soc. Christian. Achievements include patents in field; development of multi-wall carbon nanotube based gas sensors; nanocrystalline tin oxide based high sensitivity ethanol sensors; rare earth hydride thin films based optical switching devices; plasma polymerized Furan thin films; invention of methods for growing low to high aspect ratio titanium dioxide (titania) nanotube arrays on titanium foils; method to fabricate transparent nanotube array thin films; first to methods for fabricating various nanostructures like copper-oxide nano-belts, aluminum-silicon nanowires, gold-silicon composite nanowires and nanoporous oxides of iron, tin and tungsten; invention of titania nanotube array based ultra-high sensitivity hydrogen gas sensors; development of titania nanotube array photoanodes for highly efficient hydrogen production through water splitting; titania nanotube array dye sensitized solar cells; nanoporous alumina based Surface Acoustic Wave (SAW) ammonia sensors; nanoporous alumina based resistive humidity sensors. Avocations: music, reading, travel, basketball. Home: 10 Vairo Blvd Apt # 239C State College PA 16803 Office: The Pennsylvania State University 212 Materials Research Laboratory University Park PA 16802 Office Phone: 814-865-6780. Office Fax: 814-865-6780. Personal E-mail: mag_oom@yahoo.com. E-mail: dkv3@psu.edu.

**VARGO, RONALD PAUL,** information technology applications executive; b. Painesville, Ohio, Mar. 26, 1954; s. Anton M. and Ingrid E. (Olson) V.; m. Kathleen M. Martell, Nov. 20, 1976; children: Mary Christine, Kevin Matthew. BA in Econs., Dartmouth Coll., 1976; MBA, Stanford U., 1981. Various fin. positions GE, Stamford, Conn., 1976-79, Standard Oil Co., Cleve., 1981-87, dir. corp. fin., 1986-87; comml. mgr. BP Exploration, Houston, 1987-89; gen. mgr. crude oil trading BP Oil Supply Co., 1989—91; joined TRW, 1991, v.p. bus. devel. automotive electronics, v.p., treas., corp. treas., v.p. investor relations, 2001—04; v.p., treas. Electronic Data Systems Corp., 2004, co-interim CFO, 2006, CFO, 2006—. Office: EDS Corp 5400 Legacy Dr Plano TX 75024*

**VARIAN, HAL RONALD,** economics professor; b. Wooster, Ohio, Mar. 18, 1947; s. Max Ronald and Elaine Catherine (Shultzman) V.; m. Carol Johnston, Nov. 1986. S.B., MIT, 1969; MA, U. Calif.-Berkeley, 1973, PhD (NSF fellow), 1973. Asst. prof. econs. MIT, 1973-77; prof. U. Mich., 1977-95, prof. fin., 1983-95, Reuben Kempf prof. econs., 1984-95; prof. sch. bus., dean sch. info. mgmt. and sys. U. Calif., Berkeley, 1995—, Class of 1944 prof., 1996—. Siena chair in econs., U. Siena, Italy, 1990. Author: Microeconomic Analysis, 1978, Intermediate Microeconomics, 1987, Information Rules, 1998; co-editor Am. Econ. Rev., 1987-90. Guggenheim fellow, 1979-80; Fulbright scholar, 1990 Fellow AAAS, Econometric Soc.; mem. Am. Econ. Soc. Home: 1198 Estates Dr Lafayette CA 94549-2749 Office: U Calif Sims 102 South Hl Berkeley CA 94720-0001

**VARIN, ROGER ROBERT,** textile executive; b. Bern, Switzerland, Feb. 9, 1925; came to U.S., 1951; s. Robert Francois and Anna (Martz) V.; m. Annemarie Louis, May 24, 1951; children: Roger R.R., Edward C.H., Viviane A.H. BBA, Mcpl. Coll., Bern, 1944; PhD in Chemistry, U. Bern, 1951. Rsch. fellow Harvard U., Cambridge, Mass., 1951-52; rsch. assoc. E.I. DuPont De Nemours, Wilmington, Del., 1952-62; dir. rsch. Riegel Textile Corp., Ware Shoals, S.C., 1962-71; founder, chief exec. officer Varinit Corp., Greenville, S.C., 1971—. Pres. Greenville Sister City Internat., 1993; bd. dirs. Greenville Symphony Assn., 1997-2000; trustee Brevard Music Ctr., 2000—. Mem. Am. Chem. Soc., Fiber Soc., Soc. Advanced Materials and Process Engring., Rotary (pres. Greenville chpt. 1979-80), Sigma Xi. Office: Varinit Corp PO Box 6602 Greenville SC 29606-6602

**VARITEK, JASON,** professional baseball player; b. Apr. 11, 1972; Attended, Ga. Tech. Catcher Boston Red Sox, 1997—. Team USA, World Baseball Classic, 2006. Named to Am. league All-Star Team, 2005; recipient Silver Slugger award, MLB, 2005, A.L. Gold Glove, 2005. Office: Boston Red Sox Fenway Park 4 Yawkey Way Boston MA 02215*

**VARLAMOV, VLADIMIR VALENTINOVICH,** mathematics educator; b. Moscow, June 30, 1957; s. Valentin Ivanovich and Elena Pavlovna (Angelopoulo) V.; m. Ludmila Vasilyevna Verba, Nov. 15, 1983. Candidate physics and math. scis., Moscow State U., 1983. Asst. prof. dept. math. Moscow Inst. Engring. Physics, 1983-88, assoc. prof. dept. math., 1988—. Contbr. articles to profl. jours. Mem. Moscow Math. Soc., Am. Math Soc. Orthodox. Avocations: running, swimming, bicycle riding, skiing, flute. Home: 78 Parkovaya St 16-1-231 Moscow 105264 Russia Office: Moscow Inst Engring Physics Kashirskoe Shosse 31 Moscow 115409 Russia

**VARLEY, HERBERT PAUL,** Japanese language and cultural history educator; b. Paterson, NJ, Feb. 8, 1931; s. Herbert Paul and Katharine L. (Norcross) V.; m. Betty Jane Geiskopf, Dec. 24, 1960 BS, Lehigh U., 1952; MA, Columbia U., 1961, PhD, 1964; DHL (hon.), Lehigh U., 1988. Asst. prof. U. Hawaii, Honolulu, 1964-65; asst. prof. dept. East Asian Langs. and Cultures Columbia U., N.Y.C., 1965-69, assoc. prof., 1969-75, 1975-94, prof. emeritus Japanese history, 1994—, chmn. dept. East Asian Langs. and Cultures, 1983-89. Sen Soshitsu XV prof. Japanese cultural history U. Hawaii, spring 1991-93, 94—2004, prof. emeritus, 2004—. Author: The Onin War, 1967, The Samurai, 1970, Imperial Restoration in Medieval Japan, 1971, Japanese Culture, 1973, 4th edit., 2000, A Chronicle of Gods and Sovereigns, 1980, Tea in Japan: Essays on the History of Chanoyu, 1989, Warriors of Japan, As Portrayed in the War Tales, 1994; co-editor Sources of Japanese Tradition, Vol. 1, 2d edit., 2001. Bd. govs. Japanese Cultural Ctr. of Hawaii. Served with U.S. Army, 1952-54, Japan. Recipient Imperial Decoration Govt. Japan, Order of Rising Sun, Gold Rays With Rosette. Mem. Assn. Asian Studies, Japan Soc., Soc. Am. Magicians (pres. local chpt. 1983-84). Avocations: magic, piano. Home: 38 S Judd St Apt 15B Honolulu HI 96817-2609 Office: U Hawaii History Dept Sakamaki Hall A 203 2530 Dole St Honolulu HI 96822-2303 E-mail: jvarley@hawaii.edu.

**VARMA, ARVIND,** chemical engineering educator, researcher; b. Ferozabad, India, Oct. 13, 1947; s. Hans Raj and Vijay L. (Jhanjhee) V.; m. Karen K. Guse, Aug. 7, 1971; children: Anita, Sophia. BS ChemE. Panjab U., 1966; MS ChemE, U. N.B., Fredericton, Can., 1968; PhD ChemE, U. Minn., 1972. Asst. prof. U. Minn., Mpls., 1972-73; sr. research engr. Union Carbide Corp.,

Tarrytown, NY, 1973-75; asst. prof. chem. engring. U. Notre Dame, Ind., 1975-77, assoc. prof., 1977-80, prof., 1980-88, Arthur J. Schmitt prof., 1988—2003, chmn. dept., 1983-88; dir. Ctr. for Molecularly Engineered Materials, 2000—03; R. Games Slayter Disting. prof., head Purdue U. Sch. Chem. Engring., 2004—. Vis. prof. U. Wis., Madison, 1981; Chevron vis. prof. Calif. Inst. Tech., Pasadena, 1982; vis. prof. Ind. Inst. Tech.-Kanpur, 1989, U. Cagliari, Italy, 1989, 92; vis. fellow Princeton U., 1996; Piercy vis. prof. U. Minn., 2001. Co-author: Mathematical Methods in Chemical Engineering, 1997, Parametric Sensitivity in Chemical Systems, 1999, Catalyst Design, 2001; editor: (with others) The Mathematical Understanding of Chemical Engineering Systems, 1980, Chemical Reaction and Reactor Engineering, 1987; series editor: Cambridge Series in Chemical Engineering, 1996—; contbr. numerous articles to profl. jours. Recipient Tchr. of Yr. award Coll. Engring. U. Notre Dame, 1991, Spl. Presdl. award 1992, R.H. Wilhelm award AIChE, 1993, Burns Grad. Sch. award 1997, E.W. Thiele award AIChE, 1998, Chem. Engring. Lectureship award, ASEE, 2000, Rsch. Achievement award U. Notre Dame, 2001, Techs. of Yr. award Industry Week, 2005; Fulbright scholar; Indo-Am. fellow, 1988-89. Office: Purdue U Sch Chem Engring West Lafayette IN 47907 Office Phone: 765-494-4075. Business E-Mail: avarma@purdue.edu.

**VARMA, DATLA G.K.,** radiologist, researcher; b. Bobbili, Andhra, India, June 2, 1951; came to U.S., 1976; now naturalized; s. Datla V. Raju and Datla Satyavathi; m. Siva Kumari, Dec. 20, 1980; children: Datla Kirti, Datla Vivek. MBBS, Andhra Med. Coll., 1975. Diplomate Am. Bd. Radiology, Am. Bd. Nuclear Medicine. Intern King George Hosp., Visakha Patnam, India, 1974-75; resident in anat. pathology Good Samaritan Hosp., Cin., 1977-78; resident in nuclear medicine Univ. Hosp., Cin., 1978 80; resident in radiology, 1980-83; asst. prof. radiology Tulane U., New Orleans, 1983-88, med. dir. diagnostic svcs./radiology dept., 1983-89, assoc. prof. radiology, 1988-89, sect. chief body CT, 1983-89, sect. chief body MRI, 1988-89; assoc. prof. radiology U. Tex./M.D. Anderson Cancer Ctr., Houston, 1989-99, acting sect. chief MRI, 1991-99, prof. radiology, 1999—. Contbr. articles to profl. jours., chpts. to books. Avocations: sports, travel, reading. Home: 3915 Marlowe St Houston TX 77005-2045 Office: Md Anderson Cancer Ctr PO Box 57 Houston TX 77001-0057 E-mail: dvarma@di.mdacc.tmc.edu.

**VARMUS, HAROLD ELIOT,** health science administrator, educator, science researcher; b. Oceanside, NY, Dec. 18, 1939; s. Frank and Beatrice (Barasch) V.; m. Constance Louise Casey, Oct. 25, 1969; children: Jacob Carey, Christopher Isaac. BA in English, Amherst Coll., 1961; MA, Literature, Harvard U., 1962; MD, Columbia U. Med. Sch., 1966. Intern, resident Presbyn. Hosp., NYC, 1966-68; lectr. dept. microbiology U. Calif., San Francisco, 1970-72, asst. prof., 1972-74, assoc. prof., 1974-79, prof. depts. microbiology and immunology, biochemistry and biophysics, 1979—93, Am. Cancer Soc. research prof., 1984—93; clin. assoc. NIH, Bethesda, Md., 1968-70, dir., 1993—99; pres., CEO Meml. Sloan-Kettering Cancer Ctr., NYC, 2000—. Chmn. bd. on biology NRC, 1991—93; served on WHO Commn on Macroeconomics and Health; bd. dirs. Pub. Libr. Sci.; sci. bd. Grand Challenges in Global Health. Co-recipient Scientist of Yr. award, Calif. Acad. Sci., 1982, Lasker Found. award, 1982, Passano Found. award, 1983, Armand Hammer Cancer prize, GM Alfred Sloan award, Shubitz Cancer prize, 1984, Internat. award, Gardner Found., 1984, Nobel Prize in Physiology or Medicine, 1989; recipient Nat. Medal of Sci., 2002, Vannevar Bush award, NSF, 2001. Mem. NAS, Inst. Medicine, Am. Soc. Virology, Am. Soc. Microbiology, Am. Soc. Cell Biology, Am. Acad. Arts and Scis., Am. Soc. for Biochemistry and Molecular Biology. Democrat. Achievements include rsch. (with J. Michael Bishop) on the cellular origin of retroviral oncogenes. Office: Meml Sloan-Kettering Cancer Ctr 1275 York Ave New York NY 10021-6094 Business E-Mail: varmus@mskcc.org.

**VARNER, ARTHUR E.,** allergist, researcher; b. Xenia, Ohio, Mar. 18, 1966; s. Kenneth H. and Virginia L. Varner; m. Heidi Harris, Aug. 8, 1992; children: Madeleine L., Grant H., Gretchen L. BA, Miami U., Oxford, Ohio, 1988; MD, Ohio State U., 1992. Intern in internal medicine Riverside Meth. Hosp., Columbus, Ohio; allergy fellow U. Wis., Madison; allergist Allergy Diagnostic, Beachwood, Ohio, 1997—. Pollen counter. Achievements include first to relate acetaminophen use with asthma; research in decreased use of pediatric aspirin has contributed to the increasing prevalence of childhood asthma. Home: 4103 Meadowbrook Blvd University Heights OH 44118 Office: Allergy Diagnostic 23250 Mercantile Rd Beachwood OH 44122 Personal E-mail: wiscart@aol.com.

**VARNER, CARLTON A.,** lawyer; b. Creston, Iowa, July 14, 1947; BA, U. Iowa, 1969; JD magna cum laude, U. Minn., 1972. Bar: Calif. 1972. Mng. ptnr. Sheppard Mullin Richter & Hampton LLP, LA, 1991—, chmn. exec. com., 1991—98. Author: California Antitrust & Unfair Competition Law, 2nd edit., 2001, Old Wine in New Bottles: The competitor Collaboration Guidelines, 2000. Mem.: ABA (chair Exemptions & Immunities Com., Antitrust Sec.), Constl. Rights Found. (v.p.), LA County Bar Assn. (chmn. antitrust sect. 1993—94), Chancery Club of LA. Office: Sheppard Mullin Richter & Hampton LLP 333 S Hope St Fl 48 Los Angeles CA 90071-1406 Fax: 213-620-1398. E-mail: cvarner@sheppardmullin.com.

**VARNER, CHARLEEN LAVERNE MCCLANAHAN,** nutritionist, educator, administrator, dietitian; b. Alba, Mo., Aug. 28, 1931; d. Roy Calvin and Lela Ruhama (Smith) McClanahan; student Joplin (Mo.) Jr. Coll., 1949-51; BS in Edn., Kans. State Coll. Pittsburg, 1953; MS, U. Ark., 1958; PhD, Tex. Woman's U. 1966; postgrad. Mich. State U., 1955, U. Mo., 1962; m. Robert Bernard Varner, July 4, 1953. Apprentice county home agt. U. Mo., 1952; tchr. Ferry Pass Sch., Escambia County, Fla., 1953-54; tchr. biology, home econs. Joplin Sr. H.S., 1954-59; instr. home econs. Kans. State Coll. Pittsburg, 1959 63, home foods, nutrition Coll. Home Ind Arts and Sciu., Tex. Woman's U., 1963-64, rsch. asst. NASA grant, 1964-66; assoc. prof. home econs. Central Mo. State U., Warrensburg, 1966-70, adviser to Colhecon, 1966-70, adviser to Alpha Sigma Alpha, 1967-70, 72, bd. adv. Honors Group, 1967-70; prof., head dept. home econs. Kans. State Tchrs. Coll., Emporia, 1970-73; prof., chmn. dept. home econs. Benedictine Coll., Atchison, Kans., 1973-74; prof., chmn. dept. home econs. Baker U., Baldwin City, Kans., 1974-75; owner, operator Diet-Con Dietary Cons. Enterprises, cons. dietitian, 1973—, Home-Con Cons. Enterprises; adj. prof. Highland (Kans.) CC, 2004—. Active Joplin Little Theater, 1956-60. Mem. NEA, AAUW, AAUP, Mo. State Tchr. Assn., Kans. State Tchr. Assn., Am. Dietetic Assn., Mo. Dietetic Assn., Kans. Dietetic Assn., Am. Home Econs. Assn., Mo. Home Econs. Assn., Kans. Home Econs. Assn., Mo. Acad. Scis., U. Ark. Alumni Assn., Alumni Assn. Kans. State Coll. of Pittsburg, Am. Vocat. Assn., Assn. Edn. Young Children, Sigma Xi, Beta Sigma Phi, Beta Beta Beta, Alpha Sigma Alpha, Delta Kappa Gamma, Kappa Kappa Iota, Phi Upsilon Omicron, Theta Alpha Pi, Kappa Delta Pi, Kappa Phi. Methodist (organist). Home: PO Box 1009 Topeka KS 66601-1009

**VARNER, CHILTON DAVIS,** lawyer; b. Opelika, Ala., Mar. 12, 1943; d. William Cole and Frances (Thornton) Davis; m. K. Morgan Varner, III, June 19, 1965; 1 child, Ashley Elizabeth Davis. AB with distinction, Smith Coll., 1965; JD with distinction, Emory U., 1976. Assoc. King & Spalding, Atlanta, 1976-83, ptnr., 1983—. Bd. dirs. Wesley Woods Healthcare, 11th Cir. Ct. Appeals Hist. Soc.; trustee Emory U., Atlanta, 1995—, Product Liability Adv. Coun. Found., 1996—2004; mem. Adv. Com. Fed. Civil Rules, 2004—. Author: Appellate Handbook for Georgia Lawyers, 1995. Mem. Leadership Atlanta, 1984—85; mem. exec. com. Atlanta Arts Alliance, 1981—85; mem. Atlanta Symphony Chorus, 1970—74; asst. clk., elder, bd. elders Trinity Presbyn. Ch., Atlanta, 1975—88. Recipient Disting. Alumna award, Emory U. Law Sch., 1998. Fellow: Am. Coll. Trial Lawyers; mem.: ABA (mem. adv. com. fed. civil rules 2004—), Atlanta Bar Assn., Ga. Bar Assn., Phi Beta Kappa, Order of Coif. Office: King & Spalding 191 Peachtree St NE Ste 4900 Atlanta GA 30303-1740 Office Phone: 404-572-4789.

**VARNER, DAVID EUGENE,** lawyer; b. Dallas, Oct. 9, 1937; s. E.C. and D. Evelyn (Bauguss) V.; m. Joan Paula Oransky, Aug. 13, 1962; children: Michael A., Kevin E., Cheryl L. BA, So. Meth. U., Dallas, 1958, JD, 1961.

Bar: Tex. 1961, Fla. 1974, Okla., 1977, U.S. Supreme Ct. 1978. Assoc. Eldridge, Goggans, Davidson & Silverberg, Dallas, 1962-65; atty., asst. sec. Redman Industries, Inc., Dallas, 1965-66; assoc. gen. atty. Tex. Instruments, Inc., Dallas, 1966-73; sr. atty., asst. sec. Fla. Gas Co., Winter Park, 1973-76; v.p., gen. counsel, sec. Facet Enterprises, Inc., Tulsa, 1976-78, Summa Corp., Las Vegas, Nev., 1978-82; sr. v.p., gen. counsel, sec. Transco Energy Co., Houston, 1982-95; pres. The MKC Group, Houston, 1995—. Mem. royalty mgmt. adv. com. U.S. Minerals Mgmt. Svc., 1985—87. Mng. editor Southwestern Law Jour., 1960-61 Mem.: Fla. Bar Assn., Tex. Bar Assn. Office: PO Box 79571 Houston TX 77279-9571

**VARNER, JOYCE EHRHARDT,** retired librarian; b. Quincy, Ill., Sept. 13, 1938; d. Wilbur John and Florence Elizabeth (Mast) Ehrhardt; m. Donald Giles Varner, Sept. 12, 1959; children: Amy, Janice, Christian, Matthew, Nadine. BA, Northeastern Okla. State U., 1980; MLS, U. Okla., 1984. Lab. analyst Gardner Denver Co., Quincy, 1956-60; sales rep. Morrisonville, Ill., 1963-69; libr. clk. U. Ill., Urbana, 1973-75; libr. tech. asst. Northeastern Okla. State U., Tahlequah, 1976-86; asst. reference libr. Muskogee (Okla.) Pub. Libr., 1986-90; libr. Jess Dunn Correctional Ctr., Taft, Okla., 1990-98; ret., 1998; field office supr. Census 2000 Dept. of Commerce, Welling, Okla., 1998. Editor Indian Nations Audubon Nature Notes, 1977-81, 96—; contbr. articles to newspaper. Vol. Lake-Wood coun. Girl Scouts U.S.A., 1975-98, bd. dirs. 1992-98, pres., 1995-96; sec.-treas. Cherokee County Rural Water Dist. 7, 1987—; edn. chmn. Indian Nations chpt. Nat. Audubon Soc., 1989-2000, pres., 2000-04; project dir. Tahlequah Friends of the Libr., 2002-04, pres. 2004—. Recipient Thanks Badge, Lake-Wood coun. Girl Scouts U.S.A., 1990. Mem. AAUW (chair diversity com. 2000), Okla. Libr. Assn. (nominating com. 1989), Okla. Acad. Sci., Okla. Ornithol. Soc. (chmn. libr. com. 1978-88, Award of Merit 1990, pres.-elect 1994, pres. 1995-96), Alpha Chi, Beta Beta Beta, Phi Delta Kappa (Found. rep. 1984-86, historian 1992-2006). Avocations: nature study, needlecrafts, square dancing, genealogy.

**VARNER, ROBERT,** school system administrator; b. Karlsruhe, Germany, Dec. 12, 1961; s. Robert and Hisae Varner; m. Christie Branson, June 16, 1990; children: Jared, Jonathan, Jordan, Kelsie. M, Ariz. State U., Phoenix, 2000. Tchr. Cartwright Sch. Dist., Phoenix, 1995—2000, sch. adminstr., 2000—. Supporter Child with Disabilities, Phoenix; lic. min. So. Bapt., 1998—2006. Mem.: Sharing Down Syndrome Ariz. (assoc.), Tchrs. English Spkrs.Other Langs. (assoc.), Nat. Sci. Tchrs. Assn. (assoc.), Ariz. Sch. Adminstrs. (assoc.), Conservative. Baptist. Achievements include Working with hospice patients and working with children with Down Syndrome. Avocations: golf, camping, backpacking, travel. Office Phone: 623-691-4600.

**VARNER, VANCE SIEBER,** principal; b. Lewistown, Pa., Aug. 8, 1967; s. George Thomas and Kay (Sieber) V. BS, Pa. State U., 1991, MEd. Earth sci., geosci. and environ. tchr. Upper Dauphin Area High Sch., Elizabethville, Pa., 1991—. Varsity soccer coach Upper Dauphin High Sch., 1991—, asst. varsity wrestling coach, 1991—. Recipient Nat. Sallie Mae Tchr. award Student Loan Mktg. Assn., 1992. Avocations: fly fishing, hunting. Home: RR 3 Box 255 Mifflintown PA 17059-9803 Office: 2 Manor Dr Lewistown PA 17044 Business E-Mail: vsv55@mcsdk12.org.

**VARNEY, CARLETON BATES, JR.,** interior designer, columnist, educator; b. Lynn, Mass., Jan. 23, 1937; s. Carleton Bates and Julia (Raczkowskos) V.; divorced; children: Nicholas, Seamus, Sebastian. BA, Oberlin Coll., 1958; student, U. Madrid, 1957; MA, NYU, 1969; LHD (hon.), U. Charleston, 1987. Sch. tchr., 1958-59; asst. to pres. Dorothy Draper & Co., Inc., 1959-63, exec. v.p., 1963-66, pres., 1966—; dean Carleton Varney Sch. of Art & Design, Charleston, W.Va. Designer: Varney and Sons Furniture Collection Kindel Furniture Co., Carleton Varney by-the-yard decorative fabrics, dinnerware and china, crystal glassware, table and bed linen, lamps and light fixtures, ready to wear resort collection Cruzanwear, 1987, mens' wear furnishings for Rawlinson & Marking, London, 1987; Ready to wear resort coll., "A Perfect Day in Paradise", 1998, Colours Resort Collection, 2000; interior designer: Dromoland Castle, Ireland, 1963, 88, Westbury Hotel, Belgium, 1964, NY World's Fair, 1965, Clare Inn, Ireland, 1968, Greenbrier Hotel, White Sulphur Springs, W.Va., 1968-, Westbury Hotel, San Francisco, 1973, Copley Plaza Hotel, Boston, 1976, 96, Amway Grand Plaza Hotel, Grand Rapids, Mich., 1980, The Grand Hotel, Mackinac Island, Mich., 1978-, Equinox House, Manchester, Vt., 1984, Brazilian Ct. Hotel, Palm Beach, Fla., 1985, Waldorf Towers, NYC, 1985, Dawn Beach Hotel, St. Maarten, 1985, Christian Broadcasting Conv. Ctr., 1986, Met. Opera House boutique, NYC, 1985, (cruise ship) World Discoverer, 1984, Arrowwood Conv. Ctr., Purchase, NY, 1987, Boca Raton Hotel and Club, Fla., 1987, Speedway Club, Charlotte, NC, 1987, Coccoloba Plantation, Anguilla, Brit. Virgin Islands, 1987, Villa Madeleine, St. Croix, VI, 1987, Ashford Castle, Ireland, 1988, Adare Manor, Ireland, 1988, The Breakers, Palm Beach, Fla., 1989, Jackson Lake Lodge, Wyo., 1989, V.P.'s Residence, Washington, 1989, Cormorant Cove, St. Croix, VI, 1990, The Buccaneer Hotel, St. Croix, 1991, Dromoland Castle, Internat. Ctr., Ireland, 1991, West Village Golf Resort, Tokyo, 1993, Half Moon Bay Club, Jamaica, The Plaza, NY, 1997, The Hibiscus Restaurant, Palm Beach, Fla., 1999, North Shore Country Club, LI, NY, 2002, Mount Wash. Hotel and Resort, N.H., 2003, Lago Mar Resort and Club, Ft. Lauderdale, Fla., 2003-04, McJukin Corp., W.Va., 2005, Harder Hall Resort and Spa, Sebring, Fla., 2005; numerous pvt. residences; designer: White House party for celebration Israel-Egypt Peace Treaty, 1979; Palm Beach Cares fashion benefit for Am. Found. for AIDS Research, 1988, log home for Pres. and Mrs. Carter, Ellijay, Ga., 1983; color cons. Carter Presdl. Library, 1986; trustee and curator: former presdl. yacht U.S.S. Sequoia, 1982; author: numerous books including You and Your Apartment, 1960, The Family Decorates a Home, 1962 Carleton Varney Decorates Windows, 1975, Be Your Own Decorator, 1979, There's No Place Like Home, 1980, Down Home, 1981, Carleton Varney's ABC's of Decorating, 1983, Staying in Shape: An Insider's Guide to the Great Spas, 1983, Room by Room Decorating, 1984, Color Magic, 1985, The Draper Touch, 1988, Kiss the Hibiscus Goodnight, 1992, The Decorator, 1999, In The Pink, 2006; syndicated columnist: Your Family Decorator, 1968—; decorating column Familyclick.com, 2000, Inside Design column N.Y. Post, 2001; contbg. editor Good Housekeeping Mag., 1993-95; contbg. design editor Social and Personal Mag. (Ireland) 1996-; style editor Men's Style mag.; editor-at-large Hamptons Mag., 2000—. Recipient Shelby Williams award for design achievement, 1967, Tommy design award for Covington's Heraldry collection, 1989, Interior Design Hall of Fame award, 1990. Mem. Indsl. Designers Soc. Am., NY State Bd. for Interior Design, NY Athletic Club, Shannon Rowing Club (Ireland), Millbrook Golf and Tennis Club (NY). Office: Dorothy Draper & Co Inc 60 E 56th St New York NY 10022-3204 Office Phone: 212-758-2810. Business E-Mail: cvarney@dorothydraper.com *My success, I believe, is due to an ability to understand and use vibrant color appropriately, and to strive for perfection of detail in all my designs as details separate the excellent from the ordinary.*

**VARNEY, CHRISTINE A.,** federal official; Degree in Politics, Philosophy and Econs. (hon.), Trinity Coll., Dublin, Ireland, 1975; BA in Polit. Sci. and History magna cum laude, SUNY, Albany, 1977; MPA in Policy Analysis, Legislation and Rsch. magna cum laude, Syracuse U., 1978; JD cum laude, Georgetown U., 1986. Legis. asst. N.Y. Senate, Albany, 1977; econ. analyst GAO, Washington, 1978; econ. devel. dir. El Centro, Calif., 1979; dir. Neighborhood Outreach Program, San Diego, 1980-82; assoc. Surry & Morse, Washington, 1984-86, Pierson, Semmes & Finley, Washington, 1986-88; counsel Hogan & Hartson, Washington, 1990-92; chief counsel Clinton for Pres. Primary Campaign, 1992, Clinton-Gore Campaign, 1992; gen. counsel Dem. Nat. Com., 1992, Presdl. Inauguration Com., 1993; dep. asst. to President U.S., sec. to Cabinet The White House, Washington, 1993-94; commissioner FTC, Washington, 1994—97; ptnr. Hogan & Hartson LLP, Washington, 1997—, mem. exec. com. Active Women's Legal Def. Fund. Mem. D.C. Bar Assn., N.Y. State Bar Assn., Nat. Lawyer's Coun. Office: Hogan & Hartson Columbia Sq 555 Thirteenth St NW Washington DC 20004-1109 Office Phone: 202-637-6823. Office Fax: 202-637-5910. Business E-Mail: cavarney@hhlaw.com.

**VARNEY, RICHARD ALAN,** health facility administrator; b. Concord, NH, July 8, 1950; s. John Berry and Hattie Elizabeth (Harrington) V.; m. Suzanne Glaab, Dec. 31, 1983; stepchildren: Alysen Suzanne Bidle, Craig Judson Bidle. BS in Phys. Edn., U. N.H., 1972; MHA in Healthcare Adminstrn., Baylor U., 1984; diploma, Command and Gen. Staff Coll., 1986. Commd. 2d lt. U.S. Army, 1973, advanced through grades to lt. col., 1991; dep. asst. CEO Cutler Army Hosp., Ft. Devens, Mass., 1973—76; field med. asst. 38th ADA Bde., Osan Air Base, Republic of Korea, 1977—78; dep. asst. CEO 15th Med. Battalion, Ft. Hood, Tex., 1979—81; adminstrv. resident Ireland Army Hosp., Ft. Knox, Ky., 1982—83; COO, exec. officer U.S. Army Dental Activity, Ft. Knox, 1983—86; grad. instr. Army-Baylor Healthcare Program, San Antonio, 1986—90; project mgr. Office of the Army Surgeon Gen., Washington, 1990—93; ret. U.S. Army, 1993; office mgr. Aebi, Ginty, Romaker & Sprouse MD's, Inc., Lancaster, Ohio, 1993—2000; dir. gen. internal medicine program The Ohio State U. Med. Ctr., Columbus, 2000—04; dir. ops. Fairfield Dept. Health, Lancaster, 2005—. Mem. Source Selection Evaluation Bd. Champus Reform, Arlington, Va., 1987; mem. adv. com. for assoc. degree program in med. assisting Ohio U., Lancaster, 1998-2000. Adult leader Boy Scouts Am., Tex., Va. and Ohio, 1988-97, 2003—; mem. Lancaster City Bd. of Health, 1996-2001, pres. pro tem, 1999-2001; mem. Fairfield County Combined Gen. Health Dist. Bd., 2002-04. Officer US Army Med. Svc. Corps, 1973—93. Decorated Legion of Merit, Order of Mil. Med. Merit award, Expert Field Med. badge; named to Hon. Order Ky. Cols., 1989, Outstanding Young Man of Am., 1982. Fellow Am. Coll. Healthcare Execs.; mem. Ctrl. Ohio Health Adminstrs. Assn., Ohio Med. Group Mgmt. Assn., Mid-Ohio Med. Mgmt. Assn., Profl. Assn Med. Mgrs., Am. Assn. Procedural Coders, Lancaster Area Soc. for Human Resource Mrmt. (legis. rep. 1998-99, membership chair 1999—), Am. Hosp. Assn., Nat. Eagle Scout Assn., The Ret. Officers Assn., Am. Legion, Fraternal Order of Eagles, Alpha Phi Omega. Avocations: home improvement, music. Home: 1025 E 5th Ave Lancaster OH 43130-3276 Office Phone: 740-653-4489 x155. Personal E-mail: richvarneyosu@yahoo.com. Business E-Mail: rvarney@co.fairfield.oh.us.

**VARNHOLT, HEIKE,** pathologist; d. Manfred and Else Varnholt. MD, Hannover Med. Sch., Germany, 2000. Pathologist-in-tng. Mass. Gen. Hosp., Harvard Med. Sch., Boston, 2000—03; chief resident in pathology Baystate Med. Ctr./Tufts U. Sch. of Medicine, Springfield, Mass., 2003—. Contbr. articles to profl. jours. Mem.: Am. Soc. for Clin. Pathology, Rodger C. Haggitt Gastrointestinal Pathology Soc. (Travel award 2003), Arkana Pathology Informatics, Coll. Am. Pathologists (Informatics award 2004), U.S. Acad. Pathology. E-mail: heikevarnholt@yahoo.com.

**VARONE, DOUGLAS JOSEPH,** choreographer; b. Syosset, NY, Nov. 5, 1956; s. Joseph Alexander and Marie Elizabeth V. BFA, SUNY, Purchase, 1978. Dancer Limon Dance Co., NYC, 1978-79, Lar Lubovitch Dance Co., NYC, 1979-86; artistic dir. Doug Varone and Dancers, NYC, 1986—. Bd. dirs. Dova, Inc., NYC. Choreographer Rise, 1993, The Planets, 1994, Bel Canto, 1998, Sleeping with Giants, 1999, (TV films) The Planets, 1994, (films) One Last Dance, (Broadway plays) Triumph of Love, 1997, (Operas) Transatlantic, Minn. Opera, Il Viaggio a Reims, NYC Opera, Die Walkurie, Wash. Opera, Les Troyens, Met. Opera, NYC, Salome, 2004, Le Sacre du Printemps, 2004; choreographer and dir. (Operas) Orphée et Eurydice, The Barber of Seville. Guggenheim Found. fellow, 1996, NEA fellow, 1989-97, NY Found. Arts fellow, 1987; recipient Bessie award for sustained achievement in choreography, 1998, Choo-San Goh award, OBIE award spl. citation, Village Voice 2006. Mem.: Choreographers Union, Soc. Stage Directors. Office: Dova Inc Rm 4A 37 W 32nd St New York NY 10001-3804 Office Phone: 212-279-3344. E-mail: dvarone@dougvaroneanddancers.org.*

**VARPAHOVSKY, ANDREY,** computer scientist, educator; b. Moscow, July 26, 1936; s. Solomon Milikovsky and Irina Varpahovsky; m. Lina Feldman, Jan. 22, 1960; children: Fred, Katherine Bella. M, Moscow Inst. Energy, 1959; diploma, Inst. Math. Machines, Erevan, Armenia, 1971. Group leader Inst. Control Systems, Moscow, 1972—78; engr. Control Data Corp., Lexington, Mass., 1979—85; group leader Digital Equipment Corp., Marlborough, 1986—92; adv. engr. IBM, Rochester, Minn.; tchr. Worcester State Coll., Mass., 2000—. Achievements include patents in field: Worcwester State College 486 Chandler St Worcester MA 01602 Office Phone: 508-929-8560. Office Fax: 508-929-8146. Personal E-mail: avarpah@yahoo.com. E-mail: avarpahovsky@worcester.edu.

**VARRO, BARBARA JOAN,** retired editor; b. East Chicago, Ind., Jan. 25, 1938; d. Alexander R. and Lottie R. (Bess) V. BA, Duquesne U., 1959. Feature reporter, asst. fashion editor Chgo. Sun-Times, 1959-64, fashion editor, 1964-76, feature writer, 1976-84; v.p. pub. rels. Daniel J. Edelman Inc., Chgo., 1984-85; v.p. PRB/Needham Porter Novelli, Chgo., 1985-86; editor Am. Hosp. Assn. News, Chgo., 1987-94; editor spl. sects. Chgo. Tribune, 1995-2000; ret. Recipient awards for feature writing Ill. AP, 1978, 79, 80 Mem.: PEO. Home: 219 Autumn Trail N Michigan City IN 46360

**VARSHAVSKY, ALEXANDER JACOB,** molecular biologist; b. Moscow, Nov. 8, 1946; came to U.S., 1977; s. Jacob M. and Mary B. (Zeitlin) V.; m. Vera Bingham, Aug. 30, 1990; children: Roman, Anna, Victoria. BS in Chemistry, Moscow State U., 1970; PhD in Biochemistry, Inst. of Molecular Biology, Moscow, 1973. Rsch. fellow Inst. Molecular Biology, Moscow, 1973—76; asst. prof. dept. biology MIT, Cambridge, 1977-80, assoc. prof. dept. biology, 1980-86, prof. dept. biology, 1986-92; Howard and Gwen Laurie Smits prof. cell biology, divsn. biology Calif. Inst. Tech., Pasadena, 1992—. Vis. fellow Internat. Inst. for Advanced Studies, Kyoto; mem. molecular cytology study sect. NIH. Author more than 150 articles in the field of genetics and biochemistry; holder 14 patents. Recipient Novartis-Drew award, Novartis, 1998, Merit award, NIH, 1998, Gairdner Internat. award (Can.), 1999, Alfred P. Sloan Jr. prize, GM Cancer Rsch. Found., 2000, Lasker award in basic med. rsch., Albert and Mary Lasker Found., 2000, Hoppe-Seyler award, Soc. for Biochemistry and Molecular Biology, Germany, 2000, Merck award, Am. Soc. Biochemistry and Molecular Biology, 2001, Pasarow award in cancer rsch., Pasarow Found., 2001, Wolf prize in medicine, Wolf Found., Israel, 2001, Massery prize, Massery Found., 2001, Max Planck Rsch. prize, Germany, 2001, Horwitz prize, Columbia U., 2001, Wilson medal, Am. Soc. Cell Biology, 2002, Stein & Moore award, Protein Soc., 2005, March of Dimes prize devel. biology, March of Dimes Found., 2006, Gagna and Van Heck prize, Belgium, 2006, Griffuel Cancer Rsch. prize, France, 2006. Fellow AAAS, Am. Acad. Microbiology, Am. Acad. Arts and Scis.; mem. NAS, Am. Philos. Soc., European Molecular Biology Orgn. (fgn., academia Europaea). Achievements include discoveries in the fields of DNA replication, chromosome structure, ubiquitin system, and intracellular protein turnover. Office: Calif Inst Tech Divsn Biology 1200 East California Blvd Pasadena CA 91125-0001 Office Fax: 626-440-9821. Business E-Mail: avarsh@caltech.edu.

**VARTAN, MICHAEL J.,** actor; b. Boulogne-Billancourt, Hauts-de-Seine, France, Nov. 27, 1968; Various sr. mgmt. positions OSCA oilfield svcs. co.; v.p. BJ Svcs.; pres., CEO Key Energy Svcs. Inc. Actor: (TV films) Black Leather Jacket, 1988; (TV miniseries) The Mists of Avalon, 2001; (TV series) Alias, 2001—05; (films) A Man and Two Women, 1991, Stringer, 1992, Summer Strolls, 1992, Wild Flower, 1993, To Wong Foo, Thanks for Everything! Julie Newmar, 1995, The Pallbearer, 1996, Touch Me, 1997, The Myth of Fingerprints, 1997, Dead Man's Curve, 1998, Never Been Kissed, 1999, It Had to Be You, 2000, The Next Best Thing, 2000, Sand, 2000, One Hour Photo, 2002, Monster-in-Law, 2005, (guest appearances): (TV series) Fallen Angels, Spender, 1993, Friends, 1997, Ally McBeal, 2000. Avocation: hockey.*

**VARVAK, MARK,** mathematician, researcher; b. Kiev, Russia, Feb. 13, 1939; came to U.S., 1987; s. Shlyoma and Anna (Berimskaya) V.; m. Nellie Albert, Feb. 1, 1973 (div. Oct. 1983); 1 child, Alexander; m. Lidiya Zolotarenko, Aug. 30, 2002. MS in Applied Math., Ukraine U., 1969; candidate of sci., Rsch. Inst. of Structures, Kiev, 1970. Sr. rscher Rsch. Inst. of Structures, Kiev, 1963-79; sr. engr. Constrn. Authority, Kiev, 1979-86; programmer Consulting Engring. Co., N.Y.C., 1988-91; scientist Sci. Appli-

cation Internat. Corp., 1997—99, Navair Tng. Sys. Divsn., Orlando, Fla., 2002—. Contbr. more than 40 articles to profl. jours. Mem. Am. Math. Soc. Office: Training Sys Divsn 12350 Rsch Park Orlando FL 32826 Personal E-mail: varvakm@bellsouth.net.

**VARVARER, MARK A.,** otolaryngology professor; b. St. Louis, Mo., May 25, 1958; s. Peter and Mary (Michelas) V.; m. Christine R. Meyer, Oct. 12, 1985; children: Mexis, Sophie, Tessa. Degree in edn., U. Mo., Columbia, 1976—80; dental degree, U. Mo., Kansas City, 1981; MD, St. Louis U., 1986. Lic. Am. Bd. Otolaryngology, Am. Bd. Facial Plastic and Reconstructive Surgery. Instr. in otology and laryngology Harvard Sch. Medicine, Boston, 1992—94, 1996—98, assoc. prof., 2002; asst. prof. otolaryngology St. Louis U., 1994—96, prof. otolaryngology, 2003—. Dir. St. Louis U. Cancer Ctr., 2006—. Recipient William Montosonan award, Harvard Dept. Otolaryngology and Laryngology, 1994, Tchg. award, 1997. Fellow: Am. Head and Neck Soc., Am. Acad. Facial Plastic and Reconstructive Surgery, Am. Acad. Otolaryngology. Office: St Louis U Sch Medicine Dept Otolaryngology 3635 Wish at Grand Blvd Saint Louis MO 63110 Office Phone: 314-577-8887.

**VARZEGAR, MINOO,** literature educator, reading specialist; b. Kerman, Iran; d. Abdolrahim and Amjad (Vali) Varzegar; m. Saeid Fatemi, May 8; children: Delaram, Arezou. BA in English summa cum laude, U. Tehran, 1966, MA in Psychology, 1969; MA in Tchg. English, U. Tchr. Edn., 1967; MA in Tchg. ESL, U. Ill., 1971, PhD in Tchg. ESL, 1975, postgrad., 1994. Cert. tchr. English, cert. high acad. adminstrn. Asst. prof. U. Tehran, 1979—84, assoc. prof., 1984—94, prof. dept. English, 1984—97, head dept. English of Evening Classes, 1975—83, dir. Lang. Lab., 1975—80, dir. lang. ctr., 1981—83, head dept. English, 1983—97. Vis. prof. U. Ill., Champaign-Urbana, 1997-99, rsch. scholar, 1997-99; assoc. faculty Columbia U., N.Y.C., 1999-2001, exec dir PCF, 2004—; faculty English dept. Rutgers U., Newark, 1999—, William Paterson U., Wayne, NJ, 1999-2001; dir. Ctr. Testing and Psychometrics, Min. of Culture and Higher Edn., Tehran, 1975-77; mem. mng. editl. bd. and adv. bd. PCF Who's Who in The Iranian-Am. Cmty. Author: Children's English series, 1990-95, Reading Through Reading (Best Acad. Book), 1992, Testing and Measurement (Best Acad. Book), 1993, A Comprehensive Grammar of English, 1996, Testing TEFL, 1997; author/editor: Issues in Teaching English as a Second Language, 1990, English for the Students of Medicine, 1989; co-author: English for Medical Students, 1974; editor: English for the Students of Medicine (II), 1993, Novin English-Persian Dictionary, vols. I and II, 1993; co-editor: Yadvareh Persian-English Dictionary, vols. I, II, III, 1991, Yadvareh English-Persian Dictionary, vols. I and II, 1991, Yadvareh Unabridged English-Persian Dictionary, 1993, others; contbr. numerous articles to profl. jours. Mem. com. Ctr. Studying and Compiling Univ Books in Humanities Min. Culture and Higher Edn., 1984—97, mem. com. curriculum devel., 1984—97, com. for testing, 1977—79; mem. com. lang. testing Lang. Ctr., 1979—81. Recipient award for creating an Innovative Model of Reading Comprehension, U. Ill., 1975, Cert. of Appreciation for best adminstrn. U. Mich., 1998, award for extraordinary ability INS, 1998, Disting. Prof. award, 2000, Disting. Rschr. award, 2000, Woman of Achievement award BBC, 2002; U. Ill. grantee, 1975; Fulbright scholar, 1970-75, Profl. Devel. scholar TESOL, 1999; fellow in rsch. U. Ill. 1973-75. Mem. TESOL, U. Ill. Alumni Assn., Am. Assn. for Applied Linguistics, Nat. Coun. Tchrs. English, Internat. Reading Assn. Avocations: reading, painting, tennis, swimming. Home: 290 Anderson St # 6K Hackensack NJ 07601 Office: Rutgers Univ Dept English 156 Conklin Hall 175 Univ Ave Newark NJ 07102 Personal E-mail: varzegar@gmail.com.

**VASANA, SUSAN (CHUN-YE),** engineering educator; d. De-Jun and Yi-Hua Ye; m. William Vasana, Feb. 14, 2001; children: Danica Hill Chang, Anna Ye Vasana. BS, Shanghai Jiaotong U., 1983; MS, Tongji U., 1986; PhD, Queen's U., Can., 1994. Lectr. Tongji U., Shanghai, 1986—89; scientist Nat. Inst. Sci. Rsch., Montreal, Que., Canada, 1994; sr. staff engr. Motorola Inc., Boynton Beach, Fla., 1994—2002; adj. prof. Fla. Atlantic U., Boca Raton, Fla., 2000—01; prof. U. North Fla., Jacksonville, 2002—. Recipient Silver Quills award, Motorola Inc., 2000. Mem.: IEEE, Internat. Assn. Sci. and Tech. for Devel. Achievements include patents for communication device having antenna switch diversity and method therefor; method and apparatus for demodulating a frequency shift keyed signal; method and apparatus for decoding a 2-level radio signal; method in a selective call receiver for synchronizing to a multi-level radio signal; method and apparatus for baud detection in a communication device; method and apparatus for accurate synchronization using symbol decision feedback; method and apparatus for correlation detection of multi-level signals with non-standard deviations; method and apparatus for automatic simulcast correlation for a correlation detector; method and apparatus for gain normalization of a correlation demodulator. Office: U North Fla 4567 St Johns Bluff Rd S Jacksonville FL 32224

**VASCONEZ, DENNIS CORNELIUS,** secondary school educator, voice educator; s. Jose Gilberto and Mary Jane Olga (Monson) Vasconez; m. Melissa Dawn Bryan, Aug. 23, 1997; children: Caleb Luther, Ethan Glen. MusB in Edn., Simpson Coll., 1999. Vocal tchr. grades 7-12 Belle Plaine (Iowa) Schs., 1999—2000, BGM Cmty. Sch. Dist., Brook Lyn, Iowa, 2000—02; vocal tchr. grades 9-12 Ottumwa (Iowa) HS, 2002—. Mem.: Am. Choral Dirs. Assn., Iowa Choral Dirs. Assn. Avocation: singing. Office: Ottumwa High Sch 501 E 2d St Ottumwa IA 52501

**VASELL, CHRIS,** artist, filmmaker; b. Chgo., 1974; BA, U. Mich.; MFA, Art Inst. Chgo. One-man shows include It Puts the Lotion in the Basket, boom, Oak Park, Ill., 2002, Don't go outside they're waiting for you, Blum & Poe, LA, 2005, Blum & Poe, 2006, exhibited in group shows at Whitcaps, Grand Rapids Art Mus., Mich., 1997, Nippon Steel, Chgo., 1999, Chicago Drawing, Forcefield Exhibition Space, Chgo., 1999, Stray Show, boom, Chgo., 2001, Here and Now, Chgo. Cultural Ctr., Chgo., 2002, A4 vs. Letter: A show of drawings, Apt. 1R, Chgo., 2002, I See a Darkness, Blum and Poe, LA, 2003, On Paper, Nicole Klagsburn, NY, 2004, Trials and Terrors, Mus. Contemporary Art, Chgo., 2005, Having New Eyes, Aspen Art Mus., Colo., 2006, Whitney Biennial: Day for Night, Whitney Mus. Am. Art, NY, 2006. Mailing: c/o Blum and Poe 2754 S La Cienega Blvd Los Angeles CA 90034*

**VASERSTEIN, LUDMILA,** music educator; b. Odessa, Ukraine, Sept. 21, 1949; arrived in USA, 1987; d. Peter and Rozalia Ruvinsky; m. Vladimir Vassershteyn, July 8, 1972; 1 child, Gabriel. MusB, Nikolaev Coll. Music, Ukraine, 1969; MusM, Odessa State Conservatory, Ukraine, 1974. Piano tchr. Sch. of Music, Odessa, Ukraine, 1974—87, MDCC, Miami, Fla., 1987—96; music and piano tchr. Montessori Sch. of Miami Beach, No. Bay Village, Fla., 1988—2003, Gulfstream Montessori Sch., Inc., Hallandale, Fla., 2003—. Mem.: Nat. Guild of Piano Tchr. (Nat. Honor Roll 2001—03), Music Tchr. Nat. Assoc., Suzuki Assoc. of Am. Republican. Judaism. Avocations: jogging, reading. Home: 251 174th St #1202 Miami Beach FL 33160 Office: Gulfstream Montessori Sch 750 Hallandale Beach Blvd Hallandale FL 33009

**VASEY, ANN L.,** pre-school administrator, counselor; b. Cleve., May 3, 1949; d. Albert and Norma (Miller) Ringler; m. Graham C. Vasey, Feb. 20, 1972; children: Rachel Nora Vasey, Corinne Elisabeth Vasey. BS in Elem. Edn. and Early Childhood, Boston U., 1972; MEd in Counseling Psychology, Northeastern U., Boston, 1974. Lic. mental health counselor State of Mass., marriage and family counselor State of Mass., cert. clin. mental health counselor Nat. Bd. Cert. Counselors; supr. and dir. K-12 Mass. Dept. Edn., prin. pre-K-6 Mass. Dept. Edn., registered tchr. Yoga Yoga Alliance, cert. Parent Child Home Program, Parent Leadership Tng., EMDR. Adolescent and family therapist SHARE, Lowell, Mass., 1974-76; instr. Framingham (Mass.) State Coll., 1976; instr. psychol. Quinsigamond C.C., Worcester, 1978—92; founding head The Learning Experience Elem. Sch., Marlborough, 1981—88; early childhood coord. Southbridge (Mass.) Pub. Schs., 1993—; psychotherapist YOU, Inc. Family Svcs., 1995—; founding supr. Family Ctr., 2000—. Psychol. cons. Childcare Lab. Sch., Worcester, Mass., 1989—91; founding chair Family Literacy Coalition, Southbridge, 1998—; presenter Assn. Early Childhood Dirs., Oxford, 2002; ednl. and psychol. cons. HMEA Children's Svc., Hudson, 2003; team mem. comprehensive rev. and site visits

Mass. Dept. Edn., 2004, 05. Co-author: (tchrs. guide) Some Psychological Issues Concerning Adolescent Debvelopment, 1987. Mem. Mass. Cmty. Partnerships Children, Northboro; bd. mem. Ashland Cultural Coun., Ashland, Mass., 1992—98; pres. bd. dir. Early Childhood Coun., 1993—; steering com. Cmty. Connections, Southbridge, Mass., 1998—. Grantee, Mass. Dept. Edn., 1993—. Mem.: Nat. Assn. Edn. Young Children (validator), Mass. Mental Health Counselors Assn., Delta Kappa Gamma. Avocations: yoga, travel. Home: 83 Woodland Rd Ashland MA 01721-1411 Office: Southbridge Pub Sch 156 West St Southbridge MA 01550 Personal E-mail: arvasey@aol.com.

**VASHOLZ, LOTHAR ALFRED,** retired insurance company executive; b. Milw., Feb. 20, 1930; s. Alfred and Charlotte Vasholz; m. Marji Cartwright, Dec. 26, 1954; children: Julie, Ann, Eric. BS, U. Colo., 1952; M of Pub. Svc. (hon.), U. Rio Grande. ChFC. Sr. cons. Life Ins. Mktg. & Rsch., Hartford, Conn., 1966—70; v.p. N.Am. Life, Chgo., 1970—73; sr. v.p. Bankers Mut., Freeport, Ill., 1973—75; dir. sales Security Life Denver, 1975—81; v.p. Union Ctrl. Life Ins. Co., Cin., 1981—85, sr. v.p., 1985—86, mgr. Columbus, Ohio, 1986—87, sr. v.p., chief mktg. officer Cin., 1987—91, exec. v.p., corp. mktg. officer, 1991—95; chmn. Carillon Investments, 1991—95; cons. mktg. and sales to life ins. industry, 1995—. Emeritus trustee U. Rio Grande, Ohio; co-chair adv. com. Salvation Army, Coachella Valley, Calif., 2006—. Fellow Life Mgmt. Inst.; mem. Phi Delta Theta (past internat. pres., past pres. ednl. found.). Republican. Office Phone: 760-345-5052.

**VASILAKI, LINDA BOOZER,** music educator; b. Grand Rapids, Mich., Jan. 2, 1949; d. Gordon and Dianne (Demmon) Boozer; m. Yuri G. Vasilaki, Sept. 29, 1979; children: Camilla Dianne, Andrew Alten, Maria Demmon. BMus in Edn., Mich. State U., 1971; MFA, U. Iowa, 1973; EdD in Curriculum and Instrn., Argosy U., Sarasota, Fla., 2003. Cert. kindergarten-12 music tchr., 7-8 all subjects tchr., Mich., Fla.; cert. Orff, Level 1. Kindergarten-6 music cons. Grand Rapids (Mich.) Pub. Schs., 1973-75; tchr., founder Suzuki violin program Grand Rapids Bd. Edn., 1976-80; tchr. violin Nat. Music Camp, Interlochen, Mich., 1981, 82; chair music dept., orch. dir. Out of Door Acad., Sarasota, Fla., 1983—; founder, dir. Encore Fine Arts Program, Sarasota, Fla., 1988—. Tchr. viola Blue Lake Fine Arts Camp, Muskegon, 1973; violist Fla. West Coast Symphony, Sarasota, 1982—; mem. Grand Rapids Symphony, 1973-80; tchr. Suzuki Assn. Am., Sarasota, 1976—; adj. music/viola faculty Hope Coll., Grand Valley State Coll. Author: Music Lovers' Cookbook, 1983, Symbol of Liberty, 1985; editor: Out of Door Academy Cuisine, 1983; contbr. articles to profl. jours. Counselor, music therapist Indian Trails Camp for the Phys. Handicapped, Grand Rapids, 1968-69; violist Venice (Fla.) Symphony, 1991-92; former mem. faculty New Eng. Music Camp. Scholar New Coll. Music Festival, 1971, Lenox String Quartet Seminar, 1971, Banff (Can.) Centre-Fine Arts String Quartet Seminar, 1972, U. Iowa, 1972-73; Fla. Humanities grantee, summer 1995. Mem. Phi Kappa Lambda, Kappa Alpha Theta, Delta Omicron (pres. 1971), Delta Kappa Gamma. Avocations: music, reading, writing. Home: 3341 Bougainvillea St Sarasota FL 34239-5704 Business E-Mail: lvasilaki@oda.edu.

**VASILJEV, ALEXANDER VALERJOVICH,** economist, metallurgical engineer; b. Kuragata, Kazahstan, June 21, 1955; s. Valery Alexandrovich and Olga Vladimirovna Vasiljev; m. Marina Genadievna Tuzovskaya, Dec. 31, 1985; children: Olga, Nataliya. Diplomate of engring., Metall. Inst., 1977; Candidate Scis., Inst. Engring., Moscow, 1982; postgrad., Inst. Sociology Acad. Scis., Moscow, 1992; PhD in Econs., Acad. Mgmt. Russia, Moscow, 1993. Jr., then sr. scis. employee Inst. Mariupol, Ukraine, 1980-84, mgr. rsch. lab. socioecon. problems, 1985-87; mgr. socially econ. lab. Inst. Labour of Ukraine, Mariupol, 1987-90; mgr. sect. social econ. problems of port's indsl. cities Inst. Econ.-Law Rsch., Nat. Acad. Scis. Ukraine, Mariupol, 1993-98, organizer Mariupol br., 1995-97, chmn. sect. sci. coun. Olge W. Wasilievay-Cath., 1996—97; chmn. sci. coun. Inst. Econ. and Social/Cultural Rsch. Mariupol, 1989—, prof. dep. acad. mgr. staff, 2003—; prof. U. Ukraine, 2005—. Lectr. Donetsk U., 1990-91; prof. PriAzov State Tech. U., Mariupol, 1993-98, Taganrog's Inst. Mgmt. and Econs., Russia, 2001-02, Nat. U. Odessa, 2004—; vice chmn. Azov, Ukrainian Dept., Acad. Econ., Scis. and Entrepreneurship, Mariupol, 1999—, Civil Internat. Com., Tanais Reg., 2001—; rep. Azov Ukrainian Econ. Dept. Acad. Econ., Sci. and Entrepreneurship in West Europe and Am., Warsaw, 2000—; chief br. mgr. dep. acad. mgr. staff, Mariupol, 2002-03. Contbr. articles to profl. jours. Scholar Acad. Russia, 1991-92 Probationer Inst. IBMER Poland, 2000-2001; recipient cert. Frederick P. Furth Found., 1990, medal "Met. Gotey & Cafa, St. Ignatia", 1999. Mem. AAAS, Am. Biog. Inst. (rsch. bd.), N.Y. Acad. Scis., 1817 Heritage Soc. N.Y. Acad. Scis., Union Econ. Ukraine, Acad. Econ. Scis. and Entrepreneurship (bd.). Avocations: tennis, windsurfing, travel. Home: Fl519 Dovzgenko 9B St 65058 Odessa Ukraine Office: Inst Econ/Social/Cult Rsch Box 257 65001 Odessa Ukraine Office Phone: 380957292016. Personal E-mail: vasiljev2003@mail.ru. Business E-Mail: vasiljev@cic-wsc.org, committe@cic-wsc.org.

**VASILYADIS, LEON,** retired social worker; b. Tepeköy, Gökceada, Turkey, Sept. 11, 1942; s. Vasil and Tiryandafilya Vasilyadis; m. Vasiliki Berberoglu (div.); m. Rebecca Ransom-Vasilyadis, Feb. 14, 1998. BA, NYU, 1965. Case mgr. Dept. Social Svcs. City of NY, 1966—85; social worker Neighborly Sr. Svc., Clearwater, Fla., 1986—2001; svc. provider Devel. Svcs., St. Petersburg, 2001—05; ret. Recipient Svc. award, Cath. Youth Orgn., 1959, First prize, Midwest Fed. Chaparral Poets, 1995. Mem.: Pan Imbrian Benevolent Soc. (v.p. 1966—68). Democrat. Greek Orthodox. Avocations: poetry, volunteering. Home: 330 Feather Tree Dr Clearwater FL 33765

**VASILYEV, DMITRY,** research scientist; b. St.Petersburg, Russia, Dec. 26, 1976; s. Mikhail Sergeevich Lamkin and Valentina Mihaĭlovna Pavlova. MS (hon.), St. Petersburg State Tech. U., Russia, 2000. Rschr. A.F. Ioffe Physico-technical Inst., St. Petersburg, Russia, 2000—01; software engr. St. Petersburg Call Ctr., 2001—02; rsch. asst. MIT, Cambridge, Mass., 2002—. Contbr. articles to profl. jours. Fellow, MIT, 2002—03, Nat. Semiconductor, 2004—05; scholar, Internat. Soros Sci. Ednl. Program, 1998—99, 1999—2000, 2000—01. Achievements include research in model order reduction for linear and nonlinear dynamical systems. Office Phone: 617-253-1583. Personal E-mail: vasilyev@mit.edu.

**VASILYEVA, ANNA,** artist, writer; b. Kiev, Ukraine, Nov. 24, 1977; d. Tamara Balenko and Vladimir Vasylyev. Fine Art Degree, T.G. Shevchenko State Art Sch., 1997; BA in Art, Calif. State U., Northridge, 2005. Tchr. art KidsArt, Tarzana, Calif., 1999; designer, illustrator Pub. Ho. KM Academia, Kiev, 1996, All Electronics Corp., Van Nuys, Calif., 2002—; tchr. art Marina's Sch. Music and Art, Northridge, Calif., 2001; tchg. assoc. Calif. State U., Northridge, 2004—; graphic designer Big Screen Network Prodns., Westlake Village, Calif., 2005—. Exhibitions include State Fall Exhbn. Art, 1993, First Internat. Exhbn. -Presentation of Periodical Pubs. about Pets, 1995, Art Gallery of U. Kiev-Mogila Acad., 1996, Art Acad. L.A., 1999, Svitozor Gallery, 1999—2001, L.A. Valley Coll., 2000, L.A. Mission Coll., 2002, Limner Gallery, 2003, Pacific Design Ctr., L.A., 2004, Art Assn. Harrisburg's 76th Ann. Juried Exhbn., 2004; film editor, designer: Streetlight Cinema, 2004—; contbr. articles to mags. Recipient Biography Pub., The Nat. Dean's List, 2003; Campus Fee grant, 2003—. Avocations: reading, travel, horseback riding. Office: All Electronics Corp 14928 Oxnard St Van Nuys CA 91411 Office Phone: 818-904-0529. Personal E-mail: anya@artistanya.com

**VASKEVITCH, DAVID,** information technology executive; 3 children. BS in math., Computer Sci., Philosophy, U. Toronto, M in Computer Sci. With Standard Software; owner PlanDesign, Toronto, Canada; with 3Com Corp., Microsoft Corp., Redmond, Wash., 1986—, dir. U.S. mktg., 1986, gen. mgr. enterprise computing, 1993, v.p., distributed applications platform, chief architect, 1998—99, sr. v.p., developer, 1999—2000, sr. v.p. Bus. Applications Divsn., 2000—01, sr. v.p., chief tech. officer Bus. Platform, 2006—. Mem. adv. bd., Live Labs (Rsch. partnership between MSN and Microsoft Rsch.) Microsoft Corp., 2006—. Author: Client/Server Strategies: A Survival Guide for Corporate Re-engineers, 1993. While at the U. Toronto in the

1970's, he invented a typewriter-terminal-based communications messaging network that predated PC-based e-mail systems. Office: Microsoft Corp One Microsoft Way Redmond WA 98052-6399*

**VASKO, FRANCIS JOSEPH,** mathematics professor; b. Bethlehem, Pa., Mar. 23, 1952; s. Frank and Ann Vasko; m. Nancy Louise Rosenberger, July 1, 1978; 1 child, Lisa Elizabeth. MS in Math., Lehigh U., Bethlehem, Pa., 1976; MS in Indsl. Engring., Lehigh U., 1978, PhD, 1983. Math. prof. Kutztown U., Pa., 1986—. Applied math. cons. Dr.Francis Vasko, Cons., Hellertown, Pa., 1986—. Contbr. over 48 articles to profl. jours. Bd. of trustees Hellertown Libr., Pa., 1995—98. Recipient Big Brother of the yr., Big Bros./Big Sisters of the Lehigh Valley, 1994. Mem.: Sigma XI (full mem.). Achievements include research in new mathematical solution procedures for steel industry production planning and scheduling problems. Home: 510 Ellen St Hellertown PA 18055 Office: Kutztown University 170 Lytle Hall Kutztown PA 19530 Office Phone: 610-683-4417. Business E-Mail: vasko@kutztown.edu.

**VASKO, PETER THEODORE FREDERICK,** priest; b. Bklyn., Nov. 28, 1943; s. Theodore Frederick and Catherine (Buday) V. BA in Philosophy, Cath. U. Am., 1966, BD in Theology, 1969; postgrad., Duke U., 1972-73, Franciscan Studium Biblicum, Jerusalem, 1985-86. Ordained priest Roman Cath. Ch., 1987. Pub. rels. asst. Holiday Inn/Oak Grove, Durham, N.C., 1972-74; dir. devel. NAA, Charlotte, N.C., 1974-76; dir. CETA, New Orleans, 1976-78; v.p. sales Peachtree Corners Corp. Travel, Atlanta, 1978-81; bd. dirs. Franciscan Custody, Jerusalem, 1992—2001; pres. Franciscan Found. for The Holy Land, Jerusalem, 1994—. Editor photo essay See the Holy Land, 1993, One Visit to The Holy Land, 2004; editor The Holy Land Mag., 1993-95; writer, narrator video On the Road of Christ, 1994; narrator video The Life of Jesus: Scriptural Journey, 1997; guest on Mother Angelica Live, 1996, 97, 98, 02, 03, Pat Robertson 700 Club, 1996, EWTN's World Over Show, 2004, 05, 06, others; co-prodr. documentary Crisis in the Holy Land, 1994. Bd. dirs. St. Ives Soc., Jerusalem, 1992-94; guide White House Via U.S. Embassy, Jerusalem, 1992—; chaplain U.S. Marines/U.S. Consulate, Jerusalem, 1988—. Recipient Achievement in Pub. Rels. award Pub. Rels. Soc., Raleigh, 1975, Marine Security Guard Bn. Co. B Cert. of Appreciation, 1995, 99, U.S. Marine Security Detachment Comdr. Commendation award, 1999, State of Tex. Commn.: Theodore Peter F. Vasko commd. as Hon. Texan by Gov. R. Perry, 2002, Cert. of Flag Presentation of USS Ariz. by Rear Adm. Robert T. Conway, Jr., USN, Comdr., Navy Region, Hawaii, 2002, Cert. of Appreciation for Good Conduct, 2002-03, UNMC-MSG Detachment of Jerusalem, Cert. of Appreciation, MSG Det. for Outstanding Svc. as Det. Chaplain, 2003; named Jaycee of Yr., N.C. chpt., 1973, Top Ten People in Cath. Ch. Inside the Vatican mag., 2006; decorated mem. Equestrial Order of the Holy Sepulchre, 1992; order of merit Sovereign Mil. Order of The Knights Templar. Mem.: Marine Embassy Guard Assn. (mem. 2003).

**VASMATZIDIS, IOANNIS,** systems engineer; s. Prodromos and Anna Vasmatzidis; m. Hyesik Choi, Dec. 1, 1995; 1 child, AnnaMaria Choi. Diploma in mech. engring., Aristotle U. of Thessaloniki, Greece, 1988; MS in indsl. engring., U. Okla., 1990, PhD in indsl. engring., 1995. Usability engr. Pershing LLC, Jersey City, 1996—; ergonomics, project engr. BCAM Internat. Inc., Melville, NY, 1995—96; vice pres., group mgr. Pershing LLC, Jersey City, 2001—. Co-author: The Occupational Ergonomics Handbook; contbr. articles numerous profl. jours. Adv. bd. mem. Usability Profl. Group of India. Cleo-Cross Internat. Student award, U. Okla., 1993. Mem.: Usability Profl. Assn., Human Factors and Ergonomics Soc., Alpha Pi Mu Engring. Achievements include research in effects of heat strees on cognitive performance; design of the user interface for the marketspeed(TM) windows product of harrisdirect; responsible for overseeing the User interface design of the online brokerage website www.harrisdirect.com. Office: Pershing LLC A BNY Securities Group Co One Pershing Plaza Jersey City NJ 07399 Personal E-mail: vasmas@aol.com. E-mail: ivasmatzidis@pershing.com.

**VASQUEZ, GADDI H.,** ambassador, former federal agency administrator; b. Carrizo Springs, Tex., Jan. 22, 1955; m. Elaine Vasquez; 1 child, Jason. AA in Criminal Justice, Rancho Santiago C.C., 1972; BA in Pub. Svc. Mgmt., U. Redlands, 1980; DHL (hon.), U. LaVerne, 2003. Police officer City of Orange, Calif., 1975-79; coord. community rels., mgr.'s office City of Riverside, Calif., 1979-81; exec. asst. Orange County Bd. Suprs., 3d Dist., Calif., 1981-85, mem. Calif., 1987—95; area mgr. So. Calif. Edison Co., 1985; hispanic liaison Office of Gov. George Deukmejian, Calif., 1985, from dep. appointments sec. to chief dep. appointments sec. Calif., 1985-87; dir. Peace Corps, Washington, 2002—06; US rep. to UN agencies for food & agrl. US Dept. State, 2006—. Mem. Transp. Corridor Agys. Bd., 1987—, chmn. 1990-91; local agy. formation commn., 1988-93, chmn. 1990-91; mem. Calif. Film Commn., 1988-91, Calif. Coun. Criminal Justice, 1989—; founder, co-chair, Orange County Health Care Task Force, 1990—; with White House Fellowships Commn., 1990-91; co-chmn. Orange County Congestion Mgmt. Policy Task Force, 1990—; bd. dirs. Orange County Transp. Authority, 1991—, exec. com. 1992—, vice chmn. 1993—; regional advisory and planning coun., 1991—, vice chmn. 1992, chmn. 1993; official observer Armenian Independence elections, 1991. Bd. dirs. Future Leaders Am., Southwest Voter Rsch. Inst., calif. First Amendment Coalition, Orange County Boy Scout Coun., So. Area Foster Care Effort, Orange County Performing Arts Ctr., Opera Pacific; trustee Am. Coun. Young Polit. Leaders; adv. bd. Pediatric Cancer Rsch. Found, Orange County Juvenile Connection Project, Calif. Office Traffic Safety, The Salvation Army Orange County, Project AERO, Constitutional Rights Found. Orange County; community coun. Prentice Day Sch.; hon. adv. bd. Adam Walsh Ctr.; hon. bd. govs. Power Mus.; leadership coun. Orange County Points of Light. Named Officer of Yr., Am. Legion, 1977. Outstanding Young Man of Am. U.S. C.of C., 1985, One of 100 Most Influential Hispanics in U.S. Hispanic Bus. Mag., 1986-87, 88-89, 91-92, 92-93, 2002-03, Govt. Hispanic Bus. Advocate of Yr. U.S. Hispanic Champer Region I, 1991; recipient Alumni Achievement award Santa Ana Coll., 1988, Alumni of Yr.award U. Redlands, 1989, Humanitarian award NCCJ, 1989, award State Child Devel. Adv. Com., 1990, Tree of Life award Jewish Nat. Fund, 1991, Ralph E. Hudson Open Space award Landscape Architects Found., 1992, Disting. Alumni award Coun. Young Polit. Leaders, 2002, Outstanding Alumni award Am. Assn. C.C.s, 2003.*

**VASQUEZ, JO ANNE,** retired science educator; BS in biology, No. Ariz. U., 1965, MA in early childhood edn., 1968; PhD in curriculum and instrn., Kennedy-Western U., 1999. Assoc. prof. sci. and edn. Ariz. State U.; lead curriculum developer, sci. specialist Mesa Pub. Schs.; profl. devel. cons. Macmillan/McGraw Hill, 2000—. Writer Macmillan/McGraw-Hill K-6 Sci., 1998—; bd. dirs. Nat. Sci. Bd., 2002—; chair elem. sci. tchg. and assessment standards Nat. Bd. Profl. Tchg. Standards; mem. exec. bd. Nat. Acad. Sci. Ctr. for Sci., Math., and Engring. Edn.; former com. chair, reviewer Nat. Sci. Found.; cons. in field. Past pres. adv. bd. Sally Ride's TOYChallenge. Named Tchr. Yr., Nat. Environ. Assn.; recipient honoree, Nat. Assn. Latino Elected and Apptd. Officials, 2004, Gustave Oahus Elem. Sci. Tchg. award, Robert H. Carleton award, Nat. Sci. Teachers Assn., 2006. Mem.: Nat. Coun. Elem. Science Educators (past pres.), Internat. Coun. Sci. Edn. Orgn. (past pres.), Ariz. Sci. Tchrs. Assn. (past pres.), Nat. Sci. Edn. Leadership Assn. (pres.-elect), Nat. Sci. Tchrs. Assn (past mem. nat. bd. dirs., elected first Hispanic pres., Disting. Svc. to Sci. Edn. award Search for Excellence in Elem. Sci. Edn. and Supervision). Achievements include first K-12 tchr. apptd. to bd. dirs. NSF Nat. Sci. Bd. Office: Nat Sci Found 4201 Wilson Blvd Arlington VA 22230*

**VASQUEZ, JUAN FLORES,** federal judge; b. San Antonio, June 24, 1948; s. Jose and Amelia (Flores) V.; m. Mary Theresa Schultz, Aug. 22, 1970; children: Juan Jr., Jaime. BA, U. Tex., 1972; JD, U. Houston, 1977; LLM in Taxation, NYU, 1978. Bar: Tex. 1977, U.S. Dist. Ct. (so. dist.) Tex. 1982, U.S. Dist. Ct. (we. dist.) Tex. 1985, U.S. Ct. Appeals (5th cir.) 1982, U.S. Supreme Ct. 1996, U.S. Tax Ct. 1978. Acct. Coopers & Lybrand, L.A., 1972-74; tax atty. Office of Chief Coun. IRS, Houston, 1978-82, Leighton, Hood & Vasquez, San Antonio, 1987; pvt. practice San Antonio, 1987-95; judge U.S. Tax Ct., Washington, 1995—. Mem. ABA, Mex.-Am. Bar Assn.

Tex. and San Antonio, Nat. Hispanic Bar Assn., Nat. Judicial Coll., Hispanic Bar Assn. D.C., Coll. State Coll. Tex., Tex. State Bar Assn., San Antonio Bar Assn. Office: US Tax Ct 400 2nd St NW Washington DC 20217-0002

**VASQUEZ, RAMON FRANCISCO,** music educator; b. Del Rio, Tex., Mar. 7, 1972; s. Ramon Vasquez and Maria Carolina Torres. MusB, Northwestern State U. La., 1994; MusM, U. N. Tex., 1997. Asst. prof. music Auburn U., Ala. Adjudicator Nat. Trumpet Competition, Fairfax, 1999—, McKnight Artist Fellowships for Performing Musicians, Mpls., 2003. Assoc. mem. Chgo. Civic Orch., 1997. Recipient Masters Divsn. Winner, Nat. Trumpet Competition, 1997. Mem.: Internat. Trumpet Guild. Avocations: music, drum corps. Home: 3721 Chandler DR NE Minneapolis MN 55421-4434 Office: Auburn U Dept Music 101 Goodwin Hall Auburn AL 36849-5420 Personal E-mail: trptjock@aol.com.

**VASQUEZ, VICTOR R.,** chemical engineering educator; Licentiate in Chem. Engring., U. Costa Rica, San Jose, 1990; MSChemE, U. Nev., 1997, PhDChemE, 1999. Prof., rschr. U. Costa Rica, San Jose, 1991—95; assoc. prof. chem. engring. U. Nev., Reno, 1999—. Cons. Costa Rican Govt., others, San Jose, 1991—95. Sci. and tech. mem. Latino Rsch. Inst., U. Nev., Reno, 2004. Grantee, NSF, 2004—05. Mem.: AIChE. Achievements include research in development of Monte Carlo methods for uncertainty analysis. Office: Univ Nev Chem Engring Dept Mail Stop 170 Reno NV 89557 Office Phone: 775-784-6060. Personal E-mail: victor.vasquez@unr.edu.

**VASQUEZ, WILLIAM LEROY,** business educator, consultant; b. Austin, Tex., Mar. 9, 1944; s. Eliseo M. and Janie (Garcia) V. BS with distinction, Nova Southeastern U., 1983, MBA, 1985, DBA, 1992. Cert. Inst. Cert. Profl. Mgrs., 1990, Inst. Cert. Computing Profls., 1993. Svc. mgr. Data Gen. Corp., various, Latin Am., 1972-80; product mgr. Gould, Inc., Ft. Lauderdale, Fla., 1980—84, Tektronix Inc., Portland, Oreg., 1984—86, Racal-Milgo, Ft. Lauderdale, 1988—90, Citibank Internat., Ft. Lauderdale, 1991—2001; ret., 2001. Instr. City U., Portland campus, 1987-88; Maryhurst Coll., 1985-88, Nova Southeastern U. (domestic and internat.), 1988—, pres. internat. alumni assn.; instr. St. Thomas U., 1989—, Fla. Atlantic U., 1993—. Mem. VFW, Nat. Bus. Edn. Assn., U.S. Submarine Vets., Inc., Mensa. Republican. Avocations: guitar, model trains, fine arts. Home: 9788 NW 18th St Coral Springs FL 33071-5824 Office: Keiser Coll eCampus 1900 W Commercial Blvd Fort Lauderdale FL 33309 Office Phone: 954-783-7339 ext. 156, 954-351-4040. E-mail: wvasquez@earthlink.net.

**VASSALLE, MARIO,** physiologist; b. Viareggio, Lucca, Italy, May 26, 1928; came to U.S., 1958; s. Giuseppe and Antonietta (Vassalle) V.; m. Anna Maria Petrucci; children: Andrew G., Alessandra A., Massimo B., Roberto M., Francesca A. MD cum laude, U. Pisa, Italy, 1953, specialization in cardiology cum laude, 1955; doctorate honoris causa, U. Ferrara, Italy, 1990. Med. diplomate. Intern Istituto di Medicine and Cardiology U. Pisa, 1953-55, asst. Istituto di Patologia Medica, 1956-58; acting chief resident in medicine French Hosp., N.Y.C., 1958-59; trainee cardiovascular rsch. & tng. program dept. physiology Med. Coll. Ga., Augusta, 1959-60; postdoctoral fellow dept. physiology SUNY-Downstate Med. Ctr., Bklyn., 1960-61, N.Y. Heart Assn. fellow dept. physiology, 1961-62, instr., 1962, vis. asst. prof., 1964-65, asst. prof., 1965-66, assoc. prof., 1966-71, prof., 1971—; NIH fellow Physiologisches Institut U. Bern, Switzerland, 1962-64. Vis. prof. U. Ferrara, 1971, U. Vt., Burlington, 1978, Cath. Univ. Gemelli, Rome, 1984-85, SUNY at Stony Brook, 1994; assoc. editor Am. Jour. Physiology: Heart and Circulatory Physiology, 1976-80; mem. editorial bd. Circulation Rsch., 1974-80, European Jour. Pharmacology, 1985-90, Jour. Electrocardiology, 1985—; mem. editorial bd. New Trends in Arrhythmias, 1985-96, assoc. editor, 1991-96; editorial cons. Am. Jour. Physiology, Circulation, Science, Jour. Molecular Cell Cardiology, Cardiovascular Rsch; cons. NIH; mem. NIH Cardiopulmonary Study Sect., 1981-85, ad hoc mem., 1988; invited participant numerous confs., symposiums and workshops. Author (editor): Research in Phusiology, 1971, Cardiac Physiology for the Clinician, 1976, Excitation and Neural Control of the Heart, 1982; author: Diario di un Fisiologo del Cuore, 1992, Lost Emotions, 1994, The Riddle of the Mind, 1996, The Reality of the Self, 2000; editor: Chanderl McCuskey Brooks: The Scientist and the Man, 1990; author: Dunes, 2001, Twilights, 2003, Not Always, 2004, Leaves of Autumn, 2006, numerous papers, revs., chpts. and abstracts. Fulbright travel grantee, 1958-62; recipient A. and A. Sinsheimer Fund award, 1966-71, N.Y. Health Rsch. Coun. award, 1972-75. Mem. AAAS, Am. Physiol. Soc., Am. Heart Assn. (cons. on basic scis. 1969—), N.Y. Heart Assn. (bd. dirs. 1978-84), N.Y. Acad. Scis., Cardiac Muscle Soc., Cardiac Electrophysiol. Group (pres. 1972-73), Internat. Study Group for Rsch. in Cardiac Metabolism, Harvey Soc., Mex. Soc. Cardiology (hon.); Sigma Xi (pres. Downstate Med. Ctr. chpt. 1984). Roman Catholic. Home: 104 Huntington Rd Port Washington NY 11050-3511 Office: SUNY Downstate Med Ctr Box 31 450 Clarkson Ave Brooklyn NY 11203-2056 Business E-Mail: mario.vassalle@downstate.edu.

**VASSALLO, EDWARD E.,** lawyer; b. NYC, Aug. 12, 1943; BS, Columbia U., 1965, MS, 1967; JD cum laude, Fordham U., 1973. Bar: N.Y. 1974. Ptnr. Fitzpatrick, Cella, Harper & Scinto, NYC. Mem.: ABA, N.Y.C. Bar Assn., N.Y. Intellectual Property Law Assn. (pres.), Fed. Cir. Bar Assn., Internat. Trademark Assn., Am. Intellectual Property Law Assn. Office: Fitzpatrick Cella Harper & Scinto 30 Rockefeller Plz Fl 38 New York NY 10112-3800 Office Phone: 212-218-2241. Business E-Mail: eevassallo@fchs.com.

**VASSALLUZZO, JOSEPH S.,** retail company executive; BA, Pa. State U.; MBA, Temple U. Exec. v.p. growth and support svcs. Staples, Inc., Framingham, Mass., 1993, exec. v.p. growth and devel., 1993—96, pres. realty and devel. divsn., 1997—99, vice chmn., 1999—. Worked in real estate Mobil Oil Amerada Hess Corp., Am. Stores Co. Office: Staples Inc PO Box 9267 Framingham MA 01701-9265

**VASSELL, GREGORY S.,** electric utility consultant; b. Moscow, Dec. 24, 1921; came to U.S., 1951, naturalized, 1957; s. Gregory M. and Eugenia M. Wasiljeff; m. Martha Elizabeth Williams, Apr. 26, 1957; children: Laura Kay, Thomas Gregory. Dipl. Eng. in Elec. Engring, Tech. U. Berlin, 1951; MBA in Corp. Fin., NYU, 1954. With Am. Electric Power Svc. Corp., Columbus, Ohio, 1951-88, v.p. system planning, 1973-76, dir., 1973-88, sr. v.p. system planning, 1976-88; electric utility cons. Upper Arlington, Ohio, 1988—. Bd. dirs. Columbus & Southern Ohio Electric Co., 1981-88, Cardinal Operating Co.; mem. tech. adv. com. transmission FPC, 1968-70, FERC Task Force on Power Pooling, 1980-81; mem. U.S. coun. World Energy Coun. Contbr. articles to profl. jours. Fellow IEEE (life); mem. NAE, Athletic Club Columbus Home and Office: 2247 Pinebrook Rd Columbus OH 43220-4327

**VASSER, ALBERT GLENN,** lawyer; b. Pine Bluff, Ark., July 20, 1947; s. Albert P. Vasser and Bobbie Ann (Nipper) Hogan; m. Judith Jackson, Aug. 16, 1969; 1 child, Vicki Suzanne. BS in Bus. Adminstrn. with honors, U. Ark., 1969, JD, 1972. Bar: Ark., U.S. Dist. Ct. Ark., U.S. Ct. Appeals (8th cir.), U.S. Supreme Ct. From assoc. to ptnr. McKenzie, Graves, McRae, Vasser and Baler, Prescott, Ark., 1972—. Pres. Prescott (Ark.) Sch. Bd., 1985; mcpl. judge City of Prescott, Ark.; bd. dirs. S.W. Ark. Regional Health Ctr., El Dorado; bd. trustees, adminstr. Rd. First United Meth. Ch. 1st lt. U.S. Army. Recipient Spl. Justice award Ark. Supreme Ct., 1991. Fellow Am. Coll. Mortgage Attys., Ark. Bar Found. (bd. mem., pres.); mem. Ark. Bar Assn. (del. and com. chmn., pres.-elect 2004, Golden Gavel award 1984), Nevada County Bar Assn. (pres., com. mem.). Avocations: tennis, golf. Office: McKenzie McRae & Vasser 122 E 2nd St PO Box 599 Prescott AR 71857-0599

**VASSIL, JOHN CHARLES,** lawyer; b. Youngstown, OH, Mar. 3, 1930; s. Callias and Anastasia (Kyriakides) V.; m. Anita Devlin, Nov. 28, 1965; 1 son, Russell. BS in Chem. Engring., Carnegie Inst. Tech., 1952; JD, George Washington U., 1958. Bar: N.Y. 1960, U.S. Dist. Cts. (so and ea. dists.) N.Y. 1961, U.S. Ct. Appeals (2d cir.) 1965, U.S. Ct. Appeals (fed. cir.) 1982, U.S. Supreme Ct. 1961. Patent examiner U.S. Patent Office, 1955-58; ptnr. Morgan & Finnegan, LLP, N.Y.C., 1961—2001, counsel, 2002—. Lectr. in field.

Served with C.E., U.S. Army, 1953-55. Mem. ABA, Assn. Bar City N.Y., N.Y. Patent Law Assn., Am. Patent Law Assn., Am. Arbitration Assn. Home: 420 E 54th St # 36H New York NY 10022-5179 Office Phone: 212-465-8700. Business E-Mail: jcvassil@morganfinnegan.com.

**VASSILIOU, EUSTATHIOS,** chemist, consultant; b. Athens, Greece, Aug. 22, 1934; s. Theodore Vassiliou and Evlalia Porfiriou; m. Kleoniki Irene Parri; children: Theodore, Helen Apostolico, Evelyn Gearing. BSChemE, Nat. Tech. U., Athens, 1958; PhD in Chemistry, Victoria U., Manchester, Eng., 1964; postgrad., Harvard U., 1966—67. Registered patent agt. Rsch. chemist DuPont, Wilmington, Del., 1967—73, staff chemist Phila., 1973—78, rsch. assoc., 1978—85, sr. rsch. assoc. Wilmington, 1985—91, Termax Corp., Chgo., 1985—; fellow Intell. prop., 1991; pres. WTPA, Inc., Newark, Del., 1991—2003; engring. cons. in intellectual property, 2003—. Pres. PatCore, Inc., Newark, 1993—96; v.p. Health Style, Inc., Newark, 1993—97, 21st Century Rsch. Corp., Pulsbo, Wash., 1994—98. Author: (book) Physical Chemistry of Glasses. With Greek Army, 1958—60. Scholar, Greek Scholarship Found., 1960-1964, NATO, 1964. Mem.: Harvard Chemists Assn. Achievements include invention of DuPont's Silverstone coatings for cookware; co-invention Dupont's granite type Corian; more than 150 US patents in miscellaneous fields; inventions and co-inventions of crucial Termax Fasteners, especially for the automotive industry. Home and Office: 12 South Townview Ln Newark DE 19711-7419 E-mail: ev@wtpa.biz.

**VASSILOPOULOU-SELLIN, RENA,** researcher; b. Dec. 29, 1949; MD, Albert Einstein Coll. Medicine, 1974. Resident Montefiore Hosp., Bronx, 1974-77; fellow Northwestern U., Chgo., 1977-80; prof. Univ. Tex., Houston, 1980—. Fellow ACP, Am. Assn. Clin. Endocrinol.; mem. AAAS, AMA, Am. Soc. Bone and Mineral Rsch., Am. Diabetes Assn., Am. Soc. Clin. Oncology, Endo Soc. Office: Anderson Cancer Ctr 1515 Holcombe Blvd # 15 Houston TX 77030-4009

**VASSILYADI, MICHAEL,** pediatric neurosurgeon; b. Istanbul, Turkey, Nov. 25, 1961; s. Iraki and Cristal Vassilyadi; m. Anastasia Lyras, Aug. 23, 1986; children: Frank Photios, Christal, Anthony Irakli. BSc, McGill U., 1980—83, MSc, 1984—86, MD, CM, 1986—90. Diplomate Am. Bd. Pediat. Neurol. Surgery, Am. Bd. Neurol. Surgery. Med. staff Children's Hosp. of Ea. Ont., Ottawa, Canada, 1996—. Asst. prof. surgery U. of Ottawa, 1996—2003; assoc. prof. surgery and pediat. U. Ottawa, 2003—; investigator Children's Hosp. Ea. Ont. Rsch. Inst., Canada. Contbr. articles to profl. jours.; mem. editl. bd. Pediat. Neurosurgery. Ottawa chpt. dir. Think First Can. Recipient Matching Travel award, Children's Hosp. of Ea. Ont. Rsch. Inst., 1998, 2003—05, Best sci. posters, Neurol. Sciences of Que., 1995; Farquharson Rsch. scholarship, Med. Rsch. of Can., 1987, Dr. James Douglas Rsch. fellowship in Pathology, McGill U., 1985. Fellow: ACS, Am. Acad. Pediat., Royal Coll. Physicians and Surgeons Can.; mem.: Can. Pediat. Neurosurgery Group, Am. Bd. Neurol. Surgery, Am. Bd. of Pediat. Neurol. Surgery, Can. Neurosurg. Soc., Am. Soc. Pediatric Neurosurgeons, Coll. Physicians and Surgeons Ont., Coll. des Medecins du Que., Can. Med. Assn., Can. Congress Neurol. Scis., Am. Epilepsy Soc., Am. Assn. Neurol. Surgeons, Ont. Med. Assn., Internat. Soc. Pediatric Neurosurgery, Congress Neurol. Surgeons. Greek Orthodox. Achievements include research in pediatric neurosurgery. Office: Children's Hosp of Eastern Ontario 401 Smyth Rd Ottawa ON Canada K1H 8L1 Office Phone: 613-738-3985. E-mail: vassilyadi@cheo.on.ca.

**VASUDEV, BRAHM SARUP,** nephrologist; b. New Delhi, Apr. 12, 1971; MBBS, U. Pune, India, 1994. Resident Brookdale Hosp. Med. Ctr., Bklyn., 2001, chief resident in internal medicine, 2001; fellow critical care medicine Albert Einstein Coll. Medicine, N.Y., 2002—03; fellow nephrology Med. Coll. of Wis. Affiliated Hosps., Milw., 2004, fellow transplant nephrology, 2004—. Evaluator kidney transplantation Froedtert Meml. Luth. Hosp., Milw., 2004—; clin. rschr. Med. Coll. Wis., 2002—, investigator clin. trials, 2004—; instr. Med. Coll. of Wis. Affiliated Hosps., 2002—; cons. Shire Pharmaceuticals, Milw., 2003—04. Recipient Excellence award, American Transplant Congress, 2004, Young Investigator award, 2005. Mem.: Am. Soc. Nephrology (assoc.), Renal Physician Assn. (assoc.), Delhi Med. Assn. (assoc.), Indian Med. Assn. (assoc.), Am. Soc. Transplantation (assoc.). Office Phone: 414-805-9073.

**VASWANI, SHEILA ANN,** secondary school educator; b. NYC, Feb. 27, 1948; d. Elwood Stanley and Julia Zita (Sullivan) Kent; m. A. N. Vaswani; 1 child, Neela. BA in Asian Studies and Eurasian History, Hofstra U., 1972; MA in Chinese Studies, St. John's U., Jamaica, N.Y., 1977. Mng. editor County Weekly, Vt., 1979-80; secondary social studies tchr. Babylon (N.Y.) H.S., 1984—. Co-organizer adv. program Babylon (NY) HS, 1991-94, middle states evaluation com., 1991-92, human rels. seventh grade coms., 1993-94; presenter in field. Advisor Babylon (N.Y.) H.S. chpt. Nat. Honor Soc., 1989—, Home Econ. Club, Babylon, 1980—; v.p. Parents, Tchrs., Students Assn., Babylon, 1994—. Nominee Tchr. of Month award, Channel 12, 1994; named Friend of Fgn. Lang., 2003, Friend of Home Econs., 1997, Diplomate of N.Y. State Acad. Tchg. and Learning, 2000; recipient LILT award, 2003. Mem.: Registry of Outstanding Profls., L.I. Coun. for Social Studies (exec. bd. 2004, HS Tchr. of Yr. 2004), Nat. Coun. for Social Studies. Avocations: art, religion, philosophy, ethnic cooking, travel. Office: Babylon High Sch 50 Railroad Ave Babylon NY 11702-2221 Office Phone: 631-893-7910. E-mail: svaswani@babylonsd.org, svglobal@aol.com.

**VATANDOOST, NOSSI MALEK,** art school administrator; b. May 22, 1935; d. Adullah Goodar and Mahtaban (Goodar) Malek; m. Ira Varandoost, May 30, 1964; children: Debbie, Cyrus. BA, Western Ky. U., 1970. Art tchr. Met.-Davidson County Sch. Sys., Nashville, 1970-71; dir., owner Nossi Coll. Art, Goodlettsville, Tenn., 1973—. Pres. Crimson Corp.; dir. EXCEL Edn. Corp., 1980-86; vis. lectr., cons. EXCEL Bus. Inst., 1980-86. Active mem. Nat. Trust for Hist. Preservation. Mem.: NAFE, Internat. Coun. Design Schs. (pres. 1997-98), Art Inst. Nashville (founder, CEO), Art Resources of Tenn. (pres. 2000—01), Nat. Assn. of Schs. of Art and Design, Nat. Mus. Women in the Arts (charter), Hendersonville Art Guild, Hendersonville Art Coun. (com. chmn.). Club: Soroptimiste (Upper Cumberland Valley, Tenn.). Home: 104 Whirlaway Ct Hendersonville TN 37075 Office: 907 Rivergate Pkwy # E6 Goodlettsville TN 37072 Office Phone: 615-851-1088. E-mail: nossi@nossi.com.

**VATAVUK, WILLIAM MICHAEL,** chemical engineer, writer; b. Sharon, Pa., Jan. 30, 1947; s. William James and Amelia Agnes (Lenarcic) V.; m. Betsy Ann Chandler, Oct. 27, 1973; 1 child, William Chandler. B in Engring., Youngstown State U., Ohio, 1969. Registered prof. engr., NC. Chem. engr. E.I. DuPont de Nemours, Richmond, Va., 1969-70; sr. chem. engr. US EPA, Durham, NC, 1970-99; pres. Vatavuk Engring., 1999—. Author: Dawn of Peace, 1989 (Pulitzer nomination 1990), Estimating Costs of Air Pollution Control, 1990, Marketing Yourself with Technical Writing, 1992; mem. publs. com. Oilfield Jour.; inventor Vatavuk Air Pollution Control Cost Indexes; contbr. articles to profl. jour. Bd. dir. Bennett Pl. Hist. Site Support Fund, Inc., Durham, 1992—; publicity chmn. Hist. Preservation Soc. Durham, 1989-90; bd. dir. NC 4-H Devel. Fund, Raleigh, NC, 1990-93; tchr., Sunday sch. CCD, 1993. Capt. USPHS, 1970-99. Recipient NC Order of the Long Leaf Pine award, 2006. Mem. NC Farm Bur., Mercer County Hist. Soc. (life), USPHS Commd. Officers Assn. (pres. NC br. 1975-76, 84-85), Mil. Officers Assn. Am. (life), N.C. Order Lone Leaf Pine. Democrat. Roman Catholic. Avocations: reading, writing, jogging, gardening, solving puzzles. Office: 3512 Angus Rd Durham NC 27705-5404 Office Phone: 919-699-3336. Personal E-mail: wvatavuk@vatavukengineering.com.

**VATER, CHARLES J.,** lawyer; b. Pitts., Feb. 8, 1950; s. Joseph A. and Helen M. (Genellie) V.; m. Diane E. Vater, June 10, 1972; children: Allison D., Elizabeth A. BA, U. Notre Dame, 1971; JD, U. Pitts., 1975. Bar: Pa. 1975, U.S. Dist. Ct. (we. dist.) Pa. 1975, U.S. Ct. Appeals (3d cir.) 1979. Assoc. Tucker Arensberg, P.C., Pitts., 1975-80, ptnr., shareholder, 1980—. Contbr. articles to profl. jours. Mem.: Estate Planning Coun. Pitts. (bd. dirs. 1988—90, 1995—97, past pres.), Allegheny County Bar Assn. (probate coun.

1988—98, 1999—2000, chair 2006—), Phi Beta Kappa, Order of Coif. Home: 1615 Trolist Dr Pittsburgh PA 15241-2650 Office: Tucker Arensberg 1 Ppg Pl Ste 1500 Pittsburgh PA 15222-5413 Office Phone: 412-594-5556. Business E-Mail: cvater@tuckerlaw.com.

**VATER, YOURI L.,** medical educator; b. Riga, Latvia, Apr. 14, 1954; s. Eve Lazar Vater; m. Hanna Bernstein; children: Roman, Maxim (Max). MD, Riga Univ. Sch. of Medicine, Riga Latvia, 1977; PhD, U. Tartu, Estonia, 1988. Cert. sr. bd. anesthesia Israel, 1997. Rsch. fellow Riga Med. Sch., 1980—87, sr. rsch. fellow, 1987—90; dir. cardioanesthesiology dept. Heart Surgery Ctr. Sch. of Medicine Republic of Latvia, Riga, Latvia, 1980—90; residency anesthesia Univ. Tel Aviv Sacler Med. Ctr., Ichilov, 1990—97; asst. prof. U. Wash. Sch. of Medicine, Seatle, 1999—. Attending anesthesiologist U. Wash. Med. Ctr., Seatle, Wash. Contbr. articles various profl. jours. Active participant Doctors for Democracy, Tel Aviv, Israel, 1995. Lt. Israeli Mil. Forces., 1995—2004, Israel. Mem.: Am. Soc. of Transplantaion Anesthesiologists, Lavtvian Soc. of Anesthesiologists, Am. Soc. of Anesthesiologists, Israeli Soc. of Anesthesiologists. Achievements include Art Show Promotions. Avocations: travel, journalism, research in anesthesiology, art show promotion. Home: 11323- 24 th Ave NE Seattle WA 98125 Office: U Wash 1959 Pacific St POB 356540 Seattle WA 98105-6540 Office Phone: 206-598-4260. Personal E-mail: yvater@yahoo.com.

**VATNER, STEPHEN F.,** physiologist, researcher, research scientist; m. Dorothy E. Vatner, Aug. 22, 1944; children: Jonathan, Daniel, Ralph. BA, Grinnell Coll., Grinnell, Iowa, 1957—61; MD, NYU, New York, NY, 1961—65; Intern,Residence, U of VA., Charlottesville,VA, 1966—67; Postdoctoral fellow, U of WA, Seattle, WA, 1969. Cardiology. Asst. rsch. physiologist U of CA, San Diego, 1969—70, asst. prof. of medicine, 1971—72, Harvard Med. Sch., Boston, 1972—74; assoc. prof. of medicine Peter Bent Brigham Hosp.-Harvard Med. Schoolm, Boston, 1974—87; prof. of medicine Harvard Med. Sch., Boston, 1990—97; George J. Magovern prof. and dir., cardiovasc. and pulmonary rsch. inst. Allegheny U. of the Health Sciences, Pitts., 1997—99; dir. Weis Ctr. for Rsch., Henry Hood Rsch. Program, Charles B. Degenstein Prof., Penn State Coll. of Medicine, Danville, Pa., 1999—2000; u. prof. of medicine and dir. Cardiovasc. Rsch. Inst., U. of Medicine and Dentistry-New Jersey Med. Sch., Newark, 2000—01; chair, dept. of cell biology and molecular medicine UMDNJ-New Jersey Med. Sch., Newark, 2001—. Editor: (editor-in-chief) Circulation Rsch.; author (contributing author): (manuscript publications) Sci. articles in peer-reviewed jour. Recipient Established Investigatorship, AHA, 1974 -1979, Thomas L. O'Donohue Meml. Lecture in Neuropharmacology, Washington,D.C., 1997, Invited Lecture in Honor of Emeritus Prof. Andre Charlier, Unit of Cardiovasc. Physiology, Universite Catholique De Louvain, Brussels,Belgium, 1997, Hon. Prof., The fourth Mil. Med. U., Xian, China, 1998, George E. Brown Lecture, AHA, 1986, Hawthorne Lecture, Howard U., 1990, Hon. MD Degree, Kagawa Med. Sch., Kagawa,Japan, 1992, Welcome Vis. Prof., U of Nebr., 1993, Wiggers Award, Am. Physiology Soc., 1995, Fouad A. Bashour Disting. physiologist Lectr., U of TX, S.W. Med. Ctr., 1996, Konrad Witzig Meml. Lectr., The Cardiovasc. Sys. Dynamics Soc., 1996, J.R. Neely Lectr., Geisinger Clinic, Danville, PA, 1997; fellow Fellowship, The Internat. Soc. for Heart Rsch.; grantee Myocardial Hypertrophy and Heart Failure (Program Project)-Project 1 Cardiac Control in gsAlpha and 403 Mice, Nih/nhlbi (Po1 Hl59139-01), 09/15/97 - 08/31/02, Myocardial Hypertrophy and Heart Failure (Program Project) - Core A Adminstrn. of PPG, 09/15/97 - 08/31/02, Myocardial Hypertrophy and Heart Failure (Program Project) - Core B Transgenic Mouse Models for PPG, 09/15/97 - 08/31/02, Effects of Aging on Cardiovasc. Function in Primates, NIH/Aging (7RO1 AG14121-01), 08/01/97 - 07/31/02, Mechanisms of Myocardial Ischemia and Reperfusion (Program Project) - Project 2, Nih/nhlbi (1 Po1 Hl69020-01), 09/30/01 - 08/31/06, (PENDING) Integrative Mechanism in Cardiovasc. Disease (Instl. Tng. Grant), Nih/nhlbi (1T32 Hl69752-01), 07/01/02 - 06-30-07. Mem.: AHA (executive,credentials,program and nominating committees 1968), Jour. of Molecular and Cellular Cardiology (consulting editor 2000), Circulation Rsch. (consulting editor 1999), Circulation (editl. bd. mem. 1999), Circulation Rsch. (editor-in-chief 1991—99), Am. Jour. of Physiology: Heart and Circulatory Sect. (bd. of med. editors 1998), Hypertension (editl. bd. mem. 1983—89), Procs. of The Soc. for Exptl. Biology and Medicine (editl. bd. mem. 1987—), Circulation Rsch. (editl. bd. mem. 1981—87), Am. Jour. of Physiology (editl. bd. mem. 1985—90), Am. Jour. of Physiology (editl. bd. mem. 1979—81), AHA (mem. 1968), Am. Assn. of Physicians (assoc.), AHA, Keystone, CO (assoc.; co-director, sci. sessions of councils on sci. and circ. 1986), AHA, Keystone, CO (assoc.; co-director, sci. sessions of councils on sci. and circ.), Coun. on Circulation, AHA (assoc.; chmn., program com. 1982—85), Am. Soc. for Pharmacology and Exptl. Therapeutics (assoc.), Am. Soc. for Clin. Investigation (assoc.), Am. Physiol. Soc. (assoc.), Am. Fedn. for Clin. Rsch. (assoc.), Biophysical Soc. (assoc.), AHA (assoc.; bd. of directors, allegheny county 1997), AHA (assoc.; chmn., nominating com., coun. on circulation 1997—99), Am. Assn. for Accreditation of Lab. Animal Care Bd. of Trustees (assoc.), AHA, Mass. Affiliate (assoc.; v.p. 1990—92), AHA (assoc.; chmn., coun. on circulation 1990—92), AHA (assoc.; vice chmn., coun. on circulation 1988—90). Achievements include research in American Heart Association Research Achievement Award; American Heart Association, Scientific Councils Distinguished Achievment Award; National Institute of Health Merit Award. Office: UMDNJ-NJ Medical School 185 So Orange Ave - Ste G609 PO Box 1709 Newark NJ 07101-1709 Personal E-mail: vatnersf@umdnj.edu.

**VATTA, MATTEO,** medical educator, researcher; PhD, Internat. Sch. for Advanced Study, Trieste, 1997. Postdoc. fellow/assoc. Baylor Coll. Medicine, Houston, 1998—2001, instr., 1999—2001, asst. prof. pediat., 2003. Baritone/bass UN Assn. Internat. Choir, Houston, 2003. Grantee NIH, 2004—. Mem.: Heart Failure Soc. Am. (assoc.), Internat. Soc. Heart and Lung Transplantation (assoc. rsch. fellow 2001), Soc. Pediat. Rsch. (assoc.). Office: Baylor Coll Medicine 1102 Bates St FC 43004 Houston TX 77030 Office Phone: 832-824-4153. E-mail: mvatta@bcm.tmc.edu.

**VATTER, PAUL AUGUST,** business administration educator, dean; b. Boston, Sept. 14, 1924; s. August John and Elizabeth Emelia (Kunstler) V.; m. Josette Roman, July 23, 1966; children: Joel Paul, Katherine Alexandra. BA, Holy Cross Coll., 1944; MA, U. Pa., 1947, PhD, 1953; MA (hon.) Harvard U., 1970. Instr. U. Pa., Phila., 1945-53, asst. prof., 1953-58, vice dean of men, 1953-58; asst. dean Harvard U. Bus. Sch., Boston, 1958-62, assoc. prof. bus. adminstrn., 1962-70, prof., 1970-95, Lawrence E. Fouraker prof. bus. adminstrn., sr. assoc. dean, 1989-91, Lawrence E. Fouraker prof. bus. adminstrn. emeritus, 1995—; assoc. fellow Templeton Coll. Oxford (Eng.) U. Author: Quantitative Methods in Management, 1978, The Structure of Retail Trade by Size of Store, 1979, also video tapes. Office: Harvard U Bus Sch Soldiers Fld Boston MA 02163-1317 Home: 66 Sherman St Apt 204 Cambridge MA 02140-3533

**VAUDRY, J. WILLIAM, JR.,** lawyer; b. Jacksonville, Fla., Jan. 18, 1941; BBA, Tulane U., 1962, LLB, 1967. Bar: La. 1967. Mem. Lemle & Kelleher, LLP, New Orleans. Bd. editors Tulane Law Rev., 1965-67. Lt. (j.g.) USN, 1962-64. Mem. ABA, La. State Bar Assn., Order of Coif, Phi Delta Phi. Address: Lemle & Kelleher LLP Pan Am Life Ctr 21st flr 601 Poydras St New Orleans LA 70130-6029 Office Phone: 504-584-9408.

**VAUGHAN, ALDEN TRUE,** history professor; b. Providence, Jan. 23, 1929; s. Dana Prescott and Muriel Louise (True) V.; m. Lauraine A. Freethy, June 1, 1956 (div. 1981); children: Jeffrey Alden, Lynn Elizabeth; m. Virginia Mason Carr, July 16, 1983. BA, Amherst Coll., 1950; MEd, Columbia U., 1956, MA in History, 1958, PhD, 1964. Tchr. Hackley Sch., Tarrytown, NY, 1950-51, A.B. Davis High Sch., Mt. Vernon, NY, 1956-60; From history instr. to prof. Columbia U., N.Y.C., 1961—, prof. emeritus, 1994. Editor Polit. Sci. Quar., NY, 1970-71; vis. adj. prof. CUNY, Lehman Coll., NYC, 1971; vis. prof. Clark U., Worcester, Mass., 1987. Author: New England Frontier, 1965, 3d edit., 1995, American Genesis, 1975, Shakespeare's Caliban, 1991, Roots of American Racism, 1995, others; co-editor: Arden Shakespeare's The Tempest, 1999; editor Early Am. Indian Documents, 20 vols., 1977-2004;

mem. editl. bd. Ency. of the N.Am. Colonies, 1993; contbr. articles to profl. jours. including Am. Heritage, Am. Hist. Rev., New Eng. Quar. Lt. (j.g.) USNR, 1951-55. Recipient fellowship Guggenheim Found., 1973, Sr. fellowship Folger Shakespeare Libr., 1977, 89, Sr. fellowship Am. Antiquarian Soc., 1983. Mem. Am. Antiquarian Soc. (sr. fellowship), Am. Soc. for Ethnohistory, Shakespeare Assn. Am., Soc. Am. Historians (exec. sec., treas. 1965-70), Orgn. Am. Historians (program chmn. 1976), Inst. Early Am. History and Culture (coun. mem. 1985-87), Colonial Soc. Mass., Mass. Hist. Soc. Home: 50 Howland Ter Worcester MA 01602-2631

**VAUGHAN, BRAD,** engineering and design company executive; With Black & Veatch, Overland Park, Kans., 1974—, dir. devel. TransAmerica Generation Grid project, COO, BV Solutions Group, gen. ptnr., mgr. office ops. energy engring. and constrn. divsn., chief info. officer, 2003—. Office: Black & Veatch 11401 Lamar Overland Park KS 66211

**VAUGHAN, C. PORTER, III,** lawyer; b. Denver, Aug. 26, 1945; BA, Yale U., 1967; JD, U. Va., 1970. Bar: Va. 1970. Ptnr., co-head, bus. practice group Hunton & Williams LLP, Richmond, Va. Mem. editorial bd. Va. Law Rev., 1968-70. Mem.: ABA, Va. State Bar Assn. Office: Hunton & Williams Riverfront Plz E Tower PO Box 1535 Richmond VA 23218-1535 Office Phone: 804-788-8285. Office Fax: 804-788-8218. Business E-Mail: pvaughan@hunton.com.

**VAUGHAN, DAVID JOHN,** corporate financial executive; b. Detroit, July 17, 1924; s. David Evans and Erma Mildred V.; divorced; children: David John, Melissa Ann, Julia Crawford McLaughlin; m. Anne McKeown Miles, Aug. 21, 1975. AB, U. Ill., 1950. Chemist Midland Electric Colleries, Galesburg, Ill., 1950-52; pres. Varrco Distbg. Co., Peoria, 1953—, David Vaughan Investments, Inc., Peoria, 1970—. Adv. bd. Charles Schwab Inc. Trustee Eureka Coll., chmn. bd. trustees; trustee Opera Ill. Lt. USAAF, 1942-46, USAF, 1951-52, Korea. Mem. Peoria Country Club, Northport Point Club (Mich.), Peoria Skeet Club, Racquet Club, Naples Club (Fla.), Naples Bath & Tennis Club, Royal Poinciana Country Club (Naples), Masons, Shriners, Alpha Tau Omega, Phi Eta Sigma, Phi Alpha Delta. Republican. Presbyterian. Office: 5823 N Forest Park Dr Peoria IL 61614-3559 also: 824 N Birchwood Dr Northport MI 49670-9761 also: Office Comstock Bldg Winter Park FL 32789 Home: 4413 Grandview Dr Peoria IL 61614 also: 5823 N Forest Park Dr Ste 1 Peoria IL 61614-3568 Office Phone: 309-685-0033. Business E-Mail: dvaughan@dviequity.com.

**VAUGHAN, DORIS CELESTINE WALKER,** retired librarian, educator; b. Lawrenceville, Va., Aug. 21, 1930; d. Warner L. and Otelia R. (Collier) Walker; m. Clyde Wilson Vaughan Sr., Nov. 6, 1954 (dec.); children: Sharon Maria, Clyde Wilson Jr., Gregory Andre. BS, St. Paul's Coll., Lawrenceville, 1952; MLS, U. Mich., 1979. Tchr. Loudoun County Sch. System, Leesburg, Va., 1953-54, Nottoway (Va.) County Sch. System, 1954-55, Brunswick County Sch. System, Lawrenceville, 1956-70; libr. asst. Cen. State U., Wilberforce, Ohio, 1971-80, libr. reference and gifts, adj. instr., 1980-82; ret. Libr., archivist Letterkenny Army Depot, Chambersburg, Pa., 1986—87; adj. instr. Cent. State U., Wilderforce, Ohio, 1993—96; sub. tchr. Xenia Cmty. Sch., Xenia, Ohio, 1999—2005. U. Mich. fellow, 1978. Mem. AAUP, Southwestern Ohio Coun. for Higher Edn., Alpha Kappa Alpha. Democrat. Avocations: reading, cooking, writing. Home: 1062 Frederick Dr Xenia OH 45385-1649

**VAUGHAN, EDWIN DARRACOTT, JR.,** urologist, surgeon; b. Richmond, Va., May 13, 1939; s. Edwin Darracott and Blanche V. (Bashaw) V.; m. Virginia Anne Lloyd, June 30, 1962; children: Edwin Darracott III, Barbara Anderson. BS, Washington and Lee U., 1961; MD, U. Va., 1965, MS, 1969; DSc, Washington and Lee U., 1982. Diplomate Am. Bd. Urology (trustee, v.p. 1988, pres. 1989). Intern Vanderbilt U., 1965—66, asst. resident, 1966—67; chief resident in urology U. Va., 1970—71, asst. prof. urology, 1973—75, assoc. prof., 1975—78, prof., 1978; clin. rsch. fellow Columbia U., 1971—72, rsch. assoc. dept. medicine, 1972—73; James J. Colt prof. urology, chmn. dept. urology Cornell U. Med. Coll., NYC; attending urologist-in-chief NY Hosp., NYC, 1978—; sr. assoc. dean clin. affairs Cornell U. Med. Coll., NYC, 1993—2001, chmn. dept. urology, 1993—2001, exec. vice dean sr. assoc. dean clin affairs, 2005. Chief med. officer Cornell Physician Orgn., 1997-2005; sci. adv. bd. Nat. Kidney Found., 1977-81; sec-treas. Urology Coun., 1977-80, chmn., 1980-81; med. adv. bd. Coun. High Blood Pressure, 1977; acting co-chief exec. officer Columbia-Cornell Care, L.L.C., 1997; adv. coun. Nat. Diabetes and Digestive and Kidney Diseases, 2002—; bd. visitors U. Va. Editor: Seminars in Urology, 1983-95; assoc. editor Investigative Urology, 1977-78, mem. editl. bd., 1978-94, assoc. editor, 2004; mem. editl. bd. Brit. Jour. Urology, 2004; editor Campbell's Urology; assoc. editor Brit. Jour. Urology, 2004, asst. editor, 2004—; contbr. articles to profl. jours. Mem. adv. coun. Nat. Diabetes and Digestive and Kidney Diseases, 2002—; bd. visitors U. Va., 2002. Recipient Rsch. Career Devel. award NIH, 1976-78, Russell and Mary Hugh Scott award Am. Found. Urol. Disease, 1998, J.K. Latimer award NY-NJ Kidney Found., 1999, Valentine medal NY Acad. Medicine, 2000, Maurice R. Greenberg Disting. Svc. award, 2002, Good Scout award, BSA, 2002, Presdl. award Soc. Basic Sci. Rsch., 2004, Walter Reed award U. Va. Med. Sch., 2005; NIH tng. grantee, 1967-68; USPHS grantee, 1971-77; Am. Heart Assn. grantee, 1976-79 Mem. ACS, AAAS, Internat. Soc. Urology, NY Acad. Scis., Soc. Univ. Urologists, Am. Urol. Assn. (hon., chmn. rsch. com. 1980-91, treas. NY sect. 1985, v.p. NY sect. 1986, pres. NY sect. 1987, bd. dirs. 1992-97, pres.-elect 2000, pres. 2001, immediate past pres. 2002, Golden Cystoscope award 1981, Disting. Contbn. award 1992, Hugh Hampton Young award 2000), Urol. Soc. Australasia (hon.), Soc. Exptl. Biology and Medicine, Soc. Univ. Surgeons, Soc. Internat. Urology (chmn. bd. 1997—), Am. Found. Urol. Disease (pres. 1987-92, Presdl. Founder award 2004), NY Med. Surgical Soc. (pres. 2005), Soc. Basic Urol. Rsch. (Pres. award 2004), Nat. Kidney and Urol. Disease Adv. Bd. (dep. chmn.), Intersoc. for Kidney and Urol. Disease Rsch. (chmn. 1987), Am. Assn. Genito-Urinary Surgeons (Barringer medal 1993), Am. Surg. Assn., Brit. Assn. Urol. Surgeons (hon., St. Paul's medal), Japanese Urol. Soc. (hon.), Clin. Soc. Genitourinary Surgeons (pres. 2006), Sigma Chi (Significant Sig award 2000), Alpha Omega Alpha (award 1976), Omicron Delta Kappa (award 1981). Home: 1165 Park Ave Apt 6A New York NY 10128-1210 Office: 525 E 68th St New York NY 10021-4870 Office Phone: 212-746-5480. Business E-Mail: evaughan@med.cornell.edu.

**VAUGHAN, EUGENE H.,** investment company executive; b. Brownsville, Tenn., Oct. 5, 1931; s. Eugene H. Sr. and Margaret (Musgrave) V.; m. Susan Bolinger Westbrook, May 11, 1963; children: Margaret Corbin, Richard Bolinger. BA, Vanderbilt U., 1955; MBA, Harvard U., 1961. CFA, 1967. Security analyst Putnam Mgmt. Co., Boston, 1961-64; dir., dir. rsch. Underwood, Neuhaus & Co., Inc., Houston, 1964-70; pres., chief exec. officer Vaughan, Nelson & Boston, Inc., Houston, 1970-77, Vaughan, Nelson, Scarborough & McCullough, L.P., Houston, 1970—. Chmn. bd. dirs. Dreyfus Founders Asset Mgmt. Co., Denver, 1970—. Chair. Fin. Analyst Fedn., N.Y.C., 1973-74, bd. dirs., 1969-76; dir. U. Tex. Health Sci. Ctr., Houston, 2002—; pres. Houston Soc. Fin. Analysts, 1967-68; trustee exec. com. Vanderbilt U., Nashville, 1972—, St. John's Sch., Houston, 1980-85, Goodwill Industries, Houston, 1978—, United Way of Tex. Gulf Coast, 1994—; elder First Presbyn. Ch., 1976—; founding chmn., trustee Presbyn. Sch., Houston, 1986-90, Lt. USN, 1955-58. Recipient Disting. Svc. award Fin. Analyst Fedn., 1978, Humanitarian award Am. Jewish Com., 1993, Bus. Leader of Yr. award U. St. Thomas, 1996. Mem. Inst. Chartered Fin. Analysts (trustee 1986-93, chmn. 1989), Assn. for Investment Mgmt. and Rsch. (founding chmn. 1990-91, gov. 1990-93), Greater Houston Partnership (bd. dirs. 1990—, exec. com. 1993—), chair Ctr. Houston's Future 1999—), Houston Club (pres. 1983-84, bd. dirs. 1979-85, chair centennial celebration, 1992-94), Houston Country Club, Coronado Club (Houston), Houston Forum (pres. 1991-92, chmn. 1992-93), Harvard U. Bus. Sch. Club Houston (pres. 1968-69, bd. dirs. 1966-71, 86-90), Vanderbilt Club Houston (chmn. 1984—, pres. 1966-68, Disting. Svc. award 1994), Conferie des Chevaliers du

Tastevin, Belle Meade Country Club (Nashville). Republican. Avocations: travel, sailing. Home: 3465 Inwood Dr Houston TX 77019-3129 Office: Vaughan Nelson Scarborough & McCullough 600 Travis Ste 6300 Houston TX 77002

**VAUGHAN, HERBERT WILEY,** retired lawyer; b. Brookline, Mass., June 1, 1920; s. David D. and Elzie G. (Wiley) Vaughan; m. Ann Graustein, June 28, 1941 (dec. June 2002). BS cum laude, Harvard U., 1941, LLB, 1948. Bar: Mass. 1948. Assoc. Hale and Dorr, Boston, 1948-54, jr. ptnr., 1954-56, sr. ptnr., 1956-89, co-mng. ptnr., 1976-80, of counsel, 1990—2004, Wilmer Cutler Pickering Hale and Dorr, LLP, Boston, 2004—. Bd. dirs. in. com. Boston and Maine R.R., 1961—64; vis. fellow New Coll., Oxford U., 1985. Mem. standing com. Trustees of Reservations, 1986—98, chmn., 1988—92, sec., 1992—98, asst. sec., mem. adv. coun., 1998—2006, life trustee, 2004—; mem. bd. trustees Am. Friends New Coll. (Oxford U.); mem. adv. coun. James Madison Program in Am. Ideals and Instns., Princeton U. Fellow: Mass. Hist. Soc., Am. Bar Found. (life); mem.: ABA, Am. Coun. Trustees and Alumni (mem. alumni leadership coun.), Am. Coll. Real Estate Lawyers (charter mem.), Am. Law Inst., Boston Bar Assn., Mass. Bar Assn., Boston Econ. Club, Union Club (Boston), Badminton and Tennis Club. Office: Wilmer Cutler Pickering Hale and Dorr LLP 60 State St Boston MA 02109-1816 Office Phone: 617-526-6718. Business E-Mail: herbert.vaughan@wilmerhale.com.

**VAUGHAN, JACK M.,** lawyer; b. Austin, Tex., Aug. 27, 1947; BBA in Acctg., U. Tex., 1969; JD, U. Houston, 1974. Bar: Tex. 1974, CPA. Tax ptnr. Deloitte Haskins & Sells acctg.; ptnr. Fulbright & Jaworski LLP, Houston, now adminstrv. ptnr. Fellow: Coll. of Law Practice Mgmt., Texas Bar Found., Houston Bar Found. Mem. ABA, State Bar of Tex., Houston Bar Assn., Am. Inst. CPA, Tex. Soc. CPA, Assn. Legal Adminstr. Meth. Office: Fulbright & Jaworski LLP Ste 5100 1301 McKinney St Houston TX 77010-3031 Office Phone: 713-651-5151. Office Fax: 713-651-5246. Business E-Mail: jvaughan@fulbright.com.

**VAUGHAN, JAMES JOSEPH MICHAEL,** lawyer; b. Mar. 19, 1942; s. James M. and Elizabeth (McDonnell) Vaughan; m. Jeanette Rae Gerber, Aug. 5, 1967; children: Karen, Adrianne, Jennifer. BS, U. Scranton, 1963; JD, Cath. U., 1966. Bar: U.S. Dist. Ct. Md. 1979, U.S. Ct. Appeals (D.C. cir.) 1972, U.S. Ct. Claims 1973, U.S. Supreme Ct. 1977. Assoc. Dukes, Troese, et al, Chevy Chase, Md., 1969—72; atty. Assn. Am. Law Schs., Washington, 1972—76, 2001—; mem. firm Giordano, Villareale & Vaughan, Upper Marlboro, Md., 1976—2001; pvt. practice, 2001—. Mem.: Prince George's County Bar Assn., Md. Bar Assn., D.C. Bar Assn., Bar Assn. D.C., Assn. Trial Lawyers Am. Democrat. Roman Catholic. Office: Giordano Villareale and Vaughan 9300 Livingston Rd 106 Fort Washington MD 20744-4905 Office Phone: 301-248-8700.

**VAUGHAN, JOSEPH LEE, JR.,** education educator, consultant; b. Charlottesville, Va., Dec. 31, 1942; s. Joseph Lee and Ann (Doner) Vaughan; m. Mary Linda De Silva; children: Leigh Ann, Kelley, Stephen, Kathleen. BA, U. Va., 1964, MEd, 1968, EdD, 1974. Tchr. Madison (Va.) High Sch., 1965-67, Darlington Sch., Rome, Ga., 1967-69, Woodberry Forest (Va.) Sch., 1969-74; asst. prof. edn. U. Ariz., Tucson, 1974-80; prof. Tex. A&M U.-Commerce, Mesquite, 1980—. dir. programs in reading edn., 1980-86, 91-92. Dir. programs in reading edn. East Tex. State U., 1980—86; dir. Tex. Ctr. Learning Styles, 1989—95; exec. dir. Children's Inst. of Literacy Devel., Inc., 1995—2004, The Ctr. for Acad. Progress, Inc., 2004—. Co-author: Reading and Learning in Content Classrooms, 1978, 2d rev. edit., 1985, Reading and Reasoning Beyond The Primary Grades, 1986. Bd. govs. Sancta Sophia Sem., 1991-98. Mem. ASCD, Nat. Reading Conf., Internat. Reading Assn., Soc. Effective Affective Learning. Unitarian Universalist. Avocations: golf, travel, reading, antiques. Home: 447 Ridgemont Dr Heathridge TX 75126 Office: Tex A&M U-Commerce 2600 Motley Dr Mesquite TX 75150-3840

**VAUGHAN, KEITH W.,** lawyer; b. Bluefield, W.Va., Oct. 1, 1950; BA cum laude, Wake Forest U., 1972; JD cum laude, U. Ga., 1975. Bar: Ga. 1975, NC 1975, US Dist. Ct. (Eastern, Middle & Western Dists. NC), NC Supreme Ct., US Ct. Appeals (4th Cir.), US Supreme Ct. Ptnr. litigation practice group leader, mem. firm mgmt. com. Womble Carlyle Sandridge & Rice PLLC, Winston-Salem, NC, chmn. mgmt. com., mng. mem. Bd. dir. NC Assn. Def. Attys., 1985—88. Editor-in-chief Ga. Law Rev., 1974-75. Named to Bus. North Carolina's Legal Elite (Litigation). Mem. ABA, NC Bar Assn., Forsyth County Bar Assn., Ga. Bar Assn., Forsyth County Young Lawyers Assn. (pres., 1981),, Am. Inns of Ct. (Master of the Bench), Omicron Delta Kappa, Delta Sigma Rho, Tau Kappa Alpha; Fellow, Am. Coll. of Trial Lawyers Mailing: Womble Carlyle Sandridge & Rice PLLC PO Box 84 Winston Salem NC 27102 Office: Womble Carlyle Sandridge & Rice PLLC One W 4th St Winston Salem NC 27101 Office Phone: 910-721-3600, 336-721-3540. Office Fax: 336-733-8417. Business E-Mail: kvaughan@wcsr.com

**VAUGHAN, MARTHA,** biochemist, educator; b. Dodgeville, Wis., Aug. 4, 1926; d. John Anthony and Luciel (Ellingen) V.; m. Jack Orloff, Aug. 4, 1951 (dec. Dec. 1988); children: Jonathan Michael, David Geoffrey, Gregory Joshua. Ph.B., U. Chgo., Ill., 1944; MD, Yale U., New Haven, Conn., 1949. Intern New Haven Hosp., Conn., 1950-51; research fellow U. Pa., Phila., 1951-52, Nat. Heart Inst., Bethesda, Md., 1952-54, mem. research staff, 1954-68; head metabolism sect. Nat. Heart and Lung Inst., Bethesda, 1968-74; acting chief molecular disease br. Nat. Heart, Lung and Blood Inst., Bethesda, 1974-76, chief cell metabolism lab., 1974-94; dep. chief pulmonary and critical care medicine br. Nat. Heart, Lung, and Blood Inst., Bethesda, 1994—. Mem. metabolism study sect. NIH, 1965-68; mem. bd. sci. counselors Nat. Inst. Alcohol Abuse and Alcoholism, 1988-91. Mem. editl. bd. Jour. Biol. Chemistry, 1971-76, 80-83, 88-90, assoc. editor, 1992—; editl. adv. bd. Molecular Pharmacology, 1972-80, Biochemistry, 1989-94; editor: Biochemistry and Biophysics Rsch. Comms., 1990-91; contbr. articles to profl. jours., chpts. to books. Bd. dirs. Found. Advanced Edn. in Scis., Inc., Bethesda, 1979-92, exec. com., 1980-92, treas., 1984-86, v.p., 1986-88, pres., 1988-90; mem. Yale U. Coun. com. med. affairs, New Haven, 1974-80. Recipient Meritorious Svc. medal HEW, 1974, Disting. Svc. medal HEW, 1979, Commd. Officer award USPHS, 1982, Superior Svc. award USPHS, 1993. Mem. NAS, Am. Acad. Arts and Scis., Am. Soc. Biol. Chemists (chmn. pub. com. 1984-86), Assn. Am. Physicians, Am. Soc. Clin. Investigation. Home: 11608 W Hill Dr Rockville MD 20852-3751 Office: Nat Heart Lung & Blood Inst Nih Bldg 10 Rm 5N 307 Bethesda MD 20892-0001 Business E-Mail: vaughanm@nih.gov.

**VAUGHAN, MICHAEL RICHARD,** lawyer; b. Chgo., Aug. 27, 1936; s. Michael Ambrose and Loretta M. (Parks) Vaughan; m. Therese Marie Perri, Aug. 6, 1960; children: Charles Thomas, Susan Enger. Student, U. Ill., 1954-59; LLB, U. Wis., 1962. Bar: Wis. 1962. Chief atty. bill drafting sect. Wis. Legislature, Madison, 1962-68, dir. legis. attys., 1968-72; assoc. Murphy Desmond, and predecessor, Madison, 1972-73, ptnr., 1974—. Mem. Commn. Uniform State Laws, 1966—72; cons. Nat. Commn. Marijuana and Drug Abuse, 1971—73; lectr. CLE seminars. Contbr. articles to profl. jours. Warden, vestryman St. Dunstan's Episcopal Ch., 1973—78, 1980—87; mem. Wis. Episcopal Conf., 1972—76. Mem.: ABA, Dane County Bar Assn., State Bar Wis. (dir. govtl. and adminstrv. law sect. 1971—78, mem. interprofl. and bus. rels. com. 1976—89), The Club at Olde Cypress (Naples, Fla.), Nakoma Golf Club, Madison Club, U. Wis. Law Sch. Bencher Soc., Delta Kappa Epsilon. Home: 4714 Lafayette Dr Madison WI 53705-4865 Office: 2 E Mifflin St Ste 800 Madison WI 53701-2038 Office Phone: 608-257-7181. E-mail: mvaughan@murphydesmond.com

**VAUGHAN, PATRICIA ANN,** elementary school educator; b. Peoria, Ill., July 20, 1949; d. Lester Stanley and Martha Schlots Hudson; m. H. Eugene Vaughan, July 22, 1972; children: Matthew, David, Jennifer. BS, Western Ill. U., 1971. Cert. gifted certification State of Ill. Elem. tchr. Farmington Sch. Dist., Farmington, Ill., 1971—75; sub. tchr. Farmington (Ill.) and Elmwood (Ill.) Schs., 1984—92; computer gifted tchr. Elmwood Sch. Dist., 1992—94,

elem. tchr., 1994—. Local profl. devel. Elmwood Sch., Elmwood, Ill., 2001—05. Pres., v.p., treas. PEO, Elmwood, Ill., 1973—; city band mem. Elmwood Municipal Band, Elmwood, Ill., 1995—; dir. Elmwood Ednl. Found., Elmwood, Ill., 1990—; mentor Big Bros./Big Sisters, 2004—; children's choir dir., elder, organist First Presbyn. Ch., Sunday sch. tchr. Recipient Parenting award, Presbyn. Ch., 1999. Presbyn. Avocations: reading, quilting. Home: 22621 Rosenbohm Rd Elmwood IL 61529 Office: Elmwood Sch Dist 501 N Morgan Elmwood IL 61529 Office Phone: 309-742-4261. Office Fax: 309-742-4203. E-mail: pavaughan5@hotmail.com.

**VAUGHAN, SAMUEL SNELL,** editor, writer, publishing executive; b. Phila., Aug. 3, 1928; s. Joseph and Anna Catherine (Alexander) Vaughan; m. Jo LoBiondo Vaughan, Oct. 22, 1949; children: Jeffrey Marc, Leslie Jane, Dana Alexander, David Samuel. BA, Pa. State U., 1951. Deskman, King Features Syndicate, N.Y.C., 1951; asst. mgr. Doubleday Syndicate, 1952—54; advt. mgr. Doubleday, N.Y.C., 1954—56; sales mgr., 1956—58; sr. editor, 1958—68; exec. editor Doubleday, 1969—70; pub., pres. pub. div. Doubleday & Co., Inc., 1970—82, v.p. parent co., 1970—86, editor in chief, 1982—86; sr. v.p. and editor Random House, Inc., 1986—90, editor-at-large, 1990—2004. Mem. faculty, Columbia U., 1978-88; bd. dirs. Ch. Pub. Co.-Seabury Press; lectr. in field. Author: (juveniles) Whoever Heard of Kangaroo Eggs? 1957, New Shoes, 1961, The Two-Thirty Bird, 1965, (history) The Little Church, 1969, Medium Rare: A Look at the Book and Its People, 1977, (humor) Little Red Hood, 1979, The Accidental Profession, 1979, The Community of the Book, 1983, The State of the Heart, 1985; editor: Buckley: The Right Word, 1996; contbr. to N.Y. Times, Sunday Times of London, Daedalus, Am. Heritage, others. Served with USMC, 1946-48, Named Disting. Alumnus, Pa. State U., 1977, Alumni fellow. Mem. Tenafly Tennis Club, Quantuck Beach Club (Westhampton, N.Y.), Century Assn. Episcopalian. Personal E-mail: samuelsvaughan@aol.com.

**VAUGHAN, THERESE MICHELE,** insurance educator; b. Blair, Nebr., June 12, 1956; d. Emmett John and Lonne Kay (Smith) V.; m. Robert Allen Carber, Aug. 15, 1993; children: Kevin Leo Vaughan-Carber, Thomas S. Vaughan-Carber. BBA, U. Iowa, 1979; PhD, U. Pa., 1985. CPCU. Asst. prof. Baruch Coll., CUNY, 1986-87; cons. Tillinghast, N.Y.C., 1987-88; dir. ins. ctr. Drake U., Des Moines, 1988-94; ins. commr. State of Iowa, Des Moines, 1994—2004; Robb B. Kelley Disting. prof. ins. and actuarial sci. Drake U., 2005—. Bd. dirs. Endurance Splty. Holdings, Prin. Fin. Group, Nat. Coun on Corp. Ins. Chair Jour. of Ins. Regulation Bd., Kansas City, Mo., 1995-99; co-author: Fundamentals of Risk and Insurance, 1996, 99, 2003, Essentials of Insurance: A Risk Management Approach, 1995, 2001; contbr. articles to profl. jours. S.S. Huebner fellow U. Pa., 1979-82; recipient Outstanding Young Alumnus award U. Iowa, 1996; named to Iowa Ins. Hall of Fame, 2003. Mem. Nat. Assn. Ins. Commrs. (pres. 2002), Ins. Marketplace Stds. Assn. (bd. dirs. 2004—), Beta Gamma Sigma, Omicron Delta Epsilon. Avocations: hiking, biking, reading. Home: 4632 Elm St West Des Moines IA 50265-2993 Office: Drake Univ 2507 University Ave Des Moines IA 50311 Business E-Mail: terri.vaughan@drake.edu.

**VAUGHAN, THOMAS JAMES GREGORY,** historian, writer; b. Seattle, Oct. 13, 1924; s. Daniel George and Kathryn Genevieve (Browne) V.; m. Elizabeth Ann Perpetua Crownhart, June 16, 1951; children: Meagan, Margot, Stephen, Cameron. BA, Yale U., 1948; MS, U. Wis., 1950, doctoral residence, 1951-53; LittD, Pacific U., 1969; LLD, Reed Coll., 1975. Exec. dir. Oreg. Hist. Soc., Portland, 1954-90; editor in chief Oreg. Hist. Quar., 1954-89; adj. prof. Portland State U., 1968—. Chmn. bd. Salar Enterprises, Ltd.; bd. dir. Am. Heritage Pub. Co., 1976-85; film producer, 1958-99; historian laureate State of Oreg., 1989—. Author: A Century of Portland Architecture, 1967, Captain Cook, R.N, The Resolute Mariner: An International Record of Oceanic Discovery, 1974, Portland, A Historical Sketch and Guide, 1976, 2d edit., 1983, Voyage of Enlightenment: Malaspina on the Northwest Coast, 1977; editor: Space, Style and Structure: Building in Northwest America, 2 vols., 1974, The Western Shore, 1975, Ascent of the Athabasca Pass, 1978, Wheels of Fortune, High and Mighty, 1981, Soft Gold, 1982, 2d edit., 1990, To Siberia and Russian America, Vols. I, II and III, Frances Fuller Victor, 2002, others; co-editor: Siberica, 1989; mem. adv. bd. Am. Heritage Mag., 1977-90; prodr. film The Crimean War, 1994, Wellington's Last Parade, 1997, George Dewey: A Monarch of the Seas, George Catlin: the American Indians' Painter. 1st chmn. Oreg. State Com. for Humanities, NEH, 1969—; 1st chmn. Gov.'s Adv. Com. on Historic Preservation Oreg., 1970-77; sec. Oreg. Geog. Names Bd., 1958-89; adviser 1000 Friends of Oreg., 1972—; lay mem. Oreg. State Bar Disciplinary Rev. Bd., 1975-82; vice chmn. adv. panel Nat. Endowment Arts, 1975—; mem. Nat. Hist. Publs. and Records Commn. Matrix, 1975-76; historian laureate State of Oreg., 1989. With USMC, 1942-45. Decorated comdr. Order Brit. Empire; recipient Aubrey Watzek award Lewis and Clark Coll., 1975;, Edith Knight Hill award, 1977, Disting. Svc. award U. Oreg.; grantee English Speaking Union, 1961; Columbia Maritime Mus. 1st rsch. fellow, 1992, Thomas Jefferson medal, 2002. Fellow Royal Geog. Soc.; mem. Am. Assn. State and Local History (bd. dir. 1955-74, pres. 1976-78), Am. Assn. Mus. (coun., exec. com.), Nat. Trust Hist. Preservation (adv. coun.), Ctr. for Study Russian Am., Russian Acad. Scis., City Club (Portland, bd. govs.), Univ. Club (Portland, bd. govs.), The Arts Club (London). Home: 2135 SW Laurel St Portland OR 97201-2367 E-mail: goldengrove@comcast.net.

**VAUGHAN, WILLIAM WALTON,** atmospheric scientist; b. Clearwater, Fla., Sept. 7, 1930; s. William Walton and Ella Vermelle (Warr) Vaughan; m. Wilma Geraldine Stapleton, Dec. 23, 1951; children: Stephen W., David A., William D.; Robert T. BS with honors, U. Fla., 1951; grad. cert., USAF Inst. Tech./Fla. State U., 1952; PhD, U. Tenn., 1976. Cert. cons. meteorologist. Sci. asst. Air Force Armament Ctr., Eglin AFB, Fla., 1955-58, Army Ballistic Missile Agy., Huntsville, Ala., 1958-60: chief aerospace environ. div. Marshall Space Flight Center, NASA, Huntsville, 1960-76, chief atmospheric scis. div., 1976-86; rsch. prof. atmospheric sci. U. Ala., Huntsville, 1986—, dir. Rsch. Inst., 1986-94; ret., 1994. Cons. atmospheric sci. and tech. stds.; mem. adv. com. NASA. Reviewer:; contbr. articles to profl. jours. Served to capt. USAF, 1951—55. Recipient Exceptional Svc. medal, NASA, 1971. Fellow: AIAA (assoc.; standard exec. coun., Losey Atmospheric Scis. award 1980, Excellence in Aerospace Stds. award 2003), Am. Meteorol. Soc.; mem.: AAAS, Am. Geophys. Union, Stds. Engring. Soc., Sigma Xi. Office: Univ Ala Atmospheric Sci Dept Huntsville AL 35899-0001 Business E-Mail: vaughan@nsstc.uah.edu.

**VAUGHAN, WINSTON C.,** otolaryngologist, surgeon; b. Kingston, Jamaica, Sept. 2, 1964; BA in Biology with Honors, John Hopkins U., 1987; MD, Stanford Sch. Medicine, 1992. Cert. Calif., Ga. Composite State Bd. Med. Examiners, Otolaryngology. Intern, gen. surgery Stanford U. Med. Ctr. and Affiliates, 1992—93; resident, otolaryngology-head and neck surgery Stanford U. Med. Ctr., 1993—97, chief resident, dept. otolaryngology, 1997; fellow, rhinology and advanced sinus surgery Ga. Rhinology and Sinus Ctr., Savannah, Ga., 1997—98; fellow, staff surgeon Meml. Med. Ctr., St. Joseph's and Candler Hosp., Ga., 1997—98; dir., faculty. dept. otolaryngology-head and neck surgery Stanford Sinus Ctr., Stanford U. Sch. Medicine, 1998—2005; dir. Stanford Rhinology & Sinus Surgery Fellowship; dir., founder California Sinus Inst., E. Palo Alto and San Ramon, 2005—; mem., founder California Sinus Found., 2005—; otolaryngologist surgeon Stanford Hosp., Palo Alto Veterans Hosp., Lucille Packard Children's Hosp., Santa Clara Valley Med. Ctr. (Calif.). Dir. Caribbean Endoscopic Sinus Surgery Course, 2000—; mem. otolaryngology resident edn. com. Stanford U. Sch. Medicine, 1998—2002, coord.; resident cadaver dissections, 1999—2001, coord., annual otolaryngology symposium, 1999—2004, coord., endoscopic sinus surgery courses, 1999—2005; dir., scientific adv. bd., cons. Sinus Pharmacy, Santa Barbara, Calif., 2000—; cons. Bayer, Ortho-McNeil, Wallace, 1998—; GE Surgical Navigation (VTI, Boston, Mass.), 2000—, Sinus Pharma, Carpentaria, Calif., 2002—; BrainLab Surgical Navigation, 2002—04, Exploramed, 2004—; presenter in field. Reviewer Am. Jour. Rhinology, 2001—, Otolaryngology Head and Neck Surgery, 2002—; contbr. articles to profl. jours., chapters to books. Bd. trustee John Hopkins U., 1987—91; vol. physician Free Clinic, Meml. Med. Ctr., 1997—98; vol.

doctor Calif. AIDS ride, San Francisco to LA, 2000, 2004. Fellow: Am. Bd. Otolaryngology-Head and Neck Surgery, Am. Rhinology Soc. (cons. 1999—2003, bd. dir. 2004—, chmn. edn. com. 2002—04); mem.: AMA, Am. Rhinologic Assn., Am. Laryngological, Rhinological and Otological Soc., Am. Acad. Otolaryngology-Head and Neck Surgery, Caribbean Assn. Otolaryngologists, Nat. Med. Assn. Calif. Med. Assn. Achievements include pioneering the development, use and research into nebulized medications for the management of difficult chronic sinus cases since 2000. Office: California Sinus Inst and found 1900 University Ave Ste 101 East Palo Alto CA 94303 Office Phone: 650-462-3131. Office Fax: 650-322-8228.*

**VAUGHAN, WORTH EDWARD,** retired chemistry professor; b. NYC, Feb. 1, 1936; s. Royal Worth and Sylvia Marie (Fernholz) V.; m. Diane Marilyn Mayer, Aug. 9, 1969; 1 child, Wayne John BA, Oberlin Coll., 1957; MA, Princeton U., 1959, PhD, 1960. Asst. prof. chemistry U. Wis.-Madison, 1961-66, assoc. prof., 1967-76, prof., 1977—2002, prof. emeritus, 2002—. Mem. bd. advisors Am. Exchange Bank West Br., Madison, 1983-87. Author: Dielectric Properties and Molecular Behavior, 1969; editor: Digest of Literature on Dielectrics, 1974; translation editor: Dipole Moments of Organic Compounds, 1970; contbr. articles to profl. jours. Mem. Am. Chem. Soc. (pres. Wis. sect. 1968, 1998), Phi Beta Kappa Avocations: canoeing, contract bridge. Home: 501 Ozark Trl Madison WI 53705-2538 Office: Univ Wis 1101 University Ave Madison WI 53706-1322 Office Phone: 608-262-7924. Business E-Mail: vaughan@chem.wisc.edu.

**VAUGHN, CARY EDWARD,** minister, director; b. Memphis, May 16, 1971; s. Brenda Jane Vaughn; m. Lalania Star Goodman, June 26, 1992; children: Logan Star, Colton Edward. BA, Lambuth U., 1993; MSc in Orgnl. Leadership, Breyer State U., 2004. Cert. in Christian Leadership Belmont U., Tenn., 2004, in Advanced Skilltrack Christian Leadership Belmont U., Tenn., 2004, in Bivocational Ministry Leadership Belmont U., Tenn., 2005; Payroll Adminstr. HRCertification.com., Ga., 2005. Min. lay leadership Bellevue Bapt. Ch., Cordova, Tenn., 2002—, dir. lay ministry, 2002—, dir. men's ministry, 2003—, dir. new mems., 2004—, dir. career svcs., 2004—, program adminstr. spl. events, 2005—, dir. guest svcs., 2005—. Mem. Rotary Internat., Millington, Tenn., 2005—06; bd. dirs. Am. Families Assn. Discipleship Ministry, 2006; chmn. Tipton-Rosemark Acad., Millington, 2000—; ex-officio mem. Lambuth U., Jackson, Tenn., 2003—04; chmn. fundraising com. YMCA, Millington, Tenn., 2005—, bd. dirs., 2006, Chrosscheck Athletic Assn., 2006. Recipient Leadership award, Comforce, Inc., 1998, John G. Tower Disting. Alumni award, Kappa Sigma Nat. Frat., 1999, Alumnus of Yr., Lambuth U., 2000; Leadership scholarship, Kappa Sigma Nat. Frat., 1992. Mem.: Christian Educators Assn. Internat. (dir. pub. rels. Lower Miss. Valley region 2006), Assn. Christian Schs. Internat., Christian Mgmt. Assn., Harvard U. Prin. Ctr. R-Conservative. Baptist. Avocations: reading, exercise, hunting. Home: 8880 Gragg Rd Millington TN 38053-4945 Office: Bellevue Baptist Church 2000 Appling Rd Cordova TN 38016 Office Phone: 901-389-1254. Home Fax: 901-829-2994. Personal E-mail: caryvaughn@peoplepc.com. Business E-Mail: cvaughn@bellevue.org.

**VAUGHN, CLYDE A.,** career military officer; BS, S.E. Mo. State Coll., 1968; grad., U.S. Army Command and Gen. Staff Coll., 1989, U.S. Army War Coll., 1994; MPA, Shippensburg U., 1994. Advanced through grades to lt. gen. Army N.G., 2005—, numerous assignments including platoon leader, 1221st Transp. Co. Dexter, Mo., 1974—76, platoon leader Detachment 1, A Co. 1140th Engr. Battalion Charleston, Mo., 1976—78, engring. officer 1140th Engr. Battalion Sikeston, Mo., 1980—83, ops. officer 135th Engr. Group Cape Girardeau, Mo., 1984—85; comdr. Task Force 354 U.S. Army South, Panama, 1990—91; plans sect. chief N.G. bur. Army N.G., Arlingotn, Va., 1991—92, chief ops. and exercise br. N.G. bur., 1992—93, chief ops. divsn. Arlington, Va., 1997—2000, dep. dir., 2002—03; comdr. exercise support command, dep. chief staff reserve affairs N.G. U.S. Army South, Panama, 1995—97; dep. dir. ops., readiness and mobilization, office G3/G5 U.S. Army, Washington, 2000—02; asst. to chmn. of joint chiefs of staff nat. guard matters The Pentagon, Washington, 2003—05; pres., dir., N.G. bur. Army N.G., Arlington, Va., 2005—. Office: US Army NG 111 S George Mason Dr Arlington VA 22204

**VAUGHN, DONA D.,** performing company executive; b. Waynesboro, Pa., Aug. 13; d. Joseph Philip Ciano and Jayne Shearer Vaughn; m. Ronald Keith Raines, Sept. 6, 1986; 1 child, Charlotte Alessandra Vaughn Raines. AA, Brevard Coll.; BA, Wesleyan Coll.; MA, CUNY, 1986. Dir. theater devel. Marble Arch Prodns., N.Y.C., 1978—80; assoc. prof. CBS-All My Children, N.Y.C., 1981; artist-in-residence SUNY, Plattsburgh, 1983—87; dir. opera workshop Manhattan Sch. Music, N.Y.C., 1994—; stage dir., acting coach Lindemann Young Artist Devel. Program The Met. Opera, N.Y.C., 1997—; artistic dir. PORTopera, Portland, Maine, 2003—. Trustee Brevard (NC) Coll., 2000—. Office: The Manhattan Sch Music 120 Claremont Ave New York NY 10027 Personal E-mail: ddvnyc@aol.com.

**VAUGHN, DONALD C.,** engineering executive; BS in Civil Engring., Va. Poly. Inst. Registered profl. engr. Tex. Constrn. field engr. M.W. Kellogg Co., 1958, various field mgmt. positions U.S., other countries; pres. M.W. Kellogg Constructors, Inc. subs. M.W. Kellogg Co., 1980-82, chmn., CEO, pres. M.W. Kellogg Co., Houston, 1983-88; exec. v.p. Rust Internat.; sr. v.p. ops. Dresser Industries, Inc., 1992-95, exec. v.p. petroleum products and svcs., engring. svcs., 1995, pres., COO, dir.; vice chmn., mem. exec. com. Halliburton Co., Dallas, 1998—. Bd. dirs. Dresser-Rand Co., Ingersoll-Dresser Pump Co., Bredero-Shaw; mem. outside bd. dirs. Houston Exploration Co.; past chmn. U.S. sect. Turkish-U.S. Bus. Coun. Commd. officer U.S. Army Corps Engrs. Recognition Disting. Engring. Alumnus Va. Poly. Inst. Mem. Nat. Constrn. Assn., T-- Profl. Engring. So-, 25-Yr. Petroleum Industry, Va. Poly Inst Com. Excellence, Va. Tech 100 Club.

**VAUGHN, FRANCES AUSTIN,** art educator; b. Concord, NC, July 7, 1948; d. Frank Long and Mary Elizabeth (Cochrane) Austin; m. Charles Sidney Vaughn, Nov. 1980; children: Jordan Emory Sharp Jr., Catherine Marie Sharp Pursley. BS in Edn., Minot State Coll., 1976. Cert. Nat. Bd. Profl. Tchg. Stds. in Art. Chairperson art and home econs. dept. Mohall (N.D.) Pub. Schs., 1976—78; art educator K-5 Ea. Wayne Elem. Sch., Wayne County Schs., Goldsboro, NC, 1978—79; sec. to cultural arts dir. Iredell County Schs., Statesville, NC; chairperson dept. fine arts Bradwell Inst., Liberty Co. Schs. Hinesville, Ga., 1985—83; tchr. gifted K-6 Button Gwinnett/Hineshaw Sch., Liberty Co. Schs., Hinesville, 1985—91; art educator grades 8 and 9 Hillsville (Va.) Intermediate Sch., Carroll Co. Schs., 1991—92; art educator grades 6-8 Gentry Mid. Sch., Surry Co. Schs., Mount Airy, NC, 1993—. Mem. Reynolda Ho. Tchr. Adv. Bd., Winston-Salem, NC. Chmn. teamwalk March Dimes Gentry Mid. Sch.; advisor Peer Counseling Adv. Bd., Hinesville, Ga., 1987—88. Mem.: Ga. State Gifted Educators, Ga. Art Edn. Assn., N.C. Art Edn. Assn., Nat. Art Edn. Assn., Gentry Mid. Sch. Boosters Club. Moravian. Avocations: travel, landscape design, scrapbooks, walking, photography. Home: 452 Tanglewood Dr Mount Airy NC 27030 Office: Gentry Mid Sch 1915 W Pine St Mount Airy NC 27030 Office Phone: 336-786-4155. Personal E-mail: favaughn@surry.net.

**VAUGHN, GLADYS GARY,** federal agency administrator, researcher, not-for-profit exec.; b. George B. Vaughn (dec. 2000). BS, Fla. A&M U., 1964; MS in Clothing and Textiles, Iowa State U., 1968; PhD in Home Econs. Edn. and Adminstrn., U. MD.-College Park, 1974; LHD (hon.), Tuskegee U., 2006. Nat. program leader for human scis. rsch. Families, 4-H and Nutrition Unit Cooperative State Rsch., Edn. and Extension Svcs., US Dept. of Agr., Washington. Named one of Most Influential Black Americans, Ebony mag., 2006. Mem.: The Links, Inc. (pres. 2002—), Black Women's Agenda, Nat. Coalition of Black Devel. in Home Econs., Delta Sigma Theta Sorority. Office: The Links, Inc 1200 Massachusetts Ave, NW Washington DC 20005*

**VAUGHN, GLORIA C.,** state representative; b. Corpus Christi, Tex., June 25, 1936; m. James M. Vaughn; children: James, Melodie. Student, Del Mar Jr. Coll., Salvation Army Coll., N.Mex. State U. State rep. dist. 51 N.Mex.

State Legis., Santa Fe, 1996—. Mem. Bus. and Industry com. N.Mex. State Legis., Santa Fe, mem. legis. judiciary labor and human resources com. Mem.: FEMA (bd. dirs.), LVA (bd. dirs.), ARC (sec.), Salvation Army, Salvation Army (pres.), Am. Cancer Bd., Boy Scouts Am., Habitat for Humanity (bd. dirs.), Alamogordo Women's Connection. Republican. Home: 503 E 16th St Alamogordo NM 88310 Office: New Mexico State Capitol Rm 203 ICN Santa Fe NM 87503

**VAUGHN, ISSAC J.,** lawyer; b. San Francisco, Dec. 12, 1962; BS, Santa Clara U., 1984; attended, Hastings Coll. Law, 1988—89; JD, U. Mich. Law Sch., 1991. Bar: Calif. 1991. Ptnr. Wilson Sonsini Goodrich & Rosati, Palo Alto, Calif. Mem. bd. regents Santa Clara U., 1992—. Named one of Top 20 Lawyers Under 40, Calif. Law Bus., 2001, Am. Top Black Lawyers, Black Enterprise Mag., 2003. Office: Wilson Sonsini Goodrich & Rosati 650 Page Mill Rd Palo Alto CA 94304-1050 Office Phone: 650-493-9300. Business E-Mail: ivaughn@wsgr.com.

**VAUGHN, JAMES ENGLISH, JR.,** neurobiologist; b. Kansas City, Mo., Sept. 17, 1939; s. James English and Sue Katherine (Vaughn); m. Christine Singleton, June 18, 1961; children: Stephanie, Stacey. BA, Westminster Coll., 1961; PhD, UCLA, 1965. Postdoctoral rsch. fellow in brain rsch. U. Edinburgh, Scotland, 1965-66; asst. prof. Boston U. Sch. Medicine, 1966-70; head sect. molecular neuromorphology Beckman Rsch. Inst., City of Hope, Duarte, Calif., 1970—, pres. rsch. staff, 1986, chmn. divsn. neurosci., 1987—2001. Editor (assoc. editor): (Jour.) Jour. Neurocytology, 1978—86; contbr. articles to profl. jours.; mem. editl. bd. (Jour.) Synapse, 1986—; reviewer for Jour. Comparative Neurology, 1974—, Brain Research, 1976—. Recipient Alumni Achievement award, Westminster Coll., 2003; fellow Neurosci. Rsch. Program, 1969; grantee, NSF, 1983—87; rsch. grantee, NIH, 1969—99. Mem.: AAAS, N.Y. Acad. Scis., Internat. Brain Rsch. Orgn., Soc. for Neurosci. (chmn. short course 1977), Am. Assn. Anatomists, Am. Soc. Cell Biology, Sigma Xi.

**VAUGHN, JOHN ROLLAND,** auditor; b. Iola, Kans., Aug. 4, 1938; s. Ralph H. and Alice (Dille) V.; m. Doris K. Black, Sept. 4, 1960; children: Lisa Ann, Brian Douglas. BS in Bus., Emporia State U., 1960. Sr. auditor Arthur Andersen & Co., Kansas City, Mo., 1961-66; gen. auditor First Nat. Bank Kansas City, 1966-69, Commerce Bancshares, Inc., 1969-73; sr. v.p. adminstrv. svcs. divsn. Peoples Trust Bank, Ft. Wayne, Ind., 1973-77; dep. gen. auditor, v.p. Crocker Nat. Bank, San Francisco, 1978-79; v.p., gen. auditor S.W. Bancshares, Houston, 1980-83; sr. v.p., gen. auditor MCorp., Houston, 1984-87, mng. dir., 1988-89; audit dir. Banc One Corp., Dallas, 1990-92; v.p., gen. auditor St. Paul Cos., St. Paul, 1992-97; dir. internal audit Conseco Fin., St. Paul, 1998—2001; v.p., chief audit officer Calif. State Automobile Assn., 2001—02, v.p., chief risk officer, 2002—. Treas. Overland Park (Kans.) Jr. C. of C., 1965—66; outside dir. Overland Park Credit Union; contr. Ft. Wayne Bicentennial Commn., 1974—77; mem. chmns. cabinet Indianhead coun. Boy Scouts Am., 2000—01. Mem. Inst. Internal Auditors (1st v.p. Kansas City 1969-70, pres. 1970-71, midwest regional v.p. 1971-72, Twin Cities chpt. gov. 1993-97, pres. 1994-95, internat. profl. conf. com. 1995-98, internat. ednl. products com. 1999-2002, San Francisco chpt. gov. 2004—), Fin. Execs. Inst. (dir. Ft. Wayne 1976-77), Risk and Ins. Mgmt. Soc., Hartsmen, Soc. Preservation and Encouragement Barber Shop Quartet Singing in Am., Voices in Harmony Chorus, Vocal Majority Chorus, Gt. No. Union Chorus, Sigma Tau Gamma. Home: 5 Henry Ranch Dr San Ramon CA 94583

**VAUGHN, KERRI LYNN,** elementary school educator; b. Wichita, Kans., Feb. 19, 1974; d. Lee and Linda Sue Heart; m. David Vaughn, July 27, 1996; children: Rachel Renee, Samantha Lynn. BS in Elem. Edn., Kans. Newman Coll., Wichita; MA in Tchg., Friends U., Wichita. Tchr. elem. sci. Mueller Elem. Sch., Wichita, 2003—; Adj. prof. Friends U., 2005—. Mem.: Nat. Sci. Tchrs. Assn. Home: 3940 Calvert Ct Wichita KS 67217 Office: Payne Elementary School 1601 S Edwards Wichita KS 67213 Office Phone: 316-973-7850. Personal E-mail: kvaughn@usd259.net.

**VAUGHN, LINDA MARIE,** municipal official; b. Moline, Ill., Aug. 6, 1947; d. Merwin Perry and Margaret Anne Baker; m. Jeffery M. Vaughn, Aug. 16, 1969; children: Jason P., Eric M. Student, Moline Inst. Commerce, 1965. Clk. data entry Eagle Warehouse, Milan, Ill., 1966—69, Lennox Heating/AC, Marshalltown, Iowa, 1970—73, Farmall (Internat. Harvester), Rock Island, Ill., 1973—75, Ingersoll, Rockford, 1975—87; trustee Village of Machesney Park, Ill., 1987—89, clk., 1989—2001, mayor, village pres., 2001—. Guest columnist Parks Jour., 1997—; charter mem. Parks Chamber Women's Network, Loves Park, Ill., 1995; 8 gal. mem. Rock River Valley Blood Ctr. Mem. Northwestern Ill. Mcpl. Clks. Assn. (sec. 1990-92, treas. 1997-99), C. of C. (ambassador 1987—). Democrat. Roman Catholic. Avocations: writing, fishing, reading, walking. Home: 9519 Shore Dr Machesney Park IL 61115-2058 Office: Village Machesney Park 300 Machesney Rd Machesney Park IL 61115-2495

**VAUGHN, MICHAEL S.,** law educator; s. Harley (Bud) Dewitt and Judith Ann Vaughn; m. Tzu-Hsiu Nancy Vaughn, Dec. 2, 1989; 1 child, Rachel. PhD in Criminal Justice, Sam Houston State U., Huntsville, Tex., 1990—93. Prof. Ga. State U., Atlanta, 1993—, chmn. dept. criminal justice, 2002—05. Book rev. editor, Jour. Criminal Justice Edn. Acad. Criminal Justice Scis., Greenbelt, Md., 1993—96, editor, police forum police sect., 2001; editor, criminal justice rev. and internat. criminal justice rev. Ga. State U., Atlanta, 2001—; contbr., correctional health care report Civic Rsch. Inst., N.Y.C., 1999—. Contbr. articles to profl. jours. and publs.; editor: (jour.) Internat. Criminal Justice Rev. Named Outstanding Alumnus, Coll. of Criminal Justice, Sam Houston State U., 2002; recipient Outstanding Service award, Police Section, Acad. of Criminal Justice Sciences, 1998, Outstanding Paper, Acad. of Criminal Justice Scis., 1996, Outstanding Faculty Achievement award, 2004. Mem.: Am. Assn. Univ. Profs., Am. Judicature Soc., Am. Psychology-Law Soc., Am. Soc. Criminology, Acad. Criminal Justice Scis. Avocation: reading. Office: Ga State Univ Criminal Justice PO Box 4018 Atlanta GA 30302-4018 Office Phone: 404-651-3688. Business E-Mail: mvaughn@gsu.edu.

**VAUGHN, MICHAEL THAYER,** physicist, researcher; b. Chgo., Aug. 6, 1936; s. Charles Le Clair and Kathleen Inez (Thayer) V.; m. Gudrun Royek, Sept. 11, 1971 (dec. May 1984); m. Penelope Eve Reader, July 15, 1988. AB, Columbia U., 1955; PhD, Purdue U., 1960. Grad. asst. Purdue U., West Lafayette, Ind., 1955-59; rsch. assoc., instr. U. Pa., Phila., 1959-62; asst. prof. Ind. U., Bloomington, 1962-64; assoc. prof. Northeastern U., Boston, 1964-73, prof., 1973—. Vis. scientist Argonne (Ill.) Nat. Lab., 1967, U. Vienna, Austria, 1970-71, Internat. Ctr. for Theoretical Physics, Trieste, Italy, 1971, U. Southampton, Eng., 1979, 86, 93. Contbr. more than 50 articles to profl. jours. Sci. Rsch. Coun. Eng. fellow, 1979, Sci. & Engring. Rsch. Coun. Eng. fellow, 1986. Mem. AAAS, Am. Phys. Soc. Achievements include research in calculation of two-loop beta functions for renormalization of general quantum field theory, Z=0 criterion for compositeness. Office: Northeastern U Physics Dept 111 DA Boston MA 02115 Office Phone: 617-373-2954. Business E-Mail: m.vaughn@neu.edu.

**VAUGHN, NOEL WYANDT,** lawyer; b. Chgo., Dec. 15, 1937; d. Owen Heaton and Harriet Christy (Smith) Wyandt; m. David Victor Koch, July 18, 1959 (div.); 1 child, John David; m. Charles George Vaughn, July 9, 1971. BA, DePauw U., 1959; MA, So. Ill. U., 1963; JD, U. Dayton, 1979. Bar: Ohio 1979, U.S. Dist. Ct. (so. dist.) Ohio 1979, U.S. Cir. Ct. (6th cir.) 1987. Lectr. Wright State U., Dayton, 1965-67; communications specialist Charles F. Kettering Found., Dayton, 1968-71; tchr. English Miami Valley Sch., Dayton, 1971-76; law clk. to judge Dayton Mcpl. Ct., 1978-79; coordinator Montgomery County Fair Housing Ctr., Dayton, 1979-81, 85-89; atty. Henley Vaughn Becker & Wald, Dayton, 1981-90; pvt. practice Noel W. Vaughn Law Offices, Dayton, 1990—. Chmn. Dayton Playhouse, Inc., 1981—92; pres. Freedom of Choice Miami Valley, 1980—83, 1986—87; com. mem. Battered Woman Project-YWCA, 1983—84; pres. Legal Aid Soc., 1983—84; chmn. Artemis House, Inc., 1985—88, bd. dirs., 1988—97, ACLU, 1982—86,

Miami Valley Arts Coun., 1985—86, AIDS Found., 1988—90, Miami Valley Fair Housing Ctr., Inc., 1992—94, Human Race Theatre Co., Inc., 1995—2000, Housing Justice Fund, 1979—, Dayton Sister City Com., 2001—02. Recipient Order of Barristers award U. Dayton, 1979. Mem.: ABA, Ohio State Bar Assn., Ohio Fair Plan Underwriting Assn. (bd. govs. 1986—92), Dayton Bar Assn. (chmn. delivery legal svcs. com. 1983—84, family law com. 1991—, chmn. juvenile law com. 2001—03). Office: 1205 Talbott Tower 131 N Ludlow St Dayton OH 45402-1110 Office Phone: 937-222-6635.

**VAUGHN, RICHARD P.,** mathematics professor; s. Daryl Richard and Barbara Jean Vaughn; m. Paula marie Hines, Apr. 3, 1993; 1 child, Gillian Marie. BS. U. San Francisco, 1991; MA in Math., U. Calif., Davis, 1994, PhD, 1998. Residential faculty Paradise Valley CC, Phoenix, 1998—. Program coord. St. Bridget East Valley Men's Transitional Ctr., Mesa, Ariz., 2003—. Mem.: Math. Assn. Am., Chair Acad. Democrat. Roman Catholic. Avocations: fishing, puzzles. Office: Paradise Valley Cmty Coll 18401 N 32nd St Phoenix AZ 85032

**VAUGHN, ROBERT CANDLER, JR.,** lawyer; b. Winston Salem, NC, Sept. 6, 1931; s. Robert Candler and Douglas Arthur V.; m. Carolyn (Hartford), May 2, 1959; children: Patricia Anne, Robert Candler III. BS in Bus. Adminstrn., U. N.C., 1953, JD, 1955. Bar: N.C., 1955, U.S. Dist. Ct. (mid. dist.), 1959, U.S. Tax Ct., 1981. Assoc. Petree, Stockton, Robinson, and predecessor firms, Winston Salem, 1959-65, ptnr., 1965-2000. Bd. dirs. Forsyth Bank & Trust Co., Winston-Salem. Pres. United Way Forsyth County, Winston Salem, 1970-71, Forsyth County Bar Assn.; chmn. Winston Salem Coliseum and Conv. Ctr. Commn., 1974-78; bd. adv.U. NC Tax Inst., Chapel Hill; bd. dirs. Leadership Winston Salem; chmn. Winston Salem Found., 2003, Forsyth Med. Ctr. Found., 1999-01; chmn. Forsyth Tech. Coll. Found., 2006-. Lt. USN, 1955-58. Fellow Am. Bar Found., Am. Coll. Trusts and Estates Counsel (N.C.chmn. 1990-1995); mem. N.C. Bar Assn. (pres. 1985-86, bd. dirs.), U. N.C. Law Alumni Assn. (pres. 1974-75), Am. Coll. Tax Counsel, Old Town Club, Piedmont Club, Rotary. Republican. Methodist. Home: 2575 Club Park Rd Winston Salem NC 27104-2009 Office: Vaughn Perkinson Ehlinger Moxley & Stogner PO Box 25715 Winston Salem NC 27114 Office Phone: 336-794-6001. E-mail: bob.vaughn@vpems.com.

**VAUGHN, ROSALYN MAE,** academic administrator; d. Emmet and Rosie Mae Smith; children: Sherolyn Yvonne Spencer, Sonja Annette King, Rosa Leoma. BS in Elem. Edn., So. Ill. U., 1968; MA in Ednl. Leadership, Western Mich. U., 1974; PhD in Workforce Edn. Devel. and Adminstrn., So. Ill. U., 1996. Educator St. Clair County Pub. Schs., Caseyville, Ill., 1968—69, University City (Mo.) Pub. Schs., 1970—71, Calhoun County Pub. Schs., Battle Creek, Mich., 1971—72; pers. rep., trainer Ralston-Purina Co., Battle Creek, Mich., 1972—74; pub. affairs specialist Kellogg Co., Battle Creek, Mich., 1974—76; MIOSHA dir. Mich. Dept. Labor, Lansing, 1976—80; educator Escambia County Pub. Schools, Pensacola, 1980—83; mgr. Combined Ins. Co. Am., New Orleans, 1983—87; instr., rschr. Pensacola (Fla.) Jr. Coll., 1990—91; grad. internist La. Dept. Labor, Metarie, La., 1993—93; assoc. dean Jones Coll., Jacksonville, Fla., 1996—97; human resources mgr. Dynamic Ednl. Sys., Inc., Jacksonville, Fla., 1997—99; asst. prof. Barry U., Miami Shores, Fla., 1999—, adminstr. human resources devel. and adminstrn. Orlando, Fla., 2000—03; site adminstr. higher edn. leadership doctoral program Nova Southeastern U., Orlando, 2004—. Rev. panelist Family Transition Program, Fla. Dept. Health and Rehab. Svcs., Jacksonville, 1997—99; adminstrv. vol. Polk County Adult Edn. Program, Davenport, Fla., 2002—03; chairperson Mich. Commn. Employment Handicap Persons, Lansing, Mich., 1976—80; steering com., exec. bd. Ctrl. Fla. Higher Edn. Alliance, Orlando, 1999—; mem. Fla. Hosp. Diabetes Ctr., Orlando, 2000—. Recipient Diana award, Mich. Safety Conf., 1978; fellow Ill. Consortium Ednl. Opportunity Program fellow, State Ill. Dept. Edn., 1994—96; scholar State Tchrs.' scholar, 1964—68. Mem.: Ctrl. Fla. Higher Edn. Alliance (mem.-at-large 2001—), Assn. Career Tech. Educators (exec. bd. 2001—), Fla. Exec. Women (assoc.). Achievements include development of Employment Law Certification Program. Home: 6166 Stevenson Dr 205 Orlando FL 32835 Personal E-mail: rvmshrda@aol.com.

**VAUGHN, THOMAS JOSEPH,** earth science educator, administrator; b. Lawrence, Mass., Dec. 23, 1944; s. Thomas Wilbur and Dorothy Agnes (Mallon) V.; m. Priscilla Margaret Bastian, June 30, 1973; children: Matthew Thomas, Judith Diane. BA in History/Geography, Mt. Carmel Coll., Niagara Falls, Ont., Can., 1968; AM in Geography, Boston U., 1972; MEd in Secondary Ednl. Adminstrn., U. Lowell, Mass., 1977; CAGS in Computers in Edn., Lesley U., Cambridge, Mass., 1985. Cert. tchr. earth sci., geography, history, cert. gen. supr., jr.-sr. h.s. prin., Mass. Tchr. earth sci. DeSales H.S., Louisville, 1968-69; tchg. fellow Boston U., 1969-71; liberal arts prof. Bryant-McIntosh Jr. Coll., Lawrence, 1971-72; earth sci. tchr., lead sci. tchr. Arlington H.S., 1972—2004; adult edn. instr. Arlington (Mass.) Pub. Schs., 1985-90; asst. dir. project ESTEEM Harvard-Smithsonian, Cambridge, Mass., 1993; instr. earth sci. Northeastern U., Boston, 1997—; prof. environ. studies Middlesex C.C., 2004—; prof. sci. edn. U. Mass, Darmouth, 2005—. Telecom. moderator Harvard U. Sci. Tchr. Network, Cambridge, 1986-89; chair study groups for sci. edn. reform Mass. Dept. Edn., Malden, 1995—; sci. tchr. leader, 1998. Co-author: Integrating Computers in Your Classroom: Middle and Secondary Science, 1994, Harvard Smithsonian Project IMAGE, 1997; presenter in field. Lector St. Theresa's Ch., Billerica, Mass., 1975—; trustee Billerica Pub. Libr., 1993—; mem. Billerica Friends of the Libr., 1995—; bd. dirs. Tchr. Leadership Acad. Mass. Recipient Pathfinder award in tech. Mass. Dept. Edn., 1991, Sci. Educator of Yr. award for Middlesex County, Mass. Assn. Sci. Tchrs., 1998, Presdl. award for excellence in tchg. math. and sci. NSF, 2000; Disting. Alumni award U. Mass., Lowell, 2000, Boston U., 2002, Lesley U., 2005; Sally K. Lenhardt Profl. Leadership award, Lesley U., Cambridge, 2005; Tandy Tech. Scholar, 1996; inducted into Mass. Sci. Educators Hall of Fame, 1992 Fellow Tchr. Leadership Acad. Mass. (bd. dirs.); mem. NSTA, Nat. Assn. Geosci. Tchrs. (pres. New Eng. sect. 2005-06), Nat. Geog. Soc., Mass. Assn. Scis. Tchrs. (award sect.), Mass. Assn. Sci. Suprs. (pres. 2004-05), Ind. Univ. Alumni Assn. at Lowell (bd. dirs. 2005—), Alpha Omega Alpha, Gamma Theta Upsilon (local pres.). Democrat. Roman Catholic. Avocations: computers, telecommunications and internet, reading journals and books, walking. Office: Middlesex Cmty Coll Sci Dept Springs Rd Bedford MA 01730 Office Phone: 781-280-3200 3842. Personal E-mail: tomvaughn@aol.com. Business E-Mail: vaught@middesex.mass.edu.

**VAUGHN, VINCE,** actor; b. Mpls., Mar. 28, 1970; s. Vernon and Sharon Vaughn. Actor: (films) For the Boys, 1991, Rudy, 1993, At Risk, 1994, Swingers, 1996, Just Your Luck, 1996, The Lost World: Jurassic Park, 1997, The Locusts, 1997, A Cool, Dry Place, 1998, Return to Paradise, 1998, Clay Pigeons, 1998, Psycho, 1998, South of Heaven, West of Hell, 2000, The Cell, 2000, The Prime Gig, 2000, Zoolander, 2001, Domestic Disturbance, 2001; prodr.: Made, 2001; actor: Dust: An Extraordinary Correspondence, 2002, Old School, 2003, I Love Your Work, 2003, Blackball, 2003, Starsky & Hutch, 2004, Dodgeball: A True Underdog Story, 2004, Anchorman: The Legend of Ron Burgundy, 2004, The Sky Is Green, 2004, Thumbsuckers, 2005, Be Cool, 2005, Mr. & Mrs. Smith, 2005, Wedding Crashers, 2005, The Break-Up, 2006 (with Jennifer Aniston Movies-Choice Chemistry, Teen Choice Awards, 2006), Other Side of Simple, 2006; (TV films) Lies of the Heart, 1991, Sex and the Matrix, 2000, (guest appearance): (TV series) China Beach, 1989, 21 Jump Street, 1989, Hercules, 1998, Mr. Show with Bob and David, 1998, Sex and the City, 2000, Dinner for Five, 2001; guest appearance (TV series) Getaway, 2005. Named one of 50 Most Powerful People in Hollywood, Premiere mag., 2006; recipient Favorite On-Screen Match-Up (with Owen Wilson), People's Choice Award, 2006, Best On-Screen Team (with Owen Wilson), MTV Movie awards, 2006. Address: United Talent Agy Ste 500 9560 Wilshire Blvd Beverly Hills CA 90212*

**VAUGHN, WILLIAM PRESTON,** retired historian, retired educator; b. East Chicago, Ind., May 28, 1933; s. James Carl and Georgiana (Preston) V.; m. Virginia Lee Meyer, June 10, 1961; 1 child, Rhonda Louise Horton. AB, U. Mo., Columbia, 1955; MA, Ohio State U., 1956, PhD, 1961. Instr. in

history U. So. Calif., 1961-62; asst. prof. history U. N. Tex., Denton, 1962-65, assoc. prof., 1965-69, prof., 1969-91; ret., 1991. Instr. Tex. Project, Malaysia, 1986, 88. Author: Schools for All: The Blacks and Public Education in the South, 1865-77, 1974, The Antimasonic Party in the United States, 1826-43, 1983, Masonic Home and School of Texas, 2002; editor Transactions Tex. Lodge of Rsch., 1988—; contbr. articles to profl. jours. With arty. U.S. Army, 1956-57 Mem. SAR, SCV, So. Hist. Assn. (life), Historians Early Am. Republic, Blue Friars, Masons, Phi Beta Kappa, Phi Alpha Theta (manuscript competition winner 1972). Republican. Disciples Of Christ. Home: 22 CR 1602 Mount Pleasant TX 75455-8450

**VAUGHN, WILLIAM T,** corporate financial executive; b. 1947; BSc, U. of Ark. CPA. Audit mgr. Arthur Young & Co., 1974—81; contr. Marion Corp., 1981—83, Devon Energy Corp., 1983—87; v.p. fin. Devon Energy, 1987—99, sr. v.p. fin., 1999—. Mem.: Am. Inst. Cert. Pub. Accountants. Office: Devon Energy Corp 20 N Broadway Oklahoma City OK 73102

**VAUGHN, WILLIAM WEAVER,** retired lawyer; b. LA, Aug. 29, 1930; s. William Weaver and Josephine (Sweiger) V.; m. Claire Louise M'Closkey, June 2, 1962; children: Robert, Gregory, Elizabeth, Anthony, Christina, James. BA, Stanford U., 1952; LLB, UCLA, 1955. Bar: Calif. 1956. With O'Melveny & Myers, L.A., 1955-56, 57—, ptnr., 1964-96, of counsel, 1996—2002; ret., 2002. Served with U.S. Army, 1956-57. Recipient Learned Hand award Am. Jewish Com., 1991, Joseph A. Ball award for outstanding advocacy Brennan Ctr. for Justice, 1998. Fellow Am. Coll. Trial Lawyers (bd. regents 1992-95); mem. L.A. County Bar Assn. (trustee 1976-78, 80-82), L.A. County Bar Found. (bd. dirs. 1991-95), Assn. Bus. Trial Lawyers (bd. govs. 1980-82), Order of Coif, Calif. Chancery Club I(pres. 1997-98). Office: O'Melveny & Myers 400 S Hope St Los Angeles CA 90071-2899

**VAUSE, EDWIN HAMILTON,** research foundation administrator; b. Chgo., Mar. 30, 1923; s. Harry Russell and Sylvia Clair (Webster) V.; m. Harriet Evelyn Oestmann, June 30, 1951; children— Karen L., Russell E., Kurt H., Dirk C., Luke E. BS, U. Ill., 1947, MS, 1948; MBA, U. Chgo., 1952; D.Sc. (hon.), U. Evansville, 1977. Registered profl. engr., Ill. Ind. Engr., research dept. Standard Oil Co., Ind., 1948-52, asst. gen. foreman mfg. dept., 1952-57; dir. research adminstrn. Mead Johnson & Co., Evansville, Ind., 1957-60; v.p. Charles F. Kettering Found., Dayton, Ohio, 1960-66, v.p., adminstrn. dir., 1966-67, exec. v.p., 1967-71, v.p. for sci. and tech., 1971-88. Trustee The Found. Center, 1967-73; mem. adv. com. Acad. Forum, Nat. Acad. Scis. Vice-pres. Washington Twp. Bd. Edn., 1963-67; mem. Centerville-Washington Twp. Joint Planning Commn., 1967-68; mem. adv. bd. Center for Students Rights, Dayton, 1966-70; active Boy Scouts Am. Mem. Am. Inst. Chem. Engrs. (past chmn. Chgo. sect.), N.Y. Acad. Scis., Agrl. Research Inst., Nat. Industry State Agrl. Research Council. Clubs: Elks, Kiwanis (past pres.), Masons. Republican. Lutheran. Home: 11834 Calle Parral San Diego CA 92128-4534

**VAUX, HENRY JAMES, JR.,** economics professor; b. Portland, Oreg., Feb. 2, 1940; s. Henry James and Jean (Macduff) V.; m. Prindle Anders, June 19, 1964; children: Robert, Katherine. BA, U. Calif., Davis, 1962; MA, U. Mich., 1964, MS, 1968, PhD, 1973. Examiner U.S. Office Mgmt. and Budget, Washington, 1964-67; economist U.S. Nat. Water Commn., Arlington, Va., 1969-70; prof. econs. U. Calif., Riverside, 1970—, dir. water resources, 1986-93, assoc. v.p., 1992—. Pres. Nat. Inst. Water Resources, Washington, 1986-93; pres. bd. dirs. Water Edn. Found., Sacramento, 1990—; mem., chair water sci. and tech. bd. Nat. Rsch. Coun., 1994-2001; co-chair adv. bd. Rosenberg Internat. Forum, Oakland, 1996—. Recipient Nat. Leadership award Univ. Coun. Water Resource Rsch., 1994. Mem. Cosmos Club.

**VAVALA, DOMENIC ANTHONY,** research scientist, educator, retired military officer; b. Providence, Feb. 1, 1925; s. Salvatore and Maria (Grenci) V Certificate basic engring., Yale U. Army Specialized Tng. Program, 1944; BA, Brown U., 1947; MS, U. R.I., 1950; MA, Trinity U., San Antonio, 1954; PhD Physiology, Accademia di Studi Superiori "Minerva", Italy, 1957; MEd, U. Houston, 1958; DSc (hon.), Nobile Accademia di Santa Teodora Imperatrice, Rome, 1966, DMS (hon.), 1970; DPH (hon.), Nobile Accademia di Santa Teodora Imperatrice, 1983; D Pedagogy (hon.), Studiorum Universitas Constantiniana of Sovrano Ordine Constantiniano di San Giorgio, Rome, 1966; EdD (hon.), Imperiale Accademia di San Cirillo, Pomezia, Italy, 1977; LittD (hon.), Univ. Internazionale Sveva "Frederick II", Bergamo, Italy, 1979; D Health Scis. (hon.), Johnson & Wales U., 1993; LLD (hon.), Fridericus II U., Capua, Italy, 1997; MD (hon.), Frederick II U., Providence, 1999. Asst. tumor rsch. U. R.I., also asst. entomol. rsch., 1950; rsch. asst. pharmacology Boston U. Sch. Medicine, 1950—51; commd. 2d lt. med. svc. USAF, 1951, advanced through grades to lt. col., 1968; rsch. team physiologist cold injury Army Med. Rsch. Lab., Osaka Army Hosp., Osaka, Japan, 1951—52; rschr. aviation physiologist USAF Sch. Aviation Medicine, Randolph AFB, Tex., 1952—54, 3605th USAF Hosp., Ellington AFB, Tex., 1955—57, chief physiol. tng., 1957; cons. aviation physiology, flim prodr. Univ. Houston, 1956; rschr. aviation physiologist, head acad. sect. dept. physiol. tng. USAF Hosp., Lackland AFB, Tex., 1957—58; vis. prof. physiology Incarnate Word Coll., San Antonio, 1958; rschr. aviation physiologist, chief physiol. tng. comdr. 832d Physiol. Tng. Flight, 832d Tactical Hosp., Cannon AFB, N.Mex., 1958—85; adj. faculty mem. Ea. N.Mex. U., Portales, 1959—64; instr. adult edn. divsn. Clovis Mcpl. Schs., N.Mex., 1960; rschr. aviation physiologist, comdr. 15th Physiol. Tng. Flight, 824th USAF Dispensary, Kadena Air Base, Okinawa, 1965—66; rsch. scientist, directorate fgn. tech., aerospace med. divsn. Brooks AFB, Tex., 1966—68; chief R & D support and interface divsn., dep. dir. for fgn. tech., 1969—70; adj. instr. Johnson & Wales U., Providence, 1973—74; instr. humanities Johnson and Wales U., Providence, 1974—75, asst. prof. humanities, 1975—77, prof. health scis. and nutrition, 1977—93, prof. emeritus, 1999—, coord. biomed. and behavioral scis. Day Coll. divsn., 1973—75, psychology coord. vets. divsn. Coll. Continuing Edn., 1974—76, assoc. dean adj. faculty, 1975, dean faculty, 1975—77, coord. acad. devel., 1977—78, dir. mus. series, 1990—, curator Chapel Empress St. Theodora, 1992—. Pres. corp., chmn. bd. dir. Sovereign Constantinian Order of St. George, Inc., R.I., 1986—; pres. corp., chmn. bd. dir. The Noble Acad. of Empress St. Theodora of R.I., Inc., 1988—; instr. anatomy, physiology and med. terminology R.I. Hosp., Providence, 1987-90 Writer, prodr.: (TV Series) Your Body in Flight, Sta. KUHT, Houston, 1956; (TV series) Highway to Health, Okinawa, 1965; compiled and edited: Fifty Years of Progress of Soviet Medicine, 1917-67; abstractor, translator in medicine Chem. Abstracts Svc., Am. Chem. Soc., Ohio State U., 1963-74; editor: (Cath. parish newspaper) The Logos, Kadena Air Base, Okinawa, 1965-66 (1st pl. 5th Air Force chapel printed news contest); contbr. articles to profl. jours Trustee, Gov. Ctr. Schs., Providence, 1979-85; mem. scholarship com. St. Sahag and, St. Mesrob Armenian Apostolic Ch., Providence; choir master, music dir. Cannon AFB, Cath. Parish, 1958-65; received in pvt. audience Pope John Paul II, 1997. Served with AUS, 1943-44 Recipient Disting. Svc. award Clovis Jaycees, 1959, Acad. Palms Gold medal Accademia Studi Superiori "Minerva", 1960, citation, chief chaplains USAF, 1970, commendation medal USAF, 1970, chief biomed. scientist insignia, biomed. scis. corps USAF Med. Svc., 1970, spl. faculty citation Johnson and Wales U., 1981, contbr. awd. doctoral program ednl. leadership Alan Feinstein Grad. Sch., Johnson and Wales U., Providence, 1999; academician divsn. scis. Accademia di Studi Superiori "Minerva", 1960; Min. Plenipotentiary for U.S. of Nobile Accademia di Santa Teodora Imperatrice, Rome, 1967, rector pro tempore, France, 1980; decorated knight grand officer Merit Class, Sovereign Constantinian Order St. George, Rome, 1969, Knight of Grand Cross with Constantinian neckchain, Justice Class, Sovereign Constantinian Order St. George, 1969, Knight of Grand Cross Justice Class, Order St. John of Jerusalem, Knights of Malta, Bari, Italy, 1984, Knight of Grand Cross Justice Class, Order St. John of Jerusalem, Knights of Cyprus, Rhodes and Malta, Bari, 1984, Knight of Grand Cordon Justice Class, Order Teutonic Knights, Sao Paulo, 1986, Knight of Grand Cross Justice Class, Mil. Order St. Gereon, Sao Paulo, 1986, Knight of Grand Cross Justice Class, Mil. and Hospitalier Order St Jean d'Acre and St. Thomas, Capua, Italy, 1987, Knight of Grand Cross Justice Class, Mil. and Hospitalier Order St. Mary of Bethlehem, Capua, 1987; recipient Ednl. Professionalism award Domei Toastmasters Internat., 1965;

named Magnificent Rector and Pres., The Constantinian U. (Studiorum Universitas Constantiniana), Italy, 1970, Marquis of Royal Throne of Swabia of Hohenstaufen Dynasty, Prince Jean von Schwaben, Bergamo, Italy, 1984, Duke of the New Rome, Constantinople, of Imperial Dynasty of Amorium by His Imperial Highness Prince Don Francesco Amoroso d'Aragona, Capua, 2000, Citizens Citation, Hon. Vincent A. Cianci Jr., Mayor City Providence, 1995 Fellow AAAS (emeritus, life), Tex. Acad. Sci., Royal Soc. Health (London; emeritus), Am. Inst. Chemists (emeritus); mem. Assn. Mil. Surgeons U.S. (life), Nat. Assn. Doctors U.S. (founder 1958, sec.-treas. 1958-85, editor-in-chief The NADUS Jour. 1963-68), Accademia di San Cirillo Italy (hon.), N.Y. Acad. Scis., Phi Sigma, Kappa Delta Pi, Phi Kappa Phi, Alpha Beta Kappa (charter, pres. R.I. Alpha chpt. Johnson and Wales U. 1984-92), Acad. Europea for Econ. Cultural Rels. (acad. senate, medallion 2004) Home: 30 Oaklawn Ave Apt 219 Cranston RI 02920-9319

**VAWTER, MARQUIS PHILIP,** psychologist, researcher; s. Marquis Glen Miller and Geraldine Mae Ryken; m. Karen Lee Harvey, May 5, 1989. BA, U. Calif., Santa Cruz, 1973; MA, Calif. State U., Long Beach, 1978; MS in Edn., U. So. Calif., LA, 1986; PhD, Calif. Coast U., 1992. Cert. marriage and family therapist Bd. of Behavioral Sci., Calif., 1990, rehabilitation counselor Commn. Rehab. Certification, 1986; psychologist Bd. Psychology, Calif., 2000. Rsch. biochemist Beckman I; rsch. technician Long Beach Veterans Adminstrn., 1973—75; rsch. biochemist Beckman Instruments, Fullerton, Calif., 1975—80; rehab. counselor Underwriters Adjusting Co., Newport Beach, 1980—85; rehab. dir. counseling, assessment Rehab. Experts, Inc., Orange, Calif., 1986—94; postdoctoral fellow NIH, Bethesda, Md., 1994—2000; assist. profl. rschr. Dept. Psychiatry, Irvine, Calif., 2001—. Marriage and family counselor internship various mental health agencies, Orange County, 1985—90; predoctral fellowship Rijksuniversiteit, Utrecht, Netherlands, 1985—86; psychol. asst. Nat. Inst. Mental Health, Washington, 1994—96. Author: (jour. articles) Neuropsychopharmacology, Molecular Psychiatry, Schizophrenia Rsch. Fellow, U. So. Calif., 1984—85, Rijksuniversiteit, 1985; scholar, Calif. State Scholar Bd., 1969—73. Mem.: Soc. Biol. Psychiatry, Am. Assoc. Advance Sci., APA (assoc.), Am. Coll. Neuropsychopharmacology (assoc.). Achievements include patents pending for treatment and diagnosis of mental disorders; research in over 40 peer reviewed scientific publications; patents pending for NCAM and schizophrenia. Avocations: gardening, reading, travel. Office Phone: 949-824-9014.

**VAYALAKKARA, JYOTHI,** neuropsychologist, director, educator; b. Kannur, Kerala, India, July 20, 1968; d. Gangadharan Nambiar and Jayalakshmi Vayalakkara; m. Karamdas Velluva Puthiya, Apr. 23, 1990; 1 child, Jyotsna Vayalakkara Karamdas. BS in Chemistry, Calicut U., India, 1989, MA in English Lit., 1991; MS in Clin. Psychology, Nova Southeastern U., Ft. Lauderdale, Fla., 1996, PsyD, 2000; diploma in journalism, Bharatiya Vidya Bhavan, India, 1991. Cert. clin. psychologist Conn., 2004. Postdoctoral fellowship in neuropsychology New Eng. Med. Ctr., Boston, 2001—03; clin. neuropsychology fellow Tufts Med. Sch., New Eng. Med. Ctr., Boston, 2001—03; program dir., neuropsychologist Conn. Valley Hosp., Middletown, Conn., 2004—. Program dir. Conn. Valley Hosp., Middletown, 2004—; adj. psychology faculty U. Hartford, Conn., 2005—. Contbr. articles to profl. jours., chapters to books. Mem. Psychologists for Peace (PsySR), Washington, 2006—; com. mem. South Asian Womens' Network (SNEHA), Hartford, 2006—. Ann. Scholarship award, Broward Internat. Womens' Club, Fla., 1994—99. Mem.: APA (assoc.), Conn. Psychol. Assn. (assoc.), Bharatiya Vidya Bhavan (life), Asia-Pacific Coalition, Phi Theta Kappa (hon.). Avocations: writing, volunteering. Office Phone: 860-262-6049. Personal E-mail: kjjy@earthlink.net.

**VAYO, DAVID JOSEPH,** composer, music educator; b. New Haven, Mar. 28, 1957; s. Harold Edward and Joan Virginia (Cassidy) V.; m. Marie-Susanne Langille, 2002; children; Rebecca Lynn, Gordon Francis. MusB, Ind. U., 1980, MusM, 1982; D of Musical Arts, U. Mich., 1990. Prof. Nat. U., Heredia, Costa Rica, 1982-84, Nat. Symphony Youth Sch., San Jose, Costa Rica, 1982-84; asst. prof. music Conn. Coll., New London, 1988-91, Ill. Wesleyan U. Sch. Music, Bloomington, 1991-95, assoc. prof., 1995-2000, prof., 2000—. Resident artist Banff Ctr. for Arts, 1992, 94, Va. Ctr. for Creative Arts, 1994; Centrum, Port Townsend, Wash., 1996; participating composer Internat. Soc. Contemporary Music-World Music Days, Yokohama, 2001, Mexico City, 1993, Internat. Double Reed Festival, Rotterdam, The Netherlands, 1995, Internat. Trombone Festival, 1997. Composer chamber composition Signals, 1997 (commd. by Koussevitzky Music Found. and Orkest de Volharding), Symphony: Blossoms and Awakenings, 1990 (performer St. Louis Symphony, Leonard Slatkin condr. 1993), Mosaics and Webs, 2003 (commd. by Nat. Assn. Coll. Wind and Percussion Instrs.), Eight Poems of William Carlos Williams for solo trombonist, 1994 (commd. by St. Louis Symphony), piano trio Awakening of the Heart (commd. Barlow Endowment for Music Composition), 1998; works pub. by Internat. Trombone Assn. Press and A.M. Percussion Publs. John Simon Guggenheim Meml. Found. fellow, 2001; Ill. Arts Coun. fellow, 2000. Mem. ASCAP (awards 1988—), Am. Music Ctr. (copying assistance grantee 1992), Coll. Music Soc. (presenter nat. confs.), Soc. for Electro-Acoustic Music in U.S. (presenter nat. conf.), Soc. Composers (membership chmn. 1990-2000, presenter at nat. confs.), Am. Composers Forum. Avocations: athletics, popular music, travel, reading, cooking. Office: Ill Wesleyan U Sch Music PO Box 2900 Bloomington IL 61702-2900 Office Phone: 309-556-3068. E-mail: dvayo@titan.iwu.edu.

**VAZIRI, NOSRATOLA DABIR,** internist, educator, nephrologist; b. Tehran, Iran, Oct. 13, 1939; came to U.S., 1969, naturalized, 1977; s. Abbas and Tahera Vaziri. MD, Tehran U., 1966. Diplomate Am. Bd. Internal Medicine, Am. Bd. Nephrology; cert. hypertension specialist Am. Soc. Hypertension. Intern Cook County Hosp., Chgo., 1969-70; resident Berkshire Med. Ctr., Pittsfield, Mass., 1970-71, Wadsworth VA Med. Ctr., L.A., 1971-72, UCLA Med. Ctr., 1972-74; prof. medicine U. Calif.-Irvine, 1979—, prof. physiology and biophysics, 2001—, prof. biol. scis., 2006—, chief nephrology and hypertension divsn., 1977—, dir. hemodialysis unit, 1977-94, vice chmn. dept. medicine, 1982-94, chmn. dept. medicine, 1994-98, chair faculty Coll. Medicine, 1998—2002. Sr. assoc. editor Jour. Spinal Cord Medicine, 1991-2005; mem. editl. bd. Advances in Renal Replacement, 1998-02, Kidney Internat., Am. Jour. Nephrology, 1999-02, Nephron, 1999-02, Advancements in Renal Replacement Therapies, 1999-04, Internat. Jour. Artificial Organs, Spinal Cord Medicine, Jour. Renal Nutrition; contbr. articles to profl. jours. Mem. sci. adv. coun. Nat. Kidney Found., 1977—. Recipient Golden Apple award, 1977, Circle of Nephrology award, Nat. Kidney Found., 2002. Master: ACP; fellow: Am. Heart Assn. (fellow coun. high blood pressure rsch.); mem.: Assn. Profs. Medicine, Western Assn. Physicians (councilor 2003—05, pres. 2006—), Am. Paraplegia Soc. (pres. 1992—94, Donald Munro award 2002), Am. Physiol. Soc., Am. Soc. Nephrology, Alpha Omega Alpha. Home: 66 Balboa Cv Newport Beach CA 92663-3226 Office: U Calif Irvine Med Ctr Div Nephrology Dept Medicine 101 The City Dr Orange CA 92868-3201 Office Phone: 714-456-5142. Business E-Mail: ndvaziri@uci.edu.

**VAZQUEZ, AMARILIS CORRALES,** music educator; b. Havana, Cuba, Oct. 31, 1957; d. Magdaleno Jose and Dora Padron Corrales; m. Juan Francisco Vazquez, May 1, 1982; children: Amarilis Ester Vasquez, Iradis Vasquez, Jose Francisco Vasquez. BA in Sociology, Fla. So. Coll., 1979; MusM in Piano Performance, U. South Fla., 2002, Cert. Pedagogy, 2002. Exec. sec. Evangelism Explosion, Ft. Lauderdale, Fla., 1981—83; piano tchr. Lakeside Arts Acad., Lakeland, Fla., 2001—05, dir., 2003—05; adj. piano prof. Southeastern Coll., 2004—, profl. accompanist, 2003—. Co-music dir., pianist Iglesia Bautista La Promesa, Lakeland, 1987—. Vol. music tchr. Fla. Bapt. Conv., Jacksonville; vol. music educator workshops Internat. Mission Bd. of So. Bapt. Conv. Mem.: Lakeland Art Guild, Bartow Art Guild, Ridge Music Tchrs. Assn. (v.p. 2003—), Music Tchrs. Nat. Assn. Avocations: exercise, photography, art, raising roses.

**VAZQUEZ, GILBERT FALCON,** lawyer; b. Eagle Pass, Tex., Oct. 29, 1952; s. Catalina (Falcon) Vazquez. AB in Polit. Sci., Yale U., 1975; JD, Harvard U., 1978. Bar: Tex. 1978, U.S. Dist. Ct. (we. dist.) Tex. 1980, U.S.

Ct. Appeals (5th and 11th cirs.) 1981. Ptnr. Matthews & Branscomb, San Antonio, 1978-85, Akin, Gump, Strauss, Hauer & Feld, LLP, San Antonio, 1985—2003, Holland & Knight LLP, San Antonio, 2003—. Co-chmn. issues com. H. Cisneros Mayoral Campaign, San Antonio, 1981; bd. dirs. Bexar County-San Antonio United Way, 1982-87, 91—, San Antonio World Affairs Coun., 1993-96, San Antonio Mus. Assn., 1993-95; mem. exec. com. Mayor's Target 90 Commn., San Antonio, 1985-89, vice chmn., 1987-89; chmn. City of San Antonio Charter Rev. Com., 1991-93, State of Tex. Pension Rev. Bd., 1991-96, vice-chmn., 1994, chair, 1995; bd. dirs. San Antonio Zool. Soc., 1988—, mem. exec. com.(1st v.p.), 2002—; bd. dirs. Harvard Law Sch. Alumni Assn., 2002—; mem. The Pro Bono Coll. of the State Bar of Tex., 2002— Named Outstanding Young San Antonian, U.S. Jaycees, 1985, Outstanding Vol., J.C. Penny Co., 1984. Mem. ABA (internat. law sect., assoc. editor newsletter 1985-87), Nat. Assn. Bond Lawyers, Tex. Bar Assn. (governing coun. internat. law sect. 1985-88), San Antonio Bar Assn., San Antonio Young Lawyers Assn. (Outstanding Young Lawyer 1987), Hispanic Nat. Bar Assn. (regional pres. 1987-88, nat. sec. 1988-89, v.p. 1989-90), San Antonio World Trade Assn. (bd. dirs. 1987-90), Mexican C. of C. (bd. dirs. 1984-85), Greater San Antonio C. of C. (bd. dirs. 1992-95), Yale Club South Tex. (pres. 1982-85). Democrat. Roman Catholic. Avocations: community redevelopment, music, reading. Office: Holland & Knight LLP 112 E Pecan St Ste 2700 San Antonio TX 78205 Office Phone: 210-229-3000. Business E-Mail: gilbert.vazquez@hklaw.com.

**VAZQUEZ, LUIS,** electronics engineer; b. N.Y.C., Oct. 22, 1955; s. Luis Angel Vazquez and Petra Rivera; m. Adriana Babiak, Dec. 2, 1995. AS, Univ. P.R., 1976, BSEE, 1979; MA in Humanities, U. Houston-Clear Lake, 2003. Elecs. engr. U.S. Army Aberdeen Proving Ground, Md., 1982—85, NASA Johnson Space Ctr., Houston, 1985—. Author: (short stories) Marrow, From the Asylum. Forthcoming: Tidelines- An Anthology of Galveston Writers, Master thesis: The Molding of Subjugated Peoples. Mem.: INCOSE, Acad Am. Poets, Internat. Coun. Systems Engring. Roman Catholic. Achievements include design of Gun-and-Transducer Simulator; Space Shuttle In-Flight Maintenance Breakout Box; research in Paper: Line-of-Sight (LOS) Blockage and Radio Frequency (RF) Coverage Analysis for the International Space Station (ISS) MiniAERCam Project, 2nd. author. Avocations: reading, writing, travel. Office: NASA Johnson Space Center 2101 NASA Road 1 Houston TX 77058-3607 Office Phone: 281-483-7478. Business E-Mail: luis.vazquez-1@nasa.gov.

**VÁZQUEZ, MARTHA ALICIA,** federal judge; b. Santa Barbara, Calif., Feb. 21, 1953; d. Remigio and Consuelo Medina Vazquez. BA in Govt., U. Notre Dame, 1975, JD, 1978. Bar: N.Mex. 1979, admitted to practice: US Dist. Ct. (Dist. N.Mex.) 1979. Atty. Pub. Defender's Office, Santa Fe, 1979-81; ptnr. Jones, Snead, Wertheim, Rodriguez & Wentworth, Santa Fe, 1981-93; chief judge U.S. Dist. Ct. N.Mex., Santa Fe, 1993—. Democrat. Roman Catholic. Office: US Courthouse PO Box 2710 Santa Fe NM 87504-2710 Office Phone: 505-988-6330. Business E-Mail: mvazquez@nmcourt.fed.us.

**VAZQUEZ-AZPIRI, A. JAMES,** lawyer; b. Madrid, May 3, 1962; s. Hector Tomas and Iris Belinda Mary Vazquez-Azpiri; m. Yanira E. Molina, July 22, 2002; 1 child, Virginia M. MA, U. St. Andrews, Scotland, 1985, Princeton U., 1987; JD, NYU, 1992; LLM, Harvard U., 1995. Bar: Calif. 1992. Adj. atty. U.S. Commn. on Immigration Reform, Washington, 1996—97; atty. Morrison & Foerster, San Francisco, 1992—97; ptnr. Cooley Godward LLP, San Francisco, 1997—2004, Morgan, Lewis & Bockius, San Francisco, 2005—. Contbr. articles to profl. jours. Recipient C. Arthur Friedrich award, Internat. Human Rights Law Group, 1993, Wiley M. Manuel award, State Bar of Calif., 1998, Armstrong prize, Princeton U., 1997. Mem.: MLA, Royal Overseas League, Hispanic Bar Assn., Bar Assn. San Francisco, Am. Immigration Lawyers Assn., Princeton Alumni Assn., Harvard Club, Sigma Delta Pi, Phi Eta Sigma, Phi Delta Theta. Avocations: hiking, scuba diving, travel, literature. Home: 672 Sky Hy Cir Lafayette CA 94549 Office: Morgan Lewis & Bockius Spear St Tower One Market San Francisco CA 94105 E-mail: ajvazquez@morganlewis.com.

**VAZQUEZ RIVERA, ORNELA AMLIV,** psychologist; b. Malaga, Spain, Feb. 23, 1978; d. Sigfredo Vazquez Calderon and Vilma Celenia Rivera Merced. BA in Soc. Work magna cum laude, U. PR, 2001; MA, CAS in Sch. Psychology, Alfred U., NY, 2004. Lic. Sch. Psychologist NC, 2004. Intern, bilingual sch. psychologist Buffalo Pub. Schs., Buffalo, 2003—04; student svc. specialist Albemarle Rd. Elem., Charlotte, NC, 2004—. Leader Girl Scouts, Caguas, PR, 1999—2001, Charlotte, NC, 2004—. Recipient Gold Medal award, Girl Scouts, 1996. Mem.: NC Assn. of Educators, Nat. Assn. of Sch. Psychologist. Office: Charlotte Mecklenburg Schs Charlotte NC

**VAZSONYI, NICHOLAS,** foreign languages educator; b. Traverse City, Mich., May 31, 1963; s. Balint and Barbara (Whittington) V.; m. Agnes Mueller, Mar. 1, 1996; children Leah, Benjamin. BA summa cum laude, Ind. U., 1982; MA, UCLA, 1988, PhD, 1993. Legal asst. Barnes & Thornburg, Indpls., 1982-84; artistic dir. Telemusic Inc., Bloomington, Ind., 1984-86, 88-90; instr. UCLA, 1993-94; asst. prof. German Vanderbilt U., Nashville, 1994-97; assoc. prof. German U. S.C., Columbia, 1997—. Mng. editor New German Review, L.A., 1990-93. Author: Lukacs Reads Goethe: From Aestheticism to Stalinism, 1997; author; editor: Searching for Common Ground: Diskurse zur deutschen Identitat 1750-1871, 2000, Wagner's Meistersinger: Performance, History, Representation, 2003; contbr. numerous articles to profl. jours. Mem. MLA, Am. Assn. Tchrs. of German. Goethe Soc. N.Am., German Studies Assn., Phi Beta Kappa. Office: U SC German Studies Program Columbia SC 29208-0001 E-mail: vazsonyi@sc.edu.

**VAZZANA, ANDREA,** psychologist, educator; PhD, No. Ill. U., 1999. Asst. clin. prof. psychiatry NYU Sch. Medicine, NYC, 2005—. Office Phone: 212-263-8843.

**VAZZANO, FRANK PAUL,** historian, educator; b. Lorain, Ohio, July 31, 1941; s. Anthony Joseph and Dorothy Marie Vazzano; m. Charlotte Louise Schmidt, Aug. 17, 1963; children: Frank Jr., Kristen, Ann-Marie. BS, Bowling Green State U., Ohio, 1964, MA, 1965; PhD, Kent State U., Ohio, 1972. Prof. Walsh U., North Canton, Ohio, 1971—. Adj. prof. Kent State U., Stark Campus, Canton, Ohio, 1990—2001. Contbr. articles to profl. jours. Mem.: Am. Italian Hist. Assn., Ohio Acad. History, Organ. Am. Historians. Roman Catholic. Avocations: writing, gardening, sports. Home: 1043 Liberty Ln NW North Canton OH 44720 Office Phone: 330-490-7057. Business E-Mail: fvazzano@walsh.edu.

**VEACH, ROBERT RAYMOND, JR.,** lawyer; b. Charleston, S.C., Nov. 28, 1950; s. Robert Raymond and Evelyn; m. Lori Sue Erickson, May 27, 1989. Student, St. Olaf Coll., 1968-70; BS in Acctg., Ariz. State U., 1972; JD, So. Meth. U., 1975. Bar: Tex. 1975, Nebr. 1975, U.S. Dist. Ct. Nebr. 1975, U.S. Dist. Ct. (no. dist.) Tex. 1975. Temporary Emergency Ct. Appeals 1975. Acctg. instr. Sch. Bus. So. Meth. U., Dallas, 1973-74; law clk. to Hon. Joe E. Estes U.S. Dist. Ct. No. Dist. Tex.-Temp. Emergency Ct. Appeals, Dallas, 1975-76; assoc. Locke Purnell Boren Laney & Neely, Dallas, 1976-80; v.p. The Lomas & Nettleton Co., Dallas, 1980-83, Rauscher Pierce Refsnes, Inc., Dallas, 1983-87; pres. RPR Mortgage Fin. Corp., Dallas, 1985-87; sr. shareholder Locke Purnell Rain Harrell, Dallas, 1987-97; exec. v.p. Precision Imaging Solutions, Inc., Dallas, 1998—; pvt. practice Dallas, 1998—. Allied mem. N.Y. Stock Exch., 1985-87; lectr. securities and banking confs.; bd. dirs. pvt. com., 1997—; trustee CentraCore Properties Trust (NYSE-CPV), chmn. audit and fin. com., 1998-2002, 05—, chmn. bd., 2002—, chmn. corp. gov. and nominating com., 2003—. Author legal articles. Bd. dir. Washington Reg. Transplant Consortium, 1988—, Hospice Care of DC, 1989-1998, pres. bd., 1993-96; mem. Mem. Gov.'s Task Force Wash. State Housing Commn., 1982-83. Fellow Nebr. State Bar Found.; mem. ABA, State Bar of Tex., Nebr. State Bar Assn., Fed. Bar Assn., Dallas Bar Assn.

Republican. Methodist. Avocation: golf. Home: 4223 Brookview Dr Dallas TX 75220-3801 Office: 2911 Turtle Creek Blvd Ste 1240 Dallas TX 75219-6277 Office Phone: 214-520-7544. Business E-Mail: bob@veachlaw.com.

**VEACO, KRISTINA,** lawyer; b. Sacramento, Mar. 4, 1948; d. Robert Glenn and Lelia (McCain) V.; 1 child, Nina Katherine. BA, U. Calif., Davis, 1978; JD, Hastings Coll. Law, 1981. Legal adv. to commr. William T. Bagley Calif. Pub. Utilities Commn., San Francisco, 1981-86; sr. counsel Pacific Telesis Group, San Francisco, 1986-94; sr. counsel corp. and securities and pol. law AirTouch Comms., San Francisco, 1994-98; asst. gen. counsel, asst. sec. McKesson Corp., San Francisco, 1999—2006, corp. governance advisor, 2006—. Mem.: ABA, Soc. Corp. Secs. and Governance Profls. (pres. San Francisco chpt. 2001—02, mem. adv. com. San Francisco chpt., nat. bd. dirs.), San Francisco Bar Assn., Phi Beta Kappa. Office: 2470 16th Ave San Francisco CA 94116

**VEALE, SCOTT,** editor, columnist; Editor Week in Review NY Times, columnist Book Review, daily book review editor Culture Desk. Office: NY Times 229 W 43rd St New York NY 10036 Office Phone: 212-556-7872. Office Fax: 212-556-1516.*

**VEALE, TINKHAM, II,** retired chemicals executive, engineer; b. Topeka, Dec. 26, 1914; s. George W. and Grace Elizabeth (Walworth) V.; m. Harriett Alice Ernst, Sept. 6, 1941; children: Harriett Elizabeth Veale Leedy, Tinkham III, Helen Ernst Veale Gelbach. BS in Mech. Engring., Case Inst. Tech., 1937; LLD, Kenyon Coll., 1981. Registered profl. engr. With Gen. Motors Corp., 1937-38, Avery Engring. Co., 1939, Reliance Electric Co., 1940-41; asst. to pres. Ohio Crankshaft Co., 1942-46; gen. mgr. Tocco Co., 1947-51; pres. Ric Wil Corp., 1952-53, Alco Chem. Corp., 1954-56, dir., 1954-86. Spl. ptnr. Ball Burge & Kraus, investment bankers, 1957-60; chmn. bd. V. and V. Cos., Inc. and subs., Cleve., 1960-65, Alco Standard Corp. and subs., Valley Forge, Pa., 1965-86, Horsehead Industries, Inc. and subs., N.Y.C., 1981—2001, HTV Industries Inc. and subs., Cleve., 1978—; ptnr. Fair Elm Farm, 1948-2000, Kennedy Veale Stable, 1954-2000. Trustee Veale Charitable Found., 1966—. Recipient Silver Bowl award Case Inst. Tech., 1980; recipient Gold Medal Case Inst. Tech., 1982, Univ. medal Case We. Res. U., 2003. Mem. Cleve. Engring. Soc., Nat. Soc. Registered Profl. Engrs., Newcomen Soc., Phi Kappa Psi. Home: PO Box 39 Gates Mills OH 44040-0039 Office: HTV Industries Inc PO Box 295 Gates Mills OH 44040-0295 Office Phone: 440-423-4473.

**VEASEY, BYRON KEITH,** information systems consultant; b. Washington, Mar. 17, 1957; s. Columbus Jr. and Joan Marie (Ingram) V. BS in Indsl. and Sys. Engring., U. So. Calif., 1979; MBA, Ball State U., 1982; M Mgmt. in Info. Sys., U. Dallas, 1989. Cert. quality analyst Quality Assurance Inst., computing profl. Inst. for Certification of Computer Profls. CIM engr. Mason & Hanger, Amarillo, Tex., 1983-87; bus. sys. analyst E-Sys., Garland, Tex., 1987-89; consulting mgr. Deloitte & Touche, Dallas, 1989-93; sr. cons. CSC, Dallas, 1993-96; solutions mgr. AT&T, Chantilly, Va., 1996-97, Information Advantage, Vienna, Va., 1997; info. sys. cons. DMR Consulting Group, Inc., Atlanta, 1997—99, KPMG, Tampa, Fla., 1999—2000, Arthur Anderson, Dallas, 2000—01, Advance PS, Richardson, Tex., 2001—02, U. Ill., Champaign, 2002—. Mem. Dallas Heart Ball, 1991-92; mem. PM League Dallas Mus. of Art, 1992-93; bd. dirs. Dallas Wind Symphony, 1992; pres. Inst. of Indsl. Engrs., Dallas, 1992-93; v.p. programs Assn. for Sys. Mgmt., Dallas, 1991-93. Capt. USAF, 1979-82. Mem. Am. Legion. Republican. Avocations: theater, saxophone, chess, computers, travel. Home: 2424 N Tustin Ave Apt E7 Santa Ana CA 92705-1617

**VEATCH, ROBERT MARLIN,** philosopher, researcher; b. Utica, NY, Jan. 22, 1939; s. Cecil Ross and Regina V.; m. Laurelyn Kay Lovett, June 17, 1961 (div. Oct. 1986); children: Paul Martin, Carlton Elliot; m. Ann Bender Pastore, May 23, 1987. BS, Purdue U., 1961; MS, U. Calif. at San Francisco, 1962; BD, Harvard U., 1964, MA, 1970, PhD, 1971; DHL (hon.), Columbia U., 1999, Union U., 2004. Teaching fellow Harvard U., 1968-70; research assoc. in medicine Coll. Physicians and Surgeons, Columbia U., 1971-72; assoc. for med. ethics Inst. of Society, Ethics and Life Scis., Hastings-on-Hudson, NY, 1970-75, sr. assoc., 1975-79; prof. med. ethics Kennedy Inst. Ethics Georgetown U., 1979—, prof. philosophy, 1981—, dir., 1989-96; adj. prof. depts. community and family medicine and ob/gyn, 1984—. Mem. vis. faculty various colls. and univs.; mem. gov. bd. Washington Regional Transplant Consortium, 1988—; bd. dirs. Hospice Care D.C., 1989-96, 97-99, pres., 1993-95; active United Network Organ Sharing Ethics Com., 1989-95. Author: Value-Freedom in Science and Technology, 1976, Death, Dying and the Biological Revolution, 1976, rev. edit., 1989, Case Studies in Medical Ethics, 1977, A Theory of Medical Ethics, 1981, The Foundations of Justice, 1987, The Patient as Partner, 1987; (with Sarah T. Fry) Case Studies in Nursing Ethics, 1987, 3d edit., 2006, The Patient-Physician Relationship: The Patient as Partner, Part 2, 1991; (with James T. Rule) Ethical Questions in Dentistry, 1993, 2nd edit., 2004, (with Harley Flack) Case Studies in Allied Health Ethics, 1997, (with Paul DeVries and Lisa Newton) Ethics Applied, 2d. edit., 1999, (with Amy Haddad) Case Studies in Pharmacy Ethics, 1999, The Basics of Bioethics, 2000, 2d edit., 2003, Transplantation Ethics, 2000, Disrupted Dialogue, 2005; editor or co-editor: Bibliography of Society, Ethics and the Life Sciences, 1973, rev. edit., 1978, The Teaching of Medical Ethics, 1973, Death Inside Out, 1975, Ethics and Health Policy, 1976, Teaching of Bioethics, 1976, Population Policy and Ethics, 1977, Life Span: Values and Life Extending Technologies, 1979, Cases in Bioethics From the Hastings Center Report, 1982, Medical Ethics, 1989, 2d edit., 1997, Cross Cultural Perspectives in Medical Ethics, 1989, rev. edit., 2000; (with Edmund D. Pellegrino and John P. Langan) Ethics, Trust, and the Professions, 1991; (with Tom L. Beauchamp) Ethical Issues in Death and Dying, 1996, (with Hans-Martin Sass and Rihito Kimura) Advance Directives and Surrogate Decision Making in Health Care: United States, Germany, and Japan, 1998, (with Albert R. Jonsen and LeRoy Walters) Source Book in Bioethics: A Documentary History, 1998; assoc. editor Encyclopedia of Bioethics, 1998; editl. bd. Jour. AMA, 1976-86, Jour. Medicine and Philosophy, 1981—, Harvard Theol. Rev., 1975—, Jour. Religious Ethics, 1981—; editl. adv. bd. Forum on Medicine, 1977-81; contbg. editor Hosp. Physician, 1975-85, Am. Jour. Hosp. Pharmacy, 1989-99; sr. editor Kennedy Inst. Ethics Jour., 1991—; contbr. articles to profl. jours. Bd. dir. Washington Reg. Transplant Consortium, 1988-, Hospice Care of DC, 1989-1998, pres. bd., 1993-96; mem. United Network for Organ Sharing Ethics Com., 1989-95, Ad Hoc Living Donor Com., 2002-. Recipient Disting. Svc. award, United Meth. Assn., Career Achievement award, Georgetown U., 2005. Office: Georgetown U Kennedy Inst Of Ethics Washington DC 20057-0001 Office Phone: 202-687-6771. Business E-Mail: veatchr@georgetown.edu.

**VEBLEN, THOMAS CLAYTON,** management consultant; b. Hallock, Minn., Dec. 17, 1929; s. Edgar R. and Hattie (Lundgren) V.; m. Susan Alma Beaver, Sept. 1, 1950 (div. 1971); children: Kari Christen, Erik Rodli, Mark Andrew, Sara Catherine; m. Linda Joyce Eaton, Aug. 30, 1975; 1 child, Kristen Kirby. Student, U. Calif., Santa Barbara, 1950—51; BS, Calif. Poly. U., 1953; MS, Oreg. State U., 1955. Corp. v.p. Cargill, Inc., Wayzata, Minn., 1955-75; spl. asst. Sec. Interior, Washington, 1965; dir. food and agr. SRI Internat., Menlo Park, Calif., 1975-80; pres. Food Sys. Assocs., Inc., Washington, 1980-94; also bd. dirs. Food System Assocs., Inc., Washington; chmn. Enterprise Cons. and Devel., Inc., Mpls., 1990—; dir. Georgetown Cons., Inc., 1993-95; convener The Superior Bus. Firm Roundtable, 1991—; chmn. Kirby Ventures LLC, Mpls., 1997—, Wyatt Ventures, LLC, Mpls., 1999—, Northshore, LLC, Mpls., 2000—. Mem. CMC Inst. Mgmt. Cons., 1988—97, pres. Washington chpt., 1991—93. Co-author: (with M. Nichols) The U.S. Food System, 1978; (with M. Abel) Creating a Superior National Food System, 1992; author: The Way of Business: An Inquiry INto Meaning and Superiority, 2006; editor Food System Update 1986-95. Treas., bd. dirs. White House Fellows Assn., Washington, 1985; trustee Freedom from Hunger Found., Davis, Calif., 1980-99, chmn., 1986-89; bd. dirs. Patterson Sch., U. Ky., Lexington, 1976-99, Am. Near East Refugee Aid, 1994--. Recipient Presdl. Appointment White House Fellows Program, Washington, 1965.

Mem.: Coun. on Fgn. Rels., Cato Inst., Cosmos Club. Episcopalian. Avocations: canoeing, gardening. Office: Enterprise Cons and Devel Inc 2817 Lyndale Ave South Minneapolis MN 55409 Office Phone: 202-342-7640. Personal E-mail: superbizrt@aol.com.

**VECCHI, GABRIEL ANDRÉS,** geophysicist; b. Boston, Sept. 1972; s. Mario Pietro Duiglio and Frances Anne (Kosikowski) Vecchi. BA in math., Rutgers U., 1994; MS in oceanography, U. Wash., 1996, MS in applied math., 1999, PhD in oceanography, 2000. Rsch. asst. Rutgers U., IMCS, New Brunswick, NJ, 1993—94; grad. rsch. asst. U. Wash., Seattle, 1994—2000, postdoctoral rsch. asst., 2000—01; lectr. Rutgers U., New Brunswick, NJ, 2004; rsch. scientist U. Wash., Seattle, 2001—03; vis. scientist NOAA-Geophys. Fluid Dyn. Lab., Princeton, NJ, 2003—. Recipient PECASE, Exec. Office Sci. and Tech., 2002; Space grant scholarship, NASA, 1994—96. Mem.: Am. Meteorological Soc., Am. Geophysical Union. Office: NOAA Geophys Fluid Dynamics Lab Princeton Forrestal Campus Rte 1 Princeton NJ 08540 Office Phone: 609-452-6583. E-mail: gabriel.a.vecchi@noaa.gov.

**VECCHIO, ROBERT PETER,** business management educator; b. Chgo., June 29, 1950; m. Betty Ann Vecchio, Aug. 21, 1974; children: Julie, Mark. BS summa cum laude, DePaul U., 1972; MA, U. Ill., 1974, PhD, 1976. Instr. U. Ill., Urbana, 1973-76; mem. faculty dept. mgmt. U. Notre Dame, 1976—, dept. chmn., 1983-90, Franklin D. Schurz Prof. Mgmt., 1986—. Editor: Jour. of Mgmt., 1995—2000. Fellow: APA, Am. Psychol. Soc., Soc. for Indsl. and Orgnl. Psychology; mem.: Midwest Psychol. Assn., Midwest Acad. Mgmt., Acad. of Mgmt., Phi Eta Sigma, Delta Epsilon Sigma, Phi Kappa Phi. Home: 16856 Hampton Dr Granger IN 46530-6907 Office: U Notre Dame Dept Mgmt Notre Dame IN 46556

**VECCHIONE, KENNETH A.,** corporate financial executive; Grad., SUNY Albany. CFO Citicorp Credit Card; CFO, group pres. First Data Corp.; CFO AT&T Universal Card Svcs.; div. head fin. MBNA Corp., Wilmington, Del., 1998—2000; CFO MBNA Am. Bank, Wilmington, Del., 2000—; vice chmn., CFO MBNA Corp., Wilmington, Del., 2004—. Mem. Fin. Exec. Inst. Bd. dir. Del. Jewish Cmty. Ctr. Office: MBNA Corp 1100 N King St Wilmington DE 19884*

**VECCHIOTTI, ROBERT ANTHONY,** management and organizational consultant; b. N.Y.C., May 21, 1941; s. R. Lucien and Louise Victoria V.; m. Dorothea Irene Hoban, Oct. 12, 1963; children: John Robert, Rachel Irene, Sara Christine. BS, St. Peter's Coll., 1962; MA, Fordham U., 1964; PhD, St. Louis U., 1973. Lic. psychologist, Mo. Psychologist Testing and Advisement Ctr., NYU, Washington Sq. campus, 1964-65; group psychologist McDonnell Douglas, St. Louis, 1967-76, sr. bus. analyst, 1976-77, mgr. bus. planning, 1977-79; pres. Orgnl. Cons. Svcs., Inc., St. Louis, 1980—. Adj. assoc. prof. mgmt. Maryville Coll., St. Louis, 1975-81. Bd. dirs. Cath. Charities St. Louis, 1981-86, Cath. Family Svc., 1986-00, Mental Health Assn. St. Louis, 1989-05, Sta. KWMU-FM, 1989-94; trustee St. Patrick's Ctr., 2001-. With US Army, 1965-67. Fellow Soc. Indsl. and Orgnl. Psychologists; mem. APA, Rotary (past pres.). Office: Organizational Consulting Svcs Inc 230 S Bemiston Ave Ste 1107 Clayton MO 63105-1907 Office Phone: 314-863-1200.

**VECELLIO, LEO ARTHUR, JR.,** construction company executive; b. Beckley, W.Va., Oct. 26, 1946; s. Leo Arthur and Evelyn (Pais) V.; m. Kathryn Grace Cottrill, Nov. 29, 1975; children: Christopher Scott, Michael Aaron. BCE, Va. Poly. Inst. and State U., 1968; MCE, Ga. Inst. Tech., 1969; LLD, Northwood U., 1992. Sr. v.p. Vecellio & Grogan, Inc., West Palm Beach, Fla., 1973-96, pres., CEO, chmn. bd. dirs., 1996—; mng. ptnr. Deerfield Property Assocs., Palm Beach, Fla., 1988—, Vecellio Realty Co., Palm Beach, Fla., 1990—; pres. Vecellio Realty Inc., Palm Beach, Fla., 1997—; mng. ptnr. Orlando Property Assn. Ltd., 1997—, WRQ Property Assn. Ltd., 1997—; chmn., pres., CEO The Vecellio Group-Holding Co., West Palm Beach, Fla., 2002—. Pres. Vecellio Contracting Corp. and subs. (Ranger Constrn. Industries, West Palm Beach, dba Ranger Const., South, Deerfield Beach, White Rock Quarries, Miami 1990—), Fla., 1982—; founder, past dir. Gulf Nat. Bank, Sophia, W.Va., Nat. Bankers Trust, Beckley; bank dir. Raleigh County Nat. Bank (now United Nat. Bank), W.Va., 1975-87, mem. adv. bd. Sun Trust Banks. Dir. bd. dir. Econ. Coun. Palm Beach County, Fla., 1985—, chmn.-elect, 1987, chmn., 1989; gov. Northwood U., West Palm Beach, 1985—; organizer, trustee Beckley Area Found., 1985; v.p., trustee Vecellio Family Found., Beckley, 1972-96, pres., trustee, 1996—; active Mini-Grace Commn., Fla. Coun. 100, 1989—2004, vice-chmn., 1991—; commn. dir., v.p. Criminal Justice Commn.; chmn. Budget Rev. Task Force, Budget Oversight Task Force; bd. dir. Palm Beach County Cultural Coun. and Art Sch. Task Force, Fla. Coun. 100, Floridians for Better Transp., exec. com.; corporator Schepens Eye Rsch. Inst., Harvard U., 1993—; mem. engring. coun. 100 Va. Tech.; mem. pres.'s adv. bd. Ga. Inst. Tech., 2000—; trustee, chair investment com. Va. Tech. Found., 2001, exec. com., 2004-05. Capt. USAF, 1969—73. Recipient Free Enterprise medal, Palm Beach Atlantic U., 1988, Disting. Engring. Alumni award, Ga. Tech., 2002. Mem. Am. Rd. and Transp. Builders Assn. (dir. 2000, regional vice chmn. 2002-05), Flexible Pavements Assn. (found, bd. dir. 1979—), Contractors Assn. W. (bd. dir. 1975—). Clubs: Mayacoo Lakes Country (West Palm Beach), Adios Golf (Coconut Creek, Fla.), Jupiter Hills (Fla.), Everglades Club, Club Colette, Greenbrier Sporting Club Republican. Roman Catholic. Avocations: golf, boating, skiing. Home: 210 Via Del Mar Palm Beach FL 33480 Office: Vecellio Group Inc PO Box 15065 West Palm Beach FL 33416-5065 Office Phone: 561-793-2102.

**VECOLI, RUDOLPH JOHN,** retired history educator, director; b. Wallingford, Conn., Mar. 2, 1927; s. Giovanni Battista and Settima Maria (Palmerini) V.; m. Jill Cherrington, June 27, 1959; children: Christopher, Lisa, Jeremy. BA, U. Conn., 1950; MA, U. Pa., 1951; PhD, U. Wis., 1963. Fgn. affairs officer Dept. State, 1951-54; instr. history Ohio State U., 1957-59, Pa. State U., 1960-61; asst. prof. Rutgers U., 1961-65; assoc. prof. U. Ill., Champaign, 1965-67; prof. history, dir. Immigration History Rsch. Ctr., U. Minn., Mpls., 1967—2005; ret., 2005. Vis. prof. U. Uppsala, Sweden, 1970, U. Amsterdam, The Netherlands, 1988, Maria Curie-Sklodowsk U., Lublin, Poland, 1992. Author: The People of New Jersey, 1965, Foreword to Marie Hall Ets, Rosa: The Story of an Italian Immigrant, 1970, (with J. Lintelman) A Century of American Immigration, 1884-1984, (with others) The Invention of Ethnicity, 1990; contbg. author: Gli italiani fuori d'Italia, 1983, They Chose Minnesota: A Survey of the State's Ethnic Groups, 1981, Pane e Lavoro: The Italian American Working Class, 1980, Perspectives in Italian Immigration and Ethnicity, 1977, Immigrants and Religion in Urban America, 1977, The State of American History, 1970, The Reinterpretation of American History and Culture, 1973, Failure of a Dream, Essays in the History of American Socialism, 1984, Italian Americans: New Perspectives, 1985, May Day Celebration, 1988, In the Shadow of the Statue of Liberty, 1988, From Melting Pot to Multiculturalism, 1990, Studi Sull' Emigrazione, 1991, The Lebanese in the World, 1992, Swedes in America: New Perspectives, 1993, The Statue of Liberty Revisited, 1994, La Riscoperta delle Americhe, 1994, The Encyclopedia of Twentieth Century America, 1996, The Cambridge Survey of World Migration, 1995, Print Culture in a Diverse America, 1998; editor, contbg. author: The Other Catholics, 1978, Italian Immigrants in Rural and Small Town America, 1987, The Gale Encyclopedia of Multicultural Am., 1994; mem. editl. bd. Jour. Am. Ethnic History, Studi Emigrazione, America: History and Life Mid-Am., Estudios Migratorios Latino Americanos, Altreitalle; co-editor (with S. Sinke) A Century of European Migrations, 1830-1930, 1991; contbr. articles to jours. Chair history com. Statue of Liberty-Ellis Island Centennial Commn. & Found., 1983-98. With USNR, 1945-46. Decorated Knight Officer, Order of Merit (Italy), 1992; recipient Campus Major honor City of Camaiore, Italy, 1996; Newberry Libr. fellow, 1964, Am.-Scandinavian Found. fellow, 1970, NEH fellow, 1985-86; Am. Philos. Soc. grantee, 1970, Fulbright-Hays sr. rsch. scholar Italy, 1973-74; Am. Coun. Learned Soc. grantee, 1974, 86, U.S. Dept. State Travel grantee, 1977, Acad. Specialist, U.S. Info. Agy., Brazil, 1993; endowed Rudolph J. Vecoli professorship Am. immigration history, 2005. Mem. Am. Italian Hist. Assn.

(pres., mem. exec. council), Am. Hist. Assn., Orgn. Am. Historians, AAUP, Immigration History Soc. (pres., exec. council) Home: 2338 Chilcombe Ave Saint Paul MN 55108-1626 Business E-mail: vecol001@tc.umn.edu.

**VECSEY, GEORGE SPENCER,** sports columnist; b. Jamaica, N.Y., July 4, 1939; s. George Stephen and May (Spencer) V.; m. Marianne Graham; children: Laura, Corinna, David. BA in English, Hofstra Coll., 1960; LHD (hon.), Hofstra U., 1991. Sports reporter Newsday, Garden City, NY, 1960-68, NY Times, NYC, 1968-70, nat. corr., 1970-73, met., religion reporter, 1973-80, sports reporter, 1980-82, sports columnist, 1982—. Author: (with others) Naked Came the Stranger, 1969, Joy in Mudville: Being a Complete Account of the Unparalleled History of the New York Mets, 1970, One Sunset a Week: The Story of a Coal Miner, 1974, (with Loretta Lynn) Coal Miner's Daughter, 1976, (with Jacques Lowe) Kentucky: A Celebration of American Life, 1979, (with George C. Dade) Getting Off the Ground: The Pioneers of Aviation Speak for Themselves, 1978, (with Leonore Fleischer) Sweet Dreams, 1985, (with Martina Navratilova) Martina, 1985, (with Bob Welch) Five O'Clock Comes Early: A Young Man's Battle with Alcoholism, 1982, A Year in the Sun, 1989, (with Barbara Mandrell) Get to the Heart, 1991, (with Harry Wu) Troublemaker: One Man's Crusade Against China's Cruelty, 1996, (with Lorrie Morgan) Forever Yours, Faithfully, 1997, Macguire and Sosa: Baseball's Greatest Homerun Story, 1998, Subway 2000: The Dramatic Story of the First Subway Series Since 1956, 2001, Baseball, 2006; author 8 children's books; editor: The Way It Was: Great Sports Events from the Past, 1974. Recipient Disting. Writing award Am. Soc. Newspaper Editors, 1995; named NY State Sportswriter of Yr. Nat. Sportscasters and Sportswriters Assn., 1985-97. Mem. Kentuckians (bd. dirs. 1988—). Avocations: running, swimming, music, travel, languages. Office: NY Times 229 W 43rd St New York NY 10036-3959*

**VEDDER, EDDIE,** singer; b. Evanston, Ill., Dec. 23, 1965; m. Beth Liebling, June 3, 1994 (div. Sept. 2000); m. Jill McCormick, 2004; 1 child. Lead singer (band) Pearl Jam, 1991—, albums Ten, 1991—, Vs., 1993—, Vitalogy, 1994—, No Code, 1996—, Binaural, 2000, Save You, 2002, Riot Act, 2002, Pearl Jam, 2006, contbr. vocals album Temple of the Dog, 1991, Mother Love Bone, 1992, Bob Dylan Thirtieth-Anniversary Tribute, Sweet Relief: A Tribute to Victoria Williams, Shame, Judgement Night Soundtrack, 1993, Yield, 1998, Pearl Jam Live, 1999, appearances (films) Singles, 1992, Dead Man Walking, 1995.

**VEDDER, NICHOLAS BLAIR,** surgeon, researcher; b. Chgo., Mar. 27, 1955; s. Beverly Blair and Geraldine (Bovbjerg) V.; m. susan Russell Heckbert, June 26, 1978; children: Katherine Anne, Nicholas Russell. BS with distinction in Biology, Stanford U., 1977; MD, Case Western Res. U., 1981. Diplomate Am. Bd. Surgery with added qualification in hand surgery, Am. Bd. Plastic Surgery, Nat. Bd. Med. Examiners; lic. physician, Wash., Mass. Resident in surgery U. Wash., Seattle, 1981-86, NIH rsch. fellow, 1986-88, hand surgery fellow, 1990-91, asst. prof. plastic surger and orthop., 1991-95, assoc. prof., 1995—; resident in plastic surgery Mass. Gen. Hosp., Boston, 1988-90. Attending surgeon U. Wash. Hosps., 1990—, Harborview Med. Ctr., U. Wash. Med. Ctr., Children's Hosp. and Med. Ctr., VA Med. Ctr.; lectr. in field; vis. prof. Johns Hopkins U., Balt., 1991, Nat. Heart and Lung Inst., London, 1991, So. Ill. U., 1991 Contbr. numerous articles to profl. jours., chpts. to books; referee Jour. Clin. Investigation, Am. rev. of Respiratory Diseases, Jour. Surg. Rsch., Jour. Pharmacology and Exptl. Therapeutics, Jour. of trauma, Plastic and Reconstructive Surgery, Annals of Plastic Surgery. Recipient Peter Gingrass award Plastic Surgery Rsch. Coun., 1995; ACS First Prize Nat. scholar, 1987; grantee NIH, 1988-89, 89-94, 91-92, 95—, Genentech, Inc., 1991-93, Biomembrante Inst., 1993-94, Cell Therapeutics, Inc., 1995-96, CDC, G.D. Searle, Inc., 1995-96. Fellow ACS; mem. AAAS, Henry N. Harkins Surg. Soc., N.W. Soc. Plastic Surgeons, Wash. Soc. Plastic Surgeons, seattle Surg. Soc., King County Med. Soc., Wash. Med. Soc., Assn. Acad. Chmn. Plastic Surgery, Am. assn. Hand Surgery, Assn. Acad. Surgery, Am. Soc. Plastic and Reconstructive Surgeons (Robert H. Ivy award 1994), Am. Soc. Surgery or the Hand, Plastic Surgery Ednl. Found., Sigma Xi. Office: Divsn Plastic Surgery Harborview Med Ctr Univ Wash Box 359796 325 Ninth Ave Seattle WA 98104-2499

**VEDDER, RICHARD KENT,** economics professor; b. Urbana, Ill., Nov. 5, 1940; s. Byron C. and Kathleen (Fry) V.; m. Karen Pirosko, June 18, 1968; children: Virin, Vanette. BA, Northwestern U., Evanston, Ill., 1962; MA, U. Ill., 1963, PhD, 1965. Asst. prof. econs. Ohio U., Athens, 1965-69, assoc. prof. econs., 1969-74, prof. econs., 1974-85; economist Joint Econ. Com. of Congress, Washington, 1981-82; Dist. Prof. of econs. Ohio U., Athens, 1985—. Vis. prof. Claremont (Calif.) McKenna Coll., 1979-80, Econs. Inst. U. Colo., Boulder, 1977-78, 88, Washington U., St. Louis, 1995, 96; adj. fellow Am. Enterprise Inst., 2003-, dir. Ctr. for Coll. Affordability and Productivitiy, 2006; mem. Sec. of Edn.'s Commn. on Future of Edn., 2005. Author: American Economy in Historical Perspective, 1976, Can Teachers Own Their Own Schools?, 2000, Going Broke by Degree: Why College Costs Too Much, 2005; co-author: Out of Work: Unemployment and Government in Twentieth-Century America, 1993, rev. edit., 1997, The Wal-Mart Revolution. 2006. Mem. Athens Bd. Edn., 1987-91; bd. dirs. Athens Cmty. Music Sch., 1987-92, Ohio Valley Summer Theater, 2002—. Recipient rsch. grants Earhart Found., 1970, 90, Rockefeller Found., 1974, Nat. Chamber Found., 1990, fellowship Inst. for Humane Studies, Palo Alto, Calif., 1983. Mem. Am. Econ. Assn., Econ. History Assn., Rotary, U. Club. Republican. Presbyterian. Home: 7464 Ridgeview Cir Athens OH 45701-9005 Office: Ohio Univ Dept Econs Bentley Hall Annex 316 Athens OH 45701 E-mail: vedder@ohio.edu.

**VEDERNIKOV, YURI P.,** pharmacologist, educator; b. Tomsk, Russia, Aug. 3, 1937; arrived in U.S., 1991; s. Pavel D. Vedernikov and Tatjana P. Vedernikova; m. Valentina G. Budkina, Mar. 2, 1960 (dec.); 1 child, Alexander Y. Veder. MD, PhD, Sverdlovsk Med. Inst., Russia, 1963. Cert. medicine pharmacology Med. Inst., Sverdlovsk. Asst. prof. dept. pharmacology Med. Inst., Sverdlovsk, 1963—69; rschr. Inst. Plant and Animal Ecology Ural's Sci. Ctr., USSR Acad. Scis., Sverdlovsk, 1969—73; sr. rschr. All-Union Inst. Med. Info. USSR Health Ministry, Moscow, 1973—74; sr. rschr. Brain Rsch. Inst. Acad. Med. Scis., Moscow, 1974—78, sr. rschr. Cardiology Rsch. Ctr., 1978—91; rsch. instr. dept. medicine Coll. Medicine Baylor U., Houston, 1991—93, asst. prof. dept. anesthesiology and ob-gyn., 1993—95; asst. prof. U. Tex. Med. Br., Galveston, 1995—2000, assoc. prof., 2000—. Contbr. scientific papers to profl. jours. Mem.: Nitric Oxide Soc., Acad. Problems Hypoxy (academician). Achievements include patents for device for the study of mechanical properties of the vessels. Home: 21 Back Bay Cir Galveston TX 77551 Office: U Tex Med Br 301 University Blvd Galveston TX 77555-1062 Business E-mail: yvederni@utmb.edu.

**VEDROS, NEYLAN ANTHONY,** microbiologist, educator; b. New Orleans, Oct. 6, 1929; s. Phillip John and Solange Agnes (Melancon) V.; m. Elizabeth Corbett, Apr. 9, 1955; children: Sally Ann, Philippa Jane. BS in Chemistry, La. State U., 1951, MS in Microbiology, 1957; PhD, U. Colo., 1960. Postdoctoral fellow Nat. Inst. Allergy and Infectious Diseases, U. Oreg., Portland, 1960-62; microbiologist Naval Med. Research Inst., Bethesda, Md., 1962-66; research microbiologist Naval Biosci. Lab., Oakland, Calif., 1966-67; assoc. prof. med. microbiology and immunology U. Calif., Berkeley, 1967-72, prof., 1972-91, prof. emeritus, 1991—. Dir. Naval Biosci. Lab., 1968-81; mem. expert panel on bacteriology WHO, 1972-91. Bd. trustees Alameda (Calif.) Library, 1973-78. Served to comdr. M.S.C. USNR, 1952-55, 62-67. Mem.: Internat. Assn. Aquatic Animal Medicine, Internat. Assn. Microbiol. Sci., Am. Soc. Microbiology. Home: 209 Almond Way Healdsburg CA 95448 E-mail: nvedros@earthlink.net.

**VEECH, LYNDA ANNE,** musician, educator; b. Montclair, NJ, July 19, 1969; d. Robert Gerald, Sr. and Josephine Veech. B in Music Edn., Rutgers U., New Brunswick, 1991, MA in Music History, 1995; MusM in Piano Performance and Pedagogy, Westminster Choir Coll., Princeton, N.J., 1998. Cert. tchr. N.J. Faculty mem. Westminster Conservatory, Princeton, 1995—2000; pvt. studio dir. Studio of Lynda A. Veech, Verona, NJ, 1995—; faculty mem. Essex County Coll., Woodbridge, NJ, 1996—98, Caldwell

(N.J.) Coll., 2000—01; choral dir. Caldwell and West Caldwell Pub. Schs., 2000—02; music tchr. Bartle Elem. Sch., Highland Park, NJ, 2002—03; Morris Cath. HS, Denville, NJ, 2003—, chmn. Dept. Performing Arts, 2005—. Cons. freelance work, Verona, NJ, 1995—; participant Hands Across the Water Internat. Tchr. Exch. Program, Australia, 2002. Performer Ameropa Internat. Music Festival, Prague, Czech Republic, 2001, Montclair Music Festival, 2005. Bd. dirs. Music and More Booster Club, Caldwell, NJ, 2001—02; ch. musician 1st Bapt. Ch., Montclair, 2000—01; organist, choir dir. Calvary Luth. Ch., Verona, NJ, 2003—04; organist St. Luke's and All Saints Ch., Union, NJ, 2001—, 1st Reformed Ch., Pompton Plains, NJ; organist, vocalist Canticle AIDS Benefit Ensemble, NJ, 1999—2000; organist St. Anne's Ch., Hoboken, NJ, 2005—. Grantee, Rutgers U., 1991—95, Westminster Choir Coll., 1995—97. Mem.: Music Edn. Assn. (co-founder 2000—), Nat. Conf. Piano Pedagogy, Piano Tchrs. Guild, N.J. Edn. Assn., Am. Choral Dir.'s Assn., Music Educator's Nat. Conf. (treas. 1997, v.p. 1991). Roman Catholic. Avocations: reading, swimming, ballet, poetry, music. Home: 124 Sunset Ave Verona NJ 07044 Office: Morris Cath High Sch 200 Morris Ave Denville NJ 07834-1360 Personal E-mail: notenut@aol.com.

**VEECH, WILLIAM AUSTIN,** mathematics professor; b. Detroit, Dec. 24, 1938; s. Max Lincoln and Muriel Thayer Veech; m. Kathryn Lunceford, Dec. 29, 1965; children: Kathryn Muriel, Maude Elizabeth. BA, Dartmouth Coll., Hanover, NH, 1960; PhD, Princeton (NJ) U., 1963. H. B. Fine instr., Higgins lectr. Princeton U., 1963—66; asst. prof. U. Calif., Berkeley, 1966—69; from assoc. prof. to prof. Rice U., Houston, 1969—88, Milton Brockett Porter prof., 1988—2003, Edgar Odell Lovett prof., 2003—. Mem. Inst. Advanced Study, Princeton, 1968—69, Princeton, 1972, Princeton, 1976—77, Princeton, 1983—84; mem. adv. com. math. and computer sciences NSF, Washington, 1979—82; professeur associe Universite d'Aix-Marseille 2, Luminy, France, 1982, Luminy, 95, Universite de Rennes, Rennes, France, 1977; trustee Math. Scis. Rsch. Inst., Berkeley, Calif., 1989—94; vis. mem. Inst. Hautes Etudes Sci., France, 1989; disting. vis. prof. Nat. U. Singapore, Singapore, 1999. Author: A Second Course in Complex Analysis; contbr. articles to profl. jours.; mem. editl. bd. Ergodic Theory and Dynamics Sys., 1981—90, Caribbean Jour. Math., 1982, Annals of Mathematics, 1985—90. Fellow, NSF, 1960—63; Alfred P. Sloan Found. fellow, 1971—73, Woodrow Wilson Found. fellow, 1960—61, Rsch. grantee, NSF, 1969—2002. Mem.: Am. Math. Soc. (life; rep. Joint Policy Bd. Math. 1989—90, chmn. long range planning com. 1988—89, mem. exec. com. 1986—90). Republican. Episcopalian. Achievements include research in Structure Theorems in Topological Dynamics for Almost automorphic, point-distal and minimal flows; unique ergodicity in interval exchange transformations (Kronecker-Weyl Theorem Mod 2 and proof of Keane Conjecture); existence of free actions of locally compact topological groups; Ergodic theory of the Teichmuller geodesic flow and calculation of its metric entropy; first to introduce objects in dynamics now called Veech surfaces, Veech groups, Veech dichotomy and Siegel-Veech constants; introduce zippered rectangles in construction of Gauss measures on the space of interval exchange transformations. Office: Rice U Mathematics MS136 6100 S Main Houston TX 77005 Office Phone: 713-348-4881. Office Fax: 713-348-5231. Business E-mail: veech@rice.edu.

**VEEDER, DONNA CLARK,** artist; b. Nashville, Feb. 7, 1933; d. Harry Grigsby and Thelma Clayton (Black) Clark; m. Nicholas Schermerhorn Veeder, Aug. 24, 1957; children: Kristen Black Veeder Walker and Katrina Bradt Veeder Kreamer (twins). BFA, U. Ga., 1958; student in figure and portrait painting, Munson Williams Procter Sch. Art, Utica, N.Y., 1973-91. Tchr. art N.Y. Pub. Schs., Mohawk, 1960-63; portrait artist Van Hornesville, NY, 1976—2006; tchr. painting Mohawk Valley Ctr. for Arts, Little Falls, NY, 1985—99; art tchr. Owen D. Young Sch., Van Hornesville, 1984-87. Tchr. adult workshops, portrait painting Herkimer (N.Y.) County C.C., 1982-83; coord. portrait/figure class Munson Williams Proctor Sch. Art, Utica, N.Y., 1988-91, curator class show, 1990; with portrait and figure study Ctrl. Inst. Fine Arts, Beijing, 86, Picture Perfect Gallery, Canajoharie, N.Y., 1992, Selective Eye Gallery, Little Falls, N.Y., Mohawk Valley Ctr. for Arts, Little Falls, 1999-; curator Van Hornesville Artists Show, Van Hornesville Cmty. Corp., 1989, 91, 93, 95, 98, 2000, 02, 05. Co-author: (illustrated poetry) (with Robert W. Odell) Rare Friends, 1975; one-woman shows include Retrospective at 70, 2003; exhibited in group show at Mohawk Valley Ctr. for Arts, Little Falls, 2004-. Active United Meth. Ch. Van Hornesville, 1965—, Van Hornesville Cmty. Corp., 1989—. Recipient 1st pl. award Celebration of the Arts, Little Falls, 1989, Excellence award, 1991, 2d pl. oils, 1997, 1st pl. in oil award Twisted and Bent, Little Falls, N.Y., 1990, Ctrl. Adirondack Old Forge, 1994, Mohawk Valley Ctr. for Arts, Little Falls, 1995, Windings, Little Falls, N.Y., 2000, Best Interpretation Theme award Mohawk Valley Ctr. for the Arts, Little Falls, 2004, Convergence. Mem. Cooperstown Art Assn., Mohawk Valley Ctr. for Arts (com. exhbns.), Van Hornesville Artists Group (chmn. 1989-98, co-chmn. 2006), Nat. Mus. Women in Arts, Glimmerglass Opera Guild, Munson-Williams Proctor Inst., Arts Guild Old Forge, Utica Art Assn. Avocations: reading, classical music, writing poetry and essays. Home: 28 Highland Ave Little Falls NY 13365

**VEEDER, PETER GREIG,** lawyer; b. Pitts., Aug. 13, 1941; AB, Princeton U., 1963; JD, U. Pitts., 1966. Bar: Pa. 1966, D.C. 1976. Lawyer Thorp Reed & Armstrong, Pitts., 1970-99; of counsel Thorp, Reed & Armstrong LLP, Pitts., 1999—. Office: Thorp Reed & Armstrong LLP 1 Oxford Ctr 301 Grant St Fl 14 Pittsburgh PA 15219-1425 Office Phone: 412-394-7793.

**VEENEMA, RALPH JAMES,** retired urologist; b. Paterson, NJ, Dec. 13, 1921; s. Ralph Veenema and Sadie Van Dyke; m. Henriette E. Van DerMolen, Sept. 19, 1944; children: Shirley, Lois, Ralph J. Jr., Kenneth. AB, Calvin Coll., Grand Rapids, Mich., 1942; MD, Jefferson Med. Coll., Phila., 1945. Diplomate Am. Bd. Urology. Intern Paterson Gen. Hosp., NJ, 1945—46; resident in surgery U.S. Army Hosps., Alexandri La. and Jackson, Miss., 1946—48; fellow in surg. pathology Columbia Presbyn. Med. Ctr., 1978, resident in urology, 1949—52; attending urologist Presbyn. Hosp., 1957—87; chief urology Francis Delafield Hosp., 1960—72; prof. urology Columbia U. Coll. Physicians and Surgeons, NYC, 1949—87, prof. emeritus, 1987—. Contbr. articles to profl. jours. Capt. Med. Corps U.S. Army, WWII. Fellow: ACS, NY Acad. Medicine (former pres. urology sect.); mem.: Am. Urol. Assn. (awards for work in bladder cancer and prostate cancer). Avocation: beef cattle farming. Home: 40 Nelson Ave Cooperstown NY 13326

**VEGA, ANTHONY JUDE,** meteorologist, researcher; s. Alex Anthony and Carol Vega; m. Mary Juanice Fluker, Aug. 10, 1991; children: Alexandra Nicole, Victoria Marie. BA, U. New Orleans, 1987; MS, Miss. State U., 1990; PhD, La. State U., 1994. Broadcast Meteorology Miss. State U., 1990. Grad. asst. Miss. State U., Mississippi State, Miss., 1989—90; instr. Southeastern La. U., Hammond, La., 1991—91; rsch. asst. La. State U., Baton Rouge, 1991—94; asst. prof. Clarion U., Pa., 1994—99, assoc. prof., 1999—2003, prof., 2003. Author: (book) Louisiana Weather and Climate; musician: (album) The Difference. Mem. Clarion Devel. Corp., Pa., 1996—2003. Recipient Disting. Scientist, Am. Men and Women of Sci., 1997; fellow Mem., Phi Kappa Phi, 2003; grantee, NASA, 1996—99. Mem.: Pa. Geog. Soc., Nat. Weather Assn., Am. Meteorol. Soc., Assn. of Am. Geographers (climate specialty group honors dir. 1998—2005). Office: AGES Dept Clarion University Clarion PA 16214 Office Phone: 814-393-2023. Office Fax: 814-393-2004. E-mail: avega@clarion.edu.

**VEGA, FRANK J.,** newspaper publishing executive; With Gannett Co. Inc., 1978—; task force dir. to pub., circulation dir. Oakland Tribune; mem. task force to launch USA Today, 1980—82, v.p. circulation, 1982—83; asst. to pres. Mid-Atlantic Regional Newspaper Group, 1983—84; gen. mgr. El Diario-La Prensa, NYC, 1983—84; pub., CEO Cape Publications, Brevard County, Fla., 1984—91; pres. South Regional Newspaper Group, 1985—91; pres., CEO Detroit Newspaper Agy., 1991—2004; pres., pub. San Francisco Chronicle, 2005—. Office: San Francisco Chronicle 901 Mission St San Francisco CA 94103*

**VEGA, MATIAS ALFONSO,** lawyer; b. Paris, Feb. 2, 1952; s. Matias Guillermo and Colette (Lafosse) V.; m. Carmella Margarita Kurczewski, Nov. 20, 1982; 1 child, Alexandra Lafosse. AB, Yale U., 1974; JD, Harvard U., 1977. Bar: N.Y. 1978, U.S. Dist. Ct. (so. and ea. dists.) N.Y. 1979, U.S. Supreme Ct. 1984, U.S. Ct. Appeals (6th and 9th cirs.) 1985, U.S. Dist. Ct. (no. dist.) Calif. 1985. Assoc. Curtis, Mallet-Prevost, Colt & Mosle, N.Y.C. 1977-85, ptnr., 1986—. Contbr. articles to profl. jours. Mem. ABA, Am. Soc. Internat. Law, N.Y. State Bar Assn. (chmn. com. Latin Am. law, internat. law and practice sect. 1987-90), Yale Club. Republican. Roman Catholic. Home: 8 Cerf Ln Mount Kisco NY 10549 Office: Curtis Mallet-Prevost Colt 101 Park Ave Fl 34 New York NY 10178-0061 Office Phone: 212-696-6929. Personal E-mail: matvega@optonline.net. Business E-Mail: mvega@cm-p.com.

**VEGA, REINALDO,** research scientist; b. Manhattan, NY, Aug. 13, 1981; s. Juan Vega and Dawn Brocco. BS in Microelectronic Engring., Rochester Inst. Tech., Rochester, NY, 1999—2004, MS in Microelectronic Engring., 2004—06. Co-op student, microelectronics divsn. Integrated Nano-Technologies, LLC, Rochester, NY, 2001; co-op pre-profl. engr., emerging products & sige passives integration Internat. Bus. Machines, 2002, co-op pre-profl. engr., SOI device characterization, internat. bus. machines, 2003; NSF rsch. experience for undergraduates Rochester Inst. Tech., Rochester, 2004, grad. rsch. asst., tchg. asst., 2004—06. Engring. cons. Biophan Technologies, Inc., Rochester, 2005—06. Mem.: IEEE, IEEE Electron Devices Soc., RIT Microelectronic Engring. Student Assn. (grad. student advisor 2004—06, sr. design award com. mem., sr. judge 2005—06, exec. committe mem. 2005—06, process design mgr., mem. gear project 2003), RIT IEEE Student Chpt. (exec. com. mem. 2005—06). Achievements include patents pending for multi-valued logic/memory and circuits and methods thereof; metallic source/drain CMOS circuits and methods thereof. Avocations: running, golf, bicycling. Office: Univ CA 373 Cory Hall Berkeley CA 94720 Personal E-mail: beeps_and_buzzes@yahoo.com.

**VEGA, STEVE,** poet; b. N.Y.C., Nov. 13, 1949; s. Exio Ocasio Vega; children: Katherine, James-Paul Christian, Diamond Zhane. Cert. in Bus. Mgmt., Marion Bus. Coll., 1973; cert., John Marshall Law Sch., 1977; cert. in corrections and probations svcs., Chgo. Loop Coll., 1986; BA, Coll. of Comml. Sci., 1995, M in Comml. Svc., 1996, postgrad., 1997; PhD, Lord Baden-Powell Coll., Lake Geneva, Wis., 1998, fellow of Scouting degree, 2003; wilderness survival course, with APO wardogs, 1988; winter camping survival course, OKPIK, Woodstock, Ill., 1996; sea badge course, Great Lakes Navy Base, 1998. Cert. diploma pvt. investigator course US Acad. Pvt. Investigation, 2004. Adult probation officer Cook County, Ill., 1979-93; pub. safety officer, police-fireman aide Morton Grove (Ill.) emergency Svcs. and Disaster Agy., 1998—; police aide, fire rescue mem. Morton Grove (Ill.) emergency Svcs. and Disaster Agy., Homeland Security; CEO pvt. practice, 2002—. Union chief steward Cook County Adult Probation Dept., AFSCME, 1989—91; 1st v.p. AFSCME local 3486 APD officers, Chgo., 1991—92; cons. Chgo. Police Dept., FBI, U.S. Dist. Court; dep. dir. Internat. Biog. Ctr., Cambridge, England, 2000. Author: numerous poems; actor: (films) Music Box, Only the Lonely, Gladiator, Hero, Mo Money, Hoffa, Natural Born Killers, Mad Dog and Glory, Eye for and Eye (The Shadow of a Killer), Curly Sue, others; composer, rec. artist: The President Is Crying-September 11, 2001, 2001. Adult sec. coun. commn. Boy Scouts Am., Chgo., 1997, mem. ctrl. region com. Sea Scouting, 1998; vol., mem. com. City of Chgo. Health Sys. Agy., 1981—85. With USAF, 1970, with mil. aircraft command, mil. honor guard. Decorated Commendation medal USAF, 443d Svs. Squadron and Honor Guard USAF Mil. Aircraft Command, knight comdr. European Order Knighthood (Italy); named World Poet, 1987—, named one of World's Great Living Poets, 1991, The Greatest Chicagoans of the 20th Century, Chgo. Sun-Times, 1999; named to Hall of Fame, Lord Baden-Powell U., 2001; recipient Presdl. commendation, Pres. Ronald Reagan, 1987, 1988, Pres. George Bush, 1990, Arrowhead award, Boy Scouts Am., 1994, Nat. Fire Acad. Emergency Response to Terrorism cert., 2001, Presdl. Sports award, Pres. Gerald Ford, 1975. Mem.: ASCAP (composer, writer), Fraternal Order Police (officer 1988, sgt.-at-arms), Sovereign Mil. and Hospitaller Order St. George in Karinthia (titular head). Roman Catholic. Avocations: singing, composing, guitar, motorcycling, chess. Address: PO Box 221 Morton Grove IL 60053-0221 E-mail: steve_vega_records@yahoo.com, stevevegaworldpoet@yahoo.com, stevevegapoetamundial@yahoo.com.

**VEGA, SUZANNE,** singer, songwriter; b. Santa Monica, Calif., July 11, 1959; m. Paul Mills, Feb. 11, 2006. Grad., Barnard Coll., 1982. Singer, songwriter, concert performer, 1975—. Began performing in Greenwich Village coffeehouses, N.Y.C., 1975; albums include Suzanne Vega, 1985, Solitude Standing, 1987, Days of Open Hand, 1990, 99.9 F, 1992, Nine Objects of Desire, 1996, Songs in Red and Gray, 2001; songs include Cracking, Marlene on the Wall, Tom's Diner, Luka, Solitude Standing, (song for Pretty in Pink soundtrack) Left of Center; concert tours of U.S., Can., Europe and Far East, 1987. Buddhist. also: our AGF Entertainment Ltd PO Box 2036 Old Chelsea Station New York NY 10113*

**VEGH, LINDA LIBASCI,** secondary school educator; d. Alphonse Joseph and Harriet Louise Libasci; m. Joseph David Vegh, July 22, 1972; children: Joseph James, Victoria Louise. BA, U. Colo., 1973; MS, Tex. A&M U. Corpus Christi, 1994, EdD, 2000. Cert. English tchr. Colo. Dept. Edn., Tex. Edn. Agy., mid-mgmt. Tex. Bd. Educator Cert., supr. Tex. Bd. Educator Cert. Comm. craft AT&T, Colorado Springs, 1974—76, Houston, 1974—76, account exec., 1976—78; adminstrv. mgr. Mountain States Tel., Denver, 1978—80; self-employed Tupperware mgr. Denver, 1982—84; tchrs. aide Flour Bluff Ind. Sch. Dist., Corpus Christi, Tex., 1987—88, tchr. English, speech and humanities 1988—2000, supr. curriculum 2000—, mem. wdn. improvement coun., 1990—2003. Cons. to writing program U. Colo., Denver, 1981—82; adj. prof. Park Coll., Corpus Christi, 1997—98; mem. Tech. Prep. Consortium, Corpus Christi, 2000—06, Geog. Info. Sys. Task Force, Corpus Christi, 2002—06. Recipient Outstanding Tchr. of Yr., Tex. Coun. for Humanities, 1998; Phi Delta Kappa Outstanding Tchr. Scholarship, 1998. Mem.: ASCD, Tex. Assn. Secondary Sch. Prins., Tex. Soc. Suprs. Social Studies, Assn. Tex. Profl. Educators, Phi Delta Kappa, Phi Beta Kappa. Avocations: quilting, reading, puzzles, yoga. Office: Flour Bluff HS 2505 Waldron Rd Corpus Christi TX 78418 Office Phone: 361-694-9198.

**VEIGEL, JON MICHAEL,** science administrator; b. Mankato, Minn., Nov. 10, 1938; s. Walter Thomas and Thelma Geraldine (Lein) V.; m. Carol June Bradley, Aug. 10, 1962. BS, U. Washington, 1960; PhD, UCLA, 1965. Program mgr., congl. sci. fellow Office of Tech. Assessment, U.S. Congress, Washington, 1974-75; div. mgr. Calif. Energy Commn., Sacramento, 1975-78; asst. dir. Solar Energy Rsch. Inst., Golden, Colo., 1978-81; pres. Alt. Energy Corp., Rsch. Triangle Park, N.C., 1981-88, Oak Ridge (Tenn.) Associated Univs., 1988-96. Bd. dirs. Am. Coun. Energy Efficient Economy, Washington, Pacific Internat. Ctr. for High Tech. Rsch., Honolulu; cons. Sunhunner Assocs., LLC, 1996—. Contbr. articles to jours. Trustee Maryville Coll., 1990-96, Mendeleyev U., Moscow, Russia. 1st lt. USAF, 1965-68. Mem. AAAS (past mem. com. on sci. and engring. pub. policy, past chair). Avocation: photography. Office: SunRunner Assocs LLC 16259 W Spring Canyon Way Surprise AZ 85374-4961

**VEILLE, JEAN-CLAUDE,** obstetrician, educator; b. France; came to U.S., 1982; m. Ann Veille; children: Olivier, Xavier, Patrique, Robert. BS, McGill U., 1971; MD, U. Montpellier, France, 1977. Fellow in maternal-fetal medicine Oreg. Health Scis., Portland, 1982-84; from asst. prof. to assoc. prof. Case Western Res. U., Cleve., 1984-90; chief maternal, fetal medicine Case Western Reserve U., Cleve., 1989-90; assoc. prof., dir. maternal-fetal med. fellowship program Wake Forest U. Sch. Medicine, Winston-Salem, NC, 1990-95, prof., 1995—; chief maternal-fetal medicine sect., 1997—2002; chmn. dept. ob-gyn. Albany (N.Y.) Med. Ctr., 2002—. Contbr. articles to profl. jours. Grantee NIH, 1991-2002. Office: 47 New Scotland Ave Albany NY E-mail: veillej@mail.amc.edu.

**VEINOTT, ARTHUR FALES, JR.,** university educator; b. Boston, Oct. 12, 1934; m. 1960; children: Elisabeth, Michael; m. 1988. BS, BA, Lehigh U., 1956; D Eng Sc, Columbia U., 1960. From asst. prof. to assoc. prof. indsl. engring. Stanford (Calif.) U., 1962-67, prof. ops. rsch., 1967—, chmn. dept. indsl. engring., 1975-85, prof. mgmt. sci. engring., 1999—. Cons. Rand Corp., 1965, IBM Rsch. Ctr., 1968-69, 89-90; vis. prof. Yale U., 1972-73. Editor Jour. Math. Ops. Rsch., 1974-80. 1st lt. USAF, 1960-62 Guggenheim fellow 1978-79. Fellow Inst. Math. Stats.; mem. Nat. Acad. Engring., Inst. Mgmt. Sci., Ops. Rsch. Soc. Am. Achievements include development of lattice programming, qualitative theory of optimization for predicting the direction of change of optimal decisions resulting from alteration of problem parameters; structure and computation of optimal policies for supply chains and dynamic programs. Office: Stanford U Dept Mgmt Sci Engring Terman 415 Stanford CA 94305-4026

**VEITCH, BOYER LEWIS,** printing company executive; b. Phila., Oct. 20, 1930; s. Samuel Lewis and Agnes Mae (Bell) V.; m. Emmeline Barbara Smith, Nov. 22, 1952 (dec. Dec. 1994); children: William S., Nancy B., Thomas C.; m. Mary Chisholm Kiehn, Feb. 21, 1998. AB, Lafayette Coll., 1953; postgrad. Wharton Evening Sch., Acctg. and Fin., U. Pa., 1957-59. Advt. dir. Ware Bros. Co., Phila., 1956-62, v.p., 1962-69; salesman Zabel Bros. Co., Phila., 1969-75; chmn. Veitch Printing Corp., Lancaster, Pa., 1975—. Trustee Printers Disability Trust. Trustee Lafayette Coll., Easton, Pa., 1981-86, 87—, vice chmn. coll. rels. com., chmn. ann. fund, 1982-86, mem. fin. com., 1987-92, chmn. athletics and student affairs comn., 1992-97, mem. emeritus exec. com., 1997; mem. gen. adv. com. Lancaster County Career and Tech. Sch. System, 1996—; bd. dirs. Boys and Girls Club, Lancaster, 1980—, pres., 1990-92; dir. Boy's Club Lancaster Found., 1989—, pres., 1992—; elected to Boys and Girls Hall of Fame, 1999; dir. Gt. Valley Civic Assn., 1969-79; trustee Fulton Opera House Found., 1985-91, treas., 1987-89; bd. dirs. North Mus., 1992-94, Lancaster Airport Authority, 1994—, treas., 1994—; trustee PIA Disability Trust, 1994—; chmn. citizens for Schulze Com., Pa. 5th Congressional Dist., 1972-78; vestryman, sr. warden St. Peter's Ch. of Gt. Valley, 1972-78. Served with CIC, U.S. Army, 1954-56. Recipient Bronze Hope Chest award Nat. Multiple Sclerosis Soc., 1982, Nat. Svc. to Youth award Boys and Girls Clubs Am., 1992; named Small Bus. Person of Yr. Lancaster Co., 1991; named to Boys and Girls Club of Lancaster Alumni Hall of Fame, 1999, Graphic Arts Assn. Person of Yr., 2001; named Graphic Arts Assn. Person of Yr., 2001. Mem. SAR, Printing Industries Am. (dir. 1993-98), Graphic Arts Assn. (dir. 1980-98, chmn. 1990-92, Man of Yr. 2001), Lancaster C. of C. and Industry (dir. 1990-93), Lafayette Coll. Alumni Assn. (dir. 1974-78, pres. 1978-80), Pa. Economy League, Nat. Fedn. Ind. Bus., Phi Kappa Psi (past pres. and dir. chpt. alumni assn.), Ash Khan Soc. (hon.). Clubs: Hamilton (bd. dirs. 1995—), Wash Day, Lancaster Country, Avalon Yacht, Lancaster Aero., Lancaster Pirates (first mate 2001-2003, chief 2003-), Susquehanna Litho (dir. 1976-80, pres. 1979-80). Lodges: Rotary (Paul Harris fellow). Republican. Episcopalian. Home: 1044 Sylvan Rd Lancaster PA 17601-1933 Office: Veitch Printing Corp 1740 Hempstead Rd Lancaster PA 17601-5889 Personal E-mail: boygin@msn.com.

**VEITH, FRANK J.,** vascular surgeon, researcher, educator; Cert. General Surgery, 1961, Thoracic Surgery, 1968, Vascular Surgery, 1983. William J. von Liebig chmn. for vascular surgery Montefiore Med. Ctr., Bronx, NY, vice-chmn., prof. surgery, Albert Einstein Coll. Medicine, Bronx, NY. Ann. host VEITHsymposium. Contbr. more than 1,000 articles and chapters in profl. med. jours. and books.; serves on editl. bds. for four major vascular jours., editor-in-chief Vascular. Recipient Julius H. Jacobson, II, MD award for Physician Excellence, Vascular Disease Found., 2004. Mem.: Internat. Soc. for Vascular Surgery (founding sec.), Eastern Vascular Soc. (past pres.), Soc. for Vascular Surgery (past pres.). Considered role model in the field of vascular surgery; heading effort to have vascular surgery as a specialty board under the umbrella of the American Board of Specialties. Office: Montefiore Medical Ctr Med Arts Pavilion 3400 Bainbridge Ave 4th Fl Bronx NY 10467 Office Phone: 718-920-4108. Office Fax: 718-231-9811.

**VEIZER, JÁN,** geology educator; b. Pobedim, Slovakia, June 22, 1941; arrived in Can., 1973; s. Viktor and Brigita (Brandstetter) Veizer; m. Elena Ondrus, July 30, 1966; children: Robert, Andrew Douglas. Prom. Geol., Comenius U., Bratislava, Slovakia, 1964; RNDr, Comenius U., Bratislava, Slovak Republic, 1968; CSc, Slovak Acad. Sci., Bratislava, Slovakia, 1968; PhD, Australian Nat. U., Canberra, 1971. Asst. lectr. Comenius U., 1963-66; vis. rsch. scientist U. Göttingen, Fed. Republic Germany, 1972-73; rsch. scientist U. Tübingen, Fed. Republic Germany, 1973; from asst. prof. to full prof. U. Ottawa, Ont., Canada, 1973—, rsch. chair NSERC/Noranda/Can. Inst. Advanced Rsch. Ont., 1997—; prof. Ruhr U., Bochum, Germany, 1988—2004; Disting. Univ. prof. U. Ottawa, 2001—04, prof. emeritus, 2004—. Cons. NASA, Houston, 1983—86; vis. prof., scholar Northwestern U., Evanston, Ill., 1983—87; vis. fellow Australian Nat. U., 1979; vis. prof. U. Tübingen, 1974; Lady Davis professorship Hebrew U., Jerusalem, 1987. Contbr. articles to profl. jours., chapters to books. Served to jr. lt. Med., 1965—66. Named Rsch. Prof. of Yr., 1987; recipient W. Leibniz prize, German Rsch. Found., 1992; fellow Humboldt, 1980, Killam Rsch., Can. Coun., 1986—88. Fellow: Geochem. Soc. Am., Geol. Soc. Am., Geol. Survey Slovak Rep. (Gold medal 2000), Geol. Soc. Can. (Past Pres. medal 1987, Logan medal 1995), Royal Soc. Can. (Willet G. Miller medal 1991, Bancroft medal 2000); mem.: Ski Club. Roman Catholic. Avocations: reading, hiking, skiing, history. Office: Dept Earth Scis U Ottawa Ottawa ON Canada K1N 6N5 Office Phone: 613-562-5800 6461. Business E-Mail: jveizer@uottawa.ca.

**VELA, JOEL E.,** college president; b. Kerrville, Tex. BA in Social Studies, MA in Edn. and History, EdD. Pres. Palo Alto Coll., San Antonio, Mt. Hood C.C., Gresham, Oreg., 1996—2001; v.p. Rio Grande Coll. Sul Ross State U., Uvalde, Tex., 2001—. Various positions North Lake Coll., Dallas County C.C. Dist., Irving, Tex., Penn Valley C.C., Kansas City, Mo.; initiator Agribus. Inst., Mariachi Curriculum with Campanas de America. Bd. dirs. Mt. Hood Festival of Jazz, United Way; active Workforce Devel. Bd., Cath. Charities, Region 2 Workforce Quality Coun. Mem. Hispanic Mgr. C. of C., Gresham C. of C., Rotary. Office: Mt Hood Cmty Coll 26000 SE Stark St Gresham OR 97030-3300

**VELA, JOEL E.,** academic administrator; b. Mission, Tex., Apr. 16, 1949; s. Trinidad and Amelia Vela; m. Maria deJesus Romero; children: Joel Enrique, Cristina Veronica. EdD, U.Wyo., 1976. Pres. Mt. Hood C.C., Gresham, Oreg., 1996—2001; v.p. Rio Grande Coll. Sul Ross State U., Uvalde, Tex., 2001—. Pres. Kiwanis, Uvalde, 2003—04. Home: 2650 Garner Field Rd Uvalde TX 78801 Office: Sul Ross State University 400 Sul Ross Dr Uvalde TX 78801 Home Fax: 830-279-3038. Personal E-mail: jvela@sulross.edu.

**VELA, RICHARD RAUL,** literature educator; b. L.A., July 28, 1944; s. Ricardo and Lucila Vela; m. Karen Zoller, Aug. 15, 1964 (div. June 1982); 1 child, Marcos Ricardo; m. Lori Bartlett, Nov. 23, 1984 (div. June 1986). BA, U. Dallas, Irving, Tex., 1968, MA, 1970; PhD, U. N.C., Chapel Hill, 1986. Instr. Cistercian Prep. Sch., Irving, 1968—69, Westark C.C., Fort Smith, Ark., 1969—70; prof. U. N.C., Pembroke, NC, 1971—. Co-author: Shakespeare into Film, 2002; contbg. editor: Pembroke Mag., 1999, Lit. Film Quar., 2002—; fiction editor: Carlina Quar., 1980—81; contbr. chapters to books, articles to profl. jours. Pres. Rape Crisis Orgn. Robeson County, Lumberton, NC, 1993—95. Recipient Tchg. award, U. N.C. Divsn. Letters, Pembroke, 1998, Bd. Gov.'s Tchg. Excellence award, U. N.C. Sys., 2000; fellow, Danforth Found., 1978—80, Ford Found., 1978—80; scholar, Tex. Ch. Related Schs., 1962—65. Mem.: Popular Culture Assn. (area chmn. Shakespeare on film and TV S.W. chpt. 2004—). Avocations: scuba diving, photography, film collecting. Office: The University of North Carolina Dial Humanities Building Pembroke NC 28372 Office Phone: 910-521-6600. Business E-Mail: richard.vela@uncp.edu.

**VELARDE, RACHEL DAY,** choir director, vocalist, educator, small business owner; b. Bloomington, Ind., June 11, 1973; d. Mark Tyler and Dorothy Lynn Autenrieth Day; m. Arturo Velarde, June 8, 1996; children: Alessandra Tyler, Angelynn Michelle. AB, Smith Coll., Northampton, Mass., 1994; MusM in Vocal Performance, MusM in Vocal Pedagogy, Ariz. State U., 1997. Owner, instr. Velarde Voice Studio, Scottsdale, Ariz., 1993—; chorister Ariz. Opera, Phoenix, 1997—. Sec. chorus payroll Ariz. Opera, Tucson, 2002—. Singer: (oratorio alto soloist with Musica Nova) Bach/Pergolesi Psalm 51/Stabat Mater; singer: (Lady with Hat Box, Foreign Singer) (Opera in the Ozarks) Postcard from Morocco by Dominick Argento; singer: (Mother and Witch) (Ariz. Opera Outreach) Hansel & Gretel; singer: (Second Witch) (opera, Catalina Chamber Orch.) Dido & Aeneas by Henry Purcell; singer: (Tisbe) (Ariz. Opera Outreach) Cenerentola by Gioacchino Rossini; singer: (Zita) (Lyric Opera Theater of Ariz. State U.) Gianni Schicchi by Puccini. Recipient tchg. assistantship, Ariz. State U., 1994—96. Mem.: Am. Guild of Mus. Artists (sec./treas. Ariz. local chpt. A440 1998—99), Nat. Assn. Tchrs. of Singing (sec. cen.-no. chpt. 2005—), Pi Kappa Lambda Zeta Omega Chpt. Independent. Roman Catholic. Avocations: singing, reading. Office Phone: 480-221-7390. Personal E-mail: rachelvelarde@cox.net.

**VELASCO, OSCAR,** medical products executive; Tech., med. sys., nuclear medicine divsn. to lead tech. Siemens USA, 1979; v.p. svc. Northeast Zone Siemens Medical Sys. USA, Inc., now v.p., Southwest Zone Houston. Named one of Top Hispanics to Watch, Hispanic Engr. mag., 2001, 50 Most Important Hispanics in Tech., Bus., Hispanic Engineer and Info. Tech. mag., 2003, 2004, 2005. Office: Siemens Med Sys Ste 450 15600 John F Kennedy Blvd Houston TX 77032 Office Phone: 281-668-3525.*

**VELASQUEZ-GARCIA, LUIS FERNANDO,** research scientist, consultant; s. Hector Velasquez-Gutierrez and Flor Nicolasa Garcia de Velasquez. Degree in mech. engring. magna cum laude, Los Andes U., Bogota, 1998, degree in civil engring. magna cum laude, 1999; MS in Aeroanutics and Astronautics, MIT, Cambridge, Mass., 2001, PhD in Space Propulsion, 2004. Postdoctoral assoc. MIT, Cambridge, 2004—05, rsch. scientist, 2006—. Cons. Busek, Co., Natick, Mass., 2004—. Contbr. scientific papers to profl. jours. Sponsor Boston Ballet, 2005—06. Recipient Ramon de Zubiria award, Los Andes U., 1997, 1998, 1999. Mem.: Sigma Xi. Roman Catholic. Achievements include development of Highly packed electrospray emitter MEMS technology, intended for space proplusion applications, in both open and closed architectures, for doped solvents and ionic liquids as propellant; world's first MEMS Singlet Oxygen Generator for an Oxygen-Iodine Chemical Laser; high aspect ratio, re-assamblable MEMS Quadrupoles for portable, low power, fast gas analyzer technology; Carbon Nano Tube (CNT)-based field ionization / Field Emission MEMS technology for gas analyzer technology and space propulsion; patents pending for Method for 3D hand-assembled MEMS packaging to interface micro- and macro subsystems with a prescribed assembly precision, using Deep Reactive Ion Etching patterned mesoscaled deflection springs; development of micro-fabricated ionized species sensor techology using micro balances and vibrating Reed Electrometers.

**VELAZQUEZ, JOSE,** management and mathematics educator; b. NYC, Dec. 3, 1938; m. Geraldine Khaner, Aug. 31, 1963; children: Mark, Brenda. BA, Hunter Coll., 1966; MSEE, N.J. Inst. Tech., 1977; MBA, Monmouth Coll., 1972; EdD, Temple U., 1989. Physicist Columbia U., N.Y.C., 1962-65; instr. Montclair Coll., Upper Montclair, N.J., 1973-74; instr. distance learning and accelerated courses Georgian Court Coll., Lakewood, NJ, 1987—2003; program mgr., engr. Terrestrial Space Program Mgmt. Office, Monmouth, N.J., 1993-95; prof. mgmt. Bekeley Coll., N.J., 2000—. Mem. AICEA, IEEE, Langly AFB Aero Club, Phi Delta Kappa. Avocation: flying.

**VELÁZQUEZ, NYDIA MARGARITA,** congresswoman; b. Yabucoa, PR, Mar. 28, 1953; BA magna cum laude in Polit. Sci., U. PR, Rio Piedras, 1974; MA in Polit. Sci., NYU, 1976. Mem. faculty U. PR, Humacao, 1976—81; adj. prof. Puerto Rican studies CUNY Hunter Coll., 1981—83; spl. asst. Staff of US Rep. Edolphus Towns from NY, 1983; mem. City Coun., NYC, 1984—86; dir. Migration Divsn. Office Puerto Rico Dept. Labor and Human Resources, 1986—89; dir. Dept. Puerto Rican Cmty. Affairs in the US for the Commonwealth of PR, 1989—92; mem. US Congress from 12th NY dist., 1993—. Ranking minority mem. small bus. com. US Congress, 1998—, mem. fin. svcs. com. Named Woman of Yr., Hispanic Bus. Mag., 2003; recipient Small Bus. Beacon award, Nat. Small Bus. United, 2000, HerMANA award, MANA, 2002, Champion of Small Bus. Devel. award, Assn. Small Bus. Devel. Ctr., 2005. Democrat. Achievements include being the first Puerto Rican woman elected to the US Congress. Office: US Ho Reps 2241 Rayburn Ho Office Bldg Washington DC 20515-2104 Office Phone: 202-225-2361.*

**VELAZQUEZ, OMAIDA CARIDAD,** vascular surgeon, research scientist; b. Pinar del Rio, Cuba, Oct. 25, 1966; d. Telesforo and Andrea Velazquez; m. Romulo Cuy, 1991; 1 child, Peter James Cuy. MD, U. Medicine and Dentistry N.J., 1991. Lic. physician N.J. Instr. gen. surgery U. Pa. Med. Sch., Phila., asst. instr. gen. surgery, 1992—96; attending surgeon Hosp. U. Pa., Phila., 1999—. Clin. faculty gen. and vascular surgery U. Pa. Med. Sch., Phila., 1999—; adj. asst. prof. Wistar Inst., Phila., 2001—, vis. scientist, 1999—2001; attending surgeon Presbyn. Med. Ctr., Phila., 1999—, Phila. VA Med. Ctr., 2001—03, Children's Hosp. Phila., 2001—; asst. prof. surgery U. Pa. Med. Sch., 1999—, ednl. coord. vascular divsn., 2002—. Contbr. articles to sci. rsch. jours. (Joel J. Roslyn award Assn.for Acad. Surgery, 2003); external reviewer: med. jours. Recipient Scholarship for the Advancement of Med. Edn., William F. Grupe Found., Inc., 1988, 1990, Krans-Henle Meml Fund Scholarship, Kraus Henle Meml. Fund, 1989, von Liebig Found. Award for Excellence in Vascular Surg. Rsch., von Liebig Found., 2001, Residents Rsch. award, Phila. Acad. of Surgery, 1996, Young Careerist award, N.J. Bus. and Profl. Women, 1995, Surg. Student Rsch award, Assn. for Academic Surgery, 1991, Dr. Gertrude Ash Meml. award, N.J. Med. Women's Assn., 1991, Merck Manual award for highest grade in internal medicine, 1990; grantee, NIH, 2003—. Fellow: ACS; mem.: AMA, AAAS, John Morgan Soc., Internat. Acad. Clin. and Applied Thrombosis/Hemostasis, Pa. Med. Soc., Am. Soc. Angiology, Soc. U. Surgeons, Phila. Acad. Surgery, Internat. Soc. Vascular Surgery, Bus. and Profl. Women, Assn. Women Surgeons, Assn. for Acad. Surgery, Am. Surg. Assn. Found., Am. Assn. Vascular Surgery, Soc. Clin. Vascular Surgery, N.Y. Acad. Sci., N.J. Med. Sch. Alumni Assn., Sigma Xi, Alpha Omega Alpha. Office: Hosp of Univ of Pa 3400 Spruce St 4 Silverstein Philadelphia PA 19104 Office Phone: 215-662-6451.

**VELDEN, CHRISTOPHER SCOTT,** meteorologist, researcher; b. Berwyn, Ill., July 10, 1956; s. Jack Holter and Lorrie Mae Velden; m. Ann Elizabeth Hallett, June 20, 1981; children: Sara Elizabeth, Jennifer Ann. BS, U. Wis., Stevens Point, 1979; MS, U. Wis., Madison, 1982. Rsch. asst. dept. atmospheric and oceanic scis. U. Wis., Madison, Wis., 1980—82, sr. scientist Space Sci. Engring. Ctr., 1982—. Chair satellite com. Am. Meteorol. Soc., Boston, 2004—. Co-author: (textbook on hurricanes) HURRICANE! Coping with Disaster. Recipient Banner Miller Hurricane Rsch. award, Am. Meteorol. Soc., 2001, Spl. Rsch. and Achievement award, 1998, Hagemeyer Applied Tropical Rsch. award, Office Fed. Coord. for Meteorology, 2003. Mem.: Am. Meteorol. Soc. Achievements include the use of satellite data to analyse hurricanes. Avocations: travel, sports. Office Phone: 608-262-9168. E-mail: chrisv@ssec.wisc.edu.

**VELDEY, BONNIE,** special education educator; b. Mpls., Jan. 24, 1960; d. George Joseph III and Ethel Annette Acko; m. Steve Douglas Veldey, June 13, 1991; 1 child, Tyler George. AA, Inver Grove C.C., Inver Grove Heights, Minn., 1989; BA, Coll. St. Catherine, 1991; MA in Spl. Edn., St. Thomas, 1998. Sci. tchr. Roma (Tex.) Ind. Sch. Dist., 1991-92; spl. edn. tchr. Clark County Sch. Dist., Las Vegas, Nev., 1996-99; pvt. practice spl. edn. tchr. Mpls., 1999—2001; tchr. spl. edn. Mpls. (Minn.) Pub. Schs., 2001—. Democrat. Roman Catholic. Home: 4331 Minnehaha Ave Minneapolis MN 55406-3908

**VELEV, MIROSLAV N.,** electrical and computer engineer, educator; arrived in US, 1991; BSEE, Yale U., 1994, BS in Econs., 1994, MSEE, 1994; PhD in Elec. and Computer Engring., Carnegie Mellon U., 2004. Tech. assoc. info. svcs. Credit Suisse First Boston Corp., N.Y.C., 1994—95; rsch. asst. Carnegie Mellon U., Pitts., 1995—2001; pvt. practice rschr. and cons., 2003—; founder, pres., CEO, Aries Design Automation, LLC, 2005—. Mem. editl. bd.: Jour. Universal Computer Sci., 2001—, Jour. on Satisfiability, Boolean Modeling and Computation, 2003—; contbr. over 70 articles to profl. jours. Recipient Franz Tuteur Meml. prize, Yale U., 1994, EDAA Outstanding Dissertation award, 2005. Mem.: IEEE, Am. Assn. for Artificial Intelligence, Am. Soc. for Engring. Edn., Assn. for Computing Machinery.

**VELEZ, INES,** oral pathologist, educator; b. Bogota, Colombia, Apr. 15, 1946; arrived in US, 1999; d. Jose and Emilia (Marulanda) Velez; m. Eduardo Tamara (div.); children: Luis Tamara, Clara Lucia Tamara; m. Guillermo Torres, Mar. 30, 1992. DDS, Colombian Coll. Odontology, 1979; postgrad., U. Fla., 1982—84; MEd, U. Los Andes, 1989; M in Laser Dentistry, Acad. Laser Dentistry, 1997. Cert. tchr. Fla. Chair., prof. pathology Colombian Coll. Odontology, 1984—92, pres. asst., 1989—92, dir. biopsy svc., 1984—95; chair, prof., dir. biopsy svc. Columbian Sch. Medicine, 1991—98, dir. bioclinical area, 1997—98; asst. prof. to assoc. prof., dir. oral and maxillofacial pathology, dir. biopsy svc. Nova Southeastern U., Ft. Lauderdale, Fla., 2000—. Lectr. in field. Contbr. articles to profl. jours. Recipient Best Student award, Coll. Sans Facon, 1963, Colombian Coll. Odontology, 1979, Educator award, Fla. Dental Assn., 2003, Golden Apple award, Nova Southeastern U., 2003, Ctr. of Excellence award, 2004. Mem.: ADA, Broward County Dental Assn., Fla. Dental Assn., Pierre Fouchard Acad., Acad. Laser Dentistry, Columbian Acad. Oral Pathology (founder), Am. Acad. Oral and Maxillofacial Pathology, Omicron Kappa Upsilon. Home: 3524 Parkside Dr Davie FL 33328 Office: Nova Southeastern U 3200 S University Dr Fort Lauderdale FL 33328 Office Phone: 954-472-7810. Business E-Mail: ivelez@nova.edu.

**VELEZ, WILLIAM,** education educator; b. Ponce, P.R., Apr. 9, 1951; s. William Velez and Alicia Rodriguez; m. Barbara Jean Eckl, Dec. 12, 2003; children: Alfredo Joel, Marilka Rebeca. BA, U. P.R., San Juan, 1973; PhD, Yale U., 1983. Prof. U. Wis., Milw., 1981—. Author: Race and Ethnicity in the United States: An Institutional Approach, 1998, Foundations of American Higher Education, 1999. Bd. mem. Puerto Rican Found. Wis., Milw., 2001—06. Recipient Nat. Rsch. Svc. award, U. Wis.-Madison, Ctr. for Demography & Ecology, 1985—86; fellow, Ford Found., 1977—79; postdoctoral fellow, 1989—90. Mem.: Am. Sociol. Assn. (chair Latino sociology sect. 2001—02, Minority fellow 1974—77). Avocations: travel, golf. Home: 1820 N Oakland Ave Milwaukee WI 53202 Office: Univ Wis-Milwaukee 3210 N Maryland Ave Milwaukee WI 53211 Office Phone: 414-229-4388. Office Fax: 414-229-4266. Business E-Mail: velez@uwm.edu.

**VELICER, JANET SCHAFBUCH,** retired elementary school educator; b. Cedar Rapids, Iowa, Aug. 27, 1941; d. Allan J. and Geraldine Frances (Stuart) Schafbuch; m. Leland Frank Velicer, Aug. 17, 1963 (dec. Dec. 2000); children: Mark Allan, Gregory Jon, Daniel James. BS, Iowa State U., 1963, MS, 1966; cert. Elem. Edn., Mich. State U., 1976. Tchr. chemistry Prendergast High Sch., Upper Darby, Pa., 1964-65; tchr. home econs. Cardinal O'Hara High Sch., Springfield, Pa., 1965-66; substitute tchr. Pa., Mich., 1967-76; elem. tchr. Winans Elem. Sch., Waverly, Mich., 1976-78, Wardcliff Elem. Sch., Okemos, Mich., 1978-94; tchr. gifted and talented alternative program grades 4 and 5 Hiawatha Elem. Sch., Okemos, 1994-95; tchr. grade 4 Wardcliff Elem. Sch., 1995-2001; ret., 2001. Computer coord., Great Books coord.; dist. com. mem. math, computer, substance abuse, cable TV, evaluation revision Okemos Pub. Schs., Instrnl. Coun.; del. Mich. Edn. Exch. Opportunity Program, Germany, 1999. Author: (video) Wardcliff School Documentary, 1982, The Integrated Arts Program of the Okemos Elementary Schools, 1983. Citizens adv. com. to develop a five-yr. plan, 1982-83, bldg. utilization adv. com., 1983-84, cmty. use of schs. adv. com., 1984-85, strategic planning steering com., 1989-90, taking our schs. into tomorrow com., 1990-91, bonding election steering com., 1991; chmn. wellness com. Okemos Pub. Schs., 1993-95; bd. dirs. Okemos Music Patrons, 1981-86, pres., 1984-86; faculty rep. PTO; leadership coun. Nat. Instl. Clin. Application Behavioral Medicine, 1998—; chaperone Okemos HS German Club Exch., 1987, Benton Cmty. HS Spanish Club Exch., Mex., 1995, Costa Rica, 1999, Spain, 2001, 03. Recipient Classrooms of Tomorrow Tchr. award, Mich. Dept. Edn., 1990. Mem. NEA, NAFE, AARP, Nat. Ret. Tchrs. Assn., Mich. Edn. Assn., Okemos Edn. Assn. (exec. coun.), Mich. Coun. Tchrs. Math., Lansing Woman's Club (social com. 2003-04, program com. 2005—), Mich. Athletic Club, Phi Kappa Phi, Omicron Nu, Iota Sigma Pi. Democrat. Avocations: swimming, reading, hiking, travel, cultural events. Home: 2678 Blue Haven Ct East Lansing MI 48823-3804 Business E-Mail: jvelicer@msu.edu.

**VELICK, SIDNEY FREDERICK,** research biochemist, educator; b. Detroit, May 3, 1913; s. Harry Alexander and Ella (Stocker) V.; m. Bernadette Stemler, Sept. 5, 1941; children: William Frederick, Martha Elizabeth. BS, Wayne State U., 1935, PhD, U. Mich., 1938. Rsch. fellow parasitology Johns Hopkins U., Balt., 1939-40; rsch. assoc. chemistry Yale U., New Haven, 1941-45; mem. biol. chemistry dept. Washington U. Sch. Medicine, St. Louis, 1946-63, prof. biol. chemistry, 1958-64; prof., head dept. biol. chemistry U. Utah Coll. Medicine, 1964-79, prof. emeritus, 1988—. Mem. biochemistry study sect. NIH. Assoc. editor: Archives Biochemistry and Biophysics; editl. bd.: Jour. Biol. Chemistry; contbr. papers on enzyme chemistry to tech. lit. Co-founder, pres. Alliance for the Mentally Ill Utah, 1980-85. Mem. NAS, AAAS, Am. Soc. Biol. Chemists, Am. Chem. Soc., Sigma Xi. Home: 2514 S Elizabeth St # 6 Salt Lake City UT 84106

**VELISAVLJEVIC, NENAD,** physicist; b. Cuprija, Serbia, Serbia-Monteneg, Aug. 8, 1975; s. Filip and Snezana Velisavljevic. BS in Physics, Kutztown U., Pa., 1996—2000; MS in Physics, U. Ala., Birmingham, 2000—04, PhD in Physics, 2004—05. Grad. tchg. asst. dept. physics, U. Ala., 2000—01, rsch. asst., 2001—05, preparing future faculty intern, 2003—05; postdoctoral rsch. assoc. Los Alamos Nat. Lab., N.Mex., 2006—. Contbr. articles to profl. jours. Recipient Outstanding Grad. Tchg. Asst. award, Assn. Physics Tchrs., 2002, Cert. Excellence award, U. Ala., 2004; Space Grant Consortium NASA Space grant, Ala. NASA, 2003—04. Mem.: Am. Phys. Soc., Los Alamos Postdoctoral Assn.

**VELLA, CHRISTINA,** history professor; b. New Orleans, 1952; d. Mario John and Nicolina Vella; m. Robert E. Riehl, Dec. 14, 1980; children: Christie Riehl, Robin Vella Riehl. BA, La. State U., Baton Rouge, 1969; MA, U. New Orleans, 1970; PhD, Tulane U., New Orleans, 1990. Asst. prof. St. Bernard CC, Chalmette, La., 1975—83; vis. prof. Tulane U., New Orleans, 1995, adj. prof., 1991—; cons. U.S. State Dept., Washington, 1996—. Author: Intimate Enemies, 1997 (featured on cover of N.Y. Times Book Rev., 1997, nom. for Pulitzer and Nat. Book Award, adapted for opera Pontalba, 2003, Humanities Book award, 1997); co-author: The Hitler Kiss, 2002, Indecent Secrets, 2006. Recipient Award for Excellence, Am. Assn. State and Local History, 2004; grantee, L.E.H. Insts., 2002—03; Paul & Elizabeth rsch. fellow, L.A. Endowment for Humanities, 1990. Independent. Avocations: Argentine tango, jazz dance, piano. Home: 5500 Camp St New Orleans LA 70115 Office: Univ Coll Tulane Univ New Orleans LA 70118 Office Phone: 504-891-9858. Personal E-mail: vellavella@aol.com.

**VELLA, MONICA C.,** science educator; b. Queens, N.Y., Apr. 3, 1977; d. Salvina and Nazzareno Vella. PhD, Yale U., 2004. Postdoctoral assoc., Yale biotech SIG career devel. officer Yale U., New Haven, 2004—. Contbr. scientific papers to profl. jours. Recipient Hon. Mention, NSF, 2001; Grad. Rsch. fellow. Mem.: N.Y. Acad. Scis.

**VELLA, RUTH ANN,** real estate executive; b. West Chester, Pa., Aug. 18, 1942; d. Eric and Carmella Tanberg; children: Michele Francette Vella, Nicole Renae Vella. Grad., Realtor's Inst. Real estate sales assoc. Reeve Realty, Wilmington, Del., 1966-72; owner Realtor Heritage Realty, Wilmington, 1972—92; instr. sales Wilmington Coll., 1978-85; mem. faculty Del. State

Coll., 1979—; prin., owner Omega Real Estate Sch., Newark, Del., 1989—; mgr. Weichert Realtors, 1996—2002; profl. devel. coord. Prudential Fox & Roach Realtors, 2002—. Instr. Realtor's Inst., dean, 1983, asst. dean, 1983—; owner, pres. Corporate Fitness of Del., 1991—; mem. ednl. com. Del. Real Estate Commn., 2003—; spkr. in field. Real Estate Commn. 2002—06, Del. Real Estate Commn.; dir. Del. Assn. Realtors, 2004—06. Named Educator of Yr., New Castle County, 1996. Mem. New Castle County Bd. Realtors (dir. 1983-86, edn. com.), Womens Coun. Realtors (past state pres., gov.), Nat. Assn. Realtors (nat. speaker, energy conservation instr., Cert. Real Estate Broker instr.), Leading Edge Soc. Roman Catholic. Avocation: aerobics instr. and personal trainer. Office Phone: 302-999-9999. Business E-Mail: omega@realestateschool.com

**VELLACCIO, FRANK,** academic administrator; m. Cathy Vellaccio; 4 children. BS, Fordham U.; PhD in Organic Chemistry, MIT, 1974. From mem. faculty to sr. v.p. Coll. of the Holy Cross, Worcester, Mass., 1974—2003, sr. v.p., 2003—. Author (with D.S. Kemp): Organic Chemistry, 1980; contbr. articles to profl. jours. Mem.: Phi Beta Kappa. Office: Coll of the Holy Cross Office of Sr VP 1 College St Worcester MA 01610

**VELLACOTT, MAURICE,** legislator; b. Wadena, Can., Sept. 29, 1955; married; 4 children. B, Briercrest Sch.; M, Can. Theol. Sem.; D, Trinity Internat. U. Elected mem. Saskatoon Dist. Health Bd.; mem. House of Commons, Ottawa, Canada, 1997—, vice chair standing com. human resources develop. Can., dep. critic com. human resources develop. Can., mem. sub. com. status of persons with disabilities, dep. critic health, dep. critic aboriginal affairs, vice-chair com. aboriginal affairs and natural resources, co-chair all-party pro-life caucus. Mem. Can. Alliance Family Caucus, mem. ofcl. langs. com. Mem.: Sask. Landlord Assn., Sask. Taxpayers Assn., Saskatoon C. of C., Toastmasters, Can. Club Saskatoon. Conservative Party Can. Office: House of Commons Justice Bldg Ste 610 Ottawa ON Canada K1A 0A6 Address: Unit 3-844 51st St Saskatoon SK S7K 5C7 Canada E-mail: vellacott.m@parl.gc.ca.

**VELLEMAN, RUTH ANN,** retired librarian, educator; b. N.Y.C., Apr. 12, 1921; d. Joseph C. and Celia (Applebaum) Saltman; m. Moritz Velleman, June 11, 1944; children: Paul Flor, J. David, Daniel Jon. BA, Smith Coll., 1942; MS, C.W. Post Coll., 1965. Writer, cons. Human Resources Ctr. and Sch., Albertson, NY, 1963—, dir. libr. and info. svcs., 1963—87; adj. prof. Palmer Grad. Libr. Sch., C.W. Post Coll., NY, 1977—86. Author: Serving Physically Disabled People, 1979 (Ralph R. Shaw award, 1981), Meeting the Needs of People with Disabilities, 1990; contbr. articles to profl. jours. Recipient Award for Excellence in Libr. Achievement, LDA Pubs., Life Achievement award, Suffolk and Nassau County Libr. Assns., 1986. Mem.: ALA, N.Y. Libr. Assn. (Award for Svc. to Disabled 1983), Beta Phi Mu. Home and Office: Velleman Corp 92 Thompson Blvd Greenport NY 11944-3107 E-mail: mvelleman@peconiclanding.net.

**VELLEMAN, SANDRA GAYLE,** molecular biology educator, researcher; b. Malden, Mass., Feb. 2, 1959; d. William and Hilda (Gersh) V. BA with distinction in Biology, Boston U., 1981; PhD in Cell and Devel. Biology, U. Conn., 1986. NIH postdoctoral trainee connective tissue sect. U. Pa. Med. Sch., Phila., 1986-87; postdoctoral assoc. Worcester Found. Exptl. Biology, Shrewsbury, Mass., 1987-88, U. Conn., Storrs, 1988-90, asst. prof., 1990—95; prof. Ohio State U., Wooster, 1995—. Mem. AAAS, Am. Soc. Cell Biology, Soc. Devel. Biology, Poultry Sci. Assn., Sigma Xi, Phi Kappa Phi. Achievements include development of denaturing gradient gel electrophoresis to identify gene markers linked to inheritance of a lethal cartilage structural defect; research on identification on the role of skeletal muscle proteoglycans in the growth and regeneration of muscle. Office: Ohio State U Dept Animal Scis Wooster OH 44691

**VELLENGA, KATHLEEN OSBORNE,** retired state legislator; b. Alliance, Nebr., Aug. 5, 1938; d. Howard Benson and Marjorie (Menke) Osborne; m. James Alan Vellenga, Aug. 9, 1959; children: Thomas, Charlotte Vellenga Landreau, Carolyn Vellenga Berman. BA, Macalester Coll., 1959. Tchr. St. Paul Pub. Schs., 1959-60, Children's Ctr. Montessori, St. Paul, 1973-74, Children's Ho. Montessori, St. Paul, 1974-79; mem. Minn. Ho. of Reps., St. Paul, 1980-94, mem. tax. com. and rules com., 1991—94, chmn. St. Paul del., 1987—90, chmn. criminal justice div., 1987—90, mem. Dem. steering com., 1981—94, chmn. judiciary, 1991, 92, chmn. edn. fin., 1993—94. Mem. St. Paul Family Svcs. Bd., 1994-95; exec. dir. St. Paul/Ramsey County Children's Initiative, 1994-2000. Chmn. Healthstart, St. Paul, 1987-91; mem. Children, Youth and Families Consortium, 1995-99, Macalester Coll. Bd. Alumni, 1995-2001; chair Minn. Higher Edn. Svcs. Coun., 2000—05, mem. 1995—; mem. Citizens League Bd., Minn., 1999-2002, State Commn. Cmty. Svc., 2000-04; bd. dirs. Sexual Violence Ctr., 2004-06; mem. U. Minn. Out of School Time Commn., 2004; mem. H.B. Fuller Found. Bd., 2005—. Mem. LWV (v.p. St. Paul chpt. 1979), Minn. Women Elected Ofcls. (vice chair 1994). Democrat. Presbyterian.

**VELLETRI, THOMAS JOSEPH,** elementary school educator, artist; b. Rochester, N.Y., Apr. 3, 1970; s. Joseph Anthony and Faye Ann (Wray) Velletri; m. Karrie Lynn Murray, July 3, 1979; children: Samuel Thomas, Ava Grace. A in Phys. Studies, Monroe C.C., Rochester, N.Y., 1995; BS, SUNY, Brockport, 1997, MA in Liberal Studies, 2003. CPR. Tchr. phys. edn. Palmyra-Macedan Ctrl. Sch., NY, 1997—98, coach boys basketball, 1997—99; tchr. phys. ed. Rochester City Sch. Dist., NY, 1998—; coach girls basketball Brockport Ctrl. Sch., NY, 1999—2001, Rochester City Sch. Dist., NY, 2001—02; coach boys basketball Holley Ctrl. Sch., NY, 2002—05; coach indoor track Rochester City Sch. Dist., NY, 2005—. Roman Catholic. Avocation: marathon runner. Home: 24 Terrose Meadow Ln Brockport NY 14420 Office: Rochester City Sch Dist 131 W Braod St Rochester NY 14611 Office Phone: 585-235-7848. Office Fax: 585-464-6194. E-mail: tom.velletri@rcsdk12.org.

**VELLUCCI, MARGARET MARY,** librarian; b. Orangeburg, N.Y., Oct. 16, 1947; d. William James and Elizabeth Coyne; m. Leonard Thomas Vellucci, June 17, 1973 (dec. May 1978); 1 child, Kara Elizabeth. BA in Elem. Edn., Glassboro State U., 1971; MLS, Rutgers U., 1987. Substitute tchr. Old Bridge (N.J.) Twp. Sch. Dist., 1971; office worker Middlesex County Coll., Edison, N.J., 1972-75; children's libr. North Edison br. Edison Twp. Pub. Libr., 1987—93, supervising libr. Clara Barton br., 1993—. Mem. ALA, N.J. Libr. Assn. Office: Edison Twp Free Pub Libr Clara Barton Br 141 Hoover Ave Edison NJ 08837-2674

**VELOUDOS, SPIRO V.,** performing company executive, theater educator; s. Vasilios Spiro and Katherine Veloudos. BFA, Emerson Coll., Boston, 1974. Freelance actor, dir., 1974—81; artistic dir. Publick Theatre, Inc, Boston, 1981—2001; producing artistic dir. Lyric Stage Co. Boston, 1998—. Adj. faculty performing arts Emerson Coll., 2004—; adj. faculty musical theatre Boston Conservatory, 2002—04. Dir.(also outstanding production): (theatre performance) A Midsummers Night Dream; prodr.: Quilters; dir.: (theatre preformance) Sweeney Todd and Anything Goes, (theatre performance) Speed-the-Plow, Assassins, Lost in Yonkers, Never the Sinner. Mem.: Boston Study Group. Avocations: photography, music, dance. Office: Lyric Stage Co Boston 140 Clarendon St Boston MA 02116 Office Phone: 617-585-5681. E-mail: spiro_veloudos@lyricstage.com.

**VELTMAN, MARTINUS J.G.,** retired physics educator; b. Waalwijk, The Netherlands, June 27, 1931; m. Anneke Veltman; children: Helene, Hugo, Martijn. BS in math and physics, U. Utrecht, The Netherlands, 1953, MS in theoretical physics, 1956, PhD in theoretical physics, 1963. Mem. FOM, Utrecht, Netherlands, 1959—61; fellow CERN, Geneva, 1961—63, staff mem., 1963—66, cons., 1966—72; sci. assoc., 1972—73, mem. sci. policy com., 1976—81; sci. assoc., 1996—97; prof. U. Utrecht, Netherlands, 1966—81; vis. prof. U. Mich., Ann Arbor, 1980, John D. McArthur prof. of physics, 1981—97, emeritus John D. McArthur prof. of physics, 1997—; prof. U. Autonoma de Madrid, 1988—96; Lorentz prof. of physics U. Leiden,

Netherlands, 1989; Humboldt scientist Max Planck Inst., Munich, 1989—90, DESY, Hamburg, Germany, 1989—90. Postdoctoral SLAC, Stanford, Calif., 1963—64, Brookhaven Nat. Lab., L.I., NY, 1966; vis. prof. U. Paris, Orsay, France, 1968—69. Recipient High Energy and Particle Physics prize, European Physics Soc., 1993, P.A.M. Dirac Medal and Prize, Internat. Ctr. for Theoretical Physics, 1996, Nobel prize in Physics, 1999. Office: U Mich Dept Physics Randall Lab 500 E University Ave Ann Arbor MI 48109-1120*

**VELU, YOGESHWAR KARUNAKARAN,** industrial engineer, researcher; b. Bangalore, Karnataka, India, Dec. 9, 1969; s. Karunakaran Arcot Mohana Velu and PankajaSelvi Karunakaran; m. Vijayalakshmi Yogeshwar Nithyanandam; 1 child, Dhananjay Narayan. BS, Bangalore U., 1991; MS, Clemson U., 1995, Ga. Inst. Tech., 1998; PhD in Fiber and Polymer Sci., N.C. State U., 2003—03. Asst. quality control mgr. Birla Synthetics, Birlapur, Calcutta, 1991—92; rsch. engr. Ga. Inst. Tech., Atlanta, 1997—98; process engr. Nonwovens Coop. Rsch. Ctr., Raleigh, NC, 2002—03; nonwovens engr. Fleetguard, Inc, Cookeville, Tenn., 2003—04, staff rsch. engr., 2004—. Bd. dirs. Sri Venkateswara Temple, Cary, NC, 2001—02. Fellow: Textile Inst.; mem.: ASME, Fiber Soc. Office: PO Box 6001 Cookeville TN 38502-6001 Office Phone: 931-372-9851. Personal E-mail: yogivelu@yahoo.com.

**VELUCHAMY, PETHINAIDU,** marketing executive; m. Parameswari Veluchamy; children: Arun, Anu. BS in Chem., U. Madras, India; BS in Chem. Engring., Georg. State U.; PhD in Chem. Engring., U. Ill. Founder Univ. Subscription Svc., 1974; owner, chmn., CEO Creative Automation Co., 1969—. Office: Veluchamy Cos 1213 Butterfield Rd Downers Grove IL 60515

**VELURY, UMA,** finance educator, researcher; d. RameshChandra Banerjee and Jagadeeswari Banerjee Kolachina; m. Jayadev Velury, Mar. 16, 1986; 1 child, Rajiv. PhD, U. SC, Columbia. Asst. prof. U. Del., Newark, 1999—2005, assoc. prof., 2005—. Mem. editl. bd.: Rsch. in Acctg. Regulation, 2006—; contbr. articles to profl. jours. Recipient Les Chadwick Excellence in Tchg. award, Beta Alpha Psi, Del. Chpt., 2003; grantee, U. Del., 2001, Coll. Bus. and Econs., 2004, 2006. Mem.: Am. Acctg. Assn. Office: University of Delaware 223 Purnell Hall Newark DE 19716 Office Phone: 302-831-1764.

**VENABLE, ANDREW A., JR.,** library director; BBA, Va. State U., 1967; MLS, Case Western Reserve U., 1968. Rschr. Standard Oil Co. of Ohio; asst. dir. personnel Cleve. Pub. Libr., bus. mgr.- treas., head cmty. svcs., dep. dir., 1997—99, dir., 1999—, East Cleve. Pub. Libr., 1983—89, Gary Pub. Libr. Sys., Ind.; dir. libr. svcs. Vocat. Tech. Coll.; dep. dir. DC Pub. Libr. Sys., 1994—97. Mem. Ohio Libr. Coun. Named Libr. of Year, OLC, 2001. Mem.: ALA, Alpha Phi Alpha. Office: Cleve Pub Libr 325 Superior Ave, NE Cleveland OH 44114 Office Phone: 216-623-2827. E-mail: Andrew.Venable@cpl.org.*

**VENABLE, DIANE DAILEY,** retired elementary school educator; b. Sedro Woolley, Wash., June 11, 1939; d. Howard A. and LaVerne L. Dailey; m. Thomas C. Venable, June 28, 1974; 1 child, Erin Dailey. B, Simpson Coll., 1962; B of Elem. Edn., Seattle Pacific U., 1966. Tchr. elem. sch. Kent Schs., Calif., 1966—69, Seattle Schs., 1969—76, Calif. Schs., Simi Valley, 1996—98; ret., 1998. Chair 37th Dem. Assembly Dist., 1993—94; missions elder Emmanuel Presbyn. Ch., Thousand Oaks, Calif., 2000—03. Mem.: Red Hat Soc. Avocations: scrapbooks, reading, travel, golf. Home: 1024 Via Palermo Thousand Oaks CA 91320 E-mail: ddvenable@adelphia.net.

**VENAYAGAMOORTHY, GANESH KUMAR,** electrical engineer, computer engineer, educator; b. Jaffna, Sri Lanka, Feb. 25, 1972; s. Sinnathamby Nagalingam Venayagamoorthy and Neelambigai Kathiravetpillai; m. Gonasagrie Venayagamoorthy, Jan. 5, 2002. B of Engring. with honors, Abubakar Tafawa Balewa U., Bauchi, Nigeria, 1994; MS of Engring., U. Natal, Durban, South Africa, 1998, PhD, 2001. Grad. asst. Abubakar Tafawa Balewa U., Bauchi, Nigeria, 1994—94; computer engr. Sq. One Comnet, Maseru, Lesotho, 1994—95; sr. lectr. Durban Inst. Tech., Durban, Kwazulu Natal, South Africa, 1996—2002; asst. prof. U. Mo., Rolla, 2002—06, assoc. prof., 2006—. Dir. Real-Time Power and Intelligent Systems Lab., U. Mo., Rolla, 2004—. Contbr. articles to profl. jours. Recipient Young Investigator award, Internat. Neural Network Soc., 2003, Outstanding Young Engr. award, IEEE St. Louis Sect., 2004, Faculty Excellence award, U. Mo., Rolla, 2005, Outstanding Young Mem. award, IEEE Industry Applications Soc., 2005, Young Achievers award, South Inst. Elec. Engineers, 2005, Walter Fee Outstanding Young Engr. award, IEEE Power Engring. Soc., 2006; grantee, NSF, 2004, NSF Career award, 2004. Mem.: IEEE (sr.; chair St. Louis chpt. 2004—06), Inst. Elec. Engrs., Am. Soc. Engring. Edn., Internat. Neural Network Soc., South African Inst. Elec. Engrs. (sr.). Office: U Mo 132 Emerson Electric Co Hall Rolla MO 65409 Office Phone: 573-341-6641. Office Fax: 573-341-4532. E-mail: gkumar@ieee.org.

**VENCL, FREDRIC VINCENT,** biologist, researcher; b. Cleve., Nov. 27, 1949; PhD, Stony Brook U., 1977. Rsch. assoc. prof. ecology and evolution Stony Brook U., 1999—. Author: jour. articles. Grantee, NSF, 2001—06. Mem.: Assn. for Tropical Biology and Conservation. Office: Dept Ecology and Evolution Stony Brook Univ Stony Brook NY 11794-5245 Business E-Mail: fvencl@life.bio.sunysb.edu.

**VENDITTI, CLELIA ROSE See PALMER, CHRISTINE**

**VENDLER, HELEN HENNESSY,** literature educator, poetry critic; b. Boston, Apr. 30, 1933; d. George and Helen (Conway) Hennessy; 1 son, David. AB, Emmanuel Coll., 1954; PhD, Harvard U., 1960; PhD (hon.), U. Oslo, 1981; DLitt (hon.), Smith Coll., 1980, Kenyon Coll., 1982, U. Hartford, 1985, Union Coll., 1986, Columbia U., 1987, Washington U., 1991, Marlboro Coll., 1989, Yale U., 2000; DHL (hon.), Fitchburg State U., 1990, Dartmouth Coll., 1992, U. Mass., 1992, Bates Coll., 1992, U. Toronto, Ont., Can., 1992, Trinity Coll., Dublin, Ireland, 1993, U. Cambridge, 1997, Nat. U., Ireland, 1998, Wabash Coll., 1998, U. Mass, Dartmouth, 2000, Yale U., 2000, U. Aberdeen, 2000, Tufts U., 2001, Amherst Coll., 2002, Colby Coll., 2003; DHL, Bard Coll., 2005. Instr. Cornell U., Ithaca, NY, 1960-63; lectr. Swarthmore (Pa.) Coll. and Haverford (Pa.) Coll., 1963-64; asst. prof. Smith Coll., Northampton, Mass., 1964-66; assoc. prof. Boston U., 1966-68, prof., 1968-85. Fulbright lectr. U. Bordeaux, France, 1968-69; vis. prof. Harvard U., 1981-85, Kenan prof., 1985—, Porter U. prof., 2004—; assoc. acad. dean, 1987-92, sr. fellow Harvard Soc. Fellows, 1981-93; poetry critic New Yorker, 1978-99; mem. ednl. adv. bd. Guggenheim Found., 1991-01, Pulitzer Prize Bd., 1991-99; Jefferson lectr. NEH, 2004. Author: Yeats's Vision and the Later Plays, 1963, On Extended Wings: Wallace Stevens' Longer Poems, 1969, The Poetry of George Herbert, 1975, Part of Nature, Part of Us, 1980, The Odes of John Keats, 1983, Wallace Stevens: Words Chosen Out of Desire, 1984; editor: Harvard Book of Contemporary American Poetry, 1985, Voices and Visions: The Poet in America, 1987, The Music of What Happens, 1988, Soul Says, 1995, The Given and the Made, 1995, The Breaking of Style, 1995, Poems, Poets, Poetry, 1995, The Art of Shakespeare's Sonnets, 1997, Seamus Heaney, 1998, Coming of Age as a Poet, 2003, Poets Thinking, 2004, Invisible Listeners, 2005. Bd. dirs. Nat. Humanities Ctr., 1989—93. Recipient Lowell prize, 1969, Explicator prize, 1969, award Nat. Inst. Arts and Letters, 1975, Radcliffe Grad. Soc. medal, 1978, Nat. Book Critics award, 1980, Keats-Shelley Assn. award, 1994, Truman Capote award, 1996; Fulbright fellow, 1954, Guggenheim fellow, 1971-72, Am. Coun. Learned Socs. fellow, 1971-72, NEH fellow, 1980, 85, 94, 04, 05, fellow Churchill Coll., Cambridge, 1980, Charles Stewart Parnell fellow Magdalene Coll., Cambridge, 1996, hon. fellow, 1996—; NEH Jefferson Lectr. scholar US Fed. Govt., 2004-05. Mem. MLA (exec. coun. 1972-75, pres. 1980), AAAL, English Inst. (trustee 1977-85), Am. Acad. Arts and Scis. (v.p. 1992-95), Norwegian Acad. Letters and Sci., Am. Philos. Soc. (Jefferson medal 2000), Phi Beta Kappa. Home: 54 Trowbridge St 2 Cambridge MA 02138-4113 Office: Harvard U Dept English Barker Center Cambridge MA 02138-3929 Office Phone: 617-496-6028.

**VENDLINSKI, TERRY P.,** computer scientist, educator; b. San Francisco, Calif., June 13, 1970; s. Stan and Georgia Vendlinski. PhD, MIT, 2001. Educator Christian Bros. H.S., Sacramento, 1991—97; sr. rsch. assoc. UCLA, L.A., 2001—. Office: UCLA CRESST 10945 LeConte Ave Los Angeles CA 90095-7150 Office Phone: 310-206-5086.

**VENEGAS, ARTURO, JR.,** protective services official; b. San Nicolas de Ibarra, Jalisco, Mexico, Dec. 22, 1948; m. Anna Marie Venegas; children: Angela, Adriana, Anthony, Andrew. BA, San Francisco, 1978; MS in Mgmt., Calif. Poly., Pomona, 1991. Police officer Fresno (Calif.) Police Dept., 1970-75, police specialist, 1975-79, sgt., field supr., 1979, 80-85, lt., 1985-90, lt., acting divsn. comdr. adminstrv. svcs., 1990-92, dep. chief police investigations divsn., 1992-93; chief program devel., program mgr. State Office Criminal Justice Planning, Sacramento, 1979-80; chief of police Sacramento Police Dept., 1993—2006; police super session exec. Camden (NJ) Police Dept., 2006—. Mem. Calif. Atty. Gen.'s Policy Coun. on Violence Prevention; bd. dirs. Safety Ctr.; mem. exec. bd. Sacramento Safe Sts.; mem. adv. bd. Cath. Social Svcs. With U.S. Army, 1966-68. Mem. Internat. Assn. Chiefs of Police, Calif. Assn. Chiefs of Police, Calif. Peace Officers Assn. (chair law and legis. com.), Police Exec. Rsch. Forum, Ctrl. Sierra Police Chiefs Assn., FBI Nat. Acad. Assocs., Latino Peace Officers Assn., Hispanic-Am. Command Officers Assn., Am. Legion, Footprinters Internat., KC. Office: Camden Police Dept Police Adminstrn Bldg 8th & Fed St One Police Plz Camden NJ 08103*

**VENEGAS, FRANK, JR.,** construction executive; b. Detroit; Founder, chmn., CEO The Ideal Group, Inc. (formerly Ideal Steel & Builders' Supplies), 1979—; helped build Hispanic Mfg. Ctr., Detroit, 1996. Named Hispanic Businessman of Yr., US Hispanic C. of C., 2003. Office: The Ideal Group Inc 2525 Clark St Detroit MI 48209*

**VENEMAN, ANN MARGARET,** international organization executive, former secretary of agriculture; b. Modesto, Calif., June 29, 1949; d. John G. and Nita D. (Bomberger) V.; div. BA in polit. sci., U. Calif., Davis, 1970; MA in pub. policy, U. Calif., Berkeley, 1971; JD, Hastings Coll. Law, 1976. Bar: Calif. 1976, U.S. Supreme Ct. 1981. Atty. San Francisco Bay Area Rapid Transit Dist., 1976-78; dep. pub. defender Stanislaus County., Calif., 1978-80; ptnr. Damrell, Damrell & Nelson, Modesto, 1980-86; asst. to adminstr., Fgn. Agrl. Svc. USDA, Washington, 1986-87, assoc. adminstr., Fgn. Agrl. Svc., 1987-89, dep. under sec. Internat. Affairs and Commodity Programs, 1989-91, dep. sec., 1991-93, sec. of agr., 2001—05; atty. Patton, Boggs & Blow LLP, Washington, 1993—95; sec. Calif. Dept. Food and Agr., 1995—99; ptnr. Nossaman, Guthner, Knox & Elliott LLP, Sacramento, 1999—2000; exec. dir. UNICEF, 2005—. Bd. dir. Close Up Found. Office: UNICEF 3 United Nations Plz New York NY 10017*

**VENERABLE, GRANT DELBERT, II,** chemist, educator, systems scientist; b. L.A., Aug. 31, 1942; s. Grant Delbert and Thelma L. (Scott) Venerable. BS Chemistry, UCLA, 1965; MS Chemistry, U. Chgo., 1967, PhD Physical Chemistry, 1970; postdoctoral studies, UCLA Lab. Nuclear Medicine, 1971. Assoc. prof. chemistry Calif. Polytech. State U., San Luis Obispo, 1972—78; Sloan lectr. chemistry U. Calif., Santa Cruz, 1978—80; cons. software Motorola and other Cos., Cupertino, 1981—89; lectr. Coll. Ethnic Studies San Francisco State U., 1989—96; assoc. provost, assoc. v.p., prof. chemistry Chgo. (Ill.) State U., 1996—98; provo and v.p. acad. affairs Morris Brown Coll., Atlanta, 1998—2002; v.p. acad. affairs Lincoln U., Pa., 2002. Sec. State Bd. Calif. Alliance for Arts Edn., 1985—91. Author: (Book) The Discovery of Calculus of Transformations in Chemistry, 1974, The Paradox of the Silicon Savior, 1988, Managing in a Five Dimension Economy, 1999. Bd. dirs. City Quest, Chgo., 1998—2000. Recipient Achievement award, Calif. Alliance for Art Edn., 1990, Urban Edn. Achievement award, JGT Found., San Francisco, 1996. Mem.: AAAS, Am. Chem. Soc., Nat. Orgn. for Profl. Advancement of Black Chemists and Chem. Engrs., Alpha Chi Sigma. Avocations: organist, painting, swimming. Office Acad Affairs Lincoln U Box 179 Lincoln University PA 19352 Home: 300 Gaelic Way Tyrone GA 30290 Office Phone: 610-632-8300 Ext 3436. Office Fax: 610-932-1208. E-mail: ventwo@aol.com.

**VENERABLE, SHIRLEY MARIE,** retired gifted and talented educator; b. Washington, Nov. 12, 1931; d. John Henry and Jessie Josephine (Young) Washington; m. Wendell Grant Venerable, Feb. 15, 1959; children: Angela Elizabeth Maria Venerable-Joyner, Wendell Mark. PhB, Northwestern U., 1963; MA, Roosevelt U., 1976, postgrad., 1985; student in Life Long Studies, Triton C.C., River Grove, Ill., 2002. Cert. in diagnostic and prescriptive reading, gifted edn., finger math., fine arts, Ill. Tchr. Lewis Champlin Sch., 1963-74, John Hay Acad., Chgo., 1975-87, Leslie Lewis Elem. Sch., Chgo., 1988-99, Robert Emmet Sch., Chgo., 1999—; self employed tutorial programs, 1999—2003; ret., 2003. Sponsor Reading Marathon Club, Chgo., 1991—; co-creator Project SMART-Stimulating Math. and Reading Techniques John Hay Acad., Chgo., 1987-90, curriculum coord., 1985-87; creative dance student, tchr. Kathryn Duham Sch., N.Y.C., 1955-56; creative dance tchr. Doris Patterson Dance Sch., Washington, 1953-55; recorder evening divsn. Northwestern U., Chgo., 1956-62; exch. student tchr. Conservatory Dance Movements, Chgo., 1958-59; art cons. Chgo. Pub. Sch., 1967. Author primary activities Let's Act and Chat, 1991-94, Teaching Black History Through Classroom Tours, 1989-90. Solicitor, vol. United Negro Coll. Fund, Chgo., 1994; sponsor 37th Ward Reading Assn. Marathon, Chgo., 1991-94, 99; active St. Giles Coun. Cath. Women, 1985-96; vol. REAC Ctr. Programs Books, Info., Literacy and Learning, 1997-98. Recipient Meritorious award United Negro Coll. Fund, 1990, 94, Recognition award Alderman Percy Giles, Chgo., 1993, Hall of Fame award Nat. Women in Achievement, Inc. 2005. Mem. A3CD (assoc. Recognition of Svcs. award 1989), Internat. Reading Assn., Nat. Women of Achievement Assn. (Chgo. chpt.), Phi Delta Kappa, Sigma Gamma Rho (Delta Sigma grad. chpt. 1963—93, Sigma chpt. 1992, Eta Xi Sigma chpt.), Eta Xi Sigma (Pearl award for excellence in edn. 1997). Roman Catholic. Home: 1108 N Euclid Ave Oak Park IL 60302-1219

**VENETSANOPOULOS, ANASTASIOS NICOLAOS,** electrical engineer, educator; b. Athens, Greece, June 19, 1941; arrived in Can., 1968; s. Nicolaos Anastasios and Elli (Papacondilis) Venetsanopoulos. Diploma, Athens Coll., 1960; B in Elec. and Mech. Engring., Nat. Tech. U., Athens, 1965; MS, Yale U., 1966, MPhil, 1968, PhD, 1969; doctorate (hon.), Nat. Tech. U., Athens, 1994. Registered profl. engr., Greece, Ont. Asst. in instrn. engring. and applied sci. Yale U., 1966-68, research asst., 1968-69; lectr. U. Toronto, Ont., Can., 1968-69, asst. prof. elec. engring., 1970-73, assoc. prof., 1973-81, prof., 1981—, comm. communications group dept. elec. engring., 1974-78, 81-86, assoc. chmn. elec. and computer engring., 1978-79, 97—, mem. elec. and computer engring. exec. com., 1981-86, 97—, acting chmn. elec. and computer engring., 1998—99, dean applied sci. and engring., 2001—. Acad. visitor Imperial Coll. Arts and Tech. U. London, 1979-80; vis. prof. Nat. Tech. U. Athens, 1979—80, Fed. U. Tech. Lausanne, Switzerland, 1986—87, Switzerland, 1993—94, U. Florence, Italy, 1987; cons. elec. engring. Consociates Ltd.; chmn. multimedia Bell-Can., 1999—. Editor: Can. Elec. Engring. Jour., 1981—83; contbr. articles to profl. jours., chapters to books. Mem. allocations and agy. rels. com. United Cmty. Fund, Toronto, 1971—74; pres. Hellenic-Can. Cultural Soc., 1972—75; sec. gen. Greek Cmty. Met. Toronto, 1973—75. Recipient Excellence in Innovation award, Info. Tech. Rsch. Ctr. 1996; grantee Fulbright Travel, U.S., 1965, Def. Rsch. Bd. Can., 1972—75, UN, NSF, J.P. Bickell Found., Natural Scis. and Engring. Rsch. Coun. Can. Fellow: IEEE (fin. chmn. internat. symposium on circuit theory 1973, tech. program chmn. internat. conf. comm. 1978, 1986, vice-chmn. Toronto sect. 1976—77, chmn. 1977—79, assoc. editor Transactions on circuits and sys. 1985—87, guest editor spl. 1987, tech. prgram chmn. internat. conf. on acoustics speech and signal proc 1991, Millenium medal 2001—), Can. Acad. Engring., Engring. Inst. Can.; mem.: Intercultural Coun. (chmn. ednl. com. 1971—80, sr. v.p. 1977—80), Am.-Hellenic Ednl. Progress Assn. (v.p. Toronto sect. 1973—75, pres. 1975—77), N.Y. Acad. Scis., Yale Sci. and Engring. Assn., Can. Society Elec. Engring. (chmn. Toronto sect. 1975—77, nat.

dir. 1976—88, pres. 1983—86), Assn. Profl. Mech. Engrs. Greece, Assn. Profl. Elec. Engrs. Greece, Assn. Profl. Engrs. Ont., Tech. Chamber Greece, Sigma Xi. Office: U Toronto Fac Applied Sci and Engring Toronto ON Canada M5S 1A4

**VENEZIA, WILLIAM THOMAS,** school system administrator, counseling consultant; b. Jersey City, Mar. 20, 1952; s. Thomas Michael and Carmela (Crocarno) Venezia; m. Josephine DePaul. BA in History, St. Peter's Coll., 1974, postgrad., 1978-79, MA in Adminstrn./Supervision, 1984; postgrad., Jersey City State Coll., 1988-90. Cert. tchr., prin., supt., N.J.; cert. in student personnel svcs., N.J. Tchr. various schs. Jersey City Bd. Edn., 1976-92; guidance counselor P.S. # 27/Dickinson High Sch., Jersey City, 1990-92; counselor Montclair (N.J.) State Coll., 1991-92; asst. prin. Frelinghuysen Sch., Morristown, NJ, 1992-97; prin. Alexander Hamilton Sch., Morristown, 1997—2001; dir. guidance Morris Sch. Dist., 2001—02; prin. Thomas Jefferson Sch., Morristown, 2002—. Asst. football coach various schs., 1975-89; instr., adminstr. G.E.D. and A.B.E. programs Jersey City Bd. Edn., 1977-82; interim bd. sec., bus. adminstr. Weehawken Bd. Edn., 1984; mem. adv. bd. Cornerstone Sch., Jersey City, 1988-91; pre-coll. counselor UP-WARD Bound project Montclair State Coll., 1991; cons. N.J. Devils hockey team, East Rutherford, 1992, D.A.R.E. program Hudson County Prosecutor, Jersey City, 1992.h Vol. counselor Giant Steps adolescent substance abuse treatment facility; active Jersey City, 1993, Jersey City Parents' Coun. Mem. ASCD, NEA, Am. Football Coaches Assn., N.J. Edn. Assn., Assn. Adult Edn. in N.J., N.J. Assn. Sch. Bus. Officials, Hudson County Personnel and Guidance Assn., Morris Sch. Dist.Adminstrv. Assn., Iron Bound Execs. Assn., Hoboken Elks. Avocations: basketball, travel, antiques. Home. 1 Hickory St Clark NJ 07066-1924 Office: Thomas Jefferson Sch 101 James St Morristown NJ 07960 Office Phone: 973-292-2089. Business E-mail: bill.venezia@msdk12.net.

**VENEZIANO, KELLY DENISE,** psychologist; b. Phila., Apr. 28, 1976; d. Joseph Robert and Lee Bettger Morgan; m. Michael Angelo Veneziano, May 17, 2003. BA in Psychology, Rutgers U., 1998; MA in Clin. Counseling Psychology, La Salle U., 2001; Ednl. Specialist in Sch. Psychology, Rider U., 2006. Lic. profl. counselor NJ, sch. psychologist NJ. Case mgr., therapist Drenk Behavioral Health Ctr., Burlington, NJ, 2000—01; therapist CFG-CASTLE Program, Camden, NJ, 2001—05; sch. psychologist Burlington (NJ) Twp. Sch. Dist., 2005—. Mem.: NASP.

**VENINGA, JAMES FRANK,** humanities educator, editor, writer; b. Milw., Aug. 26, 1944; s. Frank and Otila Ann (Mauch) V.; m. Catherine M. Williams, Apr. 5, 1969; 1 child, Jennifer Elisa. BA, Baylor U., 1966; MTheol Studies, Harvard U., 1968; MA, Rice U., 1973, PhD, 1974. Instr. U. St. Thomas, Houston, 1971-73, asst. prof., 1974; asst. dir. Tex. Coun. for Humanities, Austin, 1975, exec. dir., 1976-97; pres., dir. Inst. for the Humanities at Salado, 1997-2000; CEO, campus dean U. Wis.-Marathon County, Wausau, 2000—. Dir. Nat. Fedn. State Humanities Couns., Washington, 1980-83; trustee Inst. for Humanities at Salado, Tex., 1980-85; vis. prof. Am. studies U. Tex., Austin, 1984; sr. lectr. Am. studies, 1986; vis. prof. Am. studies Baylor U., 1999. Author: The Humanities and Civic Imagination, 1999; editor: The Biographer's Gift, 1983, Vietnam in Remission, 1985, Standing with the Public, 1997; editor-in-chief Tex. Jour. Ideas, History and Culture, 1982-97. Recipient Baylor Man of Merit award Baylor U., 1999. 300 Country Club Rd Schofield WI 54476 Office: U Wis 518 S 7th Ave Wausau WI 54401-5362 Business E-mail: jveninga@uwc.edu.

**VENKATA, SUBRAHMANYAM SARASWATI,** engineering educator, researcher; b. Nellore, Andhra Pradesh, India, June 28, 1942; came to U.S., 1968; s. Ramiah Saraswati and Lakshmi (Alladi) V.; m. Padma Subrahmanyam Mahadevan, Sept. 3, 1971; children: Sridevi Ramakumar, Harish Saraswati. BSEE, Andhra U., Waltair, India, 1963; MSEE, Indian Inst. Tech., Madras, 1965; PhD, U. S.C., 1971. Registered profl. engr., W.Va., Wash. Lectr. in elec. engring. Coimbatore (India) Inst. Tech., 1965-66; planning engr. S.C. Elec. & Gas Co., Columbia, 1969-70; postdoctoral fellow U. S.C., Columbia, 1971; instr. elec. engring. U. Mass., Lowell, 1971-72; asst. prof. W.Va. U., Morgantown, 1972-75, assoc. prof., 1975-79; prof. U. Wash., Seattle, 1979-96; prof., chmn. dept. elec. and computer engring. Iowa State U., Ames, 1996—2002, Palmer chair prof. dept. elec. and computer engring., 2003—; dean, disting. univ. prof. Wallace H. Coulter Sch. Engring., Clarkson U., Potsdam, NY, 2004—05; v.p., exec. cons. KEMA, 2005—. Cons. Puget Sound Energy Co., Bellevue, Wash., 1980-93, GEC/Alsthom, NYC, 1991-92; series editor, bd. dirs. PWS Pub. Co., 1991-98; affiliate prof. U. Wash., Seattle, 1997-00. Author: Introduction of Electrical Energy Devices, 1987; editor, IEEE Transactions on Power Systems, 1998-00, IEEE/PES Rev. Letters, 1999-03, Internat. Jour. Sys.; mem. editl. bd. IEEE/PES/Power and Energy Mag., 2003—; patentee adaptive var compensators, adaptive power quality conditioner, distribution reliability based design software. Advisor Explorers Club, Morgantown, 1976-78; sec. Hindu Temple and Cultural Ctr. Pacific N.W., Seattle, 1990, chmn., 1991, 95; founding chmn. Hindu Temple and Cultural Ctr., Ames, Iowa, 1999—. Recipient W.Va. U. Assocs. award W.Va. U. Found., 1974, 78. Fellow IEEE (editor IEEE Trans. Power Sys. 1998-00, IEEE/PES Rev. Letters 1999-03, Internat. Jour. Sys., mem. editl. bd. IEEE/PES/Power and Energy Mag., 2003—, v.p. publs., Best Paper award 1985, 88, 91, 2005, mem. Conf. Internat. des Grands Reseaux Electriques, IEEE Press for Power Series, 1998—, Outstanding Power Engring. Educator award 1996, chmn. power engring. edn. com. 2000—, Millenneum medal 2000, Power Edn.Com. Disting. Svc. award 2005), Power Engring. Soc. IEEE (v.p. 2004—), Sigma Xi, Tau Beta Pi, Eta Kappa Nu, Rotary. Democrat. Avocations: photography, tennis, ping pong/table tennis. Home and Office: 13224 N Risky Dr Tucson AZ 85755 Office Phone: 520-797-1161. Business E-mail: ss.venkata@kema.com.

**VENKATESH, VISWANATH,** information systems professional, educator, consultant; s. Viswanath Hariharan and Subhalakshmi Viswanath. BE, Bharathiar U., Coimbatore, India, 1991; post grad., Temple U., Phila., 1993; PhD, U. Minn., Mpls., 1997. Cert. bus. process mgr. and practitioner del. Bus. Process Mgmt. Group, 2006. Asst. prof. and Tyser fellow U. Md., College Park, 1997—2002, assoc. prof. and Tyser fellow, 2002—04; prof. and George and Boyce Billingsley chair info. sys. Walton Coll. Bus. U. Ark., Fayetteville, 2004—. Dir. MBA consulting U. of Md., College Park, 2002—04; doctoral program dir. info. sys. U. Ark., Fayetteville, 2004—; assoc. editor Mgmt. Sci., Jour. Assn. of Info. Sys., Info. Sys. Rsch., MIS Quar.; invited spkr. at univs. Contbr. scientific papers to refereed profl. jours., articles. Vol. tax preparation for underprivileged, College Park, Md., 1997—2003, Fayetteville, Ark., 2004—05; donor and social supporter Lions Orgn., Chennai, Tamil Nadu, India, 1995—2006. Named Reviewer of the Yr., MIS Quar., 1999, 4th most cited article 1970-2005, Decision Scis. Jour., 2005; recipient Tchg. Innovation award, U. Md., 1998, 2001, Gen. Tchg. Excellence award, 2000, 2003, Celebrating Teachers award, 2002; grantee, NSF, Microsoft, U.S. Dept. Transportation, Veterans Health Adminstrn. Mem.: Assn. Info. Sys., Inst. Ops. Rsch. and the Mgmt. Scis. Achievements include research in technology acceptance; design of 10 different courses at the PhD, MBA, and undergraduate levels. Avocations: travel, badminton, racquetball, swimming, stamp collecting/philately. Office: Univ Ark Walton Coll of Bus Fayetteville AR 72701 Office Phone: 479 573 869. Business E-mail: vvenkatesh@vvenkatesh.us.

**VENKAYYA, RAJEEV V.,** federal agency administrator, biomedical researcher, educator; b. Dayton, Ohio, Mar. 6, 1967; BS, U. Akron, MD, Northeastern Ohio U., 1991. Resident Internal Medicine U. Mich., chief med. resident, 1994—95; fellow Pulmonary and Critical Care Medicine U. Calif., San Francisco, asst. prof. medicine; dir. High Risk Asthma Clinic San Francisco Gen. Hosp., co-dir. Med. Intensive Care Unit; founder, dir. Neomedicus, LLC, 2000—, Sapient Medical Group, Inc.; White House fellow US Dept. Energy, Washington, 2002—03; dir. Biodefense and Health White House Homeland Security Coun., 2003—; asst. to Pres. for Biological Defense Policy. Advisor San Francisco Asthma Task Force Steering Com. Contbr. articles to profl. jours. Grantee Rsch. Grant, Am. Lung Assn., 1999,

NIH, 1999. Mem.: Am. Lung Assn. San Francisco, Alpha Omega Alpha. Office: White House Homeland Security Coun 1600 Pennsylvania Ave NW Washington DC 20500 Home: 2508 Cliffborne Pl Nw Washington DC 20009-1512*

**VENNAM, VENKATA SURYA PRAKASH,** engineering educator, researcher; b. Guntur, India, Jan. 7, 1970; arrived in US, 2000; s. Chalapathi Rao and Aruna Vennam; m. Sowjanya Pamidi, Dec. 9, 1995. B of Tech., Nagarjuna U., Vijayawada, India, 1991; M of Tech., Indian Inst. Tech., Kharagpur, India, 1993; PhD, Indian Inst. Sci., Bangalore, 2000. Scientist Def. R & D Orgn., Bangalore, 1993—2000; rschr. Pa. State U., University Park, 2000—02, vis. asst. prof., 2002—. Cons. in field. Mem. rev. bd. Microwave & Optical Tech. Letters, 2002—. Recipient Young Engr. award, Indian Nat. Acad. Engring., 1999. Mem.: IEEE (sr.; mem. editl. bd. 2002—), Instn. Elect. & Telecomm. Engrs. Achievements include development of fast solvers; design of airborne ultra-low side lobe antenna. Avocations: stamp collecting/philately, chess, music, art. Business E-mail: vvp2@psu.edu.

**VENNAT, MICHEL,** former bank executive, lawyer; b. Sept. 17, 1941; m. Marie-Anne Tawil; children: Catherine, Charles-Alexandre, Frédéric-André, Michèle-Anne, Philippe-Olivier. BA magna cum laude, Coll. Jean-de-Brébeuf, Montreal, Que., Can., 1960; LL.L., U. Montreal, 1963; MA, Oxford U., Eng., 1965. Bar: Que. 1966, Paris 1995; apptd. Queen's Counsel 1983, Officer of the Order of Can., 1995. Fgn. affairs officer Dept. External Affairs, Ottawa, Ont., Canada, 1965; spl. asst. to Min. Fin., 1966-68; spl. asst. to Hon. Pierre E. Trudeau, Prime Min. of Can., 1968-70, spl. counsel, 1977; chmn. Can. Film Devel. Corp., Montreal, 1976-81; sr. ptnr. Stikeman, Elliott, Montreal, 1970-90; pres. Dumez Investments Inc., 1986-87, Westburne Internat. Industries Ltd., 1987; vice chmn. United Westburne Inc., 1990, vice chmn., CEO, 1991-93, chmn., CEO, 1993-94, also bd. dirs.; pres. Bastos du Canada Limitée, 1987—2000, also bd. dirs.; sr. ptnr. Stikeman Elliot, Montreal, 1994-2000; pres., CEO bus. devel. Bank Canada, 2000—04. Chmn. bd. dirs. Bus. Devel. Bank of Can.; lectr. in constl. law U. Montreal, 1970. Rhodes scholar, 1963-65. Mem. Barreau du Que., Barreau de Paris, Mt. Bruno Country Club, Hillside Tennis Club, Mt. Royal Club, Knowlton Golf Club, St. John Salmon Club, Montreal Badminton & Squash Club. Avocations: golf, tennis, skiing, fishing, hunting. Office Phone: 514-849-8000. Business E-mail: mvennat@iron-hill.com.

**VENNING, ROBERT STANLEY,** lawyer; b. Boise, Idaho, July 24, 1943; s. William Lucas and Corey Elizabeth (Brown) V.; m. Sandra Macdonald, May 9, 1966 (div. 1976); 1 child, Rachel Elizabeth; m. Laura Siegel, Mar. 24, 1979; 1 child, Daniel Rockhill Siegel. AB, Harvard U., 1965; MA, U. Chgo., 1966; LLB, Yale U., 1970. Bar: Calif., U.S. Dist. Ct. (no. dist.) Calif., 1971, U.S. Dist. Ct. (cen. dist.) Calif. 1973, U.S. Ct. Appeals (9th cir.) 1977, U.S. Supreme Ct. 1977, U.S. Ct. Appeals (fed. cir.) 1986, U.S. Ct. Appeals (D.C. cir.) 1987, U.S. Ct. Fed. Claims 1996. Assoc. Heller Ehrman White & McAuliffe (now known as Heller Ehrman LLP), San Francisco, 1970-73, 73-76, ptnr., 1977—, mem. exec. com., 1991-94. Vis. lectr. U. Wash., Seattle, 1973, Boalt Hall Sch. Law, U. Calif., Berkeley, 1982-85, 89, Sch. Bus., Stanford U., 1986-87. Editor Yale Law Jour., 1969-70. Early neutral evaluator U.S. Dist. Ct. (no. dist.) Calif., 1987— Fellow Am. Bar Found. (life); mem. ABA, San Francisco Bar Assn. (past chair judiciary com.), CPR Inst. for Dispute Resolution, Olympic Club. Office: Heller Ehrman LLP 333 Bush St San Francisco CA 94104-2878 Office Phone: 415-772-6158.

**VENO, RONALD JAMES, JR.,** travel industry executive; b. Malden, Mass., Feb. 3, 1963; s. Ronald James and Jeanne (Greer) V.; m. Michele Carmelina Sipala, Aug. 12, 1989; children: Erica Joan, Ronald James III. BS, Westfield State Coll., 1985; MBA, Boston Coll., Chestnut Hill, Mass., 1993. Sales rep. Quikrete Co., Everett, Mass., 1987-88; area mgr. Sunoco, Providence, 1988-94; product mgr. Collette Tours, Pawtucket, R.I., 1994-96; dir. sales and mktg. Abercrombie and Kent Overseas, Oak Brook, Ill., 1996-98, v.p. sales and mktg. Ill., 1998—. Roman Catholic. Avocations: drawing, painting, fishing. Home: 14130 S Longview Ln Plainfield IL 60544-6010 Office: Abercrombie and Kent Overseas 1520 Kensington Rd Ste 212 Oak Brook Il 60523-2156

**VENTENILLA, AURORA CURAMEN,** psychiatrist; b. San Jose, The Philippines, Nov. 7, 1939; came to U.S., 1968; d. Tereso and Petra (Patricio) Curamen; m. Doroteo Olba Ventenilla, Oct. 22, 1966; children: Anna, Enrique. MD, Manila Ctr. U., 1963. Diplomate Am. Bd. Psychiatry and Neurology. Staff psychiatrist Cleve. VA Med. Ctr., 1974—96; contract psychiatrist COMPHEALTH, Salt Lake City, 1996—; staff psychiatrist Windsor Hosp., Chagrin Falls, Ohio, 1999—2001, Fremont (Ohio) Meml. Hosp., 2000—, Ctr. for Families and Children, Parma, Ohio, 1999—. Chief of psychiatry 256 Gen. Hosp. U.S. Army Res., Parma, Ohio, 1986-92. Lt. col. U.S. Army Res., 1982-92. Decorated Army Commendation medal Operation Desert Storm, 1991. Mem. Am. Profl. Practice Assn., Assn. Philippine Physicians in Am., Assn. Philippine Physicians in Ohio. Home: 9826 Tamarack Trl Brecksville OH 44141-4109

**VENTER, J. CRAIG (JOHN CRAIG VENTER, CRAIG VENTER),** science foundation director, geneticist; b. Salt Lake City, Oct. 14, 1946; m. Claire Fraser. BS in Biochemistry, U. Calif., San Diego, 1972, PhD in Physiology and Pharmacology, 1975. Prof. SUNY, Buffalo; with Roswell Pk. Meml. Inst.; sect. and lab chief Nat. Inst. Neurol. Disorders and Stroke NIH, Bethesda, Md., 1984—92; co-founder, chair, chief scientist The Inst. for Genomic Rsch., 1992—98; co-founder, CEO, pres., chief sci. officer Celera Genomics Corp., Rockville, Md., 1998—2002; chmn. sci. adv. bd. Applera Corp., Norwalk, Conn.; chmn., co-founder, pres. The J. Craig Venter Sci. Found. Joint Tech. Ctr., 2005—, J. Craig Venter Inst.; co-founder, pres. Ctr. for the Advancement Genomics, 2003—, Inst. for Biol. Energy Alternatives, 2003—. Bd. dirs. High Tech. Coun. Md.; mem. sci. adv. bd. ValiGene; chmn., bd. trustees The Inst. for Genomic Rsch. Contbr. more than 160 articles to profl. jours. Served in U.S. Army, 1967—68. Recipient Beckman award, 1999, Chiron Corp. Biotech. Rsch. award, 1999, King Faisal Internat. award for Sci., 2000, Taylor Internat. prize in Medicine, Robarts Rsch. Inst., 2001, Gairdner award, 2002, Award for Indsl. Application of Sci., NAS, 2002. Fellow: AAAS, Am. Acad. Microbiology. Achievements include research in functional and comparative analysis of genome and gene products in viruses, eubacteria, pathogenic bacteria, archea and eukaryotes, both in plants and animals including humans; first to use automated gene sequencers; development of expressed sequence tags (ESTs); discovery of more than half of all human genes. Office: The Inst for Genomic Rsch 9712 Medical Center Dr Rockville MD 20850 also: J Craig Venture Sci Found 5 Research Pl Rockville MD 20850*

**VENTERS, HARLEY EUGENE,** lawyer; b. Okla., Nov. 12, 1922; s. Albert Harley Venters and Margaret Emily Tate; m. Anne Matilda Liccione, Oct. 4, 1946; children: Anne Eleanor, Christopher William, Harley Eugene Jr., Wanda Jean, Shelly Laura. BS, US Mil. Acad., West Point, 1946; student, Okla. U., Norman, 1941, LLB, 1953. Bar: U.S. Supreme Ct. 1971. Air cadet U.S. Army Air Corps, San Antonio, 1942—43; cadet West Point Corps Cadets, NY, 1943—46; lt. U.S. Army, 1946—50; county judge Carter County, Ardmore, Okla., 1953—54, state counsel, 1957—58; state Ho. Okla. State Legis., Oklahoma City, 1955—56; presiding judge Okla. State Indsl. Ct., Oklahoma City, 1960—61; ptnr. Venters & Venters, Oklahoma City, 1961—. Founder Okla. Interfaith Alliance. Mem.: ACLU, Sierra Club, Phi Alpha Delta. Democrat. Congregationalist. Home: 8917 N Hassett Ave Oklahoma City OK 73131 Office Phone: 405-478-1177. Personal E-mail: anneventers@yahoo.com.

**VENTI, CONNIE FRANCES,** music educator, choral director; b. Lawrence, Kans., July 6, 1946; d. Richard Harry and Frances Marie Worl; m. Arnold Louis Venti, Apr. 3, 1971; children: Joel, Christopher, Nicholas. BA, Okla. U., Iowa, 1968; MA, San Diego State U., 1991. Tchr. Lancaster (Calif.) Sch. Dist., 1968—71; staff accompanist Palomar Coll., San Marcos, Calif., 1973—2002, adj. faculty mem., 1987—2002; soloist, sect. leader 1st Presbyn.

Ch., Oceanside, Calif., 1998—2002; dir. music ministries Ch. of Resurrection, Escondido, Calif., 2002—06, choir dir., 2006—; pvt. music tchr. San Diego County, 1986—2006, Riverside County, Calif., 2006—. Mem. choir opening ceremonies Olympics, Calif., 1984; active Temecula Valley Master Chorale, 2005—. Mem.: Nat. Assn. Tchrs. Singing, Music Tchrs.' Assn. Calif. (voice chmn. south divsn. 1998—). Democrat. Roman Catholic. E-mail: cventi746@gmail.com.

**VENTIMIGLIA, VINCENT J., JR.,** federal agency administrator; married; 5 children. BA magna cum laude, Yale U.; JD, Georgetown U. Legis. asst. to Senator Gordon Humphrey US Senate Com. on Health Issues, Washington, 1985—88; dir. Capitol Hill Improvement Partnership, 1988—90; staff atty. US Sentencing Commn., 1990—94; counsel to Senator Dan Coats US Senate Labor and Human Resources Com., 1995—98; dir. Govt. Affairs Office Medtronic, Inc., 1998—2001; health policy dir. Health Policy Team Senate Health Edn. Labor and Pensions Com., 2001—05; policy dir. Senate Budget Com., 2005—06; asst. sec. for legis. US Dept. Health & Human Services, 2006—. Office: HHS 200 Independence Ave SW Washington DC 20201 Office Phone: 202-690-7627. Office Fax: 202-690-7380.

**VENTO, M. THÉRÈSE,** lawyer; b. N.Y.C., June 30, 1951; d. Anthony Joseph and Margaret (Stechert) V.; m. Peter Michael MacNamara, Dec. 23, 1977; children: David Miles, Elyse Anne. BS, U. Fla., 1974, JD, 1976. Bar: Fla. 1977, U.S. Dist. Ct. (so. and mid. dists.) Fla. 1982, U.S. Ct. Appeals (5th and 11th cirs.) 1981, U.S. Supreme Ct. 1985. Clk. to presiding justice U.S. Dist. Ct. (so. dist.) Fla., Miami, 1976-78; assoc Mahoney, Hadlow & Adams, 1978-79, Shutts & Bowen LLP, 1979-84, ptnr., 1985-95; founding ptnr. Gallwey Gillman Curtis & Vento, P.A., 1995—2004; ptnr. Shutts & Bowen, LLP, 2004—. Trustee Miami Art Mus., 1988—, v.p., 1999—; trustee The Beacon Coun., 1995-97, Law Sch. Alumni Coun., U. Fla., 1994-2004. Fellow Am. Bar Found.; mem. Dade County Bar Assn. (dir. young lawyers sect. 1978-83, editor newsletter 1981-83), Fla. Assn. for Women Lawyers, Fla. Bar Assn. (bd. govs., young lawyers div. 1983-85, civil procedure rules com. 1983-90, exec. coun. trial lawyers sect. 1996-2004), The Miami Forum (v.p. 1987-88, bd. dirs. 1989-91, co-pres. 2001-2002). Home: 3908 Main Hwy Miami FL 33133-6513 Office: Shutts & Bowen LLP 201 S Biscayne Blvd Ste1500 Miami FL 33131 Office Phone: 305-347-7318. E-mail: TVento@shutts-law.com.

**VENTO, SERGIO,** ambassador; b. May 30, 1938; m. Maria Magdalena Zelent; 2 children. M Polit. Sci., U. Rome. Cabinet sec. State Fgn. Affairs, Italy, 1963—67; 2d sec. then 1st sec. Italian Embassy, The Hague, Netherlands, 1967—70; Italian consul Buenos Aires, 1970—72; counsellor Italian Embassy, Ankara, 1972—75; with Italian Fgn. Min., 1975—79; 1st counsellor permanent Italian del. Orgn. Coop. and Devel. Eruope, 1979—85; min. plenipoteniary 2d class, 1985—87; min. fin. min., 1987—89; diplomatic counsel Italy's Prime Min., 1988; chief of mission Italian Embassy, Serbia and Montenegro, 1989—92; diplomatic counsellor Prime Min. Italy, 1992—95; amb. to France, 1995—99; permanent rep. UN, N.Y.C., 1999—2003; Italian amb. to U.S., 2003—. Italian rep. Halifax and Lyon Summits Group of Seven. Office: Embassy of Italy 3000 Whitehaven St Washington DC 20008

**VENTO-BENTE, CHRIS,** director, department chairman; b. Milw., Dec. 31, 1951; d. Frank and Helen Rose Vento; m. Ross Bente, Oct. 14, 1989. BA, Mt. Mary Coll., Milw., 1974; MS in Adminstrv. Leadership and Curriculum, U. Wis., Milw., 1988. Cert. tchr. history, Spanish secondary edn., prin. K-12, adminstr. Spanish tchr. Elmbrook Sch. Dist., Brookfield, Wis., 1974—2000; secondary coord. West Allis-West Milw. Schs., West Allis/West Milw. 2000—03, dir. instrn., 2003—. Office: West Allis West Milwaukee Schs 9333 W Lincoln Ave Milwaukee WI 53227-2303

**VENTURA, JESSE (JAMES JANOS),** former governor; b. Mpls., July 15, 1951; s. George and Bernice Janos; m. Terry Ventura; children: Tyrel, Jade. Student, North Hennepin C.C. Profl. wrestler, 1973-84; ret.; gov. State of Minn., St. Paul, 1999—2003; host The Jesse Ventura Show, 2003—. Actor starring in several films including Predator; radio talk show host. Mayor City of Brooklyn Park, Minn., 1990-95; bd. advisors Make a Wish of Minn.; vol. football coach Champlin Park H.S. Served with USN, USNR. Mem. Am. Fedn. of TV and radio Announcers, Screen Actors Guild. Independent.

**VENTURA, RODNEY,** design director, organist, conductor, accompanist; m. Jo-Ann Ferrara, Aug. 9, 1966; 1 child, Heather Flinchum. BA in Music Edn., Wagner Coll., 1966. Musical set design dir. Adirondack Ctrl. Sch., Boonville, NY, 1988—; ch. organist, choir dir. 1st Presbyn. Ch., 1989—; sch. choir accompanist Adirondack Ctrl. Sch., 1991—, Holland Patent Ctrl. Sch., Holland Patent, 1991—; condr. Voices River Mans Chorus, Lowville, 2001—. Elder 1st Presbyn. Ch., 1990—2004. Mem.: NY State Sch. Music Assn., Am. Choral Dirs. Assn.

**VENTURA, ROLAND P.,** music educator; b. Long Beach, Calif., Apr. 24, 1969; m. Angel F. Conway, Nov. 5, 1994; children: Ryan Alexander, Aurielle Rebecka. B in Music Edn., Troy (Ala.) State U., 1995, M in Music Edn., 1997. Asst. band dir. Chrales Henderson HS, Troy, 1997; asst. dir. bands S. Effingham HS and Mid. Sch., Guyton, Ga., 1997—99, Washington/Shiver Mid. Sch., Cairo, Ga., 1999—2002, Cairo HS, 1999—2002; dir. bands Salem HS, Virginia Beach, Va., 2002—; instrumental tchr. Visual and Performing Art Acad., Virginia Beach, 2004—. Musician: Thomasville (Ga.) Winds, 1999—2002, Va. Wind Symphony, 2002—, Tidewater Winds, 2005—. Mem.: Music Educators Nat. Conf. Office: Salem HS 1993 Sun Devil Dr Virginia Beach VA 23464 E-mail: roland.ventura@vbschools.com.

**VENTURI, ROBERT,** architect; b. Phila., June 25, 1925; s. Robert C. and Vanna (Lanzetta) Venturi; m. Denise Lakofski, July 23, 1967; 1 child, James Charles. Grad., Episcopal Acad., 1943; AB summa cum laude, Princeton U., 1947, MFA, 1950, DFA (hon.), 1983, Oberlin Coll., 1977, Yale U., 1979, U. Pa., 1980; Laurea Honoris Causa in Architecture, U. Rome "La Sapienza", 1994. Designer firms of Oskar Stonorov, Eero Saarinen and Assos., Louis I. Kahn, 1950—58; ptnr. firm Venturi, Cope & Lippincott, Phila., 1958—61, Venturi and Short, Phila., 1961—64, Venturi and Rauch, Phila., 1964—80, Venturi, Rauch & Scott Brown, Phila., 1980—89, Venturi, Scott Brown and Assocs., Inc., 1989—; from asst. to assoc. prof. architecture U. Pa., 1957—65; Charlotte Shepherd Davenport prof. architecture Yale, 1966—70. Author: Complexity and Contradiction in Architecture, 1966, Iconography and Electronics upon a Generic Architecture, 1996; co-author (with Denise Scott Brown and Steven Izenour): Learning from Las Vegas, 1972, with Denise Scott Brown and Steven Izenour: 2d edit., 1977;; co-author: (with Denise Scott Brown) A View from the Campidoglio, Selected Essays, 1953-84, Architecture as Signs and Systems for a Mannerist Time, 2004, author (others, also articles); prin. works include Vanna Venturi House, Phila., 1961, Guild House, 1961, Humanities Bldg., SUNY, 1972, Franklin Ct., Phila., 1972, addition to Allen Meml. Art Mus., Oberlin Coll., 1973, Inst. for Sci. Info. Corp. Hdqs., Phila., 1978, Gordon Wu Hall, Princeton U., 1980, Seattle Art Mus., 1984, The Nat. Gallery, Sainsbury Wing, London, 1986, Fisher and Bendheim Halls, Princeton U., 1986, Gordon and Virginia MacDonald Med. Rsch. Labs. (with Payette Assocs.), UCLA, 1986, Charles P. Stevenson Jr. Libr., Bard Coll., 1989, Roy and Diana Vagelos Labs. IAST (with Payette Assocs.), U. Pa., 1990, Regional Govt. Bldg., Toulouse, France, 1992, Kirifuri Resort Facilities, Nikko, Japan, 1992, Trabant U. Ctr., U. Del., Newark, 1992, Meml. Hall Restoration and Addition, Harvard U., 1992, The Barnes Found. Restoration and Renovation, Merion, Pa., 1993, Disney Celebration (Fla.) Bank, 1993, Gonda (Goldschmied) Neuroscience and Genetics Rsch. Ctr. (with Lee, Burkhart, Liu Inc.), UCLA, 1993, Princeton Campus Ctr., Princeton U., 1996, Anlyan Ctr. for Med. Rsch. and Edn., Yale U. Sch. Medicine, 1998, (with Payette Assocs.) Master Plan and Buildings for U. Mich., 1997—, Baker/Berry Libr., Dartmouth Coll., 1996, Woodmere Art Mus. addition, 2000, Biomed. Rsch. Bldg., U. Ky., 2000, Dumbarton Oaks Libr. Expansion, Washington, D.C., 2001, Stuart Country Day School Theater/Auditorium/Sanctuary, Princeton, N.J., 2001, Lehigh Valley Hosp.-

Muhlenberg, Allentown, Pa., 2002. Trustee Am. Acad. Rome, 1966—71. Decorated comdr. Order Arts and Letters (France); recipient Nat. Medal of Arts, 1992, Pritzker Architecture prize, 1991, Benjamin Franklin medal, The Royal Soc. for Encouragement of Arts, Mfrs. and Commerce, 1993, Vincent J. Scully prize, 2002; fellow Rome Prize Am. Acad., Rome, 1954—56. Fellow: AIA (award 1974, 1977, 1978), Accademia Nazionale di San Luca, Am. Acad. Arts and Scis., Am. Acad. of Arts and Letters, Royal Inc. Architects of Scotland (hon.), Royal Inst. Brit. Architects (hon.), Am. Acad. in Rome; mem.: European Acad. Scis. and Arts, Phi Beta Kappa. Office: Venturi Scott Brown & Assocs Inc 4236 Main St Philadelphia PA 19127-1603 Office Phone: 215-487-0400. Business E-Mail: venturi@vsba.com.

**VENTURINI, JUDITH ANNE,** education educator; b. Oakland, Calif. d. Arthur Francis Venturini and Germaine Junet. BS, Calif. State U., Hayward, 1969, MS in Phys. Edn., 1985, MS in Edn. Leadership, 1991; MS in Edn. Nat. U., San Jose, Calif., 1999. Practitioner of science of mind RScP. Tchr. adminstrv. intern Redwood City (Calif.) Elem. Sch. Dist., 1970—91; ednl. cons., exec. dir. Kids-at-Heart, Fremint, Calif., 1991—94; D.A.T.E. coord. Hayward Unified Sch. Dist., 1994; regional dir. Sonoma County Office of Edn., Santa Rosa, Calif., 1994—95; prin. tchr. San Jose Unified Sch. Dist., 1995—2000; spl. edn. tchr. for autistic students Santa Clara County Office of Edn., San Jose, 2001—02; adj. prof. Calif. State U., Hayward, 2000—, Nat. U., San Jose, 2000—, Nat. Hispanic U., San Jose, 2000—. Facilities chair Bay Area Career Women, San Francisco, 1987—90; chair Sonoma County Phys. Edn. Com., Santa Rosa, Calif., 1994—95; dir. Sonoma County Office of Edn. Gang Prevention Network Task Force, Santa Rosa, 1994—95. Contbr. poetry to anthologies. Bd. dirs. Ardenwood Homeowners, Fremont, Calif., 1987—88; practitioner, divinity student Ctr. of Positive Living, 2000—. Recipient multiple honors in athletics, Playmates award. Calif. Dept. Edn., 1994, Healthy Start award, 1994, 1996, award for inspirational programs for children, Housing Authority of Santa Clara County, 2000. Mem.: NEA, Calif. Tchrs. Assn. Avocations: dancesport, poetry, art, golf, writing songs. Home: 5206 Tacoma Ln Fremont CA 94555 Office: Kids-at-Heart 5206 Tacoma Ln Fremont CA 94555 Personal E-mail: junu@earthlink.net.

**VENTURINI, TISHA LEA,** professional soccer player; b. Modesto, Calif., Mar. 3, 1973; Degree in phys. edn., U. N.C. Mem. U.S. Women's Nat. Soccer Team. Mem. championship team CONCACAF, Montreal, 1994. Named Player of Yr., Mo. Athletic Club, 1994; recipient Gold medal, Centennial Olympic Games, 1996, Silver medal, World Univ. Games, 1993, Hermann trophy, 1994. Achievements include 1999 World Cup Champion. Office: c/o US Soccer Fedn 1801 S Prairie Ave # 1811 Chicago IL 60616-1319

**VENZAGO, MARIO,** conductor, music director; b. Zurich, Switzerland, 1948; m. Marianne Venzago; children: Mario, Gabriel. Studied with, Hans Swarowsky, Vienna, 1973. Music dir. Basel Symphony Orch., 1995—2003, Heidelberg Opera, 1986—89, Deutsche Kammerphilharmonie, Bremen, 1989—92, Graz Opera Ho., 1990—95, Euskadi Nat. Opera, Spain, 1998—2001, Ind. Symphony Orch., 2002—, Swedish Nat. Orch., 2003—. Guest conductor Berlin Philharmonic, Leipzig Gewandhaus Orchester, London Philharmonic, City of Birmingham Symphony, Orchestre de la Suisse Romande, Phila. Orch., Tonhalle Orchestra Zurich, Tokyo's NHK Symphony, Berlin's Komische Oper, Salzburg Festival, Hannover Radio-Philharmonie, invited by Kurt Masur, Leipzig; guest condr.: Boston Symphony, Helsinki Philharmonic, Helsinki Radio; Am. debut Hollywood Bowl, 1988, appeared N.J. Symphony, Ind. Symphony, Fla. Philharmonic, 1988; dir.: Balt. Symphony, 1995 (named artistic dir. symphony's summer festival, 2000); prin. conductor Winterthur City Orch., Lucerne Opera Ho., Orchestre de la Suisse Romande. Recipient award, Diapason d'or, awards, Grand Prix du Disque, Edison prize. Office: Ind Symphony Orch 32 E Washington St Ste 600 Indianapolis IN 46204-2919 Business E-Mail: mvenvago@IndianapolisSymphony.org.*

**VÉR, ISTVÁN LÁSZLÓ,** acoustical engineer, consultant; b. Tápiószecső, Hungary, Dec. 22, 1934; came to U.S., 1965; s. István and Erzsebet G. (Darázs) V.; 1 child, Kristina M. BSEE, Tech. U., Budapest, 1956; MSEE, Tech. U., Aachen, Germany, 1960; PhD in Acoustics, Tech. U., Munich, 1963. R&D engr. Rohde and Schwarz, Munich, 1960-65; prin. cons. BBN Techs., Cambridge, Mass., 1965—2000; ind. cons. acoustics, noise and vibration control, 2000—. Vis. scientist Indian Inst. Sci., Bangalore, India, 2005. Author: editor: Noise & Vibration Control Engineering, 1992, 2005; holder patents. Recipient U.S. Sr. Scientist award Alexander von Humboldt Found., Germany, 1978, Best Paper award Am. Soc. Heating and Refrigeration Engring., 1979. Fellow Acoustical Soc.; mem. Inst. Noise Control Engring. USA (dir. 1976-77), European Acoustics Assn. Avocations: literature, philosophy, travel, tennis. Office Phone: 978-568-0556.

**VERA NEGRON, SANDRA,** literature educator, translator; d. Luis Norberto Vera Nieves and Fredeswinda Negron Cruz. BA in English/Lit., Inter Am. U. P.R., 1993, MA in English/TESL, 1998. Translator, copywriter, proofreader Cmty. Rels. & Press Office U. P.R.-Rio Piedras Campus, 1991—93; tchr. elem. sch. ESL San Juan 3 Sch. Dist., 1995—98; instr. English E.D.P. Coll. Hato Rey Campus, 1998; lectr. English Universidad del Este, Carolina, PR, 1998—2003; instr. English Universidad Metropolitana, Cupey Campus, 1999, InterAm. U. P.R., Metropolitan Campus, 1999—2004, U. P.R., Carolina, 2000—02, Caribbean U., Carolina Campus, 2002, Universidad del Este, Carolina, PR, 2002—. Asst. translator Universidad del Este, Carolina, 2000—. Mem.: NOW, MLA, Witches Against Religious Discrimination, Internat. Fund for Animal Welfare, Am. Anti-Vivisection Soc., People for the Ethical Treatment Animals. Wicca. Avocation: literature. E-mail: saqqara@prtc.net.

**VERANO, ANTHONY FRANK,** retired banker; b. West Harrison, N.Y., Jan. 4, 1931; s. Frank and Rose (Viscomi) Verano; m. Clara Cosentino, July 8, 1951; children: Rosemarie, Diana Lynn. Student, Am. Inst. Banking, 1956-60, Bank Adminstrn. Inst., U. Wis., 1962-64, RCA Programmers Sch., 1965, Burroughs Programmers Sch., 1965, N.J. Bankers Data Processing Sch., 1966-68. With County Trust Co., White Plains, NY, 1949-61, sr. auditor, 1960-61; with State Nat. Bank Conn., Bridgeport, 1961—, auditor, 1962-79, exec. auditor, 1979—, Conn. Bank & Trust Co., 1983—; from v.p., auditor to sr. v.p., auditor Gateway Bank, Newtown, Conn., 1987-94, ret. 1996. Tchr. bank auditing Am. Inst. Banking, 1976-78. Mem. adv. bd. Norwalk Community Coll., 1968—. Served with USN, 1951-52. Mem. Bank Adminstrn. Inst. (dir. Stamford chpt. 1967-68, sec. Western Conn. chpt. 1968-69, treas. 1969-70, v.p. 1970-71, pres. 1971-72), Am. Acctg. Assn., Inst. Internal Auditors (cert. bank auditor, cert. bank compliance officer, cert. fin. svcs. auditor). Home: 224 Columbus Ave West Harrison NY 10604-2614 *It is difficult to define the elements of success. There are those who say success is achieved through drive and ambition only. However, those who have achieved their goals in life using only these two principles have probably destroyed more than they have created. Success, I feel, is achieved when drive and ambition are tempered with honesty, fairness, and respect for others. An individual must have a sense of dedication not only to his work and for those with whom he works but, most importantly, for those who work for him. This has been my philosophy in achieving my success.*

**VERBA, SIDNEY,** political science professor, academic administrator; b. Bklyn., May 26, 1932; s. Morris Harold and Recci (Salman) Verba; m. E. Cynthia Winston, June 17, 1955; children: Margaret Lynn, Ericka Kim, Martina Claire. BA, Harvard U., 1953; MA, Princeton U., 1955, PhD, 1959. Asst. prof. polit. sci. Princeton U., 1960-63, assoc. prof., 1963-64; prof. Stanford U., 1964-68, U. Chgo., 1968-72; prof. govt. Harvard U., 1972—; chmn. dept. govt., 1976-80, now Carl H. Pforzheimer U. Prof., assoc. dean Faculty Arts and Sciences, 1981—84; now dir. Harvard U. Libr. Chmn. bd. dirs. Harvard U. Press, 1991-2005; chmn. policy com. Social Sci. Rsch. Coun., 1980-86; mem. Commn. on Behavioral and Social Sciences, NRC, 1986-91; Commn. on Preservation and Access, chair com. on internat. conflict and cooperation, NRC, 1991-93; vis. com. MIT Polit. Sci. Dept.; bd. dirs. Social Sci. Rsch. Coun.; Tanner Lectr., Oxford, 1998. Author: Small Groups and Political Behavior, 1961, The Civic Culture, 1963, Caste, Race and

Politics, 1969, Participation in America, 1972 (Gladys Kammerer Award, Am. Polit. Sci. Assn., 1972), Vietnam and the Silent Majority, 1972, The Changing American Voter, 1976 (Woodrow Wilson Found. Award, Am. Polit. Sci. Found., 1976), Participation and Political Equality, 1978, Injury to Insult, 1979, Introduction to American Government, 1983, Equality in America, 1985, Elites and the Idea of Equality, 1987, Designing Social Inquiry, 1994, Voice and Equality, 1995, The Private Roots of Public Action, 2001. Recipient Johan Skytte Prize in Polit. Sci., Skytte Found., 2002, Guggenheim Fellow, 1980-81. Fellow: Am. Acad. Arts and Sciences; mem.: NAS (chair social and polit. sci. sect. 2002-), Am. Philos. Soc., Am. Polit. Sci. Assn. (exec. coun. 1971-74, v.p. 1979-81, pres.-elect 1993-94, pres. 1994-95, James Madison Award 1993, Warren Miller Award 2000), Internat. Studies Assn. (v.p. 1971-72, John Skytte prize 2002). Jewish. Office: Harvard U Libr Office Dir Wadsworth House 1340 Massachusetts Ave Cambridge MA 02138 also: Polit Sci Dept Harvard Univ 1737 Cambridge St Cambridge MA 02138 Office Phone: 617-495-4421. Business E-Mail: sverba@harvard.edu.*

**VERBIN, JEFFREY HAROLD,** lawyer; b. Chgo., July 28, 1948; s. Marvin Verbin and Eleanor (Chernoff) Cohen; m. Jacqueline Rochelle Lewis, Aug. 23, 1970; children: Matt, Dana, Alexis. BS, U. Ill., 1971; JD, Washington U., St. Louis, 1974. Bar: Ill. 1974, Calif. 1979, Ariz. 1981. With firm Altheimer & Gray, Chgo., 1974-79, Kaufman & Waring, San Diego, 1979-80, O'Connor Cavanagh Anderson Westover Killingsworth & Beshears, Phoenix, 1981—, sr. ptnr.; now mng. shareholder Greenberg Traurig LLP, Phoenix. Co-chair dinner Multiple Sclerosis Soc., Phoenix, 1992; vice chair 39th ann. testimonial dinner NCCJ, Phoenix, 1992; mem. legal and fin. com. Temple Chai, Phoenix, 1991-92. Mem. ABA (comml. fin. svcs., consumer fin. svcs., banking law and savs. instns. coms. of bus. law sect.). Ill. State Bar Assn., State Bar Ariz. chair spl. subcom. of bus. law sect., mem. legis. subcom. of bus. law sect., chair bus. law sect. 1988-89), State Bar Calif., Maricopa County Bar Assn., Order of Coif. Jewish. Avocation: sports. Office: Greenberg Traurig LLP Ste 700 2375 E Camelback Rd Phoenix AZ 85016-9000 Office Phone: 602-445-8202. Office Fax: 602-445-8100. Business E-Mail: verbinj@gtlaw.com.

**VERBINSKI, GORE,** film director; b. NYC, Mar. 16, 1964; Grad., UCLA Film Sch., 1987. Former punk band guitarist; worked on various advertising campaigns; creator of the Budweiser frogs. Dir., writer: (films) The Ritual, 1996; dir.: Mousehunt, 1997, The Mexican, 2001, The Ring, 2002, Pirates of the Caribbean: The Curse of the Black Pearl, 2003, The Weather Man, 2005, Pirates of the Caribbean: Dead Man's Chest, 2006. Recipient 4 Clio awards.*

**VERBOV, LEV FALKOVICH,** metallurgical engineer, freelance/self-employed translator, writer; b. Leningrad, Russia, Jan. 10, 1937; came to U.S., 1977; s. Falka Shevelevich and Elka Abramovna Verbova; m. Larisa Ivanovna Fedkushova, Nov. 26, 1990; 1 child, Kristina Kulbe. MS in Metall. Engring., State Polytechnic U., St. Petersburg, Russia, 1962. Sr. engr. All-Union Inst. Aluminum, Magnesium and Electrode Industry, St. Petersburg, 1962-77; engr.-scientist Aluminum Co. of Am., New Kensington, Pa., 1979-82; asst. editor Chem. Abstracts Svcs., Columbus, Ohio, 1985-87; cons. R&D scientist ECC Am., Inc., Sandersville, Ga., 1988-90; clk., team mem. Local Census Ctr., Bklyn., 1999-2000; freelance writer Bklyn., 1966—; freelance translator, 1982—. Author: (books) Commercial Star, 1999, Swan Song of Ugly Duckling, 2000; composer: Solemn Melody, 1999; patentee in field. E-mail: lverbov@aol.com.

**VERBURG, EDWIN ARNOLD,** management consultant; b. Lakehurst, NJ, Oct. 6, 1945; s. Edwin Donald Verburg and Dorothy (Orrell) Hoodless; m. Joyce Elaine Majack, Sept. 14, 1968; children: Adelle Kristine, Wendi Elizabeth. BS, Calif. Poly. U., 1968; M in City Planning, U. Calif., Berkeley, 1970; D in Pub. Adminstrn., George Washington U., 1975. Asst. planner City of Inglewood, Calif., 1970-71; planner City of Glendale, Calif., 1971-72; grad. assoc. U.S. Army Corps Engrs., Washington, 1974-75; mgr. fiscal analysis Met. Washington Coun. Govt., 1975-77; sr. program analyst U.S. Fish and Wildlife Svc., Washington, 1977-79, asst. divsn. chief, 1979-80, divsn. chief, 1980-82, asst. dir. planning and budget, 1982-86, dep. asst. dir. policy budget and adminstrn., 1986-87; dir. office of fin. U.S. Dept. Treas., Washington, 1987-88, dir. fin. svc. directorate, 1988-91, dir. fin. svc. directorate, dep. CFO, 1991-95; assoc. adminstr. adminstrn. FAA, 1995-98; prin. ptnr. Avant Mgmt. Group, Inc., 1998-99; prin., fedn. govt. svc. Kelly, Anderson & Assocs., 1999—2002, v.p., 2003—, trustee, bd. dirs., 2005—. Author: Local State and Federal Fiscal Flows, 5 Vols., 1976; contbr. articles to profl. jours. Recipient Disting. Pub. Svc. award George Washington U., Sch. Bus. and Pub. Mgmt., 1994, Sec. of Treasury Disting Svc. award, 1995, Fin. Mgmt. Svc. Commr. award, 1996. Mem. Am. Inst. Cert. Planners, Am. Planning Assn. (cert. govt. fin. mgr., Merit award Calif. chpt. 1973, First award Nat. Capital area chpt. 1980, Peer award for pub. svc. Dept. of Treasury 1990, sec. of treas. cert. appreciation 1991, Pres.'s Meritorious Svc. award 1991, Commr. Citation Fin. Mgmt. Svc. 1996, Pres. award Combined Fed. Campaign 1997), Kiwanis (Arlington chpt. bd. dirs. 1999-2001, v.p. 2001-02, pres.-elect 2002-03, pres. 2003-04, Capitol dist. lt. gov. 20th divsn. capitol dist. Kiwanis Internat. 2005-06, Hixson award 2004) Home: 538 N Oakland St Arlington VA 22203-2219 Office: Kelly Andersen & Assocs Inc 424 N Washington St Alexandria VA 22314-2312

**VERBY, JOHN EDWARD, JR.,** physician, educator; b. St. Paul, May 24, 1923; s. John E. and Amy (Martin) V.; m. Jane Verby, June 15, 1946; children: John E. III, Steve, Ruth, Karl. BA, Carleton Coll., Northfield, Minn., 1944; BS, U. Minn., 1946, MB, 1947, MD, 1948. Diplomate Am. Bd. Family Practice. Intern Hennepin County Gen. Hosp., Mpls., 1947-49; pvt. family practice Litchfield, Minn., 1949-51, 53-54; ptnr. Olmsted Med.-Surg. Group, Rochester, Minn., 1954-69; assoc. prof. U. Minn., Mpls., 1969-73, acting head family practice/community medicine asst. head, 1970-71, 71-72, mem. Grad. Sch. faculty, 1971—; prof. Dept. Family Practice/Community Health, U. Minn., 1973—. Cons. and lectr. in field; vis. prof. Welsh Nat. Sch. Medicine, Cardiff, Wales, 1977-78, N.Y. State U., Syracuse, 1988-89; developer Rural Physician Assoc. Program W.Va. Med. Sch., 1989-90. Author: Medical Examination Book in Family Practice, 1972, 4th edit., 1983; co-author: How to Talk to Doctors, 1978; contbr. articles to profl. jours. Lay liturgist Hillcrest United Mth. Ch., 1980—. With USN, 1942-45; 1st lt. U.S.Army, 1951-53. Grantee U. Minn. Hosps. and Clinics, 1985-89, Minn. Med. Found., 1980, 84, Fed. Health Professions Project, 1972-76, others; recipient Cert. Appreciation U. Minn. Bd. Regents, 1992. Fellow Am. Acad. Family Physicians (charter, Thomas W. Johnson award 1991), Am. Geriatric Soc.; mem. AMA (Physicians Recognition award 1969-85), Am. Rural Health Assn. (award 1981), Minn. Acad. Family Physicians (Tchr. of Yr. award 1988, John E. Verby award 1987), Internat. Soc. Gen. Medicine (bd. dirs. 1995-), Hennepin County Med. Soc. Home: 9609 Washburn Ave S Minneapolis MN 55431-2460

**VERCAMMEN, KENNETH ALBERT,** lawyer, prosecutor; b. Edison, NJ, Aug. 7, 1959; s. Albert Peter and Carol Ann (Rasche) V.; m. Cynthia Ann Bachenski, July 9, 1989. BS, U. Scranton, 1981; JD, Univ. Del. Law Sch., 1985. Bar: N.J. 1985, Pa. 1985, N.Y. 1986, D.C. 1987; cert. mediator N.J. Superior Ct., 1997-. Mng. atty. Cranbury, NJ, 1990—; prosecutor Township of Cranbury, Middlesex County, NJ 1991—99; spl. acting prosecutor Delaware County, Pa. District Office, Middlesex County Probation Dept., Scranton Dist. Magistrate Office, Woodbridge, East Brunswick, Metuchen, South Brunswick, Clark, Berkeley; acting assoc. prosecutor Carteret Mcpl. Ct., Middlesex County, NJ, 2000. Adj. prof. Middlesex County Coll., Edison, 1990-91, 2001; instr. criminal law and procedure and bus. law; mem. com. mcpl. ct. edn. N.J. Supreme Ct., 1990-97; spkr. litig. engagements; wills, elder law and probate. Author 132 separate law rev. and legal periodicals articles to profl. jours. including N.J. Law Jour., ABA Barrister, N.J. Lawyer, ABA Law Practice Mgmt., Dictum; editor N.J. Municipal Ct. Law Review, 1993-; author, DWI & Drug Cases, 2005. Winner of NJ State Bar Gen. Practitioner of Yr. award, 2002, Atty. of Yr. award NJ Bar Assn. Mcpl. Ct., 2006. Mem.:

N.J. State Bar Assn. (chair mcpl. ct. sect.), Middlesex Mcpl. Prosecutor's Assn. (co-chmn. mcpl. ct. practice com. 1997—, mem. bd. trustees 2000—). Avocations: cross-country running, soccer. Office: 2053 Woodbridge Ave Edison NJ 08817

**VERCAUTEREN, RICHARD FRANK,** career officer; b. Manchester, Feb. 9, 1945; s. Louis P. and Janet (Beliveau) V.; m. Gail Anne Settoon, June 3, 1972. BA in Sociology, Providence Coll., 1967; MA in Bus. Mgmt., George Washington U., 1980; MA in Internat. Studies, Georgetown U., 1996. Commd. 2d lt. USMC, 1967, advanced through grades to brig. gen., 1993; platoon comdr. 2d bn., 9th Marines, Vietnam, 1968; comdg. officer Rifle Co., Hawaii, 1971-73; mil. observer UN, Egypt, Israel, Lebanon, 1976-78; comdg. officer Spl. Task Force, S.Am., 1982; aide de camp Marine Forces Atlanic, Norfolk, Va., 1982-84; bn. comdr. 3d bn., 2nd Marines, Camp Lejeune, N.C., 1985-87; regional comdr. Embassy Guards SubSahara Africa, Nairobi, Africa, 1987-90; dep. dir. plans Hdqs., USMC, Washington, 1990-92, dir. plans, 1990-92; comdg. officer 2nd Marine Regiment, Camp Lejeune, 1992-93; comdg. gen. 1st Marine Exped Brigade, Honolulu, 1993-95; dir. stragety and plans Hdqr. USMC, 1995—. Mem. exec. bd. Capitol dist. Boy Scouts Am., Washington, 1991-92; sr. counselor Seminar XXII, MIT, Washington, 1995-96; bd. dirs. Girl Scouts U.S. Decorated Silver Star medal, Legion of Merit, Distinguished Svc. Medal; recipient Holland M. Smith award Navy League, 1982; MIT Ctr. Internat. Tech. Studies fellow in fgn. politics, 1991, fellow in nat. security studies Harvard U., 1995. Mem. Navy League (bd. dirs.), Army-Navy Club (Washington), Oahu Country Club (Honolulu), Plaza Club, Rotary. Avocations: running, golf, skiing, history, travel. Home: PO Box 222 Occoquan VA 22125-0222

**VERCELLOTTI, JOHN RAYMOND,** chemist, researcher; b. Joliet, Ill., May 2, 1933; s. Joseph Francis and Mary Teresa (Walowski) V.; m. Sharon Cecile Vergez, Sept. 3, 1966; children: Ellen Theresa, Paul Auguste. BA, St. Bonaventure U., 1955; MS, Marquette U., 1960; PhD, Ohio State U., 1963. Lectr., rsch. assoc. Ohio State U., Columbus, 1963-64; asst. prof. Marquette U., Milw., 1964-67; assoc. prof. U. Tenn., Knoxville, 1967-70; prof. Va. Poly. Inst. & State U., Blacksburg, 1970-79; vis. prof. Inst. G. Ronzoni, Milan, 1977-78; sr. scientist Gulf South Res. Inst., New Orleans, 1980-85; rsch. chemist, rsch. leader So. Regional Rsch. Ctr. USDA, New Orleans, 1985-96, collaborator, 1999—. V.p. and sr. chemist V-Labs Inc., Covington, La., 1980-85, 96—; sr. rsch. advisor Sugar Processing Rsch. Inst., Inc., New Orleans, 1996-99, 2001--; adj. prof. chemistry and physics S.E. La. U., Hammond, 1986—. Contbr. articles to profl. jours., chapters to books. U. Tenn. minority cols. grantee, 1968-70, NSF grantee, 1964—. Fellow Sigma Xi; mem. Am. Chem. Soc. (sec. 1968-90, Melville L. Wolfrom award 1994), Inst. Food Technologists. Democrat. Roman Catholic. Achievements include research on food flavor quality and agricultural commodity utilization, origin of flavor from carbohydrates, lipid oxidation products, and peptides. Home: 113 E 25th Ave Covington LA 70433-2819 Office: V-Labs Inc 423 N Theard St Covington LA 70433-2837 Office Phone: 985-893-0533. Business E-Mail: v-labs@v-labs.com.

**VERCOUTERE, WENONAH ANNREA,** research scientist; b. Santa Rosa, Calif., Aug. 11, 1970; d. Louis Charles and Mary Elizabeth Vercoutere. BS, Sonoma State U., Rohnert Park, Calif., 1995; PhD, U. of Calif., 2001. Postdoctoral rschr., gravitational biology NASA Ames Rsch. Ctr., Moffett Field, Calif., 2000—03, space life scis. rsch. scientist, 2003—. Search and rescue specialist Disaster Assistance Rescue Team, Moffett Field, 2001—06. Mem.: Am. Soc. for Gravitational and Space Biology (assoc.; bd. dirs. 2004—). Achievements include patents for single molecule detector for DNA sequence information. Office: NASA Ames Rsch Ctr Mail Stop 236-7 Moffett Field CA 94035-1000 Office Phone: 650-604-6014. Home Fax: 650-604-3159; Office Fax: 650-604-3159. Business E-Mail: wvercoutere@mail.arc.nasa.gov.

**VERCRUYSSE, RAYMOND JAMES,** director; b. Rochester, NY, Sept. 9, 1954; s. Raymond E. and Helen N. Vercruysse. BA in Econs., Iona Coll., 1977; MA in Guidance and Counseling, Cath. U. Am., 1985; EdD in Cath. Ednl. Leadership, U. San Francisco, 2004. Tchr. Power Meml. H.S., NYC, 1977—80, Bergen Cath. H.S., Oradell, NJ, 1980—81; tchr., counselor All Hallow's Inst., Bronx, 1981—87; vocat. dir. Congregation Christian Bros., New Rochelle, NY, 1987—91; pres. Bishop Kearny H.S., Rochester, NY, 1991—2000; dir. Inst. Cath. Ednl. Leadership San Francisco, 2004—. Office: Univ San Francisco 2130 Fulton St San Francisco CA 94117 E-mail: rbvercruysse@usdca.edu.

**VERDE, BRIAN JAMES,** secondary school educator; b. Columbus, Ohio, Jan. 30, 1972; s. Louis James and Elvira Sue Verde; m. Katrina Kay Eichhorn, Nov. 26, 1994; 1 child, Vincent James. BS in Edn., Ohio U., Athens, 1994; MA, Winthrop U., Rock Hill, SC, 2002. Cert. tchr. Ohio Dept. Edn., 2004. Tchr. NE Mid. Sch., Charlotte, NC, 1997—2000, Parkwood H.S., Monroe, NC, 2000—04, Bexley (Ohio) H.S., 2004—. Student coun. advisor Parkwood H.S., Monroe, 2002—04; youth for change advisor Bexley H.S., 2005—. Fellow, James Madison Meml. Fellowship Found., 2001. Mem.: NEA, Phi Alpha Theta. Home: 145 Lexington Woods Dr Granville OH 43023 Office: Bexley High School 326 S Cassingham Rd Bexley OH 43209 Personal E-mail: bverde@bexley.k12.oh.us.

**VERDE, MICHAEL L,** lawyer; b. NYC, Jan. 26, 1959; BA cum laude, Columbia Coll., 1980; JD magna cum laude, NY Law Sch., 1988. Bar: NY 1989, Maine 1992, US Dist. Ct., So. and Ea. Dist. NY 1989. Ptnr. Katten Muchin Zavis Rosenman, NYC. Mem.: ABA. Office: Katten Muchin Zavis Rosenman 575 Madison Ave New York NY 10022 Office Phone: 212-940-8541. Office Fax: 212-940-8776. E-mail: michael.verde@kmzr.com.

**VERDERBER, JOSEPH ANTHONY,** capital equipment company executive; b. Nov. 30, 1938; s. Joseph Arthur and Dorothy Louise (Buchta) V.; m. Anita Barto, Sept. 10, 1960; children: Joseph Anthony, Lisa C., Paul A. BS in Mech. Engring., MIT, 1960, MS in Mech. Engring., 1961. Registered profl. engr., Ohio. Mgr. rsch. AM Internat., Cleve., 1964-70; dir. engring. Varityper div., East Hanover, NJ, 1971-73, product mgr., 1973-77, v.p. advanced bus. devel. multigraphics div. Mt. Prospect, Ill., 1977-81, gen. mgr. imaging systems group Bedford, Mass., 1981, pres. East Hanover, NJ, 1982-88; corp. v.p. bus. devel. AM Internat., Inc., Chgo., 1988-89; pres. Am Splty. Products, Dayton, Ohio, 1989-90, Barco Graphics, Inc., Dayton, Ohio, 1990; v.p., gen. mgr. Gen. Scanning, Laser Sys. Divsn., Somerville, Mass., 1991-99; ret., 2000; CEO IBEX Process Tech., 2000. Lectr. Cleve. State U., 1962-67; chmn., SEMI New Eng. Forum, 1994-99; dir. Virtek Vision Internat., Toronto, Can. Recipient Karl Taylor Compton prize MIT, 1960; NSF fellow, 1961; named Inventor of Yr., AM Internat., Chgo., 1980. Mem. ASME, Nat. Printing Equipment and Supply Assn. (bd. dirs. 1986-88). E-mail: javerderber@yahoo.com.

**VERDERY, DAVID NORWOOD,** broadcast programming executive; b. Waco, Tex., Dec. 12, 1943; s. David Paul and Ruthe (McCawley) V.; m. Randy Lee Mahan, June 6, 1968 (div. 1970); 1 child, David Roderick. Student, Baylor U., 1961-64. Announcer KEFC, Waco, 1962-64; announcer, producer KHFI, Austin, Tex., 1964-65; announcer, prodn. dir. KIXL, Dallas, 1965-66; program dir. KVIL, Dallas, 1967, KABL, San Francisco, 1968-69; nat. program coord. The McLendon Co., Dallas, 1969-73; v.p. programming TM Programming, Dallas, 1973-80, Bonneville Broadcasting Sys., Northbrook, Ill., 1980-86; music dir. KBIG, L.A., 1985-95, asst. program dir., music dir., 1996-97, program dir., 1997; ret., 1998. Mem. Project Angel Food, L.A., 1992-94; mem. Permanent Charities Com., L.A., 1995-97, mem. Reading for the Blind, L.A., 1996-97; bd. dirs. Waco Civic Theatre, 1999-2001, v.p., 2000-01; bd. dirs. Met. Cmty. Ch., 2001-04; emperor X Royal Sovereign and Imperial Ct. of Ctrl. Tex. Empire, 2003-04. Named Adult Contemporary Music Dir. of Yr., The Gavin Report, 1992, 93. Avocations: gourmet cooking, theater, travel, musical composition, magic. Personal E-mail: wacodave@hot.rr.com.

**VERDI, ROBERT,** apparel designer, jewelry designer, television personality; b. Maplewood, NJ, Aug. 28, 1968; Grad., Fashion Inst. of Tech. Co-host Surprise by Design, Discovery Channel, 2002—03; host Full Frontal Fashion, Metro TV, 2003; guest appearances The View, Regis and Kelly, The Today Show, CNN's Headline News; co-host Emmys Live from the Red Carpet, E!, 2004; host Fashion Police, E!, 2005—. Office: E! Networks 5750 Wilshire Blvd Los Angeles CA 90036*

**VERDIER, DAVID D'OOGE,** ophthalmologist, educator; b. Grand Rapids, Mich., Jan. 22, 1949; s. Leonard D'Ooge and Anita Beatrice (Carvalho) V.; m. Beverly Deane Johnson; children: Renée Leigh, Travis D'Ooge, Eric Leonard, Nora Claire. BA in Polit. Sci., U. Mich., 1971; MD, U. Mich. Med. Sch., 1977. Resident in family practice Med. U. S.C., Charleston, 1977-80; resident in ophthalmology Pitts. Eye and Ear, U. Pitts., 1980-83; corneal and external eye fellowship U. Iowa, Iowa City, 1983-84; pvt. practice med. and surg. ophthalmology Verdier Eye Ctr. P.L.C., Grand Rapids, Mich., 1984—; clin. prof. Mich. State U. Coll. Medicine, East Lansing, 1986—. Med. dir. Mich. Tissue Bank, Lansing, Mich., 1995-98; mem. med. adv. bd. Eye Bank Assn. Am., 2003—; bd. dirs. SEECOM, 1995—, Cape Elethra Found., 2004—. Contbr. articles to profl. jours. and textbook chpts. Bd. dirs. East Grand Rapids (Mich.) Sch. Found., 1992-2000, Macatawa Bay Yacht Club, Holland, Mich., 1988-90, 94-95, Grand Rapids Art Mus., 1995-2001; bd. dirs. Macatawa Park Cottagers Assn., Holland, 1993-99, pres., 1993-98. Named to Galens Hon. Med. Soc., 1975-77. Mem. Mich. Ophthalmologic Soc. (bd. dirs. 1994-2000), Mich. State Med. Soc. (del. 1993-2000, Eye Bank Assn. Am. (med adv bd 2003—). Home: 3043 Mary St SE Grand Rapids MI 49506-3150 Office: Verdier Eye Center PLC 1000 E Paris Ave SE Ste 130 Grand Rapids MI 49546-3680

**VERDILE, VINCENT PAUL,** dean, emergency physician; b. Troy, N.Y., Aug. 13, 1955; s. Raphael Mario and Frances (Marinucci) V.; m. Louise Ann Wickware, Aug. 30, 1985. BS, Union U., 1977, MS, 1980; MD, Albany Med. Coll., 1984. Intern U. Pitts., 1984-85, resident in emergency medicine, 1985-87; assoc. med. dir. dept. pub. safety City of Pitts., 1985—93; flight physician Ctr. for Emergency Medicine, Pitts., 1988—93; chair. dept. of emergency med. Albany Med. Coll., 1993—2000, interim dean, 2000, dean, 2001—. Mem. adj. staff dept. emergency medicine Mercy Hosp., Pitts, 1987—93; med. dir., emergency med. technician Community Coll. Allegheny Coll., 1987—93; attending physician emergency dept. Presbyn.-Univ. Hosp., 1987—93; assoc. program dir. residency in emergency medicine Univ. of Pitts., 1987—93, asst. prof. medicine, 1987—93. Contbr. numerous articles to profl. jours. Mem. Soc. Acad. Emergency Medicine, Nat. Assn. Emergency Med. Svcs. Physicians (chmn. membership com. 1988—), Am. Coll. Emergency Physicians, Pa. chpt. Am. Coll. Emergency Physicians, Pa. State Med. Soc., Allegheny County Med. Soc., Am. Assn. Poison Control Ctrs. Roman Catholic. Office: Albany Med Coll Office of Dean 43 New Scotland Ave Albany NY 12208*

**VERDOORN, D.R. (SID),** food service executive; b. Albert Lea, Minn., Feb. 11, 1939; s. Cornelius Emery and Gwen (Pickell) V.; m. Carol Joyce Hoekstra, July 3, 1959; children: Jay Richard, Jeffrey Lee, James Dale. Student, Cen. Coll., Pella, Iowa. With sales C.H. Robinson Worldwide, Mpls., 1963-66, mgr. San Francisco, 1966-71, pers. dir. Mpls., 1971-75, v.p., 1975-77, pres., 1977-2000, CEO, 1977—2002, chmn., 2002—. Bd. dirs. Produce Mktg. Assocs., Newark, United Fruit and Produce, Washington. With U.S. Army, 1959-61. Republican. Avocations: hiking, water sports. Home: 28210 Woodside Rd Excelsior MN 55331-7950 Office: C H Robinson Co Inc 8100 Mitchell Rd Ste 200 Eden Prairie MN 55344-2178*

**VERDU, SERGIO,** engineering educator; b. Barcelona, Aug. 16, 1958; arrived in U.S., 1980; s. Tomas Verdu and Visitacion Lucas; m. Mercedes Paratje, Jan. 19, 1982; 1 child, Ariana. Diploma in telecom. engring., Poly. U. Barcelona, 1980; MS, U. Ill., 1982, PhD, 1984; DHL (hon.), Polytechnic U., Catalonia, 2005. Asst. prof. Princeton (NJ) U., 1984-89, assoc. prof., 1989-92, prof., 1993—. Prin. investigator U.S. Office Naval Rsch., NJ Dept. Higher Edn., U.S. Army Rsch. Office, NJ Commn. Sci. and Tech., NSF, U.S.-Israel Binational Sci. Found.; vis. prof. U. Calif., Berkeley, 1998; vis. rsch. prof. Math. Sci. Rsch. Inst., 2002. Author: Multiuser Detection, 1998, Information Theory: Fifty Years of Discovery, 1999; mem. editl. bd. Transactions on Info. Theory, 1990-94;; editor-in-chief Foundations and Trends in Comm. and Info. Theory, 2003—; contbr. numerous articles to profl. jours, chpts. to books. Recipient Nat. U. prize Ministry Edn., Spain, 1982, Presdl. Young Investigator award NSF, 1988, Frederick E. Terman award Am. Soc. Engring. Edn., 2000, Joint IEEE Comms. Info. Theory Paper award, 2007. Fellow: IEEE (Outstanding Paper award 1998, Millennium medal 2000); mem.: Info. Theory Soc. (bd. govs. 1989—99, v.p. 1995, pres. 1997, Golden Jubilee Paper award 1998, Leonard G. Abraham Paper award 2000). Office: Princeton U Dept Elec Engring Princeton NJ 08544-0001 Office Phone: 609-258-5315. Business E-Mail: verdu@princeton.edu.

**VER DUIN, D'ARLENE K.,** sociologist, researcher; b. Grand Rapids, Mich., Sept. 19, 1952; m. O. Lynn Sims, Mar. 15, 1996. BA in Sociology, U. North Tex., 1995, MPA, 1998. Rsch. scientist U. North Tex., Denton, 1999—. Author: (plays) Not Even a Goodbye, 1983. Mem. Am. Social. Assn., Pi Alpha Alpha (life), Ft. Worth Civic Orch. (pres. 1985-87) Democrat. Christian. Avocations: genealogy, needle arts, viola. Office: Univ North Tex Survey Rsch Ctr PO Box 310637 Denton TX 76203 Office Phone: 940-565-4939. Business E-Mail: dverduin@pacs.unt.edu.

**VEREB, TERESA B.,** psychiatrist; b. Poland; d. Joseph and Henryka Biskup; m. Bartholomew Vereb, Aug. 3, 1968; children: Bartholomew Jr., Teresa Tilden. MD, Acad. Medicine Warsaw 1966 Cert. stress mgmt. Am. Acad. Experts in Traumatic Stress, 2005. Resident psychiatry Hosp. Wolsky, Warsaw, 1966—68, Med. Sch. Safarik U., Kosice, Czech Republic, 1968—70, staff psychiatry, 1971—72; resident psychiatry SUNY, Buffalo, 1977—78; clin. instr. psychiatry Meyer Meml. Hosp., Buffalo, 1977—78; resident psychiatry U. Fla., Gainesville, 1978—80; pvt. practice gen. psychiatry Bradenton, Fla., 1980—; staff psychiatrist Blake Hosp., Bradenton, 1980—, Manatee Meml. Hosp., Bradenton, 1980—, chief psychiatry, sectional chief psychiatry, 1981—85, 1987—91, chairperson psychiat. sect., 2000. Active Sacred Heart Cath. Ch., Bradenton, 1980—. Named Am. Top Psychiatrist, Consumer's Rsch. Coun. Am., 2006; recipient Disting. Physician award, Fla. Med. Assn., 2005. Mem.: AMA (Physician Recognition award 1995—2002, 2005—06), Am. Acad. Experts in Traumatic Stress, Manatee County Med. Soc., Fla. Psychiat. Assn., Fla. Med. Assn. (Physician Recognition award 1995—2005, Rogeriem Pfizer Re-Commn. 1999, Am. Top Rate Physician 1999, Top Psychiatrist 2004—05, Boar Cert. for stress mgmt. 2005), Am. Psychiat. Assn. Achievements include successfully climbed Mount Kilimanjaro, 1997. Avocations: water-skiing, skiing, swimming, hiking, mountain climbing. Office: Vereb and Vereb MDs PA 5015 Manatee Ave West Bradenton FL 34209

**VEREEN, BEN,** actor, singer, dancer; b. Miami, Fla., Oct. 10, 1946; m. Nancy Vereen; children: Benjamin, Malakia, Naja, Kabara, Karon. Student, High Sch. of Performing Arts; LHD (hon.), Emerson Coll., 1977. Debut off-Broadway in The Prodigal Son, 1965; played Brother Ben in Sweet Charity, N.Y.C., Las Vegas, San Francisco, 1966, Daddy Brubeck in Can. tour, 1968, in Los Angeles co. of Hair, 1968, joined Broadway cast, 1969; played role of Judas in Jesus Christ Superstar, 1971 (Theatre World award); leading role in Pippin', 1972 (Tony award, Drama Desk award); appeared in Grind, 1985, Jelly's Last Jam, 1993, Wicked, 2005; numerous theatrical appearances, including I'm Not Rappaport, San Francisco, 1989, A Christmas Carol, 1995, 96; appeared in TV films Louis Armstrong-Chicago Style, 1976, Uptown: A Tribute to the Apollo Theatre, 1980; Pippin: His Life and Times, 1981, Breakin' Through, 1984, The Jesse Owens Story, 1984, Lost in London, 1985, The Saint in Manhattan, 1987, Jenny's Song, 1988, The Kid Who Loved Christmas, 1990, Intruders, 1992, Faraway, 2001, Feast of All Saints, 2001; created role of Chicken George in TV miniseries Roots, 1977 (TV Critics award); other TV miniseries include Ellis Island, 1984, A.D., 1985, Silk Stalkings, 1991; appeared in TV spl. Ben Vereen-His Roots, 1978,

Uptown-A Tribute to the Apollo Theatre; film appearances: Funny Lady, 1975, All That Jazz, 1979, Buy and Cell, 1989, Once Upon a Forrest, 1993 (voice only), Why Do Fools Fall in Love, 1998, I'll Take You There, 1999, The Painting, 2001, Idlewild, 2006; TV appearances: Touched by an Angel, 1997; TV series include: Tenspeed and Brown Shoe, 1980, Webster, J.J. Starbuck, 1988, Promised Land, 1996, The Jamie Foxx Show, 1996, (narrator) Vaudeville: An American Masters Special, 1997; also nightclub appearances. Chmn. Dance for Heart campaign Am. Heart Assn.; internat. chmn. Sudden Infant Death Syndrome; established Naja Vereen Meml. Scholarship Fund, 1988; founder, pres. Celebrities for a Drug-Free Am. Recipient George M. Cohan award Am. Guild Variety Artists, 1976, Image award NAACP, 1978, 79, Israel's Cultural award, 1978, Israel's Humanitarian award, 1979, Eleanor Roosevelt Humanitarian award, 1983. Mem. Actor's Equity Assn., Am. Guild Variety Artists, AFTRA, SAG. Office: care Pamela Cooper 2968 Corral Canyon Rd Malibu CA 90265-2915 *I am like the turtle--determined and will stick my neck out; turtles also teach me patience.**

**VEREEN, ROBERT CHARLES,** retired trade association administrator; b. Stillwater, Minn., Sept. 8, 1924; s. George and Leona Lucille (Made) Wihren; m. Rose Catherine Blair, Nov. 5, 1945; children: Robin, Stacy, Kim. Grad. high sch. Mng. editor Comml. West Mag., Mpls., 1946-50, Bruce Pub. Co., St. Paul, 1950-53, Nat. Retail Hardware Assn., Indpls., 1953-59; mng. dir. Liberty Distbrs., Phila., 1959-63; editor Hardware Retailing, Indpls., 1963-80; assoc. pub., dir. communications Nat. Retail Hardware Assn., 1980-84, sr. v.p., 1984-87; Vereen & Assocs., Mgmt., Mktg. Cons., 1987—. Lectr. mgmt. insts.; guest lectr. on distbn. pub.; co-founder U.S.A. Direct; co-founder, ptnr. Eurotrade Mktg., 1988—; ptnr. Hardlines Pers. Finders, 1987—. Author: (with Paul M. Doane) Hunting for Profit, 1965, The Computer Age in Merchandising, 1968, Perpetuating the Family-Owned Business, 1970, The How-To of Merchandising, 1975, The How-To of Store Operations, 1976, A Guide to Financial Management, 1976, Productivity: A Crisis for Management, 1978, Hardlines Rep Report Newsletter, 1984-94, Guidelines to Improve the Rep/Factory Relationships, 1992. Served with AUS, 1943-46. Mem. Am. Soc. Bus. Press Editors (dir., v.p. 1966-70), Soc. Nat. Assn. Publs. (dir., pres. 1970-75, chmn. journalism edn. liaison com. 1976-79), Toastmasters (v.p. treas., sec. 1955-59), Am. Hardware Mfrs. Assn. (co-founder, sec.-treas. Young Execs. Club 1958-.59, 63-65), Hardware-Housewares Packaging Expn. (founder 1960, chmn. com. packaging 1960-62, chmn. judging com. Hardware-Packaging Expn. 1975-78), Packaging Inst., Household Consumer Products Export Coun. (chmn. 1981-83), World-Wide DIY Coun. (exec. sec. 1981-99, dir. emeritus 1999—). Home and Office: 10769 Oriole Ct Indianapolis IN 46231-1006 Office Phone: 317-838-7632.

**VEREEN, WILLIAM JEROME,** uniform manufacturing company executive; s. William Coachman and Mary Elizabeth V.; m. Lula Evelyn King; children: Elizabeth King, William Coachman. BS in Indsl. Mgmt, Ga. Inst. Tech., 1963. With Riverside Mfg. Co., Moultrie, 1967—, from v.p. to exec. v.p., 1970-77, pres., 1977-84, pres., treas., CEO, 1984—; v.p., dir. Moultrie Cotton Mills, 1969—; exec. v.p. Riverside Industries, Inc., Moultrie, 1973-77, pres., 1977-84, CEO, 1984—, also dir. V.p. Riverside Uniform Rentals, Inc., Moultrie, 1971-80, pres., 1980-84, CEO, bd. dirs.; pres. Riverside Mfg. Co. (Ireland) Ltd., 1977—, Right Image Corp., Riverside Mfg. Co. GmbH, Germany, 1979—, also CEO, dir.; pres., treas., CEO G.A. Rivers Corp., Riverside Mfg. Co. (U.K.) Ltd.; pres., treas. CEO, bd. dirs. Textile Clothing Tech. Corp.; chairholder Tyner eminent scholars, prof. coll. human scis. Fla. State U., 1993-94, mem. coll. human scis. devel. bd.; bd. dirs. Ga. Power Co., Gerber Sci., Inc., Blue Cross/Blue Shield Ga., Cerulean Cos., Inc., Trade and Tourism, Ga. Rsch. Alliance, Ga. Corp. Indsl. Devel.; mem. trilateral commn. apparel labeling NAFTA; so. regional adv. dir. Bank of Am. (GA) (formerly Nations Bank, N.A.; advisor textile and apparel tariffs and quotas U.S. Dept. State Bd.; mem. World Econ. Forum, Davos, Switzerland. Bd. dirs. Moultrie-Colquitt County (Ga.) Devel. Authority, 1973-77, Moultrie-Colquitt County United Givers, 1968-75, Moultrie YMCA, 1968-75, Colquitt County Cancer Soc., 1969-73; trustee Cmty. Welfare Assn. Moultrie, 1970—, Pineland Sch., Moultrie, 1971-75, Leadership Moultrie, 1972—, Ga. Coun. Econ. Edn.; trustee Am. Apparel Edn. Found.; adv. bd. Ga. Tech. sch. of textile and fiber engring.; elder 1st Presbyterian Ch. Capt. USMCR, 1963-67. Decorated Bronze Star with combat V, Purple Heart. Mem. Internat. Apparel Fedn. (2d v.p., 1st v.p., bd. dirs., exec. com., chmn. 1991-92), Am. Apparel Mfrs. Assn. (bd. dirs. exec. com., edn. found. com., 2d vice chmn., 1990-91), Nat. Assn. Uniform Mfrs. and Distbrs. (bd. dirs. 1988-91), Am. Apparel Edn. Found. (v.p., trustee), Capital City Club (Atlanta), Commerce Club (Atlanta), World Econ. Forum, Sunset Country Club, Ga. C. of C., Elks, Kiwanis, Sigma Alpha Epsilon. Office: PO Box 460 Moultrie GA 31776-0460

**VERE HODGE, RICHARD ANTHONY,** pharmaceutical executive, consultant; b. Burnham-on-Sea, Eng., Dec. 27, 1943; s. Francis and Eleanor Mary Vere Hodge; married; 3 children. BA, Trinity Coll. Dublin, 1966; DPhil, Worcester Coll., Oxford, Eng., 1969. With Beecham Pharms. (now Glaxo-SmithKline), England, 1969—96, project mgr. human interferon project, 1974—76, chief biochemist antiviral chemotherapy project, 1981—92; loaned expert on famciclovir to World-wide Strategic Product Devel., 1993—96, assoc. dir., 1995—96; dir. Vere Hodge Anti-virals Ltd., Reigate, Surrey, England, 1996—. Cons. Pharmasset, Inc., Atlanta, 2000-05. Editor (review): (jour.) Antiviral Chemistry & Chemotherapy, 2005—; contbr. articles pub. in profl. jours., chapters to books. Founding mem. Ch. Roof Fund Com., Leigh, Reigate, Surrey, England, 1998—99. Mem. Royal Soc. Chemistry, Am. Soc. Microbiology, Internat. Soc. Antiviral Rsch. (mem. publs. com. 2006-). The Chromatography Soc. Achievements include patents for treatment of latent infection of herpesvirus, 1999. Avocations: bell ringing, gardening, hill walking. Office: Vere Hodge Antivirals Ltd Leigh Reigate Surrey RH2 8RD England Personal E-mail: averehodge@aol.com.

**VEREMEY, VOLODIMIR,** electrical engineer, researcher; s. Victor and Lyubov Veremey; m. Natalia Petrochenko, Jan. 21, 1977; 1 child, Artem. MS with honors, Kharkov State U., Ukraine, 1978; PhD in Sci, Physics and Math., Kharkov State U., 1984. Rsch. scientist Ukrainian NAS, Inst. of Radiophysics and Electronics, Kharkov, Ukraine, 1982—88, sr. rsch. scientist, 1988—2001; assoc. prof. Gebze Inst. of Tech., Gebze, Turkey, 1996—97; vis. scholar fellow Pa. State U., State College, 1997—2000; sr. scientist Xpedion Design Systems Inc., Milpitas, Calif., 2000—06, Agilent Techs., Santa Clara, Calif., 2006—. Contbr. chapters to books, over 100 articles to profl. jours. Recipient Young Scientist award, Internat. Union of Radio Sci., 1990, M.Ostrowskii Nat. Ukrainian award, Nat. Young Scientists Union Com., Kiev, Ukraine, 1991; grantee Rsch. grantee, Internat. Sci. Found., 1993, Travel grantee, 1993—94. Mem.: IEEE (ny). Avocations: tennis, skiing, martial arts. Home: 868 Transill Cir Santa Clara CA 95054 Office: Xpedion Design Systems Inc 1900 McCarthy Blvd Ste 210 Milpitas CA 95035 Office Phone: 408-449-4028. Office Fax: 408-449-4030. Personal E-mail: vladimir.space@gmail.com. E-mail: vladimirv@xpedion.com.

**VERES, BOB,** editor; b. 1952; Editor, pub. Inside Info.; editor-at-large Dow Jones Investment Advisor; editor MorningstarAdvisor.com, 2000—. Cons. TIAA-CREF, Am. Express Fin. Svc., J.P. Morgan, Inc. Author: The Cutting Edge in Financial Services, 2003. Office: Morningstar Inc 225 W Wacker Dr Chicago IL 60606

**VERES, TANIS,** elementary school educator; b. Anderson, SC, July 13, 1951; d. James H. and Dorothy M Thompson; m. George Veres; children: Joshua Bela, Jordan Armin. BA, Clemson U., 1973, MEd, 1976. Tchr. McCants Middle Sch, Anderson, SC, 1973—76, Alice Birney Middle Sch., Charleston, 1976—77, Terry Parker H.S., Jacksonville, Fla., 1977—78, Horace Man Jr. High, Miami, 1979—80, Northwood Middle Sch., Greenville, SC, 1980—83, Palmetto Middle Sch., Williamston, SC, 1983—2001; lang. arts specialist Pelzer Elem. Sch., SC, 2001—. Coach Odyssey of the Mind, Williamston, SC, 1992—96. Named Tchr. of Year, Pelzer Elem., 2004; recipient, Palmetto Middle Sch., 1996. Mem.: Internat. Raading Assn.

(Disting. Tchr. Reading 1999). Republican. Pesbyn. Avocations: reading, soccer, travel. Home: 136 Colonial Dr Pelzer SC 29669 Office: Pelzer Elem Sch 214 Lebby St Pelzer SC 29669 Office Phone: 864-947-9311. Business E-Mail: verest@anderson.k12.sc.us.

VERGARA, CAMILO JOSÉ, photographer; BA in Sociology, U. Notre Dame, 1968; MA in Sociology, Columbia U., 1977, postgrad. Co-author: Silent Cities: The Evolution of the American Cemetery, 1989; author: The New American Ghetto, 1995 (Robert E. Park award Am. Sociol. Assn., 1997), American Ruins, 1999, Unexpected Chicagoland, 2001, Twin Towers Remembered, 2001; contbr. art, Loud Paper Mag. Fellow Revson fellow, Columbia U., 1986—87, MacArthur Found. fellow, 2002.

VERGE, PIERRE, legal educator; b. Quebec City, Can., Jan. 9, 1936; s. Francis and Regina (Roy) V.; m. Colette Habel, June 29, 1963; children— Marc, Caroline, Louis. BA, Laval U., 1956, LL.L., 1959, LL.D., 1971; MA, McGill U., 1962, Cambridge U., 1977; LL.M., U. Toronto, 1968; 1971. Bar: Que. 1961, Queen's Counsel 1976. Pvt. practice law, Quebec City, Can., 1961-66; mem. faculty Laval U. Faculty of Law, 1966—, dean, 1973-77, prof. emeritus, 2003—. Commonwealth fellow St. John's Coll., Cambridge U., 1977-78 Mem. Assn. Can. Law Tchrs. (pres. 1972-73, chmn. conf. law deans 1975-76), Que. Bar, Canadian Bar, Royal Soc. Can. Home: 2542 avenue de Parc-Falaise Sillery PQ Canada G1T 1W3 Office: Cite Universitaire Universite Laval Quebec City PQ Canada

VERGHESE, ABRAHAM CHEERAN, internist, educator, writer; b. Addis Ababa, Ethiopia, May 30, 1955; came to U.S., 1980; s. George and Mary Verghese; children: Steven, Jacob. MD, Madras (India) U., 1979; MFA, U. Iowa, 1991; DSc (hon.), Swarthmore Coll., 2001. Diplomate Am. Bd. Internal Medicine, Am. Bd. Infectious Diseases, Geriatrics, and ulmonary Medicine. Intern Govt. Gen. Hosp., Madrass Med. Coll., 1979-80; resident, chief resident E. Tenn. State U., Johnson City, 1980-83, instr. in medicine, 1982-83, asst. prof. medicine, 1985-88, assoc. medicine, 1988-90; tchg. asst. medicine Boston U., 1983-85; chief infectious diseases VA Med. Ctr., Johnson City, 1986-90, asst. chief medicine, 1988-90; vis. assoc. U. Iowa, Iowa City, 1990-91; prof. medicine Tex. Tech. U., El Paso, Tex., 1991—2002; chief infectious diseases Tex. Tech. Regional Acad. Health Ctr., El Paso, 1991-97; prof. medicine, dir. Ctr. for Med. Humanities and Ethics, U. Tex. Health Scis. Ctr., San Antonio, 2002—. Author: My Own Country: A Doctor's Story of a Town and Its People in the Age of AIDS, 1994, (with others) Infection in the Nursing Home, 1990. Named Tchr. of Yr. Internat. Medicine residents and Alpha Omega Alpha E. Tenn. State U., 1989; recipient James Michener fellowship to Writer's Workshop U. Iowa. Fellow ACP (publs. coms.), Royal Coll. Physicians Can., Infectious Diseases Soc. Am., Coll. Chest Physicians; mem. Am. Geriat. Soc., Am. Fedn. for Clin. Rsch., Am. Soc. Microbiology, Soc. for Exptl. Biology and Medicine. Office: UTHSCSA Mail Code 7730 7703 Floyd Curl Dr San Antonio TX 78229 Home: 9 Inwood Fork San Antonio TX 78248

VERGNAUD, JEAN-MAURICE, science educator, researcher; b. Audincourt, Doubs, France, Dec. 3, 1932; s. Joseph and Marie-Louise (Buthod-Ruffier) V.; m. Michele Trouin, Dec. 20, 1979. MS, U. Lyon, France, 1956, PhD in Chromatography, 1965; PhD in Catalysis, U. Dijon, France, 1960. Engr. CEA, Paris, 1959, Progil, Lyon, 1960-68; prof. U. Algiers, Algeria, 1968-71, U. St. Etienne, France, 1972—. Spkr. in field. Author: Drying of Polymeric and Solid Materials, 1992, Cure of Thermosetting Resins, 1992, Dosage Forms for Controlled Release with Polymers, 1993, Liquid Transport Processes in Polymeric Materials, 1994, Assessing Bioavailability of Drug Delivery Systems, 2005, Assessing Food Safety with Polymer Packaging, 2006; mem. editl. adv. bd. Polymer Testing, Rubber Plastics and Composites, Polymer and Polymer Composites, Jour. Polymer Engring., Jour. Drying Tech.; referee Am. Assn. Pharm. Sci., 7 jours. on polymers and 2 jours. on pharmacy; contbr. over 500 articles to internat. jours. Pres. French Chem. Soc. of Lyon, 1963-68; v.p. U. St. Etienne, 1972-75. Recipient French Indsl. Soc. award, Paris, 1965, French Acad. Scis. award, Paris, 1977. Mem. Am. Chem. Soc. (George S. Whitby award 1998). Avocations: skiing, tennis, piano. Home: Rte de Chavanne Chemin de Grange Bruyas 42400 Saint Chamond France Office: Univ St Etienne 23 Dr P Michelon 42023 Saint Etienne France Personal E-mail: vergnaud.jean-maurice@wanadoo.fr.

VERHAAREN, HAROLD CARL, lawyer; b. Salt Lake City, Apr. 11, 1938; m. Cynthia Mary Hughes, Nov. 25, 1964; children: Scott Harold, Steven Robert, Jill, Brent Carl, Brian Hughes. JD, U. Utah, 1965. Bar: Utah 1965, US Dist. Ct. Utah 1965, US Ct. Appeals (10th Cir.), 1968, US Supreme Ct. 1978. Law clk. to chief justice Utah Supreme Ct., 1964-65; v.p., bd. dirs. Nielsen & Senior PC, Salt Lake City 1991—2001. Judge pro tem Small Claims Ct. Salt Lake County, 1978-85; shareholder Nielsen and Sr., 1992-. Chmn. Mt. Olympus Planning Dist., 1971-85; active Boy Scouts Am., 1967-97. Recipient Silver Beaver award Boy Scouts Am. Mem. Utah Bar Assn., Salt Lake County Bar Assn., Am. Arbitration Assn. (panel arbitrators), Delta Theta Phi, Phi Kappa Phi, Phi Eta Sigma. Mem. LDS Ch. Office: 60 E South Temple 11th Fl Salt Lake City UT 84111 E-mail: hcv@ns-law.com.

VERHALEN, ROBERT DONALD, consumer safety executive; b. Chgo., July 6, 1935; s. William Joseph and Pearl Evelyn (Anderson) V.; m. Phyllis Scandridge, Jan. 11, 1958; children: Elizabeth L., David S. BA, U. Iowa, 1963; MPH, U. N.C., 1965, DrPH, 1972. Expediter Fansteel Metall. Corp., North Chicago, Ill., 1957-58; tech. writer Collins Radio Co., Cedar Rapids, Iowa, 1958-59; rsch. aide Dept. Physics and Astronomy, Iowa City, 1960-63; sanitarian Lake County Health Dept., Waukegan, Ill., 1963-64; cons. safety mgmt. Ga. Dept. Pub. Health, Atlanta, 1965—67; instr. U. N.C., Chapel Hill, 1968-70; chief task force Pres.'s Commn. on Product Safety, Washington, 1969-70; asst. dir. Bur. Product Safety FDA, Washington, 1970-73; assoc. dir. U.S. Consumer Product Safety Commn., Washington, 1973-95; pres. Verhalen & Assocs., McLean, Va., 1995—; gen. ptnr. advotec Investment Ltd. Partnership, McLean, 1997—2001; chmn. Elmstreet Tech. Group, 1999—2003; CEO VASSOC Inst., 2002—06. Pres. Found. bd. Sch. Pub. Health U. N.C., Chapel Hill, 2000—02, guest lectr., 1975—, Walter Reed Army Med. Ctr., Washington, 1982—. Mem. editorial bd. Jour. Safety Rsch.; developer Nat. Electronic Injury Surveillance System; contbr. articles to profl. jours. Mem. bd. govs. Nat. Grad. U., 2000. Sgt. USMC, 1953-57. Mem. Am. Coll. Epidemiology, Soc. Epidemiologic Rsch., Am. Public Health Assn., Am. Statis. Assn., Sr. Exec.'s Assn. (charter), Sr. Exec. Svc. Lutheran. Avocation: sailing. Home: 640 Live Oak Dr Mc Lean VA 22101-1563 Office: Verhalen & Assocs Ste 115 1350 Beverly Rd Mc Lean VA 22101 Personal E-mail: verhalenr@aol.com.

VERHEIJ, RICHARD H., lawyer; b. Edmonton Alberta, Can., Aug. 30, 1958; BA, Case We. Reserve U., 1980, JD, 1983. Bar: Ohio 1983, U.S. Dist. Ct. Ohio (No. dist.) 1984, U.S. Ct. Appeals (sixth cir.) 1984. Assoc. Wuliger, Fadel & Beyer, 1983—84, Jacob, Medinger, & Finnegan, 1984—86; sr. corp. counsel UST, Inc., Greenwich, Conn., 1988—90, v.p., assoc. gen. counsel, 1990—95, exec. v.p., gen. counsel, 1995—. Editor: Case We. Reserve U. Law Rev., 1982—83. Mem.: ABA (mem. tort and ins. practice sect., mem. internat. litigation sect.). Assn. of Bar City of NY. Office: UST Inc 100 W Putnam Ave Greenwich CT 06830 Office Phone: 203-622-3648. Office Fax: 203-863-7250. E-mail: rverheij@usthg.com.

VERHEYEN, PETER DAVID, librarian, conservator; b. Princeton, NJ, Jan. 14, 1963; s. Egon Verheyen and Hanne Schulten; m. Hope Elizabeth Kuniholm, June 4, 1994; 1 child, Sofia Klara. BA in German Lit., Johns Hopkins U., 1985; MLS, Syracuse U. Sch. Info. Studies, 1997. Hand bookbinding apprentice Chamber of Trades, Munster, Germany, 1987; asst. conservator William Minter Bookbinding and Conservation, Chgo., 1988—91, Yale U. Libr. New Haven, 1991—92; rare book conservator Cornell U. Libr., Ithaca, NY, 1993—95; conservation libr. Syracuse U. Libr., NY, 1995—98; archival product mgr. Gaylord Bros., 1998—99; preservation and access libr. Syracuse U. Libr. Spl. Collections Rsch. Ctr, NY, 1999—. Exhbns. chair Guild Book Workers, NYC, 1990—96, publicity chair,

1998—2002, exhbns. chair, 2004—. Exhibitions include Reliures du Monde: Les Amis de la Reliure d'Art, 2nd Nat. Book and Paper Arts Biennial, Guild Book Workers, Columbia Coll. Ctr. for Book and Paper Arts, Chgo., 2000, Soc. Bookbinders Bookbinding Competition, 2003 (Harmatan Leather award, 2003), Nat. Libr. Wales, 2003, Libr. Gabrielle Roy, Quebec City, Can., 2005, Galerie des Hospices, Limoges, France, 2005; author: Springback Ledger Bindings in German Tradition, 2003; contbr. articles to profl. jours. Mem.: ALA, Can. Bookbinders and Book Artists Guild, Designer Bookbinders, Soc. Am. Archivists, Am. Inst. Conservation (cipp web, list mgr. 2002—04). Achievements include design of Tube storage unit for architectural and other oversized archival materials; development of Marcel Breuer Sketches Digization Project; Charles Eisenmann Photographs Digitization Project; Gerrit Smith Broadside Digitization Project. Office: Peter Verheyen Spl Collections Rsch Ctr Syracuse Univ Libr Syracuse NY 13244 Office Phone: 315-443-9756. Office Fax: 315-443-2671. Personal E-mail: verheyen@philobiblon.com. Business E-Mail: pdverhey@syr.edu.

VERHOEK, SUSAN ELIZABETH, botany educator; b. Columbus, Ohio, 1942; m. S.E. Williams; 1 child. *Father, Frank Henry Verhoek, 1929 Harvard graduate, earned a PhD in chemistry from the University of Wisconsin and a DPhil at Trinity College, Oxford, where he was a Rhodes Scholar. He was also a member of the Oxford Bach Choir. After a year of postdoctoral study at the University of Copenhagen, he began a long career as a professor of chemistry at The Ohio State University. Among other publications and presentations, he is co-author of several textbooks on general chemistry and currently an emeritus professor at Ohio State.* Student, Carleton Coll., 1960-62; BA, Ohio Wesleyan U., 1964; MA, Ind. U., 1966; PhD, Cornell U., 1975. Herbarium supr. Mo. Bot. Garden, St. Louis, 1966-70; asst. prof. Lebanon Valley Coll., Annville, Pa., 1974-82, assoc. prof., 1982-85, prof., 1985—. Vis. researcher Cornell U., Ithaca, N.Y., 1982-83; content cons. Merrill Pub. Co., 1987-89; vis. profl. Chgo. Bot. Garden, 1991. Author: How to Know the Spring Flowers, 1982; contbr. articles to profl. jours., newspapers, and bulls. Trustee Lebanon Valley Coll., Annville, 1979-82, 84-90, 92-98; dir. Lebanon Valley Coll. Arboretum, 1996—. Mem. Soc. for Econ. Botany (pres. 1985-86), Bot. Soc. Am., Am. Pub. Gardens Assn. Office: Lebanon Valley Coll Dept Biology Annville PA 17003-0501 Office Phone: 717-867-6178. Business E-Mail: verhoek@lvc.edu.

VERHOEVEN, PAUL, film director; b. Amsterdam, Netherlands, July 18, 1938; PhD in Maths., Physics, U. Leiden. Dir. (films) Wat Zien Ik?, 1971, Turkish Delight, 1973, Keetje Tippel, 1975, Spetters, 1981, The Fourth Man, 1983, Robocop, 1987, Total Recall, 1990, Basic Instinct, 1992, Showgirls, 1995, Starship Troopers, 1997, Hollow Man, 2000, (TV) Hitchhiker, Floris, 1969, (documentary with the Royal Netherlands Navy) Het Korps Mariniers, 1965; dir., co-screenwriter Soldier of Orange, 1979, Flesh and Blood, 1985. Office: Care Beth Swofford 9830 Wilshire Blvd Beverly Hills CA 90212-1804

VERHOFF, GLEN CHARLES, reading educator, choir director; b. Lima, Ohio, Nov. 10, 1961; s. Virgil Hubert and Anita Abnus Verhoff. AA, Ohio State U., 1982; MusB, Ohio No. U., 1985; M in Tchg., Bowling Green State U., 2004. Tchr. music Port Clinton Schs., Ohio, 1986—90, tchr. 2d grade, 1994—2004, tchr. reading, 2004—; tchr. 1st grade Parochial Schs., 1991—94; choir dir. Immaculate Conception Ch., Port Clinton, Ohio, 1990—. Mem. Playmakers Theatre, Port Clinton, Ohio. Mem.: Nat. Assn. Pastoral Musicians, Nat. Reading Assn. Roman Catholic. Avocation: collecting daylilies and hostas.

VERING, JOHN ALBERT, lawyer; b. Marysville, Kans., Feb. 6, 1951; s. John Albert and Bernadine E. (Kieffer) V.; m. Ann E. Arman, June 28, 1980; children: Julia Ann, Catherine Ann, Mary Ann. BA summa cum laude, Harvard U., 1973; JD, U. Va., 1976. Bar: Mo. 1976, U.S. Dist. Ct. (we. dist.) Mo. 1976, U.S. Ct. Appeals (8th cir.), 1977, U.S. Ct. Appeals (10th cir.), 1980, U.S. Ct. Appeals (4th cir.) 1987, Kans. 1990, U.S. Dist. Ct. Kans. 1990; arbitrator, mediator. Assoc. Dietrich, Davis, Dicus, Rowlands, Schmitt & Gorman, Kansas City, Mo., 1976-81, ptnr., 1982—88, Armstrong Teasdale LLP, Kansas City, 1989—. Editor: U. Va. Law Rev., 1974—76. Bd. dirs. Greater Kansas City YMCA Southwest Dist., 1987. Mem.: Labor and Employment Law Com. (chmn. 2003), Kansas City Metro Bar Assoc., Harvard Club (adv. bd. schs. com. Kansas City 1977—2006, v.p. 1981—82, 1992—93, pres. 1994—96). Home: 1210 W 68th Ter Kansas City MO 64113-1904 Office: Armstrong Teasdale LLP 2345 Grand Blvd Ste 2000 Kansas City MO 64108-2617 Office Phone: 816-221-3420. Business E-Mail: jvering@armstrongteasdale.com.

VERINK, ELLIS DANIEL, JR., metallurgical engineering educator, consultant; b. Peking, China, Feb. 9, 1920; s. Ellis Daniel and Phoebe Elizabeth (Smith) V.; m. Martha Eulala Owens, July 4, 1942; children: Barbara Ann, Wendy Susan. BS, Purdue U., 1941; MS, Ohio State U., 1963, PhD, 1965. Registered profl. engr., Fla., Pa., Calif. Mgr. chem. sect., sales devel. divsn. Alcoa, New Kensington, Pa., 1946-59, mgr. chem. and petroleum indsl. sales Pitts., 1965—68; prof. materials sci. and engring. U. Fla., Gainesville, 1968—, disting. svc. prof., 1984-91, prof. emeritus, 1991—; pres. Materials Cons., Inc., 1970—. Cons. Aluminum Assn., Washington, 1966-84; mem. U.S. nuclear waste tech. rev. bd., 1989-97. Author: Corrosion Testing Made Easy, The Basics, 1993; editor: Methods of Materials Selections, 1968, Material Stability and Environmental Degradation, 1988; contbr. articles to profl. jours. Pres. Gainesville YMCA, 1977. Recipient Sam Tour award ASTM, 1979, Donald E. Marlowe award Am. Soc. Engring. Edn., 1991; recipient Disting. Alumnus award Ohio State U., 1982, Disting. Faculty award Fla. Blue Key, 1983; named Tchr.-Scholar of Year U. Fla., 1979 Fellow Metall. Soc. of AIME (pres. 1984, Educator of Yr. award 1988), Am. Soc. Materials Internat., Nat. Assn. Corrosion Engrs. Internat. (bd. dirs. 1984-87, Willis Rodney Whitney award; mem. Masons, Shriners, Kiwanis, Sigma Xi, Tau Beta Pi. Republican. Presbyterian. Office: U Fla Dept Materials Sci Eng Gainesville FL 32611 Home: Apt M224 7805 NW 28th Pl Gainesville FL 32606-8659

VERKERKE, J. HOULT, law educator; b. Charlottesville, Va., 1959; BA in English and Economics, magna cum laude, Loyola Coll., Balt., 1983; MPhil in Economics, Yale U., New Haven, 1988; JD, Yale U., 1990. Economist Office Sec. US Dept. Interior, Washinton, DC, 1984; law clk. to Hon. Ralph K. Winter US Ct. Appeals 2nd Cir., New Haven, 1990—91; asst. prof. U. Va. Sch. Law, Charlottesville, 1991—96, assoc. prof., 1996—97, prof., 1997—; dir. Program Employment & Labor Law Studies, 1996—; vis. prof. U. Tex. Sch. Law, 1997. Office: U Va Sch Law 580 Massie Rd Charlottesville VA 22903-1789 Office Phone: 434-924-3463. Office Fax: 434-924-7536. E-Mail: jhv3q@virginia.edu.

VERKHOVSKY, BORIS, computer scientist, educator; PhD, USSR Acad. Scis. Wallace J. Eckert scientist IBM TJW Rsch. Ctr.; assoc. prof. Princeton U.; mem. tech. staff Bell Labs; Charles A. Dana Endowed chair professorship; prof. computer sci. NJIT, Newark. Recipient USSR Ministry of Radio-Electronics award, USSR award, Acad. Scis., Alvin Johnson award, Millennium award and Medal of Excellence. Fellow: European Acad. Scis. (v.p., bd. govs. 2004—, gov. 2002, v.p. 2003, mem. nominating com. for Nobel Prize, Blaise Pascal medal in Computer Sci. 2003). Office: NJIT Computer Sci Dept GITC 4102 University Heights Newark NJ 07102 Office Phone: 973-596-3393. Office Fax: 973-596-5777. Business E-Mail: verkhovsky@homer.njit.edu.

VERMA, ARUN K., mathematician, educator; b. Dibrugarh, India, June 1955; 3 children MSc, Dibrugarh U., India, 1977; Diploma, Indian Inst. of Tech., Kharagpur, India, 1984. Lectr. in math. Regional Engring. Coll., Silchar, Assam, India, 1984—89; rsch. assoc. Hampton U., Hampton, Va., 1989—89, vis. lectr. in math., 1989—92, asst. prof. of math., 1992—93, assoc. prof. of math., 1993—2001, prof. of math., 2001—; coord. Math. Counts Peninsula Chpt., Va., 2005—06; lead tchr. Thomson Learning Brooks/Cole Inc. Reader for AP calculus Ednl. Testing Svcs., Princeton, NJ, 1998—2004; ASEE summer faculty fellow NASA Langley Rsch. Ctr.,

Hampton, Va., 2000; U.S. EdD project cons. Ala. State U., Montgomery, Ala., 2002—03; Schev project cons. Norfolk State U., Norfolk, Va., 2002—03; faculty summer rsch. participant Oak Ridge Inst. for Sci. and Rsch., Oak Ridge, Tenn., 1993—93; lead tchr. Thompson Learning Brooks Coll., Inc., 2004—; coord. Math. Counts Peninsula Chpt., Va., 2005—. Treas. Yorktown 4th July Committe, Yorktown, Va., 2003—; elected com. mem. Internat. Baccalaureate Adv. Coun., Yorktown, Va., 2000—04; nominated com. mem. New Horizon Governors Sci. & Tech. Adv. Com., Hampton, Va., 2000—; v.p. Hindu Temple of Hampton Roads, Chesapeake, Va., 2000—. Named Leader in Edn., Hewlett-Packard Inc., 2000; recipient William C. Lowry Outstanding Math. Tchr. award, coll. level, Va. Coun. of Teachers of Math., 2001, 2002 QEM (Quality Edn. for Minorities) Excellence in Math. and/or Sci. Tchg. award, 2002. Mem.: Va. Acad. Sci. (treas. 2006—), Nat. Tech. Assn., Va. Coun. of Teachers of Math., Math. Assn. of Am., Sigma Xi. Office: Hampton U E Queen St Hampton VA 23668 Office Phone: 757-728-6983. Personal E-mail: akverma@cox.net. E-mail: arun.verma@hamptonu.edu.

VERMA, INDER M., biochemist; b. Sangrur, Punjab, India, Nov. 28, 1947; MSc in Biochemistry, Lucknow U., India, 1966; PhD in Biochemistry, Weizmann Inst. Sci., Rehovot, Israel, 1971. From asst. prof. to assoc. prof. Salk Inst. 1974-83; sr. mem. Molecular Biology & Virology Lab, 1983-85; prof. Molecular Biology, 1985-95; prof. Lab. Genetics Salk Inst. for Biol. Sciences, 1995—; Am. Cancer Soc. prof. Molecular Biology. Fellow Jane Coffin Childs Meml. Fund, 1970-73; Reverend Soloman B. Caulker Meml. fellow, 1967-70; adj. assoc. prof. U. Calif. San Diego, 1979-83, adj. prof. Biology, 1983—; March of Dimes Birth Defects Found. Franklin D. Roosevelt Investigator, 1997; mem. Virology Study Sect., 1981-85, elected mem., Inst. of Medicine, 1999. Recipient medal Outstanding Scientist N. Am. Scientists of Indian Origin, 1985-86; merit award NIH, 1987, outstanding investigator award, 1988; bd. trustees Salk Inst., 1989-91 & 94—; mem. acad. coun.. 1989—; vchmn. Fac. and Acad. coun., 1989-90 & 94-95; chmn., 1991-92 & 96-97; prof. Molecular Biology, Am. Cancer Soc., 1990; lectr. Purdue U., 1991, Sch. Med. Vanderbilt U., 1992, TATA Meml. Hosp., Bombay, India, 1992, U. Chgo., 1992, Queenstown, New Zealand, 1993, N.Y.U., 1993, Bar-Ilan U., Ramat Gan, Israel, and others. Mem. NAS (councilor, 2006-), Am. Cancer Soc., Third World Acad. Sciences, IOM, Am. Soc. for Gene Therapy (pres. 2000-2001). Office: Salk Inst Biol Studies PO Box 85800 10010 N Torrey Pines Rd San Diego CA 92186-5800 Office Phone: 619-453-4100. Business E-Mail: verma@salk.edu.*

VERMA, SATYA BHUSHAN, optometrist, educator; b. Multan, Punjab, India; s. Hari C. and Satwanti (Girdhar) V.; m. Asha C. Valecha, Dec. 28, 1974; children: Pooja, Kajal. DR OPT, Sch. Optometry GEH, Aligarh, India, 1964; BA, Delhi U., 1968; AO, U. Calif. Berkeley, 1971; OD, Pa. Coll. Optometry, 1975. Diplomate Am. Acad. Optometry, Pub. Health and Environ. Optometry. Refractionist Eye Dept. Willingdon Hosp., New Delhi, India, 1967-70; assoc. Sch. Optometry U. Calif., Berkeley, 1970-71; assoc. Pa. Coll. Optometry, Phila., 1971-75, asst. prof., 1976—. Cons. East Coast Migrant Health, Washington, 1990—. Contbr. chpts. in books and articles to profl. jours. Bd. dirs. Bridgeport-Upper Merion Lions Club, pres. 1987; chair scholarship com. AIP Found., Morrestown, N.J., 1994—; del. White House Conf. on Aging, 1995. Named Optometrist of Yr., Am. Optometric Assn., 1998; recipient Disting. Svc. award Prevent Blindness Am., 1998, Disting. Practitioner in Optometry Nat. Acads. Practice, 2000, Profl. Excellence award Coun. Indian Orgns., 2006; primary care health policy fellow DHHS, 2003. Fellow Am. Acad. Optometry (Carl C. Koch Meml. award 2002); mem. APHA (chair vision care sect.), Nat. Coun. Aging Bd. dirs. 2005—, exec. com., chair health promotion inst.), Nat. Vol. Orgn. for Ind. Living for Aging (chair 1992-94), Pa. Optometric Assn. (pres. 1996, past pres. 1997—, OD of Yr. 1997, 86, George Gottschalk Meml. award 1985), Chester-Delaware County Optometric Soc. (pres. 1982-84, OD of Yr. 1997, 86). Democrat. Hindu. Avocations: golf, tennis. Office: Pa Coll Optometry 8360 Old York Rd Elkins Park PA 19027-1516 Office Phone: 215-780-1345, 215-540-9019. E-mail: satya@pco.edu.

VERMA, SURJIT KUMAR, retired school system administrator; b. India, May 17, 1940; arrived in Canada 1966; s. Sohara Lal and Gian Devi V.; m. Raj Verma; 1 child, Soania. MEd, St. Francis Xavier U., N.S., 1975; postgrad., Dalhousie U., N.S., U. Ottawa, Ont., Can, 1979. Cert. tchr. Nova Scotia. Sci. dept. head Halifax County Bedford Dist. Sch. Bd., N.S., Canada, 1968-88, curriculum supr. N.S., 1988-94; ret., 1995. Served on C.T.F. Project Overseas Can. Teams, W.I., Nigeria, 1976, 77; mem. provincial sci. task force, biology rev. com., elem. sci. Nova Scotia Dept. Edn.; mem. Internat. Sci. Symposium, 1979; mem. selection panel PromoSci. Program. Natural Scis. and Engring. Rsch. Coun. of Can.; mem. exec. coun. N.S. Inst. Sci.; worksop presenter numerous sci. workshops. Contbr. to profl. jours. Chmn. First Metro Halifax Dartmouth Reg Sci. Fair, 1975; co-chmn. Canada Wide Sci Fair, 1984. Recipient Sci. Tchg. Achievement Recognition award, U.S. Nat. Sci. Tchrs. Assn. and Am. Gas Assn., 1993, Profl. Devel. award, N.S. Tchrs. Union, Tchg. Excellence in Sci., Tech. and Math. award, Prime Min. Can., 1993, 1994, Sci. on Display award, NASCO, 1993—94, Outstanding Achievement in Sci. Edn. award, Halifax County Sch. Bd., 1993, Surjit Verma award for tchg. excellence created in his honor, Halifax County Bedrod Dist. Sch. Bd., 1994, Michael Smith award, Industry Can., 1996, Maritimer of the Week award, Atlantic TV and Can. TV Network, 2003, Maritimer of Week award, Atlantic T.V. and Can. T.V. Network, 2003; fellow, U. Ottawa, 1979; scholar, N.S. Tchrs. Union, 1979; grad. fellow, Dalhousie U., 1980, Math. Sci. Tech. Edn. fellow, Royal Bank Queen's U., 1994, rsch. devel. grantee, Dalhousie U., 1979, Can./N.S. Tech. Devel. grantee, 1995. Mem. Nova Scotia Inst. Sci. (coun. mem.), Natural Sci. and Engring. Rsch. Coun. (mem. selection panel promosci. project). Avocations: jogging, yoga. Personal E-mail: rsverma49@yahoo.ca.

VERMEER, DONALD EUGENE, geography educator, retired; b. Oakland, Calif., Nov. 9, 1932; s. Henry Jacob and Agnes (Hertel) V.; m. Carrie Ann (Vaalburg, July 9, 1954. BA, U. Calif., Berkeley, 1954, MA, 1959, PhD, 1964. Lectr. U. Calif., Berkeley, 1961-62; asst. prof. U. Colo., Boulder, 1962-68; assoc. prof. La. State U., Baton Rouge, 1968-73, prof., 1973-88, assoc. dean, 1985-88; chmn., prof. George Washington U., Washington, 1988—96; ret., 2006. Staff mem. AID, Washington, 1977-78; pres. S.W. Social Sci. Assn., Austin, 1979-80. Editorial bd.: Exploration and Rsch., Washington, 1989—, Assn. Am. Geographers, 1985-88, Nat. Geographic Soc., 1989—; deputy editor: Social Sci. Quar., 1974—; author: The Cays of British Honduras (Belize), 1960, Man and the Earth, 1965; contbr. chpt. to book and about 75 articles to profl. jours. Capt. U.S. Army, 1954-57. Mem. AAAS, African Studies Assn., Assn. Am. Geographers, S.W. Social Sci. Assn.

VERMEER, MAUREEN DOROTHY, sales executive; b. Bronxville, N.Y., Mar. 21, 1945; d. Albert Casey and Helen (Valentine Casey) Vermeer; m. John R. Fassnacht, Feb. 11, 1966 (div. 1975); m. George M. Dallas Peltz IV, Oct. 26, 1985. Grad., NYU Real Estate Inst., 1976. Lic. real estate broker, NY. With Douglas Elliman, N.Y.C., 1965-74, mgmt. supr., 1974-78, v.p., 1978-83; real estate broker Rachmani Corp., N.Y.C., 1983-84; v.p. sales and mktg. Carol Mgmt. Corp., N.Y.C., 1984-90; v.p. mktg. The Sunshine Group, N.Y.C., 1990; v.p., sec., bd. dirs. H.J. Kalikow & Co., N.Y.C., 1991—. Mem. Real Estate Bd. N.Y. (bd. dirs., residential mgmt. com.), Assn. Real Estate Women (bd. dirs.officer, chmn. charitable fund) Republican. Presbyterian. Avocations: skiing, scuba diving. Home: 111 Broadway Norwood NJ 07648-1412 Office: H J Kalikow & Co 101 Park Ave Fl 25 New York NY 10178-0002

VERMEERSCH, DAVID ADAM, psychologist; b. Bellflower, Calif., Aug. 11, 1970; s. Frank Rennie and Doris Rae Vermeersch; m. Sharon Marie Andrews, Dec. 7, 1991; children: Jacob Adam, Ethan Andrew, Emma Baylee. PhD, Brigham Young U., Provo, Utah, 1998. Lic. psychologist Calif. Bd. of Psychology, 2006. Asst. clin. prof. counseling psychology Counseling and Career Ctr., Brigham Young U., Provo, Utah, 1998—2002; assoc. prof. psychology dept. psychology Loma Linda U., Calif., 2002—. Dir. clin. tng. dept. psychology Loma Linda U., Calif., 2005—. Author (chpt.) Encyclopedia of Psychotherapy, Psychologists' Desk Reference, Encyclopedia of Behavior Modification and Therapy, Processes in Brief Psychodynamic

Psychotherapy: Advancing Effective Practice; contbr. articles to profl. jours. Mgr., coach Yucaipa Valley Nat. Little League, Calif., 2002—06; coach Yucaipa Valley Basketball Assn., Calif., 2002—06; mem. LDS Ch., Yucaipa, Calif., 1970—2006. Mem.: APA, Soc. for Psychotherapy Rsch. Mem. Lds Ch. Achievements include member of research team that developed the Outcome Questionnaire (OQ-45), an instrument aimed at tracking patient progress throughout the course of psychological treatment. Office: Loma Linda Univ 11130 Anderson St Loma Linda CA 92350 Office Phone: 909-558-7116. Office Fax: 909-558-0171. E-mail: dvermeersch@llu.edu.

**VERMETTE, RAYMOND EDWARD,** retired health facility administrator; b. Lewiston, Maine, June 30, 1942; m. Ernestine Pero, Dec. 29, 1963; children: Tamara, Gregory. BS in Bacteriology, U. Maine, 1964; MS in Biochemistry, U. Wis., 1966; MBA, Temple U., 1973; master tchr.'s cert., Cath. Diocese Boston, 1981. Cert. in pers. mgmt., Va. Supr. animal toxicology Hazleton Labs., Vienna, Va., 1967-71; pers. mgr. Damon Clin. Lab., Phila., 1971-73, ops. mgr., 1973-75, gen. mgr. Needham Heights, Mass., 1975-90; v.p. ops. Damon Corp., Needham Heights, 1983-87, corp. v.p., 1987-89, sr. v.p., 1990—93; sr. v.p., gen. mgr. Corning/MetPath, Westwood, Mass., 1994-95; ret., 1995. Vis. lectr. fin. mgmt. and bus. adminstrn. Framingham State Coll., 1978—84; instr. mgmt. Newbury Jr. Coll., Boston, 1976—79; health care mgmt. cons., 2001—. Author: (with B. Kliman and E. Kolowrat) What You Should Know About Medical Lab Tests, 1979. V.p. fin. com., Framingham, Mass., 1982—84; mem. capital budget com. Town of Framingham, 1987; mem-elect Framingham Town Meeting, 1987—90, Govt. Study Com., 1995—97, mem. fin. com., 1997—2001; chmn. bd. religious edn. Cath. Ch., Framingham, 1981 84, co-chmn. pre-marriage preparation coun., 1981—99, organist, 1979—. Republican. Home: 2 Old Town Hwy Unit 16 East Haven CT 06512-4530

**VERMEULE, ADRIAN,** law educator; b. 1968; BA summa cum laude, Harvard Coll., Cambridge, Mass., 1990; JD magna cum laude, Harvard Law Sch., Cambridge, Mass., 1993. Bar: Washington, DC 1998. Law clk. to Hon. David B. Sentelle US Ct. Appeals DC Cir., Washington, 1993—94; law clk. to Hon. Antonin Scalia, US Supreme Ct., Washington, 1994—95; assoc. Kirkland & Ellis, Washington, 1995—96; assoc. prof. George Washington U. Nat. Law Ctr., Washington, 1996—97; asst. prof. U. Chgo. Law Sch., Chgo., 1998—2001, prof., 2001—. John M. Olin Fellow in Law Georgetown U. Nat. Law Ctr., Washington, 1996—97. Recipient Paul M. Bator award, Federalist Soc., 2003. Office: U Chgo Law Sch 1111 E 60th St Chicago IL 60637 Office Phone: 773-702-0028. E-mail: a-vermeule@uchicago.edu.

**VERMEULE, CORNELIUS CLARKSON, III,** museum curator; b. Orange, N.J., Aug. 10, 1925; s. Cornelius Clarkson, Jr. and Catherine Sayre (Comstock) V.; m. Emily Dickinson Townsend, Feb. 2, 1957 (dec. Feb. 6, 2001); children: Emily D. Blake, Cornelius Adrian Comstock. Grad., Pomfret Sch., 1943; AB, Harvard, 1949, MA, 1951; PhD, U. London, Eng., 1953; DHL (hon.), Boston Coll., 1995. Instr. fine arts, then asst. prof. U. Mich., 1953-55; asst. prof. classical archaeology Bryn Mawr (Pa.) Coll., 1955-57; curator classical art Mus. Fine Arts, Boston, 1956-96, curator emeritus, 1996—, acting dir., 1972-73, hon. visitor ancient art, 2002—; assoc. curator coins Mass. Hist. Soc., 1965-71, curator, 1971—. Lectr. fine arts Smith Coll., 1960-64, Boston U., Harvard, Wellesley Coll.; vis. prof. Yale, 1969-70, 72-73; Thomas Spencer Jerome lectr. U. Mich., 1975-76; vis. prof. Boston Coll., 1978-97; vis. prof. U. Aberdeen, Scotland, 1993; pres. Internat. Com. to Save Jewish Catacombs of Italy, 1980-84, chmn., 1984-98, dir. 1998-2000; cons. classical art Worcester Art Mus., 1998-2001. Author: (with N. Jacobs) Japanese Coinage, 1948, 2d edit., 1972, Bibliography of Applied Numismatics, 1956, The Goddess Roma, 1959, 2d edit., 1974, Dal Pozzo-Albani Drawings, 1960, European Art and the Classical Past, 1964, Drawings at Windsor Castle, 1966, Roman Imperial Art in Greece and Asia Minor, 1968, Polykleitos, 1969, Numismatic Art in America, 1971, (with M. Comstock) Greek Etruscan and Roman Bronzes, 1972, (with N. Neuerburg) Catalogue of the Ancient Art in the J. Paul Getty Museum, 1973, Greek and Roman Sculpture in Gold and Silver, 1974, Greek and Roman Cyprus, 1976, (with M. Comstock) Sculpture in Stone, 1976, Greek Sculpture and Roman Taste, 1977, Roman Art: Early Republic to Late Empire, 1978, (with A Herrmann) The Ernest Brummer Collections, Vol. II, 1979, Greek Art: Socrates to Sulla, 1980, The Jewish Experience in Roman Art, 1981, Masterpieces of Greek and Roman Sculpture in America, 1982, Greek Art: Prehistoric to Perikles, 1982, Numismatic Studies, 1983, Alexander the Great Conquers Rome, 1985, The Cult Images of Imperial Rome, 1986, Numismatic Art of the Greek Imperial World, 1987, Philatelic Art in America, 1987, (with M. Comstock) Sculpture in Stone and Bronze, 1988, (with A. Brauer) Stone Sculptures, The Greek, Roman and Etruscan Collections of the Harvard University Art Museums, 1990, (with others) Le Sport dans la Grèce Antique, 1992, Du Jeu à la Compétition, 1992, (with others) El Deporte en la Grecia Antigua, La génesis del olimpismo, 1992-93, (with others) Vase-Painting in Italy, 1993, (with others) Eye of the Beholder, Masterpieces from the Isabella Stewart Gardner Museum, 2003, Art and Archaeology of Antiquity, Vols. I-IV, 2001-04; mem. editl. bd. Minerva, 2002—. Trustee Cardinal Spellman Philatelic Mus., 1980-93. Served to 1st lt. AUS, 1943-47. Recipient Bicentennial medal Boston Coll., 1976; Fulbright fellow, 1951-53; Guggenheim fellow, 1968 Fellow AAAS, Am. Numis. Soc. (life), Royal Numis. Soc., Soc. Antiquaries; mem. Coll. Art Assn. (life), Archaeol. Inst. Am. (life) German Archaeol. Inst., Holland Soc. N.Y., Colonial Lords of Manors in Am., Mass. Hist. Soc. (hon. curator); Tavern Club (medalist 1986, Boston). Home: 47 Coolidge Hill Rd Cambridge MA 02138-5509 Office: Mus Fine Arts 465 Huntington Ave Boston MA 02115-5597 *To teach, collect and record the past, as exemplar for the present, as prologue to the future, can there be any better use of a historian's and archaeologist's professional life?*

**VERMEULEN, KEVIN J.,** publishing executive; BA, Brockport State Univ. Regional sales mgr. Miller Freeman & Gordon Pub.; dir. advertising New York Law Journal, Nat. Law Journal; assoc. publisher Law Tech. Product News; v.p. sales Nat. Law Publishing, 1996—98; v.p. & dir. nat. advertising Am. Lawyer Media, 1998—99, v.p. & group publisher, 1999—. Office: Am Lawyer Media 345 Park Ave So New York NY 10010

**VERMILLION, ROY ALAN,** secondary school educator; b. Albuquerque, N.Mex., June 18, 1959; s. James Ivan and Ruth Carol Vermillion. BS, Coll. of Idaho, Caldwell, 1981; MA, Lesley Coll., Cambridge, Mass., 1998. Cert. tchr. secondary edn. Boise State U. Nurseryman, delivery driver Molbak's Nursery, Woodinville, Wash., 1987—93; tchr. horticulture and sci. tchr. Mukilteo (Wash.) Sch. Dist., 1993—98; tchr. biology, sci., and Cisco sys. tchr. Culpeper (Va.) County H.S. and Germanna C.C., 1998—2000; biology and computer, asst. network adminstr. Belle Fourche (S.D.) Sch. Dist., 2000—02; tchr. biology and sci. Port Angeles (Wash.) H.S., 2002—. Adminstr. video conferencing network Belle Fourche Sch. Dist., 2001; selected for Sci. Edn. Partnership program Fred Hutchinson Cancer Rsch. Ctr., 2006. Recipient David C. and Mollie V. Petrie Meml. scholarship in biology, Coll. of Idaho, 1979—81, Lower Divsn. scholarship and Svc. award in biology, 1977—78. Mem.: SkiBuddies (assoc.; membership coord. 2006—), OutVentures (assoc.; bd. dirs. 2006). Democrat. Avocations: hiking, cross country skiing, kayaking, bicycling, gardening. Home: 281 Mantle Rd Sequim WA 98382 Office: Port Angeles H A 304 E Park Ave Port Angeles WA 98362 Office Phone: 360-452-7602. Personal E-mail: rvermillion@mac.com. E-mail: roy_vermillion@pasd.wednet.edu.

**VERMILYE, PETER HOAGLAND,** banker; b. NYC, Jan. 17, 1920; s. Herbert Noble and Elise Tace (Hillyer) V.; m. Lucy Shaw Mitchell, Oct. 14, 1950; children: Peter H., Dana R., Andrew R., Mary S. AB, Princeton U., 1940. V.p. pension investments J.P. Morgan & Co. and Morgan Guaranty Trust, 1940-64; ptnr. State St. Research & Mgmt., Boston, 1965-69; pres. Alliance Capital Mgmt., N.Y.C., 1970-77; sr. v.p. chief investment officer Citibank, N.Y.C., 1977-84; chmn. Baring Am. Asset Mgmt., Boston, 1984-89; sr. advisor Baring Asset Mgmt., 1990-95, Harbor Capital Mgmt., Boston 1996—2003, Fortis Investments, 2004—. Chmn. Huntington Theatre,

1989—96; bd. dirs. Engelhard Hanovia, Breadstreet Holdings Corp. Trustee Boston U., 1970—. Mem.: Brook, Somerset, Myopia. Home: 157 School St Manchester MA 01944-1236 Office: Fortis Investments 75 State St Ste 2700 Boston MA 02109

**VERMYLEN, PAUL ANTHONY, JR.,** oil industry executive; b. NYC, Dec. 5, 1946; s. Paul Anthony and Nancy Primrose (Barr) Vermylen; m. Robin S. Collins, Jan. 24, 1970; children: Robert T.C., Nancy Barr Vermylen Thornton, Sarah Morgan Vermylen Trust, Paul Anthony III. AB, Georgetown U., 1968; MBA, Columbia U., 1971. V.p. Citibank N.A., NYC, 1971-78; treas. Commonwealth Oil Refining Co., San Antonio, 1978-81, v.p. fin., CFO, 1981—82; v.p., CFO, dir. Meenan Oil Co., Inc., Syosset, NY, 1982—91, pres., 1992—2001, Meenan Oil Co., L.P., 1992—2001; chmn. Kestrel Energy Co., Inc., Huntington, NY, 2002—05; pres., bd. dirs Kestrel Energy Ptnrs. LLC, 2005—; chmn. Kestrel Heat LLC, 2006—. Bd. dirs. Petroleum Industry Rsch. Found., 1992—2002, Thermal Ventures II, Coalition Energy LLC, Downeast LNG, Inc. Bd. dirs. Huntington Arts Coun., N.Y.C., 1983—89, v.p., 1986—87, pres., 1987—89; bd. dirs. Cold Spring Harbor Whaling Mus., 1995—2000; bd. advisors Cold Spring Harbor Lab. DNA Learning Ctr., 1991—2000; bd. regents Georgetown U., Washington, 1997—2003; trustee Girls Prep. Charter Sch. N.Y.C., 2004—, bd. dirs., 2004—. Mem.: Empire State Petroleum Assn. (bd. dirs. 1994—2001), Causeway Club, N.Y. Yacht Club, Cold Spring Harbor Beach Club.

**VERNARELLI, MICHAEL JOSEPH,** economics professor, consultant, academic administrator; b. Rochester, N.Y., Nov. 24, 1948; s. S. John and Angelica Dolores (Morabito) V.; m. Joan Ann Taylor, Oct. 4, 1975; children: Jacqueline Andrea, Laurel Aileen. BA in Econs., U. Mich., 1970; MA in Econs., SUNY, Binghamton, 1974, PhD in Econs., 1978. Account analyst Travelers Ins. Co., Rochester, 1970-71; rsch. assoc. Ctrl. Adminstrn. SUNY, 1975-76; prof. econs. Rochester Inst. Tech., 1976—, chmn. dept., 1987—. Cons. econs. Rochester Downtown Devel. Corp., 1980; rsch. economist divsn. housing rsch. HUD, Washington, 1980-81, vis. scholar, 1980; pres., forensic economist Rochester Econ. Cons., 1983—; vis. prof. U.S. Bus. Sch. in Prague, 1992-96. Contbg. author: Federal Housing Policy and Desegregation, 1986. Mem. Brighton (N.Y.) Bd. Archtl. Rev., 1990-91, mem. planning bd., 1991-98. Recipient Eisenhart award Rochester Inst. Tech., 1987; grantee SUNY, Binghamton, 1974. Mem. Am. Econ. Assn., Nat. Assn. Forensic Economists, Ea. Econ. Assn., Greater Rochester C. of C. (panel mem. bus. trends com. 1987—), Omicron Delta Epsilon. Roman Catholic. Avocation: golf. Home: 133 Esplanade Dr Rochester NY 14610-3325 Office: Rochester Inst Tech Rochester NY 14623-0887 Office Phone: 585-475-2455. Personal E-mail: mjvern11@aol.com. Business E-Mail: mjvgss@rit.edu.

**VERNER, JAMES MELTON,** lawyer; b. Selma, Ala., Sept. 19, 1915; s. Singleton Foster and Jennie (Harris) V.; m. Gretchen Gores, Aug. 12, 1939; children: Ann Verner Picardo, James Singleton, William Melton. Student, Biltmore Coll., 1932—34; AB, U. N.C., 1936, JD, 1938. Bar: NC 1938, Tenn. 1947, D.C. 1950, Va. 1986. Assoc. firm Gover & Covington, Charlotte, NC, 1938; law clk. atty. gen. NC, 1938-40; atty. CAB, Washington, 1940-43; asst. gen. counsel Chgo. & So. Airlines, Memphis, 1946-47; atty. Air Transport Assn. Am., Washington, 1947-49; hearing examiner CAB, 1949-50, exec. asst. to chmn., 1950, exec. dir., 1950-53; from atty. to ptnr. Turney & Turney, 1953—60; ptnr. firm Verner, Liipfert, Bernhard, McPherson & Hand, Chartered (and predecessor firms), 1960-88; hon. mem. bd. dirs., spl. coun. Piper Rudnick Gray Cary (merged with Verner, Liipfert, Bernhard, McPherson & Hand, Chartered), Washington. Assoc. editor N.C. Law Rev., 1937—38. Former mem., chmn. policy bd. Legal Counsel for Elderly, Washington. Lt. (j.g.) USNR, 1943-46; legal officer Naval Air Transport Svc., 1945-46. Mem.: ABA, Cosmos Club (Washington), Order of Golden Fleece. Home: 900 N Taylor St # 2104-2106 Arlington VA 22203-1858 Office: Piper Rudnick Gray Cary 1200 Nineteenth St NW Washington DC 20003-6132 *My belief is that if you treat other people fairly and trust them, you will seldom be disappointed and will be the better for it.*

**VERNEY, RICHARD GREVILLE,** paper company executive; b. Providence, Aug. 24, 1946; s. Gilbert and Virginia Ruth (Piggott) Verney; m. Dorothy Howard, Aug. 26, 1967; children: Virginia F., Elizabeth I., Heather B., Eric B. AB, Brown U., 1968. Mgmt. trainee Monadnock Paper Mills, Bennington, NH, 1969-70, asst. gen. mgr., 1970, exec. v.p. 1970-76, pres., 1977-85, chmn., CEO, 1978—, Monadnock Non-Wovens, LLC, 1998—, Monadnock Specialty Coatings, LLC, 2000—. Mem. exec. com. Crotched Mt. Found., Greenfield, NH, 1974—87, trustee, 1974—, St. George's Sch., Newport, RI, 1978—93, chmn., 1985—89, hon. trustee, 1993—, Monadnock Cmty. Hosp., 1993—2000, v.p., 1997—99; trustee Nantucket Conservation Found., Inc., 1994—, pres., 1998—. Mem.: Bus. Industry Assn. N.H. (bd. dir. 1991—, mem. exec. com. 1998—2004), Boston Paper Trade Assn., Sales Assn. Paper Industry, Am. Forest and Papers Assn. (chmn. exec. bd. pulp consumers divsn. 1980—82, chmn. splty. packaging and indsl. divsn. 1984—85, chmn. cover and text exec. com. 1989—91, bd. dir. 1991—98, chmn. printing/writing exec. com. 2002—03, co-chmn. printing/writing exec. com. 2005—), N.Y. Yacht Club (N.Y.C.), Nantucket Yacht Club (Mass.), Algonquin Club (Boston). Republican. Episcopalian. Home: PO Box 145 The Verney Farm Bennington NH 03442-0145 Office: Monadnock Paper Mills Inc 117 Antrim Rd Bennington NH 03442-4205 Business E-Mail: rverney@mpm.com.

**VERNINO, STEVEN,** neurologist, researcher; PhD, Baylor Coll. of Medicine, Houston, Tex., 1992, MD, 1994. Diplomate Am. Bd. of Neurology, 2000. Assoc. prof. Mayo Clinic, Rochester, Minn., 1999—2004, U. Tex. Southwestern Med. Ctr., Dallas, 2004—. Achievements include research in Identification of antibodies that cause neurological diseases. Office: U Tex Southwestern Med Ctr 5323 Harry Hines Dallas TX 75390 Office Phone: 214-648-8816.

**VERNON, CARL ATLEE, JR.,** retired wholesale food distributor executive; b. Topeka, Aug. 15, 1926; s. Carl Atlee and Capitola May (Jarboe) V.; m. Marion Leila Colton, May 7, 1950; children— Mary Catherine, Matthew Fowler, Susan Elizabeth. BS, Yale U., 1947. Merchandising mgr. Fleming Cos., Topeka, 1957-61, dir. merchandising, 1961-66, dir. info. services, 1966-72, v.p. info. services, 1972-74, v.p. regional systems, 1974-79, sr. v.p. mktg. services Oklahoma City, 1979-88. Chmn. Shawnee County chpt. ARC, Topeka, Kans., 1957-58. Served to ensign USNR, 1944-46 Republican. Episcopalian. Avocations: golf, travel. E-mail: cavernonjr@aol.com.

**VERNON, DARRYL MITCHELL,** lawyer; b. N.Y.C., May 4, 1956; s. Leonard and Joyce (Davidson) V.; m. Lauren Lynn Bernstein, Aug. 21, 1982. BA in Math., Tufts U., 1978; JD, Yeshiva U., 1981. Bar: N.Y. 1982, U.S. Dist. Ct. (so. and ea. dists.) N.Y. 1982, U.S. Ct. Appeals (2d cir.) 1987. Assoc. Hochberg & Greenberg, N.Y.C., 1981—82; ptnr. Greenberg & Vernon, 1982—83, Law Offices of Darryl M. Vernon, 1983—; pres., ptnr. Vernon & Ginsburg, LLP, 1989—. Spkr. in field; instr. CLE courses. Contbr. articles to profl. jours. Samuel Belkin scholar, Yeshiva U., 1979. Mem. Assn. Bar City N.Y. (com. legal issues pertaining to animals), N.Y. State Bar Assn. (mem. spl. com. on animals and the law). Office: 261 Madison Ave New York NY 10016-2303 Office Phone: 212-949-7300. Business E-Mail: dvernon@vernonginsburg.com.

**VERNON, GARY WAYNE See LEVOX, GARY**

**VERNON, LILLIAN,** mail order company executive; b. 1927; d. Herman and Erna Menasche; m. Paolo Martino; children: Fred, David. DCS (hon.), Mercy Coll., Dobbs Ferry, N.Y., 1984, Coll. New Rochelle; DSc in Bus. Adminstrn. (hon.), Bryant Coll.; LLD (hon.), Baruch Coll.; LHD (hon.), Old Dominion U.; DCS (hon.), Mercy Coll.; DCS Coll. New Rochelle (hon.); D. in Bus. Adminstrn. (hon.), Bryant Coll.; LLD (hon.), Baruch Coll. Founding chmn. Lillian Vernon, Rye, NY, 1951—. Lectr. in field. Contbr. articles to profl. jours. Trustee Coll. Human Svcs., Bryant Coll.; mem. adv. bd. Giraffe Project Girl Scout Coun. Tidewater; mem. adv. bd. Women's News; mem. bd.

overseers Columbia U. Bus. Sch., NYU; mem. adv. com. Citizens Amb. Program; mem. bus. com. Met. Mus. Art; bd. govs. The Forum; mem. nat. com. The Kennedy Ctr. for Performing Arts, Washington; active The Ellis Island Reopening Com.; Bd. dirs. Westchester County, Ct. Preventive Psychiatry, Va. Opera, Children's Mus., Retinitis Pigmentosa Found. Named Va. Press Women Newsmaker of Yr., woman of Yr., Women's Direct Response Group and Westchester County Fedn. Women's Clubs, Hampton Rds. Woman of Yr., So. New Eng. Entrepreneur of Yr.; named to Acad. Women Achievers, YWCA, Direct Mktg. Assn. Hall of Fame, Conn. Women's Hall of Fame; recipient Disting. Achievement award, Lab. Inst. Merchandising, Entrepreneurial award, Women's Bus. Owners of N.Y., 1983, Bravo award, YWCA, Woman of Achievement award, Woman's NEws, Nat. Hero award, Big. Bros./Big Sisters, Legend in Leadership award, Emory U., A Woman Who Has Made a Difference award, Inter. Womens Forum, medal of honor, Ellis Island, Bus. Leadership award, Gannett Newspapers, Outstanding Bus. Leader award, Northwood Inst., Congl. Record Commendation award, Crystal award, Coll. Human Svcs., City of Peace award, Bonds of Israel, Svc. award, Sr. Placement Bur., Excellence award, Westchester Assn. Women Bus. Owners, Commendation in Cong. Record, Magnificent Seven award, Bus. and Profl. Women, Woman of Distinction award, Birmingham So. Coll. Mem.: Nat. Retail Fedn. (bd. dirs.), Women's Forum, Com. of 200, Am. Stock Exch. (listed co. adv. com.), Am. Bus. Conf. (dir.), Lotos Club. Office: Lillian Vernon Corp 445 Hamilton Ave White Plains NY 10601-1836

**VERNON, WESTON, III, (WES VERNON),** broadcaster, writer, actor; b. NYC, Aug. 23, 1931; s. Weston, Jr. and Adelaide (Neilson) V.; m. Alida Steinvoort, Oct. 5, 1951; children: Rosanne, Weston IV, Diane, John Randall. Student, Utah State U., 1949-50, Brigham Young U., 1953-54. Early broadcasting career on staff of radio stas., in Utah and Wyo., 1950-54; news and announcer KBMY, Billings, Mont., 1954-63; news dir., polit. specialist KSL Radio-TV, Salt Lake City, Utah, 1963-68; bur. chief Bonneville Internat. Corp., Washington, 1968-72; corr. CBS Radio Stas. News Svc. CBS Radio, Washington, 1972-97; host CBS Crosstalk, 1975-97. Columnist RenewAmerica.us,US AIM Report, Conservative Battleline, The High Green, The Timetable, The Accuracy In Media Report, Washington columnist Carstens Publs., Inc., guest host Dateline: Washington Radio Am. Network, 1998—; actor:. Bd. dirs. Winding-Orchard Citizens Assn., Wheaton-Glenmont, Md., 1974—77, 1986—, pres., 1975—76. Served with AUS, 1951—52. Recipient Journalism awards, Mont. A.P. Press Stas., 1960, Utah Bar Assn., 1965, Utah Broadcasters Assn., 1965—66, Nat. Press Club. Mem. SAG, AFTRA (exec. bd. Balt.-Wash. local 1997—), Am. Legion (comdr. Yellowstone Post 4 1962-63), Chesapeake Rlwy. Assn. (pres. 1992-94, bd. dirs.). Office: 1605 Billman Ln Silver Spring MD 20902-1417

**VERON, J. MICHAEL,** lawyer, writer; b. Lake Charles, La., Aug. 24, 1950; s. Earl Ernest and Alverdy (Heyd) V.; m. Melinda Anne Guidry, Jan. 2, 1993; children: John Heyd, Katharine Leigh, Dylan Michael Earl. BA, Tulane U., 1972, JD, 1974; LLM, Harvard U., 1976. Bar: La. 1974, U.S. Dist. Ct. (we. dist.) La. 1979, U.S. Dist. Ct. (ea. dist.) La. 1979, U.S. Dist. Ct. (mid. dist.) La., 1983, U.S. Dist. Ct. (ea. dist.) Tex. 1992), U.S. Ct. Appeals (5th cir.) 1981, U.S. Ct. Appeals (fed. cir.) 1996, U.S. Tax Ct. 1988. Law clk. to presiding justice La. Supreme Ct., New Orleans, 1974-75; sole practice Lake Charles, 1976-78; ptnr. Scofield, Gerard, Veron, Singletary & Pohorelsky (formerly Scofield, Gerard, Veron, Hoskins & Soileau), Lake Charles, 1978—. Instr. legal method and rsch. Boston U., 1975-76; lectr. environ. law McNeese State U., 1976-79; faculty Tulane Trial Adv. Inst., 1980; adj. prof. La. State U. Sch. Law, 1993-2000. Author: The Greatest Player Who Never Lived, 2000, The Greatest Course That Never Was, 2001; mem. bd. editors Tulane Law Rev., 1972-73, assoc. editor, 1973-74. Mem. athletic adv. com. Tulane U., 1983-86; pres. Krewe of Barataria, 1980-86. Named to La. State U. Law Ctr. Hall of Fame, 1993. Mem. U.S. Golf Assn. (sectional affairs com.), La. Golf. Assn. (bd. dirs., pres. 1990), Order of Coif, Maritime Law Assn., Lake Charles Country Club (pres. 1986). Roman Catholic. Avocations: golf, gin rummy, athletics. Home: 9 Par Dr Lake Charles LA 70605-5925 Office: Scofield Gerard Veron Singletary & Pohorelsky 1114 Ryan St Lake Charles LA 70601-5252 E-mail: mveron@sgvsp.com.

**VERONGOS, HELEN,** editor; Asst. fgn. editor, night New York Times. Office: New York Times 229 W 43d St New York NY 10036 Office Phone: 212-556-7415. Office Fax: 212-556-7278.*

**VERONICA, DEBRA CLARISSE,** principal; b. Buffalo, Sept. 17, 1966; d. John Thomas Owczarek and Dolores Pauline Evans; m. Mark David Veronica, Apr. 7, 1989; 4 children. BSc, State U. of NY at Buffalo, 1988, MSc, 1995. Cert. Teaching NY, 1996. Tchr. St. Barnabas Sch., Depew, NY, 1988—89, St. Amelia Sch., Tonawanda, NY, 1989—91, Buffalo Pub. Sch., 1991—2003; adj. prof. Canisius Coll., Buffalo, 2001—03; asst. prin. Lancaster Pub. Sch. Sys., NY, 2003—04; elem. prin. Maryvale Sch. Sys., Cheektowaga, NY, 2004—. Summer sch. prin. Sweet Home Sch., Amherst, NY, 2003; ednl. cons. Discovery Toys. Vol. tchr. St. Amelia Religious Edn. Dept., 1988—90, 1992; pres. Mother of Twins Club of Buffalo, 2002—04, corresponding sec., 2000, 2001, club adv., 2004—06. Mem.: Internat. Reading Assn., Sch. Admin. Assn. of NY State, Assn. for Supervision and Curriculum Develop., Nat. Assn. of Elem. Sch. Prin., Phi Alpha Theta, Kappa Delta Pi. Avocation: reading. Office: Maryvale Sch Sys I Nagel Dr Buffalo NY 14225

**VERONIS, GEORGE,** geophysics educator; b. New Brunswick, N.J., June 6, 1926; s. Nicholas Emmanuel and Angeliki (Efthimakis) V.; m. Anna Margareta Olsson, Nov. 8, 1963; m. Catherine Elizabeth, Jan. 29, 1949 (div. Nov. 1962); children— Melissa, Benjamin. A.B., Lafayette Coll., 1950; Ph.D., Brown U., 1954; M.A. (hon.), Yale U., 1966; DSc (hon.) Lafayette Coll. 1997. Staff meteorologist Inst. Advanced Study, Princeton, 1953-56, staff mathematician Woods Hole Oceanographic Inst., Mass., 1956-64, mem. staff, dir. geophys. fluid dynamics summer program, 1959—, assoc. prof. MIT, Cambridge, 1961-64, research oceanographer, 1964-66; prof. geophysics and applied sci. Yale U., New Haven, 1966—, Henry Barnard Davis prof., 1985—, chmn. geology and geophysics, 1976-79, dir. applied math, 1979-93. Editor Jour. Marine Rsch., 1973—; contbr. articles to profl. jours. Served with USN, 1943-46. Fellow Am. Acad. Arts and Scis., Am. Geophys. Union; mem. NAS, Norwegian Acad. Scis. (Robert L. and Bettie P. Cody award 1989, Henry Stommel Rsch. award 1997). Greek Orthodox. Office Phone: 203-432-3148. Business E-Mail: george.veronis@yale.edu.

**VERONNEAU-TROUTMAN, SUZANNE,** retired ophthalmologist; b. Coaticook, Que., Can. Oct. 30, 1928; d. Sarto Veronneau and Victorine Marcoux; m. Richard C. Troutman, July 12, 1967; stepchildren: David Troutman, Anne Troutman, Richard Troutman. BA, Coll. St. Maurice, St. Hyacinthe, Que., 1951; BSc II. U. Montreal, Que., 1952, MD, 1957; postgrad. in ophthalmology/pathology, Inst. Ophthalmology, London, 1960—61. Diplomate ophthalmology Royal Coll. Physicians of London, Royal Coll. Surgeons of Eng., lic. Med. Coun. Can., physician N.Y. State, diplomate ophthalmology Coll. of Physicians and Surgeons Province of Que., Royal Coll. of Physicians and Surgeons of Can., Am. Bd. of Ophthalmology. Sr. plastic surgery, neurosurgery resident Notre Dame Hosp., Montreal, 1957—58; resident in ophthalmology Hosp. Maisonneuve, Montreal, 1958—59; asst. in ophthalmology Hosp. Edouard Herriot, Lyon, France, 1959—60; clin. asst., OPD officer Royal Eye and Moorfields Eye Hosps., London, 1961; ophthalmic surgeon Ghandi Eye Hosp., Aligarh, India, 1962; instr. basic scis. Maisonneuve Hosp., Montreal, 1963—67; clin. asst. prof. ophthalmology SUNY Downstate Med. Ctr., Bklyn., 1971—82; clin. instr. dept. ophthalmology Cornell U. Med. Coll., N.Y.C., 1971—74, clin. asst. prof. ophthalmology, 1974—77, clin. assoc. prof. ophthalmology, 1977—98, clin. prof. ophthalmology, 1998—2000; clin. prof. emeritus Weill Med. Coll. Cornell U. N.Y.C., 2000—. Dir. strabismus clinic and orthoptics Maisonneuve Hosp., Que., 1963—67; chief ocular motility clinic Manhattan Eye Ear and Throat Hosp., N.Y.C. 1970—2000; asst. attending physician dept. ophthalmology Hosp. of the Holy Family, 1973—77, assoc. attending physician, 1977—80; asst. dir. dept. motor anomalies N.Y. Eye and Ear Infirmary, 1974—78, assoc. dir., 1978—82, assoc. attending surgeon,

1974–82; adj. attending ophthalmologist Bronx Lebanon Hosp. Ctr., 1975–77, assoc. attending ophthalmologist, 1977–79; cons. dept. ophthalmology Beth Israel Med. Ctr., 1979–87; lectr. in field. Editor, transl.: Hugonniers' textbook Strabismus, Heterophoria, Oculomotor Paralysis; author (textbook translated in French, Japanese and Portuguese) Prisms in the Medical and Surgical Treatment of Strabismus; contbr. 32 chpts. to books, articles more than 35 articles to scientific jours. Established endowment of bienniel internat. prize Pan Am. Asssn. Ophthalmology, 1991; established ann. prize Women in Ophthalmology, San Francisco, 1997; established perpetual endowment for ann. scholarships and prize dept. edn. U. Que., Montreal, 1997; established perpetual endowment for animal scholarships Dept. of Ophthalmology, U. Montréal, 2006. Recipient Residents award for outstanding tchg., N.Y. Eye and Ear Infirmary, 1970, Spl. Achievement medal, U. Montreal, 1993. Fellow: ACS (life), Royal Coll. Surgeons Can.; mem.: AMA (life), Am. Ophthalmol. Soc., Am. Acad. Ophthalmology (life Honor award 1981), Pan Am. Assn. Ophthalmology (life; bd. dirs. 1993–2003), Med. Soc. of the State of N.Y. (life), Am. Assn. Pediat. Ophthalmology and Strabismus (life; charter mem.). Home: Apt 30 A 860 United Nations Plz New York NY 10017 Personal E-mail: sveronneau@msn.com.

**VEROPOULOS, KONSTANTINOS,** computer scientist, researcher; b. Athens, Greece, Feb. 22, 1972; s. Petros Veropoulos and Georgia Kofina. BSc in Computer Sci. and Engring., Am. U. Athens, 1994; MSc in Parallel Computer Sys., U. West Eng., 1996; PhD in Machine Learning Approaches to Med. Decision Making, U. Bristol, 2001. Programmer-analyst, software developer i-con (Info. Consultants), Athens, 1994; group project supr. U. Bristol, England, 1996—2000; with Med. Imaging Rsch. Unit Dept. Human Biology U. Cape Town, South Africa, 1999—; postdoctoral scholar dept. computer sci and engring. U. Nev., Reno, 2004—06; postdoctoral rsch. assoc. divsn. atmospheric scis. Desert Rsch. Inst., 2006—. Contbr. articles to profl. jours.; author conf. procs. With Hellenic Air Forces. Mem.: IEEE, Internat. Machine Learning Soc., Hellenic Artificial Intelligence Soc. Achievements include research in interactive computer graphics; relational database programming; image processing and image recognition; medical diagnosis/prognosis computer systems; artificial neural networks; data analysis and visualization; on face categorization for face recognition algorithms; computer vision, face classification and recognition; signal processing, thermal desorption, gas chromatography, mass spectroscopy. Home: Apt 332 6200 Meadowood Mall Cir Reno NV 89502 Office: Divsn Atmospheric Scis Desert Rsch Inst 2215 Raggio Pky Reno NV 89512 Office Phone: 775-674-7155. E-mail: kvero@dri.edu.

**VERPLANK, SCOTT RACHAL,** professional golfer; b. Dallas, July 9, 1964; m. Kim Verplank; children: Scottie, Hannah, Emma, Heidi. BS in Bus., Okla. State U., 1986. Profl. golfer PGA Tour, 1986—; U.S Amateur champion, 1984; NCAA champion, 1986; winner Western Open (PGA Tour), 1985, Buick Open (PGA Tour), 1988, World Cup of Golf (individual), 1998, Reno-Tahoe Open, 2000; Ball Canadian Open, 2001. Mem. Walker Cup team, 1985, World Cup team, 1998, Ryder Cup team, 2002. Avocations: reading, kids, sports, quail hunting. Office: c/o PGA Box 109601 100 Ave of Champions Palm Beach Gardens FL 33410

**VERRECCHIA, ALFRED JOSEPH,** toy company executive; b. Providence, Feb. 19, 1943; s. Alfred Augustus and Elda Lucy (Tortolani) V.; m. Geraldine Macari, June 11, 1964; children: Michael, Michele, Melisa, Lisa. BS, U. R.I., 1967, MBA in Fin., 1971; Doctorate (hon.), Johnson & Wales U., 1991. Joined as jr. accountant Hasbro, Inc., Pawtucket, RI, 1965, v.p. fin., 1980-82, sr. v.p. fin., CFO, 1982-86, exec. v.p. fin., CFO, 1986-89, exec. v.p., 1989, pres. Hasbro mfg. svcs., 1989, co-COO, 1989, COO, domestic toys, exec. v.p. global ops., CFO, 1990—96, exec. v.p., pres., global ops., 1996—99, exec. v.p., pres., global ops and develop., 1999; exec. v.p., global ops., CFO Hasbro Inc., Pawtucket, 1999—2000; pres., COO, CFO Hasbro, Inc., Pawtucket, 2000—01, pres., COO, 2001—03, pres., CEO, 2003—. Bd. dirs. Hasbro Inc., Old Stone Corp., FM Global. Chmn. Bradley Hosp., East Providence, R.I.; pres. R.I. Pub. Expenditure Coun., Providence; bd. mem. Bd. of Govs. for Higher Edn., Providence, U. R.I. Coll. Bus., Kingston, R.I. Mem. Toy Mfrs. Am. (bd. mem.). Office: Hasbro Inc 1027 Newport Ave Pawtucket RI 02862*

**VERRILL, CHARLES OWEN, JR.,** lawyer; b. Biddeford, Maine, Sept. 30, 1937; s. Charles Owen and Elizabeth (Handy) V.; m. Mary Ann Blanchard, Aug. 13, 1960 (dec.); children: Martha Anne, Edward Blanchard, Ethan Christopher, Elizabeth Handy, Matthew Lawton, Peter Goldthwait; m. Diana Baber, Dec. 11, 1993. AB, Tufts U., 1959; LLB, Duke U., 1962. Bar: D.C. 1962. Assoc. Weaver & Glassie, 1962-64, Barco, Cook, Patton & Blow, 1964-66, ptnr., 1967, Patton, Boggs & Blow, 1967-84, Wiley, Rein & Fielding, Washington, 1984—. Adj. prof. internat. trade law/internat. bus. transaction Georgetown U. Law Ctr., Washington, 1978—, Charles Fahy Disting. adj. prof., 1993; vis. sr. lectr. internat. trade law Duke U. Law Sch., 1998—; conf. chmn. The Future of Internat. Steel Industry, Bellagio, Italy, 1984, U.S. Agenda for Uruguay Round, Airlie House, Warrenton, Va., 1986, Polish Joint Venture Law, Cracow, Poland, 1987, Internat. Steel Industry II, Bellagio, 1987, Bulgaria and the GATT, Washington, 1977; chair, spkr. Protection of Intellectual Property from Theft and Piracy Abroad Southwestern Legal Found. Fgn. Investment Symposium, 1995, chair, panel on NAFTA 2 1/2 Years Later, 1996; nat. adv. bd. Natural Resources Coun. of Maine, 2002—; panel mem. CPR Washington, 2003—. Local dir. Tufts U. Ann. Fund, 1965-69; mem. Duke Law Alumni Coun., 1972-75; trustee Internat. Law Inst., 1981—, chmn. bd. trustees, 1983-87, pres., 2002—; apptd. to roster of dispute settlement panelists World Trade Orgn., 1995, 97; chmn. adv. bd. Inst. for Advancement of Svc., 1997—; adv. com. rules U.S. Ct. Internat. Trade, 1998—; chmn. D.C. Cable Television Adv. Com., 1999—; bd. visitors Duke U. Law Sch., 2000—. Mem. ABA, Internat. Bar Assn., D.C. Bar Assn., Order of Coif, Theta Delta Chi, Phi Delta Phi, Met. Club (Washington), Chevy Chase Club (Md.), Tarratine Club (Dark Harbor, Maine). Office: Wiley Rein & Fielding LLP 1776 K St NW Washington DC 20006-2304 Office Phone: 202-719-7323. Business E-Mail: cverrill@wrf.com.

**VERRILL, F. GLENN,** advertising executive; b. N.Y.C., Dec. 17, 1923; s. Ralph Francis and Rose (Cuva) V.; m. Jean Demar, Aug. 25, 1946; children: Gary, Joan. AB, Adelphi Coll., 1949; A.M., Harvard U., 1950. With Batten, Barton, Durstine & Osborn, Inc., 1952—98, v.p., 1964; creative dir. Batten, Barton, Durstine & Osborn, Inc. (Burke Dowling Adams div.), Atlanta, 1965-70, exec. v.p., gen. mgr., 1970-71, pres., 1971-88, chmn., 1988—98, also dir. parent co. Author: Advertising Procedure, 1983, rev. edit., 1986, 88. Mem. adv. bd. U. Ga.; vice chmn. bd. overseers Coll. Bus. Adminstrn., Ga. State U.; bd. dirs. Atlanta Humane Soc., 1980-81; chmn. Advanced Advt. Inst. Atlanta, 1981; mem. Peabody award com., 1984—90; bd. dirs. Atlanta Coll. of Art, 1990. With USAAF, 1943-46. Mem. Am. Assn. Advt. Agys. (nat. dir. 1973—), Atlanta Athletic Club, Cherokee Club, Harvard Club (Atlanta). Episcopalian. Home: 1730 Winterthur Close Atlanta GA 30324 Office: BBDO Atlanta Inc Box 720717 Atlanta GA 30358

**VERRILL, JOHN HOWARD,** museum director; b. Biddeford, Maine, June 17, 1947; s. Charles Owen and Elizabeth Martha (Handy) V.; m. Carol Christine Cory, Sept. 8, 1967; 1 child, Nathan Lawrence. BA, Campbell U., 1969. Tchr. St. Mary's County Schs., Leonardtown, Md., 1969-73; sales mgr. Kable News Co., N.Y.C., 1973-79; contract adminstr. Fischbach and Moore, L.K. Comstock, Lanham, Md., 1979-83; agrl. entrepreneur Jubilee Farm, Hebron, Md., 1983-87; mus. mgr. NASA, Wallops Island, Va., 1985; exec. dir. Purnell Mus., Snow Hill, Md., 1986-93, Ea Shore of Va. Hist. Soc., Onancock, Va., 1993—. Faculty mem. Seminar for Hist. Adminstrn. at Colonial Williamsburg, 1999-2000. Editor: (book) Trustee, Board Member Handbook, 1995. Pres. Wicomico County Fair, Salisbury, Md., 1986, S.E. Shore Travel Coun., Salisbury, 1988, Lions Club, Hebron, Md., 1991; active Hist. Adminstrn. 1999-2000. Recipient Gov.'s citation, Maryland Gov. Schaeffer, 1994. Mem. Am. Assn. Mus., S. Ea Mus. Conf. (mentor 1994), Va. Assn. Mus. (mentor 1997, treas. 2004-05, v.p. 2006—), Am. Assn. State and Local History, Small Mus. Assn. (chmn. 1990, bd. dirs. 1997—), Rotary

---

Club Melfa, Va. (pres. 1995), Ea. Shore Barrier Islands Ctr. (bd. dirs. 1995—). Episcopalian (Lay Eucharistic Minister). Avocations: home restoration, gardening, boating, travel. Office: Ea Shore Va Hist Soc PO Box 193 Onancock VA 23417-0193 E-mail: kerr@esva.net.

**VERRILL, KATHLEEN WILLS,** special education educator; b. Tucson, Jan. 4, 1938; d. William Oscar Wills and Helen Louise (Boswell) Perry; m. Thomas Anthony Verrill, July 30, 1966; 1 child, Anthony Anthony. AA, Monterey Peninsula Coll., 1958; BA, San Francisco State U., 1963, MA, 1965. Tchr. educable mentally retarded Albany (Calif.) Unified Schs., 1963-70, Sch. Dist. # 49, Fairfield, Maine, 1970-73; resource tchr. Indpls. Schs., 1973-75; tchr. learning handicapped Phila. Sch. Dist., 1975-77, ednl. evaluator, 1977-79, instructional advisor, 1979-81; resource specialist San Francisco Unified Schs., 1981-82, Alameda (Calif.) Unified Sch. Dist., 1982—. Author Food Centered Curriculum for Learning Disabled, 1965. Rep. Sch. Dist. Affirmative Action com., Alameda, 1988-90. Recipient PTA Calif. Hon. Svc. award Lum Sch., 1991; named Tchr. of Yr. Alameda Sch. Dist., 1986; Crown Zellerbach Found. fellowship, 1964, edn. grant Alameda County Schs., 1964. Mem. NEA, Coun. Exceptional Children, Alameda Edn. Assn. (rep. 1989-90), Calif. Tchrs. Assn., Delta Kappa Gamma (chmn. rsch. 1988-89, pres. Delta Zeta chpt. 1992-94, exec. bd. 1994—). Avocations: travel, classical music, reading, cooking, study of artists. Office: Alameda Unified Sch Dist 1801 Sandcreek Way Alameda CA 94501-6024

**VERRILLO, RONALD THOMAS,** neuroscience educator, researcher; b. Hartford, Conn., July 31, 1927; s. Francesco Paul and Angela (Forte) V.; m. Violet Silverstein, June 3, 1950; children: Erica, Dan, Thomas. BA, Syracuse U., NY, 1952; PhD, U. Rochester, 1958. Asst. prof. Syracuse U., 1957-62, rsch. assoc., 1959-63, rsch. fellow, 1963-67, assoc. prof., 1967-74, prof., 1974-94, prof. emeritus, 1995—, assoc. dir. Inst. Sensory Rsch., 1980-84, dir., 1984-93, dir. grad. neurosci. program, 1984-93. Advisor com. on hearing, bioacoustics and biomechanics NRC. Author: Adjustment to Visual Disability, 1961 (award 1962); contbr. chpts. to books, articles to profl. jours. With USN, 1945-46. Fellow Am. Found. for Blind, 1956, NATO, 1970; grantee NSF, 1969-72, 84-87, NIH, 1972—; recipient Internat. Sensory Aids award, 1998. Fellow Acoustical Soc. Am. (Silver medal 1999); mem. Soc. for Neurosci., N.Y. Acad. Scis., Sigma Xi (Sigma award 1999). Home: 312 Berkeley Dr Syracuse NY 13210-3031 Office: Syracuse U Inst Sensory Rsch 621 Skytop Rd Syracuse NY 13244-5290 Office Phone: 315-443-4166. Business E-Mail: ron_verrillo@isr.syr.edu.

**VERRONE, PATRIC MILLER,** lawyer, writer; b. Glendale, NYC, Sept. 29, 1959; s. Pat and Edna (Miller) V.; m. Margaret Maiya Williams, 1989; children: Patric Carroll Williams, Marianne Emma Williams, Theodore Henry Williams. BA, Harvard U., 1981; JD, Boston Coll., 1984. Bar: Fla. 1984, Calif. 1988, U.S. Dist. Ct. (mid. dist.) Fla. 1984, U.S. Dist. Ct. (ctrl. dist.) Calif. 1995, U.S. Ct. Appeals (9th cir.) 1995. Assoc. Allen, Knudsen, Swartz, DeBoest, Rhoads & Edwards, Ft. Myers, Fla., 1984-86; writer The Tonight Show, Burbank, Calif., 1987-90. Adj. prof. Loyola Law Sch., LA, 1998—2000; lectr. U. Calif., LA, 2002—05. Dir. prodr., writer The Civil War-The Lost Episode, 1991; writer: The Larry Sanders Show, 1992—94, The Critic, 1993—95; prodr., writer The Simpsons, 1994—95, 2002—, Muppets Tonight!, 1995—97 (Emmy award Best Children's Program, 1998), Pinky and the Brain, 1998, Futurama, 1998—2002 (Environ. Media award, 2000, 2003, WGA award nominee, 2004, Emmy nominee, 1999, 2001, 2003, 2004, Emmy award for outstanding animated program, 2002, Writers Guild award nominee, 2004, Annie award nominee, 2004); editor: Harvard Lampoon, 1978—84, Boston Coll. Law Rev., 1983—84, Fla. Bar Jour., 1987—88, L.A. Lawyer, 1994—2005; issue editor Am. Entertainment Law Issue, 1995—2006; contbr. articles to profl. jours. including Elysian Fields Quar., White's Guide to Collecting Figures, Frank Sinatra: The Man, The Music, The Legend, Bongo Comics. Bd. dirs. Calif. Confedn. of Arts, 1994-98, Mus. Contemporary Art, 1994-95; trustee Am. Film Inst., 2005—; mem. adv. bd. Hollywood Health and Soc., 2005—. Mem. ABA (vice-chair arts, entertainment and sports law com. 1995-96), Calif. Bar, Calif. Lawyers for Arts, L.A. County Bar Assn. (sec. barristers exec. com., chmn artists and the law com., steering com. homeless shelter project, intellectual property and entertainment law sect., state appelate jud. evaluation com., legis. activity com.), Fla. Bar Assn., Writers Guild Am. West (exec. com. animation writers caucus, bd. dirs. 1999-2001, sec., treas., 2001-05, chair organizing com. 2001-05, pres. 2005—, animation writers caucus, Animation Writing award 2002), Harvard Club Lee County (v.p. 1985-86), Harvard Club So. Calif. Republican. Roman Catholic. Avocations: baseball, history. Home and Office: PO Box 1428 Pacific Palisades CA 90272-1428

**VERSACE, DONATELLA,** fashion designer; b. Reggio di Calabria, Italy, May 2, 1955; d. Antonio and Francesca V.; m. Paul Beck (div.); children: Allegra, Daniel. Degree in lit., U. Florence, Italy. Head designer Versus label Gianni Versace Group, 1978—97, vice chmn., style and image dir. N.Y.C., 1997—. Released fragrance Versace Woman, 2001. Achievements include created children's line, 1993; launched fragrance Versace Woman, 2001. Office: Gianni Versace SpA Via Ges 12 20121 Milan Italy Address: Instante Vesa srl Via Spiga 25 20121 Milan Italy Office Phone: 02 7610931. Office Fax: 02 798572.*

**VERSCH, ESTHER MARIE,** artist; b. Santa Monica, Calif., May 27, 1927; d. Claro Contreras Santellanes and Juana Hernandez; m. Chester Ray Fraelich, Nov. 14, 1943 (div. Nov. 1964); children: Joe Fraelich, Diane Fraelich Foster Viramontes; m. Terry Lee Versch, June 21, 1969; stepchildren: Fred, Roman, Joseph, Terry Jr., Michael. Student, East L.A. Coll., Pasadena City Coll. Lic. vocat. nurse. Nurse pvt. dr.'s office, L.A., 1968-69, U. So. Calif. Med. Ctr., L.A., 1963-68; artist Altadena, Calif., 1972—. Artist: (front cover) Library Services L.A., 1983, Christmas card for Western Greeting Inc., (back cover) Moccasin Tracks, 1984-85; one woman shows include Republic Fed. Savings, Altadena, Calif., Pasadena Pub. Libr., Whites Art Store and Gallery, La Canada, Calif., 1979, Windmill Gallery, 1985; group exhbns.: Women Artists of the West Internat. Exhbn. and Sale, Cody Western and Wildlife Classyc, 1979, Nat. Cowgirl Hall of Fame, Hereford, Tex., 1978, Beauty for the Beast Benefit, 1980, Ducks Unltd. Invitational Art Show, Taylor, Mich., 1986-87, Lawrence (Kans.) Indian Art Show, Mus. Anthropology, 1989-90, Snake River Showcase, Lewiston, Idaho, 1992, Women Artists of the West, 1992, 98, 99, Death Valley 49's Invitational Art Show, 1994-2000, 2001, George Ohr Cultural Arts and Cultural Ctr., Biloxi, Miss., 1998, Western and Wildlife Invitational Art Show, Estes Park, Colo., 2000, WAOW Art Show Pinedale, Wyo, 2002, Art and Music Festival, Dublin, Ohio, 2002, West Wind Gallery, Casper, Wyo., 2003-04, Pomerene Ctr. for the Arts, 2004, Zanesville Ctr. for the Arts, 2004, 05, Red River Valley Mus., Vernon, Tex., 2004, Ronald Reagan Mus., Simi Valley, Calif., 2004, Johnson Humrickhouse Mus., 2004-05, Dogwood Festival Artists Tour Studio, 2006, others; collections: Johnson Humrickhouse Mus., Coshocton, Ohio, other pvt. collections; illustrator back cover Moccasin Tracks, 1984-85. Vol. nurses aide City View Hosp., L.A., 1960-63; vol. Arroyo Rep., Pasadena, Calif., St. Luke Hosp., Pasadena, 1990-94, flu immunization ARC, 1977-78. Recipient Gold medal for watercolor San Gabriel Fine Arts, 1979, Best of Show award for watercolor Am. Indian and Western, 1990, Hon. mention San Gabriel Fine Arts, 1990, 3rd Place Watercolor Women Artists of the West Saddle Back Art Gallery, 1982. Mem. Women Artists of the West (emeritus mem., treas., asst. sec., editor West Wind, membership chmn.), Ohio Art League, Coshocton Art Guild (v.p. Juried Art Show 2004-05). Republican. Roman Catholic. Avocations: walking, gardening, sewing. E-mail: everschart@newsguy.com.

**VERSCHOOR, CURTIS CARL,** business educator, consultant; b. Grand Rapids, Mich., June 7, 1931; s. Peter and Leonene (Dahlstrom) V.; m. Marie Emilie Kritschgau, June 18, 1952; children— Katherine Anne, Carolyn Marie, John Peter, Carla Michelle. BBA with distinction, U. Mich., 1951, MBA, 1952; EdD, No. Ill. U., 1977. CPA; cert. mgmt. acctg., cert. fin. planner, cert. fraud examiner, cert. internal auditor; chartered fin. cons. Pub. accountant Touche, Ross, Bailey & Smart (C.P.A.'s), 1955-63; with Singer Co., 1963-68, asst. controller, 1965-68; controller Colgate-Palmolive Co., 1968-69; asst. controller bus. products group Xerox Corp., 1969-72; control-

---

ler Baxter Internat., 1972-73; CFO, v.p. fin. Altair Corp., Chgo., 1973-74; prof. DePaul U., Chgo., 1974-94, ledger and quill alumni rsch. prof., 1994—; pres. C.C. Verschoor & Assocs., Inc., 1981—. Part-time instr. Wayne State U., 1955-60. Author: Audit Committee Briefing: Understanding the 21st Century Audit Committee Governance Roles, 2000, Audit Committee Briefing: Facilitating New Audit Committee Responsibilities, 2001, Governance Update 2003: Impact of the New Initiatives, 2003; contbg. editor: Jour. Accountancy, 1961-62, Jour. Internal Auditing, 1985—, Strategic Fin., 1999-; editl. adv. bd. Acctg. Today, 1991—, Internal Auditor, 1993—. Trustee Hektoen Inst. Med. Rsch., Chgo., 1996—. Served with AUS, 1953-55. Recipient Elijah Watts Sells award Am. Inst. C.P.A.'s, 1953; rsch. scholar Ctr. for Bus. Ethics, Bentley Coll. Mem. AICPA, Fin. Execs. Inst., Am. Acctg. Assn., Inst. Mgmt. Accts., Inst. Internal Auditors, Nat. Assn. Corp. Dirs., Assn. Cert. Fraud Examiners, Internat. Assn. Bus. and Soc., Soc. for Bus. Ethics, Beta Gamma Sigma, Beta Alpha Psi, Delta Pi Epsilon, Phi Kappa Phi, Phi Eta Sigma. Home: 231 Wyngate Dr Barrington IL 60010-4840 Office: DePaul Univ One E Jackson Blvd Chicago IL 60604-2287 Business E-Mail: cverscho@depaul.edu.

**VERSCHUREN, ANNETTE,** retail executive; b. North Sydney, N.S., Can., 1956; Grad., Concordia U.; BBA, St. Francis Xavier U., Antigonish, N.S.; D (hon.), Mt. St. Vincent U.; LLD (hon.), St. Francis Xavier U., Antigonish, N.S. Devel. officer Cape Breton Devel. Corpn., Sydney, N.S., Canada; exec. v.p. Can. Devel. Investment Corpn.; v.p. corp. devel. Imasco Ltd.; pres., co-owner Michael's of Can., 1993—96; mem. staff to divsn. pres. EXPO Design Ctr. to Can. Divsn. pres. Home Depot, 1996—. Bd. mem. Can. Coun. Chief Execs.; chancellor Univ. Coll. Cape Breton; mem. North Am. Competitiveness Coun., 2006—, Can. Corp. Coun. on Volunteering. Bd. mem. Habitat for Humanity. Recipient Can. 125 medal. Mem.: Retail Coun. Can. (chair, Disting. Can. Retailer of Yr. 2005). Office: Home Depot Can Inc 900-1 Concorde Gate Toronto ON M3C 4H9 Canada*

**VERSFELD, LEON,** lawyer; b. South Africa, June 16, 1975; s. Johannes Hendrik and Lorraine Versfeld; m. Heather Lea Hunter, Sept. 27, 2003. BLC, U. Pretoria, South Africa, 1996, LLB, 1998; tng. diploma (hon.), Law Soc. South Africa, 1999. Bar: The High Ct. South Africa 1999, Mo. 2003, U.S Dist. Ct. Kans. 2003, U.S Dist. Ct. (we. dist.) Mo. 2003. Pharmacist asst. Link & Hyper Pharm, Pretoria, 1995—98; law clk. to Hon. NG Manitz Dept. Justice, Pretoria, 1997, law clk. to Hon. Deputy Judge Pres. P.J. Van Der Walt, 1998—99; pvt. practice Pretoria, 1999; law clerk The Wirken Law Group, P.C., Kansas City, Mo., 2000—03, assoc., 2003—. Grad. Greater Kansas City Bar Leadership Acad., 2005—06. Bd. mem. Ctrl. Youth Rugby, Kansas City, 2004—05; bd. dirs. Tru-Friends, Truman Med. Ctr., 2006; fgn. rugby player chmn. Kans. City Rugby Football Club, Kansas City, 2003—04; barrister Kans. City Met. Bar. Assn. Inn of Ct., Kansas City, 2004—05. Scholar, Delta Motor Corp., South Africa, 1994-1998. Mem.: Am. Trial Lawyers Assn., ABA, Am. Immigration Lawyer Assn., Kans. City Met. Bar Assn. Avocations: rugby, tennis, golf. Office: The Wirken Law Group PC 4740 Grand Blvd Ste 200 Kansas City MO 64112 Office Phone: 816-716-8982. Business E-Mail: lversfeld@kc.rr.com.

**VERSFELT, DAVID SCOTT,** lawyer; b. Mineola, NY, Feb. 17, 1951; s. William H. and Ruth (Gerland) V.; m. Mary Deborah Garber, Aug. 31, 1974; children: Christopher L., William S., Kathryn H. AB, Princeton U., 1973; JD, Columbia U., 1976. Bar: N.Y. 1977, U.S. Dist. Ct. (so. and ea. dists.) N.Y. 1977, U.S. Ct. Appeals (D.C. cir.) 1979, U.S. Ct. Appeals (2d and 7th cirs.) 1980, U.S. Supreme Ct. 1980, U.S. Ct. Appeals (9th cir.) 1981, U.S. Ct. Appeals (3d cir.) 1982, Ct. Internat. Trade 1990, U.S. Ct. Appeals (fed. cir.) 1994, U.S. Ct. Appeals (6th cir.) 1996. With Kirkpatrick & Lockhart LLP, NYC, 1998—2005, Kirkpatrick & Lockhart Nicholson Graham LLP, NYC, 2005—. Mem. vol. divsn. Legal Aid Soc., NYC, 1985-88, Partnership for a Drug-Free Am., 1989—. Mem. ABA, Fed. Bar Coun., Phi Beta Kappa. Office: Kirkpatrick & Lockhart Nicholson Graham LLP 599 Lexington Ave New York NY 10022-6030 Business E-Mail: dversfelt@klng.com.

**VERSHBOW, ALEXANDER R.,** ambassador; b. Boston, July 3, 1952; m. Lisa (Kaufman) Vershbow; two children. BA in Russian and East European Studies, Yale Coll., 1974; MS in Internat. Rels., Columbia U., 1976. Various fgn. svc. positions, 1977—; dir. Office of Soviet Union Affairs US Dept. State, Washington, 1988-91, prin. dep. asst. to Sec. of State for European & Can. Affairs, 1993-94, US amb. to NATO and permanent rep. to North Atlantic Coun. Brussels, 1998—2001, US amb. to Russian Fedn. Moscow, 2001—05, US amb. to Republic of Korea (South Korea) Seoul, 2005—; spl. asst. to pres. and sr. dir. European Affairs NSC, Washington, 1995-97. Contbr. articles to profl. jours. Recipient Anatoly Sharansky Freedom award Union of Couns. of Soviet Jews, 1990, 1st ann. Joseph J. Kruzel award, Sec. of Def. William Cohen, 1997, Disting. Honor award US Dept. State, 2001. Office: Am Embassy 9600 Seoul Pl Washington DC 20521

**VER STEEG, CLARENCE LESTER,** historian, educator; b. Orange City, Iowa, Dec. 28, 1922; s. John A. and Annie (Vischer) Ver S.; m. Dorothy Ann De Vries, Dec. 24, 1943; 1 child, John Charles. AB, Morningside Coll., Sioux City, Iowa, 1943; MA, Columbia U., 1946, PhD, 1950; LHD, Morningside Coll., 1988. Lectr., then instr. history Columbia U., N.Y.C., 1946-50; mem. faculty Northwestern U., Evanston, Ill., 1950—, prof. history, 1959—, dean grad. sch., 1975-86. Vis. lectr. Harvard U., 1959-60; mem. council Inst. Early Am. History and Culture, Williamsburg, Va., 1961-64, 68-72, chmn. exec. com., 1970-72; vis. mem. Inst. Advanced Study, Princeton, N.J., 1967-68; chmn. faculty com. to recommend Master Plan Higher Edn. in Ill., 1962-64; mem. Grad. Record Exam. Bd., 1981-86, chmn., 1984-86; pres. Assn. Grad. Schs., 1984-85; mem. steering com. Grad. Research Project, Consortium on Financing Higher Edn. 1981-85; working group on talent Nat. Acad. Scis., 1984-87; mem. Higher Edn. Policy Adv. Com. to OCLC, Online Computer Library Ctr., 1984-87. Author: Robert Morris, Revolutionary Financier, 1954, A True and Historical Narrative of the Colony of Georgia, 1960, The American People: Their History, 1961, The Formative Years, 1607-1763, 1964 (Brit. edit.), 1965, The Story of Our Country, 1965, (with others) Investigating Man's World, 6 vols., 1970, A People and a Nation, 1971, The Origins of a Southern Mosaic: Studies of Early Carolina and Georgia, 1975, World Cultures, 1977, American Spirit, 1982, rev. edit. 1990; sr. author: Heath Social Studies, 7 Vols., 1991, Planning at Northwestern University in the 1960s, 1993; editor: Great Issues in American History, From Settlement to Revolution 1584-1776, 1969; editl. cons.: Papers of Robert Morris, vols. I-IX, 1973-99; contbr. articles to profl. jours. With USAAF, 1942—45. Decorated Air medal with 3 oak leaf clusters; 5 Battle Stars; Social Sci. Research Council fellow, 1948-49, George A. and Eliza Gardner Howard Found. fellow, 1954-55, Huntington Library research fellow, 1955, Am. Council Learned Socs. sr. fellow, 1958-59, Guggenheim fellow, 1964-65, NEH sr. fellow, 1973; Northwestern U. Clarence L. Ver Steeg Professorship established in his honor, 1997. Mem. AAUP, Am. Hist. Assn. (nominating com. 1965-68, chmn. 1967-68, Albert J. Beveridge prize 1952, hon. mention 1991 Eugene Asher Disting. Teaching award), Orgn. Am. Historians (editorial bd. Jour. Am. History 1968-72), So. Hist. Assn. (nominating com. 1970-72). Presbyterian. Home: Apt 311 Two Arbor Ln Evanston IL 60201-4216 Office: Northwestern Univ Dept History Evanston IL 60208-0001 Business E-Mail: c-ver@nwu.edu.

**VER STEEG, DONNA LORRAINE FRANK,** nurse, sociologist, educator; b. Minot, ND, Sept. 23, 1929; d. John Jonas and Pearl H. (Denlinger) Frank; m. Richard W. Ver Steeg, Nov. 22, 1950; children: Juliana, Anne, Richard B. BSN, Stanford, 1951; MSN, U. Calif., San Francisco, 1967; MA in Sociology, UCLA, 1969, PhD in Sociology, 1973. Clin. instr. U. ND Sch. Nursing, 1962-63; USPHS nurse fellow UCLA, 1969-72; spl. cons., mem. adv. com. on physicians' assts. and nurse practitioner progs. Calif. State Bd. Med. Examiners, 1972-73; asst. prof. UCLA Sch. Nursing, 1973-79, assoc. prof. 1979-94, asst. dean, 1979-81, chmn. primary ambulatory care, 1976-87, assoc. dean, 1983-86, prof. emeritus, chair primary care, 1994-96, prof. emeritus, 1996—. Co-prin. investigator PRIMEX Project Family Nurse Practitioners, UCLA Ext., 1974—76; assoc. cons. Calif. Postsecondary Edn. Commn., 1975—76; spl. cons. Calif. Dept. Consumer Affairs, 1978; accredited visitor Western Assn. Sch. and Coll., 1985; mem. Calif. State Legis. Health Policy Forum, 1980—81; mem. nurse practitioner adv. com. Calif. Bd. RN, 1995—97; mem. Edn. Industry Interface, Info. Devel. Mktg. Sub Com., 1995—99, recruitment, 1999—2001; archivist Calif. Strategic Planning Com. Nursing/Colleagues in Caring Project, 1995—. Contbr. chpts. to profl. books, articles to profl. jours. Recipient Leadership award Calif. Area Health Edn. Ctr. Sys., 1989, Commendation award Calif. State Assembly, 1994; named Outstanding Faculty Mem., UCLA Sch. Nursing, 1982. Fellow Am. Acad. Nursing; mem. AAAS, AAUW, ANA (pres. elect Calif. chpt. 1977-79, pres. 1979-81, interim chair Calif. 1995-96), Nat. League Nursing, Calif. League Nursing, N.Am. Nursing Diagnosis Assn., Am. Assn. History Nursing, Stanford Nurses Club, Sigma Theta Tau (Alpha Eta chpt. Leadership award Gamma Tau chpt. 1994), Sigma Xi. Home: 708 Swarthmore Ave Pacific Palisades CA 90272-4353 Office: UCLA Sch Nursing Box 956917 Los Angeles CA 90095-6917 Business E-Mail: dverste@ucla.edu.

**VERSTEEG, ROBERT JOHN,** minister, actor, writer; b. Oradell, N.J., July 7, 1930; s. John Marinus and Edna Elizabeth (Ames) Versteeg; m. Sally Maude Youngblood Creel, Feb. 17, 1951 (div. Apr. 1976); children: Cassandra Lee, John Richard, Jay Russell; m. Donna Marie Stevens, June 22, 1977; 1 child, Rick. BA, Ohio Wesleyan U., 1952; MDiv, Garrett Theol. Sem., Evanston, Ill., 1955; student, Baldwin-Wallace Coll., Berea, Ohio, 1962; MA, U. N.C., 1971. Ordained to ministry Meth. Ch., 1955. Pastor Ohio Meth. Ch., 1955-62; prof., dir. drama Louisburg (N.C.) Coll., 1962-75; assoc. prof., dir. Conservatory Acting Program, Va. Commonwealth U., Richmond, 1975-76; pastor Peebles (Ohio) United Meth. Ch., 1977-79, Point Place United Meth. Ch., Toledo, 1979-82, First United Meth. Ch., Ada, Ohio, 1982-86, Oak Ilills United Meth. Ch., Cin., 1986-94, Trinity United Meth. Ch., Bowling Green, Ohio, 1994-99; writer LectionAid, 1997—99, Lectionary Homiletics, 1999—. Author: The Gracious Calling of the Lord, 1960, The Secret Life of the Good Samaritan, 1963, Whose Church is This Anyway?, 1985, Tales of Tittivillus, 1992, LectionAid, 1998, The Star Thrower, 2003; contbr. articles to profl. jours.; author, performer: (TV series) The Browning Show, 1974; Men of Faith, 1990—; (TV films) Paul A Prisoner, 1993—95; founder, dir.: Playback Theatre N.W. Ohio; Life Stage Theatrical Troupe, Inc. Named Seminarian Preacher of the Yr., Pulpit mag., 1955; named to Outstanding Young Men of Am., 1965; recipient Best Sermons award, HarperCollins, 1991; NEH fellow, 1972. Mem.: Nat. Assoc. Drama Therapy, Fellowship United Meths. in Worship, Music and Other Arts. Democrat. Avocations: reading, piano, conditioning. Home and Office: 616 Flanders Ave Bowling Green OH 43402-1519 Office Phone: 419-601-0499. E-mail: bojov@wcnet.org.

**VERTEFEUILLE, CHRISTINE SIEGRIST,** state supreme court justice; b. New Britain, Conn., Dec. 10, 1950; BA in Polit. Sci., Trinity Coll., 1972; JD, U. Conn., 1975. Pvt. practice, 1975-89; judge Conn. Superior Ct., 1989—99; adminstrv. judge Waterbury Jud. Dist., 1994-99, complex litig. judge, 1999; judge Appellate Ct., 1999-2000; assoc. justice Conn. Supreme Ct., 2000—. Alternate mem. Waterbury and New Haven (Conn.) Grievance Panels, 1985-89; faculty Conn. Judges Inst., 1989-94. Recipient Jud. award Conn. Trial Lawyers Assn., 1995. Mem. Conn. Bar Assn. (mem. exec. com. real property 1988-89). Office: Conn Supreme Ct 231 Capitol Ave Hartford CT 06106 Office Phone: 860-757-2117.

**VERTINO, ANTHONY DOMINIC,** psychologist; b. Cedar Rapids, Iowa, Feb. 26, 1970; s. Thomas Paul Vergina and Veronica An n Zelenak; m. Catherine Ann Glatz, Aug. 27, 1995; 1 child, Joseph Dominic. BS in Psychology, Loyola U., Chgo., 1992; MA in Psychology, Ill. Sch. Profl. Psychology, 1997, PsyD in Clin. Psychology, 1998. Lic. clin. psychologist Ill., registered addiction specialist, substance abuse profl. Dept. Transp. Clin. assoc. North Suburban Clinic, Skokie, Ill.; lic. clin. psychology Schwab @ the Anixter Ctr., Chgo., PsychOne, P.C., Barrington, Ill.; CEO GeroPsych Svcs. Neurobehavioral Health Connections, LLP, Mundelein, Ill., v.p., chief ops. Barrington and Mundelein. Staff cons. Kindred Hosp., Sycamore, Ill.; inservice provider Alden Nursing Homes, Ill., 2002—. Co-author: Younger Every Day, 2006. Mem.: APA. Avocations: exercise, guitar. Office: Neurobehavioral Heatlh Connections Ltd Ste 115 101 Lions Dr Barrington IL 60010

**VERTS, LITA JEANNE,** academic administrator; b. Jonesboro, Ark., Apr. 13, 1935; d. William Gus and Lolita Josephine (Peeler) Nash; m. B. J. Verts, Aug. 29, 1954 (div. 1975); 1 child, William Trigg. BA, Oreg. State U., 1973; MA in Linguistics, U. Oreg., 1974; postgrad., U. Hawaii, 1977. Librarian Forest Research Lab., Corvallis, Oreg., 1966-69; instr. English Lang. Inst., Corvallis, 1974-80; dir. spl. svcs. Oreg. State U., Corvallis, 1980-96, faculty senator, 1988-96; ret., 1996. Editor Trio Achievers, 1986, 3rd edit., 1988; contbr. articles to profl. jours. Precinct com. Rep. Party, Corvallis, 1977-80; adminstrv. bd. 1st United Meth. Ch., Corvallis, 1987-89, fin. com., 1987-93, tchr. Bible, 1978—; bd. dirs. Westminster Ho., United Campus Ministries, 1994-95; adv. coun. Disabilities Svc., Linn, Benton, Lincoln Counties, 1990-99, vice-chmn., 1992-93, chmn. 1993-94; citizen adv. bd. on Transit, 1998—, intercity steering com., 1999—, Corvallis Downtown Parking Commn., 1999—; Oreg. Longterm Care Ombudsman, 1999—. Mem. N.W. Assn. Spl. Programs (pres. 1985-86), Nat. Coun. Ednl. Opportunities Assn. (bd. dirs. 1984-87), Nat. Gardening Assn., Alpha Phi (mem. corp. bd. Beta Upsilon chpt. 1990-96). Republican. Methodist. Avocations: gardening, photography, golf. Home: 530 SE Mayberry Ave Corvallis OR 97333-1866 Personal E-mail: l.verts@comcast.net.

**VERVEER, PHILIP L.,** lawyer; b. Corvallis, Oreg. BSFS, Georgetown U., 1966; JD, U. Chgo., 1969. Bar: DC 1969, US Dist. Ct., DC 1969, US Ct. Appeals, DC Cir. 1971, US Ct. Appeals, 10th Cir. 1982, US Supreme Ct. 1986. Trial atty. Dept. Justice, Antitrust Div., 1969—77; supervisory atty. FTC, Bur. of Competition, 1977—78; chief FCC, Cable Television Bur., Broadcast Bur. and Common Carrier Bur., 1978—81; ptnr. telecom. dept. Willkie Farr & Gallagher LLP, Washington, DC. Mem.: ABA; Fed. Comm. Bar Assn. Office: Willkie Farr & Gallagher LLP 1875 K Street, NW Washington DC 20006 Office Phone: 202-303-1117. E-mail: pverveer@willkie.com.

**VERVILLE, ELIZABETH GIAVANI,** federal official; b. N.Y.C., July 13, 1940; d. Joseph and Gertrude (Levy) Giavani. BA, Duke U., 1961; LLB, Columbia U., 1964. Bar: Mass. 1965, U.S. Supreme Ct. 1970, D.C. 1980. Assoc. Snow Motley & Holt, successor Gaston Snow & Ely Bartlett, Boston, 1965-67; asst. atty. gen. Commonwealth of Mass., Boston, 1967-69; atty. advisor for African affairs U.S. Dept. State, Washington, 1979-72, asst. legal adviser for East Asian and Pacific affairs, 1972-80, dep. legal adviser, 1980-89; dep. asst. sec. state Bur. Politico-Mil. Affairs Bur. Politico-Mil. Affairs, Washington, 1989-92, sr. coord., 1992-95; dir. for global and multilateral affairs Nat. Security Coun., Washington, 1995-98; dep. dir. Critical Infrastructure Assurance Office, Washington, 2000—01; spl. rep. Bur. Narcotics and Law Enforcement, Washington, 2000—02, 2005—; acting dep. asst. sec. Bur. Internat. Narcotics and Law Enforcement, Dept. State, Washington, 2001—02, sr. advisor, 2002—05, acting dep. asst. sec., 2005—. Recipient presdl. rank of meritorious exec., 1985, 90, 2003, presdl. rank disting. exec., 1988. Mem. Am. Soc. Internat. Law, Coun. on Fgn. Rels. Home: 3012 Dumbarton Ave NW Washington DC 20007-3305 Office: Bur Internat Narcotics & Law Enforcement State Dept Washington DC 20520-0001 Office Phone: 202-647-9822.

**VERWAAYEN, BEN J.M.,** communications company executive; M in Law and Internat. Politics, State U. of Utrecht. Mgr. pub. rels. to various mgmt. positions ITT Nederland, 1975-83, exec. v.p. dir. opers., 1983-88; pres. PTT Telecom BV (Royal PTT Nederland NV), 1988-97; exec. v.p., COO Lucent Technologies, Inc., Murray Hill, NJ, 1997-99, vice-chmn., 1999—2001; CEO & bd. dir. BT Group, London, 2002—. Bd. dirs. UPS. Office: BT Group BT Centre 81 Newgate St London EC1A 7AJ England

**VERWERS, JODY ANN,** mathematics educator; b. Anchorage, Alaska, Apr. 12, 1953; d. Victor Joseph Jr. and Shirley Josephine (Guarino) Frioux; m. Robert Andrew Verwers II, Dec. 29, 1979 (div. March 14, 2005); children: Robert Andrew III, Michelle Elizabeth. BS in Math. Edn., U. Southwestern La., 1975. Cert. secondary math. tchr., La., Tex. Tchr. math. Corpus Christi Ind. Sch. Dist., Tex., 1975—82; head math. dept. Hamlin Jr. H.S., 1980—82; tchr. math. Lafayette Parish Sch., La., 1982—85, Pasadena Ind. Sch. Dist., Tex., 1985—90, Clear Creek Ind. Sch. Dist., League City, Tex., 1990—. Mem. writing com. Advanced Mathematics 7th and 8th Grade Handbooks, 1981, Geometry and Honors Geometry Curriculum Guide, 1991, 2nd edit., 1999, Geometry Credit Recovery Curriculum, 2006. Mem. Nat. Coun. Tchrs. Math., Tex. Coun. Tchrs. Math., San Jacinto Coun. Tchrs. Math. Roman Catholic. Avocations: counted cross-stitch, reading, painting. Home: 706 Lochnell Dr Houston TX 77062-2609 Office: Clear Lake HS 2929 Bay Area Blvd Houston TX 77058-1005

**VESCOVI, JASON D.,** education educator; b. Iowa City, Oct. 17, 1973; s. James C. and Anne Vescovi; m. Mercedes Barreras, June 20, 2003; 1 child, Gabriella M. BS, James Madison U., Harrisonburg, Va., 1997; MS, George Wash. U., Washington, 1999; PhD, U. Conn., Storrs, 2006. Fellow U. Toronto, Ontario, Canada, 2006; rsch. asst. U. Conn., Storrs, 2002—. Contbr. articles to profl. jours. Bd. dirs. Neag Grad. Student Assn., Conn., 2004—. Fellow, U. Conn., 2003—04, U. Toronto, 2006—; Student grant, Gatorade Sports Sci. Inst., 2005—06. Mem.: US Figure Skating Assn. (high performance evaluation com. 2003—), Nat. Strength and Conditioning Assn. (edn. com. 2001—, cert.), Am. Coll. Sports Medicine, Am. Physiol. Soc., Am. Soc. for Bone and Mineral Rsch.

**VESELINOVIČ, DRAŠKO,** stock exchange executive; b. Ljubljana, Slovenia, Feb. 26, 1959; s. Branko and Breda (Pokorn) V.; children: Eva, Gal. M of Internat. Fin., U. Ljubljana, 1986, DSc in Econs., 1996. Fgn. exch. dealer Ljubljanska Bank, fgn. exch. and internat. treasury mgr.; assoc. prof. Faculty of Econs.; fin. adviser Slovene Govt.; CEO Ljubljana Stock Exch., gen. mgr., 1993—2004. Founder The Yugoslav Stock Exch., 1989. Author: Foreign Exchange in Developed World & in Yugoslavia, 1988, Foreign Exchange Trading, 1991, Stock Exchange Handbook, 1991, 95, Options and Other Derivative Financial Instruments, 1998, Aphorisms, 1996, 2002, Foreign Exchange Act with a Commentary and By-laws, 1999; contbr.more than 200 articles to profl. jours. Mem.: Tennis Assn. Slovenia (v.p.). Avocations: tennis, music. E-mail: draskoveselinovic@yahoo.com.

**VESELL, ELLIOT SAUL,** pharmacologist, educator; b. N.Y.C., Dec. 24, 1933; s. Harry and Evelyn (Jaffe) Vesell; m. Kristen Paige Peery, Mar. 24, 1968; children: Liane Clark, Hilary Peery. AB magna cum laude, Harvard U., 1955, MD magna cum laude, 1959; DSc (hon.), Phila. Coll. Pharmacy & Sci., 1988; PhD (hon.), Philipps U., Marburg, Germany, 1991. Intern, children's med. svc. Mass. Gen. Hosp., Boston, 1959-60; rsch. assoc. Rockefeller U., NYC, 1960-62; asst. resident medicine Peter Bent Brigham Hosp., Boston, 1962-63; clin. assoc. Nat. Inst. Arthritis Metabolic Diseases, NIH, Bethesda, Md., 1963-65; head sect. pharmacogenetics Nat. Heart Inst., NIH, Bethesda, 1965-68; Evan Pugh prof. pharmacology Pa. State U., Hershey, 1968—, asst. dean grad. edn., 1973-96, chmn. dept. pharmacology Coll. Medicine, 1968—2000, Bernard B. Brodie prof., 1991—. Pfizer vis. prof.; Burroughs Wellcome vis. prof. Editor: The Life and Works of Thomas Cole, 1964, Progress in Basic and Clin. Pharmacology, 1990, others; contbr. articles to profl. jours. Recipient Von Humboldt award, 1988. Fellow: AAAS, Royal Soc. Medicine (Frohlich vis. prof. 1985); mem.: Am. Soc. Clin. Pharmacology Therapeutics (Oscar B. Hunter Meml. award 1991), Am. Coll. Clin. Pharmacology (pres. 1980—82, Disting. Investigator award 1999), Am. Soc. Pharmacology Exptl. Therapeutics (sec.-treas. 1995—98, Exptl. Therapeutics award 1971, Harry Gold award clin. pharmacology 1985), Am. Soc. Clin. Investigation, Assn. Am. Physicians, Phi Beta Kappa, Alpha Omega Alpha. Office: Pa State U Coll Medicine Dept Pharmacology PO Box 850 Hershey PA 17033-0850 Office Phone: 717-531-8285. Business E-Mail: esv1@psu.edu.

**VESELY, JEFFREY M.,** lawyer; b. Glendale, Calif., Feb. 23, 1950; BA, Univ. Calif., Santa Barbara, 1972; JD, San Fernando Valley Univ., 1975; MBA, Golden Gate Univ., 1982. Bar: Calif. 1975, US Supreme Ct. 1980. Ptnr., chmn. Tax practice Pillsbury Winthrop Shaw Pittman, San Francisco. Co-author: Distinctions Between Unitary & Nonunitary Businesses: A Practical Guide, 2001; contbr. articles to profl. jours., chapters to books. Office: Pillsbury Winthrop Shaw Pittman 50 Fremont St San Francisco CA 94105 Office Phone: 415-983-1075. Office Fax: 415-983-1200. Business E-Mail: jeffrey.vesely@pillsburylaw.com.

**VESPA, NED ANGELO,** photographer; b. Streator, Ill., May 31, 1942; s. Ned James and Evelyn Blanche (Flanigan) V.; m. Carol DeMasters, Sept. 11, 1976; 1 child, Nicole Marie; 1 son by previous marriage, James Paul. BS, So. Ill. U., 1965. Photographer Milw. Jour. Co., 1965-95, Milw. Sentinel, 1965-95; ret., 1995; freelance, 1995—. Mem. Nat. Press Photographers Assn., Wis. News Photographers Assn. (past pres.), Milw. Press Photographers. Home: 38309 Genesee Lake Rd Oconomowoc WI 53066-8614

**VESPOLI, LEILA L.,** energy executive, lawyer; b. Akron, Ohio, 1959; BS, Miami U., Ohio, 1981; JD, Case Western Res. U., 1984. Bar: Ohio 1984. From atty. to sr. atty. Ohio Edison, Akron, 1985—97; assoc. gen. counsel First Energy Corp., Akron, 1997—2000, v.p., gen. counsel, 2000—01, sr. v.p, gen. counsel, 2001—. Bd. dirs. Jersey Central Power & Light. Bd. trustees The NEOUCOM Found. Named a Women of Professional Excellence, YWCA. Mem.: Greater Cleveland General Counsel Assn., Ohio C. of C., Energy Assn. of Pa. (bd. dirs.), Edison Electric Inst., NY Utilities Assn. (bd. dirs.). Office: First Energy Corp 76 S Main St Akron OH 44308

**VESSEL, AMY MASSEY,** education educator; d. Freddie Lamonte and Carol Butler Massey; m. James Stephen Vessel; children: Brandon Edward, John Davis. BA with honors in Elem. Edn., La. Tech U., Ruston, 1992, MA in Elem. Edn., 1993; D in Elem. Edn., U. Ala., Tuscaloosa, 2000. Lic. elem. edn. La. Classroom tchr. Riser Mid. Sch., West Monroe; instr. U. Ala., Tuscaloosa, 1996—99; asst. profl. elem. edn. La. Tech U., 2000—. Bd. dirs. Jr. Aux., Ruston, 2002—, Am. Heart Assn., Ruston, 2005—06; vol., tchr. Trinity United Meth. Ch., Ruston, La., 1999—2006. Named Coll. Edn. Faculty Advisor of Yr., La. Tech U., 2003—04; recipient Outstanding Tchg. By Doctoral Student, U. Ala. Grad. Sch., 1998—99, Virgil Orr Jr. Faculty award, La. Tech U., 2006; grantee, La. Systemic Initiatives Program, 2002, 2002—03, La. Systemic Initiative Programs, 2006—. Mem.: Internat. Reading Assn. (presenter confs.), Nat. Coun. Tchrs. of Math. (presenter at meetings), Kappa Delta Pi (faculty advisor to student chpt. 2003—, nat. officer, adv. bd. mem. 1993—2006).

**VESSEY, JOHN WILLIAM, JR.,** military officer; b. Mpls., June 29, 1922; s. John William and Emily (Roche) V.; m. Avis Claire Funk, July 18, 1945; children: John William, David, Sarah. BS, U. Md., 1963; MS, George Washington U., 1967; LLD, Concordia Coll., St. Paul, 1978, U. Md., 1983, Concordia Sem., St. Louis, 1983; DMS (hon.), Norwich U., Northfield, Vt., 1985; grad., Command and Gen. Staff Coll., 1958, Indsl. Coll. Armed Forces, 1966. Commd. 2nd lt. U.S. Army, 1944, advanced through grades to gen., 1976; comdr. U.S. Army Support Command Thailand, 1970-71; chief Mil. Assistance Adv. Group Laos, 1972-73; dir. ops. Dept. Army Washington, 1973-74; comdr. 4th Inf. Div. Ft. Carson, Colo., 1974-75; dep. chief of staff-ops. Dept. Army Washington, 1975-76; comdr.-in-chief UN Command/U.S. Forces in Korea Seoul, 1976-79; comdr.-in-chief Republic of Korea/U.S. Combined Forces Command, 1978-79; vice chief of staff U.S. Army Washington, 1979-82; chmn. Joint Chiefs of Staff, 1982-85; ret. U.S. Army, 1985; presdl. emissary to Hanoi for POW/MIA matters, 1987-93. Bd. dirs. Nat. Flag Day Com.; mem. bd. visitors UMUC; chmn. bd. Ctr. Preventive Action, Def. Sci. Bd. Decorated D.S.C., Def. D.S.M., D.S.M., AF D.S.M., Navy D.S.M., Legion of Merit, Bronze Star, Air medal, Joint Svcs. Commendation medal, Army Commendation medal, Purple Heart (U.S.), Presdl.

Medal of Freedom, decorated by govts. of Austria, Belgium, Chile, Colombia, Germany, France, Greece, Honduras, Korea, Luxembourg, Norway, Pakistan, Saudi Arabia, Spain, Thailand, Uruguay; recipient State of Minn. Disting. Svc. medal, Excellence in Diplomacy award Am. Acad. of Diplomacy, Sylvanus Thayer award USMA, Alumni Achievement award and Disting. Pub. Svc. award George Washington U., Disting. Alumnus award U. Md., Golden Plate award Am. Acad. Achievement, Adm. John M. Will award N.Y. Coun. Navy League, hon. award Nat. League Families. Mem. VFW (Eisenhower medal), Assn. U.S. Army (George Marshall medal), Army Aviation Assn., U.S. Armor Assn., Coun. Fgn. Rels. (chair bd. dirs. ctr. for prevention action), Phi Kappa Phi. Lutheran.

**VESSOT, ROBERT FREDERICK CHARLES,** physicist, researcher; b. Montreal, Que., Can., Apr. 16, 1930; s. Robert Charles Ulysses and Marguerite Yvonne (Giauque) V.; m. Norma Newman Wight, Apr. 18, 1959; children: Judith Norma, Margaret Anne, Nancy Elizabeth. BA, McGill U., 1951, MSc, 1954, PhD, 1956. Mem. research staff MIT, 1956-60; mgr. Maser Research and Devel., Varian Assos., Hewlett Packard, Beverly, Mass., 1960-69; sr. physicist Harvard-Smithsonian Center for Astrophysics, Cambridge, Mass., 1969-2001, rsch. assoc., 2002—. Contbr. articles to profl. jours.; patentee in field. Served with RCAF, 1951-53. Recipient medal for outstanding sci. achievement NASA, 1978, I.I. Rabi award IEEE, 1993. Fellow Am. Phys. Soc.; mem. Eastern Yacht Club. Office: 60 Garden St Cambridge MA 02138-1516 Business E-Mail: rvessot@cfa.harvard.edu.

**VEST, CHARLES MARSTILLER,** engineering educator, former academic administrator; b. Morgantown, W.Va., Sept. 9, 1941; s. Marvin Lewis and Winifred Louise (Buzzard) V.; m. Rebecca Ann McCue, June 8, 1963; children: Ann Kemper, John Andrew. BS in Mech. Engring., W.Va. U., 1963; MS in Mech. Engring., U. Mich., 1964, PhD, 1967; degree (hon.), Mich. Tech. U., 1992, W.Va. U., 1994, Ill. Inst. Tech., 1998, U. Notre Dame, 1998, Musashi Inst. Tech., 1999, NC State U., 2002, Colo. Sch. Mines, 2005, Harvard U., 2005. Asst. prof., then assoc. prof. U. Mich., Ann Arbor, 1968—77, prof. mech. engring., 1977—90, assoc. dean acad. affairs Coll. Engring., 1981—86, dean Coll. Engring., 1986—89, provost, v.p. acad. affairs, 1989—90; pres. MIT, Cambridge, 1990—2004, pres. emeritus, prof. mech. engring., 2004—. Bd. dirs. E.I. du Pont de Nemours and Co., IBM, Math. for Am., Ithaka Harbors, Inc., Blanchette Rockefeller Neuroscis. Inst., Kavli Found., In-Q-Tel; vis. assoc. prof. Stanford (Calif.) U., 1974-75; mem. Commn. on the Intelligence Capabilities of the U.S. Regarding Weapons of Mass Destruction, 2004-05; mem. Ctr. for Strategic and Internat. Studies Commn. on Sci. Comm. and Nat. Security; mem. Mass. Gov.s Coun. on Econ. Growth and Techn. 1990-99; chmn. Presdl. Adv. Com on Redesign of Space Stat., 1993-94, chmn. U.S. Dept. Energy Task Force on Future of Sci. Programs, 1992-93; chmn. Coun. on Competitiveness, 1996-04; mem. Commn. Future Higher Edn., 2005-. Author: Holographic Interferometry, 1979, Pursuing the Endless Frontier: Essays on MIT and the Role of Research Universities, 2005; assoc. editor Jour. Optical Soc. Am., 1982-83; contbr. articles to profl. jours. Trustee Woods Hole Oceanographic Inst., 1991-2004; Univ. Corp. for Advanced Internet Devel., 2002-04; WGBH Ednl. Found., 2002-04; adv. trustee TIAX adv. bd., Environ. Rsch. Inst. Mich. Recipient Excellence in Rsch. award U. Mich., 1980, Disting. Svc. award, 1972, Disting. Visitor award U. La Plata, Argentina, 1979, Centennial medal Am Soc. Engring. Edn., 1993, Arthur M. Bueche award Nat. Acad. Engring., 2000, Nat. Leadership award Phi Kappa Psi, 1999., Pres.' award Accrediation Bd. for Engring. and Tech., 2002, U. Mich. Engring. Alumni award, 2004. Fellow AAAS, Am. Acad. Arts and Scis., Optical Soc. Am., ASME; mem. NAE, Assn. Women in Sci., Sigma Xi, Tau Beta Pi, Pi Tau Sigma. Presbyterian.

**VEST, GAYLE SOUTHWORTH,** obstetrician, gynecologist; b. Duluth, Minn., Apr. 7, 1948; d. Russell Eugene and Brandon (Young) Southworth; m. Steven Lee Vest, Nov. 27, 1971; 1 child, Matthew Steven. BS, U. Mich., 1970. Diplomate Am. Bd. Ob-Gyn. Intern in ob-gyn. Milw. County Gen. Hosp., 1974-75, So. Ill. Medicine, 1975-78; pvt. practice Chapel Hill (N.C.) Ob-Gyn., 1978-80; asst. attending physician dept. ob-gyn. U. N.C. Sch. Medicine, Chapel Hill, 1978-80; clin. assoc. dept. ob-gyn. Duke U. Med. Ctr., Durham, NC, 1978-80; pvt. practice Big Stone Gap (Va.) Clinic, 1980-88, Norwise Ob-Gyn. Assocs., Norton, Va., 1988—. Fellow: ACOG; mem.: Wise County Med. Soc., Med. Soc. Va., Va. Ob-Gyn. Soc., Christian Med. and Dental Assn. Avocations: skiing, kayaking, travel.

**VEST, GEORGE SOUTHALL,** retired diplomat; b. Columbia, Va., Dec. 25, 1918; s. George Southall and Nancy Margaret (Robertson) V.; m. Emily Barber Clemons, June 21, 1947; children—Jeannie, George, Henry BA, U. Va., 1941, MA, 1947. Fgn. service duty SHAPE and NATO, Quito, Ottawa, Paris; dir. bur. polit. mil. affairs Dept. State, asst. sec. of state for European affairs Washington, 1977-81; ambassador to European Communities Brussels, 1981-85; dir. gen. Fgn. Svc. Dept. State, Washington, 1985-89, career amb., 1987-89, ret., 1989. Served to capt. U.S. Army, 1941-46, ETO Mem. Phi Beta Kappa Episcopalian. Avocations: bicycling, gardening. Home: 5307 Iroquois Rd Bethesda MD 20816-3104

**VEST, HYRUM GRANT, JR.,** retired horticultural sciences educator; b. Salt Lake City, Sept. 23, 1935; s. Hyrum and Josephine Gwendolyn (Lund) V.; m. Gayle Pixton, Sept. 18, 1958; children: Kelly, Lani, Kari, Kamille, Kyle. BS, Utah State U., 1960, MS, 1964; PhD, U. Minn., 1967. Pathologist, agronomist U.S. Dept. Agr., Beltsville, Md., 1967-70; vegetable breeder Mich. State U., East Lansing, 1970-76; dept. head dept. hort. and landscape architecture Okla. State U., Stillwater, 1976-83; head dept. hort. scis. Tex A & M U., College Station, 1983-89; head dept. plants, soils and biometeorology Utah State U., Logan, 1989 95, assoc. dir. Utah Agrl. Experiment Sta., 1995-2000; mem. Nat. Plant Genetics Resource Bd., Washington, 1982-88; ret., 2000. Served to 1st lt. U.S. Army, 1960-63. Univ. research fellow Utah State U., 1963-64 Fellow Am. Soc. Hort. Sci. Republican. Mem. Lds Ch. Home: 368 Spring Creek Rd Providence UT 84332-9432 E-mail: gvest@cc.usu.edu.

**VEST, R. LAMAR,** church administrator; b. Belton, SC, July 24, 1940; m. Iris Vest, 1958 (dec. 2001); m. Vickie Underwood, Feb. 16, 2002; 6 children. BS, Lee U.; MA, Church of God Theological Seminary; D, Lee U. Began ministry, 1955; ordained, 1955; dir. Ch. of God Media Ministries, 1994—96, 1st asst., gen. overseer, 1996—99, presiding bishop. Chmn. Nat. Assn. Evangelicals, first-vice-chmn., second vice-chmn., bd. dir.; chmn. bd. trustee Am. Bible Soc., exec. com.; guest spkr. at various conferences, seminars, conventions, and local churches around the world. Author: (book) What a Life, The Church and Its Youth, Spiritual Renewal, The Pain and the Glory, Spiritual Balance-Reclaiming the Promise; co-author with Steven J. Land): Reclaiming Your Testimony: Your Story and the Christian Story; contbr. articles to profl. jours. State/regional youth and Christian edu. dir. for youth ministry in Okla., Calif.-Nev., and Md.-Del.-DC.; exec. leader Dept. Youth and Christian Edu. 1976—84; sec. Pentecostal Charismatic Churches NAm.; presidium Pentecostal World Fellowship; pres. Lee U., Cleve., 1984—86. Mem.: Am. Bible Soc. (trustee 1990—94, exec. com. 1994—).

**VESTAL, ALLAN W.,** dean, law educator; BA, Yale U., 1976, JD, 1979. Prof. partnership and corp. law, comml. law, and real estate Washington and Lee U. Sch. Law, 1989—2000; dean U. Ky. Coll. Law, Lexington 2000—. Practiced law for ten yrs., Wis., Iowa. Publ. (treatise with Prof. Hillman and Dean Weidner) The Revised Uniform Partnership Act; contbr. chapters to books, articles to law revs. Mem.: Am. Law Inst. Office: Coll Law U Ky Lexington KY 40506-0048 Office Phone: 859-257-1678. E-mail: vestal@email.uky.edu.

**VESTAL, JOSEPHINE BURNET,** lawyer; b. Iowa City, June 13, 1949; d. Allan Delker and Dorothy (Walker) V. Student, Williams Coll., 1970; BA, Mt. Holyoke Coll., 1971; JD, U. Wash., 1974. Bar: Wash. 1974, U.S. Dist. Ct. (we. dist.) Wash. 1974, U.S. Ct. Appeals (9th cir.) 1984, U.S. Ct. Appeals (D.C. cir.) 1984, U.S. Dist. Ct. (ea. dist.) Wash. 1993. Ptnr. Selinker, Vestal,

Klockars & Andersen, Seattle, 1974-80; assoc. Williams, Kastner & Gibbs, Seattle, 1981-87; mem. Williams, Kastner & Gibbs, PLLC, Seattle, 1988—. Mem. ABA (labor and employment sect.), Def. Rsch. Inst. (labor and employment sect.), Wash. State Bar Assn., King County Bar Assn. Office: Williams Kastner & Gibbs PLLC 4100 Two Union Sq PO Box 21926 Seattle WA 98111-3926 Office Phone: 206-233-2894. E-mail: jvestal@wkg.com.

**VESTAL, MARILYN ANITA,** writer, researcher, educator; b. Pitts., May 28, 1950; d. Elmo Foucheaux and Mary Alice (Hayes) Vestal; 1 child, Daven Remley. BS in Child and Family Devel., Va. Tech., 1974; MBA in Mgmt., Tex. Tech. U., 1980; PhD in Conflict Mgmt., Nova Southeastern U., 2001. Vol. Peace Corps, Dominican Republic, 1974-76; child devel. tng. specialist Tex. Tech. U., Lubbock, 1977-80; methods analyst supr. Cmty. Progress Coun., York, PA., 1980-81; program adminstr. East Coast Migrant Head Start Project, 1982-84; mgmt./fiscal specialist, data mgmt. project coord. Head Start Resource and Tng. Ctr., U. Md., 1984-87; exec. dir. Child Care Cons., Inc., Pa., 1987-90; mgmt. cons., mediator, 1990—. Assoc. prof. human resources mgmt. Webber Coll., 1993-97; assoc. prof. mgmt. orgn. devel. Ea. Mennonite U., 2000-03; mem. leadership faculty Mountain State U, 2004—; adj. prof. conflict resolution Nova Southeastern U., 2001-; cons. S.C. Ednl. TV, 1992-96, U. Md., Head Start Resource and Tng. Ctr., 1988-92, South Fla. C.C., 1995, Region IV Mgmt. Inst., Tuskeegee U., 1995, DHHS/Adminstrn. on Children and Families, Washington, 1991—, Wheelock Coll., 1997-98, Aspen Sys.; presenter numerous papers at confs., workshops. Mem. editl. bd.: 4th R, Assn. for Conflict Resolution, 2003—. Facilitator Wellspring Retreat, Family Enrichment Ctr., Archdiocese of Miami, 1998-2000; arbitrator Nat. Assn. Securities Dealers, 1998—; mem. Nat. Peace Corps Assn., Soc. for Human Resources Mgmt., 2001—, Consortium on Peace Rsch., EL. Devel., 2000-02, Assn. for Conflict Resolutions, 1999-; mem., bd. dirs. Child Care Cons., Inc., York, 1980-90; bd. pres. Mediation Svcs. Conflict Resolution, 2000-02; bd. dirs. Atkins House, York, 1989-90. Recipient Margaret Sangar award Planned Parenthood, 1975, Beyond War award, 1987, Cert. Recognition Dept. Interior, 1976; Head Start Rsch. scholar, 1999-2000. Mem. Broward County Mediators Assn. Roman Catholic. Avocations: tennis, travel, culture. Personal E-mail: av@anitavestal.net.

**VETRI, MARC,** chef; Cook Wolfgang Puck's Granita; chef Coco Pazzo, NYC; exec. chef Bella Blu, NYC; owner, chef Vetri Ristorante, 1998—. Recipient Best Mid-Atlantic Chef, The James Beard Found., 2005. Office: Vetri Ristorante 1312 Spruce St Philadelphia PA 19107*

**VETROCQ, MARCIA E.,** editor; BA, Princeton Univ.; MA, PhD, Stanford Univ. Prof., fine arts Univ. New Orleans, 1982—98; sr. editor Art in Am. Mag., NYC, 1998—. Co-author: The Founders & the Architects: Design of Stanford University, 1976, Domenico Tiepolo's Punchinello Drawings, 1979. Grantee Andrew and Marian Heiskell Vis. Fellow in Criticism, Am. Acad., Rome, 2004. Office: Art in America Brant Publications 575 Broadway New York NY 10012 Office Phone: 212-941-2800. Office Fax: 212-941-8885.

**VETTER, DAVID R.,** lawyer; b. Balt., Apr. 3, 1959; BA in English and economics, Bucknell U., 1981; JD, U. Fla., 1984. Bar: Fla. 1984, US Dist. Ct. Middle Dist. Fla. 1985. Atty. Robbins, Gaynor and Bronstein, Tampa, Fla., 1984—93, ptnr, 1991—93; v.p., gen. counsel Tech Data Corp., Clearwater, Fla., 1993—2000, corp. v.p., gen. counsel, 2000—03, sr. v.p., gen. counsel, sec., 2003—. Mem.: ABA, Fla. Bar Assn. Office: Tech Data Corp 5350 Tech Data Dr Clearwater FL 33760-3122

**VETTER, EVELYN M.,** librarian; b. El Paso, Tex., Jan. 29, 1947; d. George Lewis Allison and Hazel Elizabeth Whitt; m. Lon R. Vetter, June 8, 1968; 3 children. BS in Edn., Southeast Mo. State U., Cape Girardeau, 1968; MLS, U. Tex., Austin, 1971. Cert. tchr. English Mo.; tchr. speech Mo.; libr. Mo.; instructional media technologist Mo.; learning resources dir. Mo. English libr. DeSoto Pub. Schools, DeSoto, Mo., 1968—69; libr. asst. Sch. of Libr. Sci. U. Tex., Austin, 1970—71; rsch. assoc. U. Tex., 1971—73; reference libr. Mid-Continent Pub. Libr., Independence, Mo., 1973—73; br. libr., 1973—75; reference libr. Kans. City Pub. Libr., 1976—77; office mgr. L. R. Vetter, D.D.S., West Plains, 1977—88; libr. R-7 Schools, 1988—91; asst. libr. Mo. State U. (formerly S.W. Mo. State U.), 1991—93, head libr., 1993—2005, 2005—. U. libr. liaison Friends of Garnett Libr., 1992—; libr. cons. St. Mary's Regional Sch., 1990—96, grantwriter, 1986; chair assessment com. S.W. Mo. State U., 2003, chair libr. adv. com.; libr. cons. LNU-SMSU Sch. of Internat. Bus., Dalian, China, 2004—. Exhibitions include Smithsonian, 1998 (2d pl., 1998). Publicity West Plains Coun. on the Arts, Mo., 1978—79; publicity and transp. West Plains Soccer Assn.; pres., sec. and publicity Friends of West Plains Pub. Libr., 1978—85; bd. dir., grant writer and fundraising chair West Plains Adult Day Care, 1999—2001. Finalist Interstate Oratory, Interstate Forensic Assn., 1967; named Women's Collegiate Oratory Champion, Mo. Forensic Assn., 1967; recipient Team 2000 award, SW Mo. State U. - West Plains, 1996. Mem.: DAR (vice regent Ozark Spring chpt. 2004—, jr. Am. citizens contest chair), ALA (assoc.), Mo. Libr. Assn., S.W. Dist. Sch. Libr. Assn. (assoc.), S.W. Dist. Ednl. Media Assn. (assoc.; pres., sec. and program chair 1989—91), Mo. State Tchrs. Assn. (assoc.), Mo. Assn. of Sch. Librs. (assoc.), Regional Consortium for Ednl. Tech. (assoc.), Friends of Garnett Libr. (life). Office: Mo State U 304 Cleveland Ave West Plains MO 65775 Office Phone: 417-255-7945. Business E-Mail: evelynvetter@missouristate.edu.

**VETTER, LAWRENCE ANTHONY,** art educator, consultant; s. Anthony Lawrence and Lilly Vetter; m. Andrea Kay Oppelt, Jan. 12, 1968; 1 child, Rachel Tomeo. BA, Calif. State U., Fullerton, 1968, MA, 1970; postgrad., U.S. Internat. U., 1972, U. Calif., Irvine, 1974—75. Cert. coll. tchr. Calif., 1970, secondary tchr. Calif., 1975. Instr. and counselor Calif. State U. Fullerton, 1970—73, adj. lectr., 2000—; art educator Hacienda-LaPuente Unified Sch. Dist., City of Industry, 1973—; adj. lectr. Calif. Poly. U., Pomona, 2000—01. Ceramic chemistry cons. Laguna Clay Co., City of Industry, Calif., 1989—; ceramicist stoneware and porcelain vessels; keynote spkr. edn. in Hispanic cmtys. Western US Conf. of Sch. Boards and State Ednl., 2000. Vol. Calif. State Parks Sys., Dana Point, 1996. Named Nat. Outstanding Pub. Secondary Educator in the Ceramic Arts, Studio Potter Mag. N.H., 1990—91; recipient Outstanding Secondary Educator, LA County Supervisors, 1999—2000, Outstanding Advanced Placement Tchr., City of La Puente, 1996, Outstanding Secondary Tchr., U. Calif. San Diego, 2000—01, 2001—02; grantee Instrn. of Advanced Placement Art History, Hacienda-LaPuente Unified Sch. Dist., 1997, Coll. Bd./ Mellon Found., 1998. Master: Dave Hebler's Original Am. Kenpo Karate Assn. (life seventh degree black belt); mem.: NEA, Hacienda-LaPuente Unified Tchrs. Assn., Calif. Tchrs. Assn. Achievements include research in 35 stoneware glazes and 21 Raku glazes developed for international sales for Laguna Clay Company. Avocations: art, martial arts, volleyball. Home: 33472 Intera Way Dana Point CA 92629 Office: LaPuente HS 15615 East Nelson Ave La Puente CA 91744 Office Phone: 626-934-6745. Personal E-mail: lvetter@hlpusd.k12.ca.

**VETTER, VICTORIA L.,** pediatric cardiologist, educator; b. Louisville, Aug. 15, 1946; d. Albert Elmo and Mildred Irene Vetter; m. Anthony S. Jennings, June 8, 1974; children: Jennifer, Jonathan, Jason. BA in Chemistry, U. Ky., 1968, MD, 1972. Bd. cert. Am. Bd. Pediat. in Pediat. and Pediat. Cardiology. Intern pediat. Johns Hopkins Hosp., Balt., 1972—73, resident pediat., 1973—74; sr. resident pediat. Vanderbilt U. Hosp., Nashville, 1974—75; fellow pediat. cardiology The Children's Hosp. Phila., 1975—78, asst. cardiologist, 1978—82, assoc. cardiologist, 1982—89, sr. cardiologist, 1989—, dir. pediat. electrophysiology lab., 1978—95, dir. pediat. electrocardiography lab., 1978—, chief divsn. cardiology, 1993—; sr. physician dept. pediat. U. Pa. Sch. Medicine, 1989—. Instr. pediat. U. Pa. Sch. Medicine 1978, asst. prof. pediat., 1978—81, prof. pediat., 1999—; asst. prof. pediat. The Children's Hosp. Phila., U. Pa. Sch. Medicine, 1981—87, assoc. prof. pediat., 1987—99, Evelyn R. Tabas chair in pediatric cardiology, 2005—; lectr. in field. Sci. reviewer: jours. Circulation, Am. Jour. Cardiology, Jour. Am. Coll. Cardiology, Pediat. Cardiology, Pacing and Clin. Electrophysiology, Pediat. Rsch., Clin. Pediat., Annals of Internal Medicine, New Eng. Jour. Medicine, Jour. Cardiovasc. Electrophysiology, Jour. Pediat., Am. Jour.

Diseases of Children, Pediat. Emergency Care; contbr. chapters to books, articles and abtracts to jours. Grantee in field. Fellow: Am. Coll. Cardiology (mem. emergency cardiac care com. 1992—98, mem. pediat. cardiology com. 1994—96, mem. 1996 annual sci. session program com. 1995—96, mem. credentials com. 1997—2000), Am. Acad. Pediat. (mem. exec. com. pediat. cardiology subsect. 1989—92, Young Investigator award sect. on cardiology 1978); mem.: AMA, NHLBI Pediatric Network (prin. investigator 2001—), John Morgan Soc., Phila. Arrhythmia Group, Pediat. Arrhythmia Group (mem. steering com.), Phila. County Med. Soc., Internat. Registry for Drug-Induced Arrhythmias (mem. sci. adv. com.), Sudden Arrhythmia Death Syndromes Found. (mem. sci. adv. bd.), Cardiac Arrhythmias Rsch. and Edn. Found., Inc. (mem. sci. adv. bd., Heart of the Child award 1996), N.Am. Soc. Pacing and Electrophysiology (mem. annual sci. sessions program com. 1998—2001, mem. pediat. com. 1998—2001), Pediat. Electrophysiology Soc., Am. Heart Assn. Coun. on Cardiovasc. Disease in the Young (mem. exec. com. 1990—94, mem. on tng. in pediat. cardiology 1994—96, mem. com. on electrocardiography and arrhythmias 1995—97, mem. membership com. 1996—97, chair Rashkind lecture selection com.), Am. Heart Assn. (med. spokesperson), Am. Heart Assn. Southeastern Pa. Affiliate (mem. rsch. peer rev. com. 1987—92, program chairperson 1988—90, mem. exec. com. 1988—93, v.p. 1989—90, pres.-elect 1990—91, pres. 1991—92, past-pres. 1992—93, mem. bd. dirs. 1993—96, mem. bd. govs. 1994—96, mem. pediat. sub-com. cardiac support coalition 1997—, post-doctoral fellow 1976—77, 1978—79), Alpha Omega Alpha, Phi Beta Kappa. Home: 110 Willow Way Cherry Hill NJ 08034-3049 Office: The Childerns Hosp Phila 34th St & Civic Center Blvd Philadelphia PA 19104 Office Phone: 215-590-3529.

**VETTORI, PAUL MARION,** lawyer; b. Washington, Sept. 6, 1944; s. Mariano L. and Bessie (Southard) V.; m. Judith Ann Gersack, June 19, 1965; children: Joseph, Damon, Jason, Justin. BA, U. Md., Coll. Park, 1967; JD, U. Md., Balt., 1970. Bar: Md. 1970, U.S. Dist. Ct. Md. 1970, U.S. Ct. Appeals (4th cir.) 1970. Assoc. Frank, Bernstein, Conaway & Goldman, Balt., 1971-74; asst. atty. gen. Md. Atty. Gen.'s Office, Balt., 1974-75; ptnr. Shapiro, Vettori & Olander, Balt., 1975-81, Frank, Bernstein, Conaway & Goldman, Balt., 1981-91, Kenny, Vettori & Robinson, P.A., Balt., 1992-97, White, Miller, Kenny & Vettori, LLP, Towson, Md., 1997—2000, Kenny & Vettori, LLP, Towson, 2000—. Fellow Am. Coll. Trial Lawyers, Am. Bd. Trial Lawyers; mem. ABA, Md. State Bar Assn., Balt. County Bar Assn., Howard County Bar Assn., Rotary (pres.). Avocation: sports. Office: 502 Washington Ave 720 Towson MD 21204-4505 E-mail: vettori@wmkv.com.

**VEURINK, GARY R.,** chemicals executive; m. Ruth Veurink; 3 children. BSChemE, SD Sch. Mines and Tech.; graduate student in Chem. Engring., U. Mich.; grad. Advanced Mgmt. Prog., INSEAD, Fontainebleau, France; D (hon.), SD Sch. Mines and Tech., 2002. Rschr. Electro Mech. Rsch. Lab. Mich. divsn. Dow Chem. Co., 1972, global mfg. dir. engring. plastics, 1995, v.p. global purchasing, 1998, site dir. Mich. ops., bus. ops. dir. performance chems., 2000, bus. ops. leader, v.p. mfg. and engring., Chems. and Intermediates Portfolio, 2004, corp. v.p. mfg. and engring., 2004—, mem. Office of the Chief Exec., 2004—. Bd. dirs. Dow Corning Corpn., Dorinco Reinsurance Co., NAM. Pres., mem. exec. coun. Lake Huron Area Coun. Boy Scouts Am.; bd. trustees Mich. chpt. Nature Conservancy. Mem.: AIChE. Office: Dow Chem Co 2030 Dow Ctr Midland MI 48674*

**VEVERKA, DONALD VICTOR,** science educator; b. Cleve., Ohio, Sept. 2, 1956; s. Donald Clayton and Christine Joann Veverka; m. Joni Dee Ratliff, Sept. 19, 2004; 1 child, Mitchell C. BS, Ohio State U., 1978, MS, 1979; PhD, Colo. State U., 2001. Cons. self employed, Cleve., 1979—84; asst. prof. US Air Force Acad., Colo. Springs, Colo., 1994—. Rhodes scholarship selection bd. panel mem. US Air Force Acad., Colo. Springs, Colo., 2003. Contbr. articles various profl. jours. Vol. Wilson United Meth. Ch., Colo. Springs, Colo., 2000—03, Veteran's Standdown, Colo. Springs, 2003. Maj. USAF, 1984—2005. Mem.: Am. Soc. for Nutritional Scis., Soc. for Nutrition Edn., Phi Kappa Phi Nat. Honor Soc. Republican. Protestant. Achievements include patents for health promotion program "Lets Get Moving", 2001. Avocations: golf, fishing, trap and skeet. Office: USAF Acad Dept Biology 2355 Faculty Dr U S A F Academy CO 80840 Office Phone: 719-333-9670. Office Fax: 719-333-2420. E-mail: don.veverka@usafa.af.mil.

**VEYLANSWAMI, SATGURU BODHINATHA,** head of religious order; b. Berkeley, Calif., Oct. 15, 1942; Spiritual studies, Self Realization Fellowship, Vedanta Soc.; studies with Gurudeva. Mgmr. Gurudeva's Master Course Corr. Study; v.p. Gurudeva's several nonprofit corps., 1970—; tchr., counsellor younger monks N.Am., NH; pujari Murugan Temple; sr. adminstrv. positions, tchr. Innersearch Travel-Study programs; lectr. tours Mauritius, Malaysia, Singapore; lectr. Innersearch Travel Study Programs, UN Millenium Summit Religious and Spiritual Leaders, Alaska, Caribbean and Northern Europe, 1999—2001; sr. monk Kadavul Hindu Temple; World Hindu Leader Hinduism, 2001—. Devel., arch. Hindu Heritage Endowment, 1993—; creator Kauai Aloha Endowment. Named to 1st Acharya, Gurudeva's Order. Office: Kauai Aadheenam Ashram 107 Kaholalele Rd Kapaa HI 96746-9304

**VEYSEY, MICHAEL CHARLES,** lawyer; b. Aug. 17, 1944; BA, Regis Coll.; JD, Boston Coll. Cert. military judge, trial counsel JAG; various positions Gould Electronics, Inc., Eastlake, Ohio, 1980—88, sr. v.p., gen. counsel, sec., 1989—2001; sr. v.p., gen. counsel, corp. sec. Scientific-Atlanta, Lawrenceville, Ga., 2003—; Ret. col. USMC. Office: Scientific Atlanta Inc 5030 Sugarloaf Pkwy Lawrenceville GA 30044 Office Phone: 770-236-6469. E-mail: michael.veysey@sciatl.com.

**VEZEAU, TIMOTHY J.,** lawyer; BSEE cum laude, St. Louis U., 1966; JD, Georgetown U., 1971. Bar: Ill. 1972. Patent examiner US Patent Office, 1968—70; patent advisor US Office of Navel Rsch., 1971; founding ptnr. patent practice, mem. bd. dirs. Katten Muchin Rosenman LLP, Chgo. Mem.: ABA, Intellectual Property Law Assn. of Chgo., Ill. Bar Assn., Chgo. Bar Assn., Eta Kappa Nu, Pi Mu Epsilon. Office: Katten Muchin Rosenman LLP 525 W Monroe St Chicago IL 60661 Office Phone: 312-902-5516. Office Fax: 312-577-4513. E-mail: timothy.vezeau@kattenlaw.com.

**VEZERIDIS, MICHAEL PANAGIOTIS,** surgeon, educator; b. Thessaloniki, Greece, Dec. 16, 1943; came to U.S., 1974; s. Panagiotis and Sofia (Avramidis) V.; m. Therese Mary Statz; children: Peter Statz, Alexander Michael. MD, U. Athens, 1967; MA ad eundem (hon.), Brown U., 1989. Diplomate Am. Bd. Surgery. Fellow surg. rsch. Harvard Med. Sch./Mass. Gen. Hosp., Boston, 1974-77; resident U. Mass., Worcester, 1977-80; fellow surg. oncology Roswell Park Meml. Inst., Buffalo, 1980-81, attending surgeon, 1981-82; staff surgeon VA Med. Ctr., Providence, 1982-84; asst. prof. surgery Brown U., Providence, 1982-88; chief surg. oncology VA Med. Ctr., Providence, 1984—, assoc. chief surgery, 1986-98, chief surgery, 1998—; cons. in surgery R.I. Hosp., Providence, 1987—; surg. oncologist Roger Williams Med. Ctr., Providence, 1989—; assoc. chief divsn. surg. oncology Brown U., Providence, 1989—98, assoc. prof. surgery, 1988-94, prof., 1994—; prof. surgery Boston U. Sch. Medicine, 1999—. Chmn. profl. edn. com. R.I. divsn. Am. Cancer Soc., Providence, 1987-89, pres.-elect 1989-91, pres. 1991-93, del. dir. to nat. bd. dirs., 1993-96, mem. Nat. Assembly of the Am. Cancer Soc., 1997-2003, mem. internat. activities adv. com., 2003-, bd. dirs. New Eng. divsn., 1997-2005, chief med. officer New Eng. divsn., 1999-2001; chmn. R.I. State Cancer Liaison Program Am. Coll. Sugeons, 1999—, mem. commn. on cancer, 2003-, bd. dirs. Rhode Island Cancer Coun., 2004-; vis. prof. U Patras (Greece) Med. Sch., 1988; mem. sci. adv. com. Clin. Rsch. Ctr., Brown U., Providence, 1989-91. Contbr. articles to profl. jours. and chpts. in med. books. Mem. parish coun. Ch. of Annunciation, Cranston, R.I., 1989-91; vp. Hellenic Cultural Soc. Southeastern New Eng., 1987-89. Decorated Navy Commendation medal; named Profl. Fed. Employee of Yr., R.I. Fed. Exec. Coun., 1987; recipient St. George medal Am. Cancer Soc.; Named Worthy Rscr. Cancer Rsch. grantee Va, 1983-89. Fellow ACS (treas.) R.I. chpt. 1996-2000, pres.-elect 2000-2002, pres. 2002-2004); mem. Soc. Surg. Oncology, Assn. for Acad. Surgery, Am. Soc. Clin. Oncology, N.Y. Acad. Scis. (life), Soc. for Surgery Alimentary Tract,

Am. Assn. for Cancer Rsch., Collegium Internat. Chirurgiae Digestivae, Assn. Mil. Surgeons U.S., Soc. for Metastasis Rsch., New Eng. Cancer Soc., New Eng. Surg. Soc., Quidnessett Country Club. Greek Orthodox. Avocations: classical music, reading, fencing, tennis, squash, cross country skiing. Home: 50 Limerock Dr East Greenwich RI 02818-1643 Office: Univ Surg Assocs Ste 470 Two Dudley St Providence RI 02905 Office Phone: 401-331-1036. Business E-Mail: michael_vezeridis@brown.edu.

**VEZINA, GILBERT,** pediatric neuroradiologist; b. Montreal, Can., July 14, 1960; arrived in U.S., 1984; s. Jean Lorrain and Lise Vezina; m. Lise Marie Becker, Sept. 1, 2001; children: Annalise, Sophie. MD, McGill Med. Sch., Montreal, 1983. Staff radiologist dept. radiology Mass. Gen. Hosp., Boston, 1989—90, Children's Nat. Med. Ctr., Washington, 1992—; radiologist Wash. Metro Area Tuberous Sclerosis Rsch. Clinic, Fairfax, Va., 1997—. Integration panel mem. neurofibromatosis rsch. program U.S. Army Med. Rsch. and Material Command, Washington, 1997—2003; cons. Mgmt. of Myelomem-jocele Study, NIH, Bethesda, 2003—. Pres. Am. Soc. Pediat. Neuroradiology, 2001—02; vice chair radiology com. Children's Oncology Group, 2001—. Scholar, McGill Univ. (Montreal), 1978—79. Mem.: Am. Coll. Radiology, Radiological Soc. N.Am., Am. Soc. Neuroradiology. Office: Children's Nat Med Ctr Dept Radiology 111 Mich Ave NW Washington DC 20010 Office Phone: 202-884-3651. Business E-Mail: gvezina@cnmc.org.

**VEZINA, VICKY LYNNE,** middle school educator; b. Cheyenne, Wyo., June 3, 1950; d. Charles James and Wanda Louise (Byers) Seidl; m. Gary Edward Vezina, June 30, 1968; children: Jeffrey James, Michelle Annette. AS in Elem. Edn., Parkland Jr. Coll., Champaign, Ill., 1989; BS in Edn., Ea. Ill. U., 1991. Cert. tchr. K-9 in social sci. arts, gen. sci., social sci. Food demonstrator Beatrice Foods, Cheyenne, 1967; chambermaid Home Ranch Motel, Cheyenne, 1968; dog bather/groomer Shellhart's Boarding Kennels & Grooming, Cheyenne, 1968-69; parent vol. Bement (Ill.) Grad Sch., 1985-87; substitute tchr. Bement, Monticello and Cerro Gordo (Ill.) Pub. Schs., 1991—. Home bound tutor Bement H.S., 1992, 93; truancy tutor Bement Grade Sch., 1993, 94, summer tutor, 1998—; presch. tester Bement Sch. Dist., 1986-87. Chmn. membership com. Bement PTA, 1986—87; vol. Bement Sch. Dist # 5, 1985—87; tchr. Sunday sch./Bible sch. Christian Ch., Bement, 1973—79; co-chair Christian edn. com. 1st Presbyn. Ch., Monticello, 1998—2001, chair Christian edn. com., 2002, chmn. Christian Edn. Com., 2003, mem. Christian Clown Troupe, 2000—; elected elder, 2001, mem. adult choir, 1998—. Named Vol. of the Yr., Bement Sch. Dist. #5, 1987. Mem. VFW Aux., Kappa Delta Pi, Alpha Sigma Lambda, Alpha Omega. Democrat. Presbyterian. Avocations: reading, crocheting, word search puzzles, bowling, sight seeing. Home: 432 W Shumway St Bement IL 61813-1342

**VEZIROGLU, TURHAN NEJAT,** mechanical engineering educator, researcher; b. Istanbul, Turkey, Jan. 24, 1924; came to U.S., 1962; s. Abdul Kadir and Ferruh (Bürin) V.; m. Bengi Isikli, Mar. 17, 1961; children: Emre Alp, Oya Sureyya. A.C.G.I., City and Guilds Coll., London, 1946; B.Sc. with honors, U. London, 1947; D.I.C., Imperial Coll., London, 1948; PhD, U. London, 1951. Engring. apprentice Alfred Herbert Ltd., Coventry, U.K., 1945; project engr. Office of Soil Products, Ankara, Turkey, 1953-56; tech. dir. M.K.V. Constrn. Co, Istanbul, 1957-61; assoc. prof. mech. engring. U. Miami, Coral Gables, Fla., 1962-65, prof. Coral Fables, Fla., 1966—, dir. grad. studies mech. engring. Coral Gables, Fla., 1965-71, chmn. dept. mech. engring., 1971-75, assoc. dean research Coll. Engring., 1975-79, dir. Clean Energy Research Inst., 1974—. UNESCO cons., Paris; vis. prof. Middle East Tech. U., Ankara, 1969 Editor-in-chief: Internat. Jour. Hydrogen Energy, 1976—. Pres. Learning Disabilities Found., Miami, 1972-73, advisor, 1974-80. Recipient Turkish Presdl. sci. award Turkish Sci. and Tech. Research Found., 1975; named hon. prof. Xian Jiaotong U., China, 1982 Fellow AAAS, ASME, Instn. Mech. Engrs.; mem. Internat. Assn. Hydrogen Energy (pres. 1975), AIAA, Assn. Energy Engrs., Am. Nuclear Soc., Am. Soc. Engring. Edn., AAUP, Internat. Soc. Solar Energy, Systems Engring. Soc., Sigma Xi Home: 4910 Biltmore Dr Miami FL 33146-1724 Office: U Miami Clean Energy Rsch Inst PO Box 248294 Miami FL 33124-8294 Office Phone: 305-284-4666. Business E-Mail: veziroglu@miami.edu. *Hydrogen energy system will provide the world with clean and abundant energy, while doing away with pollution, acid rains and the greenhouse effect. It is a noble and worthwhile goal to strive for.*

**VIAMONTES, GEORGE I.,** psychiatrist, director; s. Jorge A. and Gloria E. Viamontes; m. Claudia D. Troesch, Mar. 14, 1990; children: George Frederick, Christopher George. BS, U. Notre Dame, Ind., 1973; MD, St. Louis U., 1990; PhD in Biology, Wash. U., St. Louis, 1979. Bd. cert. psychiatrist Am. Bd. Psychiatry and Neurology, 1996, bd. cert. addiction psychiatrist Am. Bd. Psychiatry and Neurology, 1997, bd. cert. geriatric psychiatrist Am. Bd. Psychiatry and Neurology, 1996. Regional med. dir. United Behavioral Health, Inc., St. Louis, 1995—. Editor: (profl. jour.) Psychiatric Annals, 2006; contbr. articles to profl. jours. Fellow Immunogenetics Post-Doctoral fellow, Sloan-Kettering Inst., NY, 1979—81, Am. Assn. for Geriatric Psychiatry, 1989—90. Mem.: Am. Psychiat. Assn. Conservative. Roman Catholic. Avocation: computer graphics, chess, soccer. Personal E-mail: viamonte@sbcglobal.net.

**VIANDS, DONALD REX,** plant breeder, educator; b. Riverdale, Md., Apr. 1, 1952; s. Walter Leroy and Lydia (Zeh) V.; m. Janice Ann Ruppelt, Aug. 7, 1976; children: Jamie Christopher, April Suzanne. BS in Agronomy, U. Md., 1974; MS in Plant Breeding, U. Minn., 1977, PhD in Plant Breeding, 1979. Undergrad. rsch. asst. U. Md., College Park, 1969-74; grad. rsch. asst. U. Minn., St. Paul, 1974-79; asst. prof. Cornell U., Ithaca, NY, 1979-85, assoc. prof., 1985-92, prof., 1992—, assoc. dir. acad. programs, 1995—2002, assoc. dean, dir. acad. programs, 2003—. Mem. adv. com. biotech. sci. adv. com. EPA, Washington, 1987-95; mem. steering com. N.Y. State North Country Devel. Program, 1990-99; adv. N.Y. State Forage and Grassland Coun., 1984-90, Alfalfa Crop Adv. Com., 1984-92. Contbr. articles to profl. jours., chpts. to books. Sunday sch. tchr. People's Bapt. Ch., Newfield, N.Y., 1988-2000, deacon, 1988-90, 93-98, Awana comdr., 1993-2000. Named Most Influential Faculty Mem. for Merrill Presdl. Scholar, Cornell U., 1991. Mem. Am. Soc. Agronomy (N.E. regional coord. mem. com. 1998-99), Crop Sci. Soc. Am., Am. Seed Trade Assn. (mem. minimum distance com. 1988-94), N.Am. Alfalfa Improvement Conf. (sec. 1984-86, v.p. 1986-88, pres. 1988-90), Ea. Forage Improvement Conf., Am. Forage and Grassland Coun. Republican. Achievements include development of 12 alfalfa varieties and 1 birdsfoot trefoil variety. Office: Cornell Univ Office Acad Programs 151 Roberts Hall Ithaca NY 14853-5905 Office Phone: 607-255-3081. Business E-Mail: drv3@cornell.edu.

**VIANI, JAMES LAURENCE,** lawyer; b. Kincaid, Ill., Dec. 24, 1932; s. Frank Jerome and Alfonsina V.; m. Virginia Lee Wilson, Dec. 27, 1958; children: Theresa, Diana, Deborah. BS, Millikin U., 1954; LLB, Wash. U., St. Louis, 1957. Bar: Ill. 1957, Mo. 1957. Assoc. Blackmar, Swanson, Midgley, Jones & Eager, Kansas City, Mo., 1958-59, Stinson, Mag & Fizzell, Kansas City, 1960-62; ptnr. Stinson, Mag & Fizzel, Kansas City, 1962-87, chmn. corp. dept., 1979-87, cons. ptnr., 1988-92. Br. bd. chmn. YMCA, Kansas City, 1979-81. With U.S. Army, 1957-63. Mem. ABA, Phi Kappa Phi, Order of the Coif. Republican. Avocations: hiking, reading, farming. Home: 11106 Belleview Ave Kansas City MO 64114-5115

**VIATCHENKO-KARPINSKI, SERGE,** biologist, researcher; b. Kyiv, Ukraine, May 24, 1961; s. Vsevolod Viatchenko-Karpinski and Nina Alekseeva; m. Dina Ayupova; 1 child, Alexander. MS, Kyiv State U., Phys. Dept., Ukraine, 1984; PhD in Biophysics, Bogomoletz Inst. of Physiology, Ukraine, 1995. Rsch. assoc. Bogomoletz Inst. of Physiology, Kyiv, Ukraine, 1994—95, Inst. of Neuroscience U. of Cologne, Germany, 1995—97; sr. rschr. Bogomoletz Inst. of Physiology, Kyiv, Ukraine, 1997—98; rsch. assoc. Tex. Tech U. HSC Physiology, Lubbock, 1998—2001, instr., 2001—05; rsch. assoc. prof. Med. Ctr. Ohio State U., 2006—. Mem.: Am. Heart Assn., N.Y. Acad.

of Scis., Biophysical Soc., Ukrainian Biophysical Soc., Ukrainian Physiol. Soc. Avocations: fishing, travel. Office: 505 DHLRI West 12th Ave Columbus OH 43210 Office Phone: 614-688-4250. Office Fax: 614-247-7799. Business E-Mail: serge.karpinski@osumc.edu.

**VIATER, JOHN RONALD,** investment company executive; b. Mpls., 1935; s. John Anthony and Mary Agnes (Litecky) Viater; m. Eloise Maren Johnson, Feb. 5, 1991. BA, U. Santa Ana, 1954. CEO, owner ViaCo, Lake Placid, Fla., 1956—. Pfc USMC, 1953—55, Korea. Republican. Avocations: coin collecting/numismatics, art. Home and Office: 100 Brentwood Dr N Lake Placid FL 33852

**VIAULT, RAYMOND G.,** food company executive; b. NYC, Sept. 19, 1944; m. Lucille Viault; children: Lisa, Deborah, Russell. Bachelor's degree, Brown U.; MBA, Columbia U. Pres., CEO Kraft Jacobs Suchard, Zurich, Switzerland; CEO Jacobs Suchard A.G. (acquired by Kraft Gen. Foods), 1990-93; pres. Maxwell House Coffee Co. Kraft Gen. Foods, v.p., gen. mgr. desserts divsn.; with Gen. Mills, Mpls., 1996—2004, vice-chmn., 1996—2004, also bd. dirs.; responsible for meals divsn., baking divsn. Pillsbury U.S. Bakery and Food Svc. Former bd. dirs. Cereal Ptnrs. Worldwide; bd. dirs. Newell Rubbermaid, VF Corp., Safeway Inc., 2004—. Bd. overseers Columbia Grad. Sch. Bus., N.Y.C.; trustee Lawrenceville Sch., N.J.; bd. dirs. United Way Mpls., Minn. Internat. Ctr., Technoserve. Office: PO Box 1113 One General Mills Blvd Minneapolis MN 55440-1113

**VICE, DANIEL HOY,** geologist, educator; s. Jack Hoy and Doris Lucille Vice; m. Mari Ann Poythress (div.); m. Beth Ann Van Voorst, Aug. 13, 1988. AS, Ctrl. Oreg. C.C., Bend, 1964; BS, Oreg. State U., Corvallis, 1967; MS, Ariz. State U., Tempe, 1974; EdD, Pa. State U., State College, 1996. Registered registered profl. geologist Wyo. Sampler U.S. Bur. Mines, Spokane, Wash., 1971; staff geologist Burlington No., St. Paul, 1971—74, geologist Stillings, Mont., 1974—82; cons. geologist Billings, 1982—88; part-time lectr. Pa. State U., Hazleton, 1997—98, instr. sci. divsn., 1998—. Expert witness Tech. Adv. Svc. for Attys., Blue Bell, Pa., 1997—. Contbr. articles to profl. jours. Mem.: Mont. Geol. Soc., Nat. Assn. Geosci. Tchrs., Am. Assn. Petroleum Geologists, Kiwanis. Presbyterian. Avocations: reading, hiking, fishing, lapidary work. Office: Pennsylvania State University 76 University Dr Hazleton PA 18202

**VICE, ROY LEE,** history professor; b. Lynchburg, Va., Oct. 12, 1950; s. Cline Lowell and Ruth Burchell (Newman) V.; m. Sara Pearsaul, June 2005. BA in History, BS in Physics, Carson-Newman Coll., 1972; MA in History, U. Chgo., 1976, PhD in History, 1984. Lectr. Continuing Edn. program U. Chgo., 1985-86, 87-88, rare books asst. univ. librs., 1986; asst. prof. Pacific Luth. U., Tacoma, 1986-87, Clemson (S.C.) U., 1988-90, Wright State U., Dayton, Ohio, 1990-95, assoc. prof., 1995—. Contbr. articles to profl. jours. Vol. tutor CYCLE Cabrini-Green Projects, Chgo., 1981—86; vol. lectr. LaSalle St. Ch., Chgo., 1989—98, 2000—05. With U.S. Army, 1972—74. Mem. Am. Hist. Assn., 16th Century Studies Conf. Democrat. Baptist. Home: 111 Brown St Dayton OH 45402 Office: Wright State Univ Dept History 3640 Colonel Glenn Hwy Dayton OH 45435-0001 Business E-Mail: roy.vice@wright.edu.

**VICE, SUSAN F.,** medicinal chemist; b. Oshawa, Ont., Can., Apr. 19, 1956; m. Andrew S. Thompson, Nov. 27, 1987. BS in Chemistry, U. We. Ont., London, Can., 1980; PhD, U. Waterloo, Ont., 1984. Postdoc. fellow U. Calif. Irvine, 1984—86; rsch. scientist Polysar Ltd., Sarnia, Canada, 1986—88; sr. prin. scientist Schering Plough Rsch. Inst., Kenilworth, NJ, 1988—2000; freelance tech. writer, 2001—05; mng. editor John Wiley & Sons, Inc., Hoboken, 2005—. Recipient Thomas Alva Edison Patent award, Rsch. and Devel. Coun. N.W., 2004; fellow Charles S. Humphrey grad. fellow, Guelph-Waterloo Ctr. Grad. Work in Chemistry, 1983, postdoc. fellow, Natural Scis. and Engring. Rsch. Coun., 1984—86, inds. postdoc. fellow, 1986; scholar, 1981—84. Mem.: Am. Soc. Microbiology, Editl. Freelancers Assn., Chem. Inst. Can. and Soc. Chemistry, Am. Chem. Soc. Home: 1144 Sawmill Rd Mountainside NJ 07092-2213 Personal E-mail: vicesf@yahoo.com.

**VICHIOLA, CHRISTOPHER MICHAEL,** writer, educator; b. Bridgeport, Conn., Apr. 27, 1959; s. Michael Richard and Delores (Distaci) Vichiola; m. Tracey Vichiola, Nov. 12, 1997; children: Michael, Christopher, Anthony. AS, Western Conn. State U., 1981, BA, 1983; grad., Colonel James "Bo" Gritz's Spec. Forces Green Beret On-Field Med. Surg. Sch. Cert. nursing asst. Martial arts tchr. Am. Bujinkan Dojo, Danbury, Conn., 1993—; tchr., distbr. Ctr. for Action, Kamiah, Idaho, 1997—; sales rep., safety capt. fertilizer toxic fertilizer program, power equipment specialist Home Depot, 1998—, power equipment specialist; clk. A&P Foodmart, 1999—2003; safety capt. Hazardous Waste Fertilizer Program; power equipment specialist Home Depot, 2006—. Educator, cons. Primerica Fin. Svcs., Danbury, 1997—; educator Christic Inst. Law Firm, Washington, 1995—. Author: Above the Law - The Real Story's Files, 1995, Above the Law Part II, 1995, The Real Story of Christopher Vichiola and Colonel Gritz, 1997, The Real Story of Christopher Vichiola and Colonel Gritz's Training, 1997. Educator Rev. Jesse L. Jackson's Rainbow Coalition, Washington, 1992—; Mayor Eugene Eriquez Dem. Party, Danbury, 1987—; Rep. Jack Brooks 1991—; Gov. Michael Dukakis, 1989—. Black belt in Ninjutsu, 1997; recipient Eagle award Col. James "Bo" Gritz, 1997, Spike Navy Seal Scuba badge Col. James "Bo" Gritz, 1997. Avocations: camping, scuba diving, basketball, football, martial arts.

**VICINO, THOMAS JOSEPH,** political science professor; b. Washington, July 18, 1980; s. Thomas Edward and Susann Elaine Vicino. BSc cum laude, U. Miami, 2002; MPP, U. Md., 2004, PhD, 2006. Rsch. asst. U. Md., Balt., 2002—04; asst. prof. urban affairs U. Tex., Arlington, 2006—. Contbr. articles to profl. jours. Policy analyst Citizens Planning and Housing Assn., Balt., 2003—06. Recipient Excellence in Govt. and Politics award, Howard County Exec., 1998, Frazer D. White award for Excellence in Comm. Studies, U. Miami, 1996—2002; fellow, U. Md., 2002—06; George Merrick scholar, U. Miami, 1998—2002. Mem.: Am. Polit. Sci. Assn., Urban Affairs Assn. Office Phone: 817-272-3071. Business E-Mail: thomasvicino@gmail.com.

**VICK, COLUMBUS EDWIN, JR.,** retired civil engineering design firm executive; b. Jacksonville, Fla., Nov. 8, 1934; s. Columbus Edwin Sr. and Lucretia (Dean) V.; m. Laura Kay McGowan, Mar. 28, 1964; children: Jennifer, Carolyn, Elizabeth. BSCE, N.C. State U., 1956, MSCE, 1960. Registered engr., 15 states. Rsch. asst. N.C. State Civil Engring. Dept., Raleigh, 1958-60; transp. planning engr. Harland Bartholomew & Assocs., Memphis, 1960-64, office and project mgr. Raleigh, 1964-67; prin., co-founder Kimley-Horn and Assocs. Inc., Raleigh, 1967-72, pres., 1972-92; chmn., 1992-2000. Bd. dirs. Wachovia Bank, Design Profls. Coalition Am. Cons. Engrs. Coun. Co-author: North Carolina Atlas; contbr. articles to profl. jours. Past pres., dir. N.C. State U. Engring. Found.; past pres. bd. assocs. Meredith Coll.; past dir. N.C. State U. Alumni Assn.; bd. visitors N.C. State U.; past 2d v.p. Bapt. State Conv. of N.C.; bd. dirs. Assoc. Bapt. Press, Bibl. Recorder; trustee Kenan Inst. for Engring. Tech. and Sci., Gardner Webb U., Meredith Coll.; mem. bd. advisors Wake Forest U. Sch. Divinity. Named Disting. Engring. alumnus N.C. State U., 1991. Fellow ASCE (Outstanding Young Engr. award ea. br. N.C. sect. 1966), Inst. Transp. Engrs. (Oustanding Individual Activity award so. sect. 1978, Disting. Svc. award so. sect. 1981, Lifetime Svc. award N.C. sect. 1995); mem. NSPE (Disting. Svc. award), Am. Con. Engrs. Coun., Am. Inst. Cert. Planners, Profl. Svcs. Mgmt. Assn. (Coll. of Fellow, Leonardo da Vinci award 2005), Am. Soc. Civ. Engrs. (Outstanding Engring Achievement award 1992). Baptist. Home: 2205 Nancy Ann Dr Raleigh NC 27607-3318 Office: Kimley-Horn and Assocs Inc 3001 Weston Pky Cary NC 27513-2301 Office Phone: 919-677-2002. E-mail: ed.vick@kimley-horn.com.

**VICK, EDWARD HOGE, JR.,** advertising executive; b. NYC, Feb. 27, 1944; s. Edward Hoge and Margaret Jane (Sprankle) V.; m. Nancy Jane Newcomer; Children: Joshua D., Charlie, Jane. AB, U. N.C., 1966; MS, Northwestern U., 1971. With Benton & Bowles, Inc., N.Y.C., 1971-75, Ogilvy & Mather, Inc., N.Y.C., 1975-83; exec. v.p., dir. account service Ammirati & Puris Inc., N.Y.C., 1983-85, pres., chief operating officer, 1985-90; pres., CEO Levine, Huntley, Vick & Beaver, N.Y.C., 1990-94, Young & Rubicam N.Y., 1994-96, chmn., CEO, 1997—. Author: An Examination of the Creative Process, 1971. Bd. vis. U. N.C. Decorated Bronze Star (2). Mem. Am. Assn. Advt. Agys. (bd. dirs.), Advt. Edn. Found. (bd. dirs.), St. Andrew's Soc. Republican. Presbyterian. Office: Young & Rubicam 285 Madison Ave New York NY 10017 Home: 15 E Point Ln Old Greenwich CT 06870-2403

**VICK, JAMES ALBERT,** publishing executive, consultant; b. Norwalk, Conn., Feb. 5, 1945; s. James Albert and Madeline (Mayew) V.; m. Deborah M. Ashley, Dec. 23, 1964 (div. Oct. 1974); children: James Ashley, Guy Robert; m. Susan Jane Collins, May 14, 1977; 1 child, Jonathan Scott. BS, Boston U., 1967. Dist. mgr. McGraw Hill Pub. Co., N.Y.C., 1969-75, Cahners Pub. Co., N.Y.C., 1975-79; mgr. advt. ASCE, N.Y.C., 1979-82; v.p. mktg. Bill Communications, N.Y.C., 1982-87; pub. Thomas Pub. Co., N.Y.C., 1987-95; v.p. Web Property Devel. Poppe Tyson, 1995-96; exec. v.p. sales/mktg. Lawyers Weekly Publs., Boston, 1996-98; v.p. publ. Phillips Publ./KIPI, White Plains, NY, 1998-2000; pub., staff dir. IEEE Spectrum Mag., N.Y.C., 2000—. Cons. Carvajal, Calle, Colombia, 1984, McLarens, London, 1987, 2005—06; mem. pubs. com. Am. Bus. Media, 2005—06, Bus. Publ. Audit, 2005—06. Capt. USAR, 1967-70, Vietnam. Mem.: IEEE (comms. soc., computer soc.), Soc. Nat. Assn. Publs. (bd. dirs. 2005—06), Soc. Plastics Engrs., Bus. Mktg. Assn. (cert. bus. communicator), Port Royal Golf Club, Princeton Club, Elks. Episcopalian. Avocations: golf, sailing, antique restoration. Home: 473 Judd Rd Easton CT 06612 Office: IEEE Spectrum Mag 3 Park Ave Ste 1701 New York NY 10016-5997 Fax: 212-419-7589. Office Phone: 212-419-7767. E-mail: j.vick@ieee.org, javick@att.net.

**VICK, JEFFREY HARRISON,** music educator, musician; b. Denver, Nov. 5, 1965; s. Donald James and Sharlene Marie (Savage) Vick; m. Jacquelyn Campeau, Nov. 20, 1999; 1 child, Teresa Irene. BS in Music, U. Ariz., 1989; MEd in Music, Mont. State U., 1991. Cert. music tchr. grades K-12 Mont., secondary tchr. grades 7-12, secondary tchr. music, Office of Pub. Instrn., State Mont. Music educator Bozeman (Mont.) Pub. Schs., 1990—91, Willow Creek (Mont.) Sch., 1991—92, Anderson Sch. Dist. #41, Bozeman, 1993—. Pvt. percussion tchr., Bozeman, 1989—; prin. timpanist and percussionist Bozeman Symphony Orch., 1989—, Intermountain Opera Assn., Bozeman, 1990—, Mont. Ballet Co., Bozeman, 1993—; prin. timpanist Mont. Summer Symphony, Helena, 1998—2002; libr., coach Mont. chamber music workshop Mont. State U., Bozeman, 1990—, adj. instr. music, 1992—96, adv. bd. Mont. chamber music workshop, 1998—2003; dist. and state music festival adjudicator, 1994—; clinician Internat. Conf. on Percussion Music, Tucson, 1995; founding dir. PercOrchestra, Bozeman, 2000—; mem. Flutes and Friends, 2000—. Editor (newsletter): Montana Percussion News, 1998—, composer numerous compositions for band, percussion, Balinese gamelan; numerous concerto and chamber music recitals. Recipient Individual Artist Fellowship award, Mont. Arts Coun., 1992—93. Mem.: NEA, Mont. Music Educators Assn., Music Educators Nat. Conf., Percussive Arts Soc. (sec. Ariz. chpt. 1986—87, v.p. Ariz. chpt. 1987—88, sec. Mont. chpt. 1996—), Am. Fedn. Musicians (exec. bd. local 709 1996—99, pres. local 709 1999—2002), Phi Delta Kappa (profl. rsch. grant 1999). Avocations: collecting instruments and masks, photography, world music. Home: 529 South Black Ave Bozeman MT 59715-5301 Office: Anderson Sch Dist #41 10040 Cottonwood Rd Bozeman MT 59718 Office Phone: 406-587-1305 110. Business E-Mail: jvick@metnet.mt.gov. E-mail: jvick@theandersonschool.org.

**VICK, MICHAEL (MICHAEL DWAYNE VICK),** professional football player; b. Newport News, Va., June 26, 1980; s. Brenda Boddie. Grad., Warwick High Sch., Newport News, VA, 1998; attended, Va. Tech., 2001. Football player Atlanta Falcons, 2001—. Spokesperson Boys & Girls Club of Metro Atlanta, Empty Stocking Fund. Named one of 101 Most Influential Minorities in Sports, Sports Illustrated, 2003; named to NFC Pro-Bowl, 2002, 2004—05; recipient Excellence in Sports Performance award (ESPY), 1999, Archie Griffin award, 1999. Achievements include finishing third in the balloting for the 1999 Heisman Trophy, matching the highest finish ever by a freshman in the voting. Mailing: c/o Atlanta Falcons 4400 Falcon Pkwy Flowery Branch GA 30542*

**VICK, NICHOLAS A.,** neurologist; b. Chgo., Oct. 3, 1939; MD, U. Chgo., 1965. Diplomate Am. Bd. Neurology. Intern U. Chgo. Hosps., 1965, resident in neurology, 1966-68; fellow in neurology NIH, Bethesda, Md., 1968-70; staff Evanston (Ill.) Hosp., 1975—; prof. neurology Northwestern U. Med. Sch., Evanston, Ill., 1978—. Mem.: Am. Bd. Psychiatry and Neurology (past exec. dir.). Office: Evanston Hosp Dept Neurology 2650 Ridge Ave Evanston IL 60201-1781 Office Phone: 847-570-2570. Business E-Mail: nvick@enh.org.*

**VICK, SUSAN,** playwright, educator, director, actress; b. Raleigh, NC, Nov. 4, 1945; d. Thomas B. Jr. and Merle (Hayes) V. MFA, So. Meth. U., 1969; PhD, U. Ill., 1979. Prof. drama/theatre and dir. theatre WPI, 1981—; playwright Excuse Me For Living Prodns., Cambridge, Mass., 1989—; exec. dramaturg WPI New Voices in NY Samuel French Festival, 2005; playwright Festival Fringe, Edinburgh, 1989—; dir. WPI New Voices in N.Y. Dreams Abridged, Samuel French Festival, 2004. Playwright Ensemble Studio Theatre, N.Y.C., 1981-83; founder WPI Ann. New Voices Festival of Original Plays, 1982. Editor: (2 vols.) Playwrights Press, Amherst, 1988—; playwright: When I Was Your Age, 1982, Old-Way Ames-Day, 1982, Investments, 1985, Half Naked, 1989, Quandary, 1983, Meat Selection, 1984, Give My Love to Everyone But, 1989; appeared in plays including Rip Van Winkle, 1979, Why I Live at The P.O., 1982, The Play Group, 1984-85, Present Stage, 1985, Sister Mary Ignatius Explain It All, 1986, Wipeout, 1988, Bogus Joan, 1992-93; dir. play Give My Love to Everyone But, 1990 (Edinburgh Festival); theatre editor: Sojourner The Women's Forum, 1995-98; dramatist, script cons. Clyde Unity Theatre, Glasgow, Scotland, 1992-93, 1999-2000; dir. Dreams Abridged, WPI New Voices in NY, Samuel French Festival, Chernuchin Theatre, N.Y.C., 2004. Dir., Women's Community Theatre, Amherst, 1981-84, Upstart, Wis., 1994. Faculty fellow U. Ill., 1976-77, Bd. of Trustees Award for Outstanding Tchg., WPI, 1997. Mem. U.S. Inst. for Theatre Tech., Nat. Assn. Schs. of Theatre, New Eng. Theatre Conf., Inc., Drama League, Dramatists Guild (assoc.), Soc. Stage Dirs. and Choreographers (assoc.), U.S. Inst. Theatre Tech., New England Theatre Conf., Nat. Assn. Schs. Theatre, Alpha Phi Omega (Svc. to Students award 1996). Avocations: puppets, frogs, travel. Office: WPI 100 Instit Rd Worcester MA 01609-2280 Office Phone: 508-831-5682. Business E-Mail: svick@wpi.edu.

**VICKERS, LEE LOUISE,** minister; b. Suffern, N.Y., Dec. 20, 1954; d. Chester E. and Dorothy Jean (Allen) Vickers; 1 child, Seth. Dipl. summa cum laude, We. Bapt. Coll., 1977; A in Forestry, Flathead Valley C.C., 1979, A, 1980; BA in Liberal Arts, Regents Coll., 1988. Sec.-clk. Glacier Ch., Kalispell, Mont., 1988—91; pastor Hephzibah Haven Ministry, Mont., 1991—. Poem, E Duo Unum, 1993; author: Earth and Sky, 2002. Firefighter, dept. sec. Marion (Mont.) Vol. Fire Dept., 1996—98. With U.S. Army, 1982—84. Avocations: Bee Gees fan, reading, poetry. Home: PO Box 9155 Kalispell MT 59904

**VICKERS, NANCY J.,** academic administrator; BA, Mt. Holyoke Coll., 1967, LHD (hon.), 1999; MA, Yale U., 1971, PhD, 1976. Prof. French and Italian Dartmouth Coll., 1973—87; prof. French, Italian, and comparative literature U. Southern Calif., 1987—97, dean curriculum and instrn. Coll. Letters, Arts and Scis., 1994—97; pres. Bryn Mawr Coll., 1997—. Vis. prof. Harvard U., U. Pa., UCLA; bd. dirs. Bryn Mawr Bank Corp.; bd. govs. Coun. Dante Soc. Am. Recipient Presdl. medal Outstanding Leadership and Achievement, Dartmouth Coll., 1991; fellow vis. fellow, Princeton U. Office: Bryn Mawr Coll 101 N Merion Ave Bryn Mawr PA 19010-2899

**VICKERS, ROBERT EDWIN,** retired military officer, historian, writer; b. Adams Mills, Ohio, Feb. 20, 1924; m. Annell Ross Waldrop, Jan. 18, 2002; children: Shelia Ross, Janace Nmi Chapman, Billie Ann Clark, Mark Rodgers. Postgrad., Indsl. Coll. Armed Forces, Wash., 1965—67, George Washington U., 1965—67. Advanced through grade to col. USAF, 1942, officer, pilot, sr. staff, comdr., 1942—75; founding charter dir. 8AF Hist. Soc., Hallendale, 1976—84; CEO, pres. Concierge Mgmt. Inc., Albuquerque, 1985—. Dir. awards & protocol 8AF Hist. Soc., Albuquerque, 1994—, dir., mgr. mil. reunion, 1981—85; cons. air historian Pueblo Hist. Aircraft Soc., Colo. Author: The Liberators from Wending, Remembrance of the Missing. Trustee AF Hist. Found., Washington, 1985—; internat. event chmn. 50th Anniversary WWII B-24 Gala Reunion, Ft. Worth, 1988—89; bd. dirs., cons. 8AF Meml. Mus. Found., Albuquerque, 2004—; trustee, bd. dirs. Am. Air Mus., England, Duxford AF Mus., England. Decorated Legion of Merit, ETO Campaign medal, NATO Svc. medal, Korean War and Vietnam Svc. medals, WWII Victory medal, DFC, Meritorious Svc. medal, Air Medal with oak leaf cluster, Air Force Commendation medal with oak leaf cluster, Disting. Unit citation with oak leaf cluster, Combat Readiness medal. Mem.: Air Force Assn., Mil. Officers Assn Am., 8AF Vets. (life; historian, cons. 1979—2005, N.Mex. chpt.), Dadelians (life). Republican. Avocations: history, writing, painting, golf, travel. Home: 414 Camino de la Placita #33 Taos NM 87571 Personal E-mail: duganbv@aol.com.

**VICKERS, ROGER SPENCER,** physicist, researcher, environmental artist; b. Hitchin, Hertfordshire, Eng., Nov. 13, 1937; came to U.S., 1963, naturalized, 1974; s. John Hector and Corona (McCarthy) V.; m. Solvi Loken, May 18, 1968; children: Michelle, Jacqueline Nmi. BSc with honors, Southampton U., Eng., 1959, PhD, 1963. Physicist Ill. Inst. Tech. Research Inst., Chgo., 1963-66; rsch. assoc. Stanford U., 1966-68; v.p. sci. and applications E.R.A., Inc., Houston, 1969-70; assoc. prof. elec. engring. Colo. State U., 1970-73; dir. advanced radar program SRI Internat., Menlo Park, Calif., 1973-89; dir. Environ. Mapping-Can., Vancouver, B.C., 1998—; Internat. Radar Cons. Inc., Redwood City, Calif., 2000—. Cons. NSF. Mem. IEEE. Home: 171 Main St # 252 Los Altos CA 94022 Personal E-mail: rvickers@int-radar.com.

**VICKERY, ANN MORGAN,** lawyer; b. Anderson, S.C., June 25, 1944; d. Joseph Harold and Doris (Rogers) Morgan; m. Raymond Ezekiel Vickery, Jr., June 23, 1979; children: Raymond Morgan, Philip Dickens. AB History, Mary Baldwin Coll., 1965; JD, Georgetown U., 1978. Bar: D.C. 1978. Elem. sch. tchr., Chesterfield County, Va., 1965-66; legal publs. specialist Nat. Archives and Record Svc., Washington, 1966-69; speech writing staff to Pres., rsch. asst., chief rschr., staff asst. The White House, Washington, 1969-74; summer clerk Graham & James, Washington, 1975; various positions Dept. Treasury, Washington, 1975-78; atty. Hogan & Hartson, LLP, Washington, 1978—, mng. ptnr.-D.C. office, dir. health practice group. Health group dir. Hogan and Hartson, LLP, Washington, 1991—, exec. com., 1992-95, 96-99, Washington office mng. ptnr., 1999—; outside legal counsel Nat. Hospice and Palliative Care Orgn., 1982— (named Woman of the Yr. 1986); spkr. in field. Contbr. articles to profl. jours. Dir. Hospice No. Va., Arlington, 1987-93; trustee Nat. Hospice Found., 1996—. Mem. ABA, Am. Health Lawyers Assn., D.C. Bar, Health on Wednesday, Hill & Knowlton Cmty. (director). Office: Hogan & Hartson LLP Columbia Square 555 13th St NW Ste 12E-300 Washington DC 20004-1161 Office Phone: 202-637-8605. Office Fax: 202-637-5901. Business E-Mail: amvickery@hhlaw.com.

**VICKERY, BYRDEAN EYVONNE HUGHES (MRS. CHARLES EVERETT VICKERY JR.),** retired library services administrator; b. Apr. 18, 1928; d. Roy Franklin and Margaret Cordelia (Wood) Hughes; m. Charles Everett Vickery, Jr., Nov. 5, 1948; 1 child, Camille. Student, Flat River Jr. Coll., Mo., 1946-48; BS in Edn., S.E. Mo. State Coll., 1954; MLS, U. Wash., 1964; postgrad., Wash. State U., 1969-70. Tchr. Ironton (Mo.) Pub. Schs., 1948-56; elem. tchr. Pasco (Wash.) Sch. Dist. 1, 1956-61, jr. high sch. libr., 1961-68, coord. librs., 1968-69; asst. libr. Columbia Basin Cmty. Coll., Pasco, 1969-70; head libr., dir. Instructional Resources Ctr., Pasco, 1970-78, dir. libr. svcs., 1979-87, assoc. dean libr. svcs., 1987-90, ret., 1990; owner Vickery Search & Research, Pasco, 1990-99. Chmn. S.E. Wash. Libr. Svc. Area, 1977-78, 88-90; bd. dirs. Pasco-Kennewick Cmty. Concerts, 1977-88, pres., 1980-81, 87-88, Pasco-Kennewick Cmty. Concerts, treas., 1991-99; bd. dirs. Mid-Columbia Symphony Orch., 1983-89; trustee Wash. Commn. Humanities, 1982-85; bd. mem. Arts Coun. Mid-Columbia Region, 1991-93. Author, editor: Library and Research Skills Curriculum Guides for the Pasco School District, 1967; author (with Jean Thompson), also editor Learning Resources Handbook for Teachers, 1969. Recipient Woman of Achievement award Pasco Bus. and Proffl. Women's Club, 1976. Mem. ALA, AAUW (2d v.p. 1966-68, corr. sec. 1969), Wash. Dept. Audio-Visual Instrn., Wash. Libr. Assn., Am. Assn. Higher Edn., Wash. Assn. Higher Edn., Wash. State Assn. Sch. Libr. (state conf. chmn. 1971-72), Tri-Cities Librs. Assn., Wash. Libr. Media Assn. (cmty. coll. levels chmn. 1986-87), Am. Assn. Sch. Libr. Soroptimist Internat. Assn. (rec. sec. Pasco-Kennewick chpt. 1971-72, treas. 1973-74, pres. 1978-80, v.p. 1989-90, treas. 1991, found. & awards chmn. 1995-96), Columbia Basin Coll. Adminstrs. Assn. (sec.-treas. 1973-74), Pacific N.W. Assn. Ch. Libr., Women in Comms., Pasco Bus. and Proffl. Women's Club, PEO-HJ (corr. sec. 2002-04), Farmington Presbyn. Manor (adv. bd. 2003-05), Gen. Fedn. Women's Clubs of Mo., Beta Sigma Phi, Delta Kappa Gamma, Phi Delta Kappa (sec. 1981-82, Outstanding Educator award 1983). Home: 5509 W 11th Ave Kennewick WA 99338-2138

**VICKERY, EDWARD DOWNTAIN,** lawyer; b. Ft. Worth, May 1, 1922; s. Charles Richard and Margaret May Vickery; children: Anne Vickery Stevenson, E.D. Jr. AS, North Tex. Agrl. Coll., 1941; BA, U. Tex., 1947, JD with honors, 1948. Bar: Tex. 1948, U.S. Dist. Ct. (so. dist.) Tex. 1948, U.S. Ct. Appeals (5th cir.) 1950, Bd. Immigration Appeals 1952, U.S. Supreme Ct. 1953. From assoc. to sr. ptnr. Royston, Rayzor, Vickery & Williams, Houston, 1948-55, sr. ptnr., 1955-98, of counsel, 1999—. Chmn. bd. dirs. Tradition Bankshares, Inc., Houston. Deacon First Presbyn. Ch., Houston, 1958-64, elder 1965-94; active Brazos Presbyn. Ch., 1972-77, chmn. 1976-77; bd. trustees Austin (Tex.) Presbyn. Theol. Sem., 1976-85, 86-95, vice-chmn. 1978-83, chmn. 1983-85, 89-95; bd. trustees Tex. Presbyn. Found. 1978-85 Fellow Am. Coll. Trial Lawyers, Internat. Acad. Trial Lawyers (Am. chpt.); mem. Internat. Assn. Ins. Counsel, Am. Judicature Soc., Maritime Law Assn. U.S. (exec. com. 1977-80), Nat. Soc. Supreme Ct. U.S., Tex. Assn. Def. Counsel (bd. dirs. 1965-67), Tex. Bar Found. (Houston chpt.), Tulane Admiralty Law Inst. (program, planning com., adv. bd., 1965-92), Propellor Club U.S. (nat. pres. 1965-66, 66-67, nat. first v.p. 1964-65, nat. exec. com. 1961-85, port of Houston pres. 1961-62), U. Tex. Littlefield Soc., Chancellor's Coun., T Assn., Longhorn Found., Law Sch. Found., Houston Club, Lakeside Country Club. Home: 22507 Blue Canyon Dr Katy TX 77450 Office: Royston Rayzor Vickery & Williams LLP 1001 McKinney Ste 1100 Houston TX 77002-6418 Office Phone: 713-224-8380. E-mail: ed.vickery@roystonlaw.com.

**VICKERY, RAYMOND EZEKIEL, JR.,** international business consultant, lawyer; b. Brookhaven, Miss., Apr. 30, 1942; s. Raymond Ezekiel and Clarene Helen (Dickens) V.; m. Raymond Clair Brown, Dec. 23, 1967 (div. June 1976); m. Ann Morgan, June 25, 1979; children: Raymond Morgan, Philip Dickens. AB, Duke U., 1964; postgrad., U. Sri Lanka, 1964-65; LLB, Harvard U., 1968. Assoc. Hogan & Hartson, Washington, 1968-77, prin. McLean, Va., 1985-93, Johnson & Vickery, Vienna, Va., 1977-81, Reed Smith Shaw & McClay, McLean, Va., 1981-85; asst. sec. for trade devel. U.S. Dept. Commerce, Washington, 1993-97; prin. Vickery Internat., 1977—; pvt. practice Washington, 1997—; of counsel Williams Aron & Assocs., Washington, 2002—. Adj. prof. internat. transactions George Mason U., Fairfax, Va., 1997-99. Contbr. articles to profl. jours. Del. Va. Gen. Assembly, Richmond, 1974-80; mem. Dem. Com., Farifax County, Va., 1971-93; Dem. nominee for Congress, Va., 1992; mem. State Ctrl. Com., Va., 1993; mem. Libr. Bd., Fairfax County, 1972-74. Fulbright scholar, 1964. Mem. ABA, Va. Bar Assn., D.C. Bar Assn., City Club, Phi Beta Kappa, Omicron Delta Kappa. Baptist. Avocations: fishing, horseback riding. Home: 2733 Willow Dr Vienna VA 22181-5310 Office: 1101 Pennsylvania Ave NW Washington DC 20004-2514

**VICKERY, ROBERT REMSEN,** painter; b. NYC, 1926; Student, Wesleyan Univ., Art Students League, NYC; BA, Yale Univ., 1947, MFA. Co-author (with Diane Cochrane): New Techniques in Egg Tempera, 1973; author: Robert Vickery, Artist at Work, 1979; 78 covers for Time Mag., Represented in permanent collections Met. Mus. Art, Whitney Mus., Smithsonian Instn., Corcoran Collection, NAD, Bklyn. Mus., Butler Inst. Am. Art, Chrysler Mus., Nat. Mus. Am. Art. Recipient more than 40 nat. prizes. Mem.: NAD (academician 1964—), Am. Watercolor Soc. (Dolphin fellow). Mailing: Harmon Meek Gallery Ste 309 599 Ninth St N Naples FL 34102

**VICKREY, ROBERT REMSEN,** artist; b. N.Y.C., Aug. 20, 1926; s. Claude Claire and Caroline (McKim) V.; m. Marjorie Elizabeth Alexander, Sept. 18, 1950; children: Remsen Scott, Elizabeth Nicole, Wendy Caroline, Alexander Sean. Studied with Victoria Huntley; BA, Yale U., 1947, B.F.A., 1950; student, Art Students League. Co-author: New Techniques in Egg Tempera, 1973; author: Robert Vickrey-Artist at Work, The Affable Curmudgeon, 1979; one-man shows, Midtown Galleries, N.Y.C., 1954-58, 62, 65, 69, 70, 72, Columbia (S.C.) Mus. Art, 1959, Davison Art Ctr., Wesleyan U., 1966, Va. Mus. Fine Arts, 1965, retrospective, U. Ariz. Mus. Art, 1973, San Diego Fine Arts Gallery, 1973; exhibited in nat. group shows; represented in permanent collections, Whitney Mus., Corcoran Gallery of Art, Washington, Lakeland (Fla.) Mus., Mus. Modern Art, Rio de Janeiro, Brazil, Sara Roby Found., Parrish Art Mus., Southampton, Isaac Delgado Mus., Dallas Mus., Munson-Williams-Proctor Inst., Utica, N.Y., Met. Mus. Art, NAD, Butler Inst. Am. Art, New Britain Mus. Am. Art, Gallery of Modern Art, Birmingham Mus., Spelman Coll., Newark Mus., many others; illustrator mag. covers, books. Recipient award Edward Austin Abbey mural competition, 1949, top prize Fla. Internat. Art Exhbn., 1952, 2d prize Internat. Hallmark competition, 1955, Am. Artist mag. citation, 1956, Winsor and Newton award Am. Water Color Soc., 1956, S.J. Wallace Truman prize Nat. Acad. ann., 1958, Salmagundi Club award Audubon Artists, 1971, spl. prize Internat. Biennial of Sport in Fine Arts, Mus. Contemporary Art, Madrid, 1973, Gold Medal NAD, numerous others. Mem. Audubon Artists, Am. Water Color Soc., Nat. Acad. Address: 8231 Bay Colony Dr Naples FL 34108*

**VICKSTROM, KRISTINA ROSE,** medical researcher; b. Worcester, Mass., Aug. 23, 1980; d. Steven Paul and Andrea Mary (Astrella) Vickstrom. BS in Biology: Pathogenic Microrganisms, Salve Regina U., Newport, R.I., 2002; JD, Western New Eng. Coll., Springfield, Mass., 2005. Bar: Mass. 2005. Law clk. Durchanek Law Offices, P.C., Holyoke, Mass., 2004—05; extern MA Probate & Family Ct., Springfield, Mass., 2004; project mgr. Am. Vet. Med. Frontiers, Inc., West Boylston, Mass., 2004—. Sec. West Boylston Open Space Implementation Coalition, West Boylston, 2004—; cons. Herbal BioDynamics, LLC, Worcester, Mass., 2005—. Prodr.: (plays) The Foreigner (Salve Regina U. Theatre Dept. award, 2001); mem., pres. (improvisational and acting troupe) Stagefright Theatre Co. (Stagefight Theatre Co. award, 2002). Sec. West Boylston Open Space Implementation Com., 2004—06. Recipient acad. merit scholarship, Western New Eng. Coll. Sch. of Law, 2002—05, Nat. Italian ABA, 2004, Sisters of Mercy acad. merit scholarship, Salve Regina U., 1998—2002, Campus Leadership award, 2005. Mem.: ABA (assoc.), Nat. Italian ABA (assoc.), Boston Bar Assn. (assoc.), Mass. Bar Assn. (assoc.), Student Bar Assn. (life; pres. social club 2003—04), Sigma Phi Sigma (life). Avocations: acting, travel, Broadway shows, shelter animal welfare. Home: 2 Montgomery Ave Worcester MA 01604

**VICTOR, A. PAUL,** lawyer; b. NYC, Nov. 6, 1938; s. Samuel L. and Sophie (Ostrow) V.; m. Ellen Grabois, Aug. 30, 1959; children: Stephanie, Rebecca, Diana. BBA, U. Mich., 1960, JD with distinction, 1963. Bar: N.Y. 1964, D.C. 1964. Atty. antitrust div. U.S. Dept. Justice, Washington, 1963-66; assoc. Kirkland, Ellis & Rowe, Washington, 1966-68, Weil, Gotshal & Manges, N.Y.C., 1968-72, prin., 1972—. Adj. prof. law Fordham U. Sch. of Law, N.Y.C., 1983—; mem. adv. bd. Ctr. for Am. and Internat. Law, Dallas, 1984—; bd. dirs. Toray Industries (Am.) Inc., N.Y.C., 1987—, vis. lectr. U. Mich. Law Sch., Columbia U. Law Sch., NYU Sch. of Law; presenter in field. Contbr. numerous articles to law revs., other legal pubs. regarding U.S. internat. antitrust and trade law. Mem. visitors com. U. Mich. Law Sch., 1980—2006, mem. dean's adv. com., 2006—; trustee Mass. Sch. of Law, Andover, 1989—, chmn., 1998—; sec. Japan Soc., N.Y.C., 1999-2000; bd. dirs. N.Y. chpt. Juvenile Diabetes Rsch. Found., 1994-99, 2004—. Mem. ABA (vice-chair sect. antitrust law 1994-95, mem. coun. 1983-86, 91-94, chmn. internat. antitrust com. 1982-85, 87-90, mem. internat. task force, 2005-), Internat. Bar Assn., N.Y. State Bar Assn., Order of Coif Jewish. Avocations: golf, travel, swimming. Office: Weil Gotshal & Manges LLP 767 5th Ave Fl Conc1 New York NY 10153-0119 Office Phone: 212-310-8110. Business E-mail: paul.victor@weil.com.

**VICTOR, ANN MICHELE,** musician, educator; d. Tony and Marllys Ruth Victor. MusB, Kent State U., 1977, MusM, 1979. Tchr. cert. Univ. Tex. at Austin, 1989. Instr. cello & double bass Lamar U., Beaumont, Tex., 1980—83; orch. dir. Bowie Jr. High Ector ISD, Odessa, Tex., 1990—92, Baytown Jr. Sch., Baytown, Tex., 1992—95, Alief (Tex.) ISD, 1995—97, Macario Garcia Mid. Sch., Sugar Land, Tex., 1997—2002, Sartartia Mid. Sch., Sugar Land, Tex., 2000—. Tchr., adminstrv. co-coord. U. Tex. String Project, Austin, 1985—87; prt. cello instr., 1990—; co-coord. strings orch. Houston Youth Symphony, 1999—. Fellow, AAUW, 1997. Mem.: Tex. Music Adjudicators Assn., Tex. Orch. Dirs. Assn., Tex. Classroom Tchrs. Assn., Tex. Music Educators Assn., Am. String Tchrs. Assn., Musician's Union Local 111. Baptist. Office: Sartartia Mid Sch Orch 8125 Homeward Way Sugar Land TX 77479 Personal E-mail: ann_victor@hotmail.com. E-mail: ann.victor@fortbend.k12.tx.us.

**VICTOR, MICHAEL GARY,** lawyer, physician; b. Detroit, Sept. 20, 1945; s. Simon H. and Helen (Litsky) V.; children: Elise Nicole, Sara Lisabeth. Bar: Ill. 1980, U.S. Dist. Ct. (no. dist.) Ill. 1980, U.S. Ct. Appeals (7th cir.) 1981; diplomate Am. Bd. Legal Medicine, Am. Bd. Emergency Medicine, 2003. Of counsel Bollinger, Ruberry & Garvey, Chgo., 1980—99; pres. Advocate Adv. Assocs., Chgo., 1982-95; asst. prof. medicine Northwestern U. Med. Sch., Chgo., 1982—; lectr. U. Ill., Chgo., 1999—. Dir. emergency medicine Loretto Hosp., Chgo., 1980-85, chief. sect. of emergency medicine St Josephs Hosp., Chgo., 1985-87; pvt. practice med. law Barrington, Ill, 1982-; v.p. Med. Emergency Svcs. Assocs., Buffalo Grove, Ill., 1989; v.p. MESA Mgmt. Corp.; exec. leadership coach Lee Hecht Harrison, Chgo. Author: Informed Consent, 1980; Brain Death, 1980; (with others) Due Process for Physicians, 1984, A Physicians Guide to the Illinios Living Will Act, The Choice is Ours!, 1989. Recipient Svc. awards Am. Coll. Emergency Medicine, 1973-83. Fellow Am. Coll. Legal Medicine (bd. govs. 1996-97, alt. del. to AMA House of Dels. 1996-97); Chgo. Acad. Legal Medicine; mem. Am. Coll. Emergency Physicians (pres. Ill. chpt. 1980, med.-legal-ins. coun. 1980-81, 83-84), ABA, Ill. State Bar Assn., Am. Soc. Law and Medicine, Chgo. Bar Assn. (med.-legal coun. 1981-83), AMA, Ill. State Med. Soc. (med.-legal coun. 1980-86, 88), Chgo. Med. Soc. Jewish. Home and Office: 153 Aberdour Ln Palatine IL 60067-8001 Office Phone: 847-934-8404. Personal E-mail: mgv@comcast.net.

**VICTOR, ROBERT EUGENE,** real estate company executive, lawyer; b. NYC, Dec. 17, 1929; s. Louis and Rebecca (Teitelbaum) V.; m. Dorothy Saffir, Oct. 14, 1951; children: Priscilla Saffir Victor Faubel, Pandora Saffir. LL.B., St. John's U., 1953, JD, 1968. Bar: N.Y. bar 1953, Calif. bar 1965. With firm Szold and Brandwen, N.Y.C., 1953-54; atty. Dept. Army, Phila. 1955-56; with Hughes Aircraft Co., Culver City, Calif., 1956-62; v.p., gen. counsel Packard Bell Electronics Corp., Los Angeles, 1962-70; sr. v.p., gen. counsel Cordon Internat. Corp., Los Angeles, 1970-78; also dir.; gen. counsel Am. Harp Soc., 1969-85; pres., bd. dirs. Vanowen Realty Corp., 1978-93; chmn., pres., bd. dirs. Dobere Realty, Inc., 2000—. Mem. Los Angeles County Bar Assn., Masons. Office: 722 Walden Dr Beverly Hills CA 90210-3125

**VICTOROFF, JEFF,** neurology professor, psychology professor; b. Cleveland Heights, Ohio, May 9, 1952; s. Victor and Virginia Victoroff; m. Alla Kalyenich Victoroff, June 19, 1999. BA, St. John's Coll., Annapolis, Md.,

1974; MA, U. Chgo., Ill., 1978; MD, Case Western Res. U., Cleve., Ohio, 1982. Diplomate Am. Bd. Psychiatry and Neurology. Instr. dept. neurology UCLA, 1988—90; asst. prof. neurology U. So. Calif., 1990—96, assoc. prof. clin. neurology, 1996—99, assoc. prof. clin. neurology and psychiatry, 1999—. Dir. NATO Advanced Rsch. Workshop, Psychology of Terrorism. Author: (novel) The Wild Type, 1989, (book) Saving Your Brain, 2002. Fellow: Am. Acad. Neurology; mem.: Internat. Soc. for Polit. Psychology, Am. Neuropsychiatric Assn. Office: Univ So Calif Dept Neurology Nat Rehab Ctr 7601 E Imperial Downey CA 90242 Office Phone: 310-316-0761.

**VICTORY, JEFFREY PAUL,** state supreme court justice; b. Shreveport, La., Jan. 29, 1946; s. Thomas Edward and Esther (Horton) V.; m. Nancy Clark Victory, Jan. 20, 1973; children: Paul Bradford, William Peter, Christopher Thomas, Mary Katherine. BA in History and Govt., Centenary Coll., 1967; JD, Tulane U., 1971. Bar: La. 1971. Ptnr. Tucker, Jeter, Jackson & Victory, Shreveport, 1971-82; dist. ct. judge 1st Jud. Dist. Ct., Shreveport, 1982-90; appellate judge 2d Circuit Ct. of Appeal, Shreveport, 1991-95; assoc. justice Supreme Ct. La., 1995—. Bd. dirs. La. Judicial Coll. Bd. dirs. CODAC Drug Abuse, Shreveport; mem. La. Sentencing Commn. La. NG, 1969-75. Mem. ABA, Shreveport Bar Assn., La. Bar Assn. Republican. Baptist. Avocations: tennis, motorcycles, classic cars. Office: Supreme Ct 400 Royal St New Orleans LA 70130*

**VICTORY, NANCY J.,** lawyer, former federal agency administrator; b. NYC, July 19, 1962; BA, Princeton U., 1984; JD, Georgetown U., 1988. Ptnr. Wiley, Rein & Fielding, Washington; asst. sec. for comm. & info. US Dept. Commerce, Washington, 2001—03, adminstr. Nat. Telecom. & Info. Adminstrn., 2001—03. Chair FCC Advisory Com. for the 2007 World Radiocommunication Conf., 2003—. Office: Wiley Rein Fielding LLP 1776 K St NW Washington DC 20006 E-mail: nvictory@wrf.com.

**VIDAILLET, HUMBERTO J., JR.,** physician, administrator, researcher; b. Santiago, Cuba, Sept. 24, 1954; arrived in U.S., 1968; s. Humberto J. and Caridad Vidaillet; m. Debbie Vidaillet, June 6, 1981; children: Kelsey, Daniel, Corbin. MD, U. Okla., 1981. Resident in internal medicine Mayo Clinic, Rochester, Minn., 1981-84; tng. in cardiology/electrophysiology Duke U. Med. Ctr., Durham, NC, 1984-87; dir. cardiac electrophysiology Marshfield (Wis.) Clinic, 1987—; assoc. clin. prof. medicine U. Wis. Sch. Medicine, Madison, 1994-2000, clin. prof. medicine, 2000—; dir. rsch. Marshfield Clinic Rsch. Found., 2005—. Prof. medicine U. Chile Sch. Medicine, 1994; cons. prof. medicine Inst. Med. Sci., Sch. Medicine, Medellin, Colombia, 1999; med. dir. arrhythmia svcs. St. Joseph Hosp., Marshfield, 1992—; med. dir. rsch. Marshfield Clinic; mem. hosps. and clinics bd. and authority U. Wis., 2005—; cons. in field. Contbr. articles to profl. jours. Parish coun. Our Lady of Peace Cath. Ch., Marshfield, 1996-2001; bd. dir. U. Wis. Found.; exec. com. Marshfield; vice chmn. bd. trustees Marshfield Clinic Rsch. Found., 1990-93, 2000-03, elected clin. physician rep. to bd. trustees, 2001, vice-chair, 2003—05; coord., local prin. investigator clin. trials med. rsch. dir., Marshfield Clin. Rsch. Found., 2005-, dir. med. rsch., Marshfield Clin. Rsch. Found. Am. Heart Assn. sr. investigator award, 1997, 15th Annual Gwen D. Sebold Rsch. Fellow ACP (chair internat. com. 1989-92, winner clin. paper competition 1984, 86, 87, faculty ann. sci. sessions), Am. Coll. Cardiology (mem. edn. com., faculty sci. ann. sessions sr. investigator award 2000), Am. Coll. Chest Physicians, Heart Rhythm Soc. (faculty ann. sci. sessions), mem. N.Am. Soc. Electrophysiology and Pacing (faculty ann. sci. sessions), Internat. Soc. of Internal Medicine (sci. program commn.), Inter Am. Congress Cardiology (sci. program com. 2003), Intern Am. Coll. Cardiology (US rep. to sci. com., faculty ann. sci. sessions), Human Rights Worker Internat. Office: Marshfield Clinic 1000 N Oak Ave Marshfield WI 54449-5702 Business E-mail: vidaillet.humberto@mcrf.mfldclin.edu.

**VIDAL, DAVID JONATHAN,** insurance company executive, journalist; b. Bayamón, P.R., Oct. 11, 1946; s. Jesus Maria and Ercira Audacia (Mejia) V.; m. Watuza Leal, Jan. 25, 1975; 1 child, Katalyn. AB cum laude, Princeton U., 1968; student, Sch. Advanced Internat. Studies, Washington, 1982-83; MBA, Columbia U., 1991. Reporter The Caracas (Venezuela) Daily Jour., 1969-70; reporter, news editor AP, Caracas, N.Y., Sao Paulo, 1970-73, corr. Brasilia, Brazil, 1973-75; reporter, bur. chief N.Y. Times, N.Y.C. and Rio de Janeiro, 1975-80; spl. asst., White House fellow Dept. State, Washington, 1980-81; cons. U.S. AID, Washington, 1981-82; dept. mgr. task force Pres.'s Pvt. Sector Survey on Cost Control, Washington, 1982-83; exec. dir. Nat. Commn. Secondary Schooling for Hispanics, Washington, 1983-84; dir. pub. affairs N.Y.C. Partnership, 1984-85; asst. v.p. Continental Ins., N.Y.C., 1985-95; v.p. Coun. on Fgn. Rels., N.Y.C., 1995-97; dir. rsch. global corp. citizenship The Conf. Bd., N.Y.C., 1997—; pub. Across the Board, 2001—. Adj. prof. journalism Columbia U. Grad. Sch. Journalism, N.Y.C., 1985-86; bd. dirs. Pub. Affairs Coun., Washington, 1988-95; trustee Found. for Pub. Affairs, Washington, 1989-95; mem. Contbns. Adv. Group, 1988-95, chmn., 1994-95; mem. corp. adv. group Schomburg Ctr. for Rsch. in Black Culture, 1988-95; Ad Hoc Com. on Charter Revision, 1988, Nat. Hispanic Agenda, 1988; mem. adv. group Latino Leadership Fund, 1991-95; vice-chmn. Nat. Civic League, 1999—. Author: (newspaper series) NY Times, 1980; pub. Across the Board, 2001—; contbr. articles and reports in field. Trustee N.Y. Theol. Sem., N.Y.C., 1990—; mem. Coun. Fgn. Rels.; prin. Coun. for Excellence in Govt., Washington, 1992—; dir. Coun. on Internat. Ednl. Exch., N.Y.C., 1997—2003; elder, trustee West End Presbyn. Ch., N.Y.C., 1986—. Recipient Hispanic Achievement award Wall Street chpt. IMAGE, N.Y.C., 1989; Fulbright scholar, Washington and Venezuela, 1968. Fellow Royal Soc. for Encouragement of Arts, Manufacturers and Commerce; mem. N.Y. Regional Assn. Grantmakers (dir., sec. 1988-95), Nat. Inst. Industry Assn. (corp. adv. group 1990-95), Nat. Civic League, Coun. on Fgn. Rels. Democrat. Office: The Conf Bd 845 3rd Ave New York NY 10022-6601 E-mail: david.vidal@conference-board.org.

**VIDAL, GORE,** writer; b. West Point, N.Y., Oct. 3, 1925; s. Eugene L. and Nina (Gore) V. Grad., Phillips Exeter Acad., 1943; DLitt (hon.), Brown U., 1988. Author, 1946—. Author: (novels) Williwaw, 1946, In a Yellow Wood, 1947, The City and the Pillar, 1948, The Season of Comfort, 1949, A Search for the King, 1950, Dark Green, Bright Red, 1950, The Judgment of Paris, 1952, Messiah, 1954, Julian, 1964, Washington, D.C, 1967, Myra Breckinridge, 1968, Two Sisters, 1970, Burr, 1973, Myron, 1974, 1876, 1976, Kalki, 1978, Creation, 1981 (Prix Deauville 1983), Duluth, 1983, Lincoln, 1984, Empire, 1987, Hollywood, 1990, Live From Golgotha, 1992, The Smithsonian Institution, 1998, The Golden Age, 2000, Perpetual War for Perpetual Peace, 2002, Dreaming War: Blood for Oil and the Cheney-Bush Junta, 2002 (under name Edgar Box), Imperial America, 2004, Death in the Fifth Position, 1952, Death Before Bedtime, 1953, Death Likes It Hot, 1954, The Essential Vidal, 1998; (short stories) A Thirsty Evil, 1956; (plays) Visit to a Small Planet, 1957, The Best Man, 1960, (Broadway revived 2000) Romulus, 1962, Weekend, 1968, An Evening with Richard Nixon, 1972, (essays) Rocking the Boat, 1962, Sex, Death, and Money, 1968, Reflections upon a Sinking Ship, 1969, Homage to Daniel Shays, 1973, Matters of Fact and of Fiction, 1977, The Second American Revolution, 1982 (Nat. Book Critics Circle award for criticism 1982), Armageddon?, 1987 (London), United States: Essays 1952-1992, 1993 (Nat. Book award for nonfiction 1993), The Last Empire, 2001; (films) The Catered Affair, 1956, I Accuse, 1958, The Left-Handed Gun, 1958, The Scapegoat, 1959, Suddenly Last Summer, 1959, The Best Man, 1964 (Cannes Critics prize 1964), Is Paris Burning?, 1966, The Last of the Mobile Hotshots, 1970; (teleplays) Barn Burning, 1954, Dark Possession, 1954, Smoke, 1954, Visit to a Small Planet, 1955, Dr. Jekyll and Mr. Hyde, 1955, A Sense of Justice, 1955, Summer Pavilion, 1955, The Turn of the Screw, 1955, Stage Door, 1955, A Farewell to Arms, 1955, The Death of Billy the Kid, 1955, Honor, 1956, The Indestructible Mr. Gore, 1959, Dress Gray, 1986, Billy the Kid, 1989; actor: Fellini Roma, 1978, Bob Roberts, 1992 With Honors, 1994, others, (memoirs) Screening History, 1992, Palimpsest, 1995. Mem. Pres.'s Adv. Com. on Arts, 1961-63; Dem.-Liberal candidate for U.S. Congress, 1960, candidate for Dem. nomination from Calif., 1982;

co-chmn. The New Party, 1970-71. Served with AUS, 1943-46. Named hon. citizen Ravello, Italy, 1983, Chevalier de l'Ordre des Arts et des Lettres, France, 1995. Office: Thunder Mouth Press 245 W 17th St 11th Fl New York NY 10011-5300

**VIDAL, MAUREEN ERIS,** theater educator, actress; b. Bklyn., Mar. 18, 1956; d. Louis and Lillian (Kaplan) Hendelman; m. Juan Vidal, June 25, 1974 (div. Sept. 1981); m. Guillermo Eduardo Uriarte, Dec. 22, 1986. BA, Bklyn. Coll., 1976, MS, 1981. From English tchr. to drama tchr. N.Y.C. Bd. Edn., 1976—, chair women's history dept., 1984—, dean, 1997—, drama tchr., 2002—. Mem PETA Humane Soc. Mem.: AFTRA, Gorilla Soc., Nat. Anti-Vivisection Soc. (mem. physicians' com. responsible medicine), Heights Players Theater Co. (arranger theatrical performance for residents of homeless shelters 1986—2003, exec. bd., sec. 1993—, actress), Doris Day Animal League, Delta Psi Omega. Avocations: travel, white-water rafting, scuba diving, skydiving, theater. Office: I S 318 101 Walton St Brooklyn NY 11206-4311 also: Heights Players 26 Willow Pl Brooklyn NY 11201-4513 Office Phone: 718-782-0589. E-mail: MVidal4942@aol.com

**VIDALE, JOHN EMILIO,** geologist; b. Phila., Mar. 15, 1959; s. Guido Levi and Rosemary (Jacobson) V.; 1 child, Laura. BS, Yale U., 1981; PhD, Calif. Inst. Tech., 1986. Scientist U. Calif., Santa Cruz, 1987-90, U.S Geol. Survey, Menlo Park, Calif., 1991-95; assoc. prof. UCLA, 1995-99, prof., 1999—, acting dir. Inst. Geophysics and Planetary Physics, 2002—03; interim dir., 2003—04. Editor Bulletin Seismology Soc. Am., 1988-93; contbr. articles to profl. jours. Gilbert fellow U.S. Geol. survey, 1994-95; co-recipient James B. Macelwane Young Investigator medal Am. Geophys. Union, 1994 Fellow Am. Geophys. Union (Macelwane medal 1994). Home: 10421 Colina Way Los Angeles CA 90077-2041 Office: UCLA Dept Earth & Space Sci PO Box 951567 Los Angeles CA 90095-1567 Business E-Mail: vidale@ucla.edu.

**VIDAVER, ANNE MARIE,** plant pathology educator; b. Vienna, Mar. 29, 1938; came to U.S., 1941; d. Franz and Klara (Winter) Kopecky; children: Gordon W.F., Regina M. BA, Russell Sage Coll., 1960; MA, Ind. U., 1962, PhD, 1965. Lectr. U. Nebr., Lincoln, 1965-66, asst. rsch., 1966-72, asst. prof., 1972-74, assoc. prof., 1974-79, prof. plant pathology, 1979—, interim dir. Ctr. Biotech., 1988-89, 97-00, head dept. plant pathology, 1984-2000, 2003—; chief scientist USDA's NRICGP, 2000—02. Contbr. articles to profl. jours. and books; patentee in field. Recipient Pub. Svc. award Nebr. Agri-Bus., 1977, Sci. award for excellence NAMA, New Orleans, 1991. Fellow AAAS, Am. Phytopath. Soc., Am. Soc. Microbiology; mem. Intersoc. Consortium for Plant Protection, Internat. Soc. Plant Pathology, Alliance for Prudent Use of Antibiotics. Avocations: indoor gardening, reading. Office: U Nebr Dept Plant Pathology Lincoln NE 68583-0722 Office Phone: 402-472-2858. E-mail: avidaver1@unl.edu.

**VIDAVER, ROBERT MAXWELL,** medical educator; b. Mpls., June 17, 1932; s. Robert William and Helen Mary (Ford) Vidaver; m. Virginia Moore Sewell, May 27, 1960. AB, Columbia U., 1953; MD, SUNY, 1956; MA (hon.), Dartmouth Coll., 1993. Diplomate Am. Bd. Psychiatry and Neurology, 1963. Intern in medicine U. Md., Balt., 1956—57; resident in psychiatry Yale U. Sch. Medicine, New Haven, 1957—60; asst. prof., coord. undergrad. edn. U. Md., Balt., 1962—65; state dir. psychiat. edn. Md. Dept. Health & Mental Hygiene, Balt., 1965—71; instr., asst. prof. Johns Hopkins Sch. Medicine, Balt., 1965—72; pres. First Md. Health Care Corp., Balt., 1971—72; assoc. prof. medicine and psychiatry N.J. Med. Sch., Newark, 1973—81, assoc. dean for hosp. affairs, 1979; med. dir. Martland Hosp., N.J. Med. Sch., Newark, 1974—78; prof., chmn. dept. psychiatry and behavioral sci. Ea. Va. Med. Sch., Norfolk, 1981—88; med. dir. N.H. Hosp., Concord, 1988—; prof., vice chmn. dept. psychiatry Dartmouth Med. Sch., Hanover, NH, 1988—. Bd. dirs. NH Hosp., Concord, 1988—2004. Author: Developments in Human Services' Education and Manpower, 1973; contbr. articles to profl. jours. Capt. U.S. Army, 1960—62. NY State Regents scholar, NY State Dept. Edn., Columbia U., 1949—53, NY State Profl. scholar, SUNY Coll. Medicine, 1952—56. Fellow: Am. Psychiat. Assn. (life; Disting.); mem.: U.S. Army Assn. (councillor), Alpha Omega Alpha. Episcopalian. Office: NH Hosp 36 Clinton St Concord NH 03301-2359 Office Phone: 603-271-5202. Business E-Mail: rvidaver@dhhs.state.nh.us.

**VIDELL, JARED STEVEN,** cardiologist; b. Phila., Apr. 9, 1947; s. Harry and Rose (Malken) V.; m. Cyla Trocki, Dec. 27, 1969; children: Haviv Elana, Mikhael Alon, Samara Pilar. BEd, U. Miami, 1969; DO, Phila. Coll. Osteo. Medicine, 1976. Resident and chief resident in internal medicine Atlantic City (N.J.) Med. Ctr., 1976-79; fellow in cardiovascular diseases Albert Einstein Med. Ctr., Phila., 1979-81; rsch. fellow in nuclear cardiology Deborah Heart and Lung Ctr., Browns Mills, NJ, 1981-82, dir. employee health svcs. 1982-84; asst. dir. cardiology Pritikin Longevity Ctr., Downington, Pa., 1984-87; cardiologist, dir. clin. lab. Physician Care, P.C., Towanda, Pa., 1987-90; from co-chmn. intensive care to dir. cardiac stress lab. Meml. Hosp., Towanda, 1987-90; dir. house staff, intensive/cardiac care Lower Bucks Hosp., Bristol, Pa., 1992-94; dir. house staff ICU-CCU North Phila. Health Systems, 1994-97; med. dir. North Phila. Health Sys. Girard Med. Ctr., 1997—, chmn. clin. medicine, 1997—. Med. dir. Am. Cancer Soc. chpt., 1989-90; state peer rev. KEPRO, 1989-90. Contbr. rsch. articles to profl. jours. Maj. M.C. USAR, Maj. USMC. Fellow: Am. Soc. Angiology; mem.: AMA, Nat. Assn. Managed Care Physicians, Alumni Assn. Phila. Coll. Osteo. Medicine, Phila. County Med. Soc., Pa. Med. Soc., Am. Soc. Law, Medicine and Ethics, Internat. Platform Assn., Am. Coll. Physician Execs., Internat. Soc. Endovascular Surgery, Internat. Soc. Internal Medicine, Am. Soc. Internal Medicine, Am. Coll. Chest Physicians. Avocations: squash, bicycling, cross country skiing, travel, fishing. Office: 408 N Exeter Ave Margate City NJ 08402-1868 Office Phone: 609-823-1989. Office Fax: 609-823-1989.

**VIDWANS, SMRUTI JAYANT,** microbiologist; b. India; BS in biology, MIT; PhD in microbiology, U. Calif., San Francisco, 2001. Amgen rsch. fellow Irvington Inst. Immunological Rsch., 2003; postdoctoral fellow in microbiology and immunology U. Calif., San Francisco, 2004; co-founder Phenotypica. Contbr. articles to profl. jour. Named one of Top 100 Young Innovators, MIT Tech. Review, 2004. Office: U Calif Ctr Bioentrepeneurship 185 Berry St Ste 4603 San Francisco CA 94143-1016

**VIE, RICHARD CARL,** insurance company executive; Student, St. Louis U., U. Mo. With Reliable Life Ins. Co., St. Louis, 1962-79; pres. Commonwealth Life Ins. Co., St. Louis, 1979-82; pres., chmn. bd. dirs. United Ins. Co. Am., Chgo., 1983—90; sr. v.p. bd. dirs. Unitrin, Inc., Chgo., 1990-92, pres., CEO 1992—99, chmn., pres., CEO 1999—2006, chmn., 2006—. Chmn. Life Insurers Conf., 1994; trustee Life Underwriters Tng. Coun. Bd. dirs. Concordia U. Found., 1985-94, Valparaiso U., 1995—. Lt. USN, 1958-62. Mem. The Racquet Club St. Louis, Execs. Club Chgo. Office: Unitrin Inc 1 E Wacker Dr Chicago IL 60601-1802

**VIEHE, KARL WILLIAM,** mathematics professor, lawyer, brokerage house executive; b. Allentown, Pa., Aug. 12, 1943; s. John Sage and Margaret (Higgs) V. BA in Govt. and Econs., Am. U., 1965, MA in Econs., 1968; JD, Howard U., 1981; MLT in Taxation, Georgetown U., 1982. Bar: D.C. 1983, U.S. Tax Ct. 1984, U.S. Ct. Internat. Trade 1988, U.S. Ct. Appeals (4th cir.) 1988, U.S. Ct. Appeals (D.C. cir.) 1985, U.S. Supreme Ct. 1988. Instr. math. and Russian lang. St. Albans Sch., Washington, 1968-69; pres., CEO Investment-Futures Group, Washington, 1968-84; prof. math. and stats. U. D.C., 1971—. Gen. counsel Promstroy Bank Russia, 1996-97; adj. prof. internat. law and fin. Am. U., 1972—; adj. prof. internat. law and bus. George Washington U., 1986—; internat. advt. dir. Washingtonian Mag., 1972-75; mgmt. program chmn. Fla. Inst. Tech., 1983-85; adj. faculty Internat. Law Inst., Washington, 1986—, Internat. Devel. Law Inst., Rome, 1987—; v.p., gen. counsel James A. Tilley Co., Investment Bankers, Washington, Moscow, 1994-95; chmn., CEO Horizons-Northstar Capital Mgmt. Co., Washington, 1995-97; gen. counsel U.S. Congrl. Philharmonic Orch., 1998-99; co-chmn. U.S. IRS Ann. Conf. on Current Issues in Internat. Taxation, 1986-88, Dept. Commerce Ann. Conf. on Current Issues in Internat. Trade, 1994-97; internat.

adv. bd. McGeorge Sch. Law, 1987—; presenter in field. Contbr. articles to profl. jours. Vice-chmn. bd. dirs., gen. counsel U.S. Congrl. Philharmonic Soc. Mem. ABA, Am. Econ. Assns., Am. Fin. Assn., Am. Arbitration Assn. (comml. panel, internat. panel), Washington Fgn. Law Soc. (bd. dirs.), D.C. Bar Assn., U.S. Congl. Philharmonic Soc. (vice-chmn. bd. govs.). Avocations: piano, photography, triathlons, marathons, tennis. Home: 2401 H St NW Apt 707 Washington DC 20037-2581 Office: Horizons & Northstar Capital Mgmt Co 1700 Pennsylvania Ave NW Washington DC 20006-4704

**VIEHE, RICHARD B.,** podiatrist; m. Margaret Viehe; children: Anne, Thomas, Andrew. BS, Cornell U.; MD in Podiatric Medicine, Calif. Coll. Podiatric Medicine, 1971. Resident in podiatry Lincoln Cmty. Hosp., Calif.; staff physician Children's Hosp. of Orange County; Coastal Cmtys. Hosp., Santa Ana; Coll. Hosp., Costa Mesa; Fountain Valley Cmty. Hosp.; Hoag Meml. Presbyn. Hosp., Newport Beach; St. Joseph Hosp., Orange County, & Western Med. Ctr., Santa Ana; pvt. practice Newport Ctr. Podiatry Group, Newport Beach, Calif.; dir. surgical residency Western Medical Center, Santa Ana. Bd. trustee Calif. Coll. of Podiatric Medicine, 1987—; diplomat Am. Bd. of Podiatric Surgery & Am. Bd. of Podiatric Examiners. Fellow: Am. Coll. of Foot & Ankle Surgeons; mem.: Nat. Acad. of Practice, Am. Podiatric Med. Assn. (past pres. 2002—03), Orange County Podiatric Med. Assn. (past pres.), Calif. Podiatric Med. Assn. (past pres.), Alpha Gamma Kappa, Pi Delta. Office: Newport Ctr Podiatry Group 1303 Avocado Ave Ste 195 Newport Beach CA 92660

**VIEIRA, MEREDITH,** television personality; b. Providence, Dec. 30, 1953; m. Richard Cohen June 14, 1986; children: Benjamin, Gabriel, Lily Max. BA in English (magna cum laude), Tufts U., 1975. News announcer WORC-Radio, Worcester, Mass., 1975; reporter, anchor WJAR-TV, Providence; reporter WCBS-TV, NYC, 1979-82; from reporter, Chgo. bur. to news correspondent CBS News, NYC, 1982—84; Chgo. bur. chief, contbg. nat. corr. CBS Evening News with Dan Rather, NYC, 1982—84; substitute co-anchor Morning, 1984—85; prin. corr. West 57th, 1985—89; corr., co-editor 60 Minutes, 1989—91; contbg. corr., CBS Primetime series Verdict, 1991; co-anchor CBS Morning News, 1992—93; host, chief corr. Turning Point, 1993—97; chief correspondent ABC News, NYC, 1993; co-host, moderator The View, NYC, 1997—2006; co-host Today Show, NYC, 2006—. Narrator ABC TV special Open Sesame: The Making of Arabian Nights, 2000; host 78th Ann. Miss America Pageant, 1998, Lifetime's Intimate Portrait, 1999—, ABC special The Beatles Revolution, 2000, ABC TV Network's Countdown to Oscar, 2000, Who Wants to Be a Millionaire, 2002—, co-exec. prodr., 2005—; host ABC News Spl. Fat Like Me: How to Win the Weight War, 2003. Broadway debut Thoroughly Modern Millie, 2003, cameo appearance The Stepford Wives, 2004, guest host Larry King Live, 2005, host (spl. featurette) Desperate Housewives Season 1 DVD Set, 2005, guest appearances Sports Night, 1998, Walt Disney World Christmas Day Parade, 2002, Party Planner with David Tutera, 2005, Hi-Jinks, 2005, Celebrity Jeopardy, Between the Lions (PBS), (TV series) Healthy Kids, 1998, Spin City, 2000, All My Children, 2001, General Hospital, 2003, The Practice, 2003, (talk shows) The Tonight Show with Jay Leno, Late Show with David Letterman, Late Night with Conan O' Brien, Charlie Rose and Live with Regis and Kelly, appeared in (nat. TV commercials) Bayer Aspirin, Got Milk?, featured on the cover of numerous magazines including TV Guide, Ladies Home Journal and others. Frequent contbr. several charitable foundations; co-founder, mem. sr. adv. bd. Club Mom's, 2004—. Recipient Front Page award Newswoman's Club of N.Y., 1991, Robert F. Kennedy journalism award, 1995, Woman of Yr. award, City of Hope, 2001, six Emmy awards for reporting; honored by Anti-Defamation League; Found. Am. Women Radio and T.V., 1997. Achievements include hosting more episodes as a game show host than any women in TV history. Office: ABC 320 W 66th St New York NY 10023-6304

**VIELOT, ALAIN J.,** elementary school educator; arrived in U.S., 1964; s. Kleber and Marie Claire Vielot. BA in Sociology, Howard U., 1977; MA in French Lit., Lausanne U., Switzerland, 1981, MA in Psychology, 1981; BA in Edn., Fla. Internat. U., 1993. Analyst Sociology and Psychology Think-Tank, Washington, 1982—87; tchr. Dade County Pub. Schs., Miami, Fla., 1988—; head songwriter Hilltop Records. Recipient Editor's Choice award, Nat. Libr. Poetry, 1996. Mem.: United Tchrs. Dade County, Am. Soc. Poets, Internat. Soc. Poets (Internat. Poet Merit award 1995). Roman Catholic. Avocations: football, basketball, soccer, dance, music. Home: 4841 SW 152 Ct Miami FL 33185 Office: North Miami Elem Sch 655 NE 145th St Miami FL 33163

**VIENER, JOHN D.,** lawyer; b. Richmond, Va., Oct. 18, 1939; s. Reuben and Thelma (Kurtz) V.; m. Karin Erika Bauer, Apr. 7, 1969; children: John D. Jr., Katherine Bauer Viener Riordan. BA, Yale U., 1961; JD, Harvard U., 1964. Bar: N.Y. State 1965, U.S. Supreme Ct. 1970, U.S. Dist. Ct. (so. dist.) N.Y. 1974, U.S. Tax Ct. 1975. Assoc. Satterlee, Warfield & Stephens, N.Y.C., 1964—69; sole practice N.Y.C., 1969—76; sr. ptnr. Christy & Viener, N.Y.C., 1976—98, Salans, Hertzfeld, Heilbronn, Christy & Viener, N.Y.C., 1999—2000; prin., dir. BFD Capital Beteiligungs GmbH, 2001—; mng. dir. EuCap Advisors LLC, 2004—. Founder, bd. dirs., gen. counsel Foxfire Fund, Inc., 1968—88; gen. counsel, bd. dirs. Landmark Communities, 1970—99, Am. Continental Properties Group, 1978—, NF&M Internat., Inc., 1976—2003, Singer Fund, Inc., 1979—, Immunotherapy, Inc., 1997—99, Tupper Broadcasting Group Cos., 1996—, Viener Found., 1991—; gen. counsel Nat. Cancer Found. Cancer Care, 1982—85, Troster, Singer & Co., 1970—77; bd. dirs. Gen. Financiere Immob. et Commer. S.A., 1985—89; spl. counsel fin. instns., investment banking and securities concerns; real estate and tax advisor. Bd. dirs. York Theatre Co., 1999-2001, The N.Y. Pops, 1999-2002. Mem.: Sailfish Point Golf Club, Internat. Polo Club, Palm Beach Polo Club, Washington Club, Manursing Island Club, Fairfield County Hounds, Meeker Brook Sporting Assn. Home: 1 Los Arcos Sailfish Point Stuart FL 34996 also: Old North Rd Washington CT 06793 also: 650 Park Ave New York NY 10021 Office: 620 Fifth Ave New York NY 10020-2402

**VIERCK, CHARLES JOHN, JR.,** neuroscience educator; b. Columbus, Ohio, July 6, 1936; s. Charles John and Esther (Amadon) V.; m. Cheryl Stogner; children: Kenneth Christopher, Karl Frederick. B.Sc., U. Fla., 1959, M.Sc., 1961, PhD, 1963. Postdoctoral fellow U. Pa., Phila., 1963-65; asst. prof. U. Fla., Gainesville, 1965-71, assoc. prof., 1971-77, prof., 1977—. Adj. prof. U. N.C., Chapel Hill, 1977—; dir. Ctr. Neurobiol. Scis. U. Fla., Gainesville Editor: (textbook) Basics of Neuroscience, 1974; contbr. articles to profl. jours., also chpts. to books; mem. editorial bd. Somatosensory Motor Research, Am. Pain Soc. Jour. Grantee NIH, NIMH, NSF, VA, 1966—. Mem. Soc. Neurosci., Internat. Assn. Study Pain Democrat. Avocations: jazz, golf. Office: U Fla PO Box 100244 Gainesville FL 32610-0244 Home: 6519 SW 37th Way Gainesville FL 32608-5146 E-mail: vierck@ufbi.ufl.edu.

**VIERI, CHRISTIAN,** professional soccer player; b. Bologna, Italy, July 12, 1973; s. Roberto and Nathalie V. Player Prato FC, Italy, 1989; Torino FC, Italy, 1990-93; Pisa FC, Italy, 1993; Ravenna FC, Italy, 1993—94; Venezia FC, Italy, 1994-95, Atalanta, Italy, 1995—96, 2006—, Juventus Torino, Italy, 1996—97, Atletico Madrid, Spain, 1997—98, Lazio Roma, Italy, 1998—99, Inter Milan, Italy, 1999—2005, AC Milan, Italy, 2005, Sampdoria, Italy, 2006. Mem. Italy Nat. team, 1998—, European Super Cup Champion, Juventus Torino, 1996, European Cup Winners Cup Champion, Lazio Roma, 1999. Named to FIFA 100, 2004. Mailing: Atalanta BC Corso Europa snc Ciserano 24040 Ciserano di Zingonia Italy*

**VIERMETZ, KURT F.,** banker; b. Augsburg, Bavaria, Germany, Apr. 27, 1939; came to U.S., 1985; s. Alfons and Claire (Bruck) V.; m. Felicitas Kempe, May, 1966; 1 child, Maximilian. Grad., Heilig Kreuz Coll., Germany, 1957. With Morgan Guaranty Trust Co. of N.Y., Frankfurt, Fed. Republic Germany, 1966-69; asst. v.p., Paris, 1971-82, sr. v.p. for Central Europe NYC, 1982-85; vice chmn. Morgan Guaranty Trust Co. of N.Y., 1990—; also bd. dirs. Morgan Guaranty Trust Co. of N.Y., N.Y.C.; vice chmn. J.P. Morgan & Co., Inc., 1990—2000; gen. mgr. Saudi Internat. Bank, London, 1975-77; chmn., supervisory bd. HypoVereinsbank, Munich; treas. J. P. Morgan & Co. Inc., NY; chmn. supervisory bd. Bayerishce Hypo und

Vereinsbank, AG, Munich, 1999—2003; dep. chmn., supervisory bd. Bayerishce Hypo und Vereinsbank AG, Munich, 2003—; chmn. supervisory bd. Deutsche Börse AG, Berlin, 2005—. Author books and articles on internat. fin. to profl. publs. Mem. Am. C. of C. in Germany Roman Catholic. Office: HypoVereinsbank Am Tucherpark 16 80538 Munich Germany

**VIEROW, KAREN,** mechanical nuclear engineer, researcher; d. William Frederick and Marion Christine (Christensen) V. BS in Nuclear Engring., Purdue U.; MS in Nuclear Engring., U. Calif., Berkeley; PhD in Engring., U. Tokyo, 1999. Engr. GE Nuclear Energy, San Jose, Calif., 1990-93; rschr., engr. Nuclear Power Engring. Corp., Tokyo, 1993-2000; asst. prof. Purdue U., West Lafayette, Ind., 2001—06; assoc. prof. Tex. Art U., Coll. Sta., 2006—. Vis. engr. Hitachi (Japan) Ltd., 1987-88. Recipient Tech. Program Contbn. award Toshiba Ltd., 1993. Mem. ASME (ICONE-2 tech. program dir. 1993), Japan Atomic Energy Soc., Am. Nuclear Soc., Thermal Hydraulic Divsn. Exec. Com., Japanese Soc. Multiphase Flow (Young Scientist Breakthrough award), Tau Beta Pi, Alpha Nu Sigma (pres.) Office: Tex A&M U Dept Nuclear Engring 129 Zachary 3133TAMU College Station TX 77843 Office Phone: 765-494-5746. Business E-Mail: vierow@ecn.purdue.edu, vierow@ne.tamu.edu.

**VIESSMAN, WARREN, JR.,** dean, civil engineering educator; b. Balt., Nov. 9, 1930; s. Warren and Helen Adair (Berlincke) V.; m. Gloria Marie Scheiner, May 11, 1953 (div. Apr. 1975); children: Wendy, Stephen, Suzanne, Michael, Thomas, Sandra; m. Elizabeth Gertrude Rothe, Aug. 8, 1980; children: Heather, Joshua B in Engring., Johns Hopkins U., 1952, MS in Engring., 1958, DEng, 1961. Registered profl. engr., Md. Engr. W. H. Primrose & Assocs., Towson, Md., 1955-57; project engr. Johns Hopkins U., Balt., 1957-61; from asst. to assoc. prof. N.Mex. State U., Las Cruces, 1961-66; prof. U. Maine, Orono, 1966-68, U. Nebr., Lincoln, 1968-75; sr. specialist Libr. Congress, Washington, 1975-83; prof., chmn. U. Fla., Gainesville, 1983-90, assoc. dean for rsch. and grad. study, 1990-91, assoc. dean for acad. programs, 1991—2003. Vis. scientist Am. Geophys. Union, 1970-71; Maurice Kremer lectr. U. Nebr., 1985, 2001; lectr. Harvard U. Water Policy Seminar, 1988; Wayne S. Nichols Meml. Fund lectr. Ohio State U., 1990; mem. steering com. on groundwater and energy U.S. Dept. Energy, 1979-80; mem. task group on fed. water rsch. U.S. Geol. Survey, 1985-87; mem. com. of water sci. and tech. bd. NAS, 1986-90; mem. water resources working group Nat. Coun. on Pub. Works Improvement, 1987; chmn., chief of engrs. Environ. Adv. Bd., Washington, 1991-93; chmn. solid and hazardous waste mgmt. adv. bd. State U. Sys. Fla. Co-author: Water Management: Technology and Institutions, 1984, Introduction to Hydrology, 2003, Water Supply and Pollution Control, 2005; contbr. over 167 articles to profl. jours. Mem. Water Mgmt. Com., Gainesville, 1983-88, Fla. Environ. Efficiency Study Commn., 1986-88. 1st lt. U.S. Army C.E., 1952-54, Korea. Recipient Comdr.'s award for pub. svc., U.S. Dept. Army, 1993. Diplomate Am. Acad. Water Resources Engrs. (hon. diplomate); fellow ASCE (hon. mem., Julian Hinds award 1989), Am. Water Resources Assn. (nat. pres. 1990, Icko Iben award 1983, Henry P. Caulfield Jr. medal 1996), Univs. Coun. on Water Resources (pres. 1987, Warren A. Hall medal 1994), Sigma Xi, Tau Beta Pi. Avocations: scuba diving, woodworking. Office: U Fla Coll Engring PO Box 116450 Gainesville FL 32611-6450 Office Phone: 352-392-2312. Business E-Mail: wvies@eng.ufl.edu.

**VIEST, IVAN MIROSLAV,** structural engineer, consultant; b. Bratislava, Slovakia, Oct. 10, 1922; came to U.S., 1947, naturalized, 1955; s. Ivan and Maria (Zacharova) V.; m. Barbara K. Stevenson, May 23, 1953. Ing., Slovak Tech. U., Bratislava, 1946; MS, Ga. Inst. Tech., 1948; PhD, U. Ill., 1951; doctorate (hon.), Tech. U. Kosice, 2002. Registered profl. engr., Pa. Research asst. U. Ill., Urbana, 1948-50, research assoc., 1950-51, research asst. prof., 1951-55, research assoc. prof., 1955-57; bridge research engr. Am. Assn. State Hwy. Ofcls., Nat. Acad. Scis., Ottawa, Ill., 1957-61; structural engr. Bethlehem Steel Corp., Pa., 1961-67, sr. structural cons., 1967-70, asst. mgr. sales engring. div., 1970-82; pvt. cons. structural engr. IMV Cons., 1983—. Cons. in field. Author: Composite Construction, 1958, History of Engineering Foundation, 1991, Composite Construction--Design for Buildings, 1997, Seventy-Five Years of the Lehigh Valley Section, 1997, An Immigrant's Story, 2006. Recipient Constr. award Engring. News Record, 1972, Special Achievement award, Am. Inst. Steel Constrn., 2004; named to Hall of Fame, Ga. Inst. of Tech., 1998. Fellow AAAS, Am. Concrete Inst. (Wason Rsch. medal 1956); mem. NAE, ASCE (hon., v.p. 1973-75, Rsch. prize 1958, Ernest E. Howard award 1991), Internat. Assn. Bridge and Structural Engring., Transp. Rsch. Bd. (emeritus 1999—), Czechoslovak Soc. Arts and Scis. (exec. v.p. 1992-93), Earthquake Engring. Rsch. Inst., Saucon Valley Country Club (Bethlehem). Achievements include research in steel and concrete structures including bridges and bldgs. Office Phone: 610-865-1041.

**VIETH, CHRISTOPHER W.,** former publishing executive; BS in Acctg., St. Francis U. Various fin. positions Amerada Hess Corp., 1987—95; dir. fin. Barnes and Noble, 1995—98, dir. fin. and ops., 1998—99, v.p., corp. controller, 1998—99; comptroller Dow Jones & Co., NYC, 2000—01, v.p. fin., 2001—02, v.p., treasurer, CFO, 2002—06. Mem. adv. coun. Villanova U. Ctr. for Responsible Leadership & Governance; mem. NJ Certified Pub. Accountants.*

**VIETH, WILLIAM CHAPMAN,** secondary school educator; b. Mauston, Wis., Feb. 12, 1954; s. Roland W. and Joan F. (Chapman) V.; m. Mara P. O'Neill, Dec. 29, 1979; children: Aaron Thoreau, Alexander O'Neill, Miles Darwin. BA, U. Wis., 1976, JD, 1979; BS, U. Minn., 1984, MEd, 1993. Cert. secondary English tchr. Minn. Tchr English fit Michael (Minn )-Allu swith Sch. Dist., 1984-85, Ind. Sch. Dist. 284, Wayzata, Minn., 1985—. Mem. academic standards com., Minn., 2003. Contbr. short stories and poetry to various publs. Recipient Whole Tchr. award Minn. Learning Disabilities, 1997, Golden Apple award (7). Home: 1740 Laurel Ave Saint Paul MN 55104-6128 Office: Wayzata HS 4955 Peony Ln N Plymouth MN 55446-1606 Office Phone: 763-745-6891. Personal E-mail: bill_vieth@wayzata.k12.mn.us.

**VIETOR, HAROLD DUANE,** federal judge; b. Parkersburg, Iowa, Dec. 29, 1931; s. Harold Howard and Alma Johanna (Kreimeyer) V. BA, U. Iowa, 1955, JD, 1958. Bar: Iowa 1958. Law clk. U.S. Ct. Appeals 8th Circuit, 1958-59; ptnr. Bleakley Law Offices, Cedar Rapids, Iowa, 1959-65; judge Iowa Dist. Ct., Cedar Rapids 1965-79, chief judge, 1970-79; U.S. dist. judge U.S. Dist. Ct. for So. Dist. Iowa, Des Moines, 1979-96, chief judge, 1985-92, sr. U.S. dist. judge, 1997—. Lectr. at law schs., legal seminars U.S. and Japan. Contbr. articles to profl. jours. in U.S. and Japan Served with USN, 1952-54. Mem. Iowa Bar Assn. (pres. jr. sect. 1966-67), Iowa Judges Assn. (pres. 1975-76), 8th Cir. Dist. Judges Assn. (pres. 1986-88). Office: US Dist Ct 485 US Courthouse 123 E Walnut St Des Moines IA 50309-2035

**VIETRI, LINDA SMITH,** gifted and talented educator; b. Norristown, Pa., Aug. 28, 1951; d. George John (Stepfather) and Laura MacMullen Herdegen; m. Robert Vietri, Aug. 25, 1973; children: Patrick Robert, Jeffrey Thomas, Andrew Joseph. BA in English, Ursinus Coll., 1973; MSLS, Villanova U., 1974; M of Elem. Edn., Arcadia U., 1990. Cert. elem. edn. Pa. Tchr. 4th and 5th grades Centennial Sch. Dist., Warminster, Pa., 1990—98, tchr. gifted, 1998—. Curriculum resource representative-technology Centennial Sch. Dist., 1991—93; vol. tchr. students spl. needs Gar. Nash Elem. Sch., Kulpsville, 1987—90; cmty. mentor h.s. students North Penn H.S., Lansdale, 1986—87. Coord. distribs.clothing and household items Campbell Am. M.E.Ch., Phila., 2001—05. Mem.: AAUW (assoc.), ALA (assoc.), Pa. Assn. Gifted Edn. (assoc.). Lutheran. Achievements include development of distribution of needed items to less fortunate individuals and families. Avocations: volunteer and charity work, tutoring, reading, art, travel. Home: 102 Chester Cir North Wales PA 19454 Office: Centennial Sch Dist Centennial Rd Warminster PA 18974 Office Phone: 215-441-6087. Personal E-mail: vietli@centennialsd.org.

**VIEUX, ALEX SERGE,** computer company executive, educator, journalist, entrepreneur; b. Paris, June 30, 1957; came to U.S., 1985; s. Serge and Aliette (Ackmed) V.; children: Sarah, David. Grad., Inst. d'Etudes Politiques, France, 1978; LLM, U. Paris, 1981; degree in bus., HEC, 1982; MBA, Stanford U., 1987. Cons. Arthur Andersen, Paris, 1981—85; prof. econs. U. Paris, 1983-85; US bus. corr. Le Monde, Palo Alto, Calif., 1985; chief operating officer Cats Software, Palo Alto, 1987-88; pres. Renaissance Software, Palo Alto, 1988-89; founder, chmn., CEO DASAR, Inc., Calif., 1990—; chmn., owner Etre (European Tech. Roundtable Exhbn.) and Arte (Asian Tech. Roundtable Exhbn.), 1989—; pub. Red Herring, 2004—; CEO Red Herring, Inc., 2004—. Bd. dirs. Tandem Computers (merged with Compaq), CA, Inc., Cibox, Commerce One, BVRP, Check Point Software, 1998-, madge, Thrunet and White Pajama, PC Globe, Inc., Tempe, Ariz.; exec. dir. Daum Comm., Kyriba, Qualys; vis. prof., Univ. Paris Dauphine, 1988; lectr. Univ. de Paris Sorbonne; spl. advisor, French Minister Fin., Industry and Economics, 1991-1993; pres. French Republic's Infotech Commn., 1997-99; spkr. in field. Contbr. numerous articles to profl. jours. Fulbright scholar Stanford U., 1985-86; named one of the Top 25 People Shaping a Digital Europe, Time Europe Digital 25 Avocations: tennis, chess, reading. Home: 16 Alma Ct Los Altos CA 94022-1742 Office: DASAR Inc 19 Davis Dr Belmont CA 94002 Address: 121 Avenie des Champs Elysées 75008 Paris France also: Jinyun Bldg B1101 No 43 Xizhimen Beidajie Beijing 100044 China Office Phone: 650-321-5544. Office Fax: 650-321-5597.*

**VIEZER, TIMOTHY WAYNE,** economist, investment company executive; b. Cleve., Jan. 13, 1959; s. Lawrence Stephen and Elaine Pearl (Thompson) V.; m. Jody Claire Russell, Oct. 14, 1988 (div. Aug. 1993); 1 child, Jessica Marlene; m. Joani Sue Yoakum, Sept. 21, 1996. BBA, BA with honors, Kent State U., 1982, MA in Econs., 1987, MA, 1989; PhD in Agrl. Econs., Ohio State U., 1998. CFA 2002. Administrv. asst. Arthur Andersen & Co., Cleve., 1985; corp. economist Centerior Energy Corp., Cleve., 1985-90; grad. tchg. assoc. Ohio State U., Columbus, 1990-91; grad. rsch. assoc. Nat. Regulatory Rsch. Inst., Columbus, 1991-93; asst. economist Huntington Nat. Bank, Columbus, 1991-92; portfolio analyst State Tchrs. Retirement Sys. Ohio, Columbus, 1993-99; sr. equities investment officer Sch. Employees Retirement Sys. Ohio, Columbus, 1999—. Instr. econs. Cuyahoga CC, Parma, Ohio, 1989-90; lectr. Baldwin-Wallace Coll., Berea, Ohio, 1989-90, Ohio Dominican Coll., Columbus, 1991, Capital U., 1991-95, Columbus State CC, 1992-93, Otterbein Coll., 1993-2000, Franklin U., 1994-2000, Ohio State U., 2001-. Co-author: The Soviet Occupation of Afghanistan, 1986; contbr. articles to profl. jours. Named one of Outstanding Young Men of Am. US Jaycees, 1981. Mem. Am. Econ. Assn., Am. Fin. Assn., Nat. Assn. Bus. Economists, CFA Inst. CFA Soc. Columbus, Internat. Assn. Bus. Forecasting (asst. sec. 1986, bd. dirs. 1987), Columbus Assn. Bus. Economists (past pres.), Soc. Quantitative Analysts, Chgo. Quantitative Alliance. Roman Catholic. Home: 231 E Como Ave Columbus OH 43202-1212 Office Phone: 614-222-5925. E-mail: tviezer@ohsers.org.

**VIG, VERNON EDWARD,** lawyer; b. St. Cloud, Minn., June 19, 1937; s. Edward Enoch and Salley Johanna (Johnson) V.; m. Susan Jane Rosenow, June 10, 1961; 1 child, Elizabeth Karen. BA, Carleton Coll., 1959; LLB, NYU, 1962, LLM, 1963; postdoctoral studies, Univ. Paris, Fac. de Droit, 1964. Bar: N.Y. 1962; avocat, Paris, 1992. Assoc. Cleary, Gottlieb, Steen & Hamilton, Paris, 1964, Donovan, Leisure, Newton & Irvine, N.Y.C. and Paris, 1965-72, ptnr., 1972-86, LeBoeuf, Lamb, Greene & MacRae, LLP, N.Y.C., Brussels, 1986—2001, of counsel, 2002—. Editor: NYU Law Rev. Sr. warden Grace Ch., Bklyn., 1986-2001. Mem. ABA (internat. and antitrust sects.), N.Y. State Bar Assn. (chmn. antitrust sect. 1987-88), Assn. of Bar of City of N.Y., Internat. Bar Assn., Union Internat. des Avocats, Heights Casino (bklyn.), Merriewold Club (Forestburgh, N.Y., bd. dirs. 1985-91), Phi Beta Kappa. Episcopalian. Office: LeBoeuf Lamb Greene & MacRae LLP 125 W 55th St New York NY 10019-5369 Office Phone: 212-424-8007. Business E-Mail: vvig@llgm.com.

**VIGDOR, JUSTIN LEONARD,** lawyer; b. NYC, July 13, 1929; s. Irving Barton and Ida (Devins) V.; m. Louise Martin, Mar. 8, 1952; children: Robert, Jill Vigdor-Feldman, Lisa Vigdor-Peck, Wendy Vigdor-Hess. LLB magna cum laude, St. John's U., 1951, LLM, N.Y.U., 1952. Bar: N.Y. 1951, U.S. Supreme Ct 1951, Fla. 1975. Sr. counsel Boylan, Brown, Code, Vigdor & Wilson LLP, Rochester, NY, 1958—. Bd. dirs. IEC Electronics Corp.; mem. N.Y. Uniform Law Commn., Nat. Conf. Uniform Law Commrs. Contbr. articles to profl. jours. Bd. dirs. Found. for Jewish Cmty., Ames Amzalak Meml. Trust; pres. AAA N.Y. State, Inc., Al Sigl Ptnrs. Found.; chmn. N.Y. State IOLA Fund. Served with JAGC, AUS, 1952-54. Recipient Community Svc. award N.Y. State Assn. County Clks., 1985. Fellow Am. Bar Found., N.Y. Bar Found. (Nathaniel award for cmty. svc. and profl. accomplishment); mem. Fla. Bar Assn., N.Y. State Bar Assn. (past pres. Ho. of Dels.), Monroe County Bar Assn. (past pres.), Estate Planning Coun., Am. Arbitration Assn. (nat. panel 1962—), N.Y. State C. of C. (Disting. Svc. award 1964), Irondequoit Country Club. Democrat. Jewish. Office: Boylan Brown Code Vigdor & Wilson LLP 2400 Chase Sq Rochester NY 14604 Office Phone: 585-232-5300. Personal E-mail: jvigdor@rochester.rr.com. Business E-Mail: jvigdor@boylanbrown.com

**VIGFUSSON, ROBERT JOHN,** economist; b. Gimli, Man., Canada, May 20, 1971; BSc, U. Man., Winnipeg, 1994; PhD, Northwestern U., Evanston, Ill., 2002. Rsch. asst. Bank of Can., Ottawa, Ont., 1994—96; economist Fed. Res. Bd., Washington, 2002—. Office: Fed Res Bd 20th and C St NW Washington DC 20551 Office Phone: 202-452-2335. E-mail: robert.j.vigfusson@frb.gov.

**VIGIER, FRANÇOIS CLAUDE DENIS,** city planning educator; b. Geneva, Oct. 14, 1931; s. Eugene Henri Rene and Françoise (Dupuy) V. BArch, MIT, 1955; M in City Planning, Harvard U., 1959, PhD, 1967. Architect UN Relief and Works Agy., Jordan, 1955-57; designer Town Planning Cons., Cambridge, Mass., 1957-58; mem. faculty Harvard Grad. Sch. Design, Cambridge, 1960—, prof. city planning and urban design, 1968-85, Charles Dyer Norton prof. regional planning 1985—, dir. Ctr. Urban Devel. Studies, 1987—, emeritus, 1982-86, chmn. dept. urban planning and design 1992-98. Vis. lectr. art Dartmouth Coll., 1962, 64; vis. critic urban design U. N.C., 1963; cons. Ford Found. Latin Am. program, 1964-65, Ednl. Svcs., Inc., 1966; dir. Harvard Ctr. Environ. Design Studies, 1967-69; pres. Nash-Vigier Inc., Cambridge, 1965-91. Author: Change and Apathy: Liverpool and Manchester During the Industrial Revolution, 1970, Housing in Tunis, 1987; contbr. articles to various periodicals. Decorated Knight, Order of Merit, France, 1995. Mem. Am. Inst. Cert. Planners, Am. Planning Assn. Home: 27 Fayerweather St Cambridge MA 02138-3329 E-mail: FVigier@gsd.harvard.edu.

**VIGIL, CHARLES J.,** lawyer; b. Los Alamos, N.Mex., Aug. 24, 1964; s. John Carlos and Catherine Elizabeth (Salazar) V. BBA, U. N.Mex., 1986; JD, U. Mich., 1989. Bar: N. Mex. 1989, U.S. Dist. Ct. N. Mex. 1989, U.S. Ct. Appeals (10th cir.) 1989. Atty Rodey, Dickason, Sloan, Akin & Robb, P.A., Albuquerque, 1989—. Articles editor Michigan Jour. of International Law, 1988-89. Mem. Am. Bar Assn., Albuquerque Bar Assn., N. Mex. State Bar Assn. (pres.-elect 2004) Democrat. Roman Catholic. Office: Rodey Dickason Sloan Akin & Robb PA 201 3rd St NW PO Box 1888 Albuquerque NM 87103-1888

**VIGIL, ROSE ANN,** business owner, weaver; b. Espanola, N.Mex., Feb. 24, 1965; d. Lawrence and Regina (Trujillo) Bartlett; m. Eugene David Vigil, July 25, 1987. AAS in Fibert Arts, No. N.Mex. C.C., 1995; postgrad., Coll. Santa Fe. Clerical aide No. N.Mex. C.C., Espanola, 1983-84; office mgr. trainee Branch Realty, Santa Fe, 1984-85; word processor, receptionist Legis. Edn. Study Com., Santa Fe, 1985-87; case recorder Las Cumbles Learning Ctr., Inc., Espanola, 1989-90; owner Los Vigiles Handcrafted Products, Espanola, 1990—, Los Vigiles Living Traditions Fiber Studio & Supply. Instr. N.Mex. Vocat. Tech. and Adult Edn. Conf., Albuquerque, 1992; instr. The Art

Boosters, Taos, N.Mex., 1993, Chimayo (N.Mex.) Youth Group, 1993; coord. Chimayo Arts and Crafts Festival, 1993—; weaving instr. Ghost Ranch Presbyn. Conf. Ctr., 1996. Mem. Handweavers Guild Am., Mountain Valley Wool Assn., Taos Hispanic Arts Coun. (mem. bd. 1993—), Spanish Market Vendors. Avocations: photography, dance. Home: HC 64 Box 1 Chimayo NM 87522-9748 Office Phone: 505-351-4522. E-mail: warpweave@cybermesa.com.

**VIGIL-GIRON, REBECCA,** state official; b. Taos, N.Mex., Sept. 4, 1954; d. Felix W. and Cecilia (Santistevan) Vigil; 1 child, Andrew R. AA in Elem. Edn., N.Mex. Highlands U., 1978, BA in French, 1991. Sec., project monitor, customer svc. rep. Pub. Svc. Co. N.Mex., 1978-86; sec. of state State of N. Mex, 1987—90, 1999—2006; exec. dir. N.Mex. Commn. Status of Women, 1991; electoral observer UN, Angola, Africa, 1992, Internat. Found. Electoral Sys., Dominican Republic, 1994, Equatorial Guinea, Africa, 1996, Washington, 1996. Participant AMPART, Mex., 1991. Dem. nominee U.S. Ho. Reps., 1990. Named among 100 Most Influential Hispanics in Nation, Hispanic Bus. Mag., 1990; recipient Trio Achievers award S.W. Assn. Student Assistance Programs, 1993, Gov.'s award Outstanding N.Mex. Women, 1994. Mem. Albuquerque Hispano C. of C. (membership rep., sr. sales mktg. rep., corp. rels. coord.) Democrat. Office: Office Sec of State State Capitol North Annex Ste 300 Santa Fe NM 87503

**VIGLIOTTA, MARGARET D.,** secondary school educator, art educator, artist; BA in Art Edn. cum laude, C.W. Post U., 1979; MLS, Weslyn Univ., Middletown. Conn., 1984. Permanent cert. tchr. N.Y. State, 1989. Art tchr. profoundly deaf students Mercy H.S. 75, Riverhead, NY, 1979—85; art tchr. Sachem Ctrl. Sch. Dist., Holbrook, NY, 1985—2005. Meml., sculptural Acolyte Candle Stands, St. Marks, prin. works include ceramic advent wreath on pedstal 3ft. high, ceramic chalices. Vol. Wading River Sch. Dist., 1968—92; fund raiser Boy Scouts; parent liaison com. Mid. Sch.; religiuos educator St. Mark's Parish, 1968—88, parish coun., liturgy com., 1975—2000. Mem.: Nat. Art Edn. Assn. (assoc.). Independent. Avocations: travel, crafts, reading, architecture, opera. Home: PO Box 853 Sayville NY 11782 Office Phone: 631-471-1400. Personal E-mail: pegal4@aol.com.

**VIGNALI, ROSARIO M.,** lawyer; b. Sept. 22, 1958; BA magna cum laude, City Coll., CUNY, 1979; JD cum laude, NY Law Sch., 1982. Bar: NY 1983, US Dist. Ct. So. Dist. NY, US Dist. Ct. Ea. Dist. NY, US Dist. Ct. No. Dist. NY. Ptnr. Wilson, Elser, Moskowitz, Edelman & Dicker LLP, White Plains, NYC. Mem.: ABA, Def. Rsch. Inst., NY State Bar Assn. Office: Wilson Elser Moskowitz Edelman & Dicker LLP 3 Gannett Dr White Plains NY 10604 Office Phone: 914-323-7000 ext. 4250. Office Fax: 914-323-7001. Business E-Mail: vignalir@wemed.com.

**VIGNEAULT, ALAIN,** professional hockey coach; b. Quebec City, Can., May 14, 1961; m. Josée Doucet; children: Andréanne, Janie. Player St. Louis Blues, 1981—83; head coach Can. Nat. Jr. Team, 1989-91, Trois-Rivières Draveurs, 1986—87, Hull Olympiques, 1988—92, Beauport Harfangs, 1995—97, Montreal Canadiens, 1997—2000, PEI Rocket, Charlottetown, 2003—05, Manitoba Moose (AHL), 2005—06, Vancouver Canucks, 2006—; asst. coach Ottawa Senators, 1992—95. Office: Vancouver Canucks 800 Griffiths Way Vancouver BC Canada V6B 6G1*

**VIGNERON, ALLEN HENRY,** theology studies educator, rector, auxiliary bishop; b. Mt. Clemens, Mich., Oct. 21, 1948; s. Elwin E. and Bernadine K. (Kott) V. AB in Philosophy, Sacred Heart Sem., Detroit, 1970; STL in Fundamental Theology, Pontifical Gregorian U., 1977; PhD in Philosophy, Cath. U. Am., 1987. Ordained deacon Roman Cath. Ch., 1973, ordained priest, 1975, titular bishop, 1996. Assoc. pastor Our Lady Queen of Peace Ch., Harper Woods, Mich., 1975-79; asst. prof. philosophy and theology Sacred Heart Major Sem., Detroit, 1985—; addetto of the secretariat of his Holiness the Pope The Holy See, Vatican City, 1991-94; rector, pres. Sacred Heart Major Sem., Detroit, 1994—; auxiliary bishop Archdiocese of Detroit, 1996—. Adj. prof. theology Pontifical Gregorian U., Rome, 1992-94. Roman Catholic. Office: Sacred Heart Major Sem 2701 W Chicago Detroit MI 48206-1704

**VIGNOLA, ANDREW MICHAEL, SR.,** computer company executive; b. NYC, Sept. 6, 1938; Student in bus. adminstrn., CCNY, 1956-59. Programmer trainee Citibank, NYC, 1959-60; programmer analyst Soc. Savs., Hartford, Conn., 1960-63; mgr. on-line data ctr. NCR Corp., Boston, 1963-67; cons., sr. ptnr. Computer Assistance, Inc., Hartford, 1967-72; v.p. info. sys. svc. divsn Soc. for Savs., Hartford, 1972-80; pres. Solar Svcs., Inc. subs. Soc. for Savings, 1977-80; sr. v.p., dir. info. svcs. Dime Savs. Bank, NYC, 1980-83; v.p. info. svcs. group Advest, inc., Hartford, 1983-85; pres. Cosine Inc., Meriden, Conn., 1985-90; exec. v.p., COO I.G.I.C., Great Neck, NY, 1993-99; mgmt. cons., 1999—. Former mem. faculty Conn. Savs. Sch. Fin. and Mgmt.; lectr. in field. Contbr. articles to profl. jours. Mem.: Data Processing Mgmt. Assn. (pres., chmn. bd. Hartford chpt. 1976—77). Achievements include invention of banking brokerage interface. Home: 30 Bonna St Beacon Falls CT 06403

**VIGTEL, GUDMUND,** retired museum director; b. July 9, 1925; came to U.S., 1948, naturalized, 1966; s. Arne Jonsen and Elisabeth (Petri) V.; m. Solveig Lund, 1951 (div. 1964); 1 child, Elisabeth; m. Carolyn Gates Smith, July 18, 1964; 1 child, Catherine Higdon. BFA, U. Ga., 1952, MFA, 1953; DFA (hon.), Atlanta Coll. Art, 1991. Adminstrv. asst. Corcoran Gallery Art, Washington, 1954-61, actg. dir., 1961-63; dir. High Mus. Art, Atlanta, 1963-91, dir. emeritus, 1991—. Contbr. articles and essays to profl. publs. With Royal Norwegian Air Force, 1944-45. Decorated Chevalier des Arts et Lettres, Min. of Culture, France, 1985; recipient Order of Merit 1st Class, Fed. Republic Germany, 1989, The James R. Short Lifetime Achievement award, 2003. Home: 2082 Golfview Dr NW Atlanta GA 30309-1210

**VIIL, HEINO,** retired engineer; b. Riisipere, Estonia, Dec. 18, 1919; arrived in U.S., 1951; s. Johannes Friedrich and Pauline (Jahnsohn) Viil; m. Ella Toomet, Apr. 30, 1941 (div. 1949); m. Mirdza Berzins, July 25, 1953; children: Brunolf, Silvia. PhD, Albert-Ludwigs U., Freiburg, Germany, 1950; BS, Drexel U., Phila., 1962; MS, George Washington U., 1967, SUNY, Buffalo, 1974. Preliminary engr. Proctor & Schwartz, Phila., 1951—62; rsch. engr. Robertshaw, King of Prussia, Pa., 1962—63; ops. analyst Vitro Labs., Silver Spring, Md., 1963—68; devel. engr. Bell Aerospace Co., Buffalo, 1968—74; sr. engr. Singer, Kearfott, Wayne, NJ, 1974—78; sr. mem. tech. staff ITT Def. Comm. Divsn., Nutley, NJ, 1978—94; ret., 1994. Mem.: Alpha Sigma Lambda. Home: 543 Main St Little Falls NJ 07424-2448

**VIJ, RAVI,** oncologist, researcher; s. Sunder Lal Vij; m. Kiran Raj, July 2, 2001. MBBS, Maulana Azad Med. Coll., New Delhi, 1990. Diplomate Am. Bd. Internal Medicine, Am. Bd. Oncology, Am. Bd. Hematology. Prof. BMT and leukemia Washington U. Sch. Medicine, St Louis, Mo., 2000—. Contbr. articles to profl. jours. Mem.: Am. Soc. Clin. Oncology (licentiate), Am. Soc. Hematology (licentiate). Achievements include research in bone marrow transplantation; myeloma; myelodysplastia syndrome, cmv infection. Office: Washington U Sch Medicine Campus Box 8007 660 S Euclid Saint Louis MO 63110 Office Phone: 314-454-8323.

**VIJAYAKUMAR, ASHA,** ophthalmologist; b. Chitoor, Kerala, India, July 30, 1960; d. Padmanabhan and Ammu P. Menon; m. Parakkudivilakam Vijayakumar, May 24, 1984; children: Ashvin, Roshan. B in Medicine and Surgery, Bombay U., 1985, MS in Ophthalmology, 1990. Cons. ophthalmologist Olaya Med. Ctr., Riyadh, Central Province, Saudi Arabia, 1991—96; fellow in neuro-opthalmology Henry Ford Hosp., Mich., 1997—98; fellow in cornea and refractive surgery Wayne State U., 1998—99; med. officer ophthalmology Aravind Eye Hosp., Coimbatore, Tamil Nadu, India, 1999—2001; rschr. Hosp. Sick Children and Princess Margaret Hosp., Toronto, Ont., Canada, 2001—02. Presenter in field. Contbr. revs. in field. Vol. Lions Club, 1999—2001, WHO, 1999—2001, organizer, 1999—2001, Rotary Club, Palghat, Kerala. Recipient Distinction, State Bd., 1978; scholar

North Bombay Sch. award, Welfare Soc., 1978. Mem.: Worth Am. Neuro-Ophthalmolgy Soc., Indian Ophthal. Soc., Am. Acad. Ophthalmology. Home: 1000 Central Ave Apt 131A Westfield NJ 07090

**VIJAYARAMAN, PUGAZHENDHI,** medical educator; m. Vasanthi Pugazhendhi, Dec. 10, 1993; children: Adithya Pugazhendhi, Avani Pugazhendhi. MD, JIPMER, Pondicherry, India, 1990—93. Internal Medicine Am. bd. of internal Medicine, 1997, Cardiovascualr Diseases Am. bd. of Internal Medicine, 2000, Cardiac Electrophysiology Am. bd. of Internal Medicine, 2001. Asst. prof. of internal medicine Med. Coll. Va, Va. Commonwealth U., Richmond, Va., 2002—; dir. cardiac electrophysiology divsn. McGuire VA Med. Ctr., Richmond, Va., 2002—. Dir., pacemaker, arrhythmia services McGuire VA Med. Ctr., Richmond, Va., 2002—. Contbr. articles various profl. jours. Recipient Best Outgoing Student, Madurai Med. Coll., 1989, Outstanding Academic Achievement in Cardiovasc. Medicine, Montefiore Med. Ctr., Dept. Cardiology, NY, 2000, Leo Davidoff Socs. Outstanding Achievement Tchg., Albert Einstein Coll. Medicine, Yeshiva U., NY, 1997. Mem.: Am. Heart Assn., Va. Dept. of Health (licentiate), Am. Coll. of Cardiology (assoc.). Office: McGuire Veterans Affairs Med Ctr 1201 Broadrock Blvd 111J3 Richmond VA 23049

**VIJAYARATNAM, KANAPATHIPILLAI,** civil and environmental engineer, consultant, director, educator; b. Analaitivu, Sri Lanka, May 10, 1948; arrived in Eng., 1979, naturalized, 1990; s. Kathirvelu Kanapathipillai and Parvathy Ponniah; m. Sakuntala Mylwaganam, Oct. 31, 1979. BSc in Engring. with honors, U. Ceylon, Peradeniya, 1971; M Engring., Asian Inst. Tech., Bangkok, 1977; MSc in Pub. Health (Environ.) Engring., Imperial Coll. U. London, 1982; cert. sustainable bus. challenge, World Bus. Coun. Sustainable Devel., 1999; Diploma, Imperial Coll., London, 1982; DEng, Irish Internat. U., 2004. Chartered engr., U.K. Instn. civil engring. U. Ceylon, Peradeniya, 1972; civil engr. Mahaweli Devel. Bd., Colombo, Sri Lanka, 1972-75, Renardet Engring., Singapore, 1977-80; engr. Chanton Engring. Ltd., Middlesex, 1984-85, S.P. Collins Assocs., Cambridge, U.K., 1985-86; cons. civil engr. Coulsdon, U.K., 1986-88; sr. engr. Neilcot Constrn. Ltd., Kent, U.K., 1988-90; engr. clean water bd. Binnie & Partners, Cons. Engrs., Redhill, U.K., 1990-94; sr. engr. grade 1 SMHBinnie Cons. Engrs., K.L., Malaysia, 1995-96; dep. project mgr., prin. engr. S.S.P. Consulting Engrs., Kuala Lumpur, Malaysia, 1996-97, engring. cons., 1998-99; mng. dir. Rosebury Cons., Ltd., 1999—. Exec. dir. AITA-Net (Europe), Internat. Cons. Consortium, 2001—; orig. contbr. to re-engring. of water ind. orgs., 1996, Broader Edu. Civil Engs. in 21st Century, 1995, Integrated River Basin Devel., 1977, Cost and Performance Optimization of Water Treatment System (conceptual and mathematical), 1982, Mathematical Multi-Criterion & Multi-Objective Decision Approaches to Water Resources Management, 1994, Future Direction of Civil Engring. Inst. Civil Engrs., 1995, ASCE, 2003, Sustainable Development of Infrastructure in Water and Environ. Engring., 1996, Environmentally Sound Dam and Water Power Devel., 1995, Emergence and Complexity in Urban Environmental Engring Mgmt. in 21st Century, 1999, Environ. Engring. Edn. in 21st Century, 1999, 03, and Future Dir. Tech. Edn. in Asia, 1999, Project Mgmt. Water Supply and Treatment Projects in Asia, 1995, Future Direction Engring. Edn. for a Sustainable World in the New Millenium, 2000, 03, Sustainable Water Supply for Asian City, 2001, 03, Sustainable Waste Management, 2001, leading contbr. Talking Point Forum of www.bbc.co.uk on engring., sustainable devel., environment, pub. health and pub. policy issues, 2002; contbr. numerous BBC -Have Your Say (engring. and pub. policy) forum, 2003; prof. and dean Sch. Engring. Mgmt., Sustainable Environ. Devel. and Pub. Policy Am. U. London, 2003—2006; adj. faculty Am. U. London; dean and prof. faculty engring., mgmt. and environment. Irish Internat. U., 2004-05; dir. London Engring. Sch., 2004—; exec. pres. 2005-; founder, pres., dir. gen. World Acad. Engring., 2006-; presenter in field. Contbr. articles to profl. jours. Named one of 500 Leaders of New Century, 1999, Asians in Millennium, 100 Eminent Tamils of 20th Century, Greatest Minds 21st Century, 2004—05; recipient Man of Yr. medal, Internat. Peace prize, 2005; UK Govt. scholar, 1976—77, NATO Advanced Inst. grantee, 1981, UNESCO/Colo. State U. grantee, 1981, 2004. Mem. ASCE, World Acad. Engring. (pres., dir. gen. 2006), Assn. Environ. Engring. and Sci. Profs., Royal Instn. London, Instn. Civil Engrs. London, Internat. Water Assn., Internat. Assn. Hydraulic Rsch. and Engring., Internat. Assn. Water Resources, Internat. Assn. Water Power, UNESCO Internat. Ctr. Engring. Edn., Chartered Inst. Water and Environ. Mgmt. Avocations: golf, travel, reading, writing, fine arts. Home: 1 Ashcroft Rise Coulsdon Surrey CR5 2SS England Personal E-mail: vijay@vijayaratnam.com. Business E-Mail: president@lesedu.co.uk, president@waeng.org, president@topmentor.co.uk.

**VIKAN, GARY KENT,** museum director; b. Fosston, Minn., Nov. 30, 1946; s. Franklin and Wilma (Johnson) V.; m. Elana Klausner, Sept. 12, 1971; children: Nicole, Sonia. BA, Carleton Coll., 1967; MA, Princeton U., 1970, PhD, 1976. Art mus. adminstr., curator Byzantine art Dumbarton Oaks, Washington, 1975-84; asst. dir. curatorial affairs, curator medieval art Walters Art Mus., Balt., 1985—94, dir., 1994—. Adj. prof. Johns Hopkins U. Woodrow Wilson Found. fellow, 1967-68. Mem. Byzantine Studies Counf. (governing bd. 1989—), U.S. Nat. Com. for Byzantine Studies (exec. com., 1988-92. Office: Walters Art Gallery 600 N Charles St Baltimore MD 21201

**VIKER, ERIK,** theater educator; b. West Islip, NY, Nov. 2, 1965; s. Arne and Patricia Viker; m. Brenda Fabian, May 27, 2006. BS, U. Fla., Gainesville, 1987; MFA, U. Tex., Austin, 2003. Asst. prof. theatre, tech. dir. Susquehanna U., Selinsgrove, Pa., 2003—. Freelance theatre prodn. mgr., Pa., 1997—. Mem.: Internat. Alliance Theatrical Stage Employees (mem., local 636). Libertarian. Roman Catholic. Home: 215 East Walnut St Selinsgrove PA 17870 Office: Susquehanna U 514 University Ave Selinsgrove PA 17870 Office Phone: 570-372-4548.

**VILA, ADIS MARIA,** lawyer, business government executive; b. Guines Habana, Cuba, Aug. 1, 1952; d. Calixto Vila and Adis C. Fernandez. BA with distinction, Rollins Coll., 1974; JD with honors, U. Fla., 1978; LLM with high honors, Institut Universitaire de Hautes Estudes Internationales, Geneva, 1981; MBA, U Chgo., 1997. Bar: Fla. 1979, DC 1984. Assoc. Paul & Thomson, 1979-82; White House fellow Office Pub. Liaison, Washington, 1982-83; spl. asst. to sec. state for inter-Am. Affairs Dept. State, Washington, 1983-86; dir. Office of Mex. and Caribbean Basin, Dept. Commerce, Washington, 1986-87; sec. Dept. Adminstrn., State of Fla., 1987-89; asst. sec. for adminstrn. USDA, Washington, 1989-91; vis. fellow Nat. Def. U., Washington, 1992-93; v.p. internat. devel. Vigoro Corp., Chgo., 1994-95; v.p. govt. affairs regulatory policy, Carribean & Latin Am. Nortel Networks, 1997-2000; pres., CEO Vila & Assocs., 2001—. Vis. asst. prof. Fla. Internat. U., 1993—94; mem. adv. bd. Ams. Global Asset Mgmt. Fund, 1999—; v.p. external affairs Miami Dade C.C., 2002—03; adj. faculty bus. law various not-for-profit, for profit instns., 2002—. Trustee So. Ctr. Internat. Studies, 1987—. Named one of 100 Most Influential Hispanics, 1998; Paul Harris fellow, Rotary Internat., 1983, U.S.-Japan Leadership fellow, 1991—92, Eisenhower Exch. fellow, Beca Fiore, Argentina, 1992. Mem.: Women Execs. in State Govt. (bd. dirs. 1987—89), Am. Coun. Young Polit. Leaders (bd. dirs. 1984—), Internat. Women's Forum, Coun. Fgn. Rels. (term mem. 1987—92), Dade County Bar Assn. (bd. dirs. young and lawyers sect. 1979—87). Republican. Roman Catholic. Avocations: tennis, skiing, golf, theater, art. Office Phone: 954-458-4080. E-mail: adisvila@bellsouth.net.

**VILA, ROBERT JOSEPH,** television personality, real estate developer, space designer; b. Miami, Fla., June 20, 1946; s. Roberto and Esperanza (Robles) Vila; m. Diana Barrett, Oct. 3, 1975; children: Christopher, Monica, Susannah. AA in Architecture, Miami Dade Jr. Coll., 1966; BS in Journalism, U. Fla., 1969. Editor English Lang. Cons., Stuttgart, Fed. Republic of Germany, 1971; stagehand Wurttemberg State Theatre, Stuttgart, 1972; project mgr. Barrett Assocs., Boston, 1973-74; pres. R.J. Vila, Inc., Boston, 1975-85; host This Old House Sta. WGBH-TV, Boston, 1978-89; host Bob Vila's Home Again, Cape Cod and Chgo., 1990—. Author: This Old House, 1980, Bob Vila's This Old House, 1982, Guide to Building Materials, 1986, Guide to Buying Your Dream House, 1990, Bob Vila's Tool Box, 1993, Bob

Vila's Guide to Historic Homes of New England, 1993, Bob Vila's Guide to Historic Homes of the South, 1993, Bob Vila's Guide to Historic Homes of the Mid-Atlantic, 1993, Bob Vila's Workshop, 1994, Bob Vila's Guide to Historic Homes of the Midwest and Great Plains, 1994, Bob Vila's Guide to Historic Homes of the West, 1994 (A&E Spl.), Bob Vila's Guide to Historic Homes, 1996, Bob Vila's American Home mag., 1996, Bob Vila's Complete Guide to Remodeling Your Home, 2002. Bd. dirs. Nat. Alliance to End Homlessness, Washington, Coll. Summit. Recipient Emmy award, New Eng. Region, 1979, Nat. Region, 1985. Mem.: SAG (Screen Actors Guild), AFTRA (Am. Fedn. TV Radio Artists). Roman Catholic. Avocations: sailing, fishing, bicycling, gardening, woodworking. Office: BVTV Inc 115 Kingston St Boston MA 02111

**VILADAS, PILAR,** editor; BA, Harvard Coll., 1977. With Interiors mag., 1979—81; with Progressive Architecture, 1981—88; home design editor NY Times mag., 1997—; House & Garden, 1989—93; contbg. writer Archtl. Digest, 1993—96. Author: Los Angeles: A Certain Style, 1995, Domestiticies: At Home with the NY Times Magazine, 2005; co-author: California Beach Houses: Style, Interiors, & Architecture, 1996. Office: NY Times 229 W 43rd St New York NY 10036 Office Phone: 212-556-5183. Office Fax: 212-556-7382.

**VILAR, ALBERTO W.,** investment company executive; b. Cuba, Oct. 4, 1940; BA, Washington and Jefferson Coll., 1962; MBA, Iona Coll., 1969. Co-founder, pres., profile mgr. Amerindo Investment Advisors, San Francisco, 1985—. Active in philanthropic, healthcare, and cultural endeavors; founder Alberto Vilar Global Fellows in the Performing Arts. Roman Catholic. Avocations: art, opera.

**VILCEK, JAN TOMAS,** immunologist, medical educator; b. Bratislava, Czechoslovakia, June 17, 1933; came to U.S., 1965, naturalized, 1970. s. Julius and Friderika (Fischer) V.; m. Marica F. Gerhath, July 28, 1962 MD, Comenius U., Bratislava, 1957; CSc (PhD), Czechoslovak Acad. Sci., Bratislava, 1962. Fellow Inst. Virology, Bratislava, 1957-62, head of lab., 1962-64; asst. prof. microbiology NYU Med. Ctr., N.Y.C., 1965-68, assoc. prof., 1968-73, prof., 1973—. Chmn. nomenclature com. WHO, 1981—86; mem. adv. com. Am. Cancer Soc., 1981—87, chmn., 1983; mem. sci. adv. bd. Max Planck Inst., Munich, 1987—95; pres. Vilcek Found., 2003—. Author: Interferon, 1969; editor in chief Archives of Virology, 1975-86, Cytokine and Growth Factor Revs., 1995-2005; editor: Interferons and the Immune System, 1984, Tumor Necrosis Factor: Structure, Function and Mechanism of Action, 1991, Cytokine Reference, 2000; mem. editl. bd. Virology, 1979-81, Archives of Virology, 1986-92, Infection and Immunity, 1983-85, Antiviral Rsch., 1984-88, Jour. Interferon and Cytokine Rsch., 1988—, Jour. Immunological Methods, 1986—, Natural Immunity and Cell Growth Regulation, 1986-92, Jour. Immunology, 1987-89, Lymphokine Rsch., 1987-94, Jour. Biol. Chemistry, 1988-90, ISI Atlas Sci., Immunology, 1988-89, Jour. Cellular Physiology, 1988—, Cytokine, 1989—, Biologicals, 1989-95, Acta Virologica, 1991—, Internat. Archives of Allergy and Immunology, 1992-98, Folia Biologica, 1993-96, Cellular Immunology, 1993-96, Jour. of Inflammation, 1994-97, Cytokines, Cellular & Molecular Therapy, 1998-2005; contbr. articles to profl. jours.; co-inventor of anti-inflammatory drug infliximab used in rheumatoid arthritis and Crohn's disease, other inflammatory disorders. Mem. rev. panel Israel Cancer Rsch. Fund, 1993-96; mem. fellowship rev. com. Am. Heart Assn., 1992-94. Recipient Rsch. Career Devel. award, USPHS, 1968—73, Recognition award, Japanese Inflammation Soc., 1989, Outstanding Investigator award, Nat. Cancer Inst., NIH, 1991—98, Elliott Osserman Disting. Svc. Cancer Rsch. award, Israel Cancer Rsch. Fund, 1996, Disting. Alumnus award and medal, Comenius U., Bratislava, 2001, Albert Gallatin medal, NYU, 2005; grantee, USPHS, others. Fellow AAAS; mem. Am. Soc. Microbiology, Am. Assn. Immunologists, Internat. Soc. Interferon and Cytokine Rsch. (hon. life), Czech Immunology Soc., Internat. Cytokine Soc. (hon. life, pres. 1997-98), Czechoslovak Soc. Microbiology. Office: NYU Med Ctr 550 1st Ave New York NY 10016-6402 Business E-Mail: jan.vilcek@med.nyu.edu.

**VILCHEZ, RICARDO S.,** library director; b. Masaya, Nicaragua, Jan. 20, 1953; s. Adrian Zamora and Maria M. Vilchez; children: Ricardol E., Nidia E. BA, Fordham U., 1990; MBA, CES, Managua, Nicaragua, 1998; diploma, Inst. of Christian Econs., 1982; MLS, Pratt Inst., Bklyn., 1995. With Nat. Police Nicaragua, Managua, 1968-72; presdl. asst. Govt. Nicaragua, 1972-74; libr. asst. Ctrl. Bank Libr., Managua, 1974-75; asst. presdl. office Ctrl. Bank Managua, 1975-79; libr. supervisor Fordham U., N.Y.C., 1989—. Editor (CD) Los Motivos Del Lobo, 2000. V.p. Nicaraguan Children's Found., N.Y.C., 1999—; cultural dir. Nicaraguan Support Group, N.Y.C., 1999—; pres. Comision Hispana Pro Obra Rubén Dario N.Y., 1998—. Mem. Am. Libr. Assn., Am. Soc. Info. Sci., Libr. Congress. Republican. Roman Catholic. Avocations: cultural activities, travel, walking, rare books, community activities. Home: 13 Van Pelt Ave Staten Island NY 10303-2478 Office: Fordham U 113 W 60th St New York NY 10023-7484 E-mail: rsvilchez@yahoo.com.

**VILCHEZ, VICTORIA ANNE,** lawyer; b. Tampa, Fla., Aug. 10, 1955; d. Angel and Mary Ida (Guarisco) V.; m. Louis J. Deutsch; children: Matthew Stephen Williams, Michael Paul Williams, Heather Margaret Williams. BA, Fla. State U., 1977; JD, Mercer U., 1980. Bar: Fla. 1980. Trial atty. Office Pub. Defender, Miami, Fla., 1980-83; pvt. practice, 1983—. Rep. Nat. Conf. on Women and Law, Atlanta, 1978; traffic magistrate Palm Beach County Ct., 1991-95. Vol. Cath. Home for Children, Miami, 1983-84; mem. Coun. Cath. Women; class 1994 Leadership Palm Beach County; bd. dirs. Girl Scouts coun., Palm Glades, Fla., 1995-04, first v.p., 2003-04. Recipient cert. of achievement 8th Nat. Conf. Juvenile Justice, 1981, Livingstone Hall award Juvenile Justice ABA, 1998; grantee Mercer U., 1977. Mem. Fla. Bar, Fla. Assn. Women Lawyers (sec., newsletter editor Palm Beach County chpt. 1985-86, mentor chair 2003, pres.-elect 2004-05, pres. 2005-06), Palm Beach County Bar Assn., Fla. State U. Alumni Assn., Palm Beach County Hispanic Bar Assn. (pres.-elect 1990-91, pres. 1991-92, bd. dirs. 1990—, treas. 1993-94, 94-97), Legal Aid Soc. Palm Beach (bd. dirs. 1992—, v.p. 1999-2001, pres. 2001-03), West Palm Beach Kiwanis Club, Leadership Palm Beach County (grad. 1994, bd. govs. 1999-2001). Roman Catholic. Office: Ste 401 2161 Palm Beach Lakes Blvd West Palm Beach FL 33409 Office Phone: 561-471-0001. Business E-Mail: Vilchezlaw@palmbeachbar.org.

**VILIM, NANCY CATHERINE,** advertising executive; b. Quincy, Mass., Jan. 15, 1952; d. John Robert and Rosemary (Malpede) V.; m. Geoffrey S. Horner, Feb. 16, 1992; children: Matthew Edward Cajda, Megan Catherine Cajda, Margaret Horner. Student, Miami U., Oxford, Ohio, 1970-72. Media asst. Draper Daniels, Inc., Chgo., 1972—74; asst. buyer Campbell Mithun, Chgo., 1974—75; buyer Tatham, Laird & Kudner, Chgo., 1975—77; media buyer Adcom, Inc. div. Quaker Oats Corp., Chgo., 1977—79; media supr. G.M. Feldman, Chgo., 1979—81; v.p. media dir. Media Mgmt., 1981—83; v.p. broadcast dir. Bozell, Jacobs, Kenyon & Eckhardt, Chgo., 1983—88; v.p., media mgr. McCann-Erickson, Inc., 1989—2002; broadcast supr. OMD USA, Chgo., 2002—04; sr. media buyer GSD&M, Chgo., 2004—05; media dir. Jordan, Ross & Rose, Northfield, Ill., 2005—. Judge 27th Internat. Broadcast Awards, Chgo., 1987. Co-pres. Immaculate Conception Religious Edn. Parents Club, 1995-96. Recipient Media All Star awards Sound Mgmt. Mag., N.Y.C., 1987. Mem. Broadcast Advt. Club Chgo., Mus. Broadcast Communications, NAFE. Office: JRR Advt 790 Frontage Rd Northfield IL 60093

**VILLA, JOHN KAZAR,** lawyer; b. Ypsilanti, Mich., June 9, 1948; s. John Joseph and Susie (Hoogasian) V.; m. Ellen A. Edwards, June 3, 1990. AB, Duke U., 1970; JD, U. Mich., 1973. Bar: D.C. 1973. Trial atty. U.S. Dept. Justice, Washington, 1973-77; assoc. Williams & Connolly, Washington, 1977-81, ptnr., 1981—. Author: legal treatises. Office: Williams & Connolly 725 12th St NW Washington DC 20005-5901

**VILLABLANCA, JAIME ROLANDO,** neuroscientist, medical educator; b. Chillàn, Chile, Feb. 1929; arrived in U.S., 1971, naturalized, 1985; s. Ernesto and Teresa (Hernàndez) V.; m. Guillermina Nieto, Dec. 3, 1955; children: Amparo C., Jaime G., Pablo J., Francis X., Claudio I. Bachelor in Biology, Nat. Inst. Chile, 1946; licentiate medicine, U. Chile, 1953, MD, 1954. Cert. neurophysiologist. Rockefeller Found. postdoctoral fellow in physiology John Hopkins and Harvard Med. Schs., 1959-61; Fogarty internat. rsch. fellow in anatomy UCLA, 1966-68, assoc. research anatomist and psychiatrist, 1971-72; assoc. prof. psychiatry and biobehavioral scis. UCLA Sch. Medicine, 1972-76; prof. psychiatry and biobehavioral scis. UCLA, 1976—2004, prof. neurobiology, 1977—2004, disting. prof. psychiatry and biobehavioral scis., neurobiology, 2004—. Mem. faculty U. Chile Sch. Medicine, 1954-71, prof. exptl. medicine, 1970-71; vis. prof. neurobiology Cath. U. Chile Sch. Medicine, 1974; cons. in field. Author numerous rsch. papers, book chpts., abstracts; chief regional editor Developmental Brain Dysfunction, 1988-99. Decorated Order Francisco de Miranda (Venezuela), 1987; recipient Premio Reina Sofia, Madrid, 1990, Lifetime Achievement award UCLA Sch. Medicine, 2001, Emeritus award Colegio Medico de Chile, 2004; fellow Rockefeller Found., 1959-61, Fogarty Internat. Rsch. fellow NIH, 1966-68; grantee USAF Office Sci. Rsch., 1962-65, Found. Fund Rsch. Psychiatry, 1969-72, USPHS-Nat. Inst. Child Human Devel., 1972-96, USPHS-Nat. Inst. Drug Abuse, 1981-85, USPHS-Nat. Inst. Neurol. Disorders and Stroke, 1988-92, Fgn. Scientist Traveling grant Tokyo Met. Govt., 1995. Mem. AAAS, AAUP, Sleep Rsch. Soc. (Significant Early Contbr. award 2003), Mental Retardation Rsch. Ctr., Brain Rsch. Inst., Internat. Brain Rsch. Orgn., Am. Physiol. Soc., Soc. for Neurosci., Assn. Venezolana Padres de Niños Excepcionales, Soc. Child and Adolescent Psychiatry and Neurology (Chile, hon.). Johns Hopkins Med. and Surg. Assn., Sigma Xi. Home: 200 Surfview Dr Pacific Palisades CA 90272-2911 Office: UCLA Dept Psychiatry & Biobehavioral Scis Los Angeles CA 90024-1759 Office Phone: 310-825-5195. Business E-Mail: jvillablanca@mednet.ucla.edu.

**VILLACIAN, VANESSA LUISA,** psychologist; b. Miami, Fla., Sept. 14, 1973; d. Fernando and Tania Luisa (Alvarez) Villacian; m. Robert Pagés, Dec. 23, 2004. Psy.D. utmost distinction, Carlos Albizu U., Miami, 2000. Cert. hypnotherapist. Pres. The Answers Centre, Miami, 2002—. Clin. dir. Oasis, Miami, 2005. Mem.: APA, Psi Chi. Avocation: exercise. Home: 199 Edgewater Dr Coral Gables FL 33133 Office: The Answers Centre 7171 SW 62nd Ave 301 South Miami FL 33143 Office Phone: 305-308-2178. Personal E-mail: drvpages@yahoo.com.

**VILLACORTA, YBET,** lawyer; BA, Rutgers U., 1978, MS, 1982; PhD in bioinorganic chemistry, MIT, 1987; JD, Fordham U., 1991. Bar: NJ 1992, NY 1992, DC 1999. Ptnr., patent atty. Katten Muchin Zavis Rosenman, Washington, DC. Mem.: ABA, NY Bar Assn., NJ Bar Assn., DC Bar Assn., Am. Intellectual Property Law Assn. Office: Katten Muchin Zavis Rosenman East Lobby, Ste 700 1025 Thomas Jefferson St, NW Washington DC 20007 Office Phone: 202-625-3838. Office Fax: 202-339-8292. E-mail: ybet.villacorta@kmzr.com.

**VILLAGOMEZ, TIMOTHY P.,** lieutenant governor; b. Sept. 10, 1962; s. Jose T. and Rita P. Villagomez; m. Margaret E. Keene; children: Renaesho, Jose, Rita, Juanita, Timmy. BS, San Diego U., 1987. Rep. Dist. 1 Commonwealth No. Mariana Islands Legislature, 2004—06, vice spkr., 2004—06, chmn. Pub. Utilities, Transp., and Comm. Com., 2004—06; lt. gov. Commonwealth No. Mariana Islands, 2006—. Construction & design engr. Commonwealth Utilities Corp., dep. exec. dir., exec. dir., 1990-2002; pacific regulator Micronesia Telecommunications & Cable TV Ops., 1994—2002. Chmn. Gov.'s Declaration Task Force Water State of Emergency, 1995—99, Nat. Rehab. Adv. Coun.; mem. Housing Task Force, 1999—2001, Comml. Devel. & Capital Improvement/Fed. Projects Task Force. Named Govt. Businessman of Yr., Saipan C. of C., 2000; recipient Innovation Award, Nat. Assn. State Facilities, 1998, 1999. Mem.: ASCE, Am. Gen. Contractors, Am. Pub. Power Assn., Pacific Power Assn., Pacific Island Legislatures (pres. 2004), Jr. Golf Assn. Office: Lt Gov Office of Gov Caller Box 10007 Saipan MP 96950 Office Phone: 670-664-8876. Office Fax: 670-664-2311. E-mail: tpvillagomez@itecnmi.com.*

**VILLAIRE, HOLLY HENNEN HOOD,** theater producer, director, actress, educator; b. Yonkers, NY, Apr. 11, 1944; d. John Wilson and Adele Jelonek (Deer) Hood. BA (summa cum laude), U. Detroit, 1964; MA, U. Mich., 1967. Cert. of studies Centre Dramatique Nat. du Sud Est, France, 1965. Assoc. artistic dir. Hamm & Clov Stage Co., Yonkers, NY, 1973—2001, producing artistic dir., 2001—; prodr. Olympic Arts Festival (Ensemble Studio Theatre), 1984; asst. prof. Allentown Coll. (now De Sales U.), 1991—92, Vassar Coll. 1992. Dir. grad. showcases Am. Musical and Dramatic Acad., 1992—95; screening, finals judge U. Resident Theatre Assn. Auditions, 1993—95; finals judge Region 2 Am. Coll. Theatre Festival, 1993—94; guest spkr. Disting. Artist Forum with James Earl Jones, U. Mich., 1993; guest artist, S.W. Gas Disting. Artist lectr. UNLV, Las Vegas, 1994; forum prodr. Actor's Ctr., 1996; casting cons. Stratford Festival Theatre, Conn., 1998; adj. prof. Mercy Coll., 2000—. Actor: Antony and Cleopatra (Pitts. Press award as Best Actress, 1989), (Off-Broadway) God Bless You, Mr. Rosewater, Bklyn. Acad. Music Theatre Company (BAM) dir.: Car, Berlin Festival, 1973; actor: Coming Around Again: A Concert in Tribute to Christopher Reeve, 1997; (Broadway plays) Habeas Corpus, Scapino, (theatre) On Borrowed Time, 1965, Our Town, 1966, Return the Rain, 1971, This Property is Condemned, 1972, Eyes of Chalk, 1972, Talk to Me Like the Rain and Let Me Listen, 1972; dir.: Anam, 2001, An Aisling Christmas, 2002, Anam Cara, 2003, Of Pubs and Parishes, 2004, Ardnaglass on the Air, 2005, A Touch of the Playright, 2006; prodr.: The Ring, 2006, Hispanic Heritage Cultural Weekend, 2006. Arts Alive grantee, Westchester Arts Coun. (NYSCA) 2003, 2004, 2005, 2006, NEA, 2006. Mem.: Actor's Equity Assn., AFTRA, SAG. Office Phone: 914-963-6222. Business E-Mail: hvillaire@hammandclov.org.

**VILLA-KOMAROFF, LYDIA,** molecular biologist, educator, academic administrator; b. Las Vegas, N.Mex., Aug. 7, 1947; d. John Dias and Drucilla (Jaramillo) V.; m. Anthony Leader Komaroff, June 18, 1970. BA, Goucher Coll., 1970; PhD, MIT, 1975; DSc (hon.), U. St. Thomas U., 1996, Pine Manor Coll., 1997; PhD (hon.), Goucher Coll., 1997. Rsch. fellow Harvard U., Cambridge, 1975-78; asst. prof. dept. microbiology U. Mass. Med. Ctr., Worcester, 1978-81, assoc. prof. dept. molecular genetics micro, 1982-85; assoc. prof. dept. neurology Harvard Med. Sch., Boston, 1986-95; sr. rsch. assoc. neurology Children's Hosp., Boston, 1985-95, assoc. dir. mental retardation rsch. ctr., 1987-94; prof. dept. neurology Northwestern U., Evanston, Ill., 1995—2002, assoc. v.p. rsch., 1995-97, v.p. rsch., 1998—2002; v.p. for rsch., COO, Whitehead Inst. for Biomed. Rsch. Cambridge, Mass., 2003—05; chief sci. officer Cytonome, Inc., 2005—. Mem. mammalian genetics study sect. NIH, 1982-84, mem. reviewers rsch., 1989, mem. neurol. disorders program project rev. com., 1989-94; mem. adv. bd. Biol. Sci. Directorate, NSF, 1994-99; bd. dirs. Nat. Ctr. Genome Rsch., 1995-00, TransKaryotic Therapies, 2003-05, chair 2005; mem. adv. coun. Nat. Inst. Neurol. Disorders and Stroke, NIH, 2000-04; bd. trustees Pine Manor Coll., 2004—; lectr. sr. lectr. Sloan Sch. Mgmt. MIT, 2003--05 Contbr. articles and abstracts to profl. jour.; patentee in field. Recipient Hispanic Engr. Nat. Achievement award, 1992, Nat. Achievement award Hispanic Mag., 1996; inducted Hispanic Engr. Nat. Achievement Hall of Fame, 1999; selected 50 most important Hispanics by "business & Tech., Hispanic Engr. & Info. Tech." mag. 2003; Helen Hay Whitney Found. fellow, 1975-78; NIH grantee, 1978-85, 89-96. Mem. AAAS (bd. dirs. 2000-05), Am. Soc. Microbiology, Assn. for Women in Sci., Soc. for Neurosci., Am. Soc. Cell Biology, Soc. for Advancement Chicanos and Native Ams. in Sci. (founding, bd. dir. 1987-93, v.p. 1990-93). Office Phone: 617-330-5030 ext. 354. Business E-Mail: lvk@alum.mit.edu.

**VILLANO, MARK ANTHONY,** minister; b. New Haven, Conn. s. Anthony and Mary Villano. BA, Cath. U. of Am., 1982, MDiv, 1987; MFA, U. So. Calif., 1994. Documentary dir. Human Family Edn. Cultural Inst., Pacific Palisades, Calif., 1991—95; dir. of creative develop. Paulist Prodns., Pacific Palisades, 1994—95; assoc. dir. U. Cath. Ctr. - UCLA, 1996—98,

Ohio State U.- Newman Ctr., 1998—2002; lectr. Ohio State U., 2000—02; assoc. chaplain Cath. Ctr. at Yale, 2002—; lectr. Yale U., 2004—. Bd. dirs. Paulist Prodns., 1992—98. Bd. dirs Hillhouse Scholars Program, 2002—04. Mem.: Univ. Film and Video Assn., Cath. Campus Min. Assn. Avocations: screenwriting, film theory, production. Business E-Mail: mark.villano@yale.edu.

**VILLANO, STEPHEN PAUL,** lawyer; b. Fort Meade, Md., Aug. 29, 1961; s. Michael Charles and Clair Elizabeth Villano; m. Christina Groll. BS, U. Colo., 1982; JD, Hastings Coll. Law, 1986. Assoc. Holland & Hart LLP, Denver, 1986—91, of counsel, 1997—99, ptnr., 2000—; counsel Jones Intercable, Inc., Englewood, Colo., 1992—97. Bd. dirs. Mile High chpt. ARC, Denver, 2006—. Office: Holland & Hart 555 17th St Ste 3200 Denver CO 80202 Office Phone: 303-295-8000. Office Fax: 303-295-8261.

**VILLANUEVA, DANIEL D.,** former communications executive, investment company executive; b. Tucumcari, N.Mex. children: Daniel L. Jr., James. Grad., N.Mex. State U., 1961, PhD (hon.), Calif. Lutheran U. Kicker LA Rams, NFL, Dallas Cowboys; station mgr. KMEX-TV, LA, gen. mgr., v.p., pres.; sr. v.p. Spanish Internat. Comm. Corp., 1971—86; co-founder Univision, executive positions, 1986—90; co-founder Bastion Capital Fund, 1990; ptnr. RC Fontis Partners; chmn. Integrated Water Resources. Named to Hall of Fame, Acad. TV Arts & Sciences. Office: RC Fontis Partners 55 S Lake Ave Pasadena CA 91101*

**VILLANUEVA, DANIEL L., JR.,** investment company executive; m. Judy Villanueva; 3 children. BS, Stanford U. Co-founder Radio Am., Inc., Mova, Villanueva & Associates, Inc.; pres. LA Galaxy, MLS; CEO Crown Services; ptnr. Bastion Capital Fund.; co-founding ptnr. Fontis Ventures, 2002; now ptnr. RC Fontis Partners; v.p. Villanueva Companies. Office: RC Fontis Partners 55 S Lake Ave Pasadena CA 91101*

**VILLARAIGOSA, ANTONIO R.,** mayor; b. East LA, Jan. 23, 1953; m. Corina Raigosa, 1987; children: Marisela, Prisila, Antonio Jr., Natilia Fe. BA in History, UCLA, 1977; JD, People's Coll. of Law, 1985. Mem. Calif. State Assembly, 1995—2001, Dem. whip and mem. appropriations and budget coms., majority leader, 1997, speaker, 1998—2001; city councilman, dist. 14 LA City Coun., 2003—05; mayor City of LA, 2005—. Mem. LA Met. Transp. Bd., 1990—94; nat. co-chair Kerry Presdl. Campaign, 2003—04; chair LA City Coun. Transp. Com.; bd. dirs. Met. Transit Authority. Mem. Greater Eastside Voter Registration and Edn. Project, Jobs with Peace, LAUSD Mex. Am. Edn. Commn., L.A. Ctr. for Law and Justice. Named one of 25 Most Influential Hispanics, Time Mag., 2005. Achievements include first Latino mayor for LA since Cristobal Aguilar left office in 1872. also: Ste 3200 725 S Figueroa St Los Angeles CA 90017-5432 Office: Office of Mayor City Hall 200 North Spring St Los Angeles CA 90012*

**VILLAREAL, PATRICIA J.,** lawyer; b. Sonora, Calif., Aug. 27, 1951; BA in Polit. sci., Mount Vernon Coll., 1975; JD, Harvard U., 1980. Bar: Tex. 1980. Law clk. to Judge H. Barefoot Sanders U.S. Dist. Ct. (no. dist.) Tex., 1980-82; mem. Jones Day (formerly Jones, Day, Reavis & Pogue), Dallas; ptnr. and chair, new assoc. recruiting Jones Day, Dallas. Spl. asst. Ho. Reps. Judiciary Com., 1975-77 Office: Jones Day 2727 N Harwood St Dallas TX 75201-1515 Office Phone: 214-969-2973. Business E-Mail: pjvillareal@jonesday.com.

**VILLARINI, AWILDA,** musician, composer, music educator; d. Angel Gabriel Villarini and Ana Luisa Garcia. MusM, Peabody Conservatory, Balt., 1974; profl. studies Juilliard Sch., N.Y.C., 1976; MA, NYU, 1997, PhD, 1999. Adj. prof. Coll. of New Rochelle, N.Y.C., 1982—83; piano prof. Greenwich House of Music, N.Y.C., 1982—87; musical dir. Musica Para Inst., Caquas, PR, 1987—93; adj. prof. Hostos C.C., CUNY, N.Y.C., 1996—98; tchg. fellowship NYU, N.Y.C., 1996—97; facilitator Boricua Coll., N.Y.C., 2002—03; piano prof. A Child's Voice, N.Y.C., 2003—. Musical dir. Crossover Artists, Inc., N.Y.C., 2004—; commr. Louis Vogelstein Found., NEA, Inst. de Cultura Puertorriguena. Recipient Dist. Artist award, Artist Internat., 1985, Recording prize, CRI, 1999; grant, Ford Found., 1976. Mem.: Internat. Alliance for Women in Music, Am. Music Ctr., NY Women Composers. E-mail: villariniawilda@yahoo.com.

**VILLARINO, MARIO ALBERTO,** veterinarian, researcher; b. Navojoa, Mex., Jan. 15, 1971; arrived in U.S., 1996; s. Luis Enrique Villarino and Marina Gutierrez; m. Leah A. Larsen, July 8, 2000. DVM, U. Nacional Autonoma Mexico, 1996; PhD, Tex. A&M U., 2000. Mktg. assoc. Hoechst-Mex., Mexico, 1993—94; assoc. prof. U. Nacional Autonoma Mexico, Mexico, 1994—96; tchg. asst. Tex. A&M U., Coll. Station, Tex., 1996—2000, postdoctoral rsch. assoc., 2000—03, extension rsch. assoc., 2003—. Contbr. articles to profl. jours. Fellow: U. Nacional Autonoma Mexico, 1998—2000, Tex. Agrl. Exptl. Sta., 2000—. Mem.: Assn. local de Ganaderos (adv. 1998—), Grad. Students Assn. (v.p. 1999—2000), South Tex. Aquarium Club (pres. 2000). Avocations: guitar, piano, carpentry. Home: 874 Prince Ln Rockwall TX 75087-9719 E-mail: cattletick@hotmail.com.

**VILLAROSA, SHARI,** ambassador; BA in Internat. Studies, U. NC, Chapel Hill; JD, Coll. William and Mary. Diplomat in residence East-West Ctr., Honolulu; desk officer Office Investment Affairs US Dept. State, Washington, Singapore and Indonesia desk officer, dep. dir. Office Burma, Cambodia, Laos, Thailand and Vietnam Affairs, spl. asst. to undersecretary econ. affairs, dir. Philippines, Malaysia, Brunei, Singapore Affairs, East Asia and Pacific Bur., US chargé d'Affairs in Burma Rangoon, 2005—. Office: DOS Amb 4250 Rangoon Pl Washington DC 20521-4250*

**VILLARREAL, CARLOS CASTAÑEDA,** engineering executive; b. Brownsville, Tex., Nov. 9, 1924; s. Jesus Jose and Elisa L. (Castañeda) Villarreal; m. Doris Ann Akers, Sept. 10, 1948 (dec. 1992); children: Timothy Hill, David Akers; m. June Ricchezza McElroy, Oct. 3, 2002. BS, U.S. Naval Acad., 1948; MS, U.S. Navy Postgrad. Sch., 1950; LLD (hon.), St. Mary's U., 1972. Registered profl. engr. Commd. ensign U.S. Navy, 1949, advanced through grades to lt., 1956; comdg. officer U.S.S. Rhea, 1951, U.S.S. Osprey, 1952; comdr. Mine Divsn. 31, 1953; instr. elec. engring. U.S. Naval Acad., 1954—56; resigned, 1956; mgr. marine and indsl. operation Gen. Electric Co., 1956—66; v.p. mktg. and adminstrn. Marquardt Corp., 1966—69; adminstr. Urban Mass Transit Adminstrn., Dept. Transp., Washington, 1969—73; commr. Postal Rate Commn., 1973—79; vice chmn., 1975—79; v.p. Washington ops. Wilbur Smith and Assocs., 1979—84, sr. v.p., 1984—86, exec. v.p., 1987—, also bd. dirs. Lectr. in field; mem. industry sector adv. com. Dept. Commerce; mem. sect. 13 adv. com. Dept. Transp., 1983—86. Contbr. articles to profl. jours. Mem. devel. com. Wolftrap Farm Pk. Performing Arts, 1973—78; bd. edn. St. Elizabeth Sch.; bd. dirs. Assoc. Cath. Charities, 1982—86; chmn. fin. com. Cath. Charities, USA; coun. mem. St. Elizabeth Ch., 1982—86, chmn. fin. com.; active John Carrol Soc. Decorated knight Sovereign Mil. Hospitaller Order St. John of Jerusalem of Rhodes and Malta, knight equestrian Order of Holy Sepulchre of Jerusalem, knight comdr.; recipient award Outstanding Achievement, Dept. Transp. Fellow: ASCE, Am. Cons. Engrs. Coun. (vice chmn. interna. com.); mem.: NSPE (pres. DC soc. 1986—87, bd. dirs. 1988—91), IEEE, Intelligent Transp. Soc. Am. (chmn. fin. com.), Inst. Traffic Engrs., Inst. World Politics, Internat. Bridge, Tunnel and Turnpike Assn., Washington Soc. Engrs., Transp. Rsch. Bd., Am. Rds. and Transp. Builders Assn. (chmn. pub. transp. adv. coun.), Soc. Am. Mil. Engrs., Soc. Naval Archs. and Marine Engrs., Am. Pub. Transit Assn., Army-Navy Club (pres. 1999—2004), Univ. Club. Republican. Roman Catholic. Office: Wilbur Smith Assocs 300 Williams Dr Ste 300 Fairfax VA 22031 Office Phone: 703-648-9780. Business E-Mail: cvillarreal@wilbursmith.com.

**VILLARREAL, JUNE PATRICIA,** retired sales executive; b. Atlantic City, Sept. 26, 1929; d. Edmund N. and Dorothy R. (McDowell) Ricchezza; m. Ottavio Gelmi, Dec. 16, 1954 (div. 1964); 1 child, Alessandra; m. Robert Joseph McElroy, Oct. 16, 1970 (dec. May 1974); m. Carlos Castañeda

Villarreal, Oct. 3, 2002. Student, Temple U., 1947-48, Georgetown U., 1951-53. Staff mem. Am. Consulate Gen., Milan, 1954; legis. asst. U.S. Senate, Washington, 1956; social sec. Amb. of Finland, Washington, 1958; adminstrv. asst., translator Roosevelt and Clark Lobbyists, 1958—59; legis. asst. to congressman Washington, 1960-65; sr. assoc. Gillmore M. Perry Co., Washington, 1965-76; sales exec., cons., 1980-87; ptnr. Mfrs. Representatives Internat., Washington, 1987-97; ret. Pres. Spanish-Portugese Study Group, 1994—95. Mem.: Alliance Française, D.C. League Rep. Women, Pan Am. Round Table, John Carroll Soc., Georgetown U. Alumni Assn., Equestrian Order Holy Sepulchre of Jerusalem (Lady Comdr. 2003—), Army Navy Club (Washington). Republican. Roman Catholic. Home: 4000 Cathedral Ave NW Apt 208B Washington DC 20016-5254 Personal E-mail: jprvilla@verizon.net.

**VILLARREAL, ROBERTO ESCAMILLA,** retired political science researcher, educator, administrator; b. Karnes City, Tex., Oct. 20, 1936; s. Epifanio Sr. and Antonia (Escamilla) V.; m. Norma Pedraza, June 12, 1965; children: Marco Dante, Carlo Renato, Ethel Minerva. BS, Tex. A&I U., 1962, MS, 1966; MA, U. Okla., 1972, PhD, 1975. Tchr. Pawnee Ind. Sch. Dist., Tex., 1962-63, Pharr-San Juan-Alamo Ind. Sch. Dist., Tex., 1963-66; instr. Bee County Coll., Beeville, Tex., 1967-70, U. Okla., Norman, 1970-72; chmn. Bee County Coll., Dept. Social Scis., 1972-73; dir. Bee County Coll. Fed. Programs, 1973-76; prof. U. Tex. Polit Sci. Dept., El Paso, 1976—2003, chmn., 1987—, prof. emeritus, 2003—. Advisor U. Tex. System, Austin, 1990-91; assoc. v.p. acad. affairs U. Tex., El Paso, 1991-96; exec. dir. Internat. Consortium for Health and Environ. Security, 2003— Author: Chicano Elites and Non-Elites, 1979; author/editor: Latino Empowerment, 1988, Latinos and Political Coalitions, 1991. Mem. exec. com. Hispanic Leadership Inst., El Paso, 1989— Recipient Ford Found. fellowship, 1979-71, Disting. Svc. award U. Tex., El Paso, 1985, Outstanding Achievement award in edn. Mex. Am. Bar Assn., 1991; Fulbright scholar, Mex., 1998-99; named one of 100 Most Influential Hispanics in U.S., Hispanic Bus., Mag., 1997 Mem. Nat. Assn. Chicano Studies (exec. officer 1985-86), Am. Assn. for Higher Edn. (chair Hispanic Caucus 199), Tex. Assn. Coll. Tchrs. (v.p. 1979-80, pres. 1980-82) Democrat. Roman Catholic. Home: 172 Oak Fields Dr Floresville TX 78114 Office: AFIOH/RSRH 2513 Kennedy Cir Brooks City-Base TX 78235-5226 Office Phone: 210-710-8698. Personal E-mail: revilla@tgti.net.

**VILLARRUBIA, GLENDA BOONE,** reading specialist, reading coordinator, educational consultant, educator; d. Albert Jewel and Tommie Lee Boone; m. David Daniel Villarrubia, Apr. 2, 1977; children: David Daniel Jr., Steven Joseph, John Albert. BA, Southeastern La. U., 1976, MBA, 1978. La. Teaching Certificate 1976, Reading Specialist Certification 1978, Behavior Specialist Certification 2000. Tchr. Wash. Parish Schools, Franklinton, La., 1976—79; tchr./coord. Jefferson Parish Schools, New Orleans, 1979; tchr. Ouachita Parish, Monroe, La., 1980; tchr. edn. Bogalusa City Schools, La., 1981—82, tchr., 1982—96, individualized edn. program cons., 1999—2005, individualized. program facilitator, resource teachers spl. edn., 1998—2000, dir./supr. spl. edn., 2000—01, individualized edn. program facilitator, 2001—04, compliance monitoring facilitator, 2005—. Spl. edn. cons., 2000; owner The Tchrs. Desk, 1989—99. Mem. Crisis Prevention Inst.; troop supporter Bogalusa, La., 2002—05; tiger cub leader Boy Scouts Am. Bogalusa, 1985; 4-H leader sponsor Bogalusa City Schools, 1985; beta club leader Wash. Parish Schools, 1977. Recipient Tchr. of Yr., Bogalusa City Schools, 1983, 1993, La. Dept. Edn., 1992. Mem.: Associated Profl. Educators of La., La. Pub. Sch. Rels. Assn., La. Ednl. Rsch. Assn., La. Assn. Supervision and Curriculum Devel., La. Assn. Educators, Learning Disability Assn., La. Assn. Sch. Execs., Nat. Edn. Assn., Coun. Exceptional Children, Southeastern La. Alumni Assn., Alpha Signa Tau. Avocations: travel, gardening, church, reading. Home: 21486 Hwy 436 Bogalusa LA 70427 Office Phone: 985-281-2148. Personal E-Mail: glenda90@hotmail.com.

**VILLAVECES, JAMES WALTER,** allergist, immunologist, consultant; b. San Luis Obispo, Calif., Nov. 4, 1933; s. Robert and Solita (Combariza) V. BA, UCLA, 1955; MD, U. Calif. Med. Sch., 1960. Diplomate Am. Bd. Allergy and Immunology. Intern Sawtelle VA Hosp., L.A., 1960-61; preceptorship in adult allergy L.A. County Hosp., L.A., 1964-66; fellow in allergy White Meml. CCM, L.A., 1966-67; chief allergy divsn. Ventura (Calif.) Med. Ctr., 1969-87; practice medicine specializing in allergy-immunology Ventura 1984—. Founder botanical weed allergy walks, 1970; cons. in allergy/immunology, Blue Cross, 1991-96; medical invention cons., Inventor Internat., Inc.; inventor, cons. Sprixx: Alcohol-gel Clip on Dispensers, 2001; mem. Pharmacy and Therapeutics Com., Wellpoint (Blue Cross Calif.) Inc., 1991-96; prodr. Ventura County cities street-tree guide for asthma patients; peer reviewer Blue Cross So. Calif. Wellpoint, 1980, 1994-95; cons., lectr., peer reviewer in field. Writer, prodr., editor films; contbr. articles on biology of pollens and molds of Ventura County to profl. jours.; patentee in field. Bd. dirs. Am. Lung Assn., Ventura, 1969-85, pres., 1974, advisor air pollution control com., 1971-74; judge Ventura Sci. Fair, 1970-85; lectr. in field. Recipient commendation County Bd. Suprs., Ventura, 1974; named one of Am.'s Top Physicians Consumers Rsch. Coun. Am., 2003-05. Fellow Am. Acad. Allergy, Asthma, Immunology, Am. Coll. Allergy, Asthma, Immunology; mem. Calif. Soc. Allergy-Immunology, Calif. Med. Assn., Ventura County Med. Assn., Gold Coast Tri-County Allergy Soc. (pres. 1987), Cal Club (hon.), Ventura County Sports Hall of Fame (mem. founding bd.), Mensa. Republican. Achievements include development of infection protection device for hospital and food service establishments. Avocations: writing, photography, lecturing, pistol target shooting, fishing. Home: 928 High Point Dr Ventura CA 93003-1415 Office: Dudley Profl Ctr 4080 Loma Vista Rd Ste M Ventura CA 93003-1811 Office Phone: 805-656-0453. Personal E-Mail: jvillavece@aol.com, jvillavece@yahoo.com.

**VILLELLA, EDWARD JOSEPH,** dancer, choreographer, performing arts association executive; b. LI, NY, Oct. 1, 1936; s. Joseph and Mildred (DeGiovanni) Villella; m. Janet Greschler (div.); 1 child, Roddy; m. Linda Carbonetta; children: Christa Francesca, Lauren. BS in Marine Transp., NY State Maritime Coll., 1957; LHD (hon.), Boston Conservatory, 1985, degree (hon.), Union Coll., Schenectady, N.Y., 1991; DHL (hon.), St. Thomas U., Miami, Fla., 1994, U. SC, 1997; DFA (hon.), SUNY Maritime Coll., Bronx, 1998; Doctor (hon.), Fla. Atlantic U., 2000, U. NC, Asheville, 2002, Coll. Charleston, 2002; degree (hon.), LI U., 2005. Mem. N.Y.C. Ballet, 1957, soloist, 1958—60, prin. soloist, 1960—83; artistic dir. Ballet Okla., Oklahoma City, 1983—86; founding artistic dir., CEO Miami (Fla.) City Ballet, 1985—. Vis. artist U.S. Mil. Acad., West Point, 1981—82; vis. artist Salute to Balanchine residency Harvard U., 1999—2000; vis. prof. dance U. Iowa, 1981; resident Heritage chair arts and cultural criticism George Mason U.; Dorthy F. Schmidt artist-in-residence Coll. of Arts and Letters, 2000—01. Dancer Symphony C., Scotch Symphony, We. Symphony, Donizetti Variations, Swan Lake, La Source, The Nutcracker, Agon, Stars and Stripes, The Prodigal Son, The Figure in the Carpet, 1960, Electronics, 1961, A Midsummer Night's Dream, 1962, Bugaku, 1963, Tarantella, 1964, Harlequinade, 1965, The Brahms-Schoenberg Quartet, 1966, Jewels, 1967, Symphony in Three Movements, 1972, Schéhérazade, 1975, choreographer Harlequinade, 1966, Shostakovich Ballet Suite, 1972, Shenandoah, 1975, Gayane Pas de Deux, 1972, Salute to Code, 1973, Sea Chanties, 1974, Prelude, Riffs and Fugues, 1980, dancer TV The Ed Sullivan Show, Bell Telephone Hour, Mike Douglas Show, TV spl. Harlequin, 1975 (Emmy award); co-author (autobiography): Prodigal Son, 1991. Mem. Nat. Coun. Arts, 1968—74; chmn. Commn. for Cultural Affairs, N.Y.C., 1978; bd. visitors N.C. Sch. for Arts; mem. adv. panel Nat. Endowment for Arts; trustee Wolf Trap Found. for Arts. Named Miamian of Yr., UNICO Nat., 1993, Miracle Maker, Big Bros. Big Sisters of Greater Miami, 2003; named to Fla. Artists Hall of Fame, 1997, Dance Hall of Fame, 2004; recipient Dance Mag. award, 1964, Lions of Performing Arts award, N.Y. Pub. Libr., 1987, Capezio Dance award, 1989, Gold medal, Nat. Soc. Arts and Letters, 1990, William G. Anderson Merit award, AAHPERD, 1991, Nat. Medal of Arts award, 1997, Kennedy Ctr. Honors, 1997, Cultural Soc. award, Bklyn. Ctr. for Performing Arts at Bklyn.

Coll., 1998, Am. Irreplaceable Dance Treasures: The First 100, Disting. Achievement award, U. Fla., 2005, U. Fla. Coll. Fine Arts, 2005; Robert J.H. Kiphuth fellow, Yale U., 2001, Hon. Theater Arts Br. fellow, U.S. Imperial Soc. Tchrs. Dancing, 2003.

**VILLENA-ALVAREZ, JUANITA I.,** language educator, consultant; b. Baguio, Philippines, Aug. 27; arrived in France, 1987, Spain, 1986; came to U.S., 1988; d. Juan J. V. and Milagros M.I.; m. Beda E. Alvarez, Jr., June, 1992; 1 child, Natalie Noelle. BA magna cum laude, U. Philippines, Quezon City, 1986; Magistère French Civilization, U. Paris, 1988; MA in French Lit., U. Cin., 1989, PhD in French Lit., 1994. Instr. French, Spanish U. Philippines, Quezon, 1986; grad. tchg. asst. U. Cin., 1988-93; instr. French Miami U., Oxford, Ohio, 1993; prof. French, Spanish, Global Studies U. S.C., Beaufort, 1994—, dir. liberal studies, 2003—04. Lang. cons. Software Clearing House, Cin., 1989-90, EGlobe2B, Beaufort, 2000; material devel. Judith Muyskens, Cin., 1988-90. Author: The Allegory of Literary Representation, 1997, Instructor Resources and Student Resources for Exito comml., 2001; creator more than 100 websites on teaching; contbr. article to profl. jour. Charles Phelps Taft fellow, 1993-94; recipient Rotary Amb. Goodwill Rotary Internat., 1987-88. Mem. MLA, Am. Assn. French Tchrs., S.C. Assn. Fgn. Lang. Tchrs., Alliance Française (Cin., lang. cons. 1993), French Circle (Beaufort, lang. coord. 1994—), Phi Kappa Phi. Avocations: writing, travel, translations. Office: U S C 801 Carteret St Beaufort SC 29902-4601

**VILLERS, PHILIPPE,** mechanical engineer; b. Paris, June 20, 1935; arrived in U.S., 1940, naturalized, 1946; s. Raymond and Garda (Schmidt) Villers; m. Annie Louise Young, July 13, 1957 (div. 1973); children Jocelyn Anne(dec.), Renata Jane; m. Katherine Stephan, 1973; children: Noel Stephan, Carolyn Grace. AB in Applied Scis. cum laude, Harvard U., 1955; SM in Mech. Engring., MIT, 1960. Mem. mfg. tng. program GE, 1955-58; project engr. Perkin-Elmer Corp., Wilton, Conn., 1959-62; project engr. Apollo Antenna pointings sensor Barnes Engring. Co., Stamford, Conn., 1962-65; project mgr. Advanced Products Ctr., Link Group, Gen. Precision, Inc., Binghamton, NY, 1965-67; mgr. advanced products Concord Control, Inc., Boston, 1967-69; co-founder, sr. v.p., dir. Computervision Corp., Bedford, Mass., 1969-80; founder, pres., dir. Automatix, Inc., Billerica, Mass., 1980-84; chmn. bd. Automatix Inc., Billerica, Mass., 1984-86; founder, pres., dir. Cognition Inc., 1985-88. Bd. dir. Xyvision, Inc., Wakefield, Mass., chmn., 1992—94; bd. dir. Grainpro Inc., Concord, Mass., pres. 1996—; bd. dir. Voxiva Inc., Mercy Corps, United Villages. Del. Dem. Nat. Conv., 1988, 1992; mem. Dem. Town Com., Wilton, 1963, Concord, Mass., 1978—, chmn., 1984—96; mem. Harvard Com. Univ. Resources, 1987-92; mem. various vis. coms. MIT, 1981—91; mem. vis. com. Nat. Bur. Stds., 1981—84; trustee U. Lowell, 1985—91; mem. adv. bd. Inst. Global Leadership Tufts U., Medford, Mass., 2005—; founder and pres. Families U.S.A. Founds. (formerly Villers Found.), Washington, 1981—, Bay State Retiree Vol. Coun., Concord, 1989—92. Grad. fellow, NSF, 1959—60. Mem.: ACLU (pres. com. 1981—, bd. dirs Physicians Human Rights 1991—94), ASME, IEEE, Soc. Mfg. Engrs., Unitarian-Universalist Assn. (pres. coun. 1982—86), Amnesty Internat. (bd. dirs. 1990—96, ombudsman 1992—96, mem. exec. com. 1994—96, mem. leadership coun. 1995—, coord. Concord group 15 1998—), Sigma Xi. Achievements include patents for process welding aluminum liners to steel surfaces; a horizon sensor for visible wavelength; infrared roughness testing instrument; improved thermopile construction thermal die marker; method for long term storage of a bulk biologically active commodity; solar sail applications for interpanetary probe propulsion and stabilization; method and apparatus for targetless wafer alignment; method and system for transporting and storing commodities. Home: 20 Whits End Rd Concord MA 01742-5411 Office: 200 Baker Ave Ste 309 Concord MA 01742-2170 Office Phone: 978-371-7400. Business E-Mail: pvillers@igc.org.

**VILLFORTH, JOHN CARL,** engineer, health physicist; b. Reading, Pa., Dec. 28, 1930; s. Carl and Grace L. (Fichthorn) Villforth; m. Joanne E. Heine, Sept. 12, 1953; children: Mary Jane Villforth Smith, Elaine, Jennifer Villforth Veazy. BS in San. Engring., Pa. State U., 1952, MS, 1954; MS in Physics, Vanderbilt U., 1958. Cert. Am. Bd. Health Physics. With USPHS, 1961-90; dir. Ctr. Devices and Radiol. Health, 1969-90, asst. surgeon gen., 1972-90, chief engr., 1985-89; pres. Food and Drug Law Inst., Washington, 1990—2001. Bd. dirs Vasogen Inc., EduNeering Inc. Served to capt. USAF, 1954—61, served to rear adm. USPHS, 1961—90. Decorated Disting. Svc. medal, Outstanding Svc. medal; recipient Outstanding Engring. Alumnus award, Pa. State U., 1987, Recognition award, HHS, 1987, Disting. Alumni award, FDA, 2000, Pa. State U., 2005; Univ. Alumni fellow, 2002. Mem.: USPHS Commd. Officers Assn. (chmn. bd. dirs. 1999—2000), Regulatory Affairs Profl. Soc., Internat. Radiation Protection Assn., Health Physics Soc. (pres. 1976—77, Elda Anderson award 1970), FDA Alumni Assn. (chmn. 2001—). Personal E-mail: jcvillforth@comcast.net. *Understand the problem! Too much energy is wasted and too many relationships are strained because we fail to understand the underlying problem before we embark on a solution.*

**VILLIA, MORRIS SABASTIAN,** music producer, publishing executive, writer; b. Plaquemine, La., Nov. 21, 1960; s. Morris Villia and Doretha Calloway. Student, Phillips Coll. Care initiator EMP Internat./FMP Am., New Orleans, 1985; music prod. MSV Record and Prod., New Orleans 1989—; writer/author MSV Prod. Inc., New Orleans, 1989—; exec. dir. Holographic Enterprises, 1986—; owner Sign and Logo Enterprises, New Orleans, 1997—98, MSV Record and Prod., New Orleans, La., 1990—, music cons. New Orleans, 1990—. Writer/cons. MSV Prod., Inc., New Orleans, 1990—, pub. adv., 1990—; mentor spkr. MSV Productions, Inc., New Orleans, 2000—. Author: (book) God Ghetto, 2000. Recipient hon. mention, World of Poetry, 1990, MSV Inc., 1989. Fellow: The Leukemia and Lymphoma, No. Am. Hunting Club; mem.: ASPCA. Avocations: writing, boxing. Home: PO Box 1650 Metairie LA 70004-1650 Office Phone: 504-849-1244.

**VILLINES, BENITA CURTIS,** language educator; b. Lewisburg, Tenn., June 8, 1953; d. George Edward and Edith Holbert Curtis; m. Harry Eugene Villines, May 24, 1975. BS, Mid. Tenn. State U., Murfreesboro, 1975, Med, 1981, Edn. Specialist, 1989. 5th and 6th grade tchr. Jones Sch., Lewisburg, Tenn., 1976—83; 6th-8th grade lang. arts tchr. Connelly Mid. Sch., Lewisburg, Tenn., 1983—97; 8th grade lang. arts tchr. Lewisburg Mid. Sch., 1997—. Lang. arts textbook com. Tenn. Dept. Edn., Nashville, 1997, Nashville, 2004; tech. coord. Lewisburg Mid. Sch., 1995—. Mem. vis. com. So. Assn. Schs. and Colls., Tenn., 1990. Named 21st Century Classroom Tchr., Marshall County Sch. Dist., 1998, Mid. Sch. Tchr. of Yr., 2002; Tech. grant, Tenn. Dept. Edn., 1997, Writing grant, Fed. Govt., 1998, Tech. grant, 2000. Mem.: Nat. Coun. Tchrs. English, Profl. Educators Tenn. Home: 3453 Clegg Dr Spring Hill TN 37174 Office: Lewisburg Middle Sch 500 Tiger Blvd Lewisburg TN 37091 Office Phone: 931-359-1265.

**VILLOCH, KELLY CARNEY,** art director; b. Kyoto, July 22, 1950; d. William Riley and stepdaughter Hazel Fowler Carney; m. Joe D. Villoch, Aug. 9, 1969; children: Jonathan, Christopher, Jennifer. A in Fine Arts, Dade C.C., Miami, Fla., 1971; student, Metro Fine Arts, 1973-74, Fla. Internat. U., 1985-88. Design asst. Lanvin, Miami, 1971—74, Fieldcrest, Miami, 1974-77; art dir. Advercolor, Miami, 1977-78; art dir. copywriter ABC, Miami, 1978-89; writer Armed Forces Radio & TV Network; multimedia dir. ADVITEC, 1989-91; art dir. writer Miami Write, 1979—89; owner Beach Point Prodns., 1992—; editor-in-chief L'Avenue Mag., 1998—. Lectr. Miami Dade C.C., coms. Studio Masters, North Miami, 1979-89; writer Lucent Techs., Telephonetics, Algorhythm, Inter-tel, 1997—; creative mktg. dir. Raintree Media, 2000. Prin. works include mixed media, 1974 (Best of Show 1974), pen and ink drawing, 1988 (Best Poster 1988); writer, dir., editor, prodr. (video film) Bif, 1988, Drink + Drive = Die, 1994; scriptwriter (film) The Raft, 1994, (charity video) Rosie O'Donnell, 2002; writer, dir., prodr. (pub. svc. announcement) Reading is the Real Adventure, 1990; film editor Talent Times Mag.; author: Winds of Freedom, 1994; art dir., exec. com. Miami Hispanic Media Conf., 1992, 93, 94; editor-in-chief, film editor In Grove Miami Mag., 1994-96; webmaster, web content provider, website design cons., writer, graphic artist Guru Comms., 1996; editor-in-chief L'Avenue Mag., Miami Mag., Fla. Journey and Miami Guide, 1998-99,

Paladar mag., 2002, Decasa mag., 2002, Flash Animation: Passionate Nomad-A Journey Through Cairo, 2002, Collins Ave. Mag., Markee Mag., 2006; web content provider WEBCOM; webmaster Miami Metro Mag., 2000; sr. editor Channels Intl. Mag., 2001; web site designer, multimedia dir.; creative mktg. dir. Light Sculptor Jim Morrison, 2005. State of Fla. grantee LimeLite Studios, Inc., 1990, William Douglas Pawley Found. grantee, Frances Wolfson scholar, Cultural Consortium grantee, 1993. Mem. Am. Film Inst., Phi Beta Kappa. Avocations: animation, printmaking, skin diving, boating, painting. Personal E-mail: villochk@bellsouth.net.

**VILLWOCK, KENNETH JAMES,** management company executive; b. Coral Gables, Fla., Jan. 9, 1953; s. Homer Samuel Short and Anna Villwock; m. Martha Lemus Medina, June 12, 1977; children: Theodore Elliott, Joshua James. BA, Golden Gate U., 1976; Th.M., Dallas Sem., 1980; MBA, North Tex. State U., 1985. Cert. purchasing mgr. Telemetry repair Kentron Hawaii, Ltd., Edwards AFB, Calif., 1975-76; subcontractor Dallas, 1976-80; fin. analyst, mgr. US Mktg., Unisys, Dallas, 1980-83, fin. ops. mgr., 1984-85; cash mgr. Corp. Treasury Unisys, Blue Bell, Pa., 1986-88; dir. pricing, bus. analysis U.S. Mktg., Unisys, Blue Bell, 1989; dir. fin., procurement, global customer svcs. Unisys, Blue Bell, 1990-95; dir. worldwide procurement Global Customer Svc., Unisys, Blue Bell, 1996-97; dir. Global Re-Sale Procurement, Unisys, Blue Bell, 1998-2000; pres. Emeritor, Inc., Upper Gwynedd, Pa., 2000—01; dir. global procurement Cendian Corp., Atlanta, 2001—02; CEO IEM Group, Inc., Atlanta, 2002—. Fin. planner Fin. Planning Source, Dallas, 1984-87. Youth dir. Scofield Meml. Ch., Dallas, 1979; Bible tchr. various chs., Dallas, Souderton, Pa., 1972-95; referee Whitpain Soccer Assn., Blue Bell, 1988-90; ranger Boys Brigade, Souderton, 1990-93; elder Calvary Ch. of Souderton, 1992. Staff sgt. USAF, 1971-75. Mem. Inst. of Supply Mgmt. Republican. Avocations: biblical studies, skiing, golf, tennis. Home and Office: 3003 Summit Blvd Ste 1500 Atlanta GA 30319 Office Phone: 678-485-1687, 404-460-7050. Business E-Mail: jim.villwock@iemcorp.com.

**VILMA, JONATHAN POLYNICE,** professional football player; b. Coral Gables, FL, Apr. 16, 1982; BS finance, U. Miami, 2004. Linebacker New York Jets, 2004—. Named NFL Defensive Rookie of the Yr., 2004; named to Pro Bowl, 2005. Office: New York Jets 26 Green St Newbury MA 01951-1708*

**VILSACK, THOMAS,** governor; b. Pitts., Dec. 31, 1950; adopted s. Bud and Dolly Vilsack; m. Christie Bell, Aug. 1973; children: Jess, Doug. B in History, Hamilton Coll., Clinton, N.Y., 1972; JD, Albany Law Sch., 1975. Pvt. practice, Mt. Pleasant, Iowa, 1975—87; mayor City of Mt. Pleasant, Iowa, 1987—92; mem. Iowa State Senate, 1992-98; gov. State of Iowa, 1999—. Chmn. Midwest Gov. Conf., Dem. Gov. Assn.; mem. Nat. Gov. Assn. (exec. com.). Founding mem. & former chmn. Governors Biotechnology Partnership; former chmn. Ethanol Coalition; bd. dir. United Way, Mt. Pleasant; former chmn. Midwest Governor's Conference. Mem. Mt. Pleasant C. of C. (pres.), Rotary (pres.). Democrat. Office: Office of the Governor State Capitol Bldg Des Moines IA 50319-0001 Office Phone: 515-281-5211. Office Fax: 515-281-6611.*

**VILTER, RICHARD WILLIAM, SR.,** retired internist, educator; b. Cin., Mar. 21, 1911; s. William Frederick and Clara (Bieler) V.; m. Sue Potter, Aug. 17, 1935 (dec. Aug. 2003); 1 son, Richard William, Jr. (dec.). AB, Harvard U., 1933, MD, 1937. Diplomate Am. Bd. Internal Medicine. Intern, resident internal medicine Cin. Gen. Hosp., 1937-42, founding dir. divsn. hematology/oncology, 1945-56, asst. dir. dept. internal medicine, 1953-56, dir., 1956-78; assoc. prof. medicine U. Cin. Coll. Medicine, 1948-56, Gordon and Helen Hughes Taylor prof., 1956-78, prof. medicine on spl. assignment, 1978-81, prof. medicine emeritus, 1981—, asst. dean, 1945-51; ret., 1981. Cons. VA, 1947—; cons. hematology Good Samaritan Hosp., Cin.; cons. physician Christ, Drake hosps., Cin.; mem. sci adv. bd. Nat. Vitamin Found., 1953-56; spl. cons. nutritional anemias in Egypt WHO, 1954; cons. Pan Am. Sanitary Bur. Anemias of Kashiorkor in Guatemala and Panama, 1955; mem. Am. Cancer Soc. Com. on Investigation and Therapy of Cancer, 1960-64, chmn. 1964; chmn. hematology sect. NIH, 1965-69, chmn. nat. adv. com. anemia malnutrition Rsch. Ctr. Chiengmai, Thailand, 1967-75. Assoc. editor Jour. Clin. Investigation, 1951-52; contbr. to profl. publs. Recipient Joseph Goldberger award AMA, 1960, Daniel Drake medal U. Cin., 1985, Golden Apple award U. Cin., 1985, award for excellence U. Cin., 1990, Daniel Drake Humanitarian award Acad. Medicine, Cin., 1991, 1st recipient U. Cin. Coll. Medicine Lifetime Tchg. award, 1995, Great Living Cin. award Cin. C. of C., 2005; Richard W. and Sue P. Vilter endowed professorship U. Cin. Coll. Medicine est. and funded 1999. Master ACP (past gov. Ohio bd. regents, sec. gen. 1973-78, pres.-elect 1978-79, pres. 1979-80, pres. emeritus 1984, Laureat award Ohio chpt. 2002); mem. Federated Coun. for Internal Medicine (chmn. 1979-80), Clin. and Climatol. Assn. (v.p. 1982-83), Assn. Am. Physicians, Am. Soc. Clin. Nutrition (pres. 1960-61), Am. Soc. Clin. Investigation, Ctrl. Soc. Clin. Rsch. (coun. mem. 1957-60), Am. Soc. Hematology, Am. Bd. Nutrition, Internat. Soc. Hematology, Cin. Lit. Club (pres. 1990-91), Phi Beta Kappa, Alpha Omega Alpha, Nu Sigma Nu. Home: 5 Annwood Ln Cincinnati OH 45206-1419 Office: U Cin Med Ctr Cincinnati OH 45267-0001 Office Phone: 513-558-3828. Business E-Mail: vilterr@ucmail.uc.edu.

**VIÑAS, RICHARD ROCULAN,** non-commissioned officer; s. Ricardo Villa and Ildelita Roculan Viñas; m. Lori Noelani Lee, Mar. 23, 1995; 1 child, Mikaela Lee. Grad., Mira Mesa H.S., San Diego, 1997. Commd. ensign USN, 2001; ops. specialist USS Russell, 2001—, tng. supr., 2005—06. Decorated Global War on Terrorism Expeditionary medal, Nat. Def. medal, Navy Achievement medal,, Good Conduct medal. Avocation: golf.

**VINATIERI, ADAM MATTHEW,** professional football player; b. Yanktown, South Dakota, Dec. 28, 1972; s. Paul and Judy; m. Valerie Vinatieri. BS in Fitness and Wellness, S. Dakota State. Kicker New England Patriots, 1996—2006, Ind. Colts, 2006—. Named to AFC Pro-Bowl Team, 2003—04. Achievements include kicked game winning field goal in Super Bowl XXXVI, XXXVIII; being a member of Super Bowl Champion New England Patriots, 2001, 2003, 2004. Office: Ind Colts 7001 W 56th St Indianapolis IN 46254*

**VINCE, CLINTON ANDREW,** lawyer; b. Bklyn., May 31, 1949; s. Tibor Andrew and Priscilla (Ward) V.; divorced; children: Matthew McHale, Jennifer Ann. AB, Trinity Coll., 1971; JD, Georgetown U., 1974. Bar: N.Y. 1975, U.S. Dist. Ct. (so. and ea. dists.) N.Y. 1975, U.S. Ct. Appeals (2nd cir.) 1975, D.C. 1976, U.S. Dist. Ct. D.C. 1976, U.S. Ct. Appeals (D.C. and 8th cirs.) 1976, U.S. Supreme Ct. 1979, U.S. Ct. Appeals (4th and 11th cirs.) 1984, U.S. Ct. Appeals (5th cir.) 1985, U.S. Ct. Appeals (10th cir.) 1988. Ptnr. Verner, Liipfert, Bernhard, McPherson & Hand, Washington, 1984—2001; mem. and ptnr. D.C. office Sullivan & Worcester, LLP, 2001—; mng. ptnr., dir. energy group, 2001—. Chief energy cons. City of New Orleans, 1983—; gen. counsel Southeastern Power Resources Com., Tucker, Ga., 1986—; Editor in chief: Energy Law Jour. of the EBA, 2004—05. Bd. dirs. Fed. City Coun., bd. trustees Keystone Energy. Mem.: ATLA, ABA, D.C. Bar Assn, Fed. Energy Bar Assn. (former chmn. bd. dir., chmn. Fed. Energy Law Jour. Found.), Econ. Club Washington, Cosmos Club. Avocations: sailing, skiing, tennis, literature, writing. Office: Sullivan & Worcester LLP 1666 K St NW Ste 700 Washington DC 20006 E-mail: cvince@sandw.com.

**VINCENSI, AVIS A.,** sales executive, medical educator; b. Hazardville, Conn., July 10, 1949; d. George P. Vincensi and Hilda G. (Boucher) Vincensi(dec.). AS in Bus., Holyoke (Mass.) CC, 1987. Registered diagnostic med. sonographer, radiologic tech, radiography, mammography. X-ray technologist Baystate Med. Ctr., Springfield, Mass., 1969—73, Cooley Dickinson Hosp., Northampton, Mass., 1971—73, Holyoke Hosp., 1974—87, sonographer, 1973—82; sonographer, supr. Providence Hosp., Holyoke, 1982—87; sonographer Diagnostic Imaging, Springfield, Mass., 1987—90; product specialist/product mktg. sales Corometrics Med. Sys., Wallingford, Conn.,

1991—96; diagnostic reagent rep. Sigma Diagnostics, St. Louis, 1996—2002; clin. adj. prof. Springfield Tech. CC, 1999—2002, assoc. prof., 2002—06, bd. dirs., 1999—2006, chair dept. sonography, 2002—06; staff sonographer Hartford (Conn.) Hosp., 2006—. Recipient 2 Gold medals and 1 Silver medal Tai Chi competition, 2002. Mem.: Am. Inst. Ultrasonic Medicine, Am. Registry Diagnostic Med. Sonographers. Home: 101 Acushnet Ave Springfield MA 01105-2218 E-mail: avincensi@harthosp.org.

**VINCENT, CHARLES EAGAR, JR.,** sportswriter; b. Beaumont, Tex., Mar. 24, 1940; s. Charles Eagar and Hazel Ruth (Balston) V.; m. Mary Jacquelyn Bertman, Aug. 8, 1959 (div. Jan. 1969); children: Lisa Marie, Dixie Ann, Charles Joseph, John Patrick; m. Patricia Helene Skinner, Mar. 28, 1970 (div. Apr. 1985); 1 child, Susanna Lee; m. Karen Judith Peterson, Aug. 17, 1985. Student, Victoria Coll., 1958-59. Reporter Victoria (Tex.) Mirror, 1958-59, Taylor (Tex.) Daily Press, 1959-60; sports writer Beaumont (Tex.) Jour., 1960-62; sports editor Galveston (Tex.) Tribune, 1962-63; sports writer San Antonio Express-News, 1963-69, Sandusky (Ohio) Register, 1969-70, Detroit Free Press, 1970-85, sports columnist, 1985-99. Author: Welcome to My World, 1994, Broken Wings, 1998, Men of Courage; Women of Strength, 2004; co-author: (with Richard Bak) The Corner, A Century of Memories at Michigan and Trumbull, 1999. Recipient 4th Pl. award Nat. AP Sports Editors, 1981, 5th Pl., 1989, 92, Sister Mary Leila Meml. award, 1991, Mich. Writer of the Yr. award, 1991, 97; Afro-Am. Night honoree, 1991, Mich. Columnist of Yr. award, 1991, 97; Afro-Am. Night honoree, 1991, Mich. Writer of the Yr. Nat. Sportscasters and Sportswriters, 1998. Mem.: Baseball Writers Assn. Am. Avocations: travel, cooking, genealogy. Personal E-mail: Vincentcharlie@hotmail.com.

**VINCENT, CHRISTINE,** academic administrator; m. David Chambers; 2 children. BA in visual arts, Ill. State U. Founder Cmty. & Cultural Resource Devel. Inc., N.Y.C.; dep. dir. Ford Found., N.Y.C., 1991—2001; pres. Maine Coll. Art, Portland, 2001—. Office: Office of President Maine College of Art 97 Spring St Portland ME 04101

**VINCENT, D. CHRISTOPHER,** history educator; s. Donald Cummings Vincent and LeeAnn Franco; m. Cynthia May Shaw, June 20, 1981; children: Sarah Carolyn, Kevin Stapff. BS in Bus. Adminstrn., N. Adams State Coll., Mass., 1985—91; BA in Interdisciplinary Studies, Mass. Coll. Liberal Arts, N. Adams, 1996—97; MEd, U. Phoenix, Ariz., 2000—02. Cert. social studies tchr. Mass. Bd. Edn., 1999. Computer operator Berkshire Bank and Trust, Conifer Computer Group, Pittsfield, Mass., 1981—83; computer programmer Maybary Assoc., Pittsfield, 1983—83, Berkshire Mut. Ins. Co., Pittsfield, 1984—91, mgr., automated svcs., 1991—96; history tchr. Hoosac Valley HS Adams-Cheshire Regional Sch. Dist., Cheshire, 1998—. Non credit instr., computer skills Berkshire CC, Pittsfield, 1986—88; instr., am. mgmt. courses Mass. Coll. Liberal Arts, North Adams, 1995—99. Visitation assessment com. New Eng. Assn. Schools and Colleges, North Adams, 2002—02; commdr., royal rangers outpost Assemblies of God, Pittsfield, 1994—2006; ch. treas. Christian Assembly Ch., Pittsfield, 1986—90, fin. com. mem., 2005—06. Recipient Outstanding Svc., So. New Eng. Dist. Royal Rangers, 2003, 2005, Sr. Commanders award, 2000, 2001, 2003, 2004, 2005, Sectional Commanders award, So. New Dist. Royal Rangers, 2003, 2004, Dist. Staff award, So. New Eng. Dist. Royal Rangers, 2004, 2005, Tng. Saber, 2005. Pentecostal. Avocations: sailing, camping, bicycling, travel. Home: 107 Burke Ave Pittsfield MA 01201 Office: Hoosac Valley HS 125 Savoy Rd Cheshire MA 01201 Office Phone: 413-743-5200.

**VINCENT, DAVID RIDGELY,** financial consultant; b. Detroit, Aug. 9, 1941; s. Charles Ridgely and Charlotte Jane (McCarroll) Vincent; m. Margaret Helen Anderson, Aug. 25, 1962 (div. 1973); children: Sandra Lee, Cheryl Ann; m. Judith Ann Gomez, July 2, 1979; children: Amber, Jesse Joseph Flores(dec.) 1 stepchild, Micheal Flores Jr. BSBA, Calif. State U., Sacramento, 1964; MBA, Calif. State U., Hayward, 1971; PhD, Somerset U., 1991. Cert. profl. cons. to mgmt. Sr. ops. analyst Aerojet Gen. Corp., Sacramento, 1960-66; contr. Hexcel Corp., Dublin, Calif., 1966-70; mng. dir. Memorex, Vienna, 1970-74; sales mgr. Ampex World Ops., Friebourg, Switzerland, 1974-76; dir. product mgmt. NCR, Sunnyvale, Calif., 1976-79; v.p. Boole & Babbage Inc., Sunnyvale, 1979-85; gen. mgr. Inst. Info. Mgmt., Sunnyvale Calif., Calif., 1979-85; pres., CEO The Info. Group, Inc., Santa Clara, Calif., 1985—2005; fin. advisor Ameriprise Fin. Svcs., Campbell, Calif., 2005—. Author: Perspectives in Information Management, Information Economics, 1983, Handbook of Information Resource Management, 1987, The Information-Based Corporation: Stakeholder Economics and the Technology Investment, 1990, Reengineering Fundamentals: Business Processes and the Global Economy, 1994—96; contbr. articles to profl. jours. Referee emeritus U.S. Soccer Fedn. Mem.: Inst. for Mgmt. Cons., Product Devel. and Mgmt. Assn., Am. Mktg. Assn., Nat. Investor Rels. Inst., Assn. Fin. Profl., World Future Soc., Soc. Competitive Intelligence Profl., Am. Electronics Assn., Nat. Alliance Bus. Econ., Silicon Valley Roundtable, Soc. Info. Mgmt. (treas.). Home: 2803 Kalliam Dr Santa Clara CA 95051-6838 Office: Ameriprise Fin Svcs Inc 1919 S Bascom Ave Campbell CA 95008 Office Phone: 408-963-2372. Business E-Mail: david.r.vincent@ampf.com.

**VINCENT, FRANCIS THOMAS, JR., (FAY VINCENT),** former baseball commissioner; b. Waterbury, Conn., May 29, 1938; s. Francis Thomas and Alice (Lynch) V.; m. Valerie McMahon, July 3, 1965; children: Anne, William, Edward. BA cum laude, Williams Coll., 1960; LLB, Yale U., 1963. Bar: Conn. 1963, N.Y. 1964, D.C. 1969. Assoc. Whitman & Ransom, NYC, 1963-68; ptnr. Caplin & Drysdale, Washington, 1968-78; assoc. dir. div. corp. fin. SEC, Washington, 1978; pres., chief exec. officer Columbia Pictures Industries, Inc., NYC, 1978-83, chmn., chief exec. officer, 1983-87; pres., chief exec. officer entertainment bus. sect. The Coca-Cola Co., NYC, 1987; dep. commr., chief oper. officer Major League Baseball, NYC, 1989, commr., 1989-92; pres. New England Collegiate Baseball League, 1998—2003. Non-exec. dir. Westfield Am. Mgmt. Ltd., 2002—; bd. dir. Time Warner, Inc, 1993—. Author: The Last Commissioner, 2002, The Only Game in Town: Baseball Stars of the 1930s and 1940s Talk About the Game They Loved, 2006. Trustee Williams Coll., 1970-88, Hotchkiss Sch., 1975—, Carleton Coll., 1988—. Mem. NY Athletic Club, Belle Haven Club, Phi Beta Kappa. Clubs: University, Belle Haven. Roman Catholic.*

**VINCENT, FREDERICK MICHAEL, SR.,** neurologist, educator; b. Detroit, Nov. 19, 1948; s. George S. and Alyce M. (Borkowski) Vincent; m. Patricia Lucille Condes, Oct. 7, 1972; children: Frederick Michael Jr., Joshua Peter, Melissa Anne. BS in Biology, Aquinas Coll., 1970; MD, Mich. State U. 1973. Cert. in neurology Am. Bd. Psychiatry and Neurology, 1979, Am. Bd. Electrodiagnostic Medicine, 1992, Am. Bd. Forensic Examiners, 1996, Am. Bd. Forensic Medicine, 1996, in neurology with subspecialty of clin. neurophysiology Am. Bd. Psychiatry and Neurology, 1994. Intern St. Luke's Hosp., Duluth, Minn., 1974; resident in neurology Dartmouth Med. Sch., Hanover, NH, 1975—77; instr. dept. medicine, chief resident neurology 1977—78; chief neurology sect. Munson Med. Ctr., Traverse City, Mich., 1978—84; asst. clin. prof. medicine and psychiatry Mich. State U., East Lansing, 1978—84, chief sect. neurology Coll. Human Medicine, 1984—87, clin. prof. psychiatry and internal medicine, 1989—2004, clin. prof. medicine, 1990—, clin. prof. neurology and ophthalmology, 2001—; pvt. practice Lansing, Mich., 1987—; clin. and rsch. fellow neuro-oncology Mass. Gen. Hosp., Boston, 1985; clin. fellow in neurology Harvard Med. Sch., Boston, 1985; cons. med. asst. program Northwestern Mich. Coll., Traverse City, 1983—84; neurology cons. radio call-in show Sta. WKAR, East Lansing, 1984—2000, Sta. WCMU-TV, 1981 1993—. Author: (book) Neurology: Problems in Primary Care, 1987, 2d edit., 1993; contbr. articles to profl. jours. Fellow, NSF, 1969, Nat. Multiple Sclerosis Soc., 1971. Fellow: ACP, Am. Bd. Legal Medicine, Am. Assn. Neuromuscular and Electrodiagnostic Medicine (computer electronics com. 1995—98, profl. practice com. 1999—2000, practice rev. panel 2000—03), Am. Acad. Neurology (program accreditation devel. subcom. 1993—2001), Am. Bd. Forensic Examiners, Am. Heart Assn.; mem.: Am. Coll. Legal Medicine, Am. Coll. Physician Exec., Soc. for Neuro-Oncology, Movement Disorders Soc., Am. Clin. Neurophysiology

Soc., Inuit Art Soc., Univ. Club, Alpha Omega Alpha. Independent. Roman Catholic. Avocations: art, fishing. Office: 1515 Lake Lansing Rd Ste F1 Lansing MI 48912-3752 Office Phone: 517-374-1055. Business E-Mail: vincen11@msu.edu.

**VINCENT, HAL WELLMAN,** military officer, investor; b. Pontiac, Mich., Sept. 27, 1927; s. Harold and Glenda (Wellman) V.; m. Virginia Bayler, June 9, 1951; children: David B., Dale W., Deborah K. Vincent. Student, Navy V-5 program Western Mich. Coll./Colgate U., 1945; BS in Engring., U.S. Naval Acad., 1950; postgrad., Marine Officers Basic Sch., 1950, Flight Sch., 1952, Test Pilot Sch., 1955, Navy Fleet Air Gunnery Sch., 1958, Air Force Fighter Weapons Sch., 1959, Marine Corps Command and Staff Coll., 1964, Indsl. Coll., 1969, Marine Air Weapons Tng. Unit, 1972. Commd. 2d lt. U.S. Marine Corps, 1950, advanced through grades to maj. gen., 1974; rifle and machine-gun platoon comdr. Camp Lejeune, NC, 1951; fighter pilot El Toro, Calif., 1953-54, Republic of Korea, 1953—54; test pilot Flight Test Div., Patuxent River, Md., 1955-57; ops. officer, squadron asst. and fighter pilot El Toro, 1958-59; conventional weapons project test pilot Naval Air Weapons Test Ctr., China Lake, Calif., 1960-62; squadron ops. and exec. officer El Toro and Japan, 1962-64; aviation specialist Marine Corps amphibious warfare presentation team and staff officer Quantico, Va., 1965-66; comdg. officer 2d Marine Aircraft Wing fighter-attack squadron, Beaufort, SC, 1967-68; exec. officer Marine Aircraft Group, Vietnam, 1969; logistics staff officer Fleet Marine Force Pacific, Hawaii, 1970-72; comdg. officer Marine Aircraft Group, Yuma, Ariz., 1972-73; chief of staff 3d Marine Aircraft Wing, El Toro, 1973-76; dep. chief. of staff plans and policy to Comdr. in Chief Atlantic, Norfolk, Va., 1976 78; comdg. gen. 2d Marine Aircraft Wing, Cherry Point, NC, 1978-80; dep. comdg. gen. Fleet Marine Force Atlantic, Norfolk, 1980-81; ret., 1981; pvt. investor, 1981—. Weapons test pilot; preliminary pilot, evaluator new mil. aircraft. Contbr. numerous articles on tactics and conventional weapons delivery, flight test stability and control to various mil. publs. Decorated Legion of Merit with 2 gold stars, D.F.C., Bronze Star with combat V, Air medal with star and numeral 14, Honor medal 1st class, Cross of Gallantry with gold star (Republic of Vietnam); recipient Wright Bros. Master Pilot award, 2005. Mem. SAR, Soc. Exptl. Test Pilots, Early Pioneer Naval Aviators, Marine Corps Aviation Assn., Mach 2 Club, Marbella Country Club. Achievements include invention of triple ejector rack for delivery of conventional bombs, 1961; devel. of fighter tactics in F8 and F4 aircraft, 1958-69; flew 165 models of fgn. and U.S. mil. aircraft; flew 8 models of fixed wing and helicopters on 242 combat missions; first Marine to fly MACH-2; pilot for 61 years. Personal E-mail: hwvincent@webtv.net. *In all 36 years in the service I am convinced that war is bad, and little is accomplished in the long term by warfare. However when National policy dictates a war, then we must not limit what can be done. We must win! My thought "Winning isn't everything, it's the only thing!" When I must go to battle I want to be allowed to "fight to win.".*

**VINCENT, JAMES LOUIS,** biotechnology company executive; b. Johnstown, Pa., Dec. 15, 1939; s. Robert Clyde and Marietta Lucille (Kennedy) V.; m. Elizabeth M. Matthews, Aug. 19, 1961 (div. 1998); children: Aimee Archelle, Christopher James; m. Joyce Anne Fitzgibbons, Dec. 30, 1999 (div. 2002). BSME, Duke U., 1961; MBA in Indsl. Mgmt., U. Pa., 1963; DBA (hon.), U. New Haven, 1998. Mgr. Far East divsn. Tex. Instruments, Inc., Tokyo, 1970—72; pres. Tex. Instrument Asia, Ltd., Tokyo, 1970—72; v.p. diagnostic ops., pres. diagnostics div. Abbott Labs., North Chgo., Ill., 1972—74, group v.p., bd. dirs., 1974—81, exec. v.p., COO, bd. dirs., 1979—81; corp. group v.p., pres. Allied Health and Sci. Products Co. Allied Corp., Morristown, NJ, 1982—85; CEO Biogen, Inc., Cambridge, Mass., 1985—97, 1999—2000, chmn. bd., 1997—2002; ret., 2002. Trustee Duke U., Com. for Econ. Devel.; bd. dirs. Alnylam Pharms. Recipient Young Exec. Achievement Young Execs. Club, Chgo., 1976, Disting. Alumni award Duke U., 1988, Biotech. award Wall St. Transcript, 1997. Mem. Mass. Bus. Roundtable, The Comml. Club Boston, Algonquin Club Boston, The Links (N.Y.C.). Republican. Presbyterian.

**VINCENT, JIM,** performing company executive; b. NJ; m. France Nguyen; children: Lena, Claire, June. Studied at, Wash. Sch. of Ballet, Harkness House of Ballet, N.C. Sch. of the Arts. Profl. dancer Jim Kylian's Nederlands Dans Theater, Nacho Duato's Compania Nacional de Danza in Spain; asst. artistic dir. Compania Nacional de Danza, 1990—94; concept designer, show dir. Disneyland Paris, 1997; artistic dir. Hubbard St. Dance Chgo., 2000—. Ballet master Nederlands Dans Theater II, Compa a Nacional de Danza, Opera National de Lyon. Office: Hubbard Street Dance Chgo 1147 W Jackson Blvd Chicago IL 60607*

**VINCENT, JOHN BERTRAM,** chemist, educator; b. Cape Girardeau, Mo., July 10, 1962; s. Jack Donald and Patricia Illers Vincent; m. Sharon Ellen Nevels; children: Allisa, Christina. BS, Murray (Ky.) State U., 1984; PhD, Ind. U., 1988. Postdoctoral rsch. assoc. U. Va., Charlottesville, 1988-90, NIH postdoctoral fellow, 1990-91; asst. prof. chemistry U. Ala., Tuscaloosa, 1991-96, assoc. prof., 1996-2001, prof., 2001—, faculty tchg. fellow Coll. Arts and Scis., 2002—05, pres. faculty senate, 2006—. Contbr. articles to profl. jours. Recipient Outstanding Commitment to Tchg. award U. Ala. Alumni Assn., 1999, Outstanding Honor Program Faculty award U. Ala. Honors Student Assn., 1998. Mem. Am. Diabetes Assn., Ala. Acad. Sci., Coun. on Undergrad. Rsch., Soc. Biol. Inorganic Chemistry, Am. Chem. Soc. (sec. Ala. sect. 1996-97). Presbyterian. Home: 716 53d Ct E Tuscaloosa AL 35404 Office: U Ala Dept Chemistry Tuscaloosa AL 35487-0336 Office Phone: 205-348-9203. Office Fax: 205-348-9104. Business E-Mail: jvincent@bama.ua.edu. E-mail: nevels@dbtech.net.

**VINCENT, LYNETTE SUSANNE,** music educator; b. Port Arthur, Tex., Feb. 22, 1972; d. Joseph William and Carolyn Sue Vincent. MusB, Lamar U., 1993, MusM, 1997; postgrad., U. North Tex., Denton, 2006—. Tchr. Trinity Bapt. Christian Sch., Port Arthur, Tex., 1994—96; missionary Internat. Mission Bd., So. Bapt. Conv., Amman, Jordan, 1998—2003; music instr. Nat. Music Conservatory, Amman, Jordan, 1999—2002; mid. sch. choral dir. Irving Ind. Sch. Dist., Tex., 2003—06. Singer: (chamber chorus) Aria Chamber Chorus, (solo recital) Solo concert at Dead Sea. Young Choral Artists Program grant, Irving Schools Found., 2005. Mem.: Tex. Music Educators Assn., Nat. Assn. Teachers of Singing (assoc.). Christian. Avocations: cooking, music composition, gardening.

**VINCENT, MARK See DIESEL, VIN**

**VINCENT, NORMAN FULLER,** broadcast executive; b. Boston, Oct. 5, 1930; s. Norman Harrison and Marian Bernice (Fuller) V.; m. Karen Ann Walter, June 21, 1969. BA, Denison U., 1953. Sales mgr. Sta. WMBR, Jacksonville, Fla., 1956-62; gen. mgr. Sta. WZOK, Jacksonville, 1962-66; owner, pres. Norm Vincent Sound Recording Studios, Inc., Jacksonville, 1966-75; dir. radio ops. Sta. WJCT, Jacksonville, 1975-91; announcer, narrator radio, TV film and video, talking books, 1976—. Producer, host (radio): Swing Time with Norm Vincent, 1992—. Served with USN, 1953-56; to comdr. USNR, 1958-80. Mem.: Advt. Fed. Am., Jacksonville C. of C. (armed svcs. com.), Navy League, Exch. Club, Sigma Alpha Epsilon. Republican. Episcopalian. Home: 2110 The Woods Dr Jacksonville FL 32246-1016 Office Phone: 904-221-5218. Personal E-mail: vincentswing@aol.com.

**VINCENT, NORMAN L.,** retired insurance company executive; b. Milw., July 21, 1933; s. Victor V. Vincent and Hilda I. (Boedecker) Vincent Patlow; m. Arlene Page, Jan. 31, 1953 (div. 1978); children: J. Todd, Meg; m. Donna Jean Doll, Aug. 8, 1980. BS in Bus., U. Wis., 1957; MS, Purdue U., 1958. Diplomate Am. Bd. Profl. Psychology; registered psychologist, Ill., C.P.C.U., C.L.U. Supr. agy. research State Farm Ins. Cos., Bloomington, Ill., 1960-63, dir. agy. research., 1963-66, asst. v.p. agy., 1966-69, asst. v.p. exec., 1969-70,

---

v.p. data processing, 1970-94; systems v.p., 1994-95. Pres. Bloomington Bd. Edn., 1974-77; bd. dirs. YMCA, Bloomington, 1971-85. Served with M.I. U.S. Army, 1953-55. Mem. AAAS Home: W332 N 5861 Meadowlark Ct Nashotah WI 53058-9528

**VINCENT, REGIS,** computer scientist; M of Engring., Ecole Nationale D'Ingenieurs de Brest, France, 1993; PhD, U. Nice Sophia-Antipolis, France, 1997. Sr. rsch. scientist U. Mass., Amherst, 1997—2001; sr. computer scientist SRI Internat., Menlo Park, Calif., 2001—. Achievements include patents pending for; development of in artificial intelligence for controlling over 100 autonomous robots. Office: SRI International 333 Ravenswood Avenue Menlo Park CA 94025-3493 Office Phone: 650-859-4037.

**VINCENT, RICHARD C.,** communications educator, researcher; b. Allentown, Pa., Mar. 1, 1949; s. Charles L. and Elizabeth A. Vincent; m. Christine LaCaruba, Jan. 29, 1971; children: Marisa Claire, Marielle Bryce. BA, Mansfield U., 1972; MA, Temple U., 1977; PhD, U. Mass., Amherst, 1983. Instr. Slippery Rock (Pa.) U., 1979—81; asst. prof. Western Ill. U., Macomb, 1981—83, So. Ill. U., Carbondale, 1983—86; assoc. prof. U. Hawaii-Manoa, Honolulu, 1986—2001; prof. Ind. State U., Terre Haute, 2001—. Editor: Towards Equity in Global Communication: MacBride Report Update, 1999; author: Financial Characteristics of Selected B Film Productions of Albert J. Cohen, 1980, Global Glasnost: Toward a New International Information/Communication Order?, 1992, U.S. Glasnost: Missing Political Themes in U.S. Media Discourse, 2004, International Communication: Media and Telecommunication Systems in an Era of Globalization., 2007; contbr. chapters to books, articles to profl. jours. Chartered mem. Honolulu Cmty. Media Coun., 1999—2001; del. UN & ITU's World Summit on Info. Soc., Geneva, Tunis, 2003—05. Fulbright scholar, U.S. State Dept., USIA, Dublin (Ireland) City U., 1994—95. Mem.: HCMC Freedom of Info. Day (assoc.; co-chair 2000—01), MacBride Round Table (assoc.; pres. and past pres. 1994—2000), Broadcast Edn. Assn. (assoc.; internat. divsn. rsch. chair 2006—), Am. Edn. in Journalism and Mass Comm. (assoc.; internat. divsn. sec. 2001—02, internat. divsn. rsch. chair 2002—03), Internat. Comm. Assn. (assoc.), Nat. Comm. Assn. (assoc.), Internat. Assn. Mass Comm. Rschrs. (assoc.), Union for Dem. Comm. (assoc.). Achievements include research in mass media and information and communication technologies. Office: Indiana State University Comm Dept 218 N 6th St Terre Haute IN 47809 Office Phone: 812-237-3246. Office Fax: 812-237-3217. Business E-Mail: rvincent@indstate.edu.

**VINCENT, THOMAS JAMES,** retired manufacturing executive; b. Balt., Mar. 17, 1934; s. Thomas Alonzo and Helen Gertrude (Cloman) V.; divorced; children: Wayne S., Robin K. MS, MIT, 1968. Div. gen. mgr. Fairchild Industries, St. Augustine, Fla., 1969-72; pres. T.J. Vincent Properties Ltd., St. Augustine, 1972-75, Pacific Concrete & Rock Co., Honolulu, 1975-77, Ramsey Engring. Co., St. Paul, 1977-80, Kobe Inc., L.A., 1980-84, Milchem Inc., Houston, 1984-85, York (Pa.) Internat. Corp., 1985-88, also bd. dirs., cons.; chmn., CEO Hawaii Seafood Growers, Inc., Kahuku, 1990-92. Author: Fairplan, 1962; publ.: In the Name of the Boss Upstairs, The Father Ray Brennan Story, 2004 Founder, pres. Thomas J. Vincent Found. Inc., Kaneohe, Hawaii, 1990—; founder, v.p., treas. Winter Park (Fla.) Family Health Ctr., Inc., 1995—. Named one of Outstanding Young Men in Am., Jaycees, 1965; Alfred P. Sloan fellow MIT, 1967; recipient Rsch. for Progress Achievement award, 1972. Avocations: deep sea fishing, orchid growing. Home and Office: 44-447 Kaneohe Bay Dr Kaneohe HI 96744

**VINCENTI, GENE A.,** director, consultant; b. Elizabeth, N.J., Oct. 2, 1949; s. Charles and Lucy (Diange) Vincenti; m. Regina Abrantes, July 10, 1971; children: Michael James, Jason Luis. BA, Rutgers U., Newark, 1971, MBA, 1973; Cert., Harvard Grad. Sch. Edn., Cambridge, Mass., 1990. Student asst. Kean U., Union, NY, 1968—71, offsite program mgr. Boonton, NJ, 1971; budget resource officer Rutgers U., New Brunswick, NJ, 1973—76, asst. provost, 1973—76, Newark, 1976—80, assoc. provost, 1980—2003, exec. v.p. adminstrn., 2003—. Interfunctional and team cons. Rutgers U., 1972; mem. regional bus. partnerships evaluator mid. states, 1980; mem. gov.'s mgmt. improvement agy. State of N.J., Trenton, 1982; evaluator Middle States Assn., Phila., 1985. Many other church, state and county roles; lector, Eucharistic minister, pres. parish coun. St. Thomas More Ch., Manalapan, 1989—2003; trustee Univ. Heights Sci. Park, Newark, 1990—; mem. Recreation Commn., Manalapan, NJ, 1994—2001, chmn., 1996—2001. Recipient Bus. Ptnrship award, NJ Transit, 1987; grantee, N.J. Commn. on Higher Edn., 1995. Mem.: Am. Planning Assn., Nat. Assn. Coll. and Univ. Bus. Officers, Internat. Econ. Devel. Coun. Roman Catholic. Avocations: baseball, basketball, travel. Home: 15 Mt Stream Ct Barnegat NJ 08005 Office: Rutgers Univ Ste 590 123 Washington St Newark NJ 07102

**VINCENTI, SHELDON ARNOLD,** law educator, lawyer; b. Sept. 4, 1938; s. Arnold Joseph and Mae (Burch) Vincenti; children: Matthew Lewis, Amanda Jo. AB, Harvard U., 1960, JD, 1963. Bar: Utah 1963. Sole practice law, Ogden, 1966—67; ptnr. Lowe and Vincenti, Ogden, 1968—70; legis. asst. to U.S. Rep. Gunn McKay, Washington, 1971—72, adminstrv. asst., 1973; prof., assoc. dean U. Idaho Coll. Law, Moscow, 1973—83, dean, prof. law, 1983—95, prof. law, 1995—2006; acad. dean Am. Justice Sch. Law, Paducah, Ky., 2006—. Home: 3285 W Twin Rd Moscow ID 83843-9114 Office: U Idaho Coll Law 6th & Rayburn St Moscow ID 83843

**VINCENTI, WALTER GUIDO,** aeronautical engineer, emeritus educator; b. Balt., Apr. 20, 1917; s. Guido A. and Agnes (Nicolini) V.; m. Joyce H. Weaver, Sept. 6, 1947; children— Margaret Anna, Marc Guido. AB, Stanford U., 1938, Aero. Engr., 1940. Aero. research scientist NACA, 1940-57; prof. aero. and astronautics and history of tech. Stanford U., 1957-83, prof. emeritus, 1983—. Cons. to industry, 1957—; mem. adv. panel engring. sec. NSF, 1960-63. Author: (with Charles H. Kruger, Jr.) Introduction to Physical Gas Dynamics, 1965, (with Nathan Rosenberg) The Britannia Bridge, 1978, What Engineers Know and How They Know It, 1990; also papers.; co-editor (with Milton Van Dyke) Annual Review of Fluid Mechanics, 1970-76. Served with USN, 1945-46. Recipient Gold medal Pi Tau Sigma, 1948, Engr.-Historian award ASME, 1997; Rockefeller Pub. Service award, 1956; Guggenheim fellow, 1963 Fellow AIAA; mem. Internat. Acad. Astronautics (corr.), Soc. History Tech. (Usher prize 1984, Leonardo da Vinci medal 1998), Nat. Acad. Engring., Phi Beta Kappa, Sigma Xi, Tau Beta Pi. Home: 555 Byron St #306 Palo Alto CA 94301 Office: Stanford U Stanford CA 94305 Business E-Mail: sts@stanford.edu.

**VINCI, JOHN NICHOLAS,** architect, educator; b. Chgo., Feb. 6, 1937; s. Nicholas and Nicolina (Camiola) V. B.Arch., Ill. Inst. Tech., 1960. Registered architect, Ill., Mo., Mich., Pa., NCARB. Draftsman Skidmore, Owings, Merrill, Chgo., 1960-61; with City of Chgo., 1961; stencil restorer Crombie Taylor, Chgo., 1961-62; designer Brenner, Danforth, Rockwell, Chgo., 1962-68; architect Vinci, Inc., Chgo., 1977-95; ptnr. Vinci/Hamp, Architects, Inc., Chgo., 1995—; lectr. Roosevelt U., Chgo., 1969-72, Ill. Inst. Tech., Chgo., 1977; contr. articles to profl. jours.; exhbn. designer. Bd. dirs. Music of Baroque, Chgo., 1976—87, Mies Van Der Rohe Soc., 2003—; mem. adv. com. Commn. on Chgo. Archtl. and Hist. Landmarks, 1971—83, Millennium Pk., Chgo., 2000—; exec. sec. Richard Nickel Com., Chgo., 1972—; chmn. Howard Van Doren Shaw Soc., 1994—2001; mem. Friends of the Farnsworth Ho., 2001—, Landmark Preservation of Ill. Fellow AIA; mem. Soc. Archtl. Historians, Frank Lloyd Wright Home and Studio Found., Art Inst. Chgo., The Corp. of YADDO, Chgo. Hist. Soc., Arts Club of Chgo. Roman Catholic. Home: 3152 N Cambridge Ave Chicago IL 60657-4613 Office: Vinci/Hamp Architects Inc 1147 W Ohio St Chicago IL 60622-6472

**VINE, LEO,** lawyer; b. Providence, Aug. 7, 1930; s. Morris H. and Bessie (Hazen) V.; m. Doris Kreiger, June 26, 1955; children: Harry, Marlene Vine Ross, David, Steven. AB, Brown U., 1952; JD, Harvard U., 1955. Bar: Conn. 1955, U.S. Dist. Ct. Conn. 1957, U.S. Supreme Ct. 1972. Assoc. Yudkin & Yudkin, Derby, Conn., 1957-59; pvt. practice Shelton, Conn., 1959-69; corp.

---

counsel City Shelton, 1964-67, 69-78; gen. counsel Shelton Savs. Bank, 1968—2000; ptnr. Vine & Welch, Shelton, 1969-77; gen. counsel United Meth. Homes Conn., Shelton, 1971—2000; ptnr. Winnick, Vine, Welch & Donnelly, Shelton, 1977-95; mem. Winnick, Vine, Welch, Donnelly & Teodosio, LLC, Shelton, 1995—2000; gen. counsel Shelton Econ. Devel. Commn., 1989—2000; ret. Mem. Shelton Bd. Edn., 1962-64; pres. Derby-Shelton Cmty. Chest, Naugatuck Valley, Conn., 1963-64, Beth Israel Synagogue Ctr., Derby, Conn., 1970-72; sec. Shelton Zoning Bd. Appeals; v.p. Parent Child Resource Ctr., 1992-94, pres., 1994-95, bd. dirs., 1995—. 1st lt. U.S. Army, 1955-62. Named Young Man of Yr., Shelton C. of C., 1961; recipient Gold Seal award Valley C. of C., 1987. Mem. Valley Bar Assn. (pres. Lower Naugatuck Valley 1966), Derby-Shelton Rotary Club (pres. 1964-65, Paul Harris fellow 1987-92), Phi Beta Kappa. Avocations: reading, bridge, movies, music. theater. Home: 538A North Trl Stratford CT 06614-8212 Office: Winnick Vine et al 375 Bridgeport Ave Shelton CT 06484-3844

**VINE, RICHARD,** editor; PhD in Lit., Univ. Chgo. Tchr. Art Inst. Chgo., Am. Conservatory of Music, Univ. Riyadh, Saudi Arabia, New Sch. Social Rsch., NYU; editor-in-chief Chgo. Rev.; Dialogue: An Art Jour., Columbus, Ohio; mng. editor Art in Am., NYC. Contbg. writer, lectr. in field; author: Old Nerdrum: Painting, Sketches and Drawings, 2001, Burhan Dogancay: Works on Paper, 1950-2000, 2003. Office: Art in America Brant Art Publications 575 Broadway New York NY 10012 Office Phone: 212-941-2800. Office Fax: 212-941-8885.

**VINE, STEPHEN M.,** lawyer; b. Trenton, NJ; AB magna cum laude, Harvard Univ., 1974, JD cum laude, 1977. Bar: NY 1978. Ptnr. Coudert Brothers; founding ptnr. NY Office Akin Gump Strauss Hauer & Feld LLP, 1993, now ptnr.-in-charge, NYC, head corp. and securities practice group and mem. mgmt. com. NYC. Mem.: ABA (bus. law sect.), Assn. Bar of NYC, Phi Beta Kappa. Office: Akin Gump Strauss Hauer & Feld LLP 590 Madison Ave New York NY 10022-2524 Office Phone: 212-872-1030. Office Fax: 212-872-1002. Business E-Mail: svine@akingump.com.

**VINECOUR, ONEIDA AGNES,** nurse; b. Port Arthur, Tex., Oct. 15, 1917; d. Ernest Eugene and Gertrude Mary (Wooldridge) Thorn; m. Seymour Vinecour, Jan. 14, 1943 (dec. 1976); children: Seymour Jacob, Rebecca Leah. Diploma, St. Mary's Hosp. Sch. Nursing, Port Arthur, 1939; postgrad., cert. Surg. Tech., Anesthesia, Cook County Hosp., 1939-40; postgrad. U. Chgo., 1939-40, Tex. Coll. Mines, 1943, U. Tex. Health Ctr. R.N., cert. occupational audiometric technician, occupl. spirometric technician. Operating room supr., instr. Schumpert Meml. Hosp., Shreveport, La., 1940-41; anesthetist St. Joseph Hosp., Albuquerque, 1941-42; operating room supr., instr. Lynn City Hosp. (Mass.), 1946-48; staff anesthetist St. Mary's Hosp., Port Arthur, Tex., 1951-53, in service dir., 1971-73; staff nurse Tyler County Hosp., Woodville, Tex., 1964-65; dept. head, supr. Park Pl. Hosp., Port Arthur, 1965-71; operating room supr. Mid-County Hosp., Nederland, Tex., 1973-81; staff nurse Baptist Meml. Hosp., Beaumont, Tex., 1973-81; part time staff Health Care Svcs., Port Arthur, 1983—; indsl. nurse Synpol Inc., 1984-86; staff nurse Texaco Chem. Plant, Port Arthur, 1986-92, Olsten Health Care Svcs., 1992—, staff nurse Huntsman Petro-Chem. Corp., 1996—. Served as officer U.S. Army Nurse Corps, 1942-46. Mem. Am. Nurses Assn., Mass. Nurses Assn., Tex. State Nurses Assn., Assn. Occupational Health Nurses. Republican. Methodist. Home: 2502 Glenwood Dr Port Arthur TX 77642-2639

**VINEGRAD, ALAN,** prosecutor; Graduate Magna Cum Laude, U. Pa, Wharton Sch. Bus., 1980; JD, NYU, 1984. Bar: NY, practice before: US Ct. Appeals (2nd and 3rd Cirs.), US Dist. Cts. (Eastern and So. Dist., NY). Staff acct. Price Waterhouse & Co.; clerk for Hon. Leonard B. Sand US Dist. Ct. (So. Dist.), NY, student law clerk for the Hon. Naomi Reice Buchwald; private practice Meister Leventhal & Slade, 1985—90; chief of general crimes US Atty. Office, Brooklyn, NY, 1990—94, chief of civil rights litig., 1994—97, dep. chief of the criminal divsn., 1999, chief of the criminal divsn.; chief asst. US atty.; interim US Atty. US Atty. Office, Eastern Dist., New York, 2001; ptnr., white collar def. and trial practice groups Covington & Burling, NY. Adj. prof. New York Law Sch., 1996—; guest lectr. Brooklyn Law Sch., Cardoza Sch. Law, Fordham Law Sch., Hofstra Law Sch., New York U. Law Sch., Yale Law Sch., Dept. Justice's Office of Legal Edu. Sr. editor NYU Law Review, bd. editor NY Law Journal; contbr. articles to profl. jours. and reviews. Bd. dir. Legal Aid Soc. Recipient Atty. Gen. award for Distinguished Service, Stimson Medal for Outstanding Prosecutor, US Atty. Office for Eastern Dist. of NY, Henry L. Stimson medal, Assn. Bar of City NY, 1993, Atty. General's award for Disting. Svc., 1997. Mem.: Fed. Bar Coun. (bd. trustee, chmn., com. on 2nd cir. cts.). Office: Covington & Burling 1330 Avenue of the Americas New York NY 10019 Office Phone: 212-841-1000. Business E-Mail: avinegrad@cov.com.

**VINENT-CANTORAL, AIDA R.,** mediator; b. Havana, Cuba, Nov. 8, 1948; arrived in U.S., 1959; d. Roberto M. Vinent and Carmen; m. Ennio Cantoral, Dec. 26, 1979 (div. 1981); 1 child, Alfredo Cantoral. BA, Alverno Coll., 1969; MA, Marquette U., 1971, cert. dispute resolution, 1998; cert. negotiating labor agreements, Harvard U., 2000, U. Mich., 2002, Northwestern U.; cert. mediation sys. design, U. Tex.; postgrad., U. So. Tex. Coll. Law, 2004, Fed. Mediation and Conciliation Inst., 2004. Family health asst. Milwaukee County Dept. Human Svcs. & Hosp., 1975—; human svcs. case coord. Milwaukee County Dept. Human Svcs. and Hosp., 1998—; mediator pvt. practice Milw., 1979—; mediator Milwaukee County Family Ct., 1998—, USPS, 1998—, Bus. to Bus., 1998—, CHIPS, 1997, Wis. Spl. Edn. Mediation Sys, 2001—; case mgr. Milw Co. Disability Svs., 1996—. Cons. in field Active ACR, 1998—, Wis. Assn. Homicide Investigators, 2000—; parent educator Centro Legal, Milw., 1998—. Named Human Svcs. Worker of Yr., Wis. Foster Parents, 1980. Mem.: Wis. Coun. Problem Gambling, Wis. Assn. Mediators. Republican. Address: PO Box 462 Greendale WI 53129-0462 Office Phone: 414-550-8772. E-mail: avinent@aol.com.

**VINER, PETER,** communications executive; 1 child, Christine. Profl. Mgmt., Harvard, 1980. Cert. Can. Advertising Agy. Practitioner, 1970. Pres. Telemedia Comms. Ontario, Inc., 1980-84, CKVU TV, Vancouver, 1980—84; pres., CEO CanWest Broadcasting Ltd., Toronto, 1990—93; CEO CanWest Global Comm. Corp., Toronto, 1997-99, chmn., 1999—; publisher National Post, 2001—03; exec. v.p. CanWest Global Comm. Corp., 2003—.

**VINES, HENRY ELLSWORTH, III,** accountant, lawyer, financial planner; b. Chgo., Apr. 17, 1950; s. Henry Ellsworth and Verle (Low) V.; m. Ethel Melton (div. 1977); 1 child; Tiffany Layne; m. Cindy Lou Rich, Jan. 5, 1985; 1 child, Sasha Teresa Root. BS, Menlo Sch. Bus. Adminstrn., 1972; MBA, Golden Gate Grad. Sch., 1985; CFP, Coll. Fin. Planning, Denver, 1987; JD, William F. Taft Law Sch., 1994; LLM, Wash. Sch. Law, 1998. Bar: Calif. 1996; CPA, Calif.; certified CFP. Asst. contr. Legallet Tanning, San Francisco, 1973-79; auditor Martin Schoonover & Paddock, Orange, Calif., 1980-82; tax mgr. Helsley Mulcahy & Fesler, Santa Ana, Calif., 1982-85; v.p. fin. Catalina Furniture Co., Fullerton, Calif., 1985-94; CFO Precision Concepts, Anaheim, Calif., 1987-93; pvt. practice in tax preparation Orange, Calif., 1985—; CFO M.E. Woodworking, Riverside, Calif., 1989-93, Textured Design Furniture, Anaheim, 1994-95; corp. and tax atty. in pvt. practice, Irvine, Calif., 1996—. Author: The Greatest Athlete Athlete of All Time; contbr. articles in field. Mem.: AICPA, ABA, Calif. Inst. CPAs, Irvine Spectrum Toastmasters (pres. 2000—01), San Mateo Tennis Club (pres. 1978), Foster City Tennis Club (pres. 1977). Republican. Avocations: tennis, fishing, golf. Home: 130 N Windy Pointe Orange CA 92869-2400 Office: Ste 300 8 Corporate Park Irvine CA 92606-5196

**VINES, JAMES K.,** prosecutor, lawyer; b. Dec. 1959; BS, JD, Washington & Lee U. Law clk. to Judge Robert R. Merhige, US Dist. Ct.; law clk. to Chief Justice William H. Rehnquist, US Supreme Ct., 1989—90; assoc. King & Spalding, Atlanta, 1990—93; exec. dir., gen. counsel for environ. affairs

Bridgestone/Firestone, Nashville, 1993—2000; ptnr. Baker, Donelson, Bearman & Caldwell, Nashville, 2000—02; US atty. (mid. dist.) Tenn. US Dept. Justice, 2002—. Office: US Attys Office 110 Ninth Ave S Ste A961 Nashville TN 37203*

**VINES, JOHN R.,** career military officer; BS, U. Ala.; MA, Naval War Coll. Advanced through grades to lt. gen. US Army, 2003; with 3rd Infantry Divsn., US Army Europe & Seventh Army, Ranger Dept. US Army Infantry Ctr., Ft. Benning, Ga.; comdr., specialist 1st Ranger Batallion, Hunter Army Airfield, Ga.; exec. officer 3rd Ranger Battallion, Ft. Benning, Ga., 1984—87; numerous command and staff positions Ft. Bragg, 1987—2000; comdr. 82nd Airborne Divsn., 2000—02, Coalition Task Force 82, 2002—03, Combined/Joint Task Force-180, Bagram, Afghanistan, 2003, XVIII Airborne Corps, Ft. Bragg, NC, 2003—, Multi-Nat. Corps-Operation Iraqi Freedom, Iraq, 2005—06. Decorated Def. Disting. Svc. medal, Disting. Svc. medal, Def. Superior Svc. medal, Bronze Star (with Oak Leaf cluster), Combat Infantry Badge, Master Parachutist Badge (with Bronze Svc. Star), Pathfinder Badge, Ranger Tab.

**VINET, LUC,** physicist, educator; b. Montreal, Can., Apr. 16, 1953; s. Jean and Françoise (Ouellette) V.; m. Letitia Muresan, May 19, 1989; children: Jean-François, Laurent, Stéphane, Sophie Andrée. BSc, U. Montreal, 1973, MSc, 1974, PhD, 1980; D. U. P.& M. Curie, Paris, 1979. Rsch. assoc. MIT, Cambridge, 1980—82; rsch. fellow, asst. prof., assoc. prof. U. Montreal, 1982—88, prof. physics, 1992—99; vice prin. (acad.) McGill U., Montreal, 1999—2001, provost, vice prin. (acad.), 2001—05; rector U. Montreal, 2005—. Invited prof. U. Cath. de Louvain, 1980-82; vis. scholar MIT, Cambridge, 1987; vis. prof. UCLA, 1989-90; dir. Ctr. Rsch. Math., Montreal, 1993-99; prof. physics, rector U. Montreal, 2005-. Editor: Group Theoretical Methods in Physics, 1989, Quantum Groups Integrable Models and Statistical Systems, 1993, Physics and Quantum Field Theory, 1996, Symmetries and Integrability of Difference Equations, 1996. Grantee FCAR, 1984—, NSERC, 1982—, rsch. fellow, 1982-92. Mem. APS, AMS, SIAM, CAP, CMS. Achievements include contributions in theoretical physics and mathematics - symmetry studies of difference equations; algebraic interpretation of q-special functions using quantum groups; applications of Berry potentials in the nuclear collective model; identification of Lie superalgebras as dynamical algebras in quantum mechanics; development of dimensional reduction in Yang Mills theories. Office: U Montreal Cabiner du Recteur CP 6128 SLCC Centerville Montreal PQ H3C 3S7 Canada

**VINEY, CHRISTOPHER ROBERT,** health lawyer; b. Buffalo, N.Y., May 14, 1972; s. Robert Donald and Cynthia Marie (Balcarczyk) Viney; m. Kellie Christa Bowden, Sept. 24, 2004; 1 stepchild, Ryan Marshall Glab. BA in Internat. Affairs, George Washington U., Washington, 1994; JD, Union U., Albany, N.Y., 1997. Bar: NY 1997. Judge adv. USN, Washington, 1997—2001; health lawyer Phillips Lytle, LLP, Buffalo, 2001—. Various law lectr. Various Orgns. including Erie County Med. Soc., Western NY Paralegal Assn. and Lorman Edn. Series, Buffalo, 2002—. Editor: (journal) Albany Law Review; contbr. articles to profl. jours. Founder and mem. (sax player) Phillips Lytle Music Ensemble for Nursing Homes, Buffalo, 2001—04; chairperson Phillips Lytle Vol. Crew, Buffalo, 2002—04; mem., corp. vol. coun. United Way of Erie County, Buffalo, 2002—04; intern Office of Senator Robert Dole, Washington, 1991—92; mem., governing bd. Musical Fare Theatre, Amherst, NY, 2004. Lt. USN, 1997—2001, Washington. Recipient Trial Competition - Regional Champion, Am. Trial Lawyers Assn. (ATLA), 1997. Mem.: ABA, Am. Health Lawyers Assn., Erie County Bar Assn. (health law com. mem. 2001—04), NY State Bar Assn., Justinian Soc. of Albany Law Sch. Roman Catholic. Avocations: skiing, travel, saxophone, golf. Home: 107 Crescent Ave Buffalo NY 14214 Office: Roswell Pk Cancer Inst Elm & Carlton Sts Buffalo NY 14263 Office Phone: 716-847-8400. Office Fax: 716-852-6100. E-mail: cviney@phillipslytle.com.

**VINGOE, D. GRANT,** lawyer; b. 1957; BA, Univ. Toronto, Canada, 1979; LLB, Osgoode Hall, Toronto, 1981; LLM, NYU, 1984. Bar: Ontario, Canada 1983, NY 1985. Counsel Toronto Stock Exchange, 1984—85; assoc. Kramer, Levin, Naftalis & Frankel, 1986—93, ptnr., 1994—96; ptnr., corp. dept. Dorsey & Whitney LLP, NYC, 1996—2004; ptnr., cross-border securities, fin. services regulation Arnold & Porter, NYC, 2004. Securities adv. com. Ontario Securities Commn., 1999—2001; bd. dir. Mkt. Regulation Services, Inc., Toronto, ON, Canada, 2004—. Mem.: ABA, Securities Industry Assn., Canadian Bar Assn., Canadian Soc. of NY, Americas Soc. Office: Arnold & Porter LLP 399 Park Ave New York NY 10022-4690 Office Phone: 212-715-1130. Office Fax: 212-715-1399. Business E-Mail: Grant_Vingoe@aporter.com.

**VINIAR, DAVID,** investment banker; BS in Econ. summa cum laude, Union Coll., 1976; MBA, Harvard U., 1980. Joined Goldman Sachs, 1980, ptnr., 1992-96, mng. dir., 1992—94, dep. CFO, 1994—98; CFO Goldman Sachs Group, L.P., 1999; exec. v.p., CFO Goldman Sachs, 1999—, head, fin. div. and co-head credit risk mgmt. and advisory and firm wide risk, 2001—02, head, operations, tech. and fin. div., 2002—. Bd. trustees Union Coll. Mem. bd. trustees Union Coll. Recipient CFO Excellence Award for Risk Management, CFO mag., 2001. Office: Goldman Sachs 85 Broad St New York NY 10004*

**VINICOMBE, CHARLES JAMES,** lawyer; b. Bklyn., July 12, 1962; s. James Charles and Virginia Rose V.; m. Michele Lee Buchman, Dec. 4, 1993. BA, Seton Hall U., 1984; JD, Wake Forest U., 1987. Bar: N.J.; N.C.; U.S. Dist. Ct. N.J., U.S. Dist. Ct. (mid. dist. N.C.), U.S. Ct. Appeals (3rd and 4th cirs.). Assoc. Carruthers & Roth, Greensboro, NC, 1987-89, Drinker, Biddle & Reath, Princeton, NJ, 1989-96, ptnr., 1996—. Adj. faculty Seton Hall Law Sch., Newark, 1996-97. Articles editor Wake Forest Lw Rev., 1986-87; contbr. articles to profl. jours. Law Faculty scholar Wake Forest Law Sch., Winston-Salem, N.C., 1986-87. Mem. N.J. Bar Assn., ABA, Def. Rsch. Inst., Jaycees (v.p., sec., pub. rels. dir. North Plainfield, N.J. 1980-84). Avocations: reading, hiking, fishing. Office: Drinker Biddle & Reath LLP Ste 300 105 College Rd E Princeton NJ 08540-6622 Office Phone: 609-716-6500. Office Fax: 609-799-7000. Business E-Mail: charles.vinicombe@dbr.com.

**VINIKAS, VINCENT,** historian, educator; b. Erie, Pa., Mar. 29, 1951; s. Matthias Vytautas Vinikas and Eva Aldona Damarodas. BA magna cum laude, Pa. State U., 1972; MA, Columbia U., 1974, PhD, 1983. Asst. prof. U. Ark., Little Rock, 1983—89, assoc. prof., 1989—98, prof., 1998—. Inst. fellow NEH, Ariz. State U., Tempe, 1984; conferee Newberry Libr., Smithsonian Instn., Washington, 1985; inst. fellow NEH, U. N.C., 1993; vis. prof. Karl Franzens U., Graz, Styria, Austria, 1994; inst fellow NEH, Columbia U., NY, 1998; referee/cons. St. Martin's Press, Prentice-Hall, McGraw-Hill, Houghton-Mifflin, Wadsworth. Author: (monograph) Soft Soap Hard Sell: American Hygiene in an Age of Advertisement; reviewer: Am. Hist. Rev., Jour. So. History, Jour. Social History, Jour. Econ. History, The Historian, Tech. and Culture, Ark. Hist. Quar., Jour. Am. History; contbr. articles to profl. jours.; conferee Sandage Symposium, U. Ill, 2000. Mem. ACLU, Gurdjieff Found. of Ark., Little Rock. Recipient Rsch. award, U. Ark., 1984, 1996; Pres.'s fellow, Columbia U., 1974-1975. Mem.: Am. Hist. Assn., Ark. Assn. of Coll. History Tchrs. (Biennial Essay Award 1993), Phi Alpha Theta (advisor Iota Zeta chpt.), Phi Kappa Phi (exec. bd. chpt. 134 1989—92), Phi Beta Kappa. Avocations: duplicate bridge, wilderness camping, boating. Home: 3312 W Capitol Ave Little Rock AR 72205 Office: Univ Ark History Dept Little Rock AR 72204 Office Phone: 501-569-3235. Office Fax: 501-569-3059. Business E-mail: vxvinikas@ualr.edu.

**VINING, BARBARA,** lawyer; b. Seoul, Korea, May 2, 1977; d. Martha David, JD, Bklyn. Law Sch., 2002. Atty. Pennie & Edmonds LLP, N.Y.C., 2002—04, Weil Gotshal & Manges LLP, N.Y.C., 2004—. Home: 343 East 74th St # 8I New York NY 10021 Office: Weil Gotshal Manges LLP 767 Fifth Ave Ste 3371 New York NY 10153 Office Phone: 212-310-8055. Home Fax: 212-310-8007; Office Fax: 212-310-8007. Business E-Mail: barbara.vining@weil.com.

**VINING, JOSEPH (GEORGE JOSEPH VINING),** law educator; b. Fulton, Mo., Mar. 3, 1938; s. D. Rutledge and Margaret (McClanahan) V.; m. Alice Marshall Williams, Sept. 18, 1965; children: George Joseph IV, Spencer Carter. BA, Yale U., 1959, Cambridge U., 1961, MA, 1970; JD, Harvard U., 1964. Bar: DC 1965. Atty. Office Dep. Atty. Gen., Dept. Justice, Washington, 1965; asst. to exec. dir. Nat. Crime Commn., 1966; assoc. Covington and Burling, Washington, 1966-69; asst. prof. law U. Mich., 1969-72, assoc. prof., 1972-74, prof., 1974-85, Hutchins prof., 1985—. Sir Edward Youde prof., Hong Kong, 2002. Author: Legal Identity, 1978, The Authoritative and the Authoritarian, 1986, From Newton's Sleep, 1995, The Song Sparrow and the Child, 2004. NEH sr. fellow, 1982-83, Bellagio fellow Rockfeller Found., 1997. Fellow Am. Acad. Arts and Scis.; mem. ABA, D.C. Bar Assn., Am. Law Inst. (life), Century Assn. Office: U Mich 964 Legal Rsch Ann Arbor MI 48109-1215

**VINKEN, PIERRE JACQUES,** publishing executive; b. Nov. 25, 1927; MD, U. Utrecht, 1955; postgrad., U. Amsterdam, The Netherlands, 1957-63; D (hon.), U. Paris, 1981. Staff neurosurgeon Univ. Clinic, Amsterdam, 1964-69; pres., chief editor Excerpta Medica Found., Amsterdam and Princeton, NJ, 1962-88; mng. dir. Elsevier Pub. Co., Amsterdam, 1972-78, chmn. bd. dirs., 1979-95, Reed Elsevier, London, 1993-95. Chmn. Netherlands del. Intergovernmental Unisist Conf., Paris, 1970; mem. Netherlands Unisist Commn., 1971—79, Nat. Sci. Policy Coun., The Hague, 1983—90; prof. med. database informatics U. Leyden, 1975—93; chmn. supervising bd. Halder Holdings, The Hague, Netherlands, Blue Horse Prodns., Rotterdam, Netherlands, Medialand, Amsterdam, Optas, Rotterdam, Trust Theater Co.; bd. dirs. Wereldhave Investment Co., Logica, Aalberts Industries, Revisor, Nat. Acad. Arts, Internat. Rights-Collecting and Distbns. Agys. Founder, editor-in-chief: book Handbook of Clinical Neurology, 78 vols.; editor: sci. books; contbr. articles to profl. jours. Pres. Internat. Congress Patient Counselling, 1976—79; chmn. Netherlands Commn. Bibliography and Documentation, 1972—81; dep. chmn. European Pubs. Coun.; chmn. Hiscom, Leyden, 1987—98, The Lancet, London, 1991—95; bd. dirs. Pearson, London, 1988—91, The Economist, London, 1989—92; mem. soc. adv. coun. Tinbergen Inst., Rotterdam, 1996—2000. Recipient award, Royal Netherlands Acad. Sci., 1997. Mem.: European Info. Providers Assn. (pres. 1980—83), Peruvian Soc. Psychiat. Neurology and Neurosurgery (hon.), Amsterdam Neurol. Soc. (hon.), French Neurol. Soc. (hon.), Neurol. Soc. India (hon.), Netherlands Rep. Soc. (founder 1996), Order of Orange Nassau (comdr.), Order of Netherlands' Lion (knight), Order Hipolitó Unanue (comdr.). Home: Schubertstraat 2 1077 GS Amsterdam Netherlands Personal E-mail: vinken@quicknet.nl.

**VIÑOLY, RAFAEL,** architectural firm executive; b. Montevideo, Uruguay, 1944; arrived in US, 1978; Grad. in Arch., Univ. Buenos Aires, Argentina, 1969. Founding pnr. Estudio de Arquitectura, Argentina, 1964—78; guest lectr. Univ. Wash., Harvard Univ. Grad. Sch. Design; founder, prin. Rafael Viñoly Architects PC, NYC, 1983—, established order London, 2000. Prin. works include John Jay Coll. Criminal Justice, 1988, Tokyo Internat. Forum, 1996, Univ. Chgo. Grad. Sch. Bus., Watson Inst. for Internat. Studies, Brown U., Howard Hughes Med. Inst. Janelia Farm Rsch. Campus, Va., Porter Neuroscience Rsch. Ctr. at NIH, Md., UCLA Nanosystems Rsch. Inst., Cleve. Mus. Art, Bklyn. Children's Mus., Nasher Mus., Duke U., Jazz at Lincoln Ctr., NYC, Leicester City Theatre, Performing Arts Centre, UK, also include courthouses, private residences, athletic facilities and performing arts venues; author: Rafael Viñoly, 2003. Recipient Medal of Honor, AIA NY Chapter, 1994. Fellow: AIA; mem.: NAD (academician 1994—), Japan Inst. Architects. Office: Rafael Viñoly Architects PC 50 Vandam St New York NY 10013 Office Phone: 212-924-5060. Office Fax: 212-924-5058. Business E-Mail: RafaelVinoly@rvapc.com.*

**VINROOT, RICHARD ALLEN,** lawyer, mayor; b. Charlotte, N.C., Apr. 14, 1941; s. Gustav Edgar and Vera Frances (Pickett) V.; m. Judith Lee Allen, Dec. 29, 1964; children: Richard A., Laura Tabor, Kathryn Pickett. BS in Bus. Adminstrn., U. N.C., 1963, JD, 1966. Bar: N.C. 1966. U.S. Dist. Ct. (ea., mid. and we. dists.) N.C. 1969, U.S. Ct. Appeals (4th cir.) 1969. Ptnr. Robinson, Bradshaw & Hinson, P.A., Charlotte, 1969—. Mayor City of Charlotte, 1991-95; bd. dirs. Martin-Marietta Materials Inc. Tchr. sr. h.s. sunday sch. Myers Park Presbyn. Ch., 1970—, ruling elder, 1970-76, 1978-84, 1996-2000, chmn. of session, 1984; mem. Charlotte City Coun., 1983-91. With U.S. Army, 1967-68, Vietnam. Recipient Bronze Star, 1968; named Mcpl. Leader of the Yr. Am. City & County Mag., 1995. Mem. ABA, VFW, N.C. Bar Assn., Mecklenburg County Bar Assn. (sec. 1976, bd. dir. 1970-76), Mecklenburg County Vietnam Vets. Assn., Mecklenburg County Eagle Scouts Assn., Am. Legion, Phalanx Lodge Mason. Republican. Presbyterian. Office: Robinson Bradshaw & Hinson PA 1900 Independence Ctr 101 N Tryon St Ste 1900 Charlotte NC 28246-0103

**VINSON, JAMES SPANGLER,** academic administrator; b. Chambersburg, Pa., May 17, 1941; s. Wilbur S. and Anna M. (Spangler) V.; m. Susan Alexander, Apr. 8, 1967; children: Suzannah, Elizabeth. BA, Gettysburg Coll., 1963; MS, U. Va., 1965, PhD, 1967. Asst. prof. physics MacMurray Coll., Jacksonville, Ill., 1967-71; assoc. prof. physics U. N.C., Asheville, 1971-78, prof. physics, 1974-78, chmn. dept. physics, dir. acad. computing, 1974-78; prof. physics, dean Coll. Arts and Scis. U. Hartford (Conn.), 1978-83; v.p. acad. affairs Trinity U., San Antonio, 1983-87; pres. U. Evansville, Ind., 1987-2001, pres. emeritus Ind., 2001—; pres. Nat. Sci. Ctr. Found., Augusta, Ga., 2002—. Computer cons. Contbr. articles to profl. jours. Mem. Am. Phys. Soc., World Future Soc., AAAS, Am. Assn. for Advancement of Humanities, Am. Assn. for Higher Edn., Am. Assn. Physics Tchrs., Phi Beta Kappa, Sigma Xi, Phi Sigma Kappa. Methodist. Office Phone: 706-868-3600.

**VINSON, LAURENCE DUNCAN, JR.,** lawyer; b. Gadsden, Ala., Mar. 17, 1947; BS with hons., U. Ala., Tuscaloosa, 1969; JD, U. Ala., 1973. Bar: Ala., U.S. Dist. Ct. (no., mid. and so. dists.) Ala., U.S. Ct. Appeals (11th cir.), U.S. Supreme Ct. Assoc. Bradley Arant Rose & White, LLP, Birmingham, Ala., 1973-79, ptnr., 1979—. Bar: Ala. 1973, U.S. Dist. Ct. (no. dist.) Ala. 1973, U.S. Supreme Ct. 1977, U.S. Ct. Appeals (11th cir.) 1981, U.S. Dist. Ct. (so. dist.) Ala. 1989, U.S. Dist. Ct. (mid. dist.) Ala. 1991. Chmn. Ala. Uniform Comml. Code Revisions Coms., 1991-2004. Mem. ABA, Birmingham Bar Assn., Ala. State Bar, Ala. Law Inst., Order of Coif, Phi Beta Kappa, Omicron Delta Kappa. Office: Bradley Arant Rose & White LLP One Federal Pl 1819 5th Ave N Birmingham AL 35203-2104 Business E-Mail: lvinson@bradleyarant.com.

**VINSON, VICTORIA DEAN,** middle school educator; b. Cedartown, Ga., June 19, 1952; d. BennieDean Vinson and Katherine Louise (Green) Easterwood BSEd, U. Ga., 1975; postgrad., Valdosta State U., 1976-78, Berry Coll., 1980-81, U. Maryland, Lakenheath, Eng., 1982-84, W. Ga. Coll., 1991. Cert. K-12 gifted tchr., Ga. Tchr. Tift County High Sch., Tifton, Ga., 1976-79, Elm St. Mid. Sch., Rockmart, Ga., 1980-81, 85-89, tchr. of gifted, 1991—; tchr. RAF Feltwell (Eng.)-Lakenheath Mid. Sch., 1981-84. Instr. aerobics Floyd Med. Ctr., Rome, Ga., 1985-89; tchr./asst. Baird Ballet Co., Rome, 1984-88; tchr., choreographer Rome City Ballet, 198991, Acad. Performing Arts, Cedartown, 1992-93. Mem. ASCD, NEA, Ga. Edn. Assn., Polk Edn. Assn., Nat. Coun. Tchrs. English, Ga. Supporters for Gifted, Profl. Dance Tchrs. Assn., Nat. Dance Exercise Inst. Tng. Assn., Beta Sigma Phi. Democrat. Home: 99 Seab Green Rd Cedartown GA 30125-4637 Office: Elm St Mid Sch 100 Morgan Valley Rd Rockmart GA 30153-1610

**VINSON, WILLIAM THEODORE,** lawyer; BS, USAF Acad., 1965; JD, UCLA, 1969. Bar: Calif. 1970. Judge advocate USAF, 1970-74; trial counsel Phillips Petroleum, San Mateo, Calif., 1974-75; atty. Lockheed Corp., Westlake Village, Calif., 1975-90, v.p., sec., 1990-92, v.p., gen. couns., 92-95; v.p., chief counsel Lockheed Martin Corp., Westlake Village, 1995-98; cons. Lockheed Corp., Westlake Village, 1998; dir. Siemens Govt. Svcs., Inc., 2001—. Bd. dirs. Westminster Free Clinic, 2001—. Office: 5560 E Napoleon Ave Oak Park CA 91377-4746

**VINTZILEOS, ANTHONY MARK,** obstetrician, gynecologist; b. Athens, Greece, Dec. 15, 1950; s. Mark and Barbara (Prokopiou) V.; m. Colleen Ann McBride, June 25, 1977 (div.); children: Mark, Matthew, Michael; m. Cathylynn Pike, Dec. 30, 1989; children: Barbara, William. MD, Athens U. Med. Sch. Intern Monmouth Med. Ctr., Long Branch, N.J., 1976-77; resident St. Josephs Hosp. Med. Ctr., Paterson, N.J., 1977-81; prof., chmn. Dept. Ob-gyn. and Reproductive Scis. Robert Wood Johnson Med. Sch. Maternal fetal medicine fellow U. Conn. Health Ctr., Farmington, N.J., 1981-83. Mem. Am. Coll. Ob-gyn. Home: 4 Sky High Ter Bridgewater NJ 08807-1201 Office: 125 Paterson St New Brunswick NJ 08901 Office Phone: 732-235-7628. Business E-Mail: vintziam@umdnj.edu.

**VIOLA, BILL,** artist, writer; b. NYC, Jan. 25, 1951; s. William John and Wynne Viola; m. Kira Perov; children: Blake, Andrei. BFA, Syracuse U., 1973, DFA, 1995, Sch. Art Inst. Chgo., 1997, Calif. Coll. Arts & Crafts, Oakland, 1998, Mass. Coll. Art, 1999, Calif. Inst. of the Arts, Valencia, 2000, U. Sunderland, Eng., 2000. Tech. dir. Art/Tapes/22 Video Studio, Florence, Italy, 1974-76; artist-in-residence Sta. WNET, N.Y.C., 1976-83, WXXI-TV, Rochester, NY, 1979, Sony Corp., Atsugi Labs., Japan, 1980-81, San Diego Zoo, 1984; instr. Calif. Inst. of Arts, Valencia, 1983; represented by James Cohan Gallery, N.Y.C. Solo exhbns. include The Kitchen Ctr., N.Y., 1974, Everson Mus. Art, Syracuse, N.Y., 1975, Mus. Modern Art, N.Y.C., 1979, 87, Whitney Mus. Art, N.Y.C., 1982, Musee d'Art Moderne, Paris, 1983, Mus. Contemporary Art, L.A., 1985, Fukui Prefectural Mus. Art, Fukui City, Japan, 1989, Staditsche Kunsthalle Düsseldorf, 1992, Moderna Musee, Stockholm, 1993, Museo Nacional Centro de Arte Reina Sofia, Madrid, 1993, Musee Cantonal des Beaux-Arts, Lausanne, Switzerland, 1993, Whitechapel Art Gallery, London, 1993, Tel Aviv Mus. Art, 1994, Musée d'Art Contemporain, Montreal, 1993, Centro Cultural/Banco de Brazil, Rio de Janeiro, 1994, 46th Venice Biennale, 1995, Festival d'Automne Paris, 1996, Bill Viola: A 25 Year Survey Exhbn., Whitney Mus. Am. Art, N.Y., travels to Whitney Mus. Am. Art, 1997, L.A. County Mus. Am. Art, 1998, Stedelijk Mus., Amsterdam, 1998, Mus. Pur Moderne Kunst and Shirnkunstalle Dominkankloister, Germany, 1999, San Francisco Mus. Modern Art, 1999, Art Inst. Chgo., 1999-2000, 2KM, Karlsruhe, Germany, 2000, James Cohan Gallery, N.Y., 2000, Anthony d'Offay Gallery, London, 2001, Bill Viola: Going Forth By Day, Deutsche Guggenheim Berlin, 2002; group exhbns. include De Saisset Art Gallery and Mus., Santa Clara, Calif., 1972, Whitney Mus. Am. Art, 1975-87, 89, 93, Stedelijk Mus., Amsterdam, 1984, Carnegie Mus. Art, Pitts., 1988, Kölnischer Kunstverein, Cologne, Germany, 1989, Israel Mus., Jerusalem, 1990, Musée Nat. d'Art Moderne, Ctr. Georges Pompidou, Paris, 1990, Martin Gropius Bau, Berlin, 1991, Mus. Moderne Kunst, Frankfurt, Germany, 1991, Royal Acad., London, 1993, Denver Art Mus., Columbus (Ohio) Art Mus., 1994, Anthony d'Offay Gallery, London, 1995, Mus. Modern Art, N.Y.C., 1995, Tate Gallery, London, 1995, Albright-Knox Art Gallery, 1996, Fabric Workshop, Phila., 1997, MOMA, N.Y., 1999, La Beauté, Found Cartier, 2000, Tate Modern, London, 2000, Nat. Gallery, London, 2000, James Cohan Gallery, NY, 2001; spl. screening film: Dèserts, Vienna, Austria, 1994, WhiteChapel Art Gallery, London, 2001, 49th Venice Biennale, 2001, Perth Festival, Australia, 2001, Commune di Ferrara, Italy, 2001, Musse d'Art Contemporian de Montreal, Canada, 2001; commns. include The Stopping mind, Mus. Moderne Kunst, Frankfurt, 1991, Nantes Triptych, Dèlegation aux Arts Plastiques, Nantes, France, 1992, Slowly Turning Narrative, Isnt. Contemporary Art, Phila., Va. Mus. Fine Art, Richmond, 1992, Tiny Deaths, Biennale d'Art Contemporain de Lyon, France, 1993, Dèserts, Konzerthause, Vienna, 1994, 3e Biennale d'Art contemporaire de Lyon, Musèe d'art contemporain, Lyon, France, 1995, Helaba Main Tower, Frankfurt, Germany, 2000, Gotesborgs Musiken, Sweden, 2001, Deserts, Konzerthaus, Vienna, 2001, Deserts, Carnigie Hall, New York, 2001, Deserts, Royal Festival Hall, London, 2001, Deserts, IRCAM, Centre Pomidou Main Hall, Paris, 2001, others; composer: (album) David Tudor-Rainforest IV, 1981; (video) Chott el-Djerid, Anthem, 1983, Hatsu-Yume, 1981, The Reflecting Pool, 1977-79, The Space Between the Teeth, 1976, Bill Viola: Selected Works, 1986, I Do Not Know What It Is I Am Like, 1986, The Passing, 1991, The City of Man, 1989, Nantes Triptych, 1992, Slowly Turning Narritive, 1992, Tiny Deaths, 1993, The Greetings, 1995, The Crossing, 1996, The Quintet of Remembrance, 2000, The Quintet of the Unseen, 2000, The Quintet of the Astonished, The Quintet of the Silent, 2000, Surrender, 2001, Catherine's Room, 2001, Five Angles for the Millenium, 2001, Going Forth By Day, 2002. Japan/U.S. Creative Arts fellow NEA, 1980, Rockefellor Found. Video Artist fellow, 1982, Visual Artist fellow NEA, 1983-89, Guggenheim Meml. Found. fellow, 1985, Intercultural Film/Video fellow Rockefeller Found., 1991; recipient Jury prize U.S. Film and Video Festival, 1982, Grand prize, 1983, Jury prize Video Culture/Can., 1983, Grand prize for video art, 1984, First prize for video art Athens (Ohio) Film/Video Festival, 1984, Maya Deren award Am. Film Inst., 1987, First prize Festival Internat. d'Art Video et des Nouvelles Images Electroniques de Locarno, 1987, John D. and Catherine T. MacArthur Found. award, 1989, Skowhegan medal, 1993, First prize Festival Internat. de Video, Cidade de Vigo, Spain, 1993, Medienkunstpreis, Siemens Kulturprogramm and Zentrum fur Kunst und Medientechnologie, Germany, 1993; scholar-in-residence The Getty Rsch. Inst. for History of Art and Humanities, L.A., 1998. Office: 282 Granada Ave Long Beach CA 90803 E-mail: info@billviola.edu.

**VIOLAND-SANCHEZ, EMMA NATIVIDAD,** school administrator, educator; b. Cochabamba, Bolivia, Nov. 5, 1944; came to U.S., 1961; d. Adalberto Violand and Emma Sanchez; children: James, Julia. BS, Radford U., 1966, MS, 1968; EdD, George Washington U., 1987. Postgrad. profl. lic. Tchr., counselor Am. Coop. Sch., La Paz, Bolivia, 1963, 71-76; instr. Ariz. Western Coll., Yuma, 1967-68; tchr., counselor St. Andrews Sch., La Paz, 1968-71; rschr. Instituto Boliviano Estudio Accion Social, La Paz, 1968-71; bilingual resource specialist Arlington (Va.) Pub. Schs., 1976-78, secondary project coord. Title VII, 1978-80, supr. ESOL, 1980—. Adj. prof. U. Catolica, La Paz, 1974-75; George Mason U., Fairfax, Va., 1986-94, George Washington U., Washington, 1988-97, Georgetown U., 1997—; cons. sch. dists., univs., Ministry of Edn. in Bolivia, 1976—, in El Salvador, 1996, in Escuela, Americana, San Salvador, Ministry of Devel. in Bolivia, 1996. Author: Vocational and Professional Handbook for Bolivia, 1971; contbg. author: Learning Styles in the ESL/EFL Classroom, 1995, Understanding Learning Styles in the Second Language Classroom, 1998, (monographs) Ministry of Education, 1988, National Clearinghouse for Bilingual Education, 1990, 91. Founder, pres. coun. 4606 LULAC, Arlington, 1987-96; founder chair Immigration Rights Task Force, Arlington, 1989-92; bd. trustees United Way Nat. Capital Area, Washington, 1989-94; exec. bd. Com. of 100, Arlington, 1994-95. Named one of Notable Women of Arlington, Arlington County, 1993; recipient Outstanding Dissertation award Nat. Assn. Bilingual Edn., 1988, Award Arlington County Dept. of Human Svcs., 1996; Am. fellow AAUW, 1986-87; Fulbright Sr. scholar, 1995-96. Mem. ASCD, TESOL (rsch. bd. 1979—). Avocations: travel, research, hispanic/latin american issues, consulting, sports. Office: Arlington Pub Schs 1426 N Quincy St Arlington VA 22207-3646

**VIOLANO, STELLA MARIE,** artist; b. Van Nuys, Calif., Sept. 23, 1965; d. Gayle Harold and Grace Marie Olson; m. Caesar Michael Violano, Mar. 27, 1999; children: Julia Grace, Jillian Gayle, Jenna Kathleen, Sarah Michael. AA with hon. summa cum laude, Ventura Coll., Calif., 1994—97; BA summa cum laude in Biomedical Illustration, Calif. Luth. U., Thousand Oaks, 1997—2000. Profl. fine artist SMV Studio, Thousand Oaks, Calif., 1981—; artist, photographer Visual Eyes Inc., Westlake Village, Calif., 1997. To Sleep Perchance to Dream-portrait of a homeless Jack Russell Terrier, Homeless Pets Series, Afternoon Nap- Portrait of Senior Dalmation, The Florida Cow Series, The Wildlife Series; columnists: County Connections Calif. Mag., 1990—92. Founding mem. Mt. Aire No-Kill Animal Shelter; founder Pet Helping Animals; adv. Homeless Pets. Named to design 2005 Christmas card, Almost Home Dachshund Rescue Soc., 2005; recipient 4th Pl. county profl. painting award, Adah Callahan Profl. Arts, 2004, Milford Zornes award, 18th Internat. Animals Art Exhbn., 2005, Internat. Judges award, 19th Internat. Animals on Art Exhbn., 2005. Mem.: Buenaventura Art Assn. (assoc.).

Independent. Avocations: writing, art. Studio: SMV Studio Art Helping Animals 4887 Via Aurora Newbury Park CA 91320 Office Phone: 805-402-2149. Business E-mail: info@stellaviolano.com.

**VIOLENUS, AGNES A.,** retired school system administrator; b. N.Y.C., May 17, 1931; d. Antonio and Constance Violenus. BA, Hunter Coll., 1952; MA, Columbia U., 1958; EdD, Nova U., 1990. Tchr. N.Y. State Day Care, N.Y.C., 1952-53, N.Y.C. Bd. Edns, 1953-66; asst. prin. N.Y.C. Elem. and Jr. H.S., 1966-91; student tchr. supr. dept. edn., adj. instr. CCNY, 1997. Adj. instr. computer dept. continuing edn. divsn. York Coll., N.Y.C., 1985-88, Hunter Coll., N.Y.C., 1998—; adj. instr. tchr. mentor program grad. edn. divsn. CCNY, 1990-91; reviewer instl. and instrnl. films; judge news and documentary Emmy awards NATAS, 1995, 97, 2000, 2002. Co-author: LOGO: K-12, 1980; contbr. articles to profl. jours. Mem. mid-Manhattan br. NAACP, mem. com. on Afro-Am. acad., cultural, and tech. olympics; life mem. Girl Scouts U.S., N.Y.C.; bd. visitors Manhattan Psychiat. Ctr., 1995, pres., 2000, chair 1999—; vol. advisor math., sci., computers Workshop Ctr., CCNY, 1995-97; bd. dirs. Hunter Coll. Scholarship and Welfare Fund. Recipient Dedicated Svc. award Coun. Suprs. and Adminstrs., Appreciation award Aerospace Edn. Assn., 1985, Significant Contbn. award Am. Soc. for Aerospace Edn., 1985, Leaders' Day Cert. of Appreciation, Girl Scouts U.S., 1997. Mem. ASCE, AAUW, Am. Ednl. Rsch. Assn., Assn. Advancement of Computing in Edn., Assn. Computers in Math. and Sci. Tchg., Soc. for Info. Tech. and Tchr. Edn., Assn. for Women in Sci., Nat. Tech. Assn., N.Y. Acad. Scis. (scientists in schs. program 1995), Nat. Assn. Negro Bus. and Profl. Women's Clubs (scholarship com. 1989—, family math. com. 1995, rec. sec. 1994-95, profl. award 1997), Nat. Black Child Devel. Inst. (bd. dirs. 1991—, sci. exhibit com. 1995, v.p. 1999, co-chair enterting ... com. program 1999, 2000, pub. policy com. 1991—, Bridge Bldr.'s award 1995), Schomburg Ctr. Rsch. in Black Culture Schomburg Ctr. (vols. adv. com. 1992—, bd. trustee, co-chair corp. task force on African-Am. in math., sci. and tech. 1992—, pres. 1995-98, treas. 1999-2000), Doctorate Assn. N.Y. Educators, N.Y. Alliance Black Sch. Educators, Hunter Coll. Alumni Assn. (bd. dirs. 1993—, rec. sec. 1996-99, treas. 1999—2002, named to Hall of Fame 1998), Bank St. Alumni Coun. Greater N.Y. (asst. sect. 1991-93), Wistarians Alumni Hunter Coll. (exec. com. 1990—, pres. 1990-94). Democrat. Roman Catholic. Avocations: music, genealogy.

**VIOLETTE, BANKS,** painter, sculptor; b. Ithica, NY, 1973; BFA, Sch. Visual Arts, NY, 1998; MFA, Columbia U., 2002. One-man shows include, Team Gallery, NY, 2000, 2002, 2004, LISTE, Basel, Switzerland, 2003, MW Projects, London, 2004, Galerie Rodolphe Janssen, Brussels, 2005; curator (exhibitions) Fearless Vampire Killer, ABC No Rio, NY, 1998, ZERO, Neiman Ctr. Print Studies, Columbia U., NY, 1999, Dear Dead Person, Momenta Art, Bklyn., 2001, Trans-Nat. Monster League, Derek Eller Gallery, NY, 2003; Represented in permanent collections, Whitney Mus. Am. Art, NY, Frederick R. Weisman Art Found., LA, Mus. OverHolland, Amsterdam, Mus. Modern Art, NY, Mus. Contemporary Art, LA, Musée d'Art Moderne et Contemporain, Geneva; exhibited in group shows, Lower East Side Cmty. Ctr., NY, 1997, Visual Arts Gallery, NY, 1997, 1998, Momenta Art, Bklyn., 1999, Two Friends and So On, Andrew Kreps Gallery, NY, 2000, Summer with Friends, Team Gallery, NY, 2000, Dirty Deeds Done Dirt Cheap, Contemporary Arts Ctr., Atlanta, 2001, Ghost Stories, Sandroni-Rey Gallery, Venice, Calif., 2001, Learned America, P.P.O.W., NY, 2001, Diversity Plus: Emerging Artists in a Rapid World, Visual Arts Mus., NY, 2001, Kult 48 Klubhouse, Deitch Projects, Bklyn., 2003, Flesh & Blood, Michael Steinberg, NY, 2003, An Enquiry into those Kinds of Distress which excite agreeable Sensations, Team Gallery, NY, 2003, A Matter of Facts, Nicole Klagsbrun Gallery, NY, 2003, Back in Black, Cohan Leslie and Browne, NY, 2003, Melvins, Anton Kern Gallery, NY, 2003, Return of the Creature, Kunstlerhaus Palais Thurn and Taxis Gartnerhaus, Austria, 2003, Screem, Anton Kern Gallery, NY, 2004, Penteholocaust/The Sixty-Sided Stone of the Androgyne, Peres Projects, LA, 2004, Whitney Biennial, Whitney Mus. Am. Art, NY, 2004, Noctambule, Alternative Space, Paris, 2004, Liverpool Biennial, Liverpool, England, 2004. Rema Hort Mann Found. Grant, 2000. Mailing: c/o Team Gallery 527 West 26th St New York NY 10001

**VIORST, JUDITH STAHL,** writer; b. Newark, Feb. 2, 1931; d. Martin Leonard and Ruth June (Ehrenkranz) Stahl; m. Milton Viorst, Jan. 30, 1960; children: Anthony Jacob, Nicholas Nathan, Alexander Noah. BA, Rutgers U., 1952; grad., Washington Psychoanalytic Inst., 1981. Author: (children's books) Sunday Morning, 1968, I'll Fix Anthony, 1969, Try It Again Sam, 1970, The Tenth Good Thing about Barney, 1971 (Silver Pencil award 1973), Alexander and the Terrible, Horrible, No Good, Very Bad Day, 1972, My Mama Says There Aren't Any Zombies, Ghosts, Vampires, Creatures, Demons, Monsters, Fiends, Goblins or Things, 1973, Rosie and Michael, 1974, Alexander, Who Used to Be Rich Last Sunday, 1978, The Good-Bye Book, 1988, Earrings!, 1990, The Alphabet from Z to A (with Much Confusion on the Way), 1994, Alexander, Who's Not (Do You Hear Me? I Mean It!) Going to Move, 1995, Super-Completely and Totally the Messiest, 2001, Just in Case, 2006; (poetry) The Village Square, 1965-66, It's Hard to Be Hip Over Thirty and Other Tragedies of Married Life, 1968, People and Other Aggravations, 1971, How Did I Get to Be Forty and Other Atrocities, 1976, If I Were in Charge of the World and Other Worries, 1981, When Did I Stop Being Twenty and Other Injustices, 1987, Forever Fifty and Other Negotiations, 1989, Sad Underwear and Other Complications, 1995, Suddenly Sixty and Other Shocks of Later Life, 2000, I'm Too Young to be Seventy and Other Delusions, 2005; (with Milton Viorst) The Washington Underground Gourmet, 1970, Yes Married, 1972, A Visit From St. Nicholas (To a Liberated Household), 1977, Love and Guilt and the Meaning of Life, Etc., 1979, Necessary Losses, 1986, Murdering Mr. Monti, 1994, Imperfect Control, 1998, You're Officially a Grown-Up, 1999, Grown-up Marriage, 2003; (musical) Love and Shrimp (book and lyrics), 1990; (HBO children's movie) Alexander and the Terrible, Horrible, No Good, Very Bad Day (book and lyrics), 1990, (children's stage musical) Alexander and the Terrible, Horrible, No Good, Very Bad Day, 1998, Alexander, Who's Not Not Not Not Not Gong to Move (book and lyrics), 2003. Recipient Emmy award for poems used in Anne Bancroft Spl., 1970. Jewish.

**VIORST, MILTON,** writer; b. Paterson, NJ, Feb. 18, 1930; s. Louis and Betty (LeVine) Viorst; m. Judith Stahl, Jan. 30, 1960; children: Anthony, Nicholas, Alexander. BA summa cum laude, Rutgers U., 1951; student (Fulbright scholar), U. Lyon, France, 1952; MA, Harvard U., 1955; MS, Columbia U., 1956. Reporter Bergen (N.J.) Record, 1955-56, Newark StarLedger, 1956-57, Washington Post, 1957-61; Washington corr. N.Y. Post, 1961-64; syndicated columnist Washington Evening Star, 1971-75; staff writer New Yorker, N.Y.C., 1987-93; Ferris prof. journalism Princeton (N.J.) U., 1995-96. Lectr. in field. Author: (book) Hostile Allies: FDR and deGaulle, 1965, Great Documents of Western Civilization, 1965, Fall from Grace: The Republican Party and the Puritan Ethic, 1968, Hustlers and Heroes, 1971, Fire in the Streets: America in the 1960's, 1980, Making a Difference: The Peace Corps at Twenty-Five, 1986, Sands of Sorrow: Israel's Journey from Independence, 1987, Reaching for the Olive Branch: UNRWA and Peace in the Middle East, 1990, Sandcastles: The Arabs in Search of the Modern World, 1994, In The Shadow of the Prophet: The Struggle for the Soul of Islam, 1998, What Shall I Do With This People? Jews and the Fractious Politics of Judaism, 2002, Storm from the East: The Struggle Between the Arab World and the Christian West, 2006; contbr. articles to profl. jours.; contbg. corr.: Washington Quar. Mem. nat. adv. com. Mid. East Policy Coun.; chmn. Found Investigative Journalism, 1969—78; bd. dirs. Georgetown Day Sch., 1977—80, Inst. World Affairs. Officer USAF, 1952—54. Recipient Columbia Journalism Alumni award, 1992, Human Rights award, UN Assn. DC, 2002, chevalier, Legion d'Honneur, France, 2005; scholar, Mid. East Inst.; Woodrow Wilson Sr. fellow, 1973—79, Alicia Patterson fellow, 1979. Mem.: Coun. Fgn. Rels., Author's Guild, Soc. Profl. Journalists, PEN, Am. Peace Now, Phi Beta Kappa. Personal E-mail: mviorst@aol.com.

**VIRELLA, JUAN CARLOS,** civil engineer, researcher; b. San Juan, P.R., Aug. 28, 1974; s. Juan Oscar Virella and Luz María Crespo; m. Ivelisse Berio, July 12, 1997; 1 child, Juan Carlos. PhD, U. P.R., Mayaguez, P.R., 2004.

---

Registered profl. engr., P.R. Structural engr. J.O. Virella & Assocs, Corozal, PR, 2000—; rschr. U. P.R., Mayaguez, 2004—. Grantee, NSF and EPSCOR, 2004—06. Home: Las Colinas Paseo los Robles Apt 205A Mayaguez PR 00680 Office: University of Puerto Rico at Mayaguez State road 108 Km 18 Mayaguez PR 00681 Office Phone: 787-832-4040 3295. Office Fax: 787-833-8260. Personal E-mail: vhulkster@aol.com. Business E-Mail: jvirella@uprm.edu.

**VIRKHAUS, TAAVO,** symphony orchestra conductor; b. Tartu, Estonia, June 29, 1934; came to U.S., 1949; s. Adalbert August and Helene Marie (Sild) V.; m. Nancy Ellen Herman, Mar. 29, 1969. MusB U. Miami, 1955; MusM Eastman Sch. of Music, Rochester, 1957, DMA, 1967. Dir. music U. Rochester (N.Y.), also assoc. prof. Eastman Sch., Rochester, 1967-77; music dir., condr. Duluth (Minn.) Superior Symphony Orch., 1977-94; guest condr. Rochester Philharm., Minn. Orch., Balt. Symphony, Vancouver Symphony and others, 1972—; music dir., condr. Hunstville (Ala.) Symphony Orch., 1989-2003, condr. emeritus, 2003—; guest condr. at Tallinn, Estonia, 1978, 88, 90, 92, 93, 94, 99; lectr. U. Minn.-Duluth, U. of Wis.-Superior. With U.S. Army, 1957-58, USAR, 1957-61. Recipient Howard Hanson Composition award, 1966, Am. Heritage award JFK Libr. for Minorities, 1974; Fulbright scholar, Musikhochschule, Cologne, 1963. Mem. Am. Symphony Orch. League, Condrs. Guild, Am. Fedn. of Musicians. Composer: Violin Concerto, 1966, Symphony No. 1, 1976, Symphony No. 2, 1979, Symphony No. 3, 1984, Symphony No. 4, 1989, Symphony No. 5, 1994, Violin Concerto No. 2, 1995. Republican. Lutheran. Personal E-mail: tvirkhaus@knology.net.

**VIRTEL, JAMES JOHN,** lawyer; b. Joliet, Ill., May 15, 1944, BA cum laude, Loras Coll., 1966; JD cum laude, St. Louis U., 1969. Bar: Mo. 1969, Ill. 1969. Atty. Armstrong Teasdale LLP, St. Louis, 1976—. Adj. prof. law St. Louis U., 1995-99; regent Loras Coll., Dubuque, Iowa, 1996—. Editor: St. Louis U. Law Jour., 1968-69. Fellow Am. Coll. Trial Lawyers; mem. Ill. State Bar Assn., Mo. State Bar Assn. Office: Armstrong Teasdale LLP 1 Metropolitan Sq Ste 2600 Saint Louis MO 63102-2740 Office Phone: 314-342-8088. Personal E-mail: jvirtel@sbcglobal.net. E-Mail: jvirtel@armstrongteasdale.com.

**VIRTUE, TED,** investment company executive; Grad., Middlebury Coll. Sr. v.p. Drexel Burnham Lambert; exec. v.p., head global fin., mem. mgmt. com., bus. coun., client com. Bankers Trust; pres. BT Alex. Brown Inc. (merged with Deutsche Bank), bd dirs.; pres. Deutsche Bank Alex. Brown; mem. exec. com. Deutsche Bank; CEO DB Capital Ptnrs., MidOcean Ptnrs., NYC. Bd. dirs. Noveon, Inc., Celerity Group, Inc., Ctr. Parcs UK. Office: MidOcean Ptnrs 320 Park Ave Ste 1700 New York NY 10022 Office Phone: 212-497-1400.

**VISCARDI, PETER G.,** risk management and environmental affairs executive; b. NYC, Dec. 28, 1947; s. Peter and Louise (Johnson) Viscardi; m. Margaret E. McGowan, Sept. 11, 1971 (div. 2001); children: Margaret, Peter; m. Linda M. Gawel, Sept. 26, 2003. BA, Hunter Coll., N.Y.C., 1970. CPCU. Ins. mgr. Jaffie Contracting Co., Inc., N.Y.C., 1971-73; ins. adminstr. Otis Elevator Co., N.Y.C., 1973, supr. ins. adminstrn., 1974; dir. adminstrn. Finsure divsn. Studebaker-Worthington, Inc., N.Y.C., 1975-78, corp. risk mgr./exec. v.p., chief oper. officer, 1978-80; mgr. corp. ins. Fortune Brands, Inc. (formerly Am. Brands), N.Y.C., 1980-81, mgr. corp. ins. and real estate, 1981-87, dir. corp. ins. Old Greenwich, Conn., 1987-90, dir. risk mgmt. and environ. affairs, 1990-99; cons. Shirley, NY, 2000—03; sr. mgr. Ernst & Young, 2003—04; cons., 2004—05; pres. Viscardi Risk Consulting Corp., 2005—. Mem. editl. bd.: Risk and Benefits Mag., 1987—89, 1991—92, instnl. investor adv. bd.; 1997. Mem. adv. bd. ACE Bermuda, 1999—2003. Mem.: Nat. Assn. Mfrs. (risk mgmt. and environ. quality coms. 1990—99), Am. Mgmt. Assn. (ins. and risk mgmt. coun.), Soc. CPCUs. Office Phone: 631-924-0887. E-mail: lirisk@optonline.net.

**VISCHER, HAROLD HARRY,** manufacturing executive; b. Toledo, Oct. 17, 1914; s. Harry Philip and Hazel May (Patterson) V.; m. DeNell Meyers, Feb. 18, 1938; children: Harold Harry, Robert P., Michael L. BBA, U. Toledo, 1937. With Ohio Bell Telephone Co., 1937-38; with Firestone Tire & Rubber Co., Toledo, 1948-61, nat. passenger tire sales mgr., 1953-57, dist. mgr., 1957-61; with Bandag Inc., Muscatine, Iowa, 1961-80; exec. v.p., pres. Bandag Inc. (Rubber and Equipment Sales group), 1975-80; also dir.; pres., gen. mgr. Hardline Internat., Inc., Jackson, Mich., 1980-82; chmn. Tred-X Corp., 1982—. Mem. City Council, Muscatine, 1964-76; chmn., mem. Dist. Export Council Iowa, 1964-81; chmn. Muscatine United Way, 1969-70; mem. adv. bd. Engring. Coll. Iowa State U., 1970-81; mem. Muscatine Light & Water Bd., 1979-80. Elected to Nat. Tire Dealers and Retreaders Assn. Hall of Fame, 1988, to Internat. Tire Retreading and Repairing Hall of Fame, 1990. Mem. Nat. Tire and Retreaders Suppliers Group Assn. (chmn. 1979-80, exec. com. 1977-80), Tire Retread Info. Bur. (exec. com. 1974-81), Am. Retreading Assn. (adv. bd. 1970-72), Retreading Industry Assn., Industry Man of Yr. 1979), Christian Business men's Com., Gideons. Republican. Home: 13500 Vischer Rd Brooklyn MI 49230-9022

**VISCLOSKY, PETER JOHN,** congressman, lawyer; b. Gary, Ind., Aug. 13, 1949; s. John and Helen (Kauzlaric) Visclosky; m. Anne Marie O'Keefe; children: John, Timothy. BS in acctg., Ind. U., Indpls., 1970; JD, U. Notre Dame, 1973; LLM in internat. and comparative law, Georgetown U., 1983. Bar: Ind., D.C., U.S. Supreme Ct. Legal asst. Dist. Atty.'s Office, NYC, 1972; assoc. Benjamin, Greco & Gouveia, Merrillville, Ind., 1973-76, Greco, Gouveia, Miller, Pera & Bishop, Merrillville, Ind., 1982-84; assoc. staff appropriations com. US Ho Reps., Washington, 1976-80, assoc. staff budget com., 1980-82; mem. US Congress from 1st Ind. dist., 1985—; mem. appropriations coms., subcomm. treasury, postal svc., gen. govt. and military constrn. Democrat. Roman Catholic. Office: US Ho Reps 2256 Rayburn Ho Office Bldg Washington DC 20515-1401 also: Dist Office Ste 9 701 E 83d Ave Merrillville IN 46410

**VISCOMI, FRANK JOSEPH,** pharmaceutical executive; b. Easton, Pa., Dec. 18, 1951; s. John Dominic and Catherine Viscomi; m. Janet Lynn Wilson, Sept. 29, 1979; children: Lauren Michelle, Rebecca Elizabeth. BS in Biology, Alderson Broaddus Coll., Phillipi, W.Va., 1973; MAT in Edn., Coll. NJ, Trenton, 1988, MA in Math. Physics, 1988. Biologist Colgate Palmolive Co., Piscataway, NJ, 1977—88; mgr. Johnson & Johnson Pharm. R&D, Raritan, NJ, 1988—. Tchr. Hun Sch. of Princeton, NJ, 1998—2000. Contbr. scientific papers to profl. jours.; author: 47, 2006. Mem.: Math. Assn. of Am., Mensa (life). Achievements include patents pending for Mathematical Algorythm to Calculate the Area of and Object in n-Dimensional Space; Anti-Inflammatory Agent Extracted from Milkweed Plants; Development of Laser System to Measure Corneal Opacity; Development of Laser System to Detect Tissue Degradation. Home: 82 Knapp Ave Trenton NJ 08610 Office Phone: 908-704-4750. Personal E-mail: fviscomi@aol.com.

**VISCOVICH, SIR ANDREW JOHN,** educational management consultant; b. Oakland, Calif., Sept. 25, 1925; s. Peter Andrew and Lucy Pauline (Razovich) V.; m. Roen Shirley Mulvana, Apr. 19, 1952 (div. Feb. 1985); children: Randal Peter, Andra Clair; m. Elena Beth Wong, Apr. 28, 1991; 1 child, Alison Wong. BA, U. Calif., Berkeley, 1949; MA, San Francisco State U., 1960; EdD, U. Calif., Berkeley, 1973; cert. labor dispute resolution, Golden Gate U., 1976. Assoc. supt. Oakland Unified Sch. Dist., Calif., 1970-77; supt. Palm Springs (Calif.) Unified Sch. Dist., 1976-79, Garvey Sch. Dist., Rosemead, Calif., 1979-88, Berkeley (Calif.) Unified Sch. Dist., Stockton, Calif., 1988—91; state administr. Coachella Unified Sch. Dis. Thermal, Calif., 1992—93; pres. Ctr. for Ednl. Rsch. in Adminstrn., Stockton, Calif., 1990—. Adj. prof. U. Calif., Berkeley, 1965-67, Calif. State U., Hayward, 1970-76, L.A. 1971-8; exec. dir. Marcus Foster Edn. Found., Oakland, 1975-76; cons. Spanish Ministry Edn., 1987—, Republic of China Ministry Edn., Taipei, Taiwan, 1986-89, Croatian Ministry Edn., Zagreb, 1993—, Marriott Sch. Svcs, 1992—, CSHQH, Idaho; pre-sch. dir. Oakland Unified Sch. Dist., 1974-76; asst. dir. Bay Area Bilingual Edn. League, 1971-75; dir. Bay Area Tchr. Ctr., 1974, asst. dir. Far West Ednl. Lab., 1974;

---

adj. assoc. prof. Calif. State U. at L.A.and Hayward, U. South Fla., U. Oreg., Coll. of Holy Names; exec. dir. ANRO Cons., Inc., Calif., 1973-82; nat. dir. supt. consulting svcs. Sodexho Marriott Corp., 1992-99. Author: Language Programs for the Disadvantaged, 1965, R.E.S. Plus, 1978; contbr. The School Principal, 1978. Chair United Way, Pasadena, Calif., 1985; pres. Croatian Scholarship Found., San Ramon, Calif., 1993-94. Served to ens. USNR, 1959-64. Recipient award for innovations in alternative schools Behavioral Rsch. Lab., San Francisco, 1973; named Knight of Civil Order of Merit King Juan Carlos of Spain, 1990. Mem. Am. Mgmt. Assn., Am. Assn. Sch. Adminstrs., Assn. Calif. Sch. Adminstrs., Calif. City Sch. Supts., Calif. Tchrs. Assn. (John Swett award 1978), Tau Kappa Epsilon. Avocations: golf, reading, travel, ultralite flying. Home: 3754 Fort Donelson Dr Stockton CA 95219-3211

**VISCUGLIA, JENNY LOU,** music educator; b. Englewood, Colo., Sept. 12, 1967; d. Dwight B and Lynda Lee Eames; m. Felix Alfred Viscuglia, Apr. 5, 1997; m. Andrew Norvelle, Nov. 19, 1989 (div. Sept. 27, 1996). BS in Music Edn., U. Nev., Las Vegas, 2003. Cert. nursing asst., Colo., 1986; music tchr. K-12 Nev., 2003. Cert. nursing asst. Cherry Creek Nursing Ctr., Aurora, Colo., 1986—87; class a alarm operator Regent Security, Englewood, Colo., 1987—88; waitress, asst. mgr. McCoy's Family Restaurant, Littleton, Colo., 1988—89; clerical Kelly Services, Las Vegas, Nev., 1989—90; adminstry. asst. Nathan Adelson Hospice Found., Las Vegas, Nev., 1990—95; sec. Rio Suites Hotel and Casino, Wine Cellar, Las Vegas, Nev., 1996—97; libr. Nev. Symphony, Las Vegas, Nev., 1994—98; pers. mgr., libr., clarinet sub The Las Vegas Philharm., Las Vegas, Nev., 1998—2004; k-8 music tchr. Clark County Sch. Dist., Las Vegas, Nev., 2003—. Mem. Goodsprings Citizens Adv. Coun., Goodsprings, Nev., 1998—2004; treas., mem. Goodsprings Hist. Soc., Goodsprings, 2001—04. Mem.: NEA, Music Educators Nat. Conf., Am. Orff-Schulwerk Assn., Nat. Assn. Music Educators. Avocations: travel, music, sewing. Home: Post Office Box 664 Goodsprings NV 89019 Office: Sandy Valley Elem Mid Sch Sandy Valley NV 89019 Office Phone: 702-799-0935. Personal E-mail: viscuglia@aol.com.

**VISCUSI, W(ILLIAM) G. KIP,** law and economics educator; b. Trenton, NJ, Oct. 3, 1949; s. William Edward and Evelyn (Martin) V.; m. Catherine Makdisi, Sep. 26, 1972 (div.); children: Kira Margaret, Michael Kip; m. Joni Hersch, Jan. 18, 1998. AB summa cum laude, Harvard U., 1971, MPP, 1973, AM, 1974, PhD, 1976. Prof. econs. Northwestern U., Evanston, Ill., 1976-80, 85-88; dep. dir. White House Council on Wage and Price Stability, Washington, 1979-81; prof. econs. Duke U., Durham, NC, 1981-85; John M. Olin prof. econs. U. Chgo., 1985-86; George G. Allen prof. econs. Duke U., Durham, NC, 1988-96; John M. Olin vis. prof. law and econs. Harvard Law Sch., Cambridge, Mass., 1995, John F. Cogan Jr. prof. law and econs., 1996—2006; disting. prof. law and econs. Law Sch. Vanderbilt U., Nghiville, Tenn., 2006—. Rsch. assoc. Nat. Bur. Econ. Rsch., 1978—, Nat. Commn. for Employment Policy, 1981; mem. EPA Sci. Adv. Bd., 1986—, econs. bd., 1992—, Clean Air Act, 1992—, Nat. Acad. Sci. Panel, 1978-79; cons. U.S. Gen. Acctg. Office, 1981-85, Dept. Justice, 1986-87, 89-91, U.S. Office Mgmt. and Budget, 1983; assoc. reporter Am. Law Inst., 1986-91; adj. fellow in civil justice Manhattan Inst., 1987—; inaugural spkr. Geneva Risk Econ. Lectrs., Geneva Assn. Risk and Ins., 1989; John R. Commons lectr. U. Wis., 1990; Ayne Ryde lectr. Lund U., Sweden. Author: Employment Hazards, 1979 (Wells prize 1977), Risk by Choice, 1983, Reforming Products Liability, 1991, Fatal Tradeoffs, 1992, Smoking, 1992, Rational Risk Policy, 1998, Smoke-filled Rooms: A Post-mortem on the Tobacco Deal, 2002; editor Jour. Risk and Uncertainty; contbg. editor Regulation mag.; assoc. editor Internat. Rev. of Law Econs., Geneva Papers on Risk and Ins. Theory, Jour. Regulatory Econs., Jour. Environ. Econs. and Mgmt., J Risk and Ins., Rev. Econs. and Stats., Am. Econ. Rev., Managerial and Decision Econs., Contemporary Econ. Policy. Recipient Article of the Yr. award Econ. Inquiry, 1988, Royal Econ. Soc., 1999; Book of the Yr. awards Am. Risk and Ins. Assn., 1992, 93, 94, 2000, Article award Am. Risk and Ins. Assn., 1999. Mem. Am. Econs. Assn., Econometric Soc., Am. Econ. Environ. and Resource Economists, Assn. for Pub. Policy Analysis and Mgmt., Soc. Econs. Assn. We. Econs. Assn., Am. Managerial and Decision Econs. Roman Catholic. Office: Vanderbilt Univ Law Sch 131 21st Ave South Nashville TN 37203-1181

**VISEK, WILLARD JAMES,** nutritionist, animal scientist, physician, educator; b. Sargent, Nebr., Sept. 19, 1922; s. James and Anna S. (Dworak) V.; m. Priscilla Flagg, Dec. 28, 1949; children: Dianna, Madeleine, Clayton Paul. B.Sc. with honors (Carl R. Gray scholar), U. Nebr., 1947; MSc (Smith fellow in agr.), Cornell U., 1949, PhD, 1951; MD (Peter Yost Fund scholar), U. Chgo., 1957; DSc (hon.), U. Nebr., 1980. Diplomate Nat. Bd. Med. Examiners. Grad. asst., lab. animal nutrition Cornell U., 1947-51; AEC postdoctoral fellow Oak Ridge, 1951-52; research assoc., 1952-53; research asst. pharmacology U. Chgo., 1953-57, asst. prof., 1957-61, assoc. prof., 1961-64; rotating med. intern U. Chgo. Clinics, 1957-58, 58-59, 59; prof. nutrition and comparative metabolism, dept. animal sci. Cornell U., Ithaca, NY, 1964-75; prof. clin. sci. (nutrition and metabolism) Coll. Medicine and dept. food sci. U. Ill. Coll. Agr., Urbana-Champaign, 1975—; prof. dept. internal medicine U. Ill. Coll. Medicine, Urbana-Champaign, 1986-93, prof. emeritus, 1993—. Bd. dirs. Coun. Agriculture, Sci. and Tech., 1994-97; bd. sci. advisors Coun. Sci. and Health, 1994—; Brittingham vis. prof. U. Wis. Madison, 1982-83; Hogan meml. lectr. U. Mo., 1987; mem. subcom. dog nutrition com. animal nutrition NRC-Nat. Acad. Sci., 1965-71; adv. coun. Inst. Lab. Animal Resources, NRC-Nat. Accad. Sci., 1966-69; sub-com. animal care faciltities Survey Inst. Lab. Animal Resources, 1970-76; cons., lectr. in field; mem. sci. adv. com. diet and nutrition cancer program Nat. Cancer Inst., 1976-81; mem. nutrition study sect. NIH, 1980-84; chmn. membership com. Am. Inst. Nutrition-Am. Soc. Clin. Nutrition, 1978-79, 80-83, 85; cons. VA, NSF, indsl. orgns.; Wellcome vis. prof. in basic med. scis. Oreg. State U., 1991-92; bd. sci. counselors USDA, 1989-91. Mem. editl. bd. Jour. Nutrition, 1980-84, editor, 1990-97; mem. editl. bd. Physiol. Rev., 1995-2001; contbr. articles to profl. jours. Bd. dirs. Coun. for Agrl. Sci. and Tech., 1994-97; active local Boy Scouts Am. Served with AUS, 1943-46. Recipient alumni award Nebr. 4-H, 1967, 97, alumni award U. Chgo., 1997, faculty merit award U. Ill. Coll. Medicine, 1988, Alumni Achievement award U. Nebr., 1997, U. Chgo., 1997; Nat. Cancer Inst. spl. fellow MIT, rsch. fellow Mass. Gen. Hosp., 1970-71; sr. scholar U. Ill., 1988. Fellow AAAS, Am. Inst. Nutrition (Osborne and Mendel award 1985), Am. Soc. Animal Sci. (chmn. subcom. antimicrobials, mem. regulatory agency nom. 1973-78); mem. Am. Physiol. Soc., Soc. Pharmacology and Exptl. Therapeutics, Am. Inst. Nutrition (council 1980-83, 85-86), Soc. Exptl. Biology and Medicine, Am. Soc. Clin. Nutrition, Am. Therapeutic Soc., Am. Gastroenterol. Assn., Am. Bd. Clin. Nutrition, Innocents Soc., Fedn. Am. Socs. Exptl. Biology (sci. steering group life scis. rsch. office, adv. com. 1986-92), Am. Bd. Nutrition (bd. dirs.), Am. Soc. Nutritional Scis. (Conrad Elvehjem award 1996), Nat. Dairy Coun. (rsch. adv. com. 1987-91, vis. prof. nutrition program 1991-92), Gamma Alpha (pres. 1948-49), Phi Kappa Phi (pres. 1981-82), Alpha Gamma Rho (pres. 1946-47), Gamma Sigma Delta. Presbyterian (elder). Home: 1405 W William St Champaign IL 61821-4406 Office: U Ill 190 Med Sci Bldg 506 S Mathews Ave Urbana IL 61801-3618 Office Phone: 217-244-2797. Business E-Mail: wvisek@uiuc.edu.

**VISH, DONALD H.,** lawyer, writer, photographer; b. Ft. Benning, Ga., Jan. 18, 1945; s. D. H., Jr. and Dorris (Parrish) Vish; m. Catherine Pence Hamilton, Aug. 20, 1966 (div. 1986); children: Donald Hamilton, Daphne Mershon Sullivan. BA in English, Bellarmine Coll., 1968; JD cum laude, U. Louisville, 1971. Bar: Ky. 1971, Fla. 1972. Sec., gen. counsel Gen. Energy Corp., Lexington, Ky., 1978-83; prin. Wyatt, Tarrant & Combs, Lexington, 1980-88, Frost Brown Todd, Lexington, 1988-89, 1991-98; gen. counsel Ky. Coal Producers' Self-Ins. Fund, 1992-98; sec., gen. counsel AIK Workers Compensation Fund, 1998—2004, exec. v.p., 2002—04, Middleton, Reutlinger, 2004—. Apptd. assoc. solicitor U.S. Dept. Interior, 1991—93; adj. assoc. prof. mineral law U. Ky., Lexington, 1979—85. Author: Poems and Musings, 2001, The Kentucky Anthology: 200 Years of Writing in the Bluegrass State, 2005; contbg. author: American Law of Mining, 2d edit., 1984, bd. editors and contbg. author: Coal Law and Regulation, 1983—93, Kentucky Election Law, 1995. Trustee Syre Sch., Lexington, 1980—88, chmn. bd. dir., 1986—88; mem. Blue Grass coun. Boy Scouts Am., 1988—93; apptd. gov. Ky. Registry Election Fin., 1991—93; bd. dir. Highlands Cmty. Ministries, 2001—04; bd. dirs. Ky. Shakespeare Festival, 2005—, Interfaith Paths to Peace, 2006—. Fellow: Am. Bar Found. (life); mem.: ABA (chmn. coal com., natural resources sect. 1987), Ky. Bar Assn. (mem. ethics com. 1983—85, chair residency com. 1998—2002), Fla. Bar, Energy and Mineral Law Found. (mem. exec. com. 1979—82, trustee 1979—91, trustee emeritus 1998), Am. Law Inst., Louisville Bar Found. (life), Ky. Bar Found. (life). Home: 5020 Nitta Yuma Dr Harrods Creek KY 40027 Office: Middleton Reutlinger 2500 Brown and Williamson Tower Louisville KY 40202 Office Phone: 502-584-1135. Personal E-mail: donaldvish@att.net.

**VISHNESKI, JOHN STANLEY, III,** lawyer; b. Virginia Beach, Va., Aug. 27, 1963; s. John Stanley and Antoinette Ann (Caracciolo) V.; m. Jane Estelle Beard, May 28, 1988; children: John Joseph II, Peter Anthony, Robert Thomas, Elisabeth Katharine. BA, U. Va., 1985, JD, 1988. Bar: N.D. 1988, Ill. 1988, D.C. 1989, U.S. Ct. Appeals (7th cir.) 1991, U.S. Dist. Ct. Md. 1992, U.S. Dist. Ct. D.C. 1992. Ptnr. Mayer, Brown, Rowe & Maw, Chgo. Contbr. articles to profl. jours. Elder Fair Oaks Presbyn. Ch., Oak Park, Ill., 1989—. Mem. ABA, Chgo. Bar Assn. (orch. mem. 1988—), D.C. Bar Assn., 7th Cir. Bar Assn., Raven Soc., Jefferson Soc. (pres. 1985), Phi Beta Kappa, Omicron Delta Kappa. Avocations: clarinet, wine collecting, racquetball. Office: Mayer Brown Rowe Maw Llp 230 S La Salle St Ste 400 Chicago IL 60604-1407 E-mail: jvishneski@mayerbrownrowe.com.

**VISHNIAC, ETHAN TECUMSEH,** astronomy educator; b. New Haven, Sept. 29, 1955; s. Wolf Vladimir and Helen Frances (Simpson) V.; m. Ilene Joy Busch, June 13, 1976; children: Cady Anne, Miriam Rachel. BS and BA summa cum laude, U. Rochester, 1976; MA, Harvard U., 1980. Rsch. assoc. Princeton (N.J.) U., 1980-82; lectr. U. Tex., Austin, 1982-84, asst. prof., 1984-88, assoc. prof., 1988-93, prof., 1993-98, Johns Hopkins U., Balt., 1998—. Assoc. editor Phys. Rev. Letters, 1995-97; sci. editor Astrophys. Jour., 1997—; contbr. numerous articles to profl. jours. Recipient Presdl. Young Investigator, 1985; Alfred Sloan fellow, 1986. Fellow Am. Phys. Soc.; mem. Am. Astron. Soc. (Helen B. Warner prize 1990), Internat. Astron. Union. Business E-Mail: ethan@pha.jhu.edu.

**VISHNOI, NISHEETH KUMAR,** research scientist; s. Naresh Kumar and Kanak Vishnoi. B in Tech. Indian Inst. Tech., Mumbai, India, 1999; PhD, Ga. Inst. Tech., Atlanta, 2004. Rsch. staff mem. IBM Rsch., New Delhi, 2004—06. Recipient Dirs. prize for Academic Achievement, Indian Inst. Tech., Mumbai, 1995—96, Best of IBM award, IBM Rsch., 2005; GTE fellow, Ga. Inst. Tech., 2001, Dean's fellow.

**VISHNU, ABHINAV,** research scientist; b. Moradabad, Uttar Pradesh, India, May 20, 1980; s. Vishnu Prasad and Poonam Agarwal; m. Khushbu Agarwal, Dec. 28, 2005. BS, Banaras Hindu U., Varanasi, 2002; postgrad., Ohio State U., 2002—. Intern Indian Inst. Tech., Delhi, 2000—00, Nat. U. Singapore, 2001—01; grad. rsch. assoc. Ohio State U., Columbus, 2003—06; intern IBM Corp., Austin, Tex., 2005—05; fellow Ohio State U., 2006—. Contbr. articles to profl. jours.; musician: (keyboard player) No Negative Vibrations (Best Keyboardist award, 2001). Organizer Sanskar Bharti, Hapur, Uttar Pradesh, India, 1995—97. Scholar, Ohio State U., 2002—03, 2003—06. Mem.: IEEE (assoc.). Hindu. Achievements include Design and Development of High Performance MPI on InfiniBand with multi-rail support and Fault Tolerance, currently being used by 330 organizations in more than 30 countries. Avocations: tennis, cricket, keyboards. Office: Ohio State U 395 Dreese Labs 2015 Neil Ave Columbus OH 43210 Office Phone: 614-292-5813. E-mail: vishnu@cse.ohio-state.edu.

**VISHNY, PAUL HARVEY,** lawyer; b. Chgo., Feb. 24, 1931; s. Abraham and Anna (Permut) V.; m. Michele Kopstein, June 22, 1952; children: Deborah, Renana. Miriam. JD, DePaul U., 1953. Bar: Ill. 1953, U.S. Dist. Ct. (no. dist.) Ill. 1953, U.S. Ct. Appeals (7th cir.) 1968. Ptnr. Kopstein, Vishny & Miselman, Chgo., 1957—77, D'Ancona & Pflaum, Chgo., 1977—2003; of counsel Seyfarth Shaw, LLP, Chgo., 2003—. Author: Guide to International Commerce Law, 1981, vol. 2, 1984, The Siddur Companion, 2005; editor: International Trade for the Non-Specialist, 1992, 2d edit., 1997. U.S. rep. Ctr. for Telecom. Devel., Geneva, 1985-91. Fellow Am. Bar Found.; mem. ABA, Ill. Bar Assn., Chgo. Bar Assn., Internat. Bar Assn., Fed. Comm. Bar Assn. Avocations: swimming, reading, wine. Home: 227 E Delaware Pl Chicago IL 60611-7758 Office: 131 S Dearborn St Chicago IL 60603 Office Phone: 312-460-5655. E-mail: pvishny@seyfarth.com.

**VISHWANATH, ARUN,** information scientist, educator; arrived in U.S., 1998; s. T. Vishwanath Rajagopalan and Rajagopalan Prema; m. Leslie Anne Padgett, Apr. 7, 1981. BS in Commerce and Econs., U. Bombay, India, 1994, MBA, 1996; PhD, SUNY, Buffalo, N.Y., 2001. Dir. rsch. Goldhaber Rsch. Assocs., Amhrest, NY, 1999—2004; asst. prof. Sch. Informatics U. Buffalo, 2004—. V.p. Buffalo (N.Y.) Ad Coun., 2003—; vis. asst. prof. Ind. U., Bloomington, Ind., 2001—02. Contbr. articles to profl. jours. Grantee, N.Y. Sea Grant, 2004, N.Y. State Dept. Health-Buffalo (N.Y.) Acad. Medicine, 2005, Agy. Healthcare Rsch. and Quality NIH, 2006. Mem.: Assn.Edn. in Journalism and Mass Comms., Acad. Mgmt., Internat. Comm. Assn., Brainstorm Buffalo. Office: University at Buffalo 333 Lord Christopher Baldy Hall Buffalo NY 14260 Business E-Mail: avishy@buffalo.edu.

**VISKANTA, RAYMOND,** mechanical engineering educator; b. Lithuania, July 16, 1931; came to U.S., 1949, naturalized, 1955; s. Vincas and Genovaite (Vinickas) V.; m. Birute Barbara Barpsys, Oct. 13, 1956; children: Renata, Vitas, Tadas. BSME, U. Ill., 1955; MSME, Purdue U., 1956, PhD, 1960; DEng (hon.), Tech. U. Munich, 1994. Registered profl. engr., Ill. Asst. mech. engr. Argonne (Ill.) Nat. Lab., 1956-59, student rsch. assoc., 1959-60, assoc. mech. engr., 1960-62; assoc. prof. mech. engring. Purdue U., West Lafayette, Ind., 1962-66, prof. mech. engring., 1966-86, Goss disting. prof. engring., 1986—. Guest prof. Tech. U. Munich, Germany, 1976-77, U. Karlsruhe, Germany, 1987; vis. prof. Tokyo Inst. Tech., 1983. Contbr. over 500 tech. articles to profl. jours. Recipient Sr. U.S. Scientist award Alexander von Humboldt Found., 1975, Sr. Rsch. award Am. Soc. Engring. Edn., 1984, Nusselt-Reynolds prize, 1991, Thermal Engring. award for Internat. Activity, Japan Soc. Mech. Engrs., 1994, Alumni award for Disting. Svc. U. Ill.-Urbana-Champaign, 2000; Japan Soc. for Promotion of Sci. fellow, 1983. Fellow ASME (Heat Transfer Meml. award 1976, Max Jakob Meml. award 1986, Melville medal 1988), AIAA (Thermophysics award 1979); mem. AAAS, NAE, Acad. Engring. Scis. Russian Fedn. (fgn.), Lithuanian Acad. Scis. (fgn.), Sigma Xi, Pi Tau Sigma, Tau Beta Pi. Home: 3631 Chancellor Way West Lafayette IN 47906-8809 Office: Purdue Univ 585 Purdue Mall West Lafayette IN 47907-2088 Office Phone: 765-494-5632. Personal E-mail: rviskanta@insightbb.com. Business E-Mail: viskanta@ecn.purdue.edu.

**VISNEGARWALA, FEHMIDA,** internist, educator; b. Sidhpur, Gujarat, India, May 12, 1964; arrived in U.S.; 1990; d. Saifuddin and Sarifa; m. Niranjan Iyer, Mar. 22, 1990; children: Ananth Niranjan Iyer, Avinash Hasan Iyer. MBBS, MD, Stanley Med. Coll., India, 1989. Cert. in infectious diseases Am. Bd. Of Internal Medicine. Asst. prof. medicine Baylor Coll. Medicine, Houston, 1998—, dir. edn. and rsch., 2000—04. Co-chair programs for clin. rsch. in AIDS Terry Berin Cmty., 2000—05. Grantee, NIH and Bristol Myers Squibb Found., 1999—2002. Mem.: Am. Assn. HIV Medicine. Office: Baylor College Med Path Dept 2627 Landera Ct Pearland TX 77584-9113 Office Phone: 713-798-3942. Personal E-mail: fehmiday@bcm.tmc.edu.

**VISNJIC, GORAN,** actor; b. Sibenik, Croatia, Sept. 9, 1972; m. Ivana Vrdoljak. Grad., Acad. of Dramatic Arts, Zagreb. Actor: (films) Maternal Halfbrothers, 1988, Paranoia, 1993, Welcome to Sarajevo, 1997, The Peacemaker, 1997, Rounders, 1998, Practical Magic, 1998, Committed, 2000, The Deep End, 2001, (voice) Ice Age, 2002, Doctor Sleep, 2002, Long Dark Night, 2004, Elektra, 2005; (TV films) See You, 1995, Night Watch, 1995,

Spartacus, 2004; (TV series) ER, 1999—. Recipient Vladimir Nazor award, 2005. Avocations: fencing, diving, swimming. Office: c/o United Talent Agency 9560 Wilshire Blvd Ste 5 Beverly Hills CA 90212-2400*

**VISO, OLGA,** museum director; b. Fla. MA in Art History, Emory U., 1992. Positions in dept. modern & contemporary art, office of registrar and office of dir. High Mus. Art, Atlanta, 1989—93; asst. cur. Norton Mus. Art, West Palm Beach, Fla., 1993, Hirshhorn Mus. and Sculpture Garden, Washington, 1995, assoc. cur., 1998, cur. contemporary art, 2000—03, dep. dir., 2003—06, dir., 2006—. Mem. Fed. Adv. Com. Internat. Exhibitions; co-commr., US Pavilion Venice Biennial, 2001. Arranged (exhibitions) Distemper: Dissonant Themes in the Art of the 1990s, 1996, Regarding Beauty: A View of the Late Twentieth Century, 1999—2000. Office: Smithsonian Institution PO Box 37012 Hirshhorn Mus MRC Code 350 Washington DC 20013*

**VISOCKI, NANCY GAYLE,** information services consultant; b. Dumont, N.J., May 13, 1952; d. Thomas and Gloria Visocki. BA in Math., Manhattanville Coll., 1974; MS in Ops. Rsch. and Stats., Rensselaer Poly. Inst., 1977. Rsch. asst. Coll. Physicians and Surgeons Columbia U., N.Y.C., 1974-75; programmer analyst R. Shriver Assocs., Parsippany, NJ, 1977-79; sr. tech. rep. GE Info. Svcs. Co., East Orange, NJ, 1979-81, mgr. project office Morristown, NJ, 1981-83, tech. dir., 1983-87, tech. mgr., 1988-89, area mgr. sys. devel. and consulting Parsippany, 1989-92, area tech. mgr. sys. devel. and cons., Fin. Info. Sys., 1992-93, sr. cons. info. svcs., 1993-98, project mgr. e-commerce sys. integration, 1998-2000; mgr. Major e-commerce Applications Practice, 2000—03. Active Western Hills Christian Ch., Tranquility, N.J., 1986—; vol. Women's Ctr., Hackettstown, N.J., 1989-93; class fund-raising and gift chmn. Rensselaer Poly. Inst., Troy, N.Y., 1991-95; vol. Elfun Soc., 1981—; vol. bd. dirs., treas. NJCFS Assn., 2004— Manhattanville Coll. grantee, Purchase, N.Y., 1970-71; tuition fellow Rensselaer Poly. Inst., 1975-77. Mem. NAFE, Elfun, Women of Accomplishment. Avocations: tai chi, hiking, bicycling, reading, yoga.

**VISSCHER, MARTY ORRICO,** biomedical researcher; d. Frank Paul and Elizabeth Brinkley Orrico; m. Ronald Bosman Visscher, June 10, 1972; children: Paul David, Robert Christopher. PhD, Ind. U., Bloomington, Ind., 1973; student, Xavier U., Cin., Ohio, 2005—. Postdoctoral fellow chemistry Ind. U., Bloomington, 1973—74, vis. prof. chemistry, 1974—76; asst. prof. chemistry U. Cin., 1976—78; sr. scientist R&D The Procter & Gamble Co., Cin., 1978—95; co-founder, dir. The Skin Sciences Inst. Cin. Children's Hosp. Med. Ctr., 1995—, rschr. The Skin Scis. Inst., 1995—. Mem. ADHD collaborative and task force Cin. Children's Hosp. Med. Ctr., 2002—; spkr. in field. Author: The Ideas of Chemistry, Harcourt Brace Jovanovich Inc., Laboratory Manual for The Ideas of Chemistry, Harcourt, Brace, Jovanovich, Inc., New York; contbr. chapters to books, articles to profl. jours. Mem. troop com. troop 417 Boy Scouts of Am., Cin., 1992—2006, merit badge counselor troop 417, 1996—2006; pres. Glendale Youth Sports, Cin., 1994—96, coach soccer, 1990—94; pres. Princeton Aquatics Parent Bd. Princeton City Schs., Cin., 1998—2000. Mem.: WGUC Pub. Radio, Glendale Lyceum. Achievements include patents in field. Avocations: running, fashion design, sewing, art, embroidery. Office: Cincinnati Children's Hospital Medical C 3333 Burnet Avenue Cincinnati OH 45229 Office Phone: 513-558-0393. Business E-Mail: visschmo@email.uc.edu.

**VISSER, LESLEY,** sports correspondent; b. Quincy, Mass., Sept. 11, 1953; m. Dick Stockton. BA cum laude in English, Boston Coll., 1975; PhD (hon.), Coll. Our Lady of Elms, Mass., 1995. Sports staff Boston Globe, 1974-88; feature reporter, sports staff CBS Sports, 1988—94, 2000—; corr. GameDay (now NFL Countdown), SportsCenter ESPN, Bristol, Conn., 1994-98; side-line reporter ABC, N.Y.C., 1994-00, reporter Monday Night Football, 1998-00. Sideline reporter coll. football, NFL and Super Bowl ABC, 1994—; reporter Monday Night Football, 1998—. Trustee Women's Sports Found., 1993—. Named outstanding woman sportswriter in Am., 1983, New England Newswoman of the Yr., WISE Woman of the Yr., 2002; named to the New England Sports Hall of Fame; recipient Journalism award Women's Sports Found., 1992, Pioneer award AWSM, 1999, Compass award, 2003, Pete Rozelle Radio Television award, Pro Football Hall of Fame 2006, Pop Warner Female Achievement award, 2006, Gracie Allen award Am. Women in Radio & Television, 2006 Office: CBS Sports 524 W 57th St New York NY 10019-2924*

**VISSER, RICHARD EDGAR,** minister; b. South Weymouth, Mass., Apr. 28, 1937; s. Edgar and Marjorie (McPhee) V.; m. Carol Naomi Edwards, June 21, 1958; children: Andrew, Thomas, Peter. AB, Gordon Coll., 1958, BS, 1959; BD, Gordon Div. Sch., 1962, MRE, 1965; D Ministry, Asbury Theol. Sem., 1983. Ordained to ministry Am. Bapt. Chs. in U.S.A., 1962. Pastor Acton-Milton Mills Bapt. Ch., Milton Mills, NH, 1962—65, First Bapt. Ch., Derry, NH, 1966—69; min. edn. Peters Creek Bapt. Ch., Library, Pa., 1969-73; pastor 1st Bapt. Ch., Warren, Pa., 1973-79, min. ch. edn. and music St. Albans, W.Va., 1980-83, sr. pastor Waynesburg, Pa., 1983—2003; co-pastor First Baptist Church, Warren, Pa., 2003—06; interim exec. min. Pitts. Baptist Assn., 2004—05. Pres. Clergymen's Assn. of Derry, 1967-69; founder, chmn. Pitts. Ch. Edn. Conv., 1972-73; clk. Pitts. Bapt. Assn. 1971-73; pres. Ministerial Assn., Warren, 1975-76, St. Albans, 1982-83, Waynesburg, 1988-90, 99-2001; moderator Ten Mile Assn. Waynesburg, 1985-87; pres., Ten Mile Assn. Mins. and Spouses, 2001-03; co-founder, vice chmn. Ten Mile and Monogahela Assns. Lic. Lay Pastor Tng. Program, 1988-90; chairperson Am. Bapt. Chs. Leadership Inst. Western Pa., 1993-2002; pres. Am. Bapt. Chs. of Pa. and Del., 1991-92, chmn. Sunday Sch. team, 1987-90, exec. com., 1987-94, 1997-2002, chmn. Budget Commn. 2004-05; mem. gen. bd., bd. ednl. ministries Am. Bapt. Chs. U.S.A., 1997-2002, mem. comms. com., 1999-2002, com. of 100 for Renewal, 1992-98; mem. Ministers and Missionaries Benefit Bd., 1999-2002, chmn. benefits com., 2000-02. Founder, chmn. Warren (Pa.) Community Chorus, 1974-78; pres. Warren County Health and Welfare Coun., 1975-77; chmn. Forest-Warren Counties Human Svcs. Adv. Commn., 1978-79; co. chmn. Greene County Human Svcs. Adv. Commn., Pa., 1988-96, vice chmn., 2000—02, chmn. mental health com., 2000—02, mem. sr. outreach and referral coalition, 2001-03; chmn. Greene County chpt. ARC, 1989-91; bd. dirs. Greene County Meml. Hosp., 1989—02; bd. dirs. Comty. Found. Greene County, 2000—03, vice chmn. 2001—03; mem. emergency food and shelter bd. Greene County FEMA, 1985-2003. Recipient Apollo award, Alderson-Broaddus Coll., Phillipi, W.Va., 1995. Disting. Cmty. Svc. award, Greater Waynesburg C. of C., 2002. Mem. Am. Bapt. Mins. Coun. (Excellence in Ministry award 2000, v.p. Pa. and Del. chpt. 1978-79), Rotary (v.p. Waynesburg Club 1990-91, pres. 1991-92). Avocations: walking, reading, singing. Home: Apt 204 25 Thornton Way Brunswick ME 04011 Office Phone: 814-723-1751. Personal E-mail: cvisser15370@yahoo.com. *I feel that sometimes people avoid leadership roles because they can be demanding. I do not seek leadership roles, but when I see needs and suggest possible solutions, these roles often seem to find me. I have found that an open, ordinary person such as I can make a difference and enjoy some rich rewards.*

**VISTA, JEFF PETER,** emergency medicine physician; b. Mineola, N.Y., Jan. 3, 1966; s. Reynaldo Bueta and Irenea Solmoro (Dorado) V.; m. Emily Sue Kyper, May 11, 1991; children: Andrew, Elizabeth. BA in Chemistry, W.Va. U., 1987; MD, Uniformed Svcs. U. Health Sci., Bethesda, Md., 1991. Diplomate Am. Bd. Emergency Medicine. Intern Wright State U., Dayton, Ohio, 1991-92, resident, 1992-94; mem. staff 1st Med. Group, Langley AFB, Va., 1994—, Southside Regional Med. Ctr., Petersburg, Va., 1995—, Health South Med. Ctr., Richmond, Va., 1995—. Mem. Am. Coll. Emergency Physicians. Roman Catholic. Office: 45 Pine St Langley Afb VA 23665-2025

**VISTE, ARLEN ELLARD,** chemistry professor; b. Austin, Minn., Aug. 13, 1936; s. Arthur E. and Edith L. (Kehret) V.; m. Elizabeth Ann Landbeck, June 14, 1959; children: Solveig, David, Mark. BA, St. Olaf Coll., 1958; PhD, U. Chgo., 1962. Asst. prof. chemistry St. Olaf Coll., Northfield, Minn., 1962-63; NSF fellow Columbia U., N.Y.C., 1963-64; asst. prof. Augustana Coll., Sioux Falls, SD, 1964-68, assoc. prof., 1968-73, prof., 1973—, prof. emeritus, 2002—. Contbr. articles to profl. jours. Mem. Am. Chem. Soc., Royal Soc.

Chemistry (London), S.D. Acad. Sci., Midwest Assn. Chemistry Tchrs. in Liberal Arts Colls., Phi Beta Kappa, Sigma Xi. Home: 1500 W 30th St Sioux Falls SD 57105-3622 Office: Augustana Coll Chemistry Dept Sioux Falls SD 57197-0001 Business E-Mail: arlen.viste@augie.edu.

**VISWANATHAN, GOPALAKRISHNAN,** metallurgist, researcher; b. Trichy, India, Dec. 20, 1964; arrived in U.S., 2000; s. Viswanathan Muthuswamy Iyer and Lalitha Viswanathan; m. Sivagamasundari Gopalakrishnan, Jan. 22, 1999; children: Balaji, Siddharth. MS, Bharathidasan U., Tamil Nadu, India, 1987; MS in Engring., Regional Engring. Coll., Madras, India, 1992; PhD in Metallurgy, Indian Inst. Tech., Madras, India, 1999. Lectr. Mookambigai Coll. Engring., Tamil Nadu, India, 1987—92; rschr. Indian Inst. Tech., Madras, India, 1993—99; scientist, dir. Madras, India, 1999—2000; metallurgist Controlled Thermal Tech., Phoenix, 2000—01, Superior Shot Penning Inc., Houston, 2001—. Contbr. articles to profl. jours. Mem.: Thermal Spray Soc., Am. Soc. for Materials. Achievements include establishing a treatment procedure for critical parts of a fast breeder test reactor. Home: 12919 Windfern Rd Apt 3401 Houston TX 77064 Office: Superior Shot Penning Inc 13930 Luthe Rd Houston TX 77039

**VISWANATHAN, RAMASWAMY,** physician, educator; b. Coimbatore, India, Aug. 20, 1949; came to U.S., 1972; s. Thiruvalangadu and Bhavani Krishnamurthy Ramaswamy; m. Kusum Ramakrishna, June 15, 1980; children: Vikram, Vivek, Vidya. MB, BS, U. Madras, 1972; D of Med. Sci., SUNY, 1989. Diplomate Am. Bd. Psychiatry and Neurology, geriatric psychiatry, addiction psychiatry, Am. Bd. Internal Medicine. Med. intern Bklyn.-Cumberland Med. Ctr., 1972-73; resident in internal medicine L.I. Jewish-Hillside Med. Ctr.-Queens Hosp. Ctr. Affiliation, N.Y.C., 1973-74; resident in psychiatry SUNY Health Sci. Ctr., Bklyn., 1974-77, fellow in psychosomatic medicine, 1976-78, fellow in research tng. in psychiatry, 1977-79, mem. staff, 1978—, clin. asst. prof. psychiatry, 1979-87, instr. in medicine, 1979—, clin. assoc. prof., 1987-90, assoc. prof. clin. psychiatry, 1990—, assoc. dir. med.-psychiat. liaison svc., 1981-83, 84-97, acting dir., 1983-84, dir., psychiat. liaison svc., 1998—, med. dir. Anxiety Disorders Clinic, 1982—, mem. com. cancer edn. and preventive oncology, 1983-92, dir. course on life-threatening illness, dying and death, 1984-89, dir. med. interviewing course, 1988-89, dir. doctor-patient relationship course, 1989-90, dir. intro. to clin. medicine-human dimension course, 1990-98. cons. AIDS unit, 1989—, with student examination and promotion com., 1989-94, with course dirs.' com., 1989-98; mem. exec. com. Univ. Hosp., 1992-96; internal medicine residency program rev. com. SUNY Health Sci. Ctr., 1994—; cons. Bklyn. VA Med. Ctr., 1986-89; pvt. practice medicine specializing in psychiatry, psychosomatic medicine, behavior therapy, hypnosis and sex therapy Bklyn., 1978—. Mem. task force on doctoring experience curricular reform, 1997—; Contbr. articles to profl. jours. Curriculum coun. Herricks Pub. Sch. Dist., 1992-95. Fellow ACP, Am. Psychiat. Assn. (dep. rep. Asian-Am. caucus 1996-99, RG rep. 1999—, assembly com. on procedures, 1997—, com. on consultation, liaison psychiatry and primary care edn. 1992-98, coun. on internat. affairs 1992-95, 97—, nominating com. 1997-98, assembly com. on planning 1998—, cert. excellence in med. evaluation 1999), Indian Psychiat. Soc. (life), Acad. Psychosomatic Medicine; mem. AMA, Bklyn. Psychiat. Soc. (councillor, pres. elect 1988-90, pres. 1990-92, chmn. com. on AIDS, 1990-92, chmn. on consultation-liaison psychiatry 1990-92, chmn. disaster response com. 1991-92, chmn. legis. and pvt. practice com. 1992-96, chmn. legis. com. 1996—, chmn. internat. affairs com. 1992-94), Am. Acad. Psychiatry and the Law (rsch. com. 1998—, internat. rels. com. 1999—, Assn. Advancement Behavior Therapy, Soc. Liaison Psychiatry (bd. dirs. 1986-90, 93-96, sec. 1987-88), Anxiety Disorders Assn. Am., N.Y. State Psychiat. Assn. (com. on govt. health programs 1988-94, task force on practice guidelines, legis. com., chmn. edn. com. 1992-96), Soc. Exploration Psychotherapy Integration, Indo-Am. Psychiat. Assn. (founder, life, exec. com. 1979-85, 92—, sec. 1992-94, pres.-elect 1994-96, pres. 1996-98, Sci. and Svc. award 1990). Office: SUNY Health Sci Ctr 450 Clarkson Ave # 127 Brooklyn NY 11203-2056

**VITA, MICHAEL,** economist; s. William and Marjorie Vita; m. Jean Hamilton, Oct. 9, 1993; children: Rosemary, Lily. BA, Pa. State U., University Park, 1977; MS, U. Wis., Madison, 1984; PhD, U. Wis., 1984. Economist FTC, Washington, 1984—86, dep. asst. dir. for econ. policy analysis, 1986—2000, asst. dir. for antitrust, 2000—. Office: FTC 600 Pennsylvania Ave NW Washington DC 20580 Office Phone: 202-326-3493. E-mail: mvita@ftc.gov.

**VITA, STEVEN,** poet; b. Chgo., July 16, 1960; s. John and Rosemarie V. BA in Art and English, Denison U., Granville, Ohio, 1982; MFA in English, CUNY, 1985. Founder, editor Veery, Chgo., 1991—. *"John Bayley of Oxford University analyzes, 'Vita is a poet of great promise as well as performance. He has affinities with a very distinguished kind of poet/one might call them in School of Contingency/whose doyen is of course John Ashbery."--KSUI-FM National Public Radio (NPR), Iowa City. "He is, I believe, that increasingly rare bird the true original."--Daniel Weissbort, The University of London, "The Heart of Tents." "Sir Stephen Spender, who first published W.H. Auden and whose own poetry was brought to the literary public by T.S. Eliot, calls Vita's abilities as a poet 'gifted'."--Daily Southtown.* Author: The Heart of Tents, 1991.

**VITALE, ALBERTO ALDO,** retired publishing company executive; b. Vercelli, Italy, Dec. 22, 1933; came to U.S., 1960; s. Sergio and Elena (Segre) V.; m. Gemma G. Calori, Oct. 11, 1961; children— Raffaele Robert, Alessandro David. D Econs. and Bus. Adminstrn., U. Turin, Italy, 1956, postgrad., 1956-57; postgrad. (Fulbright scholar), U. Pa. Wharton Sch. Fin., 1957-58. With Olivetti Corp. Am., 1959-72, dir. corp. planning N.Y.C., 1965-69, v.p. adminstrn., 1969-70, v.p. adminstrn., treas. N.Y.C., 1970-72; prin. officer IFI, Torino, 1972-75; exec. v.p., chief operating officer, dir. Bantam Books, Inc., N.Y.C., 1975-85, pres., 1985-87, co-CEO, 1985-86, CEO, 1986-87; pres., CEO Bantam, Doubleday, Dell Pub. Group, 1987-90, Random House, N.Y.C., 1990-96, chmn., CEO, 1998-99; chmn. supervisory bd. Random House Inc., N.Y.C., 1990—2000; ret., 2003. Bd. overseers U. Pa. Libr., 1989—; chmn. Frankfurt e.book award, 1999-2002. Mem. Assn. Am. Pubs. (dir. 1979, 86) Office: 555 5th Ave #15 New York NY 10017-2416

**VITALE, DICK,** commentator, sports writer; b. Garfield, N.J. m. Lorraine Vitale; children: Terri, Sherri. Basketball coach East Rutherford (N.J.) High Sch., 1965-71; asst. basketball coach Rutgers U., New Brunswick, NJ, 1972; coll. basketball coach U. Detroit, 1973-77, athletic dir., 1978; pro basketball coach Detroit Pistons, Auburn Hills, Mich., 1978-79; TV commentator, Sports analyst ESPN Sports, 1979—; TV commentator ABC Sports, 1987—; sports radio commentator ABC Radio Network, 1987—; sports columnist Basketball Times, 1979—, Ea. Basketball, 1979—. Radio commentator The J. P. McCarthy Show, Detroit; guest spkr., lectr. Co-author: (with Curay Kirk Patrick) Vitale: Just Your Average, Bald, One-Eyed Basketball Wacko Who Beat the Ziggy and Became a PTP'er, 1989, (with Dick Weiss) Time Out, Baby!, 1992, (with Mike Douchant) Tourney Time, It's Awesome Baby, 1994; co-author various computer games; appeared in TV commls. for Adidas, Taco Bell. Named Sports Personality of Yr., Am. Sportscasters Assn., 1989. Roman Catholic. Achievements include earning 5 sectional and 2 consecutive state championships as high sch. basketball coach.*

**VITALE, GERALD LEE,** finance company executive; b. Chgo., Apr. 3, 1950; s. Le Roy Allen and Gilda Leanora (Rasori) V. BS in Psychology, Loyola U., Chgo., 1972. Fin. mgr. Mellon Fin., Chgo., 1973-76; credit mgr. Kemper Ins. Co., Chgo., 1976-78; pres., CEO Tribune Employees Credit Union, Chgo., 1978-96. Pres. NCR Credit Union User Group, Dayton, Ohio, 1984-91; CEO, Gerald Equity Resources, Inc., 1996—; mem. adv. bd. Ill. Gov.'s Credit Union, 1993-98; dir. fin. Rush Cancer Inst., 2000-2001. Co-host Chicagoland Cable (CLTV) TV Fin. Reports, Tribune Broadcasting, 1993-96. Mem. Habitat for Humanity, 1998—, Nat. Rep. Senatorial Com., 2002; counselor youth motivation Chgo. C. of C. and Industry, 1980—97, mem. adv. bd., 1984—96; counselor Hire the Future, 1988—96; vol. Red Cloud Athletic Assn., 1993—2000, Friends of Providence-St. Mel, 1993—; mem.

Chgo. Coun. Fgn. Rels., 1995—98; mem. Coun. of 1000 Nat. Italian-Am. Found., 1995—99, Humane Soc. U.S., 1997—; mem. fin. svcs. com. Exec. Club City of Chgo., 1993—99; mem. Ctr. Study of Presidency, 1993—97, Filene Inst., 1992—96, Ill. Arts Alliance, 1996—98, George Bush Presdl. Libr. Found., 2002—, GOP Action Com., 1992—97; life mem. Rep. Nat. Com., 1977—; mem. Ill. Rep. Party, 2002—. Recipient award, Eisenhower Commn., 2002. Mem.: Fgn. Policy Rsch. Inst., Lincoln Park C. of C., Greater Garfield C. of C. (bd. dirs. 1992—95), The Carter Ctr., Am. Enterprise Inst., Nat. Assn. Investors (corp. mem. 1999—), Nat. Assn. State Chartered Credit Unions (bd. dirs. 1995—97, region V dir.), Midwest Assn. Credit Unions (bd. dirs. 1992—96), Am. Mgmt. Assn., Heritage Found., Sky Line Club, Monroe Club (bd. dirs. 1995—99). Roman Catholic. Avocations: hiking, rowing, long-distance walking. Home: 1636 N Wells St Apt 2410 Chicago IL 60614-6020 Office: GER Inc 1636 N Wells St Apt 2410 Chicago IL 60614-6020 E-mail: gerinc@aol.com.

**VITALE, THOMAS M.,** lawyer; b. NYC, Aug. 16, 1956; AB in Physics, Princeton Univ., 1977; JD, Stanford Univ., 1980. Bar: NY 1981, US Dist. Ct. (so. dist. NY) 1981. Atty. Chadbourne & Parke, NY, 1980—81, Battle Fowler, NY, 1982—85, Gaston & Snow, NY, 1985—91; ptnr. Mayer, Brown, Rowe & Maw LLP, NY, 1991—, now ptnr.-in-charge NYC Office. Assoc. editor Stanford Law Rev. Mem.: Phi Beta Kappa. Office: MayerBrown Rowe & Maw LLP 1675 Broadway New York NY 10019-5820 Office Phone: 212-506-2510. Office Fax: 212-849-5510. Business E-mail: tvitale@mayerbrownrowe.com.

**VITALO, SANDRA LYNN LIDDY,** music educator, singer; b. Livingston, N.J., Sept. 14, 1977; d. George Alan and Jeanette Liddy; m. Anthony Jason Vitalo, Feb. 28, 2004. MusB, Thje Coll. N.J., 2000; MEd, U. Phoenix, 2005. Cert. Tchr. Music K-12 N.J., 2001. Dir. choral, asst. dir. band Middletown H.S. South, NJ, 2002—, asst. dir. band, 2003—06. Working student Tall Oaks Horse Farm, Howell, NJ, 2006—; curriculum writing Middletown H.S. South, 2005—, dir. musical, 2002—. Singer (actor): (theater) N.J. Cmty. Theater. Mem.: All Shore Chorus (v.p. 2004—06, 2004—), Music Educators Nat. Conf. Office: Middletown High School South 900 Nut Swamp Road Middletown NJ 07748 Office Phone: 732-706-6111 2557.

**VITA-MORE, NATASHA,** information technology executive; b. Bronxville, N.Y., Feb. 22, 1950; d. John Simpson and Winifred Drake Clark; m. Max More, Mar. 23, 1996. BFA, U. of Memphis, 1974; MS, U. of Houston, 2006; postgrad., U. of Plymouth, Eng., 2006—. Lic.: Calif. (paralegal) 1992; cert. personal trainer Am. Muscle & Fitness, 2001, registered nutrition specialist Am. Muscle & Fitness, Calif., 2001. Founder Transhumanist Arts & Culture, LA, 1983—; sr. assoc. Foresight Inst., Palo Alto, Calif., 1995—; pres. Extropy Inst., LA, 2001—. Design prototype, Primo Posthuman. Adv. com. Alcor Life Ext. Found., Scottsdale, Ariz., 1999—; councilperson Green Party, L.A., 1991—93. Recipient First Pl., Brooks Meml. Mus. of Art, 1971. Mem.: World Transhumanist Assn. (hon. vice chmn. 2000—), Assn. of Profl. Futurists (corr.), SAG (assoc.), Women in Tech. (assoc.). Avocations: scuba diving, skiing, cycling, body sculpting. Office: Extropy Institute 10709 Pointe View Dr Austin TX 78738 Office Phone: 512-263-2749. E-mail: natasha@extropy.org.

**VITATOE, LEE ANNE,** aerospace medicine executive, aerospace physiologist; b. Omaha, Nebr., Sept. 20, 1971; d. John Montgomery and Joan Lee Green; m. David Lawrence Vitatoe, May 28, 1994. BS in health appraisal and enhancement, Miami U., 1993, MS in exercise sci., 1994. Cert. Strength and Conditioning Coach Nat. Strength and Conditioning Assn., 1996, Personal Trainer Nat. Strength and Conditioning Assn., 1995. Divsn. officer Aviation Survival Tng. Inst., Norfolk, Va., 1994—97; aeromedical safety officer Comdr., Fighter Wing Atlantic, Virginia Beach, Va., 1997—2001; operational test dir. Marine Helicopter Squadron One, Quantico, Va., 2001—05; aviation life support systems team lead Naval Air Warfare Ctr. (Code 4.6.3.3), Patuxent River, Md., 2005—. Treas. Soc. US Aerospace Physiologists, 2003—05, v.p., 2005—. Lt. comdr. USN, 1993—2005. Decorated Meritorious Svc. medal Marine Helicopter Squadron One, Navy and Marine Corps Commendation medals (2) Comdr., Fighter Wing Atlantic, Navy and Marine Corps Achievement medal Naval Aviation Survival Tng. Ctr., Meritorious Unit Commendation Marine Helicopter Squadron One, Joint Meritorious Unit Commendation medal. Mem.: Soc. of US Aerospace Physiologists (assoc.; v.p. 2005—), Aerospace Med. Assn. (assoc.), Nat. Strength and Conditioning Assn. (assoc.), Omicron Delta Kappa (assoc.), PEO (assoc.; treas. 1996—2005), Delta Gamma Frat. (assoc.; pres. 1992—93). Conservative. Methodist. Avocations: travel, cooking, knitting, bicycling. Office: Naval Air Warfare Ctr Bldg 2187 48110 Shaw Rd Ste 1240 Patuxent River MD 20670-1906 Office Phone: 301-342-8432. Personal E-mail: lee.vitatoe@navy.mil.

**VITE, FRANK ANTHONY,** realtor; b. Aurora, Ill., Feb. 9, 1930; s. Frank A. and Rose (Cosentino) V.; grad. Marmion Mil. Acad., 1948; student Sch. Mgmt., U. Notre Dame, 1958; B.A. (hon.), Hillsdale Coll., 1972; m. Barbara Ann Decio, Oct. 23, 1954; children: Bradley Scott, Mark Steven, Michael Lee, Leslie Ann, Lisa Ann. Plant engr. Lyon Metal Products, Aurora, 1951-52, purchasing agt., 1953-54; became sales mgr., exec. v.p., owner, dir. Skyline Homes, Inc., Elkhart, Ind., 1954; pres., owner B&F Realty, Inc., No. Ind. Appraisal Co., Golden Falcon Homes, Inc.; real estate broker; dir. 1st Nat. Bank, Elkhart, Ind. Trustee Hillsdale (Mich.) Coll., Holy Cross Coll., South Bend, Ind.; bd. dirs. Ind. Commn. Higher Edn. With AUS, 1952-53, Korea. Mem. Elkhart Bd. Realtors, Nat. Sales Execs. Assn., Ind. Real Estate Assn. Nat. Real Estate Brokers, Holy Name Soc. K C (4 deg.) Knight of Malta, Elks. Republican. Office: 1300 Cassopolis St Elkhart IN 46514-3248 Home: 9 Colonia Miramonte Paradise Valley AZ 85253 Office Phone: 574-264-0651.

**VITEK, REGINALD A. (REG),** lawyer; b. Bakersfield, Calif., Apr. 23, 1942; BA, San Diego State Coll., 1964; JD, UCLA, 1967. Bar: Calif. 1967, US Ct. Appeals (2d, 9th cir.), US Supreme Ct. 1976. Ptnr. bus. litigation Seltzer Caplan McMahon Vitek, San Diego. Lectr. Nat. Inst. Trial Advocacy. Mem.: ABA, State Bar Calif., San Diego County Bar Assn., Fed. Bar Assn., Assn. Trial Lawyers Am., San Diego County Trial Lawyers Assn., Assn. Bus. Trial Lawyers (founding mem. San Diego chpt.), Am. Inns of Ct., Louis M. Welsh San Diego chpt. (Master, mem. exec. com.). Office: Seltzer Caplan McMahon Vitek Symphony Towers 750 B St San Diego CA 92101 Office Phone: 858-685-3075. Office Fax: 858-702-6804. Business E-mail: vitek@scmv.com.

**VITEK, VACLAV,** materials scientist; b. Olomouc, Czechoslovakia, Sept. 10, 1940; came to U.S., 1978; s. Josef and Ruzena V.; m. Ludovita Stankovicova, Aug. 5, 1972; children: Adrian Joseph, Clementine Mary. BSc in Physics, Charles U., Prague, 1962; PhD in Physics, Czechoslovakian Acad. Scis., Prague, 1966; doctorate (hon.), Tech. U. Brno, 1999. Research assoc. dept. metall. materials sci. and research fellow Wolfson Coll., Oxford (Eng.) U., 1967-75; research officer Central Elec. Research Labs., Central Elec. Generating Bd., Leatherhead, Eng., 1975-78; prof. materials sci. and engring. U. Pa., 1978—. Vis. prof. U. Groningen, Netherlands, 1985-86. Recipient Humboldt award for sr. scientists, Germany, 1992-93, Acta metallurgica Gold medal, 1996, Mach medal Czech Acad. Scis., 1999. Fellow Inst. Physics (London), Am. Soc. Metals Internat., Metals, Minerals Materials Soc.; mem. NAE (elected 2006), Am. Phys. Soc., Materials Rsch. Soc. Office: U Pa Dept Materials Sci and Engring 3231 Walnut St Philadelphia PA 19104-6202 Business E-mail: vitek@lrsm.upenn.edu.

**VITELLO, PAUL,** journalist; m. Carol Polsky; children: Sam, Anna. BA, Trinity Coll., Hartford, Conn. Reporter New York Newsday, 1981—2005, New York Times, 2005—. Author: (articles) Recount's Silent Stunner: Gore Should Have Won, 2001, The Eleventh of Never, 2005. Office: The New York Times 3000 Hempstead Tpke Ste 200 Levittown NY 11756-1409*

**VITETTA, ELLEN S.,** microbiologist, educator, immunologist; BA, Conn. Coll.; MS, NYU, 1966, PhD, MD, 1968. Prof. microbiology Southwestern Med. Sch., U. Tex., Dallas, 1976—; dir. Cancer Immunobiology Ctr., U. Tex., Dallas, 1988—; Sheryle Simmons Patigian Disting. chair in cancer immunology Southwestern Med. Sch., U. Tex., Dallas, 1989—. Bd. sci. coun. NCI Cancer Treatment Bd., 1993; sci. adv. bd. Howard Hughes Med. Inst., 1992—; Kettering selection com. GM Cancer Rsch. Foun., 1987-88; task force NIAID in Immunology, 1989-90; mem. sci. bd. Ludwig Inst., 1983—. Mem. editl. bd.: Advances in Host Defense Mechanisms, 1983—, Annual Review of Immunology, 1991—, Bioconjugate Chemistry, 1989-93, Cellular Immunology, 1984-93, Current Opinions in Immunology, 1992—, FASEB Journal, 1987—, Internat. Jour. of Oncology, 1992—, Internat. Soc. Immunopharmacology, 1989—, Jour. of Immunology, 1975-78, Molecular Immunology, 1978-93; assoc. editor Cancer Research, 1986—; Immunochemistry sect. editor: Jour. of Immunology, 1978-82; co-editor in chief: Therapeutic Immunology, 1992—. Recipient Women's Excellence in Sci. award Fedn. Am. Soc. Exptl. Biology, 1991, Taittinger Breast Cancer Rsch. award Komen Found., 1983, Pierce Immunotoxin award, 1988, NIH Merit award, 1987—, U. Tex. Southwestern Med. Sch. Faculty Teaching award 1989, 91, 92, 93, 94, FASED Excellence in Sci. award, 1991, Abbot Clinical Immunology award Am. Soc. Microbiologists, 1992, Past State Pres. award Tex. Fed. Bus. Profl. Women's Club, 1993, Richard and Hinda Rosenthal Found. award Am. Assn. Cancer Rsch 1995, Charlotte Friend award Am. Assn. Cancer Rsch., 1995, AAAS Mentreny award, 2002. Mem. Am. Assn. Immunologists (pres. 1994), Nat. Acad. Scis., Am. Acad. Microbiology (hon.). Achievements include co-discovery of IL-4, development of immunotoxins and identification of IgD on murine B cells. Office: Univ Texas Cancer Immunobiol Ctr 6000 Harry Hines Blvd Dallas TX 75235-5303 Address: 6914 Pemberton Dr Dallas TX 75230-4260 E-mail: ellen.vitetta@utsoutheastern.edu.

**VITEV, IVAN MATEEV,** physicist, researcher; arrived in US, 1997; s. Matei Ivanov Vitev and Lilia Zlatkova Viteva; m. Sofiya Nikolova Micheva-Viteva, Jan. 14, 2000. MS, Sofia U., Bulgaria, 1995; PhD, Columbia U., N.Y.C., 2002. Cert. physics tchr. Sofia U., Bulgaria, 1995. Rsch. assoc. Iowa State U., Ames, 2002—04; J. Robert Oppenheimer fellow Los Alamos Nat. Lab., N.Mex., 2004—. Grantee, Los Alamos Nat. Lab., 2005—; J. Robert Oppenheimer fellow, 2004—. Mem.: Am. Phys. Soc. Achievements include research in theoretical nuclear physics; new states of matter; jet interactions in quark-gluon plasma. Avocations: photography, hiking. Office: Los Alamos Nat Lab Mail Stop B283 Group T-16 Los Alamos NM 87545 Office Phone: 505-665-8066. Office Fax: 505-667-1931. E-mail: ivitev@lanl.gov.

**VITEZ, MICHAEL,** reporter; b. Washington, 1957; m. Maureen Fitzgerald; children: Timmy, Sally, Jonathan. Degree, U. Va., 1979. Past reporter Hartford Courant, Washington Star, Virginian-Pilot, Norfolk; reporter Phila. Inquirer, 1985—. Co-recipient Pulitzer Prize for explanatory journalism, 1997. Office: Phila Inquirer PO Box 8263 Philadelphia PA 19101-8263

**VITKALOV, SERGEY A.,** physicist, educator; b. Zlatoust, Russia, Oct. 27, 1958; s. Anatolii I. Vitkalov and Nadezhda R. Vitkalova; m. Elena V. Furletova, July 16, 1958; children: Alexander S., Nadya S. Vitkalova. PhD, Moscow Inst. of Physics and Tech., Dolgoprudnii, 1986. Sr. rscher. P. N. Lebedev Phys. Inst., Moscow, 1986—99; rscher. U. Fla., Gainesville, 1997—98; rsch. prof. CCNY, N.Y.C., 1998—2002, prof., 2002—. Exptl. rsch. in condensed matter physics CCNY, 1998—. Author: over 40 articles in phys. jours. including Phys. Rev. Letters, Phys. Rev., others (Young Sci. award at P.N. Lebedev Inst., 1988). Recipient Career award, NSF, 2004—; grantee, Dept. of Energy, 2003—06. Mem.: Am. Phys. Soc. Achievements include discovery of dynamical destruction of electron quantum interference by electromagnetic field in conducting materials. Office: CCNY Physics Dept -J419 160 Convent Ave New York NY 10031 Office Phone: 212-650-5460. Office Fax: 212-650-6940. Business E-mail: vitkalov@sci.ccny.cuny.edu.

**VITO, RAYMOND P.,** engineering educator, researcher; BS, SUNY, Buffalo, 1964, MS, 1965; PhD, Cornell U., 1971. Postdoctoral fellow McMaster U., Canada; assoc. prof. Ga. Inst. Tech., Atlanta, 1974, assoc. dean for academic affairs, prof., Woodruff Sch. Mech. Engring.; mem. program faculty, Wallace H. Coulter Dept. Biomedical Engring. Ga. Inst. Tech. and Emory U.; pres., CEO, co-founder Medanola Medical, Inc., 2001—. Contbr. articles to profl. publs. Med. Rsch. Coun. of Can. Postdoctoral Fellowship, 1973, Nat. Aeronautics and Space Adminstrn./Am. Soc. for Engring. Edn. Summer Faculty Fellowship, 1976, 1979, Am. Soc. Mech. Engrs. Fellow, 1997, Walter H. Coulter award for Innovation and Entrepreneurship, 2002. Fellow: Am. Soc. Mech. Engrs. Achievements include 5 US Patents. Office: Ga Inst Tech Coll Engring IBB Post Office Box 0405 Rm 2308 Atlanta GA 30332 Office Phone: 404-894-2792. Office Fax: 404-894-2291. Business E-mail: raymond.vito@me.gatech.edu.

**VITRAC, JEAN-JACQUES CHARLES,** international business consultant; b. Paris, May 31, 1942; came to U.S., 1972; s. Jean Bernard Vitrac and Paulette Aimée (Buisson) Mannerheim; m. Roswitha Kahling, Sept. 11, 1965; children: Emmanuel, François, Catherine. Diploma, Faculty of Law, Aix, France, 1963; post grad. in econ. scis., Institut Superieur Sciences Economiques, Paris, 1979. Devel. officer Europe-Africa Internat. Jaycees, Geneva, 1968-70; dir. econ. affairs Internat. Jaycees, Coral Gables, Fla., 1970-72; mktg. cons. Bernard Krief Internat., Paris, 1973-79; strategy cons. Euro-PacRim Internat., Walnut Creek, Calif., 1980—. Owner Domaine Becquet Winery, Valley Springs, Calif.; chair task force on multinat. strategies Ctrl. Bank of France, Paris, 1974-78; mktg. cons. Aérospatiale, Paris, 1978; bd. dirs. Capsule Française Inc., Napa, Calif.; asst. prof. mktg. Inst. Français de Gestion, Paris, 1973-79; U.S. chmn. L'Entreprise Demain, Brussels, 1982-98; no. Calif. chmn. World Tech. Parcs Network, 1987-90, founder Export-Incubator USA, San Francisco, 2006. Author: Discover Export, 1974; co-author: Doing Business in California, 1989; editor World Tech. Execs. Network Review, 1989-90; guest columnist France-Amérique, 2005-06. Bd. dirs. E. Bay Internat. Trade Coun., 1996-97, Venetian Lakeshore, 2004-05, v.p., 2006; chair parish coun. St. Patrick's Ch., 1998, 99; trustee Mark Twain St. Joseph's Hosp. Found., 1999-2004, exec. bd. mem., pub. rels. com. co-chair, 2000-2001; elected to Calaveras County Rep. Ctrl. Com., 2001. Named knight Equestrian Order of Holy Sepulchre of Jerusalem; recipient Ambassador for Peace award Internat. Fedn. World Peace, 2006. Mem. Nat. Bus. Incubation Assn. (profl.), KC (dep. grand knight 1998, treas. 1999-2001, grand knight 2001-02, trustee 2002-04), Am. Assn. Polit. Cons., Art Renaissance Found. (hon., chair Calif. chpt. 1994—), Classical Philharm. (v.p. 1995-96), Cal-France Coun. (v.p. 1996-97), Kiwanis Internat (gov.'s cabinet, dir. com. svc. 1996-97), French War Vets. No. Calif. chpt. (pres. 1996-97), Napa Kiwanis Club (distg. pres. 1993, bd. dirs. Calif.-Nev.-Hawaii Found. 1996-98), Wine Inst., Calaveras Wine Assn., West Calaveras Rotary (founding pres. 2000-01), Jackson Rotary. Republican. Roman Catholic. Home: Becket's Ranch PO Box 467 Valley Springs CA 95252 Office: Euro PacRim Int Corp 2173 Hwy 12 East PO Box 1418 Valley Springs CA 95252-1418 Office Phone: 209-772-3469. Personal E-mail: californieusa@yahoo.fr.

**VITRANO, FRANK G.,** supermarket executive; b. 1955; With Pathmark Stores Inc., Carteret, NJ, 1972—, v.p., treas., exec. v.p., treas., CFO, 1998—2002, pres., CFO, chief adminstrv. officer, 2002—. Office: Pathmark Stores Inc 200 Milik St Carteret NJ 07008*

**VITT, DAVID AARON,** health products executive; b. Phila., Aug. 3, 1938; s. Nathan and Flora B.; m. Renee Lee Salkever, Oct. 20, 1963; children: Nadine Lori Einiger, Jeffrey Richard. BS, Temple U., 1961. Sales engr. U.S. Ray Corp., Phila., 1961-65, Midwest Am. Chgo., 1965-67, product mgr., 1967-68, product mgr. regional sales, 1968-70; dir. mktg. Valtronic & Living Wells, Bronx, NY, 1970-74; v.p., gen. mgr. dental divsn. Siemens Med. Sys. Inc., Iselin, NJ, 1974—86, past corp. v.p., gen. mgr. dental divsn.; CEO, pres. Pelton & Crane, Charlotte, NC, 1986-89; v.p. govt. sales, ret. Siemens Med. Sys., 1994; founder, pres., CEO D.A.V., Inc., 1995—; founder, co-owner RealDental.com, Denx Am., Inc., 1998; industry rep. to Am. Nat. Stds. Inst.; co. rep. U.S.-USSR Trade and Econ. Coun.; co-founder Enter Am.

Group Exec. Consultants. Bd. dirs. Am. Fund for Dental Health; apptd. mem. Charlotte Mecklenburg Cmty. Rels. Com.; mem. bd. visitors U. N.C. Charlotte; officer, mem. exec. com. Jr. Achievement. Served in USAR, 1961-68. Mem. Am. Mgmt. Assn. (bd. dirs. N.J. chpt.), Am. Mktg. Assn., Am. Dental Trade Assn. (bd. dirs.), Dental Mfrs. Am. (past pres.), Am. Acad. Dental Radiology, Charlotte Acad. C. of C. (bd. advisors), Acad. Gen. Dentists (bd. mem. found.), Masons (32d deg.), Shriners. Republican.

**VITTER, DAVID BRUCE,** senator, former congressman; b. New Orleans, La., May 3, 1961; s. Al and Audrey Vitter; m. Wendy Baldwin, 1991; children: Sophie, Lise, Airey, Jack Ba magna cum laude, Harvard U., 1983; BA/MA in History/Econs. with highest honors, Oxford U., 1985; JD with honors, Tulane U. Sch. Law, 1988. Bar: La. 1988. Bus. atty., La., 1988—99; assoc. Golden, Kingsmill and Riess, New Orleans, Duplass, Witman, Zwain and Williams, Metairie, La., Duplass, Zwain and Bourgeois, Metairie, La.; mem. La. Ho. of Reps., 1991—99, U.S. Congress from 1st. dist. La., 1999—2005, mem. transp. and judiciary com., govt. reform com., appropriations. com. Washington, 1999—2005; US Senator from La., 2005—. Adj. prof. law Tulane U., 1993—99, Loyola U., 1993—99; mem. com. security and coop. in Europe US Senate, com. commerce, sci. and transp., com. environment and public works, com. small bus. and entrepreneurship. Articles editor Tulane Law Rev., 1987-88. Lector, St. Francis Xavier Cath. Ch., Metairie, La.; Mem. Coastal Conservation Assn., Ducks Unlimited. Rhodes scholar; Recipient Legis. of Yr., Alliance for Good Govt., Lifetime Achievement award Victims & Citizens Against Crime, Republican of Yr. award Northshore Republican Men's Club, 2005. Mem. ABA, New Orleans Bar Assn., Phi Beta Kappa, Nat. Rifle Assn.; former mem. La. Bar Assn. Republican. Office: US Senate 516 Hart Senate Office Bldg Washington DC 20510 also: District Office Ste 201 2800 Veterans Blvd Metairie LA 70002 Office Phone: 504-589-2753, 202-224-4623. Office Fax: 504-589-2607, 202-228-5061.*

**VITTETOE, MARIE CLARE,** retired clinical laboratory science educator; b. Keota, Iowa, May 19, 1927; d. Edward Daniel and Marcella Matilda Vittetoe. BS, Marycrest Coll., 1950; MS, W.Va. U., 1971, EdD, 1973. Staff technologist St. Joseph Hosp., Ottumwa, Iowa, 1950-70; instr. Ottumwa Hosp. Sch. Med. Tech., 1957-70, St. Joseph Hosp. Sch. Nursing, Ottumwa, 1950-70; asst. prof. U. Ill., Champaign-Urbana, 1973-78; prof. clin. lab. scis. U. Ky., Lexington, 1978-94. Mem. Sisters of Humility of Mary, 1946—; chair Congregation of Humility of Mary; clin. lab. asst., lab. cons. 6 clinics in Haiti, 2000—. Author: Vittetoe Family Tree and Scrapbook, 2000, Peiffer-Berg Family Tree and Scrapbook, 2000, Lutz/Peiffer Family Tree Update, 2002, Vittetoe Family Tree Update, 2002; contbr. articles to profl. jours. Vol. hosp. labs., Haiti, 1999—; apptd. to advisory bd. CRUDEM Found., 2005—. Named Ky. Col., Marie Vittetoe award for excellence in svc. named for her, U. Ky., 1999; recipient Kingston award for Creative Tchg., Recognition award for svc. to edn., Commonwealth of Ky. Coun. on Higher Edn., disting. grad. award, Nat. Cath. Ednl. Assn., 1995, devel. of youth award, Iowa 4-H Found., 1996, award for devel. Best Little Lab. in Haiti, 2002. Mem. Am. Soc. for Med. Tech. (chmn. 1986-89, Profl. Achievement award 1991, Ky. Mem. of Yr. award 1994), Am. Soc. Clin. Lab. Scis., Am. Soc. Clin. Pathologists (assoc.), Alpha Mu Tau, Phi Delta Kappa, Alpha Eta. Avocations: walking, genealogy.

**VITTOR, KENNETH MARK,** lawyer; b. L.I. BS with honors, Cornell U., 1971; JD, U. Chgo., 1974. Assoc. Cahill, Gordon & Reindel, N.Y.C., 1974-80; sr. v.p., assoc. gen. counsel McGraw-Hill Cos., N.Y.C., 1980-95; sr. v.p., gen. counsel The McGraw-Hill Cos., Inc., N.Y.C., 1995—99, exec. v.p., gen. counsel, 1999—. Chmn. Libel Def. Resource Ctr., 1999-2000. Mem. Copyright, Patent and Trademark Commn., Freedom to Read Commn., Assn. of Am. Pubs., Mag. Pubs. Am. (chmn. legal affairs com.), Lawyers Commn. (chmn. libel, privacy and first amendment sub-com. 1983-86). Office: The McGraw-Hill Cos Inc 48th Fl 1221 Avenue Of The Americas New York NY 10020-1001

**VITTORI, ROBERTO,** astronaut; b. Viterbo, Italy, Oct. 15, 1964; m. Valeria Nardi; 3 children. Grad., Italian Air Force Acad., 1989; grad. undergrad. flight tng., Reese AFB, Tex., 1989; grad., U.S. Navy Test Pilot Sch., 1995; attended, U.S. Air Force Flight Safety Sch., 1997—98. Flew Tornado GR1 aircraft 155th Squadron, 50th Wing, Piacenza, Italy, 1991—94; project pilot for devel. of European aircraft EF2000 Italian Test Ctr., 1995—98; nat. rep. Beyond Visual Range Air-to-Air Missile R&D Program, 1996—98; wing flight safety officer Italian Test Ctr., 1997; tchr. aerodynamics accident investigation course Italian Air Force; astronaut Italian Space Agy. in cooperation with ESA, 1998; joined European Astronaut Corp., ESA European Astronaut Ctr., Cologne, Germany, 1998; mission specialist candidate astronaut NASA Johnson Space Ctr., Houston, 1998—, with Astronaut Office New Generation Space Vehicles Br., 2002; tng. as ld. engr. Yuri Gagarin Cosmonaut Tng. Ctr., Star City near Moscow, 2001; participated in a taxi-flight to Internat. Space Station, 2002; mem. of crew with Salizhan Sharipov and Leroy Chiao Expedition 11, 2005. Maj. Italian Air Force. Avocations: soccer, running, swimming, reading. Office: NASA Johnson Space Ctr Astronaut Office/CB Houston TX 77058

**VITTY, RODERIC BEMIS,** retired financial planner, publishing executive; b. St. Johnsbury, Vt., July 28, 1933; s. Clarence Lucian and Leota (Cobleigh) V.; m. Virginia Gable, March, 1960 (div. 1983); children: Roderic G., Virginia A., David P., Suzanne L.; m. Patricia Lyster, June 21, 1986. BS, U.S. Mil. Acad., 1955; MS in Fin. Svcs., Am. Coll., Bryn Mawr, Pa., 1977, MS in Mgmt., 1987; postgrad. exec. mgmt. program, Columbia U., 1985. CLU; chartered fin. cons.; cert. fin. planner. With Conn. Gen. Life Ins. Co. (CIGNA-Lincoln Fin. Advisor), 1960, mgr. br. office Cherry Hill, NJ, 1968—, mgr. Greater Phila. office, 1981—, mktg. gen. mgr., 1983—85, gen. mgr., regional v.p., 1985—94. Pub. owner Vt. Heritage press, Caber Pub. Ltd. Trustee St. Johnsbury Acad., Vt., 1993—, co-chair capital campaign, 1999; mem assembly of overseers Dartmouth-Hitchcock Med. Ctr.; civilian aide Sec. Army State of Vt., 2005-. Served with ref. U.S. Army, 1955-59, Pa. N.G., 1961-68. Recipient GAMA Master Agy. Builder award, 1982-92, Nat. Mgmt. awards (20), 1972-92, Outstanding Agy. awards (9), CIGNA; named to CIGNA Hall of Fame, 1998. Mem. West Point Soc. Phila. (pres. 1969-71, 89-94, emeritus, 1994), Nat. Assn. Ins. and Fin. Advisors, South Jersey Fin. Planning Coun., Internat. Assn. Fin. Planners, Soc. of Fin. Svc. Profls., So. N.J. Gen. Agts. and Mgrs. Assn. (pres. 1979-80), Nat. GAMA (regional v.p. 1986-89, treas., exec. com. 1991-94), Assn. Grads. U.S. Mil. Acad. (trustee 1992—2005, emeritus 2005-, pres. Class of 1955, 1995-2000), Army Athletic Assn., Sunnybrook Swim Club, Cherry Hill Raquet Club, Riverton Country Club, Quechee Club Vt., St. Johnsbury Country Club, Safari Club Internat., Chevaliers du Tastevin, Union League Phila., St. Andrews Soc. Vt., Masons (32 deg.), Shriners, K.T. Presbyterian. Address: Twildoon Lodge-Angell Trail PO Box 151 Quechee VT 05059-0151

**VITVITSKY, JACK,** physician assistant; b. White Plains, NY, Mar. 8, 1945; s. Alexander Jack and Helen Louise Virginia (Rider) V. BS, U. Rochester, 1968; AAS, Cuyahoga CC, Cleve., 1978; postgrad., SUNY, Plattsburgh, 1964-66, 73-74, Liberty U., 1994—. Cert. first aid and CPR instr. ARC; cert. EMT instr. N.Y.; cert. ground and flight instr., instrument instr., multi-engine instr., written test examiner FAA. Physician's asst. Planned Parenthood No. N.Y., 1979-84, Dr. David P. Gorman, Malone, NY, 1980-81, N.Y. State Dept. Corrections, Dannemora, N.Y., 1981-84, N.Y. State Office Mental Retardation and Devel. Disabilities, Tupper Lake, N.Y., 1984-85, N.Y. State Dept. Corrections, Raybrook, NY, 1985-2002; owner Adirondack Computer Testing Ctr., 1996-2005; assoc. sales rep. Primerica Fin. Svcs., Plattsburg, NY, 2002—04; bus driver Franklin County Assn. Sr. Citizens at Saranac Lake Ctr., NY, 2002—04; med. standards officer NY Army N.G., Watervliet, 2004—05. Contbr. articles to profl. jours. Active Lake Placid Vol. Ambulance Svc., Inc., 1975—, Nat. Ski Patrol System, 1975—; mem. aviation explorer program Boy Scouts Am. With U.S.Army Res., 1981-84, N.Y. Army N.G., 1984—. Mem. Am. Acad. Physician Assts. (cons. minority affairs com. 1999-2001), NY State Soc. Physician Assts., Soc. Army Physician Assts. (del. to Am. Acad. Physician Assts. Ho. of Dels.), Adirondack Soc. Physician

Assts. (sec. 1996-2004), Mid-Hudson Assn. Physician Assts., Fellowship Christian Physician Assts. (sec. 1992-97), Exptl. Aviation Assn., Aircraft Owners and Pilots Assn., US Army Flight Soc. of Flight Surgeons, NRA, Gun Owners Am., Am. Legion. Republican. Avocations: snowshoeing, skiing, writing, woodworking, equine activities. Home: 132 Old Military Rd Lake Placid NY 12946-1699 Office: 466th Med Co NYARNG 147 Warren St Glens Falls NY 12801 Personal E-mail: jackvitvitsky@juno.com.

**VITZ, PAUL CLAYTON,** psychologist, educator; b. Toledo, Aug. 27, 1935; m. Evelyn Birge; 6 children. BA high honors in Psychology, U. Mich., 1953; PhD, Stanford U., 1962. Instr. psychology Pomona (Calif.) Coll., 1962-64; asst. prof. NYU, 1965-70, assoc. prof., 1970-85, dir. psychology dept. undergrad. program, 1973-79, prof., 1985—2004, prof. emeritus, 2004—, acting dir. master's program, 1988—91, acting dir. grad. program, 1989—90. Adj. prof. John Paul II Inst. on Marriage and Family, Washington, 1990-2003, Internat. Acad. Philosophy, 1994-98; prof./sr. scholar Inst. for Psychol. Scis., 2000—; lectr. in field. Author: Psychology as Religion: The Cult of Self-Worship, 1977, 2d edit., 1994, (with A.B. Glimcher) Modern Art and Modern Science: The Parallel Analysis of Vision, 1984, Censorship: Evidence of Bias in Our Children's Textbooks, 1986, Sigmund Freud's Christian Unconscious, 1988, Faith of the Fatherless: The Psychology of Atheism, 1999; editor: (with S. Krason) Defending the Family: A Sourcebook, 1998, (with S. Felch) The Self: Beyond the Postmodern Crisis, 2006; contbr. articles to profl. jours., chpts. to books. Rsch. grantee Nat. Inst. Mental Health, 1963-64, 65-66, 66-67, Nat. Inst. Neurol. Diseases and Blindness grantee, 1970-73, 73-74, Shalom Found. grantee, 1974-78, Nat. Inst. Edn. grantee, 1983, 84-85, Dept. Edn. grantee, 1986-87. Office: Inst for the Psychol Scis Ste 511 2001 Jefferson Davis Hwy Arlington VA 22202

**VIVIO, FRANK MICHAEL,** education educator, researcher; b. Norway, Mich., Apr. 16, 1945; s. Frank Joseph and Ann Marie Vivio; m. Patricia NMN Moulas, Dec. 28, 1969; children: Frank, Nicholas, Christopher. BS, Mich. State Univ., E. Lansing, MI, 1967, MS, 1972, PhD, 1974. HS instr. Benton Harbor HS, Benton Harbor, Mich., 1967—72; asst. dir., spl. program Mich. State Univ., E. Lansing, Mich., 1974—76; planning and evalu. officer E./W. Ctr., Honolulu, 1976—80; asst. dir., ed. program Argonne Nat. Lab., Argonne, Ill., 1980—. Cons. Univ. of Alberta & World Bank, Alberta, Canada, 1980; panel mem. Nat. Acad. of Sci., Wash., DC, 1991—93. Author: (evaluation report) Internat. Atomic Energy Agy., 1984, (evaluation reports) Dept. of Energy Ed., 1986—96. Pres. Naperville Mcpl. Band, Naperville, Ill., 1997. Mem.: Naperville Mcpl. Band (section head 2001—). Avocation: music. Home: 25 W 101 Cape Rd Naperville IL 60540 Office: Argonne Nat Lab 9700 So Cass Ave Argonne IL 60439

**VIXIE SANDY, MARY DOLORES,** educational association administrator; b. San Francisco, Aug. 26, 1960; d. Orvin Leroy and Shirley Ann Vixie; m. Gary Alan Sandy, Jan. 16, 1983; children: Owen Sterling Sandy, Grayson Brooks Sandy, Bayley Jayne Sandy. BA in Philosophy, Sonoma State U., 1983; MA in Edn., U. Calif., Davis, 2005. Cons. Calif. Dept. Edn., Sacramento, 1984—86; project cons. Calif. Sch. Leadership Acad., 1986—86; assoc. in postsecondary edn. studies Calif. Post Secondary Edn. Commn., 1986—92; cons. program evaluation and rsch. Calif. Commn. Tchr. Credentialing, 1992—99, administr. tchr. devel. programs, 1999—2000, dir. profl. svcs., 2000—03; assoc. dir. tchr. edn. and pub. sch. programs Calif. State U. Office of Chancellor, Long Beach, Calif., 2004—. Panel mem. Joint Com. to Develop a Master Plan for Edn., Sacramento, 2001—02; cons. Gov. Schwarzenegger's Calif. Performance Rev., 2004—04; evaluation cons., coll. prep. math. project U. Calif., Davis, 1991—92. Contbr. articles to profl. jours. V.p. Woodland LWV, Calif., 1992; chair and mem. Curriculum Adv. Coun., Woodland Unified Sch. Dist., 1992—93; mem., bd. dirs. YMCA, 1995; mem., budget adv. com. Woodland Unified Sch. Dist., 1994—95; founder, chair Woodland Cmty. Ptnrs. for Edn., 1994—95; cub scout den leader Pack 130, Boy Scouts Am., 1997—99; chair, sch. site coun. Dingle Elem. Sch., 1998—2002; mem. Douglass Mid. Sch. Site Coun., 2002—03. Mem.: Calif. Coun. on Tchr. Edn., Am. Edn. Rsch. Assn. Democrat-Npl. Methodist. Avocations: travel, hiking, reading, photography, cooking. Office: Calif State U 6000 J St Sacramento CA 95819 Office Phone: 916-278-4178. Office Fax: 916-278-5019. Personal E-mail: msandy@calstate.edu.

**VIZARD, MICHAEL,** periodical editor; Degree in Journalism, Boston (Mass.) U. Editor PC Week, Computerworld, Digital Review; editor news InfoWorld, 1995—96, exec. news editor, 1996—99, editor-in-chief, 1999—2002; editor-in-chief CRN CMP Media, 2002—. Office: CMP Worldwide Media Networks 600 Community Drive Manhasset NY 11030-3150

**VIZCAINO, JOSE LUIS PIMENTAL,** professional baseball player; b. San Cristobal, Dominican Rep., Mar. 26, 1965; Grad. high sch., Dominican Rep. With L.A. Dodgers, 1989-90, Chgo. Cubs, 1991-93; infielder N.Y. Mets, 1994-96; with Cleve. Indians, 1996, Houston Astros, 2001—05, San Francisco Giants, 1997—2001, 2005—. Office: SBC Park 24 Willie Mays Plz San Francisco CA 94107

**VIZENOR, ERMA J.,** Native American tribal leader; b. Cass Lake, Minn. d. Albin and Norma Nordstrom; m. Dallas Vizenor (dec.). MEd, Minn. State U., Moorhead; EdD, Harvard U. Tchr.; sec.-treas. White Earth Band of Ojibwe, 1996—2002, chairwoman, 2004—. Office: White Earth Reservation PO Box 418 White Earth MN 56591 Office Phone: 218-983-3285. Office Fax: 218-983-3641.*

**VIZQUEL, OMAR ENRIQUE,** professional baseball player; b. Caracas, Venezuela, Apr. 24, 1967; Grad. high sch., Caracus. With Seattle Mariners, 1989-93; shortstop Cleve. Indians, 1994—2004, San Francisco Giants, 2004—. Recipient Winner Am. League Golden Glove, 1993-2001, named to MLB All-Star game, 1998, 1999, 2002 Office: c/o San Francisco Giants Pacific Bell Park 24 Willie Mays Plaza San Francisco CA 94107*

**VLACH, JIRI,** electrical engineering educator, researcher; b. Prague, Czechoslovakia, Oct. 5, 1922; arrived in Can., 1969; s. Frantisek and Bozena (Papouskova) V.; m. Dagmar Gutova, Oct. 22, 1949; 1 son, Martin. Dipl.eng., Tech. U. Prague, 1947, C.Sc., 1957. With Research Inst. for Radio Communications, Prague, 1948-67, head math. dept., until 1967; vis. prof. U. Ill., Urbana, 1967-69; prof. elec. engring. U. Waterloo (Ont., Can.), 1969—. Author: Computerized Approximation and Synthesis of Linear Networks, 1969, (with others) Computer Methods for Circuit Analysis and Design, 1983, 2nd edit., 1994; Basic Network Theory with Computer Applications, 1992; assoc. editor IEEE Trans. on Circuits and Systems, 1979-80, 87-88, 98—. Fellow: IEEE (life); mem.: Eta Kappa Nu. Home: 355 Craigleith Dr Waterloo ON Canada N2L 5B5 Office: U Waterloo 200 University Ave West Waterloo ON Canada N2L 6J1 Office Phone: 519-888-4567 ext 3671. Personal E-mail: jvlach@uwaterloo.ca.

**VLADECK, BRUCE CHARNEY,** academic administrator, healthcare educator; b. NYC, Sept. 13, 1949; s. Stephen Charney and Judith (Pomarlen) V.; m. Fredda Wellin, Aug. 5, 1973; children— Elizabeth Charney, Stephen Isaiah, Abigail Sarah. BA, Harvard U., 1970; MA, U. Mich, 1972, PhD in Polit. Sci., 1973. Assoc. social scientist NYC-Rand Inst., 1973-74; asst. prof. Columbia U., NYC, 1974-78, assoc. prof., 1978-79; asst. commr. health planning and resources devel. N.J. Dept. Health, Trenton, 1979-82; asst. v.p. Robert Wood Johnson Found., Princeton, NJ, 1982-83; pres. United Hosp. Fund, NYC, 1983-93; administr. HCFA, Washington, 1993-97; prof. health policy and geriatrics Mt. Sinai Med. Ctr., NYC, 1997—2004; prin. Health Scis. Adv. Svcs. Ernst & Young LLP, 2004—06; interim pres. U. Medicine and Dentistry NJ, Newark, 2006—. Mem. N.Y. State Coun. on Health Care Financing, Albany, 1978-92; mem. com. on nursing home regulation Inst. Medicine, Washington, 1983-85, chmn. com. on health care for homeless people, 1986-88, mem. prospective payment assessment com., 1986-93; mem. Nat. Bipartisan Commn. on Future of Medicare, 1997-98. Author: Unloving Care: The Nursing Home Tragedy, 1981. Contbr. numerous articles to profl. publs. Fellow N.Y. Acad. Medicine; mem. Inst. Medicine, Nat. Acad. Scis., Phi Beta Kappa. Office: U Medicine and Dentistry NJ 65 Bergen St Newark NJ 07103 Office Phone: 973-972-4400. E-mail: vladeck@umdnj.edu.

**VLADECK, JUDITH POMARLEN,** lawyer; b. Norfolk, Va., Aug. 1, 1923; BA, Hunter Coll., 1945; JD, Columbia U., 1947. Bar: NY 1947, US Supreme Ct. 1962. Assoc. Conrad & Smith, N.Y.C., 1947-51; sole practice N.Y.C., 1951-57; mem. Vladeck, Elias, Vladeck & Engelhard P.C., N.Y.C., 1957—; sr. ptnr. Vladeck, Waldman, Elias & Englehard, P.C., N.Y.C. Adj. prof. Fordham Law Sch. Mem. adv. bd. Inst. for Edn. and Rsch. on Women and Work, Cornell U.; bd. dirs. N.Y. Civil Liberties Union, 1963-68; bd. dir., counsel Tamiment Inst., Inc.; mem. advisory bd. R. Wagner Labor Archives, Tamiment Inst. Libr.; bd. dirs. lawyers' coordinating com. AFL-CIO; bd. mem. Non-Traditional Employment for Women. Recipient Hunter Coll. Profl. Achievement award, 1992, Edith Spivack award, 1998, Women of Power and Influence award NY NOW, 1998, ORT Jurisprudence award, 1996; elected to Hunter Coll. Hall of Fame, 1988; Non-Taditional Employment for Women named building Judith P. Vladeck Ctr. for Women, 1989; Margaret Brent Award, ABA 2002; Columbia Law Sch. Assoc. Medal for Excellence, 2003; NEW 25th Anniv. Equity Leadership Award, 2003, 60th Ann. NYS Human Rights Law award for Excellence, NYS Divsn. Human Rights, 2005, Peggy Browning Fund Lifetime Achievement award, 2006. Fellow Am. Bar Found., Coll. of Labor and Employment Lawyers; mem. ABA (co-chmn. labor law and equal employment coms., v.p. State Bar Assn. (labor law com.), Assn. of Bar of City of N.Y., N.Y. County Lawyers Assn., Fed. Bar Assn., Women's Bar Assn., Am. Arbitration Assn. (panel of arbitrators), Columbia Law Sch. Alumni Assn. (bd. dir.), Harlem Inst. Fashion (counsel, bd. dir.). Home: 115 Central Park W New York NY 10023-4153 Office: Vladeck Waldman Elias & Engelhard 1501 Broadway Ste 800 New York NY 10036-5560 Office Phone: 212-403-7300. Business E-Mail: jvladeck@vladeck.com.

**VLADEM, PAUL JAY,** investment advisor; b. Chgo., Apr. 5, 1952; s. Arthur I. and Elaine A. (Ascher) V.; m. Sondra Joyce Berman, Dec. 27, 1981; children: Ashley Sherree, Evan David. BSBA with honors and high distinction, U. Ill., Chgo., 1974. Lic. brokerage securities, Fla., Ill., Ariz., Conn., Ga., Ind., N.C., Colo., Md., Nev., Del., N.Y., Ohio, Calif., Utah, Mich., Mo., Mass., NJ, Pa., Tenn., Va., Oreg.; registered investment advisor; lic. ins. agt., Fla., Ill., Ind., Utah, Conn., Ariz., NY, Tenn.; CPA, Fla., Ill.; In charge acct. Peat Marwick, Fort Lauderdale, Fla., 1974-76; mgr. McGladrey & Pullen, CPA, Fort Lauderdale, 1976-85; sr. v.p. fin. Integrated Resources formerly Easter Kramer, Boca Raton, Fla., 1985-89; pres. Associated Investor Svcs., Fort Lauderdale, 1989—. Bd. dirs. Israel Bonds, Ft. Lauderdale, 1994, Jewish Family Svc., Ft. Lauderdale, 1993; chmn. CPA Com. on Israel Bonds, Ft. Lauderdale, 1994, mem. prof. adv. com., 1992—. Named One of Top Ten Brokers of Yr. Registered Rep. Mag., 1994. Mem. AICPA (personal planning divsn.), Fla. Inst. CPAs (mem. personal fin. planning com., 1985), Internat. Platform Assn. Democrat. Jewish. Avocations: tennis, basketball, attending sporting events. Home: 6508 NW 103rd Ln Parkland FL 33076-2934 Office: Associated Investor Svcs 2699 Stirling Rd Ste A200 Fort Lauderdale FL 33312-6583 Office Phone: 954-983-5600. Business E-Mail: Paul@afc-ais.com.

**VLADEM, STEVEN ALLEN,** writer, film producer, motivational speaker; b. Chgo., July 24, 1949; s. Arthur and Elaine Edythe (Ascher) Vladem. BA with honors and distinction, U. Ill., Chgo., 1970; MEd in Math., Northeastern Ill. U., Chgo., 1973; MA in Ednl. Adminstrn./Supervision, Roosevelt U., Chgo., 1975; ScD, London Sch. Applied Rsch., 1993. Tchr. math. Chgo. Bd. Edn., 1971-81, statistician and evaluator dept. rsch. and evaluation, 1979; supr. program svcs. Dept. Planning, Chgo. City Hall, 1981; coord. alt. sch. without walls program Chgo. Met. HS, 1982-87, coord. computer assisted instrn., 1987-91; developer ednl. software Chgo., 1987-92; freelance computer cons., 1987-92; writer/lectr., 1994—; prodr. Image Lost Film, 2003—. Lectr. in field; mktg. cons. Enoch Searle Prodns., 2001—, Cosmic Films, 2001—; motivational spkr. Profl. Spkrs. Bur. Internat., 2001—. Author: (poetry) The Jigsaw People, 1997; exhibitions include Gallery Art, Internat. Congress Arts and Commn., Keble Coll., Oxford U., Eng.; prodr.: Image Last Films, 2003—; exec. prodr.: (films) Gein, 2003. Mem. Internat. Parliament Safety and Peace, Palermo, Italy, 1993—95; bd. dirs. Nat. Coalition health Care Reform, 1998—; founder coun. London Diplomatic Acad., Internat. Diplomatic Acad., Albert Schweitzer Int., Chgo. Coun. Fgn. Rels.; Internat. Fellowship Christians and Jews; sec.-gen. United Cultural Conv.; hon. amb. laureates Jr. Achievement and Chgo. Assn. Bus. and Industry, 1990; support group leader, outreach vol. Nat. Keratoconus Found., L.A., 1995—; docent Tour of Old Town Old Town C. of C., Chgo., 1993; patron various arts orgns.; vol. Sight Savers Internat., Karen Or Ctr. Multi-Handicapped Blind Children, State of Ill. Transplant Program, 2003, Am. Transplant Assn., Cinema for Deaf Film Festival, 2003; judge Daniel Webster Acad. Poets Competition, 1998; nominator Col.'s Way Award. Finalist, U.S. Nat. Memory Championship, N.Y.C., 1997; named John W. Rogers Educator of the Yr., Jr. Achievement, Chgo., 1990; named to Wall of Tolerance, Civil Rights Meml. Ctr., 2003; recipient Congress Star of Distinction, Internat. Congress Arts and Comm./St. John's Coll., Cambridge U., 1992, medal of Merit, Republic of Peru, 1992, Alzheimers Rsch. award, Alzheimers Assn. Am., 2000, Internat. Peace prize, 2002, Congl. medal of Excellence, 2002, Am. medal of Honor, 2002. Mem. NATAS, Ill. Prodn. Alliance, Internat. Platform Assn. (bd. govs. internet team, red carpet com., Gold Ribbon Most Popular Artist 1995), United Writers Assn. (life fellow), World Univ. Roundtable, Toastmasters Internat., Internat. Order of Merit (Cambridge, Eng.), Daniel Webster Acad. Poets (Cert. of Merit 1995), Chrysopoets, Order of Templars of Jerusalem (knight), Lofsensic Ursinius Order (knight comdr.), World Order of St. Edn. Culture. (knight-cavalier), Am. Order Excellence, Order of San Ciriaco (count), Internat. Diplomatic Acad., Am. Legion (gold medal, sch. leadership award 1967), Rotary Club, Lions Club. Avocations: cinema, musical theatre, backgammon, architecture, world travel. Address: Profl Spkrs Bur Internat 1112 5th Ave Ste 101 Worthington OH 43085 Home: 1700 Hinman Ave Apt 2b Evanston IL 60201-4592 E-mail: stevevladem@yahoo.com.

**VLADIMIROVA, TATYANA VLADERIANA,** chemist, researcher; b. Ufa, Russia, July 12, 1955; d. Valerian Simeon Vladimirov and Appolynarya Stephen Vladimirova. Cert. in Chemistry, U. Ivanovo, Russia, 1977; postgrad., Moscow U., Russia, 1990—95. Engr. Machine Bldg. Plant, Jula, Russia, 1977—82; rsch. officer Inst. Monomiu, Jula, Russia, 1982—88, Inst. Solution Chemistry, Ivanovo, Russia, 1983—. Contbr. articles to profl. jours. Avocation: mountain climbing. Home: B Hmelnitskago St 52-26 153022 Ivanovo Russia Office: Inst Solution Chemistry Skadeucicheskaya 1 153045 Ivanovo Russia E-mail: trv@ise-ras.ru.

**VLADIMIROVICH, VINOGRADOV PAVEL,** cosmonaut; b. Magadan, Russia, Aug. 31, 1953; married; 3 children. Grad. in Dept. Airborne Vehicles, Moscow Aviation Inst., 1977. Pilot-cosmonaut, 3rd class cosmonaut Russian Fedn.; specialized in software develop for automated interactive designing systems of recoverable vehicles, develop. aerodynamics and aerodyne arrangement design models, computer graphics, 1977—83; with Head Design Bur. Rocket Space Corp., Energia, 1983; joined Energia cosmonaut corp., 1992; completed generic space tng. Yu. A. Gagarin Cosmonaut Tng. Ctr., 1992—94, complete advance test-cosmonaut tng., 1994—95; flight engr. tng. of Mir-20 and EuroMir-95 back-up crew Soyuz TM and Mir Space Station, 1995; trained for Spaceflight on Soyuz TM vehicle and Mir space e station as flight engr. Mir-22/NASA-3 and Cassiopeia programs, 1995—96; trained as flight engr. Mir-24 prime crew, 1996—97; flight engr. Soyuz TM and Mir Station, Expedition 24 (Mir-24/NASA 5. 6), 1997—98; trained for spaceflight as back-up flight engr. Mir-28, 1999—2000; trained as flight engr. Mir-29, 2000; completed tng. as test cosmonaut Internat. Space Station group, 2001—02; trained as flight engr. Internat. Space Station Taxi back-up crew 5, 2002—03; crew comdr. Internat. Space Station, Expedition-13, Soyuz TMA-8, 2006. Avocations: game sports, astronomy, history of aviaition and cosmonautics. Office: Astronaut office CB NASA Johnson Space Center Houston TX 77058*

**VLADUTIU, ADRIAN O.,** physician, educator; b. Bucharest, Romania, Aug. 5, 1940; came to U.S., 1969, naturalized 1974; s. Octavian and Veturia (Chirescu) V.; m. Georgirene D. Dietrich; children: Christina Lynn, Catherine Joy. MD, Sch. Medicine, Bucharest, 1962; PhD in Immunopathology, Sch. Medicine, Jassy, Romania, 1968. Diplomate Am. Bd. Pathology. Asst. prof. physiopathology Sch. Medicine, Bucharest, 1968-71; assoc. prof. pathology SUNY Sch. Medicine, Buffalo, 1978-81, prof. pathology, 1981—; pathologist Buffalo Gen. Hosp., 1974—2006, dir. clin. labs., 1982—2001, prof. microbiology, 1982—, prof. medicine, 1985—. Cons. Niagara Falls (N.Y.) Meml. Hosp., 1976—82; Tri-County Hosp., Gowanda, NY, 1991—93; acting head dept. pathology Buffalo Gen. Hosp., 1985—86; dir. lab. Deaconess Hosp. Buffalo, 1982—91, Columbus Meml., Buffalo, 1996—98. Author: Pleural Effusion, 1986; contbr. chapters to books, articles to profl. jours. Med. Rsch. Coun. Can. fellow, 1968, Buswell fellow, 1969; recipient rsch. prize Ministry Edn. Romania, 1965, rsch. award NIH, 1985. Fellow: ACP, Nat. Acad. Clin. Biochemistry, Coll. Am. Pathologists; mem.: Am. Soc. Investigative Pathology, Am. Assn. Immunologists. Achievements include first demonstration of the association of autoimmunity with major histocompability antigens; discovery of Buffalo thyroxine binding globulin gene. Home: 80 Oakview Dr Buffalo NY 14221-1420 Business E-Mail: vladutiu@buffalo.edu. E-mail: guthormones@yahoo.com.

**VLAHOV, DAVID,** epidemiologist; b. Washington, Aug. 31, 1952; s. William John and Helga Rose Vlahov; m. Robyn Randice Mione; children: Alexander, Alexandra Gershon. BA, Earlham Coll., 1974; BSN, MS, U. Md., 1980; PhD, Johns Hopkins U., 1988. RN 1977. Prof. epidemiology Sch. Pub. Health Johns Hopkins U., Balt., 1988—2001; dir. Ctr. for Urban Epidemiologic Studies, v.p. for rsch. N.Y. Acad. Medicine, N.Y.C., 1999—; prof. clin. epidemiology Sch. Pub. Health Columbia U., N.Y.C., 1999—. Mem. nat. adv. coun. on drug abuse Dept. HHS. Contbr. more than 500 sci. papers; editor: Jour. Urban Health, 2000—. Recipient Merit awards, NIH, 1995—2005; grantee, CDC, 1990—, NIH, 1990—, Robert Wood Johnson Found., 1990—, N.Y. Cmty. Trust, 1990—. Fellow: N.Y. Acad. Medicine, Infectious Disease Soc. of Am.; mem.: Am. Pub. Health Assn., Am. Epidemiol. Soc., Soc. for Epidemiol. Rsch. Home: 401 E 86th St Apt 12 E New York NY 10028 Office: NY Acad Medicine 1216 Fifth Ave New York NY 10029 Office Phone: 212-822-7382. Business E-Mail: dvlahov@nyam.org.

**VLAMIS, SUSAN (SUZANNE) ANNE,** editor, photographer; d. Steve Anthony and Anne Lillian Vlamis. BA in English, Long Island U., Bklyn., 1966. Intensive Film Summer Workshop NYU, 1989. Free-lance photographer, N.Y.C., 1967—72; copy asst. to features editor BRIDE'S Mag. Conde Nast, N.Y.C., 1967—68; editl. asst. Victor Riesel-Labor Columnist, N.Y.C., 1969; staff photographer The AP, N.Y.C., 1974—85, news photo editor special projects, 1998—; supervising newsfeatures photo editor AP News-Features, N.Y.C., 1985—98. Sci., health rschr. Dr. Joy C. Zagoren, PhD, N.Y.C., 1999—. Photo editor (biography) John Wayne, prodn. asst. (public access TV) Cable Doctor and Speak Out, photographer (book) Moments In Time - 50 Years of Associated Press News Photos 1985, 1st edit., The Sports 100 - The 100 Greatest Athletes of the 20th Century, 1999, One Day In Our World, Moments In Time- 60 Years of AP News Photos, The Olympics At 100, Am. Photographers, photo editor (biography) Bing Crosby, art reviewer (newspaper) The Jersey City Jour.; one-woman shows include Restoring Lady Liberty, 1986, Jazz Musicians, 1991, Commemorative Photo Exhibition 9/11, Gallery of Graphic Arts and Morning Calm Gallery, 2001, Welfare Island and other Photographs, Long Island U., 1972. V.p. of zoning com. 79th St. Neighborhood Assn., NY, 2002—03; bd. mem., v.p. Sarah Herzog Hosp., Jerusalem, 2002—. Recipient Photographers Sports award, World Press, 1975. Mem.: N.Y. Press Photographers Assn. (1st prize Feature Story for "Centennial Restoration, St. Pat's Cathedral" 1979), Am. Film Inst. (assoc.), Ocean Conservancy, Cousteau Soc., World Wild Life Found., Audobon Soc., George Eastman House N.Y.C. Colleter Club, Sierra Club. Independent. Roman Catholic. Avocations: collect fine arts and illustrated books, yoga, dance, swimming, scuba diving. Home: 405 E 82nd St New York NY 10028 Office: Associated Press 450 W 33rd St Fl 7 New York NY 10001-2606 Business E-Mail: svlamis@ap.org.

**VLAY, STEPHEN CHARLES,** cardiologist, electrophysiologist; b. N.Y.C., July 25, 1950; s. Stephen and Rose Vlay; m. Linda C. Vlay. AB, NYU, 1971; MD, Yale U., 1975. Diplomate Am. Bd. Internal Medicine, Am. Bd. Cardiovasc. Disease, Am. Bd. Clin. Cardiac Electrophysiology; testamur NASPExAM, 1997. Intern and resident in internal medicine NYU-Bellevue Med. Ctr., N.Y.C., 1975-78; fellow in cardiology Johns Hopkins Hosp., Balt., 1978-81, asst. in medicine, 1980-81; instr., asst. prof., then assoc. prof. medicine SUNY, Stony Brook, 1981-92, prof., 1992—. Dir. Stony Brook Arrhythmia Study and Sudden Death Prevention Ctr. Editor: Manual of Cardiac Arrhythmias, 1988, Medical Care of the Cardiac Surgical Patient, 1992, A Practical Approach to Cardiac Arrhythmias, 1996. Fellow ACP, Am. Heart Assn. (coun. on clin. cardiology), Am. Coll. Cardiology, Heart Rhythm Soc.; mem. N.Am. Soc. Pacing and Electrophysiology. Office: SUNY Health Sci Ctr N T17 020 Stony Brook NY 11794-0001

**VLAZNY, JOHN GEORGE,** archbishop; b. Chgo., Feb. 22, 1937; s. John George and Marie Hattie (Brezina) V. BA, St. Mary of the Lake Coll., Mundelein, Ill., 1958; STL, Pontifical Gregorian U., Rome, 1962; MA in Classics, U. Mich., 1967; MEd, Loyola U., 1972; LLD (hon.), U. Portland, 1999. Ordained priest Roman Cath. Ch., 1961, consecrated bishop Roman Cath. Ch., 1983. Assoc. pastor St. Paul of the Cross Ch., Park Ridge, Ill., 1962—63, St. Clement Ch., Chgo., 1963—68, St. Aloysius Ch., Chgo., 1968—72, pastor, 1979—81; assoc. pastor St. Sylvester Ch., Chgo., 1972—74, Precious Blood Ch., Chgo., 1974—79; faculty Quigley Prep., North Chgo., Ill., 1963—79, dean of studies, 1969—79; rector Niles Coll., Chgo., 1981—83; aux. bishop Archdiocese of Chgo., 1983—87; Episcopal vicar Vicariate I, Chgo., 1983—87; bishop Episc. Ch., Winona, Minn., 1987—97; archbishop Diocese of Portland, 1997—. Pres. Presbyteral Senate, Chgo., 1976—77; mem. Diocesan Clergy Personnel Bd., Chgo., 1981—84, chmn., 1983—84. Bd. dirs. NED, Latino Tng. Ctr., Chgo., 1980—81, Sacred Heart Sch. Theology, Hales Corners, Wis., 1986—, St. Mary's Coll., Winona, 1987—. Mem.: Nat. Conf. Cath. Bishops (various coms. 1983—), Nat. Comms. Found. (bd. dirs. 1990—). Roman Catholic. Avocations: music, running.

**VLCEK, DONALD JOSEPH, JR.,** food products executive, wholesale distribution executive, writer; b. Chgo., Oct. 30, 1949; s. Donald Joseph and Rosemarie (Krizek) V.; m. Claudia Germain Meyer, July 22, 1978 (div. 1983); 1 child, Suzanne Mae; m. Valeria Olive Russell, Nov. 11, 1989 (div. Mar. 2006); children: James Donald, Victoria Rose. BBA, U. Mich., 1971. Cert. facilitator Adizes Inst. Gen. mgr. Popps, Inc., Hamtramck, Mich., 1969-76; sr. v.p. Domino's Pizza Inc., 1978—93; pres. Domino's Pizza Distbn. Corp., Ann Arbor, Mich., 1978-93, chmn., 1993-94, also bd. dirs.; pres. Don Vlcek & Assocs., Ltd., Plymouth, Mich., 1994—; CEO Beaver Buddies, LLC, Plymouth, Mich., 2001—04; master franchisee Beaver Tails Can., Inc., Mich., Ind., Ill., Ohio, Wis.; pres. WonderPizzaUSA, 2005—, bd. mgrs., 2005—, COO, 2005—. Profl. speaker, personal coach, seminar leader, bus. cons., workshop facilitator; trustee Domino's Pizza Ptnrs. Found.; bd. dirs. RPM Pizza Inc., Gulfport, Miss., Dimango Corp., South Lyon, Mich.; sr. v.p. distbn. and tech. Domino's Ohio Commissary, Zanesville; pres. Morel Mountain Corp.; judge 1994 Duck Stamp contest U.S. Dept. Interior, Jr. Fed. Duck Stamp Contest, 1995; bd. dirs. Beaver Tails Can. Author: The Domino Effect, 1992 (Best of Bus. award ALA 1992, Soundview's Top 30 Business books of 1993), SuperVision, 1997, Job Planning and Review System Manual, 1997, 2001; (audio cassette tape series Super Vision; contbr. articles to profl. jours. Bd. dirs. Men's Hockey League of Oak Park, Mich., 1973-78; asst. coach Redford Scorpions Jr. Travel Hockey Team. Named Person of Yr. Bd. Franchises, Boston, 1981; recipient Istael award Ducks Unltd., 1992, State Major Gifts Chmn. award, 1992, 93, State Chmn.'s award, 1992, State Major Gifts award, 1994, Russ Bengal award, 2003, Mr. Producer award, 1997, 98, 2000, others. Mem. Am. Soc. of Tng. Dirs., Mich. Steelheaders Assn. (life), Ducks Unltd. (life, Domino's Pizza chpt. treas., sponsor, chmn. 1988—, Mich. state bd. dirs., life sponsor, chmn. 1989, 91-92, state trustee 1992-98, hon. trustee 2001—, chmn. exec. com. 1992-94, major gifts chmn. 1993-98, chmn. strategic devel. com. 1994, sponsor in perpetuity Grand Slam Life, Heritage sponsor, recipient Russ Bengal award, 2003), Mich. United Conservation Club (life), Whitetails Unltd. (life), Pheasants Forever (life), Midstates Masters Bowling Assn. (bd. dirs. 1976-85), Barton Hills Country Club (golf com., capt. dist. team), U. Mich. Alumni Assn. (life), Domino's Lodge/Drummond Island Wildlife Habitat Found. (pres., chmn. bd.), Vlcek Family Wildlife Found. (pres., chmn. bd.), Elks (life), Die Hard Cubs Fan Club, Greater Detroit C. of C., Profl. Spkrs. Assn. of Mich. (bd. dirs. 1997-99), Mich. Soc. Assn. Execs., Sm. Bus. Assn. Mich., Nat. Spkrs. Assn., Profl. Spkrs. Ill. (profl.), Internat. Coaching Fedn. (cert. master), Am. Soc. Tng. Dirs., Bus. Network Profls. Republican. Roman Catholic. Avocations: hunting, fishing, hockey, art, coin collecting/numismatics. Home: 9251 Beck Rd N Plymouth MI 48170-3336 Office: Don Vlcek & Assoc Ltd PO Box 701353 Plymouth MI 48170-0963 Office Phone: 734-266-2260. Personal E-mail: vlcek2@aol.com.

**VLIET, MARNI,** foundation administrator; d. James and Mary Louise Tasheff; m. Richard Wayne Vliet, Jan. 26, 1944; children: Whitney Aletia, Sasha Marie. BEd, Wichita State U., 1970, MEd, 1977. Lectr. Wichita State U., 1977—85; program cons. Kans. Health Found., Wichita, 1985—86, program officer, 1986—88, v.p. programs 1988—92, sr. v.p., 1992—96, exec. v.p. and COO, 1996, pres. and CEO, 1996—. Mem. strategic planning com. Dept. Preventive Medicine, U. Kans. Med. Sch., Wichita, 1993—94; bd. dir. Ctrs. Disease Control Found.; spkr. in field. Co-author: Public Health Reports, Community Grantmaking: A Strategic Approach; contbr. articles to jour. Founding chair Funders Concerned Against Substance Abuse, Washington, 1989—94; chair health com. Wichita Commn. on Status of Women, 1975—80, co-chair legis. com.; vice chair bd. Women's Studies Cmty. Coun., Wichita; co-founder Old Town Assn. Wichita, mem. bd.; founding chair Wichita Farm & Art Market Com., mem.; founding dir. Parent Awareness Group and Teen Awareness Day, Robinson Jr. HS, Wichita; founder, dir. Women Alive & Well I & II, Wichita; mem. exec. bd. Women's Alcohol Treatment Services, Wichita; mem. Wichita Children's Mus., Women in the Arts, Wichita; vice chair bd. Wichita Commn. on Status of Women; mem. health promotion adv. bd. Kaiser Family Found., Menlo Park, Calif., 1988—90; bd. dir. Drug Strategies, Washington, 2002—; mem. Grantmakers in Health, 1995—2001, chair bd. dirs., 1999—2001; mem. Cmty. Anti-Drug Coalitions Am., Washington, 1992—98, chair bd. dirs., 1996—98; mem. State of World Forum, San Francisco, 1998; bd. dir. Wichita Symphony Soc., 2000—, Wichita Art Mus., 2000—; mem. bd. Clearinghouse Midcontinent Founds., Kansas City, 1993—97. Recipient President's Drug Adv. Coun. Leadership award, Exec. Office Pres. U.S., 1992, Cmty. Coun. Adv. Bd. award, Wichita State U. Ctr. Women's Studies, 1996, Bd. Trustees' award, Wichita State U., 1996, Exec. of Yr. award, Clarus, 1997—98, Nat. Leadership award, Cmty. Anti-Drug Coalitions Ams., Washington, DC, 1998, Pub. Policy award, Kans. State U. Coll. Human Ecology, 2004, Women Bus. Honoree, Wichita Bus. Jour., 2004, Brotherhood/Sisterhood award, Nat. Conf. Cmty. and Justice, 55th Annual Humanitarian award, Wichita, 2005. Mem.: Coun. Founds. (assoc.), Sigma Theta Tau Internat. (adv. coun.). Avocations: reading, gardening, travel. Office: Kansas Health Found Attn Jamie Hunt Comm Prog Assoc 309 E Douglas Wichita KS 67202 Office Phone: 316-262-7676. Office Fax: 316-262-2044.

**VO, HIEU N.,** architect; b. Cantho City, Cantho, Vietnam, June 2, 1963; s. Tan T. Vo, Tiet L. Lam; m. Hanh T. none. AA, L.A. Pierce Coll., 1994; BArch (hon.), Calif. State Poly. U., 1998. Project mgr. Underwood Assocs. Architects, Decatur, Ala., 1998—99, L. Hughes Assoc. Architects, Huntsville, Ala., 2000—05, Goodrum Knowles, Inc., Huntsville, 2005—. Named to The Talent Roster for Disting. Acad. Performance, The Coll. Bd.s Coll. Scholarship Svc., 1993; recipient Concour d'Elegance, Calif. State Poly. U. Coll. of Environ. Design, 1998, Internat. Biog. Centre's 21st award for Achievement. Mem.: AIA (assoc.), Golden Key (life; California State Polytechic University, Pomona, Outstanding Achievement Scholastic and Excellent 1997). Home: 429 Barrington Hills Dr Madison AL 35758 Personal E-mail: HVO24@aol.com.

**VO, HUU DINH,** pediatrician, educator; b. Hue, Vietnam, Apr. 29, 1950; arrived in U.S., 1975; s. Chanh Dinh and Dong Thi (Pham) Vo; children: Katherine Bao-An, Karyn Bao-An, Hugh Hung. MD, U. Saigon, 1975. Diplomate Am. Bd. Pediat. Administr. bilingual vocat. tng. Cmty. Care and Devel. Svc., LA, 1976-77; resident in pediat. Univ. Hosp., Jacksonville, Fla., 1977-80; physician, surgeon, chief med. officer Lanterman Devel. Ctr., Pomona, Calif., 1980-92, chief med. staff, 1984-88, coord. med. ancillary svc., 1984-88, 91—; physician Pomona Valley Cmty. Hosp., 1988-90; asst. clin. prof. Loma Linda (Calif.) Med. Sch., 1983—; chief med. officer So. Reception Ctr. and Clinic., Norwalk, Calif., 1992-98; physician, surgeon F.C. Nelles Youth Facility, 1998—; med. dir. CTC - HGS Youth Facility, 2004—, administr., 2004—. Bd. dirs. Huu D. Vo M.D. Inc. Radio talk show host, 1997—. Nat. co-chair mem. Vietnamese Am. Cmty. U.S., 1993—95, chmn., bd. comptrs., 1998—; pres. Vietnamese Cmty. Pomona Valley, 1983—85, 1987—95, 1999—, chmn., 1993—95; bd. dirs. YMCA, Pomona, 1988—92, Sch.-Cmty. Partnership, Pomona, 1988—92, ARC, Pomona, 1995—. Mem.: AMA (Physician Recognition award 1989, 1992, 1998, 2004), Vietnamese-Am. Physicians Assn. LA and Orange County (founding mem., sec. 1982—84, bd. dirs. 1987—90), LA Pediat. Soc. Republican. Buddhist. Avocations: tennis, soccer, reading, singing, music. Office: Huu D Vo MD Inc 1182 E Holt Ave Pomona CA 91767 Office Phone: 909-623-8502. Personal E-mail: drhuuvo@hotmail.com.

**VODICKA, JASON DOUGLAS,** music educator; b. Raleigh, NC, Oct. 28, 1980; life ptnr. Derek Jon Cressman. MusB, Westminster Choir Coll., 2002. Cert. music tchr. NJ, profl. educator I Pa. Music educator Pennsbury Sch Dist., Fallsington, Pa., 2003—. William Nash scholar, Pa. Music Educators Assn., 2005. Mem.: Music Educators Nat. Conf., Am. Choral Dirs. Assn. Democrat. Office: Pennsbury HS 608 S Olds Blvd Fairless Hills PA 19030 Office Phone: 215-949-6780 70989. Business E-Mail: jvodicka@pennsbury.k12.pa.us.

**VODRA, WILLIAM WILSON,** lawyer; b. LA, Sept. 13, 1943; BA, Coll. of Wooster, 1965; JD, Columbia U., 1968. Bar: Ohio 1968, D.C. 1981. Atty. Bur. Narcotics and Dangerous Drugs/Drug Enforcement Administrn. Dept. Justice, 1971-74; atty. Office Gen. Counsel FDA Dept. Health Edn. and Welfare, 1974-79; ptnr., Pharmaceutical & Med. Tech. Practice Group Arnold & Porter, Washington, 1979—. Vice-chmn. Commn. on Federal Drug Approval Process, 1981—82; mem. Com. on Fed. Regulation of Methadone Treatment, Nat. Acad. Scis., 1992—95. Contbr. articles to profl. jours. Office: Arnold & Porter Thurman Arnold Bldg 555 12th St NW Washington DC 20004-1206 Office Phone: 202-942-5088. Office Fax: 202-942-5999. Business E-Mail: william.vodra@aporter.com.

**VOEGELI, VICTOR JACQUE,** historian, educator, dean; b. Jackson, Tenn., Dec. 21, 1934; s. Victor Jacque Voegeli and Winnie Lassiter; m. Anna Jean King, Oct. 14, 1956; children: Victor Jacque, Charles Lassiter. BS, Murray State Coll., 1956; MA, Tulane U., 1961, PhD, 1965. History tutor Tulane U., 1963-65, asst. prof., 1965-67; asst. prof. history Vanderbilt U., 1967-69, assoc. prof., 1969-73, prof. history, 1973-98, history dept., 1973-76, dean Coll. Arts and Sci., 1976-92, acting dean Coll. Arts and Sci., 1996-97, prof. emeritus, dean emeritus, 1998—. Author: Free But Not Equal: The Midwest and the Negro During the Civil War, 1967. Served with U.S. Army, 1956-58. Nat. Endowment Humanities grantee, 1969-70, 72. Mem. So. Hist. Assn. Address: 2110 Golf Club Ln Nashville TN 37215-1224

**VOEGTLIN-ANDERSON, MARY MARGARET,** music educator, small business owner; b. Seattle; d. Joseph Walter and Veronica Margaret (Conroy) Voegtlin; m. Terry Lee Anderson, Mar. 19, 1977 (div. July 20, 1982). BA cum laude, Marylhurst I., 1963; postgrad., U. Wash., 1963—65, Oakland U., 1968, Seattle Pacific U., 1982—84. Cert. std. tchg. grades K-12 Wash. Profl. cellist Oreg. Symphony, Portland, 1962—63; tchr. music and humanities Chinook Mid. Sch., Seattle, 1963—89, gifted edn. specialist, 1983—89; tchr. music, music dept. chair Highline H.S., Seattle, 1989—2004, tchr. honors English, 1989—2004; owner, tchr. Anderson Music Studio, Seattle, 2004—. Contralto soloist Mt. Baker Pk. Presbyn. Ch., 1966—68, U. Congl. Ch., Seattle, 1968—73; profl. singer Seattle Opera Co., 1968—70; vocal coach, advisor Highline Jazz Ensemble, Seattle, 1990—2004; pvt. piano, cello and voice tchr., Seattle, 1991—; astronomy club advisor Highline H.S., Seattle, 1998—2004; dir. Highline Dist. Youth Orch., 2003—04, Burien Sr. Choir, 2003; trustee Sunlight Waters Corp., 2002—; pres., owner Anderson Music Studio. Contbr. articles to profl. jours. Officer, sec. 46th Legis. Dist. Dem. Party, Seattle, 1974—78, chairperson Initiative 314 Campaign, 1975; Wash. state conv. del. Dem. Party, Olympia, 1976, Dem. precinct chairperson Seattle, 1976—77. Fulbright Scholarship grantee, Nat. Tchrs. Performance Inst., Oberlin Coll., Ohio, 1970. Mem.: NEA, Planetary Soc., Nat. Coun. Tchrs. English, Seattle Astron. Soc., Music Educators' Nat. Conf. Roman Catholic. Avocations: astronomy, reading, bicycling, writing, hiking. Personal E-mail: mvanderson03@aol.com.

**VOELLGER, GARY A.,** business consulting executive, retired air force officer; BS in Indsl. Rels. Pers. Mgmt., San Jose State U., 1967; grad., Squadron Officer Sch., 1971; M in Psychology, Peperdine U., 1976; grad., Air Command Staff Coll., Maxwell AFB, 1979, Air War Coll., 1988; cert. in Joint Flag Officer War Fighting, Maxwell AFB, 1997; cert.in sr. mgrs. govt. seminar, Harvard U., 1997. Commd. 2d. lt. USAF, 1967, advanced through grades to maj. gen., 1996; pers. officer 379th Combat Support Grp., Wurtsmith AFB, Mich., 1967-69; undergrad. navigator trng. Mather AFB, Calif., 1969-69; weapons sys. officer 46th Tactical Fighter Squadron, MacDill AFB, Fla., 1970-70; weapons syss. officer 91st Tactical Fighter Squadron, Royal Air Force Bentwaters, Eng., 1970-72; undergrad. pilot tng. Laredo AFB, Tex., 1972; F-111 transition tng. Nellis AFB, Nev., 1973-73; F-111 pilot 428th Tactical Fighter Squadron, Takhli Royal AFB, Thailand, 1973-74; F-111 instr. pilot, flight comdr., standardization and evaluation flight examiner 523rd Tactical Fighter Squadron, 27th Tactical Fighter Wing, Cannon AFB, N.Mex., 1974-79; air ops. staff officer, politico-mil. affairs officer, asst. dep. dir. Joint Nat. Security Coun. Matters Hdqs. USAF, Washington, 1980-84; comdr. 55th Tactical Fighter Squadron, Royal Air Force, Upper Heyford, Eng., 1984-87; asst. dep. comdr. ops. 20th Tactical Fighter Wing, Royal Air Force; dep. comdr. ops. 4450th Tactical Group, Nellis AFB, Nev., 1988-89, vice comdr., 1989-90; comdr. 552nd Air Control Wing, Tinker AFB, Okla. 1990-92, Coll. Aerospace Doctrine, Rsch. and Edn., Air U., Maxwell AFB, Ala., 1992-93, 43rd Air Refueling Wing, Malmstrom AFB, Mont., 1993-94, 92nd Air Refueling Wing, Fairchild AFB, Wash., 1994-95, 437th Airlift Wing, Charleston AFB, S.C., 1995-96; dir. ops. Hdqs. Air Mobility Command, Scott AFB, Ill., 1996-98; NATO force comdr. Hdqs. NATO Airborne Early Warning Force, Mons, Belgium, 1998-2000; ret. USAF; prin. Booz Allen Hamilton, O'Fallon, Ill. Decorated .D.D.S.M., Legion of Merit with oak leaf Cluster, Bronze Star medal, Meritorious Svc. medal with two oak leaf clusters, Air medal with oak leaf cluster, Armed Forces Expeditionary medal, Rep. Vietnam Gallantry Cross with Palm. Office: Booz Allen & Hamilton Inc 1728 Corporate Crossing Ste 2 O Fallon IL 62269 Office Phone: 618-622-2333. Business E-Mail: voellger_gary@bah.com.

**VOET, DONALD HERMAN,** biochemist, educator, writer; b. Amsterdam, Netherlands, Nov. 29, 1938; arrived in U.S., 1939; s. Andries and Henriette Hannah Voet; m. Judith Greenwald Voet, Jan. 30, 1965; children: Wendy Helaine, Douglas Philip. BS, Calif. Inst. Tech., 1960; PhD, Harvard U., Cambridge, Mass., 1966. Postdoc. fellow MIT, Cambridge, 1966—69; prof. U. Pa., Phila. Author: (textbook) Biochemistry, Fundamentals of Biochemistry; editor-in-chief: jour. Biochemistry and Molecular Biology Edn. Mem.: AAAS (corr.), Am. Soc. Biochemistry and Molecular Biology (corr.), Sigma Xi (corr.; sec. 1995—2000). Achievements include research in X-ray structures of proteins. Avocations: travel, backpacking, scuba diving, swimming, skiing. Office: Univ Pennsylvania Dept Chemistry 250 South 33rd St Philadelphia PA 19104 Office Phone: 215-898-6457.

**VOETSCH, BARBARA,** neurologist, researcher; b. Nürtingen, Germany, July 4, 1969; d. Karl Paul and Doris Voetsch; m. Marc A. Forgione. MD, State U. Campinas, São Paulo, 1992, PhD in Med. Scis. and Neurology, 2002. Cert. Brazilian Fed. Neurology, lic. Brazil. Intern State U. Campinas, São Paulo, Brazil, 1993—94, resident in neurology, 1994—97, stroke fellow, 1997—98; stroke rsch. fellow Harvard Med. Sch., Boston, 1999—2000; rsch. assoc. Whitaker Cardiovasc. Inst. Boston U., 2000—04, postdoctoral fellow, 2002—04, asst. prof. medicine, 2004—; coord. Stroke in the Young Clinic, State U. Campinas, São Paulo, 1997—99. Author: Thrombosis and Hemorrhage, 2002, Recent Advances in Hematology, 2004; reviewer Circulation Rsch., Stroke, Lancet, New England Jour. of Medicine; reviewer: Jour. Neurol. Scis., Circulation, Clin. Genetics, Blood Coagulation and Fibrinolysis; contbr. articles to profl. jours. Recipient Neurology award for best rsch., Brazilian Acad. Neurology, 1998, Fellow's Clin Rsch. award, Astra Zeneca Young Investigator Forum, 2000; grantee Found. for Higher Edn. and Grad. Tng., 1999—2000. Mem.: Brazilian Soc. Cerebrovascular Diseases, Brazilian Acad. Neurology, Med. Assn. São Paulo, Am. Heart Assn. (mem. stroke coun.). Avocations: tennis, volleyball.

**VOEVODSKY, VLADIMIR,** mathematician; b. Russia, June 4, 1966; BS in Math., Moscow State U., 1989; PhD in Math., Harvard U., 1992. Assoc. prof. Northwestern U., 1996—99; prof. Inst. for Advanced Study, Princeton, NJ, 2002—. Mem. Inst. for Advanced Study, Harvard U., 1992—93, 1998—2001; visiting prof. Max Planck Inst. for Math., 1996—97, Harvard U., 1996—97. Co-author: Cycles, Transfers and Motivic Homology Theories, 2000. Recipient Fields medal, 2002, rsch. grants, NSF, Clay Prize fellowship, 1999, 2000. Office: Inst for Advanced Study Sch Math Fuld 116 Einstein Dr Princeton NJ 08540 E-mail: vladimir@math.ias.edu

**VOGEL, ARTHUR ANTON,** clergyman; b. Milw., Feb. 24, 1924; s. Arthur Louis and Gladys Eirene (Larson) V.; m. Katharine Louise Nunn, Dec. 29, 1947; children: John Nunn, Arthur Anton, Katharine Ann. Student, U. of South, 1942-43, Carroll Coll., 1943-44; B.D., Nashotah House Theol. Sem., 1946; MA, U. Chgo., 1948; PhD, Harvard, 1952; S.T.D., Gen. Theol. Sem., 1969; D.C.L., Nashotah House, 1969; D.D., U. of South, 1971. Ordained deacon Episcopal Ch., 1946, priest, 1948; teaching asst. philosophy Harvard, Cambridge, Mass., 1949-50; instr. Trinity Coll., Hartford, Conn., 1950-52; mem. faculty Nashotah House Theol. Sem., Nashotah, Wis., 1952-71, asso. prof., 1954-56, William Adams prof. philosophical and systematic theology, 1956-71, sub-dean Sem., 1964-71; bishop coadjutor Diocese of West Mo., Kansas City, 1971-72, bishop, 1972-89; rector Ch. St. John Chrysostom, Delafield, Wis., 1952-56; dir. Anglican Theol. Rev., Evanston, Ill., 1964-69; mem. Internat. Anglican-Roman Cath. Consultation, 1970-90, Nat. Anglican-Roman Catholic Consultation, 1965-84, Anglican chmn., 1973-84; mem. Standing Commn. on Ecumenical Relations of Episcopal Ch., 1957-79; mem. gen. bd. examining chaplains Episcopal Ch., 1971-72. Del. Episcopal Ch., 4th Assembly World Council Chruches, Uppsala, Sweden, 1968, and others. Author: Reality, Reason and Religion, 1957, The Gift of Grace, 1958, The Christian Person, 1963, The Next Christian Epoch, 1966, Is the Last Supper Finished?, 1968, Body Theology, 1973, The Power of His Resurrection, 1976, Proclamation 2: Easter, 1980, The Jesus Prayer for Today, 1982, I Know God Better Than I Know Myself, 1989, Christ in His Time and Ours, 1982, God, Prayer and Healing, 1995, Radical Christianity and the Flesh of Jesus, 1995; editor: Theology in Anglicanism, 1985; contbr. articles to profl. jours. Vice chmn. bd. dirs. St. Luke's Hosp., Kansas City, Mo., 1971, chmn., 1973-89. Research fellow Harvard, 1950 Mem. Am. Philos. Assn., Metaphys. Soc. Am., Soc. Existential and Phenomenological Philosophy, Catholic Theol. Soc. Am. Episcopalian. Home: 4203 W 94th Terrace Apt 111 Prairie Village KS 66207 E-mail: akvogel@swbell.net.

**VOGEL, CARL E.,** communications executive; b. Oct. 18, 1957; BS in Fin. and Acctg., St. Norbert Coll., DePere, Wis. With Jones Intercable, 1983; exec. v.p. EchoStar Comm. Inc., 1994—97; CEO Star Choice Comm., 1998; chmn., CEO Primestar Inc., 1998—99; exec. v.p., COO AT&T Broadband, 1999; sr. v.p. Liberty Media Corp., 1999—2001; pres., CEO Charter Comm. Inc., 2001—05; vice chmn. EchoStar Comm. Corp., 2005—, pres., 2006—. Bd. dirs. C-SPAN, CableLabs, EchoStar Comm. Corp., 2005—. Mem.: Nat. Cable TV Assn. (bd. dirs.). Office: EchoStar Comm Corp 9601 South Meridian Blvd Englewood CO 80112 Office Phone: 303-723-1000.*

**VOGEL, CEDRIC WAKELEE,** lawyer; b. Cin., June 4, 1946; s. Cedric and Patricia (Woodruff) V. BA, Yale U., 1968; JD, Harvard U., 1971. Bar: Ohio 1972, Fla. 1973, U.S. Tax Ct. 1972, U.S. Supreme Ct. 1975. Ptnr. Vogel, Heis, Wenstrup & Cameron, Cin., 1972-96; sole practice, 1997—. Chmn. mem.'s com. Cin. Art Mus., 1987-88; chmn. auction Cin. Hist. Soc., 1985; local pres. English Speaking Union, 1979-81, nat. bd. dirs., 1981; chmn. Keep Cin. Beautiful, Inc., 1994-96; active Bravo! Cin. Ballet, 1989; chmn. Act II Nutcracker Ball, 1987-88; bd. dirs. Merc Libr., 1991-98, Cin. Preservation Assn., 1990-93, Cin. Opera Guild, 1997-99, Pro Srs., 1996-2005; vice chmn. Children's Heart Assn. Reds Rally, 1989; bd. dirs. Cin. Country Day Sch., 1983, pres. Alumni Coun. and Ann. Fund, 1983. Mem.: Fla. Bar Assn., Cin. Bar Assn., Yale Alumni Assn. (del. 1984—87), Harvard Law Sch. Assn. Cin. (pres. 1997—99, 2003—), Heimlich Inst. (trustee 1987—2001), Pro Srs. (bd. dirs. 1996—2005), Harvard Club of Cin. (bd. dirs. 1996—98, pres. 1999—2000), The Lawyers Club Cin. (pres. 1995), Cincinnatus, Cin. Yale Club (pres. 1980—81, 1996—97). Republican. Home: 3473 Forest Oak Ct Cincinnati OH 45208-1842 Office: 817 Main St Ste 800 Cincinnati OH 45202-2183 Office Phone: 513-421-4225. Personal E-mail: rvogel@iac.net.

**VOGEL, DAVID SETH,** lawyer; b. NYC, July 11, 1955; s. Joshua Selig and Muriel Rita Vogel; m. Patrice Louise Jaxon; children: Claire, Jack. AB, Amherst Coll., 1973—77; JD magna cum laude, Boston U., 1979—82. Law clerk Hon. Frank M. Johnson, Jr., 11th Circuit Ct. of Appeals, Montgomery, Ala., 1982—83; assoc. Perkins Coie Law Firm, Seattle, 1983—84; dep. prosecutor King County Prosecutor's Office, Seattle, 1984—89; assoc. Levinson Friedman Law Firm, Seattle, 1989—92; prin. Law Offices of David S. Vogel, Seattle, 1992—. Editor: Boston U. Law Rev. Pres. Vashon-Maury Island Cmty. Coun., Vashon Island, Wash., 1986—93, bd. mem., 1985—2000, Vashon Household, Vashon Island, Wash., 1996—2003; chair Vashon Town Plan Com., Vashon Island, Wash., 1992—96. Recipient Cmty. Svc. award, Vashon-Maury Island Audubon Soc., 1994, Pilchuck Audubon Soc., 1997. Mem.: ABA, Wash. Assn. Criminal Defense Lawyers, Brain Injury Assn., Wash. State Trial Lawyers Assn., Assn. of Trial Lawyers of Am., Wash. State Bar Assn., Seattle-King County Bar Assn., WSTLA Eagles. Liberal. Jewish. Avocations: fishing, hiking, camping. Office: Law Offices of David Vogel Ste 2200 821 2nd Ave Seattle WA 98104 Office Phone: 206-622-2573. Business E-Mail: dvogel@davidvogel.com.

**VOGEL, EZRA F.,** sociology educator; b. Delaware, Ohio, July 11, 1930; s. Joseph H. and Edith (Nachman) V.; m. Suzanne Hall, July 5, 1953 (div.); children: David, Steven, Eva; m. Charlotte Ikels, Nov. 3, 1979. BA, Ohio Wesleyan U., 1950; MA, Bowling Green State U., 1951; PhD, Harvard U., 1958; LittD (hon.), Kwansai Gakuin, 1980, Wittenberg Coll., 1981, Bowling Green State U., 1982, U. Md., 1983, Albion Coll., 1988, Chinese U., Hong Kong, 1992, Ohio Wesleyan, 1996; LittD (hon.), U. Mass., Lowell, 1996, Yamaguchi U., 1998, Monterrey Inst., 2002. Rsch. fellow Harvard (for work in Japan), 1958-60; asst. prof. Yale U., 1960-61; rsch. assoc., lectr. Harvard U., 1961-67, prof., 1967—2000, Henry Ford II prof. social scis., 1990—2005, emeritus, 2005—, assoc. dir. East Asian Rsch. Ctr., 1967-73, dir., 1973-77, chmn. council East Asian studies, 1977-80, dir. program on U.S.-Japan relations, 1980-87, hon. chmn. program on U.S.-Japan rels., 1988—, mem. faculty council, 1981-84, dir. Asia Ctr., 1997-99, rsch. prof., 2000—; nat. intelligence officer for East Asia Nat. Intelligence Coun., 1993-95, dir. Fairbank Ctr. East Asian Studies, 1995-99. Mem. Joint Com. on Contemporary China, 1968-75, Com. on Scholarly Communication with Peoples Republic China, 1973-75, Joint Com. Japanese Studies, 1977-79 Author: Japan's New Middle Class, 1963, Canton Under Communism, 1969, Japan As Number One, 1979, Comeback, 1985, The Impact of Japan on a Changing World, 1987, One Step Ahead in China, 1989, The Four Little Dragons, 1991, Is Japan Still Number One?, 2000; co-editor: (with Norman W. Bell) A Modern Introduction to the Family, 1960, (with George Lodge) Ideology and National Competitiveness, Living With China, 1997, (with Ming Yuan and Akihiko Tanaka) The Golden Age of the U.S.-China Japan Triangle, 2002; editor: Modern Japanese Organization and Decision-Making, 1975. Trustee Ohio Wesleyan U., 1970-75, 80-94. Served with AUS, 1951-53. Recipient Harvard faculty prize for book of year, 1970, Japan Found. prize, 1996, Japan Soc. prize 1998; Guggenheim fellow, 1972 Mem. Assn. Asian Studies (bd. dirs. 1970-72), Am. Acad. Arts and Scis. Home: 14 Sumner Rd Cambridge MA 02138-3018 Office Phone: 617-495-4014.

**VOGEL, H. VICTORIA,** psychotherapist, educator, writer, stress disorder and addiction recovery counselor; BA, U. Md., 1968; MA, NYU, 1970, MEd, 1975; MEd, postgrad., Columbia U., 1982—; cert., Am. Projective Drawing Inst., 1983; CASAC, New Sch. U. for Social Rsch., 2000. Diplomate Am. Acad. Experts in Traumatic Stress; cert. addiction recovery counselor, expert in traumatic stress, alcohol and substance abuse counselor, addictions treatment, addiction counseling alcohol and substance abuse. Art therapist Childville, Bklyn., 1962-64; tchr. Montgomery County (Md.) Jr. H.S., 1968-69; with H.S. divsn. N.Y.C. Bd. Edn., 1970—; guidance counselor, instr., psychotherapist in pvt. practice. Guidance counselor, instr., psychotherapist in pvt. practice; clin. counseling cons. psychodiagnosis and devel. studies, art/play therapy The Modern Sch., 1984—; art/play therapist Hosp. Ctr. for Neuromuscular Disease and Devel. Disorders, 1986—; employment counselor-adminstr. N.Y. State Dept. Labor Concentrated Employment Program, 1971-72; intern psychotherapy and psychoanalysis psychiat. divsn. Ctrl. Islip Hosp., 1973-75, Calif. Grad. Inst., L.A.; intern psychol. counseling and rehab. N.J. Coll. Medicine, Newark, 1979. Author: The Never Ending Story of Alcohol, Drugs and Other Substance Abuse, 1992, Variant Sexual Behavior and the Aesthetic Modern Nudes, 1992, Psychological Science of School Behavior Intervention, 1993, Joycean Conceptual Modernism: Relationships and Deviant Sexuality, 1995, Electronic Evil Eyes, 1995 (U.S. Cert. of Recognition, 1996), Psychological Paradigms of Alcohol Violence Suicide Trauma Addiction Variant Pathologies PTSD and Schizophrenia, 1999. Mem. com. for spl. events NYU, 1989; participant clin. and artistic perspectives Am. Acad. Psychoanalysis Conf., 1990, participant clin. postmodernism and psychoanalysis, 1996; aux. police officer N.Y. Police Dept., 1994—; chair bylaws com. Columbia U., 1995—. Mem.: ACA, AAAS, APA, NY Acad. Sci., Tchrs. Coll. Adminstrv. Women in Edn., Assn. Humanistic Psychology (exec. sec. 1981), Art/Play Therapy, N.Y. Art Tchrs. Assn., Am. Acad. Experts Traumatic Stress (diplomate in expert traumatic stress), Am. Soc. Group Psychotherapy and Psychodrama (publs. com. 1984—), Am. Orthopsychiat. Assn., Am. Psychol. Soc., Phi Delta Kappa (editor chpt. newsletter 1981—84, exec. sec. Columbia U. chpt. 1984—, chmn. nominating com. for chpt. officers 1986—, rsch. rep. 1986—, pub. rels. exec. bd. dirs. 1991, NYU chpt. v.p. programs 1994—).

**VOGEL, JENNIFER,** lawyer; BBA, U. Iowa; JD, U. TX Sch. Law, Austin, TX, 1987. Atty. Vinson & Elkins LLP; v.p., gen. counsel Enron Global Power & Pipelines; v.p. legal & asst. sec. Continental Airlines, Inc., Houston, 1995—2001, gen. counsel, 2001—, sr. v.p., corp. compliance officer, corp. sec., 2003—. Mailing: Continental Airlines Inc PO Box 4607 Houston TX 77210-4607 Office Phone: 713-324-2950.

**VOGEL, NELSON J., JR.,** lawyer; b. South Bend, Ind., Oct. 13, 1946; s. Nelson J. and Carolyn B. (Drzewiecki) V.; m. Sandra L. Cudney, May 17, 1969; children: Ryan C., Justin M., Nathan J. Lindsey M. BS cum laude, Miami U., Oxford, Ohio, 1968; JD cum laude, U. Notre Dame, 1971. Bar: Ind. 1971, Mich. 1971, U.S. Dist. Ct. (no. dist.) Ind. 1971, U.S. Tax Ct. 1972, U.S. Ct. Appeals (5th cir.) 1975, U.S. Ct. Claims 1980. Acct. Coopers & Lybrand, South Bend, 1969-71; assoc. Barnes & Thornburg, South Bend, 1971-76, ptnr., 1977—. Instr. U. Notre Dame, South Bend, 1971, 74-80; instr. Ind. U., South Bend, 1971-74; vice-chair Barnes & Thornburg, 2001—, mng. ptnr. South Bend office, 2001—. Trustee Project Future, St. Joseph Co., 2002—; pres. Big Bros./Big Sisters, South Bend, 1978-79; bd. pres. South Bend Regional Mus. Art, 1984-86; ethics com. Meml. Hosp., South Bend, 1986-94; bd. adv. Goshen Coll. Family Bus. program, 1993-99; bd. dirs.

Madison Ctr., 2003-06. Mem. Nat. Employee Stock Ownership Plan Assn. (sec.-treas. Ind. chpt. 1993-95), Nat. Assn. State Bar Tax Sec. (exec. com. 1982-84), Ind. State Bar Assn. (chmn. taxation sect. 1981-82, Citation of Merit 1979), Mich. Bar Assn. (tax sect.), Ind. State HS Hockey Assn., Inc. (bd. dirs. 1998-01, treas. 1998-01), Michiana World Affairs Coun. (bd. dirs. 1992-96), Michiana World Trade Club (bd. dirs. 1992-96), Mental Health Assn. St. Joseph County (bd. dirs. 1997-01), St. Joseph County C. of C. (bd. dirs. 2006-). Home: 1146 Dunrobbin Ln South Bend IN 46614-2150 Office: Barnes & Thornburg 600 1st Source Bank 100 N Michigan St Ste 600 South Bend IN 46601-1632 Office Phone: 574-233-1171. Business E-Mail: nvogel@btlaw.com.

**VOGEL, PAULA ANNE,** playwright; b. Washington, Nov. 16, 1951; d. Donald Stephen and Phyllis (Bremerman) Vogel. BA, Cath. U., 1974; doctoral studies, Cornell U., 1974-77. Instr. theatre and women's studies Cornell U., Ithaca, N.Y., 1978-81; prodn. supr. Theatre on Film & Tape, N.Y.C., 1983-85; Adele Kellenberg Seaver prof. Creative Writing Program, Brown U., Providence, 1985—. Author: (plays) Meg, 1977 (Nat. Playwright award Am. Coll. Theatre Festival), And Baby Makes Seven, 1984, Desdemona, 1985, The Oldest Profession, 1988, The Baltimore Waltz, 1992 (Obie award for best play, 1992), Hot 'N' Throbbing, 1994, The Mineola Twins, 1996, How I Learned to Drive, 1996 (Pulitzer Prize, 1998, Obie award, 1997, N.Y. Drama Critics Drama Desk award for best play, 1997, Lucille Lortel award, 1997, Outer Critics' Circle award, 1997). Recipient Bunting award, Radcliffe-Harvard Colls., 1990, Pew Charitable Trust Sr. Residency award, 1995, Laura Pels award, 1999; grantee Fund for New Am. Plays, 1994; playwright fellow NEA, 1981, 1990, Guggenheim fellow, 1995. Fellow: Am. Acad. Arts & Sciences, McDowell Colony; mem.: New Dramatists. Office: Brown U PO Box 1852 Providence RI 02912-1852*

**VOGEL, SCOTT CHARLES,** music educator; b. Mpls., Minn., Apr. 14, 1963; s. Wayne Kent Vogel and Karen Marie Vogel-Pearsal; m. Kari Ann Laine, July 25, 1992; children: Tristan, Carli, Collin. AA, No. Hennepin Cmty. Coll., 1984; BSc, Bemidji State U., 1988. Dir. bands, tchr. Princeton Pub. Schools, Minn., 1988—92, Mahnoman Pub. Schs., Minn., 1992—98, Coon Rapids H.S., Minn., 1998—. Mem.: Internat. Assn. of Jazz Educators (treas. 1992—95), Minn. Music Educators Assn., Music Educators Nat. Conf., Sons of the Am. Legion. Avocations: archery, fishing, camping, hunting. Home: 31512 104th St Princeton MN 55371 Office: Coon Rapids HS 2340 Northdale Blvd Coon Rapids MN 55433

**VOGEL, SUSAN CAROL,** nursing administrator; b. Hartford, Conn., Oct. 9, 1948; d. Morton B. and Esther (Riback) Worshoufsky. Diploma in nursing, Grace Hosp., New Haven, 1969; B in Healthcare Mgmt., U. La Verne, 1991, M in Health Adminstrn., 1994. RN, Calif.; cert. nephrology nurse, Nephrology Nurse Cert. Bd. Oper. rm. nurse New Britain (Conn.) Gen. Hosp., 1970-72; staff nurse oper. rm. Parkview Cmty. Hosp., Riverside, Calif., 1972-74; staff nurse dialysis, IV team Cedars-Sinai Med. Ctr., L.A., 1974-82; clin. nurse III dialysis UCLA, 1982-88; nurse mgr. inpatient dialysis UCLA Med. Ctr., 1988-93; adminstr. South Valley Regional Dialysis Ctr., Encino, Calif., 1993—; pres. Renal Replacement Therapies, Inc. Bd. dirs. End Stage Renal Disease Network 18, med. rev. bd., 1996—2000, treas.; chmn. bd. Renal Support Network, 2006—. Author: (with others) Review of Hemodialysis for Nurses and Dialysis Personnel, 7th edit., 2002, Vascular Access, Principles & Practices, 4th edit., 2002; editor Nephrology Nursing Jour., 2000-02. Med. rev. bd. End Stage Renal Disease Network 18, 1996-2000, treas., 2004—06; pres. Calif. Dialysis Coun., 2002-05, past pres. 2005-; trustee Am. Kidney Fund, 2005—; bd. chmn. Renal Support Network, 2006. Mem. NAFE, Am. Nephrology Nurses Assn. (pres. LA chpt. 1990-92, 96-98, nat. chair hemodialysis spl. interest group 1993-95), Nat. Kidney Found. Avocations: travel, skiing. Office: South Valley Regional Dialysis Ctr 17815 Ventura Blvd Ste 100 Encino CA 91316-3600 E-mail: svogel@svrde.com.

**VOGEL, THOMAS TIMOTHY,** surgeon, educator, lay worker; b. Columbus, Ohio, Feb. 1, 1934; s. Thomas A. and Charlotte A. (Hogan) V.; m. M.M. Darina Kelleher, May 29, 1965; children: Thomas T., Catherine D., Mark P., Nicola M. AB, Coll. of Holy Cross, 1955; MS, Ohio State U., 1960, PhD, 1962; MD, Georgetown U., 1965. Pvt. practice surgery, Columbus, 1971-2001; chmn. liturgy com., pres. parish coun. St. Catharine Parish, Columbus, 1971-73; chmn. diocesan adminstrn. com. Diocesan Pastoral Coun., Columbus, 1972-73, chmn., 1973-75; vice prefect Sodality of Holy Cross, 1953-55; mem. Ohio Bishop's Adv. Coun., Columbus, 1976-79. Clin. asst. prof. surgery Ohio State U., Columbus, 1974—; past trustee Peer Rev. Sys., Inc.; assoc. med. dir. United Health Care, Columbus, 1997-2000; cons. Rehabilitation Svcs.; commr., surveillance utilization rev. mem. Medicaid, State of Ohio, 1998-2000; assoc. med. dir. Palmetto GBA, 1999—. Contbr. articles to profl. jours. Bd. dirs. St. Vincent's Children's Ctr., 1975-83, chmn., 1981-82; past chmn. bd. trustees St. Joseph Montessori Sch. Named Knight of the Holy Sepulchre, Equestrian Order of the Holy Sepulchre of Jerusalem, 2001; recipient Layman's award. Equestrian Assn. Ga. Kiwanis, 1972. Mem. ACS, Am. Physiol. Soc., Assn. for Acad. Surgery, Ohio State Med. Assn. (del. 1993—), Sigma Xi, Delta Epsilon Sigma. Roman Catholic. Home: 247 S Ardmore Rd Columbus OH 43209-1701 Office: 621 S Cassingham Rd Columbus OH 43209-2403 E-mail: vogel.3@osu.edu.

**VOGEL, VICTOR GERALD,** medical educator, researcher; b. Bethlehem, Pa., Mar. 14, 1952; s. Victor Gerald Jr. and Margaret Moser (Smith) V.; m. Saralyn Sue Schaffner, June 25, 1977; children: Heather Marie, Christiaan Keith. Diplomate Am. Bd. Internal Medicine, Am. Bd. Preventive Medicine, Nat. Bd. Med. Examiners. Resident in internal medicine Balt. City Hosps., 1978-81; fellow in med. oncology Johns Hopkins Oncology Ctr., Balt. 1983-86; Andrew W. Mellon fellow Johns Hopkins Sch. Hygiene Pub. Health, Balt., 1984-86; asst. prof. medicine and epidemiology U. Tex./M.D. Anderson Cancer Ctr., Houston, 1986-93, assoc. prof. clin. cancer prevention, 1993-95; asst. prof. epidemiology U. Tex. Sch. Pub. Health, Houston, 1987-95; prof. medicine and epidemiology U. Pitts. Cancer Inst./Magee-Womens Hosp., 1996—, dir. MAGEE/UPCI breast cancer program, 1996—2002, dir. MAGEE/UPCI breast cancer prevention program, 2003—. Epidemiologist Tex. breast screening project Am. Cancer Soc., 1986-93; mem. data and safety monitoring bd. Women's Health Initiative, NIH, 1994—2004; bd. dirs. Nat. Surg. Adjuvant Breast and Bowel Project Found., Inc., 1997—; AMC Cancer Ctr., Denver, 1996-99; protocol chmn. Nat. Cancer Inst. Study of Tamoxifen and Raloxifene. Contbr. articles to profl. jours. Founding mem. Nat. Surg. adjuvant Breast and Bowel Project Found., Inc.; founding pres. Internat. Soc. Cancer Risk Assessment and Mgmt., 2003. Served with USPHS, 1981-83. Named Med. Vol. of Yr., Am. Cancer Soc., 1983; recipient award, 1987, career devel. award, 1990—93; fellow, Susan G. Komen Breast Cancer Found., 1990—93. Fellow Am. Coll. Preventive Medicine, ACP; mem. Am. Soc. Clin. Oncology, Am. Soc. Preventive Oncology, Christian Med. and Dental Assn., Am. Assn. Cancer Rsch. Republican. Presbyterian. Avocation: flying. Office: U Pittsburgh Cancer Inst Magee-Womens Hosp 300 Halket St Rm 3524 Pittsburgh PA 15213-3108 Office Phone: 412-641-6500. Business E-Mail: vvogel@magee.edu. E-mail: vvogel@aol.com.

**VOGEL, WERNER PAUL,** retired machine company executive; b. Louisville, June 15, 1923; s. Werner George and Emma (Bartman) Vogel; m. Helen Louise Knapp, Oct. 2, 1954. B Mech. Engring., U. Louisville, 1950. With Henry Vogt Machine Co., Louisville, 1942—86, asst. plant supt., 1957—60, plant supt., 1961—73, v.p., 1974—86; ret. Trustee City of Strathmoor, Ky., 1959—61; clk. City of Glenview Manor, Ky., 1967—73, trustee, 1974—75, treas., 1986—89; mem. advd. coun. Lindsey Wilson Coll., 1988—2003; bd. dirs. Louisville Protestant Altenheim, 1979—80, pres., 1985—90, ret. With USAAF, 1944—46. Mem.: ASME. Sigma Tau, Tau Beta Pi. Republican. Methodist. Home: 9118 Coventry Ln Louisville KY 40219

**VOGELGESANG, SANDRA LOUISE,** former ambassador, writer, consultant; b. Canton, Ohio, July 27, 1942; d. Glenn Wesley and Louise (Forry) Vogelgesang; m. Geoffrey Ernest Wolfe, July 4, 1982. BA, Cornell U., 1964; MA, Tufts U., 1965, MA in Law and Diplomacy, 1966, PhD, 1971. With Dept. State, Washington, 1975-97, policy planner for sec. state and European

Bur., 1975-80, dir. Econ Policy Office, Orgn. Econ. Coop. and Devel., 1981-82, econ. minister U.S. Embassy, Ottawa, Can., 1982-86, dep. asst. sec. Internat. Orgn. Affairs Bur., 1986-89; dep. asst. adminstr. Office Internat. Activities Environ. Protection Agy., Washington, 1989-92; with Dept. State, Washington, 1992; sr. policy advisor Agy. for Internat. Devel., 1993; US amb. to Nepal Dept. State, Washington, 1994-97; pres. Everest Assocs. and Himalaya, 1997—2004. Bd. dirs. Ctr. for Econ. Devel. and Population Activities; mem. women and conservation com. World Wildlife Fund, 1997—2004, mem. Internat. Mus. Coun., 1999—2004; bd. advisors Am.'s Soc., N.Y.C., 1986—89; mem. Pres.'s Coun. of Conf. Women Cornell U., 1998—; adv. com. Dept. of Treasury com. on Internat. Child Labor Enforcement, 1999—; mem. global coun. Internat. Mus. Women, 2004—; writer, cons. internat. devel. issues. Author: Long Dark Night of the Soul, The American Intellectual Left and the Vietnam War, 1974, American Dream-Global Nightmare: The Dilemma of U.S. Human Rights Policy, 1980. Bd. dirs. Crafts Ctr., 1999-2000. Recipient Meritorious Service awards, 1973, 74, 82, 83, 86, Disting. Honor award, 1976 Dept. State, Pres.' Disting. Service award, 1985. Mem. Council on Fgn. Relations. Office: 9009 Charred Oak Dr West Bethesda MD 20817-1923 Business E-Mail: everest.associates@erols.com.

**VOGELMAN, JOSEPH HERBERT,** scientific engineering company executive; b. NYC, Aug. 18, 1920; s. Jacob and Sabina (Weingarten) V.; m. Norma Schneider, Dec. 8, 1946; children: Jeffrey Allan, Leslie Sue, Linda Leigh. BS, CCNY, 1940; M.E.E., Poly. Inst. Bklyn., 1948, D.Elec. Engring., 1957. Registered profl. engr., N.Y., N.J. Project engr. Signal Corps Engr. Labs., Belmar, NJ, 1943-45; chief devel. br. Watson Labs., Eatontown, NJ, 1945-50; chief scientist Rome Air Devel. Center, Griffiss AFB, NY, 1951-52, chief electronic warfare lab., 1953-56, dir. communications, 1956-59; v.p., dir. Capehart Corp., N.Y.C., 1959-64; dir. electronics Chromalloy Am. Corp., N.Y.C., 1964-67, gen. mgr. pocket fone div., 1966-67, v.p., 1967-73; v.p., dir. Cro-Med Bionics Corp., 1968-73; vice chmn. bd., dir. Laser Link Corp., 1968-73; chief scientist, dir. Orentreich Found. for Advancement Sci., 1973—; pres. Vogelman Devel. Corp., 1973—. Chmn. tech. adv. com. Compupix, Inc., 1984-86. Contbr. articles to profl. jours. and encys.; patentee in field. Served with AUS, 1942-43. Recipient Outstanding Performance award USAF, 1957 Fellow AAAS, IEEE; mem. Titulaire, Societe Francaise de Electroniciens et des Radio Electriciens, N.Y. Acad. Scis., Sigma Xi, Eta Kappa Nu. Home: 48 Green Dr Roslyn NY 11576-3221 Office: 910 5th Ave New York NY 10021-4155 Personal E-mail: dr.jhv@juno.com.

**VOGELSBERG, ROSS TIMM,** education educator, researcher; b. Bryn Mawr, Pa., Feb. 23, 1945; s. Robert Wilhelm Vogelsberg and Jean Byram (Fishburn) Blanchard. BS, Colo. State U., 1968; MS, Utah State U., 1974; PhD, U. Ill., 1979. Part-time assoc. Gateways Inc., Ft. Collins, Colo., 1968; master resource tchr. Utah State U., Logan, 1972-74, assoc. dir. project, 1974-77; rsch. assoc. U. Ill., Urbana, 1977-79; project dir., asst. prof. U. Vt., Burlington, 1979-85; project dir., assoc. prof. Temple U., Phila., 1985-94; exec. dir., prof. Rural Inst. Disabilities U. Mont., Missoula, 1995—. Contbr. numerous articles to profl. jours. and chpts. in books. With U.S. Army, 1969-71, ETO. Named one of Outstanding Young Men of Am., U.S. Jaycees, 1982; recipient Svc. award United Cerebral Palsy Pa., 1986. Mem. Assn. for Spl. Edn. Tech., Am. Ednl. Rsch. Assn., Assn. for Persons Analysis, Assn. for Persons with Severe Handicaps, Nat. Soc. for Performance and Instruction, Assn. for the Advancement of Behavior Therapy, Coun. for Exceptional Children, Am. Asns. on Mental Deficiency. Office: U Mont Rural Inst 634 Eddy Ave Missoula MT 59812-0001 Office Phone: 406-243-5467.

**VOGELSONG, DIANA LOUISE,** librarian; b. Morristown, N.J., Jan. 16, 1951; d. James Howard and Doris May (Kehr) V.; m. Wallace Cutting Duncan, Jr., Apr. 24, 1976; children: Matthew, Andrea. BA, Kalamazoo Coll., 1973; MLS in Libr. and Info. Sci., U. Md., 1975; MA in Art History, Am. U., 1981. Cataloger U.S. Book Exch., Washington, 1974; searcher McKeldin Libr., U. Md., College Park, 1975; reference libr. Am. U. Libr., Washington, 1975-80, head media svcs., 1980-96, asst. univ. libr. for info. svcs., 1993—2005, acting U. Libr., 2006—. Project coord. Mus. Ednl. Site Licensing Project, Getty Art History Info. Inst., 1995-1997. Author: Guide to the Microforms Collection of the National Gallery of Art, Washington, D.C., 1990, Landscape Architecture in America: A Guide to Resources on the History and Practice of Landscape Architecture in the United States, 1997; reviewer Video Rating Guide, 1990-91; contbr. chpts. to books and articles to profl. jours. Juror Am. Film and Video Festival, 1981, 87-93, jury chairperson, 1987, 93; mem. undergrad. studies com. Am. U. Senate, 1985-91, mem. computer resources com., 1994-96, chair faculty senate com. on info. resources, 2003-2005; chair audiovisual adv. com. Consortium of Univs., Washington, 1986-88; chair Am. Univ. Libr. Faculty Coun., 1991-93, 2003-2005. Recipient Alliance Francaise prize, sr. French fellow Kalamazoo Coll.; named Outstanding Young Women of Am., 1984; Rsch. Support grantee Am. U., 1985-86. Mem. ALA (video round table 1992-94), Assn. Coll. and Rsch. Librs. (copywright com.), Consortium of Coll. and Univ. Media Ctrs. (editl. bd. Coll. and Univs. Media Rev., mem. govt. regulations and pub. policy com., ad hoc task force on copyright), Art Libraries Soc. N.Am. Regional Assn., Alpha Lambda Delta, Phi Kappa Phi, Beta Phi Mu. Avocations: gardening, dance. Office: Am Univ Libr 4400 Massachusetts Ave NW Washington DC 20016-8046 Office Phone: 202-885-3236. Business E-Mail: dvogel@american.edu.

**VOGELSTEIN, BERT,** oncology educator; b. Balt., June 2, 1949; BS in Math., U. Pa., 1970; MD, Johns Hopkins U. Sch. Medicine, 1974. Rsch. assoc. Nat. Cancer Inst., 1976—78; pediatric intern and resident Johns Hopkins U. Sch. Medicine, Balt., 1974—76, asst. prof., 1978—83, assoc. prof., 1983—89, Clayton prof. oncology and pathology, 1989—, Howard Hughes Med. Inst. investigator, 1995—. Advisor NIH Sci. Rev. Groups, Nat. Cancer Inst.; bd. reviewing editors Science; sci. editor Molecular Cell and Cancer Cell; sci. adv. bd. U, Calif., San Francisco, Cancer Ctr., GMP Genetics, Morphotek; sci. review bd. Pediatric Brain Tumor Found., US. Assoc. editor: Genes, Chromosomes and Cancer, mem. bd. reviewing editors: Sci. mag.; contbr. articles to profl. jours., 99 US patents in the field. Recipient William Allan award, Am. Soc. of Human Genetics, Alfred G. Knudson award, Nat. Cancer Inst., Anne & Jason Farber Lecture award, Am. Acad. Neurology, 1991, Internat. award, Gairdner Found., 1992, Medal of Honor, Am. Cancer Soc., 1992, Richard Lounsbery award, NAS, 1993, Baxter Rsch. award, Assn. Am. Med. Coll., 1994, laureates Passano Found., 1994, G.H.A. Clowes Meml. award, Am. Assn. Cancer Rsch., 1995, Charles S. Mott prize, GM Cancer Rsch. Found., 2000. Mem.: NAS, Am. Philosophical Soc., Inst. Medicine, Am. Acad. Arts and Scis. Achievements include revolutionizing our understanding of complex genetic mutations that occur when an normal bowel epithelial cell is transformed into a malignant cell. Office: Johns Hopkins U Sch Med Dept Oncology 424 N Bond St Baltimore MD 21231-1000*

**VOGELZANG, ALEXA RUTH,** music educator, opera singer; b. Pittsfield, Mass., Mar. 25, 1961; d. Walter and Joan Gatie Helgeland; children: Rachel Esther, Anna Kirsten. BA in Music, Calvin Coll., 1983; MusM Edn., Gordon Coll., 2005. Cert. tchr. Mass., 2004. Tchr. Lexington Pub. Schs., Mass., 1991—99; music theory instr. New Eng. Conservatory of Music, Boston, 1997—2005; tchr. Hamilton-Wenham Pub. Schs., Wenham, Mass., 1999—2000, Milton Pub. Schs., Mass., 2000—03, Danvers H.S., Mass., 2003—; dir. of music Crawford Meml. United Meth. Ch., Winchester, Mass. Music dir. Centre Stage Theater, Boston, 1995—97, Arlington Children's Theater, Mass., 1995—97, Winthrop Playmakers, Mass., 1999—2000. Singer: (Boston Lyric Opera chorus) 25 prodns. Ch. sch. tchr. and vol. Crawford Meml. United Meth. Ch., Winchester, Mass., 1994—2000. Mem.: Am. Guild of Mus. Artists, Am. Choral Dirs. Assn., Mass. Music Educators Conf., Music Educators Nat. Conf. Independent. Christian. Avocations: needlepoint, gardening, reading.

**VOGL, OTTO,** polymer science and engineering educator; b. Traiskirchen, Austria, Nov. 6, 1927; came to U.S., 1953, naturalized, 1959; s. Franz and Leopoldine (Scholz) V.; m. Jane Cunningham, June 10, 1955; children: Eric,

Yvonne. PhD, U. Vienna, 1950; Doctorate (hon.), U. Jena, Germany, 1983, Poly. Inst., Iasi, Romania, 1992, Osaka U., Japan, 1996, Slovak Acad. Scis., 2001; Doctorate (hon.), U. Leoben, Austria, 2006; PhD (hon.), U. Vienna, 2001. Instr. U. Vienna 1948-55; rsch. assoc. U. Mich., 1953-55, Princeton U., 1955-56; scientist E.I. Du Pont de Nemours & Co., Wilmington, Del., 1956-70; prof. polymer sci. and engring. U. Mass., 1970-83, prof. emeritus, 1983—; Herman F. Mark prof. polymer sci. Poly. U., Bklyn., 1983-95, prof. emeritus, 1996—. Guest prof. Kyoto U., 1968, 80, Osaka U., 1968, 96, Royal Inst. Stockholm, 1971, 87, 99, U. Freiburg, Germany, 1973, U. Berlin, 1977, Strasbourg U., 1976, Tech. U. Dresden, 1982, Wuhan U., China, 1984; Monbusho prof. Kyoto Inst. Tech., Japan, 1996; guest prof. Soviet Acad. Sci., 1973, Polish Acad. Sci., 1973, 75, Acad. Sci. Romania, 1974, 76; chmn. com. on macromolecular chemistry Nat. Acad. Sci.; cons. in field. Author: Polyaldehydes, 1967, (with Furukawa) Polymerization of Heterocyclics, 1973, Ionic Polymerization, 1976, (with Simionescu) Radical Co and Graft-polymerization, 1978, (with Donaruma) Polymeric Drugs, 1978, (with Donaruma and Ottenbrite) Polymers in Biology and Medicine, 1980, (with Goldberg and Donaruma) Targeted Drugs, 1986, (with Immergut) Polymer Science in the Next Decade, 1997, (with Kitayama and Hatada) Macromolecular Design of Polymeric Materials, My Life with Polymer Science, 2004; contbr. articles to profl. jours. Sr. fellow Japan Soc. Promotion of Sci., 1980; recipient Fulbright award, 1976, Humboldt prize, 1977, Chemistry Pioneer award, 1985, Gold medal City of Vienna, Austria, 1986, Exner medal, 1987, Mark medal, 1989, Honor Ring, City of Traiskirchen, 1989; golden hon. diploma U. Vienna, 2000, Hon. Cross of Arts and Scis., Rep. of Austria, 2000, Culture prize City of Traiskirchen, 2002, hon. medal SAS Polymer Rsch. Inst, 2003. Fellow AAAS; mem. Am. Chem. Soc. (chmn. divsn. polymer chemistry 1974, chmn. Conn. Valley sect. 1974, award applied polymer chemistry 1990, Herman F. Mark award 2000), Am. Inst. Chemistry (chmn. Pioneer Award 1985), Austrian Chem. Soc. (hon.), Japanese Soc. Polymer Sci. (hon., award 1991), N.Y. Acad. Sci., Austrian Acad. Sci., Royal Swedish Acad. Sci., Pacific Polymer Fedn. (pres.), Slovak Chem. Soc. (hon.), Croatian Chem. Soc. (hon.), Sigma Xi. Home: 12 Canterbury Ln Amherst MA 01002-3536 Office: U Mass Dept Polymer Sci and Engring Amherst MA 01003-4530 Office Phone: 413-577-1628. Personal E-mail: voglotto@aol.com. Business E-Mail: vogl@polysci.umass.edu.

**VOGLAR, INÉS ANA,** musician, educator; b. Caracas, Venezuela, Oct. 7, 1975; d. Teresa Voglar. B in Violin Performance (hon.), Duquesne U., 1999; M in Violin Performance, Carnegie Mellon U., 2001. Assoc. concertmaster Carabobo Symphony Orch., Valencia, Venezuela, 1991—96, UBS Verbier Festival Orch., Switzerland, 2002; concertmaster Duquesne Symphony Orch., Pitts., 1996—99; violinist Pitts. Opera Orch., 1998—2003, Pitts. New Music Ensemble, 1999—2003, Oreg. Symphony Orch., Portland, 2004—; violin substitute Pitts. Symphony Orch., 1999—2004. Artistic dir. Fear No Music, Portland, 2005—. Nominee All-American Scholar Collegiate award, US Achievement Acad., 1999; Libermann Scholarship, Duquesne U., 1996—99, Music Scholarship, Duquesne U. Sch. Music, 1996—99. Office: Fear No Music POBox 1262 Portland OR 97207 Office Phone: 503-227-3127. Office Fax: 503-227-3127. Personal E-mail: voglar4710@hotmail.com.

**VOGRIN, JOSEPH EDWARD, III,** lawyer; BA magna cum laude, Duquesne U., Pitts, 1969; JD, Duquesne U., 1972. Bar: Pa. 1972, U.S. Ct. Appeals (3rd cir.) 1972, US Supreme Ct. 1984. Dep. dist. atty. Dist. Atty's Office Allegheny County, Pitts., 1972—79; ptnr. Scott, Vogrin & Riester, Pitts., 1980—96, Vogrin & Riester, P.C., Pitts., 1996—2000, Meyer Darragh Buckler Bebenek & Eck, Pitts., 2000—. Program adv. com. Pa, Bar Inst. Mcpl. Solicitors, Pitts., 1999—; mem. curriculum rev. commn. Pa. Mcpl. Police Officer's Tng. Commn., Harrisburg, 2000—. Solicitor Ohio Twp. San. Authority, Pitts., 1983—, Twp. Shaler, Pitts., 1986—, Quaker Valley Coun. Govts., Pitts., 1987—, North Hills Coun. Govts., Pitts., 1989—, Boroughs Assn. Allegheny County, Pitts., 1991—92, Borough's Assn. Allegheny County, Pitts., 1994—95, Ross Twp. CSC, Pitts., 1993—; co-counsel Allegheny County and Western Pa. Assn. Twp. Commrs., Pitts., 1997—; solicitor Twp. Res., Pitts., 1998—, Borough Avalon, Pitts., 1992—2005. Mem.: Allegheny County Bar Assn. (chmn. assn. mcpl. and sch. solicitors Allegheny County 1998—99). Office: Meyer Darragh Buckler Bebenek & Eck 4850 USX Tower 600 Grant St Pittsburgh PA 15219 Personal E-mail: jvogrin@mdbbe.com.

**VOGT, ALBERT RALPH,** forester, educator, program director; BS in Forest Mgmt., Mo., 1961, MS in Tree Physiology, 1962, PhD in Tree Physiology, 1966. Instr. in dendrology U. Mo., Columbia, 1965-66; asst. prof. rsch. tree physiology Ohio State U., 1966-69, assoc. prof., assoc. chmn. rsch. and adminstrn. forestry, 1969-76, prof., chmn. dept. adminstrn. and tchg. forestry, 1976-85; prof., dir. sch. natural resources U. Mo., 1985—2003, prof. emeritus, 2003—. Mem. Mo. Forest Heritage Initiative, Gov.'s Task Force Environ. Edn., Mo. Gov.'s Energy Coalition, Mo. Citizens Com. Soil, Water, and State Parks; co-chair steering com. 3d Forestry Edn. Symposium, 1991; co-chair external rev. dept. forestry So. Ill. U., Carbondale, 1993; co-chair external rev. Sch. Forest Resources Pa. State U., 1995; chair external rev.forestry U. Wis., Madison, 1997; chair on-site S.A.F. accreditation rev. dept. forest and natural resources Purdue U., 2003. Office: U Mo Sch Natural Resources 105H Natural Resources Bldg Columbia MO 65211-0001 Office Phone: 573-882-1627. E-mail: vogta@missouri.edu.

**VOGT, DOUGLAS,** news cameraman, journalist; b. Alta., Canada, 1959; married; 3 children. Cameraman CBC-TV, BBC-TV; now with ABC News, NYC, Europe, Middle East, 1991—. Recipient three Emmy awards. Achievements include covering stories in Afganistan, Iraq, Croatia, Bosnia, and Somalia. Office: ABC News Press Rels 47 W 66th St New York NY 10023-6201 Home: Aix-en-Provence France*

**VOGT, ERICH WOLFGANG,** physicist, academic administrator; b. Steinbach, Man., Can., Nov. 12, 1929; s. Peter Andrew and Susanna (Reimer) V.; m. Barbara Mary Greenfield, Aug. 27, 1952; children: Edith Susan, Elizabeth Mary, David Eric, Jonathan Michael, Robert Jeremy. BS, U. Man., 1951, MS, 1952; PhD, Princeton U., 1955; DSc (hon.), U. Man., 1982, Queen's U., 1984; LLD (hon.), U. Regina, 1986; DSc (hon.), Carleton U., 1988, U. B.C., 1999; LLD (hon.), Simon Fraser U., 1996. Rsch. officer Chalk River (Ont.) Nuclear Labs., 1956-65; prof. physics U. B.C., Vancouver, 1965-95, prof. emeritus, 1996—, assoc. dir. TRIUMF Project, 1968-73, dir. TRIUMF Project, 1981-94, v.p. univ., 1975-81; chmn. Tri. Council B.C., 1978-80. Co-editor: Advances in Nuclear Physics, 1968—; contbr. articles to profl. jours. Decorated officer Order of Can., Order of BC; recipient Centennial medal of Can., 1967 Fellow Royal Soc. Can., Am. Phys. Soc.; mem. Can. Assn. Physicists (past pres., gold medal for achievement in physics 1988). Office: Triumf 4004 Wesbrook Mall Vancouver BC Canada V6T 2A3 Office Phone: 604-222-1047. Business E-Mail: vogt@triumf.ca.

**VOGT, HARTMUT,** education educator; b. Berlin, Oct. 18, 1923; s. Alfred and Luise (Thiele) Vogt; m. Helga Hellebrand, July 16, 1952. Cert. in tchg., U. Berlin, 1950, PhD, 1956. State tchr., Berlin, 1950-51; from lectr. to asst. prof. U. Berlin, Tübingen, Marburg, 1951-70; full prof. U. Dortmund, 1970-89, prof. emeritus, 1989—. Author: several books in field; contbr. articles to profl. jours. 1st lt. German Air Force, 1941—45. Mem.: Flying Club. Avocation: flying. Office: Univ Dortmund Emil-Figge-Strasse 50 D-44221 Dortmund 50 Germany

**VOGT, KATHLEEN CUNNINGHAM,** musician, music educator; b. Ellwood City, Pa., July 3, 1951; d. Joseph Edward and Dorothea Cunningham Vogt. BS summa cum laude in Music Edn., Duquesne U., 1973, M in Music edn., 1975. Cert. Tchr Nat. Bd., 2003. Tchr. band and choral dir. Diocese of Pitts. Schs. 1973—79; tchr. band dir. Carrick HS, 1980—84; band dir. drama tchr. Hanahan (SC) HS, 1984—2004, Sangaree Mid. Sch. Instr. percussion Duquesne U., Pitts. 1975—79; adj. prof. Charleston So. U., SC, 2001—; guest clinician and conductor, 1975—. Musician: Pitts. Symphony Orch., Charleston Symphony Orch., Lowcountry Winds, Charleston (SC) Cmty. Band. Mem. Hanahan Area Arts Coun. Mem.: Nat. Bd. Cert. Tchrs., All Berkeley County Music Educators, Nat. Band Assoc., Nat. Baton Twirling

Assn., Nat. Twirling Judges Bur. (Inducted into Baton Twirling Hall of Fame 2002), Am. Sch. Band Dirs. Assn., SC Band Dirs. Assn. (Outstanding Performance award 1985—2004, SC State Marching Band Champions 1986, 1987, 1988, 1991), SC Music Educators Assn., Music Educators Nat. Conf., Pi Lambda Theta, Phi Beta Mu. Home: 504 Greenmeadow Rd Goose Creek SC 29445 Personal E-mail: katyvogt@aol.com.

**VOGT, LORNA CORRINE,** retired librarian, small business owner; b. Rochelle, Ill., Feb. 18, 1936; d. Chester Floyd and Vera Mae (Worthington) Patton; m. Norman E. Vogt, Aug. 18, 1957; 1 child, Cindy Jean Vogt Welch. BE, No. Ill. U., 1957, MA, 1972; postgrad., Western Ill. U., 1989-90. Tchr. speech and English Harlem High Sch., Loves Park, Ill., 1957-58; tchr. English, libr. Alden-Hebron (Ill.) Jr.-Sr. High Sch., 1958-59; traffic mgr. Sta. WLBK Radio, DeKalb, Ill., 1964-65; libr. No. Ill. U., DeKalb, 1967, Malta (Ill.) Schs., 1968-71, Sycamore (Ill.) High Sch., 1971-94; ret., 1994; owner Sesquicentennial Farm. Mem. Ogle County (Ill.) Farm Bur.; presenter in field. Author: The Heritage of the Lafayette Township Schools, 1990; compiler (book) James Reed Family, 1991, William Patton Family, 1987, Lafayette Township Officers, 1993. Chmn. Books South Africa Commn., DeKalb, 1991-92; co-chmn. Literary Festival Little 7 Conf., 1991-93; chmn. bd. deacons Conglist. Ch., 1993-94, vice moderator, 1994-95; mem. Ill. Conf. United Ch. of Christ Bd., 1996-98, exec. bd., 1996-98, vice moderator Prairie Assn., 1996-97, moderator, 1997-98, United Ch. of Christ Gen. Synod, Providence, del. conf., Ill., 1999, Kansas City, Mo., 2001, Stephenson County Hist. Soc., 2002-; former mem. Assn. Gravestone Studies. Mem. NEA, Popular Culture Assn. (presenter 1989), Ill. Assn. Tchrs. English (presenter 1988-90), Nat. Coun. Tchrs. English (presenter 1991, 93), Ill. Edn. Assn., Ill. Assn. Media Edn., Midwest Gilbert and Sullivan Soc., Somerset County Pa. Hist. and Geneal. Soc., Ill. Ret. Tchrs. Assn., Ret. Tchrs. Assn. Stephenson County (sec. 2004-), Ret. Educators Assn. Sarasota, Freeport Area Camera Club, Stephenson County Hist. Soc., Alpha Sigma Alpha (life), Nat. Coun. Tchrs. English Ctr. of Excellence (co-dir., 1989-1991). Congregationalist. Avocations: writing, genealogy. Home: 3167 Sandy Pointe Dr Freeport IL 61032-2824 Personal E-mail: lornapat218@aol.com.

**VOGT, MARTHA DIANE,** lawyer; b. Albertville, Ala., Sept. 22, 1952; m. Robert A. Vogt, May 26, 1973. BA, Oakland U., 1974; JD, Wayne Law Sch., 1980. Bar: Mich. 1980, U.S. Ct. Appeals (4th cir.) 1985, Fla. 1988, U.S. Ct. Appeals (6th cir.) 1990, U.S. Ct. Appeals (11th cir.) 1996. Ptnr. Clark, Klein & Beaumont, Detroit, 1980-92, Bavol & Vogt, Tampa, Fla., 1992-95; pvt. practice Law Office of M. Diane Vogt, Tampa, Fla., 1995—. Adj. prof. Wayne Law Sch., Detroit, 1987-92; instr. U. South Fla., 1995. Author: The Silicone Solution, 1999; co-author: Lawyer Retention: Improving Job Satisfaction for Lawyers. Mem. ABA, DRI, State Bar of Mich. Assn., The Fla. Bar Assn. Office: Law Office M Diane Vogt 800 S Dakota Ave Apt 201 Tampa FL 33606-2855

**VOGT, ROCHUS EUGEN,** physicist, researcher; b. Neckarelz, Germany, Dec. 21, 1929; came to U.S., 1953; s. Heinrich and Paula (Schaefer) V.; m. Micheline Alice Yvonne Bauduin, Sept. 6, 1958; children: Michele, Nicole. Student, U. Karlsruhe, Germany, 1950-52, U. Heidelberg, 1952-53; SM, U. Chgo., 1957, PhD, 1961. Asst. prof. physics Calif. Inst. Tech., Pasadena, 1962-65, assoc. prof., 1965-70, prof., 1970—2002, R. Stanton Avery disting. svc. prof., 1982—2002, R. Stanton Avery disting. svc. prof. and prof. physics emeritus, 2002—, chmn. faculty, 1975-77, chief scientist Jet Propulsion Lab., 1977-78, chmn. div. physics, math. and astronomy, 1978-83, acting dir. Owens Valley Radio Obs., 1980-81, v.p. and provost, 1983-87. Vis. prof. physics MIT, 1988-94; dir. Caltech/MIT Laser Interferometer Gravitational Wave Observatory Project, 1987-94. Author: Cosmic Rays (in World Book Ency.), 1978, (with R.B. Leighton) Exercises in Introductory Physics, 1969; contbr. articles to profl. jours. Fulbright fellow, 1953-54; recipient Exceptional Sci. Achievement medal NASA, 1981, Profl. Achievement award U. Chgo. Alumni Assn., 1981. Fellow AAAS, A. Phys. Soc. Achievements include research in astrophysics and gravitation. Office: Calif Inst Tech 103-33 1200 E California Blvd Pasadena CA 91125-0001 Office Phone: 626-395-3800. Business E-Mail: vogt@caltech.edu.

**VOHS, JAMES ARTHUR,** health facility administrator; b. Idaho Falls, Idaho, Sept. 26, 1928; s. John Dale and Cliff Lucille (Packer) Vohs; m. Janice Hughes, Sept. 19, 1953 (dec. Oct. 1999); children: Lorraine, Carol, Nancy, Sharla; m. Eileen Galloway, Oct. 8, 2005. BA, U. Calif., Berkeley, 1952; postgrad., Harvard Sch. Bus., 1966. Employed by various Kaiser affiliated orgns., 1952—92; chmn., pres., CEO Kaiser Found. Hosps. and Kaiser Found. Health Plan, INc., Oakland, Calif., 1975—92, chmn. emeritus; chmn. bd. dirs. Holy Names Coll., 1981—92; chmn. Marcus Foster Inst., 1981—. Chmn. Fed. Res. Bank San Francisco, 1991—94. Mem. Oakland Bd. Port Commrs., 1993—96; bd. dirs. Oakland-Alameda County Coliseum Complex, 1986—96, Bay Area Coun., 1985—94, chmn., 1991—92. With U.S. Army, 1946—48. Mem.: Inst. Medicine NAS. Personal E-mail: javohs@sbcglobal.net.

**VOIGHT, CAROLYN JEAN,** administrative assistant; b. Waco, Tex., Aug. 20, 1953; d. Carroll Eugene and Wincie Iona Cannon; children: Christopher Jason Sorrels, Robyn Lynn Sorrels. BBA magna cum laude, Davenport U., 2000; MS, Cntrl. Mich. U., 2002; degree in Edn., U. Cambridge, 2003; student in Ednl. Adminstrn., Tex. A&M U., 2006—. Adj. instr. North Harris Montgomery C.C. Dist., Tomball, Tex., 1991—99; office mgr. Profl. Counseling Ctr., Lapeer, Mich., 2001—03; adminstrv. assoc. Baylor U., Waco, Tex., 2003—. Vol. Baylor U., Waco, Tex., 2003—06. Mem.: Kappa Delta Pi (assoc.). Republican. Methodist. Avocations: reading, walking, gardening. Home: PO Box 463 Waco TX 76703 Office: Baylor University One Bear Place 97020 Waco TX 76798 Office Phone: 254-710-7833. Office Fax: 254-710-8798. Business E-Mail: carolyn_voight@baylor.edu.

**VOIGHT, JACK C.,** state official; b. New London, Wisconsin, Dec. 17, 1945; s. Oscar C. and Thelma J. (Hamm) V.; m. Martha J. (Wolfe), July 14, 1973; children: Carly and Emily. BS, U. Wis., Oshkosh, 1971. Claims adjuster U.S. F and G Ins. Co., Appleton, Wis., 1971-74; ins. agy. owner Voight Ins. Agy., Appleton, Wis., 1974—; state treas. State of Wis., 1995—. Bank organizer Am. Nat. Bank, Appleton, Wis. 1992-94; real estate broker Voight Realty and Ins., Appleton, 1977-92. Pres. Appleton Northside Bus. Assn., 1982; alderman city coun., City of Appleton, 1983-83, pres., 1992-93; Sgt. U.S. Army, 1968-70. Decorated Bronze Star; named Citizen of Yr. Appleton Northside Bus. Assn., 1990. Mem. Nat. Assn. State Treas., Midwest State Treas. Assn. (pres. 1996-97); Appleton Noon Optimist Club (pres. 1980). Republican. Presbyterian. Avocations: gardening, politics. Office: State Treas Wis PO Box 7871 Madison WI 53707-7871 E-mail: jack.voight@ost.state.wi.us.

**VOIGHT, JERRY D.,** lawyer; b. Bozeman, Mont., Aug. 21, 1937; children: Janet, Jason. BS in Chem. Engring., Mont. State U., 1959; JD with hons., George Washington U., 1965. Bar: DC 1966, US Supreme Ct. 1969, US Ct. Appeals (Fed. Cir.) 1982, registered; US Patent & Trademark Office. Sr. ptnr. Finnegan, Henderson, Farabow, Garrett & Dunner LLP, Washington, 1972—; mng. ptnr. Palo Alto Office Calif. Contbr. articles to profl. jour. Named one of best lawyers in intellectual property law, Best Lawyers in Am., 2005—06. Mem.: DC Bar Assn., ABA, Am. Intellectual Property Law Assn. Avocations: skiing, collecting wood block prints. Office: Finnegan Henderson Farabow Garrett & Dunner LLP Stanford Rsch Park 700 Hansen Way Palo Alto CA 94304-1016 Office Phone: 650-849-6600. Office Fax: 650-849-6666. Personal E-mail: jerry.voight@finnegan.com.

**VOIGHT, JON,** actor; b. Yonkers, N.Y., Dec. 29, 1938; s. Elmer and Barbara (Camp) V.; m. Lauri Peters, 1962 (div. 1967); m. Marcheline Bertrand, Dec. 12, 1971 (div. 1978); children: James Haven, Angelina Jolie. BFA, Cath. U., 1960; studied with, Sanford Meisner and Samantha Harper, N.Y.C. Stage appearances include O Oysters Revue, 1961, The Sound of Music, 1961, A View from the Bridge, 1965, Romeo and Juliet, 1966, The Tempest, 1966, Two Gentlemen of Verona, 1966, That Summer-That Fall, 1967 (Theatre

World award 1967), A Streetcar Named Desire, 1973, The Hashish Club, 1975, Hamlet, 1976, The Seagull, 1992; TV appearances include Cimarron Strip, Gunsmoke; films include Fearless Frank, 1967, Hour of the Gun, 1967, Out of It, 1969, Midnight Cowboy, 1969 (Acad. award nom. best actor 1969, NY Critics Circle award 1969, L.A. Film Critics award best actor 1969, BAFTA award most promising newcomer 1969, Golden Globe award most promising newcomer 1969), Catch-22, 1970, The Revolutionary, 1970, Deliverance, 1972, The All American Boy, 1973, Conrack, 1974, The Odessa File, 1974, End of the Game, 1976, Coming Home, 1978 (Acad. award best actor 1978, Golden Globe award 1978, Cannes Internat. Film festival award 1978, NY Film Critics best actor award 1978, L.A. Film Critics award best actor 1978), The Champ, 1979 (Golden Globe award 1979), Runaway Train, 1985 (Acad. award nominee best actor 1986, London Film Critics award nominee 1986, Golden Globe best actor 1986), Desert Bloom, 1986, Eternity, 1990, The Rainbow Warrior, 1992, Heat, 1995, Mission Impossible, 1996, Rosewood, 1997, Anaconda, 1997, Most Wanted, 1997, The Rainmaker, 1997, U Turn, 1997, I Once Had a Life, 1998, Enemy of the State, 1998, Varsity Blues, 1999, A Dog of Flanders, 1999, Pearl Harbor, 2001, Lara Croft: Tomb Raider, 2001, Zoolander, 2001, Ali, 2001, Holes, 2003, Karate Dog, 2004, The Manchurian Candidate, 2004, Superbabies: Baby Geniuses 2, 2004, National Treasure, 2004; (TV films) Chernobyl: The Final Warning, 1991, The Last of His Tribe, 1992, Convict Cowboys, 1995, Boys Will Be Boys, 1997, Noah's Ark, 1999, Second string, 2002, Jasper, Texas, 2003, The Five People You Meet in Heaven, 2004, Pope John Paul II, 2005; (miniseries) Return to Lonesome Dove, 1993; actor, prodr., co-writer (films) Lookin' To Get Out, 1982, The Fixer, 1998; actor, prodr. (films) Table for Five, 1983, A Tribute to Dustin Hoffman, 1999, Noah's Ark, 1999, Second String, 2000.

**VOIGT, BARTON R.,** state supreme court chief justice; b. Thermopolis, Wyo. BA in History, MA in History, U. Wyo., JD. Atty., Thermopolis, Wyo.; former Hot Springs County atty.; former county ct. judge Gillette, Wyo.; judge Wyo. Eigth Jud. Dist., Douglas, Wyo., 1993—2001; justice Wyo. Supreme Ct., 2001—, chief justice, 2006—. Former mem. Bd. of Jud. Policy and Administration Members. Mem.: Wyo. Bar Assn. Office: Wyo Supreme Ct 2301 Capitol Ave Cheyenne WY 82001*

**VOIGT, CYNTHIA,** writer; b. Boston, Feb. 25, 1942; d. Frederick C. and Elise (Keeney) Irving; married, 1964 (div. 1972); m. Walter Voigt, Aug. 30, 1974; children: Jessica, Peter. BA, Smith Coll., 1963. High sch. tchr. English, Glen Burnie, Md., 1965-67; tchr. English Key Sch., Annapolis, Md., 1968-69, dept. chmn., 1971-79, tchr., dept. chmn., 1981-88. Author: Homecoming, 1981, Tell Me If the Lovers Are Losers, 1982, Dicey's Song, 1982 (John Newbery medal 1983), The Callender Papers, 1983 (Edgar award 1984), A Solitary Blue, 1983, Building Blocks, 1984, Jackeroo, 1985, The Runner, 1985 (Silver Pencil award 1988, Deutscher Jugend Literatur Preis 1989, ALAN award 1989), Come a Stranger, 1986, Izzy, Willy Nilly, 1986 (Calif. Young Reader's award 1990), Stories About Rosie, 1986, Sons From Afar, 1987, Tree by Leaf, 1988, Seventeen Against the Dealer, 1989, On Fortune's Wheel, 1990, The Vandemark Mummy, 1991, Orfe, 1992, Glass Mountain, 1991, David and Jonathan, 1992, The Wings of a Falcon, 1993, When She Hollers, 1994, Bad Girls, 1996, Bad, Badder, Baddest, 1997, Elske, 1999, It's Not Easy Being Bad, 2000, Bad Girls in Love, 2002, From Bad to Worse, 2003, Angus and Sadie, 2005.

**VOIGT, ELLEN,** literature educator; b. 1943; BA, Converse Coll.; MFA, U. Iowa. Prof. poetry MIT; prof. Goddard Coll., Vt.; prof. MFA program for writers Warren Wilson Coll., Asheville, NC, 1981—; Vt. State Poet, 1999—2003. Tchr. Bread Loaf Writers' Conf., Aspen Writer's Conf., Ind. Writers' Conf., Napa Writer's Conf., Catskills Writers' Conf., RopeWalk Writers' Conf. Author: (poems) Claiming Kin, 1976, The Forces of Plenty, 1983, The Lotus Flowers, 1987, Two Trees, 1992, Shadows of Heaven, 2002 (Nat. Book award finalist), (sonnet) Kyrie, 1995 (Nat. Book Critics' Circle award finalist, Teasdale Poetry prize); co-editor (with Gregory Orr): Poets Teaching Poets: Self and the World; author: The Flexible Lyric, 2001. Recipient Pushcart prize; fellow, Acad. Am. Poets, 2002; grantee, Vt. Coun. Arts, NEA, Guggenheim Found. Fellow: Am. Acad. Arts and Sciences; mem.: Acad. Am. Poets (chancellor 2003—). Achievements include developing and directing the nation's first low-residency writing program at Goddard College in 1976; the program has since been emulated by other colleges and universities. Office: Warren Wilson Coll PO Box 9000 Asheville NC 28815*

**VOIGT, JOAN (JOAN McGUIRE VOIGT),** retired literature and language professor; b. San Antonio, Oct. 27, 1933; d. Joseph Douglas and Ruth (Kelly) McG.; m. Robert Thomas Mellard, Nov. 27, 1957 (dec. Aug. 1991); children, Joseph Carmichael (dec. Nov., 1982), Travis Kelly; m. M. Gaines Voigt, May 14, 1994. BA, Mt. Holyoke Coll., 1955; MA, Trinity U., 1974. Tchr. St. Mary's Hall, San Antonio, 1964-78, headmistress, 1978-83; edn. cons. State Comptroller, Austin, 1983-84; dir. St. Mark's Sch., San Antonio, 1985-86; instr. U. Tex., 1988-90; asst. prof. English Our Lady of the Lake U., 1990—2000; ret., 2000. Commr. San Antonio Commn. on Literacy, 1986-91. Mem. exec. com. San Antonio Libr. Found., 1984-91; mem. Bexar County Hist. Commn., San Antonio, 1984-87; chmn. San Antonio Pub. Libr. Bd., 1984-90; judge Young Pegasus Poetry Competition, 1970-80, 91—; mem. Tex. Commn. on Arts, 1994-2000. Mem. Phi Beta Kappa, bd. dir. San Antonio chpt. 1980—). Presbyterian. Home: 7 Sherborne Wood San Antonio TX 78218-1771

**VOIGT, PHILIP KENNETH,** music educator; b. Smithtown, NY, Feb. 13, 1976; s. Roseann B. and Kenneth J. Voigt; m. Jennifer L. Mondolino. MusB, Ithaca Coll., N.Y., 1994—98; MA, SUNY, Stony Brook, 1999—2002, Advanced Grad. Cert. in Sch. Dist. Adminstrn., 2002—04. Cert. tchr. State of N.Y. 1998, sch. dist. adminstr. State of N.Y. 2004. Music tchr. Kings Pk Cntrl Sch. Dist., NY, 1998—99, Ctrl. Islip Union Free Sch. Dist., NY, 1999—. Coord. L.I. Summer Music Workshop, Southhampton, NY, 1995—; dir. fine and performing arts Ctrl Islip Union Free Sch. Dist., NY, 2001—; mem. adv. coun. Ea. Suffolk Bd. Coop. Ednl. Svcs., Westhampton, NY, 2002—; mem. exec. coun. N.Y. State Coun. Adminstr. for Music Edn., Islip, 2002—, Suffolk County Music Educators Assn., NY, 2003—. Roman Catholic. Avocations: jazz, theater, music. Office: Central Islip Union Free Sch Dist 545 Clayton St Central Islip NY 11722 Home: 19 Walter St 2-A Brentwood NY 11717 Office Phone: 631-348-5111. Office Fax: 631-348-5162. Personal E-mail: pvoigt@optonline.net.

**VOIGT, RICHARD,** lawyer; b. Oskaloosa, Iowa, Jan. 20, 1946; s. Franz Otto Wilhelm and Minni (Heilbrunn) V.; m. Annemarie H. Riemer, Oct. 2, 1976; children: Samuel, Nicholas. BA, Conn. Wesleyan U., 1968; JD, U. Va., 1974. Bar: Va. 1974, U.S. Dist. Ct. (ea. dist.) Va. 1979, Conn. 1981, U.S. Dist. Ct. Conn. 1982, U.S. Ct. Claims 1982, U.S. Ct. Appeals (4th cir.) 1982. Assoc. counsel regional litigation Solicitor's Office Osha Div., 1978-80; staff atty. U.S. Dept. Labor, Washington, 1974-78; prin. Siegel, O'Connor, Schiff, Zangari & Kainen, P.C., 1981-88, 87-88; ptnr. Cummings & Lockwood, Hartford, 1988—2003, McCarter & English, Hartford, 2003—. Contbg. author: ABA Treatise on Occupational Safety and Health Law, 1988; contbr. articles to profl. jours. Bd. dirs. Urban League Greater Hartford, 1984-88, Isnt. for Non-Profit Tng. and Devel., 1991-95, Hartford Proud and Beautiful, 1995—, Greater Hartford Arts Coun., 2001—. Mem. ABA (labor and employment law sect.), OSHA com., litigation sect.), Conn. Bar Assn. (labor employment law sect., employment discrimination com., com. on alternative dispute resolution). Avocations: acrylic design, history, sports. Office: McCarter & English LLP 36th Floor Cityplace I Hartford CT 06103 Office Phone: 860-275-6776.

**VOINOVICH, GEORGE VICTOR,** senator, former governor; b. Cleve., July 15, 1936; m. Janet (Allen) Voinovich; 3 children. BA in Govt., Ohio U., 1958; JD, Ohio State U., 1961; LLD (hon.), Ohio U., 1981. Bar: Ohio 1961, US Supreme Ct. 1968. Asst. atty. gen. State of Ohio, 1963-64; mem. Ohio Ho. of Reps., 1967-71; auditor Cuyahoga County, Ohio, 1971-76; commr., 1977-78; lt. gov. State of Ohio, 1979; mayor City of Cleve., 1979-89; gov. State of Ohio, 1991-98; US Senator from Ohio, 1999—; mem. fgn. rels. com.

US Senate. Pres. Nat. League Cities, 1984-85; trustee US Conf. Mayors; chmn. Midwestern Govs. Conf., 1991-92, Coun. Gt. Lakes Govs., 1992-94; chmn. Jobs for America's Graduates Program, 1995- (Nat. Leadership award 1993); mem. State and Local Govt. Coalition, 1994-; mem. com. environment and public works, US Senate, com. fgn. relations, com. homeland security and governmental affairs, chmn. com. on ethics. Recipient Tree of Life award, Jewish Nat. Found., 1981, Cert. of Merit award Ohio U., Humanitarian award NCCJ, 1986, Disting. Urban Mayor award Nat. Urban Coalition, 1987, Nat. Public Svc. award SADD, 1991, Edn. Reform Pioneer award Nat. Bus. Roundtable, 1994, George Falcon Golden Spike award, Nat. Assn. Railroad Passengers, 2000; named one of Outstanding Young Men in Ohio Ohio Jaycees, 1970; one of Outstanding Young Men in Greater Cleve. Cleve. Jaycees; named to All-Pro City Mgmt. team City & State Mag., 1987. Mem. Rep. Govs. Assn. (vice chmn. 1991-92, chmn. 1992-93), Nat. Govs. Assn. (chmn. edn. action team on sch. readiness 1991, chmn. child support enforcement work group 1991-92, mem. strategic planning task force 1991-92, mem. human resources com., co-chmn. task force on edn. 1992-93, mem. exec. com. 1993-98, co-lead gov. on fed. mandates, chmn. 1997-98), Omicron Delta Kappa, Phi Alpha Theta, Phi Delta Phi. Republican. Roman Catholic. Office: US Senate 524 Hart Sentate Office Bldg Washington DC 20510-0001 also: Central Ohio Office Rm 310 37 West Broad St Columbus OH 43215 Office Phone: 202-224-3353, 614-469-6697. Office Fax: 202-228-1382, 614-469-7733. E-mail: columbus_voinovich@voinovich.senate.gov.*

**VOITLE, ROBERT ALLEN,** dean, physiologist; b. Parkersburg, W.Va., May 12, 1938; s. Ray Christian and Ruby Virginia (Hannaman) V.; m. Linda Ellen Loveday, Dec. 5, 1975; children: Robert Allen, Elizabeth Anne, Christian Blair, Vanessa Virginia. BS, W.Va. U., 1962; MS, W.Va., 1965; PhD, U. Tenn., 1969. Asst. in poultry U. Tenn., Knoxville, 1965-69; asst. prof. physiology U. Fla., Gainesville, 1969-75, assoc. prof., 1975-79; prof., head dept. poultry Calif. Poly. State U., San Luis Obispo, 1979-81; dean Coll. Agr., Auburn U., Ala., 1981—2000, prof. poultry sci. Ala., 2000—. Cons. Columbia Bank for Coops., S.C., 1972 Contbr. articles to sci. jours. Pres., other offices Alachua County Fair Assn., Gainesville, 1969-79. Recipient Pub. Service award Alachua County Commn., 1975; recipient Tchr. of Yr. award U. Fla., 1977, Golden Feather award Calif. Poly. Inst., 1982 Mem. Poultry Sci. Assn., So. Poultry Sci. Assn., Gainesville Jaycees (JCI senatorship), Sigma Xi, Gamma Sigma Delta Clubs: Elks. Episcopalian. Home: 2247 Longwood Dr Auburn AL 36830-7105 Office: Auburn U Coll Agr Auburn AL 36849 Office Phone: 334-844-2603. Business E-Mail: rvoitle@ag.auburn.edu.

**VOJCANIN, SAVA ALEXANDER,** lawyer; b. Oak Lawn, Ill., Oct. 15, 1964; s. Jovan and Lili (Yovanovich V.); m. Valerie S. Rupich, Oct. 12, 2002; 1 child: John William Diploma, Culver Mil. Acad., 1981; BA with distinction, DePauw U., 1985; JD, Washington U., 1988. Bar: Ill. 1988, U.S. Dist. Ct. (no. dist.) Ill. 1989, U.S. Dist. Ct. (no. dist.) Tex. 1996. Assoc. Schaffenegger, Watson & Peterson Ltd., Chgo., 1988-91, Clausen Miller P.C., Chgo., 1991-98, ptnr., 1999—, shareholder, 2002—. Editor: Law, Culture and Values, 1989. Mem. Mayor's Adv. Coun. on Immigrant and Refugee Affairs, Chgo., 1992-97; trustee St. Basil Orthodox Ch. of Lake Forest, 1997—, sec. bd. trustees, 1999-2002, nominating com., 2002-. Mem.: Chgo. Bar Assn., Serbian Bar Assn. Am. (treas. 1999—2000, sec. 2000—01, v.p. 2001—02, pres. 2002—03, bd. dirs.). Orthodox. Office: Clausen Miller PC 10 S LaSalle St Chicago IL 60603-1098 Business E-Mail: svojcanin@clausen.com.

**VOJNOVIC, IGOR ZORAN,** geographer, urban planner, educator; b. Belgrade, Yugoslavia, Jan. 26, 1966; arrived in U.S., 1997; s. Zoran and Branislava Vojnovic; m. Ghada Georgis, June 10, 1999. BA, York U., Toronto, Can., 1990; MSc, U. Toronto, 1992, PhD, 1997. Instr. urban design U. Toronto, 1994—97; rsch. assoc. Intergovernmental Com. on Urban and Regional Rsch., Toronto, 1996—97; instr. urban-environmental policy Syracuse U., 1997—98; sr. urban planning and design cons. Pub. Sector Innovations, Halifax, NS, Canada, 1998—99; asst. prof. urbanenvironmental design Dalhousie U., Halifax, 1998—99; asst. prof. urbanenviron. policy Tex. A&M U., College Station, 1999—2002; prin. urban planning and design cons. Paul Raff Studio, Toronto, 2001—; assoc. prof., met. environments Mich. State U., East Lansing, 2002—. Adj. prof. govt. U. Alta., Edmonton, Canada, 2004—. Author: (monograph (in english & french) Municipal Consolidation in the 1990s, 1997; contbr. articles to profl. jours. Outreach planning and design svc. staff Dalhousie U., 1998—99, Tex. A&M U., 1999—2002, Mich. State U., 2002—06. Recipient Founders Coll. Book award, York U., 1990, Griffith Taylor Meml. award in Recognition of Acad. Excellence, U. Toronto, 1996—97, The Corps of Cadets Tchg. award, Tex. A&M U., 2002; fellow, Social Sci. and Humanities Rsch. Coun. of Can., 1993—96, Syracuse U., 1997—98; grantee, Can. Donner Found., 1998—99, Tex. A&M U., 2001, Inst. Pub. Policy and Social Rsch., 2003, Land Policy Program, 2004—, Com. Vitality Program Grant, 2005—; scholar, Province of Ont., 1990—92. Achievements include research in local policy framework for regional restructuring used as a guide in the amalgamation of Halifax Regional-Municipality; framework for municipal tax structure used for the Provincial-Municipal Service Exchange Amendments/General Work Plan and Guide to Principles. Avocations: music, saxophone. Office Phone: 517-355-7718. Business E-Mail: vojnovic@msu.edu.

**VOJT, CHRISTINE M.,** quality assurance professional, microbiologist; d. Robert H. and Patricia A. (Mully) Shafer; m. Alfred F. Vojt, Jan. 7, 1959; children: Jessica L., Zachary R., Amelia R. BS in Med. Tech., Fairleigh Dickinson U., 1981, MS in Biology, 1989. Mt (Ascp) Am. Soc. Clin. Pathologists, 1981. Med. technologist Hosp. Ctr. at Orange, NJ, 1980—84; microbiologist Revlon Rsch. Ctr., Edison, 1984—86; sr. microbiologist Mennen Co. (Colgate Palmolive), Morristown, 1986—91; lab. supr. Warner Lambert (Pfizer), Morris Plains, 1991—96; quality assurance mgr. Ortho Clin Diagnostics, Rochester, NY, 1996—2003, validation engr., 2002—05, quality assurance mgr., 2005—. Bd. dir. Pharm. Microbiology Forum, Fuquay-Varina, N.C., 1994—2001; contbg. author Parenteral Drug Assn., Wash., 1998—2000; com. mem. working group on reagent water Clin. and Lab. Standards Inst. (formerly NCCLS), Wayne, Pa., 2002—. Young leadership giving United Way, Rochester, 2001—; parish coun. St. Catherine of Siena Ch., Mendon, N.Y., 1998—2001, stewardship com., 2003—. Mem.: Am. Soc. Quality (assoc.), Am. Soc. Microbiology (assoc.), Parenteral Drug Assn. (assoc.), ASCP (assoc.). Achievements include patents for deodorant ingredients and the inhibition of microorganisms. Office: Ortho Clin Diagnostics Inc 100 Indigo Creek Dr Rochester NY 14626-5101 Business E-Mail: cmvojt@ocdus.jnj.com.

**VOJTA, PAUL ALAN,** mathematics professor; b. Mpls., Sept. 30, 1957; s. Francis J. and Margaret L. V. B in Math., U. Minn., 1978; MA, Harvard U., 1980, PhD, 1983. Instr. Yale U., New Haven, 1983-86; fellow Math. Scis. Rsch. Inst., Berkeley, Calif., 1986-87, Miller Inst. for Basic Rsch., Berkeley, 1987-89; assoc. prof. U. Calif., Berkeley, 1989-92, prof., 1992—. Mem. Inst. for Advanced Study, Princeton, 1989-90, 96-97. Author: Diophantine Approximations and Value Distribution Theory, 1987; editor: Jour. Reine Angew Math., 2004—. Recipient perfect score Internat. Math. Olympiad, 1975. Mem. Am. Math. Soc. (Frank Nelson Cole Number Theory prize 1992), Math. Assn. Am., Phi Beta Kappa, Tau Beta Pi. Avocations: skiing, computers. Office: Univ Calif Dept Math 970 Evans Hall 3840 Berkeley CA 94720-3840

**VOJTA-OSWALD, CLARICE GERTRUDE,** educational diagnostician; b. Artesian, SD, Oct. 9, 1940; d. Raymond Fenton and Bertha Grace (Bay) Connor; m. Ralph Duane Vojta, June 20, 1964 (div. Dec. 1986); m. Larry Dale Oswald, Nov. 22, 1989; children: Patrick, Susan, Sandra. BA, U. S.D., 1962; MEd, No. State U., 1982, 86, 88. Instr. music Roscoe (S.D.) Schs., 1962-63, Glenham (S.D.) Schs., 1963-65; instr. Latin Belle Fourche (S.D.) Schs., 1965-67; instr. music Dupree (S.D.) Sch., 1967-68; libr. Herreid (S.D.) Schs., 1970-74; chpt. I tchr. Timber Lake (S.D.) Schs., 1976-77; elem. tchr. Smee Schs., Wakapala, SD, 1977-88; psychol. examiner Midland (S.D.) Schs., 1988-89, Milbank (S.D.) Schs., 1989-90; ednl. diagnostician El Paso Ind. Schs., 1990—. Recipient Blue Ribbon Mobridge Art Assn., 1985. Mem. AAUW (program chmn. 1981-84), Assn. Sch. Psychologist, S.D. Counselor's

Assn., Eagles (sec. 1974-76), Moose (music chmn. 1983-85), Gamma Delta Theta (sec. 1986-88). Democrat. Roman Catholic. Avocations: painting, spectator sports, reading. Office: 5900 Enterprise Ct Apt 1E El Paso TX 79912-4751

**VOKETAITIS, ARNOLD MATTHEW,** bass-baritone, educator; b. East Haven, Conn., May 11, 1930; s. Mathew Joseph and Agnes Mary (Pilvelis) V.; m. Marion Lee Dever, June 1959 (div. 1967); children: Arnold Mathew Jr., Paul Stanley; m. Nijole Lipciute, Sept. 6, 1968. BS in Bus. Adminstrn, Quinnipiac Coll., 1954. Dir. opera program De Paul U., Chgo., 1987-89. Lectr. techniques for mus. stage, author singing technique Northwestern U., Evanston, Ill., 1986; mem. adv. panels in music and ethnic affairs Ill. Arts Coun.; mem. panel for opera and mus. theatre NEA; faculty mem. Brevard (N.C.) Summer Music Ctr., 1987, 88; artist-in-residence for opera and voice Auburn U., Ala., 1990-93; artist/mgr. for pianists, formed Keyboard Artists Internat., 1998. Condr. master classes in singing; author on voice technique; operatic debut with N.Y.C. Opera, 1958, European debut at Liceo, Barcelona, Spain, 1968; mem. Met. Opera Nat. Co., appeared with maj. operatic and symphonic orgns. in U.S., Can., Mex., Cen. Am., S.Am., Lyric Opera of Chgo., 1966-84, 89, rec. artist for Desto, Vox, Columbia, RCA; recitalist appearances on Pay-TV; classical soloist U.S. Army Band, Washington. Served as sgt. U.S. Army, 1954-56. Recipient 1st place award, Conn. Opera Assn. auditions, 1957, Rockefeller Found. award, 1964, Lithuanian Man of Yr. award, 1990, Disting. Alumni award, Quinnipiac U., 1991. Mem. AFTRA, Am. Guild Mus. Artists (life), Actors Equity. Avocations: golf, fishing, theater. Personal E-mail: avkey@juno.com. *I have felt very strongly over the years that opera was written to be enjoyed, not revered, and that it cried out to be acted as well as sung. With television's influence on the viewer, necessity became reality and my hopes are being realized.*

**VOKIC, HEATHER MAUREEN,** artist, educator; b. Euclid, Ohio, Jan. 1, 1975; d. John L. and Patricia E. Pund; m. Miroslav A. Vokic, June 21, 1997; children: Lawrence R., Alexis A., Andrew J. BS summa cum laude, Case Western Res. U., 1993; Cert. of Completion in Art Edn., Cleve. Inst. Art, 1997; MA magna cum laude, Southeastern U., Fla., 2004. Visual arts educator Ohio Dept. of Edn. Art tchr. The Andrews Sch., Willoughby, Ohio, 1997—2001; art educator Meml. Jr. H.S., Mentor, Ohio, 2002—03, Wiley Mid. Sch., University Heights, Ohio, 2003—. Exhbn. and commn., Stained Glass & Textile Work. Educator, designer Christ Luth. Ch., Willoughby, 2001—05. Recipient Silk Heros grant, Reaching Heights Found., 2004—05; Martha Holden Jennings scholar, 2005—06. Mem.: Ohio Mid. Sch. Assn. (assoc.) Lutheran. Avocations: painting, stained glass, textiles. Home: 496 E 319th St Willoughby OH 44095 Office Phone: 216-371-7270. Personal E-mail: vglassdesigns@adelphia.net. E-mail: h_vokic@chuh.org.

**VOLANAKIS, JOHN EMMANUEL,** immunologist, rheumatologist; b. Thessaloniki, Greece, Mar. 17, 1938; arrived in US, 1968, naturalized, 1978; s. Emmanuel (Manolis) John and Cleo (Agathonos) Volanakis; children: Emmanuel (Manolis) John, Marina Cleo. MD, Aristotle U., Thessaloniki, 1962; DMed, Nat. U. Athens, Greece, 1968, PhD (hon.), 2003. Cert. Bd. Internal Medicine Ministry Health, Greece, 1967. Fellow rheumatology Cleve. Met. Gen. Hosp., 1968—71; instr. dept. medicine U. Ala., Birmingham, 1971—73, asst. prof. dept. medicine, 1973—77, assoc. prof. dept. medicine, 1977—83, prof. dept. medicine, 1983—2003; pres., sci. dir. Biomedical Sciences Rsch. Ctr. Alexander Fleming, Vari, Greece, 1997—2003. Dir. rsch. component Multipurpose Arthritis Ctr., Birmingham, Ala., 1984—97. Editor: The Human Complement System in Health and Disease; contbr. articles to profl. jours. Cadet Mil. Med. Sch., 1956—61, Thessaloniki, Greece. Named Anna Lois Waters Chair of Medicine in Rheumatology, U. Ala., 1989—97; recipient Alexander von Humbolt, Rsch. award for Sr. U.S. Scientists, Alexander von Humbolt Stiftung, 1996—97; Robert M. Stecher fellow, Arthritis Found. Ohio, 1969—71, Fogarty Sr. Internat. Rsch. fellow, NIH, 1978—79. Mem.: Assn. Am. Physicians. Achievements include patents for crystals of human factor D. Avocation: literature. Home: 2900 Redmont Park C 302W Birmingham AL 35205 Office: Univ Alabama at Birmingham 1530 3rd Ave South BDB 679 Birmingham AL 35294-0012 Office Phone: 205-934-5235. Office Fax: 205-934-1477. Business E-Mail: volanaki@uab.edu.

**VOLBERG, HERMAN WILLIAM,** electronics engineer, consultant; b. Hilo, Hawaii, Apr. 6, 1925; s. Fred Joseph and Kathryn Thelma (Ludloff) V.; m. Louise Ethel Potter, Apr. 26, 1968 (dec.); children: Michael, Lori. BSEE, U. Calif., Berkeley, 1949. Project engr. Naval Electronics Lab., San Diego, 1950-56; head solid state rsch. S.C. div. Gen. Dynamics, San Diego, 1956-60; founder Solidyne Solid State Instruments, La Jolla, Calif., 1958-60; founder, v.p. electronics divsn. Ametek/Straza, El Cajon, Calif., 1960-66; founder, cons. H.V. Cons., San Diego, 1966-69; sr. scientist Naval Ocean Systems Ctr. Oahu, Hawaii, 1970-77; chief scientist Integrated Scis. Corp., Santa Monica, Calif., 1978-80; founder, pres. Acoustic Sys. Inc., Goleta, Calif., 1980-84, Invotron, Inc., Murray, Utah, 1984—; sr. scientist Reson, Inc., Santa Barbara, Calif., 1992—. Cons. Lockheed-Martin, 1985—, U. Utah Ctr. for Engring. Design, 1991; cons. on automotive underwater vehicle sonar systems Mitsui/U. Tokyo, 1992; lectr. solid state course UCLA and IBM, 1956-62; instr. Applied Tech. Inst., Columbia, Md., 1988—; contbr. to undersea acoustical rsch. and devel. programs European Union, 1990—; presenter in field Author: The Doppelganger Brane, 2004; contbr. articles to profl. jours. Mem. adv. panels for advanced sonar systems and for high resolution sonars, USN, 1970-77. 1st lt. U.S. Army, 1944-47, ETO. Recipient award of merit Dept. Navy, 1973, 94. Mem.: VFW, NRA, AAAS, IEEE (life), Math. Assn. Am., N.Y. Acad. Scis., Acoustical Soc. Am., Air Force Assn., Marine Tech. Soc., Mine Warfare Assn., U.S. Naval Inst., Libr. Congress Assocs. (charter), Planetary Assn., Old Crows, Am. Legion, Elks, Masons. Achievements include patents for device for detecting and displaying the response of tissue to stimuli, high rate neutralizer (HIRAN), crane high-voltage sensing sys. Home and Office: 41 W 6830 S Murray UT 84107-7124 Personal E-mail: hwv@aros.net.

**VOLCKER, PAUL ADOLPH,** economist, former Chairman of Federal Reserve System; b. Cape May, NJ, Sept. 5, 1927; s. Paul A. and Alma Louise (Klippel) V.; m. Barbara Marie Bahnson, Sept. 11, 1954 (dec. June 1998); children: Janice, James. AB summa cum laude, Princeton U., 1949, LLD (hon.), 1982; MA, Harvard U., 1951, LLD (hon.), 1985. Economist Fed. Res. Bank N.Y., 1952-57, pres., 1975-79; fin. economist Chase Manhattan Bank, N.Y.C., 1957-61, v.p. dir. forward planning, 1965-68; dir., Office Fin. Analysis US Dept. Treasury, Washington, 1961—63, dep. under sec. monetary affairs, 1963-65, under sec., 1969-74; chmn. bd. govs. Fed. Reserve Sys., Washington, 1979-87; chmn. James D. Wolfensohn, Inc., 1988—96. Prof. internat. econ. policy Princeton U., 1988-95, prof. emeritus, 1995—; chmn. Nat. Commn. on Pub. Svc., 1987-90, Trilateral Commn., 1990—01, Internat. House & Fin., Svcs. Vol. Corps.; chmn., Ind. Inquiry into the UN Oil for Food Programme, 2004-05, chmn. bd. trustees, Internat. Acctg. Stds. Com., 2000-06; dir. Inst. Internat. Econs. Recipient Arthur S. Fleming award, US Treasury Dept. Exceptional Svc. award, 1965, Alexander Hamilton award, 1973; Sr. fellow Woodrow Wilson Sch. Pub. and Internat. Affairs, 1974-75.

**VOLENTINE, RICHARD J., JR.,** lawyer; b. Tampa, Fla., Apr. 2, 1955; s. Richard J. Sr. and Mary Francis (Shaw) V.; m. Susan Ruth Zimmerman, May 16, 1981; children: Rachel Elizabeth, Scott Thomas, Melissa Mary. BS, Spring Hill Coll., 1977; JD, U. Ala., 1980. Bar: Ala. 1980, Mo. 1982, Fla. 1984. Staff atty. Ala. Jud. Coll., Tuscaloosa, 1980-81; staff counsel Citicorp Person-to-Person, Inc. St. Louis, 1982; regional counsel Citicorp Person-to-Person Corp., Tampa, 1982-84; asst. gen. counsel Citicorp Savs. Fla., Miami, 1984-85; assoc. counsel Nationwide Capital Corp., Atlanta, 1985-86; regional atty. FDIC, Atlanta, 1986-88; gen. counsel, v.p. Altus Bank, Mobile, Ala., 1988-90; v.p., assoc. gen. counsel Chase Home Mortgage Corp., Tampa, Fla., 1990-91; sr. v.p., chief legal officer Prudential Bank, Atlanta, 1991—2000; assoc. gen. counsel Fannie Mae, Atlanta, 2000—. Mem. ABA, Assn. Corp. Counsel, Ala. Jud. Coll. Faculty Assn. (hon.). Republican. Roman Catholic.

Avocations: playing golf and other sports, photography, writing. Home: Unit 201 3920 Riverlook Pky Marietta GA 30067 Office Phone: 404-398-6022. Business E-Mail: richard_volentine@fanniemae.com.

**VOLGIN, DENYS V.,** medical researcher; b. Melitopol, Ukraine, Apr. 19, 1973; s. Victor E. Volgin and Ludmila I. Volgina; m. Valeria Dovbik, June 12, 2003; children: Anastasia, Darya D. MS biology, chemistry (hon.), Melitopol State Pedagogical U., Ukraine, 1990—95; PhD physiology of human and animals, Bogomolets Inst. Physiology, Kiev, Ukraine, 1996—99. Asst. tchr. physiology Melitopol State Pedagogical U., Ukraine, 1995—96; postgraduate rschr. Bogomolets Inst. Physiology, Kiev, 1996—99; postdoctoral rschr. U. Pa., Phila., 1999—2002, rsch. assoc., 2002—. Recipient Faculty Career Advancement award, Am. Sleep Medicine Found., 2004; fellow Soros Fellowships, Internat. Renaissance Found., 1994, 1996. Mem.: Internat. Soc. Neurochemistry, Am. Acad. Sleep Medicine. Achievements include research in pharmacological correction of hypoxic states; study of the role of nitric oxide in central control of breathing in neonatal animals; single-cell gene expression profiling of upper airway motoneurons; study of GABAergic mechanisms in hypothalamic neurons involved in sleep/wake control, in study of hypothalmic GABAergic regulation of gene expression. Avocations: poetry, the arts. Office: Univ Pa 3800 Spruce St 209 E/Vet Philadelphia PA 19104 Office Phone: 215-898-6258. Business E-Mail: dvolgin@vet.upenn.edu.

**VOLGMAN, ANNABELLE SANTOS,** cardiologist, educator; b. Quezon City, The Philippines, Oct. 30, 1957; arrived in U.S., 1970; d. Raymundo Jocson and Purificacion Villatuya Santos; m. Keith Allen Volgman, Apr. 23, 1988; children: Robert Keith, Caroline Annabelle. BA, Barnard Coll., 1980; MD, Columbia U., 1984. Internal medicine resident U. Chgo. Hosps. and Clinics, 1984—87; cardiology fellow Northwestern Meml. Hosp., Chgo., 1987—90; asst. prof. Rush U., Chgo., 1990—2000, assoc. prof., 2001—. Cons. and spkr. in field. Contbr. articles to profl. jours. Fellow: Am. Coll. Cardiology; mem.: Am. Heart Assn. (med. chair women's legacy luncheon 2000—02, bd. dirs. 2002—, Spl. Merit award 2001—02, Women with Heart award 2005), Menomonee Club (bd. dirs. 2002—04). Avocations: running, bicycling, triathlons, reading, swimming. Office: Rush Heart Inst Ste 1159 1725 W Harrison St Chicago IL 60612 Office Phone: 312-942-6569. Business E-Mail: annabelle_volgman@rush.edu.

**VOLK, AUSTIN N.,** retired insurance company executive; b. N.Y.C., Dec. 28, 1918; s. Nicholas and Helen Volk; m. Rae Petigrue, Aug. 17, 1979; children: Deborah Saliba, John Glidden, James L.P. Glidden, Gordon G. Glidden. BA in Econ., Brown U., Providence, 1941. V.p. Nicholas Volk & Co. Inc., N.Y.C., 1946—55, pres., 1955—75, ret., 1975. Pres. Nat. Naval Res. Surface Policy Bd., Omaha, 1964—66; mem. Nat. Naval Res. Policy Bd., Washington, 1967—69. Pres. Englewood (N.J.) Cemetery Assn., 1988—; trustee, chmn. Naval War Coll. Found., 1997—99; councilman, coun. pres. City of Englewood, 1955—60, mayor, 1960—64, 1966—68; assemblyman State of N.J., Trenton, 1968—72. Capt. USNR, 1941—73, PTO, WWII, ATO, Korean War. Mem.: Navy League (pres. N.Y. coun. 1982—84, Teddy Roosevelt Leadership award 1982), Naval Order U.S. (pres. 1990—92, mem. N.Y. coun.).

**VOLK, KENNETH HOHNE,** lawyer; b. Hackensack, N.J., Nov. 8, 1922; s. Henry L. and Constance (Brady) V.; m. Joyce Geary, May 11, 1954; children: Christopher H., Cynthia. BS, U.S. Naval Acad., 1946; LLB, Yale U., 1953. Ptnr. Burlingham, Underwood, N.Y.C., 1955-92; of counsel McLane, Graf, Raulerson & Middleton, Portsmouth, N.H., 1992—. Speaker various symposia and confs. on maritime law. Assoc. editor Am. Maritime Cases; contbr. articles to profl. jours. Pres. Maritime Assocs., N.Y.C., 1967-68; chmn. bd. dirs. Seamen's House YMCA, N.Y.C., 1971-76; sec., bd. dirs. Seamen's Ch. Inst., N.Y.C., 1977-92; bd. dirs. Strawbery Banke Mus., Portsmouth, N.H.; mem. adv. bd. Tulane Admiralty Law Inst. Fellow Am. Bar Found., Am. Coll. Trial Lawyers; mem. ABA, Assn. Bar of City of N.Y., Maritime Law Assn. U.S. (exec. com. 1977-80, pres. 1990-92), Comite Maritime Internat. (titulary mem.), Quaker Hill Country Club (pres. 1976-78). Republican. Espiscopalian. Avocations: reading, hiking, fishing. Office: McLane Graf Raulerson & Middleton 100 Market St Portsmouth NH 03801 Office Phone: 603-436-2818. E-mail: kenneth-volk@mclane.com.

**VOLK, KRISTIN,** advertising agency executive; b. Phila., Feb. 26, 1953; d. Richard H. and Doris (Colasanti) V. BS in Biology, Tufts U., 1976; MPH, Boston U. Sch. Med., 1981. Rsch. technician Beth Israel Hosp., Boston, 1976; rsch. asst. Dana-Farber Cancer Inst., Boston, 1976-78; sr. rsch. asst. Beth Israel Hosp., Boston, 1978-81; rsch. supr. Schneider Parker Jakuc Advt., Boston, 1981-86; v.p., assoc. rsch. dir. HBM/Creamer, Boston, 1986-88, Della Femina McNamee, Boston, 1988-90; v.p., dir. rsch. Lawner Reingold Britton & Ptnrs., Boston, 1990-93; sr. v.p., dir. consumer insight group Arnold Fortuna Lawner & Cabot, Boston, 1993-95; exec. v.p., dir. consumer insight group Arnold Comm., Inc., Boston, 1995-99; exec. v.p., dir. strategic planning Deutsch Boston, 1999—2001; exec. v.p., chief mktg. officer Arnold Worldwide, N.Y.C., 2001—. Guest lectr. colls. and univs., Boston. Contbr. articles to profl. jours. Mem. Am. Assn. Advt. Agencies (account planning group com., chmn. conf. 1998), Ad Club N.Y. Home: 252 7th Ave Apt 15k New York NY 10001-7349

**VOLK, NORMAN HANS,** financial executive; b. NYC, Jan. 10, 1935; s. Hans and Mary (Zurl) V.; m. Karlyn Schram, Aug. 17, 1959; children: Kari, Heidi, Jenny. BA, Valparaiso (Ind.) U., 1957; MA, Marquette U., Milw., 1959. Dir. pub. rels. Wagner Coll., N.Y.C., 1961-62; asst. to owner Alan M. Wood, N.Y.C., 1962-72; sr. v.p. Bessemer Trust Co., N.Y.C., 1972-85; pres. Chamberlain & Steward, N.Y.C., 1985—. Trustee John Hartford Found., N.Y.C., 1979—. With U.S. Army, 1959-61. Mem. Univ. Club, Univ. Glee Club of N.Y.C., Doubles Club. Lutheran. Home: 445 Walton Rd Maplewood NJ 07040-1119 Office: 400 Park Ave New York NY 10022-4406

**VOLK, PATRICIA GAY,** writer, essayist; b. NYC, July 16, 1943; d. Cecil Sussman and Audrey Elaine (Morgen) Volk; m. Andrew Blitzer, Dec. 21, 1969; children— Peter Morgen, Polly Volk BFA cum laude, Syracuse U., 1964; student, Sch. Visual Arts, N.Y.C., 1968, New Sch., 1975, Columbia U., 1977-88. Art dir. Appelbaum & Curtis, N.Y.C., 1964-65, Seventeen Mag., Triangle Publs., N.Y.C., 1966-68; copywriter Doyle, Dane, Bernbach, Inc., N.Y.C., 1969-88, also sr. v.p., creative mgr., 1969-87; sr. v.p.- assoc. creative dir., 1987-88; columnist N.Y. Newsday, 1995-96; fiction instr. Yeshiva Coll. Fiction instr. Playwrights Horizon Theater Sch., Marymount Coll. Author: The Yellow Banana, 1985 (Word Beat Press Fiction Book award 1984), White Light, 1987, All it Takes, 1990, Stuffed: Adventures of a Restaurant Family, 2001; contbr. articles to N.Y. Times mag., Redbook, Allure, Mirabella, Family Circle, The New Yorker, The Atlantic, Playboy, others; contbr. short stories to popular and small press publs. and anthologies. Recipient Stephen E. Kelly award, 1983, Various Andy, Clio, Effie and One Show awards, 1970—88, Yaddo fellow, 1983, 1999, 2001—05, MacDowell fellow, 1984, 2000. Mem.: PEN, Century Assn., Author's Guild, Juliana Berner's Anglers.

**VOLK, STEPHEN RICHARD,** diversified financial services company executive, investment banker, lawyer; b. Boston, Apr. 22, 1936; s. Ralph and Miriam (Rose) V.; m. Veronica J. Brown, June 19, 1959 (dec. Feb. 1989); children: Jeffrey A., Andrew M., Michael J.; m. Diane Kemelman, Apr. 22, 1990; 1 child, Anne. Grad. cum laude, Dartmouth Coll., 1957; JD, Harvard U., 1960. Bar: N.Y. 1961. Assoc. Shearman & Sterling, N.Y.C., 1960-68, ptnr., 1968—88, dep. sr. ptnr., 1988-91, sr. ptnr., 1991—2001; vice chmn. Credit Suisse First Boston, N.Y.C., 2001—02 mem. exec. bd. and operative com., chmn., 2002—04; mem. exec. bd. Credit Suisse Group, 2003—04; vice chmn. Citigroup Inc., 2004—. Bd. dirs. ContiGroup Cos. Inc., Consol. Edison, Inc., 1996; trustee Consol Edison Co. N.Y.C., Inc.), 1998; chmn. Credit Suisse First Boston, 2002-04. Mem. dean's adv. bd. Harvard Law Sch., 1997. Fellow Am. Bar Found.; mem. Assn. Bar City N.Y., Harvard Law Sch. Assn., N.Y.C., 1999, Coun. on Fgn. Rels., Univ. Club, Phi Beta Kappa. Office: Citigroup Inc 399 Park Ave New York NY 10043

**VOLK, TIMOTHY ALAN,** youth minister; b. Pueblo, Colo., Mar. 4, 1981; s. Robert Lee and Helen Judith Volk; m. Jean Marie Thompson, June 12, 2004. Student, U. St. Mary, Leavenworth, Kans., 1999—2004. Youth min. St. Charles Borromeo Parish Diocese of Kansas City-St. Joseph, Mo., 2004—. Organizer, facilitator Project Hope Bag, Kansas City, Mo., 2004; mission trip St. Charles Parish, Kansas City, Mo. Mem.: KC Democrat. Roman Catholic. Avocations: skiing, gourmet cooking, running. Office: St Charles Borromeo Parish 900 NE Shady Lane Dr Kansas City MO 64118 Personal E-mail: timothy_volk@hotmail.com. Business E-Mail: stcharlesyouth@hotmail.com.

**VOLK, WILLIAM R.,** lawyer; b. Corpus Christi, Tex., Aug. 11, 1950; BA, Vanderbilt U., 1972; JD with honors, U. Tex., 1975. Bar: Tex. 1975. Ptnr., co-head Corp. Fin. & Securities Sect. Vinson & Elkins LLP, Austin, Tex. Fellow: Texas Bar Found. (life); mem.: ABA, Austin Bar Assn. Office: Vinson & Elkins LLP 2801 Via Fortuna, Ste 100 Austin TX 78746 Office Phone: 512-542-8609.

**VOLKEMA, MICHAEL A.,** office furniture manufacturer; Chmn., CEO Meridian Inc., Spring Lake, Mich.; pres., CEO Coro Inc., Zeeland, Mich.; Herman Miller Inc., Zeeland, 1995—2004, chmn., 2000—. Office: Herman Miller Inc 855 E Main Ave Zeeland MI 49464-0302 Office Fax: 616-654-5234.

**VOLKER, DALE MARTIN,** state legislator, lawyer; b. Lancaster, NY, Aug. 2, 1940; s. Julius J. and Loretta (O'Neill) Volker; m. Carol A. Suchyna, Nov. 28, 1970; children: Martin Andrew, Mark Dale, Meredith Ann. BA, Canisius Coll., 1963; JD, SUNY, Buffalo, 1966. Bar: NY 1967. Police officer Village of Depew, NY, 1966—72; assemblyman NY State Assembly, Albany, 1972—74; mem. NY State Senate, Albany, 1975—, Fowler and Volker, Lancaster, NY, 1978—. Mem.: Erie County Bar Assn., Eagles, Moose, Elks. Republican. Roman Catholic. Home: 92 Center Dr Depew NY 14043-1706 Office: Rm 427 State Capitol Albany NY 12247 also: 5441 Broadway Lancaster NY 14086-2123 Office Phone: 716-685-4805. Business E-Mail: volker@senate.state.ny.us.

**VOLKHARDT, JOHN MALCOLM,** food products executive; b. Chester, Pa., Apr. 13, 1917; s. George Thomas and Evelyn (Mitchell) V.; m. Linda J. Volkhardt; children: Michael, Jacqueline, Janet, Dana. AB cum laude, Brown U., 1939. Product mgr. Vick Chem. Co., N.Y.C., 1939-48; gen. mgr. Northam Warren Co., Stamford, Conn., 1948-56, Rit div. Best Foods Co., N.Y.C., 1956-58; with Best Foods div. CPC Internat. Inc., Englewood Cliffs, N.J., 1958-78, exec. v.p., 1968-71, pres., 1971-78; pres. North Am. div. CPC Internat. and exec. v.p. CPC Internat., 1978-82, group v.p., 1979; v.p. CPC, 1971-78, dir., 1977-82; pres., chmn. Full Circle Corp., Moss Creek, 1985-91; pres. Water Oak Utility, 1985-91. Dir. Storm Eye Inst., 2002—05. Chmn. bd. Keep Am. Beautiful, Inc., 1979-82, chmn. bd. trustees, 1982. Recipient Herbert Hoover award Nat. Assn. Wholesale Grocers Am.; honoree Nat. Jewish Hosp., 1976. Mem. Phi Beta Kappa.

**VOLKMAN, ALVIN,** retired physician, research scientist, educator; b. Bklyn., June 10, 1926; s. Henry Phillip and Sarah Lucille (Silverstein) V.; m. Winifred Joan Grinnell, June 12, 1947 (div. Aug. 1967); children: Karl Frederick, Nicholas James, Rebecca Jane Evans, Margaret Rose Werrell, Deborah Ann Falls; m. Carol Ann Fishel, Jan. 26, 1973 (dec. Sept. 1992); 1 child, Natalie Fishel; 1 stepchild, Jeffrey C. Moore; m. A. Suzanne Hiss, Oct. 6, 1997. BS, Union Coll., 1947; MD, U. Buffalo, 1951; D in Philosophy, U. Oxford, Eng., 1963. Diplomate Nat. Bd. Med. Examiners, Am. Bd. Pathology. Intern Mt. Sinai Hosp., Cleve., 1951-52; rsch. fellow dept. anatomy Western Res. U. Sch. Medicine, 1952-54; resident, then sr. resident, then asst. in pathology Peter Bent Brigham Hosp., Boston, 1956-60; asst. prof. pathology Columbia U. Coll. Physicians and Surgeons, 1960-66; asst. mem., then assoc. mem. Trudeau Inst., Saranac Lake, NY, 1966-67; prof. dept. pathology East Carolina U. Sch. Medicine, Greenville, NC, 1977—, acting chmn. dept. pathology, 1989-90, assoc. dean for rsch. and grad. studies, 1989-95, prof. emeritus, 1995—, ret., 1999. Mem. NIH study sect. immunological scis., 1975-79, chmn., 1977-79. Contbr. articles to sci. jours. Served to lt. USNR, 1954-56. Am. Cancer Soc. scholar, 1961-63, Arth and Rheumat Found. fellow, 1952-54. Mem. AAAS, Am. Soc. Investigative Pathology, Am. Assn. Immunologists, Am. Soc. Hematology, Reticuloendothelial Soc., Am. Soc. Microbiologists, N.Y. Acad. Scis., Soc., Leukocyte Biology (hon. life). E-mail: alvolk@cox.net.

**VOLKMAR, FRED ROBERT,** psychiatrist, educator, director; b. Highland, Ill., Mar. 26, 1950; s. Fred Harwood and Ella Josephine (Smith) Volkmar; m. Elizabeth Anne Wiesner, Sept. 2, 1984; children: Lucy Amelia, Emily Louisa. BS, U. Ill., 1972; MA, MD, Stanford U., 1976. Diplomate Am. Bd. Psychiatry and Neurology. Resident psychiatry Stanford U., Calif., 1976—80; fellow child psychiatry Yale U., New Haven, 1980—82; asst. prof. Child Study Ctr., 1982—88, assoc. prof., 1988—98, prof., 1998—, Irving B. Harris chair, 2003—, dir., chief child psychiatry Yale New Haven Hosp., 2006—. Cons. psychiatrist Benhaven Sch., New Haven, 1984—, med. dir., 1982—85; mem. sci. com. Nat. Ctr. for Clin. Infant Programs, Washington, 1985. Recipient Sandoz award, 1980, Ittelson award, Am. Psychiat. Assn., Faculty Scholar award, William T. Grant Found., 1982, Rsch. Career award, NIMH, 1983; James scholar, Laughlin fellow, 1982. Mem.: Am. Acad. Child Psychiatry, Soc. for Rsch. in Child Devel., Phi Beta Kappa. Democrat. Avocations: astronomy, photography, sailing. Office: Yale U Child Study Ctr 230 S Frontage Rd PO Box 207900 New Haven CT 06519-1124 Office Phone: 203-785-2510. Business E-Mail: fred.volkmar@yale.edu.

**VOLKOW, NORA DOLORES,** medical researcher, director; b. Mexico City, Mar. 27, 1956; m. Steven Adler. BA, Modern Am. Sch., Mexico City, 1974; MD, Nat. U. Mex., 1980; postgrad. in Psychiatry, NYU, 1980-84. Diplomate Am. Bd. Psychiatry and Neurology. Rsch. asst. Registro Nacional de Anatomia Patologica, Mexico City, 1975-76, Miles Lab. Experimental Therapeutics, Mexico City, 1977-78; intern St. Anne Psychiat. Hosp., Paris, 1979-80; residency NYU Dept. Psychiatry, 1981—84; asst. prof. U. Tex. Med. Sch., Houston, 1984-87; attending physician psychiat. unit Herman Hosp., Houston, 1985-87; assoc. scientist dept. medicine Brookhaven Nat. Lab. Upton, NY, 1987-89, assoc. chief of staff, Clinical Rsch. Ctr., 1990, dir. Nuclear Medicine, 1994—2003, dir, NIDA/DOE Imaging Ctr., 1997—2003, assoc. dir. life sciences, 1999—2003; assoc. prof. psychiatry SUNY, Stony Brook, 1991—2003, assoc. dean, Sch. Med., 1997—2003; lecturer, Psychiatry Dept. Columbia Univ.; dir. Nat. Inst. on Drug Abuse (NIDA), Washington, 2003—. Mem. Adv. Com. for Minority Tng. in Psychiatry, Washington, 1991—; mem. study sect. in clin. neuroscis. NIH, Washington, 1992—; elected mem., Inst. Medicine, 2000. Co-editor: Positron Emission Tomography in Schizophrenia Research, 1991. Named Innovator of the Yr., U.S. News and World Report, 2000; recipient Premio Robins award, U. Mex., 1978, Premio Gabino Barreza award, 1981, Laughlin fellowship, Am. Coll. Psychiatry, 1984, Scanditronix scholarship, 1985, Paul C. Aebersold award, Soc. of Nuclear Medicine, 2003. Office: Nat Inst on Drug Abuse NIH Rm 5274 6001 Executive Blvd Bethesda MD 20892-9581

**VOLL, JOHN OBERT,** history professor; b. Hudson, Wis., Apr. 20, 1936; s. Obert Frank and Ruth Olivia (Seaberg) V.; m. Sarah Lynne Potts, June 12, 1965; children: Sarah Layla, Michael Obert. AB summa cum laude, Dartmouth Coll., 1958, PhD (Ford Found. fellow), 1969; AM (Danforth fellow), Harvard U., 1960. Instr. history U. N.H., Durham, 1965-69, asst. prof., 1969-74, assoc. prof., 1974-82, prof., 1982-95, chair dept., 1988-91; prof. Georgetown U., Washington, 1995—, dep. dir. Ctr. for Muslim-Christian Understanding, 1996—2004, 2006—, dir. Ctr. for Muslim-Christian Understanding, 2004—06. Mem. history and social scis. adv. com. Coll. Bd. 1983-86, chmn. European history and world cultures achievement test com., 1985-88; tchg. fellow Harvard U., 1969. Harvard Ctr. for Middle Eastern Studies Vist. Com., 2003-05 Author: Historical Dictionary of the Sudan, 1978, 2nd edit., 1992, Islam Continuity and Change in the Modern World, 2nd edit., 1994; (with others) The Sudan: Unity and Diversity, 1985, Eighteenth Century Renewal and Reform in Islam, 1987, Sudan: State and Society in

Crisis, 1991, Islam and Democracy, 1996, Makers of Contemporary Islam, 2001; contbr. articles to profl. jours. Mem. bd. Ecumenical Ministry U. N.H., 1974-78, pres., 1975-77; chmn. social action Durham Cmty. Ch., 1974-75, mem. ch. coun., 1977-78, deacon, 1986—; Sheldon traveling fellow, 1960-61, U. N.H. summer fellow, 1969, 89, NEH fellow, 1971-72, Fulbright faculty rsch. abroad fellow, 1978-79, Inst. Advanced Studies fellow Hebrew U., 1984-85; recipient Egyptian Presdl. medal, 1991. Mem. Am. Coun. Learned Socs. (del. 1989-96, del. exec. com. 1989-92, bd. dirs. 1990-92), New England Hist. Assn. (sec. 1975-78, v.p. 1981, pres. 1982), Sudan Studies Assn. (bd. dirs. 1981-82, co-exec. dir. 1990-94), N.H. Coun. on World Affairs (bd. dirs. 1978-95), World History Assn. (bd. dirs. 2005—), Am. Hist. Assn. (chmn. program com. 1999), Mid. East Studies Assn. (bd. dirs. 1987-89, pres. 1992-93), Am. Coun. for Study of Islamic Socs. (bd. dirs. 1989—, v.p. 1989-91), N.H. Humanities Coun. (bd. dirs. 1991-95). Mem. United Ch. of Christ. Home: 4000 Cathedral Ave NW Apt 652B Washington DC 20016-5205 Office: Ctr Muslim Christian Understanding Georgetown U Washington DC 20057-0001 Office Phone: 202-687-8375. E-mail: vollj@georgetown.edu.

**VOLLA, STEVEN L.,** food products executive; Sr. v.p. Universal Health Svcs.; CEO Am. Healthcare Mgmt. Co., 1989—94; founder, non-exec. chmn. Primary Health Sys., 1994—2001; non-exec. chmn. Pathmark Stores, Carteret, NJ, 2002—. Mem. audit com. Sun Healthcare Group, Inc.; bd. dir. audit com. Brown Schs. Am., chmn.; bd. dir. Pathmark, Health Risk Mgmt. Named Turnaround Entrepreneur of Yr., Ernst & Young Inc. Mag., 1993, 1994. Office: Pathmark Stores 200 Milik St Carteret NJ 07008

**VOLLACK, LIA,** broadcast executive; Joined Sony Pictures Entertainment, 1997, sr. v.p., 1999—2000, exec. v.p., 2000, pres. worldwide music Columbia Pictures, 2002—. Named one of top women in music, Billboard, 2005. Achievements include becoming first female theatrical sound designer on Broadway. Office: Columbia Pictures 10202 West Washington Blvd Culver City CA 90232 Office Phone: 310-244-4000. Office Fax: 310-244-2626. E-mail: lia_vollack@spe.sony.com.*

**VOLLBRACHT, MICHAEL,** apparel designer, illustrator; b. Quincy, Ill., 1947; Grad., Parsons Sch. of Design, 1969. Designer Geoffrey Beene, 1969—71, Donald Brooks, 1971—73; illustrator Henri Bendel, 1973—75, Bloomingdales, 1975—80; designer, owner Michael Vollbracht Inc., 1980—85; designer Bill Blass Ltd., 2003—. Author: Nothing Sacred, 1985, 2d edit., 2000, Bill Blassan American Designer, 2002. Recipient Norman Norell award, J.C. Penney award, Coty award, 1980. Office: Bill Blass Ltd 550 7th Ave New York NY 10018 Office Phone: 212-221-6660.

**VOLLEN, ROBERT JAY,** lawyer; b. Chgo., Jan. 23, 1940; s. Ben N. and Rose (Belonsky) V.; m. Judith Paula Spector, Aug. 12, 1961; children: Steven, Neil, Jennifer. AB, U. Mich., 1961; JD, U. Chgo., 1964. Bar: Ill. 1964, D.C. 1965, U.S. Supreme Ct. 1975. Atty. appellate sect. Civil Div., U.S. Dept. Justice, Washington, 1964-65; assn. firm Schiff Hardin & Waite, Chgo., 1965-70, partner firm, 1971-72; gen. counsel BPI (Bus. and Profl. People for Pub. Interest), Chgo., 1972-83; ptnr. Schwartz & Freeman, Chgo., 1983-87. Mem. vis. com. U. Chgo. Law Sch., 1978—81. Mem. ABA (ho. of dels. 1974-76), Chgo. Council Lawyers (gov. 1972-76, 79-81). Home: 2 Kingswood Ct Deerfield IL 60015-1912 E-mail: rvollen@ameritech.net.

**VOLLMANN, WILLIAM T.,** writer; b. LA, 1959; married; 1 child. Student, Deep Springs Coll., Cornell Univ., Univ. Calif., Berkeley. Author: (short story collections) Rainbow Stories, 1989, 13 Stories and 13 Epitaphs, 1992, Butterfly Stories, 1993, The Atlas, 1996, (non-fiction) An Afghanistan Picture Show, 1992, (novels) You Bright and Risen Angels, 1987, Ice-Shirt, 1990, Whores for Gloria, 1991, Fathers and Crows, 1992, The Rifles, 1994, The Royal Family, 2000, Argall, 2001, Expelled from Eden, 2004, Rising Up and Rising Down, 2004, Europe Central, 2005 (Nat. Book award for Fiction, 2005); contbr. articles to New Yorker, Esquire, Spin, Gear, Granta, Grand Street, Outside Mag., Playboy. Recipient PEN Center USA West award for Fiction, Whiting Writers award, 1988. Home: Sacramento CA Mailing: Viking Publicity 375 Hudson St New York NY 10014*

**VOLLMER, DAVID,** museum director; Dir. Janice Mason Art Mus., Cadiz, Ky., Swope Art Mus., Terre Haute, Ind., 2001—. Office: Swope Art Mus 25 S 7th St Terre Haute IN 47807 Office Phone: 812-238-1676. E-mail: vollmer@swope.org.

**VOLLRATH, FREDERICK E.,** human resources specialist, career officer; BBA in Mgmt., U. Miami; MA in Pers. Mgmt./Adminstrn., Cen. Mich. U.; grad., U.S. Army Command/Gen. Staff, U.S. Army War Coll. Commd. 2d lt. U.S. Army, 1963, chief pers. mgmt. sect., mil. pers. divsn. Off. Adj. Gen. Vietnam, 1967—68; chief pers. svcs. divsn., then dep. adjutant gen. 4th Adjutant Gen. Co., 4th Infantry Divsn., Ft. Carson, Colo., 1972—74; adjutant gen., dep. chief of staff 4th Infantry Divsn. Ft. Carson, 1977—80; ret. U.S. Army, 1998; dir. pers. svc. support, enlisted pers. mgmt. 1st pers. cmd. U.S. Army Europe and 7th Army, Germany, 1981-84, dep. comdr. 1st pers. command, 1986-88; comdg. gen. U.S. Army Pers. Info. Sys. Command, Alexandria, Va., 1988; dir. mil. pers. mgmt. Office of Dep. Chief of Staff Pers. U.S. Army, Washington, 1995-96, dep. chief of staff for pers., 1996-98, advanced through grades to lt. gen., 1996; corp. v.p. human resources Computer Sci. Corp., El Segundo, Calif. Decorated Meritorious Svc. medal with 4 oak leaf clusters. Office: Computer Sci Corp 2100 E Grand Ave El Segundo CA 90245

**VOLLUM, ROBERT BOONE,** management consultant; b. Abington, Pa., Sept. 13, 1933; s. Charles Milton and Marion (Yocum) V.; m. Gayle Lorraine Timmerman, July 8, 1956; children: Robert Boone III, Jeffrey Charles. BS in Engring. and Sci., U.S. Naval Acad., 1955. Sr. cons., group leader Stevenson, Jordan & Harrison, Inc., N.Y.C., 1959—65; asst. to pres., plant supt., sales engr. W.L. Gore & Assocs., Inc., Newark, Del., 1965—69; gen. mgr. Philmont Pressed Steel subs. Gulf & Western Industries, Inc., Bethayres, Pa., 1969—72; gen. mgr. Air Shields divsn. Narco Sci. Industries, Inc., Hatboro, Pa., 1972—75; pres. Advanced Airflow Tech., Inc., Warminster, Pa., 1975—76, R.B. Vollum & Assocs., Huntingdon Valley, Pa., 1986—, RBV Mktg. Inc., Willow Grove, Pa., 1992—; chmn. bd. dirs., CEO SFM Technologies, Willow Grove, 1994—. Prin. mfg. cons. Sperry Corp., Blue Bell, Pa., 1976-84; dir. cons. Creative Output, Inc., Milford, Conn., 1984-86; spkr. in field. Contbr. articles to profl. jours. Bd. dirs. Upper Moreland Little League, 1965-76. Served to lt. USN, 1955-59. Fellow Am. Prodn. and Inventory Control Soc. (chpt. pres. 1984-85); mem. soc. Mfg. Engrs (sr. mem.), Computer and Automated Systems Assn. (sr. mem.). Republican. Episcopalian. Home: 525 Overlook Ave Willow Grove PA 19090-2818 Office: PO Box 206 Huntingdon Valley PA 19006-0206 Office Phone: 215-784-9011. Personal E-mail: rbvollum@rbvollum.com.

**VOLLWEILER, CHERYL P.,** lawyer; b. NYC, Dec. 4, 1963; BA, Brandeis U., 1985; JD, Hofstra U., 1988. Bar: NY 1989, NJ 1989, US Dist. Ct. Ea. Dist. NY, US Dist. Ct. So. Dist. NY, US Dist. Ct. Dist. NJ. Ptnr. Wilson, Elser, Moskowitz, Edelman & Dicker LLP, NYC. Mem.: ABA, Internat. Alliance Exec. & Profl. Women (bd. dirs.), Assn. Profl. Ins. Women (bd. dirs.), NY State Bar Assn. (co-chair toxic tort com.). Office: Wilson Elser Moskowitz Edelman & Dicker LLP 150 E 42nd St 23rd Fl New York NY 10017-5639 Office Phone: 212-490-3000 ext. 2674. Office Fax: 212-490-3038. Business E-Mail: vollweilerc@wemed.com.

**VOLMAN, DAVID HERSCHEL,** chemistry professor; b. LA, July 10, 1916; s. Carl Herman and Blanche (Taylor) V.; m. Ruth Clare Jackson, Sept. 15, 1944 (dec. Dec. 2001); children: Thomas Peter, Susan Frances, Daniel Henry. BA, UCLA, 1937, MS, 1938; PhD, Stanford U., 1940. Mem. faculty U. Calif.-Davis, 1940—41, 1946—, prof. chemistry, 1956-87, emeritus prof. chemistry, 1987—, chmn. dept., 1974-81, chmn. Acad. Senate, 1971-72; rsch. chemist OSRD, 1941-46; rsch. fellow Harvard U., 1949-50. Vis. prof. U. Wash. 1958. Editor: Advances in Photochemistry, 1983-98; mem. editl. bd.

Jour. Photochemistry and Photobiology, 1972-98; contbr. articles to profl. jours. Grantee Rsch. Corp. Am.; grantee NIH; grantee U.S. Army Rsch. Office; grantee NSF;Std. Oil Co. fellow, 1940; Guggenheim fellow, 1949-50. Mem. Am. Chem. Soc., Inter-Am. Photochem. Soc., Sigma Xi. Office: U Calif Davis Dept Chemistry 1 Shields Ave Davis CA 95616 Home: 2512 St NW 209 Washington DC 20007 Office Phone: 530-752-0960. Business E-Mail: volman@chem.ucdavis.edu.

**VOLNER, IAN D.,** lawyer; b. NYC, June 2, 1940; BA, Colgate Univ., 1962; JD (LLB), Columbia Univ., 1965. Bar: NY 1967, DC 1970. Staff atty. FCC Rev. Bd., 1968—70; ptnr., Advertising Marketing & New Media, Communications practices Venable LLP, Washington. Adj. prof. NY Law Sch., 1981—88, Catholic Univ., Univ. Md. Mem.: ABA, Fed. Comm. Bar Assn., NY State Bar Assn., DC Bar Assn., Phi Beta Kappa. Office: Venable LLP 575 7th St NW Washington DC 20004 Office phone: 202-344-4814. Office Fax: 202-344-8300. Business E-Mail: idvolner@venable.com.

**VOLOSHIN, YURY,** chemical engineer; b. Kiev, Ukraine, Aug. 14, 1976; arrived in U.S., 1990; s. Semyon and Maria Voloshin. BS in Chemistry, NYU, NYC, 2000; BE in Chem. Engring., Stevens Inst. Tech., Hoboken, NJ, 2000, MS in Chem. Engring., 2003. Process engr. Astaris, LLC, Carteret, NJ, 2000—01; rsch. asst. Stevens Inst. of Tech., Hoboken, 2001—. Presenter in field. Robert C. Stanley Grad. fellow, Stevens Inst. Tech., 2005—. Mem.: AIChE. Jewish. Achievements include research in production of hydrogen peroxide in a microreactor by direct combination method. Avocations: reading, sports. Office: Stevens Institue of Technology 1 Castle Point Hoboken NJ 07030 Office Phone: 201-216-5332. Home Fax: 201-216-8402. Office Fax: 201-216-8402. Personal E-mail: yvoloshin@yahoo.com.

**VOLPE, ANGELO ANTHONY,** retired academic administrator, chemist, educator; b. Nov. 8, 1938; s. Bernard Charles and Serafina (Martorana) V.; m. Jennette Murray, May 15, 1965. BS, Bklyn. Coll., 1959; MS, U. Md., 1962, PhD, 1966; M in Engring. (hons.), Stevens Inst. Tech., 1975. Rsch. chemist USN Ordnance Lab., Silver Spring, Md., 1961-66; from asst. prof. to prof. chemistry Stevens Inst. Tech., Hoboken, NJ, 1966-77; chmn. dept. chemistry East Carolina U., Greenville, NC, 1977-80, dean Coll. Arts and Scis., 1980-83, vice chancellor for acad. affairs, 1983-87; pres. Tenn. Technol. U., Cookeville, 1987-2000, ret., 2000, pres. emeritus, 2000—. Adj. prof. textile chem. N.C. State U., Raleigh, 1978-82; guest lect. Plastics Inst. Am., Hoboken, 1967-82. Contbr. articles to profl. jours. Recipient Ednl. Svc. award Plastics Inst. Am., 1973; named Freygang Outstanding Tchr., Stevens Inst. Tech., 1975. Mem. Am. Chem. Soc., Tenn. Acad. Scis., Sigma Xi, Phi Kappa Phi. Democrat. Roman Catholic. Avocations: golf, reading. Home: 734 Loweland Rd Cookeville TN 38501-2888 E-mail: avolpe@tntech.edu.

**VOLPE, BRUCE THOMAS,** neurologist; b. NYC, 1947; BS, Yale Coll., 1969; MD, Yale U. Sch. Medicine, 1973. Bd. cert. neurology 1980, bd. cert. internal medicine 1976. Intern U. Chgo., 1973—74, resident in internal medicine, 1974—75, Columbia Presbyn. Hosp., 1975—77; resident in neurology Cornell-NY Hosp., 1977; prof. neurology and neuroscience Weill Med. Coll., Cornell U. Burke Med. Rsch. Inst. Contbr. articles to profl. jour. Office: Burke Med Rsch Inst 785 Mamaroneck Ave White Plains NY 10605 also: Cornell U Med Ctr Dept Neurology 525 E 68th St New York NY 10021-4870 Office Phone: 914-597-2835, 914-597-2835. Office Fax: 914-597-2976. Business E-Mail: bvolpe@burke.edu.

**VOLPE, DORIS,** artist; b. Rockford, Ill., Dec. 22, 1930; d. August and Grace Adelaide Meenen; m. Samuel Volpe, Dec. 26, 1950 (dec. July 1994); children: Michael, Margaret. Group exhbns. include Art Inst. Chgo., Deer Path Gallery, Lake Forest, Ill., Gregoire Galleries, N.Y.C., Rhoda Sande Gallery, N.Y.C., Yolanda Kelly Gallery, Chgo., Peoria (Ill.) Regional Gallery, Old Orchard Shopping Ctr., Skokie, Ill., New Horizons, Chgo., Lake County Mus., Wauconda, Ill., Open Spectrum, Libertyville, Ill., Coll. Lake County, Grayslake, Ill., Neville-Sargent Gallery, Chgo., Sonnenschein Gallery, Lake Forest, Chgo. Botanic Gardens, Galleria Renata, Chgo., Clementi House Gallery, London, Millburn (Ill.) Gallery, Art in the Barn, Barrington, Ill., Art Expo, Lake Forest, Plaza del Lago, Wilmette, Ill., The Artists' Den, Valparaiso, Ind., Heirloom Gallery, Wilmette, North Shore Art League Fall Festival, Later Impressions, Chgo., Gallery 203, Chgo. Fountain Square, Evanston IL, Arts in Northbrook, Northbrook, Cantigny Fine Art Festival, Wheaton IL; solo exhbns. include Covenant Club, Chgo., 1st Fed. Savs. and Loan, Chgo., Lake County Court House, Waukegan, Ill., Kemper Group, Long Grove, Ill., The Stanley Gallery, Norfolk, Va., Univ. Club, Chgo., Chgo. Cultural Ctr. Avocations: gardening, art league activities.

**VOLPE, EDMOND L(ORIS),** retired college president; b. New Haven, Nov. 16, 1922; s. Joseph D. and Rose (Maisano) V.; m. Rose Conte, May 20, 1950; children: Rosalind, Lisa. AB, U. Mich., 1943; MA, Columbia U., 1947, PhD, 1954. Instr. NYU, 1949-54; mem. faculty CCNY, 1954-74, prof. English, 1968-74, chmn. dept., 1964-70; pres. Richmond Coll., 1974-76, Coll. S.I., NY, 1976-94; ret. Fulbright prof. Am. lit., France, 1960-61. Author: A Reader's Guide to William Faulkner, 1964, The Comprehensive College, 2001, A Reader's Guide to William Faulkner: The Novels Reissued, 2003, A Reader's Guide to William Faulkner: The Short Stories, 2004; also anthologies and coll. text books; co-editor: Eleven Modern Short Novels. Bd. dirs. S.I. United Way, 1975—, S.I. coun. Boy Scouts Am., 1977-84, S.I. Doctors Hosp., 1977-78, Snug Harbor Cultural Ctr., 1978-83, St. Vincent's Hosp. 1979—; mem. N.Y.C. Mayor's Commn. on Bias, 1986-88. With AUS, 1943-46. Recipient Commendatore Order of Merit, Republic of Italy, Cmty. Svc. award Columbian Assn. Bd. Edn., Disting. Cmty Svc award YMCA, Cmty Svc. award S.I. Women's Assn. Am. Com. on Italian Migration, Outstanding Achievement award Giuseppe Mazzini Lodge of Sons of Italy; named Educator of Yr. Am. Legion Richmond County. Mem. MLA, Am. Studies Assn., Assn. Dept. English (exec. com. 1969-71), Am. Assn. State Colls. and Univs. (task force ednl. opportunites for the aging, rsch. and liason com., com. internat. programs, health affairs com.), Am. Assn. Higher Edn., Am. Assn. Colls. for Tchr. Edn., Am. Assn. Univ. Profs., Am. Coun. Edn., Am. Studies Assn., Assn. Colls. and Univs. N.Y., Assn. Depts. of English (nat. exec. com.), Coll. English Assn. (nat. bd. dirs.), Consortium Internat. Programs, Inst. Internat. Edn., Inc., Mid. States Assn. Colls. and Schs., Andiron Club N.Y. (pres. 1972-75).

**VOLPE, JOSEPH,** former opera company general manager; b. Brooklyn, NY, July 2, 1940; m. Jean Anderson Volpe. Apprentice carpenter The Met. Opera, NYC, 1964—66, master carpenter, 1966—78, technical dir., 1978—81, assist. mgr., 1981—90, gen. mgr., 1990—2006. Author: (memoir) The Toughest Show on Earth: My Rise and Reign at the Metropolitan Opera, 2006.*

**VOLPE, JOSEPH,** Canadian government official; b. Monteleone, Puglia, Italy, Sept. 21, 1947; married; 4 children. MA in Edn., U. Toronto, Can. Mem. Can. Parliament, 1988—; parliamentary sec. to the min. health Govt. Can. 1996—98, chair standing com. on health, 1998—99, chair standing com. on natural resources and govt. ops., 1999—2000, min. human resources and skills devel., 2003—. Office: House of Commons Ottawa ON Canada K1A 0A6

**VOLPE, JOSEPH JOHN,** pediatrician, neurologist, educator; b. Salem, Mass., Dec. 17, 1938; s. John Rosario and Anne Eleanor (Femino) V.; m. Sara Lee Solov, June 2, 1980; children from previous marriage: Joanna Marie, Joseph Anthony, John Matthew. BA, Bowdoin Coll., 1960; MD, Harvard U. 1964. Diplomate Am. Bd. Pediatrics, Am. Bd. Neurology and Psychiatry with spl. competence in child neurology. Pediatric intern Mass. Gen. Hosp., Boston, 1964-65; pediatric resident, 1965-66, neurology and pediatric resident, 1968-71; rsch. assoc. Nat. Inst. Child Health and Human Devel., Bethesda, Md., 1966-68; asst. prof. pediatrics and neurology Washington U. Med. Sch., St. Louis, 1971-76, assoc. prof. pediatrics and neurology, 1976-79,

prof. pediatrics and neurology, 1979—, prof. biol. chemistry, 1980-90, dir. div. pediatric neurology, 1984-90; Bronson Crothers prof. neurology Harvard Med. Sch., Boston, 1990—; neurologist in chief Children's Hosp., Boston, 1990—. Author: Neurology of the Newborn, 1981, 4th edit., 2000; contbr. over 300 articles to profl. jours. Capt. USPHS, 1966-68. Recipient Weinstein-Goldensohn award United Cerebral Palsy Assn., 1985; rsch. grantee NIH, 1973—, March of Dimes Nat. Found., 1985-87. Mem. Nat. Acad. Scis. Inst. Medicine. Office: Children's Hosp 300 Longwood Ave Boston MA 02115-5737

**VOLPE, PETER ANTHONY,** surgeon; b. Columbus, Ohio, Dec. 17, 1936; s. Peter Anthony and Jeanette Katherine (Volz) V.; m. Suzanne Stephens, Sept. 5, 1959; children: John David, Michael Charles; m. Kathleen Ann Townsend, Mar. 28, 1978; 1 child, Mark Christopher; m. Theresa Ann Morse, Aug. 27, 2000. BA cum laude, Ohio State U., 1958, MD summa cum laude, 1961. Diplomate Am. Bd. Surgery, Am. Bd. Colon and Rectal Surgery (pres. 1988). Pvt. practice, San Francisco, 1969—; sr. ptnr. Volpe, Chui, Abel, Yee, Sternberg, San Francisco, 1987—; clin. prof. surgery U. Calif., San Francisco, 1995—. Asst. clin. prof. surgery U. Calif., San Francisco, 1972-95; chmn. dept. surgery St. Mary's Hosp. and Med. Ctr., San Francisco, 1978-90. Contbr. articles to profl. jours. Lt. USN, 1962—64. Fellow ACS (bd. govs. 1988-94), Am. Soc. Colon and Rectal Surgeons (treas. 1985-89, pres. 1990); mem. San Francisco Surg. Soc., San Francisco Med. Soc. Office: Volpe Chiu Abel and Yee Sternberg 3838 California St San Francisco CA 94118-1522 Office Phone: 415-668-0411.

**VOLPE, RALPH PASQUALE,** retired insurance company executive; b. Souderton, Pa., Sept. 20, 1936; s. Pasquale S. and Katie M. (Hartzell) Volpe; m. Marie F. Romano, Feb. 6, 1962; children: William, Anthony, Lynda. BA in Polit. Sci., Pa. State U., 1963. Claim cons. Aetna Life & Casualty Co., King of Prussia, Pa., 1964-97; litig. cons. Hartford Ins., King of Prussia, 1998—2003; ret., 2003. Bd. suprs. Upper Merion Twp., 1974—79, 1982—87, 1994—2005; chmn. Upper Merion Twp. Bd. Suprs., 1984, 1986—87, 1996—97, 2003—05, vice-chmn., 1985, 1995; 2d v.p. Montgomery County Assn. Twp. Ofcls., 1995—97, pres., 1997—99; exec. bd. Greater Valley Forge Transp. Mgmt. Assn., 1994—2003; study commn. Upper Merion Govt., 1974; exec. com. Rt. 202, 1994—2003; chmn. blue ribbon panel Montgomery County Waste Sys. Authority, 1997—98; chmn. Montgomery County Dem. Campaign, 1975, Upper Merion Dems., 1980—81. With U.S. Army, 1959—61. Recipient Good Govt. award, Upper Merion Jaycees, 1977, Excellence in Govt. Svc. award, King of Prussia C. of C., 1997, Earth Day award, Upper Merion Twp., 2004, Friend of Libr. award, Upper Merion Twp. Libr., 2005, Pub. Sector award, Greater Valley Forge Transp. Mgmt. Assn., 2005. Mem.: Southeastern Assn. Twp. Ofcls., Pa. State Assn. Twp. Suprs. (chmn. rules com. 1997—2000, chmn. resolution-legislation com. 2002—05, Pres.'s Leadership award 2006), Chapel Four Chaplains (Legion of Honor), Valley Forge Hist. Soc., Valley Forge Order Sons of Italy Am., Optimists. Republican. Roman Catholic. Home: 240 Strawberry Ln King Of Prussia PA 19406

**VOLPE, RICHARD GERARD,** insurance accounts executive, consultant; b. Sewickley, Pa., Apr. 10, 1950; s. Ralph Carl and Louise P. (Cosentino) V.; m. Janet Lynn Henne, May 10, 1986; 1 child, John Ralph. BA, Vanderbilt U., Nashville, Tenn., 1972. CPCU 1978; fellow Life Underwriting Tng. Coun. Trainee, asst. mgr. Hartford (Conn.) Ins. Group, 1973-74; v.p. sales Roy E. Barker Co., Franklin, Tenn., 1975-80; asst. v.p., product mgr. comml. ins. Nat. Farmers Union Ins., Denver, 1980-82; prin. R.G. Volpe & Assocs, Denver, 1982-85; acct. exec. Millers Mut. Ins., Aurora, Colo., 1985-89; pres, CEO AccuSure, Inc., Arvada, Colo., 1989—93; acct. exec. J.R. Misken, Inc., Denver, 1990-92, The Prudential, Colorado Springs, 1992-2001; sr. fin. rep. Principal Fin., Denver, 2001—04; comml. gen. ptnr. Planning Solutions Colo., LLC, 2004—. Edn. chmn. Insurors Tenn., Nashville, 1978-79; new candidate chmn. Mid-Tenn. chpt. CPCU, Nashville, 1979-80; cons. Bennett Nat. Bank Colo., mktg. mgr., 1989-90; cons. Colo. Plains Ins., Inc., 1987-90. Contbr. articles to profl. jours. Dem. chmn. Williamson County, Tenn., 1979; campaign mgr. legis., Franklin, 1979-98; legis. chmn. Centennial Life Underwriters, 1998, 2000, 02; del. Rep. State Caucus, 1998, 2000; mem. dist. com. Arapaho Dist., Denver Area coun. Boy Scouts Am., 2000. Named Hon. Col. Gov. Tenn., 1979; recipient Hertiage Soc., Boy Scouts of Am., 2004. Fellow Life Underwriters Tng. Coun.; mem. Soc. Property and Casualty Underwriters, Centennial Life Underwriters, Million Dollar Roundtable (qualifying mem.), South Metro Denver C. of C., Order of the Arrow, KC. Roman Catholic. Avocations: skiing, camping, hiking, bicycling, travel. Home: 10908 Snow Cloud Trl Littleton CO 80125-9210 Office: 10908 Snow Cloud Tr Littleton CO 80120 Personal E-mail: rgvolpe1@msn.com.

**VOLPÉ, ROBERT,** endocrinologist, researcher, educator; b. Toronto, Ont., Can., Mar. 6, 1926; s. Aaron G. and Esther (Shulman) V.; m. Ruth Vera Pullan, Sept. 5, 1949 (dec. Jan. 1997); children: Catherine, Elizabeth, Peter, Edward, Rose Ellen. MD, U. Toronto, 1950. Intern U. Toronto, 1950-51, resident in internal medicine, 1951-52, 53-55, fellow in endocrinology, 1952-53, NRC fellow, 1955-57, sr. rsch. fellow dept. medicine, 1957-62, McPhedran fellow, 1955-57, from asst. prof. to prof., 1962—74, prof., 1974—92, prof. emeritus, 1992—, dir. divsn. endocrinology and metabolism, 1987-92, chmn. centennial com., 1987-88; attending staff St. Joseph's Hosp., Toronto, 1957-66; active staff Wellesley Hosp., Toronto, 1966-2000, St. Michael's Hosp., Toronto, 2000—; dir. endocrinology rsch. lab. Wellesley Hosp., 1968-97, physician-in-chief, 1974-87. Trans-Atlantic vis. prof. Caledonia Endocrine Soc., 1985; Hashimoto Meml. lectr. Kyushu U., Fukuoka, Japan, 1992; K.J.R. Wightman vis. prof. Royal Coll. Physicians, Can., 1994; celebratory lectr. commemorating 200th anniversary of birth of Robert Graves, Dublin, Ireland, 1996. Author: Systematic Endocrinology, 1973, 2nd edu., 1979, Thyrotoxidosis, 1978, Auto immunity in the Endocrine System, 1981, Auto-immunity and Endocrine Disease, 1985, Thyroid Function and Disease, 1987, Autoimmune Diseases of the Endocrine System, 1990, The Autoimmune Endocrinopathies, 1999; past editl. bd. mem. Jour. Clin. Endocrinology and Metabolism, Clin. Medicine, Clin. Endocrinology, Annals Internal Medicine, Endocrine Pathology, American Journal of Physiology, Opinions in Endocrinlgy Metabolism, Thyroid; mem. editl. bd. Jour. Royal Soc. Medicine; contbr. over 320 articles to profl. jours. Nat. med. advisor Thyroid Found. Can., 1990—. Served Royal Can. Naval Vol. Res., 1943—45. Decorated officer Order of Can.; recipient Goldie medal for med. rsch. U. Toronto, 1971, Novo-Nordisk prize Irish Endocrine Soc., 1990, Commemorative medal Queen's Golden Jubilee, 2003; Med. Rsch. Coun. Can. grantee, 1960-97. Master ACP (gov. for Ont. 1978-83); fellow Royal Coll. Physicians Can. (coun. 1988-96, chmn. ann. meetings com. 1988-94, sci. program com. 1988-94, chmn. rsch. com. 1994-96, v.p. medicine 1994-96), Royal Coll. Physicians Edinburgh and London, Royal Soc. Medicine (editl. bd.); mem. AAAS, Can. Soc. Endocrinology and Metabolism (past pres., Starling prize lectr. 1985, Disting. Svc. award 1990), Toronto Soc. Clin. Rsch. (Baxter prize lectr. 1984), Can. Soc. Clin. Investigation (Disting. Svc. award 1998), Am. Thyroid Assn. (pres. 1980-81, Disting. Scientist award 1991), Assn. Am. Physicians, Assn. Can. Fedn. Clin. Rsch., Can. Med. Soc. Nuclear Medicine (Jamieson prize lectr. 1980), Can. Inst. Acad. Medicine, N.Y. Acad. Sci., European Thyroid Assn. (corr.), L.Am. Thyroid Assn. (corr.), Soc. Endocrinology and Metabolism of Chile (hon.), Caledonia Soc. Endocrinology (hon.), Japan Endocrine Soc. (hon., gold medal 1986), Order of Can. (officer), Alpine Ski Club (bd. dirs 1987-89), U. Toronto Faculty Club. Office: 600 Sherbourne Ste 211 Toronto ON Canada M4X 1W4 Office Phone: 416-926-7777. E-mail: robertvolpe@bellnet.ca. *Rigid adherence to high standards and integrity is essential. Do what is worth doing now, not tomorrow.*

**VOLPERT, RICHARD SIDNEY,** lawyer; b. Cambridge, Mass., Feb. 16, 1935; s. Samuel Abbot and Julia (Fogel) V.; m. Marcia Flaster, June 11, 1958; children: Barry, Sandy, Linda, Nancy. BA, Amherst Coll., 1956; LL.B. (Stone scholar), Columbia U., 1959. Bar: Calif. bar 1960. Atty. firm O'Melveny & Myers, Los Angeles, 1959-86, ptnr. L.A., 1967-86, Skadden, Arps, Slate, Meagher & Flom, L.A., 1986-95, Munger, Tolles & Olson, L.A., 1995—. Pub. Jewish Jour. of Los Angeles, 1985-87. Editor, chmn.: Los Angeles Bar

Jour, 1965, 66, 67, Calif. State Bar Jour, 1972-73. Chmn. cmty. rels. com. Jewish Fedn.-Coun. L.A., 1977-80; bd. dirs. Jewish Fedn.-Coun. Greater L.A., 1976-99, v.p., 1978-81; pres. Los Angeles County Natural History Mus. Found., 1978-84, trustee, 1974—, past bd. dirs., 1992-97, pres., bd. govs., 1997—; chmn. bd. councilors U. So. Calif. Law Ctr., 1979-85; vice chmn. Nat. Jewish Cmty. Rels. Adv. Coun., 1981-84, mem. exec. com., 1978-85; bd. dirs. U. Judaism, 1973-89, bd. govs., 1973-89; bd. dirs. Valley Beth Shalom, Encino, Calif., 1964-88; mem. capital program major gifts com. Amherst Coll., 1978-86; bd. dirs., mem. exec. com. L.A. Wholesale Produce Market Devel. Corp., 1978-95, v.p., 1981-93, pres. 1993-96; mem. exec. bd. L.A. chpt. Am. Jewish Com., 1967—, pres., 1999-2002, nat bd. govs., 2000-; nat. v.p., 2006-; vice-chmn. Los Angeles County Econ. Devel. Coun., 1978-81; bd. dirs. Jewish Cmty. Found., 1981—, Brandeis-Bardin Inst., 1995-2000, L.A. Chamber Orch., 2002-04; mem. Pacific S.W. regional bd. Anti Defamation League B'nai B'rith, 1964—. Named Man of Year, 1978 Fellow Am. Bar Found.; mem. Los Angeles County Bar Assn. (trustee 1968-70, chmn. real property sect. 1974-75), Los Angeles County Bar Found. (trustee 1977-80, 96-99), Calif. Bar Assn. (com. on adminstrn. justice 1973-76), Am. Coll. Real Estate Lawyers (bd. govs. 1996-99), Anglo-Am. Real Property Inst. (treas. 1995-98), Amherst Club of So. Calif. (dir. 1968-85, pres. 1972-73), City Club (L.A.). Jewish. Home: 16055 Royal Oak Rd Encino CA 91436-3913 Office: Munger Tolles & Olson 355 S Grand Ave 35th Fl Los Angeles CA 90071-1560 Office Phone: 213-683-9101. Business E-Mail: richard.volpert@mto.com.

**VOLPI, MIKE,** computer company executive; BSME, MSME, MBA, Stanford U. Former product devel. engr. and product mktg. mgr. optoelectronics divsn. Hewlett Packard; v.p. bus. devel. Cisco Systems, Inc., San Jose, Calif., 1994—, sr. v.p. bus. devel. and alliances, 1999—2000, chief strategy officer, 2000—02, chief strategy officer, v.p. internet switching and svcs. group, sr. v.p. routing tech. group, 2002—. Bd. dirs. Equinix, Inc., TIBCO Software, Opsware Inc. Office: Cisco Systems Inc 170 W Tasman Dr San Jose CA 95134

**VOLTZ, STERLING ERNEST,** physical chemist, researcher; b. Phila., Apr. 17, 1921; s. Harry John and Gertrude Irene (Derr) V.; m. Betty Morgan, Nov. 6, 1943; children: Sandra Elizabeth, Karen Lee. BA, Temple U., 1943, MA, 1947, PhD, 1952. Rsch. chemist Houdry Process Corp., Linwood, Pa., 1951-58; group leader Sun Oil Co., Marcus Hook, Pa., 1958-60; supervising engr. GE, Phila., 1960-62, cons. liaison scientist Valley Forge, Pa., 1962-68; rsch. assoc. Mobil Rsch. & Devel. Corp., Paulsboro, NJ, 1968-80, adminstrv., 1980-86; pvt. practice Media, Pa., 1986—. Contbr. articles to Jour. Phys. Chem., Jour. Am. Chem. Soc., Jour. Organic Chemistry, Analytical Chemistry, Jour. Soc. Automotive Engrs., Jour. Chem. and Engring. Data, Jour. Am. Inst. Chem. Engrs. and others. Lt. (j.g.) USN, 1943-46, ETO. Mem. AAAS, Am. Chem. Soc. (Phila. sect.), Catalysis Soc., Catalysis Club. Phila. (sec.-treas., chmn., dir. 1957-60), Am. Legion, Disabled Am. Vets., Sigma Xi. Achievements include 23 patents for Simulation of Catalytic Cracking Process, for Compatible Mixtures of Coal Liquids and Petroleum Based Fuels, for Reactivation of Automotive Exhaust Oxidation Catalyst, for Increasing Antiknock Value of Olefinic Gasoline, for Preparation of Aromatic Hydrocarbons, for Process for Dehydrocyclizing Heterocyclic Organic Compounds, for Alumina Stabilized by Thoria to Resist Alpha Alumina Formation, for Method of Treating Chromium Oxide, others; invention of plastic dry bag; co-development of commercial methanol-to-gasoline process, of fuel cell for space power applications, including first successful operation in space flight; development of catalysts and processes for petroleum and petrochemical conversions, of electronic apparatus to measure dielectric properties during oxidation reactions and establish reaction kinetics; establishment of relationship between catalytic properties, surface chemistry, and semiconductivity properties of metal oxide catalysts; research on catalytic systems for automotive emissions control including kinetic model of oxidation of carbon monoxide and hydrocarbons. Home: 6 E Glen Cir Media PA 19063-4712

**VOLZ, CHARLES HARVIE, JR.,** lawyer; b. Richmond, Va., Sept. 15, 1925; s. Charles Harvie and Mary V. (Mallory) V.; m. Constance A. Lewis, July 30, 1976; children: Charles Harvie III, Judith C. BS, U. Ala., 1950, JD, 1951. Bar: Ala. 1951, U.S. Dist. Ct. Ala., U.S. Ct. Appeals (5th cir.), U.S. Ct. Mil. Appeals, U.S. Ct. Appeals (11th cir.), U.S. Supreme Ct. 1962. Sp. agt. FBI, 1951; claim mgr. Allstate Ins. Co., 1952-54; claims atty. State Farm Ins. Co., 1954-57; ptnr. Roberts, Orme & Volz, Gadsen, Ala., 1957-59; sole practice Montgomery, 1961-63; asst. dir. Dept. Indsl. Rels., Ala., 1959-63; pnntr. Volz, Capouano, Wampold & Prestwood, 1963-84, Volz & Volz, 1984-95, Volz, Prestwood & Hanan, 1995—2001; of counsel Prestwood and Assocs., 2001—. Note editor Ala. Law Rev., 1950-51. Campaign dir. March of Dimes, 1958, Am. Cancer Soc., 1967; exec. sec. Gov.'s Com. on Employment of Physically Handicapped, 1959-62; mem. Pres.'s Com. on Employment of Physically Handicapped, 1962; bd. dirs. Montgomery chpt. Am. Cancer Soc. 2nd lt. USAAF, 1943-45. Recipient Outstanding Service award Am. Cancer Soc., 1967 Mem. ATLA (state committeeman 1973-75), Am. Arbitration Assn. (mem. nat. panel), ABA, Ala. Bar Assn., Ala. Trial Lawyers Assn., Farrah Law Soc., Montgomery Country Club, Masons, Kiwanis, Phi Alpha Delta. Methodist. Home and Office: 1638 Cobblestone Ct Montgomery AL 36117-1713 Office Phone: 334-279-8376.

**VOLZ, WILLIAM HARRY,** lawyer, educator; b. Sandusky, Mich., Dec. 28, 1946; s. Harry Bender and Belva Geneva (Riehl) V. BA, Mich. State U., 1968; MA, U. Mich., 1972; MBA, Harvard U., 1978; JD, Wayne State U., 1975. Bar: mich. 1975. Atty. pvt. practice, Detroit, 1975-77; mgmt. analyst Office of Gen. Counsel, HEW, Woodlawn, Md., 1977; from asst. prof. to prof. Wayne State U., Detroit, 1978—86, prof., 1986, dean, 1986—96; dir. Ctr. for Legal Studies Wayne State U. Law Sch., 1996-97; instr. Pa. State U., Coll. Sta., 1997—. Cons. Merrill Lynch, Pierce, Fenner & Smith, N.Y.C., 1980-83, City of Detroit Law Dept., 1982, Mich. Supreme Ct., Detroit, 1981; ptnr. Mich. CPA Rev., Southfield, 1983-85; expert witness in product liability, comml. law and bus. ethics; pres. Wedgewood Group. Author: Managing a Trial, 1982, Tiffany Pearls, 2006; contbr. articles to legal jours.; mem. editl. bds. bus. and law jours. Internat. adv. bd. Inst. Mgmt., L'viv, Ukraine, Legal counsel Free Legal Aid Clinic, Inc., Detroit 1976-96, Shared Ministries, Detroit, 1981, Sino-Am. Tech. Exch. coun., China, 1982; chair advt. rev. panel BBB, Detroit, 1988-90; pres. Mich. Acad. Sci., Arts and Letters, 1995-96, 98-2000, bd. dirs. Common Ground, Greater Detroit Alliance Bus., Olde Custodian Fund. Mem.: ABA, Players (bd. dirs.), Amateur Medicant Soc. (commissionaire 1981—85), Harvard Bus. Sch. Club Detroit, Econ. Club Detroit, Detroit Athletic Club, Beta Alpha Psi, Alpha Kappa Psi, Golden Key. Home: 3846 Wedgewood Dr Bloomfield Hills MI 48301-3949 Office: Wayne State U Sch Bus Adminstrn Cass Ave Detroit MI 48202 Office Phone: 313-577-4694. Business E-Mail: ab9241@wayne.edu.

**VOM BAUR, DAPHNE DE BLOIS,** artist; d. Francis Trowbridge vom Baur and Carolyn Bartlett Laskey; m. David Verner Hamilton, Sept. 3, 1973; children: Zoe Hamilton-vom Baur, Nerissa Alexandra Hamilton-vom Baur. BFA, Boston U., 1968. Fellow Atlantic Ctr. for Arts, New Smyrna Beach, Fla., 1986; mem. acquisitions com. S.C. Arts Commn., Columbia, SC, 1989—91. Vis. artist Susquehanna Studio, Union Dale, Pa., 1985—86. Exhbn., The Frye Mus., Seattle, 2002. Recipient Purchase award, S.C. State Art Collection, 1986. Mem.: Cosmos Club (mem. arts coun. 2001—05). Avocations: cross country skiing, swimming, opera, horses, especially the Connemara mural painting, painting. Office: Verner Gallery LLC 1 West Washington St PO Box2270 Middleburg VA 20118 Office Phone: 540-687-6875. Business E-Mail: vombaur@earthlink.net.

**VOM SAAL, WALTER,** psychology professor; b. NYC, Nov. 29, 1944; s. W. Rudolf and Jane (Towle) vom S.; children: Daniel, Laura, Jeffrey. BA, Columbia U., 1966; MA, McMaster U., 1967, PhD, 1969. Asst. prof. psychology Princeton (N.J.) U., 1969-74; assoc. prof. Millersville (Pa.) U., 1974-79, prof. psychology, 1979-86, assoc. v.p., 1986-89; provost and v.p. acad. affairs SUNY, Oneonta, 1989-94, acting pres. Plattsburgh, 1993-94,

prof. psychology, 1989—. Named Disting. tchg. fellow Commonwealth of Pa., 1979, Disting. Tchg. chair, 1979. Mem. Phi Beta Kappa. Home: 103 Elm St Oneonta NY 13820 Office: SUNY 502 Fitzelle Hall Oneonta NY 13820

**VONA, JOHN DAVID,** music educator; m. Tammy Givin, July 1, 1988; children: Philip Christopher, Courtney. B in Music Edn., Ithaca Coll., NY, 1985, M in Music Edn., 1988; cert. in Advance Study, SUNY, Brockport, 1993. Cert. educator music K-12 N.Y. State Dept. Edn., 1989, sch. dist. administr. N.Y. State Dept. Edn., 1994. Dir. band Addison (N.Y.) Ctrl. Schs., 1989—2004, tchr. music, 2004—. Judge music N.Y. State Field Band Conf., 1996—. Asst. coach basketball YMCA; asst. coach small fry football; com. chmn. Troop 61 Boy Scouts Am., Corning, NY, 2005. Named Tchr. of Yr., Addison (N.Y.) Student Coun., 2003; recipient Eagle award, Boy Scouts Am., 1980; grantee, Steuben-Alleghany BOCES, 1999. Mem.: N.Y. State Sch. Music Assn. (adjudicator 1993—), Steuben County Music Tchrs. Assn., Music Educator's Nat. Conf., Phi Mu Alpha (treas. 1983—85). Office: Addison Central Schools 7 Cleveland Drive Addison NY 14801 Office Phone: 607-359-2261. Business E-Mail: jvona@addison.wnyric.org.

**VON ARX, DOLPH WILLIAM,** food products executive; b. St. Louis, Aug. 30, 1934; s. Adolph William and Margaret Louise (Linderer) von A.; m. Sharon Joy Landolt, Dec. 21, 1957; children: Vanessa von Arx Gilvarg, Eric S., Valerie L. BSBA, Washington U., St. Louis, 1961; LHD, St. Augustine Coll., 1988. Account exec. Compton Advt., N.Y.C., 1961-64; v.p. mktg. Ralston Purina Co., St. Louis, 1964-69; exec. v.p. mktg. Gillette Personal Care Div., Chgo., 1969-72; exec. v.p. gen. mgmt. group T.J. Lipton Inc., Englewood Cliffs, NJ, 1973-87; pres., chief exec. officer R.J. Reynold Tobacco Co., Winston-Salem, NC, 1987-88; chmn., chief exec. officer Planters LifeSavers Co., Winston-Salem, 1988-91. Bd. dirs. Internat. Multi Food, Mpls., Hosp. Ptnrs. Am., Charlotte, N.C., No. Trust Fla. Corp., Miami, Cree Rsch. Inc., Durham, N.C., Ruby Tuesday Inc., BMC Fund Inc., Hosp. Ptnrs. Am., Charlotte, N.C.; chmn. Morrison's Restaurant Atlanta, 1996-98. Bd. visitors U. N.C., 1988-92; chmn. bd. trustees Wake Forest U. Grad. Sch. Mgmt., 1988-96; pres. bd. trustees N.C. Dance Theater, Winston-Salem, 1989-90; bd. dirs. Forsyth Meml. Hosp., 1988-92, Naples Conservancy, Naples Philharm. Ctr. for Arts, Fla. Arts Coun., Reynolds Mus. Am. Art, Naples Cmty. Hosp., chmn., 1994-99, bd. dirs. health care sys., chmn., 1995-2005; chmn. Regional Bus. Alliance SW Fla., Naples, Fla., 2004—. Mem. Belle Haven Club (Greenwich) (bd. dirs. 1983-87), Naples Yacht Club, Univ. Club (N.Y.C.), Linville Ridge Country Club (Linville, N.C.), Royal Poinciana Club (Naples, Fla.), Port Royal Club (Naples). Avocation: tennis. Home: 3663 Rum Row Naples FL 34102

**VON BAILLOU, ASTRID,** executive search consultant; b. Neutitschein, Czech Republic, Mar. 2, 1944; d. Karl von Baillou and Angela Stillfried; m. Dennis Hallam Bigelow, Oct. 21, 1967 (div. Oct. 1994). BA in English, Sweet Briar Coll., 1965. Creative dir. Freeman Advt., Washington, 1969-72; on-air reporter, prodr. PBS, BBC, London Weekend TV, N.Y.C., 1972-80; v.p. Sci. Program Group TV, Washington, 1980-82; pres. Cullen & Casey, N.Y.C., 1982-86; sr. v.p. Ruder Finn, N.Y.C., 1986-87; pres. Baillou Internat., N.Y.C., 1988-94; prin., mgmt. dir. Kinser & Assocs., N.Y.C., 1994-2000; ptnr. Kinser & Baillou, N.Y.C., 2000—. Home: 1245 Park Ave Apt 19F New York NY 10128-1740 Office Phone: 212-534-2161. Business E-Mail: search@kinserbaillou.com.

**VON BERNUTH, CARL W.,** lawyer, diversified financial services company executive; b. Feb. 2, 1944; BA, Yale U., 1966, LLB, 1969. Bar: N.Y. 1970, Pa. 1990. Corp. atty. White & Case, 1969-80; assoc. gen. counsel Union Pacific Corp., N.Y.C., 1980-83, dep. gen. counsel fin. and adminstrn., 1984-88, v.p., gen. counsel Bethlehem, Pa., 1988-91; sr. v.p., gen. counsel, 1991-97, sr. v.p., gen. counsel and sec. Omaha, 1997—. Mem. U. Pa. Inst. for Law and Econs. Mem. Am. Corp. Counsel Assn., Practicing Law Inst. Office: Union Pacific Corp 1416 Dodge St Rm 1230 Omaha NE 68179-0001 Home: 142 Gay Bowers Rd Fairfield CT 06824-2011

**VON BERNUTH, ROBERT DEAN,** agricultural engineering educator, consultant; b. Del Norte, Colo., Apr. 14, 1946; s. John Daniel and Bernice H. (Dunlap) von B.; m. Judy M. Wehrman, Dec. 27, 1969; children: Jeanie, Suzie BSE, Colo. State U., 1968; MS, U. Idaho, 1970; MBA, Claremont (Calif.) Grad. Sch., 1980; PhD in Engring., U. Nebr., 1982. Registered profl. engr., Calif., Nebr. Agrl. product mgr. Rain Bird Sprinkler Mfg., Glendora, Calif., 1974-80; instr. agrl. engring. U. Nebr., Lincoln, 1980-82; from assoc. prof. to prof. U. Tenn., Knoxville, 1982-90; prof. Mich. State U., East Lansing, 1990—, chmn., 1992-96. V.p. Von-Sol Cons., Lincoln, 1980-82; prin. Von Bernuth Agrl. cons., Knoxville, East Lansing, 1982—. Patentee in field. With USNR, 1970—98, Vietnam. Decorated DFC (2); recipient Disting. Naval Grad. award USN Flight Program, Pensacola, Fla., 1970. Fellow Am. Soc. Agrl. Engrs.; mem. ASCE, Irrigation Assn. (Person of Yr. 1994), Naval Res. Assn. Avocations: flying, skiing, antique tractors. Office: Mich State U Sch of Planning Design & Constrn Human Ecology Bldg East Lansing MI 48824

**VON BRANDENSTEIN, PATRIZIA,** production designer; Prodn. designer The Mirisch Agy., L.A., 1978—. Prodn. designer: (films) Heartland, 1979, Breaking Away, 1979, Ragtime, 1981 (Academy award nomination best art direction 1981), Silkwood, 1983, Amadeus, 1984 (Academy award best art direction 1984), A Chorus Line, 1985, The Money Pit, 1986, No Mercy, 1987, The Untouchables, 1987 (Academy award nomination best art direction 1987), Working Girl, 1988, The Lemon Sisters, 1990, Postcards From the Edge, 1990, Billy Bathgate, 1992, Sneakers, 1992, Leap of Faith, 1993, Six Degrees of Separation, 1993, The Quick and the Dead, 1995, Just Cause, 1995, The People vs. Larry Flynt, 1996, A Simple Plan, 1998, Man on the Moon, 1999, Shaft, 2000, It Runs in the Family, 2002, The Emperor's Club, 2002, Ice Harvest, 2006, All the King's Men, 2006, Goya's Ghosts, 2006; costume designer: (films) Between the Lines, 1977, Saturday Night Fever, 1977, A Little Sex, 1982.

**VONCANNON, BRIAN EVERETT,** writer, scriptwriter, radio personality, naturopath; s. Mary Jane and Charles Everett Voncannon. AA in Applied Sci., Ctrl. Piedmont C.C., 1998; D in Naturology, Am. Inst. Holistic Theology, 1996; D in Alternative Medicines, Open Internat. U. Alternative Medicines, 2004; D of Naturopathy, Clayton Coll. Natural Health, Birmingham, Ala., 2006. Cert. in gen. law enforcement, chem. analyst of breath, profl. trainer. Police officer Concord City Police Dept., Concord, NC, 1996—95; dep. sheriff/swat officer Cabarrus County Sheriff's Dept., Concord, NC, 1997—2002; author EveningStorm Enterprises, Midland, NC, 1997—; cmty. radio dj/rec. studio owner EveningStorm Radio, Midland, NC, 2002—. Swat officer Cabarrus County Sheriff's Dept., Concord, NC, 1998—2002. Author: (book) Chronic Fatigue Syndrome: Living with the Unknown, Shadows: Diary of a Ninja, Cherokee Blue Eyes: Keeping the Heritage Alive, Living Behind the Shield: A Modern Warrior's Path to Bravehood, Completing the Circle: The Hathcock Indian Blood, (screenplays) The Keepers, Orbit. Sound tech. First Bapt. Ch. of Locust, Locust, NC, 1985—2000. E-6 staff sgt. US Army Reserves, 1991—99, Concord, North Carolina. Decorated Army Achievement medal US Army, Disting. Honor Grad. award US Army Inf. Tng. Ctr., Ft. Benning, Ga., Cert. of Recognition for Cold War Svc. Dept. of Def., Nat. Def. Svc. medal US Army. Democrat. Baptist. Avocations: martial arts, physical fitness activities, outdoor activities, creating native American crafts, travel. Home: 13101 Pine Bluff Rd Midland NC 28107 Office: EveningStorm Enterprises 13101 Pine Bluff Rd Midland NC 28107 E-mail: eveningstorm@earthlink.net.

**VONCANNON, ERIC R.,** real estate company executive; b. Nashville, Dec. 10, 1972; s. Ted Voncannon and Ann Orman. BS in MIS, Auburn U., 1996. V.p. Graham & Co., Inc., Birmingham, Ala., 1993—; sr. sale cons. Oracle Corp., Seattle, 1998—2001. Mem. Birmingham-Jefferson County Auburn Club, 1994. Office: Grahma & Co Inc 2200 Woodcrest Pl Birmingham AL 35209 Office Phone: 205-871-7100. Office Fax: 205-871-3331. Business E-Mail: ericv@grahamcompany.com.

**VONDERBRINK, GERALD WILLIAM,** retired academic administrator, real estate manager; b. Cin. s. Richard Bernard and Marguerite Grady Vonderbrink; widowed; children: David Jerome, Diane Edwards, Philip Gerald, Joseph Paul. BSBA, Xavier U., 1950; MBA, U. Dayton, 1966. Jr. acct. Alexander Grant, Cin., 1950-51; sr. acct. Hathaway & Hathaway, Cin., 1951-54; contr. Aerosonic Instrument Co., Cin., 1954-56; fin. analyst GE, Cin., 1956-57; contr. Coll. Conservatory of Music, Cin., 1958-61; v.p. fin. affairs U. Dayton, Ohio, 1961-92, asst. exec. v.p., 1993-98. Contbr. articles to profl. jours. Pres. Ohio Assn. Coll. and Univ. Bus. Officers, 1967-68; sec./treas. Coll. Assn. Coll. and Univ. Bus. Officers, 1968-69; mem. fin. aid com. Nat. Assn. Coll. and Univ. Bus. Officers, Washington, 1978; chmn. bd. dirs. U. Dayton Libr. Advancement Assn., 1999—; treas. bd. dirs. Places, Inc., Dayton, 1999-2001; bd. dirs. Dakota Ctr., Dayton, 1999-2001, Caring Families, Inc., Dayton, 1996-2001. Cpl. U.S. Army Signal Corps, 1946-48, Japan. Democrat. Roman Catholic. Avocations: tennis, bridge.

**VONDERHAAR, BARBARA K.,** medical researcher; Grad., Clarke Coll., Dubuque, Iowa, 1965; PhD, U. Wis., Madison. Postdoctoral training in mammary gland biology NIH; now chief Mammary Biology and Tumorigenesis Lab. Ctr. Cancer Rsch., Nat. Cancer Inst., head Molecular and Cellular Endocrinology Sect., Mammary Biology and Tumorigenesis Lab.; chair Breast and Gynecologic Malignancies Faculty Nat. Cancer Inst.; co-chair Intramural Program for Rsch. on Women's Health NIH. Recipient Award for Excellence in Mentoring, Bethesda Assn. for Women in Sci., 2000, Helen F. Cserr Award for outstanding woman scientist, Mt. Desert Island Biol. Laboratories, 2004. Office: Mammary Biology and Tumorigenesis Lab Ctr Cancer Rsch 37 Convent Dr Bldg 37 Rm 1106A1 Bethesda MD 20892-4254 Office Phone: 301-435-7587. Office Fax: 301-402-0711. E-mail: bv10w@nih.gov.

**VONDERHAAR, STEVEN PAUL,** counseling administrator; s. Clarence and Marlene Vonderhaar; m. Margaret Ann Korode, June 19, 1993; children: Mollie, Sean, Claire. BA, U. Cin., 1989; MA, Xavier U., 1995; MS, Miami U., 1999. Lic. sch. psychologist Ohio Dept. Edn., nat. cert. sch. psychologist NASP, lic. sch. psychologist Ohio State Bd. Psychology. Psychol. assoc. Northkey Cmty. Care, Covington, Ky., 1993—98; sch. psychologist Milford Exempted Village Schs., 1999—; mitigation specialist S.W. Ohio, 1994—. Adj. prof. Miami U., 2004—, Xavier U., 2005—; range finder com. Ohio Dept. Edn., 2004, 05. Presenter various profl. workshops. Mem.: NASP, Ohio Sch. Psychologists Assn., SW Ohio Sch. Psychologists Assn. (pres. 2004—05), Psi Chi, Phi Kappa Tau. Avocations: reading, soccer, golf, hiking, bicycling. Office Phone: 513-831-1314.

**VON DER HEYDEN, KARL MUELLER,** retired manufacturing executive; b. Berlin, July 18, 1936; arrived in U.S., 1957, naturalized, 1967; s. Werner and Erika (Mueller) von der Heyden; m. Mary Ellen Terrell, Aug. 17, 1963; children: Ellen, Eric. Student, Free U., Berlin, 1959—61; BA, Duke, 1962; MBA, U. Pa., 1964. CPA Pa. Mgmt. trainee Berliner Bank, Berlin, 1955-57; sr. staff acct. Coopers & Lybrand, Phila., 1963-66; asst. comptr., corporate comptr. Pitney-Bowes, Inc., Stamford, Conn., 1966-74; v.p., contr. PepsiCo., Inc., Purchase, 1974-77; v.p. fin. Pepsi-Cola Co., 1977-79, v.p. mfg., 1979-80; v.p. fin., treas. H.J. Heinz Co., Pitts., 1980-83, sr. v.p. fin., CFO, 1983-89; exec. v.p., CFO RJR Nabisco Inc., NYC, 1989-93, co-chmn., CEO, 1993; pres., CEO Metallgesellschaft Corp., NYC, 1993-94; vice chmn. PepsiCo, Inc., Purchase, NY, 1996—2001; sr. advisor Clipper Group, 1994-97. Chmn. Fin. Acctg. Stds. Adv. Coun., 1995—96; bd. dirs. H.J. Heinz Co., 1983—89, Federated Dept. Stores, Inc., Aramark Corp., NYSE Group, Inc., Dreamworks Animation SKG. Trustee Duke U., Am. Acad., Berlin, Nat. Humanities Ctr. Mem.: Univ. Club N.Y.C. Office: 25 Central Park W Apt 24K New York NY 10023

**VON DER HEYDT, JAMES ARNOLD,** federal judge; b. Miles City, Mont., July 15, 1919; s. Harry Karl and Alice S. (Arnold) von der H.; m. Verna E. Johnson, May 21, 1952. BA, Albion Coll., 1942; JD, Northwestern U., 1951. Bar: Alaska 1951. Pvt. practice, Nome, Alaska, 1953—59; judge superior ct. Juneau, Alaska, 1959—66; from judge to sr. judge U.S. Dist. Ct. Alaska, 1966—; U.S. commr. Nome, 1951—; U.S. atty. divsn. 2 Dist. Alaska, 1951—53; mem. Alaska Ho. of Reps., 1957—59. Author: Mother Sawtooth's Nome, 1990, Alaska, The Short and Long of It, 2000. Pres. Anchorage Fine Arts Mus. Assn. Recipient Disting. Alumni award Albion Coll., 1995, Professionalism and Ethics award Inst. of Ct., 2005. Mem. Alaska Bar Assn. (bd. govs. 1955-59, pres. 1959-60), Am. Judicature Soc., Masons (32d degree), Shriners, Phi Delta Phi, Sigma Nu. Avocations: researching arctic bird life, creative writing, painting. Office: US Dist Ct 222 W 7th Ave Box 40 Anchorage AK 99513-7564 Office Phone: 907-677-6254.

**VON DER MEHDEN, FRED R.,** political science professor; b. San Francisco, Dec. 1, 1927; s. Fred G. and Margaret (de Valasco) von der M.; m. Audrey Eleanor Whitehead, Dec. 27, 1954; children: Laura Davis, Victoria Margaret Fredrickson. BA, U. of Pacific, 1948; MA, Claremont Grad. Sch., 1950; PhD, U. Calif. Berkeley, 1957. Mem. faculty U. Wis. Madison, 1957-68; chmn. East Asian studies U. Wis.-Madison, 1963-65, 67-68; Albert Thomas prof. polit. sci. Rice U., 1968—2000, dir. Center for Research, 1969-70, prof. studies, 1975-78, dir. program devel. studies, 1978-83; editor Rice U. Press, 1982-95; Albert Thomas prof. emeritus Rice U., 2000—. Cons. AID, 1967-78 Author: Politics of the Developing Nations, 1964, 2d edit., 1969, Religion and Nationalism in Southeast Asia, 1963, Comparative Political Violence, 1973; co-author: Issues of Political Development, 1967, The Military and Politics of Five Developing Nations, 1970, Southeast Asia 1930-1970, 1974, Religion and Modernization in Southeast Asia, 1986, Two Worlds of Islam, 1993; editor: (with R. Soligo) Issues on Income Distribution, 1975, Ethnic Groups of Houston, 1984. Mem. Mid-West Conf. Asian Affairs (pres. 1968-69), Assn. Asian Studies, Am. Polit. Sci. Assn., S.W. Conf. Asian Affairs (pres. 1976-77) Home: 12530 Mossycup Dr Houston TX 77024-4937 Office Phone: 713-348-4848. E-mail: fvdm@rice.edu.

**VON DER SCHMIDT, EDWARD, III,** neurosurgeon, veterinarian; b. Jan. 13, 1953; BS in Animal Sci., Rutgers U., 1975; DVM, Cornell U., 1979; MD, U. Medicine and Dentistry N.J., Newark, 1984. Diplomate Nat. Bd. Med. Examiners, Am. Bd. Neurol. Surgery. Veterinarian Secaucus (N.J.) Animal Hosp., 1979-82; pvt. practice vet. medicine NJ, 1980-85; gen. surg. intern Washington Hosp. Ctr., Washington, 1984-85; resident in neurosurgery George Washington U. Med. Ctr., Washington, 1985-90; pvt. practice neurosurgery Princeton (N.J.) Healthcare Ctr., 1990—. Neurosurgeon Robert Wood Johnson U. Hosp., New Brunswick, NJ, St. Peter's Med. Ctr., New Brunswick, Somerset Med. Ctr., Somerville, NJ; chief neurosurgery sect. Med. Ctr. Princeton; mem. search com. for chief divsn. neurosurgery U. Medicine and Dentistry N.J./Robert Wood Johnson Med. Sch. Mem.: AAAS, AMA, N.J. Soc. Med. Specialty (pres. 2000—02), Coun. State Neurosurgical Safety (mem. reform commit. 2001, vice chmn. N.E. quadrant 2003—), Am. Assn. Med. Transcription (bd. dirs. Ctrl. N.J. chpt.), Am. Coll. Physician Execs., Soc. Exec. Physicians, Soc. Critical Care Medicine, N.J. Neurosurgical Soc. (trustee at large 2000—, sec. treas. 1998—2000), N.Y. Acad. Sci., Middlesex Med. Soc. (sec. 2003, del.), Middlesex County Med. Soc., Med. Soc. N.J., Congress Neurol. Surgeons (mem. joint sect. disorders spine and peripheral nerves), Am. Assn. Neurol. Surgeons, Alpha Zeta (Best Freshman award). Home: 140 Hodge Rd Princeton NJ 08540-3014 Office: Princeton Healthcare Ctr 419 N Harrison St Ste 204 Princeton NJ 08540-3521

**VON DREHLE, RAMON ARNOLD,** lawyer; b. St. Louis, Mar. 12, 1930; s. Arnold Henry and Sylvia E. (Ahrens) Von D.; m. Gillian Margaret Turner, Sept. 13, 1980; children by previous marriage: Carin L., Lisa A., Courtney A. BS, Washington U., St. Louis, 1952; JD, U. Tex., Austin, 1957; postgrad. Parker Sch. Internat. Law, Columbia U., 1965. Bar: Tex. 1956, Mich. 1957, U.S. Supreme Ct. 1981. Sr. atty. Ford Motor Co., Dearborn, Mich., 1957-67; assoc., asst. gen. counsel Ford of Europe, Inc., Brentwood, Essex, Eng., 1967-75, v.p., gen. counsel, 1975-79; v.p. legal Ford Motor Credit Co., Dearborn, 1979-87; v.p., gen. counsel Am. Road Ins. Co., Dearborn, 1979-87; exec. dir. legal affairs Ford Fin. Services Group, Dearborn, 1987-91; leader in residence Walsh Coll., Mich., 1992. Panelist large complex case program Am.

Arbitration Assn., 1993—; advisor to Czech Republic Ministry of Privatization, Prague, 1993-94; leader Russian Def. Conversion Project, 1995-96; lectr. in Ea. Europe, 1995; pres. Focus Internat. LLC, 1995—. Article editor: Tex. Law Rev, 1956-57. Trustee Birmingham Unitarian Ch., 1966-67. Served to 1st lt. AUS, 1952-54, Korea. Mem. ABA, Mich. Bar Assn., Tex. Bar Assn., Internat. Bar Assn., Am. Fin. Svcs. Assn. (chmn. 1990-91, bd. dirs. 1981-91), Fin. Svcs. Coun. (bd. dirs. 1987-91), Washington U. Alumni Club Detroit (past pres.), Order of Coif, Tower Club (Tysons, Va.), Confrèrie des Chevaliers du Tastevin (France, Washington), Royal Automobile Club (London), Cosmos Club (Washington). Mem. Christ Ch. Home and Office: 519 Princess St Alexandria VA 22314-2332 E-mail: rvond2@aol.com.

**VON ESCHEN, ROBERT LEROY,** electrical engineer, consultant; b. Glasgow, Mont., Oct. 3, 1936; s. Leroy and Lillian Victoria (Eliason) Von E.; m. Carolyn Kay Frampton, Dec. 14, 1965 (dec. Feb. 1999); children: Eric Leroy, Marc Alfred. BSEE, Mont. State U., 1961; postgrad., U. Liberia, Lakeland C.C., Glendale C.C. Registered profl. engr., Pa. Hydro constrn. engr. U.S. Army Corps of Engrs., Mont., 1961-62, SD, 1961—62; hdqrs. chief engr. Eagle Constrn. Co., Colo., 1962; resident transp./distbn. elec. engr. Stanley Cons., Inc., West Africa, 1962-63, hydro cons., startup engr. Manila, West Africa, 1965-66; with Stanley Cons., 1962-68, Gilbert Assoc./United Energy Svc., 1968-92; performance based assessment program sect. engr., maintenance planning engr., condition assessment survey sect. mgr. Gilbert Assocs., Inc., Tex., 1992—. Cons. engr. fossil power plant, Ky., Colo., Mo., Korea; site project mgr., Ariz., Aruba; nuclear constrn. startup engr., Pa., Ala., Ohio; safety sys. functional inspector, Calif., Wis., Oreg.; performance based assessment program project mgr., Tex.; tech. cons. World Bank, Liberia; engring. cons. USN, Manila, 1967; founding dr. Madison Comptr. Soc., Ohio, 1983-85; v.p., dir. Boy Scouts Am., 1981-84. Founder, dir. Madison (Ohio) Computer Soc., 1983—85; v.p., bd. dirs. N.E. coun. Boy Scouts Am. Painesville, 1983—85; bd. dirs. Let's Shoot Gun Club, LLC, 2003—; Kids World Multimedia. Recipient Silver Beaver award Boy Scouts Am., 19 other awards. Mem.: AFIO, NARP, NPSE, IEEE, NRA, Tex. State Engring. Soc., Ohio State Engring. Soc., Nat. Def. Indsl. Orgn., Soc. Am. Mil. Engrs., Shriners, Masons (life). Avocations: target and skeet shooting, construction design, computers, electronics. Home: 1001 S Girl Scout Rd Amarillo TX 79124-2135 Office: BWXT Pantex LLC PO Box 30020 Amarillo TX 79120-0020

**VON ESCHENBACH, ANDREW C.,** federal agency administrator, oncologist, urologic surgeon; b. Phila., Oct. 30, 1941; BS, St. Joseph's Univ., Phila., 1963; MD, Georgetown U., 1967. Diplomate Am. Bd. Urology. Intern U. Pa./Phila. Gen. Hosp., 1967–68; resident gen. surgery Pa. Hosp., Phila., 1971—72, resident urology, 1972—75; instructor, urology U. Pa. Sch. Medicine; fellow urol. oncology U. Tex. MD Anderson Hosp., Houston, 1976—77, prof. urology, 1977—2002, chmn. dept. urology, 1983—96, cons. prof., cell biology, prof. urology, exec. v.p., chief acad. officer, dir. program ctr. Genitourinary Cancer Houston, 1997—2002, founding dir., Prostate Cancer Research Prog., 1996, v.p. for academic affairs, Roy M. and Phyllis Gough Huffington Clin. Rsch. Disting. Chair in Urologic Oncology; dir. Nat. Cancer Inst., NIH, Bethseda, Md., 2002—06; acting commr. FDA, Rockville, Md., 2005—; sr. adv. to sec. US Dept. Health & Human Services., Washington, 2006—. Founding mem. C-Change. Contbr. articles to profl. jours., books, and book chpt.; mem. edit. bd. (several jours.). Lt. comdr. U.S. Navy Medical Corps, 1968—71. Named one of 100 Most Influential People, Time Mag., 2006; recipient Julie Rogers "Spirit of Love" award, Achievement award in prostate cancer, Partners in Courage, 100 Black Men of Metropolitan Houston, Medical award of Excellence, Cancer Counseling, Certificate of Meritorious Service for outstanding contbn. to prostate disease research, Uniformed Services U. of the Health Sci. Mem.: AMA, Am. Med. Writers Assn., Soc. Surg. Oncology, Am. Urological Assn., Am. Cancer Soc. (pres.-elect 2002), Uniformed Svcs. Univ. of Health Sciences. Office: FDA Parklawn Bldg 14-71 HF-1 5600 Fishers Ln Rockville MD 20857 Office Phone: 301-827-2410. E-mail: andrew.voneschenbach@fda.hhs.gov.*

**VON FETTWEIS, YVONNE CACHÉ,** archivist, historian; b. L.A., Nov. 28, 1935; d. boyd Eugene and Georgette Louisa (Tilman) Adams; m. Maurice Lee Caché, Jan. 8, 1955 (div. 1962); children: Maurice C.B. II, Michele-Yvonne (Mrs. Vernon Young Jr.); m. Rolland Phillip von Fettweis, July 22, 1967. BA, Wagner Coll., 1954; postgrad, Am. U., 1973, Bentley Coll., 1981. Legal sec., asst. Judge, Davis, Stern, Orfinger & Tindall, Daytona Beach, Fla., 1961-66; head rec. sect., bd. dirs. 1st Ch. Christ Scientist, Boston, 1969-71, rsch. assoc., 1971-72, adminstrv. archivist, 1972-78, sr. assoc. archivist, 1979-84, records adminstr., 1984-91, div. mgr. records mgmt./orgnl. archives, 1991-92, divsn. mgr. ch. history, 1992—, divsn. mgr. ch. history and healing ministry, 1995; divsn. mgr. ch. history, 1995-96; ch. historian 1st Ch. Christ Scientist, Boston, 1996—. Cons. Christian Sci. Bd. Dirs., 1999—, pres. of Mother Ch., 2002-; mem. Religious Pub. Rels. Coun. Co-author: Mary Baker Eddy: A Lifetime of Healing, 1996, Mary Baker Eddy: Christian Healer, 1997, The New Woman and the New Church: The Lincoln Women, 2001. Trustee Ch. Hist. Trust, 1995—; exec. sec. Volusia County Goldwater campaign, Daytona Beach, 1964; mem. Christian Sci. Bd. Lectureship, 1998. Mem. Soc. Am. Archivists (editor The Archival Spirit), Automated Records and Techniques Task Force, Am. Mgmt. Assn., Orgn. Am. Historians, Ctr. for Study Presidency, Religious Pub. Rels. Coun., New Eng. Archivists, Assn. Records Mgrs. and Adminstrs. (bd. dirs. 1983—), Assn. Coll. and Rsch. Librs., Bay State Hist. League, Order Ea. Star, Order Rainbow (bd. dirs. 1972-77). Republican. Christian Scientist. Home: 147 Bosarvey Dr Ormond Beach FL 32176-6662

**VON FRAUNHOFER-KOSINSKI, KATHERINA,** bank executive, advertising executive; b. NYC; m. Jerzy Kosinski, Feb. 15, 1987 (dec. May 3, 1991). Student, St. Joseph's Convent, London, Clark's Coll. Various positions Robert W. Orr & Assocs., N.Y.C.; with traffic dept. Compton Advt., Inc., N.Y.C., 1956-63; acct. exec. J. Walter Thompson Co., N.Y.C., 1963-69; product mgr. Natural Wonder line Revlon Co., N.Y., 1969-71; pres. Scientia Factum, Inc., N.Y.C., 1971—, Polish Am. Resources Corp., N.Y.C., 1992—2000, pres., CEO, 1992—2002. Chmn. Am. Bank in Poland, 1990—2001. Co-founder Westchester Sports Club. Assoc. fellow Timothy Dwight Coll./Yale U., 1997—. Avocations: skiing, horse/polo, swimming, photography. Office: 60 W 57th St New York NY 10019-3909 Office Phone: 212-246-0128. Personal E-mail: sfi440@aol.com.

**VON FRIEDERICHS-FITZWATER, MARLENE MARIE,** researcher; b. Beatrice, Nebr., July 14, 1939; d. Paul M. and Velma B. (von Friederichs) Fitzwater; children: Richard Nielson, Kevin T. Young, James L. Nielson, Paul M. Nielson. BS, Westminster Coll., 1981; MA, U. Nebr., Omaha, 1981; PhD, U. Utah, 1987; cert. in death edn., Temple U., 1982. Various pub. rels., writing and editing positions, 1957-78; teaching fellow in comm. U. Nebr., Omaha, 1978-83, U. Utah, Salt Lake City, 1978-83; asst. prof. mass comm. U. So. Colo., Pueblo, 1983-85; prof. comm. studies Calif. State U., Sacramento, 1985—, chair comm. studies, 1996-2000; assoc. clin. prof. family practice Sch. Medicine U. Calif., Davis, 1987—, asst. adj. prof. internal medicine, 2003—, adj. asst. prof. hematology and oncology, 2005—; dir., outreach rsch. and edn. US Davis Cancer Ctr., 2000—. Condr. workshops on communication skills for health care profls. Bergan Mercy Hosp., Omaha, 1980-81, Mercy Care Ctr., Omaha, 1980-81, Am. Cancer Soc., 1981-82, Hospice of Salt Lake, Utah, 1981-82; condr. seminars, workshops and courses on health communication, death and dying, patient edn. and compliance, other related topics, 1983—; presenter in health communication various profl. orgn. meetings and confs., 1981—; dir., co-founder The Health Communication Rsch. Inst., Sacramento, 1988—. Contbr. articles to profl. jours. Trainer United Way, Sacramento, project mgr., 1986—; pres. bd. dirs. Hospice Care Sacramento, Inc., 1986-87; instr. vol. tng. program Hospice Consortium Sacramento; hospice vol. 1980—. Recipient Lifetime Achievement award Sacramento Pub. Rels. Assn., also numerous state, regional and nat. awards for writing, editing, publ. design and photography. Fellow Am. Acad. on Physician & Patient; mem. Internat. Communication Assn. (health communication div. newsletter editor 1987-89, sec. 1989-91), AAUP, Assn. Behavioral Scis. and Med. Edn., Assn. Women in Sci., Pub. Rels. Soc. Am. (bd. dirs. Calif. Capital

chpt. 1987-91), Soc. Tchrs. Family Medicine, Soc. Health Care Pub. Rels. and Mktg. No. Calif. Home: 5020 Hackberry Ln Sacramento CA 95841-4765 Office: Calif State U Communication Studies Dept 6000 J St Sacramento CA 95819-2605 Address: 3550 Watt Ave Ste 140 Sacramento CA 95821 Office Phone: 916-734-8810. E-mail: fitzm@heri.com.

**VON FURSTENBERG, BETSY,** actress, writer; b. Neiheim Heusen, Germany, Aug. 16, 1931; d. Count Franz-Egon and Elizabeth (Johnson) von F.; m. Guy Vincent de la Maisoneuve (div.); 2 children.; m. John J. Reynolds, Mar. 26, 1984. Attended Miss Hewitt's Classes, N.Y. Tutoring Sch.; prepared for stage with Sanford Meisner at Neighborhood Playhouse. Made Broadway stage debut in Second Threshold, N.Y., 1951; appeared in Dear Barbarians, 1952, Oh Men Oh Women, 1954, The Chalk Garden, 1955, Child of Fortune, 1956, Nature's Way, 1957, Much Ado About Nothing, 1959, Mary Mary, 1965, Paisley Convertible, 1967, Avanti, 1968, The Gingerbread Lady, 1970 (toured 1971), Absurd Person Singular, 1976; off Broadway appearances include For Love or Money, 1951; toured in Petrified Forest, Jason and Second Man, 1952; appeared in Josephine, 1953; subsequently toured, 1955; What Every Woman Knows, 1955, The Making of Moo, 1958 (toured 1958), Say Darling, 1959, Wonderful Town, 1959, Season of Choice, 1959, Beyond Desire, 1967, Private Lives, 1968, Does Anyone Here Do the Peabody, 1976; appeared in Along Came a Spider, Theatre in the Park, N.Y.C., 1985; appeared in film Women Without Names, 1950; TV appearances include Robert Montgomery Show, Ed Sullivan Show, Alfred Hitchcock Presents, One Step Beyond, The Mike Wallace Show, Johnny Carson Show, Omnibus, Theatre of the Week, The Secret Storm, As the World Turns, Movie of the Week, Your Money or Your Wife, Another World; writer syndicated column More Than Beauty; contbr. articles to newspapers and mags. including N.Y. Times Sunday Arts and Leisure, Saturday Rev. of Literature, People, Good Housekeeping, Art News, Pan Am Travel; co-author: (novel) Mirror, Mirror, 1988; author, illustrator Grandmothers Surprise, 2004. Avocations: tennis, painting, photography.

**VON FURSTENBERG, DIANE,** fashion designer, writer, entrepreneur; b. Brussels, Dec. 31, 1946; arrived in US, 1969, naturalized, 2002; d. Leon L. and Liliane L. (Nahmias) Halfin; m. Eduard Egon von Furstenberg, July 16, 1969 (div.); children: Alexandre, Tatiana; m. Barry Diller, Feb. 2, 2001. Student, U. Madrid, 1965-66, U. Geneva, 1966-68. Founder, pres. Diane von Furstenberg Studio, L.P., N.Y.C., 1970—; pres. Diane von Furstenberg Ltd., N.Y.C.; founder Savvy, Paris, 1985. Pioneer TV shopping with creative and live on-air selling Silk Assets collection, 1992; returns to retail as designer DIANE line of signature dresses, including the wrap, 1997. Author: Diane Von Furstenberg's Book of Beauty; Beds, 1991, The Bath, 1993, The Table, 1996, DIANE: A Signature Life, 1998; contbg. editor Vanity Fair mag., 1993. Recipient Ellis Island Medal of Honor, 1986. Mem.: Coun. of Fashion Designers of Am. (pres. 2006—). *Honesty in all ways: honest products, honest and straight approach to needs.*

**VON FURSTENBERG, GEORGE MICHAEL,** economics professor, researcher; b. Germany, Dec. 3, 1941; arrived in U.S., 1961; m. Gabrielle M. Koblitz von Willmburg, June 9, 1967; 1 child, Philip G. PhD, Princeton U., 1967. Asst. prof. Cornell U., Ithaca, N.Y, 1966-70; assoc. prof. Ind. U., Bloomington, 1970-73, prof., 1976-78, Rudy prof. econs., 1983—2006; sr. staff economist Coun. Econ. Advisors, Washington, 1973-76; div. chief rsch. dept. IMF, Washington, 1978-83; Robert Bendheim prof. econ. and fin. policy Fordham U., NYC, 2000—03; rotating econ. program dir. NSF, 2006—. Project dir. Am. Coun. Life Ins., Washington, 1976—78; sr. advisor Brookings Instn., Washington, 1978—90; vis. sr. economist planning and analysis staff Dept. State, Washington, 1989—90; Bissell-Fulbright vis. prof. Can.-Am. rels. U. Toronto, 1994—95. Contbg. author, editor: The Government and Capital Formation, 1980, Capital, Efficiency and Growth, 1980, Acting Under Uncertainty: Multidisciplinary Conceptions, 1990, Regulation and Supervision of Financial Institutions in the NAFTA Countries and Beyond, 1997; editor: Internat. Money and Credit: The Policy Roles, 1983; co-author: Learning from the World's Best Central Bankers, 1998; co-editor: Monetary Unions and Hard Pegs: Effects on Trade, Financial Development, and Stability, 2004; assoc. editor: Rev. Econs. and Stats., 1987—92, Open Econs. Rev., 1997—, Jour. Econ. Asymmetries, 2004—; contbr. articles to profl. jours. Fulbright grantee, Poland, 1991—92. Mem.: Am. Econ. Assn., N.Am. Econs. and Fin. Assn. (pres. 2000). Roman Catholic. Avocation: tennis. Office: Indiana U Dept Economics Wylie Hall Bloomington IN 47405 Office Phone: 812-855-4764. Business E-Mail: vonfurst@indiana.edu.

**VONGERICHTEN, JEAN-GEORGES,** food service executive; b. Strasbourg, Alsace; arrived in U.S., 1985; Studied with chef Paul Hueberlin, Auberge de l'Ill. Worked with Paul Bocuse L'Oasis Market, Paris; worked with master chef Louis Outhier L'Oasis, France; chef Oriental Hotel, Bangkok; opened Meridian Hotel, Singapore, Mandarin Hotel, Hong Kong, Lafayette, Boston, 1985, exec. chef N.Y.C., 1986; opened Jo Jo, 1991, Vong, N.Y.C., London, 1995, Hong Kong, 1997, Chgo., 1999, Mercer Kitchen, N.Y.C., 1998, The Lipstick Cafe, Prime, Las Vegas, Nev., 1998, Dune, Bahamas, 2000, V Steakhouse, N.Y.C., 2004, 66, 2003, Spice Market, 2005, Perry St., 2005. Author: Simple Cuisine, Jean-Georges: Cooking at Home with a Four-Star Chef, 1998, Simple to Speculate, 2000; appeared Martha Stewart Show, Live! with Regis and Kathie Lee, Today Show, Good Morning Am., Food Network, (TV series) Julia's Kitchen with Master Chefs with Julia Child, 1995. Named Jo Jo Best New Restaurant of Yr., Esquire Mag., Chef of Yr., Outstanding Chef, James Beard Found., 1998; recipient four stars for Lafayette, N.Y. Times, three stars for Jo Jo, three stars for Vong, four stars for Jean Georges, 1997, Best New Restaurant award for Jean Georges, James Beard Found., 1998. Office: Jean Georges Mgmt LLC 111 Prince St New York NY 10012

**VON GIERKE, HENNING EDGAR,** biomedical science educator, former government official, researcher; b. Karlsruhe, Germany, May 22, 1917; arrived in U.S., 1947, naturalized, 1977; s. Edgar and Julie (Braun) Von Gierke; married; 2 children. Dipl. Ing., Karlsruhe Tech., 1943, Dr. Engr., 1944. Asst. in acoustics Karlsruhe Tech., 1944—47, lectr., 1946; cons. Aerospace Med. Research Labs, Wright-Patterson AFB, Ohio, 1947—54, chief bioacoustics br., 1954—63, dir. biodynamics and bionics div., 1963—88; assoc. prof. Ohio State U., 1963—88; clin. prof. Wright State U., 1980—. Mem. com. hearing bioacoustics and biomechanics NRC, 1953—93, chmn., 1990—93, bio-astronaut com. 1959—61; mem. adv. com., flight medicine and biology NASA, 1960—61. Author numerous tech. publs., book chpts.; patentee in field. Fellow: Am. Inst. Med. and Biol. Engring., Coll. Fellows, Aerospace Med. Assn. (v.p. 1966—67, E. Liljenkrantz award 1966, A.D. Tuttle award 1974, John Paul Stapp award 2004); mem. Environ. Scis. (hon.), Acoustical Soc. Am. (pres. 1979—80, Silver medal 1981, Gold medal 1999); mem.: Internat. Acad. Astronautics, Mil. Audiology Assn. (hon.), Biomed. Engring. Soc., Inst. Noise Ctrl. Engring., internat. Acad. Aviation and Space Medicine, NAE. Achievements include research in bioacoustics, acoustics, biomechanics and bioengineering. Home: 1325 Meadow Ln Yellow Springs OH 45387-1219

**VON HAKE, MARGARET JOAN,** librarian; b. Santa Monica, Calif., Oct. 27, 1933; d. Carl August and Inez Garnet (Johnson) von Hake. BA, La Sierra U., 1955; MS in Library Sci., U. So. Calif., 1963. Tchr. Newbury Park (Calif.) Acad., 1955-60, librarian, 1957-60; circulation librarian Columbia Union Coll., Takoma Park, Md., 1962—67, library dir., 1967—, assoc. prof., 1990—2005, prof., 2005—. Mem. ALA, Md. Libr. Assn., Congress of Acad. Libr. Dirs. of Md. (pres. 1999-2000), Md. Ind. Coll.and Univ. Assn. Libr. Dirs. Round Table (chair 1996-98), Assn. Seventh Day Adventist Librs. (newsletter editor 1981-83, pres. 1989-90), Adventist Libr. Info. Cooperative Council (chair 2005—), Sligo Federated Music Club (pres. 1988-89, yearbook co-editor 2000—). Republican. Office: Columbia Union Coll 7600 Flower Ave Takoma Park MD 20912-7796 Office Phone: 301-891-4219.

**VON HILSHEIMER, GEORGE EDWIN, III,** neuropsychologist; b. West Palm Beach, Fla., Aug. 15, 1934; s. George E. Jr. and Dorothy Sue (Bridges) Von H.; m. Catherine Jean Munson, Dec. 27, 1968 (div. Oct. 1987); children:

Dana Ghermine, George E., Alexandra; m. Jonnie Mae Warner, June 29, 1991; stepchildren: Dennis Warner, Derek Warner. BA, U. Miami, 1955; PhD, Saybrook Inst., 1977. Diplomate Acad. Psychosomatic Medicine, Am. Bd. Behavioral Medicine, Am. Acad. Pain Mgmt., Am. Bd. Cert. Managed Care Providers, Am. Acad. Psychol. Treating Addiction. Nat. Register Neurofeedback. Sr. min. Humanitas, NYC, 1959-64; headmaster Summerlane Sch., North Branch, NY, 1964-69; supt. Green Valley Sch., Orange City, Fla., 1969-74; neuropsychologist Growth Insts., Twyman's Mill, Va., 1974-79, Growth Inst., DeLand, Fla., 1980-82; assoc. health profl. Maitland, Fla., 1982—2006; pvt. practice biofeedback trainer and hypnotist, 1998—. Cons. Pres. Kennedy's Commn. Nat. Vol. Svc., Juvenile Del., Migratory Labor, 1963-64, Sci. Adv. Bd. EPA, Washington, 1974-84; chmn. Cert. Bd., Internat. Coll. Environ. Medicine, 1991-94; mem. Bd. Assn. Diagnostic Efficiency and Brief Therapy, dir. curriculum, 1993-94; cons. Queen St. Psychiatric Hosp., 1982, Ont. Correctional Inst., Toronto, 1984-95. Author: How to Live With Your Special Child, 1970, Understanding Problems of Children, 1975, Allergy, Toxins and the LD Child, 1977, Psychobiology of Delinquents, 1978, Depression Is Not a Disease, 1989, Brief Therapy, 1993, Brief Therapy: Antecedent Scientific Principles, 1994; editor Human Learning, Washington, 1974-94; editor: Jour. of ANT, ANT Trails, 1998—. Mem. spl. bd. Fla. Symphony Orch., 1992-93. With mil. intelligence U.S. Army, 1957-59. Fellow Royal Soc. Health (life), Internat. Coll. Applied Nutrition, Acad. Psychosomatic Medicine; mem. Assn. Neurotrainers (pres. 1998), Toastmasters, Phi Kappa Phi, Omicron Delta Kappa, Alpha Sigma Phi. Mem. Ch. Of Brethren. Achievements include establishment of minor physical anomalies as significant predictor of physical and mental disease; demonstrated that treatment by neurofeedback significantly reduced criminal recidivism and that delinquency is a function of physical disease; demonstrated that ADHD and pain respond to neurofeedback; introduced treatment of schizophrenia by neurofeedback through Electro Dermal Response; introduced treatment of irritable bowel syndrome by neurofeedback; contributor to proof that alcoholism responds to EEG biofeedback. Office: AAT 125 S Swoope Ave Ste 109 Maitland FL 32751-5784 Office Phone: 407-644-6464. Personal E-mail: drvonh@mindspring.com.

**VON HIPPEL, ERIC ARTHUR,** innovation educator; b. Boston, Aug. 27, 1941; s. Arthur Robert and Dagmar von Hippel; m. Jessie Roberta Janjigian; children: Christiana Dagmar, Eric James. BA, Harvard U., Cambridge, Mass., 1964; MS, MIT, 1966; PhD, Carnegie-Mellon U., Pitts., 1973; D in econ. (hon.), Ludwig Maximilans Univ., 2004. Engring. mgr. Graphic Sciences, Inc., Danbury, Conn., 1966—69; cons. McKinsey and Co., N.Y.C., 1970—72; prof. Sloan School of Management, MIT, Cambridge, 1973—; head Innovation and Entrepreneurship Group. Pres. Lead User Concepts Inc, Cambridge, 1996—. Author: The Sources of Innovation, 1988, Democratizing Innovation, 2005; contbr. articles to scholarly jours. Named Sir Walter Scott Disting. Prof., Australian Grad. Sch. Mgmt., 1997—98; fellow, Canadian Inst. for Advanced Rsch., 1995—97; grantee, NSF, Alfred P. Sloan Found., 3M; Nortel Networks; NYNEX; Xerox; Bush,Boake,Allen,Bell-Atlantic. Achievements include patents for facsimile technology. Avocation: industrial archaeology. Office: MIT Rm E52-566 50 Memorial Dr Cambridge MA 02141 Business E-Mail: evhippel@mit.edu.

**VON HIPPEL, PETER HANS,** chemistry professor, researcher; b. Goettingen, Germany, Mar. 13, 1931; came to U.S., 1937, naturalized, 1942; s. Arthur Robert and Dagmar (franck) von H.; m. Josephine Baron Raskind, June 20, 1954; children: David F., James A., Benjamin J. BS, MIT, Cambridge, Mass., 1952; MS, MIT, 1953, PhD, 1955. Phys. biochemist Naval Med. Research Inst., Bethesda, Md., 1956-59; instr. asst. prof. to assoc. prof. biochemistry Med. Sch. Dartmouth Coll., 1959-67; prof. chemistry, mem. Inst. Molecular Biology U. Oreg., 1967-79, dir. Inst. Molecular Biology, 1969-80, chmn. dept. chemistry, 1980-87; rsch. prof. chemistry Am. Cancer Soc., 1989—. Chmn. biopolymers Gordon Conf., 1968; mem. trustees vis. com. biology dept. MIT, 1973—76; mem. bd. sci. counsellors Nat. Inst. Arthritis, Metabolic and Digestive Diseases NIH, 1974—78, mem. coun. Nat. Inst. Gen. Med. Scis., 1982—86, mem. dir.'s adv. com., 1987—92; bd. dirs. Fedn. Am. Socs. for Exptl. Biology, 1994—98; mem. NIH-CSR panel on boundaries for sci. rev., 1998—2003, mem. joint steering com. for pub. policy, 1998—. Mem. editl. bd. Jour. Biol. Chemistry, 1967-73, 76-82, Biochem. Biophys. Acta, 1965-70, Physiol. Revs., 1972-77, Biochemistry, 1977-80, Trends in Biochem. Soc., 1987—, Protein Sci., 1990-95; editor Jour. Molecular Biology, 1986-94; contbr. articles to profl. jours., chpts. to books. Lt. M.S.C. USNR, 1956-59. Recipient Merck award Am. Soc. Biochem. and Molecular Biology, 2000; NSF predoctoral fellow, 1953-55; NIH postdoctoral fellow, 1955-56; NIH sr. fellow, 1959-67; Guggenheim fellow, 1973-74 Fellow: Biophys. Soc., Am. Acad. Arts and Scis.; mem.: AAAS, Am. Philosophic Soc., Fedn. Am. Scientists, Nat. Acad. Scis., Biophys. Soc. (coun. 1970—73, pres. 1973—74), Am. Soc. Biochem. and Molecular Biology, Am. Chem. Soc., Sigma Xi. Home: 1900 Crest Dr Eugene OR 97405-1753 E-mail: petevh@molbio.uoregon.edu.

**VON HOFF, DANIEL DOUGLAS,** oncologist; b. Oshkosh, Wis., Apr. 29, 1947; BS, Carroll Coll., 1969; MD, Columbia U., 1973. Diplomate Am. Bd. Internal Medicine, Am. Bd. Oncology. Intern in internal medicine U. Calif., San Francisco, 1973-74, resident in internal medicine, 1974-75; med. oncology fellow Nat. Cancer Inst.; mem. faculty medicine U. Tex. Health Sciences Ctr., San Antonio, 1975—99; joined faculty U. Ariz. Health Sciences Center, 1999, prof. medicine, molecular and cell biology, and pathology, dir. Ariz. Cancer Ctr., dir. Cancer Therapeutics Program, 2003; exec. v.p., dir. translational drug devel. divsn., head pancreatic cancer rsch. program Translational Genomics Rsch. Inst. (TGen), Phoenix, 2003, now sr. investigator, dir. translational rsch. Mem. Nat. Cancer Adv. Bd., 2004—, acting chair, 2005—. Recipient Weinberg Award, Dana Farber Cancer Ctr., Harvard Med. Sch., Black Award, Ohio State U., 2003, Frances P. Bull Award, U. Mich. Comprehensive Cancer Ctr. and Divsn. Hematology/Oncology, 2003. Fellow Am. Coll. Physicians; mem. AMA, Am. Assn. Cancer Rsch. (pres. 1999-2000; Richard and Hinda Rosenthal Found. award 1997), Am. Soc. Clin. Oncology. Office: Translational Genomics Rsch Inst Ste 660 445 N 5th St Phoenix AZ 85004*

**VON HOFFMAN, NICHOLAS,** writer, retired reporter; b. N.Y.C., Oct. 16, 1929; s. Carl and Anna (Bruenn) von H.; m. Ann Byrne, 1950 (div.); children: Alexander, Aristodemos, Constantine; m. Patricia Bennett, 1979 (div.). Grad., Fordham Prep. Sch., 1948. Assoc. dir. Indsl. Area Found., Chgo., 1954-63; mem. staff Chgo. Daily News, 1963-66, Washington Post, 1966—76; columnist N.Y. Observer, 1993—; contbg. writer Archtl. Digest, 1996—. Author: Mississippi Notebook, 1964, Multiversity, 1966, We Are The People Our Parents Warned Us Against, 1968, Two, Three, Many More, 1969, Left at The Post, 1970, (with Garry Trudeau) Fireside Watergate, 1973, Tales From the Margaret Mead Taproom, 1976, Make-Believe Presidents: Illusions of Power from McKinley to Carter, 1978, Organized Crimes, 1984, Citizen Cohn, 1988, Capitalist Fools, 1992, Hoax, 2004, Devil's Dictionary of Business, 2005; also articles.

**VON HOLDEN, MARTIN HARVEY,** psychologist; b. Bronx, N.Y., May 29, 1942; s. Leon and Gertrude (Fishbein) Von H.; m. Virginia T. Brown, Dec. 17, 1971; 1 child, Mark Walter; children by previous marriage: Sandi Gwen Bitton, David Lawrence; 1 stepchild, Theresa Ann Brilli-Rogers. BA, NYU, 1964; MA, U. Toledo, 1965; D Pub. Adminstrn., NYU, 1981. Sr. psychologist N.Y. State Dept. Mental Hygiene, Rockland State Hosp., Orangeberg, 1966-67, team leader, 1970-71, dir. interdisciplinary tng. team, 1971-73; chief of service Metro Unit Harlem Valley Psychiat. Ctr., Wingdale, NY, 1973-74, dep. dir. programs, 1974-75; dep. dir. treatment svcs. Pilgrim Psychiat. Ctr., West Brentwood, NY, 1975-76; dir. Matteawan State Hosp., Beacon, NY, 1977, Ctrl. N.Y. Psychiat. Ctr., Marcy, NY, 1977-82; exec. dir. Rochester (N.Y.) Psychiat. Ctr., 1982-97; privatization project mgr. Fla. Dept. Children & Families, Tallahassee, 1997-98; from svc. team coord. to adminstr. G. Pierce Wood Meml. Hosp., Arcadia, Fla., 1998-2000; adminstr. G. Pierce Wood Meml., Arcadia, Fla., 2000—02; ops. mgmt. cons. mgr. DeSoto Juvenile Correctional Facility, 2002—06; cons. mental health Fla. Dept. Juvenile Justice, 2006—. Assoc. dir. Inst. Motivation Rsch., Croton-on-

Hudson, N.Y., 1965-73; dir. Martin H. Von Holden Assocs., motivation rsch., Fairlawn, N.J., 1970-74; cons. psychologist, group therapist Green Haven Correctional Facility, Stormville, N.Y., 1970-77; cons. psychologist, group therapist Auburn (N.Y.) Correctional Facility, 1977-94, Butler Correctional Facility, 1994-96, Willard Drug Treatment Ctr., 1997; clin. assoc. prof. dept. psychiatry Sch. Medicine, U. Rochester, 1983-97; cons. in field; spkr. in field. Contbr. articles to profl. jours. Mem. adv. comn. N.Y. State Commn. Quality Care to Mentally Disabled, 1989-97. Capt. MSC, U.S. Army, 1967-70. Recipient James Gordon Bennett prize NYU, 1964, Outstanding Achievement award United Way of N.Y. State, 1994. Fellow Am. Assn. Mental Health Adminstrs. (cert. mental health adminstr.); mem. Am. Psychol. Assn., Am. Correctional Assn., Am. Assn. Correctional Psychologists, Assn. Facility Dirs. N.Y. State Office Mental Health (pres. 1984-85), Order of Arrow, Psi Chi Jewish. Home: 1250 Peppertree Ln Port Charlotte FL 33952-1357 Office Phone: 863-990-0739. Personal E-mail: vonholden@comcast.net.

**VON KAENEL, HOWARD J.,** army officer; b. Ft. Knox, Ky., Oct. 26, 1946; BS, U.S. Mil. Acad., 1969; Rhodes Scholar, MA in Philosophy, Politics and Econs., Oxford (Eng.) U., 1973. Commd. 2d lt. U.S. Army, 1969, advanced through grades to maj. gen., with field arty., 1969, regimental / DIVARTY comdr., 1989—91; comdg. gen. III Corps Arty., Ft. Sill, Okla., 1992-94; dep. under sec. for policy Office of Sec. of Def., Washington, 1994-96; dep. dir. strategy, plans and policy directorate Office of Dep. Chief Staff for Ops. and Plans, Washington, 1996, dir. strategy, plans and policy directorate, 1996-98; mil. dep. for internat. affairs Office of Dep. Under Sec. of Army, Washington, 1998—, acting dep. under Sec. of Army for Internat. affairs, 1999. MIT seminar XXI, 1986; sr. fellow Brookings Instn., 1989. Decorated Def. DSM, Legion of Merit with 2 oak leaf clusters, Bronze Star medal with 3 oak leaf clusters, others.

**VON KALINOWSKI, JULIAN ONESIME,** lawyer; b. St. Louis, May 19, 1916; s. Walter E. and Maybelle (Michaud) von K.; m. Penelope Jayne Dyer, June 29, 1980; children by previous marriage: Julian Onesime, Wendy Jean von Kalinowski. BA, Miss. Coll., 1937; JD with honors, U. Va., 1940. Bar: Va. 1940, Calif. 1946. Assoc. Gibson, Dunn and Crutcher, L.A., 1946-52, ptnr., 1953-85, mem., chmn. exec. com., 1962—, adv. ptnr., 1985—; CEO, chmn. Litigation Scis., Inc., Culver City, Calif., 1991-94, chmn. emeritus Torrance, Calif., 1994-96, Dispute Dyamics, Inc., Torrance, Calif., 1996-2000. Instr. antitrust law So. Meth. Sch. of Law, 1982-84, bd. visitors, 1982-85; bd. dirs. W.M. Keck Found.; faculty Practising Law Inst., 1971, 76, 78-80; spkr. spl. program on antitrust litigation Columbia U. Law Sch., NYC, 1981; lawyers dels. com. to 9th Cir. Jud. Conf., 1953-67; UN expert Mission to People's Republic China, 1982. Contbr. articles to legal jours.; author: Antitrust Laws and Trade Regulation, 1969, desk edit., 1981; gen. editor: World Law of Competition, 1978, Antitrust Counseling and Litigation Techniques, 1984; gen. editor emeritus Antitrust Report. With USN, 1941-46, capt. Res. ret. Fellow Am. Bar Found., Am. Coll. Trial Lawyers (chmn. complex litigation com. 1984-87); mem. ABA (ho. of dels. 1970, chmn. antitrust law sect. 1972-73), State Bar Calif. (Anti-Trust Lawyer of Yr. award 2002), L.A. Bar Assn., U. Va. Law Sch. Alumni Assn. (mem. deans adv. coun.), Calif. Club, L.A. Country Club, La Jolla Beach and Tennis Club, Phi Kappa Psi, Phi Alpha Delta. Episcopalian. Home and Office: 12320 Ridge Cir Los Angeles CA 90049-1151 Office Phone: 310-472-1977.

**VON KAPPELHOFF, DORIS See DAY, DORIS**

**VON KLEMPERER, KLEMENS,** historian, educator; b. Berlin, Nov. 2, 1916; came to U.S., 1938; s. Herbert O. and Frieda (Kuffner) Von K.; m. Elizabeth Lee Gallaher, Dec. 19, 1953; children— Catharine Lee, James Alfred Abitur, Französisches Gymnasium, Berlin, 1934; MA, Harvard U., 1940, PhD, 1949; MA, Cambridge U., 1974. Vis. prof. Stanford U., Palo Alto, Calif., 1960; prof. history Bonn U., Fed. Republic Germany, 1963-64; L. Clark Seelye prof. history Smith Coll., Northampton, Mass., 1960-87, prof. emeritus, 1987—. Vis. prof. Amherst (Mass.) Coll., 1989, 91, 96; vis. fellow Trinity Coll., Oxford, Eng., 1982. Author: Germany's New Conservatism, 1957, Mandate for Resistance, 1969, Ignaz Seipel: Christian Statesman, 1972, German Resistance Against Hitler: The Search for Allies Abroad 1938-1945, 1992, The German Incertitudes, 1914-1945, 2000; editor: A Noble Combat. The Letters of Shiela Grant Duff and Adam von Trott, 1988, "Für Deutschland" Die Männer des 20 Juli, 1994; contbr. articles to profl. jours. Served with AUS, 1943-46, ETO Recipient Austrian Cross of Honor for Sci. and Art 1st class, 1997; Guggenheim Found. fellow, 1957-58; Fulbright fellow, 1957-58, 63-64; Overseas fellow Churchill Coll., Cambridge, Eng., 1973-74; Inst. for Advanced Study fellow, Berlin, 1986; Am. Philos. Soc. grantee, 1977-78, Am. Council of Learned Socs. grantee, 1978-79 Mem. Am. Hist. Soc. (chmn. conf. group for central European history 1982-83) Clubs: Century (N.Y.C.). Avocations: mountain climbing, hiking. Home: 23 Washington Ave Northampton MA 01060-2822 Office: Smith Coll Northampton MA 01063-0001 Office Phone: 413-585-3705. Business E-mail: kvonklem@smith.edu.

**VON KLITZING, KLAUS,** research facility administrator, physicist; b. Schroda, Poland, June 28, 1943; s. Bogislav and Anny (Ulbrich) von K.; m. Renate Falkenberg, May 27, 1971; children: Andreas, Christine, Thomas. Diploma, Tech. U. Braunschweig, 1969; PhD, U. Wuerzburg, 1972; Habilitation, 1978. Faculty mem. Tech. U., Munich, 1980-84; dir. Max Planck Inst. FKF, Stuttgart, 1985—; hon. prof. Stuggart U., 1985. Rschr. Clarendon Lab., Oxford, 1975—76, high Magnetic Field Lab., Grenoble, 1979—80. Recipient Nobel prize in physics Royal Swedish Acad. Sci., 1985. Mem.: German Physical Soc. (hon.). Achievements include discovery of the quantized Hall effect. Office: Max Planck Inst Feskörperforschung Heisenbergstr 1 D-70569 Stuttgart Germany*

**VON KOHORN, BARON RALPH STEVEN,** retired investment banker; b. Chemnitz, Germany, Dec. 14, 1919; arrived in N.Z., 1963; s. Baron Oscar and Valerie (Wirth) von K.; m. Jillian Annette Bussell, Feb. 25, 1967; children by previous marriage: Karen Janne, Kirk Steven. Student, U. So. Calif., U. Mich. Dep. chmn. various world wide bus. orgns., 1945-62; ret. Settlor von Kohorn Family Trust Controlling Genrock Group of Cos., N.Z. and Australia. Author: Abstract Paintings by Forty New Zealand Artists, 1966; What You Always Wanted to Know about Single Sideband Radio and Never Dared to Ask, 1976, VHF/FM Marine Radio, 1977, Columbia Cruises South, 1977, Columbia Cruises North, 1978, Management of a General Ancillary Licence for Clubs, 1978, Your Guide to Marine Search and Rescue, 1980; co-author, cartographer: A Cruising Man's Guide to the Marlborough Sounds, 1979, A Cruising Guide-Cape Palliser to Marlborough Sounds and Tasman Bay, 1982, The Sounds Crusing Guide, including Cape Palliser to Farewell Spit, 1986, The Cohorn Clan, 1987, The Cohorn Clan 2, 1988, New Zealand Cruising Guide-Central Area, 1989, 2d edit., 1994, 3rd edit., 1999, The Cohorn Clan 3, 1996. Founding sr. v.p., dir. Am. C. of C., 1965-74; bd. dirs. Am. Edn. Found. (Fulbright), 1965-94, Kennedy Meml. Fellowship, 1972-94, East-West Ctr., Honolulu, 1972-78; selector Eisenhower Fellowships, 1966-68, 78, 81, 86; trustee Wellington Visual Arts Trust, 1968-72, Found. for Newborn Child, 1977-96, N.Z. Oral History Archives, 1981-94, Wellington Maritime Mus., 1989-96, founder, pres.; trustee, dir. N.Z. Sports Found., 1977-85, gov., 1986-94, hon. life mem.; nat. treas. N.Z. Water Safety Coun., 1979-87, Small Boat Safety Com., 1977-90; com. chmn. N.Z. Yachting Fedn., hon. life mem. Recipient Graham Hayter trophy, 1973-74, 78-79; Lane Bryant Internat. Vol. award, 1969, Water Safety award Minister of Internal Affairs, 1987, Merit award Minister of Transport, 1987, Outstanding Vol. Svc. award Wellington, N.Z., 1987, Tribute of Appreciation award U.S. Govt., 1987, N.Z. Yacht Cruising award. Fellow Inst. Dirs. (London), N.Z. Inst. Mgmt. (counselor); mem. Royal Yachting Assn. (London, life), Past Commodores Assn. N.Z. (pres.), Internat. Order Past Commodores (internat. v.p. 1982-93, v.p. emeritus 1993—, hon. life mem., patron 1996), N.Z. Am. Assn., Wellington Planetarium Soc. (vice-chmn. 1968-73), Inst. Advanced Motorists (life, vice-chmn. 1969-73), Mus. Wellington (life, boardroom named in his honor), Nat. Press Club, Wellesley Club (Wellington), Tattersalls Club (Sydney), U. Club, Royal N.Z. Yacht Club, Royal Port Nicholson Yacht Club (life), Mana

Cruising Club (life, past commodore) Home: Herbert Gardens 186 The Terrace Wellington New Zealand Home (Summer): 122 Alexandra Parade Alexandra Headland QLD 4575 Australia

**VON MEHREN, GEORGE M.,** lawyer; b. Boston, Nov. 2, 1950; AB, Harvard U., 1972, JD, 1977; BA, Cambridge U., Eng., 1974, MA, 1985. Bar: Ohio 1977, registered: US Supreme Ct., US Ct. Appeals (6th cir.), US Dist. Ct. (No. Dist.) Ohio. Assoc. Squire, Sanders & Dempsey LLP, Cleve., 1977-86, ptnr., 1986—, co-chmn. Internat. Litig. Practice Group, 1998—. Contbr. articles to profl. jours.; spkr. in field. Mem.: ABA, Fed. Bar Assn., Ohio State Bar Assn., Union Club. Office: Squire Sanders & Dempsey 127 Public Sq Ste 4900 Cleveland OH 44114-1304 Office Phone: 216-479-8614. Office Fax: 216-479-8780. Business E-Mail: gvonmehren@ssd.com.

**VON MEHREN, ROBERT BRANDT,** retired lawyer; b. Albert Lea, Minn., Aug. 10, 1922; s. Sigurd Anders and Eulalia Marion (Anderson) von M.; m. Mary Katharine Kelly, June 26, 1948 (dec. Mar. 1985); children: Carl S., John M. (dec.), Katharine, Jane, Margaret; m. Susan Heller Anderson, Apr. 2, 1988. BA summa cum laude with philosophical oration, Yale U., 1943; LLB magna cum laude, Harvard U., 1946. Bar: N.Y. 1946, U.S. Supreme Ct. 1954. Law clk. to Judge Learned Hand U.S. Ct. Appeals (2d cir.), 1946-47; law clk. to Assoc. Justice Stanley Reed U.S. Supreme Ct., 1947-48; assoc. Debevoise & Plimpton, N.Y.C., 1946, 48-57, ptnr., 1957-93, of counsel, 1994-95, ret., 1995. Arbitrator in internat. and other matters; sr. lectr. in law Wharton Sch. U. Pa., Phila., 1985-86; legal counsel Prep. Commn. for Internat. Atomic Energy Agy., N.Y.C., 1956-57; trustee Practising Law Inst., N.Y.C., 1972-96, emeritus, 1996, pres., 1979-86, chmn. bd., 1986-96. Bd. editors Harvard Law Rev., 1944-46, Am. Jour. Internat. Law, 1981-89, hon. editor, 1990-2000; contbr. articles to profl. jours. Trustee Axe Houghton Found., N.Y.C., 1965—; bd. dirs. Legal Aid Soc., N.Y.C., 1966-70; pres. Harvard Law Sch. Assn. N.Y., 1982-83. Mem. Assn. Bar City N.Y., Internat. Law Assn. (vice chmn. 1989—, pres. Am. br. 1978-86, chmn. exec. com. 1986-92), Coll. of Comml. Arbitrators, Coun. on Fgn. Rels., Univ. Club, Century Assn. N.Y.C., The Comml. Bar Assn. Home: 925 Park Ave New York NY 10028-0210 Office: 919 3rd Ave 46th Fl New York NY 10022 Office Phone: 212-909-6588. Business E-Mail: rbvonmeh@debevoise.com.

**VON MERING, OTTO OSWALD,** anthropology educator; b. Berlin, Oct. 21, 1922; came to Switzerland, 1933, to U.S., 1939, naturalized, 1954; s. Otto O. and Henriette (Troeger) von M.; m. Shirley Ruth Brook, Sept. 11, 1954; children: Gretchen, Karin, Gregory, Hilary, Celia. Grad., Belmont Hill Sch., 1940; BA in History, Williams Coll., 1944; PhD in Social Anthropology, Harvard U., 1956. Instr. Belmont Hill Sch., Belmont, Mass., 1945-47, Boston U., 1947-48, Cambridge Jr. Coll., 1948-49; rsch. asst. lab. social rels. Harvard U., 1950-51, Boston Psychopathic Hosp., 1951-53; Russell Sage Found. fellow N.Y.C., 1953-55; asst. prof. social anthropology U. Pitts. Coll. Medicine, 1955-60, assoc. prof., 1960-65, prof. social anthropology, 1965-71; prof. child devel. and child care U. Pitts. Coll. Allied Health Professions, 1969-71; prof. anthropology and family medicine U. Fla., 1971-76, prof. anthropology in ob-gyn, 1979-84, prof. anthropology and gerontology, 1986-96, prof. anthropology and gerontology emeritus, 1998, joint prof. dept. medicine, coll. medicine, 1994-96. Lectr. Sigmund Freud Inst., Frankfurt, Germany, 1962-64, Pitts. Psychoanalytical Inst., 1960--71, Interuniv. Forum, 1967-71; tech. adviser Maurice Falk Med. Fund, 1964-75; Fulbright vis. lectr., 1962-63; Richard-Merton guest prof. Heidelberg U., Germany, 1962-63; vis. prof. Dartmouth, 1970-71; vis. lectr. continuing edn. Med. Coll. Pa., 1990-92, vis. lectr. U. Sheffield, Eng.,1995, U. Liverpool, 1995, U. Augsburg, 1997, U. Heidelberg, 1997; hon. vis. prof. U. Coll. London Med. Sch., 1997; bd. dirs. Tech. Assistance Assocs., U. Fla., 1979-84; supr. grad. study program Ctr. Gerontologic Studies, U. Fla., 1983-85, assoc. dir. 1985-86, dir. 1986-96, prof. emeritus 1998; mem. coordinating com. Geriatric Edn. Ctr. Coll. Medicine, U. Fla., 1986-96; mem. med. selection com. Coll. Medicine U. Fla., 2000—; mem. adv. bd. nursing programs Santa Fe C.C., 2001—; mem. nat. tech. expert panel on long-term care Health Care Financing Adminstrn., Washington; mem. adv. bd. Internat. Exch. Ctr. on Gerontology State U. System of Fla., 1987-92; adv. bd. Second Season Broadcasting Network, Palm Beach, Fla., 1989-92, Fla. Policy Exch. Ctr. on Aging, State U. System Fla., 1991-95, Assoc. Health Industries of Fla., Inc., Nat. Shared Housing Resource Ctr., Balt.; cons. mental hosps. Author: Remotivating the Mental Patient, 1957, A Grammar of Human Values, 1961, (with Mitscherlich and Brocher) Der Kranke in der Modernen Gesellschaft, 1967, (with Kasdan) Anthropology in the Behavioral and Health Sciences, 1970, (with Maria Alvarez) Aging, Demography and Well-Being in Latin America, 1989; (with R. Binstock and L. Cluff) The Future of Long Term Care, 1996; also articles; commentary editor: Human Organization, 1974-76; corr. editor Jour. Geriatric Psychiatry, 1990-98; mem. editl. bd. Med. Anthropology, 1976-84, Enbl. Gerontology, 1990-2005, Australasian Leisure for Pleasure Jour., 1995-2000, Jour. Cross-Cultural Gerontology, 1996-2002. Mem. nat. adv. bd. Nat. Shared Housing Resource Ctr., 1994-95; pres. Dedicated Alt. Resources for the Elderly, 1996-98; mem., bd. dirs. No. Ctrl. Fla. chpt. Alzheimer's Assn., 1996—2002; bd. dirs. Shepherd's Ctrs. Am., Gainesville, 1998-2000; adv. bd. nursing programs, Santa Fe C.C., Gainesville, 2001—. Recipient Fulbright-Hayes Travel award, 1962-63, Gerontological Pioneer award for profl. lifetime of exemplary achievement, So. Gerontological Soc., 2005; grantee Wenner-Gren Found., N.Y., 1962-63, Am. Philos. Soc., 1962-63, Maurice Falk Med. Fund, 1970-71, US-DHHS, 1979-83, Walter Reed Army Inst. Rsch., 1987-91, US-ADA/Fla. Dept. Elder Affairs, 1993-94, Rockefeller Bros. Fund, 1950-51; spl. fellow NIMH, 1971-72. Fellow AAAS, Am. Anthrop. Assn. (mem. James Mooney award com. 1978-81, vis. lectr. 1961,-62, 71-74, 91-92), Am. Gerontol. Soc., Royal Soc. Health, Acad. Psychosomatic Medicine, Am. Ethnological Soc., Soc. Applied Anthropology, Royal Anthrop. Inst.; mem. Assn. Am. Med. Colls., Assn. Anthrop. Gerontol. (pres.-elect 1991-92, pres. 1992-93), Am. Fedn. Clin. Research, Am. Public Health Assn., Canadian Assn. Gerontology, British Soc. Gerontology, So. Gerontol. Soc. (Gerontol. Pioneer honor 2005), Med. Group Mgmt. Assn., World Fedn. Mental Health, Internat. Assn. Social Psychiatry (regional counselor 1973-81), Internat. Hosp. Fedn., Myrtle Age Internat. (London). Home: 818 NW 21st St Gainesville FL 32603-1027 Office: U Fla Ctr Gerontological Studies Turlington Hall Gainesville FL 32611 Office Phone: 352-376-9512. *Three guides to conduct I value most: always search for the best fit of fact, argument, and experience. Every first remedy must be amended quickly. When the past disturbs the present, more work on the future is needed.*

**VON MOLNÁR, STEPHAN,** physics professor, director; 2 children. BS in Physics, Trinity Coll., Hartford, Conn., 1957; MS in Physics, U. Maine, Orono, 1959; PhD in Physics, U. Calif., Riverside, 1965. Mem. rsch. staff DuPont & Co., Wilmington, Del., 1959—60, IBM Thomas J. Watson Rsch. Ctr., Yorktown Heights, NY, 1965—93, mgr. coop. phenomena group, 1970—89, sr. mgr. novel structure physics, 1989—93; prof. physics, dir. ctr. materials rsch. & tech. Fla. State U., Tallahassee, 1994—. Recipient Alexander von Humboldt Sr. U.S. Scientist award, 1986. Fellow: Am. Phys. Soc.; mem.: AAAS, Materials Rsch. Soc. Office: Florida State University 406 Keen Building Tallahassee FL 32306-4351 Office Phone: 850-644-5075. Office Fax: 850-644-6504. E-mail: molnar@martech.fsu.edu.

**VON MOSCH, WANDA GAIL,** middle school educator; b. Richmond, Va., Jan. 21, 1952; d. Jesse James, Sr. and Thelma Arleen (Bruce) Perdue; m. Carl Allan Von Mosch, June 24, 1978; children: Carl Allan Jr., Sarah Ashley, Karle Danielle. BS, Longwood Coll., 1974; MS in Ednl. Leadership, Old Dominion U., 2005. Tchr. pub. schs. City of Hampton, Va., 1974-77, City of Virginia Beach, Va., 1977—. Mem., planning coun., mem. faculty coun. Gt. Neck Mid. Sch., coord. ptnrs. edn., comm. liaison; coord., forensics coach Odyssey of Mind, Gt. Neck, 1997—98; adj. instr. career switcher program Old Dominion U. Sunday sch. tchr. Va. Marine Sci. Mus., Virginia Beach, 1983—; Bethel Bible grad., tchr., 1990—; participant Malcolm Baldrige TQM procedure U.S. Congress for Ind. Learning; mem. PTA; mem. adminstrv. bd. Francis Asbury United Meth. Ch., Virginia Beach, 1986—, supt., 1991. Named Tchr. of the Yr., Walmart, 2002, Gt. Neck, 2002; recipient PTA award for Disting.

Svc., 1990. Mem.: NEA, Virginia Beach Tchr. Forum, Virginia Beach Reading Coun., Va. Math. League, Va. Reading Coun., Virginia Beach Edn. Assn., Va. Edn. Assn. Republican. Avocations: reading, cooking, music, board games, golf. Office: Great Neck Middle Sch North Great Neck Rd Virginia Beach VA 23454-1112

**VONNEGUT, KURT, JR.,** writer; b. Indpls., Nov. 11, 1922; s. Kurt and Edith Sophia (Lieber) V.; m. Jane Marie Cox, Sept. 1, 1945 (div. 1979); children: Mark, Edith, Nanette; adopted nephews: James, Steven and Kurt Adams; m. Jill Krementz, 1979, 1 child, Lily. Student, Cornell U., 1940-42, U. Chgo., 1945-47, MA in Anthropology, 1971. Reporter Chgo. City News Bur., 1946; pub. relations with Gen. Electric Co., 1947-50; free-lance writer N.Y.C., 1950-65, 74—; lectr. writers workshop U. Iowa, Iowa City, 1965-67; lectr. in English Harvard U., Cambridge, Mass., 1970; disting. prof. CCNY, 1973-74. Author: (fiction) Player Piano, 1951, Sirens of Titan, 1959, Mother Night, 1961, Cat's Cradle, 1963, God Bless You, Mr. Rosewater, 1964, Slaughterhouse-Five, 1969, Breakfast of Champions, 1973, Slapstick, or Lonesome No More, 1976, Jailbird, 1979, Deadeye Dick, 1982, Galápagos, 1985, Bluebeard, 1987, Hocus Pocus, 1990, Timequake, 1997, A Man Without a Country, 2005; (collected stories) Welcome to the Monkey House, 1968, Bagombo Snuff Box, 1999; (plays) Happy Birthday, Wanda June, 1970; (TV scripts) Between Time and Timbuktu or Prometheus-5, 1972; (essays) Wampeters, Foma and Granfalloons, 1974, Fates Worse Than Death, 1991, Timequake, 1997; (Christmas Story with illustrations by Ivan Chermayeff) Sun Moon Star, 1980; (autobiographical collage) Palm Sunday, 1981; (film appearances) Back to School, 1986, Mother Night, 1996, Breakfast of Champions, 1999 Served with inf. AUS, 1942-45. Guggenheim fellow, 1967-68. Mem. Nat. Inst. Arts and Letters (recipient Lit. award 1970). Office: c/o Donald C Farber of counsel Jacob Medinger & Finnegan LLP 1270 Avenue of the Americas New York NY 10020 Office Phone: 212-524-5035. Office Fax: 212-524-5037. Business E-Mail: dcfarber@jmfnylaw.com.

**VON PRINCE, KILULU MAGDALENE,** retired occupational therapist, sculptor; b. Bumbuli, Lushoto, Tanzania, Jan. 9, 1929; arrived in U.S., 1949; d. Tom Adalbert and Juliane (Martini). BA in Occupl. Therapy, San Jose State U., 1958, MS in Occupl. Therapy, 1972; EdD, U. So. Calif., 1980; doctorate in Higher Edn., 1978. Registered occupl. therapist; cert. work evaluator, work adjustment specialist. Commd. 2d lt. U.S. Army, 1959, advanced through grades to lt. col., staff asst. Denver, 1959-62; hand rehab. asst., hand therapy Walter Reed Army Med. Ctr., 1962-65; hand rehab. asst. occupl. therapist 97th Gen. Hosp., U.S. Army, Frankfurt, Germany, 1965-68; sr. occupl. therapist Inst. Surg. Rsch. U.S. Army, Ft. Sam Houston, Tex., 1967-70; dir. occupl. therapy clinic, sr. dir. clinics Tripler Army Med. Ctr., Honolulu, 1972-75; adminstr. occupl. therapy clinic, cons. LAMC U.S. Army, Presido, Calif., 1975; asst. evening coll. program San Jose CC, Calif., 1976-77; fellow allied health adminstrn. SUNY, Buffalo, 1978, Commonwealth U., Richmond, Va., 1978-79; staff project devel. pre-retirement program older adults De Anza Coll., Cupertino, Calif., 1980—81; project dir. Ctr. of Design, Palo Alto, 1980; part-time instr. Stroke Activity Ctr. Cabrillo Coll., Santa Cruz, Calif., 1981; dir. occupl. therapy clinics Presbyn. Med. Ctr., 1981-86; ptnr., mgr. retail store, 1986-89; dir. rehab. therapy Merrithew Meml. Hosp. Contra Costa Med. Ctr., Martinez, Calif., 1990-93; sculptor, 1993—; activity program coord. Calif. Womens Detention Facility, Chowchilla, 1994-97; ret., 1997. Co-author: Splinting of Burned Patients, 1974; producer videos: Elbow Splinting of the Burned Patient, 1970, Self-Instruction Unit: Principles of Elbow Splinting, 1971; contbr. articles to profl. jours. With U.S. Army, 1952—55. Decorated Legion of Merit; recipient Disting. Alumni Honors award San Jose State U., 1982, Best of Show award Nat. Veteran's Creative Arts Competition, Fresno Local Vet Art Show, 2004; honored by having Ballon painting to be first mosaic mural on Hwy. 168, Rotary Club, Fresno, 2006; scholar U.S. Surgeon Gen., 1972; fellow Kellogg Found., 1979. Mem.: Occupl. Therapy Assn. Calif. (v.p. 1981—84, state chair pers. 1981—84, state chair continuing edn. 1984—86, award of excellence 1986, Lifetime Achievement award 1994), Am. Occupl. Therapy Assn., Am. Soc. Hand Therapists (life), Alliance Calif. Artist. Avocations: stone sculpture, painting, kayaking, travel, fossil hunting. Home: 172 N Karen Ave Clovis CA 93612-0112 E-mail: kiluluv@aol.com.

**VON RAFFLER-ENGEL, WALBURGA (WALBURGA ENGEL),** retired language educator; b. Munich, Sept. 25, 1920; came to U.S., 1949, naturalized, 1955; d. Friedrich J. and Gertrud E. (Kiefer) von R.; m. A. Ferdinand Engel, June 2, 1957; children: Lea Maxine, Eric Robert von Raffler. DLitt, U. Turin, Italy, 1947; MS, Columbia U., 1951; PhD, Ind. U., 1953. Free-lance journalist, 1949-58; mem. faculty Bennett Coll., Greensboro, NC, 1953-55, U. Charleston (formerly Morris Harvey Coll.), W.Va., 1955-57, Adelphi U., CUNY, 1957-58, NYU, 1958-59, U. Florence, Italy, 1959-60, Istituto Postuniversitario Orgn. Aziendale, Turin, Italy, 1960-61, Bologna Center of Johns Hopkins U., 1964; assoc. prof. linguistics Vanderbilt U., Nashville, 1965-77, prof. linguistics, 1977-85, prof. emerita, sr. rsch. assoc. Inst. Pub. Policy Studies, 1985—2002, dir. linguistics program, 1978—85; chmn. com. on linguistics Nashville U. Ctr., 1978—85; Italian NSF fellow; prof. Psychol. Inst. U. Florence, Italy, 1986-87; prof. NATO Advanced Study Inst., Cortona, Italy, 1988; pres. Kinesics Internat., 1988—, ret. Vis. prof. linguistics Shanxi U., Peoples Republic China, 1988-2002; vis. prof. U. Ottawa, Ont., Can., 1971-72, Lang. Scis. Inst., Internat. Christian U., Tokyo, 1976, U. Paris, Sorbonne, 1965-67, 1978-79; grant evaluator NEH, NSF, Can. Coun.; manuscript reader Ind. U. Press, U. Ill. Press, Prentice-Hall; advisor Trinity U., Simon Frazer U.; dir. internat. seminar Cross-Cultural Comm., 1986-87; mem. Ctr. for Global Media Studies, 1999; State Dept. Italy del. to Congress of the Hague; lectr. in field; specialist in non-verbal comm. Author: Il prelinguaggio infantile, 1964, The Perception of Nonverbal Behavior in the Career Interview, 1983, The Perception of the Unborn Across the Cultures of the World, Japanese edit., 1993, English edit., 1994 (transl. into Chinese), A Traveler's Guide to Cross-Cultural Business Communications, 2000; co-author: Language Intervention Programs, 1960-75; editor, co-editor 12 books; author films and videotape; contbr. of 500 articles to profl. jours. in English, Italian, French, German, Chinese, Japanese. Grantee Am. Coun. Learned Socs., NSF, Can. Coun., Ford Found., Kenan Venture Fund, Japanese Ministry Edn., NATO, UNESCO, Finnish Acad., Meharry Med. Coll., Internat. Sociol. Assn., Internat. Coun. Linguists, Tex. A&M U., Vanderbilt U., others. Mem. AAUP, Internat. Linguistic Assn., Linguistic Soc. Am. (chmn. Golden Anniversary film com. 1974, emerita 1985—), Linguistic Assn. Can. and the U.S., Internat. Assn. for Applied Linguistics (com. on discourse analyses, sessions chmn. 1978), Lang. Origins Soc. (exec. com. 1985-97, chmn. internat. congress, 1987), Internat. Sociol. Assn. (rsch. com. for sociolinguistics, session co-chmn. internat. conf. 1983, session chmn. profl. conf. 1983), Internat. Coun. Psychologists, Internat. Assn. for Intercultural Comms. Studies, Internat. Assn. for Study of Child Lang. (v.p. 1975-78, chmn. internat. conf. Tuscan Acad. Scis., Florence, Italy 1972), Inst. for Nonverbal Comm. Rsch. (workshop leader 1981), Southeastern Conf. on Linguistics, 1980— (mem. 1985—), Semiotic Soc. Am. (organizing com. Internat. Semiotics Inst. 1981). Nat. Assn. Scholars, Tenn. Assn. Scholars (bd. dirs. 1998-99), Internat. Assn. for Intercultural Comms. Studies (panel organizer 1999), United Europe Movement (sect. chmn. 1944-45), Internat. Comm. Assn., Internat. Pragmatics Assn. Achievements include being instrumental in forcing Vanderbilt U. to enroll women on an equal basis with men. Home and Office: 2455 Brighton Oaks San Antonio TX 78231 *In the social sciences theories come and theories go. Carefully collected and objectively analyzed data are useful for generations and the cleanest research design in the lab does not equal a moderately neat design in the naturalistic setting.*

**VON RECUM, ANDREAS F.,** veterinarian, bioengineer; b. Dillingen, Bavaria, Germany, July 5, 1939; arrived in U.S., 1971; s. Bogdan Freiherr and Ilse Freifrau (von Rosenberg) von R.; m. Grudrun F. Bredenbröker-Hardt, Oct. 2, 1965; children: Derik F., Vera F., Uta F., Horst F., Thomas F., Elsa F. BS, U. Giessen, 1965; DVM, Free U. Berlin, 1968, PhD, 1969; PhD in Vet. Surgery, Colo. State U., 1974. Practitioner farm animal medicine and surgery, Meitingen, Germany, 1968-69; clin. staff small animal clinic Free U. Berlin (Germany), Coll. Vet. Medicine, 1969-72; rsch. asst. surg. lab. Colo. State U.,

Coll. Vet. Medicine, Ft. Collins, 1972-74; dir. surg. rsch. lab. Sinai Hosp. Detroit, 1975-77; prof. dept. bioengring. Clemson (S.C.) U., 1978-93, head dept. bioengring., 1982-93; chmn. bioengring. alliance S.C. Coll. Engring., Clemson U., 1984-88; scientific staff Shriners Hosp., Greenville, SC, 1989-95; prof. Hunter endowed chair bioengring. Clemson U. Coll. Engring., 1993-97; assoc. dean rsch., prof. Coll. Vet. Medicine Ohio State U., Columbus, 1997—2004; ret., 2004; founding chmn., prof. biomed. engring. dept. Ohio State U., Columbus, 2002—. Mem. coll. exec. com. Coll. Vet. Medicine, Free U., Berlin, 1970-71; adj. assoc. prof. comparative surgery Wayne State U. Sch. Medicine, Dept. Comparative Medicine, 1975-77; adj. prof. surgery U. S.C. Sch. Medicine, 1984—; Med. U. S.C., 1987-97; adj. prof. biomaterials Coll. Dentistry, U. Nijmegen, 1993—; founding chair internat. liaison com. World's Biomaterials Socs., 1996-2000; cons. in field. Editor Jour. Investigative Surg., 1991-97; patentee in field. Recipient Fulbright Scientist award, 1990-91, Alexander von Humboldt Sr. Scientist award, 1990-91; nat. and internat. fellow Biomaterials Sci. and Engring., 1996. Fellow Am. Inst. Med. and Biol. Engring.; mem. AVMA, FBSE, Blue Ridge Vet. Med. Assn. (pres. 1984), Soc. Biomaterials (asst. editor 1986—, editl. bd. 1983, program chmn. 1990, sec.-treas. 1990-92, pres. 1993-94), Internat. Soc. Artificial Internal Organs, Am. Soc. Artificial Organs, Am. Heart Assn., Acad. Surg. Rsch. (founder 1982, pres. 1982-83, newsletter editor 1982-85, Markowitz award 2004), Biomed. Engring. Soc., Am. Soc. Engring. Edn., Assn. Advancement Med. Instrumentation. Presbyterian. Home and Office: Ohio State U Coll Engring 270 Bevis Hall 1080 Carmack Rd Columbus OH 43210-1002 Office Phone: 614-292-1285. Business E-Mail: vonrecum.1@osu.edu.

**VON RHEIN, JOHN RICHARD,** music critic, journalist, writer; b. Pasadena, Calif., Sept. 10, 1945; s. Hans Walter and Elsa Maryon (Brossmann) von R. AA, Pasadena City Coll., 1965; BA in Eng., UCLA, 1967; BA in Music, Calif. State U., Los Angeles, 1970. Music reviewer Hollywood (Calif.) Citizen-News, 1968-70; music editor and critic, dance critic Akron (Ohio) Beacon Jour., 1971-77; music critic Chgo. Tribune, 1977—; prof. music appreciation Rio Hondo Jr. Coll., Calif., 1970-71. Lectr., TV host, rec. annotator. Co-author (with Andrew Porter): Bravi; contbr. articles to World Book Ency., New Grove Dictionary of Music, mags. and papers. Music Critics Assn.-Kennedy Center for Performing Arts fellow, 1972, 75; recipient Peter Lisagor award Soc. Profl. Journalists, 1999. Mem. Music Critics Assn. N.Am. (edn. com., dir. 1988), Ravinia Critics Inst. (dir. 1988). Office: Chgo Tribune Co 435 N Michigan Ave Chicago IL 60611-4066 Office Phone: 312-222-3570. Business E-Mail: jvonrhein@tribune.com.

**VON ROEDERN, BOLKO GRAF,** energy executive, researcher; b. Johannesburg, Dec. 20, 1950; arrived in US, 1979; s. Conrad Graf van Roedern and Dagmar Grafin (Lubbert) von Roedern; m. Susan Kathryn Bateman, July 6, 1982; children: Gabriele Kathryn, Meredith Margret, Christina Barbara. Diploma in physics, Tech. U. Clausthal, Germany, 1976; PhD, U. Stuttgart, 1979. Postdoctoral fellow Harvard U., Cambridge, Mass., 1979—83; sr. scientist Solar Energy Rsch. Inst., Golden, Colo., 1983—85; mgr. Glasstech Solar, Inc., Wheat Ridge, Colo., 1985—89; ptnr., co-owner MV Systems, Inc., Golden, 1989—90; sr. project mgr. Nat. Renewable Energy Lab., Golden, 1990—. Contbg. author Ency. of Energy, 2004, inventor in field. Pres. Holy Cross Luth. Ch., Wheat Ridge, 2001—03. Recipient R&D 100 award, 2003; co-finalist, World Tech. Network and The Economist, 1999. Mem.: Materials Rsch. Assn., Am. Phys. Soc., German Phys. Soc. Avocations: horseback riding, skiing, flying. Office: Nat Renewable Energy Lab 1617 Cole Blvd Golden CO 80401-3393 Office Phone: 303-384-6480. Office Fax: 303-384-6430. E-mail: bolko_von_roedern@nrel.gov.

**VON ROSEN, RÜDIGER,** stock exchange executive; b. Grocholin, June 21, 1943; Diploma, U. Frankfurt, 1970; PhD, 1973. With Deutsche Bundesbank, 1974-86; exec. vice-chmn. Fedn. German Stock Exchanges, 1986-93; speaker bd. mng. dirs. Frankfurter Wertpapierbörse AG, Frankfurt, 1990-92; mem. bd. mng. dirs. Deutsche Börse AG, Frankfurt, 1993-94, mng. dir., 1995—, Deutsche Aktieninstitut EV, Frankfurt. Hon. prof. Frankfurt U., 1998; hon. consul of Latvia, 2004—. Office: Deutsches Aktieninstitut EV Niedenau 13-19 D-60325 Frankfurt Germany Office Phone: +49-69-92915-21. E-mail: rosen@dai.de.

**VON SAUERS, JOSEPH F.,** lawyer; b. N.Y.C. s. Joseph F. and Margaret von Sauers; m. June A. von Sauers. BEE, Manhattan Coll., 1980; MBA, Pepperdine U., 1987; JD, Southwestern U., 1991; LLM, Columbia U., 1995; DBA, North Central U., 2001. Bar: Calif. 1992, D.C. 1993, Minn. 1993, Tex. 1993, Colo. 1994, U.S. Patent and Trademark Office. Contracts negotiator Hughes Aircraft Co., El Segundo, Calif., 1985-92; atty. Jones, Day, Reavis & Pogue, Dallas, 1992-94, Loeb & Loeb, LLP, L.A., 1995-97, Gray, Cary, Ware & Freidenrich, Palo Alto, Calif., 1997-98; dep. gen. coun. Roland Corp. U.S., L.A., 1998—. Active Calif. Lawyers for Arts, L.A., 1996; guest spkr. Loyola U., L.A., 1996. Contbr. articles to profl. jours. Capt. USNR. Recipient Kuwait Liberation medal Saudi Arabian/Kuwaiti Govts., 1992, 96, Joint Svcs. Commendation medal, Navy Commendation medal (2), Navy Achievement medal; Wildman scholar Southwestern U., 1987-91. Mem.: LA County Bar Assn., Naval Res. Assn. Avocations: sailing, golf, tennis.

**VON SCHACK, WESLEY W.,** utilities executive; b. NY, 1944; married. AB, Fordham U., 1965; MBA, St. John's U., Jamaica, N.Y., 1971; doctorate, Pace U., 1990. Chmn., CEO, pres. DQE, Pitts., 1986-96, ret., 1996; chmn., pres., CEO N.Y. State Electric and Gas Corp., Binghamton, 1996-99, chmn. bd. dirs., 1999—; chmn., pres., CEO Energy East Corp., Albany, NY, 1998—, lead dir. Bd. dirs. Mellon Fin. Corp., Energy East Corp., AEGIS Ins. Svcs., Inc. Trustee Gettysburg Nat. Battlefield Mus. Found.; mem. Am. Gas Assn. Found. (trustee). Office: Energy East Corp 217 Commercial St Portland ME 04101 Business E-Mail: wwvonschack@energyeast.com.

**VON SPEYER, JACQUES,** financier; b. Munich, June 12, 1950; s. Naftalie and Leah von Speyer; m. Alexa Andrea Petschek; children: Dahlia Petschek-von Speyer, Sarah Petschek-von Speyer. Degree in Internat. Fin., London Sch. Econs., 1970. Vice-chmn. Zentral Bank, Zurich, Switzerland, 1974—85; sr. advisor FDIC Mfr. Hanover Bank, Continental Ill. Bank, 1985—86; founder Seychelles Cinnamon Industry, 1986—90; chmn. Palm Beach Milk Co., 1990—94, Global Interact, 1994—99, Deerfalls Internat., Issaquah, Wash., 1999—. Amb. EEC, Brussels, 1971—73. Recipient Order Merit award, Italian Govt., 1975, Queen's medal, Hong Kong, 1977. Republican. Jewish. Achievements include invention of micro heat technology; 747 airport catering system; 1000 meter sniper scope spotting ring. Home and Office: Deerfalls Interantional 4580 Klahanie Drive South East Issaquah WA 98029 Office Phone: 425-222-0050. Home Fax: 425-222-0054; Office Fax: 425-222-0054. Personal E-mail: deerfalls@comcast.net.

**VON SPIEGEL, JANICE KRIEGER,** mathematics educator; d. Donald and Frances Krieger; m. Charles F. von Spiegel, Mar. 20, 1971; children: Heidi Robinson, Jacqueline. BA in Edn., U. Akron, 1971, MA in Edn., 2003. Tchg. cert. OH Dept. Edn., 2005. Math tchr. Akron Pub. Schs., Ohio, 1972—76; math instr. U. Akron, 1982—85; math tchr. St. Vincent-St. Mary H.S., Akron, 1985—88, Archbishop Hoban HS, Akron, 1988—. Spkr. in field. Adviser Academic Challenge Team, Akron, 1992—2004, Future Tchrs. Club, Akron, 2004—05. Mem.: Greater Akron Math. Educators Soc. (pres. 1996—2003), Math. Assn. Am., Nat. Coun. Tchrs. Math., OH Coun. Tchrs. Math. (east dist. dir. 2000—03, spkr., gen. co chair statewide conf. 1998, 2004, Outstanding Math. Classroom Tchr. East Dist. OH 1999), Pi Mu Epsilon. Home: 202 Mineola Ave Akron OH 44313 Office: Archbishop Hoban HS 1 Holy Cross Blvd Akron OH 44306 Personal E-mail: jvonspiegel@neo.rr.com. Business E-Mail: vonspiegelj@hoban.org.

**VON STACKELBERG, KATHERINE ELLEN,** environmental scientist, consultant; d. John Roderick von Stackelberg and Steffi Heuss; m. Garth Wayne Jonson, July 14, 1995; children: Sigurgeir Temple Jonson, Bryndis LeRoy Jonson. AB, Harvard U., 1988, MS, 1998, postgrad., 2000—. Sr. scientist Menzie-Cura & Assocs., Inc., Winchester, Mass., 1993—; rsch.

fellow Harvard Ctr. for Risk Analysis, Boston, 2003—. Grantee NSF and EPA, 2003—. Mem.: Soc. Environ. Toxicology and Chemistry (assoc. del. Pellston Workshop on Valuation of Ecol. Resources 2003), Soc. Risk Analysis (assoc. Student Travel award 1988). Achievements include research in evaluation of alternative air pollution control strategies for Slovak Republic through the Harvard Institute for International Development; design of contingent valuation survey to value noncancer and ecological effects of exposure to PCBs in the environment; development of probabilistic modeling tools to support risk-based decision making involving environmental contaminants. Avocations: travel, Muay Thai. Office: Menzie-Cura & Assocs Inc 8 Winchester Pl Ste 220 Winchester MA 01890 Office Phone: 781-782-6146. Home Fax: 617-783-4827; Office Fax: 781-756-1610. Personal E-mail: kvon@igc.org. E-mail: kvon@menziecura.com.

**VON STUDNITZ, GILBERT ALFRED,** state official; b. Hamburg, Germany, Nov. 24, 1950; came to U.S., 1954. s. Helfrid and Rosemarie Sofie (Kreiten) von S. BA, Calif. State U., L.A., 1972. Adminstrv. hearing officer State of Calif., Montebello, 1987-91, mgr. III driver control policy unit Dept. Motor Vehicles Sacramento, 1991-93; ops. mgr. Driver Safety Review, 1993-95; contract mgr. State Dept. Health Svcs., 1995-97; staff mgr. licensing ops. policy Dept. Motor Vehicles, Sacramento, 1997-2000; Welfare-to-Work regional mgr. State Health and Human Svcs. Agy., Sacramento, 2000; regional mgr. State Labor and Workforce Devel. Agy., 2002—. Author: Aristocracy in America, 1989; editor publs. on German nobility in U.S., 1986—. Active L.A. Conservancy, West Adams Heritage Assn., dir., 1989-91. Fellow: Internat. Soc. for Chivalric Rsch., Entente Cordiale for Chivalric and Heraldic Traditions; mem.: Nat. Assn. Managed Care Regulators, Driver Improvement Assn. Calif. (v.p. 1992—96, dir. media rels. 1996—), Calif. State mgrs. Assn., Orders and Medals Soc. Am., Sierra Club, Assn. German Nobility in N.Am. (pres. 1985—), Benicia Hist. Soc., Intertel, Mensa, Phi Sigma Kappa (v.p. chpt. 1978). Roman Catholic. Avocations: genealogy, collecting. Home: 1101 W 2nd St Benicia CA 94510-3125

**VON TERSCH, LAWRENCE WAYNE,** engineering educator, dean; b. Waverly, Iowa, Mar. 17, 1923; s. Alfred and Martha (Emerson) Von T.; m. LaValle Sills, Dec. 17, 1948; 1 son, Richard George. BS, Iowa State U., 1943, MS, 1948, PhD, 1953. From instr. to prof. elec. engring. Iowa State U., 1946-56; dir. computer lab. Mich. State U., 1956-83, prof. elec. engring., chmn. dept., 1958-65, assoc. dean engring., 1965-68, dean, 1968-89, dean emeritus, 1989—. Author: (with A. W. Swago) Recurrent Electrical Transients, 1953. Mem. IEEE; mem. Sigma Xi, Tau Beta Pi, Eta Kappa Nu, Phi Kappa Phi, Pi Mu Epsilon Home: 4822 Tacoma Blvd Okemos MI 48864-2734 Office: Michigan State U Coll Engring East Lansing MI 48823 Personal E-mail: vontersc@egr.msu.edu. E-mail: vontersch@comcast.net.

**VON VOLBORTH, ALEXIS,** geochemist, geological engineering educator; b. Viipuri, Finland, July 11, 1924; came to US 1955, naturalized; m. Nadia Hasso, 1947; children: Tatyana, Swetlana, Maria, Gregory, Anna, Nicholaus H.W., Elisabeth. PhC, U. Helsinki, 1950, PhLic and PhD in Geology-Mineralogy, 1954. Mineralogist, rsch. assoc., assoc. prof., prof. U. Nev., Reno, 1956—68; Killam vis. prof. geology, Killam rsch. prof. Dalhhousie U., Canada, 1968—72; vis. prof. NASA Lunar Sci. Inst., U. Houston, 1972—73; vis. rsch. chemist U. Calif., Irvine, 1973—76; prof. geology and chemistry N.D. State U., 1975—78; prof. geology, scientist Nuc. Radiation Ctr., Wash. State U., Pullman, 1978—79; prof. geochemistry and chemistry Mont. Coll. Mineral Sci. and Tech., Butte, 1979—94, prof. geol. engring., 1987—92, dir. accelerator lab., 1983—86, sr. radiation safety officer, 1983—86; prof. emeritus Mont. Tech./U. Mont., Butte, 1995—. Prin. investigator Stoichiometry Study Lunar Rocks, NASA, 1972-73; cons. AEC, 1961-63, NASA, 1965-73, Anaconda Co., 1968, Atomic Energy Orgn. Iran, 1975, King Abdul Aziz U., Jeddah, Saudi Arabia, 1975-76, Johns Manville Corp., Chevron, 1980-83, Pegasus Gold Inc., 1987, Placer Dome Inc., Echo Bay, Inc., 1990; U.S. rep., del. 2d Conf. on Natural Reactors, IAEC, Paris, 1977; U.S. rep. Internat. Geol. Correlation Program, 1990-96; interpreter, Russian translator in Soviet Siberia for U.S. and Can. mining cos., 1990-96. Contbr. articles to profl. jours. Traveling rsch. fellow Outokumpu Found., U. Vienna, U. Heidelberg, 1954-55, Hoover fellow Calif. Inst. Tech., 1955-56, sr. fellow Australian Acad. Sci., 1965, fellow Guggenheim Found., 1965-66; fossil Elkoceras Volborthi named in his honor. Fellow Mineral. Soc. Am., Am. Inst. Chemists; mem. Am. Chem. Soc., Am. Nuclear Soc., Soc. Econ. Geologists, Internat. Precious Metals Inst. Home and Office: PO Box 80 Dayton MT 59914-0080 Office Phone: 406-849-5830. E-mail: aalex000@centurytel.net.

**VOOGT, JAMES LEONARD,** medical educator; b. Grand Rapids, Mich., Feb. 8, 1944; married; 3 children. Student, Calvin Coll., 1962-64; BS in Biological Sci., Mich. Tech. U., 1966; MS in Physiology, Mich. State U., 1968, PhD in Physiology, 1970. Fellow, lectr. dept. physiology U. Calif., San Francisco, 1970-71; asst. prof. dept. physiology and biophysics U. Louisville Sch. Medicine, 1971-77, assoc. prof. dept. physiology and biophysics, 1977; assoc. prof. dept. physiology U. Kans. Sch. Medicine, 1977-82, prof. physiology, 1982—. Assoc. dean rsch. U. Kans. Sch. Medicine, 1982—84, chmn. dept. physiology, 1993—2001; vis. prof. Erasmus U., 1985; vice chancellor rsch. U. Kans. Med. Ctr., 2006—. Mem. editl. bd. Endocrinology, 1984-86, 89-92, Am. Jour. Physiology, 1984-88, Doody's Jour., 1995-98; ad hoc reviewer Neuroendocrinology, Sci., Biology of Reproduction, Life Scis., Jour. Endocrinology, Molecular Cellular Neuroscis., Procs. Soc. Exptl. Biology and Medicine, biochm. endocrinology study sect. NIH, 1992, reproductive endocrinology study sect., 1994-98; reviewer grants NSF; editor sci. procs. Rsch. Week, 1982-83; contbr. over 120 articles to profl. publs., 4 chpts. to books. Grantee NIH, 1972-85, 88—, NSF, 1985-86, 91-94, Ctr. on Aging, 1988, Nat. Inst. Drug Abuse, 1991-93; fellow Japan Soc. Promotion of Sci., 1993; recipient Outstanding Young Alumni award Mich. Tech. U., 1974, Honors in Edn., Med. Dental Voice, 1990, inducted Mich. Tech U Acad of Scis. and Arts, 2000. Mem. AAAS, Endocrine Soc., Internat. Soc. Neuroendocrinology (charter mem.), Am. Physiol. Soc. (pub. affairs adv. com. 1983-87) Soc. Neuroscis., Phi Kappa Phi, Sigma Xi. Office: Dept Molecular and Integrative Physiology U Kans Med Ctr 3901 Rainbow Blvd Kansas City KS 66160-0001

**VOOK, FREDERICK LUDWIG,** physicist, consultant; b. Milw., Jan. 17, 1931; s. Fred Ludwig and Hedwig Anna (Werner) V.; m. Frederica Jean Sandin, Aug. 16, 1958; children: Eric Robert, Dietrich Werner. BA with honors, U. Chgo., 1951, BS, 1952; MS, U. Ill., 1954, PhD in Physics, 1958. With Sandia Labs., Kirtland AFB East, N.Mex., 1958-94; div. supr., 1962-71; mgr. dept. research, 1971-78; dir. research, 1978-94; pvt. cons. Albuquerque, 1994—. Editor Radiation Effects in Semiconductors, 1968; co-editor: Applications of Ion Beams to Metals, 1974. Mem. coll. edvisory bd. U. Ill.; mem. policy bd. Nat. Nanofabrication Facility Cornell U.; mem. basic energy sci. adv. com. Panel on Value of Basic Rsch; mem. Okla. State Univ. Ctr. for Laser and Photonics Rsch. adv. bd. U. Chgo. and U. Ill. scholar and fellow. Fellow Am. Phys. Soc.; mem. IEEE (sr. mem.), Böhmische Physikalische Gesellschaft, Phi Beta Kappa, Sigma Xi. Office Phone: 505-884-4754. Personal E-mail: fandfvook@msn.com.

**VOOK, RICHARD WERNER,** retired physics professor; b. Milw., Aug. 2, 1929; s. Fred Ludwig and Hedwig Anna (Werner) V.; m. Julia Deskins, Sept. 7, 1957; children: Katherine, Elizabeth, Richard S., Frederick W. BA, Carleton Coll., 1951; MS, U. Ill., 1952, PhD, 1957. Staff physicist IBM Rsch. Lab., Yorktown Heights, NY, 1957—61; sr. rsch. physicist Franklin Inst. Rsch. Labs., Phila., 1961—65; assoc. prof. of metallurgy Syracuse U., NY, 1965—70, prof. of materials sci., 1970—84, prof. of physics, 1984—93, prof. emeritus, 1993—; dir. solid state sci. and tech., 1984—87, 1990—91. Physicist/chemist U. Calif. Lawrence Livermore Nat. Lab., summers 1977-81; summer faculty mem. Sandia Nat. Lab., Albuquerque, 1983, 84; bd. editors Thin Solid Films, 1985-99; cons. prof. Beijing U. Posts and Telecom., 1998-2002. Contbr. articles to profl. jours., chpts. to books. Recipient L. B. Pfeil medal and prize Metals Soc. of Great Britain, 1983. Mem. Am. Vacuum Soc., Microscopy Soc. Am., Phi Beta Kappa, Sigma Xi, Pi Mu Epsilon. Lutheran. Achievements include discovery of Auger R-factor characterization of thin film growth; development of theory of substrate-induced differential

thermal expansion strains in thin films; first observation of Stranski-Krastanov growth mode in vapor deposited thin films, first use of flash evaporation to form high Tc superconducting thin films; co-discoverer of perpendicular electric field effect in copper surface electromigration. Office: Syracuse Univ 201 Physics Bldg Syracuse NY 13244-1130 Personal E-mail: rvook@hotmail.com.

**VOORHEES, RICHARD LESLEY,** federal judge; b. Syracuse, N.Y., June 5, 1941; s. Henry Austin and Catherine Adeline (Fait) V.; m. Barbara Holway Humphries, 1968; children: Martha Northrop, Steven Coerte. BA, Davidson Coll., 1963; JD, U. N.C., Chapel Hill, 1968. Bar: N.C. 1968, U.S. Dist. Ct. (we. dist.) N.C. 1969, U.S. Tax Ct. 1969, U.S. Ct. Appeals (4th cir.) 1978, U.S. Dist. Ct. (mid. dist.) N.C. 1981. Mem., ptnr. Garland, Alala, Bradley & Gray, Gastonia, NC, 1968-80; pvt. practice Gastonia, NC, 1980-88; judge U.S. Dist. Ct., Charlotte, NC, 1988—, chief judge, 1991-98, 2006—, mem. com. on adminstrn. of magistrate judges sys., 2005—. Mem. N.C. State Rep. Exec. Com., Gaston County Rep. Com., chmn., 1979-83, U.S. Jud. Conf. Com., 1993—, case mgmt. and ct. adminstrn. com., 4th Cir. Ct. Appeals Jud. Coun., 1992-93; chmn. Gaston County Bd. Elections, Gastonia, 1985-86; alt. del. Rep. Nat. Conv., Kansas City, Kans., 1976. 1st lt. U.S. Army, 1963-65, U.S. Army Res., 1963-69. Mem. N.C. Bar Assn., Fed. Judges Assn., Dist. Judges Assn. Avocation: boating. Office: US Dist Ct WDNC 250 Fed Bldg 401 W Trade St Charlotte NC 28202-1619

**VOORHEES, STEPHANIE ROBIN FAUGHT,** retired art educator; b. Indpls., Dec. 18, 1951; d. Edward Francis and Dorothy Marie (Teague) Faught; m. James Osborn Voorhees, June 19, 1999. BFA, Montclair (N.J.) State U., 1973, postgrad., 1974-76. Substitute tchr. Woodbridge (N.J.) Twp. Bd. of Edn., 1971-73, elem. art tchr., 1973-84, 85-86; middle sch. art tchr. Colonia (N.J.) Middle Sch., 1984-85; high sch. art tchr. Woodridge HS, 1986—90; middle sch. art tchr. Avenel (N.J.) Middle Sch., 1990-94; art tchr. John F. Kennedy H.S., Iselin, NJ, 1994-98, ret., 1998. Spkr. Woodbridge River Watch, 1991; pvt. art tchr., 1983-93; yearbook advisor Woodbridge H.S., 1989-90, Avenel Mid. Sch., 1991-94, John F. Kennedy H.S., 1995-98; play set designer, 1989, 94-97. Illustrator: Care of the Lower Back, 1975, Touching All the Bases, 1993; profl. muralist. Campaign vol. Rep. Party, Woodbridge, 1992; sec. to the producer Fgn. Broadcast Svc. Dem./Rep. Nat. Convs., Miami, 1972. Recipient Gov.'s Tchr. Recognition award NJ State Dept. of Edn., 1992, Excellence in Edn. award Woodbridge C. of C., 1992. Mem. AAUW, Woodbridge Twp. Fedn. of Tchrs. (v.p. 1980-83, pres. 1983-95, cert. of merit, 1982), Art Educators of N.J., Met. Mus. of Art, Manatee County Vets. Coun. (sr. v.p.), Ecology Club (advisor 1990-94), Am. Legion Aux. 325 (historian 2000-01, treas. 2001-2003), Am. Legion (sec. 2003-, treas. post 325, sec. post 30), Cabane 880 (historian 2000-01, garde de la port 2001-02, condr. 2003—), VFW Post 10141 Ladies Aux. (life, sec. 2000, sr. v.p. 2001-03). Baptist. Avocations: singing, playing piano, dance, writing, cruise travel. Home: 16211 18th Ave E Bradenton FL 34212 Office Phone: 941-375-2269. Personal E-mail: stpvoorhs6@aol.com.

**VOORHEES, THEODORE, JR.,** lawyer; b. May 24, 1949; AB, Harvard U., 1971; JD, Catholic U., 1974. Bar: DC 1975. Ptnr. Covington & Burling, Washington, chmn. Product Liability and Toxic Tort Practice Group, co-chmn. Antitrust and Consumer Law Practice Group. Office: Covington & Burling 1201 Pennsylvania Ave NW Washington DC 20004-2401 Office Phone: 202-662-5236. Office Fax: 202-778-5236. Business E-Mail: tvoorhees@cov.com.

**VOORSANGER, BARTHOLOMEW,** architect; b. Detroit, Mar. 23, 1937; s. Jacob H. and Ethel A. (Arnstein) V.; m. Lisa Livingston, 1964; m. Catherine Hoover, Sept. 10, 1983 (dec. Dec. 2001); children: Roxanna Virginia (dec.), Matthew Ansley; m. Peggy Loar, June 5, 2004. AB cum laude, Princeton U., 1960; diplome, Fontainebleau, 1960; MArch, Harvard U., 1964; D (hon.), U. Architecture and Urbanism, Romania. Assoc. Vincent Ponte, Montreal, Que., Canada, 1964-67, I.M. Pei & Ptnrs., 1968-78, dir. Iran, 1975-78; co-chmn. Voorsanger & Mills (Architects), NYC, 1978-90; founder, prin. Voorsanger & Assocs., Architects, NYC, 1990—; founder Taylor/Voorsanger Urban Designers, 1991. Lectr. Bennington (Vt.) Coll., U. Pa., Columbia U., Harvard U.; guest critic, lectr. Yale U., Pratt Inst., CUNY, R.I. Sch. Design, U. Cin., Syracuse U., U. Tex., Arlington; mem. adv. bd. Parson Sch. Architecture; mem. archtl. rev. panel Port Authority of NY & NJ; advisor to Samsung Corp., Korea. Exhbns. include: NYU, Archtl. Assn., London, Harvard Grad. Sch. Design, Vacant Lots Housing Study, NY, Deutsches Architeckur Mus., Frankfurt, Mus. Finnish Architecture, Avery Lib. Centennial Exhbn. Columbia Univ., Helsinki, Bklyn. Mus.; major projects include: Le Cygne Restaurant, Neiman houseboat, NYU Midtown Ctr., NYU Bus. Sch. Library, La Grandeur housing, NYU dormitories, Hostos Cmty. Coll., NY; Insitalt Bklyn. Mus. masterplan internat. competition, expansion and master plan Pierpont Morgan Libr., Wethersfield Carriage Mus., Amenia, NY; Montana and Wyoming Residences; Advanced Tng. Ctr., NYU, New York Apt., NYC, Riverdale (NY) Jewish Ctr.; fellow J. Pierpont Morgan Libr., NY, Asia Soc., NY, Brody Residence, VA, Daniels/Falks Residence, Ariz., Wildcat Ridge Residence, Snowmass, Calif., Nemerever Residence, Napa, Calif.; winner competition for Nat. World War II Mus., New Orleans. Mem. vis. com. RI Sch. Design, U. Tex., Arlington; mem. Pt. Authority NY/NJ Ground Zero Archive, NY Hist. Soc.; also mem. archtl. ctr. steering com.; chmn. bd. advisors Temple Hoyne Buell Ctr., Study Am. Architecture, Columbia U., NYC, 1989—; mem. adv. bd. Parsons Sch. Architecture; chair archtl. rev. panel Port Authority NY, NJ; bd. dirs. Worldesign Found.; mem. Regent's Panel NY State U., NY State Regents' Com. on Schs; pres. NY Found. for Architecture 2000-01. 1st lt. US Army, 1960-61. Recipient Cannon prize NAD, stab. and nat. awards NYC chpt. AIA, AIA/Better Homes, Reed City Club, Interiors mag., Stone Inst., AIA/Libr., Lumen, Pratt Inst., NYU, NYC Art Commn.; competition winner Nat. WWII Mus., New Orleans. Fellow: NAD, AIA (numerous offices, including pres. N.Y.C. chpt. 1987, Nat. Honor awards, N.Y. State and NYC awards); mem.: Alumni Coun. Grad. Sch. Design Harvard (editl. bd. Harvard Design mag.), Wadawanuck Club, Century Assn., Sir John Soane Mus. Found., Archtl. League NYC (bd. dirs.), Ellis Island Yacht Club (commodore 2001—). Office: 246 W 38th St Fl 14 New York NY 10018-5805 Office Phone: 212-302-6464. Business E-Mail: bvoorsanger@voorsanger.com.

**VORA, ASHOK,** financial economist; came to U.S., 1970; s. Kevalchand and Laxmi (Mehta) V.; m. Rama Kata; children: Anjali Serena, Amit Raunak. B.Sc., U. Bombay, 1967; MBA, Indian Inst. Mgmt., 1970; PhD, Northwestern U., 1973. Asst. prof. fin. chmn. Vora Automotives Ltd., Bombay, 1963-67, chmn., 1967-70; asst. prof. fin. CUNY, 1973-80; vis. asst. prof. fin. U. Wis., Madison, 1977; vis. assoc. prof. fin. Northwestern U., Evanston, Ill., 1979-80; assoc. prof. fin. CUNY, 1980-84, prof. fin., 1984—; dir. fin. rsch. Fed. Home Loan Mortgage Corp., Reston, Va., 1987-88; vis. prof. fin. Hofstra U., Hempstead, NY, 1990-91. Cons. in field. Contbr. articles to profl. jours. Mem. Am. Econ. Assn., Am. Fin. Assn., Fin. Mgmt. Assn., So. Fin. Assn., S.W. Fin. Assn., Western Fin. Assn., Mensa, Nat. Wildlife Fedn., Beta Gamma Sigma. Office: CUNY Dept Econs 55 Lexington Ave New York NY 10010-5518

**VORA, MANU KISHANDAS,** chemical engineer, consultant; b. Bombay, Oct. 31, 1945; s. Kishandas Narandas and Shantaben K. (Valia) V.; m. Nila Narotamdas Kothari, June 16, 1974; children: Ashish, Anand. BSChemE, Banaras (India) Hindu U., 1968; MSChemE, Ill. Inst. Tech., Chgo., 1970, PhD in ChemE, 1975; MBA, Keller Grad. Sch. Mgmt., Chgo., 1985. Grad. asst. Ill. Inst. Tech., 1969-74; rsch. assoc. Inst. Gas Tech., Chgo., 1974-77; chem. engr., 1977-79, engring. supr., 1979-82; mem. tech. staff AT&T Bell Labs. (now Lucent Techs.), Holmdel, NJ, 1983-84, Naperville, Ill., 1984—; mgr. customer safisfaction, 1990-96, voice of the customer mgr., 1997-2000; pres., CEO Bus. Excellence, Inc., 2000—. Adj. prof. Ill. Inst. Tech., Chgo., 1993—; spkr. in field. Invited editor Petroleum Encyclopedia, 1980. Chmn. Save the Children Holiday Fund Drive, 1986-99; trustee Avery Coonley Sch., Downers Grove, Ill., 1987-91; pres., dir. Blind Found. for India, Naperville, 1989—. Recipient Non-Supervisory AA award Affirmative

Actions Adv. Com., 1987, 92, 97, Outstanding Contbn. award Asian Am. for Affirmative Actions, 1989, Disting. Svc. award Save the Children, 1990, Ann. Merit award Chgo. Assn. Tech. Socs., 1992. Fellow Am. Soc. for Quality (standing rev. bd. 1988—, editl. rev. bd. 1989, tech. media com. 1989, mixed media rev. bd. 1994, nat. quality month regional planning com. 1989-94, nat. cert. com. 1989-94, chmn. cert. process improvements subcom. 1990-94, testimonial awards 1995, 96, 2001, 02, exec. bd. Chgo. sect., vice chmn. sect. affairs 1993-94, sect. chmn. 1994-95, nat. dir. at large, 1996-98, nat. dir. 1998-2000, v.p. 2000-2002, vice chmn. investing in quality capital campaign, spl. award 1991, Century Club award 1992, Founders' award 1993, Joe Lisy Quality award 1994, Grant medal 2001, Lancaster medal 2005); mem. Ill. Team Excellence award (chief judge 1993-99, steering com. 1993-99, award). Hindu. Avocations: reading, photography, travel, philanthropic activities. Home: 1256 Hamilton Ln Naperville IL 60540-8373 Office: Bus Excellence Inc PO Box 5585 Naperville IL 60567-5585 Office Phone: 630-548-5531. Personal E-mail: manuvora@yahoo.com.

**VORCE-TISH, HELENE R.**, writer; d. Palmer Lemuel Vorce and Adelaide Catherine Miller; m. Charles Ronald VanBuren, Dec. 23, 1950 (div. Aug. 1967); children: Gail Rae, Karen Helene; m. William David Tish, Oct. 20, 1978 (dec.). BA in Psychology, Mich. State U., 1950, tchrs. cert. in English, 1961; M in English, U. N.Mex., 1968. Secondary tchr. English and creative writing Grant Unified Tchrs. Dist., Sacramento. Spkr. in field; instr. workshops in field. Author: (novels) The Wounds of Hate, 2001, Challenging the Forces of Hate, 2002, Fencing With Danger, 2006; regular contbr.: Foothill Times; contbr. articles to profl. jours. and popular mags. Fellow: Am. Soc. Journalists and Authors, Calif. Writers Club (bd. mem. 1999—2000). Avocations: tennis, swimming, jogging. Home: 3473 Santos Cir Cameron Park CA 95682 Office Phone: 530-677-3327. Personal E-mail: tish@directcon.net.

**VOREL, STANISLAV R.**, psychiatrist, neuroscientist; BS with honors, Bernardinus Coll., Heerlen, Netherlands, 1987; MD with honors (hon.), Rijksuniversiteit Limburg, Maastricht, The Netherlands, 1994; MS with honors (hon.), Albert Einstein Coll. Medicine, Bronx, NY, 1998, PhD (hon.) with honors, 2001. Lic. N.Y. State Bd. for Medicine, 2006. Rsch. scientist Nat. Inst. on Drug Abuse, Balt., 2001—02; resident physician in psychiatry Columbia U. / NYSPI, N.Y.C., 2002—06, fellow in addiction psychiatry, 2006—. Cons. mem. of expert panel on brain stimulation in substance abuse NIDA/NIH, Rockville, Md., 2004; invited lectr. in field. Contbr. articles to profl. jours. Brain Awareness week tchr./advisor N.Y.C. pub. schs. Recipient Outstanding Dissertation award, Am. Psychological Assn., 2003, Outstanding Resident award program, NIMH, 2004, Frieda Fromm-Reichmann award, Am. Assn. Dirs. Psychiatrics Residency Training, 2006. Mem.: Am. Psychiat. Assn. (Resident Rsch. award 2005, Young Investigator award 2006). Achievements include discovery of electrical brain stimulations with properties of retrieval cues for stored memories; research in neural circuitry underlying cocaine-seeking behavior using electrical brain stimulations; breakthrough neurobiological theories include: dopamine signals as time traces, binary coding mechanism for cocaine craving and neurobiological substrates of mental representations. Office Phone: 212-543-5447. Business E-Mail: srv2004@columbia.edu.

**VORNBERG, JAMES ALVIN**, education educator; b. Corpus Christi, Tex., Nov. 23, 1943; s. Hadley F. and Gladys O. (Smith) V.; children: Scott, Mark. BS in Edn., S.E. Mo. State U., 1965; MEd, U. Ariz., 1969, PhD, 1973. Cert. tchr., prin., supt., Mo., Tex., Ariz. Tchr. Pattonville Schs., St. Ann, Mo., 1965-66; asst. to supt. Am. Sch., São Paulo, Brazil, 1971-73; asst. prof. U. Ariz., Tucson, 1973-74; from. asst. prof. to assoc. prof. Tex. A&M U., Commerce, 1974-81, prof., 1981—, head dept., 2001—06, interim dean coll. edn. and human svcs., 2006—. Co-author: The New School Leader for 21st Century: The Principal, 2002; co-author, editor: Texas Public School Organization and Administration, 1989, 10th edit., 2006. Lt. col. USAFR, 1967-94. Office: Tex A&M U-Commerce Dept Ednl Adminstrn Commerce TX 75429

**VOROSMARTI, JAMES**, physician; b. Palmerton, Pa., Oct. 18, 1935; s. James and Ruth Smith (Mohler) V.; m. Carol Ann Schoch, June 1959; children: James III, Richard Stefan, Erika Lynn. AB, Lafayette Coll., 1957; MD, Jefferson Coll., 1961. Diplomate Am. Bd. Preventive Medicine. Jr. med. officer USN submarine base, Pearl Harbor, Hawaii, 1964-66; med. officer Deep Submergence Project, San Diego, 1966-70; post-doctoral fellow physiology dept. SUNY, Buffalo, 1970-72; exchange med. officer Inst. Naval Medicine, Gosport, Eng., 1972-75; exec. officer Naval Med. Research Inst., Bethesda, Md., 1975-78, comdg. officer, 1980-83; program mgr. Naval Med. Research, Devel. Command, Bethesda, 1978-80; med., life scis. asst. Sec. Def., Washington, 1983-86; cons. occupational medicine Rockville, Md., 1986—. Editor: Undersea Biomedical Research, 1978-82. Recipient Def. Superior Svc. medal Sec. of Def., 1986. Fellow ACP, Am. Coll. Preventive Medicine, Am. Coll. Occupational and Environ. Medicine, Am. Acad. Family Physicians; mem. Am. Physiol. Soc., Undersea Hyperbaric Med. Soc. (Shilling award 1987, past pres.). Home and Office: 16 Orchard Way S Rockville MD 20854-6130

**VORT, ROBERT A.**, lawyer; b. Newark, Sept. 24, 1943; s. Saul S. and Ruth J. (Jacobson) Vort; m. Elizabeth Hornstein, June 25, 1968 (div. Nov. 1979); m. Marcelle Greenstein, Nov. 18, 1979 (div. Jan. 1991); children: Joel, Abigail, Rebecca; m. Tina Kruh, Feb. 4, 1996; 1 child, Hannah. BS in Econs., U. Pa., 1965; JD, Columbia U., 1968. Bar: N.J. 1968, N.Y. 1970, U.S. Ct. Appeals (2d and 3d cirs. 1975), U.S. Ct. Appeals (9th cir.) 1980, U.S. Ct. Appeals (5th cir.) 1981, U.S. Ct. Appeals (fed. cir.) 1984, U.S. Dist. Ct. N.J. 1968, U.S. Dist. Ct. (so. and ea. dists.) N.Y. 1984, U.S. Supreme Ct. 1977. Law clk. to Hon. Theodore I. Botter Superior Ct. of N.J., 1968-69; assoc. Davis & Cox, 1969-71, Israel B. Greene, 1971-73; sole practitioner, 1973-82; ptnr. Balk, Goldberger, Seligsohn, O'Connor & Rhatican, 1982-84, Kirsten, Friedman & Cherin, 1986; pvt. practice, 1984-85, 87-88; ptnr. Goldberg, Mufson & Spar, West Orange, NJ, 1988-91; counsel Donald Friedman, West Orange, 1991-92; pvt. practice Tenafly, NJ, 1997—; ptnr. Pearce, Vort & Fleisig LLC, Hackensack, 2001—04; atty. pvt. practice, 2005—. Mem.: ABA (litigation sect., family law sect., legal econs. sect.), Bergen County Bar Assn., N.J. State Bar Assn. (appellate practice subcom.). Office: 2 Univ Plz Hackensack NJ 07601 Office Phone: 201-342-9501. Business E-Mail: rvort@vortlaw.com.

**VOSBECK, ELIZABETH JUST**, retired geneticist; b. Mankato, Minn., May 24, 1925; d. Frederick William and Frances Beneta (Johnson) Just; m. William Frederick Vosbeck, Aug. 2, 1947; children: Lee, William Frederick III, Lynn, Jon Scot, James Stephen. BBA, U. Minn., 1947; MS in Anatomy, George Washington U., Washington, 1965; PhD in Human Genetics, George Washington U., 1975. Mktg. rsch. tchr. Mpls. C. of C., 1947—48; embryology lab. instr., lectr., human genetics rschr. George Washington U., Washington, 1965—75; lab. dir. cell chromosome analysis Reprodn. Genetics Ctr., McLean, Va., 1976—87; ret. 1987. Grantee, NIH grantee, 1968—70. Mem.: DAR, Sigma Xi, Beta Gamma Sigma. Republican. Avocations: golf, bridge, genealogy, astrology, ice skating. Home: 7512 Fort Hunt Rd Alexandria VA 22307 E-mail: vosbeck01@aol.com.

**VOSBECK, ROBERT RANDALL**, architect; b. Mankato, Minn., May 18, 1930; s. William Frederick and Gladys (Anderson) V.; m. Phoebe Macklin, June 21, 1953; children: Gretchen, Randy, Heidi, Macklin. BArch, U. Minn., 1954. Various archtl. positions, 1956-62; ptnr. Vosbeck-Vosbeck & Assocs., Alexandria, Va., 1962-66, VVKR Partnership, Alexandria, 1966-79; exec. v.p. VVKR Inc., 1979-82, pres., 1982-88; prin. Vosbeck/DMJM, Washington and Alexandria, Va., 1989-94; v.p. DMJM Arch. and Engring., 1990-94; pvt. practice archtl. cons., 1994—. Mem. Nat. Capital Planning Commn., 1976-81, U.S./USSR Joint Group on Bldg. Design and Constrn., 1974-79; mem. Nat. Park System Adv. Bd., 1984-88. Archtl. works include Pub. Safety Ctr., Alexandria, Va., 1987, Yorktown (Va.) Visitors Ctr, 1976, Frank Reeves Mcpl. Office Bldg., Washington, 1986, Fed. Bldg., Norfolk, Va., 1979, Jeff Davis Assocs. Office Complex, Arlington, Va., 1991, Westminster Continued Care Retirement Community, Lake Ridge, Va., 1993; author: Design Matters: The Story of VVKR, 2003. Pres. Alexandria Jaycees, 1960-61; v.p. Va. Jaycees,

1962-63; pres. Alexandria Ch. of Com., 1974-75; bd. dirs. Vail Religious Found. Engring. officer USMC, 1954-56. Recipient Plaque of Honor, Fedn. Colegios Architects, Republic of Mexico, Alumni Achievement award U. Minn. Coll. Arch., 2001, hon. fellowship Colegios Architects of Spain, Royal Archtl. Inst. Can., Soc. Architects of Mex.; named Outstanding Young Man in Va., 1963, Acadamecian, Internt. Acad. Arch. Fellow AIA (bd. dirs. 1976-78, v.p. 1979-80, pres. 1981), Internat. Union Architects (coun. 1981-87), Nat. Trust Hist. Preservation. Presbyterian. Home and Office: 770 Potato Patch Dr Unit A Vail CO 81657-4462

**VOSBECK, WILLIAM FREDERICK, JR.**, architect; b. Mankato, Minn., May 13, 1924; s. William Frederick and Gladys (Anderson) V.; m. Elizabeth Just, Aug. 2, 1947; children: Lee, William Frederick III, Lynn, James Stephen. Student, U. Notre Dame, 1943, Cornell U., 1945; BArch, U. Minn., 1947. Ptnr. Vosbeck & Ward, Alexandria, Va., 1957-62, Vosbeck Vosbeck & Assos. (changed to Vosbeck Vosbeck Kendrick Redinger, Architects, Engrs., Planners), Alexandria, 1962-68; chmn. bd. dirs. VVKR, Inc., merged with Suter & Suter, Basel, Switzerland. Bd. dirs. Dominion Resources Va. Power, Crestar Fin. Corp. Prin. works include Nat. Automobile Dealers Assn. Hdqs., Am. Trucking Assn. Hdqs., Woodrow Wilson Rehab. Bldgs. and campus planning. Mem. Gov.'s Com. Employment Handicapped, 1973; trustee Va. Found. Ind. Colls., Va. Mus. Fine Arts, Va. C. of C.; vis. design critique, U. Va. Architecture; mem. Alexandra Hosp. Bd., pres., 1970, Mt. Vernon Presbyn. Ch. With USMCR, 1943—50. Recipient Wash. Acad. Sci. Nat. Capital award for achievement in arch., Nat. Rehab. Assn. citation tech. svcs., Gargoyle award, T. David Fitz-Gibbon Archt. Firm awrd, numerous honor and merit awards Va. Soc. AIA, Va. Mus. Fine Arts, Outstanding Achievement award Engring. News Record, 1977. Fellow AIA (pres. Va. chpt. 1971), Sigma Alpha Epsilon Found., Belle Haven Country Club, Cosmos Club, Rotary. Home: 7512 Fort Hunt Rd Alexandria VA 22307-1924 Office: Vosbeck Assocs 211 N Union St Alexandria VA 22314-2643 Fax: 703 683-4707. Office Phone: 703-765-5526.

**VOSE, KATHRYN KAHLER**, marketing executive, communications executive; b. Denton, Tex., Aug. 18, 1953; d. James and Martha Kahler; m. William O. Vose, June 1, 1996. BA in Sociology, Sophie Newcomb Coll. Tulane U., 1975; MA in Mass Communications, U. Minn., 1977. Health/scis. reporter The Jour.-News, Nyack, NY, 1977—83; nat. corr. Newhouse Newspapers, Washington, 1983—93; comm. dir. U.S. Dept. Edn., Washington, 1993—96; dir. comm. and mktg. Campaign for Tobacco-Free Kids, Washington, 1996—99, v.p. comm. and mktg., 1999—2000; sr. v.p., worldwide dir. anti-tobacco group Porter Novelli, Washington, 2001—02, exec. v.p., 2002—, dir. health and social mktg. practice, 2002—. Panelist Washington Week In Review; vis. fellow Woodrow Wilson Nat. Fellowship Found; adviser World Health Orgn.; bd. mem., chair mktg. com. Nat. Partnership for Women and Families; mem. steering com. for the women, tobacco and cancer initiative Nat. Cancer Inst.; mem. program and comm. coms., chmn. subcom. on comm. 11th World Conf. on Tobacco and Health; contbr. Nat. Acad. Scis. Recipient Crystal Medallion award AMA, Clarion award Assn. Women Comm., Silver Inkwell award Internat. Assn. Bus. Communicators, Mercury Grand award MerComm Internat., Thoth (2) awards Pub. Rels. Soc. Am., Assoc. Press Mng. Editors Pub. Svc. award. Mem. Nat. Press Club (pres. 1991, bd. govs.), Pub. Rels. Soc. Am. Home: 3351 Tennyson St NW Washington DC 20015-2442 Office Phone: 202-973-5800. Personal E-mail: kkahlervose@porternovelli.com.

**VOSK, TED W.**, lawyer; b. Detroit, Mich., Sept. 6, 1967; s. Stuart Allan Vosk and Susan Helen Stevens; m. Kristine Erin Kelly. BS in Physics and Math., Ea. Mich. U., 1995; Juris Doctorate, Harvard Law Sch., Cambridge, MA, 1996—99. Bar: Mass. 1999, Wash. 2000, US Dist. Ct. (we. dist.) Wash. 2003. Acting mng. dir. NSF Sci. and Tech. Ctr. on Materials and Devices for Info. Tech. Rsch., Seattle, 2002—03; assoc. Magnuson Lowell, Redmond, Wash., 2003—04; pvt. practice, cons. Bothell, Wash., 2004—. V.p. Celestial North, Bothell, 2004—; presenter, spkr. in field. On air performer (radio broadcast) Its Over Your Head. Active voter protection program Wash. State Dem. Party, Seattle, 2004; moderator Ea. Mich. U., Ypsilanti, 2005—05. Named Wash. Rising Star in Criminal Law, Wash. Law and Politics Mag., 2005; Leib scholar, Ea. Mich. U. Dept. of Physics, 1992—94, Recognition of Excellence scholar, Ea. Mich. U., 1992—94, Goldwater scholar in math., sci. and engring., Barry Goldwater Excellence in Edn. Found., 1993—95, Sandra J. Lobbestael scholar, Ea. Mich. U. Dept. of Math., 1993—94, Campus Leader scholar, Ea. Mich. U., 1994. Mem.: Assn. for Symbolic Logic, Wash. Alliance DUI Trial Lawyers, NW Acad. DUI Def., Wash. Assn. of Criminal Def. Lawyers (mem. legis. com. 2006), Math. Assn. of Am., Mensa, Sigma Pi Sigma, Phi Kappa Phi. Democrat. Avocations: astronomy, mathematics. Office: Ted Vosk Attorney at Law Seattle WA Office Phone: 425-753-6343. Office Fax: 425-820-7532. Business E-Mail: tvosk@comcast.net.

**VOSKA, KATHRYN CAPLES**, consultant, facilitator; b. Berkeley, Calif., Dec. 26, 1942; d. Donald Buxton and Ellen Marion (Smith) Caples; m. David Karl Nehrling, Aug. 15, 1964 (div. Nov. 1880); children: Sandra E. Nehrling, Barbara M. Nehrling, Melissa A. Nehrling-Holmgren; m. James Edward Voska, Aug. 31, 1985. BS, Northwestern U., 1964; MS, Nat.-Louis U., 1989. Cert. teacher, Ill.; cert. career mgmt. fellow practitioner Inst. Career Cert. Internat. Tchr. pub. schs., Northbrook and Evanston, Ill., 1964-65; acting phys. dir. YWCA, Evanston, Ill., 1975; quality control technician Baxter Travenol, Morton Grove, Ill., 1978-80; sr. quality assurance analyst Hollister Inc., Libertyville, Ill., 1980-85; info. ctr. trainer, tech. training mgr. Rand McNally, Skokie, Ill., 1985-92; cons., facilitator Capka & Assocs., Skokie and Kansas City, 1992—; dir. edn. Nat. Office Machine Dealers, 1992-94; career and mgmt. cons. Right Mgmt. Cons., Overland Park, Kans., 1994—. Pvt. practice estate conservator. Telephone worker Contact Chgo. Crisis Hotline, 1989-90; CPR instr. trainer Amer. Heart Assn., Chgo., 1977-89; aquatic dir. YMCA, Evanston, Ill., 1969-80; rep. Alumnae Panhellenic Coun., Evanston, 1969-75; grad. Leadership Overland Park, 1996, mem. 15th anniv. special task force. Mem. ASTD (bd. dirs. Kansas City chpt. 1997-99), ASCD, Soc. Human Resource Mgmt., Midwest Soc. Profl. Cons., Assn. for Mgmt. Orgn. Design, Chgo. Orgn. Data Processing Educators, Chgo. Computer Soc., Info. Ctr. Exch. of Chgo., Assn. Quality and Participation, Am. Soc. for Quality (teller KC Ill. sect. 1982-84), Internat. Soc. for Performance Improvement, Assn. Career Profls. Internat. (founding pres. Kansas City chpt. 2000-02, nat. bd. dirs. 2000—, nat. bd. v.p., pres.-elect 2002-04, nat. bd. pres. 2004-06, past pres.,k 2006—, chmn. internat. membership drive 2004), Learning Resource Network. Presbyterian. Avocations: scuba diving, swimming, hiking, camping, travel. Home: 1001 E 118th Ter Kansas City MO 64131-3828 Office: Right Mgmt Cons 7300 W 110th St Ste 800 Overland Park KS 66210-2387 Office Phone: 913-323-2309. Personal E-mail: kvoska@kc.rr.com. Business E-Mail: kathy.voska@right.com.

**VOSLOO, PAUL**, public relations executive; b. Wegberg, Germany; m. Agnieszka Joanna Wojtowicz, Sept. 30, 1995. BA in English Lit. (with honors), U. Leeds, Eng., 1983. Press officer to home sec. The Home Office, London, 1983-85; account mgr. Charles Barker, London, 1985-88; account dir. Biss Lancaster, London, 1988-89; with Burson-Marsteller, 1989-96, mng. dir. Warsaw, 1992-95, Hong Kong, 1995-96; former exec. v.p., internat. dir. Porter Novelli Internat., N.Y.C. Bd. dirs. Global Pub. Affairs Inst., 1998—. Recipient Sword of Excellence, Inst. Pub. Rels., 1987, 88; named Cons. of the Yr., Media Polska, 1994. Mem. London Inst. Eng., Inst. Pub. Rels. U.K., Internat. Pub. Rels. Assn. (Golden World award 1994, 95). Fax: 212-601-8222. E-mail: pvosloo@porternovelli.com.

**VOSS, JERROLD RICHARD**, architecture educator; b. Chgo., Nov. 4, 1932; s. Peter Walter and Annis Lorraine (Hayes) V.; m. Jean Evelyn Peterson, Aug. 21, 1954; children— Cynthia Jean, Tania Hayes. B.Arch., Cornell U., 1955; M. City Planning, Harvard U., 1959; PhD (Bus. History fellow, Univ. fellow, IBM fellow), 1971. Asst. prof. U. Calif., 1960-61; asst. prof., asso. prof. U. Ill., 1961-69; asso. prof. Harvard U., 1969-71; prof. city and regional planning Ohio State U., Columbus, 1971—, chmn. dept. city and regional planning, 1971-79; dir. Ohio State U. (Knowlton Sch. Architecture), 1981-96, prof., 1996-2000, dir., prof. emeritus 2000—. UN advisor to Govt.

Indonesia, 1964-65; social affairs officer UN Secretariat, 1970-71; project mgr. UN Task Force on Human Environment, Thailand, 1975-76; dir. rsch. and devel. UN Ctr. for Human Settlements (Habitat), 1979-81; cons. Ill. Dept. Devel., J.S. Bolles & Assocs., UN Office Tech. Cooperation, UN Devel. Program, AID, Bechtel Nat. Inc., other pvt. and pub. orgns.; mem. external examiners team United Arab U., 1992—. Author: Human Settlements: Problems and Priorities; Contbr. articles to profl. jours. Mem. pub. policy com. Smithsonian Instn., 1970-73; bd. dirs. Champaign County United Community Council, 1965-69, Columbus Theatre Ballet Assn., 1972-75. Served to 1st lt. U.S. Army, 1955-57. Mem. Acad. for Contemporary Problems (asso.), Am. Am. Inst. Planners, Am. Soc. Engring. Edn., Internat. Center for Urban Land Policy (London). Office: 190 W 17th Ave Columbus OH 43210-1320

**VOSS, LINDA I.**, finance company executive; b. Pigeon, Mich., Dec. 4, 1959; d. Edward Robert and Pearl Irene (Riffel) Ulrich; m. Timothy Allan Voss, Aug. 9, 1980; 1 child, Jason Adam. BS in Mgmt., Oakland U., Rochester, Mich., 1982; MBA in Fin., U. Mich. 1986. Student asst. Oakland U., Rochester, 1981; acct. GMAC, Detroit, 1982-84, fin. analyst, 1985-87, asst. mgr., 1988-89, mgr., 1989-90; mem. fin. staff GM, Detroit, 1990-91; credit analysis mgr. GMAC, Detroit, 1992-93, fin. planning mgr., 1993-94, asst. treas., 1995-96, fin. dir., 1996-97; CFO, exec. v.p. Nuvell Fin. Svcs./Credit Corp., Little Rock, 1997—2006; mng. dir., exec. v.p. Nat. Auto Fin. Co., Jacksonville, Fla., 2004—06; CFO, bd. dirs. GMAC Comml. Fin., NYC, 2006—. Bd. dirs. Nuvell Fin. Svcs., 1997—2006, Luth. HS, Little Rock, 2003. Author fin. software, 1988. Tchr. St. John Sunday Sch., Rochester, 1987-91; coach Rochester YMCA, 1988-91; mem. Ark. Sales Tax Adv. Com., 2000. GM fellow, 1984. Mem. Fin. Mgmt. Assn., Golden Key, Beta Gamma Sigma. Lutheran. Avocations: antiques, golf, piano. Office: GMAC Comml Fin 1290 Ave of Americas New York NY 10104 Personal E-mail: linda.voss@gm.com.

**VOSS, LISA MARIE**, music educator; b. Spokane, Wash., Sept. 25, 1967; d. Claude Clifford Olson and Margaret Fern Yetter; m. Jesse Dean Voss, July 15, 1995; children: Justin, Jordyn, Janae. BA in Music Edn., Mont. State U., Bozeman, 1990; MEd in Curriculum Instrn., Lesley U., Boston, Mass., 2004. Cert. tchr. Mont., lic. coach. Tchr. music, band/choir K-12 Turner Pub. Schs., Mont., 1993—94; tchr. gen. music, choral K-12 St. Labre Indian Sch., Ashland, Mont., 1994—96; tchr. gen. music, choir and band dir. grades 4-8 St. Charles Indian Mission Sch., Pryor, Mont., 1996—2000; tchr. music K-12 Belt Pub. Schs., Mont., 2000—02; dir. music, band, choir, guitar, keyboard grades 9-12 Gt. Falls Ctrl. Cath. H.S., Mont., 2002—. Pvt. music tchr., Billings, Broadus, Gt. Falls, 1994—; music dir. various ch. choirs, Billings and Gt. Falls, 1996—; organizer choir camp Harmony Rendezvous, Livingston, Mont., 2002—; basketball coach H.S., 1993—94; bowling coach, 1996—; golf coach H.S., 2002—. Dir.: Mont.Youth Sing, 2001, creator, hostess: Barbershop Choral Festival, 2006. Fundraiser Gt.Falls Ctrl. Cath. H.S., 2000—. Grantee, Stockman Bank, Gt. Falls, 2003, Wal-Mart, Gt. Falls, 2005. Mem.: Band Masters Assn., Am. Choral Dirs. Assn., Mont. Music Educators Assn. Roman Catholic. Avocations: golf, bowling, skiing, karaoke. Home: 329 35th Ave NE Great Falls MT 59404 Office: Gt Falls Ctrl HS PO Box 1399/121 23rd St Great Falls MT 59401

**VOSS, OMER GERALD**, farm equipment executive; b. Downs, Kans., Sept. 14, 1916; s. John and Grace (Bohlen) V.; m. Annabelle Katherine Lutz, June 30, 1940; 2 children. AB, Ft. Hays State Coll., Kans., 1937; JD, U. Kans., 1939. Bar: Kans. bar 1939. With Internat. Harvester Co., 1936-79, v.p. farm equipment div., 1962-66, exec. v.p., dir., 1966—, vice chmn., 1977-79. Served with USAAF, 1943-46 Mem.: Chicago, Commercial, Westmoreland Country.

**VOSS, PETER S.**, investment company executive; Grad., Brown Univ. CEO Security Pacific Investment Group; CEO, Europe, SE Asia Hoar Govett Cos.; Head, London merchant banking ops. Security Pacific Corp.; group exec. v.p. Bank of America; CEO, chmn. New Eng. Investment Cos. LP (now IXIS Asset Mgmt. Group NA, LP), Boston, 1992—. Bd. dir. United Way Mass. Bay. Mem.: Investment Co. Inst. (bd. dir.). Office: IXIS Asset Mgmt Group NA LP 399 Boylston St Boston MA 02116-3305 Office Phone: 617-449-2100.*

**VOSS, REGIS DALE**, agronomist, educator; b. Cedar Rapids, Iowa, Jan. 4, 1931; s. Francis Joseph and Mary Valeria (Womichil) V.; m. Margaret Anne Mitchell, Nov. 24, 1956; children: Lori Anne, John Patrick, David James. BS, Iowa State U., 1952, PhD, 1962. Lectr. profl. agronomist. Agriculturist Tenn. Valley Authority, Muscle Shoals, Ala., 1962-64; prof. Iowa State U., Ames, 1964-99, prof. emeritus, 1999—. Co-contbr. chpt. to: Fertilizer Technology and Use, 1985, Soil Testing and Plant Analysis, 1990; assoc. editor Jour. Prodn. Agr., 1988-92. Pres. FarmHouse Frat. Alumni Assn. Bd., Ames, 1990. 1st lt. USAF, 1952-56, Korea., sec. treas. Iowa State U. Retirees Assn., 2003-2004 Recipient Burlington No. Found. award Iowa State U., 1990, disting. svc. award Iowa State U. Ext., 1996, Iowa Master Farmer Exceptional Svc. award, 1998. Fellow AAAS, Am. Soc. Agronomy (bd. dirs. 1976-78, Agronomic Extension Edn. award 1984, Agronomic Achievement award 1989, Werner L. Nelson award 1992), Soil Sci. Soc. Am. (bd. dirs. 1980-83). Republican. Roman Catholic. Achievements include development of field laboratory for training of crop advisors on diagnosis of crop problems; research on effects of soil amendments on chemical indices and crop yields and economic analysis of crop yield. E-mail: rvoss@iastate.edu.

**VOSS, WILLIAM CHARLES**, retired oil company executive; b. Buffalo, Sept. 22, 1937; s. William T. and Dorathea S. (Grotke) V.; m. Marilyn Erickson, Sept. 6, 1958. Student: William, John, Douglas. AB with honors, Harvard U., 1959, MBA with honors, 1961. With Northwestern Refining Co., St. Paul Park, 1961-70, v.p. administrn., 1969-71; with Ashland Oil Inc., Ky., 1971-89, v.p. Ky., 1973-79, administrv. v.p. Ky., 1979-80, sr. v.p., group operating officer Ky., 1980-89; pres. Ashland-Warren Inc., 1979-83, APAC, Inc., 1980-82, 83-86. Mem. Am. Chem. Soc. Republican.

**VOTAW, JOHN FREDERICK, SR.**, educational association administrator, educator; b. Richmond, Va., May 9, 1939; s. Frederick Lee and Katherine (B.) V.; m. Joyce Marie Miller, June 8, 1961; children: Laura, Cynthia, Mary, John Jr. BS, U.S. Mil. Acad., 1961; MA in History, U. Calif., Davis, 1969; grad., U.S. Army Colls., 1970, grad., 1985; PhD in History, Temple U., 1991. Commd. 2d lt. U.S. Army, 1961, advanced through grades to lt. col., 1976; comdr. Company C 1st bn. 69th Armor U.S. Army, Hawaii, 1964-65; comdr. Troop A 1st Squadron 11th ACR U.S. Army, South Vietnam, 1966-67, comdr. C&C Squadron 11th ACR Fulda, Germany, 1975-77; asst. prof. history U.S. Mil. Acad., West Point, N.Y., 1970-73, asst. dean for plans and programs, 1980-81, asst. prof., 1981-82; dep. dir. U.S. Army Mil. History Inst., Carlisle Barracks, Pa., 1983-86; ret. U.S. Army, 1986; dir. First Divsn. Mus., Wheaton, Ill., 1986—2005; exec. dir. emeritus, 2005—. Adj. assst. prof. history Dominican U. (formerly Rosary Coll.), River Forest, Ill., 1991-98, adj. assoc. prof. history, 1998—; Col. Robt. R. McCormick Rsch. Ctr., Wheaton, 1991-2002; series editor Cantigny Mil. History Series, 1993-2005. Contbg. author: The D-Day Encyclopedia, 1993, The Encyclopedia of American Wars - The First World War, 1994, The European Powers in the First World War: An Encyclopedia, 1996, Encyclopedia of the Vietnam War, 3 vols., 1998, A Guide to the Study and Use of Military History, 1979, History in Dispute, vol. 5, Encyclopedia of American Military History, 3 vols., 2003, The American Expeditionary Forces in WWI, 2005; contbr. articles to profl. jours. Mem. adv. com. for the Study of Force and Diplomacy, Temple U., 1996—. Decorated Legion of Merit, Bronze Star with "V" device, Purple Heart (3 awards) and others. Mem. Am. Hist. Assn., Orgn. Am. Historians, Soc. for Mil. History (trustee 2001—), U.S. Naval Inst. (life), U.S. Army War Coll. Alumni Assn. (life), Ret. Officers Assn. (life), Disabled Am. Vets., Assn. Grads. U.S. Mil. Acad., U. Calif. Davis Alumni Assn. (life), Am. Vets. (life), Am. Legion (life), Kiwanis (Wheaton club 1986—, pres. 1991-92), Phi Alpha Theta, Phi Kappa Phi (life). Avocations: reading, writing, classical music, golf. E-mail: allons667@bigfoot.com.

**VOTAW, TY M.,** golf association commissioner; b. Salem, Ohio; children: Sam, Caroline. BS in Journalism summa cum laude, Ohio U., 1984; JD cum laude, U. NC, 1987. Atty. Taft, Stettinius & Hollister, Cin.; gen. counsel Ladies Profl. Golf Assn. (LPGA), Daytona Beach, Fla., 1991-92, spl. asst. to commr., 1992-99, v.p. bus. affairs, 1997—99, commr., 1999—. Bd. dir. Ladies Profl. Golf Assn., World Golf Found., Golf 20/20; mem. First Tee Oversight Com. Achievements include playing a key role in the establishment of the World Congress of Women's Golf. Avocations: collector of first edition books, music. Office: c/o LPGA 100 International Golf Dr Daytona Beach FL 32124-1092 Office Phone: 386-274-6200. Office Fax: 386-274-1099.

**VOTH, ALDEN H.,** political science professor; b. Goessel, Kans., May 4, 1926; s. John F. and Helena (Hildebrandt) V.; m. Norma E. Jost, Aug. 18, 1956; children: Susan, Thomas. BA, Bethel Coll., 1950; MS in Econs., Iowa State U., Ames, 1953; PhD in Internat. Rels., U. Chgo., 1959. Assoc. prof. polit. sci. Upland (Calif.) Coll., 1960-63; prof. polit. sci. San Jose (Calif.) State U., 1963-65, 67-91, prof. emeritus, 1991—. Vis. prof. polit. sci. Am. U. in Cairo, 1965-67; spkr. in field of crisis in Mid. East. Author: Moscow Abandons Israel, 1980, (with others) The Kissinger Legacy, 1984. Trustee Pomona (Calif.) Valley Am. Assn. UN, 1963; participant China Ednl. Exch., 1996. Am. U. in Cairo Rsch. grantee, 1966; Nat. Coun. on U.S.-Arab Rels. fellow, 1990—. Achievements include Organized four public seminars on the middle east crisis. San Jose, spring, 2005. Home: 1385 Kimberly Dr San Jose CA 95118-1426 Office: San Jose State U One Washington Sq San Jose CA 95192 Office Phone: 408-264-1662. Personal E-mail: ahvoth@aol.com.

**VOTH, DOUGLAS W.,** dean, educator; MD, U. Kans., 1959. Diplomate Am. Bd. Internal Medicine, 1966. Intern U. Kans. Sch. Medicine, Kansas City, 1959—60, resident in internal medicine, 1960—61, 1964—65, assoc. prof. medicine, 1971—73, prof. medicine, chair dept. and dir. residency program, 1974—84, pres. corp., 1978—84; fellow in infectious diseases Upstate Med. Ctr., Syracuse, NY, 1963—64; mem. sect. infectious diseases Kans. U. Med. Ctr., 1965—73; prof. medicine U. Okla. Sch. Medicine, 1973—74; med. dir., chief med. svc. King Fahad Hosp., Al Baha, Saudi Arabia, 1985—86; overseas advisor Royal Coll. Physicians, England, 1987—; prof. medicine U. Okla. Coll. Medicine, Oklahoma City, 1987—; acting chair dept. neurology, 1990—92, exec. dean, 1992—96; dean Faculty of Medicine and Health Scis., United Arab Emirates, 1996—2000; dir. med. edn. Sheikh Zayed Hosp., Abu Dhabi, 2000—01; dir. alumni and devel. U. Okla. Health Scis. Ctr., 2001—02; dean U. Okla. Coll. Pharmacy, Oklahoma City, 2002—. Trustee U. Presbyn. Neurol. Inst., Oklahoma City, 1994—96. Fellow: ACP, Infectious Diseases Soc. Am. Office: Univ of Okla Coll of Pharmacy PO Box 26901 Oklahoma City OK 73190 Office Phone: 405-271-6485. Business E-Mail: douglas-voth@ouhsc.edu.

**VOURVOULIAS-BUSH, ALBERTO,** arts editor; m. Jhumpa Lahiri, Jan. 15, 2001; 1 child, Octavio. PhD in Polit., Yale Univ. Program assoc., Latin Am. Coun. Fgn. Rels; staff Time Mag., dep. editor, Latin Am. Bur.; mng. editor ARTnews Mag. Co-editor: The City and The World: New York's Global Future, 1997. Office: ARTnews Magazine 48 W 38th St New York NY 10018-0042 Office Phone: 212-398-1690. Office Fax: 212-819-0394.

**VOWELL, KARMA,** arts organization fundraiser; b. Denver, Nov. 18, 1975; d. Orval and Norma Vowell. BS, U. Tulsa, Calif., 1997; MBA, Oklahoma City U., 2001. Devel. assoc. Allied Arts, Oklahoma City, 2000—04; cons. IAO, Oklahoma City, 2003—04; found. & corp. giving coord. Mid-Am. Arts Alliance, Kansas City, 2005—. Mem.: Am. Museums, Assn. Fundraising Profls. (issues and answers com. 2005—06, youth in philanthropy com. 2006, Nat. Philanthropy Day com. 2005—06), Am. Assn. Grants Profls., U. Tulsa Alumni Assn. (chair philanthropy com. Kansas City chpt. 2005—06), Delta Mu Delta. Home: 8922 McGee St Kansas City MO 64114 Office: Mid-Am Arts Alliance 2018 Baltimore Ave Kansas City MO Office Phone: 816-421-1388. Personal E-mail: kevowell@aol.com.

**VOWELL, SARAH,** writer, radio personality; b. Muskogee, Okla., Dec. 27, 1969; BA, Mont. State U., Bozeman, 1993; MA, Sch. of Art. Inst. Chgo., 1996. Former columnist Time, Salon.com, San Francisco Weekly; has contbd. to magazines and newspapers including Esquire, GQ, LA Times, The Village Voice, Spin, The NY Times Book Rev., and McSweeney's; contbg. editor This Am. Life Nat. Pub. Radio, 1996—. Guest op-ed columnist NY Times, 2005. Author: Radio On: A Listener's Diary, 1997, Take the Cannoli: Stories from the New World, 2000, The Partly Cloudy Patriot, 2003, Assassination Vacation, 2005; actor(voice): (films) The Incredibles, 2004. Office: This Am Life WBEZ Radio Navy Pier 848 E Grand Ave Chicago IL 60611*

**VOWLES, RICHARD BECKMAN,** literature educator; b. Fargo, ND, Oct. 5, 1917; s. Guy Richard and Ella (Beckman) V.; m. Ellen Noah Hudson, Aug. 1, 1942 (div. 1969); children: Elizabeth Ellen, Richard Hudson. BS, Davidson Coll., 1938; postgrad., U. N.C., 1938—39, U. Stockholm, 1939—40; MA, Yale U., 1942, PhD, 1950. Engr. Hercules Powder Co., Wilmington, Chattanooga, 1941—43; chemist Rohm & Haas, Knoxville, Tenn., 1943—44; econ. cons. War Dept., 1944; Am. vice consul Gothenburg, Sweden, 1945—46; asst. prof. English Southwestern U., Memphis, 1948—50, Queens U., N.Y.C. 1950—51; asso. prof. English U. Fla., 1951—60; prof. Scandinavian and comparative lit. U. Wis., Madison, 1960—85, prof. emeritus, 1985—, chmn. comparative lit., 1962—63, 1964—67, 1971—72, chmn. Scandinavian studies, 1977—80. Am. specialist in Scandinavia Dept. State, 1963; vis. prof. NYU, 1964, U. Helsinki, Finland, 1968, Stockholm, 1969; lectr., Sydney, Australia, 1975, Paris, 1979; master ceremonies Santa Fe Scandinavian Film Festival, 1984 Editor: Eternal Smile, 1954, Dramatic Theory, 1956, Comparatists at Work, 1968; Adv. editor: Nordic Council Series, 1965-70, Herder Ency. of World Lit; contbr. articles to profl. jours. Am.-Scandinavian Found. fellow, Stockholm, 1939-40, Lassen fellow Am. Scandinavian Found., 1986, Fulbright fellow Copenhagen, 1955-56, Strindberg fellow Stockholm, 1973, Norwegian Govt. fellow, 1978; recipient Rsch. award Swedish govt., 1978. Mem. Modern Lang. Assn., Soc. Advancement Scandinavian Study (mem. exec. com.), Internat. Comparative Lit. Assn., Am. Comparative Lit. Assn. (adv. bd.), Strindberg Soc., Phi Beta Kappa. Home: 110 S Henry St Madison WI 53703 Office Phone: 608-255-2386.

**VOYLES, C. ROBERT,** electronics executive; BSEE, post grad., S.D. Sch. Mines and Tech. Accredited sr. exec. cons. Inst. Ind. Bus., 2005. Mgr. Magnetic Peripherals, Inc.; gen. mgr. Dakota Mountain Dragway, 1978—98; mgr. engring. svcs. SCI Sys., Inc., 1987—94; v.p and founder Electronics Assembly Resource Network, Inc., 1994—. Address: 5607 Pioneer Cir Rapid City SD 57702

**VOYLES, ROBB LAWRENCE,** lawyer; b. Toledo, May 26, 1957; s. Lawrence E. and Marilyn L. (McQuade) V.; m. Loretta F. Herbert, July 19, 1980; children: Lindsay Ann, Erin Lynn. BBA in Acctg. summa cum laude, U. Dayton, 1979; JD magna cum laude, U. Mich., 1982. Bar: Tex. 1982, U.S. Dist. Ct. (no. dist.) Tex. 1982, U.S. Ct. Appeals (5th cir.) 1983, U.S. Dist. Ct. (we. dist.) Tex. 1986, U.S. Dist. Ct. (so. dist.) Calif. 1989. Assoc. Rain, Harrell, Emery, Young & Doke, Dallas, 1982-87, Baker Botts LLP, Dallas, 1987-88, ptnr., litigation dept., mem. exec. com. & ptnr. in charge Austin office Austin, Tex., 1989—. Editor U. Mich. Law Rev., 1981-82. Bd. dir. & legal counsel Greater Austin C. of C. named a Texas Super Lawyer, Texas Monthly mag. & Law & Politics mag., 2003—04; named one of Best of Bus. & Corp. Law, Austin Bus. Jour., 2004. Fellow, Tex. Bar Found.; mem. ABA (profl. liability com. litigation sect.), State Bar of Tex., Dallas Bar Assn., Dallas Young Lawyers Assn., Travis County Bar Assn., Order of Coif, Alpha Sigma Tau. Democrat. Roman Catholic. Office: Baker Botts LLP 1500 San Jacinto Ctr 98 San Jacinto Blvd Austin TX 78701-4039 Office Phone: 512-322-2626. Office Fax: 512-322-8326. Business E-Mail: robb.voyles@bakerbotts.com.

**VOYTEK, MARY SULLIVAN,** sculptor; b. Memphis, July 26, 1957; d. Herbert Dean and Mary Josphine Sullivan; m. Lawrence Voytek, June 30, 1986; children: Alexa, Zachary. BFA, Calif. Coll. of the Arts, Oakland, Calif., 1980; MFA, R.I. Sch. of Design, Providence, R.I., 1982. Vis. prof. R.I. Sch. of Design, Providence, 1980—81, Brown Univ. Providence, 1981—82; adj. prof. Fla. Gulf Coast Univ., Ft. Myers, Fla., 2000—04, asst. prof., 2004—. Pvt. cons. Fla. Gulf Coast Univ., Ft. Myers Fla., 2000—01. Pub. commns., Dream to Connect, 2004 (Fla. Arts in Pub. Pl. award), exhibitions include Matsumoto Gallery, Sanibel, Fla., 2003, TVS Internat., Atlanta, Ga., 2000, Atla. Internat. Mus. Art and Design, 2000, Gallery Camino Real, Gallery Ctr., Boca Raton, Fla., 2004, Zenith Gallery, Washington, 2005, H.W. Gallery, Naples, Fla., 2005, numerous others, Represented in permanent collections Hsinchu Mus. Art, Taiwan, Sherman Gallery, Chgo., R.I. Sch. Design Mus., numerous others. Art in pub. places bd. City of Ft. Myers, Fla., 2004—; bd. mem. Fla. Arts, Ft. Myers, Fla., 2002—05. Mem.: DAR, Internat. Sculptors Ctr. Avocations: hiking, travel. Office Phone: 239-590-7241.

**VOZZELLA, THOMAS R.,** musician, conductor, composer, organist; b. Boston, July 5, 1963; m. Cathy L Knight, July 1, 1989; 1 child, Ashley Nicole. BS, Ea. Nazarene Coll., 1986; MusM, U. La., 1996; D of Musical Arts, U. SC., 2003. Cert. in choral conducting Royal Sch. Ch. Music, Croydon, Eng. 1985. Music dir., organist various churches in the Boston and Kansas City areas, 1978—92; dir. music, organist First United Meth. Ch., El Dorado, Ark., 1993—97, Trinity United Meth. Ch., Sumter, SC, 2000—03, First Meth. Ch., Midland, Tex., 2006—; asst. prof. music Free Will Bapt. Coll., Nashville, 1997—2000, U. West Ala., Livingston, 2003—04; asst. prof. music, dept. chair Sterling Coll., Kans., 2004—05. Translator: (choral work) Tebe Poem, Hvalite, Psallite; translator, arranger: choral work Sing, Rejoice!. Grantee Bulgarian Sacred Music Rsch. Grant, U. West Ala., 2004. Mem.: Conductors Guild, Am. Choral Directors Assn., Am. Guild Organists. Personal E-mail: tvozzella@yahoo.com.

**VRABECK, KATHY,** videogame publishing executive; BA, DePauw Univ.; MBA, Ind. Univ., 1989. Sales assoc. Pillsbury Co., Quaker Oats Co., Eli Lilly & Co.; exec. v.p., global brand mgmt. Activision, 1999, exec. v.p., global pub., pres. pub., 2003—. Office: Activision, Inc 3100 Ocean Park Blvd Santa Monica CA 90405 Office Phone: 310-255-2000.*

**VRABEL, JOSEPH P.,** lawyer; b. Adams, Mass., Feb. 8, 1948; BA, Lake Forest Coll., Ill., 1970; JD, Boston Coll., 1977; Mediator Cert., Harvard U., 1997. Mass., N.Y. Shareholder atty. Cope & Wilson, PC, 1979—84; sr. ptnr. Bowditch & Dewey, 1984—2001; v.p., gen. counsel Capital Risk Mgmt., Framingham, Mass., 2001—. Adj. prof. bus. law grad.-MBA program Babson Coll. Founder Crossroads Cmty. Found.; trustee Framingham State Coll.; treas., trustee Longfellow's Wayside Inn; former chmn. United Way MetroWest; trustee MCLE; dir. John J. Tobin Found., Maynard Food Pantry, Inc.; steering com. Equal Justice Coalition; former regional dir. Am. Cancer Soc.; mem. Maynard Town Counsel. Mem.: ABA, Worcester County Bar Assn., South Middlesex County Bar Assn., Boston Bar Assn., N.Y. Bar Assn., New Eng. Bar Assn. (bd. dirs.), Mass. Bar Assn. (chmn. bldg. and ops. com. 1988—), budget and fin. com. 1992—, exec. com. 1995—, governance task force 1996—98, sec. 1998—99, dues restructuring task force 1999—2000, v.p. 1999—2000, treas. 2001—, by-law com. 2001—02, pres.-elect 2001—02, pres. 2002—03). Office: Capital Risk Mgmt 1661 Worcester Rd Ste 303 Framingham MA 01701

**VRABEL, MARK,** information resources specialist; MLS, U. Pitts., 1992. Info. resource specialist Oncology Nursing Soc., Pitts., 2006—. Contbr. articles to profl. jours. Recipient cert. of disting. svc., Doody Enterprises, Inc, 2005; Career Devel. grantee, med. informatics sect. MLA, 2003. Mem.: MLA (chair cancer librs. sect. 2006—), Am. Med. Writers Assn. Avocation: running. Office: Oncology Nursing Soc 125 Enterprise Dr Pittsburgh PA 15275 Office Phone: 412-859-6289. Office Fax: 412-859-6160. E-mail: mvrabel@ons.org.

**VRABLIK, EDWARD ROBERT,** import/export company executive; b. Chgo., June 8, 1932; s. Steven Martin and Meri (Korbel) V.; m. Bernice G. Germer, Jan. 25, 1958; children: Edward Robert, II, Scott S. BS in Chem. Engring, Northwestern U., 1956; MBA, U. Chgo., 1961; postgrad., MIT, 1970. Registered profl. engr., Ill. Dir. indsl. mktg. Eimco Corp., 1956-61; dir. indsl. mktg. and planning Swift & Co., 1961-68; v.p., gen. mgr. Swift Chem. Co., Chgo., 1968-73; pres., chief exec. officer Estech Gen. Chems. Corp., Chgo., 1973-86; pres. Kare Internat. Inc., Chgo., 1986—. Pres. Julius and Assocs., Inc., Kare Internat., Inc.; bd dirs. Potash Phosphate Inst., Consol. Fertilizers, Ltd.; mem. mgmt. com. Esmark Inc., Korbel, Inc., Mister Lawn Care, Inc. Author; patentee in field. Bd. dirs., v.p. Northwestern U. Tech. Inst.; trustee Future Farmers Am. Mem. Internat. Superphosphate Mfrs. Assn. (dir.), Am. Inst. Chem. Engrs., Fertilizer Inst. (dir.) Clubs: Butler Nat. (Oak Brook, Ill.). Lutheran. Home: 631 Thompsons Way Palatine IL 60067-4653 Office: 141 W Jackson Blvd Chicago IL 60604-2992 Office Phone: 800-852-3115. Personal E-mail: vrabliker@aol.com.

**VRANISH, JOHN MICHAEL,** electrical engineer, researcher; b. Brainerd, Minn., May 20, 1939; s. John Paul and Louise Ann (Jenkins) V.; m. Dorothy Jean Ward, June 27, 1980; children: John Christopher, Anthony Brian. BS, U.S. Mil. Acad., 1962; MSEE, George Washington U., 1973. Staff engr. robotics rsch. Naval Surface Weapons Ctr., White Oak, Silver Spring, Md., 1971-82, Nat. Bur. Standards, Gaithersburg, Md., 1982-86; staff engr. space mechanisms and space robotics Goddard Space Flight Ctr., Greenbelt, Md., 1986—. Mem. tech. task force Office of Sec. Def., 1981-82, fact finding com., 1981; cons. U.S. Congress, 1983, 87, 96; spkr. in field. Inventor capaciflector, driven ground, virtual feel 3-D sprags, carrier-less anti-backlash transmission, robotic deriveter, magnetostrictive direct drive rotary motor, spin bearings, continuously variable planetary transmission, gear bearings, flexure wedges, conformal robot gripper, stepping flexures, 3-D interactive display, screw locking clickless wrench; conformal robot gripper; holder numerous patents in field; contbr. chpts. to books, articles to various publs. Capt. U.S. Army, 1962—70. Mem. Robotics Internat. of Soc. Mfg. Engrs. (charter, award 1981). Holder world record for precision non contact robotic assembly in space; holder world record in single stage gear reduction; actuator upgrade designee, F-35 joint strike fighter. Home: 900 Truro Ln Crofton MD 21114-1207 Office: NASA/Goddard Space Flight Ctr Code 544 Greenbelt MD 20771-0001 Office Phone: 301-286-4031. Business E-Mail: john.m.vranish@nasa.gov. E-mail: jmvranish@comcast.net.

**VRATIL, JOHN LOGAN,** state legislator, lawyer; b. Great Bend, Kans., Oct. 28, 1945; s. Frank and Althea (Shuss) V.; m. Kathy Hoefer, June 21, 1971 (div. Dec. 1985); m. Anne Whitfill, Mar. 7, 1986 (div. Dec. 1992); m. Teresa Hobbs, Mar. 15, 1996; children: Alison, Andy, Ashley. BS in Edn., U. Kans., 1967; postgrad., U. Southampton, Eng., 1967-68; JD, U. Kans., 1971; postgrad., U. Exeter, Eng., 1972. Bar: Kans. 1971, U.S. Dist. Ct. Kans. 1971, U.S. Ct. Appeals (10th and 8th cirs.) 1975, U.S. Supreme Ct. 2005. From assoc. to ptnr. Bennett, Lytle, Wetzler & Winn, Prairie Village, Kans., 1972-83; with Lathrop & Gage, Overland Park, Kans., 1983—; mem. Kans. Senate from 11th dist., 1998—, v.p., 2003—. Contbr. articles to profl. jours. Mem. recreation commn. Prairie Village, 1982-83, mem. planning commn., 1983-84; v.p. Usher Mansion Hist. Found., Lawrence, Kans., 1990—. Fellow ABA Found.; mem. ABA, Kans. Bar Assn. (pres. 1995-96, gov. 1988-97), Kans. Bar Found. (trustee 1996-2002), Johnson County Bar Assn. (pres. 1979), Kans. Sch. Attys. Assn. (pres. 1985), Overland Park C of C. (bd. dirs. 1985-94, pres. 1988). Republican. Avocations: sports, hunting, reading. Office: Lathrop & Gage 10851 Mastin Blvd Ste 1000 Overland Park KS 66210-2007 Address: Kans Senate State Capitol Rm 281-E Topeka KS 66612 Office Phone: 913-451-5100. Business E-Mail: jvratil@lathropgage.com, vratil@senate.state.ks.us.

**VRATIL, KATHRYN HOEFER,** federal judge; b. Manhattan, Kans., 1949; BA, U. Kans., 1971, JD, 1975; postgrad., Exeter U., 1971-72. Bar: Kans. 1975, Mo. 1978, U.S. Dist. Ct. Kans. 1975, U.S. Ct. (we. dist.) Mo.

1978, U.S. Dist. Ct. (ea. dist.) Mo. 1985, U.S. Ct. Appeals (8th cir.) 1978, U.S. Ct. Appeals (10th cir.) 1980, U.S.C. U. Appeals (11th dist.) 1983, U.S. Supreme Ct., 1995. Law clk. U.S. Dist. Ct., Kansas City, Kans., 1975-78; assoc. Lathrop Koontz & Norquist, Kansas City, Mo., 1978-83; ptnr. Lathrop & Norquist, Kansas City, Kans., 1984-92; judge City of Prairie Village, Kans., 1990-92. Bd. dirs. Kans. Legal Bd. Svcs., 1991-92; mem. adminstrv. com. Jud. Conf. of the U.S., 2000—. Bd. editors Kans. Law Rev., 1974-75, Jour. Kans. Bar Assn., 1992—. Mem. nat. adv. bd. U. Kans. Ctr. for Environ. Edn. and Tng., 1993-95. Fellow Kans. Bar Found., Am. Bar Found.; mem. ABA (editl. bd. Judges Jour. 1996—), Am. Judicature Soc., Nat. Assn. Judges, Fed. Judges Assn., Kans. Bar Assn. (mem. bench bar com., 2005—), Mo. Bar Assn., Kansas City Met. Area Bar Assn., Johnson County Bar Assn., Assn. Women Judges, Lawyers Assn. Kansas City, Kans. State Hist. Soc., U. Kans. Law Soc. (bd. govs. 1978-81, 2005—), Kans. U. Alumni Assn. (mem. Kansas City chpt. alumni bd. 1990-92, nat. bd. dirs. 1991-96, bd. govs. Adams Alumni Ctr. 1992-95), Native Sons and Daus of Kans. (life), Jr. League Wyandotte and Johnson Counties, Order of Coif, Kans. Inn of Ct. (master 1993—, pres. 1990-96), Phi Kappa Phi. Republican. Presbyterian. Office: 511 Robert J Dole US Courthouse 500 State Ave Kansas City KS 66101-2403

**VRBKA, JUDITH MARY,** music educator; b. Osceola, Nebr., May 14, 1961; d. Charles Gregory and Wilomine Angela Kucera; m. Lynn James Vrbka, Aug. 13, 1988; 1 child, Michael Thomas. BFA in Edn., Wayne State Coll., 1983; MusM in Elem. Edn., U. Nebr., 1991. Vocal and instrumental music tchr. Dix (Nebr.) Pub. Schs., 1984—85; vocal music tchr. Shelby (Nebr.) Pub. Schs., 1985—97, vocal and instrumental music tchr., 1997—98, Rising City Pub. Schs., 1997—98, Shelby (Nebr.) Pub. Schs., 1998—99, vocal music tchr. Wilber (Nebr.)-Clatonia Pub. Sch. 1999—. Home: PO Box 284 801 S Shimerda Wilber NE 68465

**VREDENBURGH, JUDY,** youth organization executive; m. Donald Vredenburgh; 1 child. BA, U. Pa., 1970; MBA, U. Buffalo, 1975. Various positions in retail; exec. v.p., gen. mdse. mgr. Sizes Unlimited/Lerner Women; CEO Chess King; sr. v.p. March of Dimes, 1993—99; CEO and pres. Big Brothers Big Sisters of Am., 1999—. Bd. dirs. Generations United. Big Sister; bd. overseers Sch. Arts and Sciences. U. Penn. Office: Big Brothers Big Sisters of Am Nat Office 230 N 13th St Philadelphia PA 19107

**VREDEVOE, DONNA LOU,** academic administrator, microbiologist, educator, biomedical researcher; BA in Bacteriology, UCLA, 1959, PhD in Microbiology, 1963. USPHS postdoctoral fellow Stanford (Calif.) U., 1963—64; instr. bacteriology UCLA, 1963, postgrad. rsch. immunologist dept. surgery Ctr. Health Scis., 1964-65, asst. rsch. immunologist dept. surgery Ctr. Health Scis., 1964-67, asst. prof. Sch. Nursing, Ctr. Health Scis., 1967-70, assoc. prof., 1970-76; prof. Sch. Nursing, Ctr. Health Scis., 1976—, assoc. dean Sch. Nursing, 1976-78, acting assoc. dean Sch. Nursing, 1985-86, asst. dir. space planning Cancer Ctr., 1976-78, dir. space planning, 1978-90, cons. to lab. nuc. medicine and radiation biology, 1967-80, acting dean Sch. Nursing, 1995-96. Chair acad. senate UCLA, 1999—2000, vice chancellor acad. pers., 2001—. Contbr. articles to profl. publs. Postdoctoral fellow USPHS, 1963-64; Mabel Wilson Richards scholar UCLA, 1960-61; rsch. grantee Am. Cancer Soc., Calif. Inst. Cancer Rsch., Calif. divsn. Am. Cancer Soc., NIH, USPHS, Am. Nurses Found., Cancer Rsch. Coordinating Com. U. Calif., Dept. Energy, UCLA. Mem Am. Soc. Microbiology, Am. Assn. Immunologists, Am. Assn. Cancer Rsch., Nat. League Nursing (2d v.p. 1979-81), Sigma Xi, Alpha Gamma Sigma, Sigma Theta Tau (nat. hon. mem.). Office: UCLA Chancellors Office 2147 Murphy Hall PO Box 951405 Los Angeles CA 90095-1405

**VREE, ROGER ALLEN,** lawyer; b. Chgo., Oct. 2, 1943; s. Louis Gerard and Ruby June (Boersma) V.; m. Lauren Trumbull Gartside, Mar. 29, 1969; children: Jonathan Todd, Matthew David. BA, Wheaton Coll., 1965; MA, Stanford U., 1966, JD, 1969. Bar: Ill. 1969, U.S. Dist. Ct. (no. dist.) Ill. 1969. Assoc. Sidley & Austin, Chgo., 1969—75; ptnr. Sidley Austin LLP, Chgo., 1975—. Mem.: ABA. Office: Sidley Austin LLP One South Dearborn Chicago IL 60603 E-mail: rvree@sidley.com.

**VRENTAS, JAMES SPIRO,** chemical engineering professor; b. Danville, Ill., Apr. 14, 1936; s. Spiro and Evanthia (Guintonis) V.; m. Christine Mary Jarzebski, June 8, 1975; children: Catherine Eva, Jennifer Marie. BS, U. Ill., 1958; MSChE, U. Del., 1961, PhD, 1963. Rsch. engr. Dow Chem. Co., Midland, Mich., 1963-69, sr. rsch. engr., 1969-72; asst. prof. Ill. Inst. Tech., Chgo., 1972-73, assoc. prof., 1973-76, prof., 1976-80, Pa. State U., University Park, 1980-85, Dow prof., 1985—. Contbr. articles to profl. jours. Recipient William H. Walker Nat. Rsch. award AIChE, 1981, Charles Stein Materials Rsch. award, 1989. Mem. AIChE. Greek Orthodox. Achievements include development of theories for diffusion, rheology, and sorption in polymers. Home: 1705 Princeton Dr State College PA 16803-3260 Office: Pa State U 119 Fenske Lab University Park PA 16802-4400 Business E-Mail: jsv1@psu.edu.

**VROMAN, KENDAL,** investment company executive; b. 1971; BS in Applied Computer Sci., Ill. St. Univ., 1997; MBA with emphasis in Fin. Mktg., Northwestern Univ. Kellogg Sch. Mgmt., 1999. With marchFirst, Inc.; with Am. Info. Sys. Divsn. Andersen Cons. LLP; consul. Chgo. Merc. Exch. Holdings, Inc., Chgo., 2001—02, project mgr., 2002—05, dir., co-head corp. devel., 2005—. Named one of 40 Under Forty, Crain's Bus. News, 2005. Office: Chgo Merc Exch Holdings Inc 20 S Wacker Dr Chicago IL 60606 Office Phone: 312-930-1000.*

**VU, JOSEPH DUONG,** financial educator; b. Hanoi, Vietnam, Mar. 17, 1952; s. Phuong and Nhan (Trinh) V.; m. Huyen Tran T. Do, July 1, 1978; children: Christine, Daniel. BBA, Ohio U., 1973; MBA, U. Chgo., 1975, PhD in Fin., 1984. Asst. prof. Loyola U., Chgo., 1981-85, U. Ill., Chgo., 1985-88; assoc. prof. fin. DePaul U., Chgo., 1988—. Author: Investment Management, 1993. Mem. Am. Fin. Assn., Vietnamese Assn. Ill. (pres. 1993-98). Avocation: tennis. Office Phone: 312-362-5121. E-mail: jvu@depaul.edu.

**VU, QUAT THUONG,** electrical engineer; b. Vietnam, Aug. 5, 1944; came to U.S., 1988; s. Quy-Mao and Thi-Phung Vu; children: Thuong-Hien, Thuong-Duc. BSEE, U. Ngy, 1965; MSEE, Calif. Inst. Tech., 1967, PhDEE, 1970. Dean MINH-DUC U. Coll. Engring., Saigon, Vietnam, 1971-75; rschr. Hochiminh City, Vietnam, 1977-87, ENRS-CRN, Strasbourg, France, 1987-88, Calif. Inst. of Tech., Pasadena, 1989-90, Intel Corp., Santa Clara, Calif., 1990—. Achievements include two dozen patents in field. Office: Intel Corp M/S SC1-05 2200 Mission College Blvd Santa Clara CA 95052 Office Phone: 408-765-2410. Business E-Mail: quat.t.vu@intel.com.

**VUITTON, HENRY-LOUIS,** designer; b. Asnieres, Seine, France, Aug. 10, 1911; s. Gaston-Louis and Renee (Versillé) V.; m. Josette Rateau, Oct. 15, 1935; children: Colette (Mrs. Jacques Novatin), Philippe-Louis (dec.), Daniele (Mrs. Philippe Masson). Student, Cours Saint-Louis, Paris. Comml. dir. Vuitton et Vuitton, Paris, 1945-75, pres. bd. mgrs., 1975-77; pres. bd. insps. Louis Vuitton (S.A.). Author: La Malle aux Souvenirs. Decorated officer Order Nat. of Merit France; Grande Medaille d'Or du Travail; recipient Silver medal City of Paris Office: 54 Ave Montaigue 75008 Paris France*

**VUKSTA, MICHAEL JOSEPH,** surgeon; b. Pitts., Apr. 25, 1926; s. Michael and Mary Sarah (Hanulya) V.; m. Dorothy Ann Bosak, Sept. 12, 1953; children: Patricia, Michael, Carol, Janet. BA, Youngstown State U., 1949; MD, Ohio State U., 1957. Diplomate Am. Bd. Surgery. Enlisted USN, advanced through grades to capt., 1974; intern St. Elizabeth Hosp., Youngstown, Ohio, resident in gen. surgery, 1958-62; pvt. practice gen. surgery Youngstown, 1962-89; head blue team surgery Oak Knoll U.S. Naval Hosp., Oakland, Calif., 1989-93; assoc. prof. surgery NEOUCOM, Capt. USN retired. Fellow ACS, Am. Coll. Sports Medicine, Southwestern Surg. Congress; mem. Nat. Athletic Trainers Assn. (advisor). Byzantine Catholic. Home: 131 Lovett Pl Pensacola FL 32506-5265

**VULGAMORE, ALLISON,** performing arts association administrator; BMus, Oberlin Coll. Former gen. mgr., artistic admstr., mgr. ops. Nat. Symphony Orch., Washington; former gen. mgr. N.Y. Philharm. Orch., N.Y.C.; pres., mng. dir. Atlanta Symphony Orch., 1993—. Hon. dir. Oberlin Coll.; mem. arts challenge panel in music NEA. Bd. dirs. Midtown Alliance; mem. Vision 2000 Econ. Devel. Collaborative; Cultural Olympiad and opening ceremonies coord. Centennial Olympic Games, Atlanta, 1996. Am. Symphony Orch. League fellow, 1980. Mem. Atlanta Rotary. Office: Atlanta Symphony Orchestra Robert W Woodruff Arts Ctr 1293 Peachtree St NE Ste 300 Atlanta GA 30309-3552

**VULPI, FRANK JOSEPH,** music educator; b. N.Y.C., Sept. 12, 1953; s. Joseph Francis Vulpi and Celia Selesnick; m. Jennifer Mitchell Vulpi, Nov. 1, 2002. BFA, SUNY, 1975; MA, Ohio State U., 1982. Musician for dance Coll. Dance Dept., Amherst, Mass., 1978—80, Bennington Coll., Bennington, Vt., 1978; music dir. dance dept. U. NC, Greensboro, NC, 1981—. Composer various musical compositions for dance. Office: U NC Dept of Dance 221H HHP Bldg Greensboro NC 27402 Office Phone: 336-334-3064. E-mail: fjvulpi@uncg.edu.

**VULTAGGIO, DON J. (DOMINICK VULTAGGIO),** beverage company executive; b. Bklyn., Feb. 26, 1952; 1 child, Wes. Co-founder, head Ferolito, Vultaggio & Sons, Lake Success, NY, 1971—; launched Midnight Dragon Malt Liquor, 1986, Crazy Horse Malt Liquor, 1992, AriZona Iced Tea, 1992, Miss. Mud Black & Tan Beer, 1996, Miss. Mud Lager Beer, Palm Beach Malt Flavored Beverages, 1998, Blue Luna Café, 1998. Office: Arizona Beverage Co 5 Dakota Dr Ste 205 New Hyde Park NY 11042 Office Phone: 516-812-0300. Office Fax: 516-326-4988.*

**VUMBACCO, JOSEPH V.,** health services executive; BA, Bowdoin Coll.; JD, Syracuse u. Atty. Mudge, Rose, Guthrie and Alexander; sr. v.p. F&M Schaefer Corp.; exec. v.p. The Turner Corp., 1982—96, Health Mgmt. Assocs., Inc., Naples, Fla., 1996—97, pres., 1997—2001, pres., CEO, 2001—06, vice chmn., CEO, 2006—. Office: Health Mgmt Assocs Inc Ste 500 5811 Pelican Bay Blvd Naples FL 34108-2710 Office Phone: 239-597-7161. Business E-Mail: susie.brin@hma.org.

**VUOTO, ANTHONY,** corporate financial executive; BA, Princeton U.; MBA, Wharton Sch. Bus., U. Pa. Pres. consumer lending divsn. Bank One Corp., pres., COO First USA Bank; vice chmn., CFO Providian Fin. Corp., San Francisco, 2002—. Office: Providian Fin Corp 201 Mission St San Francisco CA 94105

**VURAL, VOLKAN,** Turkish diplomat; b. Istanbul, Turkey, Dec. 29, 1941; married. Grad., Ankara U. With Turkish Ministry Fgn. Affairs, 1964—; internat. officer, polit. dept. NATO Hdqrs., 1976-82; head recon. dept., envoy, dep. dir. gen. bilateral econ. aff. Ministry Fgn. Affairs, 1982-87; Turkish amb. to Tehran, 1987-88, Moscow, 1988-93; dep. under-sec., amb. spokesman Ministry Fgn. Affairs, 1993, chief advisor to prime min., dep. under-sec., 1993-95; Turkish amb. Bonn, Germany, 1995-98; rep. from Turkey to UN, 1998—2000; sec.-gen. EU Secretariat Gen. (ABGS), 2000—02; Turkish amd. Madrid, 2002—. Office: Embassy Turkey C/Rafael Calvo 18 2A-B 28010 Madrid Spain

**VYAZOVKIN, SERGEY,** chemistry professor; b. Kazan, Russia, Feb. 20, 1960; came to U.S., 1995; s. Valentin and Irma Vyazovkin; m. Sasha Vyazovkin, Oct. 1, 1983; 1 child, Polina. BS, Belorussian U., Minsk, 1982, PhD in chemistry, 1989. Rsch. prof. U. Utah, Salt Lake City, 1998—2001; prof. U. Ala., Birmingham, 2001—. Editor: Thermochim. Acta; mem. editl. bd.: Jour. Thermal Analysis and Calorimetry. Lise Meitner Rsch. fellow Austrian Rsch. Fund, 1992-93, Rsch. fellow NATO, 1994 Mem.: ACS, N.Am. Thermal Analysis Soc. (Mettler award 2004). Office: U Ala Dept Chemistry 901 S 14th St Birmingham AL 35294 E-mail: vyazovkin@uab.edu.

**VYDARENY, KAY HERZOG,** radiologist, medical educator; b. Chgo., Nov. 26, 1942; MD, U. Mich., 1968. Diplomate Am. Bd. Radiology. Intern Blodgett Meml. Med. Ctr., Grand Rapids, Mich., 1968—69; resident in diagnostic radiology Mich. State U., Grand Rapids, 1975—80; prof. radiology Emory U., Atlanta; radiologist Emory U. Hosp., Atlanta. Mem.: Am. Roentgen Ray Soc., Am. Assn. Women in Radiology, Assn. Univ. Radiologists, Am. Coll. Radiology (pres. 2001—02), Radiol. Soc. N.Am.

**VYKUKAL, EUGENE LAWRENCE,** pharmaceutical executive, director; b. Caldwell, Tex., June 26, 1929; s. Henry J. and Anna P. (Polansky) V.; m. Judith Anderson, Jan. 1, 1977; children—Anna K., Mark Roman, Laura Roman, Geni. BS in Pharmacy, U. Tex., Austin, 1952. Pharmacist Scarborough's Pharmacy, Baytown, Tex., 1952-53; pharmacist Gene Vykukal's Pharmacy, Clifton, Tex., 1953-57; with Southwestern Drug Corp. (name now Bergen Brunswig Drug Co.), 1957-86; gen. sales mgr. Southwestern Drug Corp., Dallas, 1966-67, v.p., dir. sales, 1967-75, exec. v.p., dir. sales, 1975-81, exec. v.p., 1980-81, pres., chief exec. officer, 1981-86, vice chmn., 1985-86, dir., 1966-86; asst. dean for devel., lectr. Coll. Pharmacy U. Tex., Austin, 1991—; mem. adv. coun. Pharm. Found., chmn., 1978—; sr. v.p. profl. affairs Bergen Brunswig Corp., Bergen Brunswig Drug Co., 1986—. Mem. centennial endowment com. U. Tex., 1980—; bd. dirs Baylor U. Med. Center Found., Dallas; mem. indsl. adv. coun. Coll. Pharmacy, U. Ky., 1990—. Recipient Disting. Alumni award U. Tex. Coll. Pharmacy, 1979, William J. Sheffield Disting. Alumni award U. Tex. at Austin Coll. Pharmacy, 1987, Legend of Pharmacy award U. Tex. Coll. Pharmacy Alumni Assn., 1997. Mem. Nat. Wholesale Druggists Assn. (chmn. sales mgmt. com. 1972-73, dir. 1980—, chmn. bd. 1985-86, 1st vice chmn. 1983—, chmn. exec. com. 1987—, Timothy Barry award 1990), Am. Pharm. Assn., Tex. Pharm. Assn. (long range planning com. 1983—), Wholesale Druggist Assn. Tex. (pres. 1978-79), Drug Travelers Assn. Tex. (pres. 1977-78), Sales and Mktg. Execs. Dallas (dir. 1971-72). Roman Catholic. Office: U Tex Coll Pharmacy Pharmacy Bldg Austin TX 78712-1074 E-mail: givevickacall@aol.com. *The quality of life in our great country has been enhanced by the tremendous strides made in our health care delivery system over the past three decades. To have served in the pharmaceutical segment has been very rewarding.*

**VYN, ELEANOR MEARS,** physical therapist; d. David A. and Mary A. Mears; divorced; children: Michael, Katherine, Mary. AA, Colby Jr. Coll., 1968; BS, Columbia U., 1970. Phys. therapist Kindred Hosp., Peabody, Mass., 1997—. Avocations: dance, music, art, swimming, gardening. Office Phone: 978-397-9402. Personal E-mail: elievyn@comcast.net.

**VYSKOCIL, MARY KAY,** lawyer; b. NYC, May 22, 1958; d. Gerard John and Kay Theresa (Murphy) V. BA summa cum laude, Dominican Coll., Blauvelt, N.Y., 1980; JD, St. John's U., Jamaica, N.Y., 1983. Bar: NY 1984, U.S. Dist. Ct. (so., ea. and no. dists.) N.Y. 1984, U.S. Dist. Ct. Conn. 1988, U.S. Dist. Ct. (no. dist.) Calif. 1988, U.S. Ct. Appeals (2d cir.) 1984, U.S. Ct. Appeals (3d cir. 1985), U.S. Ct. Appeals (4th and 6th cirs.) 1993, U.S. Ct. Appeals (9th cir.) 1992, U.S. Ct. Appeals (11th cir.) 1996, U.S. Supreme Ct. 1989; cert. in secondary edn., N.Y. Assoc. Simpson Thacher & Bartlett, NYC, 1983-90, ptnr., litigation dept., 1991—. Co-chair consumer subcom., gender working group 2d cir. Task Force on Racial, Ethnic and Gender Fairness, N.Y.c., 1995-97. Co-author: Modern Reinsurance Law and Practice, 1996, 2d. edit., 2000. Trustee St. Joseph's Sem., Yonkers, N.Y., 1986—, Dominican Coll., 1987—; 2nd v.p. alumni bd. dirs. St. John's U. Sch. Law, 1996—, dean search comm., 1998—. Recipient 40 Under Forty award Nat. Law Jour. 1995. Mem. Am. Bar City N.Y. (fed. cts. com. 1996-99, chair ins. com. 1993-96), ABA (co-chair subcom. ins. coverage com. of litigation sect. 1997—). Roman Catholic. Avocations: swimming, reading, travel, horseback riding. Office: Simpson Thacher & Bartlett 425 Lexington Ave New York NY 10017-3954 Office Phone: 212-455-3093. Office Fax: 212-455-2502.

**WAAGE, MERVIN BERNARD,** lawyer; b. Spirit Lake, Iowa, May 12, 1944; s. Bernard and Pearl Peterson W.; children: Love Lee, Mark Warren. BA, Northwestern Coll., Roseville, Minn., 1966; MDiv, Southwestern Sem.,

1969; JD, So. Methodist U., 1974. Bar: Tex. 1974, U.S. Dist Ct. (no. dist.) Tex. 1974, U.S. Dist. Ct. (ea. dist.) Tex. 1976, U.S. Supreme Ct. 1977, U.S. Tax Ct. 1978, U.S. Ct. Claims, 1978, U.S. Dist. Ct. (we. dist) Tex. 1988, U.S. Ct. Appeals (5th cir.) 1989. Asst. dist. atty. Denton County (Tex.) Atty.'s Office, 1974-76; pvt. practice law Denton, Tex., 1977—. Bankruptcy trustee, 1980-87, v.p. consumer bankruptcy Tex. State Bar, 2003-, course dir. Tex. State Bar advanced consumer bankruptcy course, 2004 Mem. Tex. Bar Assn., Tex. State Bar (v.p. bankruptcy com., 2002-), Tex. Bd. Legal Specialization (cert. in consumer bankruptcy 1986, cert. in bus. bankruptcy 1988). Republican. Baptist. Avocation: singing. Office: Waage 8350 S Stemmons St Denton TX 76210-2424

**WAAK, PATRICIA ANN,** political organization administrator, environmental association executive; b. Muskogee, Okla., Feb. 1, 1943; d. Boxly William and Anne Nell (Smith) W.; children: Cinira Anne Baldi, Rachel Nell Carter. Student Tulane U., 1961-62, U. Houston, 1964-65, George Mason U., 1976-77; diploma Mather Sch. Nursing, 1964. R.N., Va. notary public, N.Y. Peace Corps nurse, Maceio, Alagoas, 1966-68; staff nurse U. Wis. Children's Hosp., Madison, 1968-70; dir. counseling Planned Parenthood, Washington, 1973-75; spl. asst. Devel. Support Bur., U.S. AID, Washington, 1977-78; assoc. dir. Office of Population, AID, Washington, 1978-82; asst. dir. Ctr. for Population and Family Health, Columbia U., N.Y.C., 1982-85; dir. population Nat. Audubon Soc., 1985—, state chair, Colo. Dem. Party, 2005-; U.S. del. UN Population Commn., 1981-82; cons. Family Planning Internat., 1973, Global Com. of Parliamentarians on Population and Devel., 1984-85; project design team U.S. AID, Zimbabwe, 1985, evaluation team, Kenya, Uganda, Nigeria, 1987; NGO participant UN Mid-Decade Conf. of Women, Copenhagen, 1981; moderator global population anniversary Peace Corps Conf., 1981; mem. U.S. del. 2nd and 3d preparatory com. meetings UN Internat. Confs. on Population Devel.; mem. environ. strategy and planning commn. World Conservation Union; lectr. in field. Exec. producer (population videotape) What is the Limit, Sharing the Earth, Finding the Balance, Population and Wildlife. Mem. McGovern-Shriver Presdl. Campaign Staff, 1972; vice chmn. Arlington Democratic Com., 1974; chmn. Arlington Com. on Status of Women, 1975; dep. campaign mgr. Shriver for Pres. Com., 1976; del. Va. Dem. Conv., 1976, 82; mem. Population Task Force, 1986—; Internat. Union Conservation Nature and Natural Resources, NGO steering com. on Devel., Environment and Population; del. World Conservation Strategy Conf. Recipient Population Fellows award Population Ref. Bur., 1993. Mem. Am. Pub. Health Assn. (population sect. council, com. on women's rights), Nat. Council for Internat. Health (pub. policy com.), Assn. for Women in Devel., Nat. Women's Polit. Caucus, Soc. Internat. Devel., Women in Def. of Environment. Home: 4225 Weld Co Rd 1/2 Erie CO 80516 Office: 777 Santa Fe Ave Denver CO 80204 Business E-Mail: pwaak@coloradodems.org.

**WAALAND, IRVING T.,** retired engineer; b. Bklyn., July 2, 1927; s. Trygve and Marie Waaland; m. Helen Rita Katz, Apr. 7, 1961; children: Theodore, Neil, Elizabeth, Scott, Diane; m. Kay Williams Oct. 22, 2005 B of Aero. Engring. magna cum laude, NYU, 1953. Project engr. Grumman Corp., Bethpage, NY, 1953—74; v.p., B-2 Chief Designer Northrop Corp., Pico Rivera, Calif., 1974—93. Patentee in field. With USAF, 1946-48. Recipient Leslie E. Simon award, Am. Def. Preparedness Assn., 1990, Aerospace Engring. Leadership Award, SAE, 1993. Fellow AIAA (Aircraft Design award 1989, Aircraft Design cert. merit 1989, Wright Bros. lectr. in aeronautics 1991); mem. NAE. Office Phone: 949-583-1466.

**WAAS, GEORGE LEE,** lawyer; b. NYC, July 12, 1943; s. George and Anne Waas; m. Harriet I. Waas, July 18, 1971; children: Elaine Beth Hudgins, Amy Michelle Kinsey. BS in Journalism, U. Fla., 1965; JD, Fla. State U., 1970. Bar: Fla. 1970, U.S. Supreme Ct., 1973. Asst. atty. gen. State of Fla., 1970-71; staff atty. Fla. League of Cities, 1971; asst. to sec. and dir. labor Fla. Dept. Commerce, 1971-73; assoc. dir. continuing legal edn. Fla. Bar, 1973-74; asst. dean, instr. coll. law Fla. State U., 1974-75; atty. Fla. Dept. Health and Rehab. Services, 1977-80; ptnr. Slepin, Slepin, Lambert & Waas, 1981-86; counsel state elections Fla. Dept. of State, 1986-87; asst. atty. gen. State of Fla., Tallahassee, 1987—2003, sr. asst. atty. gen., 2003—04, special counsel to Fla. atty. gen., 2004—. *A lawyer for more than 35 years, 29 with the State of Florida, Mr. Waas has handled more than two dozen high-profile cases. Among them is the unprecedented successful prosecution of the Son-of-Sam case, resulting in an appearance on Dateline NBC. He has handled major election and voting rights cases and has argued before the U.S. Supreme Court, the Eleventh Circuit Court of Appeals, the Florida Supreme Court, and all five state district courts of appeal, with over 170 reported civil trial and appellate cases. He has published over 25 articles and chaired two Florida Bar committees and one section.* Contbr. articles to profl. jours. Bd. dirs. Big Bend Muscular Dystrophy Assn., 1980-83 (pres. 1983); mem. Leon County Cultural Resources Comn., 1985-87; mem. Gov.'s Coun. on the Voter Registration Act, 1993-96. Mem. Fla. Govt. Bar Assn. (pres. 1976-77), Fla. Bar (exec. council administr. law sect. 1981-86, chmn. 1985-86, Fla. Govt. Lawyer Sec., Claude Pepper Outstanding Govt. Lawyer award 2000), Masons, Capital Tiger Bay Tallahassee (dir. 1984-85), Fla. Bar Profl. Com. Democrat. Jewish. Home: 3797 Sally Ln Tallahassee FL 32312-1018 Office: Collins Bldg Tallahassee FL 32399-1050 Office Phone: 850-414-3662. Personal E-mail: waas01@comcast.net.

**WAAS, HARRIET ISSNER,** elementary school educator; b. Miami, Fla., July 6, 1949; d. Martin and Hildegard (Wimpfheimer) Issner; m. George L. Waas, July 18, 1971; children: Elaine Beth, Amy Michelle. BS, Fla. State U., 1971, MS, 1978. Cert. elem., reading, lang. arts, gifted-talented tchr., ESL, Fla. Elem. tchr. Leon County Schs., Tallahassee; mem. Fla. Title I Statewide Team Dist. Educators, 1997—2002, ETS/Region XIV Comprehensive Ctr. Leadership Team, Pineview. Mem. Fla. Elem. Reading Adv. Bd., 2006—. Contbr. articles to profl. jours. Recipient Extra Mile award, 1986, 1987, 1988 Mem.: SACS, Internat. Reading Assn. Home: 3797 Sally Ln Tallahassee FL 32312-1018

**WACHENHEIM, EDGAR, III,** investment company executive; b. NYC, Oct. 14, 1937; s. Edgar Jr. and Elizabeth (Lewis) W.; m. Sue Wallach, June 6, 1963; children: Lance, Kim, Chris, Amy. BA, Williams Coll., 1959; MBA, Harvard U., 1966. Securities analyst Goldman, Sachs & Co., N.Y.C., 1966-69; mng. dir. Cen. Nat. Gottesman Inc., N.Y.C., 1969-88; chmn., chief exec. officer Greenhaven Assocs., Inc., N.Y.C., 1988—. Bd. dirs. Cenro Corp., N.Y.C., Sejak, N.Y.C., Ctrl. Nat. Gottesman, Inc., N.Y.C.; pres. trustees Rye Country Day Sch., 1985-93; bd. dirs. Miriam and Ira D. Wallach Found.; trustee, treas. N.Y. Found., 1993—; trustee Skidmore Coll. 1993-2001, trustee emeritus 2001-; trustee Mus. Modern Art N.Y.C., trustee, chair exec. com. NY Pub. Libr., 1988-; chmn. Sue and Edgar Wachenheim Found. Trustee Arthur Ross Found., N.Y.C., 1978—; chmn. investment com., trustee Rye Country Day Sch., N.Y., 1985-97; bd. dirs. Miriam and Ira D. Wallach Found. Mem. N.Y. Soc. Security Analysts, Beach Point Club, Harvard Club, Century Country Club. Avocations: skiing, tennis. Office: Greenhaven Assocs Inc 3 Manhattanville Rd Purchase NY 10577-2116

**WACHMAN, MARVIN,** retired academic administrator; b. Milw., Mar. 24, 1917; s. Alex and Ida (Epstein) W.; m. Adeline Lillian Schpok, Apr. 12, 1942; children: Kathleen M., Lynn A. BS, Northwestern U., 1939, MA, 1940; PhD, U. Ill., 1942; LLD (hon.), U. Pa., 1964, Lincoln U., Pa., 1970, Del. Valley Coll. Sci. and Agr., 1973, Med. Coll. Pa., 1982, Bloomfield Coll., 1987, Albright Coll., 1991; DHL (hon.), Gratz Coll., 1973; LittD (hon.), Jewish Theol. Sem. Am., 1973, Drexel U., 1980; LHD (hon.), Colgate U., 1975, Widener U., 1976; DSc (hon.), Thomas Jefferson U., 1980; LHD, U. New Eng., 1997; DHL, Phila. Coll. Textiles and Sci., 1999. Asst. in history U. Ill., 1940-42; instr. Biarritz Am. U., Biarritz, France, 1945-46; vis. asst. prof. San Diego State Coll., summer 1948, U. Minn., 1950; assoc. prof. history U. Md. in Europe, 1952-53; from instr. to prof. Colgate U., 1954-61, dir. upper class core program, 1956-61; pres. Lincoln (Pa.) U., 1961-70; v.p. acad. affairs Temple U., 1970-73, pres., 1973-82, chancellor, 1982-2000, Dir. Salzburg Seminar in Am. Studies, 1958-60, pres. Fgn. Policy Rsch. Inst., 1983-89;

acting exec. dir. Pa. Higher Edn. Assistance Agy., 1989; acting pres. Phila. Coll. Textiles and Sci., 1991; pres. Albright Coll., 1991-92. Past chmn. Nat. Ctr. for Higher Edn. Mgmt. Sys.; specialist in Africa for State Dept., 1965, 68; mem. adv. coun. World Learning, Inc.; mem. Colgate Nat. Coun.; chmn. emeritus Collegis, Inc. Author: History of Social-Democratic Party of Milwaukee, 1897-1910, 1945, The Education of a University President, 2005; contbr. articles to profl. jours. and newspapers, also chpts. in books. Mem. adv. coun. Greater Phila. Urban Affairs Coalition, World Affairs Coun.; vice chair Fgn. Policy Rsch. Inst.; hon. dir. Phila. Contributionship; trustee emeritus Balch Inst. Ethnic Studies; mem. bd. overseers Coll. V.I.; hon. trustee Albright Coll.; hon. life trustee Temple U. With U.S. Army, 1942—46. Mem. NAACP, Am. Studies Assn. (past mem. exec. com.), AAUP (past pres. Colgate U. chpt.), Am. Hist. Assn., ACLU, Pa. Assn. Colls. and Univs. (past chmn., pres. 1993), Phi Beta Kappa. Office: Temple U Philadelphia PA 19122-6096 Office Phone: 215-204-6275. Business E-Mail: marvin.wachman@temple.edu.

**WACHOWSKI, ANDY,** film director; b. Chgo., Dec. 29, 1967; s. Ron and Lynne Wachowski; m. Alisa Blasingame, 1991. Student, Emerson Coll., Boston. Motion picture dir., writer, prodr. (With brother Larry) writer Assassins, 1995 (story, hon. mention Stockholm Film Festival); exec. prodr., writer, dir. films Bound, 1996 (Internat. Fantasy Film award 1997, nominee spl. grand prize Deauville Film Festival, hon. mention Stockholm Film Festival), The Matrix, 1999 (Saturn award for best dir., Saturn award nominee for best writer, Sierra award nominee 2000, Las Vegas Film Critics Soc. Best Original Screenplay, nominee best fgn. film Norwegian Internat. Film Festival 2000), The Matrix Reloaded, 2003; writer and exec. prodr. V for Vendetta, 2006. Office: William Morris Agy One William Morris Pl Beverly Hills CA 90212*

**WACHOWSKI, LARRY,** film director; b. Chgo., June 21, 1965; s. Ron and Lynne Wachowski; m. Thea Bloom, Oct. 30, 1993 (div. Dec. 2002). Student, Bard Coll. Motion picture dir., writer, prodr. (With brother Andy) writer Assassins, 1995 (story, hon. mention Stockholm Film Festival); exec. prodr., writer, dir. films Bound, 1996 (Internat. Fantasy Film award 1997, nominee spl. grand prize Deauville Film Festival, hon. mention Stockholm Film Festival), The Matrix, 1999 (Saturn award for best dir., Saturn award nominee for best writer, Sierra award nominee 2000, Las Vegas Film Critics Soc. Best Original Screenplay, nominee best fgn. film Norwegian Internat. Film Festival 2000), The Matrix Reloaded, 2003, The Matrix Revolutions, 2003, V for Vendetta, 2006. Address: William Morris Agy care Dave Wirtschafter One William Morris Pl Beverly Hills CA 90212*

**WACHS, JOEL,** former city councilman, foundation administrator; b. Scranton, Pa., Mar. 1, 1939; Grad. with honors, UCLA; JD, Harvard U., 1964; MA, NYU. City councilman, L.A., 1971—2001; coun. pres., pres. pro tem, chmn. revenue and taxation; mem. govt. ops., intergovtl. rels. coms., 1998; mem. govt. efficiency com., 1998; acting mayor, 1998; lectr. U. So. Calif. Law Ctr., 1999; mem. intergovtl. rels. coms.; vice-chmn. transp. coms.; chmn. govt. efficiency coms.; pres. Andy Warhol Found., NYC, 2002—. Mem. Calif. Bar Assn. Office: Andy Warhol Found 7th Fl 65 Bleeker St New York NY 10012 Office Phone: 212-387-7555. Office Fax: 212-387-7560.

**WACHS, MARTIN,** urban planning educator, author, consultant; b. NYC, June 8, 1941; s. Robert and Doris (Margolis) W.; m. Helen Pollner, Aug. 18, 1963; children: Faye Linda, Steven Brett. BCE, CUNY, 1963; MS, Northwestern U., 1965, PhD, 1967. Asst. prof. U. Ill., Chgo., 1967-69, Northwestern U., Evanston, Ill., 1969-71; assoc. prof. urban planning UCLA, 1971-76, prof., 1976-96; dir. U. Calif. Transp. Ctr., 1996-99; prof. civil and environ. engring. and city/regional planning U. Calif., Berkeley, 1996—, dir. Inst. Transp. Studies, 1999—2005; dir. transp. space and tech. group RAND Corp., Santa Monica, Calif., 2005—. Vis. disting. prof. Rutgers U., New Brunswick, N.J., 1983-84; mem. exec. com. Transp. Rsch. Bd., 1995—2004, chmn., 2000; vis fellow Oxford (Eng.) U., 1976-77. Author: Transportation for the Elderly: Changing Lifestyles, Changing Needs, 1979, Transportation Planning on Trial, 1996, also numerous articles; editor: Ethics in Planning, 1984, The Car and the City, 1992. Mem. steering com. L.A. Parking Mgmt. Study, 1976-78; bd. dirs. L.A. Commuter computer, 1978-94, mem. Calif. Commn. on Transp. Investment, 1995. Served to capt. Ordnance Corps, U.S. Army, 1967-69. Recipient Pike Johnson award Transp. Rsch. Bd., 1976, Disting. Tchg. award UCLA Alumni Assn., 1986, Disting. Planning Educator award Calif. Planners Found., 1986, W.N. Carey Disting. Svc. award Transp. Rsch. Bd., 2002, Disting. Educator award Coun. U. Transp. Ctrs., 2003; named Mem. of Yr. San Francisco chpt. Nat. Transp. Seminar, 2006; Guggenheim fellow, 1977, Humanities fellow Rockefeller Found., 1980; Rsch. lectr Soc. Sigma Xi, 2000—. Fellow: Am. Inst. Cert. Planners, Am. Coun. Edn.; mem.: ASCE, Inst. Transp. Engrs., Cosmos Club (Washington). Jewish. Home: 670 Harbor St #3 Venice CA 90291-5519 Office: RAND Corp Santa Monica CA 90401-3208 Business E-Mail: martin_wachs@rand.org.

**WACHS, SAUL PHILIP,** religious studies educator; b. Phila., Dec. 24, 1931; s. Abraham and Annette (Schaller) W.; m. Barbara Ruth Eidelman, Jan. 27, 1957 (dec. 1997); children: Sharona Rachel, Hillel Eliezer, Devorah Leah, Aviva Marcia (dec.); m. Diane Ruth Cover, Feb. 6, 2000. Hebrew tchr. diploma, Gratz Coll., 1951; BS in Edn., Temple U., 1953; BRE, Jewish Theol. Sem., 1956, B in Sacred Music, 1959, D Pedagogy (hon.), 1989; MA, Ohio State U., 1966, PhD, 1970. Dir. edn. Congregation Tifereth Israel, Columbus, Ohio, 1960-70, Park Ave Synagogue, N.Y., 1970-72; asst. prof., dir. Jewish edn. program Brandeis U., Waltham, Mass., 1972-75; dean Gratz Coll., Phila., 1975-80, Rosaline B. Feinstein prof. of Jewish edn. and liturgy, chair dept., 1980—. Bd. dirs. Jewish Edn. Assembly, N.Y.C., 1965-70, Akiba, Merion, Pa., 1975—, Beth Hillel-Beth El, Wynnewood, Pa., 1984-88, Coun. for Jewish Edn., N.Y.C., 1970-74; vis. lectr. Hebrew U., 1986-89, tutor, 1988-89, vis. rschr., 1985; vis. professorial lectr. Am. U.-George Washington U.; vis. prof. Jewish Theol. Sem. Am.; vis. instr. Coll. of Jewish Studies, Cleve., 1965-69; cons. United Synagogue Dept. Edn., 1980—, Herzlia United Schs., Cape Town, 1989—; mem. ethical adv. com. Jewish Family and Children's Svc., Phila.; vis. prof. Balt. Hebrew U., 1998-2000, U. Judaism, 1998-, Jewish Theol. Sem., 1998-. Co-author texts: Judaism, 1979, Jewish Education, 1991, also curriculum materials; contbr. articles to religious publs. Mem. Soviet Jewry com. Phila Jewish Community Rels. Coun.; bd. dirs. Akiba Hebrew Acad., 1992—. Recipient Aaron Zacks award Am. Assn. for Jewish Edn., 1959, Behrman House award for lifetime achievement Jewish Educators Assembly, 1995, Ateret Kavod award United Synagogue, Alumni award Sch. Edn. Jewish Theol. Sem. Am., 2006. Mem. ASCD, Coalition for Jewish Edn., Assn. for Jewish Studies, Assn. Instns. of Higher Learning in Jewish (past pres.), Phi Delta Kappa. Home: 346 E Lancaster Ave Apt 102 Wynnewood PA 19096-2221 E-mail: wachscover@home.com, swachs@gratz.edu. *"Happiness consists of the fulfillment of the need to be needed." (Abraham Joshua Heschel). Teaching can make a person happy because a teacher is needed.*

**WACHSBERGER, CHAIM,** lawyer; b. Tel Aviv, Sept. 15, 1951; BA, Queens Coll. CUNY, 1973; JD, Columbia U., 1976. Bar: NJ 1976, NY 1977. Ptnr. Chadbourne & Parke LLP, NYC, head, Project Fin. Practice Group, mem. mgmt. com. Contbr. articles to profl. jour. Mem.: ABA (Corp., Banking & Bus. Law Sect., Am. Bar Assn.), NJ State Bar Assn., NY State Bar Assn. Office: Chadbourne & Parke LLP 30 Rockefeller Plaza New York NY 10112 Office Phone: 212-408-5232. Office Fax: 212-541-5369. Business E-Mail: cwachsberger@chadbourne.com.

**WACHSMAN, HARVEY FREDERICK,** lawyer, neurosurgeon; b. Bklyn., June 13, 1936; s. Ben and Mollie (Kugel) W.; m. Kathryn M. D'Agostino, Jan. 31, 1976; children: Dara Nicole, David Winston, Jacqueline Victoria, Lauren Elizabeth, Derek Charles, Ashley Max, Marea Lane, Melissa Roseanne. BA, Tulane U., 1958; MD, Chgo. Med. Sch., 1962; JD, Bklyn. Law Sch., 1976. Bar: Conn. 1976, NY 1977, Fla. 1977, DC 1979, Pa. 1984, Md. 1986, Tex. 1987, US Dist. Ct. (Conn.) 1976, US Dist. Ct. (ea. and so. dists.) NY 1977, US Dist. Ct. (we. dist.) NY 1979, US Dist. Ct. (no dist.) NY 1982, US Dist. Ct. (RI) 1978, US Dist. Ct. (DC) 1981, US Dist. Ct. (ea. and we. dists.) Pa. 1990, US Ct. Claims 1990, US Tax Ct. 1990, US Ct. Internat. Trade

1990, US Ct. Appeals (2d cir.) 1976, US Ct. Appeals (DC) 1981, US Ct. Appeals (3rd cir.) 1990, US Supreme Ct. 1980, cert.: Am. Bd. Profl. Liability Attys. 1982, Nat. Bd. Trial Advocacy (Civil Trial Adv.) 1980; diplomate Nat. Bd. Med. Examiners, Am. Bd. Legal Medicine, 1982, Am. Bd. Neurol. and Orthop. Medicine and Surgery, Am. Bd. Med.-Legal Analysts in Medicine and Surgery, lic. Conn., Fla., La., Ariz., NY, Ga., Calif., Nev. Intern surgery Kings County Hosp. Ctr., Bklyn., 1962-63; resident in surgery Kingsbrook Med. Ctr., Bklyn., 1964-65; resident in neurol. surgery Emory U. Hosp., Atlanta, 1965-69; practice medicine specializing in neurosurgery Bridgeport, Conn., 1972-74; sr. ptnr. Law Offices of Harvey F. Wachsman, MD, JD, LLP, Great Neck, NY, 2001—; of counsel firm Queller, Fisher, Dienst, Serrins, Washor & Kool, LLP, NYC, of counsel; atty., pvt. practice Law Offices Harvey F. Wachsman, Upper Brookville, NY, McGehee, Pianelli & Wachsman, LLP, Upper Brookville, NY. Trustee SUNY, Melvin M. Belli Soc., Melanoma Found.; chmn. health sci. and hosp. com.; chmn., bd. dirs. Odyssey Inst. Internat.; bd. dirs. Am. Soc. Neuroimaging, 1989-1990; pres., CEO Found. Excellence & Ethics in Medicine, 1998—; mem. sponsor Trial Lawyers Pub. Justice, 1983; adj. prof. law St. John's U., Jamaica, NY, Bklyn. Law Sch., NY; adj. prof. neurol. surgery SUNY, NY, clin. asst. prof. neurology U. South Fla., Tampa; faculty mem. Practicing Law Inst., 1983; lectr. in field. Author: American Law of Medical Malpractice, Vol. I, 1980, 2d edit., 1992, American Law of Medical Malpractice, Vol. II, 1981, 2d edit., 1993, American Law of Medical Malpractice, Vol. III, 1982, 2d edit., 1994, Cumulative Supplement to American Law of Medical Malpractice, 1981, 82, 83, 84, 86, 88, American Law of Medical Malpractice, 2d edit., Vols. I, II and II, Lethal Medicine, 1993, co-author (with S. Alschuler, and Henry Holt), 1993, contbg. author Law Book Pub.: mem. editl. bd. Legal Aspects of Med. Practice, 1978-82, editl. adv. bd. mem. Lab 79; subject adv. com. Trial Mag.; editor Trial, 1981-82, 82-83, editor, northeast editor Legal Aspects Medical Practice column. Mem. 40th anniversary Israel's com. Friends of Arts' Celebration; pres., bd. trustees Nat. Grand Opera Co., 1987—92; bd. trustees Nassau County Fine Arts, 1989; v.p. Carson Scholar Fund, Balt., 1997; chmn. bd. dirs. Deja Vu Dance Co., 1985—89, Friends of Nassau County Office of Cultural Devel., 1990—92; past bd. chmn. Bd. Police Commrs. Assn. Conn., past pres.; past chmn. Newtown Bd. Police Commrs., Conn. Fellow: Am. Acad. Forensic Scis., Am. Coll. Legal Medicine Found. (bd. trustees 1988—), Assn. Trial Lawyers Am., Royal Soc. Medicine (London), Am. Coll. Legal Medicine (mem. bd. govs. 1983—84, mem. exec. coun. 1983—84, chmn. edn. com. 1983—87, chmn. 1985, mem. bd. govs. 1986—89, chmn. nat. meeting New Orleans 1988, exec. com. 1988, nat. meeting, bd. dirs. ACLM Found.), Royal Soc. Medicine, Royal Soc. Arts (London); mem.: AMA, ABA, Am. Society Law and Medicine, Tex. Bar Assn., Md. Bar Assn., Pa. Bar Assn., NY State Trial Lawyers Assn. (parliamentarian 1989—90, bd. dirs. 1990—92), NY State Acad. Trial Lawyers, Assn. Trial Lawyers Am. (NY state del. 1989—90, mem. bd. govs. 1990—92), Am. Bd. Profl. Liability Attys. (pres. 1988—), Nat. Bd. Trial Advocacy (examination devel. com. 1981, 1982, 1983, bd. dirs. 1989), Am. Assn. Advancement Sci., Scribes: Am. Society Writers on Legal Subjects, Am. Soc. Contemporary Medicine and Surgery, Conn. State Med. Soc., Nassau-Suffolk Trial Lawyers Assn., Fairfield County Med. Soc., Nassau County Bar Assn., Pa. Trial Lawyers Assn., Wis. Acad. Trial Lawyers (hon.), Tex. Trial Lawyers Assn., Md. Trial Lawyers Assn., Fla. Acad. Trial Lawyers, Conn. Trial Lawyers Assn., NY Trial Lawyers Assn., NY Acad. Scis., DC Bar Assn., Fla. Bar Assn., Conn. Bar Assn. (med. legal com.), NY Bar Assn., Congress Neurol. Surgeons, Nat. Lawyers Club, Cosmos (Washington), Cosmos Club (Washington). also: 233 Broadway New York NY 10279 Office: McGehee Pianelli Wachsman LLP 55 Mill River Rd Oyster Bay NY 11771 Office Fax: 516-624-0667. E-mail: hwachsman@quellerfisher.com. *In my pursuit of knowledge and excellence in the fields of neurosurgery and the law, I have found that arming oneself with the power of knowledge is truly the key to helping others. Let one's goal in life be to help others, and he shall always find fulfillment, challenge and hope.*

**WACHTEL, ALBERT,** writer, educator; b. NYC, Dec. 20, 1939; s. Jacob and Sarah Rose (Kaplansky) W.; m. Sydelle Farber, Mar. 9, 1958; children: Sally Rose, Seth Laurence, Stephanie Allyson, Synthia Laura, Jonathan Benjamin, Jessica Eden, Jacob Ethan. BA, CUNY, 1960; PhD, SUNY, Buffalo, 1968. Instr. SUNY, Buffalo, 1963—66, asst. to dean, 1966—68; asst. prof. U. Calif., Santa Barbara, 1968—74; prof. English, creative writing Pitzer Coll., Claremont (Calif.) Colls., 1974—. Playwright: Paying the Piper, 1968, Prince Hal, 1995; co-editor Modernism: Challenges and Perspectives, 1986; author: The Cracked Looking Glass: James Joyce and the Nightmare of History, 1992; contbr. stories, creative essays to lit. jours., newspapers, and mags. NDEA fellow, 1960-63, fellow Creative Arts Inst., U. Calif., Berkeley, 1970, NEH Summer Inst., Dartmouth Coll., 1987; Danforth Found. assoc., 1978, NEH Seminar, Cornell U., 1998. Jewish. Office: Pitzer Coll Claremont Colls Claremont CA 91711-6101 Office Phone: 909-607-3641. Business E-Mail: awachtel@pitzer.edu.

**WACHTEL, NORMAN JAY,** lawyer; b. NYC, June 1, 1941; s. A. Allen and Lillian (Rolnik) W.; m. C. Robin Fixler, June 12, 1969; children: Jonathan, Charles. AB, U. Pa., 1963, LLB, 1966; LLM, Boston U., 1967. Bar: N.Y. 1967. Assoc. Demov, Morris & Hammerling, N.Y.C., 1968-78, ptnr., 1978-87, Rogers & Wells, N.Y.C., 1987-96, of counsel, 1996—2003, Clifford Chance US LLP, N.Y.C., 2003—. Bd. advisors 1st Am. Title Ins. Co. N.Y., 1982—. Author: (chpt.) Real Estate Titles, 1984. Office: Clifford Chance US LLP 31 West 52nd St New York NY 10019 Office Phone: 212-878-8152. Personal E-mail: normanwachtel@hotmail.com. Business E-Mail: norman.wachtel@cliffordchance.com.

**WACHTEL, ESTHER,** non-profit management executive, consultant; b. June 30; m. Thomas Wachtel, Jan. 27; children: Roger Bruce, Wendy Anne, Peter James BA in Phil., Conn. Coll.; MA in Literature, Cornell U. Pres. Music Ctr. of Los Angeles County; founder, pres. The Wachtel Group, TWU, Inc. Lectr. UCLA Grad. Sch. of Mgmt. Bd. visitors George L. Graziadio Sch. of Bus. Pepperdine U.; bd. dirs. The Ventura County Mus. of History and Art; chair U. So. Calif Ctr. Philanthropy and Pub. Policy; bd. dirs. Children's Hosp. L.A. Mem.: Regency Club (bd. dirs.). Fax: 805-649-3303.

**WACHTEL, HERBERT M.,** lawyer; b. NYC, May 24, 1932; BS, NYU, 1952, LLB, 1954; LLM, Harvard Univ., 1955. Bar: N.Y. 1955, US Dist. Ct. (so. & ea. N.Y.), US Ct. Appeals (2d, 3d, 4th, 5th, 7th, 8th, 11th & Fed. cir.), US Supreme Ct. 1973. Asst. U.S. atty. U.S. Dept. Justice, so. dist. N.Y., 1955—57; ptnr., litigation dept. Wachtell, Lipton, Rosen & Katz, N.Y.C., 1965—. Editor: NYU Law Rev., 1953—54; author: N.Y. Practice Under the CPLR, 1986. Root-Tilden scholar. Fellow: Am. Bar Found., Am. Coll. Trial Lawyers; mem.: ABA, N.Y. County Lawyers Assn., Assn. Bar City of N.Y., Phi Beta Kappa, Order of the Coif. Office: Wachtell Lipton Rosen & Katz 51 W 52nd St New York NY 10019-6150 Office Phone: 212-403-1216. Office Fax: 212-403-2216. Business E-Mail: hmwachtell@wlrk.com.

**WACHTER, MICHAEL L.,** law and finance educator; b. NYC, Mar. 12, 1943; s. Abraham and Florence W.; m. Susan M. Jaffe, June 23, 1968; children: Jessica, Jonathan. BS, Cornell U., 1964; MA, Harvard U., 1967, PhD, 1970. Asst. prof. econs. U. Pa., Phila., 1969-73, assoc. prof., 1973-76, prof. econs., law and mgmt., 1976—93, William B. Johnson prof. law & econ., 1993—, co-dir. Inst. for Law and Econ., 1984—; sr. advisor Brookings Instn., Washington, 1976-90. Mem. Minimum Wage Study Commn., Washington, 1978-81; cons. U.S. Postal Svc., 1980—. Editor: Removing Obstacles to Economic Growth, 1984, Toward a New U.S. Industrial Policy, 1982; contbr. articles to profl. jours. NIH grantee, 1981-83; NSF grantee, 1974-77; 20th Century Fund grantee, 1978-82; Gen. Electric Found. grantee, 1980-83 Mem. Am. Econ. Assn., Econometric Soc., Indsl. Relations Research Assn. Office: U Pa Law Sch Inst Law & Econs 3400 Chestnut St Philadelphia PA 19104-6204

**WACHTER, SUSAN MELINDA,** finance educator, educator; b. June 22, 1943; d. Nathaniel and Edith (Dubow) Jaffe; m. Michael Lawrence Wachter, June 23, 1968; children: Jessica, Jonathan. BA, Radcliffe Coll., 1965; PhD, Boston Coll., 1974; MA (hon.), U. Pa., 1978. Lectr. Bryn Mawr Coll., Pa., 1969-72; lectr. Wharton Sch. U. Pa., Phila., 1972-74, asst. prof. fin., 1974-78,

assoc. prof., 1978-95, prof. real estate and fin., 1995—, chmn. real estate dept., 1997—99; asst. sec., policy devel. and rsch. HUD, 1999—2001; Richard B. Warley prof. fin. mgmt., 2003—. bd. dirs. Beneficial Corp., Beneficial Mortgage Corp. Author: Latin American Inflation: The Structuralist-Monetarist Debat, 1976, Inflation and Pensions, 1987; co-author: Redlining and Public Policy, 1980; co-editor: Towards a New U.S. Industrial Policy?, 1981, Removing Obstacles to Economic Growth, 1984, Real Estate Economics, 1997, Savings and Capital Formation: The Policy Options; editor: Social Security and Private Pensions: Planning for the 21st Century, 1988; bd. editors Jour. Real Estate Rsch., Jour. Am. Real Estate and Urban Econs., Jour. Housing Econs., Jour. Real Estate Fin. and Econs. Recipient Lindbach award Lindbach Soc., 1974-75; Rsch. fellow Harvard U., 1966. Mem. Am. Econ. Assn. (bd. dirs. 1984-91, pres. 1988), Lambda Alpha. Home: 355 Margo Ln Berwyn PA 19312-1453 Office: U Pa Finance Dept Philadelphia PA 19104 Office Phone: 215-898-6355. Business E-Mail: wachter@wharton.upenn.edu.

**WACHTLER, SOL,** lawyer, educator; b. N.Y.C., Apr. 29, 1930; s. Philip Henry and Fay (Sobel) W.; m. Joan Wolosoff, Feb. 23, 1952; children: Lauren Jane, Marjorie Dru, Alison Toni, Philip Henry. BA, Washington and Lee U., 1951, LLB, 1952, postgrad., 1980, LLD (hon.), 1981, New Eng. Sch. Law, 1978, Bklyn. Law Sch., 1978, Hofstra U., 1980, SUNY, 1981, Syracuse U., Dowling Coll., 1990, Thomas M. Cooley Law Sch., 1990, New. Eng. Law Sch.; LHD (hon.), LIU, Coll. of St. Rose. Bar: N.Y. 1956. Justice N.Y. State Supreme Ct., 1968-72; judge N.Y. State Ct. Appeals, Albany, 1972-84; chief judge State of N.Y., Albany, 1985-93; prof. law Touro Law Sch., 1997—. Guest lectr. Bklyn. Law Sch., Hofstra Law Sch., Yale U. Sch. Law, Albany Law Sch., St. John's Law Sch., 1968-77, USIA, Munich, Germany, 1973, Stuttgart, Germany, 1977, U. Leyden, Amsterdam, Stockholm, 1988, Madrid, 1989; chmn. NY State Fair Trial/Free Press Conf., NY State Commn. on Bicentennial of US Constitution.; bd. dirs. Confs. Chief Justices; trustee Nat Jud. Coll. Author: After the Madness, 1997, Blood Brothers, 2003; critic-at-large New Yorker mag., 1996; contbr. articles to legal jours. Councilman Town of North Hempstead, N.Y., 1963-65, chief exec., 1965-67; mem. Nassau County Bd. Suprs., 1965-67, chmn. pub. safety, 1965-67; trustee L.I. Jewish-Hillside Med. Ctr., 1970-98, L.I. U.; exec. com. North Shore L.I. Jewish Health Sys., 1998—; bd. overseers Nelson A. Rockefeller Inst. Govt., Touro Law Sch., 2002-; dist. chmn. Boy Scouts Am., 1968-69; trustee Cerebral Palsy Assn., Assn. for Help of Retarded Children, 1966-67. Mem. Am. Law Inst., Assn. N.Y. State Supreme Ct. Justices, ABA, N.Y. State Bar Assn., Nassau County Bar Assn., Order of Coif, Phi Delta Phi. Jewish. Home: 10 Stonehill Dr N Manhasset NY 11030-4438 E-mail: SWCADRE@aol.com. *As a people, we are fond of the observation that ours is a nation of laws and not of men. It too, like the words of our great laws, seems to lend security, a sense of certainty, and a predictability to the paths we travel. In the law particularly, the thought that past generations have separated right from wrong and good from evil can be comforting. Yet, here again, if we will just scratch the surface, we will find that the greatest responsibility for our national welfare does not rest with statutes carved in stone but with the principles, conscience, and morality of the individuals who constitute this generation.*

**WACHTMANN, LYNN R.,** state legislator; m. Trudy Blue; children: Cory, Aaron. Grad., Four County Joint Vocat. Sch. Owner, pres. Maumee Valley Bottlers, Inc., Napoleon, Ohio; ptnr. Culligan Water Conditioning; former councilman City of Napoleon; mem. Ho. of Reps., Ohio, 1985—98, Ohio Senate from 1st dist., Columbus, 1999—, chmn. health, human svcs. and aging com., mem. energy, natural resources, environment, highways and transp., ins., commerce and labor coms. Vol. fundraiser Crisis Pregnancy Ctrs. of N.W. Ohio, Bryan; vol. Orphan Grain Train; mem. Rep. Ctrl. Com.; Sunday sch. tchr., usher St. Paul Luth. Ch.; bd. dirs. Ohio Water Quality Assn. Named Nat. Legislator of Yr., Am. Legis. Exch. Coun., 1994, State Legislator of Yr., Nat. Retail Fedn., 1996, Legislator of Yr., Am. Legion, 2000; recipient Bobcat Legis. award, 1993, Watchdog of the Treasury award, United Conservatives of Ohio, Oustanding Freshman Legislator of Yr. award, 2000, Grad. Wall of Fame award, Four County Joint Vocat. Sch., 1997, Legislator of Yr. Defender of Life award, Ohio Right to Life, 1997, Conservation Legis. award, League of Ohio Sportsmen Nat. Wildlife Fedn., 1997, Guardian of Small Bus. award, Nat. Fedn. Ind. Bus., 1998. Mem.: NRA, Ohio Twp. Assn., Nat. Assn. Sportsman Legislators, Am. Legis. Exch. Coun. (state chmn.), Ohio Right to Life Soc., Gideon's Internat., Ohio Farm Bur., Pheasants Forever, Ducks Unlimited. Republican. Office: Rm # 040 Senate Bldg Columbus OH 43215 Office Phone: 614-466-8150.

**WACHTMEISTER, COUNT WILHELM H.F.,** diplomat; b. Vanas, Sweden, Apr. 29, 1923; s. Gustaf and Margaretha (Trolle) W.; m. Ulla Leuhusen, 1947; children: Anna, Erik. LLD, U. Stockholm, Sweden, 1946. Attache Swedish Ministry for Fgn. Affairs, 1946-47; attache Swedish Embassy, Vienna, Madrid and Lisbon, 1947-50; 2d sec. Swedish Ministry Fgn. Affairs, Stockholm, Sweden, 1950-55; 1st sec. Swedish Embassy, Moscow, 1955-58; personal asst. to UN Sec. Gen., 1958-61; head UN sect. Fgn. Ministry, Stockholm, 1962-65, dep. under-sec. polit. affairs, 1965-66; ambassador to Algeria Swedish Embassy, 1966-67; under-sec. for polit. affairs Swedish Ministry Fgn. Affairs, Stockholm, 1968-74; Swedish ambassador to U.S. Swedish Embassy, Washington, 1974-89; dean diplomatic corps in Washington, 1986-89. Sr. advisor to chmn. AB Volvo, 1989-94. Mem. Soc. Cincinnati (France), Nya Sällskapet, Swedish-Am. C. of C. (chmn. 1993-95), Sällskapet, Stockholm. Avocation: tennis. Address: Karlavagen 59A SE 11449 Stockholm Sweden Office Phone: 46-8-6603823. Fax: 46854569733.

**WACK, THOMAS E.,** lawyer; b. Mo., 1944; AB magna cum laude, Georgetown U., 1966; JD Northwestern U., 1969, Bar: Mo. 1969. Ptnr., mem. exec. com. Bryan Cave LLP, St. Louis. Program dir. Fed. Practice Com. U.S. Dist. Ct. (Mo. dist.). Fellow Am. Coll. Trial Lawyers; mem. ABA, Mo. Bar Assn. (mem. bus. torts com., mem. unfair competition com. 1990-92). Office: Bryan Cave LLP One Metropolitan Square 211 North Broadway, Ste 3600 Saint Louis MO 63102 Office Phone: 314-259-2182. E-mail: tewack@bryancave.com.

**WACKER, SUSAN REGINA,** graphics designer, consultant; b. Red Bank, NJ, Apr. 29, 1954; d. Durward Richard and Margaret Rose (Williams) Wacker; m. Edward W. Donle. BFA, Pratt Inst., 1978, cert. computer graphics/electronic pub., 2001. Asst. art dir. Lesley-Hille Inc., N.Y.C., 1975-79; art dir. Kasica, Lefton, Brown, Inc., N.Y.C., 1979-80, Marinelli & Hnath Assoc., Inc., N.Y.C., 1980-82, L'Oreal Retail Divsn., N.Y.C., 2000—02; sr. design dir. Elizabeth Arden Co., N.Y.C., 1982-99; creativie cons., pres. SRW Design, Inc., Pittsfield, Vt., 2002—. Author: Fragrances of the World/Parfums du Monde-21st Anniversary edit., 2005; exhibitions include Mus. Natural History, N.Y.C., 1997—98; photographer Fragrances of the World/Parfums du Monde, 21st Anniversary Edit., 2005. Named CPA Package of the Month Elizabeth Arden's 5th Avenue fragrance line, 1996; recipient 4 DESI awards, 1980, ANDY award, 1980, Fragrance Found. award, 1988, 1991, 1992, Silver award, N.J. Packaging Execs. Club, 1990, ADDY Excellence citation, 1991, Edison Best New Products Gold Medal award, 1991, 2 Gold awards, Nat. Paperbox & Packaging Assn., 1992, 1994, Silver Excellence award, 1993, 10 Silver Excellence awards, 1994, Silver award, Paperboard Packaging Coun., 1993, Excellence award, 1993, Mobius 1st Pl. Statuette award, 1995, Gold award, Nat. Paperboard Coun., 1995, Prix Francois 1st de L'Emballage de Luxe, 1995, OMA Gold award, 1995, Oscar de L'Emballage Prestige à Lyon, 1995, Mobius award 1st Pl. Statuette for Elizabeth Taylor's Black Pearls perfume product line/package design, 1996, OMA Gold award for Elizabeth Arden's 5th Avenue tester display, 1996, OMA Bronze award for Elizabeth Taylor's Black Pearls tester display, 1996, Lagerfeld, Jako Mdsg., 1998, Nat. Paperboard Packaging Conc. award, 1996, OMA Bronze award Lagerfeld JAKO Mdsg. Program, 1998. Mem.: Am. Inst. Graphic Arts, Fashion Group Internat. (mem. pub. rel.), Cosmetic Exec. Women Found., Internat. Perfume Bottle Assn. Achievements include patents in field. Avocations: skiing, tennis, horseback riding, photography. Office: SRW Design Inc 19 Schoolhouse Dr PO Box 567 Pittsfield VT 05762 Office Phone: 888-666-7380. E-mail: srwacker@aol.com. srwdesign@comcast.net.

**WACKER, WARREN ERNEST CLYDE,** internist, educator; b. Bklyn., Feb. 29, 1924; s. John Frederick and Kitty Dora (Morrissey) W.; m. Ann Romeyn MacMillan, May 22, 1948; children: Margaret Morrissey, John Frederick. Student, Georgetown U., 1946—47; MD, George Washington U., 1951; MA (hon.), Harvard U., 1968. Intern George Washington U. Hosp., 1951-52, resident in internal medicine, 1952-53; resident Peter Bent Brigham Hosp., Boston, 1953-55; Nat. Found. Infantile Paralysis fellow, 1955-57; investigator Howard Hughes Med. Inst., Boston, 1957-68; from faculty to prof. hygiene Harvard U., Cambridge, Mass., 1955-71, assoc. prof. medicine, 1968—71, 1971—89, Henry K. Oliver prof. hygiene emeritus, 1089—, acting master Mather House, 1974-75, acting master Kirkland House, 1975-76, master Cabot House, 1978-84; sr. med. cons. Risk Mgmt. Found., Cambridge, 1992—. Dir. health svcs. Harvard U., Cambridge, 1971-89; vis. scholar St. Mary's Hosp. Med. Sch., 1964; vis. prof. U. Tel Aviv, 1987; chmn. bd. Applied Mgmt. Sys., Burlington, Mass., 1982-97, Millipore Corp., Bedford, Mass., 1971-94. Author: Magnesium and Man, 1981; sec., editl. adv. bd. Biochemistry, 1962-76; assoc. editor Magnesium; mem. editl. bd. Toxiogical and Environ. Chemistry, 1989-2006; contbr. articles to med. and sci. jours. Vestryman St. Paul's Episc. Ch., Brookline, Mass., 1965-68, 76-79, 91-94; bd. dirs. Harvard Cmty. Health Plan, Boston, 1973-84, mem. fin. com., 1984-86, mem. corp., 1986-96; bd. dirs. Bishop Rhinelander Found., Cambridge, 1973-76, 78-84, Controlled Risk Ins. Co., 1976-78; pres. bd. overseers Peter Bent Brigham Hosp., Boston, 1979-84; trustee Brigham and Women's Hosp., Boston, 1984-89, Risk Mgmt. Found., 1979-92; mem. mgmt. bd. MIT, 1985-95; mem. corp. Mt. Auburn Hosp., Cambridge, 1986—2006; mem. adv. bd. hospitality program Episc. Diocese Mass., 1989-95. 1st lt. USAAF, 1942-45. Decorated Air medal, D.F.C., Liberation medal, Greece; named Disting. Alumnus, George Washington U., 1963; recipient Cert. of Merit, Soc. Magnesium Rsch., 1985. Mem. AMA, Am. Chem. Soc., Am. Soc. Biol. Chemistry, Am. Soc. Clin. Investigation, Mass. Med. Soc., ACP, Am. Coll. Health Assn. (pres. 1981, Boynton award 1986), Biochemistry Soc. (London), Am. Coll. Nutrition, Harvard Club (Boston), Sigma Xi, Alpha Omega Alpha. Home: 91 Glen Rd Brookline MA 02445-7764 Office: Risk Mgmt Found 101 Main St Cambridge MA 02142-1519 Office Phone: 617-679-1216. Business E-Mail: wwacker@rmf.harvard.edu.

**WACKER-B. DEBORAH,** secondary Spanish and special education educator; b. San Diego, Dec. 22, 1945; d. Robert Eugene and Marion Llewella (Bancroft) Wacker; m. William E. Calvert, Dec. 22, 1966 (div. Aug. 1984); 1 child, William E. Calvert II; m. John Steven Bertram, Mar. 8, 1985 (div. Feb. 2001). BA, Belhaven Coll., Jackson, Miss., 1967. Cert. tchr., Miss. Tex. Mid. sch. spl. edn. tchr. Killeen Ind. Sch. Dist., Tex., 1982-85; elem. sch. spl. edn. tchr., tchr. ESL, Mansfield Ind. Sch. Dist., Tex., 1985-86; jr. high sch. spl. edn. tchr., head dept. Arlington Ind. Sch. Dist., Tex., 1986-90; jr. high sch. spl. edn. tchr. Conroe Ind. Sch. Dist., Tex., 1990-92, high sch. spl. edn. tchr., 1992-93, tchr. Spanish, 1993—99; v.p. Bertram Cons., Inc., 1995—96; tchr. spl. edn. Cy-Fair Ind. Sch. Dist., Tex., 1996—97; substitute tchr. Northland Christian Sch., 1997—2003; Spanish tchr. Klein Intermediate Sch., 2000—, Alief (Tex.) Taylor H.S., 2003—. Co-sponsor Tex. Future Tchrs. Assn., Pan Am. Student Assn./Club Leon; mem. various coms. Conroe (Tex.) Ind. Sch. Dist., 1991-96 Soprano Montgomery County Choral Soc., Conroe, 1991—94, sect. leader, 1995—96; mem. Campus Site-Based Decision Making Team, 1996—97, Arlington Choral Soc., 1986—89; sponsor Tex. Future Tchrs. Am., 1995—97; mem. Houston Symphony League, 1997—2003, Houston Mus. Fine Arts, 1996—97, 1998—, Houston Mus. Natural Sci.; soprano Houston Choral Soc., 2001—. Mem.: NEA, AAUW, Alief Educators Assn. (v.p. 2004—), Klein Edn. Assn. (v.p. 2002—03), Am. Coun. Tchrs. Fgn. Lang., Conroe Edn. Assn. (pres.-elect 1990—92, exec. com. 1994—97, pres.-elect 1995—97), Tex. State Tchrs. Assn. (1st pres. 1991, spl. edn. caucus), Tex. Fgn. Lang. Assn., Internat. Club (sponsor 1995—2002). Methodist. Avocations: music, reading, travel, internet. Home: 1333 Eldridge Pkwy Apt 212 Houston TX 77077-1611 Personal E-mail: soyyarnalady@aol.com. Business E-Mail: deborah.wacker@aliefisd.net

**WACKERMANN, WILLIAM,** publishing executive; married; 3 children. Grad., Villanova U., 1989. Mktg. mgr. Bus. Week; various positions Vanity Fair, corp. mgr., 1995—96; N.Y. advt. mgr. Conde Nast Traveler, 1996—97, advt. mgr., 1997—98, assoc. pub., 1999—2000, House & Garden, 1998—99; v.p. and pub. Details mag. 2000—04, Glamour mag., 2004—. Named Mag. Pub. of Yr., Delaney Report, 2002; recipient Media Mavens award, Advt. Age, 2003. Office: Glamour Mag Conde Nast Bldg 4 Times Sq New York NY 10036-6522*

**WADDELL, DON,** professional sports team executive; m. Cheryl Waddell; 1 child, Chelsea. Player No. Mich. U. Divsn. I Hockey, 1976—80, US Nat. Team, World Champs., 1983; player, coach Goaldiggers Hockey Club, Toledo, 1985—86, Flint Spirits, 1986—88; player Los Angeles Kings, 1980—83; head coach, gen. mgr. Flint Spirits, 1988—89, gen. mgr., 1989—90; v.p., exec. com. RDV Sports, San Diego Gulls, 1990—95, head coach, 1991—92; v.p., exec. com. RDV Sports, Orlando Solar Bears, 1995—97; asst. gen. mgr. Stanley Cup Champion Detroit Red Wings, 1997—98; v.p., gen. mgr. Atlanta Thrashers, Atlanta, 1998—; asst. gen. mgr. Team USA World Championships, 1999—2000, gen. mgr., 2001—02. Named First Team Internat. Hockey League All-Star, 1982, 1986, Second Team Internat. Hockey League All-Star, 1988; named to CCHA All-Decade Team, No. Mich. U., 1970. Achievements include inducted into the No. Mich. U. Sports Hall of Fame, 1992. Office: Atlanta Thrashers 1 CNN Ctr 12th Fl S Tower Atlanta GA 30303-2762*

**WADDELL, DOUGLAS HOWARD,** family physician; b. Bluff City, TN, May 6, 1943; s. Cecil Howard and France Daisy (Boling) W.; m. Luz Isabel Chico, Jan 2, 1971; children: Amy, Christopher, Brandon. BS in Biology Chemistry, Carson-Newman Coll., Jefferson City, Tenn., 1965; MD, U. Tenn., 1969. Diplomate Am. Bd. Family Practice. Intern Baylor U. Med. Ctr., Dallas, 1970; physician, owner Launey Med. Clinic, Dallas, 1971-82, Beltline North Med. Clinic, Dallas, 1983-85, Atrium Med. Clinic, Dallas, 1985—. Fellow Am. Acad. Family Physicians; mem. Tex. Med. Assn., Dallas County Med. Soc., Tex. Acad. Family Physicians (bd. dirs. state assn., past sec., treas., v.p., pres. Dallas chpt.), Am. Coll. Occupational and Environ. Medicine. Republican. Baptist. Avocations: gardening, cooking. Home: 10473 Epping Ln Dallas TX 75229-6310 Office: Atrium Med Clinic 14645 Webb Chapel Rd Ste 111 Dallas TX 75234-3600 Office Phone: 972-247-6900.

**WADDELL, JOHN COMER,** electronics distribution company executive; b. Bridgeport, Conn., Sept. 10, 1937; s. John and Dorothy Margot (Comer) W. BA, Yale U., 1959; MBA, Harvard U., 1965. Assoc. R.W. Pressprich & Co., N.Y.C., 1965-68; ptnr. Glenn, Green & Waddell, N.Y.C., 1968-80; exec. v.p. Arrow Electronics, Inc., Melville, NY, 1969-80, chmn., CEO, 1980—86, chmn., 1986—94, vice chmn., 1994—. Mem. com. arch. & design Mus. Modern Art, NYC; mem. photographs bd. Mus. Modern Art, NYC. Joffrey Ballet; past pres. Found. for Joffrey Ballet; dir. 55th St. Dance Theater Found., Nat. Corp. Fund for Dance, Am. Arts Alliance. Officer Office of Naval Intelligence USN. Office: Arrow Electronics Inc 50 Marcus Dr Melville NY 11747-3509*

**WADDELL, M. KEITH,** human resources specialist; From v.p. to vice chmn., CFO, treas. Robert Half Internat. Inc., Menlo Pk., Calif., 1986—93, vice chmn., 1999—, CFO, 1999—, treas., 1999—. Office: Robert Half International Inc 2884 SandHill Rd Menlo Park CA 94025

**WADDELL, MARK E.,** lawyer; b. 1957; BSChemE, NJ Inst. Tech., 1979; JD, Seton Hall U., 1984. Bar: NJ 1985, NY 1985, US Ct. Appeals (Fed. Cir.), registered: US Patent & Trademark Office. Process develop. engr., 1979-83; patent atty. Hubbell Cohen, NYC, 1983—86; atty., patent law dept. Hoffmann-La Roche Inc., NYC, 1986—87; patent atty. Cohen, Pontani & Lieberman, NYC; ptnr. Bryan Cave LLP, NYC, 1991—2001, mem. exec. com & strategic planning com., chmn., Intellectual Property Practice Group; ptnr., intellectual property dept., litig. dept. Chadbourne & Parke LLP, NYC, 2001—. Spkr. in field; contbr. articles to profl. jour. Mem.: Intellectual

Property Owners Assn., Fed. Cir. Bar Assn., NY Intellectual Property Law Assn. Office: Chadbourne & Parke LLP 30 Rockefeller Plz New York NY 10112 Office Phone: 212-408-8044. Office Fax: 212-541-5369. Business E-Mail: mwaddell@chadbourne.com.

**WADDELL, WILLIAM JOSEPH,** pharmacologist, toxicologist; b. Commerce, Ga., Mar. 16, 1929; s. Daniel and Lillian Marie (Vollrath) Waddell; m. Grace Carolyn Marlowe, Oct. 19, 1974; children: William Joseph, James Glenn, Martin Christie, Amy Allison. AB in Chemistry, U. N.C., 1951, MD, 1955. Postdoctoral rsch. fellow U. N.C. Sch. Medicine, 1955-58, asst. prof. pharmacology, 1958-62, asso. prof., 1962-72, asso. prof. oral biology Dental Rsch. Ctr., 1967-69, prof., 1969-72, assoc. dir., 1968-72; prof. pharmacology U. Ky. Coll. Medicine, Lexington, 1972-77; prof., chmn. dept. pharmacology and toxicology U. Louisville, 1977-97, emeritus chmn., 1997—, prof. emeritus, 1998—. Centennial Alumni Disting. vis. prof. U. N.C. Sch. Medicine, 1979. Contbr. articles to profl. jours. Fellow: Acad. Toxicological Scis.; mem.: Soc. Toxicology, Soc. Exptl. Biology and Medicine, Internat. Soc. Study Xenobiotics, Am. Teratology Soc., Am. Physiol. Soc., Am. Soc. Pharmacology and Exptl. Therapeutics, Sigma Xi. Home: 14300 Rose Wycombe Rd Prospect KY 40059-9024 Office: U Louisville Dept Pharmacology Louisville KY 40292-0001 Business E-Mail: bwaddell@louisville.edu.

**WADDELL, WILLIAM ROBERT,** lawyer; b. Ft. Thomas, Ky., Nov. 24, 1940; s. Ewell Edward and Sara Isabel (Dean) W.; m. Linda Kay Waddle, Aug. 25, 1962; children: Robert William, Keith Edward, Alex Watson. AB, Williams Coll., 1962; JD, U. Va., 1965. Bar: Va. 1965, U.S. Dist. Ct. (ea. dist.) Va. 1966, U.S. Ct. Appeals (4th cir.) 1966, U.S. Supreme Ct. 1966, N.C. 1991. Assoc. McGuire, Woods, Battle & Boothe, Richmond, Va., 1965—69, ptnr., 1969—. Adj. faculty Sch. Law, U. Va., 1995-; bd. dirs. Cmty. Bank Virginia Beach, Va., The George Found., Alex Lee, Inc., Hickory, N.C., Downtown Rep. Club, Norfolk, Va., Greater Norfolk Corp. Author: Virginia Corporations, 2005, Dispute Resolution: A Survey, 2006; contbr. articles to profl. jours Pres. Bon Air Cmty. Assn., Richmond, 1979-80; bd. dirs., sec. Va. Advanced Tech. Assn., Richmond, 1986-96; chmn. The Steward Sch., 1985-88, Jr. Achievement of Richmond, Inc., 1989-90. Mem. ABA (comml. code com., sales subcom. 1982—, chmn. telecomm. com. 1986-90, 94-96, vice-chmn. com. on law of commerce in cyberspace 1996-98, dispute resolution com. 1990—), Order of Coif. Avocations: tennis, history, woodworking. Office: McGuireWoods LLP 1 James Ctr 901 E Cary St Richmond VA 23219 also: McGuireWoods LLP World Trade Ctr 101 W Main St Ste 9000 Norfolk VA 23510-1655 Business E-Mail: wwaddell@mcguirewoods.com.

**WADDEN, CHRISTOPHER DAVID,** food products executive; b. Ridgewood, N.J., Feb. 25, 1959; s. Robert Vincent and Mary Elizabeth (Townley) W. BSME, Tex. A&M U., 1981; MBA, Keller Grad. Sch. Mgmt., 2002. Registered profl. engr., Tex. Ind. spl. project engr. Dresser Magcobar, Houston, 1981-83; staff engr. Nabisco Brands (Nat. Biscuit Co.), Houston, 1983-84, mechanical supt. St. Louis, 1984-85, sr. project engr. East Hanover, N.J., 1985-86, shift mgr. Houston, 1986-88, ops. mgr. San Francisco, 1988-89, mfg. mgr. Chgo., 1989-91; gen. mgr. Yili Nabisco Biscuit and Food Co., Ltd., Beijing, 1991-95; pres. F.W.C. Internat., Lighthouse Point, Fla., 1995-2000; gen. mgr. Laguna Cookie Co., Tustin, Calif., 2000—01, Organic Milling Co., San Dimas, Calif., 2001—04, pres., 2005—. Contbg. author: Cookie and Cracker Manufacturing, 1990. Rep. com. mem., Lisle, Ill., 1990. Roman Catholic. Avocations: aviation, oenology, acting, writing. Office: 1035 Withsdale Pasadena CA 91105

**WADDEN, RICHARD ALBERT,** environmental engineer, educator, science administrator, consultant; b. Sioux City, Iowa, Oct. 3, 1936; s. Sylvester Francis and Hermina Lillian (Costello) Wadden; m. Angela Louise Trabert, Aug. 9, 1975; children: Angela Terese, Noah Albert, Nuiko Clare. Student, St. John's U., Collegeville, Minn., 1954-56; BSChemE, Iowa State U., 1959; MSChemE, N.C. State U., 1962; PhD in Chem. and Environ. Engring., Northwestern U., 1972. Registered profl. engr., Ill., cert. indsl. hygienist. Engr. Linde Co., Tonnawanda, NY, 1959-62, Humble Oil Co., Houston, 1962-65; instr. engring. Pahlavi U. Peace Corps, Shiraz, Iran, 1965-67; tech. adviser Ill. Pollution Control Bd., Chgo., 1971-72; asst. dir. Environ. Health Resource Ctr. Ill., Chgo., 1972-74; from asst. prof. to assoc. prof. environ. and occupational health scis. Sch. Pub. Health U. Ill., Chgo., 1972—79, prof., 1979—2003, dir., 1984-86, 88-92, dir. Office Tech. Transfer Ctr. Solid Waste Mgmt. and Rsch., 1987-92, dir. indsl. hygiene and hazardous waste tng. programs Occupl. Safety and Health Ctr., 1987—2002, prof. emeritus, 2003—. Vis. scientist Nat. Inst. Environ. Studies, Japan, 1978—79, invited scientist, Japan, 1983, Japan, 84, Japan, 88; cons. air pollution control, health implications energy devel., indoor air pollution. Author: (book) Energy Utilization and Environmental Health, 1978; author: (with P. A. Scheff) Indoor Air Pollution, 1983; author: Engineering Design for Control of Workplace Hazards, 1987; contbr. articles to profl. publs. Vis. scholar, Northwestern U., Evanston, Ill., 1997; Sr. Internat. fellow, Fogarty Internat. Ctr.-NIH, 1978—79, 1983, WHO fellow, 1984. Mem.: AIChE, Am. Conf. Govtl. Indsl. Hygienists, Am. Indsl. Hygiene Assn., Air and Waste Mgmt. Assn., Am. Acad. Indsl. Hygiene (diplomate), Am. Acad. Environ. Engrs. (diplomate), Am. Chem. Soc. Address: 816 16th St Wilmette IL 60091

**WADDEN, THOMAS ANTHONY,** psychologist, educator; b. Richmond, Va., Sept. 3, 1952; s. Thomas Antony Jr. and Mary Lloyd (Cradock) W.; m. Jan Robin Linowitz, Nov. 11, 1984; children: David Joseph, Michael James, Steven Zachary. AB magna cum laude, Brown U., 1975; PhD, U. N.C., 1981; MA (hon.), U. Pa., 1994. Psychology intern Boston VA Med. Ctr., 1980-81; instr. in psychology U. Pa. Sch. Medicine, Phila., 1981-82, asst. prof. psychology, 1982-87, assoc. psychology, 1987-91, prof. psychology, 1994—; prof. psychology, dir. clin. tng. Syracuse (N.Y.) U., 1992-93. Clin. dir. Obesity Rsch. Group, U. Pa., Phila., 1983-91, dir. Weight and Eating Disorders Program, 1994—; dir. Ctr. for Health and Behavior, Syracuse U., 1992-93. Author (with K.D. Brownell): LEARN PRogram for Weight Control, 1998; assoc. editor: Annals of Behavioral Medicine, 1990—93, mem. editl. bd.: Internat. Jour. Eating Disorders, Jour. Cons. and Clin. Psychology, Obesity Rsch.; editor (with T.B. Vanitallie): Treatment of the Seriously Obese Patient, 1992; editor: (with A.J. Stunkard) Obesity: Theory and Therapy, 1993, Handbook of Obesity Treatment, 2002; contbr. chapters to books; writer: numerous sci. papers. Recipient Nat. Rsch. Svc. award NIMH, 1983-85, Rsch. Scientist Devel. award, 1987-91, 94-2000, Midcareer Investigator award in patient oriented rsch., 2003—. Mem. APA, Soc. Behavioral Medicine (bd. dir. 1987-90), Assn. for Advancement of Behavior Therapy (New Rschr. award 1986), Acad. Behavioral Medicine, The Obesity Soc. (v.p. 2003-04, pres. 2005—), Germantown Cricket Club, Cosmos Club, Phi Beta Kappa, Sigma Xi. Democrat. Avocations: tennis, squash, music, guitar. Home: 433 Bolsover Rd Wynnewood PA 19096-1301 Office: U Pa Ste 3029 3535 Market St Philadelphia PA 19104-2641 Business E-Mail: wadden@mail.med.upenn.edu.

**WADDILL, CYNTHIA KAY,** nurse; d. Owen Lee and Epsie Adrias Sugg; m. Dale Alin Waddill, July 16, 1993; children: Stacy Kay Emfinger, Christopher Ryan Emfinger, Jamison Matthew Emfinger. ADN, U. Ark. at Little Rock, 1981—84; BSN, U. of Phoenix, 1998—2000, MSN, 2000—01; MSN FNP, Graceland U., 2001—03. Certified Nurse of the Operating Room, AORN Colo., 1994, Orthopaedic Nurse Certified, NAON, 2001. Ortho trauma charge nurse Univ. Ark. Med Sci. Campus, Little Rock, 1991—96, Shands Hosp., Jacksonville, Fla., 1996—2001; nurse Shands UF Hosp., Jacksonville, Fla., 2004—. Sr. nurse com. Ortho Trauma Practice Cons., Jacksonville, Fla., 2004—. Recipient Nat. Nurse Honor Soc., Sigma Theta Tau, 2002. Mem.: Am. Nursing Assn., Fla. Nurses Assn., Am. Acad. of Nurse Practitioners, Nat. Assn. of Orthopaedic Nurses, Sigma Theta Tau. Avocations: scuba diving, golf, fishing. Office: McLeod Orthopaedic Assocs 901 E Cheves St Ste 500 Florence SC 29501 Personal E-Mail: cbones100k@aol.com.

**WADDINGTON, RAYMOND BRUCE, JR.,** language educator; b. Santa Barbara, Calif., Sept. 27, 1935; s. Raymond Bruce and Marjorie Gladys (Waddell) W.; m. Linda Gayle Jones, Sept. 7, 1957 (div.); children: Raymond Bruce, Edward Jackson; m. Kathleen Martha Ward, Oct. 11, 1985. BA, Stanford U., 1957; PhD, Rice U., 1963; postdoctoral (Univ. fellow in Humanities), Johns Hopkins U., 1965-66. Instr. English U. Houston, 1961-62; instr. U. Kans., 1962-63, asst. prof., 1963-65; asst. prof. English lit. U. Wis., Madison, 1966-68, assoc. prof., 1968-74, prof., 1974-82; prof. English lit. U. Calif., Davis, 1982—2005. Author: The Mind's Empire, 1974, Aretino's Satyr, 2004; co-editor: The Rhetoric of Renaissance Poetry, 1974, The Age of Milton, 1980, The Expulsion of the Jews, 1994; mem. editl. bd. The Medal, 1991; sr. editor: Sixteenth Century Jour.; editor: Praeger Series on the Early Modern World. Recipient Scaglione prize for Italian Studies, 2005; Huntington Libr. fellow, 1967, 75; Inst. Rsch. in Humanities fellow, 1971-72; Guggenheim fellow, 1972-73; NEH fellow, 1977, 83; Newberry Libr. fellow, 1978; Am. Philos. Soc. grantee, 1965. Mem. Renaissance Soc. Am., Milton Soc. Am., Am. Numismatic Soc., 16th Century Soc. and Conf. (pres. 1985), Brit. Art Medal Soc., Logos Club. Home: 39 Pershing Ave Woodland CA 95695-2845 Office: U Calif Dept English Davis CA 95616 E-mail: rbwaddington@ucdavis.edu.

**WADDY, LAWRENCE HEBER,** writer; b. Sydney, Australia, Oct. 5, 1914; came to U.S., 1963; s. Percival Stacy and Etheldred (Spittal) W.; m. Laurie Hancock, July 10, 1972. BA, Oxford U., 1937, MA, 1945. Asst. master Winchester Coll. Eng., 1938—42; headmaster Tonbridge Sch., England, 1949—62; edn. officer BBC, 1962—63; chaplain The Bishop's Sch., La Jolla, Calif., 1963—67; lectr. in Greek and Latin lit. U. Calif., San Diego, 1969—80; vicar Ch. of Good Samaritan, University City, Calif., 1970—74; hon. asst. St. James By The Sea Episcopal Ch., La Jolla, 1975—. Author: Pax Romana & World Peace, 1950, Symphony, 1976, A Parish By the Sea, 1988, Shakespeare Remembers, 1994, First Bible Stories, 1994, Florence Nightingale, 1996, Bible Drama. 2004. Chaplain, British Navy, 1942-46. Recipient Drama 1st prize BBC, 1964. Republican. Episcopalian. Home: 5910 Camino De La Costa La Jolla CA 92037-6550 Personal E-Mail: lawrencewaddy@yahoo.com.

**WADDY, PATRICIA A.,** historian, architecture educator; b. Cannelton, Ind., July 29, 1941; d. Luther and Gertrude Viola (Brandyberry) W. BA, Rice U., 1963; MA, Tulane U., 1965; PhD, NYU, 1973. Vis. lectr. Carnegie-Mellon U., Pitts., 1970-71, asst. prof., 1971-77; assoc. prof. archtl. history Syracuse U., NY, 1977-91, prof., 1991—2002, disting. prof. architecture, 2002—. Vis. lectr. Cornell U., Ithaca, N.Y., 1977, vis. assoc. prof., 1980; Frederic Lindley Morgan prof. archtl. design U. Louisville, 2006. Author: Seventeenth-Century Roman Palaces: Use and The Art of the Plan, 1990 (Alice Davis Hitchcock award 1992); co-author: (with D. DiCastro and A.M. Pedrocchi) Il Palazzo Pallavicini Rospigliosi e la Galleria Pallavicini, 2000; editor Nicodemus Tessin the Younger, Traicté della decoration interieure (1717), 2002. Fulbright grantee, Rome, 1968-69; fellow Am. Acad. in Rome, 1970, Nat. Humanities Ctr., 1984-85, Samuel H. Kress sr. fellow Nat. Gallery Art, 1994-95, NEH fellow, 1998-99, Guggenheim fellow, 1999-00, Am. Coun. Learned Soc. fellow, 1978. Mem. Soc. Archtl. Historians (book rev. editor Jour. 1985-88, editor 1990-93, 2d v.p. 1993-94, 1st v.p. 1994-96, pres. 1996-98), Coll. Art Assn., Renaissance Soc. Am. Office: Syracuse U Sch Architecture Syracuse NY 13244-1250 E-mail: pwaddy@syr.edu.

**WADE, DANIEL M.,** recreational facility executive, hotel executive; With Circus Circus, Las Vegas, Nev., Holiday Casino, Las Vegas, The Maxim, Las Vegas, Aladdin Hotel, Las Vegas; v.p. ops. Harrah's Las Vegas; pres., gen. mgr. MGM Marina Hotel, Las Vegas; from various sr. level positions to vice chmn. MGM Mirage MGM Grand Hotel, Inc., Las Vegas, 1990—2001, vice chmn. MGM Mirage, 2001—.

**WADE, DIANNE ELIZABETH,** secondary school educator; b. Richmond, Va., Nov. 6, 1958; d. Allus Hess Wade and Ellen Holiday Hayden, William Carroll Johnson, Sr. (Stepfather); children: Stacy Bowman, Christine Elizabeth. BA, Carson Newman Coll., Jefferson City, Tenn., 1981; M, James Madison U., Harrisonburg, Va., 2000. Tchr. Waynesboro High Sch., Va., 1987—. Actor Waynesboro Players, 1981—2006. Actor, actor: The Man Who Came to Dinner, DeathTrap, Black Comedy, George Washington Slept Here, Nuncrackers, A Funny Thing Happened on the Way to the Forum, A Shot in the Dark, Nuncrackers, Something's Afoot, The King and I, Oliver; dir.: Inherit the Wind, The Remarkable Mr. Pennypacker, Philadelphia Story, Cole; actor: Mame, Nunsense, A Shot in the Dark, My Fair Lady, The Rainmaker, A Shot in the Dark, My Fair Lady; performer: Valley Mental Health Players; hostess Miss Stuarts Draft Pagent; singer: (cmty. choir) Waynesboro Choral Society. Choir mem. Fishersville Bapt. Ch., Va., 1981—2006, youth leader, 2000—06, children's choir dir., 1981—2005. Home: 33 Warren Cir Fishersville VA 22939 Office: Waynesboro High Sch 1200 W Main St Waynesboro VA 22980 Office Phone: 540-946-4616. Business E-Mail: dewade@waynesboro.k12.va.us.

**WADE, DWYANE,** professional basketball player; b. Chicago, Jan. 17, 1982; m. Siohvaughn Wade; 1 child. Student, Marquette U. Player Miami Heat, 2003—. Mem. U.S. Olympic Basketball Team, Athens, 2004. Named to NBA All-Rookie First team, 2004, All-NBA Second team, 2005; recipient Best Breakthrough Athlete, ESPY awards, 2005, Best NBA Player, 2006, NBA Finals MVP, 2006. Achievements include playing on NBA Championship team, 2006. Office: c/o Miami Heat American Airlines Arena 601 Biscayne Blvd Miami FL 33132*

**WADE, ED,** professional sports team executive; From pub. rels. intern to v.p., gen. mgr. Phila. (Pa.) Phillies, 1977—98, v.p., 1998—, gen. mgr., 1998—; pub. rels. asst. Houston (Tex.) Astros, 1977—79, pub. rels. dir., 1979—81, Pitts. (Pa.) Pirates, 1981—86.

**WADE, EDWIN LEE,** lawyer, writer; b. Yonkers, N.Y., Jan. 26, 1932; s. James and Helen Pierce (Kinne) W.; m. Nancy Lou Sells, Mar. 23, 1957; children: James Lee, Jeffrey K. BS, Columbia U., 1954; MA, U. Chgo., 1956; JD, Georgetown U., 1965. Bar: Ill. 1965. Fgn. svc. officer U.S. Dept. State, 1956-57; mktg. analyst Chrysler Internat., S.A., Switzerland, 1957-61; intelligence officer CIA, 1961-63; industry analyst U.S. Internat. Trade Commn., 1963-65; gen. atty. Universal Oil Products Co., Des Plaines, Ill., 1965-72; atty. Amsted Industries, Inc., Chgo., 1972-73; chief counsel dept. gen. svcs. State of Ill., Springfield, 1973-75; sr. atty. U.S. Gypsum Co., Chgo., 1975-84; gen. atty. USG Corp., 1985, corp. counsel, 1986, asst. gen. counsel, 1987, corp. sec., 1987-90, corp. sec., asst. gen. counsel, 1990-93; prin. Edwin L. Wade, 1993-95; instr. Roosevelt U., Chgo., 1995-96. Author: (books) Constitution 2000: A Federalist Proposal for the New Century, 2000, Talking Sense at Century's End: A Barbarous Time...Now What?, 2000; editor: Let's Talk Sense, A Pub. Affairs Newsletter, 1994-98. Fellow Chgo. Bar Assn. (life); mem. ABA, Ill. Bar Assn., Am. Philatelic Soc. Home: 434 Mary Ln Crystal Lake IL 60014-7257 Office: Let's Talk Sense Pub Co PO Box 2195 Crystal Lake IL 60039-2195

**WADE, ESTELLE B.,** psychologist, psychoanalyst; b. Bklyn., July 20, 1938; d. David and Selma Jobyna Schwartz; m. Donald E. Wade (div.); m. Alan L. Cantor, Apr. 3, 1992. BA, Clark U., 1959; MA, Brandeis U., 1961; PhD, Columbia U., 1971. Lic. psychologist NY, 1972, cert. profl. qualification psychology Assn. State Provincial Bds., 2001; bd. cert. found. fellow Am. Coll. Advanced Practice Psychologists, 1999. Postdoctoral fellowship in psychoanalysis Post-grad. Ctr. Mental Health, N.Y.C., 1980—83; counselor Inst. Crippled & Disabled, N.Y.C., 1961—62, N.Y.C. Dept. Hosps., Bklyn., 1962—65, Queens, 1962—65; psychology intern VA, N.Y.C., 1966—68; tchng. asst. Columbia U., N.Y.C., 1966—68; lectr. psychology CUNY, 1969—70; staff psychologist Queens County Neuropsychiatric Inst., Jamaica Heights, 1969—71; chief psychologist, 1971—81; supervising psychologist Fifth Ave. Ctr. Psychotherapy, N.Y.C., 1981—84; pvt. practice psychoanalysis & psychotherapy N.Y.C., 1977—. Host several radio programs, 1971—75. Mem. Pinewoods Folk Music Soc., 1966—75, program chair, 1971—75;

mem. Queens Ind. Democrats, Jackson Heights, 1967—69, Sloop Clearwater-NYC Chapter, 1969—75, program chair, 1973—75. Mem.: APA (program chair divsn. independent practice 1980—81, psychologist psychoanalyst practitioner, divsn. psychoanalysis 1984—), NY State Psychological Assn., Nat. Register Health Svc. Providers Psychology (platinum registrant 1994), Phi Beta Kappa. Democrat. Jewish. Avocations: classical music, opera, reading, walking. Office: 730 Fifth Ave 9th Fl New York NY 10019 Office Phone: 212-659-7799.

**WADE, GLEN,** electrical engineer, educator; b. Ogden, Utah, Mar. 19, 1921; s. Lester Andrew and Nellie (Vanderwerff) W.; m. LaRee Bailey, Mar. 20, 1945; children: Kathleen Ann, RaLee, Lisa Jean, Mary Sue. BS in Elec. Engring, U. Utah, 1948, MS, 1949; PhD, Stanford U., 1954. Research group leader, asso. prof. elec. engring. Stanford U., 1955-60; asso. dir. engring., microwave and power tube div. Raytheon Co., 1960-61, asst gen. mgr. research div., 1961-63; dir. Sch. Elec. Engring., Cornell U., 1963-66, J.P. Levis prof. engring., 1963-66; prof. elec. engring. U. Calif. at Santa Barbara, 1966—. Indsl. advisor U. R.I., 1961-63; vis. lectr. Harvard, 1963; cons. to industry, 1956—; vis. prof. Tokyo U., 1971; Fulbright-Hays lectr., Spain, 1972-73; cons. mem. Dept. Def. Adv. Group Electron Devices, 1966-73; Spl. Chair prof. Nat. Taiwan U., 1980-81, internationally renowned fgn. scholar lectureship, 1988; UN vis. prof. Nanjing Inst. Tech., 1986; UN vis. prof. S.E. U. People's Republic of China, 1989, Nat. Com. Sci. and Tech. vis. prof. U Guanajuato, Mex., 1994—; elected mem. The Electromagnetics Acad., 1990. Editor: Transactions on Electron Devices, 1961-71, IEEE Jour. Quantum Electronics, 1965-68; series editor: Harcourt Brace Jovanovich, 1964—; contbr. articles to profl. jours. U.S. del. Tech. Cooperation Program internat. meeting, 1970. Served with USNR, 1944-46. Recipient ann. award Nat. Electronics Conf., 1959, Outstanding Teaching award Acad. Senate, U. Calif., Santa Barbara, 1977, Prof. of Yr. award U. Calif. at Santa Barbara Mortar Bd. Sr. Honor Soc., 1988, Hon. Chairmanship award Twentieth Acoustical Imaging, 1992, Disting. Alumnus award Engring. Coll. U. Utah, 1998. Fellow IEEE (life; mem. adminstrv. com. profl. group election devices 1960-71, mem. publs. bd., chmn. info. processing com., mem. exec. com. 1971-72, dir. 1971-72, chmn. ednl. activities bd. 1971-72, editor proc. 1977-80, Centennial award 1984, Millennium medal 2000); mem. Am. Phys. Soc., Phi Kappa Phi, Tau Beta Pi, Sigma Xi, Eta Kappa Nu (Outstanding Young Elec. Engr. award 1955) Home: 1098 Golf Rd Santa Barbara CA 93108-2411 Office: Rm 214 Bldg 406 U Calif Santa Barbara CA Office Phone: 805-893-2508. E-mail: wade@ece.ucsb.edu.

**WADE, JAMES O'SHEA,** editor, writer; b. Atlanta, June 17, 1940; s. Richard J. and Mary Clare (O'Shea) W.; m. Linda Norman, June 19, 1971; 1 child, Christopher Scott. AB magna cum laude, Harvard U., 1962. Editor Blaisdell Pub. Co., N.Y.C., 1963-65; asst. to pres., sr. editor Macmillan Co., 1966-69; editor-in-chief World Pub. Co., 1969-71; v.p., editorial dir. David McKay Co., 1971-74; founder, pres. Wade Pub. Co., Inc., N.Y.C., 1975-78; exec. v.p. Rawson, Wade Pubs., Inc., N.Y.C., 1978-82; sr. editor Crown Pubs., Inc., N.Y.C., 1982-85, exec. editor, 1985-95, v.p., 1988-95; with Ind. Editors Group, 1996—. Mem. Century Club (N.Y.C.), Iroquois/D.U. Club (Harvard), Hasty-Pudding Inst. 1770 (Harvard U.). Democrat. Home and Office: 1565 Baptist Church Rd Yorktown Heights NY 10598-5812 Personal E-mail: jedit@optonline.net.

**WADE, JOHN CORNELIUS,** healthcare system administrator; b. Somerville, Mass., Apr. 13, 1941; s. Edward Joseph and Margaret Mary (O'Callahan) W.; m. Madeline Ann Buckley, Sept. 8, 1962 (div. May 1970); children: John Cornelius II, Madelaine Marie; m. Cheri Ann Macleod, June 11, 1971; children: Amy Katherine, Daniel Lewis. Student, Northeastern U., Boston, 1960-62; BA cum laude, Boston Coll., 1969, postgrad., 1973-78. Mgr. mgmt. info. sys. Polaroid Corp., Waltham, Mass., 1960-75, Children's Hosp., Boston, 1975-78; dir. info. systems Northwestern Meml. Hosp., Chgo., 1979-87; named dir. health data systems U. Ala. Health Systems, Birmingham, 1987; prin., nat. healthcare practice dir. Logica N.Am., Waltham, Mass.; chief info. officer St. Luke's Health Sys., Kansas City, Mo., 1993—, v.p., 1996—. Named one of Premier 100 IT Leaders, Computerworld, 2005. Fellow: Coll. Healthcare Info. Mgmt. Executives, Healthcare Info. and Mgmt. Systems Soc. Roman Catholic. Avocations: reading, gardening, world travel. Office: St Luke's Health Sys 10920 Elm Ave Kansas City MO 64134*

**WADE, JUNE BOOTH,** secondary school educator; b. St. Petersburg, Fla., Dec. 24, 1934; d. Monroe Phillippi and Julia Lenoir (Burdett) Booth; m. Charles Wade, Feb. 18, 1956; children: Susan Wade Infanzon, John Eric. BSJM, U. Fla., 1956. Tchr. English and journalism Hillsborough County Schs., Tampa, Fla. Mem. Nat. Coun. Tchrs. English, Fla. Coun. Tchrs. English, Hillsborough Coun. Tchrs. English, Ret. Educators Fla. (West Hillboraigh chpt.), Delta Kappa Gamma

**WADE, LEROY GROVER, JR.,** chemistry educator; b. Jacksonville, Fla., Oct. 8, 1947; s. Leroy Grover and Margaret Lena (Stevens) W.; m. Sandra Martinez Kooreny; children: Christine Elizabeth, Jennifer Diane. BA summa cum laude, Rice U., 1969; AM, Harvard U., 1970, PhD, 1974. Resident rsch. fellow Du Pont Chemical, Wilmington, Del., 1969; tchg. fellow in chemistry Harvard U., Cambridge, Mass., 1969-74, sr. adviser to freshmen, 1971-74; resident sci. tutor Radcliffe Coll., Cambridge, 1970-74; asst. prof. chemistry Colo. State U., Ft. Collins, 1974-80, assoc. prof., 1980-89; prof. chemistry Whitman Coll., Walla Walla, Wash., 1989—. Author: Annual Reports in Organic Synthesis, 1975-82, 8 vols., Compendium of Organic Synthetic Methods, Vols. III, IV, V, 1977, 80, 84, Organic Chemistry, 1987, 6th edit., 2005; contbr. articles to sci. jours.; reviewer profl. jours., textbooks. Mem. AAAS, Am. Chem. Soc., Am. Acad. Forensic Scis., Phi Beta Kappa (pres. chpt. 1983-84), Sigma Xi. Office: Whitman Coll Chemistry Dept Walla Walla WA 99362 E-mail: wadelg@whitman.edu.

**WADE, MICHAEL ROBERT ALEXANDER,** marketing specialist; b. NYC, June 29, 1945; s. Burton Jean and Celia (Handleman) W.; m. Carole Kay West, Aug. 25, 1974. AB, U. Chgo., 1967; postgrad. in pub. adminstrn., Am. U., 1967—71; MBA in Fin., NYU, 1975. Program analyst, mgmt. intern HUD, 1967—71; dep. dir. Mgmt. Comm. and Briefing Ctr. U.S. Price Commn., 1972; asst. exec. sec. policy coordination U.S. Cost of Living Coun., 1973—74; assoc. dir. U.S. Indochina Refugee Program, 1975—76; pres. China Trade Devel. Corp. Chgo., 1997—. Participant in Okla. oil and gas prodn. Recipient Meritorious Svc. award Exec. Office of Pres., 1972, Disting. Svc. award U.S. Cost of Living Coun., 1974. Mem. Soc. Contemporary Art, Internat. Bus. Coun. MidAm. (bd. dirs.). Office: China Trade Devel Corp 1110 Granville Dr 1st Fl Newport Beach CA 92660-6227 Office Phone: 949-759-6950. Business E-Mail: china-trade@worldnet.att.net.

**WADE, NICOLE JENNINGS,** lawyer; b. Portsmouth, Va., July 31, 1970; m. Michael Todd Wade, May 27, 1995. BA cum laude, Vanderbilt U., 1992; JD cum laude, U. Mich., 1995. Bar: Ga. 1995, US Dist. Ct. (no. dist.) Ga. 1996, US Dist. Ct. (mid. dist.) Ga. 1998, US Ct. Appeals (11th cir.) 1997, US Ct. Appeals (4th cir.) 1998. Ptnr. Powell Goldstein LLP, Atlanta, Ga., 1995—. Mem.: State Bar Ga. (chair mandatory continuing legal edn. and trial credit assistance com. 1999—2000), Bleckley Inn of Ct. (barrister 2001—03), Atlanta Bar Assn. Office: Powell Goldstein LLP 1201 W Peachtree St Atlanta GA 30309 Office Phone: 404-572-6600. Office Fax: 404-572-6999. Business E-Mail: nwade@pogolaw.com.

**WADE, REBA,** musician, educator; b. Dresden, Tenn., Apr. 30, 1938; d. John Buford and Willie Ruth (Todd) Tilley; m. Ronald Lee Wade, July 22, 1956; children: Tony Lee, Randy Neal. Student, U. Tenn., Martin, 1976-80. Tchr. pvt. studio, Martin, 1962-70, 76—, Sharon (Tenn.) Sch., 1968, Westview H.S., Martin, 1976—79, Greenfield (Tenn.) Sch., 1984-86; mgr., dir. Wade Bros., Martin, 1965-71, High Variety Show Mems., Martin, 1994—. Tchr., accompanist for students, shows, groups, auditions and on radio and TV; profl. pianist. Prodr. Wade Bros. Rec., 1969, student recs., 1988-90, 97-2005; author lyrics, music original compositions including Little Cowboy, 1963, I Love My Jesus, 1963, Christmas Time, 1964, Happy Happy Day, 1964, Love,

1964, Oh How I Love You, 1965, Dear Mis-Fortune, 1965, Red Lace, 1965, Crazy Little Feeling, 1967, All Because of Christmas Day, 1968, Mean Mean Mama, 1968, God is Like This, 1979, Little Dreams, 1992, also tnr., prodr., 1988-90, 97-2001; performer Christmas music The White House, 1997-98, Pentagon Party, 1998; performer World Wide Air Show RAF, Fairford, Eng., London, 1999; recorded 3CDs (total 32 songs and pieces on piano) Nasville, Tenn., 2000, 2001, Christmas CD (9 songs), 2003; recorded 18 songs and pieces on piano, Hilltop Rec. Studio, Nashville, 2000, 12 others, 2001, 10 more songs, 2003; prodr. five rec. sessions Hilltop Rec. Studio, Nashville, 2004; tnr. students Cerebral Palsy Telethon WBBJ TV, Jackson, Tenn., 1995-2002, 05. Active in civic affairs, 1947-; judge music festival U. Tenn., Martin, 2000-01, 2002, 2004-05, fall performance, 2000-01, 2002-03, 04, 05, Kiwanis Club Talent Show, 2000-01; active Martin Elem. Chorus, 2001; fundraiser Big Cypress Tree State Park, 2000-01, Dickson (Tenn.) Police Dept., 2000, Relay for Life, 1992-2005; invited charter mem. 1st Women's History Mus., Washington; planner, tnr. fund raiser program local fire dept. to buy new fire truck, 2000, entertainment fund raiser local town to install new lights in town, 2000; trained and provided entertainment for various charities. Recipient Vol. Svc. award State of Tenn. Recreation and Parks Assn., 2001, Companion Honor award, 2002, Salute to Greatness award, 2005; named Internat. Woman Yr., 2001, Internat. Musician, 2004, Internat. Musician Yr., 2004; nominated for Am. Medal Honor, 2002, 03-04, Lifetime Achievement award United Cultural Convention, 2005. Fellow Internat. Biog. Assn. (life, dir. deputy gen., 2006, advisor to dir. gen., 2006, Top 100 Musicians Pinnacle Achievement award, 2006, Internat. Order Merit, 2006); mem. SAI (life, social chmn. 1979), Songwriters Guild Am., Music Tchrs. Nat. Assn., Philharm. Music Club (v.p. 1983-84, pres. 1985), Am. Coll. Musicians, Dem Women, Am. Biog. Inst. (profl. women's adv. bd., 2006—, World Lifetime Achieve award, 2004, Woman of Yr., 2006, 500 Greatest Geniuses of 21st Century, 2006, Am. Medal Honor, 2006) Baptist. Achievements include being ivvited to become a charter member of the first women's history museum in Washington DC. Avocations: music writing, interior decorating and designing, travel, church and charity work. Home: 208 Melody Dr Martin TN 38237-5535

**WADE, SUZANNE L.C.,** secondary school educator; d. Clayton Charles and Louise Marguerite Connolly; m. Patrick Timothy Wade, Apr. 16, 1994; children: Brian Patrick, Emily Rose, Julia Marguerite. BS of Earth Sci. and Math., SUNY, Brockport, 1993, M of Secondary Sci. Edn., 1998. Cert. tchr. NY. Tchr. earth sci., biology Ogdensburg City Schs., NY, 1993—96, Spencerport Ctrl. Sch. Dist., NY, 1996—2000, Brighton Ctrl. Sch. Dist., Rochester, NY, 2001—. Gymnastics coach asst. SUNY, Brockport, 2002—. Roman Catholic.

**WADE, THOMAS EDWARD,** electrical engineering educator, academic administrator; b. Jacksonville, Fla., Sept. 14, 1943; s. Wilton Fred and Alice Lucyle (Hedge) W.; m. Ann Elizabeth Chitty, Aug. 6, 1966; children: Amy Renee, Nathan Thomas, Laura Ann. BSEE, U. Fla., Gainesville, 1966, MSEE, 1968, PhD, 1974. Cert. rsch. adminstr., 1992. Interim asst. prof. U. Fla., Gainesville, 1974-76; prof. elec. engring. Miss. State U., Starkville, 1976-85; state-wide dir. microelectronics rsch. lab. Miss., 1978-85; assoc. dean, prof. elec. engring. U. South Fla., Tampa, 1985—. Dir. Engring. Indsl. Experiment Sta., 1986-93, exec. dir. Ctrs. for Engring. R&D, 1985-90, mem. presdl. faculty adv. com. for rsch. and tech. devel., 1986-88, mem. fed. demonstration project com. for contracts and grants, 1986-88; mem. adv. bd. USF Exec. Fellows Program, 1987-91; chmn. evaluation task force applied rsch. grants program High Tech. and Industry Coun. State of Fla., 1988-90, vice chmn. microelectronics and materials subcoms. 1987-93, mem. telecom. subcom., 1988-89, chmn. legis. report com. FHTIC, 1989-90, chmn. U. sabbatical com., 1997-98; vice chmn. subcom. on microelectronics and materials Enterprise Fla. Innovation Partnership, 1993-94, chmn. univ. sabbatical com. 1997-98; mem. Tampa Bay Internat. Super Task Force, 1986-92, vice chmn. edn. com. 1988; dir. Fla. Ctr. for Microelectronics Design and Test, 1986-88; bd. dirs. NASA Ctr. Comml. Devel. of Space Comm. Ctr., Fla., 1990-93; bd. trustees Trinity Coll. Fla., 1997—, exec. com. 1998—, chmn. strategic planning com., 2001-; bd. trustees Toccoa Falls Coll., 2002; bd. dirs. New Tampa YMCA; rev. panel govt.-univ.-industry rsch. round table for fed. demonstration project NAS, 1988; solid state circuit specialist Applied Micro-circuits Corp., San Diego, 1981-82; sr. scientist NASA Marshall Space Flight Ctr., Huntsville, Ala., 1983; scientist Trilogy Semiconductor Corp., Santa Clara, Calif., 1984; organizer, chmn. Very Large Scale Integrated/Ultra Large Scale Integrated Multilevel Interconnection Conf., Seminar and Exhbn., editor procs., 1991—; organizer, gen. chmn. Dielectrics for Ultra Large Scale Integrated Multilevel Interconnection Conf., 1995—, Chem.-Mech.-Polish Planarization for Ultra Large Scale Integration, 1996—, Conductors for Ultra Large Scale Integrated Multilevel Interconnection Conf., 2000—; cons. in field. Author: Polyimides for Very Large Scale Integrated Applications, 1984, (U.S. Army handbook) Modern Very Large Scale Integrated Circuit Fabrication Processes, 1984, Photosensitive Polyimides for Very Large Scale Integrated Applications, 1986, Very Large Scale Multilevel Interconnection Advanced Metals Tutorial, 1996—, Very Large Scale Multilevel Interconnection Tutorial, 1987—; contr. chpts. on electronics to World Book encys., 1997; contr. over 125 articles to profl. jours. Active First Bapt. Ch., Temple Terrace, Fla., vice-chmn. bd. deacons 1989-90, chmn. bd. deacons, 1990-91, 93-94, chmn. pastor search com., 1990-91, vice-chmn. long range planning com., 1989-91, vice-chmn. pastor search com., 1994-95, dir. adult coed III Sunday sch. dept., 1993-94, ch. coun., 1994-95, ch. trustee, 1999—, mem. constn. and bylaws com., 1997-99, trustee, 1999—; treas. Tampa Palms Owners Assn., 1994-95, chmn. home decorating com., 1997; vol., United Fund, Miss. State U., 1983-85. Recipient Outstanding Engring. Tchg. award Coll. Engring. U. Fla., 1976, Outstanding Tchg. Incentive program award State of Fla., 1998, Cert. of Recognition NASA (5 times), 1981-88, Outstanding Rsch. award Sigma Xi, 1984, Outstanding Contbn. to Sci. and Tech. award Fla. Gov., 1989, 90, Outstanding Undergrad. Tchg. award U. South Fla., 1999. Mem. AAAS, NSPE, IEEE (sr. mem., guest editor periodical 1982, gen. chmn. Internat. Very Large Scale Integrated Multilevel Interconnection Conf. annually 1984-90, editor conf. procs., 1984-90, chmn. acad. affairs com. CHMT Soc., 1984-86, gen. chmn. univ./govt./industry microelectronics symposium, 1981, tech. program commn., 1994). bd. dirs. workshop on tungsten and other refractory metals 1987-90), Am. Soc. Engring. Edn. (gen. chmn. engring. rsch. coun. ann. meeting 1987, chmn. engring. rsch. coun. adminstrv. com. 1987-90, chmn. coun., 1990-92, session chmn. ann. meeting 1990, 92, bd. dirs. 1990-92, mem. nominations com. 1992-94, mem. long range planning com. 1992-95, Centennial Cert. 1992, 2d Century Cert. 1993), World Future Soc. Internat. Soc. Hybrid Microelectronics, Assn. U.S. Army (bd. dir. Suncoast chpt. 1991-93), Soc. Photo Optical Instrumentation Engring., Univ. Faculty Senate Assn. of Miss. (organizer 1985), Am. Vacuum Soc., Am. Phs. Soc., Am. Electronics Assn., Am. Inst. Physics, Nat. Coun. Univ. Rsch. Adminstrn., Soc. Rsch. Adminstrs (external rels. com. for SRA 1988-91), Fla. Engring. Soc. (v.p. edn. com. 1987-92, pres. 1989-90, bd. dirs. 1989-91, Fla. engring. found. trustee 1989-90, ann. meeting steering com. 1989-90, Outstanding Svc. to the Profession award 1992), Soc. Am. Mil. Engring., Order of Engrs., 1991, Sigma Xi (v.p. 1985), Tau Beta Pi (Fla. Alpha chpt. pres. 1969, 71, faculty advisor Miss. Alpha chpt. 1977-85, faculty advisor Fla. Alpha Gamma chpt. 1986—, Outstanding hon. soc. advisor award 1994), Eta Kappa Nu (pres. U. Fla. chpt. 1968, Org. Charter Chpt. U. South Fla. 1998, faculty adv. Kappa Xi chpt. 1996—, Outstanding Honor Soc. Adv. award 1998-99), Sigma Tau, Sigma Xi, Omicron Delta Kappa, Soc. Am. Inventors, Fla. Blue Key (v.p. 1972, sec. 1971), Epsilon Lambda Chi (founder 1970, pres. 1971). Club: Downtown Tampa Rotary (Paul Harris fellow 1987,94, 2000, perfect attendance award 1986—, chmn. com. on environ. issues 1990), Rotary Club New Tampa (organizer, charter mem., pres. 1995-96, v.p. 1996-97, mem. exec. com. 1996—, dir. internat. svc. 1997-98, sr. dir. 1998-99, 99-2001). Avocations: collecting antique furniture, carpentry, restoring antique sports cars, basketball.

**WADE, WYN CRAIG,** writer, educator; b. South Bend, Ind., July 3, 1944; s. Wyndel Calvin Wade and Ruth Marie Dishon; m. Barbara Ann Barnett, Apr. 30, 1966; 1 child, Derek Wyndel. AA, Lake Michigan Coll., 1964; BA, U. Mich., 1966; MA, U. Wis., 1971. Psychologist Wis. Divsn. of Corrections,

Madison, 1967—71, Washington County Mental Health, Montpelier, Vt., 1971—76; writer South Bend, 1976—87; vocat. evaluator Job Tng. Program, South Bend, 1987—90; dir. acad. resource ctr. Ind. U. South Bend, 1990—95; writer, tchr. Ind. Inst. Tech., South Bend, 1995—. Cons. Dallas (Tex.) Organ Works, 2000—. Author: Titanic: End of a Dream, 1979, The Fiery Cross, 1986; contbg. author: Research Papers: A Practical Guide, 2001. Mem. So. Poverty Law Ctr., Montgomery, Ala., 1987—; trustee Chad Pearson Scholarship Ind. U. South Bend, 1986—. Recipient Beckwith Lifetime Achievement award, Lake Michigan Coll., 2000, Outstanding Book award, Gustavus Myers Ctr., Boston, 1988. Mem.: AAUP, Am. Counseling Assn., Titanic Hist. Soc. (honor), Am. Theatre Organ Soc. Avocations: pipe organ performance, Gilbert & Sullivan, home remodeling, literature, art.

**WADHAMS, TIMOTHY,** consumer products company executive; BA in Economics, U. Mich., MBA. CPA Coopers & Lybrand, 1972; joined Masco Corp., Taylor, Mich., 1976, various positions MasocTech, 1984—2000, v.p. fin., CFO, 2001—04, sr. v.p., CFO, 2004—. Bd. trustees Ann Arbor Area Cmty. Found., Arbor Hospice Found.; bd. dir., M Club U. Mich.; cmty. adv. bd. Kellogg Eye Inst. Campaign. Office: Masco Corp 21001 Van Born Rd Taylor MI 48180*

**WADHWA, VIVEK,** information technology executive; b. Delhi, India; arrived in US, 1980; B in Computer Sci., Canberra U., Australia; MBA, NYU. Former v.p., information svc. Credit Suisse First Boston; former exec. v.p. & CTO Seer Technologies; founder, chmn. & CEO Relativity Technologies, Cary, NC, 1997—2005, chmn., 2005—. Pres. The Indus Entrepreneurs (NC Chapter). Office: Relativity Technologies 2300 Rexwoods Dr Ste 100 Raleigh NC 27607

**WADKINS, LANNY LANSTON,** professional golfer; b. Richmond, Va., Dec. 5, 1949; s. Jerry Lanston and Francis Ann (Burnett) W.; m. Rachel Irene Strong, Jan. 2, 1971; 1 child, Jessica. Student, Wake Forest U. Profl. golfer PGA, 1971—. Mem. numerous nat. teams including Walker Cup (2), 1969, 71, World Amateur Cup, 1970, Ryder Cup (8), 1977, 79, 83, 85, 87, 89, 91, 93, Ryder Cup Capt., 1995, World Cup (3), 1977, 84, 85, U.S. vs. Japan (2), 1982, 83, Nissan Cup, 1985, Dunhill Cup, 1986, Kirin Cup, 1987, Asahi Glass Four Tours, 1991; golf analyst, CBS Sports, 2003-. Winner 1968, 70 So. Amateur champion, Sahara Invitational, 1972, PGA, 1977, World Series of Golf, 1978, Can. PGA, 1978, Tournament Players' Championship, 1979, 82, 83, (4) 1978 Victoria PGA Championship (Australia), Can. PGA Championship, 1979 Bridgestone Open (Japan), L.A. Open, 1979, Phoenix Open, 1982, Greater Greensboro, 1983, Bob Hope Desert Classic, 1985, Doral Ryder, 1987, 1984 World Nissan Championship (Japan), Hawaiian Open, 1988, 91, Colonial Open, 1988, Anheuser Busch Classic, 1990, 1990 Fred Meyer Challenge, PGA of AmericaPlayer of Yr., 1985, Greater Hartford Open, 1992, 2000 ACE Group Classic, among others. Address: PGA America/Senior Tour 100 Ave of the Champions PO Box 109601 Palm Beach Gardens FL 33410-9601

**WADLEY, FREDIA STOVALL,** state commissioner; b. Winchester, Tenn. BS, Tenn Tech U., 1967; MD, U. Tenn., 1969; MSHPA, U. Cin., 1978. Diplomate Am. Bd. Pediats. Pediat. intern City of Memphis Hosp., 1970, pediat. resident, 1971-72; clin. instr. pediats. dept. pediats. U. Tenn. Ctr. for Health Scis., Memphis, 1973-74; pvt. practice Winchester, Tenn., 1974-75; instr. phys. assessment course dept. nursing U. Tenn., Chattanooga, 1975-76; dir. med. svcs. Dept. Health and Environ. Southeast Region, Chattanooga, 1975-80, regional dir., 1981-83; chief med. officer Dept. Health and Environ. Commr.'s Office, Nashville, 1984-87; dir. Met. Health Dept., Nashville, 1987-95; commr. Dept. Health, Nashville, 1995-97; state med. dir. Tenn. Health Srvcs. Bureau, 1997—; clin. asst. prof. dept. pediats. Meharry Med. Coll., 1985—; mem. faculty staff preventive medicine divsn. Quillen Dischner Med. Coll., 1985-87; now commr. Dept. Health, Nashville. Vol. faculty mem. dept. nursing U. Tenn. Ctr. for Health Scis., Memphis, 1977-83, U. Tenn., Knoxville, 1977-83; mem. preventive medicine resident adv. com. Meharry Family Medicine Dept., 1988—; adj. assoc. prof. nursing dept. family and cmty. health Vanderbilt U., 1988—; presenter in field. Contbr. articles to profl. jours. Mem. HSA III Task Force on Ambulatory Health Care Problems, 1977, HSA III Bd., 1981-82; mem. southeast Tenn. regional placement com. Tenn. Med. Loan Scholarship Program, 1978-79; bd. dirs. Southeast Tenn. Chpt. Kidney Found., 1981, Vol. Healthcare Sys., Inc., 1988-90, Vanderbilt AIDS Project, 1990, United Way Mid. Tenn., 1992-95, ARC, 1992; mem. Tenn. Sch. health Coalition, 1985—, Cmty. Coalition for Minority Health, 1988, Mayor's Substance Abuse Action Team, 1990; active Brentwood United Meth., Sunday Sch. tchr. 6th grade, 1984-87; chmn. Tenn. AIDS Adv. Com., 1987-88, Davidson County Child Fatality Rev. Team, 1994-95, others. Mem. AMA, APHA (Charles G. Jordan award for outstanding accomplishments in field of pub. health so. br. 1981), Southern Health Assn. (chmn. awards com. and governing coun. 1981-83, pres. 1989-90, spl. meritorious award for outstanding contbns. to orgn. and pub. health 1992), Tenn. Pub. Health Assn. (pres. 1990-91, spl. meritorious award 1993), Tenn. Health Officers, Tenn. Pediat. Soc., Tenn. Med. Assn., Nashville/Davidson County Acad. Medicine, Davidson County Pediat. Soc. Office: Health Svcs Bureau 425 5th Ave N Fl 3D Nashville TN 37247-0001

**WADLEY, M. RICHARD,** consumer products executive; b. Lehi, Utah; s. Merlyn R. and Verla Ann (Ball) W.; m. Nancy Zwiers; children: Lisa Kathleen, Staci Lin, Eric Richard, Nicole Marie. BS, Brigham Young U., 1967; MBA, Northwestern U., 1968. Brand asst. packaged soap and detergent divsn. Procter & Gamble Co., Cin., 1968-69, asst. brand mgr. packaged soap and detergent divsn., 1970-71, brand mgr. Dawn detergent, 1972-73, copy supr. packaged soap and detergent divsn., 1974-75, brand mgr. Tide detergent, 1975-77, assoc. advt. mgr. packaged soap and detergent divsn., 1977-81; corp. product dir. Hallmark Cards, Inc., Kansas City, Mo., 1982-83, corp. product dir. Ambassador Cards divsn., 1983-85; v.p., gen. mgr. feminine protection divsn. Tambrands Inc., Lake Success, NY, 1986-88; sr. v.p. Bongrain, Inc., N.Y.C., 1988-89, pres., CEO AltaDena Inc. divsn. City of Industry, Calif., 1989-91; pres. The Summit Group, 1991-93; chmn., CEO, bd. dirs. T-Chem Products Inc., Santa Fe Springs, Calif., 1993-99; CEO The Bayshore Group, 1999—. Bd. dirs. Legacy Interactive, Funosophy, Inc.; adj. prof. MBA program Pepperdine U., 1998—99. Bd. dirs. Long Beach Opera, 1993-95, L.I. Friends of the Arts, 1986-88; mem. adv. bd. Bus. Sch. Calif. State U., Long Beach. Avocations: civil war history, tennis, travel. Personal E-mail: rwbayshore@aol.com.

**WADLINGTON, W. M.,** retired commodity futures trader, financial engineer; b. Madisonville, Ky., Oct. 28, 1944; s. W. Milton and Ellen Christine (Bryan) W.; m. Anne R. Lewis, Apr. 29, 1979; children: Andrew Stephen, Michael Edward, Thomas Scott. BA, Vanderbilt U., 1967. Commd. 2d lt. U.S. Army, 1967, advanced through grades to capt., 1970, field artillery officer, 1967-78, resigned, 1978; chmn. ChartBook.com, Ltd., San Diego, 1994-98; commodity futures trader, 1978-98; ret., 1998. Pres. Scripps Ranch Villages, 1998—2004; trustee LaJolla Country Day Sch., 2000—. Decorated Silver Star. Republican. Avocations: ancient languages, computer programming, opera, weightlifting, running. Home: 10981 Twinleaf Ct San Diego CA 92131-3643

**WADLINGTON, WALTER JAMES,** law educator; b. Biloxi, Miss., Jan. 17, 1931; s. Walter and Bernice (Taylor) Wadlington; m. Ruth Miller Hardie, Aug. 20, 1955; children: Claire, Charlotte, Ian(dec.), Susan, Derek Alan. AB, Duke U., 1951; LLB, Tulane U., 1954. Bar: La. 1954, Va. 1965. Pvt. practice, New Orleans, 1954—55, 1958—59; asst. prof. Tulane U., 1960—62; mem. faculty U. Va., 1962—; prof law, 1964—, James Madison prof., 1970—2002, James Madison prof. emeritus, 2002—; prof. legal medicine Med. Sch. 1979—2002, Harrison Found. prof. 1990—92. Tutor civil law U. Edinburgh, Scotland, 1959—60; vis. Tazewell Taylor prof. law Coll. William and Mary, 1986; dir. med. malpractice program Robert Wood Johnson, 1985—91; mem. adv. com. clin. scholars program 1985—97; chmn. nat. adv. bd. Improving Malpractice Prevention and Compensation Sys., 1994—98; Disting. Health Law Tchr. Am. Soc. Law, Medicine and Ethics; trustee-at-large Edn. Commn. Fgn. Med. Grads., 1995—2003. Author (with O. Brien):

Cases and Materials on Domestic Relations, 1970, 5th edit., 2002, Family Law in Perspective, 2001; author: (with Waltz and Dworkin) Cases and Materials on Law and Medicine, 1980; editor-in-chief: Tulane U. Law Rev., 1953—54; author (with Davis, Scott, and Whitebread): Children in the Legal System, 3rd edit., 2004. Fulbright scholar, U. Edinburgh, 1959—60. Mem.: Am. Law Inst., Inst. of Medicine of NAS, Found. Advancement Internat. Med. Edn. and Rsch. (bd. dirs., sec. 2001—03). Home: 1620 Keith Valley Rd Charlottesville VA 22901-3018 Office: U Va Sch Law 580 Massie Rd Charlottesville VA 22903-1738 Office Phone: 434-924-3471. Personal E-mail: wwadlington@earthlink.net. Business E-mail: wjw@virginia.edu.

**WADLOW, JOAN KRUEGER,** retired academic administrator, retired construction executive; b. LeMars, Iowa, Aug. 21, 1932; d. R. John and Norma I. (IhLe) Krueger; m. Richard R. Wadlow, July 27, 1958; children: Dawn, Kit. BA, U. Nebr., 1953, PhD, 1963; MA, Fletcher Sch. Law and Diplomacy, 1956; cert., Grad. Inst. Internat. Studies, Geneva, 1957. Mem. faculty U. Nebr., Lincoln, 1956-79, prof. polit. scis., 1964-79, assoc. dean Coll. Arts and Scis., 1972-79; prof. polit. scis., dean Coll. Arts and Scis., U. Wyo., Laramie, 1979-84, v.p. acad. affairs, 1984-86; prof. polit. scis., provost U. Okla., Norman, 1986-91; chancellor U. Alaska, Fairbanks, 1991-99. Cons. on fed. grants; bd. dirs. Alaska Sea Life Ctr., Key Bank Alaska; mem. Commn. Colls. N.W. Assn.; pres. Lan Constrn., Inc., 1999-2004. Contbr. articles to profl. jours. Bd. dirs. Nat. Merit Scholarship Corp., 1988-97, Lincoln United Way, 1976-77, Bryan Hosp., Lincoln, 1978-79, Washington Ctr., 1986-99, Key Bank of Alaska, Alaska SeaLife Ctr.; v.p., exec. commr. North Ctrl. Assn., pres., 1991; pres. adv. bd. Lincoln YWCA, 1970-71; mem. def. adv. com. Women in the Svcs., 1987-89; mem. cmty. adv. bd. Alaska Airlines; mem. Univ. Pres.'s Mission to Israel, 1998; mem. bd. dirs. Netarts Oceanside Sanitary Dist., 2002-04. Recipient Mortar Board Tchg. award, 1976, Alumni Scholar Achievement award Rotary Internat., 1998, Alumni Achievement award U. Nebr., 2003; Seacrest Journalism fellow 1953-54, Rotary fellow, 1956-57, fellow Conf. Coop. Man, Lund, Sweden, 1956. Mem. NCAA (divsn. II pres. coun. 1997-99), Internat. Studies Assn. (co-editor Internat. Studies Notes 1978-91), Nat. Assn. State Univs. and Land-Grant Colls. (exec. com. coun. acad. affairs 1989-91, chair internat. affairs counsel 1996-97), Western Assn. Africanists (pres. 1980-82), Assn. Western Univs. (pres. 1993), Coun. Colls. Arts and Scis. (pres. 1983-84), Greater Fairbanks C. of C., Gamma Phi Beta. Republican. Congregationalist. Address: Chancellor Emerita PO Box 246 Oceanside OR 97134-0246 Personal E-mail: wadlow@hughes.net.

**WADMAN, WILLIAM WOOD, III,** educational director, technical research executive, consulting company executive; b. Oakland, Calif., Nov. 13, 1936; s. William Wood, Jr., and Lula Fay (Raisner) W.; children: Roxanne Alyce Wadman Hubbling, Raymond Alan (dec.), Theresa Hope Wadman Boudreaux; m. Barbara Jean Wadman; stepchildren: Denise Ellen Varine Skrypkar, Brian Ronald Varine. M.A., U. Calif., Irvine, 1978. Cert. program mgr. tng. Radiation safety specialist, accelerator health physicist U. Calif. Lawrence Berkeley Lab., 1957-68; campus radiation safety officer U. Calif., Irvine, 1968-79; dir. ops., radiation safety officer Radiation Sterilizers, Inc., Tustin, Calif., 1979-80; prin., pres. Wm. Wadman & Assocs. Inc., 1980—; mem. operational review team Princeton U. Rsch. Campus TOKOMAK Fusion Test Facility, 1993-94; technical project mgr. for upgrades projects Los Alamos Nat. Lab. 1994-96, tech. project mgr. for 3 projects, 1995—; mem. team No. 1, health physics appraisal program NRC, 1980—, operational readiness review team to Princeton U. Rsch. Campus TOKOMAK Fusion Test Facility, 1993-94; cons. health physicist to industry; lectr. sch. social ecology, 1974-79; dept. community and environ. medicine U. Calif., Irvine, 1979-80, instr. in environ. health and safety, 1968-79, Orange Coast Coll., in radiation exposure reduction design engring. Mason & Hanger-Silas Mason Co., Los Alamos Nat. Lab.; instr. in medium energy cyclotron radiation safety UCLBL, lectr. in accelerator health physics, 1966, 67; curriculum developer in field; subject matter expert Los Alamos Nat. Lab., Earth and Environ. Scis., Tech. Support Office. Active Cub Scouts; chief umpire Mission Viejo Little League, 1973. Served with USNR, 1955-63. Recipient award for profl. achievement U. Calif. Alumni Assn., 1972, Outstanding Performance award U. Calif., Irvine, 1973. Mem. Health Physics Soc. (treas. 1979-81, editor proc. 11th symposium, pres. So. Calif. chpt. 1977, Professionalism award 1975), Internat. Radiation Protection Assn. (U.S. del. 4th Congress 1977, 8th Congress 1992), Am. Nuclear Soc., Am. Public Health Assn. (chmn. program 1978, chmn. radiol. health sect. 1979-80), Campus Radiation Safety Officers (chmn. 1975, editor proc. 5th conf. 1975), ASTM, Project Mgmt. Inst. Club: UCI Univ. (dir. 1976, sec. 1977, treas. 1978). Contbr. articles to tech. jours. Achievements include research in radiation protection and environmental sciences; Avocations: sailing, Tae Kwon Do, wood working, numesmantics. Home: 3687 Red Cedar Way Lake Oswego OR 97035-3525 Office: 675 Fairview Dr Ste 246 Carson City NV 89701-5428 *Personal philosophy: The continuous practice of patience, openmindedness, and open communication provide the essential ingredients for a full, satisfying personal and professional life. The timing of major decisions is not a matter of heart, but the culmination of the effective use of the practices above.*

**WADSWORTH, DYER SEYMOUR,** metal products executive, treasurer, environmental services administrator; b. N.Y.C., June 16, 1936; s. Seymour and Phoebe Armistead (Helmer) Wadsworth; m. Beverley Allen Dunn Barringer, Feb. 2, 1963; children: Sophia, Jennifer. BA, Yale U., 1959; JD, Harvard U., 1962. Bar: N.Y. 1963, Pa. 1979. Assoc. Humes, Andrews & Botzow, N.Y.C., 1962-64; with Inco Ltd. and subs., N.Y.C., 1964-96; asst. gen. counsel Inco Ltd., N.Y.C., 1982-96; pres. Inco US, Inc., N.Y.C., 1993-96; chmn., CEO, treas., dir. Cass County Iron Co., Linden, Tex., 1992—; chmn. Barringer Crater Co., Flagstaff, Ariz., 1996—. Gen. counsel Sailors Snug Harbor, Sea Level, NC, 1987—2000, Baseline Fin. Svcs., Inc., N.Y.C., 1997—2000. Trustee Isaac Tuttle Fund for Aged, N.Y.C., 1968—96; bd. dirs. Frenchman Bay Conservancy, Hancock, Maine, 1997—, Amsterdam Nursing Home Corp., N.Y.C., 1982—; chmn. bd. dirs. 1986—2000. Named Trustee of the Yr., N.Y. Assn. Homes and Svcs. for Aging, 1995. Mem.: Meteoritical Soc., Yale Club Suncoast (bd. dirs. 2001—, pres. 2002—04), Union Club (N.Y.C.), Ivy League Club (Sarasota, Fla.) (bd. dirs. 2005—), Pilgrims Soc. (N.Y.C.). Home: 8466 Lockwood Ridge Rd PMB 304 Sarasota FL 34243-2951

**WADSWORTH, FRANK WHITTEMORE,** foundation administrator, literature educator; b. NYC, June 14, 1919; s. Prescott Kingsley and Elizabeth (Whittemore) W.; m. Roxalene Harriet Nevin, Oct. 22, 1943 (dec. 1979); Susan, Roxalene; m. Deborah Yohalem, Dec. 22, 1980. AB, Princeton U., 1946, PhD, 1951. Instr. English Princeton (N.J.) U., 1949-50; instr. to assoc. prof. English UCLA, 1950-61; prof. English, dean div. humanities U. Pitts., 1962-67; acad. v.p. SUNY-Purchase, 1967-78, prof. lit., 1967-89, emeritus, 1989—; nat. rep. Woodrow Wilson Nat. Fellowship Found., 1958-61, trustee, 1973—2003; vice-chmn. bd. trustees, 1992—2003; trustee Wenner-Gren Found., N.Y.C., 1970—, chmn. bd. trustees, 1977-87, vice-chmn. bd. trustees, 1992—. Author: The Poacher from Stratford, 1958; contbr. articles to publs. Served to lt. (j.g.) USNR, 1942-45. Woodrow Wilson fellow, 1946-47; Scribner fellow, 1948-49; Folger Shakespeare Library fellow, 1961; Guggenheim fellow, 1961-62 Mem. MLA, Am. Soc. Theatre Research, Malone Soc., Phi Beta Kappa Clubs: Princeton. Home: 430 Sterling Rd Harrison NY 10528-1316

**WADSWORTH, J. TRAD,** otolaryngologist, medical researcher; Diplomate Am. Bd. Otolaryngology. Asst. prof. Ea. Va. Med. Sch., Norfolk, 2001—. Office: Ea Va Med Sch 825 Fairfax Ave Ste 510 Norfolk VA 23507 Office Phone: 757-446-5934.

**WADSWORTH, JACOB ROBERT,** social studies educator; b. Springfield, Mo., Oct. 22, 1971; s. Robert Francis and Cheryl Ann Wadsworth; m. Sheri Jo Rhodes, July 31, 1998; 1 child, Madeline Claire. BS Edn., S.W. Mo. State U., Springfield, 1994; MEd, Drury U., Springfield, Mo., 2002. Cert. tchr. grades 7-12 Mo. Dept. Edn., 1994. Tchr. social studies Springfield Pub. Schs., Mo., 1995—. Asst. coach wrestling Hillcrest H.S. Wrestling Team, Springfield, 2002—. Sponsor Hillcrest H.S. Key Club, 1997—2006. Recipient Kids' Choice award, Springfield Pub. Schs. Found., 2004. Avocations: reading, running. Office: Springfield Pub Schs Hillcrest HS 3319 N Grant Springfield MO 65803 Office Phone: 417-523-4008. Business E-Mail: jwadsworth@spsmail.org.

**WADSWORTH, JOHN (JACK) SPENCER, JR.,** investment banker; b. Ft. Thomas, Ky., Sept. 12, 1939; s. John Spencer and Mary Claire (Walker) W.; m. Bette Sue Pendery, June 17, 1961; children: Elizabeth J., John S. III, Christopher W. BA in Economics, Williams Coll., 1961; MBA in Fin., U. Chgo., 1963. Exec. v.p., bd. dirs. First Boston Corp., NYC, 1963-78; joined Morgan Stanley, NYC, 1978, mng. dir., various positions US investment banking divsn., 1978—87; pres. Morgan Stanley Japan, Tokyo, 1988—93; chmn. Morgan Stanley Asia Ltd., 1993—2000, hon. chmn.; now adv. dir. Morgan Stanley; ptnr. Manitou Ventures. Bd. dirs. Pixar Inc., 2002—; chmn. bd. Littleford Bros. Inc., Florence, Ky. Trustee Asia Soc., Williams Coll.; bd. trustees Solomon R. Guggenheim Mus., NYC. Mem.: Asia Am. MultiTechnology Assn. (charter mem.). Office: Morgan Stanley 1585 Broadway New York NY 10036

**WADSWORTH, JULIE BELL,** secondary school educator; b. Balt., Md., July 28, 1952; d. Laura Smoot and Thomas Walter Bell; m. Charles Stephen Wadsworth, June 21, 1974; children: Melissa Bell, Eleanor Suzanne, Thomas Stephen. BS, Towson U., 1974. Julie Bell Wadsworth Md. State Dept. of Edn., 1996. Live-in sub.tchr. Sparks Elem. Sch., Md., 1982—94; tchr. Loch Raven Acad., Balt., 1994—. Mem. Forest Conservancy Dist. Bd. for Balt. County, Parkville, Md., 2004—06. Recipient Sci. Tchr. Recognition award, Sci. Dept., Balt. County Bd. of Edn., 2002. R-Consevative. Protestant. Avocations: canoeing, boating, walking, hiking. Home: 1812 Worthington Heights Cockeysville MD 21030 Office: Loch Raven Acad 8101 LaSalle Rd Baltimore MD 21286 Office Phone: 410-887-3518. Personal E-Mail: jwadsworth@bcps.org.

**WADSWORTH, ROBERT DAVID,** advertising executive; b. Prestbury, Cheshire, Eng., May 20, 1942; came to U.S., 1978; s. Eric and Irene (Thorpe) W.; m. Kathleen O'Meara, Dec. 13, 1968; children: Tracey, Charles Robert. BA, U. Natal, S. Africa, 1963. With Lever Bros. S. Africa, 1960-66, sr. brand mgr., 1964-66, Gen. Foods S. Africa, 1967; account exec. London Press Exch., S. Africa, 1968, Grant Advt., S. Africa, 1969; dir. then mng. dir. Cen. Advt., Johannesburg, S. Africa, 1970-73; dir. new bus. coord. McCann-Erickson, South Africa, 1973-78; sr. v.p., mng. rep., new bus. coord. McCann-Erickson, Inc., N.Y.C., 1978-82; client dir., exec. v.p. Lintas, N.Y.C., 1983-90; dir. corp. strategy, regional dir. So. Africa Lintas Worldwide, N.Y.C., 1991-97; cons. Midlothian, Va., 1998—. Home and Office: 14018 Bayport Landing Ter Midlothian VA 23112-2038

**WADSWORTH WALKER, CHERILEE,** music educator; b. Port Clinton, Ohio, Mar. 15, 1961; d. Richard Vernon Wadsworth and Joyce Marie Meter Wadsworth; m. James Edward Walker, May 2, 1996. MusB in Music Theory, Baldwin Wallace Coll., 1991; MusM in Jazz Studies, Ind. U., 1993; PhD in Music Edn., U. Okla., 2005. Musician 3d class 6th fleet USN, Naples, Italy, 1994—96, musician 2d class NATO, 1996—98; asst. prof. East Ctrl. U., Ada, Okla., 1998—2001; tchg. chmn. performing arts Ill. Ctrl. Coll., East Peoria, 2001—. Adjudicator, clinician Performing Arts Cons., Keyport, NJ, 2003—; res. musician 85th Divsn. Band, US Army, Arlington Heights, Ill., 2005—; presenter in field; spkr. in field. Contbr. articles to profl. publs.; performer: Montreux Jazz Festival, 2003, Ill. Gubernatorial Inauguration, 2003, Ft. Des Moines Meml. Pk. Dedication, 2004, Nat. Boy Scout Jamboree, 2005, WCBU 35th ann. broadcast concert, 2005. Recipient Ednl. award, Harmony Found., Inc., Minn., 2001, Commn. award, Heartland Music Found., Oklahoma City, 2001, Presentation award, Peoria World Affairs Coun., 2005. Mem.: Am. Choral Dirs. Assn., Nat. Assn. Tchrs. Singing. Office: Ill Ctrl Coll 1 College Dr East Peoria IL 61635 Office Phone: 309-694-5548. Business E-Mail: cwadsworthwalker@icc.edu.

**WADZINSKI, MARY BETH,** administrative assistant; b. Wausau, Wis., Apr. 26, 1953; d. Erwin Fredrick Hackbart and Selma Ruth Margaret Krueger; m. William R. Wadzinski, June 20, 1987 (div. June 1997); children: Bethany Dawn, Andrew William. AS, Northcentral Tech. Coll., 1973. Typist Wausau (Wis.) Abstract and Title Co., 1973-76; adminstrv. asst. Marathon County Dept. Social Svcs., Wausau, 1977—. Author poems, songs. Recipient Poet Merit award, Am. Poetry Assn., 1989, Editors Choice awards, Nat. Libr. Poetry, 1996—98, 2001, Honorable Mention award, Iliad Press, 1996—98. Mem.: America's Registry, Famous Poets Soc. (Shakespeare Trophy of Excellence 2002, Poet of Yr. medallion 2002, Diamond Homer trophy 1996, Recognition award 1998, Poet of Yr. medallion 1999, Diamond Homer trophy 1999, Recognition award 2001), Internat. Poetry Hall of Fame, Internat. Soc. Poets. Democrat. Lutheran. Avocations: shopping, garage sales, writing, singing. Home: 1113 N 6th Ave Wausau WI 54401-2747 Office Phone: 715-261-7595.

**WAELSCH, SALOME GLUECKSOHN,** geneticist, educator; b. Danzig, Germany, Oct. 6, 1907; arrived in U.S., 1933, naturalized, 1938; d. Ilya and Nadia Gluecksohn; m. Heinrich B. Gluecksohn, Jan. 8, 1943; children: Naomi Barbara, Peter Benedict. Student, U. Konigsberg, Germany, U. Berlin, 1927—28; PhD, U. Freiburg, Germany, 1932; DSc (hon.), Columbia U., 1995. Rsch. assoc. in genetics Columbia U., 1936—55; assoc. prof. anatomy Albert Einstein Coll. Medicine, 1955—58, prof., 1958—63, prof. molecular genetics, 1963, chmn. dept. genetics, 1963—76, disting. prof. emeritus. Mem. study sects. NIH. Author: contbr. numerous articles on devel. genetics. Recipient Nat Medal of Sci., Pres. Clinton, 1993, Thomas Hunt Morgan medal, Genetics Society of America, 1999. Fellow: Am. Acad. Arts & Scis., AAAS; mem.: The Royal Soc., Am. Soc. Human Genetics, Am. Soc. Naturalists, Soc. Devel. Biology, N.Y. Acad. Scis. (hon.), Genetics Soc., Am. Assn. Anatomists, Am. Soc. Zoologists, NAS, Sigma Xi. Office: Albert Einstein Coll Med Rm 827 1300 Morris Park Ave Bronx NY 10461-1926 E-mail: gradus@aecom.yu.edu.*

**WAETZMAN, LARRY SAMUEL,** diversified financial services company executive; b. Reading, Pa., Dec. 11, 1945; s. Joseph and Lilyan B. (Berliner) W.; m. Bonnie Lynn Samuels, July 27, 1969; children: Ross, Evan, Melissa. BA, Franklin & Marshall Coll., 1967; MA, U. Wis., 1968; postgrad., Nova U., Temple U., Harvard U. Lic. profl. planner, N.J. Dir. planning Borough of Norristown, Pa., 1972—74; dir. cmty. devel. Twp. of Haverford, Havertown, Pa., 1974—80; sr. planning cons. Govt. Studies & Sys., Phila., 1980—81; ptnr. Tredinnick/Waetzman Assocs., Havertown, 1981—87; prin. The Waetzman Planning Group, Ardmore, Pa., 1997—2001; pres. Waetleman Planning Group Inc., 2001—. Pres. Congregation Ner Tamid, Springfield, Pa., 1989-91; mem Hartford Twp. Planning Commn., 2004—. Served to 1st lt. U.S. Army, 1969-72. Mem. Am. Soc. Consulting Planners (pres. 1998-2000), Am. Planning Assn. (pres. ea. Pa. chpt. 1981-85), AICP, Pa. Planning Assn. (bd. dirs. 1981-85), N.J. Assn. Cons. Planners. Avocation: skiing. Home: 2725 Pine Valley Ln Ardmore PA 19003-1718 Office Phone: 610-527-0600. E-mail: lsw@waetzmanplanning.com

**WAGDY, MAHMOUD FAWZY,** engineering educator; s. Wagdy Abdel-Ghany Aly and Hekmat Mahmoud Fawzy; m. Nadia El-Gabaly, July 24, 1980; children: Sarah, Noha. BSc, Cairo U., Giza, Egypt, 1973, MSc, 1977; PhD, Kans. State U., 1983. Assoc. prof. Calif. State U., Long Beach, 1989—92, prof., 1992—. Summer faculty fellow Air Force Rsch. Lab., Dayton, Ohio, 2003. Author: (51 published papers) Research; contbr. more than 50 articles to profl. publs. Recipient 141 nternat. citations for rsch. Mem.: IEEE (chmn. LA chpt. on indsl. electronics 1992—96). Office: 8352 Brush Dr Huntington Beach CA 92647 Office: Calif State U Long Beach 1250 Bellflower Blvd Long Beach CA 90840 Office Phone: 562-985-5110. Office Fax: 562-985-5899. Business E-Mail: wagdy@csulb.edu.

**WAGENER, CHRISTINE ELIZABETH,** psychotherapist, educator; b. Alexandria, Va., Sept. 1, 1948; d. Harry F. and Elizabeth Whitmore Wagener; m. Lawrence L. Foust, Aug. 20, 1977. BA, Jacksonville U., 1970; MSW, Va.

Commonwealth U., Richmond, 1976. LCSW Tex. Clin. asst. prof. psychiatry U. Va. Med. Sch., Charlottesville, 1976—80; asst. clin. prof. psychiatry U. Tex. Med. Sch., Houston, 1980—88; pvt. practice psychotherapist Houston, 1988—. Adj. asst. prof. U. Houston Grad. Sch. Social Work, 1980—88; field instr. Va. Commonwealth U. Sch. Social Work, Richmond, 1977—80. Mem. exec. bd. Mental Health Assn., Houston, 1991—97. Mem.: NASW, Acad. Cert. Social Workers. Avocations: sailing, travel, cooking. Office: 2 Chelsea Blvd Houston TX 77006

**WAGENHEIM, KAL,** journalist, editor; b. Newark; s. Harold and Rozlon (Heller) Wagenheim; m. Olga J Wagenheim; children: David, Maria; m. Carolyn Smith Wagenheim (div.); 1 child, Jeff. Undergrad. Rutgers U., 1953—54; MA, SUNY Buffalo, 1971. Adj. prof. Columbia U. Writing Divsn., Sch. of the Arts. Author: 9 books, plays, screenplays, biography of Babe Ruth; editor: Caribbean Update Newsletter. Spec-41956 U.S. Army, 1954, Ft. Benning, Ga. Mem.: Dramatists Guild, Pen Writers Org. Avocations: reading, writing, theater. Home: 116 Myrtle Ave Millburn NJ 07041 Personal e-mail: kalwagenheim@cs.com.

**WAGES, ROBERT COLEMAN,** equity investor; b. Casablanca, Morocco, Aug. 28, 1963; came to U.S., 1963; s. Dan Sims and Sara Mae (Miller) W.; m. Tara Shamattee Sarwan, July 18, 1992; children: John Coleman, Thomas Sims; 1 stepchild, Jason Anthony Squillace. AB in Chemistry with honors, Princeton U., 1985. Cons. Oliver, Wyman & Co., N.Y.C., 1985—87; from assoc. to mng. dir. Castle Harlan, Inc., N.Y.C., 1987—2001, mng. dir., 2001—04; mng. ptnr. Litchfield Capital Ptnrs., LLC, Ballston Spa, NY, 2004—; pres. Robotics, Inc., Ballston Spa, NY, 2005—. Bd. dirs. Dearborn Risk Mgmt., Inc., N.J.; bd. dirs. Chief Execs. Network for Mfg. of the Capital Region, Inc. Mem. All Saints Episcopal Ch., vestry 1994-95, treas. 1995. Republican. Episcopalian. Avocations: sailing, travel, scuba diving, skiing. Office: Robotics Inc 2421 Rt 9 Ballston Spa NY 12020 Office Phone: 518-899-4211 x 238. Business E-Mail: rwages@litchfieldcp.com.

**WAGGONER, JAMES CLYDE,** lawyer; b. Nashville, May 7, 1946; s. Charles Franklin and Alpha (Noah) W.; m. Diane Dusenbery, Aug. 17, 1968; children: Benjamin, Elizabeth. BA, Reed Coll., 1968; JD, U. Oreg., 1974. Bar: Oreg. 1974, U.S. Dist. Ct. Oreg. 1975, U.S. Ct. Appeals (9th cir.) 1980, U.S. Tax Ct. 1979, U.S. Supreme Ct. 1979. Clk. to presiding justice Oreg. Supreme Ct., Salem, 1974-75; assoc. Martin, Bischoff & Templeton, Portland, Oreg., 1975-78, ptnr., 1978-82, Waggoner, Farleigh, Wada, Georgeff & Witt, Portland, 1982-89, Davis Wright Tremaine, Portland, 1990—. Contbr. articles to profl. jours. Fulbright scholar U. London, 1968-69. Mem. ABA, Oreg. Bar Assn., Multnomah Bar Assn., Reed Coll. Alumni Assn. (v.p. 1988, pres. 1989, bd. mgmt.) Alzheimers Assn. of Columbia-Willamette (v.p. 1992, pres. 1993), Order of Coif, Phi Beta Kappa. Democrat. Avocations: woodworking, calligraphy. Office: Davis Wright Tremaine 1300 SW 5th Ave Ste 2300 Portland OR 97201-5682 Office Phone: 503-778-5326. Business E-Mail: jimwaggoner@dwt.com.

**WAGGONER, KATHLEEN ALICE,** psychotherapist; b. St. Louis, Jan. 10, 1954; d. William Dale Jerry Siebe and Doris Ilene Hanson; m. Robert Douglas Clark, July 24, 1974 (div. 1980); children: Angel Mae, Andrew Miles, Jason Allen; m. Curtis Lee Waggoner, Jr., Sept. 6, 1981; children: Amanda Jane, Kathleen Lee, Elizabeth Anne, Kathleen Rose. AA, St. Louis CC, 1983; BS, Southeast Mo. State, 1989, MA, 2003. Cert. NCC, LPC. Tchr. Cinemon Bear Day Care, Cape Girardeau, Mo., 1985—87; supr. infant toddlers San Jose Hosp., Calif., 1989—91; pvt. cons. Molene, Ill., 1991—93; clin. staff Pathways Cmty. Supports, Cape Girardeau, 1995—97, Cmty. Counseling Ctr., Cape Girardeau, 1999—. Pres. WELA, 2002—; sec. Sedgewickville Luth. Ch., Mo., 2004—. E-2 USN, 1973—76, Key West, Fla. Mem.: ACA. Personal e-mail: katecila@hotmail.com.

**WAGGONER, LAWRENCE WILLIAM,** law educator; b. Sidney, Ohio, July 2, 1937; s. William J. and Gladys L. Waggoner; m. Lynne S. Applebaum, Aug. 27, 1963; children: Ellen, Diane. BBA, U. Cin., 1960; JD, U. Mich., 1963; PhD, Oxford U., Eng., 1966. Assoc. Cravath, Swaine & Moore, N.Y.C., 1963; prof. law U. Ill., Champaign, 1968-72, U. Va., Charlottesville, 1972—74, U. Mich., Ann Arbor, 1974-84, Lewis M. Simes prof. law, 1987—. Dir. rsch., chief reporter joint editorial bd. for Uniform Trust and Estate Acts, 1986-94, dir. rsch., 1994—, mem. joint editl. bd. uniform trust and estate acts; reporter restatement (3d) of property, 1990—; adviser restatement (3d) of trusts, 1993—. Author: Uniform Trust and Estate Statutes, 2006—, California and Uniform Trust and Estate Statutes, 2006—, Family Property Law: Wills, Trusts, and Future Interests, 4th edit., 2006. Served to capt., U.S. Army, 1966-68. Fulbright scholar Oxford U., 1963-65. Mem. Am. Law Inst., Am. Coll. Trust and Estates Counsel, Internat. Acad. Estate and Trust Law. Office: U Mich Law Sch 625 S State St Ann Arbor MI 48109-1215 Business E-Mail: waggoner@umich.edu.

**WAGGONER, PAUL EDWARD,** agricultural scientist; b. Appanoose County, Iowa, Mar. 29, 1923; s. Walter Loyal and Kathryn (Maring) W.; m. Barbara Ann Lockerbie, Nov. 3, 1945; children— Von Lockerbie, Daniel Maring S.B., U. Chgo., 1946; MS, Iowa State Coll., 1949, PhD, 1951. From asst. to chief scientist Conn. Agrl. Expt. Sta., New Haven, 1951-71, vice dir., 1969-71, dir., 1972-87, disting. scientist, 1987—. Mem. panels on policy implications of global warming NAS, 1989-91; chmn. sci. adv. bd. Giant Sequoia Nat. Monument, 2001-02. Contbr. articles to profl. jours. Served to capt. USAAF, 1943-46 Guggenheim fellow, 1963 Fellow AAAS (chmn. climate changes and water resources com. 1986-89), Am. Phytopath. Soc.; mem. NAS, Am. Meteorol. Soc. (Outstanding Achievement in Biometeorology award 1967), Conn. Acad. Sci. and Engring., Recipient of the Anton-de- Bary Medal, 1996, Grads Club. Achievements include rsch. in mathematical simulation of plant disease epidemics, hydrologic role of foliar pores, climate change on agriculture and water resources, how much ten billion can spare for nature. Home: 314 Vineyard Point Rd Guilford CT 06437-3255 Office: Conn Agrl Expt Sta PO Box 1106 New Haven CT 06504-1106 Personal E-Mail: agwagg@comcast.net.

**WAGGONER, ROBERT,** chef; Studied with Michael Roberts, Trumps, 1981—83; studied with Jacques Lameloise, Charles Barrier, Pierre Gagnaire, Gerard Boyer, Mark Meneau, France; studied with Jean Paul Coupal, Caracas, Venezuela. Owner restaurant Le Monte Cristo, France; chef with Jean Pierre Silva Le Vieux Moulin, Beaune, 1991; chef Turnberry Isle, Fla., 1993, The Wild Boar, Nashville, Charleston Grill, 2002—. Guest appearances fine dining establishments James Beard Ho., N.Y.C. Appeared (TV series) Gourmet Getaways with Robin Leach, Great Chefs of the South, Nashville's Talk of the Town, Ralph Emery Show, The Food Network's In Food Today, appearances with food reporter Burt Wolf (TV series) The Travel Channel, CNN, PBS Stas. nationwide, host Salute to Southern Chefs. Supporter nat. relief hunger charity Share our Strength. Office: Charleston Grill Charleston Pl Hotel 244 King St Charleston SC 29401

**WAGLE, A. TINA,** education educator, researcher; d. Datta and Sue Wagle. BA, Colgate U., Hamilton, NY, 1996; MA, Middlebury Coll., Vt., 1999; PhD, SUNY, Buffalo, 2003. Cert. in secondary Spanish tchg. NY, 2000. Tchr. Portsmouth Abbey Sch., RI, 1996—99; instr. Canisius Coll., Buffalo, 2000—03; asst. prof. Daemen Coll., Amherst, 2002—03; prof. SUNY Empire State Coll., 2003—. Bilingual edn. adv. com. mem. Buffalo Pub. Schools, 2004—; redesign team mem. Grover Cleve. HS, Buffalo, 2005—. Bd. trustees Cath. Charities of Western NY, Buffalo, 2005—. Mem.: Am. Ednl. Rsch. Assn. Office: SUNY Empire State Coll 617 Main St Buffalo NY 14221 Office Phone: 716-853-7700. Home Fax: 716-853-7713. Business E-Mail: tina.wagle@esc.edu.

**WAGMAN, ROBERT JOHN,** journalist, writer; b. Chgo., Nov. 11, 1942; s. Albert Alan and Rosamond (Horner) Wagman; m. Carol Ann Mueller, Jan. 30, 1965; children: Jennifer, Patricia, Marilyn. AB, St. Louis U., 1966, MA, 1968, JD, 1971. Analyst Dun & Bradstreet, 1965-67; with CBS News, 1967-71, 74-77; asst. to dean St. Louis U. Sch. Law, 1971-74; Washington bur. chief

N.Am. Newspaper Alliance, 1977-80, Ind. News Alliance, 1980-82; columnist Newspaper Enterprise Assn., 1980-95. Sr. corr. Soccertimes, VP, Washington, SMA Global. Author, co-author Hubert Humphrey, The Man and His Dream, 1978, Citizens Guide to the Tax Revolt, 1979, Asbestos: The Silent Killer, 1982, Lord's Justice, 1985, Instant Millionaires, 1986, The Nazi Hunters, 1988, The First Amendment Book, 1991, 2d edit., 1996, World Almanac Guide to the Supreme Court, 1993, Blood Oath, 1994, Hong Kong, 1997, And Beyond, 1997; editor: World Almanac of U.S. Politics, 1994—2000. Recipient Thomas Stokes award in Journalism. Business E-Mail: Mobilewag@aol.com.

**WAGNER, ALAN CYRIL,** television and film producer, consultant, performing arts educator; b. N.Y.C., Oct. 1, 1931; s. Joseph and Isabelle (Chanson) W.; m. Martha Celia Dreyfus, Mar. 11, 1956; children: David Mark, Susan Jill, Elizabeth Celia. BA, Columbia U., 1951, MA in English, 1952. Mgr. network programs Benton & Bowles, Inc., N.Y.C., 1957-61; dir. program devel. CBS, N.Y.C., 1961-68, v.p. program devel. Hollywood, Calif., 1968-73, v.p. program planning and devel. N.Y.C., 1973-75, v.p. nighttime programs, 1975-78, v.p. programs, 1978-82; pres., chief exec. officer The Disney Channel, N.Y.C., 1982-83; pres., CEO Alan Wagner Prodns., Inc., N.Y.C., 1983—; exec. v.p. feature and TV devel. and prodn. Grosso-Jacobson Entertainment Corp., N.Y.C., 1985-90; pres. Boardwalk Entertainment, N.Y.C., 1990-97, chmn., 1997—. Sr. program cons. Todays Cath. Cable Network, 1999—; creative cons. concert series Ctrl. Vantage, Syntague, N.Y.C., 2004—; adj. assoc. prof. visual arts NYU, 1993—98; lectr. Met. Opera Guild, CUNY, Wagner Soc. Prodr., dir., host program Living Opera, Stas. WNYC-WNYC-FM, N.Y.C., 1958-68; host radio broadcasts N.Y.C. Opera Co., 1978-80; panelist, commentator Met. Opera broadcasts, 1996—; contbr., Opera News, 2001—; Playbill, 2004—; exec. prodr. film Reunion at Fairborough, 1985; prodr. TV pilot We're Puttin' on the Ritz, 1986; author: Prima Donnas and other Wild Beasts, 1961; exec. con. The Gunfighters, Diamonds; supervising prodr. Cop Talk: Behind the Shield, 1988, 89, True Blue, TV movie and series, 1989, A Family for Joe, TV movie and series, 1989-90, TV series Counterstrike, 1990-93, Top Cops, 1989-94; exec. prodr. TV movies Spenser: Ceremony, Spenser: Pale Kings and Princes, 1993, Spenser: The Judas Goat, Spenser: A Savage Place, 1994, Wounded Heart, 1995, Hearts Adrift, Reasons of the Heart, 1996, TV series The Marriage Counselor, 1994. Lt. (j.g.) USNR, 1953-57. Recipient Evelyn Burkey Meml. award Writers Guild Am., 1983, Silver Circle award NATAS, 1999. Mem. Brit. Acad. Film and TV Arts, Wagner Soc. N.Y., Columbia U. Alumni Assn. Avocations: opera, other music, sound reproduction, baseball, other sports. Office: Boardwalk Entertainment 210 E 39th St New York NY 10016-2754 *A decent and abiding respect for the opinions and talents of the creative community on one hand, and the consuming community on the other, has always served as the necessary framework for any decision making in both my professional and personal life. The doers and the thinkers are crucially important, but no more so than those for whom they do and think. If I can serve as an effective middle man, a good part of my life's objective is realizable.*

**WAGNER, ALEXANDER JOHANNES,** physicist, educator; m. Heather Jean Ummel-Wagner, Oct. 10, 2000. Diploma in Math., U. Bielefeld, Germany, 1990, diploma in Physics, 1990; MS in Physics, U. Bielefeld, 1994; PhD in Theoretical Physics, Oxford U., Eng., 1997. Postdoctoral rsch. asst. MIT, Cambridge, Mass., 1998—99, U. Edinburgh, Scotland, 2000—02; asst. prof. N.D. State U., Fargo, 2002—. Presenter in field. Achievements include research in lattice boltzmann; spinodal decomposition; viscoelasticity. Office: ND State Univ Dept Physics Administration Dr Box 5566 Fargo ND 58105-5566 Office Phone: 701-231-9582. Business E-Mail: alexander.wagner@ndsu.edu.

**WAGNER, ALLAN RAY,** psychology professor; b. Springfield, Ill., Jan. 6, 1934; s. Raymond August and Grace (Johnson) W.; m. Barbara Rae Meland, Nov. 21, 1959, (dec. Nov. 1994); children: Krystn Rae, Kathryn Rae. BA, U. Iowa, 1956, MA, 1958, PhD, 1959; MA hon., Yale U., 1970. Asst. prof. psychology Yale U., New Haven, 1959-64, assoc. prof., 1964-69, prof., 1970-89, chmn. psychology dept., 1983-89, James Rowland Angell prof. psychology, 1990—, chmn. philosophy dept., 1991-93, dir., divsn. of the soc. sci., 1992-98. Cons. NIMH, 1968-71; mem. Pres. Biomed. Research Panel, 1975-76; adv. bd. Cambridge Ctr. Behavioral Studies, 1982-2000; mem. psychobiology panel NSF, 1984-85, com. on basic research in behavioral and social scis. NRC, 1984-87. Author: Reward and Punishment, 1965; assoc. editor: Learning and Motivation, 1969-74, Animal Learning and Behavior, 1972-74; editor: Jour. Exptl. Psychology, 1974-81, Quantitative Analyses of Behavior, Vol. 3, 1982, Vol. 4, 1983, Vol. 7, 1988. Fellow, NSF, 1958, NIMH, 1963; grantee, NSF, 1960—2004. Fellow APA (Disting. Scientific Contbn. award 1998-99), AAAS (mem. coun. 1988-91), Soc. Exptl. Psychologists (Howard Crosby Warren medal 1991), Am. Psychol. Soc.; mem. NAS, Psychonomic Soc., So. Quantitative Analysis of Behavior (sec. 1983-92), Ea. Psychol. Assn. (bd. dirs. 1985-88), Sigma Xi, New Haven Lawn Club. Home: 1405 Ridge Rd North Haven CT 06473-3051 Office: Yale U Dept Psychology PO Box 208205 New Haven CT 06520-8205 Office Phone: 203-432-4691. Business E-Mail: allan.wagner@yale.edu.

**WAGNER, AMY,** oceanographer; BS in Marine Scis., Tex. A&M U., Galveston, 1998; MS in Oceanography, Tex. A&M U., College Station, 2002. Phys. scientist Naval Oceanog. Office, Stennis Space Ctr., Miss., 1998—2000. Mem.: Am. Geophys. Union. Office: Texas A&M U Dept Oceanography College Station TX 77843-3146 Office Phone: 979-845-1056. Office Fax: 979-845-6331. E-mail: amyw@ocean.tamu.edu.

**WAGNER, ANN LOUISE,** ambassador, former political organization executive; m. Ray Wagner; children: Raymond III, Stephen, Mary Ruth. BSBA, U. Mo., 1984. Mem. com. Lafayette Twp.; chmn. com. St. Louis County Republican Ctrl. Com.; mem. Mo. Fedn. Republican Women; dir. ho. and senate redistricting commn. Mo. Rep. Party, 1991, chmn. Jefferson City, 1999—2001; Mo. state exec. dir. Bush/Quayle Campaign, 1992; advisor Ashcroft for Senate Campaign, 1994; 2nd congl. dist. chair Dole for Pres. Campaign, 1996; co-chmn. Rep. Nat. Com., Wash., 2001—05; US amb. to Luxembourg US Dept. State, 2005—. Mem.: Republican Nat. Conv. Midwestern State Chmn.'s Assn. (com. on arrangements 2000, del. 2000, del. chmn. 2000). Office: Am Embassy Luxembourg Unit 1410 APO APO AE 09126

**WAGNER, ANNICE MCBRYDE,** judge; b. D.C. BA, JD, Wayne State U. Administrative aide to pres. Barnstable County Mental Health Assn.; with Houston and Gardner; gen. counsel Nat. Capital Housing Authority; people's counsel D.C.; assoc. judge Superior Court D.C., 1977-90, D.C. Ct. Appeals, 1990—94, 2005—, chief judge, 1994—2005. Mem. bd. directors Conference of Chief Justices; mem. bd. trustees United Planning Organization, 1979—, v.p. bd. trustees, 1988—; chair Task Force On Gender Bias In The Courts, D.C. Judicial Conference Arrangements Com., Com. On Selection & Tenure of Hearing Commissioners; mem. teaching team, trial advocacy workshop Harvard U. Office: DC Ct of Appeals 500 Indiana Ave NW Ste 6000 Washington DC 20001-2131*

**WAGNER, ARTHUR WARD, JR.,** lawyer; b. Birmingham, Ala., Aug. 13, 1930; s. Arthur Ward and Lucille (Lockheart) W.; m. Ruth Shingler, May 11, 1957; children: Celia Wagner Minter, Julia Wagner Dolce, Helen Wagner McAfee. BSBA, U. Fla., 1954, JD, 1957. Bar: Fla. 1957, U.S. Dist. Ct. (so. dist.) Fla. 1957, U.S. Dist. Ct. (mid. dist.) Fla. 1975. Ptnr. Wagner & McAfee, P.A., West Palm Beach, Fla., 1959-2000; ret., 2000—. Lectr. in field. Author: Art of Advocacy; Jury Selection, 1981; co-author: Anatomy of Personal Injury Lawsuit I & II, 1968 and 1981. Mem. 15th Jud. Nominating Com., Palm Beach City, 1979—82, 4th Dist. Nominating Commn., Palm Beach City, 1982—86; mem. pres.'s coun. U. Fla.; vestry Holy Trinity Parish, v.p., 2002—; bd. dirs. chmn. U. Fla. Found., 2004—, chmn. 2005—06. Fellow Internat. Acad. Trial Lawyers, Am. Coll. Trial Lawyers, Internat. Soc. Barristers, Am. Bd. Trial Advs.; mem. Assn. Trial Lawyers Am. (pres.

1975-76, hon. life trustee Roscoe Pound Found.), So. Trial Lawyers Assn. (pres. 1991), U. Fla. Law Coll. Alumni (mem. bd. govs.). Democrat. Episcopalian. Personal E-mail: wrwagner8553@aol.com.

**WAGNER, AUREEN PINTO,** psychologist, educator; d. Baptist and Winifred Pinto; m. Scott C. Wagner, June 25, 1994; 2 children. BA, St. Agnes Coll., Mangalore, India, 1981; MA, Mysore U., India, 1983; PhD, U. Iowa, 1989. Lic. psychologist NY. Clin. intern Yale U. Child Study Ctr., New Haven, 1988—89; postdoctoral fellow Brown U., Providence, 1989—91; asst. prof. psychiatry/psychology U. Rochester (NY) Sch. Medicine and Dentistry, 1991—98; founder, dir. Lighthouse Press, Inc., Rochester, 1998—2006, The Anxiety Wellness Ctr., Rochester, 2006—; clin. assoc. prof. neurology U. Rochester (NY) Sch. Medicine and Dentistry, 2003—. Mem. profl. adv. bd. Tourette Syndrome Assn. Rochester, 1997—; dir. OCD and Anxiety Consultancy, Rochester, 2002—; mem. sci. adv. bd. Obsessive Compulsive Found., New Haven, 2005—; internat. spkr. in field. Author: Up and Down the Worry Hill: A Children's Book about Obsessive-Compulsive Disorder and its Treatment, 2000 (Reader's Preference Editors' Choice Award, 2003), What to Do When Your Child Has Obsessive-Compulsive Disorder: Strategies and Solutions, 2002, (manual) Treatment of OCD in Children and Adolescents, 2003, Worried No More: Help and Hope for Anxious Children, 2002, 2d edit., 2005. Grantee J.N. Tata scholar, Tata Found., Bombay, India, 1984—88; Lady Meherbai Tata scholar, Lady Meherbai Tata Edn. Trust, Bombay, India, 1984—88, Robert J. Haggerty Rsch. scholar, U. Rochester Sch. of Medicine, 1995, Nat. Merit scholar, Govt. of the State of Karnataka, India, 1981—83. Mem.: APA, Genesee Valley Psychol. Assn. (chmn. newsletter com 2005—), Anxiety Disorders Assn. Am., Obsessive Compulsive Found. Roman Catholic. Achievements include development of conceptual framework to explain treatment of OCD to children. Avocations: travel, gardening, choral music, walking. Office: 2300 Buffalo Road #100B Rochester NY 14624 Office Phone: 585-594-4770. Personal E-mail: aureen@rochester.rr.com.

**WAGNER, BARBARA LEE,** musician; b. Lockport, N.Y., Feb. 5, 1937; d. Richard Lee and Flora May McCarthy; m. William George Wagner, June 15, 1957 (dec. Apr. 17, 2003); children: Molly Heller-Wagner, Carrie Martin. BFA, SUNY, Buffalo, 1958; studies with Raymond Harvey, Buffalo, 1988—95; studies with Karl Richter, Munich Conservatory, 1974. Condr. Orchard Pk. Chorale, NY, 1975—79; dir. vocal activities Nichols Mid. Sch., Buffalo, 1977—97, Nichols Upper Sch., Buffalo, 1997—2001, Buffalo Sem., 2001—03; artistic dir. Buffalo Gay Men's Chorus, 2001—. Music dir. Peace Odyssey Concert Choir, 1989; guest condr. City of Good Neighbors Chorale, 1992; condr. Freudig Singers, 1998. Condr.: premier of Requiem by Kurt Vonnegut and Edgar Grana, 1988; co-author: Singing the Living Tradition, 1993. Min. music Unitarian Universalist Ch., Buffalo, 1963—; music dir. Temple Beth Am. Choir, Williamsville, NY, 1964—78, Unitarian Universalist Gen. Assembly Choir, 1986, 1992. Recipient award for Choral Excellence, Buffalo Philharm. Orch., 2002, Erie County Music Educators, 2002, NY State Pride Agenda award for cmty. svc., 2005. Mem.: Wednesday Morning Musicale, Erie County Music Educators Assn., N.Y. State Sch. Music Assn., Music Educators Nat. Assn., Am. Choral Dirs. Assn., Am. Guild Organists (sub-dean Buffalo chpt.), Unitarian Universalist Musicians Network (chair new hymns supplemental task force 2003, former v.p., former exec. bd., program chair), Chromatic Club (former bd. dirs.). Democrat. Avocations: reading, gardening. Home: 9 John Brian Ln Buffalo NY 14227 Office: Unitarian Universalist Ch 695 Elmwood Ave Buffalo NY 14222 Office Phone: 716-885-2136. Personal E-mail: wagschoir@aol.com.

**WAGNER, BILLY,** professional baseball player; b. Tannersville, Va., July 25, 1971; m. Sarah Wagner. Student, Ferrum Coll. Baseball player Houston Astros, 1995—2003, Phila. Phillies, 2003—05, NY Mets, 2005—. Mem. Team USA, World Baseball Classic, 2006. Recipient Rolaids Relief Man Award, 1999. Achievements include holds the single-season NCAA record for most strikeouts per nine innings (19.1 in 1992); Division III mark for most career K's (327 in 182.1 innings); fewest hits allowed per game (1.58 in 1992); NL All-Star 1999, 2001, 2003 and 2005. Office: NY Mets 123-01 Roosevelt Ave Flushing NY 11368*

**WAGNER, BRUCE STANLEY,** marketing professional; b. San Diego, Aug. 1, 1943; s. Robert Sheldon and Janet (Lowther) Wagner; m. Elizabeth Pearsall Winslow, Oct. 4, 1975; children: Sage Elizabeth, Alexander Winslow. BA, Dartmouth Coll., 1965; MBA, U. Pa., 1984. Sr. v.p. Grey Advt., Inc., N.Y.C., 1967-81; exec. v.p., chief oper. officer Campaign '76 Media Comm., Inc., Washington, 1975-76; exec. v.p., bd. dirs. Ross Roy, Inc., Bloomfield Hills, Mich., 1981-91, Ross Roy Group, Inc., Bloomfield Hills, 1991—94; v.p. mktg. and comms. ITT Automotive Inc., Auburn Hills, Mich., 1995-99; pres. Wagner & Co., Ltd., Birmingham, Mich., 1999—2000; v.p. mktg. and corp. comms. MSX Internat. Inc., Southfield, Mich., 2001—03; pres. Wagner & Co., Ltd., Birmingham, 2004—. Mem. parents bd. Bucknell U., pres. parents bd., 1999—2000, mem. bus. adv. bd., chmn., 2003—. Mem.: Am. Assn. Advt. Agys. (chmn., bd. govs. Mich. coun. 1985—86, bd. govs. ctrl. region 1988—94), Wharton Alumni Assn. (chmn. 1983—85), Birmingham Athletic Club, Orchard Lake Country Club, Detroit Athletic Club, Wharton Club Mich. (bd. dirs. 1985—90). Office: Wagner & Co Ltd 975 Arlington Rd Birmingham MI 48009-1684

**WAGNER, CHARLENE BROOK,** secondary school educator; b. LA; d. Edward J. and Eva (Anderson) Brook; children: Gordon, Brook, John. BS, Tex. Christian U., 1952; MEd, Sam Houston U., 1973; postgrad., U. Tex., Austin, 1975, Tex. A&M U., 1977. Sci. educator Spring Branch Ind. Sch. Dist., Houston, 1970-98; ret., 2000; dir. CompuKidZ, Houston, 1998—2000; cons. Scott Foresman, Addison Wesley, Ginn, Houston, Cons. Scott Foresman Pub. Co., Houston, 2000-01; owner Sci. Instrnl. Sys. Co., 1988—; dir. Compukidz. Mem. Houston Symphony League, 1992, Mus. Fine Arts, Mus. of Art of Am. West, Houston, 1989, Mus. Natural Scis., Women's Christian Home, Houston, 1991; mem. Houston Grand Opera Guild, mem. exec. bd. 1999-2000, rec/corr. sec.; social chmn. Encore, 1988; mem. Magic Circle Rep. Women's Club. Mem.: AAUW, NAFE, NEA, Internat. Platform Assn., Spring Branch Edn. Assn., Tex. State Tchrs. Assn., Heather and Thistle Soc., Wellington Soc. for Arts (Houston chpt.), Clan Anderson Soc., Art League Houston, Shepherd Soc., Watercolor Arts Soc. (Houston), Houston Highland Games Assn., Space City Ski Club. Episcopalian. Avocations: painting, watercolor media. Home: 2670 Marilee Ln Apt B54 Houston TX 77057-4264 E-mail: wagner2670@aol.com.

**WAGNER, CHERI J.,** business owner; b. Mar. 9, 1963; Owner, mgr. Wagner Constrn., Lake Arrowhead, Calif., 1980-94, Blind Ambitions, Skyforest, Calif., 1994—. Mem. C. of C., Soroptomist, Nat. Fedn. Ind. Bus., Humane Soc., Arrowhead Bldg. Contractors Assn., Mountain Women's Assn. E-mail: poker4me247@msn.com.

**WAGNER, CHRISTIAN NIKOLAUS JOHANN,** materials engineering educator; b. Saarbrucken-Dudweiler, Germany, Mar. 6, 1927; arrived in U.S., 1959, naturalized, 1969; s. Christian Jakob and Regina (Bungert) W.; m. Rosemarie Anna Mayer, Apr. 5, 1952; children—Thomas Martin, Karla Regine, Petra Susanne. Student, U. Poitiers, France, 1948-49; Licence es Sci., U. Saar, Ger., 1951, Diplom-Ingenieur, 1954, Dr.rer.nat., 1957. Research asst. Inst. fur Metallforschung, Saarbrucken, 1953-54; vis. fellow M.I.T., 1955-56; research assoc. Inst. fur Metallforschung, 1957-58; teaching, research asst. U. Saarbrucken, 1959; asst. prof. Yale U., New Haven, Conn., 1959-62, assoc. prof., 1962-70; prof. dept. materials engring. UCLA, 1970-91, prof. emeritus, 1991—, chmn. dept., 1974-79, asst. dean undergrad. studies Sch. Engring. and Applied Sci., 1982-85, acting chmn., 1990-91. Vis. prof. Tech. U., Berlin, 1969, U. Saarbrücken, 1979—80. Contbr. articles to profl. jours. Recipient U.S. Sci. Humboldt award, U. Saarbrucken, 1989—90, 1992. Fellow Am. Soc. Metals Internat.; mem. Am. Crystallographic Assn., Minerals, Metals and Materials Soc. Home: 37621 Golden Pebble Ave Palm Desert CA 92211-1430 Office: UCLA 6532 Boelter Hl Los Angeles CA 90095-0001 Personal E-mail: cwagner@dc.rr.com.

**WAGNER, CURTIS LEE, JR.,** judge; b. Nov. 8, 1928; m. Jeanne E. Allen (dec.); children: Curtis L. III, Rex A. Student, Tenn. Poly. Inst., 1947-49; LLB, U. Tenn., 1951. Bar: Tenn. 1952. Assoc. Kramer, Dye, McNabb and Greenwood, Knoxville, Tenn., 1951-54; atty.-adv. gen. crimes and fraud sect. Criminal Divsn. Dept. Justice, Washington, 1954-56; trial atty. Dept. Justice, Washington, 1954-60; assigned to Ct. of Claims sect. Civil Divsn., Washington, 1956-60; spl. asst. comms., transp. and utilities JAG Dept. Army, Washington, 1960-64; chief Regulatory Law Divsn., Washington, 1964-74; adminstrv. law judge FERC, Washington, 1974-79, chief adminstrv. law judge, 1979—. Mem. civilian lawyer career com., 1960-74; chmn. JAG incentive awards com. 1960-74; mem. Army Staff Awards Bd., 1964-74, Army Environ. Policy Council, 1972-74. Dist. commr. Nat. Capital Area coun. Boy Scouts Am., 1967-69; mem. Bd. Govts. Watergate of Alexandria Condo, 1996—; commr. Alexandria Redevel. and Pub. Housing Commn., 1996-2000; mem. waterfront com. City of Alexandria, 2005—. Decorated Meritorious Civilian Svc. award, Exceptional Civilian Svc. award; recipient citation for outstanding performance Dept. Army, 1961-74, Scouter's Tng. award Boy Scouts Am., 1965, Scoutmaster's Key, 1966, Commr.'s Key, 1968, Commr.'s Arrowhead Honor, 1966, Silver Beaver award 1969. Mem. Order of Arrow, Annapolis Yacht Club. Methodist. Office: Fed Energy Regulatory Commn 888 1st St NE Washington DC 20426-0002 Office Phone: 202-502-8500. Business E-Mail: curtis.wagner@ferc.gov.

**WAGNER, CYNTHIA GAIL,** editor, writer; b. Bethesda, Md., Oct. 3, 1956; d. Robert Cheney and Marjory Jane (Kletzing) W. BA in English, Grinnell Coll., 1978; MA in Comms., Syracuse U., 1981. Editl. asst. The Futurist/World Future Soc., Bethesda, Md., 1981—82, staff editor, 1982-85, asst. editor, 1985-91, sr. editor, 1991-92, mng. editor, 1992—. Editor: (newsletter) Futurist Update, 2000—, (book) Foresight, Innovation, and Strategy: Toward a Wiser Future, 2005; columnist: 3-2-1 Contact, 1994; contbr. Encyclopedia of the Future, 1995, The 21st Century, 1999; contbg. writer/music reviewer BeaversonIdol.com., 2004—. Mem. Theatre Comm. Group, Washington Shakespeare Reading Group. Avocation: theater. Office: The Futurist World Future Soc 7910 Woodmont Ave Ste 450 Bethesda MD 20814-3066 Business E-Mail: cwagner@wfs.org.

**WAGNER, DAVID,** computer scientist, educator; b. 1974; AB in Mathematics, Princeton U., 1995; MS in Computer sci., U. Calif., Berkeley, 1999, PhD in Computer sci., 2000. Assist. prof. computer sci. U. Calif., Berkeley, Calif. 1998—. Mem. org. com. Ctr. for Discrete Mathematics & Theoretical Computer Sci., Rutgers U., Piscataway, NJ; mem. prog. com. Operating Systems Design & Implementation Symposium, 2004; co-chair IEEE Security & Privacy Conference. Co-author: (numerous scientific publications including) Cryptoanalysis of the Cellular Encryption Algorithm, 1997, Cryptanalysis of Some Recently-Proposed Multiple Modes of Operation, 1998, TAZ Servers and the Rewebber Network: Enabling Anonymous Publishing on the World Wide Web, 1998, Slide Attacks, 1999, The Boomerang Attack, 1999, Practical Techniques for Searches on Encrypted Data, 2000, Intercepting mobile communications: the insecurity of 802.11, 2001, Securing Wireless and Mobile Networks: Is It Possible?, 2002, Private Circuits: Securing Hardware against Probing Attacks, 2003, Analyzing Internet Voting Security, 2004. Named Best Academic Researcher, Information Security Mag.; named one of Brilliant 10, Popular Science mag., 2002; grantee Sloan Rsch. Fellowship. Expert in the field of security, wireless security, sensor network security, cryptography. Discovered flaw in Secure Sockets Layer security tool built into Netscape Navigator (with Ian Goldberg), cryptanalyzed the CMEA algorithm used in cellphones (with Bruce Schneier). Invented new form of cryptanalysis called "slide attack" (with Alex Biryukov). Office: U Calif Computer Sci Dept 387 Soda Hall #1776 Berkeley CA 94720

**WAGNER, DONALD BERT,** health facility administrator; b. York, Pa., July 27, 1930; s. Bert Daniel and Mary Elizabeth (Roelke) W.; m. Janet Louise Bankert, July 12, 1952; children: Kimberly, Susan, David, John. Student, Franklin & Marshall, 1948-50; BS in Phys. Therapy, Columbia U., 1952; MHA, Baylor U., 1960. Commd. 2d lt. USAF, 1952, advanced through grades to brig. gen., 1982; physical therapist Randolph AFB, San Antonio, 1952-55; asst. adminstr. USAF/RAF S. Ruislip, London; adminstr. USAF/RAF Bentwaters, Ipswich, England, 1955-58; various adminstrv. roles USAF Hosps. and Commands, Europe and U.S., 1958-73; dep. comdr. USAF Sch. Health Care Sci., Wichita Falls, Tex., 1973-75; adminstr. Wilford Hall Med. Ctr., San Antonio, 1975-79; chief med. svc. corps Office Surgeon Gen. USAF, San Antonio, 1979-82; dep. surgeon gen. USAF Med. Svc. Ctr., San Antonio, 1981-82, ret., 1982; adminstr., assoc. v.p. M. D. Anderson/U. Tex. Cancer Ctr., Houston, 1982-85; chief exec. officer Meml. Southwest Hosp., Houston, 1985-91; v.p. Meml. Hosp. System, Houston, 1985-91, internal cons., interim hosp. CEO, 1991—2005; mem. adv. bd. Grad. Program in Healthcare Adminstrn. Texas Women's U., Houston. Adj. prof. Baylor and Trinity U., San Antonio, 1975-82; assoc. prof. U. Houston, St. Louis U., 1982-88; exec. officer Woodlands Hosp., Angleton-Danbury Hosp., Prevention and Recovery Ctr., Bellville Hosp., MHHS Long Term Acute Care Hosp., MH S.E. Hosp.; cons., El Salvador, Nicaragua, China, Saudi Arabia, Japan, Korea, 1991-02. Bd. dirs. Hospice at the Med. Ctr., 1982-2001, Child Advocates, Houston, 1985-89, Kidney Found., Houston, 1985-88, Westland YMCA, Houston, 1985-88, 90-94, Ft. Bend County YMCA, 1998-2003, Greater Houston Hosp. Coun., 1983-87, Sam Houston area Alzheimer's Assn. 1990-94; mem.n. external adv. bd. Sch. Allied Health, U. Tex. Med. Br.; mem. adv. bd. gradrogram healthcare adminstrn. Tex. Women's U., Houston. Named Disting. Alumnus Baylor U. Program in Healthcare Adminstrn., 1993. Fellow Am. Coll. Healthcare Execs. (edn. com., ethics com., comm. com.), Royal Soc. Health; mem. Am. Hosp. Assn. (bd. dirs. hosp. rsch. and edn. found. 1990—), Tex. Hosp. Assn. Assn. Mil Surgeons U.S (Ray F. Brown award 1982 Outstanding Sr. Level Healthcare Exec. Regents award 1991, Regents Lifetime Achievement award 2004), Am. Mgmt. Soc. Republican. Methodist. Avocation: music. Home and Office: 1746 Carriage Way Sugar Land TX 77478-4201 Office Phone: 281-980-5613.

**WAGNER, DOROTHY MARIE,** retired senior creative designer, artist; b. Chgo., Jan. 12, 1926; d. William Christopher and Margaret Frances (Rowell) W. Student, Kalamazoo Coll., 1943-45; BS, Western Mich. U., 1947; BFA, Art Ctr. Coll. Design, L.A., 1962. Dir. electroencephalography lab. Bronson Hosp., Kalamazoo, 1945-51; dir. EEG lab. Terr. Hosp., Kaneohe, Hawaii, 1951-55, UCLA Med. Ctr., 1955-60; sr. creative designer GM Tech. Ctr. Styling, Warren, Mich., 1962-82. Cons. in EEG, Army Hosp., Honolulu, 1950-55; dir. sales and rental gallery Pt. Huron (Mich.) Mus., 1989-93, art and painting instr., 1992-96. Recipient Best of Show award Ea. Mich. Internat. Art Show, 1992, 1st pl. award, 1988, 89, 94. Mem. Blue Water Art Assn. (pres. 1990-96), Orion Art Ctr. Episcopalian. Avocations: horseback riding, showing in dressage, breeding and raising racing greyhounds, water color and acrylic painting, stained glass design and fabrication. Home: 14841 Pine Knoll Rd Capac MI 48014-1913 E-mail: dot@glis.net.

**WAGNER, ELLYN SANTI,** retired mathematics educator; BS, No. Ariz. U., 1971, MA, 1974; postgrad., George Mason U., 1980-82. Cert. tchr., Va. Tchr. math. Flagstaff (Ariz.) Pub. Schs., 1972-76, head math. dept., 1974-76; asst. prof. math. No. Va. C.C., Annandale, Va., 1976—2004. Participant Writing Across the Curriculum Workshops, Annandale, 1992-93. Recipient recognition for outstanding contbns. to edn. No. Va. C.C. Alumni Fedn., 1993. Mem. Am. Math. Assn. Two-Yr. Colls., Va. Math. Assn. Two-Yr. Colls. (regional v.p. 1989-91, coord. spring conf. 1992), Phi Kappa Phi. Avocations: classical piano, ballroom dancing.

**WAGNER, ERIC ARMIN,** retired sociologist; b. Cleve., May 31, 1941; s. Armin Erich and Florence (Edwards) W. AB, Ohio State U., 1964; MA, U. Fla., 1968, PhD, 1973. Instr. sociology Ohio U., Athens, 1968-73, asst. prof., 1973-75, assoc. prof., 1975-83, prof., 1983-97, chmn. sociology and anthropology, 1974-78, 1986—91, 1994—97, vice chmn. faculty senate, 1982—84, prof. emeritus, 1997. Contbr. articles to profl. jours. Dir. Planned Parenthood of Southeast Ohio, 1990-96, pres. 1992-94. Mem. Internat.

**WAGNER, FLORENCE ZELEZNIK,** retired telecommunications industry executive; b. McKeesport, Pa., Sept. 23, 1926; d. George and Sophia (Petros) Zeleznik; m. Francis Xavier Wagner, June, 18, 1946; children: Deborah Elaine Wagner Franke, Rebecca Susan Wagner Schroettinger, Melissa Catherine Wagner Good, Francis Xavier, Robert Francis. BA magna cum laude, U. Pitts., 1977, MPA, 1981. Sec. to pres. Tube City Iron & Metal Co., Glassport, Pa., 1944-50; cons. Raw Materials, Inc., Pitts., 1955; gen. mgr. Carson Compressed Steel Products, Pitts., 1967-69; ptnr. Universal Steel Products, Pitts., 1970-71; gen. mgr. Josh Steel Co., Braddock, Pa., 1971-78; owner Wagner's Candy Store, Mt. Lebanon, Pa., 1979-80; borough sec./treas. Borough of Pennsbury Village, Allegheny County, Pa., 1980-88; ptnr. Tele-Communications of Am., Burgettstown, Pa., 1984-86; trustee Profit-Sharing Trust, Pension Trust Josh Steel Co., Burgettstown, 1986-88, Consol, Inc., Upper St. Clair, 1989—. Mem. Foster Parents; sec. Sch. Bd. St. Bernard Cath. Elem. Sch., Mt. Lebanon, Pa., 1995—98; vol. Pitts.-Carlow GED Literacy program, 1997—98, Upper St. Clair Libr.; Mem. Jefferson Twp. Planning Commn.; mem. Washington County, Pa. Mem. AAUW, Pitts. Symphony Soc., Pitts. Ballet Theater Guild, Soc. Pub. Adminstrn. (founder U. Pitts. br.), Acad. Polit. Sci., U.S. Strategic Inst., Southwestern Pa. Sec. Assn., Alpha Sigma Lambda (past treas., sec., pres.). Republican. Home: 1611 Upper Saint Clair Dr Pittsburgh PA 15241-2648 Personal E-mail: fwagner@libcom.com.

**WAGNER, FREDERICK REESE,** retired language educator; b. Phila., Apr. 15, 1928; m. Barbara Alexander Brady, May 9, 1959 (div. 1968); 1 child, Christopher A. BA summa cum laude, Duke U., 1948, MA, 1949, PhD, 1971. Advt. mgr. Prentice-Hall, Inc., N.Y.C., 1955-57; promotion mgr. Harper & Row, N.Y.C., 1957-65; instr. English Duke U., Durham, NC, 1967-69; asst. prof. Hamilton Coll, Clinton, NY, 1969-73, assoc. prof., 1973-78, prof. English, chmn. dept., 1978-90, prof. English, 1990-95, ret., 1995. Author: Famous Underwater Adventurers, 1962; Submarine Fighter of the American Revolution, 1963; Patriot's Choice: The Story of John Hancock, 1964; Robert Morris, Audacious Patriot, 1976. Mem. Thoreau Soc. (pres. 1984-86), Hawthorne Soc., Phi Beta Kappa. Home: 2160 Bleecker St Apt A-215 Utica NY 13501

**WAGNER, FREDERICK WILLIAM (BILL WAGNER),** lawyer; b. Daytona Beach, Fla., Apr. 13, 1933; s. Adam A. and Nella (Schroeder) W.; m. Ruth Whetstone; children: Alan Frederick, Darryl William, Thomas Adam. BA, U. Fla., 1955, LLB with honors, 1960. Bar: Fla. 1960, U.S. Supreme Ct. 1967, D.C. 1989; cert. civil trial lawyer, Fla. Bar; cert. aviation lawyer, Fla. Bar. Pvt. practice law, Miami, Fla., 1960-63, Orlando, Fla., 1963-65, Tampa, Fla., 1965—; ptnr. Nichols, Gaither, Beckham, Colson, Spence & Hicks, Tampa, 1965-67; ptnr., shareholder Wagner, Vaughan McLaughlin & Brennan, P.A., 1967—. Mem. Gov.'s Jud. Nominations Commn., 1971-72, Constnl. Jud. Nominations Commn., 1972-75; mem. Fla. Bd. Bar Examiners, 1974-77, emeritus mem., 1995—; chmn. Civil Procedure Rules Com. Fla. Bar, 1977-78; bd. govs. Fla. Bar, 1978-83; trustee Roscoe Pound Inst., 1984-92; mem. civil jury instrn. com. Fla. Supreme Ct., 1985-2003. Contbr. articles to profl. jours. 1st lt. USAF, 1955-57. Fellow Am. Bar Found., Am. Coll. Trial Lawyers, Internat. Acad. Trial Lawyers, Am. Bd. Trial Advcs.; mem. ATLA (bd. govs. 1973-80, 84-89, chmn. pub. affairs dept. 1984-89, treas. 1982-84, v.p. 1986-87, pres.-elect 1987-88, pres. 1988-89), Am. Inns of Ct. Found. (trustee 1996-2000), Acad. Fla. Trial Lawyers (bd. dirs. 1965-84, pres. 1972-73), Bay Area Trial Lawyers Assn. (v.p. 1966-68), Am. Law Inst. (coun. 1993—), Lawyer-Pilots Bar Assn., Fla. Bar Found., U. Fla. Alumni Assn., Nat. Bd. Trial Advocacy (cert. civil), Assn. Personal Injury Lawyers, Australian Lawyers Alliance, Pan European Orgn. Personal Injury Lawyers, So. Trial Lawyers Assn., Nat. Transp. Safety Bd. Bar Assn., Tampa Bay Trial Lawyers Assn. Democrat. Methodist. Home: 901 Mariner Way Tampa FL 33602-5759 Office: Wagner Vaughan McLaughlin & Brennan 601 Bayshore Blvd Ste 910 Tampa FL 33606-2786 Office Phone: 813-225-4000. Business E-Mail: BillWagner@WagnerLaw.com.

**WAGNER, GERALDINE MARIE,** nursing educator, consultant; b. Renton, Wash., Apr. 12, 1948; d. Ernest F. and Vera P. (Temiraeff) W. AA, Pasadena City Coll., 1970; BA cum laude, Calif. State U., Northridge, 1977; BSN, Calif. State U., L.A., 1982; MEd summa cum laude, Azusa Pacific U., 1993. Cert. pub. health nurse, Calif. Dept. Health Svcs. In utilization mgmt. Blue Cross, Woodland Hills, Calif., 1987-88, Healthmarc, Pasadena, Calif., 1988-90; nursing educator, asst. dir. vocat. nursing program Casa Loma Coll., L.A., 1991-92, dir. program planning and devel., and coord. continuing edn. Lake View Terrace, 1992-93; dir. vocat. nursing program Glendale (Calif.) Career Coll., 1994-95; with patient care rev. svcs. U. So. Calif. U. Hosp., L.A., 1996—; med.-legal nurse cons., 2000—. Docent Mission La Purisima Concepcion. Capt. Nurse Corps, U.S. Army, 1979-84. Mem.: VFW, Civil War Preservation Trust, Calif. Mission Studies Assn., Assn. for Women in Math., Fellowship Cath. Scholars, Nat. Assn. Cath. Nurses, Computer Using Educators, Nat. Coun. Tchrs. Math., Am. Math. Soc., Blue Army Our Lady Fatima, Nat. Maritime Hist. Soc., Soc. Cath. Social Scientists, Civil War Soc., Order of Preachers, Mil. Officer Assn. Am., U.S. Naval Inst., Cath. War Vets, Res. Officers Assn. U.S., Army Nurse Corps Assn., AMVETS, Assn. U.S. Army, Inst. Religious Life, Assn. Hebrew Catholics, Disabled Am. Vets., Am. Legion, Sigma Theta Tau, Pi Lambda Theta. Roman Catholic. Home: 924 Rock Rose Ln Lompoc CA 93436 Office Phone: 805-735-3575. E-mail: srgmwagnerop@earthlink.net, srgmwagnerop@verizon.net.

**WAGNER, HAROLD A.,** retired gas industry executive; b. Oakland, Calif., Nov. 12, 1935; s. Harold A. and Lurline Frances (Madsen) Wagner; m. Marcia Kenaston, July 17, 1956; children: Sandra Wagner Boye, Kristi Wagner Schwiering, Tracey, Eric. BS in Mech. Engring., Stanford U., 1958, SEP, 1982; MBA, Harvard U., 1963. Regional sales mgr. ind. gases U.K. Air Products & Chems., Allentown, Pa., 1963—70; mgr. GM ind. gases U.S. Air Products & Chems., 1970—76; regional sales mgr. GM Ind. Gases Continental Europe, 1976—80, GM Ind. Gases U.S., 1980—81; v.p. sales ind. gases div. FM, 1981—82; v.p. corp. planning Air Products & Chems., 1982—87, v.p. bus. div. chems., 1987—88; pres. AP Europe, 1988—90, exec. v.p., 1990—91, pres., COO, 1991—92, past chmn. pres., CEO; chmn., pres., CEO, dir. Air Products and Chems., 1992—2001, chmn., CEO, dir., ret.; chmn. Agere Systems, 2001—. 1st lt. USAF, 1958-61. Avocations: squash, photography. Home: 4031 Savannah Trl Santa Rosa CA 95404-8897

**WAGNER, JAMES MILLER,** funeral director; b. Louisville, Ky., June 3, 1965; s. William Henry and Jane (Miller) Wagner. Funeral dir., Hanover Coll., 1988. Apprentice, funeral dir., embalmer Highlands Funeral Home Inc., Louisville, 1989—; funeral dir. Bosse Funeral Home, Inc., Louisville, 1995—. Sec. bd. dirs. Louisville Hist. League, 1989—99. Mem.: Falls Cities Funeral Dirs. Assn., Rotary Club Louisville. Roman Catholic. Avocation: history. Home: 3501 Illinois Ave #A16 Louisville KY 40213 Office: Bosse Funeral Home Inc 1355 Ellison Ave Louisville KY 40204 Office Phone: 502-451-8440.

**WAGNER, JAMES WARREN,** academic administrator, engineering educator; b. Washington, July 12, 1953; s. Robert Earl and Bernice (Bittner) W.; m. Debbie Kelley, July 31, 1976; children: Kimberly Renee, Christine Kelley. BSEE, U. Del., 1975; MS, Johns Hopkins U., 1978, PhD, 1984. Electronics engr. U.S. FDA, Washington, 1975-84; asst. prof. Johns Hopkins U., Balt., 1984-88, assoc. prof., 1988-93, 1997-93, chmn. dept. materials scis. and engring., 1993-97; prof. materials sci. and engring., dean Case Sch. Engring. Case Western Res. U., Cleve., 1998—2000, provost, 2000-01, interim pres., 2001—02; pres. Emory U., Atlanta, 2003—. Contbr. articles to profl. jours. Elder Presbyn. Ch. U.S.A.; bd. mem. Carter Ctr., Ga. Rsch. Alliance, SunTrust Banks, Metro Atlanta C. of C. Mem. IEEE, Optical Soc. Am., Laser & Electro-Optics Soc. Presbyterian. Achievements include scientific contributions to the field of optical metrology applied to materials characterization, especially advanced holographic and laser-based ultrasonic methods. Office: Emory Univ Office of the Pres Atlanta GA 30322

**WAGNER, JODY M.,** treasurer; b. Canton, Ohio; m. Alan L. Wagner; children: Rachael, Jason, Elizabeth, Maxwell. Degree in econs., Northwestern U., Evanston, Ill., 1977; grad. degree in law, Vanderbilt U., Nashville, 1980. Bar: Tenn. 1980, Va. 1984. With Kaufman and Canoles PC, Norfolk, Va., 1981—2002; state treas. Va., 2002—. Office: Commonwealth of Va Dept of Treasury 101 N 14th St Richmond VA 23218 Office Phone: 804-371-6013. Business E-Mail: jody.wagner@trs.virginia.gov.

**WAGNER, JOHN LEO,** lawyer, retired judge; b. Ithaca, NY, Mar. 12, 1954; s. Paul Francis and Doris Elizabeth (Hoffschneider) W.; m. Marilyn Modin, June 18, 1987. Student, U. Nebr., 1973-74; BA, U. Okla., 1976, JD, 1979. Bar: Okla. 1980, Calif. 1999, U.S. Dist. Ct. (we. dist.) Okla. 1980, U.S. Dist. Ct. (no. and ea. dists.) Okla. 1981, U.S. Dist. Ct. (ctrl. dist.) Calif. 2000, U.S. Ct. Appeals (10th cir.) 1982. Assoc Franklin, Harmon & Satterfield Inc., Oklahoma City, 1980-82; ptnr. Franklin, Harmon & Satterfield, Inc., Oklahoma City, 1982; assoc. Kornfeld, Franklin & Phillips, Oklahoma City, 1982-85, ptnr., 1985; magistrate judge U.S. Dist. Ct. No. Dist. Okla., Tulsa, 1985-97; dir. Irell & Manella LLP Alt. Dispute Resolution Ctr., Newport Beach, Calif., 1997—2005. Pres. U. Okla. Coll. Law Assn., 1991-92. Fellow Am. Coll. Civil Trial Mediators, Internat. Acad. Mediators, Fed. Magistrate Judge's Assn. (dir. 10th cir. 1987-89); mem. ABA, 10th Cir. Edn. Com., Okla. Bar Assn., Council Oak Am. Inn of Cts. (pres. 1992-93), Jud. Conf. U.S. (com. ct. adminstrn. and case mgmt. 1992-97), CPR-Georgetown Commn. Ethics and Standards in ADR. Republican. Office: Judicate West ADR 1851 E 1st St Ste 1450 Santa Ana CA 92705 Office Phone: 800-488-8805. Business E-Mail: jwagner@wagneradr.com.

**WAGNER, JUDITH BUCK,** investment firm executive; b. Altoona, Pa., Sept. 25, 1943; d. Harry Bud and Mary Elizabeth (Rhodes) B.; m. Joseph E. Wagner, Mar. 15, 1980; 1 child, Elizabeth. BA in History, U. Wash., 1965; grad., N.Y. Inst. Fin., 1968. Registered Am. Stock Exch., N.Y. Stock Exch., investment advisor. Security analyst Morgan, olmstead, Kennedy & Gardner, L.A., 1968-71, Boettcher & Co., Denver, 1972-75; pres. Wagner Investment Mgmt., Denver, 1975—. Chmn. The Women's Bank, N.A., Denver, 1977-94, organizational pres., 1975-77; chmn. Equitable Bankshares Colo., Inc., Denver, 1980-94; pres. Equitable Bank of Littleton, Colo., 1985; lectr. Denver U., Metro State, 1975-80. Author: Woman and Money series Colo. Woman Mag., 1976, moderator "Catch 2" Sta. KWGN-TV, 1978-79. Pres. Bit Sisters Colo., 1977-82, bd. dirs., 1972-83; bd. fellows U. Denver, 1985-90; bd. dirs. Red Cross, 1980, Assn. Children's Hosp., 1985, Colo. Health Facilities Authority, 1978-84, Jr. League Cmty. Adv. Com., 1979-82, Bros. Redevel., Inc., 1979-80; mem. agy. rels. com. Mile High United Way, 1978-81, chmn. United Way Venture Way, 1978-81, chmn. United Way Venture Grant com., 1980-81; bd. dirs. Downtown Dener, Inc., 1988-95; bd. dirs., v.p., treas. The Women's Found. Colo., 1987-91; treas., trustee, v.p. Graland Country Day Sch., 1990-97, pres., 1994-97; trustee Denver Rotary Found., 1990-95, Hunt Alternatives Fund, 1992-97; trustee The Colo. Trust, 1998—, chmn., 2003-05. Recipient Making It award Cosmopolitan Mag., 1977, Women on the Go award, Savvy Mag., 1983, Minouri Yasoui award, 1986, Salute Spl. Honoree award, Big Sisters, 1987; named one of the Outstanding Young Women Am., 1979, Woman Who Makes A Difference award Internat. Women's Forum, 1987, Maverick Thinker award Urban Park, 2003; named Disting. Citizen award U. Colo., 2005. Fellow Assn. Investment Mgmt. & Rsch.; mem. Women's Forum Colo. (pres. 1979), Women's Found. Colo., Inc. (bd. dirs. 1986-91), Denver Soc. Security Analysts (bd. dirs. 1976-83, v.p. 1980-81, pres. 1981-82), Colo. Investment Advisors assn., Rotary (treas. Denver chpt. found., pres. 1993-94), Leadership Denver (Outstanding Alumna award 1987), Pi Beta Phi (pres. U. Wash. chpt. 1964-65). Office: Wagner Investment Mgmt Inc Ste 240 3200 Cherry Creek South Dr Denver CO 80209-3245 Office Phone: 303-777-1800.

**WAGNER, LAWRENCE M.,** diversified financial services company executive; Exec. v.p., COO The Hillman Co., Pitts., pres., CEO. Bd. mem. Black Rock Inc. Vice chair, v.p. Pa. Economy League; bd. mem. Allegheny County United Way. Office: The Hillman Company 1900 Grant Bldg Pittsburgh PA 15219

**WAGNER, LESLIE,** lawyer; b. Houston, July 18, 1953; d. Jacob and Geraldine (Harris) W. BA cum laude, U. Tex., 1975; JD, U. Houston, 1980. Bar: Tex. 1980, U.S. Dist. Ct. (so. dist.) Tex. 1981. Trial atty. civil rights EEOC, Houston, 1981—84; pvt. practice Houston, 1984—85, 1987—88, 2004—; dir. law placement U. Houston Law Ctr., 1985—87; employee rels. atty, sr. employee rels. analyst The Meth. Hosp. System, Houston, 1985—97; employee rels. cons. Prudential Fin., Houston, 1997—2003; equal employment affirmative action cons., 2004—. Cons. EEOC, Houston, 1984—; v.p., treas. Houston Soc. Healthcare Human Resources Adminstrns., 1995-97; dir., gen. counsel Hematology/Oncology Assistance Resource Coalition, 1995-2002. Editor: U. Houston Law Rev., 1979, assoc. editor, 1980. Mem. health and edn. com. Jewish Cmty. Ctr., Houston, 1983-85; polit. cons. Houston, 1984-85. Named Honors Day Honoree U. Tex., 1971; Arts and Scis. scholar U. Tex., 1971-74. Mem. ABA (com. employee and labor rels. 1983-85, employment rights com. gen. practice sect. 1986), ATLA, Houston Bar Assn., Tex. Young Lawyers Assn. (job fair com.), Tex. Hosp. Assn., Soc. of Human Resources Mgmt., Nat. Assn. Law Placement (careers com. 1986-87, minority placement com. 1987), Am. Studies Assn., Houston Festival Dancers (treas. 1976-77), Eta Phi Sigma. Democrat. Avocations: creative writing, dance, reading. Home: 5407 Wigton Dr Houston TX 77096-4005 Personal E-mail: leslie.wagner@earthlink.net.

**WAGNER, LINDSAY JEAN,** actress; b. L.A., June 22, 1949; d. Bill Nowels and Marilyn Louise (Thrasher) W.; m. Alan Rider (div.); m. Michael Brandon, Dec. 1976 (div.); m. Henry Kingi, 1981 (div.); children: Dorian Henry, Alex Nathan; m. Lawrence Mortorff, 1990 (div.). Student, U. Oreg., 1967. Tchr. acting children Founders Sch. Los Angeles, 1975. Actress numerous TV shows Universal Studios, Universal City, Calif., 1971-74; motion picture picture appearances include: Two People, 1972, The Paper Chase, 1973, Second Wind, 1976, Nighthawks, 1981, Martin's Day, 1984, Ricochet, 1991, Frog and Wombat, 1998, A Light in the Forest, 2002, Buckaroo, 2005, The Surfer King, 2006; TV series include The Bionic Woman, 1976-78, Jessie, 1984, Peaceable Kingdom, 1989; appeared in TV miniseries Scruples, 1980, Princess Daisy, 1983, The Dead of the Night, 1989, Voices of the Heart, 1990, To Be the Best, 1991; TV films include: The Two Worlds of Jennie Logan, 1979, The Incredible Journey of Dr. Meg Laurel, 1979, I Want to Live, 1983, Two Kinds of Love, 1983, Callie and Son, 1983, Passion, 1984, This Child is Mine, 1985, The Other Lover, 1985, Nightmare at Bitter Creek, 1988, The Taking of Flight 847, 1988, Shattered Dreams, 1990, Babies, 1990, Fire in the Dark, 1991, She Woke Up, 1992, Treacherous Crossing, 1992, To Be the Best, 1992, A Message from Holly, 1992, Nurses on the Line: The Crash of Flight 7, 1993, Men Who Hate Women & Women Who Love Them, 1994, Once in a Lifetime, 1994, Bionic Ever After?, 1994, Fighting for My Daughter, 1995, A Mother's Instinct, 1996, Sins of Silence, 1996, Their Second Chance, 1997, Contagious, 1997, Frog and Wombat, 1998, The Fourth Horseman, 1998, Thicker Than Water, 2005; author book, video, film: (with others) Lindsay Wagner's New Beauty: The Acupressure Facelift; co-author: The High Road to Health, 1990; spokesperson for Select Comfort Sleep Number Bed. Office: ICM c/o Sylvia Gold 8942 Wilshire Blvd Beverly Hills CA 90211-1934*

**WAGNER, MARTHA JO,** lawyer; b. Chgo., Apr. 6, 1951; d. Joseph Richard and Mary Marjorie W. BA summa cum laude, U. Md., 1979; JD cum laude, Georgetown U., 1982. Bar: DC 1982, Pa. 1985, Ga. 1997, U.S. Dist. Ct. D.C. 1983, U.S. Dist. Ct. (we. dist.) Pa. 1985, U.S. Ct. Appeals (3d cir.) 1985. Motions clk. DC Ct. Appeals, Washington, 1982-83; atty. Pension Benefit Guaranty Corp., Washington, 1983-85; assoc. Reed, Smith, Shaw & McClay, Pitts., 1985-88, Kilpatrick & Cody, Washington, 1988—91, ptnr., 1991, Kilpatrick & Stockton, Atlanta and Washington, 1999; ptnr., employee benefits practice Venable LLP, Washington. Editor (lead articles): The Tax

Lawyer; contbr. articles to profl. jours. Fellow Am. Coll. Employee Benefits Counsel; mem. ABA (co-chmn. Employee Benefits Com., Labor & Employment Law sect.), State Bar Ga., DC Bar Assn., Phi Beta Kappa, Phi Kappa Phi, Phi Alpha Theta. Democrat. Office: Venable LLP 575 7th St NW Washington DC 20004 Office Phone: 202-344-4002. Office Fax: 202-344-8300. Business E-Mail: mjwagner@venable.com.

**WAGNER, MARY MARGARET,** library and information scientist, educator; b. Mpls., Feb. 4, 1946; d. Harvey F.J. and Yvonne M. (Brettner) W.; m. William Moore, June 16, 1978; children: Lebohang Y.C., Nora M. BA, Coll. St. Catherine, St. Paul, 1969; MLS, U. Wash., 1973; PhD, U. Minn., 2003. Asst. libr. St. Margarets Acad., Mpls., 1969-70; libr. Derham Hall High Sch., St. Paul, 1970-71; youth worker The Bridge for Runaways, Mpls., 1971-72; libr. Guthrie Theater Reference and Rsch. Libr., Mpls., 1973-75; asst. br. libr. St. Paul Pub. Libr., 1975; prof. dept. info. mgmt. Coll. St. Catherine, St. Paul, 1975—. Del. Minn. Gov.'s Pre-White House Conf. on Librs. and Info. Svcs., 1990; mem. Minn. Pre-White House Program Com., 1989-90, Continuing Libr. Info. and Media Edn. Com. Minn. Dept. Edn., Libr. Devel. and Svcs., 1980-83, 87-2002; mem. cmty. faculty Met. State U., St. Paul, 1980—; mem. core revision com. Coll. St. Catherine, 1992-93, faculty budget adv. com., 1992-95, faculty pers. com., 1989-92, 2001-04, acad. computing com. 1991-96, ednl. policies com., 1998-01; chair curriculum subcom. Minn. Vol. Cert. Com., 1993—. Contbr. articles to profl. jours. Bd. dirs. Christian Sharing Fund, 1976-80, chair, 1977-78. Grantee U.S. Embassy, Maseru, Lesotho, Africa, Brit. Consulate, Maseru, Fed. Inst. for Mus. and Libr. Scis., various founds.; Upper Midwest Assn. for Intercultural Edn. travel grantee Assoc. Colls. Twin Cities. Fellow: Higher Edn Consortia for Urban Affairs (bd. dirs. 1998—); mem. ALISE (chair internat. rels. com. 2001—03), ALA (libr. book fellows program 1990—91), Minn. Ednl. Media Orgn., Minn. Libr. Assn. (pres. 1981—82, chair continuing edn. com. 1987—90, steering com. Readers Adv. Roundtable 1989—91), Spl. Libr. Assn., Am. Soc. Indexers, Am. Soc. Info. Sci. Office: Coll St Catherine Dept Info Mgmt 2004 Randolph Ave Saint Paul MN 55105-1750 Office Phone: 651-690-6843. Business E-Mail: mmwagner@stkate.edu.

**WAGNER, MARY S.,** education center administrator; b. Jamestown, N.D., May 13, 1948; d. Thomas Charles Heydweiller and Lila Mae Clemens; m. David Wagner (div.); children: Kristen, James. BS, Cameron U., 1982; MBA, Okla. City U., 1984; graduate, Army Mgmt. Staff Coll., 1995; EdD, Nova Southeastern U., 1998. Cert. tchr. Okla., 1982. Adminstrv. asst. Electronics Command, Ft. Monmouth, NJ, 1972—74, Army Audit Agy., Frankfurt, Germany, 1974—80, Civilian Pers. Office, Ft. Sill, Okla., 1980—83; guidance counselor Army Edn. Ctr., Germany, 1983—86; test specialist Military Entrance Processing Sta., Springfield, Mass., 1986—88; vocat. aptitude battery, 1988—90; edn. svcs. officer 415 Base Support, Bn. Kaiserslautern, Germany, 1990—96, Western Corridor, Republic of Korea, 1996—97, Area Support Group, Kuwait, 1997—. Named Vol. of Yr., Boy Scouts Am., 1986; recipient Outstanding Svc. award, Area Support Group, Kuwait, 2005, Commdrs. medal, U.S. Army, 1991. Avocations: reading, travel, cooking. Office: Area Support Group Kuwait Edn ASG Kuwait APO AE 09366 Business E-Mail: mary.wagner@arifjan.arcent.army.mil.

**WAGNER, MELINDA,** musician, composer; b. Phila., 1957; m. James Saporito; children: Benjamin, Olivia. Grad., U. Chgo., U. Pa. Studied with Richard Wernick, George Crumb, Shulamit Ran, Jay Reise. Instr. U. Pa., Swarthmore Coll., Syracuse U., Hunter Coll. Works performed by: Chgo. Symphony, Am. Composers Orchestra, Chamber Music Soc. of Lincoln Ctr., Ill. Chamber Orchestra, Oakland East Bay Symphony; commissioned works: Barlow Found., Fromm Found. Harvard U., Mary Flagler Carey Charitable Trust, Chgo. Symphony Orchestra, N.Y. New Music Ensemble, Am. Brass Quintet; composer Falling Angels, commissioned by Chgo. Symphony Orchestra, premiered in 1993, performed by Am. Composers Orchestra, 1995, Chgo. Symphony, 1996, Concerto for Flute, Strings, and Percussion (Pulitzer prize in Music 1999), commissioned and premiered by Paul Lustig Dunkel and Westchester Philharmonic, 1998, Extremity of Sky, premiered by Emanuel Ax, Chicago Symphony Orch., 2003. Fellow Guggenheim Meml. Found., Howard Found., 1996; resident fellow MacDowell Colony, Yaddo; grantee Ill. Arts Coun., N.Y. State Coun. on Arts; recipient three ASCAP Found. Young Composer awards. Mem. ASCAP (panelist ASCAP Deems Taylor Competition, ASCAP Found. Morton Gould Grants to Young Composers Program; recipient numerous ASCAP Standard Special awards).

**WAGNER, NORMAN JOSEPH, III,** chemical engineering educator, researcher; b. Phila., Aug. 7, 1962; s. Norman Joseph and Gertrude Eugene (Mamrod) Wagner; m. Sabine Banerjee, Dec. 21, 1990. BS, Carnegie Mellon U., 1984; PhD, Princeton U., 1989. Collaborator Los Alamos Nat. Lab., US Dept. Energy, 1986—96, dir.'s postdoctoral, 1990; NATO postdoctoral fellow U. Konstanz, Germany, 1988-89; asst. prof. U. Del., Newark, 1991-95, assoc. prof., 1995—99, prof., 1999—, Alvin B. and Julia O. Stiles prof., 2005—. Rschr. Ctr. for Molecular and Engring. Thermodynamics, 1995—; guest prof. Inst. Polymer Physics, Swiss Fed. Inst. of Tech., Zurich, Switzerland, 1997, Dept. Physics, U. Konstanz, Germany, 1997—98; Robert W. Vaughan Lectureship Calif. Inst. Tech., 1998; vis. scholar Dept. Physics, U. Rome, 2004. Sect. editor Current Opinion in Colloid & Interface Science, 2001—, editl. bd. Rheologica Acta, 2001—, Journal of Polymer Science Part B: Polymer Physics, 2002—, Particles & Particle Systems Characterization, 2004—, Journal of Rheology, 2005—; contbr. articles to profl. jours. Named to Upper St. Clair HS Alumni Hall of Fame, 2002; recipient Presdl. Young Investigator Award, NSF, 1991, DuPont Young Faculty Award, 1995, 1996, 1997, Fulbright Sr. Scholar Award, 1997, Paul A. Siple Meml. Award, 2002. Mem.: AAAS, Neutron Scattering Soc. of Am., Materials Rsch. Soc., Am. Physical Soc., Am. Soc. Engring. Edn., Am. Chem. Soc. (Local Sect. Award, Del. Sect. 2006), Soc. Rheology, Am. Inst. Chem. Engrs., Fulbright Soc., Delta Phi Alpha. Achievements include patents in field of Shear Thickening Fluid Containment in Polymer; Advanced Body Armor Utilizing Shear Thickening Fluids, 2005. Office: U Del Dept Chem Engring 224 Colburn Lab Newark DE 19716 Office Phone: 302-831-8079. Office Fax: 302-831-4466. E-mail: wagnernj@udel.edu.*

**WAGNER, PAUL ANTHONY, JR.,** education educator; b. Pitts., Aug. 28, 1947; s. Paul A. and Mary K. Wagner; children: Nicole S., Eric P., Jason G., Emily Ryanne. BS, N.E. Mo. State U., 1969; MEd, U. Mo., 1972; MA in Philosophy, 1976, PhD in Philosophy of Edn., 1978. Internat expeditor electromotive div. GM, La Grange, Ill., 1970-71; instr. Moberly (Mo.) Jr. Coll., 1972-73, U. Mo., Columbia, 1973-78, acting dir. instl. rsch. and planning, 1990-92, dir. univ. self study, 1991-92; instr. Mo. Mil. Acad., 1978-79; prof. edn. and philosophy U. Houston-Clear Lake, Atrium Ctr. Disting. Rsch. Prof., 1980, Chancellor's Disting. Svc. Prof., 1985, dir. Inst. Logical and Cognitive Studies, 1980—, dir. Project in Ethics, 1989—, chmn. Dept. Edn. Found., 2003—. Judge Sears Intercollegiate Ethics Bowl, Dallas, 1998; pres. Wagner & Assoc. Ednl. Consulting, 1988-93; dir. Tex. Ctr. for Study Profl. Ethics in Tchg., 1988-95; rsch. assoc. Ctr. for Moral Devel., Harvard U., 1985-86; vis. scholar Stanford U., Palo Alto, Calif., 1981; cons. total quality mgmt. Golden Gate U., 1992-93, M.D. Anderson Cancer Ctr. and Hosp., 1992-93, U. Houston-Victoria, 1993; cons. strategic planning Houston Chronicle Newspaper, 1997; chair So. Accreditation of Coll. and Sch. steering com. U. Houston, Clear Lake, 1990-93, pres. faculty senate, 1999-2001; chair planning and budgeting com., 1996-98, chair, Univ. Life com., 2003-2007, Houston Tenneco Marathon, 1992-94; steering com. Trilateral Conf. and Supershow Greater Houston Partnership, 1994-95; cons., ethics trainer Am. Leadership Forum, 1995-98; chair Tchr. Cert. Coun. 2000-; planning com. Tex. Ethics in Govt. Ann. Conf., 1995-98; adj. prof. ethical theory U. Houston, 2000—; faculty exec. com. U. Houston Sys., 1999-2001, chair univ. life com., 2003—; faculty senate exec. comm., 1999— dept. chair Ednl. Found., 2003—; mem. doctoral faculty, 2005—, mem. grad. faculty, 1990—; adj. prof. bus. mgmt. U. Houston, Victoria, chmn. edn. dept., 2003—; cons. in field Author: (with F. Kierstead) The Ethical Legal and Multicultural Founds. of Teaching, 1992, Understanding Professional Ethics, 1996, Wagner-Kierstead Moral Self-Assessment Protocol, 2d edit., 2002; contbr. articles to profl. jours. on sci. edn., mgmt. theory and philosophy of edn.;

Mem. editl. bd. Jour. of Thought, 19815, Focus on Learning, 1982-85; editorial cons. Instrnl. Scis., 1981-83; editorial assoc. Brain and Behavioral Scis., 1985. Vice-chmn. Human Rights Com., Columbia, Mo., 1978-79; Sunday sch. tchr. Mary Queen Cath. Ch., Friendswood, Tex., 1979-85; founding bd. dir. Bay Area Symphony Soc., 1983-85; capital campaign com. Soc. Prevention Cruelty to Animals, 1989-91; publicity com. Am. Cancer Soc., Houston chpt., 1989-92; cons. in strategic planning M.D. Anderson Cancer Ctr. vol. divsn., 1992-93; steering coun. City of Houston Emerging Bus. Conf., 1994-95, Trilateral Conf., Greater Houston Partnership, 1994-95; active Houston Bus. Promise; chair strategic planning com. Leadership Houston, 1996-98; bd. dirs. Houston Vol. Ctr., Leanna Sprainno Dance Co., 1999-2002, Baker Inst., 1998-2001, chair, 1999-2001; bd. dirs. Hope Village Friendswood, Tex.; ann. leadership briefing com. Rice U., 2001-03; mem. Linda Lorelle Scholarship Com., 1995—, Project Grad Coordinating Coun., 1994-96, pres., 1995-96; emcee, expert commentator for pub. TV, Channel 8, Houston, 1989-2002. Sgt. Mo. N.G.; 1970-76; mem. choir Queen of Angels Cath. Ch., Dickinson, Tex., 2003—. Recipient Cert. of Appreciation, City of Columbia, 1978; K.E. Graessle scholar, 1968, Mo. Peace Studies Inst. grantee, 1971. Mem. AAUP, Assn. Applied and Profl. Ethics, Am. Assn. Pub. Adminstrs. (ethics com.), Am. Philos. Assn., Assn. Philosophers in Edn. (exec. bd., v.p.), Philosophy of Edn. Soc. (exec. sec.-treas., hospitality chair 1995-96), Am. Ednl. Studies Assn., Philosophy Sci. Assn., S.W. Philosophy Edn. Soc., Tex. Network for Tchr. Tng. in Philosophy for Children (bd. dirs. 1983-90), Tex. Ctr. for Ethics in Edn. (bd. dirs. 1990-98), Tex. Ednl. Found. Soc. (pres. 1995-98), Tex. Assn. Coll. Tchrs., So. Assn. Colls. Coord., Houston Bar Assn. (steering coun. NAFTA Conf. 1993-94), Informal Logic Assn., Leadership Houston, Friends Hermann Pk., Clearlake Cir. (chair 1979-85), Phi Delta Kappa, Kappa Delta Pi. Roman Catholic. Avocations: running, reading, opera, ballet. Home: RR 4 Box 217 Navasota TX 77868-9413 Office: U Houston 2700 Bay Area Blvd Rm 338 Houston TX 77058-1002 Office Phone: 281-283-3571. Business E-Mail: wagner@cl.uh.edu.

**WAGNER, PAULA,** film producer; b. Youngstown, Ohio; m. Robin Wagner (div.); m. Rick Nicita, 1984. BFA in Drama, Carnegie-Mellon U. Agent Creative Artist Agy.; cofounder (with Tom Cruise) Cruise/Wagner Productions, 1993—, prodr., ptnr. Actress on & off Broadway, (TV miniseries) Loose Change, 1978; co-author: Out of Our Father's House; prodr.: (films) Mission: Impossible, 1996, Without Limits, 1998, Mission: Impossible II, 2000, Vanilla Sky, 2001, The Last Samurai, 2003, Suspect Zero, 2004, Elizabethtown, 2005, Ask the Dust, 2006, Mission: Impossible III, 2006; exec. prodr.: The Others, 2001, Narc, 2002, Shattered Glass, 2003, War of the Worlds, 2005. Bd. trustees Carnegie-Mellon U.; bd. dir. Nat. Film Preservation Found., UCLA Sch. Theater, Film and TV. Co-recipient Nova award for outstanding achievement by new or emerging prodr. in theatrical motion pictures, Producer's Guild, 1997.

**WAGNER, RAYMOND THOMAS, JR.,** lawyer, legal association administrator; b. St. Louis, June 8, 1959; s. Raymond T. and Loretto (Muenster) W.; m. Ann L. Trousdale, Feb. 20, 1987. BA, St. Louis U., 1981, MBA, 1984; JD, U. Mo., Kansas City, 1985; LLM in Taxation, Washington U., St. Louis, 1993. Bar: Mo. 1985, Ill. 1986, U.S. Supreme Ct. 1989, U.S. Tax Ct. 1989. Legal rsch. and writing instr. U. Mo., Kansas City, 1983-84; law clk. to chief justice Mo. Supreme Ct., Jefferson City, 1985-86; assoc. Gilmore & Bell, St. Louis, 1986-87, Suelthaus & Kaplan P.C., St. Louis, 1987-89; gen. counsel Mo. Dept Revenue, 1989-90; counsel to gov. State of Mo., Jefferson City, 1990-91; dir. revenue Mo. Dept. Revenue, 1991-93; counsel Armstrong Teasdale Schlafly & Davis, St. Louis, 1993; dir. revenue Ill. Dept Revenue, Springfield, 1993-95; legal and legis. v.p. Enterprise Rent-A-Car, St. Louis, 1995—; mcpl. judge City of Ballwin, Mo., 1999—. Adj. prof. law LLM taxation program sch. law Washington U., St. Louis, 1993—; adj. prof. tax law Fontbonne U., St. Louis, 2002-03; chmn. Gov.'s Ethics Com., 1991-92, Mo. Hwy. Reciprocity Commn., 1991-93; commr. Multistate Tax. Commn., 1991-93, Mo. Mil. Adv. Commn., 1991-93; mem. IRS Oversight Bd., 2003-, chmn., 2004-. Precinct capt. Gravois Twp., Webster Groves, 1988; bd. dirs. Shelter the Children, St. Louis, 1988-95; bd. dirs. Foster Care Coalition St. Louis, 1995-2002, pres. 1998-2000; chmn. platform com. Mo. Rep. Conv., 1992; exec. bd. dirs. St. Louis U. Sch. Bus.; mem. chancellor's coun. U. Mo., St. Louis, 1998—. Mem. ABA, Ill. Bar Assn., Mo. Bar Assn., Bar Assn. Met. St. Louis (chmn. law student svcs. com. 1986-87, chmn. social com. 1987-88, mem. exec. com. young lawyers assn. 1988-89, co-chmn. adminstrv. law com., govt. liaison com. young lawyers sect. 1989-90, chmn. legis. com. 1991-2004, legal svcs. oversight commn. 2001-), Regional Commerce and Growth Assn. (vice chair pub. policy coun. 1996, chair pub. policy coun. 1998-2000, vice chair govt. affairs exec. com. 2000-02), Associated Industries Mo. (bd. dirs. 1996-2003), Mo. C.of C. (bd. dirs. 1998-2004). Republican. Roman Catholic. Avocation: running. Office: Enterprise Rent-A-Car 600 Corporate Park Dr Saint Louis MO 63105-4204 Office Phone: 314-512-5000. E-mail: rwagner@erac.com.

**WAGNER, RICHARD,** retired professional sports team executive, athletics consultant; b. Central City, Nebr., Oct. 19, 1927; s. John Howard and Esther Marie (Wolken) W.; m. Gloria Jean Larsen, May 10, 1950; children—Randolph G., Cynthia Kaye. Student, pub. schs., Central City. Gen. mgr. Lincoln (Nebr.) Baseball Club, 1955-58; mgr. Pershing Mcpl. Auditorium, Lincoln, 1958-61; exec. staff Ice Capades, Inc., Hollywood, Calif., 1961-63; gen. mgr. Sta. KSAL, Salina, Kans., 1963-65; dir. promotion and sales St. Louis Nat. Baseball Club, 1965-66; gen. mgr. Forum, Inglewood, Calif. 1966-67; asst. to exec. v.p. Cin. Reds, 1967-70, asst. to pres., 1970-74, v.p. adminstrn., 1975, exec. v.p., 1975-78, gen. mgr., 1977-83, pres., 1978-83, Houston Astros Baseball Club, 1985-87; spl. asst. Office of Baseball Commr., 1988-93; asst. to chmn. Major League Exec. Coun., 1993-94. Pres. RGW Enterprises, Inc., Phoenix, 1978-97. Served with USNR, 1945-47, 50-52. Named Exec. of Yr., Minor League Baseball, Sporting News, 1958. Republican. Methodist.

**WAGNER, RICHARD E.,** economist, educator; b. Jamestown, ND, Apr. 28, 1941; s. Herbert and Dorothy Mae King; m. Barbara Helen (Westgate) W., June 9, 1962; children: Stephanie Wagner Tice, Valerie Wagner Smith. AA, Fullerton (Calif.) Jr. Coll., 1961; BS, U. So. Calif., 1963; PhD, U. Va., 1966. Asst. prof. econs. U. Calif., Irvine, 1966-68, Tulane U., New Orleans, 1968-73; prof. econs. Va. Poly. Inst. and State U., Blacksburg, 1973-79, Auburn (Ala.) U., 1979-81, Fla. State U., Talahassee, 1981-88; Holbert L. Harris prof. econs. George Mason U., Fairfax, Va., 1988—. Sr. fellow, chmn. acad. adv. bd. Pub. Interest Inst., Mt. Pleasant, Iowa, 1995—. Author: Democracy in Deficit, 1977, To Promote the General Welfare, 1989, The Economics of Smoking, 1991, Trade Protection in the United States, 1995; editor: Public Choice and Constitutional Economics, 1988, Charging for Government, 1991, Limiting Leviathan, 1999, Federalist Government in Principle and Practice, 2001, Politics, Taxation, and The Rule of Law, 2002. Mem. Am. Econ. Assn., So. Econ. Assn. (exec. com. 1987-88), Internat. Inst. Pub. Fin., Internat. Soc. New Inst. Econs., Pub. Choice Soc. Home: 11845 Clara Way Fairfax Station VA 22039 Office: George Mason U Dept Econs Fairfax VA 22030 Office Phone: 703-993-1132. Business E-Mail: rwagner@gmu.edu.

**WAGNER, ROBERT,** actor; b. Detroit, Feb. 10, 1930; m. Natalie Wood, Dec. 28, 1957 (div. Apr. 27, 1962); m. Marion Marshall Donen; 1 child, Kate; remarried Natalie Wood, July 16, 1972 (dec. Nov. 29, 1981); 1 child, Courtney; m. Jill St. John, 1990. Films include: Halls of Montezuma, The Frogmen, Let's Make It Legal, With a Song in My Heart, What Price Glory?, Stars and Stripes Forever, The Silver Whip, Titanic, Star of Tomorrow, Beneath the 12-Mile Reef, Prince Valiant, Broken Lance, White Feather, A Kiss Before Dying, The Mountain, The True Story of Jesse James, Stopover Tokyo, In Love and War, Say One For Me, Between Heaven and Hell, The Hunters, All the Fine Young Cannibals, Sail a Crooked Ship, The Longest Day, The War Lover, The Condemned of Altona, Harper, Banning, The Biggest Bundle of Them All, The Pink Panther, The Curse of the Pink Panther, Winning, The Affair, The Towering Inferno, Critical List, Dragon: The Bruce Lee Story, Overdrive, 1997, Austin Powers-International Man of

Mystery, 1997, Wild Things, 1998, No Vacancy, 1999, Love and Fear, 1999, The Kidnapping of Chris Burden, 1999, Austin Powers: The Spy Who Shagged Me, 1999, Crazy in Alabama, 1999, Forever Fabulous, 2000, The Calling, 2001, Jungle Juice, 2001, Austin Powers in Goldmember, 2002, El Padrino, 2004, Little Victim, 2005, Hoot, 2006 (voice) Everyone's Hero, 2006; starred in TV series It Takes a Thief, Switch!, Hart to Hart (Golden Globe nominee), Lime St.; produced, starred in TV series Madame Sin; formed Robert Wagner Prodns.; other TV appearances include: Streets of San Francisco, The Ox-Bow Incident, Gun In His Hand, And Man Created Vanity, The Enemy on the Beach, Runaway Bay, How I Spent My Summer Vacation, Name of the Game, City Beneath the Sea, Cable Car Mystery, To Catch a King, Cat on a Hot Tin Roof, Indiscreet, 1988, Seinfeld, 1990, Becoming Dick, 2000, The Retrievers, 2001, Rocke's Red Glare, 2000-01; Movies of the Week There Must Be a Pony, Love Amongst Thieves, This Gun for Hire. Office: Robert Wagner Fan Club PO Box 370790 Reseda CA 91337 Home: 8687 Melrose Ave West Hollywood CA 90069-5701*

**WAGNER, ROBERT EARL,** retired agronomist; b. Garden City, Kans., Mar. 6, 1921; s. Fay Arthur and Margaret (Longbottom) W.; m. Bernice Bittner, Aug. 7, 1948; children— Robert Earl, James Warren, Douglas Alan. BS, Kans. State Coll., 1942; MS, U. Wis., 1943, PhD, 1950. Forage crops specialist Ft. Hays Expt. Sta., Hays, Kans., 1943—45; assoc. agronomist Plant Industry Sta., U.S. Dept. Agr., Beltsville, Md., 1945—48, rsch. agronomist, asst. project leader pasture and range project, 1951—54, rsch. agronomist, project leader we. pasture and range project, 1954—56; prof., head dept. agronomy U. Md., 1956—59; regional dir. Am. Potash Inst., 1959—66; v.p. Am. Potash Inst., Found. Internat. Potash Rsch., 1966—67; dir. Coop. Ext. Svc., U. Md., 1967—75; pres., bd. dirs. Potash Inst., 1975—77, Potash and Phosphate Inst., 1977—88, pres. emeritus, 1988—; chmn., bd. dirs. Potash & Phosphate Inst. Can., 1975—88; pres., bd. dirs. Found. for Agronomic Rsch., 1980—87; owner Wagner Performance Cattle, Stone Mountain, Ga., 1985—. Bd. dirs., mem. exec. com. Internat. Fertilizer Devel. Ctr., 1975-98; chmn. Nat. Ext. Com. on Orgn. and Policy; mem. U.S. del. 7th Internat. Grassland Congress, New Zealand. Author tech., popular publs.; Editor: Proc. Sixth Internat. Grassland Congress. Chmn. fin. com. Parks Springs Retirement Cmty., 2005—06. Recipient Medallion award Am. Forage and Grassland Coun., Disting. Grasslander award, 1994; award Md. Farm Bur.; Disting. Svc. award in agr. Kansas State U., 1985, Disting. Alumnus award, 1990; Cert. of Disting. Citizenship, State of Md.; Robert E. Wagner Efficient Agr. award established in his honor; Disting. Grasslander award Am. Forage and Grassland Coun., 1994; named to Am.'s Registry of Outstanding Profls., 2003. Fellow AAAS, Am. Soc. Agronomy (chmn. grassland com., exec. com., bd. dirs., pres. N.E. br.), Crops Sci. Soc. Am., Soil Sci. Soc. Am.; mem. Grassland Coun. (pres.), Am. Soc. Range Mgmt., Cosmos Club (Washington), Atlanta Athletic Club, Sigma Xi, Alpha Zeta, Gamma Sigma Delta, Phi Kappa Phi Presbyterian. Home: 1495 Parkview Blvd Stone Mountain GA 30087-1016 Office: 655 Engineering Dr Norcross GA 30092-2822

**WAGNER, ROBERT WALTER,** photographer, communications educator, educator, film producer, consultant; b. Newport News, Va., Nov. 16, 1918; s. Walter George and Barbara Anne Wagner; m. Betty Jane Wiles, Nov. 21, 1948; children: Jonathan R., Jeffrey A., Jennifer J. BSc, Ohio State U., 1940, MA, 1941, PhD, 1953. Motion picture writer-dir. Office War Info., N.Y.C. and Washington, 1942-43; writer-dir. Office Coord. Interam. Affairs for South and Ctrl. Am., 1943-44; chief info. Divsn. Mental Hygiene, Ohio Dept. Pub. Welfare, 1944-46; dir. divsn. motion pictures Ohio State U., Columbus, 1946-58, prof. comms., photography and cinema, 1960—, chmn. dept. photo-cinema, 1966-74. Pres. Univ. Film Found., 1979-85; writer, dir. James Thurber's Columbus Town, 1990, Images of the Depression, 1990; writer, prodr. TV series The Last of the Silents, 1975; internat. coms. comms.; bd. dirs. Am. Film Inst., 1974-81; mem. faculty U. So. Calif., 1958-59, U. P.R., 1961, 66, 68, San Jose State U., 1967, Ariz. State U., 1971, Concordia U., Montreal, 1980, 81, Danish Nat. Film Sch., 1983, 94, Emerson Coll., Boston, 1987. Author film series: Series of Motion Picture Documents on Communication Theory and New Educational Media, 1966; co-author: The American Tintype, 1999; editor: Education of Film Maker, 1975; co-producer: Cognizant Media, Studio City, Calif., 1997, The View from Malabar, 2000; curator: The Art of Humane Propaganda, Columbus Mus. of Art, 2001, Pioneers of The American Tintype, Columbus Mus. of Art, 2003, Photography in The Midwest, Encl. of The Midwest, 2005; author: Not On Your Tintype, 2005. Recipient Disting. Svc. award Columbus Cmty. Film Coun., 1986, Disting. Svc. award Ohio State U., 1988, Ohiana Pegasus award, 1985; Ency. Brit. fellow, 1953; Sr. Fulbright fellow, Peru, 1976. Fellow Soc. Motion Picture and TV Engrs. (Eastman Gold Medal award 1981); mem. Acad. TV Arts and Scis. (Disting. Svc. award 1966), Univ. Film/Video Assn. (bd. editors jour. 1975-85, editor jour. 1956-75), Internat. Congress Scis. Cinema and TV (v.p. 1964-82), Assn Ednl. Comm. and Tech. (bd. editors jour. 1976—), Torch Club (Columbus, pres. 1996). Home: 1353 Zollinger Rd Columbus OH 43221-2939 E-mail: profwags@aol.com.

**WAGNER, ROBIN SAMUEL ANTON,** stage and set designer; b. San Francisco, Aug. 31, 1933; s. Jens Otto and Phyllis Edna (Smith-Spurgeon) W.; children: Kurt, Leslie, Christie. Student, Calif. Sch. Fine Arts, 1953-54. Pres. Scarab Prodns., Inc., 1975—; prof. theatre arts Columbia U., 1988—; sr. v.p. The Design Edge, 1989—. Adv. com. Broadway Theatre Inst. Set designer (Broadway plays) The Condemned of Altona, 1966, Galileo, 1967, The Trial of Lee Harvey Oswald, 1967, Hair, 1968, Lovers and Other Strangers, 1968, The Cuban Thing, 1968, The Great White Hope, 1968, Promises Promises, 1968, The Watering Place, 1969, My Daughter, Your Son, 1969, Gantry, 1970, The Engagement Baby, 1970, Lenny, 1971 (Drama Desk award, outstanding set design, 1971), Jesus Christ Superstar, 1971, Inner City, 1971, Sugar, 1972, Lysistrata, 1972, Seesaw, 1973, Full Circle, 1973, Mack & Mabel, 1974. The Fifth Dimension with Jo Jo's Dance Factory, 1974, A Chorus Line, 1975, Hair, 1977, On the Twentieth Century, 1978 (Tony award, best scenic design, 1978, Drama Desk award, outstanding scenic design, 1978), Ballroom, 1978, Comin' Uptown, 1979, 42nd Street, 1980, Dreamgirls, 1981 (Drama Desk award, outstanding set design, 1982), Merlin, 1983, Song and Dance, 1985, Teddy & Alice, 1987, Chess, 1988, Jerome Robbins' Broadway, 1989, City of Angels, 1989 (Tony award, best scenic design, 1990, Drama Desk award, outstanding set design, 1990), Crazy for You, 1992, Jelly's Last Jam, 1992, Angels in America: Millennium Approaches, 1993, Angels in America: Perestroika, 1993, Victor/Victoria, 1995, Big, 1996, The Life, 1997, Side Show, 1997, Saturday Night Fever, 1999, Kiss Me, Kate, 1999 (Tony award, best scenic design, 2000, Drama Desk award, outstanding set design of a musical, 2000), The Wild Party, 2000, The Producers, 2001 (Tony award, best scenic design, 2001, Drama Desk award, outstanding set design of a musical, 2001), Flower Drum Song, 2002, The Boy From Oz, 2003, Never Gonna Dance, 2003, A Chorus Line, 2006, (plays) Resurrection Blues, 2006, (off-Broadway) Putting It Together, Hamlet 50, In White America, View from the Bridge, Mahogony, The Prodigal, Between Two Thieves, Cages. Mem. adv. bd. Nat. Corp. Theatre Fund, Theatre Adv. Coun. for City of N.Y.; mem. art adv. com. N.Y. Internat. Festival of the Arts; bd. trustees N.Y. Shakespeare Festival. Recipient Theatre World award, 1975, Outer Circle Critics award, 1978, 90, 92, 00, Maharam award, 1973, 75, 82, Lumen award, 1975, Dramalogue award, 1980, Boston Critics award, 1974, 92, award for excellence in theatre Ensemble Studio Theatre, 1990, Dora award, 1995, New Eng. Theatre Conf. 1996 Lifetime Achievement award, En Garde Arts honoree, N.Y.C., 1996. Mem. United Scenic Artists Elected to The Theatre Hall of Fame, 1999. Office: Robin Wagner Studio 890 Broadway New York NY 10003-1211

**WAGNER, ROD,** library director; b. Oakland, Nebr., Sept. 14, 1948; s. Francis Lynn and Doris Jean (Egbers) W.; m. M. Diane Kennedy, June 14, 1969; children: Jennifer, Brian, James. BA Social Sci. Edn., Wayne (Nebr.) State Coll., 1970; MA Polit. Sci., U. Nebr. Lincoln, 1971; MA Libr. Sci., U. Mo., 1981. Rsch. coord. Nebr. Libr. Commn., Lincoln, 1972, planning, evaluation, rsch. coord., 1972-73, adminstrv. asst., 1973-74, dep. dir., 1974-87, dir., 1988—. Bd. dirs. Nebr. Universal Svcs., 1998-2006. Mem. state govt. coun. Nebr. Info. Tech. Commn., 1999—. With U.S. Army N.G.,

1970-77. Mem. ALA (contbr. yearbook 1981-84), Assn. Specialized and Cooperative Libr. Agys. (bd. dirs. 1998-2000), Nebr. Libr. Assn. (pres.-elect 1993-94, pres. 1994-95), Chief Officers State Libr. Agys., Western Coun. State Libs. (pres. 1992-93). Presbyterian. Home: 3205 W Pershing Rd Lincoln NE 68502-4844 Office: NE Libr Commn 1200 N St Ste 120 Lincoln NE 68508-2023 Office Phone: 402-471-4001. Business E-Mail: rwagner@nlc.state.ne.us.

**WAGNER, ROSE MARY,** retired librarian; b. Stuttgart, Germany, Sept. 20, 1941; came to the U.S., 1948; d. Alfred Ferdinand and Lina (Hemminger) Bauer; m. Robert John Wagner, Aug. 27, 1966. BA with distinction, U. Mich., 1963, MA, 1966; MA in Libr. and Info. Sci., Rosary Coll., 1985. Head translation dept. Hill, Steadman and Simpson, Chgo., 1975-85; asst. chief libr. Sargent & Lundy Engrs., Chgo., 1985-87; law libr. Goldberg, Kohn et al, Ltd., Chgo., 1987-88; coms. libr. Chgo. Pub. Libr., 1988—89, coms. libr., project dir., 1989—90, reference libr., 1990—95, head fgn. lang. info. ctr., 1995—2004, head fgn. lang. and lit., 2003—04; ret., 2004. Mem. ALA, MLA. Avocations: skiing, tennis, swimming, painting, drawing. Home: 9640 S Longwood Dr Chicago IL 60643-1608

**WAGNER, ROY,** anthropology educator, researcher; b. Cleve., Oct. 2, 1938; s. Richard Robert and Florence Helen (Mueller) W.; m. Brenda Sue Geilhausen, June 14, 1968 (div. Dec. 1994); children: Erika Susan, Jonathan Richard. AB, Harvard U., 1961; AM, U. Chgo., 1962, PhD, 1966. Asst. prof. anthropology So. Ill. U., Carbondale, 1966-68; assoc. prof. Northwestern U., Evanston, Ill., 1969-74; prof. U. Va., Charlottesville, 1974—, chmn. dept., 1974-79. Mem. cultural anthropology panel NSF, Washington, 1981-82. Author: (novels) Habu, 1972, The Invention fo Culture, 1975, Lethal Speech, 1978, Symbols That Stand for Themselves, 1986, An Anthropology of the Subject, 2001. Social Sci. Research Council faculty research grantee, 1968; NSF postdoctoral research grantee, 1979. Fellow Am. Anthropol. Assn. Avocation: flying hot air balloons. Home: 726 Cargil Ln Charlottesville VA 22902-4302 Office: U Va Dept Anthropology University Station Charlottesville VA 22906

**WAGNER, RUTH JOOS,** elementary school educator; b. L.A., June 1, 1933; d. Walter Joos and Ruth McKenzie (Edwards) J.; m. Gerald Dayton Wagner, Dec. 17, 1960; 1 child, Gregory Dayton. BA, UCLA, 1955, MA, 1976. Cert. primary Tchr., Calif. Kindergarten tchr. Inglewood (Calif.) Unified Sch. Dist., 1955—59, 1963—93, Coronado (Calif.) Unified Sch. Dist., 1959-62; pres. Rainbow West Assocs., L.A., 1986—. Ball chmn. League for Crippled Children, L.A., 1984, pres., 1988; bd. trustees L.A. Orthopaedic Hosp. Found., 1996-98; bd. dirs. L.A. Orthopaedic Hosp., 1998—; pres. League for Crippled Children, 2003-04; docent Getty Mus., 1997— Named Tchr. of Yr., Inglewood Sch. Dist., 1984. Mem. NEA, Calif. Tchrs. Assn, Inglewood Tchrs. Assn., Greater L.A. Zoo Assn., World Affairs Coun., Lake Arrowhead Country Club. Republican. Episcopalian. Avocations: tennis, watercolor painting. Home: 2117 Eric Dr Los Angeles CA 90049-1816

**WAGNER, SAMUEL ALBIN MAR,** recording industry executive, educator; b. Brighton, Colo., Feb. 23, 1942; s. Jacob Doer and Leota Garnet (Wilson) W.; m. Donna Dee Person, Mar. 20, 1987; children: Kurt, Andrea, Autumn, Jan, Arthur. BA in History, U. Colo., 1964, MA in History, 1965; STB (MTS) in History of World Religions, Harvard U., 1968; cert. in archival adminstrn., U. Denver, 1978. cert. records mgr. 1983; cert. archivist 1994. Archival asst. Harvard U. & Harvard Bus. Sch., 1965-68; asst. curator we. hist. collections U. Colo., 1968-70; sr. asst. archivist Cornell U., Ithaca, NY, 1971-73; editor Brighton Blade, Ft. Lupton Press, Colo., 1973-77; city archivist City of Providence, 1978-80; state records analyst Wyo. State Archives, Cheyenne, 1979-83; pres. Records Mgmt. Cons. Internat., 1983—; records mgr. Ft. Collins (Colo.) Police Dept., 1984-87; pub. records adminstr. State RI, Providence, 1987-90; asst. prof. master archival studies program U. BC, Vancouver, Canada, 1990-93; editor Mo. State Archives, Jefferson City, 1994-96; prodr. community access Sta. JCTV, Jefferson City, 1994-96; chief NJ Bur. Records Mgmt., Trenton, 1996—; pres. Historic Rsch. Svcs., Jefferson City, Trenton, 1994—. Instr. Chapman, U., 1981-87, Colo. State U., 1985-87, Lincoln U., 1995-96, U. BC, 1990-93; speaker in field. Author: Brighton Reflections, 1976, Adams County: Crossroads of the West, 1977, Directory of Automated Records Management Systems, 1985-91, Crossroads of the West: A History of Brighton and the Platte Valley, 1977; editor The Fort Lupton Story, 1977, Adams County Colorado: A Centennial History, 2002, Moving Archives, 2002; contbr. articles to profl. jours. Officer, bd. dirs. Adams County Hist. Soc., 1973-77; county historian Adams County, Brighton, 1976-77; mem. Brighton Human Rels. Commn., 1977-78; bd. dirs. Brighton Bicentennial Com., 1975-76, Ft. Lupton Bicentennial Com., 1975-76, RI RSVP, 1978-80, mem. RI Pub. Records Adv. Coun., 1987-90, RI Hist. Records Adv. Bd., 1987-90; chmn. info. profls. task force Freedom of Info. and Privacy Assn., 1991-93; chmn. oral history project Cole County Hist. Soc., 1996. Recipient Hist. Preservation award Adams County Hist. Soc., 1978, award Freedom of Info. and Privacy Assn., 1993; grantee Ethnic Heritage Project Colo. Humanities Coun., 1977, Humanities and Social Scis. U. BC, 1993, Nat. Historic Pub. & Records Commn., 1988-92; Ford Found. fellow, 1964-65. Mem. Assn. Records Mgrs. and Adminstrs. (pres. No. Colo. chpt. 1984-85, v.p. Ocean State chpt. 1987-90, bd. dirs., editor Vancouver chpt. 1991, bd. dirs. Ctrl. NJ chpt. 2000-, pres. 2002-), records mgmt. standards and glossary task forces, mem. Yr. 1985, microcomputer/PC industry action com., chmn. 1984-86, editor Software Dir. 1985-91, co-chmn. tech. applications com. 1989-90, chmn. Archives ISG 1997-99, ISG mid-year seminar program com. 1998-2002, mgr. edn. sector 1999-2002), Inst. Cert. Records Mgrs. (regional coord., exam proctor, grader 1982-, cert. records mgr. 1983), Soc. Am. Archivists (com. automated records and techniques 1990-94, select com. task force on automated records and techniques 1994-98, chmn. MicroMARC users group 1994-96, rep. joint SAA-ARMA Com. 1995-97), Nat. Assn. Govt. Archivists an Records Adminstrs., Archives Assn. B.C. (freedom of info. and privacy legis. com. 1990-93), Assn. Can. Archivists (electronic records select com. 1991-93, Acad. Cert. Archivists (outreach com. 1996-98, mem. commn. on future of archival enterprise 1999-2000), Pub. Sector Mgrs. Assn., Am. Civil Liberties Union, Nature Conservancy, Am. Hist. Soc. of Germans from Russia (charter mem.), Mid-Atlantic Regional Archives Conf. (program com. 1999-2000, 2002-). Democrat. Unitarian Universalist. Avocations: history, art, photography, filmmaking. Home: 387 N 6th Ave Brighton CO 80601 Office Phone: 609-530-3204. Business E-Mail: albin.wagner@sos.state.nj.us.

**WAGNER, SANDRA M.,** lawyer; b. Utica, N.Y., Feb. 9, 1952; BA, St. Lawrence U., Canton, N.Y., 1974; JD, U. San Diego, 1977. Bar: Calif. 1981, U.S. Dist. Ct. (no. dist.) Calif. 1981, U.S. Tax Ct. 1981. Assoc. Law Offices Timothy A. Tosta, San Francisco, 1981—83, Law Offices Jesse W. Jack, San Jose, Calif., 1983—87; ptnr. Froman and Wagner LLP, San Diego, 1999—2003; pvt. practice Cupertino, Calif., 1987—89, San Diego, 1990—98, 2003—. Author: AILA's 12th Annual California Chapters Conference Handbooks, AILA's 15th and 16th Annual California Chapters Conference Handbooks. Cub Scout leader Boy Scouts Am., Solana Beach, Calif., 1991—97, Boy Scout leader, 1994—. Recipient Scout Leader Recognition award, Del Mar Solana Beach Optimist Club, 1993, 1994, 1998, Dist. award Merit, Boy Scouts Am., 1996, Silver Beaver award, 2002. Mem.: Am. Immigration Lawyers Assn. (chair San Diego chpt. 2002—03, vice chmn. San Diego chpt. 2006—), Order of Arrow (mem. election com. 1999—), Rotary (mem. svc. com. 2000—), Sigma Delta Pi. Avocations: camping, backpacking, rock climbing, music. Office: 12625 High Bluff Dr Ste 302 San Diego CA 92130 Business E-Mail: swagner@wagnerimmigrationlaw.com.

**WAGNER, THOMAS EDWARD,** academic administrator, educator; b. Lexington, Ky., Dec. 6, 1937; s. Thomas Caney and Gaynell (Waggoner) W.; m. Susan Adell Brant, Sept. 3, 1960; children: Brant, Brian, Jennifer. BS, U. Cin., 1962; MA, Miami U., Oxford, Ohio, 1967; EdD, U. Cin, 1973. Tchr. Finneytown Sch. Dist., Cin., 1962—67; admissions officer U. Cin., 1967—70, summer sch. dean, 1970—73, asst. to pres., 1973—74, asst. v.p., 1974—77, vice provost faculty affairs, 1977—85, sr. vice provost, 1985—91,

dean for undergrad. and student affairs, 1987—91, v.p. student affairs and svcs., 1991—94, prof. planning, 1983—2000, prof. emeritus, 2000—. Mem. adv. com. The Collegeboard, N.Y.C., 1989-91. Author 3 books; contbr. articles to profl. jours and chpts. to books. Bd. dirs. Charter Com., Cin., 1985-88, Inroads, Cin., 1990-96, Presbyn. Child Welfare Agy., 1992-98, Buckhorn Children's Ctr., 1992-98; mem. steering com. Cin. Youth Collaborative, 1988-91; active Fernald Citizens Adv. Bd., 1993—. With USAFR, 1955-63. Fulbright fellow, 1992, USIA rsch. fellow, 1997. Fellow Ctr. for Dispute Resolution, Soc. for Values in Higher Edn. Presbyterian. Avocations: reading, sports, photography. Home: 1086 W Galbraith Rd Cincinnati OH 45231-5612 Office: Univ Cin Sch of Planning PO Box 210016 Cincinnati OH 45221-0016

**WAGNER, TODD,** Internet company executive; Grad., Ind. U., U. Va. CPA Tex. Co-founder, CEO broadcast.com. (now Yahoo! Broadcast), 1995—; co-owner, CEO 2929 Entertainment. Founder Todd Wagner Found., 2000—; founder, co-chmn. Content Partners, LLC; bd. trustees Am. Film Inst., Tribeca Film Inst.; spkr. in field. Guest appearances on CNBC and CNN, featured in Wall Street Journal, Fortune, NY Times, Business Week and Variety, actor, exec. prodr. (films) Akeelah and the Bee, 2006; exec. prodr.: (TV series) Star Search, 1983, The Benefactor, 2004; (films) Searching for Debra Winger, 2002; exec. prodr.: (films) Godsend, 2004; exec. prodr.: (films) Criminal, 2004, Enron: The Smartest Guys in the Room, 2005, The Jacket, 2005, Good Night, and Good Luck, 2005; exec. prodr.: (films) One Last Thing..., 2005; exec. prodr.: (films) The War Within, 2005, Herbie Hancock: Possibilities, 2006, The Architect, 2006, Diggers, 2006; exec. prodr.: (films) Fay Grim, 2006. Bd. dir. After-School All Stars Dallas. Named Man of Yr., 2000, Social Entrepreneur of Yr., Dallas Cu. for Nonprofit Mgmt., 2002, Kappa Sigma Man of Yr., 2003; named one of Forbes' Richest Americans, 2006; recipient Trailblazer Award, Dallas Film Festival, 2004, Dallas CASA's Champion of Kids, 2005, First Star Visionary award. Office: Yahoo Broadcast 2914 Taylor St Dallas TX 75226-1908 also: Todd Wagner Found 3008 Taylor St Dallas TX 75226 E-mail: twagner@2929entertainment.com.*

**WAGNER, WILLIAM GERARD,** dean, information scientist, consultant, physicist, investment manager; b. St. Cloud, Minn., Aug. 22, 1936; s. Gerard C. and Mary V. (Cloone) W.; m. Janet Agatha Rowe, Jan. 30, 1968 (div. 1978); children: Mary, Robert, David, Anne; m. Christiane LeGuen, Feb. 21, 1985 (div. 1989); m. Yvonne Naomi Moussette, Dec. 4, 1995. BS, Calif. Inst. Tech., 1958, PhD (NSF fellow, Howard Hughes fellow), 1962. Cons. Rand Corp., Santa Monica, Calif., 1960-65; sr. staff physicist Hughes Research Lab., Malibu, Calif., 1960-69; lectr. physics Calif. Inst. Tech., Pasadena, 1963-65; asst. prof. physics U. Calif. at Irvine, 1965-66; assoc. prof. physics and elec. engring. U. So. Calif., L.A., 1966-69, prof. depts. physics and elec. engring., 1969—, dean div. natural scis. and math. Coll. Letters, Arts and Scis., 1973-87, dean interdisciplinary studies and developmental activities, 1987-89, spl. asst. automated record services, 1975-81; founder program in neural, informational & behavioral scis., 1982—. Chmn. bd. Malibu Securities Corp., L.A., 1971—; cons. Janus Mgmt. Corp., L.A., 1970-71, Croesus Capital Corp., L.A., 1971-74, Fin. Horizons Inc., Beverly Hills, Calif., 1971—; allied mem. Pacific Stock Exch., 1974-82; fin. and computer cons. Hollywood Reporter, 1979-81; mem. adv. coun. for emerging engring. techs. NSF, 1987-89; cons. Wagner Tech. Solutions, L.A., 2001—. Contbr. articles on physics to sci. publs. Richard Chase Tolman postdoctoral fellow, 1962—65. Mem.: Am. Phys. Soc., Nat. Acad. Security Dealers, Sigma Xi. Home: 183 Beloit Ave Los Angeles CA 90049-3007 Office: U So Calif Hedco Neurosci Bldg Los Angeles CA 90089-0001 Office Phone: 213-740-7839. Business E-Mail: wwagner@usc.edu.

**WAGO, MILDRED HOGAN,** retired municipal official; b. N.Y.C., Aug. 16, 1918; d. Andrew James and Gunhild (Olsen) Hogan; m. Charles Leonard Wago, Nov. 24, 1949 (dec.); children: Linda G., Richard Herbst, Charlene C., and William Decker. Grad. bus. sch., White Plains, N.Y. Clk. Met. Life Ins. Co., N.Y.C., 1938-50; publican Town of North Castle, Armonk, NY, 1960—2001. Mem. N.Y. State Assn. Receivers and Collectors (v.p. 1983-2001), Westchester County Assn. Receivers and Collectors (v.p., pres. 1987—), Nat. Assn. Exec. Females. Republican. Home: 3 Wago Ave Armonk NY 10504-1447

**WAGONER, ANNA MILLS S.,** prosecutor; b. 1949; BA, Agnes Scott Coll.; JD, Wake Forest U. Assoc. Woodson, Linn, Sayers, Lawther, Short and Wagoner, 1985—87, ptnr., 1987—90; chief judge Dist. 19-C, NC, 1990—2001; US atty. (mid. dist.) NC US Dept. Justice, 2001—. Office: US Attys Office PO Box 1858 Greensboro NC 27402*

**WAGONER, BRENT LEE,** director, coach; b. Bowling Green, Ky., Aug. 4, 1968; s. Charles Lee and Doris Jean (Petty) Wagoner. BA in Social Studies, We. Ky. U., Bowling Green, 1990, rank II in Spl. Edn., 1994, rank I in Ednl. Leadership, 2005. Spl. edn. instr. East Hardin Mid. Sch., Glendale, Ky., 1992—97, tchr. social studies, 1997—2004, curriculum/instrn. assessment coord., 2004—. Participant Ky. Tchr. Forum, 2004—.

**WAGONER, DAVID EVERETT,** lawyer, arbitrator; b. Pottstown, Pa., May 16, 1928; s. Claude Brower and Mary Kathryn (Groff) W.; children: Paul R., Colin H., Elon D., Peter B., Diana F.; m. Jean Morton Saunders; children: Constance A., Jennifer L., Melissa J. BA, Yale U., 1950; LLB, U. Pa., 1953. Bar: D.C. 1953, Pa. 1953, Wash. 1953. Law clk. U.S. Ct. Appeals (3d cir.), Pa., 1955-56; law clk. U.S. Supreme Ct., Washington, 1956-57; ptnr. Perkins & Coie, Seattle, 1957-96. Panel mem. of arbitration forum worldwide including People's Republic of China, B.C. Internat. Comml. Arbitration Ctr., Hong Kong Internat. Arbitration Centre, London Ct. Internat. Arbitration, AAA's Internat. Ctr. Dispute Resolution, CPR Inst. Dispute Resolution. Mem. teh. com. Mepl. League Seattle and King County, 1958—, chmn., 1962-65; mem. Seattle schs. citizens coms. on equal ednl. opportunity and adult vocat. edn., 1963-64; mem. Nat. Com. Support Pub. Schs.; mem. adv. com. on community colls., to 1965, legislature interim com. on edn., 1964-65; mem. community coll. adv. com. to state supt. pub. instrn., 1965; chmn. edn. com. Forward Thrust, 1968; mem. Univ. Congl. Ch. Council Seattle, 1968-70; bd. dirs. Met. YMCA Seattle, 1968; bd. dirs. Seattle Pub. Schs., 1965-73, v.p., 1966-67, 72-73, pres., 1968, 73; trustee Evergreen State Coll. Found., chmn. 1986-87, capitol campaign planning chmn.; trustee Pacific NW Ballet, v.p. 1986. Served to 1st lt. M.C., AUS, 1953-55 Fellow Coll. Comml. Arbitrators, Am. Coll. Trial Lawyers (mem. ethics coms., legal ethics com.), Chartered Inst. Arbitrators, Singapore Inst. Arbitrators; mem. ABA (chmn. standing com. fed. jud. improvement, chmn. appellate advocacy com., mem. com. on separation of powers and jud. independence), Wash. State Bar Assn., Seattle-King County Bar Assn., Acad. Experts, Swiss Arbitration Assn., Nat. Sch. Bds. Assn. (bd. dirs., chmn. coun. Big City bds. edn. 1971-72), English-Speaking Union (v.p. Seattle chpt. 1961-62), Chi Phi. Office: Internat Arbitration Chambers US BankCtr 1420 5th Ave Fl 22 Seattle WA 98101-4087 Home: 1633 Broadmoor Dr E Seattle WA 98112-3747 Office Phone: 206-224-2872. Personal E-Mail: email@davidwagoner.com.

**WAGONER, DAVID RUSSELL,** writer, educator; b. Massillon, Ohio, June 5, 1926; s. Walter Siffert and Ruth (Banyard) W.; m. Patricia Lee Parrott, July 8, 1961 (div. June 1982); m. Robin Heather Seyfried, July 24, 1982; children: Alexandra Dawn, Adrienne Campbell. BA in English, Pa. State U., 1947; MA in English, Ind. U., 1949. Instr. English DePauw U., 1949-50; instr. Pa. State U., 1950-53; asst. prof. U. Wash., 1954-57, assoc. prof., 1958-66, prof., 1966—, prof. emeritus, 2006—. Elliston lectr. U. Cin., 1968; editor Poetry NW, 1966-02; poetry editor Princeton U. Press, 1977-81, Mo. Press, 1983— Author: (poetry books) Dry Sun, Dry Wind, 1953, A Place to Stand, 1958, The Nesting Ground, 1963, Staying Alive, 1966, New and Selected Poems, 1969, Working Against Time, 1970, Riverbed, 1972, Sleeping in the Woods, 1974, Collected Poems, 1976, Who Shall Be the Sun?, 1978, In Broken Country, 1979, Landfall, 1981, First Light, 1983, Through the Forest, 1987, Walt Whitman Bathing, 1996, Traveling Light: Collected and New Poems, 1999, The House of Song, 2002, Good Morning and Good Night, 2005; (novels) The Man in the Middle, 1954, Money, Money, Money, 1955, Rock, 1958, The Escape Artist (also film 1982), 1965, Baby, Come on Inside, 1968, Where is

My Wandering Boy Tonight?, 1970, The Road to Many a Wonder, 1974, Tracker, 1975, Whole Hog, 1976, The Hanging Garden, 1980; editor: Straw for the Fire: From the Notebooks of Theodore Roethke, 1943-63, 1972. Recipient Morton Dauwen Zabel prize Poetry mag., 1967, Blumenthal-Leviton-Blonder prize, 1974, 2 Fels prizes Coordinating Coun. Lit. Mags., 1975, Tietjens prize, 1977, English-Speaking Union prize, 1980, Sherwood Anderson award, 1980, Ruth Lilly Poetry prize, 1991, Levinson prize, 1994; Union League Prize, 1987, Pacific N.W. Booksellers award, 2000; Guggenheim fellow, 1956, Ford fellow, 1964, Nat. Inst. Arts and Letters grantee, 1967, Nat. Endowment for Arts grantee, 1969 Mem. Acad. Am. Poets (chancellor 1978—2000), Soc. Am. Magicians, Nat. Assn. Blackfeet Indians (asso.) Home: 5416 154th Pl SW Edmonds WA 98026-4348 Office: U Wash PO Box 354330 Seattle WA 98195-4330 E-mail: renogawd@aol.com.

**WAGONER, JENNINGS LEE, JR.,** historian, educator; b. Winston-Salem, NC, July 26, 1938; s. Jennings Lee and Carolyn Nelme (Phifer) W.; m. Shirley Canady, Aug. 12, 1962; children: David Carroll, Brian Jennings. BA, Wake Forest U., Winston-Salem, N.C., 1960; MAT, Duke U., Durham, N.C., 1961; PhD, Ohio State U., 1968. Tchr. High Point Pub. Schs., NC, 1960-62; instr. Wake Forest U., 1963-65; tchg. assoc. Ohio State U., Ohio, 1965-68; from asst. prof. to prof. history of edn. U. Va., Charlottesville, Va., 1968—2005; dir. Ctr. for Study Higher Edn., 1975-85, chmn. leadership and policy studies, 1985-87; disting. prof. Curry Sch. Edn. U Va., Va., 1987, William C. Parrish Jr. Endowed prof. Va., 1994—96; prof. emeritus, 2005—. Vis. research scholar Harvard U., 1972, U. Calif., Berkeley, 1984; vis. prof. Monash U., Melbourne, Australia, 1992. Author: Thomas Jefferson and the Education of a New Nation, 1976, Jefferson and Education, 2004; co-author: American Education: A History, 1996, 3d edit., 2004; co-editor: Changing Politics of Education, 1978: editl. bd. History of Edn. Quar., Ednl. Studies jour.; contbr. articles to profl. jours. Recipient Disting. Prof. award Univ. of Va. Alumni Assoc., 1996, Sesquicentennial fellow U. Va., 1972, 84, 90. Mem. History of Edn. Soc. (p. divsn. 1983-85, bd. dirs. 1979-81), Am. Ednl. Rsch. Assn. (v.p. divsn. F 1981-83), Orgn. Am. Historians, Am. Ednl. Studies Assn. (bd. dirs.), Assn. Study Higher Edn., Raven Soc., Outward Bound, Kappa Delta Pi, Phi Delta Kappa, Omicron Delta Kappa (faculty advisor), Golden Key Nat. Honor Soc. Avocations: hiking, fishing, canoeing. Home: 468 Dry Bridge Rd Charlottesvle VA 22903-7456 Office: U Va 405 Emmet St Charlottesville VA 22903

**WAGONER, RALPH HOWARD,** academic administrator; b. Pitts., May 30, 1938; s. Richard Henry and Charlotte (Stevenson) W.; m. Wilma Jo Staup, Dec. 21, 1961; children: Amanda Jane, Joseph Ryan. AB in Biology, Gettysburg Coll., 1960; MS in Ednl. Adminstrn., Westminster Coll., 1963; PhD, Kent State U., 1967; postgrad., MIT, 1973, Dartmouth Coll., 1979. Prin., tchr., coach Williamsfield (Ohio) Elem. and Jr. High Sch., 1960-62; dir. elem. edn. Pymatuning Valley (Ohio) Local Schs., 1962-64, asst. supt. instrn., 1964-65; acad. counselor, asst. to dean coll. Kent (Ohio) State U. 1965-66, instr. edn., 1966-67; asst. prof. Drake U., Des Moines, 1967-70, assoc. prof., 1970-71, chmn. dept. elem. edn., 1968-70, chmn. dept. tchr. edn., 1970-71, acad. adminstrn. intern Am. Council Edn., Office of Pres., 1971-72, asst. to pres., 1972-77, dir. devel., 1975-77; v.p. pub. affairs and devel., prof. Western Ill. U., Macomb, 1977-87, pres., 1987-93, Augustana Coll., Sioux Falls, SD, 1993—2000, Lutheran Ednl. Conf. of N.Am. Adj. prof. San Francisco Theol. Sem., 1971; mem. senate Drake U., 1968-77; sponsor interhall council Western Ill. U., 197893, mem. BOG/UPI task force on incentives for faculty excellence, co-chmn., faculty mentor, 1985-93; cons. in field. Co-author: (with L. Wayne Bryan) Societal Crises and Educational Response: A Book of Readings, 1969, (with Robert L. Evans) The Emerging Teacher, 1970, (with William R. Abell) The Instructional Module Package System, 1971, Writing Behavioral Objectives or How Do I Know When He Knows, 1971; contbr. articles to profl. jours. Chmn. Mid-Ill. Computer Consortium, 1980, 85, Western Ill. Corridor of Opportunity, 1987-93; mem. Pres.' Regional Adv. Coun., 1977-87; mem. investments com. McDonough County YMCA; mem. exec. com. Macomb Area Indsl. Corp.; trustee Robert Morris Coll., 1983-88, Chgo. and Carthage, Ill., 1983-88; bd. dirs. Ill. Coun. Econ. Edn., 1987-93, McDonough County United Way Dr., 1980-82; bd. trustees The Cornerstone Found. LSS of Ill., 1990-96; mem. Sioux Falls Tomorrow Task Force, 1993-94; bd. dirs. S.D. Symphony, 1993—, Edn. Telecomms. State of S.D., 1993—, Sioux Falls Devel. Found., 1993—, Children's Inn, 1993—, Sioux Valley Physicians Alliance, 1995—, LECNA, 1996—; life trustee Lutheran Social Svcs., 1996—. Recipient Man of Yr. award Andover Rotary Club, 1964, Quax Honor award, 1969-70, Disting. Alumni award Gettysburg (Pa.) Coll., 1991; named McDonough County Citizen of Yr., Elks, 1982. Fellow Am. Coun. Edn. (cons. fund raising 1984-87); mem. Am. Assn. State Colls. and Univs. (com. econ. devel. 1988, com. on athletics 1987), Ednl. Computing Network (chmn. policy bd. 1985-87), Assn. Midcontinent Univs. (coun. dels. 1987-93), Gateway Conf. (coun. dels. 1987-93), Coun. for Advancement and Support of Edn. (discussion leader, speaker, 1975, 77, 80, 84, 86, 91, 92, 93, 94, Citation award 1981, 83, Grand award 1982, Bronze award 1985, Silver award 1986), Macomb C. of C. (exec. com., bd. dirs.), Ill. Chamber Econ. Devel. Policy Task Force, Blue Key (hon.), Omicron Delta Kappa, Phi Eta Sigma (hon.), Phi Mu Alpha. Lodges: Rotary. Lutheran. Office: Augustana Coll 2001 S Summit Ave Sioux Falls SD 57197-0001 Home: 6512 Evergreen Acres Dr Wentworth SD 57075-7316

**WAGONER, RICK (G. RICHARD WAGONER JR.),** automotive executive; b. Wilmington, Del., Feb. 9, 1953; BS in Econs., Duke U., 1975; MBA, Harvard U., 1977. Analyst in treas.'s office, mgr. Latin Am. financing, dir. Can. and overseas borrowing, dir. capital analysis and investment GM Corp., N.Y., 1977-81, treas. Sao Paulo, Brazil, 1981-84, exec. dir. fin., 1984-87, v.p., fin. mgr., 1987-88, group dir. strategic bus. planning, 1988-89, v.p fin. Zurich, Switzerland, 1989-91, pres. Brazil, 1992-93, head Worldwide Purchasing Group, 1993-94, exec. v.p., pres. N. Am. ops., 1994-98, pres., COO, 1998—2000, pres., CEO, 2000—03, chmn., CEO, 2003—. Bd. dirs GM Corp., 1998—. Chmn. bd. visitors Fuqua Sch. Bus. Duke U.; trustee Detroit County Day Sch. Mem. Soc. Automotive Engrs. (mem. VISION 2000 exec. com.). Office: GM Corp 300 Renaissance Ctr Detroit MI 48265-0001*

**WAGONER, ROBERT VERNON,** astrophysicist, educator; b. Teaneck, NJ, Aug. 6, 1938; s. Robert Vernon and Marie Theresa (Clifford) W.; m. Lynne Ray Moses, Sept. 2, 1963 (div. Feb. 1986); children: Alexa Frances, Shannon Stephanie; m. Stephanie Brewster, June 27, 1987. BME, Cornell U., 1961; MS, Stanford U., 1962, PhD, 1965. Rsch. fellow in physics Calif. Inst. Tech., 1965-68, Sherman Fairchild Disting. scholar, 1976; asst. prof. astronomy Cornell U., 1968-71, assoc. prof., 1971-73; assoc. prof. physics Stanford U., 1973-77, prof., 1977—2004, emeritus prof., 2005—. George Ellery Hale disting. vis. prof. U. Chgo., 1978; mem. Com. on Space Astronomy and Astrophysics, 1979-82, theory study panel Space Sci. Bd., 1980-82, physics survey com. NRC, 1983-84; grant selection com. NSERC (Can.), 1990-93; mem., Kavli Inst. Particle Astrophysics cosmology, 2004—; mem. visitors com. divsn. astron. scis. NSF, 2005 Contbr. articles on theoretical astrophysics and gravitation to profl. jours., mags.; co-author Cosmic Horizons, 1982; patentee in field. Sloan Found. rsch. fellow, 1969-71; Guggenheim Meml. fellow, 1979; grantee NSF, 1973-90, 2000-03, NASA, 1982-99. Fellow Am. Phys. Soc.; mem. Am. Astron. Soc., Internat. Astron. Union, Tau Beta Pi, Phi Kappa Phi Office: Stanford U Dept Physics Stanford CA 94305-4060 Office Phone: 650-723-4561. Business E-Mail: wagoner@stanford.edu.

**WAGONER, RUTH R,** education coach; b. Louisville, Ky., Feb. 25, 1950; d. Joseph Edward and Patricia Jane Richardson; m. James Reagan Wagoner, Aug.18, 1973; 1 child: Amanda Lee. PhD, Univ. of KY, Lexington, KY, 1994; MA, Western KY Univ., Bowling Green, KY, 1973; BA, Bellarmine Univ., Louisville, KY, 1971. Prof. Bellarmine Univ., Louisville, 1973—. Ed. coach Bellarmine Mock Trial, Louisville, 1985—. Recipient Reynoldson Award, Am. Mock Trial Assoc./ Des Moines, Iowa, 1987, 1991, Neal Smith Award, 1993, Reynoldson Award, 1994, 1998—99. Mem.: Am. Mock Trial Assoc. (exec. comm.- sec. 2002—04). Home: 3115 Brownsboro Rd Louisville KY 40206 Office Phone: 502-452-8417. E-mail: rwagoner@bellarmine.edu.

**WAGONER, WALTER DRAY, JR.,** lawyer; b. New Haven, Dec. 25, 1942; s. Walter D. and Mariana (Parcells) Wagoner; m. Rosa Nilda Morales, Jan. 22, 1980; children: David, William Carlos, Brenda, Lisa. BA, Yale U., 1965, LLB, 1970. Bar: Conn. 71, U.S. Dist. Ct. Conn. 71. Staff atty. New Haven Legal Assistance Assn., 1970—74, mng. atty., 1974—76, dir. legal edn., 1976—78; sole practice New Haven, 1978—. Chmn. New Haven City Commn. Cultural Affairs, 1977—79; trustee Conn. Pub. TV, 1977—83, U.S. Bankruptcy Ct. for Dist. Conn., 1983—87. Mem. Conn. Bar Assn., Loizenos Club (hon.). Democrat. Office: 840 Elm St New Haven CT 06511-4010 Office Phone: 203-624-7759. E-mail: wdwagoner@yahoo.com.

**WAGSTAFF, BARBARA JANE,** marketing executive; b. Beaumont, Tex., Feb. 18, 1934; d. Martin Dempsey and Elberta Parker (McKim) Wagstaff; m. D. Lee Dye, May 14, 1983. Student, Sam Houston State U., 1952—54, So. Meth. U., 1955, UCLA, 1960. Advt. mgr. Home Furniture, Dallas; account exec. Sta. KFOX-AM-FM Radio, Long Beach, Calif.; advt. mgr. WAADE Realty chain, Inland Empire, Calif.; advt. account exec. Sta. KNBC-TV, San Diego; dir. advt. svcs. Visitor Publs., Honolulu, 1975—81; Hawaii sales mgr. Image Internat. Ltd., Auckland, New Zealand; co-owner, mng. dir. Fine Art Galleries of Hawaii, Kamuela, 1989—99. Active Main St. Waimea, Hawaii; pres., moderator Imiola Congl. Ch., Waimea; choir mem. 1st Parish Congl. Ch., 2001—; founding bd. dirs., v.p Nat. Women's Polit. Caucus, San Diego; steering com. bd. Hawaii Visitors Industry Edn. Com., Honolulu, NOW, San Diego; bd. dirs., com. chair Waimea Outdoor Cir.; active No. Hawaii Traffic Planning Com.; choir mem. Seacoast Cmty. Chorus, 2004—05. Mem.: Advt. and Sales Club (San Diego) (bd. dirs. 1964—70). Independent. Congregationalist. Avocations: reading, art, travel, photography. Home: PO Box 194 Moody ME 04054 Office Phone: 936-327-7550.

**WAH, BENJAMIN WAN-SANG,** electrical and computer engineering educator; b. Hong Kong, Sept. 7, 1952; s. Hsien-Feng and Chi-Ching (Wong) W.; m. Christine Hai-Ling Lee, Nov. 4, 1981; children: Catherine Lih-Lien, Elaine Yin-Lien. BSEE, Columbia U., 1974, MSEE, 1975; MS in Computer Sci., U. Calif., Berkeley, 1976, PhD, 1978. Asst. prof. elec. engring. Purdue U., West Lafayette, Ind., 1979-84, assoc. prof. elec. engring., 1984-85; assoc. prof. elec. and computer engring. U. Ill., Urbana-Champaign, 1985-89, prof. elec. and computer engring., 1989—, Robert T. Chien disting. prof. engring., 1998—2003, Franklin W. Woeltge endowed prof. elec. and computer engring., 2004—. Program dir. NSF, Washington, 1988-89; Fujitsu vis. chair prof. intelligence engring. U. Tokyo, 1992; McKay vis. prof. U. Calif., Berkeley, 1994. Author: Algorithms for the Satisfiability Problem, 1998; editor: Computers for Artificial Intelligence Applications, 1986 (Best Seller, Computer Soc. Press 1987, 88); contbr. articles to profl. jours. Recipient Lifetime Achievement award, R.T. Yeh, 2004. Fellow ACM, AAAS, IEEE (co-founder jour. 1988, editor-in-chief IEEE Trans. on Knowledge and Data Engineering, 1993-96), Soc. for Design and Process Sci.; mem. IEEE Computer Soc. (bd. govs. 1989-93, 96-97, treas. 1997, 2nd v.p. publs. 1998, 1st. v.p. publs. 1999, pres. 2001, Tech. Achievement award 1998, W. Wallace-McDowell medal, 2006), Pan Wen Yuan Found. (Outstanding Rsch. award, 2006). Avocations: bicycling, building computers, tennis. Office: Univ Ill Rm 456 CSRL 1308 W Main St Urbana IL 61801-2307 Office Fax: 217-244-7175. Business E-Mail: wah@uiuc.edu.

**WAHEED, KHURRAM,** electrical engineer, electronics engineer, educator; s. Abdul-Waheed Khawaja and Najma Waheed; m. Ayesha Khurram, Sept. 12, 1998; children: Rafay Khurram, Iqra Khurram. BSEE, U. Engring. and Tech., Lahore, Pakistan; MSEE, Mich. State U., 2000, PhD in Elec. Engring., 2003. Asst. prof. San Diego State U., 2003—04, adj. faculty, 2004—; lead RF sys. engr. Tex. Instruments, Dallas, 2004—. Contbr. articles to profl. jours. Fellow, Semiconductor Rsch. Corp., 2000, U. Mich., 2001—02. Mem.: IEEE (mem. circuits and sys. conf. rev. coms. 2001, mem. vlsi sys. and applications tech. com. 2002, mem. neural networks tech. com. 2002, fellowship 2001, Student Paper award 2001, Vol. award 2000). Achievements include patents for self-programmable chip; patents pending for blind multi-user detection CDMA systems; adaptation on deep-submicron VLSI using the hybrid stochastic gradient. Office: Texas Instruments Inc 12500 TI Blvd MS 8723 Dallas TX 75243 Office Phone: 214-567-7140. E-mail: khurramwaheed@ieee.org.

**WAHL, DONALD J.,** counseling administrator; BS in Transp., Travel & Tourism, St. Louis U., 1974; MA in Counseling Psychology cum laude, Chapman U., 1977; PhD in Counselor Edn. magna cum laude, St. Louis U., 1985. Lic. profl. counselor Mo., 1995, counselor Nat. Bd. Cert. Counselors, 1995, cert. group psychotherapist Nat. Registry Cert. Group Psychotherapists, 1996. Activities therapist St, Louis U., 1977—98; instr. Bevo Long and Nottingham Cmty. Schs., 1991—98; counselor, cons. Cath. Family Svcs., 1999, dir. Kenrick cmty. group program, 1999—2002; crisis counselor NW R-I Sch. Dist., Jefferson County, 1999—2002; dir. Youth Violence Prevention Project, St. Louis, 2002—, Family Therapy Program, 2003—. Adj. prof. dept. behavioral scis. St. Louis C.C., 1999; adj. prof. U. Mo.; presenter in field. Prodr.: (website) Youth Violence Prevention Project. Cons. Youth Violence Prevention Project, 2002—06; mem. Children's Behavioral Health Coalition, 2003—06. 1st lt. USAF, 1974—76. Grantee, USAF, 1973-72. Mem.: Partnership Against Violence Network, Am. Group Psychotherapy Assn., Am. Mental Health Counselors Assn. Achievements include development of Youth Violence Prevention Program Selection Tool. Office Phone: 314-652-6004 3013. Personal E-mail: jeffcoproject@hotmail.com.

**WAHL, ROSEMARIE,** biologist, educator; d. Arnold Spencer and Rosemary Doyle Wahl; m. Michael Leroy Tumlinson, May 31, 1992; m. Miroslav Synek (div.); children: Mary Rose Synek, Thomas Robert Synek. BS, MIT, 1956; MS, U. Chgo., 1961, PhD, 1967. Instr. U. Ill., Chgo., 1965—66; asst. prof. Tex. Christian U., Ft. Worth, 1967—72; assoc. prof. St. Mary's U., San Antonio, 1976—83, prof., 1983—, chair dept. biol. scis., 1979—2004. Vis. asst. prof. U. Tex., Austin, 1972—75; chief advisor health professions St. Mary's U., 1979—2004, chair premed./predental adv. com., 1979—2004. Mentor, advisor on biotechnology, mayor, city ofcl. City of San Antonio, 1984—95. Recipient Disting. Faculty award, St. Mary's U. Sch. Sci., Engring and Tech., 1986. Mem.: Tex. Genetics Soc., Tex. Assn. Advisors for Health Professions (mem. exec. com.), Am. Soc. Microbiology, Sigma Xi. Avocations: travel, culture, welfare of children and veterans. Office: St Marys U Dept Biol Scis 1 Camino Santa Maria San Antonio TX 78228 Office Phone: 210-431-8064. Business E-Mail: rwahl@stmarytx.edu.

**WAHL, WILLIAM BRYAN,** marketing professional, real estate company officer; b. Aurora, Colo., Dec. 17, 1963; s. Harold Edward Wahl and Dianne (Fowler) Armstrong. BBA in Mgmt., St. Edward's U., 1987; MBA in Gen. Bus., Kent Coll., 1991; PhD in Bus., U. San Moritz, 1999. Asst. store mgr. Handy Dan, Austin, Tex., 1981-88; real estate broker Powell/Armstrong Realty, Austin, 1985—88, S&W Realty, Austin, 1988—; nat. mktg. dir. Am. Home Products, Austin, 1988—; pres. Wahl Success Systems, Austin, 1989—, project mgr. applied materials, 1995—98; procurement mgr. Dell Computer Corp., 2000—; pres. O.H.S. Prodns., 2000—; Brigadier Group LLC, 2003—; Am. Healthcare Options LLC, 2003—. Bd. dirs Pahl Enterprises, Austin, 1988—. Named Outstanding Citizen, Berkeley Davis, Inc., Berkeley, Calif., 1988. Mem. Austin Assn. Life Underwriters, Austin Bd. Realtors, Tex. Assn. Realtors, Nat. Assn. Realtors, Nat. Assn. Life Underwiters, Mktg. and Distributive Edn. Roman Catholic. Avocations: black belt in taekwondoe, golf, weightlifting. Home: 1206 Greenlawn Blvd Round Rock TX 78664-6918

**WAHLBERG, MARK,** actor; b. Dorchester, Mass., June 5, 1971; s. Donald and Alma Wahlberg; children: Ella Rae, Michael. Singer (albums with Marky Mark and the Funky Bunch) Music for the People, 1991, You Gotta Believe, 1992; Appeared in films Renaissance Man, 1994, The Basketball Diaries, 1995, Fear, 1995, Boogie Nights, 1997, Traveller, 1997, The Big Hit, 1998, Three Kings, 1999, The Corruptor, 1999, The Yards, 1999, The Perfect Storm, 2000, The Planet of the Apes, 2001, Rock Star, 2001, The Truth About Charlie, 2002, The Italian Job, 2003, I Heart Huckabees, 2004, Four Brothers,

2005, Invincible, 2006, The Departed, 2006; (TV movies) The Substitute, 1993; exec. prodr.: (films) Juvvies, 2004, (TV series) Entourage, 2004-. Office: Cortina Bus Mgmt PO Box 610287 Newton MA 02461*

**WAHLBERG, PHILIP LAWRENCE,** former bishop; b. Houston, Jan. 18, 1924; s. Philip Lawrence and Ella Alieda (Swenson) W.; m. Rachel Conrad, June 1, 1946; children: David, Christopher, Pauli, Sharon. AA, Tex. Luth. Coll., 1942, DD (hon.), 1963; BA, Lenoir Rhyne Coll., Hickory, N.C., 1944, DD (hon.), 2005; MDiv, Luth. Theol. Sem., Columbia, S.C., 1946. Ordained to ministry United Luth. Ch. in Am., 1946. Pastor St. Luke Luth. Ch., Thunderbolt, Ga., 1946-50, Redeemer Luth. Ch., Wilmington Island, Ga., 1946-50, St. Mark Luth. Ch., Corpus Christi, Tex., 1950-59; pres. Tex.-La. Synod, United Luth. Ch. Am., Austin, Tex., 1959-62; bishop Tex.-La. Synod, Luth. Ch. Am., Austin, Tex., 1963-87; acting dir. devel. Luth. Outdoor and Retreat Ministries Southwest, 1987-88; legis. liaison Tex. Impact, Austin, 1989-91; interim coord. Regional Ctr. for Mission Evang. Luth. Ch. in Am. Dallas, 1991-92; mem. devel. staff Luth. Sem. Program in Southwest, 1992—2005; mem. com. on appeals, also chmn. Evang. Luth. Ch. in Am., 1988-95, hearing officer, 1995-98. Also mem. exec. coun. Luth. Ch. in Am., N.Y.C., 1980-87, chmn. com. on legal matters, 1984-87; mem. mgmt. com. Divsn. for Mission in N.Am., N.Y.C., 1972-80, chmn., 1972-76; bd. dirs. Bd. Am. Missions, N.Y.C., 1963-72, chmn., 1968-72; bd. dirs. Luth. Sch. Theology, Chgo., 1967-87. Author articles in religious jours., sermons; author theol. cassette, 1973. Named Disting. churchman Tex. Luth. Coll., 1978; Disting. Alumnus, Lenoir Rhyne Coll., 1962; named Man of Year, Thunderbolt, Ga. C. of C., 1950. Democrat. Avocations: winemaking, golf, choral singing. Office: 5804 Cary Dr Austin TX 78757-3108

**WAHLHEIM, PAUL STEVEN,** emergency physician; b. Sacramento, Sept. 30, 1968; s. Charles Aurther and Jacquline Ann Wahlheim; m. DeAnna Renee Wahlheim, July 28, 1998; children: Michaela, Cheyenne. MD, SUNY, Albany, 2000; Med. Surgeon, Universidad Autonoma de Guadalajara, Mex., 1997. Chief resident N.Y. Med. Coll., Valhalla, 2000—01; emergency physician SUNY, Albany, 2000—; attending emergency medicine E.M. Paver Emergency Physicians, Phoenix, 2001—. Mentor Covenant House, 1999—. Fellow: Am. Coll. Emergency Physicians (chpt. bd. dirs. 2005—06). Avocations: basketball, cooking, water sports.

**WAHLQUIST, ANDREW FOLKMAN,** government affairs executive; b. Ogden, Utah, Jan. 29, 1940; s. Keith Campbell and Ruth (Folkman) W.; m. Myrna Helen Kasparek, July 13, 1962; children: Kristin Diane, Andrea Katherine. BS in Comm., U. Utah, 1963. Asst. news dir. KCPX-TV & Radio, Salt Lake City, 1959-67; pub. relations asst. U.S. Steel, Pitts., 1967-72; nat. coord., Let's Clean Up Am. Office Sec. Interior, Washington; spl. asst. The White House, Washington, 1973-74, deputy asst. adminstr., 1974—76; pres. Commemorative Mktg., Washington, 1976; chief of staff to Senator John Warner US Congress, Washington, 1979-86; v.p. govt. relations, v.p. corp. relations Greenwich Air Services, Miami; v.p. bus. devel. Kellstrom Industries; ptnr. Alcalde & Fay, Arlington, Va., 2002—. Dir. Wolf Trap Assocs., Vienna, Va., 1995; mem., Salt Lake City C. of C.; commr. Va. Port Authority, Norfolk, 1994-97; guest lectr. U. Va., George Mason U., Am. U. Producer, writer (documentary) Utah Hoover Commission, 1970 (Utah Broadcasters award 1970), Scrapbook of a Grand Old Lady, 1968 (1st pl. award Utah Broadcasting 1968). Dir. Claude Moore Colonial Farm, McLean, Va., 1980—; dir. emeritus Fairfax (Va.) Symphony, 1980—; adminstr. Am. Revolution Bicentennial. Recipient George Washington medal Freedoms Found., Valley Forge, Pa., 1972, Man of Yr. award Utah Jaycees, Salt Lake City, 1966. Mem. Pub. Rels. Soc. Am., Soc. Profl. Journalists, Army and Navy Club Washington. Republican. Mem. Lds Ch. Office: Alcalde & Fay 2111 Wilson Blvd Ste 850 Arlington VA 22201-3058 Office Phone: 703-841-0626. Office Fax: 703-243-2874. E-mail: wahlquist@alcalde-fay.com.

**WAHOSKE, MICHAEL JAMES,** lawyer; b. Ripon, Wis., June 4, 1953; children: Jennifer, John. BA with highest honors, U. Notre Dame, 1975, JD summa cum laude, 1978. Bar: Minn. 1978, U.S. Dist. Ct. Minn. 1979, U.S. Ct. Appeals (7th cir.) 1979, U.S. Ct. Appeals (8th and 9th cirs.) 1980, U.S. Ct. Appeals (10th cir.) 1982, U.S. Supreme Ct. 1982, U.S. Ct. Appeals (6th cir.) 1988, U.S. Ct. Appeals (fed. cir.) 1989, U.S. Ct. Appeals (D.C. cir.) 1992, U.S. Ct. Appeals (4th cir.) 1994, U.S. Ct. Appeals (11th cir.) 1996, Supreme Ct. of Winnebago Tribe of Nebr., 1996. Law clk. to judge Luther M. Swygert U.S. Ct. Appeals (7th cir.), Chgo., 1978-79; law clk. to chief justice Warren E. Burger U.S. Supreme Ct., Washington, 1979-80; assoc. Dorsey & Whitney, Mpls., 1980-85, ptnr., chmn., appellate practice, 1986—. Adj. prof. law U. Minn., Mpls., 1981-83. Exec. editor U. Notre Dame Law Rev., 1977-78; co-editor: Freedom & Education: Pierce v. Society of Sisters Reconsidered, 1978. Recipient Vol. Recognition award Nat. Assn. Attys. Gen., 1993, Spl. Recognition award, 2003; Supreme Ct. Reception honors State and Local Legal Ctr., 1991, 92, 93, 95. Fellow: Am. Acad. Appellate Lawyers; mem.: FBA, ABA (standing com. on Amicus Briefs 1997—2002), Hennepin County Bar Assn., Minn. Bar Assn., U.S. Ct. Appeals (8th cir.) Bar Assn., Phi Beta Kappa. Office: Dorsey & Whitney LLP Ste 1500 50 S Sixth St Minneapolis MN 55402-1498 Office Phone: 612-340-8755. Office Fax: 612-340-2868. Business E-Mail: wahoske.michael@dorsey.com.

**WAHWEAH, LINDA MCNEIL,** insurance agent, writer; b. Albuquerque, Apr. 2, 1955; d. Ernest Neil and Elizabeth Ann (Murane) Lemke; m. Eugene Gerald Wahweah, Feb. 14, 1979 (div. June 2001). Bus., Cannon's Internat. Bus. Coll., 1976. Legal sec. Manpower Gen. Dynamic, San Bernardino, Calif., 1980—82; ins. c.s.r. p.l. and comml. Ctrl. City Ins. Agy., San Bernardino, 1982—84; ins. office mgr. Bankers Life Ins., Riverside, Calif., 1984—85; ind. ins. agt. Am. Family Life Ins., Redlands, Calif., 1986—98; civil rights adv. Walker River Palute Tribe, Schurz, Nev., 1989—95; freelance writer Native Am. Civil Rights, San Clemente, Calif., 1996—2003; chronical specialist Native Am. Civil Union, San Bernardino, West Cajon, Calif., 2000—03. Promotor specialist Karaoke of Inland Empire, San Bernardino, 2000—03; council mem. Native Am. Civil Rights Union, 1992—95, founder, 1993. Author: Poetry's "Guardian" Best Poems and Poets of 2003. Lobbyist Walker River Piaute Tribe, Schurz, Nev., 1993—95, civil rights adv. San Clemente, 1995—96. Named World Champion Amateur Poet, Internat. Soc. Poets, 2002, No. Am. Poet of Merit, Internat. Libr. Poetry, 2002, New Country Female Vocalist, CCMA of Inland Empire, 1999; recipient Editor's Choice award, Internat. Libr. Poetry, 2003, Outstanding Achievement in Poetry award, Internat. Soc. Poets, 2004, Poet of Merit award, Internat. Soc. Poetry, 2005. Mem.: ACLU, San Bernardino County Bar Assn., European Soc. Lit., Humane Soc., Am. Poetry Assn., Am. Lit. Guild, N.Am. Fishing Club. Democrat. Ch. Of Christ. Avocations: writing, karaoke, cooking, sewing. Office Phone: 909-648-4112. Personal E-mail: wllply9@aol.com.

**WAIDE, ROBERT BRUCE,** ecologist, researcher; s. Kenneth Johnson Waide and Margaret Bruening; m. Valli Marie Rivera, Jan. 7, 1991; children: Valiangelic Fernandez, Dayanara Fernandez. BS, U. Ill., Urbana, 1969; MS, U. Wis., Madison, 1974; PhD, U. Wis., 1978. Dir. Inst. for Tropical Ecosystem Studies, San Juan, PR, 1992—97; exec. dir. LTER Network Office, Albuquerque, 1997—. Editor: (book) The Food Web of a Tropical Rain Forest. Grantee, NSF, 1997—. Mem.: Ecol. Soc. of Am. (life). Achievements include research in the Luquillo long term ecological research program. Avocations: golf, birdwatching, hiking. Office: University of New Mexico Department of Biology MSC03 2020 Albuquerque NM 87131-0001 Office Phone: 505-277-2649.

**WAILAND, GEORGE,** lawyer; b. Munich, Mar. 14, 1947; came to U.S. 1951; s. Max and Bella (Grylak) W.; m. Adele M. Rosen, Aug. 20, 1972; children: J. Zachary, William J. BS, NYU, 1969, JD, 1972. Bar: N.Y. 1973, U.S. Supreme Ct. 1976, U.S. Dist. Ct. (so., ea. dists.) N.Y. 1973, U.S. Dist. Ct. (no. dist.) N.Y. 1981, U.S. Claims Ct. 1979, U.S. Tax Ct., 1979, U.S. Ct. Appeals (2d cir.) 1973, U.S. Ct. Appeals (fed. cir.) 1982, U.S. Ct. Appeals (4th cir. and 9th cir.) 1986, U.S. Ct. Appeals (7th cir.) 1987. Assoc. Cahill Gordon & Reindel LLP, N.Y.C., 1972-80, ptnr., 1980—. John Norton Pomeroy scholar NYU, 1970. Home: 1050 Park Ave New York NY 10028-1031 Office: Cahill Gordon & Reindel LLP 80 Pine St Fl 17 New York NY 10005-1790 Office Phone: 212-701-3212. Business E-Mail: gwailand@cahill.com.

**WAINIO, MARK ERNEST,** insurance company consultant; b. Virginia, Minn., Apr. 18, 1953; BA, Gustavus Adolphus Coll., 1975. Cert. safety profl., assoc. loss control mgmt., assoc. risk mgmt., assoc. claims, CPCU. Carpenter ABI Contracting Inc., Virginia, 1975-77; co-owner Mesabi Builders, Albuquerque and Eveleth, Minn., 1977-79; sr. engring. rep. Aetna Life & Casualty, Albuquerque, 1979-86; loss control specialist CNA Ins. Cos., Albuquerque, 1986-91, loss control cons., 1991-94, mgr. loss control svcs., 1994-95, dir. loss control svcs., 1995-97, asst. v.p. loss control svcs., 1997-98, RSKCo a bus. unit, CNA Risk Mgmt., Albuquerque, 1998—99; asst. v.p. client svcs. RSKCo Cons. Svcs., Albuquerque, 1999—2003; client svc. dir. CNA Risk Control, Albuquerque, 2003—04, consulting dir., 2004—. Owner MEW Safety and Risk Mgmt., 1989—; pres. MW Enterprises, 1990—. Mem. Am. Soc. Safety Engrs., CPCU. Avocations: golf, fishing, hunting, swimming, Karate. Office: CNA 8500 Menaul Blvd NE Ste B560 Albuquerque NM 87112-1273 E-mail: mark.wainio@cna.com.

**WAINIO, MARSHA DIANNE,** school system administrator; b. Crystal Falls, Mich., June 20, 1953; d. Melvin George and Elaine Helen Johnson; m. Roy William Wainio, July 23, 1973. BA in Liberal Studies, Calif. State U., Chico, 1980. Cert. adminstr. Calif. Tchr. Cascade Union Elem. Sch. Dist., Anderson, Calif., vice prin., coord. curriculum and instrn.; dir. North State profl. devel. Tehame County Dept. Edn., Red Bluff, Calif.; prin. Orland (Calif.) Unified Sch. Dist., asst. supt. Mem.: AAUW (v.p. membership 1984 88), Shasta Cmty. Concert Assn. (pres. 1997), Assn. Calif. Sch. Adminstrs. (region I pres. 1998—99, mem. region 4 North State conf. 1999—2002, mem. legis. action com. 1999—2003), Soroptimist (scholarship chmn. 1993—99), Rotary (Camp Royale coord. 2005—06), Phi Kappa PHi. Republican. Lutheran. Avocations: music, cooking, travel. Office: Orland Unified Sch Dist 1320 6th St Orland CA 95963

**WAINIO, MELODY F.,** registrar; b. Coshocton, Ohio, Feb. 25, 1948; d. Francis W. and Dorothy M. Burkhart; m. Edwin A. Wainio, July 20, 1985; m. Robert H. Vaughn, Sept. 7, 1968 (div. 1983); children: Eric R. Vaughn, Bryan S. Vaughn. AA, Lakeland C.C., Mentor, OH, 1982; BS in Tech. Edn., U. Akron, 1987; MSEd, Capella U., 2003. Adj. instr. Bryant and Stratton Coll., Richmond Heights, Ohio, 1990—90, full-time instr., 1990—91, faculty advisor, 1991—98, assoc. dean instrn. Willoughby Hills, Ohio, 1998—2003, dean student svcs., 2003—05, registrar, 2005—. Mem.: ASCD, Nat. Acad. Advising Assn. Home: 181 Meriden Rd Painesville OH 44077 Office: Bryant and Stratton Coll 27557 Chardon Rd Wickliffe OH 44092 Personal E-mail: mwainio@ameritech.net. E-mail: mfwainio@bryantstratton.edu.

**WAINSCOTT, JAMES LAWRENCE,** steel industry executive; b. LaPorte, Ind., Mar. 31, 1957; s. James J. and Frances J. (Cunningham) W. BS magna cum laude, Ball State U., 1979; MBA U. Notre Dame, 1987. CPA, Ind.; cert. mgmt. acct.; cert. internal auditor; cert. info. systems auditor; chartered fin. analyst. Sr. auditor Geo. S. Olive & Co., CPAs, Indpls. and Valparaiso, Ind., 1979-82; fin. mgr. Midwest div. Nat. Steel Corp., Portage, Ind., 1982-88, mgr. pension investments, Pitts., 1988-90, asst. treas., asst. sec., Pitts., 1991-92; treas., asst. sec., Mishawaka. Ind., 1993-95, v.p. & treas. AK Steel Holding Corp., Middletown, OH, 199598, CFO, AK Steel Holding Corp., 1998-99, sr. v.p., CFO, 1999-2003, pres. & CEO, 2003—, chmn. 2006—; cons. Edward J. Wainscott, CPA, LaPorte, Ind., 1982; instr. acctg. Purdue U.-Westville, 1980-82, Valparaiso U., 1980-84. Advisor Jr. Achievement, 1984; vol. Am. Cancer Soc., Valparaiso Income Tax Assistance Program, Valparaiso Community/Univ. Campaign; pres., treas. Midwest Steel Employees Fed. Credit Union; pres. Midwest Steel Employees Assn.; mem. Ball State U. Cardinal Connection; mem. N.W. Ind. Open Housing Council; chmn. dean's adv. council Valparaiso U.; bd. dirs. Youth Svc. Bur. St. Joseph County; chmn. fin. com. Good Shepherd Parish, Cin., 1999-2001. Mem. Ind. CPA Soc. (chmn. chpt. activities com. 1985-86, chpt. bd. dirs. 1983-86, chpt. pres. 1984-85, chmn. chpt. task force, pres. award 1994, state bd. dirs. 1987-90), Nat. Assn. Accts. (chpt. bd. dirs. 1982-86, chpt. pres. 1983-84; Past Pres. award 1984), Am. Inst. CPA's, Inst. Mgmt. Acctg., Inst. Internal Auditors, Inst. Chartered Fin. Analysts, Assn. for Investment Mgmt. and Rsch., Chgo. Soc. Fin. Analysts, U. Notre Dame Exec. MBA Alumni Assn., Mensa, Blue Key, Golden Key, Intertel, Delta Sigma Pi. Roman Catholic. Avocations: music, chess, coin collecting, sports, travel. Office: AK Steel Holding Corp 703 Curtis St Middletown OH 45043 Home: 8099 Carnaby Ln Cincinnati OH 45249-1567*

**WAINSTEIN, KENNETH L.,** federal agency administrator, former prosecutor; b. Alexandria, Va., 1962; BA in Govt. and Internat. Rels., U. Va., 1984; JD, U. Calif., Berkeley, 1988. Corr., caseworker Office Congressman Carl D. Perkins, Washington, 1984; paralegal securities sect. Cleary, Gottlieb, Steen & Hamilton, Washington, 1984—85; summer assoc. for litigation, environ., tax and labor teams Hunton & Williams, Washington, 1986; summer assoc. for litigation, corp. and labor depts. Gibson, Dunn & Crutcher, Washington, 1987; law clk. for Hon. Thomas Penfield Jackson U.S. Dist. Ct. D.C., Washington, 1988—89; asst. U.S. atty. (So. dist.) NY US Dept. Justice, 1989—92, line prosecutor, dep. chief homicide sect. Washington, 1994—99, prin. asst. U.S. atty. DC, 1999—2000, interim U.S. atty. DC, 2001, dir. Exec. Office U.S. Attorneys, 2001—02; gen. counsel FBI, Washington, 2002—03, chief of staff, 2003—04; interim U.S. atty. DC US Dept. Justice, 2004—05, US atty. Washington, 2005—06, asst. atty. gen. for nat. security, 2006—. Mem.: Phi Beta Kappa. Office: US Dept Justice 950 Pennsylvania Ave NW Washington DC 20530*

**WAINWRIGHT, DALE V.,** state supreme court justice; b. Tenn. m. Debbie Wainwright; 3 children. Studied, London Sch. of Economics, 1981; BA, Howard U., 1983; JD, U. Chgo. Law Sch., 1988. With Andrews & Kurth, Houston, Haynes & Boone, Houston; dist. judge. Harris County, 1999—2002; justice Tex. Supreme Ct., Austin, 2002—. Mem. Am. Law Inst., Tex. Commn. on Jud. Efficiency. Co-founder Aspiring Youth Program; bd. mem. Houston Volunteer Lawyers Program, Texas Young Lawyers Assn.; former pres. Houston Young Lawyers Assn. Recipient Legal Excellence award, NAACP, 2000. Fellow: Houston Bar Found., Tex. Bar Found.; mem.: ABA, Houston Bar Assn., State Bar Tex. Office: Tex State Supreme Ct PO Box 12248 Austin TX 78711 Office Phone: 512-463-1332.*

**WAINWRIGHT, DAVID STANLEY,** patent agent; b. New Haven, May 23, 1955; s. Stanley Dunstan and Lillian (Karelitz) W.;m. Catherine Demetra Kefalas, Aug. 11, 1984; children: Maxwell Stanley Hector, Eric George Alexander. BSc in Physics with 1st class honors, Dalhousie U., Halifax, N.S., 1976; MSc in Physics, U. BC, Vancouver, 1979. Registered patent agt., U.S., Can. Model plant supr., scientist, technician Moli Energy Ltd., Maple Ridge, BC, Canada, 1978-84, project leader cell devel., 1984-88, cell devel. mgr., 1988-90, 1990-92, mgr. intellectual property, 1992-98; patent agt. Ballard Power Sys., Burnaby, BC, 1998—2005; sr. patent agent Cardiome Pharma Corp., Vancouver, Canada, 2000—06; IP specialist Questair Techs. Inc., Burnaby, Canada, 2006—. Contbr. articles to profl. jours. Mem. Patent and Trademark Inst. Can. Home: 2585 W 1st Ave Vancouver BC Canada V6K 1G8 Office: Questair Technologies Inc 6961 Russell Ave Burnaby BC Canada V5J 4R8 Office Phone: 604-453-6896. Business E-Mail: wainwright@questairinc.com.

**WAINWRIGHT, GEORGE L., JR.,** state supreme court justice; b. Wilson County, NC, Dec. 10, 1943; s. George Sr. and Susan Wainwright; m. Carol McChesney; children: Kennon, Ashton. AB in Political sci., U. N.C., 1966; JD, Wake Forest U., 1984. Agribusiness and real estate positions, Wilson, 1966-81; atty. Wheatly, Wheatly, Nobles & Weeks, Beaufort, NC, 1984-90; judge Dist. Ct., 1991—94; resident Superior Ct. judge for N.C. Jud. Dist. 3B,

1994—98; justice NC Supreme Ct., 1999—. Served in U.S. Coast Guard Reserve, 1966—72. Morehead scholar, 1966. Mem. N.C. Bar Assn., Lookout Rotary Club. Presbyterian. Office: Supreme Ct NC Justice Bldg PO Box 1841 Raleigh NC 27602-2170*

**WAINWRIGHT, PAUL EDWARD BLECH,** construction company executive; b. Annapolis, Md., Jan. 28, 1917; s. Richard and Alice Sorrel (Blech) W.; m. Helen Mae Rogers, July 10, 1941; children— Richard, Paul Edward Blech, John. BS in Civil Engring., Va. Mil. Inst., 1938. Cost engr. Turner Constrn. Co., N.Y.C., 1938-40, cost engr., asst. supt., 1945-46; cost. engr. for contractors Pacific Naval Air Bases, Honolulu, 1940-42; with Dillingham Corp., Honolulu, 1946-82, asst. v.p., then v.p., 1961-69, group v.p. constrn., 1969-82; cons. constrn. Honolulu, 1982—. Bd. dirs. Hawaii Visitors Bur., 1967, Goodwill Industries Hawaii, 1965-70; pres. Citizens Adminstrn. of Justice Found., 1968, Hawaii Epilepsy Soc., 1975. Served with AUS, 1942-45. Decorated Legion of Merit, Bronze Star, Air medal. Mem. Am. Soc. Mil. Engrs., Beavers, Gen. Contractors Assn. Hawaii (pres. 1966), Hawaii C. of C. (dir. 1964-65), Waikiki Yacht Club, Outrigger Canoe Club. Republican. Episcopalian. Home: 4301 Providence Point Pl SE Issaquah WA 98029-6270

**WAIT, CHARLES VALENTINE,** banker; b. Albany, NY, May 28, 1951; s. Newman Edward Jr. and Jane Caroline (Adams) W.; m. Candace Ellin Hollar, May 27, 1978; children: Charles Valentine Jr., Christopher David, Alexandra Dallas Wait. BA, Cornell U., 1973; cert. in banking, Rutgers U., 1981; LHD (hon.), SUNY Empire State Coll., 2001. Asst. v.p. The Adirondack Trust Co., Saratoga Springs, NY, 1974, treas., 1978-81, sec., treas., 1981-84, pres., 1984—. Trustee NY Bus. Devel., 1997-2003; mem Saratoga County Indsl. Devel. Agency, 1998-2006; mem. Yaddo Corp., Saratoga Springs, 1996-2004, sec., asst. treas., 1997-2004, sec./ treas., 1997-2004; class A dir. Fed. Res. Bank NY, 2003— Chmn. Saratoga Springs City Ctr. Authority, 1983—89; trustee Skidmore Coll., Saratoga Springs, NY, 1984—2002, Nat. Mus. Dance, Saratoga Springs, 1987—2002, Charles R. Wood Found., 1991—98, NY Racing Assn., Saratoga Hosp., 2003—04, Nat. Mus. Racing, 1988—91, v.p., 1989—91; treas. Saratoga Care, Inc., 2002—04; chmn. Face of the Future Capital Campaign. Named Outstanding New Yorker, NY State Jaycees, 1984, Disting. Citizen, Saratoga Springs Sr. Citizens, 2002; recipient Pvt. Sector Initiative award, Pres. Ronald Reagan, Commitment to Cmty. award, NY State Bus. Coun., 1983, Liberty Bell award, Saratoga County Bar Assn. for cmty. svc., Good Scout award, Twin Rivers Coun., 1997, Sam Walton Bus. Leader award, 1997, Exec. of Yr. award, Capital Dist. Bus. Rev., 1999, Denis Kemball-Cook award, 2003, Lucy Skidmore Scribner award, Skidmore Coll., Saratoga Springs, 2003, J. Michael O'Connell Cmty. Svc. award, Saratoga Jaycees, 2004; Paul Harris fellow Dist. 7190, 1997. Mem. Ind. Bankers Assn. of N.Y. State (bd. dirs., sec. 1986-87), N.Y. Bankers Assn. (bd. dirs. 1987, treas. 1995—, chmn. 1997-99), N.Y. State Bankers Retirement System (trustee 1987-95, vice chmn., chmn. 1992-94), Am. Inst. Banking (Counsel of Yr. 1976), Greater Saratoga C. of C., Pillar Soc. Republican. Home: 658 N Broadway Saratoga Springs NY 12866-1624 Office: The Adirondack Trust Co 473 Broadway Saratoga Springs NY 12866-2262 Office Phone: 518-584-5844.

**WAIT, GEORGE WILLIAM,** sales executive; b. Balt., Oct. 23, 1958; s. Frank H., Jr. and Betty (Cartwright) Wait; m. Susan Erwin, Oct. 16, 1982; children: J. Stokes, Hannah S., C. Sam, Addy M. BSBA, Western Carolina U., 1982. From sales rep. to regional sales asst. Gen. Mills Inc., Kinston, N.C., 1982-85, dist. sales mgr. Charlotte, N.C., 1985-87, product sales mgr. Mpls., 1987-89, mgr. promotions and merchandising Raleigh, N.C., 1989-90, regional merchandising mgr., 1990—, regional tri healthway dir., 1992—, mgr. bus. devel., 1993—, corp. ops. mgr. Cary, N.C., 1995—. Author: How to Approach Meaningful Reduction, 2002; guest columnist: Cary News, 2001. Head coach '84 Explorers Soccer Team, 1990—; pres. A. V. Baucom-Elem. Sch. PTO, Apex, NC, 1991—93; mem. Indian Guides YMCA, 1991—, mem. youth com., 1995—; asst. scout master Boy Scouts Am., 1996—; mem. adv. com. Wake County Bd. Edn., 1996—, chmn. adv. coun., 1997—99; chmn. Dist. 8 adv. coun. Wake County Sch. Bd., 2003—; pres. Davis Dr. Mid. Sch., 1997—98, 1998—99; pres. PTA, 1997—99; chmn. Wake County Fun Festival, Apex Adv. Coun. Bd. Edn., 1997—99; area v.p. Wake County PTA Coun., 1998—99; mem. Wake County Health Schs. Task Force, 2003—; pres. Salem MS Athletic Booster Club, 2004. Named to order of Arrow, Boy Scouts Am., 1999; recipient Seal of the Wake county BOE, Wake County Pub. Sch., 2003. Mem.: Grocery Mfrs. Retail Assn., KC (3d degree), Lambda Chi Alpha. Republican. Roman Catholic. Avocations: golf, weightlifting, reading, swimming. Office: Gen Mills Inc PO Box 4349 Cary NC 27519-4349 Office Phone: 919-319-0469. Business E-Mail: george.wait@genmius.com.

**WAIT, SAMUEL CHARLES, JR.,** academic administrator, educator; b. Albany, N.Y., Jan. 26, 1932; s. Samuel C. and Margaret M. (Cassedy) W.; m. Carol D. Petrie, June 6, 1957; children: Robert J., Alison R. BS in Chemistry, Rensselaer Polytechnic Inst., 1953, MS in Physical Chemistry, 1955, PhD in Physical Chemistry, 1956. Postdoc. teaching fellow U. Minn., 1958-59; visiting asst. prof. Carnegie Inst. Tech., 1959-60; rsch. sci. Nat. Bur. Standards, 1960-61; from asst. prof. to prof. of chemistry Rensselaer Poly. Inst., Troy, N.Y., 1961—, from asst. dean of sci. to assoc. dean of sci., 1974—, acting dean of sci., 1978-80, 88-89, 2005—. Dir. Cooperative Coll. Sci. Improvement Program, Troy, 1972-73, Rsch. Participation for High Sch. Tchrs., Troy, 1962-67; asst. dir., prof. M of Sci. in Natural Sci. Program, Troy, 1962-74. Author: Scattering of Laser Radiation, 1971; contbr. articles to profl. jours. Pres. dist. 2 Niskayuna (N.Y.) Fire Co., 1970-72, mem. 1966—; mem. Niskayuna Bd. Fire Commrs., 1978-83; trustee Dudley Obs., 1978—, v.p., 1980-91, pres., 1991-2001; mem. math., sci. and tech. adv. com. Schenectady County C.C., 1976—, chmn., 1977-78; vice chmn. Schenectady County Fire Bd., 1978-99; mem. Schenectady County Hazardous Materials Team, 1991-2002. Recipient Disting Faculty award Rensselaer Alumni Assn., 1988, Alumni Key award, 1994, Rensselaer Alumni Admission award of excellence, 1993, Rensselaer Alumni Assn. Albert Fox Demers medal, 1997, Rensselaer Alumni Fellow award, 2003, Disting. Svc. award Rensselaer Alumni Assn., 2005; named fellow Rsch. Corp., 1954-55, Eastman Kodak Co., 1955-56; Fulbright scholar, 1956-58. Mem. Am. Chem. Soc., Rensselaer Premed. Soc., Sigma Xi, Alpha Epsilon Delta, Phi Theta Kappa. Office: Rensselaer Poly Inst 1C 05 Sci Ctr 110 8th St Troy NY 12180-3522 Office Phone: 518-276-6305. Business E-Mail: waitsc@rpi.edu.

**WAITE, BARBARA L. (PIXIE),** lawyer; b. Columbus, Miss., July 7, 1952; BA summa cum laude, Memphis State Univ., 1980; JD, Georgetown Univ., 1984. Bar: DC 1984, DC Ct. Appeals 1985, US Dist. Ct. (DC, Ariz.), US Ct. Internat. Trade 1985, US Ct. Appeals (DC, Fed. cir.) 1985, US Supreme Ct. 1989. Ptnr., Copyright & Unfair Trade practice Venable LLP, Washington, 2000—. Editor (mng.): Am. Criminal Law Rev. Mem.: Copyright Soc. USA. Office: Venable LLP 575 7th St NW Washington DC 20004 Office Phone: 202-344-4811. Office Fax: 202-344-8300. Business E-Mail: blwaite@venable.com.

**WAITE, CHARLES MORRISON,** food products executive; b. Chgo. Oct. 1, 1932; s. Norman and Lavinia M. (Fyke) W.; m. Barbara Chowning Wham, Aug. 21, 1954; children: Susan R., Charles M., John B., David T. BA, Yale, 1954; MBA, Harvard, 1958. Mgr. planning and analysis Standard Fruit & Steamship Co., New Orleans, 1958-62, v.p., exec. v.p., 1969-72, dir., 1972-76; div. mgr. Standard Fruit Co., La Ceiba, Honduras, 1962-69; dir. Standard Fruit Tropical Charities Inc., 1970-76; sr. v.p. Castle & Cooke, Inc. Honolulu, 1972-76; exec. v.p. Castle & Cooke Foods, San Francisco, 1974-76; pres. United Fruit Co., Boston, 1976-77; sr. v.p. United Brands Co., Boston, 1976-77; pres. Genoa Packing Co., Boston, 1977-78, Catelli Foods, Inc., 1979-90, Howard Foods Inc., Danvers, Mass., 1990—, also bd. dirs. Bd. dirs. Rock of Ages Corp., Barre, Vt., Swenson Granite Co., Concord, N.H. Served to 1st lt. USAF, 1955-57. Mem. Zeta Psi. Clubs: Harvard (Boston). Republican. Episcopalian. Home: 520 Cherry Valley Rd Gilford NH 03249-7841 Office: Howard Foods Inc 5 Ray St Danvers MA 01923-3531

**WAITE, CHARLES PRESCOTT,** entrepreneur; b. Manchester, Conn., Mar. 30, 1930; s. Earl M. and Virginia (Clark) W.; m. Catherine Corbett, Apr. 21, 1951 (div. Feb. 1985); children: Charles P. Jr., David C., Catherine C., Patricia C.; m. Angela Peterson, Feb. 16, 1985. BS, U. Conn., 1957; MBA, Harvard U., 1959. V.p.m. Am. Research & Devel. Corp., Boston, 1960-66; ptnr., pres. Greylock Mgmt. Corp., Boston, 1966—. Bd. dirs. Stellar Computer Corp., Newton, Mass., Floating Point Systems, Beaverton, Oreg., Micom Sytems, Simi Valley, Calif., Data Input Output Corp., Kirkland, Wash., Lumber Mutual Ins. Co., Framingham, Mass. Trustee Kenyon Coll., Gambier, Ohio, 1985—, Dana Hall Sch., Wellesley, Mass., 1974-84. Served to lt. col. U.S. Army, USAR, 1951-73. Republican. Congregationalist. Clubs: Algonquin (Boston), Harvard (Boston and N.Y.C.). Avocation: travel. Home: 85 E India Row Boston MA 02110-3320 Office: Brett Levy 40 Court St Boston MA 02108-2202

**WAITE, DENNIS VERNON,** brokerage house executive, consultant; b. Chgo., Aug. 26, 1938; s. Vernon George and Marie G. Waite; m. Christine Rene Hibbs; 1 child, Kip Anthony. BA, U. Ill., 1968; MS in Journalism, Northwestern U., 1969. Fin. reporter, columnist Chgo. Sun-Times, Chgo., 1969-76; asst. prof. Northwestern U., Evanston, Ill., 1978-79; assoc. prof. Mich. State U., East Lansing, 1979-82; ptnr. Fin. Rels. Bd., Inc., Chgo., 1982-90, sr. ptnr., 1991-97, sr. counselor, 1997—. Reporter, producer econ. affairs Sta. WTTW-TV, Sta. WBBM-TV, Chgo., 1973-76; adj. faculty English, Coll. of DuPage, 1998—2004. Mem. editorial adv. bd. alumni relations U. Ill., Chgo., 1980-84, 90-94. With USAF, 1956-60, PTO. Rutgers U. fellow, 1972. Mem. Medill Alumni Assn. (bd. dirs. 1989-92). Avocations: reading, writing, history, Tae Kwon Do. E-mail: dennis_waite@yahoo.com.

**WAITE, DOUGLAS JOHN,** chaplain; b. Puyallup, Wash., June 21, 1950; s. John Harold and Nancy Geraldine Waite; m. Gail Marie Anderson, Aug. 28, 1971; children: Briana Marie, Lauren Beth Fox, David Akira, Mae Ying, Jonathan Douglas. BA, U. Wash., Seattle, 1972; MDiv, Fuller Theol. Sem., Pasadena, 1978, D in Ministry, 1994. Ordained Elder United Meth. Ch., Wash., 1982. Pastor Avon United Meth. Ch., Mt. Vernon, Wash., 1978—84; br. chaplain U.S. Marine Corps, 1st Force Svc. Support Group, Camp Pendleton, Calif., 1984—86; hosp. chaplain U.S. Naval Hosp., Yokosuka, Japan, 1986—89, Rota, Spain, 1993—96; aircraft carrier command chaplain USS Nimitz (Cvn-68), Bellingham, Wash., 1989—92; command chaplain Whidbey Island Naval Air Sta., Oak Harbor, Wash., 1996—98; aircraft carrier command chaplain USS Abraham Lincoln (Cvn-72), Everett, Wash., 1998—2001; dep. chaplain of coast guard U.S. Coast Guard Hdqs., Washington, 2001—03; pacific area chaplain U.S. Coast Guard, Alameda, Calif., 2003—06; naval surface and air force chaplain U.S. Navy, Coronado, Calif., 2006—. Author: (rsch. work) Defence Communities Mag., 1996, (rsch. article) Navy and Marine Corp Times, 1996, (autobiography) By the Grace of God (Desktop Publishing, 2003). Twice chaplain of U.S. senate for the day U.S. Coast Guard, Washington, 2003, prayer with pres. George W. Bush, 2003, chaplain at the pentagon attack, 2001, chaplain at world trade ctr. attack New York, NY, 2001, chaplain at hurricane katrina/rita disaster New Orleans, 2005. Capt. USN, 1972—2006. Decorated Three Nat. Def. Svc. medals Dept. of Def., SW Asia Svc. medal, Armed Forces Expeditionary medal, Global War on Terrorism medal, Humanitarian Svc. medal, Navy Achievement medal U.S. Navy, Liberation medal Kuwait, Two Navy and a Coast Guard Commendation medal U.S. Navy, U.S. Coast Guard, Three Meritorious Svc. medals; recipient 9-11 medal, Dept. of Transp., 2002. Mem.: Mil. Officers Assn. of Am., Mil. Chaplains Assn., Ducks Unlimited, Blackpoint Gamebird Club. United Methodist. Achievements include research in Generation X in the Military. Avocations: hunting, dog training, fishing, jogging, boating. Home Fax: 510-437-3774.

**WAITE, LAWRENCE WESLEY,** osteopathic physician, educator; b. Chgo., June 27, 1951; s. Paul J. and Margaret E. (Cresson) W.; m. Courtnay M. Snyder, Nov. 1, 2002; children: Colleen Alexis, Rebecca Maureen, Alexander Quin. BA, Drake U., 1972; DO, Coll. Osteo Medicine and Surgery, 1975; MPH, U. Mich., 1981. Diplomate Nat. Bd. Osteo. Med. Examiners; bd. cert. family practice, holistic medicine, neuromusculoskeletal medicine, Osteopathic Manipulative Medicine. Intern Garden City Osteo. Hosp., Mich., 1975—76; practice gen. osteo. medicine Garden City, 1979—82, Battle Creek, 1982—96, La Crosse, Wis., 1996—2004; emergency rm. physician, 2004—; sect. head Onalaska Family Practice, 1999—2002, coord. rsch., chmn. dept., 1996—99, chmn. integrative medicine edn./rsch. com., 2002—04, vice chair, dept. integrative medicine, 2004. Cons. Nat. Bd. Examiners Osteo. Physicians and Surgeons, 1981—88, 1998—; chief med. examiner Calhoun County, 1991—93; preceptor U. Wis. Med. Sch., 1997—2000, assoc. clin. prof., 2000—, Mich. State U. Coll. Osteo. Medicine, East Lansing, 1979—97, Lakeview Gen. Osteo. Hosp., Battle Creek, Mich., 1983—87; mem. profl. adv. coun. Good Samaritan Hosp., Battle Creek, 1982—83; exec. bd. Primary Care Network, 1994—96; assoc. clin. prof. Des Moines U. Coll. Osteo. Medicine, 2002—05; mem. evaluations registry Commn. on Osteo. Coll. Accreditation, 2006—. Writer TV program Cross Currents Ecology, 1971; editor radio series Friendship Hour, 1971-72 Bd. dirs. La Crosse YMCA, 2000-03; Internat. Log Rolling Assn., 2000-04; cert. judge U.S. Log Rolling Assn., 2006—; bd. dirs., instr. Hospice Support Services, Inc., Westland, Mich., 1981-86; exec. bd. officer Battle Creek Area Urban League, 1987-91; bd. dirs., mem. exec. com. Clearwater Farm Found., Inc., 1999-04; vestryman St. Thomas Episcopal Ch., 1990-93; bd. mem. Eagle Bluff Environ. Learning Ctr., Lanesboro, 2003-; leader Boy Scouts Am.; bd. sec. Internal Soc. Complementary Alternative Medicine Rsch., 2004-05. Served to lt. comdr. USN, 1976-79. U. Wis. fellow, Madison, 2003-04; State of Iowa scholar, 1969. Mem. AMA, APHA, Population Inst. (population action coun. 1984-99, Internat. Soc. Complementary Medicine Rsch. (sec. 2001 2003), Nat. Eagle Scouts Assn. (life), Am. Osteo. Assn., S. Ctrl. Osteo. Assn. (officer, state del. 1983-96), Am. Acad. Osteopathy, Bermuda Hist. Soc. (life), Brotherhood St. Andrews (life). Avocations: geography, medieval history, genealogy. Home and Office: 2110 Evenson Dr Onalaska WI 54650-8772 Office Phone: 608-397-6678. Business E-Mail: lwwaite@wisc.edu.

**WAITE, STEPHEN HOLDEN,** lawyer; b. Rochester, NY, Dec. 5, 1936; s. Richard Holden and Judith H. (Lapp) Waite; m. Sarah T. Caswell, Aug. 20, 1960 (dec. Mar. 1996); m. Martha Gay Stewart, Jan. 4, 1997; children: Sarah T., Richard H. BA, Amherst Coll., 1958; JD, Yale U., 1961. Bar: NY 1961. Mem. firm Nixon, Hargrave, Devans & Doyle, Rochester, NY, 1961-69; v.p., counsel Lincoln First Banks Inc., Rochester, 1969-73; sr. v.p., 1977-83, exec. v.p., 1978-81, CFO, 1973-81; sr. v.p. Schlegel Corp., 1981-82; mem. firm Harris, Beach, Wilcox, Rubin & Levey, Rochester, 1982-88, Underberg & Kessler, Rochester, 1988—. Past chmn. Rochester Area Hosp. Assn.; mem. strategic planning commn. Monroe Cmty. Hosp.; past bd. dirs., treas. Hosp. Trustees N.Y. State; past bd. dirs., past chmn. Ctr. Govtl. Rsch.; treas. Planned Parenthood Rochester/Syracuse Region; bd. dirs. Planned Parenthood Rochester/Syracuse region, Mercy Flight Ctrl., Inc.; past bd. dirs. Highland Hosp., Monroe County Long Term Care, Inc., Rochester Regional Rsch. Libr. Coun., Hosp. Assn. N.Y. State, Health Futures for Rochester, Harley Sch., Hearing and Speech Ctr. Rochester. With U.S. Army, 1962. Mem.: Monroe County Bar Assn., N.Y. State Bar Assn., Country Club Rochester. Home: 68 N Main St Pittsford NY 14534 Office: 300 Bausch and Lomb Pl Rochester NY 14604 Office Phone: 585-258-2826.

**WAITES, ROBERT GUINN,** utilities executive; b. Laurel, Miss., July 12, 1950; s. Robert Leland Waites and Ida Doris (Gordon) Robinson; m. Lynda Gay Tubertini, Nov. 25, 1972; children: Julie G. Burran, Andrea G. BS, U. So. Miss., 1972; JD, Miss. Coll., 1976. Commd. 2d lt. U.S. Army, 1972, advanced through grades to capt., 1980, res., 1980; legal counsel Miss. House Reps., Jackson, 1976-89, Legis. Environ. Protection Coun., Jackson, 1989-90; dep. dir. Miss. Pub. Utilities Staff, Jackson, 1990-96, exec. dir., 1996—. Mem. ABA, Miss. State Bar Assn., Miss. Rep. Party, Kappa Sigma (Outstanding Mem. award 1972). Methodist. Avocations: golf, biking. Home: 179 Apple Blossom Dr Brandon MS 39047-7686 Office: Miss Pub Utilities Staff 550 High St Jackson MS 39201-1113

**WAITKUS, JAY,** writer; b. Grosse Pointe Farms, Mich., Oct. 7, 1968; s. Gerald C. Waitkus and Sara W. Kent. BS, Charter Oak State Coll., New Britain, Conn., 2003; MA, Fla. Atlantic U., 2005. Freelance journalist Sun-Sentinel, Palm Beach Post, South Fla. Bus. Jour., others, Fla., 1998—2001. Author: (novels) In the Depths of Shadows, 2003, Dividing Line, 2006, short stories, (plays) The Fallen Angel's Redeemer, 2002. Founding sponsor Disabled Vets. LIFE Meml. Found., Washington; Christian missionary, ch. planter Bapt. Ch. Palm Beach, Fla., 1997—98. Named Writer of Month, Gulf Coast Writers Assn., 2002. Mem.: Nat. Writers Assn., Nat. Geog. Soc. Conservative.

**WAITS, THOMAS ALAN,** composer, actor, singer; b. Pomona, Calif., Dec. 7, 1949; s. Frank W. and Alma (Johnson) McMurray; m. Kathleen Patricia Brennan, Aug. 10, 1980; children: Kellesimone Wylder, Casey Xavier, Sullivan Blake. Composer 20 albums including Closing Time, 1973, The Heart of Saturday Nite, 1974, Nighthawks at the Diner, 1975, Small Change, 1976, Foreign Affairs, 1978, Blue Valentine, 1979, Heart Attack and Vine, 1980, One From the Heart, 1981, Swordfishtrombones, 1983, Rain Dogs, 1985, Anthology, 1985, Frank's Wild Years, 1987, Big Time, 1988, Bone Machine, 1992, Night on Earth, 1992, The Black Rider, 1993, Beautiful Maladies, 1998, Mule Variations, 1999 (Grammy Award, 1999), Alice, 2002, Blood Money, 2002, Real Gone, 2004; composer (film scores) One from the Heart, 1983, Streetwise, 1985, Night on Earth, 1991; co-author music and songs (with Kathleen Brennan) for Night on Earth, 1991, End of Violence, 1997, Bunny, 1999, Liberty Heights, 2000, Big Bad Love, 2002, Pollock, 2002, Dead Man Walking, film American Heart; composer songs and music for The Black Rider opera, Hamburg, Germany, 1990; composer songs and music, writer (with Kathleen Brennan) Alice Avant Garde opera, Hamburg, 1992, opera Woyzeck (recipient Italian Drama Critics award for Best Musical, 2003), Copenhagen, 2000; actor (musical) Frank's Wild Years, 1986, (stage play) Demon Wine, 1989; appeared in films Paradise Alley, 1978, The Outsiders, 1983, Rumble Fish, 1983, The Cotton Club, 1984, Down by Law, 1986, Ironweed, 1987, Candy Mountain, 1987, Big Time, 1988, Cold Feet, 1989, The Bearskin, 1991, Queen's Logic, 1991, At Play in the Fields of the Lord, 1991, Bram Stoker's Dracula, 1992, Short Cuts, 1993, Mystery Men, 1999, Coffee & Cigarettes, 2003. Recipient Acad. Award nomination Best Song Score for One from the Heart, 1983; Grammy award for best alternative album Bone Machine, 1992, Grammy award for Mule Variations as best contemporary folk music, 2000, Dramalogue award for actor Demon Wine, Danish Theater award for Woyzeck as best musical, 2001. Mem. ASCAP (Founders award for career achievement in songwriting 2001), Musicians Union Local 47, SAG, AFTRA, Motion Picture Acad. Office: care Howard Grossman 10960 Wilshire Blvd Ste 2150 Los Angeles CA 90024-3807

**WAITT, THEODORE W. (TED WAITT),** venture capitalist, former computer company executive; b. Sioux City, Iowa, Jan. 18, 1963; m. Joan Waitt; 4 children. Attended, U. of Iowa; PhD (hon.), U. of SD. Co-founder Gateway Inc., Poway, 1985, pres., 1985—96, 2001—04, CEO, 1993—99, 2001—04, chmn., 1993—2005; founder, chmn., CEO Avalon Capital Group. Founder, chmn. Waitt Family Found., 1993—; chair Waitt Inst. for Historical Discovery, Waitt Inst. for Violence Prevention, Waitt Inst. for Scientific Breakthroughs; trustee Salk Inst., 2005—; chmn., Founding Fathers campaign Family Violence Prevention Fund. Named one of Ten Outstanding Young Americans, U.S. Jr. C. of C., Forbes' Richest Americans, 2005, 2006; recipient Young Entrepreneur of the Year award, U.S. Small Bus. Assn.

**WAJENBERG, ARNOLD SHERMAN,** retired librarian, educator; b. Indpls., Apr. 11, 1929; s. Henry and Hazel L. (Johnson) W.; m. Joyce E. Dunham, Sept. 6, 1952; 1 child, Earl S. BA, Butler U., Indpls., 1951, MA, 1953, U. Chgo., 1955. Cataloger U. Chgo. Library, 1953-69; catalog librarian U. Ill. Chgo., 1969-74, asst. catalog librarian Champaign-Urbana, 1974-78, prin. cataloguer, 1979-94; retired, 1994; prof. library adminstrn. U. Ill., Champaign-Urbana. Prin. educator, Ill. Tng. Program for Implementation of Anglo-Am. Cataloguing Rules, 2d edit., 1979-80; mem. editorial policy com. Dewey Decimal, 1981-92; Ill. rep. cataloging adv. com., Online Computer Libr. Ctr. 1979-82, cataloging and database svcs. adv. com., 1989-92. Author: FLC FEDLINK AACR 2 Cataloging Manual for Federal Libraries, 1981; contbr. articles to profl. jours. Mem. ALA (com. on cataloging: description and access 1981-86, mem.-at-large exec. com. cataloging and classification sect. 1982-86) Avocations: walking, science fiction. Home: 240 Donald Dr Goffstown NH 03045-6214

**WAJER, RONALD EDWARD,** management consultant; b. Chgo., Aug. 31, 1943; s. Edward Joseph and Gertrude Catherine (Rytelny) W.; m. Mary Earlene Hagan, July 5, 1969; children: Catherine, Michael. BSIE, Northwestern U., 1966; MBA, Loyola U., Chgo., 1970. Project engring. mgr. Procter & Gamble, Chgo., 1966-67; indsl. engring. mgr. Johnson & Johnson, Bedford Park, Ill., 1967-71; project mgr. Jewel Cos., Franklin Park, Ill., 1971-73; divsn. engring. mgr. Abbott Labs., North Chicago, Ill., 1973-79; pres. bus. engring. divsn. R.E. Wajer & Assocs., Northbrook, Ill., 1979—. Contbr. articles to profl. jours. Sec. Downtown Redevel. Commn., Mt. Prospect, Ill., 1977-78; fundraising vol. Maryville Acad., Des Plaines, 1985—; bd. dirs. Lattof YMCA, Des Plaines, 1994-96; profl. advisor Sch. for New Learning, DePaul U., 1994—; mem. indsl. sector com. Lincoln Found. for Bus. Excellence, 1997-99. Recipient Cmty. Svc. award Chgo. Lighthouse for the Blind, 1989, Cert. of Merit, Village of Mt. Prospect, 1978. Mem. Inst. Indsl. Engrs. (cmty. svc. chmn. 1984), Inst. Mgmt. Cons. (cert., exec. v.p., bd. dirs. 1987-94), Assn. Mgmt. Cons. (ctrl. regional v.p. 1985-87), Midwest Soc. Profl. Cons., Northwestern Club Chgo. Roman Catholic. Office: Bus Engring 5 Revere Dr Ste 200 Northbrook IL 60062-8000 Office Phone: 847-824-0809. Business E-Mail: rewajer@busmengg.com

**WAJERT, SEAN PETER,** lawyer; b. Chester, Pa., Feb. 2, 1960; s. John Max and Kathleen Francella (Gorand) W.; m. Lisa Marie. AB magna cum laude, Harvard U., 1981; JD cum laude, U. Pa., 1984. Bar: Pa. 1984, US Dist. Ct. Ea. Dist. Pa. 1986, US Ct. Appeals 3rd Cir. 1985, US Ct. Appeals 10th Cir. 1986. Law clk. to Hon. Arlin M. Adams US Ct. Appeals 3rd Cir., Phila., 1984-85; assoc. Pepper, Hamilton & Scheetz, Phila., 1985-87, Hoyle, Morris & Kerr, Phila., 1988-91, ptnr., 1992-95; of counsel Dechert Price & Rhoads (now Dechert LLP), Phila., 1995—97, ptnr., 1997—, chair firm mass torts & product liability practice group. Adj. prof. U. Pa. Law Sch., 1990-98, Thomas O'Boyle hon. lectr.-in-law, 1999-2000. Editor in chief: U. Pa. Law Rev., 1983-84. Vol. Congl. campaign., Phila., 1988, Bucks City, 1989. James Finnegan Fellow, 1979; recipient Am. Jurisprudence Award, 1982, Edwin R. Keedy Award, 1984, John H. Maurer Meml. Prize, 1984. Mem. ABA, Pa. Bar Assn., Phila. Bar Assn., Def. Rsch. Inst., Order of Coif. Republican. Roman Catholic. Office: Dechert LLP Cira Centre 2929 Arch St Philadelphia PA 19104-2808 Office Phone: 215-994-2387. Office Fax: 215-994-2222. Business E-Mail: sean.wajert@dechert.com.

**WAJSGRAS, DAVID C.,** manufacturing executive; m. Teena Wajsgras; 3 children. BS in Acctg., U. Md., College Park; MBA in Fin., Am. U. CPA. CFO Maserati Automobile, Balt.; sr. auditor Coopers & Lybrand; contr. Constellation Investments, C.G.I.; from contr. to v.p. fin. UNC Inc., Annapolis, Md.; various sr. fin. positions AlliedSignal, Inc., Morristown, NJ, 1992—97; corp. contr. Engelhard Corp., Iselin, NJ, 1997—99; v.p. contr. Lear Corp., Southfield, Mich., 1999—2002, sr. v.p., CFO, 2002—05, exec. v.p., CFO, 2005—06; CFO, sr. v.p. Raytheon Corp., Waltham, Mass., 2006—. Mem.: Fin. Execs. Inst. Office: Raytheon Corp 870 Winter St Waltham MA 02451-1449*

**WAKE, DAVID BURTON,** biology professor; b. Webster, SD, June 8, 1936; s. Thomas B. and Ina H. (Solem) W.; m. Marvalee Hendricks, June 23, 1962; 1 child, Thomas Andrew BA, Pacific Luth. U., 1958; MS, U. So. Calif., 1960, PhD, 1964. Instr. anatomy and biology U. Chgo., 1964-66, asst. prof. anatomy and biology, 1966-69; assoc. prof. zoology U. Calif., Berkeley, 1969-72, prof., 1972-89, John and Margaret Gompertz prof., 1991-97, prof. integrative biology, 1989—2003, prof. emeritus integrative biology, 2003—, faculty rsch. lectr., 2004; prof. grad. sch., 2005—. Dir. Mus. Vertebrate Zoology U. Calif., Berkeley, 1971-98; curator Herpetology Mus. Vertebrate Zoology, U. Calif., 1969-; vis. Alexander Agassiz prof. Mus. Comparative Zoology, Harvard U., 2002. Author: Biology, 1979; co-editor: Functional Vertebrate Morphology, 1985, Complex Organismal Functions: Integration and Evolution in the Vertebrates, 1989. Recipient Quantrell Tchg. award U. Chgo., 1967, Outstanding Alumnus award Pacific Luth. U., 1979, Joseph Grinnell medal Mus. Vertebrate Zoology, 1998, Henry S. Fitch award Am. Soc. Ichthyologists and Herpetologists, 1999, Joseph Leidy medal Acad. Nat. Sci. Phila., 2006, Berkeley Citation award U. Calif., 2006; grantee NSF, 1965—; Guggenheim fellow, 1982. Fellow AAAS, Am. Acad. Arts and Scis.; mem. NAS, NRC (bd. biology 1986-92), Am. Philos. Soc., Internat. Union for Conservation of Nature and Natural Resources (chair task force on declining amphibian populations 1990-92), Am. Soc. Zoologists (pres. 1992), Am. Soc. Naturalists (pres. 1989), Am. Soc. Ichthyologists and Herpetologists (bd. govs.), Soc. Study Evolution (pres. 1983, editor 1979-81), Soc. Systematic Biology (coun. 1980-84), Herpetologist's League (Disting. Herpetologist 1984). Home: 999 Middlefield Rd Berkeley CA 94708-1509 Business E-Mail: wakelab@uclink.berkeley.edu.

**WAKE, MADELINE MUSANTE,** academic administrator, nursing educator; Diploma, St. Francis Hosp. Sch. Nursing, 1963; BS in Nursing, Marquette U., 1968, MS in Nursing, 1971; PhD, U. Wis., Milw., 1986. Clin. nurse specialist St. Mary's Hosp., Milw., 1971-74, asst. dir. nursing, 1974-77; from dir. continuing nursing edn. to provost Marquette U., Milw., 1977—2002, provost, 2002—. Mem. devel. team Internat. Classification for Nursing Practice, Geneva, 1991-99. Chmn. bd. dirs. Trinity Meml. Hosp., Cudahy, Wis., 1991-96; bd. dirs. Blood Ctr. Wis., 2003-. Recipient Profl. Svc. award Am. Diabetes Assn.-Wis. affiliate, 1978, Excellence in Nursing Edn. award Wis. Nurses Assn., 1989; named Disting. Lectr. Sigma Theta Tau Internat., 1991. Fellow: Am. Acad. Nursing; mem.: ANA, Am. Assn. Colls. and Univs., Vis. Nurs Assn. Wis. (bd. dirs.), Am. Assn. Coll. Nursing (bd. dirs. 1999—2002). Office: Marquette Univ O'Hara Hall Milwaukee WI 53201-1881 Office Phone: 414-288-7511.

**WAKE, MARVALEE HENDRICKS,** biology professor; b. Orange, Calif., July 31, 1939; d. Marvin Carlton and Velvalee (Borter) H.; m. David B. Wake, June 23, 1962; 1 child, Thomas A. BA, U. So. Calif., 1961, MS, 1964, PhD, 1968. Tchg. asst., instr. U. Ill., Chgo., 1964, asst. prof., 1966—69; lectr. U. Calif., Berkeley, 1969—73, asst. prof., 1973—76, assoc. prof., 1976—80, prof. zoology, 1980—89, chmn. dept. zoology, 1985—89, chmn. dept. integrative biology, 1989—91; 1999—2002, assoc. dean Coll. Letters and Sci., 1975—78, prof. integrative biology, 1989—2003, Chancellor's prof., 1997—2000, prof. of the Grad. Sch., 2004—. Mem. NAS/NRC Bd. on Sustainable Devel., 1999-99, NSF Bio Adv. Commn., 1997-2002; Smithsonian Sci. Commn., 2001-02. Editor, co-editor: Hyman's Comparative Vertebrate Anatomy, 1979, The Origin and Evolution of Larval Forms, 1999, Ecology and Evolution in the Tropics, 2005; co-author: Biology, 1978; contbr. articles to profl. jours. NSF grantee, 1978—; Guggenheim fellow, 1988-89. Fellow: AAAS (chair Biology Sect. G 1998), Calif. Acad. Sci. (trustee 1992—98, hon. trustee 1998—), Am. Acad. Arts and Scis.; mem.: Internat. Soc. Vertebrate Morphology (pres.-elect 2004—07), Am. Inst. Biol. Sci. (pres. 2005), World Congress of Herpetology (sec. gen. 1994—97), Internat. Union Biol. Scis. (U.S. nat. com. chmn 1992—95, sec. gen. 1994—2000, pres. 2000—04), Soc. Integrative Comparative Biology (pres. 2001—03), Am. Soc. Ichthyologists and Herpetologists (bd. govs. 1978—, pres. 1984). Office: U Calif Dept Integrative Biology 3060 VLSB Berkeley CA 94720-3140 E-mail: mhwake@socrates.berkeley.edu.

**WAKE, RICHARD W.,** food products executive; b. 1953; BS, U of Illinois. With Aurora Eby-Brown Co., Inc., 1975—, co-pres., bd. dir. Naperville, Ill., 1983—. Office: 280 Shuman Blvd Ste 280 PO Box 3067 Naperville IL 60566-7067

**WAKE, THOMAS G.,** food products executive; Co-pres. Eby-Brown Co., Naperville, Ill., co-chief exec., 1983—. Office: Eby Brown Co 280 Shuman Blvd Ste 280 Naperville IL 60563-2578*

**WAKEFIELD, DAN,** writer, scriptwriter; b. Indpls., May 21, 1932; s. Benjamin H. and Brucie (Ridge) W. BA, Columbia U., 1955; Nieman fellow, Harvard U., 1963-64. News editor Princeton (N.J.) Packet, 1955; staff writer Nation mag., 1956-59; free lance writer, 1959—; contbg. editor The Atlantic Monthly, 1968-80; staff Bread Loaf Writers Conf., 1964, 66, 68, 70, 86; contbn. writer GQ mag., 1992—; columnist Beliefnet.com, 2000—. Vis. lectr. U. Mass., Boston, 1965-66; vis. lectr. journalism U. Ill., 1968; writer-in-residence Emerson Coll., 1989-92; writer in residence Fla. Internat. U., 1995—. Creator, story cons. TV show James at 15, 1977-78, Heartbeat, 1988; author: Island in the City: The World of Spanish Harlem, 1959, Revolt in the South, 1961, Ananthology, 1963, Between the Lines, 1966, Supernation at Peace and War, 1968, Going All the Way, 1970 (Nat. Book Award nomination), Starting Over, 1973, All Her Children, 1976, Home Free, 1977, Under the Apple Tree, 1982, Selling Out, 1985, Returning: A Spiritual Journey, 1988, The Story of Your Life: Writing a Spiritual Autobiography, 1990, New York in the Fifties, 1992, Expect a Miracle, 1995, Creating from the Spirit, 1996, How Do We Know When It's God? A Spiritual Memoir, 1999; contbg. editor Atlantic Monthly, 1969-80; editor: The Addict: An Anthology, 1963; (documentary) New York in the Fifties, 2000; (teleplay) The Innocents Abroad (Mark Twain) for PBS, 1983; writer, co-prodr. TV movie The Seduction of Miss Leona, 1980; screenplay Going All the Way, 1997 (selection Sundance Film Festival 1997). Bernard DeVoto fellow Bread Loaf Writers Conf., 1957, Rockefeller Grant in Creative Writing, 1968; short story prize, Nat. Council of Arts, 1968. Mem. Authors Guild Am., Writers Guild Am., Nat. Writers Union, Vestry of King's Chapel.

**WAKEFIELD, STEPHEN ALAN,** lawyer; b. Olney, Ill., Oct. 18, 1940; s. George William and Blanche Lucille (Sheesley) Wakefield; m. Patrica Ann McGuire, Nov. 29, 1980; 1 child, Mark;children from previous marriage: Melissa Hawley, Tracy, Stephen Alan Jr. LLB, U. Tex., Austin, 1965. Bar: Tex. 1965. Assoc. Baker & Botts, Houston, 1965—70, ptnr., 1974—84, sr. ptnr., chmn. energy dept., 1986—89; atty. Fed. Power Commn., Washington, 1970—72; dep. asst. sec. energy programs Dept. Interior, Washington, 1972—73, asst. sec. energy and minerals, 1973—74; asst. adminstr. Fed. Energy Office, Washington, 1973—74; vice chmn., gen. counsel United Energy Resources, Inc., Houston, 1985-86; pres. United Gas Pipe Line Co., Houston, 1985—86; exec. v.p. MidCon Corp., 1985—86; gen. coun. Dept. Energy, Washington, 1989—91; ptnr. Akin, Gump, Strauss, Hauer & Feld, L.L.P., 1991—97; sr. v.p., gen. coun. So. Co., Atlanta, 1997—2001, sr. counsel, 2001—. Bd. visitors M. D. Anderson Cancer Ctr.; bd. govs. Robert Packard Ctr. ALS Rsch. Johns Hopkins U. Mem.: Tex. Bar Assn., Capital City Club (Atlanta). Home: 201 Blackland Dr NW Atlanta GA 30342-4405 Office: Southern Co Ste 1400 270 Peachtree St NW Atlanta GA 30303-1263 Office Phone: 404-506-0553. Personal E-mail: sawakefield@mindspring.com. Business E-Mail: sawakefi@southernco.com.

**WAKEFIELD, TIMOTHY STEPHEN (TIM WAKEFIELD),** professional baseball player; b. Melbourne, Fla., Aug. 2, 1966; m. Stacy Wakefield. Student, Fla. Tech. Pitcher NY-Pa. League, Welland, 1989, Carolina League, Salem, 1990, So. League, South Carolina, 1991, 93, Am. Assn. League, Buffalo, 1991-92, 94, Pitts. Pirates, 1992-93, Internat. League, Pawtucket, 1995, Boston Red Sox, 1995—. Donates money to the Make-A-Wish Foundation for every strikeout and win. Named Nat. League Rookie of the Yr. The Sporting News, 1992, Am. League Comeback Player of the Yr., 1995; inducted into the Sunshine State Conference Hall of Fame, 1998 Placed 3rd in Cy Young voting, 1995. Won 16 games first year with Boston Red Sox leading them to division title. Longevity and consistency have helped him become one of the top pitchers in Red Sox history. Office: c/o Boston Red Sox Fenway Pk 4 Yawkey Way Boston MA 02215-3409*

**WAKEMAN, FREDERIC EVANS, JR.,** historian, educator; b. Kansas City, Kans., Dec. 12, 1937; s. Frederic Evans and Margaret Ruth (Keyes) Wakeman; m. He Lea Liang; children: Frederic Evans III, Matthew Clark, Sarah Elizabeth. BA, Harvard Coll., 1959; postgrad., Institut d'Etudes Politiques, U. Paris, 1959-60; MA, U. Calif., Berkeley, 1962, PhD, 1965. Asst. prof. history U. Calif., Berkeley, 1965-67, assoc. prof., 1968-70, prof., 1970-89, Haas prof. Asian Studies, 1989—, dir. Ctr. Chinese Studies, 1972-79; humanities research prof., vis. scholar Corpus Christi Coll., U. Cambridge, Eng., 1976-77, Beijing U., 1980-81, 85. Acad. adviser U.S. Ednl. Del. for Study in China; chmn. Joint Com. Chinese Studies Am. Coun. Learned Socs./Social Sci. Rsch. Coun.; sr. adviser Beijing office NAS; pres. Social Sci. Rsch. Coun., 1986-89, chmn. com. on scholarly comm. with China, 1995-2000; dir. Inst. East Asian Studies, Berkeley, 1990-2001; vis. prof. U. Heidelberg, Germany, 2000; hon. prof. China People's U. Author: Strangers at the Gate, 1966, History and Will, 1973, The Fall of Imperial China, 1975, Conflict and Control in Late Imperial China, 1976, Ming and Qing Historical Studies in the People's Republic of China, 1981, The Great Enterprise, 1986, Shanghai Sojourners, 1992, Policing Shanghai, 1995, Shanghai Badlands, 1996, China's Quest for Modernization, 1997, Reappraising Republican China, 2000, Spymaster, 2003. Harvard Nat. scholar, 1955-59; Tower fellow, 1959-60; Fgn. Area fellow, 1963-65; Am. Coun. Learned Socs. fellow, 1967-68; Guggenheim fellow, 1973-74; NRC fellow, 1985. Fellow: Am. Acad. Berlin; mem.: Shanghai Acad. Social Scis. (fgn.), Am. Philos. Soc., Am. Hist. Assn. (pres.), Am. Acad. Arts and Scis. Home: 460 Boca Ratan Dr Lake Oswego OR 97034 Office: U Calif Inst East Asian Studies Berkeley CA 94720-0001 Office Phone: 510-643-9496. Business E-Mail: jingcha@socrates.berkeley.edu.

**WAKOSKI, DIANE,** poet, educator; b. Whittier, Calif., Aug. 3, 1937; d. John Joseph and Marie Elvira (Mengel) W. BA in English, U. Calif., Berkeley, 1960. Writer-in-residence Mich. State U., East Lansing, 1976—, Univ. disting. prof., 1990—. Vis. writer Calif. Inst. Tech., 1972, U. Va., 1972-73, Wilamette U., 1973, Lake Forest Coll., 1974, Colo. Coll., 1974, U. Calif., Irvine, 1974, Macalester Coll., 1975, U. Wis., 1975, Hollins Coll., 1974, U. Wash., 1977, Whitman Coll., 1976, Emory U., 1980-81, U. Hawaii, 1978. Author: Coins and Coffins, 1962, Discrepancies and Apparitions, 1966, Inside The Blood Factory, 1968, The George Washington Poems, 1967, The Magellanic Clouds, 1969, The Motorcycle Betrayal Poems, 1971, Smudging, 1972, Dancing On The Grave of A Son Of A Bitch, 1973, Trilogy, 1974, Virtuoso Literature For Two and Four Hands, 1976, Waiting For the King of Spain, 1977, The Man Who Shook Hands, 1978, Cap of Darkness, 1980, The Magician's Feastletters, 1982, The Collected Greed: Parts I-XIII, 1984, The Rings of Saturn, 1986, Emerald Ice: Selected Poems 1962-87, 1988 (William Carlos Williams prize 1989), Medea The Sorceress, 1991, Jason the Sailor, 1993, The Emerald City of Las Vegas, 1995, Argonaut Rose, 1998, The Butcher's Apron: New & Selected Poems, 2000. Named Univ. Disting. Prof., Mich. State U., 1990, Author of Yr., Mich. Libr. Assn., 2003; recipient award, Mich. Arts Found., 1989, Disting. Faculty award, Mich. State U., 1989; grantee Cassandra Found., 1970, N.Y. State Cultural Coun., 1971—72, Guggenheim Found., 1972—73, Fullbright, 1984, Mich. Arts Coun., 1988. Office: Mich State U 207 Morrill Hall East Lansing MI 48824-1036 E-mail: dwakoski@aol.com.

**WAKS, JAY WARREN,** lawyer; b. Newark, Dec. 6, 1946; m. Harriet, Aug. 27, 1969; children: Jonathan Warren, Allison Lindsay. BS, Cornell U., 1968, JD, 1971. Bar: N.Y. 1972, U.S. Ct. Appeals (2 cir.) 1972, U.S. Dist. Ct. (no. dist.) N.Y. 1972, U.S. Dist. Ct. (so. dist.) N.Y. 1973, U.S. Dist. Ct. (ea. dist.) N.Y., 1973, U.S. Ct. Appeals (3d cir.), U.S. Ct. Appeals (2d cir.), U.S. Ct. Appeals (D.C. cir.), 1983, U.S. Dist. Ct. D.C. 1985, U.S. Supreme Ct. 1991. Law clk. to Hon. Inzer B. Wyatt U.S. Dist. Ct. So. Dist. N.Y., 1971-72; assoc. Kaye, Scholer, Fierman, Hays & Handler, N.Y.C., 1972-80; ptnr. Kaye Scholer LLP, N.Y.C., 1981—, chmn. employment and labor law practice/litigation, chmn. ADR practice group, mem. e-commerce practice group and internat. practice group; Kevin Becraft Lectr. Cornell U., ILR Sch., Inst. for Workplace Studies. Bd. dirs., exec com., gen. counsel Legal Momentum; advisor restatement of the law third-employment law Am. Law Inst., 2004—. Bus. Watch columnist Nat. Law Jour., 1990—; contbg. author numerous articles to profl. jours. Chair Work in Am. Inst., 2002—04; nat. chmn. Cornell Law Sch. ann. fund Cornell U., 2001—04, chmn. 20th, 25th and 30th reunion campaigns Cornell Law Sch., former nat. co-chair Cornell Law Sch. dean's spl. leadership com. Class of '68, major gifts com., co-chair, 2002; chair Cornell U. Coun., 2005—; employment disputes com. CPR Internat. Inst. for Conflict Prevention and Resolution, 1988—, chair, 1991—, mem. CPR exec. com.; bd. dirs. Fed. Bar Found., 2004—; mem. exec. com., chair program com. Fed. Bar Coun.; chmn. adv. coun. Cornell Law Sch., chmn., 2004—; exec. com. mem. coun. Cornell U., 2000—. Named Among Nation's Best Litigators in Employment Law, The Nat. Law Jour., 1992, Among Best Lawyers in NY and Among 7 Best Corp. Side Labor/Employment Lawyers, N.Y. mag., 1995, Among NY Area's Best Lawyers, 2005, Top of the Docket column for success in high-profile public sector case, Am. Lawyer, 2002, Among #1 Employment Def. Lawyers in NY, Chambers USA Guides, 2003—; recipient recognition for svc. to diversity efforts, Cornell Black Alumni Assn.; profiled in Cornell Law Forum, 2004, profiled online, Cornell ILR Sch., 2005, 2006. Fellow Am. Bar Found., Coll. Labor and Employment Lawyers; mem. ABA (spkr. ann. meetings sect. labor and employment), State Bar Calif. (assoc.), N.Y. State Bar Assn. (co-chair employment alternative dispute resolution com., labor and employment law sect., exec. com. 1995-99), Am. Law Inst., Assn. Bar of City of N.Y. (chmn. labor and employment law com. 1990-93), Fed. Bar. Coun. (sustaining). Avocations: swimming, tennis, skiing, fitness training, travel. Office: Kaye Scholer LLP 425 Park Ave New York NY 10022-3506 Office Phone: 212-836-8558. Business E-Mail: jwaks@kayescholer.com.

**WAKSCHLAG, MILTON SAMUEL,** lawyer; b. Omaha, July 4, 1955; s. Fishel and Stefa (Kleiner) W.; m. Laurie S. Weinzweig, June 15, 1980; children: Tmima, Shira, Efraim. BA, Loyola U., 1977; postgrad., Rabbi Brisk Rabbinical Coll., 1977; JD, U. Chgo., 1980; LLM in Taxation, DePaul U., 1987. Bar: Ill. 1980. Assoc. Borge and Pitt, Chgo., 1980-85, ptnr., 1986, Katten Muchin Rosenman LLP, Chgo., 1987—, chair, pub. fin. dept., chair, fin. products group, mem. pro bono com. Adv. com. on svcs. to disabled, Ill. Atty. Gen's Office; prin. faculty mem. nat. tng. seminar, Govt. Fin. Officers Assn.; co-chair Bond Buyer's Ninth Ann. Midwest Pub. Fin. Conf.; nat. conf. chmn., Ctr. Bus. Intelligence; spkr. in field. Author: Important Developments During the Year: Tax Exempt Financing, 1989; contbr. papers in field. Founder, v.p., bd. dirs., trustee Keshet: Jewish Parents of Children with Spl. Needs, 1984—; trustee Lincolnwood Dist. Pub. Libr., 1988-89; bd. dirs. Brisk Rabbinical Coll., 1990-2006. Recipient Pro Bono Svc. award, Katten Muchin Rosenman LLP, Guardian of Hope award, Keshet, 2006. Mem. ABA (chmn. com. on tax-exempt fin., 1999-2001), Nat. Assn. Bond Lawyers (mem. steering com. bond attys.' workshop). Office: Katten Muchin Rosenman LLP 525 W Monroe St Chicago IL 60661 Office Phone: 312-577-8897. Business E-Mail: milton.wakschlag@kattenlaw.com.

**WAKSMAN, BYRON HALSTED,** immunologist, educator, medical association administrator; b. N.Y.C., Sept. 15, 1919; s. Selman A. and Bertha (Mitnik) W.; m. Joyce Ann Robertroy, Aug. 11, 1944; children: Nan, Peter. BS, Swarthmore Coll., 1940; MD, U. Pa., 1943. Intern Michael Reese Hosp., Chgo., 1944; fellow Mayo Found., 1946-48; NIH fellow Columbia U. Med. Sch., 1948-49; assoc., then asst. prof. bacteriology and immunology Harvard Med. Sch., 1949-63; rsch. fellow, then assoc. bacteriologist (neurology) Mass. Gen. Hosp., 1949-63; prof. microbiology Yale U., 1963-74, prof. pathology, 1974-78, chmn. dept., 1964-70, 72-74, prof. pathology and biology, 1979-89; v.p. rsch. programs Nat. Multiple Sclerosis Soc. N.Y.C., 1979—87, v.p. rsch. and med. programs, 1987-89; adj. prof. pathology NYU, 1979—, rsch. prof. biomedicine and sci. edn., 2002—, dir. (ad interim) programs for prep. edn. sci. and medicine, 2002—03, sr. advisor collaborative edn. programs, 2003—; vis. scientist in neurology Harvard U., 1990—. Mem. expert panel immunology WHO, 1963—83; microbiology fellowships panel and study sect. mem. NIH, 1961—69; bd. trustees Found. for Microbiology, 1968—, pres., 1970—2000, chmn. bd. trustees, 2001—; bd. trustees Biosis, 1988—91; dir. sci. writing fellowships program Marine Biol. Lab., Woods Hole, Mass., 1990—95; Humboldt prof. Max Planck Inst., Martinsried, 1991—92; dir. European Initiative for Communicators Sci., 1992—95; chmn. bd. Sci.

Counsellors Nat. Inst. Aging, 1977—79. Contbr. articles to profl. jours.; editor: Progress in Allergy/Chemical Immunology, 1962—; mem. editl. adv. bd.: Cellular Immunology, 1970—95, Immunol. Comms., 1970—95, Inflammation, 1975—90, assoc. editor: Bacteriol. Revs., 1963—67, Jour. Immunology, 1962—66, Internat. Archives Allergy and Applied Immunology, 1962—95. Served as psychiatrist AUS, 1944-46. Fellow Am. Acad Arts and Scis.; mem. Am. Assn. Immunologists (councillor 1965-70, pres. 1970-71), Brit. Soc. Immunology, Am. Soc. Microbiology (councillor 1967-71), Am. Acad. Microbiology, Am. Acad. Neurology, Am. Neurol. Assn. Home: Brookhaven at Lexington 1010 Waltham St Apt 462 Lexington MA 02421 Office Phone: 781-862-3839. Business E-mail: bwaksman@partners.org.

**WAKUMOTO, YOSHIHIKO,** electronics company executive, grants executive; b. Tokyo, June 4, 1931; s. Yoshitaro and Fumie (Oka) W.; m. Reiko Tanaka, Mar. 28, 1959; children: Yoshiaki, Yoshiyoshi. BA, Tokyo U., 1955; postgrad., Columbia U., 1960-61. Dep. mgr. license negotiation Toshiba Corp., Tokyo, 1964-67, mgr. overseas mfg. ops., 1967-72, mgr. fin. divsn., 1972-74, gen. mgr. internat. fin. divsn., 1974-81, gen. mgr. internat. affairs divsn., 1981-88, v.p., dep. group exec.-internat. staff group, 1988-91, exec. v.p. for corp. planning, info. sys. and group cos., 1991-95, exec. v.p. for internat. rels., 1995-96, advisor, 1996—2001; exec. dir. Japan Found. Ctr. for Global Partnership, Tokyo, 1996—2002; spl. asst. to the pres. The Japan Found., 2002—05. Mem., Japan Nat. Com. United World Colls., 1996—2002; dir. The Am. Studies Found., 1997—; chairperson CARE Japan, 2003—; pres. Japan Assn. for Cultural Exch., 2004—. Co-author: Foreign Exchange Risk and International Financial Strategy, 1973, The Run-up of 21st Century, 1991; translator: Management By Exception, 1968. Mem. Internat. House of Japan, Japan Internat. Affairs, Fgn. Corr. Club Japan (assoc.). Home: 3-43-18 Hongo Bunkyo-ku Tokyo 113-0033 Japan Office: Japan Assn for Cultural Exch 1-11-28 Akasaka Minato-ku Tokyo 107-0052 Japan E-mail: waksan@tcn-catv.ne.jp.

**WALBERG, HERBERT JOHN,** psychologist, educator, consultant; b. Chgo., Dec. 27, 1937; s. Herbert J. and Helen (Bauer) W.; m. Madoka Bessho, Aug. 20, 1965; 1 child, Herbert J. III. BE in Edn. and Psychology, Chgo. State U., 1959; ME in Counseling, U. Ill., 1960; PhD in Ednl. Psychology, U. Chgo., 1964. Instr. psychology Chgo. State U., 1962—63, asst. prof., 1964—65; lectr. edn. Rutgers U., New Brunswick, NJ, 1965—63; asst. prof. edn. Harvard U., Cambridge, Mass., 1966—69; assoc. prof. edn. U. Ill., Chgo., 1970—71, prof., 1971—84, rsch. prof., 1984—, external examiner, 1981. External examiner, 1981; ednl. cons. numerous orgns.; external examiner Monash U., 1974, 76, Australian Nat. U., 1977; speaker in field; former coord. worldwide radio broadcasts on Am. Edn. Voice of Am., USIA, Office Pres. U.S., cons. Ctr. for Disease Control U.S. Pub. Health Svcs., 1985-90. Author, editor 40 books; chmn. editl. bd. Internat. Jour. Ednl. Rsch., 1985—; contbr. over 350 articles to profl. jours., chpts. to books. Mem. Chgo. United Edn. Com., also other civic groups, 1971-86; bd. dirs. Family Study Inst., 1987; chmn. bd. dirs. Heartland Inst., 1995. Nat. Inst. Edn. rsch. grantee, 1973, NSF rsch. grantee, 1974, March of Dimes rsch. grantee, 1976, numerous others. Fellow AAAS, Am. Psychol. Assn., Royal Statis. Soc.; mem. Internat. Acad. Edn. (founding), Am. Ednl. Rsch. Assn., Assn. for Supervision and Curriculum Devel., Brit. Ednl. Rsch. Assn., Nat. Soc. for Study Edn., Evaluation Rsch. Soc., Internat. Acad. Scis., Phi Delta Kappa (Disting. Rsch. award U. Chgo. chpt. 1971, cert. of recognition 1985), Phi Kappa Phi (hon.). Lutheran. Avocation: travel. Home: 180 E Pearson St Apt 3607 Chicago IL 60611-2135 Office: U Ill 1040 W Harrison St Chicago IL 60607-7129 Office Phone: 312-505-0528. Personal E-mail: hwalberg@yahoo.com.

**WALBERT, KATE,** writer, educator; b. Aug. 13, 1961; Lectr. writing Yale U. Author: Where She Went, 1998 (N.Y. Times Notable Book, 1998), The Gardens of Kyoto, 2001, Our Kind: A Novel in Stories, 2004 (Nat. Book Award finalist, 2004); contbr. articles to newspapers. Recipient NEA Fellowship, Conn. Commn. on Arts Fellowship. Office: Yale U 63 High St PO Box 208302 New Haven CT 06520-8302 E-mail: kate.walbert@yale.edu.

**WALBESSER, HENRY HERMAN,** computer science educator; b. Buffalo, May 9, 1935; s. Henry Herman and Florence (Schoenl) W.; m. Diane L. Walker, Aug. 16, 1958; children: Henry, Kathleen, James. BS, SUNY, Buffalo, 1958; MA, U. Md., 1960, PhD, 1965; DSc, U. of the Republic, Uruguay, 1976. Asst. prof. U. Tex., Austin, 1961-63; assoc. dir. AAAS, Washington, 1963-68; assoc. prof. U. Md., College Park, 1968-76, assoc. dean/assoc. provost, 1971-76, prof., chair Catonsville, 1976-92, prof. emeritus, 1992—; prof. Baylor U., Waco, Tex., 1992—, dean, 1992—96; COO, provost Henry Cogswell Coll., Everett, Wash., 2005—, provost, COO, 2005—. Author: Evaluation Model, 1965, Integrity and Higher Education, 2001, A Brief Primer on Teaching: For New University Personnel, 2002, Imagination, 2003, An Introduction to Data Analysis for Computer Scientists and Engineers, 2003; co-author: Descriptive Data Analysis, 1991, Inferential Data Analysis, 1994; contbr. articles to profl. jours. Active adv. bd. Gov.'s Econ. Devel. Office, Annapolis, Md., 1988-91, Strecker Mus., Waco, 1992-2006, Lyric Opera of Waco, 1997-2006; worker Habitat for Humanity, Waco, 1996—. Fulbright-Hays fellow, 1967, 68, SEAMEO fellow, 1981, 82, OECD fellow, 1988. Fellow: AAAS; mem.: Nat. Hist. Soc. Democrat. Baptist. Avocations: bioinformatics, history of university presidents, gardening. Home: PO Box 1428 Hewitt TX 76643 Office: Henry Cogawall Coll Reed Hall 3002 Colby Ave Everett WA 98201 Office Phone: 254-644-0841. Personal E-mail: HHWalbesser@aol.com.

**WALBURN, JOHN CLIFFORD,** mental health services professional; b. Marion, Ind., Apr. 6, 1945; s. Rex Raymond and Norma Jane (Clifford) W.; m. Linda Sue Spall, Sept. 21, 1968 (div. Dec. 1987); 1 child, Geoffrey Jacob; m. Mitzi Lynn Johnson, June 20, 1991; 1 child, Abigail Rae. BS, Ball State U., 1969, MA, 1975; JD, I.U., Indpls., 1991. Bar: Ind. 1992. Planner Metro. Planning Commn., Muncie, Ind., 1970-72; dir. adult svcs. Del. County Assn. for Retarded, Muncie, Ind., 1972-76; exec. dir. Fayette-Union Assn. for Retarded, Connersville, Ind., 1976-83; cons. Ind. Protection and Advocacy, Indpls., 1984-86; case mgr. Ind. Dept. Mental Health, Indpls., 1986-87; exec. dir. Cardinal Mgt., New Castle, Ind., 1987-2000; founding ptnr. Creative Human Resource Solutions, New Castle, Ind., 1998—; exec. dir. Cmty. Alternative, Southeast Divsn. of Rescare, Jeffersonville, Ind., 2000—. Ofcl. Ind. Spl. Olympics, 1973—; chmn. Ind. Residential Mgmt. Com., 1991—; cons. DLG Cons. and Mktg. Svc., Ind., 1992; treas. Cmty. Action, So. Ind. Co-author: Feldman/Walburn Habilitation System, 1988; photo, drawing artist, 1978—. Treas. cmty. action, So. Ind., Madison Area C. of C.; bd. dirs. Arts Coun. of So. Ind., 2004-. With USN, 1965-67. Named Ky. Col., Commonwealth of Ky., 1978. Mem. Am Assn. Mental Retardation (bd. dirs. 1991-98), Ind. Assn. Rehab. Facilities (bd. dirs. 1996—, Pres.'s award 1998), Madison Area C. of C. Avocations: sports, playing/listening to music, movies, art, reading fiction. Home: 2559 So College Hill Dr Hanover IN 47243-9177 Office: RES-CARE Twenty-Five-O-One Pl 6200 E Hwy 62 Ste 675 Jeffersonville IN 47130 Business E-Mail: jwalburn@rescare.com.

**WALCH, TIMOTHY GEORGE,** library director; b. Detroit, Dec. 6, 1947; s. George Louis Walch and Margaret Mary (Shields) DeSchryver; m. Victoria Irons, June 24, 1978; children: Thomas Emmet, Brian Edward. BA, U. Notre Dame, 1969; PhD, Northwestern U., 1975. Assoc. dir. Soc. Am. Archivists, Chgo., 1975-79; grants analyst Nat. Hist. Publ. Commn., Washington, 1979-81; budget analyst Nat. Archives, Washington, 1981-82, editor Prologue, 1982-88; asst. dir. Hoover Presdl. Libr., West Branch, Iowa, 1988-93, dir., 1993—. Author: Catholicism in America, 1989, Pope John Paul II, 1989, Parish School, 1996, reprinted, 2003, others; editor: Herbert Hoover & Harry S Truman, 1992, Immigrant America, 1994, At the President's Side, 1997, Herbert Hoover & Franklin D. Roosevelt, 1998, Uncommon Americans, 2003, and others; assoc. editor: U.S. Cath. Historian, 1983—; guest columnist Cedar Rapids Gazette, 1996-2006; contbr. History News Svc., 2002—. Recipient Journalism award U.S. Cath. Press Assn., 1986, 1st place publ. award Nat. Assn. Govt. Communicators, 1988, U.S. Archivist's award Nat. Archives, 1993, Iowa Gov.'s Vol. award, 1995, 97, Dominican Veritas Forum award, 1996, Harris fellow, Rotary Internat., 2005, Rogus Lecture, U. Dayton,

1999, Williams Lecture, La. State U., Shreveport, 2000, Hatfield Lecture, Oreg. Hist. Soc., 2003. Mem. Orgn. Am. Historians, U.S. Cath. Hist. Soc., State Hist. Soc. Iowa (trustee 2005—), Rotary Internat. Home: 65 N Westminster St Iowa City IA 52245-3833 Office: Hoover Presdl Libr PO Box 488 West Branch IA 52358-0488 Office Phone: 319-643-6029. Personal E-mail: Twalch47@aol.com. Business E-mail: timothy.walch@nara.gov.

**WALCHER, ALAN ERNEST,** lawyer; b. Chgo., Oct. 2, 1949; s. Chester R. and Dorothy E. (Kullgren) W.; children: Dustin Alan, Michael Alan, Christopher Ray. BS, U. Utah, 1971, cert. in internat. rels., 1971, JD, 1974. Bar: Utah 1974, U.S. Dist. Ct. Utah 1974, U.S. Ct. Appeals (10th cir.) 1977, Calif. 1979, U.S. Dist. Ct. (cen. dist.) Calif. 1979, U.S. Ct. Appeals (9th cir.) 1983, U.S. Dist. Ct. (ea., no., and so. dists.) Calif. 1994. Sole practice, Salt Lake City, 1974-79; ptnr. Costello & Walcher, L.A., 1979-85, Walcher & Scheuer, 1985-88, Ford & Harrison, 1988-91, Epstein Becker & Green, 1991-2003; sole practice, 2003-; judge pro tem Los Angeles Mcpl. Ct., 1986-91; dir. Citronia, Inc., Los Angeles, 1979-81. Trial counsel Utah chpt. Common Cause, Salt Lake City, 1978-79. Robert Mukai scholar U. Utah, 1971. Mem. Soc. Bar and Gavel (v.p. 1975-77), ABA, Fed. Bar Assn., Los Angeles County Bar Assn., Century City Bar Assn., Assn. Bus. Trial Lawyers, Phi Delta Phi, Owl and Key. Home: 17933 Sunburst St Northridge CA 91325-2848 Office Phone: 310-344-6570. Personal E-mail: alan1002@earthlink.net.

**WALCHER, KATHLEEN,** state official; b. Sept. 20, 1948; Clk. of ct. of Common Pleas, Huron County; civil sheriff deputy; deputy clk.; state rep. State of Ohio, 58th Dist., 2002—. Mem.: Juvenile and Family Law (vice-chair), Econ. Devel. and Tech., County and Twp. Govt., Agr. and Natural Resources. Republican. Office: 77 South High St 12th Fl Columbus OH 43215-6111

**WALCOTT, CHARLES,** neurobiology and behavior educator; b. Boston, July 19, 1934; s. Charles Folsom and Susan (Cabot) W.; m. Jane Clayton Taylor, Aug. 14, 1976; children: Thomas Stewart, Samuel Cabot. AB, Harvard U., 1956; PhD, Cornell U., 1959. Asst. prof. div. engring. and applied physics Harvard U., Cambridge, Mass., 1961-65; asst. prof. biology Tufts U., Medford, Mass., 1965-67; assoc. prof. dept. biology SUNY, Stony Brook, 1967-74, prof. dept. biology, 1974-81; prof., exec. dir. Cornell Lab. of Ornithology, Ithaca, NY, 1981-93, Louis Agassiz Fuertes dir., 1992-95; prof. neurobiology and behavior Cornell U., 1981—; dir. divsn. biol. scis., 1998-99, assoc. dean of the univ. faculty, 2000—03, dean of univ. faculty, 2003—. Cons., dir. Elem. Sci. Study, Watertown, Mass., 1961-67; dir. 3-2-1-Contact, Children's TV Workshop, N.Y.C., 1978—80; dir. L.A. Fuertes. Contbr. many rsch. papers to sci. jours. Dir. sci. TV, Mass. Audubon, Lincoln, 1959—61. Avocations: gardening, sailing, photography. Home: 84 Besemer Hill Rd Ithaca NY 14850-9636 Office: Cornell U Dept Neurobiology Behavior W255 Seeley Mudd Hall Ithaca NY 14853 Office Phone: 607-254-4382. Business E-Mail: cw38@cornell.edu.

**WALCOTT, JOHN L.,** communications executive; b. Paterson, NJ, Aug. 29, 1949; s. Henry Richards Jr. and Katharine McCauley (Fearing) W.; m. Nancy Bittles, Aug. 11, 1973; children: Jennifer James, Allison Tierney, Elizabeth Bittles. BA, Williams Coll., 1971. With Redwood (NJ) News, 1972, The Record, Hackensack, NJ, 1972—77; econ. corr., nat. polit. corr., chief diplomatic corr. Newsweek, 1977—86; nat. security corr. Wall St. Jour., 1986—89; fgn. editor, nat. editor US News & World Report, 1989—96; fgn. editor, news editor Knight Ridder, Inc., 1997—2002, bur. chief, 2002—06, The McClatchy Co., Washington, 2006—. U.S. Rep. U.N. Conf. on Media, Igls, Austria, 1983; mem. Georgetown U. Sch. Fgn. Svc. Leadership Seminar, Washington, 1985; profl. lectr. Georgetown U. Sch. Fgn. Svc., 1996—; bd. advisors SmartBrief, Inc., 1997—. Co-author: (with David C. Martin) Best Laid Plans: The Inside Story of America's War Against Terrorism, 1988. Named Disting. Friend, Georgetown U. Sch. Fgn. Svc., 1985—; recipient Edward Weintal prize Georgetown U., 1988, Edwin M. Hood award Nat. Press Club, 1983, Freedom of the Press award, 1995, Overseas Press Club award, 1983, 84, Newspaper Guild of N.Y. award, 1985, Nat. Headline award, 2005. Mem. Overseas Writers Club (pres. 1986-88), White House Correspondents Assn., Gridiron Club, Sigma Delta Chi. Presbyterian. Office: McClatchy Newspapers One Metro Ctr Ste 1000 700 12th St NW Washington DC 20005-3994 Business E-Mail: jwalcott@mcclatchydc.com.

**WALD, BERNARD JOSEPH,** lawyer; b. Bklyn., Sept. 14, 1932; s. Max and Ruth (Mencher) W.; m. Francine Joy Weintraub, Feb. 2, 1964; children: David Evan, Kevin Mitchell. B.B.A. magna cum laude, CCNY; J.D. cum laude, NYU, 1955. Bar: N.Y. 1955, U.S. Dist. Ct. (so. dist.) N.Y. 1960, U.S. Dist. Ct. (ea. dist.) N.Y. 1960, U.S. Ct. Appeals (2d cir.) 1960, U.S. Supreme Ct. 1971. Mem. Herzfeld & Rubin, P.C. and predecessor firms, N.Y.C., 1955—. Mem. ABA, N.Y. State Bar Assn., Assn. Bar City N.Y., N.Y. County Lawyers Assn. Office: Herzfeld & Rubin PC 40 Wall St Ste 5400 New York NY 10005-2301 Office Phone: 212-471-8475. Business E-Mail: bwald@herzfeld-rubin.com.

**WALD, CATHERINE,** writer; b. Port Chester, N.Y. d. Arnold Myron Wald and Edith Zukosky; m. Reb Steven Cole, Aug. 26, 1984; children: Benjamin, Nina. Student, Wesleyan U., 1972—74; BA cum laude in French, Barnard Coll., 1976. Adminstrv. asst. CBS Records, NY, 1979—81; editor AIG, N.Y.C., 1981—83; editl. dir. Brecker & Merryman, N.Y.C., 1983—84; sr. editor Philip Morris, N.Y.C., 1984—85, Avon Products, N.Y.C., 1985—87; freelance author Mohegan Lake, NY, 1987—. Cons. in field; lectr. in field; creator rejectioncollection.com. Author: The Resilient Writer: Tales of Rejection and Triumph, 2005 (Outstanding Book award, 2006); contbr.: The Practical Writer: From Inspiration to Publication, 2004; translator: Childish Things, 1994; contbr. column in newspaper, articles to mags. Vol. tchr. Westchester Residential Opportunities, White Plains, NY, 2004—. Recipient Eleanor Keller French prize, Barnard Coll., 1976, 5 awards, Internat. Assn. Bus. Communicators, 1982—97, Second prize, Writer's Digest, 1994, Gold award, Women in Comms. Clarion Awards, 2002. Mem.: Westchester Arts Councils Artist Roster, Journalism and Women Symposium, Am. Soc. Journalists and Authors. Avocations: writing, opera, walking. Office: C Wald rejectioncollection.com PO Box 443 Shrub Oak NY 10588 Office Phone: 914-528-3309. E-mail: cathy@writerwald.com.

**WALD, DOUGLAS L.,** lawyer; b. Sept. 16, 1954; AB, Harvard Univ., 1975, JD, 1979. Bar: D.C. 1979. Law clk. Judge William H. Timbers, US Ct. Appeals, 2d Cir., 1979—80; ptnr., chmn. Antitrust Com. Arnold & Porter, Washington, 1980—. Contbr. articles to profl. jours. Office: Arnold & Porter 555 Twelfth St NW Washington DC 20004-1206 Office Phone: 202-942-5112. Office Fax: 202-942-5999. Business E-Mail: douglas_wald@aporter.com.

**WALD, MICHAEL LEONARD,** economist; b. Balt., Jan. 5, 1951; s. Leonard Marvin and Frances (Kosinski) Wald; m. Marlena Malmstedt, June 10, 1972. BA, Am. U., 1972; MPA, U. Ga., Athens, 2006. Mgr. Woodward and Lothrop Dept. Store, Washington, 1972-75, Hecht Co., Washington, 1975-76; store mgr. W.J. Sloane & Co., Washington, 1976-77; economist U.S. Bur. Labor Stats., Balt., 1977-85, Washington, 1985-86, Atlanta, 1986-96, S.E. regional economist, 1996—. Lectr. fed. compensation issues. Mem. editl. bd. HR Atlanta, 1993—95; contbr. articles to profl. jours.; reviewer Monthly Labor Rev., 1992—, peer reviewer ACA Jour., 1995—99. Bd. dirs. Athens (Ga.) Habitat for Humanity, 1990—93; venue mktg. liaison mgr. 1996 Centennial Olympic Games. Recipient Commr.'s award for Outstanding Mgmt. Performance, 2000, Sec.'s Exceptional Achievement award, 2001. Mem.: Labor and Employee Rels. Assn., Atlanta Econ. Club (officer 2003—04), Atlanta Labor and Employment Rels. Assn. (bd. mem. 2005, bd. dirs. 2005—), Nat. Assn. Bus. Econ., Atlanta Compensation Assn. (v.p. 1992—94, pres. 1996), Pi Alpha Alpha, Phi Kappa Phi, Alpha Tau Omega. Avocations: reading, home improvement, travel. Home: 5015 Fawn Valley Dr Loganville GA 30052-3879 Office: US Bur Labor Stats 61 Forsyth St SW Ste 7t50 Atlanta GA 30303-8817 Office Phone: 404-331-3415. Business E-Mail: wald.michael@bls.gov.

**WALD, NIEL,** public health educator; b. N.Y.C., Oct. 1, 1925; s. Albert and Rose (Fischel) W.; m. Lucienne Hill, May 24, 1953; children: David, Phillip. AB, Columbia U., 1945; MD, NYU, 1948. Sr. hematologist Atomic Bomb Casualty Commn., Hiroshima, Japan, 1954-57; head biologist health physics divsn. Oak Ridge Nat. Lab., 1957-58; med. rsch. and tchg. specializing in radiation medicine and cytogenetics Pitts., 1958—; mem. faculty U. Pitts. Grad. Sch. Pub. Health and Med. Sch., 1958—2004, prof. radiation health, 1962-91, prof. environ. and occupl. health, 1991—2004, prof. radiology, 1965—2004; prof. human genetics U. Pitts., 1991—2004, prof. emeritus, 2004—; chmn. dept. radiation health U. Pitts. Grad. Sch. Pub. Health and Med. Sch., 1969-76, 77-89, chmn. dept. occupl. health, 1975-76, chmn. dept. indsl. environ. health scis., 1976-77. Dir. radiation medicine dept. Presbyn.-Univ. Hosp., 1966—; med. dir. Clin. Cytogenetics Lab., U. Pitts., 1982-99, chmn. Radiation Safety Com. 1960-2005, radiation cytogenetics cons., 1999—; dir. U.S. Dept. Energy postdoctoral fellowship program in radiation scis., 1997-2004; cons. U.S. NRC Office of Nuc. Materials Safety and Safeguards, mem. adv. panel for decontamination of Three Mile Island Nuc. Power Sta. Unit 2, 1981-93, cons. adv. com. on reactor safeguards, 1989-94; mem. U.S. working group on health effects, U.S.-USSR Joint Coordinating Com. for Civilian Nuc. Reactor Safety, 1989-92; cons. USN, nuc. industries and utilities; chmn. radiol. health study sect. USPHS, 1967-71; mem. Nat. Coun. Radiation Protection and Measurements, 1969-81, consociate mem., 1981—; mem. Gov. Pa. Adv. Com. Atomic Energy Devel. and Radiation Control, 1966-84, chmn., 1974-76; mem. Pa. Dept. Environ. Protection adv. com. on low level radioactive waste disposal, 1985—; mem. U.S. nuc. tech. adv. group Internat. Stds. Orgn., 2003-. Contbr. numerous articles to sci. and med. publs. Vol. U.S. Citizens Def. Corp. Air Warden Svc., 1943—45, capt. USAF, 1952—54. Recipient Health Physics Faculty Rsch. award U.S. Dept. Energy, 1992-95. Mem. Health Physics Soc. (pres. 1973-74), Am. Pub. Health Assn. (governing coun. 1971-73, program devel. bd. 1973-74), Radiation Rsch. Soc. (assoc. editor jour. 1965-68), Soc. Nuc. Medicine (assoc. editor jour. 1959-69), Am. Soc. Human Genetics, Am. Coll. Occupl. & Environ. Medicine, AAAS, AMA, Internat. Soc. Hematology. Achievements include research in the diagnosis and treatment of accidental human radiation injury, in human radiation dosimetry by automatic image analysis of radiation-induced chromosome aberrations, in the cytogenetics of murine radiation-induced leukemia and in health studies of irradiated human populations in U.S., Japan and Russia. Office: U Pitts Grad Sch Pub Health A-744 Crabtree Hl Pittsburgh PA 15261-0001 Office Phone: 412-624-2735. Business E-Mail: wald@pitt.edu.

**WALD, PATRICIA MCGOWAN,** retired federal judge; b. Torrington, Conn., Sept. 16, 1928; d. Joseph F. and Margaret (O'Keefe) McGowan; m. Robert L. Wald, June 22, 1952; children: Sarah, Douglas, Johanna, Frederica, Thomas. BA, Conn. Coll., 1948; LLB, Yale U., 1951; HHD (hon.), Mt. Vernon Jr. Coll., 1980; LLD, LLD, Hofstra U., 1991, New Eng. Coll., 1991, Vermont Law Sch., 1995; LLD, Yale U., 2001. Bar: D.C. 1952. Clk. to Hon. Jerome Frank U.S. Ct. Appeals, 1951—52; assoc. Arnold, Fortas & Porter, Washington, 1952—53; mem. D.C. Crime Commn., 1964—65; atty. Office of Criminal Justice, 1967—68; Neighborhood Legal Svc., Washington, 1968—70; co-dir. Ford Found. Project on Drug Abuse, 1970, Ctr. for Law and Social Policy, 1971—72, Mental Health Law Project, 1972—77; asst. atty. gen. for legis. affairs U.S. Dept. Justice, Washington, 1977—79; judge U.S. Ct. Appeals (D.C. cir.), 1979—99, chief judge, 1986—91; judge Internat. Criminal Tribunal for Former Yugoslavia, The Hague, Netherlands, 1999—2001. Bd. dirs. Am. Constn. Soc., 2002—. Author: Law and Poverty, 1965; co-author: Bail in the United States, 1964, Dealing with Drug Abuse, 1973; bd. editors: ABA Jour., 1978—86; contbr. articles to profl. jours. Mem. Commn. on Intelligence Capabilities of the US Regarding Weapons of Mass Destruction, 2004—05; trustee Ford Found., 1972—77, Phillips Exeter Acad., 1975—77, Agnes Meyer Found., 1976—77, Conn. Coll., 1976—77; active Carnegie Coun. on Children, 1972—77; bd. dirs. Mental Disability Rights Internat., 2002—. Recipient Lifetime Achievement award, The Am. Lawyer, 2004. Mem.: ABA-Ctrl. and Ea. European Law Inst. (exec. bd. 1994—99), Am. Constitution Soc. (bd. dirs. 2004—), Am. Philos. Assn., Inst. Justice Initiative, Am. Acad. Arts and Scis., Am. Law Inst. (coun. mem. 1979—, exec. com. 1985—99, 2d v.p. 1988—93, 1st v.p. 1993—98), Open Soc. Inst. (chair justice initiative 2002—04), Phi Beta Kappa. Office: 2101 Connecticut Ave NW Washington DC 20008 Personal E-mail: patwald2@cs.com.

**WALD, PETER ALLEN,** lawyer; b. 1953; AB magna cum laude, Brown U., 1974; JD magna cum laude, Harvard U., 1977. Bar: Calif. 1979. Law clk. to Hon. James R. Browning US Ct. Appeals (9th Cir.), 1977—78; ptnr. Latham & Watkins LLP, San Francisco, 1996—; global dept. chair, litig. dept. and chair, Bay Area litig. dept. Notes editor Harvard Law Rev., 1977. Named one of Top 10 Trial Lawyers in Am., Nat. Law Jour., 2006. Mem.: Phi Beta Kappa. Office: Latham & Watkins LLP Ste 2000 505 Montgomery St San Francisco CA 94111-2562 Business E-Mail: peter.wald@lw.com.*

**WALD, RICHARD CHARLES,** media consultant, educator; b. NYC; s. Joseph S. and Lily (Forstate) W.; m. Edith May Leslie; children: Matthew Leslie, Elizabeth Tole, Jonathan Simon. BA, Columbia U., 1952, MA, 1953; AB, Clare Coll., Cambridge, 1955. From reporter to mng. editor NY Herald Tribune, 1951—66; asst. mng. editor Washington Post, 1967; exec. v.p. Whitney Comm. Corp., NYC, 1968; pres. NBC News, 1968-77; asst. to chmn. bd. Times-Mirror Co., LA; sr. v.p. ABC News, 1978—99, sr. v.p. editl. quality, 1993—99, now cons.; Fred Friendly Prof. Journalism Columbia U., 1999—. Annotator: (with James Bellows) The World of Jimmy Breslin, 1967; chmn. bd. Columbia Daily Spectator. Mem. adv. bd. Knight Fellowship, Stanford U.; bd. dir. Correspondents Fund, Ctr. For Comm. Mem.: Fedn. Am. Scientists. Office: Columbia Sch Journalism 2950 Broadway New York NY 10027 also: ABC News 47 W 66th St New York NY 10023-6290 E-mail: richard.c.wald@abc.com.

**WALD, ROBERT LEWIS,** lawyer; b. Worcester, Mass., Sept. 9, 1926; s. Lewis and Freda Ann (Rosenfield) W.; m. Patricia Ann McGowan, June 22, 1952; children: Sarah Elizabeth, Douglas Robert, Johanna Margaret, Frederica Nora, Thomas Robert. AB, Harvard U., 1947; LLB, Yale U., 1951. Bar: Mass. 1951, D.C. 1959, U.S. Ct. Appeals (4th cir.) 1957, U.S. Supreme Ct. 1957, U.S. Ct. Appeals (D.C. cir.) 1959, U.S. Ct. Appeals (6th cir.) 1971. Clerk to Judge Irving R. Kaufman U.S. Dist. Ct. (so. dist.) N.Y., 1951-52; asst. to gen. counsel, chief div. export trade FTC, Washington, 1954—56; ptnr. Wald, Harkrader & Ross and predecessors, Washington, 1961—87, Nussbaum & Wald, Washington, 1989—96; sr. counsel Baach Robinson & Lewis, Washington, 1996—. Dir., trustee Washington Lawyers' Com. for Civil Rights, Urban Affairs and predecessor, 1969—, co-chmn., 1976—78; dir. Romanian-Am. Enterprise Fund, 1994—97, chmn., 1994—96; dir. Global Rights and predecessor, 1991—, Frederic B. Abramson Mem. Found., 1998—; hon. dir. Capital Area Immigrants' Rights Coalition, 1999—; dir. Internat. Sr. Lawyers Project, 2001—; bd. mgmt. trustees Internat. Assn. Women Judges, 1997—; bd. advisors Internat. Women Judges Found., 1997—. Served to lt. USNR, 1944-46, 52-53. Mem. ABA, D.C. Bar Assn. Home: 2101 Connecticut Ave NW Washington DC 20008-1728 Office: Baach Robinson & Lewis 1201 F St NW Ste 500 Washington DC 20004 Office Phone: 202-833-8900. E-mail: robert.wald@beachrobinson.com.

**WALD, SYLVIA,** artist; b. Phila., Oct. 30, 1915; Student, Moore Inst. Art, Sci. and Industry. One-woman shows include U. Louisville, 1945, 49, Kent State Coll., 1945, Nat. Serigraph Soc., 1946, Grand Central Moderns, N.Y.C., 1957, Devorah Sherman Gallery, Chgo., 1960, New Sch., 1967, Book Gallery, White Plains, NY, 1968, Benson Gallery, Bridgehampton, L.I., 1977, Knoll Internat., Munich, 1979, Amerika Havs, Munich, 1979, Aaron Berman Gallery, N.Y.C., 1981, Hirschtladler Gallery, 1994, New Britain (Conn.) Mus., 1994, Dongah Art Gallery, Seoul, Korea, 1995, Hanlim Art Gallery, Daejun, 1995-96, Kwangju City Art Mus. Pusan, Korea, Dong Shin U., Kwangju, 1996, Chosun U. Mus., Kwangju City, 2001, Chosun Univ. Mus. Art, Kwangju, Korea, 2002, 05, Tenri Gallery, N.Y.C., 2004, 05; exhibited in group shows at Nat. Sculpture Soc., 1940, Sculpture Internat., Phila., 1940, Chgo. Art Inst., 1941, Bklyn. Mus., 1975, Libr. of Congress, 1943, 52, 58, Smithsonian Instn., 1954, Internat. Print Exhbn., Salzburg and Vienna, 1952,

2d Sao Paulo Biennial, 1953, N.Y. Cultural Ctr., 1973, Mus. Modern Art, N.Y.C., 1975, Benson Gallery, Bridgehampton, L.I., 1982, Dumon-Landis Gallery, New Brunswick, N.J., 1982-83, Suzuki Gallery, N.Y.C., 1982, Sid Deutch Gallery, N.Y.C., 1983, Aaron Berman Gallery, N.Y.C., 1983, Full House Gallery, Kingston, N.J., 1984, Nabi Gallery, Sag Harbor, N.Y., 1989, Worcester Mus., 1991, Boston Mus. Fine Arts, 1991, Hirschl & Adler Gallery, N.Y.C., 1993, Parrish Mus., Southampton, 2002, Tenri Galleru, NYC, 2005, 2x13 Gallery, 2006, Korea Gallery, 2006, others; represented in permanent collections Aetna Oil Co., AAUW, Ball State Tchrs. Coll., Bibliotheque Nat., Paris, Bklyn. Mus., Howard U., State U. Iowa, Libr. of Congress, U. Louisville, Nat. Gallery, Mus. Modern Art, Phila. Mus., N.C. Mus., Rose Mus. Art at Brandeis U., Whitney Mus., N.Y.C., Finch Coll. Mus., N.Y.C., U. Nebr., Ohio U., U. Okla., Princeton, Victoria and Albert Mus., Walker Gallery, Worcester (Mass.) Art Mus., Guggenheim Mus., N.Y.C., Grunewald Mus., UCLA, Rutgers Mus., N.J., Aschenbach Collection Mus., San Francisco, Grunewald Coll. Mus. UCLA, Wellesley Coll.; acquisitions Yale U. Art Gallery, 1998, Cleve. Mus., 1998; contbr. articles to profl. jours. Address: 417 Lafayette St New York NY 10003-7005

**WALD, WAYNE A.,** lawyer; b. Queens, NY, Dec. 18, 1962; BS magna cum laude, SUNY, Albany; JD, NYU, 1989. Bar: NY 1990. Ptnr. Katten Muchin Zavis Rosenman, NYC. Office: Katten Muchin Zavis Rosenman 575 Madison Ave New York NY 10022 Office Phone: 212-940-8508. Office Fax: 212-940-8776. E-mail: wayne.wald@kmzr.com.

**WALDA, JOHN D.,** educational association administrator, lawyer; b. Ft. Wayne, Ind., June 14, 1950; s. David William and Martha (Lefever) W.; m. Julie Inskeep, Aug. 3, 1974; children: Laura, Kirk. AB, Ind. U., 1972, JD, 1975. Bar: Ind. 1975, U.S. Dist. Ct. (no. and so. dists.) Ind. 1975, U.S. Ct. Appeals (7th cir.) 1977, U.S. Ct. Appeals (6th cir.) 1987, U.S. Dist. Ct. (we. dist.) Mich. 1991. Ptnr. Barrett & McNagny, Ft. Wayne, 1975—2001; chmn. Clarian Health Ptnrs., Inc., 1996—2004, dir., 1996—2004, Assn. Governing Bds. of Univs. & Colls., 2000—04, vice chmn., 2000—02, chmn., 2002—03; exec. dir. Fed. Rels. Ind. U. Sys., 2002—04; sr. v.p. Fed. Rels. BoseTreacy Assoc. LLC; ptnr. Bose McKinney & Evens LLP; pres. Nat. Assn. Coll. and Univ. Bus. Officers, 2006—. Dir. Ft. Wayne Newspapers, Inc., 1990—; master of the bench Am. Inns of Ct.; gen. counsel Journal-Gazette (Ft. Wayne). Pres. bd. trustees Ind. U., 1990—; first chmn. Ind. Lottery Commn., 1989; bd. dirs. Ft. Wayne Civic Theatre, Ft. Wayne Mus. of Art; active Allen County Parks & Recreation Bd., Headwaters Park Commn.; bd. dirs., v.p. Jr. Achievement Northeast Ind.; Dem. candidate for U.S. House of Reps. 1978, 80. Fellow Ind. Bar Found.; mem. ABA (house of dels. 1983-86), Ind. State Bar Assn., (chmn. young lawyers sect. 1983-84), JUNTO Club of Ft. Wayne (pres.). Democrat. Avocations: skiing, backpacking, golf. Office: Barrett & McNagny PO Box 2263 Fort Wayne IN 46801-2263 also: Nat Assn Coll and Univ Bus Officers 2501 M St, NW, Ste 400 Washington DC 20037 Office Phone: 202-861-2500. E-mail: john.walda@nacubo.org.*

**WALDECK, JOHN WALTER, JR.,** lawyer; b. Cleve., May 3, 1949; s. John Walter Sr. and Marjorie Ruth (Palenschat) W.; m. Cheryl Gene Cutter, Sept. 10, 1977; children: John III, Matthew, Rebecca. BS, John Carroll U., 1973; JD, Cleve. State U., 1977. Bar: Ohio 1977. Product applications chemist Synthetic Products Co., Cleve., 1969-76; assoc. Arter & Hadden, Cleve., 1977-85, ptnr., 1986-88, Porter, Wright, Morris and Arthur, Cleve., 1988-90, ptnr. in charge, 1990-96; ptnr. Walter & Haverfield LLP, Cleve., 1996—, mem. exec. com., 2003—. Bd. advisors Litigation Mgmt., Inc., 2000—04. Chmn. Bainbridge Twp. Bd. Zoning Appeals, Chagrin Falls, Ohio, 1984-94; trustee Greater Cleve. chpt. Lupus Found. Am., 1978-91, sec., 1979-86; trustee LeBlond Housing Corp., Cleve., 1990-96, sec., 1996, Univ. Circle, Inc., 1993-97, Fairmount Ctr. for Performing and Fine Arts, Novelty, Ohio, 1993-96, sect., 1994-95; bd. dirs. Geauga County Mental Health Recovery Svc. Bd., Chardon, Ohio, 1988-97, treas., 1991-93, vice-chmn., 1993-95, chmn., 1995-97; mem. bd. advisors Palliative Care Svcs., Cleve. Clinic Cancer Ctr., 1989-91. Mem. Ohio State Bar Assn. (real property sect. bd. govs. 1992), Greater Cleve. Bar Assn. (real property, corp. banking sect, co-chair real estate law inst. 1990, 95, 96). Roman Catholic. Avocations: beekeeping, gardening, jogging. Home: 18814 Rivers Edge Dr W Chagrin Falls OH 44023-4968 Office: Walter & Haverfield LLP suite 3500 1301 E Ninth St Cleveland OH 44114 Office Phone: 216-781-1212. Business E-Mail: jwaldeck@walterhav.com.

**WALDEN, DANA,** broadcast executive; BA in Comm., U. So. Calif. Formerly with Bender, Goldman & Helper; former v.p. mktg. Arsenio Hall Comm., Paramount; former sr. v.p. media and corp. rels. 20th Century Fox TV, v.p. current programming, 1994—96, former v.p. drama, former sr. v.p. drama, former exec. v.p. drama devel., co-pres., 1999—. Named one of 100 Most Powerful Women in Entertainment, Hollywood Reporter, 1999—2005. Mem.: Hollywood Radio and TV Soc. (v.p. 2003—). Office: 20th Century Fox TV 10201 W Pico Blvd Bldg 88 Rm 29 Los Angeles CA 90035*

**WALDEN, GREG,** congressman; b. The Dalles, Oreg., Jan. 10, 1957; s. Paul Walden; m. Mylene Walden; 1 child. BS in Journalism, U. Oreg., Eugene, 1981. Press sec. Staff of US Rep. Denny Smith of Oreg., 1981—84, chief of staff, 1984—86; owner Columbia Gorge Broadcasters, Inc., The Dalles, 1986—; mem. Oreg. State Ho. Reps., 1989-95, majority leader, 1991-93; mem. Oreg. State Senate, 1995-97, asst. majority leader, 1995-97; mem. US Congress from 2nd Oreg. dist., 1999—, mem. energy and commerce com., vice chmn. oversight and investigations subcommittee, mem. resources com., chair forests and forest health subcommittee, dep. majority whip, 2002—. Owner MSW Comm. Bd. dirs., exec. com. Assn. Oreg. Industries; bd. dirs. Oreg. Health Scis. Found. Named Outstanding Young Oregonian, Oreg. Jaycees, 1991, Legislator of Yr., Nat. Rep. Legislators Assn., 1993, Agr. Retailers Assn., Ctrl. Oreg. Visitors Assn., Nat. Assn. Home Care, Nat. Rural Health Assn., Oreg. Assn. Home Care, Oreg. Rural Electric Coop. Assn., Hero of the Taxpayer, Ams. for Tax Reform, Friend of the Shareholder, Am. Shareholders Assn., Oreg. Person of Yr., Dorchester Conf., Perfect Voter, Info. Tech. Industry, Guardian of Small Bus., Nat. Fedn. Ind. Bus., Friend of the Pear Industry, N.W. Pear Industry, Friend of the Farm Bur., Oreg. Farm Bur., Protector of Property Rights, Property Rights Alliance, Champion of Small Bus., Small Bus. Survival Com.; recipient Legislator of Yr., Safari Club Internat., Benjamin Franklin award, 60+ Assn., Pub. Svc. award, Am. Coll. Nurse-Midwives, Thomas Jefferson award, Food Distribrs. Internat., Disting. Svc. award, Forest Counties and Schs. Coalition, Champion award, League of Pvt. Property Owners, Congl. Champion award, Nat. Assn. Svc. and Conservation Corps, Wheat Adv. award, Nat. Assn. Wheat Growers, Appreciation award, Oreg. Nat. Guard, Sr. Legis. Achievement award, Seniors Coalition, Spirit of Enterprise award, US C. of C., Golden Bulldog award, Watchdog of the Treasury. Mem. Hood River C. of C., Nat. Fedn. Ind. Bus., Elks, Rotary, Republican. Episcopalian. Office: US Ho Reps 1210 Longworth Ho Office Bldg Washington DC 20515 Office Phone: 202-225-6730.*

**WALDEN, JAMES WILLIAM,** accountant, educator; b. Jellico, Tenn., Mar. 5, 1936; s. William Evert and Bertha L. (Faulkner) Walden; m. Eva Sue Selvia, Jan. 16, 1957 (dec. Aug. 1988); 1 child, James William; m. Hattie Nan Lamb, Jan. 6, 1990 (div. June 1992); m. Janet Faulkner, Aug. 12, 1993 (div. May 2001); m. Louise Davis, Apr. 28, 2004. BS, Miami U., Oxford, Ohio, 1963; MBA, Xavier U., Cin., 1966. CPA, Ohio. Tchr. math. Middletown (Ohio) City Sch. Dist., 1963-67, Fairfield (Ohio) High Sch., 1967-69; instr. accounting Sinclair Community Coll., Dayton, Ohio, 1969-72, asst. prof., 1972-75, assoc. prof., 1975-78, prof., 1978-89, prof. emeritus, 1991—. Cons., public acct.; mem. adj. faculty in acctg. Capital U., 1980—. Group comdr., fin. officer and chief staff Ohio wing CAP; bd. dirs. Frankin Cmty. Svcs.; bd. dir. Franklin Food Pantry. With USAF, 1954—59. Mem.: Ohio Soc. CPAs, Greater Hamilton Estate Planning Coun., Nat. Soc. Pub. Accts., Pub. Accts. Soc. Ohio (pres. S.W. chpt. 1985—86), Springboro C. of C. (bd. dirs., treas.), Kiwanis (pres. Springboro chpt.), Butler County Torch Club, Lions, Rotary, Am. Legion (life), Beta Alpha Psi. Home: PO Box 469 Springboro OH 45066-0469 Office: Sinclair C C 265 N Main St Springboro OH 45066-9255 Office Phone: 937-748-3736. E-mail: jwalden@one.net.

**WALDEN, JENNIFER LEE,** plastic surgeon; b. Austin, Tex., Nov. 17, 1971; d. Richard M. and Shirley T. Walden. BA, U. Tex., Austin, 1994, MD, 1998. Intern U. Tex., Galveson, 1998—99, resident in plastic surgery, 1999—2003; aesthetic surgery fellow Manhattan Eye, Ear and Throat Hosp., NYC, 2003—04, asst. attending, 2004—, Lenox Hill Hosp., NYC, 2004—. Co-dir. Nat. Student Rsch. Forum. Contbr. articles to profl. jours. Med. mission vol. surgeon Austin Smiles, 2005—06; med. vol. NYC Dept. of Health Med. Res. Corps. Recipient Mavis P. Kelsey Excellence in Medicine award, Kelsey Seybold Found., Houston, 1998, Hermann Barnett Meml. award, U. Tex., 1998, Janet M. Glasgow Meml. award, Am. Med. Women's Assn., 1998, Merck Manual award, Merck and Co., 1998, Best Sci. Exhibit award, Am. Soc. for Aesthetic Plastic Surgery, 2004; Vaughn Found. scholar, U. Tex., 1995—97, Isabella H. Brackenridge scholar, 1996, 1998, Donald P. Duncan Meml. scholar, 1997. Mem.: ACS (assoc.; plastic and maxillofacial surgery adv. coun. 2002—03), NY Med. Soc., NY County Med. Soc., Northeastern Soc. Plastic Surgeons, Assn. Women Surgeons, Am. Soc. Plastic Surgeons, Alpha Omega Alpha (Tex. alpha chpt. pres. 1997—98), Pi Beta Phi (ednl. enrichment chair 1993—94). Office: 50 E 71st St New York NY 10021 Office Phone: 212-288-9009. Office Fax: 212-737-8340. E-mail: drjenniferwalden@hotmail.com.

**WALDEN, JOHN,** retail executive; married; 5 children. B, U. Ill.; M, Northwestern U.; JD, Ill. Inst. Tech. Former exec. Storage Tech. Corp., Ameritech Corp.; former pres., COO Peapod, Inc., Skokie, Ill.; pres. Best Buy.com subs. Best Buy Co., Inc., 1999—2003; exec. v.p. human capital and leadership, 2002—05, exec. v.p. customer bus. group, 2005—. Office: Best Buy Co Inc 7601 Penn Ave S Minneapolis MN 55423 Office Phone: 612-291-1000. Office Fax: 612-292-4001.

**WALDEN, SHELTON HARRISON,** radio personality, educator; s. Herman B. Walden and Sarah Louise Harrison. BA in Polit. Sci., Fordham U., 1984. Radio broadcaster, N.Y.C., 1986—. Prodr., radio host, journalist Walden's Pond. Mem.: Fighting 69th Rep. Club (pres. 2005—06). Home and Office: 65 W 96th St #24C New York NY 10025 Office Phone: 212-209-2984. E-mail: shelton@waldenspond.com.

**WALDENBERG, ALAN S.,** lawyer; b. Mineola, NY, June 19, 1953; BS magna cum laude, U. Md., 1974; JD cum laude, Harvard U., 1978. CPA Md., 1976; bar: NJ 1978, US Dist. Ct. NJ (inactive) 1978, NY 1979, US Tax Ct. 1981. Ptnr., mem. exec. com. Schulte Roth & Zabel LLP, NYC. Contbr. articles to profl. jour.; spkr. in field. Mem.: NY Bar Assn. (Taxation Sect.). Office: Scultz Roth & Zabel LLP 919 Third Ave New York NY 10022 Office Phone: 212-756-2000. Office Fax: 212-593-5955. Business E-Mail: alan.waldenberg@srz.com.

**WALDERA, WANDA FRANCES,** artist; b. Southport, Conn., May 8, 1952; d. Clifford O. and Isabella (DeMattia) W.; m. Stephen Warren French, Oct. 19, 1990. BFA, San Jose State U., 1983, MFA, 1988. One-woman shows include Freightdoor Gallery, Santa Clara U., 1983, San Jose State U., 1988, San Jose City Coll., 1990, Mission Coll., Santa Clara, 1991, San Jose Inst. Contemporary Art, 1991, 96,; two-person shows include Univ. YWCA, Berkeley, Calif., 1997, Union Gallery, San Jose, Calif.; exhibited in group shows San Jose Mus. Art, 1987, 88, San Jose Inst. Contemporary Art, 1987, 96, 2000, San Jose State U., 1989, 95, Fong & Spratt Gallery, 1989, 90, 91, Sun Gallery, 1990, L.A. Artcore, 1990, San Jose City Coll., 1991, Davis Art Ctr. 1991, San Francisco State U. Union Gallery, 1993, Berkeley Art Ctr., Calif., 1997, Quan Yin Gallery, Oakland, 1998 NCJW Womens Gallery, Santa Monica, 1994, Art Space, San Antonio, Tex., 1995, also others. Treas. adv. bd. Inst. Contemporary Art, San Jose, 1992—96.

**WALDERA, WAYNE EUGENE,** crisis management executive; b. Cayuga, N.D., Mar. 23, 1930; s. Bernard Cyril and Eleanor Nee (Kugler) W.; m. Eva Jenzene Personius, Jan. 13, 1958; children: Anthony, Lori, Mia, Shauna. BSBA, N.D. State U., 1952. With Gamble-Skogmo, 1954-88; pres. Gamble div. Gamble-Skogmo, Mpls., 1972-88; pres., CEO Retail Resource Co., Mpls., 1988-89, Amdura Corp., Denver, 1989-92, also bd. dirs.; chmn. Sullivan Waldera, Inc., Mpls., 1992-93; prin., CEO Waldera & Co. Inc., Mpls., 1993—. 1st lt. USAF, 1952-54. Home: 12125 62nd St Waconia MN 55387-9411 Office: Waldera & Co Inc 700 Twelve Oaks Ctr Dr Ste 208 Wayzata MN 55391-1435 E-mail: wwaldera@uswest.net.

**WALDHAUSEN, JOHN ANTON,** retired surgeon, retired editor; b. NYC, May 22, 1929; s. Max. H. and Agnes H. (Stettner) W.; m. Marian Trescher, June 4, 1957; children: John H., Robert Rodney, Anthony Gordon Scarlett. BS magna cum laude, Coll. Great Falls, 1950; MD, St. Louis U., 1954. Diplomate Am. Bd. Surgery, Am. Bd. Thoracic Surgery. Intern Johns Hopkins Hosp., 1954-55, resident, 1955-57; clin. asst. Nat. Heart and Lung Inst., NIH, 1957-59; resident Hosp. U. Pa., 1959, Ind. U. Med. Ctr., 1960-62; practice medicine specializing in cardiothoracic surgery Indpls., 1962-66, Phila., 1966-70; mem. staff Milton S. Hershey Med. Ctr., Hershey, Pa., 1969-96. From instr. to asst. prof. Ind. U. Med. Ctr., 1962—66; assoc. prof. surgery U. Pa., Phila., 1966—70; prof. surgery Pa. State U. Coll. Medicine/Milton S. Hershey Med. Ctr, 1966—83, chmn. dept. surgery 1969—94, sr. mem. grad. faculty, 1970—94, interim provost, dean, 1972—73, assoc. dean health care, 1973—75, assoc. dean and dir. Univ. Physicians, 1993—96, J.W. Oswald prof., 1983—99, J.W. Oswald prof. emeritus, 1999—; trustee U. Great Falls, Mont., 2001—04. Mem. editl. bd. Jour. Cardiovasc. Surgery 1985-93, Jour. Pediatric Surgery, 1972-78, Jour. Thoracic and Cardiovasc. Surgery, 1982, editor, 1994-2000; cons. editor Archives of Surgery, 1972-74; contbr. chpts. to books and articles to med. jours. Recipient Career Devel. award USPHS, 1964. Fellow AAAS; mem. AMA, ACS (chpt. pres. 1974-75, gov. 1979-85, chmn. adv. coun. cardiothoracic surgery 1992-97), Am. Acad. Pediat., Am. Assn. Surgery of Trauma, Am. Coll. Cardiology (sec. 1981-82, trustee 1984-89, mem. editl. bd. jour. 1983, assoc. editor 1986-89), Am. Fedn. Clin. Rsch., Am. Heart Assn., Am. Physiol. Soc., Am. Soc. Artificial Internal Organs, Am. Assn. Thoracic Surgery (1st v.p. 1990-91, pres., 1991-92), Am. Surg. Assn. (1st v.p. 1984-85), Ctrl. Surg. Assn., Internat. Cardiovasc. Soc. (chpt. recorder 1969-74), Am. Assn. Thoracic Surgery (pres. 1977-78), Thoracic Surgery Dirs. Assn. (pres. 1977-79), Societe International de Chirurgie (membership chmn. 1987-92, treas. 1992-94), Soc. Clin. Surgery (treas. 1971-80, v.p. 1981-82, Pres. 1982-83), Soc. Surg. Chairmen, Soc. Thoracic Surgeons, Soc. Univ. Surgeons, Soc. Vascular Surgery, So. Surg. Assn., Sigma Xi, Alpha Omega Alpha. Home: 515 Bridgeview Dr Lemoyne PA 17043 Office: Pa State U Coll Med MS Hershey Med Ctr PO Box 850 Hershey PA 17033-0850 Office Phone: 717-531-8330. Personal E-mail: jwaldhausen@aol.com.

**WALDINGER, ROBERT JON,** psychiatrist; b. Omaha, Mar. 1, 1951; s. David and Miriam (Passman) W.; m. Jennifer Abby Stone, May 26, 1986; children: Daniel Cane, David Stone. AB, Harvard U., 1973, MD, 1978. Diplomate Am. Bd. Psychiatry and Neurology. Fellow in psychol. rsch. McLean Hosp., Belmont, Mass., 1982-85, asst. dir. residency tng., 1985-90; dir. tng. Mass. Mental Health Ctr., Boston, 1990-96; rsch. assoc. Judge Baker Children's Ctr., Boston, 1997—2003; assoc. prof. psychiatry Harvard Med. Sch., 2003—. Mem. faculty Boston Psychoanalytic Inst., 1987—; cons. Harvard U. Health Svc., Cambridge, Mass., 1984—. Author: Psychiatry for Medical Students, 1984, Effective Psychotherapy with Borderline Patients, 1987. Knox fellow Harvard U., 1973. Fellow Am. Psychiat. Assn. (Falk fellow 1980-82). Democrat. Mem.: Office: Brigham and Women's Hosp 1249 Boylston St Boston MA 02215-5794 Office Phone: 617-525-6133.

**WALDKOETTER, RAYMOND OLIVER,** psychologist, consultant; b. Indpls., Oct. 25, 1928; s. Raymond Oliver Waldkoetter, Sr. and Viola Simmons Waldkoetter; m. Mary Frances McBane, Sept. 25, 1953; children: Lisa K. Keenan, Greta A. Banner, Eric R., William H., Janet M. Turko, Olivia E. BS in Edn., Ind. U., 1951, MS in Edn., 1955, EdD in Psychol. Studies, 1963. Cert. psychologist Ind. Health Professions Bur. Dir. student activities U. Toledo, 1957—59; expatriate tutor Techiman Tng. Coll., Abetifi, Ghana, 1959—60; counselor Testing Bur. Depauw U., Greencastle, Ind., 1960—61;

rsch. psychologist Enlisted Evaluation Ctr., Ft. Harrison, Ind., 1961—63, tech. advisor, 1965—73; dean of students Shepherd Coll., Shepherdstown, W.Va., 1963—64; sr. rsch. psychologist Army Rsch. Inst., Alexandria, Va., 1974—82; consulting psychologist U.S. Army Soldier Support Ctr., Ft. Harrison, 1982—93; pvt. practice Greenwood, Ind., 1993—. Mem. bd. advisors The Monroe Inst., Faber, Va., 1986—. Capt. USMC, 1951—59. Recipient Harry Greer award, Internat. Mil. Testing Assn., USN, 1983, Comdrs. award for Civil Svc., Dept. of the Army, 1993. Mem.: APA, Masons, Phi Delta Kappa, Theta Xi. Methodist. Achievements include personnel rating form design; sound-wave acoustic therapy; occupational analysis for performance enhancement. Avocations: reading, parapsychology, travel. Home: 906 S Haven Rd Greenwood IN 46143-2623

**WALDMAN, AMY,** journalist; BA, Yale U., 1991. Freelance journalist, prof. U. Western Cape, South Africa, 1992—94; editor, writer Washington Monthly; editor Washington Post; metro desk reporter NY Times, 1997—2002, co-bur. chief New Delhi, 2002—05; nat. corr. Atlantic Monthly, Washington, 2005—. Recipient Disting. Feature Writing award, NY Newspaper Pub. Assn., Front Page award, Newswomen's Club NY, Overseas Press Club award for best bus. reporting in newspapers, 2006. Office: The Atlantic Monthly 600 New Hampshire Ave NW Washington DC 20037 Office Phone: 202-266-6000.*

**WALDMAN, CAROL,** dentist; Grad. in Esthetic Dentistry, Las Vegas Inst. Advanced Dentistry, 1997; grad. in Occlusion & Diagnosis & Treatment of Diseases of Temporal-Mandibular Joint, Dawson Centre Advanced Dental Studies. Sr. instr. Continuing Edn. Dept., Cosmetic Dentistry U. Toronto, 1998; asst. dir. & instr. New Millennium Dentistry. Mem.: Am. Acad. Cosmetic Dentistry, Toronto Acad. Cosmetic Dentistry (pres.-elect). Office: 808 York Mills Rd Toronto ON Canada Office Phone: 416-445-6000. Business E-Mail: cwaldman@cosmeticdentistry.net.

**WALDMAN, DANIEL,** lawyer; BA, Harvard U., 1977; JD, Columbia U., 1980. Bar: D.C. 1980. Clk. to Judge William A. Norris U.S. Ct. Appeals (9th cir.), 1980-82; assoc. Arnold & Porter, Washington, 1982—87, ptnr., 1987—96; gen. counsel Commodity Futures Trading Commn., Washington, 1996—99; ptnr., Derivatives Practice Group Arnold & Porter, Washington, 1999—. Office: Arnold & Porter 555 Twelfth St NW Washington DC 20004-1206 Office Phone: 202-942-5804. Office Fax: 202-942-5999. Business E-Mail: dan.waldman@aporter.com.

**WALDMAN, MICHAEL,** economist, educator; b. Paterson, N.J., May 12, 1955; s. Henry and Nettie Waldman; m. Karen Voris, July 9, 1982 (div. Jan. 1992); m. Lisa Berki, July 18, 1999; children: David Henry, Emma Nicole. BS in Econs., MIT, 1977; PhD in Econs., U. Pa., 1982. From asst. prof. to prof. econs. UCLA, 1983-93; prof. econs. Cornell U., Ithaca, NY, 1991-97, Charles H. Dyson prof. in mgmt., 1997—. Vis. prof. econs. Yale U. Sch. Orgn. and Mgmt., New Haven, 1989—90, U. Chgo. Grad. Sch. Bus., 1997—99. Co-editor Jour. Econ. Perspectives, 2000—; assoc. editor Quar. Jour. Econs., 2000—; contbr. articles to profl. jours. Mem.: Western Econ. Assn., Soc. Labor Economists, Royal Econ. Soc., Econometric Soc., Am. Econ. Assn. (program com. 2004). Office: Cornell U Johnson Grad Sch Mgmt Sage Hall Ithaca NY 14853 Business E-Mail: mw46@cornell.edu.

**WALDMAN, SEYMOUR MORTON,** lawyer; b. N.Y.C., Aug. 6, 1926; s. Louis and Bella B. Waldman; m. Lois Citrin, Aug. 5, 1951; children: David, Daniel, Michael, Ellen. BA, Columbia U., 1948, LLB, 1950. Bar: N.Y. 1950, U.S. Ct. Appeals (1st, 2d, 3d, 4th, 5th, 6th and D.C. cirs.), U.S. Dist. Ct. (so. dist.) N.Y., U.S. Dist. Ct. (ea. dist.) N.Y., U.S. Supreme Ct. 1956. From assoc. to ptnr. Waldman & Waldman, N.Y.C., 1950—82; ptnr., of counsel Vladeck, Waldman, Elias & Engelhard, P.C., 1982—2005. Village atty. Village of Croton-on-Hudson, NY, 1972—2005. Chair zoning bd. appeals Village of Croton-on-Hudson, 1962—72; trustee Hosp. Joint Diseases Orthopaedic Inst., 1968—93. With USN, 1944—46. Mem. ABA, N.Y. State Bar Assn., Phi Beta Kappa. Avocation: tennis. Office: Vladeck Waldman Elias & Engelhard PC 1501 Broadway Ste 800 New York NY 10036-5560

**WALDMANN, THOMAS ALEXANDER,** medical researcher, physician; b. NYC, Sept. 21, 1930; s. Charles Elizabeth (Sipos) Waldmann; m. Katharine Emory Spreng, Mar. 29, 1958; children: Richard Allen, Robert James, Carol Ann. AB, U. Chgo., 1951; MD, Harvard U., 1955; PhD (hon.), U. Med. Sch., Debrecin, Hungary, 1991. Diplomate Am. Bd. Allergy and Immunology. Intern Mass. Gen. Hosp., Boston, 1955—56; clin. assoc. Nat. Cancer Inst. NIH, Bethesda, Md., 1956—58, sr. investigator, 1958—68, head immunophysiology sect., 1968—73, chief metabolism br., 1971—. Cons. WHO, 1975, 78; bd. dirs., v.p. Found. for Advanced Edn. in Scis., Bethesda, 1980—2002, treas., 1988—90, v.p., 1990—92; William Dameshek vis. prof. U. Calif., Irvine, 1984; mem. med. adv. bd. Howard Hughes Med. Inst., 1987—93; vis. com. mem. Harvard Med. Sch., Boston, 1988—94; mem. sci. adv. com., chmn. Mass. Gen. Hosp., 1992—96; chmn. sci. adv. bd. Health-Care Investment Corp., Princeton, NJ, 1986—2003. Author: Plasma Protein Metabolism, 1970; contbr. articles to profl. jours. With USPHS, 1956—58, 1959—63, 1975—94. Named Man of Yr., Am. Leukemia Soc., 1980; recipient Henry M. Stratton medal, Am. Hematology Soc., 1977, G. Burroughs Mider award, NIH, 1980, Disting. Svc. medal, Dept. Health and Human Svcs., 1983, Abbott Lab. award in Clin. and Diagnostic Immunology, Am. Soc. Microbiology, 2002, Debrecen prize, Debrecen Med. Sch., Hungary, 2005. Fellow: Am. Acad. Allergy (Bela Schick award 1974, John M. Shelton award 1984, Lila Gruber prize 1986, Simon Shubitz prize 1987, CIBA-GEIGY Drew award 1987, Milken Family Med. Found. Disting. Basic Scientist prize 1991, Artois Latour Internat. Rsch. prize 1991, Bristol-Myers Cancer prize 1992, Paul Ehrlich medal 1997); mem.: NAS (chmn. 1985—), Clin. Immunology Soc. (pres. 1988), Am. Soc. Clin. Investigation (mem. editl. bd. 1978—80, 1983—88), Assn. Am. Physicians, Hungarian Acad. Scis. (hon.), Inst. Medicine, Am. Acad. Arts and Scis. Achievements include research in defining of structure of multisubunit IL-2 receptor; identifying novel cytokine IL-15; discovery of forms of IL-2R-directed therapy using alpha and beta-emitting radionuclide chelate versions of humanized monoclonal antibodies (Zenapax) for treatment of cancer; analysis of immunoglobulin gene rearrangements to define clonality and classifying human lymphoid neoplasia; discovery of intestinal lymphangeictasia and allergic gastroenteropathy. Office: Nat Inst Health 10 Center Dr Bethesda MD 20892-1374 Office Phone: 301-496-6656. Business E-Mail: tawald@helix.nih.gov.

**WALDMEIR, PETER NIELSEN,** retired journalist; b. Detroit, Jan. 16, 1931; s. Joseph John and Helen Sarah (Nielsen) W.; m. Marilyn C. Choma; children— Peter William, Patti Ann, Lindsey Marilyn, Christopher Norman. Student, Wayne State U., 1949-58. From mem. staff to sports columnist Detroit News, 1949—72, gen. columnist, 1972—2004; ret., 2004. Pres. Old Newsboys Goodfellow Fund, Detroit, 1988; mem. city coun. Grosse Pointe Woods, Mich., 2005. With USMC, 1951-53. Recipient Headliners award Nat. Headliners Club, 1971, SDX Lifetime Achievement award, 2000; named Mich. Sports Writer of Yr., Nat. Sportscasters and Sportswriters, 1967, 69, 71; Heart award Variety Club Internat., 1985; inducted Mich. Journalism Hall of Fame, 2000. Mem. Sigma Delta Chi. Roman Catholic. Personal E-mail: pwaldmeir@aol.com.

**WALDO, JAMES CHANDLER,** lawyer; b. Seattle, Oct. 23, 1948; s. Burton Chandler and Margaret (Hoar) W.; m. Sharon B. Waldo; children: Sara K., William K., John J. Grad., Whitman Coll., 1970; JD, Willamette U., 1974. Bar: Wash. 1974, U.S. Ct. Appeals (9th cir.) 1976. Exec. asst. Dept. of Labor, Washington, 1974-76; asst. U.S. atty. Justice Dept., Seattle, 1976-79; of counsel ESTEP & LI, Seattle, 1979-80; ptnr. Gordon, Thomas, Honeywell, Malanca, Peterson & Daheim LLP, Seattle, 1981—. Chmn. N.W. Renewable Resources Ctr., Seattle, 1984-97, Wash. State Energy Strategy Com., 1991-93; spl. counsel on Water for Gov., 2001—04. Trustee Western Wash. U., 1981-93. Recipient Outstanding Alumnus of Yr. Whitman Coll., 1994, Dir.'s award Wash. Dept. Fisheries, 1986, Pres.'s award Assn. Wash. Bus., 1988, Outstanding Citizen award Western Assn. Fish & Wildlife Agys., 1987, Merit award, Am. Water Works Assn., 2005. Mem. Am. Water Works Assn. (Award of Merit 2005). Office: Gordon Thomas Honeywell Malanca Peterson & Daheim LLP PO Box 1157 Tacoma WA 98401-1157 Office Phone: 253-620-6541.

**WALDO, ROBERT LELAND,** retired insurance company executive; b. Pittsville, Wis., Sept. 1, 1923; s. Elmer Harley and Edith Viola (Senter) W.; m. Elaine Anne Jossie, June 4, 1947; children: Daniel Robert, Thomas Parker, Susan Jeanne. BA, U. Wis., 1949, JD, 1951. Assoc. atty. Foley & Lardner, Milw., 1951-59; asst. sec., asst. gen. counsel Wis. Gas Co., Milw., 1959-69; v.p., gen. counsel Verex Corp. and Subss., Madison, Wis., 1969-72; exec. v.p., sec. Verex Corp. and subs., Madison, Wis., 1972-78, pres., chief operating officer, 1978-82, pres., chief exec. officer, 1982-85, chmn., chief exec. officer, 1985-86. Served as sgt. U.S. Army, 1943-46, ETO. Mem. Wis. Bar Assn., Dane County Bar Assn., Mortgage Ins. Co.'s Am. (pres. 1980-82), Maple Bluff Country Club. Republican. Methodist. Avocations: travel, golf. Home: 818 Charing Cross Rd Madison WI 53704-6010

**WALDOCK, WILLIAM DAVID,** aerospace transportation executive; b. Ft. Worth, Tex., Aug. 4, 1952; s. Wallace Gordon and Annabelle (Wolfe) W.; m. Barbara A. Wisler, Sept. 14, 1974; children: Andrew, Kathleen. BA in History, U. Fla., 1975; student, Miami-Dade Coll., Miami, Fla., 1977-78; M of Aero. Sci. with honors, Embry-Riddle Aero. U., 1982; postgrad., Kennedy-Western U. Prof. aero. sci. Embry-Riddle Aero. U., Prescott, Ariz., 1982—, chief investigator aircraft accidents, 1991—, assoc. dir. Ctr. Aerospace Safety Edn., 1986—, dir. Robertson Aviation Safety Ctr., 1995—. Pres., chief cons. Sys. Safety, Inc., Prescott, 1990—; cons. Am. West Airlines, Phoenix, 1996-99; presenter numerous safety confs. Contbr. articles to profl. publs.; guest various T.V. shows. Lt. comdr. USCG, 1975-96, ret. Mem. SAFE Assn. (Gen. Spruance award for Outstanding Contbns. to Safety Through Edn. 1990), Aircraft Owners and Pilots Assn., Aircraft Rescue and Firefighting Working Group, Am. Soc. Safety Engrs., World Safety Orgn. (cert.), Internat. Soc. Air Safety Investigators (pres. Ariz. chpt. 1987—). Achievements include over 150 field investigations; research in accident history. Office: Embry-Riddle Aero U Bldg 21 3700 Willow Creek Rd Prescott AZ 86301-3721 Office Phone: 928-777-6956. Personal E-mail: wwaldock@msn.com.

**WALDREP, B. DWAIN,** education educator; b. Decatur, Ala., Oct. 11, 1954; s. Emmett N. and Melva Jo Waldrep; m. Phyllis M. Morgan, June 9, 1971; 1 child, Matthew N. BA, Southeastern Bible Coll., 1984; MA, U. Ala., 1985; MABS, Dallas Theol. Sem., 1991; PhD, Auburn U., 2001. Prof. Southeastern Bible Coll., Birmingham, Ala., 1990—; adj. prof. U. of Ala., 2002—. Contbr. articles to profl. jours. Specialist 5 U.S. Army, 1971—76, US and Korea. Mem.: So. Hist. Assn., Ala. Hist. Assn. Office Phone: 205-970-9231.

**WALDRON, GERARD J.,** lawyer; b. Nov. 20, 1960; BA, U. Va., 1982; M in Pub. Policy, with honors, Duke U., 1990, JD with high honors, 1990. Bar: Pa. 1990, DC 1997. Staff for US Rep. Edward Markey (D-MA) US Ho. of Reps, Washington, 1982—85, staff, sub-com. energy, 1985—87, staff, sub-com. telecom., 1987, sr. counsel, sub-com. telecom., 1991—95; law clk. for Judge Dickson Phillips US Ct. Appeals (4th cir.), Washington, 1990—91; ptnr., Comm. Practice Group Covington & Burling, Washington. Author: Keep States Off the Net Backbone: Only the FCC Has Authority to Regulate Interstate Web Traffic, 2000, FCC Clarifies Telemarketing Rules, 2005. Office: Covington & Burling 1201 Pennsylvania Ave NW Washington DC 20004-2401 Office Phone: 202-662-5360. Office Fax: 202-662-6291. Business E-Mail: gwaldron@cov.com.

**WALDRON, JEREMY JAMES,** law educator; b. Invercargill, Southland, New Zealand, Oct. 13, 1953; s. Francis Herbert and Joyce Annette (Ainge) W.; m. Helen McGimpsey, Jan. 26, 1974 (div. Oct. 1989); 1 child, Samuel James. BA with honors, U. Otago, New Zealand, 1974, LLB with honors, 1978; DPhil, Oxford U., 1986. Bar: New Zealand 1978. Asst. lectr. philosophy U. Otago, 1975-78; fellow in polit. theory Lincoln Coll., Oxford, Eng., 1980-82; lectr. in polit. theory U. Edinburgh, Scotland, 1982-87; prof. law U. Calif., Berkeley, 1987—96; Laurence S. Rockefeller Univ. prof. of politics Princeton U., 1996—97; Maurice and Hilda Friedman prof. law Columbia U., NYC, 1997—2004, Univ. prof., 2005—06, NYU, 2006—. Editor: collection of essays Theories of Rights, 1984, Nonsense Upon Stilts, 1987; author: (textbook) The Law, 1990, (monograph) The Right to Private Property, 1988; contbr. articles to profl. jours. Avocations: romance, music, travel. Home: 19 Edwards Pl Princeton NJ 08540-5113 Office: NYU Sch Law 40 Washington Sq S, 411K New York NY 10012 Office Phone: 212-998-6573. Office Fax: 212-998-4894. E-mail: jeremy.waldron@nyu.edu.*

**WALDRON, KAREN,** development, construction, and management company executive; m. Shawn Ricci. Chairperson/sr. v.p. F&W Mgmt.; pres. Bent Tree Farm Ltd., The Ctr. at Walnut Grove; chairperson, CEO Fralin and Waldron, Inc., Roanoke, Va. Mem. bd. visitors Radford U.; mem. exec. bd. Roanoke Valley Horse Show; pub. bd. dirs., chair Va. Horse Ctr. Avocations: horse industry, Pilates instruction, yoga, dance. Office: Fralin and Waldron Inc Ste 200 PO Box 24018 3130 Chaparral Dr Roanoke VA 24018

**WALDRON, THEODORE CHARLES,** physician; b. West Hazleton, Pa., June 3, 1946; s. Leonard Raymond Waldron; m. Gloria Jean Koziel, June 24, 1978; children: Theodore Leonard, Diane Christopher. BS in Biology, Alliance Coll., 1968; D of Osteopathy, Phila. Coll. Osteopathic Medicine, 1978. Diplomate Am. Osteo. Coll. Gen. Practice; diplomate Nat. Bd. Examiners of Osteo. Medicine and Surgery; diplomate State Bd. Osteo. Examiners; cert. gen./family practice; lic. Pa., S.C. Gen. practice medicine, Conyngham, Pa., 1979-00; chief family practice dept. Hazleton St. Joseph Med. Ctr., 1989-90; physician specialist II White Haven (Pa.) Ctr., 1993-96; disability physician specialist Pa. Dept. Labor and Industry Bur. Disability Determination, Wilkes-Barre, 1996—; med. dir. Lattimer ICF-MR Facility, 1995—2000. Med. dir. Hazleton Nursing & Geriatric Ctr., Mountain City Convalescent Ctr., Hazleton, 1983-91; occupational health physician Workmed, Hazleton, 1991-93. Dir. vector control for Lycoming, Clinton, Snyder and Union counties, Pa. following Hurricane Agnes flooding, 1972. Served as sgt. USAR, N.G., 1969-76. Mem. Am. Osteopathic Assn., Pa. Osteopathic Med. Assn., Osteopathic Coll. Family Practice, Pa. Osteopathic Gen. Practice Soc., S.C. Osteopathic Med. Assn. Republican. Roman Catholic. Avocations: fishing, photography, gardening, electronics, science. Home: 146 Hickory Rd Sugarloaf PA 18249-9556 E-mail: twaldron@gmpexpress.net.

**WALDROP, FRANCIS NEIL,** physician; b. Asheville, N.C., Oct. 5, 1926; s. Troy Lester and Emma Louise (Ballard) W.; m. Eleanor Dorothy Wickes, June 10, 1950; children: — Mark Lester, Barbara Louise. AB, U. Minn., 1946; MD, George Washington U., 1950. Intern George Washington U. Hosp., Washington, 1950-51; resident St. Elizabeth's Hosp., Washington, 1951-54, med. officer, 1951-71; dir. manpower and tng. programs NIMH, Rockville, Md., 1972-75; dep. administr. Alcohol, Drug Abuse and Mental Health Adminstrn., HEW, Rockville, 1975-79; ret., 1979. Clin. prof. psychiatry George Washington U. Recipient Superior Service award HEW, 1962, Disting. Service award, 1964 Fellow Am. Psychiat. Assn. (Vestermark award 1980). Achievements include research, publs. in field. Home: 1775 Elton Rd Silver Spring MD 20903-1726

**WALDROP, ROSMARIE,** writer; b. Kitzingen, Germany, Aug. 24, 1935; arrived in U.S., 1958; d. Josef and Friederike Sebald; m. Keith Waldrop, Jan. 20, 1959. Student, U. Wurzburg, 1954—56, U. Freiburg, 1957—58; MA, U. Mich., 1960, PhD, 1966. Asst. prof. Wesleyan U., 1964—70. Vis. writer Southeastern Mass. U., 1977; vis. lectr. Tufts U., 1979—81; vis. assoc. prof. Brown U., 1977—78, 1983, 97. Author: The Hanky of Pippin's Daughter, 1987, Reluctant Gravities, 1999, A Form of Taking It All, 2001, Lavish Absence: Recalling and Rereading Edmond Jabes, 2002, Blindsight, 2003, Dissonance (If you are interested): Collected Essays, 2005, Curves to the Apple, New Directions, 2006, translator books and poems. Recipient Writer's

award, Lila Wallace Readers Digest, N.Y.C., 1999—2002; fellow, NEA, 1994; grantee, Found. for Contemporary Performance Arts, 2003; scholar, Brown U. Fellow: Am. Acad. Arts & Sciences; mem.: PEN. Home: 71 Elmgrove Ave Providence RI 02906

**WALEK, DAVID B.,** lawyer; b. Ft. Monmouth, N.J., May 18, 1954; s. Walter J. and Charlotte H. (Haag) W.; m. Elizabeth R. Gibson; children: Christopher, Emily, Merritt. BA cum laude, Yale U., 1976; JD, Harvard U., 1980. Bar: Mass., 1980. Assoc. Ropes & Gray, Boston, 1980-89, ptnr. corp. dept., 1989—, co-head tech. co. practice group. Lectr. Sloane Sch. Mgmt., MIT. Chmn. Artists for Humanity, Boston. Mem.: ABA, Boston Bar Assn. Office: Ropes & Gray 1 International Pl Boston MA 02110-2624 Home: 279 South Ave Weston MA 02493 Office Phone: 617-951-7388. Office Fax: 617-951-7050. Business E-Mail: david.walek@ropesgray.com.

**WALEN, HARRY LEONARD,** historian, lecturer, author; b. Winchester, Mass, June 26, 1915; s. Harry Leonard and Alice (Garland) W.; m. Elizabeth Rowe Benson, June 26, 1939; children: Harry Benson, Kimball Frederick, Robert Leonard. AB cum laude, Harvard U., 1937, AM, 1942. Tchr. Los Alamos Ranch Sch., N.Mex., 1937-42, head English dept. N.Mex., 1939-42; tchr. English Groton Sch., Mass., 1942-46; instr. English, faculty marshal Newton Jr. Coll., 1946-51; tchr. English and journalism Newton HS, Newtonville, Mass., 1946-51, administr., 1951-55; directing editor secondary sch. English textbooks Ginn and Co., Boston, 1955-61; prin. Needham HS, Mass., 1961-72, career and post secondary guidance counselor Mass., 1972-79. Mem. Regional Interviewing Com. for Overseas Grants and Fellowships, 1961-84; mem. planning com. Task Force on High Sch. Graduation Requirements, Mass Dept. Edn., 1976-80. Author: (books) The Family Travel-Camper, 1955, (with E. Gordon and others) Types of Literature, American Literature, (with English Literature, 1964, The Memory Book of the New England Association of Teachers of English, 1981, The Sons of the American Revolution 1962-82: An Historical Anthology, 1984, Images and Perceptions, 1996, The Birds of Budapest, 2004; (monographs) English Learning Environments, 1972, History of the Order of Founders and Patriots of America, 1982, Centennial History, 1996; co-author Alluring Rockport, rev. edit. 1986, The Little Old Meeting House and How It Grew; (poetry) Images and Perceptions, 1996; editor The English Leaflet, 1947-54; cons. editor on career edn. New Voices Series, 1978; poet laureate, Rockport, 1998, 99-; contbr. chpts., articles, poems to books, profl. jour. and periodicals. Alderman City of Newton, Mass., 1961-72; corp. mem. USS Mass. Meml. Com., Inc., 1972—, bd. dir., 1984-91, honorary dir., 1995—; chmn. edn. com. N.E. Conf. NCCJ, 1972-82, mem. study mission to Israel, 1974; vice chmn. New Eng. Conf. on Quality of Life, Boston, 1973; mem. Newton Regional Adv. Manpower Planning Bd., 1973-77; pres. counseling svc. YMCA, Greater Boston, 1976-7; chmn. Newton Highlands Bd. Christian Edn., 1974-75; pres. bd. trustees weekday ch. sch.; 1st Congl. Ch., Rockport, Mass., ch. historian, 1982-2002; del. Mass. Conf. United Ch. Christ, 1989-96. John Hay fellow, 1965; Mass. Dept. Edn. Commonwealth fellow, 1971; recipient citation U.S. Commr. Edn., 1971, citation New Eng. Assn. Schs. and Colls., 1984, cert. of Appreciation, City of Newton, 1971, Service award, YMCA, 1978. Mem. Nat. Council Tchr. English (assoc. chmn. nat. conv. 1965, chmn., co-founder Emeritus Assembly 1979-83, various other coms. and offices, Citation 1969), Nat. Assn. Secondary Sch. Prin., Headmasters Assn. (life), New Eng. Assn. Tchr. English (life, past pres., chmn. ann. C. S. Thomas award com. 1975-96, historian 1978—, Thomas award 1978), Mass. Secondary Sch. Prins. Assn. (diploma standards com. 1973-78, Bronze plaque 1974), Mass. Council Tchr. English (co-founder), Mass. Schoolmasters Club (past pres., hon. life), MENSA, Friends of Jackson Homestead, Newton Hist. Soc. (life, past pres.), Los Alamos (N.Mex.) Hist. Soc. (life), Sandy Bay Hist. Soc. (pres. 1983-86), Greater Boston Guidance Club (hon.), Nat. Gavel Soc., New Eng. Hist. and Geneal. Soc., SAR (pres. state 1979-81, nat. trustee 1981-83, historian gen. 1983-86, sec. Mus. Bd. 1982-88, Minuteman award 1985), Gen. Soc. Mayflower Descs. (mem. nat. exec. com. 1990-93), Mass. Soc. Mayflower Descs. (gov. 1985-88, dep. gov. gen. 1988-93), Pilgrim John Howland Soc. (pres. 1987-99, pres. emeritus 1999—, led pilgrimage to Eng., 1989), Mass. Huguenot Soc. (pres. 1990-92, nat. del. 1983-92), Descs. Colonial Clergy, Soc. Colonial Wars, Navy League US (life), Sons and Daus. of 1st Settlers of Newbury (pres. 1982-84), Piscataqua Pioneers (pres. 1990-91), Order of Crown of Charlemagne, Order Founders and Patriots (nat. treas. 1978-81, dep. gov. gen. 1981-84, exec. com. 1992-2000, councillor gen. Mass. 1984—, NH, 1987-90, 93—, gov. 1992-95, councillor gen. 1993—, Nat. Disting. Svc. award 1996), Boston Athenaeum, Harvard Club, Boston Authors Club (pres. 1995-96), English Lunch Club (pres. 1975-82), Friday Evening Club (most venerable 1979-86), Sandy Bay Yacht Club, Masons (32d degree, 50-Yr. award). Home: 16 Rockrimmon Rd Kingston NH 03848-3037

**WALENDOWSKI, GEORGE JERRY,** accounting and business educator; b. Han-Minden, Germany, Mar. 25, 1947; arrived in US, 1949; s. Stefan (dec.) and Eugenia (Lewandowska) W. AA, LA City Coll., 1968; BS, Calif. State U., LA, 1970, MBA, 1972; cert., Inst. Mgmt. Accts., 2004. Cert. community coll. instr. acctg. and mgmt., Calif. Acct. Unocal (formerly Union Oil Co. Calif.), LA, 1972-76, data control supr., 1976-78, acctg. analyst, 1978-79; sr. fin. analyst Hughes Aircraft Co., El Segundo, Calif., 1979-83, fin. planning specialist, 1983-84, program controls specialist, 1984-86, bus. mgmt. specialist, 1986-92, bus. analyst, 1993-95. Adj. instr. bus. math. L.A. City Coll., 1976-80, acctg., 1980-97, 99—, mem. acctg. adv. com., 1984, 87, 89, 99, acctg. and bus. Pasadena City Coll., 1996-2001, 2003—; reviewer conf. papers. Contbr. articles to profl. jours. Mem. commn. Rep. Pres. Task Force, 1986. Recipient Medal of Merit, Rep. Presdl. Task Force, 1984, cert. of merit, named registered life mem. commn., 1986, named Honor Roll life mem., 1989; recipient Vice-Presdl. Cert. of Commendation, Rep. Nat. Hall of Fame, 1992, Rep. Congl. cert. of Appreciation, 1993, Rep. Congl. Order of Freedom award Nat. Rep. Congl. Com., 1995, Recognition award LA chpt. Strategic Leadership Forum, 1983. Mem.: High Potentials Soc., Mysterium Soc., Internat. High IQ Soc., Midwest Fin. Assn. (program rev. com. 2002), Ea. Fin. Assn. (program rev. com. 2000), Soc. Advancement Mgmt. (editl. rev. bd. Advanced Mgmt. Jour. 1999—, selection com. mem. Internat. Conf. 2000), Nat. Bus. Edn. Assn., Am. Acctg. Assn. (competitive manuscript com. 1997—98, reviewer tchg. curr. sect. 1998, tchg. and curriculum sect. two-yr. coll. issues com. 1998—99), Inst. Mgmt. Accts. (author's cir. L.A. chpt. 1980, mem. editl. adv. bd. Strategic Fin. and Mgmt. Acctg. Quarterly 2002—, Robert Half author's trophy 1980, cert. of appreciation 1980, 1983), Acad. Mgmt. (reviewer social issues in mgmt. divsn. 1991, mgmt. edn. and devel. divsn. program rev. com. 1998, 1999, reviewer bus. policy and strategy divsn. 2002—04, reviewer for acad. of mngmt. learning & ed. Jour. 2003, Tchg. and Cirriculum Innovative Tchg. award com. 2004—05, Bus. Policy and Strategy Divsn. Outstanding Reviewer award 2004), Delta Pi Epsilon (proposal reviewer 2005), Beta Gamma Sigma. Republican. Roman Catholic. Home: 426 N Citrus Ave Los Angeles CA 90036-2632 Office: LA City Coll 855 N Vermont Ave Los Angeles CA 90029 Personal E-mail: geowalen@sbcglobal.net.

**WALES, GWYNNE HUNTINGTON,** retired lawyer; b. Evanston, Ill., Apr. 18, 1933; s. Robert Willett and Solace (Huntington) W.; m. Janet McCobb, Feb. 8, 1957; children — Thomas Gwynne, Catherine Anne, Louise Carrie. AB, Princeton U., 1954; JD, Harvard U., 1961. Bar: N.Y. 1962. Assoc. White & Case, N.Y.C., 1961-69, ptnr., 1969-2000, resident ptnr. Brussels, 1969-75, Ankara, Turkey, 1998-2000. Served with USN, 1954-58. Mem.: Am. Law Inst. (life) Round Hill (Greenwich, Conn.). Home: 1406 Brookside Dr Fairfield CT 06824

**WALES, JIMMY DONAL (JIMMY DONAL "JIMBO" WALES),** Internet company executive; b. Huntsville, Ala., Aug. 7, 1966; m. Christine Wales; 1 child, Kira. Attended, Auburn U.; attended PhD programs in finance, U. Ala., Ind. U. Faculty mem. U. Ala., Ind. U.; futures and options trader Chgo. Options Assocs., Chgo.; founder Nupedia.com, 1999—2000; CEO Bomis, Inc., San Diego, 2000—01; founder Wikipedia (Parent orgn.-Wikimedia Found., Inc.), 2001—, Wikimedia Found. Inc., St. Petersburg, Fla., 2003—,

pres., dir., chmn. bd. trustee, 2005—; founder Wikia, 2004—. Nominee Rave award in Technology, WIRED, 2005; recipient 100 Most Influential People, Time Mag., 2006. Office: Wikimedia Found Inc 204 37th Ave N Saint Petersburg FL 33704*

**WALES, ROSS ELLIOT,** lawyer; b. Youngstown, Ohio, Oct. 17, 1947; s. Craig C. and Beverly (Bromley) W.; m. Juliana Fraser, Sept. 16, 1972; children: Dod E., J. Craig. AB, Princeton U., 1969; JD, U. Va., 1974. Bar: Ohio 1974, U.S. Dist. Ct. (so. dist.) Ohio 1974, U.S. Ct. Appeals (5th cir.) 1979. Assoc. Taft, Stettinius & Hollister, Cin., 1974-81, ptnr., 1981—. Pres. U.S. Swimming, Inc., Colorado Springs, 1979-84, U.S. Aquatic Sports, Inc., Colorado Springs, 1984-88, 94-98; dir. Child Welfare League Am., 2003-, treas., 2005-06, chmn.-elect, 2006—. Pres. Cin. Active to Support Edn., 1987-88; chmn. sch. tax levy campaign, Cin., 1987; trustee The Childrens Home Cin. 1987—, v.p., 1995-98, pres., 1998-02; bd. dirs., sec., v.p. FINA Bur., 1988-2000; trustee Cin. State Tech. and C.C., 1994—, sec. 1995-98, vice-chmn., 1998-00, chair 2000-02; pres. Cin. Arts Sch., 2000-01; sec. Greater Cin. Arts and Edn. Ctr., 1996-05; mem. Anti-Doping Rev. Bd., U.S. Anti-Doping Agy., Colo. Springs. Mem. ABA, Ohio Bar Assn., Cin. Bar Assn., Internat. Swimming Fedn. of Lausanne, Switzerland (sec. 1988-92, v.p. 1992-2000). Presbyterian. Office: 425 Walnut St Ste 1800 Cincinnati OH 45202-3957 Office Phone: 513-357-9351. Business E-Mail: wales@taftlaw.com

**WALES, WALTER D.,** physicist, researcher; b. Oneonta, N.Y., Aug. 2, 1933; s. Walter D. and Anna Laura (Brockway) W.; m. Margaret Irene Keiter, June 19, 1955; children: Stephen Dirk, Carolyn Sue. BA, Carleton Coll., 1954; MS, Calif. Inst. Tech., 1955, PhD, 1960. Instr. physics U. Pa., Phila., 1959-62, asst. prof., 1962-64, assoc. prof., 1964-72, prof., 1972—, chmn. dept. physics, 1973-82, assoc. dean, 1982-87, acting dean, 1987-88, assoc. dean, 1988-92, dep. provost, 1992-95, interim dean, 1996-98, ombudsman, 1999-2001, interim assoc. provost, 2002—04; assoc. dir. Princeton (N.J.)-Pa. Accelerator, 1968-71; staff physicist AEC, 1972-73. Fellow Am. Phys. Soc.; mem. Am. Assn. Physics Tchrs. Achievements include research in exptl. particle physics. Home: 404 Drew Ave Swarthmore PA 19081-2406 Office: 209 S 33rd St Philadelphia PA 19104-6317 Office Phone: 215-898-7942. Business E-Mail: wales@physics.upenn.edu.

**WALGREN, DOUG,** lawyer, former congressman; b. Dec. 28, 1940; married. BA, Dartmouth Coll.; LL.B., Stanford U. Bar: Pa., Calif. Staff atty. Neighborhood Legal Services; individual and corp. practice law, 1969-76; chmn. subcom. on sci. rsch. and tech. 98th-100th Congress from 18th Dist. Pa.; chmn. subcom. on commerce, consumer protection and competitiveness 101st Congress; of counsel Drinker Biddle & Reath LLP, Washington, 2002—. Bd. mem. Nat. Ctr. for Rehabilitation Med., NIH, Ctr. Organ Recovery and Edn. Named Nat. Sci. Found. Legislator of Yr., 1989. Mem.: Calif. Bar Assn., Pa. Bar Assn. Office: Drinker Biddle & Reath LLP Ste 1100 1500 K St NW Washington DC 20005-1209 Office Phone: 202-842-8806. Business E-Mail: douglas.walgren@dbr.com.

**WALGREN, FRANCES J.,** art appraiser; MA in Art History, Queens Coll., NY, 1985; attended, Parsons Sch. Design, NY, Am. Coll., Paris. With Christie's, NYC, 1991—; specialist in books and manuscripts, dept. head, N.Am. Catalogued and auctioned the Fox-Bute Set of Audubon's Birds of America (2000) for $8 million, a world auction record for any printed book. Office: Christie's/NY 20 Rockefeller Plz New York NY 10020 Office Phone: 212-636-2665. Office Fax: 212-636-4928. Business E-Mail: fwahlgren@christies.com.

**WALI, MOHAN KISHEN,** environmental scientist, forester, educator; b. Kashmir, India, Mar. 1, 1937; came to U.S., 1969, naturalized, 1975; s. Jagan Nath and Somavati (Wattal) W.; m. Sarla Safaya, Sept. 25, 1960; children: Pamela, Promod. BS, U. Jammu and Kashmir, 1957; MS, U. Allahabad, India, 1960; PhD, U. B.C., Can., 1970. Lectr. S.P. Coll., Srinagar, Kashmir, 1963-65; rsch. fellow U. Copenhagen, 1965-66; grad. fellow U. B.C., 1967-69; asst. prof. biology U. N.D., Grand Forks, 1969-73, assoc. prof., 1973-79, prof., 1979-83, Hill rsch. prof., 1973; dir. Forest River Biology Area Field Sta., 1970-79, Project Reclamation, 1975-83; spl. asst. to univ. pres., 1977-82; staff ecologist Grand Forks Energy Rsch. Lab. U.S. Dept. Interior, 1974-75; prof. Coll. Environ. Sci. and Forestry SUNY, Syracuse, 1983-89, dir. grad. program environ. sci., 1983-85, prof. Sch. Natural Resources, 1990—, dir. Sch. Natural Resources, assoc. dean Coll. Agr., 1990-93; dir. Environ. Sci. Grad. program Ohio State U., Columbus, 2001—. Vice chmn. N.D. Air Pollution Adv. Coun., 1981-83; co-chair IV Internat. Congress on Ecology, 1986. Editor: Some Environmental Aspects of Strip-Mining in North Dakota, 1973, Prairie: A Multiple View, 1975, Practices and Problems of Land Reclamation in Western North America, 1975, Ecology and Coal Resource Development, 1979, Ecosystem Rehabilitation-Preamble to Sustainable Development, 1992; co-editor Agriculture and the Environment, 1993; sr. editor Reclamation Rev., 1976-80, chief editor, 1980-81; chief editor Reclamation and Revegetation Rsch., 1982-87; contbr. articles to profl. jours. Recipient B.C. Gamble Disting. Tchg. and Svc. award, U. ND, 1977. Fellow AAAS, Am. Acad. Scis. India; mem. Ecol. Soc. Am. (chmn. sect. internat. activities 1980-84), Bot. Ecol. Soc., Can. Bot. Assn. (dir. ecology sect. 1976-79, v.p. 1982-83), Am. Soc. Agronomy, Am. Inst. Biol. Sci. (gen. chmn. 34th ann. meeting), Internat. Assn. Ecolog (co-chmn. IV Internat. Congress Ecology), Internat. Soc. Soil Sci., N.D. Acad. Sci. (chmn. editl. com. 1979-81), Sigma Xi (nat. lectr. 1983-85, pres. Ohio State chpt. 1993-94, pres. Syracuse chpt. 1984-85, Outstanding Rsch. award U. N.D. chpt. 1975). Office: Ohio State U Sch Environ and Natural Resources 2021 Coffey Rd Columbus OH 43210-1044 Business E-Mail: wali.1@osu.edu.

**WALK, LOUIS BERNARD,** physician; b. Lacona, Iowa, Apr. 8, 1930; s. William J. Walk and Veronica M. Endres. BS, Drake U., 1953, MS, 1958; DO, Coll. Med. and Surgery, Des Moines, 1966. Diplomate Am. Bd. Family Practice. With med. dept. US Army, 1967—75; resident in family medicine William Beaumont Med. Ctr., El Paso, Tex., 1970—73; solo practice family practice clinic Silvis, Ill., 1975—96; physician Iowa, Ill., Mo., Nebr., 1997—. Bd. dirs. Illini Hosp., Silvis, 1986—89. Brigadier gen. spl. forces U.S. Army, 1969—70, Vietnam. Named one of Am.'s Top Family Doctors, Am. Consumer Rsch. Coun., 2004—05. Mem.: Am. Acad. Family Physicians, Assn. Mil. Surgeons US, Alpha Omega Alpha. Home: 21517 Arbor St Elkhorn NE 68022 Office Phone: 308-381-2224. Fax: 308-381-0793.

**WALKE, DAVID MICHAEL,** business advisory, consulting and research executive; b. Mt. Vernon, N.Y., Dec. 30, 1954; s. Charles Philip and Elinor Mae (Denner) W.; m. Linda Susan Berkover, Nov. 26, 1978; children: Evan Matthew, Hilary Rose. BS in Acctg., Syracuse U., 1976. Account exec. Ecom Cons., Inc., N.Y.C., 1976-79, Anametrics, Inc., N.Y.C., 1979-81, Ruder, Finn & Rotman, Inc., N.Y.C., 1981-82; prin. Morgen-Walke Assocs., Inc., N.Y.C., 1982—2000, mng. ptnr.; CEO, dir. FINDS/SVP consulting, 2001—. Mem. Nat. Investor Rels. Inst., Gilda's Club Westchester (bd. dirs.).

**WALKEN, CHRISTOPHER,** actor; b. Astoria, N.Y., Mar. 31, 1943; s. Paul Walken; m. Georgianne Thon, 1969. Attended Hofstra U., studied with Wynn Handman, Actors Studio. Stage appearances include Broadway, off-Broadway and regional theatres throughout U.S. and Can.; Broadway debut in J.B. 1959; other stage appearances include Best Foot Forward, West Side Story, Macbeth, The Lion in Winter (Clarence Derwent award 1966), Hamlet, The Rose Tatoo (Theatre World's Most Promising Personality 1966-67), Romeo and Juliet, The Seagull, 2001, The Night Thoreau Spent in Jail (Joseph Jefferson award 1970-71), Kid Champion (Obie award 1975), Miss Julie, Sweet Bird of Youth, Hurlyburly, 1984, Cinders, 1984, A Bill of Divorcement, 1985, Coriolanus, 1988, Othello, 1992, (also playwright) Him, 1995, Mother Courage, 2006; films include The Anderson Tapes, 1971, Next Stop Greenwich Village, The Sentinel, 1977, Roseland, 1977, Annie Hall, 1977, The Deer Hunter, 1978 (N.Y. Film Critics Best Supporting Actor award 1978, Acad. award Best Supporting Actor 1979), Last Embrace, 1979, Dogs of War, 1981, Heavens Gate, 1980, Pennies From Heaven, 1981, The Happiness

Cage, 1982, The Dead Zone, 1983, Brainstorm, 1983, A View to a Kill, 1984, At Close Range, 1986, Deadline, 1987, Puss in Boots, 1988, The Milagro Beanfield War, 1988, Biloxi Blues, 1988, Communion, 1989, King of New York, 1990, Homeboy, 1991, The Comfort of Strangers, 1991, McBain, 1991, All American Murder, 1992, Batman Returns, 1992, True Romance, 1993, A Business Affair, 1994, Wayne's World II, 1994, Pulp Fiction, 1994, Search and Destroy, 1995, Nick of Time, 1995, The Addiction, 1995, The Prophecy, 1995, The Funeral, 1996, Basquiat, 1996, The Wild Side, 1996, Things To Do in Denver When You're Dead, 1995, Last Man Standing, 1996, Touch, 1997, Mousehunt, 1997, Excess Baggage, 1997, Suicide Kings, 1997, Sleepy Hollow, 1999, Blast From the Past, 1999, Kiss Toledo Goodbye, 1999, Vendetta, 1999, Antz (voice), 1998, Illuminata, 1998, New Rose Hotel, 1998, The Prophecy II, 1998, Trance, 1998, Scotland PA, 2001, Joe Dirt, 2001, America's Sweethearts, 2001, Chelsea Walls, 2001, The Affair of the Necklace, 2001, Jungle Juice, 2001, Poolhall Junkies, 2002, The Country Bears, 2002, Plots with a View, 2002, Catch Me If You Can, 2002 (Best Actor in Supporting Role, British Acad. Film Award (BAFTA) 2003), Kangaroo Jack, 2003, Gigli, 2003, The Rundown, 2003, Man on Fire, 2004, Envy, 2004, The Stepford Wives, 2004, Around the Bend, 2004, Wedding Crashers, 2005, Domino, 2005, Click, 2006; TV films include Sarah, Plain and Tall, 1991 (Emmy nominee), Skylark, 1993, Scam, 1993; The Opportunists, 1999, The Prophecy III: The Ascent, 1999, Sarah, Plain and Tall: 3, 1999; (TV series) Saturday Night Live (Am. Comedy award 2001), Naked City, 1958, Hawaii Five-O, 1968, Kojak, 1973; (TV mini-series) Julius Caesar, 2002. Recipient Best Supporting Male Performance (True Crime: NYC), Spike TV Video Game awards, 2005.*

**WALKER, ALICE,** writer; b. Eatonton, Ga., Feb. 9, 1944; d. Willie Lee and Minnie (Grant) W.; m. Melvyn R. Leventhal, Mar. 17, 1967 (div. 1976); 1 dau., Rebecca Walker Leventhal, 1970. Attended, Spelman Coll.; BA, Sarah Lawrence Coll., 1966; PhD (hon.), Russell Sage U., 1972; DHL (hon.), U. Mass., 1983. Co-founder, pub. Wild Trees Pr., Navarro, Calif., 1984-88. Writer in residence, tchr. black studies Jackson State Coll., 1968-69, Tougaloo Coll., 1970-71; lectr. literature Wellesley Coll., 1972-73, U. Mass., Boston, 1972-73; disting. writer Afro-American studies dept. U. Calif., Berkeley, 1982; Fannie Hurst Prof. of Literature Brandeis U., Waltham, Mass., 1982; cons. Friends of the Children of Miss., 1967. Author: Once, 1968, The Third Life of Grange Copeland, 1970, Five Poems, 1972, Revolutionary Petunias and Other Poems, 1973 (Nat. Book award nomination 1973, Lillian Smith award So. Regional Coun. 1973), In Love and Trouble, 1973 (Richard and Hinda Rosenthal Found. award Am. Acad. and Inst. of Arts and Letters 1974) Langston Hughes: American Poet, 1973, Meridian, 1976, Goodnight, Willie Lee, I'll See You in the Morning, 1979, You Can't Keep a Good Woman Down, 1981, The Color Purple, 1982 (Nat. Book Critics Circle award nomination 1982, Pulitzer Prize for fiction 1983, Am. Book award 1983; movie Steven Spielberg, The Color Purple), In Search of Our Mothers' Gardens, 1983, Horses Make a Landscape Look More Beautiful, 1984, To Hell With Dying, 1988, Living By the Word: Selected Writings, 1973-1987, 1988, The Temple of My Familiar, 1989, Her Blue Body Everything We Know: Earthling Poems, 1965-1990, 1991, Finding the Green Stone, 1991, Possessing the Secret of Joy, 1992, (with Pratibha Parmar) Warrior Marks, 1993, (with others) Double Stitch: Black Women Write About Mothers & Daughters, 1993, Everyday Use, 1994, Alice Walker Banned: The Banned Works, 1996, Everything We Love Can Be Saved: A Writer's Activism: Essays, Speeches, Statements and Letters, 1997, The Same River Twice, 1997; editor: I Love Myself When I'm Laughing... And Then Again When I'm Looking Mean and Impressive, 1979, By The Light of My Father's Smile, 1998, The Way Forward is With a Broken Heart, 2000, Absolute Trust in the Goddess of the Earth: New Poems, 2003. Recipient first prize Am. Scholar essay contest, 1967, O. Henry award for Kindred Spirits, 1986, Nora Astorga Leadership award, 1989, Fred Cody award for lifetime achievement Bay Area Book Reviewers Assn., 1990, Freedom to Write award PEN Ctr. USA West, 1990; Bread Loaf Writer's Conf. scholar, 1966; Merrill writing fellowship, 1967; McDowell Colony fellowship, 1967, 77-78; National Endowment for the Arts grantee, 1969, 77; Radcliffe Inst. fellowship, 1971-73; Guggenheim fellow, 1977-78. Achievements include introducing the word "womanist". Address: Random House Inc 1745 Broadway #B1 New York NY 10019-4305

**WALKER, ALLEN LYON,** engineer; b. Wellsboro, Pa., Jan. 30, 1943; s. Joseph Dewitt and Louise (Thompson) W.; m. Jean Barbara Hickson, Aug. 11, 1979 (div. Jan. 1985); 1 child, Iain Lyon Walker; m. Mary Ann Knowlton Walker, Jan. 30, 1987. A in Engine. Mech., Williamsport (Pa.) Tech. Inst., 1963; Grad., U.S. Army Aviation Sch., 1970, U.S. Army Test Pilots Sch., 1970, U.S. Army Comd./Gen. Staff, 1975, Ft. Leavenworth, Kans., 1991. Lic. comml. pilot, FAA. Exptl. lab. tech. Ille Electric Corp., Williamsport, 1963-65; commd. 2nd lt. U.S. Army, 1965, advanced through grades to maj., 1966, ret., 1995; tool engr. Ingersoll Rand Corp., Painted Post, N.Y., 1965-66; aviator, test pilot U.S. Army, Vietnam, 1966-68, aircraft maintenance officer Europe, Germany, 1969-72, co. comdr., 1969-72; maintenance engr. Ingersoll Rand Corp., Painted Post, N.Y., 1972-75; logistics mgr. Bell Helicopter Internat., Kermanshah, Iran, 1975—77; base supply mgr. Gen. Devices/Grumman, Isfahan, Iran, 1977—79; field engr. Northrop Grumman Corp., Phila., 1980—. Adv. Army of the Rep. of Vietnam, Anh-Khe, 1967, English instr., 1967. Author treatise, 1990. Founding warden Internat. Order of St. Vincent, Holy Nativity, Rockledge, Pa., 1992-98, life mem.; dist. commr. Cradle of Liberty coun. Boy Scouts Am., Phila., 1994-99, coun. commr., 1999-2004, adv. coun., 2004—. Maj. U.S. Army, 1966-72, Vietnam, Europe. Decorated Bronze Star, Air medal, Meritorious Svc. medal; recipient Silver Beaver award, Boy Scouts Am., award of merit, Cradle of Liberty coun. Boy Scouts Am., Disting. Commr. award, Daniel C. Beard Masonic Scouter's award, Boy Scouts Am.; James E. West Found. fellow. Mem.: SAR, Soc. Logistics Engrs. (vice-chmn. 1982—85), Mil. Order of Loyal Legion of U.S. (Allied Masonic degrees steward 2004), Lyons Family Assn. (v.p. 1972—75), Brit. Officers Club of Phila. (sec. 1990—93), Knight Masons (jr. warden 2005), York Rite Sovereign Coll. (Phila. gov. 2005—06), Royal Order Scotland, Nat. Sojourners, Knights Templar, Shriners (comdr. Legion of Honor 2000), Masons (past master 2001—03, 32d degree, freemason). Republican. Episcopalian. Avocations: genealogy, scouting, astronomy. Office: Naval Inventory Control Pnt 700 Robbins Ave Philadelphia PA 19111-5008 Home: 40 North Hill Ter Mansfield PA 16933

**WALKER, AMBER MICHELLE,** military officer; b. Ocala, Fla., Sept. 16, 1982; d. Keith Edward and Debra Faye Raub; m. Michael Scott Walker, June 19, 2004. BSc in Mech. Engine., Aero Sys., US Mil. Acad., 2004; student, U. Oxford, 2004—. Lt. US Army, Killeen, Tex., 2004—. Decorated Nat. Def. Svc. medal US Army, Global War on Terror Svc. medal, Parachutist badge US Army Airborne Sch.; scholarship, Rhodes Trust, 2003, 2004. Mem.: ASME, Soc. Women Engrs., Phi Kappa Phi. Office: Univ Oxford Dept Engineering Science Parks Rd Oxford OX1 3PJ England Personal E-mail: amber.m.walker@us.army.mil. Business E-Mail: amber.walker@eng.ox.ac.uk.

**WALKER, ANN YVONNE,** lawyer; b. San Francisco, Sept. 26, 1954; d. C. Richard and Athene (Henderson) Walker. BS with distinction in Math., Stanford U., 1976, JD, 1979. Bar: Calif. 1979. Assoc. Wilson, Sonsini, Goodrich & Rosati, Palo Alto, Calif., 1979-86, ptnr., 1986—. Violinist, bd. dirs. Redwood Symphony Orch., 1985—. Mem.: ABA (mem. fed. regulation securities com. 1992—, mem. com. lawyer bus. ethics 1993—, mem. standing com. professionalism 1996—99, chair 1997—2001, mem. bus. law sect. publs. bd. 2000—04, mem. bus. law sect. coun. 2001—05, mem. standing com. tech. and info. sys. 2005—), Palo Alto Area Bar Assn., Santa Clara County Bar Assn., Calif. State Bar Assn. (mem. corps. com. 1992—96, chair 1995—96, mem. exec. com. bus. law sect. 1996—, vice chair 1998—99, chair 1999—2000, advisor 2000—05, co-chair coun. state bar sects. 2001—02, advisor emeritus 2005—), Phi Beta Kappa. Office: Wilson Sonsini Goodrich and Rosati 650 Page Mill Rd Palo Alto CA 94304-1050 Office Phone: 650-320-4643. Business E-Mail: awalker@wsgr.com.

**WALKER, ANNETTE,** retired counseling administrator; b. Birmingham, Ala., Sept. 20, 1953; d. Jesse and Luegene (Wright) W. BS in Edn. Huntingdon Coll., 1974; MS in Adminstrn. and Supervision, Troy State U., 1977, 78, MS in Sch. Counseling, 1990, AA in Sch. Adminstrn., 1992; diploma, World Travel Sch., 1990; diploma in Cosmetology, John Patterson Coll., 1992; MEd in higher Edn. Adminstrn., Auburn (Ala.) U., 1995. Cert. tchr., adminstr., Ala.; lic. cosmetologist, Ala.; lic. funeral dir., Ala. Tchr. Montgomery (Ala.) Pub. Sch. System, 1976-89, sch. counselor, 1989—2000; lit. tchr. Fed. Bur. of Justice, 1997—2000; ret., 2000; acad. advisor Cmty. Coll. of Air Force; acad. counselor Maxwell Air Force Base, Ala., guidance counselor edn. office, 2001—. Tchr. Fed. Govt., 1997—, U.S. Bur. Justice, 1997—; gymnastics tchr. Cleveland Ave. YMCA, 1971-76; girls coach Montgomery Parks and Recreation, 1973-76; summer sch. sci. tchr. grades 7-9, 1977-88; chmn. dept. sci. Bellingrath Sch., 1987-90, courtesy com., 1987-88, sch. discipline com., 1977-84; recreation asst. Gunter AFB, Ala., 1981-83; calligraphy tchr. Gunter Youth Ctr., 1982; program dir. Maxwell AFB, Ala., 1983-89, vol. tchr. Internat. Officer Sch., 1985—, Adult Laubach Reading Prog., Ala. Goodwill Amb., 1985—, day camp dir., 1987, calligraphy tchr., 1988; trainer internat. law for sec. students, Ala., 1995—; leader of workshops in field; sales rep. Ala. World Travel, 1990—; behavior aid Brantwood Children's Home, 1996—; computer tchr. hs diploma program Montgomery County Sch., 1995—; behavior aide Brantwood Children's Home, 1995—; hotel auditor, 1995—; Am. del. to China, People to People Internat., 1998; acad. advisor C.C. of Air Force, Maxwell AFB, Ala., 2002—. Mem. CAP; vol. zoo activities Tech. Scholarship Program for Ala. Tchrs. Computer Courses, Montgomery; bd. dirs. Cleveland Ave. YMCA, 1976—80; sponsor Belle-Howe chpt. Young Astronauts, 1986—90, Pate Howe chpt., 1991—92; judge Montgomery County Children Festival Elem. Sci. Fair, 1988—90; bd. dirs. Troy State U. Drug Free Schs., 1992—; chmn. Maxwell AFB Red Cross-Youth, 1986—88; goodwill amb. sponsor to various families (award 1989, 95); State of Ala. rep. P.A.T.C.H.-Internat. Law Inst., 1995; founder Okinawa, Japan chpt., bd. dirs. People to People Internat., 2000; tchr. Naraha Jr. High, Beulah Bapt. Ch., Montgomery. Named Tchr. of the Week, WCOV-TV, 1992, Ala. Tchr. in Space Program, summer, 1989, Local Coord. Young Astronaut Program, 1988, Citizen Amb. to China, People to People Internat., 1999; recipient Outstanding High Sch. Sci./Math. Tchr. award, Sigma Xi, 1989, Most Outstanding Youth Coun. Leader award, Maxwell AFB Youth Ctr., 1987, Outstanding Ala. Goodwill Amb. award, 1989, 1995, Tchr. of Yr. award, Paterson Sch., 1990, Career Infusion award (Most Appreciated Tchr. award), 1987, Montgomery Pub. Sch., 1982, 1984, Earthwatch Ednl. award, Israel, 1997, 20 Class award, Maxwell AFB Internat. Fgn. Officer Program, 25 Class award, 2003, 30 Class award, 2005, Ala. Goodwill Amb. award, Maxwell AFB Inernat. Officer Program 30 Class award, 2005; Fulbright scholar, Japan, 1999. Mem. NEA, Internat. Platform Assn., People to People Internat. (founder, bd. trustees, organizer, pres. Ala. chpt. 1998), Nat. Sci. Tchrs. Assn., Ala. Sch. Counselors, Montgomery Sch. Counselors Assn., Montgomery County Ednl. Assn., Space Camp Amb., Huntingdon Alumni Assn. (sec.-treas.), Ala. Goodwill Amb., Montgomery Capital City Club, Young Astronauts, Ea. Star, Japan Friends of Fulbright Meml. Fund Tchr. Prog., Water Watch, Montgomery, AL, Zeta Phi Beta, Chi Delta Phi, Kappa Pi. Avocations: international travel, calligraphy, international food, cruising. Personal E-mail: Awalker2001@yahoo.com.

**WALKER, ANTOINE DEVON,** professional basketball player; b. Chgo., Aug. 12, 1976; 1 child, Crystal. Student, U. Ky., 1996. Forward Boston Celtics, 1996—2003, 2005, Dallas Mavericks, 2003—04, Atlanta Hawks, 2004—05, Miami Heat, 2005—. Named to 1996-97 NBA All Rookie First Team. Avocations: dance, bowling, video games. Office: c/o Boston Celtics 151 Merrimac St Ste 5 Boston MA 02114-4714*

**WALKER, AUDREY THAYER,** social worker, psychotherapist; b. Quincy, Mass., June 29, 1935; d. Paul Clifton and Dorothy Ritchie Thayer; m. David A. Walker, Aug. 21, 1982; children: Elizabeth Penniman Billett Bilhartz, Matthew Thayer Billett. AB, Wheaton Coll., 1957; MSS/MSW, Smith Coll., 1959. Cert. social worker, LICSW D.C., cert. diplomate in clin. social work. Caseworker Ch. Home Soc., Boston, 1959—61; caseworker, family therapist Family Svc. Agy. of Sacramento, 1961—63; chief psychiat. social worker, supr. dept. psychiatry George Washington U., 1969—90, adj. assoc. prof., 1971—, dir. social work tng., 1975—90; adj. assoc. prof. Smith Coll. Sch. for Social Work, Northampton, Mass., 1971—2003; pvt. practice clin. social worker, psychotherapist, 1990—; adj. faculty Counseling and Psychiat. Svcs., Georgetown U., 1993—2005; field faculty advisor Smith Coll. Sch. for Social Work, Northampton, Mass., 1996—2003, adj. assoc. prof., 2006—. Adj. faculty, cons. Clin. Social Work Inst., 1999—2006; co-leader theoretical integrative seminar Smith Coll. Sch. for Social Work, 2003—. Co-sponsor Life Cycle Courses George Washington U. Dept. Psychiatry, Washington Psychoanalytic Inst., 1975—85; co-chair benefit ann. lectures Smith Coll. Sch. for Social Work Alumni Assn., Washington, 1978—88. Named Disting. Practitioner, Nat. Acads. of Practice, 2005; recipient Day-Garreit award for significant and maj. contbns. to social work, Smith Coll. Sch. Social Work, 2005; Grad. Study scholar, Episcopal Ch. of Am., Youth Svcs. Divsn., 1957-1959, Sr. Class Grad. Study awardee and scholar, Wheaton Coll. Sr. Class, 1957. Mem.: Nat. Academics of Practice (disting. practitioner, social work 2005—), Wash. Psychoanalytic Inst., Am. Group Psychotherapy Assn. (full clin. mem. 1982—2004), Smith Coll. Sch. for Social Work Alumni Assn. (Greater Washington chpt. steering com. 1974—93, co-chair Psychoanalytic Jour. Club 1975—76), Greater Washington Soc. for Clin. Social Work (v.p. profl. affairs 1990—94, bd. mem.-at-large, advisor 1994—2005, continuing edn. com. 1995—, founding chair consultation svcs. com. 1997—98, ad hoc ethics com. 2006—, Cert. of Appreciation 1991—97, 2002—04), Nat. Membership Com. on Psychoanalysis in Social Work (Washington area chair 1997—2003), Smith Coll. Club (Washington) (bd. dirs. 1983—87), Pi Gamma Mu, Democrat. Unitarian. Avocations: study group: the brain and psychoanalysis, travel, reading/book clubs, theatre, ballet/dance. Home: 4416 Q St NW Washington DC 20007 Office: 3 Washington Cir NW Ste 406 Washington DC 20037 Office Phone: 202-331-1547. Business E-Mail: audrey.walker@msb.edu.

**WALKER, BARBARA DODSON,** cultural organization administrator, educator; b. Washington, Jan. 18, 1930; d. Joseph Norman Dodson and Naomi Althea Neal; m. James Dent Walker; children: James Dent, Barbara Ann Brissett, Althea Elizabeth Davi, Susan Victoria. BS, Miner Tchrs. Coll., Washington, 1951; EdM, Fed. City Coll., Washington, 1972. Cert. tchr. Tchr. DC Pub. Sch., Washington, 1951—83; rec. sec. Afro-Am. Hist. and Geneal. Soc., Washington, 1989—92, nat. pres., 1993—. Dir. Fedn. of Geneal. Socs., 1997—; coun. mem. Assn. Study of African-Am. Life and History, 2002—; mem. DC Hist. Records Adv. Bd., 2003—. Contbr. book and periodical indexes, articles to profl. jours., chapters to books. Recipient Dist. Svc. award, Afro-Am. Hist. and Geneal. Soc., 1989, DC Geneal. Soc., 2001. Mem.: Nat. Geneal. Soc., Hist. Soc. of Washington. Avocations: reading, collecting books, music boxes, angels. Home: 1320 Sheperd St NW Washington DC 20011 Office: Afro-Am Hist & Geneal Soc PO Box 73067 Washington DC 20056-7306

**WALKER, BARBARA HILLS,** secondary school educator; b. Pitts., Apr. 7, 1946; d. Wesley E. and Anne Margaret (Baker) Hills; m. George William Walker, Dec. 22, 1967; children: Kelley, George, Joshua, Zachary. BA, U. Mich., 1968. Cert. biology, gen. sci. secondary tchr., N.Y. Tchr. Batavia (N.Y.) High Sch., 1988; biology tutor Genesee (N.Y.) Community Coll. Owner, prin., Holiday Hollow, Pembroke, N.Y., 1993—. Mem. Leonard Nimoy Fan Club (founder, v.p. 1983-86, pres. 1985-95). Republican. Presbyterian. Avocations: reading, crafts, carpentry, sewing. Home: 1410 Main Rd Corfu NY 14036-9758

**WALKER, BEATRIZ ALEM,** language educator; b. Montevideo, Uruguay, 1958; permanent resident, 2002; d. Miguel Ronald and Nela Flor de Liz Alem; m. Jack C Walker, 1979; children: Ana Maria Parker, Amanda, Ashley Trevino, J.C. BAS, Abilene Christian U., 1996; MEd, Abilene Christian U., 1999; MA in romance languages, Tex. Tech. U., 2002, student. Tchg. cert. Abilene Christian U., 1997, cert. of proficiency in english U. Mich., 1979,

Alianza Cultural Uruguay, 1979, bi-lingual sec. cert. 1977. Spanish instr. Abilene Ind. Sch. Dist., Abilene, Tex., 1997—99, Abilene Christian U., 1999—; grad. asst. to cert. officer Abilene Christian U., Dept. Edn. 1996; asst. with spanish lags Abilene Christian U., Dept. Fgn. Languages, 1996; translator for channel 5 Montevideo, Uruguay, 1991—92; bilingual sec. to Dr. Dan C. Coker Abilene Christian U., Dept. Missions, 1982—83; bilingual sec. La Iglesia de Cristo, 1977—79. Cons. culture and lang. Bridges to the World, Abilene; state textbook rev. panel me. Tex. Edn. Agy., Austin, 2000. Recipient Nat. Honor Soc., Phi Eta Sigma, ACU Chpt., 1995, Sigma Delta Pi, Tex. Tech. Chpt., 2000. Mem.: Am. Assn. teachers of Spanish and Portugese, Am. Coun. Tchg. of Fgn. Languages, Phi Delta Kappa. Avocations: travel, writing, photography.

**WALKER, BETTE,** automotive executive; BS in Bus. Mgmt., U. NH; student, Bosotn U.; completed Global Leadership Executive Development Program, Harvard U. Tech. dir. Latin Am. Digital Equip. Corp.; IT exec. auto. sector safety restraint sys. AlliedSignal, Inc.; v.p., CIO, energy & chassis divsn. Delphi Corp., Troy, Mich., 1997—. Office: World Hdqrs 5725 Delphi Dr Troy MI 48098-2815*

**WALKER, BETTE M.,** information technology executive; BS in Bus. Mgmt., U. NH. Various positions most recently info. tech. dir. Latin Am. Digital Equipment Corp.; head of info. tech. automotive sector's safety restraint systems divsn. AlliedSignal Inc., head of info. tech. aerospace sector's comml. avionics divsn.; chief info. officer energy & chassis divsn. Delphi Corp., Troy, Mich., 1997, exec. dir. global bus. services and ops., now v.p., chief info. officer. Named one of Premier 100 IT Leaders, Computerworld, 2005. Office: VP & CIO Delphi Corp 5725 Delphi Dr Troy MI 48098-2815

**WALKER, BEVERLY ANN,** minister, health facility administrator; b. Baltimore, Md., Mar. 17, 1950; d. Morris Allen and Mary Estelle Johnson; children: Tyrone Anthony Jeffries, Towanda Tonette Fortune, Bernard Alexander Jeffries, Charlotte Shrae Young, Harold Lawrence. BA, Va. Sem. and Coll., 1998; M. Religious Edn., Andersonville Bapt. Sem., 2000, DRE, 2002; MDiv, Va. U.-Lynchburg, 2005. Supr. ins. processing Va. Health Svcs. Found., Charlottesville, 1982—95; pastor North River Bapt. Ch., Bridgewater, Va., 1983—2001; founder Va. Women in Ministry, Charlottesville, 1990—95; moderator Berean Bapt. Assn., Bridgewater, 1994—98; founder God Called and Chosen Vessels, Stuarts Draft, 2002—; pastor Rising Sun Bapt. Ch., North Garden, 2004—. Counselor Harrisonburg Jail, Va., 1998—2001; bd. dirs. Helping Hand Ministry, Harrisonburg, 2002—. Contbr.: ch. adminstrn. book and handbook Decently and In Order. Mem. NAACP, Harrisonburg, Va., 1985. Recipient Female Ministerial award, Shenandoah Valley Hit Newspaper, 1994, Outstanding Svc. award, Va. Women in Ministry, 1995. Mem.: Hampton's Min. Conf., Bapt. Gen. Conf., Va. Bapt. Conf., Berean Valley Bapt. Assn. (life). Liberal. Baptist. Avocations: travel, reading, singing, dance, exercise. Home: 2410 Berkshire Pl Apt 42 Charlottesvle VA 22901-2444 Office Phone: 434-972-1800. Personal E-mail: beverlyrnrd3@aol.com.

**WALKER, BILLY J.,** bank executive; b. Mar. 4, 1931; Student, Jacksonville U.; grad., Harvard U., La. State U. Joined Atlantic Nat. Bank, Jacksonville, 1948, various positions to pres.; CEO, 1974-76; pres., CEO Atlantic Bancorp., Jacksonville, 1976; chmn., CEO First Union Nat. Bank Fla.; vice chmn. First Union Corp., Charlotte, N.C., 1991—. Bd. dirs. Ctr. for World Capitalism, North Fla. Coun.-Boy Scouts Am., Citizens Against Crime, James Madison Inst. for Pub. Policy Studies, St. Luke's Hosp. affiliate Mayo Clinic; chmn. bd. trustees, mem. exec. com. bd. dirs. Jacksonville U.; chmn. Tournament Players Championship Charities. Recipient Brotherhood award Nat. Conf. Christians and Jews, 1983. Office: First Union Corp 1 First Union Ctr Fl 40 Charlotte NC 28288

**WALKER, BONNIE LEE,** small business owner; b. Erie, Pa., July 17, 1939; d. Ray Morse and Alice Bertha (Akerly) Theuret; m. Robert L. Walker, Sept. 27, 1958 (div. May 1978); 1 child, April Leanne Walker Cope; m. George William Knott, Apr. 4, 1980. BA, U. Md., 1965; MEd, Bowie (Md.) State U., 1975; PhD, U. Md., 1979. Registered yoga instr. Prince George's County (Md.) Schs., 1965-76; curriculum developer Gallaudet U., Washington, 1976-78; asst. prof. Bowie State U., 1978-81; rschr. JWK Internat., Annandale, Va., 1981-84, project dir., 1985-86; project coord., sys. analyst Inter Am. Rsch. Assocs., Rosslyn, Va., 1984-85; pres. Bonnie Walker & Assocs., Bowie, Md., 1986—. Prin. investigator Nat. Inst. on Aging, 1990, 92, 95, 97, 2004, Ctrs. for Disease Control, Atlanta, 1993-94 Author: Basic English Grammar, 1981, Basic English Composition, 1982, Life Skills English, 1983, Injury Prevention for Young Children, 1995, Injury Prevention for the Elderly, 1995, Fire Safety in Nursing Facilities, 1996, Sexuality and the Elderly, 1997, Basic English, 2000, Using CBI and the Web to Train Board and Care Providers, 2003; editor: The Wit and Wisdom of an Old Muskrat Trapper, 2005; contbr. Cup of Comfort for Teachers, 2004. Fellow VA Ctr. for Creative Arts, Sweet Brier Coll., 1995, 96, 97, 99, 2001 Mem. Bowie Women Tennis Club (pres., sec. 1990-95), United Meth. Ch Mem. Ch. of God. Avocations: tennis, yoga, painting. Home and Office: Bonnie L Walker & Assocs 210 Country Club Dr Rehoboth Beach DE 19971-1872 Personal E-mail: bonnie4101@aol.com.

**WALKER, BONNIE LOU,** social studies educator; b. Scranton, Pa., Dec. 8, 1973; d. Jesse Crussell Howell and Esther Mae Altemier; m. Jeffrey William Walker, Oct. 5, 1996; children: Amaya Dian, Rylie Grace. BSc in Social Studies Edn., Lock Haven U., Lock Haven, U., 1995, cert. in Driver's Edn., 1997. Cert. tchr. social studies Pa. Dept. Edn., tchr. driver's safety Pa. Dept. Edn. Tchr. social studies Cowanesque Valley H.S. No. Tioga Sch.Dist., Westfield, Pa., 1996—. Adv. student coun. Cowanesque Valley H.S. No. Tioga Sch. Dist., 1998—2005, adv. com. Cowanesque Valley H.S., 2006; coach various teams. Named Adv. of Yr., Dist. 7 PASC, 2005. Mem.: NEA, Pa. Edn. Assn., No. Tioga Edn. Assn. (rep. 1996—), Delta Kappa Gamma. Democrat. Office: Cowanesque Valley High School 51 North Fork Rd Westfield PA 16950

**WALKER, BRIAN C.,** manufacturing executive; Pres., N. Am. Herman Miller, Inc., 1999—2003, pres., COO, 2003—04, pres., CEO, 2004—, bd. dir., 2003—05. Office: Herman Miller 855 E Main Ave Zeeland MI 49464-0302 Office Phone: 616-654-3000. Office Fax: 616-654-5234.

**WALKER, CARLENE MARTIN,** state senator; BS, Brigham Young U., 1969. Supr. coding & data entry the Wirthlin Group, 1982-86; cons. D.K. Shifflet & Assocs., 1987-88; ptnr., mgr. Covecrest Properties, 1978-99; dir. adminstrn. Energy Lock, Inc., 1992-99; tech. recruiter Manpower Tech., 1999-2000; mem. Utah State Senate, Salt Lake City, 2001—. Cons. Wash. Times Newspaper, 1987-88. Bd., chair fundraising com. Granite Edn. Found., 1989-90; chmn., founder of the bd. Repub. Womens Political Action Com. Office: 4085 E Prospector Dr Salt Lake City UT 84121

**WALKER, CAROL MCRANEY,** mathematics professor, consultant; b. Jackson, Miss., May 25, 1952; d. Robert Rex and Hilda Grafton McRaney; m. David James Walker, July 26, 1974; children: Allison McRaney, Carol Ann. BA in Math. Miss. State U. Starkville, 1973; MEd in Math., Delta State U. Cleveland, Miss., 1976. Tchr. Jackson Pub. Schs., 1973—79; instr. math. Hinds CC, Raymond, Miss., 1980—. Cons. Thomson Higher Edn., Belmont, Calif., 2004—05. Author: (test bank) Test Bank for Tussy and Gustafson's Elementary Algebra, 3d edit.; Test Bank for Tussy and Gustafson's Intermediate Algebra, 3d edit. Pres. PTSA Wilkins Elem., Jackson, 1990—92, Peeples Mid. Sch., 1996—97, Forest Hill HS, Jackson, 1997—2000; adopt a sch. coord. Alta Woods United Meth. Ch. and Lester Elem., Jackson, 1995—2001; pres. Jackson Assn. Talented and Gifted, 1995—96; adminstrv. bd. Alta Woods United Meth. Ch., Jackson, 1993—2006; sec., treas. Hinds

CC, Raymond, Miss., 1994—96. Mem.: Hinds CC Edn. Assn. (treas. 2005—06), Delta Kappa Gamma Tau chpt. (pres. 2004—06). Methodist. Avocations: reading, walking. Office: Hinds CC PO Box 1100 Raymond MS 39154 Office Phone: 601-857-3244.

**WALKER, CHARLES D.,** astronaut; b. Bedford, Ind., Aug. 29, 1948; s. Donna Lake Walker; m. Susan Y. Flowers; 1 child. BS in Aero. and Astronautical Engring., Purdue U., 1971; DSc (hon.), St. Louis Coll. Pharmacy, 1985. Civil engring. technician, land acquisition specialist, forest firefighter U.S. Forest Svc.; design engr. Bendix Aerospace Co.; project engr. Naval Sea Systems Command; test engr., Aft Propulsion Subsys. for Space Shuttle orbiters McDonnell Douglas Corp., 1977, original mem. Space Mfg. Team (laster Electrophoresis Ops. in Space, EOS), chief test engr., payload specialist, EOS commercialization project, 1979—86, spl. asst. to pres. Space Systems Co., 1986; sr. mgr., space programs bus. devel. and mktg. Boeing Co. Ops., Washington. Industry mem. numerous NASA task forces; mem. NRC Space Applications Bd.; faculty course advisor, lectr. Internat. Space U., 1988; nat. panel mem. NASA/Industry Manned Flight Awareness Program, NASA/Industry Edn. Initiative; bd. dirs. Challenger Ctr. Space Sci. Edn.; trainer various NASA astronaut crews; astronaut Space Shuttle missions 41-D, 51-D and 61-B; chmn. organizing com. World Space Congress, 1992. Contbr. articles to profl. jours. and mags., chapters to books. Bd. mem. Astronauts Meml. Found.; vol. chmn., bd. dirs. Spacecause. Named Ky. Col., Commonwealth of Ky., 1990; recipient Space Flight medals, NASA, 1984—85, Aerospace Laurels award, Aviation Week and Space Tech. Mag., 1985, Engring. Astronaut Alumnus award, Purdue U. Schs. Engring., Lindbergh award, AIAA, St. Louis sect., 1986. Mem.: Assn. Space Explorers (bd. dirs.), Nat Space Soc. (bd. dirs., past pres.). Achievements include patents for electrophoresis apparatus with flow control. Office: Astronaut Office/CB NASA Johnson Space Ctr Houston TX 77058

**WALKER, CHARLES DODSLEY,** conductor, organist; b. N.Y.C., Mar. 16, 1920; s. Marshall Starr and Maude Graham (Marriott) Walker; m. Janet Elizabeth Hayes, May 30, 1949 (dec. Feb. 1997); children: Peter Hayes, Susan Starr; m. Elizabeth Ann Phillips, Jan. 14, 2001. BS, Trinity Coll., 1940; AM, Harvard U., 1947. Organist, choirmaster Am. Cathedral, Paris, 1948-50, Ch. of the Heavenly Rest, N.Y.C., 1951-88; music dir. Blue Hill Troupe, Ltd., N.Y.C., 1955-90, Chapin Sch., N.Y.C., 1961-85; mem. organ faculty Union Theol. Sem., N.Y.C., 1962-73, NYU, N.Y.C., 1968-80; dean, music dir. Berkshire Choral Inst., Sheffield, Mass., 1982-91; organist, choirmaster Trinity Episcopal Ch., Southport, Conn., 1988—. Contbr. articles to profl. jours. Lt. comdr. USNR, 1942—46. Named Artist of Yr., Fairfield Arts Coun., 2004; recipient Disting. Alumnus award, Cathedral Choir Sch., 1988. Fellow: Am. Guild Organists (nat. pres. 1971—75); mem.: Canterbury Choral Soc. (founder, condr. 1952—), Am. Fedn. Musicians, St. Wilfrid Club, Bohemians. Avocations: travel, photography. Home: 160 W 96th St Apt 15N New York NY 10025-9212 Office: Trinity Episcopal Ch 651 Pequot Ave Southport CT 06890-1416 Office Phone: 203-255-0454. Personal E-mail: dodsley@aol.com.

**WALKER, CHARLES HENRI,** lawyer; b. Columbus, Nov. 11, 1951; s. Watson Hershel and Juanita Elizabeth (Webb) W.; m. Amanda Tressel Herndon, June 27, 1981; children: Katrina Della, Allison Lyles, Carlton Wesley. BA magna cum laude, Tufts U., 1973; JD, Emory U., 1976. Bar: Ohio 1976. Assoc. Bricker & Eckler LLP, and predecessors, Columbus, 1976-81, sr. counsel, 1982—. Bd. dirs. Salesian Boys Club, Columbus, 1983-89, Planned Parenthood Cen. Ohio, Columbus, 1984-85, Life Care Alliance, 1993—, Ctrl. Ohio Transit Authority, 1994—2000; mem. sports arena com. City of Columbus, 1989; chmn. Tufts Alumni Admissions Program, 1986—; legal advisor Ohio Mock Trial Advocacy Program, 1988-92; pres., bd. dirs. I-670 Corridor Devel. Corp., 1993—98. Fellow ABA; mem. Nat. Bar Assn., Ohio Bar Assn. (com. profl. conduct and legal ethics, 1988—92), Columbus Bar Assn., Nat. Assn. R.R. Trial Counsel, Columbus Acad. Alumni Assn. (past pres.), Sigma Phi Phi. Democrat. Roman Catholic. Clubs: Athletic, President's (Ohio State U.). Home: 40 E Frankfort St Columbus OH 43206-1041 Office: Bricker & Eckler LLP 100 S 3rd St Columbus OH 43215-4291 Office Phone: 614-227-2339. Office Fax: 614-227-2390. E-mail: cwalker@bricker.com.*

**WALKER, CHARLES URMSTON,** retired university president; b. Bolivar, Pa., June 20, 1931; s. Charles William and Frances May (Urmston) W.; m. Cherie Hall Duckworth, Aug. 7, 1959; children: Douglas Leland, Christy Lynn. BA, U. Pitts., 1953; MA, Columbia U., 1958; PhD, Stanford U., 1964; LLD (hon.), Kanto Gakuin U., 1979; LHD (hon.), Linfield Coll., 1992. Asst. prof. English Rockford (Ill.) Coll., 1958-61; dept. head, residence dir. Menlo Coll., Menlo Park, Calif., 1961-64; v.p., dean Hamline U., St. Paul, 1964-70; pres. Russell Sage Coll., Troy, NY, 1970-75, Linfield Coll., McMinnville, Oreg., 1975-92, pres. emeritus, 1992—; ednl. cons., 1992—; dir. managed programs Ford Family Found., Roseburg, Oreg., 1993-98. Bd. dirs. 1st Fed. Savs. & Loan, McMinnville, Wespro Ins. Co., Oreg. Mut. Ins. Co.; mem. Univ. Pres. Initiative, IIE/USIA/NATO, Brussels, 1991. Bd. dirs. South Tillamook County Libr., 1994, pres., 2004; pres. Neskowin (Oreg.) Chamber Music; co-chair bldg. com. First Bapt. Ch., McMinnville; trustee, vice chair Ford Family Found.; chair Oreg. Cultural Trust, pres. Found. Better Oreg.; bd. dirs. Tillamook County Futures Coun., 2005; v.p. Hillside Found., 2003—. Warg scholar U. Pitts., 1949-51; Univ. fellow Stanford U., 1963-64; Hill Found. grantee, St. Paul, 1970; Paul Harris fellow Rotary Internat., 1987; recipient Community Svc. award Troy, N.Y. Troy C. of C., 1975, First Citizen award McMinnville, Oreg., 1989; named Man of Yr., Troy C. of C., 1975. Mem. Univ. Club (Portland), Rotary (past pres. McMinnville). Home: 1324 SW Gilorr St Mcminnville OR 97128-6617 E-mail: cwalkc@oregoncoast.com.

**WALKER, CHARLS EDWARD,** economist, consultant; b. Graham, Tex., Dec. 24, 1923; s. Pinkney Clay and Sammye D. (McCombs) W.; m. Harmolyn Hart, June 24, 1949; children: Carolyn, Charls Edward. BBA, U. Tex., 1947, MBA, 1948; PhD in Econs., U. Pa., 1955. Instr. fin. U. Tex., 1947-48, asst. prof., then assoc. prof., 1950-54; instr. fin. U. Pa. Wharton Sch., 1948-50; fin. economist Fed. Res. Bank Phila., 1953; with Fed. Res. Bank Dallas, 1954-61, v.p., econ. adviser, 1958-61; economist Republic Nat. Bank Dallas, 1955-56; asst. to sec. treasury, 1959-61; exec. v.p. Am. Bankers Assn., N.Y.C., 1961-69; under sec. treasury, 1969-72; dep. sec., 1972-73. Adj. prof. U. Tex., Austin, 1986-96, Tex. A&M U., 2000-2003; bd. dirs. Nat. Coun. Econ. Edn.; chmn., CEO Charls E. Walker Assocs., Inc., 1973-96; disting. vis. prof. Emory U., 2000-02. Co-editor: The Bankers Handbook, New Directions in Federal Tax Policy, The Consumption Tax: A Better Alternative, 1987, Intellectual Property Rights and Capital Formation, 1988, The U.S. Savings Challenge, 1990; contbr. articles to profl. jours. and newspapers, chpts. to books. Founder, chmn. emeritus Am. Coun. for Capital Formation; co-founder, chmn. exec. com. Com. on the Present Danger, 1976; chmn. Pres.'s adv. coun. on minority enterprise, 1973-75; co-chmn. Presdl. Debates, 1976; founder chmn. Bretton Woods Com. chmn. Ronald Reagan's Task Force on Tax Policy, 1980; sr. advisor Ctr. for Deliberative Polling, U. Tex., 1996-; Stanford U., 2003-. Recipient Alexander Hamilton award U.S. Dept. Treasury, Urban League award, Baker award for Exemplary Svc. to Econ. Edn., 1991, Disting. Svc. award, 2002, Pro Bono Meritas award Coll. Liberal Arts U. Tex., 2003; named Disting. Alumnus, U. Tex., 1994. Mem.: Coun. Fgn. Rels., Sea Island (Ga.) Club, Congl. Club (Bethesda, Md.), Burning Tree Club. Home: 10120 Chapel Rd Potomac MD 20854-4143 Home (Winter): 105 Biltmore Saint Simons Island GA 31522 What's good for the public interest ultimately is good for every person, business, or other group in the nation. This, combined with modern application of the Golden Rule, about sums it up.

**WALKER, CLARENCE WESLEY,** lawyer; b. Durham, N.C., July 19, 1931; s. Ernie Franklin and Mollie Elizabeth (Cole) W.; m. Ann-Heath Harris, June 5, 1954; children: Clare Ann, Wesley Gregg. AB, Duke U., 1953, LL.B., 1955. Bar: N.C. 1955. Assoc. Mudge Stern Baldwin & Todd, 1955-59; ptnr. Kennedy, Covington, Loddell & Hickman, Charlotte, N.C., 1960-. Bd. dirs. Lawyers Mut. Liability Ins. Co., Legal Services Corp. N.C., Oakwood Homes Corp. Glendale Group, Ltd.; lectr. N.C. Bar Found. Continuing Legal Edn. Insts., N.C. Jud. Planning Com., 1978-79; pres. Pvt. Adjudication Found.

---

Chmn. bd. mgrs. Charlotte Meml. Hosp. and Med. Ctr., 1981-87; trustee N.C. Ctrl. U., 1979-83; vice-chmn. Charlotte-Mecklenburg Hosp. Authority, 1988-99; adv. bd. Ctrl. Piedmont Paralegal Sch.; trustee Carolinas Healthcare Found., Charlotte Country Day Sch., 1977-81; state chmn. Nat. Found. March of Dimes, 1968-70; chmn. Charlotte Park and Recreation Commn., 1970-73; bd. dirs. Charlotte Symphony, 1965-71, Bethlehem Ctr., 1975-77, N.C. Recreators Found., 1973-75; adv. bd. Charlotte Children's Theatre, 1972; bd. dirs. Charlotte C. of C., 1970-72; bd. visitors Duke U. Law Sch.; dir., gen. campaign chmn. United Way Ctrl. Carolinas, 1985. Fellow Am. Bar Found.; mem. N.C. Bar Assn. (pres. 1978-79, gov. 1971-75), ABA (state del. 1980-89, assembly del. 1989-97, bd. govs. 1997-2000, chair audit com. 2000—) 26th Jud. Dist. Bar Assn., Mecklenburg Bar Found. (trustee), Am. Law Inst., Order of Coif, Phi Eta Sigma, Phi Beta Kappa. Democrat. Methodist. Home: 1047 Ardsley Rd Charlotte NC 28207-1815 Office: Kennedy Covington Lobdell & Hickman Hearst Tower 47th Fl 214 N Tryon St Charlotte NC 28202

**WALKER, COREAN JONES,** evangelist; b. Marion, Ind., Mar. 27, 1952; d. Arthur Lee and Millie Mae Jones; 1 child, Jennifer Nicole. Diploma, Marion HS, Marion, Ind., 1970; diploma word processing, Ind. Bus. Coll., Marion, Ind., 1987—89. Evangelist. Dist. coord. Ind. One Ch. One Child, Marion, Ind., 1991—92; dir., fin. coord. Caring Hands Ministry, Marion, Ind., 1997—2003; editor-light centennial New Light Bapt. Ch., Marion, Ind., 2001—02; pub. rels. and mktg. mgr. In His Presence Internat. Ministry. Author: Walk With Me Lord, 2002, Inspirations of Love, 2003; editor: (newsletter) Light Centennial, 2001. Exec. sec. B for City Coun., Marion, Ind., 2003; founder Arthur Lee Jones- Millie Mae Jones Ministries; group leader Purpose Driven Women; founder His Women Outreach Ministry, active In The Way Ministries; bd. dirs. Faith Tabernacle Outreach Ministries, Am. Bus. Women, Grant County Chaplaincy Bd., Grant County Sheriff's Dept. Recipient Corean Walker Day Proclamation, City of Muncie, James P. Carey-Mayor, 1991, Ind. One Ch. One Child, Elaine Walters/South Bend Mar, 1991, Cert. of Recognition, Famous Poets-Mark Schramm/ Talent, Oreg., 2001, Editor's Choice award, Internat. Libr. Poetry, 2005. Baptist. Starting "Caring Hands" a ministry that has helped 1,600 children have a nice Christmas- also in helping 250 children with Easter baskets. Assisting in adoptions for special needs children; intercessor for Kids Hope; assistance directory of Crowned With His Glory Ministries. Home: 2125 So Florence St Marion IN 46953 Office Phone: 765-668-8871. Personal E-mail: evancjw@yahoo.com.

**WALKER, CRAIG MICHAEL,** lawyer; 2 children. BA, Williams Coll., 1969; JD, Cornell U., 1972. Bar: N.Y. 1973, U.S. Dist. Ct. (so. dist.) N.Y. 1975, U.S. Ct. Appeals (2d cir) 1975, U.S. Supreme Ct., 1976. Assoc. Alexander and Green, N.Y.C., 1972—80, ptnr., 1980—86, chmn. litigation dept., 1985—86; ptnr. Walter, Conston, Alexander, and Green P.C., N.Y.C., 1987—89, Rogers and Wells, LLP, N.Y.C., 1990—99, Clifford, Chance, Rogers and Wells, LLP, NYC, 2000—02; spl. trial counsel Clifford Chance US, LLP, NYC, 2002—03; ptnr., spl. trial counsel Walker Law, LLP, Pound Ridge, NY, 2004—. Contbr. author: New York Forms of Jury Instruction, 1992; contbr. articles to profl. journals. Fellow Am. Bar Found.; mem. ABA, N.Y. State Bar Assn., Def. Rsch. Inst., Fed. Bar Coun. Democrat.

**WALKER, DALE MAXWELL,** city official; b. Big Rapids, Mich., Dec. 18, 1947; s. Lewis M. and Hilma I. (Windquist) W.; m. Joanne Kay Richmond, June 22, 1968; children: Christina Elizabeth, Heather Marie. BS, Ferris State U., 1970; MBA, Ctrl. Mich. U., 1981. Cert. govt. fin. mgr., credentialed city mgr. Dir. fin. City of Owosso, Mich., 1970-74; internal auditor John Wesley Coll., 1974—76; corp. treas. Mich. Bapt. Homes, Detroit, 1976-77; dir. fin. City of Cadillac, Mich., 1977—. Pres. Gospel Bookstore, Inc., Cadillac, 1983-98; bd. dirs. Workplace Ministry, 2001-05. Bd. dirs. Wexford County United Way, 1980-82, Shiawassee County United Way, 1971-72; sec.-treas. Cadillac Police and Fire Retirement System, 1977-87, bd. dirs. 1987—; chmn. Mcpl. Employees Retirement System, Mich., 1997—. Fellow Govtl. Fin. Officers Assn. U.S. and Can. (Profl. Achievement award 1984-2005); mem. Mich. Mcpl. Fin. Officers Assn. (bd. dirs. 1983-85), Internat. City Mgrs. Assn., Mich. Mcpl. Treas. Assn., Mcpl. Treas. Assn. U.S. and Can. (bd. dirs. 1982-84), McGuires Golf Club. Republican. Baptist. Avocations: golf, swimming, reading. Home: 901 Lincoln St Cadillac MI 49601-2035 Office: 200 N Lake St Cadillac MI 49601-1829 Office Phone: 231-775-0181. E-mail: finance@cadillac-mi.net.

**WALKER, DANIEL,** museum director; BA, Bowdoin Coll.; MA, Harvard U. Assoc. curator to curator Ancient, Near Ea. and Far Ea. Art Cin. Art Mus., 1975—88; head Islamic Dept. Met. Mus. Art, NYC, 1988—2005, Patti Cadby Birch Curator in Charge, Dept. Islamic Art, 1997—2005; dir. The Textile Mus., Washington, 2005—. Curator (exhibitions) Flowers Underfoot: Indian Carpets of the Mughal Era, Met. Mus. Art, 1998. Office: The Textile Mus 2320 S St NW Washington DC 20008-4088

**WALKER, DANIEL REUBEN,** surgeon; b. Provo, Utah, June 14, 1969; s. Alton Jay and Sheila Hamilton Walker; m. Anjenette Dustin, Dec. 21, 1991; children: Pearl Faith, Carmen Megumi, Lily Grace, Andrew Alonzo, Soren Kyle, Kjirstina Joy. BS, Brigham Young U., 1993; MS, Idaho State U., 1995; MD, Uniformed Svc. U. of the Health Sci., 1999. Lic. Licensure Idaho State Bd. of Medicine. Intern USAF, Travis AFB, Calif., 1999—2001, flight surgeon Tokyo, 2001—05, resident San Antonio, 2005—. Pastoral coord., Japan, 2001—05. Maj. USAF. Decorated Meritorious Svc. Medal USAF.

**WALKER, DAVID ALAN (DAVID ALAN WALKER),** finance educator; b. York, Pa., Jan. 5, 1941; s. Arthur Benjamin and Alva (Strasbougher) Walker; m. Audrey Thayer, Aug. 21, 1982; children: Matthew Billett, Elizabeth Penniman Bilhartz. BA, Pa. State U., 1962; MS, Iowa State U., 1964, PhD, 1968. Asst. prof. Pa. State U., 1968-70; economist FDIC, 1970-76, 78-80; vis. assoc. prof. Northwestern U., 1976-77; dir. rsch. Office Comptroller Currency, 1977-78; assoc. prof. Georgetown U., 1980-82, prof., 1982-92, assoc. dean, 1985-87, John A. Largay prof., 1992—. Chair governing bd. Credit Rsch. Ctr., 1997-05; dir. Capital Mkts. Rsch. Ctr., 1989-2005; mem. quality assessment team Israel Coun. Higher Edn., 2005; cons. in field. Co-author textbooks; editor Jour. Fin. Rsch., 1981-87; co-editor Jour. Small Bus. Fin., 1992-95; mem. editl. bd. Jour. Fin. Rsch., Fin. Mgmt., J.F.Q.A., Fin. Rev., Quar. Rev. Econ. and Fin., Jour. Small Bus. Fin.; contbr. articles to profl. jours. NDEA fellow, 1962-64. Mem. Am. Econ. Assn., So. Fin. Assn. (bd. dirs.), Ea. Fin. Assn. (bd. dirs.), Fin. Mgmt. Assn. (v.p. 1990-91, pres. 1994-95, trustee 1995-2005, chair bd. trustees 1999-2005), Beta Gamma Sigma. Republican. Home: 4416 Que St NW Washington DC 20007 Office: Georgetown U Sch Bus Washington DC 20057-0001 Office Phone: 202-687-4582. E-mail: walkerd@georgetown.edu.

**WALKER, DAVID ELLIS, JR.,** communications educator, minister, consultant; b. Richmond, Va., Oct. 5, 1938; s. David Ellis and Laura Eloise (Vaughan) W.; m. Sandra Suzanne Barnes, Feb. 3, 1964; children: David Ellis III, Virginia Suzanne Walker Frizzell, Cindy Poole Key, Michelle Poole Clark. BA, David Lipscomb U., 1960; MA, U. Fla., 1961, PhD, 1969. Ordained to ministry Ch. Christ, 1954. Instr. Jacksonville (Fla.) U., 1963-65; min. Ch. of Christ, 1954—; prof. Middle Tenn. State U., Murfreesboro, 1965—. Acting chmn. dept. speech Middle Tenn. State U., 1984, 1990, dir. debate, 1965-70, pres. faculty senate, 1983-84; coord. comm. studies,1969-81, 97-99; cons. in field. Editor Jour. of NonTraditional Education, 1992-96; contbr. articles to profl. jours. Grad. fellow U. Fla., 1961-63; grantee Mid. Tenn. State U., 1967, 72, 77-78, 88-90, 92-94, David Walker scholar Mid. Tenn. State U., 1993—. Mem. NEA, Tenn. Comm. Assn. (v.p. 1973-74, 2002-03), Tenn. Intercollegiate Forensic Assn. (pres. 1966-67, exec. sec. 1967-68), So. States Comm. Assn., Tenn. Edn. Assn., Pi Kappa Delta (gov. province of S.E. 1966-68), Phi Kappa Phi (chpt. treas. 1989-90). Avocations: reading, walking. Home: Ste 202 910 Murfreesboro Rd Franklin TN 37064 Office: Mid Tenn State U Dept Of Speech And Theatre Murfreesboro TN 37132-0001 Business E-Mail: dwalker@mtsu.edu.

---

**WALKER, DAVID MICHAEL,** federal official; b. Birmingham, Ala., Oct. 2, 1951; s. David Sellers and Dorothy Ann (West) W.; m. Mary Carmel Etheredge, June 12, 1971; children: Carol Marie, James Andrew. BS in Acctg., Jacksonville U., 1973; Sr. Exec. Govt. Cert., Harvard U., 1986; PhD in Bus. Adminstrn. (hon.), Bryant Coll., 2002; PhD in Pub. Svc. (hon.), Lincoln Meml. U., 2004; PhD in Civil Laws (hon.), Jacksonville U., 2006. CPA, Fla., Tex. Sr. auditor Price Waterhouse & Co. and Coopers & Lybrand, Jacksonville, Fla., 1973-76; dir. personnel Coopers & Lybrand, Atlanta and Houston, 1976-79; Ea. regional mgr. Source Svcs. Corp., Washington, 1979-83; acting exec. dir. and dep. exec. dir. Pension Benefit Guaranty Corp., Washington, 1983-85; dep. asst. sec. US Dept. Labor, Washington, 1985-87, asst. sec. for pension and welfare benefit programs, 1987-89; ptnr., global mng. dir. human capital svcs. practice Arthur Andersen LLP, Atlanta, 1989-98; US comptroller gen. US Govt. Accountability Office, Washington, 1998—. Author: Retirement Security-Understanding and Planning Your Financial Future, 1996; co-author: Delivering on the Promise: How to Attract, Manage and Retain Human Capital, 1998; contbr. articles, editl. adv. bd. numerous profl. jours. Gov. bd. Internat. Orgn. Supreme Audit Instns. chmn. strategic planning, acctg., reporting; chmn. U.S. Intergovtl. Audit Forum; chmn. U.S. Joint Fin. Mgmt. Improvement Program, Ctr. Continuous Auditing. Recipient numerous pub. svc., profl. and industry awards for outstanding svc. and contbns. Mem. AICPA Group of 100 (past chmn. employee benefit plans com.), Nat. Acad. Pub. Adminstrn., Nat. Acad. Social Ins., Coun. for Excellence in Govt., Concord Coalition, Sons of Am. Revolution, Cosmos Club. Roman Catholic. Home: 9061 Tower House Pl Alexandria VA 22308-2758 Office: US Govt Accountability Office 441 G St NW Ste 700 Washington DC 20548-0001 Office Phone: 202-512-5500. E-mail: walkerd@gao.gov.

**WALKER, DEBRA BESS,** lawyer; b. Carthage, Ill., May 27, 1960; d. Roy Francis and Marianna Emily (Johnson) W. BS in Accountancy, U. Ill., 1982, JD, 1987. Bar: Ill. 1987; U.S. Dist. Ct. (no. dist.) Ill. 1987. CPA McGladrey & Pullen, Champaign, Ill., 1983-84; atty. Williams & Montgomery, Chgo., 1987-93, Brydges Riseborough, Chgo., 1993-96, Clausen Miller, P.C., Chgo., 1996—. Adv. bd. mem. Bd. of Visitors (1993-96) and chmn. and bd. dirs. Recent Alumni Adv. Bd. (1995-97), U. Ill. Coll. of Law. Recipient Outstanding Woman Law Grad. award U. Ill. Coll. of Law, 1987, Outstanding Recent Alumni award, U. Ill. Coll. of Law, 1997. Mem. Women's Bar Assn. Ill. (1st v.p. 1997-98, pres. 1998-99), North Mich. Ave. Bus. and Profl. Women's Network (pres. 1990-91, Woman of Achievement 1994), Ill. State Bar Assn., Chgo. Bar Assn., Ill Bar Found. (bd. dirs., 2000—), Ill. Supreme Ct. Com. on Professionalism. Democrat. Methodist. Avocations: athletics, dance, singing, theater, movies. Office: Clausen Miller PC 10 S Lasalle St Ste 1600 Chicago IL 60603-1098 Office Phone: 312-606-7839. Business E-Mail: dwalker@clausen.com.

**WALKER, DEWARD EDGAR, JR.,** anthropologist, educator; b. Johnson City, Tenn., Aug. 3, 1935; s. Deward Edgar and Matilda Jane (Clark) W.; m. Candace J. Arroyo; children: Alice, Deward Edgar III, Mary Jane, Sarah, Daniel, Joseph Benjamin. Student, Ea. Oreg. Coll., 1953-54, 56-58, Univ. of the Americas, 1958-59; BA in Anthropology with honors, U. Oreg., 1960-61, PhD in Anthropology, 1964; postgrad., Wash. State U., 1962. Asst. prof. anthropology George Washington U., Washington, 1964-65, Wash. State U., Pullman, 1965-67, research collaborator, 1967-69; assoc. prof., chmn. dept. Sociology/Anthropology, lab. dir. U. Idaho, Moscow, 1967-69; prof. U. Colo., Boulder, 1969—, research assoc. in population process program of inst. behavioral sci., 1969-73, assoc. dean Grad. Sch., 1973-76. Founder, v.p. Walker Rsch. Group, Ltd., Boulder, Colo., 1995. Founder, co-editor Northwest Anthropol. Rsch. Notes, 1966—; editor, Plateau Vol.: Handbook of North American Indians, 1971-98; author, co-author 150 books; contbr. over 250 articles to profl. jours. Mem. tech. steering panel Hanford Environ. Dose Reconstrn. Project, 1988-95, Basalt Waste Isolation Project, Hanford, 1986-88; advisor Native Am. affairs. With U.S. Army, 1954-62. Fellow NSF, 1961, NDEA, 1961-64. Fellow Am. Anthropol. Assn. (assoc. editor Am. Anthropologist 1973-74), Soc. Applied Anthropology (hon. life, exec. com. 1970-79, treas. 1976-79, chmn. 1960-2000, cons., expert witness, editor Human Orgn. 1970-76, High Plains Applied Anthropology rschr.); mem. AAAS, Am. Acad. Polit. and Social Scis., N.W. Anthropol. Conf. Avocations: geology, mining, ranching. Home: PO Box 4147 Boulder CO 80306-4147 Office: U Colo PO Box 233 Boulder CO 80309-0233 Office Phone: 303-492-6719. E-mail: walkerde@colorado.edu. *I have been both lucky and happy to have had the opportunities to do so many wonderful things in my life as an anthropologist.*

**WALKER, DONALD EZZELL,** retired academic administrator; b. Springfield, Mo., July 13, 1921; s. Edward Everett and Cecilia (Ezzell) W.; m. Ann Lathrop, Dec. 17, 1943; 1 son, Craig Lathrop. AB, U. So. Calif., 1943, M.Th., 1947; PhD, Stanford U., 1954; L.H.D. (hon.), Southeastern Mass. U., 1973. Recreational dir. club work All Nations Found., Los Angeles, 1941-42, Wilshire Meth. Ch., Los Angeles, 1942-43; asst. minister Vincent Meth. Ch., Los Angeles, 1943-44; minister Encinitas Meth. Ch., 1945-47; teaching asst. Stanford U., 1947-49; instr. sociology San Diego State Coll., 1949-51, asst. prof. sociology, 1951-54, assoc. dean students, counseling, 1954-56, dean counseling, 1956-58, v.p. acad. affairs, 1968-71, acting pres., 1971-72; dean of students San Fernando Valley State Coll., Northridge, Calif., 1958-60; pres. Idaho State U., 1960-64; dean of students Sonoma State Coll., Rohnert Park, Calif., 1964-66; vice chancellor student affairs U. Calif., Irvine, 1966-68, sr. lectr. Grad. Sch. Administrn., 1967-68, fellow Univ. Coll., 1967-68; pres. Southeastern Mass. State U., N. Dartmouth, 1972-83; chancellor Grossmont-Cuyamaca Community Coll. Dist., El Cajon, Calif., 1983-92; ret., 1992. Author (with others) Readings in American Public Opinion, The Effective Administrator: A Practical Approach to Problem-Solving, Decision-Making, and Campus Leadership, 1979; Never Try to Teach a Pig to Sing: Wit and Wisdom for Leaders, 1996; contbr. articles to profl. jours. Home: 8661 Lake Murray Blvd Apt 19 San Diego CA 92119-2842

**WALKER, DONALD MURRAY,** minister; b. Lansing, Mich., Oct. 10, 1938; s. Paul H. and Margaret V. (Holloway) W.; m. Jacquelyn Touchstone, June 7, 1958; children: Donalyn Renee Scoggins, S. Denise Walker. BS, Lee U., 1977; MA, Ashland U., 1978; MDiv, Ch. of God Theol. Sem., 1980; EdD, Southeastern Nova U., 1983. Ordained to ministry Ch. of God, 1968. Evangelist Ch. of God, Minot, N.D., 1958-60, state dir. youth and Christian edn. Indpls., 1960-64, pastor S.C., 1964-70, state dir. youth and Christian edn. Mich., 1970-74, Ohio, 1974-78, Tenn., 1978-82; pres. Northwest Bible Coll., Minot, 1982-86; state overseer Ch. of God, N.D., S.D., 1984-86, asst. dir. gen. edn. dept. Cleveland, Tenn., 1986-88, state overseer Ind., 1988-93, Tenn., 1993-98, mem. exec. coun., 1994-98; pres. Ch. of God Theol. Sem., Cleveland, Tenn., 1998—2002; state adminstry. bishop No. Ga. Ch. of God, 2002—, mem. exec. coun., 2002—. Chmn. Ch. of God Chaplains Commn., Cleveland, 1990-94; mem. bldg. com. Internat. Ch. of God World Hdqs., 2002-2005; mem. world mission bd. Ch. of God, 2002—. Bd. dirs. chmn. bldg. com. Lee U., 1994-98. Home: 1845 Partridge Rd NW Cleveland TN 37312-2128 Office: No Ga Ch of God Exec Office 962 Parkside Walk Ln Lawrenceville GA 30043 While there are many issues and crises in life that we often do not understand our attitude toward our faith in God and His mercy can never be dictated by our circumstances.

**WALKER, DORETTA ANITA,** director; b. Memphis, Tenn., Feb. 21, 1942; d. Elgin and Mary Ella Walker. BS, So. Ill. U., 1970; cert. reading specialist, Harris Stowe Tchrs. U., 1978; MEd, Nat. Coll. Edn., 1989. Cert. officer African Meth. Episc. Ch., 2004. Mem. Divsn. Curriculum Com., St. Louis, Chpt. I Staff Devel. Planning Com., St. Louis; mem. curriculum com. SAT-MMA, St. Louis; coord. After Sch. Tutorial Program, St. Louis. Named to Wall Tolerance, 2005; recipient Shining Star award, 2004, Tchr. Appreciation award, Urban League of Metro, St. Louis, 1990. Mem. NAACP, Nat. Bethou Edn. Alumni, So. Ill. U Alumni Assn., The Symner Alumni Assn. (life), Tu Gamma Delta. Democrat. Avocations: travel, photography, jazz. Home: 3026A N Taylor Ave Saint Louis MO 63115

**WALKER, DORIS ISAAK,** writer, historian, educator; b. Cleve. d. Alphonse Charles and Rose Emma (Gibbons) Isaak; children: Brent Evan Walker, Blair Dana Walker; m. Jack Pierson Smith, 2001. BA, Case Western Reserve U.; postgrad., Northwestern U., U. Calif., Irvine. Publs. editor Brunswick Corp., Chgo.; pub. rels. mgr. Dana Point (Calif.) Harbor, 1970-84; field rsch. writer Kessler Esch., L.A., Calif., 1984-89. Instr. Calif. history South Orange County Coll. Dist.; lectr. in field. Author: A Guide Book of Philatelic-Numismatic Covers, 1970, Dana Point Harbor/Capistrano Bay: Home Port for Romance, 1981, 4th edit., 1995, The Whales of Capistrano Bay, 1982, Sections of Orange, 1989, Orange County Adventures with Children, 1997, The Heritage of San Clemente, 2000, Coastal Reflections, 2001, Mission Viejo: The Ageless Land, 2005, Orange County Then and Now, 2006; contbr., editor, photographer newspapers, mags. Commr. Orange County Hist. Commn., 1994—; founder, coord. Dana Point Festival of Whales, 1975-84. Recipient more than 100 awards including Am. History award DAR, Clarion award, Unique Coverage award, Women in Comm., Woman of Distinction award Capistrano Bay Area, Soroptimist Internat., Crisis Comm. Award Internat. Coun. Indsl. Editors, cert. of recognition Calif. State Senate; named Orange County Woman of Achievement in Comm., YMCA. Mem. AAUW (pres. San Clemente-Capistrano Bay br.), Nat. Fedn. Press Women (Nat. first place history book award), So. Calif. Media Profls. (pres. 2006), Calif. Press Women (pres. Orange County dist., state sec.), Dana Point Hist. Soc. (hon. life, co-founder, dir.), San Juan Capistrano Hist. Soc. (dir.), Orange County Hist. Soc. (dir.), Dana Point Lighthouse Soc. (hon. life), Friends of Libr. (hon. life). Avocations: travel, photography. Office: PO Box 546 Dana Point CA 92629-0546 Office Phone: 949-496-6677. Personal E-mail: homeports@aol.com.

**WALKER, DOUGLAS C.,** banker; b. Bethelaham, Pa. BA, Princeton U., 1970; MBA, Harvard U., 1978. Asst. v.p. J.P. Morgan, 1970-76; gen. ptnr. Brown Bros. Harriman & Co., N.Y.C. Bd. dirs. Asten Group, Inc., Magee Reiter Automotive, Inc., Nat. Lands Trust. Bd. dirs. U. Pa. Mus., Acad. Natural Scis. Office: Brown Bros Harriman & Co 1531 Walnut St Philadelphia PA 19102-3098

**WALKER, DUARD LEE,** medical educator; b. Bishop, Calif., June 2, 1921; s. Fred H. and Anna Lee (Shumate) Walker; m. Dorothea Virginia McHenry, Aug. 11, 1945; children: Douglas Keith, Donna Judith, David Cameron, Diane Susan. AB, U. Calif., Berkeley, 1943, MA, 1947; MD, U. Calif., San Francisco, 1945. Diplomate Am. Bd. Microbiology. Intern, U.S. Naval Hosp., Shoemaker, Calif., 1945—46; asst. resident internal medicine Stanford U. Service San Francisco Hosp., 1950—52; assoc. prof. med. microbiology and preventive medicine U. Wis., Madison, 1952—59, prof. med. microbiology, 1959—88, prof., chmn. med. microbiology, 1970—76, Paul F. Clark prof. med. microbiology, 1977—88, prof. emeritus, 1988—, prof., chmn. med. microbiology, 1981—88. Cons. Naval Med. Rsch. Unit, Gt. Lakes, Ill., 1958—74; mem. microbiology tng. com. Nat. Inst. Gen. Med. Scis., 1966—70; mem. nat. adv. Allergy and Infectious Diseases Coun., 1970—74; mem. adv. com. on blood program rsch. ARC, 1978—79; mem. study group on papovaviridae Internat. Com. on Taxonomy of Viruses, 1976—90; mem. vaccines and related biol. products adv. com. FDA, 1985—89; mem. rev. panel postdoct. rsch. fellowships for physicians Howard Hughes Med Inst., 1990—93. Mem. editl. bd. Infection and Immunity, 1975—83, Archives of Virology, 1981—83, Microbial Pathogenesis, 1985—90. Served to lt. (j.g.) USNR, 1943—46, served to capt. USNR, 1953—55. Fellow NRC postdoctoral virology, Rockefeller Inst. Med. Rsch., N.Y.C., 1947—49, USPHS immunology, George Williams Hooper Found., U. Calif., San Francisco, 1949—50. Fellow: Infectious Diseases Soc. Am., Am. Acad. Microbiology, Am. Pub. Health Assn.; mem.: Arts and Letters, Wis. Acad. Sics., Am. Soc. Virology, AAUP, Reticuloendothelial Soc., Soc. Exptl. Biology and Medicine, AAAS, Am. Soc. Microbiology, Am. Assn. Immunologists, NAS. Home: 618 Odell St Madison WI 53711-1435 Office: U Wis Med Sch 600 Highland Ave Madison WI 53792-1510 Office Phone: 608-233-9279. Personal E-mail: dlwalke1@facstaff.wisc.edu.

**WALKER, EDWARD KEITH, JR.,** retired management consultant, retired military officer; b. Annapolis, Md., Jan. 23, 1933; s. Edward Keith and Miriam (Whitmore) W.; m. Carol Ann Turner, June 12, 1954 (dec. June 14, 2002); children: Lynn Walker Streett, Wendy Louise. BS, U.S. Naval Acad., 1954; postgrad., Armed Forces Staff Coll., 1966; MBA in Fin. Mgmt., George Washington U., 1970. Commd. ensign U.S. Navy, 1954, advanced through grades to rear admiral, 1981; force supply officer COMSUBLANT Norfolk, Va., 1975—78; exec. officer SPCC Mechanicsburg, Pa., 1978—80; comdr. Naval Supply Ctr., Puget Sound, Bremerton, Wash., 1980—81; Atlantic Fleet supply officer CINCLANTFLT Norfolk, 1981—83; asst. comptroller Navy Dept., Washington, 1983—84; comdr. Naval Supply Systems Command and 35th chief supply corps Washington, 1984—88; v.p. adminstrn. and corp. strategy Resource Cons. Inc., Vienna, Va., 1989—2000, v.p. emeritus, 2000—. Vice chmn. bd. dirs. Herley Industries. Decorated D.S.M., Legion of Merit (3 awards); recipient Def. Superior Service medal, 1983 Mem. Vinson Hall Corp. (bd. dirs., chmn. 2003), Naval Acad. Found. (trustee), U.S. Navy Meml. Found. (bd. dirs., trans.), Supply Corps Found. (past pres.), Supply Corps Assn. (past pres.), U.S. Naval Inst., Am. Soc. Naval Engrs., Naval Submarine League, Naval Order U.S. (life), Surface Navy Assn. (life), Navy League U.S. (life), Naval Acad. Alumni Assn. (life), Mil. Officers Assn. (life), N.Y. Yacht Club, Chesapeake Yacht Club. Republican. Episcopalian. Home: 3520 Saylor Pl Alexandria VA 22304-1831 *There is no greater satisfaction than to see your people succeed, and then to insure they get the credit.*

**WALKER, EDWARD S., JR.,** former ambassador; b. Abington, Pa., June 13, 1940; s. Edward Stanley and Rosabel Dunlop (Gould) W.; m. Wendy Jane Griffiths, Apr. 7, 1973; Kathryn Erica, Christopher James. BA, Hamilton Coll., 1963; MA, Boston U., 1965. Joined Fgn. Svc., Dept. State, Washington, 1967; polit. officer Am. Embassy, Tel Aviv, 1969-73; staff asst. Nr. Ea. affairs US Dept. State, Washington, 1974-75; Arabic lang. trainee Fgn. Svc. Inst., Lebanon, Tunis, Egypt, 1975-77; polit. officer Am. Embassy, Damascus, Syria, 1977-79; spl. asst. Pres.'s personal rep., Washington, 1980-82; exec. dir. Office of Dep. Sec. US Dept. State, Washington, 1982-84; mem. Royal Coll. Def. Studies, London, 1984-85; dep. asst. sec. Bur. Near East Affairs US Dept. State, 1988-89, U.S. amb. to United Arab Emirates Abu Dhabi, 1989-92; dept. permanent rep. to UN, N.Y.C., 1993-94; U.S. amb. to Egypt US Dept. State, Cairo, 1994-97, U.S. amb. to Israel Tel Aviv, 1997—99, asst. sec. for Near Ea. Affairs Washington, 2000—01; pres., CEO Mid. East Inst., Washington, 2001—. With U.S. Army, 1962-65. Decorated Order of Independence (Abu Dhabi); recipient Superior Honor award Dept. State, 1975, Meritorious Honor award, 1976, Disting. Civilian Svc. award Dept. Def., 1997. Episcopalian. Office: Middle East Inst 1761 N St NW Washington DC 20036

**WALKER, FLOYD LEE,** lawyer; b. Kiefer, Okla., Mar. 27, 1919; s. Willis and Sarah Josephine (McFarl) W.; children by previous marriage: Mary Lea Walker Byrd, Cheryl Sue Walker Newman, James M.; m. Virginia Gifford Raines, Oct. 8, 1971. LLB, Tulsa U., 1949. Bar: Okla. 1949. Claims atty. Standard Ins. Co., Tulsa, 1949-53; pvt. practice Tulsa, 1953—. 1st lt. USAAF, 1942-45. Decorated DFC, Air medal with 3 oak leaf clusters. Fellow Am. Coll. Trial Lawyers; mem. ABA, ATLA, Okla. Bar Assn. (bd. govs. 1979-82), Tulsa County Bar Assn. (pres. 1973), Okla. Trial Lawyers Assn. Home: 1502 S Boulder Ave Apt 7B Tulsa OK 74119-4022 Office: 900 Oneok Plz Tulsa OK 74103

**WALKER, FRANKLIN CURTIS,** federal agency administrator; b. Sept. 10, 1945; s. Howard and Edna Walker; m. Judy Provins, May 29, 1967; children: Mark, Kathy, Phillip. BS in Biology, N.Mex. State U., 1972. Park ranger White Sands Nat. Monument Nat. Park Svc., 1970-72, park ranger Jefferson Nat. Expansion Meml., 1972-73, park ranger Gulf Islands Nat. Seashore, 1973-77, naturalist south dist. Yellowstone Nat. Park, 1977-80, chief of interpretation Carlsbad Caverns Nat. Park, 1980-85, park supt. Ft. Clatsop Nat. Meml., 1985-90, supt. Nez Perce Nat. Hist. Park Idaho, Oreg., Wash.,

Mont., 1990-98, supt. Saguaro Nat. Park Tucson, 1998—. 1st lt. U.S. Army, 1967-69. Office: Saguaro Nat Park 3693 S Old Spanish Trl Tucson AZ 85730-5601 Home: PO Box 254 Yellowstone National Park WY 82190-0254

**WALKER, GEORGE HERBERT, III,** former ambassador, retired investment banking company executive; b. St. Louis, Mar. 16, 1931; s. George H. and Mary (Carter) W.; m. Sandra E. Canning, Dec. 23, 1955 (div. Oct. 1962); children: Mary Elizabeth, Wendy, Isabelle; m. Kimberly Gedge, July 27, 1968 (div. Jan. 1977); children: George H. IV, Carter; m. Carol Banta, Feb. 21, 1987. BA, Yale U., 1953; LL.B., Harvard U., 1956. Bar: Conn. 1956. Gen. ptnr. G.H. Walker & Co. (later G.H. Walker, Laird Inc.), 1961-74; sr. v.p., also bd. dirs. White, Weld & Co. Inc., 1974-75; chmn. bd. dirs. G.H. Walker & Co., 1973-74; exec. v.p. Stifel Nicolaus & Co., 1976-78, pres., CEO, 1978-92, chmn., 1982—2001, chmn. emeritus, 2001—; US amb. to Hungary US Dept. State, Budapest, 2003—06. Civilian aide to sec. U.S. Army for Ea. Mo., 1973-80; bd. dirs. Laidlaw Corp., Laclede Steel Co., Eck-Adams Corp.; bd. govs. Midwest Stock Exch., 1982-88. Bd. dirs. Downtown St. Louis Inc., 1975-90, chmn., 1984-86; bd. dirs. Webster U., chmn. bd., 1987-92; trustee Mo. Hist. Soc., St. Louis Children's Hosp., 1972-92, Jefferson Nat. Expansion Meml. Assn., 1992; vestryman St. Ann's Ch., Kennebunkport, Maine; mem. Mo. Rep. Ctrl. Com., 1983—; adv. bd. St. Louis Area coun. Boy Scouts Am., 1989—; trustee investment trust Episcopal Diocese of Mo.; hon. bd. dirs. Anti-Drug Abuse Edn. Fund, Inc., 1990—; bd. dirs. St. Louis Zoo, 1992. With USAF, 1956-58. Mem. Rotary (St. Louis club). E-mail: walkergh@stifel.com.

**WALKER, GEORGE KONTZ,** law educator; b. Tuscaloosa, Ala., July 8, 1938; s. Joseph Henry and Catherine Louise (Indorf) W.; m. Phyllis Ann Sherman, July 30, 1966; children: Charles Edward, Mary Neel. BA, U. Ala., 1959; LLB, Vanderbilt U., 1966; AM, Duke U., 1968; LLM, U. Va., 1972; postgrad. (Sterling fellow), Law Sch. Yale U., 1975-76. Bar: Va. 1967, N.C. 1976. Law clk. U.S. Dist. Ct., Richmond, Va., 1966-67; assoc. Hunton, Williams, Gay, Powell & Gibson, Richmond, 1967-70; pvt. practice Charlottesville, Va., 1970-71; asst. prof. Law Sch. Wake Forest U., Winston-Salem, NC, 1972-73, assoc. prof. Law Sch., 1974-77, prof. Law Sch., 1977—, mem. bd. advisors Divinity Sch., 1991-94; Charles H. Stockton prof. internat. law U.S. Naval War Coll., 1992-93. Vis. prof. Marshall-Wythe Sch. Law, Coll. William and Mary, Williamsburg, Va., 1979-80, U. Ala. Law Sch., 1985; cons. Naval War Coll., 1976—, Nat. Def. Exec. Res., 1991—, Naval War Coll., Internat. Law Dept. Adv. Bd., 1993—. Author: The Tanker War, 1980-88, 2000; contbr. articles to profl. jours. With USN, 1959-62, capt. USNR, ret. Woodrow Wilson fellow, 1962-63; decorated Order of the long Leaf Pine; recipient Joseph Branch Alumni Svc. award, Wake Forest, 1988, Meritorious Unit Commendation, USN, 1993; named Hon. Atty. Gen. N.C., 1986. Mem.: ABA, Internat. Inst. Humanitarian Law, Maritime Law Assn., Am. Law Inst., Am. Judicature Soc., Internat. Law Assn. (exec. com. Am. br. 2001—), Am. Soc. Internat. Law (exec. coun. 1988—91), N.C. Bar Assn. (v.p. 1997—98), Va. Bar Assn., Order of Barristers (hon.), Piedmont Club, Phi Delta Phi, Sigma Alpha Epsilon, Phi Beta Kappa, Order of the Coif (hon.). Democrat. Episcopalian. Home: 3321 Pennington Ln Winston Salem NC 27106-5439 Office: Wake Forest U Sch Law PO Box 7206 Winston Salem NC 27109-7206

**WALKER, GEORGE THEOPHILUS, JR.,** composer, music educator, pianist; b. Washington, June 27, 1922; s. George Theophilus Sr. and Rosa (King) W.; children: Gregory, Ian. MusB, Oberlin Coll., 1941; student of Rudolf Serkin, Rosario Scalero; Artist Diploma, Curtis Inst. music, 1945; D of Mus. Arts, U. Rochester, 1957; DFA (hon.), Lafayette Coll., 1982; MusD (hon.), Oberlin Coll., 1983; student of, Nadia Boulanger; MusD (hon.), Curtis Inst. Music, 1997; DHL (hon.), Montclair State U., 1997; MusD (hon.), Bloomfield Coll., 1997; DFA (hon.), Spelman Coll., 2001. Instr. Dillard U., New Orleans, 1953-54; instr. Dalcroze Sch. Music, N.Y.C., 1960-61, New Sch. Social Research, N.Y.C., 1961; instr. to assoc. prof. Smith Coll., Northampton, Mass., 1961-68; assoc. prof. U. Colo., Boulder, 1968-69; disting. prof. Rutgers U., Newark, 1976-92, prof. emeritus, 1992. Concert pianist Nat. Concert Artists, N.Y.C., 1950-53, Columbia Artists, N.Y.C., 1959-60; adj. prof. Peabody Inst. Johns Hopkins U., Balt., 1975-78; disting. prof. U. Del., Newark, 1975-76. Composer: Sonata for 2 Pianos (Harvey Gaul prize 1963), numerous sonatas, cantatas and concertos, Concerto for Cello and Orch., 1982, Sinfonias for Orch. Bd. dirs. Am. Bach Found., 1988; mem. Mary Flagler Cary Trust Commn., 1998. Recipient award Am. Acad. and Inst. Arts and Letter, 1982, Koussevitsky award, 1988, Pulitzer prize, 1996, L.J. Govs. award 1997, Koussevitsky award 1998, Mary Flagler Cary Charitable Trust award, 1998, Dorothy Maynor Arts Citizens award, 2000, A.I. duPont award Del. Symphony, 2001, Classical Roots award Detroit Symphony, 2001; grantee Smith Coll., U. Colo., Rutger U. Rsch. Coun., NEA, N.J. State Coun. for Arts; Fulbright fellow, 1957, John Hay Whitney fellow, 1958, Guggenheim fellow, 1969, 88, Rockefeller fellow, 1971, 74; Disting. scholar U. Rochester, 1996; commd. N.Y. Philharm., Kennedy Ctr., Cleve. Orch., Boston Symphony, N.J. Symphony, Am. Guild of Organists; inducted Am. Classical Music Hall of Fame, 2000. Mem. ASCAP, Am. Acad. Arts and Letters (mem.-elect), Am. Bach Found. (bd. dirs. 1988), Am. Symphony League. Democrat. Avocations: tennis, photography, music. Home: 323 Grove St Montclair NJ 07042-4223 Personal E-mail: gtwalker@verizon.net.

**WALKER, GEORGE W.,** bishop; Sr. bishop African Meth. Episcopal Zion Ch., Farmington. Named one of 100 Most Influential Black Americans, Ebony mag., 2004. African Meth Episcopal Zion Episcopal Residence PO Box 483 Farmington CT 06034*

**WALKER, GLORIA LEE,** training services executive; b. Oklahoma City, Dec. 31, 1942; d. Russell Holland and Ethel Wanita (Kierig) Walker; m. Thomas William Rupprath, June 3, 1966 (div. Feb. 1995); children: Robert Rupprath, John Rupprath. BA in Sociology, U. S.C., 1965; MS in Elem. Edn., U. Nebr., 1971; EdD in Adminstrn., Fla. Atlantic U., 1986. Ops. rsch. analyst U.S. Bur. Mines, Washington, 1988-90; employment devel. specialist IRS, Dallas, 1991-92; pres. AMERITRAIN, Dallas/Lubbock, Tex., 1992—. Author: Training a Diversified Workforce, 1993, Developing Training Materials, 1995, Instructing Diversified Employee, 1995, Seminars in Training, 1995.

**WALKER, GORDON BEVERLEY MOORE, JR.,** business educator; b. N.Y.C., Oct. 10, 1944; s. Gordon Beverley Moore and Nancy Holton Walker; m. Jane Edwards, June 15, 1977 (div. Sept. 1983); 1 child, Emma; m. Nancy Niebuhr, Mar. 22, 1984; children: Hugh Curran, Ian Moore. BA, Yale U., 1966; MBA, U. Pa., 1976, PhD, 1982. Assoc. prof. Sloan Sch. Mgmt., MIT, Cambridge, Mass., 1981-86, Wharton Sch., U. Pa., Phila., 1986-91, Sch. of Orgn. and Mgmt., Yale U., New Haven, 1991-93; prof., chair Cox Sch. of Bus., So. Meth. U., Dallas, 1993—. Cons. in field; bd. dirs. Alico, Inc. Co-author: Modern Competitive Strategy, 2003, 2d edit., 2006; contbr. articles to profl. jours. 1st lt. USMC, 1967-70. Decorated Bronze star; recipient numerous grants including NSF, 1987-89, 95-97. Mem.: Am. Sociol. Assn., Acad. Mgmt., Yale Club of Dallas (pres. 2001—02, 2003—05). Home: 331 Ridgebriar Dr Richardson TX 75080-1920 Office: Cox Sch Bus So Meth U Dallas TX 75275-0333 Office Phone: 214-768-2191. Business E-mail: gwalker@mail.cox.smu.edu.

**WALKER, GORDON DAVIES,** government official, writer, lecturer, consultant; b. Logan, Utah, July 10, 1944; s. Rudger Harper and Fawn Lucile (Davies) W.; m. Carlene Martin, June 5, 1968; children— Kimberly Anne, Kelly Anne, Gordon Davies Jr., Bradford Martin AB, Brigham Young U., 1968; MBA, Harvard U., 1971. Project dir. Becker Research Co., Boston, 1969-71; dir. mktg. Am. Nat. Enterprises, Salt Lake City, 1971-72; v.p., dir. Sweetwater Properties, Salt Lake City, 1972-76; gen. ptnr. Covecrest Properties, Salt Lake City, 1976—; spl. asst. to sec. HUD, Washington, 1981-82, dep. under sec., 1983-86; cons. real estate, fin. Commerce Cons., Washington, 1986-87; pres., chief exec. officer Deseret Fed. Savs. and Loan, Salt Lake City, 1987-88; pres. U.S. Resources, Inc., Phoenix, 1988-92, also bd. dirs.; pres. Energy Lock Inc., Salt Lake City, 1992—2002; exec. dir. Utah chpt. Alzheimer's Assn., 2002—06; dir. housing cmty. devel. State of Utah,

2003—. Author: Finance Your Own Way to Success, 1980; Develop Your Way to Success, 1981; Hottest New Ideas of the 1980's, 1982. Rep. state del., Salt Lake City, 1974; del. Rep. Nat. Conv., 1988 Mem. Nat. Assn. Realtors Mem. Lds Ch.

**WALKER, GRAHAM CHARLES,** biology professor; b. Boston, Feb. 8, 1948; s. Charles Bertram and Margaret Elizabeth (Biehn) W.; m. Janet Elizabeth Haliburton, May 30, 1970; 1 child, Gordon Andrew. BSc with honors, Carleton U., Ottawa, Ont., Can., 1970; PhD, U. Ill., 1974. Asst. prof. biology MIT, Cambridge, Mass., 1976-80, assoc. prof. biology, 1980-86, prof. biology, 1986—. Rsch. prof. Howard Hughes Med. Inst., 2002—, Am. Cancer Soc., 2003—. Co-author: DNA Repair and Mutagenesis; editor-in-chief Jour. Bacteriology, 1991-2001, editor, 1985-91; editl. bd. Mutation Rsch., Amsterdam, Netherlands, 1982—; editl. bd. DNA Repair, 2002—, contbr. articles to Procs. NAS USA, Cell, Microbiology Rev., Jour. Bacteriology. Housemaster McCormick Hall, MIT, Cambridge, 1986-92, Margaret MacVicar Faculty fellow MIT, 1992-2002, John Simon Guggenheim Meml. fellow, 1984, Woodrow Wilson fellow, 1970; recipient Rita Allen Career Devel. award, 1978-83, Howard Hughes Med. Inst. grantee in biology, 2002. Fellow Am. Acad. Arts & Scis.; mem. Am. Acad. Microbiology, Am. Soc. for Microbiology, Genetics Soc. Am., Am. Chem. Soc., Environ. Mutagen Soc. Achievements include discovery of umuDC analogs on plasmid pKM101; demonstration of repetoire of SOS genes; demonstrated critical role of exopolysaccharide in nodule invasion by Rhizobium meliloti; cloning and analysis of roles of UmuDC in UV mutagenesis; demonstrated RecA-mediated cleavage activates UmuD, second symbiotically active exopolysaccharide in R. meliloti. Office: MIT Biology Dept 77 Massachusetts Ave Cambridge MA 02139-4307 Business E-Mail: gwalker@mit.edu.

**WALKER, HENRY GILBERT,** health care executive, consultant; b. Gowanda, NY, Feb. 16, 1947; s. Henry George and Grace Dayton (Moore) W.; m. Elaine Ruth Darbee, July 18, 1970 (div. Dec. 1979); 1 child, Matthew Case; m. Patricia Ann Andrade, May 14, 1983; children: Michael David, Christopher John. BS in Indsl. Engring., Cornell U., 1969; MBA, U. Chgo., 1975. Evening adminstr. Rush-Presbyn. St-Luke's Med. Ctr., Chgo., 1973-75; mgmt. cons. Booz, Allen & Hamilton, Chgo., 1975-79; regional adminstr., v.p. S.W. Community Health Service, Albuquerque, 1979-83, adminstr., v.p., 1983-86; exec. v.p. Presbyn. Healthcare Services, Albuquerque, 1986-92; pres., CEO Tucson Med. Ctr., 1992—95, Health Ptnrs. of Ariz., 1995—97, Providence Health System, Seattle, 1997—2004; ptnr. Andrade Walker Consulting, LLC, Bellevue, Wash., 2004—. Bd. dirs. Park Dist., Elmhurst, Ill., 1978, 1979; mem. Dist. III Cmty. Action Com., Albuquerque, 1985; divsn. chmn. United Way of Albuqueque, 1985, 1988. Recipient Hosp. Survey award U. Chgo., 1975, Bachmeyer award U. Chgo., 1975, Outstanding Midshipman award Cornell U., 1969; named one of Emerging Healthcare Leaders, Healthcare Forum, 1985, 86, Healthcares Up and Comers, Modern Healthcare Mag., 1987. Mem.: Healthcare Forum (bd. dirs., chmn.), N.Mex. Hosp. Assn. (chmn. bd. dirs. 1983—85, treas.). Democrat. Presbyterian. Avocations: reading, hiking, skiing.

**WALKER, HERSHEL O.,** history educator; b. Andrews, Tex., Dec. 30, 1957; s. H. O. Jr. and Betty Ann Walker; m. Mary H. Walker; children: Allison Robinson, Jesse K., Shawn M. BA, Tex. Tech. U., Lubbock, 1981; MA, Tex. A&M U., College Station, 1995. Cert. secondary tchr. Tex. Edn. Agy. Tchr. world and U.S. history grades 9-12 Giddings Ind. Sch. Dist., Tex., 1981—. Office: Giddings HS PO Box 389 Giddings TX 78942-0389

**WALKER, HOWARD ERNEST,** lawyer; b. Mobile, Ala., Mar. 3, 1944; s. Ernest W. and Denise (Kearney) W.; m. Michelle Anne Pinsonneault, June 20, 1992. BA, U. Ill., 1966; JD, Boston U., 1974. Bar: R.I. 1974. Assoc. Hinckley, Allen & Snyder, Providence, 1974-80, ptnr., 1980—2004. Trustee Providence Pub. Libr., 1978-2000, pres., 2002—, vice chmn. programs; trustee R.I. Wild Plant Soc., 1995-97—; trustee R.I. Civic Chorale & Orchestra, 1988-95; dir. South Shore Mental Health Ctr., 1997—, v.p. 2000—; trustee and sec. Hopkinton Land Trust, 2002—; sec., Mem. Hopkinton Planning Bd., 2002—, sec., 2003-04. Lt. USNR, 1967-71. Mem. ABA, R.I. Bar Assn. (mem. ad hoc com. on future of law practice, chmn. superior ct. bench/bar com. 1990-93, 94-95, Dorothy Lohmann Cmty. Svc. award 2003), Maritime Law Assn. of US, Phi Kappa Phi, Phi Beta Kappa. Avocations: western Americana, natural history. Home: 39A Berrie Ln PO Box 118 Rockville RI 02873-0118 Office: PO Box 299 Hope Valley RI 02832 Office Phone: 401-539-6767. Business E-Mail: hewlaw@hughes.net.

**WALKER, IRVING EDWARD,** lawyer; b. Balt., Jan. 31, 1952; s. Bertram and Mildred (Shapiro) W.; children: Brandon Harris, Aaron Seth, Emily Celeste. BA, Duke U., 1973; JD, U. Md., 1978. Bar: Md. 1978, US Dist. Ct. Md. 1978, US Ct. Appeals (4th cir.) 1980, US Supreme Ct. 1995, US Ct. Appeals (3d cir.) 2001. Assoc. Frank, Bernstein, Conaway & Goldman, Balt., 1978-85, ptnr., 1986-91; prin. Miles & Stockbridge, Balt., 1991-2001; ptnr. Saul Ewing LLP, Balt., 2001—. Chmn. Bankruptcy & Creditors Rights Group, 1991-2000, vice chmn. bankruptcy and reorganization dept., 2006—. Contbg. author: Bankruptcy Deskbook, 1986. Bd. dirs. Jewish Cmty. Ctr. Greater Balt., 1986-88, Temple Emanuel of Balt., Inc., 1996-2002, Homeless Persons Representation Project, 2005—, Etz Chain Ctr., 2005—. Mem. ABA, Md. Bar Assn., Bar Assn. Balt. City (chmn. bankruptcy and bus. law com. 1989-90), Am. Bankruptcy Inst., Bankruptcy Assn. Dist. Md. (pres. 1992-93, chmn. Balt. chpt. 1989-91), Order of Coif. Avocation: weightlifting. Office: Saul Ewing LLP 500 E Pratt St Baltimore MD 21202 Business E-Mail: iwalker@saul.com.

**WALKER, JAMES ELLIOT CABOT,** physician; b. Bryn Mawr, Pa., Sept. 28, 1926; s. Arthur Meeker and Sylvia (Cabot) W.; m. Audrey Crowder Wakeman, July 11, 1965; children— Holly Barnwell, James Elliot Cabot. BA, Williams Coll., 1949; MD, U. Pa., 1953; MS in Hygiene, Harvard U., 1966. Intern and resident in medicine U. Wis., 1953, U. Mich., 1954-55, Peter Bent Brigham Hosp., 1958-60, assoc. dir., sr. assoc. dept. medicine Boston; also research asst., lectr. Harvard U. Med. Sch., 1959-65, prof. medicine and soc. and clin. planner, 1965-68, chmn. dept. clin. medicine, 1968-72; chmn. dept. community medicine U. Conn. Med. Sch., Farmington, 1972-86, prof. medicine, 1968-92, prof. medicine emeritus, 1992—. Vis. prof. St. Thomas' Hosp., London, 1975-76, Harvard Med. Sch., Cambridge, Mass., 1986-87; pres. Northeast Can./Am. Health Coun., 1978-87; dir. Ctr. for Internat. Cmty. Health Studies, 1981-86; assoc. dir. Traveler's Ctr. on Aging, 1987-98; chmn. Alzheimers Coalition of Conn., 1992-94; med. dir. Avery Heights Retirement Cmty., 1992-98; warden St. John's Ch., West Hartford, Conn., 1994-00; chmn. bd. Conn. Cmty. Care Inc., 1998-2001; chmn. bd. Duncaster Inc., 2000-02. Author articles, monograph in field. Served with Am. Field Service, 1945; to capt. M.C. U.S. Army, 1955-58. Fellow ACP, AGS. Home: 79 Bayberry Hill Rd Avon CT 06001-2800 Office: U Conn Health Ctr Farmington CT 06032 E-mail: jecwalker@comcast.net.

**WALKER, JAMES HARPER,** retired security firm executive, writer; b. Cleve., Ohio, Jan. 29, 1936; s. Roy Hubert and Susie May Walker; m. Barbara Jean Woods, Feb. 15, 1962; children: James Randolph, Mark Lawrence, John Ireland. BA, Lake Erie Coll., 1968. Charter life underwriter Ohio, 1971. Agt., staff mgr., sales mgr. Monumental Ins. Co, Cleve., 1962—72; police officer, detective Waite Hill (Ohio) Police Dept., 1974—81; asst. chief police Huron Rd., East Cleve., 1981—84; area mgr. The Wackenhut Corp., Louisville, 1985—94; ret. Author: (novel) Man In Blue (Lib. of Congress award), Inside Your Local Police, (children short story) Bushytail the Squirrel. Dir. save a sight fund Lions Club, Willoughby, Ohio, 1976—78; mem. police fellowcraft team Masonic Lodge, Willoughby 302, Ohio, 1976—81. Staff sgt. U.S. Army, 1953—56. Recipient Hon. Cert., Internat. Soc. Poets, 1994. Mem.: Masons. Independent-Republican. Avocations: golf, travel. Home: 44 Pfrimmers Chapel Rd Corydon IN 47112 Personal E-Mail: jwalk010@aol.com.

**WALKER, JANE STEWART,** small business owner, publishing executive, educator; b. Connersville, Ind., July 9, 1938; d. George Sinks and Cornelia Stewart Tatman; m. Frank Dilling Walker, Aug. 25, 1979; m. Guy Thomas

Connelly (div.); children: Kevin Connelly, Katherine Connelly. BA, Sweet Briar College, Va., 1960. Asst. tchr. The Children's Corner, Indpls., 1971—75; historic interpreter Conner Prairie Pioneer Settlement, Noblesville, Ind., 1975; staff asst. Hist. Landmarks Found. Ind. Indpls., 1975—78; classified ads, credit and purchasing Topics Newspapers, 1978—80; staff edn. docent Children's Mus., 1981—88; part owner News Examiner Co., Connersville, 1991—93, Winchester (Ky.) Sun, 1991—2005, Comml. Printing Svc., Connersville, Ind., 1989—. Dir. and v.p. Tatman, Inc., Connersville, Ind., 1983—; sec. and pres. Found. Hand Rsch. and Edn., Indpls., 1988—94; dir. and v.p. Walker Family Found., 1993—. Author: The Encyclopedia of Indianapolis, 1994. State co-chair Phillips Acad. Nat. Centennial Fund Dr., Andover, Mass., 1977—79; dir. and pres. Coleman Adoption Svcs., 1982—88; chmn. fin. devel. Arthritis Found. Ind., 1989—97; mem. alumni coun. Phillips Acad., Andover, Mass., 1984; bd. dir. Sweet Briar Coll., Va., 1999—2006, vice chair. bd. dir., 2003—06. Co-recipient Humanitarian of Yr., Arthritis Found. Ind., 1998. Mem.: Sweet Briar Alumnas Club of Ind. (co-pres. 1990—), Univ. Park Country Club. Avocations: photography, golf, reading, travel. Office: 7361 Eaton Ct University Park FL 34201

**WALKER, JEFFREY CLEMENS,** venture capitalist; b. Knoxville, Tenn., Sept. 22, 1955; s. William Clemens and Joyce Hazel (Harkins) W.; m. Suzanne Marie Connelly, Apr. 27, 1984; children: Courtney, Ryan, Morgan, Hunter. BS, U. Va., 1977; MBA, Harvard U., 1981. CPA, Tex.; cert. mgmt. acct., Tex. Sr. auditor cons. Arthur Young & Co., Houston, 1977-79; assoc. Chem. Bank, NYC, 1981-82, v.p., 1982-83; ptnr. Chase Capital Ptnrs., NYC, 1984-87, mng. ptnr., 1988—95; co-founder, gen. ptnr. JP Morgan Ptnrs. at JP Morgan Chase & Co., 1984—, vice-chmn., mng. ptnr., 1988—, dir., 1995—. Bd. dirs. Timothys, Inc., Toronto, Monet Corp., NYC, Guitar Ctr., LA, Metroplex Corp., NJ, Doaneroducts, Mo., Metakote, Lima, Ohio, Chase Asia Fund, NYC, Chase Equity Ptnrs, NYC, Thomas Jefferson Found. (Monticello), JP Morgan Chase Found.; dir. Domain, 1-800-Flowers, Metroplex, Doane Pet Care, House of Blues, Metokote, Axis Ins. and Guitar Center; chmn., NPower NY, Finance Com., U. Va.; serves on adv. bd., Solera Capital; mem.Investment Com., JPMorgan Partners Asia, JP Morgan Private Equity Partners Select, and JPM organ Horizon Funds Mem. Young Pres. Orgn.; chmn. Bd. Edn., Wilton, Conn.; bd. dirs. WPA Theatre, NYC; pres. of bd. of trustees, McIntire Sch., U. Va. Endowment, chmn., Finance Com.; dir., NYC Investment Fund, Lincoln Center Film Soc., The Big Apple Circus, The Internat. Center of Photography, Wilton Y; bd. trustees, Morgan Library and St. Luke's School Mem. AICPA, Nat. Venture Capital Assn., Nat. Assn. Small Bus. Investment Cos. (bd. govs., vice chmn.), Silver Spring Country Club, Golf Club of Purchase, Pawling Mountain Hunt Club, wilton Riding Club, Beta Gamma Sigma. Republican. Unitarian Universalist. Home: 360 New Canaan Rd Wilton CT 06897-3331 Office: JP Morgan Ptnrs 1221 Ave of the Americas New York NY 10020 Office Phone: 212-899-3400. Office Fax: 212-899-3401.

**WALKER, JENNIE LOUISE,** not-for-profit fundraiser, consultant; b. Ft. Hood, Tex., Nov. 27, 1962; d. Homer Lee and Jennie Louise (Smith) Walker; m. Philip Jerome King, Apr. 23, 1994 (div. Mar. 1999). BA in Speech Comm., Columbus State U., Ga., 1984, postgrad., 1985, Mercer U., Macon, Ga., 1987-90. Intern Senator Mack Mattingly, Washington, 1984, Congressman Richard Ray, Washington, 1984; rsch. asst. Robinson Humphrey Co., Inc., Atlanta, 1985-89; mktg. asst. Norrell Corp., Atlanta, 1989-90; dir. rsch. Carter Ctr., Inc., Atlanta, 1990-94, Boys & Girls Clubs Am., Atlanta, 1994-2000; dir. philanthropic initiatives WEBMD Found., Inc., Atlanta, 2000; assoc. dir. Global Philanthropists Cir. Synergos Inst., NYC, 2000—02; pres., CEO Jennie Walker Co., Inc., NYC, 2001—04, J. Walker, Inc., 2004—. Mem. adv. bd. The Found Ctr., Atlanta, 1997—2000, Found. Ctr., Atlanta, 1997—2000. Vol. Atlanta Project, 1992, Sta. WPBA-TV, Channel 30, Musicians on Call N.Y., 2001—, Lyric Chamber Music Soc. N.Y., 2000—; mem. adv. bd. Ga. Addiction Pregnancy and Parenting Family Enrichment Ctr, 1994—96; mem. Music Mgrs. Forum U.S., 2003—; vol. World Hunger Yr., 2004—, Richard Ray for Congress Campaign Com., 1984. Mem.: DAR, NARAS (assoc.), Nat. Assn. Recording Industry Profls., Nashville Songwriters Assoc. Internat., Women in Music (mem. 2002—), Assn. Ind. Music Pubs., Assn. Ind. Music Publ., Nat. Acad. Popular Music, Spl. Libr. Assn., Soc. Competitive Intelligence Profls., Am. Prospect Rsch. Assn. (pres. Ga. chpt. 1993—94, 1996—97), Nat. Acad. Songwriters, Broadcast Music, Inc., Ga. Music Industry Assn. (bd. dirs. 1991—93, publicity chair 1991—93, v.p. 1992—93, 1995—98, bd. dirs. 1995—2000, fundraising chair 1995—2000, pres. 1998—2000, pres. emeritus, advisor 2000—, Pres. award for vol. svc. 1997), Nat. Soc. Fundraising Exec., Columbus State U. Alumni Assn. Methodist. Avocations: songwriting, singing. Office: 435 W 57th St #15-S New York NY 10019 Office Phone: 212-541-7456. Business E-mail: jennie@jenniewalker.com

**WALKER, JERALD CARTER,** academic administrator, minister; b. Bixby, Okla., May 22, 1938; s. Joseph Carter and Trula Tosh (Jackson) W.; m. Virginia Canfield, Apr. 14, 1963; children: Elisabeth Katherine, Anne Carter. BA in Sociology, Oklahoma City U., 1960; BD, U. Chgo., 1964; D of Religion, Sch. Theology at Claremont, 1966; LHD (hon.), Shiller U., 1994. Ordained to ministry Meth. Ch., 1964. Dir., campus minister Campus Christian Assn., Chgo., 1961-64; minister of outreach Temple Meth. Ch., San Francisco, 1965-66; chaplain, assoc. prof. religion Nebr. Wesleyan U., Lincoln, 1966-69; pres. John J. Pershing Coll., Beatrice, Nebr., 1969-70; v.p. univ. rels., assoc. prof. Southwestern U., Georgetown, Tex., 1970-74; pres. Baker U., Baldwin, Kans., 1974-79, Oklahoma City U., 1979-97, chancellor Okla., 1997—. Ednl. adv. to bd. China. Tianjin U. Commerce, People's Republic of China; participant Okla. Ann. Conf. of United Meth. Ch. Co-author: The State of Sequoyah: An Impressionistic View of Eastern Oklahoma, 1985; contrib. chpt. books, articles to profl. jours. Bd. dirs., past chmn. Okla. Ind. Coll. Found. Recipient Alumni Recognition award Nebr. 4H Club, 1970, Okla. 4H Club, Disting. Alumnis award Oklahoma City U., 1974, Outstanding Citizen award Dist. 575 Rotary Internat., 1990, Award for Excellence Asia Soc. Okla., 1990, Humanitarian award for Okla/Ark. region NCCJ, 1992, Nat. Police Adminstrn. award for promotion or peace and order Rep. of China, 1992, Francis Asbury award for fostering United Meth. Ministries in Higher Edn., 1994, Excellent Leader award Mgmt. Devel. Inst. Singapore, 1996, Benjamin Franklin award Downtown Olka. City Sertoma Club, 1992, Excellent Leader award Mgmt. Devel. Inst. of Singapore, 1996, Nat. Medal of Honor Cherokee Nation, 2000; inducted to Okla. Higher Edn. Hall of Fame, 1999. Mem. Nat. Assn. Schs. and Colls. of United Meth. Ch. (past pres.), Nat. Assn. Colls. and Univs. (bd. dirs.). Office: Oklahoma City U 6826 E 112th St S Bixby OK 74008-2062

**WALKER, JEWETT LYNIUS,** clergyman, church official; b. Beaumont, Tex., Apr. 7, 1930; s. Elijah Harvey and Ella Jane (Wilson) W.; m. Dorothy Mae Croom, Apr. 11, 1965; children: Cassandra Lynn, Jewett L., Kevin, Michelle, Ella, Betty Renne, Kent, Elijah F. BA, Calif. Western U., 1957; MA, Kingdom Bible Inst., 1960; B Religious Edn., St. Stephens Coll., 1966, DD, 1968; LLD, Union Bapt. Sem., 1971; postgrad., St. Paul Sch. Theology, 1979, Southwestern Bapt. Theol. Sem., 1985-86; grad., Nat. Planned Giving Inst., 1981, Philanthropy Tax Inst., 1982; DD, Clinton Jr. Coll., 1992. Ordained to ministry African Methodist Episcopal Zion Ch., 1957. Pastor Shiloh A.M.E. Zion Ch., Monrovia, Calif., 1961-64, Martin Temple A.M.E. Zion Ch., L.A., 1964-65, 1st A.M.E. Zion Ch., Compton, Calif., 1965-66, Met. A.M.E. Zion Ch., L.A., 1966-73, Logan Temple A.M.E. Zion Ch., San Diego, 1973-74, Rock Hill A.M.E. Zion Ch., Indian Trail, NC, 1974-79, Bennettsville A.M.E. Zion Ch., Norwood, NC, 1979-86, Price Meml. A.M.E. Zion Ch., Concord, NC, 1986-89, Mt. Zion A.M.E. Zion Ch., Hickory Grove, SC, 1989-91, NewHope AME Zion Ch., Lancaster, SC, 1991—92, Mt. Zion A.M.E. Zion Ch., Lancaster, SC, 1992—2001, Mt. Moriah A.M.E. Zion Ch., Richburg, SC, 2001—03, New Hope A.M.E. Zion Ch., Lancaster, SC, 2003—. Sec.-treas. dept. home missions, brotherhood pensions and relief African Methodist Episcopal Zion Ch., Charlotte, N.C., 1974-92; mem. exec. bd. Prophetic Justice Unit Com. Nat. Coun. Chs., co-chairperson pers. com.; mem. World Meth. Coun., del. 14th World Conf Author: Is There a Man in the House, 1975, Lets Get Serious about Missions, 1991, Issues Facing the Ministry, 1991, The Denominational Dollar, 1992, also articles. Chmn.

Minority Affairs Adv. Com., Mecklenburg County; trustee Clinton Coll., dir. planned giving, 1992; trustee Rock Hill, Lomax-Hannon Coll., Greenville, Ala., Union Bapt. Theol. Sem., Birmingham, Ala.; bd. mgrs. McCrorey br. YMCA; pres. Am. Ch. Fin. Svc. Corp., Carolina Home Health Svc. Inc., Meth. Life Ins. Soc. Inc., bd. trustees State N.C. Coll. Found., Inc., 1987, del. Presbyn. Ptnrs. in Ecumenism Nat. Coun. Chs. Christ, 1986, pres., 1988—; pres. Walker Funeral Home Inc. (formerly The House of Irma Funeral Home), Concord, Am. Ch. Econ. Devel. Corp.; del. Presbyn. Ch. U.S. Gen. Assembly, 1985; mem. citizens parole accountability com. Mecklenburg County, Charlotte, 1993; mem. planned giving adv. bd. Livingston Coll., Salisbury, N.C.; pres. Jewett L. Walker & Assocs.; chmn. minority affairs adv. com. Mecklenburg County; com. mem. Charlotte Mecklenburg Citizen Parole Accountability Com., 1994, vice chmn., 1998; pres. Pardue St. Apts. Inc., Lancaster, S.C., 1997—; Am. Ch. Econ. Devel. Corp., 1999; elected to jud. coun. African Meth. Episcopal Zion Ch., 2000; mem. adv. bd. Mechanics and Farmers Bank, Charlotte, 2001 Fellow Nat. Assn. Ch. Bus. Adminstrs., Ch. Bus. Adminstrn., Presbyn. Ch. Bus. Adminstrn. Assn.; mem. NAACP (life), Nat. Soc. Fund Raising Execs., Am. Bible Soc. (state dir. vols., N.C. and S.C. dir. vol.), Nat. Spkrs. Bur., Christian Ministries Mgmt. Assn., Am. Soc. Assn. Execs., Funeral and Cremation Soc. South, Inc. (founding mem. 1998), Shriners, Masons (33 deg.), Prince Hall Affiliation. Republican. Home: 910 Bridlepath Ln Charlotte NC 28211-2022 Office: 4501 Walker Rd Charlotte NC 28211-2047

**WALKER, JOAN H.,** marketing and communications executive; m. George Walker. BA, Rutgers U., New Brunswick, 1968, MA in Sociology, 1973. Sr. exec. mktg. and govt. N.J. State Govt., 1973-83; pres. Richmann & Ptnrs., 1983-88; exec. v.p. Saatchi & Saatchi, 1988-90; mng. dir. mktg. comm. NYNEX Corp., 1990-93; pres., CEO Bozell Pub. Rels., N.Y.C., 1993-96; ptnr. Bozell Sawyer Miller Group, 1996; sr. v.p. corp. comm. Ameritech, Chgo., 1996-99; sr. v.p. global pub. affairs Monsanto (merged with Pharmacia & UpJohn, now Pharmacia), Skolie, Ill., 1999—2002; exec. v.p. corp. mktg. and comm. Qwest Comm. Internat., 2002—. Dir. Qwest Found.; mem. bd. trustees Colo. Symphony Orch. Office: Qwest Comm Internat 1801 California St Denver CO 80202 E-mail: Joan.H.Walker@am.pnu.com.

**WALKER, JOHN LOCKWOOD,** lawyer; b. Atlanta, Sept. 3, 1952; s. James William and Doris (Camp) W.; m. Caroline Asher Walker, Jan. 16, 1952; children: Ann Caroline, John Lockwood Jr., Elizabeth Davis, Lindsay Eleise. BA, Duke U., 1974, JD, 1977. Atty. legal div. bd. govs. FRS, Washington, 1977-79; assoc. Simpson Thacher & Bartlett LLP, NYC, 1979-84, ptnr., 1984—. Chmn. Richina Pacific Ltd. Bd. dirs., vice chmn. Fin. Svcs. Vol. Corps. Mem. Coun. on Fgn. Rels., Met. Club of Washington, Univ. Club (N.Y.C.), Chevy Chase (Md.) Club, Bedford (N.Y.) Golf and Tennis Club, Sankaty Head Golf Club (Nantucket, Mass.). Episcopalian. Office: Simpson Thacher & Bartlett LLP 425 Lexington Ave Fl 8 New York NY 10017-3954 E-mail: JWalker@stblaw.com

**WALKER, JOHN MERCER, JR.,** federal judge; b. NYC, Dec. 26, 1940's. John Mercer and Louise (Mead) W.; m. Cristy West, June 20, 1980 (div. Apr. 1983); m. Katharine Kirkland, Feb. 14, 1987. BA, Yale U., 1962; JD, U. Mich., 1966. Bar: NY 1969, U.S. Dist. Ct. (so. dist.) N.Y. 1971, US Ct. Appeals (2d cir.) 1972, US Supreme Ct. 1977, US Ct. Appeals (D.C. cir.) 1982. Maxwell Sch. Pub. Adminstrm. fellow, state counsel Republic of Botswana, Africa, 1966-68; assoc. Davis, Polk and Warwell, NYC, 1969-70; asst. U.S. atty. criminal divsn. (So. dist.) NY US Dept. Justice, NYC, 1971-75; assoc. to ptnr. Carter, Ledyard and Milburn, NYC, 1975-81; asst. sec. enforcement ops. US Dept. Treasury, Washington, 1981-85; judge U.S. Dist. Ct. (so. dist.) N.Y., 1985-89, US Ct. Appeals (2nd cir.), New Haven, 1989—, chief judge, 2000—. Adj. prof. NYU Law Sch., 1995—; gen. counsel Nat. Coun. on Crime and Deliquency, N.Y.C., 1977-81; chmn. Fed. Law Enforcement Tng. Ctr., Washington, 1981-85; spl. counsel Adminstrv. Conf. U.S., Washington, 1986-92; mem. budget com. jud. conf. Inst. Jud. Adminstrn., 1992—, dir., 1992—. Del. Rep. Nat. Conv., Detroit, 1980. With USMCR, 1963-67. Recipient Alexander Hamilton award Sec. of Treas., Washington, 1985, Secret Service Honor award, 1985. Mem. ABA, D.C. Bar Assn., Assn. Bar City of NY, Fed. Judges Assn. (pres. 1993-95). Republican. Episcopalian. Office: US Cir Ct 157 Church St New Haven CT 06510-2100*

**WALKER, JOHN SEIBELS,** artist; b. Columbia, SC, Nov. 12, 1960; s. George Rivers Pinckney and Harriet Moore Walker; m. Karen Louise Dyndiuk, Nov. 22, 1985. BA in Studio Arts, U. of South, 1983; apprentice study in classical realism, Atelier Lack, Mpls., Minn., 1991. 19th & early 20th century art dealer; instr. Charles Cecil Studios, Florence, Italy, 1991—; portraitist, fine artist Charlotte, NC, 2000—. Mem.: Am. Soc. Classical Realism, Am. Soc. Portrait Artists (finalist). One-man shows John Seibels Walker Studios Ste 30 118 East Kingston Ave Charlotte NC 28203 Office Phone: 704-338-9613. Office Fax: 704-338-9019. E-mail: jseibelswalker@hotmail.com, john@johnseibelswalker.com.

**WALKER, JONI CAROL,** secondary school educator; b. Greybull, Wyo., Dec. 16, 1968; d. John Murray and Marlys Jean Good; m. Sean W. Walker, June 16, 2001; children: Jett, Javin. B. Black Hills State U.; Mm. Grand Canyon U. Tchr. Guernsey High Sch., Wyo., 1993—94, Powell Mid. Sch., 1994—2001, Big Piney High Sch., 2001—. Office: Big Piney High Sch PO Box 769 Big Piney WY 83113 Office Phone: 307-276-3324. E-mail: walkerjoni@yahoo.com.

**WALKER, JUANITA MOFFETT,** retired secondary school educator; b. Edwards, Miss., Jan. 31, 1939; d. Fred Douglas and Matlean Allen Moffett; m. Tommy Lewis, June 11, 1962; children: Tommy Jr., Edward, Roland. AA, Utica Jr. Coll., Miss. 1959; BA, Jackson State U., 1961; MA, Purdue U., 1975; postgrad., Black Hills State U., Spearfish, SD, Ind. U. Cert. tchr. Miss., S.D., counselor Ind. Tchr. Burgland H.S., McComb, Miss., 1961, Oglala Cmty. H.S., Pine Ridge, SD, 1962—69, Wirt H.S., Gary, Ind., 1969—71, West Side H.S., Gary, Ind., 1971—78; counselor Pulaski Mid. Sch., Gary, Ind., 1978—82, Bailly Mid. Sch., Gary, Ind., 1982—91, Edison Mid. Sch. Gary, Ind., 1991—2001. Testing coord. Bailly and Edison Mid. Schs., 1982—95; dept. chmn. Edison Mid. Sch., 1991—2001; chmn. guidance career day Bailly Mid. Sch., 1982—90. Author: Church Folk, 2001; co-host (TV series) MUH, 2002—04. Historian Gary Civic Chorale, 1980—2003; founder, pres. Gary Writers Workshop, 2001—03; active Friends of Libr., Gary, 2000—04, Little Zion M.B. Ch. Mem.: Alpha Kappa Alpha. Avocations: singing, playing keyboards, travel, public speaking, reading. Phone: 601-201-6913.

**WALKER, JUDY LOU,** special education educator, director; d. Charles Emil and Carolyn Hazel Carlson; m. Bernard Dee, July 8, 1989; children: Jaycie, Brendan. BA in Liberal Studies, Biola U., La Mirada, Calif., 1988; MS in Elem. Edn., Chadron State Coll., Nebr., 1996. Cert. profl. tchr. Nebr. Substitute tchr. Kimball Pub. Schs., Nebr., 1989—90, Title I tchr., 1990—92, asst. volleyball coach, 1990—94, asst. basketball coach, 1990—94, Title I dir., 1992—. AWANA leader Kimball Evang. Free Ch., 2000—01, leader TruthQuest, 2004—. Nominee Title I Disting. Schs. award, 1997—98, 1998—99. Mem.: NEA, Nebr. State Edn. Assn., Kimball Edn. Assn., Internat. Reading Orgn. Avocations: reading, sports, scrapbooks. Office: Mary Lynch Elem Sch 1000 E 6th St Kimball NE 69145 Office Phone: 308-235-4696.

**WALKER, KARA,** artist; b. Stockton, Calif., Nov. 26, 1969; BA in Painting/Printmaking, Atlanta Coll. Art, 1991; MFA in Painting/Printmaking, R.I. Sch. Design, 1994. One-woman shows include Gallery 100, Atlanta, 1991, Ctr. Curatorial Studies, Bard Coll., Annandale-on-Hudson, NY, 1995, Nexus Contemporary Arts Ctr., Atlanta, 1995, Wooster Gardens/Brent Sikkema, NYC, 1995, 1998, Bernard Toale Gallery, Boston, 1996, Huntington Beach Arts Ctr., Calif., 1997, U. Chgo., 1997, Contemporary Arts Ctr., Cin., 1997, Henry Art Gallery, U. Wash., Seattle, 1997, The Carpenter Ctr., Harvard U., Cambridge, Mass., 1997, San Francisco Mus. Modern Art, 1997, The Forum, St. Louis, 1998, Vienna State Opera House, Austria, 1998, The Print Ctr., Phila., 1998, Galleri Index, Stockholm, 1998, Contemporary Arts

Mus., Houston, 1999, Calif. Coll. Arts and Crafts, Oliver Art Ctr., Oakland, 1998, Brent Sikkema, NY, 1998, McKinney Ave. Contemporary, Dallas, 1999, Des Moines Art Ctr., 2000, The Emancipation Approximation, Tel Aviv Mus. Art, 2001, Disturbing Allegories, Vanderbilt U. Fine Arts Gallery, Tenn., 2001, American Primitive, Brent Sikkema Gallery, NYC, 2001, Nat Turner's Revelation (an Important Lesson from our Negro Past You Will Likely Forget to Remember), Galerie Max Hetzler, Berlin, 2002, For the Benefit of All the Races of Mankind (Mos' Specially the Master One, Boss), Germany, 2002, Mannheimer Kunstverein, Germany, 2002, Internat. Bienal of Sao Paolo, Brazil, 2002, An Abbreviated Emancipation, U. Mich. Mus. Art, 2002, Narratives of a Negress, Tang Tchg. Mus. and Art Gallery, Skidmore Coll., 2003, Drawings, Brent Sikkema, 2003, Excavated from the Black Heart of a Negress, Studio Mus., Harlem, 2003, Centro Nazionale per le Arti Contemporanee, Rome, 2003, Fibbergibbet and Mumbo Jumbo, Fabric Workshop and Mus., Phila., 2004, Grub for Sharks: A Concession to the Negro Populace, Tate Liverpool, 2004, Museo de Arte Carrillo Gil, Mexico City, 2005, Event Horizon, New Sch. U., 2005, Song of the South, REDCAT, LA, 2005, exhibited in group shows at New Visions Gallery, Atlanta, 1991, MU Gallery, Boston, 1993, Sol Koffler Gallery, Providence, 1994, Paul Morris Gallery, NYC, 1995, Mills Gallery, Boston, Inst. Contemporary Art, 1996, Greg Kucera Gallery, Seattle, 1997, Stephen Friedman Gallery, London, 1998, Looking Forward Looking Backward, Elaine L. Jacob Gallery, Wayne State U., 1999, Istanbul Biennial: The Passion and the Wave, 1999, This Is Not the Place, Ramapo Coll. NJ, 2000, Blurry Lines, John Michael Kholer Arts Ctr., Wis., 2000, The Print World, Ljubljana Biennial, Slovenia, 2001, The Americans, Barbican Art Galleries, London, 2001, Form Follow Fiction, Castello di Rivoli Museo d'Arte Contemporanea, 2001, Moving Pictures, Solomon R. Guggenheim Mus., NYC, 2002, Telling Tales: Narrative Impulses in Recent Art, 2002, Tempo, MoMAQNS, NYC, 2002, Black President: The Art and Legacy of Fela Anikulapo-Kuti, New Mus., NYC, 2003, Comic Release: Negotiating Identity for a New Generation, Carnegie Mellon U., 2003, Provocations, Bronx Mus. Art, 2004, Monument to Now, DESTE Found. Contemporary Art, Athens, Greece, 2004, Fairy Tales Forever: Internat. Homage to H.C. Andersen, Copenhagen, 2005, Kiss the Frog! The Art of Transformation, Nat. Mus. Art, 2005, Getting Emotional, Inst. Contemporary Art, Boston, 2005, The Shadow, Vestsjaellands Kunstmuseum, Denmark, 2005, The World is a Stage, Mori Art Mus., Tokyo, 2005, Trials and Terrors, Mus. Contemporary Art, 2005, numerous others; author: Freedom, A Fable, A Curious Interpretation of the Wit of a Negress in Troubled Times; contbr. articles to profl. jours. Recipient MacArthur fellow, John D. and Catherine T. MacArthur Found., Lucelia Artist award, Smithsonian Am. Art Mus., 2004; fellow Individual Artist's fellow, Art Matters, Inc.; scholar Presdl. scholar, Atlanta Coll. Art, Ida Blank Ocko scholar. Office: c/o Sikkema Jenkins & Co 530 West 22d St New York NY 10011*

**WALKER, KAREN D.,** lawyer; b. Tampa, Feb. 24, 1968; BS in Comm. studies, Fla. State U., 1990; JD with high honors, U. Fla. Coll. Law, 1993. Bar: Fla. 1993, US Dist. Ct. (no. and So. Districts Fla.) 2000. Ptnr. Holland & Knight LLP, Tallahassee, ptnr., pub. policy and regulation group, mem., govt. contracts team, mem., Nat. Def., Homeland Security and Govt. Procurement Team; mem., telecommunications team; mem. com. Holland & Knight LLP. Mng. editor U. Fla. Law Review, 1991—92, title standards editor, 1992—93. Chair bd. dirs. United Way of the Big Bend, Inc. Mem.: Tallahassee Women Lawyers, Tallahassee Bar Assn., Order of the Coif, ABA (chair, young lawyers divsn., com. on women in the profession 2000—01, mem., standing com. on pub. edn. 2000—02, chair, young lawyers divsn., com. on women in the profession 2001—02, Fla. state chair pub. contract law sect. state/local procurement divsn 2002—, mem. sect. on pub. utilities, comm., and transportation law, chair IT procurement com.), Fla. Bar (mem. adminstrv. law sect.). Office: Holland & Knight LLP 315 S Calhoun St Ste 600 Tallahassee FL 32301 Office Phone: 850-425-5612. Business E-Mail: karen.walker@hklaw.com.

**WALKER, KELLEY,** painter; b. Columbus, Ga., 1969; BFA, Univ. Tenn., Knoxville, 1995. Exhibited in group shows at Paula Cooper Gallery, NYC, 2003, Curious Crystals of Unusual Purity, PS1 Contemporary Art Ctr., 2004, Tuesday Is Gone, Club 22, Tbilisi, Ga., 2004, La Lettre Volée, F.R.A.C. Franche-Comté Musée des Beaux-Arts de Dole, 2004, Galerie Peter Kilchmann, Zurich, Switzerland, 2004, Last One On is a Soft Jimmy, curated by Kelley Walker, Paula Cooper Gallery, NYC, 2004, La Salle de Bains, Lyon, France, 2005, Situational Prosthetics, New Langton Center for the Arts, San Francisco, Calif., 2005, Log Cabin, Artists Space, NYC, 2005, 7th Shorjah Biennial, United Arab Emirates, 2005, Invisible Hands and the Common Good, Champion Fine Art, LA, 2005, Bridge Freezes Before Road, Barbara Gladstone Gallery, 2005, Crash/Cars, Museo de Arte Contemporanea de Vigo (MARCO), Vigo, Spain, 2005, Whitney Biennial, Whitney Mus. Art, 2006.*

**WALKER, KELLYE L.,** lawyer; b. Little Rock, Aug. 16, 1966; BS, La. Tech. U., 1987; JD, Emory U., 1992. Atty. Boult, Cummings, Conners & Berry PLC, Nashville; assoc. Chaffe, McCall, Phillips, Toler & Sarpy LLP, New Orleans, 1995—98, ptnr., 1998—2000; mem., counsel Hill & Barlow LLP, Boston, 2000—03; sr. v.p., gen. counsel, sec. BJ's Wholesale Club Inc., Natick, Mass., 2003—. Achievements include Developed "Women in Bus. Series" at Chaffe, McCall, Phillips, Toler & Sarpy LLP. Office: BJ's Wholesale Inc One Mercer Rd Natick MA 01760-0023

**WALKER, KENNETH LYNN,** lawyer; b. New Haven, Nov. 22, 1948; s. John Charles and Virginia Clare (Lovett) W.; m. Suzanne Kay Thompson, Jan. 27, 1979; children: Katherine Leslie, Caroline Leigh, Christine Lynn. BA, Coe Coll. 1969; MA, New Sch. Social Research, 1973; JD, U. Iowa, 1975. Bar: Ohio. Assoc. Baker & Hostetler, Cleve., 1975-79; atty. Cole Nat. Corp., Cleve., 1979-84; sr. group counsel TRW, Inc., Cleve., 1984-91; v.p.; gen. coun. sec. Varity Corp., 1991-97; v.p. gen. counsel. Sealy Corp., 1997-2000, sr. v.p., gen. counsel 2000—. Editor Jour. Corp. Law, 1974-75. Mem. ABA, Ohio Bar Assn., Cleve. Bar Assn. Office: Sealy One Office Parkway at Sealy Dr Trinity NC 27370 Business E-Mail: kwalker@sealy.com

**WALKER, KIM A.,** lawyer; BA, U. Va., 1988; JD, Columbia U., 1991. Spl. counsel, Intellectual Property Dept. Willkie Farr & Gallagher LLP, NYC. Mem.: ABA, Black Entertainment and Sports Lawyers Assn., Internat. Trademark Assn., Assn. Bar of City NY (mem. Com. Entertainment Law 2004—). Office: Willkie Farr & Gallagher LLP 787 Seventh Ave New York NY 10019 Office Phone: 212-728-8776. E-mail: kwalker@willkie.com.

**WALKER, LARRY A.,** secondary school educator; b. LA, Dec. 30, 1942; s. Basil and Marjorie Walker; m. Mary Clare Walker, Feb. 11, 1967; children: Stephen, Gregory, Megan. BA, San Fernando Valley State, Northridge, Calif.; MA, UCLA, 1966. Chemistry and oceanography tchr. Notre Dame HS, Sherman Oaks, Calif., 1966—67; chemistry tchr. Calabasas HS, Calif., 1977—. Cons., spkr., presenter in field. 20km race walk team US Olympics, 1976, 1980. Roman Catholic. Avocations: photography, poetry, fishing, hiking, singing. Office: Calabasas High Sch 22855 Mulholland Hwy Calabasas CA 91302

**WALKER, LAURIE SHANNON,** psychologist, counselor; b. Harrisburg, Pa., Apr. 29, 1958; d. Don Lockwood Lucas and Muriel Mae Schmidt; m. James Robert Walker, Aug. 29, 1982; children: Adrienne, Alexis, Alyssa. BA, Dickenson Coll., Carlisle, Pa., 1980; MS, Millersville U., Pa., 1993; doctoral student, Union Inst. and U., Cin., 2001—. Lic. psychologist 1997, profl. counselor. Counselor Craig & Associates, York, Pa., 1992—95; psychologist Tressler Luth. Svcs., Mechanicsburg, Pa., 1995—98, Mazzihi & Sullivan, 1995—98, Guidance Associates of Pa., Camp Hill, 1998—99; pvt. practice Laurie S. Walker, M.S., L.P.C., Loveland, Colo., 1999—. Contbr. articles to profl. jours. and periodicals. Group facilitator R25 Sch. Dist., Loveland, Colo., 2002—. Mem.: APA. Democrat. Avocations: reading, writing, film and theatre reviewing. Office: Laurie S Walker MS LPC Ste B 2114 Lincoln Ave Loveland CO 80538 Home: PO Box 1842 Berthoud CO 80513-1842

**WALKER, LAWRENCE HOWARD, JR.,** music educator, department chairman; b. Phila., Feb. 26, 1955; s. Lawrence Walker Sr. and Daisy Walker; m. Sheila Patricia Roberts, July 18, 1981; children: Lauren, Iris. BS, Va. State U., 1978, MEd, 1981. Cert. tchr. Va. Tchr. Chesterfield Sch., Va., 1978, Fairfax Co. (Va.) Pub. Sch., 1978—. Dept. chair Fairfax (Va.) Pub. Sch., camp dir. Home: 13314 Lockgate Pl Herndon VA 20171-4028

**WALKER, LELAND JASPER,** civil engineer; b. Fallon, Nev., Apr. 18, 1923; s. Albert Willard and Grayce (Wilkinson) W.; m. Margaret Frances Noble, Jan. 21, 1946; children: Thomas, Margaret, Timothy. BS in Civil Engring, Iowa State U., 1944; D. Eng. (hon.), Mont. State U., 1983. Engr. with various govtl. depts., 1946-51, 53-55; v.p. Wenzel & Co. (cons. engrs.), Great Falls, Mont., 1955-58; pres., chmn. bd. No. Engring. and Testing, Inc., Great Falls, 1958-88. Pres. Ind. Labs. Assurance Co., 1977-79; bd. dirs. Applied Tech., Inc. Pres., trustee Endowment and Rsch. Found. Mont. State U., 1969-82, Mont. Deaconess Hosp., Great Falls, 1959-67. McLaughlin Rsch. Inst. Biol. Scis., 1989-92, Mont. Sch. Deaf and Blind Found., 1984—; trustee Rocky Mountain Coll., 1977-80, Dufresne Found., 1979-87; chmn., bd. dirs. Mont. Tech. Svcs. Adv. Coun. adv. coun. Engring. Coll. Mont. State U.; bd. dirs. Mont. State Fair, Engring. Socs. Commn. on Energy, 1977-79, Mont. Bd. Sci. and Tech., 1983-88, Great Falls Chamber Found., 1989-91, trustee Great Falls Public Libr. Found., 1995-2001. Named to Mont. Engrs. Hall Fame, 2003. Fellow ASCE (pres. 1976-77), AAAS, Cons. Engrs. Coun. (pres. Mont. 1971), Accrediting Bd. Engring. and Tech. (v.p. 1978-79, pres. 1980-83); mem. Nat. Acad. Engring., Am. Coun. Ind. Labs. (hon., sec. 1973-76), Meadowlark Country Club, Pachyderm Club (bd. dirs., v.p. 1992-94), Chi Epsilon (nat. hon.), Tau Beta Pi (hon.). Republican. Methodist. Home: 1200 32nd St S Apt 9 Great Falls MT 59405-5333

**WALKER, LOIS VIRGINIA,** multimedia designer, educator, poet, editor; b. Wheaton, Ill., Oct. 23, 1929; d. Earl William and Gertrude Johanna (Wuster) W.; m. Nicolas N.K. Kittrie, Apr. 20, 1951 (div. 1957). Student, Coll. of Emporia, Kans., 1948-49; BA, U. Kans., 1951, BS, 1954; postgrad., Columbia U., N.Y.C., 1957-59. Cert. elem. edn. tchr., N.Y. Tchr. Dist. 17, Hicksville, N.Y., 1954-86; freelance artist, 1974—; tchr. Taproot Workshop Inc., Stony Brook, NY, 1994—. Mem. decentralization panel N.Y. State Coun. Arts, 1989-91; host radio shows Adelphi U., Garden City, N.Y., 1980-94; treas. L.I. Poetry Collective, Huntington, N.Y., 1988-2001, co-chmn., 1991-2001. Editor Xanadu and Process, 1979-2001; author numerous poems. Mem. Environ. Def. Fund, 1985—. Mem. Poetry Soc. Am., Nat. League Am. Pen Women, Art League of Long Island, Friends of Poets and Writers, N.Y. State Ret. Tchrs. Assn. (life), L.I. Women's Coalition Inc., Sierra Club, Nature Conservancy. Avocations: travel, music, dance, lectures. Home: 149 Harbor S Amityville NY 11701-3820 Personal E-mail: loisvwalker@aol.com.

**WALKER, LORENE,** retired elementary school educator; b. Clovis, N.Mex., July 27, 1911; d. Jessie H. and Tille Eula (Harlan) Black; m. Carl Westley Walker, June 9, 1934; children: Wesley, Charles. BS, N.Mex. State U., 1933; M of Family Life, Ctrl. Wash. U., 1959, postgrad., 1956—74. Tchr. home econs. Floyd Sch., near Portales, N.Mex., 1933-34, Navajo Meth. Mission, Farmington, N.Mex., 1947-48; home agt. ext. svc. Wash. State Coop. Ext. Svc., Yakima, 1948-56; family life, counseling tchr. West Valley Sch., Yakima, 1956-71, spl. elem. reading tchr., 1971-75; tour organizer, leader Mission Tour, Yakima, 1966-98; trainer missioners United Meth. Ch., Yakima, 1998—. Coord. 4-H camps, fairs and programs Wash. Coop. Ext. Svc., Yakima, 1950-56. Chairperson Experiment for Internat. Living, Yakima Valley Rep. Women's Club, 1966-87; docent, tour leader Yakima Valley Mus., 1976—; trustee Found. Pacific Northwest United Meth. Ch., 1984—; pres. Columbia River dist. United Meth. Ch., 1987-88, chairperson global missions, 1993-94; chair Tour With a Mission, 1966-1993; del. World Meth. Conf., Brighton, Eng., 2001. Mem. AAUW (treas. 1962-66, bd. dirs., chair internat. rels. 1962-89; spl. honor award 1989), United Meth. Women (pres. 1987-89, active local, dist. confs. Pacific N.W. Conf., spl. recognition 1989), Wesleyan Svc. Guild Meth. Women. (officer 1964-68), Yakima Woman's Century Club (active local orgns.), Ret. Tchrs. Assn. (active local orgns.), Alpha Delta Kappa (pres. 1967-69). Achievements include donating profit from tours to schools, hospitals and other charities. Avocations: gardening, travel, needlecrafts, international political and cultural news. Home: 101 N 48th Ave Apt 25A Yakima WA 98908-3179

**WALKER, LORENZO GILES,** surgeon, educator; b. Phila., June 29, 1957; s. Manuel Lorenzo and Romaine Yvonne (Smith) W.; m. Yvonne Ruiz; children: Zachary Giles, Benjamin Lee, Cassidy Leigh. BA cum laude, U. Pa., 1978; MD, Harvard U., 1982. Diplomate Am. Bd. Orthopaedic Surgery, Nat. Bd. Med. Examiners; lic. surgeon, Mass., Calif.; cert. added qualification hand surgery, 1993; recertified orthopedic surgery and hand surgery, 2003. Intern in surgery New Eng. Deaconess-Harvard Surg. Svc., Boston, 1982-83, asst. resident in surgery, 1983-84; resident in orthop. surgery Harvard U., Boston, 1985-88; fellow in hand surgery UCLA Med. Sch., 1988-89, asst. clin. prof. orthop. surgery Calif., 1988—; attending physician dept. orthop. Hand Clinic Calif., 1996-98; ptnr. Ventura Orthop. Hand and Sports Med. Group, Calif., 1994-98; solo practice hand surgery, 1998—. Staff physician St. John's Plasant Valley Hosp., Camarillo, Calif., St. John's Regional Med. Ctr., Oxnard, Calif., Cmty. Meml. Hosp., Ventura, Calif.; attending physician, cons. Sepulveda, Calif. VA Hosp.; presenter in field. Cons. reviewer Clin. Orthopaedics and related Rsch., 1990-92; contbr. numerous articles to profl. jours. Vol. Spl. Olympics, Ventura, 1994-96, Direct Relief Internat., Santa Barbara, Calif., 1994-96, Ventura County Rescue Mission, 1994-98. Recipient Cert. of Appreciation, Am. Heart Assn., 1994; UCLA faculty fellow, 1988-89. Mem. Am. Soc. for Surgery of the Hand, Am. Assn. for Hand Surgery, AMA, Calif. Med. Assn., Calif. Orthopaedic Assn., Calif. Ringside Physician, Ventura County Med. Soc., Internat. Soc. Aquatic Medicine, Western Orthopaedic Assn., Orthopaedic Overseas, UCLA Hand Club, Arthroscopy Assn. N.Am., Alpha Epsilon Delta, Onyx Honor Soc., Philomathean Soc. Avocations: photography, scuba diving, sports memorabilia, fishing, travel. Office Phone: 805-485-7764.

**WALKER, LUCY DORIS,** secondary school educator, writer; b. Ridgeway, NC, May 6, 1951; d. Edgerton Verl and Mary Ellen (Williams) Plummer; m. William A. Walker Jr., June 21, 1969 (div. Aug. 1974); 1 child, Lucretia Marie. BA in English Edn., Fairleigh Dickinson U., 1975; MA in Theater Arts, Montclair State U., 1977. Cert. English and theater arts tchr., N.J. Tchr., dir., actor, writer Ctr. Modern Dance Edn., Hackensack, NJ, 1978; writer, dir. Am. Theater Actors, NYC, 1978-79; tchr. multicultural hub Ctr. Internat. Studies, Cultural Events, Teaneck HS, Teaneck, NJ, 1979—; coord. Teaneck Arts Acad. at Teaneck HS, Teaneck, NJ, 2002—. Artistic dir. Teaneck H.S. dance ensemble, 1989—; program coord. African and African-Am. Studies Resource Ctr., 1990—; instructional leader for fine and performing arts, coord. Teaneck Arts Acad. Writer and choreographer various plays, 1979-95. Recipient Acad. Achievement award Fairleigh Dickinson U. Opportunities Program, 1974, Black Heritage award Nat. Assn. Negro Bus. & Profl. Women's Clubs, 1991. Mem. NEA, NJ Edn. Assn. Democrat. Baptist. Avocations: sewing, gardening, hiking, painting, music. Home: 363 Washington Pl Englewood NJ 07631-3232 Office: Teaneck HS 100 Elizabeth Ave Teaneck NJ 07666-4713 E-mail: plumwalk@msn.com.

**WALKER, LULA NORIEGA,** educational association administrator; b. Alexandria, Va., Nov. 20, 1944; d. Eugene and Ruth Elizabeth (Lowe) Noriega; m. James J. Walker Sr., Sept. 29, 1979; children: Lynn, James, Melvin, Sean, Ronald; m. Jim Patterson. BS in Agrl. and Tech., U. N.C., 1966; MLS, SUNY, Stony Brook, 1976; PD, L.I. U., 1982. Cert. sch. adminstr., N.Y.; cert. English tchr. N.Y. Tchr. High Point (N.C.) Pub. Schs.; chairperson, English tchr. Westbury (N.Y.) Pub. Schs.; asst. prin. N. Babylon (N.Y.) Pub. Schs. Mem. SANYS, ASCD. Home: 139 Craig Ave Freeport NY 11520-1532

**WALKER, MAMIE ODENA,** retired secondary school educator; b. Statesville, NC, Mar. 12, 1940; d. Ernest Glen Sr. and Annie Louise Allison; m. William Paul Walker Jr.; 1 child, Daryl L. BS, Livingstone Coll., Salisbury, NC, 1963; MS in Tchg., Cath. U. Am., Washington, 1971. Cert. in day care

I and II Prince George's CC, MD, 1982. Sci. tchr. Elm City (NC) Pub. Schs., 1963—64, Mackin Cath. HS, Archdiocese of Washington, 1965—67, Washington Pub. Schs., 1967—69, 1971—74, 1988—2002; ret. 2002; lab. asst. Howard U. Coll. Medicine, Washington, 1965—67. Mem. adv. com. Sickle Cell Disease Assn., Washington, Am. Physiol. Soc.; mem. Cool Spring Terrace Assn., Adelphi, Md., 2002—; v.p. Washington Inter Alumni Coun. United Negro Coll. Fund, 1988—. Named Outstanding Biology Tchr., Nat. Assn. Biology Tchrs., 1973, 1993. Mem.: Livingstone Coll. Alumni Assn. (v.p. Washington chpt.), Delta Sigma Theta (Geraldine P. Woods award). Democrat. Avocations: cooking, reading, gardening, singing, public speaking. Home: 8410 Rambler Dr Adelphi MD 20783

**WALKER, MARK A.,** lawyer; b. NYC, June 24, 1941; s. Joseph and Eleanor (Junger) W.; m. Tania Khodjamirian; children: Marie, Andrew. BA, Stanford U., 1963; LLB, Yale U., 1966. Bar: N.Y. 1967, U.S. Dist. Ct. (so. dist.) N.Y. 1977. Assoc. Cleary, Gottlieb, Steen & Hamilton, Paris, Brussels and N.Y., 1966-75, ptnr. NYC, 1975—2005, mng. ptnr., 2005—. Mem. Assn. Bar City N.Y. Office Phone: 212-225-2240. E-mail: mwalker@cgsh.com.

**WALKER, MARTIN ALAN,** journalist; b. Durham, England, July 23, 1947; came to U.S., 1978; s. Tom and Dorothy (McNeill) W.; m. Julia Watson, 1978; children: Kate, Fanny. MA, U. Oxford, 1966-69; student, Harvard U., 1969-71. Former journalist, bur. chief The Guardian, Washington, 1988; editor English lang. ops. UPI, Washington, 2004—. Guest lectr. Columbia Univ, UCLA, NYU, Univ. Toronto, Pitts. Author: The National Front, 1978, Power of the Press, 1982, The Walking Giant, 1986, Martin Walker's Russia, 1988. Named Reporter of Yr., U.K. Press, 1986, 87, 97, Fgn. Journalist of Yr. Krokodil, Moscow, 1988; Brackenbury scholar U. Oxford, 1966-69; Harkness fellow Harvard U., 1969-71, Am. Polit. Sci. Assn. fellow, 1971-72, policy fellow, Woodrow Wilson Internat. Ctr. for Scholars, Washington, sr. fellow, World Policy Inst., New Sch., NYC. Mem. White House Press Assn. Avocation: cross country skiing. Office: UPI 1510 H St NW Washington DC 20005

**WALKER, MARY L.,** lawyer; b. Dayton, Ohio, Dec. 1, 1948; d. William Willard and Lady D. Walker; child, Winston Samuel. Student, U. Calif., Irvine, 1966-68; BA in Biol. Scis./Ecology, U. Calif., Berkeley, 1970; postgrad., UCLA, 1972-73; JD, Boston U. Law Sch., 1973. Bar: Calif. 1973, U.S. Supreme Ct. 1979, U.S. Dist. Ct. (no., ctrl., ea. and so. dists.) Calif. Atty. So. Pacific Transp. Co., San Francisco, 1973-76; assoc. Richards, Watson & Gershon, LA, 1976—77, ptnr. 1979-82, ptnr., chair environ. dept. San Francisco, 1989-91; prin. dep. asst. atty., environment and natural resources divsn. U.S. Dept. Justice, Washington, 1982-84; dep. solicitor U.S. Dept. Interior, Washington, 1984-85; asst. sec. for environment, safety and health U.S. Dept. Energy, Washington, 1985-88; spl. cons. to chmn. bd. Law Engring. Inc., Atlanta, 1988-89; v.p., West Coast and the Pacific Law Environ., Inc., San Francisco, 1989; ptnr. Luce, Forward, Hamilton & Scripps, San Diego, 1991-94; ptnr. and chair San Diego Environ. Law Group Brobeck, Phleger & Harrison, LLP, San Diego, 1994—2001; gen. counsel and chief of ethics U.S. Dept. Air Force, U.S. Dept. Defense, Washington, 2001—. U.S. commr. InterAm. Tropical Tuna Commn., 1988—95; mem. adv. bd. Floresta, Inc.; instr. natural resources law U. Calif., San Diego. Author of opinion pieces on environ. regulation, energy policy and nuclear power. Bd. dirs. Endowment for Cmty. Leadership, 1987—2000, Global Involvement Through Edn., 1998—2001; chair, environ. com. San Diego C. of C., 1993—94; adv. bd. Endowment for Cmty. Leadership, Washington. Named Outstanding Young Women of Am., 1984; recipient Women Who Mean Business award, Inaugural award for Law, San Diego Bus. jour., 1994. Mem. Calif. Bar Assn., San Diego Bar Assn., BIOCOM (bd. dirs. 1991-2001, pres. 1994, chair/co-chair environ. and safety com., 1991-2001), Profl. Women's Fellowship-San Diego (co-founder, bd. dirs. 1996-2001, pres. 1996-97), World Affairs Coun., Renaissance Women. Republican. Office: Air Force Gen Counsel Rm 4E856 1740 Air Force Pentagon Washington DC 20330-1740 Office Fax: 703-693-9355, 703-697-3796. E-mail: maryl.walker@pentagon.af.mil.

**WALKER, MATTHEW,** radiologist; s. Patricia Walker; m. Karen Tamburro; children: Grace Elizabeth, Owen Patrick. MD, Jefferson Med. Coll., Phila., 1994. Asst. prof. radiology Feinberg Sch. of Medicine, Northwestern U., Chgo., 2001—06, assoc. prof. radiology, 2006—. Chief neuroradiology Feinberg Sch. of Medicine, Northwestern U., Chgo., 2003—06. Achievements include research in Neurovascular imaging with CT and MR. Office: Northwestern Radiology 676 N St Clair St Ste 1400 Chicago IL 60611 Office Phone: 312-695-1292.

**WALKER, MICHAEL ANGUS,** economist, director; b. Corner Brook, Nfld., Can., Sept. 11, 1945; m. Janet Walker; children: Margot, Joel. BA, St. Francis Xavier U., 1966; MA, U. Western Ont., 1967, PhD, 1971. Instr. U. Western Ont., Canada, 1968—69; with Bank of Can., 1969—72; instr. Carleton U., Canada, 1971; with Fed. Dept. Fin., Canada, 1973—74; exec. dir. The Fraser Inst., Vancouver, B.C., Canada, 1974—2005, sr. fellow, 2005—; pres. The Fraser Inst. Found., 2005—. Bd. dirs. Mancal Corp., Canaccord Capital Inc., The Milton and Rose D. Friedman Found. Office: The Fraser Inst 4th Floor 1770 Burrard St Vancouver BC Canada V6J 3G7 Office Phone: 604-688-0221. Business E-mail: michaelw@fraserinstitute.ca.

**WALKER, MICHAEL CHARLES, SR.,** retired services executive; b. Rochester, N.Y., Mar. 4, 1940; s. Charles Boyle and Evelyn Ester (Young) W.; m. Patricia Ann Camelio, Feb. 2, 1963; children: Michael Charles Jr., Lynn, Lea, Matthew. BA, U. Colo., 1962; MBA, Columbia Pacific U., 1982, DBA, 1984. Adminstrv. trainee Lincoln Rochester (N.Y.) Trust Co., 1962-64, mktg. officer, 1964-68; asst. v.p. Lincoln First Bank of Rochester, 1968-72, v.p., 1972-77; pres. M.C. Walker Co., Inc., Spencerport, NY, 1977-80; CEO, PRCC, Rochester, 1980—89; pres., CEO Presbyn. Homes and Svcs. Genesee Valley, Inc., Rochester, 1999—2002. Lectr. SUNY, Brockport, 1982—89; v.p., dir. Kilian and Caroline Schmitt Found., Rochester, 1985—; mem. adv. bd. Chase Manhattan Bank, Rochester, 1989—92; trustee Rochester Hearing and Speech Ctr., 1989—95, chmn., 1993—94; bd. dirs. Genesee Region Home Care Assn., Rochester, 1990—2000; trustee Greater Rochester C. of C., 1981—89. Author: Introduction to Bank Marketing Research, 1969, rev. edit., 1972, Practical Handbook of Marketing Definitions, 1970, 2d edit., 2004, Marketing to Seniors, 2004; contbr. articles to profl. jours. Leader task force Spencerport Ctrl. Schs. Bd. Edn., 1977, 80-81, 85; chmn. Monroe County Svs. Bond Com., Rochester, 1972-97; mem. United Way Evaluation Team, 1990-94; bus. adv. bd. SUNY, Brockport, 1993—2004; mem. N.Y. State Bd. Profl. Med. Conduct, 1993—; profl. adv. com. Self Help for Hard of Hearing, 1994-96; trustee Nazareth Coll., 2005—. Recipient Pres.'s Geneseekers award, Rochester Area C. of C., 1979, Innovation of Yr. award, NYAHSA, 1989, Cmty. Svc. award, Self Help for Hard of Hearing, 1997, Patriotic Svc. award, U.S. Treasury, 1997. Mem. Am. Mktg. Assn. (pres. Rochester chpt. 1969-70), N.Y. State Bankers Assn. (pres. residential mortgage com. 1975-76), N.Y. Assn. Homes and Svcs. for Aging (various coms.), Rochester Rotary, Am. Legion. Episcopalian. Avocations: golf, reading, travel, physical fitness.

**WALKER, MINERVA E. GILARA,** poet, retail executive; b. Dauphin County, Pa., June 23, 1924; d. Daniel Snavely Ensminger and Nora Alice Hostetter; m. Stanley Michael Gilara, July 11, 1942 (div. Aug. 1972); children: Jerry, Stanley, Paul, Connie; m. John Henry Walker, Nov. 25, 1976 (dec. June 1993); 1 child, Tina. Student, Harrisburg Area C.C. Freelance writer, reporter Lebanon (Pa.) Daily News, 1954—60; hostess, retail advt. Welcome Wagon Internat., Hummelstown, Pa., 1958—60; tour guide, pub. rels. Indian Echo Caverns, Hummelstown, 1967—72; staff writer Middletown (Pa.) Press and Jour., 1960—66; retail rep. Svc. Advantage, Indpls., 1994—2000, Office Max, Shaker Heights, Ohio, 2000—04. Lutheran. Avocations: poetry, writing, art, travel, needlecrafts. Home: 28905 229th Pl SE Black Diamond WA 98010 Personal E-mail: minervawalker@comcast.net.

**WALKER, MORT,** cartoonist; b. El Dorado, Kans., Sept. 3, 1923; s. Robin A. and Carolyn (Richards) W.; m. Catherine Prentice, Aug. 24, 1985; children: Greg, Brian, Polly, Morgan, Marjorie, Neal, Roger, Whitney, Cathy, Jr., Priscilla. Student, Kansas City Jr. Coll., 1941-42, Washington U., St. Louis, 1943-44; BA, U. Mo., 1948; LL.D., William Penn Coll., 1981. Designer Hallmark Greeting Cards, 1941; editor Dell Pub. Co., 1948-49; free lance cartoonist Saturday Evening Post, other popular mags., 1948-50. Scholar in residence Mo. U., 1992. Comic strip artist King Features, 1950—; creator Beetle Bailey, 1950, Hi and Lois, 1954, Sam's Strip, 1961, Boner's Ark, 1968, Sam and Silo, 1977, The Evermores, 1982, Betty Boop and Felix, 1984, (for United Features) Gamin and Patches, 1987; author: Most, 1971, Land of Lost Things, 1973, Backstage at the Strips, 1975, The Lexicon of Comicana, 1981, The Best of Beetle Bailey, 1984, The Coconut Crew, 1997, (autobiography) Mort Walker's Private Scrapbook, 2001; contbr. 92 paperback collections. Mem. Pres.'s Com. to Hire Handicapped, People to People Com. Exhbn. touring group show Met. Mus. Art, N.Y.C., 1951; chmn. Nat. Cartoon Mus. Served to 1st lt. AUS, 1943-46, ETO. Decorated chevalier Order Arts and Letters (France), 2000; recipient Outstanding Cartoonist award The Banshees, 1955, Il Secolo XIX award (Italy), 1972, Adamson award (Sweden), 1975, 88, Segar award, 1977, 4th Estate award Am. Legion, The Jester, 1979, Power of Printing, 1977, NCS Golden T-Square award, 1999, Disting. Civilian Svc. award U.S. Army; named Man of Yr. NCCJ, 1988. Mem. Nat. Cartoonists Soc. (pres. 1959-60, Reuben award 1953, Best Humor Strip award 1966, 69, named to Hall Fame, Nat. Cartoon Mus. 1989), Artists and Writers, Newspaper Features Coun. Authors Guild, Soc. Illustrators, Nat. Press Club, Silvermine Club (Norwalk, Conn.), Greenwich Country Club, Quechee Club, Kappa Sigma (named Man of Yr. 1988). Office: care King Features Syndicate 888 7th Ave New York NY 10019 *If I enjoy my own life that's one thing. But if I can help others enjoy their lives more, many lives are made more enjoyable.*

**WALKER, OLENE S.,** former governor; b. Ogden, Utah, Nov. 15, 1930; d. Thomas Ole and Nina Hadley (Smith) W.; m. J. Myron Walker, 1957; children: Stephen Brett, David Walden, Bryan Jesse, Lori, Mylene, Nina, Thomas Myron. BA, Brigham Young U., 1954; MA, Stanford U., 1954; PhD, U. Utah, 1986; HHD (hon.), Weber State U., 1997. V.p. Country Crisp Foods, 1969-92; mem. Utah Ho. of Reps. Dist. 24; lt. gov. State of Utah, 1993—2003, gov., 2003—05. Mem. Salt Lake Edn. Found. bd. dirs. 1983-90; dir. community econ. devel.; mem. Ballet West, Sch. Vol., United Way, Commn. on Youth, Girls Village, Salt Lake Conv. and Tourism Bd.; mem. adv. coun. Weber State U. Mem. Nat. Assn. Secs. of State (Western chmn., nat. lt. gov.'s conf., pres. 1997-98). Republican. Mem. Lds Ch. Achievements include becoming first female elected to office of governor of Utah.*

**WALKER, PATRICIA ANN,** special education educator; b. Medford, Oreg., July 29, 1962; d. Oran C. Chastain and Sadimae J. Chastain-Jones, Benjamin Jones (Stepfather); m. John Walker; 1 child, Robert Owen. BS in Elem. Edn., So. Oreg. State Coll., 1985. Store mgr. 7-Eleven Store, Costa Mesa, Calif., 1986—90; sales rep. Mclanes So. Calif., San Bernardino, 1990—93, Sales Mark, Santa Fe Springs, Calif., 1993—98; substitute tchr. San Diego City Union Sch. Dist., 2000—02; spl. edn. pre-k tchr. Escondido Union Sch. Dist., Calif., 2002—. Recipient Nicolaysen Ctr. Employee of the Yr. award, Escondido Union Sch. Dist., 2004-05, Nicolaysen Ctr. Educator of the Yr. award, Escondido Elem. Educators Assn., 2004-05; grantee, Delta Kappa Gamma, 1981; scholarship, Ben Ziri Caravan of the Alhambra, 2001, Found. of Devel. Disabilities Peterson, 2001. Mem.: Nat. PTA, Coun. for Exceptional Children, Escondido Elem. Educators Assn., Autism Soc. of Am. (San Diego chpt.). Avocations: swimming, spending time with my son. Home: 4250 Don Way San Diego CA 92117 Office: Escondido Union School District 1330 E Grand Ave Escondido CA 92027-3099 Office Phone: 760-432-2168. Personal E-mail: pwalker714@yahoo.com.

**WALKER, PATRICIA ANN DIXON,** retired elementary school educator, real estate rehabilitator; b. Somerset, Pa., Nov. 26, 1937; d. Telford Miles and Bernice Irene Dixon; m. Paul J. Kuty, Nov. 2, 1957 (div. Nov. 1974); 1 child, Paul Dixon Kuty; m. James William Walker, Mar. 23, 1991. BS in Elem. Edn., Ind. State Coll., 1960; MA in Elem. Edn., Trenton State Coll., 1966. Tchr. grade 1 Neshaminy Sch. Dist., Langhorne, Pa., 1960—93; real estate investor Phila., 1985—. Vol. tutor NAACP, Bucks County, Pa., 1967—68; mem. Levittown Hist. Preservation Com., 2002—; committeewoman Dem. Party, Bucks County, 1974—78; chair Dem. Assn. Middletown Twp., Bucks County, 1974—75. Recipient Gift of Time tribute, Am. Family Inst. Valley Forge, 1992. Mem.: Homeowners Assn. Phila., Neshaminy Fedn. Ret. Tchrs., Pa. Assn. Sch. Retirees (mem. Bucks County chpt.). Avocation: travel. Home: 24 June Rd Levittown PA 19056 Office Phone: 215-945-4239.

**WALKER, PAUL R.,** lawyer; b. Bronx, NY, Feb. 6, 1945; AB, U. Notre Dame, 1966; LLB, U. Pa., 1969. Bar: N.Y. 1970, Calif. 1972. Former ptnr. Paul, Hastings, Janofsky & Walker, L.A.; ptnr., chmn. real estate practice group, mem. mgmt. com. & mng. ptnr. LA office Dewey Ballantine LLP, LA. Office: Dewey Ballantine LLP Suite 2600 333 S Grand Ave Los Angeles CA 90071-1530 Office Phone: 213-621-6200. Office Fax: 212-621-6201. Business E-Mail: pwalker@deweyballantine.com.

**WALKER, PETER,** landscape architect; BS in Landscape Arch., U. Calif., Berkeley, 1955; postgrad., U. Ill., 1956; M in Landscape Arch., Harvard U., 1957. Resident Am. Acad. in Rome, 1991; co-founer Sasaki, Walker Assocs., Inc., 1957—75; prin., consulting prin., chmn. The S.W.A. Group, 1975—83; founder, prin. Peter Walker & Ptnrs. Landscape Arch. Inc., Berkeley, Calif., 1983—. Instr. landscape arch. Harvard U. Grad. Sch. Design, 1958—59, adj. prof., 1976—91, acting dir. Urban Design Program, 1977—78, chmn. dept. landscape arch., 1978—81, Charles Eliot chair, 1992; vis. critic MIT, 1959; dir. The S.W.A. Group Summer Sch., 1973—83; chmn. dept. landscape arch. U. Calif., Berkeley, 1997—99; guest lectr. and spkr. in field. Co-author: Invisible Gardens: The Search for Modernism in the American Landscape; mem. editl. bd.: Landscape Arch., 1988—91. Named co-winner, World Trade Ctr. Site Meml. Competition, 2003; named to Inst. Honor, AIA, 1992. Fellow: Inst. for Urban Design, Am. Soc. Landscape Archs. Office: Peter Walker and Ptnrs 739 Allston Way Berkeley CA 94710

**WALKER, PETER JOHN CHARLES,** science foundation director; b. Kendal, Cumbria, Eng., May 30, 1955; s. Brian Wolson and Nancy Walker; m. Ceri Jane Knapper, Jan. 23, 1984; children: Gareth, Megan, Gwilym. BSc, Sheffield U., Eng, 1973; PhD, Sheffield U., Eng., 1981. Dir. Disaster Policy Dept, IFRC, Geneva, 1991—2000, Regional Office, IFRC, Bangkok, 2000—02, Feinstein Internat. Ctr., Tufts U., Medford, Mass., 2002—. Editor: (annual review) World Disasters Report. Mem., adv. bd. humanitarian accountability project HAP Internat., Geneva, 2002. Achievements include development of Sphere International standards in disaster response; Code of Conduct for relief workers. Office: Tufts U Feinstein Internat Ctr Ste 4800 200 Boston Ave Medford MA 02155 Office Phone: 617-627-3361.

**WALKER, PHILIP CHAMBERLAIN, II,** health facility administrator; b. Big Spring, Tex., July 7, 1944; s. Philip Chamberlain and Mary Catherine (St. John) W.; m. Linda Jane Holsclaw, Jan. 21, 1978; children: Shannon M., Meghan M. BA, Cen. Wash State Coll., 1970; MS, U. Idaho, 1971. Exec. dir. Multnomah Found. for Med. Care, Portland, Oreg., 1972-81; chief exec. officer Peer Rev. Orgn. for Wash. State, Seattle, 1981-84; dir. Preferred Provider Orgn. devel. Provident Life and Accident, Chattanooga, 1984-88; v.p. Maxicare Health Plans, LA, 1988-91; v.p., gen. mgr. Maxicare Health Plans Midwest, Chgo., 1991-92; pres. Health Plus, Peoria, Ill., 1992—; CEO, chmn. bd. HCH Adminstrn., Peoria, Ill., 1992-98; sr. v.p. Health Care Horizons, Albuquerque, 1992-98; exec. v.p. Proctor Health Sys., 1998—. Bd. dirs. RMR Group, HCH Adminstrn., Health Care Horizons; cons. in field. Contbr. articles to profl. jours. Bd. dirs. Boys and Girls Club of Greater Peoria, 2003—; v.p. Boys and Girls Club Peoria, 2004—06; Ctrl. Ill. regional adv. bd. Multiple Sclerosis Assn., 2002—04; chmn. Hult Health Edn. Ctr., 1999—2003, bd. dirs., Cancer Ctr. for Healthy Living, 2001—03, Heart of Ill.

United Way, 2004—. With USAF, 1961—66, Vietnam. Mem.: Creve Coeur Club (bd. govs., pres.). Office: 5409 N Knoxville Ave Peoria IL 61614 Office Phone: 309-689-8600. Business E-Mail: phil.walker@proctor.org.

**WALKER, RADFORD,** web architect; b. Pueblo, Colo., Apr. 12, 1957; s. Frank M. and Marian F. Walker; m. Sharon L. Stevens, Dec. 27, 1980; children: Rader Steele, Tova Sidnee Ann, Nyssa Radell Turney, Tacita Wynn Tansey. BS, Wichita State U., 1979; MS, U. Colo., 1992. Lab. asst. Dr. Paul Tasch, Wichita, Kans., 1978; asst. staff mgr. Southwestern Bell, St. Louis, 1979-82; sys. analyst Mountain Bell, Denver, 1983-87; mem. tech. staff U S WEST, Denver, 1988-92, sr. mem. tech. staff, 1994-97; mem. tech. staff U S WEST Advanced Tech., Boulder, Colo., 1993; sr. info. tech. architect Qwest, Thornton, Colo., 1998—. Editor newspaper Above The Line, 1989-96; exec. editor newspaper The Walker Squaker, 1994—; contbr. articles to profl. jours. Bd. dirs. Metro Wastewater Reclamation Dist., Denver, 1997-2001, Arabian Acres Metro Dist., 2004—; commr. Thornton Devel. Authority, 1997-2001; mem. city coun. City of Thornton, 1997-2001; fair dir. Denver Metro Region Sci. Fair, Eastlake, Colo., 1997-2000; bd. dirs. Thornton Arts Sci. Hist. Cultural Orgn., 1997-2001; mem. North Front Range Trnasp. Alternatives Feasibility Study, Denver, 1999; bd. dirs., judge Colo. Sci. and Engring. Fair, 1985—. NSF grantee, 1978; recipient Outstanding Young Man of Am. award V.I.P. Awards Ltd., 1985. Mem. IEEE Computer Soc., Am. Assn. Artificial Intelligence, Assn. Computing Machinery (chair Denver chpt. 1990-92), Platte Valley Model R.R. Club (pres. 1984—, past sec., Logo Design award 1989). Avocations: model railroading, lapidary, paleontology, nascar auto racing. Office: Qwest 1005 17th St Rm 1090 Denver CO 80202 E-mail: radford@walkersquawker.net.

**WALKER, RANDALL H.,** air transportation executive; b. Boulder City, Nev. m. Terry Walker; 6 children. BS in Acctg. magna cum laude, Brigham Young U. Budget analyst Clark County (Nev.) Mgr.'s Office; bus. mgr. Las Vegas Met. Police Dept.; dep. city mgr. City of Las Vegas; Las Vegas rep. to Nev. State Legislature; asst. county mgr. Clark County, dir. dept. fin.; dep. dir. Clark County Dept. Aviation, now dir. Office: c/o McCarran Internat Airport PO Box 11005 Las Vegas NV 89111-1005

**WALKER, RANDOLPH MEADE,** minister; b. Heathsville, Va., Mar. 24, 1950; s. Levi Robeson and Elsie Tolson Walker; m. Deloris Adair Walker; children: Jennifer Michelle, John Randolph. BA, Hampton U., 1972; MA, U. Memphis, 1976, PhD, 1990; LLD, LeMoyne-Owen Coll., 2002; MDiv, Memphis Theol. Sem., 2004. Pastor Pilgrim Rest Bapt. Ch., Henning, Tenn., 1976—82; sales exec. AC-DELCO Divsn. GM Corp., Memphis, 1972—86; pastor New Phila. Bapt. Ch., Memphis, 1982—96; assoc. prof. LeMoyne-Owen Coll., Memphis, 1987—2002; pastor Castalia Bapt. Ch., Memphis, 1998—. Bd. mem. Shelby County Hist. Com., Memphis, 2002—. Mem. NAACP, Memphis, 1976—, Urban League, Inc., Memphis, 1982—, Kiwana's Inst., Memphis, 2002—. Recipient Svc. award, Memphis Theol. Sem., 2003. Mem.: So. Conf. of African Am. Studies, Memphis Bapt. Ministerial Assn., West Tenn. Hist. Soc. Democrat. Baptist. Avocations: baseball, football, basketball, reading, writing. Office: Castalia Bapt Ch 1540 Castalia St Memphis TN 38114 Office Phone: 901-276-7295. E-mail: rmwalker@midsouth.rr.com.

**WALKER, RAYMOND JOHN,** physicist; b. LA, Oct. 26, 1942; s. Raymond Osmund and Marie Dorothy (Peterman) W. BS, San Diego State U., 1964; MS, UCLA, 1966, PhD, 1973. Rsch. assoc. U. Minn., Mpls., 1973-77; rsch. geophysicist Inst. Geophysics and Planetary Physics UCLA, 1977—; prof. in residence Inst. Geophysics and Planetary Physics and Dept. Earth and Space Sci., 1999—. Mgr. planetary plasma interactions node, 1990-, and project scientist, 1992-96, NASA Planetary Data System; mem. numerous coms. on space physics and the mgmt. of space physics data NRC and NASA. Contbr. articles to profl. jours. Mem. AAAS, Am. Geophys. Union (chair info. tech. com. 1990-92, Edward A. Flinn III award 1996), Am. Astron. Soc. (div. Planetary Sci.). Achievements include research in magnetospheric physics, in planetary magnetospheres, in global magnetohydrodynamic simulation of solar wind-magnetosphere interaction, in data management, in magnetic field modeling. Home: 11053 Tennessee Ave Los Angeles CA 90064-1936 Office: UCLA IGPP 405 Hilgard Ave Los Angeles CA 90095-1567 Office Phone: 310-825-7685. Business E-Mail: rwalker@igpp.ucla.edu.

**WALKER, RICHARD BRIAN,** chemistry professor; b. Quincy, Mass., May 14, 1948; s. George Edgar and Eva Mary (Taylor) W. BS in Biochemistry, U. So. Calif., 1970; PhD in Pharm. Chemistry, U. Calif., San Francisco, 1975. Rsch. assoc. Oreg. State U., Corvallis, 1975-76, U. Wash., Seattle, 1976-78; lectr. U.S. Internat. U., San Diego, 1978-81, Hamdard Sch. Pharmacy, New Delhi, India, 1981-82; rsch. scientist Biophysica Found., San Diego, 1982-83; assoc. prof. chemistry U. Ozarks, Clarksville, Ark., 1983-84; asst. to assoc. prof. chemistry U. Ark., Pine Bluff, 1984-96, prof. chemistry, 1996—. Prin. investigator minority biomed. rsch. support program NIH, Bethesda, Md., 1986—; project dir. Ark. Systemic Sci. Initiative; chair U. Ark. Pine Bluff Instl. Rev. Bd., 2003-; rev. in field. Contbr. articles to profl. jours. Coord. home Bible fellowship The Way Internat., Pine Bluff, 1984-99; judge Ctrl. Ark. Sci. Fair, Little Rock, 1986—. NIH rsch. grantee, 1986, 89, 93. Mem. Am. Chem. Soc., Am. Acad. Scis., Am. Assn. Pharm. Scientists, Sigma Xi (sec.-treas. ctrl. Ark. chpt. 2005-06, v.p. 2007-08). Avocations: fishing, golf, skiing. Office: 1200 University Dr Pine Bluff AR 71601-2799 Home: 2401 Lakeview Rd Apt K3 North Little Rock AR 72116-9410 Office Phone: 870-575-8894. Business E-Mail: walker_r@uapb.edu.

**WALKER, RICHARD HAROLD,** pathologist, educator; b. Cleve., Dec. 2, 1928; s. Harold Deford and Bernice Margaret (Wright) W.; m. Carolyn Franklin, Sept. 28, 1951; children: Bruce, Lynn, Cara. Lora, DS, Emory U., 1950, MD, 1953. Intern City of Memphis Hosps., 1953-54; resident in pathology Coll. Medicine U. Tenn., Memphis, 1954-55, 57-59, prof. pathology, 1966-70; Am. Cancer Soc. clin. fellow U. Tenn. Coll. Medicine, 1957-59; med. dir. blood bank and transfusion svc. City of Memphis Hosps., Memphis, 1961-70; chief of blood bank and transfusion service William Beaumont Hosp., Royal Oak, Mich., 1970-95, med. dir. Sch. Med. Tech., 1970-91. Clin. prof. pathology Sch. Medicine Wayne State U., Detroit, 1982-95. Contbr. articles on blood transfusion, blood group genetics and transfusion medicine to med. jours. Capt. USNR ret. Recipient Murray Thelin Humanitarian award Memphis chpt. Nat. Hemophilia Found., 1968. Mem. AMA, Coll. Am. Pathologists, Am. Soc. Clin. Pathologists (Disting. Svc. award 1977, Ward Burdick award 1992), Am. Assn. Blood Banks (pres. 1976-77, John Elliott Meml. award 1986), Tenn. Assn. Blood Banks (L.W. Diggs award 1986), Internat. Soc. Blood Transfusion, Am. Soc. for Histocompatibility and Immunogenetics. Republican. Presbyterian. Home: 4204 Fleet Landing Blvd Atlantic Beach FL 32233-4590

**WALKER, RICHARD HENRY,** lawyer; b. Wilmington, Del., Dec. 29, 1950; s. Henry H. and Mary L. (Meister) W.BA, Trinity Coll., 1972; JD cum laude, Temple U., 1975. Bar: Pa. 1976, U.S. Supreme Ct. 1977, N.Y. 1978, D.C. 1981. Law clk. to Hon. Collins J. Seitz U.S. Ct. Appeals (3rd cir.), Wilmington, Del., 1975-76; assoc., ptnr. Cadwalader, Wickersham & Taft, N.Y.C., 1976-91; regional dir. N.E. office U.S. SEC, N.Y.C., 1991-95, gen. counsel Washington, 1996-98, dir. enforcement, 1998—2001; global gen. counsel Deutsche Bank, 2001—. Bd. dir. MBIA Inc., 2006—; mem. legal adv. com. NYSE. Trustee Am. Folk Art Mus. Recipient Presdl. Rank Disting. Svc. award, SEC, 1997, Disting. Svc. award. Fellow Am. Bar Found.; trustee SEC Historical Soc.; mem. Phi Beta Kappa

**WALKER, RICHARD HUGH,** orthopaedic surgeon; b. Elgin, Ill., Jan. 29, 1951; m. Wendy Allen; children: Ashley Elizabeth, Blake Allen, Emily Paige. AB cum laude, Occidental Coll., 1973; MD, U. Chgo., 1977. Diplomate Nat. Bd. Med. Examiners, Am. Bd. Orthopaedic Surgery. Jr. resident in surgery UCLA, 1977-79; jr. resident in orthopaedic surgery Stanford (Calif.) U., 1979-81, sr. resident, 1981-82, chief resident, 1982-83; clin. instr. divsn. orthop. surgery, sect. lower extremity reconstructive surgery Scripps Clinic, La Jolla, Calif., 1983—, co-dir. lower extremity reconstructive surgery fellowship, divsn. orthopaedic surgery, 1989—, assoc. head. divsn. orthopaedic surgery, 1990-97, chmn. dept. surgery, 1998—, v.p. surg. svcs., 2001—. Staff physician dept. surgery Green Hosp. of Scripps Clinic, La Jolla, 1983—, mem. exec. com., 1994—2001, chief of staff, 1995—97; Team physician San Diego Padres, 1983—86, team physician, 1995—99; Clin. instr. dept. orthopaedics and rehab. U. Calif., San Diego, 1983—; asst. clin. prof., 1992—; Mem. bd. dir. Scripps Clinic Med. Group, La Jolla, 1992—, mem. exec. com., 1998—, med. dir. surg. specialties, 1998—2001, mem. joint exec. bd., 1992—93. Cons. reviewer Clin. Orthopaedics and Related Rsch., 1989—, Jour. Bone and Joint Surgery, 1994—; contbr. articles to profl. jours. Mem. AMA, ACS, Am. Acad. Orthopaedic Surgeons, We. Orthopaedic Assn. (program chmn. San Diego chpt. 1994-95, treas. 1995-96, v.p. 1996-97, pres. 1997-98, Resident Paper award 1983), Calif. Orthopaedic Assn., Assn. Arthritic Hip and Knee Surgery (charter mem. 1991), Am. Assn. Hip and Knee Surgeons, Assn. Bone and Joint Surgeons (Nicholas Andry Rsch. award 1997). Office: Scripps Clinic Divsn Orthop Surgery 10666 N Torrey Pines Rd La Jolla CA 92037-1092 Office Phone: 858-554-9882. Business E-Mail: rwalker@scrippsclinic.com.

**WALKER, RICHARD K.,** lawyer; b. Knoxville, Tenn., Oct. 21, 1948; BA with honors, U. Kans., 1970, JD, 1975; student, U. Bonn, Germany; grad. student, U Tübingen, Germany. Bar: Ariz. 1975, D.C. 1977, U.S. Supreme Ct. 1977. Asst. prof. law U. S.C., 1977-81, assoc. prof. law, 1981-82; ptnr. Bishop, Cook, Purcell & Reynolds, Washington, 1981-90, Winston & Strawn, Washington, 1990-93; dir. Streich Lang, Phoenix, 1993-2000; ptnr. Quarles & Brady Streich Lang, Phoenix, 2000—. Bd. trustees Ariz. Theatre Co., 1995-2001, 04-; bd. dirs. Phoenix Cmty. Alliance, 2001—. Fulbright Direct Exch. scholar. Mem. ABA, Labor and Employment Law Sec. (mem. equal employment opportunity law com. and devel. of the law under the NLRA com., 1979—), Litigation Sec. (mem. class actions and derivitive suits com. and trial pratice com., 1998—, mem. employment rels. and labor law com., 1979—), Ariz. Assn. Def. Counsel (bd. dirs. 1997-2000). Office: Quarles & Brady Streich Lang LLP Renaissance One 2 N Central Ave Phoenix AZ 85004-2345 Office Phone: 602-229-5219. E-mail: rwalker@quarles.com.

**WALKER, ROBERT F.,** social studies educator; b. Van Nuys, Calif., Sept. 9, 1977; s. Carol Walker. BA, U. Calif., Davis, 2000; MA in History, Stanford U., Calif., 2002; MA in Ednl. Tech., Calif. State U., Northridge, 2005. Cert. single subject tchg. credential in Social Studies Calif. State U., 2003. Social studies tchr. Bishop Alemany HS, Mission Hills, Calif., 2003—04, Acad. Canyons, WSHUHD, Santa Clarita, Calif., 2004—. Mem.: Internat. Soc. Tech. in Edn., Nat. Coun. Social Studies, Nat. Hist. Assn. Green Party. Office: Acad Canyons 26455 Rockwell Canyon Rd Santa Clarita CA 91355 Office Phone: 661-362-3056.

**WALKER, ROBERT HARRIS,** historian, writer, editor; b. Cin., Mar. 15, 1924; m. Grace Burtt; children: Amy, Rachel, Matthew. BS, Northwestern U., 1945; MA, Columbia U., 1950; PhD, U. Pa., 1955. Edn. specialist U.S. Mil. Govt., Japan, 1946-47; instr. Carnegie Inst. Tech., 1950-51, U. Pa., 1953-54; asst. prof., dir. Am. studies U. Wyo., 1955-59; asso. prof. George Washington U., 1959-63, prof. Am. civilization, 1963-94, dir. Am. studies program, 1959-66, 68-70. First dir. edn. and pub. programs NEH, 1966-68; fellow Woodrow Wilson Internat. Ctr., 1972-73, Rockefeller Rsch. Ctr., 1979, Hoover Instn., Huntington Libr., 1980; specialist grants to Japan, Germany, Thailand, Iran, Greece, Israel, Brazil, China, People's Republic of Korea, Hong Kong, 1964-91; Fulbright lectr., Australia, New Zealand, Philippines, 1971, Sweden, France, West Germany, Norway, all 1987; Am. Coun. Learned Socs. alt. del. UNESCO Gen. Info. Program, 1978—; co-founder Algonquin Books, 1982. Author: Poet and Gilded Age, 1963, Life in the Age of Enterprise, 1967, American Society, 1981, 2d edit., 1995, Reform in America (nominated for Pulitzer prize in history), 1985, (with R.H. Gabriel) Course of American Democratic Thought, 3d edit., 1986, Cincinnati and the Big Red Machine, 1988, Everyday Life in Victorian America, 1994; editor, compiler: American Studies in the U.S., 1958, American Studies Abroad, 1975, Reform Spirit in America, 1976, 85, American Studies: Topics and Sources, 1976, Friends of Raoul Wallenberg, 1987-1997, 1998; editor: Am. Quar., 1953-54; sr. editor: Am. Studies Internat., 1970-80, Am. studies series for Greenwood Press, 1972—, over 100 vols. Founding mem. Japan-U.S. Friendship Commn., 1977-80; founding pres. Friends of Raoul Wallenberg Found., 1987-99. With USNR, 1943-46, 50. Mem. Am. Studies Assn. (nat. pres. 1970-71), Cosmos Club, Phi Beta Kappa. Office: 200 Riverside Blvd #4J New York NY 10069-0907

**WALKER, ROBERT R.,** music educator; b. Electra, Tex., Oct. 23, 1963; s. Bobby Walker and Jan Kaspar; m. Elizabeth Pond, Aug. 23, 1986; children: Emily Hamilton, Bo Hamilton, Katherine, Hannah, Michael, Matthew, Bryan. MusB, Emporia State U., 1992, MusM, 1995. Cert. interactive TV instr. Kellogg C.C. Music instr. Kellogg C.C., Battle Creek, Mich., 1995—2001; dir. music Labette C.C., Parsons, Kans., 2001—. Recipient Disting. Faculty award, Labette C.C., 2005, Exemplory Online Course Design award, Kans. Blackboard Users Group, 2003. Mem.: Am. Choral Directors Assn. (assoc.). Home: 2812 Stevens Parsons KS 67357 Office: Labette CC 200 South 14th St Parsons KS 67357 Office Phone: 620-820-1021. Business E-Mail: robertw@labette.edu.

**WALKER, ROBERT SMITH,** former congressman; b. Bradford, Pa., Dec. 23, 1942; s. Joseph Erdman and Rachael Viola (Smith) W.; m. Sue Ellen Albertson, Apr. 13, 1968. Student William & Mary, 1960—61; BS in Edn., Millersville U., Pa., 1964; MA in Polit. Sci., U. Del., 1968; LLD (hon.), Franklin & Marshall Coll., 1998. Tchr. Penn Manor High Sch., Lancaster, Pa., 1964-67; legis. asst. to Congressman Edwin D. Eshleman, 1967-74, administrv. asst., 1974-76; mem. 95th-104th Congresses from 16th Pa. dist., Washington, 1977-96, chmn. House Com. Sci.; vice chmn. house budget com., chmn. house Rep. leadership, 1995-97; chief dep. minority whip, 1989-95; spkr. pro tempore, 1996; chmn. Wexler & Walker Pub. Policy Assocs., Washington, 1997—. Adv. bd. Innerlink, 2001; chmn. Commn. on the Future of the U.S. Aerospace Industry, 2001—02; mem. Nat. Academies Aeronautics and Space Engring. Bd., 2004—, Pres.'s Commn. on the U.S. Postal Svc., 2003, Pres.'s Commn. on Space Exploration, 2004; polit. analyst Fox News, 2005—. Co-author: Congress-The Pennsylvania Dutch Representatives, 1774-1974, Can You Afford This House, 1978, House of Ill Repute, 1987, Space: The Free Market Frontier, 2003, Crossroads: The Future of American Politics, 2003; columnist: UPI; contbr. articles to profl. jours. Trustee Aerospace Corp., 1997-2005, vice chmn., 2004-05, chmn., 2006; active Space Found., 2004—. Susquehanna Valley Ctr. Pub. Policy, 1998—. With Pa. NG, 1967-73, bd. dirs. Space Devel., 2001—, Zero G, 2005. Pa. Nat. Guard, 1967—73. Recipient NASA Disting. Svc. medal, 1996, NASA Disting. Pub. Svc. medal, 2004; fellow Millersville U., 1996-2001, Franklin & Marshall Coll., 1997-2001. Mem. Am. League of Lobbyists (bd. dirs. 2000-04). Republican. Presbyterian. Office: Wexler & Walker Pub Policy Assocs 1317 F St NW Ste 600 Washington DC 20004-1157 Office Phone: 202-638-2121. Business E-Mail: walker@wexlerwalker.com. *The revolution sweeping politics, economics, culture and technology will produce new opportunities but at the same time will demand a new way of thinking about our economy and our society. The wealth of information available to each individual means that government and business must think in terms of individualized approaches.*

**WALKER, ROGER GEOFFREY,** geology educator, consultant; b. London, Mar. 26, 1939; s. Reginald Noel and Enfield Annie Walker; m. Gay Parsons, Sept. 18, 1965; children: David John, Susan Elizabeth. BA, Oxford U., Eng., 1961, DPhil in Geology, 1964. NATO postdoctoral fellow in geology Johns Hopkins U., Balt., 1964-66; from asst. to assoc. prof. McMaster U., Hamilton, Ont., Canada, 1966-73, prof. geology, 1973-98, prof. emeritus, 1998—. Tchr. profl. short courses on various aspects of oil exploration in clastic reservoirs, Can., U.S., Brazil, Australia, Japan, Italy, Venezuela, Norway; grant selection com. earth scis. sect. Nat. Scis. and Engring. Rsch. Coun. Can., 1981-84; Judd A. & Cynthia S. Oualline Centennial lectr. U. Tex., Austin, 1986; vis. scientist Denver Rsch. Ctr., Marathon Oil Co., Littleton, Colo., 1973-74, Amoco Can. Petrol Co., Calgary, Alta., 1982; vis. fellow Australian Nat. U., Canberra, 1981; vis. prof. Fed. U. Ouro Preto, Brazil, 1987, 89-91, Fed. U. Rio Grande do Sul, Brazil, 1992; adj. prof. U. Regina, 1997—; pres. Roger Walker Cons., Inc., 1997—. Editor: Facies Models, 1979, 3d edit., 1992; contbr. over 140 articles to profl. jours. Recipient oper. and strategic grants Nat. Scis. and Engring. Rsch. Coun. Can., 1966—. Fellow: Royal Soc. Can.; mem.: Internat. Assn. Sedimentologists (Henry Clifton Sorby medal 2002), Can. Assn. Univ. Tchrs., Soc. Sedimentary Geology (Francis J. Pettijohn medal 1997), Soc. Econ. Paleontologists and Mineralogists (hon.; assoc. editor 1970—78, pres. eastern sect. 1975—76, coun. for mineralogy 1979—80), Am. Assn. Petroleum Geologists (Disting. lectr. 1979—80, Disting. Educator award 1999), Can. Soc. Petroleum Geologists (Link award 1983, R.J.W. Douglas Meml. medal 1990), Geol. Assn. Can. (assoc. editor 1977—80, Past Pres.'s medal 1975, Disting. Svc. award 1994, Logan medal 1999). Achievements include research in sedimentary facies analysis, sedimentology of turbidites, quantitative basin analysis, sedimentology of Western Canadian Cretaceous clastic wedge. Home and Office: Roger Walker Cons 83 Scimitar View NW Calgary AB Canada T3L 2B4 Business E-Mail: walkerrg@telus.net.

**WALKER, RONALD CRAIG,** artist, educator; b. Oxnard, Calif., Sept. 3, 1958; s. Richard Scott and Nancy Bell Walker; m. Erin Marie Mahoney, June 20, 1992; children: Ryley, Colin. AA in Fine Arts, Ventura Coll., 1979; BS in Edn., Ctrl. Mo. State U., 1981, MA, 1984; MFA, U. Kans., 1992. Art instr. Learning Tree U., Thousand Oaks, Calif., 1992—93, Tacoma C.C., Gig Harbor, Wash., 1993—94, Bethel Sch. Dist., Spanaway, Wash., 1994—95, San Juan Unified Sch. Dist., Sacramento, 1996—. Gallery dir. Buenaventura Art Assn., Ventura, Calif., 1986—87; juror Calif. State Fair, Sacramento, 1999. Curator Ventura Arts Coun., Calif., 1988, judge, 1989, 1991; Buenaventura Art Assn., Ventura, Calif., 1984, Laredo Ctr. for the Arts, Tex., 2002. Mem.: NEA, Roseville Arts Ctr., Calif. Arts League. Avocation: walking. Office: San Juan Unified Sch Dist 7940 Mariposa Ave Citrus Heights CA 95610

**WALKER, RONALD EDWARD,** psychologist, educator; b. East St. Louis, Ill., Jan. 23, 1935; s. George Edward and Marnella (Altmeyer) W.; m. Aldona M. Mogenis, Oct. 4, 1958; children: Regina, Mark, Paula, Alexis. BS, St. Louis U., 1957; MS, Northwestern U., 1959, PhD, 1961. Lectr. psychology Northwestern U., 1959-61; faculty dept. psychology Loyola U., Chgo., 1961—, asst., then assoc. prof., 1961-68, prof., chmn. dept., 1965—73, prof. emeritus, 1999—, acting dean Coll. Arts and Scis., 1973-74; dean Loyola U. (Coll. Arts and Scis.), 1974-80, academic v.p., 1980-81, sr. v.p., dean faculties, 1981-89, exec. v.p., 1989-99. Cons. VA, Chgo., 1965-74; Am. Psychol. Assn.-NIMH; vis. cons., 1969; vis. scientist Am. Psychol. Assn. NSF, 1968; Cook County (Ill.) rep. from Ill. Psychol. Assn., 1969-72; cons.-evaluator North Cen. Assn., 1986-99. Contbr. articles to profl. jours. Bd. trustees St. Francis Hosp., Evanston, Ill., 1986—92, Chgo. Archdiocesan Sems., 1985—97, Loyola Acad., Wilmette, Ill., 1987—93, St. Louis U., 1988—97; bd. dirs. Holy Family Villa Nursing Home, Lemont, Ill., 2002—05. Recipient Disting. Psychologist of Yr. award Ill. Psychol. Assn., 1986. Home: Unit 5I 1630 Sheridan Rd Wilmette IL 60091-1835 Business E-Mail: rwalker@luc.edu.

**WALKER, RONALD HUGH,** retired management consultant; b. Bryan, Tex., July 25, 1937; s. Walter Hugh and Maxine (Tarver) W.; m. Anne Lucille Collins, Aug. 8, 1959; children: Lisa, Marjorie, Lynne. BA, U. Ariz., 1960. With Allstate Ins. Co., Pasadena, Calif., 1964-67, Hudson Co., 1967-69; asst. to sec. interior, 1969-70; founder, 1st dir., staff asst. to Pres. U.S. White House Advance Office, 1970-72; spl. asst. to Pres., 1972-73; dir. Nat. Park Service, Washington, 1973-75; cons. Saudi Arabia, 1975; assoc. dir. World Championship Tennis, 1975-77; pres. Ron Walker & Assocs., Inc., Dallas, 1977-79; sr. ptnr., mng. dir. Korn/Ferry Internat., Washington, 1979—2001; ret., 2000. Bd. dirs., chmn. Guest Svcs. Inc., Mullin Cons., Inc., Vinson & Co.; chmn. NOVAVAX, 1999-2005. Bd. dirs. U.S.S. Arizona Found. and Memorial; mem. Nat. Pk. Svc. Dirs. Coun.; founder, chmn. emeritus Order of Raft, 1972; spl. presdl. del. to Prime Min. Indira Gandhi's funeral New Delhi, 1984; spl. presdl. del. to Games of XXIV Olympiad Seoul, 1988; trustee Nat. Outdoor Leadership Sch., Nat. Fitness Found., Pres.'s Coun. on Phys. Fitness and Sports, 1981—85; bd. dirs. NCAA Found., mem. exec. com., mem. adv. bd.; bd. dirs. Meridian Internat.; mem. Ctr. for Study of Presidency, 1988—95; chmn. Freedom Found. at Valley Forge, 1989—2000; trustee Ford's Theater, Washington; men's chair Project Hope Ann. Ball, 1989, 1990, 1991; chmn. ann. dinner Boys and Girls Clubs Am., 1993; chmn. 50th Presdl. Inauguration, Dedication Richard Nixon Libr., Birthplace, 1990, bd. dirs., 1990; nat. chair Celebrities and Sports for Bush-Quayle; mem. over-site com. U.S. Rowing, 1993; mem. com. Preservation of White House, 1973—75; mem. Nat. Pk. Adv. Bd., 1973—75, Nat. Pk. Found., 1973—75, John F. Kennedy Ctr. for Performing Arts, 1973—75, Friends of Nancy Hanks Ctr.; bd. trustees Mridian House Internat., 1992—; mem. USA Gymnasium Found., 1993—99; trustee U. Ariz. Found.; chair Nat. Pk. Found. Alumni Assn.; bd. dirs Saquaro Nat. Park; mem. adv. bd. Nat. Park Sys., 2004—; vol. Nixon/Agnew Campaign, 1968, transition and inauguration team, 1969; vice chmn. Pres.'s Commn. on Bicentennial U.S. Constn., 1985—88; mem. Coun. for Excellence in Govt., 1988—; mgr., CEO Rep. Nat. Conv., 1984, sr. advisor, 1988, 1992, 1996, 2000, 2004, Bush/Quayle Presdl. Campaign, 1988, Bush/Cheney Presdl. Campaign, 2000, 2004, Bush/Cheney Inauguration; hon. chmn. Cheney Inaugural Activities; coord. v.p. debate Cheney and Lieberman, 2000, Cheney and Edwards, 2004; mem. leadership adv. bd. NCAA; bd. dirs. Grand Teton Nat. Pk. Found., Saquaro Nat. Pk. Found. Capt. U.S. Army, 1961—64. Recipient Disting. Citizen award U. Ariz., 1973, Outstanding Svc. award Dept. Interior, 1975, Centennial Medallion award U. Ariz., 1989, Ellis Island Congl. medal of honor, 1992, Lincoln medal Ford's Theater, 2002. Mem. NCAA (bd. dirs. 1992-2003, exec. com. 1992-2003, adv. bd.), Boone. Club of Washington, Met. Club of Washington, Congl. Country Club, Georgetown Club, City Club of Washington, Univ. Club. of N.Y., Burning Tree Club, Phi Delta Theta (named to Hall of Fame, 1991). Republican. Methodist. Home (Winter): 13535 Placita Montanas de Oro Tucson AZ 85755 E-mail: roadrunnerrhw@aol.com.

**WALKER, RONALD R.,** editor, educator, writer; b. Newport News, Va., Sept. 2, 1934; s. William R. and Jane Marie (King) W.; m. O. Diane Mawson, Apr. 16, 1961; children: Mark Jonathan, Steven Christopher. BS, Pa. State U., 1956; postgrad., Harvard U., 1970-71. Reporter, news editor, sr. editor, editorial page editor, mng. editor San Juan Star (P.R.), 1962-73, Washington columnist, 1982-84, city editor, 1984-87; instr. journalism Pa. State U., State College, 1973-74; asst. prof. Columbia U. Grad. Sch. Journalism, N.Y.C., 1974-76; editor The Daily News, V.I., 1976-77; press sec. Gov. V.I., 1978-79; spl. asst., chief of staff Rep. James H. Scheuer, U.S. Congress, 1980-82, Resident Commr. Jaime B. Fuster, U.S. Congress, 1987-92; spl. asst., press sec. Resident Commr. Antonio J. Colorado, 1992-93; ind. profl. writer, weekly columnist editl. page San Juan Star, 1993—; regular columnist St. John Times, 1997—. Contbr. articles to nat. mags. and jours. including The Nation, The N.Y. Times, The Washington Post, and others. Served with U.S. Army, 1957-59. Nieman fellow in journalism Harvard U., 1970-71. Mem. Soc. Nieman Fellows, Leica Hist. Soc. Address: PO Box 1358 St John VI 00831-1358 Personal E-Mail: rrwalker340@earthlink.net.

**WALKER, RONALD TRACY,** retired personnel director; b. North Wilkesboro, N.C., July 27, 1937; m. Nena Watkins; children: Randy, Kirk. Student, Wilkes C.C., Wake Forest U. With CMI Industries Inc., Elkin, NC, 1967-99, plant human resource mgr.; ret. 1999; mem. N.C. Ho. of Reps., 1999—. Commr. Wilkes County, 1978-96, past mem. region "D" coun. govts.; regional econ. devel. coun., indsl. park coun., chmn. regional transp. com., mem. regional adv. com. to WNCREDC, liaison Advantage West and region "D" coun. govts.; past chmn. region "D" coun. govts Wilkes County, northwestern housing authority; past mem. bd. edn., 1972-76, airport authority; past vice-chmn., chmn. Wilkes County Commrs.; past bd. dirs. Blue Ridge Water Assn.; pres. Northwestern Devel. Assn.; trustee Health Ins. N.C. Assn. County Commrs.; mem. N.C. Regional Econ. Devel. Commn.; apptd. mem. N.C. Adv. Coun. Vocat. and Technical Edn., 1972-76, N.C. Dept. Correction, 1984-92; Rep. candidate for N.C. Commr. of Labor, 1996; candidate N.C.

House, 1998, 2000, N.C. House of Rep., 2001-, With USAF, 1955-59. Recipient Leadership award Western N.C., 1996. Office Phone: 919-733-5935. Personal E-mail: tracyw@ncleg.net.

**WALKER, ROSLYN ADELE,** retired museum director; b. Memphis, Tenn., July 26, 1944; Student Gen. Studies, U. Poitiers, France, 1965; BS in Art Edn. with high honors, Hampton U., 1966; MA in History of Art, Indiana U., 1969, PhD in History of Art, 1991. Registrar Mus. African Art, Washington, 1968-69; conservator Univ. Art Gallery U. Mass., Amherst, 1969-70; temporary registrar Fed. Dept Antiquities Nat. Mus., Lagos, Nigeria, 1970; curator of collections Inst. African Studies U. Idaban, Nigeria, 1973-75; curator ethnographic art collection Univ. Mus. Ill. State U., Normal, 1975-81, interim adminstr., 1975, adminstr., 1975-77, dir., 1977-81; curator Nat. Mus. African Art Smithsonian Instn., Washington, 1981-93, sr. curator, 1993-97, dir., 1997—2002; sr. curator The Arts of Africa, the Pacific and the Americas Dallas Mus. Art, Margaret McDermott curator African art. Rsch. asst. Mus. Modern Art, N.Y.C., 1971-72, guest curator African Women/African Art, The African-Am. Inst., N.Y.C., 1976, Lakeview Mus. Arts and Scis., Peoria, Ill., 1981; instr. in primitive art U. Mass., Amherst, 1969-70, in African decorative art USDA Grad. Sch., Washington, 1984. in Art in Africa, Dept. Art History, U. Md., College Park, 1990; vis. lectr. Afro-Am. Art, Ind. U., Bloomington, 1970-71, lectr. 1971-72, summer program, U. Idaban, Nigeria, 1974; asst. prof. Art Dept., Ill. State U., Normal, 1975-81. Author: (with Roy Sieber) African Art in the Cycle of Life, 1987, Olowe of Ise: A Yoruba Sculptor to Kings, 1998; contbr. catalogs for exhibitions of African Art to Royal Acad. of Arts, London, 1995, Guggenheim Mus. N.Y. and Afro-Am. Hist. and Cultural Mus., Phila., 1996; contbr., reviews, essays and articles to profl. jours. and mags. Mem. visual arts and crafts adv. panel Washington Commn. on the Arts. Recipient Ford Found. Fgn. Study grant, 1965, Faculty Rsch. grant, U. Mass., 1970, Fgn. Lang. fellowship Ind. U., Bloomington, 1971, Grant in Aid, Ind. U., 1972, Rsch. Fund grant (collections-based), Smithsonian Instn., Washington, 1994; named Twenty Yr. Student, Hampton U., 1986. Mem. Arts Coun. African Studies Assn. (past bd. dirs.), ArTable, Assn. Art Mus. Dirs.

**WALKER, SALLY BARBARA,** retired glass company executive; b. Bellerose, NY, Nov. 21, 1921; d. Lambert Roger and Edith Demerest (Parkhouse) W. Diploma, Cathedral Sch. St. Mary, 1939; AA, Finch Jr. Coll., 1941. Tchr. interior design Finch Coll., 1941-42; draftsman AT&T, 1942-43; with Steuben Glass Co., N.Y.C., 1943—, exec. v.p. 1959-62, exec. v.p. ops., 1962-78, exec. v.p. ops. and sales, 1978-83, exec. v.p., 1983-88, ret., 1988. Pres. 116 E. 66th St. Corp. Mem. Fifth Ave. Assn., Rockaway Hunting Club, Lawrence Beach Club, Colony Club, English-Speaking Union, Garden Club of Lawrence, City Garden Club of N.Y.C. Republican. Episcopalian. Home: 4031 Kenneth Pike #93 Greenville DE 19807

**WALKER, SANDRA KAY,** theater educator; b. Topeka, Sept. 6, 1952; d. Norman Woodrow and Ernestine Lee Humphrey; m. Wayne Wesley Walker, May 17, 1978; children: Justin Wesley, Jodie Davis, Jessica Dawn. BA, Southeastern Okla. State U., Dumat, 1978. Cert. tchr. Okla. Tchr., Okla., 1978—85, Meeker, Okla., 1986—87, Davenport Pub. Schs., 1994—. Named World Champion Ribbon Runner, NSRP, 1994. Mem.: NEA, Okla. Edn. Assn. Avocations: gardening, rodeo, jewelry. Office: Davenport Pub Schs 413 Broadway Davenport OK 74026

**WALKER, SCOTT ALLEN,** theater and language arts educator, theater director; b. Salem, Oreg., Mar. 5, 1965; s. Lewis Ira and Gloria Anne Walker; m. Gretchen Elizabeth Wehe; children: Brennan Scott, Tristan James. BS in Secondary Edn., Western Oreg. State Coll., Monmouth, 1988. Cert. std. secondary edn. Oreg. Tchr. Milwaukie (Oreg.) HS, 1992—. State/chpt. dir. Internat. Thespian Soc., Cin., 2000—03; pres. Oreg. Theatre Arts Assn., 2001—03. Recipient Rex Rabold Meml. award, Oreg. Thespians, 2001, Melba Day Sparks-Henning award, 2003. Office: Milwaukie HS 11300 SE 23d Ave Milwaukie OR 97222 Office Phone: 503-353-5840.

**WALKER, SUE ALBERTSON,** retired school system administrator, educational consultant; b. Bloomsburg, Pa., May 1, 1943; d. Robert Wilson Albertson and Sara Porter; m. Robert Smith Walker, Apr. 13, 1968. BS in Edn., Millersville State Coll., Pa., 1964; MLS, Syracuse U., 1967. Cert. instrnl. II, curriculum and instrn. Pa. Sch. libr. Benton (Pa.) Area Sch. Dist., 1964—68; media coord. Fairfax (Va.) County Sch. Dist., 1968—73; libr. supr. Sch. Dist. of Lancaster, Pa., 1973—88, dir. curriculum, 1988—99. Adj. faculty Millersville U., 1983—85, Drexel U., Phila., 1984—91; libr. cons., East Petersburg, Pa., 1980—; del., mem. steering com. Pa. Gov.'s Conf. on Librs., Harrisburg, 1976; del. White Ho. Conf. on Librs., Washington, 1978; advisor Gov.'s Adv. Coun. on Librs., Harrisburg, 1983—88. Author: Standards of Practice for Teachers, 2004. Chair Millersville U. Coun. Trustees, 1997—; sec. Lancaster Found. Ednl. Enrichment, 1999—; co-chair Millersville U. 150th Anniversary Celebration, 2002—. Named Outstanding Contbr., Pa. Sch. Librs. Assn., 1988. Mem.: ASCD, ALA, Am. Assn. Sch. Librs. (bd. dirs. 1986—89, conf. co-chair 1986), Phi Delta Kappa (Disting. Educator 1986). Republican. Presbyterian. Avocations: reading, travel, volunteer work. Home: 6065 Parkridge Dr East Petersburg PA 17520

**WALKER, SUZANNAH WOLF,** language educator; b. Akron, Ohio, May 3, 1954; d. Robert Patton and Katherine Jane (Guglielmi) Wolf Jr.; m. Timothy Gordon Walker, Dec. 23, 1988 (div. Dec. 21, 1992). BA in Secondary Edn., U. Akron, 1976; MA in Pub. Rels., Kent State U., 1987. Tchr. English, Spanish Cuyahoga Falls (Ohio) City Sch., 1977—96; tchr. English DOD Dependents Sch., Wurzburg, Germany, 1981—82; tchr. English, Spanish Canton (Ohio) City Schs., 1999—. Mem. supt. adv. com. Cuyahoga Falls City Sch., 1995, bldg. rep., 1992—95, Canton City Schs., 2000—03. Pub. rels. intern Ronald McDonald House, Cleve., 1985. Mem.: NEA, Canton Profl. Educators Assn. (mem. exec. com. 2003—), N.E. Ohio Fgn. Lang. Assn., Ohio Fgn. Lang. Assn., Cuyahoga Falls Edn. Assn., Ohio Edn. Assn. Home: 3430 E Prescott Cir Cuyahoga Falls OH 44223 Office Phone: 330-454-7717.

**WALKER, SUZANNE ROSS,** mathematics and education educator; b. Johnston, RI, Aug. 14, 1960; d. Raymond Henry Ross and Matilda Marion DeChristofaro; m. Paul Joseph Walker, Feb. 17, 1990; 1 stepchild, William Braeden Pierce. BA in Math./Math Edn. magna cum laude, Providence Coll., 1982, EdM in Guidance Counseling summa cum laude, 1992. HS math tchr. Bay View Acad., East Providence, RI, 1983—85, LaSalle Acad., Providence, 1985—87, Woonsocket Edn. Dept., RI, 1987—, math curriculum coord., 1998—. Math instr. Hall Inst. Tech. Sch., Pawtucket, RI, 1993—90; adj. faculty mem. calculus RI Coll., 1987—; advisor advanced placement calculus class Woonsocket HS, 1997—; prof. Providence Coll., 2000—, math prof., 2006—. Chairperson Johnston H.S. Class of 1978, RI, 1988—. Mem.: Am. Math. Soc., Am. Tchrs. Math., R.I. Math Tchrs. Assn. (advisor to student math team), Nat. Coun. Tchrs. Math., Math. Assn. Am., Phi Sigma Tau, Pi Mu Epsilon. Roman Catholic. Avocations: aerobics, yoga, walking, movies, music. Home: 39 Roger Williams Dr Greenville RI 02828 Office: Woonsocket HS 777 Cass Ave Woonsocket RI 02895 Office Phone: 401-767-4730. Personal E-mail: suzy814@msn.com.

**WALKER, TAMMIE LEIGH,** music educator; d. Dennis Edwin Behr and Elaine Rita Creager; m. Timothy Lynn Walker, July 29, 1995; children: Sophia Marian, Bennett Chad, Lucy Isabel, Grace Tammie. DMA in Piano Performance, U. Ill., 2001. Tchg. asst. U. Ill., Champaign-Urbana, 1995—98; assoc. prof. music Western Ill. U., Macomb, 1998—. Musician: performances in continental U.S., Hawaii, and Western Europe. Scholar, U. Wis., 1991—95. Fellow: Ill. State Music Tchrs. Assn. (coord. music competitions 2002—); mem.: Coll. Music Soc., Music Tchrs. Nat. Assn., Pi Kappa Lambda, Phi Kappa Phi. Democrat. Methodist. Avocations: travel, camping, cooking, running. Home: 426 W Jackson St Macomb IL 61455 Office: Western Illinois Univ Browne Hall 219 1 University Cir Macomb IL 61455 Office Phone: 309-298-1237. Fax: 309-298-1665. Business E-Mail: tl-walker4@wiu.edu.

**WALKER, THOMAS CARLTON,** music educator; b. Rochester, Minn., Apr. 10, 1936; s. Carl and Ethel Walker; m. Alleen Logsdon, Aug. 24, 1964; children: Kurt, Craig, Garett, DeAnna. Attended, St. Paul Bible Coll., 1956; MusB, Greenville Coll., 1958; attended, U. Ariz., 1962-63, MusM, 1967; advanced grad. study, U. Mo., 1976. Cert. C.C. tchg. cert. Ariz., 1987, lic. life ins. Ariz., massage therapy Ariz. Music instr. Phoenix Christian HS, 1960—62, Elfrida Elem., Valley Union HS, Elfrida, Ariz., 1963—67; music dept. chair Ctr. Coll., McPherson, Kans., 1967—81; choral conductor McPherson Coll., Kans., 1972—73, 1974—75; min. of music Free Meth. Ch., McPherson, 1967—73, 1974—75; music dept. chair Bartlesville Wesleyan Coll., Bartlesville, Okla., 1981—83; music instr. Phoenix Christian HS, Phoenix, 1983—85; dir. music Epworth United Meth. Ch., Phoenix, 1986—91; music instr. Glendale C. C., Glendale, Ariz., 1991—92; instr. Maricopa County Traffic Survival Sch., Phoenix, 1985—97; dir. music, choir Bethel Bapt. Ch., Phoenix, 1991—99; dir. music Lakeview United Meth. Ch., Sun City, Ariz., 1999—. Massage therapist Self Employed, Ariz., 1989—; conductor Overseas Touring Choir, 1979; choir conductor Free Meth. World Convocation, Indpls., 1979; coll. rep. Watson Colloquium-Free Meth. Ch. World Headquarters, Winona Lake, Ind., 1980; music dir. ch. & youth camps in Calif., Ariz., Kans., Ark. & Ill.; vocal & coral cons. McPherson Theatre Guild; mem. facilities planning com. McPherson Free Meth. Ch. Composer: Five Songs of Thanksgiving, 1967. With U.S. Army Air Defense Command Choral Group, 1958—60. Sgt. U.S. Army, 1958—60. Named Outstanding Educator of Am., Outstanding Educators of Am., 1972. Mem.: Ariz. Music Educators Assn., Am. Choral Dir. (life), Music Educators Nat. Conf. (life), Internat. Massage Assn. Meth. Avocation: antiques. Home: 4140 W Hayward Ave Phoenix AZ 85051 Office Phone: 623-974-5821.

**WALKER, THOMAS H.,** industrial designer; b. Hattiesburg, Miss., Nov. 11, 1950; s. Thomas Ray and Mary Ella (Bennett) W.; m. Cynthia Kay Sherer, June 5, 1993; children: Ty, Kelly, Rachel, Stacey. BS in Engring., Miss. State U., 1972, MBA, U. West Fla., 1982; postgrad., Nat. Def. U., 1987-88, Harvard U., 1990, Fed. Exec. Inst., 1992. Registered profl. engr., Va. Indsl. engr. Navy Pub. Works Ctr., Norfolk, Va., 1973-75, Atlantic Divsn. Naval Facility Engring. Commn., Norfolk, Va., 1975-76; supervisory gen. engr. Naval Comm. Sta., Exmouth, Australia, 1976-78; indsl. engr. Western Divsn. Naval Facility Engring. Commn., San Bruno, Calif., 1978-79; head facilities mgmt. Navy Pub. Works Ctr., Pensacola, Fla., 1979-82, Subic Bay, The Philippines, 1982-85; dep. dir. facilities mgmt. USMC, Washington, 1985-89; asst. commr. GSA, Washington, 1989-92, dep. asst. commr., Gamma Beta Phi, 1992-93, asst. regional adminstr. pub. bldgs. Kansas City, Mo., 1993-99; asst. regional adminstr. Pub. Bldgs. Svc., Atlanta, 1999—2006; sr. dir. govt. programs Opus Corp., Atlanta, 2006—; bldg. devel. and design executive, 2006—. Bd. dirs. Kansas City BOMA. Coach Little League Baseball, Fairfax, Va., 1986-92, Girls Softball Team, Lees Summit, Va., 1995. cub scout den father Boy Scouts Am., Fairfax, 1987-88. Miss. State U. Disting. Engring. fellow, 1992; recipient Arthur S. Fleming award Washington Jaycees, 1989, Presdl. rank award, 1996, v.p. Hammer award, 1996. Mem. NSPE, Va. Soc. Profl. Engrs., Bldg. Owners and Mgrs. Assn. (mem. govt. rels. com. 1991—, chmn. 1993—, mem. corp. facilities com. 1991—, nat. adv. coun. 1995—), Nat. Mem. of Yr. 1997, Atlanta Svc. award 2000, Bd. Chmn.'s award 2006), Internat. Facilities Mgmt. Assn. (mem. pub. sector com. 1991—, Golden Cir. award 1991), Sr. Execs. Assn., Phi Kappa Phi, Alpha Pi Mu, Gamma Beta Phi, Sigma Lambda Chi. Methodist. Avocation: golf. Home: 595 Kings Grant Walk Roswell GA 30075-5528 Office: 925 North Point Pkwy Ste 305 Alpharetta GA 30005 Office Phone: 770-663-5316. Business E-Mail: tom.walker@opuscorp.com

**WALKER, THOMAS RAY,** city aviation commissioner; AB in Art, Dartmouth Coll., 1970; BArch, Ill. Inst. Tech., 1977. Project mgr. Lohan Assocs., 1977-86; v.p. design and constrn. The Chgo. Dock and Canal Trust, 1986-91; exec. dir. Pub. Bldg. Commn. of Chgo., 1991-95; commr. dept. transp. City of Chgo., 1995-99; commr. Chgo. Dept. of Aviation, City of Chgo., 2000—. Prin. works include Soldier Field World Cup renovation, Chgo., Wright Coll. Addition, Chgo. Pub. Schs. capital improvement program, Cityfront Ctr., Chgo., MarketTower Officer Bldg., Indpls., Episcopal Sch. of Dallas Libr./Fine Arts addition, Frito-Lay Nat. Hdqs., Plano, Tex. Vice chmn. Chgo. Area Transp. Study; commr. State St. Commn.; mem. com. Newhouse arch. fellowship program Chgo. Arch. Found.; mem. Chgo. Planning Commn.; mem. selection com. cmty. svc. fellowship Chgo. Cmty. Trust; mem. TRB steering com. Conf. Transp. Issue in Large U.S. Cities; mem. Conf. Minority Transp. Officials; trustee Chgo. Music and Dance Theater; chmn. leadership coun. Met. Open Cmtys.; co-chmn. adv. bd./housing com. Met. Planning Coun. 1st lt. USAF, 1970-72. Mem. Intelligent Transp. Soc. of Am. (bd. dirs.), Nat. Assn. City Transp. Ofcls. (chmn.), Nat. Orgn. Minority Architects, Urban Land Inst., Lambda Alpha Internat. Office: O'Hare Internat Airport Dept of Aviation PO Box 66142 Chicago IL 60666-0142

**WALKER, TIMOTHY CRAIG,** transportation executive; b. Huntington, W.Va., Jan. 16, 1945; s. John Paul and Marjorie Frances (Withers) W. BA, Northwestern U., 1967; B of Fgn. Trade, Am. Grad. Sch. Internat. Mgmt., 1968. Mgmt. trainee to dir. OIM/internat. mktg. ops. NCR Corp., Dayton, Ohio, 1968—79; v.p. mktg. Do-Ray Lamp Co., Inc., Colorado City, Colo., 1979—87; v.p. sales and mktg. Truck-Lite Co., Inc., Jamestown, NY, 1984—; pres., COO Truck-Lite Internat., Inc., 1990—, also bd. dirs. Recruiter Am. Grad. Sch. Internat. Mgmt., 1971—. Bd. dirs. Valley Human Resources, United Way Agy., 1980-84, Goodwill Industries of Pueblo, Colo., 1983-84; mem. Working Group for U.S. Dept. Commerce MOSS Talks. Recipient Pres.'s award 1st alumnus Am. Grad. Sch. Internat. Mgmt., 1976, award for excellence in internat. advt., 1968; named to Automotive Hall of Fame. Mem. Transp. Safety Equipment Inst. N.Am. (chmn. mktg. and statis. com. 1980-82), European Transport Maintenance Coun. (bd. dirs. 1991-93), Heavy Duty Bus. Forum (bd. dirs.), Heavy Duty Mfrs. Assn. (bd. govs. 1987-95, sec. 1990-91, 95-96, vice chmn. 1997, chmn. 1998), Overseas Automotive Coun. (bd. dirs.), Pueblo Area C. of C. (transp. com. 1981-84), Coun. Fleet Specialists (mfrs. liaison com. 1989-91), 500 Automotive Execs. Club. Republican. Presbyterian. Home: PO Box 1263 Jamestown NY 14702-1263 Office: Truck-Lite Co PO Box 387 Jamestown NY 14702-0387 Office Phone: 716-665-6214. Personal E-mail: tcwbhx@aol.com. Business E-Mail: twalker@truck-lite.com.

**WALKER, TODD A.,** music educator, football coach; b. Jamestown, NY, Apr. 29, 1965; s. Richard and Marcia Walker; m. Amy Walker, July 6, 2001; children: Grace, Ally. BS in Music Edn., Edinboro U. Pa., 1987; MS in Spl. Edn., SUNY, 1993. Music edn. cert. K-12 NY State Edn. Dept., 1987, spl. edn. K-12 NY State Edn. Dept., 1993. Vocal music instr. Mt. Morris (NY) Ctrl. Schs., 1987—89, Caledonia-Mumford MS/HS, NY, 1989—. Musical dir., prodr. Caledonia-Mumford HS, 1989—2002, varsity football asst. coach, 1992—, varsity baseball coach. Named Outstanding Music Educator - Choral Music, Rochester Phiharm. Orch., 2000, NY State Football Champions, 1993, 1994, 1995, 2003. Mem.: NY State Baseball Coaches Assn., NY State Football Coaches Assn., Music Educator's Nat. Conf., Phi Delta Kappa. Republican. Roman Catholic. Office: Caledonia-Mumford MS/HS 99 North Street Caledonia NY 14423 Office Phone: 585-538-6811 1119.

**WALKER, VALAIDA SMITH,** university administrator, retired; d. Samuel and Rosa (Lee) Smith. BS in Math. and Phys. Edn., Howard U., Washington, 1954; MEd in Spl. Edn., Temple U., 1970, EdD in Spl. Edn., 1973. Jr. H.S. math. tchr., Balt., 1955-58, Albuquerque, 1964-65; tchr. emotionaly disturbed and socially maladjusted children Phila. 1965-66; demonstration tchr., 1968-70; tchg. assoc., coord./supr. resource rm. tchr. tng. program Temple U., Phila., 1970-72; commr. mental retardation Southeastern region Dept. Pub. Welfare, Commonwealth Pa., 1973-74; program dir. Woodhaven Ctr. Mentally Retarded Temple U., Phila., 1974-76, chairperson dept. spl. edn., 1980-83, assoc. dean Coll. Edn., 1983-84, assoc. vice provost undergrad. programs, 1984-90, interim vice provost adminstrn., 1987-90, acting v.p. student affairs, 1990-92, prof. dept. spl. edn., 1974—, v.p. student affairs, 1992—. Past mem. steering com., chairperson cmty. svcs. task force subcom. Pres. Com. on Mental Retardation; exec. advisor Caribbean Assn. Mental Retardation, 1982-89; mem. adv. panel on spl. edn. Commonwealth Pa.,

1985-93; hearing office Pa. Dept. Edn., 1978-91; gov.'s apointee Profl. Stds. and Practices Commn., 1980-83; field reader U.S. Office Edn., Bur. Handicapped, 1980-93; expert witness Pennhurst State Instn. Ct. Case, 1973-74. Bd. dirs. Elwyn Insts., 1983—, chairperson edn. com. William Penn Adult Cmty. Sch. Adv. Bd., 1976; bd. mem. Rebecca Gratz Assn., Phila. Recipient svc. award Chapel of Four Chaplains, cert. of honor Alumni Assn. Temple U., Phila., 1990, Svc. award Kappa Alpha Phi, Phila., 1995; named Spl. Educator Yr., Sigma Pi Epsilon Delta, 1983, Tchr. of Yr. Sigma Pi Epsilon Delta, Phila., 1995. Fellow Am. Assn. Mental Retardation (pres.-elect, program chair 1986-87, pres. 1987-88). Baptist.

**WALKER, VAUGHN R.,** federal judge; b. Watseka, Ill., Feb. 27, 1944; s. Vaughn Rosenworth and Catharine (Miles) W. AB, U. Mich., 1966; JD, Stanford U., 1970. Intern economist SEC, Washington, 1966, 68; law clk. to the Hon. Robert J. Kelleher US Dist. Ct. Calif., LA, 1971-72; assoc. atty. Pillsbury Madison & Sutro, San Francisco, 1972-77, ptnr., 1978-90; judge US Dist. Ct. (no. dist.) Calif., San Francisco, 1990—, chief judge, 2004—. Mem. Calif. Law Revision Commn., Palo Alto, 1986-89; bd. advisors Law and Econs. Ctr., George Mason U., 1999—. Dir. Jr. Achievement of Bay Area, San Francisco, 1979-83, St. Francis Found., San Francisco, 1991-97, 98—, Woodrow Wilson Found. fellow U. Calif., Berkeley, 1966-67. Fellow Am. Bar Found.; mem. ABA (jud. rep., antitrust sect. 1991-95), Lawyers' Club of San Francisco (pres. 1985-86), Assn. Bus. Trial Lawyers (dir. 1996-98), Am. Law Inst., Am. Saddlebred Horse Assn., San Francisco Mus. Modern Art, Bohemian Club, Olympic Club, Pacific-Union Club. Office: US Dist Ct 450 Golden Gate Ave San Francisco CA 94102-3482

**WALKER, W. JACK,** retired small business owner; b. Sept. 30, 1919; s. John Wesley Walker, Mattie Alma (Gilbert) Walker; m. Loraine Walker; 1 child, Gayle Walker Threet. BBA, U. Tenn., 1940; DHL (hon.), Knoxville Coll., 1988. Owner W.Jack Walker Rolling Store, 1946—51, Walker Market, Knoxville, Tenn., 1954—78; cons. Ernest Youngblood Assocs., Knoxville, 1978—. Bd. govs. Club LeConte, 1977—; bd. dirs. St. Mary's Health Sys., Inc., Cmty. Found. East Tenn., Wellness Cmty. Knoxville, Child & Family Svcs., Salvation Army, Presbyn. Homes of Tenn., Inc., Tenn. Valley Agrl. & Indsl. Fair, v.p. exec. com., 1984—; chmn. investment com. Monday Found., 1990—; bd. dirs. Sr. Citizens Home Assistance Svcs., Pellissippi State C.C. Found., Union Planters Bank, 1990—, Blount Hearing and Speech Found.; deacon Ctrl. Bapt. Ch. Bearden; chmn. bd. First Tenn. Bank, Knoxville, Tenn., 1977—86. With U.S. Coast Guard. Named Retailer of Yr., Tenn. Retail Merchants Assn., 1977, Salesman of Yr., 1978; recipient Outstanding Leadership award, ARC, 1968, Outstanding Svc. award, Castle Heights Mil. Acad., 1980, Pres.'s award, Knoxville Area Urban League, 1987, Disting. Svc. award, Arthritis Found., 1988, Book of Golden Deeds award, Knoxville Exch. Club, 1985, Brotherhood-Sisterhood award, Nat. Conf. Christians and Jews, 1987. Mem.: Masons (32d degree), YMCA Knoxville (Red Triangle award, Man of Yr. 1968), U. Tenn. Pres.'s Club, Rotary Club Knoxville. Office: Ernest Youngblood Assocs 1810 Ailor Ave Ste E Knoxville TN 37921 Home: 801 Vanosdale Rd # 100 Knoxville TN 37909-2497

**WALKER, W. LAURENS,** law educator; b. Spartanburg, SC, 1937; AB, Davidson Coll., NC, 1959; JD, Duke U., 1963; SJD, Harvard U., 1970. Bar: Ga. 1964, DC 1966, NC 1972, Va. 1983. Assoc. Sutherland, Asbill & Brennan, Atlanta, 1963, 1965—67; asst. prof. U. NC, Charlotte, 1968—69, assoc. prof., 1969—73, prof., 1973, Kenan rsch. prof., 1974—75, Paul B. Eaton prof., 1976—78; prof. U. Va. Sch. Law, Charlottesville, 1978—84, T. Munford Boyd prof., 1984—, Class of 1963 rsch. prof., 1990—92, Hunton & Williams rsch. prof., 1995—98, John V. Ray rsch. prof., 2000—03, now Caddell & Chapman rsch. prof. U. Va., Charlottesville, 1977—78. Co-author: Procedural Justice: A Psychological Analysis, 1975, Social Science in Law: Cases and Materials, 1985. Co-recipient Biennial Disting. Contbn. Award, Am. Psychology-Law Soc., 1988. Mem.: Phi Beta Kappa. Office: U Va Sch Law 580 Massie Rd Charlottesville VA 22903-1789 Office Phone: 434-924-3834. E-mail: wlw4q@virginia.edu.

**WALKER, WALDO SYLVESTER,** biologist, educator, academic administrator; b. Fayette, Iowa, June 12, 1931; s. Waldo S. and Mildred (Littelle) W.; m. Marie J. Olsen, July 27, 1952 (div.); children: Martha Lynn, Gayle Ann; m. Rita K. White, June 16, 1984. BS cum laude, Upper Iowa U., Fayette, 1953; MS, U. Iowa, 1957, PhD, 1959; D of Sci. (hon.), Upper Iowa U., 2004. Mem. faculty Grinnell (Iowa) Coll., 1958, assoc. dean coll., 1963-65, chmn. div. Natural Scis., 1968-69, dean of adminstrn., 1969-73, exec. v.p., 1973-77, dean coll., 1973-80, provost, 1977-80, exec. v.p., 1980-90, exec. v.p. and treas., 1988-90, v.p. for coll. svcs., 1990-95, prof. biology, 1968-2001, prof. emeritus, 2001—. Research assoc. U. B.C. Dept. of Botany, 1966-67. Author articles on plant physiology, ultrastructural cytology. Served with U.S. Army, 1953-55. Fellow NSF Sci. Faculty, 1966-67; recipient NSF research grants, 1960-63, 68. Mem. Am. Assn. Colls., Am. Conf. Acad. Deans (nat. chmn. 1977-78), Am. Assn. Higher Edn., Sigma Xi. Home: 1920 Country Club Dr Grinnell IA 50112-1130 Address: Grinnell Coll PO Box H2 Grinnell IA 50112-0805 E-mail: walkerws@iowatelecom.net.

**WALKER, WALTER FREDERICK,** professional basketball team executive; b. Bradford, Pa., July 18, 1954; m. Linda Walker. Diploma, U. Va.; MBA, Stanford U., 1987; BA, U. Va., 1976. Chartered Fin. Analyst. Player Portland (Oreg.) Trail Blazers, 1976-77, Seattle SuperSonics, 1977-82, pres., CEO, 1994—; player Houston Rockets, 1982-84; with Goldman Sachs and Co., San Francisco, 1987-94; prin. Walker Capital, Inc., San Francisco, 1994. Mem. USA gold medal World Univ. Games basketball team, 1973; broadcaster basketball Raycom Network, 1989-94; cons. Seattle SuperSonics, 1994. Bd. dirs. Advanced Digital Info. Corp., Drexler Tech. Corp. Named 1st team Acad. All-Am. U. Va.; named to Pa. State Sports Hall of Fame. Nat. trustee Boys and Girls Clubs of Am. Office: Seattle SuperSonics 351 Elliott Ave W Seattle WA 98119-4101 E-mail: wwalker@sonics-storm.com.

**WALKER, WILLA R.,** performing arts association administrator; d. Bernard and Molka Rouder; m. Andrew S. Walker, June 23, 1991; 1 child, Abby. BA, N.Y. U., N.Y.C., 1974; post grad., Brandeis U., Waltham, Mass., 1975—78. Dir. Carnegie Hall Internat. Am. Music Competition, N.Y.C., 1980—86; asst. to artistic dir. Carnegie Hall, 1980—86; orch. mgr. Buffalo Philharmonic Orch., 1986—98; dir. advocacy programs and spl. events ArtServe Mich., Southfield, 1999—99; mgr. edn. program and Kielstein-Laredo-Robinson Internat. Trio award Chamber Music Soc. Detroit, Farmington Hills, 2003—. Cons. and grant writer Cultural Affairs Dept. City of Detroit, 1999—2003, Detroit Zoo, 1999—2003, Detroit Symphony, 1999—2003. Contbr. articles to arts publs., record liner notes (Grammy nomination, 1981). Bd. mem. Franklin Cmty. Svcs., 1998, 1997. Doctoral Rsch. fellow, Smithsonian Inst., 1978—79. Mem.: Chamber Music Am., Am. Symphony Orch. League.

**WALKER, WILLIAM BOND,** painter, retired librarian; b. Brownsville, Tenn., Apr. 15, 1930; s. Marshall Francis and Mary Louise (Taylor) W. BA, State U. Iowa, 1953; M.L.S., Rutgers U., 1958. Librarian-trainee Donnell br. N.Y. Public Library, N.Y.C., 1955-57; reference librarian/cataloger Met. Mus. Art, N.Y.C., 1957-59; chief librarian Bklyn. Mus., 1959-64; supervisory librarian Library of Nat. Collection Fine Arts and Nat. Portrait Gallery, Smithsonian Instn., Washington, 1964-80; Arthur K. Watson chief librarian Thomas J. Watson Library, Met. Mus. Art, N.Y.C., 1980-94; ret., 1994. Adj. lectr. Columbia U. Sch. Library Service, 1987-88. Author: annotated bibliography American Sculpture, 18th-20th Century, 1979; retrospective exhbn. paintings, 1954-96, Pittsfield, Mass., 1996-97; solo and group exhbns. Columbia County, N.Y., Berkshire County, Mass., Rochester, N.Y., 1997-2003. Mem. ALA, Art Librs. Soc. N.Am (charter; pres. 1975, Disting. Svc. award, 1992), Geneal. and Biog. Soc. (corr.), Phi Beta Kappa. Home: 54 Queechy Lake Dr PO Box 237 Canaan NY 12029-0237 E-mail: lakequeechy@taconic.net.

**WALKER, WILLIAM EASTON,** surgeon, educator, lawyer; b. Glasgow, Scotland, Aug. 7, 1945; came to U.S., 1969; s. William Telfer and Josephine Blair (Easton) W.; m. Mary Fraley Cooley, June 23, 1973; children— Sarah Cooley, Blair Easton, Denton Arthur Cooley, William Easton, II MD, Glasgow U., Scotland, 1968; PhD, Johns Hopkins U., 1975; JD, South Tex. Coll Law, 1993. Diplomate Am. Bd. Surgery, Am. Bd. Thoracic Surgery, Am. Bd. Vascular Surgery. Intern, resident Johns Hopkins U., Balt., 1969-75; resident Vanderbilt U., Nashville, 1975-79; assoc. prof., dir. div. thoracic and cardiovascular surgery U. Tex. Med. Sch., Houston, 1979-94. Cons. M.D. Anderson Hosp., Houston, 1979—. Recipient Harwell Wilson award Vanderbilt U., Nashville, 1979 Fellow ACS, So. Surg. Assn., Royal Coll. Surgeons, Am. Coll. Cardiology; mem. Am. Assn. Thoracic Surgery, Coun. Fgn. Rels., Houston Country Club, Belle Meade Country Club, Cosmos Club (Washington), Krewe of Endymion (New Orleans), Phi Beta Kappa, Sigma Xi. Republican. Presbyterian. Avocations: law, bridge, Wagner, World War I history, cooking. Home and Office: 2831 Sackett St Houston TX 77098-1125 Office Phone: 713-520-0021. E-mail: wwalker19@houston.rr.com.

**WALKER, WILLIAM HAMILTON,** civil engineer, educator; b. Brookline, Mass., Dec. 28, 1934; s. William A. and Ingeborg (Thorkilsen) W.; m. Shirley Ann Ackerman, Nov. 3, 1962; children: William Franklin, John Hamilton. BS, U. Mass., 1956; MS, U. Ill., 1958, PhD, 1963. Rsch. asst. U. Ill., Urbana, 1956-61, instr. civil engring., 1961-63, asst. prof., 1963-68, assoc. prof., 1968-90, prof., 1990—99, assoc. head dept., 1985—, prof. emeritus, 1999—. Cons. to various govt. agys. and industry, 1965—. Contbr. articles to profl. jours. Trustee Windsor Park Fire Protection Dist., Champaign, Ill., 1972—. Mem. ASCE (pres. cen. Ill. sect. 1984); mem. Am. Soc. for Engring. Edn., Sigma Xi, Tau Beta Pi, Phi Kappa Phi. Presbyterian. Avocations: photography, videography, travel, bird watching. Home: 2402 Melrose Dr Champaign IL 61820-7607 Office: U Ill 205 N Mathews Ave Urbana IL 61801-2350 Office Phone: 217-333-6948. Business E-Mail: whwalker@uiuc.edu.

**WALKER, WILLIAM O., JR.,** pediatrician; b. Meridian, Miss., Feb. 27, 1954; s. William Otis and Miriam Wilkerson Walker; m. Patricia Lathrop, June 7, 1975; children: William Lathrop, Kathryn Ryan. MD, Tulane U., New Orleans, 1979. Diplomate Am. Bd. of Pediat., 1984. Assoc. prof., pediat. U. of Wash. Sch. of Medicine, Seattle, 2001—; dir. develomental behavioral pediat. fellowship Dept. of Pediat., U. of Wash. Sch. of Medicine, Seattle, 2002—. Col. U.S. Army, 1979—2001. Fellow: Am. Acad. of Cerebral Palsy and Devel. Medicine, Am. Acad. of Pediat.; mem.: Child Neurology Soc. Office: Children's Hosp Med Ctr 4800 Sand Point Way NE M2-8 Seattle WA 98105 Office Phone: 206-987-2204. Office Fax: 206-987-3824. E-mail: william.walker@seattlechildrens.org.

**WALKER, WILLIAM TIDD, JR.,** investment banker; b. Detroit, Sept. 5, 1931; s. William Tidd and Irene (Rhode) W.; m. Patricia Louise Frazier, Sept. 10, 1953; children: Donna Louise, Carol Ann, Sally Lynn, Alyssa Jane. Student, Stanford, 1950. Stockbroker William R. Staats & Co., Los Angeles, 1952-57, sales mgr., 1957-58, syndicate partner, 1958-65; sr. v.p. Glore Forgan, William R. Staats Inc., N.Y.C., 1965-68; partner, exec. com. Lester, Ryons & Co., Los Angeles, 1968; exec. v.p. Bateman Eichler, Hill Richards Inc., Los Angeles, 1969-85. Pres., CEO WTW Inc.; chmn., CEO Walker Assocs.; bd. dirs. Digid, Inc., Health Scis. Group, Inc.; chmn. King-Thomason Group, Inc., Supralife Internat., Stone Mountain Data Ctrs. Inc., Desert Health Products Inc.; adv. mem. Am. Stock Exch., 1981—. With USAF, 1949-52. Mem. Securities Industry Assn. (dir. nat. syndicate com., chmn. Calif. dist. 10), Pacific Coast Stock Exch. (bd. govs. 1971-72), Investment Bankers Assn. (nat. pub. rels. com. 1966—), Bond Club L.A. (pres. 1973), Calif. Yacht Club. Office: Walker Assocs PO Box 10684 Beverly Hills CA 90213-3684 Office Phone: 310-276-8783.

**WALKER, WILLIAM WOODARD, JR.,** management consultant, telecommunications technology executive; b. Montevideo, Uruguay, Aug. 2, 1950; s. William Woodard and Jane (Wootton) W. BA in Polit. Sci., U. N.C., Chapel Hill, 1973; MBA, Coll. of William & Mary, 1978. Acct. mgr. Jarvis Corp., Alexandria, Va., 1978-80; mgmt. cons. Daniel Penn Assocs., Schuykill Haven, Pa., 1981-82; mktg. exec. Sprint Corp., McLean, Va., 1982-84; pres. Woodard Walker Assocs., Inc., Vienna, Va., 1984—. Dir. bd. of dirs. coun. of co-owners The Colonies Condominium, McLean, 1992-94. Mem.: Soc. Telecomm. Cons., Friends Assisting the Nat. Symphony Orch., Washington (exec. com. 1996—97). Met. Club Washington. Republican. Episcopalian. Avocations: tennis, bicycling. Home: 8145 Skelton Cir Falls Church VA 22042 Office Phone: 703-760-7833. E-mail: woodwalk@mindspring.com.

**WALKER, WOODROW WILSON,** retired lawyer, real estate investor, farmer; b. Greenville, Mich., Feb. 19, 1919; s. Craig Walker and Mildred Chase; m. Janet K. Keiter, Oct. 7, 1950; children: Jonathan Woodrow, William Craig, Elaine Virginia. BA, U. Mich., 1940; LLB, Cath. U., 1950. Bar: D.C. 1950, U.S. Supreme Ct. 1958, Va. 1959. Operator family farm, 1937-39; dir. Libr. of Congress Fed. Credit Union, 1957-60; atty. Am. law div. legis. reference Libr. Congress, Washington, 1951-60; pvt. practice, Arlington, Va., 1960-2000. Counsel, bd. dirs. Calvary Found., Arlington, 1970-85, first pres., 1972; judge moot ct. George Mason Law Sch., 1986; owner-operator Walker Farm Front Royal, Va., 1972—. Co-author rsch. publs. for U.S. Govt.; featured in Washington Post. V.p. Jefferson Civic Assn., Arlington, 1955-61; pres. Nellie Custis PTA, Arlington, 1960-61; sec. Arlington County Bd. Equalization Real Estate Assessment, 1962, chmn. 1963; com. chmn. Arlington Troop 108 Boy Scouts Am., 1964-69; mem. Arlington County Pub. Utilities Commn., 1964-66, vice chmn., 1965-66; pres. Betschler Class Adult Sunday Sch., Calvary United Meth. Ch., Arlington, 1965. Served with U.S. Army, 1943-45, PTO. Cited for notable deed in conduct of his legal duties Washington Post, 1996. Mem. ABA, Arlington County Bar Assn., Va. Farm Bur., Va. Cattleman's Assn, Independent, Methodist. Home and Office: 2822 Pi Scot Dr Arlington VA 22202-2301

**WALKER BONNER, LINDA CAROL,** music educator; b. Nashville, Tenn., Aug. 18, 1953; d. John Louis and Caronia Walker; m. Divorced; children: Jordan Bonner III, Angela Jonelle Bonner. BS, Tenn. State U., 1975; M, Vanderbilt U., 1977. Music specialist Williamson County Schools, Franklin, Tenn., 1976—. Contbr. articles to profl. jours. Vol. Habitat For Humanities, Nashville, 2000—05; v.p. Missionary Soc., Nashville, 2002—05. Mem.: WCEA (life; minority rep. 1986—92), TEA (life; minority affairs com. 1988—90). Home: 756 Garrison Dr Nashville TN 37207 Office: Grassland Elem Sch 6803 Manley Ln Brentwood TN 37027 Office Phone: 615-472-4480. Personal E-mail: lcwbonner@comcast.net. E-mail: lindab1@wcs.edu.

**WALKER NEVE, DIANA,** singer, voice educator; d. Ellis Roy Walker and Beth Swenson; m. Charles Montgomery Neve, Jr.; stepchildren: Meisha E. Neve, Charles M. Neve, III, Robert B. Neve, Mariah A. Neve, Isaiah A. Neve 1 child, Nicholas Pietro Joseph Neve. MusB Performance Highest Honors, U. Mo.-Kansas City Conservatory Music, 1977, MusM Performance High Honors, 1979. Coloratura soprano soloist St. Louis Opera, 1983—84, N.Y.C. Opera, 1983—90; soprano recitalist Carnegie Hall, Carnegie Recital Hall, N.Y.C., 1983—94, Town Hall (Winners Cir. Series), N.Y.C., 1984; soprano concert recitalist Internat. Art Song Festival, Petit Jean, Ark., 1985—86; coloratura soprano soloist Bklyn. Philharm., 1985—86, Balt. Renaissance Opera, 1985—86, Miami Chamber Symphony, Fla., 1986, Chattanooga Opera, 1986, Seattle Opera, 1985—87, Handel Festival Soc., Washington, 1987—88, Utah Opera, Salt Lake City, 1987—88, Chgo. Opera Theatre, 1989, Nat. Ballet Can., Toronto, 1985—89, Lyric Opera Kansas City, Mo., 1985—96, L'Opera de Nice, France, 1989; singing prin. role of Carlotta and Madame Firmin in Phantom of the Opera Live Entertainment Corp Can., Toronto, 1991—95; coloratura soprano soloist Roanoke Opera and Symphony, Va., 1994—96; guest artist The Vocal Majority (Award Winning Male Choir), Dallas, 1998—99; classical/musical theatre concert performer Utah Arts Coun., Salt Lake City, 1998—. Tchr. voice, Salt Lake City, 1997—; guest artist prof., lectr. Brigham Young U., Provo, Utah, 1995—2000; guest artist prof. U. Mass., Amherst, 1983, U. Hawaii, Honolulu and Hilo, 2002—03. Vocalist (with David Glen Hatch): CD Broadway Classics, vocalist (with Mormon Symphony & Youth Chorus): CD You'll Never Walk Alone, soprano

soloist: CD A Mormon Tabernacle Choir Christmas; actor: (documentaries) The Earthquake Zone, (and singer): (films) Look at Me (Innovation in Film award, Kans. City Film Festival, 1997); soundtrack soloist: films The Ghost of Dickens Past, soundtrack artist: films Cold Mountain, guest artist: soap opera Another World, 1984. Guest artist performer The Nat. Assn. of Christians and Jews, Salt Lake City and other cities, Utah, 1993—94, Hugh O Brian Youth Found., Honolulu, 1994—95; vocal rec. guest artist Sweet Songs of Liberty CD Benefit for 9/11 Victims by MoV'N Pictures, Inc., Salt Lake City and N.Y.C., 2001; guest artist performer Com. to Elect Mit Romney for Gov. of Mass.; soprano soloist Mormon Tabernacle Choir, Salt Lake City, 1988—90; guest artist performer Utah State Penitentiary, Salt Lake City, 1997—99. Recipient 2d Pl., Naefger Competition, 1978, Met. Opera Young Artist Awards, 1979, Internat. Am. Music Competition at Carnegie Hall, 1983, Alumni Achievement award, U. Mo.-Kansas City Conservatory Music, 1985, Gov.' s Artist award, Gov. Michael Leavitt, Utah, 2000; grantee Monetary award for Career Devel., The Sullivan Found., N.Y.C., 1980—85, Monetary award for Film Project, Nat. Endowment for Arts, 1993; scholarship, Music Acad. West, Santa Barbara, Calif., 1977, fellowship, Tanglewood Music Festival, Mass., 1978, scholarship, Banff Sch. Music, Alta., Can., 1979, Aspen Summer Music Festival, 1979. Mem.: Can. Actors Equity, Nat. Assn. Tchrs. Singing (won 3 student contests Kansas City Conservatory Music 1977—79), Am. Guild Musical Artists, Actors Equity. Republican. Mem. Lds Ch. Avocations: travel, scuba diving, camping, horseback riding, violin. Home: 2763 Evergreen Ave Salt Lake City UT 84109 Personal E-mail: charles_diana@comcast.net.

**WALKER TUCKER, DANA,** lawyer; b. St. Louis, Oct. 23, 1963; d. Donald Edward and Mary Louis Walker; m. Mark Avery Tucker, May 29, 1998; 1 child, Jackson Miles Tucker. BS, U. Mo., 1986; JD (scholar 1991-94), St. Louis U., 1994. Bar: Mo. 1995, Ill. 2003. With Husch and Eppenberger, St. Louis, 1994—96, Banks and Assocs., 1996—2000; atty. Gary, Williams, Parenti, et. al., Stuart, Fla., 2000—02; atty., ptnr. Fox Galvin LLC, St. Louis, 2002—. Adj. prof. Washington U. Law Sch., 2004—. Mem.: Bar Assn. Met. St. Louis, Mound City Bar Assn., Def. Resource Inst., Nat. Bar Assn., Delta Sigma Theta. Democrat. Baptist. Office: Fox Galvin LLC #1 Memorial Dr Saint Louis MO 63102 Office Phone: 314-588-7000. Home Fax: 314-588-1965; Office Fax: 314-588-1965. Personal E-mail: dtucker@foxgalvin.com.

**WALKINSHAW, NICOLE M.,** performing arts educator; B in Com. Processes & Disorders, U. Fla., 1988—92, B, 1988—92; M in Social Foundations in Multicultural Edn., Fla. Atlantic U., 2004—05. Cert. in Adolescent Young Adulthood/English Lang. Arts U.S. Nat. Bd. Edn., Fla., 1992. Educator Nova HS, Davie, Fla., 1992—. S.t.a.r. mentoring program dir. Nova HS, 1996—, broadway series interactive achievers program dir., 2001—, e.a.g.l.e. tolerance tng. initiative program dir., 2002—. Facilitator (seminar) Integrating Literary Circles Across the Curricular Disciplines, Honae vs Tatamya: Exploring the Multifaceted & Mystical World of Japan; editor: (pub.) SNAPSHOT Entertainment Newsletter. Fundraiser project dir. Until There's A Cure, Davie, 1997—98; youth vol. coord. Read Across Am., Davie, 2002—05; fundraiser project coord. Broadway Cares Equity Fights A.I.D.S., Davie, 2003—05; vol. supr. Kids In Distress, Davie, 2003—05. Recipient Broward's Best, Broward County Sch. Bd., 2003, Alumni Assn. Appreciation award, U. Fla., 2004; Team Mentor grant, Citibank, 2002—03, Fulbright Meml. Fund. scholar, 2002. Mem.: NEA, Fla. Edn. Assn., Nat. Assn. Multicultural Edn., Fla. Humanities Coun., So. Poverty Law Ctr. Avocations: writing, travel, cinematic & arts appreciation. Office: Nova HS 3600 College Ave Davie FL 33314 Office Phone: 754-323-1650.

**WALKLEY, MARY L.,** voice and music educator; b. Storm Lake, Iowa, Oct. 17, 1947; d. Leonard Leroy Gustafson and Betty Angelyne Barnes; m. Robert Wayne Gustafson, Feb. 10, 1965 (div. Feb. 11, 1983); children: Robert Scot, Andrea Lynn Jenkins. MusB in performance, U. of Tampa, Fla., 1983. Cert. level V speech level singing Instr. Seth Riggs Speech Level Singing Internat., 2000. Founder and dir., pre-coll. music program U. of Tampa, Fla., 1983—93; fine arts dir. Tampa Prep. Sch., 1983—96, 1983—97; founder and music dir. The Broadway Theatre Project, 1990—; founder and program dir. The Speech Level Singing Inst., L.A., 1998—2002; guest artist and workshop presenter Internat. Thespian Assn., Tampa, 1998—. Vocal cons. Busch Gardens Entertainment, Tampa, Fla., 1998—. Musician (arranger): (vocal arrangements, orchestrations) Broadway Theatre Project. Grantee study with Seth Riggs, Benedict Found., 1997. Mem.: NARAS, Nat. Assn. of Teachers of Singing, Inc. Avocations: travel, reading, singing, piano. Home: 775 NE 76th Street Miami FL 33138 Office: FloridaSings 775 NE 76th Street Miami FL 33138 E-mail: mary@floridasings.com.

**WALKOWIAK, VINCENT STEVEN,** lawyer; b. Apr. 22, 1946; s. Vincent Albert and Elizabeth (Modla) W.; m. Linda Kae Schweigert, Aug., 1968; children: Jenifer, Steven. BA, U. Ill., 1968, JD, 1971. Bar: Ill. 1971, Minn. 1971, Tex. 1981, U.S. Ct. Appeals (8th cir.) 1971, (5th cir.) 1982, U.S. Dist. Ct. (ea., we., so., and no. dists.) Tex. 1982. Assoc. Dorsey, Marquart, Windhorst, West & Halladay, Mpls., 1971-74; ptnr. Fulbright & Jaworski LLP, Houston, 1982—. Prof. Fla. State U., Tallahassee, 1974-76, So. Meth. U., Dallas, 1976-84. Editor: Uniform Product Liability Act, 1980, Trial of a Product Liability Case, vol. 1, 1981, vol. 2, 1982, Preparation and Presentation of Product Liability, 1983, Attorney Client Privilege in Civil Litigation, 3d edit., 2004. Office: Fulbright & Jaworski LLP 2200 Ross Ave Ste 2800 Dallas TX 75201-2784 Office Phone: 214-855-8037. E-mail: vwalkowiak@fulbright.com.

**WALKUP, HUGH ROBERT,** education adminstrator; b. Harlingen, Tex., Nov. 9, 1943; s. Robert Hugh and Berniece Janet (Neurenschwader) W. BA magna cum laude, Harvard U., 1965; MEd, U. Wash., 1975, PhD, 1986. Dir. Summerhill Secondary, Seattle, 1969-73; head resident U. Wash., Seattle, 1973-76; rschr. Seattle Sch. Dist., 1976-78; dir. Seattle Vets. Action Ctr., 1978-82, Administrn. Human Resources, Seattle, 1982-86; mgr. data analysis Social and Health Svcs., Olympia, Wash., 1986-88; assoc. dir. Higher Edn. Coordinating Bd., Olympia, 1988-94; dir. Washington Goals Zooo, Olympia, 1994—. 1st lt. U.S. Army, 1966-68, Vietnam. Office: Goals Zooo/OSPI Old Capitol Bldg # Ms-47200 Olympia WA 98504-0001

**WALKUP, ROBERT E.,** mayor; b. Ames, Iowa, Nov. 14, 1936; m. Beth Walkup; 3 children; 2 stepchildren. BS in Indsl. Engring., Iowa State U. Exec. Rockwell Internat., Fairchild Republic; vice exec. Hughes Aircraft Co.; mayor City of Tucson, Ariz., 1999—. Chmn. Greater Tucson Econ. Coun.; founder, first chmn. Ariz. Space Commn.; vol. Tucson Cmty. Food Bank; co-founder Pima-Santa Cruz County Sch.-to-Work Program; co-founder El Centro Cultural de las Americas. Capt. U.S. Army. Republican. Avocations: playing guitar, sketching, studying astronomy, restoring antique cars and motorcycles. Office: City Hall 255 W Alameda St Tucson AZ 85701-1362 Fax: 520-791-4213. Business E-Mail: email_mayor@mail.ci.tucson.az.us.*

**WALL, BARBARA WARTELLE,** lawyer; b. New Orleans, Sept. 30, 1954; d. Richard Cole and Ruth Druhan (Power) Wartelle; m. Christopher Read Wall, June 21, 1980; 2 children. BA, U. Va., 1976, JD, 1979. Bar: N.Y. 1980, U.S. Dist. Ct. (so. and ea. dists.) N.Y. 1980. Assoc. Satterlee & Stephens, N.Y.C., 1979—85; asst. gen. counsel Gannett Co., Inc., Arlington, Va., 1985—90, sr. legal counsel, 1990—93, v.p., sr. legal counsel, 1993—2004, v.p. assoc. gen. counsel, 2004—. Mem.: ABA (past chair forum comm. law), Assn. Bar City of N.Y., N.Y. State Bar Assn. Republican. Episcopalian. Home: 5026 Tilden St NW Washington DC 20016-2334 Office: Gannett Co Inc 7950 Jones Branch Dr Mc Lean VA 22102-0320 Office Phone: 703-854-6951. Business E-Mail: bwall@gannett.com.

**WALL, BRIAN RAYMOND,** forest economist, business consultant, researcher; b. Jan. 26, 1940; s. Raymond Perry and Mildred Beryl (Pickert) W.; m. Joan Marie Nero, Sept. 1, 1962 (div. Aug. 1990); children: Torden Erik, Kirsten Noel. BS, U. Wash., 1962; MF, Yale U., 1964. Forestry asst. Weyerhaeuser Timber Co., Klamath Falls, Oreg., 1960; inventory forester

West Tacoma Newsprint, Steilacom, Oreg., 1961-62; timber sale compliance forester Dept. Nat. Resources, Kelso, Wash., 1963; rsch. forest economist Pacific N.W. Rsch. Sta., USDA Forest Svc., Portland, Oreg., 1964-88; cons., 1989—. Co-founder, bd. dirs. Cordero Youth Care Ctr., 1970-81; owner Brian R. Wall Images and Communications; Nikken ind. distbr. Sage Mentor Lifestyles; owner Sage Mentors Bus. Consultancy; cons. to govt. agys., Congress univs., industry, small bus.; freelance photographer. Co-author: An Analysis of the Timber Situation in the United States, 1982; contbr. articles, reports to profl. publs., newspapers. Interviewed and cited by nat. and regional news media. Recipient Cert. of Merit U.S. Dept. Agr. Forest Svc., 1982. Mem. ACLU, Soc. Am. Foresters (chmn. Portland chpt. 1973, Forester of Yr. 1975), Conf. of Western Forest Economists Inc. (founder, bd. dirs. 1988-91, treas. 1982-87), Portland Photographic Forum, Common Cause, Oregon Economists Assn., Nat. Audubon Soc., Amnesty Internat., Zeta Psi. Home: 6160 SW Alice Ln # 204 B Beaverton OR 97008 Personal E-mail: brwall01@cs.com.

**WALL, CHARLES R.,** lawyer; BA in Hist., Grinnell Coll., Iowa, 1967; JD, U. Mo. Law Sch., 1970. Assoc. and ptnr. Shook, Hardy & Bacon, Kans. City, Mo., 1970—90; v.p.,assoc. gen. coun. Philip Morris Co. Inc., NYC, 1990—94, sr. v.p. litig., 1994—95, dep. gen. coun., 1995—2000; sr. v.p., gen. coun. Altria Grp., Inc. (formerly Philip Morris Co. Inc.), NYC, 2000—. Mem.: bd. dirs. NY City Opera, Neurosciences Inst., La Jolla, Calif. Office: Altria Group Inc 120 Park Ave New York NY 10017 Office Phone: 917-663-5000.

**WALL, CHRISTOPHER READ,** lawyer; b. Norfolk, Va., Oct. 6, 1952; s. Maurice E. Wall and Marilyn (Murrah) Hardin; m. Barbara L. Wartelle, June 21, 1980. BA summa cum laude, Yale U., 1974; BA, Oxford U., 1976; JD, U. Va., 1979. Bar: N.Y. 1980, U.S. Dist. Ct. (so. dist.) N.Y. 1980, U.S. Ct. Internat. Trade 1985, D.C. 1986, U.S. Dist. Ct. D.C. 1986, U.S. Ct. Appeals (fed. cir) 2002. Ptnr. Winthrop, Stimson, Putnam & Roberts and Pillsbury Winthrop LLP, NYC & Washington, 1979—2005; ptnr., co-chmn. Internat. Trade practice Pillsbury Winthrop Shaw Pittman, Washington, 2005—. Contbr. articles to profl. jours. Vice chmn & past chmn. Swedish-Am. C. of C.; chmn. trade & investment adv. com. British-Am. Bus. Assn. Mem. ABA (chmn. spl. adv. com. internat. activities, vice chmn. internat. law & practice sect., co-chmn. internat. litigation com.), Assn. of Bar of City of N.Y., DC Bar, Phi Beta Kappa. Office: Pillsbury Winthrop Shaw Pittman 2300 N St NW Washington DC 20037 Office Phone: 202-663-9250. Office Fax: 202-663-8007. Business E-Mail: cwall@pillsburylaw.com.

**WALL, CLARENCE VINSON,** state legislator; b. Athens, Ga., Oct. 17, 1947; s. Clarence Jacob and Fannie Lucile (Clark) W.; m. Linda Gail Mason, Dec. 6, 1969 (div. 1980); 1 child, Jeffrey Vinson. Grad. high sch., Lawrenceville, Ga., 1965. Rep. Ga. Ho. of Reps., Lawrenceville, 1973-82, 85-96. Staff sgt. Ga. Nat. Guard, 1967-73. Republican. Baptist. Home: 3750 S Arville St Apt 135 Las Vegas NV 89103

**WALL, DELLA,** human resources specialist, manufacturing executive; Various positions SupeRx Drug Stores, Kroger Mfg., 1971—2000; v.p. deferred benefits Kroger Co., Cinn., 2000—01, v.p. compensation and benefits, 2001—03, corp. v.p. human resources, 2003—04, group v.p. human resources, 2004—. Bd. dirs. Profit Sharing Coun. Office: Kroger Co 1014 Vine St Cincinnati OH 45202-1100 Office Phone: 513-762-4000. Office Fax: 513-762-1160.

**WALL, EDWARD MILLARD,** environmental consulting executive; b. Newburyport, Mass., Dec. 17, 1929; s. Millard Edward and Edith Noyes (Carter) W.; m. Jean Titus, Jan. 27, 1951 (dec. 1989); children: Karen, Kenneth, Kathryn; m. Gertrude Knott, Nov. 18, 1992. BSME, Tufts U., 1951; MBA, Xavier U., 1962. Cert. hazardous materials mgr. Tech. service engr. Goodyear Tire, Akron, Ohio, 1951-53; mgr. engine test facilities Gen. Electric, Cin., 1956-62; mir. mfg. Williams Mfg., Portsmouth, Ohio, 1962-74; sr. project mgr. N-Ren Corp., Cin., 1975-78; v.p. mfg. Nelson Electric, Tulsa, 1979-88; v.p. Techrad Environ. Svcs., Oklahoma City, 1988-92, pres., 1992-97; retired, 1997. Mem. Vo-Tech Edn. Adv. Com., Tulsa, 1982-88. Lt.(j.g.) USNR, 1953-56. Mem. ASME, NSPE, Am. Prodn. and Inventory Control Soc. (cert.), Am. Mgmt. Assn. Lodges: Rotary, Masons. Republican. Presbyterian. Avocations: golf, swimming. Home: 165 Francis Dr NE Port Charlotte FL 33952

**WALL, FREDERICK THEODORE,** retired chemistry professor; b. Chisholm, Minn., Dec. 14, 1912; s. Peter and Fanny Maria (Rauhala) W.; m. Clara Elizabeth Vivian, June 5, 1940; children: Elizabeth Wall Ralston, Jane Vivian Wall. B.Chemistry, U. Minn., 1933, PhD, 1937. Mem. faculty chemistry dept. U. Ill., 1937-64, dean grad. coll., 1955-63; prof., chmn. dept. chemistry U. Calif., Santa Barbara, 1964-66, vice chancellor rsch., 1965-66; vice chancellor grad. studies and research, prof. chemistry U. Calif. at San Diego, 1966-69; exec. dir. Am. Chem. Soc., Washington, 1969-72; prof. chemistry Rice U., Houston, 1972-78. Pres. Assn. Grad. Schs., 1961; trustee Inst. Def. Analyses, 1962-64; mem. governing bd. Nat. Acad. Scis.-NRC, 1963- 67. Author: Chemical Thermodynamics, 1958; editor Jour. Phys. Chemistry, 1965-69. Mem. Am. Chem. Soc. (Pure Chemistry award 1945, dir. 1962-64), Finnish Chem. Soc. (corr.), Am. Acad. Arts and Scis., Nat. Acad. Scis. Achievements include early work on Monte Carlo computer simulation of macromolecular configurations and of basic reaction probabilities. E-mail: ftwall@worldnet.att.net.

**WALL, JAMES MCKENDREE,** minister, editor; b. Monroe, Ga., Oct. 27, 1928; s. Louie David and Lida (Day) W.; m. Mary Eleanor Kidder, Sept. 11, 1953; children: David McKendree, Robert Kidder, Richard James Harold, Ga. Inst. Tech., 1945-47; BA, Emory U., 1949, MDiv, 1955, LHD (hon.) 1985; MA, U. Chgo., 1960; LittD (hon.), Ohio No. U., 1969; DHL (hon.), Willamette Coll., 1978; DD (hon.), MacMurray, 1981; DHL (hon.), Coe Coll., 1987; DHL (hon.), Elmhurst Coll., 1999. Ordained to ministry United Meth. Ch., 1954. Staff writer, sports dept. Atlanta Jour., 1948-50; asst. minister East Lake Meth. Ch., Atlanta, 1953; asst. to dean students Emory U., Atlanta, 1954-55; pastor North Ga. Conf. Moreland, Luthersville Meth. Chs., Ga., 1955-57, Bethel United Meth. Ch., Chgo., 1957-59; mng. editor Christian Adv. mag., Park Ridge, Ill., 1959-63, editor, 1963-72, Christian Century mag., Chgo., 1972-99, sr. contbg. editor, 1999—. Author: Church and Cinema, 1971, Three European Directors, 1973, Winning the War, Losing Our Soul, 1991, Hidden Treasures: Searching for God in Modern Culture, 1997; author, editor: Theologians in Transition, 1981, A Century of the Century, 1987, How My Mind Has Changed, 1991. Del. Dem. Nat. Conv., 1972, 76, 80, 92, 96, 2000; mem. Dem. Nat. Com., 1976-80, Dem. State Cen. Com., 1974-86, Pres. Commn. White House Fellowships, 1976-80. Served to 1st lt. USAF, 1950-52. Mem. Alpha Tau Omega, Omicron Delta Kappa, Sigma Delta Chi. Home: 451 S Kenilworth Ave Elmhurst IL 60126-3928 Office: Christian Century 104 S Michigan Ave Ste 700 Chicago IL 60603-5905 E-mail: jimwall165@aol.com.

**WALL, JAMIE LYNN,** elementary school educator; b. Hoboken, NJ Aug. 2, 1976; d. Ivan and Dolores Morin; m. Kevin Wall, Mar. 24, 2000; 1 child, Aidan. BA in Math. Edn., Caldwell Coll., Caldwell, N.J., 1998. Cert. tchr. math. N.J. Dept. Edn., 1999. Eighth grade math tchr. Brooklawn Mid. Sch., Parsippany, NJ, 1998—, lead math. tchr., 2002—; math tutor Caldwell Coll., Caldwell, NJ, 1999—2003. Conf. spkr. and workshop presenter in field. Recipient, Caldwell Coll. scholar, 1995—98, Edn. Assn. award, Caldwell Coll., 1997; scholar, Caldwell Coll. scholar, 1994—98, Edward J. Bloughstein Disting. scholar, 1994. Mem.: ASCD, Caldwell Coll. Edn. Assn. (sec. / treas. 1995—97), N.J. Edn. Assn., Nat. Assn. of Math. Tchrs. N.J., Nat. Coun. of Teachers of Math., Alpha Chi, Kappa Delta Epsilon, Delta Epsilon Sigma. Business E-Mail: jwall@pthsd.k12.nj.us.

**WALL, JENNIFER GREY,** assistant principal; b. South Boston, Va., Aug. 12, 1973; d. Sarah Snow and Robert Thompson Wall. BS, Va. Tech., 1994, MA in Curriculum and Instrn., 2000. Lic. ednl. leadership. Tchr. math

Blacksburg Mid. Sch., Va., 1994—2005, Dublin Elem. Sch., Va., 2005—. Math dept. chair Blacksburg Mid. Sch., 1997—2005, bldg. mentor coord., 2000—05, sch. improvement co-chair, 2001—04, team leader, 2003—05; math mentor coach Montgomery County Schools, Christiansburg, Va., 2004—05; profl. devel. presenter, Va., 1997—2005. Band mem. Blacksburg Cmty. Band, 1994—2001. Recipient Leila Stalker Math. Tchr. of the Yr., Blue Ridge Coun. of Teachers of Math., 2000; Hatcher Meml. scholarship, Va. Tech Math. Dept., 1991—93, Nat. Sci. Scholars, Nat. Dept. of Edn. 1991—93, Future Educator scholarship, Phi Delta Kappa, 1991. Mem.: VAESP, ASCD, Va. Coun. Tchrs. Math., Phi Delta Kappa, Pi Mu Epsilon, Phi Kappa Phi, Phi Beta Kappa. Avocations: music, walking. Home: 705 McBryde Dr Blacksburg VA 24060 Office: Dublin Elem Sch 600 Dunlap Rd Dublin VA 24084 Office Phone: 540-643-0337. Personal E-mail: jwall.vt@verizon.net.

**WALL, KATHY ELLIOTT,** secondary school educator; b. Kershaw, S.C., Nov. 13, 1955; d. Alton Leonard and Myrtle Mildred Elliott; m. Ronald Lee Wall, June 19, 1976; children: Noel E., Elliott Lee, Oliver Lawrence. BMus, Furman U., Greenville, S.C., 1978; MEd, U. S.C., 1983. Cert. tchr. S.C. Tchr. Heath Springs (S.C.) Elem. Sch., 1978—85, Andrew Jackson Mid. Sch., Kershaw, SC, 1985—99, Andrew Jackson H.S., Kershaw, SC, 1992—. Keyboard accompanist Covenant Bapt. Ch., Lancaster, SC, 2001—; children and youth music dir. First Bapt. Sch., Kershaw, 1990—2001; interim music dir. Heath Springs Bapt. Sch., 1980—84. Vol. Meals on Wheels, Kershaw, 1999—. Mem.: Palmetto State Tchrs. Assn., Music Educators Nat. Conf. Home: PO Box 91 Kershaw SC 29067

**WALL, LINDA AMANDA,** economics educator; b. Roanoke, Va., Oct. 9, 1948; d. Paul Kenneth and Annie Treva (Brillheart) Ferris; m. Maynard Burl Honaker Jr. (dec.); children: Krista Renea Bowen, Rhonda Kay Bowling; m. Norman Wayne Wall, May 15, 1993. BS in edn. vocational home econ., Concord Coll., Athens, W.Va., 1969; MA in commn., W. Va. U., 1980. Educator Stonewall Jackson HS, Charleston, W.Va., 1969—71, Glenwood Jr. HS, Princeton, W.Va., 1985—98, Pikeview HS, Princeton, W.Va., 1999—. Adv. Family, Career, Cmty. Leaders of Am., Glenwood and PikeView H.S., Princeton, W.Va., 1985—, Mercer County Bd. of Health, Food Svc., Princeton, W.Va., 1996—98; dept. chair Family and Consumer Sci. Dept., Pikeview H.S., Princeton, W.Va., 1999—. Grant writer: various financial grants. Coord. for cmty. charities Family Career Cmty. Leaders of Am., Princeton, W.Va., 1990—; coord. Pam Hawkins Walk-a-thon, Princeton, W.Va., 1997—2004, St. Judes, Princeton, 1997—. Nominee Character Educator for W.Va., 2004, Outstanding Woman in W.Va., 2005, 2006; named State Secondary Family and Consumer Sci Tchr. of Yr. for W.Va., 2004—05, Tchr. of Yr., Pike View HS, 2005; recipient 110% Club, Mercer County Schs., 2004—05, Nat. Honor's Roll, Outstanding Am. Tchrs., 2005—06. Mem.: W.Va. Assn. Family and Consumer Sci. (sec at 2003—04), Assn. Career and Tech. Edn., Alpha Delta Kappa (sec. 1995—2003, v.p. 2003—05). Republican. Bapt. Avocations: piano, antiques, cooking, exercise, travel. Home: 200 Sparrow St Princeton WV 24740 Office: Pikeview HS 3566 Eads Mill Rd Princeton WV 24740 Office Phone: 304-384-7586. E-mail: lwall@access.k12.wv.us.

**WALL, M. DANNY,** finance company executive; BArch, N.D. State U., 1963. Exec. dir. Urban Renewal Agy., Fargo, ND, 1964-71, Salt Lake City Redevel. Agy., 1971-75; dir. legis. Office U.S. Senator Jake Garn, Washington, 1975-78; minority staff dir. Senate Com. for Banking, Housing and Urban Affairs, Washington, 1979-80, staff dir., 1980-86, Rep. staff dir., 1987; chmn. Fed. Home Loan Bank Bd./Fed. Home Loan Mortgage Corp., Washington, 1987-89; dir. Office Thrift Supervision (formerly Fed. Home Loan Bank Bd.), 1989-90; fin. svcs. cons., 1990—2003; sr. v.p. Dougherty Funding LLC, 1997—2003; pres. Capmark Bank. Office Phone: 801-567-2686. Business E-Mail: dan_wall@capmark.com.

**WALL, MATTHEW J., JR.,** surgeon, research scientist; b. June 22, 1958; s. Matthew J. and Anne V. W.; m. Barbara M. Wall; children: Christopher Matthew, Patrick Joseph. BS, Rice U., Houston, 1980; MD, Baylor Coll. Medicine, Houston, 1984. Diplomate Am. Bd. Surgery, Am. Bd. Thoracic Surgeons, Am. Bd. Surg. Critical Care. Resident gen. surgery Baylor Affiliated Hosp., Houston, 1984-89, resident cardiothoracic surgery, 1989-91; asst. prof. surgery Baylor Coll. Medicine, Houston, 1991-95, assoc. prof. surgery, 1995—2004, prof. Michael E. DeBakey dept. surgery, 2004—, dep. program dir. thoracic surgery residency, 1999—; program dir. surg. critical care residency, 1999—2004; dir. trauma and critical care svcs. Ben Taub Gen. Hosp., Houston, 1993-99, dep. chief surgery, 1993—, exec. dir. trauma and critical care, 2000—, chief thoracic surgery, 2000—. Contbr. chpts. to books, articles to jours. Fellow ACS (pres.-elect South Tex. 2005-06, chmn. com. on trauma 2002—), Am. Assn. Surgery Trauma, Soc. Thoracic Surgeons; mem. AAAS, Assn. Academic Surgery, Soc. Surg. Soc., Harris County Med. Soc.

**WALL, WILLIAM D.,** federal judge; BA, Rutgers U., 1971; JD, Fordham U., 1977. Special asst. NY Atty. Gen. Office State Prosecutor, 1977—79; atty. to ptnr. Farrell Fritz, 1979—2000; magistrate judge US Dist Ct. (Eastern Dist. NY), 2000—. Bd. dirs. Molloy Coll.; bd. sponsors Mercy Medical Ctr. Mem.: NY Bar Assn., Nassau County Bar Assn., ABA. Office: US Courthouse 824 Federal Plaza Central Islip NY 11722-4450

**WALLACE, ANDERSON,** lawyer, educator; b. Cleve., Sept. 24, 1939; s. Anderson and Agatha Lee (Culpepper) Wallace; m. Kristine Lee Gough; children: Anderson III, Whitney, Nicole Belcher. BA, George Washington U., 1962, JD, 1964, LLM, 1966. Bar: Tex. 68, U.S. Dist. Ct. (no. dist.) Tex. 68, U.S. Ct. Claims 68, U.S. Tax Ct. 68, U.S. Ct. Appeals (5th cir.) 68, U.S. Supreme Ct. 71, U.S. Ct. Appeals (11th cir.) 81. Program mgmt. asst. NASA, Washington, 1962—64; atty. U.S. Dept. Treasury, Washington, 1964—66; tax atty. Price Waterhouse & Co., Atlanta, 1966—67; tax ptnr. Jackson, Walker, Winstead, Cantwell & Miller, Dallas, 1967—84; dir. in charge tax dept. Baker, Mills & Glast, P.C., Dallas, 1984—93; pres. Anderson Wallace Jr., P.C., Attys., Dallas, 1993—. Instr. Sch. Law So. Meth. U. Trustee S.W. Mus. Sci. and Tech., Dallas, 1974—, Girls Found. Dallas Inc.; chmn. Inst. on Employee Benefits, Southwestern Found., 1976. Mem.: ABA. Office: 3328 Purdue Ave Ste 100 Dallas TX 75225-7635 Office Phone: 214-739-1714. E-mail: awallacejr@sbcglobal.net.

**WALLACE, ANDREW GROVER,** internist, educator, dean; b. Columbus, Ohio, Mar. 22, 1935; s. Richard Homes and Eleanor Bradley (Grover) W.; m. Kathleen Barrick Altvater, June 22, 1957; children: Stephen Andrew, Michael Bradley, Kathleen Claude. BS, Duke U., 1958, MD, 1959. Diplomate Am. Bd. Internal Medicine. Intern medicine Duke U. Hosp., Durham N.C., 1959-60, asst. resident, 1960-61; fellow NIH, Bethesda, Md., 1961-63; chief resident medicine Duke U., Durham, 1963-64, asst. prof., 1965-67, assoc. prof., 1967-71, chief, divsn. cardiology, 1970-81, prof. medicine, 1971—, Walter Kempner prof. medicine, 1973; vice chancellor health affairs, chief exec. officer Duke U. Hosp., Durham, 1981-87; v.p. health affairs Duke U., 1987-90; dean Dartmouth Med. Sch., Hanover, NH, 1990—2000. V.p. for health affairs Dartmouth Coll., 1990-98; cons. program com., cardiology adv. com. and pharmacology study sect. Nat. Heart and Lung Inst., cardiovascular merit rev. bd. VA. Co-author: (with R.S. Williams) Biological Effects of Physical Activity, 1989; mem. editl. bd. Am. Jour. of Physiology, 1965-70, Jour. of Pharmacology and Exptl. Therapeutics, 1966-71, Jour. of Molecular and Cellular Cardiology, 1970-75, Jour. of Clin. Investigation, 1973-78. Pres. Durham YMCA Swim Assn., 1975-77; bd. dirs. Durham C. of C.; co-chmn. Nat. Jr. Olympics, 1976. Markle scholar, 1965-70 Mem. AAAS, AAMC, NAS, Inst. of Medicine, Am. Fedn. for Clin. Rsch. (coun.) Am. Soc. Internal Medicine, Am. Soc. Clin. Investigation, Am. Heart Assn. (coun. on clin. cardiology), Am. Physiol. Soc., Biomed. Engring. Soc., Soc. Med. Adminstrs., Assn. Am. Med. Colls. (adv. com. electronic residency 1992-94, generalist initiative 1993-95, mission and orgn. 1994-2000, exec. coun. 1996-98), N.H. Med. Soc., So. Soc. Clin. Investigation. Home: 2112 Faucette Mill Rd Hillsborough NC 27278-7553

**WALLACE, ANTHONY FRANCIS CLARKE,** anthropologist, educator; b. Toronto, Ont., Can., Apr. 15, 1923; s. Paul A.W. and Dorothy Eleanor (Clarke) W.; m. Betty Louise Shillott, Dec. 1, 1942; children: Anthony, Daniel, Sun Ai, Samuel, Cheryl, Joseph. BA, U. Pa., 1948, MA, 1949, PhD, 1950; L.H.D. (hon.), U. Chgo., 1983. Instr. anthropology Bryn Mawr Coll., 1948-50; asst. instr. anthropology U. Pa., research sec. Behavioral Research Council, 1951-55; research asst. prof. U. Pa., 1952-55, vis. assoc. prof., 1955-61, prof., 1961—, chmn. dept., 1961-71, Geraldine R. Segal prof. Am. social thought, 1980-83, Univ. prof. anthropology, 1983-88, prof. emeritus, 1988—. Sr. rsch. assoc. anthropology Eastern Pa. Psychiat. Inst., 1955-60, dir. clin. research, 1960-61, med. research scientist, III, 1961-80; mem. tech. adv. com. N.J. Psychiat. Inst., 1958; cons. disaster studies NRC, 1956-57; cons. Phila. Housing Authority, 1952; mem. rsch. adv. com. Commonwealth Mental Health Research Found., 1960-61, U.S. Office Edn., 1965-68; mem. behavioral scis. study sect. NIMH, 1964-68; mem. NRC, 1963-66; mem. various adv. coms. NIMH, 1962—; mem. social sci. adv. council NSF, 1969-72 Author: King of the Delawares: Teedyuscung, 1700-1763, 1949, Culture and Personality, 1961, rev. edit., 1970, Religion: An Anthropological View, 1966, Death and Rebirth of the Seneca, 1970, Rockdale: The Growth of an American Village in the Early Industrial Revolution, 1978, new. edit., 2004, Social Context of Innovation, 1983, new ed., 2003. St. Clair, 1987, The Long, Bitter Trail, 1993, Jefferson and the Indians, 1999, Revitalizations and Mazeways, 2003, Modernity and Mind, 2005 Bd. mgrs. Founds. Fund for Research in Psychiatry, 1969-71. Served AUS, 1942-45. Recipient Bancroft prize in Am. History, 1979, Dexter prize in History of Technology, 1989, Caroline Bancroft prize in history, 2000; Guggenheim fellow, 1978-79 Fellow Am. Anthrop. Assn. (pres. 1971-72,); mem. Nat. Acad. Scis., Am. Philos. Soc., Am. Acad. Arts and Scis. Home: 4139 Upper Valley Rd Parkesburg PA 19365-1607 Office: Univ Pa Dept Anthropology 33rd and Spruce Sts Philadelphia PA 19104

**WALLACE, ARDELIA LESLENE,** elementary school educator; d. Robert J. and Billie Loyce Turner; m. Kenneth Carson Wallace, Oct. 26, 1946; 1 child, Carson Wayne. BS, SW Tex. State U., San Marcos, Tex. Cert. Tchr. State Bd. of Educators, Tex., 1997. Fifth grade tchr. Dripping Springs ISD, Dripping Springs, Tex., 1999—. Mem.: ATPE. D-Conservative. Achievements include Innovative Teaching Award for 2004. Avocations: reading, gardening. Office Phone: 512-858-4903 207.

**WALLACE, ARTHUR, JR.,** retired college dean; b. Muskogee, Okla., June 12, 1939; s. Arthur and Edna (Collins) W.; m. Claudina Young, Oct. 4, 1969 (div. Nov. 2002); children: Dwayne, Jon, Charles. BS, Langston U., 1960; MS, Okla. State U., Stillwater, 1962, PhD, 1964. Dir. commodity rsch. Gen. Foods Corp., White Plains, NY, 1964-67; v.p., sr. economist Merrill Lynch & Lionel D. Edie & Co., N.Y.C., 1968-71; econ. cons. Wall St. fin. instns. Group IV Econs., N.Y.C., 1972-76; mgr. U.S. and Can. econs. Internat. Paper Co., N.Y.C., 1976-78, chief economist, 1978-82, dir. corp. affairs and policy analysis, 1982-83, corp. sec. Purchase, NY, 1983-87, v.p., corp. sec., 1987-93; pres. Internat. Paper Co. Found., 1983-93; dean coll. bus. San Francisco State U., 1993-98; ret.

**WALLACE, BARBARA BROOKS,** writer; b. Soochow, China, Dec. 3, 1922; arrived in U.S., 1938; d. Otis Frank and Nicia Brooks; m. James Wallace, Jr., Feb. 27, 1954; 1 child, James V. BA, UCLA, 1945. Script sec. Foote, Cone & Belding, Hollywood, Calif., 1946-49; tchr. Wright MacMahon Secretarial Sch., Beverly Hills, Calif., 1949-50; head fund drive Commerce and Industry Divsn. ARC, San Francisco, 1950-52. Author: Claudia, 1969 (Nat. League Am. Pen Women Juvenile Book award, 1970), Andrew the Big Deal, 1970, The Trouble with Miss Switch, 1971, Victoria, 1973, Can Do, Missy Charlie, 1974, The Secret Summer of L.E.B. (Nat. League Am. Pen Women Juvenile Book award, 1974), Julia and the Third Bad Thing, 1975, Palmer Patch, 1976, Hawkins, 1977, Peppermints in the Parlor, 1980 (William Allen White award, 1983), The Contest Kid Strikes Again, 1980, Hawkins and the Soccer Solution, 1981, Miss Switch to the Rescue, 1981, Hello, Claudia, 1982, Claudia and Duffy, 1982, The Barrel in the Basement, 1985, Argyle, 1987, 1992, Perfect Acres, Inc., 1988, The Twin in the Tavern, 1993 (Edgar award Mystery Writers Am., 1994), Cousins in the Castle, 1996, Sparrows in the Scullery, 1997 (Edgar award, 1998), Ghosts in the Gallery, 2000, Secret in St. Something, 2001, Miss Switch Online, 2002, The Perils of Peppermints, 2003. Mem.: Authors Guild, Children's Book Guild of Washington, Alpha Phi. Episcopalian. Home: 6251 Old Dominion Dr Apt 436 Mc Lean VA 22101-4810 E-mail: bbwallace@cox.net.

**WALLACE, BARRON F.,** lawyer; b. Beaumont, Tex., 1964; BA in history, U. Tex., Austin, 1986; JD, U. Mich., 1989. Bar: Tex. 1990. Ptnr., co-head, pub. fin. sect. Vinson & Elkins LLP, Houston. Bd. dirs. Tex. Lyceum Assn., Fourth Ward Redevelopment Authority; mem. Tex. C-Bar Adv. Bd. Mem. Ctr. for Houston's Future, 2004 Edn. Policy Com. Greater Houston Partnership, Tex. Rising Stars 2004; bd. dirs. Park People. Named one of Am. Top Black Lawyers, Black Enterprise mag., 2003; recipient Tex. Rising Star, Tex. Super Lawyers Rising Stars Edn. mag., 2004, Outstanding Texan award, Black Leg. Caucus, 1999, 2001. Mem.: Tex. Bar Found., Nat. Assn. Bond Lawyers (vice chair gen. law com.), State Bar Tex. (mem. adminstrv. and pub. law section). Office: Vinson & Elkins LLP Ste 2300 First City Tower 1001 Fannin St Houston TX 77002-6760 Office Phone: 713-758-4810. Office Fax: 713-615-5076. Business E-Mail: bwallace@velaw.com.

**WALLACE, BEN,** professional basketball player; b. White Hall, Ala., Sept. 10, 1974; m. Chanda Wallace. Student, Va. Union, 1996. Basketball player Wash. Bullets, 1996—99, Orlando Magic, 1999—2000; forward-ctr. Det. Pistons, 2000—06, Chgo. Bulls, 2006—. Mem. USA Team. Named NBA Defensive Player of Yr., 2002, 2003, 2005, 2006; named to NBA All-Defensive Team, 2002, 2003, 2004, 2005. Achievements include being a member of NBA Champion Detroit Pistons, 2004. Office: Chgo Bulls United Ctr 1901 W Madison St Chicago IL 60612-2459*

**WALLACE, BOB (ROBERT EUGENE WALLACE JR.),** lawyer; b. NYC, Mar. 1, 1956; s. Robert E. Wallace Sr. and Vivian A. (High) Wallace; m. Julia Wallace; children: Grant, Eric. BA in Am. Studies, Yale U., 1978; JD, Georgetown U., 1981. Bar: Mo. 1981, Pa. 1991. Legal intern NFL, N.Y.C., 1980; assoc. Guilfoil, Petzall & Shoemake, St. Louis, 1981—91; asst. to the pres., gen. counsel Phila. Eagles, 1991—94; exec. v.p., gen. counsel St. Louis Rams, 1995—. Adj. prof. law St. Louis U., 1986-88. Bd. govs. downtown YMCA, St. Louis, 1985-88; bd. dirs. Payback, Inc., Urban League of Greater St.Louis, Operation Excel, Amateur Athletic Assn., St. Louis, 1985-88, Sports Lawyers Assn., St. Louis Sports Commn. Recipient Dist. Service award St. Louis Pub. Schs., St. Louis, 1985-88. Mem. ABA (sports lawyer div.), Met. Bar Assn. (exec. com. young lawyers sect., chmn. media com. 1983-86). Democrat. Avocations: sports, reading, bike riding. Office: St Louis Rams One Rams Way Earth City MO 63045 Office Phone: 314-982-7265. Business E-Mail: bwallace@rams.nfl.com.

**WALLACE, BRADFORD F.,** music educator; b. Effingham, Ill., July 17, 1980; s. Gary Lynn and Susan Elizabeth Wallace. MusB, Ea. Ill. U., 2003. Band dir. Effingham HS, 2003—. Home: 401 N 4th Apt B Effingham IL 62401 Office: Effingham HS 1301 W Grove Effingham IL 62401 Office Phone: 217-540-1100. Business E-Mail: wallaceb@effingham.k12.il.us.

**WALLACE, BRIAN MARK,** music educator; b. Pascagoula, Miss., July 8, 1975; s. Dan Lester Wallace and Paula Ann Bennett; m. Laurie Ann Gowen, June 8, 2002. B in Music Edn., U. Mo., Saint Louis, 2002, M Vocal Music Edn., 2005—. Cert. Choral Vocal Edn. Grades K-12 Mo. Dept. Elem. and Secondary Edn., 2002. Vocal music tchr. Marvin Elem. Sch., St. Louis, 2002—03, 2004—05; choir dir. Ritenour HS, St. Louis, 2003—04; co-owner, operator W&W Prodns., St. Louis, 1994—2001; choir dir. Orchard Farm HS and Mid. Sch., St. Charles, Mo., 2005—. Music minister Beggy Hills Bapt. Ch., St. Charles, Mo., 2000—03; chorus dir. Maryland Heights Cmty. Chorus, Mo., 2001—03; chorus mem. Union Ave. Opera Theatre, Saint Louis, Mo., 2001, Saint Louis Symphony Chorus, Mo., 2002—04; cast mem. Opera Theatre Saint Louis, Mo., 2001. Puppeteer FBC Harvester Puppet Team, Saint Charles, Mo., 2003—; choir mem. FBC Harvester Adult Choir, Saint Charles, Mo., 2003—. Mem.: Nat. Assn. Music Edn., Am. Choral Dirs. Assn. So. Bapt. Avocations: music, reading, travel. Home: 1455 Mohican Trail Saint Charles MO 63304 Office Phone: 636-250-5421. Business E-Mail: bwallace@ofsd.k12.mo.us.

**WALLACE, CAROL,** editor at large; b. Chgo. BS in Comm., U. Ill., 1971. With Phila. Daily News, Rochester Times-Union, Tribune Pub. Co., N.Y. Daily News, N.Y.C., 1979—82; sr. writer People Mag., N.Y.C., 1982—85, sr. editor, 1985—88, 1990—92, asst. mng. editor, 1991—94, dep. mng. editor, 1994—97, mng. editor, 1997—2002; editor at large Time Inc., N.Y.C., 2003—. Writer, host The Wallace Report for Daytime, Heart/ABC Women's Network, 1982—84; editor Us Mag., 1988—90. Co-author: The Portable Best Friend, 1996. Recipient Front Page award, Newswomen's Club N.Y., 1982.

**WALLACE, CHRISTOPHER,** broadcast television correspondent; b. Chgo., Oct. 12, 1947; s. Mike and Norma (Kaphan) W.; m. Lorraine Smothers, Oct. 4, 1997; children: Peter Farrell, Margaret Coleman, Andrew Farrell, Catherine Farrell, Sarah Smothers, Remick Smothers. BA, Harvard U., 1969. Nat. reporter Boston Globe, 1969-73; polit. reporter Sta. WBBM-TV, Chgo., 1973-75; investigative reporter Sta. WNBC-TV, NYC, 1975-78; polit. reporter NBC News, Washington, 1978-81; anchor Today Show, 1982, NBC Nightly News (Sunday), 1982—84, 1986—87; chief corr. White House, 1982-89; anchor Meet the Press, 1987—88; sr. corr. Prime Time Live, ABC-TV, 1989-98; substitute host Nightline, ABC-TV; chief corr. 20/20 ABC-TV, Washington, 1998—2003; host FOX News Sunday with Chris Wallace, FNS, FOX News Channel, 2003—. Covered presdl. campaigns and Democratic and Republican conventions, 1980, 84, 88. Reporter, writer: documentaries NBC The Migrants, 1980, Protection For Sale: The Insurance Industry, 1981, Nancy Reagan, The First Lady, 1985. Recipient Peabody award U. Ga., 1978, Emmy award NATAS, 1981, 90, award Overseas Press Club, 1981, Humanitas Found. award, 1981, Investigative Reporters and Editors award U. Mo. Sch. Journalism, 1990, 95, George Polk award, 1992, Columbia-DuPont award, 1997. Office: FOX News Channel 1211 Avenue of the Americas New York NY 10036

**WALLACE, CURTIS WILBERN, JR.,** music director, organist; b. Roanoke, Va., Apr. 30, 1962; s. Curtis Wilbern and Shirley Jean Wallace. BA in Sacred Music, Roanoke Coll., 1984. Organist Midland Bapt. Ch., Vinton, Va., 1977—80; music dir. Our Lady Perpetual Help Cath. Ch., Salem, Va., 1980—85; dir. music ministries Holy Redeemer Cath. Ch., Coll. Park, Md., 1985—87; organist, choir master St. Mark's Luth. Ch., Roanoke, 1988—90; dir. music St. Margaret Mary Cath. Ch., Winter Park, Fla., 1990—. Dir. music ministries divsn. Nat. Assn. Pastoral Musicians. Prodr.: (St. Margaret Mary Choir CD) Sounds of Christmas, 2002, Taizé Prayer, 2003, Jubilate Deo, 2005. Mem.: Am. Guild Organists. Republican. Roman Catholic. Achievements include leading St. Margaret Mary Catholic Church pilgrimage to Rome, Italy in November 2003. Avocations: aquarium fish, travel. Home: 648 Tuskawilla Point Lane Winter Springs FL 32708-4902 Office: St Margaret Mary Catholic Ch 526 Park Ave N Winter Park FL 32789-3208 Office Phone: 407-628-2346. Office Fax: 407-647-4492. Personal E-mail: curtiswallace@cfl.rr.com. Business E-Mail: curtis@stmargaretmary.org.

**WALLACE, DANIEL,** writer; b. Birmingham, Ala., 1959; m. Laura Wallace; 1 child, Henry. Attended, Emory U., USC. With trading co., Nagoya, Japan; bookstore mgr. Chapel Hill, NC; illustrator. Author: Big Fish: A Novel of Mythic Proportions, 1998, Ray in Reverse, 2000, Watermelon King, 2003, Crossroads, 2004; contbr. stories to mags. Big Fish adapted to film by Tim Burton. Office: Penguin Publicity 375 Hudson St New York NY 10014 E-mail: daniel@danielwallace.org.

**WALLACE, DANNY P.,** library and information scientist, educator; b. Monett, Colo., Oct. 23, 1950; s. Harold and Willa Wallace; m. Connie J. Van Fleet; children: Robyn Solomon, Elizabeth. PhD, U. Ill., Urbana-Champaign, 1984. Assoc. dean, prof. La. State U., Baton Rouge, 1985—95; dir., prof. Kent State U., Ohio, 1996—2000; dir. U. Okla., Norman, 2000—05, prof., 2000—. Editor: Reference and User Svcs. Quar.; author: (book) Library Evaluation: A Casebook and Can-Do Guide. Mem.: ALA (com. accreditation 2003—), Okla. Libr. Assn. (chair-elect libr. edn. divsn. 2006—), Am. Soc. Info. Sci. and Tech. (mem. editl. bd. jour., Doctoral Dissertation scholar 1984), Assn. Libr. and Info. Sci. Edn. (bd. dirs. 1998—2001, 2003—04, Doctoral Students' Dissertation award 1986, Tchg. Excellence award 2000), Reference and User Svcs. Assn. (bd. dirs. 1991—2006). Office: Univ Oklahoma 401 W Brooks Rm 120 Norman OK 73019 Office Phone: 405-325-3921.

**WALLACE, DEE,** actress; b. Kansas City, Mo., Dec. 14, 1948; d. Robert Stanley and Maxine (Nichols) Bowers; m. Christopher Stone, June 28, 1980 (dec.); m. Skip Belyea; 1 child, Gabriella. BA, U. Kans., 1971. Actress feature films The Christmas Visitor, Secret Admirer, Cujo, E.T., Jimmy the Kid, The Howling, 10; actress ABC movies of the week Eminent Domain, Hostage Flight, A Whale for a Killing; actress CBS movies of the week An Enemy Among Us, Sin of Innocence, The Sky is No Limit, Happy, Surprise, Surprise, The Five of Me, Young Love, First Love; actress NBC movies of the week Wait Til Your Mother Gets Home, Child Bride of Short Creek, Skeezer; actress CBS After School Special Dad's Out of a Job; actress ABC After School Special Run Don't Walk; actress CBS series Police Story, Together We Stand/Nothing is Easy, Lou Grant; actress stage prodns. including Annie Get Your Gun, Oklahoma, My Fair Lady, Applause, Butterflies are Free, Middle of the Night. Spkr. in field; mgr. DWS Acting Studio, Burbank, Calif. Appeared in films including Nevada, 1997, Mutual Needs, 1997, Black Circle Boys, 1997, Bad As I Wanna Be: The Dennis Rodman Story, 1998, Flamingo Dreams, 1998, To Love, Honor and Betray, 1999, Invisible Mom II, 1999, Pirates of the Plain, 1999, Out of the Black, A Month of Sundays, Dead Canaries, Spice of Life, Total Rex, Abominable, Expiration Date, others; appeared on TV shows Cold Case, 2005, Crossing Jordan, 2005, Sons and Daughters, 2005. Fundraiser Actors and Others for Animals, L.A., 1980—, Amanda Found., L.A., 1986, 87; co-host, fundraiser Children's Hospital Telethon, Sta. KCET, L.A., 1985—; spokesperson Nat. Assn. of Children of Alcoholics, 1987—. Mem. Screen Actors Guild, Actors Equity, AFTRA. Methodist. Avocations: dance, singing. Office Phone: 818-876-0386. E-mail: totoent@aol.com.

**WALLACE, DERRICK DONNELL,** construction executive, accountant; b. Orlando, Fla., Nov. 4, 1953; s. Theressa (Wallace) Williams; m. Robin Joy Abrams, Nov. 18, 1978 (div. Nov. 1981); children: Daunte, Deja. BS in Acctg., Fla. A&M U., 1975. Staff acct. Price Waterhouse & Co., CPA, Tampa, Fla., 1975-77; chief acct. Tuttle-White Constructors, Inc., Orlando, Fla., 1977-79; pres. Construct Two, Inc., Orlando, 1979—. Chmn. Pvt. Industry Coun. Cen. Fla., Orlando, 1983—. Commr. Mayor Commn. of the Arts, Orlando, 1988, Youth Opportunities Commn., Orlando, 1989—; mem. Ptnrs. in Edn., Orange County Sch. System, 1988—. Recipient Outstanding Svc. award AMVETS, 1987, Outstanding Achievement award Greater Fla. Minority Devel. Coun., 1988, Up and Comer award, 1989. Mem. NAACP, Greater Fla. Fair Bd. (bd. dirs. 1988—), Greater Orlando C. of C. (bd. dirs. 1988—), Fla. A&M U. Alumni Assn. (v.p. 1988—). Republican. Avocations: tennis, swimming. Office: 30 S Ivey Ln Orlando FL 32811-4222*

**WALLACE, DESIREE,** investigational drug pharmacist, pharmacy educator; d. Divinia and Russell Wilkinson; m. Craig Wallace; children: Joshua children: Isabella. PharmD, U. So. Calif., 1996. Investigational drug pharmacist Loma Linda U. Med. Ctr., Calif., 1999—; asst. prof. pharmacy practice Loma Linda U. Sch. Pharmacy, Calif., 2002—. Pharmacist cons. Timebandits Inc., Loma Linda, 1996—; mem. instl. rev. Loma Linda U., 1999. Contbr. articles to profl. jours. Bd. dirs. Am. Cancer Soc., Upland, Calif., 1997—99. Achievements include research in ginko biloba and acetazolamide prophylaxis for acute mountain success. Business E-Mail: dwallace@ahs.llumc.edu.

**WALLACE, DON, JR.,** law educator; b. Vienna, Apr. 23, 1932; s. Don and Julie (Baer) Wallace; m. Daphne Mary Wickham, 1963; children: Alexandra Creed, Sarah Anne, Benjamin James. BA with high honors, Yale U., 1953; LL.B. cum laude, Harvard U., 1957. Bar: N.Y. 1957, D.C. 1978, U.S. Supreme Ct. Assoc. Fleischmann, Jaeckle, Stokes and Hitchcock, N.Y.C., 1959-60, Paul, Weiss, Rifkind, Wharton and Garrison, N.Y.C., 1957-58, 60-62; rsch. asst. to faculty mem. Harvard Law Sch., Cambridge, Mass., 1958-59; regional legal adv. Middle East AID, Dept. State, 1963-65, dep. asst. gen. counsel, 1965-66; assoc. prof. law Georgetown U. Law Ctr., Washington, 1966-71, prof., 1971—2002; chmn. Internat. Law Inst., Washington, 1969—; adj./emeritus prof. Georgetown U. Law Ctr., Washington, 2002—. Cons. AID, 1966-70, UN Centre on Transnat. Corps., 1977-78; counsel Wald, Harkrader & Ross, Washington, 1978-86, Arnold & Porter, 1986-89, Shearman & Sterling, 1989-98, Morgan, Lewis & Bockius, 1998—; legal advisor State of Qatar, 1979-82; chmn. adv. com. on tech. and world trade Office of Tech. Assessment, U.S. Congress, 1976-79; mem. Sec. of State's Adv. Com. on Pvt. Internat. Law, 1979—; mem. U.S. del. UN Conf. on State Succession in Respect of Treaties, Vienna, 1978; mem. U.S. del. new internat. econ. order working group UN Commn. Internat. Trade Law, Vienna, 1981—; vis. com. Harvard Law Sch., 1996-97; mem. panel of judges World Trade Orgn., 1996-2000. Co-author: Internat. Business and Economics: Law and Policy; author: International Regulation of Multinational Corporations, 1976, Dear Mr. President: The Needed Turnaround in America's International Economic Affairs, 1984; editor: A Lawyer's Guide to International Business Transactions, 1977-87; contbr. numerous articles on internat. trade and law to profl. jours., books revs. on law and bus. to profl. jours. Coord. Anne Arundel County (Md.) Dem. Nat. Com., 1972-79; sec. Chesapeake Found., 1972-73; nat. chmn. Law Profs. for Bush and Quayle, 1988, 92, for Dole and Kemp, 1996; v.p., bd. govs. UNIDROIT Found., Rome, 1997—. Fulbright fellow, 1967, Eisenhower Exch. fellow, 1976. Mem. ABA (chmn. sect. internat. law 1978-79, ho of dels. 1982-84, mem. adv. bd. Ctrl. European and Eurasian Law Initiative), Am. Law Inst., Repub. Nat. Lawyers Assn., Internat. Law Assn., Shaybani Soc. of Internat. Law (v.p.), Cosmos Club, Met. Club, Acad. Coun. European Ctr. Peace and Devel. (Belgrade). Home: 2800 35th St NW Washington DC 20007-1411 Office: Georgetown U Law Ctr 600 New Jersey Ave NW Washington DC 20001-2022 E-mail: wallace@ili.org.

**WALLACE, DONALD JOHN, III,** rancher; b. Houston, May 17, 1941; s. D. J., Jr. and Doris Jill (Gano) Wallace; m. Patricia Anne McShane, Sept. 3, 1964 (div. 1984); children: Donald John IV, Megan; m. Nena Jo Isenhower, June 1, 1985 (div. 1989); 1 child, Andrew; m. Kay Fulkerson, May 31, 1997. BBA in Mktg., Texas A&M U., 1963. Regional sales dir. Orkin Exterminating Co., Inc., Dallas, 1977-79, br. mgr., 1979-80, dist. mgr., 1980-83, comml. region mgr., 1983-85, regional sales dir., 1985-86; owner Omega Telex, Dallas, 1986-88; rancher Valley View, Tex., 1988—. Mem. Tex. Structural Pest Control Bd., Austin, 1983—84; leader Big Mineral Trail Riders Club Boy Scouts Am.; bd. dirs. Frank Buck Zoo, Gainesville, Tex., 1997—98; pres. Frank Buck Zool. Soc.; bd. dirs. North Tex. Med. Found., Gainesville Econ. Devel. Corp. Republican. Roman Catholic. Avocations: hiking, fishing, hunting, skiing, horseback riding. Home: 1034 Trails End Valley View TX 76272-6114 Personal E-mail: donandkay@cooke.net.

**WALLACE, DOUGLAS C.,** geneticist, educator; PhD in Microbiology and Human Genetics, Yale U. Prof., dir. Ctr. for Molecular Medicine Emory U. Sch. Medicine, Atlanta, 1990—2002; Donald Bren prof. biol. scis. and molecular medicine U. Calif., Irvine, 2002—; dir. Ctr. for Molecular, Mitochondrial Medicine and Genetics, U. Calif., 2002—. Author of more than 270 rsch. papers published in various jours. including Cell, Science, Nature, Procs. of Nat. Acad. of Scis., New Eng. Jour. Medicine. Co-recipient Passano award (with Guiseppi Attardi), 2000; recipient Rsch. award for Medical Rsch. in Alzheimer's Disease, Metropolitan Life Found., 2000. Fellow: Am. Acad. Arts and Scis.; mem.: NAS, Am. Soc. Human Genetics (William Allan award 1994). Office: U Calif Biological Chemistry Dept 2028 Hewitt Hall Irvine CA 92697

**WALLACE, EDWARD CORBETT,** lawyer; s. Edward Corbett Wallace; m. Pamela S. Falk; children: Richard Falk-Wallace, William Gerety Falk-Wallace. BA cum laude, Columbia U., 1971, MA, 1973; JD, Fordham U., 1977. Bar: NY 1977, US Dist. Ct. (so. dist.) NY 1980, US Ct. Appeals (2d cir.) 1994. Chief of staff to Pres. City Coun., NYC, 1983-86; v.p. Boston Properties, NYC, 1986-91; counsel Lankenau, Kovner & Kurtz, NYC, 1991-92; ptnr. Phillips, Nizer, Benjamin, Krim & Ballon, NYC, 1992; now shareholder, govt. and adminstrv. law dept. Greenberg Traurig, LLP, NYC. Councilmen.-at-large, NNY, 1981-83; mem. law com. Mcpl. Arts Soc. Office: Greenberg Traurig LLP MetLife Bldg 200 Park Ave New York NY 10166 Office Phone: 212-801-9200. Office Fax: 212-801-6400. Business E-Mail: wallacee@gtlaw.com.

**WALLACE, EMILY MITCHELL,** writer, editor, educator; d. George Lafayette and Prewitt Carlisle (Evans) Mitchell; m. Gregory Merrill Harvey, June 14, 1969; m. Robert Arthur Wallace, June 8, 1954 (div. 1964). BA, Southwest Mo. State, 1958; MA, Bryn Mawr Coll., 1959, PhD, 1965. Tutor, history and lit. Curtis Inst. of Music, Phila., 1957—58, chair English dept., 1976—78, 1979—83; tchr. lit. Shipley Sch., Bryn Mawr, Pa., 1959—60; instr. to asst. prof. U. Pa., Phila., 1962—67; vis. assoc. prof. Swarthmore Coll., Pa., 1967—68, 1969—70; leader interdisciplinary seminar Yale U., New Haven, 1979; rsch. assoc. Ctr. Visual Culture Bryn Mawr Coll., 2003—. Mem. sponsoring com. Marianne Moore Fund for Poetry, Bryn Mawr Coll., 1975—; mem. adv. com. Rosenbach Mus. and Libr., Phila., 1980—; curriculum cons. Cooper Union of Art, Sci. and Tech., NY, 1984—85; interdisciplinary rsch. scholar in poetry and visual arts; writer photographic essays and multimedia lectrs. scholarly and acad. audiences, double-screen lectrs. confs. and symposium miles and [?]. Author (book) A Bibliography of William Carlos Williams, 1969; guest editor (periodical) W.C. Williams Review, Centennial Issue, 1983, PAIDEUMA (Spcl. James Laughlin Vol.), 2002; author: (photo essay) Youthful Days and Costly Hours: The Education of Ol' Ez and Billy Williams at Penn, U. Pa. Conf. Papers, 1983, Athena's Owls: The Education of Marianne Moore and Hilda Doolittle, Bryn Mawr '09 in Poesis, 1985, Some Friends of Ezra Pound in the Yale Rev., 1986, Saffron Honey: A Love Song by William Carlos Williams, The Idea and The Thing in Modernist American Poetry, 2001, Why Not Spirits?-The Universe is Alive, in Ezra Pound and China, 2003. Mem. bd. dirs. Am. Found., Bok Tower, Fla., 1976—86; shareholder The Libr. Co., Phila., 1981—; lifetime mem. Friends of the Bryn Mawr Coll. Libr., Pa., 1996—; mem. Yale Libr. Assocs., Franklin Inn., Phila. Fellow, AAUW, 1968—69; Workman Traveling fellowship, Bryn Mawr Coll., Eng., France, Italy, 1961—62, Inaugural Beinecke fellow, Yale U., 1987, Everett Helm Vis. fellow, Lilly Libr., Ind. U., 2003. Mem.: Modern Lang. Assn., Harvard Humanities Ctr. Faculty Arts and Scis., Conn. Acad. Arts and Sci., Assn. Lit. Scholars and Critics, Emily Dickinson Soc., H.D. Soc., Ezra Pound Soc., William Carlos Williams Soc. (first pres.), Marianne Moore Soc., Wallace Stevens Soc., Henry James Soc., Ernest Hemingway Soc., Merion Cricket Club. Democrat. Avocations: chess, music, travel, gardening, tennis. Home: 1939 Panama St Philadelphia PA 19103-6609 Office Phone: 610-718-0503. Personal E-mail: emwallace@aol.com.

**WALLACE, F. BLAKE,** retired aerospace transportation executive, retired mechanical engineer; b. Phoenix, Jan. 10, 1933; BMechE, Calif. Inst. Tech., 1955; MS in Engring., Ariz. State U., 1963, PhD in Engring., 1967. Preliminary design engr. Pratt & Whitney, East Hartford, Conn., 1955-59; chief engr. advanced tech. Garrett Corp., Phoenix, 1959-80; mgr. advanced plans and programs Aircraft Engine Group GE, Evendale, Ohio, 1981-83; gen. mgr. Allison div. GM, Indpls., 1983-93, v.p., 1987-93; chmn. & CEO Allison Engine Co., Indpls., 1993-95; ret., 1995. Author numerous tech. papers. Fellow AIAA (chmn. air breathing propulsion tech. com. 1977-78, Air Breathing Propulsion award 1991), U.S. Advanced Ceramic Assn. (chmn. 1987-89).

**WALLACE, GLADYS BALDWIN,** librarian; b. Macon, Ga., June 5, 1923; d. Carter Shepherd and Dorothy (Richard) Baldwin; m. Hugh Loring Wallace Jr., Oct. 14, 1941 (div. Sept. 1968); children: Dorothy, Hugh Loring III. BS in

---

Edn., Oglethorpe U., 1961; MLS, Emory U., 1966; EdS, Ga. State U., 1980. Libr. pub. elem. schs., Atlanta, 1956-66; libr. Northside HS, 1966-87, Episc. Cathedral St. Philip. Author: The Time of My Life, 1994, Just a Moment, a Book of Poetry, 2005, Glorious Grass, 1999; contbg. author: Trees of Atlanta. Mem. High Mus. Art, Madison-Morgan Cultural Ctr. Recipient Poet of Merit award, 1999; Ga. Dept. Edn. grantee, 1950, NDEA grantee, 1963, 65. Mem.: Am. Assn. Univ. Women, Atlanta Hist. Soc., Am. Assn. Ret. Persons, Atlanta Bot. Garden, Ga. Women of Achievement. Home: NC 6 136 Peachtree Memorial Dr NW Atlanta GA 30309-1096

**WALLACE, HARRY LELAND,** lawyer; b. San Francisco, June 26, 1927; s. Leon Harry and Anna Ruth (Haworth) W.; m. Marilyn D. Wallace (dec. June 13, 2005); 1 child, Mary Ann Wallace Frantz. AB in Govt.; BS in Bus, Ind. U., 1949; JD, Harvard U., 1952. Bar: Wis. 1953. Law clk. U.S. Supreme Ct. Justice Sherman Minton, Washington, 1952-53; assoc. firm Foley & Lardner, Milw., 1953-61, partner, 1961-96, retired, 1996; officer and/or dir. various corps. Treas. Mequon-Thiensville Sch. Bds., 1966-67, 71-73, pres., 1965-66, 67-71, 73-75; bd. dirs. Milw. County Assn. for Mental Health, 1970-76, Milw. Mental Health Found., 1983-94; chmn. financing policies com. Gov.'s Commn. on Edn., 1969-70; mem. Gov.'s Task Force on Sch. Financing and Property Tax Reform, 1972-73; chmn. Gov.'s Commn. on State-Local Rels. and Fin. Policies, 1975-76; trustee Pub. Policy Forum, 1976-92, sec., 1984-86, pres., 1986-88. With USN, 1945-46. Mem. Wis. Bar Assn., Am. Law Inst., Phi Beta Kappa, Beta Gamma Sigma, Delta Tau Delta. Clubs: Milwaukee. Methodist. Home: 1913 Somerset Ln Northbrook IL 60062-6067 Personal E-mail: lelandwallace@comcast.net.

**WALLACE, HENRY JARED, JR.,** lawyer; b. Pitts., Oct. 26, 1943; s. Henry Jared and Jane (Bowman) Wallace. BA, Harvard U., 1965, JD, 1968. Bar: Pa. 1969, U.S. Supreme Ct. 1973. With Reed Smith, Pitts., 1968—94; pvt. practice Pitts., 1995—. Served with U.S. Army, 1968-70. Mem. Duquesne Club, Fox Chapel Golf Club, Harvard-Yale-Princeton Club (Pitts.). Home and Office: 149 Ridgeview Dr New Kensington PA 15068-9389

**WALLACE, J. CLIFFORD,** federal judge; b. San Diego, Dec. 11, 1928; s. John Franklin and Lillie Isabel (Overing) Wallace; m. Virginia Lee Schlosser, 1957 (dec.); m. Elaine J. Barnes, Apr. 8, 1996 (dec.); m. Dixie Jenee Robison Zenger, Apr. 2, 2001. BA, San Diego State U., 1952; LLB, U. Calif., Berkeley, 1955. Bar: Calif. 1955. With Gray, Cary, Ames & Frye, San Diego, 1955—70; judge U.S. Dist. Ct. (so. dist.), Calif., 1970—72, U.S. Ct. Appeals (9th cir.), San Diego, 1972—96, chief judge, 1991—96, sr. judge, 1996—. Contbr. articles to profl. jours. Stake pres. San Diego East LDS Ch., 1962—67, regional rep., 1967—74, 1977—79. With USN, 1946—49. Mem.: Inst. Jud. Adminstrn., Am. Bd. Trial Advocates. Mem. Lds Ch. Office: US Ct Appeals 9th Cir 940 Front St Ste 4192 San Diego CA 92101-8918 *My principles, ideals and goals and my standard of conduct are embodied in the Gospel of Jesus Christ. They come to fruition in family life, service, industry and integrity and in an attempt, in some small way, to make my community a better place within which to live.*

**WALLACE, JANE HOUSE,** retired geologist; b. Ft. Worth, Aug. 12, 1926; d. Fred Leroy and Helen Gould (Kixmiller) Wallace. AB, Smith Coll., 1947, MA, 1949; postgrad., Bryn Mawr Coll., 1949—52. Geologist U.S. Geol. Survey, 1952—97; chief Pub. Inquiries Offices, Washington, 1964—72, spl. asst. to dir., 1974—97, dep. bur. ethics counselor, 1975—97, Washington liaison Office of Dir., 1978—97; ret., 1997. Recipient Meritorious Service award Dept. Interior, 1971, Disting. Svc. award, 1976, Sec.'s Commendation, 1988, Smith Coll. medal, 1992. Fellow Geol. Socs. Am., Washington (treas. 1963-67); mem. Sigma Xi (assoc.)

**WALLACE, JESSE WYATT,** pharmaceutical scientist; b. Canton, Ga., Jan. 24, 1925; s. Jesse Washington and Lula (Wyatt) W.; m. Myra Brown, Jan. 2, 1949; children: Karin, Kimberly, Stephen, David. BBA magna cum laude, U. Ga., 1954; postgrad., U. Pa., 1959; MS, Ga. Inst. Tech., 1960; postgrad., U. Va., 1978, MIT, 1984. Chmn. svc. groups Ga. Tech, Atlanta, 1953-57; adminstrv. mgr. Am. Viscose Corp., Marcus Hook, Pa., 1957-61; various exec. positions FMC Corp., Phila., 1961-85; pres., dir. Wallco Internat. Corp., Wilmington, Del., 1985-89, 96—; v.p., sec. Pharm. Svc. and Tech., Inc., Woodbury, NJ, 1989-95. Adv. bd. Pharm. Tech. Conf., 1986—99. Editor: Controlled Release Systems, 1988; contbr. Encyclopedia, 1989; contbr. articles to profl. jours; author (manual) Problem Solver, 1980. Vice chmn. Ch. Deacons, Wilmington, 1969-71; v.p., bd. dirs. Wilmington Gideons, 1969-71; v.p., bd. dirs. ACA Acad., 1971-73; founder, vice chmn. Del. Family Found., 1990-99. Lt. USN, 1943-46, 50-53. Recipient Publ. award Pharm. Technology, 1989. Fellow Acad. Pharm. Scis., Am. Assn. of Pharm. Scientists; mem. Internat. Platform Assn., La. Fedn. Internat. Pharm., Am. Assn. Pharm. Scientists, Mensa, Delta Sigma Pi (life), Delta Mu Delta. Republican. Avocations: reading, golf, travel, racquetball. Office: Wallco Internat Corp 1106 Grinnell Rd Wilmington DE 19803-5126

**WALLACE, JOHN E.,** state supreme court justice; b. Pitman, NJ, 1942; m. Barbara Wallace; 5 children. BA in Political sci., U. Del., 1964; JD, Harvard U. Sch. of Law, 1967. Atty. Trustees of Penn Central Transportation Co., Montgomery, McCracken, Walker & Rhoads, Phila.; partner Atkinson, Myers, Archie & Wallace; municipal judge Wash. Township, Gloucester County; judge NJ Superior Ct., 1984—92, judge appellate div., 1992—2003; justice NJ Supreme Ct., 2003—. Former mem. NJ Supreme Ct. Task Force for Minority Concern; mem. NJ Ethics Commn., Jud. Advisory Com. on Americans with Disabilities Act, Supreme Ct. Special Com. on Matrimonial Litigation, Appellate Div. Rules Com.; former chmn. Supreme Ct. Ad Hoc Com. on Admissions. Coach Washington Twp. H.S. Served to rank of captain U.S. Army, 1968—70. Mem.: ABA, Garden State Bar Assn. (Van J. Clinton award 2002), NJ State Bar Assn., Nat. Bar Assn., Camden County Bar Assn., Gloucester Bar Assn. Office: Richard J Hughes Justice Complex 25 Market St PO Box 970 Trenton NJ 08625*

**WALLACE, JOHN LOYS,** retired aviation services executive; b. Decatur, Tex., July 31, 1941; s. John K. and Flora Viola (Lumsden) Montgomery W.; m. Linda M. Jackson, May 18, 1962; children— John, Amy Lynn, Katherine Lea, Elizabeth D'Ann Student, U. Tex.-Arlington, 1961-65, North Tex. State U., Denton, 1960-61. V.p. acctg. svcs. Gen Airmotive, Dallas, 1975-77, v.p. fin., 1977-80, exec. v.p., gen. mgr. Gen Aviation div., 1980-82; exec. v.p fin., adminstrn. Aviall, Dallas, 1982-85; exec. v.p., chief oper. officer Aviall, Inc., Dallas, 1985-89, pres. Gen. Aviation Svcs. div., 1989-93; ret., 1993. Mem. Fin. Execs. Inst., North Dallas C. of C., U.S./Mex. C. of C. (bd. dirs.), Chif Exec.'s Round Table, Cotton Creek Club, Delta Sigma Phi. Republican. Presbyterian. Avocations: gardening, fishing, golf. Home: 3651 Pinehurst Cir Gulf Shores AL 36542-9052

**WALLACE, JOHN MITCHELL MAVER** See DUFFY-KING, JAN

**WALLACE, JOYCE IRENE MALAKOFF,** internist; b. Phila., Nov. 23, 1940; d. Samuel Leonard and Henrietta (Hameroff) Malakoff; m. Lance Arthur Wallace, Aug. 30, 1964 (div. 1974); 1 dau. Julia Ruth; m. Arthur H. Kahn, Oct. 7, 1979 (div. 1986); 1 son, Aryeh N. Kahn. AB, Queens Coll., CUNY, 1961; postgrad., Columbia U., 1962-64; MD, SUNY, 1968. Diplomate Am. Bd. Internal Medicine. Intern St. Vincent's Hosp. Med. Ctr. N.Y.C. 1968-70; practice medicine N.Y.C., 1970-71; resident Manhattan VA Hosp., N.Y.C., 1972, Nassau County Med. Ctr., East Meadow, N.Y., 1972-73; practice medicine North Conway, NH, 1973—74; practice medicine specializing in internal medicine N.Y.C., 1976—; med. dir. FROST'D Primary Care, 1999—2003. Mem. attending staff Nassau County Med. Ctr., 1974, St. Vincent's Hosp. and Med. Ctr., N.Y.C., 1977—; asst. prof. medicine Mt. Sinai Med. Sch., N.Y.C.; pres. Found. for Rsch. on Sexually Transmitted Diseases, Inc., 1986-89, exec. and med. dir., 1989-2003. Fellow ACP, N.Y. Acad. Medicine; mem. Am. Med. Women's Assn., N.Y. County, N.Y. State Med. Socs.

---

**WALLACE, JULIA DIANE,** newspaper editor; b. Davenport, Iowa, Dec. 3, 1956; d. Franklin Sherwood and Eleanor Ruth (Pope) W.; m. Doniver Dean Campbell, Aug. 23, 1986; children: Emmaline Livingston Campbell, Eden Jennifer Campbell. BS in Journalism, Northwestern U., 1978. Reporter Norfolk Ledger-Star, Va., 1978-80, Dallas Times Herald, 1980-82; reporter, editor News sect. USA Today, Arlington, Va., 1982-89, mng. editor spl. projects, 1989-92; mng. editor Chgo. Sun-Times, 1992-1996; exec. editor Statesman Jour., Salem, Oreg., 1996—98; mng. editor Ariz. Republic, Phoenix, 1998—2000, Atlanta Jour.-Constitution, 2001—02, editor, 2002—. Mem. Am. Soc. Newspaper Editors. Mailing: Atlanta Journal-Constitution PO Box 4689 Atlanta GA 30302*

**WALLACE, LINDA KAY,** mathematics professor; d. John Edward and Marion Sue Wallace. BS, Radford U., 1989, MS, 1991. Educator Prince William County Pub. Sch., Manassas, Va., 1991—98, math. instrnl. specialist, 1998—2001, algebra readiness coord., 2001—06; math. coord. Roanoke City Pub. Schs., Va., 2006—. Ednl. cons. Casio, Inc., Dover, NJ, 2004—. Mem.: Nat. Coun. Tchrs. Math. (assoc.), Nat. Coun. Suprs. Math. (assoc.), Phi Delta Kappa (assoc.; pres. chpt. 1448 2004—05, Outstanding Student of Yr. 1991). Office: 40 Douglass AveNW Roanoke VA 24012 Office Phone: 540-853-6052. Office Fax: 703-441-4497. E-mail: wallaclk@pwcs.edu.

**WALLACE, MARK ALLEN,** hospital administrator; b. Oklahoma City, Apr. 24, 1953; s. William Howell and Mollie Marie (Godsy) W.; children: Emily, Benjamin. BS, Okla. Bapt. U., 1975; MS, Washington U., St. Louis, 1978. Adminstrv. asst. Bapt. Med. Ctr., Oklahoma City, 1975-77; adminstrv. resident Meth. Hosp., Houston, 1977-78; asst. v. Tex. Meth. Hosp., Houston, 1978-80, v.p., 1980-83, sr. v.p., 1983-89; pres., CEO Tex. Children's Hosp., Houston, 1989—. Adj. instr. Washington U., 1984—; adj. asst. prof. Tex. Womans U., Houston, 1983—; bd. dirs., chmn. fin. com., treas. Greater Houston Hosp. Svc. Corp., 1986-90; bd. trustees, Nat. Assn of Children's Hospitals and Related Institutions Contbr. articles to profl. jours. Chmn. campaign drives United Way, Houston, 1984, 86, corporate walk for Juvenile Diabetes Found. Walk to Cure Diabetes, 2000; class chmn. alumni vision for excellence and growth for future campaigns Okla. Bapt. U., 1982; bd. dirs. Tex. Gulf Coast chpt. March of Dimes Birth Defects Found., 1985-91, Zoological Society of Houston, Sam Houston Area Coun. of the Boy Scouts, World Health & Golf Assn., Greater Houston Partnership (vice-chair Flood Control Task Force), Greater Houston Community Found.; bd. governors, Houston Forum; active mem. Second Baptist Ch., Houston, Young Presidents' Orgn., and Houston Country Club Recipient Emerging Leaders in Health Care award Healthcare Forum Mag. and Korn/Ferry Internat., 1987. Fellow Am. Coll. Healthcare Execs. (com. on membership, subcom. on recruitment 1990—, Robert S. Hudgens Meml. award, 1992, Young Healthcare Exec. of Yr., 1992); mem. Am. Heart Assn. (med. adv. com. 1990-91), Healthcare Forum (pres. emerging leaders alumni group 1988-91), Am. Hosp. Assn., Tex. Hosp. Assn. (bd. dirs., bd. dirs. polit. action com. 1988—, chmn. bd. trustees, 1998-1999), Greater Houston Hosp. Coun. (bd. dirs. 1991—, chmn. 1993-1994), Houston Area Health Care Coalition, Childrens Hosp. Assn. Tex. (pres. 1992—, chmn. 2002-2003), Tex. Gulf Coast Arthritis Found. (bd. dirs. 1990-91). Republican. Baptist. Office: Tex Children's Hosp 6621 Fannin St Houston TX 77030 also: PO Box 300630 Houston TX 77230-0630*

**WALLACE, MARK RAYMOND,** physician; b. Seattle, Feb. 22, 1955; s. George Warren and Grace Joann (Balch) W.; m. Kathleen Cornell, Jan. 19, 1985; 1 child, Luke Randall. BA in Chemistry, Whitman Coll., Walla Walla, Wash., 1977; MD, St. Louis U., 1981. Diplomate Am. Bd. Internal Medicine, sub-bd. Infectious Diseases; cert. added competence in clin. tropical medicine. Intern Med. Ctr. Hosp. of Vt., Burlington, 1981-82; resident U. Wash., Seattle, 1982-84; staff physician Naval Hosp., Long Beach, Calif., 1984-85, head internal medicine dept., 1986-87, fellow in infectious diseases San Diego, 1987-89, staff physician, 1989-90, head HIV unit, 1990-93, dir. infectious disease fellowship, 1993—, head infectious disease, 1998—. Author/co-author numerous jour. articles and abstracts. Capt. USN, 1984—. Decorated Navy Commendation medal, Meritorious Svc. medal; Nat. Merit scholar, 1973. Fellow ACP, Infectious Disease Soc. Am.; mem. AMA, Am. Soc. Microbiology (Weigelt-Wallace award in clin. medicine named in his honor 1992), Physicians Assn. for AIDS Care, Phi Beta Kappa, Alpha Omega Alpha. Avocation: fishing. Office: Naval Med Ctr San Diego CA 92134 Address: 685 Palm Spring Dr Ste 2A Altamonte Springs FL 32701

**WALLACE, MICHELE,** writer, educator; b. NYC, Jan. 4, 1952; d. Robert Earl Wallace and Faith Ringgold; m. Eugene Nesmith, Dec. 22, 1989 (div. Nov. 2002). BA, CCNY, 1974, MA in English, 1990; PhD in Cinema Studies, NYU, 1998. Asst. prof. English CUNY, 1989—91; assoc. prof. English, women's studies and film CUNY and CUNY Grad. Ctr., 1991—97, prof., 1998—2006. Pres. Art Without Walls, 1974. Author: Black Macho and the Myth of the Superwoman, 1979, Invisibility Blues: Pop to Theory, 1990, Black Popular Culture, 1992, Dark Designs and Visual Culture, 2004; columnist: The Village Voice, 1996; editor: Women in Art, 1971; mem. editl. bd.: Social Identities, Souls; contbr. to newspapers and popular mags. including Ms., The Village Voice, The Nation, The N.Y. Times, Art Forum, Art In America. Founding mem. Nat. Black Feminist Orgn., 1974; pres. Women Students and Artists for Black Art Liberation, 1970—76. Mem.: PEN, MLA, Oscar Micheaux Soc., Soc. Cinema Studies, Am. Studies Assn., Phi Beta Kappa. Office Phone: 212-650-6367. Personal E-mail: olympiax@aol.com. Business E-Mail: mfw28@cornell.edu.

**WALLACE, MIKE (MYRON LEON WALLACE),** newscaster, television personality; b. Brookline, Mass., May 9, 1918; s. Frank and Zina (Sharfman) Wallace; m. Lorraine Perigord, 1955 (div. 1983); children: Peter(dec.), Christopher, Pauline; m. Mary Yates, June 28, 1986. BA, U. Mich., 1939; LHD (hon.), U. Mass., 1978; LLD (hon.), U. Mich., 1987, U. Pa., 1989. Associated with radio, 1939—; TV, 1946—; commentator CBS-TV, 1951—55, TV interviewer, reporter, 1951—; CBS news corr., 1963—; corr., co-editor 60 Minutes, CBS, 1968—. Numerous TV appearances include Night Beat, 1956—57, The Mike Wallace Interview, 1957—60, anchor Biography, 1959—61 (George Foster Peabody award, 1962), CBS Reports: 1968, 1993, presenter Mike Wallace Then and Now, 1990, co-anchor Watergate: The Secret Story, 1992, In the Killing Field of America, 1995 (Robert F. Kennedy Journalism award grand prize and TV first prize, 1996, George Foster Peabody award, 1995); author: Mike Wallace Asks, 1958; co-author (with Gary Paul Gates): (memoir) Close Encounter, 1984, Between You and Me: A Memoir, 2005. Naval comm. officer USN, 1943—46. Named Broadcaster of Yr. Internat. Radio and TV Sco., 1993; named to TV Acad. Hall of Fame, 1991; recipient Robert Sherwood award, 19 ATVAS Emmy awards, Disting. Achievement award, U. So. Calif. Sch. Journalism, Robert F. Kennedy Journalism award in Internat. broadcast category, George Foster Peabody award for 60 Minutes. The CIA's Cocaine, 1993, Alfred I. DuPont Columbia U. Journalism award, 1972, 1983, 1999, Carr Van Anda award, 1977, Thomas Hart Benton award, 1978, Paul White award, Radio/TV News Directors Assn., 1991, Lifetime Achievement Emmy, 1993, Fred Friendly First Amendment award, Quinnipiac Coll., 2002, honored for lifetime contribution to radio and TV, Chgo. Mus. Broadcast Comm., 1989. Mem.: Soc. Profl. Journalists, Century Assocs., Sigma Delta Chi.*

**WALLACE, NICOLLE (NICOLLE DEVENISH),** former federal official; b. Orinda, Calif. m. Mark Wallace. BA, U. Calif., Berkley; MA, Medill Sch. of Journalism, Northwestern U. With Calif. Assembly Rep. Caucus, 1997—98, Calif. Rep. Party, 1998; former press aide to CEO Scripps.com; former secretary to Gov. Jeb Bush State of Fla.; former communications dir. Fla. State Tech. Office; spl. asst. to Pres. & dir. of media affairs The White House, Washington, 2000—05, asst. to Pres. for comm., 2005—06. Communications dir. Bush-Cheney '04 campaign.

**WALLACE, NORA ANN,** lawyer; b. Phila., May 24, 1951; AB, Vassar Coll., 1973; JD cum laude, Harvard U., 1976. Bar: N.Y. 1977. Mem. Willkie Farr & Gallagher, N.Y.C. Trustee Vassar Coll., Bklyn. Acad. Music, Bklyn. Acad. Music Endowment Trust; bd. dirs. Joseph Collins Found. Office: Willkie Farr & Gallagher 787 7th Ave New York NY 10019-6099

**WALLACE, PAULA S.,** academic administrator; 3 children. BA, Furman U.; MEd, EdS, Ga. State U. Co-founder Savannah Coll. Art and Design, 1979, pres., 2000—. Author of children's books. Mem. Skidaway Island United Meth. Ch., Savannah, Ga. Film and Videotape Commn., Ga. C. of C.; bd. dirs. B. B. & T. Bank, Nat. Mus. Women in the Arts. Recipient Oglethorpe Bus. and Profl. Women award, James T. Deason Human Rels. award; named Outstanding Young Woman of Am., Ky. Col.; named to Savannah Bus. Hall of Fame. Office: Savannah Coll Art and Design PO Box 3146 622 Drayton St Savannah GA 31402-3146 Office Phone: 912-525-5200.

**WALLACE, PETER MARSDEN,** radio producer, commentator, writer; b. Parkersburg, W.Va., Aug. 15, 1954; s. Aldred Pruden and Margaret Anne (Yoak) Wallace; m. Bonita Lucille Shock, Oct. 15, 1977 (div. 2005); children: Meredith Anne, Matthew Edward. AB in journalism/advt., Marshall U., 1976; ThM, Dallas Theol. Sem., 1984. Editor W.Va. Hillbilly, Richwood, W.Va., 1976-79; editl. asst. Dallas Theol. Sem., 1981-84; editl. mgr. Walk Thru the Bible Ministries, Atlanta, 1984-85, editl. dir., 1985-90; sr. copywriter & broadcast prodr. Larry Smith & Associates, Atlanta, 1990—2001; exec. prodr. Day 1 radio program (formerly The Protestant Hour), Atlanta, 2001—, host, 2005—; v.p. Alliance for Christian Media. Mem. Faith & Values Media Mem. Coun.; bd. trustees Nat. Interfaith Cable Coalition, 2005—. Author: What Jesus Is Saying to You Today, 1994, What the Psalmist is Saying to You Today, 1994, What God Is Saying to You Today, 1995, Psalms for Today, 2001, TruthQuest Devotional Journal, 2002, Old Testament for Today, 2003, Out of the Quiet: Responding to God's Whispered Invitations, 2004; co-author: The West Virginia Picture Book, 1979; contbr. articles to religious magazines; editor: The Daily Walk Bible, 1987. Recipient Outstanding Young Men Am. Award, US Jaycees, 1984. Democrat. Avocations: reading, camping. Office: Day 1 Ste 300 644 W Peachtree St Atlanta GA 30308-1925 Office Fax: 404-815-0495. E-mail: pwallace@day1.net.

**WALLACE, R. H., JR.,** lawyer; b. Livingston, Tex., Oct. 9, 1943; BS, U.S. Naval Acad., 1966; JD, Baylor U., 1973. Bar: Tex. 1973, US Dist. Ct. (no., so., ea. we. dist. Tex.), U.S. Ct. Appeals (5th cir.), US Supreme Ct.; cert. civil trial & criminal law Tex. Bd. Legal Specialization. Atty. criminal div., appellate sect. US Dept. Justice, 1973—76; asst. U.S. atty. US Dept. Justice, No. Dist. Tex., 1976-84, dep. chief criminal div., 1983-84; mem., comml. litig. practice, mng. ptnr. Shannon Gracey Ratliff & Miller LLP, Fort Worth. Faculty mem. Nat Inst. Trial Advocacy. Fellow Am. Coll. Trial Lawyers; life fellow Tex. Bar Found.; mem. ABA, Nat. Assn. Criminal Def. Lawyers, State Bar Tex., Tex. Assn. Def. Counsel. Office: Shannon Gracey Ratliff & Miller Ste 3800 777 Main St Fort Worth TX 76102 Office Phone: 817-336-9333. Office Fax: 817-336-3735. Business E-Mail: rhwallace@shannongracey.com.

**WALLACE, RASHEED,** professional basketball player, marketing professional; b. Sept. 17, 1974; s. Jackie Wallace; m. Fatima Sanders, July 18; 3 children. Attended, U. N.C. Prof. basketball player Washington Wizards, 1995—96, Portland Trailblazers, 1996—2004, Atlanta Hawks, 2004, Detroit Pistons, 2004—; CEO Dir. Hit Studios, Phila., 2002—. Founder Rasheed A. Wallace Found., Phila., 1997. Named to NBA All-Star Team, 2000, 2001. Achievements include being a member of NBA Championship Team, 2004. Office: c/o Detroit Pistons 2 Championship Dr Auburn Hills MI 48326*

**WALLACE, RICHARD,** editor, writer; b. Bronxville, N.Y., May 25, 1947; m. Elisabeth Beeftink, May 24, 1969; 1 child, Eric B. BA, Columbia U., 1974. Reporter, editor, contbr. varius industry and bus. pubs., Electronic News, EE Times, 1976-92; editor-in-chief Electronic Engring. Times, Manhasset, NY, 1992—98; editor, dir. EE Times, 1998—. Office: CMP Media LLC Electronic Engring Times 600 Community Dr Ste 1 Manhasset NY 11030-3875

**WALLACE, RICHARD P.,** computer company executive; BSEE, Univ. Mich.; M engring. mgmt., Santa Clara Univ. Engring. positions Ultratech Stepper, Cypress Semiconductor; mgmt. positions KLA-Tencor Corp., 1988—95, sr. engr. mgr. Wisard San Jose, Calif., 1995—98, v.p., gen. mgr. Mirage group, 1998—99, group v.p., 1999—2000, exec. v.p., 2000—05, pres., COO, 2005, CEO, 2006—. Office: KLA-Tencor Corp 160 Rio Robles San Jose CA 95134*

**WALLACE, ROBERT BRUCE,** retired surgeon; b. Washington, Apr. 12, 1931; s. William B. and Anne E. W.; m. Betty Jean Newel, Aug. 28, 1955; children: Robert B., Anne E., Barbara N. BA, Columbia U., 1953, MD, 1957. Diplomate Am. Bd. Surgery, Am. Bd. Thoracic Surgery. Chmn., prof. dept. surgery Mayo Clinic and Mayo Med. Sch., Rochester, Minn.; bd. govs. Mayo Clinic, 1968-79; prof. dept. surgery Georgetown U. Sch. Medicine, 1980—96, chmn. dept. surgery, 1980-95, surgeon and chief univ. hosp., 1980-95; retired, 1996. Trustee Mayo Found., 1970—78; chmn. sci. adv. com. LeDucq Found., 2000—05. Mem. ACS (bd. govs. 1975-79), Am. Surg. Assn., Soc. Clin. Surgery, Am. Assn. Thoracic Surgery (pres. 1994-95), Internat. Cardiovascular Soc., Soc. Vascular Surgery, Thoracic Surgery Found. Rsch. & Edn. (bd. dirs. 1993-2001, pres. 1998-2001). Home: 1322 Darnall Dr Mc Lean VA 22101-3009 E-mail: rbwallace@cox.net.

**WALLACE, ROBERT EARL,** geologist; b. N.Y.C., July 16, 1916; s. Clarence Earl and Harriet (Wheeler) W.; m. Gertrude Kivela, Mar. 19, 1945; 1 child: Alan R. BS, Northwestern U., 1938; MS, Calif. Inst. Tech., 1940. PhD, 1946. Geologist US Geol. Survey, various locations, 1942-98. regional geologist Menlo Park. Calif., 1970-74, chief scientist Office of Earthquakes, Volcanoes and Engring., 1974-87, emeritus, 1987-98; asst. and assoc. prof. Wash. State Coll., Pullman, 1946-51; prof. emeritus U. Nev., Reno, 1998—2003. Adv. panel Nat. Earthquake Prediction Evaluation Coun., 1980-90; adv. com. Stanford U. Sch. Earth Sci., 1972-82; engring. criteria rev. bd. San Francisco Bay Conservation and Devel. Commn., chmn. 1981-92. Contbr. articles to profl. jours. Recipient Alfred E. Alquist award Calif. Earthquake Safety Found., 1995. Fellow AAAS, Geol. Soc. Am. (chmn. cordillidan sect. 1967-68, Career Contbn. award Structural Geology and Tectonics, 2002), Earthquake Engring. Rsch. Inst. (hon. 1999), Calif. Acad. Scis. (hon.); mem. Seismol. Soc. Am. (medalist 1989) Avocations: birdwatching, amateur radio, painting.

**WALLACE, SAMUEL TAYLOR,** health system administrator; b. Blytheville, Ark., Sept. 2, 1943; m. Sara Billow, Apr. 30, 1992. BS, U. Mo., 1965; M.H.A., Washington U., St. Louis, 1970. Asst. administr. Hillcrest Med. Ctr., Tulsa, 1969-75; administr. St. Luke's Meth. Hosp., Cedar Rapids, Iowa, 1975-81, pres., 1981-95, Iowa Health Sys., Des Moines, 1995—. Bd. dirs Vol. Hosp. Am., Dallas, 1982-94, Iowa Kidf Charities, 2001-; chmn. bd. dirs Vol. Hosp. Iowa, Cedar Rapids, 1983-87; bd. dirs Greater Des Moines Partnershp, 1996—, Physician Mgmt. Resources, 1996—2000, Health Enterprise of Iowa, 1995-2000; mem. Cedar Rapids coun. Boy Scouts Am., 1983, Mid-Iowa coun., 1995—. Served to capt. M.S.C. U.S. Army, 1965-68, Vietnam. Recipient Silver Beaver award Boy Scouts Am., 1980, Silver Antelope award, 1992; James E. West fellow, 1994, Dist. Eagle Scout, 2002. Fellow Am. Coll. Healthcare Execs. (Iowa bd. regents 1982-84, 88-95, interim gov. Dist. 5 1999-2000); mem. Iowa Hosp. Assn. (dir. 1982-85). Lodges: Rotary (Cedar Rapids pres. 1986-87). Republican. Methodist. Office: Iowa Health Sys 1200 Pleasant St Des Moines IA 50309-1406

**WALLACE, TERESA LYNN,** art educator; b. Springfield, Mo., Dec. 8, 1962; d. Joe Mack and Lanora Nadine Sanders; m. Richard Everett Wallace, June 6, 1986; children: Hannah Kate, Allison Rae. BA in Elem Edn., Coll. Ozarks, 1986; art cert., Southwest Mo. State U., 2002. Art tchr. Couch Sch., Myrtle, Mo., 1999—2001, Alton Elem. Sch., Alton, Mo., 2002—. V.p. Parent Tchr. Orgn., Alton, 1999; co-creator art scholarships, Alton, 2001. Prin. works

include (paintings) The Wailing Wall, Harlin Mus., 1997—, French City Sidewalks, 2001, Mexico, 2003, Mexico Moment, 2004, Open Air Market, Art Show, 1998—, Visions of China, West Plains, Mo., 2000—. Leader PTO, Youth Cmty. Betterment, Alton, 1999. Outstanding Achievement honoree, Internat. Reading Assn., 2005. Baptist. Avocations: flute, reading.

**WALLACE, THOMAS C.,** editor, publishing executive; b. Vienna, Dec. 13, 1933; came to U.S., 1938; s. Don and Julia (Baer) W.; m. Lois Kahn, July 19, 1962 (div. May 2000); 1 son, George Baer; m. Barbara Shortt, Nov. 12, 2000. Grad., Peddie Sch., 1951; BA, Yale U., 1955, MA in History, 1957. Editor G.P. Putnam Sons, N.Y.C., 1959-63; with Holt, Rinehart & Winston, N.Y.C., 1963-81, editor-in-chief gen. books divsn., 1968-81; v.p., sr. editor Simon and Schuster, N.Y.C., 1981; editor W.W. Norton, N.Y.C., 1982-87; v.p. Wallace Lit. Agy., N.Y.C., 1987-98; pres. T. C. Wallace, Ltd., N.Y.C., 1998—. Bd. dirs. Roger Klein Found. Mem. PEN, Yale Club, Century Assn. (N.Y.C.). Home: c/o Century Club 7 W 43d St New York NY 10036 Office: Ste 2005 215 Park Ave S New York NY 10003 Office Phone: 212-254-0300. Personal E-mail: tcwallace2@aol.com.

**WALLACE, THOMAS J.,** editorial director; married; 3 children. Grad. Harvard U., 1972. Various editl. positions NY Times and Newsday; editor-in-chief Conde Nast Traveler, NYC, 1990—2005; editl. dir. Conde Nast Pubs. Inc., NYC, 2005—. Office: Conde Nast Pubs 4 Times Sq 17th Fl New York NY 10036-6561

**WALLACE, TIMOTHY R.,** manufacturing executive; b. 1954; Grad., So. Meth. U., 1975. Joined Trinity Industries, 1975, v.p., 1984, sr. v.p., 1989, COO railcars and containers segment, chmn., pres., CEO, 1996—. Bd. dirs. VIAD Corp., Phoenix. Office: Trinity Industries 2525 Stemmon Freeway Dallas TX 75207

**WALLACE, WALTER C.,** lawyer, government official; b. NYC, Mar. 25, 1924; m. Frances Helm, Apr. 5, 1963; 1 dau. Laura. BA magna cum laude, St. John's U., Hillsdale, N.Y., 1948; LLB with distinction, Cornell U., 1951. Bar: N.Y. 1952, Calif. 1954, D.C. 1975, U.S. Dist. Ct. (no. dist.) Calif. 1954, U.S. Ct. Appeals (9th cir.) 1954, D.C. 1975, U.S. Dist. Ct. D.C. 1975, U.S. Ct. Appeals (D.C. cir.) 1975. Assoc. Cahill, Gordan & Reindel, N.Y.C., 1951-54; exec. asst. Sec. of Labor, Washington, 1955-60, asst. sec. of labor for manpower and employment, 1960-61; gen. counsel Presdl. R.R. Commn., Washington, 1961; v.p. labor rels. Hudson Pulp & Paper Corp., N.Y.C., 1963-73; pres. Bituminous Coal Operators Assoc., Washington, 1974-75; ptnr. Ables & Wallace, Washington, 1977-80; prin. Law Offices Walter C. Wallace, N.Y.C., 1981-82; mem. Nat. Mediation Bd., Washington, 1982—chmn., 1983, 85, 88. U.S. del. Internat. Labor Orgn. Conf. on Labor Rels. in Timber Industry, Geneva, 1958; asst. to cabinet com. on oil imports chaired by John Foster Dulles, 1958. Mem. bd. editors Cornell Law Quar., 1950-51. Bd. dirs. Nat. Safety Coun., Washington, 1974-75; asst. to chmn. United Givers Fund, Washington, 1956, mem. admission and allocations com., 1957-58. Staff sgt. U.S. Army, 1943-45, ETO. Decorated Bronze Star; recipient Presdl. commendation Pres. Eisenhower, Washington, 1961, Disting. Svc. award United Givers Fund, 1956, Disting. Svc. award Nat. Mediation Bd., 1990. Mem. Calif. Bar Assn., N.Y. State Bar Assn., D.C. Bar Assn., Order of Coif. Republican. Roman Catholic. Home: 55 Central Park W New York NY 10023-6003

**WALLACE, WILLIAM, III,** engineering executive; b. Bklyn., June 7, 1926; s. William and Ruth (Fitch) W.; m. Dorothy Ann Reimann, Aug. 2, 1969 (dec.); 1 child, Andrew William. B.E.E., Union Coll., 1947. Registered prof. engr., 22 states. Test engr. Gen. Electric Co., Schenectady, 1947; engr. Ebasco Services Inc., N.Y.C., 1948-67, chief elec. engr., 1967-70, mgr. projects, 1970-73, v.p. Atlanta office Norcross, Ga., 1973-76, exec. v.p. N.Y.C., 1976-80, dir., pres., chief exec. officer, 1980-82, chmn., chief exec. officer, 1982-86, also bd. dirs.; cons., 1986—. Bd. dirs. McNab Corp. Chmn. bd. advisors Sch. engring., N.C. State U., 1986-89; mem. adv. bd. trustees Union Coll., 1997-2000; trustee Poly. Prep. Country Day Sch., 1990-2002; trustee Saddle River Day Sch.; deacon West Side Presbyn. Ch., Ridgewood, N.J., 1988-90, 96-2000, elder, 1990-93, trustee, 2000-2003. Mem. IEEE (sr.), NSPE, N.J. State Soc. Profl. Engrs., World Rehab. Fund (bd. dirs. 1986-96), N.Y.C. C. of C. and Industry (bd. dirs. 1980-88), Delta Upsilon (vice chmn. Ednl. Found. 1986-95). Republican. Home and Office: 84 Buckhaven Hl Upper Saddle River NJ 07458

**WALLACE, WILLIAM EDWARD,** thoracic surgeon; BS, Stephen F. Austin State U., 1972; MS, Tex. Tech. U., Lubbock, 1974; MD, U. North Tex. Health Sci. Ctr., Forth Worth, 1980. Diplomate Nat. Bd. Med. Examiners, in surgery and surg. critical care Am. Bd. Surgery, Am. Bd. Thoracic Surgery. Intern Tulsa Regional Med. Ctr., 1980—81; resident in gen. surgery Dallas-Fort Worth Med. Ctr., Grand Priarie, Tex., 1981—85; fellow in cardiothoracic-vascular surgery Tex. Heart Inst., Houston, 1985—86, 1989—90; pvt. practice Forth Worth, 1986—. Physician, bd. dirs. Osteo. Med. Ctr. Tex., Fort Worth, 2000—03, chief of staff, 1993—2000; clin. asst. prof. U. North Tex. Health Sci. Ctr., Fort Worth, 1987—; adj. prof. Cardiovasc. Rsch. Inst., 2001—. Contbr. articles to sci. jours. Fellow: Am. Osteo. Assn., Am. Coll. Health Sci., Am. Coll. Chest Physicians; mem.: Soc. Critical Care Medicine, Tex. Med. Found., Tex. Med. Assn. Office: 4315 Booth Callaway Rd Ste 311 North Richland Hills TX 76180 Business E-Mail: wwallace@med-edge.com. E-mail: william.wallace@heartplace.com.

**WALLACE DE CORNWALL, CLINTON H.,** media consultant; b. Montego Bay, Jamaica; s. E. Herbert Wallace and Elbemire Violette Forbes; m. Marina Olga-Yvonne Wallace De Cornwall. Dec. 1995. BS in Comm., NYU, 1995; MA in Media, Canterbury U., U.K., 2002. Notary pub. Calif., cert. French Lit. U. De Paris. Media rels. asst. Warlock Records, N.Y.C., 1992—93; news rmt. asst. NBC News, 1993—94; media cons. Antoine Breton and Assocs., Paris, 1994—; co-founder Photoglobo, Strausbourg, France, 1999—2003; staff photographer Globe Photos Inc., N.Y.C., 1999—2003; corr. Euroimagen, Madrid, 2002—03; media cons. D'ouzio and Assocs., Beverly Hills, Calif., 2000—03, Fusion Publicity, West Hollywood, 2001—, Verbana and Assocs., Burbank, 2002—, Amplified Pub. Relats., 2003—04. Founder Photmundo Internat., Granada, Spain, 1993. Editor: Talawah Jours., 1999, Brazil Expire, 2002; photographer Latin Style, 2001. Fellow: Hon. Order Ky. Cols.; mem.: Am. Fedn. Televison and Radio Artists, Mus. of Making Music. Avocations: photography, travel, archaeology, French literature, writing. Office Phone: 310-585-4637.

**WALLACE DOUGLAS, JEAN,** conservationist; b. Des Moines, Iowa, June 30, 1920; d. Henry A. and Ilo Wallace; m. Wallace Leslie Douglas, Oct. 12, 1946; children: David, Joan, Ann. BA, Connecticut Coll., 1943. Pres. Wallace Genetic Found., Washington, D.C., 1965—. Past bd. dirs. America The Beautiful, Am. Bird Conservancy, Cornell Lab. of Ornithology, The Land Inst., Wallace House Birthplace, The Accokeek Found., Am. Farmland Trust, Concern, Henry A. Wallace Inst. for Alternative Agr. Office: Wallace Genetic Found Ste 221 4910 Massachusetts Ave NW Washington DC 20016-4358

**WALLACH, ALAN,** art historian, educator; b. Bklyn., June 8, 1942; s. Israel and Vivian (Esner) W.; m. Phyllis Rosenzweig, Jan. 3, 1988. BA, Columbia U., 1963, MA, 1965, PhD, 1973. Assoc. prof. Kean Coll., Union, NJ, 1974-89; Ralph H. Wark prof. art and art history, prof. Am. studies Coll. William and Mary, Williamsburg, Va., 1989—. Vis. prof. UCLA, 1982-83, Stanford (Calif.) U., 1987, CUNY, 1988, U. Mich., 1993, U. Del., 2006; co-curator Nat. Mus. Am. Art, Washington, 1991-94. Author: (with William Truettner) Thomas Cole: Landscape into History, 1994; Exhibiting Contradiction: Essays on the Art Museum in the United States, 1998; mem. editl. bd. Am. Quar., 2000-03; contbr. articles to profl. jours. Sr. Postdoctorate Rsch. award Smithsonian Inst., 1985-86. Mem. Am. Studies Assn., Coll. Art Assn. (bd. dirs. 1996-2000), Assn. Art Historians (pres. 2009 Belmont Rd NW Washington DC 20009-5449 Office: Coll William and Mary Dept Art and Art History Williamsburg VA 23187-8795 Office Phone: 757-221-2530. Business E-Mail: axwall@wm.edu.

**WALLACH, ANNE JACKSON See JACKSON, ANNE**

**WALLACH, ELI,** actor; b. Bklyn., Dec. 7, 1915; s. Abraham and Bertha (Schorr) W.; m. Anne Jackson, Mar. 5, 1948; children: Peter Douglas, Roberta Lee, Katherine Beatrice. AB, U. Tex., 1936; MS in Edn, CCNY, 1938; student, Neighborhood Playhouse Sch. of Theatre, 1940; doctorate (hon.), Emerson Coll., Boston, Sch. Visual Arts, 1991. Corp. member, dir. Neighborhood Playhouse Sch. Theatre. Actor, 1945—; Broadway plays include Antony and Cleopatra, 1948, Mr. Roberts, 1949-50, Rose Tatoo, 1950-52, Camino Real, 1953, Mademoiselle Colombe, 1953, Teahouse of the August Moon, 1954-55, London prodn., 1954, Major Barbara, 1956, Rhinoceros, 1961, Luv, 1964, Promenade All, 1972, Twice Around the Park, 1983, Opera Comique, Kennedy Ctr. Performing Arts, 1987, The Flowering Peach, Fla., 1987, Broadway, 1994, Cafe Crown, 1989; appeared off-Broadway prodn. Typists and the Tiger, 1962-63, London prodn., 1964, Saturday, Sunday, Monday, 1974, (with wife and 2 daus.) Diary of Anne Frank, 1977-78, Visiting Mr. Green, 1997; off-Broadway in Tennessee Williams Remembered, 1999; on tour Down the Garden Paths, 1998-99; appeared in: nat. tour co. Waltz of the Toreadors, 1973-74; appeared in TV film Executioner's Song, 1982, Murder By Reason of Insanity, 1985, Monday Night Mayhem, 2000, TV series Batman, 1966, Kojak, 1973, Highway to Heaven, 1984, Our Family Honor, 1985, L.A. Law, 1986, Law & Order, 1990, The Education of Max Bickford, 2001-02, TV miniseries Christopher Columbus, 1985, The Education of Max Bickford, 2002; motion pictures include Baby Doll, 1955, The Misfits, 1960, The Victors, 1962, Lord Jim, 1964, How To Steal a Million, The Good, the Bad and the Ugly, 1973, Crazy Joe, 1973, Movie, Movie, 1976, Sam's Son, 1985, Tough Guys, 1986, Rocket to the Moon,1986, Nuts, 1987, The Impossible Spy, 1987, Godfather III, 1990, The Two Jakes, 1990, Article 99, Mistress, 1991, Night and the City, 1991, Honey, Sweet Love, 1993, Two Much, 1995, The Associate, 1996, Keeping the Faith, 2000, (TV movie) Monday Night Mayhem, 2002, Mystic River, 2003; author: The Good, The Bad, and Me: In My Anecdotage, 2005. Served to capt. Med. Adminstrn. Corps AUS, World War II. Recipient Donaldson, Theatre World, Variety, Antoinette Perry, Drama League awards, Brit. Film Acad. award, 1956, Disting. Alumnus award U. Tex., 1989. Original mem. Actors Studio. Office: Paradigm Talent Agency 500 5th Ave Fl 37 New York NY 10110-3799

**WALLACH, ERIC JEAN,** lawyer; b. NYC, June 11, 1947; s. Milton Harold and Jacqueline (Goldschmidt) W.; m. Miriam Grunberger, Mar. 21, 1976; children: Katherine, Emily, Peter. BA, Harvard U., 1968, JD, 1972. Bar: N.Y. 1973, U.S. Dist. Ct. (so. and ea. dists.) N.Y. 1973, U.S. Dist. Ct. (no. dist.) N.Y. 1989, U.S. Ct. Appeals (2nd cir.) 1973, (3d cir.) 1996, U.S. Tax Ct. 1976. Assoc. Webster & Sheffield, N.Y.C., 1972-77, Rosenman & Colin, N.Y.C., 1977-80, ptnr., 1981-96, mem. mgmt. com., 1993-96, chmn. employment practice group, 1985-96; ptnr., chmn. employment practice group Kasowitz, Benson, Torres & Friedman LLP, N.Y.C., 1996—. Arbitrator Internat. Ct. Arbitration, Am. Arbitration Assn., others; presenter, chmn. CLE programs, Practising Law Inst., Cambridge Inst. Mem. editl. bd. You and the Law, 1992-96; contbr. articles to profl. jours. Sec.-treas. Art Dealers Assn. Am., Inc., N.Y.C., 1985-96; trustee C.G. Jung Found. for Analytical Psychology; trustee Am. Jewish World Svc., Inc., N.Y.C., 1989-97, chmn., 1995-97; dir. N.Y. Jr. Tennis League. Named to NY Super Lawyers. Mem. Harvard Club N.Y.C. (admissions com. 1992-94), Sunningdale Country Club, Poughkeepsie Tennis Club. Democrat. Avocations: sports, travel, reading. Home: 940 Park Ave New York NY 10028 also: 16 Buttonwood Ln Rhinebeck NY 12572-3510 Office: Kasowitz Benson Torres & Friedman LLP 1633 Broadway New York NY 10019 Office Phone: 212-506-1750. Business E-Mail: ewallach@kasowitz.com.

**WALLACH, HOWARD FREDERIC,** psychiatrist; b. Chgo., Sept. 4, 1923; s. Leo and Mildred (Ebert) W.; m. Laurie Rochelle Gettleman, Sept. 15, 1945 (div. July 1968); children: Joan, John, Richard; m. Gloria Bunny Jackman, July 14, 1968; children: Rand, Steve, Beth. MD, U. Ill., Chgo., 1946; M.Social Psychiatry, UCLA, 1969. Diplomate Am. Bd. Psychiatry and Neurology. Intern Cook County Hosp., Chgo., 1946—47, resident internal medicine, 1947—49; pres Mount Sinai Hosp. Med. Rsch. Found., 1952—64; asst. clin. prof. psychiatry UCLA, 1968—80, assoc. clin. prof., 1980—; chief allied mental health Brentwood VA Hosp., L.A., 1970—72; chief psychiatry Sepulveda VA Hosp., L.A., 1972—74; pvt. practice L.A. Bd. govs. Cedars-Sinai Med. Ctr., L.A., 1985—, mem. exec. com., 2000—; cons. VA Med. Ctr., L.A., 1982-90; developer maj. high rise apts., Chgo., 1951-64. Contbr. articles to profl. jours. Sec. Am. Psychiat. Found., Washington, 1990-99; bd. dirs. Nat. Mus. Health and Medicine, Washington, 1989-99; v.p. Jewish Family Svc. of L.A., 1997-98; bd. dirs., pres. Young Men's Jewish Charities, Chgo., 1951-62; mem. Cook County Blue Ribbon Commn., 1959-63. 1st lt. U.S. Army, 1943-46. Recipient Bronze award Boys Clubs of Am., 1962, Pres.'s Spl. Achievement award So. Calif. Psychiat. Soc., 1991. Fellow Am. Coll. Psychoanalysts, Am. Psychiat. Assn. (exec. com. 1982-88), Am. Acad. Psychoanalysis; mem. Calif. Psychiat. Assn. (pres. 1986-88), So. Calif. Psychiat. Soc. (pres. 1979-80, mem. coun. 1975-83), Alpha Omega Alpha. Avocations: photography, computers, golf, walking, presidential manuscript collecting. Office: 2080 Century Pk E Ste 1809 Los Angeles CA 90067-2001 Office Phone: 310-553-2833. Personal E-Mail: hfwallach@gmail.com.

**WALLACH, IRA DAVID,** lawyer, corporate financial executive; b. N.Y.C., June 3, 1909; s. Joseph and Della (Kahn) W.; m. Miriam Gottesman, Dec. 25, 1938. BA, Columbia U., 1929, JD, 1931, LLD (hon.), 1983, U. Maine, 1983. Bar: N.Y. 1932. Practiced in N.Y.C. 1932-45; exec. v.p. Gottesman & Co., Inc. (name changed to Central Nat.-Gottesman Inc. 1984), N.Y.C., 1952-56, pres., CEO, 1956-74, chmn., CEO, 1974-79, chmn., 1979-2001, sr. vice chmn., 2001—, also bd. dirs. Exec. v.p. Ctrl. Nat. Corp., N.Y.C., 1952-56, pres., CEO, 1956-74, chmn., CEO, 1974-79, chmn., 1979—; exec. v.p. Eastern Corp., Bangor, Maine, 1951-52; pres. Sejak Corp., N.Y.C., dir., exec. v.p. Cenro Corp., N.Y.C. Pres. D.S. and R.H. Gottesman Found., 1956—, bd. dirs. 1941—; chmn., dir. Miriam and Ira D. Wallach Found., 1956—; co-founder, chmn. emeritus East West Inst., 1981—; bd. dirs. Internat. Peace Acad., People for the Am. Way Found. Lt. USNR, 1943-46. Mem. Am. Bar Assn., Assn. of Bar of City of N.Y., N.Y. Co. Lawyers Assn. Home: 5 Sherbrooke Rd Scarsdale NY 10583-4429 Office: 3 Manhattanville Rd Purchase NY 10577-2116

**WALLACH, KENNETH L.,** paper company executive; b. NYC, 1946; m. Susan Wallach. BA, Harvard Coll., 1968, JD, 1972. Chmn., pres., CEO Ctrl. Nat.-Gottesman Inc., Purchase, NY, 1998—. Mem. regional adv. bd, J.P. Morgan Chase. Trustee Am. Mus. Natural History; dir. 92d St. Y, Syracuse Pulp and Paper Found., Nat. Book Found. Office: Ctrl Nat-Gottesman Inc 3 Manhattanville Rd Purchase NY 10577*

**WALLACH, LESLIE ROTHAUS,** architect; b. Pitts., Feb. 4, 1944; s. Albert and Sara F. (Rothaus) W.; m. Susan Rose Berger, June 15, 1969; 1 child, Aaron. BS in Mining Engring., U. Ariz., 1967, BArch, 1974. Registered arch., Ariz.; registered contractor, Ariz. Prin. Line and Space LLC, Tucson, 1978—. Mem. awards jury Sunset mag., 1997, Ariz. Homes of Yr., 1997, L.A. AIA; keynote spkr. various confs. Rep. projects include Ariz. Sonora Desert Mus. Restaurant Complex, Tucson, Elgin Elem. Sch., Ariz., Hillel Student Ctr. U. Ariz., Tucson, Boyce Thompson Southwestern Arboretum Vis. Ctr., Superior, Ariz., Ban Perdo Riparian Ctr., Sierra Vista, Ariz., Nat. Hist. Trails Ctr., Casper, Wyo., 2002, Vis. Ctr. and Arboretum, Flagstaff, Ariz., 2001, Regional Libr., Phoenix, 2002, Poetry Ctr. for U. Ariz., 2003, New Regional Libr. U. Ariz., Phoenix, 2006; contbr. Sunset Mag., Architecture Mag. and Fine Homebuilding; pub.: Space and Society (Italy), Hinge (Hong Kong), Wallpaper (London); exhibited at U. Ariz., AIA Nat. Conv., Washington, The Dutch Jour., Objekt, 2003; interview and profile pub. in Architecture and Urbanism, 2006. Bd. dirs Tucson Regional Plan, Inc.; pres. Civitas Sonoran (The Environ. Design Coun. of the U. of Ariz. Coll. of Arch.). Recipient Roy P. Drachman Design award, 1982, 85, 93, 2001, Electric League Ariz. Design award, 1987, 88, Gov. Solar Energy award, 1989, Desert Living awards citation, 1991, Ariz. Architect's medal, 1989, Disting. Alumni award U. Ariz., 1998, also 45 additional design awards, including 4 received in 1995, winner

$25,000 prize, nat. Endowment of the Arts, 2002, Coll. of Architecture Alumni of Yr., U. Az., 2001. Fellow AIA (Ariz. Honor award 1989, 92, 96, AIA/ACSA Nat. Design award 1991, Western Mountain region Design award 1992, 96, CA AIA/Phoenix Homes and Gardens Home of the Yr. Honor award 1992, 96, Western Region Silver medal 1996, design award, 2004); mem. SAC AIA (past pres., Design award 1985, 88, 90), Western Mountain Region AIA (named Firm of Yr. 1999), Tex. AIA (jury mem. design awards, 2005—). Achievements include being selected as the architect to design the 300 acre Desert Learning Center Campus and new visitor center in Red Rock Canyon, Nevada. Office: Line and Space 627 E Speedway Blvd Tucson AZ 85705-7433 Office Phone: 520-623-1313. E-mail: studio627@lineandspace.com.

**WALLACH, MAGDALENA FALKENBERG (CARLA WALLACH)**, writer; b. Brussels; d. Carl Albert and Renee Antoinette (Meunier) Falkenberg; m. Philip Charles Wallach, Mar. 5, 1950. Student, Columbia U., Hunter Coll., New Sch. for Social Rsch. Ptnr. Williams-Falkenberg Advt. Assocs., Inc., N.Y.C., 1951-55. Author: Reluctant Weekend Gardener, 1971, Interior Decorating with Plants, 1976, Gardening in the City, 1976, Garden in a Teacup, 1978; contbr. articles to N.Y. Times, Glamour, Working Woman, Greenwich Time, Stamford Adv. others. Former bd. dirs. ARC, NYC; active Bruce Mus., 1987-2001, chmn. spl. events 75th anniversary gala, chmn. Renaissance Ball, bd. dirs., also other fundraising activities; founder Greenwich Adult Day Ctr., bd. dirs., v.p., chair annual fund raiser. Mem. Nat. League Am. PEN Women (pres. Greenwich br. 1987-92, Owl award 1996), Authors Guild, Garden Writers Assn., English-Speaking Union (past bd. dirs. Greenwich br.), Alliance Francaise, Nat. Inst. Social Scis. Roman Catholic. Avocations: gardening, reading, travel, music, theater. Home: 126 W Lyon Farm Dr Greenwich CT 06831-4352.

**WALLACH, MARK IRWIN**, lawyer; b. May 19, 1949; s. Ivan A. and Janice (Grossman) W.; m. Karla L. Wallach, 1996; children: Kerry Melissa, Philip Alexander; stepchildren: Daniel Kanter, Rachel Kanter, Adam Kanter. BA magna cum laude, Wesleyan U., 1971; JD cum laude, Harvard U., 1974. Bar: Ohio 1974, U.S. Dist. Ct. (no. dist.) Ohio, 1974, U.S. Ct. Appeals (6th cir.) 1975, U.S. Supreme Ct. 1985. Law clk. U.S. Dist. Ct., Cleve., 1974-75; assoc. Baker & Hostetler, Cleve., 1975-79; chief trial counsel City of Cleve., 1979-81; assoc. Calfee, Halter & Griswold, Cleve., 1981-82, ptnr., 1982—, co-chmn. litigation dept., 2004—. Mem. fed. ct. adv. com. U.S. Dist. Ct. (no. dist.) Ohio, 1991-95; chmn. bd. trustees Ohio Group Against Smoking Pollution, 1986-90; trustee Cleve. chpt. Am. Jewish Com., 1986—, sec. 1989-91, v.p., 1991-95, pres., 1995-97; bd. trustees Citizens League of Greater Cleve., 1978-79, 87-92. Author: Christopher Morley, 1976. Pres. Wesleyan Alumni Club, Cleve., 1983-87, 92-2006; trustee Lyric Opera, Cleve., 1995-2006, pres., 1996-98, Ratner Schs., 1994-96; pres. Performing Arts Together, 1997-2001; trustee The Sculpture Ctr. 2001—, Cleve., 2006—, sec., 2006—, pres., 2001—; trustee Bellefaire Jewish Children's Bur., 2001-06. Mem. ABA, Ohio Bar Assn., Fed. Bar Assn., Cuyahoga County Law Dirs. Assn., The Cleve. Racquet Club, Greater Cleve. Bar Assn., The Club at Soc. Ctr. Avocations: reading, bicycling, space exploration, politics. Home: 2758 Claythorne Rd Shaker Heights OH 44122-1938 Office: Calfee Halter & Griswold 1400 McDonald Investment Ctr 800 Superior Ave E Ste 1800 Cleveland OH 44114-2688 Office Phone: 216-622-8344. Business E-Mail: mwallach@calfee.com.

**WALLACH, MORTON L.**, scientist; s. Herman and Helen Wallach; children: Bonalynn, Richard, Hillary. BS in Chemistry, Wayne State U., 1951—55, PhD in Phys. Chemistry, 1955—59. Soi. advisor & tech. operation mgr. Polysar, Inc., Leominster, Mass., 1987—90; pres./ceo PEL Associates, Groton, Conn., 1975—. Expert Teltech Network of Experts, Mpls., 1990—; v.p. Ocean Tech. Found., 2000—; initial affiliate U. of Conn., Groton, Conn., United States, 2001—. Author (25 pubs. & five books): (science & technology) PEL Ann. Update: Recent Progress in Polymer/Plastics Tech. Recipient Gold Innovation prize Sensors, CQIA, 2004, Silver Innovation prize for smart coating, Ronal Reagan award for leadership in bus. and entrepreneurship; fellow Fulbright, State Dept., USA, 1960. Mem.: Licensing Executives Soc., Conn. Tech. Coun., Soc. of Plastics Engineers, Am. Chem. Soc. Achievements include invention of novel sensors, coatings, plastics, polymer films; first to Polymer Films, Polymer Blends; patents pending for Novel Sensors; New Smart Coatings; development of light scattering theory and applications to polymers and colloids; patents for novel stents for angioplasty, port security. Avocations: swimming, travel. Home: 23 Wildwood Rd Groton CT 06340 Office: PEL Associates 1084 Shennecossett Rd Groton CT 06340 Office Phone: 860-448-6522. E-mail: mlwallach@pelassociates.com.

**WALLACH, NOLAN R.**, mathematician, consultant; b. Bklyn., N.Y., Aug. 3, 1940; s. Morris and Pauline Wallach; m. Barbara Hawkins, Apr. 25, 1965; children: Dana, Pamela. BS, U. Maryland, 1962; MA, Wash. U., St. Louis, Mo., 1963, PhD, 1966. Instr. U. of Calif., Berkeley, 1966—69; asst. prof. math. Rutgers U., New Brunswick, NJ, 1969—70, assoc. prof. math., 1970—72, prof. math., 1972—86, Hermann Weyl prof. math., 1986—89; prof. math. U. Calif.-San Diego, La Jolla, 1989—. Cons. Ctr. for Comm. Rsch., La Jolla, 1995—; mem. Mat. Math. Com., 1985—92. Author: (book) Real Reductive Groups I, II, 1988, Continuous Cohomology, 2d edit., 1999; editor: Mathematics: Theory and Applications, 2001—; co-editor: Annals of Math., 1997—2003. Recipient Sloan fellowship, Alfred Sloan Found., 1972—74, Linback award for rsch. excellence, 1977. Fellow: Am. Acad. Arts and Scis.; mem.: Am. Math. Soc. (mem. editl. com. 1991—93, editor bull. 1995—98, mem. coun. 1999—2002). Office: U Calif San Diego Dept Math La Jolla CA 92093 Business E-Mail: nwallach@ucsd.edu.

**WALLACH, PATRICIA**, councilman, retired mayor; b. Chgo. m. Ed Wallach; 3 children. Grad., Pasadena City Coll. Mem. city coun. City of El Monte, Calif. 1990-92, mayor, 1992-99, elected mem. of city coun., 2002. Ret. tchr.'s aide Mountain View Sch. Dist. Past trustee El Monte Union High Sch. Dist., L.A. County High Sch. for the Arts; amb. of goodwill Zamora, Michoacan, Mex., Marcq-en-Baroeul, France, Yung Kang, Hsiang, Republic of China, Minhang, Peoples Republic of China; bd. dirs. Cmty. Redevel. Agy., El Monte Cmty. Access TV Corp.; mem. PTA, Little League Assns.; del. Foothill Transit. Mem. League of Calif. Cities, San Gabriel Valley Coun. of Govts., Independent Cities Assn., U.S./Mex. Sister Cities Assn., Sister Cities Internat., Women of the Moose, El Monte Women's Club. Office Phone: 626-580-2001.

**WALLACH, STEVEN ERNST**, lawyer, pilot; b. N.Y.C., Mar. 21, 1944; s. Eduard Herbert Wallach and Karin (Wassermann) Grunebaum; m. Stefany Gay Rosehill (div. Oct. 1990); children: Shelby Karin, Shawna Beth; m. Geri Joan Grieco, Nov. 21, 1992. BS, USAF Acad., 1965; MS summa cum laude, U. So. Calif., 1971; JD magna cum laude, U., 1986. Bar: Fla. 1986, D.C. 1988, U.S. Dist. Ct. (so. dist.) Fla. 1987, U.S. Dist. Ct. (mid. dist.) Fla. 1989, U.S. Dist. Ct. Ariz. 1989; cert. airline transport pilot, 1969; bd. cert. aviation law, 1998. Systems analyst Hughes Aircraft Co., L.A., 1971-72; airline capt. Eastern Air Lines, Miami, 1972-91; atty. Barwick, Dillian & Lambert P.A., Miami Shores, Fla., 1987-96; atty., ptnr. Thornton Davis & Murray, P.A., Miami, 1996-98. Aviation mgmt. cons. PRC Speas, Lake Success, N.Y., 1977-83, TRAMCO, Cambridge, Mass., 1972-77, A.V. lawyer, 1997, Steven Wallach Assoc., 1998—. Trustee Karin Grunebaum Cancer Found., Cambridge, 1979—; chmn. Karin Grunebaum Cancer Rsch. Found., Cambridge, 2004—. Capt. USAF, 1965—70. Decorated DFC, 5 air medals. Avocation: flying. Home: 2600 S Ocean Blvd Apt 21-E Boca Raton FL 33432

**WALLACK, JOEL JEFFREY**, psychiatrist; b. Newark, June 8, 1946; BA in Psychology, U. Wis., 1968; MD, U. Medicine of N.J., 1974. Diplomate Am. Bd. Psychiatry and Neurology, Nat. Bd. Med. Examiners. Intern in medicine St. Vincent's Hosp., N.Y.C., 1974-75; resident in psychiatry St. Luke's Hosp., N.Y.C., 1975-78; fellow in consultation psychiatry Montefiore Hosp. and Med. Ctr., Bronx, N.Y., 1978-79; sr. fellow in consultation psychiatry Mt. Sinai Med. Ctr., N.Y.C., 1979-80; faculty dept. psychiatry, 1980-82; dir. consultation psychiatry Beth Israel Med. Ctr., N.Y.C., 1982-92; dep. dir. dept. psychiatry Bellevue Hosp. NYU, N.Y.C., 1992—96; chmn. dept. psychiatry

Cabrini Med. Ctr., N.Y.C., 1996—. Editor: AIDS Update, 1992; contbr. articles to profl. jours. and books. Fellow Am. Psychiat. Assn. (disting.), Acad. Psychomatic Medicine, Am. Coll. Psychiatrists; mem. Assn. Acad. Psychiatry, Soc. Liaison Psychiatry (sec., pres. 1994), Am. Psychosomatic Soc. Office: Cabrini Med Ctr 227 E 19th St New York NY 10003

**WALLACK, RINA EVELYN**, lawyer; b. Pitts.; d. Erwin Norman and Gloria A. (Schacher). AD in Nursing, Delta Coll., 1973; BS cum laude in Psychology, Eastern Mich. U., 1980; JD cum laude, Wayne State U., 1983. Registered nurse Mich.; bar: Calif. 1983. Psychiat. head nurse Ypsilanti (Mich.) State Hosp., 1973-77, instr., nursing educator, 1977-80; teaching asst. contracts Wayne State U., Detroit, 1981-83; legal asst. Wayne County Prosecutor's Office, 1982-83; atty. NLRB, L.A., 1983-86, dir. employee rels. legal svcs. Paramount Pictures Corp., L.A., 1986-89, v.p., 1989-98, v.p., sr. counsel, 1998-2002, sr. v.p., 2002-; Contbr. articles to profl. jours. Instr. ARC, Mich., 1978-80. Recipient Am. Jurisprudence Book award, 1983. Mem. ABA, L.A. County Bar Assn., Am. Trial Lawyers Assn., Mich. Bar Assn., Calif. Bar Assn., Order of Coif. Avocations: shooting, movies, dancing, reading, photography.

**WALLACK, STANLEY S.**, healthcare administrator; b. Sept. 6, 1941; BA, Antioch Coll., 1964; PhD in Econs., Washington U., St. Louis, 1969. Mem. faculty U. Ill., Champaign; dep. asst. dir. Congl. Budget Office for Health Income Assistance, Washington, 1971-75; dir. divsn. health resources U.S. Office Asst. Sec. for Planning and Evaluation, HEW, 1971-75; mem. faculty, exec. dir. Schneider Inst. for Health Policy, Brandeis U., Waltham, Mass.; chmn. bd. dirs., CEO LifePlans, Inc., 1993-97. Developer Social Health Maintenca Orgn.; prin. investigator Health Policy Rsch. Consirtium/HCFA; dir. Pew Doctoral Program; co-dir. Kaiser Found. Ctr. for State Svcs.; co-prin. investigator NIDA Ctr. for Drug Abuse Svcs. Rsch. Contbr. articles to profl. publs. Office: PO Box 549110 415 South St # MS035 Waltham MA 02454-9110 E-mail: wallack@brandeis.edu.

**WALLEM, PAUL SIGURD**, financial planner; b. Ottawa, Ill., Mar. 14, 1934; s. Sigurd and Bertha Wallem; m. Joan B. Wallem, Aug. 12, 1956; children: Jeffery, Linda, Stephen. BS, U. Ill., 1956. CFP. Terr. and sales mgr. Internat. Harvester Co., Chgo., 1958-66, export mgr., 1966-68; pres. Wallem Internat., Belvidere, Ill., 1969-86; owner Wallem Assocs., Rockford, Ill., 1986—. Chmn., bd. trustees Highland Hosp., Belvidere, 1977-79; founding dir. Vintage Wings and Wheels Mus., Poplar Grove, Ill., 1996—. 1st lt. U.S. Army, 1956-58. Republican. Methodist. Avocation: aviation. Office: Wallem Assocs 6068 Palo Verde Dr Rockford IL 61114

**WALLER, EDWARD MARTIN, JR.**, lawyer; b. Memphis, July 2, 1942; s. Edward Martin and Freda (Lazarov) W.; m. Laura Jayne Rhodes, June 18, 1982; children: Lauren, Jonathan, Melissa. BA, Columbia U., 1964; JD, U. Chgo., 1967. Bar: Fla. 1967. Assoc. Fowler, White, Boggs, Banker, P.A., Tampa, Fla., 1967-72, ptnr., 1972—. Mem.: ABA (banking and fin. transactions com. 1978—82, co-chmn. 1983—87, coun. 1990—92, litig. sect. standing com. professionalism chmn. 1995—97, budget officer 1999—2000), Bay Area Legal Svcs. (bd. dirs. 2003—, pres. 2006—), Hillsborough County Bar Assn., Fla. Bar Assn., Fla. Supreme Ct. Commn. on Professionalism. Democrat. Jewish. Office: Fowler White Boggs Banker PO Box 1438 Tampa FL 33601-1438 Office Phone: 813-222-1137.

**WALLER, EPHRAIM EVERETT**, retired association executive; b. Sioux City, Iowa, Aug. 10, 1928; s. Everett and Ruth Emma (Little) W.; m. Virginia Louise Harper, Oct. 3, 1959. BA, U. Iowa, 1951, MA, 1959; grad., Strategic Intelligence Sch., 1955, Army Security Agy. Sch., 1962, Nat. Cryptologic Sch., 1966, Commd. and Gen. Staff Coll., 1966; grad. with honors, State Dept. Fgn. Svc. Inst., 1967, Turkish Lang. Sch., 1968; grad., Indsl. Coll. Armed Forces, 1972; EdD with honors, U. S.D., 1981. Cert. fgn. area specialist, cryptologist. Commd. 2d lt. U.S. Army, 1951, advanced through grades to lt. col., 1967, ret. 1979; exec. dir. Midwest Agrl. Chem. Assn., Sioux City, Iowa, 1981—95; ind. cons. in field Sioux City, 1996—. Mem. sci. and regulatory oversight coun. Am. Crop Protection Assn., Washington, 1990-95; mem. interregional coord. coun. Joint Body U.S. Regional Agrl. Assns., Dawson, Ga., 1991-95 Contbr. articles to profl. jours. Mem. coms. 1st Congrl. Dist., Sioux City, 1937— Decorated Bronze Star, Cross of Gallantry with Silver Star, Legion of Merit with oak leaf cluster, Chinese and Vietnamese Honor medals, Meritorious Svc. medal with oak leaf cluster, Joint Svc. Commendation medal with oak leaf cluster, Army Commendation medal with oak leaf cluster, Army Gen. Staff badge, Vietnamese Combat Merit medal; Asia Found. scholar U. Iowa; recipient Outstanding Leadership in the Industry award Am. Crop Protection Assn., 1995, Leadership in Cmty. and Pub. Edn. award Am. Crop Protection Assn., 1993-94, Dedication and Svc. to Agrl. Industry award Ill. Fertilizer and Chem. Assn., 1987, Dean Roy Exceptional Svc. award Midwest Agrl. Chem. Assn., 1985, Industry Vision award Mid Am. Crop Protection Assn., 1995, Significant Svc. to Agr. and Agrl. Chem. Industry award So. Crop Protection Assn., 1981-95, Don Kenna Excellence in Coalition Bldg. and Pub. Rels. award Fertilizer and Ag-Chem. Affiliated Assns., 1994. Mem. Ret. Officers Assn., Siouxland C. of C. (com. 1981-95), Interprofit. Inst., Scottish Rite, Masons, Eastern Star, Phi Delta Kappa, Delta Sigma Rho Avocations: swimming, hiking, travel, stamp collecting/philately, writing. Home: 2847 Valley Dr Sioux City IA 51104-4071

**WALLER, EUNICE MCLEAN**, retired elementary school educator; b. Lillington, N.C., June 29, 1921; d. Absolom and Mary W. (Tucker) McLean; m. William DeHomer Waller, Aug. 9, 1958; m. Henry W. Ferguson, June 29, 1942 (div. June 1954). BS summa cum laude, Fayetteville (N.C.) State U., 1942; MS in Edn., U. Pa., 1952; 6th yr. Cert., U. Vt., 1965. Tchr. Harnett H.S., Dunn, NC, 1942—46, Shawtown H.S., Lillington, NC, 1946—56; demonstration tchr. Fayetteville State U., NC, 1956—58; tchr. 2d and U. Elem. Sch., Washington, 1958—60; tchr., asst. to prin. Fitch Elem. Sch., Washington, 1960—62; 7th grade tchr. Sarah Nance Elem. Sch., Columbia, SC, 1963—64; tchr. 8th grade Clark Lane Mid. Sch., Waterford, Conn., 1969—93; ret., 1993. Instr. dept. edn. Conn. Coll., New London, 1970—2001. Corporator Lawrence Meml. Hosp., New London; commr. ethics City Coun. of New London, Conn., 1990—2001; mayor, dep. mayor Dem. Town Com., New London, 1986—88; Civil Rights commr. City New London, 2006—; state convener State of Conn. Nat. Coun. Negro Women, Inc. sects., Washington, 2006—; v.p. NAACP, New London, 1990—2001; pres. Nat. Coun. Negro Women, New London, 1993—2000; trustee Mitchell Coll., New London, Waterford Country Sch., Conn. Named Woman of the Yr., Nat. Coun. Negro Women, 1993; recipient Lifetime Achievement award, W.E.B. DuBois, 1999, Cmty. Svc. award for outstanding achievement, Opportunities Industry Coun., 1983, Dr. E.E. Smith Highest Honors award, Fayetteville State U., 1942; grantee, NSF, 1965. Mem.: NEA (life; Conn. state div. 1984—88), Conn. Edn. Assn. (Pub. Relations Achievement award 1988), New London Lions (v.p. 1989—99). Democrat. Baptist. Avocations: civic volunteer, civil rights activitst.

**WALLER, GARY FREDRIC**, language educator, poet; b. Auckland, N.Z., Jan. 3, 1944; came to U.S., 1983; s. Fred and Joan Elsie (Smythe) W.; m. Jennifer Robyn Denham, July 2, 1966 (div. 1980); children: Michael, Andrew; m. Kathleen Ann McCormick, Nov. 12, 1988; one child, Philip. BA, U. Auckland, 1965, MA, 1966; PhD, Cambridge U., Eng., 1970. Donaldson Bye fellow Magdalene Coll., Cambridge, Eng., 1967-69; assoc. prof. English U. Auckland, New Zealand, 1969-72, Dalhousie U., N.S., Can., 1972-78; head, prof. English Wilfrid Laurier U., Waterloo, Can., 1978-83; head, prof. lit. and cultural studies Carnegie Mellon U., Pitts., 1983-92; dean arts and scis., prof. lit. and cultural studies U. Hartford, West Hartford, Conn., 1992-95; provost, v.p. acad. affairs, prof. lit. and cultural studies Purchase (N.Y.) Coll. SUNY, 1995—2004, prof. lit. and cultural studies Purchase (N.Y.) Coll., 2005—. Author: The Strong Necessity of Time, 1976, The Triumph of Death, 1977, Pamphilia to Amphilanthus, 1977, Dreaming America, 1979, Mary Sidney Countess of Pembroke, 1979, Sir Philip Sidney and the Interpretation of Renaissance Culture, 1984, Sixteenth Century Poetry, 1986, 2d edit., 1993, Reading Texts, 1986, Lexington Introduction to

Literature, 1987, Shakespeare's Comedies, 1991, Reading Mary Wroth, 1991, The Sidney Family Romance, 1993, Edmund Spenser: A Literary Life, 1994, Lady Mary Sidney's Antonie and a Discourse of Life and Death, 1996; (poems) Other Flights, Always, 1991, Impossible Futures Indelible Pasts, 1983 Office: Purchase Coll Acad Affairs Purchase NY 10577

**WALLER, GARY WILTON**, administration educator, minister; b. Ft. Worth, July 16, 1948; s. Robert Preston and Lillian Lee (Taylor) W.; m. Cindy Ann Dollar, Jan. 3, 1975; children: Stephanie, RyAnn. BS in Phys. Edn., Baylor U., 1970; MRE, Southwestern Bapt. Theol. Sem., Ft. Worth, 1972, PhD, 1979, U. North Tex., 1992. Ordained to ministry, Bapt. Ch., 1979. Min. music and youth North Cleburne Bapt. Ch., Cleburne, Tex., 1970-72; min. edn. Trinity Bapt. Ch., Ft. Worth, 1972-74, Gambrell Street Bapt. Ch., Ft. Worth, 1978-82; min. edn. and evangelism North Ft. Worth Bapt. Ch., 1974-78, 1st Bapt. Ch., Waco, Tex., 1982-84; prof. administrn. Southwestern Bapt. Theol. Sem., Ft. Worth, 1984—2006, dean distance learning, 1984—2006; v.p. instnl. effectiveness Rockbridge Sem., Springfield, Mo., 2006—. Em. Com. To Nominate Coordinating Bds., Dallas, 1983-84; trustee Latham Springs Encampment, Aquilla, Tex., 1971-72, 76-78. Trustee Castleberry Ind. Sch. Dist., Ft. Worth, 1977-79; pres. bd. Aerials Gymnastics, Arlington, Tex., 1991-94. Fellow Scarborough Inst.; mem. So. Bapt. Religious Educators (v.p. 1995), Tarrant Bapt. Religious Educators (pres. 1981), Bapt. Religious Educators S.W., Am. Mgmt. Assn., Castleberry Alumni Assn. (treas. 1978-80, Outstanding Ex award 1978), Woodhaven Country Club. Avocation: golf. Office: Southwestern Bapt Theol Sem PO Box 22487 Fort Worth TX 76122-0001 Business E-Mail: gwaller@swbbts.edu.

**WALLER, HAROLD MYRON**, political science professor; b. Detroit, Oct. 12, 1940; s. Allan L. and Lillian R. (LeVine) W.; m. Diane Carol Goodman, June 28, 1966; children: Sharon, Dahvi, Jeffrey. SB, MIT, 1962; MS, Northwestern U., 1966; PhD, Georgetown U., 1968. Asst. prof. McGill U., Montreal, 1967-71, assoc. prof., 1971-93, prof., 1993—, chmn. polit. sci. dept., 1969-74, 89-90, acting chmn., 1980-81, 86-87, assoc. dean (acad.) faculty arts, 1991-94, acting dean faculty arts, 1994-95, chair N.Am. studies program, 2003—04. Pres. McGill Assn. Univ. Tchrs., Montreal, 1978-79; fellow Jerusalem Ctr. Pub. Affairs, 1980—; dir. Can. Ctr. Jewish Univ. Studies, Montreal, 1980—; vis. scholar Hudson Inst., Washington, 2004-05. Co-author: Maintaining Consensus: The Canadian Jewish Polity in the Postwar World, 1990; co-editor: Canadian Federalism: From Crisis to Constitution; contbg. editor: Middle East Focus; mem. editorial bd. Jewish Political Studies; chmn. editorial bd. Viewpoints; contbr. numerous articles to profl. jours. and books in field. Com. chmn. Can. Jewish Congress, Montreal, 1971-74; chair, nat. exec. Can. Profs. for Peace in Middle East, Toronto, 1975-85; pres. Akiva Sch., Montreal, 1984-85; com. chmn. Jewish Edn. Council, Montreal, 1986-88. Recipient Nat. Jewish Book award Jewish Book Coun., N.Y.C., 1991; Grad. fellow NSF, Washington, 1965-66, Leave fellow Social Sci. Humanities Rsch. Coun., Ottawa, 1981-82. Mem. Am. Polit. Sci. Assn., Can. Polit. Sci. Assn., Assn. Jewish Studies, Assn. Sociol. Study of Jewry, Assn. Israel Studies, Faculty Club, Sigma Xi, Pi Sigma Alpha. Jewish. Avocations: travel, athletics, reading, politics. Office: McGill U Dept Polit Sci 855 Sherbrooke St W Montreal PQ Canada H3A 2T7 Office Phone: 514-398-4806. Business E-Mail: harold.waller@mcgill.ca.

**WALLER, JOHN HENRY, JR.**, state supreme court justice; b. Mullins, SC, Oct. 31, 1937; s. John Henry and Elnita (Bass) Waller; m. Jane McLaurin Cooper, Nov. 16, 1963 (div.); children: John Henry III, Melissa McLaurin; m. Debra Ann Meares, May 9, 1981; children: Ryan Meares, Rand Ellis. AB in Psychology, Wofford Coll., 1959; LLB, JD, U. S.C., 1963. Mem. SC Ho. of Reps., 1967—77, asst. majority leader, 1973—74, majority leader, 1975—76; mem. SC Senate, 1977—80; judge SC Cir. Ct., 1980—94; assoc. justice SC Supreme Ct., 1994—. Capt. U.S. Army, 1959—60. Recipient Disting. Svc. award, Municipal Assn. of S.C., 1968. Mem.: Millins Rotary Club (1st pres.), Shriners, Masons. Avocations: woodworking, golf, water sports, skiing. Office: SC Supreme Ct Supreme Court PO Box 11330 Columbia SC 29211-1330*

**WALLER, JOHN LOUIS**, anesthesiologist, educator; b. Loma Linda, Calif., Dec. 1, 1944; s. Louis Clinton and Sue (Bruce) W.; m. Jo Lynn Marie Haas, Aug. 4, 1968; children: Kristina, Karla, David. BA, So. Coll., Collegedale, Tenn., 1967; MD, Loma Linda U., 1971. Diplomate Am. Bd. Anesthesiology. Intern Hartford (Conn.) Hosp., 1971—72; resident in anesthesiology Harvard U. Med. Sch.-Mass. Gen. Hosp., Boston, 1972—74, fellow, 1974—75; asst. prof. anesthesiology Emory U. Sch. Medicine, Atlanta, 1977—80, assoc. prof., 1980—86, chmn. dept. anesthesiology, 1986—2000, prof., 1986—2001, prof. emeritus, 2001—; chief anesthesiology Henry W. Hosp. Atlanta, 1986-94, med. dir., 1993-95; assoc. v.p. info. svcs. Woodruff Health Scis. Ctr., 1995-97; chief info. officer Emory U. System Healthcare, Atlanta, 1995-97; prof. anesthesiology Med. U. S.C., Charleston, 2002—, chmn. dept. anesthesia and perioperative medicine, 2002—05, dir. med. informatics, 2005—. Cons. Arrow Internat., Inc., Reading, Pa., 1988—; mem. adv. com. on anesthetic and life support drugs FDA, Washington, 1986—92; numerous vis. professorships and lectures. Contbr. articles to med. jours. Maj. M.C., USAF, 1975-77. Recipient cert. of appreciation Office Sec. Def., 1983. Fellow: Am. Coll. Chest Physicians, Am. Coll. Anesthesiologists; mem.: Assn. Cardiac Anesthesiologists, Soc. Acad. Anesthesia Chmn. (councillor 1989—), Assn. Univ. Anesthesiologists, Internat. Anesthesia Rsch. Soc. (trustee 1984—2002, sec. 1996—98, chair 1998—2000), Soc. Cardiovascular Anesthesiologists (pres. 1991—93), Am. Soc. Anesthesiologists. Avocations: fishing, sailing, swimming. Office: Med U SC Dept Anes and Perioperative Medicine 167 Ashley Ave Ste 525 Ste 301 Charleston SC 29425 Business E-Mail: wallerj@musc.edu.

**WALLER, MARY BELLIS**, educational consultant, researcher; b. Milw., May 18, 1940; d. Ernest Anthony and Hazel Mary (Addie) Bellis; m. Michael I. Waller, May 9, 1987 (dec. Nov. 1996); children: Eric B. Griswold, Andrew D. Griswold, Megan E. Griswold Simone BS, U. Wis., Milw., 1969, MS, 1971, PhD, 1992. Coord. Wis. Coalition for Ednl. Reform, Milw., 1971-74; instr. U. Wis., Milw., 1974-77; exec. dir. Worker Rights Inst., Milw., 1977-87; adj. prof. Nat. Coll. Edn., Evanston, Ill., 1981-96; preceptor, clin. program coord. U. Wis.-Parkside, Kenosha, 1987-96; Wis. lead cons. Emprise Designs, 1993-97; psychotherapist, dir. outreach programs Achievement Assocs., Ltd., 1998—; clin. assoc. prof. U. Wis., Milw., 2002—. Cons. on drug-affected children; ctr. scientist Ctr. for Addiction and Behavioral Health Rsch., 1996—; pres. Program Devel. and Evaluation, 1993—, Priority Group, Inc., 1998—. Author: Crack-Affected Children: A Teacher's Guide, 1993, Lady of the Manor: Medieval Cooking with Herbs, 1994; author numerous articles on drug-affected children. Mem. ASCD, NAEYC, Am. Ednl. Rsch. Assn., Assn. Tchr. Educators, Phi Delta Kappa (Disting. Svc. award 1992). Home: 8316 N Regent Rd Milwaukee WI 53217-2736 Office Phone: 414-352-2213. Personal E-mail: mwaller@execpc.com.

**WALLER, PETER WILLIAM**, public relations executive; b. Kewanee, Ill., Oct. 1, 1926; s. Ellis Julian and Barodel (Gould) Waller; m. Anne-Marie Appelius van Hoboken, Nov. 10, 1950; children: Catherine, Hans. BA with honors, Princeton U., 1949; MA with honors, San Jose State U., 1978. Bur. chief Fairchild Publs., San Francisco, 1953-55; freelance writer Mountain View, Calif., 1956-57; pub. rels. coord. Lockheed Missiles and Space, Sunnyvale, Calif., 1957-64; info. mgr. 1st missions to Jupiter, Saturn, Venus NASA Ames Rsch. Ctr., Mountain View, 1964-83, mgr. pub. info., 1983-95; cons. NASA-Ames Galileo, Lunar Prospector, 1996-97; prodr. space films PacPAW Assoc., 1998—. Speechwriter to pres. Lockheed Missiles and Space, 1960—64. Prodr.: (documentaries) Jupiter Odyssey, 1974 (Golden Eagle, 1974); prodr., writer NASA Aero. program, 1984; contbr. articles to profl. jours., encyclopedias. Cons. preservation Lake Tahoe Calif. Resources Agy., Sacramento, 1984. Mem.: No. Calif. Sci. Writers Assn., Sierra Club. Democrat. Congregationalist. Avocations: skiing, travel, architecture, construction, hiking. Home: 3655 La Calle Ct Palo Alto CA 94306-2619 Personal E-mail: pwaller@sbcglobal.net.

**WALLER, ROBERT JAMES,** writer; b. Aug. 1, 1939; s. Robert Sr. and Ruth W.; m. Georgia Ann Wiedemeier (div. 1997); 1 child, Rachael. Student, U. Iowa, 1957-58, U. No. Iowa, 1958; PhD, Ind. U., 1968. Prof. mgmt. U. No. Iowa, Cedar Falls, 1968-91, dean bus. sch., 1979-85. Author: Just Beyond the Firelight: Stories & Essays, 1988, One Good Road is Enough: Essays, 1990, The Bridges of Madison County, 1992, Slow Waltz in Cedar Bend, 1993, Old Songs in a New Cafe: Selected Essays, 1994, Border Music, 1995, A Thousand Country Roads: An Epilogue to the Bridges of Madison County, 2002, High Plains Tango, 2005; recorded album The Ballads of Madison County, 1993, Puerto Vallarta Squeeze, 1996. Recipient Literary Lion award New York Public Library, 1993. Office: care Aaron Priest Literary Agy 708 3rd Ave Fl 23 New York NY 10017-4201

**WALLER, ROBERT REX,** ophthalmologist, educator, foundation administrator; b. N.Y.C., Feb. 19, 1937; s. Madison Rex and Sally Elizabeth (Pearce) W.; m. Sarah Elizabeth Pickens, Dec. 27, 1963; children: Elizabeth, Katherine, Robert Jr. BA, Duke U., 1958; MD, U. Tenn., 1963. Diplomate Am. Bd. Ophthalmology (dir. 1982—, vice chmn. 1988-89, chmn. 1989—). Intern City of Memphis Hosps., 1963-64; resident in internal medicine Mayo Grad. Sch. Medicine, Rochester, Minn., 1966-67, resident in ophthalmology, 1967-70, faculty, 1970—; assoc. prof. ophthalmology Mayo Clinic, Rochester, Minn., 1974-78, prof., 1978—; chmn. dept. ophthalmology Mayo Med. Sch., Rochester, Minn., 1974-84, cons., 1970—, bd. govs., 1978-93, chmn., 1988-93; trustee Mayo Found., Rochester, 1978—, pres., CEO, 1988-98, pres. emeritus, 1999—. Chmn. bd. trustees Healthcare Leadership Coun., Washington, 1999—2001, mem. bd. trustees, 2001—. Contbr. chpts. to books, articles to profl. jours. Elder 1st Presbyn. Ch., Rochester, 1975-78; mem. Rochester Task Force on Pub. Assembly Facilities, 1983-84. Recipient Ocuplastic Surgery fellow U. Calif. San Francisco, 1973. Mem. AMA, Minn. State Med. Assn., Zumbro Valley Med. Assn., Am. Acad. Ophthalmology, Am. Ophthalmol. Soc., Orbital Soc., Am. Soc. Ophthalmic Plastic and Reconstructive Surgery, Minn. Acad. Ophthalmology and Otolaryngology, Memphis Country Club, Old Baldy Golf Club, Augusta Nat. Golf Club, Alpha Omega Alpha, Delta Tau Delta. Presbyterian. Avocations: golf, travel, photography. Home: 199 Greenbriar Dr Memphis TN 38117-3238 E-mail: RWaller@mayo.edu.*

**WALLER, STACEY,** psychologist; b. Charleston, W. Va., Feb. 12, 1974; d. Clarence V and Glenna J Waller. BA, W. Va. U., 1996; MA, Western Mich. U., 2000, PhD, 2004. Lic. Psychologist. Post doctoral fellow W. Va. U., 2002—04; clin. psychologist W. Va. U. Med. Corp., 2004. Contbr. articles to profl. jours. Mem.: Am. Psychological Assn. Office: W Va U Dept Behavioral Medicine and Psychiatry 930 Chestnut Ridge Rd Morgantown WV 26506 Business E-Mail: swaller@hsc.wvu.edu.

**WALLER, STEPHEN,** air transportation executive; b. 1949; Student, New Zealand U., 1970-74. Courier, country mgr., european mktg. mgr. DHL Airways, Inc., London, 1975-80, Tehran, Iran, 1975-80, v.p. field svcs. Redwood City, Calif., 1980-93, sr. v.p. Network Trans. divsn., 1994—. Office: Dhl 1200 S Pine Island Rd Ste 170 Plantation FL 33324-4469

**WALLER, WILLIAM LOWE, JR.,** state supreme court justice; b. Miss., Feb. 9, 1952; s. Bill and Carroll (Overton) Waller; m. Charlotte Brawner, Aug. 4, 1979; children: William, Jeannie, Clayton. BA in Bus., Miss. State U., 1974; JD, U. Miss., 1977; grad., U.S. Army War Coll. Bar: Miss. 1977. Ptnr. Waller and Waller, 1977-97; judge City of Jackson, Miss., 1995-96; justice Miss. Supreme Ct., Jackson, 1998—, presiding justice, 2004—. Chmn. Miss. Pub. Defenders Task Force, 2000-05; mem. Study Commn. on the Miss. Jud. Sys.; chmn. Supreme Ct. Rules Com., 2001-. Deacon First Bapt. Ch., Jackson, Miss.; B.G., IRR., 2004. With USAR. 2004. Recipient Chief Justice award, 2005. Mem. ABA, Miss. Bar Assn. (chmn. Lawyer Referral Service 1987-89), Miss. Trial Lawyers Assn. (bd. mem. 1979-82), Hinds County Bar Assn. (Jud. Innovation award 2003-04), Jackson Young Lawyers Assn., Christian Legal Soc., Am. Legion, Miss. Nat. Guard Assn. (sec., chmn. legis. com., bd. dirs., nat. guard Miss. Army 1975-2004). Office: PO Box 117 Jackson MS 39205-0117*

**WALLER, WILMA RUTH,** retired secondary school educator, retired librarian; b. Jacksonville, Tex., Nov. 15, 1921; d. William Wesley and Myrtle (Nesbitt) W. BA with honors, Tex. Woman's U., 1954, MA with honors, 1963, MLS with honors, 1976. Tchr. English Dell (Ark.) High Sch., 1953-54, Jefferson (Tex.) Ind. Schs., 1954-56, Tyler (Tex.) Ind. Schs., 1956-68; librarian Wise County Schs., Decatur, Tex., 1969-71, Thomas K. Gorman High Sch., Tyler, 1971-74, Sweetwater (Tex.) Ind. Sch. Dist., 1974-86; ret. Lectr., book reviewer for various clubs. Active in past as vol. for ARC, U. Tex. Health Ctr. Ford Found. fellow, 1959; recipient Delta Kappa Gamma Achievement award, 1992. Mem. UDC, Smith County Ret. Sch. Pers., Bible Study Group, Delta Kappa Gamma. Republican. Baptist. Avocations: reading, gourmet cooking, piano, writing. Home: 1117 N Azalea Dr Tyler TX 75701-5206

**WALLERSTEIN, MITCHEL BRUCE,** dean, educator; b. N.Y.C., Mar. 8, 1949; s. Melvin Julian and Rita Helen (Nomburg) W.; m. Susan Elyse Perlik, June 29, 1974; children: Matthew, Leah. AB, Dartmouth Coll., 1971; MPA, Syracuse U., 1972; MS, MIT, 1977, PhD, 1978. Assoc. dir. Internat. Food Policy Program MIT, Cambridge, Mass., 1978-83, lectr. dept. polit. sci., 1978-83; asst. prof. dept. polit. sci. Holy Cross Coll., Worcester, Mass., 1979-81; exec. dir. office internat. affairs NRC, NAS, Washington, 1983-89, dep. exec. officer, 1989-93; dep. asst. sec. of def. U.S. Dept. Def., Washington, 1993-97; disting. rsch. prof. Nat. Def. U., Washington, 1998; v.p. John D. and Catherine T. MacArthur Found., Chgo., 1998—2003; dean, prof polit. sci. and pub. adminstrn. Maxwell Sch. Citizenship and Pub. Affairs, Syracuse U., NY, 2003—. Adj. prof. Sch. Advanced Internat. Studies, Johns Hopkins U., Washington, 1992-98; adj. prof. Sch. Fgn. Svc., Georgetown U., Washington, 1989-93. Author: Food for War - Food for Peace: The Politics of U.S. Food Aid, 1979; author, dir. reports in field including multiple NAS reports on tech. transfer and nat. security. Recipient Sec. Def. medal for Outstanding Pub. Svc., 1997, 98. Mem. AAAS, Internat. Inst. Strategic Studies, Coun. Fgn. Rels. Democrat. Office: Maxwell Sch Citizenship and Pub Affairs Syracuse Univ 200 Eggers Hall Syracuse NY 13244-1020 Office Phone: 315-443-3461. Office Fax: 315-443-3385. Business E-Mail: mwallers@maxwell.syr.edu.

**WALLERSTEIN, RALPH OLIVER,** physician; b. Dusseldorf, Germany, Mar. 7, 1922; arrived in U.S., 1938, naturalized, 1944; s. Otto R. and Ilse (Hollander) Wallerstein; m. Betty Ane Christensen, June 21, 1952; children: Ralph Oliver, Richard, Ann. AB, U. Calif., Berkeley, 1943; MD, U. Calif., San Francisco, 1945. Diplomate Am. Bd. Internal Medicine. Intern San Francisco Hosp., 1945—46, resident, 1948—49, U. Calif. Hosp., San Francisco, 1949—50; research fellow Thorndike Meml. Lab., Boston City Hosp., 1950—52; chief clin. hematology San Francisco Gen. Hosp., 1953—87; mem. faculty U. Calif., San Francisco, 1952—, clin. prof. medicine, 1969—, prof. emeritus of medicine. Bd. govs. Am. Bd. Internal Medicine, 1975—83, chmn., 1982—83. Photographer (exhibitions) U. Calif., San Francisco. Capt. M.C. U.S. Army, 1946—48. Decorated Outstanding Civil Svc. medal; recipient ACP gov. award, 1977—87, chmn. bd. govs. 1980—81, regent 1981—87, pres. 1988—89), AMA, Western Assn. Physicians, Western Soc. Clin. Rsch., Internat. Soc. Hematology, Calif. Acad. Medicine, Inst. Medicine, Am. Assn. Blood Banks, Am. Soc. Internal Medicine, Am. Fedn. Clin. Rsch., Am. Clin. and Climatol. Assn., San Francisco Med. Soc., Am. Soc. Hematology (pres. 1978), Gold Headed Cane Soc. Republican. Jewish.

**WALLERSTEIN, ROBERT SOLOMON,** retired psychiatrist; b. Berlin, Jan. 28, 1921; s. Lazar and Sarah (Guensberg) Wallerstein; m. Judith Hannah Saretsky, Jan. 26, 1947; children: Michael Jonathan, Nina Beth, Amy Lisa. BA, Columbia U., 1941, MD, 1944; postgrad., Topeka Inst. Psychoanalysis, 1951-58. Assoc. dir., then dir. rsch. Menninger Found., Topeka, 1954-66; chief psychiatry Mt. Zion Hosp., San Francisco, 1966-78; tng. and supervising analyst San Francisco Psychoanalytic Inst., 1966—; clin. prof. U. Calif. Sch. Medicine, Langley-Porter Neuropsychiat. Inst., 1967-75, prof., chmn. dept. psychiatry, also dir. inst., 1975-85, prof. dept. psychiatry, 1985-91, prof.

emeritus, 1991—, ret. Vis. prof. psychiatry La. State U. Sch. Medicine, New Orleans Psychoanalytic Inst., Pahlavi U., Shiraz, Iran, 1977, Fed. U. Rio Grande do Sul, Portol Alegre, Brazil, 1980; mem., chmn. rsch. scientist career devel. com. NIMH, 1966—70; fellow Ctr. Advanced Study Behavioral Scis., Stanford, Calif., 1964—65, 1981—82, Rockefeller Found. Study Ctr., Bellagio, Italy, 1992. Author: 20 books; mem. editl. bd.: numerous profl. jours.; contbr. 360 articles to profl. jours. With U.S. Army, 1946—48. Recipient Heinz Hartmann award, N.Y. Psychoanalytic Inst., 1968, Disting. Alumnus award, Menninger Sch. Psychiatry, 1972, J. Elliott Royer award, U. Calif., San Francisco, 1973, Outstanding Achievement award, No. Calif. Psychiat. Soc., 1987, Mt. Airy gold medal, 1990, Mary Singleton Sigourney award, 1991, Outstanding Contbn. to Psychoanalytic Edn. award, Internat. Fedn. Psychoanalytic Edn., 1999. Fellow: ACP, Am. Orthopsychiat. Assn., Am. Psychiat. Assn., Am. Coll. Psychoanalysts; mem.: Group Advancement Psychiatry, Mex. Psychoanalytic Assn. (hon.), Brit. Psycho-Analytic Soc. (hon.), Internat. Psychoanalytic Assn. (v.p. 1977—86, pres. 1985—89, hon. v.p. 1999—), Am. Psychoanalytic Assn. (pres. 1971—72), Phi Beta Kappa, Alpha Omega Alpha. Home: 290 Beach Rd Belvedere CA 94920-2472 Office Phone: 415-435-3417.

**WALLEY, BYRON See CARD, ORSON SCOTT**

**WALLEY, JAMES MARVIN, JR.,** engineering executive, management consultant, real estate company executive; b. Orange, Calif., Oct. 25, 1947; s. James Marvin Sr. and Edna Amelia (Rohr) W.; m. Marynelle Lorimer Walley, Apr. 28, 1990; children: Charlotte, Elizabeth, Edward, Joseph. BSCE, Tulane U., 1970, MSCE, George Washington U., 1974; MBA in Fin., U. So. Miss., 1980. Registered profl. engr., Tex., Va.; cert. property mgr., lic. broker. Commd. ensign USN, 1970, advanced through grades to lt. comdr. Civil Engr. Corps, served in Vietnam, 1970-71, resigned, 1981; exec. v.p. SPW, Inc., Dallas, 1981-84; chief ops. officer, ptnr. Montgomery Cos., Inc., Dallas, 1984-87; sr. v.p. Law Engring., Inc., Dallas, 1988-94; pres., COO Cura, Inc., Dallas, 1995. Pres., CEO Geo. Marine, Inc., 1996; v.p. Archon Group, 1997—. Vice chmn., chmn. ARC, 1985, sec.; councilman University Park City, 1998-2002. Rear Admiral Civil Engr. Corps, USN Res. Fellow: ASCE; mem.: Soc. Am. Mil. Engrs., Seabee Meml. Scholarship Assn. (pres. 2001—03), Leadership Dallas Alumni (pres. 1986), Tulane Alumni Coun. Assn. (pres. 1989), Salesmanship Club Dallas, Masons (32d Degree, KCCH). Republican. Roman Catholic. Avocations: golf, skiing. Address: RADM CEC USNR 600 E Las Colinas Blvd Ste 400 Irving TX 75039

**WALLFESH, HENRY MAURICE,** communications executive, writer; b. N.Y.C., June 15, 1937; s. David Shibe and Rose (Silk) W.; m. Suzanne Krakowitch, Dec. 26, 1960; children: Saundra Kay, Gerald Bruce. Grad. indsl. and labor rels., Cornell U., 1958. Editor, co-pub. Indsl. Rels. News, N.Y.C. and Stamford, Conn., 1960-67; pres., chief exec. officer RAI div. Hearst Bus. Communications, N.Y.C., 1968-91, sr. v.p., editor at large, 1991; pres. Whale Communications, Inc., Stamford, Conn., 1992—. Pres. Indsl. Rels. Inst., Stamford, 1964-67; founder, bd. dirs. Internat. Soc. Pre-Retirement Planners, 1975-88; bd. dirs. VSOP Mktg., Boston. Author: Implications of the Age Discrimination in Employment, 1977, When a CEO Retires, 1978. Bd. dirs. Aging in Am., N.Y.C., 1985-90, N.Y.C. Anti-Defamation League, 1987-93; mem. alumni bd. dirs. Cornell Inst. Labor Rels., 1995—99. Capt. inf. USAR, 1958-67. Recipient Corp. Achievement award Nat. Assn. for Sr. Living Industries, 1990; inducted into Internat. Soc. Pre-Retirement Planners Hall of Fame, 1988. Mem. Roxbury Swim and Tennis Club (bd. dirs. 1975-78), Cornell Club. Jewish. Avocations: tennis, theater, writing. Home and Office: 341 Biltmore Ln Somerset NJ 08873-6004 Personal E-mail: hswhale@aol.com.

**WALLIN, JAMES PETER,** lawyer; b. Huntington, NY, May 9, 1958; s. Jerome Peter and Margaret Mary (Gilvarry) W.; children: James Peter Jr., Thomas George, Katherine Grace, Sarah Elizabeth. BA in Econs., SUNY, Stony Brook, 1980; JD, N.Y. Law Sch., 1983. Bar: N.Y. 1984. Counsel Alliance Capital Mgmt., N.Y.C., 1982-86; assoc. Cole & Dietz (now Winston & Strawn), N.Y.C., 1986-87; counsel The Dreyfus Corp., N.Y.C., 1987-88; gen. counsel Yamaichi Capital Mgmt. Inc., N.Y.C., 1988-92, Yamaichi Internat. (Am.) Inc., N.Y.C., 1992-94, Evergreen Asset Mgmt. Corp., 1994-97; dir. Governance Group Morgan Stanley Investment Mgmt., NYC, 1997—2005; sr. v.p., chief admin. officer Alliance Bernstein Fixed Income, 2006—. Faculty Practicing Law Inst., N.Y.C., 1992—. Author: (seminar materials) Broker Dealer Regulation, 1992. Avocations: aviation, skiing, sailing. Home: PO Box 90 Cold Spring Harbor NY 11724-0090

**WALLIN, LELAND DEAN,** artist, educator; b. Sioux Falls, SD, Oct. 14, 1942; s. Clarence Forrest and Leona Mae (McInnis) W.; m. Meredith Maria Hawkins, Mar. 26, 1977; 1 child, Jessica Hawkins. Student, Columbus Coll. Art and Design, 1961-62; BFA in Painting, Kans. City Art Inst., Mo., 1965; MFA in Painting, U. Cin. with Cin. Art Acad., 1967. Prof. drawing, painting, sculpture St. Cloud State U., Minn., 1967-86; prof. Queens Coll., CUNY, Flushing, NY, 1983-84; prof., coord. MFA painting Marywood U., Scranton, Pa., 1985-90; prof. painting and drawing East Carolina U., Greenville, NC, 1992—; advisor Painting Guild, 1993—. Lectr. Carnegie-Mellon U., Pitts., 1988; curator Philip Pearlstein Retrospective Exhibit, Scranton, 1988; juror Belin Arts Grant Com., Waverly, Pa., 1986—; vis. prof. painting East Carolina U., Greenville, 1992-93; judge, juror No. Nat. Art Competition, 1993. One-man shows include Mpls. Coll. Art and Design, 1978, Harold Reed Gallery, 1983, Gallery Henoch, NYC, 1991, exhibited in group shows at Bklyn. Mus., 1983, Greenville County Mus. Art, SC, 1983, Huntsville Mus. Art, 1994, San Bernardino County Mus. Internat., Calif., 1995, Contemporary Realism, Phila., 1996, Ctr. Arts, Loredo, Tex., 1997 (Internat. First Pl. award, 1997), 1999 (Internat. First Pl. award, 1999), Contemporary Realism, Phila., 1998, Downey (Calif.) Mus. Art, 1998, Palm Springs Desert Mus., 1999, Fine Arts Ctr., Sacramento, 1999, Bellevue Art Mus., Wash., 2001, Morris Mus. Art, Ga., 2001, Huntsville Mus. Art, Ala., 2002, Miss. Mus. Art, 2002. Represented in permanent collections represented in various collections; contbr. articles to profl. jours. Named Outstanding Tchr., East Carolina U., 1994, 1995; recipient Scholar-Tchr. award for Coll. Fine Arts and Comm., East Carolina U. Sch. Art and Design, 2005—, numerous rsch. awards, East Carolina U., 1994—. Home: 218 York Rd Greenville NC 27858-5601

**WALLING, CHEVES THOMSON,** chemistry professor; b. Evanston, Ill., Feb. 28, 1916; s. Willoughby George and Frederika Christina (Haskell) W.; m. Jane Ann Wilson, Sept. 17, 1940; children— Hazel, Rosalind, Cheves, Janie, Barbara AB, Harvard, 1937; PhD, U. Chgo., 1939. Rsch. chemist E.I. duPont de Nemours, 1939-43, U.S. Rubber Co., 1943-49; tech. aide Office Sci. Research, Washington, 1945; sr. rsch. assoc. Lever Bros. Co., 1949-52; prof. chemistry Columbia U., N.Y.C., 1952-69; Disting. prof. chemistry U. Utah, Salt Lake City, 1970-91, prof. chemistry emeritus, 1991—. Author: Free Radicals in Solution, 1957, Fifty Years of Free Radicals, 1995; also numerous articles. Fellow AAAS; mem. Nat. Acad. Scis., Am. Acad. Arts and Scis., Am. Chem. Soc. (editor jour. 1975-81, James Flack Norris award 1970, Lubrizol award 1984) Home: 222 Gilson Rd PO Box 537 Jaffrey NH 03452-0537 Office Phone: 603-532-6557.

**WALLING, DONOVAN ROBERT,** editor, writer; b. Kansas City, Mo., Jan. 9, 1948; s. Donovan Ernest and Dorothy Jane (Goyette) W.; m. Diana Lynn Eveland, Oct. 19, 1968 (dec. 1991); children: Katherine Anne, Donovan David, Alexander James. BS in Edn., Kans. State Tchrs. Coll., 1970; MS, U. Wis., Milw., 1975. Cert. tchr., adminstr., Wis., Ind. Tchr. Sheboygan (Wis.) Area Sch. Dist., 1970-81, 83-86, coord. lang. arts and reading, 1986-91; tchr. Dept. Def. Dependents Schs., Zweibruecken, Germany, 1981-83; dir. instrnl. svcs. Carmel (Ind.)-Clay Schs., 1991-93; dir. publs. Phi Delta Kappa Internat., Bloomington, Ind., 1993—. Mem. adj. faculty U. Wis., Oshkosh, 1986-91, Silver Lake Coll., Manitowoc, Wis., 1987-91. Author: Complete Book of School Public Relations, 1982, How To Build Staff Involvement in School Management, 1984, Teachers as Leaders, 1994, Rethinking How Art Is Taught, 2000, Visual Knowing, 2005, Teaching Writing to Visual, Auditory, and Kinesthetic Learners, 2006; also numerous articles. Mem. ASCD, Nat. Coun. Tchrs. English, Internat. Reading Assn., Phi Delta Kappa (v.p. Cen. Ind.

chpt. 1992-93). Avocations: writing, painting. Office: Phi Delta Kappa Internat PO Box 789 Bloomington IN 47402-0789 Office Phone: 800-766-1156. Business E-Mail: dwalling@pdkintl.org.

**WALLINGFORD, ANNE,** freelance/self-employed writer, marketing professional, consultant; b. Chgo., June 29, 1949; d. Lester Arlyn and Roseanne (Jones) W. BS in Edn., Chgo. State U., 1975. Cert. elem. and mid. sch. tchr., Ill. Profl. dressmaker Annie's Original's, Chgo., 1968-72; instr., asst. prin., St. Bonaventure Sch., Chgo., 1972-81; instr., chair sci. dept. Our Lady of Lourdes Sch., Chgo., 1981-87; product designer, catalog mgr. FSC Ednl., Inc., Mansfield, Ohio, 1988-91; interim dir. pub. rels. Shelby Meml. Hosp., 1991-92; founder, dir. Anne Wallingford WordSmith, Chgo., 1992—. Instr. English lit. and bus. writing North Ctrl. Tech. Coll., 1991-92; catalog/project developer ETA, 1992-95, Sargent-Welch, 1993-2002, Basic Sci., 2003—; permissions editor McGraw-Hill, 2000—; tech. writer United Sci., 2002—; cons. in field. Contbr. articles to profl. jours. and newspapers. Active The Vol. Ctr., Mansfield, 1992-93, steering com. Wright Community Ctr., 1991; treas. Wolfram St. Block Club, Chgo., 1975-78. Recipient Gold award Adler Planetarium, Chgo., 1985. Mem. Nat. Writers Union, Chgo., Women in Pub. (Individual Excellence in Prodn., 1994, 95), Soc. Tech. Communicators, Profl. Freelance Assn. (founder, pres., 1991-92), Editl. Freelancers Assn., Mensa. Avocations: telecommunications, reading, theater, museums.

**WALLINGTON, PATRICIA MCDEVITT,** computer company executive; b. Phila., July 29, 1940; d. James J. and Mary (Eschbach) McDevitt; m. William R. Wallington; 1 child, Colleen Kydis. BA, U. Pa., 1975; MBA, Drexel U., 1978; postgrad. mgmt. devel., Harvard U., 1981. Project mgr. Fidelity Mut., Phila., 1965-72, Penn Mut. Ins. Co., Phila., 1972-77; mgr. info. systems Sun Info. Svcs., Phila., 1977-81; dir. info. systems Sun Exploration & Prodn. Co., Dallas, 1981-87; sr. v.p., chief info. officer Mass. Mut. Life Ins. Co., Springfield, 1987-89; corp. v.p., chief info. officer Xerox Corp., Rochester, NY, 1989—99; pres. CIO Assocs., Sarasota, Fla., 2000—. Mem. MBA adv. bd. Baylor U., Waco, Tex., 1986-88; bd. dirs. FINA, Inc., Middlesex Mut. P&C Co. Mem. adv. bd. Handicap Ctr.-HUP, Phila., 1978-80; v.p. fin. Girls Club Dallas, 1986-87. Named one of Top 100 Women in Tech., 1994, Hall of Fame, 1997, CIO mag., 1997. Mem. Soc. for Info. Mgmt.

**WALLIS, BEN ALTON, JR.,** lawyer; b. Llano County, Tex., Apr. 27, 1936; s. Ben A. and Jessie Ella (Longbotham) W.; children from previous marriage: Ben a. III, Jessica; m. Joan Mery, 1987. BBA, U. Tex., 1961, JD, 1971; postgrad., Law Sch. So. Meth. U. Bar: Tex. 1966, U.S. Dist. Ct. (no. dist.) Tex. 1971, U.S. Ct. Appeals D.C. 1974, U.S. Dist. Ct. D.C. 1975, U.S. Dist. Ct. (we. dist.) Tex. 1975, U.S. Dist. Ct. (no. dist.) Calif. 1983, U.S. Ct. Appeals (5th cir.) 1975, U.S. Ct. Appeals (8th cir.) 1980, U.S. Ct. Appeals (11th cir.) 1981, U.S. Dist. Ct. (ea. dist.) Wis. 1983, U.S. Supreme Ct. 1974. Pvt. practice, Llano, 1966-67, Dallas, 1971-73; investigator, prosecutor State Securities Bd. Tex., 1967-71; v.p. of devel. Club Corp. Am., Dallas, 1973; assoc. counsel impeachment task force U.S. Ho. of Reps. Com. on Judiciary, Washington, 1974; prin. Law Offices of Ben Wallis, P.C., San Antonio, 1974—. Chmn. Nat. Land Use Conf., 1979-81; mem. Gov.'s Areawide Planning Adv. Com., 1975-78; pres. Inst. Human Rights Rsch., 1979-2000. Mem.: FBA, ATLA, Coll. of State Bar of Tex., State Bar Tex. (former chmn. agr. tax com.), D.C. Bar Assn., San Antonio Bar Assn., Delta Theta Phi, Delta Sigma Pi. Republican. Baptist. Office: 7800 W IH 10 Ste 130 San Antonio TX 78230 Office Phone: 210-525-1500. Business E-Mail: wallislaw@sbcglobal.net.

**WALLIS, CARLTON LAMAR,** librarian; b. Blue Springs, Miss., Oct. 15, 1915; s. William Ralph and Tellie (Jones) W.; m. Mary Elizabeth Cooper, Feb. 22, 1944; 1 child, Carlton Lamar. BA with spl. distinction, Miss. Coll., 1936; MA, Tulane U. 1946; B.L.S., U. Chgo., 1947; L.H.D., Rhodes Coll., Memphis, 1980. English tchr., coach Miss. Pub. Schs., 1936-41; teaching fellow Miss. Coll. and Tulane U., 1941-42; chief librarian Rosenberg Library, Galveston, Tex., 1947-55; city librarian Richmond, Va., 1955-58; dir. Memphis Pub. Library, 1958-80, ret., 1980. Author: Libraries in the Golden Triangle, 1966; contbr. articles to library jours. Trustee Belhaven Coll., 1978-82, Nat. Ornamental Metal Mus., 1989—. Served as chief warrant officer AUS, 1942-46. Decorated Bronze Star. Mem. ALA (chmn. library mgmt. sect. 1969-71), Pub. Library Assn. (dir. 1973-77), Tex. Library Assn. (pres. 1952-53), Va. Library Assn., Southwestern Library Assn. (exec. bd. 1950-55), Southeastern Library Assn. (chmn. pub. library sect. 1960-62), Tenn. Library Assn. (pres. 1969-70, Distinguished Service award 1979, Intellectual Freedom award 1998). Presbyterian (elder). Club: Egyptian (pres. 1973-74). Home: 365 Kenilworth Pl Memphis TN 38112-5405

**WALLIS, DIANA LYNN,** artistic director; b. Windsor, Eng., Dec. 11, 1946; d. Dennis Blackwell and Joan Williamson (Gatcombe) W. Grad., Royal Ballet Sch., Eng., 1962-65. Dancer Royal Ballet Touring Co., London, 1965-68; ballet mistress Royal Ballet Sch., London, 1969-81, dep. ballet prin., 1981-84; artistic coord. Nat. Ballet of Can., Toronto, 1984-86, assoc. artistic dir., 1986-87, co-artistic dir., 1987-89; free-lance prod., tchr. London; dep. artistic dir. English Nat. Ballet, London, 1990-94; artistic dir. Royal Acad. Dance, 1994—. Fellow Imperial Soc. Tchrs. Dancing. Office Phone: 0207 326 8012. Business E-Mail: lwallis@rad.org.uk.

**WALLIS, ERIC G.,** lawyer; b. Astoria, NY, Jan. 8, 1950; AB magna cum laude, U. Pacific, 1972; JD, U. Calif., Hasting Coll. of Law, 1975. Bar: Calif. 1975. Mem. Crosby, Heafey, Roach & May PC, Oakland, Calif., 1982—. Editl. assoc. Hastings Law Jour., 1974-75. Mem. ABA (sect. litigation), State Bar Calif., Alameda County Bar Assn. Office: Crosby Heafey Roach & May PC 1999 Harrison St Fl 26 Oakland CA 94612-3520 E-mail: ewallis@chnm.com.

**WALLIS, JIM,** religious speaker, activist, writer; b. Detroit, June 4, 1948; m. Joy Carroll, Oct. 25, 1997; children: Luke, Jack. BA, Mich. State U., 1970; grad., Trinity Evang. Div. Sch., Deerfield, Ill. Founder, editor-in-chief, exec. dir. Sojourners, 1971—; convener, pres. Call to Renewal, 1995—. Vis. fellow Inst. Politics, Harvard U., 2002. Author: Call to Conversion, 1981, The Soul of Politics: A Practical and Prophetic Vision for Change, 1994, Who Speaks for God? A New Politics of Compassion, Community, and Civility, 1996, Faith Works, 2000, God's Politics: Why the Right Gets It Wrong and the Left Doesn't Get It, 2005. Named one of 50 Faces for America's Future, Time mag., 1979. Office: Sojourners Ste 200 3333 14th St NW Washington DC 20010-2319 Office Phone: 202-328-8842.

**WALLIS, JUDITH LYNN,** science educator; b. Belen, N.Mex., Aug. 12, 1956; d. Tex Eldon and Elaine Marie Wallis. M, U. Nebr., Kearney, 1981. Sci. tchr. Coachella Valley H.S., Thermal, Calif., 1984—. Cset writer Calif. Dept. Edn., Sacramento, 2002—04. Recipient Tchr. of Yr., Coachella Valley H.S., 1995, 1996. Office: Coachella Valley high School 83800 Airport Blvd Thermal CA 92274 Office Phone: 760-399-5183. Personal E-Mail: jujuwal@aol.com. E-mail: jwallis@coachella.k12.ca.us.

**WALLIS, RICHARD FISHER,** physicist, researcher; b. Washington, May 14, 1924; s. William F. and Alberta (Sigelen) W.; m. Mary Camilla Williams, Aug. 20, 1955; children: Maria Fisher, Sylvia Camilla. BS, George Washington U., 1945, MS, 1948; PhD, Cath. U. Am., 1952. Postdoctoral fellow (U. Md.), College Park, 1951-53; chemist Applied Physics Lab. Johns Hopkins U., Silver Spring, Md., 1953-56; physicist Naval Rsch. Lab., Washington, 1956-66, 67-69, head semiconductors br., 1958-66, 67-69; prof. physics U. Calif., Irvine, 1966-67, 69—, prof. emeritus, 1993—; chmn. dept. physics U. Calif., Irvine, 1972-75, 80-83. Vis. prof. U. Paris, 1975-76, 79, 85. Author: (with Maradudin and Dobrzynski) Handbook of Surfaces and Interfaces, 1980, (with Balkanski) Many-Body Aspects of Solid State Spectroscopy, 1986, (with Balkanski) Semiconductor Physics and Applications, 2000; editor: Lattice Dynamics, 1965, Localized Excitations in Solids, 1968 (with Stegeman) Electromagnetic Surface Excitations, 1986, (with Birman and Sebenne) Elementary Excitations in Solids, 1992; contbr. articles to profl. jours. Served with U.S. Army, 1945-46. Recipient Pure Sci. award Naval

Rsch. Lab., 1964, Disting. Alumni Achievement award George Washington U., 1991. Fellow Am. Phys. Soc., AAAS; mem. Philos. Soc. Washington, Phi Beta Kappa, Sigma Xi Home: 2635 Alta Vista Dr Newport Beach CA 92660-4102 Office: U Calif Dept Physics Irvine CA 92697-0001

**WALLISON, FRIEDA K.,** lawyer; b. N.Y.C., Jan. 15, 1943; d. Ruvin H. and Edith (Landes) Koslow; m. Peter J. Wallison, Nov. 24, 1966; children: Ethan S., Jeremy L., Rebecca K. AB, Smith Coll., 1963; LLB, Harvard U., 1966. Bar: N.Y. 1967, D.C. 1982. Assoc. Carter, Ledyard & Milburn, N.Y.C., 1966-75; spl. counsel divsn. market regulation SEC, Washington, 1975; exec. dir., gen. counsel Mcpl. Securities Rulemaking Bd., Washington, 1975-78; ptnr. Rogers & Wells, N.Y.C. and Washington, 1978-83, Jones, Day, Reavis & Pogue, N.Y.C. and Washington, 1983-98; mem. Govtl. Acctg. Standards Coun., Washington, 1984-90, Nat. Coun. on Pub. Works Improvement, Washington, 1985-88; vice chair environ. fin. adv. bd. EPA, 1988-92. Contbr. articles to profl. jours. Fellow Am. Bar Found.; mem. N.Y.C. Bar Assn.

**WALLMANN, JEFFREY MINER,** author; b. Seattle, Dec. 5, 1941; s. George Rudolph and Elizabeth (Biggs) W. BS, Portland State U., 1962; PhD, U. Nev., 1998. Pvt. investigator Dale Sys., N.Y.C., 1962-63; asst. buyer, mgr., pub. money bidder Dohrmann Co., San Francisco, 1966-69; dir. pub. rels. London Films, Cinelux-Universal, Trans-European Publs., 1970-75; editor-in-chief Riviera Life mag., 1975-77; instr. U. Nev., Reno, 1990—, Regis U. 2003—. Instr. U. Nev., Las Vegas, 1998—, chair gen. studies; instr. U. Phoenix, 2001—, Regis U., 2003—. Author: The Spiral Web, 1969, Judas Cross, 1974, Clean Sweep, 1976, Jamaica, 1977, Deathtrek, 1980, Blood and Passion, 1980, Brand of the Damned, 1981, The Manipulator, 1982, Return to Conta Lupe, 1983, The Celluloid Kid, 1984, Business Basic for Bunglers, 1984, Guide to Applications Basic, 1984, The Western: Parables of the American Dream, 1999, (under pseudonym Leon DaSilva) Green Hell, 1976, Breakout in Angola, 1977, (under pseudonym Nick Carger) Hour of the Wolf, 1973, Ice Trap Terror, 1974, (under pseudonym Margaret Maitland) The Trial, 1974, Come Slowly, Eden, 1974, How Deep My Cup, 1975, (under pseudonym Amanda Hart Douglass) First Rapture, 1972, Jamaica!, 1978, (under pseudonym Grant Roberts) The Reluctant Couple, 1969, Wayward Wives, 1970, (under pseudonym Gregory St. Germain) Resistance # 1: Night and Fog, 1982, Resistance #2: Magyar Massacre, 1983, (under pseudonym Wesley Ellis) Lonestar on the Treachery Trail, 1982, numerous others, (under pseudonym Tabor Evans) Longarm and the Lonestar Showdown, 1986, (under pseudonym Jon Sharpe) Trailsman 58: Slaughter Express, 1986, numerous others in Trailsman series, also others under pseudonyms; co-author: (under pseudonym William Jeffrey) Duel at Gold Buttes, 1980, Border Fever, 1982, Day of the Moon, 1983, The Western: Parables of the American Dream, 1999; contbr. articles and short stories to Argosy, Ellery Queen's Mystery Mag., Alfred Hitchcock's Mystery Mag., Zane Grey Western, Venture, Oui, TV Guide. Mem. Mystery Writers Am., Sci. Fiction Writers Am., We. Writers Am., Nat. Coun. Tchrs. English, Crime Writers Am., Nev. state Coun. Tchrs. English, Esperanto League N.Am., We. Lit. Assn., Internacia Soc. Amikeco Kaj Bonvolo, Sci. Fiction Rsch. Assn., Internat. Assn. Fantastic in the Arts, We. Lit. Assn. Office: care of Barry Malzberg PO Box 61 Teaneck NJ 07666-0061

**WALLOT, JEAN-PIERRE,** archivist, historian; b. Valleyfield, Que., Can., May 22, 1935; s. Albert and Adrienne (Thibodeau) W.; m. Denyse Caron; children: Normand, Robert, Sylvie. BA, Coll. Valleyfield, 1957; lic. es lettres, U. Montreal, 1957, MA in History, 1957, PhD in History, 1965; D (hon.), U. Rennes, France, 1987, U. Ottawa, Can., 1996. Reporter Le Progres de Valleyfield, 1954—61; from lectr. to prof. history U. Montreal, 1961—65, dept. chmn., 1973—75, vice-dean studies faculty arts and scis., 1975—78, vice-dean rsch. Faculty Arts and Scis., 1979—82, academic v.p., 1982—85. Nat. archivist, Can., 1985-97; historian Nat. Mus. Man, Ottawa, Ont., 1966-69, assoc. prof. U. Toronto, 1969-71; prof. Concordia U., Montreal, Que., 1971-73; vis. prof. U Ottawa, 1997—; dir. Ctr. de Rsch. en Civilisation Canadienne-Francaise, 2000—; dir. Etude Assn. Ecole Pratique des Hautes Etudes en Scis. Sociales, Paris, 1975, 79, 81, 83, 85, 87, 89, 94. Author: French and American Intrigues in Canada, 1965; author: (with John Hare) Imprints in Lower Canada, 1967; author: Confrontations, 1971; author: (with G. Paquet) Patronage and Power in Lower Canada, 1973; author: A Quebec that Changed, 1973; editor (with R. Girard): Memoires de J.E. McComber, bourgeois de Montréal, 1981; editor: (with J. Goy) Evolution and Ruptures in the Rural World, 1986; editor: Identity Constructs and Social Practices, 2002, The Non-Existent Debate: The Pepin-Robarts Commission, 2003, Linguistic Governance, 2005. Pres. internat. adv. com. on Memory of the World UNESCO, 1993—98. Decorated officer Order Arts et Lettres, France; officer Order of Can., 1991; recipient Marie Tremaine medal, 1973, Tyrrell medal, 1982, Royal Soc. Centenary medal, 1994, Jacques Ducharme prize, 1997, Queen's Jubilee medal, 2002; Faculty of Arts and Scis. U. de Montreal Merit medal, 2004. Fellow Royal Soc. Can. (sect. pres. 1985-87, pres. 1997-99); mem. Am. Antiquarian Soc., Acad. des Lettres du Quebec, Inst. d'Histoire l'Amerique Francaise (pres. 1973-77), Can. Hist. Assn. (pres. 1982), Assn. Can.-Francaise l'Avancement Scis. (pres. 1981-83, emeritus mem.), Assn. Archivists Que., Can. Archivists, Internat. Coun. on Archives (v.p. 1988-92, pres. 1992-96, pres. emeritus). Roman Catholic. Office: U Ottawa CRCCF PO Box 450 Sta A Ottawa ON Canada K1N 6N5 Office Phone: 613-562-5710. Business E-Mail: jpwallot@uottawa.ca.

**WALLPHER, LUIS ANTONIO,** small business owner, painter, writer; b. La Paz, Bolivia, Apr. 30, 1948; s. Luis Humberto Wallpher and Hortensia Gonzalez; m. Monica Vivado De Wallpher, Oct. 13, 1991; children: John L., Anthony, Andy. BFA, Md. Inst. Coll. of Art. Owner Wallpher Galleries of Fine Arts, LaPaz, Bolivia. Author: En La Brecha Cultural, 2005. Councilman Municipal House, LaPaz, Bolivia, 1996; pres., founder Falange Democratica Boliviana, LaPaz, Bolivia, 1998; founder Momimiento Haciendo Patria. Recipient Mare of La Paz, 1994. Mem.: Am. Inst. of Conservation of Monuments. Avocations: tennis, movies, painting.

**WALLS, GEORGE RODNEY,** lawyer; b. New Orleans, Sept. 30, 1945; s. Preston Rodney and Bobbe Cleo (Sharp) W.; m. Nancy Ellen Smith, June 29, 1974; children: Scott Christian, Brian Cannon. BA, U. Md., 1967, JD, 1970. Bar: Md. 1971, D.C. 1971, U.S. Dist. Ct. D.C. 1971, U.S. Supreme Ct. 1977. Assoc. counsel GAC Fin. Inc., Allentown, Pa., 1970-73; sr. atty. Quality Inns Internat., Inc., Silver Spring, Md., 1973-76; gen. counsel, sec. Suburban Bancorp., Bethesda, Md., 1976-86; sr. assoc. gen. counsel, corp. sec. Sovran Fin. Corp., Norfolk, Va., 1986-90; sr. assoc. gen. counsel C&S/Sovran, Norfolk, Va., 1990-91; asst. gen. counsel NationsBank Corp./Bank of Am., Charlotte, N.C., 1991—. Mem. Md. Bar Assn., DC Bar Assn., Soc. Corp. Secs. and Govt. Profls., Assn. Corp. Counsel. Presbyterian. Home: 12425 Pine Valley Club Dr Charlotte NC 28277-4023 Office: Bank of Am NCI 007 20 01 100 N Tryon St Charlotte NC 28255-0001 E-mail: gwalls@carolina.rr.com, george.walls@bankofamerica.com.

**WALLS, JAMES DOUGLAS,** minister; b. Washington, Aug. 1, 1931; s. George Washington and Emma (Benson) W.; m. Donna Marie Payne, June 16, 1962; children: Quentin Douglas, Janice Marie. Student, Washington Bible Inst., 1957-61; DD, Faith Evangelistic Christian Coll., Detroit, 1990, So. Calif. Sch. Ministry, Inglewood, 1991; HHD (hon.), Faith Evang. Christian Schs., Detroit, 1991. Ordained to ministry Ch. of God, 1960. Pastor Ch. of God, Xenia, Ohio, 1968—; mem. program and planning com., nominating com. Nat. Assn. Ch. of God, West Middlesex, Pa., 1983-89, coord. nat. preachers clinic, 1986—2000, mem. mass comm. bd., 1988-92, mem. ch. rels. bd., 1989-93, chief ops. officer, 2000—. Chair. bd. dirs. Women's Abuse of Substance Intervention Tactics, 1990-94 Editor Words of Truth, 1972-84, Xenia Herald, 1988-2000. Mem. Cumberland Ridge Civic Assn., Columbus, Ohio, 1971—. With U.S. Army, 1952-54. Mem. Urban Christian Leadership Assn., Xenia Area Assn. Chs., African Am. Ministerial Alliance, Ohio State Ch. of God Missionary Bd. Home: 3032 Pine Valley Rd Columbus OH 43219-1643

**WALLS, MARTHA ANN WILLIAMS (MRS. B. CARMAGE WALLS),** publishing executive; b. Gadsden, Ala., Apr. 21, 1927; d. Aubrey Joseph and Inez (Cooper) Williams; m. B. Carmage Walls, Jan. 2, 1954; children: Byrd Cooper, Lissa Walls Vahldiek. Student pub. schs., Gadsden. Pres., dir. Walls Newspapers, Inc., 1969-70; sec., treas., dir. Summer Camps, Inc., Guntersville, Ala., 1954-69; CEO, pres., dir. So. Newspapers, Inc., Houston, 1970—; pres., dir. So. Newspapers of Ala., Inc., Scottsboro. V.p., dir. Ft. Payne (Ala.) Newspapers, Inc.; dir. Galveston Newspapers, Inc.; dir. Monroe (Ga.) Newspapers, Inc.; bd. dirs. Jefferson Pilot Corp., Greensboro, N.C., 1990-98, Jefferson-Pilot Life Ins. Co., 1990-98, Jefferson Pilot Comm., 1990-98. Bd. dirs. Montgomery Acad., 1970-74. Mem.: Soc. Profl. Journalists. Episcopalian. Office: 5701 Woodway Ste 300 Houston TX 77057 Personal E-mail: mwalls@sninews.com.

**WALLS, ROBERT HAMILTON, JR.,** lawyer; b. Austin, Tex., May 19, 1960; s. Robert Hamilton Sr. and Anita L. (Hoffman) W.; m. Nancy R. Ghormley, Aug. 11, 1984. BBA in Petroleum, U. Tex., 1983, JD, 1985. Bar: Tex. 1985. Assoc. Vinson & Elkins, Houston, 1985—; dep. gen. coun. Enron Corp., Houston, 1992—2002, exec. v.p. & gen. coun., 2002—. Mem. ABA, Houston Bar Assn. Office: Office of Gen Coun Enron Corp 1400 Smith St PO Box 1188 Houston TX 77251-1188

**WALLS, WILLIAM WALTON, JR.,** management consultant; b. Phila., Oct. 3, 1932; s. William Walton and Mary Crown (Elliott) W.; m. Nina Catherine deAngeli, July 1, 1961; 1 child, Deborah. BSME, Swarthmore Coll., 1959. With Boeing Helicopters, Phila., 1959-96, v.p. light helicopter joint venture, 1988-91, v.p. devel. programs, 1991-92, v.p. rsch. and engring., 1992-96; small high-tech. bus. cons. Ridley Park, Pa., 1996—. Cons. in field. Chmn. aerospace adv. coun. Pa. State Coll., 1974-79; mem. NATO Indsl. Advisors Group, 1988-93; mem. bd. advisors Rotocraft Ctr. Excellence, Rensselaer Polytech. Inst., 1982-84 Mem. Am. Helicopter Soc. (pres. 1988-89, chmn. 1989-90). Republican. Avocations: travel, computers, classical music, exercise. Home: 502 Harrison St Ridley Park PA 19078-3208 Personal E-mail: wwwallsjr@comcast.net.

**WALLSKOG, JOYCE MARIE,** nursing educator, retired psychologist; b. Melrose Park, Ill., Apr. 20, 1942; BSN, Alverno Coll., 1977; MSN, U. Wis., Milw., 1982; PhD, Marquette U., Milw., 1992. RN, Wis.; lic. psychologist; diplomate Am. Coll. Forensic Examiners. Staff nurse St. Mary's Hill Hosp., Milw., 1977—78, Waukesha (Wis.) Meml. Hosp., 1978—80, clin. nurse specialist, 1980—87; asst. prof. nursing Marquette U., Milw., 1986—2005; psychotherapist Psychiat. Assocs. Comprehensive Services, Ltd., Milw., 1982—85; nurse psychotherapist Counseling and Wellness Ctr., Waukesha, 1982—2005; adv. practice nurse prescriber, 1995—2005; guest lectr. Concordia U., Milw., 2005. Cons. Alverno Coll., Milw., 1983-84, Health Care Cons., Sussex, Wis., 1985—; coord. Waukesha Premenstrual Syndrome Program, 1980—; nurse psychotherapist Stress Mgmt. and Mental Health Svcs., Waukesha, 1991-94; co-founder Turning Point Mental Health and Cons. Svcs., Waukesha, 1994—; advanced practice nurse prescriber, 1995—. Contbr. articles to profl. jours. Bd. dirs. Waukesha County Mental Health Assn., 1982; mem. Waukesha County Unified Svcs., 1984; adv. bd. Northwest Rehab. Ctr., 1992-94; advisor Resolve Through Sharing, 1986-2001, Women's Health Svcs., 1987-2001; advisor Parish Nurse Program. Mem. APA, ANA (coun. psychiat. and mental health nursing), Wis. Nurses Assn. (rep. Wis. Coalition on Sexual Misconduct by Psychotherapists and Counselors 1988-93), Delta Upsilon Sigma, Phi Lambda Delta. Personal E-mail: wallskogj@aol.com.

**WALLS PERRY, J(OYCE) LORRAINE,** elementary school educator; b. Washington, Pa., Aug. 23, 1948; d. William K. and Minnie (Crockett) W.; m: Robert L. Perry; 1 child, Lisa Michelle. BA, Point Park Coll., Pitts., 1971; MA in Teaching, U. Pitts., 1972, cert. in curriculum and supervision, 1995. Cert. elem. and early childhood tchr. Pa., elem. prin. Instructional teacher leader, elem tchr. Pitts. Bd. Edn., 1988-92, resource tchr. elem. and mid. sch. social studies, 1992—2000; v.p. Belmar Elem. Sch., Pitts., 2000—02, ret., 2002; ednl. cons., 2002—. Tchr.-in-Residence fellow U. Pitts., 1992-93. Holmes group scholar, 1992-93. Mem. TESA. Home: 3594 Harlow Pl Pittsburgh PA 15204-1143 Personal E-mail: raine823@msn.com.

**WALMER, EDWIN FITCH,** retired lawyer; b. Chgo., Mar. 24, 1930; s. Hillard Wentz and Anna C. (Fitch) W.; m. Florence Poling, June 17, 1952; children: Linda Diane Walmer Dennis, Fred Fitch. BS with distinction, Ind. U., 1952, JD with high distinction, 1957. Bar: Wis. 1957, U.S. Dist. Ct. (ea. dist.) Wis. 1957. Assoc. Foley & Lardner, Milw., 1957-65, ptnr., 1965-90, ret., 1990. Served to 1st lt. U.S. Army, 1952-54. Recipient Cal. C. Chambers award Culver (Ind.) Mil. Acad., 1948. Fellow Am. Coll. Trust and Estate Counsel; mem. Order of Coif, Dairymen's Country Club (Boulder Junction, Wis.), Vineyards Country Club (Naples, Fla.), Phi Eta Sigma, Beta Gamma Sigma. Republican. Congregationalist. Avocations: golf, fishing.

**WALMSLEY, JAMES NAYLOR,** hydroponic farming executive; b. Rockford, Ill., Sept. 6, 1929; s. James A. and Louella H. (Gage) W.; m. Ann Walmsley (divorced); children: Dana, Lauren, Michael, Daryl Lynn; m. Helga Walmsley (div.); children: Kristen V., Tanya J. Student, George Washington, 1950-52, Loyola U., 1953-55, Northwestern U., 1955. Investment banker Hornblower & Weeks, Chgo., 1955-61; pres. Manin Internat. Inc., Chgo., 1961-72, Jinga Hydroponic Farms Ltd., Chgo., 1972—, Bahedeshar Ltd., tech. R & D, Clarksburg, W.Va., 1995—; mng. dir. Manin Internat., Inc., Las Vegas, Nev., 2000—. Active Points of Light Found., Children Def. Fund; rep. W.Va. Rep. Presdl. Roundtable, 2001; hon. chmn. grassroots campaign Rep. Hdqrs., 2002. With USN, 1949-53. Recipient Internat. Am. award, 1987. Mem. Royal Horticulture Soc. Am. Horticulture Soc., N.Y. Acad. Scis. The Heritage Found. Republican. Avocations: travel, art, reading. Office: Bahedeshar Ltd 728 Milford St Clarksburg WV 26301 Office Phone: 304-622-7600.

**WALMSLEY, JUDITH ABRAMS,** chemistry professor; b. Oak Park, Ill., Feb. 6, 1936; d. Kenneth Frederick and Edna Martha (Grau) Abrams; m. Frank Walmsley, Aug. 29, 1959; children: Katherine Ellen, Susan Jennifer. BA in Chemistry, Fla. State U., 1958; PhD in Chemistry, U.N.C., 1962. Rsch. scientist Owens-Ill., Inc., Toledo, 1963-66; rsch. assoc., instr. Mich. State U., East Lansing, 1979-80; sr. rsch. assoc. U. Toledo, 1974-87; assist. prof. U. Tex., San Antonio, 1987-93, assoc. prof., 1993—2000, prof., 2000—, chair dept., 2001—05. Instr. U. Toledo, 1968-69, 75-77, 83-87. Patentee in field; author lab. manuals, 1985; contbr. articles to profl. jours. Recipient rsch. grants Rsch. Corp., U. Tex., 1988-90, NIH, 1990—, DeArce Biomed. Rsch., U. Toledo, 1984-87. Mem. Am. Chem. Soc., AAAS, Sigma Xi, Phi Beta Kappa, Phi Kappa Phi, Delta Gamma. Presbyterian. Avocations: reading, sewing, swimming. Office: Dept Chemistry U Tex San Antonio San Antonio TX 78249-0698 Business E-mail: judith.walmsley@utsa.edu.

**WALMSLEY, PRISCILLA HELEN,** computer company executive; d. Bruno Joseph and Agnes Marie Walmsley; life ptnr. Douglas Michael Kimble. BS, U. Va., Charlottesville, Va., 1990. Software developer Platinum Tech. Inc., McLean, Va., 1990—95, dir. devel., 1995—99; v.p. devel. XMLSolutions Corp., McLean, 1999—2002; mng. dir. Datypic, Traverse City, Mich., 2002—. Mem. working group W3C, Cambridge, Mass., 1999—2004. Author: Definitive XML Schema, 2001, XML in Office 2003, 2003, XQuery, 2006. Mem.: Sierra Club (sec. 2001—06, comm. membership 2001—06), Mensa. Personal E-mail: pwalmsley@datypic.com.

**WALP, SUSAN JANE,** illustrator, educator; b. Allentown, Pa., 1948; BA, Mount Holyoke Coll., 1970; attended, Boston U. Sch. Fine Arts, 1968, NY Studio Sch. Drawing, Painting and Sculpture, 1969—71, Skowhegan Sch. Painting and Sculpture, 1971. Faculty mem. painting Internat. Sch. Art, Montecastello di Vibio, Italy, 1979—99; vis. assist. prof. Dartmouth Coll., Dept. Studio Art, Hanover, NH, 1996—. Exhibited in group shows at Metropolitan Show, Denver Art Mus., 1974, Artists Choose Artists, Lake George Arts Project, 1982, Nature Morte: A Current View, NY Studio Sch., 1993, Objects of Personal Significance, Knoxville Mus. Art, 1996—98, Tex. Tech Lubbock, 1989—98, Hunter Mus. Art, 1996—98, Tarble Art Ctr., 1996—98, Am. Acad. Invitational Exhibition of Painting & Sculpture, AAAL, 1999, Intimate Visions, SUNY, Cortland, 2001, one-man shows include Victoria Munroe Fine Art, NY, 1994, Fischabach Gallery, 1996, Hackett Freedman Gallery, San Francisco, 1999, 2000. Recipient Soc. Illustrators Award, 1984, Am. Illustration Award, 1984; fellow Guggenheim Meml. Found., 2004. Office: Dept Studio Art Dartmouth Coll Hanover NH 03755 E-mail: Susan.J.Walp@dartmouth.edu.

**WALPIN, GERALD,** lawyer; b. NYC, Sept. 1, 1931; s. Michael and Mary (Gordon) W.; m. Sheila Kainer, Apr. 13, 1957; children: Amanda Eve, Edward Andrew, Jennifer Hope. BA, CCNY, 1952; LLB cum laude, Yale Law Sch. 1955. Bar: N.Y. 1955, U.S. Supreme Ct. 1965, U.S. Ct. Appeals (2d cir.) 1960, (6th cir.) 1969, (3d cir.) 1976, (8th cir.) 1982, (9th cir.) 1983, (llth cir.) 1983, (7th cir.) 1984, U.S. Ct. Claims 1984. Law clk. to Hon. E.J. Dimock US Dist. Ct. (so. dist.) NY, NYC, law clk. to Hon. F.P. Bryan, 1955-57; asst. US atty., chief spl. prosecutions US Atty. Office, NYC, 1960-65; sr. ptnr. Katten Muchin Rosenman, LLP, predecessor firms, NYC, 1965—2002, chmn. litigation dept., 1985-96, counsel, 2002—. Adv. com. Fed. Ct. So. Dist. NY, 1991-98; co-chmn. lawyers divsn. Anti-Defamation League, NY, 1994-97; bd. dirs. Ctr. Individual Rights, 1997—; pres. Fed. Bar Coun., 2002-04. Editor Yale Law Jour., 1953-54, mng. editor, 1954-55; contbr. articles to profl. jours. Pres. Parker Jewish Inst. for Health Care and Rehab., New Hyde Park, N.Y., 1987-90, trustee, 1979—; bd. dirs. Fund for Modern Cts., N.Y.C., 1985-91; mem. law com. Am. Jewish Com., 1980-90; mem. Com. for Free World, N.Y.C., 1983-91, trustee, mem. exec. com. United Jewish Appeal Fedn. Jewish Philanthropies, N.Y.C., 1984-86; mem. Nassau County Crime Commn., 1970; pres. Kensington Civic Orgn., Gt. Neck, N.Y., 1972-73. Recipient Quality of Life award United Jewish Appeal Fedn., 1978, Human Rels. award Am. Jewish Com., 1982, Gift of Life award Jewish Inst. Geriatric Care, 1987, Learned Hand award Am. Jewish Com., 1990, Human Rels. award Anti-Defamation League, 1998. Mem. ABA, Fed. Bar Coun. (chmn. modern cts. com. 1989, v.p. 1991-95, chmn. bench and bar liaison com. 1994-95, vice chmn. 1995-97, chmn. bd. dirs. 1997-99, pres. 2002-04, pres. emeritus 2004—), Federalist Soc. (chmn. litigation sect. 1996-99, mem. bd. visitors 1999—), Univ. Club. Republican. Jewish. Home: 875 Park Ave New York NY 10021-0341 Office: Katten Muchin Rosenman LLP 575 Madison Ave Fl 20 New York NY 10022-2511 Office Phone: 212-940-7100. Business E-Mail: gerald.walpin@kattenlaw.com. *My life should be an appropriate response to God and this country for providing me with the opportunities I have had: Contribution to our society and strengthening of our country's steadfast opposition to discrimination for or against anyone based on race, religion or sex.*

**WALPOLE, JIM (JAMES R. WALPOLE),** lawyer; b. Oswego, NY, Aug. 31, 1944; s. Richard and Margaret Mary Walpole; children: Sarah, Mark, Ethan. BA, John Carroll U., 1966; JD, Case Western Res. U., 1969. Bar: Ohio 1969, D.C. 1971, Ill. 1994. U.S. Ct. Appeals (D.C., 3d, 4th, 7th, 8th and 11th cirs.), U.S. Supreme Ct. 1973. Trial atty. U.S. Dept. Justice, Washington, 1971-74; asst. gen. counsel Am. Mining Congress, Washington, 1975—; ptnr. Holland & Hart, Washington, 1979—85, Chadbourne & Parke, Washington, 1985-92; v.p. environment, safety & health FMC Corp., Chgo., 1992-95; asst. gen. counsel Sears Roebuck & Co., Chgo., 1995—2001; gen.counsel NOAA, Washington, 2002—. Mem. adv. com. U.S. C. of C., Washington, 1987-92; adj. prof. environ. law Cath. U., Washington, 1975-79. Author publs. in field. Bd. dirs. Griffin Theater Co. Roman Catholic. Avocations: civil war, fishing. Office: NOAA 1401 Constitution Ave NW Washington DC 20230

**WALRATH, HARRY RIENZI,** retired minister; b. Alameda, Calif., Mar. 7, 1926; s. Frank Rienzi and Cathren (Michlar) W.; m. Dorothy B. Maxter, June 24, 1961; 1 son, Gregory Rienzi. AA, City Coll., San Francisco, 1950; BA, U. Calif., Berkeley, 1952; MDiv, Ch. Div. Sch. of Pacific, 1959. Ordained deacon Episcopal Ch., 1959, priest, 1960. Dist. exec. San Mateo area Boy Scouts Am., 1952-55; curate All Souls Parish, Berkeley, Calif., 1959-61; vicar St. Luke's, Atascadero, Calif., 1961-63, St. Andrew's, Garberville, Calif., 1963-64; assoc. rector St. Luke's Ch., Los Gatos, 1964-65, Holy Spirit Parish, Missoula, Mont., 1965-67; vicar St. Peter's Ch., Litchfield Park, Ariz., 1967-69; also headmaster St. Peter's Schs., Litchfield Park, Ariz., 1967-69; chaplain U. Mont., 1965-67; asst. rector Trinity Parish, Reno, 1969-72; coord. counciling svcs. Washoe County Coun. Alcholism, Reno, 1972-74; adminstr. Cons. Assistance Svcs., Inc., Reno, 1974-76; pastoral counselor, contract chaplain Nev. Mental Health Inst., 1976-78; contract mental health chaplain VA Hosp., Reno, 1976-78; mental health chaplain VA Med. Ctr., Reno, 1978-83, staff chaplain, 1983-85, chief chaplain svc., 1985-91, triage coord. mental health, ret., 1991. Per diem chaplain Washoe Med. Ctr., Reno, 1993; assoc. priest Trinity Episcopal Ch., Reno, 1995; assoc. Mountain Ministries, Susanville, Calif., 1995—. Author: God Rides the Rails-Chapel Cars on American Railroads at the Turn of the Century, 1994. Dir. youth Paso Robles Presbytery; chmn. Diocesan Commn. on Alcoholism; mem. clergy team Episcopal Marriage Encounter; chaplain Make A Wish Found., 1998-2000; mem. at-large Washoe dist. Nev. area coun. Boy Scouts Am., scoutmaster troop 73, 1976, troop 585, 1979-82, asst. scoutmaster troop 35, 1982-92, assoc. adviser area 3 Western region, 1987-89, regional com. Western Region, 1989-90; lodge adviser Tannu Lodge 346, Order of Arrow, 1982-87; docent coun. Nev. Hist. Sch., 1992; South Humboldt County chmn. Am. Cancer Soc.; trustee Cmty. Youth Ctr., Reno. With USNR, 1944-46. Decorated Pacific Theatre medal with star, Am. Theatre medal, Victory medal, Fleet Unit Commendation medal; recipient dist. award of merit Boy Scouts Am., St. George award Episc. Ch., Boy Scouts Am., Silver Beaver award Boy Scouts Am., 1986, Founders' award Order of the Arrow, Boy Scouts Am., 1995; performance awards VA-VA Med. Ctr., 1983, 84; named Arrowman of Yr., Order of Arrow, Boy Scouts Am. Cert. substance abuse counselor, Nev. Mem. Ch. Hist. Soc., U. Calif. Alumni Assn., Nat. Model R.R. Assn. (life), Sierra Club Calif., Missoula Coun. Chs. (pres.), Rotary, Alpha Phi Omega. Democrat. Home: 4822 Ramcreek Trl Reno NV 89509-8029 E-mail: v7t11@aol.com.

**WALRATH, PATRICIA A.,** state legislator; b. Brainerd, Minn., Aug. 11, 1941; d. Joseph James and Pansy Patricia (Drake) McCarvill; m. Robert Eugene Walrath, Sept. 1, 1961; children: Karen, Susan, David, Julie. BS, Bemidji State U., 1962; MS, SUNY, Oswego, 1975. Cert. secondary math. tchr., N.Y., Mass. Programmer analyst Control Data Corp., Mpls., 1962-65; crewleader dept. commerce U.S. Census, Middlesex County, Mass., 1979-80; selectman Town of Stow, Mass., 1980-85; invic. math. Hale Jr. High Sch., Stow, 1981-82; instr. math. Johnson & Wale Coll. Hanscom AFB, Bedford, Mass., 1983-84, test examiner, 1983-84; state rep. 3d Middlesex dist. State of Mass., Boston, 1985—. Many coms. including most recently; chmn. com. long term debt and capital expenditures Mass. Ho. of Reps., 1997—2001, asst. whip, floor chair, 2001—04, chmn. healthcare financing com., 2005—. Chmn. Mass. Indoor Air Pollution Commn., Boston, 1987-88; mem. Stow Dem. Com., 1988—. Recipient Disting. Svc. award Auburn N.Y. Jaycees, 1976. Mem. LWV (pres. 1973-76, dir. 1977-78), Mass. Legislators' Assn., Mass. Dem. Leadership Coun. (v.p. 1991-92, co-chmn. 1993-94, treas. 1995-99), Mass. Women's Legis. Caucus (chair 1986). Roman Catholic. Avocations: gardening, stamp collecting/philately, travel. Home: 20 Middlemost Way Stow MA 01775-1363 Office: State Capital RM 236 Boston MA 02133 Office Phone: 617-722-2430. Business E-Mail: Rep.PatriciaWalrath@hou.state.ma.us.

**WALSH, ALEXANDRA M.,** lawyer; b. 1972; BA summa cum laude, Bowdoin Coll., 1995; JD, Stanford Univ., 2001. Bar: Md. 2004. Law clk. U.S. Ct. Appeals (D.C. cir.), Washington, 2001—02; assoc. Latham & Watkins, Washington, 2003—; law clk. to Hon. Stephen G. Breyer U.S. Supreme Ct., Washington, 2003—04; assoc. Baker Botts, Washington, 2004—. Mem.: Order of the Coif. Office: Baker Botts LLP The Warner 1299 Pennsylvania Ave Washington DC 20004-2400

**WALSH, CHARLES RICHARD,** retired banker; b. Bklyn., Jan. 30, 1939; s. Charles John and Anna Ellen Walsh; m. Marie Anne Goulden, June 24, 1961; children: Kevin C., Brian R., Gregory M. BS, Fordham U., 1960; MBA, St. John's U., 1966, D of Comml. Scis. (hon.), 1985. V.p. Mfrs. Hanover Trust Co., Hicksville, NY, 1974-80, sr. v.p. 1980-86, exec. v.p. 1986-90, group exec., mem. mgmt. com., 1990-92; exec. v.p., group exec. Chem. Banking Corp., Hicksville, NY, 1992-95, The Chase Manhattan Corp., 1995-97; ret., 1997. Bd. dirs. Mastercard Internat.; bd. dirs., former chmn. Eastern States Monetary Svcs., Lake Success, N.Y., 1978-88; former pres., CEO, bd. dirs. The Bankcard Assn., Hicksville, 1988-91. Vice chmn. adv. bd. St. John's U., 1982—; sustaining mem. Rep. Nat. Com., 1978—. With USAR, 1960, 61-62. Mem. N.Y. State Bankers Assn. (former bd. dirs., mem. gov. coun., chmn. consumer banking divsn.), Am. Bankers Assn. (mem. govt. rels. coun., chmn. bank card divsn., mem. exec. com., former mem. comms. coun. and chmn. edn. coun.), Am. Mgmt. Assn., N.Y. Credit and Fin. Mgmt. Assn., Soc. Cert. Consumer Credit Execs. (cert.), Beta Gamma Sigma, Omicron Delta Epsilon, North Hempstead Country Club, Gov.'s Club Kiawah Island (S.C.), Kiawah Island Club. Republican. Home: 31 Fieldstone Ln Oyster Bay NY 11771-3122 also: 107 Goldeneye Dr Kiawah Island SC 29455-5773

**WALSH, CHRISTINE ANN,** cardiologist; b. Bklyn., Dec. 31, 1947; d. Martin and Loretta (Lesniewski) Kull; m. Sean Michael Walsh, June 10, 1978; children: Kathleen, Sean, Stephen. BS, Fordham U., 1969; MD, Yale U., 1973. Diplomate Am. Bd. Pediatrics, Am. Bd. Critical Care Medicine, Am. Bd. Pediatric Cardiology. Intern, then resident Babies Hosp., N.Y., Columbia-Presbyn. Med. Ctr., N.Y.; fellow in pediatric cardiology Columbia U., N.Y., asst. prof. Coll. Physicians and Surgeons N.Y.C., 1980-84; asst. prof. Albert Einstein Coll. of Medicine, N.Y.C., 1984-91; asst. attending physician N.C. Bronx Hosp., 1984—; asst. attending pediatrician Jacobi Med. Ctr., Bronx, 1984—; dir. Pediat. Dysrhythmia Ctr. Montefiore Med. Ctr., Bronx, 1984—, from asst. to assoc. attending pediatrician, 1984-98, attending pediatrician, 1998—, chief sect. pediatric. cardiology, 2002—; assoc. prof. pediat. Albert Einstein Coll. of Medicine, Bronx, 1991-98, prof., 1998—, co-chair admissions com., 1998—. Cons. Adult Arrhythmia Svc., Montefiore Med. Ctr., Pacemaker Ctr., epilepsy unit, Cranio-facial Ctr.; postdoctorate in cardiac electrophysiology and phramcology Columbia U. Coll. Physicians and Surgeons, N.Y.C., 1978—80. Editor: Adolescent Medicine, State of Art Revs., Adolescent Cardiology; contbr. articles to profl. jours. Bd. dirs. Velo-Cardio-Facial Syndrome Ednl. Found., N.Y.C., 1995—. Grantee, Albert Einstein Interdivisional, 1995, 1999. Fellow: Am. Acad. Pediat., Am. Coll. Cardiology; mem.: N.Y. Soc. Pediatric Critical Care Assn., Am. Heart Assn., Pediat. Electrophysiology Soc., Pediatric Cardiology Soc. (treas. 1987—88, sec. 1988—89, v.p. 1989—90, pres. 1990—91), Heart Rhythm Soc., Assn. Yale Alumni Medicine (sec.), Phi Beta Kappa. Avocations: gardening, skiing, scuba diving, piano, camping. Home: PO Box 238 Flushing NY 11363-0238 Office: Montefiore Med Ctr 111 E 210th St Bronx NY 10467-2401 Office Phone: 718-741-2310.

**WALSH, CRAIG T.,** composer, educator; b. Somerville, N.J., Apr. 11, 1971; MusB, Mannes Coll. Music, N.Y.C., 1993; MFA, Brandeis U., 1995, PhD, 1999. Asst. prof. U. N.C., Greensboro, 1998—2001, U. Ariz., Tucson, 2001—. Composer: (music) Zook (Nat. Assn. Composers award, 2000), Schism for clarinet and violin (Lee Ettelson Composer's award Music Tchrs. Nat. Assn., 2000), Lines for piano solo, Terma for soprano and digital media (Eric Siday Musical Creativity award Internat. Computer Music Assn., 2004), Pipeline Burst Cache for cello and digital media (Morton Gould Young Composer's award ASCAP, 1999), Bugaboo for chamber orchestra (Wellesley Composers Conf. award, 2002), 0 To 33 In 1098.5 For Clarinet, Violin, And Piano (Salvatore Martirano Internat. Composition award), Pipeline Burst Cache for cello and digital media (Concorso Internazionale Luigi Russolo, 1999). John Simon Guggenheim Meml. fellow, 2002. Mem.: Coll. Music Soc., Internat. Assn. Computer Music, Soc. Electro-Acoustic Music. Office: U Ariz Sch Music and Dance Tucson AZ 85721-0004 Office Phone: 520-521-1655. Business E-Mail: ctwalsh@email.arizona.edu.

**WALSH, DANIEL J.,** medical products executive; MBA in Exec. Mgmt., St. John's U., NYC. CPA NY. With US Dept. Def., Loral Corpn.; dir., sr. mgr. mgmt consulting divsn. PricewaterhouseCoopers, 1986—93; corp. compliance officer Smiths Grp., PLC, 1993—2003; v.p., chief compliance officer Sci.-Atlanta, Inc., 2003—05; exec. v.p., chief ethics and compliance officer Cardinal Health, 2005—. Office: Cardinal Health 7000 Cardinal Pl Dublin OH 43017*

**WALSH, DAVID GRAVES,** lawyer; b. Madison, Wis., Jan. 7, 1943; s. John J. and Audrey B. Walsh; married; children: Michael, Katherine, Molly, John. BBA, U. Wis., 1965; JD, Harvard U., 1970. Bar: Wis. Law clk. Wis. Supreme Ct., Madison, 1970-71; ptnr. Walsh, Walsh, Sweeney & Whitney, Madison, 1971-86; ptnr.-in-charge, pres. Foley & Lardner, Madison, 1986—95. Pres., bd. regents U. Wis., 2003—; bd. dirs. Nat. Guardian Life, Madison, Thompson Investment Mgmt., Inc., Alkar-Rapidpak, Inc.; lectr. U. Wis., Madison, 1974-75, 77-78; pres. U. Wis. sys. bd. regents, 2005-. Chmn. State of Wis. Elections Bd., Madison, 1978. Lt. USN, 1965-67, Vietnam. Recipient Disting. Bus. Alumnus award U. Wis. Sch. Bus., 1997. Maple Bluff Country Club (Madison) (pres. 1987). Roman Catholic. Avocations: tennis, golf, fishing. Home: 41 Fuller Dr Madison WI 53704-5962 Office: Foley & Lardner PO Box 1497 Madison WI 53701-1497 Office Phone: 608-258-4269. Business E-Mail: dwalsh@foley.com.

**WALSH, DAVID JOSEPH,** pediatric neurologist, educator; b. St. Louis, Oct. 5, 1946; s. Joseph Lloyd and Dorothy Ann Walsh. BS, Georgetown U., 1968; MD, Med. U. S.C., 1973. Diplomate Am. Bd. Psychiatry and Neurology, Am. Bd. Pediat. Asst. prof. neurology and pediat. Jacksonville Health Edn. Program, U. Fla., Jacksonville, 1981—82; asst. prof. pediat. and neurology U. Kans., Kansas City, 1982—88; pvt. practice Allegheny Neurol. Assoc., Pitts., 1988—90; asst. prof. neurology Med. Coll. Wis., Milw., 1990—2000; assoc. prof. neurology St. Louis U., St. Louis, 2000—. Program dir. pediat. residency U. Kans., Kansas City, 1982—87; program dir. pediat. neurology residency program Med. Coll. Wis., Milw., 2001—03; chief med. staff, divsn. neurology Children's Hosp., Milw., 2001—04; chief sect. child neurology St. Louis U., St. Louis, 2004—. Author: (short story) Upping the Ritalin. Pres. Epilepsy Found. S.E. Wis., Milw., 1994—2000; chair profl. adv. bd., 1992—2004; profl. adv. bd. Epilepsy Found., St. Louis. Lt. USNR, 1974—76. Fellow: Am. Acad. Neurology; mem.: Assn. U. Profs. Neurology, Harvard Med. Alumni Assn., Med. U. S.C. Alumni Assn., Child Neurology Soc. Independent. Roman Catholic. Avocations: Aikido, opera, travel. Office: Cardinal Glennon Children's Hosp 1465 S Grand Blvd Glennon Hall Rm 502 Saint Louis MO 63104 Office Phone: 314-268-4105. E-mail: walshdj@slu.edu.

**WALSH, DENNIS P.,** federal agency administrator; m. Barbara A. O'Neill; children: Steven, Rose. BA in Govt. summa cum laude, Hamilton Coll., 1975; JD cum laude, Cornell Law Sch., 1983. Atty.-advisor NLRB Hdqrs., 1984—87; field atty. region 4 NLRB, 1987—89, chief counsel to Margaret A Browning, 1994—97, chief counsel to Wilma B. Liebman, 1997—2000, mem., 2000—01, 2002—04; assoc. Spear, Wilderman, Borish, Endy, Browning & Spear, Phila., 1989—94; mem. NLRB, 2006—. Business E-Mail: dennis.walsh@nlrb.gov.

**WALSH, DENNY JAY,** reporter; b. Omaha, Nov. 23, 1935; s. Gerald Jerome and Muriel (Morton) W.; m. Peggy Marie Moore, Feb. 12, 1966; children by previous marriage— Catherine Camille, Colleen Cecile; 1 son, Sean Joseph. B.J., U. Mo., 1962. Staff writer St. Louis Globe-Democrat, 1961-68; asst. editor Life mag., N.Y.C., 1968-70, assoc. editor, 1970-73; reporter N.Y. Times, 1973-74, Sacramento Bee, 1974—. Served with USMC, 1954-58. Recipient Con Lee Kelliher award St. Louis chpt. Sigma Delta Chi, 1962; award Am. Polit. Sci. Assn., 1963; award Sigma Delta Chi, 1968; Pulitzer prize spl. local reporting, 1969; 1st prize San Francisco Press Club, 1977; Beacon award for lifetime achievement, 1st Amendment Coalition, 2004. Office: Sacramento Bee 21st & Q Sts Sacramento CA 95816 Office Phone: 916-321-1189. Business E-Mail: dwalsh@sacbee.com.

**WALSH, DIANA CHAPMAN,** academic administrator, sociologist, educator; b. Phila., July 30, 1944; d. Robert Francis and Gwen (Jenkins) Chapman; m. Christopher Thomas Walsh, June 18, 1966; 1 child, Allison Chapman. BA in English, Wellesley Coll., 1966; MS in Journalism, Boston U. Sch. of Pub. Comm., 1971; PhD in Health Policy, Boston U., 1983; LHD (hon.), Boston U, 1994, Amer. Coll. of Greece, Athens, 1995, U. Mass., Amherst, 1999; LHD, Northeastern U., 2003. Dir. info., edn. Planned Parenthood League, Newton, Mass., 1971—74; sr. program assoc. Dept Pub. Health, Boston, 1974—76; assoc. dir. Boston U. Health Policy Inst., 1985—90; prof. Sch. Pub. Health, Sch. Medicine, Boston U., 1987—90, adj. prof. pub. health, 1990—; Florence Sprague Norman and Laura Smart Norman prof., chair dept. health and social behavior Harvard Sch. Pub. Health, 1990—93, adj. prof., 1993—; pres. Wellesley Coll., 1993—. Author: (book) Corporate Physicians, 1987; editor: Women, Work and Health: Challenges to Corporate Policy, 1980, (book series) Industry and Health Care, 1977—80; co-author: Payer, Provider, Consumer, 1977; contbr. articles to profl. jours. Bd. dirs. Planned Parenthood League of Mass., 1974—79, 1981—85, bd. overseers, 1993—94; trustee Occupl. Physicians Scholarship Fund, 1987—94, WGBH Ednl. Found., 1993—2000. Recipient Book of the Yr. award, Am. Jour. Nursing, 1980; fellow, Kellogg Nat. fellow, 1987—90. Mem.: AHA, AAAS, Consortium on Financing Higher Edn., State Street Corp. (chair 2003—04), Mass. Pub. Health Assn., Soc. for the Study of Social Problems, Am. Sociol. Assn. Avocations: gender and health, social policy, writing, skiing. Office: Wellesley Coll Office of the Pres 106 Central St Wellesley MA 02481-8268 Office Phone: 781-283-2237, E-mail: president@wellesley.edu.*

**WALSH, DIANE,** pianist; b. Washington, Aug. 16, 1950; d. William Donald and Estelle Louise (Stokes) W.; m. Henry Forbes, 1969 (div. 1979); m. Richard Pollak, 1982. MusB, Juilliard Sch. Music, 1971; MusM, Mannes Coll., 1982. N.Y.C. debut Young Concert Artists Series, 1974; founding mem. Mannes Trio, 1983-94; solo appearances include: Kennedy Ctr. for Performing Arts, Washington, 1976, Met. Mus., N.Y.C., 1976, Wigmore Hall, London, 1980, Merkin Concert Hall, 1989, Miller Theatre, 1994, 96; with Mannes Trio: Lincoln Ctr.'s Alice Tully Hall, Libr. of Congress, 1987; appeared with maj. orchs. worldwide, including St. Louis Symphony, Indpls. Symphony, San Francisco Symphony, Am. Symphony, Austin (Tex.) Symphony, Bavarian Radio Symphony of Munich, Berlin Radio Symphony, Radio Symphony Frankfurt, Radio Symphony Stuttgart; has toured Europe, N.Am., S.Am., C.Am., Russia; Marlboro Festival, 1982, Bard Festival, 1990-99, Santa Fe (N.Mex.) Festival, 1995; recs. for Nonesuch Records, 1980, 82, Book-of-Month Records, 1985, Music and Arts, 1990, CRI, 1991, Koch, 1995, Biddulph Records, 1998, Stereophile, 1998, Newport Classic, 1998, Sony, 2000, Bridge, 2004; artistic dir. Skaneateles Festival, 1999-2004; mem. piano and chamber music faculty Mannes Coll. Music, 1982—. Recipient 3d prize Busoni Internat. Piano Competition, Italy, 1974, 2nd prize Mozart Internat. Piano Competition, Salzburg, Austria, 1975, 1st prize Munich Internat. Piano Competition, 1975, Naumburg Chamber Music award, 1986, Classical Recording Found. award, 2004, Classical Internet award, 2004; NEA grantee, 1981. Office Phone: 212-580-0210.

**WALSH, DOLORES ANN GONCZO (LORRY WALSH),** special education educator; b. Detroit, Sept. 3, 1933; d. Joseph John and Dolores (Carey) Gonczo; m. Bernard Waldrup, Aug. 23, 1958 (div. 1980, dec. 2000); children: Elizabeth, Carey, Leslie, Bernard III; m. Deleon Walsh, Sept. 3, 1982 (dec. 1990). Student, Barat Coll., 1951-52; PhB, U. Detroit, 1955; MPS, Manhattanville Coll., 1978. Tchr. 2d grade East Detroit (Mich.) Pub. Schs., 1955-58; tchr. 4th grade Birmingham (Ala.) Schs., 1958-59, St. Franics Xavier Sch., Birmingham, 1959-62; homebound tchr. Greenburg Ctrl. 7, Hartsdale, NY, 1969-73, tchr. spl. edn., 1973-91; ret., 1991. Tchr. English, China, 1998; mem. Middle States Evaluating Team of High Schs., 1082-90. Dist. leader Dem. Party Greenburgh, 1981-91; sec. Greenburgh Health Cen. Bd., Greenburgh, N.Y., 1986-91; leader Girl Scouts U.S., 1968-69; CCD tchr. Convent of Sacred Heart, Greenwich, Conn.; vol. West Valley Art Mus., 1992-2001, Cath. Ctr., 1998—. Mem. Ariz. Alumnae of Sacred Heart (pres. 2001-03), Delta Zeta. E-mail: lorry2@quik.com.

**WALSH, DON,** engineer, consultant; b. Berkeley, Calif., Nov. 2, 1931; s. J. Don and Marguerite Grace (Van Auker) W.; m. Joan A. Betzmer, Aug. 18, 1962; children— Kelly Drennan, Elizabeth McDonough BS, U.S. Naval Acad., 1954; MS, Tex. A&M U., 1967, PhD, 1968; MA, San Diego State U., 1968. Commd. ensign USN, 1954, advanced through grades to capt., 1974, officer-in-charge Bathyscaph Trieste Trieste, 1959-62, comdr. in USS Bashaw, 1968-69; dir. Inst. Marine and Coastal Studies, prof. ocean engring. U. So. Calif., L.A., 1975-83; pres., CEO Internat. Maritime, Inc., 1976—; mng. dir. Deep Ocean Engring., Inc., 1990—2000, also bd. dirs. Dir. Ctr. for Marine Transp. Studies, U. So. Calif., 1980-83, Coastal Resources Ctr., 1990-94; trustee USN Mus. Found., 1989—; mem. Nat. Adv. Com. on Oceans and Atmosphere, 1979-85; bd. govs. Calif. Maritime Acad., 1985-95; pres. Parker Diving, 1989-94. Editor, contbr.: Law of the Sea: Issues in Ocean Resource Management, 1977, Energy and Resources Development of Continental Margins, 1980, Energy and Sea Power: Challenge for the Decade, 1981, Waste Disposal in the Oceans: Minimizing Impact, Maximizing Benefits, 1983; editor Jour. Marine Tech. Soc., 1975-80; mem. editorial bd. U.S. Naval Inst., 1974-75. Bd. dirs. Charles and Anne Lindbergh Found., 1996-2005. Decorated Legion of Merit (2); Woodrow Wilson Internat. Ctr. for Scholars fellow, 1973-74. Fellow Marine Tech. Soc., Acad. Underwater Arts and Scis., Explorers Club (hon. life, bd. dirs. 1994-2000, Explorers Medal, 2001); mem. AAAS, Soc. Naval Archs. and Marine Engrs., Am. Soc. Naval Engrs., Navy Inst., Adventurers Club (hon. life), Am. Geog. Soc. (hon. life), Nat. Acad. Engring. Home and Office: Internat Maritime Inc 14758 Sitkum Ln Myrtle Point OR 97458-9726 Personal E-mail: imiwalsh@worldnet.att.net, imiwalsh@mac.com.

**WALSH, DOUGLAS SHAWN,** medical association administrator, dermatologist, director, military officer; b. Cin., May 18, 1961; s. Gerald Peter and Geraldine Lee Walsh; m. Anocha Kansorn, July 1, 2004. BS summa cum laude in Biology, Mt. St. Mary's Coll., 1983; MS in Biology and Exptl. Medicine, St. Thomas Inst. Adv. Studies, Cin., 1985; MD, George Washington U., 1989. Diplomate Am. Bd. Dermatology, Nat. Bd. Med. Examiners, ACLS, Advanced Trauma Life Support, good clin. practices; med. lic. Md., 1990-, Pa., 1993-, Hawaii, 1995-98, Thailand, 2001-2002, Ga., 2003-, drug enforcement adminstrn., 1995-. Commd. 2d lt. U.S. Army, 1986, advanced through grades to col., 1993; intern Walter Reed Army Med. Ctr., Wash., 1989-90, resident in dermatology, 1992-95; chief dept. combat casualty and clin. rsch. divsn. surgery Walter Reed Army Inst. Rsch., Wash., 1990-92, med. rsch. fellow, 1994-95, rsch. investigator divsn. exptl. therapeutics, 1995; clin. investigator dept. immunology US Army med. component Armed Forces Rsch. Inst. Med. Scis., Bangkok, 1990-92, asst. chief, 1995—97, chief dept., 1997—2001, sr. clin. investigator, 2001—02; chief dermatology svc. dept. medicine Eisenhower Army Med. Ctr., Ft. Gordon (Augusta), Ga., 2002—05, chief dept. clin. investigation, 2003—05; asst. chief dept. clin. trials Walter Reed Army Inst. Rsch., Silver Spring, 2005—06. Rsch. asst. dept. molecular virology Gamble Inst. Med. Rsch., Cin., 1984-85; rschr. in microbial genetics George Washington U. Sch. Medicine, 1986-87; cons. in dermatology Walter Reed Army Med. Ctr., 1995—; clin. cons. Leonard Wood Meml. Ctr for Leprosy Rsch., Cebu City, Philippines, 1996—; mem. Instl. Animal Care and Use Com. Armed Forces Rsch. Inst. Med. Scis., Bangkok, 1996—; adj. assoc. clin. prof. dept. medicine sect. dermatology Med. Coll. Ga., Augusta, 2003—; adj. assoc. prof. dept. dermatology Uniformed Svcs. U. Health Scis., Bethesda, 2004-. Contbr. numerous articles to profl. jours. Decorated Army Commendation medal, 1995; Armed Forces Health Professions scholar, 1985-89; Frederick Mohs grantee Nat. Skin Cancer Found., 1993-94; grantee Dermatology Found., 1994-95. Fellow Am. Acad. Dermatology; mem. AMA (mem. com. on phys. plant resources for accreditation 1987) Am. Soc. Microbiology, Binford-Dammin Soc. for Infectious Disease Pathologists, Am. Soc. Tropical Medicine and Hygiene, Soc. Investigative Dermatology, Am. Fedn. Clin. Rsch., Monsignor Tierney Honor Soc., Delta Epsilon Sigma, Beta Beta Beta. Office: Walter Reed Army Inst Rsch Dept Clin Trials Silver Spring MD 20910 Business E-Mail: douglas.s.walsh@us.army.mil.

**WALSH, EDWARD F.,** social studies educator; b. Buffalo, Oct. 25, 1965; s. John and Betty Walsh; m. Nicoletta Walsh; children: Connor, Gabriella. M in Edn., SUNY, Buffalo, 1995. Cert. 7-12 grade tchr. N.Y. State, 1989. Social studies tchr. Depew H.S., NY, 1990—, Lancaster H.S., NY, 1995—. Asst. cub master Boy Scouts Am., Clarence, NY, 2004—06. Mem.: World History Assn. Avocations: travel, camping, reading. Office: Lancaster High Sch 1 Forton Dr Lancaster NY 14086 Office Phone: 716-686-3255. E-mail: ewalsh@lancaster.wnyric.org.

**WALSH, EDWARD JOSEPH,** food products executive, cosmetics executive; b. Mt. Vernon, NY, Mar. 18, 1932; s. Edward Aloysius and Charlotte Cecilia (Borup) W.; m. Patricia Ann Farrell, Sept. 16, 1961; children: Edward Joseph, Megan Simpson, John, Robert. BBA, Iona Coll., 1953; MBA, NYU, 1958. Sales rep. M & R Dietetic Labs., Columbus, Ohio, 1955-60; with Armour & Co., 1961-71, Greyhound Corp., 1971-87; v.p. toiletries div. Armour Dial Co., Phoenix, 1973-74, exec. v.p., 1975-77; pres., CEO Armour Internat. Co., Phoenix, 1978-84; pres. The Dial Corp. (formerly Armour-Dial Co.), Phoenix, 1984-87, chief exec. officer, 1984-87; pres., chief exec. officer Purex Corp., 1985; chmn., chief exec. officer The Sparta Group Ltd., Scottsdale, Ariz., 1988—. Bd. dirs. Guest Supply Inc., New Brunswick, NJ, 1988—2001, WD-40 Co., San Diego, 1988—2004, Nortrust Holding Corp., Phoenix, No. Trust Bank of Ariz., N.A., Inc., Matrixx Initiatives, Inc., Phoenix; mem. bd. advisors Brother to Brother Internat., 1988—2001, Universal Tech. Inst., Phoenix, 1996—2004; dir. Exec. Svc. Corp. Ariz., 1996—2000. Trustee Scottsdale Meml. Health Found., 1995-98; pres. Mt. Vernon Fire Dept. Mems. Assn., 1960-61. Served with U.S. Army, 1953-55, Germany. Recipient Loftus Lifetime Achievement award, Iona Coll., 2004. Mem. Am. Mgmt. Assn., Nat. Meat Canner Assn. (pres. 1971-72), Cosmetic, Toiletries and Fragrance Assn. (bd. dirs. 1985—87), Nat. Food Processors Assn. (bd. dirs.). Republican. Roman Catholic. Office: The Sparta Group Ltd 6623 N Scottsdale Rd Scottsdale AZ 85250-4421

**WALSH, GEORGE WILLIAM,** publishing company executive, editor, author; b. N.Y.C., Jan. 16, 1931; s. William Francis and Madeline (Maass) W.; m. Joan Mary Dunn, May 20, 1961; children— Grail, Simon. BS, Fordham U., 1952; MS, Columbia U. Sch. Journalism, 1953. Copy editor, reporter Cape Cod Standard-Times, Hyannis, Mass., 1955; communications specialist IBM, N.Y.C., 1955-58; editorial trainee Time, Inc., 1958-59; writer-reporter Sports Illus., N.Y.C., 1959-62; book editor Cosmopolitan, N.Y.C., 1962-65, mng. editor, 1965-74; editor-in-chief, v.p. Ballantine Books div. Random House, N.Y.C., 1974-79, Macmillan Pub. Co., N.Y.C., 1979-85; pub. cons., 1985—. Author: Gentleman Jimmy Walker, 1974, Public Enemies, 1980, Damage Them All You Can--Robert E. Lee's Army of Northern Virginia, 2002, Whip the Rebellion--Ulysses S. Grant's Rise to Command, 2004. Served with AUS, 1953-55. Mem. Assn. Am. Pubs. Clubs: Univ. (N.Y.C.); Pamet Harbor Yacht and Tennis (Truro, Mass.). Roman Catholic. Personal E-mail: edchief@verizon.net.

**WALSH, GERALDINE FRANCES,** nursing administrator; b. Phila., July 3, 1946; d. Raymond S. and Marie Ruth (Lipsett) Lore; m. Harry G. Walsh, Jan. 29, 1966; children: Michael, Gregory. AA, No. Va. Community Coll., 1979; BS, St. Joseph's Coll., Windham, Maine, 1987; MS, St. Joseph's Coll., 2006. Cert. in nursing adminstrn.; cert. dir. nursing adminstrn. long term care; lic. nursing home adminstr. Charge nurse, asst. head nurse Parkview Hosp., Phila., 1968-73; staff nurse JFK Med. Ctr., Edison, 1973-76; clin. nursing supr., charge nurse med.-surg. Loudoun Hosp. Ctr., Leesburg, Va., 1976-88; asst. dir. nursing Loudoun Long Term Care Ctr., Leesburg, 1988-95; dir. nursing Inova Cameron Glen Care Ctr., Reston, Va., 1995-99, Integrated Health Svcs. No. Va., 1999—2003, Genesis Woodmont Healthcare and Rehab. Ctr., 2003—. Recipient Nursing Achievement award. Fellow Nat. Assn. Dirs. Nursing; mem. ANA, NAFE, Nat. League Nursing, Va. League Nursing, Va. Nurses Assn., Am. Coll. Healthcare Execs. (student assoc. mem.), Assn. Healthcare Adminstrs. of Nat. Capitol Area, Va. Organ. Nurse Execs. Address: 208 Birdie Rd Locust Grove VA 22508-5116 Personal E-Mail: walshge@attglobal.net. Business E-Mail: geri.walsh@genesishcc.com

**WALSH, JAMES JOSEPH,** lawyer; b. New Orleans, June 21, 1948; s. Francis Michael and Violet (Young) W.; m. Priscilla Robson Ferris, Oct. 12, 1972; children: Caitlin Marian, Alison Robson. BA, La. State U., 1970, JD, 1975. Bar: La. 1975, Mich. 1977, U.S. Ct. Appeals (6th cir.) 1981, U.S. Supreme Ct. 1991. Law clk. Mich. Ct. Appeals, Detroit, 1975-77; assoc. Bodman LLP, Detroit, 1977—84, ptnr., 1984—. Counsel Outdoor Advt. Assn. Mich. Editor: La. Law Rev., 1975. Named to Hall of Fame, La. State U. Law Sch., 1988. Mem. State Bar Mich., Washtenaw County Bar Assn., Detroit Athletic Club, Mich. C. of C., Jefferson City Buzzards. Avocations: fishing, gardening, golf. Home: 8025 Mast Rd Dexter MI 48130-9301 Office: Bodman LLP 110 Miller Ave Ste 300 Ann Arbor MI 48104-1339 Office Phone: 734-930-0237. Business E-Mail: jwalsh@bodmanllp.com.

**WALSH, JAMES THOMAS (JIM WALSH),** congressman; b. Syracuse, NY, June 19, 1947; s. William F. Walsh; m. DeDe Ryan; 3 children. BA in Hist., St. Bonaventure U., 1970. Agrl. ext. agt. Peace Corps, Nepal, 1970-72; mktg. exec. telecom. co., 1974-88; exec.-in-residence telecom. inst. SUNY Inst. Tech. Utica-Rome, 1986-87; mem. Common Coun., Syracuse, NY, 1977-85, pres., 1986-88; mem. US Congress from 25th NY dist., 1989—, mem. appropriations com., chmn. mil. quality of life and vets. affairs subcommittee, chmn. Friends of Ireland, 1995—, co-chair US-Irish Interparliamentary Grp., co-founder, co-chair Congl. Hearing Health Caucus. Bd. mem. Erie Canal Mus., Vera Ho., Everson Mus. Recipient Flax Trust award, 1997, Bobby Sands award, Ancient Order Hibernians, 1998, Ellis Island Medal of Honor, Nat. Ethnic Coalition Orgns., 2002, Legislator of Yr. award, Congl. Fire Svcs. Inst., 2003, Willis H. Carrier award, Ctr. Excellence in Environ. Systems, 2003. Republican. Roman Catholic. Office: US Ho Reps 2369 Rayburn Ho Office Bldg Washington DC 20515-3225 Office Phone: 202-225-3701.*

**WALSH, JOAN,** editor-in-chief; Freelance writer; with In These Times, Chgo., Santa Barbara News & Review; news editor Salon.com, San Francisco, 1998—99, v.p. news, 1999—2003, v.p., co-mng. editor, 2003—04, sr. v.p., editorial ops., 2003—04, editor-in-chief, 2005. Office: Salon Media Group 101 Spear St 203 San Francisco CA 94105-1517 Office Phone: 415-645-9200. Business E-Mail: jwalsh@salon.com.

**WALSH, JOHN,** television show host, missing children and victims' rights advocate; b. Auburn, NY, Dec. 26, 1945; m. Revé Drew Walsh, 1971; children: Adam(dec.), Megan, Callahan, Hayden. Former hotel marketer. Author: Tears of Rage, 1997, No Mercy, 1998, Public Enemies: The Host of America's Most Wanted Targets the Nation's Most Notorious Criminals, 2001; host (TV series) America's Most Wanted, 1988—, The John Walsh Show, 2002—04, creator The New America's Most Wanted: America Fights Back, appeared in (TV) Springfield's Most Wanted, 1995, Safety Patrol, 1998, American Crime Fighter: E! True Hollywood Story, 2000, Inside TV Land: Cops on Camera, 2002, Laci Peterson: E! True Hollywood Story, 2004, co-host Hawaii's Missing Kids: Eyes of the Innocent, 2004, actor & exec. prodr. (TV films) Smart Kids, 1994, If Looks Could Kill: The John Hawkins Story, 1996 (films) Jesuit Joe, 1991, Wrongfully Accused, 1998, Press Run, 1999, Grey Owl, 1999; narrator (films) The Safe Side, 2004. Founder Adam Walsh Child Resource Ctr., Straight Shooter; bd. dir. Nat. Ctr. for Missing and Exploited Children, chief exec. officers coun., nat. adv. bd., spokesperson. Named one of 50 Most Beautiful People in World, People mag., 1996, 100 Americans Who Changed History, CBS Portraits; recipient US Marshals Man of Yr. award, 1988, Spl. Recognition award, US Atty. Gen., honored in Rose Garden 4 times by 3 US Presidents, FBI Man of Yr. award, 2000. Achievements include being instrumental advocate in passage of Missing Children Act of 1982, and Missing Children's Assistance Act of 1984; testified over 55 times before Congress and state legislatures on crime, missing children and victims' issues. Office: Americas Most Wanted PO Box Crime TV Washington DC 20016-9126*

**WALSH, JOHN ALFRED,** retired social worker; b. N.Y.C., N.Y., June 4, 1927; s. Joseph Thomas and May Catherine (Moran) Walsh; m. Gwendolyn Ann Stockton, Apr. 13, 1952; children: Ralph, Carl, Nils. BA cum laude, St. Mary's U., Balt., 1949; M in Social Svc., Fordham U., 1954. Lic. clin. social worker, nursing home administr., marriage/family therapist. Social worker Cath. Charities, Bklyn., 1949—56; supr. after care clinics Ancora (N.J.) Psychiat. Hosp., 1956—57; dir. social svc. Trenton (N.J.) Psychiat. Hosp., 1958—68; asst. supt. Hunterdon Devel. Ctr., Clinton, NJ, 1968—91; ret. Author: (pamphlet) Fabulous Rosts, 1982. V.p. Warren County Hist. Soc., Belvidere, NJ, 1990—. assn. Hunterdon Devel. Ctr., Clinton, 1991—; mem. bd. edn. Belvidere Sch. Dist., 1991—2001. Capt. U.S. Army, 1953—66. Avocation: collecting stamps and post cards. Home: 703 Oxford St Belvidere NJ 07823 E-mail: jaw703@aol.com.

**WALSH, JOHN CHARLES,** metallurgical engineer, director; b. Indpls., Sept. 8, 1924; s. John Charles; children: Michael S., Carolyn Ann, Anne D. BS, Notre Dame U., 1949. Auditor Herdrich Boggs & Co., Indpls., 1949—78; with P.R. Mallory & Co., Inc., 1978—; pres. Walgang Co. Inc., Indpls., 1970—. V.p., treas. P.R. Mallory & Co., 1971. With USMCR, 1943—45. Mem. Fin. Execs. Inst., Ind. Hist. Soc., Econ. Club, Notre Dame Club, Rotary. Home: 4974 Shadow Rock Cir Carmel IN 46033-9500 Office: 160 W Carmel Dr Ste 265 Carmel IN 46032

**WALSH, JOHN L.,** energy executive; BA, MBA, Harvard Univ. Mgmt. positions through v.p. AmeriGas indsl. gas div. UGI Corp., 1981—86; v.p. spl. gases, pres. process gas solutions No. Am., pres. process Plants BOC Group PLC, 1986—2001, exec. dir., CEO indsl. & spl. products div., 2001—05; pres., COO UGI Corp., 2005—; bd. dir. AmeriGas Propane, 2005—, UGI Utilities. Office: UGI Corp 460 N Guelph Rd King Of Prussia PA 19406 Mailing: UGI Corp PO Box 858 Valley Forge PA 19482*

**WALSH, JOSEPH MICHAEL,** magazine distribution executive; b. NYC, Jan. 19, 1943; s. John Redmond and Bridget Judith (Donovan) W.; m. Theresa Rose Vericker, Oct. 3, 1964; children—Joseph, Matthew, Teresa Ann, John, James. BBA in Acctg., Iona Coll., 1964. With Peat, Marwick, Mitchell & Co., C.P.A.s, N.Y.C., 1964-70, audit supr., until 1970; asst. to chmn. bd. and pres. Cadence Industries Corp., West Caldwell, NJ, 1970-71, v.p., 1971-74, exec. v.p., 1974-87; pres. subs. Curtis Circulation Co., 1972-74, chmn., chief exec. officer, 1982—; pres. Data Services for Health, 1976-77, U.S. Pencil and Stationery Co., 1977-79, Perfect Subscription Co. (parent Perfect Sch. Plans, Perfect Telephone Plan, Moore Cottrell and Keystone Readers Service), 1980-83. Mem. AICPA, N.Y. State Soc. CPAs, K.C. Office: Curtis Circulation Co 730 River Rd New Milford NJ 07646-3048 Office Phone: 201-634-7400. E-mail: jwalsh@curtiscirc.com.

**WALSH, JOSEPH RICHARD,** lawyer; b. Atlanta, May 10, 1951; s. Joseph Radamaker and Meta Lucille (Cole) Walsh; m. Elisabeth Clare Kane, July 27, 1980; children: Lindsay Carolyn, Dana Elisabeth, Cameron Marisa. B in Indsl. Engring., Ga. Inst. Tech., 1973; JD, U. Ga., 1976; ML in Taxation, Georgetown U., 1984. Bar: Ga. 1976, U.S. Dist. Ct. (no. dist.) Ga. 1976, U.S. Ct. Appeals (5th cir.) 1976, Va. 1978, U.S. Ct. Appeals (4th cir.) 1978, DC 1979, U.S. Ct. Appeals (11th cir.) 1982, U.S. Claims Ct. 1983, U.S. Tax Ct. 1983, Calif. 1984, U.S. Dist. Ct. (no. dist.) Calif. 1984, U.S. Ct. Appeals (9th cir.) 1984. Indsl. engr. So. Rlwy. Sys., Atlanta, 1973—74; atty. ICC, Washington, 1977—78, atty., asst. rail merger coord., 1979—84; assoc. Fulbright & Jaworski, Washington, 1978—79; counsel Bank Am. Nat. Assn., San Francisco, 1984—85, sr. counsel, 1985—98, asst. gen. counsel, 1998—2006; pvt. practice law Orinda, Calif., 2006. Counselor Athens (Ga.) Legal Aid and Defender Soc., 1976; instr. comml. law San Francisco Law Sch., 1987—92. Co-author: (book) Federal Regulatory Process: Practice and Procedure, 1981. Campaign vol. Jimmy Carter Presdl. Campaign, NH, 1976. Named Outstanding Young Men Am., U.S. Jaycees, 1982; Nat. Merit scholar, Ga. Inst. Tech., 1969, NSF grantee, 1972. Mem.: ABA, World Affairs Coun., Assn. Corp. Counsel, Am. Inst. Indsl. Engrs., San Francisco Leasing Lawyers Forum, San Francisco Bar Assn., Calif. Bar Assn., Va. Bar Assn., Fed. Bar Assn., Ga. Bar Assn., DC Bar Assn., Calif. Nature Conservancy, Sierra Club, Commonwealth Club Calif., Lawyers Club San Francisco), Alpha Pi Mu, Tau Beta Pi, Phi Kappa Phi. Office: 65 Rheem Blvd Orinda CA 94563 Business E-Mail: jrichardwalsh@comcast.net.

**WALSH, JOSEPH THOMAS,** law educator, retired state supreme court justice; b. Wilmington, Del., May 18, 1930; s. Joseph Patrick and Mary Agnes (Bolton) W.; m. Madeline Maria Lamb, Oct. 6, 1955; children: Kevin, Lois, Patrick, Daniel, Thomas, Nancy. BA, LaSalle Coll., 1952; LLB, Georgetown U., 1955. Bar: D.C. 1955, Del. 1955. Atty. Ho. of Reps., Dover, Del., 1961-62; chief counsel Pub. Svc. Commn., Dover, 1964-72; judge Del. Superior Ct., Wilmington, 1972-84; vice chancellor Ct. of Chancery, Wilmington, 1984-85; justice Del. Supreme Ct., Wilmington, 1985—2003. Adjunct prof. Widener U. Sch. of Law, 2003—. Capt. U.S. Army, 1955-58. Democrat. Roman Catholic.

**WALSH, KERRI LEE,** Olympic athlete; b. Aug. 15, 1978; d. Tim and Margie. BA in Am. studies, Stanford U., 1999. Player BVA Tour, 2001, FIVG Internat. Tour, 2001—, AVP Tour, 2003—; beach volleyball player Team USA, Sydney Olympic Games, 2000, Team USA, Athens Olympic Games, 2004. Named First Team All-Am., 1995—99, Pro Beach Volleyball Rookie of the Yr., 2001, AVP Best Offensive Player, 2003, AVP Most Valuable Player, 2003, AVP Team of the Yr. (With Misty May), 2003. Achievements include being the second person in history named First Team All-American four years in a row, Stanford U., 1995-1999; winning FIVB World Champions with partner Misty May, 2002, 2003; winning global gold medal (with Misty May) in Athens Olympic games, beach volleyball, 2004. Office: c/o USOC One Olympic Plz Colorado Springs CO 80909

**WALSH, LAWRENCE EDWARD,** lawyer; b. Port Maitland, N.S., Can., Jan. 8, 1912; came to U.S., 1914, naturalized, 1922; s. Cornelius Edward and Lila May (Sanders) W.; m. Mary Alma Porter; children: Barbara Marie, Janet Maxine (Mrs. Alan Larson), Sara Porter, Dale Edward, Elizabeth Porter (Mrs. Joseph Wells). AB, Columbia U., 1932, LLB, 1935; LLD, Union U., St. John's U., 1975, Suffolk U., 1975, Waynesburg Coll., 1976, Vt. Law Sch. 1976. Bar: N.Y. 1936, D.C. 1981, Okla. 1981, U.S. Supreme Ct. 1951. Spl. asst. atty. gen. Drukman Investigation, 1936—38; dep. asst. dist. atty. N.Y. County, 1938—41; assoc. Davis Polk Wardwell Sunderland & Kiendl, 1941—43; asst. counsel to gov. N.Y., 1943—49; counsel to gov., 1950—51; counsel Pub. Svc. Commn., 1951—53; gen. counsel, exec. dir. Waterfront Commn. of N.Y. Harbor, 1953—54; U.S. judge So. Dist. N.Y., 1954—57; U.S. dep. atty. gen., 1957—60; ptnr. firm Davis, Polk & Wardwell, 1961—81; counsel firm Crowe & Dunlevy, Oklahoma City, 1981—. Ind. counsel Iran/Contra investigation, 1986-93; chmn. N.Y. State Moreland Commn. Alcoholic Beverage Control Law, 1963-64; pres. Columbia Alumni Fedn., 1968-69; dep. head with rank of amb. U.S. del. meetings on Vietnam, Paris, 1969; counsel to N.Y. State Ct. on Judiciary, 1971-72; 2d cir. mem. U.S. Cir. Judge Nominating Commn., 1978-80. Author: (Book) Firewall The Iran-Contra Conspiracy and Cover-Up, 1997, The Gift of Insecurity, 2003. Trustee emeritus Columbia U., Mut. Life Ins. Co., N.Y. Recipient medal for excellence Columbia U., 1959, Law Sch., Columbia U., 1980, John Jay award Columbia Coll., 1989. Fellow Am. Bar Found., Am. Coll. Trial Lawyers; mem. Am. Law Inst., ABA (pres. 1975-76), N.Y. State Bar Assn. (pres. 1966-67), Oklahoma County Bar Assn., Okla. State Bar Assn., Internat. Bar Assn., Assn. of Bar of City of N.Y., N.Y. County Lawyers Assn., Fed. Bar Coun., Law Soc. Eng. and Wales (hon.), Can. Bar Assn. (hon.), Mex. Bar Assn. (hon.), Century Assn., Oklahoma City Golf and Country Club, Beta Theta Pi. Presbyterian. Home: 1902 Bedford Dr Oklahoma City OK 73116-5306 Office: 1800 Mid Am Towers Oklahoma City OK 73102 Office Phone: 405-235-7789.

**WALSH, LOUISA MARCY,** medical researcher, researcher; b. Charleston, S.C., Apr. 8, 1960; d. Norman Sinkler and Marcy Stoney Walsh. MD, Med. U. SC, Charleston, 1986; BS, U. of the South, Sewanee, Tenn., 1982. Med.

dir. AstraZeneca, LP, Wilmington, Del., 1998—2006, dir. clin. rsch., 2006—. Contbr. articles to profl. jours. Vol. Phila. Cares, 2004. Mem.: Drug Info. Assn., Internat. Soc. Pharmacoepidemiology. Office: AstraZeneca LP 1800 Concord Pike Wilmington DE 19850-5437 Office Phone: 302-886-5380.

**WALSH, M. EMMET,** actor; b. Ogdensburg, NY, Mar. 22, 1935; BBA, Clarkson Coll., 1958; student, Am. Acad. Dramatic Arts, 1959-61. Appeared in films including Chasing 3000, The Man in the Chair, Raising Arizona, Ordinary People, The Milagro Beanfield War, Romeo and Juliet, Winterdance, My Best Friend's Wedding, Twilight, A Time To Kill, Albino Alligator, Free Willy II, Snow Dogs, Music of Chance, White Sands, Narrow Margin, The Mighty Quinn, Clean and Sober, Harry and The Hendersons, Fletch, Missing in Action, Back to School, Blood Simple, Blade Runner, Silkwood, Sundown, Brubaker, Raise the Titanic, Fast Walking, Reds, The Jerk, Straight Time, At Long Last Long, Serpico, What's Up Doc?, They Might Be Giants, Midnight Cowboy, End of the Road, Cannery Row, Slap Shot, Cold Turkey, The Traveling Executioner, Alice's Restaurant, Airport '77, Wild Wild West, Christmas in the Clouds, Poor White Trash, Random Hearts, Iron Giant, Skirty Winner, Queen of Hearts, Baggage, Me and Will, Erasable You, Carrot Top, A Time to Kill, Chairman of the Board, Retroactive, The Killing Jar, Portraits of Innocence, Criminal Hearts, Panther, Camp Nowhere, Dead Badge, Probable Cause, Glass Shield, Relative Fear, Cops and Robbersons, Bitter Harvest, Wilder Napalm, Equinox, Naked Truth, Killer Image, Red Scorpion, Chattahoochee, Thunderground, Catch Me If You Can, War Party, Sunset, No Man's Land, The Best of Times, Wildcats, Critters, The Pope of Greenwich Village, Grandview-USA, Raw Courage, Scandalous, Escape Artist, Back Roads, Bound for Glory, Nickelodeon, Mickey & Nicky, The Fish That Saved Pittsburgh, Kid Blue, Prisoner of 2nd Avenue, The Gambler, Get to Know Your Rabbit, Escape From the Planet of the Apes, Little Big Man, Loving, Stiletto, Christmas With The Kranks, Racing Stripes, Bitter Harvest, Greener Mountains, Inn Trouble, Man in the Chair; (TV shows) include Frasier, Sandy Duncan Show, Bonanza, Mind of the Married Man, The Rockford Files, All in the Family, Bob Newhart Show, The Waltons, Little House on the Prairie, Early Edition, Tales from the Crypt, Home Improvement, The Outer Limits, X Files, The Abduction of Kari Swenson, Resting Place, The Woman Who Willed a Miracle, The Guardian, Tracy Ullman's Trailer Tales, Charlie Lawrence, Ed, Gideon's Crossing, Night Visions, Cover Me, NYPD Blue, Monster, Men in White, Nightmare in Big Sky Country, The Tracey Ullman Show, Dogs, The Lottery, The Mixed Up Files Of..., The Jackie Thomas Show, Wild Card, Four Eyes and Six Guns, Grey Fox, The Nerd, Love and Lies, Fourth Story, The Flash, Unsub, Brotherhood of the Rose II, Murder Ordained I & II, Amazing Stories, Broken Vows, Hero in the Family, The City, Deliberate Stranger, The Right of the People, Twighlight Zone, The Hitchhiker, You Are the Jury, Vanishing America, After Mash, Night Partners, High Noon Two, East of Eden I & II, Helinger's Law, French-Atlantic Affair, Countdown to Superdome, Dear Detective, Mrs. R's Daughter, James at Fifteen, Red Alert, A Question of Guilt, No Other Love, Panic On Page One, Skag, The Gift, Mississippi, Starsky and Hutch, Mary Hartman, Gibbsville, Tony Randall Show, Nancy Walker Show, Kate McShane, Joe & Sons, The Cop and the Kid, Brahmins, McMillan & Wife, N.Y.P.D., Baretta, Don Rickles Show, Nichols, Texas Wheeler, Crime Club, Prudential's "On Stage," The Doctors, Outlaws, Jimmy Stewart Show, Men at Law, Dr. Dan, Love of Life, Amy Prentiss, The Law, Arnie, Julia, Con Sawyer; HBO series includes The Mind of the Married Man; Broadway includes That Championship Season, Does the Tiger Wear a Necktie?, The Beauty Part, Buried Child, Royal Nation Theatre, London, 2004; Off Broadway shows include Shepherds of the Shelf, Blackfriars Theatre, 1961, The Old Glory, The Outside Man, Am. Pl. Theatre, 1964, Death of the Well Loved Boy, St. Marks Playhouse, 1967, Three From Column "A", Theatre 73, 1968, Are You Now or Have You Ever Been, L.A. Ford's Theatre, D.C., 1975, Marathon '93, Ensemble Studio Theatre, 1993; Off-Off-Broadway shows at New Theatre Workshop, The Loft, Tamarack, Actors Studio, The Playbox, Ensemble Studio Theatre, The Pub. TheatreNYSF; regional theatre shows at Theatre of Living Arts, Phila., 1965, Studio Arena, Buffalo, 1966, Long Wharf Theatre, New Haven, 1967, Cin. Playhouse in Pk., 1995, La Jolla Playhouse, 1999, Arena Stage, D.C., 2000; summer stock shows at Coll. Theatre, Am. Acad. Dramatic Arts, 1954-61, Bucks County Playhouse, New Hope, Pa., 1962, Brattleboro Summer Theatre, Vt., 1963, Caravan Theatre, Dorset, Vt., 1964, U. Ky., 1966, Berkshire Theatre Festival, Stockbridge, Mass., 1967-70, Vt. Summer Theatre Festival, Johnson, 1974, U. Tulsa, 1983, Santa Barbara Theatre Festival, 1985, U. Vt., 1992; voices include The Civil War, Baseball, The Way West, The West, King of The Hill, Wild Thornberry, Muriel's Christmas Carol, Big Guy and Rusty, The Simpsons, The New Scooby Doo.

**WALSH, MARIE LECLERC,** nurse; b. Providence, Sept. 11, 1928; d. Walter Normand and Anna Mary (Ryan) Leclerc; m. John Breffni Walsh, June l8, 1955; children: George Breffni, John Leclerc, Darina Louise. Grad., Waterbury Hosp. Sch. Nursing, Conn., 1951; BS, Columbia U., 1954, MA, 1955. Team leader Hartford (Conn.) Hosp., 1951-53; pvt. duty nurse St. Luke's Hosp., N.Y.C., 1953-57; sch. nurse tchr. Agnes Russel Ctr., Tchrs. Coll. Columbia U., N.Y.C., 1955-56; clin. nursing instr. St. Luke's Hosp., N.Y.C., 1957-58; chmn. disaster nursing ARC Fairfax County, Va., 1975; course coord. occupational health nursing U. Va. Sch. Continuing Edn., Falls Church, 1975-77; mem. disaster steering com. No. Va. C.C., Annandale, 1976; adj. faculty U. Va. Sch. Continuing Edn., Falls Church, 1981; disaster svcs. nurse ARC, Wichita, Kans., 1985-90, disaster svcs. nurse Seattle-King County chpt. Seattle, 1990-96; ret. Rsch. and statis. analyst U. Va. Sch. Continuing Edn. Nursing, Falls Church, l975; rsch. libr. Olive Garvey Ctr. for Improvement Human Functioning, Inc., Wichita, 1985, Sec. Dem. party, Cresskill, N.J., 1964-66; county committeewoman, Bergen County, N.J., 1965-66; pres., v.p., Internat. Staff Wives, NATO, Brussels, Belgium, 1978-80; election officer, supr. Election Bd., Wichita, 1987, 88; v.p. McLean Newcomers, 1997-99, pres., 1999-2000. Mem. AAAS, AAUW, N.Y. Acad. Sci., Pi Lambda Theta, Sigma Theta Tau. Avocations: travel, gardening. Home: 8800 Prestwould Pl Mc Lean VA 22102-2231

**WALSH, MATHEW M.,** construction executive; Grad., St. Ignatius Coll. Prep. Sch., U. Notre Dame. CEO, pres. Walsh Group, Inc., Chgo. Mem. Union League Club. Office: Walsh Group Inc 929 W Adams St Chicago IL 60607-3021

**WALSH, MATTHEW M.,** real estate developer; b. 1946; Attended, Univ. Notre Dame, So. Bend, Ind. Chmn., CEO The Walsh Constrn. Group. Mem. Nat. Constrn. Indus. Roundtable. Mem. bd. St. Ignatius Coll. Prep. Sch., Union League Club, Univ. Notre Dame. Office: Walsh Group 929 W Adams St Chicago IL 60607*

**WALSH, MICHAEL J.,** lawyer; b. Portland, Oreg., Sept. 4, 1932; s. Frank M.J. and Elisemary (Derbes) W.; m. June Griffin, Nov. 28, 1959; children: Molly, Erin, Kathryn (dec.); Anne. BA, U. Portland, 1954; JD, Georgetown U., 1959. Bar: D.C. 1959, Oreg. 1959, U.S. Ct. Appeals (fed. and 9th cirs.) 1959, U.S. Tax Ct. 1959, U.S. Supreme Ct. 1968. Law ck. to presiding justice Oreg. Supreme Ct., Salem, 1959-60; mng. ptnr. Rankin, Walsh, Ragen and Roberts, Portland, 1960-75; pvt. practice Portland, 1976—81; ptnr. Walsh and Conolly, Portland, 1982-83; of counsel McEwen, Hanna, Gisvold and Rankin, Portland, 1983-85, Bullivant, Houser, Bailey, Pendergrass, & Hoffman, Washington, 1985—. Chief judge Employees Compensation Appeals Bd. US Dept. Labor, Washington, 1985—2003, sr. counsel Adminstrv. Appeals Bd., 2003—04; legal counsel Reagan-Bush '84, Nat. Hdqs., Washington, 1983—84. Chmn. legal dev. March of Dimes, 1967; chmn. admissions Georgetown U., Oreg., 1972-83; trustee Christie Sch., 1974-78; trustee Cath. Charities Oreg., 1966-72, pres. 1971; trustee Parry Ctr. for Children, 1967-73, v.p. 1970-71; trustee Portland Tennis Ctr. Assn., 1972-83, pres. 1976-82; bd. dirs. Portland Traffic Safety Commn., 1981-83. Served with JAGC, USAF, capt. res. Mem. Am. Judicature Soc., Am. Trial Lawyers Assn., Nat. Assn. Coll. and Univ. Attys., Am. Arbitration Assn., D.C. Bar Assn., Oreg. Bar Assn.

(mem. various coms.), Multnomah County Bar Assn., Portland C. of C. (bd. dirs. 1975-78, chmn. legis. coun. 1975), John Carroll Soc., Thomas More Soc. Clubs: Georgetown Univ. (Oreg.) (pres. 1966). Home: 3273 Sutton Pl NW # B Washington DC 20016-3537

**WALSH, MICHAEL P.,** mechanical engineer; m. Evelyn Walsh. BS, Manhattan Coll., 1966; postgrad., Princeton U., 1970. Dir. motor vehicle pollution control Dept. Air Resources, NYC, 1970—74, U.S. Environ. Protection Agy., 1974—81; independent technical cons., 1981—. Co-chair mobile source advisory subcom. EPA. Author: (bimonthly publ.) Car Lines. Named MacArthur fellow, John D. and Catherine T. MacArthur Found., 2005. E-mail: mpwalsh@igc.org.*

**WALSH, MICHAEL S.,** lawyer; b. Chgo., Sept. 29, 1951; AB, Colgate U., 1973; MBA, Cornell U., 1975; JD, So. Meth. U., 1978. Bar: Ill. 1978, US Dist. Ct. (no. dist.) Ill. 1978, U.S. Ct. Appeals (fed. cir.) 1983, U.S. Ct. Appeals (9th cir.) 1985. Mem. Jenner & Block, Chgo. Mem. ABA, Ill. State Bar Assn., Chgo. Bar Assn. Office: Jenner & Block One IBM Plz Chicago IL 60611-3608 E-mail: mwalsh@jenner.com.

**WALSH, MICHAEL THOMAS,** historian, musician; b. Balt., Dec. 1, 1978; s. John Michael and Annette Mary Walsh. BA magna cum laude, Loyola Coll., Balt., 2000; MA, PhD, U. Md., Balt., 2002—. Profl. musician self employed, Balt., 1998—; tchg. asst. history U. Md., 2002—03, tchg. asst. polit. sci., 2003—05, acadmic advisor 2003—, tchg. asst. history, 2005—. Contbr. ency. entries. Sustaining mem. Rep. Nat. Com.; pres. Rep. Presdl. Task Force. Mem.: Orgn. Am. hist., Am. Hist. Assn., Pi Sigma Alpha, Phi Alpha Theta. Republican. Roman Catholic. Avocations: music, reading, sports, swimming. Personal E-mail: mwalsh3@umbc.edu.

**WALSH, NAN,** artist, painter, sculptor, consultant; b. NYC, Nov. 4, 1932; d. Joseph Edward and Mary Ellen (White) Heinl; m. Albert Anthony Walsh, July 10, 1954 (dec. Oct. 9, 2002); children: Maryellen, Nanette, Mark, Gregg (dec.). BS in Elem. Edn., Fordham U., 1954; postgrad., Nat. Acad. Sch. Fine Arts, Art Life Studio Inc., White Plains and Portchester, N.Y., 1984-94, V.K. Jonynas, L.I., N.Y., 1968-88, Art Ctr. No. N.J., 1996—2002. Fashion model Martha Clyde, N.Y.C., 1951-54; tchr. Yonkers (N.Y.) Pub. Schs., 1953-55; gallery dir. Mamaroneck Artists Guild, Larchmont, NY, 1988-95; fine artist, art juror, cons., 1995—. Membership juror Mamaroneck Artists Guild, Larchmont, 1982-84, membership juror chair, 1996-98, mem. adv. bd., 1996-98; mem. Ctr. for Contemporary Printmaking, 1998—. One-woman shows and juried exhbns. Westchester and N.Y.C., 1976—; works represented in corp. and pvt. collecitons. Hostess chairperson Citizens for John Lindsay, Gracie Mansion, N.Y., 1970; mem. Studio Twelve, pres., show chair, 1972-80; mem. Katonah Mus. Art. Recipient numerous 1st place awards for art. Mem. Nat. League Am. Penwomen (corr. sec. and membership chair 1992-96), Nat. Mus. Women in the Arts, N.Y. Soc. Women Artists, Guild Creative Art, N.J. Artists Equity, Mamaroneck Artists Guild (v.p 1982, 83, membership chair 1992-95 Fordham U. Art Club (show chair 1965-80). Avocations: gardening, bridge, tennis, swimming, travel.

**WALSH, NICOLAS EUGENE,** rehabilitation services professional, educator; b. Mpls., July 1, 1947; s. Leonard Cyril and June Alice Walsh; m. Wendy Sarah Allnutt, June 1, 1973; children: Meghan, Rorey, Katlin, Alaine. BS, USAF Acad., 1969; MS, Marquette U., 1974; MD, U. Colo., 1979. Asst. prof. naval sci. Marquette U., Milw., 1972—74; from asst. prof. to assoc. prof. rehab. medicine U. Tex. Health Sci. Ctr., San Antonio, 1982—89, prof., chmn. rehab. medicine, 1989—, exec. assoc. dean Sch. Medicine, 1999—2000, disting. prof., 2001—. Dir. Am. Bd. Phys. Medicine and Rehab., Rochester, Minn., 1994—2006, sec., 1996—98, chmn., 1998—2005; pres., CEO Rehab Physician Group, 1998—2001. Author book chpts.; editor: Rehabilitation of Chronic Pain, 1991; editor-in-chief Archives of Phys. Medicine and Rehab., Chgo., 1994—2000; mng. editor: Rehabilitation Medicine: Principles and Practices, 2005. Named Health Care Profl. of Yr., Gov.'s Com. for Disabled Persons, 1989; recipient Excellence in Rsch. award, Am. Jour. Phys. Medicine and Rehab., 1991. Fellow: Am. Acad. Phys. Medicine and Rehab. (Richard and Hinda Rosenthal Found. award 1991, Zieter lectr. 2003), Am. Bd. Pain Medicine (v.p. 1993—94, sec. 1994—96); mem.: Phys. Medicine and Rehab. Edn. and Rsch. Found. (pres. 1993—2000, Excellence in Rsch. award 1991), Assn. Acad. Physiatrists (v.p. 1993—95, pres. 1996—98). Office: U Tex Health Sci Ctr Mail Code 7872 7703 Floyd Curl Dr San Antonio TX 78229-3900 Office Phone: 210-567-5350. Business E-Mail: walshn@uthscsa.edu.

**WALSH, PATRICK CRAIG,** urologist; b. Akron, Ohio, Feb. 13, 1938; s. Raymond Michael and Catherine N. (Rodden) W.; m. Margaret Campbell, May 23, 1964; children—Christopher, Jonathan, Alexander. AB, Case Western Res. U., 1960, MD, 1964. Intern in surgery Peter Bent Brigham Hosp., Boston, 1964-65, asst. resident in surgery, 1965-66; asst. resident in pediatric surgery Children's Hosp. Med. Center, Boston, 1966-67; resident in urology UCLA Med. Ctr., 1967-71; dir., chmn. James Buchanan Brady Urol. Inst., urologist-in-chief Johns Hopkins Hosp., Balt., 1974—2004; prof., dir. dept. urology Johns Hopkins U. Sch. Medicine, 1974—2004, prof. urology, 2004—. Contbr. articles to med. jours. Served to comdr. M.C. USN, 1971-73. Recipient Charles F. Kettering medal GM Cancer Rsch. Found., 1996. Mem. Soc. Univ. Surgeons, Am. Assn. Genitourinary Surgeons, Clin. Soc. Genitourinary Surgeons, Am. Urol. Assn., Endocrine Soc., Am. Surg. Assn. Inst. Medicine of NAS, Alpha Omega Alpha. Roman Catholic. Office: Johns Hopkins Med Inst 600 N Wolfe St Baltimore MD 21287-0005 Office Phone: 410-955-6101.*

**WALSH, PAUL S.,** food products executive; b. Manchester, May 15, 1955; married; 1 child. Grad., Manchester Polytechnic. Fin. planning and acct. mgr. Grand Metropolitan, Watney, Mann and Truman Brewers, 1982—86; fin. dir. Grand Metropolitan (merged with Guinness UDV in 1997), Watney, Mann and Truman Brewers, 1986; CFO Inter-Continental Hotels, 1987—88, CFO, food divsn., 1989—92; pres., pres., CEO Pillsbury Co., Mpls., 1992—2000; COO, CEO Guinness UDV Diageo plc, London, 2000—01, CEO, 2000—. Bd. dir. Grand Metropolitan, 1995; bd. dirs. Diageo, 1997—, Burger King Corp.; non-exec. dir. Centrica plc, 2003—, Fed. Express Corp., General Mills, Inc.; gov. Henley Mgmt. Centre. Mem.: Chartered Inst. Mgmt. Accountants, Scotch Whisky Assn. (dir.). Office: Diageo plc 8 Henrietta Pl London W1G ONB England*

**WALSH, PETER JOSEPH,** physics professor; b. N.Y.C., Aug. 21, 1929; s. Peter and Mary Ellen (Kelly) W.; m. Rosemarie Imundo, May 13, 1952; children: Kathleen, Mary Ellen, Susan, Carole, Karen. BS, Fordham U., 1951; MS, N.Y.U., 1953, PhD, 1960. Research physicist Westinghouse Elec. Co., Bloomfield, NJ, 1951-60; supervisory physicist Am. Standard, Piscataway, NJ, 1960-62; prof. Fairleigh Dickinson U., 1962-93; prof. emeritus, 1993—. Vis. rsch. scientist MIT, 1977; vis. prof. electronics and elec. engring. U. Sheffield, 1978-79; NASA fellow U. Santa Clara, 1980; Am. Soc. Engring. Edn. Navy fellow Naval Rsch. Labs., 1981, 82, 86, NASA Langley, 1987, Air Force fellow Hanscom AFB, 1988, Kirtland AFB, 1990; vis. prof. U. Genoa, 1984; vis. scholar Stanford U., 1984-85, cons. physics to 20 labs., 1963—; chmn. bd. trustees EMS Edn. Corp., 1982—. Author: Dark Side of Knowledge, articles in field. Mem. Am. Phys. Soc., AAAS, N.J. Acad. Sci., Sigma Xi (sec. 1969) Home: 40 Saint Josephs Dr Stirling NJ 07980-1224 Personal E-mail: peterj@gowebway.com.

**WALSH, PETER JOSEPH,** marketing professional; b. Newport, RI, Jan. 22, 1948; s. Alexander Ronald and Mary (O'Connell) W.; m. Virginia Diana Santore, May 11, 1978 (div. May 1992); children: Bridget, Peter, Lara, Elizabeth, Vanessa. BA, Santa Clara U., 1970; MA, Johns Hopkins U., 1978. V.p. Noblemet Internat., N.Y.C., 1978-80; mktg. dir. Multi-Arc Scientific Coatings, St. Paul, Minn., 1980-88; sr. v.p. Projects Devel., Inc., N.Y.C., 1988-91; pres. Kiser Rsch., Inc., Washington, 1990-93; v.p. Sonalysts, Inc., Waterford, Conn., 1993—. Bd. dirs. Conn. Tech. Coun., 2002—. Bd. dirs. Portsmouth Abbey Sch. Alumni, Portsmouth, RI, 1996—2000, Mystic Coast and Country, 2002—, Newport Internat. Film Festival, 2006—. Roman Catholic. Avocations: tennis, golf, running. Office: Sonalysts Inc 215 Parkway N Waterford CT 06385-1209 Home: 4 Barney Ct Newport RI 02840

**WALSH, PHILIP CORNELIUS,** retired mining executive; b. Harrison, NJ, May 23, 1921; s. Philip Cornelius and Frances (Prendergast) Walsh; m. Alexandra Somerville Tuck, May 19, 1945 (dec. Sept. 1993); children: Eugenie Philbin Flaherty, Philip C.C., Frances Cummings, Alexander Tuck, Nicholas Holladay, Elizabeth Lovering; m. Peggy Flanigan McDonnell, Oct. 13, 1996. BA, Yale U., 1943; member of the Class of 1944. With W.R. Grace & Co., Lima, Peru and N.Y.C., 1946-71; v.p. parent co., chief operating officer Latin Am. group, 1961-71, group exec. corp. adminstrv. group, 1970-71; v.p. Cerro Corp., 1972-74, Newmont Mining Corp., 1974-80; chmn. bd. Foote Mineral Co., Exton, Pa., 1979-80; dir. Cyprus Minerals Co., 1980—85; vice chmn. St. Joe Minerals Corp., 1980-85; chmn. bd. Chilean Lithium Co. Ltd., 1980-94; dir. T. Rowe Price Assocs., Inc., 1986—2000; ret., 2000. Past dir. Peabody Coal Co., Piedmont Mining Co.; bd. advisors Fond Elec.; mem. Nat. Strategic Minerals and Metals Program Adv. Commn. Mem. Harding Twp. Bd. Edn., NJ, 1960—66, Harding Twp. Com., 1966—72, police commr., 1966—72; trustee Morristown Meml. Hosp., 1969—79; vis. com. Colo. Sch. Mines, Global Sys. and Cultures. 1st lt. U.S. Army. Decorated Silver Star, Purple Heart. Mem.: AIME (Saunders gold medal 1992, Disting. Mem. award 1993), Am. Soc. (hon. dir.), Pan Am. Soc. U.S. (past vice chmn.), Am. Assn. Order of Malta (past chancellor), Fed. Assn. Order of Malta, Edgartown Golf Club, Essex Hunt Club, Edgartown Yacht Club (commodore 1993—95), Racquet and Tennis Club, Somerset Hills Country Club, Sigma Xi, Phi Beta Kappa. Republican. Roman Catholic. Home: Pleasant Valley Peapack NJ 07977 Personal E-mail: knobbyiv@aol.com.

**WALSH, ROBERT K.,** dean; m. Kathie Walsh; 4 children. AB, Providence Coll., 1964; JD, Harvard U., 1967. Bar: Calif. 1967, Ark. 1979. Assoc. McCatchen, Black, Verleger & Shea, L.A., 1967-70; asst. prof. Villanova (Pa.) U., 1970-71, assoc. prof., 1971-73, prof., 1973-76; ptnr. Friday, Eldredge & Clark, Little Rock, 1981-89; dean, prof. Wake Forest Sch. Law, Winston-Salem, NC, 1989—. Bd. trustees Nat. Assn. Law Placement Found., Am. Inns of Ct. Found. Mem. ABA (chair Accreditation Com. 1984-86, chair Standards Rev. Com. Sect. Legal Edn. 1991—, Central European and Eurasian Law Initiative Adv. Coun.), N.C. Bar Assn. (chair bar bench and law schs. com. 1990-92, v.p., bd. govs. 1994-95). Office: Wake Forest Sch Law Dean's Office PO Box 7206 Winston Salem NC 27109-7206 Office Phone: 336-758-5436. Office Fax: 336-758-4632.

**WALSH, SCOTT WESLEY,** reproductive physiologist, researcher; b. Wauwatosa, Wis., July 23, 1947; s. Virgil C. and Harriet E. (Jacobson) W.; m. Cynthia Lee Sorenson, Oct. 10, 1981 (div. Mar. 1987); m. Margaret Ann Dahmus, Apr. 16, 1994. BS with honors, U. Wis., 1970, MS, 1972, PhD, 1975. Asst. prof. U. N.D. Sch. Medicine, Grand Forks, 1975-76; asst. to assoc. scientist Oreg. Primate Ctr., Beaverton, 1976-80; asst. prof. Oreg. Health Scis. U., Portland, 1978-80, Mich. State U., E. Lansing, 1980-85; assoc. prof. U. Tex. Health Sci. Ctr., Houston, 1985-90; prof. Va. Commonwealth U. Med. Ctr., Richmond, 1990. Grant reviewer Nat. Inst. Child Health and Human Devel., Washington, 1988—. Mem. editl. bd. Jour. Soc. Gynecol. Investigation. Named to Dean's Tchg. Excellence List, U. Tex. Health Sci. Ctr., 1989; recipient Shannon award Nat. Inst. Child Health and Human Devel., NIH, grantee 1983—, Grant-in-aid Am. Heart Assn., 1999-2002. Mem. Soc. for Gynecologic Investigation, Am. Physiol. Soc., Endocrine Soc., Soc. for Study Reprodn., Soc. for Free Radical Biology and Medicine, Internat. Soc. for Study Hypertension in Pregnancy. Achievements include discovery of imbalance of increased thromboxane, decreased protacyclin and increased lipid peroxides, decreased antioxidants in placentas obtained from women with pregnancy-induced hypertension. Office: Va Commonwealth U Med Ctr Dept Ob-Gyn PO Box 980034 Richmond VA 23298-0034

**WALSH, THOMAS CHARLES,** lawyer; b. Mpls., July 6, 1940; s. William G. and Kathryne M. Walsh; m. Joyce Williams, Sept. 7, 1968; children: Brian Christopher, Timothy Daniel, Laura Elizabeth Smith. BS in Commerce magna cum laude, St. Louis U., 1962, LLB cum laude, 1964. Bar: Mo. 1964, U.S. Dist. Ct. (ea. dist.) Mo. 1964, U.S. Ct. Appeals (8th cir.) 1968, U.S. Supreme Ct. 1971, U.S. Ct. Appeals (6th cir.) 1972, U.S. Ct. Appeals (5th cir.) 1974, U.S. Ct. Appeals (9th cir.) 1980, U.S. Ct. Appeals (7th cir.) 1982, U.S. Ct. Appeals (9th cir.) 1987, U.S. Ct. Appeals (4th cir.) 1989, U.S. Ct. Appeals (11th and fed. cirs.) 1992, U.S. Ct. Appeals (2d and 10th cirs.) 1993. Jr. ptnr. Bryan, Cave, McPheeters & McRoberts, St. Louis, 1964-73; ptnr. Bryan Cave LLP, St. Louis, 1974—; mem. exec. com. Bryan Cave LLP, St. Louis, 1980-96. Mem. 8th Cir. Adv. Com., 1983-86. Bd. dirs. St. Louis Symphony Soc., 1983-95. With U.S. Army, 1965-66; lt. USNR, 1966-71. Fellow Am. Coll. Trial Lawyers, Am. Acad. Appellate Lawyers; mem. Mo. Bar Assn., St. Louis Bar Assn., Am. Law Inst., Mo. Athletic Club, Bellerive Country Club. Roman Catholic. Office: Bryan Cave LLP 1 Metropolitan Sq 211 N Broadway Saint Louis MO 63102-2750 Office Phone: 314-259-2284. Business E-mail: tcwalsh@bryancave.com.

**WALSH, THOMAS FRANCIS, JR.,** producer, writer, director; b. NYC, Aug. 15, 1956; s. Thomas Francis and Catherine Alice (May) W.; m. Adriana Mia Stastny, Oct. 19, 1996; children: Barron, Arielle, Thomas III. BFA, NYU, 1977. Pres. Tom Walsh Prodns. Inc., N.Y.C. and Del., 1977-89; chmn., CEO I.D.L. Inc., N.Y.C. and Calif., 1989-91, Wonderland Dream Factory Inc., Calif. and Del., 1991-93, Enteraktion Inc. and Enteraktion Studios, Inc., L.A., 1993—, also prodr., dir. 8 new entertainment web series, prodr., dir. Kidsline (TV), 2002—. Prodr.: (feature film) Denial, 1991; (CD-ROM) The Arrival, 1996; exec. prodr.: (TV) We Dare You!, 1982, House to House, 1982, Mismatch, 1979; prodr., dir.: The Whole Truth, 1977, (TV) Global Trade with Toms Travis, 2002; prodr., dir., writer (TV) 14 Stories, 2002, Newsoes, 2003, (TV) Tower of Madness, 2004, (TV) Seawhawk, 2004, (TV) The Kernies, 2005 (TV) Los Opolis; created and developed more than 175 creatures and characters for TV, movies and computer animation Scholar Helena Rubenstein Co., N.Y.C., 1976-77; recipient 1st prize for best TV show Conn. Assn. Profl. Communicators, 1974, Bronze and Silver awards Nat. Forensic League, 1977, Kate Garland award NYU/Columbia Pictures, 1976. Mem. Psi Upsilon (Delta chpt.), Alpha Epsilon Rho. Avocations: boating, diving, trains. Office: Enteraktion Studios Sound City Center Stages 15466 Cabrito Rd Van Nuys CA 91406 Home: 1015 9th St Apt 104 Santa Monica CA 90403 Business E-Mail: tomwalsh@enteraktion.com.

**WALSH, THOMAS JOSEPH,** ophthalmologist; b. NYC, Sept. 18, 1931; s. Thomas Joseph and Virginia (Hughes) W.; m. Sally Ann Maust, June 21, 1958; children: Thomas Raymond, Sara Ann, Mary Kelly, Kathleen Meghan. BA, Coll. Fordham, 1954; MD, Bowman Gray Med. Sch., 1958; degree in Mgmt., Yale U., 1998. Intern St. Vincent's Hosp., N.Y.C., 1958-59; resident ophthalmology Bowman Gray Med. Sch., Winston-Salem, NC, 1961-64; fellow neuro-ophthalmology Bascom Palmer Eye Inst., Miami, Fla., 1964-65; practice medicine specializing in neuro-ophthalmology Stamford, Conn., 1965—; dir. neuro-ophthalmology service, asst. prof. ophthalmology and neurology Yale Sch. Medicine, New Haven, 1965-74, assoc. prof., 1974-79, prof., 1979—, also bd. permanent officers; dir. ophthalmology Stamford Hosp., 1978-83; mem. staff St. Joseph Hosp., Yale New Haven Hosp. Cons. to surgeon gen. army in neuro-ophthalmology Walter Reed Hosp., Washington, 1966—, VA Hosp., West Haven, 1965—, Silver Hill Found., New Canaan, Conn., 1974—; adj. prof. Dartmouth Med. Sch.; telemedicine bd. ORBIS Internat.; cons. mem. of bd. Obis Internat.; lectr. in field. Contbr. articles to various publs. Adv. bd. Stamford Salvation Army, 1972-92; med. bd. Darien Nurses Assn., Conn., 1972—; surgeon Darien Fire Dept., 1969—. With AUS, 1959-61. Decorated Knight of Malta; Centennial fellow Johns Hopkins, 1976; named one of Top Opthalmologists, Best Doctors.com, 2004 Mem. AMA, Conn., Fairfield County med. socs., Acad. Ophthalmology, Oxford Ophthal. Congress, Acad. Neurology, Am. Assn. Neurol. Surgeons, Internat. Neuro-Ophthalmology Soc., Soc. Med. Cons. to Armed Forces, Cosmos Club (Washington), Darien County Club, Yale Club (N.Y.C.), Lions, Army-Navy Club, Orbis Internat. (cybermedicine bd. mem.). Office: Yale

---

Dept Ophthalmology PO Box 208061 330 Cedar St Stamford CT 06520-8061 Office Phone: 203-785-6444. Personal E-mail: twalsh13@optonline.net. Business E-mail: thomas.walsh@yale.edu.

**WALSH, W. TERENCE,** lawyer; b. Toledo, Ohio, Nov. 18, 1943; s. Walter James and Ann (Gifford) W.; m. Patricia Jane Walker, Dec. 17, 1966; children: Christopher O'Brien, Ryan Kerrick, Ann Elisabeth. AB, Brown U., 1965; JD, Emory U., 1970. Bar: Ga., 1971, U.S. Dist. Ct. (no dist.) Ga., 1971, U.S. Ct. Appeals (11th cir.), 1971, U.S. Supreme Ct., 2003. Assoc. Alston, Miller & Gaines, Atlanta, 1970-76, ptnr., 1976-83; ptnr., litig. trial practice group Alston & Bird LLP, Atlanta, 1983—. Lectr. various seminars on bus. litig., appellate procedure, juvenile law, ethics, and professionalism. Contbr. articles to profl. jours. Co-founder Truancy Intervention Project, 1991—; chmn. Kids In Need of Dreams, Inc., 1993-; bd. dirs. Family Connection Partnership, 2000-, Georgians for Children, 1993-2003, The Bridge, 1994-99, Ga. Justice Project, 1987-97, Juvenile Justice Fund, 2000—, Ga. Acad., 1999-2002; bd. dirs. Atlanta Legal Aid Soc., Inc., 1976-98, pres., 1997; chmn. Capital Area Mosaic, 1994-96; chmn. sch. bd. Christ the King Sch., 1982-84; alumni trustee Brown U., 1994-2001; chmn. State Bar Com. on Children and the Cts., 1996—; bd. dirs. Child Placement Project Adv. Bd. Supreme Ct. Ga., 2000—. Recipient cmty. svc. award Martin Luther King, Jr. Ctr. for Nonviolent Social Change, 1995. Fellow: Ga. Bar Found.; mem.: ABA (juvenile justice sect., Livingston Hall Juvenile Justice award 1999), Atlanta Bar Assn. (Leadership award 2005), Gate City Bar Assn., Atlanta Bar Assn. (bd. dirs. 1987—93, pres. 1991—92, Charles E. Watkins award 1994, S. Phillip Heiner award 1994, David Pollard award 1995), State Bar Ga. (bd. govs. 1979—99, pres. young lawyers sect. 1980—81, H. Sol Clark award 1987, Chief Justice's award for cmty. svc. 1998), Emory Law Alumni Assn. (exec. com. 1990—98, Disting. Law Alumnus award 2000). Avocations: sports, gardening, reading. Office: Alston & Bird LLP One Atlantic Ctr 1201 W Peachtree St NW Ste 4200 Atlanta GA 30309-3449 Office Phone: 404-881-7161. Office Fax: 404-253-8884. Business E-Mail: twalsh@alston.com.

**WALSH, WILLIAM ALBERT,** management consultant, retired military officer; b. Gilman, Ill., Aug. 15, 1933; s. Lawrence Eugene and Myrtle R. (Mulder) W.; m. Joan Elizabeth Kennedy, Dec. 28, 1957; children: Kathryn, Michael, Julie. BS in Commerce, U. Notre Dame, 1955; MS in Mgmt. with distinction, U.S. Naval Postgrad. Sch., Monterey, Calif., 1962; MS in Internat. Affairs with honors, George Washington U., 1972. Commd. ensign U.S. Navy, 1955, advanced through grades to rear adm., 1981; exec. asst. to dep. chief naval ops. (Surface Warfare), Washington, 1974-76; comdg. officer USS Juneau, San Diego, 1976-78; comdr. Amphibious Squadron Three, San Diego, 1978-79; head plans and policy div., comdr. rapid deployment naval forces Comdr. in Chief U.S. Pacific Fleet, Honolulu, 1979-81; comdr. Amphibious Group Eastern Pacific, San Diego, 1981-82; dir. surface warfare div. Office Chief Naval Ops., Pentagon, Washington, 1983-85; ret., 1985; pres. Air/Space Am., San Diego, 1986-89, W.A. Walsh Enterprises, 1990—. Decorated Legion of Merit with 2 gold stars, Bronze Star, Navy Commendation medal U.S.; Disting. Service Order 2d Class Vietnam

**WALSH, WILLIAM ARTHUR, JR.,** lawyer; b. Washington, Mar. 17, 1949; children: Jesse Creighton, Patrick McKay. BS in Econs. and Fin., U. Md., 1972; JD, U. Richmond, 1977. Bar: Va. Ptnr. Hunton & Williams LLP, Richmond, Va., 1977—. Adv. bd. for law rev. U. Richmond. Trustee, bd. dirs. Va. Commonwealth U. Real Estate Found.; mem. Va. Commonwealth U. Real Estate Circle of Excellence. Mem. Va. Bar Assn., Am. Coll. Real Estate Lawyers. Home: 4705 Leonard Pky Richmond VA 23226-1337 Office: Hunton & Williams LLP Riverfront Plz East Tower 951 E Byrd St Richmond VA 23219-4074 Office Phone: 804-788-8378. Business E-Mail: wwalsh@hunton.com.

**WALSH, WILLIAM DESMOND,** investor; b. NYC, Aug. 4, 1930; s. William J. and Catherine Grace (Desmond) W.; m. Mary Jane Gordon, Apr. 5, 1951; children: Deborah, Caroline, Michael, Suzanne, Tara Jane, Peter. BA, Fordham U., 1951; JD, Harvard U., 1955. Bar: NY 1955. Asst. US atty. So. dist. NY, NYC, 1955-58; counsel NY Commn. Investigation, NYC, 1958-61; mgmt. cons. McKinsey & Co., NYC, 1961-67; sr. v.p. Arcata Corp., Menlo Park, Calif., 1967-82; chmn. Sequoia Assocs. LLC, 1982—; pres., CEO Atacra Liquidating Trust, 1982-88. Chmn. bd. dir. Neuroscis. Inst./Scripps, Americscape, Inc., Cornelius, Oreg., Creativity Inc., Van Nuys; bd. dir. URS Corp., San Francisco, Am. Ireland Fund, Boston. Mem. bd. overseers Hoover Inst.; co-chmn. dean's adv. bd. Harvard Law Sch.; trustee emeritus Fordham U. Mem. NY State Bar Assn., Harvard Club (NYC and San Francisco), Fordham Club No. Calif., Knights of Malta. Home: 279 Park Ln Atherton CA 94027-5448 Office Phone: 650-321-9400. Office Fax: 650-321-9412. Business E-Mail: sequoiaassociates@gmail.com.

**WALSH, WILLIAM L., JR.,** lawyer; b. Boston, June 21, 1941; BS, Boston Coll., 1965; JD, Cath. U. Am., 1968. Bar: Va. 1968, D.C. 1971. Trial atty. Naval Supply Systems Commd., 1968-71, dep. counsel, 1974-77; asst. counsel Naval Ordinance Systems Commd., 1971-74; staff asst. to Commn. on Govt. Procurement, 1972; asst. gen. counsel Navy, 1977-78; navy legal mem. Def. Acquisition Regulation Coun., 1977-78; chief counsel NASA's George C. Marshall Space Flight Ctr., 1978-81; ptnr., Govt. Contracts practice Venable LLP, Vienna, Va. Mem. adv. bd. George Mason Univ. Sch. Mgmt., Nat. Ctr. for Tech. & the Law; past chmn. Govt. Affairs com., No. Va. Tech. Council; bd. dir., past gen. counsel Fairfax County C. of C. Mem. ABA (chmn. Small Bus. com., Fed Regulations com.), Fed. Bar Assn., Va. State Bar Assn, DC Bar Assn., Fairfax County Bar Assn., Arlington County Bar Assn. Office: Venable LLP Suite 300 8010 Towers Crescent Dr Vienna VA 22182 Office Fax: 703-760-1685, 703-821-8949. Business E-Mail: wlwalsh@venable.com.

**WALSHE, AUBREY PETER,** political science professor; b. Johannesburg, Jan. 12, 1934; s. Aubrey John and Joan Kathleen (Evans) W.; m. Catherine Ann Pettifer, Jan. 28, 1957; children: Sally, Jane, Dominic, Emma. BA, Wadham Coll., Oxford, Eng., 1956, MA, 1959; PhD, St. Antony's Coll., Oxford, 1968. Vis. asst. prof. U. Notre Dame, Ind., 1962-63, asst. prof. dept. govt. and internat. studies Ind., 1967-71, dir. African studies Ind., 1971-77, assoc. prof. Ind., 1971-77, prof. Ind., 1977—. Sr. assoc. fellow St. Antony's Coll., Oxford, 1972-73; dir. ann. Missionary Inst. on Sub-Saharan Africa, U.Notre Dame, 1969—; lectr. and cons. in field; found. mem. So. African Rsch. Archival Project;l mem. N.Am. Support Com., Ecumenical Dialogue of Third World Theologians. Contbr. articles to profl. jours.; author: The Rise of African Nationalism in South Africa, 1971, 2d edit. 1988, Black Nationalism in South Africa: A Short History, 1975, Church Versus State in South Africa, 1983, Prophetic Christianity and the Liberation Management in South Africa, 1997; contbr. revs. to numerous jours.; occasional reader: U. Calif. Press, U. Notre Dame Press, Rev. of Politics, Social Scis. and Humanities Rsch. Coun. of Can., Ottawa, Ind. U. African Studies Pubs. Com., Cath. Inst. for Internat. Rels., London, U. Queensland, Australia. Mem. edn. com. cath. Inst. for Internat. Rels.; London; adv. bd. Storypoint Ctr., Presbyn. Ch. U.S.A., N.Y.C.; cons. Nat. Coun. of Chs. of Christ, Convocation of the Kairos Document: Challenge to the Ch. in South Africa. Walsh-Price fellow Ctr. for Mission Studies, Maryknoll, N.Y., 1980-81, Helen Kellogg Inst. for Internat. Studies fellow, 1983, Inst. for Internat. Peace Studies fellow, 1987; MacArthur Found. grantee, 1989-90; recipient Sheedy award for Excellence in Tchg, U. Notre Dame, 2004. Ecumenical Christian. Home: 1037 N Niles Ave South Bend IN 46617-1249 Office: Univ Notre Dame Dept Govt Notre Dame IN 46556

**WALSH MITCHELL, DIANA,** school psychologist, consultant; d. T. and D. Walsh. BA, Hofstra U., 1997; MA, Adelphi U., 1999; MS in Edn., Fordham U., 2002, Profl. Diploma in Sch. Psychology, 2002; D in Psychology, Fairleigh Dickinson U., 2005. Cert. sch. psychologist N.Y. State Edn. Dept., 2002. Sch. psychologist Pub. Sch., Hewlett, NY, 2002—03; psychometrician Schneider Children's Hosp., New Hyde Park, NY, 2002—04; cons. NY, 2004—; sch. psychologist NY, 2004—. Cons. Pvt. Sch., Kew Gardens, NY; presenter in field. Mem.: NASP, APA, N.Am. Assn. for the Study of Obesity, NY Assn. Sch. Psychologists. Personal E-mail: dianawmitchell@aol.com.

---

**WALSH-PIPER, KATHLEEN A.,** museum director; b. Chgo., Aug. 17, 1947; d. James Clement and Jane (Burnham) W.; m. Michael G. Rubin, May 17, 1969 (div. 1978); m. Rubin H. Piper, Dec. 19, 1987. BA, Washington U., St. Louis, 1969, MA in Art History, 1973; postgrad., St. Louis U. Cert. tchr., Mo. Tchr. St. Louis Archdiocesan Schs., 1970-73; asst. prof. Mo. Bapt. Coll., St. Louis, 1973; tchr. Hazelwood Jr. High Sch., St. Louis, 1974-77; mus. tchr. St. Louis Art. Mus., 1976, coord. rsch. ctr., 1977-80; asst. dir. mus. edn. Art. Inst. Chgo., 1980—85; dir. edn. Terra Mus. Am. Art, Chgo., 1985-88; head dept. tchr. and sch. programs Nat. Gallery Art, Washington, 1988—95; cultural specialist U.S. Info. Agency, 1995; dir. edn. and pub. progs. Dallas Mus. Art, Tex., 1995—2002; dir. U. Ky. Art Mus., Lexington, 2002—. Mus. guest scholar J. Paul Getty Mus., Malibu, Calif., 1997. Author: Teachers Guide to the Art Institute of Chicago, 1984, Image to Word: Art and Creative Writing, 2002; contbr. articles to profl. jours. Robert E. Smith fellowship Nat. Gallery of Art, 1994. Mem. Nat. Art Edn. Assn. (regional mus. educator 1984, nat. mus. educator 1985, dir. mus. divsn. 1992—), Am. Assn. Mus. (chair midwest edn. ccom. 1983-84). Avocation: writing. Office: U Ky Art Mus 116 Singletary Ctr Rose St and Euclid Ave Lexington KY 40506-0241 Office Phone: 859-257-1152. E-mail: kwpiper@email.uky.edu.

**WALSKE, M(AX) CARL, JR.,** physicist; b. Seattle, June 2, 1922; s. Max Carl and Margaret Ella (Fowler) W.; m. Elsa Marjorie Nelson, Dec. 28, 1946; children: C. Susan, Steven C., Carol A. (dec.). BS in Math. cum laude, U. Wash., 1944; PhD in Theoretical Physics, Cornell U., 1951. Staff, asst. theoretical divsn. leader Los Alamos Sci. Lab., 1951-56; dep. rsch. dir. Atomics Internat., Canoga Park, Calif., 1956-59; sci. rep. AEC in U.K., London, 1961-62; theoretical physicist RAND Corp., 1962-63; sci. attache U.S. missions to NATO and OECD, Paris, 1963-65; staff mem. Los Alamos Sci. Lab., 1965-66; asst. to sec. def. for atomic energy Dept. Def., 1966—73, chmn. military liaison com. to atomic energy commn.; pres., COO Atomic Indsl. Forum, Inc., Washington, 1973-87. Chmn. Upper Hood Canal Watershed Mgmt. Com., 1994-2000; budget steering com. Kitsap County, 1996, budget com., 1997-99, participant strategic planning, 1997, planning commn., 1998-2000. Lt. (j.g.) USNR, 1943-51. Recipient Disting. Civilian Svc. medal Dept. Def. Fellow Explorers Club, Am. Phys. Soc.; mem. Am. Nuc. Soc., Phi Beta Kappa, Sigma Xi. Home: PO Box 370 Silverdale WA 98383-0370 E-mail: cwalske@wavecable.com. *To seek out positions which appeared the most challenging and personally satisfying; to gain my reward through self-respect rather than public recognition; to expend extra effort as an offset to my limitations.*

**WALSMITH, CHARLES RODGER,** psychologist, educator; b. Denver, May 19, 1926; s. Joseph Francis and Florence Ophelia (Smith-Brown) W.; children: Karen Frances, Cynthia Ann, Erik Konrad. BA, U. Denver, 1956, MA, 1962; postgrad., U. Wash., 1968-76; PhD, Stanton U., 1976. Rsch. psychologist Pers. Tng. and Rsch. Ctr., Maintenance Lab., USAF, Lowery AFB, Denver, 1956; rsch. assist. U. Colo. Med. Ctr., Denver, 1956-57, rsch. assoc., 1957-64; assoc. prof. psychology North Pk. Coll., Chgo., 1965-66; sr. human engring. analyst, psychoacoustics Boeing Co., Seattle, 1965-68; instr. psychology dept. behavioral scis. Bellevue (Wash.) C.C., 1968-87, chmn. dept., 1968-75, 79-82, Phi Theta Kappa advisor, 1981-87, instr., chmn. dept. emeritus, 1987—. Resident trainer Gestalt Inst. of Can., Lake Cowichan, B.C., summers 1969-71, assocs., 1969—; dir. Gestalt Inst. of Wash., Bellevue, 1970—. Dem. precinct chmn. Renton, Wash., 1966-68. With USNR, 1944-46. Chancellor's Ednl. scholar U. Denver, 1956. Mem. NEA, Phi Beta Kappa, Psi Chi. Home: Gestalt House 14909 SE 44 Pl Bellevue WA 98006 Office Phone: 425-747-8278. Personal E-mail: crwalsmith@netzero.net.

**WALSS, RODOLFO J.,** obstetrician, gynecologist, artist; b. Monclova, Coahuila, Mex., June 13, 1945; came to U.S., 1992; s. Rodolfo and Maria Consuelo W.; m. Maria Eugenia Aurioles, Dec. 17, 1967; children: Eugenia, Consuelo, Rodolfo, Patricia, Leonardo. MD, U. Coahuila (Mex.), Torreón, 1970. Diplomate Am. Bd. Ob-Gyn. Intern Ohio Valley Med. Ctr., Wheeling, W.Va., 1973-74; resident U. W.Va. Ohio Valley Med. Ctr., Wheeling, W.Va., 1974-77; prof. obstetrics faculty of medicine U. Coahuila (Mex.), Torrón, 1978-92, prof. gynecology faculty of medicine, 1982-92; chief ob-gyn svc. Mexican Social Security Inst., Torrón, 1986-90, chief divsn. ob-gyn., 1990-92; ob-gyn. Women Healthcare Group, Brownsville, Tex., 1992—2003; chief ob-gyn. Columbia Valley Regional Med. Ctr., Brownsville, 1994-97, mem. edn. com., 1997—; pvt. practice Brownsville, 1997—; vice chief of state, 2003; chief of staff Valley Regional Med. Ctr., 2004. Contbr. 22 articles to profl. jours. Fellow Am. Coll. Ob-Gyn., ACS; mem. Am. Soc. Reproductive Medicine, AMA, Tex. Med. Assn. Avocation: painting. Home: 24 Summit Dr Brownsville TX 78521-3610 Office: Ste 205 4770 N Expressway Brownsville TX 78520 Office Phone: 956-350-0838. E-mail: rodolfowalss@aol.com.

**WALSTON, RODERICK EUGENE,** federal official; b. Gooding, Idaho, Dec. 15, 1935; s. Loren R. and Iva M. (Boyer) W.; m. Margaret D. Grandey; children: Gregory Scott W., Valerie Lynne W. AA, Boise Jr. Coll., 1956; BA cum laude, Columbia Coll., 1958; LL.B. scholar, Stanford U., 1961. Bar: Calif. 1961, U.S. Supreme Ct. 1973. Law clk to judge U.S. Ct. Appeals 9th Cir., 1961-62; dep. atty. gen State of Calif., San Francisco, 1963-91, head natural resources sect, 1969-91, chief asst. atty. gen. pub. rights div., 1991-99; spl. dep counsel Kings County, Calif., 1975-76; gen. counsel Metropolitan Water Dist. So. Calif., 2000—02; dep. solicitor U.S. Dept. Interior, 2002—; of counsel Best, Best and Krieger, LLP, Walnut Creek, Calif., 2005. Mem. environ. and natural resources adv. coun. Stanford (Calif.) Law Sch. Contbr. articles to profl. jours.; bd. editors: Stanford Law Rev., 1959-61, Western Natural Resources Litigation Digest, Calif. Water Law and Policy Reporter; spl. editor Jour. of the West. Co-chmn. Idaho campaign against Right-to-Work initiative, 1958; Calif. rep. Western States Water Coun., 1986—; environ. and natural resources adv. coun., Stanford Law Sch. Astor Found. scholar, 1956-58; Nat. Essay Contest winner Nat. Assn. Internat. Rels. Clubs, 1956, Stanford Law Rev. prize, 1961; recipient Best Brief award Nat. Assn. Attys. Gen., 1997; named Pub. Lawyer of Yr., Calif. State Bar, 2004 Mem. ABA (chmn. water resources com. 1988-90, vice chmn. and conf. chmn. 1985-88, 90—), Contra Costa County Bar Assn., U.S. Supreme Ct., Hist. Soc., Federalist Soc., World Affairs Coun. No. Calif. Office: Best Best and Krieger LLP 2033 N Main St Walnut Creek CA 94596 Office Phone: 925-977-3304. Business E-Mail: roderick.walston@bbklaw.com.

**WALT, MARTIN,** physicist, educator; b. West Plains, Mo., June 1, 1926; s. Martin and Dorothy (Mantz) W.; m. Mary Estelle Thompson, Aug. 16, 1950; children: Susan Mary, Stephen Martin, Anne Elizabeth, Patricia Ruth. BS, Calif. Inst. Tech., 1950; MS, U. Wis., 1951, PhD, 1953. Staff mem. Los Alamos Sci. Lab., 1953-56; research scientist, mgr. physics Lockheed Missiles and Space Co., Palo Alto (Calif.) Rsch. Lab., 1956-71; dir. phys. scis., 1971-86, dir. research, 1986-93; cons. prof. Stanford U., 1986—. Mem. adv. com. NRC, NASA, Dept. Def.; Calif. Lawrence Berkeley Lab. Author 2 books; contbr. articles to sci. jours. Served with USNR, 1944-46. Wis. Research Found. fellow, 1950-51; AEC fellow, 1951-53 Fellow Am. Geophys. Union, Am. Phys. Soc.; mem. Am. Inst. Physics (bd. govs.), Fremont Hills Country Club. Home: 12650 Viscaino Ct Los Altos Hills CA 94022-2517 Office: Stanford U Starlab Packard 352 Stanford CA 94305 Office Phone: 650-723-2690. Business E-Mail: walt@nova.stanford.edu.

**WALT, STEVEN DAVID,** law educator; b. Rochester, Minn., Mar. 10, 1954; s. Alexander Jeffrey and Irene (Lapping) W. BA cum laude, Kalamazoo Coll., 1976; MA in philosophy, U. Chgo., 1979, PhD in philosophy, 1984; JD, Yale U., 1988. Bar: NY 1988. Asst. prof. philosophy Calif. Inst. Tech., Pasadena, 1983-85; asst. prof. law Wharton Sch. Bus., U. Pa., Phila., 1988-90, U. San Diego, 1990-92, assoc. prof., 1992—93; prof. U. Va. Sch. Law, Charlottesville, 1992— Vis. assoc. prof. U. Va. Sch. Law, 1992—93; mem. editl. bd. Legal Theory. Co-author (with R. Jordan and W. Warren): Commercial Law, 2000, Secured Transactions in Personal Property, 2000; co-author: (with C. Gillette) Sales Law: Domestic and International, 2002; co-editor (with J. Kraus): The Jurisprudential Foundations of Corporate and Commercial Law, 2000. Mem.: Am. Soc. Polit. & Legal Philosophy. Office: U Va Sch Law 580 Massie Rd Charlottesville VA 22903-1789 Office Phone: 434-924-7930. E-mail: sdw6a@virginia.edu.

**WALTER, BURL LEROY, JR.,** retired music educator; b. Lawrence, Kans., Aug. 15, 1933; s. Burl Leroy and Ruth Christian Walter; m. Evelyn Ruth Shaline, Mar. 26, 1956; children: Burl Leroy III, Ellen Ruth. BS, NW Mo. State U., Maryville, 1956. Music educator Hopkins Pub. Schools, Hopkins, Mo., 1955—56; army bandsman 22nd Army Band, San Francisco, 1956—58; music educator Macksburg H.S., Macksburg, Iowa, 1958—60, Schleswig H.S., Schleswig, Iowa, 1960—63; musician Glenn Houpt Trio and Symphony Orch., Sioux City, Iowa, 1963—64; music educator Kings Canyon Unified Sch. Dist., Reedley, Calif., 1964—2000; lectr. Calif. State U., Fresno, Calif., 1974—75. Mem. Kings Canyon Edn. Assn., 1965; treas. Fresno-Madera Music Edn. Assn., Calif., 1965; v.p. Calif. Band Directors Assn., Calif., 1968; mem. Calif. Teachers Assn., Calif., 1965, Fresno Dixieland Soc., Calif., 1985, Percusive Arts Soc., Calif., 1965, Local 210 Musicians Union, Calif., 1965. Pfc U.S. Army, 1956—58, San Francisco. Named Outstanding Music Educator, Fresno-Madera Music Edn. Assn., 1996—97, Outstanding Band Dir., 1997, Outstanding Music Educator, Calif. Music Educators Assn., 1988, 1996, State of Calif., 1996; named to Hall Of Fame, Reedley C. of C., 1999; recipient Man of Yr., 1997, Disting. Svc. award, Calif. Band Dirs. Assn., 1968, Lifetime Svc. award, Calif. Band Dirs., 2001. Home: 1425 E St Reedley CA 93654

**WALTER, CARMEL MONICA,** security firm executive, writer; b. Dublin, July 24, 1943; arrived in U.S., 1961; d. Albert and Anastatia Woods; m. Michael William Walter, June 15, 1963; children: Coleen, Daniel, Eileen. BS magna cum laude, Madonna U., Livonia, Mich., 1987. Co-founder, co-owner Am. Security Alarm Co., Madison Heights, Mich., 1969—72, Alarm Supply Co., Inc., Livonia, Mich., 1969—89, founder, owner Milford, NJ, 2001—. Intro.and product tng. for first wireless security sys. Resldent Sentry, Madison Heights, 1967—72; co-owner CMD Co., Flemington, NJ, 1989—2002; established ongoing comprehensive tech. support sys. Alarm Supply Co., Milford, 2003—. Co-author (with Michael Walter): (security products and application manual) The Security Store. Mem. cert. nat. emergency response teams emergency support function #13 public safety and security Am. Bd. for Certification in Homeland Security, Springfield, Mo., 2005. Mem.: Am. Coll. Forensic Examiners Inst. (cert. homeland security-II), Kappa Gamma Pi. Roman Catholic. Avocations: travel, golf, theater, cooking, interior design. Office Phone: 908-995-2449. Business E-Mail: alarmsply@aol.com. E-mail: carmelwalter@aol.com.

**WALTER, DEBORAH,** elementary school educator; b. Orangeburg, S.C., Feb. 10, 1955; d. Eugene Robert and Charlotte Willard Walter. AA, St. Mary's Coll., Raleigh, N.C, 1975; BS in Elem. Edn., U. Va., 1977; MA in Early Childhood Edn., Oglethorpe U., 1986. Tchr. Wade Hampton Acad., Orangeburg, 1977—80, Brumby Elem. Sch., Marietta, Ga., 1982—87, Dept. of Def. Dependents Overseas Schs., Schweinfurt, Germany, 1987—94, S.C. Dept. of Def. Elem. and Secondary Schs. Laurel Bay Site, Beaufort, 1994—. Mem., vice chmn. Sch. Adv. Coun., Schweinfurt, 1988—93; study group facilitator Study of Tchg., Schweinfurt, 1991—94; drama coach, dir. Schweinfurt Elem. Sch., 1992—94; chair Sch. Improvement Team, Beaufort, 1995—2001; grade level chair Elliott Elem. Sch., Beaufort, 2001, Beaufort, 2004—05. Vol. Friends of the Libr., Beaufort, 1994—2005; Sunday sch. tchr. Cmty. Bible Ch., Beaufort, 2000—05. Named Tchr. of Yr., Brumby Elem. Sch., 1987, S.C./Ft. Stewart DDESS, 2005; recipient Tchr. award, Laurel Bay Schs., Beaufort, 1998; Tommy Wannamaker scholar, Wade Hampton Acad., 1973. Mem.: Alpha Delta Kappa (publicity chair 2004—05). Avocations: travel, hiking. Home: 2703 Palm Dr Beaufort SC 29902 Office Phone: 843-846-6982.

**WALTER, HAROLD MARK,** lawyer; b. Balt., 1957; BA, Franklin Marshall Coll., 1979; JD, U. Md., 1982. Bar: Md. 1983, N.Y. 1997, U.S. Dist. Ct. Md. 1990, U.S. Dist. Ct. (so. and ea. dists.) N.Y. 1997, U.S. Dist. Ct. D.C. 2004, U.S. Ct. Appeals (4th cir.) 1992, U.S. Ct. Appeals (3d cir.) 1997, U.S. Supreme Ct. 1995, DC 2005. Law clk. Ct. Spl. Appeals, Md., 1982—83; ptnr. Tydings & Rosenberg LLP, Balt., 1983—. Steering com. industrywide litig. Def. Rsch. Inst. Named one of Top Ten Most Winning Attys., The Nat. Law Jour., 2002. Mem.: ABA (forum com. entertainment and sports industries), N.Y. State Bar Assn., Md. State Bar Assn., Balt. (Md.) County C. of C. Office: Tydings & Rosenberg LP 100 East Pratt St Baltimore MD 21202 Office Phone: 410-752-9720. Business E-Mail: hwalter@tydingslaw.com.

**WALTER, HEATH ALLEN,** music educator; b. Brush, Colo., May 9, 1970; s. Merle Dennis and Evelyn Elanor Walter. BA, Doane Coll., Crete, Nebr., 1992; MA, Western Ill. U., Macomb, 2002. Cert. tchr. U. North Colo. Greeley, 1993. Choral dir. Windsor Mid. and H.S., Colo., 1994—97, Windsor H.S., 1997—2000, Wheat Ridge H.S., Colo., 2002—06, Cherry Creek H.S., Greenwood Village, Colo., 2006—. Gov. Colo. All State Choir, 2004—. Named Outstanding Am. Tchr., NHR, 2006. Mem.: Music Educators Nat. Conf., Am. Choral Dirs. Assn. Office: Cherry Creek H S 9300 Union Ave Greenwood Village CO 80111

**WALTER, HUGO GÜNTHER,** humanities educator, poet; b. Phila., Mar. 12, 1959; s. Paul and Elli R. Walter. BA, Princeton U., 1981; MA in Humanities, Old Dominion U., 1989; MA in Lit., Yale U., 1983, MPhil in Lit., 1984, PhD in Lit, 1985; PhD in Interdisciplinary Humanities, Drew U., 1996. Adj. instr. Yale U., New Haven, 1981-85, Old Dominion U., Norfolk, Va. 1988-89; asst. prof. Washington and Jefferson Coll., Washington, Pa., 1989-92, Fairleigh Dickinson U., Madison, NJ, 1992-96, Kettering U., Flint, Mich., 1996-99; assoc. prof. Berkeley Coll., White Plains, 1999—. Vis. asst. prof. Rhodes Coll., Memphis, 1986-87, U. Mo., Columbia, 1987-88. Author: (poetry) The Fragile Edge, 1988, Velvet Rhythms, 1989, Amber Blossoms and Evening Shadows, 1990, Golden Thorns of Light and Sterling Silhoucttcs, 1991, Waiting for Babel Trophesion of Sunflower Dreams, 1992, Along the Maroon-Prismed Threshold of Bronze-Pealing Eternity, 1992, The Light of the Dance Is the Music of Eternity, 1993, Dusk-Gloaming Mirrors and Castle-Winding Dreams, 1994, Amaranth-Sage Epiphanies of Dusk-Weaving Paradise, 1995, 2d edit., 1996, A Purple-Golden Renascence of Eden-Exalting Rainbows, 2001, (monographs) The Apostrophic Moment in 19th and 20th Century Lyric Poetry, 1988, Space and Time on the Magic Mountain: Studies in the 19th and 20th Century European Literature, 1999. Mem. Acad. Am. Poets, Internat. Soc. Poets. Avocations: music, painting. Home: 157 Loomis CT Princeton NJ 08540-3438 Personal E-mail: hwalprin@aol.com.

**WALTER, INGO,** economics professor; b. Kiel, Germany, Apr. 11, 1940; arrived in U.S.; 1950; s. Hellmuth and Ingeborg (Moeller) W.; m. Jutta Ragnhild Dobernecker, June 28, 1963; children: Carsten Erik, Inga Maria. AB summa cum laude, Lehigh U., 1962, MS, 1963; PhD, NYU, 1966. Asst. prof. econs. U. Mo., St. Louis, 1965-67, assoc. prof., chmn. dept., 1967-70; prof. econs. and fin. Stern Sch. Bus. Adminstrn. NYU, N.Y.C., 1970—, assoc. dean academic affairs, 1970-79, chmn. internat. bus. and fin. depts., 1980-85, Dean Abraham L. Gitlow chair, 1987-90; Charles Simon chair, dir. NYU Ctr., 1990—2003; Seymour Milstein chair fin., corp. governance and ethics, dir. NYU Global Bus. Inst., 2003—06. Prof. internat. mgmt. (joint appt.) INSEAD, Fontainebleau, France, 2005-2005; cons. in field. Author: editor 28 books including Secret Money, 1985, 2d edit., 1990, Global Banking, 3d edit., 2003, Universal Banking in the United States, 1994, Street Smarts, 1997, High Finance in the Euro-Zone, 2000, Mergers and Acquisitions in Financial Services, 2004, Governing the Modern Corporation, 2006; contbr. articles to profl. jours. Recipient Bernhard Harms medal, 1992; Ford Found. fellow, 1974-76, Rockefeller Found. fellow, 1977-78. Mem. Am. Econ. Assn., Am. Fin. Assn., Acad. Internat. Bus., Royal Econ. Soc. So. Econ. Assn., Phi Beta Kappa, Beta Gamma Sigma, Omicron Delta Epsilon. Home: 77 Club Rd Montclair NJ 07043-2528 Office: NYU Stern Sch Bus 44 W 4th St New York NY 10012-1106 E-mail: iwalter@stern.nyu.edu.

**WALTER, J. JACKSON,** management consultant, foundation administrator; b. Abington, Pa., Nov. 6, 1940; s. Joseph Horace and Edith Wilson (Jackson) W.; m. Susan Draude, Feb. 3, 1978; 1 child, Allison K. AB, Amherst Coll., Mass., 1962; LLB, Yale U., New Haven, 1966. Sec. Fla. Dept. Bus. Regulation, Tallahassee, 1976-79; dir. US Office Govt. Ethics, Washington,

1979-82; pres. Nat. Acad. Pub. Adminstrn., Washington, 1982-84, Nat. Trust Historic Preservation, Washington, 1984-92; exec. dir. Waterford Found., Va., 1996-98. Chmn. Amendment I, Inc., 2000—06. Co-author: America's Unelected Government, 1983. Contbr. articles to profl. jours. Mem. Nat. Acad. Pub. Adminstrn., Met. (Washington) Club. Office Phone: 540-882-4116.

**WALTER, JESS,** writer; m. Anne Walter; children: Brooklyn, Ava, Alec. Co-author (with Christopher Darden): In Contempt, 1996; author: Every Knee Shall Bow, 1995 (PEN Center West lit. nonfiction award finalist, 1996), Over Tumbled Graves, 2001 (NY Times Notable Book), Ruby Ridge (re-release of Every Knee Shall Bow), 2002, Land of the Blind, 2003, Citizen Vince, 2005 (Washington Post Best Book of Yr., 2005, Edgar Allan Poe award for best novel Mystery Writers Am., 2006), The Zero, 2006. Home: Spokane WA Mailing: HarperCollins Author Mail 10 E 53rd St New York NY 10022*

**WALTER, JOHN FREDERICK,** historical researcher, genealogist; b. Bklyn., Sept. 27, 1939; s. William O. and Madeline (Dittrich) W.; m. Margaret Killeen, Feb. 9, 1963; children: Mark, Michael, Robin, Brian. Student, St. John's U., 1955-61. Records mgr. Ladenburg Thalmann & Co., N.Y.C., 1961-76, W.R. Family Assocs., N.Y.C., 1976-94; dir., owner Inst. for Civil War Rsch., Middle Village, NY, 1994—. Author: The Confederate Dead in Brooklyn. Merit badge counselor Boy Scouts Am., Middle Village, 1990—. Sgt. U.S. Army Res., 1961-65. Mem. Nat. Geneal. Soc., Co. Mil. Historians, Assn. Profl. Genealogists, Cartophilic Soc. Great Britain. Roman Catholic. Avocations: walking, volleyball, racquetball, cigarette card collecting. Home and Office: 79-13 67 Dr Middle Village NY 11379 E-mail: icwrjohn@aol.com.

**WALTER, KENNETH GAINES,** library director; b. Atlanta, Mar. 14, 1932; s. Gaines Winningham and Freddie Lou (Thigpen) W.; m. Eva Lou McClelland, June 10, 1965; children: Regina Eileen, Kevin Michael. BA, Emory U., 1954, MS, 1958; postgrad., U. Vienna, Austria, 1962; MSLS, U. N.C., Chapel Hill, 1966; EdD, U. Ga., 1995. Asst. cataloging libr. Ohio U., Athens, 1961-65, head cataloging libr., 1965-68, faculty rep. Bapt. Student Union New Haven, 1965-68; asst. dir. libr. U.S.C., Columbia, 1968-75; dir. libr. Ga. So. U., Statesboro, 1975-84; dir. libr. svcs. So. Conn. State U., New Haven, 1985-97, dir. libr. svcs. emeritus, 1997—. Cons. libr. strategic planning, budgeting, evaluation of book collections; faculty advisor Delta Tau Delta, Statesboro, 1976-83; book reviewer Libr. Jour., 1970-78. Contbr. articles to profl. jours. Mem. Conn. State U. Sys. Lib. Autom. RFP com., 1991-93, lib. dirs. com., 1985-97, Conn. Coun. Acad. Lib. Dirs., 1989-97 (emeritus mem. 1997—), Interagy. Libr. Planning Com., Hartford, Conn., 1986-89; mem. com. in-state svc. Conn. Acad. Lib. Dirs., 1985-89; mem. cataloging bd. New Haven Colony Hist. Soc., 1987-89; mem. Statesboro-Ga. So. Community Chorus, 1980-84; chmn. bd. suprs. CORE Credit Union, Statesboro, 1978-81. Staff sgt. U.S. Army, 1956-57. Recipient scholarship Emory U., 1950-53; Fulbright scholar, 1961-62; grantee Austrian Govt., 1961-62. Mem. ALA (life), Ga. Acad. Libr. Dirs., Ga. regents com. 1975-83 (sub com. coop. purchasing, 1978-1980, autom., 1980-1983, a/v 1975-1978), Assn. Coll. and Rsch. Librs., Libr. Adminstrn. and Mgmt. Assn., Reference and User Svcs. Assn., Southeastern Libr. Assn., Ga. Libr. Assn., Conn. Libr. Assn., Cen. Ga. Assoc. Librs. (pres. 1980-82), East. Ga. Libr. Triangle (pres. 1976-83), Ga. Acad. Sci., Ga. Assn. Coll. and Rsch. Librs. (pres. 1983), Rotary (New Haven), Sigma Gamma Epsilon, Beta Phi Mu, Phi Delta Kappa, Delta Tau Delta. Baptist. Avocations: camping, rock collecting, stamp collecting/philately, woodworking. Home: 512 Wallingford Rd Cheshire CT 06410-2844

**WALTER, MARK R.,** investment company executive; JD, Northwestern Univ. Mng. ptnr. Liberty Hampshire Co.; CEO Guggenheim Capital LLC, Chgo. Trustee Solomon R. Guggenheim Mus., NYC. Office: Guggenheim Capital LLC 227 W Monroe St Chicago IL 60606

**WALTER, PATRICIA L.,** psychotherapist, consultant; b. Logansport, Ind., Mar. 15, 1935; d. William Marion and Doris May (Duddleston) Sievers; m. Raymond C. Walter Jr., Mar. 28, 1968; m. Keith A. Erny (div.); children: Rodney Erny, Jeffrey Erny, Mark Erny, Troy Erny. BS in Edn., Ind. U., 1973, MS in Edn. & English, 1976, MS in Counseling, 1984. Cert. English tchr., lic. mental health counselor Ind., cert. nat. cert. addictions prevention specialist III, forensic counselors 1998. Tchr. English Logansport Sch. Corp., Ind., 1973—97; psychotherapist Four County Counseling, Peru, 1993—2000; high sch. counselor Logansport Cmty. Schs., 1997—2003; mental health cons. Texas Migrant Headstart, Kokomo, 2004—; psychotherapist RAJ Clinic, Logansport, 2004—. Coord. Adminstrv. Counsel, Logansport, 2001—03; coach Acad. Competitions, 1987—98, Girls 6th Grade Basketball, 1975—78. Vol. First Call Home Health and Hospice, 2004. Mem.: Call County Carousel, Am. Mental Health Counselors Assn., Kiwanis (sec. 1997—98, pres. 2005—), Zeta Tau Chapter of Sigma Phi Gamma Sorority. Republican. Avocations: golf, ballroom dancing, reading, exercise, gardening. Home: 5209 Canterbury Ln Logansport IN 46947

**WALTER, PAUL HERMANN LAWRENCE,** chemistry professor; b. Jersey City, Sept. 22, 1934; s. Helmuth Justus and Adelaide C. J. (Twardy) W.; m. Grace Louise Carpenter, Aug. 25, 1956; children: Katherine Elizabeth Walter Bousquet, Marjorie Allison Walter Moran. BS, MIT, 1956; PhD, U. Kans., 1960. Rsch. scientist DuPont Cen. Rsch. Dept., Wilmington, Del., 1960-67; prof. chemistry Skidmore Coll., Saratoga Springs, NY, 1967-96, chair chemistry and physics, 1975-85, prof. emeritus, 1996—. Translator: (book) Foundations of Crystal Chemistry, 1968; contbr. articles to profl. jours. Fellow Chem. Inst. Can.; mem. AAAS, AAUP (pres. 1984-86), Am. Chem. Soc. (bd. dirs. 1991-99, chmn. 1993-95, pres.-elect 1997, pres. 1998, Radding award 2002), Soc. Quimica de Mexico (hon.). Presbyterian. Achievements include patents in field. Home: 3 Benedictine Retreat Savannah GA 31411-1624 E-mail: phlw@alum.mit.edu.

**WALTER, PETER,** biochemist; b. Berlin; Diploma in Chemistry, Free U. Berlin, 1976; MSc in Organic Chemistry, Vanderbilt U., 1977; PhD in Cell Biology, Rockefeller U., 1981. Prof., chmn. dept. biochemistry & biophysics U. Calif., San Francisco; investigator Howard Hughes Medical Inst. Harvey lectr. Rockefeller U., 1996; Feodor-Lynen lectr. Mosbach Kolloquium, 1998. Co-author: Molecular Biology of the Cell, 2002, Essential Cell Biology, 2003. Recipient Searle Scholar award, 1983, Passano award, 1988, Eli Lilly award, 1988, Alfred P. Sloan award, 1989, Merit award, Nat. Insts. Health, 1990, Wiley Prize biomedical sciences, 2005. Fellow: Am. Acad. Microbiology, Am. Acad. Arts and Scis.; mem.: NAS, European Molecular Biology Orgn. (assoc.). Office: U Calif San Fransisco Dept Biochemistry & Biophysics Genentech Hall N312 600 16th St San Francisco CA 94143-2200 Office Phone: 415-476-5017. Office Fax: 415-476-5233. Business E-Mail: walter@cgl.ucsf.edu.*

**WALTER, ROBERT D.,** health products executive; b. Columbus, OH, July 13, 1945; m. Peggy McGreevey, 1967; children: Matthew, Blane, Peter. BMechE, Ohio U., 1967; MBA, Harvard U., 1970; Ph.D (hon.), Ohio U., 1997. Engr. N. Am. Rockwell, 1968; founder Cardinal Foods Inc. (acquired by Roundy's Inc. 1988), Dublin, Ohio, 1971-88; founder, CEO Cardinal Distribution, Dublin, Ohio, 1979—94; CEO Cardinal Health, Inc. (formerly Cardinal Distribution), Dublin, Ohio 2004—2006, chmn., 2006—. Bd. dirs Viacom Inc., Am Express; bd. trustees Battelle Meml. Inst., Ohio U. Trustee Battelle Meml. Inst. Recipient Christopher Columbus award, Greater Columbus C of C, 2001. Avocations: golf, running, skiing. Office: Cardinal Health Inc 7000 Cardinal Pl Dublin OH 43017-1092*

**WALTER, ROBERT IRVING,** retired chemistry professor; b. Johnstown, Pa., Mar. 12, 1920; s. Charles Weller and Frances (Riethmiller) W.; m. Farideh Asghari, Oct. 17, 1973. AB, Swarthmore Coll., Pa., 1941; MA, Johns Hopkins U., Balt., 1942; PhD, U. Chgo., 1949. Instr. U. Colo., 1949-51, U. Conn., 1953-55; rsch. assoc. Rutgers U., 1951-53; assoc. physicist Brookhaven Nat. Lab., 1955-56; mem. faculty Haverford Coll., 1956-68, prof. chemistry, 1963-68; prof. U. Ill., Chgo., 1968—, prof. emeritus, 1990—.

Vis. lectr. Stanford (Calif.) U., winter 1967; acad. guest U. Zurich, 1976; U.S. NAS exch. visitor to Romania, 1982, 88. Mem. Adv. Council Coll. Chemistry, 1966-70. Served with USNR, 1944-46. Grantee U.S. Army Signal Research and Devel. Lab., NIH, NSF, Dept. Energy; NSF fellow, 1960-61 Fellow AAAS; mem. Am. Chem. Soc. (vis. scientist div. chem. edn. 1964-73), Sigma Xi. Achievements include special research preparation, proof of structure, chemical and physical properties of stable aromatic free radicals, C1 reactions and mechanisms in heterogeneous catalysis, reactions of porphyrin bases. Home: 2951 Central St Unit 308 Evanston IL 60201-1284

**WALTER, SHERYL LYNN,** lawyer; b. Morris, Ill., July 18, 1956; d. C. Frank and Margaret (Juhl) W. BA in History cum laude, Grinnell (Iowa) Coll., 1978; JD cum laude, U. Minn., 1984; MPA John F. Kennedy Sch. of Govt., Harvard U., 2003. Bar: Minn. 1984, U.S. Dist. Ct. Minn. 1987, U.S. Ct. Appeals (8th cir.) 1987, D.C. 1989, U.S. Dist. Ct. D.C. 1989, U.S. Ct. Appeals (D.C. cir.) 1989. Law clk. to presiding judge 3d Jud. Dist. of Minn., Rochester, 1984-85; law clk. to Chief Judge Donald P. Lay U.S. Ct. Appeals (8th cir.), St. Paul, 1985-87; assoc. Mayer, Brown & Platt, Washington, 1987-89; gen. counsel Nat. Security Archive, Washington, 1989-94, Assn. Records Review Bd., Washington, 1994-95, Commn. Protecting and Reducing Govt. Secrecy, Washington, 1995-97, dep. spl. counsel U.S. Senate Vets. Affairs com., 1997-98; minority staff dir., chief counsel U.S. Senate Jud. Com., Youth Violence Subcom., 1998-2000; with Office of Legis. Affairs U.S. Dept. of Justice, 2000—03, acting asst. atty. gen., 2001, chief of staff Office of Intelligence & Policy Rev., 2003—. Cons. Amnesty Internat., Washington, 1988-89. Mem. ABA (vice chmn. adminstrv. law sect. govt. info. subcom. 1990-96), D.C. Bar Assn. (steering com., adminstrv. law sect. 1990-97), Am. Soc. Access Profls. (bd. dirs. 1990-98, pres. 1996-97), Brit.-Am. Security Info. Coun. (bd. dirs. 1994-2000), Lawyers Alliance for World Security (bd. dirs. 1994-2000). Office: US Dept Justice 9th and Pennsylvania Ave NW Washington DC 20530

**WALTER, THOMAS BERNARD,** music educator, conductor; b. Neenah, Wis., Apr. 23, 1952; s. Michael Milton and Marie Helen Walter; m. Susan Jane Eastman, Aug. 9, 1974; children: Aaron Thomas, Alexandria Suzanne. MusB, St. Norbert Coll., De Pere, Wis., 1974; MusM in Edn., U. Miami, Coral Gables, 1980. Music educator Menasha Pub. Schs., Wis., 1974—, coord. k-12 music, 1990—, dir. choral studies, 2001—. Accompanist Chaminade Women's Chorus, Appleton, Wis., 1974—79, music dir., 1980—; dir. music St. John the Bapt. Cath. Ch., Menasha 1978—2000; coord. children's honor choir Wis. Choral Director's Assn., Appleton, 2001; coord. music St. Mary Cath. Ch., 2002—; mem. steering com. Fox Cities H.S. Choral Festival, 2004—; soloist holiday concert Boy Choir Orgn., 1993, 2004. Music dir. Menasha Civic Chorale, Wis., 1974—77, Liberty Choir, Appleton, 1976—80; facilitator Appleton Med. Ctr. Sing For The Cure choral project, 2002; music dir. Colors of Christmas gospel choir Fox Cities Performing Arts Ctr., 2004. Recipient Excellence in Edn. award, Menasha Pub. Schools, 1981, 1994. Mem.: Nat. Assn. Pastoral Musicians (assoc.), Music Educators Nat. Conf. (assoc.), Am. Choral Directors Assn. (assoc.), Wis. Choral Directors Assn. (assoc.). Roman Catholic. Avocations: travel, swimming, reading, history. Home: 3341 White Birch Ln Appleton WI 54915 Office: Menasha HS 420 7th St Menasha WI 54952 Office Phone: 920-967-1800 4533. E-mail: waltert@mjsd.k12.wi.us.

**WALTER, VIRGINIA ANN,** information scientist, educator; b. Fargo, ND, Apr. 15, 1943; d. Roland and Vivian Kerber; children: Eva Mitnick, Sarah. BA in World Lit., San Francisco State U., 1964; PhD, U. So. Calif., 1984. Prof. Info. Studies Dept. U. Calif., L.A., 1990—; coord. children's svcs. L.A. (Calif.) Pub. Libr., 1987—90. Contbr. articles to profl. jours. Mem.: Assn. Libr. Svc. to Children (pres. 2000—01, Disting. Svc. award 2004). Office: UCLA Information Studies Department Box 951520 220 GSEIS Bldg Los Angeles CA 90095-1520 Office Phone: 310-206-9363.

**WALTER, VIRGINIA LEE,** psychologist, educator; b. Temple, Tex., Oct. 30, 1937; d. Luther Patterson and Virginia Lafayette (Wilkins) W.; m. Glen Ellis, 1958 (div.); children: Glen Edward, David Walter; m. Robert Reinehr, 1963 (div.); 1 son, Charles Allen; m. Robert Bruininks, 1975 (div.). BS, U. Tex.-Austin, 1959, M.Edn., 1967; postgrad. internship program in spl. Edn. Adminstrn., 1970; Ed.D., U. Houston, 1973. Prof. ednl. psychology dept. ednl. psychology U. Minn., Mpls., 1973-85; pres. Sch. Resource Ctr., Austin, Tex., 1985-90; tchr. Llano Pub. Schs., 1988-97; dir. Walter Resources, 1998—. Chmn. State Adv. Coun. for Inservice Tng. Regular Classroom Tchrs., 1977-79; cons. spl. ednl. various sch. dists., state depts. and agys. Editl. cons.: Jour. Ednl. Psychology, 1979, Reading Rsch. Quar., 1982; assoc. editor: Exceptional Children, 1979-84; assoc. editor Teaching Exceptional Children, 1985-89; contbr. articles to profl. jours., papers to profl. confs. Named Minn. Spl. Educator of Yr., 1978; recipient Svc. award Internat. Coun. Exceptional Children, 1978; HEW Office of Human Devel. Svcs. grantee, 1976-80; Dept. Edn. contractee, 1980-83 Mem. Coun. for Exceptional Children, Nat. Assn. Children with Learning Disabilities (dir. Minn. chpt. 1978-80), Nat. Assn. Retarded Citizens, AAUP, Assn. Supervision and Curriculum Devel. Home and Office: 7108 Running Rope Austin TX 78731-2128

**WALTER, W. EDWARD,** hotel executive, corporate financial executive; Ptnr. Trammell Crow Residential Co.; pres. Bailey Capital Corp.; from sr. v.p. acquisitions to exec. v.p., CFO Host Marriott Corp., Bethesda, Md., 1996—2003, exec. v.p., 2003—, CFO, 2003—. Office: Host Marriott Corp 6903 Rockledge Drive Ste 1500 Bethesda MD 20817

**WALTER, WILLIAM G.,** consumer products company executive; V.p., gen. mgr. Specialty Chemicals Group FMC Corp., 1997—2000, exec. v.p., 2000—01, chmn., pres. CEO, 2001—. Dir. Internat. Paper Co., 2005—. Mem. The Business Roundtable; mem. exec. comm. The Philadelphia Chamber of Commerce. Office: c/o FMC 1735 Market St Philadelphia PA 19103

**WALTERMIRE, THOMAS ALLEN,** finance company executive; b. Balt., Oct. 30, 1949; s. William Everett and Emma (Barack) W.; m. Shirley Jean Flinn, June 16, 1972; children: Todd Andrew Barack Waltermire, Kevin Adam Davis Waltermire, Heidi Alexis Nicole Waltermire. BS, Ohio State U., 1971; MBA, Harvard U., 1974. Mgr. corp. fin. B.F. Goodrich Co., Akron, Ohio, 1975-76; asst. treas., 1977-78; asst. contr., 1978-80; dir. planning, analysis chem. group B.F. Goodrich Co., Cleve, 1980, dir. purchasing div., 1981-84, v.p. comml. svcs., 1984, pres. elastomers and latex div. Cleve., 1985-89, v.p. investor rels., 1989—93; CFO Geon Co., Cleve., 1993—97, COO, 1997—99, CEO, 1999—2000, PolyOne Corp. (Geon and M.A. Hanna merger), Cleve., 2000—05. Vice chmn., bd. dirs. NorTech; mem. Ohio Third Frontier Adv. Bd.; chmn. Ohio Polymer Strategy Coun. Bd. dirs., exec. com. Ohio Bus. Roundtable; bd. dirs. Greater Cleve. Partnership, Vols. Unlimited, Cleve. Orchestra, Ohio State U. Assn., 2003, Nat. Inventors Hall of Fame; chmn. Ohio State U. Assn., 1999—2001; mem. Ohio State U. Alumni Adv. Coun. Republican. Methodist.

**WALTERS, ARTHUR SCOTT,** neurologist, educator, clinical research scientist; b. Balt., Feb. 20, 1943; s. Charles Henry and Jean Vivian (Scott) W.; m. Bokyun Kim, May 18, 1985 (div. Oct. 1992); m. Lesley J. Gill, Dec. 19, 1992. BA, Kalamazoo Coll., 1965; MS, Northwestern U., 1967; MD, Wayne State U., 1972. Diplomate Am. Bd. Psychiatry and Neurology; diplomate Am. Bd. Sleep Medicine. Intern Oakwood Hosp., Dearborn, Mich., 1972-73; resident in neurology SUNY Downstate Med. Ctr., Bklyn., 1976-79; movement disorder fellow Neurol. Inst., NYC, 1982-84; asst. prof. neurology Robert Wood Johnson Med. Sch., U. Medicine & Dentistry NJ, New Brunswick, 1984-91, assoc. prof. neurology, 1991-99, clin. prof. neurology, 1999—; asst. chief divsn. neurology Lyons VA Med. Ctr., NJ, 1985-89, neurology cons., 1994-99; prof. neurosci. Seton Hall U. Sch. Grad. Med. Edn., South Orange, NJ, 1999—; NJ Neurosci. Inst., Edison, 1999—. Nat. chmn. med. adv. bd. Restless Legs Syndrome Found., 1992-98; organizer Internat. Restless Legs Study Group, 1992—; head Restless Legs Syndrome and Periodic Limb Movement Coun. for the Nat. Sleep Found., 1994-96;

neurology cons. Coney Island Hosp., Bklyn., Bklyn. Jewish Hosp., 1980-81; presenter in field. Contbr. articles to profl. publs., chpts. to books; organizer symposia. Named Rschr. of Yr. in medicine Seton Hall U. Sch. Grad. Med. Edn., 2003-04, Michael S. Aldrich hon. lectr. in sleep medicine for outstanding contbns. to patient care, rsch. and edn. U. Mich., 2006; grantee UMDNJ, 1984-86, VA RAG, 1985-86, Sandoz Corp., 1985-88, VA Merit Rev., 1989-98, Clemente Found., 1994-95, Purdue Pharma, 2000—, NIH, 2002. Fellow Am. Acad. Neurology, Am. Acad. Sleep Medicine; mem. AAAS, Am. Neurol. Assn., Sleep Rsch. Soc., Movement Disorder Soc., NJ Acad. Scis., NJ Sleep Soc. (sec. 1995-96, treas. 1996-97, v.p. 1998-99). Office: NJ Neuro Sci Inst JFK Med Ctr 65 James St Edison NJ 08820-3947 Office Phone: 732-321-7000 ext. 68177. E-mail: artumdnj@aol.com.

**WALTERS, BARBARA JILL,** broadcast journalist; b. Boston, Mass., Sept. 25, 1931; d. Lou and Dena (Selett) Walters; m. Robert Katz, June 21, 1955 (div. 1958); m. Lee Gruber, 1963 (div. 1976); 1 adopted child, Jacqueline; m. Merv Adelson, 1986 (div. 1992). BA in English, Sarah Lawrence Coll., 1953, LHD (hon.), Ohio State U., Marymount Coll., 1975, Wheaton Coll., 1983, Temple U., Hofstra U., Ben-Gurion U. Former producer WNBC-TV; former writer CBS News; then with Stas. WPIX and CBS-TV; writer, reporter-at-large Today Show, 1961—63, regular panel mem., 1964—74, co-host, 1974—76; moderator syndicated program Not For Women Only, 1972—76; founder, pres. Barwall Productions, NYC, 1976—; newscaster ABC Evening News (now ABC World News Tonight), 1976—78; host The Barbara Walters Spls., 1976—; co-host ABC TV news show 20/20, 1984—99, anchor, 1999—2004; host The 10 Most Fascinating People, 1993—; co-exec. prodr., co-owner, co-host The View, ABC, NYC, 1997—; exec. prodr. The Iyanla Show, 2001. Contbr. NBC Radio Network. Contbr. ABC programs Issues and Answers; author: (book) How to Talk With Practically Anybody About Practically Anything, 1970; contbr. to Reader's Digest, Good Housekeeping, Family Weekly. Honorary chair Nat. Assn. Help for Mentally Retarded Children, 1970. Named Woman Yr. Comm., 1974, Broadcaster Yr., Internat. Radio and TV Soc., 1975, Woman Yr., Theta Sigma Phi; named one of Am.'s 75 Most Important Women, Ladies' Home Jour., 1970, 200 Leaders Future, Time Mag., 1974, 10 Women Decade, Ladies' Home Jour., 1979, Most Important Women, Roper Report, 1979, Women Most Admired Am. People, Gallup Poll, 1982, 1984, Am.'s 100 Most Important Women, Ladies' Home Jour., 1983, America's 100 Most Important Women of the Century, Good Housekeeping, 2000, Ladies' Home Journal, 2000; named to 100 Women of Accomplishment, Harper's Bazaar, 1967, 1971, Museum of Television and Radio, Los Angeles, 2004; recipient Award Yr., Nat. Assn. TV Program Execs., 1975, Daytime Emmy award, Nat. Acad. TV Arts and Scis., 1975, Emmy award, 1980, 1982, 1983, Daytime Emmy award for outstanding talk show, 2003, Mass Media award, Am. Jewish Com. Inst. Human Relations, 1975, Barbara Walters' Coll. Scholarship in Broadcast Journalism established in her honor, Ill. Broadcasters Assn., 1975, Matrix award, N.Y. Women in Comm., 1977, Hubert H. Humphrey Freedom prize, Anti Defamation League B'nai B'rith, 1978, Pres.'s award, Overseas Press Club, 1988, inducted Hall of Fame, Acad. TV Arts and Scis., 1990, Lowell Thomas award, Marist Coll., 1990, Lifetime Achievement award, Internat. Women's Media Found., 1991, saluted, Am. Mus. Moving Image, 1992, Lifetime Achievement award, Women's Project and Prodn., 1993, honored for contbn. to broadcast journalism, Mus. TV and Radio, 1996, George Foster Peabody award for her interview with actor Christopher Reeve, 1996, Muse award, NY Women in Film and TV, 1997, Lifetime Achievement award, Daytime Emmy Awards, 2000, Nat. Acad. TV Arts and Scis., 2000, Silver Satellite award, Am. Women Radio and TV, Sherry Landing Leadership award, The Hollywood Reporter, 2005. Achievements include first woman to co-anchor the Network News, 1976; interviewed every U.S. president and first lady since Nixon; conducted several historic interviews including the Nov. 1977 joint interview with Egyptian President Anwar Sadat and Israel's Prime Minister Menachem Begin; hour-long primetime interview with Cuba's President Fidel Castro, June 9, 1977 and a second interview 25 years later in 2002; conducted the first interview with Monica Lewinsky, which became the highest-rated news program, 48.5 million viewers, ever broadcast by a single network, 1999. Office: The View 320 W 66th St New York NY 10023-6304

**WALTERS, BILL,** retired state senator; b. Paris, Ark., Apr. 17, 1943; s. Peter Louis and Elizabeth Cecelia (Wilhelm) W.; m. Joyce Leslie Garrett Moore, Jan. 9, 1964 (div. 1970); children: Jamie, Sherry Ann; m. Shirley Ann Dixon, Aug. 20, 1971; 1 child, Sandra. BS, U. Ark., 1966, JD, 1971. Bar: Ark. 1971, U.S. Dist. Ct. Ark. 1971. Asst. prosecuting atty. 12th Jud. Dist. Ark., Ft. Smith, 1971-74; pvt. practice Greenwood, Ark., 1975—; mem. Ark. Senate, Little Rock, 1982-2000. Bd. dirs., sec.-treas. Mineral Owners Collective Assn. Ark., Greenwood; former v.p., bd. dirs Sebastian County Abstract & Title Ins. Co., Greenwood and Ft. Smith, Ark.; mem. Ark. Real Estate Commn., Ark. Abstract and Title Commn. Committeeman Rep. Ctrl. Com. Ark., Ft. Smith, 1980; search pilot CAP, Ft. Smith. Decorated Silver Medal of Valor; recipient Cert. of Honor Justice for Crime's Victims, 1983. Mem. Ark. Bar Assn., South Sebastian County Bar Assn. (pres. 1991-94), Profl. Landmen's Assn. Roman Catholic. Home: PO Box 280 Greenwood AR 72936-0280 Office: 1405 W Center Greenwood AR 72936-3200 Office Phone: 479-996-2122. Business E-Mail: waltlaw@waltlaw.net.

**WALTERS, CHRISTOPHER KENT,** lawyer; b. Bryn Mawr, Pa., Oct. 10, 1942; s. Lester K. and Margaret (Becker) W.; m. Teri R. Simon, Nov. 23, 1980. AB, Princeton U., 1964; JD, U. Mich., 1967. Bar: Pa. 1967, U.S. Supreme Ct. 1980. Ptnr. Reed Smith LLP, Phila., 1980—2005, sr. pro bono counsel, 2005—. Capt. U.S. Army, 1968-70, Vietnam. Office: Reed Smith LLP 2500 One Liberty Pl Philadelphia PA 19103 Office Phone: 215-851-8100. E-mail: cwalters@reedsmith.com.

**WALTERS, CHRISTOPHER MATCHETTE,** music director; b. Findlay, Ohio, Apr. 6, 1980; s. Joseph Matchette Walters, III and Patricia Ellen Kelley. MusB, Vanderbilt U., 2002, MEd, 2003; M in Sacred Music, Emory U., 2005. Cert. K-12 vocal/gen. music tchr. Tenn., 2003, Ga., Ill., 2005. Dir. music Conyers (Ga.) Presbyn. Ch., 2003—05; vocal music dir. Jacksonville High Sch., Turner Jr. High, Ill., 2005—. Music intern Belmont United Meth. Ch., Nashville, 2002—03. Composer, condr.: choral cantata debut recital The Lord is My Rock!. Mem.: Nat. Assn. for Tchrs. of Singing, Nat. Assn. for Music Edn., Chorus Am., Am. Guild Organists, Am. Choral Dirs. Assn., Pi Kappa Lambda, Phi Mu Alpha (music dir. 1999—2002), Pi Delta chpt.). Democrat. Avocations: composing, songwriting. Home: 1062 W College Jacksonville IL 62650 Office: 1211 North Diamond St Jacksonville IL 62650 Office Phone: 217-243-4384 1118. Business E-Mail: cwalters@jax117.morgan.k12.il.us.

**WALTERS, DANIEL RAYMOND,** political columnist; b. Hutchinson, Kans., Oct. 10, 1943; s. Howard Duke and Glenna Lucille (Hesse) W.; m. Doris K. Winter, June 16, 1995; children: Danielle, Staci. Mng. editor Hanford (Calif.) Sentinel, 1966-69, Herald News, Klamath Falls, Oreg., 1969-71, Times-Standard, Eureka, Calif., 1971-73; polit. writer and columnist Sacramento (Calif.) Union, 1973-84; polit. columnist, state editor Capitol Bur., Sacramento Bee, 1984—. Author: The New California: Facing the 21st Century, 1986; founding editor Calif. Polit. Almanac, 1989. Office: The Sacramento Bee 925 L St Ste 600 Sacramento CA 95814-3763

**WALTERS, DELORES MAXINE,** anthropologist; d. Hubert N. Walters and Constance M. Quinn. BS, CCNY, N.Y.C., 1966, BSN, Columbia U., N.Y.C., 1968; PhD, CUNY, N.Y.C., 1987. With Vis. Nurse Svc. NY & Hosp. Joint Diseases, 1972—76; rsch. assoc. Human Rels. AreaFiles, 1987—88; dir. African, Latin, Asian, Native Am. Cultural Ctr. Colgate U., 1997; cmty. advocate, 1997—2002; cmty. rsch. specialist Nat. Underground R.R. Freedom Ctr., Cin., 2002—06; asst. prof. No. Ky. U., 2002—. Vis. asst. prof. Colgate U., 1988—95, Syracuse U., NY, 1988—95, U. Pacific, 1988—95; cons. in field. Dir.: (video) Murshidat: Female Primary Health Care Workers Transforming Society in Yemen, 1999. Capt. USAF, 1970—72, Tachikawa, Japan. Fellow, Am. Inst. Yemeni Studies, 1994, 1996; grantee, Fulbright Found., 1983, 1996, Dutch Embassy, Yemen, 1996—99. Avocations: bicycling, photography, travel, gardening.

**WALTERS, GEORGE O.,** lawyer; b. Hazel Park, Mich., Nov. 11, 1930; s. George O. and Theodora (Tanis) Walters; m. Audrey Grace McEvoy, June 4, 1955; children: Mary Forness, Joseph, John, Kathryn Geiger. BA, U. Mich., 1952, JD, 1955. Bar: Mich. 1955, U.S. Dist. Ct. (we. dist.) Mich. 1957. Assoc. White & Block, Grand Rapids, Mich., 1957-62; lawyer sole practice Ludington, Mich., 1962-65; prosecuting atty. Mason County, Ludington, 1963-64; asst. city atty. City of Grand Rapids, 1965-67, dep. city atty., 1967-68, city atty., 1969-72; ptnr. White, Smitter & Walters, Grand Rapids, 1972—99; pvt. practice, 1999—. Commr. Grand Rapids Bldg. Authority, 1973—. Chmn. Rep. Organ. Mason County, 1964. With U.S. Army, 1956-57. Avocations: golf, swimming. Home: 502 Mulford Dr SE Grand Rapids MI 49507-3518 Office: 3737 Lake Eastbrook Blvd Grand Rapids MI 49546 Office Phone: 616-975-1899.

**WALTERS, GLEN ROBERT,** retired banker; b. Mpls., Sept. 11, 1943; s. Sterling Thomas and Mildred Eunice (Parkinson) W.; m. Gail Elvira Engelsen, June 11, 1966; children — Nicole Marie, Brent Aaron, Hillary Renee. BA, U. Minn., Mpls., 1965, postgrad., 1965-67; banking degree, Rutgers U., New Brunswick, NJ, 1982. Comml. banker 1st Nat. Bank, Mpls., 1967-83, sr. v.p. human resources, 1983-90; sr. v.p. Firstar Bank Minn., Mpls., 1990-2001, US Bank, Mpls., 2001—05. Served to sgt. USNG, 1967-73 Republican. Presbyterian.

**WALTERS, JEAN MARIE,** personal growth educator; b. St. Louis, Feb. 7, 1941; d. James Blaine Davenport and Helen Elizabeth (Vosbrink) Davenport; m. John E. Walters, Sept. 26, 1959 (div. Oct. 1975); m. Marvin Lucy, Aug. 13, 1988 (div. Jan. 2002); children: Steven John, Debra Jean, Jeffrey Scott, Cynthia Leigh D of Metaphys., Coll. of Metaphys., 1977; cert. reality therapist, Inst. Reality Therapy, 1982; DDiv, Ch. of Metaphys., 1977, Universal Life Ch., 1980. Personal growth cons., St. Louis, 1978—; tchr. personal growth Maryville U., St. Louis, 1988—, St. Louis C.C., 1992—. Host Positive Moments, McKenna-Walters Psychotherapy, Radio Sta. KXOK, 1985; founder, pres. PSI Bus. Cons., St. Louis, 1980-85, Mind Dynamics, St. Louis, 1980-83; founder, v.p. Found. for Transformation, pres. Spiritual Transformation Found., St. Louis, 1999—; lectr. in field. Author: (novels) Game of Life, Dreams & Symbology of Life, Look, Ma, I'm Flying, Choosing Health, Set Yourself Free, Evolution: The Master Plan; columnist: St. Louis Globe Dem., 1983—84, St. Louis Home Mag., 1985, St. Louis Fax Daily, 1999—2003; prodr.: Transformation Radio; columnist: Yes You Can, 1999—, host syndicated radio show: Positive Moments, 2000—01. Bd. dirs., regional dir. Sch. Metaphysics, Springfield, Mo. Mem.: Nat. Spkrs. Assn., Mo. Spkrs. Assn. Avocations: travel, writing, decorating, creative activities. Office Phone: 314-991-8439. E-mail: jean@spiritualtransformation.com.

**WALTERS, JEFFERSON BROOKS,** musician, retired real estate broker; b. Dayton, Ohio, Jan. 20, 1922; s. Jefferson Brooks and Mildred Frances (Smith) W.; m. Mary Elizabeth Espey, Apr. 6, 1963 (dec. July 22, 1983); children: Dinah Christine Basson, Jefferson Brooks; m. Carol Elaine Clayton Gillette, Feb. 19, 1984. Student, U. Dayton, 1947. Composer, cornetist, Dayton, 1934—; real estate broker, 1948-88; ret., 1988. Condr., composer choral, solo voice settings of psalms and poetry Alfred Lord Tennyson; composer Crossing the Bar (meml. performances U.S. Navy band), 1961; composer The Yorktown Grand March (Good Citizenship medal SAR, 1988). Founder Am. Psalm Choir, 1965; apptd. directed giving officer Kettering (Ohio) Med. Ctr., 1982—85. With USCGR, 1942—45, PTO, ETO. Mem.: SAR (life), Masons (32d degree). Brethren Ch. Home: 4113 Roman Dr Dayton OH 45415-2423

**WALTERS, JOHN P.,** federal official; b. 1952; m. Mary Walters; children: Michaela, Rebecca. BA, Mich. State U.; MA, U. Toronto. Acting asst. dir. and program officer div. edn. programs NEH, 1982—85; asst. to sec. U.S. Dept. Edn., 1985—88; chief of staff Office Nat. Drug Control Policy, Washington, 1989—91, dep. dir. supply reduction, 1991—93, dir., 2001—; pres. Philanthropy Roundtable, 1996—2001. Vis. fellow Hudson Inst., 1993; instr. polit. sci. Mich. State U., Boston Coll. Co-author (with William J. Bennett & John J. Di Iulio Jr.): Body Count: Moral Poverty and How to Win America's War Against Crime and Drugs, 1996. Pres. New Citizenship Program. Office: Office Nat Drug Control Policy 750 17th St NW Washington DC 20503*

**WALTERS, JOHNNIE MCKEIVER,** lawyer; b. Hartsville, SC, Dec. 20, 1919; s. Tommie Ellis and Lizzie Lee (Grantham) W.; m. Donna Lucile Hall, Sept. 1, 1947; children: Donna Dianne Walters Gent, Lizbeth Kathern Walters Kukorowski, Hilton Horace, John Roy. AB, Furman U., 1942, LLD, 1973; LLB, U. Mich., 1948. Bar: Mich. 1948, N.Y. 1955, S.C. 1961, D.C. 1973. Atty. office chief counsel IRS, Washington, 1949-53; asst. mgr. tax div. law dept. Texaco, Inc., N.Y.C., 1953-61; ptnr. firm Geer, Walters & Demo, Greenville, SC, 1961-69; asst. atty. gen. tax div. Dept. Justice, Washington, 1969-71; commr. IRS, 1971-73; ptnr. firm Hunton & Williams, Washington, 1973-79, Leatherwood Walker Todd & Mann, P.C., Greenville, 1979-95; exec. v.p., gen. counsel Colonial Trust Co., Greenville, 1996—2004. Bd. dirs. Textile Hall Corp., Greenville, Colonial Trust Co. Mem. S.C. Coun. on Competitiveness, 1987—91, S.C. Ethics Commn., 2005—. With USAF, 1942—45. Fellow Am. Coll. Tax Counsel (founding regent), Am. Coll. Trust and Estate Counsel, Am. Bar Found., S.C. Bar Found. (bd. dirs. 1988-92); mem. ABA (taxation sect.), S.C. Bar (chmn. taxation sect. 1983-84), Rotary (pres. local club 1968-69). Republican. Baptist. Home: 125 Hummingbird Ridge Greenville SC 29605-5305 E-mail: jwalters1804@charter.net.

**WALTERS, MARIAN R.,** research administrator; b. Washington, 1948; PhD, U. Houston, 1975. Prof. physiology Tulane U. Sch. Medicine, New Orleans, 1980—2004, dir. tuxcoe leadership core, 1999—2004, dir. of grad. studies in physiology, 1983—2004; assoc. dean rsch. and grad. studies Penn State U., Harrisburg, 2004—. Chair endocrinology and metabolism sect. Am. Physiol. Soc., 1995—98; coun. mem. Soc. for Exptl. Biology and Medicine, 2001—. Author: (book chapter) Encyclopedia of Hormones: Calcium Regulating Hormones. Office: Penn State Harrisburg 777 W Harrisburg Pike Middletown PA 17057

**WALTERS, MARJORIE ANNE,** interior designer, consultant; b. Flushing, N.Y., Dec. 5, 1925; d. Walter Bowne Williams, Florence Clara (Bach) Williams; m. Robert Leslie Walters, Sept. 17, 1949; children: Robert Bowne(dec.), Richard James. BS, Coll. William & Mary, 1947; AA, N.Y. Sch. Interior Design, 1958. Owner, pres. M.W. Walters, Interiors, Hohokus, NJ, 1958—86; pres. N.J. Ridgewood Art Inst., 1980—86; owner, pres. M.W. Walters, Interiors, Richfield Springs, NY, 1986—. Dir. Art & Program Commn., Richfield Springs, 1993—; chmn. Baker's Beach Art & Programs Commn., Richfield Springs; exec. dir. Cooperstown N.Y. Art Assn. 1986—90. Smithy-Pioneer Gallery, Cooperstown, N.Y., 2001—. Pres. Richfield Springs Hist. Assn., 1997—; v.p. Richfield Springs Libr. Bd., 1999—; sec. zoning bd. of appeals Town of Richfield Springs, 1999—; organizer of restoration and dedication of hist. town clock of 1918 Richfield Springs, NY, 2005. Recipient Cmty. Svc. award, Richfield C. of C., 1994, Good Citizenship award, DAR, 1994, Good Neighbor award, WBUG AM/FM, 1994, Ostego 2000 Historic Landmark award, Ostego County, 2006. Mem.: Nat. Mus. Women in Arts (charter mem.), Internat. Visual Artists (Eng.), Lake and Valley Garden Club (pres. 1998—2000). Avocations: landscape painting, flower arranging, swimming, skiing. Home and Office: 217 Walters Way Richfield Springs NY 13439 Office Phone: 315-858-0027. E-mail: mbwalt@aol.com.

**WALTERS, MARK DOUGLAS,** obstetrician, gynecologist; b. Toledo, July 21, 1954; s. Donald Walters; m. Virginia Walters; children: Samantha, Maxwell, Zoe. BS in biology, U. Cincinnati, 1976; MD, Ohio State U., 1980. Cert. Am. Bd. Ob-Gyn. Intern Tufts U. Sch. Medicine, Boston, 1980—81; resident in ob-gyn., 1981—84; asst. prof. dept. ob-gyn. U. Tex. Health Sci. Ctr., San Antonio, 1984—90; assoc. prof. dept. reproductive biology and ob-gyn. Case Western Reserve U. Sch. Medicine, Cleve., 1990—93; med. dir. Women's Health Ctr. U. Hospitals of Cleve., 1990—93; chief gynecology sect. VA Med. Ctr., Cleveland, 1992—93; vice-chmn. dept. ob-gyn., head

sect. gen. gynecology, dir. urogynecology The Cleve. Clinic Found., 1993—, dir. fellowship program in urogynecology/reconstructive pelvic surgery, 1997—. Author: (book) Clinical Urogynecology, 1993, Urogynecology and Reconstructive Pelvic Surgery, 3d edit., 2006. Recipient Am. Resident Tchg. award, MetroHealth Med. Ctr., 1996, 1999, 2000, 2002. Fellow: Am. Coll. of Obstetricians and Gynecologists; mem.: Cleve. Soc. of Ob-gyn., Soc. of Gynecologic Surgeons, Am. Urogynecology Soc., Jour. of Gynecologic Surgery (editl. bd.), Internat. Urogynecology Jour. (editl. bd.). Office: Cleve Clinic Found Dept Ob-gyn 9500 Euclid Ave Desk A81 Cleveland OH 44195 E-mail: walterm@ccf.org.

**WALTERS, MATTHEW PAUL,** recreational facility executive, consultant; b. Columbus, Ohio, Aug. 3, 1977; s. Thomas Edward and Kathy Ann Walters. BA, Ottawa U., 2002; MBA in concentration mktg., U. La Verne. Mktg., and pub. rels. Artist Direct, Encino, Calif., 1998—2000; owner Adventure Ventures, Tempe, Ariz., 1998—. Vol. plan creator Good Samaritan Hosp., Phoenix, 2001. Mem.: IndUS Entrepreneur. Republican. Roman Catholic. Avocations: running, basketball. Personal E-mail: matt.walters@ptk.org, avziee@hotmail.com.

**WALTERS, MILTON JAMES,** investment banker; b. Hornell, NY, May 21, 1942; s. James Henry and Frances Eleanor (Simmons) W.; m. Caroline Houck, May 24, 1963; children: Melissa Ann, Gregory Thomas, Timothy Allen. BA, Hamilton Coll., 1964. Trainee Mfrs. Hanover, 1964-65; with A.G. Becker Inc., N.Y.C., 1965-84; mng. dir. Smith Barney, N.Y.C., 1978—84, Prudential Securities, N.Y.C., 1997-99; pres. Tri-River Capital, 1988—. Bd. dirs. Decision One, Frederick's of Hollywood, Sun Healthcare Group. Trustee Hamilton Coll., Clinton, N.Y., 1983-88, Friends Acad., Locust Valley, N.Y., 1981-91 Mem. Nat. Assn. Corp. Dirs., Nat. Assn. Cert. Valuation Analysis, Econ. Club N.Y. Republican. Presbyterian. Office: Tri-River Capital PO Box 128 New York NY 10150-0128 Office Phone: 212-581-5777. Business E-Mail: mjw@tririv.com.

**WALTERS, ROBERT ANCIL,** physicist, mathematician; b. Russell Springs, Ky., Mar. 12, 1915; s. Robert Edmund Lee and Talitha Margaret (Wilson) W.; m. Etha Jane McKinley, Feb. 2, 1943; 1 child, Robert Ancil II; m. Sandra Faye Roy, June 29, 1969; 1 child, Forrest Wayne. BS, Western Ky. U., 1941; postgrad., George Washington U., 1943-45, Agrl. Grad. Sch., 1947-48, Am. U., 1951-52. H.S. asst. prin. Russell County Bd. Edn., 1941-42; physicist, head exterior ballistics U.S. Naval Weapons Lab., Dahlgren, Va., 1942-59; pres. Walters Ins. and Investment Counselor, Dahlgren, 1948-80; engr., head systems planning U.S. Naval Space Surveillance, Dahlgren, Va., 1959-69; R&D specialist, physicist interdisplinary math. cons. U.S. Naval Warfare Lab., Dahlgren, 1969-75. Pres. Navel Weapons Lab. Fed. Credit Union, Dahlgren, 1968-74; bd. examiners Potomac River Naval Com., Washington, 1953-56; biology lab. instr. Western Ky. U., Bowling Green, 1935-36. Chmn. Old Dominion Eye Bank, Richmond, Va., 1975-76; co-chair Dem. Party, Ky., 1937-42; pres. Nat. Fedn. Fed. Employees, Washington, 1963-69. Recipient Nat. Quality award Nat. Assn. Life Underwriters, 1976; named Ky. Col., gov. of Ky., 1976, Outstanding Citizen of Yr., VFW, 1981, Guest of Honor King George County Fall Festival, 1994. Mem.: Lions Internat. (dep. dist. gov. 1976—77, Disting. Svc. award 1975, Melvin Jones fellow 2001, cert. for disting. leadership and svc. 2005). Baptist.

**WALTERS, ROBERT C.,** lawyer; b. Gene Autry, Okla., Mar. 28, 1958; BA, U. Tex., 1980, JD, 1983. Bar: Tex. 1983, U.S. Supreme Ct., U.S. Ct. Appeals, Fifth and Ninth Cir., U.S. Dist. Ct., No., So., and Ea. Dist. Tex. Adminstrv. ptnr. Vinson & Elkins LLP, Dallas. Office: Vinson & Elkins LLP 3700 Trammell Crow Ctr 2001 Ross Ave Dallas TX 75201-2975 Office Phone: 214-220-7704. E-mail: rwalters@velaw.com.

**WALTERS, RONALD OGDEN,** mortgage banker; b. Holcombe, Wis., July 13, 1939; s. Ogden Eugene and Josephine Ann (Hennekens) W.; m. Margaret Ellen Weisheipl, July 14, 1962; children — Laurie, Cheryl, Michael, Patrick Student, U. Wis., 1959-62. Mgr. Thorp Fin., LaCrosse, Wis., 1962-65, regional mgr. Milw., 1965-69, ITT Consumer Fin. Corp., Milw., 1969-74, sr. v.p. Brookfield, Wis., 1974-90, exec. v.p. adminstrn., 1990-92; CEO Ideal Fin. Corp., Brookfield, 1993—, USA Funding Corp., Brookfield, Wis., 1993—. Mem. Wis. Fin. Services Assn. (pres. 1980) Republican. Roman Catholic. Avocations: boating, fishing, hunting. Home: 812 Back Bay Delafield WI 53018-1528 also: 17035 W Wisconsin Ave Brookfield WI 53005-5734 Office Phone: 262-938-9259. Business E-Mail: rwalters@usafundingcorp.com.

**WALTERS, ROSS A.,** federal judge; BA in History, Pa. State U., 1971; JD with high distinction, U. Iowa, 1977. Law clk. to Judge William C. Hanson US Dist. Ct. (So. Dist. Iowa), 1977—79; assoc. Herrick and Langdon, Des Moines, 1979—82, ptnr., 1982—90; judge Iowa Dist. Ct. (Jud. Dist. 5-C), 1990—94; magistrate judge US Dist. Ct. (So. Dist.) Iowa, 1994—, chief magistrate judge, 1998—2005. Chief magistrate judge US Dist. Ct. (So. Dist.) Iowa, 1998—2005. Bd. editors, contemporary studies project leader Iowa Law Rev. Legal officer, adminstrv. div. officer US Navy Reserve, 1971—74, aboard USS Oklahoma City. Office: US Courthouse Rm 440 123 E Walnut St Des Moines IA 50309-2035

**WALTERS, SCOTT TIMOTHY,** psychologist, educator; b. Junction City, Kans., Apr. 12, 1971; s. James and Candace Walters; m. Kelli Beth Donoho, Sept. 29, 2002. BA, Biola U., 1993; PhD, U. N.Mex., 2002. Asst. prof. psychology U. Tex. Southwestern Med. Ctr., 2003, asst. prof. behavioral sciences, 2002—. Author: (textbook) Anytown Economics, 2002, Talking with College Students About Alcohol: Motivational Strategies to Reduce Abuse, 2005; editor: Treating Substance Abuse: Theory and Technique, 2003. Named Outstanding Tchg. Assoc., U. N.Mex, 1999, Outstanding Grad. Rschr., Sigma Xi, 2000; recipient New Investigator award, Intl Conf. for Treatment of Addictive Behaviors, 2000, Disting. Student in Psychology award, Nat. Inst. Alcohol Abuse and Alcoholism, 1993; fellow Nat. Rsch. Svc. award, 1997—2001; Regents Endowed fellow, U. N.Mex, 1999. Mem.: APA (David Pilon tng. scholar 2001), Rsch. Soc. on Alcoholism, Motivational Interviewing Network of Trainers, Psi Chi. Achievements include research in effective drug and alcohol interventions for college students and young adults; design of Website development, e.g., www.e-toke.com and www.e-chug.com. Office: U Tex Sch Pub Health 5323 Harry Hines V8112 Dallas TX 75390-9128 Office Phone: 214-648-1519. Office Fax: 214-648-1081. E-mail: scott.walters@utsouthwestern.edu.

**WALTERS, SHERWOOD GEORGE,** management consultant, educator; b. Detroit, May 9, 1926; s. George Henry and Helen (Parker) Walters; m. Alexandra Sielcken, Sept. 4, 1952; children: Margaret Taylor Clifford, Karen Chapin, George Alexander II, Virginia Sherwood McFee. *Father, Lt. Commander USNR. Grandparents: George A. Walters, lawyer, newsman, public servant, inventor of stop and go traffic light system, driver's license law, Negligent Homicide Act, Sheriff, Deputy Police Commissioner, Councilman, Detroit. Served Public Safety Committee for Presidents Coolidge and Hoover, editorial/features writer, Detroit Free Press, News and Journal, Vice Council General Hankow, China. Ethelwyn Taylor Walters, first woman to serve US Federal District Court. Vice-President, Detroit Federated Woman's Club, President, Salvation Army, member, DAR. Grandchildren: George A. Walters, III, junior, Georgia Tech; Cassandra Jo Walters, sophomore, Abraham Baldwin College, University of Georgia. Uncle, Herbert Richards Noxon, creator official US portrait of Uncle Sam, hung in Smithsonian Institution. Sister, Virginia Walters Rider, New Canaan Ct. VP: Women's Clug, Historical and Political Science.* BA in Econs. and History cum laude, Western Md. Coll., 1949; MS in Internat. Trade, History, Columbia U., 1950, MBA with distinction, 1953; PhD in Govt. with distinction, NYU, 1960, cert. specialist in Latin Am. affairs, 1960. From instr. to assoc. prof. econs. sociology mktg. Coll. Bus. Econs., Lehigh U., Bethlehem, Pa., 1950—60; pres., dir. S.G. Walters Assocs., 1952—; exec. v.p., dir. ctrs., retail planning mgr., devel. projects mgr. Mobil Oil, NYC, 1960-65; mgr. comml. mktg. Chem. Plastics divsn., exec. officer mktg. dir. Gen. Tire & Rubber Internat. Plastics Co., Akron, Ohio, 1965-70; prof. Rutgers U. Bus. Sch., Newark, 1970—93, prof.

emeritus mgmt. studies, 1993—; founding dir. interfunctional mgmt. program Rutgers U., Newark, 1970-88; founding dir. PhD mgmt. program, chmn. orgn. ops. mgmt. dept. Rutgers U. Grad Sch. Bus. Adminstrn., Newark. Former rsch. instr. US Small Bus. Devel. Coun.; former co-dir. E.I. DuPont de Nemours Interdisciplinary Rsch. Team; dir. various internat. programs in mgmt., banking and sci. Internat. Labor Orgn., UN Indsl. Devel. Orgn., US Dept. State, NSF, Romania, Puerto Rico, Sweden, Northern Ireland, France, 1971—2004, UN Devel. Orgn., U.S. State Dept., NSF, 1971—2004; founder Nat. Sci. Found. Industry, 1987—2004; spkr., moderator, advisor in field. Author (with Cmte. on Retailing, et al.): Principles of Retailing, 1955, Principles of Marketing, 1961; author: (with M.D. Snider, M.L. Sweet) Readings in Marketing, 1962; co-author (with Morris L. Sweet and Max D. Snider): (seminal books) Marketing Management Viewpoints Commentary and Readings, 2d edit., 1970; co-author: (with Morris L. Sweet) Mandatory Housing Finance Programs, A Comparative International Analysis, 1975; co-author: (with Denis O. Gray) Managing the Industry University Cooperative Research Centers: A Guide for Directors and Other Stakeholders, 1998; prodr., dir., participant (cmty. sponsored radio program) Breakfast with the Walters, WEST/NBC, Easton, Pa., 1953—57; contbr. over 188 articles, govt. rsch. reports in field. Adviser Nat. Rep. Congl. Com. on Tax Reform, 2001; mem. govs. commn. energy task force NJ, 1975—76; mem. Jud. Com. Energy Safety Stds., 1975—76, Com. Liquified Natural Gas, 1975—76; chmn. Subcom. Forecasting Demand and Supply Liquified Gas, 1975, 1976; mem. NJ R&D Coun., 1984—93; chmn. U/Indsl. Partnerships, John Von Neumann Ctr., Princeton U., 1986; hon. chmn. bus. adv. coun. Nat. Rep. Congl. Com., 2003—04; elder, trustee, co-dir. Christian Edn. Com. Topsail Presbyn. Ch., Hampstead, NC. From pvt. to 1st lt. Inf., Quartermaster Corps U.S. Army, 1944—47, North Atlantic, Murmansk, PTO. Recipient Founders Day award, NYU, 1960, Prof. of Yr., Rutgers Grad. Sch. Bus., 1976, Christian R. and Mary F. Lindback Excellence in Tchg. award, Rutgers U., 1983, Rep. Presdl. Legion of Merit medal, 1994, Excellence award, NSF, 2004, Bd. Trustees Alumni award, McDaniel Coll. (formerly Western Md. Coll.), 2003, 2004, Bd. Trustess Alumni award, 2005, Businessman of Yr. Winner from NC award, Bus. Adv. Coun., Nat. Rep. Congl. Com., DC, 2005, Dr. S. George Walters Cons. Excellence award named in his honor, Rutgers Bus. School, 1991—; DuPont fellow, 1951, Spl. Studies scholar, Ford Found., Harvard U. Bus. Sch., Cambridge, Mass., 1956. Fellow: Acad. Polit. Sci.; mem.: SAR, S.R., Newcomen Soc., Beta Gamma Sigma (sec., treas., pres. Lehigh chpt. 1953—60, sec., treas., pres. Rutgers chpt. 1970—88). Avocation: deep sea fishing. Home: 110 Topsail Watch Ln Hampstead NC 28443-2728 Office Phone: 910-329-0663. Office Fax: 910-329-0824. Personal E-mail: s.george.walters@worldnet.att.net.

**WALTERS, STEVEN ANTHONY**, small business owner, consultant; b. Laurel, Miss., Aug. 4, 1961; s. Cleborne Boone and Maxine Nix Walters. BEd, U. So. Miss., Hattisburg, 1980—83. Lic. master barber cosmetology State La., 1989. Owner, stylist Hairitage Salon & DaySpa, Houma, La., 1990—. Image cons. A Crowning Touch, Houma 1983—2005; pageant cons. Min. music Little Caillou Bapt. Ch., Chauvin, La., 2003—05. Recipient Mr. United Am. award, United Am. Pageant Sys., 2005, Mr. Plus Am. Amb., 2005, Mr. Global amb., 2005, America's Mr. US, 2006. Home: 707 Central Ave Houma LA 70364 Office: Hairitage Salon & Day Spa 707 Central Ave Houma LA 70364 Personal E-mail: sawalters79@bellsouth.net.

**WALTERS, SUE FOX**, broadcast executive, accountant; b. Louisville, June 9, 1941; d. Thomas Burke and Reva Crick Fox; m. Hugh Alexander Walters (dec. 2001); children: Thomas Wade Walters, Alexandra Walters Ebling. Student, N.C. State U., Ky. Wesleyan Coll. Acct., paralegal for fin. instns. and firms; ct. adminstr. 45th Jud. Cir. Ct., Ky.; v.p., treas. Alexander and Assocs., CATV cons. firm, Greenville, Ky.; corp. adminstr., pub. corp. Bellevue, Wash.; sr. acctg. specialist Japanese/Am. Automotive Mfg. Co., Bowling Green, Ky.; land developer. Pres., Jr. Woman's Club Greenville, 1964-65, Woman's Club of Greenville, 1976-78; vice gov. 2d dist. Ky. Fedn. Women's Clubs, 1980. Avocations: historical preservation, design, antiques, dogs, flying. Home: 151 N Main St Greenville KY 42345-1503 Office Phone: 270-338-4237.

**WALTERS, WILLIAM BEN**, chemistry professor; b. Highland, Kans., Apr. 26, 1938; s. Ben Guthrie and Dolly Varden (Shaw) W.; m. Barbara Lulu Sternaman, Aug. 5, 1962; children: Katharine, David. AS, Highland Coll., 1957; BS, Kans. State U., 1960; PhD, U. Ill., 1964. Asst. prof. MIT, Cambridge, 1965-70; assoc. prof. chemistry U. Md., College Park, 1970-77, prof., 1977—, assoc. chmn. dept., 1982-86. Vis. prof. U. Louvain, Belgium, 1978; chair U. Senate, 1999-00; mem. physics adv. com. Grand Accelerateur Nat. d lons Lourds, 2003-2006. Recipient Nuclear Chemistry award Am. Chemical Soc., 2001; Guggenheim fellow Oxford U., 1986-87, Von Humboldt fellow Univ. Mainz, 2001-02, 06. Mem. Am. Phys. Soc., European Phys. Soc., Am. Chem. Soc. (chmn. div. nuclear chemistry 1986), Rotary (bd. dirs. College Park 1990-91, 2000—). Office: U Md Dept Chemistry College Park MD 20742-0001 Office Phone: 301-405-1801. E-mail: wwalters@umd.edu.

**WALTHER, ADRIAAN**, retired physics professor; s. George F. J. A. Walther and Gerrigje A. Van Donk; m. Trudy C. Huygen, May 14, 1960; children: Peter J., Ellen G. Sousa. Ph.D, Tech. U. Delft, Netherlands, 1959. Chief scientist Diffraction Ltd., Inc., Bedford, Mass., 1960—72; prof. physics WPI, Worcester, Mass., 1972—2001; ret., 2001.

**WALTHER, DALE JAY**, lawyer; b. Elko, Nev., Oct. 15, 1948; s. Harold V. and Beryl H. W.; m. Kazue Mori, Sept. 25, 1975; children— Kent, Brian, Nolan, Lisa, Curtis, Katie. B.A., Northwestern U., 1972; postgrad., Notre Dame U. summer law program, Japan, 1974; J.D., Calif. Western Sch. Law, 1975 Bar Alaska 1975 Assoc. Law Offices Murphy Clark, Anchorage, 1975-80; ptnr. Clark, Walther & Flanigan, Anchorage, 1980-93; ptnr. Walther & Flanigan, Anchorage, 1993—. Mem. Anchorage Bar Assn., Alaska Bar Assn., ABA, Order of Barristers, Am. Arbitration Assn., Phi Alpha Delta. Lodge: Elks. Home: PO Box 100428 Anchorage AK 99510-0428 Office: Walther & Flanigan 1029 W 3rd Ave Ste 250 Anchorage AK 99501 Office Phone: 907-279-9999.

**WALTHIE, THEO H.**, chemicals executive; Grad. summa cum laude in Chem. Engring., Tech U. Delft, Netherlands. Mem. spl. assignments prog. Dow Europe, 1970—72, prodn. engr. chlorinated solvents plant Terneuzen, Netherlands, 1972—74, various purchasing positions Rotterdam, Netherlands, 1974—78; bus. mgr. Dow Chem. Iberica, 1978—82; mgr. hydrocarbon feedstock supplies Dow Europe, Horgen, Switzerland, 1982—86, bus. v.p. hydrocarbons, 1986—89, v.p. polyurethanes, 1989—91, mgr. thermosets bus. grp., 1991—92, mgr. automotive grp., 1992—95, global v.p. hydrocarbons and energy, 1995—2000; bus. grp. pres. hydrocarbons and energy Dow Chem. Co., 2000—, mem. Office of the Chief Exec., 2006—. Mem.: Assn. Petro-Chem. Producers Europe (pres. 1998, mem. steering com. 1997, pres. 1998), Internat. Isocyanate Inst. (pres.), European Isocyanate Producers Assn. (v.p.). Office: Dow Chem Co 47 Bldg Midland MI 48067

**WALTNER, BEVERLY RULAND**, artist; b. Kansas City, Mo.; d. Harry George and Ruth Anna (Laitner) Waltner, Jr. Student Columbia U., 1950-51, Yale U., 1951-53; B.A., U. Miami, Fla., 1955; M.F.A., No. Ill. U., 1968; postgrad. Kent State U., summer 1968. Tchr. art pub. schls. N.Y., Fla., Mo., Ill., 1960-65; instr. art Barry Coll., Miami Shores, Fla., 1969-70; artist-designer, Coral Gables, Fla., 1972—; One-woman shows: Art Gallery, No. Ill. U., DeKalb, 1968, Lyons Meml. Library, Point Lookout, Mo., 1968, Jewish Community Ctr. Gallery, Kansas City, Mo., 1969; juried exhbns. include: New Horizons in Painting, North Shore Art League, 1966, 68, Chautauqua Exhbn. Am. Art, 1968-73, 78, 10th Midwestern Biennial, Joslyn Mus., 1968, Mid-Am. I, Nelson Gallery and St. Louis Mus., 1968, Nat. Soc. Painters in Casein and Acrylic, 1969, 70, 72, 73, Ark. Nat., Ark. State U., 1970, 35th Ann. Mid-Yr. Show, Butler Inst. Am. Art, 1970, Am. Exhbn. Am. Painting, Soc. Four Arts, 1971, 74, IV and V Ann. Pan. Am. Exhbns., 1972, 73; represented in permanent collections: No. Ill. U., Arlen Realty Mgmt., Inc., Alexander Muss and Sons, Equitable Life Assurance Soc. of A., Gen. Devel.

Corp., Zuckerman-Vernon Corp., also numerous pvt. collections. Recipient 1st place award Ann. Chautauqua Exhbn. of Am. Art, 1968, Louis E. Selden award, 1972; top award New Horizons in Painting Show, 1966, honorable mention, 1968. Mem. Artists Equity Assn., Cultural Execs. Council Profl. Artists Guild (treas. 1977-78, v.p. 1978-79, editorial staff newsletter 1977—79), Chautauqua Art Assn., Coral Gables C. of C. (cultural affairs com. 1979). E-mail: bob98@bellsouth.net.

**WALTON, ALAN GEORGE**, venture capitalist; b. Birmingham, Eng., Apr. 3, 1936; s. Thomas George and Hilda (Glover) W.; m. Jasmin Yvonne Christensen, Sept. 1, 1958 (dec. Nov. 1970); children: Kimm A., Keir D.A.; m. Elenor Jean McElliott, Aug. 6, 1977; children: Kristin M., Sherri L. PhD, U. Nottingham, Eng., 1960, DSc, 1973; LLD (hon.), U. Nottingham, Eng., 2005. Rsch. assoc. Ind. U., Bloomington, 1960-62; asst. prof. chemistry Case Western Res. U., Cleve., 1962-66, assoc. prof., 1966-69, assoc. prof. macromolecular sci., 1969-71, prof., 1971-81, dir. lab. for biol. macromolecules, 1972-81; pres., CEO Univ. Genetics Co., 1981-86, chmn., 1986-87; sr. ptnr. Oxford Biosci Ptnrs., Westport, Conn., 1987—; chmn. Oxford Biosci. Corp., 1992—. Vis. lectr. biol. chemistry Harvard Med. Sch., 1971; mem. Pres. Carter's Task Force on Sci. and Tech.; U.S. project officer Rudjer Boskovic Inst., Zagreb, Yugoslavia, 1967—75; bd. dirs. Acadia Pharma, Alexandria R.E.I.T. Applied Cell Tech.; chmn. Avalon Therapeutics; co-founder The Inst. for Genomic Rsch., 1994; co-founder, past bd. mem. Human Genome Scis., Inc.; emeritus dir. Research!America. Author: Formation and Properties of Precipitates, 1967, Biopolymers, 1973, Structure and Properties of Amorphous Polymers, 1980, Polypeptide and Protein Structure, 1981, Recombinant DNA, 1981, Yearbook of Genetic Engineering and Biotechnology, 1983, 85, 88, (biography) Beneath This Gruff Exterior There Beats a Heart of Plastic, 2000, How to Make Money Investing in Biotechnology, 2005. Bd. dirs. Friends of Nottingham U. Recipient Israel State medal, 1972, Case Inst. Centennial Scholar medal, 1981. Mem. Nat. Venture Capital Assn., Sigma Xi (Research award 1973), Pi Kappa Alpha. Home: 11 Beachside Common Westport CT 06880 Office: Oxford Biosci Corp 315 Post Rd W Westport CT 06880-4739 Business E-mail: awalton@oxbio.com.

**WALTON, ALICE LOUISE**, bank executive; b. Newport, Ark., Oct. 7, 1949; d. Sam and Helen (Robson) Walton BBA, Trinity U., 1971; D. of Bus. Adminstrn. (hon.), S.W. Bapt. U., 1988. Investment analyst First Commerce Corp., New Orleans, 1972-75; dir., v.p. investments Walton Enterprises, Bentonville, Ark., 1975—; retail & investment broker E.F. Hutton Co., New Orleans, 1975-79; vice chair, investment dir. Walton Bank Group, Bentonville, Ark., 1982-88; founder, former pres., chair, CEO Llama Co./Llama Asset Mgmt. Co., Fayetteville, Ark. Mem. dean's adv. coun. U. Ark. Coll. Bus. Adminstrn., Fayetteville, 1989-90. Bd. trustees Amon Carter Mus., Ft. Worth, Tex. Named Disting. Bus. Lectr. Ctr. State U., Edmond, Okla., 1989, Arkansan of Yr., Ark. Easter Seals Soc., 1990; named one of Top 100 Women in Ark., Ark. Bus., 1995, Top 200 Collectors, ARTnews mag., 2006, Forbes Richest Americans, 2006. Mem.: Northwest Ark. Coun. (first chairperson 1990). Achievements include #13 on Forbes' World's Richest People List, 2005.*

**WALTON, ANDRE**, psychologist, consultant; s. Christiane Harvey; m. Robin Walton. BA, Open U., England; PhD, U. Nev., Reno, Nev., 2005. CEO CT Audio Group of Cos.; exec. dir. Found. Relevant Edn. About the Law, Las Vegas, Nev. Exec. dir. Project R.E.A.L., Las Vegas, 2005—06. Office Phone: 702-388-7527. Personal E-mail: walton_andre@hotmail.com.

**WALTON, ANTHONY JOHN (TONY WALTON)**, set designer, illustrator, writer; b. Walton on Thames, Eng., Oct. 24, 1934; s. Lancelot Henry Frederick and Hilda Betty (Drew) W.; m. Julie Andrews, May 10, 1959 (div. 1968); 1 child, Emma Kate; m. Genevieve LeRoy, Sept. 12, 1991; 1 stepchild, Bridget. Student, Oxford Sch. Tech. Art and Commerce, 1949-52, Slade Sch. Fine Art, London, 1954-55. Designer settings, costumes for theater prodns., London, off-Broadway, 1957-60, Broadway, 1961—; Broadway prodns. include Pippin, 1972 (Tony award 1972-73, Drama Desk award 1972-73), Shelter, 1973 (Drama Desk award 1972-73), Chicago, 1975, Sophisticated Ladies, 1981, The Real Thing, 1984, Hurlyburly, 1984, I'm Not Rappaport, 1985, House of Blue Leaves, 1986 (Tony award 1985-86), Drama Desk award 1985-86), Front Page, 1986, Social Security, 1986 (Drama Desk award 1985-86), Anything Goes, 1987, Grand Hotel, 1989, Six Degrees of Separation, 1990, The Will Rogers Follies, 1991, Death and the Maiden, 1992, Conversations with My Father, 1992, Four Baboons Adoring the Sun, 1992, Guys and Dolls, 1992 (Tony award 1991-92, Drama Desk award 1991-92), Tommy Tune Tonight, 1992, She Loves Me, 1993, A Grand Night for Singing, 1993, Laughter on the 23rd Floor, 1993, Picnic, 1994, A Christmas Carol, N.Y.C., 1994, Company, 1995, Moonlight, 1995, A Fair Country, 1996, A Funny Thing Happened on the Way to the Forum, 1996, The Shawl, 1996, Make Someone Happy, Bay St. Theater Festival, 1997, Not Waving, 1997, Steel Pier, 1997, King David, 1997, 1776, 1997; The Cripple of Inishmaan, 1998; Noel & Gertie, 1998; House, 1998; Ashes to Ashes, 1999; Annie Get Your Gun, 1999; On Raftery's Hill, 2000 (Dublin and London); If Love Were All, 1999; Taller Than a Dwarf, 2000, Uncle Vanya, 2000, The Man Who Came To Dinner, 2000, Our Town, 2002, Blithe Spirit, 2002, I'm Not Rappaport, 2002, Nobody don't Like Yogi, 2003, The Boy Friend, 2003, Princesses, 2004, Well, 2006; dir., designer The Importance of Being Earnest, 1996, Major Barbara, 1997, Where's Charley?, 2004, After the Ball, 2004; dir. Noel Coward in Two Keys Bay St. Theater Festival, 1996; dir. Missing Footage, 1999; dir., co-writer, costume designer Oops! The Big Apple Circus Stage Show, 1999; ballets, principally San Francisco Ballet Co., Am. Ballet Theatre, Peter and the Wolf, Dance Theatre of Harlem "St. Louis Woman", 2003, Lincoln Ctr., N.Y.C.; films include Mary Poppins, A Funny Thing Happened on the Way to the Forum, Murder on the Orient Express, The Wiz, All That Jazz (Acad. award with Philip Rosenberg 1980), Prince of the City, Star 80, The Glass Menagerie, 1987, Regarding Henry, 1991, Our Town, 2003; operas in London, 1963-68, Spoleto, Italy, 1965, Santa Fe, 1975, San Francisco, 1992, Chgo., 1993; author: Adelie Penguin in Wonders, 1981; illustrator (books) Wonders, 1981, The Importance of Being Earnest, 1973, Lady Windemere's Fan, 1973, Popcorn, 1972, God Is a Good friend, 1969, Witches Holiday, 1971, Dumpy the Dump Truck, 2000, The Great American Musical, 2006, and 11 more books in the continuing series. Served with RAF, 1952-54. Recipient Emmy award Death of a Salesman, 1986; named to Theatre Hall of Fame, 1991; elected to Interior Design Hall of Fame, 1993. Mem.: Acad. Motion Picture Arts and Scis., Costume Designers Guild Calif. United Scenic Artists. Office: care Martino ICM 40 W 57th St New York NY 10019-4001

**WALTON, CAROLE LORRAINE**, clinical social worker; b. Harrison, Ark., Oct. 20, 1949; d. Leo Woodrow Walton and Arlette Alegra (Cohen) Armstrong. BA, Lambuth Coll., Jackson, Tenn., 1971; MA, U. Chgo., 1974. lic. clin. social worker. Social worker Community Mental Health, Flint, Mich., 1971-72, clin. social worker Westchester, Ill., 1974-76; dir. self-travel program Chgo. Assn. Retarded Citizens, 1972. council family svcs. Inner Harbors Psych. Hosp., Douglasville, Ga., 1976-83; sr. mental health clinician Northside Mental Health Ctr., Atlanta, 1983—; pvt. practice clin. social work Atlanta, 1997—2001. Mem.: NASW, Ga. Soc. for Clin. Work (pres. 1981—82, 1993—95, ethics co-chair 2003—05). Avocation: tennis. Office: Northside Mental Health Ctr 1140 Hammond Dr Ste J-1075 Atlanta GA 30328-7145 Office Phone: 770-842-3761.

**WALTON, CHARLES MICHAEL**, civil engineering educator; b. Hickory, N.C., July 28, 1941; s. Charles O. and Virginia Ruth (Hart) W.; m. Betty Grey Hughes; children: Susan, Camila, Michael, Gantt. BS, Va. Mil. Inst., 1963; MCE, N.C. State U., 1969, PhD, 1971. Research asst. N.C. State U., Raleigh, 1967-71; transp. planning engr. N.C. Hwy. Commn., Raleigh, 1970-71; asst. prof. civil engring. U. Tex., Austin, 1971-76, assoc. prof., 1976-83, prof., 1983—, Bess Harris Jones Centennial prof. natural resource policy studies, 1987-91, Ernest H. Cockrell Centennial chair engring., 1991-93, Ernest H. Cockrell Centennial chair engring., 1993—, chmn. dept. civil engring., 1988-96. Transp. cons., 1970—; assoc. dir. Ctr. for Transp. Rsch. U. Tex., 1980-88; chmn., exec. com. Transp. Rsch. Bd., NRC, 1991,

Disting. Lectr., 1994. Contbr. articles to profl. jours. Past chmn. Urban Transp. Commn., Austin. Recipient Disting. Engring. award N.C. State U., 1995, Joe J. King Profl. Engring. Achievement award U. Tex. at Austin, 1995-96, W.N. Carey Jr. Disting. Svc. award Transp. Rsch. Bd., 1998, George S. Bartlett award AASHTO, Transp. Rsch. Bd., ARTBA, 2000, Disting. Contbns. to Univ. Transp. Edn. and Rsch. award Coun. Univ. Transp. Ctrs., 2005; named to Am.'s Top 100 Pvt. Sector Transp. Design and Constrn. Profls. of 20th Century, 2004, Am. Rd. and Transp. Builders Assn. 2005. Fellow ASCE (Harland Bartholomew urban planning award 1987, Frank M. Masters transp. engring. award 1987, James Laurie prize 1992, Francis C. Turner lectr. 1999, Outstanding Projects and Leaders award, 2005), Inst. Transp. Engrs.; mem. NSPE, NAE, Intelligent Transp. Soc. Am. (tech. coord. coun., past chair bd. dirs., past chair tech. coord. coun.), Am. Rd. and Transp. Assn. (western v.p., past pres. edn. divsn., 1st vice chair; named to Am.'s Top 100 Pvt. Sector Transp. Design and Constrn. Profls. of 20th Century), Am. Rd. and Transp. Builders Assn. (sr. vice chmn.), Soc. Automotive Engrs., Urban Land Inst., Inst. for Ops. Rsch. and Mgmt. Scis., Soc. Am. Mil. Engrs., Internat. Rd. Fedn. (bd. dirs.), Internat. Rd. Ednl. Found. (bd. dirs.), Austin C. of C. (Leadership Austin program). Democrat. Methodist. Home: 3404 River Rd Austin TX 78703-1031 Office: U Tex Dept Civil Engring Dept Civil Engring ECJ Hall Ste 6 3 Austin TX 78712 Office Phone: 512-471-1414. Business E-Mail: cmwalton@mail.utexas.edu.

**WALTON, CHRISTY R.**, philanthropist; b. Feb. 1949; m. John Thomas Walton (dec. June 27, 2005); 1 child, Lukas. Mem. bi-nat. advisory bd. San Diego Natural History Mus., former mem. bd. trustees; co-founder Harborside Sch., San Diego, 1996. Named one of Forbes Richest Americans, 2005—06.*

**WALTON, CONRAD GORDON, SR.**, retired architect; b. Houston, June 18, 1928; s. John Edward and Evelyn Lucile (Gordon) W.; m. Rilda Ellen Akin, Dec. 10, 1954; children: Conrad Gordon Jr., Evelyn Coleman, Roberta Agnes. BS (Walsh scholar), Rice U., 1951; postgrad., U. Houston, 1955. Registered architect, Tex., NCARB, ret. Past pres. DCW Architects, Inc. Mem.: AIA (emeritus). Home: 9014 Springview Ln Houston TX 77080-1755

**WALTON, CONSTANCE WILLIAMS**, music educator; b. Pasadena, Calif., June 30, 1919; d. Milo Beyer and Helen Woodbridge Williams; m. Donald Rech Walton, June 14, 1941; children: David Woodbridge, Robert Williams. BM Piano and Composition, Phila. Conservatory of Music, 1939; tchrs. cert., U. of the Arts Julliard Composers Workshop, 1960—61. Tchr. of piano and composition, 1941—. Performer Ensemble Group of Schubert Club, Fairfield County, Conn., 1990—; dir. Musica Planti, Greenwich, Conn., 1995—. Composer: (Flute Solo) Qumran, Preludes and Postludes for Organ; composer: (Five songs for treble voices based on Mother Goose Rhymes), Sonata II for violin and piano. Chmn. prayer chain First Congregational Ch., Greenwich, Conn., 2001—; supt. Sunday Sch. Diamond Hill Meth. Ch., Conn., 1958—60, pres. women's soc. Recipient 1st prize for composition religious music, First Congl. Ch. 300th Ann. celebration competition, 1966, Citation from Conn. Gov. for Career, 1996. Mem.: Nat. League of Am. Pen Women (pres. Pioneer br. 1992—93), Schubert Club of Fairfield, Conn. (chmn., chmn. performers workshop 1995—96). Avocations: reading, bible study, swimming, walking. Home: 36 Old Wagon Rd Old Greenwich CT 06870

**WALTON, DAN GIBSON**, lawyer; b. Houston, Mar. 26, 1950; s. Dan Edward and Lucy Frances (Gibson) W.; m. Martha Sandlin, June 24, 1972; children: Cole Gibson, Emily Wyatt. BA with honors, U. Va., 1972; JD with honors, U. Tex., 1975. Bar: Tex. 1975, U.S. Dist. Ct. (so. dist.) Tex. 1977, U.S. Ct. Appeals (D.C. cir.) 1975, U.S. Ct. Appeals (5th cir.) 1981, U.S. Supreme Ct. 2001; bd. cert. in civil trial law. Law clk. to hon. Malcolm R. Wilkey D.C. Ct. Appeals (D.C. cir.), 1975-76; assoc. Vinson & Elkins LLP, Houston, 1976-82, ptnr., 1982—, co-head Litig. Sect. Bd. dirs. The Meth. Hosp., Houston; pres.-elect State Bar Tex., 2006—. Bd. dirs. Tex. Equal Access to Justice Found., 2000-06, State Bar of Tex., 1999-2002, South Tex. Coll. Law, Houston, 1994—, Briarwood Sch./Brookwood Cmty., Houston, 1991—, Alley Theatre, 2003—; trustee St. John's Sch., Houston, 1997-2005, Good Samaritan Found., 1998—, Cullen Trust for Health Care, 2002—; chancellor Tex. Ann. Conf., United Meth. Ch., 1996—; admission commn. U.S. Dist. Cts. for So. Dist. Tex.; chair U.S. Magistrate Judge Merit Selection Com. Fellow Am. Bar Found., Tex. Bar Found., Houston Bar Found. (chair 1994), Houston Bar Assn. (pres. 1998-99), Garland Walker Am. Inn of Ct. (master), Am. Bd. Trial Advocates (assoc.), Internat. Soc. Barristers, Internat. Assn. Def. Counsel, Tex. Assn. Def. Counsel. Avocations: golf, skiing. Office: Vinson & Elkins LLP 2300 First City Tower 1001 Fannin St Ste 3201 Houston TX 77002-6706 Office Phone: 713-758-2026.

**WALTON, DEWITT TALMAGE, JR.**, dentist; b. Macon, Ga., May 25, 1937; s. DeWitt T. Sr. and Jimmie (Braswell) W.; m. Joan Robinson, June 11, 1960; children: Jimmie Walton Paschall, Gwen N., Gayle Walton Smith, Joy A. BS, Howard U., 1960, DDS, 1961. Pvt. practice, Macon, 1963—. Chmn. dental adv. com. Ga. Dept. Med. Assistance; dental svcs. adv. com. Dept. Physical Health, Ga. Dept. Human Resources; adv. bd. dirs. Wachovia Bank, Macon-Warner Robins area; bd. dirs. The Ga. Dept. Cmty. Affairs Fin. chmn. Boy Scouts Am., Piedmont/Creek Dist., 1978-80, exec. bd., 1978-82, v.p. exec. com., 1983-84; apptd. Bibb County Bd. Edn., 1969-73; vice chmn. Macon-Bibb County Transit Authority, 1981-87; bd. dir. exec. com. Devel. Corp. Mid. Ga., 1984-91; sec.-treas. Urban Devel. Authority, Macon-Bibb County, 1984-87; trustee Macon Heritage Found., 1983-87; bd. dirs. Ctrl. Ga. Speech and Hearing Ctr., 1984-87, Boys' Club Macon, Inc., 1986, 87, 88, The Grand Opera House, 1988, 89, 90, Booker T. Washington Ctr., 1993, Pub. Edn. Found., 1995—, Douglass Theater, 1995—; mem. oversight com. Minority Bus. Assistance Program, 1984, 911 native Bibb County Commn. on Excellence in Edn., 1984; trustee United Way Macon-Bibb County, 1985, 86, 87; deacon, elder, treas. Washington Ave. Presbyn. Ch.; active Downtown Coun., Coalition for Polit. Awareness, So. Poverty Law Ctr., NAACP; mem. "Cmty. Hero"-torchbearer Olympic Torch Relay for 1996 Olympic games, Atlanta; advisory bd. Wachovia Bank, Macon, Warner-Robins, 1999—; apptd. bd. dirs. Ga. Dept. Cmty. Affairs, 1999—, Cmty. Found. Ctrl. Ga., 2001—. With U.S. Army, 1961-63. Recipient Cert. of Appreciation State Bar of Ga., Citizenship award Bibb County Voter's Registration League, Inc., 1977, Cmty. Svc. award NAACP, 1982, Cmty. Svc. award Alpha Kappa Alpha Sorority, 1982, Meritorious Svc. award United Negro Coll. Fund, 1983, Comml. Bldg. of Yr. award Macon Heritage Found., 1983, Faithful Svc. award Bibb County Dept. Family and Children's Svcs., 1983-90, Lifetime Achievement award for cmty. svc., Boys' and Girls' Clubs, 2002, Citation Macon-Bibb County Beautification Clean Cmty. Comm., 1983-84, Cert. appreciation Macon-Bibb County Econ. Opportunity Coun., 1984, Outstanding Svc. award So. Poverty Law Ctr., 1984, Proclamation Mayor George Israel Svc. on Macon-Bibb County Transit Authority, 1984, Outstanding Alumni award Coll. Dentistry Howard U., 1985, award for Outstanding Svc. Macon-Bibb County Urban Devel. Authority, 1987, award for Outstanding Svc. Macon-Bibb County Transit Authority, 1987, cert. Appreciation Close-Up Found., 1988, cert. Appreciation Ga. Dental Edn. Found., 1988, Cmty. Svc. award United Way Macon-Bibb County, 1988, cert. Disting. Svc. Devel. Corp. Middle Ga., 1990, Continuous Corp. Support award Entrepreneurship and Black Youth Program U. Ga., 1990, cert. Recognition Outstanding Svc. So. Poverty Law Ctr., 1990, cert. Appreciation Keep Macon-Bibb Beautiful Commn. and Cherry Blossom Festival, 1990, James E. Carter award Ga. Dental Soc., 1993; named Olympic Torchbearer, 1996. Fellow Acad. Gen. Dentistry (Membership award 1983-85), Acad. Dentistry Internat., Am. Coll. Dentists, Ga. Dental Assn. (hon.), Internat. Coll. Dentists, Pierre Fauchard Acad.; mem. AAAS, ADA (alt. del. Ga. 1989-91, life mem.), Am. Analgesic Soc., Am. Endodontic Soc., Am. Fund Dental Health, Am. Sch. Health Assn., Am. Soc. Dentistry for Children, Nat. Dental Assn. (life), Nat. Rehab. Assn., Ga. Dental Soc. (pres., 1978, Citizenhip award 1979-80, Humanitarian award 1981-82, James E. Carter Jr. award 1993), North Ga. Dental Soc. (pres. 1978-79), Cen. Dist. Dental Soc. (peer rev. com., legis. com., alt. del. to Ga. Dental Assn. 1982, 83, 84, del. 1984, 85, 86, 87), Bibb County Dental Soc. (charter), Acad. Continuing Edn., Fed. Dentaire Internat. (life), Pres'. Club

Howard U. (life), Am. Running and Fitness Assn. (life), Greater Macon C. of C. (bd. dirs. 1995-97), Macon Tracks, Sigma Pi Phi, Omega Psi Phi (life). Presbyterian. Avocations: walking, jogging, aerobics, coin collecting/numismatics, real estate. Home: 2988 Malibu Dr Macon GA 31211-2609

**WALTON, G. CLIFFORD,** physician; b. Richmond, Va., Jan. 5, 1968; s. Eugene Marion and Mary Ann (McNabb) W.; m. Tami Marie Daniel, June 26, 1998. BS summa cum laude, Hampden-Sydney Coll., 1990; MD, Med. Coll. Va., 1994. Intern Med. Coll. Va., Richmond, 1994-95; resident Blackstone (Va.) Family Practice, 1995-97; pvt. practice, Kenbridge, Va., 1997-99, Richmond, 1996—. Med. examiner Va. Dept. Health, Powhatan, 1996—; mem. housestaff coun. Med. Coll. Va., 1995-97. Sci. fair judge Southside Va. H.S., Farmville, 1988-97. Mem. AMA, Am. Acad. Family Physicians, Med. Soc. Va., Phi Beta Kappa, Sigma Xi, Omicron Delta Kappa. Avocations: baseball card collecting, gardening, photography. Home: 1640 Jeter Rd Powhatan VA 23139-6907 Office: Patient First 12101 South Chalkley Rd Chester VA 23831 Office Phone: 804-796-3636.

**WALTON, GERALD WAYNE,** retired university official; b. Union, Miss., Sept. 11, 1934; s. Willie Jay and Ruby Elizabeth (Williamson) W.; m. Juliet Katherine Hart, Aug. 26, 1960; children: Katherine Hart, Dorothy Elizabeth, Margaret Stevens. AA, East Central Jr. Coll., 1954; BS, U. So. Miss., 1956; MA, U. Miss., 1959, PhD, 1967. Tchr. asst. U. Miss., 1956-59, instr. English, 1959-62, asst. prof., 1962-67, assoc. prof., 1967-70, prof., 1970-99, assoc. dean Coll. Liberal Arts, 1970-76, dean, 1976-82, assoc. vice chancellor for acad. affairs, 1982-94, interim vice chancellor for acad. affairs, 1994-96, provost, 1996-99. Contbr. articles to profl. jours. Vice-pres. Oxford Human Rels. Coun., 1968; mem. adminstrv. bd. Oxford U. Meth. Ch., chmn. bd. trustees, 1971-72, lay leader, 1999-2001; bd. dirs. Yoknapatawpha Arts Coun., 1980-81; sec.-treas. So. Lit. Festival, 1965; sec. U. Miss. Friends of Libr.; v.p. U. Miss. Friends Mus. bd. trustees Miss heritage Trust. Tri-Univ. fellow in linguistics U. Nebr., 1969-70. Mem. MLA, Am. Dialect Soc., Miss. Folklore Soc., Friends of Arts in Miss., Miss. Assn. English Tchrs. (sec. 1968), Miss. Inst. Arts and Letters (sec. 1979-80), Nat. Coun. Tchrs. English, William Faulkner Soc., Miss. Hist. Soc., Oxford-Lafayette County Heritage Soc., So. Studies Adv. Coun., Rotary (sec.), Golden Key, Phi Kappa Phi, Sigma Tau Delta, Omicron Delta Kappa. Home: 106 Ole Miss Dr Oxford MS 38655-2615 E-mail: gww@olemiss.edu.

**WALTON, HELEN,** philanthropist; m. Sam M. Walton (dec. 1992, founder of Wal-Mart) BA, U. Okla. Co-owner Arvest Bank; founder (with Sam M. Walton) Walton Family Found., 1987; contbr. Walton Family Arts Center. Mem. bd. trustees Univ. Osarks, 1975—. Known for philanthropic contributions, specifically to Arkansas and education. Named one of World's Richest People, Forbes, 2001—04, Forbes Richest Americans, 2006. Office: Walton Family Found PO Box 2030 Bentonville AR 72712

**WALTON, JAMES MELLON,** investment company executive; b. Pitts., Dec. 18, 1930; m. Ellen Carroll; 4 children. BA, Yale U.; MBA, Harvard U. With Gulf Oil Corp., Phila., Houston, Pitts., Tokyo, Rome, 1958-67; pres. Carnegie Inst., Pitts., 1968-84, Carnegie Mus. Natural History and Mus. of Art, Pitts., 1968-84, Carnegie Library, Pitts., 1968-84; life trustee, pres. emeritus Carnegie Inst. and Carnegie Library, Pitts., 1984—. Vice chmn. bd. dirs. MMC Group Inc.; bd. dirs. New Ireland Fund, Inc. Mem. sponsoring com. Penn's Southwest Assn.; trustee emeritus Carnegie-Mellon U.; treas. Carnegie Hero Fund Commn.; dir. World Affairs Coun. of Pitts., One Hundred Friends of Pitts. Art; trustee Sarah Scaife Found. Inc., Extra Mile Found.; chmn. Vira I. Heinz Endowment; mem. Cultural Dist. Devel. Com. Lt. U.S. Army, 1954-56. Office: 525 William Penn Way Ste 3902 Pittsburgh PA 15219-1710 E-mail: jmwa@earthlink.net.

**WALTON, JIM,** news network executive; BA in Radio, TV and Film, U. Md., 1981. Video journalist CNN, Atlanta, 1981-83; tape editor CNN Sports, Atlanta, 1983-85, exec. prodr., 1985-97; pres. CNN/SI, Atlanta, 1997—2000, CNN Networks/USA, Atlanta, 2000; pres. & COO CNN News Group, Atlanta, chmn. & CEO, 2003—. Olympic prodr. 1984 L.A. Games, remote prodr., sr. prodr. Office: CNN 1 CNN Ctr NW Atlanta GA 30303-2762

**WALTON, JIM CARR,** bank executive; s. Sam Moore and Helen Walton; m. Lynne Walton; 4 children. Grad., U. Ark. Pres., chmn., CEO Arvest Bank, Bentonville, Ark. At-large exec. com. mem. Ark. Coun. Econ. Edn.; mem. nat. bd. advisors Children's Scholarship Fund; mem. dean's exec. adv. bd. Sam M. Walton Coll. Bus. Named one of World's Richest People, Forbes, 2001—, Forbes Richest Americans, 2006. Office: 125 W Central Ste 218 Bentonville AR 72712*

**WALTON, JON DAVID,** lawyer; b. Clairton, Pa., Sept. 18, 1942; s. Thomas Edward and Matilda Lucy (Sunday) W.; m. Carol Jeanne Rowland, Sept. 15, 1964; children: David Edward, Diane Elizabeth. BS, Purdue U., 1964; JD, Valparaiso U., 1969. Bar: Pa. 1969. Atty. U.S. Steel Corp. (now USX Corp.), Pitts., 1969-73; asst. gen. counsel Harbison-Walker Refractories, Pitts., 1973-75, gen. counsel, 1975-81, v.p., gen. counsel, 1981-83; regional gen. counsel Dresser Industries, Inc., Pitts., 1983-86; gen. counsel, sec. Allegheny Ludlum Corp., Pitts., 1986-90, v.p., gen. counsel, sec., 1990-96, Allegheny Techs. Inc., Pitts., sr. v.p., gen. counsel, sec., sr. v.p., chief legal and admin. officer, 2001—03; exec. v.p. human resources, chief legal and compliance officer, gen. counsel, corp. sec., 2003—. Trustee Westminster Coll., 1997—; pres., bd. dirs. Music for Mt. Lebanon, 1996-2002, Pitts. Youth Golf Found., 1991-2001, United Way of Allegheny County, 2002-, NAM, 2002-, Pitts. Symphony Orchestra, 2003-; clk. of session Southminster Presbyn. Ch., 1998-2001, 04-. Mem. ABA, Pa. Bar Assn., Allegheny County Bar Assn., Am. Soc. Corp. Secs. (former pres. regional group), Am. Corp. Counsel Assn., Am. Arbitration Assn. (panel arbitrators), Duquesne Club, Valley Brook Country Club, Rolling Rock Club. Home: 137 Hoodridge Dr Pittsburgh PA 15228-1803 Office: Allegheny Technologies Inc 1000 Six PPG Pl Pittsburgh PA 15222-5479 Office Phone: 412-394-2836. Business E-Mail: jwalton@alleghenytechnologies.com.

**WALTON, LARS TIMOTHY,** director, consultant; b. Southfield, Mich., Jan. 29, 1981; s. James Stephen and Dorcas Ann Walton. BA in Polit. Sci., U. Calif., Berkeley, 2002. Clk. Ho. Rep. Policy Com., Washington, 2003—04; policy asst. Congressman Christopher Cox, Washington, 2004—05, polit. dir., 2005; asst. dir., fed. rels. U. Calif., Irvine, 2005—. Campaign mgr. Cox for Congress, Newport Beach, Calif., 2005; exec. dir. Congl. Leadership Fund, Newport Beach, Calif., 2005. Intern White Ho., Washington, 2002—03. Mem.: Chi Psi. Republican. Office: Univ Calif 120 J Administration Irvine CA 92697-3175 Office Phone: 949-824-8686. Office Fax: 949-824-2095.

**WALTON, MADALYN CAROL,** music educator; b. Alexandria, La., Nov. 5, 1949; d. Willie James Walters and Dona Maxine Self; m. Thomas L. Walton, June 14, 1969; children: Suanne Marie, Alicia René. B in Sacred Music, Gulf-Coast Bible Coll., Houston, 1972; MEd, U. So. Miss./McNabb., 1988. Cert. Nat. Bd. Cert. Tchr., 2003. Choral tchr. Rolla (Mo.) HS, 1983—84, St James (Mo.) HS, 1984—88; elem. music tchr. Davenport (Fla.) Elem., 1988—90, Hillcrest Elem., Lake Wales, Fla., 1990—. Contbr. editor (book) Polk County Curriculum Guide Grades K-5, 1999. Min. of music First United Meth. Ch., 1998—2001. Mem.: Fla. Music Edn. Assn., Music Educators Nat. Conf. Republican. Mem. Ch. Of God. Avocations: scrapbooks, church music, travel, theater. Home: 736 Hunt Dr Lake Wales FL 33853 Office: Hillcrest Elem 1051 State Rd 60E Lake Wales FL 33853 Office Phone: 863-678-4055. E-mail: madalyn_walton@allvantage.com.

**WALTON, MORGAN LAUCK, III,** lawyer; b. Woodstock, Va., July 30, 1932; s. Morgan Lauck Jr. and Frances (Allen) W.; m. Jeannette Freeman Minor, Mar. 4, 1961; children: Morgan Lauck IV, Charles Lancelot Minor, Christopher Allen, Laura Cathlyn Hirschfeld. BA, Randolph-Macon Coll., 1953; LLB, U. Va., 1959. Bar: Va. 1959, N.Y. 1959, U.S. Ct. Appeals (2d cir.) 1959, U.S. Dist. Ct. (ea. and so. dists.) N.Y. 1960, U.S. Dist. Ct. (we. dist.) Va.

1988. Assoc. Donovan Leisure Newton & Irvine, N.Y.C., 1959-68, ptnr., 1968-84; counsel FDIC, Washington, 1989-90, asst. gen. counsel, 1990-97; dir. Advice Co., Sausalito, Calif., 2005—; ret. Contbr. articles to profl. jours. Trustee Randolph-Macon Acad., Front Royal, Va., 1987-92, trustee emeritus, 2002—; trustee Unitarian Ch. Shenandoah Valley, Shenandoah Valley Music Festival, Woodstock, 1986-87; chmn. bd. All Souls Ch., NYC, 1974-76; active Shenandoah County Dem. Com., 1999—; assoc.dir. Lord Fairfax Soil and Water Dist., 2004-05, dir., 2005-06. With US Army, 1953-56. Mem. Univ. Club (N.Y.C.), Collectors Club, Order of Coif, Phi Beta Kappa. Democrat. Home and Office: 908 Kern Springs Rd Woodstock VA 22664-3216 Personal E-mail: jwalton@shentel.net.

**WALTON, ORTIZ MONTAIGNE,** musician, sociologist; b. Chgo. m. Kara Dozier. Student, Hartt Sch. Music, 1951-54, Mannes Sch. Music, 1954-55; BS in Psychology, Roosevelt U., 1966; MA in Sociology, U. Calif., Berkeley, 1970, PhD in Sociology, 1973. Musician Hartford, New Haven, Springfield, Bridgeport Symphony Orchs., 1951-54, Buffalo Philharm. Orch., 1954-57, Boston Symphony Orch., 1957-63; program coord. Chgo. Assn. Retarded Children, 1964-66; musician Cairo (Egypt) Symphony, 1963-64. Prin. investigator Soc. Survey of Alcohol and Drug Use among Adolescents and Young Adults Nat. Inst. Alcohol Abuse and Alcoholism, 1977-79; asst. dir. Chgo. Fedn. Settlement Houses, 1964-66; instr. Dept. African-Am. Studies U. Calif. Berkeley, 1974-76; faculty Wright Inst. of Berkeley Grad. Sch., 1974-75; mem. bd. of studies in sociology U. Calif. Santa Cruz, 1975; career and guidance counseling Opportunities Industrialization, Oakland, Calif., 1967-68; cons. alcohol, drugs and youth criminal justics Merritt Coll., Oakland, 1979, curriculum devel., 1973; program devel., talent recruitment Today's Artists, Berkeley, 1979. Solo recitals (contrabass) include U. Buffalo, 1956, Merkin Concert Hall, N.Y.C., 1987, Weil Recital Hall at Carnegie Hall, N.Y.C., 1987, Bklyn. Acad. Music, 1988, YMCA Harlem Branch, 1988, Rutgers U., New Brunswick, N.J., 1989. Lehman Coll., N.Y.C., 1989, Cheyney, U. Pa., 1990, Chgo. State U., 1993; composer: Fantasy to Duke Ellington for solo contrabass, 1968, Scale Method for contrabass, 1981, Resonance for contrabass and piano, 1983, Sonata for contrabass and piano, 1985; recordings: (with Ishmael Reed) Black Box, Nat. Philharmonic Orchestra London, The Walton Statement for Contrabass and Orch. (by Arthur Cunningham), 1987, Art of the Bass Viol: Music of the Baroque Era, 1991; author: Music: Black, White and Blue, 1972, Toward a Non-Racial Society, 1997, others. Active mayoral campaign Harold Washington, Chgo., 1983. U. Calif. Berkeley Grad. fellow, 1968-72; Nat. Inst. Mental Health fellow, 1968-72; Ford Found. dissertation grant 1970-71; Inst. Community and Race Relations grant U. Calif. Berkeley, 1970-71. Mem. Am. Sociol. Assn., Internat. Soc. Bassists, Chamber Music Am. Home: 1129 Bancroft Way Berkeley CA 94702-1849 Office Phone: 510-649-0504.

**WALTON, REGGIE BARNETT,** judge; b. Feb. 8, 1949; m. Debra Walton; 1 child, Danon. BA, W.Va. State Coll., 1971; JD, Am. U., 1974. Staff atty. Defender Assn. Phila., 1974-76; asst. U.S. atty. Office of U.S. Atty., Washington, 1976-80, chief career criminal unit, 1979-80; assoc. judge Superior Ct. D.C., 1981—89, 1991—2001; exec. asst. U.S. atty. Office of U.S. Atty., Washington, 1980-81; dep. presiding judge criminal divsn. Superior Ct. D.C., 1986-89; assoc. dir. Office Nat. Drug Control Policy, Exec. Office of Pres., Washington, 1989-91; sr. White House advisor for crime, 1991; U.S. dist. judge U.S. Dist. Ct. for D.C., Wasington, 2001—. Mem. U.S. Dept. Justice and ABA Ctrl. and East European Law Initiative Reform Project, Irkutsk, Russia, 1996; instr. SEAK, Inc., 1993, 97, Criminal Practice Inst., Washington, 1996, 97, Ctrl. and East European Law Inst., ABA, 1996, Harvard U., 1994—; mem. faculty Nat. Jud. Coll., Reno, Nev., 1999—; George Washington U. Law Ctr., 1992—; instr. Nat. Inst. Trial Advocacy, Georgetown U. Law Sch., Washington, 1983—, U.S. Dept. Justice, 1993, ABA Traffic Ct. Sem., Washington, 1984, 87; presiding guest lectr. Lincoln U., Jefferson City, Mo., 1991, Albany (Ga.) State Coll., 1991; lectr. U.S. Atty.'s Office, Washington, 1979-81, D.C. Bar Assn., 1980, Graterford (Pa.) State Prison, 1974-76; mem. jud. coun. Cir. Ct. D.C., 2004—; chmn. commn. Nat. Prison Rape Reduction, 2004— Contbr. articles to profl. jours. Active Big Brothers; mem. task force on interscholastic programs D.C. Pub. Schs., 1987; hon. mem. Capital Ballet Guild, Inc., 1989; mem. D.C. Cares, Inc., 1990; mem. Nat. Ctr. for Missing and Exploited Children, bd dirs., 1990-91; bd. dirs. Robert A. Shuker Scholarship Fund., Inc., 1993— Hillcrest Children's Ctr., 1994-96; co-chmn. pub. safety com. D.C. Agenda Project, Fed. City Coun., 1995—. Recipient Dean's award Washington Coll. Law, 1989, Disting. Svc. award Young Lawyers sect. Bar Assn. D.C., 1989, H. Carl Moultrie award D.C. br. NAACP, 1989, Sec.'s award Dept. Vets. Affairs, 1990, James R. Waddy Meritorious Svc. award W.Va. State Coll. Nat. Alumni Assn., 1990, County Spotlight award Nat. Assn. Counties, 1990, William H. Hastie award Jud. coun. Nat. Bar Assn., 1993, Honorable Robert A. Shuker Meml. award Nat. U.S. Attys. Assn., 1997, Friendship award Best Friends Found., 1998, Disting. Alumni award Am. U., 1999, Angel award Bridging the Gap Tri-County Inc., Mt. Sinai Bapt. Ch., 2000, North Star award Washington Coll. of Law, Am. U., 2000, among others. Mem. ABA (lawyer competency com. 1984-87, del. nat. conf. state trial judges 1986), D.C. Bar Assn. (criminal instrns. com. 1984-86), Washington Bar Assn., Nat. Inst. Trial Advocacy Advocates Assn., Am. Inns of Ct. Republican. Office: US Dist Ct for DC 333 Constitution Ave NW Washington DC 20001-2131 E-mail: waltonrb@dcsc.gov.

**WALTON, ROB (SAMUEL ROBSON WALTON),** discount department store chain executive; b. Tulsa, 1944; s. Sam Moore and Helen Walton; m. Carolyn Walton (div.); 3 children. Student, Coll. of Wooster; BA in Acctg., U. of Arkansas, 1966; JD, Columbia U., 1969. Formerly with Conner, Winters, Ballaine, Barry & McGowen; with Wal-Mart Stores Inc., Bentonville, Ark., 1969—, sr. v.p., 1978-82, also bd. dirs., vice chmn. bd., 1982-92, chmn., 1992—. Trustee Wooster Coll. Named one of World's Richest People, Forbes Mag., 2005, Forbes Richest Americans, 2006. Avocations: bicycling, pheasant hunting. Office: Wal-Mart Stores Inc 702 SW 8th St Bentonville AR 72716-6299*

**WALTON, ROBERT LEE, JR.,** plastic surgeon; b. Lawrence, Kans., May 30, 1946; s. Robert L. and Thelma B. (Morgan) W.; m. Elisabeth K. Beahm, Oct. 7, 2000; children: Marc, Morgan, Lindsey. BA, U. Kans., 1968; MD, U. Kans., Kansas City, 1972. Diplomate Am. Bd. Surgery, Am. Bd. Plastic Surgery. Resident in surgery Johns Hopkins Hosp., Balt., 1972-74, Yale-New Haven (Conn.) Hosp., 1974-78; chief of plastic surgery San Francisco Gen. Hosp., 1979-83; prof. and chmn. dept. plastic surgery U. Mass. Med. Ctr., Worcester, 1983-94; prof., chmn dept. plastic surgery U. Chgo., 1994—2004, prof. dept. plastic surgery, 2004—. Contbr. articles to profl. jours. Founder Projecto Mira Found. for Handicapped Children, Santurce, P.R., 1990. Mem. ACS, Am. Assn. Plastic Surgeons, Am. Soc. Plastic and Reconstructive Surgery, Am. Soc. Reconstructive Microsurgery, Alpha Omega Alpha. Office: Ste 400 2913 N Commonwealth Ave Chicago IL 60657 Office Phone: 773-702-4111, 773-702-4111. Personal E-mail: notlaw72@sbcglobal.net. Business E-Mail: rwalton@surgery.bsd.uchicago.edu.

**WALTON, RODNEY EARL,** lawyer; b. Corvallis, Oreg., Apr. 28, 1947; s. Ray Daniel Jr. and Carolyn Jane (Smith) W. BA, Coll. of Wooster, 1969; JD, Cornell U., 1976; MA in History, Fla. Internat. U., Miami, 2001. Bar: Fla. 1976, U.S. Dist. Ct. (so. dist.) Fla. 1976, U.S. Supreme Ct. 1980, U.S. Ct. Appeals (11th cir.) 1981. Assoc. to jr. ptnr. Smathers & Thompson, Miami, Fla., 1976-87; ptnr. Kelley, Drye and Warren, Miami, 1987-93; atty. Heinrich Gordon Hargrove Weihe & James, P.A., Ft. Lauderdale, 1994-97. Adj. instr. U.S. mil. history Fla. Internat. U., 2001, adj. instr. modern U.S. history, 2003—04, 2006. Sec. bd. dirs. Kings Creek Condominium Assn., Miami, 1984-89, treas., 1984, pres., 1990-91. 1st lt. U.S. Army, 1969-73, Vietnam. Decorated Bronze Star. Mem. ABA, Fla. Bar. Republican. Methodist. Avocations: travel, reading, tennis, history. Home: 7985 SW 86th St Apt 430 Miami FL 33143-7014 Personal E-mail: rodneyearlwalton@aol.com.

**WALTON, SHIRLEY DAWN,** retired medical technician; b. Jamestown, N.Y., Dec. 12, 1935; d. Kenneth Everett and Wilma Alene Lewis; m. Okley Homa Walton, May 3, 1963 (dec.); 1 child, William W. Cert. respiratory care practioner Fla., 1993. Trainee Women's Christian Hosp., Jamestown, 1956—61; nurse's aid St. Joseph's Hosp., Tampa, Fla., 1963—64, cardiology technician, 1964—74; cardiology tech. U. Hosp., Tampa, 1975—82, respiratory therapist, 1982—88; cardiology tech. East Pasco Med. Ctr., Zephyrhills, Fla., 1988—98; ret., 1998. Methodist. Home: 6801 Woodsman Dr Zephyrhills FL 33544 Personal E-mail: wwaltonz@aol.com

**WALTON, STANLEY ANTHONY, III,** lawyer; b. Chgo., Dec. 10, 1939; s. Stanley Anthony and Emily Ann (Pouzar) W.; m. Karen Kayser, Aug. 10, 1963; children: Katherine, Anne, Alex. BA, Washington and Lee U., 1962, LLB, 1965. Bar: Ill. 1965, U.S. Dist. Ct. (no. dist.) Ill. 1966, U.S. Ct. Appeals (7th cir.) 1966. Ptnr. Winston & Strawn, Chgo., 1965-89, Sayfarth Shaw Fairweather, Chgo., 1989-96. Trustee Village of Hinsdale (Ill.), 1985-89; bd. dirs. Washington and Lee Law Sch., Lexington, Va., 1975-78, bd. dirs. univ. alumni, 1983-87, pres., 1986-87; bd. dirs. UNICEF, Chgo., 1983; pres. Hinsdale Hist. Soc., 1979-81, 2001—, St. Isaac Jogues PTA, 1980; sec. Hinsdale Cmty. Svc., 2000—; bd. dirs. Hinsdale Ctrl. Found., 2000—. Mem. Ill. State Bar Assn., Phi Alpha Delta, Hinsdale Golf Club. Republican. Roman Catholic. Home and Office: 6679 Snug Harbor Dr Willowbrook IL 60527 Office Phone: 630-887-9216.

**WALTON, WILLIAM W., JR.,** surgeon; b. Richmond, Va., Sept. 24, 1944; s. William and Lucille (Webb) W.; m. Helen Whitehurst, June 29, 1969; children: David, Jennifer. BS, Davidson Coll., N.C., 1966; MD, U. Va., Charlottesville, 1970. Internship U. Ky., Lexington, 1970—75; surgeon Lexington Clinic, Ky., 1977—. Bd. dirs. Lexington Clinic, 1979—86, v.p., 1994—2000; pres. St. Joseph Hosp., Lexington, 2002—. Maj. USAF, 1975—77. Recipient Tchg. award, U. Ky., 2002. Fellow: Am. Coll. Surgeons. Republican. Presbyterian. Avocations: fishing, boating. Home: 2020 Blannon Rd Lexington KY 40502 Office: Lexington Clinic 1221 S Breakway Lexington KY 40509 Business E-Mail: wwait@lexclinic.com.

**WALTRIP, DARRELL LEE,** race car driver; b. Owensboro, Ky., Feb. 5, 1947; s. Leroy and Margaret Jean (Evans) Waltrip; m. Stephanie Hamilton Rader, Aug. 15, 1969; children: Jessica Leigh, Sarah. Student, Ky. Wesleyan Coll. Driver for Junior Johnson & Assocs., Rick Hendrick Motor Sports; owner Darrell Waltrip Honda Volvo, 1994—. Author (with Jade Gurss): DW: A Lifetime Going Around in Circles, 2004; (with Jay Carty) Darrell Waltrip: One on One: The Faith That Took Him to the Finish Line, 2004; actor(voice): (films) Cars, 2006, Talladega Nights: The Ballad of Ricky Bobby, 2006. Named Driver of Yr., Nat. Motorsports Press Assn., 1977, Olsonite Driver of Yr., 1979, winner, Winston Cup, 1982, Nat. Assn. Stock Car Auto Racing Championship, 1985, Winston Cup Championship, 1981, 1982, 1985, Coca Cola 600, 1985, 1988, 1989, Wrangler 500, 1985, Bisch 500, 1986, Budweiser 400, 1986, Holly Farms 400, 1986, Goody's 500, 1987, 1988, 1989, Motorcraft 500, 1989, Daytona 500, 1989, Champion Spark Plug 500, 1991. Mem.: Nat. Assn. Stock Car Auto Racing. Republican. Presbyterian. Achievements include being the top motor sport money winner worldwide with more than 7.5 million dollars.*

**WALTRIP, MICHAEL,** professional race car driver; b. Owensboro, Ky., Apr. 30, 1963; m. Elizabeth Waltrip; children: Caitlin Marie, Margaret Carol. Stock car racer, 1981—. Recipient Most Popular Driver awards, NASCAR Dash Series, 1983, 1984. Achievements include Mini-Modified divsn. track championship Ky. Motor Speedway, 1981; NASCAR Touring Goody's Dash Series, 1982-84, including series title 1983; NASCAR Winston Cup Series, 1985—, including 2d-place in Rookie of Yr. race, 1986; 2d-place 1988 Miller 500 at Pocono; NASCAR Busch Series Grand Nat. divsn. career includes 7 victories, 11 poles. Avocations: golf, tennis. Office: 222 Raceway Dr Mooresville NC 28117-6510

**WALTRIP, ROBERT L.,** environmentalist, funeral company executive; b. Austin, Tex., 1931; BBA in Mgmt., U. Houston, 1954. With Heights Funeral Home, 1954—62; founder, chmn. bd. Service Corp. Internat., Houston, 1962—, CEO, 1962—2005; founder, chmn. bd. dirs. Waltrip Enterprises Inc., Houston, 1982—; with Tanknology Corp. Internat., Houston, 1988—, Tanknology Environ. Inc., Houston, 1989—. Office: Service Corp International 1929 Allen Pky Houston TX 77019-2507 also: Tanknology Environ Inc 5225 Hollister St Houston TX 77040-6205

**WALTUCK, DAVID,** chef, restaurant owner; m. Karen Waltuck. Student, CCNY, Culinary Inst. Am. Lunch chef La Petite Ferme; chef, co-owner (SoHo, Grand St) Chanterelle, N.Y.C., 1979—89, chef, co-owner (TriBeCa, Harrison St.), 1989—. Recipient James Beard Found. award, 2004. Office: Chanterelle 2 Harrison St New York NY 10013-2810

**WALTZ, JOSEPH MCKENDREE,** neurosurgeon, educator; b. Detroit, July 23, 1931; s. Ralph McKinley and Bertha (Seelye) W.; m. Janet Maureen Journey, June 26, 1954; children: Jeffrey McKinley, Mary Elaine, David Seelye, Stephen McKendree; m. Marilyn Liska, June 5, 1967; 1 child, Tristana McKendree. Student, U. Mich., 1950; BS, U. Oreg., 1954, MD, 1956. Diplomate Am. Bd. Neurol. Surgery. Surg. intern U. Mich. Hosp., 1956-57, gen. surg. resident, 1957-58, clin. instr. neurosurgery, 1960-63; neurosurg. assoc. St. Barnabas Hosp., N.Y.C., 1963—; assoc. dir. Inst. Neurosci., 1974—, dir. dept. neurol. surgery, 1977—2002; attending Neurosci. Inst. Our Lady of Mercy, 1998—. Assoc. cons. in neurosurgery Englewood (N.J.) Hosp., 1964—; assoc. prof. neurosurgery NYU Med. Str., 1974—; asst. prof. dept. surgery (neurosurgery) N.Y. Coll. Osteo. Medicine, 1989—; mem. alumni bd. U. Mich. Med. Ctr., 1995; dir. Med. Ct. Graphics. Author: (chpt.) Cryogenic Surgery, Neurology, 1982, Advances in Neurology, 1983, Textbook of Stereotactic and Functional Neurosurgery, 1997; contbr. articles to profl. jours. Mem. sci. adv. bd. Dystonia Med. Research Found., 1980—; trustee St. Barnabas Hosp., 1980—. Served to capt. M.C. AUS, 1958-60. Recipient Bronze award Am. Congress Rehab. Medicine, 1967, World Svc. Svc. award Rotary, Disting. Trustee award United Hosp. Fund, 1995. Mem. AMA, Am. Paralysis Assn., World Soc. Stereotactic and Functional Neurosurgery, Congress Neurol. Surgeons, Math. Assn. Am., Internat. Neural Network Soc., Soc. for Cryobiology, N.Y. State Med. Soc., Bronx County Med. Soc., N.Y. State Neurosurg Soc., Nat. Ski Patrol, Phi Beta Pi. Achievements include spl. rsch. on neurophysiology and treatment of epilepsy, basal ganglia disorders, abnormal movement disorders, cerebral palsy, also neurosurg. application stereotactic thalamic surgery and spinal cord stimulation. Home: Four B Island South 720 Milton Rd Rye NY 10580-3258 Office: 150 Purchase St Ste 7 Rye NY 10580 Office Phone: 914-967-6577. Personal E-mail: joemwaltz@aol.com.

**WALTZ, KATHLEEN M.,** publishing executive; b. Mar. 6, 1954; m. Bill Raffel, 1990; stepchildren: Jamie, Jenny. BA, DePaul U.; postgrad., Northwestern U. Telemarketer Chgo. Tribune, 1973, mgr. recruitment advt., 1987, dir. customer satisfaction, 1990—93, dir. classified advt., 1990—95, v.p./dir. of developing bus., 1995—97; v.p., gen. mgr. Sun-Sentinel Co., Fla., 1997—98; CEO, pres., pub. Daily Press, Newport News, Va., 1998—2000, Orlando Sentinel Comm., 2000—. Bd. dirs. United Way. of Va. Peninsula, Peninsula Allice for Econ. Devel. WHRO Found. and Greater Peninsula Now; bd. dirs., exec. com. Hampton Roads Partnership; ABC/NAA liaison com., sr. exec. resource corps. Coll. of William and Mary. Mem. So. Newspapers Pub. Assn. (diversity com.). Avocations: travel, golf, gardening. Office: Orlando Sentinel 1000 N Garland Ave Orlando FL 32801

**WALTZ, KATHY,** publishing executive; m. Bill Raffel; stepchildren: Jamie, Jenny. BA in Liberal Arts, DePaul U.; postgrad., Northwestern U., 1991. Dir. classified advt., dir. customer satisfaction Chgo. Tribune, 1973—97, v.p., dir. developing businesses, 1995—97; v.p., gen. mgr. Sun-Sentinel Co., Ft.

Lauderdale, Fla., 1997—98; pres., pub., CEO Daily Press, Hampton Roads, Va., 1998—2000, Orlando (Fla.) Sentinel, 2000—. Avocations: gardening, golf, history, travel. Office: Orlando Sentinel Comms 633 N Orange Ave Orlando FL 32801

**WALTZ, SUSAN,** political scientist, educator; Former chmn. Amnesty Internat., London, England, 1993-98; prof. internat. pub. policy Gerald Ford Sch. Pub. Policy U. Mich., Ann Arbor, 2001—. Bd. dirs. Am. Friends Svc. Com., 2000—. Office: Ford Sch Public Policy Michigan U 611 Tappan St Ann Arbor MI 48109 Office Phone: 734-615-8683. Business E-Mail: swaltz@umich.edu.

**WALTZER, GARRETT J.,** lawyer; b. Nashville, 1961; BA, Colorado College, 1983; JD, University of California, Los Angeles School of Law, 1987. Bar: Calif. 1987. Law clerk to the Hon. Ferdinand F. Fernandez, U.S. Dist. Ct. for Central Dist. of Calif., 1987—88; ptnr. Skadden, Arps, Slate, Meagher & Flom LLP. Office: Skadden 525 University Avenue Suite 1100 Palo Alto CA 94301

**WALUMBWA, FRED OCHIENG,** business educator; s. John Lumbwa Onyango and Florence Aoko Lumbwa; m. Vivian Achieng Omondi, Oct. 31, 1974; 1 child, John-Henry Ochieng. PhD, U. Ill., 2002. Cert. tchr. Kenya Nat. Exam. Coun., 1990. Lectr. U. Nebr., Lincoln, 2002—03, vis. asst. prof., 2003—. Personal asst., pub. rels. officer Kenya Nat. C. of C. and Industry and Milligan and Co., Nairobi, 1993—95. Contbr. articles to profl. jours. Bd. dirs. Lakeside, Kisumu, Nyanza, Kenya, 0199—2005. Recipient Grad. fellowship, U. Ill., 1999, Outstanding Performance as Pres. award, African Stduent Orgn., U. Ill., 1999, Outstanding Sec. Gen. award, 1997; MBA Fellowship award for cmty. svc. leadership, U. Ill., 1995. Mem.: Nat. Acad. of Mgmt. (life; reviewer 2000—05, Cert. of Appreciation 2003).

**WALZ, ANGELA,** retired secondary school educator; b. Salt Lake City; d. Albert Richard and Emma (Boehnke) Riedel; m. Marvin Gideon Walz, Nov. 21, 1967; children: Gregory Marvin, Richard David. BS, U. Utah, 1959; student, BYU, 1963—81, Utah State U., 1985, Boston U., 1987—92, U. San Diego, 1994—97, U. Minn., 1994, U. Md., 1997—99. Sec. LDS ch. music com. Kelly Girl Agy., 1955—64; admin. asst. BYU and music dept. U. Utah Ednl. Rsch., 1960—61; sec. Am. Embassy, Germany, 1964—65; H.S. bus. tchr. Granite H.S., Salt Lake City, 1961—64; bus. tchr. DoDDS, Baumholder, Germany, 1954—94; team mem. Dept. Def. Overseas Sch., Germany, 1995—2000; bus. work edp. tchr. DoDDS Overseas Sch., Hanau, Germany, 1994—2001. Mem. curriculum develop. com. Dept. Def. Dependent Sch., Wiesbaden, Germany, 1995—2000, Washington, 1995—2000; prin. adv. bd. Baumholder H.S., 1990—91; admin. asst. music programs Ch. of Jesus Christ Latter Day Saints, Salt Lake City, 1956—64. Singer various musical prodns. Mem. cmty. choral groups Rheinlandpfalz Internat. Choir, Germany, 1961—90; ch. pianist and organist Latter Day Saints Ch., 1953—2005. Named Outstanding FLBA adv., Future Bus. Leaders of Am., 1990; recipient Outstanding Tchr. award, Bitburg Sch. Dist., 1971, Baumholder Sch. Dist., 1991, Hanau Sch. Dist., 1995. Republican. Ch. Jesus Christ. Avocations: music, swimming, skiing, travel, community involvement. Home: 477 East Peak Ridge Way Draper UT 84020

**WALZ, LEO R.,** conductor; b. Denver, Colo., Sept. 10, 1960; s. Edward and Edna Walz. MusM, Colo. State U., 1985; MusD, U. Miami, 1992. Conductor, music dir. The Alhambra Orch., Miami, Fla., 1990—2000; tchr. Miami-Dade Pub. Sch., Miami, Fla., 1997—; conductor So. Fla. Youth Symphony, Miami, Fla., 2000—. Guest conductor, Romania, Russia, Bulgaria, Ukraine. Mem.: Conductors Guild, Am. Symphony Orch. League. Achievements include founder, The Alhambra Orch. Miami Fla. 1990. Home: 6261 Sunset Dr G8 Miami FL 33143

**WALZ, THOMAS,** biology professor; b. Basel, Switzerland, Nov. 4, 1967; s. Dieter and Dorothea Walz. PhD, U. Basel, Switzerland, 1996. David Phillips rsch. fellow U. Sheffield, England, 1998—99; asst. prof. Harvard Med. Sch., Boston, 1999—2004, assoc. prof., 2004—; adj. assoc. prof. U. Tex. Med. Br., Galveston, 2004—. Dir. Harvard Med. Sch., 2002—. Office: Harvard Med Sch 240 Longwood Ave Boston MA 02115 Office Phone: 617-432-4090.

**WALZER, MICHAEL,** political science professor; b. NYC, Mar. 3, 1935; s. Joseph P. and Sally (Hochman) W.; m. Judith Borodovko, June 17, 1956; children: Sarah, Rebecca. BA, Brandeis U., 1956; PhD, Harvard U., 1961. Fulbright fellow Cambridge (Eng.) U., 1956-57; asst. prof. Princeton U., 1962-66; faculty Harvard U., 1966-80, prof. govt., 1968-80; prof. Sch. Social Scis., Inst. Advanced Study, Princeton, N.J., 1980—. Editor, Dissent Magazine; author: The Revolution of the Saints, 1965, Obligations: Essays on Disobedience, War and Citizenship, 1970, Political Action, 1971, Regicide and Revolution, 1974, Just and Unjust Wars, 1977, Radical Principles: Reflections of an Unreconstructed Democrat, 1980, Spheres of Justice: A Defense of Pluralism and Equality, 1983, Exodus and Revolution, 1985, Interpretation and Social Criticism, 1987, The Company of Critics: Social Criticism and Political Commitment in the Twentieth Century, 1988, What It Means To Be an American, 1993, Thick and Thin: Moral Argument at Home and Abroad, 1994, (with David Miller) Pluralism, Justice, and Equality, 1995, On Toleration, 1997; Arguments From the Left, 1997, Reason Politics and Passion, 1999, Exilic Politics in the Hebrew Bible, 2001, War Politics and Morality, 2001, Arguing About War, 2004, Politics and Passion, 2005; editor: (with others) The Jewish Political Tradition, Vol. I, 2000, Vol. II, 2003; contbg. editor New Republic, 1976—; mem editl bd, Philosophy and Public Affairs, Political Theory. Id. govt. Hebrew U., Jerusalem, 1975 ; trustee Brandeis U., 1983-88; chmn. faculty adv. cabinet United Jewish Appeal, 1977-81. Home: 103 Linwood Cir Princeton NJ 08540-3625

**WALZER, NORMAN CHARLES,** economics professor; b. Mendota, Ill., Mar. 17, 1943; s. Elmer J. and Anna L. Walzer; m. Dona Lee Maurer, Aug. 22, 1970; children: Steven, Mark. BS, Ill. State U., Normal, 1966; MA, U. Ill., 1969, PhD, 1970. Rsch. asst. Dept. Cities and Villages Mcpl. Problems Com., Springfield, Ill., 1974-84; vis. prof. U. Ill., Urbana, 1977-78; prof. econs. Western Ill. U., Macomb, 1978—, interim dean coll. bus. and tech., 1993-95. Author: Cities, Suburbs and Property Tax, 1981, Government Structure and Public Finance, 1984; editor: Financing State and Local Governments, 1981, Rural Community Economic Development, 1991; co-editor: Financing Local Infrastructure in Non Metro Areas, 1986, Financing Economic Development in The 1980s, 1986, Financing Rural Health Care, 1988, Rural Health Care, 1992, Rural Community Economic Development, 1992, Local Economic Development: International Trends and Issues, 1995, Community Visioning Programs: Practice and Principles, 1996, Public-Private Partnerships for Local Economic Development, 1998, Cooperative Approach to Community Economic Development, 2000, Local Government Innovations, 2000, American Midwest: Managing Change in Rural Transition, 2003, Cooperatives and Development: Applications for the 21st Century, 2003. Mem. Am. Econs. Assn., Ill. Econs. Assn. (pres. 1979-80), Mid-Continent Regional Sci. Assn. (pres. 1985-86). Office: Western Ill U Ill Inst Rural Affairs 518 Stipes Hall Macomb IL 61455

**WAMBACH, ABBY (MARY ABIGAIL WAMBACH),** Olympic athlete; b. June 2, 1980; Grad., Univ. of Florida. Mem. U.S. Nat. Soccer Team, 2001—; professional soccer player Washington Freedom, 2002—03; mem. U.S. Women's Olympic Soccer Team, Athens, 2004. Named WUSA All-Star game MVP, 2002, WUSA Rookie of the Year, 2002, WUSA First Team All-Star, 2003, MVP Founders Cup Champions match, 2003; named to WUSA All-Star Team, 2002—03. Achievements include member of U.S. Women's Gold medal Soccer Team, Athens Olympic games, 2004; scored overtime game winning goal in Olympic gold medal game, Athens Olympic games, 2004; member of Founders Cup Championship Team, Washington Freedom, 2003. Office: c/o US Soccer Federation 1801 S Prairie Ave Chicago IL 60616

**WAMBAUGH, JOSEPH A., JR.,** author; b. Pitts., Jan. 22, 1937; s. Joseph Aloysius and Anne (Malloy) W.; m. Dee Allsup, Nov. 26, 1955; children: Mark (dec.), David, Jeannette. BA, Calif. State Coll., L.A., 1960; MA, Calif. State Coll., Los Angeles, 1968. Police officer, L.A., 1960-74. Author: The New Centurions, 1971, The Blue Knight, 1972, The Onion Field, 1973 (Edgar Allan Poe award Mystery Writers Am. 1974), The Choirboys, 1975, The Black Marble, 1978, The Glitter Dome, 1981, The Delta Star, 1983, Lines and Shadows, 1984 (Rodolfo Walsh prize Internat. Assn. Crime Writers 1989), The Secrets of Harry Bright, 1985, Echoes in the Darkness, 1987, The Blooding, 1989, The Golden Orange, 1990, Fugitive Nights, 1992, Finnegan's Week, 1993, Floaters, 1996, Fire Lover, 2003 (Edgar Allan Poe award Mystery Writers Am. 2003). Served with USMC, 1954-57. Recipient Grand Master award, Mystery Writers Am., 2004. Personal E-mail: copbooks@cox.net.

**WAMBOLD, RICHARD LAWRENCE,** manufacturing executive; b. Wilbraham, Mass., Jan. 19, 1952; s. Richard A. and Virginia M. (Reid) W.; m. Patricia Bentley, Aug. 24, 1974; children: Lauren, Carolyn, Robin. BA, U. Tex., 1974, MBA, 1977. From systems cons. to strategic planning mgr. Tenneco, Inc., Houston, 1977-81, asst. to chmn. and chief exec. officer, 1981-84, pres. Tenneco Ventures Inc., 1984-88, v.p. corp. planning and devel., 1988—; exec. v.p., gen. mgr. Internat. Bus. Group, J.I. Case Co., Racine, Wis., 1988—99; chmn. and CEO Pactiv Corp., 1999—. Mem. Nat. Venture Capital Assn., Bus. Roundtable, Comml. Club Chgo. Avocation: sailing. Office: J I Case 700 State St Racine WI 53404-3392 also: Headquaters 1900 West Field Court Lake Forest IL 60045

**WAMP, ZACHARY PAUL,** congressman; b. Ft. Benning, Ga., Oct. 28, 1957; m. Kim Watts; 2 children. Student, U. NC, Chapel Hill, 1977—78, student, 1979—80, U. Tenn., 1978—79. Chmn. Hamilton County Rep. Party, 1987; regional dir. Tenn. Rep. Party, 1989; v.p. Charter Real Estate Corpn., 1989-92; comml. and indsl. real estate broker Fletcher Bright Co., 1992-94; mem. US Congress from 3rd Tenn. dist., 1995—, mem. appropriations com., founder, co-chmn. Congl. Fitness Caucus. Bd. dirs. United Negro Coll. Fund, Am. Diabetes Assn., Boy Scouts Am., Chattanooga Urban League. Named Chattanooga Bus. Leader of Yr., Chattanooga Bus. Jour., 1993; recipient Disting. Svc. award, Chattanooga C. of C., Brainerd-East Hamilton County Br., 1999, Energy Leadership award, US Energy Assn. and Johnson Controls, Inc., 2003. Republican. Baptist. Office: US Ho Reps 1436 Longworth Ho Office Bldg Washington DC 20515 Office Phone: 202-225-3271.

**WAMPLE, ROBERT LEE,** research scientist, director; b. Dover, Del., Aug. 29, 1944; s. Irvin Martin and Bertha Louella Wample; m. Pamela Price Wample; children: Robert Lee, Jeffrey Paul. BS, U. Idaho, Moscow, 1971; PhD, U. Calgary, Can., 1976. Prof., rsch. scientist Irrigated Agr. Rsch. and Ext. Ctr., Wash. State U., Prosser, 1986—2000; chair and dir. Dept. Viticulture and Enology and Viticulture and Enology Rsch. Ctr., Calif. State U., Fresno, 2000—. Owner EdgeKnoll Consulting, Clovis, Calif., 1990—; ex-officio bd. mem. Am. Vineyard Found., Napa, Calif., 2001—; advisor Ctrl. Calif. Wine Growers, Fresno, Calif., 2004—; mem. Glassy Winged Sharpshooter, Pierces Disease Adv. Bd., Sacramento, 2004—, Calif. Raisin Mktg. Bd., Fresno, Calif., 2004—05; pres. Am. Soc. of Enology and Viticulture, Davis, Calif., 2005—. Assoc. editor Am. Jour. Enology and Viticulture, 2000—06; author: (over 100 rsch. publs.) Plant Physiology, Am. Jour. of Enology and Viticulture, Jour. Am. Soc. for Horticulture Sci., Plant and Soil, Physiologia Plantarum, Hortscience, Acta Horticulturae. Mem. Rotary Internat., Fresno, Calif., 1995—2006. Sgt. USMC, 1962—66. Recipient Chateau Ste Michelle Disting. Prof. of Viticulture, Wash. State U., Stimson Ln. Vineyards and Estates, 1995—2000, Industry Svc. award, Wash. Assn. of Wine Grape Growers, 1999, Claude Laval, Jr. award for Innovative Tech. and Rsch., Calif. State U., Fresno, 2005—06, Cert. of Recognition for Rsch., Scholarship and Creative Activities, 2005—06, Julio Gallo Chair of Viticulture and Enology, E&J Gallo Winery, 2000—; Post-Graduate Scholarship, NRC of Can., 1974—76. Mem.: Am. Soc. of Enology and Viticulture (2d v.p. 2003—04, 1st v.p. 2004—05, pres. 2005—06, Outstanding Rsch. Paper 1993), AAAS (assoc.). Achievements include patents for Use of plant hormones to stimulate reproductive development in Pinus species; Use of load-cell technology to estimate yield in trellised fruit crops; patents pending for Use of Near Infrared Spectroscopy to non-destructively measure wine grape fruit quality in the field. Office: Calif State Univ Fresno 2360 E Barstow Ave Fresno CA 93740-8003 Office Phone: 559-278-7179. Business E-Mail: rwample@csufresno.edu.

**WAMUTISO, KINEENE,** humanities educator; b. Kitui, Kenya, Sept. 5, 1959; s. Mutiso Kivuve and Ndulu (Nzoka) Mutiso; m. Jane Chepkoech Koe, July 20, 1994; 1 child, Mutiso. BA with honors, U. Nairobi, Kenya, 1983, MA, 1985, PhD, 1996. Lectr. Hankuk U. Fgn. Studies, Seoul, South Korea, 1985-88; warden U. Nairobi, 1990—, lectr. Coll. Humanities and Social Scis., 1989-96; sr lect. Coll. of Humanities and Social Scis. U Nairobi, 1996—. Examiner Kenya Nat. Examination Coun., Nairobi, 1990—; curriculum developer Kenya Inst. Edn., Nairobi, 1990—; lectr. Kenyatta U., 1988-89; vis. lectr. U. Nat. du Rwanda, 1991-94. Author: Mizan Yangu, 1986, Unakiki wa Malenga wa Mvita, 1986, Swahili-Korean-English Dictionary of Proverbs, 1988, Catharsis, 1992, Uhakiki wa Visiki, 1997; editor: Utamaduni wa Mkorea, 1987; contbr. articles to profl. jours. Recipient Cert. of Recognition, Ministry of Edn., 1990; U. York scholar, 1987; grantee Internat. Cultural Soc., 1991, Deutsche Stiftung für Internat. Entwicklung, 1991, Codesria, 1992, Deutscher Akademischer Austauschdienst, 1994. Mem. Kenya Writers Assn., Kenya Oral Lit. Assn., Kenya Nat. Commn. UNESCO, Korean Found., Coun. for Devel. of Social Sci. Rsch. in Africa. Avocations: writing, travel, movies, cultures. Home: PO Box 13316 Nairobi Kenya Office: U Nairobi Dept Linguistics & African Langs Nairobi Kenya

**WAMUTOMBO, DIKEMBE MUTOMBO MPOLONDO MUKAMBA JEAN JACQUE See MUTOMBO, DIKEMBE**

**WAN, FREDERIC YUI-MING,** mathematician, educator; b. Shanghai, Jan. 7, 1936; arrived in U.S., 1947; s. Wai-Nam and Olga Pearl (Jung) W.; m. Julia Y.S. Chang, Sept. 10, 1960. SB, MIT, 1959, SM, 1963, PhD, 1965. Mem. staff MIT Lincoln Lab., Lexington, 1959—65; instr. math. MIT, Cambridge, 1965—67, asst. prof., 1967—69, assoc. prof., 1969—74; prof. applied math. and math. U. Wash., Seattle, 1983—95; prof. math. mech. and aero. engring. U. Calif., Irvine, 1995—. Chmn. Dept. Applied Math. U. Wash. 1984-88, divsn. dean scis. Coll. Arts and Scis., 1988-92; vice chancellor rsch., dean grad. studies U. Calif. Irvine, 1995-2000, faculty athletics rep., 2000-04, dir. math. and computational biology grad. program, 2006—; program dir. divsn. math. sci. NSF, 1986-87, divsn. dir., 1993-94; mem. MIT Ednl. Coun. for B.C. Area Can., 1974-83; trustee NSF Inst. Pure and Applied Math., chmn., 1999-2001; cons. in field Assoc. editor Jour. Applied Mechanics, 1991-95, Can. Applied Math. Quar., Studies in Applied Math., Jour. Dyn. Discrete, Continuous and Impulsive Sys., 1994-97, Natural Resource Modeling 1985-88, Internat. Jour. Solids & Structures, 1996-2005, Jour. Mechanics of Material and Structures, 2005—; contbr. articles to profl. jours. Killam Sr. fellow, 1979; recipient Sloan Found. award, 1973, Phys. Scis. Tchg. Excellence award U. Calif. 2004-06, Chancellors award, 2006. Fellow AAAS, ASME; mem. Russian Acad. Natural Scis. (fgn.), Am. Acad. Mechanics (sec. fellows 1984-90, pres. 1993-94), Soc. Indsl. and Applied Math., Can. Applied Math. Soc. (coun. 1980-83, pres. 1983-85, Arthur Beaumont Disting. Svc. award 1991), Am. Math. Soc., Math. Assn. Am., Sigma Xi (pres. U. Calif. Irvine chpt. 2005—). Home: 22 Urey Ct Irvine CA 92612-4077 Office: U Calif Irvine Dept Math Rm 267 MST Bldg Irvine CA 92697-3875 Business E-Mail: fwan@uci.edu.

**WAN, JULIA CHANG,** retired science educator; b. Hong Kong, Oct. 13, 1937; d. Charles S.Y. and Lucy (Wong) Chang; m. Frederic Y.M. Wan, Sept 10, 1960. BA, Wellesley Coll., 1960, MA, 1970; EdD, Boston Coll., 1978. Mem. staff Bio Rsch. Inst., Cambridge, Mass., 1960-64; physics tchr. Watertown (Mass.) H.S., 1970-73; sci. dir. Watertown Pub. Schs., 1973-79; curriculum coord. Fed. Way Sch. Dist., Fed. Way, Wash., 1979-83; asst. supt.

Bainbridge Island (Wash.) Sch. Dist., 1983-93; program dir. NSF, Washington, 1993-95; dir. Ctr. for Excellence in Sci. and Math. Edn. Calif. State U., Fullerton, 1995-2000. Mem. accreditation com. N.W. Assn. Schs. and Colls., Boise, Idaho, 1981-95; mem. edn. opportunity coun. AAAS, Washington, 1995-99; bd. dirs. Challenger Ctr., Alexandria, Va., 1997-2000. Author: Designing School Health Education Curricula, 1992, 2d edit. 1995; contbr. articles and revs. to sci. mags. Bd. dirs. NOW, 1985-88; mem. Commn. on Asian-Am. Affairs, Olympia, Wash., 1990-93; bd. trustees Girls, Inc., Orange County, Calif., 1995-2000. Recipient award profl. excellence We. Wash. U. Bellingham, 1988, exemplary program award Met. Life Found., N.Y.C., 1989; grantee: NSF (numerous), Arlington, Va., 1989-2000, Beckman Found., Irvine, Calif., 1998-2000. Mem. ASCD, Am. Ednl. Rsch. Assn., Nat. Sci. Tchrs. Assn. E-mail: Jwan@fullerton.edu.

**WAN, JULIN,** materials scientist; s. Bengen Wan and Qimei Gu; m. Rui Gu, July 16, 1996. PhD, Tsinghua U., Beijing, 1995. Asst. prof. Tsinghua U., Beijing, 1995—97; rsch. scientist and lectr. Toyama U., Japan, 1997—98; postdoc rsch. assoc. U. Calif., Davis, 1998—2002; materials scientist GE Global Rsch. Ctr., Niskayuna, NY, 2002—. Mem.: Minerals, Metals and Materials Soc., Materials Rsch. Soc., Am. Ceramic Soc., Sigma-Xi. Home: 3 Tintagel Way Rexford NY 12148 Office: GE Global Rsch Ctr One Rsch Cir Niskayuna NY 12309 Office Phone: 518-387-4067. E-mail: wan@research.ge.com.

**WAN, MING,** computer scientist, researcher; s. Yueqin Shi and Xianrong Wan; m. Lan Yao, Oct. 3, 1972; children: Ori M. Huang, Erana. BS, Nanjing U., 1990, MS, 1993; PhD, Tsinghua U., 1996. Cert. Nat. 6-Level English cert. Nat. Edn. Dept, China, 1990. Rsch. asst. Nanjing U., Nanjing, Jiangsu, China, 1990—93, counselor undergraduate program, computer sci. dept., 1991—93; rsch. asst. Tsinghua U., Beijing, 1993—96; post doctoral assoc. SUNY, Stony Brook, 1997—99, rsch. asst. prof., 1999—2000; sr. rschr. Viatronix Inc., Stony Brook, 1999—2000, The Boeing Co., Seattle, 2000—. Cons. Inst. Geography, Chinese Academia Sinica, Beijing, 1992—93, Chinese Acad. Architecture Sci., Beijing, 1993—94, Nanjing Kemei High Tech. Corp., Jiangsu, 1994—95; com. mem. Internat. Workshop Vol. Graphics, 2001—; Internat. Symposium on Visual Computing, 2006. Recipient Best Performance award, 2004. Achievements include patents for medical imaging and visualization system, in the application of virtual colonoscopy; patents pending for Boeing Invention Disclosure entitled Distributed Tempero-Spatial Query Service; design of a commercial eal-Titme 3D virtual colonoscopy system on PC at Viatronix Inc; development of practical 3D medical imaging and visualization systems on both PC and SGI workstations, cooperated with Hospital 301 and other leading hospitals in China. Personal E-mail: mwan00@yahoo.com.

**WAND, MARTIN,** ophthalmologist, educator; m. Karen Egger; children: Andrew, Christopher, Bradford. BS, Yale U., New Haven, 1963, MD, 1968. Diplomate Am. Bd. of Ophthalmology, 1976, recertified 2003. Pres. New Eng. Ophthal. Soc., Boston, 1997—98; trustee McLean Health Ctr., Simsbury, Conn., 2000—05; councilor Am. Glaucoma Soc., San Francisco, 2000—05; clin. prof. ophthalmology U. Conn. Sch. Medicine, Farmington, Conn., 2000—; dir. Am. Bd. Ophthalmology, Phila., 2001—; trustee Am. Acad. Ophthalmology, San Francisco, 2006—, vice-chair, coun., 2006—. Contbr. over 100 articles to profl. jours., chapters to books. Lt. commdr. U. S. Pub. Health Svc., 1970—72, Ctr. for Disease Control. Fellow: Am. Acad. Ophthalmology (Honor award 1985, Sr. Honor award 1996, Secretariat award 2003); mem.: Chandler-Grant Soc., Am. Eye Study Club, Am. Glaucoma Soc., New Eng. Ophthal. Soc. Office: Cons Ophthalmologists 499 Farmington Ave Farmington CT 06032 Office Phone: 860-678-0202.

**WAND, PATRICIA ANN,** librarian; b. Portland, Oreg., Mar. 28, 1942; d. Ignatius Bernard and Alice Ruth (Suhr) W.; m. Francis Dean Silvernail, Dec. 20, 1966 (div. Jan. 19, 1986); children: Marjorie Lynn Silvernail, Kirk Dean Silvernail. BA, Seattle U., 1963; MAT, Antioch Grad. Sch., 1967; AMLS, U. Mich., 1972. Vol. Peace Corps, Colombia, S.Am., 1963-65; secondary tchr. Langley Jr. High Sch., Washington, 1965-66; asst. libr. Wittenberg U. Libr., Springfield, Ohio, 1967-69; secondary tchr. Caro (Mich.) High Sch., 1969-70; assoc. libr. Coll. of S.I. (N.Y.) Libr., 1972-77; head, access svcs. Columbia U. Librs., N.Y.C., 1977-82; asst. univ. libr. U. Oreg., Eugene, 1982-89; univ. libr. The Am. U., Washington, 1989—. Cons. Bloomsburg (Pa.) U. Libr., 1990, Banco Ctrl., Ecuador, 1998, Am. U. Sharjah, UAE, 1999-2002; bd. dirs. CAPCON, 1997-2003, chair, 2002-03; bd. dirs. ERIC Clearinghouse on Higher Edn. Adminstrn. Contbr. articles to profl. jours. Pres. West Cascade Returned Peace Corps Vols., Eugene, 1985-88; v.p. Friends of Colombia, Washington, 1990—; speaker on Peace Corps, 1965—, libr. and info. svcs., 1979—; bd. mem. Nat. Peace Corps Assn., 2005—. Honors Program scholarship Seattle U., 1960-62, Peace Corps scholarship Antioch U., 1965-66; recipient Beyond War award, 1987, Fulbright Sr. Lectr. award Fulbright, 1989, Disting. Alumnus award Sch. of Info. and Libr. Studies, U. Mich., 1992. Mem. ALA (chmn. com. on legislation 1997-98, coun. 2001-04, internat. rels. com. 2004—), Assn. Coll. and Rsch. Librs. (chair budget and fin. bd. dirs. 1987-89, 2001-04, chair WHCLIS task force 1989-92, chair govt. rels. com. 1993-94, chair internat. rels. com. 1996-98), On-line Computer Librs. Ctr. (adv. com. on coll. and univ. librs 1991-96), D.C. Libr. Assn. (bd. dirs. 1993-98, pres. 1996-97, Disting. Svc. award 2003). Home: 4854 Bayard Blvd Bethesda MD 20816-1785 Office: Am Univ Libr 4400 Massachusetts Ave NW Washington DC 20016-8046 Office Phone: 202-885-3237.

**WANDEL, SHARON LEE,** sculptor; b. Bemidji, Minn., Mar. 19, 1940; d. Roy J. and Bonnie (Englund) Opsahl; m. Thaddeus Ludwik Wandel, Oct. 17, 1970; children: Holly, Erika. BA, Gustavus Adolphus Coll., 1962; MSW, Columbia U., 1965; Cert. in Arts Mgmt., SUNY, Purchase, 1993. Caseworker Manhattan State Hosp., N.Y.C., 1963-64; caseworker/unit duty officer Bur. Soc. Svc., N.Y.C., 1965-67; teaching asst. dept. medicine NYU Med. Ctr., N.Y.C., 1967—71. Adv. bd. Lamia, Inc., NYC, 1999—2003. One-woman shows at Silvermine Guild of Artists, New Canaan, Conn., 1993, 97, 2000, Pen and Brush, NYC, 1994, Clark Whitney Gallery, Lenox, Mass., 1994, James Cox Gallery, Woodstock, NY, 1994, 96, Cortland Jessup Gallery, Provincetown, Mass., 1998, NYC, 2000, 02, Gallery Marya, Osaka, Japan, 1999, Laura Barton Gallery, Westport, Conn., 2000, Firehouse Gallery, Damaviscotta, Maine, 2000, Gallery Irohane, Osaka, Japan, 2001; exhibited in group shows at Nat. Acad. Design, NYC, 1988, 90, 92, 94-95, 97-2000, 04-06, Cortland Jessup Gallery, Provincetown and NYC, 1998-2002, Canyon Ranch, Lenox, Mass. 1999-2003, Chesterwood, Lenox, Mass., 2000-01, Butler Inst. Am. Art., Youngstown, Ohio, 2000, Cavalier Gallery, Nantucket, Mass., 2001, Berkshires Bot. Garden, Mass., 2001, Paesaggio Gallery, West Hartford, Conn., 2001-04, Leighton Gallery, Blue Hill, Maine, 2001-06, Munson Gallery, Chatham, Mass., 2002-06, Sakai (Japan) City Mus., 2002, Craven Gallery, Martha's Vineyard, Mass., 2002-06, Berta Walker Gallery, Provincetown, Mass., 2002, Elan Fine Arts, Rockport, Maine, 2003-05, 2006, Clarke Galleries, Stowe, Vt., 2003-06, Palm Beach, Fla., 2003-04, NYC, 2003-04, Westchester Arts Coun., White Plains, NY, 2004, Gallery Yellow, Cross River, N.Y., 2006; permanent collections at Art Students League, Westinghouse Corp. Collection, Pitts., Nat. Acad. Design, Housatonic Mus., CT, C. of C., Toyamura, Japan, Pfizer Corp. Collection, Armonk, NY; commns. include two 8' bronze figures for Ihilani Resort, Kapolei, Hawaii, 1993, 2 5" figures Silvermine Galleries, 1993. Mem. rsch. com. Arthritis Found., N.Y.C., 1968-69. Recipient N.Am. Sculpture Exhbn. 2d place, 1991, Three River Arts Festival (Carnegie Inst.) Purchase award, 1990, Hakone Open Air Mus. (Japan) 3d and 4th Rodin Grand Prize Exhbn. Excellent Maquettes, 1990, 92, Matrix Gallery 1st prize for sculpture, 1990, Ariel Gallery Internat. Competition Group Show award, 1989, Salmagundi Club McReynolds award, 1989, Barret Coleco award, 1988, 1st place nat. competition Sundance Gallery, Bridgehampton, N.Y., 1997; Vt. Studio Ctr. fellow, 2000; elected Nat. Academician Nat. Acad. Design, 1994. Mem. Silvermine Guild of Artists (Solo Show award 1992), N.Y. Soc. Woman Artists (past pres.), Knickerbocker Artists USA, The Pen and Brush (Meisner award 1990, Solo Show award 1993), Nat. Acad. Design (elected nat. academician 1994, Cleo Hartwig award 1990), Nat. Sculpture Soc. (Meisner award 1994, Hexter award 1993, Spring award 1991, Meiselman award 1990), Audubon Artists

(Chaim Gross Found. award 1993), Sculptors Guild (past bd. dirs.). Avocations: travel, cooking, reading. Studio: PO Box 314 Croton On Hudson NY 10520-0314 E-mail: wandel_s@hotmail.com.

**WANDER, HERBERT STANTON,** lawyer; b. Cin., Mar. 17, 1935; s. Louis Marvin and Pauline (Schuster) W.; m. Karen Woloshin, Aug. 2004; children: Daniel Jerome, Susan Gail, Lois Marlene. AB, U. Mich., 1957; LLB, Yale U., 1960. Bar: Ohio 1960, Ill. 1960. Law clk. to judge US Dist. Ct. (no. dist.) Ill., 1960—61; ptnr. Pope Ballard Shepard & Fowle, Chgo., 1961—78, Katten Muchin Rosenman LLP, Chgo., 1978—. Trustee Michael Reese Found., 1991-; bd. dir. Tel. & Data Systems, Chgo., 1968-, Advance Ross Corp., 1991-96; mem. legal adv. com. to the bd. gov. NY Stock Exch., 1989-92; mem. legal adv. bd. Nat. Assn. Securities Dealers, Inc., 1996-99; co-chair SEC Adv. Com. on Smaller Pub. Cos., 2004; spkr. in field. Editor: (jour.) Bus. Law Today, 1992-93; editor-in-chief: (jour.) The Bus. Lawyer, 1993-94; contbr. numerous articles to profl. jour. Bd. dir. Jewish Fedn. Met. Chgo., 1972—, pres., 1981-83; bd. dir. Jewish United Fund, 1972—, pres., 1981-83, chmn. pub. affairs com., 1984-87, gen. campaign chmn., 1993; former regional chmn. nat. young leadership cabinet United Jewish Appeal; vice-chmn. large city budgeting conf. Coun. Jewish Fedns., 1979-82, bd. dir., 1980—, exec. com., 1983-84. Mem. ABA (sec. bus. law sect. 1992-93, vice-chair 1993-94, chair-elect 1994-95, chair 1995-96, apptd. to commn. on multidisciplinary practice 1998, mem. task force on atty. client privilege, 2004, mem. task force on fedl. sentencing guidelines, 2004, co-chair sec. adv. com. on smaller pub. cos., 2004), Ill. State Bar Assn., Chgo. Bar Assn., Yale Law Sch. Assn. (exec. com. 1982-86), Std. Club, Econ. Club, Northmoor Country Club, Phi Beta Kappa. Home: 70 Prospect Ave Highland Park IL 60035-3329 Office: Katten Muchin Rosenman LLP 525 W Monroe St Ste 1700 Chicago IL 60661-3693 Business E-Mail: hwander@kattenlaw.com.

**WANDERS, HANS WALTER,** banker; b. Aachen, Germany, Apr. 3, 1925; came to US, 1929, naturalized, 1943; s. Herbert and Anna Maria (Kusters) W.; m. Elizabeth Knox Kimball, Apr. 3, 1949; children: Crayton Kimball, David Gillette. BS, Yale U., 1947, Ea. Inst. Tech., 1949; postgrad. Grad. Sch. Banking, Rutgers U., 1961-64. With GE, 1947-48, Libbey-Owens-Ford Glass Co., 1948-53, Allied Chem. Co., 1953-55, McKinsey & Co., Inc., 1955-57; from asst. cashier to v.p. No. Trust Co., Chgo., 1957-65; v.p. Nat. Blvd. Bank, Chgo., 1965-66, pres., 1966-70; exec. v.p. Wachovia Bank & Trust Co., N.A., Winston-Salem, NC, 1970-74, chmn., 1977-85, vice chmn., 1985-88, also bd. dirs.; pres. Wachovia Corp., Winston-Salem, 1974-76, 85-87, chmn., 1977-85, vice chmn., 1987-88, also bd. dirs.; pres., chief exec. officer 1st Wachovia Corp. Services, Inc., Winston-Salem, 1986-88, ret., 1988; dir. Exxon Supply Co., 1989-94, Goody's Mfg. Corp., 1989-94, Gulf Resources, Inc., 1989-92, Turnpike Properties, Inc., 2001—. Chmn. Winston-Salem Found. Com., 1981-82; bd. dirs. NC Textile Found., NC Engring. Found., Inc., 1971-88; trustee, mem. exec. com. Salem Coll. and Acad., 1986-91, Tax Found., 1982—, vice chmn., 1984-86, chmn., 1986-88, chmn. exec. com., 1989; mem. bd. visitors Fuqua Sch. Bus., Duke U., 1978-89, NC Japan Ctr., 1982—; mem. nat. corps. com. United Negro Coll. Fund; mem., chmn. NC Bd. Econ. Devel., 1989-93; corporator Belmont Hill Sch., 1996—. Lt. USNR, 1943-46, 51-53. Mem. Am. Bankers Assn. (chmn. mktg. divsn. 1979-80, dir. 1971-73), Assn. Res. City Bankers, Conf. Bd. (So. regional adv. coun.), Assn. Bank Holding Cos. (bd. dirs., exec. com. 1981-83), Chgo. Club, Commonwealth Club Chgo., Twin-City Club Winston Salem, Old Town Club Winston-Salem, Roaring Gap Club NC Home: 10 Graylyn Pl Winston Salem NC 27106 Office: Wachovia Corp 420 W 4th St Ste 202-A Winston Salem NC 27101-2837 Office Phone: 336-732-5923.

**WANDYCZ, PIOTR STEFAN,** historian, educator; b. Krakow, Poland, Sept. 20, 1923; s. Damian Stanislaw and Stefania (Dunikowska) W.; m. Maria Teresa Chrzaszcz, Aug. 13, 1963; children: Anna, Joanna, Antoni. BA, Cambridge U., 1948, MA, 1952; PhD, London U., 1951; MA (hon.), Yale U., 1968; DHC, Wroclaw U., 1993, Sorbonne U., Paris, 1997, Jagiellonian U., 2000, Cath. U. Lublin, 2004. Instr. to assoc. prof. history Ind. U., 1954-66; fellow Harvard's Russian Rsch. Ctr., 1963-65; assoc. prof. history Yale U., 1966-68, prof., 1968-89, chmn. Russian and East European coun., 1974-76, 81-83, Bradford Durfee prof., 1989-97, prof. emeritus, 1997—. Vis. prof. history Columbia U., 1967, 69, 74 Author: Czechoslovak-Polish Confederation and Great Powers, 1956, France and Her Eastern Allies, 1962, Soviet-Polish Relations, 1969, The Lands of Partitioned Poland, 1974, United States and Poland, 1980, August Zaleski, 1980, Polska i Zagranica, 1986, The Twilight of French Eastern Alliances, 1988, Z Dziejow dyplomacji, 1988, Polish Diplomacy 1914-1945, 1988, The Price of Freedom, 1992, 2nd edit., 2001, Die Freiheit und ihr Preis, 1993, Pod zaborami, 1994, Cena wolnosci, 1995, 2d edit., 2003, Laisves Kaina, 1997, Stredni Evropa v Dejinach, 1998, Tsenata na svoboda, 1999, Z Pilsudskim i Sikorskim, 1999, Il prezzo della liberta, 2001, O Federalizmie i emigracji, 2003, Pax Europaea, 2003; co-author: Historia Europy Srodkowo-Wschodniej, 2000, Histoire de l'Europe du Centre-Est 2004, Tsina Slobody, 2004, A Szabaeag Ara, 2004, Aleksander Skrzynski, 2006; contbr. articles to profl. jours.; mem. editl. bd. Slavic Rev., Internat. History Rev., Polish Rev., Polin., East European Politics and Society. Served as 2d lt. Polish Army, 1942-45. Decorated Comdr.'s Cross of Polonia Restituta; recipient Alfred Jurzykowski Found. award in history, 1977; fellow Guggenheim Found., Ford Found., Rockefeller Found., Am. Philos. Soc., Am. Coun. Learned Socs., Social Sci. Rsch. Coun., Internat. Rsch. and Exchs. Bd. Mem. AAAS (Wayne Vucinich prize 1989), Am. Hist. Assn. (George Louis Beer prize 1962, 89), Polish Hist. Assn. (), Polish Acad. Arts and Scis., Polish Acad. Scis., Polish Inst. Arts and Scis. (pres. 1999—), Polish Soc. Abroad (A. Lenkszewicz prize 1991, Oscar Halecki History award 1997), Czechoslovak Acad. of Scis. (Hlavka medal 1992, A. Gieysztor prize 2004), Czechoslovak Soc. Arts and Scis. Home: 27 Spring Garden St Hamden CT 06517-1913 Office: Yale U Dept History New Haven CT 06520-8324 Office Phone: 203-432-1382. Business E-Mail: piotr.wandycz@yale.edu.

**WANEBO, HAROLD J.,** surgeon, educator; b. Denver, Feb. 12, 1935; s. Clifford P. and JoAnn (Curtin) W.; m. Claire Anne Wanebo, Oct. 27, 1964; children: John Eric, Michael David, Jacqueline Elise. BS, Regis Coll., 1957; MD, U. Colo., 1961. Intern Cornell Med. divsn. Bellevue Hosp., N.Y., 1961-62, resident N.Y., 1962-63; surg. resident U. Calif. Med. Ctr., San Francisco, 1963-65, 67-69; fellow in tumor immunology Meml. Sloan-Kettering Cancer Ctr., N.Y., 1965-67, sr. surg. fellow N.Y., 1971-73, clin. instr. attending surgeon N.Y., 1973-74, assoc. N.Y., 1973-77, asst. attending surgeon N.Y., 1974-77, assoc. scientist N.Y., 1977-83, cons. clin. immunology svc. N.Y., 1977-90; instr. surgery Cornell U.-N.Y. Hosp. Med. Ctr., 1973-75, asst. prof. surgery, 1975-77; chief divsn. surg. oncology Med. Ctr., prof. surgery U. Va., Charlottesville, 1977-87; prof. surgery, dir. surg. oncology Brown U., Providence, R.I., 1987—; chief surgery Roger Williams Med. Ctr., Providence, 1987—. Editor: Hepatic and Biliary Cancer, 1987, Common Problems in Cancer Surgery, 1990, Colorectal Cancer, 1993, Surgery for Gastrointestinal Cancer, 1996; contbr. numerous chpts. to books and articles to profl. jours. Maj. U.S. Army, 1969-71, Vietnam. Decorated Bronze star; recipient Commendation medal V device. Mem. ACS, Am. Assn. Cancer Edn., Am. Assn. Cancer Rsch., Am. Assn. Immunologists, Am. Cancer Soc. (Jr. Faculty Clin. Fellowship award 1974-77), Am. Surg. Assn., Am. Soc. Clin. Oncology, Am. Assn. Vol. Physicians, Med. Soc. State of N.Y., Med. Soc. R.I., Med. Soc. Va., Nafzigger Surg. Soc., New Eng. Surg. Soc., N.Y. Acad. Scis., N.Y. Surg. Soc., Soc. Surgery of Alimentary Tract, Soc. Surg. Oncology, Soc. Univ. Surgeons, Southeastern Surg. Congress, Soc. Surg. Assn., Soc. Head and Neck Surgery, Albemarle County Med. Soc. Office: Roger Williams Med Ctr 825 Chalkstone Ave Providence RI 02908-4728 Office Phone: 401-456-2464. Business E-Mail: hwanebo@rwme.org.

**WANEK, WILLIAM CHARLES,** public relations executive; b. Ridgewood, N.Y., Oct. 21, 1932; s. William John and Anna (Benes) W.; m. Robbie Gene Fairbanks, Feb. 14, 1974; children: William Robert, Jennifer Leigh. BA in English, CCNY, 1954; MA in Psychology, The New Sch. Social Rsch., N.Y.C., 1982. Asst. editor Soap Chem. Spltys. Mag., N.Y.C., 1956-58; editor in chief Maintenance Supplies Mag., N.Y.C., 1958-60; acct. exec. O.S. Tyson & Co. Inc., N.Y.C., 1960-62; dir. advt. and pub. rels. Pa. Glass Sand Corp.,

---

N.Y.C., 1962-64; sr. acct. exec. McCann-Erickson Inc., N.Y.C., 1964-66; acct. supr. Burson-Marsteller Assocs., N.Y.C., 1966-71; exec. v.p. Gibbs & Soell Inc., N.Y.C., 1971—. With U.S. Army, 1954-56. Mem. Am. Agrl. Editors Assn., Nat. Agri-Mktg. Assn. (bd. dirs. ea. chpt. 1974-76), Nat. Assn. Farm Broadcasters. Presbyterian. Avocations: horticulture, classical music, theater, reading, swimming. Office: Gibbs & Soell Inc 600 3rd Ave Fl 6 New York NY 10016-1903

**WANG, AIXUE,** translator, writer; b. Taoyuan, Hunan, China; arrived in U.S., 1988; s. Gaokun Wang and Yunhuang Xia; m. Lingling Li, May 7, 1986; 1 child, Haoming. MA, U. Houston, 1990, PhD, 1995. Tchr. No. 4 HS Taoyuan, 1976—82; instr. Beijing Coll. Internat. Rels., 1984—88; tchg. asst. U. Houston, 1988—95; internat. program specialist and adj. prof. English William Woods U., Fulton, Mo., 1995—2002; freelance translator, writer St. Paul, 2002—. Author: A Comparison of the Dramatic Work of Cap Yu and J. M. Synge, 1999; translator (to Chinese): 1850 "The Prelude" (Wordsworth), 2004. Home and Office: 5046 Eastwood Mounds View MN 55112 Office Phone: 651-283-8655. Personal E-mail: wangax@hotmail.com.

**WANG, ALBERT HUAI-EN,** lawyer; b. Tainan, Taiwan, Feb. 21, 1967; s. Tien-Yu Wang and Shiu-Yin Chen. BA in Bus. Econs. magna cum laude, MA in Bus. Econs. magna cum laude, UCLA, 1990; JD, Cornell U., 1994. Bar: NY 1995. Tax specialist KPMG Peat Marwick, LA, 1990-91; tchr. asst. Cornell Law Sch., 1993; assoc. Willkie Farr & Gallagher LLP, NYC, 1994-99, Schulte Roth & Zabel LLP, NYC, 1999—2001; ptnr., head of China practice Phillips Nizer LLP, NYC, 2001—. Legal counsel, adv. coun. Asian Am. Bus. Devel. Ctr., NYC, 1999—2002; dir. Baldor Splty. Foods, Inc., 2001—. U. Calif. regent scholar, 1986-90, Alumni scholar UCLA, 1986, Departmental scholar, 1989. Mem.: ABA, Am. C. of Tax, Asian Fin. Soc. (adv. coun. mem. 2002—), Orgn. Chinese Ams. (NY chpt. adv. coun.), US-China Lawyers Soc. (bd. dirs. 2002—), Chinese Fin. Soc. (dir., legal counsel 2000—02), NY State Bar Assn., Chinese Am. Voters Assn. of Queens (dir. NY chpt. 1999—2001), Asia Soc., China Inst., Phi Beta Kappa, Omicron Delta Epsilon, Phi Delta Phi. Democrat. Avocation: languages. Office: Phillips Nizer LLP 666 Fifth Ave New York NY 10103-0084 Home: 13810 Franklin Ave Apt 5n Flushing NY 11355-3305 Office Phone: 212-977-9700. Business E-Mail: awang@phillipsnizer.com.

**WANG, ALBERT JAMES,** violinist, educator; b. Ann Arbor, Mich., Nov. 19, 1958; s. James and Lydia (Ebenhoch) Wang; m. Bridget Renee Becker, June 30, 1987 (div. 2000); children: Ona Lenore, Kevin Lewis. MusB, Ind. U., 1979; MusM, U. Mich., 1981; DMA, Am. Conservatory, 1993. Prin. second violin Baton Rouge Symphony Orch., 1981-82; first violin Valcour String Quartet, Baton Rouge, 1981-82, Loyola String Quartet, 1982-83; mem. Lyric Opera Chgo. Orch., 1982—; mem. Orch. Ill., Chgo., 1982-88; prin. 2d violin Internat. Symphony Orch., Port Huron, Mich., 1984; 1st violin Internat. String Quartet, Port Huron, 1984; concertmaster, soloist Chgo. Chamber Orch., 1985-88, Chgo. Philharm., 1985—; mem. Grant Park Symphony Orch., Chgo., 1986-87; concertmaster, soloist Birch Creek Music Festival, Wis., Woodstock (Ill.) Mozart Festival Orch., 1988-90; concertmaster Rockford (Ill.) Symphony Orch., 1990-91, Northwestern Music Festival Orch., 1990—; soloist, concertmaster Pro Musica Orch. of Mauritius, 1992-93; soloist, concertmaster China tour Classical Symphony Orch., 1994, 95; soloist, concertmaster Midwest Symphony Orch., 1995-96; music dir. Baroque Masterplayers, 1994—; soloist, concertmaster Met. Arts Orch., 1995-98. Artist-in-residence St. Clair Coll., Port Huron, 1984, Elgin C.C., 1994—97; lectr. Am. Conservatory Music, Chgo., 1994—92; Fulbright lectr. Francois Mitterand Conservatory of Music, Quatre Bornes, Mauritius, 1992—93; asst. prof. violin Roosevelt U., 1993—2002; adj. asst. prof. violin Wheaton (Ill.) Coll., 1997—2000; adj. asst. prof. violin Moody Bible Inst., Chgo., 1997—2000; v.p. sales and mktg. Music Edn. Publs., Inc., Coral Springs, Fla., 1997—98. Numerous solo, recital and chamber music appearances and master classes throughout U.S., Can., France, Mauritius and China; recs. and broadcasts by Mauritian Nat. Radio and WFMT Chgo. Fine Arts Sta., PBS, Nat. Pub. Radio, and Chinese Nat. Radio and TV; numerous world premiers; recs. on New World Records and with Slavic Projection Ensemble; N.Y. recital debut at Carnegie Hall, 1998; adjudicator for state and nat. music competitions; contbr. articles and revs. to profl. jours. Vol. ARC, Literacy Vols. Am., Chgo. Pub. Librs., United Way; bd. advisors Prism Music Festival, 1984—, Am. Chamber Symphony, 1985, Symphony II, 1992-94. Fulbright grantee, 1992-93; recipient 1st prize Ann Arbor (Mich.) Symphony Competition, 1976, Soc. Am. Musicians Competition, Chgo., 1984, Internat. Concerts Atlantique Competition, N.Y.C., 1989, Chgo. Park Dist. Competition, 1991, 2nd prize Biennial Adult Artist Competition, 1992, Helmuth Fuchs Performance award 1998; selected to Arts Am. Touring Artist Roster, 1993; finalist Lilly Fellows Program in Humanities and the Arts, Valparaiso U., 1994, Harry and Sarah Zeizer Fellowship and prize; recipient Leo Sowerby medal, 1994; Christian Performing Artists' fellow. Mem. ASCAP, Am. Fedn. Musicians, Am. String Tchrs. Assn., Coll. Music Soc., Chamber Music Am., Am. Music Ctr., Music Tchrs. Nat. Assn., Christian Performing Artists' Fellowship. Avocations: powerlifting, fishing, travel, woodworking. Home: 6110 N Glenwood Ave Chicago IL 60660-1804 Office: Lyric Opera Chgo 20 N Wacker Dr Chicago IL 60606-2806 Office Phone: 312-332-2244. Personal E-mail: aw_dma@hotmail.com.

**WANG, AN-YI (ANNE) CHOU,** real estate broker; b. Taipei, Taiwan, Aug. 9, 1946; arrived in U.S., 1984; d. Chin-Yung and Fei-Ying Chou; m. An Tai Wang, Apr. 14, 1971; 1 child, Stewart Sei-Yu. BA in Journalism, Nat. Cheng Chi U., 1970. Analyst Ctrl. Daily News, Taipei, 1970; reporter China Daily News, Taipei, 1970—71, Taiwan Times, Kaohsiung, Taiwan, 1971—72; chief editor Gen. Instrument of Taiwan Ltd., Taipei, 1972—77; reporter, chief editor Broadcasting Co. of China, Taipei, 1977—84; reporter Ctrl. Daily News, San Francisco, 1984—86, Internat. Daily News, San Francisco, 1986—87; sales rep. Century 21-City Properties, San Francisco, 1987—94; broker, owner Evergreen Realty, San Francisco, 1995—. Author (short story): Heart of Women, 1984; author: (essay) Stories of Artist, 1980, Group Image of Journalists and Pub. Opinion, 1981. Mem.: San Francisco Assn. Realtors, San Mateo County Assn. Realtors, Calif. Assn. Realtors. Avocations: photography, travel, reading. Home: 2266 34th Ave San Francisco CA 94116 Office: Evergreen Realty 2124 Taraval St San Francisco CA 94116 Office Phone: 415-682-2888. Personal E-mail: evergree@pacbell.net.

**WANG, ARTHUR CHING-LI,** judge, law educator; b. Boston, Feb. 4, 1949; s. Kung Shou and Lucy (Chow) W.; m. Wendy F. Hamai, May 22, 1976 (div. 1981); m. Nancy J. Norton, Sept. 1, 1985; children: Alexander Xinglin, Sierra Xinan. BA, Franconia Coll., 1970; JD, U. Puget Sound, 1984. Bar: Wash. 1984. Printer Carmel Valley (Calif.) Outlook, 1970-73; project coord. Tacoma (Wash.) Cmty. House, 1973-76; rsch. analyst Wash. Ho. of Reps., Olympia, 1977-80, mem., 1981-94; of counsel Davies Pearson, P.C., Tacoma, 1984-94; mem. Pers. Appeals Bd., Olympia, 1994—96; chief admnstrv. law judge Wash. Office Admnstrv. Hearings, 1997—; judge Wash. Ct. Appeals, 2000—. Adj. prof. U. Puget Sound Law Sch., Tacoma, 1987, Seattle U. Law Sch., 1995—98; chmn. commerce and labor com. Wash. Ho. Reps., Olympia, 1985—88, chmn. revenue com., 1989—92, chmn. ho. capital budget com., 1993—94; chair Nat. Chinese Am. Polit. Caucus, 1994. Adv. editor U. Puget Sound Law Review, 1983-84. Vista vol. Tacoma Urban League, 1973—74; del. Dem. Nat. Conv., 1976; bd. dirs. Pierce County AIDS Found., 1999—2005, pres., 2002; bd. dirs. Planned Parenthood of Western Wash., 2001—, chair, 2005—. Named Chinese Am. Man of Yr., Seattle Chinese Post, 1991, Legislator of Yr., Wash. Health Care Assn., 1992, Alumni of Yr., U. Puget Sound Law Sch. Alumni Assn., 1993; recipient Exemplary Leadership award, Wash. State Access to Justice Bd., 1999, Profl. Excellence award, Wash. Assn. Asian Am. Profls., Seattle, 2001, State Leadership award, Wash. State Combined Fund Dr., 2003. Democrat. Avocation: birding. Home: 3319 N Union Ave Tacoma WA 98407-6043 Business E-Mail: awang@oah.wa.gov.

**WANG, BAOLIANG (BOB WANG),** applications scientist, researcher; b. Xinji, Hebei, China, Jan. 9, 1963; came to U.S., 1988; s. Yuzhuang and Shuyin (Yang) W.; m. Haiying Li, May 15, 1987; children: George, May. BS, Nankai U., 1982; PhD, U. Ill., Chgo., 1993. Lectr. Hebei Tchrs. U., 1985—88;

---

postdoctoral rschr. U. Ill., Chgo., 1993—; sr. applications scientist, applications rsch. mgr. Hinds Instrument, Inc., Hillsboro, Oreg., 1995—. Recipient 2 R&D 100 awards. Achievements include research in polarization modulation instrumentation; investigation of vibrational Zeeman effect using magnetic vibrational circular dichroism; Fourier transform infrared-vibrational circular dichroism spectroscopy; invention of a highly sensitive birefringence measurement system known as EXICOR; measurement of optical rotation. Home: 16254 NW Joscelyn St Beaverton OR 97006-7258 Office Phone: 503-690-2000. E-mail: bwang@hindsintrument.com.

**WANG, BIXIANG,** mathematician; BS, Lanzhou U., China, 1988, MS, 1991, PhD, 1994; MS, McMaster U., Can., 2003. Postdoctoral rschr. Beijing Inst. Applied Physics and Computational Math., 1994—96; asst. prof. Tsinghua U., Beijing, 1996—97; rsch. fellow U. Complutense de Madrid, 1997—98; postdoctoral rschr. Brigham Young U., Provo, Utah, 1998—99, vis. asst. prof., 1999—2000, U. Kans., Lawrence, Kans., 2003—05; asst. prof. N.Mex Inst. Mining and Tech., Socorro, N.Mex., 2005—. Contbr. over 35 articles to profl. jours. Fellow, Spanish Ministry Edn. and Sci., 1997—98; scholar, German Academic Exch. Svc., 1998, McMaster U., 2001—02, Natural Scis. and Engring. Rsch. Coun. Can., 2002—04. Mem.: Soc. Indsl. and Applied Math., Am. Math. Soc. Office: New Mexico Institute of Mining and Tech 801 Leroy Place Socorro NM 87801 Office Phone: 505-835-5787.

**WANG, CHAO-CHENG,** mathematician, engineer; b. Peoples Republic of China, July 20, 1938; came to U.S., 1961; s. N.S. and V.T. Wang; m. Sophia C.L. Wang; children: Ferdinand, Edward. BS, Nat. Taiwan U., 1959; PhD, Johns Hopkins U., 1965. Registered profl. engr., Tex. Asst. prof. Johns Hopkins U., Balt., 1966-68, assoc. prof., 1968-69; prof. Rice U., Houston, 1968-79, Noah Harding prof., 1979—, chmn. math. sci. dept., 1983-89, chmn. mech. engring. and materials sci., 1991-94. Author numerous books in field; contbr. articles to profl. jours. Named Disting. Young Scientist Md. Acad. Sci., 1968. Mem. ASME, Soc. Natural Philosophy (treas. 1985-86), Am. Acad. Mechs. Office: Rice Univ Dept Mech Engring Materials Sci Houston TX 77251

**WANG, CHAOLI,** electronics engineer; s. Jiahua Wang and Shuqing Chen. B in Engring., Fuzhou U., Fujian, China, 1998, M in Engring., 2001; student, The Ohio State U., Columbus, Ohio, 2001—. Grad. rsch. assoc. The Ohio State U., Columbus, 2002—. Visualization rsch. fellow Oak Ridge Nat. Lab., Tenn., 2004—06. Contbr. articles to profl. jours. Recipient Sci. and Tech. award, Fujian Province, 2002; fellow, The Ohio State U., 2001; scholar, Nokia, 2000; Fuguang scholarship, Fuzhou U., 1996—97, ASTRO fellowship, Oak Ridge Nat. Labs., 2005—06. Mem.: IEEE, Assn. Computing Machinery, Pi Kappa Pi, Upsilon Pi Epsilon. Achievements include research in the application of human perception in multiresolution volume visualization; development of integrated services platform for real estate information based on geographic information system. Office: The Ohio State University 395 Dreese Labs 2015 Neil Avenue Columbus OH 43210 Office Phone: 614-292-4029.

**WANG, CHARLES B.,** professional sports team executive, former computer company executive; b. Shanghai, Rep. China, Aug. 19, 1944; arrived in U.S., 1952; BS in Math., Queens Coll., 1967. Programming trainee Columbia U. Riverside Rsch. Inst., Islandia, NY; v.p. sales Std. Data Corp.; CEO Computer Assocs., Islandia, 1976—2000, chmn., 1980—2002, chmn. emeritus; owner, CEO NY Islanders, Uniondale, 1999—, Bridgeport Sound Tigers; co-owner NY Dragons (arena football). Author: Techno Vision, 1994, Techno Vision II: Every Executive's Guide to Understanding and Mastering Technology and the Internet, 1997. Founder The Smile Train; active Nat. Ctr. for Missing and Exploited Children, Make-A-Wish Found. Avocations: cooking, basketball. Address: NY Islanders Nassau Veterans Meml Coliseum 1255 Hempstead Turnpike Uniondale NY 11553*

**WANG, CHEN CHI,** electronics executive, real estate company executive, diversified financial services company executive; b. Taipei, Taiwan, Aug. 10, 1932; came to U.S., 1959, naturalized, 1970; s. Chin-Ting and Chen-Kim Wang; m. Victoria Rebisoff, Mar. 5, 1965; children: Katherine Kim, Gregory Chen, John Christopher, Michael Edward. BA in Econs., Nat. Taiwan U., 1955; BSEE, San Jose State U., 1965; MBA, U. Calif., Berkeley, 1961. With IBM Corp., San Jose, Calif., 1965-72; founder, CEO Electronics Internat. Co., Santa Clara, Calif., 1968-72, owner, gen. mgr., 1972-81; reorganized as EIC Group, 1981-2000; chmn. bd., CEO EIC Investment Corp., 1982—2004; dir. Systek Electronics Corp., Santa Clara, 1970-73; founder, sr. ptnr. Wang Enterprises (name changed to Chen Kim Enterprises 1982), Santa Clara, 1974-75, Hanson & Wang Devel. Co., Woodside, Calif., 1977-85; chmn. bd. Golden Alpha Enterprises, San Mateo, Calif., 1979-99; mng. ptnr. Woodside Acres-Las Pulgas Estate, Woodside, 1980-85; founder, sr. ptnr. DeVine & Wang, Oakland, Calif., 1977-83, Van Heal & Wang, West Village, Calif., 1981-82; founder, chmn. bd. EIC Fin. Corp. (now EIC Investment Corp.), Redwood City, Calif., 1985-90; chmn. bd. Maritek Corp., Corpus Christi, Tex., 1988-89; chmn. EIC Internat. Trade Corp., Lancaster, Calif., 1989-90, EIC Capital Corp., Redwood City, 1990-91. Mng. mem. Sixtieth West, LLC, 1997—2004, Land Investment Co. Calif., LLC, 1998—, Aceh Capital, LLC, 1998—. Author: Monetary and Banking System of Taiwan, 1955, The Small Car Market in the U.S., 1961. Served to 2d lt. Nationalist Chinese Army, 1955-56. Mem. Internat. Platform Assn., Tau Beta Pi. Mem. Christian Ch. Home: 195 Brookwood Rd Woodside CA 94062-2302 Office: ACE Group Head Office Bldg 2055-2075 Woodside Rd Redwood City CA 94061-3355 Office Phone: 650-364-3330. Business E-Mail: chenwang@acecapgroup.com.

**WANG, CHEN-KU,** retired library director; b. Peiping, China, July 18, 1924; s. Bing-fong Wang and Fong-gen Hsia; m. Shuo-fen Wang, Aug. 15, 1946; children: Pei-chi, Sheng-shiang, Sheng-Wen. MA, Peabody Coll. Tchrs., 1959; LLD (hon.), Ohio U., 1988. Prof. Nat. Taiwan Normal U., Taipei, 1960-94; dir. Nat. Ctrl. Libr., China, 1977-89, ret., 1994. Dir. Ctr. for Chinese Studies, 1977—89. Author: Selection and Acquisition of Library Materials, 1978; hon. editor Jour. Libr. and Info. Sci., 1975—. Decorated knight comdr. Silvestri, Vatican; recipient Disting. Svc. award Chinese-Am. Libr. Assn.and Libr. Assn. China, 1986, 87. Mem. Libr. Assn. China (pres. 1992-97, hon. pres. 2003-06).

**WANG, CHI HUA,** chemist, education educator; b. Beijing, Apr. 18, 1921; arrived in U.S., 1948; s. Wen Ru and Liu Shih Wang; m. Nancy Yang Wang; 1 child, Fong. BS, St. John's U., Shanghai, 1945; MS, Fu-Jen U., Peking, 1947; PhD, St. Louis U., 1951. Instr. in chemistry Brandeis U., 1953—55, asst. prof., 1955—60, assoc. prof. of chemistry, 1960—62; sr. scientist Arthur D. Little Inc., Cambridge, 1962—64; assoc. prof. in chemistry Wellesley Coll., 1964—68, dir. molecular biology program, 1966—68; assoc. prof. of chemistry U. of Mass., Boston, 1968—70, prof. of chemistry, 1971—99, prof. of chemistry emeritus, 1999—. Cons. Arthur D. Little Inc., Mass., 1964—80; vis. prof. of chemistry The Chinese Acad. of Sci., Taiwan U., Tsing-hua U., Taipei, 1966, The PhotoChemistry Inst., The Chinese Acad. of Sci., Beijing, 1980, Jilin U., 1980, Chinese Acad. of Sci., Beijing, 1983, The Chinese Acad. of Sci., Organic Chemistry Inst., Chengdu, 1985, The Grad. Sch., The Chinese Acad. of Sci., Beijing, 1987, 91, 94. Contbr. numerous articles to various jours., 1953—90; author: (book) An Intro. to the Fundamentals of Phys. Organic Chemistry, 1990. Grantee, Brandeis U., 1951—53. Avocation: Oriental art. Home: 106 Pleasant St Lexington MA 02421

**WANG, CHIA PING,** physicist, researcher; b. The Philippines; came to U.S., 1963, naturalized; (parents Chinese citizens). s. Guan Can and Tah (Lin) W. BS, U. London, 1950; MS, Brit. U. Malaya in Singapore (now U. Singapore), 1951; PhD in Physics, Brit. U. Malaya (now U. Singapore) and U. Cambridge, 1953; DSc in Physics (hon.), U. Singapore, 1972. Asst. lectr. U. Malaya, Singapore, 1951—53; prof. physics, 1956—58, head electron physics divsn., 1955—58; prof. physics, 1958—58, head electron physics divsn., 1955—58; head electron physics Lanchow (China) Atomic Project, 1958; faculty Hong Kong U., Chinese U., Hong Kong, 1958, prof. physics, 1959—63, acting head physics, math. depts., 1959; rsch. assoc. lab. nuc. studies Cornell U., Ithaca, NY, 1963—64; assoc. prof. space sci. and applied physics Cath. U. Am., Washington, 1964—68; assoc. prof. physics Case Inst. Tech., Case Western Res. U., Cleve., 1966—70; vis. scientist, vis. prof. Cavendish Lab., U. Cambridge (Eng.), Inst. Theoretical Physics, U. Louvain (Belgium), Cosmic Ray Lab., U.S. Naval Rsch. Labs. (concurrently U. Md.) MIT, 1970—75; rsch. physicist radiation lab. U.S. Army Natick (Mass.) R & D Command, 1975—, Steering com. sci. and tech. directorate U.S. Army Natick R & D Command, 1993—; steering com. nuc. physics divsn. Nankai U., Tientsin, 1956-58; vis. scientist, vis. prof. U. Cambridge (Eng.), U. Leuven, Belgium, U.S. Naval Rsch. Labs., U. Md., MIT, 1970-75. Co-author: Atomic Structure and Interactions of Ionizing Radiations with Matter in Preservation of Food by Ionizing Radiation, 1982; contbr. over 80 articles to profl. jours. Recipient Outstanding Performance award Dept. Army, 1980, Quality Increase award, 1980, Sustained Superior Performance awards, 1990, 96. Mem. AAAS, Am. Nuc. Soc., Am. Phys. Soc., Inst. Physics London (chartered physicist), N.Y. Acad. Scis., Sigma Xi. Achievements include pioneering research in nucleon sub-structure (now often referred to as parton), established quantum fluctuating 3-quark-many-qq-bar (called Ylon, later known as Valence Quarks, Sea Quarks) nuclear sub-unit structure from MIT/SLAC/CERN deep inelastic electron-neutrino-nucleon scattering experiments; multiparticle production, cosmic radiation, picosecond time to pulse-height conversion, thermal physics, power law of laser steel melting, microwaves absorption and scattering, initiating cosmic-ray extensive air shower research in China; visualizing with Otto Frisch the sinusoidal interference laser light waves in Frisch's laser interferometer. Office: US Army Natick Lab/MIT 28 Hallett Hill Rd Weston MA 02493-1753 Office Phone: 781-899-6751. Personal E-mail: chiapingwang@yahoo.com. Business E-Mail: plinmarcus@alumni.tufts.edu.

**WANG, CHUNG SHAN,** physicist; b. Fukien, China, Dec. 16, 1937; came to U.S., 1964; s. Pey-jen and I-jen (Liu) W.; m. Kaiwen K. Mao, June 2, 1969 (div. Sept. 1988); children: Alicia K., Jason K. BS, Nat. Cheng Kung U., 1962; MS, U. Idaho, 1966, PhD, 1969. Asst. prof. SUNY, Albany, 1969-77; staff scientist Systems and Applied Sci. Corp., College Park, Md., 1977-78; rsch. staff Tech. Svc. Corp., Silver Spring, Md., 1978-79; tech. staff Tex. Instruments, Inc., Suitland, Md., 1979-81; sr. physicist Vitro Corp., Rockville, Md., 1981-99, BAE Sys., Rockville, Md., 2000—03; ret., 2003. Contbr. articles to profl. jours. Mem. Am. Geophys. Union. Avocation: ballroom dancing. Home: 12 Sebastiani Blvd Gaithersburg MD 20878-4120 E-mail: chung.wang@baesystems.com.

**WANG, CHUNSHENG,** chemical engineer, educator; s. Qingzhao Wang and Xiujuan Lin; m. Yan Tian; 1 child, Yiran. PhD, Zhejiang U., China, 1995. Rsch. scientist Ctr. Electrochem. Sys. & Hydrogen Rsch. Tex. A&M U., College Station, 1999—2003; asst. prof. Ctr. Mfg. Rsch. & Dept. Chem. engring. Tenn. Technol. U., Cookeville, 2003— Asst. prof. Tenn. Technol. U., Cookeville, Tenn., 2003. Author: Journal of The Electrochemical Society (TTU Chpt. Sigma Xi Rsch. Award, 2006). Sect. chair Electrochem. Soc. Grantee, NASA, 2001-2003, Nat. Sci. Found., 2006-2007, Army Rsch. Office, 2006-2009. Mem.: Sigma Xi. Achievements include invention of NASA tech. brief, Patent Application and software Release award. Office: Tenn Tech U 115 W 10th St Cookeville TN 38505 Office Phone: 931-372-3678. Office Fax: 931-372-6345. Business E-Mail: cswang@tntech.edu.

**WANG, DAVID,** finance educator; BBA, Feng Chia U., Taiwan, 1994; MS in Bus. Adminstrn., San Francisco State U., 2000; D of Bus. Adminstrn., Golden Gate U., 2003. Adj. prof. of fin. Golden Gate U. San Francisco, Calif., 2002—04; asst. prof. of fin. Hsuan Chuang U., Hsinchu, Taiwan, 2004—, dir. of academic program devel., 2004—05. Internat. affairs com. mem. Decision Sciences Inst., 2005—; editl. adv. bd. mem. Internat. Rsch. Jour. of Fin. and Economics, 2005—, Internat. Bull. of Bus. Adminstrn., 2005—; cons. Info. Ctr. on Schools Abroad, Taipei Pub. Libr., Taiwan, 2005— Author: (journal article) Journal of Academy of Business and Economics, Vol. 5, No. 2, pp. 53-61, Journal of American Academy of Business, Cambridge, Vol. 6, No. 1, pp. 272-277 (Best Author Award, 2005), Corporate Finance Review, Vol. 9, No. 3, pp. 33-38, Journal of Academy of Business and Economics, Vol. 3, No. 1, pp. 79-86, Journal of American Academy of Business, Cambridge, Vol. 5, No. 1&2, pp. 203-209. Recipient Rsch. Award, Hsuan Chuang U., Taiwan, 2005, Tutoring Award, 2005; grantee Rsch. Grant, 2004-2005, 2005-2006, Nat. Sci. Coun., Taiwan, 2004-2005. Mem.: Taiwan Fin. Assn., Fin. Engring. Assn. of Taiwan, Internat. Assn. of Fin. Engineers, Decision Sciences Inst., Global Assn. of Risk Professionals, Assn. for Fin. Professionals, Fin. Mgmt. Assn. Internat., Am. Fin. Assn. Achievements include research in Author of several journal articles in the field of financial engineering. Office: Hsuan Chuang University 48 Hsuan Chuang Road Hsinchu 300 Taiwan Office Phone: 886-3-5302255 ext.2265. Office Fax: 886-3-5391235. E-mail: dwang@hcu.edu.tw.

**WANG, DELIANG,** computer scientist, educator; b. He County, China, Jan. 27, 1963; came to U.S., 1988; s. Shiwu Wang and Xianzheng Song; m. Ping Bai, Jan. 19, 1991 BS, Peking U., Beijing, 1983, MS, 1986; PhD, U. So. Calif., 1991. Asst. rsch. fellow Inst. Computing Tech. Academia Sinica, Beijing, 1986—87; rsch. asst. U. So. Calif., L.A., 1988—90; asst. prof. Ohio State U., Columbus, 1991—96, assoc. prof., 1997—2001, prof., 2001—. Vis. scientist Harvard U., Cambridge, 1998-99 Assoc. editor (jour.) Neurocomputing, 1995—, Neural Computing and Applications, 1996—, IEEE Trans. Neural Networks, 1998—; contbr. articles to profl. jours NSF rsch. initiation award, 1992, Office of Naval Rsch. young investigator awardee, 1996 Fellow IEEE; mem. Internat. Neural Networks Soc. (pres. 2006), IEEE Signal Processing Soc., IEEE Computational Intelligence Soc Achievements include contributions to temporal sequence learning/processing, revealing learning mechanisms in anuran visual perception and oscillatory associative memory; co-discovered mechanism of selective gating and co-originated LEGION networks; applying LEGION networks to visual and auditory scene analysis. Office: Ohio State U Dept Computer Sci and Engring 2015 Neil Ave Columbus OH 43210 Office Phone: 614-292-6827. E-mail: dwang@cse.ohio-state.edu.

**WANG, DESHENG,** cardiologist, physiologist, researcher; arrived in US, 2002; m. Wen Zheng. MD, PhD, Wuhan U., Hubei, China, 2000. Advanced from resident to chief resident Sch. Medicine, Wuhan U., 1989—95, asst. prof., 1995—2001, assoc. prof., 2001—06; rsch. assoc. Sch. Medicine, W.Va. U., Morgantown, 2002—. Recipient Lian Bang Med. awards, Sch. Medicine, Wuhan U., 1999—2000, 2d prize Sci. and Tech. Advancement award, Govt. Hubei Province, 2001, 1st prize Sci. and Tech. Advancement award, 2003. Mem.: Soc. Neurosci., Sigma Xi. Office: West Va Med Sch Medical Center Dr Morgantown WV 26505 Office Phone: 304-293-5241. Business E-Mail: dwang@hsc.wvu.edu.

**WANG, DONG,** chemist, researcher; arrived in U.S., 1999; s. LiBin Wang and ShuRong Jiang; m. Ling Gong, Dec. 26, 2001. BS, Peking U., Beijing, 1999; PhD, Rutgers U., 2004. Grad. rsch. asst. Rutgers U., Newark, 1999—2004, tchg. asst., 2001—02; post doctoral rschr. U. Houston, 2004—. Contbr. articles to profl. jours. Excallance fellowship, Rutgers U., 1999. Mem.: Am. Chem. Soc., Sigma Xi. Achievements include research in rigid-rod sensitizers for functionalization of titanium dioxide nanoparticles. Home: 10555 W Jewell Ave Bldg 13 Apt 206 Lakewood CO 80232 Office: Nat Renewable Energy Lab Mail Stop 3216 1617 Cole Blvd Golden CO 80401 Office Phone: 303-384-6796. E-mail: dong_wang@nrel.gov.

**WANG, FREDERICK MARK,** pediatrician, ophthalmologist, educator; b. NYC, Feb. 17, 1948; Student, Harvard U., 1968; MD, Yeshiva U., 1972. Diplomate Am. Bd. Ophthalmology, Am. Bd. Pediats., Nat. Bd. Med. Examiners. Intern in pediats. H.C. Moffitt-U. Calif. San Francisco Hosps., 1972-73; resident in pediats. Bronx Mcpl. Hosp. Ctr.-Albert Einstein Coll. Medicine, 1973-74; resident in ophthalmology, 1976-79; Heed fellow in ophthalmology and strabismus Children's Hosp. Nat. Med. Ctr., Washington, 1979-80; asst. prof. ophthalmology Albert Einstein Coll. Medicine, Bronx, 1980-82, asst. clin. prof., 1982-85, clin. prof., 1985-95, clin. prof., 1995—, asst. prof. pediats., 1980-82, asst. clin. prof. pediats., 1982-92; dir.

---

pediat. ophthalmology and strabismus svc. Montefiore Med. Ctr., Bronx, 1980-90. Cons. ophthalmologist Children's Evaluation & Rehab. Ctr., Rose Kennedy Ctr. for Rsch. in Mental Retardation and Human Devel., Bronx, 1980—, Craniofacial Ctr., Montefiore Med. Ctr., Bronx, 1980—; attending physician in ophthalmology Bronx Mcpl. Hosp./Montefiore Med. Ctr., 1980—; asst. attending physician in ophthalmology North Ctrl. Bronx Hosp., 1980-98; attending physician Strabismus Svc., N.Y. Eye & Ear Infirmary, N.Y.C., 1982-99, attending surgeon, 1999—; sci. reviewer Jour. Am. Acad. Ophthalmology, 1980-86; mem. profl. adv. bd. Found. for Children with Learning Disabilities, N.Y.C., 1983-89; mem. sci. adv. bd. The Glaucoma Found., N.Y.C., 1986-92; mem. profl. adv. bd. Nat. Assn. for Visually Handicapped, N.Y.C., 1988—; coord. pediat. sect. Greater N.Y. Ophthalmology Clin. Lectr. Series, 1990-93; mem. Velo-Cardio-Facial Syndrome Ednl. Found., 1994—, nominating com., 1995—. Mem. editl. bd. Jour. Pediat. Ophthalmology and Strabismus, 1998—; contbr. articles to profl. jours., chpts. to books. Referee, U.S. Soccer Fedn. Maj. med. officer USAF, 1974-76. Mem. Am. Acad. Pediats., Am. Acad. Ophthalmology, Am. Assn. for Pediat. Ophthalmology and Strabismus, N.Y. Soc. for Pediat. Ophthalmology and Strabismus (program chmn. 1987-89, pres. 1990-92), N.Y. Soc. for Clin. Ophthalmology (corr. sec. 1988-90, membership chmn. 1990-91, program chmn. 1991-92, pres. 1992-93), N.Y. Acad. Medicine (sec. sect. on ophthalmology 1993-94, sect. chmn. 1995-96), Alpha Omega Alpha. Avocations: fishing, chess, swimming, soccer refereeing. Office: Pediat Ophthalmology NY 30 E 40th St New York NY 10016-1201 Office Phone: 212-684-3980.

**WANG, GUANGSHUN,** educator; b. Yangzhou, Jiangsu, China; s. Zhengyun and Xiulan Wang; m. Xia Li; children: Shuona, Annie. PhD, Simon Fraser U., Burnaby, Canada, 1997. Asst. prof. U. Nebr. Med. Ctr., Omaha 2002—. Fellow, Fla. State U., Tallahassee, 1997—99, NIH, Bethesda, Md., 1999—2002. Office: UNMC Eppley Institute 986805 Nebraska Medical Center Omaha NE 68198-6805 Office Phone: Fax: 402-559-4651. E-mail: gwang@unmc.edu.

**WANG, GUANGYA,** ambassador, international organization official; b. Jiangsu Province, China, Apr. 1950; married; 1 child. Studied, Student Ctr. of British Coun., Wales Atlantic Untied Coll. and London Sch. Econ. and Polit. Sci., United Kindgom of Great Britain and Northern Ireland, 1972—75, John Hopkins U., 1981—82. Sect. mem., dept. of translation and interpretation Ministry of Foreign Affairs, 1975—77, third sec. and then dep. divsn. chief, dept. internat. orgns. and conf., 1983—88, counselor and then dep. dir., dept. internat. orgns. and conf., 1992—93, dir., dept. of internat. orgns. and conf., 1993—98, asst. min. foreign affairs, 1998—99, vice min. foreign affairs, 1999—2003; staff mem. to attache Chinese Mission to UN, 1977—81, attache, 1982—83, counselor, 1988—92, amb. and perm. rep, 2003—. Office: 350 East 35th St New York NY 10016 Office Phone: 212-655-6100, 212-655-6191. Office Fax: 212-634-7626, 212-481-2998.*

**WANG, GUILING,** education educator, researcher; d. Zhaoen Wang and Xiuqin Li; m. Xuefeng Cao, June 24, 1998; 1 child, Sarah Angela Cao. PhD, MIT, 2000. Rsch. assoc. Princeton U., 2000—01; asst. rsch. scientist NASA and U. Md., Greenbelt, 2001—02; asst. prof. U. Conn., Storrs, 2003—. Assoc. editor Am. Geophys. Union, Washington, 2004—. Author: (book chapter) Encyclopedia of Atmospheric Sciences, Annual Review of Environment and Resources; contbr. articles to profl. jours. Grantee, NOAA, 2003—, NASA, 2003—, 2004—, NSF, 2005—. Mem.: Am. Geophys. Union, Am. Meteorol. Soc. Achievements include discovery of the existence of multiple biosphere-atmosphere equilibrium states in climate models. Office: Univ of Conn 261 Glenbrook Rd Storrs Mansfield CT 06269-2037 Office Phone: 860-486-5648. E-mail: gwang@engr.uconn.edu.

**WANG, GWO JAW,** orthopedic surgery educator; Lillian T. Pratt prof. and chmn. orthopedic surgery U. Va. Sch. Medicine, Charlottesville, 1992—2000; pres. Kaohsiung Med. U., Taiwan, 2000—06. Recipient U. Va. Pres.'s Report award, 1992, Otto Aufranc award, Hip Soc. and Am. Acad. Orthop. Surgeons, 1992, 1997, Stinchfield award, 1986, Nicholas Andry award, 1998. Office: Kaohsiung Med Univ 100 Shih Chuan 1st Rd Kaohsiung Taiwan Office Phone: 886-7-311-7820. Office Fax: 886-7-3212062. Business E-Mail: gwojaw@cc.kmu.edu.tw.

**WANG, HANRONG,** law librarian, educator, library and information scientist; arrived in US, 1998; d. Changqing Wang and Xianhua Yang; m. Zhanen Mo; 1 child, Chuyuan Mo. BA, Huazhong Normal U., 1989; MLS, MEd, U. So. Miss., 2000. Asst. prof. Zhanjiang (China) TVU, 1989—98; asst. prof. Jacksonville (Ala.) State U., 2000—06, assoc. prof., 2006—. Contbr. articles to profl. jours. Mem.: ALA, Ala. Rsch. Libr. Assn., Ala. Libr. Assn. Achievements include research in librarianship and technology. Office: Houston Cole Library Jacksonville State University Jacksonville AL 36265 Office Phone: 256-782-5250. Business E-Mail: hwang@jsu.edu.

**WANG, HONG,** engineer, researcher; b. Qianjiang, Hubei, China, June 27, 1963; s. Chuanzhong Wang, Qiande Liu; m. Lili Yu; 1 child, Yu. B Engring., Wuhan U. of Hydraulic and Elec. Engring., Hubei, China, 1983; M Engring., Wuhan U. of Hydraulic and Elec. Engring., Hubei, China, 1986; D Engring., Wuhan U. of Hydraulic and Elec. Engring., Hubei, China, 1991; PhD, Mich. Tech. U., 2001. Lectr. Wuhan U. of Hydraulic and Elec. Engring., Hubei, China, 1986—92, assoc. prof., 1992—95; vis. scholar dept. mining and geol. engring. U. Ariz., Tucson, 1995—96; rsch. asst. dept. mech. engring.-engring.-mechanics/mining engring. Mich. Tech. U., Houghton, 1996—2001; postdoctoral rschr. dept. mech. engring. Johns Hopkins U., Balt., 2001—04; postdoctoral rschr. Oak Ridge Nat. Lab., Oak Ridge, Tenn., 2004—. Visiting Engineer Geo-Eng Australia PTY LTD, Morwell, Victoria, Australia, 1994—94; Field Engineer The 9th Hydroelectric Constructional Bureau, Qinzheng, Guizhou, China, 1990—90. Author: (journal) Acta Materialia, 2004, Wear, 2002, Journal of the Mechanics and Physics of Solids, 2002, Wear, 2001, (Ph.D. Dissertation) Mechanics of Material Removal during the Formation of Single-Grit Rotating Scratch with a Conical Tool, 2001, (journal) International Journal of Rock Mechanics and Mining Science, 1997, (book) Properties of Fissured Rock Mass and Constructional Mechanics of Tunnel System, 1993 (The First Class Award of Science and Technology Progress, Wuhan Univ. of Hydr. and Elec. Eng., 1995), Mechanics of Jointed and Fractured Rock, 1992 (The First Class Award of Science and Technology Progress, Wuhan Univ. of Hydr. and Elec. Eng., 1994), (journal) Journal of Hydraulic Engineering, 1993, (D.E. Dissertation) Statistical Fracture Mechanical Analysis and Joint Network Simulation Technique of Rocks, 1991, (journal) Sichuan Water Power, 1991 (The Third Class Award of Science and Technology Progress, The Ministry of Electric Industry, China, 1992), Site Investigation Science and Technique, 1990, Journal of Yangtze Institute of Science Research, 1990 (The Third Class Award of Science and Technology Award, The Ministry of Water Conservancy, China, 1994), Journal of Wuhan Univerity of Hydr. and Elec. Eng., 1989, Chinese Journal of Rock Mechanics, 1988, Fracture and Strength of Rock and Concrete, 1986. Mem.: ASME, Am. Ceramic Soc., Soc. Exptl. Mech., Sigma Xi. Home: 244 N Purdue Ave #101 Oak Ridge TN 37830 Office: Oak Ridge Nat Lab Metals and Cermaics Divsn PO Box 2008 Oak Ridge TN 37831 Office Phone: 865-574-5601. Office Fax: 865-574-6098. Business E-Mail: wangh@ornl.gov.

**WANG, HONG-WEI,** biologist; b. Fushun, Liaoning Province, China, Jan. 27, 1974; s. Baoxin Wang and Shuzhi Yu; m. Wennan Liu, Nov. 21, 1977. PhD, Tsinghua U., Beijing, 2001. Fellow LBNL, Berkeley, Calif., 2001—06, scientist, 2006—. Achievements include research in Cryo-electron microscopy of macromolecule complexes.

**WANG, JAW-KAI,** bioengineering educator; b. Nanjing, Jiangsu, China, Mar. 4, 1932; arrived in U.S., 1955; s. Shuling and Hsi-Ying (Lo) W.; m. Kwang Mei Chow, Sept. 7, 1957 (div. Oct. 1989); children: Angela C.C., Dora C.C., Lawrence C.Y.; m. Bichuan Li, Sept. 25, 1999. BS, Nat. Taiwan U., 1953; MS in Agrl. Engring., Mich. State U., 1956, PhD, 1958. Registered

---

profl. engr., Hawaii. Faculty agrl. engring. dept. U. Hawaii, Honolulu, 1959-93, assoc. prof., chmn. dept. agrl. engring., 1964-68, prof., chmn. dept. agrl. engring., 1968-75, prof. biosys. engring., 1994—2000, prof. molecular biosciс. dept., 2000—02; prof. emeritus U. Hawaii-Manoa, Honolulu, 2004—, dir. Aquaculture Program, 1990-96; spl. asst., Internat. Rsch. Dept., Office of Internat. Cooperation and Devel. U.S. Dept. Agr., 1988; pres. Aquaculture Tech., Inc., 1990—; academic cons. Chinese Acad. Fishery Scis., 2004—, chief sci. advisor, fishery, machinery and instrument rsch. inst., 2004—, chief tech. expert, rsch. inst. fisheries machinery and instrument, 2005—, mem. nat. open lab. for control of aquaculture water quality, 2005—. Co-dir. internat. sci. and edn. coun. USDA; vis. assoc. dir. internat. programs and studies office Nat. Assn. State Univs. and Land-Grant Colls., 1979; vis. prof. Nat. Taiwan U., 1964-65, 2000-01, U. Calif., Davis, 1980; hon. prof. coll. pharmacology Tianjing U., China, 2003; cons. U.S. Army Civilian Adminstrn., Ryukus, Okinawa, 1965, Internat. Rice Rsch. Inst., Philippines, 1971, Pacific Concrete and Rock Co. Ltd., 1974, AID, 1974, Universe Tankships, Del., 1980-81, World Bank, 1981, 82, ABA Internat., 1981-85, Internat. Found. for Agrl. Devel./World Bank, 1981, Rockefeller Found., 1980, Orizaba, Inc., 1983, Agrisys./FAO, 1983, Info. Processing Assocs., 1984, County of Maui, 1984, 85, Dept. of State, 1985, Alexander and Baldwin, 1986; mem. expert panel on agrl. mechanization FAO/UN, 1984-90; sr. fellow East-West Ctr. Food Inst., 1973-74; dir. Info. Sys. and Svcs. Internat., Inc., 1986-90; mem. bd. on agr. and natural resources The Nat. Acads., 2004—; panel mem. Vietnam Edn. Found., 2004-06; acad. cons. Chinese Acad. Fishery Scis., 2004-06; mem. bd. agrl. and natural resources Nat. Acads., 2004-06. Author: Irrigated Rice Production Systems, 1980; editor: Taro-A Review of Colocasia Esculenta and its Potentials, 1983; mem. editl. bd. Aquacultural Engring., 1982—. Recipient Exemplary State Employee award State of Hawaii, 1986, State of Hawaii Disting. Svc. award Office of Gov., 1990. Fellow Am. Soc. Agrl. Engrs. (chmn. Hawaii sect. 1962-63, chmn. grad. instrn. com. 1971-73, various coms., Engr. of Yr. 1976, Tech. Paper award 1978, Kishida Internat. award 1991), Am. Inst. Med. and Biol. Engring.; mem. NAE, Aquaculture Engring. Soc. (pres. 1994-95), Sigma Xi, Gamma Sigma Delta (pres. Hawaii chpt. 1974-75), Pi Mu Epsilon. Office: U Hawaii MBBE Dept 1955 East West Rd Honolulu HI 96822 Office Phone: 808-956-8154. Personal E-Mail: jawkai@gmail.com. Business E-Mail: jawkai@hawaii.edu. To be allowed a continuing search for truth even when you are doubting its existence, is to be blessed.

**WANG, JEFFREY C.,** surgeon; b. Mitchell, SD, July 30, 1965; s. YuSan and Linda Wang; m. Christina Jennet Lee, June 28, 1992; children: Christopher Jeffrey, Benjamin Jeffrey. BS, Stanford U., Calif., 1987; MD, U. Pitts., 1991. Chief spine surgery UCLA Comprehensive Spine Ctr., 1997—. Office: UCLA Comprehensive Spine Center 1250 16th Street Suite 745 Santa Monica CA 90404 Office Phone: 310-319-3334. Office Fax: 310-319-5055.

**WANG, JIA,** research scientist; b. Wenzhou, Zhejiang, China, Dec. 25, 1968; came to the U.S., 1990; p. KeQiang Wang and DanPing Cai. BA, Wenzhou Tchrs.' U., 1988; MS, Ft. Valley State U., 1992; PhD, UCLA, 1996. Sr. statistician Applied Mgmt. and Planning Group, L.A., 1995-97; asst. dir., sr. rsch. assoc. Ctr. for Pacific Rim Studies UCLA, 1997—2002, sr. rsch. and project dir. Ctr. for Study of Evaluation, 2003—. Cons. The World Bank, Washington, 1997—, WHO, Geneva, Switzerland, 1999-2002. 1st author: (book) Measuring Country Performance on Health: Selected Indicators for 115 Countries, 1999; contbr. articles to profl. jours. Univ. fellow UCLA, 1992-96. Mem. AAAS, Am. Ednl. Rsch. Assn., Comparative and Internat. Edn. Soc. Avocations: reading, hiking, travel. Office: Pub Works Inc 90 North Daisy Ave Pasadena CA 91107 E-mail: jiawang@ucla.edu.

**WANG, JIAN,** materials scientist, researcher; b. Weiyuan, Sichuan, China, Mar. 3, 1971; s. Fengyan Wang and Shufen Deng; m. Lingyun Zhu, Apr. 16, 1974. BS, Peking U., Beijing, China, 1992, PhD, 1998. Postdoctoral fellow U. Tex., Austin, 1999—2001; rsch. assoc. Boston U., 2001—04; scientist Nanostellar, Menlo Park, Calif., 2004—. Contbr. articles to profl. jours. Am. Chem. Soc., Jour. of Physical Chemistry, to profl jours. Co-founder Austin Peking U. Alumni Assn. Mem.: Am. Chem. Soc. Achievements include development of nanocatalyst formulation and synthesis for automobile exhaust control in a nanotechnology start up co; patents pending in field. Avocations: reading, badminton, ping pong/table tennis, classical music. Office: 3603 Haven Ave Menlo Park CA 94025 Office Phone: 650-368-1010. Business E-Mail: jwang@nanostellar.com.

**WANG, JIANLIN,** civil engineering educator; PhD, U. Minn., Mpls., 2004. Post-doctoral assoc. U. Minn., Minneapolis, 2004—05; rsch. assoc. assoc. U. Fla., Gainesville, 2005—06. Recipient Neville G.W. Cook Award, U. Minn., 2004; fellow, Third MIT Conf., 2005; Sommerfield Fellowship, U. Minn., 2000, Young Rschr. Fellowship, US Assn. Computational Mechanics, 2003. Mem.: Internat. Assn. Boundary Element Methods, Assn. Asphalt Paving Technologists, Sigma Xi. Achievements include development of a fast pavement cracking simulator and pavement design tool; a fast algorithm for modeling of composite and functionally graded materials. Office: U Fla 365 Weil Hall PO Box 116580 Gainesville FL 32611 Office Phone: 352-392-9537 ext. 1480.

**WANG, JIN,** research scientist; s. Lianru Wang and Yuliang Zhang; m. Xiaoyan Guo; 1 child, Jerry. Ph D, U. So. Calif., L.A., Calif., 1995. Scientist Ctr. for Monitoring Rsch., Arlington, Va., 1995—2000; network solution specialist Hewlett Packard Co., Reston, Va., 2000—. Contbr. articles to profl. jour. Fellow, Keck Found., 1997. Mem.: Am. Geophys. Union, IEEE. Achievements include research in artificial intelligence application in seismic network; optimum array signal processing; IP telephony monitoring and network performance management. Home: 43087 Claremorris Way South Riding VA 20152 Office: Hewlett & Packard Co 10700 Parkridge Blvd Reston VA 20191 Office Phone: 703-476-3087.

**WANG, JINLIN,** chemical engineer; b. Beijing, Apr. 12, 1957; s. Longji Wang and Enting Cai; m. Lifu Jiang, Mar. 15, 1986; children: Yuhong, John Yuming. BSE, Beijing Inst. Chem. Tech., 1982; PhD in Chem. Engring., Purdue U., 1995. Postdoctoral fellow Bisco Inc., Itasca, Ill., 1996—97; rsch. chemist Cargill Inc., Wayzata, Minn., 1997—98; sr. materials analyst Intel Corp., Chandler, Ariz., 1998—. Presenter in field. Contbr. articles to profl. jours. Mem.: The Soc. of Rheology. Achievements include research in packaging materials and processes developments for microelectronic packages, especially flip chip packaging technology; rheology and wettability of packaging materials; solder joint reliability; metrology developments. Avocations: reading, table tennis. Office: Intel Corp 5000 W Chandler Blvd Chandler AZ 85226 Business E-Mail: jinlin.wang@intel.com.

**WANG, JIONGJIONG,** neuroscientist, educator; b. Jinhai Wang and Fengxian Fu; m. Bo Peng, Dec. 22, 1998; 1 child, Eric. BS, Fu Dan U., Shanghai, 1993; PhD, U. Sci and Tech. China, Beijing, 1998. Staff scientist U. Pa., Phila., 2001—03, asst. prof., 2003—. Fellow Inst. on Aging, U. Pa., Phila., 2004—; cons. Hong Kong Rsch. Grants Coun., 2004—. Contbr. chapters to books. Fellow, Gordon Rsch. Conf., 2002; grantee, Thrasher Rsch. Fund, 2004, NIMH, 2005; scholar, Fu Dan U., 1990—93, Hongkong Dong's Found., 1997. Mem.: Cognitive Neurosci. Soc., Organ. Human Brain Mapping (Student Stipend award 1999), Soc. Magnetic Resonance in Medicine (Student Stipend award 2000—03). Achievements include patents pending for multi-contrast hemodynamic imaging using arterial spin labeling. Avocations: music, reading, sport, movie, travel. Office: Univ Pa 3 W Gates 3400 Spruce St Philadelphia PA 19104 Office Phone: 215-614-0631. Office Fax: 215-349-8260. E-mail: wangj3@mail.med.upenn.edu.

**WANG, JOHN,** not-for-profit company executive; b. Taipei, Taiwan, July 29, 1947; s. Stephen and Marcelle Wang; m. Lilly Ying, Jan. 9, 1989; children: Christina, Scott. BA, Queens Coll. N.Y.C., 1972. Urban planner developer. City Planning, N.Y.C., 1972—80; freelance writer/cons., 1980—85; exec. dir. Chinese Am. Local Devel. Corp., N.Y.C., 1985—90; pres. John Wang Assocs., N.Y.C., 1990—94, Asian Am. Bus. Devel. Ctr., N.Y.C., 1994—

Mem. N.Y. State Small Bus. Adv. Bd., 1990—93, 1995—98; del. White House Conf. on Small Bus., 1995; mem. adv. coun. Lower Manhattan Devel. Corp., N.Y.C., 2002—. Organizer Empire State Bldg. Lighting in Honor of Lunar New Year, 2000—03. Staff sgt. USAF, 1966—69. Named an Everyday Hero, Newsday, 2002; journalism fellow, Columbia U., 1980—81. Avocations: photography, fishing. Office: Asian Am Bus Devel Ctr 150 Lafayette St New York NY 10013

**WANG, JOHN CHENG HWAI,** communications engineer, researcher; b. Beijing, Feb. 12, 1934; s. Hwa Lung and Shu Shiang (Shia) W.; m. Rosa Jenny Chu, Sept. 9, 1967; children: Sophia, Maria, Nina, Amy. BS, U. Md., 1959; MS, U. Pitts., 1968. Engr. Chesapeake Instrument Corp., Shadyside, Md., 1959-64; rsch. scientist Rsch. Ctr. U.S. Steel Corp., Monroeville, Pa., 1964-67; asst. prof. Pa. State U., New Kensington, 1967-69; rsch. engr. FCC, Washington, 1969—. Cmn. working party ionospheric propogation, Internat. Telecom. Union (ITU), Geneva, 1983-. Contbr. articles to profl. jours. Fellow IEEE. Avocations: astronomy, bridge, chinese history. Office: FCC 445 12 St SW Washington DC 20554-0001 Office Phone: 202-418-2435. Business E-Mail: john.wang@fcc.gov.

**WANG, JOHN XIAOWU,** computer company executive; b. Hefei, Anhui, China, July 6, 1958; arrived in U.S. 1982; s. Zhi Dao Wang and Xian Zhen Fang; m. Lin Hu, Aug. 24, 1985; children: Fanny, Kathy, Bill. B in Physics, U. Sci. and Tech. China, Hefei, 1982; MS, NYU, 1984, PhD in Physics, 1990. Sr. engr. Micromath, Salt Lake City, 1990-92; chmn., chief engr. Poly Software Internat. Ltd., Salt Lake City, 1992-95, pres., CEO, 1995—; software engr. Pearl River, NY, 2000—. Contbr. articles to profl. jours. James Arthur fellow, NYU, 1990. Home: 7 Kerry Ct Pearl River NY 10965-3034 Business E-Mail: wang@polysoftware.com.

**WANG, JOSEPHINE L. FEN,** physician; b. Taiwan, China, Jan 2, 1948; came to U.S., 1974; d. Pao-San and Ann-Nam (Chen) Chao; m. Chang-Yang Wang, Dec. 20, 1973; children: Edward, Eileen. MD, Nat. Taiwan U., Taipei, 1974. Diplomate Am. Bd. Pediatrics, Am. Bd. Allergy and Immunology. Intern Nat. Taiwan U. Hosp., 1973-74; resident U. Ill. Hosp., Chgo., 1974-76; fellow Northwestern U. Med. Ctr., Chgo., 1976-78; instr. pediatrics, 1978—; cons. Holy Cross Hosp., Chgo., 1978—, Meth. Hosp. Ind., 1979—, St. Anthony Hosp., 1985—, Christ Hosp., 1995—. Fellow Am. Coll. Allergy; mem. AMA, Am. Acad. Allergy. Office: 9012 Connecticut Dr Merrillville IN 46410-7170 also: 4901 W 79th St Burbank IL 60459-1554

**WANG, JUI HSIN,** biochemistry educator; b. Beijing, Mar. 16, 1921; arrived in U.S., 1946; s. Lieh and Sun Li (Sun) W.; m. Yen Chan Yang, Apr. 2, 1949 (dec. 1993); children: Jane, Nancy. BS, Nat. S.W. Assoc. U., Kunming, China, 1945; PhD, Washington U., St. Louis, 1949; MA (hon.), Yale U., 1960. Postdoctoral fellow radiochemistry Washington U., 1949-51; mem. faculty Yale U., New Haven, 1951-72, prof. chemistry, 1960-62, Eugene Higgins prof. chemistry, 1962-65, Eugene Higgins prof. chemistry and molecular biophysics, 1965-72; Einstein prof. sci. SUNY, Buffalo, 1972—. Rschr. molecular structure and biochem. activity, superconductivity. Contbr. articles to profl. jours., chpts. to books. Guggenheim fellow Cambridge U., 1960-61. Fellow AAAS, Am. Acad. Arts and Scis.; mem. Am. Chem. Soc., Am. Soc. Microbiology, Yale Chemists Assn., Am. Soc. for Biochemistry and Molecular Biology, Am. Phys. Soc., Biophys. Soc., Am. Assn. Cancer Rsch., Academia Sinica, Materials Rsch. Soc., Am. Assn. Cancer Rsch., Sigma Xi. Home: 755 Renaissance Dr Apt 206 Williamsville NY 14221-8046 Office: SUNY Dept Chemistry Buffalo NY 14260-0001 Business E-Mail: juiwang@buffalo.edu.

**WANG, KAIHONG,** mechanical engineer, researcher; MS, So. Ill. U., Carbondale, 2004; PhD, Va. Tech, Blacksburg, 2004. Mfg./mech. engr. Capital Steel and Iron Inc., Beijing, 1990—98; mech. engr. AREVA NP Inc., Lynchburg, Va., 2005—. Mech. design/mfg. processes Capital Steel and Iron Inc., Beijing, 1990—98; structural analysis AREVA NP Inc., Lynchburg, Va., 2005—. Rsch. Assistantship Va. Tech, 2000—04, So. Ill. U., 1998—2000. Mem.: AIAA, ASME, Soc. for Exptl. Mechanics. Office: AREVA NP Inc 3315 Old Forest Rd OF-50 Lynchburg VA 24501 Office Phone: 434-832-4653. Office Fax: 434-832-2831.

**WANG, KIM,** commissioner, librarian; m. Harry Wang; children: Elaine, Steve, Leslie. BA in History, U. Colo.; MLS, U. Calif., Berkeley. Former libr. U. So. Calif., Hughes Aircraft; property mgr. and real estate broker. Mem. Nat. Mus. & Libr. Services. Bd., Inst. Mus. & Libr. Services, Washington, 2004—. V.p. La Terrazza Homeowners Assn.; former parks and recreation commr., planning commn. mem. City of Rancho Palos Verdes; bd. mem. Torrance Calif. Bd.; mem. Cultural Arts Commn., Torrance, Calif.; trustee Marymount Coll., Palos Verdes, Calif.; former bd. mem. Am. Heart Assn., Torrance. Mem.: AARP, AAUW (Torrance br.), LWV (Torrance br.), Am. Contract Bridge League, Torrance Sister City Assn., Torrance Hist. Soc., Torrance Hist. Assn., Torrance Chamber Toastmasters, Torrance Area C. of C. Office: Inst Mus and Libr Svcs 1100 Pennsylvania Ave NW Washington DC 20506

**WANG, LEI,** biochemist; b. China; BS in organic chemistry, Peking U., 1994, MS in physical chemistry, 1997; PhD in bioorganic chemistry, U. Calif., Berkeley, 2002. Postdoctoral rschr. biochemistry U. Calif., San Diego, 2002—. Contbr. articles to profl. jour. Named one of Top 100 Young Innovators, MIT Tech. Review, 2004; recipient Grand prize, Collegiate Inventors Competition. Nat. Inventors Hall Fame, Young Scientist prize, Amersham Biosciences, 2003; Merck fellow, Damon Runyon Cancer Rsch. Found., 2002. Office: The Salk Inst 10010 N Torrey Pines Rd La Jolla CA 92037 Business E-Mail: lewang@ucsd.edu.

**WANG, LIJUN,** chemical engineer, educator; b. Zongyang, Anhui, China, Mar. 20, 1971; m. Xiao Zhou, Apr. 21, 1977. B in Chem. Engring., Zhengzhou U., China, 1994; MS in Chem. Engring., South China U. Tech., Guangzhou, 1997; PhD in Engring., Nat. U. Ireland, Dublin, 2001. Lic. profl. chem. engr., Nebr. Bd. Engrs. and Architects, 2005, cert. energy mgr., Assn. Energy Engrs., 2006. Rsch. assoc. U. Calif., Davis, 2002; asst. prof. U. Nebr., Lincoln, 2002—06. Contbr. articles to profl. jours. Mem.: AIChE. Office: University of Nebraska-Lincoln BSE 233 L W Chase Hall East Campus Lincoln NE 68583 Office Phone: 402-472-4574. Office Fax: 402-472-6338. Personal E-mail: l_j_wang@yahoo.com. E-mail: lwang5@unl.edu.

**WANG, LU-HAI,** medical educator, biochemist; b. Tonan Jien, Yuin Lin Shien, Taiwan, Sept. 2, 1947; s. Bun-Chin Wang and Tsoo Huang; m. Mei-Hui Teng; children: Sophia F., Sandra T. PhD, U. Calif., Berkeley, 1976. Postdoctoral fellow Univ. Calif., Berkeley, 1976—77, Rockefeller U., N.Y.C., 1977—79, asst. prof., 1979—85, assoc. prof., 1985—88; assoc. prof. with tenure The Mt. Sinai Sch. Medicine, NYC, 1988—92, prof., 1992—. Study sect. mem., reviewers reserve NIH, Bethesda, Md., 1988—; sci. cons. Nat. Health Rsch. Inst., Taipei, Taiwan, 1996; hon. prof. Peking Union Med. Coll., China, 1998; rschr. of molecular oncogenesis in field; bd. mem. oncogene rsch., edn. bd. The Mt. Sinai Sch. Medicine, NYC, 1986—90. Recipient Jr. Faculty award, Am. Cancer Soc., 1979, Career Rsch. Devel. award, NIH; scholar Am. Leukemia Soc. Mem.: Soc. Chinese Biochemists in Am. (virology edn. bd. 1997—, chief edn., biotech. & biopharm divsn. 2005—05), Am. Soc. Advancement Scis., N.Y. Acad. Sci., Am. Soc. Microbiology. Office: Mount Sinai Sch Medicine Dept Microbiology 1 Gustave Levy Pl New York NY 10029 Office Phone: 212-241-3795.

**WANG, MIN,** electronics engineer; b. Qishan, Shaanxi, China, Sept. 20, 1977; arrived in U.S., 1999; s. Enquan Wang and Huanqin Li; m. Jiang-Jiang Cheng, Aug. 30, 2003. BS, Tsinghua U., Beijing, 1999; MSEE, U. Wash., 2001, PhDEE, 2004. Pre-doctal rsch. assoc. U. Wash., Seattle, 1999—2004; software engr. Intel Corp., Hillsboro, Oreg., 2003; rschr. Intel Corp. - Intel Rsch., Seattle, 2003; sr. signal integrity engr. Intel Corp., Folsom, Calif.,

2004—. Mem.: IEEE (Best Paper award 2002, 2006). Home: 4453 Lick Mill Blvd Santa Clara CA 95054 Mailing: Intel Corp 2200 Mission College Blvd MS SC12-108 Santa Clara CA 95054 Office Phone: 408-765-7127. E-mail: min.wang@intel.com.

**WANG, MINGYU,** hydrologist, environmental scientist; B in Hydrogeology, Liaoning Tech. U., China, 1982; M in Hydrogeology, China U. of Geoscis., 1988; PhD, U. Ariz. Cert. Ground Water Profl. Nat. Ground Water Assn., USA, 2002. Lectr. & rsch. hydrogeologist Liaoning Tech. U., Fuxin, Liaoning, China, 1988—95, assoc. prof., 1995—96; vis. rsch. scientist U. of Ariz., Tucson, 1996—97; sr. project scientist US EPA's Ctr. for Subsurface Modeling Support, Ada, Okla., 2000—. Contbr. articles to profl. jours. Mem. of editl. bd. Jour.: Hydrogeology and Engring. Geology, Beijing, 2002—; oversea expert reviewer Nat. Natural Sci. Found. of China (NSFC), Beijing, 2004—. Named to Hundreds of Talents list, Chinese Acad. Scis., 2005; recipient Extraordinary Ability Outstanding Scientist, US Govt., 2003, Sr. Tech. Leader, Shaw Environ., Inc., 2004, Pres. award for Excellence, ManTech Environ. Tech., Inc, 2001, Nat. Outstanding Rsch. award, Chinese Govt., 1995, Excellent Grad. Student, China U. of Geoscience Beijing, 1988. Mem.: Nat. Ground Water Assn. (NGWA), Internat. Assn. of Hydrogeologists (IAH), Am. Geophys. Union. Achievements include research in Practical & Cost-Effective Discrete Fracture Fluid Flow-Equivalent Continuum Approach; Practical & Cost-Effective Discrete Fracture Network Fluid Flow Approach; Groundwater protection optimal management; Control of groundwater bursting into mines; Pumping test design in fractured rocks; integrated and systematic groundwater modeling approach. Office: EPA's Ctr Subsurface Modeling 919 Kerr Research Dr Ada OK 74820 Office Phone: 1-580-436-8656. Office Fax: 1-580-436-8718. Personal E-mail: mingyuwpan@yahoo.com. E-mail: wang.mingyu@epa.gov.

**WANG, NANCY,** pathologist, educator; b. An-Wei, China, Sept. 2, 1944; m. Tingchung Wang; children: Jessie, Melissa. BS, Nat. Taiwan U., 1966; MS, U. Minn., 1968, PhD, 1978. Diplomate Am. Bd. Med. Genetics. Instr. Dept. Pathology & Lab. Med. U. Minn., Mpls., 1978-79, asst. prof., 1980-82, Dept. Pathology, Tulane Med. Sch., 1982-83, assoc. prof., 1984-86, U. Rochester, NY, 1986-93, prof. NY, 1993—. Mem.: Am. Assn. Human Genetics. Office Phone: 585-275-6597. Business E-Mail: nancy_wang@urmc.rochester.edu.

**WANG, NING,** education educator; b. Jingzhou, China, Dec. 25, 1971; PhD, U. Chgo., 2002. Rsch. assoc. U. of Chgo. Law Sch., 2002—05; asst. prof. Ariz. State U., Tempe, 2005—. Summer Fellow, Ctr. for Advanced Study in Behavioral Sci., 2006. Office: Sch of Global Studies Ariz State Univ 675 S Myrtle Ave Tempe AZ 85287-4802 Office Phone: 480-727-0738. Office Fax: 480-727-8292. Business E-Mail: ningwang@asu.edu.

**WANG, PEILING,** information scientist, educator; d. Yongping and Junming Wang. PhD, U. Md., College Park, 1987—94. Libr., dir. AREC Info. Ctr. U. Md., 1990—95; assoc. prof. U. Tenn., Knoxville, 1995—. Contbr. articles to profl. jours. Recipient Best JASIST Paper award, Am. Soc. Info. Sci. & Tech., 1999, Outstanding Tchr. award, 2005; grantee Scholarship, Fo-Kuang Hsi lai, 1989; Rsch. & Demonstration grant, Inst. Mus. & Libr. Svcs., 2005. Mem.: ASIST (Outstanding Tchg. Info. Sci. award 2005), ALISE (Rsch. grant 2005). Office: Univ Tenn Knoxville 1345 Circle Park Dr Knoxville TN 37996 Office Fax: 865-974-4967. Business E-Mail: peilingw@utk.edu.

**WANG, PERRY C.,** chemist, researcher; s. Jingcheng Wang and Enlan Hao; m. Linda J. Jin, July 12, 1983; 1 child, Alice Y. BS, Shandong U., Jinan, China, 1981; MS, Oreg. State U., Corvallis, Oreg., 1991, PhD, 1995. Sr. scientist U.S. EPA Rsch. Lab, Ada, Okla., 1995—2000; rsch. chemist Abbott Labs., Abbott Park, Ill., 2000—. Recipient President's award, ManTech Environ. Tech, 1999. Mem.: Am. Soc. Mass Spectrometry, Am. Chem. Soc. Office Phone: 847-937-6737.

**WANG, QIGUI,** materials engineer, researcher; b. Funing, Jiangsu, China, Nov. 23, 1960; arrived in U.S., 1997, permanent resident, 1999; s. Chengchao and Yun (Guo) Wang; m. Jiaping Zhang, Mar. 3, 1961; 1 child, Weike. Bachelor in Sci. and Engring., Nanjing Inst. of Tech., Nanjing, Jiangsu, China, 1982; MSc in Sci. and Engring., SE U., Nanjing, Jiangsu, China, 1987; PhD, U. Queensland, Brisbane, Australia, 1997. Lectr. Nanjing (Jiangsu) Inst. of Tech., China, 1982—87; asst. prof. SE U., Nanjing, Jiangsu, China, 1988—92; vis. rsch. scientist Fed. U. of Rio Grande do Sol(UFRGS), Porto Alegre, Brazil, 1992—94; rsch. scholar Australian Government's Coop. Rsch. Ctr. (CAST), Brisbane, Queensland, Australia, 1994—97; postdoctoral rsch. scientist Worcester (Mass.) Poly. Inst., 1997—99; sr. rsch. engr. Aerotek, Saginaw, Mich., 1999—2000; sr. materials engr. Gen. Motors Corp, Saginaw, Mich., 2000—. Consulting engr. Metall. Machinery Plant of Jiangsu Province, Nanjing, China, 1982—87; sr. consulting engr. Nanjing (Jiangsu) Non-Ferrous Metals Corp, China, 1987—89, Nanjing Motors Corp., Nanjing, Jiangsu, China, 1989—92. Contbr. articles to profl. jours., 1997. Named for The Best Rsch. Work, The Sci. and Tech. Com. of Jiangsu Province, China, 1991; recipient OPRS Scholarship, Australian Edn. Dept., 1994-1997, CAST Rsch. Scholarship, The U. of Queensland, Australia, 1994-1997, Rsch. Fellowship, Brazilian Rsch. Coun. (CNPq), 1992-1994, Rsch. Found. of Rio Grande do Sul (FAPERGS), Brazil, 1992-1994, The Best Undergraduate Thesis award, The State Edn. Com. of China, 1982. Mem.: Am Foundrymen's Soc., Am. Soc. Materials Internat. (chpt. sec. 2001, vice chair 2002), The Minerals, Metals & Materials Soc. Achievements include Chinese patent. Avocations: coin collecting/numismatics, stamp collecting/philately, travel.

**WANG, QIN,** computer engineer, researcher; b. Lishui, Zhejiang, China, Jan. 15, 1973; d. Jixu Wang and Xuewen Chen; m. Ying Hu. PhD, Iowa State U., 1998—2001. Rsch. asst. Iowa State U., Ames, Iowa, 1998—2001; principle software engr. EMC, Hopkinton, Mass., 2001—. Contbr. articles to profl. jours. (Best Thesis Award, 1998). Recipient PACE, Iowa State U., 1998, ABD, 2001, Best Grad. award, Zhejiang Province, 1995, 1998, Best Thesis award, 1995, 1998, Siemens prize, Siemens Inc., 1996, Nari award, Chinese State Power, 1997, Outstanding Student award, Zhejiang Univ., 1991—94; scholar Grad. Coll. scholar, Iowa State U., 1998—2001, First Level Outstanding Student Scholarship, Zhejiang Univ., 1991—94. Mem.: IEEE, Soc. Women Engrs., Nat. Scholars Honor Soc., Delta Epsilon Iota, Tau Beta Pi, Sigma Xi. Personal E-mail: qwanghz@yahoo.com.

**WANG, SHEN K.,** orthopedist, surgeon; b. Nanjing, China, Sept. 5, 1922; s. Chun-Hwa Wang and Chih-Hwa Liu; m. Eleanor Chao-Chih Wang, Sept. 5, 1946; children: Cathy S., Colbert L. MD, Nat. Cent. U., Chungking, China, 1946, Harvard U., 1957. Asst. resident in orthop. surgery, Boston, 1946—57; asst. resident Children's Med. Ctr., Boston, 1957—95. Leader Cub Scout, Barrackville, W.Va., 1957—59. Home and Office: 1232 Bell Run Rd Fairmont WV 26554-1407 Office Phone: 304-363-2693. Personal E-mail: shenkwang@hotmail.com.

**WANG, SHIH-HO,** electrical engineer, educator; b. Kiangsu, China, June 29, 1944; arrived in US, 1968; BEE, Nat. Taiwan U., Taipei, 1967; MEE, U. Calif., Berkeley, 1970, PhD in Elec. Engring., 1971. Asst. prof. elec. engring. U. Colo., Colo. Springs, 1973-76, Boulder, 1976-77; asst. prof. electrical engring. U. Md., College Park, 1977-78, assoc. prof., 1978-84; prof. U. Calif., Davis, 1984—. Cons. Lawrence Livermore (Calif.) Nat. Lab., 1986-88; scientific officer Office Naval Research, Arlington, Va., 1983-84. Assoc. editor Internat. Jour. Robotics and Automation, 1986—90. Served to 2d lt. China Air Force, Taiwan, 1967-68. Mem. IEEE (hon. mention award control systems soc. 1975). Office: Univ Calif Dept Elec Computer Engring Davis CA 95616 Business E-Mail: shwang@ucdavis.edu.

**WANG, SHUNZHU,** humanities educator, researcher, translator; b. Yaancheng, China, June 21, 1957; arrived in U.S., 1992; s. Decai Wang and Jinbao Xu; m. Aiping Chen, Feb. 13, 1980; 1 child, Ying. BA in English Lang. and Lit., Suzhou U., China, 1980; MA in English Edn., Wayne State U., 1994; PhD in Comparative Lit., Purdue U., 2001. Tchr. Yancheng (China) H.S., 1980—84; lectr., program coord. Yancheng Inst. Edn., 1984—89; assoc. dir.

English dept. Nanjing (China) Coll. Comm., 1989—92; tchg. asst. Bennington (Vt.) Coll., 1999—. Referee Mosaic (acad. jours.), 2000—. Author: Contemporary Western Rhetoric, 2 vols. (in Chinese), 1998; contbr. articles to profl. jours. Mem.: MLA, Am. Coun. Tchg. Fgn. Langs., Am. Comparative Lit. Assn. Office: Bennington Coll Rte 67A Bennington VT 05201 E-mail: shunzhu@bennington.edu.

**WANG, SUSAN S.,** manufacturing executive; BA in Acctg., U. Tex.; MBA, U. Conn. CPA, Calif. With Price Waterhouse & Co., N.Y.C.; various fin. and acctg. mgmt. positions Xerox Corp., Westvaco Corp.; dir. fin. Solectron Corp., Milpitas, Calif., 1984, v.p. fin., CFO, 1986, sr. v.p., 1990—, also bd. dirs. Mem. adv. bd. YWCA, Santa Clara County; chairperson Fin. Exec. Rsch. Found. Recipient Top Women in Industry award YWCA; named one of San Francisco Bay Area's most powerful corp. women. Mem. AICPA, N.Y. State Soc. CPA, Fin. Execs. Inst. Office: Solectron Corp 777 Gibraltar Dr Milpitas CA 95035-6328

**WANG, TIANSHU,** music educator, musician; b. Shenyang, China, Feb. 12, 1969; arrived in US, 1993; d. Guan Wang and Jue Yu; m. Jian Xu, Aug. 8, 1993; children: Kevin Yilun children: David Yakun. MusB, Shanghai Conservatory Music, China, 1991; MusM, U. Ariz., 1995, D in Musical Art, 1999. Lectr. Shanghai Conservatory Music, 1991—93; vis. asst. prof. Sweet Briar (Va.) Coll., 1999—2002; asst. prof. Capital U., Columbus, Ohio; prof. of piano Shenyang (China) Conservatory of Music. Recipient Best Performance award, The Tcherepnin Soc. NY, 1989, First prize, Green Valley Piano Competition, 1993, Nat. Young Artist Piano Competition, 1995. Mem.: Coll. Music Soc., Music Tchrs. Nat. Assn., Phi Beta Delta. Home: 958 Gray Dr Pickerington OH 43147 Office: Capital Univ 1 College and Main Columbus OH 43209 Office Phone: 614-236-6410. Business E-Mail: twang@capital.edu.

**WANG, TING,** mechanical engineering educator; BSME, Tatung Inst. Tech., Taipei, Taiwan, 1977; MSME, SUNY, Buffalo, 1981; PhD in Mech. Engring., U. Minn., 1984. Dir. Energy Conversion and Conservation Ctr., U. New Orleans; prof. dept. mech. engring.; dir. gas turbine lab. Clemson (S.C.) U. Contbr. articles to profl. publs. Endowed chair Jack and Reba Matthy Energy Rsch. Fellow ASME; mem. gas turbine com., heat transfer com., biomass and alternative fuels com., George Westinghouse Silver medal 1998). Achievements include research in gas turbine application, integrated gasification combined cycle, mist/steam cooling for advanced turbine systems, heat transfer enhancement and drag reduction on micro-structured surfaces, impingement cooling on a moving surface, turbulent and transitional flows, energy conservation in residential housing. Office: Energy Conversion & Conservation Ctr Univ New Orleans New Orleans LA 70148-2220 Business E-Mail: twang@uno.edu.

**WANG, TZA-HUEI (JEFF WANG),** engineering educator; m. Yahui Peng, Apr. 25, 1998; children: Michelle, Erica. BS, Nat. Taiwan U., Taipei, 1992, MS, 1994; PhD, UCLA, 2002. Project leader Taiwan Semiconductor Mfg. Co., Hsinchu, Taiwan, 1996—98; grad. rsch. asst. UCLA, 1998—2002; asst. prof. Johns Hopkins U., Balt., 2002—. Proposal rev. panelist NIH, Bethesda, Md., NSF, Arlington, Va. Editor: Jour. Nanomedicine: Nanotechnology, Biology and Medicine; contbr. scientific papers to profl. jours. Named to U.S. del., 1st U.S.-China Nanotechnology Forum, 2004; recipient Best Paper award, World Congress Chinese Biomedical Engrs., 2002, Faculty Early Career Devel. award, NSF, 2006, Pres.'s award, Nat. Taiwan U.; grantee, Johns Hopkins U., 2003, NIH, 2003, NSF, 2004, 2006, Applied Physics Lab., 2006; St. Paul Found. scholar, 2000. Mem.: AAAS, IEEE, ASME, World Assn. Chinese Biomedical Engrs. Achievements include research in single QDs detect DNA; new nanosensor uses quantum dots to detect DNA sequences; new DNA technique; patents for method for determining standard cycle time of a stage dynamically; biosensors and methods for their use; patents pending for semiconductor quantum-dot based inorganic/organic hybrid biosensor for homogenous separation-free detection of biomolecules; first to ultrasensitive detection of DNA of specific sequences and point mutations, which often serve as biomarkers for cancer diagnostics, at the most fundamental (single-moelcule) level; use of nanocrystals (quantum dots) as biosensors for cancer diagnostics; development of highly sensitive and quantitative bioanalytical platform that enables measurements of gene expression of single cells. Office: Johns Hopkins U 108 Latrobe 3400 N Charles St Baltimore MD 21218 Office Phone: 410-516-7086. Office Fax: 410-516-7254.

**WANG, VERA,** fashion designer; b. NYC, June 27, 1949; d. Cheng Ching Wang; m. Arthur Becker, June 22, 1989; children: Cecilia, Josephine. BA in Art History, Sarah Lawrence Coll., New York, 1978. Various positions including accessories editor, European editor, sr. fashion editor Vogue mag., NYC, 1969—85; design dir. Ralph Lauren Women's Wear, NYC, 1987-89; prin. Vera Wang Bridal House Ltd., NYC, 1990—; expanded to ready-to-wear, fragrance, eyewear, footwear, fine jewelry, and a home collection. Designer for Olympic figure skaters including Nancy Kerrigan's silver medal performance at the 1994 Olympics. Costume designer (films) The Parent Trap, 1998, First Daughter, 2004; author: Vera Wang on Weddings, 2001. Recipient Womenswear Designer of the Yr., Coun. Fashion Designers Am., 2005. Achievements include first to successfully fuse high style and fashion with the tradition and symbolism of the bridal industry; designing wedding and red carpet gowns for Hollywood's elite. Office: Vera Wang Bridal House 225 W 39th St Fl 10 New York NY 10018-3103 Office Phone: 212-575-6400.

**WANG, WAYNE,** film director; b. Hong Kong, Jan. 12, 1949; arrived in U.S., 1967; m. Cora Miao. Student, Calif. Coll. Arts and Crafts. Dir., writer: A Man, a Woman, and a Killer, 1975, Blue in the Face, 1995, Chinese Box, 1997; dir., writer, prodr., editor: Chan is Missing, 1982; dir., prodr.: Dim Sum: A Little Bit of Heart, 1985; dir.: Slamdance, 1987, Dim Sum Take Out, 1988, Eat a Bowl of Tea, 1989, Life is Cheap...But Toilet Paper is Expensive, 1989, The Joy Luck Club, 1993, Smoke, 1995, Anywhere But Here, 1999, Maid in Manhattan, 2002, Because of Winn-Dixie, 2005, Last Holiday, 2006; prodr. Lanai-Loa, 1998; dir., writer, prodr. Center of the World, 2001. Office: 916 Kearny St San Francisco CA 94133 also: ICM c/o Bob Walker 40 W 57th St Fl 16 New York NY 10019-4001*

**WANG, WILLIAM KAI-SHENG,** law educator; b. NYC, Feb. 28, 1946; s. Yuan-Chao and Julia Ying-Ru (Li) W.; m. Kwan Kwan Tan, July 29, 1972; 1 child, Karen You-Chuan. BA, Amherst Coll., 1967; JD, Yale U., 1971. Bar: Calif. 1972. Asst. to ump. partner Gruss & Co., N.Y.C., 1971-72; asst. prof. law U. San Diego, 1972-74, asso. prof., 1974-77, prof., 1977-81, Hastings Coll. Law, U. Calif., San Francisco, 1981—. Vis. prof. law U. Calif., Davis, 1975—76, Hastings Coll. Law, U. Calif., 1980, UCLA, 1990, Villanova U., 1999, Bklyn. Law Sch., 2000, Leiden (Netherlands) U., 2004; cons. White Ho. Domestic Policy Staff, Washington, 1979; chair investment policy oversight group, bd. participant Law Sch. Admissions Coun.; nat. adjudicatory coun. NASD; mem. then chair com. on audit and assn. investment policy Assn. Am. Law Schs., 1995—98. Co-author: Insider Trading, 2d edit., 2005; mem. editl. bd.: Internat. and Comparative Corp. Law Jour.; contbr. articles to newspapers, mags., profl. jours. Mem. State Bar Calif., Am Law Inst. Home: 455 39th Ave San Francisco CA 94121-1507 Office: U Calif Hastings Coll Law 200 McAllister St San Francisco CA 94102-4978 Office Phone: 415-565-4666. Business E-Mail: wangw@uchastings.edu.

**WANG, WILLIAM WEIQI,** physician; b. Shanghai, China, June 3, 1962; arrived in U.S., 1989; s. Junmin Wang and Shanlai Gan. MD, Shanghai Med. U., 1985; PhD, U. Medicine and Dentistry N.J., Newark, 1995. Fellow NIMH, Bethesda, Md., 1995—96; rsch. assoc. Baylor Coll. Medicine, Houston, 1997—98; resident psychiatry Washington U., St. Louis, 1998—2002; attending psychiatrist SSM Healthcare, St. Louis, 2002—; clin. instr. St. Louis U. Med. Sch., 2003—. Bd. dir. Impact Group, LLC. Author: Psychiatry Pearls of Wisdom, 1999, Psychiatry for the Boards, 2002; contbr. articles to profl. jours. Recipient Clin. Rec. award, Shanghai Bur. Pub. Health, 1988.

Mem.: AMA, So. Med. Assn., Am. Psychiat. Assn. Avocations: fine arts, poetry, history. Office: 255 Spencer Rd Saint Peters MO 63376 Office Phone: 636-916-4144. E-mail: wwwang@rocketmail.com.

**WANG, X. T. (XIAOTIAN WANG),** psychologist, educator; b. Beijing, Oct. 10, 1957; arrived in U.S., 1987; s. Zhong Wang, Nancy Zilin Tian; m. Ying Shi, May 19, 1957; 1 child, Geng. M in Patho-physiology, Jinan U., China, 1985; MA in Physiol. Psychology, Beijing Med. U., 1991; PhD, N.Mex. State U., 1993. Lectr. Jinan U. Med. Sch., Guangzhou, Guangdong, China, 1986—87; grad. asst. N.Mex. State U., 1987—93; asst. prof. U. SD, Vermillion, 1993—98, assoc. prof., 1998—2003, prof., 2003—. Vis. scientist Max Planck Inst., Berlin, 1998—99, 2004; vis. prof. Hong Kong U. Sci. and Tech. Sch. Bus. and Mgmt., Hong Kong, 2000—01, Peking U., Beijing, 2004—06. Mem. editl. bd.: Jour. Behavioral Decision Making, 2002—, guest editor: Jour. Bioeconomics, 2001—02; expert cons. Chinese Natural Sci. Found., Psychologica Sinica, 2005—; contbr. chapters to books, 18 articles to profl. jours. Grantee, NSF, 1999—2003, James McDonnell Found., 2000; scholar Nat. Grad. scholar, Dept. Edn. China, 1982. Mem.: Human Behavior and Evolution Soc. (Young Investigator award 1992), Soc. for Judgement and Decision Making, Psychonomic Soc., Acad. Mgmt., Behavioral and Brain Scis. (assoc.). Home: 849 Valley View Dr Vermillion SD 57069 Office: Univ SD 414 East Clark St Vermillion SD 57069 Office Phone: 605-677-5183. Business E-Mail: xtwang@usd.edu.

**WANG, XING,** power systems engineer; b. Haerbin, Heilongjiang, China, June 25, 1970; arrived in U.S., 2001; s. Shaohu Wang and Jianshan Mao; m. Ying Xiao. PhD, Bruncl U., London, 2001. Power systems engr., rschr. Electric Power Rsch. Inst., Beijing, 1991—96, team leader energy mgmt. sys., 1997—98; power systems engr. Alstom Esca Corp., Bellevue, 2001—. Recipient China Nat. award sci. and tech., 1997. Mem.: IEEE Power Engring. Soc. (sr.). Office: Alstom Esca Corp 11120 NE 33rd Pl Bellevue WA 98004 Home: 17305 NE 18th Pl Bellevue WA 98008-3140 Personal E-mail: xingwang@yahoo.com. Business E-Mail: xing.wang@tde.alstom.com.

**WANG, XINSHING,** lawyer; b. Da Tong, Shan Xi, China, May 20, 1975; arrived in US, 1997; d. Zhifang Wang and Fumei Zhang; m. Jiachen Tian, Jan. 9, 1999; 1 child, Caleb Y. Tian. BS, Peking U., Beijing, China, 1997; MS, U. Kans., Lawrence, 1999, JD, 2002. Rsch. asst. Higuchi Biosci. Ctr., Lawrence, 1997—99; pateht atty. Lathrop & Gage, LC, Kansas City, Mo., 2002—05, NYC, 2005—. Corp. gen. counsel, dir. Christian Worldwide Worship Ministries, Omaha, 2002—05. Active Lawrence Chinese Evang. Ch., 2002—05. Mem.: ABA, US-China Lawyers Soc. (bd. dirs. 2005—06). Avocations: fishing, tai chi. Office: Ste 1847 230 Park Ave New York NY 10169

**WANG, XIUYING,** agricultural engineer, researcher; d. Shangyi Wang and Hu Cheng; m. Chengwen Chen, Nov. 29, 1972; 1 child, Emma Chen. PhD, Purdue U., 2004. Post doctoral rsch. assoc. Blackland Rsch. and Ext. Ctr., Temple, Tex., 2004—06, rsch. asst. prof., 2006—. Contbr. articles to profl. jours. Home: 1617 Canyon Creek Dr Apt#133 Temple TX 76502 Office: Blackland Rsch and Extension Ctr 808 E Blackland Rd Temple TX 76502 Office Phone: 254-774-6105. Office Fax: 254-770-6561. Business E-Mail: swang@brc.tamus.edu.

**WANG, XUDONG,** network architect, researcher; PhD, Ga. Inst. Tech., 2003. Rschr. Shanghai Jiao Tong U., Shanghai, 1993—97; rsch. asst. Ga. Inst. Tech., Atlanta, 1998—2003; sr. rschr. Kiyon, Inc., Ja Lolla, Calif., 2003—05, network arch. and r&d leader, 2005—. Tech. reviwer Maj. IEEE Journals on Comm. and Networking, 2002—. Editor: Elsevier Jour. Ad Hoc Networks; guest editor: IEEE Wireless Comm. Jour. Ad Hoc Networks. Recipient Shanghai Sceience and Tech. Progress award, Shanghai Mcpl. Govt., 1997. Mem.: ACM, IEEE. Achievements include research in multi-channel TDMA MAC for wireless mesh networks; patents pending for single-channel TDMA MAC for Wi-Fi wireless mesh networks; scalable MAC with Layer-2 Routing for UWB wireless mesh networks; multichannel TDMA wireless communications; invention of mesh routers with Multi-channel MAC; first to develop TDMA MAC over IEEE 802.11 for wireless mesh networking; study wireless mesh networks. Office: 4225 Executive Sq Ste 290 La Jolla CA 92037 Office Phone: 858-453-3491.

**WANG, YANBIN,** physicist, researcher; s. Wenzhang Wang and Zhenying Liu; m. Mei Wang; children: Vania Wen, Erik Feng. PhD, SUNY, Stony Brook, 1991. Asst. rsch. prof. Ctr. High Pressure Rsch., Stony Brook, 1994—96; beamline scientist Ctr. Advanced Radiation Sources, Chgo., 1996—2000, sr. rsch. assoc., 2001—. Editor: Center for Advanced Radiation Sources 5460 S Ellis Ave Chicago IL 60637 Office Phone: 630-252-0425. Office Fax: 630-252-0436. Business E-Mail: wang@cars.uchicago.edu.

**WANG,** cardiologist, educator, medical researcher; b. Tangshan, China, May 12, 1923; arrived in U.S.; 1949; s. Yu-Shen and Jun-Rong (Bo) Wang; m. Helen S. Huang; children: Dale, Cynthia, Jennifer, Heather. MB, Nat. Shanghai Med. Coll., 1948; MD, Harvard U., 1952. Diplomate Am. Bd. Internal Medicine, cert. cardiovasc. diseases. Intern, resident Mass. Gen. Hosp., Boston, 1952—57, fellow in cardiology, 1957—58; fellow in cardiovasc. physiology Mayo Found., Rochester, Minn., 1958—59; dir. cardiac catherization lab., program dir. cardiovasc. fellowship tng. U. Minn. Hosp., 1959—86; from instr. to prof. cardiology U. Minn. Med. Sch., Mpls., 1959—93, prof. emeritus, 1993—. Contbr. chapters to books, articles to profl. jours. Bd. dirs. Minn. Mus. Art, St. Paul, 1984—90, MacPhail Music Ctr., 2002—05; bd. dirs. China Ctr. U. Minn.; session elder House of Hope, Presbyn. Ch., St. Paul. Capt. MC USAF, 1954—56. Recipient Lifetime Educator award, U. Minn. Med. Sch. Cardiology, 1999. Fellow: AAAS, ACP, Am. Heart Assn. (pres., bd. dirs. Minn. chpt. 1973-74, com., Internat. program com., Gt. Plains com., Lifetime Achievement award 2004), Am. Coll. Cardiology; mem.: Am. Fedn. Clin. Rsch., Assn. Univ. Cardiologists, Alpha Omega Alpha. Achievements include development of rate-pressure product as an index of cardiac work and coronary blood flow; research in cardiovascular response to exercise in normal subjects and in heart disease; in vivo assessment of cardiac valve protheses; treatment of adult congenital heart disease and of coronary disease in diabetes mellitus. Office: FUMC MMC 508 420 Delaware St SE Minneapolis MN 55455-0374 Office Phone: 612-625-5949. Business E-Mail: wangx002@umn.edu.

**WANG, YING,** chemistry and physical science researcher; b. ZiYang, Sichuan, China, Jan. 7, 1966; arrived in U.S., 2001; d. Jinlan Xiong; m. Chengyong Wang, Jan. 15, 1990; children: Jiayu, Joshua. Degree in chemistry, S.W. Normal U., Chongqing, China, 1987; PhD, Hunan U., 1997. Tchr. S.W. Normal U., 1990—94, prof., 1997—98; rschr. Hunan U., Changsha, 1994—97, Swiss Fed. Inst. Environ. Sci. and Tech., Kastaniebaum, 1998—99, Weizmann Inst. Sci., Rehovot, Israel, 1999—2001, Wayne State U., Detroit, 2001—04, U. Mich., Ann Arbor, 2004—. Recipient Disting. Post-doctoral award, Weizmann Inst. Sci., 1999—2001; Wilhelm-Simon scholar, Ctr. for Excellence in Analytical Chemistry ETH, 1998. Mem.: Material Rsch. Soc., Am. Chem. Soc., Sigma Xi. Achievements include design of fluorescence image and label polymer; optical fiber and chemical sensors. Personal E-mail: ying05wang@yahoo.com.

**WANG, YINMIN,** materials scientist, educator; s. Zhenhua Wang and Aixiang Sheng. BS, Nat. U. of Def. Tech., China, 1987; MS in Materials, Shanghai Jiao Tong U., China, 1994, Johns Hopkins U., Balt., 1999, MS in Computers, 2003, PhD in Materials, 2003. Harold Graboske fellow Lawrence Livermore Nat. Lab., Livermore, Calif., 2004—06, staff scientist, 2006—. Reviewer panel Singapore Sci. and Engring. Rsch. Coun., Singapore, 2004—; reviewer various jours. Contbr. articles to profl. jours. Recipient CMS Excellence in Publ. awards, Lawrence Livermore Nat. Lab., 2005—06, MRS medal, Materials Rsch. Soc., 2002; Disting. Harold Graboske fellow, Lawrence Livermore Nat. Lab., 2004—05. Mem.: TMS (assoc.), Materials Rsch. Soc. (assoc.). Achievements include discovery of discovery of using bimodal nanostructure to achieve high strength and high ductility in nano-structured materials; patents pending for high strength and high performance nanostructured materials and the method of making the same; research in finding of superplastic behavior in carbon nanotubes; ultrahigh strength nanostructured materials under shock loading; fast mass transport in sub-2nm carbon nanotube pores.

**WANG, YOUCHENG,** information technology educator; PhD, U. Ill. Rsch. asst., project mgr. U. Ill., Urbana-Champaign, 1999—2003; prof. info. tech. and tourism U. Ctrl. Fla., Orlando, 2003—. Cons. U. Ctrl. Fla., Orlando, 2003—06. Author: (book) Advanced English for Science and Technology, The Kaleidoscope of the American Society.; editor: (guest editor) International Jour. of Hospitality Management. Grantee, Elkhart County Conv. and Visitors Bur., 2003, Assn. Travel Mktg. Executives, 2006, Visit Fla., 2006; scholar, U. Purdue, 1997-1999, U. Ill., 1999-2003. Mem.: Internat. Soc. Travel and Tourism Educators, Hospitality Info. Tech. Assn., Hospitality Fin. and Tech. Profls., Internat. Coun. on Hotel, Restaurant, and Instl. Edn., Travel and Tourism Rsch. Assn.

**WANG, YUCONG,** engineering executive; s. Hezhang and Lingmei Wang; m. Lin Cao, July 4, 1987; children: Linda J., Daniel J. BS, Shanghai Jiaotong U., 1982, MS, 1984; PhD, Mich. Tech., 1990; MBA, Ctrl. Mich. U., 2000. Faculty Shanghai Jiaotong U., 1984—87; sr. engr. advanced mfg. engring. GM Powertrain, Saginaw, Mich., 1990—96, staff engr. materials engring., 1996—99; prin. engr. leader Surface Engring. and Tribology Ctr., GM, Pontiac, Mich., 1999—2006, program mgr. China tech. mgmt., 1999—; pres. Detroit Chinese Engrs. Assn., Detroit, 2005—. Adj. prof. engring. Oakland U., Mich.; guest prof. Shanghai Jiaotong U. Author over 60 articles to tech. publs. Vice chmn. Tri-City Am. Chinese Assn., Saginaw, Mich., 1992—93. Recipient Appreciation award, U.S. Dept. of Energy, 2002, Herman H. Doehler award, N.Am. Diecasting Assn., 2005, Asian Am. Engr. of Yr. award, Chinese Inst. of Engrs., USA, 2005. Fellow: ASM Internat. (Saginaw Valley chpt. vice-chmn. 1998—99, chmn. 1999—2000, 5-Star chpt. award 2000); mem.: Am. Soc. Materials, Nat. Soc. of Collegiate Scholars (life), Beta Gamma Sigma (life). Achievements include invention of 35 Patents In Automotive Engineering, Materials Engineering, Surface Engineering and Tribology Areas. Office: GM Corp 895 Joslyn Ave Pontiac MI 48340 Office Phone: 248-857-2073. Business E-Mail: yucong.wang@gm.com.

**WANG, YUFENG,** science educator; arrived in U.S., 1995; d. Qiancai Wang and Jinzhu Chen. BS in Genetics, Fudan U., Shanghai, China, 1993; MS in Stats. and Genetics, Iowa State U., 1998, PhD in Bioinformatics and Computational Biology, 2001. Grad. asst. Iowa State U., Ames, 1995—2001; rsch. scientist Am. Type Culture Collection, Manassas, Va., 2001—03; asst. prof. U. of Tex., San Antonio, 2003—. Author to profl. jours. albums. Fellow James Cornette Rsch. fellowship, Iowa State U., 2001. Mem.: Am. Statis. Assn., Internat. Soc. Computational Biology, Genetics Soc. Am. Achievements include research in functional divergence and age distribution of human gene families, computational approach in drug discovery, evolutionary and population genetics of infectious diseases. Office: University of Texas San Antonio Dept of Biology 6900 N Loop 1604 West San Antonio TX 78249 Home: 12222 Vance Jackson Rd Apt 1538 San Antonio TX 78230-5947 Office Phone: 210-458-6492. Business E-Mail: ywang@utsa.edu.

**WANG, YUHANG,** science educator; b. Xian, China, Nov. 3, 1968; s. Zhizhong Wang and Helan Cheng; m. Yiqun Bai; children: Clara, Ella. PhD, Harvard U., Cambridge, Mass., 1997. Rsch. faculty II Ga. Inst. Tech., Atlanta, 1997—99, assoc. prof., 2002—; asst. prof. Rutgers U., New Brunswick, NJ, 2000—02. Mem.: Am. Meteorol. Soc., Am. Geophys. Union. Office: Ga Inst Tech 311 Ferst Dr Atlanta GA 30332-0340 Office Phone: 404-894-3995. Office Fax: 404-894-5638. E-mail: yuhang.wang@eas.gatch.edu.

**WANG, YU-PING,** computer science educator, engineering educator; arrived in US, 1996, permanent resident, 2003; s. Jinxuan Wang and Aiqing Zhao; m. Ping Xie; children: Aubrey, Macie. PhD, Xi'an Jiaotong U., China, 1996—96. Sr. rsch. engr. Perceptive Sci. Instrument Inc., League City, Tex., 2000—01, Advanced Digital Imaging Rsch., LLC, League City, 2001—03; asst. prof. computer sci. and elec. engring. U. Mo., Kansas City, 2003—. Contbr. articles to profl. jours. Rsch. grantee, U. Mo. Mem.: IEEE (mem. machine learning for signal processing tech. com. 2006—). Achievements include research in image processing and biimaging analysis. Office: U Mo 5100 Rockhill Rd Kansas City MO 64110 Office Phone: 816-235-5223. Office Fax: 816-235-5159. Business E-Mail: wangyup@umkc.edu.

**WANG, ZHI,** biomedical researcher; b. Lanchou City, Ganshu, China, June 2, 1950; m. Xia Zhang, June 24, 1953; 1 child, Ruibing. MD, Xi'an Sch. Medicine, 1981. Action dir., asst. prof. Tufts U. Sch. Medicine, Boston, 1999—2000; dir., prof. Boston U. Sch. Medicine, 2001—. Recipient Assn. Rsch. award, Am. Laryngol. Assn., 1994; grantee, NIH, 2001. Fellow: Am. Acad. Otolaryngology Head and Neck Surgery. Achievements include research in less side-effects in cancer treatment/surgery. Office: Boston Univ Sch Medicine 88 E Newton St D616 Boston MA 02118 Home: 9 Hialeah Lane Framingham MA 01701 Office Phone: 617-414-1590. Personal E-mail: zhiw@hotmail.com. Business E-Mail: zwang@bu.edu.

**WANGARD, GREGG,** chef; b. Wis. m. Kelly Wangard. Studied, Wauesha Tech. Coll., Wis. Apprentice Am. Culinary Fedn.; intern Rosewood Caneel Bay Resort, St. John, US Virgin Islands; chef de cuisine Caroina Restaurant, Kohler, Wis., The Immigrant Room & Winery Bar, The Am. Club; head, culinary ops. Ocean and Vine Restaurant, Loews Santa Monica Hotel, 2004—. Named one of LA's Rising Stars, StarChefs.com, 2006. Avocations: bicyeling, bunketball, tennis, Green Bay Packers. Office: Ocean and Vine at the Loews Santa Monica Hotel 1700 Ocean Ave Santa Monica CA 90401 Office Phone: 310-458-6700.*

**WANG-BIRNBAUM, RUTH DEBORAH,** secondary school educator, director; b. N.Y.C., July 4, 1961; d. Leonard and Sabine Wang; m. Stuart C. Birnbaum, July 31, 1988. BA, Bklyn. Coll., 1982, MA, 1985; postgrad., NYU, 1985. Cert. secondary edn. tchr. N.Y. Dept. Edn., supr. and adminstrn. N.Y. State Dept. Edn., 2002. Tchr., advisor Shulamith HS, Bklyn., 1982—2004; asst. prin. Ma'ayanot Yeshiva H.S., Teaneck, NJ, 2004—. Mem.: Nat. Coun. Tchrs. English. Democrat. Avocations: reading, swimming, cooking, skiing. Personal E-mail: rdwbirnbaum@hotmail.com.

**WANGENSTEEN, STEPHEN LIGHTNER,** surgery educator; b. Mpls., Aug. 30, 1933; s. Owen Harding and Sarah (Davidson) W.; m. Lita Laura Lindley, Sept. 12, 1935; children: Christine, Stephen, Philip, William. BA, BS, U. Minn., 1955; MD, Harvard U., 1958. Diplomate Am. Bd. Surgery. Resident surgeon Columbia-Presbyn. Hosp., N.Y.C., 1958-65; asst. prof./assoc. prof. surgery U. Va., Charlottesville, 1967-72, prof. surgery U. South Fla., Tampa, 1987—. Dep. chmn. dept. surgery, 1989-90. Contbr. articles to profl. jours. Fellow ACS; mem. Am. Surg. Assn., So. Surg. Assn., University Surgeons, Halsted Soc., Field Club (Sarasota, Fla.). Avocations: boating, horses, cooking, gardening. Home: 82 Red Bank Rd Rembert SC 29128-9635 Personal E-mail: stephen@hunterhorse.com.

**WANGER, EUGENE GILKISON,** retired lawyer; b. Chgo., May 16, 1933; s. Eugene Miles and Roka Gilkison Wanger; m. Marilyn Rose Morris, July 14, 1962. AB cum laude, Amherst Coll., Mass., 1955; JD, U. Mich., Ann Arbor, 1958. Bar: Mich. 1958, U.S. Supreme Ct. 1968. Assoc. Fraser, Trebilcock, Davis & Foster, Lansing, Mich., 1958—61, Snyder Loomis & Ewert, Lansing, 1962—65; city atty. Lansing, 1965—67; prin. Wanger Law Offices, Lansing, 1968—95. Author: Michigan Constitutional Death Penalty Ban; contbr. articles to profl. jours. Del. Ingham County Hist. Commn., 1971—81, Mich Constl. Conv., 1961—62; nat. bd. dirs. Am. Truck Hist. Soc., 1987—2002; mem. Ingham County Bd. Commrs., Mich., 1965—73, chmn. 1972; pres. Ingham County Hist. Commn., 1977—78; co-chmn. Mich. Com. Against Capital Punishment, 1972—. Recipient Legacy of Life award, Ctrl.

United Meth., Detroit, 2000, conf. rm. in state office bldg. named in his honor, 2001. Mem.: ABA (mem. death penalty com. sect. on individual rights and responsibilities), State Bar Mich. (past vice chmn. com. constl. law, Champion of Justice award 2005), Am. Judicature Soc., Hist. Soc. Mich. (life), Mich. Supreme Ct. Hist. Soc. (life), Mich. Bar Found. (life). Republican. Congregational. Avocations: magic, collecting books.

**WANGLER, WILLIAM CLARENCE,** retired insurance company executive; b. Buffalo, Dec. 7, 1929; s. Emil A. and Viola M. (Roesser) W.; m. Carol B. Sullivan, Aug. 17, 1957; children: Jeffrey W., Eric J. BS, SUNY, Cortland, 1951. Claims adjuster Liberty Mut. Ins. Co., Buffalo, 1954-60, claims supr. Miami, Fla., 1960-65, home office examiner Boston, 1965-68, asst. claims mgr. Cleve., 1968-69, claims mgr. Cleve, 1969-73, div. claims service mgr. Pitts., 1973-79, div. claims mgr., 1979-86, v.p. asst. gen. claims mgr. adminstrn. Boston, 1986-94, ret., 1994. Pres. Claims Mgrs. Counsel, Cleve., 1970; chmn. Nationwide Intercompany Arbitration, Cleve., 1969-70. Loaned exec. Mass. Bay United Way, Boston, 1964; account exec. Pitts. United Way, 1985-86. Served to capt. USMC, 1951-54. Republican. Roman Catholic. Home: 64 Trout Farm Ln Duxbury MA 02332-4609 E-mail: vcwangler@webtv.net.

**WANGSGARD, CHRIS PRINCE,** lawyer; b. Ogden, Utah, July 16, 1941; s. Scott Maughn and Elizabeth (Prince) W.; m. Erica Gwilliam, June 25, 1979; children: Kirk, Sten, Dane. BS, U.S. Military Acad., 1963; JD, U. Utah, 1972. Bar: Utah 1972, U.S. Dist. Ct. (Utah) 1972, U.S. Ct. Appeals (10th cir.) 1972. Commd. 2d lt. U.S. Army, 1963, advanced through grades to capt., resigned, 1969; atty. Van Cott, Bagley, Cornwall & McCarthy, Salt Lake City, 1972-91, ptnr., 1977-91, Parsons Behle & Latimer, Salt Lake City, 1991—. Adj. prof. Coll. of Law U. of Utah, 1983-87. Mem. Am. Inns of Ct. (Master of the Bench). Office: Parsons Behle & Latimer 201 S Main St Ste 1800 Salt Lake City UT 84111-2218 Office Phone: 801-536-6782. Business E-Mail: cwangsgard@pblwest.com.

**WANI, MANSUKHLAL CHHAGANLAL,** chemist; b. Nandurbar, Maharastra, India, Feb. 20, 1925; came to U.S., 1958, naturalized, 1977; s. Chhagnalal Kikabhai and Maniben Chhaganlal (Shah) W.; m. Ramila Mansukhlal Dalal, Dec. 4, 1954; 1 child, Bankim M. BS with honors, St. Xavier's Coll., Bombay U., 1947, MS, 1950; PhD, Ind. U., 1962. Lectr. chemistry Bhavan's Coll., Bombay, 1951-58; rsch. asst. Ind. U., Bloomington, 1958-61; rsch. assoc. U. Wis., Madison, 1961-62; prin. scientist Rsch. Triangle Inst., Rsch. Triangle Park, NC, 1962—. Inventor anticancer drugs. Recipient B.F. Cain Meml. award Am. Assn. Cancer Rsch., 1994, City of Medicine award Durham, N.C., 1994, Award of Recognition Nat. Cancer Inst., 1996, Charles E. Kettering prize GM Cancer Rsch. Found., 2000, Ranbaxy Rsch. award. Mem. AAAS, Am. Chem. Soc., Am. Soc. Pharmacognosy, N.Y. Acad. Scis., India Assn. (pres. 1970-72), Hindu Soc. (dir. 1976-81), Assn. Indians in Am., Indo-Am. Forum, Sigma Xi, Phi Lambda Upsilon. Democrat. Avocations: reading, travel, sports. Home: 2801 Legion Ave Durham NC 27707-1921 Office: Rsch Triangle Inst 3040 W Cornwallis Rd Research Triangle Park NC 27709-2194 Office Phone: 919-541-6685. Business E-Mail: MCW@rti.org.

**WANK, GERALD SIDNEY,** periodontist, educator; b. Bklyn., Jan. 20, 1925; s. Joseph and Sadie (Ikowitz) W.; m. Gloria Baum, June 4, 1949; children: David, Stephen, Daniel. BA, NYU, 1945, DDS, 1949; cert. in orthodontia, Columbia U., 1951, cert. in periodontia, 1956. Intern Bellevue Hosp., 1949-50; pvt. practice N.Y.C., Great Neck, N.Y., 1949—; instr. dept. periodontia, oral medicine NYU Dental Sch., 1956-63, asst. clin. prof. dept. periodontia, 1963-67, asst. prof. periodontia, oral medicine, former postgrad. dir. periodontal-prosthesis dept. fixed partial prosthesis, 1970—, clin. assoc. prof. periodontia and oral medicine, 1970-77, clin. prof. dept. periodontia and implantology, 1977—, postgrad. dir. periodontia, 1968-71, Disting. prof. periodontics, 2002; lectr. periodontology Harvard U. Sch. Dental Medicine, 1971—74; vis. lectr. N.Y.C. C.C. Sch. Dental Hygiene, 1960-65, Albert Einstein Coll. Medicine, 1967-96; sr. attending staff North Shore U. Hosp., 1974-77, sr. asst. attending divsn. surgery, 1977—. Cons. orthodontic panel N.Y. State, N.Y.C. depts. health, 1953-80; cons. periodontal prosthesis, Goldwater Meml. Hosp., N.Y.C.; former postgrad. instr. 1st Dist. Dental Soc. Postgrad. Sch., dist. claims com.; lectr. in field; mem. admissions N.Y. U. Coll. Dentistry, 1975-86, chmn. fund raising, 1976-77; cons. N.Y. VA Hosp., 1996—. Contbr. to: Practice of Periodontia, 1960, Dental Clinics of North America, 1972, 81, Manual of Clinical Periodontics, 1973; contbr. articles to profl. jours. Capt. USAF, 1953-55. Recipient Alumni Meritorious Service award NYU, 1981, Coll. Dentistry Alumni Achievement award NYU, 1983, Disting. Prof. Periodontics award NYU Coll. Dentistry, 2002, named to Leaders in Am. Sci., 1963-64. Fellow APHA, Acad. Gen. Dentistry, N.Y. Acad. Dentistry (life), Internat. Coll. Dentistry (life), Am. Coll. Dentistry (life), Am. Acad. Oral Medicine (pres. N.Y. sect. 1971-72); mem. N.Y. Coll. Dentists (dir.), ADA, Dental Soc. N.Y.C. (dir. 1st dist., chmn. ethics com. 1985-86, peer rev. com.), Fedn. Dentaire Internat., Am. Assn. Dental Schs., N.Y. State Pub. Health Assn., AAUP, Pan Am. Med. Assn. (life), AAAS, ADA, Am. Acad. Periodontology, Sci. Rsch. Soc. Am., Northeastern Soc. Periodontia (life), Am. Acad. Dental Medicine, Acad. Gen. Dentistry, Internat. Acad. Orthodontia, Am. Assn. Endodontists (life), Am. Acad. Periodontia (life), Am. Acad. Oral Medicine (life), NYU Coll. Dentistry Alumni Assn. (dir., sec. 1973-74, v.p. 1974-75, pres. 1976-77), Am. Assn. Endodontists, NYU Coll. Dentistry Dental Assocs. (charter), Acad. Oral Rehab. (hon.), First Dist. Dental Soc. (program chmn. 1984, chmn. continuing edn. 1983, sec., 1985, v.p. Eastern Dental Soc. br. 1986, pres.-elect 1987, pres. br. 1988, bd. dirs. 1989—, Meritorious Svc. award 1997), NY County Dental Soc. (peer rev. com.), Am. Acad. Osseointegration (life), NYU Gallatin Assocs., Alumni Fedn. NYU (dir. 1976-81), N.Y. County Dental Soc. (Dist. Claims Com.), Soc. of the Torch, Masons, Century Club, NYU Club, Fresh Meadow Country Club, Omicron Kappa Upsilon (life), Alpha Omega. Jewish. Home and Office: 40 Bayview Ave Great Neck NY 11021-2819 Office: 30 E 40th St New York NY 10016-1201 Personal E-mail: g.wank@aol.com.

**WANKAT, PHILLIP CHARLES,** chemical engineering educator; b. Oak Park, Ill., July 11, 1944; s. Charles and Grace Wankat; m. Dorothy Nel Richardson, Dec. 13, 1980; children: Charles, Jennifer. BS in Chem. Engring., Purdue U., 1966, MS in Edn., 1982; PhD, Princeton U., 1970. From asst. prof. to C.L. Lovell disting. prof. chem. engring Purdue U., West Lafayette, Ind., 1970—, head freshman engring. 1987-95, interim dir. continuing engring. edn., 1996, head interdisciplinary program, 2000—04. Cons. pharm. firm, 1985-94. Author: Large Scale Ads and Chromatog, 1986, Equil Staged Separations, 1988, Rate Controlled Separations, 1990, Teaching Engineering, 1993, The Effective, Efficient Professor, 2002; patentee in field. With AUS, 1962-64. Recipient award in Separations Sci. and Tech., Am. Chem. Soc., 1994. Mem. AIChE, Am. Soc. Engring. Edn. (Union Carbide Lectr. award 1997), Am. Chem. Soc. Avocations: fishing, canoeing, camping. Office: Purdue U Dept Chem Engring 480 Stadium Mall Dr West Lafayette IN 47907-2100 Business E-Mail: wankat@ecn.purdue.edu.

**WANKE, RONALD LEE,** lawyer; b. Chgo., June 22, 1941; s. William F. and Lucille Wanke; m. Rose Klonowski, Oct. 23, 1987. BSEE, Northwestern U., 1964; JD, DePaul U., 1968. Bar: Ill. 1968. Assoc. Wood, Dalton, Phillips, Mason & Rowe, Chgo., 1968-71, ptnr., 1971-84, Jenner & Block, Chgo., 1984--. Lectr. John Marshall Law Sch., Chgo., 1985-94; mem. adv. com. intellectual property program, U. Chgo. Law, 2001-03. Contbr. chpt. to book, articles to Software Law Jour., 1987, Internat. Legal Strategy, 1995. Office: Jenner & Block One IBM Plz Ste 4400 Chicago IL 60611-7603 Office Phone: 312-222-9350.

**WANN, LAYMOND DOYLE,** retired petroleum research scientist; b. Magazine, Ark., Apr. 25, 1924; s. Vernon Cecil and Emma (McCrary) W.; m. Betty Lou Brown, Nov. 6, 1948; children: Jacqueline, Lyndall Doyle. BS in Physics (Phi Eta Sigma scholar), Okla. State U., 1949, MS, 1950. With Conoco Inc., Ponca City, Okla., 1951-84, sr. rsch. scientist, 1957-60, rsch. group leader, 1960-81, assoc. rsch. dir., 1981-84, staff scientist, 1984-85, ret., 1985. Cons. in disciplines of phys. Contbr. articles on elec. and radioactive well-logging, elec. design to profl. jours. Patentee in field. Mem. Mcpl. Airport Bd., Ponca City. Served with AUS, 1942-46; ETO. Decorated Bronze Star. Mem. Am. Petroleum Inst. (chmn. well logging subcom.), IEEE, Aircraft Owners and Pilots Assn., Seaplane Pilots Assn., VFW, Am. Legion, Phi Kappa Phi, Pi Mu Epsilon, Sigma Pi Sigma. Republican. Episcopalian (vestryman). Home: 1501 Monument Rd Ponca City OK 74604-3522 Office: 1000 S Pine St Ponca City OK 74601-7509 E-mail: ldwann@yahoo.com.

**WANN, MICHAEL STEPHEN,** music educator; b. Balt., Md., July 5, 1950; s. William Richard and Mildred Naomi Wann; 1 child, Michael Joseph. BS in Music Edn., Towson State U., Md., 1976; MEd, Loyola Coll., 1991; MusM in Edn., Peabody Conservatory @ Johns Hopkins U., 1995. Cert. tchr. Md., 1991. Band dir. Instrumental Program of Md., Lanham, Md., 1976—79, Archbishop Curley High, Baltimore, Md., 1979—80; instrumental music tchr. Balt. County Pub. Schs., Towson, Md., 1981—97, Howard County Pub. Schs., Ellicott City, Md. Curriculum com. mem. Howard County Pub. Schs., 1998—2001; chmn. of the bd. Cmty. Music Ctr. of Md., Inc, Columbia, Md., 1999—. Musician: (TV series) Marriage in the Family. Mem.: Percussive Arts Soc., Am. Fedn. of Musicians, Md. Band Dirs. Assn, Music Educators Nat. Conf. Avocations: golf, tennis, reading, painting. Home: 8332 Ridgely Oak Rd Baltimore MD 21234 Office: Northfield Elementary School 9125 Northfield Rd Ellicott City MD 21042 Business E-Mail: mwann@mail.howard.k12.md.us.

**WANNER, ERIC,** foundation executive; b. Wilmington, Del., Mar. 14, 1942; s. Edwin and Isabel Smith (Speakman) W.; m. Patricia Attix, June 13, 1964 (div. 1976); children: Noel Edwin, Erin Cole; m. Carla Francesca Seal, June 18, 1983; children: Lindzay Elizabeth. BA, Amherst Coll., 1963; PhD, Harvard U., 1969. Asst. to assoc. prof. Harvard U., Cambridge, Mass., 1968-76; behavioral sci. editor Harvard U. Press, Cambridge, Mass., 1976-82; program officer Alfred P. Sloan Found., N.Y.C., 1982-84, v.p., 1984-86; pres. Russell Sage Found., N.Y.C., 1986—. Trustee Ctr. for Advanced Study in Behavioral Scis., 1993-99; bd. dirs. Dogan Found., Paris, Am. Acad. Polit. Social Sci. Author: Remembering, Forgetting and Understanding Sentences, 1974; editor: Language Acquisition: the State of the Art, 1982; contbr. articles to profl. jours. Fulbright fellow Sussex U., Brighton, Eng., 1979, N.Y. Inst. for Humanities fellow, NYU, 1985-93, Am. Acad. Arts and Scis. fellow, 1994—. Mem.: Century Assn., Sigma Xi. Office: Russell Sage Found 112 E 64th St New York NY 10021-7383 Business E-Mail: ew@rsage.org.

**WANNIER, MARIO MARC-ANTOINE,** oil industry executive, multimedia specialist, director; b. Basle, Switzerland, Sept. 16, 1951; arrived in U.S., 2000; s. Willy Wannier and Aurelie Wannier-Bourquard; m. Clemencia Bello, Jan. 6, 1975; children: Catherine, Marianne. Vordiplomexamen, Basle U., Switzerland, 1973, Diplomexamen, 1975, PhD in Earth Scis., 1979. Asset mgr. Sarawak Shell Berhad, Miri, Malaysia, 1994—99; subsurface projects mgr. Shell Oil Co., Houston, 2000—. Author (dir.): Destination Miri: A Geological Tour, 1998 (Multimedia CD Title of Yr. award Pikom-Computimes IT, 1999), Northern Sarawak's National Parks and Giant Caves. Designer geol. exhbn. on the jura mountains Musee d'Histoire, Delemont, Switzerland, 1973—75. With Swiss AF, 1971—78. Office Phone: 281-544-2628. Personal E-mail: mwannier@yahoo.com.

**WANNSTEDT, DAVID RAYMOND,** college football coach, former professional football coach; b. Pitts., May 21, 1952; m. Jan Wannstedt; children: Keri, Jami. Grad., U. Pitts., 1974. Player Green Bay Packers, 1974; grad. asst. U. Pitts., 1975—76; receivers & spl. teams coach, 1977—78; defensive line coach Okla. State U., 1979-82, U. So. Calif., 1983-85; def. coord. U. Miami, 1986-89, Dallas Cowboys, 1989-93; head coach Chgo. Bears, 1993-98; asst. head coach Miami Dolphins, 1999-2000, head coach, 2000—04, U. Pitts. Panthers, 2004—. Named to NCAA 2nd team All-East, NFL Coach of the Year UPI, Football News, 1994; inducted into Western Pa. Hall of Fame, 1990. Office: U Pitts Football Team PO Box 7436 Pittsburgh PA 15213 Office Phone: 412-648-8711.

**WANTLAND, WILLIAM CHARLES,** retired bishop, lawyer; b. Edmond, Okla., Apr. 14, 1934; s. William Lindsay and Edna Louise (Yost) W. BA, U. Hawaii, 1957; JD, Okla. City U., 1967; D in Religion, Geneva Theol. Coll., Knoxville, Tenn., 1976; DD (hon.), Nashotah House, Wis., 1983, Seabury-Western Sem., Evanston, Ill., 1983. With FBI, various locations, 1954-59, Ins. Co. of N.Am., Oklahoma City, 1960-62; law clk.-atty. Bishop & Wantland, Seminole, Okla., 1962-77; vicar St. Mark's Ch., Seminole, 1963-77, St. Paul's Ch., Holdenville, Okla., 1974-77; presiding judge Seminole Mcpl. Ct., 1970-77; atty. gen. Seminole Nation of Okla., 1969-72, 75-77; exec. dir. Okla. Indian Rights Assn., Norman, 1972-73; rector St. John's Ch., Oklahoma City, 1977-80; bishop Episcopal Diocese of Eau Claire, Wis., 1980-99; interim bishop of Navajoland, 1993-94; ret., 1999. Adj. prof. Law Sch. U. Okla., Norman, 1970-78; instr. canon law Nashotah House, 1983-97, 2004—; mem. nat. coun. Evang. and Cath. Mission, Chgo., 1977-90; mem. Episcopal Commn. on Racism, 1990-92, Episcopal Indian Ministries, 1990-95, Standing Commn. on Constn. and Canons, 1992-95; assisting bishop Diocese of Dallas, 2002—04, of Ft. Worth, 2000—. Author: Foundations of the Faith, 1982, Canon Law of the Episcopal Church, 1984, The Prayer Book and the Catholic Faith, 1994; co-author: Oklahoma Probate Forms, 1971; contbr. articles to profl. jours. Pres. Okla. Conf. Mcpl. Judges, 1973; v.p. South African Ch. Union, 1985-95; trustee Nashotah House, Wis., 1981—, chmn., 1992-98; bd. dirs. SPEAK, Eureka Springs, Ark., 1983-89; Wis. adv. com. US Civil Rights Commn., 1990-91; support com. Native Am. Rights Fund, 1990—; mem. City Coun. of the City of Seminole, Okla., 2002-. vice mayor, 2003-04, 05-; co-chmn. Luth.-Anglican-Roman Cath. Commn. of Wis., 1989-95; pres. Wis. Episc. Coun., 1995-97, Wis. Coun. Chs., 1985-86; mem. Living Ch. Found., 1981-02; bd. dirs. Seminole Nation Hist. Soc. 1999-; mem. adv. bd. Seminole Hist. Soc., 2003-. Recipient Most Outstanding Contbn. to Law and Order award Okla. Supreme Ct., 1975, Outstanding Alumnus award Okla. City U., 1980, Wis. Equal Rights Coun. award, 1986, Manitou Ikwe award Indian Alcoholism Coun., 1988, Episcopal Synod Pres.'s award, 1995, 2004. Mem. Okla. Bar Assn., Okla. Indian Bar Assn., Oklahoma City Law Sch. Alumni Assn. (pres. 1968), Ct. Indian Offenses Seminole Nation Okla. (chief magistrate). Democrat. Episcopalian. Avocations: canoeing, skin-diving, cross country skiing. Personal E-mail: puca382@mbo.net. *If we truly believe that God reigns, we will so order our lives that such a belief is clearly reflected in all that we do and say; further, such a belief will shape our relations, not only with all other people, but all of God's created order.*

**WANTZ, KATHY LYNN ZEPP,** school nurse; d. Garland Edgar and Barbara Purdie Zepp; m. Stephen Albert Wantz, Apr. 8, 1979; children: Elizabeth Ann Chaney, Ashley May. RN, Catonsville C.C., 1979. RN Md., Md. From nurse's aid to in-svc. dir. WNCC, 1975—80; charge nurse Carroll County Gen. Hosp., 1980—86; residential client coord. Carroll County ARC, 1986—87; sch. nurse Carroll County Pub. Schs., 1987—91; staff nurse Critical Care Nursing Agy.-CCN, Inc., 1987—92; charge nurse PACU Carroll County Gen. Hosp./Dixon Outpatient Surg. Ctr., 1992—98; sch. nurse Carrolltowne Elem./Regional Spl. Edn. Ctr., 1998—. Lectr./presenter in field. Vol. Relay for Life, Md. Coop. Ext. Svc.; mem. Carrolltowne PTA, Carroll-towne Social Com.; former sec. and amb. attendant Pleasant Valley Cmty. Fire Dept.; former Sun. sch. tchr. and supt., choir mem. St. Mary's Union Ch. of Christ. Named Md. Sch. Health Nurse of the Yr., Md. Assn. Sch. Health Nurses, 2004—05; recipient Spirit award, Carroll County Gen. Hosp. Mem.: Sch. Nurse Assn. Carol County, Carroll County Edn. Assn., Md. State Tchrs. Assn., Md. Assn. Sch. Health Nurses, Nat. Assn. Sch. Health Nurses. Republican. United Ch. Of Christ. Avocations: reading, gardening, scuba diving, snorkeling, travel.

**WAPIENNIK, CARL FRANCIS,** manufacturing executive, planetarium and science institute administrator; b. Donora, Pa., Oct. 10, 1926; s. Karl and Rose (Kidzinski) W.; m. Elva Louise Bartron, Nov. 27, 1953; children: Carl Eric, Ellen Louise. BS, U. Pitts., 1953. Prodn. supr. RCA, Canonsburg, Pa., 1953—54; staff physicist Buhl Planetarium and Inst. Popular Sci., Pitts.,

1954—64, exec. dir., 1964—82; owner, operator Work-O-Art Miniatures (small mfg. firm), 1983—2003. Patentee means for controlling liquid flow. Mem. Rostraver Twp. Planning Commn., 1965-67; mem. adv. bd. Allegheny C. of C. (formerly North Side Pitts. C. of C.), 1966-67, dir., 1968-73, pres., 1970; mem. adv. coun. Salvation Army, 1978-82; bd. dirs. Bapt. Homes, Pitts., 1982-94; chmn. Rostraver Twp. Mcpl. Water Authority, 1990-94. With USNR, 1945-46. Recipient Man of Yr. award in sci. Pitts. Jaycees, 1969. Mem. Pitts. Bapt. Assn. (dir. 1976-82, 1976-82), Phi Beta Kappa, Sigma Pi Sigma. Home: 602 Salem Church Rd Belle Vernon PA 15012-2906

**WARAKOMSKI, ALPHONSE WALTER JOSEPH, JR.,** sales executive, marketing professional; b. N.Y.C., Apr. 1, 1943; s. Alphonse Walter and Mary (Dupnock) Warakomski. BS in Chemistry, St. Bonaventure, 1968; MBA in Mktg., Keller Grad. Sch., 1981. Chemist, lab. mgr. Purification Sci. Geneva, NY, 1968—73; applications engr. Pollution Control Industries, Stamford, Conn., 1973; mgr. sales Kopper's Environ. Elements, Balt., 1974; mktg. specialist, regional mgr. Union Carbide Linde, Chgo., 1975—79; sales engr. Dorr Oliver, Chgo., 1980—81; dir. mktg. and sales Linde AG Lotepro, Valhalla, NY, 1981—2000; ptnr. Mixing and Mass Transfer Techs., Inc., 2000—. Contbr. articles to profl. jours. Mem.: AIChE, Am. Chem. Soc., Water Environment Fedn., Internat. Ozone Assn., Am. Water Works Assn. Home: 8833 N Congress Apt 818 Kansas City MO 64153 Office Phone: 816-665-1931. Business E-Mail: awarakomski@m2ttech.com.

**WARBERG, WILLETTA,** concert pianist, music educator; b. Twin Falls, Idaho, June 2, 1932; d. George William Warberg and Ethel Margaret (Sargent) Warberg-Chandler; m. David Jacob Bar-Illan, Sept. 3, 1954 (div.); children: Daniela, Jeremy Oscar. Student, Colo. Women's Coll., 1950-51, Aspen Music Camp, 1951; studied with, Rudolph Firkusny, 1951-53; BS, Manches Coll. Music, N.Y.C., 1954. Assoc. food editor Look mag., N.Y.C., 1956-61; food editor Status mag., N.Y.C., 1961-62, Ladie's Home Jour., N.Y.C., 1964-66; photog. stylist Gourmet mag., N.Y.C., 1961-64, freelance writer, photog. stylist, 1965-75; pres., owner Willetta Enterprises, advt. agy., Twin Falls, 1976-84; food columnist, music and arts critic Times News, 1978-87; duo-piano ptnr. with Robert Starer, N.Y.C., Woodstock, 1991—2000; piano coach Saugerties, NY, 1991—. Made feasibility study of restaurant situation in Israel, U.S. Dept. State ICA Point 4 Program, Washington and Israel, 1960; artist-in-residence Holy Cross Concert Series, Kingston, N.Y., 1994—. Concert pianist, Idaho, Oreg., Utah, Wash., Colo., N.Y.C., N.Y. State, 1940—; author: Cooking from Scratch, 1976, Space Age Cookery, 1977; syndicated food columnist Willetta Says, 1978-87; contbr. food and sci. articles to Cosmopolitan, Modern Maturity, Esquire, Sun Valley, Sci. Digest, also other mags. Bd. dirs. N.W. Opera Assn., 1984-87; pres. bd. dirs. Woodstock Lyric Theatre, 1994-2000; v.p. bd. dirs. Woodstock Chamber Orch., 1993—; chmn. Friends of the Maverick Concerts Inc., Woodstock, N.Y., 1999—. Winner Rocky Mountain talent search contest Salt Lake Tribune and Salt Lake Telegram, 1949. Mem. Nat. Fedn. Music Clubs, Music Tchrs. Nat. Assn. (cert.), Kingston Music Soc. Avocations: designing and sewing clothes, painting still lifes, swimming, developing recipes, writing.

**WARBLE, CHARLES EDWARD,** materials scientist; b. Goshen, Ind., 1931; s. Harry Earlston and Thelma Viola Warble; m. Yvonne Valerie Cole, Dec. 1986 (div. May 1990); m. Agnes Martha Kardos, June 12, 1958 (dec. Dec. 1980); children: Brian Ellery(dec.), Stephen Earlston. BSc in Geology, Wayne State U., 1954; DSc of Materials Sci., Flinders U., 1987. Cartographer U.S. Army Map Svc., Washington, 1956—60; geologist, geophysicist Country Rds. Bd., Melbourne, Victoria, Australia, 1961—62; exptl. officer,sr. rsch. scientist Commonwealth Sci. & Indsl. Rsch. Orgn., Melbourne, 1962—86; sr. rsch. assoc. Arizona State U., 1982—83; cons. Melbourne, 1987—88, Phoenix, San Diego, 1988—92; assoc. devel. engr. U. Calif. San Diego, 1992—97; sr. mfg. processing engr. Corning OCA, Garden Grove, Calif., 1997—99; cons. Irvine, Calif., 1999—2001; rsch. fellow U. Sci. and Philosophy, Blacksburg, Va., 2001—02; cons. Irvine, 2003—. Contbr. articles to profl. jours. Vol. Companion Hospice, Orange County, Calif., 2002—. Recipient John Lysaght Inventors Award, 1972; fellow, Japanese Govt., 1979, Lawrence Berkeley Lab., 1983, 1985. Achievements include patents in field. Avocations: ballroom dancing, hiking, photography, inline skating, percussionist.

**WARBURTON, RALPH JOSEPH,** architect, educator, engineer; b. Kansas City, Mo., Sept. 5, 1935; s. Ralph Gray and Emma Frieda (Niemann) W.; m. Carol Ruth Hychka, June 14, 1958; children: John Geoffrey, Joy Frances W. Tracey. BArch, MIT, 1958; MArch, Yale U., 1959, M.C.P., 1960. Registered arch., Colo., Conn., Fla., Ill., La., Md., NJ, NY, Tex., Va., DC; registered profl. engr., Conn., Fla., NJ, NY; registered cmty. planner, Mich., NJ; lic. interior designer, Fla. With various archtl. planning and engring. firms, Kansas City, Mo., 1952-55, Boston, 1956-58, NYC, 1959-62, Chgo., 1962-64; chief planning Skidmore, Owings & Merrill, Chgo., 1964-66; spl. asst. for urban design HUD, Washington, 1966-72, cons., 1972-77; prof. architecture, archtl. engring. and planning U. Miami, Coral Gables, Fla., 1972-2000, chmn. dept. architecture, archtl. engring. and planning, 1972-75, assoc. dean engring. and environ. design, 1973-74, dir. grad. urban and regional planning program, 1973-75, 81, 87-93, prof. emeritus, 2000—. Advisor govt. Iran, 1970, govt. France, 1973, govt. Ecuador, 1974, govt. Saudi Arabia, 1985; cons. in field, 1972—, lectr., critic design juror in field, 1965—; mem./chmn. Coral Gables Bd. Archs., 1980-82. Author: Space for Urban Activity, 1960; assoc. author: Man-Made America: Chaos or Control, 1963; editor: New Concepts in Urban Transportation, 1968, Housing Systems Proposals for Operation Breakthrough, 1970, Focus on Furniture, 1971, National Community Art Competition, 1971, Defining Critical Environmental Areas, 1974; contbg. editor: Progressive Architecture, 1974-84; editl. adv. bd.: Jour. Am. Planning Assn., 1983-88, Planning for Higher Edn., 1986-94, Urban Design and Preservation Quar., 1987-94; contbr. over 130 articles to profl. jour.; mem. adv. panel Industrialization Forum Quar., 1969-79, archtl. portfolio jury Am. Sch. and Univ., 1993. Mem. Met. Housing and Planning Coun., Chgo., 1965-67; mem. exec. com. Yale U. Arts Assn., 1965-70; pres. Yale U. Planning Alumni Assn., 1983-89; mem. ednl. adv. com. Fla. Bd. Architecture, 1975; mem. grievance com. The Fla. Bar, 1996-99; mem code commn.'s Nat. Fire Protection Assn., 1998-. Recipient W.E. Parsons medal Yale U., 1960; recipient Spl. Achievement award HUD, 1972, commendation Fla. Bd. Architecture, 1974, Fla. Trust Hist. Preservation award, 1983, Group Achievement award NASA, 1976; Skidmore, Owings & Merrill traveling fellow MIT, 1958; vis. fellow Inst. Architecture and Urban Studies, NYC, 1972-74; NSF grantee, 1980-82. Fellow AIA (nat. housing com. 1968-72, nat. regional devel. and natural resources com. 1974-75, nat. sys. devel. com. 1968-73, bd. dirs. Fla. S. chpt. 1974-75, Edn. Leadership award Miami chpt. 2000, Test of Time Design award Fla. Assn. 2002), ASCE (archtl. engring. and structural engring. insts.), Fla. Engring. Soc. (bd. dirs. 1984-85, Miami chpt. bd. dirs. 1982-83, 84-85), Nat. Acad. Forensic Engrs.; mem. Am. Inst. Cert. Planners (exec. com. dept. environ. planning 1973-74), Am. Soc. Engring. Edn. (chmn. archtl. engring. divsn. 1975-76), Dade Heritage Trust (Cmty. Svc. award 2002), Nat. Sculpture Soc. (allied profl.), Nat. Soc. Archtl. Engrs. (founding), NSPE, Nat. Trust Hist. Preservation (principles and guidelines com. 1967), Am. Soc. Landscape Archs. (hon., chmn. design awards jury 1971, 72), Am. Planning Assn. (Fla. chpt. award excellence 1983), Am. Soc. Interior Designers (hon.), Omicron Delta Kappa, Sigma Xi, Tau Beta Pi. Home and Office: 2825 Cascade Dr Plano TX 75025-4106 Office Phone: 214-495-9892. Personal E-mail: ProfRJWarc@aol.com. *My contribution to society is made through comprehensive determination, design and development activity leading to habitats most suited to the optimum continuing progress of mankind.*

**WARCH, RICHARD,** former academic administrator; b. Hackensack, N.J., Aug. 4, 1939; s. George William and Helen Anna (Hansen) W.; m. Margot Lynn Moses, Sept. 8, 1962; children: Stephen Knud, David Preston, Karin Joy. BA, Williams Coll., 1961; B.D., Yale Div. Sch., 1964; PhD, Yale U., 1969; postgrad., U. Edinburgh, 1962-63; H.H.D., Ripon Coll., 1980. Asst. prof. history and Am. studies Yale U., 1968-73, asso. prof., 1973-77; asso. dean Yale Coll.; dir. summer plans Yale U., 1976-77; asso. dir. Nat. Humanities Inst., New Haven, 1975-76; v.p. acad. affairs Lawrence U.,

Appleton, Wis., 1977-79, pres., 1979—2004. Cons. Nat. Humanities Faculty; ordained to ministry United Presbyn. Ch. in U.S.A., 1968; dir. Bank One of Appleton. Author: School of the Prophets, Yale College, 1701-1740, 1973; editor: John Brown, 1973. Rockefeller Bros. Theol. fellow, 1961-62 Mem. Am. Studies Assn., Soc. for Values in Higher Edn., Winnebago Presbytery. Clubs: Rotary.

**WARD, AARON,** professional hockey player; b. Windsor, Ont., Can., Jan. 17, 1973; Attended, U. Mich. Defenseman Detroit Red Wings, 1993—2001, Carolina Hurricanes, 2001—06, NY Rangers, 2006—. Achievements include being a member of Stanley Cup Champion Detroit Red Wings, 1997, 1998, Carolina Hurricanes, 2006. Office: NY Rangers 2 Pennsylvania Plaza New York NY 10121*

**WARD, ALAN S.,** lawyer; b. Wilmington, Del., Jan. 1, 1931; s. Gilbert Hughes and Sarah Anna (Sparks) W.; m. Mariette S. Schneider, Apr. 4, 1959; children: Kathryn Ann Ward Koch, Guy Gilbert, Carolyn Alice. AB, Wesleyan U., 1952; JD, U. Chgo., 1955. Bar: Del. 1955, U.S. Supreme Ct. 1959, N.Y. 1962, D.C. 1964. Law clk. to judge U.S. Dist. Ct., Wilmington, Del., 1955-56; trial atty. Antitrust divsn. Dept. Justice, Washington, 1956-61, asst. chief spl. litigation sect., 1960-61; assoc. Breed, Abbott & Morgan, N.Y.C., 1961-63; ptnr. Hollabaugh & Jacobs, Washington, 1963-70; dir. Bur. Competition, FTC, Washington, 1970-73; ptnr. Baker & Hostetler LLP, Washington, 1973-2000; mem. mng. com. Baker & Hostetler, Washington, 1977-87. Lectr. law George Washington U., 1967-70; lectr. profl. assns Mem. bd. trustees Wesleyan U., 1986-89. Mem. ABA (chmn. antitrust com. litigation sect. 1986-87), Assn. of Bar of City of N.Y., Bar Assn. D.C., Del. Bar Assn., Wesleyan U. Alumni Assn. (chmn. 1983-86), Univ. Club, Union Club (N.Y.C.), Union Club (Cleve.), Columbia County Club (Chevy Chase, Md.), Farmington Country Club (Charlottesville, Va.). Republican. Methodist. Avocations: squash, golf, tennis, sailing. Home: 3577 Hamlet Pl Chevy Chase MD 20815-4822 Office: Baker & Hostetler LLP 1050 Connecticut Ave NW Washington DC 20036-5304 E-mail: award@bakerlaw.com, mitalward@aol.com.

**WARD, BESS B.,** oceanographer, educator; BS in Zoology, Michigan State U., East Lansing, 1976; MS in Biological Oceanography, U. Wash., Seattle, 1979, PhD in Biological Oceanography, 1982. Postgrad. rsch. biologist, Inst. Marine Resources, Scripps Instn. Oceanography U. Calif., San Diego, 1982—84, asst. rsch. oceanographer, Inst. Marine Resources, Scripps Instn. Oceanography, 1984—89, chair food chain rsch. group, Scripps Instn. Oceanography, 1987—88, assoc. mem. Ctr. Molecular Genetics, 1987—91, asst. prof. marine sci. Santa Cruz, 1989—91, assoc. prof. marine sci., 1991—95, prof., chair ocean sci. dept., 1995—98; prof. oceanography Princeton U., Princeton, NJ, 1998—. Visiting scientist Max Planck Inst. für Limnologie, Germany, 1993; disting. visiting biologist Woods Hole Oceanographic Instn., 1996. Fellow: Am. Acad. Arts & Sciences, Am. Geophysical Union, Am. Acad. Microbiology; mem.: AAAS, Am. Soc. Limnology & Oceanography (G. Evelyn Hutchinson medal 1997). Office: Princeton U Dept Geosciences M51 Guyot Hall Princeton NJ 08544

**WARD, BEVERLY ALLEN,** church administrator, music educator; b. Charleston, SC, Jan. 13, 1935; d. Homer Allen and Pearl Vivian (Wilson) Ward. BA in music cum laude, Furman U., 1957; MusM, Eastman Sch. Music, 1960. Fellow Coll. Ch. Musicians, Washington, 1963; instr. theory and organ Am. Conservatory Music, Chgo., 1964—69; organist/choirmaster/dir. music St. James Episcopal Cathedral, Chgo., 1965—69; admin. asst./organist dir. First Congl. Ch., Hendersonville, NC, 1978—94; dir. music/adminstr. St. James Episcopal Ch., Hendersonville, 1994—2000; organist/choirmaster St. Mary's Episcopal Ch., Asheville, NC, 2001—03; interim adminstrn/musician First Congl. Ch., Hendersonville, 2004—05. Music dir. Carolina Chamber Singers, Hendersonville, NC, 1981—96. Orchestrator Passion Cantata: Forsaken of Man (ISowerby) ms and performance, 1987; composer: (organ composition) Crucifier: Lift High the Cross, 1982. 1st lt. U.S. Army, 1957—59. Decorated Commendation ribbon US Army. Mem.: Am. Anglican Musicians, Am. Guild Organists (dean WNC chpt. 1982—84, 1990—92). Republican. Episc. Home: 1402 Fifth Ave W Hendersonville NC 28739

**WARD, BILL,** musician; b. Birmingham, England, May 5, 1948; Founding mem., drummer Black Sabbath, 1969—80, 1983, 1994, 1997—. Musician: (albums) Ward One: Along the Way, 1985, When the Bough Breaks, 1997, Two Hands Clapping, 1999; musician: (with Black Sabbath) Black Sabbath, 1970, Paranoid, 1971, Master of Reality, 1971, Black Sabbath, vol. 4, 1972, Sabbath Bloody Sabbath, 1973, Sabotage, 1975, Technical Ecstasy, 1976, Never Say Die!, 1978, Heaven & Hell, 1980, Born Again, 1983, Sabbath Stones, 1996, Reunion, 1998. Named to Rock and Roll Hall of Fame, 2006. Office: Sanctuary Records Group Ltd Sanctuary House 45-53 Sinclair Rd London W14 0NS England*

**WARD, BRENDA ROBINSON,** social worker; b. Gastonia, NC, Nov. 12, 1954; d. Elvin Franklin and Annie Sue (Clemmer) Robinson; m. Robert Crawford Ward, Aug. 29, 1981; children: Lauren Clemmer, Thomas Crawford. BSW, NC State U., 1977; MSW, U. N.C., 1980. LCSW NC. Social worker I Broughton Hosp., Morganton, NC, 1977—78; social worker II Smoky Mtn. Area Mental Health, Dillsboro, NC, 1980—81, Cherry Hosp., Goldsboro, NC, 1981—83; social worker III Piedmont Behavioral Health-care, Concord, NC, 1983—91, local mental health unit coord., 1991—97, clin. social work specialist Kannapolis, NC, 1997—2002; clin. coord. Lifeworks Oupatient Program Rowan Reg. Med. Ctr., 2002—. Mem.: Cabarus County Mental Health Assn., NASW. Office: Lifeworks Outpatient Prgm Rowan Reg MC 612 Mocksville Ave Salisbury NC 28144

**WARD, CAM,** professional hockey player; b. Sherwood Park, Atla., Can. Feb. 29, 1984; Goalie Lowell Lock Monsters (AHL), 2004—05, Carolina Hurricanes, 2005—. Recipient Conn Smythe Trophy, 2006. Achievements include being a member of Stanley Cup Champion Carolina Hurricanes, 2006; tying the record for playoff wins by a rookie goalie, 2006. Office: Carolina Hurricanes RBC Ctr 1400 Edwards Mill Rd Raleigh NC 27607*

**WARD, CHARLES A.,** federal agency administrator; b. Huntsville, Ala., Oct. 14, 1931; s. Hosie and Barbara Ward; 1 child, Pamela A. BA, Talladega Coll., 1954. Distbn. clk. Post Office Dept., Chgo., 1954—65, foreman mails, 1966—68, gen. foreman, 1968—70; mgr. quality control U.S. Postal Svc., 1973—78, mgr. distbn., 1973—80, officer-in-charge Ft. Lauderdale, Fla., 1980, sect. ctr. mgr., postmaster Binghamton, NY, 1980—82, acting mgr. sect. com. Va., 1982, mgr. sect. ctr., postmaster Memphis, 1982—84, Greensboro, NC, 1984—87. Mem. United Negro Coll. Fund; co-chair Combined Fed. Campaign, Memphis; mem. Piedmont Interfaith Coun.; bd. dirs. Broome County Urban League, Binghamton, NY, United Way; bd. visitors Oak Ridge Mil. Acad.; bd. advisers Francis Home, Inc.; mem. Shepherds Ctr. Greensboro, McIver Ednl. Ctr., Hayes-Taylor YMCA, United Svc. for Older Adults. Mem.: NAACP, Greensboro Housing Coalition, So. Poverty Law Ctr., Nat. Assn. Postmasters of US, Nat. League Postmasters, Nat. Assn. Ret. Fed. Employees, Nat. Postal Supvs., Midwest Assn. Sickle Cell Anemia, United Negro Coll. Fund, N.C. A&T Aggie Club, Greensboro Civitan Club, Rotary, Talladega Coll. Alumni Club, Omega Psi Phi. Home: 219 Village Ln Unit E Greensboro NC 27409-2523

**WARD, CHARLES RAYMOND,** systems engineer; b. Lansing, Mich., Oct. 23, 1949; s. George Merrill and Dorothy Irene (Hupp) W.; m. Sarah Hopkins Eddy, June 23, 1979; children: Katherine Emily, Rachel Elizabeth. BS in Math., Purdue U., 1971; MSEE, Naval Postgrad. Sch., 1977. Commd. ensign USN, 1971, advanced through grades to lt. commdr., served on USS Barbel 1972-75, served on USS James Madison, 1978-81, served on USS Alabama, 1983-85; strategic navigation project mgr. Strategic Systems Programs, Arlington, Va., 1985-91; surveillance towed array sensor sys., mgr. sys. engring. Govt. Info. Sys. divsn. TRW, McLean, Va., 1991-95; integrated undersea surveillance sys., mgr. internat. programs TRW, San Diego, 1995-2000; integrated undersea surveillance, mgr. fixed surveillance Command,

Control and Intelligence divsn. TRW, 2000—02; asst. program mgr. sys. integration Command Control and Intelligence Divsn. Northrop Grumman Mission Sys., 2002—04; program mgr. Maritime Surveillance Sys., Def. Mission Sys. Divsn., Northrop Grumman Mission Sys., 2004—. Editor: Trident Navigation Standard Operating Procedures, 1991, Acoustic Warfare Operating Doctrine, 1992, Surveillance Towed Array Sensor Passive User's Guide, 1994. Chmn. grounds com. Burke (Va.) United Meth. Ch., 1989-97, chmn. worship com., 1993-94; chmn. Camp Va. site adv. com., 2001—; chmn. Julian Retreat Ctr. Task Force, 2002—. Mem. IEEE, Eta Kappa Nu, Sigma Xi. Republican. Achievements include research in automatic depth and pitch control for a near surface submarine. Office: Northrop Grumman Mission Systems 1843 Hotel Circle S San Diego CA 92108-3320 E-mail: chuck.ward@ngc.com.

**WARD, CHARLIE,** professional basketball player; b. Thomasville, Ga., Oct. 2, 1970; Student, Tallahassee C.C., Fla., Florida State U. Basketball player N.Y. Knicks, 1994—2004, Phoenix Suns, 2004—. Heisman Trophy, 1993, Coll. Football Player of the Yr. award Sporting News, 1993; named to Coll. All-America First Team Sporting News, 1993; Coll. Football Hall of Fame, 2006. Office: c/o Phoenix Suns 201 E Jefferson St Phoenix AZ 85004

**WARD, CHESTER LAWRENCE,** physician, consultant; b. Woodland, Calif., June 8, 1932; s. Benjamin Briggs and Nora Elizabeth Ward; m. Sally Diane Ward, Dec. 10, 1960; children: Katharine, Leanne. BA, U. Calif., Santa Barbara, 1955; MPH, U. Calif., Berkeley, 1966; MD, U. So. Calif., 1962; grad., Indsl. Coll. Armed Forces, 1978. Commd 2d lt., inf. U.S. Army, 1954, advanced through grades to brig. gen., 1980; surgeon 5th Spl. Forces, Ft Bragg, NC, Vietnam, 1963-64; chief aviation medicine, preventive medicine and aeromed. consultation service Ft. Rucker, Ala., 1967-68; surgeon Aviation Brigade and USA Vietnam Aviation Medicine Cons., 1968-69; flight surgeon Office of U.S. Army Surgeon Gen., 1970-71; physician The White House, Washington, 1971-75, 76; dir. environ. quality rsch. U.S. Army Med. Rsch. and Devel. Commd., 1975-76; comdr. Womack Army. Hosp., 1978—80; surgeon XVIII Airborne Corps, Ft. Bragg, 1978-80; comdr. William Beaumont Army Med. Ctr., El Paso, Tex., 1980-82; med. dir. Union Oil Co., Schaumburg, Ill., 1982-83, dir. domestic medicine L.A., 1983-84; exec. dir. continuing med. edn. and clin. prof. emergency medicine U. So. Calif. Sch. Medicine, L.A. 1984-85; dir., health officer Dept. Pub. Health, Butte County, Calif., 1985-95; cons., contractor, pvt. practice medicine, 1996—; med. dir. NorCal EMS, 2001—05. Trustee, pres. Oroville Union HS Dist., 1998—2002; chmn. Citizen's Bond Oversight Com., 2003—05; apptd. by Gov. Wilson Calif. Commn. Emergency Med. Svcs., past commr. Decorated DSM, Legion of Merit (2), Bronze Star, Air medal (5). Fellow: Aerospace Med. Assn., Am. Coll. Preventive Medicine (past regent); mem.: No. Calif. Emergency Med. Svcs. Inc. (governing bd. 1987—2006, dir.), Calif. Med. Assn. (past del.), Butte-Glenn County Med. Soc. (past pres.), Mil. Officers Assn. (past chpt. pres.). Personal E-mail: tvldoc@sbcglobal.net.

**WARD, CHRISTOPHER,** computer scientist, researcher; b. London, Eng., Aug. 17, 1959; s. Michael Ward and Jean Mary Potter; m. Kathleen M McWilliams, Sept. 1, 1990; children: Keegan D McWilliams-Ward, Eva J McWilliams-Ward, Christina C McWilliams-Ward. BSc in Computer Sci., U. Hertfordshire, Eng., 1983; MSc in Computer Sci., U. Fla., Gainesville, 1985, PhD in computer Sci., 1987. Asst. prof. Auburn U., Ala., 1988—93; assoc. prof. Hunter Coll., CUNY, NYC, 1993—96; sr. mem., tech. staff and group head Sarnoff Corp., Princeton, NJ, 1996—2000; rsch. staff mem. IBM T.J. Watson Rsch. Ctr., Hawthorne, NY, 2000—. Author: (textbook) Computer Organization and the MC 68000; contbr. articles to profl. jours. Mem. bd. edn. Glen Ridge Sch. Dist., NJ, 2001—. Recipient Presdl. Recognition award, U. Fla., 1985, Authors award, Auburn U., 1993, Achievement award, Sarnoff Corp., 1998, Rsch. award, IBM Corp., 2005—06. Mem.: IEEE (sr.), Internat. Broadcasters Conv. (coun. mem. 1997—2000), Assn. Computing Machinery, Upsilon Pi Epsilon (chpt. pres. 1987—88). Achievements include patents in field. Office: IBM TJ Watson Research 19 Skyline Drive 1S-D60 Hawthorne NY 10532 Office Phone: 914-784-7186. Personal E-mail: christopher_ward@ieee.org. Business E-Mail: cw1@us.ibm.com.

**WARD (BAILEY), DAISY DALE,** writer; b. Dayton, Ohio, June 12, 1931; d. Ennis and Cora Dale (Greene) Ward; m. James Arrelaus Bailey, June 26, 1965 (dec. Dec. 27, 1999); m. Charles Morris Gilham, Dec. 25, 1949 (dec. Feb. 11, 1961); children: James Craige Bailey, Angelia Dale Wood, Linda Yvette Gilham, Lisa Yvonne Matthews. BA, Goddard Coll.; JD, The Am. Sch. of Law. Counselor Camp Fire Girls, Atlanta, 1968—69, cmty. bd., 1969—70; mem. Aux. to the Med. Assn. of Ga., Atlanta, 1970—91, AMA Aux., Inc, Atlanta, 1970—91; rec. sec. Emory U. Woman's Club, Atlanta, 1972—73, Aux. to the Nat. Med. Assn., Inc, Washington, 1986—87; pres.-elect Aux. to the Atlanta Med. Assn., Atlanta, 1974—75, Aux. to the Nat. Med. Assn., Inc, Washington, 1987—88; pres. Aux. to the Atlanta Med. Assn., Atlanta, 1975—76, Aux. to the Nat. Med. Assn., Inc, Washington, 1988—89, region iii v.p., 1975—76; treas. Aux. to the Nat. Med. Assn., Inc., Washington, 1981—84; hon. chair SW Cmty. Hosp. Charity Ball, Atlanta, 1982; vice chair Emory U. Woman's Investment Club, Atlanta, 1983—84, chair, 1984—85; 2nd v.p. Aux. to the Nat. Med. Assn., Inc., Washington, 1985—86; bd of dirs. Aux. to the Nat. Med. Assn., Inc, Washington, 1981—, NAACP Atlanta Chpt., Atlanta, 1986—90, Habitat for Humanity, Atlanta, 1989—91; mem. of the bd. Nat. Cancer Inst., Washington, 1988—89; chair bd. of dirs. Aux. to Nat. Med. Assn., Inc, Washington, 1989—90; bd. mem. Black Elected County Ofcls. Main Project, Atlanta, 1989—90; parliamentarian Aux. to the Nat. Med. Assn., Inc, Washington, 1990—91; bd. of trustees Sr. Citizen Svcs., Atlanta, 1985—87; mem. Atlanta chpt. CARATS, Inc., 1980—, pres. Atlanta chpt., 1986. Chair-advisory coun. Aux. to the Atlanta Med. Assn., Atlanta, 1976—77; mem Aux. to the Atlanta Med. Assn., Inc., 1968—; chair pres.' coun. Aux. to the Nat. Med. Assn., Inc, Washington, 1995—96. Author: (book) The Perfect Law of Liberty. Mem. Youth Svc. Guild, Columbus, Ohio, 1963—68; pres. Juliett Federated Clubs, Newark, Ohio, 1962—64; apptd. to bi-racial panel Gov. of Ga., Atlanta, 1987; bd. of trustees Trinity AME Ch., Atlanta, 1992—; v.p. Atlanta Phys. Medicine & Rehab. Svcs., Inc, 1982—90. Recipient Proclamation, Atlanta City Coun., 1988, Appreciation, Habitat for Humanity-Atlanta, 1991, Trustee of the Yr., Trinity AME Ch., 2002, Pillar of Strength award, Aux. to the Atlanta Med. Assn., Inc, 2002, Appreciation, Aux. to the Nat. Med. Assn., Inc, 1989, Achievement, Region III Aux. to the Nat. Med. Assn., Inc, 1989, Proclamation, Gov. of Ga., 1989, Exceptional Cmty. Leadership Local-State-National, Group Of Concerned Women, 1988, Key To The City of Orlando, Mayor of Orlando, Fla., 1989, Appreciation award, Nat. Mar. of Dimes, 1989, Svc. award, Aux. to the Nat. Med. Assn., Inc, 1989, Ga. State Med. Assn., 1989, Region V Aux. to the Nat. Med. Assn., Inc, 1989, NAACP, 1990, Nefertiti Outstanding Achievement award, Soc. Docta, Inc., 2002, Atlanta (Ga.) Appreciation award, 2002. Mem.: Ohio State U. Presidents Club, Ohio State U. Faculty Club, Alpha Kappa Alpha Sorority. Avocations: writing, travel, reading. Personal E-mail: daisydward@aol.com.

**WARD, DAVID,** academic administrator, educator; b. Manchester, Eng., July 8, 1938; arrived in U.S., 1960; s. Horace and Alice (Harwood) Ward; m. Judith B. Freifeld, June 11, 1964; children: Michael J.H., Peter F.B. BA, U. Leeds, Eng., 1959, MA, 1961; MS, U. Wis., 1961, PhD, 1963; LittD, U. Leeds, 1992. Lectr. Carleton U., Ottawa, Ont., 1963—64; asst. prof. Univ. B.C., Vancouver, 1964—66, U. Wis., Madison, 1966—67, assoc. prof., 1967—70, prof., 1970—, chmn. geography dept., 1974—77, assoc. dean Grad. Sch., 1980—88, provost and vice chancellor acad. affairs, Andrew Clark prof. geography, 1989—94, chancellor, 1994—2000; pres. Am. Coun. on Edn., Washington, 2000—. Mem. exec. com. Argonne Nat. Lab., Ill., 1990—93; dir.-at-large Social Sci. Rsch. Coun., 1991—93; mem. Kellogg Commn. on Future of Land Grant Univs.; chair Internet 2, Consortium Advances Network Devel.; mem. coun. UN U., 2004—; mem. Sec. of Edn.'s Commn. on Future of Edn., 2005. Author: Cities and Immigrants, 1970, Geographic Perspectives on Americas Past, 1978, Poverty Ethnicity and the American City, 1989, Landscape of Modernity, 1992; contbr. articles to profl. jours. Fellow Guggenheim fellow, 1976, Einstein fellow, Hebrew U., 1980, Fulbright fellow, Australian Nat. U., 1979. Fellow: Am. Acad. Arts and Scis.;

mem.: Assn. Am. Geographers (pres. 1989). Office: Am Council on Edn One Dupont Circle NW Washington DC 20036-1193 Office Phone: 202-939-9311. Business E-Mail: president@ace.nche.edu.

**WARD, DAVID ALLEN,** sociology educator; b. Dedham, Mass., June 21, 1933; s. Theodore Allen and Jessie Miller (Ketchum) W.; m. Carol Jane Barton, June 15, 1957 (div. 1964); children: Douglas Allen, Andrew Barton; m. Reneé Ellen Light, Mar. 10, 1967. BA, Colby Coll., 1955; PhD, U. Ill., 1960. Asst. prof. Wash. State U., Pullman, 1960-61; asst. research sociologist UCLA, 1961-64; assoc. prof. U. Minn., Mpls., 1965-68, prof., 1968—2002, chmn. dept. sociology, 1984-88, 92-95. Chmn. Salzburg (Austria) Seminar in Am. Studies, 1977; cons. jud. com. U.S. Ho. Reps., Washington, 1984. Co-author: Women's Prison, 1965, Prison Treatment, 1971; co-editor: Delinquency, Crime and Social Process, 1969, Confinement in Maximum Custody, 1981; editorial cons. Jour. Criminal Law and Criminology, 1968-97. Mem. Mpls. Civilian Police Rev. Bd., 1991-94. Liberal Arts fellow Harvard U. Law Sch., 1968-69; Fulbright research fellow, 1971-72; research fellow Norwegian Fgn. Office, Oslo, 1976. Mem.: Am. Soc. Criminology, Am. Sociol. Assn. (chmn. sect. criminology 1976—77). Office: Univ of Minn Dept of Sociology 909 Social Sci Bldg Minneapolis MN 55455

**WARD, DAVID HENRY (DAVE WARD),** television news reporter, anchorman; b. Dallas, May 6, 1939; s. H.M. and Mary Ward; m. Glenda Lois Odom, Nov. 10, 1959 (div.); children: Linda Ann, David H.; m. Debra Rene Holland, Apr. 25, 1974 (div.); children: Jonathan H., Christopher H. Student, Tyler Jr. Coll., Tex., 1957—59. Announcer Sta. KGKB, Tyler, 1958—60; program dir. Sta. WACO (Tex.), 1960—62; news dir. Sta. KNUZ, Houston, 1962—66; news reporter, photographer, writer, prodr. Sta. KTRK-TV, 1966—. Freelance writer, prodr., cons. Chmn. pub. affairs adv. bd. Houston Bus. Coun.; pub. info. com. Am. Cancer Soc.; pres. bd. dirs. Easter Seal Soc., Harris, Ft. Bend counties; committeeman Houston Livestock Show and Rodeo, 1997—98. Named Man of Yr., Houston Sertoma Club, 1974, TV Personality of Yr., Am. Women in Radio and TV, 1983, Best TV Anchor, Houston Press, 1995, 1996, 2001; recipient Best TV Newscast award, Tex. UPI, 1968, 1972, 1973—80, TV Svc. award, Houston Jaycees, 1982. Mem.: Houston Press Club, Sigma Delta Chi. Baptist. Office: Channel 13 PO Box 13 3310 Bissonnet St Houston TX 77005-2195

**WARD, DAVID SCHAD,** scriptwriter, film director; b. Providence, Oct. 24, 1947; s. Robert McCollum and Miriam (Schad) W.; children: Joaquin Atwood, Sylvana Soto. BA, Pomona Coll., 1967; M.F.A., UCLA, 1970. Scriptwriter: films include Steelyard Blues, 1971, The Sting, 1973 (Acad. award best original screenplay 1973), The Milagro Beanfield War, 1988, (with Nora Ephron and Jeff Arch) Sleepless in Seattle, 1993 (Academy award nominee Best Original Screenplay 1993), (with John Eskow, Ted Elliott and Terry Rossio) The Mask of Zorro; writer, dir. films include Cannery Row, 1981, Major League, 1989, King Ralph, 1991, The Program, 1993, Major League II, 1995, Down Periscope, 1996. Mem.: Acad. Motion Picture Arts and Scis., Dirs. Guild Am. Office: c/o Ben Smith 8942 Wilshire Blvd Beverly Hills CA 90211

**WARD, DAVID WAYNE,** physicist, researcher; b. Houston, Tex., Sept. 21, 1970; s. David Gerald and Barbarra Cox Ward; m. Sabine Margaret Volkmer, June 15, 2006; m. Vannessa Ann Warren, Jan. 20, 1989 (div. May 1, 1991); m. Candy Miller, Jan. 1, 1993 (div. Mar. 1, 1995); m. Rebecca Elizabeth Slenker, May 19, 1995 (div. Feb. 1, 2002); 1 child, Christina Ann. BS Physics, Coll. of Charleston, Charleston, SC, 1999; PhD in Phys. Chemistry, MIT, Cambridge, Mass., 2005. Boatswains mate 2nd class U.S. Navy, Little Creek, Va., 1992—96; pres. and founder Ward, Ward, and Smith LLP, Charleston, SC, 1997—99; postdoctoral fellow Harvard U., Cambridge, Mass., 2005—06; pres. and founder Piffany, Inc., Somerville, Mass., 2006—. Dir. ChildrenAtWar.org, Somerville, Mass., 2006—. Author: (plays) Surely You're Mad, Mr. Feynman Or 8.00 Physics For Girls!, Crash, He Said She Said, (short stories) Rabbit Rabbitus, Lorca and the Sandman, Artificial Intelligence Sentinel-911, The Automaton. Founder and prin. investigator for methods to reduce the worlds small arms inventory. ChildrenAtWar.org, Somerville, Mass. 2006. E5 USN, 1992—96, Little Creek, Va. Decorated Liberation of Kuwait Medal Kingdom of Saudi Arabia, Meritorious Svc. Medal U.S. Navy, Meritorious Unit Commendation, Armed Forces Svc. Medal, Navy E Ribbon, Chief of Naval Ops. Letter of Commendation; fellow Truman Fellowship Finalist, Sandia Nat. Laboratories, 2005; scholar Quattrochi Scholarship, Coll. of Charleston, 1998. Mem.: Optical Soc. Am., Am. Phys. Soc., Phi Kappa Phi. Achievements include invention of Polaritonics, an intermediate regime between electronics and photonics in which phonon-polaritons are used as the infor. carrier in active and passive polaritonic circuits; patents pending for A robust and cost-effective method for the destruction of small arms; research in Single molecule microscopy and spectroscopy, biophysical modelling, computational electrodynamics, ultrafast signal processing, polaritonics, infor. theory, population growth, disarmament; design of Piffany search engine; discovery of Discovered the physical origins of negative refraction; development of Developed FDTD simulations for the polariton regime; first to Co-Inventor, along with Wei Min and Xiaoliang Sunney Xie, of homodyne amplified resonance Rayleigh polarized scattering (HARRPS) microscopy; discovery of that the limits to growth as dictated by the power input from the sun will be realized within the next 1000 years; patents pending for Ranking search results with readability formulae; Homodyne amplified resonant rayleigh polarized scattering (HARRPS) a new horizon for single molecule sci. and tech; web browser module For readability and context identification or adjustment; Multiferroic crystals that affect a negative index of refraction; All-optical high-speed dielectric-semiconductor hybrid photonic switches bases on photonic bandgap and spatio-temporal pulse shaping tech; Sys. and methods for automated categorization of an uncategorized corpus. Office: Harvard U 12 Oxford St M027 Cambridge MA 02138 Office Phone 617-496-0747 E-mail david@davidward.org

**WARD, DEBRA YVETTE,** elementary school educator; b. Petersburg, Va., Dec. 6, 1960; d. Willie Lee and Corinne Richardson Dillard; m. Jerald Vittoro Ward, Feb. 17, 1989; children: Eric Michael, Yvette Corinne. BA, Va. Tech, 1983; MEd in Adminstrn., Lamar U., 2002. Cert. prin., tchr. Elem. tchr. Beaumont (Tex.) Ind. Sch. Dist., 1995—. Tchr. Triumph Ch., Beaumont, 1995—99, 2002—. Mem.: BAABSE, TAABSE, NEA, ACSD, Tex. Edn. Assn., Phi Delta Kappa (fin. sec. 2003—05, pres. 2005—), Zeta Phi Beta (treas. 2003—). Home: 5280 Sunset Beaumont TX 77705 Office Phone: 409-833-3831. E-mail: dydw83@aol.com.

**WARD, DOREE MAXINE,** secondary school educator; b. Des Moines, Iowa, Oct. 17, 1955; d. Jeane and Wesley Ward. BSE in Edn., Drake U., 1977, MSEd, 1997. Tchr. Thomas Jefferson H.S., Council Bluffs, Iowa, 1978—82; tchr./coach Floyd Valley H.S., Alton, Iowa, 1982—84, Newton H.S., Newton, 1987—. Del. to Russia and Hungary People to People Internat., 1993. Del. Russia and Hungary People to People Internat., 1993. Mem.: Iowa Assn. of Safety Edn. (pres. 1994—2002), Iowa State Edn. Assn. Avocations: swimming, horseback riding, softball, basketball. Home: 515 E 10th St S Newton IA 50208 Office: Newton High School 800 E 4th St S Newton IA 50208 Business E-Mail: wardd@newton.k12.ia.us.

**WARD, ERICA ANNE,** lawyer, educator; b. Okiyama, Japan, Oct. 20, 1950; d. Robert Edward and Constance Regina (Barnett) Ward; m. Ralph Joseph Gerson, May 20, 1979; children: Stephanie Claire Gerson, Madeleine Ward Gerson. BA, Stanford U., 1972; JD, U. Mich., 1975. Bar: Calif. 1975, DC 1976, US Ct. Appeals (5th and DC cir.) 1977, Temp. Emergency Ct. Appeals 1983, Mich. 1989. Assoc. Wilmer, Cutler & Pickering, Washington, 1975—77; staff counsel US Senate Ethics Com., Washington, 1977—78; exec. asst. gen. counsel Dept. Energy, Washington, 1978—79; counsellor to dep. sec., 1980; assoc. dir. energy and natural resources, domestic policy staff White House, Washington, 1980—81; counsel Skadden, Arps, Slate, Meagher & Flom., Washington, 1981—87; ptnr. 1987; adj. prof. law U. Mich., Ann Arbor, 1984—85; Editor Mich. Law Rev., 1975; commr. Mackinac Is. State Pk. Commn., Mich., 1989—95. Recipient Outstanding Svc. medal, Dept.

Energy, 1981. Mem.: Women's Bar Assn. DC, ABA, U. Mich. Law Sch., Cranbrook Ednl. Cmty., Children's Hosp. Mich. Democrat. Jewish. Office: Skadden Arps Slate Meagher Flom 1440 New York Ave NW Ste 600 Washington DC 20005-6000 Office Phone: 202-371-7050. Business E-Mail: eward@skadden.com.

**WARD, GEOFFREY CHAMPION,** writer, editor; b. Newark, Ohio, Nov. 30, 1940; s. Frederick Champion and Rachel Duira (Baldinger) W.; m. Diane Raines; children: Nathan, Kelly; 1 stepchild, Garrett. BA, Oberlin Coll., 1962, DHL (hon.), 2004, Wilkes U., 1995. Sr. picture editor Ency. Britannica, Chgo., 1964-68; co-founder, editor Audience mag., Boston, 1969-73; mng. editor Am. Heritage Mag., N.Y.C., 1976-78, editor, 1978-82. Author: Lincoln's Thought and the Present, 1978, Treasures of the Maharajas, 1983, Before the Trumpet: Young Franklin Roosevelt, 1882-1905, 1985, A First-Class Temperament: The Emergence of Franklin Roosevelt, 1989 (Nat. Book Critics Cir. award, Francis Parkman prize Soc. Am. Historians, L.A. Times biography prize, Ohioana award), The Civil War: An Illustrated History, 1990, American Originals: The Private Worlds of Some Singular Men and Women, 1991; (with Diane Raines Ward) Tiger Wallahs, Encounters with the Men Who Tried to Save the Greatest of the Great Cats, 1993, Baseball: An Illustrated History, 1994, Closest Companion: The Unknown Story of the Intimate Friendship between Franklin Roosevelt and Margaret Suckley, 1995, The West: An Illustrated History, 1996, (with Michael Nichols) The Year of the Tiger, 1998, Not for Ourselves Alone: Elizabeth Cady Stanton and Susan B. Anthony, 1999, Jazz: A History of America's Music, 2000, (with Dayton Duncan) Mark Twain, 2001, Unforgivable Blackness: The Rise and Fall of Jack Johnson, 2004 (Anisfield/Wolf Book award, 2005); editor: The Best American Essays of 1996; (TV documentaries) Huey Long, 1985, Thomas Hart Benton, 1989, Lindbergh, 1990, Nixon, 1990 (Writer's Guild Am. award), The Civil War, 1990 (Emmy award), Reminiscing in Tempo, 1991, Empire of the Air, 1992, The Kennedys, 1992 (Emmy award), George Marshall and the American Century, 1993, Baseball, 1994 (Emmy award), Daley: The Last Boss, 1995, The West, 1996, Theodore Roosevelt, 1996 (Emmy award), Thomas Jefferson, 1997, Frank Lloyd Wright, 1998, Not for Ourselves Alone, 1999, Jazz, 2000, (with Dayton Duncan) Mark Twain, 2001, Unforgivable Blackness: The Rise and Fall of Jack Johnson, 2005 (Emmy award, Writers Guild award); contbr. articles to mags., jours. Bd. dirs. Save the Tiger Fund. Recipient Christopher awards for The Statue of Liberty, Theodore Roosevelt, Not For Ourselves Alone, Mark Twain, The Civil War, New Eng. Booksellers Assn. award, Am. Booksellers award, Lila Acheson Wallace Readers Digest writers award. Mem. Soc. Am. Historians (Friend of History award), Orgn. Am. Historians, Serengeti Club, Writers Guild Am. East Inc., Century Assn. Home: 17 C 290 W End Ave New York NY 10023-8106 Office: Brandt &Hochman care Carl Brandt 1501 Broadway Ste 2310 New York NY 10036-5689

**WARD, GEORGE FRANK, JR.,** international programs executive, ambassador; b. Jamaica, N.Y., Apr. 9, 1945; s. George Frank and Hildegard Louisa (Evans) W.; m. Peggy Elizabeth Coote, June 12, 1965; 1 child, Pamela Ward Priester. BA, U. Rochester, 1965; MPA, Harvard U., 1980. U.S. vice consul Am. Consulate, Hamburg, Germany, 1970-72; ops. officer Office Sec. State, Washington, 1972-74; U.S. consul Am. Consulate Gen., Genoa, Italy, 1974-76; polit. officer Am. Embassy, Rome, 1976-77, exec. asst., 1977-79, polit. officer Bonn, Germany, 1984—85, dep. chief mission, 1989—92; polit.-mil. officer US Dept. State, Washington, 1980-84, 1985—88, prin. dep. asst. sec. Bur. Internat. Orgn., 1992-96, US amb. to Namibia, 1996-99, US coord. for humanitarian assistance to Iraq, 2003; v.p., dir. profl. tng. program US Inst. Peace, Washington, 1999—2005; sr. v.p. internat. programs World Vision, 2005—. Capt. USMC, 1965-69, maj. USMCR, 1969-78. Decorated Vietnamese Cross Gallantry, Naval Commendation medal with combat V; recipient Presdl. Meritorious Svc. award, 1992, 1994, Disting. Honor award, U.S. State Dept., 1992. Fellow: Phi Beta Kappa; mem.: Am. Fgn. Svc. Assn., Washington Inst. Fgn. Affairs, Cosmos Club. Anglican. Home: 3404 Walnut Hill Ct Falls Church VA 22042-3546 Business E-Mail: gward@worldvision.org.

**WARD, GEORGE TRUMAN,** architect; b. Washington, July 24, 1927; s. Truman and Gladys Anna (Nutt) W.; m. Margaret Ann Hall, Sept. 10, 1949; children: Carol Ann Ward Dickson, Donna Lynne Ward Solomon, George Truman, Robert Stephen. BS, Va. Poly. Inst., 1951, MS, 1952; postgrad., George Washington U., 1966. Registered profl. arch., Va., Md., D.C., W.Va., Ohio, N.J., Del., N.C. Archtl. draftsman Charles A. Pearson, Radford, Va., 1950; head archtl. sect. Hayes, Seay, Mattern & Mattern, Radford and Roanoke, 1951-52; with Joseph Saunders & Assocs., Alexandria, Va., 1952-57, assoc. arch., 1955-57; ptnr. Vosbeck-Ward & Assocs., Alexandria, 1957-64, Ward/Hall Assocs., Fairfax, 1964—. Dir. Crestar Bank/Greater Washington Region, 1967-99. Pres. PTA Burke (Va.) Sch., 1970-71; mem. bd. mgrs. Fairfax (Va.) County YMCA, 1964-76; chmn. adv. com. Coll. Arch., Va. Poly. Inst., 1984-90; bd. dirs. mem. investment com. Va. Tech. Found., Inc., 1986-91, 93-98; pres. Springfield Rotary Found., 1978-79; chmn. county adv. bd. Salvation Army, 1978-79, 89-95, co-chmn. Fairfax County Salvation Army Capital Campaign, 1991-95; mem. Gen. Bd. Va. Bapts., deacon, moderator; mem. bd. vis. Va. Poly. Inst. & State U., 1984-87; trustee Fairfax County Pub. Schs. Edn. Found., Inc. With AUS, 1946-47. Paul Harris fellow; recipient Disting. Svc. award Va. Tech. Alumni Assn., 1988; recipient William H. Ruffner medal Va. Tech., 1996, VSAIA William C. Noland award, 1998, Va. Tech. Coll. Arch. and Urban Studies Lifetime Contbn. award, 1998. Fellow Coll. AIA; mem. AIA (corp., charter Octagon Soc.), No. Va. Soc. AIA (chmn. polit. action com. 1991-93, Disting. Svc. award 1990, treas. Va. Soc. 1994-98, Outstanding Achievement award 1996), Rowe Fellowship (charter mem. 1988), Alumni Assn. Va. Poly. Inst. & State U. (bd. dirs., v.p. 1992, pres. 1994), Interfaith Forum on Religion, Art and Arch., Va. Found. for Arch. (trustee), Va. Assn. Professions, Va. C. of C., No. Va. Angus Assn. (pres. 1987-88), Va. Tech. Alumni Assn. (hon., life, bd. dirs. Disting. Svc. award 1988), Masons, Shriners, KT, Rotary (charter mem., pres. Springfield 1973-74, Disting. Svc. award dist. 7610 1995), Tau Sigma Delta, Omicron Delta Kappa, Phi Kappa Phi, Pi Delta Epsilon, Ut Prosim. Baptist. Office: Ward Hall Assoc AIA Ste 300 12011 Lee Jackson Memorial Hwy Fairfax VA 22033-3310 E-mail: gtward@wardhall.com.

**WARD, HARRY MERRILL,** history professor; b. West Lafayette, Ind., July 30, 1929; s. Hiley L. and Agnes Ward. Student, U. Ill., 1947-49; BA, William Jewell Coll., 1951; MA, Columbia U., 1954, PhD, 1960. Social investigator N.Y.C. Dept. Welfare, 1958-59; asst. prof. Georgetown (Ky.) Coll., 1959-61; from asst. to assoc. prof. Morehead (Ky.) State U., 1961-65; vis. assoc. prof. So. Ill. U., 1967-68; assoc. prof. history U. Richmond, Va., 1965-77, prof. history, 1977—, William Binford Vest prof. history 1993-99, William Binford Vest prof. history emeritus, 1999—. Cons. in field. Author: The United Colonies of New England, 1643-1690, 1961, Department of War, 1781-1795, 1962, 1981, Unite or Die: Intercolony Relations, 1690-1763, 1971, Statism in Plymouth Colony, 1973, Duty, Honor or Country: General George Weedon and the American Revolution, 1979, Richmond: An Illustrated History, 1985, 1988, Charles Scott and the Spirit of '76, 1988, Major General Adam Stephen and the Cause of American Liberty, 1989, Colonial America, 1607-1763, 1990, American Revolution: Nationhood Achieved, 1763-1788, 1994, General William Maxwell and the New Jersey Continentals, 1997, The War for Independence and the Transformation of American Society, 1999, Between the Lines: Banditti of the American Revolution, 2002, George Washington's Enforcers: Policing the Continental Army, 2006; co-author: Richmond During the Revolution, 1775-1783, 1977; contbr. articles to profl. jours. With USMC, 1951—53. Recipient Fraunces Tavern Mus. Book award, 1990, Scholar award in history, Va. Social Sci. Assn., 1992, History prize for disting. achievement, Soc. of the Cin. in the State of N.J., 2004. Fellow: Pilgrim Soc.; mem.: Am. Hist. Assn., So. Hist. Assn., Orgn. Am. Historians (Council). Office: U Richmond Dept History Richmond VA 23173-0180 Office Phone: 804-289-8345. Business E-Mail: kfugett@richmond.edu.

**WARD, HARRY PFEFFER,** hematologist, retired academic administrator; b. Pueblo, Colo., June 6, 1933; s. Lester L. and Alysmai (Pfeffer) W.; m. Betty Jo Stewart, Aug. 20, 1955; children— Stewart, Leslie, Elizabeth, Mary Alice,

Amy. AB, Princeton U., 1955; MD, U. Colo., 1959; MS, U. Minn., 1963. Intern Bellevue Hosp., N.Y.C., 1959; resident Mayo Clinic, Rochester, Minn., 1960-63; practice medicine specializing in hematology; chief medicine Denver VA hosp., 1968-72; dean, asso. v.p. U. Colo. Sch. Medicine, 1972-78, prof. medicine, 1972; chancellor U. Ark. Med. Sci., Little Rock, 1979-2000, chancellor emeritus, 2000—. Clin. investigator VA, 1964-67 Chmn. Assn. Acad. Health Ctr., 1993-94. Mem. ACP, AMA, Am. Fedn. Clin. Research, Central Soc. Clin. Investigation, Am. Soc. Hematology, Internat. Soc. Hematology, Western Soc. Clin. Research. Home: 369 Valley Club Cir Little Rock AR 72212-2900 Office: U Ark Med Scis 4301 W Markham St Little Rock AR 72205-7101 E-mail: hpward1@msn.com.

**WARD, HILEY HENRY,** journalist, educator; b. Lafayette, Ind., July 30, 1929; s. Hiley Lemen and Agnes (Fuller) W.; m. Charlotte Burns, May 28, 1951 (div. 1971); children: Dianne, Carolee, Marceline, Laurel; m. Joan Bastel, Aug. 20, 1977. BA, William Jewell Coll., 1951; MA, Berkeley Bapt. Div. Sch., 1953; MDiv, McCormick Theol. Sem., Chgo., 1955; student, Northwestern U., 1948, 54, 56-57; PhD, U. Minn., 1977. News asst. Christian Advocate, 1953-55; editor jr. publs. David C. Cook Pub. Co., 1956-59; editor Record, Buchanan, Mich., 1960; religion editor Detroit Free Press, 1960-73; asst. prof. journalism Mankato (Minn.) State U., 1974-76; assoc. prof. journalism Wichita (Kans.) State U., 1976; prof. journalism Temple U., Phila., 1977-96, prof. emeritus, 1997—, dir. news-editorial sequence, journalism dept., 1977-80, chmn. dept., 1978-80. Instr. journalism Oakland U., Rochester, Mich., evenings 1963-66. Author: Creative Giving, 1958, Space-age Sunday, 1960, Documents of Dialogue, 1966, God and Marx Today, 1968, Ecumania, 1968, Rock 2000, 1969, Prophet of the Black Nation, 1969, The Far-out Saints of the Jesus Communes, 1972, Religion 2101 A.D., 1975, Feeling Good About Myself, 1983, Professional Newswriting, 1985, My Friend's Beliefs: A Young Reader's Guide to World Religions, 1988, Reporting in Depth, 1991, Magazine and Feature Writing, 1993, Mainstreams of American Media History, 1997; editor: Media History Digest, 1979-94; exec. editor: Kidbits, 1981-82; book editor: Editor and Publisher, 1989-98; contbr. articles to profl. jours., feature articles to newspapers and mags.; also short stories and poems. Religious Pub. Rels. Coun. fellow, 1970; recipient citation Religious Heritage Am., 1962, Leidt award Epsic. Ch., 1969, citation U.S. Am. Revolution Bicentennial Adminstrn., 1976, Text and Acad, Authors citation, 1997. Mem. Religion Newswriters Assn. (pres. 1970-72), Am. Soc. Journalists and Authors, Am. Journalism Historians Assn. (bd. dirs. 1994-96, Kobre lifetime achievement award 1999), Overseas Press Club. Home: PO Box 399 1263 Folly Rd Warrington PA 18976-1422 E-mail: bastel@voicenet.com.

**WARD, HINES, JR.,** professional football player; b. Seoul, Republic of Korea, Mar. 8, 1976; s. Hines Ward Sr. and Kim Young-hee; m. Simone Ward; 1 child, Jaden. BA in consumer economics, U. Ga., 1997. Wide receiver Pitts. Steelers, 1998—. Named MVP, Super Bowl XL, 2006; named to NFL Pro-Bowl, 2001—04. Achievements include being a member of Super Bowl XL Champion Pittsburgh Steelers, 2006; being the first Korean-American Super Bowl MVP, 2006. Office: c/o Pittsburgh Steelers 3400 S Water St Pittsburgh PA 15203*

**WARD, HORACE TALIAFERRO,** federal judge; b. LaGrange, Ga., July 29, 1927; m. Ruth LeFlore (dec.); 1 son (dec.). AB, Morehouse Coll., 1949; MA, Atlanta U., 1950; JD, Northwestern U., 1959. Bar: Ga. 1960. Instr. polit. sci. Ark. A.M. and N. Coll., 1950-51, Ala. State Coll., 1951-53, 55-56; claims authorizer U.S. Social Security Adminstrn., 1959-60; assoc. firm Hollowell Ward Moore & Alexander (and successors), Atlanta, 1960-69; individual practice law Atlanta, 1971-74; judge Civil Ct. of Fulton County, 1974-77, Fulton Superior Ct., 1977-79; U.S. Dist. Ct. judge No. Dist. Ga., Atlanta, 1979-93; sr. judge U.S. Dist. Ct. No. Dist. Ga., Atlanta, 1993—. Lectr. bus. and sch. law Atlanta U., 1965-70; dep. city atty., Atlanta, 1969-70, asst. county atty., Fulton County, 1971-74 Former Trustee Friendship Baptist Ch., Atlanta; mem. Ga. adv. com. U.S. Civil Rights Commn., 1963-65; assisting lawyer NAACP Legal Def. and Edn. Fund, Inc., 1960-70; mem. Jud. Selection Commn., Atlanta, 1972-74, Charter Commn., 1971-72; mem. Ga. Senate, 1964-74, jud. com., rules com., county and urban affairs com.; mem. State Democratic Exec. com., 1966-74; former bd. dirs. Atlanta Legal Aid Soc.; bd. dirs Atlanta Urban League, Fed. Defender Program, No. Dist. Ga.; trustee Met. Atlanta Commn. on Crime and Delinquency, Atlanta U.; Fledgling Found. Mem. Am. Bar Assn., Nat. Bar Assn. (chmn. jud. council 1978-79), State Bar Ga., Atlanta Bar Assn., Gate City Bar Assn. (pres. 1972-74), Atlanta Lawyers Club, Phi Beta Kappa, Alpha Phi Alpha, Phi Alpha Delta, Sigma Pi Phi. Office: US Dist Court 1252 US Courthouse 75 Spring St SW Atlanta GA 30303-3309 Office Phone: 404-215-1330.

**WARD, JAMES A.,** lawyer; b. Waukesha, Wis. BA in Polit. Sci., Carroll Coll., Waukesha, 1971; JD, So. Meth. U., 1974. Bar: Wis. 1974, U.S. Dist. Ct. (ea. and we. dists.) Wis. 1974, U.S. Supreme Ct. 1979. Atty. Krause & Ward, Waukesha, 1974-78; sole practitioner Waukesha, 1978-80; atty. Congdon, Ward & Walden, S.C., Waukesha, 1981—2002; sole practitioner, 2003—. Mem. Waukesha County Bd. Adjustment, 1992—. Mem. Rotary Office: 161 W Wisconsin Ave Pewaukee WI 53072-2400 Office Phone: 262-691-3000. E-mail: james@jwardlaw.com.

**WARD, JOE HENRY, JR.,** retired lawyer; b. Childress, Tex., Apr. 18, 1930; s. Joe Henry and Helen Ida (Chastain) W.; m. Carlotta Agnes Abreu, Feb. 7, 1959; children: James, Robert, William, John. BS in Acctg., Tex. Christian U., 1952; JD, So. Meth. U., 1964. Bar: Tex. 1964, Va. 1972, D.C. 1974; CPA, Tex. Mgr. Alexander Grant & Co. CPA's, Dallas, 1956-64; atty. U.S. Treasury, 1965-68; tax counsel U.S. Senate Fin. Com., 1968-72; pvt. practice Washington, 1972-83; asst. gen. counsel, tax mgr. Epic Holdings, Ltd. and Crysopt Corp., 1983-87; pvt. practice Washington and Va., 1987-95; ret., 1995. Lt. USNR, 1952-56. Mem.: AICPA, Univ. Club. Home: 2639 Mann Ct Falls Church VA 22046-2721

**WARD, JONATHAN P.,** former service company executive; b. May 6, 1954; BSChemE, U. N.H., 1976; grad. advanced mgmt. program, Harvard Bus. Sch. With R.R. Donnelley, 1977—2001, pres. Merchandise Media and Fin. Svcs. bus. units, mng. comml. printing operation, v.p. dir. Spartanburg, S.C., mfg. divsn., exec. v.p. Comml. Print Sector, 1995—97, pres., COO, 1997—2001; pres., CEO ServiceMaster, Downers Grove, Ill., 2001—02, chmn., CEO, 2002—06. Dir. Metromail Corp., Siegwerk Inc. USA, J. Jill Group Inc., First Horizon. Trustee Goodman Theatre, Chgo.; dir. Chgo. Youth Ctrs., Evanston Northwestern Hosp. Mem.: Nat. Assn. Mfr., Direct Mktg. Assn.*

**WARD, KATHLEEN ANNE,** radiologist; b. Chgo., Ill., Oct. 8, 1950; d. Charles Joseph and Anne Loretta (Cannon) W.; m. Mark Steven Reiter; children: Elizabeth, Daniel. BS in Chemistry, Mundelein Coll., Chgo., 1971; MS in Biol. Chemistry, U. Ill., Chgo., 1977; MD, Loyola U., 1981. Bd. cert. Nat. Bd. Med. Examiners, Am. Bd. Radiology, lic. Ill. Intern in internal medicine Michael Reese Hosp. and Med. Ctr., Chgo., 1981—82; resident in diagnostic radiology Loyola U. Med. Ctr., Maywood, Ill., 1982—85, fellow in computed tomography and ultrasound, 1985—86; radiologist Meyer Med. Group, S.C., Chgo., 1986—95, Suburban Radiologists, S.C., Western Springs, Ill., 1996—2002; mem. active staff LaGrange (Ill.) Meml. Hosp., 1996—2002; mem. assoc. staff GlenOaks Hosp., Glendale Heights, Ill., 2000—02; attending radiologist Loyola U. Med. Ctr., Maywood, Ill., 2004—. Reviewer Am. Jour. Roentgenology, 2005—; clin. asst. prof. dept. radiology Loyola U., Stritch Sch. Medicine, Maywood, 2004—05, asst. prof. dept. radiology, 2005—. Author: (book chpt.) Immune System Genetics and Regulation, 1978; contbr. articles to profl. jours. Parent co-chair Ann. Giving Fund, Morgan Park Acad., 1995—96; bd. dirs. Morgan Park Acad., Chgo., 1997—2001, S.W. Suburban Youth Symphony Orch., 1998—99; hon. chair Salute to Excellence, Morgan Park Acad. Fundraiser, 1997. Recipient Scholastic Achievement award, Am. Med. Women, 1981. Fellow: Am. Coll. Radiology (ultrasound clin. image reviewer clin. evaluation subcom. 1997); mem.: Radiol. Soc. N.Am. (local sci. exhibits com. 1985, local tech. exhibits com. 1994—96), Ill. Radiol. Soc. (membership com. 2001—02, 2003—), Chgo. Radiol. Soc. (exec. com. 1995—, v.p. 1998—99, pres.-elect

---

1999—2000, pres. 2001—02, past pres. 2001—), Am. Roentgen Soc., Am. Inst. Ultrasound in Medicine, Am. Assn. for Women Radiologists (membership com. 1995—96, awards com. 1999, bylaws com. 2000, chair bylaws com. 2000, v.p. 2000, pres.-elect 2001, pres. 2002, awards com. 2002—, immediate past pres. 2003, chair awards com. 2005), Alpha Omega Alpha. Office: Loyola U Med Ctr Dept Radiology Bldg 103 Rm 0047 2160 S 1st Ave Maywood IL 60153

**WARD, KEN, JR.,** journalist; Environ. reporter Charleston (WV) Gazette. Recipient Edward J. Meeman award for environ. reporting, Scripps Howard Found., 2006. Mem.: Soc. Environ. Journalists (chair First Amendment task force 2002—, David Stolberg Meritorious Svc. award 2004). Office: The Charleston Gazette 1001 Virginia St E Charleston WV 25301 Office Phone: 304-348-1702. Office Fax: 304-348-1233. E-mail: kward@wvgazette.com.*

**WARD, LESLIE ALLYSON,** journalist, editor; b. LA, June 3, 1946; d. Harold Gordon and Marilyn Lucille (Dahlstead) W.; m. Robert L. Biggs, 1971 (div. 1977); m. Colman Robert Andrews, May 26, 1979 (div. 1988); m. John P. Lindsay, Oct. 10, 2003. AA, Coll. San Mateo, 1966; BA, UCLA, 1968, MJ, 1971. Reporter, researcher L.A. Bur. Life mag., 1971-72; reporter, news asst. L.A. bur. N.Y. Times, 1973-76; sr. editor New West mag., L.A., 1976-78, 79-80; L.A. bur. chief US mag., 1978-79; Sunday style editor L.A. Herald Examiner, 1981-82, editor-in-chief Sunday mags., 1982-83, Olympics editor, 1984, sports editor, 1985-86, sr. writer, 1986; sr. editor L.A. Times Mag., 1988-90; travel editor L.A. Times, 1990—2003. Democrat. Office: LA Times Times Mirror Sq Los Angeles CA 90053

**WARD, LEWIS EDES,** mathematician, educator; b. Arlington, Mass., July 20, 1925; s. Lewis E. Sr. and Mary C. (Ball) W.; m. Grace J. Ward, Jan. 31, 1949; children: Lawrence, Dinah, Michael. AB, U. Calif., Berkeley, 1949; MS, Tulane U., 1951, PhD, 1953. Instr. U. Nev., Reno, 1953-54; asst. prof. U. Utah, Salt Lake City, 1954-56; rsch. mathematician USN, China Lake, Calif., 1956-59; lectr. UCLA, 1957-59; assoc. prof. U. Oreg., Eugene, 1959-65, assoc. dean, 1966-69, prof., 1965-91, prof. emeritus, 1991—. Author: Topology, 1972; contbr. articles to profl. jours. Mem. Math. Assn. Am. (vis. mathematician, 1960-64), Am. Math. Soc. (organizer spl. sessions, 1980, 82), Oregon Acad. Sci. (vis. scientist, 1962-64). Avocations: hiking, skiing. Office: U Oreg Dept Math Eugene OR 97403 Business E-Mail: lward@darkwing.uoregon.edu.

**WARD, LLEWELLYN ORCUTT, III,** oil industry executive; b. Oklahoma City, July 24, 1930; s. Llewellyn Orcutt II and Addie (Reisdorph) W.; m. Myra Beth Gungoll, Oct. 29, 1955; children: Casidy Ann, William Carlton. Student, Okla. Mil. Acad. Jr. Coll., 1948-50; BS, Okla. U., 1953; postgrad., Harvard U., 1986. Registered profl. engr., Okla. Dist. engr. Delhi-Taylor Oil Corp., Tulsa, 1955-56; ptnr. Ward-Gungoll Oil Investments, Enid, Okla., 1956—; owner L.O. Ward Oil Ops., Enid, 1963—; chmn., CEO Ward Petroleum Corp. Mem. Okla. Gov.'s Adv. Coun. on Energy; rep. to Interstate Oil Compact Commn.; dir. Hydril Corp; chmn., CEO Ward Petroleum Corp. Chmn. Indsl. Devel. Commn., Enid, 1968—; active YMCA; mem. bd. visitors Coll. Engring., U. Okla.; mem. adv. coun. Sch. Bus., trustee Phillips U., Enid, Univ. Bd., Pepperdine, Calif.; Okla. chmn. U.S. Olympic Com., 1986—; Rep. nat. committeeman from Okla., 1982-88; mem. Pres.'s adv. com. on arts Kennedy Ctr. Served with C.E., U.S. Army, 1953-55. Named Chief Roughneck of Yr., Lone Star Steel, 1999. Mem. Ind. Petroleum Assn. Am. (chmn. 1996-98), Okla. Ind. Petroleum Assn. Am. (pres., bd. dirs.), Nat. Petroleum Coun., Enid C. of C., U. Okla. Coll. Engring. Disting. Grads. Soc., Am. Bus. Club (pres. 1964), Masons, Shriners, Rotary (pres. Enid 1990-91), Alpha Tau Omega. Methodist. Home: 900 Brookside Dr Enid OK 73703-6941 Office: 502 S Fillmore St Enid OK 73703-5703 Office Phone: 580-234-3229.

**WARD, LOUIS EMMERSON,** retired physician; b. Mt. Vernon, Ill., Jan. 19, 1918; s. Henry Ben (Pope) and Aline (Emmerson) Ward; m. Nan Talbot, June 5, 1942; children: Nancy, Louis, Robert, Mark; m. Marian Mansfield, Jan. 27, 1979. AB, U. Ill., 1939; MD, Harvard, 1943; MS in Medicine, U. Minn., 1949. Intern Ill. Research and Ednl. Hosp., Chgo., 1943; fellow medicine Mayo Found., 1946—49; cons. medicine, rheumatology Mayo Clinic, 1950—83, chmn. bd. govs., 1964—75. Contbr. articles to profl. jours. Vice chmn. bd. trustees Mayo Found., 1964—76; past bd. dirs. Fund for Republic, Ctr. for Study Dem. Instns., Arthritis Found., Northwestern Bell Telephone Prin. Fin. Group; mem. Nat. Coun. Health Planning and Resource Devel., 1976—83. With M.C. U.S. Army, 1944—46. Recipient Achievement award, U. Ill., 1968, Disting. Alumnus award, Mayo Found., 1983. Master: Am. Coll. Rheumatology; mem.: So. Minn. Med. Assn., Zumbro Valley Med. Soc., Minn. Med. Soc., Ctrl. Soc. Clin. Rsch., Nat. Soc. Clin. Rheumatologists, AAAS, AMA, Phi Beta Theta, Alpha Omega Alpha, Sigma Xi, Phi Beta Kappa. Home: Apt 916 211 2nd St NW Rochester MN 55901-2820

**WARD, MICHAEL J.,** rail transportation executive; b. Balt., Sept. 2, 1950; BS, U. Md., 1972; MBA, Harvard U., 1976. Rsch. analyst Chessie Sys., Balt., 1977—80, mgr., coord. analysis-fin., 1980—81, mgr. bus. rsch. Cleve., 1981—82, dir. nat. accts., 1982—84, asst. v.p. coal mktg., 1984—85, Balt., 1984—86; v.p. coal mktg. CSX Distbn. Svcs., Balt., 1986—88; v.p. coal CSX Transp., Jacksonville, 1988—94, gen. mgr. C&O Bus. Unit, v.p. coal Huntington, W.Va., 1994—95, sr. v.p. fin. Jacksonville, 1995—96, CFO, 1995—98, exec. v.p. fin., 1996—98, exec. v.p. coal and merger planning, 1998—99, exec. v.p. coal svc. group, 1999—2000, exec. v.p. ops., 2000, pres., 2000—03, CEO, 2002—03; pres. CSX Corp., Jacksonville, 2002—, chmn., pres., CEO, 2003—. Bd. dirs. Ky. Coal Coun., Ashland, Inc., CSX Corp. Bd. dirs. Ctr. Energy Econ. Devel., Take Stock in Children. Mem.: Fla. Coun. 100, Assn. Am. Railroads (bd. dirs.). Phi Kappa Phi, Beta Gamma Sigma. Office: CSX Corp 500 Water St C 900 Jacksonville FL 32202*

**WARD, MONICA,** social sciences educator; BA in Polit. Sci., U. Calif., LA, 1989; MEd, Chapman U., Orange, Calif., 2005. Social sci. tchr. Poly H.S., Riverside, Calif., 1999—2000, Martin Luther Kind H.S., 2001—. Tchr. 6th grade Rivera Elem. Sch., Riverside, 1995—99. Mem.: Nat. Coaches Fedn., Calif. Interscolastic Fedn. (meet mgmt. 2005—06), Calif. Coun. Social Studies, Nat. Coun. Social Studies.

**WARD, PERRY W.,** college president; BS, Miles College; MSW, PhD, U. Ala. Pres. Lawson State Cmty. Coll., 1987—; exec. dir. basic edn. Birmingham (Ala.) Pub. Schls., 1979-87, dir. fed. programs adminstrn., 1975-79; adj. prof. U. Ala. Grad. Schl. Soc. Work, 1977-82; dir. emerg. schl. aid act program Miles Coll., 1973-75, assoc. dir. emerg. schl. assistance progam 1972-73, instr. adult edn. program, 1969-71. Cons. in field. Bd. dirs. U. Ala., Health Svcs. Found.; Birmingham Urban League (pres.), Ala. Coll. Assn. (pres.), Central Ala. Athletic Assn. (v.p.); mem. Pres.'s roundtable; participant AACC Pres. Acad. Fellow I-D-E-A Acad. Disting. Educators award; recipient Kermit Mathison Ounstanding Cmty. Coll. Administrator award, NAACP Boy Scouts Am. Appreciation award, Headstart Recognition for Outstanding Svc. award. Bd. dir. Compass Bk. Ala.; mem. Leadership Birmingham, Leadership Ala., C. of C. Birmingham Edn. roundtable, Nat. bd. Am. Assoc. Cmty. Colls. (regional accreditation coms.). Office: Lawson State Com Coll 3060 Wilson Rd SW Birmingham AL 35221-1717

**WARD, PETER ALLAN,** pathologist, educator; b. Winsted, Conn., Nov. 1, 1934; s. Parker J. and Mary Alice (McEvoy) Ward. BS, U. Mich., 1958; MD, U. Mich. Med. Sch., 1960. Diplomate Am. Bd. Anatomic Pathology, 1964, Am. Bd. Immunopathology, 1983. Intern Bellevue Hosp., NYU, N.Y.C., 1960—61; resident dept. pathology U. Mich. Med. Sch., Ann Arbor, 1961—63; postdoctoral fellow Scripps Clinic and Rsch. Found., divsn. Exptl. Pathology, La Jolla, Calif., 1963—65; chief immunology br. Armed Forces Inst. Pathology, Wash., 1965—71; prof. dept. pathology U. Conn. Health Ctr., Farmington, 1971—80, prof. and chmn. dept. pathology, 1973—80; prof. and chmn. dept. of pathology U. Mich. Med. Sch., Ann Arbor, 1980—2005, interim dean, 1982—85. Mem. pathology study sect. NIH, Bethesda, Md., 1974—76, chmn. pathology study sect., 1976—78; mem. rsch. rev. com. NHLBI/NIH, Bethesda, Md., 1978—82; sci. adv. bd. Armed Forces Inst.

---

Pathology, Wash., 1978—83; cons. VA Hosp., Ann Arbor, 1980—; first Godfrey D. Stobbe prof. of pathology U. Mich. Med. Sch., 1987—; bd. dir. Univs. Associated for Rsch. and Edn. in Pathology, Inc., 1988—90; disting. faculty lectr. U. Mich. Biomedical Rsch. Coun., Ann Arbor, 1989—; pres.-elect U.S./Can. Acad. Pathology, Inc., 1991—92, pres., 1992—93; past pres. and chair nominating com. U.S./Can. Acad. of Pathology, Inc., 1993—94; mem. Inst. Lab. Animal Resources, 1993—96; coun. chair Inst. Lab. Animal Rsch. Coun., 1999—; chmn. nominating com. Soc. Med. Consultants to the Armed Forces, 1989—93; mem. Inst. Medicine/NAS, 1990—; trustee Am. Bd. Pathology, 1988—97, bd. dirs., 1996—97, life trustee, 1998—; treas. Soc. Leukocyte Biology, 2000—03, pres., 2004—05; bd. dirs. Fedn. Am. Socs. for Exptl. Biology, 2004—. Capt. M.C U.S. Army, 1965—67, Armed Forces Inst. Pathology, Wash. Recipient R & D Achievement award, U.S. Army, 1969, Meritorious Civilian Svc. award, 1970, Parke-Davis award, Am. Soc. Exptl. Pathology, 1971, Borden Rsch. award, U. Mich. Med. Sch., 1990, Merit award, NIH, 1990-97, Nat. Pres. award in recognition of leadership as pres., Mich. State Med. Soc., 1992, Rous-Whipple award, Am. Soc. Investigative Pathology, 1996, Lifetime Nat. Assoc., Nat. Academies Sci., 2001, Gold-Headed Cane award, Am. Soc. Investigative Pathology, 2001, J. Burns Amberson Lectr., Am. Thoracic Soc., 2003, Disting. Svc. award, Assn. Pathology Chairs, 2004, Chugai award for excellence in mentoring and scholarship, Am. Soc. Investigative Pathology, 2005. Fellow: AAAS, Am. Heart Assn. (fellow, coun. on cardiopulmonary, perioperative & critical care 2003); mem.: Inst. Lab. Animal Rsch. Coun. (coun. chair 1999—), Assn. Pathology Chairmen (rsch. com. mem. 1982), Am. Soc. Investigative Pathology (rep. to faseb bd./faseb fin. com. 2004), Am. Thoracic Soc. (sci. adv. com. 1989), Am. Bd. Pathology (pres. 1996—97), Am. Assn. Immunologists (nominating com. 1992), Am. Assn. for Advancement of Sci., U.S. and Can. Acad. Pathology, Inc., NIH (mentored scientist spl. emphasis panel 2001), Nat. Heart, Lung, and Blood Inst. (com. mem. 1990, rev. com. 1990), Mich. Thoracic Soc., A. James French Soc. Pathologists (charter mem.), Am. Soc. Clin. Investigation. Achievements include patents for sulfatides as anti-inflammatory compounds, U.S. Patent No. 5, 486, 536; compositions and methods for the treatment of sepsis, U.S. Patent No. 6, 673, 346. Office: Univ Mich Med School 1301 Catherine M5240 Med Sci 1 Ann Arbor MI 48109-0602 Office Phone: 734-763-6384. Office Fax: 734-763-4872. Business E-Mail: pward@umich.edu.

**WARD, R. LAWRENCE,** lawyer; b. Kans. City, Kans., May 19, 1936; BBA, Univ. Mo., Kans. City, 1959, JD, 1961. Bar: Mo. 1961, US Dist. Ct. (Kans., we. Mo., ea. Mich. dist.), US Ct. Appeals (8th, 10th cir.), US Supreme Ct. Firm chmn. & chmn. bus. litigation group Shugart Thomson & Kilroy, Kans. City, Mo. Mem. Mo. 16th Cir. Judicial Commn., 1979—85, Mo. Appellate Judicial Commn., 1992—97. Trustee Donnelly Coll. Named one of Top Ten Trial Lawyers in Am., Nat. Law Jour., 1994, Top Ten Kans. City Legal Leaders, Daily Record, 2004; recipient Lon O. Hocker Mem. Trial Lawyer award, Mo. Bar Found., Purcell Professionalism award, 1997, Herbert Hartley award, Am. Judicial Soc., 2001. Fellow: Am. Bar Found., Am. Coll. Trial Lawyers; mem.: ABA (Mo. state del. to Ho. Del. 1992—98), Mo. Bar (mem. bd. gov. 1973—77), Kans. City Met. Bar Assn. (pres. 1983, Lifetime Achievement award 1997). Office: Shugart Thomson & Kilroy 12 Wyandotte Plz 120 W 12th St Kansas City MO 64105 Office Phone: 816-374-0571. Office Fax: 816-374-0509. Business E-Mail: lward@stklaw.com.

**WARD, RICHARD HURLEY,** director, dean, writer; b. NYC, Sept. 2, 1939; s. Hurley and Anna C. (Mittasch) W.; children from a previous marriage: Jeanne M., Jonathan B.; m. Michelle Pierczynski, June 15, 1987; 1 child: Michelle Sophia. BS, John Jay Coll., CUNY, 1968; M in Criminology, U. Calif., Berkeley, 1969, D in Criminology, 1971. Detective NYC Police Dept., 1962—70; coord. student activities John Jay Coll., NYC, 1970—71, dean students, 1971—75, v.p., 1975—77, vice chancelor, 1977—93; assoc. chancellor and prof. internat. criminology U. Ill., Chgo., 1993—98; exec. dir. Office Internat. Criminal Justice, 1985—99; exec. v.p. MBF Edn. Group, Malaysia, 1996—97; dean Coll. Criminal Justice, Sam Houston State U., Huntsville, Tex., 1999—2006, assoc. v.p. rsch. and spl. programs, 2006—. Vis. prof. Zagazig U., Egypt, Egyptian Police Acad., 1986, East China Inst. Politics and Law, Shanghai, 1990-91; lectr., various confs. in China, Egypt, Russia, Italy, Eng., Peru, Germany, Saudi Arabia, Finland, Taiwan, Vietnam, Turkey, Korea, United Arab Emirates and U.S., 1983—. Author: (with others) Police Robbery Control Manual, 1975; Introduction to Criminal Investigation, 1975, (with Robert McCormack) An Anti-Corruption Manual for Administrators in Law Enforcement; Quest for Quality, 1984; gen. editor Foundations of Criminal Justice, 46 vols., 1972-75; editor: (with Austin Fowler) Police and Law Enforcement, Vol. I, 1972; Police and Law Enforcement, Vol. II, 1975; (with Harold Smith) International Terrorism: The Domestic Response, 1982, International Terrorism: Operational Issues, 1988; co-author: (with James Osterburg) Criminal Investigation: A Method for Reconstructing the Past, 1992, 4th edit., 2004, (with K. Kiernan and D. Mabrey) Introduction to Homeland Security, 2006. Mem. Mayor of Chgo.'s Blue Ribbon Pannel on Police Promotion; varsity baseball coach U. Ill., Chgo., 1980-82, John Jay Coll. Criminal Justice, CUNY, 1971-72; chief investigator Mayor's Commn. Police Integrity, 1998; mem. Houston Crime Lab. Com., 2005. Cpl. USMC, 1957-61. Recipient Leonard Reisman award John Jay Coll. Criminal Justice, 1968, Alumni Achievement award, 1978, Richard McGee award U. Calif., Berkeley Sch. Criminology, 1971, Friendship medal Peoples Republic of China, 1994, Hans Mattick award III. Acad. Criminology, 1999; Justice Dept. fellow U. Calif., Berkeley, 1971. Mem. ASPA, Acad. Criminal Justice Scis. (pres. 1977-78, Founder's award 1985), Internat. Assn. Chiefs of Police (emsn. edn. and tng. sect. 1974-75), Sigma Delta Chi. Office: Sam Houston State U Houston Police Dept Crime Lab Coll Criminal Justice Huntsville TX 77341 Office Phone: 936-294-4650. Business E-Mail: ward@shsu.edu.

**WARD, RICHARD JOSEPH,** university dean, educator, author; b. Beverly, Mass., Nov. 7, 1921; s. Ralph Woodbury and Margaret (Lyons) W.; m. Cecilia Butler, Sept. 1, 1951; children: Timothy, Mary, Richard, Christopher. BS, Harvard U., 1945; MA, U. Mich., 1948, PhD, 1958. Dir. planning AID Mission to Jordan, 1961-63; chmn. econ. dept. C.W. Post Coll., L.I. U., 1960-61, 63-65; chief planning Bur. for Near East and South Asia, AID, 1965-69; mgr. internat. cons. Peat, Marwick, Mitchell & Co., Washington, 1969-75; dean U. Mass. Coll. Bus., Dartmouth, 1975-87, dean, dir. rsch., prof., 1990-96, Chancellor prof. emeritus, 1996; dir. U.S. Internat. U. Sch. Bus., London, 1988-89; cons. in field. Author: Principles of Economics, 1967, Development Problems, 1973, The Palestine State, 1978, Development Horizon '80, 1980; editor: The Challenge of Development, 1967, Grampas Are For All Seasons, 2005; contbr. articles to profl. jours. Bd. dirs. Indsl. Found., 1976-82; bd. dirs. Jr. Achievement, 1977-99, also past pres.; mem. exec. com. World Congress on Violence and Human Co-existence. Lt. USNR, WWII. Recipient Disting. Svc. award AID, Jordan Mission, 1963, Univ. Svc. award U. Mass. Alumni Assn., 1983, Gov.'s Citation for Svc., 1987; Harvard fellow Ford Found., 1957. Mem. Assn. Social Econs. (pres. 1970-71), Ea. Econ. Assn. (exec. com.), Am. Econ. Assn., Harvard Club (pres. 1984-87, regional bd. dirs.S.E. Mass. and R.I. 1989-92), U.S. Signatory/Found. for Human Co-Existence. Home: 20 Pleasant St South Dartmouth MA 02748-3813 Office Phone: 508-992-5554. Personal E-mail: wardjrichard@comcast.net.

**WARD, RICHARD VANCE, JR.,** management consultant; b. Montreal, Quebec, Canada, June 19, 1929; s. Richard Vance Ward and Isobel Eugene Mosley; m. Elizabeth Anne Gareau, Aug. 15, 1953; children: Carolyn, Jennifer, Philip, Karen, Katherine. BSc, McGill U., Montreal, 1951; diploma in bus. adminstrn., U. Western Ont., London, Can., 1952. Indsl. engr. CIL Inc., Montreal, Canada, 1952-63, prodn. mgr., 1963-65; prodn. dir. ICI Am. Inc., Stamford, 1965-73, CIL Inc., Montreal, Canada, 1973-76, v.p. 1976-84; pres. CIL Corp. of Am., Stamford, Conn., 1984-89, Ward Assoc. Mgmt. Cons., 1989—. Chmn., pres., dir. Friends of McGill, Inc., NYC; bd. dirs. Chlorine Inst. Washington, mem. exec. com., 1984—86; bd. dir. Cornwall Chem. Inc., CIL Corp. Am., Cansco Chems. Inc., Canada. Mem. Chem. Mfrs.

Assn., Friends of McGill U. (dir, pres.), Sr. Men's Club (dir., pres.), SCORE (chmn.), Exchange Club (dir.). Avocations: sailing, hiking, curling, skiing. Home: 45 Brushy Ridge Rd New Canaan CT 06840-4207 Personal E-mail: wardllc@aol.com.

**WARD, ROBERT,** composer, educator, conductor; b. Cleve., Sept. 13, 1917; s. Albert E. and Carrie (Mollenkopf) W.; m. Mary Raymond Benedict, June 19, 1944; children: Melinda, Johanna, Jonathon, Mark, Timothy. B.Mus., Eastman Sch. Music, 1939; cert., Juilliard Grad. Sch. Music, 1946; student composition with, Bernard Rogers, Howard Hanson, Frederick Jacobi, Aaron Copland; conducting with, Albert Stoessel, Edgar Schenkman; D.F.A., Duke, 1972; Mus.D., Peabody Inst., 1975; D.F.A., U. N.C., Greensboro, 1992. Tchr. Juilliard Sch. Music, 1946-56; mng. editor, exec. v.p. Galaxy Music Corp., until 1967, dir., 1967—; exec. v.p. Highgate Press, 1967; pres. N.C. Sch. Arts, Winston-Salem, 1967-74, tchr. composition, 1974-79; prof. composition Duke U., Durham, NC, 1978-87, Mary Duke Biddle prof. music, 1978-87; composer Mus. Natural Sci., NC, 1999—. Chmn. bd. Triangle Music Theater Assocs. Composer: 1st Symphony, 1942, Hush'd Be the Camps Today, 1943, Second Symphony, 1947, First Sonata for Violin and Piano, 1950, Third Symphony, 1951, Fourth Symphony, 1958, Arioso and Tarantelle, Violin and Piano, 1955, Fantasia for Brass Choir and Timpani, 1956, Prairie Overture, 1957, Divertimento for Orchestra, 1961, Earth Shall Be Fair, 1960, He Who Gets Slapped (Pantaloon) (opera in 3 acts); opera in 4 acts The Crucible, 1962 (Pulitzer Prize in music); Hymn and Celebration (for orch.), 1962; for orch. Invocation and Toccata, 1963; opera in 2 acts The Lady From Colorado, 1964; Let the Word Go Forth, 1965; cantata Sweet Freedom's Song, 1965, Hymn To The Night, 1966; First String Quartet, 1966, Sacred Songs for Pantheists, 1966, Festive Ode, 1966, Fiesta Processional, 1967, Antiphony for Winds, 1967 Concerto for Piano and Orchestra, 1968, Four Abstractions, 1977; opera Claudia Legare, 1974; Fifth Symphony-Canticles for America, 1976, Sonic Structure (for orch.), 1980; opera Abelard and Heloise, 1981, Minutes Till Midnight, 1982, Dialogues for Violin, Cello and Orchestra, 1983, Concerto for Saxophone and Orchestra, 1984, Raleigh Divertimento for Wind Quintet, 1986, Festival Triptych, 1987, Sixth Symphony, 1988, First Symphonic Set for the New South, 1988, Fanfare, 1988, Second Symphonic Set, 1988, Appalachian Ditties and Dances, 1988, 5x5, 1989, Images of God, 1989, Ballet Music on The Scarlet Letter, 1990, Second Sonata for Violin and Piano, 1990, Bath County Rhapsody, 1991, Serenade for Mallarmé, 1991, By The Way of Memories for Orchestra, 1997, one act opera Roman Fever, 1993, Love's Seasons, 1994, song cycle Sacred Canticles, 1994, The Hill Song, 1996, Brass Ablaze for British Brass Band, 1996, Night Under the Big Sky for Wind Quintet and Piano, 1997, Echoes of America, Trio for Clarinet, Cello and Piano, 1997, Cherish Your Land-Chorus, 2000, Bayou Rhapsody, 2001, Cherish Your Land, 2001, Dialogues: A Triple Concerto for Violin, Cello and Piano and Orch., 2002, Seventh Symphony, 2003, Nonet arrangement of Raligh Divertimento, 2003, A Friend of Napoleon, 2005. Bd. dirs. Martha Baird Rockefeller Fund for Music, 1971-82, Am. Symphony Orch. League, 1977-89, Nat. Inst. Music Theatre, 1977-85; mem. music com. Henry St. Settlement; bd. dirs. Durham Arts Coun. Served with AUS, 1942-46. Decorated Bronze Star; MacDowell Colony fellow, 1938; recipient Juilliard Pub. award, 1942, Fine Arts award State of N.C., 1975, Gold Baton award Am. Symphony Orch. League, 1991, Disting. Faculty Alumnus award U. N.C., 1992, A.I. DuPont award of Del. Symphony, 1995; Alice M. Ditson fellow Columbia U., 1944, Guggenheim fellow, 1950, 52, 66-67; Am. Acad. Arts and Letters grantee, 1964. Mem. Nat. Acad. Arts and Letters. Home: The Forest at Duke 2701 Pickett Rd # 4022 Durham NC 27705-5688 Office Phone: 919-493-8468.

**WARD, ROBERT ALLEN, JR.,** advertising executive; b. Summit, N.J., Sept. 25, 1937; s. Robert Allen and Edith Allen (Edith) Seiberling; m. Nancy Prescott, Oct. 3, 1964; children: Victoria, Jennifer, Robert. BA, Yale U., 1959. Electronics analyst and account exec. U.S. Trust Co., N.Y.C., 1959-62; v.p., dir. Progressive Mktg. Svcs., N.Y.C., 1962-63, Coin Depot Corp., Elizabeth, NJ, 1963-68; pres. J.S. Riley Co., Wayne, NJ, 1964-70; pres., dir. C.G.W. Enterprises, Butler, NJ, Carelli, Glynn & Ward Advt. Co., 1969-95, All Hours Answering Svc., Pompton Lakes, NJ, 1969-93; v.p., dir. N.J. Exch., 1969-93; v.p. direct Anserve Inc., 1993—. Pres., dir. B.E.K. Inc., real estate mgmt. co., Wayne, N.J., Litho Four Printers, 1970-88, Healthserve, 1996—; dir. Devon Pubs., Butler, N.J., 1977-78; owner 1250 Rt # 23 LLC, 817 Ringwood Ave. LLC. Pres. Kinnelon PTA, N.J., 1972-73; councilman Kinnelon Borough Coun., 1978-83; police commr., Kinnelon, 1978-83; mem. Kinnelon Drug Adv. Coun., 1978-83; vestry St. David Episc. Ch., Kinnelon, 1969-72, 78-87, 90-93, sr. warden, 1978-87; bd. dirs. Morris Area Coun. Girl Scouts U.S.A., 1977-80, Morris Land Conservancy, 2002—, Inner City Ensemble, 1983-90; bd. dirs. Willing Hands, 1989—, chmn., 2000—; mem. sports awards dinner com. North Jersey March of Dimes, 1986-90; chmn. Yale Alumni Schs. Commn., 1984—; dir. Morris Land Conservancy, 2002—; mem. Christmas Cove Improvement Assn. With USMC, 1959-60, served to capt. USAR and NYNG, 1960-72. Mem. No. N.J. Advt. Club (bd. dirs 1970-72), Commerce and Industry Assn. of N.J. (Penpac bd. dirs. 1990), N.J. Home Builder Assoc. (bd. dirs. 1967-70), Bank Mktg. Assn., Hugueuot Soc., S.A.R., Inner City Ensemble/NJ.J. Dance Troupe (bd. dirs. 1983-89), Yale Club (trustee, v.p. 1981—, pres. 1993-96, Montclair), Smoke Rise Club (Kinnelon), Smoke Rise Paddle Tennis Club (pres. 1988—). Republican. Home: 393 Ski Trl Kinnelon NJ 07405-2247 Office: Anserve 1250 State Rt 23 Butler NJ 07405-2002 Office Phone: 973-838-2242. E-mail: robert_ward@amserve.com.

**WARD, ROBERT EDWARD,** retired political science professor, academic administrator; b. San Francisco, Jan. 29, 1916; s. Edward Butler and Claire Catherine (Unger) W.; m. Constance Regina Barnett, Oct. 31, 1942; children: Erica Anne, Katherine Elizabeth. BA, Stanford U., 1936; MA, U. Calif.-Berkeley, 1938, PhD, 1948. Instr. in polit. sci. U. Mich., 1948-50, asst, prof, polit. sci., 1950-54, assoc. prof., 1954-58, prof., 1958-73, Stanford U., 1973-87, dir. Center for Research in Internat. Studies, 1973-87. Cons. in field; advisor Center for Strategic and Internat. Studies, Washington, 1968-87 Author: Modern Political Systems: Asia, 1963, Political Modernization in Japan and Turkey, 1964. Mem. nat. council Nat. Endowment for Humanities, Washington, 1968-73; mem. Pres.'s Commn. on Fgn. Lang.-Internat. Studies, 1978-79; chmn. Japan-U.S. Friendship Commn., 1980-83; mem. Dept. Def. Univ. Forum, 1982-87. Served to lt. (j.g.) USN, 1942-45. Decorated Legion of MErit, 1945; recipient Japan Found. award Tokyo, 1976, Order of Sacred Treasure (Japan), 1983 Fellow Am. Acad. Arts and Scis.; mem. Am. Polit. Sci. Assn. (pres. 1972-73), Assn. Asian Studies (pres. 1972-73), Social Sci. Research Council (chmn. 1969-71), Am. Philos. Soc. Home: Box 8129 501 Portola Rd Portola Valley CA 94028

**WARD, ROBIN A.,** mathematics professor; b. Bryn Mawr, Pa., Jan. 26, 1965; d. Hugh J. Ward and Regina Dorothy Cruice; m. Christopher Michael DelConte, Aug. 21, 1999; children: Sienna Olivia DelConte, Sophia Arabella DelConte. BA, U. Va., Charlottesville, 1997. Asst. prof. Calif. Poly. State U., San Luis Obispo, 1997—2000, U. Ariz., Tucson, 2000—. Ednl. cons. NASA, Lancaster, Calif., 1998—2002. Author: Numeracy and Literacy. Recipient Outstanding Tchg.a Award, U. Ariz., 2005; fellow, NASA and ASEE1, 1998, 1999; grantee Edn. grantee, NASA, 1998—2002, PT3 grantee, US Dept Edn., 2000—04. Mem. AWM, RCML, NCTM. Home: 728 N Campbell Ave Tucson AZ 85719 Office: U Ariz PO Box 210069 Tucson AZ 85721 Office Phone: 520-621-1124. Office Fax: 520-626-7877. E-mail: raward@email.arizona.edu.

**WARD, RODMAN, JR.,** lawyer, director; b. Wilmington, Del., Apr. 8, 1934; s. Rodman and Dorcas (Andrews) W.; m. Susan Speakman Hill, Oct. 10, 1959; children: Margery Ward Garnett, Emily Ward Neilson, Rodman III, Jennifer Ward Oppenheimer. BA, Williams Coll., 1956; LLB, Harvard U., 1959. Bar: Del. 1959, D.C. 1959. Partner Prickett, Ward, Burt & Sanders, Wilmington, 1967-79, Skadden, Arps, Slate, Meagher & Flom, Wilmington, 1979—2002, of counsel, 2002—. Bd. dirs. WMB Holdings, Inc. Author: (with Folk and Welch) Folk on the Delaware General Corporation Law, 1987; contbr. Trustee Winterthur Mus. Gardens and Libr., exec. com. chmn. acad. affairs com.; bd. dirs. The Del. Art Mus.; exec. com., bd. dirs. The Garden

Conservancy. Capt. USAF, 1960—63. Fellow: Am. Coll. Trial Lawyers; mem.: ABA, Am. Judicature Soc., Assn. of Bar of City of N.Y., D.C. Bar Assn., Am. Bar Found. (life), Del. State Bar Assn. (pres. 1989—90), Am. Law Inst., Vicmead Hunt Club, Wilmington Country Club, Wilmington Club. Home: 52 Selborne Dr Wilmington DE 19807-1216 Office: PO Box 636 Wilmington DE 19899-0636 Office Phone: 302-651-3000. Business E-mail: rward@skadden.com.

**WARD, ROGER COURSEN,** lawyer; b. Newark, June 19, 1922; s. Waldron Merry and Aline Toppin (Coursen) W.; m. Katharine More Stevens, Oct. 22, 1949; children: James Olney, Alexander More. Grad., Phillips Exeter Acad., 1940; AB, Princeton U., N.J., 1943; LL.B., Columbia U., N.Y.C., 1949. Bar: N.J. 1949. Law clk. to justice N.J. Supreme Ct., 1951; since practiced in Newark, Morristown, Montclair, NJ; ptnr. Pitney, Hardin, Kipp & Szuch, 1959-91, counsel, 1991-92, Schwartz, Tobia, Stanziale, Sedita & Campisano, LLP, 1993—2005, McElroy Deutsch, Mulvaney & Carpenter, LLC, 2005—. Bd. advisors Am. Inst. Law Tng. Within Office, Phila. 1986-88, Law Hiring and Tng. Report, Chgo., 1983-88. Bd. dirs. United Hosps. Newark, 1965-78, pres., 1973; trustee, v.p. Newark Mus. Assn., 1969-92; bd. dirs. Better Bus. Bur. Greater Newark, 1970-84; mem. Summit Zoning Bd. Adjustment, 1966-70; trustee Eye Inst. N.J., 1973, Pingry Sch., 1966-68, Summit YMCA, 1960-62, Newark Council Social Agys., 1956-60; vice chmn. Newark Mayor's Commn. on Youth, 1958-60. Served to lt. (j.g.) USNR, 1943-46, PTO, ETO. Harlan Fiske Stone scholar Columbia U., 1949. Mem. Essex County Bar Assn., Short Hills (N.J.) Club, Phi Beta Kappa. Office: McElroy Deutsch Mulvaney and Carpenter LLP Gateway Three Ctr 100 Mulberry St Newark NJ 07102-4079 Office Phone: 973-565-2019. Business E-mail: rward@mdmc-law.com.

**WARD, RONALD R.,** lawyer; b. Sacramento, June 12, 1947; BA, Calif. State U., 1973; JD, U. Calif., 1976. Bar: Calif. 1977, Wash., U.S. Dist. Ct. Calif. (No. Dist.) 1979, U.S Dist Ct. (We. Dist.) Wash., U.S. Ct. Appeals (9th cir.). Asst. atty. gen. State of Wash., 1979—82; atty., shareholder Levinson Friedman PS, Seattle, 1982—2005, Jones & Ward, PLLC, Seattle, 2005—. Vol. reading tutor, tchr. asst. Hawthorne Sch., Seattle, mem. parent bd., mem. annual giving steering com.; mem. long-range planning com. Holy Names Acad., Seattle; bd. trustees N.W. Chamber Orch. Named Super Lawyer, 2003—. Mem.: ABA (mem. Ho. of Dels. 2004—, mem. commn. for renaissance of idealism in the profession, mem. standing com. on pro bono and pub. svc.), Am. Bd. Trial Advocates, Loren Miller Bar Assn., Nat. Bar Assn. (Disting Svc. award 1994), Assn. Trial Lawyers Am., Wash. State Trial Lawyers Assn. (mem. bd. govs. 1989—96, co-chmn. Seattle downtown roundtable 1993—96, v.p. west 1994—96, Spl. Pres. Recognition award 1995), State Bar Calif., Fed. Bar Assn., Wash. State Bar Assn. (mem. bd. govs. 2002—03, pres.-elect 2003—04, pres. 2004—05), King County Bar Assn. Office: Jones & Ward PLLC 1000 Second Ave Ste 4050 Seattle WA 98104-1023 Office Phone: 206-957-1273. Office Fax: 206-957-1275. E-mail: rrw@joneswardlaw.com.

**WARD, ROSCOE FREDRICK,** engineering educator; b. Boise, Idaho, Dec. 5, 1930; s. Roscoe C. W. and Alice E. (Ward); m. Julia Duffy, June 8, 1963; children: Eric R., David C. Student, U. Oreg., 1949-50; BA, Coll. of Idaho, 1953; postgrad., U. Wash., 1955-57; BS, Oreg. State U., 1959; MS, Wash. State U., 1961; Sc.D., Washington U., St. Louis, 1964. Registered profl. engr., Ohio. Asst. prof. civil enring. U. Mo., Columbia, 1963-65, Robert Coll., Istanbul, Turkey, 1965-67; assoc. prof. civil engring. Asian Inst. Tech., Bangkok, 1967-68; assoc. prof. civil engring., assoc. dean Sch. Engring. U. Mass., Amherst, 1968-75; prof. Bogazici U., Istanbul, 1974-75; br. chief biomass energy Dept. Energy, Washington, 1975-79; interregional advisor UN/World Bank, 1979-83; dean Sch. Applied Scis. Miami U., Oxford, Ohio, 1983-88, prof. paper and chem. engring. Sch. Engring. and Applied Scis., 1983—. Vis. scientist Csir, Republic of South Africa, 1990-91. Contbr. chapters to books, articles to profl. jours. Fellow: ASCE. Home: 4818 Bonham Rd Oxford OH 45056-1423 Business E-mail: wardrf@muohio.edu.

**WARD, RUSSELL AVERY,** sociology educator; b. Rochester, N.Y., June 16, 1947; s. Eldred Ovenshire and Carol (Gannett) W.; m. Marjorie Morgan, Nov. 20, 1971; 1 child, Matthew Morgan. B.A. in Chemistry, U. Rochester, 1969; M.S. in Sociology, U. Wis.-Madison, 1971, Ph.D. in Sociology, 1974. Asst prof. sociology SUNY-Albany, 1974-80, assoc. prof., 1980—89, prof., 1989—, chair, 2003—. Author: The Aging Experience, 1984, Health in Aging, 1987, The Environment for Aging, 1988; contbr. articles to profl. jours. Bd. mem. Colonie Sr. Svcs. Ctr. and Sr. Adv. Network, 1995—. Ford fellow U. Wis., 1973. Fellow Gerontol. Soc. Am.; mem. Am. Sociol. Assn., Phi Beta Kappa. Avocations: travel; photography. Office: SUNY Dept Sociology 1400 Washington Ave Albany NY 12222-0100 Business E-mail: r.ward@albany.edu.

**WARD, SELA,** actress; b. Meridian, Miss. d. Granberry Holland and Annie Kate Ward; m. Howard Sherman May 23, 1992; 2 children. BA, U. Ala. Actor: (TV series) Emerald Point, N.A.S., 1983-84, Cameo By Night, 1987, Sisters, 1991—96 (Emmy award for Lead Actress in Drama Series 1994), Once and Again, 1999-2002 (winner lead actress in a drama series, Emmy award 2000, winner lead actress in a drama series, Golden Globe award 2001), House, 2005-; (TV films) The King of Love, 1987, Bridesmaids, 1989, The Haunting of Sarah Hardy, 1989, Rainbow Drive, 1990, Child of Darkness, Child of Light, 1991, Double Jeopardy, 1992, Killer Rules, 1993, Almost Golden: The Jessica Savitch Story, 1995 (winner lead actress in drama movie Cableace award 1996), The Rescuers: Stories of Courage: Two Women, 1997, Catch a Falling Star, 2000, Suburban Madness, 2004; (films) Rustler's Rhapsody, 1985, Nothing in Common, 1986, Steele Justice, 1987 Hello Again, 1987, The Fugitive, 1993, My Fellow Americans, 1996, 54, 1998, 54, 1998, Runaway Bride, 1999, The Reef, 1999, The Badge, 2002, Dirty Dancing: Havana Nights, 2003, The Day After Tomorrow, 2004; prodr. (Lifetime cable network) documentary Changing Face of Beauty, 2000, Lifetime "Intimate Portrait", 2001. Office: 289 S Robertson Blvd Ste 469 Beverly Hills CA 90211-2834

**WARD, SOLVEIG MARIA,** marketing professional; b. Stockholm, Aug. 22, 1954; d. Ingvar Erik and Inga Kronman; m. Edward L. Ward, Jan. 20, 1997; children: Johan Fredrick Mahrs, Lars Richard Mahrs. MSEE, Royal Inst. of Tech., Stockholm, 1977. Sales engr. Asea Ab, Vasteras, Sweden, 1977—80; supr. dept. sales ASEA SA de CV, Mexico City, 1980—82; product mktg. mgr. Abb (Asea) Ab, Vasteras, 1982—92; mgr. consulting engring. ABB Inc., Coral Springs, Fla., 1992—99, product mgr. Allentown, Pa., 1999—2002; dir. product mktg. RFL Electronics Inc., Boonton Twp., NJ, 2002—. Mem.: IEEE. Achievements include patents for high speed single pole trip logic for use in protective relaying. Office: RFL Electronics Inc 353 Powerville Rd Boonton NJ 07005 Office Phone: 973-334-3100. Office Fax: 973-334-3863. Business E-Mail: solveig.ward@rflelect.com.

**WARD, SPRING TINA,** history and political science educator; b. Hagerstown, Md., Nov. 28, 1956; d. Raymond Leon and Opal Dorothy (Spade) Ward; m. Robin L. Brna, Dec. 16, 1989. MA, U. Keele, Eng. Mus. dir. City of Hagerstown, Md., 1981—86; dir. pub. rels. YMCA Greater Balt., Balt., 1986—91; asst. prof. history and polit. sci. Hagerstown C.C., 1991—. Clk. session Covenant Ch., 2002—; bd. trustees Hagerstown C.C. Found., 2002—, Leadership Hagerstown, 1999—, Hagerstown Commn. for Women, 1998—2001. Mem.: Washington County Higher Edn. Assn. (co-pres. 1998—2002), LWV (bd. trustees 1993—2002, dir. pub. rels. 1994—). Office: Hagerstown Cmty Coll 11400 Robinwood Dr Hagerstown MD 21742

**WARD, STEPHEN M., JR.,** computer company executive; BSME, Calif. Polytech. State U., San Luis Obispo. Joined IBM Corp., Tucson, 1978; v.p. info. tech., gen. mgr. IBM ThinkPad; gen. mgr. IBM's Global Indsl. Sector; chief info. officer, v.p. bus. transformation IBM Corp., sr. v.p., gen. mgr. regional systems group Armonk, NY, 2003—04; sr. v.p., gen. mgr. personal sys. group IBM, Armonk, NY, 2004—05; CEO Lenovo Group Ltd., Purchase,

NY, 2005, cons., 2005. Past bd. dir. e2open; bd. dir. Carpenter Technology Corp. Recipient NY Ten Award, Exec. Coun., 2005. Office: Lenovo Group Ltd The Centre at Purchase 1 Manhattanville Rd Purchase NY 10577*

**WARD, SUSAN SPRINKLE,** organist; b. Asheville, N.C., June 17, 1954; d. John Robert and Edna Muse Sprinkle; m. Roger Ervin Ward, Aug. 10, 1974; children: Jonathan Michael, Alyssa Lynn. MusB in Edn., Mars Hill Coll., 1976. Music assoc., youth min. Grace Bapt. Ch., Asheville, NC, 1976—85; music assoc., children's choir coord. Biltmore Bapt. Ch., 1985—91; music assoc., organist Fla. St. Bapt. Ch., Greensboro, 1991—97; staff accompanist U. N.C., Greensboro, 1994—99; music assoc., organist First Bapt. Ch., Gastonia, 1999—2001; staff accompanist Wingate U., 1999—2001; music assoc., organist First Bapt. Ch., Southern Pines, 2001—. Children's music cons. Lifeway Pub., Nashville, 1985—2001, Bapt. State Conv., Raleigh, NC, 1985—. Charter mem. N.C. Bapt. Singers, 1984—. Mem.: N.C. Bapt. Singers (assoc.; sect. leader 1995—2000), Am. Guild English Handbell Ringers (assoc.), Am. Choral Dirs. Assn. (assoc.), Choristers Guild (assoc.; ea. N.C. chpt. pres. 2004—), Delta Omicron (assoc.). Liberal. Baptist. Avocations: travel, working with children. Home: 3104 Shopton Dr Apex NC 27502 Office: First Bapt Ch So Pines 200 E New York Ave Southern Pines NC 28387 Office Phone: 910-692-8750. Office Fax: 910-693-1161. Personal E-mail: s_p_ward@yahoo.com.

**WARD, THOMAS,** research scientist; PhD, U. Calif., Santa Barbara. Rschr. Harvard U., Cambidge, Mass., 2003—05. Mem.: Am. Phys. Soc. Office Phone: 310-825-1087.

**WARD, TOM L.,** energy executive; BBA, U. Okla., 1981. Pres., COO, dir. Chesapeake Energy Corp., 1989—2006; CEO, chmn. bd. dirs. Riata Energy, Inc., 2006—. Bd. trustees Anderson U., Ind. Named one of Forbes' Richest Americans, 2006. Office: Riata Energy, Inc Ste 1600 1601 Northwest Expressway Oklahoma City OK 73118 Office Phone: 405-753-5500.*

**WARD, VANESSA GAYLE,** religious organization administrator, minister, consultant; b. Omaha, Mar. 24, 1953; d. Lillard William and Marcella Louise Loftin; m. Keith Dewayne Loftin, Sept. 29, 1973; children: Keith Dewayne Ward Jr., Torrey Glenn, Juana Chon-Ta', Va'Chona Reayle. Grad., Saul David Alinsky Leadership Tng. Inst., 2000; student, Gen. Dist. Ann. Sch. of Prophet, 1995. Overseer and CEO The Body of Christ Internat. (TBOC), Omaha, 2004—; founder and lead organizer Concerned Chs. and Citizens United (CCCU), Omaha, 2004—; founder, lead organizer 4Ward Leap. Founding pastor Afresh Anointing Ch., Omaha, 2002—, Spirit of God AME Zion Ch., Omaha, 1997—; cons. Luth. Metro Ministries ELCA, Omaha, 2002—, Evang. Covenant Ch., Omaha, 2003—; cmty. vol. Infinia Nursing Home, Omaha, 2004—, Maple Crest Nursing Home, Omaha, 1996—. Singer (dancer): (the musical) Working:. Cmty. activist; mem. Luth. Nebr. Senate Outreach (ELCA); steering com. Exec. Offices of Weed & Seed (North Omaha), Omaha, 2002; co-chair Omaha Together One Cmty. (OTOC), Omaha, 2002; pres. Ctrl. Pk. Neighborhood Assn., Omaha, 2000. Recipient, Exec. Offices of Weed and Seed award, 2003, Neighborhood Improvement grantee, 2000, Unsung Hero award, 2005. Mem.: Habitat for Humanity, Nat. Coun. of Negro Women. Office: The Body of Christ (TBOC) International 4757 N 24th St Omaha NE 68110 Office Phone: 402-451-6813.

**WARD, VERNON GRAVES,** retired internist; b. Palisade, Nebr., Mar. 5, 1928; s. Charles Bennett and Mildred Belle (Graves) W.; m. Eleanore Mae Farstveet, Aug. 28, 1952; children: Margo, Alison, Barry. BA, Nebr. Wesleyan U., 1948; MD cum laude, U. Nebr., Omaha, 1954. Diplomate Am. Bd. Internal Medicine. Instr. in anatomy Columbia U., N.Y.C., 1948—50; intern U. Wis., Madison, 1954—55, resident internal medicine, 1955—58, chief resident, physician, 1957—58; fellow in neurophysiology and psychosomatic medicine U. Okla., Oklahoma City, 1960—61; asst. clin. prof. medicine U. Wis., Madison, 1961—62; pvt. practice internal medicine Kearney, Nebr., 1962—67; asst. prof. U. Nebr. Coll. Medicine, Omaha, 1967—69; assoc. clin. prof. medicine U. Nebr., Omaha, 1969—; pvt. practice internal medicine Omaha, 1969—2005; ret. Chmn. dept. internal medicine Clarkson Hosp., Omaha, 1976-78, 96-98. Contbr. articles to profl. jours. including JAMA, Nebr. State Med. Jour., Wis. State Med. Jour., Am. Heart Jour., Postgrad. Medicine. Pres. Nebr. chpt. Arthritis Found., 1969-71. Lt. commdr. USNR, 1958-60. Recipient Cmty. Based Tchg. award ACP-ASIM, 2000; named Hutton Traveling Scholar Coll. of Physicians, 1965. Fellow ACP, Am. Coll. Rheumatology; mem. AMA, Nebr. State Med. Soc., Omaha Med. Soc., Am. Soc. Internal Medicine (Cmty.-Based Tchg. award 2000), Am. Psychosomatic Soc., Nebr. Soc. Internal Medicine (pres. 1980-82, Disting. Internist award 1990), Phi Kappa Phi, Alpha Omega Alpha (pres. Nebr. chpt. 1984-85), Phi Chi (grand sec.-treas. 1986—2006, co-chmn. nat. conv. Omaha 1953, emeritus trustee 2006—), Phi Kappa Tau. Republican. Lutheran. Home: 302 N 54th St Omaha NE 68132-2813

**WARD, WILLIAM E.,** career military officer; b. Balt. m. Joyce Ward; 2 children. BA in Polit. Sci., Morgan State U., 1971; student, US Army Infantry Sch., 1976; MA in Polit. Sci., Pa. State U., 1979; grad., US Army Command & Gen. Staff Coll., 1982—83, US Army War Coll., 1991—92. Commd. 2d lt. U.S. Army, advanced through grades to lt. gen., 2002; rifle platoon leader A Co., 3rd Bn. 325th Infantry 82nd Airborne divsn., Ft. Bragg, NC, 1971—72, anti-tank platoon leader, 1972—74, liaison officer, 1974; rifle platoon leader B Co. 1st Bn., 17th Infantry, 2nd Infantry Divsn. 8th Army, Republic of Korea, 1974—76; instr. then asst. prof. social scis. U.S. Mil. Acad., West Point, NY, 1978—82; logistics staff officer 210th Field Arty. Group US Army Europe & 7th Army, Herzo Base, Germany, 1983-85, exec. officer US Army Community Activity Aschaffenburg, Germany, 1985—86, exec. officer 1st bn. (mechanized), 7th infantry, 3rd divsn., 1986—87; commd. 5th bn. 9th Inf. Rgt. 6th Infantry Divsn., Ft. Wainwright, Alaska, 1988—91; commd. 2d Commando Brigade 10th Mt. Divsn., Ft. Drum, 1992—94; exec. officer to vice chief of staff US Army, Washington, 1994—95; dep. dir. ops. Nat. Mil. Command Ctr., The Joint Staff (J-3), Washington, 1995-96; asst. divsn. comdr. for support 82d Airborne Divsn., Ft. Bragg, 1996-98; chief, Office Mil. Ops. Am. Embassy, Cairo, 1998—99; comdr. 25th Inf. Divsn. U.S. Army Hawaii, Ft. Shaffer, Hawaii, 1999—2000; vice dir. ops. The Joint Staff, Washington, 2000—02; comdr. Stabilisation Force, Operation Joint Force, Sarajevo, Bosnia-Herzegovina, 2002—03; dep. commdg. gen., chief of staff US Army Europe & 7th Army, 2003—; spl. security coord. for Mid. East US Dept. State, 2005—. Decorated Def. Superior Svc. medal with oak leaf cluster, Disting. Svc. medal, Legion of Merit with 2 oak leaf clusters, Def. Meritorious Svc. medal, Meritorious Svc. medal with 6 oak leaf clusters, Joint Service Commendation medal, Army Commendation medal with three oak leaf clusters, Army Achievement medal with oak leaf cluster, Presdl. Order of Merit (Arab Rep. of Egypt). Achievements include participation in OPERATION RESTORE HOPE in Mogadishu, Somalia, 1992-93.

**WARD, WILLIAM FRANCIS, JR.,** real estate investment broker; b. Everett, Mass., Aug. 23, 1928; s. William Francis and Helen (Schriber) W.; m. Elaine L. Wilson, June 11, 1950 (dec. Oct. 1993); children: Jeffrey W., Gary T., Michelle A., Gregory W., Suzanne M.; m. Marie-Louise Buchheit, Nov. 5, 1994. BS, U.S. Mil. Acad.; 1950; MBA, Harvard U., 1956; LLB, La Salle U., 1966; LLD (hon.), So. Vermont U., 1996; HHD (hon.), N.Y. Coll. of Podiatric Medicine, 2003. Commd. 2d lt. U.S. Army, 1950; resigned, 1956; econ. analyst E.I. duPont de Nemours & Co., Inc., Wilmington, Del., 1956-58; sec. N.Y. State Bridge Authority, Poughkeepsie, 1958-60; div. contbr., dir. mktg. svcs. GAF Corp., N.Y.C., 1960-63; asst. to pres. Grosset & Dunlap, Inc., 1963-65, v.p., 1965-67; contr. Dun & Bradstreet, 1967-71, v.p., 1968-71; chmn. bd., pres. Dun-Donnelley Pub. Corp., 1971-77; exec. v.p. Am. Cancer Soc.; from v.p., treas. to pres. Gestam, Inc., 1981-86; chief Army Res., 1986-91, comdr. U.S. Army Res. Command, 1990—91; chmn., pres. Realicam, 1995—. Bd. dirs. Quotron Electronics, Inc, Premier Nat. Bank, Eastern Savs. Bank, Apple Bank for Savs., Corinthian Broadcasting, Greater N.Y. Bank for Savs.; trustee All-City Funds; mem. adv. bd. Astoria Fin. Bank, Podia Ins. Co.; mem. faculty Dutchess C.C., 1958-60, NYU Sch. Commerce, 1960-64; trustee N.Y.C. Foot Clinics, 2004—. Pres. Ramapo Central Sch. Dist., 1966-72, 1982-87; mem. facilities and planning bd. Good Samaritan

Hosp., 1980-85; chmn. United Way, Rockland County, 1992-94; county chmn. Citizen for Kennedy and Johnson, 1960; Dem. candidate for Ho. of Reps., 1962; chmn. Young Citizens for Johnson and Humphrey, 55 counties NY, 1964; exec. v.p. Am. Cancer Soc., 1976-81; bd. dirs. NYC divsn. Aerospace Edn. Found., U.S. Army War Coll. Found., West Point Fund, 1979, Franciscan Sisters of the Poor Found., 1980-92; trustee NY Mil. Acad. 1982-86, 91-96, trustee emeritus, 1996—; trustee Assn. Grads. U.S. Mil. Acad., 1993-2003, trustee emeritus, 2003—, exec. com., 1996-2003; chmn. audit com., 1996—; trustee Hist. Soc. Rockland County, 1993-95, NY Coll. Podiatric Medicine, 2000, chmn. bd. trustees, 2004—. Capt. AUS, 1950-54; to maj. gen. USAR 1978-91. Decorated D.S.M. with 1 oak leaf cluster, Legion of Merit, Meritorious Svc. medal with oak leaf cluster, Air medal with 3 oak leaf clusters, Army Commendation medal with oak leaf cluster, Purple Heart, Army Achievement medal. Mem. West Point Soc. (Washington chpt., Space Coast chpt., N.Y. chpt., pres. 1974-76), Antrim Players, Soc. Harvard Engrs. and Scientists, Fin. Execs. Inst., Newcomen Soc., Res. Officers Assn. Am. Friends of Viet Nam (nat. chmn.), VFW, Am. Legion, Knight of Holy Sepluchre, Disabled Am. Vets., Pilgrim Soc., Army and Navy Club, Squadron "A" Club, Univ. Club (N.Y.), Harvard Club (Washington), Nat. Press Club. Roman Catholic. Home: Summit View Farm 341 17A PO Box 150 Goshen NY 10924-0150 also: 1271 Continental Ave Melbourne FL 32940 E-mail: wward@hvc.rr.com.

**WARD-BROWN, DENISE,** sculptor, educator; BFA cum laude, Temple U., 1975; MFA summa cum laude, Howard U., 1984. Assoc. prof. U. Washington, St. Louis, 1991—. One-woman shows Cinque Gallery, N.Y.C., 1984, Washington Project for the Arts, Washington, 1984, Bozeman, Mont., 1986, O St. Gallery, Washington, 1989, Montgomery Coll., Tacoma Park, Md., 1989, Fitzpatrick Gallery, Washington, 1989, U. Md., Princess Anne, Md., 1991, Pierce-Arrow Gallery, St. Louis, 1993, St. Louis Art Mus., 1995, Margaret Harwell Art Mus., Poplar Bluff, Mo., 1998; group exhbns. include Corcoran Mus. Art, Washington 1987, George Washington U., 1987, U. Richmond, Va., 1987, Shippee Gallery, N.y.C., 1987, Strathmore Arts Ctr., Rockville, md., 1988, Rockville Arts Ctr., 1989, Notre Dame Coll., Balt., 1989, No. Va. C.C., Arlington, 1989, The Kunstrum, Washington, 1990, Montgomery Coll., Tacoma Park, Md., 1990, Smithsonian-Anacostia Mus., Washington, 1990, Art St. Louis, 1992, Lindenwood Coll., St. Louis, 1993, Murray State U. Eagle Gallery, 1993, Portfolio Gallery, St. Louis, 1994, U. Wis., Eau Claire, 1994, U. Md., College Park, 1994, St. Louis Design Ctr., 1996, Gene Pool & Assocs., N.Y.C., 1996, Smithsonian Instn., 1996, numerous others. Study grantee Penland (N.C.) Sch. Crafts, 1973, Haystack Mt. Sch. Crafts, Deer Isle, Maine, 1973, 74, Howard U./Ford Found., 1982, 83, Vt. Studio Sch., Johnson, 1986, Geog. Devel. grantee Washington D.C. Commn. on the Arts and Humanities, 1984, 85; Individual Artist grantee Washington D.C. Commn. on the Arts and Humanities, 1986, 87, 89, 91, Mbari, Ritual and Rememory, Regiona Artists' Projects grantee, 1994; Fulbright scholar African Rsch. Program, Ghana, others. Office: Dept Sculpture Sch Art Washington U Camp Box 1031 1 Brookings Dr Saint Louis MO 63130-4862 Fax: 314-935-8412. E-mail: ddwardb@art.wustl.edu.

**WARDEN, GAIL LEE,** healthcare executive; b. Clarinda, Iowa, May 11, 1938; s. Lee Roy and Juanita (Haley) W.; m. Lois Jean Johnson, Oct. 9, 1965; children: Jay Christopher, Janna Lynn, Jena Marie. BA, Dartmouth Coll., 1960; MHA, U. Mich., 1962; PhD in pub. adminstrn., Cent. Mich. U., 1995. Adminstrv. asst. Blodgett Meml. Ctr., Grand Rapids, Mich., 1962; adj. Dewitt Hosp., Ft. Belvoir, Va., 1963-65; exec. v.p./COO Rush-Presbyn.-St. Luke's Med. Ctr., Chgo., 1965-74; exec. v.p. Am. Hosp. Assn., Chgo., 1976-81; pres., CEO Group Health Coop. Puget Sound, Seattle, 1981-88, Henry Ford Health Sys., Detroit, 1988—2003, pres. emeritus, 2003—. Past chmn. Am. Hosp. Assn., HRET, Steering Com. Transformational Leadership Project in Health Mgmt. Edn. and Practice; former chmn. Nat. Quality Forum; chair Nat. Ctr. Healthcare Leadership, IOM Com. on Future Emergency Medicine in US, Detroit Wayne County Health Authority; bd. dirs. Comerica Bank, Nat. Rsch. Corp.; mem. RAND Health Bd. Advisors; dir. emeritus Nat. Com. on Quality Assurance, former chmn.; former mem. Bd. Health Care Svcs., Inst. Medicine, Com. Quality Health Care in Am., Fed. Adv. Commn. Consumer Protection and Quality in Health Care Industry, Nat. Commn. Civic Renewal, Pew Health Professions Comms., IOM, gov. coun.; vice chair bd. dirs. Rosalind Franklin U. Medicine and Sci.; chair campaign com., mem. dean's adv. bd. U. Mich. Sch. Pub. Health. Contbr. articles to profl. jours. Former bd. dirs. Robert Wood Johnson Found., 1965; bd. dirs. Citizens Rsch. Coun. Mich.; chair Detroit Zoological Soc.; former mem. bd. dirs. Detroit Econ. Growth Corp.; former mem. Detroit Met. Wayne County Airport Commn.; former chmn. Greater Detroit Area Health Coun.; bd. dirs. Bon Secours Cottage Health Svcs., co-chair capital campaign; past mem. Fed. Adv. Commn. on Consumer Protection and Quality in the Health Care Industry. Capt. USAR. Named one of Ten Outstanding Young Men in Chgo., Jr. Assn. Commerce and Industry, 1968; named on e of 100 Most Powerful People in Healthcare, Modern Healthcare, 2002-04; recipient Nat. Health Care award, B'nai B'rith Internat., 1992, CEO award Am. Hosp. Assn.'s Soc. for Healthcare Planning and Mktg., 1993, Gold Medal award, Am. Coll. Health Care Execs., 1999; first recipient Thompson Vis. Fellowship award, Yale, Health Quality award, Nat. Com. Quality Assurance, Disting. Svc. award, AHA, Walter J. McNerney Fellowship award for Health System Improvement, HRET. Mem. APHA, NAS Inst. Medicine (governing coun.), Am. Coll. Hosp. Adminstrs. (named Young Adminstr. of Yr. 1972), Am. Healthcare Systems, Inst. Healthcare Improvment, Nat. Resource Ctr. on Chronic Care Integration, Alpha Chi Rho. Office: Henry Ford Health System 1 Ford Pl Detroit MI 48202-3450

**WARDEN, JOHN LEHMAN,** lawyer; b. Evansville, Ind., Sept. 22, 1941; s. Walter Wilson and Juanita (Veatch) W.; m. Phillis Ann Rodgers, Oct. 27, 1960; children: Anne W. Clark, John L., W. Carson. AB, Harvard U., 1962; LLB, U. Va., 1965. Bar: N.Y. 1966, U.S. Ct. Appeals (2d cir.) 1966, U.S. Dist. Ct. (so. and ea. dists.) N.Y. 1967, U.S. Ct. Appeals (10th cir.) 1971, U.S. Supreme Ct. 1972, U.S. Ct. Appeals (D.C. cir.) 1980. Assoc. Sullivan & Cromwell, N.Y.C., 1965-73, ptnr., 1973—. Commr. US Antitrust Modernization Commn., 2004—. Editor-in-chief: Va. Law Rev., 1964-65. Hon. trustee U. Va. Law Sch. Found.; trustee Am. Ballet Theatre. Fellow Am. Coll. Trial Lawyers; mem. ABA, Am. Law Inst., NY State Bar Assn., Assn. Bar City NY, NY County Lawyers Assn., Knickerbocker Club, Down Town Assn. Club, Doubles Club, Bedford Golf and Tennis Club, Lyford Cay Club. Republican. Episcopalian. Office: Sullivan & Cromwell 125 Broad St Fl 28 New York NY 10004-2489 Office Phone: 212-558-3610. E-mail: wardenj@sullcrom.com.

**WARDEN, RICHARD DANA,** government labor union official; b. Great Falls, Mont., Dec. 10, 1931; s. Robert Dickinson and Helen (Leach) W.; m. Barbara Freeman; children from previous marriage: Denise, Michael, Joseph, Jerome. BA, U. Mont., 1957, MA, 1958. Reporter, then state editor Gt. Falls (Mont.) Tribune, 1959-61; legis. asst. to U.S. Senator Lee Metcalf of Mont., 1962-63; adminstrv. asst. to U.S. Congressman James G. O'Hara of Mich., 1963-67; dep. dir. Office Civil Rights, HEW, 1967-68; legis. rep. AFL-CIO, 1969-70; dir. Washington Research Project Action Council, 1970-72; asst. legis. chmn. UAW, 1972—75, legis. dir., 1975-77, 79-91, ret., 1991. Asst. sec. legis. HEW, 1977-79 Served with USN, 1950-54. Congressional fellow, 1961-62; recipient Pub. Affairs Reporting award Am. Polit. Sci. Assn., 1960 Home: 211 Marina Dr Lewes DE 19958

**WARDEN, WALDIA ANN,** archdiocese official, director; b. New Orleans, Jan. 15, 1933; d. Walter Emmer and Lydia Eugenie (LeBlanc) W BS, St. Mary's Dominican Coll., 1961; MS Dietetics, St. Louis U., 1964; JCL, Cath. U. Am., 1988. Joined Dominican Sisters, Congregation of St. Mary, Roman Cath. Ch., 1953, coun. mem., 1976-84, 96-2004. Tchr. elem. schs., 1954—62; instr. foods and nutrition Dominican Coll., New Orleans, 1964—66, chmn. home econs. dept., 1966—69, asst. dean students, 1969—75, chmn. dept. home econs., 1975—78, chmn. Coll. Planning Coun., 1972—76; dir. Rosaryville Ctr., Ponchatoula, La., 1979—81; pres. St. Mary's Dominican Coll. New Orleans, 1983—86; defender Bond for Tribunal Archdiocese of New Orleans, 1989—2005; dir. Rosaryville Spirit Life Ctr., 2005—. Pres. St. Mary's Dominican H.S., 1990-94; coord. First Ct. Met. Tribunal, Archdiocese

of New Orleans, 1994-2005 Trustee St. Mary's Dominican Coll., 1973-79, 83-86, 90-93; bd. regents Our Lady of Holy Cross Coll., New Orleans, 1992-98; bd. dirs. Henriette deLille Mid. Sch. for Girls, 2000-04, chair, 2004-05 Mem. La. Dietetic Assn. (editor jour. 1966-68), La. Leadership Conf. Women Religious, Am. Dietetic Assn., Am. Home Econs. Assn., Canon Law Soc. Am., Dominican Leadership Conf. (cluster coordination com. 2002-06, chair reconclauration subcom. 2002-06) Home: 39003 Rosaryville Rd Ponchatoula LA 70454-7001 Office Phone: 225-294-5039. Personal E-mail: dawaldia@aol.com.

**WARDER, LAWRENCE A.,** federal agency administrator; b. Akron, Ohio; m. Dianne Warder; 2 children. BS, U. Akron; MBA, Kent State U., 1969. CPA, cert. mgmt. acct., mgmt. cons. Pilot plant operator Gen. Tire and Rubber Co., supr. fin. sys.; cons. Touche Ross & Co., Clev., 1969—70, Detroit, 1970—77, ptnr., 1977—81; mng. dir. Ctrl.-S.W. Group, Dallas, 1981—92, mgr. NY and N.E. region, 1992—96; dir. ops. cons. Deloitte Cons. LLP, 1996—98, head European ops. London, 1998—2000, global dir. ops., 2000—01, NYC, 2001—02; cons. to sys. chancellor U. Tex., 2002—05, cons. instl. audit and compliance com.; with O'Donnell Found., Dallas, Austin Ind. Sch. Dist.; CFO US Dept. Edn., Washington, 2006—. Office: US Dept Edn 400 Maryland Ave SW Washington DC 20202*

**WARDER, MICHAEL YOUNG,** academic administrator; b. Buffalo, June 29, 1946; s. Thomas Grayston and Norma A. (Young) W.; m. Cheryl Lynn Gilkerson, Feb. 8, 1975; children: Maureen, Amy, Michael Jr. BA, Stanford U., 1968. Tchr. Drew Sch., San Francisco, 1968—69; pres. Internat. Re-edn. Found., San Francisco, 1970—73; sec.-gen. Internat. Conf. on Unity of Scis., N.Y.C., 1974—79; pres., pub. Newsworld Commn., N.Y.C., 1976—79; dir. adminstrn. Heritage Found., Washington, 1980—83; exec. v.p. Ethics and Pub. Policy Ctr., Washington, 1983—84, The Rockford Inst., Ill., 1985—95; v.p. devel. Claremont Inst., Calif., 1995—2001; exec. dir. So. Calif. Children's Scholarship Fund, 2001—05; vice chancellor Pepperdine U., Malibu, Calif., 2005—. Radio commentator (bi-weekly) Sta. WNIJ-FM NPR Affiliate, DeKalb, Ill., 1991—95; del. leader People to People, USSR, 1991, Rockford Inst., Lithuania, Latvia, Estonia, 1994; del. leader to London Claremont Inst., 1996, del. leader to Hong Kong, 97, del. leader to Israel, 98, del leader to Rome, 2000; guest TV programs Politically Incorrect/ABC, Fox News Channel, MSNBC, others; spkr. in field; polit. analyst in field. Op-ed columnist The Wall Street Jour., USA Today, L.A. Times, The Chgo. Tribune, Chgo. Sun Times, San Francisco Chronicle, San Diego Union Tribune, St. Louis Post Dispatch, Indpls. Star, 1985—; host/prodr. (TV weekly public affairs show) Stateline Newsmakers, 1990-92; columnist (weekly) Rockford Register Star, 1991-92. Recipient Silver Dome award Ill. Broadcasters Assn., 1993, 95, 96; grantee Earhart Found., 1988. Mem.: So. Calif. Grant Makers, L.A. World Affairs Coun., Phila. Soc., Coun. for Nat. Policy, Americanism Ednl. League (bd. dirs.). Republican. Avocations: travel, history, geography. Office: Pepperdine U 24255 Pacific Coast Hwy Malibu CA 90263 Office Phone: 310-506-4486. Business E-Mail: michael.warder@pepperdine.edu.

**WARDER, RICHARD CURREY, JR.,** dean, mechanical aerospace engineering educator; b. Nitro, W.Va., Sept. 30, 1936; s. Richard Currey and Edith Irene (Moser) W.; m. Carolyn Strickler, Mar. 7, 1964 (div. Dec. 1978); children: Jennifer, Jeffrey W.; m. Marjorie Dianne Forney, Jan. 10, 1981. BS, S.D. Sch. Mines, 1958; MS, Northwestern U., 1959, PhD, 1963. Registered profl. engr., Mo., Tenn. Asst. prof. Northwestern U., Evanston, Ill., 1963-65; mgr. energy processes research Litton Industries, Beverly Hills, Calif., 1965-68; assoc. prof. mech. and aerospace engring. U. Mo., Columbia, 1968-72, prof., 1972-94, James C. Dowell prof., 1989-94, chmn. mech. aerospace engring., 1988-94; dean U. Memphis Herff Coll. Engring., 1994—. Program mgr., head resources sect. NSF, Washington, 1974-76; mem. Engring. Accreditation Commn., 2003—; cons. to industry U.S. govt. Bd. dirs. Columbia Montessori Soc., 1971-73; bd. dirs. Columbia Soccer Club, 1976-80, pres., 1978-80; referee Maj. Indoor Soccer League, 1979-83. Fellow: ASME, AIAA (assoc.); mem.: AAAS, Am. Soc. Engring. Edn., Am. Phys. Soc. Methodist. Office Phone: 901-678-4306.

**WARDLAW, KIM A. MCLANE,** federal judge; b. San Francisco, July 2, 1954; m. William M. Wardlaw Sr., Sept. 8, 1984. Student, Santa Clara U., 1972—73, Foothill C.C., Los Altos Hills, Calif., 1973—74; AB in Comm summa cum laude, UCLA, 1976, JD with honors, 1979. Bar: Calif., U.S. Dist. Ct. (ctrl. dist.) Calif. 1979, U.S. Dist. Ct. (so. dist.) Calif. 1982, U.S. Dist. Ct. Nev. 1985, U.S. Dist. Ct. (no. dist.) Calif. 1992, U.S. Dist. Ct. Mont. 1993, U.S. Dist. Ct. Minn. 1994, U.S. Dist. Ct. (no. dist.) Ala. 1994, U.S. Dist. Ct. (so. dist.) Miss. 1995, U.S. Supreme Ct. Law clk. U.S. Dist. Ct. Ctrl. Dist. Calif., 1979—80; assoc. O'Melveny and Myers, 1980—87, ptnr., 1987—95; judge U.S. Dist. Ct. Calif., LA, 1995—98, U.S. Ct. Appeals (9th cir.), 1998—. Presdl. transition team Dept. Justice, Washington, 1993; mayoral transition team City of LA, 1995—; bd. govs. UCLA Ctr. for Comm. Policy, 1994—, vice-chair, 1994—; cons. in field. Co-author: The Encyclopedia of the American Constitution, 1986; contbr. articles to profl. jours. Pres. Women Lawyers Pub. Action Grant Found., 1986—87; founding mem. LA Chamber Orch., 1992—; active Legal Def. and Edn. Fund Calif. Leadership Coun., 1993—; active Blue Ribbon of LA Music Ctr., 1993—; del. Dem. Nat. Conv., 1992. Named one of Most Prominent Bus. Attys. in LA County, LA Bus. Jour., 1995; recipient Buddy award, NOW, 1995. Mem.: NOW, ABA, Orgn. Women Execs., Assn. Bus. Trial Lawyers (gov. 1988—), LA County Bar Assn. (trustee 1993—94), Women Lawyers Assn. LA, Calif. Women Lawyers, Mex.-Am. Bar Assn. LA County, Hollywood Womens Polit. Com., Downtown Women Ptnrs., City Club Bunker Hill, Breakfast Club, Chancery Club, Phi Beta Kappa. Office: US Ct Appeals 9th Cir 125 South Grand Ave Pasadena CA 91105*

**WARDLOW, BENJAMIN FRANKLIN, III,** sales executive; b. Lebanon, Ohio, Sept. 17, 1946; s. Benjamin Franklin Wardlow II and Blanche Lee Hardwick; m. Barbara Ann Wardlow, Sept. 17, 2002. BS, U. Cin., 1984. Corp. sales mgr. Marquette Mfg., Minn., 1968—76; br. mgr. Netherland Rubber Co., Charlestow, W.Va., 1976—78; airline acct. adminstr. Gen. Elec., Cin., 1978—81; sales mgr. Twyman Templeton Co., Columbus, 1981—87; owner A/C Sys., Cin., 1987—93; sales exec. Keidel Supply, 1993—. With U.S. Army, Vietnam. Mem.: Disabled Veterans Am., Lexington Valley Scottish Rite, Lebanon Elks, Montgomery Lodge F & AM. Republican. Quaker. Avocations: golf, marathon running, tennis.

**WARDRIP, ELIZABETH JANE,** retired librarian; b. Lawrenceburg, Ind., Dec. 12, 1925; d. Estal Joseph Ackerman and Dorothy Leona Unthank; m. Schuyler Clark Wardrip, Dec. 20, 1953 (div. Dec. 24, 1981); children: Gregory Clark, Elizabeth Jane, Margaret Louise, Laura Anne, Mary Ann. BS in Gen. Studies, Columbia U., 1951; MLS, U. Md., 1972. Cert. libr. Md., 1972. Libr. adult svcs. Prince George's County Meml. Libr. Sys., Hyattsville, Md., 1972—92, ret., 1992. Fellow, U. Rochester, 1951. Mem.: DAR (regent 1999—2001). Democrat. Roman Catholic. Avocations: reading, theater, travel, museums, art galleries. Home: 6103 Sutters Place Bowie MD 20720

**WARDROPPER, IAN BRUCE,** museum curator, educator; b. Balt., May 11, 1951; s. Bruce Wear and Joyce (Vaz) W.; stepmother: Nancy Hélène (Palmer) W.; m. Laurel Ellen Bradley, May 22, 1982 (div. 1996); 1 child, Chloe Bradley; m. Sarah Anne McNear, June 21, 1997. BA, Brown U., 1973; MA, NYU, 1976, PhD, 1985. Asst. curator European sculpture Art Inst. Chgo., 1982-85, assoc. curator European decorative arts and sculpture, 1985-89, Eloise W. Martin curator European decorative arts and sculpture, and classical art, 1989-2001; Iris and B. Gerald Cantor curator in charge dept. European sculpture and decorative arts Met. Mus. Art, N.Y.C., 2001—05, chmn., 2005—. Adj. instr. Drew U., NJ, 1982; vis. asst. prof. Northwestern U., Evanston, Ill., 1986, Sch. of Art Inst. Chgo., 1988; guest scholar J. Paul Getty Mus., Malibu, Calif., 1995; Rhoades lectr. U. Chgo., 1997; exhbns. panelist NEA, 1993, creation and presentation panelist, 98, indemnity panelist, 1998—2001. Co-author: European Decorative Arts in the Art Institute of Chicago, 1991, Austrian Architecture and Design beyond Tradition in the 1990s, 1991, News from a Radiant Future: Soviet Porcelain from the Collection of Craig H. and Kay A. Tuber, 1992, Chiseled with a Brush:

Italian Sculpture, 1860-1925, from The Gilgore Collections, 1994, From the Sculptor's Hand: Italian Baroque Terracottas from the State Hermitage Museum, 1998; contbr. articles to profl. jours. NEA fellow, 1976-77, Chester Dale fellow Met. Mus. Art, 1978-79; Kress Found. rsch. grantee, Paris, 1979-81, Am. Philos. Soc. grantee, 1991; named Chicagoan of the Yr. in Arts Chicago Tribune, 1994. Mem. Phi Beta Kappa. Office: Met Mus Art 1000 Fifth Ave New York NY 10028-0198 Office Phone: 212-879-5500 ext. 4980. Business E-Mail: Ian.wardropper@Metmuseum.org.

**WARD-STEINMAN, DAVID,** composer, music educator, pianist; b. Alexandria, La., Nov. 6, 1936; s. Irving Steinman and Daisy Leila (Ward) W.-S.; m. Susan Diana Lucas, Dec. 28, 1956 (div. 1993); children: Jenna, Matthew; m. Patrice Dawn Madura, May 28, 2001. MusB cum laude, Fla. State U., 1957; MusM, U. Ill., 1958, DMA, 1961; studies with Nadia Boulanger, Paris, 1958-59; postdoctoral vis. fellow, Princeton U., 1970. Grad. instr. U. Ill., 1957-58; mem. faculty San Diego State U., 1961—2003, prof. music, 1968—, disting. prof. music, emeritus prof., 2004, dir. comprehensive musicianship program, 1972—2003, composer in residence, 1961—, univ. rsch. lectr., 1986-87. Faculty Eastman Sch. Music Workshop, 1969, Coll. Music Soc. Nat. Inst. for Music in Gen. Studies, U. Colo., 1983-84, Calif. State Summer Sch. for the Arts, Loyola Marymount U., 1988; Ford Found. composer in residence Tampa Bay (Fla.) Area, 1970-72, Brevard Music Ctr., N.C., 1986; acad. cons. U. North Sumatra (Indonesia), 1982; concert and lecture tour U.S. Info. Agy., Indonesia, 1982; master tchr. in residence Atlantic Ctr. for the Arts, New Smyrna Beach, Fla., 1996; vis. artist in residence Victorian Ctr. for the Arts, Melbourne, Australia, 1997, faculty Coll. Mus. Soc. Nat. Insts., San Diego, 1999, 2001, 2003, Ind. 2003; adj. prof. music Ind. U., Bloomington, 2004—. Composer: Symphony, 1959, Prelude & Toccata for orch., 1962, Concerto No. 2 for chamber orch., 1962, ballet Western Orpheus, 1964, Cello Concerto, 1966, These Three ballet, 1966, The Tale of Issoumbochi chamber opera, 1968, Rituals for Dancers and Musicians, 1971, Antares, 1971, Arcturus, 1972, The Tracker, 1976, Brancusi's Brass Beds, 1977; oratorio Song of Moses, 1964; Jazz Tangents, 1967, Childs Play, 1968; 3-act opera Tamar, 1977; Golden Apples, 1981; choral suite Of Wind and Water, 1982; Christmas cantata And In These Times, 1982; Moiré for piano and chamber ensemble, 1983, And Waken Green, song cycle on poems by Douglas Worth, 1983, Olympics Overture for orchestra, 1984, Children's Corner Revisited, song cycle, 1984, Summer Suite for oboe and piano, 1984, Quintessence for double quintet and percussion, 1985, Chroma concerto for multiple keyboards, percussion and chamber orch., 1985, Winging It for chamber orchestra, 1986, Elegy for Astronauts for orchestra, 1986, What's Left for piano, 1987, Gemini for 2 guitars, 1988, Intersections II: Borobudur, Under Capricorn, 1989, Voices from the Gallery, 1990, Cinnabar for viola and piano, 1991, Seasons Fantastic for chorus and harp, 1992, Cinnabar Concerto for Viola and Chamber Orchestra, 1993, Night Winds Quintet # 2 for woodwinds, 1993, Double Concerto for Two Violins and Orchestra, 1995, Prisms and Reflections (3rd Piano Sonata), 1996, Millennium Fanfare for symph. orch., 2000, Millennium Dances for symph. orch., 2001, FIESTA! for symphony orch., 2002, FLIGHT! for 2 Pianos, 2002; recs. include Fragments from Sappho, 1969; Duo for cello and piano, 1974, Childs Play for bassoon and piano, 1974, The Tracker, 1989, Brancusi's Brass Beds, 1984, concert suite from Western Orpheus, 1987, Sonata for Piano Fortified, 1987, Moiré, 1987, 3 Songs for Clarinet and Piano, 1987, Concerto #2 for Chamber Orchestra, 1990, Prisms and Reflections, 1999, Cinnabar, 1999, Sonata for Piano Fortified, 1999, Night Winds, 1999, Borobudur, 1999, Cello Concerto, 2000, Cinnabar Concerto, 2000, Chroma Concerto, 2000, I Am the Wind for voice and chamber ensemble, 2002, Skyline and Under Capricorn, 2005, Songs of the Seasons, 2006; commd. by Chgo. Symphony, Joffrey Ballet, San Diego Ballet, San Diego Symphony, numerous others; author: (with Susan L. Ward-Steinman) Comparative Anthology of Musical Forms, 2 vols, 1976, Toward a Comparative Structural Theory of the Arts, 1989. Recipient Joseph H. Bearns prize in Music Columbia U., 1961, SAI Am. Music award, 1962, Dohnanyi award Fla. State U., 1965, ann. BMI awards, 1970—, Broadcast Music prize, 1954, 55, 60, 61; named Outstanding Prof., Calif. State Univs. and Colls., 1968, Outstanding Alumnus of Yr., Fla. State U., 1976; Fulbright sr. scholar La Trobe U. and Victorian Coll. Arts, Victorian Arts Ctr., Melbourne, Australia, 1989-90. Mem. Coll. Music Soc. (nat. bd. for composition 1991-93), Broadcast Music, Inc., Soc. of Composers, inc., Nat. Assn. of Composers U.S.A., Golden State Flying Club. Presbyterian. Office: San Diego State U Dept Music San Diego CA 92182 Business E-Mail: dwardste@mail.sdsu.edu.

**WARDY, JOE,** former mayor; b. El Paso, Tex., 1953; s. Joe and Mary Rodriguez Wardy; m. Delores Prouse Wardy; children: Kaleb, David. B in fin., U. of Tex. at El Paso, 1976. With Herman/Miles Trucking, Inc., 1985, ptnr., pres.; COO Miles Group, Inc., 2000; mayor City of El Paso, Tex., 2003—05. Mem. Frank Manning Little League Com.; pres. Franklin Football Booster Club; mem. Tex. Assn. of Football Ofcls.; exec. com. Greater El Paso C. of C.; chmn. El Paso Leadership and Rsch. Coun.; adv. bd. Liberty Mutual Ins. Southwest; bd. dir. North Am. Transp. Alliance, Candlelighters of El Paso; exec. com. Tex. Motor Transp. Assn.; mktg. and mgmt. adv. bd. U. of Tex. at El Paso; v.p. at large Am. Trucking Assn. Office: Joe Wardy, Mayor of El Paso 2 Civic Ctr Plaza, 10th Fl El Paso TX 79901

**WARE, BENNIE,** academic administrator; b. Ponca City, Okla., Sept. 21, 1946; s. Clyde Elmer and Lois Aliene (Smith) W.; m. Sheridan Lee Welch, May 28, 1967 (div. 1976); 1 child, Winston Arthur; m. Claudia Borman, Dec. 21, 1979 (div. 1998); children: Jeffrey Bright, Amelia Marie; m. Eleanor Gallagher, Mar. 7, 1998. BS in Chemistry, Okla. State U., 1968; PhD in Biophys. Chemistry, U. Ill., 1972. Asst. prof. chemistry Harvard U., Cambridge, Mass., 1972-75, assoc. prof., 1975-79; prof., chmn. dept. chemistry Syracuse U., 1979-84, Kenan prof. sci., 1984-91, v.p. rsch., 1989-92, v.p. rsch., computing, 1992—. Contbr. articles to profl. jours. Grantee NSF, 1972, 74, 77, 80, 83, 86, 89, NIH, 1972, 74, 76, 77, 79, 81, 84, 86; Alfred P. Sloan fellow, 1976-80. Fellow AAAS; mem. Phi Beta Kappa, Phi Kappa Phi. Achievements include invention of electrophoretic light scattering; first to combine laser light scattering and fluorescence photobleaching recovery to distinguish mutual and tracer diffusion; first to apply laser Doppler velocimetry to protoplasmic streaming. Home: 333 Berkeley Dr Syracuse NY 13210-3041 Office: Syracuse Univ 3-014D Ctr Sci And Tech Syracuse NY 13244-0001 Office Phone: 315-443-2492. Business E-Mail: brware@syr.edu.

**WARE, BRENDAN JOHN,** retired electrical engineer and utility executive; b. Dublin, Aug. 27, 1932; arrived in U.S., 1959, naturalized, 1967; m. Jane Mills Orth, Oct. 7, 1961; children: Michael, Henry, Frieda. B.E. with honors, Nat. U. Ireland, Dublin, 1954. Various engring. positions Am. Elec. Power Service Corp., N.Y.C., 1960-76, mgr. elec. research and tech. svcs. Columbus, Ohio, 1976-96. Contbr. articles to profl. jours. Fellow: IEEE. Roman Catholic.

**WARE, CHARLOTTE ETHEL,** retired elementary school educator; b. Phila., Aug. 2, 1931; d. Charles Edward and Helen (Whelan) Ware; 1 child, Jonathan Bryson Ware. BS in Edn., U. Colo., Boulder, 1972; MA, U. No. Colo., Greeley, 1989. Dept. supr. Opinion Rsch. Corp., Princeton, 1952-61; clk. teller, collection dept. United Bank of Denver, 1961-65; commencement clk. IV U. Colo., Boulder, 1965-70; substitute tchr. St. Vrain Sch. Dist. REI-J, Longmont, Colo., 1972-73, Sch. Dist. 1, Denver, 1973-83, Sch. Dist. 9R, Durango, Colo., 1985-88; tchr. St. Columba Sch., Durango, 1988—93. Filmed law enforcement crisis intervention training Durango Cable Access TV, 2003—; tutor St. Columbia Sch., 2005—06. Prodr.: Crisis Intervention Training, 2003. Vol. Denver Ctr. Theatre Co.; Theatre Assocs. Group, Inc., phonathon chmn., Denver, 1983; active Sacred Heart and St. Columba Jail Ministry, Durango, 1995—, Mental Health Summit Partnership Crisis Intervention Planning Com., Durango, 2002—; criminal justice coordinating com. Mercy Med. Ctr. Aux, Durango, 2000—, Meth Forum, 2004—; active Nat. Alliance for the Mentally Ill S.W. Colo., 2003—, treas., 2004-, bd. dirs., 2006-, St. Columba Social Justice Com., 2006-. Recipient Cmty. Builder award, Mental Health Summit Partnership, 2003, Crisis Intervention Star award, Nat. Alliance for the Mentally Ill S.W. Colo., 2004. Mem. St. Columba Altar and Rosary Soc. (treas. 1986-88, past pres., v.p.), Cath. Daus. Am. (past regent), Bus. and Profl. Women's Club (v.p. Boulder chpt. 1964), DAR (Sarah Platt Decker chpt. chaplain 2006—), Pi Lambda Theta (pres. 1982), Phi Delta Kappa. Roman Catholic. Avocations: reading, swimming, writing. Home: 950 E 32nd St 204 Durango CO 81301-6029

**WARE, D. CLIFTON,** vocalist, educator; b. Newton, Miss., Mar. 15, 1937; s. Durward Clifton and Emma Edna (Blount) W.: m. Elizabeth Jean Oldham, June 20, 1958; children: Jon Clifton, David Michael, Stephen Alan. BA, Millsaps Coll. 1959; MusM, U. So. Miss., 1962; MusD, Northwestern U., 1970. Voice instr. U. So. Miss., Hattiesburg, 1964-69; prof. voice and pedagogy U. Minn., Mpls., 1970—; chmn. Roy A. Schuessler Vocal Arts Ctr., 1970—. Clinician, cons., adjudicator. Author: (book, song collection and video) Voice Adventures, 1988, (text, song collection, audio cassette, CD) Adventures in Singing, 1995, 2d edit., 1998, 3rd edit., 2004, Basics of Vocal Pedagogy, 1998, The Singer's Life: Goals and Roles, 2005; made recs. St. Nicolas, 1977, Paul Bunyan, 1988, Vocal Explorations: The Bad, the Good, and the Other, 2003; tenor soloist opera, oratorio, recitals. Mem. Nat. Assn. Tchrs. Singing (pres. Minn. chpt. 1972-73, 81-82, found 1995—), Nat. Opera Assn. (pres. 1978-79), Pi Kappa Lambda, Phi Kappa Delta, Phi Mu Alpha Sinfonia, Pi Kappa Alpha. Avocations: travel, hiking, reading.

**WARE, FREDERICK,** internist, educator, nephrologist; b. Omaha, June 16, 1928; s. Frederick John and Clara Louise (Abbott) Ware; m. Charlott Rae Johnson, Sept. 15, 1978; children: Andrea Johnson, Nicholas Harper; m. Elizabeth Diane Thomas (div.); children: Frederick, Mary(dec.), Sally, Tom, Dana. BSc with high distinction, U. Nebr., Lincoln, 1949; MS, U. Nebr., Omaha, 1953; PhD, U. Nebr., 1956, MD cum laude, 1956. Diplomate Am. Bd. Internal Medicine, 1965, Am. Bd. Nephrology, 1976. Co-founder, ptnr. Internal Medicine Assocs., Omaha, 1970—91; prof. internal medicine U. Nebr. Coll. Medicine, Omaha, 1968—91, prof. physiology-biophysics, 1968—91, acting chief nephrology, 1976—87, prof. emeritus, 1991—. Med. dir. Renal Disease Ctr. Clarkson Hosp., Omaha, 1973—91; med. dir. Woodman & World Life Ins. Security, Omaha, 1976—; co-founder, med. dir., pres. Nebr. Organ Recovery Sys., Omaha, 1977—2004. Capt. USAF, 1959—61. Named Disting. Alumnus, U. Nebr. Coll. Medicine, 2003, Legend of Clarkson, Clarkson Hosp., 2005; recipient Golden Apple award, U. Nebr. Coll. Medicine, 1970; Conkling scholar, 1950. Fellow: ACP; mem.: Alpha Omega Alpha, Sigma Xi, Phi Beta Kappa. Avocations: carpentry, classical music, reading. Home: 6040 Mary Nelson Ln Fort Calhoun NE 68023

**WARE, GEORGE HENRY,** botanist; b. Avery, Okla., Apr. 27, 1924; s. Charles and Mildred (Eshelman) W.; m. June Marie Gleason, Dec. 21, 1955; children: David, Daniel, Patrick, John. BS, U. Okla., 1945, MS, 1948; PhD, U. Wis., 1955. Asst. prof. Northwestern State U. of La., Natchitoches, 1948-56, assoc. prof., 1956-62, prof. U. Conservation Sect., No. La. Supplementary Edn. Ctr., Natchitoches, 1967-68; dendrologist Morton Arboretum, Lisle, Ill., 1968-92; adminstr. Urban Vegetation Lab., 1986-92, rsch. fellow in dendrology, 1992-94, dendrologist emeritus, rsch. assoc., 1995—. Vis. prof. U. Okla., Norman, 1957, 61, 63-64; adj. prof. Western Ill. U., 1972-85; ext. faculty George Williams Coll., Downers Grove, Ill., 1969-76, Nat. Coll. Edn., Evanston, Ill., 1972-76, adj. prof. Aurora U., 2003—. Trustee nomination caucus Coll. of DuPage, Glen Ellyn, Ill., 1974-78; bd. dirs. Kane-DuPage Soil and Water Conservation Dist., 1969-81, DuPage Environ. Commn., 1992—; Openlands Project, 1996—; pres. La. Acad. Scis., 1966-67; dir. La. State Sci. Fair, 1966. With USN, 1942-46. Recipient Gold Seal award, Nat. Coun. State Garden Clubs, 1991, Am. Forests Urban Forestry Rsch. medal, 1994, Lifetime Svc. award, Nat. Urban and Cmty. Forestry Adv. Coun., 1995, Hutchinson medal, Chgo. Botanic Garden, 1997, Morton J. Colman award, Am. Nursery and Landscape Assn., 1998, award of merit, Am. Assn. Botanic Gardens and Arboreta, 2000, Liberty Hyde Bailey award, Am. Horticultural Soc., 2002, Conservation Leadership award, Openlands Project, 2005. Mem.: Am. Forests, Nature Conservancy, Ill. Arborist Assn. (pres. 1987—88), Am. Assn. Bot. Gardens and Arboreta, Internat. Soc. Arboriculture (Pres. Commendation award 2000), Southwestern Assn. Naturalists (treas. 1963—69). Office: Morton Arboretum Lisle Ill. 60532-1293 Office Phone: 630-719-2413. Business E-Mail: gware@mortonarb.org.

**WARE, GWENDOLYN C.,** retired counseling administrator; m. Roy Ware, Mar. 28; 1 child, Sonja (Ware) Lucca. BA in English magna cum laude, U. Ark., Pine Buff, 1970; MEd in Secondary Counseling with honors, U. Nev., Las Vegas, 1975. English instr. Clark County Sch. Dist., Las Vegas, 1971—77, guidance counselor, 1977—95, scholarship and coll. prep counselor, 1996—2003, ret., 2003. Fin. aid/scholarship workshop presenter Clark County Sch. Dist., Las Vegas, 1997—2003; coll. preparation workshop facilitator and presenter Kappa Alpha Psi Kappa League, Las Vegas, 2002—. Mem. Black Cmty. Orgn. Network, Las Vegas, 1988—2005. Mem.: AAUW, NAFE, Clark County Sch. Counselors' Assn., Western Assn. Coll. Admissions Counselors, Sickle Cell Anemia Found. (scholarship rev. and selection 1987—88), Phi Delta Kappa (2nd v.p. membership 1997—99, Mem. of Yr. 1997).

**WARE, J(OE) ANTHONY,** cardiologist; b. Topeka, Dec. 12, 1952; s. Joe F. and Jane C. (Casper) Ware; children: Gabriel, Rachel, Emily. BS summa cum laude, Washburn U., 1974; MD, Kans. U., 1977. Diplomate Am. Bd. Internal Medicine, Am. Bd. Cardiovasc. Disease. Intern, resident Baylor Coll. Medicine, Houston, 1977-81, chief resident, 1981, clin. fellow in cardiovasc. disease, 1981-84; rsch. fellow Beth Israel Hosp., Med. Sch. Harvard U., Boston, 1984-86, assoc. prof. medicine, 1986-97; Sidney L. & Miriam K. Olson prof. cardiology Albert Einstein Coll. Medicine and Montefiore Med. Ctr., N.Y.C., 1997-2001, chief cardiovasc. divsn., 1997-2001; v.p. cardiovasc. rsch. and clin. investigation Eli Lilly and Co., Indpls., 2001—. Dir. CCU Beth Israel Hosp., Med. Sch. Harvard U., 1992—93, dir. vascular biol. unit, 1992—97. Author, editor: book Angiogenesis in Cardiovascular Disease, 1999; contbr. articles to profl. jours. Fellow: Am. Coll. Cardiology; mem.: Molecular Medicine Soc., Assn. Profs. Cariology, Assn. Univ. Cardiologists, Am. Soc. Clin. Investigation, Am. Heart Assn., Am. Soc. Cell Biology, Am. Soc. Hematology, Assn. Am. Physicians, Interurban Clin. Club. Office: Eli Lilly Corp Ctr DC 0520 Indianapolis IN 46285 Office Phone: 317-651-1034. E-mail: jaware@lilly.com.

**WARE, JON DEAN,** retail executive; b. Springfield, Ill., Nov. 14, 1935; s. Claude Richard and Dorothy Elizabeth (Smith) W.; m. June L. Lamar, Aug. 12, 1956; children: William Bradley, Todd Richard. BS in Edn., Ea. Ill. U., 1958. Lab. analyst USI, Tuscola, Ill., 1957; tchr. Daytona Beach (Fla.) Sch. Sys., 1958-59; warehouse mgr. Warlubco, Inc., Jacksonville, Ill., 1959-62; supr. Ware Oil Co., Jacksonville, 1962-64, constrn. mgr., 1965-72, purchasing mgr., constrn. mgr., v.p., 1972-77, pres., 1972—2002; ret., 2002. Mem. bd. trustees Ill. Coll., treas., mem. exec. bd. Mem. Petroleum Marketers Am. (pres. 1997), Ill. Petroleum Marketers (pres. 1987). Republican. Methodist. Avocations: golf, tennis, hunting, boating. Home: 1553 Mound Ave Jacksonville IL 62650-2255

**WARE, MARILYN,** ambassador, former utilities company executive; b. Lancaster, Pa., Nov. 4, 1943; d. John III and Marian Ware; children: Mark Strode, Amy Strode, Scott Strode. D of Pub. Services.; Thaddeus Stevens Coll. Tech.; 1998; LittD (hon.), Franklin & Marshall Coll., 2003. Vice-chmn. Am. Water Works Co., Inc., Voorhees, NJ, 1984-88, chmn., 1988—2003, chmn. emeritus Vorhees, NJ, 2003; US amb. to Finland US Dept. State, Helsinki, 2005—. CEO Ware Family Offices, Strasburg, Pa., 1991; dir. CIGNA Corp., Phila., 1993-2005, IKON Office Solutions, Malvern, Pa., 2000—2005, Am. Enterprise Inst., Washington, 1994, PENJERDEL Coun., Phila.; mem. Nat. Infrastructure Advisory Coun., 2002, Pew Oceans Commn., 2000-03 Editor: The Oxford Press, Lancaster, Pa., 1978-82. Trustee Nat. Osteoporosis Found., Washington, 1996-2000, U. Pa. Health Sys., Phila., 1991—; Gannon U., Erie, Pa., 1996-2000, Nat. Coun. of Conservation Fund, Washington, 1999—; Eisenhower Exch. Fellowships, Phila., 1995—; chmn. exec. com., 2000; founding mem., bd. dirs. Lancaster Farmland Trust, 1987—; founder, adv. bd. dirs. Janus Sch., Mt. Joy, Pa., 1991—; v. sec. Oxford Found., Strasburg, 1981—; chmn. Tom Ridge for Gov. Campaign,

Harrisburg, Pa., 1993-94, Rep. Com. of Lancaster County, 1978-80, Woman for Bush, Pa., 1987-88; mem. Rep. State Com. of Pa., 1985-90. Recipient Samuel S. Baxter Meml. award Water Resources Assn., 2000, Paradigm award Greater Phila. C. of C., 1999, Dir.'s Choice award Nat. Women's Econ. Alliance Found., 1992; named Bus. Leader of Yr., Rep. Caucus, Pa. Ho. of Reps., 1993, Disting. Daus. of Pa., Gov. Tom Ridge, 2000. Office: Am Embassy 5310 Helsinki Pl Washington DC 20521*

**WARE, PAUL F., JR.,** lawyer; b. Boston, Feb. 24, 1944; AB, U. Notre Dame, 1966; LLB, U. Pa., 1969. Bar: Mass. 1969, U.S. Supreme Ct. 1973, D.C. 1974. Law clk. to Hon. Andrew Caffrey U.S. Dist. Ct., 1969-70; asst. U.S. atty. Dept. Justice, Washington, 1970-73, spl. asst. U.S. atty., 1973-74; spl. asst. atty. gen. Commonwealth of Mass., Boston, 1982-83; atty. Goodwin, Procter & Hoar, Boston; ptnr. Goodwin Procter LLP, Boston, 1978—, and chmn., litig. dept., mem. exec. com. Clin. assoc. instr. Harvard Law Sch., Cambridge, Mass., 1976, trial advisor, 1977-80, 83-88; mem. faculty Mass. Continuing Legal Edn., 1990; active U.S. Magistrate Selection Panel; trial counsel Iran Contra Investigation, 1992-93. Fellow Am. Coll. Trial Lawyers; mem. ABA, Mass. Bar Assn., Boston Bar Assn. Office: Goodwin Procter LLP Exchange Pl 53 State St Boston MA 02109-2803 Office Phone: 617-570-1280. Office Fax: 617-523-1231. Business E-Mail: pware@goodwinprocter.com.

**WARE, RICHARD ANDERSON,** foundation executive; b. N.Y.C., Nov. 7, 1919; s. John Sayers and Mabelle (Anderson) W.; m. Lucille Henney, Mar. 20, 1942 (div. 1972); children: Alexander W., Janet M., Bradley J., Patricia E.; m. Beverly G. Mytinger, Dec. 22, 1972. BA, Lehigh U., 1941; M in Pub. Adminstrn., Wayne State U., 1943; D in Social Sci. (honoris causa), Francisco Marroquin U., Guatemala, 1988. Research asst. Detroit Bur. Govt. Research, 1941-42; personnel technician Lend-Lease Adminstrn., Washington, 1942-43; research asso. to asst. dir. Citizens Research Council, Detroit, 1946-56; sec. Earhart and Relm Founds., Ann Arbor, Mich., 1951-70, trustee, pres., 1970-84, trustee emeritus, pres. emeritus. Prin. dep. asst. sec. def. for internat. security affairs, Washington, 1969-70; cons. Office Asst. Sec. Def., 1970-73; dir. Citizens Trust Co., 1970-87. Vice pres. Ann Arbor United Fund and Cmty. Svcs., 1968, pres., 1969; asst. dir. Mich. Joint Legis. Com. on State Reorgn., 1950-52; sec. Gov.'s Com. to Study Prisons, 1952-53; com. to chmn. Ann Arbor City Planning Commn., 1958-67; mem. Detroit Com. on Fgn. Rels., 1971-87; mem. Woodrow Wilson Internat. Center for Scholars, 1977-85; vis. com. divsn. social scis. U. Chgo., 1977-85; mem. adv. com. The Citadel, 1977-85; mem. adv. coun. internat. studies program Fletcher Sch., Tufts U., 1979-85; trustee Greenhills Sch., 1973-80, Ann Arbor Area Found., 1977-83, Inst. Pub. Policy Analysis, 1985-2003, Inst. Polit. Economy, 1985—2005, Ctr. for Study Social and Polit. Change Smith Coll., 1988—2005, Pequawket Found., 1989—, Intercollegiate Studies Inst., 1996—; polit. analyst Rep. Nat. Com., Washington, 1964; bd. dirs. The Liberty Fund, Inc., Indpls., 1980—2004, Bd. Fgn. Scholarships, 1984-90, chmn., 1987-89. With USAAF, 1943-46. Recipient Civilian Meritorious Service medal Dept. Def., 1970; Paul Harris fellow Rotary, 1997. Fellow Mont Pelerin Soc.; mem. Govtl. Research Assoc. (trustee, v.p. 1955-56), Am. Polit. Sci. Assn., Ann Arbor Club, North Conway Country Club, Cosmos Club (Washington), Phi Beta Kappa, Phi Alpha Theta Congregationalist. Home: PO Box 310 Intervale NH 03845-0310 Office: 2200 Green Rd Ste H Ann Arbor MI 48105-1569

**WARE, SUSAN W.,** historian; b. Wash., DC, Aug. 22, 1950; d. Charles Kline and Charlotte McConnell Wolfe; m. Donald R. Ware, June 10, 1972. BA, Wellesley Coll., 1968—72; MA, Harvard U., 1973, PhD, 1978. Asst. to assoc. prof. NYU, 1986—95; hon. vis. scholar Radcliffe Coll., 1996—97; editor, Notable Am. Women Radcliffe Inst. for Advanced Study, Harvard U., 1997—2005; vis. lectr., history Harvard U., 2002—05. Adv. bd. Schlesinger Libr., Cambridge, Mass., 1988—97, Franklin and Eleanor Roosevelt Inst., Hyde Park, NY, 1986—; assoc. Clio, Inc., Charlotte, Vt., 1996—; exec. bd. Soc. of Am. Historians, N.Y.C., 1990—2002. Author: (books) Beyond Suffrage: Women in the New Deal, 1981, Letter to the World: Seven Women Who Shaped the Am. Century, 1998; editor: Forgotten Heroes: Inspiring Am. Portraits from our Leading Historians, 1998; author: Holding Their Own: Am. Women in the 1930s, 1982, Ptnr. and I: Molly Dewson, Feminism, and New Deal Politics, 1987, Still Missing: Amelia Earhart and the Search for Modern Feminism, 1993, It's One O'Clock and Here Is Mary Margaret McBride! A Radio Biography, 2005. Home: 16 Hilliard St Cambridge MA 02138 Office: Radcliffe Inst for Advanced Study 10 Garden St Cambridge MA 02138 Personal E-mail: sdware@aol.com.

**WARE, THADDEUS VAN,** retired government official; b. High Point, N.C., Mar. 31, 1935; s. Elsec and Irene (Myers) W.; m. Doretha Ardella Lee, June 18, 1960; children— Kimberly Melissa, Chrystal Lynn. BA cum laude, Va. Union U., 1957; JD, Howard U., 1960. Bar: Va. bar 1961, D.C. bar 1970, U.S. Supreme Ct. bar 1970. Gen. atty. Office of Solicitor, Dept. Labor, 1961—66; trial counsel Chief Counsel's Office, Fed. Hwy. Adminstrn., 1966—69; staff asst. to Pres. Richard M. Nixon, 1969—70; chief adminstrv. judge, chmn. Bd. Contract Appeals, Dept. Transp., 1987—2003; ret., 2003. Appt. bd. contract appeals Dept. Trans., 1970. Served with AUS, 1960-61. Mem. Va., D.C., U.S. Supreme Ct., Fed. Bar Assns., Urban League, NAACP, Bd. Contract Appeals Judges Assn. (pres. 1988-89), Alpha Phi Alpha, Sigma Delta Tau, Alpha Kappa Mu (Disting. Career Svc. award). Home: 2213 Parallel Ln Silver Spring MD 20904-5446

**WARE, THERESA,** reading specialist, educator; b. Bklyn., Feb. 1, 1961; d. Donald Thomas and Vivian Sawyer; m. Dwight David Ware, Oct. 10, 1987; children: Dwight David II, Aaron Alexander. BS, U. Md., Ea. Shore, 1984; MEd in Reading, Bowie State U., Md., 2000. Cert. Tchr., Reading Specialist Md. State Dept. of Edn., 1997, Notary Pub. Md., 1988. Classroom tchr. DC Pub. Schs., Washington, 1990—97, Prince Georges County Pub. Schs., Upper Marlboro, Md., 1997—98; reading initiative tchr. Montgomery County Pub. Sshs.; reading specialist Montgomery County Pub. Schs., Silver Spring, Md., 2001—, staff devel. tchr., 2001—. Mem. Montgomery County Coun. of the Internat. Reading Assn., Silver Spring 1998—2005; del. Md. State Tchrs. Assn., Silver Spring, 1999—2000; v.p. Montgomery County Coun. of the Internat. Reading Assn., Silver Spring, 2003—04. Mem.: Alpha Kappa Alpha Sorority. Roman Catholic. Avocations: reading, travel. Office: Montgomery County Pub Schs Divsn Acad Support FSP 4910 Macon Rd Ste 204 Rockville MD 20852

**WARE, WILLIAM BRETTEL,** education educator; b. Glen Ridge, N.J., June 17, 1942; s. Howard Brettel and Helen Burd (Dickson) W.; m. Andrea Lou Gartley, June 24, 1967 (div. May 1989); children: Emily Dickson, Matthew Brettel, Erin Johanna Ware; m. Barbara Ann McClave Reynolds, Dec. 26, 1991; adopted children: Dianne Catherine, Kristin Elise. AB, Dartmouth Coll., 1964; MA in Tchg., Northwestern U., 1965, PhD, 1968. Classroom tchr. Chgo. Pub. Schs., 1964-65; asst. prof. U. Fla., Gainesville, 1968-73, assoc. prof., 1973-76, prof. 1976-78, U. NC, Chapel Hill 1978—, prof. social work, 2004—. Contbr. chpts. to books and articles to profl. jours. Mgr. youth soccer team Ctrl. Carolina Youth Soccer Assn., Chapel Hill, 1980-86. Recipient J. Minor Gwynn professorship Sch. Edn., U. N.C., 1994-95, Chancellor's Award for Disting. Tchg., 1995. Mem. Am. Ednl. Rsch. Assn., Nat. Coun. on Measurement in Edn., N.C. Assn. for Rsch. in Edn. (bd. dirs., pres. 1996-97, treas. 1998—). Home: 907 Bayberry Dr Chapel Hill NC 27517-8378 Office: Sch Edn Univ North Carolina Cb # 3500 Chapel Hill NC 27599-3500

**WAREHAM, ELLSWORTH EDWIN,** cardiothoracic surgeon, educator; b. Avinger, Tex., Oct. 3, 1914; s. Dayton and Goldie Leah Wareham; m. Barbara Nell Nix, May 7, 1950; children: Martin, Robert, Julie, John, Scott. An. Can. Jr. Coll., Coll. Heights, Alta., 1931–33, at, 1935–36, Can. Union Coll., Lacombe, Alta., 1936; MD, Loma Linda U., Calif., 1942; LLD (hon.), Andrews U., Berrien Springs, Mich., 1971. Cert. Am. Bd. of Surgery, 1954, Am. Bd. of Thoracic Surgery, 1955. Intern Seattle Gen. Hosp., 1942—45; indsl. surgeon Good News Bay Mining Co., Platinum, Alaska, 1942—45; resident fellow in surgery Loma Linda U. Med. Ctr., Calif., 1947—50; resident

surgery Bellevue Hosp. Columbia U., NYC, 1950—52; resident thoracic and cardiovasc. surgery Queens Med. Ctr., NYC, 1952—53; resident cardiovasc. surgery svcs. St. Francis Hosp. Cardiac Children, Roslyn, NY, 1954—55; prof. surgery Loma Linda U., 1964—2006, prof. emeritus surgery, 2006—; chief cardiothoracic surgery Loma Linda U. Med. Ctr., 1964—86; acting chmn. dept. of surgery Loma Linda U., 1973—75; staff Loma Linda U. Med. Ctr., 1964—86, Riverside Gen. Hosp., Calif., 1973—75; prof. cardiac surgery King Saud U., Riyadh, Saudi Arabia, 1986—88; admin. dir. Hong Kong Heart Ctr., 1988—. Surgeon and dir., Loma Linda U. mission to Pakistan, India, Thailand and Formosa U.S. Dept. of State, 1963; surgery team Govt. of Greece, Athens, 1967—73; organizer heart surgery affiliation Evangelismos Hosp. and Loma Linda U. Sch. Medicine, 1970—76; surgeon, heart team Loma Linda U., China, 1981. Performer: (films) Atrial Septal Defect, 1964 (Golden Eagle Cine award, Venice Film Festival, 1964); contbr. articles to profl. jours. Lt.(j.g.) USN, 1945—47, PTO. Recipient Outstanding Educator of Am., 1970, award for svc. to people of Pakistan, City of Karachi, 1963, Medallion award for svc. to Greek People, Evangelismos Hosp., Athens, 1967, Golden Medal of Health, Republic of Vietnam, 1974, Outstanding Alumnus, Loma Linda U. Sch. of Med., 1974, Outstanding Contbn. to Medicine, San Bernardino County Med. Soc., 1986, Outstanding Achievement award in medicine, Ministry of Def. and Aviation, Saudi Arabia, 1986, Pres. Commendation, US, 1984, Alumnus of the Yr., Loma Linda U., 1994, Outstanding Contbn., Pasadena divsn., Am. Heart Assn., 1999. Fellow: Am. Coll. of Cardiology, Am. Coll. Surgeons; mem.: AMA, Western Assn. of Thoracic Surgery, Pacific Coast Surg. Assn., Am. Assn. for Thoracic Surgery, San Bernardino County Med. Soc., Calif. Med. Assn., Soc. of Thoracic Surgeons, Alpha Omega Alpha. Republican. Adventist. Achievements include development of heart surgery programs in Greece, Saudi Arabia, Hong Kong, developing countries. Mailing: Box 1068 Loma Linda CA 92354

**WAREHAM, JOHN P.,** medical products executive; MS in Pharmacy, Creighton U.; MBA, Washington U. Various positions SmithKline, 1968—79, pres., Norden Labs., 1979—84; v.p., diagnostics sys. group Beckman Coulter, Fullerton, Calif., 1984—93, pres., COO, 1993—98, CEO, 1998—. Mem., adv. coun. Keck Grad. Inst. of Applied Life Scis.; mem., chief exec. roundtable U. Calif., Irvine; mem. Ctr. for Corp. Innovation; mem., bd. trustees Mfrs. Alliance/MAPI; dir.; past chmn. AdvaMed; bd. dirs. Steris Corp., 2000—, Beckman Coulter, Fullerton, Calif., 1993—, chmn., bd. dirs., 1999—. Office: Beckman Coulter 4300 N Harbor Blvd Fullerton CA 92834

**WAREHAM, RAYMOND NOBLE,** brokerage house executive; b. Rochester, NY, Nov. 20, 1948; s. Simon Harold and Barbara (Snell) W.; m. Cornelia Lee Clifford, June 28, 1975; children: Ellinor Park, Laura Stewart, Cornelia Ashley. BS in Indsl. Engring., Northwestern U., 1970; MBA, Harvard U., 1975. With J.P. Morgan & Co., NY, 1975-80, mgr. dir., head banking industry group NY, 1988-92, head-corp. fin. Tokyo, 1980-85; exec. dir. J.P. Morgan Securities Ltd., London, 1986-87; mng. dir. corp. fin. dept. J.P. Morgan Securities, N.Y.C., 1992-98; sr. portfolio mgr. Sanford C. Bernstein Alliance Capital, N.Y.C., 1999—; sr. mng. dir., 1999—. Trustee Am. Sch., Tokyo, 1982-85; elder Brick Presbyn. Ch., NYC, 1989-92; bd. dir. Brick Ch. Day Sch., 1989-92, Juvenile Diabetes Found., 1997-98; pres. bd. trustees Spence Sch., NYC, 1995-2001; Life trustee, 2002-; Lt. Supply Corps, USN, 1970-73. Mem. DERU (Northwestern hon.), Naval War Coll. Found., Union Club (NY), Duxbury (Mass.) Yacht Club, Century Club (Harvard Bus. hon.). Republican. Avocations: sports, antique furniture. Home: 1148 5th Ave New York NY 10128-0807 Office: Alliance Capital/Sanford C Bernstein 17th Fl 1345 Ave of Americas New York NY 10105-0096

**WAREN, STANLEY ARNOLD,** academic administrator, performing company executive; b. NYC, Mar. 22, 1919; s. Maurice and Minnie (Rosen) W.; m. Florence Rigal, Nov. 21, 1949; 1 child, Mark BSS., CCNY, 1938; MA, Columbia U., 1939, PhD, 1953. Exec. producer, dir. theatre, 1953-70; prof., chmn. dept. speech and theatre CCNY, 1967-72; prof., exec. officer Ph.D. program theatre CUNY, 1972-81, v.p.; provost, dep. pres. Grad. Sch., 1981-84; dir. Ctr. for Advanced Study in Theatre Arts, NYC, 1979-82, 84-86. Reviewer NEH, 1978—91; advisor humanities com. Bklyn. Acad. Music, NYC, 1980—81; spl. edn. cons. Dougle Image Theatre, NYC, 1982—90; mem. adv. coun. Roundabout Theatre, NYC, 1985—93; Fulbright-Hayes vis. prof. Nat. Taiwan U., 1986—87; vis. prof. Shanghai Drama Inst., 1988; USIS grant, lectr., Hong Kong, 88, Ctr. for Living and Learning, Marymount Manhattan, 1998—2006, New Sch. U., 2000—03. Dir. musical The Chess King (Taiwan) 1987, Old B Hanging on the Wall (Shanghai), 1988, Judas, Mexico (NY), 1989, Seasoned Citizens Theare Co., 2003-06. Bd. dirs. Women's Inter. Art Ctr., NYC, 1978-82; mem. grants panel NYC Dept. Cultural Affairs, 1979; bd. dirs. Frank Silvera Workshops for Writers, NYC, 1979-81. Served to capt. USAF, 1942-46 Grantee Herman Goldman Found., 1980-82, NEH, 1980-81, NY Coun. Humanities, USIA/Arts Am., Singapore, 1990. Mem. AAUP, Assn. for Theatre in Higher Edn., Soc. Stage Dirs. and Choreographers, Profl. Staff Congress CUNY, The Drama League (mem. awards nominating com. 1997—). Clubs: The Century Assn. (resident 1984—). Democrat. Avocations: art, tennis, swimming. Home: 465 W End Ave #11D New York NY 10024-4926 Office: Theatre PhD Program Grad Sch 365 5th Ave New York NY 10016-4309

**WARENSKJOLD, DOROTHY,** singer, educator; d. William Earl and Mildred Lorrayne (Stombs) Warenskjold. BA, Mills Coll., 1943. Soprano San Francisco Opera Co., 1949—58, Columbia Artists Mgmt., N.Y.C., 1950—72; adj. prof. UCLA, Westwood, 1984—97, 1999; master class instr. numerous orgns., 1999—. Singer numerous recs. Named Woman of Yr., Opera Guild, 1988. Mem.: Nat. Assn. Tchrs. of Singing (adv. bd. 2004—). Achievements include 1st American singer asked to appear at the Rebild Festival in Denmark. Home: 7716 Oakview Ln Lenexa KS 66216 Personal E-mail: dwkc1@yahoo.com.

**WARES, ARSALAN,** mathematics professor; b. Dhaka, Bangladesh, Feb. 20, 1968; s. Shamsul and Amera Wares. PhD in Math. Edn., Ill. State U., Normal, 2001. Asst. prof. U. Man., Winnipeg, Manitoba, Canada, 2001—04, Valdosta State U., Ga., 2004—. Home: 1016 Williams Street Valdosta GA 31601 Office: Valdosta State University 1500 North Patterson St Valdosta GA 31698 Office Phone: 229-333-5787.

**WARFEL, M(ARTHA) KAY,** speech pathology/audiology services professional; b. Lancaster, Pa., Mar. 2, 1955; d. Orlene Dickenhart and Martha (Herr) W.; m. George Jay Malley, Jr., Sept. 21, 1978 (div. 1979); m. C. Robert Paul III, Aug. 15, 1987; 1 child, Thomas Matthew Warfel Paul. BS in Speech Pathology/Audiology, Pa. State U., Univ. Pk., 1976; MEd in Speech Pathology, U. Oregon, Eugene, 1979; MBA in Mktg., Iona Coll., New Rochelle, N.Y., 1986; PhD in Health Adminstrn., Kennedy-Western U., Thousand Oaks, Calif., 2004. Cert. clinician. Speech lang. pathologist Lancaster-Lebanon #13, East Petersburg, Pa., 1970—78, Douglas ESD, Roseburg, Oreg., 1979—80, Bethel Sch. Dist. #52, Eugene, 1980—81, NY Bd. Edn., Bronx, 1981—93, Sch. Dist. Lancaster, Pa., 2003—04, Avon Grove Sch. Dist., West Grove, 2004—. Speech pathologist Eugene Speech and Hearing Ctr., 1980; speech cons. Margaret Chapman Sch., Hawthorne, N.Y., 1988-89; instr. sensory impairments Manhattan Coll., Riverdale, N.Y., 1987-88; adj. instr. lang. disorders of children Coll. New Rochelle, N.Y., 1988-89; with press The Athletics Congress, Indpls., 1981-88; press officer 1988 USA Men's and Women's Olympic Track and Field Teams, 1988. Contbr. dissertation. Vol. Rep. Nat. Com., Lancaster, 1972, Spl. Olympics, 1976-83, Lane County Prisons, Eugene, 1979; bd. dirs. Meml. Meth. Early Childhood Ctr., advt. chairperson, 1994—. Mem. Am. Speech-Lang.-Hearing Assn., Am. Mktg. Assn., Coun. Exceptional Children, N.Y. Speech-Lang.-Hearing Assn. Republican. United Methodist. Avocations: gardening, jogging, reading, raising poultry, cross stitch. Personal E-mail: kaypsu76@kennett.net.

**WARFIELD, GERALD ALEXANDER,** composer, writer; b. Ft. Worth, Feb. 23, 1940; s. George Alexander and Geraldine (Spencer) Warfield. Student, Tex. Christian U., 1958-61; BA, N. Tex. State U., 1963, MMus, 1965; postgrad., Tanglewood, 1963—64; MFA, Princeton U., 1967. Instr. Princeton U., 1968-71; assoc. dir. Index New Mus. Notation, N.Y.C.,

1971-75. Lectr. contemporary music notation; mem. conf. com. Internat. Conf. New Mus. Notation, Belgium, 1974; chmn. program com. 2d Nat. Conf. Music Theory, 1977. Author: A Beginner's Manual of Music 4B, 1967, Layer Analysis: A Primer of Elementary Tonal Structures, 1976, Writings on Contemporary Music Notations, 1977, How to Write Music Manuscript, 1977, The Investor's Guide to Stock Quotations, 1982, How to Buy Foreign Stocks and Bonds, 1984, How to Read Financial News, 1986, No Nonsense Guides to the Stock Market, Mutual Funds, Tax-Free Bonds, 1999, Managing Your Stock Portfolio, Money Market Funds, 1993; co-author: Grove's Dictionary of Music and Musicians, 1976; author (with others): Layers Dictation, 1978, Export-Import Financing, 1986, Feng Shui Revealed, 1997; editor: Longman Music Series, 1976—85; contbr. articles to profl. jours.; composer: Variations and Metamorphoses, 1973 (1st prize Ariz. Cellos Soc.), filmstrip introduction Musical Notation, 1976, Fantasy Quintet, 1978 (2d prize New Music Young Ensembles). Adv. bd. Boyce Ditto Pub. Libr., 2005—. Mem.: Broadcast Music Inc., Coll. Music Soc. (coun., conf. chmn. 1981), Am. Composers Alliance (treas. 1979—96), Soc. Composers, Inc. (chmn. exec. com. 1972—74, conf. chmn. 9th Ann. Conf. 1974, founding editor Jour. Music Scores, gen. mgr. 1977—2000, 2002—). Home: 410 SW 4th Ave # 4 Mineral Wells TX 76067-5840 Personal E-mail: geraldwarfield@cox-internet.com.

**WARFIELD, WILLIAM LEONARD,** musician, composer, educator; b. Balt., Md., Mar. 2, 1952; s. William Leonard and Margaret Anna Belle Warfield; m. Carol Beth Heft, Mar. 11, 1954. MMus, Manhattan Sch. Music, 1994. Asst. prof., jazz trumpet U. N. Fla., Jacksonville, Fla., 1995—96; assoc. prof. music Lehigh U., Bethlehem, Pa., 1996—; freelance trumpeter, arranger, composer, conductor Bill Warfield Music, N.Y.C., NY, 1980—. Composer (Bill Warfield's Big Band): (CD rec.) NYC Jazz, 1990; composer: (with Dave Stryker) Nomad, 1995; composer: Beneath the Stacks, 2002, Le Jazz Hot, 2003; prodr.: (CD rec.) A Faceless Place, 2005, The City Never Sleeps, 1994; conductor: Bitches Brew, 2003. Recipient William Borden award outstanding accomplishment in jazz and comml. trumpet, Manhattan Sch. of Music, 1994, Frank Hook Asst. Professorship award, Lehigh U., 2000; Franz and Class of 68 grantee, 2000. Mem.: Internat. Assn. Sch. of Jazz, Nat. Acad. Recording Arts and Scis., Lehigh Valley Jazz Repertory Orch. (founding dir. 1996—). Home: 400 W 43rd St New York NY 10036 Office: Lehigh U Zoellner Arts Ctr 420 Packer Ave Bethlehem PA 18015 E-mail: wlw@lehigh.edu.

**WARFORD, PATRICIA,** psychologist; d. Eldon J. Jameson and Rosa Kirschenman; m. Gary W. Warford, Sept. 5, 1955; children: Candice C. Zaniewski, Nathanael A. BS, S.D. State U., 1991; MS, George Fox Coll., 1993, D of Psychology, 1996. Lic. psychologist Oreg. Bd. Psychologist Examiners, 1998. Psychologist Western Psychol. & Counseling, Beaverton, Oreg., 1994—98, Yamhill County Adult Mental Health, McMinnville, 1998—2000, pvt. practice, Newberg, 2001—; co-owner Life Estrategies Domestic Abuse Program, McMinnville, 2005—. Faculty State Victims Assistance Acad., Salem, Oreg., 2004—; presenter Boston Coll., Boston, 2002, George Fox U., Newberg, 2004. Co-author: (training manual chapter) Trauma Bonding. Oregon State Victims Assistance Academy Training Manual Number 2002-VF-GX-KO23 awarded by the Office for Victims of Crime, Office of Justice Programs, U.S. Department of Justic, 2004. Appointee Oreg. Gov.'s Coun. Domestic Violence, Salem, 2004. Mem.: APA, Tri-County Batterers Intervention Providers, Yamhill County Domestic Violence Task Force. Office: 1013 N Springbrook PO Box 3279 Newberg OR 97132 Office Phone: 503-554-8172. Office Fax: 877-892-6114.

**WARGA, JACK,** mathematician, educator; b. Warsaw, Dec. 5, 1922; came to U.S., 1943, naturalized, 1949; s. Herman and Czarna (Lichtenstein) W.; m. Faye Kleinman, Feb. 27, 1949; children—Charna Ruth Schakow, Arthur David. Student, Brussels U., 1939-40; BA, Carleton Coll., 1944; PhD, NYU, 1950. Assoc. mathematician Reeves Instrument Corp., N.Y.C., 1951-52; Chief engring. computing sect. Republic Aviation Corp., Farmingdale, NY, 1952-53; head math dept. Burroughs Corp., Pasadena, Calif., 1954-56; mgr. math dept. Avco Research and Devel., Wilmington, Mass., 1957-66; prof. math. Northeastern U., Boston, 1966-93, prof. emeritus, 1993—. Author: Optimal Control of Differential and Functional Equations, 1972, expanded Russian transl., 1977; contbr. articles to profl. jours. Served with AUS, 1944-46. Weizmann Meml. fellow, 1956-57 Fellow AAAS; mem. Am. Math. Soc., Soc. Indsl. and Applied Math. (editor Jour. on Control and Optimization 1963-89). Home: 7356 Falls Rd W Boynton Beach FL 33437-6316 E-mail: warga@neu.edu.

**WARGO, LOVETTA LYNN,** medical educator, physical therapist, writer; d. Lewis and Patsy Elaine Hickman; m. George Peter Wargo, July 24, 1998; 1 child, Davey Henry Addams. AAS, J. Sargent Reynolds, 1998. Respiratory Therapy Advance Practice Commonwealth of VA State Bd. for CC, 1998, PALS Provider Am. Heart Association, 2002, BLS Instructor Am. Heart Association, 2002, Heartsaver First Aid Instructor Am. Heart Association, 2004, Registered Respiratory Therapist Nat. Bd. for Respiratory Care, 1999, Respiratory Therapy Commonwealth of Va., 1998, Respiratory Therapy Technology J. Sargeant Reynolds CC/ Va., 1997, Respiratory Therapy Assisting J. Sargeant Reynolds CC/ Va., 1997, Certified Respiratory Therapy Technician Nat. Bd. for Respiratory Care, 1998, ACLS Instructor Am. Heart Assn., 2002, ACLS Provider Am. Heart Assn., 2002, PALS Instructor Am. Heart Association, 2002. Educator Riverside Regional Med. Hosp., Newport News, Va., 1998—; item writer Nat. Bd. Respiratory Care, Lenexa, Kans., 2002—, Am. Assn. Cirtical-Care Nurses, Aliso Viejo, Calif., 2003. Mem.: Seaford Women's Club (assoc.), Phi Theta Kappa (assoc.). Achievements include invention of medical education tools. Office: Riverside Regional Medical Hospital 500 J Clyde Morris Blvd Newport News VA 23601

**WARIN, ROGER E.,** lawyer; b. Des Moines, June 14, 1945; s. Roger Francis and Mary (Gray) Warin; m. Diane Whyte-Warin, May 31, 1974; children: Elizabeth, Patricia, Christopher, Michael. BA, Creighton U., 1967; JD, Georgetown U., 1970. Bar: Nebr. 1970, DC 1971. Law clk. for Judge Oliver Gasch US Dist. Ct., DC, Washington, 1970-71; assoc. Steptoe & Johnson LLP, Washington, 1971-77, ptnr., litig. & ins. dept., 1978—, mem. exec. com. Adj. prof. ins. law Am. U., Washington, 1978—81; bd. mem. Washington Lawyers Com. for Civil Rights. Contbr. articles to profl. jour.; spkr. in field. Fellow: Am. Coll. Trial Lawyers; mem.: ABA (Litig., Tort & Ins. Practice Sect.). Avocation: skiing. Office: Steptoe & Johnson LLP 1330 Connecticut Ave NW Ste 700 Washington DC 20036-1704 Office Phone: 202-429-6280. Office Fax: 202-429-3902. Business E-mail: rwarin@steptoe.com.

**WARINER, JEREMY,** Olympic track and field athlete; b. Irving, Tex., Jan. 31, 1984; Student, Baylor Univ. Mem. U.S. Olympic Track Team, Athens 2004. Named Mondo Outdoor Track Athlete of the Yr., USA Track Coaches Assoc., 2004. Achievements include winning gold medal, 400m, Athens Olympic games, 2004; being NCAA Champion, Indoor 400m, Indoor 4x400m relays, Outdoor 400m, Outdoor 4x400m relay, 2004. Office: c/o USOC 1 Olympic Plaza Colorado Springs CO 80909

**WARING, GEORGE ORAL, III,** ophthalmologist, surgeon; b. Buffalo, Feb. 21, 1941; s. George Oral Waring and Mary Jane Fitzpatrick-Waring; children from previous marriage: George IV, John Timothy, Joy Waring-Harty, Matthew. BS cum laude, Wheaton Coll., Ill., 1963; MD, Baylor Med. Coll., Houston, 1967. Diplomate Am. Bd. Ophthalmology (assoc. examiner, 1980, 89). Rotating intern Ben Taub Gen. Hosp., Houston, 1967—68; resident Willis Eye Hosp. and Rsch. Inst., Phila., 1970—73, head fellow in corneal and external disease, 1973—74; staff physician Hosp. Ship Hope, Natal, Brazil, 1973; asst. prof. U. Calif., Davis, 1974—79, assoc. prof., 1979; surg. dir. Sacramento Valley Eye Bank, 1976—79; staff physician Emory Clinic, Inc., Atlanta, 1979—82, clinic ptnr., 1982—2002, with, 2002—; med. dir. Emory Vision Correction Ctr., 1994—2001; founding surgeon InView Vision (formerly Emory Vision), 2001—; pvt. practice Atlanta, 2004—. Affiliate scientist Yerkes Regional Primate Rsch. Ctr. Emory U. Sch. Medicine, Atlanta, 1982—92, assoc. prof., 1979—83, prof., dir. regractive surgery, 1983—2004, clin. prof., 2006—; rsch. assoc. French Ministry Rsch. & Tech.,

1992; Fogarty sr. internat. fellow US NIH, 1992; vis. prof. Ain Shams U., Cairo, 1992—93; chmn. dept. ophthalmology, dir. rsch. dept. El-Magrabi Eye Hosp. and Med. Ctr., Jeddah, Saudi Arabia, 1992—95; cons. Summit Tech., 1990—95, Chiron Corp., 1993—2005, Nidek, Inc., 2001—; mem. sci. adv. bd. Calhoun Vision, 2002—; mem. sci. adv. bd., clin. investigator AcuFocus, 2005—. Mem. editl. bd.: Am. Jour. Ophthalmology, 1981—87, mem. consultative bd.; 1987—97; mem. editl. bd. Jour. Refractive Surgery, 1985—87; assoc. editor: Jour. Refractive Surgery, 1987—88, editor-in-chief; 1989—, mem. editl. bd.: numerous jours.; contbr. chapters to books, articles to profl. jours. Lt. USPHS. Co-recipient Emmy award, NATAS, 1977; recipient Hon. medal, Ain Shams U., 1989, Barraquer prize, Internat. Soc. Refractive Keratoplasty, 1992, Buasch and Lomb Visionary award, 2004; grantee, NIH, 1978—81, 1980—, 1980—91, others, U. Calif., Davis, 1973—76, 1982—83, 1987—88, others, various industries; Pew Found. scholar, 1971—72, Training grantee, NIH, 1971. Fellow: ACS (mem. com. applicants 1991), Eye Bank Assn. Am. (mem. constitution and by-laws com. 1984—86, mem. program com. 1985, mem. adv. bd.), Royal Coll. Ophthal-mologists, Am. Acad. Ophthalmology (mem. interprofessional edn. com. 1978—81, mem. instrn. adv. com. 1978—81, cons. 1983—, Life Achievement Honor award 2004, Physician's Recognition award 1976, 1980—82), Explorer's Club; mem.: AMA (mem. ophthalmology program com. 1975—79, Physician's Recognition award 1989—95), Willis Eye Hosp. Ex-Resident's Soc., Soc. Heed Fellows (mem. Heed award nomination com. 1983—84, 2000—04, chmn. 2004, Outstanding Ophthalmologist 1978, 1979), Saudi Ophthal. Soc., Paton Corneal Transplant Soc., Internat. Soc. Refractive Surgery of Am. Acad. Ophthalmology (trustee 1981—89, editor Jour. Refractive Surgery 1989—, Lifetime Achievement award in Refractive Surgery 1997), Egyptian Soc. Ocular Implants and Refractive Surgery (hon.), Internat. Ophthalmic Microsurgery Study Group, Ga. Soc. Ophthalmology (mem. pub. edn. com. 1981—84, mem. govtl. com. 1988—89, mem. laser com. 1991—92), Dekalb Med. Soc., Coun. Refractive Surgery Quality Assurance, Castroviejo Cornea Soc. (mem. exec. com. 1981—85, program chmn. 1983—85, Castroviejo medal 2004), Assn. Rsch. Vision and Ophthal-mology (mem. cornea sect. com. 1985—88, chmn. cornea sect. com. 1987—88), Am. Ophthal. Soc., Commd. Officers Assn. USPHS, Am. Eye Study Club (emeritus mem. 1988—). Avocations: art, kayaking, mountain climbing, scuba diving, sailing. Home: 36 Willow Glen Atlanta GA 30342 Office: INView 301 Perimeter Ctr N Ste 600 Atlanta GA 30346 Office Fax: 404-250-9006.

**WARING, WALTER WEYLER,** literature and language professor; b. Sterling, Kans., May 13, 1917; s. Walter Wray and Bonnie Laura (Weyler) W.; m. Mary Esther Griffith, Feb. 8, 1946; children: Mary Laura, Helen Ruth, Elizabeth Anne, Claire Joyce. BA, Kans. Wesleyan U., 1939; MA, U. Colo., 1946; PhD, Cornell U., 1949. Tchr., English and chemistry Belleville (Kan.) High Sch., 1939-41; instr. U. Colo., Boulder, 1941-42, 46-47; mem. faculty Kalamazoo Coll., 1949—, prof. English, 1955-85, prof. emeritus, 1985—, chmn. dept., 1953-78, dir. humanities, 1978-83. Ednl. TV lectr.; vis. prof. Kenyon Coll., 1984-86, 90-91. Painter watercolors; author: Thomas Carlyle, 1978, also articles. Served to 1st lt. AUS, World War II, PTO. Decorated Legion of Merit. Mem. Phi Beta Kappa. Home: 8794 Keller Rd Delton MI 49046-8728 E-mail: weylerwaring@cs.com.

**WARING, WILLIAM WINBURN,** pediatric pulmonologist, educator; b. Savannah, Ga., July 20, 1923; s. Antonio Johnston and Sue Ann (Winburn) W.; m. Nell Pape Williams, July 19, 1952; children: William Winburn, Benjamin Joseph, Antonio Johnston, Peter Ayraud, Patrick Houstoun Grad., Hotchkiss Sch., Lakeville, Conn., 1942; student, Yale U., 1942-43; MD, Harvard U., 1947. Diplomate Am. Bd. Pediatrics (subbd. of pediatric pulmonology 1985-89). Intern Children's Hosp., Boston, 1947-48; intern, then resident Johns Hopkins Hosp., Balt., 1948-52; practice medicine specializing in pediatrics Jacksonville, Fla., 1955-57; instr. dept. pediatrics Sch. Medicine, Tulane U., New Orleans, 1957-58, asst. prof., 1958-61, assoc. prof., 1961-66, prof. emeritus, 1966—, Jane B. Aron Prof. Pediatrics, 1987-96. Dir. Pediat. Pulmonary Ctr., New Orleans, 1969-88, Cystic Fibrosis Ctr., Tulane U., New Orleans, 1988-88; chmn. profl. tng. com. Cystic Fibrosis Found., 1978-86; cons. La. State Handicapped Children's Assn., 1963-88; mem. pulmonary diseases adv. com. NIH, 1978-80. Co-author: Pro Parvulis: On Behalf of the Little Ones. A History of the Department of Pediatrics, Tulane Medical School, 1834-2003, 2003; co-author, editor: Practical Manual of Pediatrics, 1975, 2d edit., 1982; editor: Harriet Lane Handbook: A Manual for Pediatric House Officers, 1952, Hospital Pediatric Manual, 1958; contbg. author books on pediatric pulmonary disease, also articles in field; assoc. editor Am. Jour. Diseases of Children, 1989-91; mem. editl. bd. Pediatric Pulmonology, 1985-94. Served to capt. M.C., U.S. Army, 1952-54. Recipient Rsch. Career Devel. award, NIH, 1970—72, Edwin L. Kendig, Jr. award for outstanding achievement in pediatric pulmonology, 2004. Fellow Am. Acad. Pediatrics (exec. com. 1966-71, Edwin L. Kendig Jr. award), Am. Coll. Chest Physicians; mem. Am. Pediatric Soc., Am. Thoracic Soc. (v.p. 1977). Clubs: Boston, So. Yacht, Wyvern (New Orleans). Republican. Roman Catholic. Avocations: fly fishing, running, computers. Home: 123 Walnut St Apt 905 New Orleans LA 70118-4846 Office: Tulane U Sch of Medicine Dept of Pediatrics 1430 Tulane Ave New Orleans LA 70112-2699 E-mail: wwaring@bellsouth.net.

**WARITZ, RICHARD STEFAN,** toxicologist, researcher; b. Portland, Oreg., Apr. 1, 1929; s. Anton John and Theresa (Stegelmaier) W.; m. Ruth Evelyn White, June 7, 1950; children: Joyce E., Gary S., Sharon J., Carol L. BA, Reed Coll., 1951; PhD, Stanford U., 1957. Diplomate Am. Bd. Toxicology, Acad. Toxicological Scis. Sr. rsch. scientist E.I. DuPont de Nemours & Co., Wilmington, Del., 1957-64, mgr. inhalation toxicology, 1964-72, mgr. bio-scis., 1972-75; sr. toxicologist Hercules Inc., Wilmington, 1975-80, mgr. toxicology, 1980-92; pres. BioSante Internat., Inc., 1992—2005. Grad. toxicology edn. adv. bd. Rutgers U., Piscataway, N.J., 1980-2005, vis. prof. toxicology, 1993-2005; life scis. adv. bd. U.S. Army, Aberdeen, Md., 1982-92; toxicology peer rev. bd. U.S. Army Ctr. for Health Promotion and Preventive Medicine, 1992—; vis. prof. toxicology Rutgers U., 1993-2005. Contbr. articles to profl. jours. Mem.: Am. Chem. Soc., Am. Conf. Govtl. Indsl. Hygienists, Am. Indsl. Hygiene Assn., Internat. Union Toxicol. Socs. (councillor 1983—88), Soc. Toxicology (treas. 1981-85, pres. Mid-Atlantic chpt. 1989). Roman Catholic. Avocations: golf, fishing, bowling. Home: 2613 Turnstone Dr Wilmington DE 19808-1638 E-mail: waritztox@verizon.net.

**WARMAN, EDUARDO NORBERTO,** research scientist; arrived in US, 1985; s. Israel Miguel and Renee Celia Warman; m. Berta Estela Feingold, Dec. 14, 1984; children: Cynthia, Leo, Max. Licenciado, U. Buenos Aires, 1985; PhD, Case Western Res. U., 1992. Staff scientist Medtronic, Mpls., 1994—99, sr. prin. scientist, 1999—. Medtronic tech. fellow, Sci. and Tech. Bd., 2000. Achievements include patents in field; patents pending in field. Office: Medtronic 7000 Central Ave NE Minneapolis MN 55432 Office Phone: 763-514-3569.

**WARMAN, LYNNETTE R.,** lawyer; b. Willmar, Minn., Oct. 1, 1955; BA, U. Nebr., 1983; JD, Creighton U., 1986. Bar: Nebr. 1986, Tex. 1987, US Ct. Appeals 5th Cir., US Dist. Ct. No. Ea., We. & So. Districts Tex. Shareholder Jenkens & Gilchrist, P.C., Dallas, head bus. devel. Mem.: ABA, Tex. Bar Assn., Dallas Bar Assn. (bankruptcy sect.), John C. Ford. Am. Inn of Ct., Am. Bankruptcy Inst. Office: Jenkens & Gilchrist PC 1445 Ross Ave Ste 3700 Dallas TX 75202-2799 Office Phone: 214-855-4792. Office Fax: 214-855-4300. Business E-mail: lwarman@jenkens.com.

**WARMBROD, CATHARINE PHELPS,** educational researcher, consultant; b. Lost Nation, Iowa, July 2, 1929; d. Paul Edward and Ruth Dorthea Phelps; m. J. Robert Warmbrod, Jan. 30, 1965. BA, U. Iowa, 1952; MS, U. Ill., 1965, advanced cert. in edn., 1967. Head supr. student tchrs. in bus. edn. U. Ill., Urbana, 1966-67; chmn. office adminstrn. Columbus (Ohio) State Community Coll., 1970-77; rsch. specialist NCRVE Ohio State U., Columbus, 1977-88, rsch. specialist emeritus, 1988—; prin. Warmbrod Ednl. Svcs., Columbus, 1988-2001. Bd. dirs. Nat. Assn. Industry/Edn. Cooperation, Buffalo, 1980-88. Author: Retraining and Upgrading Workers, 1983; contbr.

to profl. publs.; editor: VocEd Insider for Tech. Edn., 1981. Bd. dirs. Ohio Women, Inc., Columbus, 1986—92, Friendship Village, Dublin, Columbus, 1990—2004. Mem. Am. Vocat. Assn. (policy com. 1980-83), Assn. Faculty and Profl. Women Ohio State U. (pres. 1984-85), Am. Assn. Cmty. Colls., Am. Tech. Edn. Assn., Delta Pi Epsilon. United Methodist. Office: Warmbrod Ednl Svcs 3853 Surrey Hill Pl Columbus OH 43220-4778 Business E-Mail: warmbrod.2@osu.edu.

**WARNATH, MAXINE AMMER,** psychologist, arbitrator; b. NYC, Dec. 3, 1928; d. Philip and Jeanette Ammer; m. Charles Frederick Warnath, Aug. 20, 1952; children: Stephen Charles, Cindy Ruth. BA, Bklyn. Coll., 1949; MA, Columbia U., 1951, EdD, 1982. Lic. psychologist Oreg. Various profl. positions Hunter Coll., U. Minn., U. Nebr., U. Oreg., 1951-62; asst. prof. psychology Oreg. Coll. Edn., Monmouth, 1962-77; assoc. prof. psychology, chmn. dept. psychology & spl. edn. Western Oreg. U., Monmouth, 1978-83, prof., 1983—96, prof. emeritus, 1996—. Dir. organizational psychology program, 1983—96; pres. Profl. Perspective Internat., Salem, Oreg., 1987—; cons., dir. Orgn. R&D, Salem, Oreg., 1983—87; seminar leader Endeavors for Excellence program. Author: Power Dynamism, 1987. Mem.: APA (com. pre-coll. psychology 1970—74), Western Psychol. Assn., Oreg. Psychol. Assn. (pres. 1980—81, pres.-elect 1979—80, legis. liaison 1977—78), Oreg. Acad. Sci., N.Y. Acad. Scis., Am. Psychol. Soc. Office: Profl Perspectives Internat PO Box 2265 Salem OR 97308-2265 Office Phone: 503-371-6451. Personal E-Mail: mwarnath@comcast.net. Business E-Mail: warnatm@wou.edu.

**WARNE, ALAN M.,** adult education educator, consultant; b. Pierre, SD, Aug. 24, 1945; s. Maynard L. and Ione P. Warne; m. Joan Caulfield, Sept. 7, 1996; children: Alan, Jr. M., Andrea W. White, Amy N. BA in Polit. Sci., Ariz. State U., 1963—67; MA in Ednl. Psychology, Ea. Ky. U., 1969—70; EdD in Continuing Edn., Temple U., 1972—78. Fgn. student advisor Ariz. State U., Tempe, 1966—68; dir. internat. student services U. of Ky., 1968—71; dir. office of internat. services Temple U., 1971—77; exec. dir. Phila. Coun. for Internat. Visitors, 1977—81, Nat. Coun. for Internat. Visitors, Washington, 1981—85; chief exec. officer/vice pres. for programs People to People Internat., Kans. City, Mo., 1986—99; pres. & ceo Entrepreneurial Edn. Found., Kans. City, Mo., 2000—; sr. program mgr. Med. Ctr. U. Kans., Kans. City, 2002—. Mng. dir. The Brain Inc., Kans. City, Mo., 2000—; planning cons. Kauffman Ctr. for Entrepreneurial Leadership, Kans. City, Mo., 2000; academic program cons. Rockhurst U., Kans. City, Mo., 2000; mem. continuing med. edn. adv. com. U. Kans., 2002—, mem. continuing med. ctr. statewide adv. bd. and governing com., 2002—; peer grant reviewer U.S. Dept. Edn., 2005—. Contbr. curriculum guide Expo 92 (Kans. City-Seville), nat. profl. newsletter Mgmt./Program Planning Articles, admissions guide - internat. student A Model for the Edn. of Fgn. Students. Bd. mem./arts com. Mayor's UN Day Com., Kans. City, Mo., 1990—96; site planning com. Kans. City Sch. Dist., Kans. City, Mo., 1990—91; bd. mem./vice chair Nat. Coun. for Internat. Visitors, Washington, 1978—81; founding bd. mem. Consortium for Internat. Citizen Exch., Washington, 1981—85, Caruthers' Arts Alliance, Kans. City, Mo.; scholarship committees rep. U. of Mo., Kans. City, Mo., 1986—2005; pres./vice pres. Pk. U. Bd. of Visitors, Parkville, Mo., 1995—2001. Recipient Del. Leader - Baltic Nations, Ambassadors, Inc., 1999, Thematic Specialist -Citizen Initiatives (6-US Cities), Inst. of Internat. Edn., 1981; grantee Ednl. Travel Grant, Republic of China Ministry of Edn., 1975. Fellow: Rotary Club Internat. (ednl./scholarship/planning committees 1999—2006); mem.: Soc. Govt. Meeting Profls., Assn. of Internat. Educators (regional chair, coord. of nat. job registry, exec. com. 1967—2000), Kans. City Club (membership com. 1993—2006). Avocations: volunteerism, travel, cinema, theater, organizational development. Home: 431 West 70th St Kansas City MO 64113 Office: U Kans Med Ctr 3901 Rainbow Blvd Kansas City KS 66160-7108 Office Phone: 913-588-4487. Personal E-mail: kcawarne@aol.com. Business E-Mail: awarne@kumc.edu.

**WARNECKE, JOHN CARL,** architect; b. Oakland, Calif., Feb. 24, 1919; s. Carl I. and Margaret (Esterling) W.; children by previous marriage: John Carl, Rodger Cushing, Margaret Esterling, Frederic Pierce. AB, Stanford U., 1941; MA, Harvard U., 1942. Asso. Miller & Warnecke, architects, 1944-46; prin. John Carl Warnecke, AIA, 1947-58; partner Warnecke & Warnecke, 1954-62; pres., dir. design John Carl Warnecke & Assoc., 1958—. Works include U.S. Naval Acad. Master Plan, Michelson and Chauvenet Halls, Annapolis, Md., U. Calif. at Santa Cruz Master Plan and Library, Lafayette Sq., Washington, Georgetown U. Library, Washington, Kaiser Center for Tech., Pleasanton, Calif.; bldgs., Stanford U., Hawaii State Capitol, Honolulu, Philip A. Hart Senate office bldg., USSR Embassy, Hennepin Govt. Center, Mpls., J.F. Kennedy Meml. Grave, Arlington Nat. Cemetery, Va., Neiman Marcus and Bergdorf Goodman Stores, Logan Airport, Boston, Am. Hosp, Paris, The Sun Co. Hdqrs, Radnor, Pa., King Abdulaziz U. Med. Center, Jedda, Saudi Arabia, Yanbu Town Ctr. Master Plan, Hilton Hotel & Casino, Atlantic City. Mem. Fine Arts Commn., Washington, 1963-67. Recipient Arnold Brunner prize in architecture Nat. Inst. Arts and Letters, 1957; also 70 nat., regional awards for excellence. Fellow AIA; Mem. NAD (assoc., 1958-94, academician, 1994-) Office: 300 Broadway St San Francisco CA 94133-4587 also: 1707 H St NW Ste 1100 Washington DC 20006-3919 also: 462 Broadway New York NY 10013-2618 also: 1180 S Beverly Dr Los Angeles CA 90035-1153 also: Warnecke-Sonoma Vineyard 13427 Chalk Hill Rd Healdsburg CA 95448-9043

**WARNER, BARRY GREGORY,** ecologist, educator; b. Cambridge, Ont., July 20, 1955; s. Gregory O. and Alma (Jansen) W. B in Environ. Studies, U. Waterloo, 1978, MS, 1980; PhD, Simon Fraser U., Burnaby, Can., 1984. Rsch. assoc. prof. U. Waterloo, Ont., 1985-89, rsch. assoc. prof. Ont., 1989-91, assoc. prof. geography Ont., 1991-96, prof. biology, earth sci. and geography Ont., 1996—; dir. Wetlands Rsch. Inst., 1991—; U. Neuchatel. Vis. prof. U. Neuchatel, 1993, U. Franche-Comte, Bescon, France, 2002; chair Can. Nat. Wetlands Working Group, 1993—; bd. dirs. Internat. Mire Conservation Group. Editor: Methods in Quaternary Ecology, 1990; co-editor: Wetlands: Envirgradients, Boundaries and Buffers, 1996; contbr. articles to profl. jours. Postdoctoral fellow Natural Scis. and Engring. Rsch. Coun. of Can., 1984-85, rsch. fellow, 1985-90; fellow Suisse Nat. Res. Fond, 1993; Sr. Scientist Fellowship, Ministere de la Recherche, France. Fellow Geol. Assn. Can., Soc. Wetland Scientists (pres., v.p. 2000-2003). Office: U of Waterloo Wetlands Rsch Ctr Waterloo ON Canada N2L 3G1 Office Phone: 519-888-4567 3607. Business E-mail: bwarner@uwaterloo.ca.

**WARNER, BRIAN HUGH See MANSON, MARILYN**

**WARNER, CAROLYN G.,** musician, music educator; b. Winnipeg, Man., Can., Apr. 19, 1951; arrived in U.S., 1975; d. Alfred and Gertrude Gadiel; m. Stephen David Warner, June 1, 1980; 1 child, Ari M. BA, U. Toronto, Ont., Can., 1971, MA, 1972; postgrad., Paris Conservatory Music, 1975. Violinist, pianist Buffalo Philharm., 1975—79, Cleve. Orch., 1979—. Adj. prof. chamber music Cleve. Inst. Music, 1987—; artistic dir. Cleve. Duo and James Umble, 1994—, James V young person's performing ensemble, Cleve., 1998—2003. Transcriber: classical music scores, musician: recordings Cappella, Dana and Klavier labels. Grantee, Ohio Arts Coun., 1984—, Arts Midwest, 1987—; Can. Coun. Career grantee, 1972—75. Mem.: Am. Fedn. Musicians, Coll. Music Soc., Chamber Music Am. Avocations: jogging, gardening, boating, organizing benefit concerts. Home: 17500 Shelburne Rd Cleveland Heights OH 44118 Office: Cleve Orch Severance Hall Euclid Ave Cleveland OH 44106

**WARNER, CHARLES COLLINS,** lawyer; b. Cambridge, Mass., June 19, 1942; s. Hoyt Landon and Charlotte (Collins) W.; m. Elizabeth Denny, Aug. 24, 1964; children: Peter, Andrew, Elizabeth. BA, Yale U., 1964; JD cum laude, Ohio State U., 1970. Bar: Ohio 1970. Assoc. Porter, Wright, Morris & Arthur and predecessor, Columbus, 1970-76, ptnr., 1976—, also mgr. labor and employment law dept., 1988-92. Pres. Peace Corps Svc. Coun., Columbus, 1974—76, Old Worthington (Ohio) Assn., 1976—78, Worthington Ednl. Found., 1994—96, Opera Columbus, 1999—2001, Alliance for Quality Edn., Worthington, 1987—89; chmn. lawyers sect. United Way, Columbus,

1983—84; mem. alumni adv. coun. Ohio State U., 1998—2004; vp Chamber Music Columbus, 2004—06. Fellow: Ohio Bar Found., Coll. Labor and Employment Lawyers, Am. Bar Found., Columbus Bar Found. (trustee 1996—, v.p. 2006—); mem.: Ohio State U. Alumni Advisory Coun., Yale Club (pres. 1979—81), Lawyers Club, Capital Club, Nat. Coun. Ohio State U. Coll. Law (pres. 2002—04), Ohio State U. Law Alumni Assn. (pres. 1996—97, Disting. Svc. award 2003), FBA, Ohio Assn. Civil Trial Attys. (exec. bd. 1988—97, Frank Hurd Mem. of Yr. award 1998), Ohio Mgmt. Lawyers Assn. (chair 2004—06), Columbus Bar Assn. (bd. govs. 1982—93, pres. 1991—92, Cmty. Svc. award 2003), Ohio Met. Bar Assn. (pres. 1991—92), Ohio State Bar Assn. (chmn. fed. cts. com. 1992—94, coun. of dels. 1993—), ABA (exec. com. Met. Bar Caucus 1992—94, chmn. state and local bar ADR com. 1995—98, co-chair EEO com. 2000—02). Avocations: clarinet, singing, tennis. Home: 145 E South St Columbus OH 43085-4129 Office: Porter Wright Morris & Arthur 41 S High St Ste 2800 Columbus OH 43215-6194 Office Phone: 614-227-2013. E-mail: cwarner@porterwright.com.

**WARNER, CHARLES DAVID, III,** academic administrator; b. Hagerstown, Md., Feb. 2, 1957; s. Charles David Jr. and Ivy Ella Warner; m. Debra Jean Teter, May 25, 1985; children: Betsy, Molly, Charles. B in Music Edn., Shepherd Coll., 1980; M in Music Edn., Towson U., 1985; EdD, Va. Poly. Inst. and State U., 1999. Prof. music Hagerstown C.C., Md., 1989—2001, chair humanities divsn., 2000—03, dir. instrn., 2003—04; exec. dir. Univ. System Md., 2004—. Author: Opinions of Administrators, Faculty, and Students Regarding Academic Freedom and Student Artistic Expression, 2001. Mem. NEA, Phi Kappa Phi. Republican. Lutheran. Avocations: sailing, reading. Home: 17729 Bluebell Dr Hagerstown MD 21740 Office: Univ Sys Md Hagerstown Edn Ctr 32 W Wash St Hagerstown MD 21740 Office Phone: 240-527-2727. Office Fax: 240-527-2781. Business E-Mail: dwarner@hagerstown.usmd.edu. E-mail: d.warner@myactv.net.

**WARNER, CHARLES HENRY, JR.,** architect; b. Tucson, May 2, 1952; s. Charles Henry and Joan Ruth (Boone) W.; BS in Environ. Design, U. Okla., 1974; BS in Architecture, 1975; M in Architecture, 1975; m. Mary L. Briggs, Mar. 22, 1974; 1 dau., Rebecca Gayle. Elec. designer/project mgr. Binnicker Assos., Oklahoma City, 1975-77; project mgr. Jones Hester Bates Reik, Oklahoma City, 1977; project architect Howard & Porch Inc., Oklahoma City, 1977-79; prin.-in-charge prodn. Quentin Remy Assocs., Norman, Okla., 1979-82; sole propr. CHW Assocs., 1982-86; sr. architect Bohm-Nees Bus. Space Design, 1986—; cons. in field. Youth soccer referee. Recipient Reynolds Aluminum Co. award, 1973. Registered architect, Okla. Mem. AIA, Nat. Council Archtl. Registration Bds., South Can. Amateur Radio Soc. Democrat. Methodist. Clubs: Demolay, Masons (32 deg.). Author instructional publs. for U. Okla. archtl. courses. Office: 55 E Nationwide Blvd Columbus OH 43215-2512

**WARNER, C(HARLES) ROBERT,** mathematics professor; b. Toronto, Ont., Can., Aug. 24, 1931; came to U.S., 1955; s. Charles Joseph Sr. and Dorothy C. (Soucy) W.; m. Anne Woolever, Aug. 16, 1971. BA, U. Toronto, 1955; MS, U. Rochester, N.Y., 1957, PhD, 1962. Instr. U. Conn., Storrs, 1958-59; asst. prof. Mich. State U., East Lansing, 1962-64; U. Md., College Park, 1964-69, assoc. prof., 1989—. Invited vis. scholar St. Lawrence U., 1985, 88; lectr. in field. Contbr. articles to Jour. Functional Analysis, Pacific Jour. of Math., Jour. of Math. Analysis and Applications, Proc. Am. Math. Soc., Trans. Am. Math. Soc., Math. Ann. Mem. Am. Math. Soc., Math. Assn. Am. Office: U Md Dept Maths College Park MD 20742-0001

**WARNER, CHRISTOPHER HUGH,** psychiatrist; b. Steubenville, Ohio, Apr. 2, 1974; s. William Norman and Diana Lynn Warner; m. Carolynn Marie Stocum, Mar. 3, 1997; children: Jacob Thomas, Aaron Christopher, Matthew Dylan. BS, U.S. Mil. Acad., West Point, NY, 1996; MD, Uniformed Svcs. U. of Health Sci., Bethesda, Md., 2000. Lic. physician Ind., 2000, diplomate Am. Bd. of Family Practice, 2005. Resident in family practice and psychiatry Walter Reed Army Hosp., Washington, 2000—05; chief resident NCC Family Practice-Psychiatry, Washington, 2003—05; divsn. psychiatry 3rd Inf. Divsn., Fort Stewart, Ga., 2005—. Maj. U.S. Army, 1992—, Fort Stewart, Ga. Decorated Bronze Star US Army; named Martin Fenton Nat. Resident of the Yr., Assn. of Medicine and Psychiatry, 2005, Resident Tchr. of the Yr., Soc. of Tchrs. of Family Medicine, 2005; recipient Award for Outstanding Leadership in Psychiatry, Assn. of Acad. Psychiatry, 2004, George Ginsberg Award for Accomplishment in Edn. and Tng. in Psychiatry, Am. Assn. of Dirs. of Psychiat. Residency Tng., 2004, Gen. Graves B. Erskine Award for Most Outstanding Resident, Walter Reed Army Med. Ctr., 2005, Al Glass Award for Outstanding Leadership in Mil. Psychiatry, 2005. Mem.: Assn. for Acad. Psychiatry (assoc.), Am. Psychiat. Assn. (assoc.; regional chpt. jr. devel. officer 2005), Am. Acad. of Family Physicians (assoc.). Christian. Achievements include research in examining the ethics training of psychiatric residents; on eating disorders in military recruits; on depression in military recruits; on the characteristics and effacacy of FP/Psych trained individuals; on leadership development in medical residency training. Home: 373 Steeple Chase Ln Richmond Hill GA 31324 Office: Division Mental Health Bldg 601E Fort Stewart GA 31314 Office Phone: 912-767-2620. E-mail: christopher.h.warner@us.army.mil.

**WARNER, DEBORAH COURTNEY,** artist, educator; b. Phila., Aug. 14, 1947; d. Halsey Feraud Warner and Irene Courtney. BS in Art Edn. cum laude, Moore Coll. Art, Phila., 1969; MEd in Art Edn., Temple U., Phila., 1972; MFA in Fiber, Temple U., 1973. Art tchr. Wagner Jr. HS, Phila. Sch. Dist., 1969—70; mem. faculty Moore Coll. Art and Design, Phila., 1970—, prof., 1985—, dean, 1990—93, chair, prof. textile design dept., 1994—. Dir. summer sessions undergrad. program, coll. prep. program, h.s. program Moore Coll. Art and Design, 1970—71, mem. faculty art edn. dept., dir. young artist workshop, 1970—74, mem. faculty textile design dept., 1974—, asst. dean design group, textile design, fashion design, interior design depts., 1979—80, chair textile design dept., 1977—82, faculty rep. to bd. mgrs., 2005—; mem. crafts adv. panel Pa. Coun. on the Arts, 1978—81; lectr., leader workshops in field; vis. artist Skidmore Coll., Saratoga Springs, NY, 1974—78; juror Mass. Grants to Individuals, Artists Found., Boston, 1980, NY Guild Handweavers, NYC, 1981, Pa. Guild Craftsmen, 1984, Phila. Guild Handweavers, 1990; guest artist Rochester Inst. Tech., NY, 1981. One-woman shows include Phila. Art Alliance, 1972, Mirick, Pearson, Ilvonen, Batcheler, AIA, Phila., 1974, Hadler/Rodriquez Gallery, NYC, 1976, 1979, Objects Gallery, San Antonio, 1983, Miller/Brown Gallery, San Francisco, 1983, Moore Coll. of Art Galleries North, Kimmel Ctr., Pa., 2002, exhibited in group shows at Phila. Mus. Art, 1977, Newark Mus., 1978, Phila. Coll. Textiles and Sci., 1980, U. Pa., Phila., 1982, Nat. Craft Showroom, NY, 1986, The Soc. for Art in Crafts, Pitts., 1987, Mus. Art and Design, Helsinki, Finland, 2000, Nat. Craft Gallery, Kilkenny, Ireland, 2005, numerous others, Represented in permanent collections Daphne Farago Collection, Mus. Fine Arts, Houston, Wilmington (Del.) Trust, Psychiat. Insts. Am., Washington, Gotass-Larsen Shipping Firm, NYC, Romanek-Golub, Chgo., Newcombe Hosp., Vineland, NJ, Arrowmont Sch. Art and Craft, Gatlinburg, Tenn., SmithKline Beecham, Phila., Security Pacific Nat. Bank, LA, Hyatt Regency Hotels, San Antonio, Austin, Tex., Bishop Eustace Sch., Pennsauken, NJ, McNeil Pharm., Spring House, Pa., Brendler Dove Archtl. Offices, San Antonio, US News and World Report Offices, Washington, Griffin Ctr., Culbro Corp., Winsor, Conn., PennWalt Bldg. Lobby, Goldman Sachs, Phila., ARA Tower, ARA Svcs., Inc., Amburn and Jarosinski Architecture and Interior Design. Recipient hon. mention, Leeway Found., 1997, Disting. Alumnae award, Moore Coll. Art and Design, 1999, Lindback Disting. Tchg. award, Moore Coll. Art, 2001; artist fellow, Nat. Endowment for the Arts, 1979, faculty devel. grantee, Moore Coll. Art and Design, 1982, 1998, 2002, 2005. Address: 3121 W Coulter St Philadelphia PA 19129-1001 E-mail: dcwarner3121@aol.com.

**WARNER, DENNIS ALLAN,** psychology professor; b. Idaho Falls, Idaho, Apr. 27, 1940; s. Perry and Marcia E. (Finlayson) W.; m. Charyl Ann DeHart, Dec. 12, 1962; children: Lisa Rae, Sara Michelle, David Perry, Matthew Arie. BS, Brigham Young U., 1964; MS with honors, U. Oreg., 1966, PhD, 1968.

Asst. prof. edn. Wash. State U., Pullman, 1968-72, assoc. prof. edn., 1972-78, prof. edn., 1978-85, dir. tchr. edn., 1983-85, prof., chmn. ednl. counseling psychology, 1985-93, interim dir. Partnership Ctr., 1993—94, 2004—06, prof. ednl. leadership and counseling psychology, 1994—, assoc. dean Coll. Edn., 1999—2005, exec. assoc. dean Coll. Edn., 2006—; dir. H.S. equivalency program, 2004—. Vis. assoc. prof. psychology U. Idaho, Moscow, 1971. Author: Interpreting and Improving Student Test Performance, 1982; contbr. articles to profl. jours. Postdoctoral research assoc. U. Kans., 1976-77. Fellow: APA; mem.: Phi Delta Kappa. Mem. Lds Ch. Home: 645 SW Mies St Pullman WA 99163-2057 Office: Wash State Univ Coll Edn Cleveland Hl Rm 160B Pullman WA 99164-2114 Office Phone: 509-335-1738. E-mail: dawarner@wsu.edu.

**WARNER, DON LEE,** dean emeritus; b. Norfolk, N.B., Jan. 4, 1934; s. Donald A. and Cleo V. (Slagel) W.; m. Patricia Ann Walker, Feb. 24, 1957; children: Mark J., Scott Lee. BS in Geol. Engring., Colo. Sch. Mines, 1956, MSc in Geol. Engring., 1961; PhD in Engring. Sci., U. Calif., Berkeley, 1964. Registered profl. engr., Mo.; geologist, Mo., Miss., Tex. Geol. engr. Gulf Oil Corp., Casper, Wyo., 1956, Calif. Exploration Co., Guatemala, 1957-58; civil engr. U.S. Forest Svc., Gunnison, Colo., 1958-59; teaching asst. Colo. Sch. Mines, Golden, 1959-61; rsch. asst. U. Calif., Berkeley, 1962-64; rsch. geologist and engr. U.S. Pub. Health Svc., Cin., 1964-67; chief, earth scis. Ohio Basin Region Fed. Water Pollution Control Adminstrn., 1967-69; prof. geol. engring. U. Mo., Rolla, 1969-92, prof. emeritus geol. engring., 1992—, dean emeritus Sch. Mines and Metallurgy, 1992—, chmn., geol. engring., 1980-81, dean Sch. Mines and Metallurgy, 1981-93. Bd. dirs. Underground Injection Practices Coun., 1985-89; mem. adv. com. to Sec. of Interior for Mineral Resources Rsch., 1985-92. Author: Subsurface Wastewater Injection, 1977. Special award scholarship Colo. Sch. Mines, 1951-56, grad. fellowship Colo. Sch. Mines, 1959-51, rsch. fellowship U. Calif., 1962-64; recipient Best Paper award Am. Water Works Assn., 1971. Fellow Geol. Soc. Am.; mem. Am. Inst. Profl. Geologists (cert.), Am. Assn. Petroleum Geologists, Geol. Soc. Am., Nat. Ground Water Assn. (sci. award 1984, disting. lectr. 1986), Blue Key, Soc. Petroleum Engrs., Scabbard and Blade, Theta Tau, Tau Beta Pi. Avocations: fishing, boating, tennis, golf. Office: Univ Mo Sch Materials Energy and Earth Resources 1870 Miner Cir Rolla MO 65409-0001 E-mail: dlw@fidmail.com.

**WARNER, DOUGLAS ALEXANDER, III,** banker; b. Cin., June 9, 1946; s. Douglas Alexander Jr. and Eleanor (Wright) W.; m. Patricia Grant, May 13, 1977; children: Alexander, Katherine, Michael. BA, Yale U., 1968. Officer's asst. J.P. Morgan & Co. Inc., N.Y.C., 1968-70; asst. treas. J.P. Morgan & Co., Inc., N.Y.C., 1970-72, asst. v.p., 1972-75; v.p. Morgan Guaranty Trust Co., N.Y.C., 1975-85; sr. v.p. J.P. Morgan & Co. Inc., N.Y.C., 1983-87, exec. v.p., 1987-89; mng. dir. Morgan Guaranty Trust Co., N.Y.C., 1989-90, pres., 1990-95, chmn., pres., CEO, 1995—, also bd. dirs. Bd. counselors Bechtel Group, Inc.; bd. dirs. GE Co., Anheuser-Busch Cos., Ltd.; chmn. bd. of overseers and mgrs. Meml. Sloan-Kettering Cancer Ctr.; mem. The Bus. Coun. Trustee Pierpont Morgan Libr. Mem. Links Club, River Club, Meadowbrook Club (L.I.). Avocations: golf, skiing, shooting.

**WARNER, EMILY HANRAHAN HOWELL,** retired pilot, writer; b. Oct. 30, 1939; m. Julius "Jay" Warner. BA in English, Souther U., Baton Rouge, La. Kindergarten and elem. sch. tchr.; flight instr. Clinton Aviation Co., 1961—67, rose to positions of chief pilot and flight sch. mgr., 1967—73; pilot Frontier Airlines, 1973—86, Continental Airlines, 1986—88, United Parcel Svc., 1988—90; aviation safety inspector FAA, 1990—2002, aircrew program mgr., 1992—2002. Bd. dirs. Internat. Air Mus., Dayton, Ohio. Author: (children's books) Lily of Watts- A Birthday Discovery, 1969, Lily Takes A Giant Step, (biography) Weaving the Winds, 2003. Co-founder Northeast Women's Ctr., Denver; active with Congress of Racial Equality, ACLU, NAACP. Named to Colo. Aviation Hall Fame, 1983, Nat. Women's Hall Fame, Seneca Falls, NY, 2001; recipient Amelia Earheart award as the Outstanding Woman in US Aviation, 1973. Mem.: Colo. Aviation Hist. Soc., Internat. Soc. Women Airline Pilots (founder), Ninety-Nines: Internat. Orgn. Women Pilots. Achievements include uniform installed in Smithsonian Inst. Air and Space Mus., 1976; first woman hired as pilot by major US airline, 1973.

**WARNER, H. TY,** entrepreneur, manufacturing executive; b. Chgo., Sept. 3, 1944; s. Harold and Georgia Warner. Student, Kalamazoo Coll. Salesman Dakin Toys, Applause Inc., San Francisco; founder, owner, pres. Ty Inc., Westmont, Ill., 1985—; owner Four Seasons, NYC, 1999—, San Ysidro Ranch, 1999—, Four Seasons Biltmore, 2000—, Sandpiper Golf Course, 2003—. Named one of World's Richest People, Forbes Mag., 2005, Forbes' Richest Americans, 2006. Achievements include invention of Beanie Babies. Office: Ty Inc 280 Chestnut Ave Westmont IL 60559

**WARNER, HAROLD CLAY, JR.,** banker, investment company executive; b. Knoxville, Tenn., Feb. 24, 1939; s. Harold Clay and Mary Frances (Waters) W.; m. Patricia Alice Rethorst, Sept. 1, 1961; children: Martha Lee, Carol Frances. BS in Econs, U. Tenn., 1961, PhD, 1965. Asst. to pres. First Fed. Savs., Savannah, Ga., 1965-67; v.p. and economist No. Trust Co., Chgo., 1967-73; sr. v.p. and chief economist Crocker Nat. Bank, San Francisco, 1974-79, sr. v.p. liability mgmt., 1979-82; exec. v.p., dir. fixed income mgmt. BA Investment Mgmt. Corp., 1982-84, dir., pres., COO, 1984-86; dir., pres. Montgomery St. Income Securities, Inc., 1984-86; sr. v.p. Bank of Am., San Francisco, 1982-86; chmn. BA Investment Mgmt. Internat., Ltd., 1985-86; pres. Arthur D. Gimbel, Inc., San Mateo, Calif., 1986-87; exec. v.p., chief investment officer Riggs Nat. Bank Washington, 1987-88; chmn. Riggs Investment Mgmt. Corp., 1988-89; sr. v.p., chief economist Bank of Calif. San Francisco, 1989-93; pres., chief investment officer MERUS Capital Mgmt., San Francisco, 1989-93; pres. Govett Asset Mgmt. Co., 1993-95, Govett Fin. Svcs. Ltd., 1993-95; pres., COO Fisher Investments, Inc., Woodside, Calif., 1996; pres. Warner Fiduciary Counsel, LLC, San Francisco, 1997; 1st v.p., sr. dir. portfolio mgmt. Mellon Pvt. Wealth Mgmt., San Francisco, 1998—. Lectr. dept. econs. U. Tenn., 1962-63, Grad. Sch. Bus., Loyola U., Chgo., 1969-73; lectr. Pacific Coast Banking Sch., U. Wash., 1978-79. Chmn. bd. trustees Children's Hosp. and Rsch Ctr. Found. NDEA fellow, 1961-64 Mem. Burlingame Country Club, Pacific-Union Club, Phi Gamma Delta, Phi Eta Sigma, Beta Gamma Sigma, Omicron Delta Kappa, Phi Kappa Phi. Home: PO Box 2449 Yountville CA 94599-2449 Office: 525 Market St 35th Flr San Francisco CA 94105-2743 Office Phone: 415-951-4102. Business E-Mail: warner.hc@mellon.com.

**WARNER, ISIAH MANUEL,** chemistry professor; b. DeQuincy, La., July 20, 1946; s. Humphrey and Irma (St. Romain) W.; m. Della Blount, June 1, 1968; children: Isiah Jr., Chideha, Edward. BS chemistry, Southern Univ., 1968; PhD, Univ. Wash., 1977. Teaching asst. Univ. Wash., Seattle, 1973-75, rsch. asst., 1975-77; asst. prof. Tex. A&M Univ., College Station, Tex., 1977-82; assoc. prof. Emory Univ., Atlanta, 1982-86, prof., 1986, 1987-92; Philip W. West prof., analytical and environ. chem. La. State Univ., Baton Rouge, 1992—, chair, dept. chem., 1994—97, Boyd prof., chem., 2000—, vice chancellor, strategic initiatives, 2001—. Cons. Nat. Sci. Found., 1980—, Coca Cola, Atlanta, 1984-92, Nat. Insts. Health, Bethesda, Md., 1979—, Eli Lilly & Co., Indpls., 1988, 89; rsch. prof., Howard Hughes Med. Inst., 2002-. Contbr. articles to profl. jours. Recipient Charles Holmes Herty award, 1992, Benedetti Pichler award, 1994, NY SAS gold medal, 1991, Presdl. Young Investigator award, 1984, outstanding tchr. award, 1993, Am. Assn. for Advancement of Sci. Lifetime Mentor award, a Fulbright fellowship for rsch., teaching in Kenya, Howard Hughes Med. Inst. grant, 2002, ACS award for encouraging disadvantaged students into the sciences, Am. Chem. Soc., 2003. Mem. Am. Chem. Soc., Nat. Orgn. Black Chemist and Chemical Engrs., Soc. Applied Spectroscopy, Internat. Chemometrics Soc. (N.Am. chpt.), Nat. Rsch. Coun. Chem. Sci. Roundtable 1996-2001, Sigma Xi. Avocations: racquetball, chess, cards. Office: La State Univ Dept Chemistry Baton Rouge LA 70803-0001 Office Phone: 225-388-2829. Office Fax: 225-578-3971. E-mail: iwarner@lsu.edu.

**WARNER, JACK,** paper company executive; Grad., Washington & Lee U. Chmn. emeritus Gulf States Paper Corp., Tuscaloosa, Ala. Founder & curator Westervelt-Warner Mus. Am. Art, Tuscaloosa. Named one of Top 200 Collectors, ARTnews Mag., 2004. Avocation: Collector of 19-century Am. and European art; Impressionism. Mailing: Westervelt Warner Mus of Young Am 8316 Mountbatten Rd Tuscaloosa AL 35406

**WARNER, JOANNE MARIE,** theater educator; d. Nelson Raymond and Mary Edith Warner; m. Perry Lynne Patton, Dec. 31, 1989; children: Taylor Warner Patton, Jackson Warner Patton. BA, Siena Heights U., Adrian, Mich., 1983. Cert. tchr. elem. sch. Mich., 2002. Coord. ednl. outreach coord. Siena Heights U., 2004—, adj. faculty, 2004—. Tchr. Creative Stages, Lake Somerset, Mich., 2000—; spkr. in field. Prodr.: (plays) Siena Heights Youth Theatre. Arts advocacy Americans For The Arts, Bklyn., Mich. Mem.: Am. Alliance Theatre in Edn. Independent. Avocations: travel, writing. Home: 14373 Limerick Lane Somerset MI 49281 Office: Siena Heights University 1247 Siena Heights Drive Adrian MI 49221 Office Phone: 1-517-264-7890. Home Fax: 1-517-688-5361. Personal E-mail: joannewarner@comcast.net. Business E-Mail: jwarner1@sienaheights.edu.

**WARNER, JOANNE RAINS,** nursing educator, associate dean; b. Sioux Falls, S.D., June 27, 1950; d. Arnold D. and Arlene M. (Lawrence) W.; children: David Warner, Isaac Daniel. BA, Augustana Coll., 1972; MA, U. Iowa, 1976; D of Nursing Sci., Ind. U., 1990. Vis. nurse Delaware County Vis. Nurse Assn., Muncie, Ind., 1976-77; cons. Ind. State Bd. Health, Indpls., 1977-78; instr. Briar Cliff Coll., Sioux Falls, 1981-82; adj. faculty Okla. Bapt. U., Shawnee, 1985; assoc. prof. Ind. U., Indpls., 1990, assoc. dean for grad. programs, 2000—. Mem. exec. com. Friends Com. on Nat. Legis., Washington, 1992—; fellow Primary Health Care Policy, Washington, 1996; bd. trustees Earlham Coll. Campaign mgr. Doug Kinser for State Rep. Ind. House Dist. 54, 1988-94; exec. com., mem. New Castle (Ind.) Healthy City Com., 1989-99; chair residential drive Am. Cancer Soc., New Castle, 1989; mem. ANA, Assn. Cmty. Health Nurse Educators (bd. dirs.), Ind. Polit. Sci. Assn. (v.p. 1993-94,. pres. 1994-95). Mem. Soc. Of Friends. Office: Ind U 1111 Middle Dr Indianapolis IN 46202 Home: 3736 NE 36th Ave Portland OR 97212-1834 Office Phone: 317-274-3115.

**WARNER, JOHN ARNAN,** state supreme court justice; b. Great Falls, Mont., Jan. 22, 1943; s. James Arnan and Cleo (Schaedler) W.; m. Katherine Warner; children: Matthew, Marion, Ann, Jeffrey, Jonathan, Katherine. BA, U. Mont., 1965, LLB, 1967. Bar: Mont. 1967, U.S. Dist. Ct. Mont. 1967, U.S. Ct. Appeals (9th cir.) 1982. Law clk. Mont. Supreme Ct., Helena, Mont., 1967-68; ptnr. Bosch, Kuhr, et al, Havre, Mont., 1968-88; atty. City of Havre, 1984-88; dist. judge 12th Judicial Dist., Mont., 1988—2003; justice Mont. Supreme Ct., 2003—. Former chmn. Supreme Ct. Sentence Review Div.; former mem. Dist. Ct. Council; former chmn. Mont. Jud. Standards Commn.; mem. teaching staff Commn. on Cts. of Limited Jurisdiction; mem. Supreme Ct. Commn. to Review Canons of Jud. Ethics. Past pres. Mont. Swimming, Inc.; past chmn. Hill Top Recovery Bd.; past bd. dirs Mont. AAU; del. Mont. Officials Assn. Mem. ABA, Mont. Bar Assn. (trustee 1980-88, pres. 1987-88, mem. jud. relations com.), 12th Judicial Dist. Bar Assn. (past pres.), Def. Rsch. Inst., Lions (past pres. Havre chpt. swim team). Roman Catholic. Avocations: fishing, hunting, hiking. Office: Mont Supreme Ct Justice Bldg PO Box 203003 Helena MT 59620-3003 Office Phone: 406-444-5494. Business E-Mail: jwarner@mt.gov.

**WARNER, JOHN EDWARD,** advertising executive; b. Troy, N.Y., Mar. 26, 1936; s. George Edward and Ann Frances (Teson) W.; m. Anne Elizabeth Hibbard, Sept. 19, 1959; children: Matthew J., Barbara A., Peter J., Christopher J. BS in Chemistry and Philosophy, Coll. Holy Cross, 1957. Promotion mgr. Union Carbide Corp., N.Y.C., 1957-62; acct. exec. McCann-Erickson, Inc., N.Y.C., 1962-64; pres. Warner, Bicking & Fenwick, Inc., N.Y.C., 1964-84; chmn. Warner, Bicking, Morris & Ptnrs. Inc., 1984-97; pres. Transworld Advt. Agy. network, 1987-97, Quatrefoil, Inc., 1998—. Bd. dirs. Thomas Pub. Co., N.Y.C. Author: (non-fiction) Decorating Time Savers by Jack Warner, 2001, (fiction) Tom Never's Ghost, 2006. Home: 706 Hillcrest Rd Ridgewood NJ 07450-1110 E-mail: jawarner@optonline.net.

**WARNER, JOHN HILLIARD, JR.,** technical services company executive; b. Santa Monica, Calif., Mar. 2, 1941; s. John Hilliard and Irene Anne (Oliva) W.; m. Helga Magdalena Farrington, Sept. 4, 1961; children: Tania Renee, James Michael BS in Engring. with honors, UCLA, 1963, MS in Engring., 1965, PhD in Engring., 1967. Mem. staff Marquardt Corp., Van Nuys, Calif., 1963; mem. faculty West Coast U., LA, 1969-72; mem. staff TRW Sys. Group, Redondo Beach, Calif., 1967-70, sect. mgr., 1970-73; mem. staff Sci. Applications Internat. Corp., San Diego, 1973-75, asst. v.p., 1975-77, 1977-80, corp. v.p., 1980-81, sr. v.p., 1981-87, sector v.p., 1987-89, exec. v.p., 1989-96, bd. dirs., 1988—2006, corp. exec. v.p., 1996—2005, chief adminstrv. officer, 2003—06, exec. v.p., 2005—. Cons. Rand Corp., Santa Monica, 1964—66; bd. dirs. AMSEC LLC, Mimix Broadband. Contbr. articles to profl. jours Trustee Scripps Health, 2001—; bd. dirs. Corp. Dirs. Forum, 2001- AEC fellow, 1963, 66, NSF fellow, 1964, 65 Mem. AIAA, NDIA, Nat. Assn. Corp. Dirs., Healthcare Info. and Mgmt. Sys. Soc., Assn. U.S. Army, Air Force Assn., Armed Forces Comm. and Electronics Assn., Navy League U.S., La Jolla Chamber Music Soc. (bd. dirs. 1990-97, adv. bd. 1998-2001), San Diego C. of C. (bd. dirs. 2000-04), Calif. C. of C. (bd. dirs. 2000—), Calif. Bus. Roundtable, Sigma Nu, Tau Beta Pi Methodist. Avocations: bicycling, golf, fishing, music. Office: SAIC 10260 Campus Point Dr San Diego CA 92121-1522

**WARNER, JOHN J.P.,** orthopedist; s. Richard and Gloria Diane (Marmar) Warner; m. Geraldine Vanhissel; children: Brooke, Lauren, Christina, Ben. BA magna cum laude, Colgate U., Hamilton, NY, 1978; MD with honors, U. Rochester, NY, 1982; MA (hon.), Harvard U., Cambridge, 2004. Diplomate Am. Bd. Orthop. Surgery. Instr., asst. orthop. surgery Harvard Med. Sch., Boston, 1988; from asst. prof. to assoc. prof. orthop. surgery U. Pitts. Sch. Medicine, Pitts., 1990—98; assoc. prof. dept. orthop. surgery Mass. Gen. Hosp./Brigham and Women's Hosp., Boston, 1999—2004, prof. dept. orthop. surgery, 2004—. Lectr., spkr. in field; asst. team physician NFL NY Giants, 1989—90; head team physician Central Cath. HS Football, Pa., 1991—98, Pitts. Golden Triangles Jr. Olympic Volleyball Club, 1992—93; head football team physician Pitts. Marauders, 1993—94; head swim team physician, volleyball team orthop. cons. U. Pitts., 1993—98; head tennis team physician Point Park Jr. Coll., 1993—98. Contbr. articles to profl. jours., chapters to books. Award com. Orthop. Rsch. and Edn. Found., 2000—; Recipient John J. Joyce award, Internat. Arthroscopy Assn., 1993, Tchg. award, U. Pitts. Graduating Sr. Orthop. Residents, 1998; Rsch. grant, Bristol-Myers, Squibb, and the Commonwealth Fund, 1992—93, OREF, 1994—96, Am. Assn. Orthop. Surgeons, 1996, ORLAC, 2000, Arthroscopy Assn. N.Am., 2003—05, Ednl. grant, Smith and Nephew Endoscopy, 2000—03, Mitek, Johnson & Johnson, 2001—02, Sulzer Orthop., 2001, Arthrex, 2002, Aircast Corp., 2002, Tornier, 2003, Pfizer Inscope Orthop. fellow, 2005—06. Mem.: New Eng. Shoulder and Elbow Soc. (founder, v.p., founding mem. hand/shoulder sect. 2004—), New Eng. Orthop. Soc. (Kilfoyle award 2004), Am. Orthop. Assn. (com. for Zimmer Annual Travel awards 1999—2000), Am. Orthop. Soc. for Sports Medicine, Orthop. Rsch. Soc. (program com. 1998, 2001), Am. Shoulder and Elbow Surgeons (com. on first open meeting 1997, rsch. and awards com. 1997—2000, chmn. com. on exch. fellows 1998—2001, membership com. 2004—, Neer award 1994, 1999), Arthroscopy Assn. N.Am. (rsch. and awards com. 1997—2000, rsch. com. 2002—, edn. com. 2003—, rsch. com., chmn. 2004, O'Connor award 2001), Am. Coll. Sport Medicine, Am. Acad. Orthop. Surgeons (com. on shoulder and elbow 1998—2001, ednl. program com. 1998—2003, program com. 2001—05, chmn. annual meeting 2004), Acad. Orthop. Soc., La. Orthop. Soc., Am. Coll. Physician Execs. (assoc.), Alpha Omega Alpha, Phi Beta Kappa. Avocations: golf, skiing. Home: 471 Wellesley St Weston MA Office: Mass Gen Hosp Yawkey Bldg 55 Fruit St Boston MA 02114-3108

**WARNER, JOHN WILLIAM,** senator; b. Washington, Feb. 18, 1927; s. John William and Martha Stuart (Budd) W.; m. Catherine Conover Mellon, Aug. 7, 1957 (div. 1973) children: Mary Conover, Virginia Stuart, John William IV.; m. Elizabeth Taylor, Dec. 4, 1976 (div. Nov. 7, 1982); m. Jeanne Vander Myde, Dec. 15, 2003 BS Engring., Washington and Lee U., 1949; LL.B., U. Va., 1953. Law clk. to Hon. E. Barrett Prettyman US Ct. Appeals (DC cir.), 1953-54; spl. asst. to U.S. atty. US Dept. Justice, 1956-57, asst. U.S. atty., 1957-60; ptnr. Hogan & Hartson, 1960-68; owner, operator Atoka Cattle Farm, 1961—94; under sec. USN, Washington, 1969-72, sec., 1972-74; adminstr. Am. Revolution Bicentennial Adminstrn., 1974-76; US Senator from Va., 1979—. Chmn. armed services com.; mem. com. on homeland security & govtl. affairs, environment and pub. works coms., rules and adminstrn. com., nat. Rep. senatorial com.; rep. to sec. def., Law of the Sea Talks, 1969-73, prin. US negotiator & signatory, Incidents at Sea Exec. Agreement, 1970-72, exec. branch rep., Am. Revolution BiCentennial Adminstrn., 1974-76, US del. to 12th Spl. Session of UN Gen. Assembly, 1982, observer, Geneva Arms Control Talks, 1985 Served with USNR, 1944-46; USMC, 1951-52; USMCR, 1952-64. Recipient Edmund S. Muskie Disting. Pub. Svc. award, Ctr. for Nat. Policy, 1999, Harry S. Truman award, Nat. Guard Assn. of the US, 2000, James Forrestal Meml. award, Nat. Def. Industrial Assn., 2000, Wings of Liberty award, Aerospace Industries Assn., 2001, VFW Congl. award, VFW, 2001, Arthur T. Marix Congl. Leadership award, The Retired Officer Assn., 2001, Leadership award, Pvt. Sector Coun., 2003, Spirit of Hope award, United Svc. Organizations, 2003, Congl. Am. Spirit Medallion, Nat. D-Day Mus., 2004. Mem. DC Bar Assn., Am. Legion, Veterans Fgn. Wars (Va. chpt.). Republican. Episc. Office: US Senate 225 Russell Senate Bldg Washington DC 20510-0001 also: Federal Bldg Rm 235 180 West Main St Abingdon VA 24210-2844 Office Phone: 202-224-2023, 276-628-8158. Office Fax: 202-224-6295, 276-628-1036.*

**WARNER, KARL K.,** former prosecutor; b. 1952; BS, U.S. Mil. Acad.; JD, W.Va. U. Gen. counsel to 10th Mountain Div. U.S. Army, 1994—96; legal counsel to Multi-Nat. Force Joint Chiefs of Staff, Haiti, 1994—95, legal counsel to two chmn., joint chiefs staff, 1996—98; gen. counsel U.S. Spl. Ops. Command, 1998—2001; U.S. atty. (So. dist.) W.Va. U.S. Dept. Justice, 2001—05.

**WARNER, KENNETH E.,** dean, public health educator, consultant; b. Washington, Jan. 25, 1947; s. Edgar W. Jr. and Betty (Strasburger) W.; m. Patricia A. Hilty, 1, 1977; children— Peter, Andrew AB, Dartmouth Coll., 1968; MPhil, Yale U., 1970, PhD, 1974. Lectr. dept. health mgmt. and policy Sch. Pub. Health, U. Mich., Ann Arbor, Mich., 1972—74, asst. prof., 1974—77, assoc. prof., 1977—83, prof., 1983—, chmn., 1982—88, 1992—95, Richard D. Remington Collegiate prof. pub. health, 1995—2001, dir. Tobacco Rsch. Network, Avedis Donabedian Disting. Univ. prof. pub. health, 2001—, dean, 2005—. Cons., Washington, 1976—95, Office on Smoking and Health, USPHS, Rockville, Md., 1978—, Inst. Medicine, Nat. Acad. Scis., Washington, 1984—, numerous additional pub. and pvt. orgns.; mem. bd. sci. counselors divsn. cancer prevention and control Nat. Cancer Inst., Bethesda, Md., 1985—89. Author: (with Bryan Luce) Cost-Benefit & Cost Effectiveness Analysis in Health Care, 1982; contbr. articles to profl. jours. Trustee Am. Lung Assn., Mich., Lansing, 1982; mem. subcom. on smoking Am. Heart Assn., Dallas, 1985—87; mem. com. on tobacco and cancer Am. Cancer Soc., N.Y.C., 1984-92; bd. dirs. Am. Legacy Found., 1999-2003. Hon. Woodrow Wilson fellow, 1968; W.K. Kellog Found. fellow, 1980-83; vis. scholar Nat. Bur. Econ. Research, Stanford, Calif., 1975-76; recipient Surgeon Gen.'s medallion Dr. C. Everett Koop, 1989. Fellow Assn. Health Svcs. Rsch.; mem. APHA (leadership award 1990), Inst. Medicine, Phi Beta Kappa. Office: U Mich Dept Health Sch Pub Health 109 Observatory St Ann Arbor MI 48109-2029 Office Phone: 734-763-5454. Business E-Mail: kwarner@umich.edu.

**WARNER, KENNETH WILSON, JR.,** editor, publishing executive; b. Chgo., Dec. 22, 1928; s. Kenneth Wilson and Ann S. (Knapp) W.; m. Deborah Ann Bollo, Dec. 28, 1982 (div. Apr. 1995); 1 child, Joseph; children by previous marriages: Sara, Seth, Katharin. BS Ed., No. Ill. State Teachers Coll., 1950. Staff editor Bldg. Supply News, Chgo., 1953-56; staff editor Elec. Merchandising, 1956-60; free-lance writer Sarasota, Fla., 1960-66; editor Gunsport Mag., Alexandria and Falls Church, Va., 1966-67, Gunfacts Mag., Arlington, Va., 1968-70, pub., 1968-70; exec. editor Am. Rifleman, Nat. Rifle Assn., Washington, 1971-78, asst. dir. publs. div., 1972-78; editor Am. Hunter, 1973-78, Am. Rifleman, 1976-78; dir. publs. NRA, Washington, 1977-78; editor in chief Gun Digest, Knives Annual-Krause Publs., Inc., Greenville, W.Va., 1979-99; editor, pub. Knives Digest Two Knife Guys Pub., Inc., Chattanooga, 2000—01; pres. Knifeware, Inc., Greenville, W.Va. Cons. firearms and cutlery cos.; co-founder Am. Knife and Tool Inst., 1997. Author: The Practical Book of Knives. 1976; The Practical Book of Guns, 1978. Editor: The Bolt Action, 1976. Contbr. articles to profl. jours. Capt. U.S. Army. 1951-53. Recipient Cutlery Hall of Fame; inducted into Am. Bladesmith Soc. Hall of Fame, 1996. Mem.: NRA (life), Knifemaker's Guild Am. (assoc.). Office: Prin Office PO Box 52 Greenville WV 24945-0052 Office Phone: 304-832-6878. Personal E-Mail: knifeware@earthlink.net.

**WARNER, KERSTIN JULIANNA,** gifted and talented educator; d. Kerstin and John Warner; m. Louis Weinberg, June 23, 1995; 1 child, Sofia Weinberg. BS in Fine Art, Vassar Coll., Poughkeepsie, N.Y., 1986; MS in Spl. Edn., Bank St. Coll. Edn., 1994. Cert. tchr. K-8, spl. edn. 1-12, art 1-12 Conn.; tchr. elem. K-6, art 1-12, spl. edn. 1 - 12 NY. Asst. tchr. St. Anne's Sch., Bklyn., 1987—90; tchr. spl. edn. preschool The League Sch., Bklyn., 1990—92; 2d grade tchr. Berkeley Carroll Sch., Bklyn., 1992—95; tchr. gifted St. Paul Pub. Schs., 1995—99, Bedford Mid. Sch., Westport, Conn., 1999—. Coach mock trial team Bedford Mid. Sch., Westport, 2002—; book discussion trainer Westport Pub. Libr., 2001—; Conn. chair Nicholas Green award, 2005—. Pres. Vassar Club of Fairfield County, Westport, Conn., 2002—. Recipient Golden Apple Achiever award, Ashland, 1998; Inter-district Archaeology Program, Conn. Assn. for the Gifted, 2004—05. Mem.: ASCD, Nat. Assn. for Gifted Children (state coord., chairperson Nicholas Green award 2006—), Conn. Assn. for the Gifted, Nat. Coun. Tchrs. Math., Vassar Club (pres. 2002—). Democrat. Avocations: creative writing, drawing, international travel. Office: Bedford Middle School 88 North Ave Westport CT 06880 Office Phone: 203-341-1582. E-mail: kerstin_warner@westport.k12.ct.us.

**WARNER, KURT (KURTIS WARNER),** professional football player; b. Burlington, Iowa, June 22, 1971; m. Brenda Warner; 4 children. BA in Comm., No. Ill. U. Quaterback Iowa Barnstormers (Arena Football League), 1995—97, Amsterdam Admirals (NFL Europe), 1998, St. Louis Rams (NFL), 1998—2004, N.Y. Giants, East Rutherford, NJ, 2004—05, Arizona Cardinals, 2005—. Founder First Things First Found., 1999—. Named NFL MVP, 1999, 2001, Super Bowl XXXIV MVP, 2000; named to, NFL Pro-Bowl, 1999—2001. Achievements include led NFL in passing touchdowns, 1999, 2001, passing yards, consecutive; quarterback Super Bowl Championship Team, Super Bowl XXXIV, 2000; tied the NFL record with six consecutive 300-yard passing games during 2000-01 season; set record for highest rated passer in NFL history, 2002; holds Super Bowl record with 414 passing yards; only player in NFL history to record perfect passer rating of 158.3 twice in his career. Office: 8701 S Hardy Dr Tempe AZ 85284*

**WARNER, M. RICHARD,** paper and forest products company executive; b. Lufkin, Tex., Nov. 8, 1951; s. M.L. and Gladys (Hester) W.; m. Elizabeth Denman, July 28, 1973; children: Virginia Lee, Richard Denman. BBA, Baylor U., 1974, JD, 1975. Pvt. practice, Lufkin, 1976-83; with office of gen. counsel Temple-Eastex Inc., Diboll, Tex., 1983-84; with office of trans. Temple-Inland Inc., Diboll, 1984-86, treas., v.p., gen. coun., chief adminstrv. officer, 1986—, pres., 2004—. Bd. dirs. Peoples Nat. Bank, Lufkin, Lumbermans Investment Corp., Austin, Tex., Guaranty Fed. Savs. Bank, Dallas. Bd. dirs. Diboll Booster Club, 1986—; pres. Temple-Inland Found., Diboll, 1986—. Mem. State Bar of Tex., Angelina County Bar Assn. (sec.-chair. 1976), Angelina County Young Lawyers Assn. (pres. 1980), Baylor Law Alumni Assn. (bd. dirs. 1985—). Avocations: hunting, fishing, golf. Office: Temple-Inland Inc 303 S Temple Dr Diboll TX 75941-2419*

**WARNER, MARK ROBERT,** former governor; b. Indpls., Ind., Dec. 15, 1954; s. Robert and Margaret Warner; m. Lisa Collis; children: Madison, Gillian, Eliza. BA, George Washington U., 1977; JD, Harvard U., 1980. Founding ptnr. Columbia Capital Corp., Alexandria, Va., 1989; gov. State of Va., Richmond, 2001—06. Chmn. Va. State Dem. Party, 1993—95; mem. Dem. Nat. Com., 1993—95; chmn. Nat. Gov. Assn., 2004—05. Founding chmn. Va. Health Care Found.; creator SeniorNavigator.com; founder TechRiders, Va. High-Tech Partnership; co-chmn. Va. Cmtys. in Schs. Found.; mem. Old Presbyn. Meeting House; past bd. dirs. Va. Union U., George Washington U., Appalachian Sch. Law, Va. Found. for Ind. Colls., Va. Math and Sci. Coalition. Democrat. Presbyn.*

**WARNER, MATTHEW DOUGLAS,** executive recruiter; b. Portland, Oreg., Mar. 11, 1980; s. Phillip Douglas Warner and Linda Sue Bay-Warner. AA, Thomas Edison State Coll., 2000. Pers. supr. Adecco Employment Svcs., Vancouver, Wash., 1999—2001, br. tng. specialist Melville, NY, 1999—2000; sr. recruiter Comprehensive HR, Portland, Oreg., 2001—01; staffing mgr. Hire Source, Inc., Vancouver, 2001—03; recruitment specialist Parkway Exec. Search and Staffing Svcs., Vancouver, 2003—05, br. mgr., 2005—06, sr. br. mgr., 2006—. Prof. human resources SHRM/HRCI, 2001—. Del. state conv. Wash. State Dems., Seattle, 2004. Avocation: volunteerism. Home: 1021 West 38th St Vancouver WA 98660 Office Phone: 360-514-9308. Personal E-mail: mattwarner@yahoo.com.

**WARNER, MINER HILL,** investment banker; b. N.Y.C., Aug. 13, 1942; s. Bradford Arnold and Nancy (Hill) W.; m. Ellen C. Murphy, Mar. 18, 1972; children— Alix Mallet-Prevost, Lily Wolcott. AB, Harvard U., 1964; C.E.P., Institut d'Etudes Politiques, Paris, 1963; M.Sc. in Econs., London Sch. Econs., 1965; LL.B., U. Pa., 1968; postgrad., NYU. Grad. Sch. Bus. Adminstrn., 1971-73. Bar: N.Y. 1969. Assoc. Shearman & Sterling, N.Y.C., 1968-71; assoc. Salomon Bros. Inc., N.Y.C., 1971-73; v.p. Salomon Bros. Internat. Ltd., London, 1974-78; v.p., mgr. Salomon Bros. Inc., N.Y.C., 1979-87; dir. Merrill Lynch & Co., N.Y.C., 1988-92; pres. Pub. Resources Internat., N.Y.C., 1992-95, chmn., 1996—. Adv. dir Coun. of the Americas, 1991-93. Mem. Pres.'s Pvt. Sector Survey on Cost Control, Washington, 1982-83; mem. coun. Grad. Theol. Union, Berkeley, Calif., 1998-; vestryman St. John's Ch., Fishers Island, N.Y., 1980-99, sr. warden, 1994-99; regent Cathedral of St. John the Divine, N.Y., 1995-97, trustee, 1997—, mem. exec. com.; English-Speaking Union U.S. bd. dirs., mem. exec. com., 2002-06, mem. task force Gen. Theol. Sem., N.Y., 2000-02; pres. Pilgrims; trustee N.Y. Hist. Soc., 1985—, chmn. 1994-99, chmn. emeritus, 1999—; trustee Hispanic Soc. Am., 2005-. Decorated Order of St. John of Jerusalem. Mem. Pub. Securities Assn. (guaranteed loan com. 1980-86), Mayflower Soc. (former gov.), Brook Club (sec.), River Club, Links Club, Met. Club (Washington), Fishers Island Club, Hay Harbor Club (Fishers Island) (former dir.), Econ. Club N.Y. Republican. Episcopalian. Home: 148 E End Ave New York NY 10028-7503 Office: Pub Resources Internat 780 3d Ave Ste 2805 New York NY 10017-2024

**WARNER, PATRICIA ANN,** secondary school educator; b. Wooster, Ohio, Dec. 21, 1949; d. Kent Branson and Irene Mae (Graves) W. BA in English, Coll. of Wooster, 1972, MAT in English, 1973. Cert. tchr. Ohio; nat. bd. cert. tchr. adolescence and young adulthood English lang. arts. Instr. in English Orrville (Ohio) H.S., 1974—, Wayne Col., Orrville, Ohio, 1988-91. Named Orrville (Ohio) City Schs. Tchr. of Yr., 1987-88, Jennings Scholar Jennings Found., 1994-95. Mem. NEA, NCTE, Ohio Council of Tchrs. of English and Language Arts. Office: Orrville HS 841 N Ella St Orrville OH 44667-1154

**WARNER, PAUL MICHAEL,** federal judge, former prosecutor; b. 1952; BA, Brigham Young U., 1973, JD, 1976, MPA, 1984. Atty. judge advocate general's corps USN, 1976—82; asst. atty. gen. State of Utah, Salt Lake City, 1982—83; asst. US atty. Dist. Utah US Dept. Justice, Salt Lake City, 1983—94, US atty., 1996—2006; magistrate judge US Dist. Ct., Salt Lake City, 2006—. With USNR, 1976—82, advanced through ranks to col. Nat. Guard, 1983—, Utah. Office: US Dist Ct 350 S Main St Salt Lake City UT 84101*

**WARNER, PETER DAVID,** publishing executive; b. Phila., Aug. 15, 1942; s. Robert and Myra (Spector) W.; m. Ruth Bluestein (div. 1982); m. Jill Sansone, 1983; children: Emily, Cynthia, Nicholas. BA, NYU, 1964. Asst. dir. membership and devel. Mus. Modern Art, N.Y.C., 1973-76; editor, promotion dir. Book-of-the-Month Club, N.Y.C., 1976-79; pres. Thames and Hudson, N.Y.C., 1979—. Author: Loose Ends, 1972, Lifestyle, 1986. Mem. The Writers Room (bd. dirs.), The Century Assn. Office: Thames & Hudson Inc 500 5th Ave New York NY 10110-0002

**WARNER, ROBERT MARK,** dean, archivist, historian; b. Montrose, Colo., June 28, 1927; s. Mark Thomas and Bertha Margaret (Rich) W.; m. Eleanor Jane Bullock, Aug. 21, 1954; children: Mark Steven, Jennifer Jane. Student, U. Denver, 1945; BA, Muskingum Coll., 1949, LL.D. (hon.), 1981; MA, U. Mich., 1953, PhD, 1958; H.H.D. (hon.), Westminster Coll., Pa., 1981; L.H.D. (hon.), DePaul U., 1983. Tchr. high sch., Montrose, Colo., 1949-50; lectr. dept. history U. Mich., 1958-66, assoc. prof., 1966-71, prof., 1971-97, prof. emeritus, 1997—, prof. Sch. Info. 1974-97, emeritus, 1997—, dean Sch. Info. and Library Studies, 1985-92, univ. historian, 1992—, interim dir. Univ. Libraries, 1988-90; asst. in rsch. Bentley Hist. Libr., 1953-57, asst. curator, 1957-61, asst. dir., 1961-66, dir., 1966-80; archivist of U.S., 1980-85. Mem. exec. com. Bentley Hist. Libr., 1988—; bd. visitors Libr. Sci., Case Western Res. U., 1976-80, chmn., 1980-84, Maxwell Sch. Govt., Syracuse U., 1982-87; chmn. Gerald R. Ford Presdl. Libr. Bldg. Com., 1977-79; bd. dirs., sec. Gerald R. Ford Found., 1987—; trustee Woodrow Wilson Internat. Ctr. for Scholars, 1980-85, chmn. fellowship com. 1983-85; chmn. Nat. Hist. Publs. and Records Commn., 1980-85; mem. exec. com. Internat. Coun. on Archives, 1984-88; pres. 2d European Conf. on Archives, 1989; comptroller gen. U.S. Rsch. and Edn. Adv. Com., 1988-2000; rsch. adv. com. Online Computer Libr. Ctr., 1990-93; bd. govs. Clements Libr., 1988-90, 93—2004, Clark Hist. Libr. Ctrl. Mich. U., 1987—; vis. prof. UCLA, 1993. Author: Chase S. Osborn, 1860-1949, 1960, Profile of a Profession, 1964, (with R. Bordin) The Modern Manuscript Library, 1966, (with C.W. Vanderhill) A Michigan Reader: 1865 to the Present, 1974, (with F. Blouin) Sources for the Study of Migration and Ethnicity, 1979, Diary of a Dream: A History of the National Archives Independence Movement, 1980-1985, 1995. Served with U.S. Army, 1950-52. Recipient Disting. Svc. award Muskingum Coll., 1990, Disting. Svc. award Nat. Hist. Pub. and Records Commn., 1992. Fellow Soc. Am. Archivists; mem. Am. Hist. Assn. (council 1981-85), Orgn. Am. Historians, ALA (council 1986-91), Assn. for Library and Info. Sci. Edn., Presbyn. Hist. Soc. (bd. dirs. 1987-91), Am. Assn. State and Local History, Hist. Soc. Mich. (trustee 1960-66, v.p. 1972-73, pres. 1973-74), Soc. Am. Archivists (mem. council 1967-71, sec., exec. dir. 1971-73, v.p. 1974-75, pres. 1976-77), Am. Antiquarian Soc., Phi Alpha Theta, Beta Phi Mu. Clubs: U. Mich. Research. Lodges: Rotary. Presbyterian. Home: 1821 Coronada St Ann Arbor MI 48103-5066 Office: U Mich Sch Info 550 E University Ave Ann Arbor MI 48109-1092 Business E-Mail: archlib@umich.edu.

**WARNER, ROBERTA ARLENE,** retired accountant, financial services executive; b. Binghamton, N.Y., Dec. 31, 1938; d. Murrilan Earl and Ethel Margaret (Bell) W. BA, SUNY, Binghamton, 1960; MBA, Ind. U., 1962, MHA with highest distinction, 1973. CPA, N.Y.; lic. nursing home adminstr., N.Y. Sr. acct. Arthur Young & Co., CPA, Buffalo, 1962—66; acctg. supr. Children's Hosp., Buffalo, 1966—68; contr. King Manor Nursing Homes-Ave. Bldg. Corp., Buffalo, 1968—71; asst. dir. health fin. Hosp. Assn. N.Y. State, Albany, 1973—80, dir. health fin., 1980—93, Healthcare Assn. N.Y. State, Albany, 1994—97, dir. data analysis and stds., 1997—98; pres. Roberta A. Warner Cons, 1999—2003, ret., 2003. Author articles in field. Trustee Ednl. Found. of Am. Women's Soc. CPA, Am. Soc. Women Accts., 1985-87. Fellow Healthcare Fin. Mgmt. Assn.; mem. AICPA, Am. Acctg. Assn., Am. Soc. Women Accts. (pres. Buffalo chpt. 1967-68), Am. Women's Soc. CPA, N.Y. State Soc. CPA, Ind. U. Alumni Assn. (life), SUNY Binghamton Alumni Assn. (life), Grange. Methodist. Home: 569 NY Rte 79 Windsor NY 13865-2714

**WARNER, ROLLIN MILES, JR.,** economics educator, real estate broker; b. Evanston, Ill., Dec. 25, 1930; s. Rollin Miles Warner Sr. and Julia Herndon (Polk) Clarkson. BA, Yale U., 1953; cert. in law, Harvard U., 1956; MBA, Stanford U., 1960; cert. in edn. adminstrn., U. San Francisco, 1974. Lic. real estate broker Real Estate Cert. Inst., Calif. Asst. to v.p. fin. Stanford U., 1960-63; instr. history Town Sch., San Francisco, 1963-70, instr. econs. and history, dean, 1975—; prin. Mt. Tamalpais, Ross, Calif., 1972-74; dir. devel. Katharine Branson Sch., Ross, 1974-75. Author: America, 1986, Europe, 1986, Africa, Asia, Russia, 1986, Greece, Rome, 1981, Free Enterprise at Work, 1986. From scoutmaster to summer camp cmnor. Boy Scouts Am., San Francisco, 1956—. Served to lt. USNR, 1953—55, Korea, Pacific, Vietnam. Recipient Silver Beaver award Boy Scouts Am., 1986, Town Sch. for Boys medal Town Sch. Alumni Coun., 1995. Mem.: U.S. Naval Inst., Marines Meml. Assn., South End Rowing Club (San Francisco), San Francisco Yacht Club (Belvedere, Calif.), Grolier Club NY. Office: Town Sch 2750 Jackson St San Francisco CA 94115-1195 E-mail: warnerrollinm1960@alumni-gsb.stanford.edu.

**WARNER, SCOTT DENNIS,** investment banker; b. York, Pa., July 13, 1963; s. Earl Dennis and Sandra Glee (Barnhart) W. SB in Elec. Engring., MIT, 1986, SB in Computer Sci. and Engring., 1986, SM in Elec. Engring. and Computer Sci. 1986; MBA in Fin., U. Chgo., 1990. Intern IBM Corp., Yorktown Heights, NY, 1983-86; fin. analyst Merrill Lynch & Co., NYC, 1986-88, assoc., 1990-94, v.p., 1994-95; assoc. Goldman, Sachs & Co., NYC, 1989; v.p. Lipper & Co. L.P., NYC, 1995-98, Gerard Klauer Mattison & Co., Inc., NYC, 1998—2002; pres. Internat. Capital LLC and Warner Capital, S.e.c.s., Luxembourg, 2003—05, Internat. Capital LLC, London, 2006—. Nat. Merit scholar, 1981, ROTC scholar, 1981, teaching asst. scholar MIT, 1985, 86; Leon C. Marshall scholar U. Chgo., 1988. Mem. Nat. Eagle Scout Assn., Delta Upsilon Frat. Republican. Presbyterian. Office: Internat Capital LLC 17 Cranley Mews London SW7 3BX England Personal E-Mail: scottdwarner@yahoo.com.

**WARNER, TOKESHA L.,** health facility administrator; d. Johnny W. and Mary M. (Wilson) Warner; children: Raina children: Stefan Wright. BA, Earlham Coll., 1996; postgrad., Walden U., 2002—. Event coord., Nashville, 1996—98; program coord. Vanderbilt Children's Hosp., Nashville, 1999—2003. Co-chmn. diversity workgroup Assn. Univ. Ctrs. on Disabilities, Silver Spring, Md., 2003—04; chmn. football program Tenn. Police Athletic League, Nashville, 2002—03. Independent. Avocations: creative writing & poetry, photography, hist. of colonial America. E-mail: tokesha.warner@vanderbilt.edu.

**WARNER, WILLIAM HAMER,** mathematician; b. Pitts., Oct. 6, 1929; s. John Christian and Louise (Hamer) W.; m. Janet Louise West, June 29, 1957; 1 dau., Katherine Patricia. Student, Haverford Coll., 1946-48; BS, Carnegie Inst. Tech., 1950, MS, 1951, PhD, 1953. Research asso. grad. div. applied math. Brown U., Providence, 1953-55; asst. prof. dept. aerospace engring. and mechanics U. Minn., Mpls., 1955-58, asso. prof., 1958-68, prof., 1968-95, prof. emeritus, 1995—. Author: (with L.E. Goodman) Statics, 1963, Dynamics, 1964; contbr. articles to profl. jours. Mem.: Soc. Natural Philosophy, Math. Assn. Am., Soc. Indsl. and Applied Math., Am. Math. Soc. Office: Univ Minn 107 Akerman Hall 110 Union St SE Minneapolis MN 55455-0153 E-mail: warner@aem.umn.edu.

**WARNER, WILLIAM KENT, JR.,** religious organization administrator, consultant; b. Chgo., June 14, 1933; children: William Kent III, Robert David, Steven Bradley. BA in Theology, Wheaton Coll., 1953; MA summa cum laude, Columbia Internat. U., S.C., 1954; MS, U. Ill., Urbana, 1960; PhD, U. Iowa, Iowa City, 1972. Ordained Evang. Free Ch. Am., 1954. Missionary, tchr. and prin. Tchg. Tng. Inst., Zimbabwe, 1955—59; founder dir. publ. house, 1961—67; founder, exec. dir. CCOSA, Wheaton, Ill., 1969—. Prin. Tchg. Tng. Inst., Zimbabwe, 1959; founder, pub. Pub. House, Harare, 1961—67; founder, exec. dir. CCOSA, 1969—. Avocations: writing, speaking, table tennis. Office: CCOSA c/o M Mahoney CPA/MBA 496 E Roosevelt Ste 110 Wheaton IL 60187 E-mail: drwkwarner@hotmail.com.

**WARNKE, GORDON E.,** lawyer; b. Wetaskiwin, Alta., Canada, Nov. 3, 1957; BS, U. Alta., 1978, LLB, 1981; SJD, Harvard Univ., 1984. Bar: NY 1984. Co-mng. ptnr., mem. exec. com., co-chmn. tax group Dewey Ballantine LLP, NYC. Mem.: ABA (past chmn. com. on affiliated & related corp.), NY State Bar Assn. (mem. exec. com.), Assn. of the Bar of the City of NY. Office: Dewey Ballantine LLP 1301 Ave of the Americas New York NY 10019-6092 Office Phone: 212-259-6070. Office Fax: 212-259-6333. Business E-Mail: gwarnke@dbllp.com.

**WARNOCK, JOHN EDWARD,** computer company executive; b. Salt Lake City, Oct. 6, 1940; BS in Math. and Philosophy, U. Utah, 1961, MS in Math., 1964, PhD in Elec. Engring. and Computer Sci., 1969; DSc (hon.), Univ. Utah. With Evans & Sutherland Computer Corp., Computer Scis. Corp., IBM; prin. scientist Xerox Palo Alto Rsch. Ctr., Calif., 1978-81; co-founder, chmn. Adobe Sys., Inc., San Jose, Calif., 1982—, CEO, 1982—2000. Bd. dir. Octavo Corp. Patentee in field; contbr. articles to profl. jours. and industry mags.; spkr. in field. Bd. mem., past chmn. Tech Mus. Innovation; mem. entrepreneurial bd. adv. com. Am. Film Inst. Recipient Computer Achievement award Assn. for Computing Machinery SIGGRAPH, 1989, Tech. Excellence award Nat. Graphics Assn., 1989, ACM Software Sys. award, 1989, Lifetime Achievement award for tech. excellence, PC Mag., 1989, J. Anderson Disting. Achievement award, 1991, Disting. Alumnus award U. Utah, 1995, Cary award Rochester Inst. Tech., 1995, Fellow award, Computer History Mus., 2002; named to Computer Reseller News Hall of Fame, 1998. Fellow ACM; mem. NAE, Utah Info. Tech. Assn. Office: Adobe Sys Inc 345 Park Ave San Jose CA 95110-2704*

**WARNOCK, WILLIAM REID,** lawyer; b. Detroit, July 25, 1939; s. William G. and Margery E. (Ford) W.; m. Sandra L. Klarich, Dec. 27, 1961; children: Cheryl Lynn, Laura Ellen. BBA, U. Mich., 1961, JD with distinction, 1964. Bar: Ill. 1964, U.S. Dist. Ct. (no. dist.) Ill. 1965, U.S. Supreme Ct. 1972, Mich. 1995. With Ross & Hardies, Chgo., 1964-70; regional counsel U.S. Dept. HUD, Chgo., 1970-73; ptnr. Roan & Grossman, Chgo., 1973-82; sole practice Chgo., 1982-85; ptnr. Siegel & Warnock, Chgo., 1985-91; of counsel Donovan & Olsen, Chgo., 1991; pres. William R. Warnock P.C., LaGrange, Ill., 1992—2002, Three Rivers, Mich., 2002—03. Cons. Ill. Dept. Bus. and Econ. Devel., Chgo., 1977-78, Ill. Housing Devel. Authority, Chgo., 1973-78, Council State Housing Financing Agys., Washington, 1975-78; past pres., chmn. Atty.'s Title Guaranty Fund, Inc., Chgo., 1986-88, also bd. dirs. 1976—2003. Author: (legal references) Land Use and Zoning, 1974-88, Ward on Title Examination, 1975, Illinois Real Property Service: Real Estate Exchanges, 1988, Environmental Law and the Real Estate Lawyer, 1989-90. Mem. Ill. State Bar Assn., Am. Coll. Real Estate Lawyers. Republican. Methodist. Avocations: boating, woodworking. Personal E-mail: warnockwr@aol.com.

**WARPEHA, RAYMOND LEONARD,** surgeon, educator; b. Mpls., Dec. 5, 1934; s. Frank Joseph and Sophie Helen (Fryzlewicz) Warpeha; m. Ivy Lee Kloth; children: Katherine, John, Joseph, Frank. BS, U. Minn., 1956, DDS, 1958; MD, Northwestern U., 1965, PhD in Anatomy. 1966. Cert. Am. Bd. Surgery, 1971, plastic surgery Am. Bd. Surgery, 1973. Instr. anatomy Northwestern U. Med. Sch., Chgo., 1963—65, instr. surgery, 1969—72; asst. prof. surgery and anatomy Loyola U. Stritch Sch. Medicine, Maywood, Fla., 1973—75, assoc. prof. surgery and anatomy, 1975—80, prof. surgery and anatomy, 1981—2000, prof. emeritus, 2000—. Cons. surgery Cook County Hosp., Chgo., 1970—72; founder, dir. Burn Ctr. Loyola U. Hosp., 1972—91; dir. surg. anatomy dept. surgery Loyola Med. Sch., 1972—2000. Author: 59 articles and 9 book chpts., Clinics of Plastic Surgery North America, 1981; mem. editl. bd.: Chgo. Medicine. Chmn. Ill. Burn Surgeons adv. group Ill. Dept. Med. Svcs., Springfield, 1973—80; chmn. burn surgeons adv. group Divsnl. Med. Svcs., Washington, 1975; mem. bd. trustees Ill. Trauma Soc.;

trustee Am. Soc. Maxillofacial Surgery. Recipient award for Lifetime Med. Contbns. and Pub. Svc. to Burn and Fire Victims and Survivors, Knapp Burn Found., Chgo., 1999; postdoctoral Am. Heart Assn. fellow, Northwestern Med. Sch., 1962—63. Fellow: Am. Coll. Surgeons (chmn. membership com. Dist. 3 1995—99); mem.: Am. Soc. Plastic and Reconstructive Surgeons, Soc. Head and Neck Surgeons, Am. Assn. Plastic Surgeons, Am. Soc. Maxillofacial Surgeons, Am. Burn Assn., Chgo. Soc. Plastic Surgery (pres. 1983—84, treas. 1981—82, v.p. 1982—83). Roman Catholic. Avocations: fishing, botany. Office: Loyola Med Ctr Dept Surgery 2160 S First Ave Maywood IL 60153

**WARREN, ALICE LOUISE,** artist; b. Springfield, Mass., May 7, 1927; d. Roland D. and Ella May (McGrath) Eaton Von Der Lancken; m. John Homer Warren, June 5, 1948 (dec. Jan. 1988); children: John David (dec.), Daniel Wayne. Student, N.Y. Sch. Writing, 1952-55, Mansion House Art Sch., 1969, 70, 71; grad., Nat. Landscape Inst., 1960, Famous Writers Sch., 1965; Cert., United UMA Sch., 1967. Home nursing cert.; cert. home health aide paramedical. Nurses aide ARC, Springfield, 1942-45; vol. nurses aid, 1943—44; hot-line councilor Check Line, West Springfield, Mass., 1945-46; freelance columnist New England Homestead, Springfield, 1960-63; freelance columnist, editor Garden Page Woman's Circle, Horticulture mags. Author, photographer: (booklet) Evergreen Shrubs, 1964. solo art exhbns. Mercy Hosp., Arts Unltd. Gallery, 1997, Bay State Med., Springfield, Mass., 1999; featured artist Barnes and Noble Bookstore, Oct. 1999, Westfield Antheneum, 2000; on-line exhbns. MindsIsland.com, 2002, ArtRepsart.com, 2002--, Art-Exchange.com, 2003--. Recipient Bill Curtin award for watercolor, 1983. Mem. Amherst Writers & Artists Inst., Springfield Art League, Scriptures Writers, Mass. Writers Guild (treas. 1963), Tobacco Valley Artists Assn. Avocations: painting, travel, photography, reading. E-mail: artislalaw@comcast.nct.

**WARREN, ALVIN CLIFFORD, JR.,** law educator; b. Daytona Beach, Fla., May 14, 1944; s. Alvin Clifford and Barbara (Barnes) Warren; m. Judith Blatt, Aug. 20, 1966; children: Allison, Matthew. BA in English, Yale U., 1966; JD, U. Chgo., 1969. Bar: Conn. 1970, Pa. 1975. Asst. to assoc. prof. law U. Conn., West Hartford, 1969-73, assoc. prof., Duke U., Durham, NC, 1973-75, prof. U. Pa., Phila., 1975-80, prof. Harvard Law Sch., Cambridge, Mass., 1980—98, Ropes & Gray prof., 1998-, dir. fund for tax and fiscal rsch. policy, 1985-. Vis. assoc. prof., U. Pa., 1974-75; vis. prof. Harvard Law Sch., 1979-80. Author: Integration of Individual and Corporate Income Taxes, 1993; contbr. articles to law journals. Mem.: ABA (tax sect.). Office: Harvard Law Sch 1563 Massachusetts Ave Cambridge MA 02138 Office Phone: 617-495-3186. Office Fax: 617-496-4880. E-mail: warren@law.harvard.edu.

**WARREN, ARETE BERNICE,** art historian; b. Chgo., July 23, 1946; d. Lyle Dwight Swartz and Phyllis Elizabeth Coffman; m. William Bradford Warren, Sept. 20, 1985. BA, Northwestern U., 1968; MA, U. N.C. Chapel Hill, 1970. Cert. secondary sch. tchr. Ill. Rsch. asst. Victoria and Albert Mus., London, 1970—73; lectr. Tate Gallery, London, 1973; coord. program/edn. Cooper-Hewitt Mus., N.Y.C., 1973—74; exec. dir. Royal Oak Found., N.Y.C., 1974—82; asst. to dir. N.C. Mus. Art, Raleigh, 1982—85; ind. writer, lectr., 1985—. Chmn. N.Y. com. Am. Mus. in Britain, 1995—, U.S./U.K. coun. chmn., 1999—, trustee, 2004—; mem. Mayor's Commn. for Protocol, City of N.Y., 1995—2002; mem. steering com. N.Y. Bot. Garden, 1995—97; mem. N.Y. State Bd. for Hist. Preservation, 1998—, N.Y. State Empire Plaza Art Commn., 2000—; lectr. in field. Co-author: Glass Houses, 1988; contbr. articles to profl. jours. V.p. Royal Oak Found., Inc., 1982—86, sec., 1986—90, bd. dirs., 1987—93; bd. dirs., mem. strategic planning com. Keep N.C. Beautiful, Inc., 1983—85; trustee Preservation League N.Y. State, 1990—96, 1998—2004, trustee coun., 1996—98, 2004—, exec. com., 1998—2006; bd. visitors/nat. adv. coun. Ackland Art Mus., U. N.C., Chapel Hill, 1991—2005, chmn., 1996—2000; mem. coun. of fellows Morgan Libr., N.Y.C., 2003—. Mem.: Internat. Coun. Mus., Am. Assn. Mus., Soc. Archtl. Historians, Millbrook (N.Y.) Garden Club, Sharon (Conn.) Country Club, Garden Club Am. (zone III N.Y. rep. 1999—2001, vice chmn. zones I, II, III, IV 2001—03, nat. chmn. 2004—06, garden history and design com.), Women's Nat. Rep. Club (bd. govs. 1989—92, pres. 1990—91), Colony Club. Avocations: gardening, writing, travel, cooking. Home: 520 E 86th St New York NY 10028

**WARREN, ARTHUR LEE,** secondary school educator, school system administrator; b. Newark, N.J., Sept. 6, 1947; s. Arthur and Mattie Nate Warren; m. Marvine Marshall, Oct. 10, 1970; children: Jeremy Lee, Ashlee Kathryn. BA, Rutgers U., 1978; MEd, Kean U., 1988. Cert. Administr./Supr. NJ., 1978, Tchr. History NJ., 1988. History tchr. Fords Jr H.S., NJ, 1978—81; tchr. Woodbridge H.S., NJ, 1984—88, vice prin., 1989—93, prin., 1996—; tchr. John F. Kennedy H.S., Iselin, NJ, 1988—89; prin. Ross St. Elem. Sch., Woodbridge, NJ, 1993—96, Fords Mid. Sch., Fords, NJ, 1995—96. Trustee Principal's Ctr. for the Garden State, Coll. of N.J., Ewing, NJ, 2004—; Prodigal Found., Woodbridge, NJ, 2000—. Com. mem. Citizen's Adv. Com., Plainfield, NJ, 1975—78, Census 2000, Twp. of Woodbridge, NJ, 1999—2000. Recipient Prin. of the Yr., N.J. Prins. & Suprs. Assn., 2000. Mem.: Nat. Assn. Secondary Sch. Prins., Assn. for Supervisory and Curriculum Devel., Nat. Assn. of Secondary Prins., N. J. Prins., Kappa Betta Pi. Office: Woodbridge HS Samuel Lupo Pl Woodbridge NJ 07095 Office Phone: 732-602-8600. Office Fax: 732-602-8612. Business E-mail: arthur.warren@woodbridge.k12.nj.us.

**WARREN, CHARLES DAVID,** library administrator; b. Martin, Tenn., June 12, 1944; s. Charles Alton and Evelyn (Bell) W.; children: Aaron David, Meredith Hild, Julia Myers. BS, U. Tenn., 1967; MS, U. Ill., Urbana, 1969. cert. pub. library adminstr. Dir. Shiloh Regional Library, Jackson, Tenn., 1969-72, Cumberland County Pub. Library, Fayetteville, NC, 1973-79; exec. dir. Richland County Pub. Library, Columbia, SC, 1979—. Bd. dirs. Civic Music Assn., Fayetteville, NC, 1977-79, Fayetteville Symphony, 1973-78, Fayetteville Arts Commn., 1975; v.p. Friends of Librs. U.S.A., 1994—; mem. Columbia Coord. Coun., 1987-88; chmn. Richland County History Commn., 1987-93; mem. John Cotton Dana Awards Commn., 1994-99. Recipient Lucy Hampton Bostick award, 1993, S.C. Pub. Administr. Yr. award, 1993; named Young Man of Yr., Fayetteville Jaycees, 1977, S.C. Libr. of Yr., 1991, Internat. Fedn. Librs., 1997-2001, Order of Silver Crescent, 1999. Mem. ALA (pres. Jr. Member Roundtable 1977, chmn. awards com. 1984), Southeastern Libr. Assn. (pres. pub. libr. sect. 1978), S.C. Libr. Assn. (bd. dirs. 1980), Friends Libraries USA (bd. dirs. 1992-), Southeastern Libr. Network (bd. dirs. 2002-), Rotary, Kiwanis, Beta Phi Mu. Democrat. Episcopalian. Home: 619 King St #806 Columbia SC 29205 Office: Richland County Pub Libr 1431 Assembly St Columbia SC 29201-3101

**WARREN, CHRISTOPHER COLLINS,** professional football player; b. Silver Spring, Md., Jan. 24, 1968; Degree in psychology, Ferrum Coll. Running back Seattle Seahawks, 1990-98, Dallas Cowboys, 1998—. Selected to Pro Bowl, 1993-94. Office: Phila Eagles 3501 S Broad St Philadelphia PA 19148

**WARREN, DANIEL CHURCHMAN,** health facility administrator; b. Washington, Sept. 23, 1939; s. Walter Thomas and Laura Katherine W.; m. C. Frederica Lessing, June 5, 1958; 1 child, Christopher C. BS, Roanoke Coll., 1960; MD, Med. Coll. Va., 1964; MPH, U. N.C., 1971; MMAS, U.S. Army Command & Gen. Coll., 1974. Diplomate Nat. Bd. Med. Examiners, Am. Bd. Preventive Medicine, lic. physician VA; ordained Anglican Cath. priest 2002. Intern Georgetown U. Hosp., 1964-65; resident in surgery Med. Coll. Va., 1967-68, William Beaumont Gen. Hosp., 1968-69; resident in preventive medicine Walter Reed Army Inst. Rsch., 1971-73; commd. 2d lt. U.S. Army, 1965, advanced through grades to col., 1986; ret. HealthAm. Va. 1986; pvt. practice travel, 1987-89; dir. Peninsula Health Dist., Newport News, Va., 1990—2001; warden Holyrood Sem., 2001—; rector St. Matthews Anglican Cath. Ch., 2002—; warden Scott Sch. Theology, 2003—. Clin. asst. prof. family and cmty. medicine Ea. Va. Med. Sch., Norfolk; cons. Riverside Regional Med Ctr., Newport News. Active Gloucester County Rep. Com., 1987-96, chmn. 1992-95, Gloucester County Redistricting Adv. Com., 1991,

2001; hon. chmn. Combined Va. Campaign United Way the Va. Peninsula, 1992. Fellow: Am. Coll. Preventive Medicine; mem.: Med. Soc. Va., Mid-Tidewater Med. Soc., Ret. Officers Assn., Cremona Fiddlers. Republican. Anglican. Avocation: English and Virginia history. Office: 215 Main St Newport News VA 23601 Business E-Mail: dwarrenmd@cox.net.

**WARREN, DAVID HARDY,** psychologist, educator; b. Chelsea, Mass., July 28, 1943; s. Roland Leslie and Margaret (Hodges) W.; m. Katherine V. Warren; children: Michael Jonathan Warren, Gabriel Kristopher Coy. AB in Psychology, Yale U., 1965; PhD in Child Devel, U. Minn., 1969. Prof. psychology U. Calif., Riverside, 1969—, dean Coll. Humanities and Social Scis., 1977-85, dir. Univ. honors program, chair dept. psychology, 1992-94, exec. vice chancellor, 1994—2003. Author: Blindness and Early Childhood Development, 1977, 84, Blindness and Children: An Individual Differences Approach, 1994; contbr. articles to profl. jours.

**WARREN, DAVID LILES,** educational association executive; b. Goldsboro, N.C., Sept. 15, 1943; s. James Hubert and Katherine (Liles) W.; m. Ellen Elizabeth LeGendre, Mar. 1, 1969; children— Jamison, Mackenzie, Katrin BA in English, Wash. State U., 1965; M. Urban Studies, Yale U., 1970, M.Div., 1970; PhD, U. Mich., 1976; LittD, Elmhurst Coll., 1994, Moravian Coll., 1994; LLD, Rider U., 1996, Mt. Union Coll., 1997, Centre Coll., 1997, Mercer U., 1998, Franklin and Marshall Coll, 1999; Doctor of Public Service, Rocky Mountain Coll., 1999; LLD, Ky. Wesleyan Coll., 2000; LHD, U. of New Haven, 2001; LittD, Middlebury Coll., 2001. Gen. sec. Dwight Hall, Yale U., New Haven, 1969-76, bd. dirs., 1976—; assoc. dir. community relations Yale U., New Haven, 1976-78; sr. v.p.; provost Antioch U., N.Y.C. and Yellow Springs, Ohio, 1978-82; chief adminstry. officer City of New Haven, 1982-84; pres. Ohio Wesleyan U., Delaware, 1984-93, Nat. Assn. Ind. Colleges and Universities, Washington, 1993—. Cons. to hosps., sch. systems, colls., univs.; bd. dirs. Delaware County Bank; chmn. NCAA Pres. Commn., Div. III, 1990-92. Contbr. chpts. to books, articles to Yale Alumni Mag. Mem. NEw Haven Bd. Alderman, 1973-75; vice chmn. New Haven Commn. on Poverty, 1981-82; pres. North Coast Athletic Conf., 1988-90; justice of peace New Haven Dem. Party, 1974-76; state chmn. People to People, 1987; chmn. Gov.'s Task Force on Dep. Registrar, 1987; chmn. Ohio Five Coll. Commn., 1985-95, Campus Compact Nat. Exec. Com., 1987-88; bd. dirs. U.S. Health Corp., Coun. Ethics and Econs.; exec. com. Great Lakes Colls. Assn., Ctrl. Ohio Symphony Orch.; chmn. Ohio Ethics commn. Fulbright scholar Wash. State U., 1965-66; Rockefeller fellow Yale U., 1966; disting. Centennial Alumnus Wash. State U. Mem. Am. Assn. Higher Edn., Assn. Ind. Colls. Univs. (sec. 1987-88), Univ. Club (Columbus, Ohio), Grad. Club (New Haven), Cosmos Club (Washington), Phi Beta Kappa. Democrat. Presbyterian. Avocations: jogging, writing, tennis. Office: Nat Assn Ind Colls & Univs 1025 Connecticut Ave NW Ste 700 Washington DC 20036-5409 Office Phone: 202-785-8866.

**WARREN, DAVID P.,** stock exchange executive; BA, Wesleyan U.; MBA, Yale Sch. Mgmt., 1988. Investment banker CS First Boston, 1987—95; dep. treas. State of Conn., 1995—98; CFO Long Island Power Authority (LIPA), 1998—2000; chief adminstry. officer NASDAQ Stock Market, Inc., NYC, 2001, CFO, 2001—. Office: NASDAQ Stock Market Inc 1 Liberty Plz New York NY 10006 Office Phone: 212-401-8742. Office Fax: 212-401-1024.

**WARREN, DEAN STUART,** artist; b. Mpls., June 30, 1949; s. Jefferson Trowbridge and Dorothy Ann (Edin) Warren; m. Betty Sharon Poe, Aug. 14, 1971; children: Jeremy, Adam. BFA, Fla. Atlantic U., 1973; MA, Northwestern State U., 1975; MFA, Stephen F. Austin State U., 1980. Instr. art Cisco (Tex.) Jr. Coll., 1976-78; staff craftsworker Walt Disney Show Prodn. Walt Disney World, Lake Buena Vista, Fla., 1981-83, staff craftsworker staff shop, 1983, property craftsworker, 1983-87, artist preparator animation dept., 1987—; lead prodn. artist Marvac, Inc., Seminole County, Fla., 1983. Founder Dean S. Warren Studio, 1991—; cons. children's edn. program Mt. Dora (Fla.) Ctr. Arts; instr. Bok Tower Gardens Edn. Ctr. Workshop, Lake Wales, Fla., 1996. Author: Runemaster, 1991; Youth Art Symposium, U. Ctrl. Fla., 1993, Children's Art program Atlantic Ctr. Arts, 1995, Edn. Ctr., 1996, one-man shows include Ormond Beach (Fla.) Meml. Art Gallery and Gardens, 1987, U. Ctrl. Fla. Art Gallery, Orlando, 1991, Harris House Atlantic Ctr. Arts, New Smyrna Beach, Fla., 1993, D'Ars Studio Gallery, Milan, 2000, numerous group shows including most recently, exhibited in group shows at Warehouse Gallery, Orlando, 1999—2000, D'Ars Studio Gallery, Milan, 1999—2002, Crealdé Sch. Art Sculpture Garden, Winter Park, 2000, 2003, Walt Disney World, 2000, Alice and William Jenkins Gallery, Crealdé Sch. Art, 2001, Banca Popolare di Milano, Bergamo, Italy, 2001, Postart Gallery, Milan, 2002, Galleria Blanchaert, 2002, Church St. Gallery Contemporary Art, Orlando, 2003, Deland (Fla.) Mus. Art, 2004, Art 6 Gallery, Richmond, Va., 2005. Recipient award, U. Ga. Bot. Gardens, Athens, 1980, Valencia CC, 1983, Arts on The Park, Lakeland, Fla., 1995; Artsits in Schs. grantee, Tex. Commn. Arts, 1980. Mem.: Order of Meroyingian Dynasty, Order of Crown of Charlemagne. Home: 8069 Wellsmere Cir Orlando FL 32835-5361 Personal E-Mail: wwwarrenitaly@aol.com.

**WARREN, DIANE,** lyricist; Staff writer Jack White, 1983; founder, owner RealSongs, LA. Author over 100 top ten pop songs including I'll Never Get Over You (Getting Over Me), How Do I Live, I Don't Want to Miss a Thing, If You Asked Me To, Don't Turn Around, Set The Night To Music, I'll Still Love You More, Because You Loved Me (Grammy award, song written specifically for a motion picture or TV, 1996), Rhythm of the Night, Nothing's Gonna Stop Us Now, Unbreak My Heart, Music of My Heart, My First Night With You (Nashville Songwriters Assn. Internat. award, superior creativity in the words and music of a song, 2000), I Will Get There (Nashville Songwriters Assn. Internat. award, superior creativity in the words and music of a song, 2000), There You'll Be, and many others. mem. PETA; founder David S Warren Weekly Entertainment Series, Jewish Home for the Aging; donor Wildlife Waystation, 100th Ann. Life Found., The Lange Found. Named Songwriter of Yr., Nat. Acad. Songwriters, 1996, No. 1 Pop Songwriter of Yr., Am. Songwriter Awards, 1997, Songwriter of Yr., Nashville Songwriters Assn. Internat., 2000; named to Songwriters Hall of Fame, 2001, Hollywood Walk of Fame, 2001; recipient Songwriter of Yr., Am. Soc. Composers, Authors & Publishers, 1990, 1991, 1993, 1998, 1999, Billboard, George and Ira Gershwin award, outstanding musical achievement, 1998, New Millennium Visionary award, Am. Cinema Awards Found., 1999, Legacy award, Orgn. For the Needs of the Elderly, 1999, Dream Maker's Cir. Award, Dream Found., 2000, Lifetime Achievement award, Bill Gavin Heritage Found., 2000, Angel award, Angels on Earth, 2000, Musician's Adv. award, Am. Soc. Young Musicians, 2001, Telly award, Found. for a Better Life, 2003. Achievements include songs features in over 80 motion pictures. Office: Realsongs 6363 W Sunset Blvd Fl 8 Hollywood CA 90028-7330 Mailing: c/o The Chasen Co 8899 Beverly Blvd Ste 405 West Hollywood CA 90048*

**WARREN, DONALD JOHN,** retired surgeon, educator; b. New Haven, NY, Jan. 23, 1924; s. John Walls and Jane Margaret (Pendorf) W.; m. Muriel Celia Beach, June 24, 1944 (div. 1980); children: Douglas, Mark, Barbara; m. Betty V. Jones, Apr. 3, 1982. BA, SUNY, Syracuse, 1945, MD, 1947. Cert. surgery. Intern Syracuse U. Hosp., 1947-48; resident in surgery Millard Fillmore Hosp., Buffalo, 1952-56; gen. surgeon USAF, 1956-66, 80-84, ret., 1984; pvt. practice, 1966-75, 1985-88; ret., 1988. Gen. surgeon VA, 1975-80; asst. prof. surgery U. Calif., Davis, 1973-75; asst. clin. prof. surgery, U.S.D., 1977-80. Fellow: ACS. Home: 1616 79th Pl Lubbock TX 79423-2402 Personal E-Mail: wbettyvan@aol.com.

**WARREN, DONALD WILLIAM,** medical and dental educator; b. Bklyn., Mar. 22, 1935; s. Sol B. and Frances W.; m. Priscilla Girardi, June 10, 1956; children: Donald W. Jr., Michael C. BS, U. N.C., 1956, DDS, 1959; MS, U. Pa., 1961, PhD, 1963; D in Odontology (hon.), U. Kuopio, Finland, 1991. Asst. prof. dentistry U. N.C., Chapel Hill, 1963-65, dir. Craniofacial Ctr. 1963-2000, assoc. prof., 1965-69, prof., 1969-80, chmn. dept. dental ecology, 1970-85, Kenan prof., 1980—2004, Kenan prof. emeritus, 2004—, rsch. prof. otolaryngology, 1985—2004; ret. Cons. NIH, Bethesda, Md., 1967-2000, R.

J. Reynolds-Nabisco, Winston-Salem, N.C., 1986-99. Contbr. articles to profl. jours. Recipient Honor award Am. Cleft Palate Assn./Craniofacial Assn., 1992, O. Max Garner award U. N.C. Bd. Govs., 1993, honors award Angle Orthodontic Soc., 1998. Fellow AAAS, Internat. Coll. Dentists, Am. Speech and Hearing Lang. Assn. (Editors award 1998, Honors award 2003), Internat. Assn. Dental Rsch., Acoustical Soc. Am., Am. Cleft Palate Assn. (pres. 1981-82, Disting. Svc. award 1984), Am. Cleft Palate Edn. Found. (pres. 1976-77). Avocations: horse related activities, running, farming. Home: PO Box 1356 Southern Pines NC 28388-1356 Business E-Mail: don_warren@dentistry.unc.edu.

**WARREN, ELIZABETH A.,** law educator; 1 child, Amelia Warren Tyagi. BS, U. Houston, 1970; JD, Rutgers U., 1976. Bar: NJ, Tex. Lectr. law Rutgers Sch. Law, Newark, 1977—78; asst. prof. law U. Houston Law Ctr., 1978—80, assoc. dean academic affairs, 1980—81, assoc. prof. law, 1981—83; rsch. assoc. Population Rsch. Ctr. U. Tex., Austin, 1983—87; prof. law U. Tex. Sch. Law, 1983—87, Conoco Faculty Prof. in Law, 1985—86, Jay H. Brown Centennial Fellow in Law, 1986—87; prof. law U. Pa. Law Sch., Phila., 1987—90, William A. Schnader Prof. Comml. Law, 1990—95; Leo Gottlieb prof. law Harvard Law Sch., Cambridge, Mass., 1995—. Vis. assoc. prof. law U. Tex. Sch. Law, 1981—82; vis. prof. law U. Mich., 1985; Robert Braucher Vis. Prof. Comml. Law Harvard U., 1992—93; proposal reviewer NSF, 1985—; bd. editors Am. Bankruptcy Law Jour., 1989—92; editl. adv. bd. Little Brown & Co. Law Sch. Divsn. (now Aspen Press), 1990—; com. on jud. edn. Fed. Jud. Ctr., 1990—99; bd. trustees Am. Bankruptcy Bd. Certification, 1992—96; exec. com. Nat Bankruptcy Conf., 1993—95, 2002—05; advisor German Govt. Task Force on Bankruptcy Reform, 1993; reporter, cons., sr. advisor Nat. Bankruptcy Rev. Commn., 1995—97; regular commentator All Things Considered program Nat. Pub. Radio. Co-author: (books) As We Forgive Our Debtors: Consumer Credit and Bankruptcy in America, 1989 (Silver Gavel Award, ABA, 1990), The Law of Debtors and Creditors, 1991, 1996, 2001, Secured Transactions: A Systems Approach, 1995, 1998, 2000, 2003, Comml. Law: A Systems Approach, 2003, The Fragile Middle Class: Americans in Debt, 2000 (Scholarship Award, Am. Coll. Consumer Fin. Services Lawyers, 2000); co-author: (with Amelia Warren Tyagi) The Two-Income Trap: Why Middle-Class Mothers and Fathers Are Going Broke, 2003; author: numerous books chapters and jour. articles. Named one of 50 Most Influential Women Attorneys, Nat. Law Jour., 1998; recipient Frankel Publ. Award for Outstanding Writing, 1982, Commedation for Svc., Am. Bankruptcy Bd. Certification, 1998, Brown Award for Jud. Scholarship and Edn., Fed. Jud. Ctr., 1998, Champion of Consumer Rights Award, Nat. Assn. Consumer Bankruptcy Attorneys, 2000, Excellence in Edn. Award, Nat. Conf. Bankruptcy Judges, 2001, Lawrence P. King Award, Comml. Law League Am., 2002, Outstanding Tchr. Award, U. Houston Law Ctr., 1981, L. Hart Wright Teaching Excellence Award, U. Mich. Sch. Law, 1986, Harvey Levin Award for Excellence in Tchg., U. Pa. Sch. Law, 1989, 1992, Lindback Award for Disting. Tch., U. Pa., 1994, Albert A. Sacks-Paul A. Freund Award for Tchg. Excellence, Harvard Law Sch., 1997. Fellow: Am. Coll. Bankruptcy (Commendation for Outstanding Pub. Svc. 1998); mem.: Assn. Am. Law Schools (chair comml. and related consumer law sect. 1983—84, chair comml. law workshop 1984, planning com. conf. on tchg. contract law 1989, profl. devel. com. 1988—91, chair debtor-creditor sect. 1989—90, chair legislation com. debtor-creditor sect. 1990—93), Am. Law Inst. (exec. com. coun. 1994—95, US Adviser, Transnat. Insolvency Project 1995—, mem. nominating com. 1995—, exec. com. coun. 1998—, 2nd v.p. coun. 2000—04). Office: Harvard U Law Sch Hauser 200 Cambridge MA 02138

**WARREN, IRWIN HOWARD,** lawyer; b. NYC, May 16, 1950; s. Milton and Shirley (Glatman) W.; m. Elizabeth Vogel, Aug. 11, 1974. BA, Columbia U., 1971, JD, 1974; Harlan Fiske Stone Scholar. Bar: NY, 1975, US Ct. Appeals (2nd (1979), 1st (1980), 4th (1981), 3rd (1982), 8th (1985), 5th (1996), 6th (1996) cirs.), US Dist. Ct. (So. and Ea. dists.), 1975. Assoc. Weil, Gotshal & Manges LLP, NYC, 1974-82, ptnr., co-head bus. and securities litigation dept., 1982—. Spkr. in field; litigation sect. rep. US Jud. Conference's Civil Rules Styles Com., 2003—. Contbr. articles to profl. jours. and publs. Mem. ABA (lectr., tchr., co-author of articles, co-chair, ethics subcommittee of committee on corp. counsel, sect. of litigation 1984-85, co-chair of com. on class actions and derivative suits, sect. of litigation 1986-89, mem. sect. of litigation task force on ancillary bus. activities of lawyers 1989-94, dir., divsn. III - programs, sect. of litigation 1989-90, divsn. dir., divsn. VI - sect. of litigation The Profession 1991-92, co-chair of securities litigation com., sect. of litigation 1990-91, co-chair of the ethics and professionalism com., sect. of litigation 1992-95, mem., coun. of the sect. of litigation 2004—, mem., sect. of litigation fed. practice task force 2000-2004); life mem. Fellows of the Am. Bar Found. 1990-. Office: Weil Gotshal & Manges LLP 767 5th Ave New York NY 10153-0023 Office Phone: 212-310-8648.

**WARREN, J. RICHARD,** editor, retired humanities educator; b. Sanford, Apr. 27, 1925; s. Ralph Moore Warren and Demarius Kate Musson-Warren; m. Mabel Martin, Aug. 21, 1949; children: Barbara Anne Tucker, J. Richard Jr., Mary Jane Cowen. BA in French, Stetson U., Deland, Fla., 1949, MA in Secondary Sch. Guidance, 1951; PhD in Music Edn. Supervision and Adminstrn., Fla. State U., Tallahassee, 1961; at: Tex. A&M U., Bryan, U.Ill., Urbana, Ctrl. Signal Corps Sch., Camp Crowder, Mo., Marbach Tutoring Inst. Fgn. Langs., Frankfort, Germany, Biarritz Am. U., France, U. Fla., Gainesville, Fla. State U., Tallahassee, U. W. Fla., Pensacola. Cert. edn. adminstrn. and supervision Fla., 1951, music Fla., 1951, French Fla., 1951, coll. academic adminstrn. and supervision Fla., 1961. Tchr. music Washington County H.S., Chipley, Fla., 1950—53, Bay H.S., Panama City, 1952—59, Fla. State U., Tallahassee, 1959—61, Brevard C.C., Cocoa, 1961; cons. fine arts curriculum Fla. Dept. Edn. Instrnl. Svcs., Tallahassee, 1961—67; dean humanities Fla. Jr. Coll., Jacksonville, 1967—70; dir. continuing edn. Jacksonville U., 1970—72, dean humanities Piedmont Coll., Charlottesville, Va., 1972—73; dean humanities, divsn. dir. and chmn. fine and performing arts dept. Okaloosa-Walton C.C. (now Okaloosa-Walton Coll.), Niceville, Fla., 1973—93; ret. 1993; exec. officer Fla. League of the Arts, Inc., 1993—. Min. music First Meth. Ch., New Smyrna Beach, Fla., 1950—51, First Baptist Ch., Chipley, 1951—53, First Meth. Ch., Panama City, 1953—59, First Baptist Ch., Merritt Island, 1961, Southside Baptist Ch., Jacksonville, 1970—72; tchr. summer sch. Fla. State U., Tallahassee, 1952—59; clinician music camp Bapt. Harmony Bay, 1952—59; cons. Duval Magnet Sch., Jacksonville, 1970—72, Mattie Kelly Arts Ctr., Destin, 1975—90; editor Arts & Humanities jour. of Fla. League Arts, Niceville, 1993—. Contbg. editor: Fla. Sch. Bull., 1961—68; contbr. articles to profl. jours. Deacon Southside Bapt. Ch., Jacksonville, Fla.; mem. First Bapt. Ch., Vaparaiso, Fla.; ednl. and choir cons. Cath. Ch., Panama City, Fla., St. Augustine Diocese, Jacksonville, Fla. Sgt. Signal Corps U.S. Army, 1943—47, ETO. Mem.: Fla. League Arts, Fla. Vocal Music Assn. (life; past pres.), Fla. Music Educators Assn. (life), Music Educators Nat. Conf. (life), Rotary (J.U. rep. 1970—72), Kiwanis (pres. Valparaiso chpt. 2005—, Cir. K advisor Okaloosa-Walton Coll. chpt., Legion of Honor), Lions, Lambda Chi Alpha (founder Stetson U. chpt.), Pi Kappa Lambda. Avocations: gardening, piano, writing. Home: 2408 Edgewater Dr Niceville FL 32578-2304

**WARREN, JACK DUANE,** professional society administrator, historian, writer; b. Washington, Aug. 3, 1962; s. Jack Duane Warren and Margaret Glenn; m. Janet Louise Tew, Sept. 30, 1989; children: Emily Rose, Audrey Louise, Jack Duane III. Exec. dir. Soc. of Cincinnati, Washington, 2004—. Author: The Papers of George Washington, 1998, The Presidency of George Washington, 2000. Office: Soc of Cincinnati 2118 Massachusetts Ave NW Washington DC 20008

**WARREN, JACK HAMILTON,** retired diplomat, banker, trade policy advisor; b. Apr. 10, 1921; m. Hilary J. Titterington; children: Hilary Warren Nicolson, Martin, Jennifer Warren Part, Ian. Student, Queens U., Kingston, Ont., Can., 1938-41. Joined Dept. External Affairs, Canada, 1945; assigned London, 1948-51; fin. counsellor Washington, 1952—54, NATO, Paris, 1954—57; asst. dep. minister trade and commerce Ottawa, 1958-64; dep. minister, trade and commerce, 1964-68; dep minister industry, trade &

commerce, 1968-71; high commr. to U.K., 1971-75; ambassador to U.S., 1975-77; Can. coord. Gatt multilateral trade negotiations, 1977-79; vice-chmn. Bank of Montreal, 1979-86; prin. trade policy advisor Govt. Que., 1986-94; dir. Alternate Canadian Internat. Monetary Fund, Internat. Bank for Reconstruction & Development, Washington. Served with Royal Canadian Navy, 1941-45; officer Order of Can., 1982. Recipient Pub. Svc. Outstanding Achievement award, 1976. Home: Ottawa 301 C-997 N River Rd Ontario Canada K1K 3V5

**WARREN, JAMES I.,** lawyer; b. Trenton, NJ, Dec. 7, 1950; BA, Stanford U., 1971; JD, NYU, 1975, LLM, 1979, MS in Acctg., 1980. CPA; bar: NJ 1976, NY 1979. Ptnr., co-chmn. tax dept. Reid & Priest; chmn., Nat. Utility Tax Practice Group Price Waterhouse Cooper; sr. tax ptnr., Nat. Energy Tax Svc. Practice Group Deloitte & Touche; ptnr., tax, benefits, trusts & estates dept. Thelen Reid & Priest LLP, 2003—. Spkr. in field. Office: Thelen Reid & Priest LLP 875 Third Ave New York NY 10022-2001 Office Fax: 212-603-2001, 212-603-2072. Business E-Mail: jwarren@thelenreid.com.

**WARREN, JAMES RONALD,** retired museum director, journalist; b. Goldendale, Wash., May 25, 1925; stepson H.S. W.; m. Gwen Davis, June 25, 1949; children: Gail, Jeffrey. BA, Wash. State U., 1949; MA, U. Wash., 1953, PhD, 1963. Adminstrv. v.p. Seattle Community Coll., 1965-69; pres. Edmonds Community Coll., Lynnwood, Wash., 1969-79; dir. Mus. of History and Industry, Seattle, 1979-89. Lectr. in field. Author history books; columnist Seattle Post Intelligencer, 1979-92, Seattle Times, 1992-96. Served with U.S. Army, 1943-45, ETO, prisoner-of-war, Germany. Mem. VFW, Am. Ex-POW Assn., 42d (Rainbow) Div. Vets., Rotary, also others. Home and Office: 3235 99th Ave NE Bellevue WA 98004-1803 Personal E-mail: jrgwarren@msn.com.

**WARREN, JENNIFER ELIZABETH,** family nurse practitioner; b. Clovis, N.Mex., Nov. 13, 1964; d. Ronald Dwayne and Lillian Ann (Reed) Carter; m. Johnny Lynn Warren Jr., May 18, 1991. BSN, West Tex. State U., 1988; MSN-FNP, West Tex. A&M U., 1998. RN, Tex.; cert. family nurse practitioner. Clin. asst. Northwest Tex. Hosp., Amarillo, 1987—88; neonatal ICU nurse Meth. Children's Hosp., Lubbock, Tex., 1988—98, Covenant Med. Ctr., Lubbock, 1999—2000; family nurse practitioner Covenant Family Health Care Ctr., 2000—03, Garza County Health Clinic, Post, Tex., 2003—05, Spur (Tex.) Clinic, 2005—. Family nurse practitioner Primestaff, 2004—, Physicians Network Svcs., 2001—05. Spur (Tex.) Clinic, 2005—. Mem. Am. Acad. Nurse Practitioners, Tex. Nursing Assn., Endometriosis Assn. (organizer/contact, Lubbock leader 1993—), South Plains Nurse Practitioners Assn. Democrat. Methodist. Avocations: gardening, cross stitch, latch hook, swimming. Home: 1002 W 10th St Post TX 79356-2450 Office: Spur Clinic 907 E Hill Spur TX 79370 Office Phone: 806-271-3306. Office Fax: 806-495-3576, 806-271-4256. Personal E-mail: jewarren@caprock-spur.com. Business E-Mail: jewarren@teamumc.com.

**WARREN, JOHN COOLIDGE,** educational administrator; b. Boston, May 16, 1956; s. William Bradford and Mary-Elizabeth (Coolidge) W.; m. Laura Parker Appell, June 18, 1983; children: Ethan Reynolds Appell, Amanda Pfaltzgraff Appell. BA, Stanford U., 1978, MA, 1980, MEd, Harvard U., 1991, EdD, 1994. Tchr. history Robert Louis Stevenson Sch., Pebble Beach, Calif., 1979-81, Milton Acad., Mass., 1981, chmn. dept. history, 1992-95, acad. dean, 1995—2001, spl. asst. head sch., 2001—06; head sch. St. Mark's Sch., 2006—. Faculty cons. Ednl. Testing Svc., Princeton, 1990—, William Joiner Ctr., Boston, 1992—; editl. cons. Longman Inc., White Plains, NY, 1991—. Editor: America's Intervention in Vietnam, 1987. NEH fellow, 1985, advanced doctoral fellow, Harvard U., 1993. Mem. Am. Hist. Assn., Orgn. Am. Historians, Assn. Asian Studies, World Affairs Assn., Boston Athenaeum, Colonial Soc. Mass., Mass. Hist. Soc., Phi Beta Kappa. Avocations: canoeing, fishing. Home and Office: St Mark's Sch 25 Marlborough Rd Southborough MA 01772 Office Phone: 617-898-1798.

**WARREN, JOHN WILLIAM,** professional society administrator; b. Clarksville, Ark., June 27, 1927; s. Frederick H. and Fannie Emiline (Casey) W.; m. Marguerette Christine Cohoon, Oct. 9, 1948 (dec. Dec. 1987); children: Catherine Gail, Carolyn Anne, Eve Colette; m. Anna Jane Taylor, Feb. 10, 1990. BA, Abilene Christian U., 1949; MA, U. Ark., 1951; PhD, U. Tenn., 1961. Instr. U. Tenn., Knoxville, 1954—61; assoc. prof. David Lipscomb Coll., Nashville, 1961—62; prof., chmn. English Tenn. Tech. U., Cookeville, 1962—88; assoc. exec. dir. Phi Kappa Phi, Baton Rouge, 1988—92, exec. dir., 1992—99, exec. dir. emeritus, 1999—; v.p. Assn. Coll. Honor Socs., 1999—2001, pres., 2001—03. Author Ofcl. Lit. Map of Tenn., 1976; author: Tennessee Belles-Lettres-Guide to Tennessee Literature, 1976. Mem. Rotary (Cookeville pres. 1972-73), Phi Kappa Phi (Tenn. Tech. U. chpt. pres. 1980, SE region v.p. 1982-88, nat. bd. dirs. 1982-88). Republican. Mem. Ch. of Christ. Avocations: gardening, travel. Personal E-mail: pkpjwarren@aol.com.

**WARREN, KATHERINE VIRGINIA,** art gallery director; b. Balt., Aug. 10, 1948; d. Joseph Melvin and Hilda Virginia (Thiele) Heim; m. David Hardy Warren; 1 child, Gabriel Kristopher Coy; 1 stepchild, Michael Jonathan Warren. BA, U. Calif., Riverside, 1976, MA, 1980. Asst. curator Calif. Mus. Photography, Riverside, 1979-80, acting dir., 1980-81, asst. dir., curator of edn., 1981-84; dir. univ. art gallery U. Calif., Riverside, 1980—2003, ret., 2003—. Bd. dirs. Riverside Arts Found., 1980-89, chmn. bd., 1986-88. Marius De Brabant fellow U. Calif., 1977-79. Mem. Am. Assn. Mus., Western Mus. Conf. Office: Sweeney Art Gallery U Calif Riv Side Riverside CA 92521-0001

**WARREN, KELCY L.,** energy executive; b. Gladewater, Tex., Nov. 9, 1955; s. Hugh Brinson and Bertie (Robinson) W. BSCE, U. Tex., Arlington, 1978. Pipeline design engr. Lone Star Gas Co., Dallas, 1978-81; pres., chief oper. officer Cornerstone Natural Gas, Inc., Dallas, 1993—96; pres. Energy Transfer Partners, Dallas, 1996—2004, co-chmn., co-CEO of gen. ptnr., 2004—. Mem. Natural Gas Transp. Assn., Natural Gas Soc. North Tex. (pres. 1981—), Energy Club Dallas (bd. dirs. 1985—). Office: Energy Transfer Partners 2838 Woodside St Dallas TX 75204*

**WARREN, MAREDIA DELOIS,** music educator; b. Odis Franklin and Mary Velma Lewis; m. Charles Augustus Warren, July 9, 1966; children: John Charles, Maredia Dionne. B in Music Edn. magna cum laude, Howard U., 1965; MA, Columbia U., 1967, EdD, 1989. Tchr. elem. music Hartford Pub. Schs., 1965—66; adj. faculty Herbert H. Lehman Coll., CUNY, 1972—79, Fairleigh Dickinson U., 1975—79, Montclaire State U., 1984—93; tchr. music grades K-6 Teaneck Pub. Schs., NJ, 1979—87; dir. vocal music Teaneck H.S., 1987—99; asst. prof. music educator William Paterson U., Wayne, NJ, 1999—2000; assoc. prof., coord. music edn. N.J. City U., Jersey City, 2000—. Condr. N.J. All-State Chorus, N.J. State Music Tchrs. Assn., 1994, 2006, Mass. ACDA Women's Honor Choir, Amherst, Mass., 2003, Cape Cod H.S. Festival, 2005; dir. music, organist Presbyn. Ch. Teaneck, 1995—; presenter Choral Music Workshop, Ghana, 1995; presenter in field. Bd. mem., cons. Bergen County Divsn. Hist. and Cultural Affairs, 2002—; People to People amb. to China, 1998. Named Disting. Secondary tchr., Princeton U., 1993; recipient Trailblazer award in arts and culture, Nat. Coalition of 100 Black Women, 2005. Mem.: NEA (life), Coll. Music Soc., N.J. Music Educators Assn., Am. Choral Dirs. Assn., Am. Orff Schulwerk Assn., Orgn. Am. Kodaly Educators, Music Educators Nat. Conf. (collegiate advisor 2003—), N.J. Am. Choral Dirs. Assn. (Repertoire and Standards chair multicultural 1999—2003, bd. mem.), N.J. Edn. Assn. (life), Alpha Kappa Alpha, Inc. Office: NJ City Univ 2039 Kennedy Blvd Jersey City NJ 07305 Office Phone: 201-200-2158. E-mail: mdlwarren@aol.com.

**WARREN, MARIE ANTOINETTE,** elementary school educator; b. L.A., July 21, 1965; d. Kazmer Anthony Wolkensperg and Janette Mary Hudgins; m. Brian Keith Warren, Sept. 26, 1983; children: Anthony Brian, Brianna Marie. AA, St. Clair County C.C.; BSc in Edn., Ctrl. Mich. U.; MS in Child Devel., Mich. State U.; degree in Ednl. Leadership, Oakland U. Cert. elem.

tchr. Mich., 1990, in administrv. leadership in edn. Mich., 2005. Tchr. elem. sch. Port Huron (Mich.) Area Sch. Dist., 1991—. Mem. bd. edn. Trinity Luth. Sch., Port Huron. Mem.: Am. Youth Soccer Assn. (bd. dirs., child advocate). Office Phone: 810-984-6528.

**WARREN, MARK EDWARD,** cruise line executive, lawyer; b. Rochester, Minn., Nov. 26, 1951; s. Edward Joseph and Eunice (Golberg) W.; m. Jasmine Margaret Syracuse, Feb. 18, 1984; children: Natalie, Stephanie. Cert., Instituto de Estudios Europeos, Madrid, 1972; BA, Gustavus Adolphus Coll., St. Peter, Minn., 1974; JD, U. Minn., 1977. Bar: Calif. 1977, U.S. Dist. Ct. (no. and cen. dists.) Calif. 1978, U.S. Ct. Appeals (9th cir.) 1985, U.S. Dist. Ct. (ea. dist.) Calif. 1986, U.S. Dist. Ct. (so. dist.) Calif. 1987, D.C. 1989, U.S. Supreme Ct. 1989, U.S. Ct. Appeals (D.C. cir.) 1989, U.S. Dist. Ct. (D.C. dist.) 1989, U.S. Dist. Ct. Md. 1991, Va. 1992. Assoc. Gibson, Dunn & Crutcher, L.A., 1977-78; spl. asst. to v.p. Walter Mondale The White Ho., Washington, 1979-80; assoc. Gibson, Dunn & Crutcher, L.A., 1980-84, ptnr. L.A. and Washington, 1985-93; sr. v.p., gen. counsel Princess Cruises, L.A., 1993-96; pres. The Gt. Am. Sta. Found., Washington, 1997-99; exec. v.p., gen. counsel NCL Corp., Miami, Fla., 2003—. Mem. U. Minn. Law Alumni Assn. (bd. dirs. 1990-98), U.K. P&I Club (bd. dirs. 1995-96, bd. dirs. West of Eng. chpt. 2005—). Office: 7665 Corporate Center Dr Miami FL 33126

**WARREN, MELISSA ALLISON,** lawyer; BA magna cum laude, Duke U., Durham, N.C., 1983; JD cum laude, U. Pa. Law Sch., 1988. Bar: Md. 1988. Ptnr. bus. transactions, securities, practices Venable LLP, Balt., 2001—. Office: Venable LLP 1800 Mercantile Bank & Trust Bldg 2 Hopkins Plz Baltimore MD 21201 Office Phone: 410-244-7695. Office Fax: 410-244-7742. Business E-Mail: mawarren@venable.com.

**WARREN, RICHARD WAYNE,** obstetrician, gynecologist; b. Puxico, Mo., Nov. 26, 1935; s. Martin R. and Sarah E. (Crump) W.; m. Rosalie J. Franzoia, Aug. 16, 1959; children: Lani Marie, Richard W., Paul D. *Daughter Lani Marie, MD 1988, University of Minnesota, was a resident in OB-GYN at Valley Medical Center, San Jose, California. She specializes in ob-gyn and is a partner in the Warren Medical Corp. Son Paul Douglas, MD 1991, Harvard University, was a resident in orthopedic surgery at Texas Tech University. A fellow in foot and ankle surgery in Galveston, Texas and a joint replacement fellow in Boston. His practice is in orthopedic surgery in Virginia Beach, Virginia. Wife Rosalie L. and son Richard W. manage the Warren Medical Corp. Son Richard W. teaches in the Evergreen School District, San Jose, California.* BA, U. Calif., Berkeley, 1957; MD, Stanford U., Calif., 1961. Diplomate Am. Bd. Ob-Gyn. Intern Oakland (Calif.) Naval Hosp., 1961-62; resident on ob-gyn. Stanford Med. Ctr., 1964-67; pvt. practice specializing in ob-gyn. Mountain View, Calif., 1967—. Mem. staff Stanford Hosp., El Camino Hosp.; pres. Warren Medical Corp.; assoc. clin. prof. ob-gyn. Stanford Sch. Medicine. Contbr. articles to profl. jours. With USN, 1961-64. Fellow Am. Coll. Ob-Gyn.; mem. AMA, Am. Fertility Soc., Am. Assn. Gynecologic Laparoscopists, Calif. Med. Assn., San Francisco Gynecol. Soc., Peninsula Gynecol. Soc., Assn. Profs. Gynecology and Obstetrics, Royal Soc. Medicine, Shufelt Gynecol. Soc. Santa Clara Valley. Home: 102 Atherton Ave Menlo Park CA 94027-4021 Office: 2500 Hospital Dr Mountain View CA 94040-4106 Office Phone: 650-961-8111.

**WARREN, RICK DUANE,** minister, writer; b. San Jose, Calif., Jan. 28, 1954; s. James Russell and Dorothy Nell (Armstrong) W.; m. Elizabeth Kay Lewis, June 21, 1975; children: Amy Rebecca, Joshua James, Matthew David. BA, Calif. Bapt. Coll., 1977; MA of Divinity, Southwestern Bapt. Theol. Sem., 1979; D of Ministry, Fuller Theol. Sem., 1989. Youth evangelist Calif. So. Bapt. Convention, Fresno, 1970-74; assoc. pastor First Bapt. Ch., Norwalk, Calif., 1974-76; asst. to pres. Internat. Evangelism Assn., Fort Worth, 1977-79; founding pastor Saddleback Valley Cmty. Ch., Mission Viejo, Calif., 1980—; founder Pastors.com. Lectr. Saddleback Ch. Growth Seminars. Author: The Purpose-Driven Church, 1995, Personal Bible Study Methods, 1997, The Power to Change Your Life, 1998, Answers to Life's Difficult Questions, 1999, Planned for God's Pleasure, 2002, The Purpose-Driven Life, 2002 (Gold Medallion award, ECPA Book of the Yr. 2003), The Emerging Church, 2003, Daily Inspiration for the Purpose-Driven Life, 2004. Named Outstanding Preacher of 1977, McGregor Found; named one of 100 Most Influential People of 2005, Time mag. Mem. No. Am. Soc. for Ch. Growth. Baptist. Office: Saddleback Valley Comm Ch 24194 Alicia Pky Ste M San Juan Capistrano CA 92691-3927 also: Pastors.com 20 Empire Dr Lake Forest CA 92630-2244*

**WARREN, ROBERT LEE,** dentist, educator; b. Boone, NC, July 20, 1943; s. John Floyd and Maude Elizabeth (Roark) Warren; m. Deborah Andrews; children: Blaire, Robert, Debin. BS in Biology, Appalachian State U., 1965; postgrad., Duke U., 1967; DDS, U. NC, 1972. Instr. biology and chemistry West H.S., North Wilkesboro, NC, 1965—68; gen. practice dentistry Boone 1972—. Adj. asst. prof. dept. operative dentistry U. NC Sch. Dentistry, Chapel Hill, 1972—79, adj. asst. prof. dept. fixed prosthodontics, 1982—84, adj. asst. prof. operative dentistry, 1987—97. Mem. Watauga County Bd. Edn. Nat. Sci. fellow, Duke U. Master: Acad. Gen. Dentistry (bd. dirs.); mem.: ADA, First Dist. Dental Soc., NC Dental Soc., Boone C. of C., U. NC Dental Alumni Assn. (bd. dirs.), Tar Heel Dental Study Club (pres.), Delta Sigma Delta. Republican. Baptist. Avocations: tar heel sports, show horses, sports cars. Home: 127 Alan Dr Boone NC 28607 Office: R Lee Warren 142 Doctors Dr Boone NC 28607-5018

**WARREN, ROBERT STEPHEN,** lawyer; b. Pasadena, Calif., Dec. 9, 1931; s. Harry Ludwig and Maxine Winifred (Hopkins) W.; m. Betty Lou Soden, June 11, 1955 (dec. Sept. 1991); children: Kimberly Ann, Stephen Hopkins; m. Anna Marie Pretzel, Dec. 28, 1993. BA in Econs., U. Southern Calif., 1953, LLB, 1956. Bar: Calif. 1956, Del., U.S. Ct. Appeals (9th cir.), U.S. Dist. Ct. (ctrl. dist.) Calif., U.S. Ct. Mil. Appeals, U.S. Dist. Ct. (so. dist.) Calif., U.S. Dist. Ct. (ea. dist.) Calif., U.S. Dist. Ct. (no. dist.) Calif., U.S. Dist. Ct. Wyo., U.S. Dist. Ct. Colo., U.S. Dist. Ct. (ea. dist.) Wash., U.S. Supreme Ct. From assoc. to ptnr. Gibson, Dunn & Crutcher, L.A., 1956, 59—. Contbr. articles to profl. jours.; assoc. editor Southern Calif. Law Rev.; speaker in field. Mem., former chair bd. councilors U. So. Calif. Law Ctr.; past pres., exec. com. mem. Western Justice Ctr. Found. 1st It. U.S. Army, 1957—59. Recipient Learned Hand award Am. Jewish Com., 1988, Shattuck-Price award Los Angeles County State Bar Assn., 1989, Joseph A. Ball award Brennan Ctr. for Justice/NYU, 1997, Trial Lawyer Hall of Fame award Calif. State Bar Assn., 1998. Mem. Am. Coll. Trial Lawyers, Am. Bus. Trial Lawyers, Order of Coif, City Club on Bunker Hill, Phi Beta Kappa. Republican. Presbyterian. Avocations: hiking, reading, tennis. Office: Gibson Dunn & Crutcher 333 S Grand Ave Ste 4400 Los Angeles CA 90071-3197 Office Phone: 213-229-7326. Business E-Mail: rwarren@gibsondunn.com.

**WARREN, ROSANNA,** poet; b. Fairfield, Conn., July 27, 1953; d. Robert Penn Warren and Eleanor Clark; m. Stephen Scully, 1981; children: Katherine, Chiara; stepson, Benjamin. BA summa cum laude, Yale U., 1976; MA, Johns Hopkins U., 1980. Pvt. art tchr., 1977-78; clerical worker St. Martin's Parish, N.Y.C., 1977-78; asst. prof. English Vanderbilt U., Nashville, 1981-82; vis. asst. prof. Boston U., 1982-88, asst. prof. English and modern fgn. langs., 1989-95, assoc. prof. English 1995—, Emma MacLachlan Metcalf prof. humanities, 2000—. Poetry cons., contbg. editor Partisan Rev., 1985-98; poet-in-residence Robert Frost Farm, 1990. Author: The Joey Story, 1963, Snow Day, 1981, Each Leaf Shines Separate, 1984, Stained Glass, 1993, Departure, 2003; editor, contbr.: The Art of Translation: Voices from the Field, 1989; editor: Eugenio Montale's Cuttlefish Bones, 1993, Satura, 1998; translator (with Stephen Scully) Euripides' Suppliant Women, 1995, poetry anthologies include In Time, 1995, From This Distance, 1996, Springshine, 1998; contbr. to periodicals including Agni Rev., Am. Poetry Rev., Antioch Rev., Atlantic Monthly, Chelsea, Chgo. Rev., Georgia Rev., Nation, New Republic, New Yorker, N.Y. Times, Paris Rev., Threepenny Rev., Partisan Rev., Ploughshares, Southern Rev., Washington Post. Recipient McLaughlin English prize Yale U., 1973, Charles E. Clark award Yale U., 1976, Nat. Discovery award in poetry 92nd St. YMHA-YWCA, 1980, Newton Arts Coun. award, 1983, Lavan Younger Poets prize Acad. Am. Poets, 1992,

Lamont Poetry prize Acad. Am. Poets, 1993, Lila Wallace Writers' Fund award, 1994, Witter Bynner prize in poetry Acad. Arts and Letters, 1994, May Sarton award New Eng. Poetry Club, 1995, Pushcart prize, 2004, 06, award of merit in poetry Am. Acad. Arts and Letters, 2004, Ellen Maria Gorrissen Berlin prize Am. Acad. Berlin, 2006; named Scholar of House Yale U., 1975-76; Yaddo fellow, 1980, Lannan Found. fellow, 2005; Ingram Merrill grantee, 1983, 93; Guggenheim fellow, 1985-86; Am. Coun. Learned Socs. grantee, 1989-90. Fellow: Am. Acad. Arts and Sci.; mem.: PEN, ALTA, MLA, Acad. Am. Poets (chancellor 1999—2005), Assn. Literary Scholars and Critics (v.p. 2004, pres. 2005).

**WARREN, RUSS C.,** artist, educator; b. Washington, Dec. 29, 1951; s. Thomas Wayne and Dona Marie Warren; m. Carolyn Bolen Warren, Oct. 22; children: Tasha, Tanya Marie Haggard. BFA, U. N.Mex., 1973; MFA, U. Tex., San Antonio, 1977. Prof. art Davidson (N.C.) Coll., 1978—. Home: 841 Wolf Trap Rd Charlottesville VA 22911

**WARREN, RUSSELL FREDERICK,** orthopedist; b. Burlington, Vt., June 18, 1939; MD, SUNY, Syracuse, 1966. Bd. cert. orthopedic surgery. Intern St. Lukes Hosp. Ctr., NYC, 1966—68; resident orthopedic surgery Hosp. for Spl. Surgery, NYC, 1970—73, surgeon in chief, 1993—2003, surgeon-in-chief emeritus, 2003; fellow in shoulder surgery Columbia Presbyn. Med. Ctr., NYC, 1977; prof. surgery, chmn. divsn. orthopaedic surgery Weill Med. Coll., Cornell U.; physician New York Giants. Past pres. Am. Shoulder and Elbow Soc., 1994—95, Am. Orthopaedic Soc. for Sports Medicine, 1994—95. Recipient Neer award for shoulder rsch., 1989, 1995, 2005, O'Donohue award for sports medicine rsch., 1982, 1991, 1994, Humana award for sports medicine, 1992. Achievements include research in shoulder and knee instability; ligament reconstruction and arthroscopy; joint replacement-knee and shoulder; rotator cuff disease and sports injuries. Mailing: Hosp for Spl Surgery 535 E 70th St New York NY 10021 Office: Belaire Bldg 1st Fl 525 E 71st St New York NY Office Phone: 212-606-1178. Business E-Mail: warrenr@hss.edu.

**WARREN, RUSSELL GLEN,** educational consultant; b. Balt., Apr. 29, 1942; s. Clarence N. and Kathryn (Butler) W. BBA, U. Richmond, 1964; PhD, Tulane U., 1968. Asst. prof. to assoc. prof. U. Richmond, Va., 1971—74, dean, 1974—76, asst. v.p. to asst. pres., 1976—78; v.p. acad. affairs U. Montevallo, Ala., 1978-84, James Madison U., Harrisonburg, Va., 1984-90, v.p. acad. affairs, acting pres., 1986—87; pres. N.E. Mo. State U., Kirksville, 1990—94; disting. prof. econs., mgmt. Hardin-Simmons U., Abilene, Tex., 1995-97, dir. Ctr. for Rsch. Tchg. and Learning, 1995-97; exec. v.p., provost Mercer U., Macon, Ga., 1997—2002; prof. econs. So. Wesleyan U., 2003—06; pvt. practice cons. Kiawah Island, SC, 2006—. Chmn., adv. bd. Coll. Humanities, Social Sci. Coll. Charleston, SC, 1999—2002. Author: Antitrust in Theory and Practice, 1976, Carpe Diem, 1995. Bd. dirs. Va. Rural Devel. Corp., Richmond, 1988-90, Am. Coll. Bldg. Arts, 2005—; v.p. Kiawah Island Cmty. Assn., 2005-2006. Capt. U.S. Army, 1969—71. Named One of Outstanding Young Men of Va., Va. Jaycees, 1976. Mem.: Am. Coun. on Edn. (coun. of fellows), Am. Assn. Colls. and Univs. (bd. dirs. 1994—95). Methodist. Avocations: golf, collecting cars. Home and Office: 175 Marsh Island Dr Kiawah Island SC 29455 E-mail: kiawahwarren@cs.com.

**WARREN, RUSSELL JAMES,** investment banker, consultant; b. Cleve., July 28, 1938; s. Harold Fulton and Agnes Elmenah (Hawkswell) Warren; m. Doris Helen Kenyeres, June 6, 1964. BS, Case We. Res. U., 1960; MBA, Harvard U., 1962. CPA Ohio. With Ernst & Whinney, Cleve., 1962—87, ptnr. in charge merger and acquisition svcs., 1976—87, pres. TransAction Group, 1987—. Bd. dirs. Seneca Capital Mgmt., Inc. Co-author: (book) Implementing Mergers and Acquisitions in the Financial Services Industry, 1985; assoc. editor: Jour. Corp. Growth, 1986—87, mem. editl. bd.; 1988; contbg. editor: Jour. Buyouts and Acquisitions, 1984—86; contbg. author: venture capital financing study conducted in five countries for Asian Devel. Bank, Malaysia, Indonesia, Pakistan, Sri Lanka, Thailand, 1986. Trustee Case We. Res. U., 1980—2005, chmn. audit com., 1991—2005; trustee Cleve. Bot. Garden, 1995—2002, We. Res. Hist. Soc., 1996—2002, chmn. investments com., 1999—2002; trustee Cmty. Improvement Corp. Summit, Medina and Portage Counties, 1992—2000, Cascade CDC, 1992—2000, Brit.-Am. C. of C., Great Lakes Region, 2001—05; dir. Univ. Tech., Inc., 1986—88; adv. bd. Shaker Investments, 1992—; v.p. M&A Internat. Inc., 1990—91, pres., 1992; bd. zoning appeals City of Lyndhurst, 1978—, chmn., 1980—82, 1991—93, 2000—01, 2006—; mem. vis. com. Case Sch. Engring., 1990—2004, Weatherhead Sch. Mgmt., 1998—2004; deans advisory coun. Case Sch. Engring., 2005—, Weatherhead Sch. Mgmt., 2005—; trustee Town Hall of Cleve., 2005—, Fairmont Presbyn. Ch., 1987—93, elder, 1991—93. Mem.: AICPA, Cleve. World Trade Assn., Cleve. Com. Fgn. Rels., Assn. Corp. Growth, Ohio Soc. CPAs, Harvard Club NYC, Catawba Island Club, Mayfield Country Club, Union Club, Jesters. Office: The TransAction Group 500 Hanna Bldg Cleveland OH 44115 Office Phone: 216-348-1666.

**WARREN, SHIRLEY M.,** respiratory therapist; d. Martin Edgar Davis and Grace Marie Collins; m. Charles Earnest Holmes (div.); stepchildren: Charles Jr., Zann; m. Gary Don Warren, Jan. 2, 1984; children: Byron Keith, Dena Nicole, Theophilus Terrell. Attended, El Centro C.C., 1976, Calif. Coll. Health Sci., 1989. Cert. Respiratory Therapy Practioner Tex. Dept. State Health Svc., 1988. Respiratory therapist Baylor Med. Ctr., Dallas, 1974—81, 1990—91, Meth. Med. Ctr., Dallas, 1981—84, S.W. Med. Ctr., Dallas, 1984—90; respiratory therapist practioner Lancaster Med. Ctr., Tex., 1990—96, Vencor Hosp., Dallas, 1994—2003, Respiratory Assocs., Arlington, Tex., Ingenium Resources, Arlington, wellness care with the elderly; educator respiratory therapy Our Children's Ho., Dallas, 1999—2005. Pastor's aide, usher, mem. com. Bayside Ch. Living God, Dallas. Home: 210 Indian Trail Cedar Hill TX 75104

**WARREN, STEPHEN THEODORE,** human geneticist, educator; b. Grosse Point, Mich., Nov. 30, 1953; s. Theodore Stephen and Frances (Fedo) W.; m. Karen Lee Pierce, Aug. 27, 1978; 1 child, Thomas. BS, Mich. State U., 1976, PhD, 1981. Diplomate Am. Bd. Med. Genetics. Grad. asst. Mich. State Univ., East Lansing, 1976-81; rsch. assoc. Univ. Ill., Chgo., 1981-83, instr., 1983-85; asst. prof. Emory U. Sch. of Medicine, Atlanta, 1985-91, assoc. prof., 1991-93, W.P. Timmie prof. human genetics, 1993—, chmn. dept. human genetics, 2001—; investigator Howard Hughes Med. Inst., 1992—2002. Vis. scientist European Molecular Biol. Lab., Heidelberg, Germany, 1984.; cons. Ctrs. for Disease Control, Atlanta, 1988-89, NIH, Bethesda, Md., 1989—; collaborator Ctr. D'Etude du Polymorphysme Humain, Paris, 1989—. Editor-in-chief Am. Jour. Human Genetics, 2000—; mem. editl. bd. Human Molecular Genetics, Am. Jour. Human Genetics, Cytogenetics, Cell Genetics, Mammalian Genome, others; contbr. chpts. to books and more than 200 articles to profl. jours. Recipient Sigma Xi prize Mich. State Sigma Xi, East Lansing, 1981, NIH fellowship NIH, Bethesda, 1982, Basil O'Connor award March of Dimes, 1987, 1986, Albert E. Levy award Emory Univ., Atlanta, 1987, William Rosen Rsch. award Nat. Fragile X Found., 1996; inductee Nat. Inst. Child Health and Human Devel. Hall of Fame Honor, 2003. Fellow Am. Coll. Med. Genetics; mem. Am. Soc. Human Genetics (nominating com. 1991, awards com. 1992—, bd. dirs. 1997—, William Allan award 1999), Am. Soc. Biochemistry and Molecular Biology, Am. Soc. Microbiology, Genetics Soc. Am., Am. Soc. Human Genetics (pres.-elect, 2004), Human Genome Orgn., Inst. Medicine., Nat. Academies. Achievements include research in molecular genetic studies of the fragile X syndrome and other human genetic diseases. Home: 2305 Kimbrough Ct Atlanta GA 30350-5635 Office: Emory Univ Sch Medicine 301 Whitehead Bldg 615 Michael St Atlanta GA 30322-4218

**WARREN, WILLIAM BRADFORD,** lawyer; b. Boston, July 25, 1934; s. Minton Machado and Sarah Ripley (Robbins) W.; children: John Coolidge, Sarah; m. Arete B. Swartz, Sept. 20, 1985. AB magna cum laude, Harvard U., 1956, LLB cum laude, 1959. Bar: N.Y. 1960. Assoc. Dewey Ballantine, N.Y.C., 1959-68; ptnr. Dewey Ballantine, LLP, 1968—2002, of counsel, 2002—. Lectr. Inst. Fed. Taxation, NYU, So. Fed. Tax Inst., Practicing Law Inst. Pres. Cintas Found., N.Y.C.; bd. dirs. St. John's Coll., Annapolis and

Santa Fe; bd. dirs. John Carter Brown Libr., Providence; adv. bd. dirs. Met. Opera Assn., N.Y.C. Mem. Am. Law Inst., Am. Coll. Trust and Estate Counsel (former regent), Acad. Am. Poets (bd. dirs., vice chair), Internat. Acad. Estate and Trust Law (former exec. com.), N.Y. State Bar Assn. (chmn. com. taxation of trust and estates sect. 1980-83), Assn. Bar City N.Y., Soc. Mayflower Descs., Harvard Club, Knickerbocker Club, Century Club, Grolier Club (past pres.). Home: 520 E 86th St New York NY 10028-7534 Office: Dewey Ballantine LLP 1301 Avenue Of The Americas New York NY 10019-6022 Office Phone: 212-259-8700. Business E-Mail: wwarren@dbllp.com.

**WARREN, WILLIAM KERMIT,** retired editor; b. Harlem, Ga., May 27, 1941; s. William Kermit and Willie Garnell (Thaxton) Warren; m. Nancy Carolyn Andrews, Sept. 5, 1964; children: Wendy Karen, William Kermit. BA in Journalism, U. Ga., 1964. Reporter Augusta Ga. Chronicle, Ga., 1964-65; reporter Chattanooga Times, Tenn., 1965-66, reporter, city editor Tenn., 1971-80; mng. editor Roanoke (Va.) Times & World News, 1980-95; electronic pub. cons., 1995-98; prin. New City Media, Blacksburg, Va., 1998-99. Served to capt USAF, 1966—70. Recipient Best Feature Story Award, Ga AP, 1964. Mem.: AP Managing Eds Asn, Sigma Delta Chi. Episcopalian. Avocation: reading.

**WARREN, WILLIAM L.,** lawyer; b. Trenton, N.J., Mar. 14, 1948; BA, Colgate U., 1969; JD, NYU, 1973. Law clk., Hon. John R. Bartels US Dist. Ct. (ea. dist.), NYC, 1974; litigation assoc. Dewey Ballantine, NYC, 1975-81; ptnr. Warren Goldberg Berman & Lubitz, Princeton, NJ, 1982-87, Cohen Shapiro Polisher Shiekman & Cohen, Lawrenceville, NJ, 1987-95; ptnr., chair, NJ environ. law group Drinker Biddle & Reath LLP, Princeton, 1995—; mng. ptnr., mem. mngmt com. Office: Drinker Biddle Reath LLP Ste 300 105 College Rd E Princeton NJ 08540-6622 Office Phone: 609-716-6603. Office Fax: 609-799-7700. Business E-Mail: william.warren@dbr.com.

**WARREN ELLISON, TASHEAYA L.,** tax attorney; b. Portland, Oreg., Dec. 28, 1972; d. Johnnie R. and Ella F. Warren; m. Scott R. Ellison, June 21, 2002; 1 child, Thaddeus L. BA, U. of Oreg., 1994, JD, 1997; LLM in Taxation, Georgetown U., 1999. Bar: Calif. 2000, Oreg. 1997, D.C. 2000. Sr. assoc. PricewaterhouseCoopers LLP, Washington, 1999—2001; atty. advisor assoc. Chief Counsel Internat. to the IRS, Washington, 2001—. Mem.: ABA (tax sect.), Nat. Bar Assn. (membership chair Greater Washington Area chapt. women lawyers divsn. 2002—04). Home: Ste 100-285 1220 L St NW Washington DC 20005 Office: 1111 Constitution Ave NW Rm 4560 Washington DC 20204

**WARRICK, EMORY LAWRENCE,** retired education educator; b. Montgomery, July 29, 1928; s. Edward Lawrence and Ruth Grey Warrick; m. Sylvia Anne Saunders, Dec. 23, 1954; children: Aleta Ann, Julienne Dell, Emory L. Jr., Elizabeth Grey(dec.). BA, Mill Sap Coll., Miss., 1951; MS, U. Miss., 1957; MA, U. Ga., 1972. Bd., chorus dir. various secondary schs., Miss., Tenn., Ga., 1952—68; prof. sociology and criminal lus Valdosta (Ga.) State Coll., 1972—76; prof. sociology Ga. Mil. Acad., Moudy AFB, 1976—81; program coord. Family Support Ctr., Moody AFB, Valdosta, Ga., 1981—90; ret., 1990. Marriage/family therapist pvt. practice, 1952—80. Mem.: NEA, Soutern Sociological Soc., Kiwanis. Episcopal. Avocations: reading, writing. Home: 314 E Park Ave Valdosta GA 31602-3034

**WARRICK, KIMBERLEY KAYE,** language educator, social studies educator; b. Lake Wales, Fla., Apr. 13, 1963; d. Bonnie Dawn and Edward Milo Dunagin (Stepfather); m. Robert Kelly Warrick, Nov. 30, 1986 (div. Apr. 0, 1995); 1 child, Kalegh Rebekah. BA, Capital U., 1989; MA, Ohio State U., 1999. Cert. elem. tchr. Mont., Ohio, learning disablities tchr. Mont., Ohio. Tchr. kindergarten/kindergarten afterschool program Columbus Torah Acad., Ohio, 1990—96, tchr. resource/ESL, 1990—96, tchr. 1st grade, 1990—96; tchr. 6th grade English/Social Studies Groveport Madison Local Schs., Ohio, 1996—2003; tchr. spl. edn. 8th grade Bozeman Pub. Schs., Mont., 2003—05, tchr. spl. edn. 9th grade, 2005—. English curriculum com. Bozeman Pub. Schs., Mont., 2004—05. Facilitator Tchr. for Civic Edn., Bozeman, Mont., 2004—05; del. Mont. Rep. Party State Conv., Big Sky, 2004. Mem.: Phi Delta Kappa (pres. MSU chpt. 2006), Coun. Tchr. Cert. Profl. Develop. (state bd. pub. edn. 2005—), Nat. Coun. for History Educators, Bozeman Edn. Assn. (bldg. rep. 2004—05), Gallatin County Rep. Women. Avocations: reading, volleyball, needlepoint. Office: Bozeman HS 205 N 11th Ave Bozeman MT 59715 Office Phone: 406-522-6241. Office Fax: 406-522-6222. Business E-Mail: kwarrick@bozeman.k12.mt.us.

**WARRING, DOUGLAS FRANKLIN,** education educator, psychologist, director; b. Braham, Minn., Aug. 16, 1949; s. Herbert Franklin and Maxine (Anderson) W.; m. Tonya Huber, Aug. 8, 2004; children: Jana, Leah, Noah. BA, Bethel Coll., 1971; MA in Teaching, Coll. St. Thomas, 1975; PhD, U. Minn., 1983. Lic. social studies tchr., secondary sch. prin., Minn.; lic. psychologist, Minn. Instr. bus. Inver Hills C.C., Inver Grove Heights, Minn., 1980-83; instr. psychology Concordia Coll., St. Paul, 1983; asst. prof. psychology U. Minn., Waseca, 1982-84; asst. prof. edn. U. St. Thomas, St. Paul, 1984-90; dir. tchr. edn. Coll. St. Thomas, St. Paul, 1989-90, assoc. dean, 1990-95; prof. in edn. and psychology Univ. St. Thomas, 1996—. Mem. bd. examiners Nat. Coun. on Accreditation for Tchr. Edn., 1998—. Jour. Critical Issues in Curriculum & Instrn., 1999-2004, Jour. Action in Tchr. Edn., 2000—. Mem. Curriculum Com. Bloomington, Minn., 1985-89; vice chair Planning, Evaluation and Reporting Com., Bloomington, 1985-87, chair, 1988-89. Served with USAR. Named one of Outstanding Young Men of Am., 1985. Mem. APA, ASCD, Am. Assn. Tchr. Edn. (exec. bd., pres. Minn. chpt. 1985, nat. resolutions com. 1988, nat. rsch. com. 1997), Minn. Assn. Tchr Edu. (exec. bd. 1984-93, pres. 1990-92), Minn. Human Rels. Assn., Internat. Coun. of Edn. for Teaching (life), Internat. Soc. for Tchr. Edn., Am. Legion, Met. Wrestling Ofcls. Assn. (v.p. 1982-86), Minn. Assn. Supervision and Curriculum Devel. (bd. dirs. 1994-2004), Soc. Psychol. Study of Social Issues, World Coun. Curriculum Instrn. Office: U St Thomas 1000 La Salle Ave Minneapolis MN 55403-2009 Home: 2698 Lake Ct Mounds View MN 55112-4106 E-mail: dfwarring@stthomas.edu.

**WARRINGTON, GEORGE D.,** rail transportation executive; b. Sept. 19, 1952; BA cum laude, Syracuse U., 1974, MPA, 1975. Asst. to dir. divsn. commuter svcs. N.J. Dept. Transp., 1975-77; asst. to commr., 1977-80; dep. exec. dir./chief of staff N.J. Transit Corp. Ops., 1980-88; v.p., gen. mgr. N.J. Transit Rail Ops., 1988-90; dep. commr. N.J. Dept. Transp., 1990-92; exec. dir., pres. Del. River Port Authority and Port Authority Transit Corp., 1992-94; pres. N.E. Corridor Strategic Bus. Unit, Nat. R.R. Passenger Corp. (Amtrak), 1994-98, pres., CEO, 1998—2002; exec. dir. N.J. Transit Corp., 2002—. Bd. dirs. Phila. Belt Line R.R., U. Del. Intermodal Transp. Assn., Mineta Internat. Inst. Surface Transp. Policy Studies; mem. adv. bd. Voorhees Transp. Ctr. Bloustein Sch. Planning and Pub. Policy Rutgers U. Recipient Salzberg Medallion, Syracuse U. Office: NJ Transit Corp One Penn Plaza E Newark NJ 07105-2246 Fax: 202-906-2850.

**WARRINGTON, WILLARD GLADE,** retired university official; b. Macomb, Ill. Oct. 24, 1920; s. Henry K. and Farie V. (Prather) W.; m. A. Irene Windser, Aug. 9, 1945 (dec. 1969); m. Janette Moffatt Cooper, Apr. 26, 1972; children: David, Steven, Douglas, Jane Ann, Stephen Cooper. B.Ed., Western Ill. State Tchrs. Coll., 1941; MS, U. Ill., 1949, MS, 1950, E.D.D. 1952. Tchr. public high schs., Ill., 1941-42, 45-48; mem. faculty Mich. State U., 1952-58, dir. office evaluation services, 1958-74, asso. dean Univ. Coll., 1974-78, acting dean Univ. Coll., 1978-80, dir. undergrad. univ. div., 1980-85, dir., prof. emeritus, 1986—. Cons. edn.; Ford Found. cons. U. Philippines. Contbr. articles on ednl. measurement to profl. publs.; editorial bd.: Ednl. and Psychol. Measurement, 1968-85. Active Boy Scouts Am., 1957-68. Served to lt. col. USAAF, 1942-45. Mem. Nat. Council on Measurement in Edn. (pres. 1973-74), Am. Ednl. Research Assn., Assn. for Gen. and Liberal Studies (sec.-treas. 1973-79) Methodist. Home: 1211 Ascot Pl Haslett MI 48840

**WARRIOR, DELLA C.,** academic administrator, art educator; BA in Sociology, Northeastern State U.; MA in Edn., Harvard U. Pres. Inst. Am. Indian Arts, Santa Fe, devel. dir. CEO Otoe-Missouria Tribe, 1989—92; exec. bd. mem. World Indigenous Nations Higher Edn. Consortium; mem. U.S. Pres. Bd. Adv. on Tribal Coll. & U., 2002—.

**WARRIOR, PADMASREE,** communications executive; BSChemE, Indian Inst. Tech., New Delhi, India; MSChemE, CornellU. Joined Motorola, Inc., Schaumburg, Ill., 1984, v.p., gen. mgr., energy sys. group, corp. v.p., chief technology officer, semiconductor products sector, v.p., 1999, corp. officer, 2000, sr. v.p., 2003—05, chief tech. officer, 2003—, exec. v.p., 2005—. Gen. mgr. Thoughtbeam, Inc. (subsidiary of Motorola); mem. coun. digital economy Tex. Gov.; mem. rev. panel Tex. Higher Edn. Bd.; dir. Ferro Corp. Recipient Women Elevating Sci. and Tech. award, Working Woman Mag., 2001. Office: Motorola Inc 1303 E Algonquin Rd Schaumburg IL 60196 Office Phone: 847-576-5000.*

**WARSH, KEVIN MAXWELL,** bank executive; b. Apr. 13, 1970; m. Jane Lauder. BA, Stanford U., 1992; JD, Harvard U., 1995. Exec. dir., v.p. mergers & acquisitions, investment banking dir. Morgan Stanley & Co., Inc., 1996—2002; spl. asst. to Pres. for econ. policy Nat. Econ. Coun., Washington, 2002—06; mem. bd. govs. Fed. Res. Sys., Washington, 2006—. Office: Fed Res Sys 20th St & Constitution Ave NW Rm 2010 Washington DC 20551 Office Phone: 202-452-3200. Office Fax: 202-452-2611.*

**WARSHAW, ALLEN CHARLES,** lawyer; b. Harrisburg, Pa., Aug. 27, 1948; s. Julius and Miriam (Nepove) W.; m. Shirley Anne Ness, Aug. 23, 1970; children: Christopher James, Andrew Charles, William Robert. BA, U. Pa., 1970; JD, Villanova U., 1973. Bar: Pa. 1973, U.S. Dist. Ct. (ea. and mid. dists.) Pa. 1974, U.S. Ct. Appeals (3d cir.) 1975, U.S. Supreme Ct. 1977, Calif. 1978. Staff atty. Office Atty. Gen., State of Pa., Harrisburg, 1973-79, chief civil litig., 1979-85, dir. civil law, 1985-86; ptnr. Duane, Morris & Heckscher, Harrisburg, 1986—2002; shareholder Klett, Rooney, Lieber & Schorling, Harrisburg, 2002—06; chief counsel Dept. Pub. Welfare Commonwealth of Pa., 2006—. Past pres. Mechanicsburg Soccer Assn.; Dem. committeeperson Cumberland County; past bd. dirs. Mechanicsburg Area Sch. Dist.; bd. dirs. Planned Parenthood Susquehanna Valley, vice chair. Fellow: Am. Bar Found.; mem.: ABA, FBA, ABA Coun. Appellate Lawyers, Am. Bankruptcy Inst., Pa. Bar Assn., Dauphin County Bar Assn., Wildcat Found. (bd. dirs.). Home: 1035 Mccormick Rd Mechanicsburg PA 17055-5970 Office: Klett Rooney Lieber & Schorling 17 N Second St 15th Fl Harrisburg PA 17101 Office Phone: 717-783-2800. Business E-Mail: acwarshaw@klettrooney.com, awarshaw@state.pa.us.

**WARSHAW, ANDREW LOUIS,** surgeon, researcher; b. NYC, Feb. 18, 1939; s. David and Florence (Rand) W.; m. Brenda Rose Flavin, Jan. 4, 1986; children: Jordan, Abigail, Daniel; stepchildren: Heather, Gretchen, Brenda. AB, Harvard U., 1959, MD, 1963. Diplomate Am. Bd. Surgery. Intern in surgery Mass. Gen. Hosp., Boston, 1963-64, resident in surgery, 1964-65, 67-70, rsch. fellow in medicine, 1970, chief resident in surgery, 1971; clin. assoc. in gastroenterology NIH, Bethesda, Md., 1965-67; from instr. surgery to prof. surgery Harvard Med. Sch., Boston, 1972-90, Harold & Ellen Danser prof. surgery, 1990-97, W. Gerald Austen prof. surgery, 1997—; assoc. chief surg. svcs. Mass. Gen. Hosp., Boston, 1990-97, chief gen. surgery, 1992-97, chmn. dept. surgery, surgeon-in-chief, 1997—. Editor: Pancreatitis, 1989, Current Practice of Surgery, 1993, The Pancreas, 1998; contbr. more than 400 articles to med. jours., revs.; contbr. to 8 med. ednl. films, videos; editor-in-chief Surgery, 1997—. Trustee Mass. Gen. Hop., Boston, 1999—. Lt. comdr. USPHS, 1965-67. Mem. ACS (pres. Mass. chpt. 1991-92, gov. 1997-2003, health policy steering com. 2001-, 1st v.p. 2004-), Am. Bd. Surgery (chmn. 1992-93, dir. 1985-93), New Eng. Surg. Soc. (pres. 1993-94), Soc. for Surgery of Alimentary Tract (pres. 1997-98), Internat. Assn. Pancreatology (pres. 1998-), Boston Surg. Soc. (pres. 1999-2000), Halsted Soc. (pres. 2002-03). Avocations: photography, fly fishing. Office: Mass Gen Hosp White 506 Boston MA 02114 Business E-Mail: awarshaw@partners.org.

**WARSHAW, CAROLE KLEIN,** education educator, consultant; d. Irving and Frieda Patlis Klein; m. Gerald Jay Warshaw, June 9, 1956; children: Ms. Jodie Sharon Arrington, Howard Gary, Dr. Joel David. BA, Hunter Coll., N.Y.C., 1957; MS in Spl. Edn., Hofstra U., 1976; Profl. Diploma- Adminstrn., St. John's U., Queens, N.Y., 1987, Ed.D. 1993. Cert. elem. sch. tchr. N.Y.C. Bd. Edn., 1957, asst. prin. N.Y.C. Bd. Edn., 1989, adminstrn./supr. N.Y. State Dept. Edn., 1987, clin. edn. trainer Fla. Dept. Edn., 2000. Tchr. N.Y.C. Bd. Edn., Queens, 1957—84, tchr. trainer, 1984—89, dir. testing, 1989—90; assoc. prof. Lynn U., Boca Raton, Fla., 1994—, coord. master's program, 1994—, coord. evening edn. programs, 1994—. Liaison to dept. of edn. Lynn U., Boca Raton, 1995—; cons. Florence Fuller Child Devel. Ctrs., Boca Raton, 1999—, Toussaint L'Ouverture H.S., Delray Beach, Fla., 2001—; clin. supervision trainer Fla. Dept. Edn., Boca Raton, 1999—. Contbr. articles to profl. jours. V.p. Coalition of Boynton Beach (Fla.) Residents, 1992—94, Temple Beth Emeth, Bklyn., 1964—65; pres. Palm Shores Homeowners Assn., Boynton Beach, 1993—94. Impact II grantee, N.Y.C. Bd. Edn., 1981. Mem.: Coun. Adminstrs. and Suprs., Coun. for Exceptional Children, Phi Delta Kappa, Kappa Delta Pi (counselor 1997—). Independent. Hebrew. Avocations: bridge, travel, music. Office: Lynn U 3601 N Military Trl Boca Raton FL 33431 Office Phone: 561-237-7088. Personal E-mail: jecawa@adelphia.net. Business E-Mail: cwarshaw@lynn.edu.

**WARSHAW, MARVIN D.,** conductor, educator, musician; b. Norman Maurice Warshaw and Heartha Joyce Levinson; m. Carol A. Pendleton, May 25, 1986. M in Musical Arts, Yale U., 1980. Pers. mgr., libr., prin. violist, soloist New Haven Symphony Orch., 1977—; pvt. lessons tchr. Wesleyan U., Middletown, Conn. 1997—; faculty instr. Ednl. Ctr. for the Arts, New Haven, 1997—; strings tchr. Coop. H.S. for the Arts and Humanities, New Haven, 1999—2004; condr. Greater New Haven Concert Orch., 2001—; founding mem., mgr. Wall St. Chamber Players, 1980—; orch. pers. mgr., libr. violist Bellingham Festival, 2004—. Head orch. libr. Aspen (Colo.) Music Festival, 1981—98. Office: New Haven Symphony Orch 70 Audubon St New Haven CT 06510

**WARSHAW, STANLEY IRVING,** federal official, consultant; b. Boston, Nov. 5, 1931; s. Alec and Sarah (Laserson) W.; m. Wanda Faye Capino, Feb., 12, 1992; 1 child from previous marriage, Karen Beth. BS in Ceramic Engring. Ga. Tech. Inst., 1957; Sc.D. in Ceramics, M.I.T., 1961; grad., Advanced Mgmt. Program, Harvard Bus. Sch., 1978. Sr. scientist research div. Raytheon Co., Waltham, Mass., 1961-64; with Am. Standard, Inc., New Brunswick, N.J., 1964-75, gen. mgr. engring. and devel., 1972-75; dir. Ctr. for Consumer Product Tech., Nat. Inst. Stds. and Tech. (formerly Nat. Bur. Stds.), Washington, 1975-80, dir. Office Product Standards Policy, 1981-86, assoc. dir., 1987-89, dir. Office Standards Svcs. Gaithersburg, Md., 1989-93; sr. policy advisor for stds. and tech. U.S. Dept. Commerce, Gaithersburg, 1994-99. Served to capt. U.S. Army, 1951-53. Fellow N.Y. Acad. Scis., Washington Acad. Scis. Home: 11783 Haddon Pkwy Boynton Beach FL 33437-1665 Office Phone: 561-740-4045. E-mail: swarshaw@adelphia.net.

**WARSHAWSKY, ISIDORE,** physicist, consultant; b. NYC, May 27, 1911; s. Morris and Esther (Sherman) W. BS cum laude, CCNY, 1930. Physicist Nat. Adv. Com. Aeronautics, Langley Field, Va., 1930-42, chief instrumentation sect. Cleve., 1942-50; chief instrument rsch. br. Nat. Adv. Com. Aeronautics/ NASA, Cleve., 1950-72; instrumentation cons. NASA, Cleve., 1972-90, ret., 1990, disting. rsch. cons. (unsalaried), 1990-95. Author: (textbook) Foundations of Measurement and Instrumentation, 1990; author 10 NACA/NASA tech. reports; contbr. 20 articles to sci. jours. and books. Fellow Instrument Soc. Am.; mem. Am. Phys. Soc., Am. Vacuum Soc., Phi Beta Kappa.

**WARSHAWSKY, MARK JOEL,** human resources specialist, former federal agency administrator; b. Chgo., Mar. 26, 1958; s. Arthur and Dorothy (Chislof) W.; m. Laura Beth Margolis, June 28, 1987; children: David,

Hannah, Avi, Sarah. BA, Northwestern U., 1979; PhD, Harvard U., 1984. Actuary Combined Ins., Chgo., 1979-80; rsch. asst. Nat. Bur. Econ. Rsch., Cambridge, Mass., 1981-82; tutor Harvard U., Cambridge, 1983-84; economist Fed. Res. Bd., Washington, 1984-88; dir. Fed. Res. Bd. Credit Union, 1988—89; sr. economist Fed. Res. Bd., 1989—92; sr. economist employee plans and exempt orgns. IRS, 1992—95; dir., strategic and pension rsch. Teachers Ins. & Annuity Assoc. Coll. Retirement Equity Fund, N.Y.C., 1995—98; dir. rsch. Teachers Ins. & Annuity Assoc. Coll. Retirement Equity Fund Inst., N.Y.C., 1998—2001; dep. asst. sec., econ. policy, microeconomic analysis US Dept. Treasury, Washington, 2002—04, asst. sec., econ. policy, 2004—06; dir. retirement rsch. Watson Wyatt Worldwide, Inc., Arlington, Va., 2006—. Contbr. articles to profl. jours; author/editor several books. Trustee Actuarial Found., 2000—02. Sloan scholar Harvard U., 1983-84. Mem. Am. Econ. Assn., Am. Risk and Ins. Assn., Nat. Assn. Bus. Economists, Nat. Assn. Soc. Ins. Republican. Jewish. Office: Watson Wyatt Worldwide Inc 901 N Glebe Rd Arlington VA 22203

**WARTELL, MICHAEL ALAN,** academic administrator; b. Albuquerque, Nov. 4, 1946; s. Richard H. and Betty D. (Davis) Wartell; m. Ruth E. Beachy, Dec. 3, 1977; children: Justin Davis, Richard Harrison. BS, U. N.Mex., 1967; MS, Yale U., 1968, PhD, 1971. Asst. prof. chemistry Met. State Coll., 1971—75, assoc. prof., chmn. dept., 1975—78; dean sch. natural scis., prof. chemistry James Madison U., 1979—84; provost, v.p. acad. affairs Humboldt State U., Arcata, Calif., 1984—89, prof. chemistry, 1984—94; chancellor Ind U. - Purdue U., Ft. Wayne, 1994—. Mem. U.S. Army Sci. Bd., 1981—87; participant various study groups on chem. warfare, decontamination, biodefense; cons. U.S. Army, IRT Corp., Sandia Nat. Labs., SRI Internat., JAYCOR, HERO, Boeing Elecs., Battelle; mem. Def. Intelligence Agy. Sci. Adv. Com., 1984—; chmn. bd. visitors Def. Systems Mgmt. Coll., Ft. Belvoir, Va., 1984—, chair, 1985—. Co-author: Engineering Education and A Lifetime of Learning, 1975, Introduction to Chemistry, 1975, Fundamentals of Chemistry, 1980; contbr. articles to profl. jours. Bd. dirs. Humboldt State U. Found., 1984—. Fellow: Am. Acad. Forensic Scis.; mem.: Kappa Nu Epsilon, Am. Assn. Univ. Adminstrs. (evaluation task force 1978—79, stds. and rev. com. 1983—84), Am. Phys. Soc., Am. Chem. Soc., Phi Kappa Phi, Phi Beta Kappa, Sigma Xi. Jewish. Office: Ind U Purdue U 2101 E Coliseum Blvd Fort Wayne IN 46805-1445 E-mail: wartell@ipfw.edu.

**WARTH, ROBERT DOUGLAS,** history professor; b. Houston, Dec. 16, 1921; s. Robert Douglas and Virginia (Adams) W.; m. Lillian Eleanor Terry, Sept. 18, 1945. BS, U. Ky., 1943; MA, U. Chgo., 1945, PhD, 1949. Instr. history U. Tenn., Knoxville, 1950-51; instr. Rutgers U., Newark, 1951-54, asst. prof., 1954-58; vis. prof. Paine Coll., Augusta, Ga., 1960; asso. editor Grolier, Inc., N.Y.C., 1960-62, 63-64; lectr. Hunter Coll., N.Y.C., part time, 1962-63; asso. prof. S.I. C.C., 1964-68; prof. history U. Ky., Lexington, 1968-92, prof. emeritus history, 1992—. Pres. So. Conf. Slavic Studies, 1982-83 Author: The Allies and the Russian Revolution, 1954, Soviet Russia in World Politics, 1963, Joseph Stalin, 1969, Lenin, 1973, Leon Trotsky, 1977, Nicholas II: The Life and Reign of Russia's Last Monarch, 1997. Served with AUS, 1943-44. Sr. scholar award So. Conf. Slavic Studies, 1992. Mem. Am. Hist. Assn., Am. Assn. Advancement Slavic Studies, AAUP Office: U Ky Dept History Lexington KY 40506-0001 Home: 2069 Fontaine Rd Apt 4 Lexington KY 40502

**WARTHAN, HELEN PATRICIA,** retired secondary school educator; b. Alexandria, Va., June 14, 1941; d. Anthony John and Elizabeth Radcliff (Etchison) Trovato. BS, Fairmont State Coll., W.Va., 1964; MEd, Tex. A&M U., 1969; postgrad., Fla. State U., Tallahassee, 1966-70, U. Ga., 1971-73, SUNY, 1984-87. Tchr., counselor Carrabelle (Fla.) HS, 1964-70; tchr., chmn. dept. sci. Towers HS, Decatur, Ga., 1970—99; ret., 1999; edn. cons., 2000—. Cons. and presenter in field. Pres. Decatur Civic Chorus, 1975—76, 1986—87, 2000—01, 2006—, treas., 1979—80, sec., 2002—03, patron chair, 1990—92, Mary Clark award chair, 1998—, sec., 2002—03; resource agt. Weather Edn. Am. Meteorol. Assn., 1991—, mem. minority scholarship com., 1993—2005, tchr. in residence, 1993; vol. Meals-on-Wheels, 2000—; asst. treas. Oakhurst Presbyn. Ch., 1999—. Named Tchr. of the Yr., Ga. Tchrs. Assn., 4th Dist., 1976, Dekalb County Tchr. of the Yr., 1985; recipient C.L. Chandler award, Atlanta Am. Meteorol. Assn., 1997; Benedum Acad. scholar, 1959—64. Mem.: ASCD, AAAS, Atlanta Am. Meterological Soc., Am. Meteorol. Soc., Am. Geologic Assn. (named Regional Tchr. of the Yr. 1998), Bd. Sch. and Popular Meteorol. and Oceanographic Edn., Internat. Oceanographic Found., Nat. Oceanographic Soc., Nat. Sci. Tchrs. Assn., Nat. Assn. Biology Tchrs., Ga. Sci. Tchrs. Assn. (Tchr. of the Yr. award 12th dist. 1988, 1997), Nat. Earth Sci. Tchrs. Assn. (regional dir. 1987—91), Sci. Tchrs. Assn. Rockdale and Dekalb (pres. 1980, 1987, Sci. Tchr. of the Yr. 1984—85, 1986—87), Dekalb-Decatur Ret. Tchrs. Assn., Ga. Assn. Ret. Tchrs. Episcopalian. Home: 1470 Stoneleigh Cir Stone Mountain GA 30088-3436 Personal E-mail: pwart@aol.com.

**WARTHEN, HARRY JUSTICE, III,** lawyer; b. Richmond, Va., July 8, 1939; s. Harry Justice Jr. and Martha Winston (Alsop) W.; m. Sally Berkeley Trapnell, Sept. 7, 1968; children: Martha Alsop, William Trapnell. BA, U. Va., 1961, LLB, 1967. Bar: Va. 1967, U.S. Ct. Appeals (4th cir.) 1967, U.S. Dist. Ct. (ea. dist.) Va. 1969. Law clk. to judge U.S. Ct. Appeals (4th cir.), Richmond, Va., 1967-68; assoc. Hunton & Williams, Richmond, 1968—. Lectr. in field U. Va. Law Sch., Charlottesville, 1975—77. Trustee exec. com. Hist. Richmond Found., 1986-95, 96-2005, pres., 2000-02; trustee Woodrow Wilson Birthplace and Mus., 1997-2003, 05-; dir. exec. com. Preservation Alliance of Va. (now part of APVA Preservation Va.), 1991-97, pres., 1994-96; Va. rep. bd. advisors The Nat. Trust for Historic Preservation, 2003—; dir. The Corp. for Jefferson's Poplar Forest, 2005-; elder, trustee endowment fund Grace Covenant Presbyn. Ch.; moderator Hanover Presbytery, Presbyn. Ch (USA). 1988. Lt U.S. Army. 1962 61. Fellow Am. Coll Trust and Estate Counsel, Va. Law Found.; mem. Va. Bar Assn. (chmn. sect. on wills, trusts and estates 1981-89), Antiquarian Soc. Richmond (pres. 1977-78, 98-99), Country Club Va., Deep Run Hunt Club. Republican. Home: 1319 Shallow West Rd Manakin Sabot VA 23103-2305 Office: Hunton & Williams Riverfront Plz E Tower 951 E Byrd St Richmond VA 23219 Office Phone: 804-788-8414. Business E-Mail: hwarthen@hunton.com.

**WARTLUFT, DAVID JONATHAN,** retired librarian, minister; b. Stouchsburg, Pa., Sept. 22, 1938; s. Cleaver Milvard and Dorothy (Stump) W.; m. Joyce Claudia Dittmer, June 15, 1963 (div. Sept. 1988); children: Elizabeth Marie, Deborah Joy, Rebecca Janet, Andrew Jonathan. AB (Trexler scholar), Muhlenberg Coll., 1960; MDiv (Danforth scholar), Luth. Theol. Sem., Phila., 1964; MA (scholar), U. Pa., 1964; MS (Lilly Found. scholar), Drexel U., 1968; DD, Luth. Theol. Sem., Phila., 2003. Asst. chaplain, instr. religion Springfield Coll., Mass., 1962-63; ordained minister Luth. Ch., 1964; pastor Jerusalem Luth. Ch., Allentown, Pa., 1964-66; cataloger, reference libr. Luth. Sem. Phila., 1966-68, asst. libr., 1968-77, dir. libr., 1977—2002, chaplain, 1978-79, dir. 1st yr. field edn., 1979-81, 82-83, 1985—2002; interim pastor New Jerusalem (Pa.) Luth. Ch., 2003—04, New Bethel Union Ch., Pa., 2004, Maiden Creek (Pa.) Union Ch., 2005—06, Friedens Luth. Ch., Stony Run, Pa., 2006—. Comms. com. Northeastern Pa. Synod, 1967—78; archivist Northeastern Pa. Synod, Luth. Ch. Am., 1970—87; conv. com. Northeastern Pa. Synod, 1976; v.p. Luth. Archives Ctr., Phila., 1979—85, 1998—2005, bd. dirs.; libr. cons. Gurkul Luth. Ch., Madras, India, 1989, Huria Kristen Batak Protestant Sem., Pematang Siantar, Sumatra, Indonesia, 1989, Luther Sem., Adelaide, Australia, 1996; chair archives adv. bd. Evang. Luth. Ch. Am., 2000—03; adv. bd. Resource Ctr. Northeastern Pa. Synod, 2003—; archivist Northeastern Pa. Synod, Evang. Luth. Ch. Am., 1988—91, 2002—. Editor: Teamwork, 1970—84, The Periodical, 1979—84, Luth. Hist. Soc. Eastern Pa.; author: (book indexes) Luther in Mid Career (H. Bornkamm), 1983, Theodicy in the Old Testament (J. Crenshaw), 1983, The Roots of Anti-Semitism (H. Obermann), 1984, The Book of Revelation: Justice and Judgment (E.S. Fiorenza), 1985, Rediscovering Paul (N.R. Peterson), 1985, The Opponents of Paul in Second Corinthians (D. Georgi), 1986, Psychological Aspects of Pauline Theology (G. Theissen), 1986, Ethics of the New Testament (W. Schrag), 1987, Israel's Praise (W. Brueggemann), 1987, Commitment to Unity (W.K. Gilbert), 1988, Paul and His Letters (L. Keck),

1988, Finally Comes the Poet (W. Bruggemann), 1989, Community and Commitment (G. Rupp), 1989, Protest and Praise (J.M. Spenser), 1990, After the Absolute (L. Swidler), 1990, Greeks, Romans and Christians (L. Swidler), 1990, The New Era in Religious Education (P. Babin), 1991, A Commentary on the Book of Amos (S. M. Paul), 1992, The Book of Revelation (J. Roloff), 1993, What is Scripture? (W.C. Smith), 1993, Jesus in the Gospels (R. Schnackenburg), 1995, Amos (Jeremias), 1998, World Religions in America (J. Neusner), 1999, Revolution and Renewal (Campolo), 2000, Nicholas Lyra: The Senses of Scripture (Krey and Smith), 2000, Beleaguered Rulers (W. May), 2001, Practical Theology for Black Churches (D.P. Andrews), 2003, Approaches to Auschwitz (Roth and Rubenstein), 2003, PostColonial Imagination and Feminist Theology (Kwok, p-l), 2004, Discerning the Divine (Callen, B.L.), 2004, Foundations of Christian Worship, 2006, Science and Scripture, 2006; contbr. articles to profl. jours. Mem.: Drexel U. Grad. Sch. Libr. and Info. Sci. Alulmni Assn. (bd. dirs. 1978—80), Mid. States Assn. (accreditation visitor), Assn. Uniting Religion and Art (chmn. membership com., treas. 1995—2002), Paradise Falls Luth. Assn. (chmn. religious activities 1985—86, bd. dirs. 1985—87), Assn. Theol. Schs. in US and Can. (selection panel for libr. grants), Luth. Hist. Conf. (com. on scholarly rsch. and pub. 1981—, constl. revision com. 1984—86, membership chair 1994—96, editor essays and reports 1996—2000, bd. dirs., treas., 1988-94 1996—2002), Coun. on Study Religion (liaison com. 1974—77, nominating com. 1978—80, liaison com. 1981—82), Coun. Nat. Libr. and Info. Assn. (counselor 1978—81), Southeastern Pa. Theol. Librs. Assn. (sec. 1970—73, chair planning com. 1986—89), Am. Theol. Libr. Assn. (exec. sec., editor procs. 1971—81, bd. dirs. 1991—94, recording sec. 1995—97, devel. officer 1998—99), Luth. Hist. Soc. Ea. Pa. (life; bd. dirs. 1991—94, v.p. 1994—99), Beta Phi Mu, Phi Sigma Tau, Eta Sigma Phi. Democrat. Personal E-mail: djwartluft@aol.com. Business E-mail: dwartluft@ltsp.edu. *By God's grace I am freed to live a life of joyful service in gratitude.*

**WARTMAN, STEVEN A.,** medical association administrator; Grad., Cornell U., 1966; MD, Johns Hopkins U., 1970, PhD Sociology, 1979. Diplomate Am. Bd. Internal Medicine. Dir. med. svs., chmn. medicine Mount Sinai Med. Ctr., Miami Beach; prof. medicine U. Miami; sr. residency in internal medicine Baltimore City Hosp.; intern in internal medicine Stanford U. Med. Ctr.; resident in internal medicine Yale-New Haven Hosp.; prof. medicine Albert Einstein Coll. Medicine; physician-in-chief L.I. Jewish Med. Ctr.; with Edward Meilman Disting. Chair Medicine; dir. Ctr. Quality Rsch. North Shore-L.I. Jewish Health Sys.; dean U. Tex. Med. Sch. San Antonio, 2000—05; pres. Assn. Acad. Health Centers, Washington, 2005—. Contbr. more than 120 peer-reviewed jour. articles, abstracts, chapters to books. Recipient Leadership and Achievement award, Soc. Gen. Internal Medicine, 1997, Excellence award, U.S. Health Resources and Svcs. Adminstrn., 1999; fellow Internat. in Health Care, Yugoslavia, 1969, Primary Care Policy, USPHS, 1991; scholar Henry Luce, Indonesia, 1975—76, Robert Wood Johnson Clin., Johns Hopkins U., 1976—78. Fellow: ACP; mem.: Alpha Omega Alpha, Phi Beta Kappa. Office: Assn Academic Health Centers Ste 720 1400 Sixteenth St NW Washington DC 20036*

**WARWICK, DIONNE,** singer; b. East Orange, N.J., Dec. 12, 1940; m. Bill Elliott (div. 1975); children: David, Damon. Student, Hartt Coll. Music, Hartford, Conn. As teen-ager formed Gospelaires and Drinkard Singers, then sang background for rec. studio, 1966; debut, Philharmonic Hall, N.Y. Lincoln Center, 1966; appearances include London Palladium, Olympia, Paris, Lincoln Ctr. Performing Arts, N.Y.C.; records include Don't Make Me Over, 1962, Walk On By, Do You Know The Way to San José, What The World Needs Now, Message To Michael, I'll Never Fall In Love Again, I'll Never Love This Way Again, Deja Vu, Heartbreaker, That's What Friends Are For; albums include Valley of the Dolls and Others, 1968, Promises, Promises, 1975, Dionne, 1979, Then Came You, Friends, 1986, Reservations for Two, 1987, Greatest Hits, 1990, Dionne Warwick Sings Cole Porter, 1990, Hidden Gems; The Best of Dionne Warwick, Vol. 2, 1992, (with Whitney Houston) Friends Can Be Lovers, 1993, Dionne Warwick and Placido Domingo, 1994, Aquarela Do Brasil, 1994, From the Vaults, 1995, Sings the Bacharach and David Songbook, 1995, Dionne Sings Dionne, 1998, I Say a Little Prayer for You, 2000; TV appearance in Sisters in the Name of Love, HBO, 1986; screen debut Slaves, 1969, No Night, So Long, also, Hot! Live and Otherwise; co-host: TV show Solid Gold; host: TV show A Gift of Music, 1981; star: TV show Dionne Warwick Spl. Founder Dionne Warwick Scholarship Fund, 1968, charity group BRAVO (Blood Revolves Around Victorious Optimism), Warwick Found. to Help Fight AIDS; spokeswoman Am. Sudden Infant Death Syndrome; participant U.S.A for Africa; Am. Amb. of Health, 1987. Recipient Grammy awards, 1969, 70, 80; NAACP Key of Life award, 1990.

**WASAN, DARSH TILAKCHAND,** academic administrator, chemical engineer, educator; b. Sarai, Salah, West Pakistan, July 15, 1938; came to U.S., 1957, naturalized, 1974; s. Tilakchand Gokalchand and Ishari Devi (Obhan) W.; m. Usha Kapur, Aug. 21, 1966; children: Ajay, Kern. BSChemE, U. Ill., 1960; PhD, U. Calif., Berkeley, 1965. Asst. prof. chem. engring. Ill. Inst. Tech., Chgo., 1964-67, assoc. prof., 1967-70, prof., 1970—, chmn. dept., 1971-77, 78-87, acting dean, 1977-78, 87-88, v.p. rsch. and tech., 1988-91, provost, 1991—, provost and sr. v.p., 1995-96, v.p., internat. and Motorola chair, 1996—. Cons. Inst. Gas Tech., 1965-70, Chgo. Bridge & Iron Co., 1967-71, Ill. EPA, 1971-72, NSF, 1971, 78-79, 87-89, Nelson Industries, 1976—, B.F. Goodrich Chem. Co., 1976-78, Exxon Rsch. & Engring. Co., 1977-89, Stauffer Chem. Co., 1980-88, ICI Ams., 1988-92, Westinghouse Savannah River Co., 1995-2004, Monsanto, 1999-2004; Procter & Gamble lectr. U. Cin. Editor-in-chief Jour. colloid and Interface sci.; mem. publs. bd. Chem. Engring. Edn. Jour.; mem. adv. bd. Jour. Separations Tech., Current Opinion in Colloid and Interface Sci., Jour. of Dispersion Sci. and Tech.; contbr. articles to profl. jours. Recipient Donald Gage Stevens Disting. Lectureship award Syracuse U., 1991, Jakob J. Bikerman Lectureship award Case Western U., 1994, Robert Gilpin Lectr. award Clarkson U., 1995, MacMoran Disting. Lectureship award Tulane U., 1996, Sidney Ross lectr. award, 1996, Bonnet Dodge Disting. Lectureship award Yale U., 1998, Dinesh O. Shah Lectureship award U. Fla., 2004, Norman N. Li Disting. Lectureship award Wayne State U., 2005; Spl. citation U.S. FDA, 2000. Fellow AIChE (Ernest Thiele award 1989, Thomas Baron award in fluid-particle systems 2002, Alpha Chi Sigma award for chem. engring. rsch. 2005); mem. AAAS, NAE, Am. Chem. Soc. (award in colloid chemistry 2000, Langmuir Lectureship award 2004), Am. Soc. Engring. Edn. (Western Electric award 1972, 3M Lectureship award chem. engring. divsn. 1991), Fine Particles Soc. (pres. 1976-77, Hausner award 1982), Sigma Xi. Home: 8705 Royal Swan Ln Darien IL 60561-8433 Office: Ill Inst Tech 3300 S Federal St Chicago IL 60616-3793 Office Phone: 312-567-3001. Business E-Mail: wasan@iit.edu.

**WASCH, WILLIAM KARL,** gerontologist, consultant; b. Mt. Vernon, N.Y., May 11, 1931; s. Karl F. and Lina M. (Krauth) W.; m. Susan Beck Wasch, Aug. 23, 1958; children: Christina, William K. Jr., Heidi, Frederick. BA with honors, Wesleyan U., 1952; MS in Bus., Columbia U., 1953. Fin. analyst Std. Oil of N.J., N.Y.C., 1956-59; mktg. rep. Esso Std., N.Y.C., 1959-61; mktg. economist Sinclair Refining Co., N.Y.C., 1961-64; dir. devel. and alumni rels. Wesleyan U., Middletown, Conn., 1965-84; pres. William K. Wasch Assocs., Middletown, 1985—. Builder accessible housing; host CPTV In Our Prime, 2004—05. Author: Home Planning for Your Later Years, 1996. Trustee Wesleyan U., Middletown, 1997-2000, Nat. Coun. on Aging, Inc., Washington, 1994-96, 98-2005, leadership coun., 2006-, host CPTV show, In Our Prime, 2005, Seabury Retirement Cmty., Bloomfield, Conn., 1984-2002; chair Middletown Sr. Affairs Comm., 1996-2002; alt. del. White House Conf. on Aging, 2005; host PBS Nat. Show In Our Prime, 2006. Lt. j.g. USNR, 1953-56. Mem. Hartford Club, Adelphic Ednl. Fund (sec., treas.), Am. Assn. for Support of Ecological Initiatives (sec., treas.), Phi Beta Kappa. Episcopalian. Avocation: squash. Home and Office: 150 Coleman Rd Middletown CT 06457-5065 Office Phone: 860-346-2967. Business E-Mail: wkwasch@snet.net.

**WASDEN, LAWRENCE,** state attorney general; m. Tracey Wasden; children: Sean, Ashley, Cassidy, Blake. B.A., BYU, 1982; JD, U. Idaho, 1985. Bar: Idaho 1985. Dep. pros. atty. Canyon County, Idaho; dep. atty. gen. Idaho State Tax Commn.; dep. chief of staff State of Idaho, Boise, chief of staff to atty. gen., atty. gen., 2003—. Mem.: Idaho State Bar (founding mem., immediate past chmn. govt. and pub. lawyers sect.). Republican. Office: Office Atty Gen PO Box 83720 700 W Jefferson St Boise ID 83720*

**WASENDORF, RUSSELL R., SR.,** brokerage house executive; Dir. pub. affairs Am. Soybean Assn.; head Wasendorf & Son Co., 1980—, Wasendorf & Assoc., Inc.; chmn., CEO Peregrine Fin. Group, Inc., 1980—. Founder Stocks, Futures and Options mag., 2001, Ctr. Futures Edn.; ptnr. Allen's New Am. Cafe, Chgo. Author: (books) Commody Trading: The Essential Primer, 1985, All About Futures From The Inside Out, 1992, All About Commodities From The Inside Out, 1992, All About Options from the Inside Out, 1992, All About Managed Futures From The Inside Out, 1993, The Complete Guide To Single Stock Futures, 2003. Office: PFG Inc 190 S LaSalle St 7th Fl Chicago IL 60603 Office Phone: 800-333-5673.*

**WASHBURN, DAVID THACHER,** lawyer; b. Claremont, NH, May 2, 1930; s. Walter Henry and Josephine Emmeline (Dana) W.; m. Joycemarie Springer, June 10, 1957 (div. Dec. 1975); children: Margaret Dana, David Thacher Jr., Robert Springer, John Putnam. BA, U. Vt., 1952; JD, NYU, 1955. Bar: N.Y. 1956, D.C. 1970, U.S. Supreme Ct 1970. From assoc. to ptnr. Paul, Weiss, Rifkind, Wharton & Garrison, N.Y.C., 1955—95, of counsel, 1996—. Adj. prof. CUNY Law Sch., 1997-98. Trustee Rye Neck Bd. Edn., Mamaroneck, N.Y., 1971-73, Cambridge (Mass.) Coll., 1980-88, The Yard, N.Y.C., 1986-95, ARIA Found., Inc., Williston, Vt., 1991—; trustee, mem. exec. com. Rare Ctr. for Tropical Conservation, Phila., 1979-80; dir. Sanctuary for Families, Inc., N.Y.C., 1994-2003, mem. exec. com., treas. 1995-2000. Mem. ABA, N.Y. State Bar Assn., Assn. of Bar of City of N.Y., The Coffee House, Westchester Country Club. Home: 10 W 66th St New York NY 10023-6206 Office: Paul Weiss Rifkind Wharton & Garrison Fl 2 1285 Ave of the Americas New York NY 10019-6064 Office Phone: 212-373-3301. Business E-Mail: dwashburn@paulweiss.com.

**WASHBURN, DONALD ARTHUR,** retired transportation executive, investor; b. Mankato, Minn., Sept. 24, 1944; s. Donald and Geraldine Helen (Pint) W.; m. Christine Carvell, Aug. 24, 1968; children: Timothy, Abigail. BBA cum laude, Loyola U., Chgo., 1971; MBA, Northwestern U., 1973, JD cum laude, 1978. Bar: Ill. 1978. With prodn. mgmt. dept. J.T. Ryerson/Inland Steel, Chgo., 1963-68; asst. to the pres. G.B. Frank, Inc., 1969-70; cons. Intec, Inc., 1970-72; mktg. mgmt., atty. Quaker Oats, Co., 1972-79; sr. cons. Booz, Allen & Hamilton, 1979-80; from corp. v.p. to exec. v.p. Marriott Corp., Washington, 1980-90; sr. v.p. N.W. Airlines, Mpls., 1990-94, exec. v.p. 1994-98; pres. emeritus N.W. Cargo, 1997—98; chmn. N.W. Aerospace Tng. Corp., 1996—98. Bd. dirs. LaSalle Hotel Properties, Greenbrier Cos., Inc., Key Tech., Inc., Amedisys, Inc., Draper & Kramer, Inc., LAGA, Inc., Victor Plastics, Inc., Paulson Oil Co., LAI Co., Inc.; law bd. Northwestern U., alumni adv. bd. Kellogg Grad. Sch.; adv. bd. Spell Capital Ptnrs. Fund II, LP, Fund III, LP. Contbr. articles to profl. jours. Mem. nat. bd. dirs. Stand for Children, Friends of the Children; bd. dirs. Portland Citizens Crime Commn., Citizens Common. on Homeless, Oreg. Bus. Assn., Stand for Children (nat. bd.); dir. emeritus Childrens Cancer Rsch. Fund. Mem.: ABA, Ill. Bar Assn., Alpha Sigma Nu, Beta Sigma Sigma. Unitarian Universalist.

**WASHBURN, GLADYS HAASE,** retired church musician, educator, director; b. San Antonio, Feb. 19, 1919; d. Henry August and Rosa Sophie (Sundermeyer) Haase; m. Jost Brainard Washburn, Dec. 29, 1942 (dec.); children: Yvonne Rosalind, Henry Brainard, Diane Louise. Tchg. cert. in piano/organ, St. Louis Coll. Music, 1940. Cert. piano St. Louis Coll. Music, 1940. Ch. pianist Friedens Evang. Ch., 1932—38; organist, choir dir. St. Martin's Ch., High Ridge, Mo., 1939—40; choir dir. Bethany Evang. and Ref. Ch., San Antonio, 1940—42, organist, choir dir. New Orleans, 1952—53, St. Paul's Evang. and Ref. Ch., Corpus Christi, Tex., 1944—51, Bethlehem United Ch. of Christ, Buffalo, 1964—70, First Congl. United Ch. of Christ, Dwight, Ill., 1970—72, St. Michael's Episcopal Ch., Independence, Mo., 1985—92; dir. jr. choir Bethlehem Evang. and Ref. Ch., Buffalo, 1956—61; interim organist, choir dir. St. Paul's and St. Marks Ch., Buffalo, 1963, Village United Ch. of Christ, Blue Springs, Mo., 1992—93; interim organist chs. Greater Kansas City area, 1993—97; ret., 1997. Cons. chs. seeking organists, Buffalo, Blue Springs, Mo. Organ recitalist S.W. Conf. Nat. PTA Meeting, San Antonio, 1941, 1942; accompanist Harlandale Sch. Dist., San Antonio, 1941, 1942. Recipient Cert. in Ministry in Music, United Ch. Christ, 1992. Mem.: Am. Guild Organists. Republican. United Ch. Of Christ. Avocations: sewing, cooking, reading. Home: 300 SW 19th Terr Blue Springs MO 64015

**WASHBURN, JERRY MARTIN,** accountant, corporate executive; b. Powell, Wyo., Dec. 31, 1943; s. Roland and Lavon (Martin) W.; divorced; children: Garth, Gavin, Kristina; m. Mary Scatterday. BS in Acctg., Brigham Young U., 1969. CPA, Wash., Idaho, Oreg. Staff acct. Arthur Andersen & Co., Seattle, 1969-70, from sr. auditor to audit mgr. Boise, Idaho, 1971—79; v.p. contr. Washburn Musicland, Inc., Phoenix, 1980-82; mgr., ptnr. Washburn Enterprises, Phoenix, 1977-90; pres. Total Info. Systems, Inc., Phoenix, 1984-90; v.p. KJ Mktg., Inc., Phoenix, 1990-91; dir. mktg. IPRO, Inc., Phoenix, 1991-94; assoc. Perfect Strategies, Inc., Phoenix, 1994—95; v.p., CFO Global Indsl. Products, Inc., Scottsdale, Ariz., 1995—96. Pres., CEO OneSource Techs., Inc., Scottsdale, 1996-2002, dir., chmn. 1999; ptnr. Tatum Ptnrs. LLP, 2002—; mng. mem. Ptnrs. Resource Mgmt., LLC, 2003-05; founding dir. Internat. and Commerce Bank, Phoenix, 1985-86; chmn. audit com. 1source Techs., 2000-03, AmeriFirst Found., 2004. Mem. AICPA, Inst. Internat. Auditors (pres. Boise chpt. 1974, bd. dirs. Boise and Portland chpts. 1975-77), Am. Mgmt. Soc., Wash. Soc. CPAs. Independent. Office: Tatum Partners LLP PO Box 25881 4800 N Scottsdale Rd Scottsdale AZ 85255 Personal E-mail: washburn3@cox.net. Business E-Mail: jerry.washburn@tatumpartners.com.

**WASHBURN, JOAN THOMAS,** small business owner; b. N.Y.C., Dec. 26, 1929; d. Frank B. and Josephine (Hartman) Thomas; m. Alan Lindsay Washburn, Sept. 26, 1953; children: Brian, Susan. BA, Middlebury Coll., Vt., 1951. Asst. Kraushaar Gallery, N.Y.C., 1951—53; dir. pub. rels. Wadsworth Atheneum, Hartford, Conn., 1953—55; dir. contemporary art Graham Gallery, N.Y.C., 1955—67; asst. Coorder-Ekstrom Gallery, N.Y.C., 1967—69; dir. Am. painting dept. Sotheby Parke-Bernet, N.Y.C., 1973—75; pres., dir. Washburn Gallery, N.Y.C., 1971—. Mem. Art Dealers Assn. (bd. dirs., v.p. 1991—) Home: 20 W 57th St New York NY 10019-3917 Office Phone: 212-397-6780. Personal E-mail: jwashburn@earthlink.net.

**WASHBURN, JOHN ROSSER,** entrepreneur; b. Hopewell, Va., July 24, 1943; s. Winthrop Doane and Mary Virginia (Overstreet) W.; m. Rebecca m. Wells, Sept. 1991; 1 child, Amanda Ashley Washburn; stepchildren: Eric Joseph Harrison, Leo M. Cicone, Suzann R. Weldon. Student, Louisburg Jr. Coll., 1963-64, U. Richmond Ext., 1967-69, Williams Coll., 1985, Stanford U., 1986-87. Asst. mgr. Liberty Loan Corp., Richmond, Va., 1965-67; loan interviewer Ctrl. Fidelity Bank, Richmond, Va., 1967-69; regional credit/sales supr. Moores Bldg Supplies, Inc., Roanoke, Va., 1969-74; corp. credit mgt. Owens & Minor, Inc., Richmond, 1974-88; fin., investment cons. JA-GO Enterprises, Richmond, 1982-98; prin. agt., owner Washburn Ins. and Fin. Svcs. Group, Richmond, 1996—2005. Instr., lectr. investment fin., credit mgmt. Washburn Enterprises, 1970—; sec.-treas. Multi-Enterprises, Inc., Richmond, 1988-98; indl. agt. N.Y. Life Ins. Co. Richmond, 1994-98; dir., v.p. Forbes Clin. Rsch. Group, Richmond, 1995-2005; exec. sr. v.p. E-Com Cons., Inc., Richmond, 1998—; charter mem., ptnr. Nations Bus. Cons. Group, Tysons Corner, Va., 1998-2003; pres., CEO Washburn & Assocs., 2003—; sr. v.p. Am. Wellness Alliance Immune Health Mgmt. Group LLC, 2005—. Active YMCA, 1979—, Am. Mus. Nat. History, 1982—, Nat. Rep. Congl. Com., 1980—, U.S. Def. Com., 1987—; info. svcs. officer, dept. homeland security, USCG Aux., 2005-; mem. Credit Rsch. Found. Mem. Internat. Platform Assn., Nat. Assn. Credit Mgmt. (Appreciation cert. for outstanding svc. 1980-81, pres. ctrl. Va. sect. 1979-80, chmn. legis. com.

1977-79, dir. 1983—), Am. Mgmt. Assn., Nat. Wildlife Fedn., Nat. Assn. Life underwriters (Nat. Quality award 1996, 97), Va. Assn. Life Underwriters, Am. Pharmacists Assn., Congressional Club, Hopewell Yacht Club. Episcopalian. Office: Washburn Enterprises PO Box 477 Dutton VA 23050-0477 Office Phone: 804-725-2614. Business E-Mail: jack@washburnandassociates.com.

**WASHBURN, PHOEBE,** artist; b. Poughkeepsie, NY, 1973; BFA cum laude, Newcomb Coll., Tulane U., New Orleans, 1996; MFA, Sch. Visual Arts, NYC, 2002. Exhibitions include Family, Radiance Gallery, Greensboro, 1997, Breakout, Rosetree Gallery, New Orleans, 1997, Artist's Eye, Greensboro Artists' League, NC, 1998, Tree, Silverwood St., Phila., 1999, Shape Things to Come, Forma Gallery, NYC, 1999, Integrated Aesthetics, SVA Satellite Gallery, Brooklyn, 2001, All You Can Eat, Visual Arts Gallery, NYC, 2002, Slice and Dice, 2004, Beginning Here: 101 Ways, 2004, Everyday Materials, Westside Gallery, NYC, 2002, DNA @ DNA, DNA Gallery, Provincetown, Mass., 2002, Art NY, kunstraume auf Zeit, Austria, 2002, Ctr. Curatorial Studies Mus., Bard College, 2003, Mixture Gallery, Houston, Tex., 2003, Rubbish, Cuchifritos, NYC, 2004, Weatherspoon Art Gallery, Milan, 2004, PS1, LI City, 2004, AIM 22: Artist in Marketplace, Bronx Mus., 2004, Make It Now, Sculpture Ctr., LI, 2005, Bench, Kunsthalle St. Gallen, Switzerland, 2005, Strange Architecture, Catherine Clark Gallery, San Francisco, 2005, Greater NY 2005, PS1, 2005, Makes for My Billionaire Status, Kantor, Feuer Gallery, LA, 2005, Has No Secret Surprise, UCLA, Hammer Mus., 2005, Kemper Mus., Kansas City, 2006, Studio Visit, Exit Art, NYC, 2006, Lipstick Bldg., 53rd and 3rd, NYC, 2006, one-woman shows include LFL Gallery, NYC, 2002, 2004, Rive U. Gallery, Houston, Tex., 2003, Faulconer Gallery, Grinnell U., IA, 2003, Ierimonti Gallery, Milan, 2004. Recipient Rusty Collier Meml. award in studio art, Tulane U., 1996, AAAL award, 2005. Office: c/o Zach Feuer Gallery 530 W 24th St New York NY 10011 Office Phone: 212-989-7700. Office Fax: 212-989-7720.*

**WASHBURN, STEWART PUTNAM,** management consultant; b. Claremont, N.H., Apr. 6, 1929; s. Walter Henry and Josephine (Dana) W.; m. Josephine F. Foster, Aug. 20, 1960 (dec. 1980); children: Patricia, Alice. BS in Commerce and Econs., U. Vt., 1951; MBA, Harvard U., 1953. Cert. comml. lender. V.p. Worcester County Nat. Bank, Worcester, Mass., 1955-74; v.p., sr. loan officer First Nat. Bank, New Bedford, Mass., 1974-77; sr. v.p., sr. loan officer Durfee Attleboro Bank, Fall River, Mass., 1977-90; mgmt. cons. in comml. lending Fall River and Dartmouth, Mass., 1990—. Dir. Bristol Workforce Investment Bd., Fall River, 1982—, chmn., 1987-99; dir. Southeastern Econ. Devel. Corp., Taunton, Mass., 1983—, treas., v.p., pres., 1995-98; dir. Jobs for Fall River 1981—, chair loan com. 1997—; mem. coun., mem. loan com. New Bedford Econ. Devel. Coun.; mem. town mtg., mem. fin. com. Dartmouth, Mass. With U.S. Army, 1953-55. Mem. Inst. Mgmt. Cons. (treas. New Eng. chpt. 1997-2001), Risk Mgmt. Assn. (life, bd. govs. N.E. chpt. 1973-75, chmn. credit policy roundtable 1989, Spl. Svc. award 1989). Avocations: bowling, gardening, fishing. Home and Office: 5 Middle St Dartmouth MA 02748-3427 Office Phone: 508-993-1044. Personal E-mail: spwashburn@verizon.net.

**WASHINGTON, ALLYN JARVIS,** writer; b. Manchester, Conn., July 15, 1930; s. Joseph Senior and Ruby Moore Washington; m. Mildred Irene Jones, June 7, 1958; 1 child, Joanne Washington Baron 1 stepchild, Margaret Ann Schroeder. BS, Trinity Coll., Hartford, Conn., 1953; ScM, Brown U., 1956. Instr. Trinity Coll., 1955—57, Boise (Idaho) Jr. Coll., 1957—58; prof. Dutchess C.C., Poughkeepsie, NY, 1958—79, acting exec. dean, 1974—75; textbook author Addison-Wesley pub., Boston, 1964—. Author: Basic Technical Mathematics with Calculus, 1964, 8th edit., 2005, Technical Calculus with Analytic Geometry, 1966, 4th edit., 2002, Introduction to Technical Mathematics, 1969, 4th edit., 1988. Sgt. U.S. Army, 1950—51. Allyn J. Washington Ctr. Sci. and Art bldg. named in his honor, Dutchess C.C., 2000. Mem.: NY State Math. Assn. Two Yr. Colls. (pres. 1974—75, award for exemplary svc. 1978), Math. Assn. Am., Am. Math. Assn. Two Yr. Colls., Phi Beta Kappa. Avocations: bridge, travel, stamp collecting/philately. Home and Office: 160 Starling Cir Grass Valley CA 95945 E-mail: allynjw@foothill.net.

**WASHINGTON, CECILE FERNANDO,** career planning administrator; m. Karen M. Mclean, Mar. 22, 1998; children: Jason M., Cecil F. BBA, Edward Waters Coll., Fla.; MS, Nova Southeastern U., Fla., 1998—2000. Cert. ednl. specialist Nova Southeastern U., 2002, Notary Fla. Sec. State, 2005. Career devel. coord. Fla. A&M U., Tallahassee, 2004—. Mem. com. Tallahassee & African Sister Cities Coalition, Inc., 2004. Mem.: Nat. Achievers Soc., Multimedia Ednl. Resource Learning & Online Tng., Nat. Assn. Colls. Employers, Fla. Career PA, Bros. Acad. Home: 3488 Barnstaple Dr Tallahassee FL 32317 Office: Fla A&M U Tallahassee FL 32307 Personal E-mail: cecilewashington@yahoo.com. Business E-Mail: cecile.washington@famu.edu.

**WASHINGTON, CLARENCE EDWARD, JR.,** insurance company executive; b. New Orleans, Nov. 20, 1953; s. Clarence Edward and Alice Mildred (Jones) W.; m. Denise Sandra Agard, June 29, 1985. BS cum laude, Xavier U., 1983. Mgr. Time Saver, Inc. New Orleans, 1972-79; budget, fin. analyst Equitable Life Assurance, N.Y.C., 1983-84; actuarial asst. Prudential Life Assurance, Newark, 1984-87; pension mgr. Am. Internat. Life, N.Y.C., 1987—. Mem. Am. Mus. Natural History (assoc.). Democrat. Roman Catholic. Office: Am Internat Life 80 Pine St Fl 13 New York NY 10005-1702

**WASHINGTON, DENNIS R.,** contracting company executive; b. Spokane, Washington, 1934; Equipment operator Guy F. Atkinson Co., Alaska; with King & McLaughlin Construction Co.; founder Washington Construction Co., Missoula, Mont., 1964; chmn., pres., CEO Morrison-Knudsen, 1999; chmn. Washington Group Internat., Inc. (formerly Morrison-Knudsen), Boise, Idaho. Founder Dennis & Phyllis Washington Found., 1998. Named one of Forbes' RIchest Americans, 2006; recipient Entrepreneurial award, Montana Ambassadors, Moles award outstanding achievement construction, Am. Soc. Civil Engineers, Lewis and Clark Pioneer award, Mont. Acad. Disting. Entrepreneurs, Golden Plate award, Acad. Achievement, Metal of Honor, Nat. Ethnic Coalition Organizations. Mem.: Horatio Alger Assn. (Norman Vincent Peale award), Am. Acad. Of Achievement. Office: Washington Group Internat Inc 720 Park Blvd Boise ID 83729 Mailing: The Dennis and Phyllis Washington Found PO Box 16630 Missoula MT 59808-6630 Office Phone: 208-386-5000. Office Fax: 208-386-7186.*

**WASHINGTON, DENZEL,** actor; b. Mt. Vernon, N.Y., Dec. 28, 1954; m. Pauletta Pearson, June 25, 1983; children: John David, Katia, Malcolm and Olivia. BA in Journalism, Fordham U.; student, Am. Conservatory Theatre, San Francisco. With N.Y. Shakespeare Festival, Manhattan Theatre Club, New Fed. Theatre. Actor: (stage prodns.) Coriolanus, 1979, Spell No. 7, The Mighty Gents, Richard III, One Tiger to a Hill, Ceremonies in Old Dark Men, When the Chicken Comes Home to Roost (Audelco award), A Soldier's Play (Obie award 1981), Checkmates, 1988, Split Second, Julius Caesar, 2005; (feature films) Carbon Copy, 1981, A Soldier's Story, 1981, Power, 1986, Cry Freedom, 1987, For Queen and Country, 1988, The Mighty Quinn, 1989, Glory, 1989 (Golden Globe award 1989, Acad. award 1990, NAACP Image award 1990), Heart Condition, 1990, Mo' Better Blues, 1990, Ricochet, 1991, Mississippi Masala, 1992, Malcolm X, 1992, Much Ado About Nothing, 1993, Philadelphia, 1993, The Pelican Brief, 1993, Crimson Tide, 1995, Virtuosity, 1995, Devil in a Blue Dress, 1995, Courage Under Fire, 1996 (NAACP Image award 1997), The Preacher's Wife, 1996, Fallen, 1998, He Got Game, 1998, The Siege, 1998, The Bone Collector, 1999, The Hurricane, 2000 (nominee Best Actor Acad. award 2000, Golden Globe award for Best Performance by Actor in Motion Picture Drama 2000), Remember the Titans, 2000, Training, Day, 2001 (Best Actor Acad. award 2002, nominee Golden Globe award for Best Performance by Actor in Motion Picture Drama 2002), John Q, 2002, Out Of Time, 2003, Man on Fire, 2004, The Manchurian Candidate, 2004, Inside Man, 2006; actor, dir. prodr. The Antwone Fisher Story, 2002; (TV Movies) Wilma, 1977, License to Kill, 1984, The George McKenna Story, 1986; (TV miniseries) Flesh and Blood, 1979; regular (TV series) St. Elsewhere, 1982-88. Spokesperson Boys and Girls Clubs Am.

Recipient Harvard Found. award, 1996; Am. Conservatory Theater scholar; named one of 50 Most Powerful People in Hollywood Premiere mag., 2002-06. Avocations: basketball, reading, cooking.*

**WASHINGTON, DONALD W.,** prosecutor; b. 1955; m. Yvonna Malonson; children: Tiffany, Greg, Donny. BS in Mech. Engring., U.S. Mil. Acad., 1977; JD, S. Tex. Coll. Law, 1989. Assoc. Alexander & McEvily, Houston, 1990—91; gen. litig. counsel Conoco Inc., 1993—96, div. counsel, Gulf of Mex. divsn., 1993—96; ptnr. Jeansonne and Redmondet, Lafayette, La., 1996—2001; U.S. atty. (we. dist.) La. US Dept. Justice, Shreveport, La., 2001—. U.S. Army, 1977—82 USAR, 1983—87. Office: US Attys Office 300 Fannin St Ste 3201 Shreveport LA 71101*

**WASHINGTON, ERIC T.,** judge; b. New Jersey, 1953; BA, Tufts U., 1976; JD, Columbia U. Sch. of Law, 1979. Assoc. Fulbright and Jaworski, Houston and Washington, 1979—82, 1985—87; legis. dir., counsel Rep. Michael Andrews, 1983—85; spl. corp. counsel Washington, 1987—88; prin. dep. corp. counsel, 1988—90; ptnr. Hogan & Hartson, Washington, 1990-95; judge Superior Ct., 1995—99, D.C. Ct. Appeals, 1999—2005, chief judge, 2005—. Former co-chair, strategic planning leadership council DC Courts; mem. Standing Com. on Fairness and Access to Courts, Access to Justice Commn. Mem.: DC Bar Assn. (mem. criminal justice act counsel for child abuse and neglect com., mem. standing com. on federal judiciary). Office: DC Ct Appeals 6th Fl 500 Indiana Ave NW Fl 6 Washington DC 20001-2138 E-mail: ewashington@dcca.state.da.us.*

**WASHINGTON, GARRETT LLOYD,** language educator; b. Kansas City, Mo., June 21, 1980; s. Larry Joseph and Ellie Jean Washington; m. Camille Ottombre, July 16, 2005. BA in Asian Studies, Rice U., 2002; M in History, U. of Paris VIII, 2004. Profl. rugby player Clube Desportivo do Universidade do Oporto, Porto, Portugal, 2002—03; instr. English Lycee Rene Cassin, Noisiel, Paris, 2003—04; teng. asst. Purdue U., West Lafayette, Ind., 2005—. Transl. dept. fgn. langs. and lits. Purdue U., West Lafayette, 2005—. Contbr. articles conf. papers to profl. jours. Mem.: Midwest Assn. of Interpreters and Transls., Am. Hist. Assn., N.W. Ind. Exiles Rugby Club (Newcomer of the Yr. 2004-2005). Office Phone: 765-496-1704.

**WASHINGTON, GLORIA DUNN,** secondary school educator; d. Percy and Eleanor McCoy Dunn; m. Leroy Roosevelt Washington; children: Cheryl Lynn Ford, Gloria Candacy, Daphne Dena Reddick. BA, Baber-Scotia Coll., 1966; MA, U. South Fla., 1978, Edn. Specialist, 1981. Tchr. Newfane Ctrl. Sch., NY, 1966—67, Auburndale H.S., Fla., 1976—97, North Ctrl. Adult Sch., Auburndale, 1980—88, Lakeland Sr. H.S., Fla., 1997—. Youth dir. St. Mark, Lakeland, Fla., 1985—; founder/sponsor Unified Culture Club, Lakeland, 1991—; co-chair English curriculum for English tchrs. Polk County, 1997. Editor: (poems) Polk County Poetry Contest Booklet; co-author: (curriculum) English Curriculum for North Central Adult School, 1984-1985. Chairperson adminstrv. coun. St. Mark United Meth. Ch., Lakeland, 1996—2004. Named English Tchr. Yr., Polk County Coun. Tchrs. English, 1995—96, 1999—2000, 2003—04, 2004—05. Mem.: Delta Kappa Gamma (pres. 1998—2000, Plague-Outstanding Pres. 2000), Phi Delta Kappa (publicity 2003—). St. Mark United Meth. Achievements include est. Peace and Unity Walk, 1999-. Avocations: reading, writing, playing the piano, collecting clocks. Office: Lakeland High School 726 Hollingsworth Rd Lakeland FL 33813 Office Fax: 863-499-2917. Personal E-mail: gjwash1@acninc.net. E-mail: gloria.washington@polk-fl.net.

**WASHINGTON, ISAIAH,** actor; b. Houston, Aug. 3, 1963; m. Jenisa Marie Washington, Feb. 14, 1999; 3 children. Attended, Howard U. Actor: (films) The Color of Love, 1991, Land Where My Fathers Died, 1991, Strictly Business, 1991, Alma's Rainbow, 1994, Crooklyn, 1994, Stonewall, 1995, Clockers, 1995, Girl 6, 1996, Dead Presidents, 1995, Get on the Bus, 1996, Love Jones, 1997, Mixing Nia, 1998, Bulworth, 1998, Rituals, 1998, Out of Sight, 1998, True Crime, 1999, A Texas Funeral, 1999, Veil, 2000, Romeo Must Die, 2000, Dancing in September, 2000, Kin, 2000, Tara, 2001, Exit Wounds, 2001, Sacred Is the Flesh, 2001, Welcome to Collinwood, 2002, Ghost Ship, 2002, Hollywood Homicide, 2003, This Girl's Life, 2003, Blood on a Happy Face, 2004, Wild Things 2, 2004, Dead Birds, 2004, Trois 3: The Escort, 2004, The Moguls, 2005, Step Up, 2006; guest appearances (TV series) Law & Order, 1991, Homicide: Life on the Street, 1994, Lifestories: Families in Crisis, 1994, NYPD Blue, 1995, New York Undercover, 1996, Living Single, 1996, High Incident, 1997, Ally McBeal, 1998, Soul Food, 2002, Touched by an Angel, 2001; actor: (TV films) Strapped, 1993, Mr. & Mrs. Loving, 1996, Soul of the Game, 1996, Joe Torre: Curveballs Along the Way, 1997, Always Outnumbered, 1998; (TV series) Grey's Anatomy, 2005— (Outstanding Actor in a Drama Series, NAACP Image Awards, 2006). Office: Gray's Anatomy / ABC-TV Los Feliz Tower, 4th Fl 4151 Prospect Ave Los Angeles CA 90027 also: c/o Innovative Artists 1505 10th St Santa Monica CA 90401*

**WASHINGTON, JAMES WINSTON, JR.,** artist, sculptor; b. Gloster, Miss., Nov. 10, 1909; s. James and Lizie (Howard) W.; m. Janie R. Miller, Mar. 29, 1943. Student, Nat. Landscape Inst., 1944-47; D.F.A., Center Urban-Black Studies, 1975. Tchr. summer class N.W. Theol. Union Seattle U., 1988. One man shows U.S.O. Gallery, Little Rock, 1943, Foster-White Gallery, Seattle, 1974, 78, 80, 83, 89 (also at Bellevue Art Mus., 89), Charles and Emma Frye Art Mus., Seattle, 1980, 95, Mus. History and Industry, Seattle, 1981; exhibited in group shows Willard Gallery, N.Y.C., 1960-64, Feingarten Galleries, San Francisco, 1958-59, Grosvenor Gallery, London, Eng., 1964, Lee Nordness Gallery, N.Y.C, 1962 Woodside Gallery, Seattle, 1962-65, Foster-White Gallery, Seattle, 1974, 76, 89, 92, Smithsonian Instn., 1974, San Diego, 1977, others; retrospective exhbn. Bellevue Art Mus., 1974, Wazhington 1989; represented in permanent collections Seattle, San Francisco, Oakland art museums, Seattle First Nat. Bank, Seattle Pub. Libr. YWCA, Seattle, Kinear Jr. H.S., Seattle World's Fair, Expo 70 Osaka, Japan, Whitney Mus. Am. Art, N.Y.C.; commd. sculpture: Bird With Covey, Wash. State Capitol Mus., Olympia, 1983, Obelisk with Phoenix and Esoteric Symbols of Nature in granite, Sheraton Hotel Seattle, 1982, Life Surrounding the Astral Alter, In Matrix, owner T.M. Rosenblume, Charles Z. Smith & Assocs., Seattle, 1986, The Oracle of Truth (6 1/2 ton sculpture) Mt. Zion Bapt. Ch., Seattle, 1987, commd. sculptures King County Arts Commn., 1989, Bailey Gatzent Elem. Sch., Seattle, 1991, Twin Eaglets of the Cosmic Cycle (Quincy Jones), 1993, Fountain of Triumph (Bangasser Assocs. Inc.), 1992-93, Seattle, 1993-94, 94-95, Child in Matrix, 1995, Blunt Tail Owl, 1996, Bunny Rabbit and Robbin, 1996; author book of poetry Poems of Life, 1997 (Internat. Hall of Fame Nat. Soc. Poets). Passover leader Mt. Zion Baptist Ch., Seattle, 1974-87; founder James W. Washington, Jr. and Mrs. Janie Rogella Washington Found. Recipient Spl. Commendation award for many contbns. to artistic heritage of state Gov., 1973, plaque City of Seattle, 1973, plaque Benefit Guild, Inc., 1973, arts service award King County Arts Commn., 1984, cert. of recognition Gov. of Wash., 1984, Editor's Choice award Outstanding Achievement in Poetry Nat. Libr. Poetry, 1993; named to Wash. State Centennial Hall of Honor, Wash. State Hist. Soc., 1984; home and studio designated historic landmark (city and state), 1991; Dr. James W. Washington Jr. and Mrs. Janie Rosella Washington Found. established, 1997. Mem. Internat. Platform Assn., Internat. Soc. Poets (life, awards 1993), Profl. Artists Phila., Masons (33d degree). Home: 1816 26th Ave Seattle WA 98122-3110

**WASHINGTON, KAREN,** librarian, educator; b. Spanishtown, St. Catherine, Jamaica, Jan. 4, 1971; d. Louis and Patricia Mclean; m. Cecile Washington, May 23, 1998; children: Jason Moore, Cecil. BS, Nova Southeastern U., Florida, 1995—97, MS, 1998—2000, Degree in Ednl. Specialist, 2001—02. Cert. tchr. Fla., 1998, Ga., 2003. Libr. Fla. A&M U., Tallahassee, 2004—. Bd. dirs Tallahassee and African Sister Cities Coalition, Inc., 2004. 3M Tech. grant, AASL, 2004. Mem.: PDK. Home: 3488 Barnstaple Dr Tallahassee FL 32317 Home Fax: 850-877-6107. Personal E-mail: kmmwash@yahoo.com. Business E-mail: karen.washington@famu.edu.

**WASHINGTON, KERRY,** actor; b. Bronx, NY, Jan. 31, 1977; BFA theatre, George Washington Univ., 1998. Actor: (TV films) Magical Make-Over, 1994; (films) Our Song, 2000, 3D, Save the Last Dance, 2001, Lift, 2001, Take the A Train, Bad Company, 2002, United States of Lelan, 2003, The Human Stain, 2003, Sin, 2003, Against the Ropes, 2004, Strip Search, 2004, She Hate Me, 2004, Ray, 2004, Sexual Life, 2005, Mr. & Mrs. Smith, 2005, Fantastic Four, 2005, Wait, 2005, Little Man, 2006. Nominee Best Female Actress, Ind. Spirit Awards, 2002.*

**WASHINGTON, LAWRENCE J., JR.,** chemicals executive; BSChemE, MSChemE, U. Detroit. Mgr. environ. svcs. Dow Chem. Co., Midland, Mich., 1980—87, gen. mgr. western divsn. Pittsburgh, Calif., 1987—90, v.p. Dow North Am. Midland, Mich., 1990—94, corp. v.p. human resources rep., 1994—, corp. v.p. environ., health & safety, and pub. affairs, 1997—. Served for four years USAF. Mem.: Univ. Detroit Mercy (advisory bd. mem.), Mich. Tech. Univ. (advisory bd. mem.), Chem. Bank & Trust Co. (bd. dirs.), Dorinco Reinsurance Co. (bd. dirs.), Liana Ltd. (bd. dirs.).

**WASHINGTON, MALIVAI,** retired professional tennis player, foundation administrator; b. Glen Cove, NY, June 20, 1969; Student, U. Mich. Pres. MaliVai Washington Found., Jacksonville, Fla. Winner Fed. Express Internat., Memphis, 1992, US Clay Cts. Championships, Charlotte, NC, 1992, Australian Open, 1994, Ostrava Open, Czech Republic, 1994, XL Bermuda Open, 1996; finalist Wimbledon, England, 1996; mem. US Davis Cup Team, 1993, 96, 97. Named One of 50 Most Beautiful People in World, People Mag., 1994; recipient Rookie of Yr. award, Tennis Mag., 1990, Leadership Award, Arthur Ashe Athletic Assn., 1998, Otis Smith Civic Award, Fla. Sports Awards, 2001. Achievements include Named All-American NCAA, 1988-89; ranked 6th, US Tennis Assn., 1993; ranked 177th, 1999; represented US Olympic team in singles and doubles, Atlanta, 1996. Office: MaliVai Washington Found 2933 N Myrtle Ave Ste 101 Jacksonville FL 32209

**WASHINGTON, MARCEL MAURICE,** statistician, researcher; b. Paterson, NJ, July 6, 1978; s. Daphne Pines. Cert., DeVry Inst., North Brunswick, N.J., 1999. Priority client rep. Merrill Lynch, Pierce Fenner & Smith, Ewing, NJ, 1999—2002; team lead N.J. Pub. Interest Rsch. Group, New Brunswick, NJ, 2003—. CEO Mozaic Entertainment, 2003. Actor: (films) Midnight, 2003; author: Tiny the Turtle & Friends, 2005. CEO Found. Estates & Culture, 2004. Avocation: kickboxing. Home and Office: 652 Johnstone St Perth Amboy NJ 08861

**WASHINGTON, MARCUS D.,** history educator; b. Dayton, Ohio, Oct. 28, 1951; m. Marcia B. Gober, July 17, 2000; 1 child, Eric Collier. BS, Knoxville Coll., 1973. Tchr. Osborne HS, Marietta, Ga., 1998—. Mem. Ben Hill United Meth. Ch.

**WASHINGTON, MICHELE,** educational consultant; BA in Edn., Capitol U., 1978, MA in Edn. and Counseling, 1993. Instr., counselor, reading tutor Oakland Cmty. Jr. Coll., St. Louis, 1975—88; counselor student career planning, advisement, sexual harassment, tchr. Dallas Ind. Sch. Dist., 1988—90; instr. Dallas CC Dist., 1990—99; owner Elehcims Art Works, Lewisville, Tex., 2000—. Spkr., presenter in field. Bd. dirs. YWCA, Womens Halfway House; program devel. com. Pheonix House. Mem.: ASTD.

**WASHINGTON, REGINALD LOUIS,** pediatric cardiologist; b. Colorado Springs, Colo., Dec. 31, 1949; s. Lucius Louis and Brenette Y. (Wheeler) W.; m. Billye Faye Ned, Aug. 18, 1973; children: Danielle Larae, Reginald Quinn. BS in Zoology, Colo. State U., 1971; MD, U. Colo., 1975. Diplomate Nat. Bd. Med. Examiners, Am. Bd. Pediat., Pediatric Cardiology. Intern U. Colo. Med. Ctr., Denver, 1975—76, resident in pediat., 1976-78, chief resident, instr., 1978-79, fellow in pediatric cardiology, 1979-81, from asst. prof. pedit. to assoc. clin. prof. pediat., 1982—2005, clin. prof. pediat., 2005—; staff cardiologist Children's Hosp., Denver, 1981-90; v.p. We. Cardiology Assocs., Divsn. for Fetal, Pediatric and Adult Congential Heart Disease, Denver, 1990—2004; med. dir. Rocky Mountain Pediatrix Cardiology, Denver, 2004—; chief of staff Presbyn./St. Lukes Med. Ctr., 1999-2001. Admissions com. U. Colo. Sch. Medicine, Denver, 1985-89; chmn., bd. dirs. Coop. Health Care Agreements, 1994-98; chmn. dept. pediatrics Presbyn./St. Lukes Med. Ctr, Denver, 1996-99, 2003-05, pres.-elect med. staff, 1997-99, chmn. ethics com., 2003-06; adv. coun. Nat. Heart Lung Blood Inst., NIH, 1996-986 Cons. editor Your Patient and Fitness, 1989-92; mem. editl. bd. Jour. Pediats., 2004—. Chmn. Coop. Health Care Agreements Bd., State of Colo., 1994-98; adv. bd. dirs. Equitable Bank of Littleton, Colo. 1984-86; bd. dirs. Rocky Mountain Heart Fund for Children, 1984-89, Rainbo Ironkids, 1989-95, Ctrl. City Opera, 1989-95, Cleo Parker Robinson Dance Co., 1992-94, Nat. Coun. Patient Info. and Edn., 1992-98, Children's Heart Alliance, 1993-94, Colo. State U. Devel. Coun., 1994-2003, Caring for Colo. Found., 1999-2001; nat. bd. dirs. Am. Heart Assn., 1992-96; trustee Denver Ctr. Performing Arts, 1994—, Regis U., 1994-99; mem. Gov.'s Coun. Phys. Fitness, 1990-91; bd. govs. Colo. State U., 1996-2004, pres., 2001-03; trustee Colo. Trust, 2002-; trustee Helen Bonfils Found., 2003—. Recipient William E. Morgan Alumnus Achievement award Colo. State U., 2004, Cardiologist of Yr., HCA, 2004; named Salute Vol. of Yr. Big Sisters of Colo., 1990; honoree NCCJ, 1994, Physician of Yr., Nat. Am. Heart Assn., 1995. Fellow Am. Acad. Pediat. (cardiology subsect., chmn. sports medicine and fitness com. 2000-2004, chmn. task force on obesity 2003—), Am. Coll. Cardiology, Am. Heart Assn. (coun. on cardiovasc. disease in the young, exec. com. 1988-91, nat. devel. program com. 1990-94, vol. of yr. 1989, pres. Colo. chpt. 1989-90, Torch of Hope 1987, Gold Heart award Colo. chpt. 1990, bd. dirs. Colo. chpt., exec. com. Colo. chpt. 1987-2000, grantee Colo. chpt. 1983-84, mem. editl. bd. Pediat. Exercise Scis. 1988-2002), Soc. Critical Care Medicine; mem. Am. Acad. Pediat. Perinatology, Am. Acad. Pediat./Pediat. Cardiology (exec. com. 1996-2001), N.Am. Soc. Pediat. Exercise Medicine (pres. 1986-87), Colo. Med. Soc. (chmn. sports medicine coun. 1993-94), Leadership Denver 1990, Glenmoor Golf Club. Democrat. Roman Catholic. Avocations: golf, fishing. Office: Rocky Mountain Pediat Cardiology 10103 Ridgegate Pkwy Ste 107 Lone Tree CO 80124 Office Phone: 303-860-9933. E-mail: rlwash@aol.com.

**WASHINGTON, STROTHER LEE, JR.,** mechanical engineer, design engineer; b. Charlottesville, Va., Feb. 9, 1952; s. Strother Lee and Peachie Frances Washington; m. Lillian Juanita Young, May 20, 1978; 1 child, Keyana Latrice. BSME, U. Va., 1974; MS, Johns Hopkins U., 1979. From prin. engr. to mech. design mgr. Northrop Grumman, Annapolis, Md., 1990—98, mech. engring. mgr., 1999—. Mentor Worthy, Balt., 1998—; coach Amatuer Athletic Union, Balt., 1990—; asst. track coach Bowie (Md.) State U., 1998—2000. Recipient Outstanding Svc. award, United Way, 1995. Mem.: ASME, Am. Design Drafting Assn., Nat. Soc. Black Engrs., Alpha Phi Alpha. Democrat. Baptist. Achievements include invention of modular bouyant fairing panel, translating desktop assembly, connector saver for anphenol connector. Avocations: photography, Antique tools, sports, music, auto restoration. Home: 2085 Ingleside Ct Crofton MD 21114 Office: Northrop Grumman Aviation Blvd Gate 1 Baltimore MD 21203

**WASHINGTON, WARREN MORTON,** meteorologist; b. Portland, Oreg., Aug. 28, 1936; s. Edwin and Dorothy Grace (Morton) W.; m. LaRae Herring, July 30, 1959 (div. Aug. 1975); children: Teri, Kim, Marc (dec.), Tracy; m. Jona Ann, July 3, 1978 (dec. Jan. 1987); m. Mary Elizabeth Washington, Apr., 1995. BS in Physics, Ore. State U., 1958, MS in Meteorology, 1960; PhD in Meteorology, Pa. State U., 1964; degree (hon.), Oreg. State U., 2006. Dir. of climate and global dynamics div. Nat. Center Atmospheric Research, Boulder, Colo., 1978-95; affiliate prof. meteorology oceanography U. Mich. at Ann Arbor, 1968-71; mem. Nat. Adv. Com. for Oceans and Atmospheres, 1978-84. Mem. sec. of energy adv. bd. U.S. Dept. Energy, 1990-93. Contbr. articles to meteorol. jours. Mem. Boulder Human Relations Commn., 1969-71; mem. Gov.'s Sci. Adv. Com., 1975-78. Recipient Disting. Alumni award Oreg. State U., 1991, E.B. Lemon Disting. Alumni award Pa. State U., 1991, Le Verrier medal Soc. Meteorol. France, 1995, Bonfils-Stanton Found. award, 2000, Vollum award Reed Coll., 2005; inductee NAS portrait collection African Am. in Sci., Engring., and Medicine, 1997; named Sigma Xi Disting. lectr.,

1998-99. Fellow AAAS (bd. dirs.), Am. Meteorol. Soc. (pres. 1994, Anderson award 2000); mem. NAE, Am. Philosophy Soc., Am. Geog. Union, Nat. Sci. Bd. (chmn. 2002-06). Home: 725 Pinehurst Ct Louisville CO 80027-3285 Office: PO Box 3000 Boulder CO 80307-3000

**WASHKEWICZ, DONALD E.,** manufacturing executive; b. Cleve. m. Pam Washkewicz; children: Dawn, Tiffany, Bryan. BME, Cleve. State U., 1972; MBA, Case Western Res. U., Cleve., 1979. Lic. profl. engr., OH. With Parker Hannifin Corp., Cleve., 1972—, from engr. to gen. mgr. Parflex Divsn., 1972—82, v.p. ops. fluid connectors group, 1994-97, v.p., pres. hydraulics group, 1997-2000, COO, 2000—01, pres., 2000—, CEO, chmn., 2001—. Bd. Mfr. Alliance/MAPI. Bd. Greater Cleve. Growth Assn., Cleve. Tomorrow. Recipient Disting. Alumni Award, Cleve. State U., 2002, Ellis Island Medal Honor, 2003. Mem.: Nat. Assn. Mfr., Nat. Soc. Profl. Engr. Office: Parker Hannifin Corp 6035 Parkland Blvd Cleveland OH 44124-4141*

**WASICK, MARY ANN,** retired librarian; b. Milw., July 19, 1946; d. Julius John and Florence Elizabeth (Brockway) W. BS in Edn., U. Wis., Milw., 1969; MA in Libr. Sci., U. Wis., Oshkosh, 1972; postgrad., U. Wis., 1969—. Tchr., libr. Milw. Pub. Schs., 1969-71; administry. grad. asst. U. Wis., Oshkosh, 1971-72; libr. West Allis (Wis.) Pub. Libr., 1972—2001. Reviewer in field. Bd. dirs. West Allis Hist. Soc., 1991-93; publicity chair Fountain Art Fair West Allis Art Alliance, 1991. Mem.: Honeybee Quilters (pres. 2004), Am. Classical League, U. Wis. Milw. Alumni Assn. (life), U. Wis.-Oshkosh Alumni Assn. (life), Wis. Quilters Inc., Embroiderer's Guild Am. (program chmn. 1989—90, pres. Greater Milw. chpt. 2003, pres. Badger chpt. 2005). Avocations: quilting, embroidery, collecting depression glass, travel, art shows. Home: 1310 S 98th St West Allis WI 53214-2641

**WASIK, BARBARA HANNA,** psychologist, educator; b. Douglas, Ga., May 29, 1942; d. Frank Joseph and Josephine (Nahoom) Hanna; m. John L. Wasik, June 24, 1966; children—John Gregory, Mark Timothy, Joseph Jr. AB, U. Ga., 1963; MA, Fla. State U., 1965, PhD, 1967. Lic. psychologist, N.C. Postdoctoral research fellow Duke U., Durham, N.C. 1967-68; dir. research Ford Found. grant, Durham, NC, 1968-69; from asst. prof. to assoc. prof. U. N.C., Chapel Hill, 1969-77, prof., 1977—; William R. Kenan Jr. disting. prof., 2003—, assoc. dean Grad. Sch., 1972-75, chmn. div. human devel. and psychol. services, 1975-77, assoc. dean Sch. Edn., 1977-83, 1988—92, sr. investigator Child Devel. Ctr., 1972—. Mem. commn. NAS, 1998—2000; co-facilitator Nat. Forum Home Visiting, 1999—. Assoc. editor Jour. Applied Behavior Analysis, 1972; mem. editorial bd. Behavioral Assessment, 1984-85; contbr. chpts. to books and articles to profl. jours. Mem. N.C. Psychological Assn. (sec. 1982-85, pres. 1988-89), Am. Psychol. Assn. (divsn. 25 sec-treas. 1983-86, coun. rep. 1994-99, bd. edn. affairs 1999-2001, chair bd edn. affairs 2001), Soc. Research in Child Development, Southeastern Psychol. Assn., Assn. Advancement Behavior Therapy. Democrat. Roman Catholic. Home: 609 Brookview Dr Chapel Hill NC 27514-1402

**WASKO-FLOOD, SANDRA JEAN,** artist, educator; b. NYC, Mar. 12, 1943; d. Peter Edmund and Margaret Dalores (Kubek) Wasko; m. Michael Timothy Flood, June 28, 1969. BA, UCLA, 1965, postgrad., 1968-69, Calif. State U., Northridge, summer 1968; student, Otis Art Inst., L.A., 1969, Marie Kaufman, Rio de Janeiro, 1970-72, Museo de Arte Moderno, 1970-73, Foothill Coll., Los Altos, Calif., 1973-74, Claremont (Calif.) Coll., 1975, U. Wis., Janesville, 1977, Beloit (Wis.) Coll., 1977-78, U. Wis., 1977-78; grad. etching student, Warrington Colescott. Instr. printmaking Washington Women's Arts Ctr., 1983; artist-in-residence U. Md., College Park, 1985; instr. printmaking Arlington (Va.) Arts Ctr., 1984-85; prof. St. Mary's (Md.) Coll., 1985; instr. printmaking Arlington County Lee Arts Ctr., 1989-97; workshop coord. cultural affairs div. Arlington County Cultural Affairs, 1989-97; printmaking instr. Home Studio, Alexandria, Va., 1987—; founder, pres. Living Labyrinths Peace, Inc., 2005—. Condr. workshops Washington Performing Arts Soc., 2002—; founder, pres., bd. dirs. Living Labyrinths for Peace, Inc., 2005—. One woman shows include Wisconsin Women in the Arts Gallery, Madison, 1977, Mbari Art, Washington, 1981, Miya Gallery, Washington, 1981, Slavin Gallery, Washington, 1982, Stuart Mott House, Washington, 1983, Washington Printmakers Gallery, 1986, 88, 91, St. Peter's Ch., N.Y.C., 1989, Montana Gallery, Alexandria, Va., 1991, Montpelier Cultural Arts Ctr., Laurel, Md., 1992, Gallery 10, Washington, 1994, 96, Sch. 33, Balt., 1996; mus. and internat. shows include Boston Printmakers: The 39th North Am. Print Exhbn., Framingham, Mass., Jan.-Mar., 1986, Internat. Graphic Arts Found. and Silvermine Guild Arts Ctr., New Canaan, Conn., Feb., 1988, Prints: Washington, The Phillips Collection, Washington, Sept.-Oct., 1988, Contemporary Am. Graphics, Book Chamber Internat., Moscow, 1990, Gallery 10 Artists of Washington D.C. Vartai Gallery, Lithuania, 1994, Peninsula Fine Arts Ctr., Newport News, Va., 1995-96, Riva Sinistra Arte, Florence, Italy, 1997, Contemporary Art Ctr. Va., Virginia Beach, 2000, Charles Sumner Sch. Mus., Washington, D.C., 2001, numerous others; juried shows include Washington Women's Arts Ctr.: Printmakers VII show, 1985, Washington Women's Arts Ctr., 1981, 82, Seventh Ann. Faber Birren Color Show Nat. Juried Open Exhibit, Stamford, Conn., 1987, Acad. of the Arts 25th Ann. Juried Exhbn., 1989, Fla. Printmakers Nat., 1994, S.W. Tex. State U., 1995, Peninsula Fivie Arts Ctr., Newport News, Va., 1998, Washington Women Artists, Women's Caucus for Art, 2001, Rockville Art Place, Md., 2002, Internat. Photography, 2003, and numerous others; invitational shows include Office of the Mayor, Mini Art Gallery, Washington, "Glimpses: Women Printmakers", 1981, Pyramid Paperworks, Balt., 1984, Gallery 10 "Nightmare Show": Washington, D.C., 1987, The Intaglio Process, The Benedicta Art Ctr. Gallery, St. Joseph, Minn., 1988, Women's Caucus for Art, Washington Artists in Perspective, Westbeth Gallery, N.Y.C., 1990, 91, Wesley Theol. Sem., 1992, Balt. City Hall, N.Am. Print Alliance, 1993, The Five Elements Women's Caucus For Art, 1994, WPA/Corcoran Auction, 1999, Washington Theological Union, Washington, 1999, Cannon Rotunda, U.S. House of Reps., Washington, 2000, Charles Sumner Sch. Mus., Washington, 2001, Washington Women Artists Marching into the Millennium, Women's Caucus for Art, 2001, Anne C. Fisher Gallery, Wash., 2005 and numerous others; galleries: Slavin Gallery, Washington, D.C., 1981-83, Washington Printmakers Gallery, Washington, 1985-96, White Light Collaborative, N.Y.C., 1988-89, Montana Gallery, Alexandria, Va., 1989-91, Gallery 10, Washington, 1992-97, Charleuoix Gallery, Albuquerque, NM, 1999, and numerous others; collections include Nat. Mus. of Women in the Arts, Washington, Corcoran Gallery of Art, Washington, Museo de Arte Moderno, Buenos Aires, Cultural Found., USSR, Coll. Notre Dame, Balt., Potomac Hosp., Woodbridge, Md.; dir. Labyrinths for Peace 2000, U.S. Capitol, 2002; featured artist Kali Guide: A Directory of Resources for Women, 2d reprint, 2002. Pres. Washington Area Printmakers, Washington, D.C., 1985-86; pub. rels. dir. Washington Women's Arts Ctr., 1980; bd. dirs. Washington Women's Arts Ctr., 1981-82; program chair D.C. chpt. Women's Caucus for Art, 1998—; founding mem. the Labyrinth Soc., 1998-; spl. projects dir. Labyrinth Soc., 2000; cons. Labyrinth Making and Products. Recipient Award of Honorable Mention Nat. Gallery of Art, 1989, Best of Show, Artists Equity Exhibit, Gallery 901, Washington, 1997; grantee Friends of the Torpedo Factory Art Ctr., Alexandria, Va., 1989, DC Commn. on Arts and Humanities Summer Edn. and Sports Program Artist in Schs., 2000, 01, 05, Wash. Performing Arts Soc., 2002-06; individual artists fellow Va. Commn. for Arts, 1990. Mem.: Arts/Sci. Collaborative, Inc. (N.Y.C.), Artists Using Sci. and Tech. (San Francisco), YLEM, The Labyrinth Soc., Washington Sculpture Group, Am. Print Alliance, Md. Printmakers, Women's Caucus for Art, So. Graphics Coun., Pyramic Atlantic, Nat. Print Orgn., Corcoran Gallery/Washington Project for the Arts. Avocations: classical music, hiking, reading. Studio: Living Labyrinths Peace Ctr 57 N St NW Washington DC 20001-1254 Home: 2229 Lake Ave Baltimore MD 21213-1015 Office Phone: 703-217-6706. Personal E-mail: waskoart@cox.net.

**WASMER, CARMENIA ANN,** language educator; b. White Plains, N.J., Sept. 23, 1934; d. Peter and Catherine (Chioma) Medure; m. John David Wasmer, Apr. 12, 1958; children: Michael, Christopher. BA with honors, Douglass Coll., 1956; MLS, Rutgers U., New Brunswick, N.J., 1966; MA, William Paterson Coll., 1982. Cert. ESL tchr., English, French, Spanish tchr., reading specialist, ednl. media specialist, profl. libr., N.J.; cert. braillist ARC.

Tchr. Spanish and French Bergenfield (N.J.) High Sch., 1956-61; River Dell Jr.-Sr. High Sch., Oradell, N.J., 1961-62; sch. libr. Holdrum Sch., Rivervale, N.J., 1964-67; part-time libr. Ridgewood (N.J.) Libr., 1971—2003; ESL tchr. Westwood (N.J.) Regional Schs., 1980—98. Adj. instr. ESL, Bergen Community Coll., Paramus, N.J., 1988—; coord. ESL tchr. intern program Fairleigh Dickinson U., Teaneck, N.J., 1991. Active ARC, Ridgewood, N.J., 1973-76; chmn. PTO, Paramus, 1975-78; leader Cub Scouts, Paramus, 1975-77; vol. Cath. Charities, Paramus, 1975-76, Literacy Vols. Am., 1998—; pres. bd. dirs. Sipporta Village Coop., Inc., 2001—. Leopold Schepp Found. scholar, N.Y.C., 1953, 54, 55. Mem. NEA, N.J. Edn. Assn., Bergen County Edn. Assn., Westwood Edn. Assn. (chair philanthropic fund 1992-98), N.J. Bilingual/ESL Tchrs. Assn., Beta Phi Mu, Kappa Delta Pi, Pi Lambda Theta. Avocations: travel, reading. Home: 189 Forest Ave # 313 Paramus NJ 07652-5325

**WASMER, PEDRO E.,** technology leasing company executive; b. Santiago, Cuba, 1940; Grad., Balt. Poly. Inst., 1958; BS in civil engring., U. Md., 1962; M in Latin Am. Studies, Am. U., 1964. Positions in civil engring., 1962—64; positions with IBM, Honeywell, 1964—74; joined DPF, Inc., 1974; founder Somerset Investment Services, 1980, St. James Leasing, Ltd., 1989; founder, CEO Somerset Capital Group, Ltd., 1996—. Bd. dirs. Bridgeport Regional Bus. Coun. Bd. dirs. Coun. Churches of Bridgeport, U. Md. Found. Inc.; bd. visitors U. Md. Clark Sch. Engring. Mem.: Equipment Leasing Assn. (bd. dirs.). Office: Somerset Capital Group Ltd Ste 301 1087 Broad St Bridgeport CT 06604 Office Phone: 203-394-6182. Office Fax: 203-394-6192. E-mail: pedro.wasmer@somersetcapital.com.*

**WASMUTH, CARL ERWIN,** retired physician, lawyer; b. Pitts., Feb. 16, 1916; s. Edwin Hugo and Mary Blanche (Love) W.; m. Martha Conn., Aug. 25, 1939; children: Carl Erwin; m. Gertrude White Ruth, June 19, 1984; m. Wilhelmina Waterman Devine, May 12, 1990. BS, U. Pitts., 1935, MD, 1939; LLB, Cleve.-Marshall Law Sch., 1959. Diplomate Am. Bd. Anesthesiology. Bar: Ohio 1959. Intern Western Pa. Hosp., Pitts., 1939-40; fellow anesthesiology Cleve. Clinic Found., 1949-51, mem. emeritus staff, 1976—; pvt. practice medicine Dry Run, Pa., 1942-45, Scottdale, Pa., 1945-49; mem. dep. anesthesia Cleve. Clinic, 1951—, head dept., 1967-69; asso. prof. law Cleve.-Marshall Law Sch., 1959-66; adj. prof. Cleve. Marshall Law Sch., 1966-73. Author: Anesthesia and the Law, 1961, Law for the Physician, 1966, Law and the Surgical Team, 1968; Editor: Legal Problems in the Practice of Anesthesiology, 1973; contbg. editor: Hale's Anesthesiology; editorial bd.: Med. World News; Contbr. articles to profl. jours. Trustee Cleve.- Marshall Law Sch., chmn., 1969-71; bd. dirs. Scottdale Hosp. Found; chmn. bd. govs. Cleve. Clinic, 1969-71; trustee Cleve. Clinic Found., 1969-76, v.p., 1973-76; trustee Cleve. Clinic Edni. Found., 1969-76, v.p., 1973-76; chmn. bd. trustees, pres. Cleve. Marshall Ednl. Found., 1972-81; bd. overseers Coll. Law, Cleve. State U., 1972-76; vis. com. Coll. Law, Case-Western Res. U., 1973-76; trustee United Torch Svcs.; hon. trustee Tucson Symphony Soc., 1983-84, 88; trustee Santa Cruz Med. Found., 1977, pres., 1978; bd. govs. Ohio World Trade Center; trustee Cancer Center Cleve., Ohio Coll. Podiatric Medicine, 1976, Am. Coll. Legal Medicine Research Found., 1984—; mem. U. Ariz. Found., 1978, World Congress Med. Law, 1967—, Keynoter 3d World Congress, 1971; sec. Commn. Med. Malpractice, HEW, 1972-73; vestryman St. Francis-in-the-Valley Episcopal Ch., Green Valley, 1990-93. Named Distinguished Eagle Scout Nat. Council Boy Scouts Am., 1977; named Outstanding Citizen Eagle Cuyahoga council, 1976; Citizen of Year Cleve. Area Bd. Realtors, 1976 Fellow: ACP, Law Sci. Acad., Am. Coll. Chest Physicians, Am. Coll. Legal Medicine (pres. bd. govs. 1966—69), Am. Coll. Anesthesiologists; mem.: ABA, AAAS, AMA, NRC, Cleve. Bar Assn., Cuyahoga County Bar Assn., Ohio Bar Assn., Transplantation Soc. (charter) Cleve. Acad. Medicine, Com. Cadaver Utilization, Nat. Acad. Sci., N.Y. Acad. Scis., Ohio Med. Assn., Acad. Anesthesiology (chmn. program com. 1967), World Fedn. Anesthesiologists (vice chmn. Am. del. 1967), Internat. Anesthesia Rsch. Soc., Cleve. Soc. Anesthesiologists (pres. 1963), Ohio Soc. Anesthesiologists (dir. 1960—69), Am. Soc. Anesthesiologists (dir., pres. 1968, spkr. ho. of dels.), Ariz. Sr. Acad., Gainey Ranch Golf Club (Scottsdale), Old Pueblo Club, The Lakes Club, Mt. Kenya Safari Club (Nanyuki, Kenya), Pleasant Valley Country Club, Tucson Club, Country Club of Green Valley, Lions (past pres. local clubs), Masons, Delta Theta Phi, Phi Rho Sigma. E-mail: cwasmuth@cox.net.

**WASOW, OMAR,** Internet company executive; BA in Race and Ethnic Rels., Stanford U., Calif., 1992. Coord. voter registration Freedom Summer '92, 1992; asst. dir. Strictly Bus., 1992—93; founder, owner New York Online, 1993—; internet analyst NewsChannel4, NYC, 1995—; exec. dir. BlackPlanet.com at Community Connect, NYC, 1999—. Co-chair Coalition for Ind. Pub. Charter Schs.; bd. dirs. N.Y. Software Indusry Assn., World-Studio, The Refugee Project. Fellow Next Generation Leadership program, Rockefeller Found. Office: NBC 30 Rockefeller Plz New York NY 10112 also: BlackPlanet (dot) com Community Connect 205 Hudson St New York NY 10013*

**WASS, HANNELORE LINA,** educational psychology educator; b. Heidelberg, Germany, Sept. 12, 1926; came to U.S., 1957, naturalized, 1963; d. Hermann and Mina (Lasch) Kraft; m. Irvin R. Wass, Nov. 24, 1959 (dec.); 1 child, Brian C.; m. Harry H. Sisler, Apr. 13, 1978. BA, Tchrs. Coll., Heidelberg, 1951; MA, U. Mich., 1960, PhD, 1968. Tchr. W. Ger. Univ. Lab. Schs., 1958-60; mem. faculty U. Mich., Ann Arbor, 1958-60, U. Chgo. Lab. Sch., 1960-61, U. Mich., 1963-64, Eastern Mich. U., 1965-69; prof. ednl. psychology U. Fla., Gainesville, 1969-92, prof. emeritus, 1992—, faculty assoc. Ctr. for Gerontol. Studies Gainesville. Cons., lectr. in thanatology. Author: The Professional Education of Teachers, 1974, Dying-Facing the Facts, 1979, 2d edit., 1988, 3d edit., 1995, Death Education: An Annotated Resource Guide, 1980, vol. 2, 1985, Helping Children Cope With Death, 1982, 2d edit., 1984, Childhood and Death, 1984; founding editor (jour.) Death Studies, 1977-92; cons. editor: Ednl. Gerontology, 1977-92, (book series) Death Education, Aging and Health Care, 1980-96; contbr. approximately 200 articles to profl. jours. and chpts. in books. Mem. Am. Psychol. Assn., Gerontol. Soc., Internat. Work Group Dying, Death and Bereavement (bd. dirs.), Assn. Death Edn. and Counseling. Home: 6014 NW 54th Way Gainesville FL 32653-3265 E-mail: wass@nersp.nerdc.ufl.edu.

**WASSELL, STEPHEN ROBERT,** mathematics professor, researcher; b. Santa Monica, Calif., Jan. 17, 1963; s. Desmond Anthony and Catherine Ann (Stephens) W. BS in arch., U. Va., 1984, MS in math, 1987, PhD in math., 1990, M in computer sci., 1999. Programmer, analyst UNISYS, McLean, Va., 1984-85, graphics artist, 1986; tutor summer transition program U. Va., Charlottesville, 1987-88, tchg. asst., 1986-90; asst. prof. math. Sweet Briar (Va.) Coll., 1990-96, assoc. prof. math., 1996—2002, prof. math., 2002—, dept. chmn., 1996—97, 1999—2002, 2004—05. Prof. of record Ctr. for the Liberal Arts, U. Va., 1991; vis. asst. prof. math., U. Va., Charlottesville, 1992, vis. assoc. prof. computer sci., 1998-99; doctoral cons., Charlottesville, 1989-90. Author: (with Kim Williams) On Ratio and Proportion, 2002; editor: The Golden Section, 2003, (with Branko Mitrovic) Villa Cornaro, 2006. Recipient Grad. assistantship award U. Va., 1986-90; Gordon T. Whyburn fellow, 1985-86. Mem. AAUP (Sweet Briar chpt. sec.-treas. 1993-99), Am. Math. Soc., Math. Assn. Am., Am. Solar Energy Soc., Sigma Nu (Beta chpt. treas. 1985-86). Achievements include patents for solar powered lawnmower, solar shed, ear muffs. Office: Sweet Briar Coll Dept Math Scis Sweet Briar VA 24595 Home: PO BOX 1112 Sweet Briar VA 24595 Office Phone: 434-381-6214. Business E-mail: wassell@sbc.edu.

**WASSENICH, LINDA PILCHER,** retired health facility administrator; b. Washington, Aug. 27, 1943; d. Mason Johnson and Vera Bell (Stephenson) Pilcher; m. Mark Wassenich, May 14, 1965; children: Paul Mason, David Mark. BA magna cum laude with honors, Tex. Christian U., Fort Worth, 1965; MSW, U. N.C., Chapel Hill, 1970. Licensed advanced practitioner, cert. social worker, Tex. Counselor family ct. Dallas County Juvenile Dept., 1970-73, 75-76; dir. govt. rels. Vis. Nurse Assn., Dallas, 1980-84, exec. officer of hospice, 1984-85; exec. dir. Incest Recovery Assn., Dallas, 1985-86; assoc. exec. dir. Lone Star Coun. Camp Fire, Dallas, 1986-89; exec. v.p. Vis. Nurse Assn. Found., Dallas, 1989-91; dir. policy and resource devel. Vis. Nurse Assn. Tex., 1992-99; ret. Field instr. U. Tex. Arlington Sch. Social Work, 1993-99. Contbr. articles to profl. publs. Mem. Leadership Dallas 1988—89; bd. dirs. Women's Coun. Dallas County, 1986—95, 1999—2001, pres., 1992—93; mem. adv. bd. Maternal Health and Family Planning Dallas, 1990—94; chmn. Dallas County Welfare Adv. Bd., 1991—95; bd. dirs. United Way of Met. Dallas, 1992—94, Youth Impact Ctrs., Dallas, 1993—94; trustee Simmons Family Found., Dallas, 2000—; mem. cmty. coun. Greater Dallas, 2004—; chair governance com. Human Rights Initiative of North Tex., Dallas, 2004—; chair adv. coun. Dallas Area Agy. on Aging, 2005—. Recipient Heart award Lone Star Coun. Camp Fire USA, 1990, Laurel award AAUW, Dallas, 1995, Valuable Alumna award Tex. Christian U. Alumni Assn., 2003, Women of Spirit award Am. Jewish Congress, Dallas, 2005; named Field Inst. of Yr., U. Tex. Arlington Sch. Social Work, 1999, Golden Rule award finalist JC Penney, 2000. Mem.: LWV (bd. dirs. Dallas 1974—80, pres. 1995—99, bd. dirs. Tex. 1999—, Tex. v.p. pub. rels. 2001—, Myrtle Bales Bulkley award 2000, Pres. award 2005), NASW (co-chmn. Dallas unit 1981—82, chair Tex. nominating com. 1990—92, Tex. bd. dirs., Social Worker of Yr. award 1988, Lifetime Achievement in Social Work award 2002), Assn. Fundraising Profls. (bd. dirs. Dallas chpt. 1994—97, v.p. governance 1995—96, cert., Outstanding Fund Raising Exec. of Yr. 1999), Acad. Cert. Social Workers. Home: 5221 Pebblebrook Dallas TX 75229-5504

**WASSER, DENNIS MATTHEW,** lawyer; b. Bklyn., Aug. 27, 1942; BA with honors, U. Calif. LA, 1964; JD, U. So. Calif., 1967. Bar: Calif. 1968, cert.: State Bar Calif. Bd. Legal Specialization (specialist in family law). Ptnr. Wasser, Cooperman & Carter, LA. Lectr. in field; co-instr. advanced profl. program family law U. So. Calif., 1989; instr. U. Calif. LA. Contbr. articles to profl. jours. Mem.: ABA, Am. Acad. Matrimonial Lawyers, LA County Bar Assn. (chmn. 1984, mem. exec. com. family law sect. 1978—88), Beverly Hills Bar Assn. (chmn. family law sect. 1978—79). Office: Wasser Cooperman & Carter Ste 1200 One Century Plz 2029 Century Park E Los Angeles CA 90067 Office Phone: 310-277-7117. Office Fax: 310-553-1793.*

**WASSER, HENRY,** retired American literature and sociology educator; b. Pitts., Apr. 13, 1919; s. Nathan and Mollie (Mendelson) W.; m. Solidelle Felicité Fortier, Aug. 20, 1942; children: Michael Frederick (dec.), Eric Anthony (dec.), Frederick Anthony, Felicity Louise. BA, MA, Ohio State U., 1940; PhD, Columbia U., 1951. Teaching fellow George Washington U., 1940-42; analyst USAAF intelligence, 1941-43; chemist Goodyear Synthetic Rubber Co., 1943-45; from tutor to assoc. prof. City Coll., CUNY, 1946-66; prof. English, dean faculties Richmond Coll., CUNY, 1966-73; v.p. for acad. affairs Calif. State U., Sacramento, 1973-74; prof. English Coll. S.I., CUNY, 1974-89; dir. Center for European Studies, Grad. Sch. CUNY, 1979-93, prof. emeritus of sociology and English, 1989—. Fulbright prof. U. Salonika, Greece, 1955-56; Higher Edn. Seminar assoc. Columbia U., 1961—, co-chair, 1982-87, chair, 1987-89; mem. Colloquium on Higher Edn., Yale U., 1974-75; Fulbright prof. Am. Lit. U. Oslo, 1962-64, dir., prof. Am. Inst., 1963-64; vis. prof. U. Sussex, Eng., 1972, U. Salonika, 1955-56; lectr. in field, Sweden, Norway, Eng., Germany, Poland, Yugoslavia, Italy, Turkey, Greece, Bulgaria; Fulbright prof. Am. Lit. and Civilization U. Bergen, Norway, 1989-90, U. Aveiro, Portugal, 1993; steering com. Internat. Conf. Higher Edn., 1989-; rsch. scholar comparative higher edn. CUNY, 1989—. Author: The Scientific Thought of Henry Adams, 1956, (with others) Higher Education in Western Europe and North America: A Selected and Annotated Bibliography, 1979, American Literature and Language: A Selected and Annotated Bibliography, 1980; editor: (with Sigmund Skard) Americana Norvegica; Norwegian Contributions to American Studies, 1968, (with others) The Compleat University, 1983, Problems of the Urban University: A Comparative Perspective, 1984, Impact of Changing Labor Force on Higher Education, 1987; editor (with Ulrich Teichler) German and American Universities: Mutual Influences, 1992, Diversification in Higher Education: A Comparative View, 1999; mem. bd. editors History of European Ideas, 1986—, guest editor, summer, 1987; guest editor Higher Edn. Policy, spring, 1994, contbr. articles to newspapers and profl. jours. Faculty trustee CUNY, 1981-86, trustee emeritus, 1986—; bd. dirs. Scandinavian Seminar, 1978-86, sec., 1980-83, vice chmn., 1983-86. Recipient Am. Scandinavian Found. award, 1969, 71, German Acad. Exch. Svc. award, 1973, 80, Swedish Info. Svc. award, 1979, Norwegian Ministry of Culture award, 1983, NEH award, 1984, Foscolo medal U. Pavia, Italy, 1986, German Marshall Fund award, 1985, 87, Atheneum medal U. Pavia, Italy, 1988, Disting. Senator award CUNY Faculty Senate, 1994. Mem. Am. Studies Assn. (pres. Met. N.Y. chpt. 1961-62, mem. nat. exec. coun. 1968-74), Melville Soc. Am. (historian 1969-74), MLA, Am. Scandinavian Found. (fellow 1971), Internat. Assn. Univ. Profs. English, Assn. Upper Level Colls. and Univs. (2d v.p. 1971-72), Assn. for World Edn. (internat. coun.), Phi Beta Kappa (sec. City Coll. chpt. 1957-62, 64-67, pres. CUNY Acad. for Humanities and Scis. 1991-2004, exec. dir. 2004-), Henry Adams Soc. (exec. coun. 1994—, pres. 1999-2003, dir. 2004-), Mass. Hist. Soc. (fellow 2001). Home: 333 E 34th St Apt 16C New York NY 10016-4950 also: 5517 Fieldston Rd Bronx NY 10471-2503 Office: CUNY Academy Grad Sch 365 Fifth Ave New York NY 10016-4309 Office Phone: 212-817-7944. E-mail: hwasser@gccuny.edu.

**WASSER, LAURA ALLISON,** lawyer; b. LA, May 23, 1968; d. Dennis Wasser. BA, U. Calif. Berkeley, 1991; JD, Loyola Law Sch., 1994. Bar: Calif. 1994. Ptnr. Wasser, Cooperman & Carter, LA. V.p. fin. devel., bd. dirs. Harriet Buhai Ctr. Family Law. Mem.: LA County Bar Assn., Beverly Hills Bar Assn. Office: Wasser Cooperman & Carter Ste 1200 One Century Plz 2029 Century Park E Los Angeles CA 90067 Office Phone: 310-277-7117. Office Fax: 310-553-1793.*

**WASSERBURG, GERALD JOSEPH,** geology and geophysics educator; b. New Brunswick, NJ, Mar. 25, 1927; s. Charles and Sarah (Levine) W.; m. Naomi Z. Orlick, Dec. 21, 1951; children: Charles David, Daniel Morris. Student, Rutgers U., 1946—48; BS in Physics, U. Chgo., 1951, MSc in Geology, 1952, PhD, 1954, DSc (hon.), 1992; Dr. Hon. Causa, Brussels U., 1985, U. Paris, 1986; DSc (hon.), Ariz. State U., 1987; Dr. (hon.), U. Rennes, 1998; DSc (hon.), U. Turin, Italy, 2000. Rsch. assoc. Inst. Nuc. Studies U. Chgo., 1954-55; asst. prof. Calif. Inst. Tech., Pasadena, 1955-59, assoc. prof., 1959-62, prof. geology and geophysics, 1962-82, John D. MacArthur prof. geology and geophysics, 1982—2001, prof. emeritus, 2001—. Served on Juneau Ice Field Rsch. Project, 1950; cons. Argonne Nat. Lab., Lamont, Ill., 1952-55; former mem. U.S. Nat. Com. for Geochem., com. for Planetary Exploration Study, NRC, adv. coun. Petroleum Rsch. Fund, Am. Chem. Soc.; me. lunar sample analysis planning team (LSAPT) manned Spacecraft Ctr., NASA, Houston, 1967-71, chmn., 1970; lunar sample rev. bd., 1970-72; mem. Facilities Working Group LSAPT, Johnson Space Ctr., 1972-82; mem. sci. working panel for Apollo missions, Johnson Space Ctr., 1971-73; advisor NASA, 1968-88, phys. scis. com., 1971-75, mem. lunar base steering com., 1984; chmn. com. for planetary and lunar exploration, mem. space sci. bd. NAS, 1975-78; chmn. divsn. Geol. and Planetary Scis., Calif. Inst. Tech., 1987-89; vis. prof. U. Kiel, Fed. Republic of Germany, 1960, Harvard U., 1962, U. Bern, Switzerland, 1966, Swiss Fed. Tech. Inst., 1967, Max Planck Inst., Mainz and Heidelberg, Fed. Republic of Germany, 1989, others; invited lectr., Vinton Hayes Sr. fellow Harvard U., 1980, Jaeger-Hales lectr. Australian Nat. U., 1980, Harold Jeffreys lectr. Royal Astron. Soc., 1981, Ernst Cloos lectr. Johns Hopkins U., 1984, H.L. Welsh Disting. lectr. U. Toronto, 1986, Danz lectr. U. Wash., 1989, Goldschmidt Centennial lectr. Norwegian Acad. Sci. and Letters, 1989, Lindsay lectr. Goddard Space Flight Ctr., 1996, other lecturshipss; plenary spkr. 125th Anniversary Geol. Soc. Sweden, 1996; 60th Anniversary Symposium spkr. Hebrew U., Jerusalem, 1985, 75th Anniversary Symposium spkr., 2000; Lezione Magistrale, Umbria Libri, Perugia, 2003. Served with U.S. Army, 1944-46. Decorated Combat Inf. badge; recipient Group Achievement award NASA, 1969, Exceptional Sci. Achievement award NASA, 1970, Disting. Pub. Svc. medal NASA, 1973, J.F. Kemp medal Columbia U., 1973, Profl. Achievement award U. Chgo. Alumni Assn., 1978, Goldschmidt medal Geochem. Soc., 1978, Disting. Pub. Svc. medal with cluster NASA, 1978, Wollaston medal Geol. Soc. London, 1985, Sr. Scientist award Alexander von Humboldt-Stiftung, 1985, Crafoord prize Royal Swedish Acad. Scis., 1986, Holmes medal, 1987, Regents fellow Smithsonian Inst., Gold medal Royal Astron. Soc., 1991; named Hon. Fgn. fellow European Union Geoscis., 1983. Fellow Am. Acad. Arts and Scis., Geol. Soc. London (hon.), Am. Geophys. Union (planetology sect., Harry H. Hess medal 1985), Geol. Soc. Am. (life, Arthur L. Day medal 1970), Meteoritical Soc. (pres. 1987-88, Leonard medal 1975), Geochemical Society and the European Assn. for Geochemistry, 1996; mem. Nat. Acad. Scis. (Arthur L. Day prize and lectureship 1981, J. Lawrence Smith medal 1985), Norwegian Acad. Sci. and Letters, Am. Phil. Soc. Achievements include research in geochemistry and geophysics and the application of the methods of chemical physics to problems in the earth scis. Major researches have been the determination of the time scales of nucleosynthesis, connections between the interstellar medium and solar material, the time of the formation of the solar system, the chronology and evolution of the earth, moon and meteorites, the establishment of dating methods using long-lived natural radio-activities, the study of geologic and cosmic processes using nuclear and isotopic effects as a tracer in nature, the origin of natural gases, and the application of thermodynamic methods to geologic systems. Office: Calif Inst Tech Divsn Geol & Planetary Scis Pasadena CA 91125-2500 Business E-Mail: gjw@gps.caltech.edu.

**WASSERMAN, BARRY L(EE),** architect; b. Cambridge, Mass., May 25, 1935; s. Theodore and Adelaide (Levin) W.; m. Wilma Louise Greenfield, June 21, 1957 (div. 1971); children: Tim Andrew, Andrew Glenn; m. Judith Ella Michalowski, Apr. 22, 1979. BA, Harvard U., 1957, M. Arch., 1960. Registered architect, Calif. Assoc. John S. Bolles Assocs., San Francisco, 1960-69; prin. Wasserman-Herman Assocs., San Francisco, 1969-72; prin., dir. Office Lawrence Halprin U Assocs., San Francisco, 1972-76; dep. state architect State of Calif., Sacramento, 1976-78, state architect, 1978-83; prof. dept. architecture, dir. Inst. Environ. Design, Sch. Environ. Design Calif. State Poly. U., Pomona, 1983-87, chair dept. architecture, Coll. Environ. Design, 1988-96, prof. emeritus, 1997—. Program advisor Fla. A&M U., Tallahassee, 1981—83; adv. com. Interior Design Program Calif. State U., Sacramento, 2004—; bd. dirs. Environ. Coun. Sacramento; mem. City of Sacramento Plng. Commn., 2004—; cons. in field. Architect Wasserman House, San Rafael, Calif., 1963 (AIA-Sunset Mag. award of Merit 1965-66), Anna Waden Library, San Francisco, 1969 (AIA award of Merit 1970), Capitol Area Plan, Sacramento, 1977 (Central Valley chpt. AIA Honor award 1979), co-author: Ethics and the Practice of Architecture, 2000. Recipient Awards citation Progressive Architecture 26th awards Program, 1979, Octavius Morgan award Calif. Architects Bd., 2000. Fellow AIA (chmn. architecture in govt. com., 1979, bd./dir. environ. coun. Sacramento, 2004—) Democrat. Jewish. Home: 6456 Fordham Way Sacramento CA 95831-2218 E-mail: blw2@mindspring.com.

**WASSERMAN, BURTON,** artist, educator; b. Bklyn., Mar. 10, 1929; s. Louis and Matilda (Kravitz) W.; m. Sarah Frances Masher, Nov. 2, 1950; 1 child, Marc. BA, Bklyn. Coll., N.Y., 1950; MA, Columbia U., N.Y.C., 1954, EdD, 1958. Art tchr. various pub. schs., L.I., N.Y., 1954-59; prof. art Rowan U., Glassboro, NJ, 1960—2004, prof. emeritus, 2000—. Prin. art exhibition critic Art Matters, Phila., 1981—. Author: Exploring the Visual Arts, Modern Painting: The Movements, The Artists, Their Work, Bridges of Vision: The Art of Prints and the Craft of Printmaking; (with Sarita Rainey) Basic Silkscreen Printmaking, Crayon Resist Techniques; exhibited in various group shows; represented in permanent collections Phila. Mus. Art, N.J. State Mus., Stedelijk Mus., Amsterdam, Macedonian Ctr. for Contemporary Art, Thessaloniki Greece, numerous colls., cos., and pvt. collections. With U.S. Army, 1951-53. Recipient 1st prize Huntington Twp. Art League, 1956, L.I. Art Tchrs. Ann. Exhbn., 1957, 3d prize Hofstra U. Ann. Art Exhbn. L.I. Artists, 1956, 57, Brickhouse purchase prize Norfolk (Va.) Mus. Art and Scis., 1965; Kelsey Purchase prize N.J. State Mus., 1966, Ryan purchase prize, 1967; purchase prize USIA, 1970, hon. citation and Liberty Bell award City of Phila., 1992; grantee State of N.J., Rowan Coll. N.J., 1977, 78, 80, 83, 84, 86, 92. Mem. Phila. Art Alliance (bd. dirs. 1978-83); Artists Equity (past nat. pres. 1971-73). Avocations: reading, travel. Home: 204 Dubois Rd Glassboro NJ 08028-1225 Personal E-mail: burtwasserman@verizon.net.

**WASSERMAN, DAVID H.,** medical educator, researcher; b. New Orleans, Aug. 24, 1957; m. Doris S. Wasserman; children: Micah Joseph, Mira Rose. BSc in Kinesiology, UCLA, 1979, MSc in Kinesiology, 1981; PhD in Physiology, U. Toronto, 1985. Rsch. asst. dept. respiratory physiology and medicine UCLA, 1979—81, tchg. asst. gen. physiology dept. kinesiology, 1980—81; tchg. asst. gen. physiology dept. physiology U. Toronto, 1982—84; rsch. assoc. dept. molecular physiology and biophysics Vanderbilt U. Sch. Medicine, Nashville, 1985—87, lab. instr. med. sch. physiology dept. molecular physiology and biophysics, 1986—88, course coord., lectr. exercise physiology dept. molecular physiology and biophysics, 1986—, rsch. instr. dept. molecular physiology and biophysics, 1987—88, asst. prof. dept. molecular physiology and biophysics, 1988—92, lectr. tutorials in physiology dept. molecular physiology and biophysics, 1989—90, lectr. metabolic regulation in vivo dept. molecular physiology and biophysics, 1989—, lectr. history physiology dept. molecular physiology and biophysics, 1991—92, assoc. prof. dept. molecular physiology and biophysics, lectr. med. sch. physiology dept. molecular physiology and biophysics, 1992—98, lectr. interdisciplinary grad. program physiology dept. molecular physiology and biophysics, 1992—94, course coord., instr. tutorials in profl. physiology dept. molecular physiology and biophysics, 1995—. Lectr. in field. Mem. editl. bd.: Am. Jour. Physiology: Endocrinology and Metabolism, 1992—, Jour. Applied Physiology, 1996—, assoc. editor: Metabolism, 1996—; contbr. articles to profl. jours. Mem.: European Assn. for Studies in Diabetes, Juvenile Diabetes Found. Internat. (bd. dirs. Tenn. chpt. 1995—, chmn. govt. rels. com. Tenn. chpt. 1996—), Am. Physiol. Soc. (mem. program adv. com. 1988—92, head org. com. interactions endo. and cardiovasc. sys. health/disease 1989—91, sec./treas. endocrinology and metabolism sect. 1992—95, mem. organizing com. integrated biology of exercise 1993—), Am. Coll. Sports Medicine, Am. Diabetes Assn. (mem. rsch. coun. on exercise 1988—, co-advisor tech. report on diabetes and exercise 1993—94, mem. grant rev. panel 1993—96). Office: Vanderbilt U Med Sch Dept Molec Physio & Biophys Light Hl Rm 702 Nashville TN 37232-0001

**WASSERMAN, EDWARD ARNOLD,** psychology professor; b. LA, Calif., Apr. 2, 1946; s. Albert Leonard and May (Sabin) W. BA, UCLA, 1968; PhD, Ind. U., 1972. Postdoctoral fellow U. Sussex, Brighton, Eng., 1972; from asst. prof. to prof. psychology U. Iowa, Iowa City, 1972-83, prof., 1983—, Stuit prof. exptl. psychology, 1997—. Pres. faculty senate U. Iowa, 1997-98; vis. scientist CNRS, Marseille, France, 1999. Contbr. articles to profl. jours., chpts. to books; assoc. editor several jours. Bd. dirs. Big Bros., Big Sisters, Johnson County, Iowa, 1982-85 Ind. U. fellow, 1968, U. Iowa fellow, 1975, 82, NAS fellow, former USSR, 1976, James Van Allen Natural Scis. fellow, 1994-95. Fellow APA, Am. Psychol. Soc.; mem. Psychonomic Soc., Midwestern Psychol. Assn., Soc. Exptl. Psychologists, Phi Beta Kappa. Office: U Iowa Dept Psychology Iowa City IA 52242

**WASSERMAN, HARRIET M.,** academic administrator; BS in chemistry, U. Wash. Assoc. dean., dir. info. tech. services Seattle Ctrl. Cmty. Coll. Named one of Premier 100 IT Leaders, Computerworld, 2005. Office: Seattle Ctrl Cmty Coll 1701 Broadway Seattle WA 98122 Office Phone: 206-344-4344. E-mail: hwasse@sccd.ctc.edu.*

**WASSERMAN, PAUL,** library and information science professor; b. Newark, Jan. 8, 1924; s. Joseph and Sadie (Ringelescu) W.; m. Krystyna Ostrowska, 1973; children: Jacqueline R., Steven R. BBA, Coll. City N.Y., 1948; MS in L.S., Columbia, 1949, MS, 1950; PhD, U. Mich., 1960; postgrad., Western Res. U., 1963-64. Advt. mgr. Zuckerberg Co., N.Y.C., 1946-48; asst. to bus. libr. Bklyn. Pub. Library, 1949-51, chief sci. and industry div., 1951-53; librarian, asst. prof. Grad. Sch. Bus. and Pub. Adminstrn., Cornell U., 1953-56, libr., assoc. prof., 1962-65; librarian prof., 1962-65; dean U. Md. Coll. Library and Info. Scis., 1965-70, prof., 1970-97, prof. emeritus, 1997—. Vis. prof. U. Mich., summers 1960, 63, 64, Asian Inst. Tech., U. Hawaii, U. Hong Kong, summer 1988, Chulalongkorn U., Bangkok,

1990, U. Wash., summer 1991, U. Wis., summer 1992, C.W. Post Coll., L.I. U., 1993, Inst. Sci. and Tech. China, Beijing, 1996; Isabel Nichol lectr. Denver U. Libr. Sch., 1968; market rsch. cons. Laux Advt., Inc., 1955-59, Gale Rsch. Co., Detroit, 1959-60, 63-64; rsch. planning cons. Ind. U. Sch. Bus., 1961-62; cons. to USPHS as mem. manpower tng. rev. com. Nat. Libr. Medicine, 1966-69, Ohio Bd. Regents, 1969, Omngraphics Inc., 1988-91, VITA, summer 1991; dir. Documentation Abstracts, Inc., 1970-73, v.p., 1971-73; Fulbright prof. Warsaw U., 1993-94; rsch. project dir. Kellogg Study, 1996-98. Author: Information for Adminstrators, 1956, (with Fred Silander) Decision Making, 1958, Measurement and Evaluation of Organization Performance, 1959, Sources of Commodity Prices, 1960, 2d edit., 1974, Sources for Hospital Administrators, 1961, Decision Making: An Annotated Bibliography, supplement, 1958-63, 1964, Librarian and the Machine, 1965; Book rev. editor: Adminstrv. Sci. Quar, 1956-61; editor: Service to Business, 1952-53, Directory of University Research Bureaus and Institutes, 1960, Health Organizations of the U.S. and Canada, 1961, and 2d to 4th edit., 1977, Statistics Sources, 1962 and 4th to 8th edits., 1984, (with Bundy) Reader in Library Adminstration, 1968, Reader in Research Methods in Librarianship, 1969; mng. editor: Mgmt. Information Guide Series, 1963-83, Consultants and Consulting Organizations, 1966, 4th edit., 1979, 5th edit., 1982, Who's Who in Consulting, 1968, 2d edit., 1974, Awards, Honors and Prizes: A Sourcebook and Directory, 1969, 2d edit., 1972, 4th edit. Vol. 1, 1978, International and Foreign Awards, 1975, New Consultants, 1973-74, 76-77, 78-79, Readers in Librarianship and Information Science, 1968-78, Ency. Bus. Information Sources, 1971, 3d edit., 1976, 4th edit., 1980, 5th edit., 1983, Library and Information Services Today, 1971-75, Consumer Sourcebook, 1974, 2d edit., 1978, 3d edit., 1980, 4th edit., 1983; series editor: Contributions in Librarianship and Information Science, 1969-99; coordinating mgmt. editor. Information Guide Library, 1971-83, The New Librarianship-A Challenge for Change, 1972; mng. editor: Museum Media, 1973, Library Bibliographies and Indexes, 1975, Ethnic Groups in the United States, 1976, 2d edit., 1982, Training and Development Organizations, 1978, 2d edit., 1983, Speakers and Lecturers: How to Find Them, 1979, 2d edit., 1982, Learning Independently, 1979, 2d edit., 1983, Recreation and Outdoor Life Directory, 1979, Law and Legal Information Directory, 1980, 2d edit., 1982, Ency. Health Info. Sources, 1986, Ency. Sr. Citizen Info. Sources, 1987, Ency. Pub. Affairs Info. Sources, 1987, Ency. Legal Info. Sources, 1987; mem. editorial bd. Social Scis. Citation Index, Inst. Scientific Info., 1972-95, Jour. Library Adminstrn., 1979-89, Social Sci. Info. Studies, 1979—, 1991 Education for Info.: The Internat. Rev. of Education and Tng. in Library and Info. Sci., 1983-88, The Best of Times: A Personal and Occupational Odyssey, 2000, New York from A to Z, 2002, Washington DC from A to Z, 2003, Weasel Words, The Dictionary of American Doublespeak, 2005. Active U.S. Com. on Edn. and Tng. for Internat. Fedn. for Info. and Documentation, 1993-94. Served with U.S. Army, 1943-46. Decorated Purple Heart, Bronze Star; recipient ALA Ref. Svcs. Divsn./Gale Rsch. Bus. Libr. award, 1997; Fulbright scholar, Sri Lanka, 1986-87, Poland, 1995. Mem. AAUP, ALA, Am. Soc. Info. Sci., Spl. Librs. Assn. (editor, chmn. publ. project., Disting. Mem. award bus. divsn. 1996—). Home: 4940 Sentinel Dr Apt 203 Bethesda MD 20816-3552 Office: U Md Coll Info Studies College Park MD 20742-0001 E-mail: pw11@umail.umd.edu.

**WASSERMAN, RICHARD LAWRENCE,** pediatrician, educator; b. Bklyn., Oct. 28, 1948; s. Isidore and Gladys (Glazer) W.; m. Tina D. Rice; children: Jonathan A., Leslie R. BS in Chemistry, Haverford Coll., 1970; PhD, CUNY, 1975; MD, U. Tex. Southwest, Dallas, 1977. Diplomate Am. Bd. Pediatrics, Am. Bd. Allergy and Immunology. Intern Children's Hosp. Phila., 1977-78, resident in pediatrics, 1978-79, fellow in immunology, 1979-80; rsch. assoc. in immunology Rockefeller U., N.Y.C., 1980-82; asst. prof. pediatrics and microbiology U. Tex. S.W. Med. Ctr., Dallas, 1982-88, asst. clin. prof. pediatrics, 1988-99, assoc. clin. prof. pediatrics, 1999—; asst. chief pediatrics Baylor U. Med. Ctr., Dallas, 1989; dir. Immunology Clinic Children's Med. Ctr., Dallas, 1983—2003. Adj. attending physician Mt. Sinai Hosp., N.Y.C., 1981-82; cons. Am. Assn. Blood Banks, Arlington, Va., 1983-95; test devel. com. Nat. Bd. Med. Examiners, 1992—; med. dir. pediatric allergy and immunology Med. City Children's Hosp., Dallas, 1994—; chmn. Am. Lung Assn. Tex., Dallas, 1999-2000. Pres. Hobart Coll. Alumnae Coun., 2000-01; overseer Jewish Inst. Religion, Hebrew Union Coll., Cin., 2000— Fellow Am. Assn. Allergy, Asthma and Immunology; mem. Am. Assn. Immunologists, Clin. Immunology Soc., Am. Acad. Allergy Asthma and Immunology (chmn. pub. reln. 1999-2001, med. infomatics 2002-04), So. Soc. for Pediatric Rsch. (coun. 1986-87, Founder's award 1988), Greater Dallas Pediat. Soc. (pres. 1999), Phi Beta Kappa Zeta. Home: 7153 Lavendale Ave Dallas TX 75230-3650 Office Phone: 972-566-7788.

**WASSERMAN, RICHARD LEO,** lawyer; b. Balt., Aug. 6, 1948; s. Jack B. and Claire (Gutman) W.; m. Manuele Delbourgo, May 13, 1973; children: Alexander E., Lauren E. AB, Princeton U., 1970; JD, Columbia U., 1973. Bar: N.Y. 1975, Md. 1978, U.S. Dist. Ct. (so. and ea. dists.) N.Y. 1975, U.S. Dist. Ct. Md. 1978, U.S. Ct. Appeals (2d cir.) 1975, U.S. Ct. Appeals (4th cir.) 1979, U.S. Supreme Ct. 1982. Law clk. to hon. Roszel C. Thomsen U.S. Dist. Ct. Md., Balt., 1973-74; assoc. Proskauer Rose Goetz & Mendelsohn, N.Y.C., 1974-78, Venable LLP, Balt., 1978-81, ptnr., Bankruptcy & Creditors' Rights practice, 1982—. Bd. dirs. Legal Aid Bur., Inc., 2004—. Co-author, editor in chief: Bankruptcy Appeals Manual, 1998; editor: Bankruptcy Appeals Manual, 2d edit., 2005. Fellow Am. Coll. Bankruptcy, Md. Bar Found.; mem. ABA (bus. bankruptcy com.), Md. Bar Assn. (sec. coun. bus. law sect. 1989-92), Bar Assn. Balt. City (chmn. banking, bankruptcy and bus. law com. 1987-88), Bankruptcy Bar Assn. Dist. Md. (bd. dirs. 1988—, pres. 1990-91), Assn. Bar City N.Y., Am. Bankruptcy Inst., Princeton U. Alumni Assn. Md. (bd. dirs. 1980-98, pres. 1985-87), Suburban Club Baltimore County (bd. govs. 1982-89, 94-98, 2d v.p. 1986-87, sec. 1987-88, pres.-elect 1994-95, pres. 1995-97). Democrat. Jewish. Avocations: tennis, golf, hiking. Office: Venable LLP 1800 Mercantile Bank & Trust Bldg 2 Hopkins Plz Baltimore MD 21201 Office Phone: 410-244-7505. Office Fax: 410-244-7742. Business E-Mail: rlwasserman@venable.com.

**WASSERMAN, ROBERT HAROLD,** biology professor; b. Schenectady, Feb. 11, 1926; s. Joseph and Sylvia (Rosenberg) W.; m. Marilyn Mintz, June 11, 1950; children: Diane Jean, Arlene Lee, Judith Rose. BS, Cornell U., 1949, PhD, 1953; MS, Mich. State U., 1951. Research assoc. AEC project U. Tenn., Oak Ridge, 1953-55; sr. scientist med. div. Oak Ridge Inst. Nuclear Studies, 1955-57; assoc. prof. phys. biology N.Y. State Vet. Coll., Cornell U., 1957-63, prof., 1963—, James Law prof. physiology, 1989-97, James Law prof. emeritus, 1998—, acting head phys. biology dept., 1963-64, 71, 75-76, chmn. dept. /sect. physiology, 1983-87, mem. exec. com. div. biol. sci., 1983-87. Vis. fellow Inst. Biol. Chemistry, Copenhagen, 1964-65; chmn. Conf. on Calcium Transport, 1962; co-chmn. Conf. on Cell Mechanisms for Calcium Transfer and Homeostasis, 1970; mem. adv. bd. Vitamin D Symposia, 1976—; adv. bd. Symposia Calcium-Binding Proteins, 1977-2001, chmn., 1977; food and nutrition bd. NRC; cons. NIH, Oak Ridge Inst. Nuclear Studies; pub. affairs com. Fedn. Am. Socs. Exptl. Biology, 1974-77; chmn. com. MPI, NRC; pre-doctoral fellowship panel Howard Hughes, 1999-2000, 03. Bd. editors: Calcified Tissue Research, 1977-80, Procs. Soc. Exptl. Biol. Medicine, 1970-76, Cornell Veterinarian, Jour. Nutrition; contbr.: articles to profl. jours. Served with U.S. Army, 1944-45. Recipient Mead Johnson award, 1969, Andre Lichtwitz prize INSERM, 1982, W.F. Neuman award Am. Soc. Bone and Mineral Rsch., 1990, Merit award NIH, 1993-96, Brown U. Rsch. award, 2004; Guggenheim fellow, 1964-65, 72, fellow NSF-OECD, 1964-65. Fellow Am. Inst. Nutrition, mem. Am. Physiol. Soc., Soc. Exptl. Biology and Medicine, AAAS, Nat. Acad. Scis., Sigma Xi, Phi Kappa Phi, Phi Zeta Home: 207 Texas Ln Ithaca NY 14850-1758 Business E-Mail: rhw2@cornell.edu.

**WASSERMAN, STEPHEN IRA,** allergist, immunologist, educator; b. LA, Dec. 17, 1942; m. Linda Morgan; children: Matthew, Zachary. BA, Stanford U., 1964; MD, UCLA, 1968. Diplomate Am. Bd. Internal Medicine, Am. Bd. Allergy and Immunology. Intern, resident Peter B. Brigham Hosp., Boston, 1968-70; fellow in allergy, immunology Robert B. Brigham Hosp., Boston, 1972-75; asst. prof. medicine Harvard U., Boston, 1975-79, assoc. prof.,

1979, U. Calif.-San Diego, La Jolla, 1979-85, prof., 1985—, chief allergy tng. program Sch. Medicine, 1979-85, chief allergy div. Sch. Medicine, 1985-93, acting chmn. dept. medicine, 1986-88, chmn. dept. medicine, 1988-2000, Helen M. Ranney prof., 1992—2001, chief allergy tng.program Sch. Medicine, 2001—05. Co-dir. allergy sect. Robert B. and Peter B. Brigham Hosps., 1977-79; dir. Am. Bd. Allergy and Immunology; dir. Am. Bd. Internal Medicine., chair, 1999-2000. Contbr. articles to profl. jours. Served to lt. comdr. USPHS, 1970-72, San Francisco. Fellow Am. Acad. Allergy and Immunology (pres. 1997-98); mem. Am. Soc. Clin. Investigation, Assn. Am. Physicians, Am. Assn. Immunologists, Collegium Internationale Allergologicum, Phi Beta Kappa, Alpha Omega Alpha. Office: U Calif San Diego Stein Clin Rsch Bldg Rm 244 9500 Gilman Dr MC 0637 San Diego CA 92093-0637

**WASSERMAN, STEVE,** literary agent; b. Vancouver, Wash., Aug. 3, 1952; s. Abraham and Ann (Dragoon) W.; m. Michelle Krisel, Mar. 7, 1982 (div. Dec. 2001); children: Claire, Paul, Isaac; m. Jodi Faith Cahn, Aug. 11, 2002; 1 child, Mira. AB in Criminology, U. Calif., Berkeley, 1974. Asst. editor City Mag. of San Francisco, 1975—76; dep. editor opinion sect. L.A. Times, 1977—83; editor-in-chief New Republic Books The New Republic, NYC, 1984—87; pub., editl. dir. Hill and Wang divsn. Farrar, Straus and Giroux Inc., NYC, 1987—90; pub. The Noonday Press divsn. Farrar, Straus and Giroux Inc., NYC, 1987—90; editl. dir. Times Books divsn. Random House, NYC, 1990—96; editor L.A. Times Book Rev., 1996—2005; mng. dir. Kneerim & Williams at Fish & Richardson, NYC, 2005—. Cons. editor The Threepenny Rev., Berkeley, Calif., 1980—86, Tikkun, Oakland, Calif., 1986—90; founder, co-dir. L.A. Inst. for Humanities, U. So. Calif., 1998—2005; Donald and Doris Fischer lectr. Grad. Sch. of Journalism U. Calif. Berkeley, 1999; instr., master profl. writing program U. So. Calif., 2000—05; co-dir. L.A. Times Festival of Books, 1997—2005; chair Pulitzer Prize Nominating Jury for Gen. Nonfiction, 2000; mem. Pulitzer Prize Nominating Jury for Fiction, 2003; bd. dirs. Nat. Book Critics Cir., 1997—2005; mem. jury lit. prizes Commonwealth Club Calif., 2001—. Contbr. articles and revs. to mags. and newspapers. Mem. PEN Office: Kneerim & Williams at Fish & Richardson Citigroup Ctr 52nd Fl 153 E 53rd St New York NY 10022-4611 Office Phone: 212-641-2267. E-mail: wasserman@fr.com.

**WASSERMAN, SUSAN VALESKY,** accountant, artist, yoga instructor; b. St. Petersburg, Fla., June 5, 1956; d. Charles B. Valesky and Jeanne I. (Schulz) Morgan; m. Fred Wasserman, III, May 19, 1990; 1 child, Sara Elisabeth. BS in Merchandising, Fla. State U., Tallahassee, 1978; CPA Fla.; ChFC, cert. yoga tchr. Fla. Inst. for Integrated Yoga Studies, 2002, yoga therapist Integrated Yoga Therapy, 2004. Store mgr. Levi Straus Inc., San Francisco, 1979; pvt. practice acct. St. Petersburg, 1980—; acct., tax and fin. planning specialist Barber, Stowe & Co., St. Petersburg, 1997—98; owner White Egret Yoga Studio, South Pasadena, Fla., 2002—. Exhibitions include Longboat Key (Fla.) Art Ctr., 1993, Fla. Suncoast Water Color Soc., Sarasota, 1994, South Pasadena Artspring, 1999—2000 (Judges award, 1998), 2005. Mem.: Internat. Assn. Yoga Therapists, Suncoast Yoga Tchrs. Assn. (treas.), Yoga Alliance. Home and Studio: 7015 Grevilla Ave S Saint Petersburg FL 33707-2050 Office: 5800 4th St N Saint Petersburg FL 33703-1402 Office Phone: 727-347-7354. E-mail: yogisue@tampabay.rr.com.

**WASSERMAN, WILLIAM PHILLIP,** lawyer; b. LA, Sept. 13, 1945; s. Al and Ceil (Diamond) W.; married; children: Sam, George. BA, U. Calif., Berkeley, 1967; JD, U. Calif., 1971. Bar: Calif. 1971, U.S. Tax Ct. 1971. Ptnr. Ernst & Young LLP, Los Angeles, 1970—. Lectr. in field; participant in numerous programs, confs., and workshops in field in field. Mem. Editorial adv. bd.: Real Estate Taxation: A Practitioner's Guide, 1984—, Federal Tax Annual: Real Estate, 1982; contbr. numerous articles to profl. jours. Mem. ABA (nat. chmn Tax Sect. com. on real estate problems 1985-87), State Bar Calif., Los Angeles County Bar Assn., Calif. Bd. Legal Specialization (cert. taxation law specialist). Office: Ernst & Young LLP 725 S Figueroa St Los Angeles CA 90017-5524

**WASSERMAN-SCHULTZ, DEBBIE,** congresswoman; b. Forest Hills, N.Y., Sept. 27, 1955; BA in Polit. Sci., U. Fla., 1988, MA, 1990. Mem. Fla. Ho. of Reps., 1992—2004, US Congress from 20th Fla. dist., 2005—; mem. Ho. Judiciary com. Mem. Gov.'s Commn. on Edn., 1996—; mem. legis. adv. coun. So. Regional Edn. Bd., 1995—; bd. dirs. Fla. Distance Learning Network, 1994; mem. Classrooms First Task Force, 1993. Recipient award for outstanding family advocacy Dade County Psychol. Assn., 1993, Giraffe award Women's Advocacy Majority Minority, 1993, Legis. Svc. award Fla. Assn. Women Lawyers, 1993, Quality Floridian award Fla. League of Cities, 1994, AMIT Woman of Yr. award, 1994, Outstanding Legislator of Yr. award Fla. Fedn. Bus. and Profl. Women, 1994, Rosemary Barkett award Acad. Fla. Trial Lawyers, 1995, Woman of Vision award Weizmann Inst. Sci., others; named one of 25 Most Unstoppable Women, South Fla. Mag., 1994. Mem. Omicron Delta Kappa. Democrat. Jewish. Avocations: bowling, golf, politics, old houses. Office: US House of Representatives 118 Cannon House Office Bldg Washington DC 20515-0920 also: 10100 Pines Blvd Pembroke Pines FL 33026 Office Phone: 202-225-7931.

**WASSERSTEIN, BRUCE,** investment banker; b. NYC, Dec. 25, 1947; s. Morris and Lola Wasserstein; 5 children. BA with honors, U. Mich., 1967; MBA with high distinction, Harvard U., 1971, JD cum laude, 1971; diploma in law, Cambridge U., 1972. Assoc. Cravath, Swaine & Moore, N.Y., 1972-77; mng. dir. The First Boston Corp., N.Y.C., 1977-88; pres. Wasserstein, Perella and Co., N.Y.C., 1988—2000; exec. chmn. Dresdner Kleinwort Wasserstein, NYC, 2000—01; CEO Lazard LLC, Paris, 2001—; chmn. bd. Am. Lawyer Media, 1997—; owner The Daily Deal, 1999—, New York Magazine, 2003 ; chmn. Wasserstein & Co., 2001—. Author: Corporate Finance Law; Big Deal: Mergers and Acquisitions in the Digital Age, 2000 rev. edit. Mem. SEC Adv. Comm. Tender Offers; mem. vis. com. Harvard Law Sch., Harvard Bus. Sch., U. Mich., Columbia Journalism Sch., Cambridge U. Bus. Sch. Mem. Coun. on Fgn. Rels. Democrat. Office: Lazard LLC 30 Rockefeller Plaza New York NY 10020

**WASSHAUSEN, DIETER CARL,** botanist; b. Jena, Germany, Apr. 15, 1938; came to U.S., 1950, naturalized, 1957; s. Heinz P. and Elizabeth A. (Mueller) W.; m. Merrilee M. Locklin, Dec. 23, 1961; children— Lisa A., David B. BS, George Washington U., 1962, MS, 1965, PhD, 1972. Science curator dept. botany Smithsonian Instn., Washington, 1969-76; chmn., curator dept. botany Nat. Mus. Natural History, Washington, 1976—. Recipient Smithsonian Research Found. awards, 1974, 75, Wildenow medal, 1979 Mem. Am. Soc. Plant Taxonomists, Internat. Assn. Plant Taxonomy, Neotropical Field Botanists assn., Am. Inst. Biol. Scis., AAAS, Assn. Tropical Biology, Sigma Xi. Presbyterian. Achievements include research on systematics of neotropical Acanthaceae, floristic studies in Gramineae of Brazil, floristic studies in Begoniaceae, revision of Nat. List Sci. Plant Names. Home: St James Plantation 2931 Legends Dr Southport NC 28461 Office: Nat Mus Natural History 10th St and Constitution Ave NW Washington DC 20560-0001 Office Phone: 202-633-0944. Personal E-mail: dmwasshausen@aol.com.

**WASSMER, RUDOLF ANDREAS,** entrepreneurial engineer; b. Berne, Switzerland, Nov. 27, 1941; s. Hans Erich and Margaretha Katharina (von Mandach) W.; m. Janine Antoinette Georgine Koch, Aug. 24, 1978; 1 child, Alexandra Janine. Diploma mech. engring., Fed. Inst. of Tech., 1967; diploma, European Inst. Bus. Administrn., 1971. Jr. project engr. internat. Polysius, Paris, 1968; del. project engr. SungShin Cement, Seoul, 1969-70; with Swiss Aluminium Ltd., Zuerich, 1971-72; cons. Portland Cement Werk, 1973; works engr. Würenlingen AG, 1973-74; tech. dir., engr. Fla. 1974-76; mem. staf Cementia Engring and Cons., Zurich, 1976-78, sr. engr. internat., 1981-87, 92; works dir., improvement plan Bamburi Portland Cement Co. Ltd., Kenya, 1978-81; entrepreneurial engr. Swiss secretariatia Holdit, Leadership and Devel. Activities Inlasaahowal, Zurich, 1987—. Capt. Swiss Army Res., 1964-91. Mem. INSEAD (alumnus), ETHZ, Swiss Engring. and Arch.,

Eur Ing Feani (cert.), Seoul Club, Mobasa Club. Avocation: sports. Office: Holdit & Studio HQ Holdit & Studio P-C-W Hdqs 4th floor Asylstrasse 64 8032 Zurich Switzerland Office Fax: 41 40 44 3830975.

**WASSMER, THEODORE MILTON,** artist; b. Salt Lake City, Feb. 23, 1910; s. Theodore James and Hester Sadie (Hall) W.; m. Julia Farnsworth Lund, Dec. 8, 1945 (dec. May 1996). Student, Art Students League, N.Y.C. 1947-51; student under Raphael Soyer, Am. Art Sch., N.Y.C., 1949-51. Employed by engraving and wholesale hardware cos., Salt Lake City, 1925-42; artist W.P.A., 1946-52, Woodstock, NY, 1952-85, Salt Lake City, 1985—. Apprentice to Florence E. Ware painting murals for the WPA, 1934-39. More than 3,000 works are in museums, colls., schs. and pvt. collections in U.S., Europe and Japan; with wife donated more than 1,500 works to Springville Mus. of Art, Snow Coll., Brigham City Mus.-Gallery, Fairview Mus. of History and Art and Nora Eccles Harrison Mus. Art, Utah; solo show at Albany (N.Y.) Inst. History and Art, 1974; other solo shows in Alaska, Ariz., Tex., Utah, Fla., N.Y. and Calif.; Salt Lake City Arts Ctr., 1999, So Ho Gallery, 2002, Alice Gallery Utah Arts Coun., 2004, Art Access Gallery, Salt Lake City, 2005; exhibited with 4 other artists over 80, 1994; solo show of 50 recent works at Myra Powell Gallery, Ogden, Utah, 1997; works reproduced in various publs. Sgt. U.S. Army Air Force, 1942-45. Springville Mus. Art honored his 80th yr. with reception and 60-yr. retrospective show, 1930-90, showing 100 of his works and issuing a 24-page catalog; recipient Michael O. Leavitt Gov. award, 2000. February 23, 2005 proclaimed Theodore Milton Wassmer Day. Avocation: collecting art. Home: 130 S 1300 E Apt 501 Salt Lake City UT 84102-1779

**WASSNER, STEVEN JOEL,** pediatric nephrologist, educator; b. NYC, Dec. 16, 1946; s. Abraham and Clara (Weitzner) W.; m. Enid K. Kling, June 11, 1972; children: Adam Jacob, Nancy Shane. BS, CCNY, 1968; MD, NYU, 1972. Diplomate Am. Bd. Pediatrics, Am. Bd. Pediatrics Nephrology. Intern, resident Children's Hosp. L.A., 1972-74, fellow in pediatric nephrology, 1974-75; rsch. fellow in pediatric nephrology UCLA, 1975-77; asst. prof. pediat. Pa. State U. M.S. Hershey Med. Ctr., Hershey, 1978-83, assoc. prof., 1983-91, prof., 1991—, vice chmn. dept., 1989-99, dir. med./pediat residency program, 1989—94, vice chmn. edn., 1999—, chief divsn. pediat. nephrology and hypertension, 1978—, chief divsn. pediatric nephrology and diabetes, 1991-99, dir. pediat. residency program, 1988—2006, vice-chmn. edn., 2000—, interim chief divsn. endocrinology, 2006—. Vis. prof. human biochemistry Hebrew U., Hadassah Hosp., 1985-86; dir. Pediatric Diabetes Svc., 1998-99. Contbr. articles to med. jours. Mem. adv. bd. Kidney Found. South Ctrl. Pa., Harrisburg, 1980-90, sci. adv. coun. for pediatric nephrology/urology Nat. Kidney Found., 1986-92, Harrisburg com. for Hebrew U.; bd. dirs. Jewish Family Svc., Harrisburg, 1979-85, pres., 1983-85; bd. dirs. United Jewish Fedn., 1983-85, 94-97, Yeshiva Acad., 1987-90. Recipient Rsch. Career Devel. award NIH, 1983; Musclar Dystrophy Assn. grantee, 1979-81, Disting. Educator award, 2005; Sr. Internat. fellow Fogarty Internat. Ctr. NIH, 1985. Fellow Am. Acad. Pediatrics (exec. com. sect. on nephrology, chair program subcom. 1998-2002, chmn. exec. com. sect. on nephrology 2002-06), Am. Bd. Pediatrics; mem. Am. Pediatrics Soc., Am. Soc. Nephrology, Internat. Soc. Nephrology, Am. Soc. Pediatrics Nephrology, Internat. Soc. Pediatric Nephrology, Internat. Pediatric Nephrology Assn. (counsellor 1989-95). Office: MS Hershey Med Ctr PO Box 850 Hershey PA 17033-0850 Office Phone: 717-531-5707. Business E-Mail: swassner@psu.edu.

**WASSON, BARBARA HICKAM,** music educator; b. Spencer, Ind., Feb. 12, 1918; Student, DePauw U., 1937-38; BA, Vassar Coll., 1939; MusM, Chgo. Mus. Coll., 1944; postgrad., Ind. U., 1962-63. Founder, co-dir. Wasson Piano Studios, Dayton, 1946—; instr. Cedarville Coll., Dayton, Ohio, 1970-72; adj. prof. Wright State U., Dayton, Ohio, 1973-78; asst. prof. U. Cin., 1982-87; prof. Wright State U., 2005—. Instr. U. Dayton, Ohio, 2004—. Named Cert. Tchr. of Yr., Western Dist. of Ohio, 1998, 2001, Family of Yr., Ohio Fedn. Music Clubs, 2002; recipient Family of Yr. award Ohio Fedn. Music Clubs, 2002; MTNA Found. fellow, 2004. Fellow Music Tchrs. Nat. Assn.; mem. Ohio Music Tchrs. Assn. (pres. 1980-82, chmn. western dist. 1976-78), Calif. Assn. Bilingual Edn. (chmn. cpt. 2005-06, Tchr. of Yr. 2006), Dayton Music Club (pres. 1989-91), Mu Phi Epsilon (pres. Dayton alumnae chpt. 1986-88), Dayton Piano Tchrs. Study Club (v.p. 2004-2006). Home: 9620 Belfry Ct Dayton OH 45458-4157 Office Phone: 937-885-3983. Personal E-mail: wassonpno@aol.com.

**WASSON, JAMES WALTER,** aircraft electronics manufacturing company executive; b. Pitts., Dec. 9, 1951; s. George Frederick and Dolores Helen (Weurl) W.; m. Evelyn Fay Gonzales, Dec. 28, 1974; children: Robert, Brian. AST, Pitts. Inst. Aeronautics, 1972; BSET, Northrop U., Inglewood, Calif. 1981; MBA, U. Phoenix, Mesa, 1988, govt. contracts mgmt. cert., 1989; PhD in Internat. Bus., Stamford Hill U., London, 2005. Avionics technician various cos., 1972-74; electronics prodn. mgr. Ostgaard Industries, Gardena, Calif., 1974-75; sr. avionics design engr. Allied Signal Garrett Airesearch Aviation Co., L.A., 1975-81; v.p. engring., co-founder Avionics Engring. Svcs., Inc., Tucson, 1980-81; sr. tech. specialist Northrop Aircraft Div., Hawthorne, Calif., 1981-84; prog. mgr. McDonnell Douglas Helicopter Co., Mesa, Ariz., 1984-93; exec. v.p., co-founder Leading Edge Technologies, Inc., Mesa, 1991-95; mgr. bus. devel. McDonnell Douglas Helicopter Sys., Mesa, 1993-95; dir. advanced tech. devel. Smiths Aerospace, Inc., Grand Rapids, Mich., 1995—2004; chief tech. officer BAE Sys., Johnson City, NY, 2004—. Adj. prof. ops. mgmt., contract mgmt., program mgmt., proposal devel., strategic mgmt., mktg., tech. mgmt., rsch. projects U. Phoenix Online Campus, 1990-2005, chair Grad. Bus. and Mgmt. Coll., U. Phoenix, W. Mich. Campus, 2000-2004, acad. cabinet, 2001-2003; cons. in field. Author: Avionics Systems Operation and Maintenance, 1993, Business Opportunities in Artificial Intelligence, 1988; contbr. articles to profl. journ. Inventor in field Com. chem. industry adv. bd. Northrop U., 1981; chmn. bd. dirs., pres. Alta Mesa Community Assn., 1989; organizer Boy Scouts Am., Mesa, 1988. Named Engr. of Yr., Northrop U., 1980; recipient Disting. Alumnus award Pitts. Inst. Aeronautics, 1981, U. Phoenix, 1996; named to Hall of Fame, Career Colls. Assn., 1991. Mem. AIAA, IEEE, NSPE, Soc. Automotive Engrs., Army Aviation Assn. (chpt. v.p. 1988-91, treas. 1993-95), Nat. Def. Indsl. Assn., Assn. U.S. Army, Am. Helicopter Soc. (chmn. avionics com. 1990), Assn. Avionics Educators, Rotorcraft Industry Tech. Assn. (bd. dirs. 1998-99), Crystal Springs Country Club (fin. com. 2000-01). Republican. Roman Catholic. Avocations: flying, scuba diving, hiking, golf, camping. E-mail: james.wasson@baesystems.com.

**WASSON, JEFFREY,** music educator; b. Evanston, Ill., Aug. 24, 1948; s. Newton Oliver and Hilda Crowell Wasson. MusB, Northwestern U., 1970, MusM, 1973, PhD, 1987. Instr. music Northwestern U., Evanston, Ill., 1980-85; asst. prof. music Barat Coll., Lake Forest, Ill., 1986-92; dir. music St. Mary of the Angels, Chgo., 1992-97. Barat Coll. Lake Forest, Ill., 1987—, assoc. prof. music, 1992-99, prof. music, 1999-2001, Barat Coll. DePaul U., 2001—02; prof. musicianship DePaul U., Chgo., 2002—. Vis. prof. music, Northwestern U., 1990, 93; bd. mem. New Music Chgo., 1987, 92-94, v.p., 1987-88, pres., 1988-92; bd. dirs. Ars Musica Chgo., 2000-05, v.p., 2003-04, pres., 2004—; NEH summer seminar participant Brandeis U., 1995, Boston U., 2000; lectr. Yale U., U. Leuven, Belgium, U. Mich., Ann Arbor, U. Minn., U. Mich. State U., Loyola U. of Chgo., U. Nebr. Editor: A Compendium of American Musicology, 2000; contbr. articles to profl. jours., chpts. to books. Summer seminar grantee NEH, U. Rochester (declined). Mem. NARAS, Am. Musicol. Soc., Am. Guild Organists, Internat. Musicol. Soc., Coll. Music Soc., Organ Hist. Soc., Club Internationale, Phi Kappa Lambda. Episcopalian. Avocations: fine art collecting, Lionel trains. Office: DePaul Univ School Music 804 W Belden Ave Chicago IL 60614-3296 Office Phone: 773-325-4378.

**WASSON, STEVEN,** music educator, piano technician; b. Dayton, Ohio, June 17, 1946; s. Audley Jackson and Barbara Hickam Wasson; m. Emmagene Phyllis Goss, Nov. 27, 1971. MusB, Eastman Sch. Music, Rochester, New York, 1969; MusM, Eastman Sch. Music, 1971; D of Musical Arts, Coll. Conservatory of Music, Cin., 2000. Pvt. music tchr. Wasson Music Studio,

Rochester, 1970—72, Milw., 1972—73, Dayton, Ohio, 1974—, piano technician, 1985—. Lectr. in field. Musician: Commemorative Dedications, Op. 40, Smoke And Steel, Op. 15 (Louis Lane prize Eastman Sch. Music, 1968), Paraphrases, Op. 39. Ch. coun. sec. Resurrection Evang. Luth. Ch., Centerville, Ohio, 1989—90. Mem.: BMI (assoc.), Am. Music Ctr., Assn. Wels And Els Composers (assoc.), Am. Composers Forum (assoc.), Am. Coll. Musicians (assoc.), Music Tchrs. Nat. Assn. (assoc.; Ohio state composition chmn. 1983—84). Republican. Avocations: reformation theological studies, linguistics, gardening, bowling. Home and Office: Wasson Music Studio 415 Corona Ave Dayton OH 45419-2606 E-mail: drswssnmuscstd@aol.com.

**WASTBERG, OLLE M.,** cultural organization administrator; b. Stockholm, May 6, 1945; s. Erik and Greta (Hirsch) W.; m. Inger Claesson, Feb. 21, 1968; children: David, Elias. BA, U. Stockholm, 1972. Tchr. polit. sci. U. Stockholm, 1967-68; journalist polit. dept. Expressen, 1968-71; editor-in-chief, 1994-95; rsch. fellow Bus. and Soc. Rsch. Ctr., 1971-76; pres. Aktieframjandet, 1976-82; mem. Parliament, 1976-82; pres. Swedish Newspaper Promotion Assn., 1983-91; undersec. of state for fin. affairs Ministry of Fin., Stockholm, 1991-93; pres. bd. Nordic Investment Bank, 1992-94, Swedish Broadcasting Corp., 1996-99; consul gen. for Sweden in NY, 1999—2004; dir. gen. Swedish Inst. Bd., 2005—. Dir. Stockholm Stock Exchange, 1977-82, 88-92; group of 10 deputies IMF, 1991-93; Swedish del. meeting of ministries of fin., 1992; mem. govt. com. on S. Africa consumer politics and stock market; pres. Bertil Ohlin Inst., 1996-2000. Author books on African problems, immigration politics and econ. topics; contbr. articles to profl. jour. Polit. sec. Liberal Youth Sweden, 1966, v.p., 1996-71; bd. Liberal Party, 1972-93, 97-2000, pres. exec. com., 1982-83; bd. dir. Friends of Hebrew U. of Jerusalem. Recipient Gold medal Swedish Mktg. Group, 1982; Swedish Man of the Yr., NY, 2003. Home: Bellmansgatan 6 11820 Stockholm Sweden Office: Swedish Inst Skeppbron 2 16391 Stockholm Sweden Office Phone: +4684537810. Business E-Mail: olle@wastberg.se.

**WASTERLAIN, CLAUDE GUY,** neurologist; b. Courcelles, Belgium, Apr. 15, 1935; s. Desire and Simone (De Taeye) W.; m. Anne Marguerite Thomsin, Feb. 28, 1967; 1 child, Jean Michel. Cand. Sci., U. Liege, 1957, MD, 1961; LS in Molecular Biology, U. Brussels, 1969. Resident Cornell U. Med. Coll., NYC, 1964-67, instr. neurology, 1969-70, asst. prof., 1970-75, assoc. prof., 1975-76, UCLA Sch. Medicine, 1976-79, prof., 1979—2005, vice-chair dept. neurology, 1976—, disting. prof., 2005—; chief neurology svc. VA Med. Ctr., Sepulveda, Calif., 1976—. Attending neurologist UCLA Ctr. Health Scis., 1976—; chair neurology Greater LA VA Health Care Sys., 1998—. Author, editor: Status Epilepticus, 1984, Neonatal Seizures, 1990, Molecular Neurobiology and Epilepsy, 1992, Progressive Nature of Epileptogenesis, 1996, Status Epilepticus: Mechanism Management, 2006; contbr. articles to med. jours. William Evans fellow, U. Auckland, New Zealand, 1984; recipient N.Y. Neurol. Soc. Young Investigator award, 1965, Rsch. Career Devel. award NIH, 1973-76, Worldwide AES award for rsch. in epilepsy, 1992, Golden Hammer Tchg. award, 1996, Amb. for Epilepsy, Internat. League Against Epilepsy, 2003. Fellow Am. Acad. Neurology; mem. Am. Neurol. Assn., Am. Soc. Neurochemistry (coun. mem. 1991-97), Internat. Soc. Neurochemistry, Am. Epilepsy Soc., Royal Soc. Medicine. Avocations: tennis, skiing, jazz, theater. Office: West LA Va Med Ctr 11301 Wilshire Blvd Los Angeles CA 90073 Office Phone: 310-268-3595. Business E-Mail: wasterla@ucla.edu.

**WASYLYNA, VICTOR J.,** lawyer; s. Myron and Mary Wasylyna. BS in Chem. Engring., Ohio State U., Columbus, 1996; JD, Case Western Res. U., Cleve., 2003. Bar: Ohio Supreme Ct., U.S. Patent and Trademark Office. Assoc. Thompson Hine LLP, Dayton, Ohio, 2003—. Mem.: ABA, Dayton Intellectual Property Law Assn., Am. Intellectual Property Law Assn. Office: Thompson Hine LLP 10 W Second St Dayton OH 45402 Office Phone: 937-443-6812.

**WATABE, NORIMITSU,** biologist, marine biologist, educator; b. Kure, Hiroshima, Japan, Nov. 29, 1922; came to U.S., 1957; s. Isamu and Matsuko (Takamatsu) W.; m. Sakuko Kobayashi, Dec. 12, 1952; children: Shoichi, Sachiko. BS, 1st Nat. High Sch., Tokyo, 1945; MS, Tohoku U., Sendai, Japan, 1948, DSc, 1960. Rsch. investigator Fuji Pearl Co., Mie-ken, Japan, 1948-52; instr. Prefect U. Mie, Tsu, Mie-ken, 1952-55, asst. prof., 1955-59; rsch. assoc. Duke U., Durham, N.C., 1957-70; assoc. prof. U. S.C., Columbia, 1970-72, prof. biology and marine sci., 1972-93, disting. prof., 1993-94, disting. prof. emeritus, 1994—. Cons. Ford Found., 1968; vis. prof. U. Bonn, Germany, 1976-77; dir. Electron Microscopy Ctr., 19770-95; cons. in field. Author: Studies on Pearls, 1959; editor: Mechanisms of Mineralization, 1976, Mechanisms of Biomineralization, 1980, Hard Tissue Mineralization and Demineralization, 1991; assoc. editor, Jour. Morphology, 1999—; contbr. articles to profl. jours. Recipient Pearl Rsch. award Elmer W. Ellsworth, 1952, Alexander Von Humboldt award Govt. of Germany, Russel award U. SC, 1981; grantee NIH, 1971-76, NSF, 1973-95. Fellow AAAS; mem. Am. Micros. Soc. (life). Avocations: music, piano playing. Office: Dept Biol Sci U South Carolina Columbia SC 29208-0001

**WATANABE, AUGUST MASARU,** physician, educator, retired science association director; b. Portland, Oreg., Aug. 17, 1941; s. Frank H. and Mary Y. W.; m. Margaret Whildin Reese, Mar. 14, 1964; children: Nan Reiko, Todd Franklin, Scott Masaru. BS, Wheaton Coll., Ill., 1963; MD, Ind. U., 1967. Diplomate Am. Bd. Internal Medicine. Intern Ind. U. Med. Center, Indpls., 1967-68, resident, 1968-69, 71-72, fellow in cardiology, 1972-74; clin. assoc. NIH, 1969-71; clin. instr. medicine Georgetown U. Med. Sch., Washington, 1970-71; mem. faculty Ind. U. Sch. Medicine, Indpls., 1972—2003, prof. medicine and pharmacology, 1978—2003, chmn. dept. medicine, 1983-90; dir. Regenstrief Inst. for Health Care Ind. U. Sch. of Medicine, Indpls., 1984-90; from v.p. to group v.p. rsch. labs. Eli Lilly & Co., Indpls., 1990-94, v.p., pres. labs, 1994-95; exec. v.p. sci. and tech. Eli Lilly and Co., Indpls., 1996—2003; chmn. bd. BioCrossroads, 2003—. Mem. pharmacology study sect. NIH, 1979-81, chmn., 1981-83; cardiovasc.-renal adv. com. FDA, 1982-85; mem. com. A, Nat. Heart, Lung and Blood Inst., 1984-88, chmn., 1986-88; bd. dirs. QuatRx, Endocyte, Reliant, Kalyrsys, Ambrx; cons. in field. Contbr. articles to profl. jours.; editorial bds. sci. jours. Bd. dirs. Ind. U. Found., 1989—, Indpls. Symphony Orch., 1994—, Regenstrief Found., 1995—. NIH grantee, 1972-92. Fellow ACP, Am. Coll. Cardiology, Am. Heart Assn. (councils on clin. cardiology and circulation, research rev. com. Ind. affiliate 1978-82, research and adv. com. North Central region 1978-82, adv. com. cardiovascular drugs 1976-79, chmn. com. 1979-81, chmn. program com. council on basic sci. 1982-84, chmn. com. on sci. sessions programs 1985-88, bd. dirs. 1985-88), Am. Coll. Cardiology (govt. relations com. 1979-81, trustee 1982-87); mem. Am. Fedn. Clin. Research (councilor Midwest sect. 1976-77, chmn.-elect Midwest sect. 1977-78, chmn. sect. 1978-79, chmn. sect. nominating com. 1979-80), Am. Soc. Clin. Investigation, Am. Soc. Clin. Pharmacology and Therapeutics, Am. Soc. Pharmacology and Exptl. Therapeutics (exec. com. div. clin. pharmacology 1978-81), Cardiac Muscle Soc., Central Soc. Clin. Research (councillor 1983-86, pres.-elect 1989, pres. 1990), Internat. Soc. Heart Research, Assn. Am. Physicians, Assn. Profs. of Medicine, Sigma Xi. Office: BioCrossroads Baker and Daniels Bldg 300 N Meridian St Ste 950 Indianapolis IN 46204

**WATANABE, CORINNE KAORU AMEMIYA,** judge, state official; b. Wahiawa, Hawaii, Aug. 1, 1950; d. Keiji and Setsuko Amemiya; m. Edwin Tsugio Watanabe, Mar. 8, 1975; children: Traciann Keiko, Brad Natsuo, Lance Yoneo. BA, U. Hawaii, 1971; JD, Baylor U., 1974. Bar: Hawaii 1974. Dep. atty. gen. State of Hawaii, Honolulu, 1974-84, 1st dep. atty. gen., 1984-85, 87-92, atty. gen., 1985-87; assoc. judge Hawaii Intermediate Ct. Appeals, Honolulu, 1992—. Mem. ABA, Hawaii Bar Assn. Office: Hawaii Intermediate Ct Appeals 426 Queen St 2d Fl Honolulu HI 96813

**WATANABE, KEN,** actor; s. Koide, Niigata, Japan, Oct. 21, 1959; m. Kaho Minami, Dec. 2005; 2 children from previous marriage. Actor: (films) Setouchi shonen yakyu dan, 1984, Kekkon annai mystery, 1985, Tampopo, 1985, Umi to dokuyaku, 1986, Bakumatsu jyunjyoden, 1991, Rajio no jikan, 1997, Kizuna, 1998, Supêsutoraberâzu, 2000, Oboreru sakana, 2001, Sennen no koi-Hikaru Genji monogatari, 2001, Hi wa mata noboru, 2002, T.R.Y.,

2003, The Last Samurai, 2003 (Acad. Award nomination for best supporting actor, 2004), Year One in the North, 2005, Batman Begins, 2005, Memoirs of a Geisha, 2005; (TV series) Kimitachi ga ite boku ga iru, 1992, Ikebukuro West Gate Park, 2000, Hojo Tokumune, 2001, Suna no utsuwa, 2004. Mailing: c/o Roar 2400 Broadway Santa Monica CA 90404*

**WATANABE, KYOICHI A(LOYSIUS),** pharmacology educator, chemist; b. Amagasaki, Hyogo, Japan, Feb. 28, 1935; s. Yujiro Paul and Yoshiko Francisca (Hashimoto) W.; m. Krystyna Lesiak; children: Kanna, Kay, Kenneth, Kim, Kelly, Katherine. BA, Hokkaido U., 1958, PhD, 1963. Lectr. Sophia U., Tokyo, 1963; rsch. assoc. Sloan-Kettering Inst., N.Y.C., 1963—66, assoc., 1968—72, 1972—81, prof., 1981—95; rsch. fellow U. Alta., Edmonton, Canada, 1966—68; assoc. prof. Cornell U. Med. Coll., N.Y.C., 1972—81, prof. pharmacology, 1981—98; dir. organic chemistry Codon Pharm., Inc., Gaithersburg, Md., 1996—98; v.p. R&D Pharmasset Inc., Tucker, Ga., 1998—; vis. prof. chem. dept. Emory U., 2003—. Study sect. NIH, Washington, 1981-84. Recipient Szalecki medal, Wojzkowa Akademia Medyczna, 1989, Marie Sklodowka Curie medal, Polish Chem. Soc., 1993, František Šorm Meml. award, Czech Acad. Scis., 2002. Mem. Polish Chem. Soc. (hon.), Russian Acad. Sci. (bd. sci. cons. Engelhardt Inst. Molecular Biology 1994-97). Achievements include rsch. in total synthesis of nucleoside antibiotics, novel heterocycle ring transformation, C-nucleoside chemistry, antiviral and anticancer nucleosides, intercalating agents, modified oligonucleotides, triplex DNA for gene repair.

**WATANABE, MAMORU,** internist, researcher; s. Takazo and Nao W.; m. Marie Watanabe, June 1, 1974; 1 child, David. MD, McGill U., 1957, PhD, 1963. Intern Royal Victoria Hosp., Montreal, 1957—58, resident in medicine, 1958—63; prof. medicine U. Alta., Edmonton, 1967—74, U. Calgary, Alta., 1974—97, head internal medicine Alta., 1974—76, assoc. dean edn. Alta., 1976—80, assoc. dean research Alta., 1980—81, acting dean medicine Alta., 1981—82, dean faculty medicine Alta., 1982—92, prof. emeritus Alta., 1997—. Fellow Royal Coll. Physicians and Surgeons (Can.). Home: 162 Pumpridge Place SW Calgary AB Canada T2V 5E6 Office: U Calgary 3330 Hospital Dr NW Calgary AB Canada T2N 1N4 Office Phone: 403-220-8725. Business E-Mail: watanabe@ucalgary.ca.

**WATANABE, MARK DAVID,** pharmacist, educator; b. Santa Monica, Calif., Dec. 7, 1955; s. Jack Shigeru and Rose Nobuko (Iida) W. BA in Chemistry, U. Calif., Irvine, 1977, BS in Biol. Sci., 1978; PharmD, U. Calif., San Francisco, 1982, PhD in Pharm. Chemistry, 1990. Lic. pharmacist Calif., Oreg., Ill., Mass. Pharmacy intern various locations, San Francisco, 1979-82; pharmacist Kaiser Permanent, San Francisco, 1981-87; clin. scis. rsch. fellow in psychiat. pharmacy U. Tex., Austin, 1987-89; clin. asst. prof. pharmacy practice U. Ill., Chgo., 1989-98. Rsch. asst. U. Calif., San Francisco, 1980-87; clin. pharmacy cons. Ill. Dept. Mental Health & Devel. Disabilities, 1994-98; med. sci. mgr. Bristol-Myers Squibb, 1998-99; clin. pharmacy specialist Alameda Co., Calif., 1999-2003; asst. clin. prof. clin. pharmacy, U. Calif., San Francisco, 1999-2003; asst. clin. specialist Northeastern U., 2003—. Regents scholar U. Calif., San Francisco, 1979-82; recipient Excellence in Teaching award Long Found., San Francisco, 1984. Mem.: Am. Pharm. Assn., Am. Soc. Health-Sys. Pharmacists, Am. Coll. Clin. Pharmacy, Mensa, Rho Chi. Unitarian Universalist. Avocations: individual and fitness sports, reading, travel, music. Office: Northeastern U Sch Pharm 206 Mugar Boston MA 02115 Office Phone: 617-373-8172. Business E-Mail: m.watanabe@neu.edu.

**WATANABE, SATOSHI PATTEN,** economist, researcher; b. Koriyama, Fukushima, Japan, Oct. 19, 1966; s. Keiki Watanabe, Mieko Watanabe; m. Nicole Michelle Patten; children: Sean Lucas children: Daichi Joseph. BA, Weber State U., 1990, cert. in gerontology, 1990; MA in Econ., Columbia U., 1993, MEd, 1997, MA in Stats., 1999, MPhil, PhD, Columbia U., 2000. Lectr. Manhattan Coll., Riverdale, NY, 1998; stat. data analyst City of N.Y., 1998—99; rsch. assoc. Am. Inst. Rsch., Arlington, Va., 1999—2000, rsch. scientist, 2000—01, sr. rsch. scientist, 2001—02; asst. prof. Rsch. Ctr. for Univ. Studies, U. Tsukuba, Japan, 2002—04, assoc. prof. Rsch. Ctr. for Univ. Studies, 2004—. Bd. dirs. Policy Rsch. and Analysis Network for Japan, Washington, 1999—; cons. World Bank, Washington, 2000—01. Contbr. articles to profl. jours. Mem.: Soc. Labor Economists, Am. Econ. Assn., Phi Kappa Phi. Unitarian Universalist. Avocations: travel, guitar, marathons. Office: U Tsukuba 3-29-1 Otsuka Bankyo-ku Tokyo 112-0012 Japan Office Fax: 703-527-4661. E-mail: swatanabe@mbaib.gsbs.tsukuba.ac.jp.

**WATCHORN, WILLIAM ERNEST,** venture capitalist; b. Toronto, Ont., Can., Aug. 8, 1943; s. Roy Elgin and Josephine (Swyrida) W.; m. Maureen Emmett, Dec. 28, 1967; 1 child, Meghan. Chartered Acct., Toronto, 1967. Mgr. fin. planning Found. Group of Cos., Toronto, 1968-70; cons. Regional Master Planning Study, Malaysia, 1970-72; controller Selkirk Holdings, Ltd., Toronto, 1972-75; corp. contr. Torstar Corp., Toronto, 1975-78; v.p. fin. Canwest Capital Corp., Winnipeg, Man., 1978-82; exec. v.p. Kaiser Resources Ltd., Vancouver, B.C., 1982; sr. v.p., CFO, Fed. Industries Ltd., Winnipeg, 1982-88; pres., CEO, Fed. Industries Indsl. Group, Winnipeg, 1989-91; CEO, Ensis Corp., Inc., Winnipeg, 1991-97; founder, pres., CEO Ensis Growth Fund Inc., Ensis Mgmt. Inc., Winnipeg, 1997—; pres., CEO Altura Growth Fund (EVCC) Inc., Altura Mgmt., Inc., Vancouver, BC, Canada, 2002—04. Bd. dirs. Ensis Growth Fund Inc., Winnipeg Airports Authority Inc.; mem. Manitoba Bus. Coun.; assoc. Asper Sch. Bus., U. Man. Bd. dirs. C.D. Howe Inst., Toronto, Can. Stds. Assn. Fellow Man. Inst. Chartered Accts.; mem. Can. Inst. Chartered Accts., Winter Club, St. Charles Country Club. Avocations: squash, golf, tennis. Home: 6453 Southboine Dr Winnipeg MB Canada R3R 0B7 Office: Ensis Growth Fund Inc 200 Graham Ave Ste 1120 Winnipeg MB Canada R3C 4L5 Office Phone: 204-949-3710. Business E-Mail: watchorn@ensis.mb.ca.

**WATED, GUILLERMO,** psychology educator; s. Guillermo F. and Eugenie Wated. BS in Bus. Adminstrn., U. Miami, Coral Gables, 1992, MBA, 1994; MS, Fla. Internat. U., Miami, 1999, PhD in Indsl. Orgnl. Psychology, 2002. Instr. Fla. Internat. U., 2002—05; asst. prof. psychology Barry U., 2005—. Cons. Skyversity, Inc., Miami, 2000—04. Contbr. articles to profl. jours. Mem.: APA, Soc. Tchg. Psychology, Soc. Indsl./Orgnl. Psychology. Office: Barry Univ Psychology Dept 11300 NE 2d Ave Miami FL 33161

**WATERBURY, JOHN,** academic administrator, political science professor, writer; PhD in Pub. Law and Govt., Columbia U., 1968. Asst. prof. polit. sci. U. Mich., 1968; mem. Am. Univs. Field Staff, Cairo, 1971—77; prof. politics and internat. affairs Woodrow Wilson Sch. Pub. and Internat. Affairs, Princeton U., NJ, dir. Ctr. Internat. Studies NJ; pres. Am. U. of Beirut, 1998—. Vis. prof. U. of Aix-Marseilles III, 1977—78; editor World Politics jour. Princeton U., 1992—98. Author: Commander of the Faithful: The Moroccan Political Elite-a Study in Segmented Politics, Vol. 2, 1970, North for the Trade: The Life and Times of a Berber Merchant, 1972, Egypt: Burdens of the past, Options for the Future, 1978, Hydropolitics of the Nile Valley, 1979, Egypt of Nasser and Sadat: The Political Economy of Two Regimes, 1983, Exposed to Innumerable Delusions: Public Enterprise and State Power in Egypt, India, Mexico, and Turkey, 1993, Nile Basin: National Determinants of Collective Action, 2002; co-editor: Patrons and Clients, 1977; co-author: Middle East in the Coming Decade: From Wellhead to Well-Being, 1978; co-editor: The Political Economy of Risk and Choice in Senegal, 1987; co-author: Political Economy of the Middle East: State, Class, and Economic Development, 1990; co-editor: Political Economy of Public Sector Reform and Privatization, 1990, Peasants and Politics in the Modern Middle East, 1991; co-author: Core and Periphery: A Comprehensive Approach to Middle Eastern Water, 1997; contbr. articles to profl. jours. Office: Am U of Beirut Office of the Pres PO Box 11-0236 Riad El Solh 1107 2020 Lebanon Office Phone: 961 1 350000. Office Fax: 961 1 744474. E-mail: waterbury@aub.edu.lb.*

**WATERBURY, LARRY,** physician, educator; b. Ft. Worth, May 30, 1937; m. Marcia Winkelman, 1968. Student, Princeton U., 1955-57, S.W. Tex. Coll., 1957-58; MD, U. Tex., Galveston, 1962. Diplomate Am. Bd. Internal

Medicine, Am. Bd. Hematology, Am. Bd. Oncology. Intern U. Okla. Hosps., Oklahoma City, 1962-63; resident internal medicine parkland Meml. Hosp., Dallas, 1965-67; instr. dpet. Medicine U. Tex., Dallas, 1969-70; from instr. to assoc. prof. medicine Johns Hospkins U., Balt., 1970-82, assoc. prof. medicine, 1982—, assoc. prof. oncology, 1986—. Asst. chief physician Balt. City Hosps., 1970—, dir. blood bank, 1970-73; chief divsn. hematology, oncology Francis Scott Key Med. Ctr., Balt., 1978—; mem. adv. com. Johns Hopkins Home Health Care Hospice, 1995—. Author: Hematology for the House Officer, 1981, 4th edit., 1996, (chpt.) Clinical Pathology, 1973, Complications of Neoplastic Disorders, 1979, Guide to Hematologic Disorders, 1980; co-author: (chpt.) Clinical Anesthesia, Vol. 3, 1968; author, co-author: (chpt.) Principles and Practice of Medicine, 19th edit., 1976, Principles of Ambulatory Medicine, 3d edit., 1991, 6th edit., 2003; contbr. articles to profl. jours. With U.S. Army Spl. Forces, 1963-65, Vietnam. Mem. Am. Soc. Hematology, Am. Soc. Clin. Oncology. Home: 5713 Visitation Way Baltimore MD 21210-1348 Office: Johns Hopkins Bayview Med Ctr Bayview Campus Divsn Hematology Oncology 4940 Eastern Ave Baltimore MD 21224-2735 E-mail: lawaterbur@aol.com.

**WATERER, BONNIE CLAUSING,** retired secondary school educator; b. Toledo, Sept. 25, 1940; d. Kermit Henry and Helen Ethel (Waggoner) Clausing; m. Louis P. Waterer, June 17, 1961; children: Ryan, Reid. BS in Home Econs. Edn., Ohio State U., 1962; MA in Home Econs. Edn., San Jose State U., 1966. Tchr. James Lick H.S., San Jose, 1963-67, 1973-76; adult edn. instr. Met. Adult Edn. Program, San Jose, 1968-75; home econs. instr. Independence H.S., San Jose, 1976-99, home econs. dept. chair, 1976-80; home econs. coord. East Side Union H.S. Dist., San Jose, 1980-99, coord. coll. and career resource ctrs., 1995-99, ret., 1999—. Child care occupations instr. Ctrl. County Occupl. Ctr., San Jose, 1989-99; child devel. instr. Evergreen Valley Coll., San Jose, 1995. Bd. dirs. NAMI Yavapai County, Ariz., 2001—, West Yavapai Guidance Clinic, 2005—; mem. Family Resource Ctr. adv. coun. Yavapai Regional Med. Ctr., 2004—. Mem.: AAUW (v.p. Prescott br. 2004—06), Home Econs. Tchrs. Assn. Calif. (pres. 1989—91, Outstanding Tchr. award 1987), Calif. Assn. Family and Consumer Sci. (Tchr. of Yr. award 1994), Am. Assn. Family and Consumer Sci., Phi Upsilon Omicron, Delta Kappa Gamma (sec. Prescott br. 2002—06), Omicron Nu. Democrat. Methodist. Avocations: travel, computers, cooking, sewing. Home: 1052 Vantage Pt Cir Prescott AZ 86301 E-mail: bh2oer@aol.com.

**WATERHOUSE, KEITH,** urologist, educator, retired surgeon; b. Derby, UK, May 10, 1929; arrived in U.S., 1953, naturalized, 1964; s. Arthur Reginald and Marion (Tock) Waterhouse; m. Anne Therese Milotzky, Jan. 14, 1955; children: Katherine-Anne, Vincent, Maria-Ursula, Isabelle, Christopher. BA, Cambridge U., Eng., 1950; MD, Oxford U. Med. Sch., Eng., 1953; MA, Cambridge U., Eng., 1957. Cert. urology 1964. Intern Bklyn. Hosp., 1953—54; resident Kings County Hosp., Bklyn., 1957—59; instr. surgery SUNY, Bklyn., 1959—61, asst. prof. urology, 1961—62, assoc. prof. urology, 1962—65, prof. surgery, 1965—84, chmn. dept. urology, 1969—84, prof. emeritus, 1984—. Dir. urology Kings County Hosp., 1962—84; urologist-in-chief Downstate Med. Ctr., Bklyn., 1962—84; chmn. Residency Rev. Com., 1975—76, Registry Genito Urinary Pathology, 1975—76. Contbr.: 86 articles to med. jours., mem. editl. bd.: 6 med. jours. including Jour. Urology, Urology, Nephrology, and Urologic Radiology. Capt. Royal Army Med. Corps, 1955—57, Berlin. Recipient Valentine medal, NY Acad. Medicine, 1992, William Bureau award, NJ Acad. Medicine, 1973. Fellow: Royal Coll. Surgeons, Am. Coll. Pediatrics, Am. Coll. Surgeons; mem.: Clin. Soc. Genito Urinary Surgeons, Australian Urol. Soc. (hon.), Italian Urol. Soc. (hon.), Panamanian Urol. Soc. (hon.), Am. Soc. Genito Urinary Surgeons, Am. Urol. Soc., S.W. Fla. Archaeol. Soc. (pres. 1989—90, dir. 1987—93). Personal E-mail: rkwivhs@aol.com.

**WATERMAN, CHRISTOPHER,** dean; MusB in Composition and Electric Bass, Berklee Coll. Music; PhD in Anthropology, U. Ill. Assoc. prof. music U. Wash., head ethnomusicology program, chair African studies prof.; rept. dept. world arts and cultures UCLA, 1996—, chair dept., 1997, acting dean, 2002—04, dean Sch. Arts and Arch., 2004—. Author: Juju: A Social History and Ethnography of an African Popular Music, 1990; co-author: American Popular Music: From Minstrelsy to MTV, 2002. Recipient Ethel Curry Disting. Lectureship in Musicology, U. Mich. Achievements include cited by Rolling Stone magazine for his innovative course on world popular music, 1992. Office: UCLA Sch Arts and Arch Box 951427 303 E Melnitz Los Angeles CA 90095-1427

**WATERMAN, DANIEL,** mathematician, educator; b. Bklyn., Oct. 24, 1927; s. Samuel and Anna (Robson) W.; m. Mudite Upesleja, Nov. 4, 1960; children: Erica, Susan, Scott. BA, Bklyn. Coll., 1947; MA, Johns Hopkins U., 1948; PhD, U. Chgo., 1954. Research assoc. Cowles Commn. Research in Econs., Chgo., 1951-52; instr. Purdue U., West Lafayette, Ind., 1953-55, asst. prof., 1955-59, U. Wis.-Milw., 1959-61; prof. Wayne State U., Detroit, 1961-69, Syracuse (N.Y.) U., 1969-96, prof. emeritus, 1996—, chmn. math dept., 1988-94. Cons. Martin-Marietta, Denver, 1960-61; rschr. in real and Fourier analysis, rsch. prof. Fla. Atlantic U., 1997—. Author: Homeomorphisms in Analysis, 1997; editor: Classical Real Analysis, 1985: contbr. articles to profl. jours. Fulbright fellow U. Vienna, 1952-53 Mem. Math. Assn. Am., Am. Math. Soc. (coun. mem.-at-large 1975-78), JMAA (assoc. editor 1997—), Radovi Matematicki (editl. advisor 1986—), Sigma Xi. Home: 7739 Majestic Palm Dr Boynton Beach FL 33437-5413 E-mail: fourier@adelphia.net.

**WATERMAN, ELLEN K.,** director; b. Chattanooga; children: Jennifer W., Meghan K. BA in Psychology, Rosemont Coll., Pa., 1965; MA in Info. and Learning Techs., U. Colo., 1996. Dir. Inst. U. Denver U. Coll., 1987—92; dir. prodn. Jones Internat. U., Englewood, Colo., 1993—94; dir. distance learning Regis U., Denver, 1996—2006. Bd. trustees, v.p. Denver Botanic Gardens, 1978—90; trustee Betty Ford Alpine Gardens, Vail, Colo., 1993—96. Contbr. articles to profl. jours. Recipient Excellence cert., Nat. U. Continuing Edn. Assn., 1990, 1992; grantee, US Dept. Edn., 2000—02. Mem.: Internat. Soc. for Performance Improvement. Avocation: gardening. Office: Regis Univ SPS 3333 Regis Blvd - Code K18 Denver CO 80221 Business E-Mail: ewaterma@regis.edu.

**WATERMAN, MICHAEL SPENCER,** mathematics professor, biology professor; b. Coquille, Oreg., 1942; s. Ray S. and Bessie E. Waterman; m. Vicki Lynn Buss, Chgo (div. 1977); 1 child, Tracey Lynn BS, Oreg. State U., 1964, MS, 1966; MA, Mich. State U., 1968, PhD, 1969. Assoc. prof. Idaho State U., Pocatello, 1969-75; mem. staff Los Alamos Nat. Lab., 1975-82, cons., 1982—; prof. math. and biology U. So. Calif., L.A., 1982—, U. So. Calif. Assocs. Endowed Chair, 1991—. Vis. prof. math. U. Hawaii, Honolulu, 1979-80; vis. prof. structural biology U. Calif. San Francisco, 1982; vis. prof. Mt. Sinai Med. Sch., NYC, 1988; 150th anniversary vis. prof. Chalmers U., 2000; Aisenstadt chair U. Montreal, 2001 Author: Introduction to Computational Biology, 1995; editor: Mathematical Methods for DNA Sequences, Calculating the Secrets of Life, 1995, Genetic Mapping and DNA Sequencing, 1996, Mathematical Support for Molecular Biology, 1999; Annals of Combinatorics, Methodology and Computing in Applied Probability, Genomics, Computational Methods in Science and Technology, Acta Biochimica et Biophysica Sinca; editor-in-chief: Jour. Computational Biology; contbr. articles to profl. jours. Recipient Internat. award, Gardner Found., 2002; fellow, Guggenheim Found., 1995; grantee, NSF, 1971, 1972, 1975, 1988—Los Alamos Nat. Lab., 1976, 1981, Sys. Devel. Found., 1982—87, NIH, 1986—99, Sloan Found., 1990—91. Fellow AAAS, Am. Acad. Arts and Scis. Inst. Math. Stats.; mem. NAS, French Acad. Sci., Am. Statis. Assn., Soc. Math. Biology, Soc. Indsl. and Applied Math. Office: U So Calif Dept Biol Sci Los Angeles CA 90089-1340

**WATERMAN, ROBERT A.,** lawyer; b. LA, Jan. 4, 1954; m. Leslie Waterman; 2 children. BA summa cum laude, Calif. State U., Long Beach, 1976; JD, U. Calif., Berkeley, 1979. Bar: Calif. 1979. Mem. McCutchen, Doyle, Brown & Enersen, San Francisco; ptnr. Latham & Watkins, San

Francisco, 1993—97; sr. v.p., gen. counsel HCA, Nashville, 1997—. Assoc. editor Calif. Law Rev., 1977-78, note and comment editor, 1978-79. Mem. State Bar Calif. Office: HCA Inc 1 Park Plaza Nashville TN 37203

**WATERS, ALICE,** executive chef, restaurant owner, writer; b. Chatham, N.J., Apr. 28, 1944; 1 child. Grad. in French Cultural Studies, U. Calif., Berkeley, 1967; postgrad., Montessori Sch., London; degree (hon.), Mills Coll., Oakland, Calif., 1994. Exec. chef, owner Chez Panisse, Berkeley, Calif., 1971—, Chez Panisse Cafe, Berkeley, Calif., 1980—, Cafe Fanny, Berkeley, Calif., 1984—. Mem. adv. bd. U. Calif., Berkeley; active The Garden Project, San Francisco; spkr. in field of food safety and health. Author: Chez Panisse Menu Cookbook, Chez Panisse Vegetables, (storybook and cookbook for children) Fanny at Chez Panisse. Developer Martin Luther King Jr. Mid. Sch. Edible Schoolyard, Berkeley. Named Best Chef in Am., James Beard Found., 1992, Best Restaurant in Am., 1992, Humanitarian of Yr., 1997, Mother of Am. Cooking, N.Y. Times; named one of 10 Best Chefs in the World, Cuisine et Vins du France, 1986; recipient Spl. Achievement award, James Beard Found., 1985, Restaurant and Bus. Leadership award, Restaurants and Instns. Mag., 1987, Barbar Boxer Top Ten Women award, 1991, Le Tour du Monde en 80 Toques, Metziner & Varaut, 1991, Nat. Edn. Diplomate award, 1996. Office: Chez Panisse 1517 Shattuck Ave Berkeley CA 94709-1598*

**WATERS, BETTY LOU,** newspaper reporter, writer; b. Texarkana, Tex., June 13, 1943; d. Chester Hinton and Una Erby (Walls) W. AA, Texarkana Jr. Coll., 1963; BA, East Tex. State U., 1965. Gen. assignment reporter Galveston County Pub. Co., Galveston and Texas City, 1965-68; news and feature writer Ind. and Daily Mail, Anderson, S.C., 1968-69; reporter Citizen-Times newspaper, Asheville, N.C., 1969-74; edn. and med. reporter News Star World Pub. Co., Monroe, La., 1974-79; reporter, writer Delta Democrat Times, Greenville, Miss., 1980-89; staff writer Tyler (Tex.) Morning Telegraph, 1990—. Named Citizen of Yr., Sigma Sigma chpt. Omega Psi Phi, 2001; recipient hon. mentions, Tex. AP, 1966, news media award, N.C. Easter Seal Soc., 1973, 1st place award for articles, La. Press Women's Contest, 1978, 1st place for interview, 1979, for gen. news, Miss. Press Assn., 1983, 3d place award for feature writing, 1984, for investigative reporting, 1988, 1st place for best series of articles, 1990, Sch. Bell award for outstanding series, 1997, award for outstanding edn. series, Tex. State Tchrs. Assn., 1998, Tex. Coll. Women Changing the World award, 2000, Sch. Bell award for outstanding continuous coverage, Tex. State Tchrs. Assn., 2004. Mem. Sigma Delta Chi.

**WATERS, CHRIS HAROLD,** literature and language professor, poet; b. Wilmington, N.C., Nov. 8, 1926; s. Harold Carlton and Theodora Beatrice (Baring-Gould) Waters; m. Lenore Paley Waters (div.); children: Gwyneth, Jennifer; m. Dora Vera Mancinelli, Aug. 12, 1979; 1 child, Matthew. AB, Harvard Coll., Cambridge, Mass., 1949; MA, U. Wash., Seattle, 1954, PhD, 1956. Instr. Salisbury Sch., Conn., 1951—52; tchg. asst. U. Wash., Seattle, 1952—55; instr. to asst. prof. Coll. William and Mary, Williamsburg, Va., 1955—60; asst. prof. Carlton Coll., Northfield, Minn., 1960—62; prof. U. R.I., Kingston, 1962—91, prof. emeritus, 1991—. Co-founder, head South County French Speaking Union, RI, 1982—; co-founder Paul Claudel Soc. Author: Senegal, Poems on Africa, 1999, Hatteras Symphony, Poems, 2001, Outer Banks Sonata, Poems, 2004. Pfc. U.S. Army, 1945—46. Mem.: R.I. Fgn. Lang. Assn., Am. Assn. Tchrs. French, African Lit. Assn. Avocations: tennis, bicycling, swimming. Home: PO Box 233 Saunderstown RI 02874

**WATERS, DONALD JOSEPH,** data processing executive; b. Balt., Sept. 16, 1952; s. Richard Hunter and Annette Catharine (Hannan) W.; m. Beverly Ann Brent, Apr. 5, 1974; children: Laura Elizabeth, Sarah Elizabeth. BA, U. Md., 1973; M Phil, Yale U., 1976, PhD, 1982. Resource specialist Yale Computer Ctr., New Haven, 1982-84; dir. computer services Yale Sch. Mgmt., New Haven, 1984-87; head, systems office Yale U. Library, New Haven, 1987-92, dir., libr. and adminstrv. systems, 1992-93, assoc. univ. librarian, 1993-97; dir. Digital Libr. Fedn., Coun. Libr. & Info. Resources, New Haven, 1997-99; program officer Andrew W. Mellon Found., N.Y., 1999—. Author: Strange Ways and Sweet Dreams: Afro-American Folklore From the Hampton Institute, 1983. Fellow AAAS; mem. Am. Soc. Info. Sci. Roman Catholic. Avocations: jazz, rowing, cabinet making. Home: 40 Overbrook Rd Madison CT 06443-1834 Office: 140 E 62nd St New York NY 10021-8124 Office Phone: 212-500-2470.

**WATERS, JENNIFER NASH,** lawyer; b. Bridgeport, Conn., Dec. 21, 1951; d. Lewis William and Patricia (Cousins) W.; m. Todd David Peterson, Sept. 19, 1981; children: Elizabeth, Andrew. BA, Radcliffe, 1972; JD, Harvard, 1976. Bar: D.C. 1977, U.S. Supreme Ct. 1980. Clk. U.S. Ct. Appeals (D.C. cir.), Washington, 1976-77; assoc. Jones, Day, Reavis & Poque, Washington, 1977-79, Crowell & Moring, Washington, 1979-83, ptnr., 1983—. Mem. ABA (ho. of dels. 1997-99), Fed. Energy Bar Assn. (bd. dirs. 1988-99, v.p. 1994-95, pres. 1996-97). Office: Crowell & Moring LLP 1001 Pennsylvania Ave NW Fl 10 Washington DC 20004-2505

**WATERS, JOHN,** film director, writer, actor; b. Balt., Apr. 22, 1946; s. John Samuel and Patricia Ann (Whitaker) W. Student, NYU, 1966. Speaker various colls., comedy clubs, U.S., Europe, Australia, 1968—. Writer, dir. films Roman Candles, 1966, Eat Your Makeup, 1968, Mondo Trasho, 1969, Multiple Maniacs, 1970, Pink Flamingos, 1972, Female Trouble, 1974, Desperate Living, 1977, Polyester, 1981, Cry-Baby, 1990, Serial Mom, 1994, Pecker, 1998, Cecil B. DeMented, 2000; writer, dir., actor film Hairspray, 1987; actor Something Wild, 1988, Homer and Eddie, 1990, Sweet and Lowdown, 1999, 21 Jump Street, 1990, Divine Trash, In Bad Taste, 1999, Blood Feast 2: All U Can Eat, 2002, Each Time I Kill, 2002; author: Shock Value, 1981, Crackpot, 1986, Trash Trio, 1988, Director's Cut, 1997; contbr. articles to N.Y. Times, Art. Film, other mags. Fund raiser AIDS Action Balt.; spokesperson Anti-Violence Campaign, N.Y.C., 1991. John Waters Day named in his honor State of Md., 1985; John Waters Week named in his honor City of Balt., 1988. Mem. AFTRA, SAG, Dirs. Guild Am., Writers Guild Am., Acad. Motion Picture Arts and Scis. Avocation: study of extreme catholic behavior before the reformation. Address: care CAA 9830 Wilshire Blvd Beverly Hills CA 90210

**WATERS, JOHN B.,** lawyer; b. Sevierville, Tenn., July 15, 1929; s. J. B. and Myrtle (Paine) W.; m. Patsy Temple, Apr. 8, 1953; children: John B., Cynthia Beth BS, U. Tenn., 1952, JD, 1961; D in Environ. Sci. (hon.), Milligan Coll., 1993. Bar: Tenn. 1961, U.S. Dist. Ct. (ea. dist.) Tenn. 1961, U.S. Supreme Ct. 1969, U.S. Dist. Ct. D.C. 1970. Of counsel Long, Ragsdale & Waters, P.C., Knoxville, Tenn.; mng. ptnr. Waters and Co. Investment Mgmt., 1993—. Mem. hearing coun. Bd. Profl. Responsibility Supreme Ct., 1974—80, 1995—2001, Fed. co-chmn. Appalachian Regional Commn., 1968—71; chmn. Sevier County Indsl. Bd., Sevierville Libr. Found.; mem. Gov.'s Com. Econ. Devel.; Tenn. rep. to So. Growth Policies Bd., 1970—74; appointed dir. by Pres. Reagan TVA, Knoxville, 1984, appointed chmn. bd. dirs. by Pres. Bush, 92; bd. dirs. Inst. Nuc. Power Ops., 1985—93; trustee East Tenn. Bapt. Hosp., Knoxville; mem. Tenn.-Tombigbee Waterway Authority, 1993—2000; bd. dirs. East Tenn. Found.; chmn. Leadership Sevier, 1996—2001. Author: Downbound, The Memoirs of John B. Waters, Jr., 2004. Dir. Friends of Great Smoky Mountain Nat. Pk. Lt. USN, 1952—55. Fellow Am. Bar Found.; mem. Tenn. Bar Assn. (pres. 1983-84), Sevier County Bar Assn. (past pres.). Republican. Baptist. Home: Waters Edge 405 Burridge Dr Sevierville TN 37862-3202 also: 119 Commerce St Sevierville TN 37862-3524 Office Phone: 865-453-1051. Business E-Mail: jbwaters@esper.com.

**WATERS, JOHN W.,** minister, educator; b. Atlanta, Feb. 5, 1936; s. Henry and Mary Annie (Randall) W. Cert., U. Geneva, Switzerland, 1962; BA, Fisk U., 1957; STB, Boston U., 1967, PhD, 1970. Ordained to ministry Bapt. Ch., 1967. Min. religious edn. Ebenezer Bapt. Ch., Boston, 1965-67, assoc. min., 1967-69; min. Myrtle Bapt. Ch., West Newton, Mass., 1969, Greater Solid Rock Bapt. Ch., Atlanta, 1980—2005, sr. min. emeritus, 2005—. Prof. Interdenominational Theol. Ctr., Atlanta, 1976-86, trustee, 1980-83, adj. prof.

---

2005-; bd. dirs. Habitat for Humanities, Atlanta, 1984-90; chmn. South Atlanta Joint Urban Ministries, 1983-93; chairperson Coun. Overseers New Era Bapt. Conv. Ctr., 1996-2001; pres. Clayton County Ministers Conf., 2000 Contbr. articles to profl. jours. Mem. Va. Highlands Neighborhood Assn., Atlanta, 1977-87, Butler St. YMCA, 1980-86, South Atlanta Civic League, 1983, others; treas. Prison Ministries with Women, Inc.; v.p. South Met. Ministries Fellowship, Atlanta, 1990-94. Fund for Theol. Edn. fellow, 1965-67, Nat. Fellowship Fund fellow, 1968-70, Rockefeller doctoral fellow, 1969. Mem. AAUP (chpt. pres. 1971-72), Am. Acad. Religion, Soc. Bibl. Lit., Blacks in Bibl. Studies, New Era Missionary Bapt. Conf. Ga., So. Bapt. Conv., Am. Legion Home: 1516 Niskey Lake Trl SW Atlanta GA 30331-6318 Address: PO Box 310416 Atlanta GA 30331 Personal E-mail: jwwatersphd@yahoo.com. *In life, each of us faces a variety of choices. The choices made determine our destiny, fate. When more of us assume responsibility and accountability for the choices made, the world in which we live will be decisively better.*

**WATERS, KAREN RIGSBY,** music educator; b. Murfreesboro, Tenn., Nov. 22, 1976; d. Marvin Leonard and Brenda Kaye Rigsby; m. James Paul Waters, Dec. 20, 2003. MusB, Tenn. Tech U., 1999. Lic. tchr. Tenn., 1999. Music specialist Sumner County Schs., Hendersonville, Tenn., 1999—2000, Dekalb County Schs., Smithville, Tenn., 2000—01, St. Bernard Acad., Nashville, 2001—03, St. Edward Sch., Nashville, 2003—. Choir dir. St. Edward Mass Choir, Nashville, St. Edward Show Choir, Nashville, 2003—; choral dir. St. Bernard Acad. Choir, Nashville, 2001—03; band dir. St. Bernard Acad. Band, Nashville, 2001—02; pvt. music instr. Self-employed, Nashville. Mem. Child's Best Interest, Nashville, 2003—04, Music Row Democrats, Nashville, 2004, First Bapt. Ch., Hendersonville, Tenn., 1999—2004. Scholar Music Achievement scholar, Tenn. Tech U., 1995—99. Mem.: Women's Coalition Parental Rights, Coalition Parental Rights, Mid. Tenn. Elem. Music Edn. Assn., Tenn. Music Educator Assn., Music Educators Nat. Conf., Mu Phi Epsilon (alumni sec. 1997—99). Baptist. Avocations: travel, reading, movies, golf. Office: Saint Edward School 190 Thompson Ln Nashville TN 37211 Office Phone: 615-833-5770.

**WATERS, LOU,** news correspondent; b. Mpls., July 7, 1938; s. Louis Joseph and Anne Marie Riegert; m. Martha Lee Morin, Feb. 15, 1975; children: Scott, Christopher, Alexander. Student, U. Minn. Reporter Sta. KDWB, Mpls., 1959, Sta. WWTC, Mpls., Sta. KFWB, L.A., Sta. WLBS-FM, N.Y.C., Sta. KNEW, San Francisco; reporter, anchor Sta. KVOA-TV, Tucson, news dir., Sta. KCST-TV, San Diego; asst. sta. mgr., evening anchor Sta. KOLD-TV, CBS, Tucson; co-anchor CNN Today CNN, Atlanta, 1980—89, co-anchor Earlyprime, 1991—. Avocations: golf, photography, music.

**WATERS, MARY A.,** literature and language professor; d. John Elvin and Myrtle Waters; m. Noel Phipps, May 31, 1994. BU, U. Calif., Davis, 1994—2001. Faculty fellow U. Calif., 2001—03; vis. prof. Temple U., Phila., 2003—04; asst. prof. Wichita State U., Kans., 2004—. Author: British Women Writers and the Profession of Literary Criticism, 1789-1832, 2004. Grantee Seminar grant, Nat. Endowment for Humanities, 2005; Travel grant, Fulbright Program, 1997—98. Mem.: MLA, North Am. Soc. Study Romanticism, Phi Kappa Phi Honor Soc. Avocation: dance. Office: Wichita State Univ 1845 Fairmount Wichita KS 67260-0014 Business E-Mail: mary.waters@wichita.edu.

**WATERS, MARY CATHERINE,** sociology educator; b. Bronx, NY, Nov. 18, 1957; d. Michael Francis and Margaret Mary (O'Carroll) W.; m. Ric W. Bayly, Sept. 10, 1993. BA in Philosophy, Johns Hopkins U., 1978; MA in Sociology, U. Calif., Berkeley, 1981, MA in Demography, 1983, PhD in Sociology, 1986. Acting instr. Dept. Sociol. U. Calif., Berkeley, 1983—85; asst. prof. Dept. Sociol. Harvard U., Cambridge, Mass., 1986-90, John L. Loeb assoc. prof., 1991—93, prof., 1993—, chmn. Dept. Sociol., 2001—05; prof. Harvard Coll., Cambridge, Mass., 1999—2004. Mem. immigration coun. Social Sci. Rsch. Coun., NYC, 1994; bd. dirs. Population Assn. Am., 2005—; cons. US Census Bur., Washington, 1993—95, adv. com. profl. associations, 1999—2005; cons. Bklyn. Children's Mus., 1994—98; cons. radio coverage of immigration WGBH Radio; cons. exhibits on African Am. history, immigration Strong Mus. of History, Rochester, NY, 1994; cons. project on social context of Puerto Rican child health and growth Wellesley Coll. Ctr. Rsch. on Women, 1995—97; internat. adv. bd. Ethnicities; consulting editor Am. Jour. Sociology, 1995—98; editl. bd. mem. Internat. Migration Rev. Author: (books) From Many Strands: Ethnic and Racial Groups in Contemporary America, 1990, Ethnic Options: Choosing Identities in America, 1990, Black Identities: West Indian Immigrant Dreams and American Realities, 1991 (Mira Komorovsky award Ea. Sociol. Soc., Otis Dudley Duncan award, Am. Sociol. Assn., Best Book in Ethnic Incorporation Am. Polit. Sci. Assn., Disting. Book award Cornell U. Ctr. Study Inequality, Thomas and Znaniecki award best book internat. migration Am. Sociol. Assn., 1999); co-editor (with Peggy Levitt): The Change Face of Home: The Transnational Lives of the Second Generation, 2002; co-editor: (with Joel Perlmann) The New Race Question: How the Census Counts Multiracial Individuals, 2002; co-editor: (with Fiona Devine) Social Inequalities in Comparative Perspective, 2003; co-editor: (with Philip Kasinitz and John H. Mollenkopf) Becoming New Yorkers: Ethnographies of the New Second Generation, 2004; contbr. articles to profl. jour., chapters to books. Bd. trustees Russell Sage Found., 2002—07; adv. bd. Ctr Rsch. on Immigration U. Houston; mem. Rsch. Network on Transition to Adulthood MacArthur Found., 2001—. Recipient Gertrude Jaeger prize, U. Calif. Berkeley, 1984, Hoopes award excellence in teaching, 1990, 1996, George R. Kharl award excellence in teaching, 1991, Shannon award, Nat. Inst. Child Health and Human Development, 1995—97; fellow Walter Channing Cabot Faculty, 2003—04; grantee Radcliffe Inst. Advanced Study, 2005—06; vis. scholar Russell Sage Found., 1991—92; Guggenheim fellow, 1993—94. Fellow Am. Acad. Arts and Sciences; mem.: Regional Sci. Assn., Soc. for Study of Social Problems, Sociol. Rsch. Assn., Am. Philosophical Soc., Population Assn. Am., Ea. Sociol. Soc. (chair Candace Rogers award com. 1994, disting. contribution to scholarship com. 2002), Am. Sociol. Assn. (nom. com. mem. sect. race and ethnic minorities 1992, coun. mem. sect. race and ethnic minorities 1994—96, nom. com. mem. sect. race and ethnic minorities 1995, coun. mem. sect. population 1995—97, nominations com. 1995—97, chair sect. internat. migration, Thomas and Znaniecki Book Award Com. 2000). Democrat. Office: Dept Sociology Harvard Univ 540 William James Hall Cambridge MA 02138-2044 Office Phone: 617-495-3947. Office Fax: 617-496-5794. E-mail: mcw@wjh.harvard.edu.

**WATERS, MAXINE,** congresswoman; b. St. Louis, Aug. 15, 1938; d. Remus and Velma (Moore) Carr; m. Sidney Williams, July 23, 1977; children: Edward, Karen. Grad. in sociology, Calif. State U., L.A.; doctorate (hon.). Spelman Coll., NC Agrl.& Tech. State U., Morgan State U. Former tchr. Head Start. Mem. Calif. Assembly from dist. 48, 1976-91, Dem. caucus chair, 1984; mem. U.S. Congress from 35th Calif. dist., 1991—; mem. Banking, Fin., Judiciary, Urban Affairs com., Ho. subcom. on banking, capitol subcom. on banking, employment and tng. subcom. on vets., veterans affairs com., banking and fin. svcs. com., ranking house subcom. on gen. oversight and investigations; chair Congl. Black Caucus. Mem. Dem. Nat. Com., Dem. Congrl. Campaign com.; del. Dem. Nat. Conv., 1972, 76, 80, 84, 88, 92, mem. rules com. 1984; mem. Nat. Adv. Com. for Women, 1978—; bd. dirs. TransAfrica Found., Nat. Women's Polit. Caucus, Ctr. Nat. Policy, Clara Elizabeth Jackson Carter Found. Spellman Coll., Nat. Minority AIDS Project, Women for a Meaningful Summit, Nat. Coun. Negro Women, Black Women's Agenda; founder Black Women's Forum; dep. City Councilman David Cunningham, 1973-76, chief dep. Minority Whip; mem. Congl. Children's Working Group, Congl. Progressive Caucus, Dem. Nat. Com.; chair Dem. Caucus Spl. Com. election Reform; vice chair Steering Com. Mem. Calif. Peer Counseling Assn., Nat. Com. Econ. Conversion and Disarmament; mem. bd. Ctr. Study Sport in Soc., L.A. Women's Found. Named one of 100 Most Influential Black Americans, Ebony mag., 2006. Democrat. Office: US Ho Reps 2344 Rayburn Ho Office Bldg Washington DC 20515-0535 also: 10124 S Broadway Ste 1 Los Angeles CA 90003 Office Phone: 202-225-2201, 323-757-8900. Office Fax: 202-225-7854, 323-757-9506.*

---

**WATERS, RICHARD,** retired publishing executive; b. Sterling, Mass., May 13, 1926; s. Sherman Hoar and Viola (Arnold) W.; m. June Hollweg Dorer, Aug. 27, 1949; children: Karl (dec.), Kurt, Kris. BA, Hobart Coll., 1950, LLD hon., 1970; MBA, Harvard U., 1951. Assoc. acct. Hunter & Weldon, N.Y.C., 1953-55; exec. v.p., CFO Reader's Digest Assn., Pleasantville, NY, 1955-77; assoc. dean Harvard U. Bus. Sch., Boston, 1977-81; pres., CEO Sporting News, St. Louis, 1981-90, ret., 1990. Bd. dirs. Republic Nat. Bank, N.Y., Spectrum Pet Care, Inc. Trustee Hobart Coll., 1971-91, William Smith Coll., 1971-91; regional v.p. Associated Industries N.Y. State, Albany, 1965-79; chmn. bd. Westchester Heart Assn., Port Chester, N.Y., 1975-76; bd. dirs., vice-chmn. Gateway chpt. Nat. Multiple Sclerosis Soc., St. Louis, 1995-95, chmn., 1996-98, chair emeritus 1999—; mem. St. Louis Sports Commn., 1985—; hon. trustee Hobart and William Smith Colls., 1992—; bd. dirs. Buddy Fund, St. Louis, 2001—. With USN, 1944-46, PTO; 1st lt. USAF, 1951-53. Mem. Baseball Writers Assn. Am. Clubs: Old Warson Country, St. Louis Club. Republican. Home: 20 Somerset Downs Saint Louis MO 63124-1007 E-mail: somersetdw@aol.com.

**WATERS, ROBERT FRANCIS, JR.,** music educator, writer; s. Robert and Evelyn Waters. BA, U. N.C., 1978, MusB, 1982; MusM, U. Md., 1995, PhD, 2002. Faculty Montgomery Coll., Rockville, Md., 1997—2002; asst. prof. music Shorter Coll., Rome, Ga., 2002—04; faculty N.C. Sch. Arts, Winston-Salem 2005. Asst. adj. prof. music Wake Forest U., Winston-Salem, 2004—, Guilford Coll., Greensboro, NC, 2005—06; vis. faculty Adama Mickewicz U., Poznan, Poland, 1989. Editl. asst.: Center Study in 19th Century Music, 1994; contbr. columns in Washington Post;, musician piano recitals; contbr. articles to profl. jours. Nat. Senatorial scholarship, 1992. Fellow: Music Critics Assn. N.Am.; mem.: Am. Musicol. Soc. (finalist Irving Lowens award 1996, 2002). Avocations: tennis, skiing, theater, dance. Home: 4309 McCarron Ct Greensboro NC 27406

**WATERS, ROGER ALLEN,** music educator; b. Atlanta, Ga., June 12, 1949; s. John Clarence Waters, Virginia Elizabeth Waters; m. Sandra Lynn Smith, Aug. 12, 1978; children: Michael Allen, Melody Elizabeth. BMus, Ga. State U., 1973, MMus, 1981. Lic. min. Salem Bapt. Ch. Dir. choral activities Southwest DeKalb H.S., Decatur, Ga., 1976—82; min. music High Point Bapt. Ch., Covington, Ga., 1982—89, Salem Bapt. Ch., McDonough, Ga., 1989—. Instr. voice Ga. Perimeter Coll., Clarkston, Ga., 1998—2005; music dir., condr. Covington/Conyers Choral Guild, Covington, Ga., 1985—. Bd. dirs. Covington/Conyers Choral Guild, Covington; deputized sheriff DeKalb County Sheriff's Dept., Decatur, 1970—. Staff sgt. USAF, 1967—73. Mem.: Ga. Music Educators Assn., Am. Choral Dirs. Assn. (state pres. 1991—93), Music Educators Nat. Conf., Nat. Assn. Tchrs. Singing. Republican. Avocations: golf, tennis, mint collectibles, scale trains. Home: 1996 Gibralter Way Conyers GA 30012 Office Phone: 770-957-4543.

**WATERS, RONALD V., III,** candy company executive; m. Ann Waters. BA in History & Economics, Trinity Coll.; M in Acctg., NYU. Ptnr. KPMG Peat Marwick; v.p. fin. & adminstrn. Gillette Co., 1993—99, v.p., controller, 1999, v.p. fin. & strategic planning, Grooming & Batteries, 1998—99; sr. v.p., CFO William Wrigley Jr., Inc., Chgo., 1999—2003, COO, 2004—. Bd. dir. The Joffrey Ballet, 2003—, treas., chmn. fin. com., co-chmn., 2004; bd. dir. HNI Corp., 2002—, Greater N. Mich. Ave. Assn., Goodman Theatre, Latin School of Chgo. Office: William Wrigley Jr Co 410 N Michigan Ave Chicago IL 60611

**WATERS, RONALD W.,** theology studies educator, church administrator, pastor; b. Kokomo, Ind., July 23, 1951; s. Ronald Lee and Carolyn Elizabeth (Myers) W.; m. Norma Lee Grumbling Waters, June 16, 1973; 1 child, Melinda Ronee Waters. BA magna cum laude, Ashland (Ohio) Coll., 1973; MA in Comms. with high honors, Wheaton (Ill.) Coll., 1975; MDiv with high honors, Ashland (Ohio) Theol. Seminary, 1985; postgrad., Asbury Theol. Seminary, 1993—2002. Ordained elder Brethren Ch., 1986; lic. minister, 1985-86. Asst. to dir. Bd. of Christian Edn. The Brethren Ch., Ashland, Ohio, 1971-74; mng. editor of publs. Brethren Pub. Co., Ashland, Ohio, 1975-78, asst. to dir. and gen. mgr., 1978-80, exec. dir., 1980-82; dir. of Denom. Bus. The Brethren Ch. Nat. Office, Ashland, Ohio, 1982-84; cons. in mgmt. and computer applications, 1984-85; pastor Mt. Olive Brethren Ch., McGaheysville, Va., 1985-89; dir. Brethren Ch. Ministries The Brethren Ch. Nat. Office, Ashland, Ohio, 1989-95; asst. prof. evangelism Ashland Theol. Sem., 1996-2001; cons. for evangelism and ch. growth The Brethren Ch. Nat. Office, Ashland, Ohio, 1996-2001; pastor Hammond Ave. Brethren Ch., Waterloo, Iowa, 2002—. Bd. dirs. corp. sec Brethren Printing Co., Ashland, 1989-96; mem. mission bd. Brethren Ch. Southeastern Dist., 1987-89; mem., sec. exec. bd. Ctrl. Dist., The Brethren Ch., 2002—; mem. statement of faith task force Gen. Conf. Brethren Ch., 1981-84, polity com. 1986-91, 2004—; bd. ref. congl. adv. The Andrew Ctr., Elgin, Ill., 1994-97; founder, tchr. Young Adult Sunday Sch. class Park St Brethren Ch., Ashland, 1990-93; adv. com. Ashland Theol. Sem., 1990-95; mem. evangelism mgmt. team New Life Ministries, Mt. Joy, Pa., 1992-2001; adj. prof. Bethany Theological Seminary, 2002—; spkr. in field. Author: Promise for the Future, 1993, Leader's Manual for Inviting and Welcoming New People, 1995; editor: The Brethren Evangelist mag., 1975-78, New Beginnings mag., 1995-97; contbg. editor LIFE products mag., 1998-99; contbr. numerous articles to religious jours.; webmaster, www.newlifeministries-nlm.org, 2000—. Mem. adv. coun. World Relief Corp., Wheaton, Ill., 1990-92; dir. vol. ministries Park St. Brethren Ch., 1998-99; sec.-treas. Ohio dist. Mission Bd., 1996-2001. Mem. Am. Soc. Ch. Growth, Nat. Assn. Brethren Ch. Elders, Black Hawk Assn. Evangelicals (pres. 2005—). Mem. Brethren Ch. Office: Hammond Ave Brethren Ch 1604 Hammond Ave Waterloo IA 50702

**WATERS, SYLVIA,** dance company artistic director; BS in Dance, The Juilliard School, studied with Antony Tudor and Martha Graham; PhD (hon.), State U. N.Y., Oswego, 1997. Prin. dance Alvin Ailey Am. Dance Theater, N.Y.C., 1968—74; artistic dir. Alvin Ailey Repertory Ensemble, N.Y.C., 1974—. Panelist Nat. Endowment for the Arts, N.Y. State Council on the Arts.

**WATERS, TIMOTHY J.,** lawyer; b. Santa Rosa, Calif., Apr. 18, 1943; BS, U. San Francisco, 1965; JD with honors, George Washington U., 1968. Bar: Va. 1968, D.C. 1973. Atty. FTC, Washington, 1968-73, asst. to dir. Bur. Competition, 1971, asst. to Chmn., 1972; ptnr., mem. firm exec. mgmt. com., co-ptnr.-in-charge DC Office McDermott, Will & Emory, Washington. Mem. D.C. Bar, Va. State Bar,U.S. Ct. Appeals for D.C., Third, Forth, Ninth Cir., U.S. Supreme Ct.

**WATERS, WILLIAM CARTER, III,** retired internist, educator; b. Atlanta, Dec. 12, 1929; s. William Carter and Nannie Ellen (Starr) W.; m. Sarah Ann Bankston; children: William Carter IV, Sarah Walker Waters McEntire. AB, Emory U., 1950, MD, 1958. Diplomate Am. Bd. Internal Medicine (internal medicine and nephrology). Resident in internal medicine Grady Meml. Hosp./Emory U., Atlanta, 1958-60, 61-62; fellow in nephrology New Eng. Med. Ctr., 1960-61; practice medicine specializing in internal medicine and nephrology, Atlanta, 1962—2002; from instr. to assoc. prof. Emory U. Sch. Medicine, 1962-70, clin. assoc. prof., 1970-85, clin. prof., 1985—. Chief staff internal medicine Piedmont Hosp., Atlanta, chmn. bd., 1991-94; 1st chmn. bd. Promina Health Sys., Atlanta, 1994-96; med. dir. internal medicine divsn. Multiple Sclerosis Clinic, Atlanta, 2005—. Contbr. articles to med. jours. Chmn. Piedmont Hosp. Found., 2002—05, chmn. bd. visitors, 2004—. With USAF, 1951—52. Fellow ACP (master: gov. for Ga.); mem. AMA, Med. Assn. Ga., Med. Assn. Met. Atlanta, Am. Soc. Nephrology, S.E. Clin. Club, Atlanta Country Club, Piedmont Driving Club, Big Canoe Club. Methodist. Personal E-Mail: drwaters@mindspring.com.

**WATERSTON, ROBERT HUGH,** medical educator, researcher, medical geneticist, department chairman; b. Detroit, Sept. 17, 1943; BSE, Princeton U., N.J., 1965; PhD, MD, U.Chgo., 1972. Postdoctoral fellow divsn. cell biology MRC Lab Molecular Biology, Cambridge, England, 1972—74; intern in pediatric medicine Children's Hosp. Med. Ctr., Boston, 1974—75; postdoctoral fellow divsn. cell biology MRC Lab Molecular Biology, Cambridge, England, 1975—76; asst. prof. dept. anatomy and neurobiology Washington U., St. Louis, 1976—89; asst. prof. genetics Washington U. Sch. Medicine, St. Louis, 1980—81, assoc. prof. genetics, 1981—87, prof. genetics, 1987—91, prof. and acting head dept. genetics, 1991—93, James S. McDonnell prof. and chmn. dept. genetics, 1993—2003, head, dept. genetics Seattle, dir., Genome Sequencing Ctr., chmn. dept. genome sci., 2002—; William B. Gates III endowed chair biomed. scis., 2003—. Founder Genome Sequencing Ctr., St. Louis; ad hoc mem. Molecular Cytology Study Sect., 1977, 83; regular mem. Molecular Cytology Study Sect., NIH, 1987—88, chmn., 1989—91; mem. NIH, 1985—86, mem. adv. coun., Molecular Cytology Study Sect., mem. nat. adv. coun. for human genome rsch., 1998—2002; mem. fellowship rev. subcom. Muscular Dystrophy Assn., 1982—87, mem task force on genetics, 1983; mem. organizing com. Fourth Internat. C. elegans Meeting, Cold Spring Habor, NY, 1985. Contbr. over 80 articles to profl. jours.; mem. editl. bd. Jour. Cell Biology, 1988—91. Named NIH predoctoral trainee, 1968—71, Am. Heart Assn. Established Investigator, 1980—85; recipient Beadle award, Gen. Soc. Am., Dan David Prize, Peter H. Raven Lifetime award, 2000, Internat. Gairdner award, 2002, Alfred P. Sloan, Jr. prize, GM Cancer Rsch. Found., 2003, Genetics prize, Peter Gruber Found., 2005; fellow Am. Cancer Soc. (postdoctoral), 1972—74, Muscular Dystrophy Assn. (postdoctoral), 1975—76, John Simon Guggenheim, 1985—86; grantee, NIH, 1997—99, 1998—2001, Merck & Co., 1994—99. Fellow: Am. Acad. Arts & Sciences; mem.: NAS, Am. Soc. Cell Biology: STS, Genetics Soc., Alpha Omega Alpha, Sigma Xi. Address: Washington U Sch Medicine Dept Genetics Box 357730 Seattle WA 98101 Office Phone: 206-685-7347. Office Fax: 206-221-4692. Business E-Mail: waterston@gs.washington.edu.*

**WATERSTON, SAMUEL ATKINSON,** actor; b. Cambridge, Mass., Nov. 15, 1940; s. George Chychele and Alice Tucker (Atkinson) W.; m. Lynn Louisa Woodruff, Jan. 26, 1976; children: Graham C., Elisabeth F., Katherine B.; child by previous marriage: James S. BA, Yale U., 1962; student, Sorbonne, Paris, 1960-61. Theatrical appearances include: Indians, Oh Dad Poor Dad, Halfway Up the Tree, Lunch Hour, Hamlet, The Tempest, Measure for Measure, Much Ado About Nothing (Obie, Drama Desk awards), Benefactors, 1986, A Walk in the Woods, 1988, Abe Lincoln in Illinois, 1993-94 (Drama League award 1994), Shakespeare & Szekspir, 1994; film appearances include: The Great Gatsby, 1975, Rancho Deluxe, 1976, Capricorn One, 1978, Interiors, 1978, Sweet William, 1978, Heaven's Gate, 1979, Eagle's Wing, 1983, The Killing Fields, 1984 (Acad. nomination best leading actor), Warning Sign, 1985, Savages, Hopscotch, 1980, Hannah and Her Sisters, 1986, Just Between Friends, 1986, The Devil's Paradise, September, 1987, Welcome Home, 1989, Crimes and Misdemeanors, 1990, Captive in the Land, 1990, Crimes and Misdemeanors, The Man in the Moon, 1991, Mindwalk, 1991, Serial Mom, 1994, Nixon, 1995, The Proprietor, 1996, Shadow Conspiracy, 1997, Le Divorce, 2003; TV films include: Much Ado About Nothing, 1974, The Glass Menagerie, 1975, Diabolique, 1975, Friendly Fire, 1978, Oppenheimer, 1982, Exiled, 1998, A House Divided, 2000, The Matthew Shepard Story, 2002; TV series Q.E.D., 1982, Terrorist on Trial: The United States vs. Salim Ajami; TV miniseries appearance: Oppenheimer, 1980, 82, Gore Vidal's Lincoln, 1988, Nightmare Years, 1989, Lost Civilizations, 1995 (Emmy award for best documentary 1996), Thomas Jefferson, 1997; regular TV series Q.E.D., 1979, I'll Fly Away, NBC-TV, 1991-93 (Emmy award nomination, Lead actor, Drama, 1993), I'll Fly Away: Then and Now, PBS, 1993 (Emmy nomination, Lead Actor - Special, 1994), Law and Order. 1994— (Screen Actors Guild award, 1999), Miracle at Midnight, 1998. Law and Order: Special Victims Unit, 1999, (documentary) Unfinished Journey, 1999. Mem. Actors Equity Assn., Screen Actors Guild, AFTRA Address: care Addis/Wechsler & Assocs 955 Carrillo Dr Fl 3 Los Angeles CA 90048-5400

**WATFORD, DOLORES,** elementary school educator; b. Feb. 26, 1951; BS in Edn., U. Hartford, 1973; MA in Psychol. Remedial Reading, Tchrs. Coll. Columbia U., 1974; MS in Spl. Edn., LI U., 1990, MS in Edn., 1993, profl. diploma in Sch. Adminstrn., 1997. Tchr. asst. Dalton Sch., Manhattan, NY, 1974—76; tchr. Pub. Sch., Conn., 1976—77; elem. tchr. Pub. Sch. 169, Bklyn., 1981—85; reading tchr. Pub. Sch. 167, Bklyn., 1985—2005; tchr. Pub. Sch. 191, Bklyn., 1985—99, Pub. Sch. 255, Bklyn., 1999—. Sec. Sch. Leadership Team, Bklyn., 2004—05. Pres. Bklyn. Reading Council, 2002. Recipient Svc. award, Bklyn. Reading Coun., 2004. Mem.: Internat. Reading Assn., NY State Reading Assn. (v.p. 2005—). Avocations: singing, aerobics, volleyball, reading. Home: One Rundle Ct Hempstead NY 11550 Personal E-mail: doloresbrc2002@msn.com.

**WATJEN, THOMAS ROS,** insurance company executive; With investment and corp. fin. depts. Aetna Life and Casualty, 1981-84; ptnr. Conning and Co., ins. cons. firm, 1984-87; mng. dir. responsible for ins. practice group Morgan Stanley & Co., 1987-94; exec. v.p.; CFO Provident Cos., Inc., Chattanooga, 1994—97, vice chmn., fin., 1997—99; exec. v.p.; fin. UnumProvident Corp., Chattanooga, 1999—2002, vice chmn., COO, 2002—03, pres., CEO, 2003—. Office: Unum Provident Corp One Fountain Sq Chattanooga TN 37402 E-mail: twatjen@unumprovident.com.*

**WATKIN, VIRGINIA GUILD,** retired lawyer; b. Clinton, Mass., July 28, 1925; d. George Cheever and Dorothy Louise (Springer) Guild; m. Donald M. Watkin, June 22, 1946; children: Henry M., Mary Ellen, Edward G., Ann Kymry. BA, Wellesley Coll., 1946; LLB, Columbia U., 1949; LLD (hon.) Norwich U., 1986. Bar: N.Y. 1949, D.C. 1952, Mass. 1963, U.S. Ct. Appeals (D.C. cir.) 1952, U.S. Supreme Ct. 1954, U.S. Dist. Ct. Mass. 1968, U.S. Ct. Appeals (1st cir.) 1968, U.S. Ct. Appeals (9th cir.) 1976, U.S. Ct. Appeals (4th cir.) 1980, U.S. Ct. Fed. Claims 1983, U.S. Ct. Appeals (5th cir.) 1993. Assoc. Covington & Burling, Washington, 1952-58; assoc. counsel Mass. Crime Commn., 1963-64; from assoc. to ptnr. Herrick, Smith, Donald, Farley & Ketchum, Boston, 1966-74; ptnr. Covington & Burling, Washington, 1974-2000; ret., 2000. Bd. vis. Columbia U. Sch. Law; bd. overseers Wellesley Coll. Stone Ctr. for Develop. Svcs. and Studies, 1989—, Wellesley Coll. Ctr. for Rsch. on Women, 1990—. Author: Taxes and Tax Harmonization in the Central American Common Market, 1967; contbr. articles to profl. jours. Trustee Northfield (Mass.) Mt. Hermon Sch. Bd., 1978-83, Norwich U., Northfield, U., 1977-90, Wellesley Coll., 1989—. Mem. ABA, Am. Law Inst., D.C. Bar Assn. (pres. 1993—), Soc. Woman Geographers, Columbia Law Sch. Alumni Assn. (regional v.p.), Wellesley Coll. Alumnae Assn. (bd. dirs. 1985-88), Cosmos Club. Home: 3001 Veazey Ter NW Washington DC 20008-5454 Office: Covington & Burling PO Box 7566 1201 Pennsylvania Ave NW Washington DC 20044-7566

**WATKINS, ANN ESTHER,** mathematics professor; b. L.A., Jan. 10, 1949; d. Rex Devere and Burnice Gordine (Duckworth) Hamilton; m. William Earl Watkins, Oct. 5, 1973; children: Mary Ann, Barbara Lee. BA, Calif. State U., Northridge, 1970, MS, 1972; PhD, UCLA, 1977. Instr. math. Los Angeles Pierce Coll., Woodland Hills, Calif., 1975-90; prof. math. Calif. State U., Northridge, 1990—. Editor: (with Albers, Rodi) New Directions in Two Year College Mathematics, 1985; co-author: (with Landwehr) Exploring Data, 1986, 2d edit., 1994, (with Landwehr, Swift) Exploring Surveys, 1987, (with Albers, Loftsgaarden, Rung) Statistical Abstract of Undergraduate Programs in the Mathematical Sciences and Computer Science, 1992 (with Scheaffer, Gnanadesikan, Witmer) Activity-Based Statistics, 1996, 2d edit., (with Scheaffer, Cobb) Statistics in Action, 2004; assoc. editor: American Mathematical Monthly, 1996-2000; editor Coll. Math. Jour., 1989-94; co-editor: (with Apostol, Mugler, Scott and Sterrett) A Century of Calculus, Part II, 1992; mem. editl. bd. Jour. Statis. Edn., 1992-95; mem. adv. bd. Math. Horizons mag., 1992-2001. Grantee NSF, 1987-90, 92—. Fellow Am. Statis. Assn.; mem. Math. Assn. Am. (2d v.p. 1987-88, pres. 2001-03, chair So. Calif. sect. 1988-89, gov. So. Calif. sect. 1995-98), Nat. Coun. Tchrs. Math. Business E-Mail: ann.watkins@csun.edu.

**WATKINS, BIRGE SWIFT,** real estate investment executive; b. Grand Rapids, Mich., May 2, 1949; s. Robert Goodell and Betty Jane (Swift) W.; m. Elizabeth Beverly Price, Nov. 28, 1985; children: Elizabeth Porter, Benjamin Thorne Swift, Robert William MacIntosh. BA, Alma Coll., 1971; MBA,

London Bus. Sch., 1981; MPA, Harvard U., 1989. Staff asst. to Pres. of U.S., Washington, 1974-77; congl. press sec. U.S. Ho. of Reps., Washington, 1977; v.p. Arbor Internat. Inc., McLean, Va., 1980-81; asst. office dir. AID, Washington, 1982-88; asst. dir. Pres.'s Task Force on Internal Pvt. Enterprise, Washington, 1983-85; dep. asst. sec. USDA, Washington, 1989-90; dir. investor outreach Resolution Trust Corp., Washington, 1991-94; ptnr. Benton Resources, Washington, 1994-95; mng. dir. Thornfalcon Internat., 1996-99; sr. v.p. Lifecare Mgmt. Ptnrs., 1999—2002, Friedman, Billings, Ramsey Group, Inc., 2002—03; v.p. Landmark Atlantic Holdings, LLC, 2003—. Cons. Washington Campus Inc., 1977, Va. Med. Assocs. Inc., Springfield, 1988, U.S.C. of C. Mem. campaign staff Reagan-Bush campaign, Washington, 1980, Bush for President, 1988; mem. transition team office of Pres.-elect Bush, 1988; chmn. bd. trustees Partnership Warrenton Found.; bd. dirs., founder John Singleton Mosby Found. and Mus., Land Trust of Va.; coun. mem. Town of Warrenten, Va., 2002--. Avocations: skiing, running, contemporary art. Home: 832 Blackwell Rd Warrenton VA 20186-2216 Office: Arlington VA Office Phone: 703-998-5200.

**WATKINS, BRENDA L.,** music educator; b. Norfolk, Va., Apr. 18, 1946; d. Rosser Lee and Constance Norsworthy Jones; m. Claude William Watkins, Nov. 1, 1964; 1 child, Kimberly Lynn, Cynthia Anne, Katherine Lee. Student, William & Mary Coll., 1964, Old Dominion U., 1964-68. Adminstrv. asst. Va. Nat. Bank, Norfolk, 1964-71; pre-sch. tchr. asst. Westwood Hill Bapt. Ch., Virginia Beach, 1972-74; pre-sch. music tchr. Bellamy Manor and Broad Bay Manor, Virginia Beach, 1993-96; music tchr. Court House Pre-Sch., Virginia Beach, 1994-97, Great Neck Pre-Sch., Virginia Beach, 1994-97; ind. music tchr. Music and Arts Music, Chesapeake, Va., 1998—. Author, editor: Childhood Memories, 1994. Vol. info. desk Assn. for Rsch. and Enlightment, Virginia Beach, 1999. Mem. Music Tchrs. Nat. assn., Tidewater Music Tchrs. Assn., Order of Ea. Star (Kempsville chpt.), Ladies Oriental Shrine N.Am. (Zulekia Ct. #35), U.S. Amateur Ballroom Dancers Assn., Inc., Va. Dept. Game and Inland Fisheries (cert. boat safety). Lutheran. Avocations: writing, music, boating, walking. Home: 612 Cardamon Ct Virginia Beach VA 23464-1901

**WATKINS, CAROL A.,** special education educator; b. Norfolk, Va., Dec. 7, 1954; d. Bernard Melvin and Jean Everton Dixon; m. William Stanley Watkins, Jr., July 23, 1954; children: William Stanley Watkins III, Bryce Reid. MEd, Va. Commonwealth U., 1986. Postgrad. prof. tic. Commonwealth of Va., 2003. Tchr./ spl. edn. New Kent County Pub. Schools, New Kent, 1984—95; dept. chair Hanover County Pub. Schools, Mechanicsville, Va., 1995—2002, 2003—. Fellow Grad. student tuition, Va. Commonwealth U., 1983-1984; grantee Project Unite Grant, Commonwealth of Va., 1994-1995. Avocations: volunteer- lewis ginter botanical gardens, consultant with the pampered chef*, old church community center member, ptsa faculty representative. Home: 8099 Candleberry Drive Mechanicsville VA 23111 Office: Lee-Davis HS 7052 Mechanicsville Turnpike Mechanicsville VA 23111 E-mail: cwatkins@hanover.k12.va.us.

**WATKINS, CAROLE S.,** human resources specialist, medical products executive; b. 1960; BA in Bus., Franklin U., Columbus, Ohio. With O.M. Scott & Sons, Lazarus, Huntington Banks; mem. staff Ltd. Brands, Columbus, Ohio, 1989—96; v.p. human resources Pharm. Distbn. Cardinal Health, Inc., Columbus, Ohio, 1996—2000, sr. v.p. pharm. distbn. and provider svcs., 2000, exec. v.p. human resources, 2000, chief human resources officer. Office: Cardinal Health 7000 Cardinal Pl Dublin OH 43017

**WATKINS, CHARLES BOOKER, JR.,** mechanical engineering educator; b. Petersburg, Va., Nov. 20, 1942; s. Charles Booker and Haseltine Lucy (Thurston) W. BS in Mech. Engring. cum laude, Howard U., 1964; MS, U. N.Mex., 1966, PhD, 1970. Registered profl. engr., D.C. Mem. tech. staff Sandia Nat. Labs., Albuquerque, 1964-71; asst. prof. dept. mech. engring. Howard U., Washington, 1971-73, prof., chmn. dept. mech. engring., 1973-86; prof. mech. engring. CCNY, 1986—, dean Sch. Engring., 1986—99; dir. CREST Ctr., 2002—. Cons. U.S. Army, U.S. Navy, NSF, pvt. industries, 1984-85. Rsch. grantee NSF, USN, Nuclear Regulatory Commn., Dept. Energy, NASA; Sandia Labs. doctoral fellow; NDEA fellow. Fellow ASME, AIAA (assoc.); mem. AAAS, Soc. Automotive Engrs. (Ralph R. Teetor award 1980), Am. Soc. Engring. Edn., Am. Soc. Safety Engrs., Sigma Xi, Omega Psi Phi, Tau Beta Pi. Home: 130 Buckingham Dr Hackensack NJ 07601 Office: CCNY Sch Engring Convent Ave New York NY 10031

**WATKINS, CURTIS WINTHROP,** artist; b. Pontiac, Mich., Apr. 9, 1946; s. Robert James and Arvella Marquitta (Chenoweth) W.; m. Gayle Lynn Blom, Dec. 19, 1975; 1 dau., Darcy Ann. Student, Ann Arbor Art Ctr., 1964-66, Kendall Sch. Design, 1966-68, Kraus Hypnosis Ctr., 1966, 70, Arons Ethical Hypnosis Tng. Ctr., 1977. Illustrator, instr. Ann Arbor Art Ctr. 1969-71; owner, dir. Hypno-Art Rsch. Ctr. and Studio, Howell, Mich., 1971—. Research on visualization process of subconscious by doing art work under hypnosis; lectr. hypnosis convs. and schs. One-man shows include LeVern's Gallery, 1969, Rackham Gallery, 1973, Hartland Gallery, 1974, Platt Gallery, 1975, Detroit Artists Guild Gallery, 1975, Golden Gallery, 1977, Cromaine Gallery, 1982, Driggett Gallery, 1982, Mill Gallery, 1983, Walnut Street Gallerya, 1983, Merrill Gallery, 1986, Corbino Gallery, 1986, VanAntwerp, 1991; group shows include Mich. All-State Show, 1980, Mich. State Fine Arts Exhibit, 1980, Washington Internat., 1981, Lansing (Mich.) Art Gallery, 1981, Capitol City Arts Show, 1981, Mich. Ann., 1981, Mich. Ann., 1982-83; illustrator: Handbook of Hypnotic Techniques, 1988. Bd. dirs. 9th Ann. Hartland Art Show, 1975, Livingston Arts and Crafts Assn., 1977-79, Hartland Art Coun., 1974-78. Recipient Dr. Garland H. Fross award, 1989, numerous awards of excellence in art. Mem. Internat. Soc. Artists, Assn. Advance Ethical Hypnosis, Am. Assn. Profl. Hypnologists, Internat. Soc. Profl. Hypnosis, Internat. Platform Assn. Presbyterian. Home: 1749 Pinckney Rd Howell MI 48843-7874 Office Phone: 517-546-6648.

**WATKINS, DEAN ALLEN,** electronics executive, educator; b. Omaha, Oct. 23, 1922; s. Ernest E. and Pauline (Simpson) W.; m. Bessie Ena Hansen, June 28, 1944; children— Clark Lynn, Alan Scott, Eric Ross. BS, Iowa State Coll., 1944; MS, Calif. Inst. Tech., 1947; PhD, Stanford, 1951. Engr. Collins Radio Co., 1947-48; mem. staff Los Alamos Lab., 1948-49; tech. staff Hughes Research Labs., 1951-53; asso. prof. elec. engring. Stanford, 1953-56; prof., dir. Electron Devices Lab., 1956-64, lectr. elec. engring., 1964-70; co-founder, pres., chief exec. officer, dir. Watkins Johnson Co., Palo Alto, Calif., 1957-67, chmn., chief exec. officer, dir., 1967-80, chmn., dir., 1980-2000. Cons. Dept. Def., 1956-66; mem. White House Sci. Coun., 1988-89. Patentee in field; contbr. articles to profl. jours. Legis. chmn.; dir. San Mateo County Sch. Bds. Assn., 1959-69; gov. San Francisco Bay Area Coun., 1966-75; Rep. precinct capt. Portola Valley, 1964; vice chmn. San Mateo County Fin. Com., 1967-69; mem. Calif. Rep. Ctrl. Com., 1964-68; trustee Stanford, 1966-69; regent U. Calif., 1969-96, chmn., 1972-74; mem. governing bd. Sequoia Union H.S. Dist., 1964-68, chmn., 1967-68; mem. governing bd. Portola Valley Sch. Dist., 1958-66; mem. bd. overseers Hoover Instn. on War, Revolution and Peace, Stanford, 1969—, chmn., 1971-73, 85-86; adv. policy commn. Santa Clara County Jr. Achievement; trustee Nat. Security Indsl. Assn., 1965-78. Served from pvt. to 1st lt. C.E., O.R.C. AUS, 1943-46. Fellow IEEE (7th region Achievement award 1957, Frederik Philips award 1981), AAAS; mem. Am. Phys. Soc., Am. Mgmt. Assn., Western Electronic Mfrs. Assn. (chmn. San Francisco coun. 1967, v.p., dir.), Calif. C. of C. (dir. 1965-92, treas. 1978, pres. 1981), Nat. Acad. Engring., Mounted Patrol San Mateo County (spl. dep. sheriff 1960-70), San Mateo County Horsemen's Assn., San Benito County Farm Bur., Calif. Cattlemen's Assn., Delta Upsilon. Clubs: Palo Alto, Calif. (Palo Alto), University (Palo Alto); Shack Riders (San Mateo County); Commonwealth (San Francisco); Rancheros Visitadores.

**WATKINS, ESTHER SHERROD,** secondary school educator, school librarian; b. Port Gipson, Miss., June 4, 1939; d. Raphael Sherrod and Carrie Powell Sherrod Peterson; m. John H. Watkins (dec.); children: Sharene Watkins Tolbert, MD, John Timothy. BA, Tougaloo Coll., Miss., 1960—64; Calif. tchng. credential, Calif. State U. Los Angeles, 1966—72; MA, U. of San Francisco, 1978—79. Sch. reading coord. Samuel Gompers Mid. Sch.,

Los Angeles, 1968—69, English/reading tchr., 1963—69; English tchr. Robert Frost Mid. Sch., Granada Hills, 1969—79, Sun Valley Mid. Sch., 1979—84; sch. writing coord. Verdugo HS, Tugunga, 1984—95; English tchr. Verdugo Hills HS, 1984—95, libr., 1995—2001. Del. NEA, 2000—01; active union mem. UTLA, 1995—2001. Author: Using Novels to Help High School Students to Cope, 1979. Elder Pasadena Christian Ch., 1969—; nat. bd. Delta Sigma Theta. Recipient 5 awards for fostering excellence in writing, L.A. Sch. Dist. Mem.: YWCA, Delta Sigma Theta. Achievements include serving as interim counselor co-dept. chair, reading compter coord. and training tchr. supr. Office Phone: 818-371-4096.

**WATKINS, GEORGE DANIELS,** physics professor; b. Evanston, Ill., Apr. 28, 1924; s. Paul F. and Lois V. (Daniels) W.; m. Carolyn Lenore Nevin, June 19, 1949; children: Lois Roberta, Paul Brent, Ann Romaine. BS, Randolph-Macon Coll., 1943; D.Sc. (hon.), 1976; MA, Harvard U., 1947, PhD, 1952. Research physicist Gen. Electric Research Lab., Schenectady, 1952-75; adj. prof. Rensselaer Poly. Inst., 1962-65, SUNY-Albany, 1969-72; Sherman Fairchild prof. physics Lehigh U., Bethlehem, Pa., 1975-95, prof. emeritus, 1995—; chmn. Gordon Research Conf. on Defects in Semiconductors, 1981; mem. solid state adv. com. Oak Ridge Nat. Lab., 1980-85. Mem. editl. bd. Phys. Rev. B, 1978-82; contbr. articles to profl. jours. Served to lt. (j.g.) USNR, 1943-46. NSF fellow, 1966-67; named Virginian of Yr. Va. Press Assn., 1980; recipient Alexander von Humboldt sr. U.S. Scientist award, 1983, 91. Fellow Am. Phys. Soc. (Oliver E. Buckley award 1978), AAAS, Nat. Acad. Scis. Democrat. Unitarian Universalist. Business E-Mail: gdw0@lehigh.edu.

**WATKINS, H. THOMAS,** biopharmaceutical company executive; B, Coll. William & Mary; MBA, U. Chigo. Grad. Sch. Bus. With Arthur Anderson Co., 1974; mgmt. cons. McKinsey and Co., Inc., 1979—85; bus. unit dir., physicians office diagnostics Abbott Labs., 1985—88, divisional v.p., pharma. products divsn., 1988—93; divisional v.p., sector gen. mgr., benchtops sys. Abbott Diagnostics Divsn., 1993—94, area v.p., Asia/Pacific, 1994, pres., Japanese subs., corp. v.p., 1996—99; v.p. Abbott Healthsystems, 1998; pres. TAP Pharma. Products Inc. (jointly owned by Abbott Labs. abd Takeda Pharma. Co. Ltd., 1998—2004; CEO, bd. dir. Human Genome Sciences, Inc., Rockville, Md., 2004—. Bd. dir. Lake Forest Hosp. Found. and Lake Forest Hosp., Ill.; trustee William & Mary Bus. Sch. Found., Coll. William & Mary, Williamsburg, Va. Office: Human Genome Sciences Inc 14200 Shady Grove Rd Rockville MD 20850 Office Phone: 301-309-8504. Office Fax: 309-309-8512.

**WATKINS, HAROLD ROBERT,** minister; b. Wauseon, Ohio, July 30, 1928; s. Orra Lynn and Florence Margaret (Bruner) W.; m. Evelyn Norma Earlywine, June 18, 1950; children: Mark Edwin, Nancy Jo Watkins. AB, Bethany Coll., 1950; MDiv, Lexington Theol. Sem., 1997; DD, Phillips U., 1985, Christian Theol. Sem., Indpls., 1995; BD, Coll. of Bible, 1953. Ordained minister Disciples of Christ, 1950. Min. Park Ave. Christian Ch., Tucson, 1953-56, First Christian Ch., Tuscaloosa, Ala., 1956-57; gen. ch. adminstr. Bd. Ch. Extension of Disciples of Christ, Indpls., 1958-95, pres., 1980-95, pres. emeritus, 2004—; mem. faculty Lexington Theol. Sem., 1996-97, 98-99, interim pres., 2001. Chmn. bd. dirs. Discipledata, Inc., Indpls., 1980—94; bd. dirs. United Church Ins. Co. Author: Continuity, Conservation and The Cutting Edge, 2005. Trustee Bethany (W.Va.) Coll., 1976—, Nat. City Christian Ch. Corp., Washington, 1981—; bd. dirs. Ecumenical Ch. Loan Fund, Geneva; pres. World Conv. Chs. of Christ, Nashville, 1988-92; bd. dirs. United Ch. of Christ Ins. Bd., 1997—. Recipient Outstanding Alumnus award Bethany Coll., 1975. Mem. Interfaith Forum on Religion, Art and Arch. (dir. officer 1979-95, pres. 1981-82, Elbert M. Conover award 1989). Home: 7402 Somerset Bay Apt 118 Indianapolis IN 46240-3495 Office Phone: 317-251-2977. Personal E-mail: hwatkins28@aol.com.

**WATKINS, HAYS THOMAS,** retired railroad executive; b. Fern Creek, Ky., Jan. 26, 1926; s. Hays Thomas Sr. and Minnie Catherine (Whiteley) W.; m. Betty Jean Wright, Apr. 15, 1950; 1 son, Hays Thomas III. BS in Acctg., Western Ky. U., 1947; MBA, Northwestern U., 1948; LLD (hon.), Baldwin Wallace Coll., 1975, Alderson Broaddus Coll., 1980, Coll. of William and Mary, 1982, Va. Union U., 1987. CPA, Ill., Ohio. With C. & O. Ry. Cleve., 1949-80, v.p. fin., 1964-67, v.p. adminstrv. group, 1967-71, pres., CEO, 1971—73, chmn. bd., CEO, 1973—80; with B. & O. R.R., 1964-80, v.p. finance, 1964-71, pres., CEO, 1971—73, vice chmn. bd., CEO, 1973—80; chmn., CEO Chessie System, Inc., 1973—80; pres. and co-CEO CSX Corp. (merger of Chessie System, Inc. and Seaboard Coast Line Industries, Inc.), Richmond, Va., 1980—82, chmn. bd., CEO, 1982—89, chmn. bd., 1989-91; chmn. emeritus, 1991—. Vice-rector bd. visitors Coll. William & Mary, 1984-87, rector, 1987-93. With AUS, 1945-47. Named Man of Yr., Modern R.R. mag., 1984; recipient Excellence in Mgmt. award Industry Week mag., 1982. Mem. Nat. Assn. Accts., Am. Inst. C.P.A.'s. Clubs: Commonwealth (Richmond, Va.); Country of Va. (Richmond). Home: 22 Lower Tuckahoe Rd W Richmond VA 23238-6108 Office: CSX Corp 901 E Cary St Ste 1605 Richmond VA 23219 Office Phone: 804-782-1411.

**WATKINS, JAMES DAVID,** federal official, military officer; b. Alhambra, Calif., Mar. 7, 1927; s. Edward Francis and Louise Whipple (Ward) Watkins; m. Sheila Jo McKinney, Aug. 19; 1950 (dec. Sept. 1996); m. Janet L. McDonough, June 17, 2000; children: Katherine Marie, Laura Jo, Charles Lancaster, Susan Elizabeth, James David, Edward Francis stepchildren: John Christopher McDonough, Sean Charles McDonough, Robert Edward McDonough, Siobhan McDonough. BS, U.S. Naval Acad., 1949; MSME, Navy Postgrad. Sch., 1958; LHD (hon.), Marymount Coll., 1982, N.Y. Med. Coll., 1988; DSc (hon.), Dowling Coll., 1983, U. Ala., 1991; LLD (hon.), Cath. U. Am., 1985, Mt. Sinai Sch. Medicine, 1993, Calif./ U. Pa., 1994; DS (hon.), Coll. William and Mary, 1999. Commd. ensign USN, 1949, advanced through grades to adm., 1979, comdg. officer U.S.S. Snook, 1964-66, exec. officer U.S.S. Long Beach, 1967; head submarine/nuclear power distbn. control br. Bur. Naval Pers., Dept. Navy, Washington, 1969-71, dir. enlisted pers. div., 1971-72, asst. chief naval pers. for enlisted pers. control, 1972-73; comdr. Cruiser-Destroyer Group 1 USN, 1973-75; dep. chief naval ops. manpower Dept. Navy, Washington, 1975-78, chief of naval pers., 1975-78, chief Bur. Naval Pers., 1975-78; comdr. U.S. Sixth Fleet USN, 1978-79; vice chief naval ops. Dept. Navy, Washington, 1979-81, comdr.-in-chief U.S. Pacific Fleet, 1981-82, chief naval ops., 1982-86; ret. USN, 1986; chmn. Presdl. Commn. Human Immunodeficiency Virus Epidemic, 1987-88; sec. Dept. Energy, Washington, 1989-93; pres. Joint Oceanographic Instn., 1993-2000, Consortium Oceanographic Rsch. and Edn., 1993-2001. Chmn. Presidentially Apptd. Commn. Ocean Policy, 2001—04. Decorated DSM with 1 gold star, Legion of Merit with 2 gold stars, Bronze Star medal with combat v; recipient Disting. Alumni award, Naval Postgrad. Sch., 1958, Chmn.'s award, Am. Assn. Engring. Socs., 1991, Disting. Grad. award, U.S. Naval Acad., 2001, Scientific Am. 50 award, 2004, Senator. John H. Chafee Coastal Stewardship award, 2005, Internat. Sea Keepers award, 2005, Lifetime Achievement award, Nat. Marine Sanctuary Found., 2006. Mem.: Knights of Malta. Roman Catholic.

**WATKINS, JAMES KELLEY,** retired urologist; b. Milford, Mich., Mar. 25, 1930; s. Ralph Nelson and Georgia Eileen Watkins; m. Janet Elizabeth Weber, Dec. 29, 1956; children: Katherine Harrison, William, Christopher, Bridget Hannock. AB in History, U. Mich., Ann Arbor, 1952, MD, 1959. Diplomate Am. Bd. Urology. Head dept. urology Butterworth Hosp., Grand Rapids, Mich., 1973—74; renal transplant surgeon St. Mary's Hosp., Grand Rapids, 1973—94; chief of staff Ferguson Hosp., Grand Rapids, 1992—94; ret. Mem. Gerontology Network, Grand Rapids, 1996—2005. Bd. dirs., mem. allocations com. United Way, Grand Rapids, 1989—92; trustee YMCA, Grand Rapids. Lt. (j.g.) USN, 1952—55. Recipient Holloway scholar, USN, 1948—52. Fellow: ACS; mem.: Kent Med. Found. (pres. 1990), Kent County Med. Soc. (pres. 1989, editor monthly bull. 1989—2005). Democrat. Roman Catholic. Avocations: rowing, running, golf, bicycling, tennis. Home: 252 Paarl St NW # 3D Grand Rapids MI 49503

**WATKINS, JERRY WEST,** retired oil company executive, lawyer; b. Vernon, Tex., Dec. 10, 1931; s. Terrell Clark and Daisy (West) W.; m. Elizabeth Jill Cole, Sept. 3, 1955. Student, Hendrix Coll., 1949-50, La. Poly. Inst., 1950-51; JD, U. Ark., 1954. Bar: Ark. 1954. Law clk. Supreme Ct. Ark., Little Rock, 1954-55; with Murphy Oil Corp., El Dorado, Ark., 1955-89, sec., gen. atty., 1966-71, sec., gen. counsel, 1971-88, v.p., dir., 1975-88, exec. v.p., 1991-92, also bd. dirs., 1975-89. CEO, bd. dirs. Ocean Drilling and Exploration Co., New Orleans, 1989-91; mem. Ark. Bd. Law Examiners, 1969-74; bd. dirs. Simmons First Bank of El Dorado, N.A., Simmons First Nat. Corp. Mem. Barton Libr. Bd., El Dorado, 1966—89; trustee Ark. State U., 1982—87; bd. dirs. South Ark. Arts Ctr., El Dorado, 1979—82, 1985—88, Warner Brown Hosp., El Dorado, 1984—87, South Ark. Med. Sys., 1987—89, Presbyn. Found. Ark., 1998—, Union County Cmty. Found., 2001—. Mem. ABA, Ark. Bar Assn., Union County Bar Assn. Home: 111 Watkins Dr El Dorado AR 71730-2752

**WATKINS, JOAN MARIE,** osteopath, physician; b. Anderson, Ind., Mar. 9, 1943; d. Curtis David and Dorothy Ruth (Beckett) W.; m. Stanley G. Nodvik, Dec. 25, 1969 (div. Apr. 1974). BS, West Liberty State Coll., 1965; Cert. of Grad. Phys. Therapy, Ohio State U., 1966; DO, Phila. Coll. Osteo., 1972; M of Health Professions Edn., U. Ill., Chgo., 1986; MPH, U. Ill., 1989. Diplomate Osteo. Nat. Bds., Am. Bd. Preventive Medicine, Am. Bd. Occupl. and Environ. Medicine, Am. Bd. Emergency Medicine. Resident in phys. medicine and rehab. U. Pa., 1973—74; emergency osteo. physician Cooper Med. Ctr., Camden, 1974-79, Shore Meml. Hosp., Somers Point, NJ, 1979-81, St. Francis Hosp., Blue Island, Ill., 1981-82, Mercy Hosp. and Med. Ctr., Chgo., 1982-90, dir. emergency ctr., 1984-88; resident in occupl. and preventive medicine U. Ill., 1988-90; corp. med. dir. occupl. health svc. Univ. Cmty. Hosp., Tampa, 1992—. Fellow Am. Coll. Occupl. and Environ. Medicine, Am. Soc. Preventive Medicine, Fla. Assn. Occupl. and Environ. Medicine (pres. 1999-2001). Avocations: sailing, needlecrafts, swimming. Home: 4306 Harbor House Dr Tampa FL 33615-5408 Office: Univ Community Hosp Occupational Health Svcs 3100 E Fletcher Ave Tampa FL 33613-4613 Office Phone: 813-390-6558. Office Fax: 813-615-7711.

**WATKINS, JOE BILL,** lawyer; b. Llano, Tex., July 21, 1943; BA, U. Tex., 1965, LLB with high honors, 1965. Bar: Tex. 1968. Exec. asst. to atty. gen. State of Tex., 1973—74; ptnr., head Pub. Policy Sect. Vinson & Elkins LLP, Austin, Tex. Fellow: Am. Leadership Forum. Office: Vinson & Elkins LLP Ste 100 2801 Via Fortuna Austin TX 78746 Office Phone: 512-542-8460. E-mail: jwatkins@velaw.com.

**WATKINS, JOHN B.,** lawyer; b. Feb. 4, 1956; BA, Johns Hopkins Univ., 1977; JD, Univ. Mich., 1981. Bar: Md. 1981, DC 1988. Ptnr., vice chmn. Corp. dept. Wilmer Cutler Pickering Hale & Dorr, Baltimore. Mem.: ABA, Md. Bar Assn. Office: Wilmer Cutler Pickering Hale & Dorr 100 Light St Baltimore MD 21202 Office Phone: 410-986-2820. Office Fax: 410-986-2828. Business E-mail: john.watkins@wilmerhale.com.

**WATKINS, JOHN FRANCIS,** management consultant; b. Alhambra, Calif., May 21, 1925; s. Edward F. and Louise (Ward) W.; divorced; children—Stephen, Katherine, John Francis, William. BSCE, U. Tex., Austin, 1947. With Earle M. Jorgensen Co., Lynwood, Calif., 1947-90, sr. v.p. adminstrn., 1978-90, ret.; owner John F. Watkins Assocs., Pasadena, Calif., 1990—. Pres. bd. Poly. Sch., Pasadena, 1978—80, Holy Family Sch., 1994—2002; adv. bd. mem. Serra H.S., Verbum Dei H.S., Dolores Mission Sch., 1996—; mem. Coll. Sci. and Engring. Coun. Loyola Marymount U.; adv. bd. Bishop Mora Salesian H.S., 1994—; mem. Cath. Edn. Found. Archdiocese L.A., 1995—; St. Gabriel pastoral region bd. dirs. Cath. Charities, 1994—; bd. dirs. Boys Republic, Chino Hills, Calif., 1970—, pres., 1977—80; bd. dirs. St. Luke Hosp., Pasadena, 1979—86, chmn. bd., 1982—86; bd. dirs. Econ. Literacy Coun. Calif., 1980—87, Pasadena Mus. of History, 1990—99. Mem. U.S. Navy League (nat. bd. dirs. 1989—, pres. Pasadena coun. 1992-93), Calif. Club, Annandale Golf Club, Serra Club (pres. 1995-97), Valley Club (San Marino, Calif.), Twilight Club (pres. 2002-03). Republican. Roman Catholic. Home and Office: 410 California Ter Pasadena CA 91105-2419 E-mail: jwatkins@pacificnet.net.

**WATKINS, JOHN GOODRICH,** psychologist, educator; b. Salmon, Idaho, Mar. 17, 1913; s. John Thomas and Ethel (Goodrich) W.; m. Evelyn Elizabeth Browne, Aug. 21, 1932; m. Doris Wade Tomlinson, June 8, 1946; m. Helen Verner Huth, Dec. 28, 1971; children: John Dean, Jonette Alison, Richard Douglas, Gregory Keith, Rodney Philip, Karen Stroobants, Marvin R. Huth. Student, Coll. Idaho, 1929-30, 31-32; BS, U. Idaho, 1933, MS, 1936; PhD, Columbia U., 1941. Instr. high sch., Idaho, 1933-39; faculty Ithaca Coll., 1940-41; prof. Auburn U., 1941-43; assoc. prof. Wash. State U., 1946-49; chief clin. psychologist U.S. Army Welch Hosp., 1945-46; clin. psychologist VA Hosp., American Lake, Wash., 1949-50; chief clin. psychologist VA Mental Hygiene Clinic, Chgo., 1950-53, VA Hosp., Portland, Oreg., 1953-64; prof. psychology U. Mont., Missoula, 1964-84, prof. emeritus, 1984—, dir. clin. tng., 1964-80. Lectr. numerous univs.; clin. assoc. U. Oreg. Med. Sch., 1957; pres. Am. Bd. Examiners in Psychol. Hypnosis, 1960-62. Author: Objective Measurement of Instrumental Performance, 1942, Hypnotherapy of War Neuroses, 1949, General Hypnotherapy, 1960, The Therapeutic Self, 1978, (with others) We, The Divided Self, 1982, Hypnotherapeutic Techniques, 1987, rev. edit., 2006, (with others) Hypnoanalytic Techniques, 1992, (with others) Ego States: Theory and Therapy, 1997, Adventures in Human Understanding, 2001, Emotional Resonance, 2005; contbr. articles to profl. jours. Mem. Internat. Soc. Clin. and Exptl. Hypnosis (co-founder, pres. 1965-67, recipient awards 1960-65), Soc. Clin. and Exptl. Hypnosis (pres. 1969-71, Morton Prince award), Am. Psychol. Assn. (pres. divsn. 30 1975-76, recipient award 1993), Phi Delta Kappa. Home and Office: 8258 Greenwood Pl Longmont CO 80503 Office Phone: 303-652-6556. Office Fax: 303-652-6525. *For a complete life one needs a job, a love, a friend, and an enemy. My "enemies" are injustice, war, poverty, illness, and suffering, not people. Make your existence as meaningful as possible. Enjoy life fully, and when it comes time to leave, have no fear or regrets. Seek to leave this world a little better off because you lived. These are my values. Would that I were mature enough always to live up to them.*

**WATKINS, JULIA ANNE,** healthcare educator, researcher; b. Evanston, Ill., Sept. 24, 1956; d. Jewell Benton and William Benson Watkins. BA, U. Calif., Santa Barbara Calif., 1980; MPH, U. SC., Columbia, S.C., 1996; Grad. Cert. in Drug & Alcohol Studies, U. SC., 1994—96; PhD, U. SC., 1999. Registered Respiratory Therapist Nat. Bd. of Respiratory Care, 1984, cert. Respiratory Therapy Tech. Nat. Bd. Respiratory Care, 1982. Adj. faculty Appalachian State U., Boone, NC, Walden U., Minneapolis, Minn., 2000—02; outcomes data mgr. St. Joesephs/Candler, Savannah, Ga., 2001—03; prof. of record Calif. Coll. for Health Scis., National City, Calif., 2002—03; asst. prof. U. North Fla., Jacksonville, Fla., 2003—. reviewer for nat. registry of evidence-based programs and practices MANILA Cons. Group, Inc., McLean, Va., 2005—; collaborating rsch. scientist for addictive health behaviors rsch. inst. U. Fla., Gainesville, 2004—; faculty rsch. assoc., ctr for rsch. on substance abuse U. North Fla., Jacksonville, Fla., 2003—04; reviewer of manuscripts European Jour. of Social Psychology, Hoboken, NJ, Substance Abuse Treatment, Prevention & Policy, London, 2005—, The Internat. Jour. of Interactive Tech. and Smart Edn., Leicester, United Kingdom, Eating and Weight Disorder Jour., Rome, 2003—; reviewer of textbooks Profl. Resources, Jacksonville, Fla., 2003—. Contbr. scientific papers to profl. jour. Del. com. mem. Am. Heart Assn., Jacksonville, Fla., 2005—06; adv. bd. mem. City of Jacksonville Childhood Obesity Coalition, Jacksonville, Fla., 2005—06; Profl. Resource Center, Jacksonville, Fla. Grantee Brooks Coll. of Health Rsch. Professorship, Brooks Coll. of Health, 2004—, Summer Tchg., U. North Fla., 2006, Summer Proposal Devel., 2005, Summer Scholarship, 2004; Faculty Fellow, 2006. Mem.: North Am. Assn. for the Study of Obesity (assoc.), APA (assoc.), Acad. for Eating Disorders (assoc.), APHA (assoc.). Avocations: swimming, running, travel. Office: Univ N Florida 4567 St Johns Bluff Rd S Jacksonville FL 32224 Office Phone: 904-620-1468. E-mail: jwatkins@unf.edu.

**WATKINS, M(ARTHA) ANNE,** family practice nurse practitioner; b. Vicksburg, Mich., Feb. 9, 1961; d. George H. and Coleene M. (Shearer) W. ADN, S.W. Mich. Coll., 1984; BSN, U. Mich., 1988, MSN, 2003. RN, Mich. Staff nurse Lee Meml. Hosp., Dowagiac, Mich.; clin. nurse II thoracic intensive care U. Mich. Hosps., Ann Arbor; emergency nurse Lee Meml. Hosp., Dowagiac, Mich.; critical care nurse Mercy Meml. Hosp., St. Joseph, Mich.; house supr. Lee Meml. Hosp., Dowagiac, Mich., dir. med. surg. pediat., 1995, v.p. patient care svcs., 1996—2001; family nurse practioner Planned Parenthood Mid Mich. Alliance, Benton Harbor, Mich., 2004—. Mem. Phi Theta Kappa. Home: 303 Mcphil Dr Dowagiac MI 49047-1012 Office: Planned Parenthood Mid Mich Alliance 1161 E Napier Benton Harbor MI 49022 Office Phone: 269-926-2042.

**WATKINS, NANCY ANN,** music and art educator; b. Copperhill, Tenn., Oct. 30, 1960; d. Robert Glenn and Mary Ann Collis; m. Randall David Watkins, June 12, 1982; children: Jason David, Carrie Ann. B in Music Edn., West Ga. Coll., Carrollton, 1982; M in Early Childhood Edn., North Ga. Coll., Dahlonega, 1993; edn. specialist, Piedmont Coll., 2004. Piano tchr. Epworth Elem. Sch., Ga., 1982—83, West Fannin Middle Sch., Blue Ridge, Ga., 1982—83; pvt. piano tchr. Blue Ridge, 1982—87, 1989—2003; elem. tchr. Fannin County Bd. Edn., Blue Ridge, 1992—. Mem.: Ga. Music Educator's Assn., Profl. Assn. Ga. Educators. Home: 2530 Sugar Creek Rd Blue Ridge GA 30513 Office: Blue Ridge Elem Sch 224 E Highland St Blue Ridge GA 30513

**WATKINS, SARA,** musician; b. June 8, 1981; Mem. bank Nickel Creek; with Sugar Hill Records, 1999—. Musician: (recordings) Nickel Creek, 2000 (Cert. Gold, 2002, 2 Grammy nominations, 2001), This Side, 2002 (Cert. Gold, 2003, Grammy award for Contemporary Folk Album, 2003), (CD) Ten From Little Worlds, Not All Who Wander Are Lost, G.I.gantic, Faraway Land, Let it Fall, 26 Miles, More Than Words, Pickin' on ZZ Top, Philadelphia Folk Festival: 40th Anniversary, Telluride Bluegrass Festival: Reflection, Vol. 1, This is Americana, Vol 1: A View From Sugar Hill, Pickin' on the Rolling Stones, Prancer Returns, Further Down the Old Plank Road. Named Southwest Regional champions, Pizza Hut Internat. Bluegrass Music Showdown, 1994, Ariz. State Fiddle Champion, 1996, Emerging Artist of Yr., IBMA, 2000, Instrumental Group of YR., 2001; named one of Five Music Innovators for the Millennium, Time mag., 2000. Office: Q-Prime 131 S 11th St Nashville TN 37206

**WATKINS, STEPHEN EDWARD,** accountant, publishing executive; b. Oklahoma City, Sept. 1, 1922; s. Ralph Bushnell and Jane (Howell) W.; m. Suzanne Fowler, Aug. 16, 1976; children— Elizabeth Ann Watkins Racicot, Stephen Edward, Jr. BBA, U. N.Mex., 1944. C.P.A., N.Mex. With Peat, Marwick, Mitchell & Co., 1944-67; pres. The New Mexican daily newspaper, Santa Fe, 1967-78, 90—; pvt. practice pub. acctg. Santa Fe, 1978—. Vestryman Ch. of Holy Faith; trustee St. Vincent Hosp., 1979-85, Orchestra Santa Fe, 1976-82, Hist. Santa Fe Found. (pres. 1990). Mem. AICPA, Sons of Am. Revolution, Rotary. Home: 1325 Don Gaspar Ave Santa Fe NM 87505-4627 Office: 223 E Palace Ave Santa Fe NM 87501-1947

**WATKINS, TIONNE (T-BOZ),** singer; b. Des Moines, Apr. 26, 1970; 1 child, Chase Rolison. Singer, mem. TLC, 1991—. Actor: (films) House Party 3, 1994; host: (TV series) One World Music Beat, 1998—2001; prodr.: ATL, 2006; singer: (solo albums) Touch Myself, 1996, My Getaway, 2001. Recipient Grammy for "Creep, 1995. Office: LaFace Records One Capital City Plz 3423 Piedmont Rd NE Atlanta GA 30305-1754*

**WATKINS, WESLEY WADE,** retired congressman; b. DeQueen, Ark., Dec. 15, 1938; s. L. V. and Mary J. W.; m. Elizabeth Lou Rogers, June 9, 1963; children: Sally, Martha, Wade. BS, Okla. State U., 1960, MS, 1961. With USDA, Washington, 1961; asst. dir. admissions Okla. State U., 1963-66; exec. dir. Kiamichi Econ. Devel. Dist. of Okla., 1966-68; founder, owner commn. and land devel. bus., 1968-76; mem. Okla. Senate, 1975-76, U.S. Congress from 3d Okla. Dist., 1977—91, 1997—2002; mem. ways and means com., human resources suncom., budget com.; pres. World Export Services, Stillwater, Okla., 1991—96. Pres. Higher Edn. Alumni Council of Okla.; Okla. chmn. Nat. Future Farmers Am. Found.; mem. Okla. Health Planning Council.; Pres. Ada (Okla) Growth and Devel. Assn. Served with Air N.G., 1960-66. Recipient Nat. Security Leadership award U.S. Air N.G., 1967, Okla. 4-H Alumni Recognition award, 1978, Disting. Alumnus award Okla. State U. Alumni Assn., 1978, others; named Policymaker of the Yr. Am. Vocational Assn., One of 3 Outstanding Young Men in Okla., Okla. Jaycees, 1968; named to Okla. State U. Hall of Fame, 1989. Mem. C. of C. Clubs: Masons, Lions. Republican. Presbyterian.

**WATKINS, WILLIAM, JR.,** electric power industry executive; b. Jersey City, Aug. 12, 1932; s. William James and Willie Ree (Blount) W.; m. Sylvia I. Mulzac, Oct. 16, 1955; children: Cheryl, Rene, Linda. BBA, Pace U., 1954; MBA, NYU, 1962; postgrad. advanced mgmt. program, U. Mich., 1979; postgrad. exec. program, Edison Electric Inst., 1988. Staff asst. Consol. Edison Co. N.Y., N.Y.C., 1957-64; sys. mgr. Volkswagen Am., Englewood Cliffs, N.J., 1964-71; v.p. dir. adminstrn. New Eng. Power Svc. Co., Westboro, Mass., 1972-82, v.p., dir. human resources, 1986-92; v.p., dist. mgr. Narragansett Electric Co., Providence, 1982-86, exec. v.p., 1992-97; retired. Bd. dirs. Peerless Precision Corp., Lincoln, R.I., 1982-91; mem. bd. advisors Sarasota Pvt. Bank, Fleet Fin. Group, 2001. Chmn. R.I. Urban Project, Providence, 1984, R.I. Coun. for Econ. Edn., Providence, 1984; mem. Gov.'s Commn. on Health Care Reform, 1993-94; trustee R.I. Hosp., 1995-96, Lifespan, 1996-99, Roger Williams U., Bristol, R.I., 1991-94; bd. dirs. R I Hosp. Fin. Corp., Providence, 1987-91, inroads, 1993-97, Leadership R.I., 1993-95, NCCJ, 1993-97; mem. resource and devel. commn. Episcopal Diocese Mass., 1988-92; chmn. bd. trustees RISD, 1998-2000. Recipient Cmty. Svc. award Urban League R.I., 1986, Paris V. Sterett award John Hope Settlement House, 1987, Small Bus. Adminstrn. Adv. of the Yr. award, 1994; named Developer of Yr., Am. Econ. Devel. Coun., 1996. Mem. N.E. Econ. Developers Assn. (bd. dirs. 1993-97), R.I. Urban Bankers Assn., Kappa Alpha Psi, Sigma Pi Phi. Avocations: swimming, biking, hiking, travel, golf. Home: 5114 87th Ct E Bradenton FL 34211-3743 E-mail: wwatkin5114@aol.com.

**WATKINS, WILLIAM D.,** computer hardware company executive; BS in Polit. Sci., U. Tex. Exec. Domain Tech., 1990-96; sr. v.p. Conner Peripherals, 1996-98; COO, exec. v.p. Seagate Technology, Milpitas, Calif., 1998—2000, COO, pres. Scotts Valley, Calif., 2000—04, pres., CEO, 2004—. Avocation: racing. Office: Seagate Tech 920 Disc Dr Scotts Valley CA 95066*

**WATLER, PAUL C.,** lawyer; b. Beaumont, Tex., June 23, 1954; BJ, Univ. Tex., 1976, JD, 1981. Bar: Tex. 1981, cert.: Tex. Bd. Legal Specialization (civil trial law). Shareholder, commml. litigation Jenkens & Gilchrist, Dallas. Named a Tex. Super Lawyer; named one of Top Dallas / Fort Worth Lawyers, D Mag. Fellow: Tex. Bar Found.; mem.: ABA, Libel Def. Resource Ctr. Media Law Resource Ctr., Coll. of State Bar Tex., State Bar Tex., Dallas Bar Assn., Freedom of Information Found. Tex. (past pres., James Madison award). Office: Jenkens & Gilchrist Ste 3200 1445 Ross Ave Dallas TX 75202-2799 Office Phone: 214-855-4393. Office Fax: 214-855-4300. Business E-Mail: pwatler@jenkens.com.

**WATLEY, NATASHA,** Olympic athlete; b. Canoga Pk., Calif., Nov. 27, 1981; d. Edwin and Carolyn. Grad., UCLA, 2003. Mem. U.S. Nat. Team, 2002—. U.S. Women's Softball Team, Athens Olympic Games, 2004. Named NFCA First Team All-Am., 2000, 2001, 2002, 2003, MVP of ISF World Championships, 2002, Pac-10 Player of the Yr.; 2003; recipient Honda award for Top College Female Athlete, 2003. Achievements include invention of mem. Gold medal U.S. Nat. Team, ISF World Championships, 2002, Pan Am. Games, 2003, Athens Olympic Games, 2004; mem. NCAA Champion UCLA Bruins, Women's Coll. World Series, 2003.

**WATNE, ALVIN L.,** retired surgeon, educator; b. Shabbona, Ill., Jan. 13, 1927; m. Diana Folio, Dec. 3, 1966; children: Carrie, Matthew, Andrew, Valerie. BS, U. Ill.-Chgo. Coll. Medicine, 1950, MD, 1952, MS, 1956. Diplomate: Am. Bd. Surgery. Intern Indpls. Gen. Hosp., 1952-53; resident U. Ill. Research and Edn. Hosps., Chgo., 1954-58; assoc. cancer surgeon Cancer Research, Roswell Park, Buffalo, NY, 1958, assoc. chief cancer research, 1959; assoc. prof. surgery W.Va. U., 1962-67, prof., 1967-72, acting chmn. dept. surgery, 1973-75, prof., chmn. dept. surgery, 1975-86, U. Ill., Peoria, 1986-91; dir. Cancer Ctr. of Ga., 1991-94; assoc. dir. dept. surgery Ga. Bapt. Med. Ctr., 1994-97. Cons. surgery VA, Clarksburg, W.Va., 1963-2005, vice-chmn. bd., Univ. Ill. Found., 2005 Author: Gardner's Syndrome, 1977, (2d edit.), 1979, Melanoma of Head and Neck, 1981, Polyposis Coli, 1982. Pres. W. Va. div. Am. Cancer Soc., 1967-68, 80—, v.p., 1981. Recipient Hektoen Gold medal AMA, 1958; recipient Hektoen Silver medal AMA, 1960 Mem. ACS (pres. W.Va. chpt. 1972-73, chmn. local com. 1978—, gov. 1985—), Southeastern Surg. Congress (councilor 1980—), Soc. Surg. Oncology (exec. council 1980), Soc. Head and Neck Surgeons (pres. 1982), Am. Cancer Soc. (dir.-at-large 1985—)

**WATNE, DARLENE CLAIRE,** county official; b. Minot, N.D., Feb. 11, 1935; d. Charles A. and Anna Marie Widdel (Fjeld) W.; m. Clair A. Watne, Mar. 27, 1954; children: Carmen, Steven, Nancy, Matthew. Court reporting diploma, Minot (N.D.) Bus. Coll., 1975; grad., Real Estate Inst., 1991. Cert. residential real estate specialist, N.D. Exec. sec. Grand Exalted Ruler Elks, Minot, ND, 1964-75; pres. Bus. Coll., Minot, 1974-76; ct. reporter N.W. Judicial Dist., Minot, 1976-90; real estate broker Watne Realtors Better Homes & Gardens, Minot, 1990-99; mem. N.D. Senate from 5th dist., Bismark, 1994—2001; commr. Ward County, ND, 1994—. Active Joint Civil Svcs. to the Poor, 1995-2001. Bd. dirs. ARC, Salvation Army, Red Cross; numerous state polit. interim senate coms. Named Minot Woman of Distinction in Bus. and Industry, 1993, Liberty award ND Bar Assn., 2000, named Citizen of Yr. ND Builders Assn., 2001. Republican. Avocations: reading, laking. Home: 520 28th Ave SW Minot ND 58701-7065

**WATNE, DONALD ARTHUR,** retired accountant, educator; b. Gt. Falls, Mont., Jan. 18, 1939; BA with high honors, U. Mont., 1960, MA, 1961; PhD, U. Calif., Berkeley, 1977. CPA, Oreg. Acct. Piquet & Minihan, Eugene, Oreg., 1961-65; mgr. capital investment analysis Weyerhaeuser Co., Tacoma, 1965-68; mktg. rep. IBM Corp., Portland, Oreg., 1968-70; dir. EDP Ctr. in Concejo Mcpl., Barquisimeto, Venezuela, 1971-72; prof. acctg. Portland State U., 1976-2001, prof. emeritus, 2001—. Vis. prof. Xiamen (Fujian, People's Rep. China), 1985-86, U. Otago, Dunedin, New Zealand, 1985-86, U. Newcastle, Australia, 1985-86; cons. in field; acctg. qualifications com. Oregon State Bd. Acctg., 1989-98, CPE com., 1998-2001 Author: (with Peter B.B. Turney) Auditing EDP Systems, 2d edit. 1990; contbr. chpts. to books, articles to profl. jours. Del. to Soviet Union citizen amb. program People to People Internat., 1990; active Tng. the Trainers Program, Vilnius, Lithuania, 1993; trustee, treas. First Unitarian Ch. of Portland, 2002—; mem. bd. stewards First Unitarian Ch. of Portland Found., 2002—, treas., 2004— Mem.: AICPA, Oreg. Soc. CPAs, Mensa, Mazamas Mountain Climbing Club. Home: 2826 NE 26th Ave Portland OR 97212-3503 E-mail: dawatne@msn.com.

**WATROS, CYNTHIA,** actress; b. Lake Orion, Mich., Sept. 2, 1968; d. Bruce and Nancy Watros; m. Curtis Gilliland, 1996; 2 children. Student, Macomb CC, Mich.; BFA, Boston U. Actor: (films) Cafe Society, 1995, His and Hers, 1997, Mercy Streets, 2000, Yellow Bird, 2001, P.S. Your Cat is Dead, 2002, Duane Incarnate, 2004, American Crude, 2005, Just Pray, 2005; (TV series) The Guiding Light, 1994 (Daytime Emmy award, 1998), Titus, 2000, Drew Carey Show, 2002—04, Lost, 2005— (Outstanding Performance by an Ensemble in a Drama Series, Screen Actors Guild award, 2006). Avocations: snow skiing, dancing. Address: care Innovative Artists 1505 10th St Santa Monica CA 90401 Mailing: care Touchstone TV Prodn Bldg #343 500 S Buena Vista Burbank CA 91521*

**WATROUS, ROBERT THOMAS,** academic director; b. Cleveland, Apr. 20, 1952; s. Frank Thomas and Marie Anne (Kmeicik) W.; m. Robin Joyce (Braun), Mar. 14, 1981 (div. 1993); 1 child, Michael Francis; m. Susan J. (Rupp), Mar. 8, 2003. BS, U. Dayton, Ohio, 1974, MS, 1977. Dir. student ctr. for off campus cmty. rels. U. Dayton, Ohio, 1974—76, resident dir., 1976—78; dir. of housing St. Bonaventure U., Olean, NY, 1978—81; asst. dean of student life housing U. Pa., Kutztown, 1981—86, dir. commuter and jud. affairs, 1986—2004, dean, student svcs. and campus life, 2004—. Faculty senate Kutztown U. Pa. 1986-89, 92-95; mem. Pa. Task Force on Intergroup Behavior in Higher Edn., 1991-94; trainer Pa. Interagy. Task Force on Civil Tension, Harrisburg, Pa., 1989-2001; exec. coun. Adult Learners Consortium, Bloomsburg, Pa., 1990-91; mem. Lehigh Valley Svc. Learning Consortium, 1994—. Bd. mgr. Tri Valley YMCA, Fleetwood, Pa., 1983-94; adv. bd. Crossroads, Kutztown, 1989-94; bd. dir. Jr. Achievement of Berks County, Reading, Pa., 1990, Reading, Pa., 1990, Reading and Berks Coun. YMCA, 1992-96; mem. Leadership Berks, Reading, 1990; bd. dir. Leadership Berks, 1995—, sec. 1998-99, pres., 2000-04; co-founder Leading Sch. Bd., 1994—; mem. Leadership Alliance Berks, 2004-, YMCA cultural diversity and internat. awareness com., 1994—; mem. Berks County Conflict Resolution Task Force, 1996-2004; v.p. Fleetwood Activities Booster Club, 1998-2002, pres., 1999-2001. Mem. Nat. Assn. Student Pers. Adminstr. (profl. affiliate), Hawk Mt. Coun. Boy Scouts Am. (sustaining mem.), Berks County C. of C. (sch. bd. governance com. 1993-2000), Fleetwood Youth Soccer Club (v.p., pres. 1999), Fleetwood Youth Basketball Assn. (coach 1995-96), Leadership Alliance of Berks, 2003-, Greater Reading Leadrership Alliance, 2004-. Avocations: golf, sports, gardening. Business E-Mail: watrous@kutztown.edu.

**WATSON, ANTHONY L.,** health facility executive; b. 1942; Supervising pub. health adviser dept.health edn. and welfare Ctr. for Disease Control, Pub. Health Svc., 1966-70; dep. dir. Comprehensive Health Planning Agy., N.Y.C., 1970-76, Health Planning, N.Y.C., 1976—85; exec. v.p., COO HIP Health Plan of N.Y., 1985—91, chmn., CEO, 1991—. Mem. Community Council of Greater N.Y.; pres, CEO The N.Y. Urban Coalition. Mem. Am. Health Planning Assn., Am. Hosp. Assn. Office: HIP Health Plan of NY 55 Water St New York NY 10041*

**WATSON, ARTHUR DENNIS,** federal official; b. Brownsville, Pa., May 11, 1950; s. Arthur Francis and Margaret Teresa (Mastile) Puglia, John Leslie Watson (Stepfather); m. Kathleen Frances Zaccardo, July 16, 1983; 1 child, Fiona Kathleen. BSBA, U. Richmond, 1972; MS in Bus.-Govt. Rels., Am. U., 1977, MA in Lit., 1979; PhD in English Lang. and Lit. Cath. U., 1987. Statis. asst. U.S. Postal Svc. Hdqrs., Washington, 1972—73, economist assoc., 1973—74, staff economist, 1974—77, mktg. analyst, 1977; rate analyst U.S. Postal Rate Commn., Washington, 1977—79; dir. pub. affairs, 1979—82; pub. affairs officer ICC, Washington, 1982—89, dep. dir. pub. affairs, 1989—93, assoc. dir. congl. and pub. affairs, 1993—95; dir. media affairs surface transp. bd. Dept. Transp., Washington, 1996—. Pres. Arthur D. Watson and Co., Clifton, Va., 1983—; Washington corr. Linn's Stamp News, Sidney, Ohio, 1983—84. Contbr. articles to profl. jours. With USCG, 1972—78. Recipient Meritorious Svc. medal, USCG Res., 1989, Pub. Svc. award, ICC, 1989, Spl. Achievement award, Surface Transp. Bd., 1999, Merger Response Team Performance award, 2000, Performance award for media and pub. affairs, 2000, Second Pl. award, Internat. Plastic Modelers Soc. (No. Va. divsn.), 2000, Merger Response Team Performance award, Surface Transp. Bd., 2001, Agy. Performance award Merger team, 2001, Performance award for website enhancements, 2002, Performance award for media and pub. affairs, 2002. Mem.: Assn. Transp. Law Profls., E. Clairborne Robins Sch. Bus. Alumni Assn. Roman Catholic. Avocations: classical music, reading, writing, model building, travel. Home: 6521 Rockland Dr Clifton VA 20124-2415 Office: Surface Transp Bd 1925 K St NW Ste 845 Washington DC 20423-0001

**WATSON, BERNARD CHARLES,** foundation administrator, educator; m. Lois Lathan, July 1, 1961; children: Barbra, Bernard Jr. BS, Ind. U., 1951; MEd, U. Ill., 1955; PhD, U. Chgo. 1967; postdoctoral work, Harvard U.,

1968; LHD (hon.), Allen U., 1981, LaSalle U., 1987, Spring Garden Coll., Elizabethtown Coll, Beaver Coll., 1988, Harris-Stowe State Coll., Morris Brown Coll., 1989, Millersville U., 1991, N.C. Ctrl. U., 1999; LLD (hon.), Lincoln U., 1974, Fla. Meml. Coll., 1984, Temple U., 1986, Med. Coll. Pa., 1986, Tuskegee U., 1991, Lincoln U., 1992, Morgan State U., 1992, Phila. Coll. Pharmacy and Sci., 1994, Bethune-Cookman Coll., 1995; HHD (hon.), Wilberforce U., 1979; DFA, Univ. of the Arts, 1992; D of Pedagogy, Drexel U., 1992. Tchr., prin. Roosevelt Jr. and Sr. H.S., Gary, Ind., 1955-65; staff assoc. Midwest Adminstrn. Ctr. U. Chgo., 1965-67; assoc. supt. innovative programs Sch. Dist. Phila., 1967-68, dep. supt. for planning, 1968-70; prof. chmn. dept. urban edn. Temple U., Phila., 1970-75, also prof. social foundations Coll. Edn. and prof. urban studies Coll. Liberal Arts, 1970-75, v.p. acad. adminstrn., 1976-81; presdl. scholar, 1994—; pres., CEO William Penn Found, Phila., 1982-93; chmn. HMA Found., Phila., 1994-97. Bd. dirs. Comcast Corp., First Union Bancorp North, First Union Bank, Keystone AAA Club, Keystone Ins. Co., Phila. Contributionship; assoc. edn. Grad. Sch. Edn. Harvard U., 1970-72, mem. vis. com., 1981-87; mem. vis. com. dept. Afro-Am. studies Harvard Coll., 1974-78. Author: In Spite of the System: The Individual and Educational Reform, 1974; editor in chief Cross Reference: A Jour. Pub. Policy and Multi-Cultural Edn., 1976-79, Testing Its Origin, Use and Misuse, 1997, Colored, Negro, Black: Chasing the American Dream, 1997; contbr. numerous articles to profl. jours., chpts. to books. Mem. steering com., mem. exec. com. Nat. Urban Coalition, 1973-89; vice chmn. Nat. Adv. Coun. Edn. Professions Devel., 1967-70, Pa. Coun. on Arts, 1986-93; mem. Nat. Coun. Ednl. Rsch., 1980-82, William T. Grant Found. Commn. Work, Family and Citizenship, 1987-88; sr. vice chmn. bd. trustees Nat. Urban League, 1983-96; vice chmn. bd. dirs. Pa. Conv. Ctr. Authority, 1986—; trustee Thomas Jefferson U., 1993-95; sec. bd. N.J. State Aquarium, 1988-93; chmn. Ave. the Arts Inc., 1992—; mem. fed. judiciary nominating com. Pa., 1981-89; bd. dirs. Friends of the Nelson Mandela Children's Fund, 1996—, Marian Anderson Hist. Soc., 1998—; mem. adv. com. Frederick D. Patterson Rsch. Inst., 1998—; chmn. bd. dirs. Barnes Found., 1999—. Recipient numerous honors and awards for leadership in edn., the arts, and civil rights. Mem. Am. Philosophical Soc., Am. Acad. Polit. and Social Sci., Phi Delta Kappa, Kappa Delta Pi.

**WATSON, BETTY,** artist; b. Passaic, N.J., Feb. 19, 1928; d. Joseph Francis and Doris Lillian (Wilcox) Rean; m. Robert Watson; children: Winthrop, Caroline Watson Keens. Student, Phoenix Sch. of Design, N.Y.C., 1946, Pa. Acad. Fine Arts, 1947, Art Students League, N.Y.C., 1947, 48, 49-51; BA, Wellesley Coll., Mass., 1949; postgrad., NYU, 1950-51; MFA, U. N.C., 1965. Asst. in art Barnard Coll., N.Y.C., 1949-51; asst. to Ferdinand Roten, Art Dealer Balt., 1952; instr. art Calif. State U., Northridge, 1968-69. One-woman shows include U. NC, Greensboro, 1962, East End Gallery, Provincetown, Mass., 1965, Place Gallery, Provincetown, Mass., 1966, Newsweek Gallery, NYC, 1966, Galley Saint, Norfolk, Va., 1966, Elliott U. Ctr., 1972, High Point NC Theatre and Exhbn. Ctr., Morehead Gallery, 1982, GAL Gallery, Greensboro, 1993, Francis Marion U., SC, 1995, Jackson Libr. U. NC, Greensboro, 2000, retrospective exhbn. Green Hill Ctr. for NC Art, Greensboro, 2006; exhibited in group shows at Nat. Acad. Design, NYC, Am. Gallery, NYC, A.M. Sachs Gallery, NYC, Beilin Gallery, NYC, Waverly Gallery, NYC, Jack Tanzer Gallery, NYC, Grand Rapids Mich. Art Mus., Provincetown Mass. Art Assn., NC Mus. Art, Raleigh, Montclair (NJ) Arts Mus., South Eastern Ctr. Contemporary Art, Winston-Salem, NC, Calif. State U., Northridge, Collector's Gallery at NC Mus. Art, Raleigh, Weatherspoon Mus., U. NC, Greensboro, Ctr. for Creative Leadership, Greensboro, NC, 305 West Cameron Gallery, Chapel Hill, NC, Corp. Art Directions, NYC, 1991-95; author: Betty Watson Paintings: Five Decades, 1999. Mem. Phi Beta Kappa. Home: 4321 Galax Trail Greensboro NC 27410

**WATSON, BRENDA BENNETT,** insurance company executive; b. Decatur, Ga., Aug. 26, 1940; d. Robert Joseph and Clarissa Mae (Weekes) Bennett; m. James H. Pair Jr., Apr. 4, 1969 (div. Aug. 1993); children: Richard S. Pair, Randall J. Pair, Ronald G. Pair; m. James Leigh Watson, Sept. 9, 1995. Student, DeKalb Coll., 1971. Lic. property and casualty agt., Fla., Ga., Okla., Tenn., Tex. Underwriter W. K. Stringer Co., Atlanta, 1961-65, Tharpe & Assocs., Atlanta, 1965-68; sr. v.p. Alexander - Howden, Atlanta, 1968-82; exec. v.p., ptnr. Pair Underwriting Mgrs. Inc., Atlanta, 1982-86; pres. Walkingstick-LaGere-Pair Underwriting Mgrs., Inc., Chandler, Okla., 1986-88; exec. v.p., dir. LaGere-Walkingstick Ins. Agy., Chandler, Okla., 1988—. Exec. v.p. Nat. Am. Ins. Co., Chandler, Okla., 1987—, Austin, Tex. 1999—; exec. v.p., bd. dirs. Chandler Ins. Ltd., Cayman Islands, 1985—. Dir., past pres. Gateway to Prevention and Recovery, 1994-98. Mem. Nat. Assn. Ins. Women (pres. Atlanta chpt. 1978-79, Woman of Yr. 1979-80). Republican. Episcopalian. Office: Wells Fargo Bank Bldg 2028 E Ben White Blvd Ste 200 Austin TX 78741 E-mail: bwatson@naico.com.

**WATSON, CATHERINE ELAINE,** journalist; b. Mpls., Feb. 9, 1944; d. Richard Edward and LaVonne (Slater) W.; m. Al Sicherman (div.); children: Joseph Sicherman, David Sicherman. BA in Journalism, U. Minn., 1966; MA in Teaching, Coll. of St. Thomas, 1971. Reporter Mpls. Star Tribune, 1966-72; editor Picture mag., 1972-78, Travel sect., 1978—2004; editor in chief Galena (Ill.) Gazette, 1990-91. Instr., online mentor Split Rock Arts Program, U. Minn., 1996-2006; sr. travel editor Star Tribune, 2001-04. Author: Travel Basics, 1984, Roads Less Traveled: Dispatches from the Ends of the Earth, 2005 (named Best Book Soc. Am. Travel Writers - Ctrl. States, 2001); contbr. articles to newspapers and travel mags. and books. Recipient Newspaper Mag. Picture Editor's award Pictures of Yr. Competition, 1974, awards for writing and photography Soc. Am. Travel Writers, 1983-2004, Photographer of Yr. award, 1990, Alumna of Notable Achievement award U. Minn. Coll. Liberal Arts, 1994; rsch. grant Jerome Found./Gen. Mills Found., 2004; named Lowell Thomas Travel Journalist of Yr., 1990, Lowell Thomas Bronze awards 1994, 96, 2003. Mem. Am. Newspaper Guild, Soc. Am. Travel Writers, Phi Beta Kappa, Alpha Omicron Pi.

**WATSON, CHARLES M.,** financial consultant; b. Ft. Sill, Okla., May 6, 1952; s. Wendell D. and Saraethel Watson; m. Mary E. Green, May 22, 1976; children: Angie, Emily. BS, U. Okla. U., 1974. V.p. corp. accts. Coulter Corp., Hialeah, Fla., 1979—97; dir. integrated health networks Beckman Coulter, Brea, Calif., 1997—2003; fin. advisor Smith Barney, Red Bank, NJ, 2004—. Founder Monmouth Network, Middletown, NJ, 2004—; chmn. How Firm a Foundation, Middletown, 2005—; profl. tennis tchr. USPTA; stewardship chmn. vestry Christ Ch., Middletown, 2004—06. Mem.: No. Monmouth C. of C., Rotary (sgt.-at-arms Red Bank Club 2005—). Episcopalian. Avocation: Karate. Office: Smith Baney 55 Broad St Red Bank NJ 07701

**WATSON, DENNIS WALLACE,** microbiologist, educator; b. Morpeth, Ont., Can., Apr. 29, 1914; came to U.S., 1938, naturalized, 1946; s. William and Sarah (Verity) W.; m. Alicemay Whittier, June 15, 1941; children: Catherine W., William V. BSA, U. Toronto, 1934; MS, Dalhousie U., 1937; PhD, U. Wis., 1941, DSc (hon.), 1981. Rsch. assoc. U. Wis., 1942, asst. prof., 1946-49; vis. investigator Rockefeller Inst., 1942; investigator Connaught Lab. Med. Rsch. U. Toronto, 1942-44; assoc. prof. U. Minn., Mpls., 1949-52, prof., 1953-63, head dept. microbiology, 1964-84, Regents prof. microbiology, 1980-84, Regents prof. emeritus, 1984—. Vis. prof. Med. Sch. U. Wash., 1950; mem. Commn. Immunization Armed Forces Epidemiology Bd., 1946-59; bd. sci. counselors, divsn. biol. standards NIH, 1957-59, allergy and immunology study sect., 1954-58; chmn. tgn. grant com. Inst. Allergy and Infectious Diseases, 1964, adv. coun., 1967-71; microbiology panel Office Naval Rsch., 1963-66 Mem. editl. bd. Infection and Immunity, 1971-72; editl. cons. Medcom Faculty Medicine, 1973— Bd. dirs Nat. Found. Infectious Diseases, 1976-81; vice chmn. Nat. Soc. Microbiology Found., 1973. With AUS, 1944-46. Recipient Rsch. Career award USPHS, 1962-63; Spl. Rsch. fellow, 1960-61 Mem. AAAS, Am. Assn. Immunologists, Am. Chem. Soc., Am. Acad. Microbiology (vice chmn. bd. govs. 1967), Am. Soc. Microbiology (pres. 1969, v.p. Found. 1972-73), Internat. Endotoxin Soc. (hon., life), Soc. Exptl. Biology and Medicine (coun. 1977-79, pres. 1976-77), Lancefield

Soc., Sigma Xi, Phi Zeta. Home: 2106 Hendon Ave Saint Paul MN 55108-1419 Office: U Minn Med Sch Dept Microbiology PO Box 196 Minneapolis MN 55440-0196 E-mail: watsondw651@msn.com.

**WATSON, DIANE EDITH,** congresswoman; b. LA, Nov. 12, 1933; d. William Allen Louis and Dorothy Elizabeth (O'Neal) Watson. AA, L.A. City Coll., 1954; BA, UCLA, 1956; MS, Calif. State U., L.A.; PhD, Claremont Grad. Sch., 1987. Tchr., sch. psychologist L.A. Unified Sch. Dist., 1960-69, 73-74; assoc. prof. Calif. State U., L.A., 1969-71; health occupations specialist Bur. Indsl. Edn., Calif. Dept. Edn., 1971-73; mem. L.A. Unified Sch. Bd., 1975-78, Calif. Senate from dist. 26, 1978-98, chairperson health and human svcs. com.; US amb. to Micronesia US Dept. of State, 1999-2001; mem. U.S. Congress from 33d Calif. dist., 2001—, mem. govt. reform com. and internat. rels. com. Mem. Legis. Black Caucus, edn. com., budget and fiscal rev. com., criminal procedure com., housing and land use com. Calif State Sen.; del. Dem. Nat. Conv., 1972—; mem. Dem. Nat. Com.; mem. exec. com. Nat. Conf. State Legislators Author: Health Occupations Instructional Units-Secondary Schools, 1975, Planning Guide for Health Occupations, 1975; co-author: Introduction to Health Care, 1976. Recipient Mary Church Terrell award, 1976, Brotherhood Crusade award, 1981, Black Woman of Achievement award NAACP Legal Def. Fund, 1988; named Alumnus of Yr., UCLA, 1980, 82. Mem. Calif. Assn. Sch. Psychologists, L.A. Urban League, Calif. Tchrs. Assn., Calif. Commn. on Status Women. Democrat. Roman Catholic. Office: US Ho Reps 125 Cannon HOB Washington DC 20515-0533 also: 4322 Wilshire Blvd Ste 302 Los Angeles CA 90010 Office Phone: 202-225-7084. Fax: 202-225-2422. Office Phone: 323-965-1422. Office Fax: 323-965-1113.*

**WATSON, DOC (ARTHEL LANE WATSON),** vocalist, guitarist, banjoist, recording artist; b. Deep Gap, N.C., Mar. 2, 1923; s. General Dixon and Annie (Greer) Waston; m. Rosa Lee Carlton; children: Eddy Merle(dec.), Nancy Ellen. Ind. rec. artist, touring performer. First appearance Boone (N.C.) Fiddler's Conv., rec. artist Folkways in 1960's, signed with Vanguard Records, 1964, recorded for United Artists, Columbia, Poppy, Sugar Hill, Verve and Flying Fish labels; performer: Newport Folk Festival, 1963, Smithsonian Inst., White House, 1980, Carnegie Hall, 1985; toured in Africa for Dept. State, 1970, also Europe and Japan, albums (many with Merle Watson) Southbound, Red Rocking Chair, The Guitar Album, Riding the Midnight Train (Grammy award for Best Traditional Folk album, 1986), Portrait, Songs for Little Pickers, On Praying Ground (Grammay award for best traditional folk album, 1990); performer (music): (films) Places in the Heart. Recipient Grammy award, 1973, 1974, 1979, 1986, 1990, N.C. award. State of N.C., 1985, Carolina prize N.Y. Times Corp., 1985, Grammy award for Best Traditional Folk Rec., 1990, Nat. Medal of Arts, Pres. of U.S. with NEA, 1997, Nat. Heritage award, NEH, 1988, Grammy award for Lifetime Achievement, 2004. Office: care Folklore Prodns 1671 Appian Way Santa Monica CA 90401-3258 Fax: 310-458-6005. E-mail: info@folkloreproductions.com.

**WATSON, DONALD CHARLES, JR.,** cardiothoracic surgeon, educator; b. Fairfield, Ohio, Mar. 15, 1945; s. Donald Charles and Pricilla H. Watson; m. Susan Robertson Prince, June 23, 1973; children: Kea Huntington, Katherine Anne, Kirsten Prince. BA in Applied Sci., Lehigh U., 1968, BSME, 1969; MSME, Stanford U., 1969; MD, Duke U., 1972. Diplomate Am. Bd. Thoracic Surgery, Am. Bd. Surgery. Intern Stanford U. Med. Ctr., Calif., 1972-73, resident in cardiovasc. surgery Calif., 1973-74, resident in surgery Calif., 1976-78, chief resident in heart transplant Calif., 1978-79, chief resident in cardiovasc. and gen. surgery Calif., 1978-80; clin. assoc. surgery br. Nat. Heart and Lung Inst., 1974-76, acting sr. surgeon, 1976; assoc. cardiovasc. surgeon dept. child health and devel. George Washington U., Washington, 1980-84, asst. prof. surgery, asst. prof. child health and devel., 1980-84, attending cardiovasc. surgeon dept. child health and devel., 1984-89, assoc. prof. surgery, 1984-89; assoc. prof. pediats. U. Tenn.-Memphis, 1984-90, prof. surgery 1990—2006, prof. pediats., 1990—2006, chmn. cardiothoracic surgery, 1984-99, assoc. chief med. officer, 1999—2001. Mem. staff Le Bonheur Children's Med. Ctr., Memphis, 1984—2006, chmn. cardiothoracic surgery, 1984-99; cons. in field; instr. advanced trauma life support; profl. cons., program reviewer HHS. Contbr. chpts., numerous articles, revs. to profl. publs. Bd. dirs. Internat. Children's Heart Found., Child Health Alliance Mid-South. Served to lt. comdr. USPHS, 1974-76. Smith Kline & French fellow Lehigh U., 1967; NSF fellow Lehigh U., 1968; univ. interdepartmental scholar and univ. scholar Lehigh U., 1968. Fellow Am. Coll. Cardiology, Am. Coll. Chest Physicians (forum cardiovasc. surgery, coun. critical care), Southeastern Surg. Congress, Am. Acad. Pediats. (surgery sect.), ACS; mem. Assn. Surg. Edn., Am. Assn. Thoracic Surgery, Soc. Thoracic Surgeons, So. Thoracic Surg. Assn., Am. Thoracic Soc., Assn. Acad. Surgery, Internat. Soc. Heart Transplantation, Am. Fedn. Clin. Rsch., Found. Advanced Edn. in Scis., Andrew G. Morrow Soc., Norman E. Shumway Soc. (multiple bd. dirs.), Coun. on Cardiovasc. Surgery Am. Heart Assn., Soc. Internat. di Chirrg., AAAS, N.Y. Acad. Sci., AMA, NIH Alumni Assn., Stanford U. Med. Alumni Assn., Stanford U. Alumni Assn., Lehigh U. Alumni Assn., Smithsonian Assocs., Sierra Club, U. Tenn. Pres.'s Club, LeBonheur Pres's Club, U.S. Yacht Racing Assn., Pilots Internat. Assn., Nat. Assn. Flight Instrs., Aircraft Owners and Pilots Assn., Order Ky. Cols., Crescent Club, Phi Beta Kappa, Tau Beta Pi, Pi Tau Sigma, Phi Gamma Delta. Republican. Presbyterian. Achievements include established a regional referral center for the treatment of congenital heart disease. Avocations: golf, sailing, mountain climbing, flying. Office Phone: 828-277-0677. E-mail: dcwbusi@aol.com, dwutmem@aol.com.

**WATSON, DONALD RALPH,** architect, dean, writer, artist; b. Providence, Sept. 27, 1937; s. Ralph Giles W. and Ethel (Fletcher) Pastene; m. Marja Palmqvist, Sept. 8, 1966 (div. Jan. 1984); children: Petrik, Elise; m. Judith Criste, Jan. 3, 1986 (dec. Oct. 8, 2000). AB, Yale U., 1959, BArch, 1962, MEd, 1969. Lic. architect Nat. Council Archtl. Registration Bds. Architect Peace Corps, Tunisia, 1962-64; archtl. cons. Govt. of Tunisia, 1964-65; pvt. practice, Trumbull, Conn., 1969—; dean Sch. Architecture, Rensselaer Poly. Inst., Troy, NY, 1990-95, prof., 1990—2001. Frederick C. Baker vis. prof. U. Oreg., 1995; chmn. environ. design program, Yale U., 1979-90; vis. prof. Yale U., 1995-2000. Author: Designing and Building a Solar House, 1977, Energy Conservation Through Building Design, 1979, Climatic Design, 1983, Energy Design Handbook, 1993; editor-in-chief Time Saver Standards: Architectural Design Data, 1997, 2005, Time-Saver Standards: Urban Design, 2003. Bd. dirs. Save the Children Fedn., 1979-82. Recipient Honor Design award Conn. Soc. Architects, 1974, Honor Design award region AIA, 1978, 84, 1st award Owens Corning Energy Conservation Bldg. Design Program, 1983, Excellence in housing award Energy Efficient Bldg. Assn., 1988, Lifetime Achievement award Passive and Low Energy Architecture, 1990, Best in Show Watercolors, Soc. Creative Artists, 1999, Green Bldg. Design award NESEA, 2002, Disting. Prof. award ACSA, 2002, James Haecker Disting. Leadership award, Archtl. Rsch. Centers Consortium, 2004; Assn. of Collegiate Schs. of Archtecture/Am. Metals Climax rsch. fellow, 1967-69; rsch. fellow Rockefeller Found., 1978. Fellow: AIA. Home and Office: 54 Larkspur Dr Trumbull CT 06611-4652

**WATSON, DOUG,** information technology executive; Asst. v.p. mgmt. info. sys. Bacardi-Martini; v.p. info. sys., chief info. officer Bacardi USA Inc. Miami, Fla. Named one of Premier 100 IT Leaders, ComputerWorld, 2003. Office: Bacardi USA Inc 2100 Biscayne Blvd Miami FL 33137-5028 Office Phone: 305-573-8511. Office Fax: 305-573-7507.

**WATSON, E BRUCE,** science educator; b. Nashua, N.H., Oct. 16, 1950; m. M. Susan Watson; 1 child, Jonah. Student, Williams Coll., 1968—69; BA in Geology, U. NH., 1972; PhD in Geochemistry, MIT, 1976. Postdoctoral fellow Carnegie Inst., 1976-77; from asst. to full prof. Rensselaer Polytechnic Inst., Troy, NY, 1977—, chmn. dept. earth and environ. scis., 1990-95, Inst. prof. sci., 1995—. Vis. scientist Max Planck Inst. Chemistry, Mainz, Germany, 1984; original mem. highly-cited rschrs. ISI Thomsen Sci.; Qualline lectr. U. Tex. at Austin, 2004. Assoc. editor Geochimica et Cosmochimica Acta, 1985-88; editor petrology and geochemistry Neues

Jahrbuch fur Mineralogie, 1988-96; editor Chem. Geology, 1991-95; mem. editl. bd. Geochimica et Cosmochimica Acta, 1997—; contbr. articles to profl. jours., chpts. to books. Vis. rsch. fellow Macquarie U., Australia, 1981, geochemistry fellow European Assn. Geochemistry and Geochem. Soc.; named Disting. alumnus U. N.H., 1999. Fellow AAAS, Am. Geophys. Union (fellows com. 1992-95, nominating com. 1997-98, R.A. Daly lectr. 1999, W.H. Bucher medal); Mineral. Soc. Am. (pres. 1998), Geol. Soc. Am. (Arthur L. Day medal 1998); mem. NAS, Geochem. Soc. (budget com. 1990, councilor 1991-94, F.W. Clarke medal 1983, V.M. Goldschmidt award 2005), ISI Thomsen Sci. (original mem.). Office: Rensselaer Polytechnic Inst 110 8th St Troy NY 12180-3522 Office Phone: 518-276-8838. Business E-Mail: watsoe@rpi.edu.

**WATSON, EASTER JEAN,** psychotherapist, financial program consultant; b. Leland, Miss., U.S.A., Mar. 15, 1948; d. Tom and Louise B. Watson; m. Boisie Lee Watson, Oct. 24, 1965 (div. Apr. 1983); children: LaTonia Deonnette, Lorenzo Tomas, Derek Ondrea(dec.). BA in Sociology & Minority Studies, U. Notre Dame, 1974; MSW, Atlanta U., 1987. Psycho-therapist Oak Park & River Forest Mental Health Ctr., Ill., 1991—92; program cons. child welfare program Assn. House of Chicago, Chicago, Ill., 1993—94; exec. dir. Easter Watson, MSW & Assoc., Chicago, Ill., 1994—95; child welfare admin. Kinara Com. Svcs., Chicago, Ill., 2000—01; psycho-therapist cons. Self employed, Chicago, Ill., 2001—03; asst. dir. of child welfare YMCA of Metro, Chicago, Ill., 1996—2000. Cons. alternative sch. Chgo. Pub. Sch., Mgmt. Planning Inst., Chgo., 2001—; field instr. Chgo. State U., Chgo., 2001—, Nat. Louis U., Chgo., 2001—, Roosevelt U., 2001. Coord. (parent conference) The Power of Parents, 2003. Mem. Operation PUSH, Chgo., 1996—. Grantee, U. Notre Dame, 1972. Protestant. Home: 8049 South Sacramento Ave Chicago IL 60652 Office: Holistic Comprehensive Proffl Svs Inc 10630 South Western Ave Chicago IL 60642 Personal E-mail: eastwats@aol.com.

**WATSON, ELIZABETH MARION,** protective services official; b. Phila., Aug. 25, 1949; d John Julian and Elizabeth Gertrude (Judge) Herrmann; m. Robert LLoyd Watson, June 18, 1976; children: Susan, Mark, David. BA in Psychology with honors, Tex. Tech. U., 1971. With Houston Police Dept., 1972-92, detective homicide, burglary and theft, 1976-81, lt. records div. northeast patrol div., 1981-84, capt. inspections div., auto theft div., 1984-87, dep. chief west patrol div., 1987-90, police chief, 1990-92; with Austin, Tex. Police Dept., 1992—, police chief, 1992—. Mem. adv. bd. S.W. Law Enforcement Inst., Richardson,Tex., 1990—. Mem. editorial bd. Am. Jour. Police, 1991—. Mem. Internat. Assn. Chiefs of Police (mem. major cities chiefs, mem. civil rights com.), Police Exec. Rsch. Form, Tex. Police Chiefs Assn. Roman Catholic. Home: 725 County Road 136b Kingsland TX 78639-3943

**WATSON, EMILY,** actress; b. London, Jan. 14, 1967; m. Jack Waters, 1995. Grad., Bristol U. Motion picture and stage actress. Films include Breaking the Waves, 1996 (nominee Best Actress Oscar 1997, nominee Golden Globe award 1997, Robert award 1997, N.Y. Film Critics Circle award 1996, Nat. Soc. Film Critics award 1996, L.A. Film Critics Assn. New Generation award 1996, European Film award 1996, others), The Mill on the Floss, 1997, Metroland, 1997, The Boxer, 1997, Hilary and Jackie (nominee Best Actress Oscar 1999, nominee Golden Globe award 1999), The Cradle Will Rock, 1999, Angela's Ashes, 1999, Trixie, 2000, Gosford Park, 2001 (SAG award outstanding performance by the cast, 2002), In Search of the Assasin, 2001, Equilibrium, 2002, Punch-Drunk Love, 2002, Red Dragon, 2002, Equilibrium, 2002, Blossoms and Blood, 2003, (voice) Back to Gaya, 2004, The Life and Death of Peter Sellers, 2004, Separate Lies, 2005, (voice) Corpse Bride, 2005, Wah-Wah, 2006. Office: c/o SAG 5757 Wilshire Blvd Los Angeles CA 90036-3635*

**WATSON, EMMA,** actress; b. Oxford, England, Apr. 15, 1990; Actor: (films) Harry Potter and the Sorcerer's Stone, 2001, Harry Potter and the Chamber of Secrets, 2002, Harry Potter and the Prisoner of Azkaban, 2004, Harry Potter and the Goblet of Fire, 2005; appearances (TV) The Oprah Winfrey Show, 2002, The Tonight Show with Jay Leno, 2002. Office: c/o Leavesden Studios PO Box 3000 Leavesden WD2 7LT England*

**WATSON, EVELYN EGNER,** radiation scientist; b. Corbin, Ky., Dec. 15, 1928; d. Edgar Mattison and Bertha Mae (Mayfield) Egner; m. Earl Greene Watson, Nov. 10, 1953; children: Nancy Eileen, Philip Allen. AA, Cumberland Coll., 1946; student, Lincoln Meml. U., 1947-48; BA, U. Ky., 1949; postgrad., U. Tenn., 1968. Math. and sci. tchr. Lynch (Ky.) High Sch., 1949-50; office mgr. Whitley County Sch. System, Williamsburg, Ky., 1950-53; sr. lab. tech. Radiation Internal Dose Ctr. Oak Ridge (Tenn.) Assoc. Univs., 1961-71, scientist, 1971-79, program mgr., 1979-89, program dir., 1989-94; cons. internal dosimetry Tenn., 1994—. Lectr. in field; cons. USFDA, Rockville, Md., 1983-88. Assoc. editor Jour. Nuclear Medicine 1981-86; editor newsletter Soc. Nuclear Medicine S.E. chpt., 1988-99; co-author: MIRD Primer, 1988; contbr. articles to profl., chpts. to books. Bd. dirs. Youth Haven, Oak Ridge, Tenn., 1970-74, Clinch River Home Health, Clinton, Tenn., 1988-94. Recipient Excellence in Tech. Transfer award Fed. Lab. Consortium, 1985, Lifetime Scientific Achievement award Assn. Women in Sci., 1993. Mem. Soc. Nuclear Medicine (med. internal radiation dose com. 1980—, chmn. 1994—, Marshall Brucer award for Disting. Svc. to S.E. chpt. 1999), Health Physics Soc. (Disting. Svc. award 1981, treas. 1976-77, Lifetime Achievement award 1994), European Assn. Nuclear Medicine, Nat. Coun. on Radiation Protection and Measurements (sci. com. 1986-98), Sigma Xi. Mem. Ch. of Christ. Avocations: reading, word puzzles, handicrafts. Home: 104 New Bedford Ln Oak Ridge TN 37830-8289 E-mail: eew72@comcast.net.

**WATSON, GAIL H.,** retired librarian; b. Hattiesburg, Miss., May 12, 1941; d. Robert Elkin and Virginia Lucille (Swann) Hill; m. Tommy Gene Watson, June 4, 1963; children: James Todd, Thomas Gregory. BA, U. So. Miss., 1963; M in Librarianship, U. S.C., 1975; MEd, Tenn. State U., Nashville, 1983. Tchr. Hawkins Jr. H.S., Hattiesburg, 1963-64, Seminary (Miss.) H.S., 1965-66; libr. Bush River Elem. Sch., Newberry, S.C., 1973-74, Prosperity (S.C.) Elem. Sch., 1974-76; tchr. Franklin County H.S., Winchester, Tenn., 1977-83; libr. South/J.D. Jackson Jr. H.S., Cowan, Tenn., 1983—2003; ret., 2003. Mem. SACS rev. teams, Tenn., 1985—. Tenn. Dept. Edn. grantee, 1995. Mem. ALA, Soc. for Promotion of Christian Knowledge, Franklin County Librs. (chair 1998-2003), Franklin County Ret. Tchrs. Assn. (pres. 2006-09), Delta Kappa Gamma (pres. 2006—), Kappa Delta. Democrat. Episcopalian. Avocations: reading, travel. Home: 143 S Carolina Ave Sewanee TN 37375-2405 Personal E-mail: gailwatson@bellsouth.net.

**WATSON, GARY ALAN,** management consultant; b. Terre Haute, Ind., Dec. 2, 1948; s. James Ralph and Lois Levine (Lowe) Watson; m. Linda Largen Watson, Aug. 5, 1972; children: Betsy, Andrew. BS in Speech Edn., Ind. State U., Terre Haute, Ind., 1970, MS in Speech Comm., 1972; student, U. Louisville, 1983. Cert. tchr. Ky. Instr. Fla. Coll., Tampa, Fla., 1972—73; tchr. Jefferson County Pub. Schs., Louiseville, Ky., 1973—94; tchr. instrnl. resources, 1994—2000; educator Ky. Dept. Edn., Frankfort, Ky., 2000—03; prin., owner Helping Support Educators Inc., Louisville, 2004—. Adj. lectr. Ind. U. Southeast, New Albany, Ind., 1973—94; coach literacy Jefferson County Pub. Schs., 2003—; cons. in field. Adv. com. Louisville (Ky.) Writing Project, 1996—2000; elder Douglass Hills Ch. Christ, Louisville. Recipient Tchr. award, Louisville (Ky.) Cmty. Found., 1990, 1992, 1994. Mem.: Ky. Cols. Home and Office: Helping Support Educators Inc 2614 Wilburlook Ln Louisville KY 40220

**WATSON, GEORGE HENRY, JR.,** broadcaster, journalist; b. Birmingham, Ala., July 27, 1936; s. George Henry and Grace Elizabeth (Carr) W.; m. Ellen Havican Bradley, July 13, 1979; children: George H., III, Ellen Havican BA, Harvard U., 1959; MS, Columbia U., 1960. Reporter Washington Post, 1960-61; corr. ABC News, 1962-75, Moscow bur. chief, 1966-69, London bur. chief, 1969-75, v.p., Washington bur. chief, 1976-80; v.p., mng. editor

Cable News Network, 1980; v.p. news ABC News, N.Y.C., 1981-85, exec. in charge ABC News Viewpoint, 1981-85, v.p., Washington bur. chief, 1985-93, sr. contbg. editor, 1993-2001; freelance broadcast journalist. Served with U.S. Army, 1958. Recipient Peabody award, 1982, DuPont Columbia award, 1983, nat. news Emmy award, 1984. Mem. Radio Television News Dirs. Assn., Soc. Profl. Journalists, Nat. Press Club, Overseas Press Club (award for best television documentary 1971, citation for excellence 1974), Nat. Press Club, Com. to Protect Journalists, Fgn. Policy Assn., Cosmos Club. Personal E-mail: ghwjr727@hotmail.com.

**WATSON, GEORGE W.,** energy executive; BSEE, Queen's U., Kingston, Can., 1970, MBA in Fin. Mktg., 1972; grad. advanced mgmt. program, Harvard U., 1988. With Can. Imperial Bank Commerce, Toronto; asst. gen. mgr. worldwide, oil and gas divsn. Calgary, 1981; dir. fin. Dome Petroleum, v.p. fin.; v.p., treas. Amoco Can.; pres., CEO Intensity Resources, 1988-90; CFO TransCanada, 1990-93, pres. 1993-99, CEO, 1994-99; ptnr. Northridge Can. Inc., 1999—2002. CEO Critical Control Solutions Corp.; chmn. bd. dirs. Badger Daylighting Inc.; chmn. Zebas Energy Corp., Calgary Olympic Devel. Assn.; bd. dirs. Can. Spirit Resources Corp., Teekay LNG LLP, Repeat Seat Ltd., Recap Energy Inc., Signal Energy Corp. Bd. dirs. Queen's U., TGS N. Am. Real Estate Investment Trust. Address: PO Box 122 Niagara Falls Canada L2E 6S8 Office Phone: 403-705-7510. Business E-mail: george.watson@criticalcontrol.com. E-mail: georgewwatson@shaw.ca.

**WATSON, GEORGIANNA,** retired librarian; b. Lock Haven, Pa., Feb. 18, 1949; d. George and Anna (Eisenhower) Rhine; children: Sharga Nicolle, George Winfield-Martin. BS in Edn., Lock Haven State U., 1971; MLS, Brigham Young U., Provo, Utah, 1978; M in Pub. Adminstrn., John Jay Coll. Criminal Justice, N.Y.C., 1986. Lic. realtor NY. Tchr. Mifflin County Sch. Dist., Lewistown, Pa., 1971—72; libr. Shiprock Boarding Sch. Bur. Indian Affairs, N.Mex., 1972—79, libr. Ft. Sill Indian Sch. Lawton, Okla., 1979—80; libr. U.S. Mil. Acad., West Point, 1980—83, head pub. svcs., libr., 1983—2006; ret. Owner The Paint Pony, Walden, NY; weekly talk show host WTBQ Radio; real estate salesperson Exclusively Equine Properties, Goshen, NY, 2006—. Mem. Am. Quarter Horse Assn., Internat. Arabian Horse Assn., Am. Paint Horse Assn., N.Y. State Horse Coun. (Mid-Hudson dir.), Pi Alpha Alpha. Republican. Home: 8 St Michaels Ln Walden NY 12586-2466 Office: Exclusively Equine Properties LLC 349 Sarah Wells Tr Goshen NY 10924 Office Phone: 845-294-4224. Personal E-mail: gwatso@huc.rr.com.

**WATSON, HARLAN L(EROY),** federal agency administrator, physicist, economist; b. Macomb, Ill., Dec. 17, 1944; s. Joseph Carroll and Helen Louise (Sanders) Watson; m. Sharon Ann Rinkus Diguette, Apr. 22, 1977. BA in Physics, Western Ill. U., 1967; PhD in Physics, Iowa State U., 1973; MA in Econs., Georgetown U., 1981. Postdoctoral fellow Argonne (Ill.) Nat. Lab., 1973-75; project scientist, tech. sr. scientist B-K Dynamics, Inc., Rockville, Md., 1975-78; tech. staff TRW Energy Systems Planning Group, McLean, Va., 1978-80; profl. staff mem. subcom. on energy nuclear proliferation and govt. processes Com. on Govtl. Affairs, U.S. Senate, Washington, 1980-81; tech. and sci. cons. Com. on Sci. and Tech., U.S. Ho. of Reps., 1981-86; rep. energy and environ., coord. Com. on Sci., Space and Tech., U.S. Ho. of Reps., 1986-89; sci. adviser to sec. Dept. Interior, Washington, 1989-93, dep. asst. sec. for sci.-water and sci., 1989-90, prin. dep. asst. to sec. for water and sci., 1990-93; rep. spl. asst. subcom. energy, com. sci., space, tech. U.S. Ho. of Reps., Washington, 1993-95, staff dir. subcom. energy and environment, com. sci., 1995—2001; sr climate negotiator, spec rep US Dept State, Washington, 2001—. Contbr. articles to profl jours. Home: 6719 Tomlinson Ter Cabin John MD 20818-1328 Office: 2201 C St NW Rm 4330 Washington DC 20520-0001 E-mail: WatsonHL@state.gov.

**WATSON, JACK CROZIER,** retired state supreme court justice; b. Jonesville, La., Sept. 17, 1928; s. Jesse Crozier and Gladys Lucille (Talbot) W.; m. Henrietta Sue Carter, Dec. 26, 1958; children: Carter Crozier (dec.), Wells Talbot. BA, U. Southwestern La., 1949; JD, La. State U., 1956; completed with honor, Appellate Judges Seminar, NYU, 1974, Sr. Appellate Judges Seminar, 1980. Bar: La. 1956. Atty. King, Anderson & Swift, Lake Charles, La., 1956—58; prosecutor City of Lake Charles, 1960; asst. dist. atty. Calcasieu Parish, 1961—64; ptnr. Watson & Watson, Lake Charles, 1961—64; judge 14th Jud. Dist., La., 1964—72; judge ad hoc Ct. Appeals, 1st Cir., Baton Rouge, 1972—73; judge Ct. Appeals, 3d Cir., Lake Charles, 1973—79; assoc. justice La. Supreme Ct., New Orleans, 1979—96, ret., 1996; of counsel Baggett, McCall, Burgess, Watson & Gaughan, Lake Charles, 2004—. Faculty advisor Nat. Coll. State Judiciary, Reno, 1970, 73; adj. prof. law summer sch. program in Greece, Tulane U., 1988-00, 05-06; adj. prof. law So. U., Baton Rouge, 1998-99; del. NEH Seminar, 1976; La. del to Internat. Conf. Appellate Magistrates, The Philippines, 1977; mem. La. Jud. Coun., 1986-92. 1st lt. USAF, 1950-54. Mem. ABA, La. Bar Assn., S.W. La. Bar Assn. (pres. 1973), Law Inst. State of La., La. Coun. Juvenile Ct. Judges (pres. 1969-70), Am. Judicature Soc., S.W. La. Camellia Soc. (pres. 1973-74), Am. Legion (post comdr. 1963), Lake Charles Yacht Club (commodore 1974), Blue Key, Sigma Alpha Epsilon, Phi Delta Phi, Pi Kappa Delta. Democrat. Baptist. Home (Summer): Grand West Village Leadville CO 80461 Office Phone: 337-478-8888.

**WATSON, JAMES DEWEY,** molecular biologist, educator; b. Chgo., Apr. 6, 1928; s. James Dewey and Jean (Mitchell) W.; m. Elizabeth Lewis, 1968; children: Rufus Robert, Duncan James. BS, U. Chgo., 1947; PhD in Zoology, Ind. U., 1950; DSc (hon.), U. Chgo., 1961, Ind. U., 1963; LLD (hon.), U. Notre Dame, 1965; DSc (hon.), L.I. U., 1970, Adelphi U., 1972, Brandeis U., 1973, Albert Einstein Coll. Medicine, 1979, Hofstra U., 1976, Harvard U., 1978, Rockefeller U., 1980, Clarkson Coll., 1981, SUNY, 1983; MD (hon.), U. Buenos Aires, Argentina, 1986; DSc (hon.), Rutgers U., 1988, Bard Coll., 1991, U. Cambridge, 1993, Fairfield U., 1993, U. Stellenbosch, 1993, U. Oxford; MD, Charles Univ., Prague, 1998; DSc (hon.), Washington Coll., 1999, U. Judaism, 1999, U. Coll. London, 2000, U. Wesleyan U., 2000, Wilson U., 2001, Dartmouth, 2001, Trinity Coll., Dublin, 2001. Rsch. fellow NRC, U. Copenhagen, 1950-51; Nat. Found. Infantile Paralysis fellow Cavendish Lab., Cambridge U., 1951-52, 55-56; sr. rsch. fellow biology Calif. Inst. Tech., 1953-55; asst. prof. biology Harvard U., 1955-58, assoc. prof., 1958-61, prof., 1961-76; dir. Cold Spring Harbor Lab., NY, 1968-93, pres. NY, 1994—2003, chancellor NY, 2003—; assoc. dir. Nat. Ctr. for Human Genome Rsch., NIH, 1988-89, dir. Nat. Ctr. for Human Genome Rsch., 1989-92. Newton-Abraham vis. prof. Oxford U., 1994. Author: Molecular Biology of the Gene, 1965, 4th edit., 1986, The Double Helix, 1968, (with John Tooze) The DNA Story, 1981, (with others) The Molecular Biology of the Cell, 1983, 2d edit., 1989, 3d edit. 1994, (with John Tooze and David Kurtz) Recombinant DNA, A Short Course, 1983, 2d edit., 1992, A Passion for DNA, 2000, Genes, Girls and Gamow, 2001, DNA: The Secret of Life, 2003. Named Hon. fellow Clare Coll., Cambridge U., hon. knight of Brit. Empire, 2002; recipient (with F.H.C. Crick) John Collins Warren prize Mass. Gen. Hosp., 1959, Eli Lilly award in biochemistry Am. Chem. Soc., 1959, Albert Lasker Prize Am. Pub. Health Assn., 1960, (with F.H.C. Crick) Rsch. Corp. prize, 1962, (with F.H.C. Crick and M.H.F. Wilkins) Nobel prize in medicine, 1962, Presdl. Medal of Freedom, 1977, Kaul Found. award for excellence, 1993, Nat. Biotech. Venture award, 1993, Copley Medal, 1993, Charles A. Dana award, 1994, Lomonosov medal Russian Acad. Sci., 1995, Nat. medal of Sci., 1997, Liberty medal City of Phila., 2000, Benjamin Franklin medal for disting. achievement in scis. Am. Philos. Soc., 2001, Gairdner award for merit, 2002, Lotos Club Medal of Merit, 2004. Mem. NAS (Carty medal 1971), Am. Philos. Soc., Am. Assn. Cancer Rsch., Am. Acad. Arts and Scis., Am. Soc. Biol. Chemistry, Royal Soc. (London), Acad. Scis. Russia, Danish Acad. Arts and Scis. Achievements include co-discovery of Double-Helix DNA. Office: Cold Spring Harbor Lab PO Box 100 Cold Spring Harbor NY 11724-0100*

**WATSON, JASON BRADLEY,** not-for-profit developer; b. Washington, May 19, 1977; s. Robert Bradley and Janet Arletta Watson; m. Kristina Bernice Friesen, Aug. 14, 1999; 1 child, Cassidy. BA, Drake U., 1998; ThM, Christian Bible Coll., Rocky Mount, NC, 2004; MEd, Lynchburg Coll., 2006. Rsch. asst. Dr. Myron Marty, Des Moines, 1996—98; tchr. Clinton

Christian Sch., Upper Marlboro, Md., 1998—2001; asst. program dir. Patrick Henry B&G Plant, Brookneal, Va., 2001—02, program dir., 2002—04, exec. dir., 2004—. Lifetime mem. Answers in Genesis-Creation Mus., Ky.; charter mem. Nat. Constn. Ctr., Phila.; mem. Nat. Trust Hist. Preservation, Washington. Recipient Xerox award for Humanities and Social Scis., 1994. Mem.: Christian Mgmt. Assn., Va. Assn. Children's Homes (cert. in childcare), Pi Sigma Alpha, Phi Alpha Theta. Republican. Baptist. Avocations: baseball, lighthouses, reading. Home and Office: 860 Red Hill Rd Brookneal VA 24528

**WATSON, JENNY,** family and consumer sciences educator; b. Radford, Va., Nov. 4, 1979; d. E.R. Watson, Jr. and Janice South Watson. BS, Bridgewater Coll., 2001. Cert. family and consumer scis. tchr. Am. Assn. of Family and Consumer Scis., 2001, tchr. Va., 2002. Tchr. family and consumer scis. Grayson County Career & Tech. Edn. Ctr., Independence, Va., 2003—; state coord. Va. FCCLA Alumni & Assocs., 2005—. Newsletter editor Va. FCCLA, 1995—2001, cons., 1997—, bd. dirs., 2003—. Recipient Outstanding Svc. award, Bridgewater Coll., 2001, Nat. FCCLA Master Adviser, Family, Career, and Cmty. Leaders of Am. (FCCLA), Outstanding New Educator award, 2005, New Achiever award, 2006. Mem.: Va. FCCLA (alumni and assoc. execc. bd., pres., pres.-elect, past pres., reporter 1997—2005, state exec. coun. 2003—, master advisor), Va. Assn. of Family and Consumer Scis. (bd. dirs. 1998—2001, 2006—), Va. Assn. of Tchrs. of Family and Consumer Scis. (Outstanding New CTE LEducator 2005), Assn. of Career and Tech. Edn., Am. Assn. of Family and Consumer Scis. (nat. 2d vice chair 1999—2000).

**WATSON, JERRY CARROLL,** advertising executive; b. Greenville, Ala., Aug. 22, 1943; s. William J. and Georgia Katherine (Mixon) W.; m. Judith Zeigler Brooks, Sept. 16, 1988; 2 child, Theodore William, Hunter Brooks. BS, U. Ala., Tuscaloosa, 1967; MS, U. Va., 1995. Staff writer Phillips, Eindhoven, The Netherlands, 1967-68; mgr. mktg. Fuller & Dees Mktg., Montgomery, Ala., 1968-70; v.p. Nat. Student Mktg., Washington, 1970-73; pres. Coll. & Univ. Press, Washington, 1973-80; ptnr. Direct Response Consulting Svcs., McLean, Va., 1981-96. Bd. dirs. Foxhall Corp., The Art Co., Mustique Co. Founding mem. Am. Inst. Cancer Rsch. Mem. Direct Mktg. Assn., Non-Profit Mailer Fedn., Promotional Mktg. Assn., Nature Conservancy, Sierra Club, Falls Church (Va.) C. of C. (bd. dirs.). Avocations: forestry, gardening, astronomy, photography. Home: 850 Dolley Madison Blvd Mc Lean VA 22101-1821 Office: Direct Response Cons Svcs 6849 Old Dominion Dr Ste 300 Mc Lean VA 22101-3791 E-mail: watson@drcs.com, watson@mouselink.net.

**WATSON, JESSICA LEWIS,** writer; b. Urbana, Ill., June 16, 1964; d. Jane Eileen Lewis; m. Bruce S. Watson, Aug. 9, 1986 (div. Apr. 2003). BA in English, U. Ill., 1987; Diploma in Am. Lit., U. Liege, 1988; MA in English, Baylor U., 1994. Social worker Roundhouse, Champaign, Ill., 1988-89; cmty. liaison Krannert Ctr. for the Performing Arts, Urbana, Ill., 1989-90; freelance, writer and author Waco, also Champaign, Ill., 1990—; lectr. in English Baylor U., Waco, Tex., 1996-98; English instr. U. Ill., Urbana, 1988. Author: Bastardy as a Gifted Status in Chaucer and Malory, 1996, Illegitimacy Empowered, 1994.; contbr. articles to profl. jours. Singer Austin Civic Chorus, Tex., 1996-2000. Recipient Literary Touring Program award Tex. Commn. on the Arts, Temple, Longview, Ft. Hood, 1994-97, Helen Chambers Poetry award Baylor U., Waco, 1994; grantee Aspen Writers Found., Colo., 1992. Avocations: modern dance, swimming, playing and singing classical music. Home: 1206 W Columbia Ave Champaign IL 61821 Personal E-mail: jessicabulty@yahoo.com.

**WATSON, JOANN FORD,** theology studies educator; b. Ashland, Ohio, Apr. 11, 1956; d. Laurence Wesley and Edna Lucille (Garber) Ford; m. Duane Frederick Watson, June 2, 1984; 1 child, Christina Lucille. BA, DePauw U., 1978; MDiv, Princeton Theol. Sem., 1981; PhD, Northwestern U., 1984. Ordained to ministry Presbyn. Ch. Asst. prof. hist. theology Ashland (Ohio) Theol. Sem., 1984-86, assoc. prof. theology, 1989-95, chair dept. ch. history and theology, 1989—95, 2003—, H.R. Gill prof. theology, 1996—; chaplain Grady Meml. Hosp., Atlanta, 1986-87; co-pastor Tri-Ch. Parish United Meth. Chs. Northwestern, NY, 1987-89; pastor Camroden Presbyn. Ch., Rome, NY, 1987-89; parish assoc. First Presbyn. Ch., 1985—86. Clergy commr. del. Gen. Assembly Presbyn. Ch., 1995; parish assoc. First Presbyn. Ch., Ashland, 2004—05. Author: Manna for Sisters in Christ, 1989, Mutuality in Christ, 1991, Meditations in Suffering, 1993, Study of Karl Barth's Doctrine of Man and Woman, 1995, Sister to Sister, 1998, Healed to Serve, 2001, Selected Spiritual Writings of Anne Dutton Vol. 1: Letters, 2003, Hymns, Poetry, Memoirs, Discourses, Vol. II, 2004, Vol. III, 2006, Autobiography, 2006. Mem. Hospice Ashland County chpt., 1989—93; assoc. mem. Women's Symphony League, Ashland Symphony Orch., 1989—94; missionary vol. Mother Teresa's Missionaries of Charity, Calcutta, 1988. Recipient Outstanding Faculty Mentor of Yr. award, Ashland Sem., 2004, Disting. Alumni Hall of Fame award, Ashland H.S., 2005; Northwestern U. fellow, 1982—84. Mem.: Am. Acad. Religion, Soc. Bibl. Lit., Nat. Assn. Presbyn. Clergywomen, Presbyn. Women in Leadership, Internat. Assn. Women Mins. (mem. exec. bd., trustee 1990—95), Phi Beta Kappa (Outstanding Faculty Mentor award 2001, 2002, Women's Achievement award, Ashland County, Ohio 2003, Outstanding Faculty Mentor award 2004, 2005), Alpha Lambda Delta. Republican. Avocations: travel, music, water sports. Office: Ashland Theolog Sem 910 Center St Ashland OH 44805-4007 Office Phone: 419-289-5182. Business E-Mail: jwatson@ashland.edu.

**WATSON, JOHN ALLEN,** lawyer; b. Ft. Worth, Sept. 18, 1946; s. John and Mary (Barlow) W.; m. Patricia L. Clardy, Oct. 24, 1946; 1 child, Virginia E. BA, Rice U., 1968; JD, U. Tex., Austin, 1971. Bar: Tex. 1971. Assoc. Fulbright & Jaworski, Houston, 1971-78, ptnr., 1978—. Mem. ABA. Office: Fulbright & Jaworski LLP 1301 McKinney St Ste 5100 Houston TX 77010-3031 Office Phone: 713-651-5151. E-mail: jwatson@fulbright.com.

**WATSON, JOHN LAWRENCE, III,** former trade association executive; b. Rome, Ga., Jan. 14, 1932; s. John Lawrence and Mary (Cowen) W.; m. Dorothy Palmer McLanahan, Aug. 9, 1958; children: Mary Palmer Watson Gard, Valerie Catherine Watson Bilbrough, John Lawrence IV. BS, Auburn U., 1954. Trader-over the counter J.C. Bradford & Co., Atlanta, 1957-58; with Robinson Humphrey & Co., Atlanta, 1958-64; dept. head-over the counter, 1964-74, dir. equity trading, 1974-83, dir. capital markets, 1983-85; pres. Security Traders Assn., N.Y.C., 1985-96, ret., 1996. Past mem. bd. visitors Babcock Sch. Mgmt. Wake Forest U.; past chmn. Parent's Coun. Wofford Coll.; life trustee Pace Acad.; former trustee Securities Industry Found. for Econ. Edn.; pres. trustees The City Ch., N.Y., 2005-. Named Man of Yr., Equities mag. Mem. Nat. Assn. Securities Dealers (dist. chmn. 1982, bd. govs. 1983-85), Am. Mus. Fin. History (trustee), Capital City Club, Piedmont Driving Club (Atlanta), Ponte Vedra Club, Sawgrass Country Club (Ponte Vedra), Univ. Club (N.Y.C.). Home: 505 Ponte Vedra Blvd Ponte Vedra Beach FL 32082-2317

**WATSON, JOHN S.,** oil company executive; b. Oct. 1956; BA, U. of Calif., Davis, 1978; MBA, U. of Chicago, 1980. Mgr. credit card, products, investor relations Chevron, 1993—95; pres. Chevron Canada, Ltd., 1996—98; dir. Caltex Corp.; v.p. strategic planning Chevron Corp., 1998—2001; v.p. fin., CFO, 2001—. Office: Chevron Corp 6001 Bollinger Canyon Rd San Ramon CA 94583-2324

**WATSON, JOYCE MORRISSA,** forensic and clinical psychologist; d. Joseph Morris and B. Joyce Watson; 1 child, Matthew Joseph. BA, Maryville Coll., 1985; MSc summa cum laude, Troy State U., 1989; D magna cum laude in Psychology, Forest Inst. Profl. Psychology, 1994. Cert.: Fed. Bur. Prisons (fed. law enforcement officer) 1996; lic. psychologist Dept. Health, Fla., 1996. Sr. psychologist Fla. Dept. Corrections, Zephyrhills, 1995—96, regional mental health cons. Ft. Lauderdale, 1997—2000, dir. mental health Tallahassee, 1999—2002; staff psychologist, fed. law enforcement officer Fed. Bur. Prisons, Sumterville, Fla., 1996—97; dir. Sarasota Psychol. Svcs., Fla., 2002—. Faculty U. Sarasota, Tampa, 1997—2000; adv. coun. Governor's Commn. Mental Health and Substance Abuse, Tallahassee,

1999—2000; coun. mem. Fla. State Mental Health Planning Coun., Tallahassee, 1999—2001; bd. mem. hosp. North Fla. Reception Ctr. Hosp., Lake Butler, 1999—2001; presenter in field. Author jour. articles, book articles, essays in book. Vol. tchr. Fruitville Elem. Sch., Sarasota, 1989; vol. Bright Beginnings, Sarasota, 2003—05, Little League, Sarasota, 2005. Recipient Exceptional Performance award, Dept. Justice, Time-Off award, Bureau of Prisons; grantee, Pfizer, Glaxo Wellcome. Mem.: APA, Fla. Psychol. Assn., Soc. Personality Assessment. Avocations: show dogs, music, water sports. Office: J Morrissa Watson PsyD 4411 Bee Ridge Rd #353 Sarasota FL 34233 Business E-Mail: morrissawatson@aol.com.

**WATSON, JULIAN** See BLAKE, BUD

**WATSON, KATHY,** political organization administrator; b. Skowhegan, Maine; Owner Kathy Watson Co.; mem. Pittsfield Rep. Com., 1982—; Somerset County Rep. Com., 1982—; vice chmn. Maine Rep. Party, 1986-88, 94-98, chmn., 1998—. Co-chmn. Maine women for Reagan/Bush, 1984; county chair Reagan for Pres., 1988, McKernan for Gov., 1990, Snowe for Congress, 1990, 92, Cohen for U.S. Senate, 1990, Snowe for Senate, 1994; mem. Bush adv. com., 1992; del. Rep. Nat. Conv., 1988, 92, 96; mem. rules com. Rep. Nat. Com., 1992, 96. Bd. dirs. Sr. Connections/Bridges. Mem. Assoc. Gen. Contractors Am.

**WATSON, KENNETH MARSHALL,** physics professor; b. Des Moines, Sept. 7, 1921; s. Louis Erwin and Irene Nellie (Marshall) W.; m. Elaine Carol Miller, Mar. 30, 1946; children: Ronald M., Mark Louis. BS, Iowa State U., 1943; PhD, U. Iowa, 1948; ScD (hon ), U. Ind., 1976. Rsch. assoc. Naval Rsch. Lab., Washington, 1943-46; staff Inst. Advanced Study Princeton (N.J.) U., 1948-49; rsch. fellow Lawrence Berkeley (Calif.) Lab., 1949-52, staff, 1957-81; asst. prof. physics U. Ind., Bloomington, 1952-54; assoc. prof. physics U. Wis., Madison, 1954-57; prof. physics U. Calif., Berkeley, 1957-81, prof. oceanography, dir. marine physics lab. San Diego, 1981-93. Cons. Sci. Application Corp., 1981-2004; mem. U.S. Pres.'s Sci. Adv. Com. Panels, 1962-71; adviser Nat. Security Coun., 1972-75; mem. JASON Adv. Panel, 1959-2001; sci. adv. bd. George C. Marshall Inst., 1989—. Author: (with M.L. Goldberger) Collision Theory, 2004; (with J. Welch and J. Bond) Atomic Theory of Gas Dynamics, 1966; (with J. Nutall) Topics in Several Particle Dynamics, 1970; (with Flatté, Munk, Dashen) Sound Transmission Through a Fluctuating Ocean, 1979. Mem.: Nat. Acad. Scis. Home: Unit 2008 8515 Costa Verde Blvd San Diego CA 92122-1150 Office: U Calif Marine Physics Lab La Jolla CA 92093-0213 Office Phone: 858-534-6620. E-mail: kmw@mpl.ucsd.edu.

**WATSON, KIMBERLY,** music educator, pianist; b. Midwest City, Okla., Sept. 21, 1970; d. John and Jane Howell. MusM, U. Okla., 1995. Cert. music tchr. Okla. Music Teachers Assn., 1991. Music instr. Okla. Bapt. U., Shawnee, 1995—. Pianist Immanuel Bapt. Ch., Norman, 1991—. Editor: (newsletter) Oklahoma Music Teacher. Canine handler Okla. Search and Rescue Dogs, Oklahoma City, 2000—. Mem.: Am. Assn. Med. Transcriptionists, Nat. Piano Teachers Guild, Music Teachers Nat. Assn., Okla. City Obedience Tng. Club, OkPaws, Pi Kappa Lambda. Office: Okla Baptist U 500 W University #61257 Shawnee OK 74804 Office Phone: 405-878-2300. Business E-Mail: kim.watson@okbu.edu.

**WATSON, MELINDA S.,** social studies educator; b. Spartanburg, SC, Dec. 11, 1974; d. Samuel Boyd and L. Jane (Pitts) Sexton; m. David Lee Watson, June 26, 1999. BS in Edn., Lander U., Greenwood, S.C., 1997. Cert. tchr. S.C. Tchr. sgl. edn. Northwood Mid. Sch., Taylors, SC, 1998—2002; tchr. social studies Belton Mid. Sch., Belton, SC, 2002—, yearbook staff advisor, 2002, sch. improvement coun., 2005—. Presenter in field. Named Tchr. of the Yr., Belton Mid. Sch., 2004—05, Top Tchr., Northwood Mid. Sch., 2001; grantee Sch.-wide Character Edn. grantee, 2000. Mem.: Palmetto State Tchrs. Assn., S.C. Coun. for Social Studies, S.C. Mid. Sch. Assn. Avocations: travel, computers, scrapbooks, history, music. Office: Belton Middle School 102 Cherokee Rd Belton SC

**WATSON, MICHAEL THOMAS,** biology educator; b. May 14, 1973; MS in Biomed. Engring., Boston U., 1996; MS in Edn., U. Bridgeport, 2001; MS in biology, C.C.S.U., 2001. Rsch. technician Neurogen, Branford, Conn., 1996-97; biomed. engr., sales and tech. support KENT Sci. Corp., Litchfield, Conn., 1997—2000; tchr. math., biology Watertown High Sch., 2001—; prof. math. U. Bridgeport, 2004—. Avocations: reading, golf, basketball. Office: Watertown H S 324 French St Watertown CT 06795-2528 Personal E-Mail: mwatson514@msn.com.

**WATSON, NOEL G.,** construction executive; b. Bison, SD, 1936; BSChemE, U. N.D., 1958; postgrad., Colo. Sch. Mines, 1958-60. With AMAX Inc., 1962-65, Jacobs Engring. Group, Pasadena, Calif., 1960-62, 1965—, pres., 1987—2002, CEO, 1992—, chmn., 2004—. Office: Jacobs Engineering Group PO Box 7084 1111 S Arroyo Pkwy Pasadena CA 91109*

**WATSON, OLIVER LEE, III,** aerospace engineer, manufacturing executive; b. Lubbock, Tex., Sept. 18, 1938; m. Judith Valerie Horvath, June 13, 1964; 1 child, Clarke Stanford. BSEE, U. Tex., 1961; MSEE, Stanford U., 1963; MBA, Calif. State U., Fullerton, 1972; cert., U. So. Calif., 1980. Mgr. ballistic analysis Rockwell Internat. autonetics Divsn., Anaheim, Calif., 1973-78, mgr. minuteman systems, 1978-83, mgr. preliminary engring., 1983-84; mgr. analysis group autonetics divsn. Rockwell Internat., Anaheim, Calif., 1984-85, mgr. aircraft sys. autonetics dept., 1985-93, dep. dir. integrated product devel. N.Am. aircraft aircraft modification divsn., 1993-94, dep. dir. engring. N.Am. aircraft modification divsn., 1994-96; dep. dir. engring. comm. and combat sys. divsn. Boeing N.Am., Anaheim, 1996-98; skills, process and metrics mgr. Comm. and Battle Mgmt., Anaheim, 1998-99; process, metrics and tools dir. Anaheim Site Engring., Integrated Def. Sys., Anaheim, Calif., 1999—, 2001—. Lectr. engring. Calif. State U., Fullerton, 1981—90, guest prof., 2005, mem. indsl. adv. bd., 1994—, vice-chmn., 1995—97; adv. com. Accreditation Bd. for Engring. and Tech., 2000; sec. Elec. Engring. Indsl. Adv. Bd., 2001—; spkr. in field. Co-author Digital Computing Using Fortran IV, 1982; Fortran 77, A Complete Primer, 1986; contbg. author: The World's Best Shortest Stories, 2001. Bd. dirs. Olive Little League, Orange, 1980; vol. Stanford U. Engring. Fund, Orange County, Calif., 1983, regional chmn. 1984-86, So. Calif. chmn. 1986-91; mem. Stanford Assocs., 1988—. Recipient Stanford Assocs. Centennial Medallion award, 1991; fellow N.Am. Aviation Sci.-Engring., L.A., 1962-63, Inst. Advancement Engring., L.A., 1976. Mem. IEEE (sr., sec. v.p. 1974-75, sect. chmn. 1975-76), Nat. Mgmt. Assn. (exec. advisor for fin. Boeing Anaheim chpt. 2002), Jaycees (v.p. Orange chpt. 1973-74), Rockwell-Calif. State U. Alumni Club (v.p. 1993, pres. 1993-94), Lido Sailing Club. Republican. Avocations: sailing, swimming, humor writing, scriptwriting, reading. Office: Boeing NAm C3ISR PO Box 3105 MC-CA92 Anaheim CA 92803-3105

**WATSON, PATRICIA PULLUMS,** school system administrator; b. Chgo., June 3, 1949; d. James and Aletha (Pearline) Pullums; m. Charles Michael Watson, Aug. 10, 1985; 1 child, Kevyn Charles. BA, Chgo.State U., 1973; MS in Edn. and Reading, Chgo. State U., 1981; MA in Adminstrn. and Supervision, Gov.'s State U., University Park, Ill., 1997; postgrad., Ill. State U., 2004—. Cert. tchr. Ill. Tchr. Theodore Herzl Sch., Chgo., 1973—74; program dir. Accounters Cmty. Ctr., Chgo., 1974—83, asst. exec. dir., 1989—98, exec. dir., 1998—2002, pres., CEO, 2002—03; head tchr., asst. prin. Accounters Prep. Acad., Chgo., 1980—89; tchr., dept. chair., program coord. Cullen Elem. Sch., Chgo., 1991—98; asst. prin. Shoesmith Elem. Sch., Chgo., 1998—. Mem. People To People Citizen Amb. Program, Spokane, Wash., 1997—. Grantee grant, Chgo. Found. for Edn., 1996. Mem.: NAACP, Chgo. Area Alliance Black Sch. Educators, Assn. Supervision and Curriculum Devel., Nat. Assn. Secondary Sch. Prins., Nat. Coun. Negro Women, Internat. Reading Assn., Nat. Alliance Elem. Sch. Prins., Chgo. Prins. and Adminstrs. Assn., Chgo. Asst. Prin. Assn., Phi Delta Kappa, Delta Sigma Theta. Avocation: golf. Office Phone: 773-535-1764. Office Fax: 773-535-1877. Personal E-Mail: wats1612@sbcglobal.net. E-Mail: ppwatson@cps.k12.il.us

**WATSON, PATTY JO,** anthropology educator; b. Superior, Nebr., Apr. 26, 1932; d. Ralph Clifton and Elaine Elizabeth (Lance) Andersen; m. Richard Allan Watson, July 30, 1955; 1 child, Anna Melissa MA, U. Chgo., 1956, PhD in Anthropology, 1959. Archaeologist-ethnographer Oriental Inst.-U. Chgo., 1959—60, rsch. assoc., archaeologist, 1964—70; instr. anthropology U. So. Calif., Los Angeles, 1961, UCLA, 1961, L.A. State U. 1961; asst. prof. anthropology Washington U., St. Louis, 1969—70, assoc. prof., 1970—73, prof., 1973—2004, Edward Mallinckrodt disting. univ. prof., 1993—2004, prof. emerita, 2004—; faculty affiliate anthropology U. Mont., 2003—. Mem. rev. panel NSF, Washington, 1974-76; fellow Ctr. Advanced Study in Behavioral Scis., Stanford, Calif., 1981-82, 91-92. Author: The Prehistory of Salts Cave, Kentucky, 1969, Archaeological Ethnography in Western Iran, 1979; author: (with others) Man and Nature, 1969, Explanation in Archeology, 1971, Archeological Explanation, 1984, Girikihaciyan, A Halafian Site in Southeastern Turkey; author: (editor) Archeology of the Mammoth Cave Area, 1974, Prehistoric Archeology Along the Zagros Flanks, 1983; co-editor: The Origins of Agriculture, 1992, Of Caves and Shell Mounds, 1996, Archaeology of the Middle Green River Region, Kentucky, 2005. Recipient Arthur Holly Compton Faculty Achievement award Washington U., St. Louis, 2000, Peter H. Raven award for lifetime achievement Acad. Sci. St. Louis, 2002; grantee NSF, 1959-60, 68, 70, 72-74, 78-79, NEH, 1977-78, Nat. Geog. Soc., 1969-75, Southeastern Arch. Conf. Lifetime Achievement award, 2004. Fellow Am. Anthropol. Assn. (editor for archaeology 1973-77, Disting. Lectr. award 1994, Disting. Svc. award 1996), AAAS (chair sect. H 1991-92); mem. Cave Rsch. Found., Am. Acad. Arts and Scis., Am. Philos. Soc., Soc. Am. Archaeology (exec. com. 1974-76, 82-84, editor Am. Antiquity 1984-87, Fryxell medal 1990), Assn. Paleorient (sci. bd.), Nat. Speleological Soc. (hon. life, editorial bd. bull. 1979—, sci. award), Archaeol. Inst. Am. (Gold Medal for Disting. Archaeol. Achievement 1999), Nat. Acad. Scis. Business E-Mail: pjwatson@artsci.wustl.edu.

**WATSON, PAUL,** photojournalist, correspondent; Photographer The Toronto Star, 1986—, Africa bur. chief, 1992—94, Asian bur. chief, 1994—98; staff writer L.A. Times, 1998—, South Asia bur. chief New Delhi, 2001—. Recipient Robert Capa gold medal for photography, 1993, Nat. Newspaper award for spot news photography, 1994, Pulitzer Prize for spot news photography, 1994, Nat. Newspaper award for internat. reporting, 1996, George Polk award for internat. reporting, 1999, 2000, Freedom of Press award, Nat. Press Club, 2000. Office: D 7/10 Vasant Vihar New Delhi India Fax: 91-11-2617-7-709. E-mail: paulrwatson@yahoo.com.

**WATSON, PAULA D.,** retired librarian; b. N.Y.C., Mar. 6, 1945; d. Joseph Francis and Anna Julia (Miksza) De Simone; m. William Douglas Watson, Aug. 23, 1969; children—Lucia, Elizabeth AB, Barnard Coll., 1965; MA, Columbia U., 1966; MSLS, Syracuse U., 1972. Libr. reference U. Ill., Urbana, 1972—77, libr. city planning and landscape architecture, 1977—79, head documents libr., 1979—81; asst. dir. gen. svcs. U. Ill. Libr., Urbana, 1981—88, acting dir. gen. svcs., 1988—93, dir. ctrl. pub. svcs., 1989—93, asst. libr., 1993—95, dir. electronic info. svcs., 1995—2004, dir. scholarly comm., 2003—04; ret., 2004. Author: Electronic Journals: Acquisition and Management, 2003, E-Publishing Impact on Acquisition and Interlibrary Loan, 2004; contbr. articles to profl. jours. N.Y. State Regents fellow Columbia U., N.Y.C., 1965-66; Council on Library Resources profl. edn. and tng. for librarianship grantee, 1983 Mem. ALA (sec. univ. librs. sect. ALA-Assn. Coll. and Rsch. Librs. 1989-91, com. on instnl. coop., chair pub. svcs. dirs. group, 1997-99, mem. com. inst. coop./OCLC virtual electronic libr. steering com.), Ill. Library Assn. Avocation: gardening. Home: 715 W Delaware Ave Urbana IL 61801-4806

**WATSON, PETER S.,** former federal agency administrator; married. LLB, Auckland U.; LLM, McGill U.; MIBA, West Coast U. Pvt. practice internat. and bus. law, L.A., Washington, 1976, 78-88; spl. advisor to Pres. Overseas Pvt. Investment Corp.; dir. Asian affairs NSC, Washington, 1989-91; commr. U.S. Internat. Trade Commn., 1991—96, vice chmn., 1992-94, chmn., 1994-96; sr. advisor Armitage Associates, L.C.; counsel Pillsbury Winthrop LLP; pres., CEO Overseas Private Investment Corp., 2001—05, Dwight Group, 2005—. Vis. prof. St. Peter's Coll., Oxford U., The Brookings Instn.; bd. trustees Woodrow Wilson Internat. Ctr. for Scholars, bd. visitors Peter F. Drucker Grad. Sch. of Mgmt. at Calremont Graduate U., Friend of Aukland U.; mem. advisory bd., Georgetown U. Journal of Internat. Law; didting. lecturer Georgetown U. McDonough Sch. Bus., co-chair Ar. Internat. Apointements Com. ABA; mem. Coun. Fgn. Relations Author Completeing the World Trading System: Proposals for a Millenium Round, 1999, Free Trade: Risks and Rewards, 2000, The Economic Arsenal in the War Against Terrorism, 2002; Co-author National Conformity Assessment Schemes: Non-Tariff Trade Barriers in Information Technology, 1999; Contbr. articles to profl. jours. Recipient New Zealand Order of Merit, 2002 Republican. Office: The Brookings Instn 1775 Massachusetts Ave NW Washington DC 20036

**WATSON, RALPH EDWARD,** internist, educator; b. Cin., Apr. 4, 1948; s. John Sherman and Evelyn (Moore) W.; m. Demetria Renee Sept. 9, 1972; children: Ralph Edward, Monifa. BS, Xavier U., 1970; MD, Mich. State U. 1976. Diplomate Am. Bd. Internal Medicine; cert. clin. hypertension specialist. Intern U. Cin. Med. Ctr., 1976-77, resident in internal medicine, 1977-79, asst. clin. prof. internal medicine, 1980-88; asst. prof. internal medicine Mich. State U., East Lansing, 1988-94, assoc. prof., 1994—. Attending physician in hypertension clinic Mich. State U., 1988-91, assoc. dir. hypertension clinic, 1991-94, dir. hypertension clinic, 1995—, program dir. transitional yr. residency, 1990-96, assoc. program dir. internal medicine residency, 1996-2003; mem. U.S. HHS Office Minority Health Resource Person Network. Fellow ACP, Internat. Soc. Hypertension in Blacks, Am Assn. Black Cardiologists; mem. Nat. Med. Assn., Am. Soc. Internal Medicine, Lansing Area Am. Heart Assn. (bd. dirs.), Am. Soc. Black Cardiologists (chair rsch. com.), Am. Soc. Hypertension, Xavier U. Alumni Assn., Alpha Omega Alpha. Office: Mich State U 338B Clinical Ctr East Lansing MI 48824-1313 Office Phone: 517-353-4811.

**WATSON, RAYMOND COKE, JR.,** engineering executive, academic administrator; b. Anniston, Ala., Aug. 31, 1926; BS, Jacksonville State U.; MSE, U. Ala.; MS, U. Fla.; MBA and PhD in Engring. Sci., Calif. Coast U. Chief engr. Dixie Svc. Co., 1948-54; head dept. physics and engring. Jacksonville State U., 1954-60; v.p. engring. and rsch. Teledyne Brown Engring., 1960-70, chief engr., chief scientist, 1990—2001; dir. continuing edn., engring. and math. U. Ala., Huntsville, 1970-76; pres., prof. engring. and math. Southeastern Inst. Tech., Huntsville, 1976—; owner RC Watson & Assocs., 1980—; pres., CEO Vision Techs. Kinetics, 2000—03. Adj. assoc. prof. U. Ala., Huntsville, 1961-70. Contbr. more than 450 articles and reports to profl. jours. Chmn. elec. engring. adv. bd. Ala. A&M U. Recipient NASA Pub. Svc. award; NSF Sci. Faculty Fellow. Mem. IEEE, AIAA, Optical Soc. Am., Ops. Rsch. Soc. Am., Inst. Mgmt. Sci., Internat. Soc. Optical Engrs., Inst. Indsl. Engrs. Achievements include research in defense systems, space systems and electro-optics. Home: 1801 Inspiration Ln SE Huntsville AL 35801-1150 Office: RC Watson & Assocs PO Box 1485 Huntsville AL 35807 Office Phone: 256-726-3995. Business E-Mail: ray.watson@tbe.com. E-mail: rxxwatson@aol.com.

**WATSON, REBECCA WUNDER,** federal agency administrator, lawyer; b. Chgo., Feb. 17, 1952; d. David Hart and Shirley May (Dahlin) Wunder; m. Keith C. Thomson, Oct. 6, 1979 (div. Dec. 1989); m. Gregory B. Watson, Jan. 20, 1996. BA, U. Denver, 1974, MA in LS, 1975, JD, 1978. Bar: Bar: Wyo. 1978, Colo. 1989, D.C. 1995, Mont. 1995. Law clk. U.S. Dist. Ct. for Dist. Wyo., Cheyenne, 1978-80; assoc., then ptnr. Burgess & Davis, Sheridan, Wyo., 1980-88; pvt. practice, Denver, 1988-90; asst. gen. counsel for energy policy US Dept. Energy, Washington, 1990-93; of counsel Crowell & Moring, Washington, 1993-95; ptnr. Gough Shanahan Johnson & Waterman, Helena, Mont., 1995—2002; asst. sec. land & minerals mgmt. US Dept Interior, Washington, 2002—. Contbr. author: ABA Natural Resource Law Handbook, 1993; contbr. articles to law jours. Mem. ABA (chmn. natural resource com. sect. adminstrv. law 1994-97, chmn. pub. lands com. sect. natural resources,

energy and environ. law 1997-99), Wyo. Bar Assn., Mont. Bar Assn., Phi Beta Kappa. Republican. Avocations: cooking, reading, travel, hunting. Office: US Dept Interior Land and Materials Mgt 1849 C St NW Washington DC 20240 Home: 72 W Ranch Trl Morrison CO 80465-9503 Office Phone: 202-208-6734. E-mail: Rebecca_Watson@ios.doi.gov.

**WATSON, RICHARD THOMAS,** lawyer; b. Lakewood, Ohio, Aug. 21, 1933; s. Thomas Earl Watson and Sara Lucille (Whapham) Hadfield; m. Judith C. Briggs, Aug. 6, 1960; children: David, Andrew, Susan (dec.). AB, Harvard U., 1954, JD, 1960. Bar: Ohio 1960. Assoc. Spieth, Bell, McCurdy & Newell, Cleve., 1960, ptnr., 1965, mng. ptnr., 1987—. Bd. dirs. numerous corps. Chancellor Episcopal Diocese of Ohio, Cleve., 1986—; mem. Harvard U. com. on univ. resources, 1992—; bd. trustees Cleve. Mus. Art, 1991—. Mem. Union Club Cleve. Office: Spieth Bell McCurdy & Newell 925 Euclid Ave Ste 2000 Cleveland OH 44115-1408 Office Phone: 216-696-4700. E-mail: richardtwatson@att.net.

**WATSON, ROBERT FRANCIS,** lawyer; b. Houston, Jan. 9, 1936; s. Louis Leon and Lora Elizabeth (Hodges) W.; m. Marietta Kiser, Nov. 24, 1961; children: Julia, Melissa, Rebecca. BA, Vanderbilt U., 1957; JD, U. Denver, 1959. Bar: Colo. 1959, U.S. Dist. Ct. (no. dist.) Tex. 1967, U.S. Supreme Ct. 1968, Tex. 1973, U.S. Ct. Appeals (5th cir.) 1973, U.S. Dist. Ct. (so. dist.) Tex. 1980, U.S. Ct. Appeals (11th cir.) 1981. Law clk. U.S. Dist. Ct. Colo. 1960-61; trial atty. SEC, Denver, 1961-67, asst. regional adminstr. Ft. Worth 1967-72, regional adminstr., 1972-75; ptnr. Law, Snakard & Gambill, P.C., Ft. Worth, 1975-98, of counsel, 1998—2005, shareholder, 2005—; exec. v.p., gen. counsel First Command Fin. Svcs., Inc., Ft. Worth, 1998—2005. Counsel City of Ft. Worth Police Investigation Commn., 1975; spl. counsel Office Atty. Gen. State Ariz., 1977-78. Contbr. articles to profl. jours. Mem. Ft. Worth Crime Commn., 1987-93. Honoree 27th Ann. Rocky Mountain State-Fed.-Provincial Securities Conf. Fellow: Coll. of State Bar Tex., U. Denver Law Sch. Alumni Coun., Tex. Bar Found. (life), Colo. Bar Assn. (life), Tarrant County Bar Assn., Ft. Worth Club; mem.: ABA, Tarrant County Bar Found., Tex. Bus. Law Found. (bd.dirs. 1988—93), State Bar Tex., Fed. Bar Assn., Shady Oaks Country Club (Ft. Worth), Phi Delta Phi. Republican. Presbyterian. also: Law Snakard & Gambill PC 1600 W 7th St Ste 500 Fort Worth TX 76102-3819 Office Phone: 817-878-6374. Business E-Mail: bwatson@lawsnakard.com.

**WATSON, ROBERT JOE,** retired health facility administrator, retired career officer; b. Wellington, Kans., Nov. 12, 1934; s. Charles Bruce and Marguerite B. (Scholes) W.; m. Ursula Eschenroeder, Dec. 26, 1983; children: Stephanie Watson-Zollinger, Stacy Watson Bruce, Susannah Watson Gold; stepchildren: Jurgen Wanke, Claudia Beeck. MS in Edn., Kans. State Tchrs. Coll., 1963; MBA, U. Hawaii, 1969; MHA, George Washington U., 1973, EdD, 1976; student, Command-Gen. Staff Coll., 1973, U.S. Army War Coll. 1986. Commd. 2nd lt. U.S. Army, 1963, advanced through grades to col. 1989; stationed at Tripler Army Med. Ctr., Honolulu, 1967-69, USARV Surgeons Office, Long Binh, Vietnam, 1969-70, Surgeon Gen.'s Office, Washington, 1970-74, Walter Reed Med. Ctr., Washington, 1974-76, Acad. Health Svcs., Ft. Sam Houston, Tex., 1976—80, 68th Med. Group, Ziegenberg, Germany, 1980-82, U.S. Army Hosp., Ft. Riley, Kans., 1982-84, 34th Gen. Hosp., Augsburg, Germany, 1984-87; assoc. dean USA Med. Field Svc. Sch., Ft. Sam Houston, Tex., 1987—89; assoc. dir. Student Health Ctr. U. Fla., Gainesville, 1989—2005; ret., 2005. Fellow Am. Coll. Healthcare Execs. (adv., regent 1982-84). Episcopalian. Avocations: tennis, golf, gardening.

**WATSON, ROBERT JOSE,** professional sports team executive; b. L.A., Apr. 10, 1946; m. Carol; children: Keith, Kelley. Student, Harbor Jr. Coll. Wilmington, Calif. Baseball player Astros, Houston, 1965-79; gen. mgr., 1993-95; baseball player Red Sox, Boston, 1979, Yankees, N.Y.C., 1980-82; gen. mgr., 1996—; baseball player Braves, 1982-84; coach, instr. Oakland, 1984-88; asst. gen. mgr. Astros, Houston, 1988-93; gen. mgr. Team USA, World Baseball Classic, 2006—; also v.p. in charge of discipline Major League Baseball. All-star Nat. League, 1973. Office: Major League Baseball 31st Fl 245 Park Ave New York NY 10167*

**WATSON, ROBERT WINTHROP,** poet; b. Passaic, N.J., Dec. 26, 1925; s. Winthrop and Laura Berdan (Trimble) W.; m. Elizabeth Ann Rean, Jan. 12, 1952; children: Winthrop, Caroline. BA, Williams Coll., 1946; postgrad., U. Zurich, 1947; MA, Johns Hopkins, 1950, PhD in English, 1955. Instr. English Williams Coll., 1946, 47-48, 52-53, Johns Hopkins, 1950-52; mem. faculty U. N.C., Greensboro, 1953—, prof. English, 1963-90. Vis. poet, prof. English Calif. State U., Northridge, 1968-69 Author: (poetry) A Paper Horse, 1962, Advantages of Dark, 1966, Christmas in Las Vegas, 1971, Selected Poems, 1974, Island of Bones, 1977, Night Blooming Cactus, 1980, The Pendulum: New and Selected Poems, 1995; (novels) Three Sides of the Mirror, 1966, Lily Lang, 1977, (art book) Betty Watson Paintings, 1999; co-founder The Greensboro Rev., 1966. Swiss-Am. exch. fellow, 1947; grantee Nat. Endowment for Arts, 1973; recipient Am. Scholar Poetry prize, 1959, Lit. award Am. Acad. Inst. Arts Letters, 1977. Home: 4321 Galax Trail Greensboro NC 27410

**WATSON, RONALD LYNN,** theater educator; b. Pasadena, Tex., May 4, 1964; s. Jeffrey Ward Watson and Nelda Joyce Elliot. BFA, SW Tex. State U., 1987; MA, Baylor U., Waco, Tex., 1987. Dir. of theatre Alief-Taylor H.S., Houston, 2001—05; instr. of theatre San Antonio Coll., 2005—. U.i.l. tech. design contest state dir. U. Interscholastic League, Austin, Tex., 2006—. Dir.: (theatre production) A Flea In Her Ear. Mem.: Tex. Ednl. Theatre Assn. Office: San Antonio Coll 1300 San Pedro Ave San Antonio TX 78212 Office Phone: 210-785-6098.

**WATSON, RUBIE S.,** museum director; BS in archaeology and anthropology, U. Calif., Berkeley; MS in Anthropology, Rice U.; PhD in Social Anthropology, London Sch. Econs. Assoc. prof. anthropology, acting dir. Asian Studies program U. Pitts.; assoc. curator Peabody Mus. Archeology & Ethnology, sr. lectr. dept. anthropology Harvard U. Cambridge, Mass., 1992-95, assoc. dir., then Howells dir. Peabody Mus., 1995—. Author several books including Inequality Among Brothers: Class and Kinship in South China, 1985; editor: Memory, History, and Opposition under State Socialism, 1994; co-editor: Marriage and Inequality in Chinese Society, 1990, Harmony and Counterpoint: Ritual Music in Chinese Context, 1996. Fellow: Am. Acad. Arts. & Sci. Office: Peabody Mus Archeology Harvard U 11 Divinity Ave Cambridge MA 02138-2019

**WATSON, S. MICHELE,** school nurse; b. Selma, Ala., Apr. 21, 1965; d. Kenneth and Linda (Bishop) Wilds; m. H. Alan Watson, May 30, 1987. AAS, Cleveland State Community Coll, Tenn., 1987, AS, 1985. RN, Tenn. ICU staff Meml. Hosp., 1987-88; emergency rm. staff Cleveland (Tenn.) Cmty. Hosp., 1988; team leader Bradley Meml. Home Health, Cleveland, 1988-2001; sch. nurse Cleveland City Schs., 2001—06. Home: 316 Mountain Crest Dr La Follette TN 37766 Business E-Mail: watson343@bellsouth.net.

**WATSON, S.A.,** lawyer, retired judge; b. Hot Springs, Ark., July 11, 1942; s. Sterl A. and Naomi Pauline (Thrasher) W.; m. Wanda Batt, May 2, 1968; children: Angel Watson Brothers, Clinton Jeremy. JD, U. Ala., 1966. Bar: Ala. 1967, U.S. Dist. Ct. Ala. 1968, U.S. Supreme Ct. 1970. Assoc. Humphrey, Lutz & Smith, Huntsville, Ala., 1967-68; asst. dist. atty. 23d Jud. Cir., Huntsville, Ala., 1968-69, chief asst. dist. atty., 1969-72, dist. judge, 1972-74, cir. judge, 1974-87; ptnr. Hornsby, Watson, Hornsby and Blackwell, Huntsville, Ala., 1988—. Chair Madison County jud. commn. 23d Jud. Cir. 1978-83; faculty advisor Nat. Jud. Coll., Reno, 1982-87; spl. judge Ala. Ct. Criminal Appeals, Montgomery, 1983; spl. justice Ala. Supreme Ct., Montgomery, 1996-97; mem. faculty trial advocacy tng. program La. State U. Law, 1996, 97, 99, 2001. Home: 1929 Cherry Tree Rd Gurley AL 35748-9318 Office: Hornsby Watson Hornsby and Blackwell 1110 Gleneagles Dr SW Huntsville AL 35801-6404

**WATSON, SAMUEL RAY,** academic administrator; b. Lynchburg, Va., Mar. 23, 1948; s. Kelly Wilson and Russell (Johnson) W.; m. Peggy Anne Mundy, June 14, 1969; children: Derek Ray, Deidre Dianne. BS, Va. Poly. Inst. and State U., 1970, MA, 1975, EdS, 1984; postgrad., U. S.C., 1986-90. Cert. tchr. adminstr., Va., S.C. Jr. high math. tchr. Martinsville City Pub. Schs., 1970-80, asst. prin. jr. high sch., 1980-84, prin. jr. high sch., 1984-86; prin. middle sch. Lady's Island Mid. Sch., Beaufort, S.C., 1986-90; math. tchr. Battery Creek High Sch., Beaufort, 1990-91; asst. prin. Dinwiddie (Va.) County High Sch., 1991-94; asst. supt. Dinwiddie (Va.) County Pub. Schs., 1994—. Bd. dirs., cert. shelter mgr. ARC, 1991—; pres. Dinwiddie cpt. Am. Cancer Soc., 1992-93. Mem. ASCD, Nat. Assn Secondary Sch. Prins., Va. Assn. Secondary Sch. Prins., Civitan, Phi Delta Kappa. Methodist. Avocations: computers, reading, water sports. Home: 1839 Ramblewood Rd Petersburg VA 23805-2900 Office Phone: 804-541-6400. Business E-Mail: rwatson@hopewell.k12.va.us.

**WATSON, SHARON GITIN,** psychologist; b. N.Y.C., Oct. 21, 1943; d. Louis Leonard and Miriam (Myers) Gitin; m. Eric Watson, Oct. 31, 1969; 1 child, Carrie Dunbar. BA cum laude, Cornell U., 1965; MA, U. Ill., 1968, PhD, 1971. Psychologist City N.Y. Prison Mental Health, Riker's Island, 1973-74, Youth Services Ctr., Los Angeles County Dept. Pub. Social Services, L.A., 1975-77; dir. clin. services, 1978, dir. Youth Services Ctr., 1978-80; exec. dir. Crittenton Ctr. for Young Women and Infants, L.A., 1980-89, Assn. Children's Svcs. Agys. of So. Calif., L.A., 1989-92, L.A. County Children's Planning Coun., 1992-99; cons. L.A. County Chief Adminstrv. Office, 2001—04, Edn. Coordinating Coun., 2004—; mem. L.A. City Commn. for Children, Youth and Their Families, 2000—, L.A. County Children's Planning Coun., 2001—. Mem. L.A. delegation Pres.'s Summit for Am.'s Future, 1997. Mem. Commn. for Children's Svcs. Family Preservation and Family Support Policy Com., 1989—99, Interagy. Coun. Child Abuse and Neglect Policy Com., 1993—99, Mayor's Com. on Children, Youth and Families, 1993—95; bd. dirs. Adolescent Pregnancy Childwatch, 1985—89, L.A. Ednl. Partnership, 1999—2003, LISC Health Sector, 1996—99, L.A. Roundtable for Children, 1988—94; trustee L.A. Ednl. Alliance for Restructuring Now, 1992—99. Mem.: APA, Assn. Children's Svcs. Agys. So. Calif. (sec. 1981—83, pres. elect 1983—84, pres. 1984—85), Calif. Assn. Svcs. for Children (sec.-treas. 1983—84, pres. elect 1985—86, pres. 1986—87), U.S. Figure Skating Assn. (chmn. sanctions and eligibility 1993—96, membership com. 1996—99, strategic planning com. 2000—02, regional vice chmn. competitions com. 2000—02, sec. 2002—, bd. dirs. 1992—, mem. exec. com. 2002—, nat. competition judge), U.S. Olympics Com. (Jr. Olympics com. 1998—2000), Pasadena Figure Skating Club (pres. 1985—87, 1989—90), So. Calif. Inter-Club Assn. of Figure Skating Clubs (vice chair 1989—91, chair 1991—93). Home and Office: 4056 Camino Real Los Angeles CA 90065-3928 E-mail: sharonla12@aol.com.

**WATSON, SOLOMON BROWN, IV,** lawyer, publishing executive; b. Salem, N.J., Apr. 14, 1944; s. Solomon Brown and Denise Amelia W.; m. Bernadette Aldrich, Mar. 18, 1967 (div.); children: Katitti Madrid, Kira Pallis (twins); m. Brenda J. Wilson, Apr. 28, 1984. BA in English, Howard U., 1966; JD, Harvard U., 1971. Bar: Mass. 1972, N.Y. 1977. Assoc. Bingham, Dana & Gould, Boston, 1971-74; with legal dept. The N.Y. Times Co., N.Y.C. 1974—76, asst. sec., 1976—79, corp. sec., asst. gen. counsel, 1979-89, gen. counsel, 1989-90, v.p., gen. counsel 1990-96, sr. v.p., gen. counsel, sec., 1996—2005, sr. v.p., chief legal officer, 2006—. Active Vols. Legal Svc., Jobs for Youth Inc., until 1989; v.p. N.Y. Vietnam Vets. Leadership Program, Inc., until 1992, Agent Orange Assistance Fund, Vets. Adv. Bd. Lt. U.S. Army, 1966-68. Decorated Bronze Star with oak leaf cluster, Army Commendation medal with oak leaf cluster and V; recipient Nat. Equal Justice award Legal Def. Fund, 2002. Mem. ABA (com. on corp. law depts., mem. task force on corp. responsibility 2002—), Nat. Bar Assn., Assn. Bar City N.Y., Mass. Bar Assn., Newspaper Assn. Am. (mem. legal affairs com.), N.Y. Stock Exch. Office: NY Times Co 229 W 43rd St New York NY 10036-3959 Office Phone: 212-556-7534. Business E-Mail: watsons@nytimes.com.

**WATSON, STANLEY ELLIS,** clergyman, small business owner; b. New Orleans, July 25, 1957; s. Joseph and Dorothy (Jones) W. EdB, Jarvis Christian Coll., Hawkins, Tex., 1977; MRE, Tex. Christian U., Ft. Worth, 1979; spl. edn., So. U. A&M, Baton Rouge, 1986; grad., U.S. Acad. Port Investigation, 1991; DD (hon.), Charter Ecumenical Ministries, 1994; student in Christian Counseling, Christian Bible Coll. and Sem., 2005—. Cert. tchr.; registered notary Mich.; lic. pvt. investigator, La. Asst. min. Jarvis Christian Coll., Hawkins, Tex., 1974-77; tchr. pub. sch., Daingerfield, Tex., 1977-78; sr. pastor Truevine Christian Ch., 1977—79; asst. min. Park Manor Christian Ch., Chgo., 1980-81; asst. mgr. K- Mart, Shreveport, La., 1981-82; min. United Christian Ch., Jackson, Miss., 1982-83; tchr. pub. sch., Napoleonville, La., 1986-87, Zachary, La., 1987-88; min. Vt. Christian Ch., Flint, Mich., 1988—92, sr. pastor, 1990; assoc. min. Buena Vista Bapt. Ch., St. James, La. Owner, mgr. Watson Diversified Fin. Co., 1989—, Watson Detective Agy., Donaldsonville, La., 1992—; v.p. DVY Sys., Inc., 1997—; CEO Watson and Julien Cmty. Mission, Inc., Donaldsonville, La.; clin. pastoral counseling, christian counseling, 2001.e Mem. NAACP, NEA. Recipient Presdl. citation Nat. Assn. for Equal Opportunity in Higher Edn.; Christian Women's fellow, 1975-77, St. Louis Bd. fellow, 1977-79, Tex. Christian U. Brite Div. Sch. scholar, 1977; Jarvis Christian Coll. cert. of Honor and Merit, 1974-77; named Rev. Stanley Watson Day City of Flint, Mich., 1989, Disting. Alumnus, Jarvis Christian Coll., 1995. Mem. Nat. Assn. Investigative Specialists, Am. Inst. Profl. Bookeepers, Am. Fin. Coord. Assn. (fin. coord.), Christian Counselors Assn., Nat. Assn Investigative Specialist, Nat. Assn. Federated Tax Preparers, Am. Soc. Notaries, Aircraft Owners and Pilots Assn. Coun. for Exceptional Children, Forgotten Man Ministries, Jarvis Christian Coll. Alumni Assn. (v.p.), NAACP, Urban League of Flint, Urban Coalition of Greater Flint, Flint C. of C., Internat. Reading Assn., NEA, Am. Sailing Assn., Phi Beta Sigma, Kappa Delta Pi. Mem. Tex. Christian U. Alumni Assn. Democrat. Avocations: beekeeping, collecting coins, stamps, sports cards, coffees. Home and Office: PO Box 668 Donaldsonville LA 70346-0668 Office Phone: 225-717-1633. E-mail: jarvis19771@yahoo.com.

**WATSON, STEWART CHARLES,** construction executive; b. Brock, Sask., Can., Sept. 17, 1922; s. Samuel Henry and Elva Jane (St. John) W.; m. Irene Lillian Ahrens, Aug. 4, 1943; children: Judith Gail (Mrs. David Stafford), Wendy Carolyn (Mrs. Roy Amuso), Ronald James, Candyce Louise. Student, U. Buffalo. With Acme Steel & Malleable Iron Works, Buffalo, 1940—42, Acme Hwy. Products, Buffalo, 1946—55, internat. mktg. mgr., 1955—69; pres. Watson-Bowman Assocs. Inc., Buffalo, 1970—, Kinematics, 1984—. Chmn. bd. Air Stewart Inc.; Internat. lectr. on kinetics of civil engring. structures; mem. U.S. Transp. Rsch. Bd.; bd. dirs. Internat. Bridge of Peace for Bering Strait Crossing. With AUS, 1943-45, ETO. Fellow Am. concrete Inst. (dir. 1984—, Delmar Bloehm award 1984, Charles S. Whitney medal 1987, hon. mem.); mem. ASTM, NAS, Internat. Jts. and Bearings Rsch. Coun. (chmn. 1988—), Internat. Activities Commn., Masons (32 degree), Shriners. Home: 3 Chicory Ln East Amherst NY 14051

**WATSON, THOMAS STURGES,** professional golfer; b. Kansas City, Mo., Sept. 4, 1949; s. Raymond Etheridge and Sarah Elizabeth (Ridge) W.; m. Linda Tova Rubin, July 8, 1973 (div.); children: Margaret Elizabeth, Michael Barrett. BS, Stanford U., 1971. Profl. golfer, 1971—. Winner Western Open, 1974, 1977, 1984; winner Byron Nelson Tournament, 1975, 78, 79, 80; winner Brit. Open, 1975, 77, 80, 82, 83; winner, U.S. Open, 1982; winner World Series, 1975, 80; winner Andy Williams San Diego Open, 1977, 80; winner El Prat, 1977; winner Masters, 1977, 81; winner Bing Crosby Nat. Pro-Am Golf Tournament, 1977, 78; winner Tucson Open, 1978, 84; winner Colgate Hall of Fame Classic, 1978, 79; winner Anheuser Busch Golf Classic, 1978; winner Meml. Tournament, 1979; winner Heritage Classic, 1979, 83; winner Tournament of Champions, 1979, 80, 84; Los Angeles Open, 1980, 82; Greater New Orleans Open, 1980, 81; Dunlop Phoenix, 1980, Atlantic Classic, 1981; Nabisco Championship, 1987, Hong Kong Open, 1992; Recipient Vardon Trophy, 1977, 78, 79, Byron Nelson award, 1977-78, 79-80; named to Ryder Cup Team, 1977, 81, 83, 89 (elected capt. 1992—); named Player of Year Profl. Golf Assn., 1977, 78, 79, 80, 82, 84; elected to PGA

World Golf Hall of Fame, 1988, Kans. Golf Hall of Fame, 1991, William H. Richardson award 1990. Mem. U.S. Golf Assn., Profl. Golfers Assn., Golf Course Supts. Assn. of Am. (Old Tom Morris award 1992), Butler Nat. Golf Club, Shadow Glen Club, Preston Trails Golf Club, Oakwood Country Club, Par Club, Blue Hills Country Club, Kansas City Country Club, Royal and Ancient Golf Club St. Andrews. Achievements include being the leading money winner PGA, 1977-80, 84. Address: PGA PO Box 109601 100 Ave of Champions Palm Beach Gardens FL 33418-3665 Office: Tom Watson Designs 1901 W 47th Pl Mission KS 66205

**WATSON, WILLIAM DOUGLAS,** astrophysicist; b. Memphis, Tenn., Jan. 12, 1942; s. William Douglas and Antoinette Lovejoy Watson; m. Paula D. DeSimone, Aug. 23, 1969; children: Lucia Anne, Elizabeth Lovejoy. BS in Physics, MIT, 1960—64, PhD in Physics, 1964—68. Rsch. assoc. Ctr. Radioastronomy & Space Rsch., Cornell U., Ithaca, NY, 1970—72; asst. prof. physics, asst. prof. astronomy U. Ill., Urbana, 1972—74, assoc. prof. physics, assoc. prof. astronomy, 1974—77, prof. physics, prof. astronomy, 1977—2002, rsch. prof. physics, 2002—. Home: 715 W Delaware Ave Urbana IL 61801 Office: Univ Ill Loomis Lab 1110 W Green St Urbana IL 61801 Office Phone: 217-333-7240.

**WATSON-BOONE, REBECCA A.,** dean, researcher, library and information scientist, educator; b. Springfield, Ohio, Mar. 7, 1946; d. Roger S. and Elizabeth Boone; m. Dennis David Ash, 1967 (div. 1975); m. Frederick Kellogg, 1979 (div. 1988); m. Peter G. Watson-Boone, May 26, 1989. Student, Earlham Coll., 1964-67; BA, Case Western Res. U., 1968; MLS, U. N.C., 1971; PhD, U. Wis., 1995. Asst. reference libr. Princeton (N.J) U., 1970-76; head cen. reference dept. U. Ariz., Tucson, 1976-83, assoc. dean Coll. Arts and Scis., 1984-89. Loaned exec. Ariz. Bd Regents, 1988 89; pres. Ctr. for Study of Info. Profls., 1995—2002. Author: Constancy and Change in the Worklife of Research University Librarians, 1998; contbr. articles to profl. jours. Mem. ALA (div. pres. 1985-86, councilor 1988-92), NAFE, Assn. for Libr. and Info. Sci. Edn. Mem. Religious Soc. Of Friends. Office: 30 Camino de la Vina Vieja Placitas NM 87043 Business E-Mail: rebeccawb@earthlink.net.

**WATT, DOUGLAS (BENJAMIN WATT),** writer, drama critic; b. N.Y.C., Jan. 20, 1914; s. Benjamin Douglas and Agnes Rita (Neimann) W.; m. Ray Mantel, Nov. 5, 1937 (div.); children— Richard David, James Douglas; m. Ethel Madsen, Aug. 13, 1951; children— Patricia, Katherine. AB, Cornell U., 1934. Copy boy N.Y. News, 1936-37, radio columnist, 1937-40, drama reporter, 1940-71, sr. drama critic, 1971-87, critic-at-large, 1987-93; staff writer New Yorker mag., 1946-95; profl. song writer; columnist Small World, 1955-70. Nominating com. Tony Awards, Pulitzer Awards, Theater World Awards; co-founder Drama Desk; chmn. Astarre Awards. Pres. Hampton Animal Shelter, 1965-79. Served with USAAF, World War II. Mem. ASCAP, N.Y. Drama Critics Circle (pres. 1975-77) Clubs: Dutch Treat (N.Y.C.) (bd. govs.). Home: 27 W 86th st New York NY 10024-3615 E-mail: patricia_watt@msn.com. *To say one has achieved success, except perhaps in isolated instances, is an exercise in vanity and contrary to man's experience. At best, some satisfaction can be gained in one's career, and then almost always because of intense effort.*

**WATT, DWIGHT, JR., (ARTHUR DWIGHT WATT JR.),** computer programming and microcomputer specialist; b. Washington, Jan. 25, 1955; s. Arthur Dwight and Myrtle Lorraine (Putnam) W.; m. Shari Elizabeth Gambrell, July 30, 1988. BA, Winthrop U., 1977, MBA, 1979; EdD, U. Ga., 1989. Cert. computer and internet profl. Inst. Cert. Computer Profls., Microsoft; cert. home fire arms safety, NRA; cert. A+ personal computer technician, CompTIA; cert. sys. engr., sys. adminstr., office user specialist instr.; i-net plus cert. Comptia; Network + cert.; cert. network adminstr. and acad. instr., Comptia; Server + cert. CompTIA. Data processing instr. York Tech. Coll., Rock Hill, SC, 1977-78; computer ctr. asst. Winthrop U., Rock Hill, SC, 1976-79; data processing instr. Brunswick (Ga.) Coll., 1979-80; system operator, asst. programmer Sea Island (Ga.) Co., The Cloister, 1981; pvt. practice data processing cons. Swainsboro, Ga., 1981; computer programming/microcomputer specialist instr. Swainsboro Tech. Inst., 1981-96; sr. programmer/analyst Policy Mgmt. Sys. Corp., Columbia, SC, 1996-97; microcomputer specialist instr. Athens Tech. Coll.-Elbert County Campus, Elberton, Ga., 1997-2001; chmn. IT dept. Heart of Ga. Tech. Coll., Dublin, 2001—05; instr. Peirce Coll., Phila., 2005—; CIO Ga. Healthcare Sys., Atlanta, 2001; instr. So. Wesleyan U., Central, SC, 2005—. Chmn. exec. bd. computer curriculum Ga. Dept. Tech. and Adult Edn., 1990-92, 2002-05, exec. bd. computer curriculum, 1994-96, vice chair, 2000-02, CIS cons. for curriculum, 2006—; chmn. East Ctrl. Ga. Consortium for Computer Occupations, 1990-96; co-facilitator CIS curriculum rev. and update Ga. Tech. Colls., 2001; spkr. in field; cons. in field. Author: District Revenue Potential and Teachers Salaries in Georgia, 1989, Structured COBOL for Technical Students, 1998; co-author: District Property Wealth and Teachers Salaries in Georgia, 1990, Factors Influencing Teachers Salaries: An Examination of Alternative Models, 1991, Local Wealth and Teachers Salaries in Pennsylvania, 1992, School District Wealth and Teachers' Salaries in South Carolina, 1993, Test Yourself A+ Certification Practice Exams, 1998, GDTAE CIS Curriculum Standards and Guides Revision Problems, 2001. Chmn. Emanuel County chpt. ARC, Swainsboro, 1989-90, 92-93, bd. dirs., 1989-96; pres. United Meth. Men. Swainsboro, 1984-86; trustee Greater Swainsboro Tech. Inst. Found., Inc., 1995-96; bd. dirs. Emanuel Arts Coun., 2004—. Recipient Nat. Tech. Tchr. of Yr. finalist award Am. Tech. Edn. Assn., 1994; Olympic Cmty. Hero Torchbearer, 1996 Mem. Inst. Cert. Computing Profls., Ga. Bus. Edn. Assn. (dir. dist. 1 1986, 96, dist. sec.-treas. 1993-95, dist. 1 dir.-elect 1995-96, Dist. 1 Postsecondary Tchr. Yr. 1985, State Postsecondary Tchr. Yr. 1995), Profl. Assn. Ga. Educators, Swainsboro Jaycees (Outstanding Young Citizen 1985, treas. 1984-89, pres. 1987-88, pres. S.E. Ga. Jaycee Fair 1995, treas. S.E. Ga. Jaycee Fair 1993-94), Ga. Jaycees (v.p. area C 1988-89, chaplain 1989-90, dir. region 4 1990 91, chmn. state shooting edn. 1991-92, chair Internat. BB Gun Match Championship 1999, co-chair match 2000, treas. match 2002), U.S. Jr. C. of C. (nat. rep. shooting edn. program 1992-95, Shooting Edn. State Program Mgr. Yr. 1992, webmaster Internat. BB Gun Championship match 1999—), Swainsboro-Emanuel County C. of C. (webmaster 2002—), Ga. Kiwanis (tech. chair, webmaster 2002—), Emanuel Artist Guild (v.p. 2003—05), Swainsboro Kiwanis (bd. dirs. 2005—, webmaster, 2003—). Methodist. Home: PO Box 1637 206 Hereford Rd Swainsboro GA 30401 Personal E-Mail: dwight-watt@att.net.

**WATT, JOSEPH MICHAEL,** state supreme court justice; b. Austin, Tex., Mar. 8, 1947; m. Cathy Watt; children: Justin, Christopher, Jennifer, Michael. BA in History, Tex. Tech U., 1969; JD, U. Tex., 1972. Bar: Tex. 1972, Okla. 1974. Pvt. practice, Altus, Okla., 1972-85; judge Dist. Trial Ct., 1985-91; gen. counsel to gov. State of Okla., Oklahoma City, 1991-92; justice Okla. Supreme Ct., Okahoma City, 1992—2003, chief justice, 2003—. Liaison to Okla. Bar Assn. Okla. Supreme Ct., 1997—98; mem. Appellate Div. of Ct. on Judiciary, 1997—98, Truth in Sentencing Commn., Supreme Ct. Long Range Planning Commn.; chmn. Supreme Ct. Com. for Time Standards. Mem. Okla. Bar Assn. Office: Okla Supreme Ct State Capitol Rm 245 Oklahoma City OK 73105 Fax: 405-521-6982. Office Phone: 405-521-3848. E-mail: joseph.watt@oscn.net.*

**WATT, KENNETH EDMUND FERGUSON,** zoology educator; b. Toronto, July 13, 1929; s. William Black Ferguson Watt and Irene Eleanor (Hubbard) Dodd; m. Genevieve Bernice Bendig, Oct. 28, 1955; children: Tanis Jocelyn, Tara Alexis. BA in Hon. honor, U. Toronto, 1951; PhD in Zoology, U. Chgo., 1954; LLD, Simon Fraser U., 1973. Biometrician Rsch. div. Dept. Lands and Forests, Ont., Canada, 1954-57; sr. biometrician Can. Dept. Agr., Ottawa, Ont., 1957-60; head, statis. rsch. and svcs. Canadian Dept. Forestry, Ottawa, 1960-63; from assoc. prof. to prof. Dept. Zoology, U. Calif., Davis, 1963-93. Author: Ecology and Resource Management, 1968, Principles of Environmental Sciences, 1973, Understanding the Environment, 1982, Taming the Future, 1991. Recipient Gold medal Entomol. Soc., 1969. Achievements include development of new approach to forecasting future based on exhaustive statistic testing of nonlinear math. equations to long runs of historical data; discovery that change through time in real world systems violates Markov principles. Home: 2916 Quail St Davis CA 95616-5711 Office: U Calif Dept Evolution & Ecology Davis CA 95616 Office Phone: 530-750-3253. Personal E-mail: kenwatt@sbcglobal.net. *The actual causes of present events are much further back in time than most people suspect. Failure to understand this is why forecasting is such a disaster area.*

**WATT, LINDA E.,** former ambassador; married; 2 children. BA, Vanderbilt U., 1973; MA, U. N.Mex., 1975. With Dept. of State, 1976—, Managua, London, San Jose, Quito, Moscow; polit. advisor U.S. So. Command, Miami; U.S. amb. to Panama U.S. Dept. State, 2002—05.

**WATT, MELVIN LUTHER,** congressman, lawyer; b. Steele Creek, NC, Aug. 26, 1945; m. Eulada Paysour; children: Brian, Jason. BS in Bus. Adminstrn., U. NC, Chapel Hill, 1967; JD, Yale U. Law Sch., 1970; degree (hon.), NC A&T State U., Johnson C. Smith U., Bennett Coll. Atty. Ferguson, Stein, Watt, Wallas, Adkins, & Gresham, 1971-92; mem. NC State Senate, 1985-86; co-owner East Towne Manor, 1989—; mem. US Congress from 12th NC dist., 1993—, mem. fin. svcs. com., mem. judiciary com., ranking minority mem. comml. and adminstrv. law subcommittee, mem. Congl. Black Caucus, 2004—, mem. joint econ. com. Pres. Mecklenburg County Bar. Active Ctrl. Piedmont CC Found., Legal Aid of Southern Piedmont, NC NB Cmty. Devel. Corpn., Auditorium-Coliseum-Civic Ctr. Authority, United Way, Mint Mus., Family Housing Svcs., Pub. Edn. Forum, Dilworth Cmty. Devel. Assn., Cities in Schs., Housing Authority Scholarship Bd., Morehead Scholarship Selection Com.; bd. visitors Johnson C. Smith U. Named one of 100 Most Influential Black Americans, Ebony mag., 2006. Mem. NAACP (life), NC Assn. Black Lawyers, NC Acad. Trial Lawyers, Charlotte C. of C. (sports action coun.), West Charlotte Bus. Incubator, Inroads Inc., Phi Beta Kappa. Democrat. Presbyterian. Office: US Ho Reps 2236 Rayburn Ho Office Bldg Washington DC 20515-3312 Office Phone: 202-225-1510.*

**WATT, STEPHANIE DENISE,** musician, educator, department chairman; d. Edmund Hudson and Joan Elizabeth (Patterson) Watt. BFA in Music Performance, LI U., 1984, MA in Composition and Performance, 1988, MS in Computer Sci. and Engring., 1999. Adj. asst. prof. music LI U., C.W. Post Campus, Brookville, NY, 1988—97, assoc. prof. music, 1997—; adj. asst. prof. music Suffolk County CC, Ammerman Campus, Selden, NY, 1988—97; adj. asst. prof. music Dowling Coll., Oakdale, NY, 1989—91; guest lectr. in music history Alvin Ailey Am. Dance Sch., NYC, 1996—98. Founder EastWest Sch. Performing Arts, NY, 1979—2006; coord. seminar abrus. LI U. Chamber Music Program, Brookville, 1994—97; dir. piano studies LI U., C.W. Post Campus, 1988—, co-dir. student concert series, 1990—96, dir. theory studies, 1999—; adjudicator LI Philharm. Young Artist Piano Competition, 1994—2004, Music Lovers Club Young Artist Competition, 1994—2006, 8th and 9th NY Young Artist Piano and Violin Competition, 2005, 06; piano master classes Müvészeti Szakközepiskola és Gimnázium, Szombathely. Author: Information Theory Analyses of Bach Chorales and a Learning Classifier System, 1999; musician: (CD recording on Capstone Records) Duo for Cello and Piano by Allen Brings, 2006; dancer (dance exhbn.) Argentine Tango & Salsa Exhbn.; performer: Camerata Pro Musica, 2000, Carnegie Hall, 2005, The Hecksher Mus. Art, 2005, Park Ave. United Meth. Ch., 2005, Brick Gallery, 2005, LI U., C.W. Post Campus, 2005, 2006, Clarinet & Piano Concert, 2006, Concert Tour of Hungary, Communidad de Palermo Symphony Orch., 2006; guest artist, clinician LI Choral Festival and Inst., 2004, 2005, (DuoLeo performace) Weill Hall Carnegie Hall, NYC, 2005, Park Ave. United Meth. Ch., 2005, LI U., C.W. Post Campus, Brookville, 2005, 2006, (DuoLeo performace and solo performance) Brik Gallery, Catskills, NY, 2005, (Martino and Watt duo performace) Steinway Hall, NYC, 2006, Blueport Libr., 2006, LI Philharm. Choir, 2006, (DuoLeo performace one-woman shows) The Heckscher Mus. Art, Huntington, NY, 2005; dancer (dance exhbns.) Babylon Village Fair, NY, 2005, New Life Cmty. Ch., Sachem, NY, 2006, LI U., C.W. Post, 2006; featured Strings mag., 2002; contbr. articles to profl. confs. Recipient First Pl. award Foxtrot Exhbn., Kings Ball Dancesport Championships, SI, NY, 2001, First Pl. award Am. Tango Exhbn., 2001, First Pl. award Viennese Waltz Exhbn., Stardust Ball Competition, Melville, NY, 2002, First Pl. award Open Tango Exhbn., Stardust Ball, Melville, NY, 2002, Cert. of Recognition music performance, Mayor of Inc. Village of Hempstead, 1995, Second Pl. award slow waltz exhbn., NJ Open Championships, Rutherford, 2003, Third Pl. award Dance Team Exhbn., Northeastern Open Championships, Weston, Conn., 2003. Mem.: AAUW (assoc.), NY State Music Assn. (assoc.), Coll. Music Soc. (assoc.), Phi Eta Sigma. Achievements include research in the history of the tango and its political influence in Argentina. Office: LI U CW Post Campus 720 Northern Blvd Greenvale NY 11548 Office Phone: 516-299-2474. Office Fax: 516-299-2884. Personal E-mail: stefani1435@aol.com.

**WATTEL, HAROLD LOUIS,** economics professor; b. Bklyn., Sept. 30, 1921; s. David Max and Carolyn (Abrams) W.; m. Sara Gordon, Sept. 1, 1946; children: Karen, Jill. BA, Queens Coll., 1942; MA, Columbia U., 1947; PhD magna cum laude, New Sch. Social Research, 1954. Jr. economist WPB, 1942; economist Dept. Agr., 1946; econ. cons. Boni, Watkins & Mounteer, 1952; economist Bur. Bus. and Community Research, Hofstra U., 1954, 57, dir., 1957-58; prof. econs. Bur. Bus. and Community Rsch., Hofstra U., 1957-86, prof. emeritus, 1986—, chmn. dept. econs., 1957-61, chmn. div. bus., 1961—, dean Sch. Bus., 1965-73. Econ. cons. to consumer counsel Staff Gov. N.Y., 1956—58; cons. N.Y. State Moreland Commn. on Alcoholic Beverage Control Law, 1963—64, Legislative Refernce Bur. U. Hawaii, 1966, Schenley Industries, 1967—, Ralston Purina Co., 1967—, Am. Can Co., 1965—; econ-metric Nat. Millinery Planning Bd., 1959—70; ednl. cons, U.S. Merchant Marine Acad., Kings Point, 1972; cons. Bulova Watch Co., 1975—82. Author ann. publ.: The Millinery Industry; Editor: Planning in Higher Education, 1975, Chief Executive Officer Compensation, 1978, The Gross Personal Income Tax, 1981; Contbr. chpts. to books, encys., dictionaries, also reports; Editor, contbr.: L.I. Bus., 1954-59. Mem. Comprehensive Health Planning Coun., 1970-75; bd. dirs., v. p., N.Y. State unit Am. Lung Assn.; pres. Nassau-Suffolk unit; bd. dirs. Comprehensive Health Planning Coun., Nassau-Suffolk, N.Y., N.Y. State Citizen Coun., Regional Med. Program Nassau-Suffolk, consumer rep., bd. dirs. Island Peer Rev. Orgn., 1990; treas. Parodneck Found.; chair Pronet Citizens Advocacy Ctr., 1997—. Lt. USNR, 1942-46. Edn. fellow, 1949; Hazen Found. fellow, 1952; Ford Found. regional fellow, 1960 Mem. AAUP (chpt. pres. 1953), Middle Atlantic Assn. Colls. Bus. Adminstrn. (pres. 1970-71), Am., Met. econs. assns., N.Y. State Environ. Health Assn. (v.p.), Island Peer Rev. Orgn. (consumer/AARP rep. 1990—), Pi Gamma Mu, Omicron Chi Epsilon, Beta Gamma Sigma (hon. assoc.). Home: 181 Shepherd Ln Roslyn Heights NY 11577-2525 Office: Hofstra U Dept Econ Hempstead NY 11550 E-mail: phdhlw@juno.com.

**WATTENMAKER, RICHARD JOEL,** archivist, director; b. Phila., Feb. 22, 1941; s. Nathan H. and Frances (Rynes) W.; m. Eva Augusta Oscarsson, June 25, 1968; children: Adrian Ezra, Barnaby Leo. BA, U. Pa., 1963; MA, NYU Inst. Fine Arts, 1965, PhD, 1972; student, The Barnes Found., 1959-66. Dir. Rutgers U. Art Gallery, New Brunswick, NJ, 1966-69; chief curator Art Gallery Ont., Toronto, Canada, 1969-73; dir. Chrysler Mus., Norfolk, Va., 1979-80, Flint (Mich.) Inst. Arts, 1980-88, Archives of Am. Art, Smithsonian Instn., Washington, 1990—2005, sr. scholar, 2006—. Lectr. Barnes Found., 1991-92. Author: The Art of Charles Prendergast, 1968, The Art of Jean Hugo, 1973, Puvis de Chavannes and the Modern Tradition, 1975, The Fauves, 1975, The Dutch Cityscape in the 17th Century and it's Sources, 1977, William Glackens' Beach Scenes at Bellport, 1988, Dr. Albert C. Barnes and The Barnes Foundation, 1993, Maurice Prendergast, 1994. Trustee Intermus. Conservation Lab., Oberlin, Ohio, 1982-88. Recipient Founders Day award NYU, 1972 Office: Smithsonian Instn Archives of Am Art Victor Bldg Ste 2200 MRC937 PO Box 37012 Washington DC 20013-7012 Office Phone: 202-275-1922. Office Fax: 202-275-1955. Business E-mail: wattenmakerr@si.edu.

**WATTERS, ANN OLIVA,** psychologist, educator; d. George Verdelli II and Dorothy Austin Oliva; m. Thomas A. Watters, Aug. 30, 1975; children: Andrew George, Michael Thomas. BA in English, U. Calif., Berkeley, 1974; MA in English Lit., Washington U., St. Louis, 1976; MA in Health Psychology, Calif. Sch. Profl. Psychology, 1997, PhD in Psychology, 1999. Lectr. rhetoric and English Stanford U., Calif., 1987—; pvt. practice clin. psychology San Mateo, Calif., 1999—; asst. clin. prof. psychiatry U. Calif., San Francisco, 2005—. Author, editor: Global Exchange: Reading/Writing in a World Context, 2005; co-author: Creating America: Reading & Writing Arguments, 4th edit., 2005, Writing for Change: A Community Reader. Chair bd. dirs. San Mateo Med. Ctr. Found. Mem.: AAUP, APA, Calif. Psychol. Assn. Office: 101 S San Mateo Dr # 303 San Mateo CA 94401 Office Phone: 650-342-3843. Fax: 650-375-8398. E-mail: watters@stanford.edu.

**WATTERS, EDMOND CLAIR,** ophthalmologist, educator; b. Natrona Heights, Pa., Dec. 25, 1942; s. John Lomnet and Maribelle (Good) Watters; m. Comly Colwell Watters, Dec. 27, 1966; children: Christine, Jennifer, Edmond. BS Coll. William and Mary, 64; MD, George Washington U., 1968. Diplomate Am. Bd. Ophthalmology. Intern Mercy Hosp., Pitts., 1968—69; resident in ophthalmology U. Pitts., 1971—74; ophthalmologist E.H. Konnerdoll, Tarntum, Pa., 1974—77; ophthalmologist, pres. Western Pa. Surg. Eye Assn., Pitts., 1977—97, Western Pa. Surg. Eye Assn./UPMC, Pitts., 1997—. Chief ophthalmology sect. U. Pitts. Med. Ctr., St. Margaret's, 1989—, pres. med. staff, 2000—; bd. dirs. St. Margaret Found., Pitts., 1990—; assoc. clin. prof. ophthalmology U. Pitts. Elder Fox Chapel (Pa.) Presbyn. Ch., Fox Chapel, 1996—99. Capt. U.S. Army, 1969—71. Decorated Bronze Star (3). Fellow: ACS; mem.: AMA, Pa. Med. Soc., Allegheny County Med. Soc., Am. Soc. Cataract and Refractive Surgeons, Pitts. Ophthalmology Soc., Pa. Acad. Ophthalmology. Republican. Presbyterian. Avocations: golf, fishing, hunting, gardening, sailing. Home: 300 Windmere Dr Pittsburgh PA 15238 Office Phone: 412-782-5900.

**WATTERS, EDWARD MCLAIN, III,** lawyer; b. 1943; s. Edward and Lucy F. (Disston) W.; m. Susan Secor, May 12, 1979; children: Jennifer Susan, Ann Elizabeth. BA cum laude, Yale U., 1965; JD cum laude, U. Pa., 1970. Bar: Pa. 1970. Ptnr. Pepper Hamilton LLP, Phila., 1977—. Lectr. programs on estate planning and will drafting Pa. Bar Inst. Bd. dirs. Children's Cruise and Playground Soc. Pa., Sanitarium Playgrounds of NJ, others. Lt. USNR, 1965-75; chair Decedents Estate Adv. Com. to Pa. Legislature's Joint State Govt. Commn. Fellow Am. Coll. Trust and Estate Counsel (com. state laws); mem. ABA, Phila. Bar Assn., Pa. Bar Assn. (past chmn. legis. com. probate sect.), Phila. Estate Planning Coun. (past pres.), Yale Club of Phila., Penn Club, Merion Golf Club. Office: Pepper Hamilton LLP 400 Berwyn Park 899 Cassatt Rd Berwyn PA 19312-1183 Office Phone: 610-640-7809. E-mail: watterse@pepperlaw.com.

**WATTERS, RICHARD DONALD,** lawyer; b. Midland, Mich., May 3, 1951; s. Donald Wayne and Madalyn Bird (Tinetti) W.; m. Ann Elizabeth Hutchison, May 24, 1975; children: Kelly E., Nathan Paul. BS in Indsl. Engring., Bradley U., 1973; JD cum laude, St. Louis U., 1976. Bar: Mo. 1976, U.S. Dist. Ct. (we. and ea. dists.) Mo. 1976, Ill. 1977, U.S. Ct. Appeals (8th cir.) 1981; cert. healthcare mediator. Assoc. Lashly & Baer, P.C., St. Louis, 1976-81, ptnr., 1981—, dept. chmn., 1989—. Instr. St. Louis U. Sch. Law, 1977-79. Chmn., pres. United Cerebral Palsy Assn. St. Louis, 1985-88; bd. dirs. Canterbury Enterprises, sheltered workshop, St. Louis, 1988-94, participant Leadership St. Louis, 1988-89; ethics com. DePaul Health Ctr., 1990—. Mem. Am. Health Lawyers Assn., Mo. Soc. Hosp. Attys. (bd. dirs. 1988-94, pres. 1990-91), Mo. Bar Assn. (vice chmn. health and hosp. com. 1988-90), Bar Assn. Metro. St. Louis (co-chmn. med.-legal com.). Republican. Avocation: sailing. Office: Lashly & Baer PC 714 Locust St Saint Louis MO 63101-1699 Office Phone: 314-621-2939. Business E-Mail: rdwatters@lashlybaer.com.

**WATTLETON, FAYE (ALYCE FAYE WATTLETON),** educational association administrator, advocate; b. St. Louis, July 8, 1943; d. George and Ozie (Garrett) Wattleton; m. Franklin Gordon (div.); 1 child, Felicia. BS in Nursing, Ohio State U., 1964; MS in Maternal and Infant Health Care, Columbia U., 1967; LHD (hon.), St. Paul's Coll., 1985, Spelman Coll., 1986; LLD (hon.), Northeastern Univ. Law Sch., 1990; LHD (hon.), Long Island Univ., 1990, U. Pa., 1990, Bard Coll., 1991; HHD (hon.), Oberlin Coll., 1991; LLD (hon.), Wesleyan Univ., 1991; LHD (hon.), Hofstra U., 1992, Haverford Coll., 1992, Meadville-Lombar Sem./U. Chicago, 1992; D in Pub. Svc. (hon.), Simmons Coll., 1993. Tchr. Miami Valley Hosp. Sch. Nursing, Dayton, Ohio, 1964-66; asst. dir. Montgomery County Combined Pub. Health Dist., Dayton, 1967-70; exec. dir. Planned Parenthood, Dayton, 1970-78; pres. Planned Parenthood Fedn. Am., Inc., NYC, 1978-92, Ctr. for Advancement of Women, NYC, 1995—. Author: How to Talk to Your Child About Sexuality, 1986, Life on the Line, 1996. Bd. dirs. Pardee Rand Grad. Sch., Quidel Corp., Savient Pharm., Jazz at Lincoln Ctr., Well Choice Inc., Eisenhower Fellowship, UNA/USA; trustee Columbia U. Recipient Am. Humanist award, 1986, John Gardner award, 1987, APHA award of excellence, 1989, Humanitarian award Congrl. Black Caucus Found., 1989, Claude Pepper Humanitarian award Internat. Platform Assn., 1990, Pioneer of Civil Rights and Human Rights award Nat. Conf. Black Lawyers, 1990, Florina Lasker award NY Civil Liberties Union Found., 1990, Whitney M. Young Jr. Svc. award Boy Scouts Am., 1990, Ministry of Women award Unitarian Universalist Women's Fed., 1990, Spirit of Achievement award Albert Einstein Coll. Medicine Yeshiva U., 1991, 20th Anniversary Advocacy award Nat. Family Planning and Reproductive Health Assn., 1991, Women of Achievement award Women's Projects and Prodn., 1991, Margaret Sanger award, 1992, Jefferson Pub. Svc. award, 1992, Dean's Disting. Svc. award Columbia Sch. Pub. Health, 1992, Fries prize, 2004; named one of Best Mgrs. of Non-Profit Orgns. in Am. Bus Week, Outstanding Mother Nat. Mother's Day Com., 1997; named to Nat. Women's Hall of Fame, 1993. Office: Ctr for Advancement of Women 25 W 43rd St Ste # 1120 New York NY 10036 Office Phone: 212-391-7718. Business E-Mail: fwattleton@advancewomen.org.

**WATTLEWORTH, ROBERTA ANN,** physician; b. Sioux City, Iowa, Dec. 26, 1955; d. Roland Joseph and Elizabeth Ann (Ahart) Eickholt; m. John Wade Wattleworth, Nov. 7, 1984; children: Adam, Ashley. BS, Morningside Coll., Sioux City, 1978; D of Osteopathy, Coll. Osteo. Medicine/Surgery, Des Moines, 1981; M.Healthcare Adminstrn., U. Osteo. Med. and Health Scis., Des Moines, 1999; MPH, Des Moines U., 2004. Intern Richmond Heights (Ohio) Gen. Hosp., 1981-82, resident in anesthesiology, 1982-84; anesthesiologist Doctor's Gen. Hosp., Plantation, Fla., 1984-85; resident in family practice J.F. Kennedy Hosp., Stratford, NJ, 1985-87; educator family practice U. Osteo. Medicine and Health Scis., Des Moines, 1987-89; family practitioner McFarland Clinic, P.C., Jewell, Iowa, 1989-94; lectr. family practice Osteopath. Med. Ctr., Des Moines U., 1999—, prof. chair dept. family medicine, 2003—. Med. dir. nursing home Bethany Manor, Story City, Iowa, 1990-99, Jewell Vol. Fire and Rescue Squad, 1990-99. Bd. dirs. Heartland Sr. Svcs., 1995—99, Iowa Rural Health Assn. Named Nat. Outstanding Osteo. Educator of Yr., Nat. Student Osteo. Med. Assn., 2001—02. Fellow Am. Coll. Osteo. Family Physicians; mem. Am. Osteo. Assn., Am. Med. Dirs. Assn. (sec.-treas. Iowa chpt. 1997-99), Am. Coll. Osteo. Family Physicians (pres.-elect 2000-01, pres. 2001-02, Physician of Yr. 2004-05), Soc. Tchrs. Family Medicine. Lutheran. Avocations: gardening, cooking, painting. Office: 3200 Grand Ave Des Moines IA 50312-4104 Office Phone: 515-271-7816. E-mail: Roberta.Wattleworth@dmu.edu.

**WATTS, ANTHONY LEE,** bank executive; b. Griffin, Ga., Jan. 24, 1947; s. Edgar Lee and Eula Mae (Benton) W.; m. Barbara Malinda Harp, Oct. 11, 1969; children: Natalie Paige, Barbara Leigh, Melanie Marie. AA, Gordon Mil. Coll., 1967; ABJ, U. Ga., Atlanta, 1969. Conventional loan rep. Fed. Nat. Mortgage Assn., Atlanta, from 1971, asst. regional appraiser, quality control and property mgr., to 1976; v.p., dir. bus. svcs. Ticor Mortgage Ins. Co., Atlanta, 1976-82; v.p. regional sales and exec. v.p. Ticor Indemnity Co., 1982-85; sr. v.p., regional mgr. Ticor Mortgage Ins. Co., Atlanta, 1984, sr. v.p., ea. divsn. mgr., 1984-85; pres. Mt. Vernon Fed. Savs. Bank, Dunwoody,

Ga., 1985-95, Mt Vernon Fin. Corp., 1993-95; prin., dir. Banc Mortgage Fin. Corp., 1996-99, vice chmn., co-CEO, 1999—2002, co-pres., 2003—04; ret., 2004. Lectr. to trade access. Bd. dirs. Ga. Spl. Olympics; elder, bd. Peachtree Christian Ch. With U.S. Army, 1969—71. Decorated Bronze Star; Paul Harris fellow, 1987. Mem. Rotary (past pres. Dunwoody club), Cherokee Town and Country Club (pres. 2002-03), Gridiron Club of U. Ga., Phoenix Soc. (bd. trustees).

**WATTS, CARL DOUGLAS,** music educator; b. Carloconta, Mo., Mar. 5, 1945; s. Gordan and Deby Watts; m. Janet Watts, Sept. 30, 1995; 4 children. MusB, Ctrl. Mo. State U., 1966, MusM, 1970. Tchr. band Oak Grove (Mo.) Schs., 1966—75; tchr. band, dir. fine art Blue Springs (Mo.) Schs., 1978—2000; tchr. band Bishop Miege H.S., Shawnee Mission, Kans., 2000—. Office: Bishop Miege High Sch 5041 Reinhardt Dr Shawnee Mission KS 66205

**WATTS, CLAIRE A.,** retail executive; b. Feb. 26, 1960; BA in Marketing, U. Cin. With Limited Stores, Lands End, May Dept. Stores; divisional merchandising mgr. product devel. Wal-Mart Stores Inc., Bentonville, Ark., 1997—2001, sr. v.p. product devel., 2001—03, exec. v.p., product devel., apparel, & home merchandising, 2003—. Office: Wal-Mart Stores Inc 702 SW 8th St Bentonville AR 72716*

**WATTS, CLAUDIUS ELMER, III,** retired military officer; b. Bennettsville, SC, Sept. 22, 1936; s. Claudius Elmer and Blanche Robey (Wannamaker) Watts; m. Patricia Jane Sims, July 23, 1960; children: Claudius Elmer IV, Patricia Watts Heck. AB in Polit. Sci., The Citadel, 1958; postgrad. (Fulbright scholar), London Sch. Econs. and Polit. Sci., 1958-59; MBA, Stanford U., 1967. Commd. officer USAF, 1958, advanced through grades to lt. gen., 1986, comdr. 438th Mil. Airlift Group McGuire AFB, NJ, 1979-80, comdr. 63d Mil. Airlift Wing Norton AFB, Calif., 1980-82, asst. dep. chief staff plans Mil. Airlift Command Scott AFB, Ill., 1982-83, dep. chief staff plans Mil. Airlift Command, 1983-84; dir. budget Hdqrs. U.S. Air Force, Washington, 1984-85; sr. mil. asst. to dep. sec. def. U.S. Dept. Def., Washington, 1985-86; compt. USAF, Washington, 1986-89; pres. Citadel, Charleston, SC, 1989-96; ret., 2000. Former adv. coun. grad. sch. bus. Stanford U.; former bd. visitors Air U.; former chmn. peer rev. teams, mem. coun. NCAA Coun.; former trustee Aerospace Edn. Found.; bd. dirs., chair audit com. Cmty. First Bank S.C.; bd. dirs. Crescent Mortgage Co., Carolina Fin. Corp. Past trustee Palmetto Partnership; past chmn. Marion Sq. Commn.; former bd. dirs., mem. fin. com. Air Force Aid Soc.; mem. bd. advisors Am. Leadership Found. Decorated Def. Disting. Svc. medal, USAF Disting. Svc. medal, Legion of Merit with oak leaf cluster, DFC with two oak leaf clusters, Air medal with 10 oak leaf clusters, Gallantry Cross with Palm, Vietnamese Svc. medal with 2 svc. stars Vietnam; Paul Harris fellow, Rotary. Mem.: VFW, Mil. Officers Assn. Am., Am. Soc. Mil. Comptrs., Airlift Assn., Air Force Sgts. Assn., Air Force Assn., Am. Legion, Order of Daedalians, Mil. Order World Wars. Methodist. Avocations: golf, reading. Office: 229 Country Club Ln Charleston SC 29412-2208 Business E-Mail: wattsc@a.tadel.edu.

**WATTS, DAVID H.,** construction company executive; b. Newark, 1938; Grad., Cornell U., 1960. Pres., CEO Ford, Bacon & Davis, Inc, Granite Constrn. Inc., Watsonville, Calif., 1987—2003; chmn. Granite Contrn. Inc., Watsonville, Calif., 1999—. Office: Granite Constrn Inc PO Box 50085 Watsonville CA 95077-5085

**WATTS, DORIS EARLENE,** retired librarian; b. Palatka, Fla., Jan. 7, 1923; d. Charles Franklin and Elouise A.C. (Hagler) Foster; m. Fernand Cortez Watts, Aug. 30, 1950 (dec. 1955); children: Varick Steven, Franklin Cortez. AB, Howard U., 1950; postgrad., Cath. U. Am., 1960-61, postgrad., 1965. Clk. War Dept., Washington, 1942-46, VA, Washington, 1949; editorial clk. Dept. Army, Washington, 1950-52, clk., 1953-59, Dept. Commerce, Washington, 1959; with ICC, Washington, 1959—, librarian to 1983. Recipient Spl. Achievement award ICC, 1983; recipient Spl. Achievement award, 1984 Mem. ALA, Delta Sigma Theta. Democrat. Methodist. Home: 2502 Perry St NE Washington DC 20018-3133

**WATTS, EMILY STIPES,** retired English language educator; b. Urbana, Ill., Mar. 16, 1936; d. Royal Arthur and Virginia Louise (Schenck) Stipes; m. Robert Allan Watts, Aug. 30, 1958; children: Benjamin, Edward, Thomas. Student, Smith Coll., 1954-56; AB, U. Ill., 1958, MA (Woodrow Wilson Nat. fellow), 1959, PhD, 1963. Instr. English U. Ill., Urbana, 1963-67, asst. prof., 1967-73, assoc. prof., 1973-77, prof., dir. grad. studies dept. English, 1977—2005, prof. emerita, 2005—; bd. dirs. U. Ill. Athletic Assn., chmn. 1981-83; mem. faculty adv. com. Ill. Bd. Higher Edn., 1984—, vice chmn., 1986-87, chmn., 1987-88. Author: Ernest Hemingway and The Arts, 1971, The Poetry of American Women from 1632 to 1945, 1977, The Businessman in American Literature, 1982; contbg. editor: English Women Writers from the Middle Ages to the Present, 1990; contbr. articles on Jonathan Edwards, Anne Bradstreet to lit. jours. John Simon Guggenheim Meml. Found. fellow, 1973-74 Mem. AAUP, Am. Inst. Archaeology, Assn. Lit. Scholars Critics, Authors Guild, Ill. Hist. Soc., The Phila. Soc., Phi Beta Kappa, Phi Kappa Phi. Presbyterian. Home: 1009 W University Ave Champaign IL 61821-3317

**WATTS, GINNY (VIRGINIA C. WATTS),** artist; b. Chester, Pa., Jan. 24, 1931; d. Edwin Swoope Craig and Ruth Irene Tonge; m. Lynch S. Watts, Jr., July 21, 1951 (wid.); children: L. Kenneth, Karen Elizabeth Watts Dick, Monica Faye Watts Malandruccolo, Dawn Ellen Watts Eller; m. Alfred E. Meeds, May 5, 1948 (div. Nov. 1950); children: Brenda Joyce Meeds Parker, Edwin Lewis, Michael Alfred. Student, Del. Tech. and C.C., Georgetown, 1998—99. County coord. Easter Seals, Wilmington, Del., 1985-86; resident advisor Dept. Mental Retardation Kencrest Svcs., Dover, 1986-87, program mgr., 1987-90; fine arts instr. Del. Tech. and C.C., Georgetown, 1998—2002—. Instr. workshops Millsboro Art Gallery, 2000; exhibited in group shows at Del. Art Ctr., 1942—, Del. Tech. and C.C., 1997—, Millsboro Art League and Gallery, Del., 1997—, Fine Arts Event, Rehoboth Beach, Del., 2000, Geyers Art Gallery, Milford, Del., 2000, 01, 2002, others; artist oil, graphite and watercolor paintings, 1942—; group mural: wall of Art Gallery/Del. Tech. C.C., 1998; mural for lobby of Presentations, 2000; fine art work exhibited in offices of U.S. Sen. from Del.; contbr. articles to area newspapers. Vice-pres. Adult Art League, Del. Tech. C.C., 1997—; bd. dirs. Millsboro Art League, 1998—, pres., 2001—; mem. Sussex County Arts Coun., 1997—, Nat. Mus. Women in the Arts; bd. advisors Del. adult plus program Del. Tech. and C.C.; pres. Adult PLUS Art League, 1998—; pres. Millsboro Art League, 2001-. Recipient Excellence of Artistic Achievement award DAPA and Del. Tech. C.C. award for excellence Del. Tech. C.C., 2006. Avocations: swimming, hiking, bicycling, camping, gardening. Personal E-mail: vrcmw@aol.com.

**WATTS, HAROLD WESLEY,** economist, educator; b. Salem, Oreg., Sept. 30, 1932; s. Elton and Clarine W.; m. Doris A. Roth, Sept. 28, 1951 (div. 1973); children—Michael Lee, Suzanne, Jane Marie, Kristin. BA, U. Oreg., 1954; MA, Yale U., 1956, PhD, 1957. From instr. to assoc. prof. Yale U., New Haven, 1957-63; from assoc. prof. to prof. econs. U. Wis., Madison, 1963-76, dir. Inst. Research on Poverty, 1966-71; prof. econs. and pub. policy Columbia U., N.Y.C., 1976-98, prof. econs. and pub. policy emeritus, 1998—, dir. Pub. Policy Rsch. Ctr., 1988-93; sr. fellow Mathematica Policy Research Princeton, N.J., 1979-92; sr. rsch. assoc. Urban Inst., 1994-95. Recipient Paul Lazarsfeld award, 1980; Guggenheim fellow, 1975 Fellow Assn. Pub. Policy Analysis and Mgmt., Econometric Soc.; mem. Am. Econ. Assn., L.I. Wine Coun. (pres. 2000-02, sec. 2004-06). Democrat. Home: 144 Bay Ave Greenport NY 11944-1404 Office: Ternhaven Cellars PO Box 758 Greenport NY 11944 Office Phone: 631-477-8737. Business E-mail: harold@ternhaven.com.

**WATTS, HELENA ROSELLE,** military analyst; b. East Lynne, Mo., May 29, 1921; d. Elmer Wayne and Nellie Irene (Barrington) Long; m. Henry Millard Watts, June 14, 1940; children: Helena Roselle Watts Scott, Patricia

Marie Watts Foble. BA, Johns Hopkins U., 1952, postgrad., 1952—53. Assoc. engr. Westinghouse Corp., Balt., 1965—67; sr. analyst Merck, Sharp & Dohme, Westpoint, Pa., 1967—69; sr. engr. Bendix Radio divsn. Bendix Corp., Balt., 1970—72; sr. scientist Sci. Applications Internat. Corp., McLean, Va., 1975—84; mem. tech. staff The MITRE Corp., McLean, 1985—94; ret., 1994. Adj. prof. Def. Intelligence Coll., Washington, 1984-85. Contbr. articles to profl. jours. Mem. IEEE, AAAS, AIAA, Nat. Mil. Intelligence Assn., U.S. Naval Inst., Navy League U.S., Air Force Assn., Assn. Former Intelligence Officers, Assn. Old Crows, Mensa, N.Y. Acad. Sci. Republican. Roman Catholic. Avocations: photography, reading.

**WATTS, J. C., JR.,** former congressman, retired professional football player; b. Eufaula, Okla., Nov. 8, 1957; m. Frankie Watts; 5 children. BA in Journalism, U. Okla., 1981. Profl. football player Ottawa and Toronto Teams Can. Football League, 1981-86; youth min. to assoc. pastor Sunnylane So. Bapt. Ch., Del City, 1987-94; mem. Okla. Corp. Commn., 1990—95, chmn., 1992—95; mem. U.S. Congress from 4th Okla. dist., 1995—2003; mem. armed svcs. com.; mem. special oversight panel on terrorism; chmn. GOPAC, 2003—. Mem. Nat. Drinking Water Adv. Coun.; mem. electricity com. Nat. Assn. Regulatory Utility Commrs; hon. co-chmn. Rep. Nat. Conv., 2000. Bd. of rep. Fellowship of Christian Athletes, Okla.; leader Orphan Found. of Am., Boy Scouts of Am.; guest preacher; co-chair Coalition for AIDS Relief in Africa. Named Most Valuable Player (Orange Bowl), 1980, 1981; named to Orange Bowl Hall of Fame, 1992. Republican. Address: GOPAC 600 13th St Ste 790 Washington DC 20005

**WATTS, JILL MARIE,** history educator; b. Pomona, Calif., May 28, 1958; d. Thomas H. and Doris Ruth (Hohlfeld) W. BA in History, U. Calif., San Diego, 1981; MA in History, UCLA, 1983, DPhil in History, 1989. Asst. prof. Weber State U., Ogden, Utah, 1989-91, Calif. State U. San Marcos, 1991-94, assoc. prof., 1994—96, dir. history program, 1994, 1995—96, prof. history, 2002—, and assoc. dept. chair, 2005—. Author: God, Harlem USA: The Father Divine Story, 1992, Mae West: An Icon in Black and White, 2001, Hattie McDaniel: Black Ambition, White Hollywood, 2005; editl. adv. bd. Jour. Popular Culture, 2005—, contbr. articles to profl. publs. (Theodore Salautos award). Carey McWilliams fellow, 1986-87, Rosecrans fellow, 1986-87, Inst. for Am. Cultures fellow, 1986-87, Cornell U. Soc. for Humanities fellow, 1994-95. Mem. Am. Hist. Assn., Orgn. Am. Historians, Am. Studies Assn., Western Assn. Women Historians, Oral History Assn., Popular Culture Assn., Am. Culture Assn. Office: Calif State U History Program San Marcos CA 92096-0001 Business E-Mail: jwatts@csusm.edu.*

**WATTS, JOHN S., JR.,** insurance company executive; BA in English, UCLA. Various mgmt. positions HealthNet, Northwestern Nat. Life Ins. Co.; regional dir. LA sales office Blue Cross of Calif., 1995—97, gen. mgr. large grp. svcs., 1997; acting sr. v.p. UNICARE comml. accounts large grp. divsn. ea., so. and ctrl. regions WellPoint Health Networks Inc.; sr. v.p. large group divsn. Blue Cross and Blue Shield of Ga. (subs. WellPoint Health Networks, Inc.) 2001—03, pres. CEO 2003; pres. CEO nat. accounts strategic bus. unit WellPoint, Inc. Indpls.; pres., CEO comml. and consumer bus. strategic bus. unit WellPoint, Inc. Office: WellPoint Inc 120 Monument Cir Indianapolis IN 46204

**WATTS, LINDA SUSAN,** humanities educator; BA, U. Del., 1981, MA in History, 1983; MA in Am. Studies, Yale U., 1986, PhD in Am. Studies, 1989. Instr. history and Am. studies U. Del., Newark, 1981—83; instr. English and Am. studies Yale U., New Haven, 1984—86, coord. sr. essays and projects in Am. studies, 1987—89; vis. asst. prof. English, Am. studies, and Afro-Am. studies Wesleyan U., Middletown, Conn., 1989—90; asst. prof. Drake U., Des Moines, 1990—95, asst. prof., assoc. dir. women's studies program, 1992—93, assoc. prof. English, 1995—96, assoc. prof. English, assoc. dean Coll. of Arts and Scis., 1996—99; prof. Am. studies, dir. interdisciplinary arts and scis. program U. Wash., Bothell, 1999—2001, prof. Am. studies, interdisciplinary arts and scis. program, 2001—. Author: (book) Rapture Untold: Gender, Mysticism, and 'The Moment of Recognition' in the Writings of Gertrude Stein, 1996, Gertrude Stein: A Study of the Short Fiction, 1999; contbr. book The World Is Our Home: Society and Culture in Contemporary Southern Writing, articles to profl. jours. HIV/AIDS cmty. edn. instr. ARC, Des Moines, 1992—99, HIV/AIDS instr. trainer, 1996—99; vol. literacy tutor Adult Literacy Ctr., Des Moines, 1990—98; vol. mus. visitor svcs. Experience Music Project, Seattle, 2000—01; vol. AIDS Greater Des Moines, 1992—93, SELFHELP Crafts of the World, Des Moines, 1992—94; vol. curriculum cons. and co-instr. Operation Peer Helper, ARC Youth Program, Des Moines, 1993—93; vol. edn. com. mem. AIDS Project of Greater Des Moines, 1993—95; chair HIV/AIDS edn. program com. ARC, Des Moines, 1994—95, vol. mem. HIV/AIDS edn. program com., 1995—99; vol. planning com. mem. World AIDS Day Observance, State of Iowa, Des Moines, 1997—98. Finalist Woodrow Wilson Dissertation Grant in Women's Studies, Woodrow Wilson Found., 1988, Ill.-Nat. Women's Studies Assn. Manuscript award, 1990; nominee Poet of the Yr., Internat. Soc. Poets, 2001; named Semi-Finalist N.Am. Open Poetry Contest, Internat. Libr. of Poetry, 2000, Internat. Libr. Poetry, 2001; recipient Editor's Choice Award for Outstanding Achievement in Poetry, poetry.com, 2000, Internat. Poet of Merit award, Internat. Soc. Poets, 2002, Open Poetry Competition award, King County Pub. Art Program, State of Wash., 2000; Grad. fellow, U. Del., 1981—83, Grad. Sch., Yale U., 1983—87, Marcia Brady Tucker fellow, 1984—85, Sterling fellow, Yale U., 1983—84. Mem.: Phi Beta Kappa, Phi Alpha Theta, Phi Kappa Phi, Phi Kappa Phi. Office: Univ Wash Bothell Box 358511 11136 NE 180th St Bothell WA 98011-8246 E-mail: lswatts@u.washington.edu.

**WATTS, MARY ANN,** retired elementary school educator; b. Harrisburg, Pa., Sept. 13, 1927; d. Major Allan and Ellana Susan (Robinson) Brown; m. Spencer R. Watts, June 23, 1951; children: Shelley Lynn, Allison Dee, Howard Allan. BS, Cheyney U., 1949; postgrad., Temple U., 1965—67, Pa. State U., 1969—72, student, 2003—. Tchr. Harrisburg Sch. Dist., 1949-51, 59-69, Balt. Sch. Dist., 1951-57, Reading (Pa.) Sch. Dist., 1969-89. Mem. sch. dist. dress and discipline code com., 1977-79. Corr. Hamburg Item. Bd. dirs. Pa. State Assn. Boroughs, mem. resolutions and policy com.; mem. Bernville Borough Coun., 1976-2003, v.p., 1988-93, 96-98; sec., treas. Berks County Borough Assn., 1977-2003; Reach to Recovery vol. Am. Cancer Soc. Recipient Disting. Alumna award for achievement in govt. and politics Cheyney U., 1999. Mem. Pa. State Edn. Assn. (life), Pa. Assn. Sch. Retirees, Reading Assn. Sch. Retirees, Bernville Woman's Club (pres. 1978-80, 86-88, Woman of Yr. 1985, Grange Cmty. Svc. award 1988), Pa. State U. Alumni Assn., Cheyney Alumni Assn. Democrat. Mem. United Ch. of Christ.

**WATTS, MIKAL C.,** lawyer; b. Corpus Christi, Tex., July 17, 1967; BA with high honors, U. Tex., 1987, JD, 1989. Bar: Tex. 1989, U.S. Dist. Ct., So. and Ea. Dists. Tex. Atty. for Hon. Thomas R. Phillips, Chief Justice of Supreme Ct., Tex., 1989—90; assoc. David L. Perry & Assocs., Corpus Christi, 1990—91, ptnr., 1991, Perry & Haas, L.L.P., 1991—97; founder Harris & Watts, P.C., 1997, Watts & Heard, L.L.P., 2001; founder, ptnr. Watts Law Firm, L.L.P., 2002—. Named one of 40 Under 40, Nat. Law Jour., 2002, 2005; recipient Niemann Cup, 1989. Mem.: ABA (mem. Tort and Insurance Practice Com.), Coll. of State Bar of Tex., Reynaldo G. Garza Am. Inn of Ct. (charter mem.), Corpus Christi Young Lawyers Assn., Tex. Trial Lawyers Assn. (mem. bd. dirs.), Attys. info. Exchange Group (co-chair Chrysler Minivan Liftgate Latch Litig. Subgroup), Assn. Trial Lawyers of Am., Corpus Christi Bar Assn. Office: Tower II Bldg 14th Fl 555 N Carancahua St Corpus Christi TX 78478 Office Phone: 361-887-0500. E-mail: mcwatts@wattslawfirm.com.

**WATTS, NAOMI,** actress; b. Shoreham, Kent, Eng., Sept. 28, 1968; d. Peter Watts. Spl. envoy on HIV/AIDS UN, 2006—. Actor: (films) For Love Alone, 1986, Flirting, 1991, Matinee, 1993, Wide Sargasso Sea, 1993, Gross Misconduct, 1993, The Custodian, 1993, Tank Girl, 1995, Children of the Corn IV: The Gathering, 1996, Persons Unknown, 1996, Under the Lighthouse Dreaming, 1997, Dangerous Beauty, 1998, A House Divided, 1998, Strange Planet, 2001, Ellie Parker, 2001, Down, 2001, Mulholland Drive, 2001, The Ring, 2002, Plots with a View, 2002, Rabbits, 2002, Ned Kelly,

2003, Le Divorce, 2003, 21 Grams, 2003 (Acad. Award nomination for best actress, 2004, Screen Actors Guild Award nomination for best actress, 2004), We Don't Live Here Anymore, 2004, The Assassination of Richard Nixon, 2004, I Heart Huckabees, 2004, Ellie Parker, 2005, The Ring Two, 2005, Stay, 2005, King Kong, 2005; (TV films) Bermuda Triangle, 1996, Timepiece, 1996, The Christmas Wish, 1998, The Hunt for the Unicorn Killer, 1999, The Wyvern Mystery, 2000, The Outsider, 2002; (TV miniseries) Brides of Christ, 1991; (TV series) Home and Away, 1991, Sleepwalkers, 1997. Mailing: Creative Artists Agy 9830 Wilshire Blvd Beverly Hills CA 90212-1825*

**WATTS, OLIVER EDWARD,** engineering company executive; b. Hayden, Colo., Sept. 22, 1939; s. Oliver Easton and Vera Irene (Hockett) W.; m. Charla Ann French, Aug. 12, 1962; children: Erik Sean, Oliver Eron, Sherilyn. BS, Colo. State U., 1962. Registered profl. engr., Colo., Calif.; profl. hand surveyor, Colo. Crew chief Colo. State U. Rsch. Found., Ft. Collins, 1962; with Calif. Dept. Water Resources, Gustine and Castaic, 1964-70; land and water engr. CF&I Steel Corp., Pueblo, Colo., 1970-71; engring. dir. United Western Engrs., Colorado Springs., Colo., 1971-76; ptnr. United Planning and Engring Co., Colorado Springs, 1976-79; owner Oliver E. Watts, Cons. Engr., Colorado Springs, 1979—. Dir. edn. local Ch. of Christ, 1969-71, deacon, 1977-87, elder, 1987-96. 1st lt. C.E., AUS, 1962-64. Recipient Individual Achievement award Colo. State U. Coll. Engring., 1981. Fellow ASCE (life; v.p. Colorado Springs br. 1975, pres. 1978); mem. NSPE (pres. Pike's Peak chpt. 1975, sec. Colo. sect. 1976, v.p. 1977, pres. 1978-79, Young Engr. award 1976, Pres.'s award 1979), Cons. Engrs. Coun. Colo. (bd. dirs. 1981-83), Am. Cons. Engrs. Coun., Profl. Land Surveyors Colo. Cons. Engrs. Coun. (del. 1980—), Colo. State U. Alumni Assn. (v.p., dir. Pike's Peak chpt. 1972-76), Lancers, Lambda Chi Alpha. Home: 7195 Dark Horse Pl Colorado Springs CO 80919-1442 Office: 614 Elkton Dr Colorado Springs CO 80907-3514

**WATTS, ROBERT ALLAN,** publisher, lawyer; b. July 4, 1936; s. Richard P. and Florence (Hooker) W.; m. Emily Stipes, Aug. 30, 1958; children: Benjamin H., Edward S., Thomas J. Student, DePauw U., 1954-55; BA, U. Ill., 1959, JD, 1961. Bar: (Ill.) 1961. Assoc. Stipes Pub. Co., Champaign, Ill., 1962-67, ptnr., editor, 1967—. Treas. Planned Parenthood, 1976-80; mem. Pres.'s Coun., U. Ill.; pres. Friends of Libr., U. Ill., 1980-82; treas. Campaign Rep. Party, 1976-80;; bd. dirs. local United Way, 1972-81, City of Champaign Libr. Found., 1993-. Mem. Ill. Bar Assn., U. Ill. Found., Nat. Acad. Arts (bd. dirs. 1983-89), Champaign Country Club, Saugatuck Yacht Club (commodore), Lake Shore Bath & Tennis Club (pres. 1983-85). Home: 1009 W University Ave Champaign IL 61821-3317 Office: Stipes Publishing Co 204 W University Ave Champaign IL 61820-3912

**WATTS, ROBERT GLENN,** retired pharmaceutical executive; b. Norton, Va., Apr. 28, 1933; s. Clifford Amburgey and Stella Lee (Cornette) Watts; m. Doris Juanita Slaughter, Aug. 29, 1953 (dec. 1980); children: Cynthia L. Watts Waller, Robert Glenn, Kelly L.; m. Sara Lowry Childrey, Aug. 20, 1982; 1 child. Matthew R. Alexander 1 stepchild, J. Eric Alexander. BA, U. Richmond, 1959. Dir. ops. A.H. Robins Co., Inc., Richmond, Va., 1967-71, asst. v.p., 1971-73, v.p., 1973-75, sr. v.p., 1975-79, exec. v.p., 1979-92; ret., 1992. Bd. dirs. Little Oil Co., BB&T Bank, Fidelity Group. Mem. Pvt. Industry Coun., Richmond, 1983—; sec. YMCA, Richmond, 1984—; bd. dirs. United Way, Richmond, 1982—. With USN, 1952—56. Mem.: Met. Richmond C. of C. (chmn. 1985—86). Epsicopalian. Home: 2409 Islandview Dr Richmond VA 23233-2525 E-mail: RGW433@aol.com.

**WATTS, RONALD LESTER,** retired military officer; b. Seneca, Mo., June 27, 1934; s. Lester N. and Naomi (Montgomery) W.; m. Anita Abelquist, Sept. 26, 1981; 1 child, Christina; children by previous marriage— Elizabeth Ann, Ronald Allen BS in Edn., Pitts. State U., 1956; MS in Polit. Sci., Auburn U., 1976. Commd. officer U.S. Army, 1956, advanced through grades to lt. gen. 1987; asst. div. comdr. 1st Inf. Div., Ft. Riley, Kans., 1981-83; comdg. gen. U.S. Army Readiness, Fort Meade, Md., 1983; dep. comdg. gen. 1st U.S. Army, Fort Meade, Md., 1983-84; comdg. gen. 1st Inf. Div., Ft. Riley, Kans., 1984-86; chief staff Hdqrs. Forces Command, Ft. McPherson, Ga., 1986-87; commdg. gen. VII Corps, 1987-89, ret., 1989; pres. Watts Leadership Devel. Svcs., Greensboro, Ga., 1990—. Decorated D.S.M. with oak leaf cluster, Legion of Merit with 2 oak leaf clusters, Bronze Star, Air medal with 10 oak leaf clusters and V device, Combat Inf. badge, Def. Superior Svc. medal with cluster. Home: 1512 Raphis Royale Blvd Englewood FL 33633 Office Phone: 706-453-9367.

**WATTS, ROSS LESLIE,** finance educator; b. Hamilton, Australia, Nov. 10, 1942; came to U.S., 1966; s. Leslie R. and Elsie B. (Horadam) W. m. Helen Clare Firkin, Jan. 15, 1966; children: Andrew David, James Michael. B. Commerce with honors Commonwealth Govt. scholar 1960-65), U. Newcastle, Australia, 1966; MBA Ford Found. fellow 1967-68, U. Chgo., 1968, PhD, 1971. Audit clk. Forsythe & Co., Newcastle, Australia, 1960-64, acct., 1964-66; instr. Grad. Sch. Bus., U. Chgo., 1969-70; asst. prof. Simon Sch. Mgmt., U. Rochester (N.Y.), 1971-78, assoc. prof., 1978-84, prof., 1984-86; endowed chair Rochester Telephone Corp., 1986-98; William H. Meckling prof. U. Rochester (N.Y.), 1998—2005; prof. Sloan Sch. MIT, Cambridge, Mass., 2005—. Prof. commerce U. Newcastle, 1974-76; hon. prof. City U. Hong Kong, 1996—, Xiamen U., China, 1999—; disting. lectr. Hong Kong U. Sci. and Tech., 1994—; vis. prof. MIT, 2002; cons. in field. Contbr. articles on acctg. rsch. to profl. jours.; assoc. editor Jour. Acctg. Rsch., 1972-78, Jour. Fin. Econs., 1974-89, Australian Jour. Mgmt., 1976-81; co-editor Jour. Acctg. and Econs., 1979—; editor Jour. Acctg. Abstracts, 1995-97; dir., editor Acctg. Rsch. Network, 1997—; mem. adv. bd. Midland Corp. Fin. Jour., 1983-88, Continental Bank Jour. of Applied Corp. Fin., 1988-94, Bank Am. Jour. Applied Corp. Fin., 1994—; mem. editorial bd. Contemporary Acctg. Rsch., 1983-85; cons. editor Asia Pacific Jour. Acctg. Econs., 1998—. Recipient Notable Contbn. award AICPA, 1979, 80, award Alpha Kappa Psi Found., 1985. Mem. Am. Acctg. Assn. (Outstanding Educator award 2000, Seminal Rsch. award 2004), Am. Fin. Assn., Inst. Chartered Accts. in Australia. Home: 22 Park St Arlington MA 02474 Office: MIT Sloan Sch 50 Memorial Blvd Cambridge MA 02142-1347 Office Phone: 617-253-2668. Business E-Mail: rwatts@mit.edu.

**WATTS, STEPHEN HURT, II,** lawyer; b. Lynchburg, Va., Feb. 21, 1947; s. James Owen Jr. and Sarah Webb (Key) W.; m. Beverley Allan Brockenbrough, July 16, 1969 (div. 1986): children: Day Lowrey, Stephen Hurt Jr.; m. Sally Yates Wood, May 24, 1986 (div. 1995); m. Mollie Crawford Talbott; March 24, 1999. BA, Washington & Lee U., 1968; JD, U. Va., 1972. Bar: Va. 1972, W.Va. 1973. Law clk. Taylor, Michie & Callahan, Charlottesville, Va., 1970-72; assoc. Spilman, Thomas, Battle & Klostermeyer, Charleston, W.Va., 1972-75; ptnr. Watts & Watts, Lynchburg, Va., 1975-77; v.p., counsel Commonwealth Gas Pipeline Corp., Richmond, 1977-81; gen. counsel Commonwealth Natural Resources, Inc., Richmond, 1980-81; assoc. McGuire Woods LLP (formerly McGuire, Woods, Battle & Boothe, LLP), Richmond, 1981-83, ptnr., 1983—. Bd. dirs. Lower Fan Civic Assn. Richmond, 1987-91, TheatreVirginia, Richmond, 1992-93, Va. Oil and Gas Assn., 1993; pres., bd. dirs. Studio Theatre Richmond, 1991-93; chmn. outreach com. Grace and Holy Trinity Episcopal Ch., Richmond, 1993. Mem. ABA, Va. State Bar (all attys. commn.), chm. 1995-96), Fed. Energy Bar Assn. Office: McGuire Woods LLP One James Center 901 E Cary St Richmond VA 23219-4057 E-mail: swatts@mcguirewoods.com.*

**WATTS, SUSAN HELENE,** theater educator; d. Howard Harold and Madelyn Rebecca (Moore) Watts. BA, Mich. State U., 1963; MS, U. Kans., 1984. Tchr. Douglas County Schs., Castle Rock, Colo., 1964—74; owner/mgr. Old Bank Cafe, Oskaloosa, Kans., 1976—80; tchr. Valley Falls H.S., 1984—86; instr. Highland C.C., 1986—89; tchr. Oskaloosa H.S., 1986—89; communication coord./actor Omaha Magic Theatre, 1989—90; instr/divsn. chair McCook C.C., 1990—. Charter mem. Leadership McCook, 1990—; bd. mem. S.W. Nebr. Cmty. Theater Assn., 1990—2001; mem. Nebr. Transfer Initiative, 1995—; chair local integrity subcom. North Ctrl. Accreditation Com., 1998—2001; adv. bd. Bright Beginnings, 1997—2001; mem. Campus Pres.'s Adv. Coun., 1993—97. Actor: (plays) Marvin's Room, Pools Paradise, Morning's At Seven, (stand up comedy) An Evening with Cassandra; author: (humor column) Dear Cassandra; dir.: (over sixty plays and musicals) (Outstanding Kans. Theatre Tchr., 1983). Banquet com. writer/performer McCook C. of C., 1998—2002; mem. goal setting task force McCook City Coun., 1998—98; mem. McCook Humane Soc., McCook, 1995—2003; bd. dirs. SpringFest, 1998—2000. Named Outstanding Kans. Theatre Tchr., Assn. Kans. Theatre, 1983. Mem.: NEA, Soc. Stage Dir. Choregraphers, Mid-Plains Edn. Assn., Nebr. State Edn. Assn., Kiwanis, Alpha Delta Kappa, Delta Kappa Gamma. Avocations: golf, gardening. Office: McCook Cmty Coll 1205 E Third Mc Cook NE 69001 Office Phone: 308-345-8173.

**WATTS, THOMAS PARRISH,** history educator, consultant; m. Judy Marie Griffith, Nov. 24, 1968; 1 child, Shelly Dawn Watts-Dognazzi. BS, U. of So. Miss., Hattiesburg, 1971; MEd, U. of So. Calif., L.A., 1978; M of Strategic Studies, Nat. Def. U., Washington, 1994. Nat. bd. cert. profl. tchr. Nat. Bd. for Profls. Tchg. Stds. Bn. comdr. 1313th Transp. Ocean Port Bn., Seattle, 1990—92; mil. adviser to sec. of def. Office of the Sec. of Def., Washington, 1992—93; mil. adviser to U.S. amb. U.S. Mission to NATO, Brussels, 1994—97; dir., instr. U.S. Army War Coll., Carlisle Barracks, Pa., 1997—99; dep. dir. Miss. Dept. of Human Svcs., Jackson, Miss., 1999—2000; tchr. Am. history Madison Mid. Sch., Miss., 2000—. Editor: (ednl. package) Tracing Our Trace (Nat. Geog. Soc. grant, 2002). Col. U.S. Army, 1971—99. Decorated Legion of Merit, Def. Meritorious Svc. Medal, Army Meritorious Medals (4), Joint Svc. Commendation Medal, Army Commendation Medal (4) US Def. Dept. and US Army; named Disting. Mem. of U.S. Army Transp. Corps' Rgt., 2006, Gilda - Lehrman History Tchr. of Yr. for Miss., Gilda - Lehrman History Inst., 2005, 2002 - 2003 Tchr. of Yr., Madison County Sch. Dist., 2003. Mem.: VFW (life), Miss. Hist. Soc., Nat. Def. Transp. Assn., Am. Legion, Nat. Assn. of Social Studies Educators. Independent. United Methodist. Avocations: history, travel. Office: Madison Midd Sch 1365 Mannsdale Rd Madison MS 39110 Office Phone: 601-605-4171. Home Fax: 601-853-2254; Office Fax: 601-853-2254. Personal E-mail: tomw1048@aol.com Business E-Mail: twatts@madison.k12.ms.us.

**WAUD, ROGER NEIL,** economist, educator; b. Detroit, Mar. 26, 1938; s. Othneil Stockwell and Mary Josephine (Gough) Waud; children: Heather, Neil. BA, Harvard U., 1960; MA, U. Calif., Berkeley, 1962; PhD (Ford Found. fellow), U. Calif., Berekley, 1965. Asst. prof. bus. econs. Grad. Sch. Bus. U. Chgo., 1964-69; assoc. prof. econs. U. N.C., Chapel Hill, 1969-72, prof., 1972-97, prof. emeritus, 1997—; sr. economist, bd. govs. Fed. Res. Sys., Washington, 1973-75; prof., dir. grad. econs. program Va. Tech., 1997—2002. Cons. Dept. Labor; mem. adv. bd. Taxpayers Ednl. Coalition, 1981; rsch. assoc. Nat. Bur. Econ. Rsch., 1982—92; mem. N.C. Energy Policy Coun., 1986—92; vis. prof. Duke U., 1992—94. Author: Macroeconomics, 5th edit., 1992, Microeconomics, 5th edit., 1992; mem. editl. bd. So. Econ. Jour., 1970—73, Studies Econs. and Fin., 1995—97; contbr. articles to profl. jours. Mem.: So. Econ. Assn. (exec. com. 1977—79), Am. Econ. Assn.

**WAUGAMAN, RICHARD MERLE,** psychiatrist, educator; b. Easton, Pa., Apr. 27, 1949; s. Charles Hoffmeier and Ruth Alviene (Melee) W.; m. Elisabeth Leone Pearson, June 20, 1970; children: Adele Marie, Garrett Dennis. AB, Princeton U., 1970; MD, Duke U., 1973. Cert. psychiatry, 1978, psychoanalysis, 1984. Resident in psychiatry Sheppard-Pratt Hosp., Towson, Md., 1973-76; mem. faculty Washington Sch. Psychiatry, 1983-96; grad. Washington Psychoanalytic Inst., 1984, tng. and supervising analyst, 1989-2001, tng. and supervising analyst emeritus, 2001—; from clin. instr. to clin. assoc. prof. Georgetown U. Sch. Medicine, Washington, 1978-92, clin. prof. psychiatry, 1992—; staff psychiatrist Chestnut Lodge, Rockville, Md., 1986-99. Cons. psychiat. residency program Nat. Naval Med. Ctr., Bethesda, Md., 1994—96; adj. prof. psychiatry Uniformed Svcs. U. of Health Scis., 1999—; reader Folger Shakespeare Libr. Contbr. articles to profl. jours. Mem. Washington Psychoanalytic Soc., Am. Psychoanalytic Assn. (exec. coun. 1993-97, com. on certification 1998-2002), Internat. Psychoanalytic Assn., Am. Psychiat. Assn., Cosmos Club. Home: 8109 Horseshoe Ln Potomac MD 20854-3834 Office Phone: 301-654-9771. Personal E-mail: rwmd@comcast.net.

**WAUGAMAN, RICHARD WILLIAM,** sales executive; b. Freedom, Pa., Aug. 29, 1958; s. Harry and Bonita (Reed) Waugaman. Student, Robert Morris Coll., 1984. Cert. travel agt. Purchasing coord. Integrated Supply Network, Lakeland, 1993—98; contract sales rep. The Ledger (A N.Y. Times Co.), Lakeland, Fla., 1998—. Avocations: travel, collecting. Office: The Ledger (A N Y Times Co) 300 West Lime St Lakeland FL 33802 Personal E-mail: PandaBear1958@att.net.

**WAUGH, JOHN STEWART,** chemist, educator; b. Willimantic, Conn., Apr. 25, 1929; s. Albert E. and Edith (Stewart) W.; married 1983; children: Alice Collier, Frederick Pierce. AB, Dartmouth Coll., 1949; PhD, Calif. Inst. Tech., 1953; ScD (hon.), Dartmouth Coll., 1989. Rsch. fellow in physics Calif. Inst. Tech., 1952-53; mem. faculty MIT, Cambridge, 1953—, prof. chemistry, 1962—, Albert Amos Noyes prof. chemistry, 1973-88, inst. prof., 1989—, emeritus, 1996—. Vis. prof. U. Calif.-Berkeley, 1963-64, Max Planck Inst., Heidelberg, 1972; sr. fellow Alexander von Humboldt-Stiftung; vis. scientist Harvard U., 1976; mem. chemistry adv. panel NSF, 1966-69, vice chmn., 1968-69; mem. rev. com. Argonne Nat. Lab., 1970-74; mem. sci. and edn. adv. com. Lawrence Berkeley Lab., 1980-86; exchange visitor USSR Acad. Scis., 1962, 75; mem. vis. com. Tufts U., 1966-69, Princeton, 1973-78; mem. fellowship com. Alfred P. Sloan Found., 1977-82; Joliot-Curie prof. École Supérieure de Physique et Chemie, Paris, 1985, 96; lectr. in field. Author: New NMR Methods in Solid State Physics, 1978; editor: Advances in Magnetic Resonance, 1963-87; assoc. editor: Jour. Chem. Physics, 1963-67, Spectrochimica Acta, 1964-78; mem. editl. bd. Chem. Revs., 1978-82, Jour. Magnetic Resonance, 1989—, Applied Magnetic Resonance, 1989—. Recipient Irving Langmuir award, 1976, Gold Pick Axe award, 1976, Pitts. award Spectroscopic Soc. Pitts., 1979, Wolf prize in chemistry, Wolf Found., 1984, Pauling medal, 1985, Calif. Inst. Tech. disting. alumnus award, 1987, Killian award, 1988, ISMAR prize, 1989, Richards medal, 1992, Evans award, 1994, Ea. Analytical Symposium award 1996, Russell Varian prize, 2006; Sloan fellow, 1958-62, Guggenheim fellow, 1963-64, 72; Sherman Fairchild scholar Calif. Inst. Tech., 1989. Fellow: AAAS, Am. Phys. Soc. (chmn. divsn. chemistry and physics 1983—84); mem.: NAS, Slovenian Acad. Sci. and Arts (fgn. corr.), Nat. Magnetic Resonance Soc. India (hon.), Internat. Soc. Magnetic Resonance (coun. mem. 1989—95, exec. com. 1996—, v.p. 1997—, pres. 1999—2002), Sigma Xi, Phi Beta Kappa. Office: MIT 6-233 77 Massachusetts Ave Cambridge MA 02139-4307 Office Phone: 617-253-1901. Business E-Mail: jswaugh@mit.edu.

**WAUGH, THEODORE ROGERS,** orthopedic surgeon; b. Montreal, Sept. 21, 1926; s. Theodore Rogers and Anne Maude (Lawlor) W.; children: Susanne Rogers, Margaret Stewart, Theodore Rogers. BA, Yale U., 1949; MD, CM, McGill U., 1953; DMS, U. Goteborg, Sweden, 1968. Diplomate Am. Bd. Orthop. Surgery. Intern Royal Victoria Hosp., Montreal, 1953-54; asst. resident in pathology McGill U., 1954-55; asst. resident in surgery NYU Bellevue Med. Ctr., 1955-56; asst. resident, resident, fellow N.Y. Orthop. Hosp., Columbia U., 1958-62, instr., clin. asst. prof. orthop. surgery, 1962-68; asst. attending Presbyn. Hosp., N.Y.C., NY, 1962-68; prof., chief divsn. orthop. surgery U. Calif., Irvine, 1968-78; prof., chmn. dept. orthop. surgery NYU Med. Ctr., 1978-96, emeritus prof., 1997—. Adj. prof. surgery Dartmouth U. Sch. Medicine, 1998-2003, adj. prof. orthopaedics, 2003—. Contbr. numerous articles to profl. jours. Capt., M.C. USAF, 1956-58. Fellow ACS, Royal Coll. Surgeons (Can.), Am. Acad. Orthop. Surgeons, Scoliosis Rsch. Soc., Assn. Bone and Joint Surgeons, Am. Orthop. Assn., Am. Orthop. Soc. Sports Medicine; mem. Nat. Soc. Colonial Wars (sec. 2005-06), 20th Century Orthpedic Club, Alpha Omega Alpha. Presbyterian. Achievements include developing designer surgical devices used in orthopaedic surgery. Office: Dartmouth-Hitchcock Med Ctr One Medical Center Dr Lebanon NH 03756 E-mail: trwmd3@adelphia.net.

**WAUGH, WILLIAM HOWARD,** physician, research scientist; b. N.Y.C., May 13, 1925; s. Richey Laughlin and Lyda Pearl (Leamer) W.; m. Eileen Loretta Garrigan, Oct. 4, 1952; children: Mark Howard, Kathleen Cary, William Peter. Student, Boston U., 1943, W.Va. U., 1944; MD, Tufts U., 1948, postgrad., 1949—50. Cardiovascular rsch. trainee Med. Coll. Ga., Augusta, 1954-55, asst. rsch. prof. physiology, 1955-60, assoc. medicine, 1957-60; assoc. prof. medicine U. Ky., Lexington, 1960-69; Ky. Heart Assn. Chair in cardiovascular rsch. Ky. Heart Assn., Lexington, 1963-71; prof. medicine U. Ky., Lexington, 1969-71; prof. medicine and physiology East Carolina U., Greenville, 1971—2001, rsch. prof. physiology, 2001—04, prof. emeritus, 2001—. Head renal sect. U. Ky. Coll., Lexington, 1960-68; chmn. dept. clin. scis. East Carolina U., Greenville, 1971-75, chmn. policy and rev. com. on human rsch., 1972-90. Contbr. articles to profl. jours. With AUS, 1943-46; capt. USAF, 1952-54. Fellow ACP; mem. AAAS, Am. Physiology Soc., Am. Heart Assn., Am. Soc. Nephrology, Microcirculatory Soc. Achievements include basic advances in excitation contraction coupling in vasc. smooth muscle; basic advances in autoregulation of renal blood flow and urine flow; adj. therapy in acute lung edema; noncovalent antisickling agents and amino acid nutrient in sickle cell hemoglobinopathy; oral citrulline as dietary supplement in man; daily intermittent peritoneal dialysis. Home: 119 Oxford Rd Greenville NC 27858-4954

**WAVLE, JAMES EDWARD, JR.,** pharmaceutical company executive, lawyer; b. N.Y.C., July 19, 1942; s. James Edward and Florence Marie (Kehoe) W.; children from previous marriage: James Edward, William Patrick, Robert Thomas, Stephanie Elizabeth; m. Elizabeth Edith Symons Tallett; 1 child, Christopher Andrew; stepchildren: James E. Tallett, Alexander M. Tallett. BA, Adelphi U., 1964; JD, Georgetown U., 1967; LLM, NYU, 1968. Bar: N.Y. bar 1967. With Warner-Lambert Co., Morris Plains, N.J., 1968-87, internat. counsel, 1971-74, assoc. gen. counsel, 1974-77, v.p., gen. counsel, 1977-80, sr. v.p., gen. counsel, 1980-81; corp. sr. v.p. and pres. Parke-Davis Group, 1982-87; pres., CEO Centocor Inc., Malvern, Pa., 1987-92; chmn. Dioscor Inc., Stockton, N.J., 1993-97; chmn., pres., CEO Therics, Inc., Princeton, NJ, 1997—2003. Mem. ABA, Lookaway Golf Club, Stamford Yacht Club.

**WAWRYTKO, SANDRA ANN,** humanities educator; b. Chgo., Oct. 18, 1951; d. Stanley Andrew Wawrytko and Alyce Valerie Cioch-Wawrytko; m. Charles Wei-hsun Fu, Sept. 29, 1994 (dec. Oct. 15, 1996). BA in Philosophy, Knox Coll., 1972; MA in Philosophy, Washington U., 1975, PhD in Philosophy, 1976. Instr. Washington U. St. Louis, 1973—77; prof. San Diego State U., 1980—. Vis. prof. Chinese Culture U., Yangmingshan, Taiwan, 1984, Fo Guang Buddhist Coll., Kaohsiung, Taiwan, 1990—2004; prin. investigator San Diego State U. Lang. Acquisition Rsch. Ctr., San Diego, 1994—2003; vis. prof. U. San Diego, San Diego, 1978—81; founder, exec. dir. Internat. Soc. for Philosophy and Psychotherapy; founder, pres. Charles Wei-hsun Fu Found. Author: The Undercurrent of Feminine Philosophy in Eastern and Western Thought, 1981, CRYSTAL: Spectrums of Chinese Culture Through Poetry, 1995; editor: North American Institute of Zen Buddhist Studies, Rethinking the Curriculum: Toward an Integrated Interdisciplinary Education, 1990, The Problem of Evil, 2000, (book series) Asian Thought and Culture, Philosophy and Psychotherapy; co-author: The Buddhist Religion, 1996; narrator: interactive CD-ROM Crystals of Chinese Culture, 2000; author (and editor): Saving the Elephant: Asian Encounters with Imperialism, Orientalism, and Gloablization, 2004. Edn. rep. San Diego Sister City Program, Yantai, China, 1985; bd. dirs. San Diego Chinese Hist. Soc. and Mus., 2002—; pres. Charles Wei-hsun Fu Found., San Diego, 1997—. Recipient univ. fellowship, Washington, U., 1974—75, Humanities Advancement Poetry Contest award, Humanities Advancement Com., 1983. Mem.: World Congress of Logotherapy (sec.-gen. 1982—85), Internat. Soc. for Chinese Philosophy (sec., exec. bd. mem. 1990—2003), Phi Beta Delta (governing bd. 2002—06), Phi Beta Kappa (Faculty Lectr. No chpt. 2002—03). Avocations: poetry, translating classical Chinese poetry, collecting Asian art and books, creating culinary adventures. Office: San Diego State U Dept Philosophy San Diego CA 92182-0303 E-mail: wawrytko@mail.sdsu.edu.

**WAWRZASZEK, SUSAN V.,** university librarian; MSLS, SUNY Buffalo. With Brandeis U., Mass., 1995—, assoc. univ. libr. Mass., 2002—03, acting univ. libr. Mass., 2003—05, univ. libr. Mass., 2005—. Office: Brandeis U Mailstop 045 PO Box 549110 Waltham MA 02454-9110 Office Phone: 781-736-4700. Office Fax: 781-736-4719. E-mail: wawrzaszek@brandeis.edu.*

**WAX, ADAM,** biomedical engineer, educator; b. N.Y.C., Feb. 11, 1970; s. Arnold S. and Bonny Lee Wax; m. Jodi Ann Princenthal, June 27, 1999; children: Jessica children: Rachel. BSEE, Rensselaer Poly. Inst., 1993; BS in Physics, SUNY, Albany, 1993; PhD in Physics, Duke U., 1999. Postdoctoral fellow MIT, Cambridge, Mass., 1999—2002; asst. prof. dept. biomed. engring. Duke U., Durham, NC, 2002—. Contbr. articles to profl. jours.; assoc. editor Applied Optics, 2004—, patentee in field. Recipient Ralph E. Powe Jr. Faculty Enhancement award, Oak Ridge Associated Univs., 2003, Career award, NSF, 2004, Excellence in Tchg. and Rsch. award, Capers and Marion McDonald, 2006; NRSA fellow, NIH, 2000—02. Mem.: Biomed. Engring. Soc., Am. Assn. Cancer Rsch., Optical Soc. Am. (chair mem. and edn. svcs. coun. 2006—, bd. dirs. 2006—).

**WAX, AMY LAURA,** law educator; BS summa cum laude, Yale U., 1975; MD cum laude, Harvard U., 1981; JD, Columbia U., 1987. Bar: NY 1988. Resident in neurology NY Hosp.-Cornell Med. Ctr., 1982—85; cons. neurologist Bronx Cross County Clinic, NY, 1985—87, Brooklyn North Med. Group, 1985—87; law clk. to Hon. Abner J. Mikva US Ct. Appeals, DC Cir., 1987—88; asst. to solicitor gen. Office of Solicitor Gen., US Dept. Justice, Washington, DC, 1988—94; assoc. prot. U. Va. Law Sch., 1994—99, prof., 1999—2000, Class of 1948 prof. scholarly rsch. in law, 2000—01; vis. prof. U. Pa. Law Sch., Phila., 2000, prof. law, 2001—. Contbr. articles to profl. jours. Office: U Pa Law Sch 3400 Chestnut St Philadelphia PA 19104 Office Phone: 215-898-5638. Office Fax: 215-994-0496. E-mail: awax@law.upenn.edu.

**WAX, ARNOLD,** physician; b. Bklyn., Mar. 11, 1949; s. Emanuel and Eleanor (Greenfield) W.; m. Francine Wax; children: Erin, Rachael, Adam, Benjamin. BS in Pharm. Scis., Columbia U., 1971; MD, SUNY, Buffalo, 1976. Diplomate Nat. Bd. Med. Examiners, Am. Bd. Internal Medicine, Am. Bd. Quality Assurance and Utilization Rev. Physicians, Am. Acad. Pain Mgmt.; lic. physician, Fla., Calif., N.D., Minn., N.Y., Nev., Ariz. Intern. resident Millard Fillmore Hosp., Buffalo, 1976-79; clin. asst. instr. SUNY, 1977-79; instr. medicine U. Rochester, NY, 1979-81; dir. internal medicine U. N.D., Grand Forks, 1982-83, clin. asst. prof., 1982-85; pvt. practice Las Vegas, Nev., 1987—. Mem. staff Sunrise Hosp., Las Vegas, Desert Springs Hosp., Las Vegas, Nathan Adelson Hospice, Las Vegas, So. Hills Hosp., Spring Valley Hosp. Contbr. articles to profl. jours. Grantee So. Nev. Cancer Rsch. Found., Ea. Coop. Oncology Group, Gynecol. Oncology Group, North Ctrl. Cancer Treatment Group, S.W. Oncology Group. Fellow Am. Coll. Physicians; mem. AMA, Am. Cancer Soc. (fellow 1979), Am. Soc. Clin. Oncology, Am. Coll. Physicians (gov. State of Nev.), Nev. Oncology So. (v.p.), Nev. Med. Soc., Clark County Med. Soc. (trustee, peer rev. com., treas.), Nev. Peer Rev. Orgn., U. Nev. Las Vegas Found., Nev. Dance Theater, Nev. Opera Theater, Las Vegas Symphony, Nev. Inst. Contemporary Art, Lied Mus., Allied Arts Coun., James Platt White Soc., U. Buffalo Found., Rho Chi (Bronze medal 1971). Home: 2224 Chatsworth Ct Henderson NV 89074-5309 Office Phone: 702-952-1251. Business E-Mail: arnold.wax@usoncology.com. E-mail: arnoldwax@cox.net.

**WAX, BENJAMIN,** physical education educator, consultant; b. Amory, Miss., June 29, 1968; s. Benjamin and Mae Francis Wax; m. Cynthia Wax, July 30, 1993; 1 child, Dominique. AS, Itawamba CC, Fulton, Miss., 1988; BS, Miss. State U., Starkville, 1991, MS, 1993; PhD, Miss. Oxford, 1999. Instr. Miss. State U., Starkville, 1991—92, Lafayette County Sch., Miss., 1992—93, strength coach, 1992—93; instr. U. Miss., Oxford, 1993—98;

owner Curves for Women, Greenville, 1996—99, Columbus, 1996—99, Oxford, 1996—99; asst. prof. Miss. Valley State U., Itta Bena, 1999—2002, assoc. prof., 2003—; dir. Health and Fitness Ctr., 2003—; co-founder, pres. Premier Lady Internat. Inc., 2005. Fitness cons. Sweat Fitness Club, Oxford, 2000—03; phys. edn. activities coord. sci. program Miss. Valley State U., 2001—, fitness cons., 2002—; dir. Ladies Rx Internat., 2004. Presenter (at profl. meetings). Recipient Minority Nat. Academic Achievement award, 1997, Minority Assoc. Academic award, 1989—91, academic excellence, Alliance for Graduate Education in Mississippi, 2003. Mem.: Nat. Strength and Conditioning Assn., Am. Physiol. Soc., Am. Coll. of Sports Medicine. Office: MS Valley State University box 7270 14000 Hwy 82W Itta Bena MS 38941 E-mail: bjwax_2000@yahoo.com.

**WAX, NADINE VIRGINIA,** retired bank executive; b. Van Horne, Iowa, Dec. 7, 1927; d. Laurel Lloyd and Viola Henrietta (Schraer) Bobzien; divorced; 1 child, Sharlyn K. Wax Munns. Student, U. Iowa, 1970-71; grad. Nat. Sch. Real Estate and Fin., Ohio State U., 1980-81. Jr. acct. McGladrey, Hansen, Dunn (now McGladrey-Pullen Co., CPAs), Cedar Rapids, Iowa, 1944-47; office mgr. Iowa Securities Co. (now Wells Fargo Mortgage Co.), Cedar Rapids, 1954-55; asst. cashier Mchts. Nat. Bank (now U.S. Bancorp.), Cedar Rapids, 1956-75; asst. v.p. Mchts. Nat. Bank (now U.S. Bancorp), Cedar Rapids, 1976-78, v.p., 1979-90; ret., 1990. Vol. St. Luke's Hosp. Aux., Cedar Rapids, 1981—85, SCORE, 1999—2006; bd. dirs., treas. Kirkwood C.C. Facilities Found., 1970—2006; bd. dirs. treas. Kirkwood C.C. 1984—91; trustee Indian Creek Nature Ctr., Cedar Rapids, 1974—2006, pres., 1980—81; mem. Linn County Regional Planning Commn., 1982—92, Cedar Rapids-Marion Fine Arts Coun., 1994—97; bd. suprs. Compensation Commn. for Condemnation, 1987—92; bd. dirs. Am. Heart Assn., Cedar Rapids, 1983—94; mem. Iowa Employment and Tng. Coun., Des Moines, 1982—83. Recipient Outstanding Woman award, Cedar Rapids Tribute to Women and Industry, 1984. Mem. Fin. Women Internat. (state edn. chmn. 1982-83), Am. Inst. Banking (bd. dirs. 1968-70), Soc. Real Estate Appraisers (treas. 1978-80), Linn County Bankers Assn. (pres. 1979-80), Cedar Rapids Bd. Realtors, Cedar Rapids C. of C. (bus.-edn. com. 1986-91), Cedar Rapids Country Club. Lutheran. Avocations: travel, reading, walking. Home: 147 Ashcombe SE Cedar Rapids IA 52403-1700

**WAX, WILLIAM EDWARD,** photojournalist; b. Miami, Fla., Dec. 7, 1956; s. Ira and Rita (Gunshor) W. AS, Berry Coll., Rome, Ga., 1976; BS in Engring., U. Fla., 1983. With Ind. Fla. Alligator, Gainesville, Fla., 1977-79; staff photographer Gainesville (Fla.) Sun, 1979-87; photo cons. N.Y. Times regional newspapers, 1984—; freelance photographer Miami, 1987—; pres. Wax & Co. Inc., Miami Beach, Fla., 1989—, Waxcom, Miami Beach, Fla., 1996—. Owner Studio SoBe, Miami Beach, 1992—; faculty So. Short Course in News Photography, 1985—; lectr. in field. Named Photographer of Yr., NPPA/U. Mo. and Nikon, 1980, So. Photographer of Yr., 1980, Regional Photographer of Yr., 1979, 82, 85; nominated Pulitzer prize, 1979, 89, STC Internat. Design, 1996-97; recipient Mark of Excellence, Sigma Delta Chi, 1978, Best of Show award Atlanta Seminar on Photojournalism, 1982, Best of Show and Silver medal Hearst awards, 1978, Design Gold award Fla. Tech. Writers Assn., 1992, Design award, Gold award, Excellence award Soc. Tech. Comm. Internat. Tech. Art Competition, 1993, 94, 97-03, Best of Show, 1994, 98, 01, Disting. Design award, 1993, 97, 99-03, Excellence Design award, 1993, 98, 99, Design Excellence awards and award of merit, 1995, 00, Best of Show award Ann. Report Fla. Pub. Rels., 1995, Gold, Silver and Bronze awards Fla. Mag. Assn., 1994, 96-04, Merit award STC, 1995, Apex Design awards 1996-04, Global award/Ann. Report, 1996, Maggie award Best Newsletter in the West, 2004, Healthcare Advt. award, 2002-04, SIAA awards, 2004. Mem. Nat. Press Photographers Assn., Fla. Mag. Assn., Profl. Photographers Assn., Nikon Profl. Svcs., Fla. Press Photographers Assn. Office: Wax & Co 350 Lincoln Rd Ste 516 Miami FL 33139-3148 Office Phone: 305-674-9542.

**WAXENBERG, JAY DAVID,** lawyer; b. NYC, Aug. 29, 1956; s. Milton J. and Edith (Balter) W.; m. Gayle D. Waxenberg, Mar. 3, 1985; children: Michael Ian, Alex Evan. BA, SUNY, Stony Brook, 1978; JD, Boston U., 1981; LLM in Taxation, NYU, 1987. Bar: N.Y. 1982. Estate adminstr. U.S. Trust Co., NY, 1981-84; assoc., personal planning dept. Proskauer Rose LLP, NYC, 1984-90, partner & chmn. personal planning dept., 1991—, exec. com. mem. Faculty mem. Fordham U. Sch. Law, continuing edn. program Estate Planning Beyon d the Basics; faculty mem. Practising Law Inst. Introduction to the Adminstration of New York Estates, 1991; lectr. in will drafting. Contbr. author: Estate Tax Techniques/Tax Responsibilities, 1988. Mem. ABA (Marital deduction com.), N.Y. Bar Assn. (com. on estate planning), Assn. of Bar of City of N.Y. (spl. com. on estate and gift taxation); fellow Am. Coll. of Trust & Estates Counsel. Office: Proskauer Rose LLP 1585 Broadway Fl 27 New York NY 10036-8299

**WAXLER, BEVERLY JEAN,** anesthesiologist, physician; d. Isadore and Ada Belle (Gross) Marcus; m. Richard Norman Waxler, Dec. 24, 1972; 1 child, Adam R. BS in Biology, No. Ill. U., 1971; MD, U. Ill., Chgo., 1975. Diplomate Am. Bd. Anesthesiology, Am. Bd. Pathology. Intern dept. pathology Northwestern U., Chgo., 1975—76, resident, 1976—79; instr. Rush Presbyn. St. Luke's Med. Ctr., Chgo., 1979—81; asst. prof. pathology Loyola U., Maywood, Ill., 1981—84; resident dept. anesthesiology Stroger Hosp. Cook County (formerly Cook County Hosp.), Chgo., 1984—87; attending anesthesiologist Stroger Hosp. Cook County, Chgo., 1987—; chmn. divsn. postanesthetic care Stroger Hosp. of Cook County, Chgo., 2004—; clin. asst. prof. U. Ill., Chgo., 1988—95; asst. prof. Rush Med. Coll., Chgo., 1996—. Contbr. articles to profl. jours. Grantee, Varlen Corp., 1982; Nat. Rsch. Svc. fellow, Nat. Cancer Inst., 1980. Mem. AAAS, Ill. Soc. Anesthesiologists, Chgo. Soc. Anesthesiologists, Am. Soc. Anesthesiologists, Internat. Anesthesia Rsch. Soc. (B. B. Sankey Anesthesia Advancement award 1989), Sigma Xi. Office: Stroger Hosp Cook County Dept Anesthesiology 1901 W Harrison St Chicago IL 60612 Office Phone: 312-864-2140. Business E-Mail: bwaxler@rush.edu.

**WAXMAN, ALLEN,** pharmaceutical executive; Grad., Dartmouth Coll., NH, Harvard Law Sch. Clk. Staff of Hon. Thomas Penfield Jackson of US Dist. Ct., Washington; ptnr. Williams & Connolly, LLP, Washington; sr. asst. gen. counsel, chief litig. Pfizer, Inc., 2003—05, sr. v.p., assoc. gen. counsel, 2005, gen. counsel. Chmn. bd. Thurgood Marshall Acad., Washington; adj. prof. law Georgetown U. Law Ctr.; mem. US policy government com. Pfizer, Inc. Mem.: Equal Justice Works (bd. mem., officer). Office: Pfizer Inc 235 E 42nd St New York NY 10017*

**WAXMAN, ANITA,** theater producer; Prodr. (plays) Mrs. Klein, Below the Belt, Wild Honey (Drama Desk award nomination), The Foreigner, Music Man, 2000-01, One Flew Over the Cuckoo's Nest, 2001 (Tony award for Best Revival of a Play), Noises Off, 2001-02, Top Dog/Underdog, 2002 (Tony award for Best Play and Pulitzer Prize), The Elephant Man, 2002, Flower Drum Song, 2002-03, Gypsy, 2004 (Tony award for Best Revival of a Musical), Bombay Dreams, 2004—; co-prodr. (plays) Present Laughter (Tony award nomination), Breaking the Code, Circle & Bravo, Long Day's Journey Into Night, Annie get Your Gun, Mr. & Mrs. Nobody. Founder Noah's Ark Found.; creator Passin-Waxman Ctr., Moscow. Office: Waxman Williams Entertainment 260 W 44th St Ste 500 New York NY 10036-3900

**WAXMAN, BRUCE I.,** lawyer; b. N.Y.C., July 30, 1942; m. Sarah Jane Elpern, Mar. 17, 1974. BS, Cornell U., 1964; JD, Columbia U., 1967. Bar: D.C. 1970. Atty. Am. Fedn. of Govt. Employees, Washington, 1970—72; exec. dir. D.C. Pub. Employee Rels. Bd., 1972—80; dir. collective bargaining Assn. of Flight Attendants, Washington, 1980—82; atty. U.S. Dept. Commerce, Washington, 1983—2000; assoc. gen. counsel Exec. Office of Immigration Rev. U.S. Dept. Justice, Washington, 2000—. Capt. U.S. Army, 1967—69. Mem.: Soc. Fed. Labor Relations Professionals, Fed. Bar Assn. Office: US Dept Justice Exec Office for Immigration Rev 5107 Leesburg Pike Ste 2600 Falls Church VA 22041

**WAXMAN, HENRY ARNOLD,** congressman; b. LA, Sept. 12, 1939; s. Louis and Esther (Silverman) W.; m. Janet Kessler, Oct. 17, 1971; children: Carol Lynn, Michael David. BA in Polit. Sci, UCLA, 1961, JD, 1964. Bar: Calif. 1965. Mem. Calif. State Assembly, 1969-74, U.S. Congress from 30th Calif. dist. (formerly 29th), 1975—; interm. commerce subcom. on health and environment, 1979-94; ranking minority mem. govt. reform & oversight com. Pres. Calif. Fedn. Young Democrats, 1965-67. Mem. Calif. Bar Assn., Guardians Jewish Home for Aged, Am. Jewish Congress, Sierra Club, B'nai B'rith, Phi Sigma Alpha. Democrat. Office: US Ho Reps 2204 Rayburn Ho Office Bldg Washington DC 20515-0530

**WAXMAN, RONALD,** computer engineer; b. Newark, Nov. 28, 1933; s. Benjamin and Rose (Lifson) W.; m. Pearl Latterman, June 19, 1955; children: David, Roberta, Benjamin. BSEE, N.J. Inst. Tech., 1955; MEE, Syracuse U., 1963. Engr. IBM, Poughkeepsie, NY, 1955-56, 58-64, East Fishkill, NY, 1964-70, Poughkeepsie and Kingston, NY, 1970-80, sr. engr. Manassas, Va., 1980-87; prin. scientist U. Va., Charlottesville, 1987-97; cons. pvt. practice, Reston, Va., 1997—. IEEE rep. and tech. advisor to Internat. Elec. Commn. U.S. tech. activities group for internat. design automation stds., 1994—98; steering com. very high speed integrated circuits hardware description lang. VHDL Users Group, 1987—91; panel for assessment of Nat. Inst. Stds. and Tech. Measurement and Stds. Labs. NRC, 2002—; presenter in field. Contbr. articles to profl. jours. 1st lt. USAF, 1956-58. Fellow IEEE, IEEE Computer Soc. (bd. govs. 1994-99, 96-98, 2000-02, chmn. fellows evaluation com. 1995-96, chmn. audit com., 1997, founder, chmn. design automation stds. subcom. 1983-88, steering com. 1989-2003, chmn. design automation tech. com. 1988-90, steering com. 1991—, vice-chmn. tech. activities bd. 1991-92, 99, chmn. awards com. 1993, disting. visitor 1986-88, chmn. disting. visitor program 2004—, v.p. activities bd. 1994, v.p. tech. activities, 1998, Meritorious Svc. cert. 1988, Disting. Svc. cert. 1994, TAB Pioneer award 1989, 3d. Millennium medal 2000), Internat. Fedn. Info. Processing Orgns. (CS rep. 2000—, sec. tech. reps. com., 2000—, vice chmn. 2004—, Outstanding Svc. award 2005, chmn. 2006—), Assn. for Computing Machinery (spl. interest group DA). Achievements include patents in field. Personal E-mail: r.waxman@computer.org.

**WAXMAN, SETH PAUL,** lawyer; b. Hartford, Conn., Nov. 28, 1951; s. Felix H. and Frieda (Goodman) W.; m. Debra F. Goldberg, Mar. 20, 1977; children: Noah, Sarah, Ethan. AB summa cum laude, Harvard U., 1973; JD, Yale U., 1977. Bar: D.C. 1978, U.S. Dist. Ct. D.C. 1979, U.S. Ct. Appeals (D.C. cir.) 1979, U.S. Ct. Appeals (1st cir.) 2000, (2d cir.) 1998, (3d cir.) 1983, (4th cir.) 1982, (5th cir.) 1997, (6th cir.) 1998, (7th cir.) 1998, (8th cir.) 1998, (9th cir.) 1982, (10th cir.) 1998, (11th cir.) 1989, U.S. Ct. Appeals (fed. cir.) 1998, U.S. Supreme Ct. 1982. Law clk to Judge Gerhard A. Gesell, Washington, 1977-78; ptnr. Miller Cassidy Larroca & Lewin, Washington, 1978-94; assoc. dep. atty. gen. U.S. Dept. Justice, Washington, 1994-96, dep. solicitor gen., 1996-97, acting dep. atty. gen., 1997, solicitor gen., 1997-2001; ptnr. Wilmer, Cutler, Pickering, Hale and Dorr, LLP, 2001—. Disting. vis. from practice Georgetown U Law Ctr., 2001—; vis. prof. Georgetown U Law Ctr., 2001; vis. fellow Harvard U. JFK Sch. Govt., 2001; dir. Supreme Ct. Inst., Georgetown U. Law Ctr.; chmn. Legal Affairs Mag., 2004—06. Editor Yale Law Jour., The Combatant Detention Trilogy Through the Lenses of History, 2005; contbr. articles to profl. jours. Prin. Coun. for Excellence in Govt.; trustee Supreme Ct. Hist. Soc.; overseer Harvard U.; bd. dirs. Nat. Found. for Jewish Culture; trustee Bruce J. Ennis Found. Named hon. spl. agt., FBI, 2001; named one of 75 Best Lawyers in Washington, Washingtonian mag., 2002; recipient Pro Bono Publico award, ABA, 1988, Edmund J. Randolph award, U.S. Dept. Justic, 2001, Benjamin L. Cardozo Cert. of Merit, Anti-Defamation League, 1987, Thomas Jefferson Found. medal in law, U. Va., 2002, Pursuit of Justice award, Internat. Assn. Jewish Lawyers and Jurists, 2001, BYU Rex Lee Advocacy Award, 2002; fellow Michael C. Rockefeller, Harvard U., 1973—74. Master: Edward Coke Appellate Inn Court; fellow: Am. Acad. Arts & Sciences, Am. Coll. Trial Lawyers, Am Acad. Appellate Attys., Am. Bar Found.; mem.: Am. Law Inst. Office: Wilmer Cutler Pickering Hale and Dorr LLP 2445 M St NW Washington DC 20003-1420 Office Phone: 202-663-6000. Fax: 202-663-6000. E-mail: seth.waxman@wilmerhale.com.

**WAXMAN, STEPHEN GEORGE,** neurologist, neuroscientist; b. Newark, Aug. 17, 1945; s. Morris and Beatrice (Levitch) Waxman; m. Merle Applebaum, June 25, 1968; children: Matthew, David. AB, Harvard U., 1967, PhD, 1970, MD, 1972; MA (hon.), Yale U., 1986. Rsch. fellow in neurosci. Albert Einstein Coll. Medicine, Bronx, NY, 1970—72; clin. fellow Boston City Hosp., 1972—75; asst. prof. neurology Med. Sch. Harvard U., Boston, 1975—77, assoc. prof., 1977—78; prof. Stanford U., 1978—86, vice chmn. dept. neurology, 1981—86, neuroscis. program, 1981—86; chief neurology unit Palo Alto VA Hosp., Calif., 1978—86; chmn. dept. neurology Yale U., New Haven, 1986—, Bridget Marie Flaherty prof. neurology, neurobiology and pharmacology, 1986, 2005—; chief neurology Yale-New Haven Hosp., 1986; dir., Ctr. for Neuroscience and Regeneration Rsch. Yale U. Med. Sch. Vis. asst. prof. biology MIT, Cambridge, 1975—77, vis. assoc. prof., 1977—78; vis. prof. U. Coll. London, 1998—, Inst. Neurology, Queen Square, England, 1998—; vice chmn. dept. neurology Stanford U., 1981—86, chmn. neuroscis. program, 1982—86; mem. adv. bd. Regeneration Programs VA, Washington, 1982—86; mem. sci. adv. com. Nat. Spinal Cord Injury Assn., 1982—87, Paralyzed Vets. Am., 1981—91; dir. Ctr. Rsch. Neurol. Disease VA Med. Ctr., West Haven, Conn., 1986—; mem. corp. Marine Biol. Labs., Woods Hole, Mass., 1988; mem. sci. adv. coun. Am. Paralysis Assn., 1988—92; mem. bd. sci. counselors NINDB, 1990—92; mem. bd. neurosci. and behavior Inst. Medicine, 1990; Geschwind vis. prof. Harvard U., 1996; dir. PVA/EPVA Neurosci. Rsch. Ctr. VA Hosp., West Haven, 1986—; numerous vis. lectureships. Author: Spinal Cord Compression, 1990, Correlative Neuroanatomy, 1995, 2d edit., 2000, The Axon, 1995, Diseases of the Spinal Cord, 2000, Form and Function in the Brain and Spinal Cord, 2001; editor: Physiology and Pathobiology of Axons, 1978; editor-in-chief: The Neuroscientist; editor-in-chief Neurosci. Letters; editor: Jour. Physiology; assoc. editor: Muscle and Nerve, Jour. Neurol. Scis., mem. editl. bd.: Brain, Ann. Neurology, Trends in Molecular Medicine, Brain Rsch., Internat. Rev. Neurobiology, Jour. Neurol. Rehab., Devel. Neurosci., Jour. Neurotrauma, Neurobiology of Disease, Cerebrovascular Disease, Synapse, Restorative Neurology and Neurosci.; editor: Jour. of Physiology. Named Nat. Multiple Sclerosis Soc. established investigator, 1987; recipient Trygve Tuve Meml. award, NIH, 1973, Rsch. Career Devel. award, 1975, Disting. Alumnus award, Albert Einstein Coll. Medicine, 1990; rsch. fellow, Univ. Coll., London, 1969. Fellow: NAS, Am. Acad. Neurology (Wartenberg award 1999, Dystel prize 2003), Am. Heart Assn. (stroke coun.), Inst. Medicine, Royal Soc. Medicine (Gt. Britain); mem.: Nat. Multiple Sclerosis Soc. (Reingold award 2005), Am. Univ. Profs. Neurology, Assn. Rsch. in Nervous and Mental Diseases (trustee, pres. 1992), World Fedn. Neurology, Am. Neurol. Assn. (councillor 1980), Soc. Neurosci., Internat. Brain Rsch. Orgn. (U.S. nat. sec.), Dana Alliance for Brain Initiatives, Am. Soc. Cell Biology. Office: Yale U Sch Medicine 33 Cedar St New Haven CT 06519-2314 Business E-Mail: stephen.waxman@yale.edu.

**WAXMAN, WENDY,** set designer; b. Hartford, Conn. BA, Case Western Reserve U. Prop stylist, prodr. commercials; design dir. Food Network, 1994—. Design dir. 30 Min. Meals, Good Food Fast, Essence of Emeril, Emeril Live, Sara's Secrets, Passion for Dessert with Jacques Torres, Molto Mario, How to Boil Water, Sweet Dreams. Office: TV Food Network GP 1180 Ave of Americas 11th Fl New York NY 10036*

**WAXSE, DAVID JOHN,** judge; b. Oswego, Kans., June 29, 1945; s. I. Joseph and Mary (Poole) W.; m. Linda Schilling (div.); children: Rachel, Ryan, Rebecca; m. Judy Pfannenstiel, May 29, 1982; 1 child, Elayna. BA, U. Kans., 1967; teaching cert., Columbia U., 1968, JD, 1971. Bar: Kans 1971, U.S. Ct. Appeals (10th cir.) 1971, U.S. Supreme Ct. 1975, U.S. Ct. Appeals (8th Cir.) 1998. Dean of students Intermediate Sch. 88, N.Y.C., 1968-70; legal edn. tchr. Peter Cooper Sch., N.Y.C., 1970-71; assoc. Payne & Jones, Olathe, Kans., 1971-74, ptnr., 1974-84; of counsel Shook, Hardy & Bacon, Overland Park, Kans., 1984-86, ptnr., 1986-95; shareholder Shook, Hardy & Bacon

---

P.C., Overland Park, 1993-95; ptnr. Shook, Hardy & Bacon L.L.P., Overland Park, Kans., 1995-99; shareholder Shook, Hardy & Bacon P.C., Overland Park, 1993-95, v.p., asst. gen. counsel, 1995-99; U.S. magistrate judge Kansas City, 1999—. Mcpl. judge City of Shawnee, Kans., 1974-80; atty. City of DeSoto, Kans., 1972-79; adj. prof. U. Kans. Sch. Law, Lawrence, 1981-82; mem. juv. code adv. com. Kans. Jud. Coun., 1979-83, guardianship adv. com., 1982-83, atty. fees adv. com., 1986-87; mem. Civil Justice Reform Act Adv. Com., U.S. Dist. Ct. for Dist. Kans., 1991-95; mem. Kans. Commn. on Jud. Qualifications, 1992-99, vice-chmn. 1994-97, chair, 1997-99; v.p. Kans. Legal Svcs., Inc., 1980-82, pres., 1985-87; bd. advisors Kans. Coll. Advocacy, 1979-80; bd. trustees, Lawyer's Com. Civil Rights Under Law, 1997-99. Author: (with others) Kansas Employment Law, 1985, Litigating Employment Law Cases, 1987, Kansas Employment Law Handbook, 1991, supplements, 1992, 95, Kansas Annual Survey, 1990-2000; contbr. articles to profl. jours. Mem. Kan. Gov.'s Adv. Com. on Criminal Justice, 1974-77; mem. Kans. Justice Commn., 1997-99; gen. counsel Western Mo. Dist. ACLU, 1976-78, 86-97, v.p., 1983-86, nat. bd. dirs., 1979-86, 91-99, chmn. children's rights com., 1980-86; mem. AIDS Pol. Network, 1987-99, med. treatment issues com., 1991-96, constn. com., 1991-99; mem. med./tech. com. AIDS Coun. Greater Kans. City, 1986-98, ethics com. consortium Midwest Bioethics Ctr., 1990-2002; bd. dirs. Parents Anonymous Kans., 1978-83, pres., 1979; bd. dirs., mem. fin. com. Kans. Com. for Prevention Child Abuse, 1980-83. Fellow Am. Bar Found.; Kans. Bar Found.; mem. ABA (chmn. children's rights com. and family law sects. 1985-86, mem. ho. of dels. 2000—, professionalism com. 2000-05, bd. of editors The Profl. Lawyer, 2000-05), Am. Judicature Soc. (bd. dirs. 1997-2003, adv. com. for ctr. for judicial conduct 1997—), Kans. Bar Assn. (chmn. legal aid com. 1978-83, bd. govs. 1988—, v.p. 1996-97, pres.-elect 1997-98, pres. 1998-99, mem. ABA ho. dels. 2000—, Pres.' Outstanding Svc. award 1982), Kans. City Met. Bar Assn., Johnson County Bar Assn. (chmn. legal aid com. 1975-82, 92-96), Earl E. O'Connor Am. Inn of Ct. (counselor, pres.-elect 2002, pres. 2003). Office: U S Courthouse 500 State Ave Rm 219 Kansas City KS 66101-2400 E-mail: judge_waxse@ksd.uscourts.gov.

**WAY, BARBARA HAIGHT,** retired dermatologist; b. Franklin, NJ, Dec. 27, 1941; d. Charles Padley and Alice Barbara (Haight) Shoemaker; m. Anthony Biden Way; children: Matthew Shoemaker Way, Sarah Shoemaker Way. AB in Music cum laude, Bryn Mawr Coll., 1962, postgrad., 1963-64; MD, U. Pa., 1968. Diplomate Am. Bd. Dermatology. Systems engr. IBM, Balt., 1962—63; mem. dean's staff Bryn Mawr (Pa.) Coll., 1963—64; med. intern U. Wis. Hosps., Madison, 1968—69, resident in dermatology, 1969—72; physician emergency rm. St. Francis Hosp., La Crosse, Wis., 1969—72, founder dept. dermatology, 1972; asst. prof. dept. dermatology Tex. Tech U. Sch. Medicine, Lubbock, 1972—73, from asst. clin. to assoc. clin. prof., 1973—74, asst. prof., assoc. chair, 1974—76, assoc. prof., chair, 1976—81, assoc. clin. prof., 1981—92; clin. prof. Tex. Tech. U. Health Scis. Ctr., Lubbock, 1995—2005, founder, dir. dermatology residency tng. program, 1978—81, pvt. practice, 1973—74, 1981—2006; acting dir. Lubbock City Health Dept., 1982—83; ret., 2006. Courtesy staff Covenant Hosp., Lubbock, subsect. chief, 1992, 94; courtesy staff Covenant Lakeside Hosp., Lubbock, mem. credentials com., 1990, 92, 94, 95, founding dir. phototherapy unit, 1990-91, 93, mem. exec. com., 1991, 93, 98, chief dermatology sect., 1991, 93, 98. Alumna admissions rep. Bryn Mawr Coll., 1972-75, 87-96; mem. selection com. outstanding physician Lubbock chpt. Am. Cancer Soc., 1991-94, chmn., 1991; bd. dirs. Tex. Tech. U. Med. Found., 1987-89, Double T. Connection, 1988-90. Fellow Am. Acad. Dermatology (reviewer jour.); mem. Tex. Dermatol. Soc. (chmn. roster com. 1980), Tex. Med. Assn. (mem. sexually transmitted diseases com. 1986-90, mem. coun. pub. health 1990-92, vice councillor dist. III 1992-98, councillor dist. III 1998-2000, chmn. reference com. fin. and orgnl. affairs ann. session 1992), Lubbock County-Garza County Med. Soc. (mem. various coms. 1980-2000, chmn. sch. and pub. health com. 1983, mem. bd. censors 1983-85, chair 1985, sec. 1986, v.p. 1987, liaison with Tex. Tech. U. Health Scis. Ctr. com. 1988-91, co-chmn. pub. rels. com. 1988-89, alt. Tex. Med. Assn. del. 1988-89, del. 1990-95, 98-2000, pres.-elect 1989, pres. 1990, chmn. ad hoc bylaws com. 1991-94, chmn. Hippocratic award 1991), Women's Dermatologic Soc. (founding sec.). Personal E-mail: anthony.way@ttuhsc.edu.

**WAY, DANNY,** professional skateboarder; b. Portland, Ore., Apr. 15, 1974; Skateboarder H-Street, 1988—90, Blind, 1990—91; founder, skateboarder Plan B, 1991—. Named Skater of Yr., 1991, 2004. Achievements include being the first person to build and use a skateboarding megaramp, 2003; setting a distance record of 75 feet, 2004; jumping over the Great Wall of China using a megaramp, 2005. Office: c/o Plan B 1410 Vantage Ct Vista CA 92081*

**WAY, E(DWARD) LEONG,** pharmacologist, toxicologist, educator; b. Watsonville, Calif., July 10, 1916; s. Leong Man and Lai Har (Shew) Way; m. Madeline Lu, Aug. 11, 1944; children: Eric, Linette. BS, U. Calif., Berkeley, 1938, MS, 1940; PhD, U. Calif., San Francisco, 1942. Pharm. chemist Merck & Co., Rahway, NJ, 1942; instr. pharmacology George Washington U., 1943-46, asst. prof., 1946-48; asst. prof. pharmacology U. Calif., San Francisco, 1949-52, assoc. prof., 1952-57, prof., 1957-87, prof. emeritus, 1987—, chmn. dept. pharmacology, 1973-78. USPHS spl. rsch. fellow U. Berne, Switzerland, 1955-56, China Med. Bd.; rsch. fellow, vis. prof. U. Hong Kong, 1962-63; Sterling Sullivan disting. vis. prof. Martin Luther King U., 1982; hon. prof. pharmacology and neurosci. Guangzhou Med. Coll., 1987; mem. adv. com. Pharm. Rsch. Mfrs. Assn. Found., 1968-98; mem. coun. Am. Bur. for Med. Advancement in China, 1982; bd. dirs. Li Found., 1970—, pres., 1985-98, bd. dirs. Haight Ashbury Free Clinics, 1986-93; Tsumura prof. neuropsychopharmacology med. sch. Gunma U., Maebashi, Japan, 1989-90; sr. staff fellow Nat. Inst. on Drug Abuse, 1990-91; rschr. on drug metabolism, analgetics, devel. pharmacology, drug tolerance, drug dependence and Chinese materia medica. Editor: New Concepts in Pain, 1967, (with others) Fundamentals of Drug Metabolism and Drug Disposition, 1971, Endogenous and Exogenous Opiate Agonists and Antagonists, 1979; mem. editl. bd. Clin. Pharmacology, Therapeutics, 1975-87, Drug, Alcohol Dependence, 1976-87, Progress in Neuro-Psychopharmacology, 1977-91, Research Communications in Chem. Pathology and Pharmacology, 1978-91, Alcohol and Drug Dependence, 1986-91, Asian Pacific Jour. Pharm., 1985—, Jour. Chinese Medicine, 1993—; contbr. numerous articles and revs. to profl. publs. Recipient Faculty Rsch. Lect. award, U. Calif., San Francisco, 1974, San Francisco Chinese Hosp. award, 1976, Cultural citation and Gold medal, Ministry of Edn., Republic of China, 1978, Nathan B. Eddy award, Coll. on Problems in Drug Dependence, 1979, Mentorship award, 2004, Chancellor's award for pub. svc., U. Calif., 1986, Disting. Alumnus award, U. Calif., San Francisco, 1990, Asian Pacific Am. Systemwide Alliance award, 1993, Lifetime Achievement award, Chinese Hist. Soc., 2001. Fellow Am. Coll. Neuropsychopharmacology (life, emeritus), Am. Coll. Clin. Pharmacology (hon.), Coll. on Problems of Drug Dependence (exec. com. 1978-92, chmn. bd. dirs. 1978-82, Nathan B. Eddy award 1979, Mentorship award 2004); mem. AAAS, Am. Soc. Pharmacology, Exptl. Therapeutics (bd. editors 1957-65, pres. 1976-77, Torald Sollman award 1992), Fedn. Am. Socs. Exptl. Biology (exec. bd. 1975-79, pres. 1977-78), Am. Pharm. Assn. (life, Rsch. Achievement award 1962), AMA, Soc. Aid and Rehab. Drug Addicts (Hong Kong, life), Western Pharmacology Soc. (pres. 1963-64), Japanese Pharm. Soc. (hon.), Coun. Sci. Soc. Pres.' (exec. com. 1979-84, treas. 1980-84), Chinese Pharmacology Soc. (hon.), Academia Sinica (academician). Office: U Calif Dept Cellular and Molecular Pharmacology 1210 S San Francisco CA 94143-0001 Office Phone: 415-476-2722.

**WAY, HELEN SUE,** science educator; d. Joseph O. and Helen P. Fair; m. Gary H. Way; children: Timothy D., Christopher S. BS in Geology, Okla. State U., Stillwater, 1968, MS in Geology, 1983; postgrad., Phillips Theol. Sem., Tulsa, Okla., 2007—. Tchr. Stillwater H.S., Okla., 1968—72; geol. tech. various cos., 1972—95; adj. instr. U. St. Gregory's U., Shaawnee, 1998—. Adj. instr. Rose State Coll., Mid-West City, Okla., 1995—2000. Author: Transitional Science. Keader Boy Scouts Am., Shawnee. Lutheran. Office: St Gregory U 1900 W MacArthur Shawnee OK 74804

---

**WAY, JACOB EDSON, III,** museum director; b. Chgo., May 18, 1947; s. Jacob Edson Jr. and Amelia (Evans) W.; m. Jean Ellwood Chappell, Sept. 6, 1969; children: Sarah Chappell Quiroga, Rebecca Stoddard, Jacob Edson IV. BA, Beloit Coll., 1968; MA, U. Toronto, 1971, PhD, 1978; postgrad., Episcopal Theol. Sem. S.W., 2005—. From instr. to assoc. prof. Beloit (Wis.) Coll., 1972—85; dir. Logan Mus. Anthropology, Beloit, 1980-85, Wheelwright Mus. Am. Indian, Santa Fe, 1985-89; interim dir. N.Mex. Mus. Natural History, Albuquerque, 1990-91; exec. dir. Space Ctr. Internat. Space Hall of Fame, Alamogorgo, N.Mex., 1991-94; dir. N.Mex. Farm and Ranch Heritage Mus., 1994-99; cultural affairs officer State of N.Mex., Santa Fe, 1997—2003; realtor Margo Cutler, Ltd., Santa Fe, 2003—05. Evaluator Nat. Park Service, Denver, 1986. Contbr. articles to profl. jours. Mem. Nuke Watch, Beloit, 1983-84; cultural affairs officer State of N.Mex., 1997-2003. Research grants Wis. Humanities Com., 1984, NSF, 1981; grantee Cullister Found., 1978-84; fellow U. Toronto, 1971. Mem. Am. Assn. Mus., Am. Assn. Phys. Anthropology, Can. Assn. for Phys. Anthropology, N.Mex. Assn. Mus. (pres. 1994-96), Soc. Am. Archaeology, Wis. Fedn. Mus. (adv. bd. 1982-85). Avocations: camping, skiing, fishing, reading, horseback riding. Personal E-mail: jeway@earthlink.net.

**WAY, STEPHEN L.,** insurance company executive; Ins. broker Willis Faber & Dumas, London, 1964—68, Stewart Smith Inc., London, 1968—69, Bradstock Blunt & Crawley, London, 1969—70, Stewart Smith Inc., NYC, 1970—74; founder, chmn. HCC Holdings Inc., Houston, 1974—, pres., 1974—96, 2003—. Bd. dir. Del Monte Fresh Produce. Office: HCC Holdings Inc 13403 Northwest Freeway Houston TX 77040*

**WAY, THOMAS PAUL,** computer scientist, educator, magician; b. Bethesda, La., Sept. 21, 1962; s. Stanley Howard and Laura Pelland Way; m. Laura Yule Kerst, Nov. 5, 1991; children: Emma Russell Kerst, Amelia Brandford Kerst, Edward Swanson Kerst. BA in Film and TV, U. Md., College Park, 1984; MS in Computer Sci., U. Del., Newark, 1997, PhD in Computer Sci., 2002. With Villanova (Pa.) U. Software cons.; sec. AgoraNet, Inc., Wilmington, Del. Magician Magic Tom. Unitarian Universalist. Achievements include research in Nanocompilers. Avocations: running, comedy writing. Office: Villanova U 800 Lancaster Ave Villanova PA 19085 Office Phone: 610-519-5033. Business E-Mail: thomas.way@villanova.edu.

**WAYANS, DAMON,** actor; b. NYC, Sept. 4, 1960; s. Howell and Elvira Wayans; m. Lisa Thorner, Apr. 24, 1984 (div. May 21, 2000); children: Damon Jr., Michael, Cara Mia, Kyla. Actor: (TV appearances) Saturday Night Live, 1985—86, Triple Cross, 1985, Take No Prisoners: Robert Townsend and His Partners in Crime, 1988, The Mutiny Has Just Begun: Robert Townsend and His Partners in Crime, III, 1989: (TV series) One Night Stand, 1989, In Living Color, 1990—92 (Emmy Outstanding writing in variety program, 1990, 1991, Outstanding individual in variety program, 1991), Damon (also exec. prodr.), 1998, My Wife and Kids (also exec prodr., writer), 2001—05; (films) Beverly Hills Cop, 1984, Hollywood Shuffle, 1987, Roxanne, 1987, Colors, 1988, I'm Gonna Git You Sucka, 1988, Punchline, 1988, Earth Girls Are Easy, 1989, Look Who's Talking Too (voice), 1990, The Last Boy Scout, 1991, Mo' Money (also prodr., writer), 1992, Last Action Hero, 1993, Blankman (also exec. prodr., writer), 1994, Major Payne (also exec. prodr., writer), 1995, Celtic Pride, 1996, Great White Hype, 1996, Bulletproof, 1996, The Great White Hype, 1996, Goosed, 1999, Harlem Aria (also prodr.), 1999, Bamboozled, 2000, Marci X, 2003, Behind the Smile, 2004; host: (TV series) Premium Blend, 2005—06.*

**WAYANS, KEENEN IVORY,** actor, producer; b. NYC, June 8, 1958; s. Howell and Elvira Wayans; m. Daphne Polk, June 16, 2001; 5 children: Jolie Ivory Imani, Keenen Ivory Jr., Nala, Bella, Daphne Ivory. Student Tuskegee Inst., Ala. Actor: (films) Star 80, 1983, The Glimmer Man, 1996, (TV films) For Love and Honor, 1983, (TV series) For Love and Honor, 1983; actor, prodr. (films) Don't Be a Menace to South Central While Drinking Your Juice in the Hood, 1996; actor, writer: (films) Hollywood Shuffle, 1987; actor, dir., prodr.: (films) Scary Movie, 2000, Little Man, 2006; actor, dir., writer: (films) I'm Gonna Git You Sucka, 1988, A Low Down Dirty Shame, 1994; actor, exec. prodr., writer: (films) Most Wanted, 1997; dir.: (films) Scary Movie 2, 2001; dir., writer, creator: (TV series) In Living Color, 1990-94 (Emmy award for outstanding variety, music or comedy series, 1990); dir., prodr., writer: (films) White Chicks, 2004; exec. prodr., host: (TV series) The Keenen Ivory Wayans Show, 1997-98; prodr., writer (TV films) Hammer, Slammer, & Slade, 1990, (comedy sketch) Eddie Murphy Raw, 1987; writer: (films) The Five Heartbeats, 1991.*

**WAYANS, MARLON,** actor, film producer, writer; b. NYC, July 23, 1972; s. Howell and Elvira Wayans; children: Amai Zachary, Shawn Howell. Grad.: Howard U. Actor: (films) I'm Gonna Git You Sucka, 1988, Mo' Money, 1992, Above the Rim, 1994, The Sixth Man, 1997, Senseless, 1998, Requiem for a Dream, 2000, (voice) The Tangerine Bear, 2000, Dungeons & Dragons, 2000, The Ladykillers, 2004; (TV series) In Living Color, 1990—94, (voice) Waynehead, 1996—97, (prodr., writer): (films) Don't Be a Menace to South Central While Drinking Your Juice in the Hood, 1996, Scary Movie 2, 2001, White Chicks, 2004, Little Man, 2006, (dir., prodr., writer): (TV series) The Wayans Brothers, 1995—99; writer (films) Scary Movie, 2000, Scary Movie 3, 2003, Scary Movie 4, 2006. Office: William Morris Agy One William Morris Place Beverly Hills CA 90212*

**WAYANS, SHAWN,** actor, film producer, writer; b. NYC, Jan. 19, 1971; s. Howell and Elvira Wayans. Actor: (films) I'm Gonna Git You Sucka, 1988, New Blood, 1999; (TV series) In Living Color, 1990—94, (voice) Waynehead, 1996—97, (dir., prodr., writer) The Wayans Brothers, 1995—99, (prodr., writer): (films) Don't Be a Menace to South Central While Drinking Your Juice in the Hood, 1996, Scary Movie, 2000, White Chicks, 2004, Little Man, 2006, (co-exec. prodr., writer) Scary Movie 2, 2001; writer (films) Scary Movie 3, 2003, Scary Movie 4, 2006. Office: William Morris Agy One William Morris Pl Beverly Hills CA 90212*

**WAYBURN, EDGAR,** internist, environmentalist; b. Macon, Ga., Sept. 17, 1906; s. Emanuel and Marian (Voorsanger) W.; m. Cornelia Elliott, Sept. 12, 1947; children: Cynthia, William, Diana, Laurie. AB magna cum laude, U. Ga., 1926; MD cum laude, Harvard U., 1930. Hosp. tng. Columbia-Presbyn. Hosp., N.Y.C., 1931-33; assoc. clin. prof. Stanford (Calif.) U., 1933-65, U. Calif., San Francisco, 1960-76; practice medicine specializing in internal medicine San Francisco, 1933-1985; mem. staff Pacific Presbyn. Med. Ctr., San Francisco, 1959-86, chief endocrine clinic, 1959-72, vice chief staff, 1961-63, hon. staff, 1986—. Editor: Man Medicine and Ecology, 1970, Your Land and Mine, 2004; contbr. articles to profl. and environ. jours. Mem. Sec. of Interior's Adv. Bd. on Nat. Park System, 1979-83, mem. world commn. on protected areas Internat. Union for Conservation Nature and Natural Resources; leader nat. campaigns Alaska Nat. Interest Lands Conservation Act; trustee Pacific Presbyn. Med. Ctr., 1978-86; bd. dirs. Garden Sullivan Hosp., 1965-80; chmn. People For a Golden Gate Nat. Recreation Area, 1971-2005; mem. citizens' adv. commn. Golden Gate Nat. Recreation Area, San Francisco, 1974-2003, leader nat. campaigns, 1955-90; prin. citizen advocate Redwood Nat. Park, 1968, 78; dir. The Antarctica Project, 1993-2003; mem. adv. bd. Pacific Forest Trust; hon. chmn. Tuolomne River Preservation Trust, 1983-1985; prin. adv. Enlargement of Mt. Tamalpais State Pk.; leader campaign to establish Golden Gate Nat. Recreation Area, 1972. Maj. USAF, 1942-46. Recipient Douglas award Nat. Pks. and Conservation Assn., 1987, Leopold award Calif. Nature Conservancy, 1988, Fred Packard award Internat. Union Conservation Nature, 1994, Laureate of Global 500 Roll of Honour award U.N. Environment Programme, 1994, 1st Conservation award Ecotrust, 1994, Albert Schweitzer prize, 1995, Presdl. Medal of Freedom, 1999. Fellow ACP (laureate); mem. AMA, Am. Soc. Internal Medicine, Calif. Med. Assn. (del. 1958-83, Recognition award 1986, Leadership and Loyalty awards 1986), San Francisco Med. Soc. (pres. 1965, Resolution of Congratulations 1986), Sierra Club (pres. 1961-64, 67-69, John Muir award 1972, hon. pres. 1993—), Sierra Club Found. (dir. 1960-87, pres. 1971-78, hon. pres. 1998—), Fedn. Western Outdoor Clubs (pres. 1953-55). Avocations: exploration, hiking.

**WAYLAND-SMITH, ROBERT DEAN,** retired banker; b. Oneida, NY, July 2, 1943; s. Robert and Prudence Cragin W.-S.; m. Kathleen Anne Schultz, Aug. 24, 1968 (dec. Oct. 1999), m. Linda M. Amendola, July 21, 2002; children: Kristin, Debra. BA in Econs., U. Rochester, 1965. Mgr. equipment svc. Strong Meml. Hosp., Rochester, NY, 1965-67; mgmt. trainee Chase Lincoln First Bank, N.A., Rochester, 1967-68; mgr. mcpl. securities, 1968-81, mgr. portfolio mgmt. depart., 1981-84, mgr. fin. and investment svc. dept., 1984-87, mgr. trust and fin. svc. dept., 1987-88; pres. and CEO Rochester region Chase Manhattan Bank, N.A., 1988-93, upstate trust and investment divsn. exec., 1993-98; ret., 1998. Mem. adv. bd. Roberts Wesleyan Coll., Rochester, 1989-99; mem. adv. coun. J.W. Jones Sch. Bus. SUNY, Geneseo, 1990-99. Trustee Ctr. for Govtl. Rsch., 1985—; dir. Greater Rochester Visitors Assn., 1990-93, Rochester Downtown Devel. Corp., 1991-93, United Neighborhood Ctrs., Greater Rochester Found., 1992-2002; mem. fin. execs. adv. bd. Coll. Bus. Rochester Inst. Tech., 1994-97; mem. United Way Greater Rochester Corp., 1998-2003; bd. dirs. Oneida Cmty. Mansion House, 1988—; bd. dir. Via Health, 1999-2001; bd. govs. The Genesee Hosp., 1992-2001; mem. bd. trustees Rochester Inst. Tech., 2003—; chair coll. coun. SUNY Coll. Geneseo, 1999—; bd. dirs. Rochester Enterprise, 2004—. Fellow: Assn. for Investment Mgmt. and Rsch.; mem.: Greater Rochester Met. C. of C. (bd. dirs. 1992—95), Greater Rochester Ind. Practice Assn. (bd. dirs. 2000—), Rochester Soc. Security Analysts, Oak Hill Country Club, Genesee Valley Club (treas. 2002—05, pres. 2005). Avocations: golf, gardening, reading. Office: JP Morgan Chase One Chase Sq Rochester NY 14643 Office Phone: 585-258-5517. Business E-Mail: robert.d.wayland-smith@chase.com.

**WAYLONIS, JEAN LYNNETTE,** elementary school educator; b. Brookville, Pa., Mar. 9, 1953; d. Leslie Edwin Gray and Lillian Wanita Bryant; m. Anthony John Waylonis, June 16, 1973; children: Anthony James, Ellen Claire. BS in child devel. and early childhood edn., Pa. State U., 1971—75; MA in early childhood spl. edn., George Wash. U., 1997—99. Postgraduate Professional License Va. Dept. of Edn., 2000. Pre-kindergarten tchr. Norfolk Pub. Schools, Norfolk, Va., 1976—78; dir. Subic Bay Naval Base Nursery Sch. Assn., Philippines, 1979—81; family adv. Family Advocacy Ctr., Subic Bay Naval Base, Philippines, 1981—82; multi-age inclusion tchr. FCPS - Belvedere Elem., Falls Church, Va., 1989—. Mentor Fairfax County Pub. Schools, Falls Ch., Va., 1992—99; trainer Project Realign, Washington, 1995—98; cons./trainer/presenter Collaborative Inclusion Project Team, Washington, 1992—99; presenter Fairfax County Pub. Schools, Fairfax, Va., 1992—. Composer: (song) Five Little Bunnies; contbr. article George Mason U. TAC Newsletter. Presenter Child Day Care Coun., Richmond, Va., 1997. Recipient Outstanding Leader award, Girl Scout Coun. Nation's Capital, 1996, Exceptional Inclusion Tchr., Va. Divsn. of Early Childhood, 1995; grant, Coun. for Exceptional Children, 1995. Mem.: AAUW (assoc.), NEA (assoc.), Nat. Assn. for Educators of Young Children (assoc.). Catholic. Avocations: sewing, travel. Home: 7201 Galgate Dr Springfield VA 22153 Office: FCPS - Belvedere Elementary School 6540 Columbia Pike Falls Church VA 22041 Personal E-mail: waylonis@erols.com. E-mail: jean.waylonis@fcps.edu.

**WAYMAN, JOSEPH MCKELDEN,** editor, researcher; b. Strasburg, Va., Mar. 22, 1927; s. Joseph McKelden Wayman and Cathryn Bernice Loomis. Def. contract classes, UCLA, 1964—67; BS, Va. Tech., 1952. Gen. duty assignments Am. Safety Razor Yorkville Paper Co., N.Y.C., 1952—54; statis. compiler U.S. Census Bur., Washington, 1954—56; mail distbn. U.S. Post Office, U.S. Gen. Svcs. Adminstrn., San Francisco, 1956—58; item mgr. USAF, San Bernardino, Calif., 1958—62, price analyst L.A., 1962—84; editor Grandstand Baseball Ann., Downey, Calif., 1985—. Contbr. chapters to books. With USAF, 1945—47. Mem.: Baseball Reliquary, Inc., Pacific Coast League Hist. Soc., Soc. for Am. Baseball Rsch. (pub. pitching W-L records Nat. League, 1890-1899 1996). Democrat. Methodist. Avocations: stamp collecting/philately, walking, baseball. Office: Grandstand Baseball Ann PO Box 4203 Downey CA 90241 Office Phone: 562-806-2734.

**WAYMAN, ROBERT PAUL,** computer company executive; b. Chgo., July 5, 1945; s. Lowell Roger and Dorothy Emma (Francke) Wayman; m. Susan O. Humphrey; children: Jennifer, Allison, Grant, Kirsten, Clayton. BS in Sci. Engring., Northwestern U., Evanston, Ill., 1967, MBA, 1969. Cost acct., Instrument Divsn. Hewlett-Packard Co., Loveland, Colo., 1969—71, mgr. cost accounts, 1971—73, divsn. contr. Palo Alto, Calif., 1973—76, instrument grp. contr., 1976—83, dep. corp. contr., 1981—84, corp. contr., 1984, CFO, 1984—, v.p., 1987—88, sr. v.p., 1987—92, exec. v.p., 1992—, interim CEO, 2005. Bd. dirs. Hewlett-Packard Co., 1993—2002, 2005—, CNF, Inc., Sybase, Inc.; mem. Policy Coun. of the Tax Found. Dir. Cultural Initiatives of Silicon Valley; mem. adv. bd. Northwestern U. Kellogg Sch. Mgmt. Mem. Fin. Execs. Inst., Coun. Fin. Execs. of the Conf. Bd., Private Sector Coun. Office: Hewlett-Packard Co 3000 Hanover St Palo Alto CA 94304-1181*

**WAYNE, EARL ANTHONY,** ambassador, former federal agency administrator; b. 1950; married; 2 children. BA, U. Calif., Berkeley; MA, Princeton U., Stanford U.; MPA, Harvard U., 1984. Joined Fgn. Svc., 1975, various positions; spl. asst. to sec. US Dept. State, 1981—83; first sec. US Embassy, Paris, 1984—87; nat. security corr. Christian Sci. Monitor, 1987—89; dir. regional affairs U.S. Amb. at Large for Counter-Terrorism, 1989—93; dir. Western European affairs Nat. Security Coun., 1991—93; dep. chief mission U.S. Mission to European Union, 1993—96; dept. asst. sec. for Europe and Can. US Dept. State, Washington, 1996—97, prin. dep. asst. sec. for European affairs, 1997—2000, asst. sec. for econ. & bus. affairs, 2000—06, interim under sec. for econ. bus. and agrl. affairs, 2005, US amb. to Argentina Buenos Aires, 2006—. Recipient Presdl. Disting. Svc. award, 2001, Disting. Honor award, US Dept. State, 2005, Presdl. Meritorious Svc. award. Office: US Embassy 3130 Buenos Aires Pl Washington DC 20521

**WAYNE, JUNE CLAIRE,** artist; b. Chgo., Mar. 7, 1918; d. Albert and Dorothy Alice (Kline) LaVine. DFA (hon.), Rutgers U., 2005. Indsl. designer, N.Y.C., 1939-41; radio writer, mem. staff sta. WGN, Chgo., 1942-43; founder, 1959; since dir. Tamarind Lithography Workshop, Inc. (funded by Ford Found.), Los Angeles; Tamarind Inst., U. N.Mex., 1970—. Mem. vis. com. Sch. Visual and Environ. Studies, Harvard, 1972-74, chancellors adv. com., arts mgmt. program Grad. Sch. Adminstrn., U. Calif. at Los Angeles, 1969-80, Calif. Confederation of Arts adv. bd., 1988, Calif. State U. dept. of art adv. coun., Long Beach, 1988, Rutgers U. Mason Gross Sch. Arts prof. of rsch. printmaking and paper, New Brunswick, NJ, 2002-. Contbr. articles to profl. publs.; subject TV programs.; Numerous one-woman exhbns., 1935—, latest being, Art Mus., U. N.Mex., 1968, Cin. Art Mus., 1969, Iowa Art Mus., U. Iowa, 1970, Grunwald Graphics Arts Found., U. Calif. at Los Angeles, 1971, Municipal Art Gallery, Barnsdall Park, LA, 1973, Van Doren Gallery, San Francisco, 1974, La Demeure, Paris, 1974, Musée de Brest, France, 1976, Montgomery Gallery, Pomona Colls., Calif., 1978, Ariz. State U. Galleries, 1978, ICA travelling exhbn., Rennes, 1976, Nancy, 1977, Brussels, 1978, Reims, 1978, Lyons, 1979, Neuberger Mus., Purchase, NY, 1997, Skirball Mus., Cin., 1998, LA County Mus. Art, 1998, Palm Springs Desert Mus., Calif., 1999, A.R.T. Gallery, NY, 2003, Rutgers U., Newark, 2005, The Armory Ctr. for Arts, Pasadena, Calif., 2005, Stedman Gallery, Newark, 2005, Mason Gross Galleries, New Brunswick, NJ, 2006, Birmingham Mus. and Art Gallery, UK, 2006, Tama Art U. Mus., Tokyo, 2006; rep. permanent collections, Library of Congress, The British Mus., London, Mus. Modern Art, NYC, Art Inst. Chgo., Houghton Library at Harvard, Smithsonian Instn., Rosenwald Collection, The Victoria and Albert Mus., London, Nat. Gallery Art, NY Pub. Library, Cin. Art Mus., Pasadena (Calif.) Mus. Art, Phila. Mus. Art, Phila. Print Club, Birmingham Mus. and Art Gallery, Walker Art Center, Mpls., Zimmerli Art Mus., New Brunswick. Bd. dirs. Grunwald Center Graphic Arts, 1965-80. Recipient numerous prizes, 1950—, latest being Prix de la Biennal Internat. de L'Estampe d'Epinal, France, 1971; Purchase Prize Biennal d'Epinal, 1973; Golden Eagle Cine award and Acad. award nomination for film Four Stones for Kanemitsu, 1974; Silver Life Achievement award YWCA, 1983; Communicator award Women in Media, 1983; Woman of the Year, Palm Springs Desert Mus., 1999; Zimmerli award Women in Arts Com., Coll. Arts Assn., 2003; Mason Gross Sch. Disting. Svc. Arts award, 2004. Mem. Writers Guild Am., Women in Film, AFTRA, Women's Caucus for Art, Soc. Am. Graphic Artists, Soc. Washington Printmakers, LA Printmakers Soc., The Trusteeship, Internat. Women's Forum. Address: 1108 Tamarind Ave Los Angeles CA 90038-1906

**WAYNE, KYRA PETROVSKAYA,** writer; b. Crimea, USSR, Dec. 31, 1918; arrived in U.S., 1948, naturalized, 1951; d. Prince Vasily Sergeyevich and Baroness Zinaida Fedorovna (Fon-Haffenberg) Obbolensky; m. George J. Wayne, Apr. 21, 1961; 1 child, Ronald George. BA, Leningrad Inst. Theatre Arts, 1939, MA, 1940. Actress, concert singer, Russia, 1939-46; actress, 1948-59; enrichment lectr. Royal Viking Line cruises, Alaska-Can., Greek Islands-Black Sea, Russia/Europe, 1978-79, 81-82, 83-84, 86-8, 88. Author: Kyra, 1959, Kyra's Secrets of Russian Cooking, 1960, 1993, The Quest for the Golden Fleece, 1962, Shurik, 1971, 1992, The Awakening, 1979, The Witches of Barguzin, 1975, Max, The Dog that Refused to Die, 1979 (Best Fiction award Dog Writers Assn. Am., 1980), Rekindle the Dreams, 1979, Quest for Empire, 1986, Li'l Ol' Charlie, 1989, Quest for Bigfoot, 1996, Pepper's Ordeal, 2000, The Chaperone, 2006. Founder, pres. Clean Air Program, Los Angeles County, 1971—72; mem. Seattle Art Mus.; mem. women's coun. Sta. KCET-Ednl. TV; mem. Monterey County Symphony Guild, 1989—91, Monterey Bay Aquarium, Monterey Peninsula Mus. Art, Friends of La Mirada, Fresno Art Mus., Fresno Met. Mus., Valley Children's Hosp. Served to lt. Russian Army, 1941—43. Decorated Red Star, numerous decorations USSR; recipient award, Crusade for Freedom, 1955—56, Los Angeles County, 1972, Merit award, Am. Lung Assn. Los Angeles County, 1988, award of Merit, Congress Russian Ams., 1999. Mem.: Seattle Art Mus., Idyllwild Sch. Music, Carmel Music Soc. (bd. dirs. 1992—94), Authors Guild, Soc. Children's Book Writers, PEN, Fresno Philharm., UCLA Affiliates (life), L.A. Lung Assn. (life, pres. and founder clean air program 1972—74), Art and Theatre Assn. (trustee 1987), Friends Lung Assn. (pres. 1988), UCLA Med. Faculty Wives (pres. 1970—71, dir. 1971—75), Club 25, Los Angelenos Club (life). Home: 25875 Canyon Rd NW Poulsbo WA 98370 Office Phone: 360-779-4480. Personal E-mail: kyrapwayne@aol.com. Personal philosophy: I believe in total loyalty. Loyalty to one's family and friends, to one's colleagues and to one's country. In my case - to my chosen country, the U.S.A.

**WAYNE, LESLIE,** reporter; Spl. projects reporter NY Times, bus. day reporter. Recipient Bus. Reporter of Yr. award, Knight-Bagehot, 1997. Office: NY Times 229 West 43rd St New York NY 10036 Office Phone: 212-556-7192. Office Fax: 212-556-1448.*

**WAYNE, STEPHEN J.,** government educator, writer; b. NYC, Mar. 22, 1939; s. Arthur G. and Muriel Wayne; m. Cheryl Beil, May 22, 1982; children: Jared B., Jeremy B. BA with honors, U. Rochester, 1961; MA, Columbia U., 1963, PhD, 1968. Instr. polit. sci. U.S. Naval Postgrad. Sch., 1963-65; instr. politics and govt. Ohio Wesleyan U., 1966-68; asst. prof. to prof. politics and pub. affairs The George Washington U., 1968—88; prof. govt. Georgetown U., Washington, 1989—. Presenter and lectr. in field. Author: The Legislative Presidency, 1978, The Road to the White House, 1980, 7th edit., 2004, (with George C. Edwards) Presidential Leadership: Politics and Policy Making, 1985, 7th edit., 2006 (with Cal MacKenzie, David O'Brien and Richard L. Cole) The Politics of American Government, 1995, 3d edit., 1999; editor: Investigating the American Political System: Problems, Methods, and Projects, 1974, (with George C. Edwards) Studying the Presidency, 1983, (with Clyde Wilcox) The Quest for National Office, 1992, (with Wilcox) The Election of the Century and What It Tells Us about the Future of American Politics, 2002, Is This Any Way to Run a Democratic Government?, 2004; appeared on 3 one-hour programs on presidency Every Four Years, sta. WHYY-TV, PBS, 1980; election night analyst ARD-German TV, 1992; contbr. numerous articles, chpts. and book revs. to books and profl. jours. Office: Georgetown U Dept Govt 37th And O NW Washington DC 20057-0001 Office Phone: 202-687-5908. Business E-Mail: waynes@georgetown.edu.

**WAYNICK, CATHERINE ELIZABETH MAPLES,** bishop; b. Nov. 13, 1948; d. Sevedus A. and Janet E. (Wilcox) Maples; m. Larry Wade Waynick, Nov. 28, 1968; 2 children. Student, Ctrl. Mich. U., 1966—68; BA in Religious Studies, Madonna Coll., 1981; MDiv, St. John's Provincial Sem., Plymouth, MI, 1985; DD (hon.), The Gen. Sem., NYC, 1998. Ordained deacon, 1985, priest, 1986; rector All Saints' Parish, Pontiac, Mich., 1994—97; consecrated bishop, 1997; bishop Episcopal Diocese of Indpls., 1997—. Mem. bd. Bexley Hall Sem., Rochester, NY. Office: Episcopal Diocese Indpls 1100 W 42nd St Indianapolis IN 46208 Office Phone: 317-926-5454. Office Fax: 317-926-5456.

**WAYTE, ALAN (PAUL WAYTE),** lawyer; b. Huntington Park, Calif., Dec. 30, 1936; s. Paul Henry and Helen Lucille (McCarthy) W.; m. Beverly A. Bruen, Feb. 19, 1959 (div. 1972); children: David Alan, Lawrence Andrew, Marcia Louise; m. Nancy Kelly Wayte, July 5, 1975. AB, Stanford U., 1958, JD, 1960. Bar: Calif. 1961, U.S. Dist. Ct. (so. dist.) Calif. 1961, U.S. Supreme Ct. 1984. Ptnr. Adams, Duque & Hazeltine, LA, 1966-85, Dewey Ballantine, LA, 1985—2004; of counsel DLA Piper Rudnick Gray Cary LA, 2004—. Mem. L.A. County Bar Assn. (chmn. real property sect. 1981-82), Am. Coll. Real Estate Lawyers (bd. govs. 1989—, pres. 1994), Am. Coll. Mortgage Attys., Anglo-Am. Real Property Inst. (bd. govs. 1989-91), L.A. Philharm. Assn. (exec. com. bd. dirs. 1973—), Chancery Club, Calif. Club (L.A.), Valley Hunt Club (Pasadena). Office: DLA Piper Rudnick Gray Cary Suite 2300 550 S Hope St Los Angeles CA 90071 Office Phone: 213-330-7734. Office Fax: 213-330-7534. Business E-Mail: alan.wayte@dlapiper.com. E-mail: awayte@ix.netcom.com.

**WAZIRI, GHAUS GHULAM,** diplomat; b. Kabul, Afghanistan, Mar. 3, 1935; arrived in U.S., 1981; s. Abdul Wadood and Noorj-ehan Waziri; m. Anisa Barak Waziri, Nov. 25, 1963; children: Omar, Homaira, Zahra. B in Law and Polit. Sci., Kabul U., Afghanistan, 1957; grad. degree in Law and Polit. Sci., Sorbonne U., Paris, 1968—70. Afghan del. UN, NYC, 1962—65; dir. law and treaties Dept. Fgn. Ministry, 1966—67, dep. dir. econ. rels., 1970—72; 1st sec., charge d'affairs Embassy Afghanistan, Beijing, 1973—77, Dacca, Bangladesh, 1980—81; dir. Inst. Diplomacy, Ministry Fgn. Affairs, 1977—80. Author: Afghan-Soviet War I and II, 1982, Afghanistan at High Crisis, 2004, Shelter, 2004. Dept. dir. Afghanistan Resistant Groups, Peshawar, Pakistan, 1981—88; dir., polit. advisor, pres. Peshawar based Afghan Govt., 1988—91; chief cabinet, advisor Former King Afghanistan, Rome, 1992—2000. Sgt. Afghan Mil. Infantry, 1957—59. Mem.: ACLU, Carter Ctr. Peace, Health, Acad. Polit. Sci. Avocations: music, travel, literature, studying philosophy. Home: 2941 W Lowell Ave Apt 198 Tracy CA 95377 Home Fax: 209-836-8825.

**WEAGRAFF, PATRICK JAMES,** psychology professor, writer; b. Buffalo, May 27, 1940; s. Harry Edward and Donnabelle (O'Brien) W.; children from a previous marriage: Michael, Patrick Jr., Kim Marie, Susan Lynn; m. Sandra Weagraff, Sept. 19, 1993; 1 stepchild, Nicholas Turner. BS, SUNY, Buffalo, 1963; MEd, U. Md., 1965; EdD, UCLA, 1970, PhD, 1971. Cert. psychology, post secondary edn., secondary edn., ednl. adminstrn., drug and alcohol counseling. Assoc. dir. U.S. Peace Corps, Lagos, Nigeria, 1965-68; ednl. adminstr. Calif. Dept. Edn., Sacramento, 1971-75; assoc. commr. edn. Mass. Dept. Edn., Boston, 1975-76; psychologist Sierra View Mental Health, Auburn, Calif., 1978-81; chief clin. svcs. Calif. Dept. Mental Health, Sacramento, 1981-93; clin. dir. St. Joseph's Hosp., Stockton, Calif., 1993-95; prof. psychology Profl. Sch. Psychology, Sacramento, 1993-98; assoc. prof. Nat. U., Stockton, Calif., 1983-99; mng. SP Behavioral Health LLC. Author 9 books including Careers in Focus, 1993, Communications, 1993, Public Service Occupations, 1993, Construction Occupations, 1993, Decision Making, 1995, Making Decisions Work, 1997. Trustee Crossroads Inc., Sacramento, 1982-90; bd. dirs. Golden Empire Scouts, Sacramento, 1985-91; trustee Western Inst. Therapeutic Studies, 1996—. Edn. Profession Devel. Act fellow UCLA, 1970. Mem. Phi Delta Kappa, Epsilon Pi Tau. Jewish. Avocation: classic cars. Home: PO Box 25756 Miami FL 33102-5756 E-mail: p.j.weagraff@yahoo.com.

**WEAKLAND, REMBERT G.,** retired archbishop; b. Patton, Pa., Apr. 2, 1927; s. Basil and Mary (Kane) Weakland. AB, St. Vincent Coll., Latrobe, Pa., 1948, DD (hon.), 1963, LHD (hon.), 1987; MS in Piano, Juilliard Sch. Music, 1954; postgrad., Columbia U., 1954—56, PhD in Musicology, 2000; LHD (hon.), Duquesne U., 1964, Belmont Coll., 1964, Cath. U. Am., 1975, Xavier U., Cin., 1988, DePaul U., 1989, Loyola U., New Orleans, 1991, Villanova U., 1992, Dayton U., 1993, Marian Coll., Fond du Lac, Wis., 1995, St. Anselm Coll., Manchester, N.H., 1996, St. Norbert Coll., De Pere, Wis., 1996, U. San Francisco, 1997, Scholastica Coll., 1998; HHD (hon.), St. Ambrose U., Davenport, 1990, Aquinas Inst. Theology, St. Louis, 1991, St Mary's Coll., Notre Dame, Ind., 1994; LLD (hon.), Cardinal Stritch Coll., Milw., 1978, Marquette U., 1981, Loyola U., Chgo., 1986, U. Notre Dame, 1987, Mt. Mary Coll., Milw., 1989, John Carroll U., Cleve., 1992; LLD (hon.), Fairfield U., 1994; D of Sacred Music (hon.), St. Joseph's Coll., Rensselaer, Ind., 1979; DST of Sacred Music (hon.), Jesuit Sch. Theology, Berkeley, Calif., 1989; DST (hon.), St. John's U., Collegeville, Minn., 1991, Santa Clara U., 1991; DST (hon.), Yale U., 1993; DD (hon.), Lakeland Coll., Sheboygan, 1991, Ill. Benedictine Coll., Lisle, Ill., 1992, Regis Coll., Toronto, 1993, Trinity Coll., Hartford, 1996, Trinity Lutheran Sem., Columbus, Ohio, 1998; D of Ministry (hon.), Catholic Theol. Union, Chgo., 1999. Joined Benedictines Roman Cath. Ch., 1945, ordained priest 1951. Faculty music dept. St. Vincent Coll., 1957—63, chmn., 1961—63, chancellor chmn. of bd. of Coll., 1963—67; elected co-adjutor archabbot, 1963; abbot primate Benedictine Confederation, 1967—77; archbishop Archdiocese of Milw., 1997—2002, archbishop emeritus, 2002—. Mem.: Ch. Music Assn. Am. (pres. 1964—66), Am. Guild Organists. Roman Catholic. Office: PO Box 070912 Milwaukee WI 53207-0912

**WEAKLEY, CLARE GEORGE, JR.,** insurance company executive, theologian, entrepreneur; b. Dallas, Apr. 14, 1928; s. Clare George and Louise (Cunningham) Weakley; m. Jean C. Burrow, July 20, 1962; children from previous marriage: Clare George III, Carol J.(dec.), Charles E. BBA, So. Meth. U., 1948, ThM, 1967. Ordained to ministry Christian Cmty., 1977. With Employers Ins., Dallas, 1948-52; owner Weakley & Co., Dallas, 1952-2001. Founder, pres. Am. Svc. Found., Inc., 1967—, Cornerstone Ministries, 1982—, Small Bus. Assn., Inc., 1988—, Christian Cmty., 1977—, founder, leader; vis. prof. western bus. theory and Christian ethics St. Petersburg (Russia) Internat. Mgmt. Inst. (formerly Leningrad Internat. Mgmt. Inst.), 1990—. Author: In God We Trust, 1997, God 101, 1998; author, editor: The Wesley Library Series for Today's Reader, The Nature of Kingdom, 1976, The Nature of Spiritual Growth, 1977, The Nature of Revival, 1987, The Nature of Salvation, 1988, The Nature Holiness, 1988. Republican. Home: 13731 Goldmark Dr Apt 1207 Dallas TX 75240-4220 Office: Christian Cmty 13731 Goldmark Dr #1207 Dallas TX 75240 E-mail: clare@christian-community.org, weakley_co@earthlink.net.

**WEALE, MARY JO,** artist; b. Lexington, Ky., Feb. 26, 1924; d. James William Whitehouse and Mary Gladys (Eblen) Lindley; m. Donald Arthur Danford, Nov. 22, 1945 (div. Nov. 1960); children: Rebecca Jo Danford Burkhardt, James Arthur; m. William Bruce Weale, June 20, 1963 (dec. May 2003); step-children: Margot, Bruce Preston. BS, U. Ky., 1945; MS, Fla. State U., 1963, PhD, 1968. Comml. artist, Paducah, Ky., 1954-60; extension agt. U. Ky., Springfield, Ky., 1961-62; asst. to assoc. prof. Fla. State U., Tallahassee, 1965-73, prof., chmn., 1973-85, prof., 1985-90; watercolor artist J/B Assocs., Tallahassee, 1968—. Visiting grad. prof. numerous univs. and colls., 1968-88; watercolor workshops Walt Disney World, Ctr. Profl. Devel., Fla. State U., Internat. Inst. Foreign Study. Author: Rendering for Interior Designers, 1965, Watermedia: The Technical/Creative Edge, 1990; co-author: (with Weale and Croake) Environment Interiors, 1982-96; watercolor works featured in Internat. Wildlife Art News Yearbook, 1992, Florida Wildlife, 1991; contbr. articles to profl. jours; one women exhibits include Chez Pierre, 1996, FSU Pres. Command Performance, 1992, Kennedy Douglas Ctr. for Arts, 1986, Ed Ball Wabulla Springs State Park, 1987, 90, 92, Gallery of Art, Hawaii, 1992, Univ. Ctr. FSU, Fla. League of Cities, 2000, FSU Univ. Ctr., 2002. Founder 10 Artists Ltd., Tallahassee, 1987. Recipient fellowship, Fla. State U., 1962-63, Effie I. Raitt, 1963-64, Attingham Park British Nat. Trust, 1970; recipient grant Fla. State U., State of Fla., 1971, 75, 78. Mem. Am. Soc. Interior Designers (Medalist award 1986), Interior Design Educators Coun. (emeritus, placement chmn. 1971-85), Fla. Watercolor Soc. (life, signature mem., editor newsletter 1989-91, sec. 1992-94), So. Watercolor Soc. (sec. 1981-83), Ga. Watercolor Soc. (life mem.), Tallahassee Watercolor Soc. (various offices), Phi Kappa Phi, Omicron Nu, Phi Upsilon Omicron, Gallery Art, Panama City, Fla., Nuance Gallery, Tampa, Fla. Democrat. Episcopalian. Avocations: sewing, travel, music, reading, raising greenhouse orchids and plants. Home and Office: J/B Assocs 1102 Sarasota Dr Tallahassee FL 32301-5727 Office Phone: 850-877-3094. E-mail: weale1@earthlink.net.

**WEAR, JEAN ANN,** accountant; b. Wheeling, W.Va., Oct. 19, 1959; d. Robert J. and Bertha Ann (Beltz) Loth; m. Mark E. Wear, May 21, 1983; children: Sean Michael, Aaron Patrick. BSBA in Acctg., West Liberty State Coll., 1981. CPA. Staff auditor Wheeling Dollar Bank and Trust Co., 1981—84; asst. mgr. Citizens Fidelity Bank and Trust Co., Lexington, Ky., 1985; internal auditor, investment acct. Bradford Nat. Life Ins. Co., Lexington, 1985—87; v.p. fin., CFO Concordia Mut. Life Assn., Downers Grove, Ill., 1987—93; contr., sec. Zurich Life Ins. Co. Am., Schaumburg, Ill., 1993—95; mgr. sys. controls Met Life Ins. Co., Aurora, Ill., 1995—. Mem. Oswego (Ill.) Jaycees, 1990-92. Mem. AICPA, Ill. Soc. CPA, Inst. Mgmt. Accts., Inst. Internal Auditors, Am. Mgmt. Assn. Republican. Lutheran. Avocations: ice skating, music, piano, flute, reading, crafts/sewing. Office: MetLife NSC 177 S Commons Dr Aurora IL 60504-4173

**WEARLY, WILLIAM LEVI,** retired manufacturing executive; b. Warren, Ind., Dec. 5, 1915; s. Purvis Gardner and Ethel Ada (Jones) W.; m. Mary Lou Riddle, Mar. 8, 1941; children: Patricia Ann, Susan, William Levi, Elizabeth. BS, Purdue U., 1937, Dr Engring. (hon.), 1959. Student career engr. C.A. Dunham Co., Michigan City, Ind., 1936; mem. elec. design staff Joy Mfg. Co., Franklin, Pa., 1937-39, v.p., gen. sales mgr., 1952-56, exec. v.p., 1956-57, pres., dir., 1957-62; v.p., dir. Ingersoll-Rand Co., 1964-66, exec. v.p., 1966-67, chmn., chief exec. officer, 1967-80, chmn. exec. com., 1981-85. Dir. ASA Ltd., Med. Care Am.; trustee LMI; speaker engring. groups. Author tech. publs. relating to mining; patentee in field. Bd. dirs. Boys Clubs Am. Mem. NAE, IEEE, AIME, Nat. Acad. of Engring., C of C., Sky Club N.Y.C., Blind Brook Golf Club, Desert Forest Golf Club, Minikahda Club, Ariz. Club, Masons, Shriners, Eta Kappa Nu, Tau Beta Pi, Beta Theta Pi. Republican. Methodist. Mailing: PO Box 1072 Carefree AZ 85377-1072 Personal E-mail: wwearly@peoplepc.com.

**WEARN, WILSON CANNON,** retired media executive; b. Newberry, S.C., Oct. 7, 1919; s. George F. and Mary (Cannon) W.; m. Mildred Colson, Feb. 21, 1948; children: Jean Wearn Held, Joan Wearn Gilbert, Wilson Cannon Jr. B.E.E., Clemson U., 1941. Engr. Westinghouse Electric Corp., Pitts., 1941, FCC, Washington, 1946-48; assoc. cons. electronic engr. firm Weldon & Carr, Washington, 1948-50; ptnr. Vandivere, Cohen & Wearn (cons. engrs.), Washington, 1950-53; with Multimedia Broadcasting Co., Greenville, S.C., 1953-68, organizer of corp., 1953, became corp. officer, 1960, pres., 1964-77, Multimedia, Inc., Greenville, 1977-81, chief exec. officer, 1978-84, chmn. bd., 1981-89, chmn. emeritus Greenville, 1989-95. Instr. electronic engring. Clemson U., 1946. Mem. S.C. Hosp. Adv. Council, 1969-71; bd. dirs. Family and Children Service of Greenville County, 1967-69, pres., 1969; bd. dirs. Newspaper Advt. Bur., 1981-85; trustee Greenville Symphony Assn., 1960-62, 71-77, pres., 1977; trustee Greenville Hosp. System, 1964-70, chmn., 1968-70; trustee Broadcast Rating Council, 1969-73, chmn., 1971-73; trustee Clemson U. Found., 1973-79, pres., 1979; trustee Presbyn. Coll., F.W. Symmes Found. Served to capt. Signal Corps, AUS, 1941-45, PTO. Decorated Bronze Star; recipient Outstanding Alumni award Clemson U., 1972 Mem. Nat. Assn. Broadcasters (chmn. bd. 1975-77), S.C. Broadcasters Assn. (pres. 1967), Greater Greenville C. of C. (pres. 1972), Nat. Assn. Securities Dealers (bd. govs. 1985-88), Kiwanis (Greenville), Poinsett Club (Greenville), Augusta (Ga.) Nat. Golf Club. Presbyterian (elder). Personal E-mail: mcwearn@msn.com.

**WEART, SPENCER RICHARD,** historian; b. Detroit, Mar. 8, 1942; s. Spencer Augustus and Janet (Streng) W.; m. Carole Ege, June 30, 1971; children: Lara Kimi, Spencer Gen. BA, Cornell U., 1963; PhD, U. Colo., 1968. Postdoctoral fellow Calif. Inst. Tech., 1968-71, U. Calif., Berkeley, 1971-74; dir. Ctr. for History Physics, Am. Inst. Physics, College Park, Md., 1974—. Author: Scientists in Power, 1979, Nuclear Fear, 1988, Never at War, 1998, Discovery of Global Warming, 2003; contbr. articles to profl. jours. Recipient Andrew Gemant award Am. Inst. of Physics, 1994 Fellow AAAS. Home: 12 Buena Vista Dr Hastings On Hudson NY 10706-1104 Office: Am Inst Physics One Physics Ellipse College Park MD 20740-3843 Office Phone: 301-209-3174. E-mail: sweart@aip.org.

**WEARY, PEYTON EDWIN,** retired medical educator; b. Evanston, Ill., Jan. 10, 1930; s. Leslie Albert and Conway Christian (Fleming) W.; m. Janet Edsall Gregory, Aug. 23, 1952; children: Terry, Conway Christian, Carolyn Fielder. BA, Princeton U., 1970; MD, U. Va., 1955. Diplomate: Am. Bd. Dermatology (dir. 1978-88, pres. 1987-88). Intern, case Western Res. U. Hosps., Cleve., 1955-56; rotating intern Univ. Hosp. Cleve., 1955-56; asst. resident dermatology U. Va., Charlottesville, 1958-60, resident dermatology, 1960-61, instr. dept. dermatology, 1961-62, asst. prof., 1962-65, asso. prof., 1965-70, prof., chmn. dept. dermatology, 1970-93; mem. staff Univ. Hosp., mem. cancer com., 1974—98, ret., 2001, prof. emeritus, 2001—. Univ. Hosp. house staff, 1960-61, clin. staff, 1965-66, pres. clin. staff, 1966-67; co-chair Nat. Coun. on Skin Cancer Prevention, Fed. Coun. on Skin Cancer Prevention, 1997-2001, Ctr. for Disease Control, 1997-2000. Mem. editorial bd. Jour. Am. Acad. Dermatology, 1978-87; editorial adv. bd. Skin and Allergy News, 1978—; contbr. articles to profl. jours. Bd. dirs. Lupus Found. Am., 1980-84; trustee, mem. exec. com. Dermatology Found., 1975-79; pres. Albermarle County unit Am. Cancer Soc., 1967-69. Served from 1st lt. to capt., M.C. U.S. Army, 1956-58. Recipient Walter Reed Disting. Achievement award U. Va. Alumni Assn., 2001 Master: Am. Acad. Dermatology (hon. bd. dir. 1973—76, pres. 1993—95, elected master in dermatology 2000, Gold medal 1990); mem.: Coun. Med. Splty. Socs. (bd. dir. 1989—92, sec. 1992—95), Am. Bd. Med. Spltys. (v.p. 1988, pres.-elect 1989, pres. 1990—92, Disting. Svc. award 1999), Raven Soc., So. Med. Assn., Med. Soc. Va. (Cmty. Svc. award 2001), Albermarie County Med. Soc., Dermatology Found., Am. Dermatol. Assn. (bd. dir. 1987—93, pres. 1992—93), Assn. Profs. Dermatology (sec.-treas. 1976—79), Soc. Investigative Dermatology (bd. dir. 1976—81, v.p. 1985, hon. mem. 1996), Va. Dermatol. Soc. (sec.-treas. 1965—71), Nat. Assn. Physicians Environ. (pres. 1995—97), Alpha Omega Alpha, Sigma Xi. Presbyterian. Home: 204 Magnolia Dr Charlottesville VA 22901

**WEATHERBY, DONALD ALAN,** telecommunications industry executive, writer; b. Columbus, Ohio, Dec. 11, 1954; s. Virgil Byron and Janet JoAnn Weatherby. Student, Columbus State C.C. Mainframe sys. adminstr. Contract to Bell Labs., Columbus, 1981—86; ops. mgr. AT&T Labs., Reynoldsburg, Ohio, 1996—. Sys. developer and implementation AT&T Labs., Reynoldsburg, 1996—2002. Author: (tech. mgmt.) Geekology 101: Managing the Aliens, Your Computer Support Staff, 1999, (novels) The Star Spangled Specter, 1995; composer: (jazz rock lit.fusion) Plush Hush CD - Generation Y, 2000. Recipient Vol. award, Ohio Legal Rights Svc. - State of Ohio, 1999. Mem.: MUFON (assoc.; data specialist 1999—2002, award for creation of MUFON Web database 2001). Unitarian Universalist. Avocations: writing macabre fiction, astronomy, UFO researcher, jazz-literary music. Home: 7485 E National Rd South Charleston OH 45368-8770 Personal E-mail: geekology@worldnet.att.net.

**WEATHERLY, ALVIS MORRISON, JR.,** retired association developer; b. Atlanta, Nov. 19, 1925; s. Alvis Morrison and Frances Louise (Stocks) W.; m. Mary Elizabeth Hyndman, Dec. 27, 1947; children: Mary Ann Weatherly Cobb, Elizabeth Louise Weatherly Williamson, Alvis Morrison III. Student, Ga. Inst. Tech., 1942-44; BBA, U. Ga., 1947; LLB, Atlanta Law Sch., 1952. Treasury cashier for Ga. So. Bell Te. Co. (now BellSouth), Atlanta, 1948-82; devel. dir. Atlanta Area Coun. Boy Scouts Am., 1984-93. Author, editor: History of Georgia Jaycees 1921-1962, 1962. Club pres., dist. pres., state chmn., state treas., state historian Ga. Jaycees, 1955-63, past asst. coun. comm., coun. adv. bd.; instr. commr. conf. Boy Scouts Am., 1982, coun. commr. sci., wood badge, asst. course dir., nat. exec. tng. inst., pres. basic training course class, coun. encampment chief, 1976, mem. exec. bd. Altanta area coun.; past dean Coll. of Commr. Sci., 1980-1983; Jr. Achievement, Atlanta, 1951, 63; loaned exec. Atlanta United Appeal, 1964, 65; mem. Selective Svc. Bd., Atlanta, 1964-74; mem. staff Atlanta Olympics, 1996; del. 17th World Meth. Conf., Rio de Janeiro, 1996; bd. dirs., past pres. Ga., Nat. Meml. Day Assn. and Ave. of Flags; adv. bd. Hist. Oakland Found., past adminstrv. bd. mem., usher, Funeral and Meml. Guild, past sec. fin. com., past tchr. youth Sunday sch., past mem. adult Sunday sch. class, trustee, past ch. sch. membership cultivation supt., past asst. ch. sch. supt., past mem. commn. on edn., past mem. evangelism commn., past adminstrv. bd. mem. Peachtree Rd. United Meth. Ch. Sgt. USAAC, 1946, WWII; 1st lt. USAFR, 1961 Named Jaycee of Yr. North DeKalb chpt., Jaycees, Outstanding Dist. Pres.-Ga., Key Man of Ga., Hal Salfen Outstanding State Com. Chmn., M. Keith Upson Outstanding State V.P.; recipient Silver Beaver award, Boy Scouts Am., 1974, James E. West fellow, 1996, Whitney M. Young Jr. Svc. in Urban Scouting award, 1996, Scout Show honoree, 1996, Dist. Award of Merit, Disting. Commr. award, Vigil honor, Order of the Arrow, Spirit of Yr. 1st class, 2001, Internat. Scouter's award 35 Yr. Vet. Scouter, Willing Svc. banner, WSB Radio, Atlanta, 1974, 1976, Cert., Indian Creek Garden Club, Atlanta, Cross of Mil. Svc., United Daus. of the Confederacy, Cross and Flame award, Peachtree Rd. United Meth. Ch., 21 Alive Cmty. Svc. award, Atlanta WXIA-TV, 2005. Master Mason (50 Yr. pin, Daniel Carter Beard Masonic Scouter award); mem. SAR (past pres. Atlanta chpt., War Svc. medal, Meritorious Svc. medal, Silver Good Citizenship medal), Rotary (bd. dirs., treas. Sandy Springs club, bd. dirs., sec., v.p. Smyrna-Cumberland club, sgt.-at-arms, bd. dirs., treas., sec., past pres. Buckhead Atlanta Club, Paul Harris fellow, Will Watt fellow, Otis Jackson fellow, Tom Slaughter fellow, Cmty. Svc. award, Svc. Above Self award, Rotarian of Yr., Rotary Found. Dist. Svc. award, Buckhead (Atlanta) Boy of Yr.), Tel. Pioneers of Am., Shrine, 1st Families of Ga., SCV (War Svc. medal), Mil. Order of Stars and Bars (past comdr.), Huguenot Soc. in Town of Manakin in Colony of Va. (past state pres.), Jamestowne Soc. (past 1st Ga. Co. Gov.), Sons and Daus. of the Pilgrims (past 2d dep. gov.), Sons and Daus. of Antebellum Planters (founding), Order of Indian Wars of U.S., Soc. of Descs. of Washington's Army at Valley Forge, Gen. Soc. War of 1812, Sons of Revolution (2d v.p.), Order of Washington, Soc. Colonial Wars in State of Ga., Magna Charta Barons, Magna Charta Dames and Barons (past state chmn.), Sovereign Colonial Soc., Ams. Royal Descent, Colonial Order of the Crown, Soc. Descs. of Knights of the Most Noble Order of the Garter, Plantagenet Soc., Old Guard of Gate City Guard (past comdt. col.), Hancock medal, Charles Gavin Trophy, The Dr. George Turnbull Pursley award, Guardsman Yr. Award 2002, 2004), Scabbard and Blade, Gridiron Secret Soc., Buckhead 50 Club (Atlanta Buckhead Boy of Yr. 2002), Am. Legion (Post 140), Atlanta Chpt. Mil. Officers Assn. Am., Sigma Nu, Beta Gamma Sigma (past pres. Atlanta chpt.), Alpha Phi Omega, Delta Sigma Pi, Omicron Delta Kappa (alumni). Home: 710 Starlight Ln NE Atlanta GA 30342-2838

**WEATHERLY, ROBERT STONE, JR.,** banker; b. Birmingham, Ala., May 12, 1929; s. Robert Stone and Gladys (Manning) W.; m. Mary Anne Burr, May 1, 1954; children: Robert Stone, III, Henry, William. AB, Princeton U., 1950; LL.B., Harvard U., 1953. grad. advanced mgmt. program, 1972. Bar: Ala. 1953. Assoc. firm Burr, McKamy Moore & Thomas, Birmingham, 1955-62; asst. gen. atty. Vulcan Materials Co., Birmingham, 1962-69, v.p. chems. div. Wichita, Kans., 1969-71, treas., 1971-74, v.p. and controller, 1974-77, pres. metals div. Birmingham, Ala., 1977-87, pres. Middle East div., 1982-87; chmn., chief exec. officer Jefferson Fed. Savings, Birmingham, 1987-91; dir., sec. All Seasons Travel, Birmingham, 1991—. Disting. lectr., practitioner U. Ga. Served with U.S. Army, 1953-55. Mem. Nat. Assn. Accts.

(cert. mgmt. acct.), Beta Gamma Sigma. Clubs: Country of Birmingham, Chattooga (Cashiers, N.C.). Presbyterian. Home: 4608 Old Leeds Rd Birmingham AL 35213-1802 Office: All Seasons Travel 120 Office Park Dr Birmingham AL 35223-2422

**WEATHERMON, SIDNEY EARL,** elementary school educator; b. Abilene, Tex., Jan. 20, 1937; s. Sidney Elliot Weathermon and Evelyn Marie (Landreth) Parker. BA, U. Colo., 1962, MA, 1968, EdD, 1976. Cert. K-12 reading tchr., elem. edn. tchr., K-12 reading specialist. Tchr. grades 3-6 Jefferson County Pub. Schs., Colo., 1963—66; tchr. grades 5-6 Boulder Valley Pub. Schs., Colo., 1962—63, tchr. reading, 1968—71, consortium dir. right-to-read project Louisville Mid. Sch., 1974—75, coord. comm. skills program Vocat.-Tech. H.S., 1976, K-12 dist. reading specialist, 1971—85, chpt. 1 tchr. grades 1-6, 1985—89, coord. chpt. 1 kindergarten project, 1985—89, tchr. grade 1, 1989—95. Instr. U. Colo., Boulder, 1971-72, U. No. Colo., Greeley, 1977; adj. faculty Regis U., Denver, 1972-95, dept. edn. instr., 1982. Contbr. articles to profl. jours. Recipient Celebrate Lit. award, Boulder Coun. Internat. Reading Assn., 1986, IBM Corp. Tchr. of Yr. award, 1989, Colo./Nat. Educator, Milkin Family Found., 1990; NDEA fellow, 1966-68. Mem. NEA, Internat. Reading Assn., Colo. Edn. Assn., Boulder Valley Edn. Assn. (chair tchr. adv coun., assoc. rep., tchrs. rights and activities commn., negotiations team, profl. leave com.), Phi Delta Kappa (certs. of recognition 1987, 90), Kappa Delta Pi. Democrat. Avocation: southwest Indian art. Home: 449 S Shore Dr Osprey FL 34229-9657 E-mail: drsidw@comcast.net.

**WEATHERS, MILLEDGE WRIGHT,** retired economics professor; b. Augusta, Ga., May 11, 1926; s. Robert Edward Lee and Margaret Elizabeth (Johnson) W.; m. Anna-Maria Helene von Bertrab; children: Helene, Martin, Margarete, Benjamin. BA, George Washington U., 1949, MA, 1957; doctor oeconomiae publicae, U. Munich, 1961. Rsch. analyst U.S. Dept. Air Force, Washington, 1951-57. Gen. Electric Co., Santa Barbara, Calif., 1961-62; asst. practice cons. Munich, 1962-64; cons. Gesellschaft fuer Anlagewerte, Munich, 1964-66; sr. staff analyst Lockheed-Ga. Co., Marietta, 1966-68; prof. econs. Adrian (Mich.) Coll., 1968-91. Contbr. articles to profl. jours. With U.S. Army, 1944-46. Mem. Am. Econs. Assn., Assn. for Evolutionary Econs., Nat. Tax Assn., Economists for Peace and Security, Kappa Sigma. Avocations: music, walking. Home: 930 Lincoln Ave Adrian MI 49221-3230 Personal E-mail: Mweathers@adrian.edu.

**WEATHERSBY, GEORGE BYRON,** management company executive; b. Albany, Calif., Dec. 9, 1944; s. Byron and Fannie A. W.; m. Linda Rose Scheirer, June 29, 1979; children: Deborah Jane, Geoffrey Byron. BS, U. Calif., Berkeley, 1965, MS, 1966, MBA, 1967, MS, Harvard U., 1968, PhD, 1970; DHL (hon.), U. San Francisco, 1987; LLD (hon.), U. So. Ind., 1992. Mem. faculty, assoc. dir. analytical studies, dir. Ford Found. rsch. program U. Calif., Berkeley, 1969-72; spl. asst. to U.S. Sec. of State Washington, 1972-73; dir. rsch. Nat. Commn. on Financing Higher Edn., Washington, 1973-74; assoc. prof. mgmt. Harvard U., Cambridge, Mass., 1974-78; commr. higher edn. State of Ind., 1977-83; pres. Curtis Pub. Co., 1983-86, New UPI Inc., Washington, 1985-86; corp. v.p. fin. Ontario Corp., Muncie, Ind., 1986-88, pres., 1988-91, also bd. dirs.; ptnr. Founders Court Inc., Princeton, NJ, 1991-93; independant cons., 1975—; pres. Oxford Mgmt. Corp., 1993-98, Cambridge Parallel Processing, 1994-98, Electronic Retailing Syss. Internat., 1996-98; pres., CEO, bd. dirs. Am. Mgmt. Assn., N.Y.C., 1998—2002; chmn., CEO Genesys Corp., LLC, 2002—. CEO, Quisic, Inc., 2001-02; chmn. bd. dirs. Otis Conner Cos., 1984-86, Curtis Media Corp., 1984-86, Curtis Internat. Ltd., 1985-86, Prince Gardner, Inc., 1991-93, Alma Industries, 1992-93, Hanes Holding Co., 1992-93; bd. dirs. Holcim (US) Inc., Farm Fans Inc., Delta Consol. Industries, Cambridge Parallel Processing, Advanced Retail Mktg., ERS, Inc., AOI Med., Inc. Author: Financing Postsecondary Education in the U.S, 1974, Colleges and Money, 1976; contbr. numerous articles to profl. jours.; cons. editor: Jour. Higher Edn., 1974—; exec. editor: Change mag., 1980-84. Bd. dirs. Nat. Ctr. for Higher Edn Mgmt. Sys., 1980-83, U.S.A. Group, 1989—96; mem. steering com. Edn. Commn. of States, 1978-82; mem. Ind. Com. Humanities, 1981-87; trustee U. So. Ind., 1985-91, Park Tudor Sch. Indpls., 1986-91, Butler U., 1987-93; mem. adv. coun. Invest in New Zealand, 1991-2001, MicroNets, 2005-; mem. adv. coun. for leadership and mgmt. for U.S. Dept. State, 2004-06. Calif. Regents scholar, 1963-65; NSF fellow, 1966-67; AEC fellow, 1966-67; Kent fellow, 1967-70; White House fellow, 1972-73; named 1 of 100 Outstanding Young Leaders in Higher Edn. Change Mag., 1978, 1 of Top 100 CEOs, C10 Mag., 2000. Mem. Am. Mgmt. Assn., Am. Coun. Edn., Ops. Rsch. Soc. Am., Inst. Mgmt. Scis., Econometrica, Young Pres. Orgn. Republican. Business E-Mail: gweathersby@genesysllc.com.

**WEATHERSPOON, TERESA GAYE,** professional basketball player; b. Jasper, Tex., Dec. 8, 1965; Grad., La. Tech. Inst., 1988. Guard Blusto, Italy, 1988—89, 1990—93, Magenta, Italy, 1989—90, Como, Italy, 1996—97, CSKA, Russia, 1993—95, WNBA - N.Y. Liberty, N.Y.C., 1997—2003, L.A. Sparks, 2004—. Named, NCAA Women's Basketball Team Decade, 1980, La. State Player of Yr., 1988, Kodak All-Am., 1987, 1988, WNBA defensive player of yr., 1997, 1998, WNBA All-Star, 1999—2002; named to All-WNBA 2nd team, 1997—2000; recipient Gold medals, World Championship, 1986, Goodwill Games, 1986, World Univ. Games, 1987, Broderick Cup, Wade Trophy, became first player in WNBA history to record 1,000 career assists. Office: c/o Los Angeles Sparks 555 N Nash St El Segundo CA 90245

**WEATHERSTONE, SIR DENNIS,** retired bank executive; b. London, Nov. 29, 1930; s. Henry Philip and Gladys (Hart) W.; m. Marion Blunsum, Apr. 4, 1959; children: Hazel, Cheryl, Gretel, Richard Paul Student, Northwestern Poly., London, 1946-49. Sr. v.p. Morgan Guaranty Trust Co. N.Y., N.Y.C., 1972-77, exec. v.p., 1977-79, treas., 1977-79, vice chmn., 1979-80, chmn. exec. com., 1980-86; pres. J.P. Morgan & Co., Inc. (formerly Morgan Guaranty Trust Co. N.Y.), N.Y.C., 1987-90, chmn., chief exec. officer, 1990-95. Staff mem. Internat. Monetary Fund, 1970-94, dep. dir. rsch., 1987-94; bd. dirs. GM Corp., 1986-2001, Merck & Co., Inc., 1991-2001, L'Air Liquide, NY Stock Exch., 2003-05; mem. bd. banking supervision Bank of Eng., 1995-2001; sr. fellow Inst. for Internat. Economics. Trustee Alfred P. Sloan Found., Internat. Acctg. Standards Com. Found. Decorated Knight Comdr. Order Brit. Empire. Office: Inst for Internat Econ 1750 Massachusetts Ave NW Washington DC 20036 Office Phone: 212-720-7691.*

**WEATHERUP, ROY GARFIELD,** lawyer; b. Annapolis, Md., Apr. 20, 1947; s. Robert Alexander and Kathryn Crites (Hesser) W.; m. Wendy Gaines, Sept. 10, 1977; children: Jennifer, Christine. AB in Polit. Sci., Stanford U., 1968, JD, 1972. Bar: Calif. 1972, U.S. Dist. Ct. 1973, U.S. Ct. Appeals (9th cir.) 1975, U.S. Supreme Ct. 1980. Assoc. Haight, Brown & Bonesteel, LA, Santa Ana, 1972—78, ptnr., 1979—2003, Lewis Brisbois Bisgaard & Smith, LA, 2004—. Judge Moot Ct. UCLA, Loyola U., Pepperdine U.; arbitrator Am. Arbitration Assn.; mem. com. Book Approved Jury Instrns. LA Superior Ct. Mem. ABA, Calif. Acad. Appellate Lawyers, LA County Bar Assn., Town Hall Calif. Republican. Methodist. Home: 17260 Rayen St Northridge CA 91325-2919 Office: Lewis Brisbois Bisgaard & Smith 221 N Figueroa St Los Angeles CA 90012 Office Phone: 213-250-1800. E-mail: royweatherup@aol.com.

**WEAVER, BARBARA FRANCES,** librarian, consultant; b. Boston, Aug. 29, 1927; d. Leo Francis and Nina Margaret (Durham) Weisse; m. George B. Weaver, June 6, 1951; 1 dau., Valerie S. Clark. BA, Radcliffe Coll., 1949; MLS, U. R.I., 1968; EdM, Boston U., 1978. Head libr. Thompson (Conn.) Pub. Libr., 1961-69; dir. Conn. State Libr. Svc. Ctr., Willimantic, 1969-72; regional adminstr. Ctrl. Mass. Regional Libr. Sys., Worcester, 1972-78; asst. commr. of edn., state libr. State of N.J., Trenton, 1978-91; dir. R.I. Dept. State Libr. Svcs., Providence, 1991-96; chief info. officer State of RI, 1996—2001; govt. cons. in tech. mgmt., orgnl. devel. and libr. adminstrn., 2001—. Lectr. Simmons Coll., Boston, 1976-78. Mem. Conn. Libr. Assn.

**WEAVER, CARLTON DAVIS,** retired oil industry executive; b. Grantsville, W.Va., May 27, 1921; s. Arley Ezra and Grace (Davis) Weaver; m. Nancy Mason McIntosh, Mar. 21, 1951; 1 child, Nancy Mason. BS in Engr. Mines, W.Va. U., 1948. Office engr. E.I. du Pont de Nemours & Co., 1941-42, tech. service rep., 1948-51; with Ashland (Ky.) Oil, Inc., 1951-81, exec. asst., 1960-67, v.p., 1967-72, sr. v.p., 1972-81, group oper. officer, 1976-81, pres. Ashland Resources Co. div., 1970-74; chmn. bd. Ashland Coal, Inc., 1981-84, Ven-Black, Inc., 1983-86. Chmn. vis. com. Coll. Mineral and Energy Resources W.Va. U., 1967—80. Served to 1st lt. USMCR, 1942—46, served to maj. USMCR, 1952—53. Home: 64 Surfsong Rd Kiawah Island SC 29455-5753 also: PO Box 578 White Sulphur Springs WV 24986-0578 Office: 1409 Winchester Ave Ashland KY 41101-7555 E-mail: carltondweaver@charter.net, buckweav@charter.net.

**WEAVER, CHARLES LYNDELL, JR.,** marketing executive, educational consultant; b. Canonsburg, Pa., July 5, 1945; s. Charles Lyndell and Georgia Lavelle (Gardner) W.; m. Ruth Marguerite Uxa, Feb. 27, 1982; children: Charles Lyndell III, John Francis. BArch, Pa. State U., 1969; cert. in assoc. studies, U. Florence, Italy, 1968. Registered architect, Pa., Md., Mo., Va., Mass., Ga.; cert. Nat. Coun. Arch. Registration Bd.; cert. designee, Design Build Inst. Am., 2002. With Celento & Edson, Canonsburg, part-time 1966-71; project architect Meyers & D'Aleo, Balt., 1971-76, corp. dir., v.p., 1974-76; ptnr. Borrow Assocs.-Developers, Balt., 1976-79, Crowley/Weaver Constrn. Mgmt., Balt., 1976-79; pvt. practice arch. Balt., 1976-79; cons., project mgr. U. Md., College Park, 1979-80; corp. cons. architect Bank Bldg. & Equipment Corp., Am., St. Louis, 1980-83; dir. archtl. and engring. svcs. Ladue Bldg. and Engring. Inc., St. Louis, 1983-84; v.p., sec. Graphic Products Corp.; pres. CWCM Inc. Internat., 1987-2000. Dir. K-12 Edn. Market Ctr. and sr. program mgr. Sverdrup Corp., 1989-95; prin. Benham Internat. Eurasia, 1995, v.p., dir. mktg. and bus. devel. The Benham Group, St. Louis, 1995-96; v.p. Chiodini Assocs., 1997-98; asst. lectr. Washington U., 1997-2000, 01-; cons. Stifel Cap. Start Up Venture Capital Fund; ops. mgr., generations cons. Stifel Capco Venture Capital, 1998; dir. mktg. sys. The Maiman Co., 1998-99; dir. edn. program mgmt. The Integral Group, Atlanta, 1999-2001; vis. Alpha Rho Chi lectr. Pa. State U., 1983; vis. lectr. Washington U. Lindenwood Coll., 1987, Wentworth Inst., Boston, Am. Assn. Cost Engrs., So. Fla., 1994, with U. Houston, 2002; mem. panel Am. Univ. Architects Conv., 1983; v.p. program mgmt. and ednl. facilities Kennedy Assoc. Inc.; participant K-12 Nat. Summit, San Diego, 2002; URS Corp. dep. project mgmt. Phila. Sch. Improvement Team, 2003-04; demonstration ednl. facilities East Orange, New Brunswick, Trenton and Vineland, NJ; preconstrn. svcs. coord.-design/build Joseph, Jingoli and Sons, East Orange, Trenton & Vineland Abbott Demonstration Schs.; spkr. and presenter in field Contbr. Planning Guide for Maintaining Facilities, U.S. Dept. Edn. Project bus. cons. Jr. Achievement, 1982-85, 2001-2003; mem. cluster com., advisor Explorer Program, 1982-85; mem. Design Build Inst. Am., 1998—, splty. contractor task force chmn., 2000-02. Recipient 5 brochure and graphic awards Nat. Assn. Indsl. Artists, 1973; 1st award Profl. Builder/Am. Plywood Assn., 1974; Honor award, 2 articles Balt. chpt. AIA, 1974; Better Homes and Gardens award Sensible Growth, Nat. Assn. Home Builders, 1975; winner Ridgely's Delight Competition, Balt., 1976. Mem. ASCD, AACE (conv. spkr. So. Fla. sect. 1994), Vitruvius Alumni Assn., Pa. State Alumni Assn., AIA, Constrn. Specifications Inst., Am. Assn. Sch. Adminstrs. (nat. coun., panel moderator 1994), Coun. Ednl. Facilities Planners, Assn. Sch. Bus. Ofcls., Alpha Rho Chi (nat. treas. 1980-82, dir. nat. found. treas. 1989-97), Optimists Internat. Office: Bldg 4 Ste 216 3131 Princeton Pike Lawrenceville NJ 08648 Business E-Mail: cweaver@jingoli.com.

**WEAVER, CHRISTOPHER E.,** naval officer; BS, U.S. Naval Acad., 1971; MPA, George Washington U.; Disting. Grad., Indsl. Coll. of Armed Forces. Commd. ensign USN, 1971, advanced through ranks to rear adm.; various assignments to comdg. officer USS Spruance (DD 963), U.S. Naval Sta., Norfolk, Va.; Commandant Naval Dist., Washington; comdr. Navy Installations Command USN, Washington. Home: 712 Warrington Ave SE Washington DC 20003 Office: Comdr Navy Installations Command CP5 Ste 480 2000 Navy Pentagon Washington DC 20350-2000

**WEAVER, CLIFFORD LEE,** retired lawyer, winery owner; b. Chgo., Mar. 11, 1945; s. Thomas E. and Thera A. (Ramey) Cash; m. Donna Rae Florence, Aug. 20, 1966; 1 child, Megan R. AB with honors, U. Chgo., 1966, JD with honors, 1969. Bar: Ill. 1969, U.S. Dist. Ct. (no. dist.) Ill. 1969, U.S. Ct. Appeals (7th cir.) 1969, U.S. Supreme Ct. 1975. Sr. clk. U.S. Ct. Appeals, Chgo., 1969-71; assoc. Ross & Hardies, Chgo., 1971-75, ptnr., 1976-83, Burke, Weaver & Prell, Chgo., 1983-99, mng. ptnr., 1990-99; owner, operator Azienda Agricola Le Miccine vineyard and winery, 1996—. Gen. counsel N.W. Water Commn., 1978—99, DuPage River Commn., DuPage County, Ill., 1987—99, Lake County (Ill.) Forest Preserve, 1991—99; village atty. Village of Bannockburn, Ill., 1977—99, Village of Northbrook, 1977—99, Village of Glencoe, Ill., 1978—99, Village of Hinsdale, Ill., 1985—99, Village of Libertyville, Ill., 1990—99. Co-author: Special Districts in Illinois, 1977, City Zoning, 1979; contbr. numerous articles to profl. jours. Trustee Kenilworth (Ill.) Libr. Dist., 1987-89; mem. Kenilworth Zoning Bd., 1985-2006. Mem.: ABA, Order of Coif, Phi Beta Kappa. Republican. Home: 144 Woodstock Ave Kenilworth IL 60043-1262 Office Phone: 847-256-7258. E-mail: clw@lemiccine.com.

**WEAVER, CONSTANCE,** communications executive: Various mgmt. positions in product mgmt., mktg. and corp. planning McGraw Hill; exec. dir. unit Bus. Week; leadership positions with responsibility for investor rels. and fin. comms. Microsoft Corp., MCI Comms.; v.p. investor rels. AT&T Corp., Bedminster, NJ, 1996—2002, exec. v.p. pub. rels., mktg. comms. and brand, 2002—. Bd. dirs. Applied Digital Solutions, Inc., New Jersey Performing Arts Ctr., Somerset Hills YMCA, Atlanta Symphony Orch., Nat. Coun. La Raza; grant com. mem. Monterey Peninsula Found.; corp. rep. Ford's Theatre Bd. Gov's., Wash., DC. Bd. dirs. Somerset Hills YMCA, N.J. Performing Arts Ctr. Mem.: Nat. Investor Rels. Inst. (former dir.), NJ300, Fin. Women's Assn., Arthur W. Page Soc., The Wisemen. Office: AT&T Corp 1 AT&T Way Bedminster NJ 07921

**WEAVER, DELBERT ALLEN,** retired lawyer; b. Shoshone, Idaho, May 28, 1931; s. Arlo Irving and Kate Rosamond (McCarter) W.; m. Jeanne Carol Alford, June 1959; children: Tobin Elizabeth, Michael Andrew, Matthew Stewart, Edward Malcolm. BA, U. Oreg., 1953, LLB, 1956. Bar: Oreg. 1956, U.S. Dist. Ct. Oreg. 1956, U.S. Ct. Appeals (9th cir.) 1968. Ptnr. Weaver & Oram, Eugene, Oreg., 1956-59; dep. atty. City of Portland, Oreg., 1959-68; assoc. Winfree, Latourette, Murphy, et al., Portland, 1968-71; stockbroker Dupont Glore Forgan, Portland, 1971-73; securities examiner corp. div. State of Oreg., Salem, 1973-75, dep. commr. corp. div., 1975-80; pvt. practice Portland, 1980-87; counsel Schwabe, Williamson & Wyatt, Portland, 1987-90, sr. ptnr., 1991-96; pvt. practice Portland, 1996-2000; counsel Dunn, Carney, Portland, 2000—04; ret., 2005. Personal E-mail: dweaver1091@charter.net.

**WEAVER, DIANNE JAY,** lawyer; b. Kansas City, Mo., June 28, 1944; d. Thomas G. and Anna Jeanette Jay; m. Benjamin J. Weaver, Sept. 16, 1970; children: Jay, Jenny, Scott, Elizabeth. BS, U. Kans., 1965; JD, Ind. U., 1970. Bar: Ind., Fla., Colo.; bd. cert. trial lawyer. Ptnr. Weaver & Weaver, P.A., Ft. Lauderdale, Fla.; of counsel Krupnick Campbell Malone Roselli Buser Slama & Hancock P.A., Ft. Lauderdale; ptnr. Harrell & Johnson, P.A., Jacksonville, 2002—. Speaker in field. Contbr. articles to profl. jours. Trustee Civil Justice Found.; bd. dirs. Trial Lawyers for Pub. Justice; chmn. publicity com. Civil Justice Found. Fellow Roscoe Pound Found. (life); mem. ATLA (bd. govs., sec.), Acad. Fla. Trial Lawyers (bd. dirs.), So. Trial Lawyers Assn. (bd. govs.), Fla. Bar Assn. (chair trial advocacy com.), Fed. Bar Assn., Broward County Women Lawyers Assn. (founding pres.). Office: Harrell & Harrell PA 4735 Sunbeam Rd Jacksonville FL 32257 Office Phone: 904-251-1111. Business E-Mail: dweaver@forjustice.com.

**WEAVER, EARL D.,** theater educator; b. Maywood, Calif., Aug. 24, 1956; s. Earl Douglas Weaver and Celia Faye Hyatt; life ptnr. Thomas G. Keetch. AA in Journalism, East LA C.C., 1977; BA in Theatre and Dance, U. Redlands, Calif., 1979; MFA, U. Calif., Irvine, 1990. Asst. prof. theatre Point Pk. U., Pitts., 1992—98; instr. theatre Las Positas C.C., Livermore, Calif., 2000—01; asst. prof. theatre U. Ctrl. Fla., Orlando, 2003—. Mng. dir. Theatre Factory, St. Louis, 1991—92. Dir.: (theatre production) Sunday in the Park with George (Outstanding Dir./Am. Coll. Theatre Festival, 1998), Tintypes (Outstanding Dir./Am. Coll. Theatre Festival, 1997). Recipient Outstanding Photography award, Internat. Libr. Photography, 2004—05. Mem.: Assn. Theatre Higher Edn. (assoc.), United Faculty Fla. (assoc.), Southeastern Theatre Conf. (assoc.), Nat. Educators Assn. (assoc.), Nat. Assn. Schs. Theatre (assoc.), Ednl. Theatre Assn. (assoc.), Actors Equity Assn. (assoc.). D-Liberal. Avocations: travel, photography. Office: University of Central Florida 12501 Research Parkway Suite 180 Orlando FL 32816 Office Phone: 407-823-3638. E-mail: eweaver@mail.ucf.edu.

**WEAVER, ELIZABETH A.,** state supreme court justice; b. New Orleans; d. Louis and Mary Weaver. BA, Newcomb Coll.; JD, Tulane U. Elem. tchr. Glen Lake Cmty. Sch., Maple City, Mich.; French tchr. Leelanau Sch., Glen Arbor, Mich.; pvt. practice Glen Arbor, Mich.; law clk. Civil Dist. Ct., New Orleans; atty. Coleman, Dutrey & Thomson, New Orleans; atty. title specialist Chevron Oil Co., New Orleans; probate and juvenile judge Leelanau County, Mich., 1975—86; judge Mich. Ct. Appeals, 1987—94; justice Mich. Supreme Ct., Lansing, 1995—. Chief justice Mich. Supreme Ct., 1999—2000, re-elected, 2002—; chief justice Pat Rellected Superior Ct. Justice, 2002—; instr. adm. dept. Ctr. Mich. U.; mem. Mich. Com. on Juvenile Justice, Nat. Conv. State Adv. Groups on Juvenile Justice for U.S.; chair Gov.'s Task Force on Children's Justice, Trial Ct. Assessment Commn., Office Juvenile Justice and Delinquency Prevention; jud. adv. bd. mem. Law and Orgnl. Econs. Ctr. U. Kans.; treas. Children's Charter of Cts. of Mich. Chairperson Western Mich. U. CLE Adv. Bd.; mem. steering com. Grand Traverse/Leelanau Commn. on Youth; mem. Glen Arbor Twp. Zoning Bd.; mem. charter arts north Leelanau County; mem. citizen's adv. coun. Arnell Engstrom Children's Ctr.; mem. cmty. adv. com. Pathfinder Sch. Treaty Law Demonstration Project; active Grand Traverse/Leelanau Mental Health Found. Named Jurist of Yr., Police Officers Assn. of Mich.; named one of five Outstanding Young Women in Mich., Mich. Jaycees; recipient Eastern award, Warren Easton Hall of Fame, Lifetime Dedication to Children award, Mich. Champions in Childhood Injury Prevention, 2000, Recognition award for outstanding svc. to Mich. children and families, Gov. Engler and Family Independence Agy., 2000, Profls. award, Mich. Assn. Drug Cts., 2002, Mary S. Coleman award, Ctr. for Civic Edn. Through Law, 2002. Fellow: Mich. State Bar Found.; mem.: ABA, Antrim County Bar Assn., Leelanau County Bar Assn., Grand Traverse County Bar Assn., La. Bar Assn., Nat. Coun. Juvenile and Family Judges, Mich. Bar Assn. (chair CLE adv. bd., chair crime prevention ctr., chair juvenile law com.), Delta Kappa Gamma (hon.). Office: Mich Supreme Ct 3300 Grandview Plz 10850 E Traverse Hwy Traverse City MI 49684-1364*

**WEAVER, FRANKLIN THOMAS,** retired newspaper executive; b. Johnstown, N.Y., Oct. 11, 1932; s. Edwin K. and Bertha J. (Wendt) W.; children: Thomas, James, Michael, David, Tammy, Kelly, Anna; m. Joyce W. Phelps, Oct. 23, 1991. BA with high honors in Journalism, Mich. State U., 1954. Advt. sales rep. Grand Rapids Press, Mich., 1955-64; controller Muskegon (Mich.) Chronicle, 1964-66; mgr. Bay City (Mich.) Times, 1966-73, Jackson (Mich.) Citizen Patriot, 1973-84, pub., 1984—99; ret. Mem.: Mich. Press Assn. (pres. 1991), Newspapers Assn. Am., Greater Jackson C. of C., Ella Sharp Mus. (pres. 1995—96), Jackson Country Club.

**WEAVER, HOWARD C.,** newspaper executive; b. Anchorage, Oct. 15, 1950; s. Howard Gilbert and Lurlene Eloise (Gamble) W.; m. Alice Laprele Gauchay, July 16, 1970 (div. 1974); m. Barbara Lynn Hodgin, Sept. 16, 1978. BA Johns Hopkins U., 1972, MPhil Cambridge U., 1993. Reporter, staff writer Anchorage Daily News, 1972—76, columnist, 1979—80, mng. editor, 1980—83, editor, 1983—95; editor, owner Alaska Advocate, 1976—79; asst. to pres. McClatchy Newspapers, 1995—97, editor of editl. pages, 1997—2001; v.p. news The McClatchy Co., 2001—. Internat. co-chair Northern News Svc., 1989—94; disting. lectr. journalism U. Alaska, Fairbanks, 1991. Pulitzer Prize juror, 1988, 1989, 1994, 1995, 2002; bd. visitors John S. Knight Fellowship Stanford U.; Pulitzer Prize juror, 2003. Recipient Pulitzer prize, 1976, 1989, Headliner award, Press Club of Atlantic City, 1976, 1989, Gold medal, Investigative Reporters and Editors, 1989, Pub. Svc. award, AP Mng. Editor's Assn., 1976, 1989. Mem.: Investigative Reporters and Editors, Am. Soc. Newspaper Editors, Upper Yukon River Press Club (pres. 1972), Alaska Press Club (bd. dirs. 1972—84), Sigma Delta Chi (Nat. award 1989). Avocations: hockey, travel, opera.

**WEAVER, JANET S.,** editor; m. Mark Weaver; children: Sam, Rachel. B in journalism, U. Mo., 1984. Reporter, asst. city editor Stuart (Fla.) News, 1986—89; from reporter to dep. mng. editor/features and sports Virginian-Pilot, Norfolk, Va., 1989—94; mng. editor The Wichita (Kans.) Eagle, 1994—97, Sarasota (Fla.) Herald-Tribune, 1997—99, exec. editor, 1999—2003; dean faculty Poynter Inst., St. Petersburg, Fla., 2003—04; mng. editor The Tampa Tribune, Fla., 2004—05, exec. editor, v.p. Fla., 2005—. Mem.: Am. Soc. Newspaper Editors (bd. dirs.). Office: Tampa Tribune 202 S Parker St Tampa FL 33606

**WEAVER, JOHN BORLAND,** musician, department chairman, composer; b. Palmerton, Pa., Apr. 27, 1937; s. David Williams and Bertha Brownlee (Borl) W.; m. Marianne Carol Gruhn, Apr. 30, 1942; children: Jonathan Kirk, Kirianne Elizabeth. Diploma, Curtis Inst. Music, Phila., 1959; M in Sacred Music, Union Theol. Sem., 1968; MusD (hon.), Westminster Coll., 1995, MusD (hon.), 1995, Curtis Inst. Music, 2003. Head organ dept. Curtis Inst. Music, 1972 2003; chmn. organ dept. Manhattan Sch. Music, 1983-84, Juilliard Sch. Music, N.Y.C., 1986—2004. Mem. faculty Westminster Choir Coll., Princeton, N.J., 1970-72, Union Theol. Sem. Sch. Sacred Music, 1970-73 Organist, choirmaster, Holy Trinity Lutheran Ch., N.Y.C., 1959-70, Temple Beth-El, Manhattan Beach, N.Y., 1970-80; dir. music, Madison Ave. Presbyn. Ch., N.Y.C., 1970—2005; solo organ recitalist, U.S., Can., Western Europe, U.K., Brazil; composer: Psalm 100, 1958, Toccatafor Organ, 1959, Epiphany Alleluias, 1967, Rhapsody for Flute and Organ, 1968, Good Christian Men, Rejoice, 1978, Introit for Pentecost, Fantasia for Organ, Passacaglia on a Theme by Dunstable, all 1981, The Joyful Feast, 1988, Psalm 46, 1989, Dialogues for Flute and Organ, 1991, Prayer for Transfiguration Day, 1991, Prelude and Fugue in E Minor, 1994, Prayer From Psalm 139, 1995, Variations on Three Hymn Tunes, 1997, Restore Us, O Lord of Hosts, 1995; contbr. articles to jours. including Reformed Liturgy and Music. Served with AUS, 1961-63. Decorated Army Commendation medal; recipient Disting. Svc. in the Field of Music award, Peabody Conser. Johns Hopkins U., 1989. Mem.: Presbyn. Mus. Musicians (pres. 1984—86), Am. Guild Organists (voted Internat. Performer of Yr., NYC chpt. 2005), N.Am. Acad. Liturgy, St. Wilfrid Club (NYC). Home: 23 Rowell Rd West Glover VT 05875 Office Phone: 802-525-4491. Personal E-mail: marianneweaver@juno.com. *By hard work and good fortune I have been able to do that which I decided, at ten, to do with my life.*

**WEAVER, JOHN CARL,** chemist, educator; b. Gibson, Ohio, Aug. 5, 1908; s. William Edwin and Rena Belle (Emerson) W.; m. Marian Louise King, 1940; children: John K., Susan E. BS in Chemistry, Denison U., 1930; MA in Chemistry, U. Cin., 1933, PhD in Chemistry, 1935. Instr. chem. engring. U. Cin., 1935—36; chemist Sherwin Williams Co., Cleve., 1936—73, dir. rsch., 1968—73, consultant, 1974—79; adj. prof. Case We. Res. U., Cleve., 1980—. Mem. utilization rsch. adv. com. USDA, 1962-69, founding mem. Western Reserve Frontiers of Chemistry adv. bd., 1941-74, coord., supr. Sherwin William catalyst lab. on Western Reserve campus. Developer dehydrated castor oil, 1938; editor Jour. of Coatings Tech., 1963-72. Fellow ASTM (hon. bd. dirs. 1977-80, tech. com. ops. 1976-77, chmn D-14 1984-89), Fedn. Socs. Coatings Tech. (Heckel award 1976), Am. Chem. Soc., Sigma Xi. Avocation: genealogy. Office: Case Western Res U 541 Kent Smith Bldg Cleveland OH 44106 Home: 2181 Ambleside Dr Cleveland OH 44106

**WEAVER, KENNETH NEWCOMER,** geologist, state agency administrator; b. Lancaster, Pa., Jan. 16, 1927; s. A. Ross and Cora (Newcomer) W.; m. Mary Elizabeth Hoover, Sept. 9, 1950; children: Wendy Elaine, Matthew Owen. BS, Franklin and Marshall Coll., 1950; MA, Johns Hopkins U., 1952, PhD, 1954. Instr. geology Johns Hopkins, 1953- 54; ops. analyst Ops. Rsch. Office, Washington, 1954-56; chief geologist, then mgr. geology and quarry dept. Medusa Portland Cement Co., Wampum, Pa., 1956-63; dir., state geologist Md. Geol. Survey, Balt., 1963-92; chmn. Md. Land Reclamation Com., 1978-92. Gov.'s rep. Interstate Oil Compact Commn., Interstate Mining Compact Commn.; mem. outer shelf adv. com. U.S. Dept. Interior; chmn. Md. Topographic Mapping Com.; mem. com. on surface mining and reclamation NAS, 1978, vice chmn. com. on disposal of excess spoil, 1980-81, mem. com. on geologic mapping, 1983, liaison mem. Bd. earth scis., 1982-88, mem. com. on water resources rsch., 1989-92, chmn. com. on abandoned minelands rsch. priorities, 1987; mem. subcom. on mgmt. of maj. underground constrn. projects Nat. Acad. Engring.; mem. Md. Commn. on Artistic Property, 1988-92. With U.S. Maritime Svc., 1944—46, with AUS, 1954—56. Recipient John Wesley Powell award USGS, 1994; named hdqr. bldg. The Kenneth N. Weaver Bldg. Md. Geol. Survey, 1994. Fellow Geol. Soc. Am. (sec. N.E. sect. 1985-2001), AAAS (sr.); mem. Am. Assn. Petroleum Geologists (Ea. sect., George V. Cohee Pub. Svc. award 1991), Am. Inst. Mining Engrs., Am. Inst. Profl. Geologists (editor 1983-84, Martin Van Couvering Meml. award 1992), Am. Geol. Inst. (governing bd. 1973, exec. com. 1989-90, medal in memory of Ian Campbell 2001), Am. Water Rsch. Assn., Geol. Soc. Washington, Assn. Am. State Geologists (pres. 1973, hon. mem. 1992), Johns Hopkins Club (Balt.). Republican. Presbyterian (elder). Office: Md Geol Survey 2300 St Paul St Baltimore MD 21218-5210 Home: 2525 Pot Spring Rd Unit S322 Lutherville Timonium MD 21093-2862 Office Phone: 410-554-5532. Personal E-mail: kweaver418@aol.com.

**WEAVER, LINDA MARIE,** pharmacist, education educator; d. John William and Lorraine Marie Miller; m. Daniel Jacob Weaver. BA in Edn. and Spanish, Western Mich. U., 1974; BS in Pharmacy, Ferris State U., 1984; PharmD, Midwestern U., Chgo. Coll. of Pharmacy, 2000. Registered Pharmacist Mich., 1984. Ambulatory pharmacist Perry Drugs, Midland, Mich., 1984—87, Revco Drugs, Tucson, 1987—89, Walgreens Drug, Tucson, 1989—93; compliance officer Ariz. State Bd. of Pharmacy, Phoenix, 1993—99; clin. hosp. pharmacist John C. Lincoln Hosp., Phoenix, 1999—2001; med. sci. liaison Wyeth Pharmaceuticals, Scottsdale, 2001—03; med. liaison Abbott Labs., Scottsdale, 2003—04, clin. sci. mgr., 2004—. Adj. faculty mem. Midwestern U. Coll. of Pharmacy, Glendale, Ariz.; instr. Rio Salado C.C., Phoenix, 1997—98, Ariz. Pharmacy Assn., 1987—; adv. bd. mem. SCP Comm., Inc., Phoenix, 2001—01. Vol. Am. Diabetes Assn., Scottsdale, 1994—2004, Am. Heart Assn., Scottsdale, 1994—2004, Am. Cancer Assn., Scottsdale, 1994—2004. Recipient Golden Key Nat. Honor Soc., Mich. State U., 1981, Rho Chi Honor Soc., Midwestern U., 2000. Mem.: Am. Soc. of Health Sys. Pharmacists (licentiate), Am. Colleges of Clin. Pharmacists (licentiate), Am. Pharmacists Assn. (licentiate; del. 2001—03), Ariz. Pharmacy Assn. (licentiate; co-chair profl. affairs com. 1999—2000, maricopa rep. 2001—02, 2nd v.p. 2002—03, cert. of appreciation for outstanding svc. to Ariz. pharmacy assn. 2000, exec. bd. mem. award 2005). Avocations: scuba diving, cooking, jazz, travel, wine tasting. Home: 6120 E Gold Dust Ave Scottsdale AZ 85253 Office: Abbott Laboratories 6120 E Gold Dust Ave Scottsdale AZ 85253 Office Phone: 480-951-0366. Personal E-mail: lwpharmd@juno.com.

**WEAVER, LOIS JEAN,** physician, educator; b. Wheeling, W.Va., May 23, 1944; d. Lewis Everett and Ann Weaver. BA, Oberlin Coll., 1966; MD, U. Chgo., 1970. Pulmonary fellow Northwestern U., Evanston, Ill., 1975-77; trauma fellow U. Wash. Harborview Hosp., Seattle, 1977-79, research assoc., instr. medicine, 1979-81, clin. asst. prof. medicine, 1983—; clin. research fellow Virginia Mason Med. Research Ctr., Seattle, 1981-82; mem. med. staff Swedish Hosp., Seattle, 1984-92. Pulmonary cons. Fred Hutchinson Cancer Research Inst., Seattle, 1984-86, regional med. advisor and med. cons., disability quality br. Social Security, Seattle, 1985—. Contbr. sci. articles to profl. jours. La Verne Noyes scholar U. Chgo., 1966; Parker B. Francis fellow Northwestern U., 1975. Mem. AMA, Wash. Lung Assn., Sigma Xi. Avocations: gardening, music. Home: PO Box 2098 Kirkland WA 98083-2098 Office: 701 5th Ave Ste 2900 MIS 105 Seattle WA 98104-7075

**WEAVER, LUCILLE MAE,** retired elementary school educator, radiological technician; b. Lairdsville, Pa., Dec. 16, 1927; d. Frederick Thomas and Edna Lucille (Vandine) Tebbs; m. Carl Allen Weaver, Aug. 6, 1950; children: Craig Allen, Cynthia Ann, Christine Allison. BA, Lycoming Coll., 1968; M in elem. edn., Penn. State and In-Svc., 1978. Med. sec. Radiologists Office, Williamsport, Pa., 1945—51; reg. radiologist tech. Radiologist Office, Williamsport, Pa., 1951—57; part time tech. Divine Providence Hosp., 1961—68; tchr. Williamsport Area Sch. Dist., 1969—93; ret. Coun. pres., sec. and com. chair St. Mark's Luth. Ch. Mem.: Pa. Soc. Ret. Educators, DAR (hon. regent, registrar), Woman's Club Williamsport. Republican. Luth. Avocations: crafts, travel, gardening, quilting. Home: 401 Lincoln Ave Williamsport PA 17701

**WEAVER, LYNN EDWARD,** academic administrator, consultant, editor; b. St. Louis, Jan. 12, 1930; s. Lienous E. and Estelle F. (Laspe) W.; m. JoAnn D., 1951 (div. 1981); children: Terry Sollenberger, Gwen, Bart, Stephen, Wes; m. Anita G. Gomez, Oct. 27, 1983. BSEE, U. Mo., 1951; MSEE, So. Meth. U., 1955; PhD, Purdue U., 1958. Devel. engr. McDonnell Aircraft, St. Louis, 1952-53; aerophysics engr. Convair Corp., Ft. Worth, 1953-55; instr. elec. engring. Purdue U., Lafayette, Ind., 1955-58; assoc. prof., then prof., dept. head U Ariz., Tucson, 1959-69; assoc. dean coll. engring. U. Okla., Norman, 1969-70; exec. asst. to pres. Argonne Univs., Chgo., 1970-72; dir. sch. nuclear engring. and health physics Ga. Inst. Tech., 1972-82; dean engring., disting. prof. Auburn (Ala.) U., 1982-87; pres. Fla. Inst. Tech., Melbourne, 1987—2002, pres. emeritus prof. elec. engring., 2002—. Cons. Ga. Power; bd. dirs. DBA Systems, Inc., Melbourne, Fla.; chmn. pub. affairs coun. Am. Assn. Engring. Soc., Washington, 1984-87; bd. adv. Ctr. for Sci., Tech. and Media, Washington; chmn. Ind. Colls. and Univs. Fla., 1999-2001. Author: (textbook) Reactor Dynamics & Control, State Space Techniques, 1968; exec. editor Annals of Nuclear Energy; contbr. numerous articles to tech. jours. U.S. rep. World Fedn., Engring. Orgn. Engring. Edn., 1981-86; bd. dirs. myregion..org, 2001-. Served to lt. USAF, 1951-53. Recipient Mo. Honors award for disting. svc. in engring., 1996. Fellow Am. Nuclear Soc.; mem. IEEE (sr.), Am. Soc. Engring. Edn., Sigma Xi, Eau Gallie Yacht Club. Republican. Roman Catholic. Avocations: tennis, jogging. Office: Fla Inst Tech 150 W University Blvd Melbourne FL 32901-6975 Office Phone: 371-674-8099. E-mail: lweaver@fit.edu.

**WEAVER, MICHAEL ALAN,** music educator; b. West Chester, Pa., Oct. 11, 1962; s. Joseph Edward and Evelyn Edwards Weaver; m. Cathy Gail Cooper, Jan. 8, 1993; children: Alex Zygmunt, Vance Zygmunt. Assoc. in Gen. Studies, Chaminade U. of Honolulu, 1987; MusB in Music Edn., East Carolina U., 1996, MusM in Performance and Suzuki Pedagogy, 1998; MusD in Performance, Fla. State U., 2003. Lic. tchr. music K-12 NC Dept. of Pub. Instrn., 1996, Dept. of Pub. Instrn., NC, 2003. Cert. Suzuki violin tchr. Suzuki Assn. of the Americas, Colo., 1998, Suzuki viola tchr. Suzuki Assn. of the Americas, Colo., 1998. Mil. policeman, enlisted USMC, Kaneohe Bay, Hawaii, 1983—88, counterintelligence specialist Camp Lejeune, NC, 1988—93; pvt. violin and viola tchr. Elizabeth City, NC, 1994—; sect. and asst. prin. viola Long Bay Symphony, Myrtle Beach, SC, 1996—99; intern, sect. violist NC Symphony, Raleigh, NC, 1997; grad. tchg. asst. viola and music history East Carolina U., Greenville, NC, 1997—98; gen. asst. and counselor NC Suzuki Inst., Greenville, NC, 1997—99; substitute tchr. New Hanover County Schools, Wilmington, NC, 1998—99; propr., repairman Weaver's Bowed Instruments Sales and Repair, Elizabeth City, NC, 1999—; u. fellow Fla. State U., Tallahassee, 1999—2001; substitute violinist/violist Tallahassee Symphony Orch., Tallahassee, 1999—2002; orch. libr. Fla. State U. Summer Music Camps, Tallahassee, 2000, orch. camp coord., 2002—03; acting prin. violist Pensacola Symphony, Pensacola, Fla., 2000; prin. violist Albany Symphony Orch., Albany, Ga., 2000—02; grad. tchg. asst. in viola Fla. State U. Music, Tallahassee, 2001—02; u. fellow Fla. State U., Tallahassee, 2002—03; sect. violist Tallahassee Symphony Orch., Tallahassee, 2002—03; asst. prof., strings and music edn. Elizabeth City State U., Elizabeth City, NC, 2003—; substitute violist Wilmington Symphony Orch., Wilmington, NC, 2003—. Coord. cert. program NC Am. String Teachers Assn., Greenville, 2004—; violist, lectr. 4th Ann. Hawaii Internat. Conf. Arts and Humanities, 2006. Contbr. articles to profl. jours. Mem., music ministry Salem Bapt. Ch., Elizabeth City, NC, 2004, Bradfordville First Bapt. Ch., Tallahassee, 2000—04. Staff sgt. USMC, 1983—93, Parris Island, Camp Lejeune, Kaneohe Bay, Okinawa. Decorated Good Conduct medals USMC, Navy Achievement Medal, Navy and Marine Corps Overseas Svc. Medal, Joint Mil. Unit Award, Nat. Def. Svc. Medal; recipient All Am. Scholar Collegiate Award, East Carolina U., 1994—96; fellow, Fla. State U., 1999—2003; grantee Perkins String Quartet Project, James J. and Mamie Richardson Perkins Trust, 1998, Fla. State U., 2001; Gravely Found. scholar, East Carolina U., 1996. Mem.: Music Educators Nat. Conf. (faculty advisor 2004), Suzuki Assn. of the Americas, Violin Soc. of Am., Am. Viola Soc., Am. String Teachers Assn. (student chpt. pres. 1998—98, musical dir., condr. student chpt. symphony orch.), Golden Key (life), Omicron Delta Kappa (life), Pi Kappa Lambda Music Honors Soc. (life). Avocations: travel, fishing, scrimshaw. Home: 705 Flora Street Elizabeth City NC 27909 Office: Elizabeth City State University 1704 Weeksville Road Elizabeth City NC 27909 Office Phone: 252-335-3363. E-mail: maweaver@mail.ecsu.edu.

**WEAVER, MICHAEL GLENN,** pharmacist; b. Tuscola, Ill., Sept. 11, 1955; s. Glen H. and Margaret I. (Long) W.; m. Catherine A. (Paynic), Sept. 30, 1978; children: Jennifer L., Michelle R., Gregory M. BS, St. Louis Coll. of Pharmacy, 1978; MBA, So. Ill. U., 1989. Registered pharmacist Ill. Clin. coordinator, staff pharmacist St. Elizabeth Med. Ctr., Granite City, Ill., 1975-87; dir. pharmacy Freeport (Ill.) Meml. Hosp. (now Freeport Health Network), 1987-92, dir. pharmacy and info. systems, 1992-97, dir. info. and telecom. svcs., 1997—2002; dir. pharmacy Freeport Health Network, 2002—; dir. Ill. Bd. Pharmacy, 1995-99, AeroComputing, Inc., 2001—02. Allocations com. United Way of N.W. Ill., 2000-, bd. dirs. 2006-, Girl Scouts, Green Hills, 2005-. Mem.: Am. Coll. Healthcare Execs., Ill. Coun. Hosp. Pharmacists (dir. ednl. affairs 1991—94, dir. orgnl. affairs 2004—05, pres.-elect 2005—06), Ill. Pharm. Assn., Am. Soc. Hosp. Pharmacists, Kiwanis (dir. 2005- Lincoln-Douglas chpt. 2002—, v.p. 2003—04, pres. elect 2004—05, pres. 2005—), Delta Sigma Theta, Beta Gamma Sigma, Phi Kappa Phi. Republican. Mem. United Church of Christ. Avocations: computer, music, tennis, swimming, racquetball. Home: 1346 Carriage Hill Ln Freeport IL 61032-6168 Office: Freeport Health Network 1045 W Stephenson St Freeport IL 61032-4899 Personal E-mail: mgw01@aol.com. Business E-mail: mweaver@fhn.org.

**WEAVER, MICHAEL JAMES,** lawyer; b. Bakersfield, Calif., Feb. 11, 1946; s. Kenneth James and Elsa Hope (Rogers) W.; m. Valerie Scott, Sept. 2, 1966; children: Christopher James, Brett Michael, Karen Ashley. AB, Calif. State U., Long Beach, 1968; JD magna cum laude, U. San Diego, 1973. Bar: Calif., 1973, U.S. Dist. Ct. (so. dist.) Calif. 1973, U.S. Ct. Appeals (9th cir.) 1975, U.S. Supreme Ct. 1977. Law clk. to chief judge U.S. Dist. Ct. (so. dist.) Calif., San Diego, 1973-75; with Latham & Watkins, San Diego. Judge pro tem San Diego Superior Ct.; master of the Bench of the Inn, Am. Inns of Ct., Louis M. Welch chpt.; lectr. Inn of Ct., San Diego, 1981—, Continuing Edn. of Bar, Calif., 1983—, Workshop for Judges U.S. Ct. Appeals (9th cir.), 1990; mem. task force on establishment of bus. cts. sys. Jud. Coun. Calif., 1996-97; adv. com. U.S. Ct. Appeals (9th cir.), 2006—. Editor-in-chief: San Diego Law Rev., 1973; contbr. articles to profl. jours. Bd. dirs., pres. San Diego Kidney Found., 1985-90; bd. dirs. San Diego Aerospace Mus., 1985-97; trustee La Jolla (Calif.) Playhouse, 1990-91. lt. USNR, 1968-74. Fellow Am. Coll. Trial Lawyers; mem. San Diego Assn. Bus. Trial Lawyers (founding mem., bd. govs.), San Diego Def. Lawyers Assn. (dir.), Am. Arbitration Assn., 9th Cir. Jud. Conf. (del. 1987-90), Calif. Supreme Ct. Hist. Assn. (bd. dirs. 1998—), Safari Club Internat. (San Diego chpt.), San Diego Sportsmen's Club, Coronado Yacht Club. Republican. Presbyterian. Avocations: reading, flying, skiing. Office: Latham & Watkins 600 West Broadway Ste 1800 San Diego CA 92101-8197 Business E-Mail: mike.weaver@lw.com.

**WEAVER, MOLLIE LITTLE,** lawyer; b. Alma, Ga., Mar. 11; d. Alfred Ross and Annis Mae (Bowles) Little; m. Jack Delano Nelson, Sept. 12, 1953 (div. May 1970); 1 dau., Cynthia Ann; m. 2d, Hobart Ayres Weaver, June 10, 1970; stepchildren: Hobart Jr., Mary Essa, Robert. BA in History, U. Richmond, 1978; JD, Wake Forest U., 1981. Bar: N.C. 1982, Fla. 1983; Cert. profl. sec.; cert. adminstrv. mgr. Supr., Western Electric Co., Richmond, Va., 1952-75; cons., owner Cert. Mgmt. Assocs., Richmond, 1975-76; sole practice, Ft. Lauderdale, Fla., 1982-86, Emerald Isle, N.C., 1986-89, Richmond, 1989—. Author: Secretary's Reference Manual, 1973. Mem. adv. coun. to Bus. and Office Edn., Greensboro, N.C., 1970-73, adv. com. to bus. edn. Va. Commonwealth U., Richmond, 1977. Recipient Key to City of Winston-Salem, N.C., 1963; Epps award for scholarship, 1978. Mem. ABA, N.C. Bar Assn., Fla. Bar Assn., Word Processing Assn. (v.p., founder Richmond 1973-75), Adminstrv. Mgmt. Soc. (com. chmn. Richmond, 1973-75), Phi Beta Kappa, Eta Sigma Phi, Phi Alpha Theta. Republican. Home: 12301 Renwick Pl Glen Allen VA 23059-6959 E-mail: Legal311@aol.com.

**WEAVER, MURIEL MARGARET,** music educator; b. Dayton, Ohio, Apr. 22, 1943; d. Robert Flower and Dixie Faye (Wakeman) McKibben; m. Fredrick Daniel Weaver, June 5, 1965; children: Meva Anne, Kelly Marie, Christopher Ryan, Melissa Faye. BA cum laude, Miami U., Oxford, 1965, MEd, Mt. St. Joseph, Cin., 1986. Music tchr. Trotwood-Madison (Ohio) Pub. Sch., 1965-73, Worthington Pub. Sch., Chillicothe, Ohio, 1975-76, Chillicothe Pub. Sch., 1983—. Pvt. practice tchr. music, Dayton and Chillicothe, 1960—. Violinist Dayton Symphony Orch., 1962—73, Columbus Symphony Orch., 1973—75, Portsmouth Cmty. Orch., 2005—; dir. Agapé Handbell Choir, Chillicothe, 1976—; dir. choir Walnut St. United Meth. Ch., 1980—; co-dir. Chillicothe Cmty. Chorus, 1981—91; founder, coord. Chillicothe String Ensemble, 1994—. Fellow NEA, Chillicothe Educator's Assn., Ohio Music Educator's Assn., Am. Guild English Handbell Ringers, Am. String Tchrs. Assn., Phi Beta Kappa, Delta Omicron. Clubs: Chillicothe Raquet, Miriam-Rebekah Circle. Republican. Methodist. Avocations: tennis, raquetball, camping.

**WEAVER, PEGGY (MARGUERITE MCKINNIE WEAVER),** plantation owner; b. Jackson, Tenn., June 7, 1925; d. Franklin Allen and Mary Alice (Caradine) McKinnie; children: Elizabeth Lynn, Thomas Jackson III, Franklin A. McKinnie. Student, U. Colo., 1943-45, Am. Acad. Dramatic Arts, 1945-46, S. meisner's Profl. Classes, 1949, Oxford U., 1990, 91. Actress, 1946-52; mem. staff Mus. Modern Art, N.Y.C., 1949-50; woman's editor radio sta. WTJS-AM-FM, Jackson, Tenn., 1952-55; editor, radio/TV Jackson Sun Newspaper, 1952-55; columnist Bolivar (Tenn.) Bulletin-Times, 1986—2000; chmn. Ho. of Reps. of Old Line Dist., Hardeman County, Tenn., 1986—91, 1994—97. Pres. Hardeman County chpt. Assn. Preservation of Tenn. Antiquities, 1991—95; charter mem. adv. bd. Tenn. Arts Commn., Nashville, 1967—74, Tenn. Performing Arts Ctr., Nashville, 1972—; chmn. trustees br. Tenn. Libr. Assn., Nashville, 1973—74; Henry County regional chmn. Opera Memphis, 1979—91; mem. nat. coun. Met. Opera, N.Y.C., 1980—92, Tenn. Bicentennial Com., Hardeman County, 1993—96; bd. sec. Memphis Brooks Mus. League, 1997—98; docent Dixon Gallery and Gardens, Memphis; founder Paris-Henry County (Tenn.) Arts Coun., 1965. Mem. DAR, Nat. Soc. Colonial Dames Am. (chmn. Memphis Town com. 2002-04), Oxford Alumni Assn. N.Y., English Speaking Union (London chpt.), Jamestown Soc., Crescent Club, Dilettantes. Methodist. Avocations: horseback riding, travel, theater. Office: 402 Heritage Plantation Hickory Valley TN 38042 Office Phone: 731-764-6009. Business E-Mail: pweaver@heritagecompanies.net.

**WEAVER, PETER DAVID,** bishop, religious organization administrator; b. Greenville, Pa., Jan. 15, 1945; s. Adolph Peter and Dorothy Selina (Barbor) W.; children: Rebecca Hope, Sarah Joy, Rachel Faith. ThD, Boston U., 1975; MDiv, Drew U., 1969; BA, W.Va. Wesleyan U., 1966. Ordained deacon and elder United Meth. Ch. Pastor Whitaker (Pa.) U. Meth. Ch., 1971-77; sr. pastor Smithfield United Ch., Pitts., 1977-88, First United Meth. Ch., Pitts., 1988-96; bishop United Meth. Ch., Phila., 1996—2004, pres. coun. of bishops, 2003—, bishop, New Eng. conference Boston, 2004—. Adj. faculty Drew U., Madison, N.J., 1980's, Pitts. Theol. Seminary, 1990's; co-founder, pres. Bethlehem Haven, Pitts., 1981-88; chair mission divsn. Gen. Coun. on Ministries United Meth. Ch., Dayton, Ohio, 1992-96. Bd. dirs. YMCA, Pitts., 1978-88, Goodwill Industries, Pitts., 1981-93, One Voice Against Racism, Pitts., 1990-96, Vintage Inc., Pitts., 1989-96; trustee W.Va. Wesleyan Coll., Buckannon, 1980-96, Drew U., 1996—, Wesley Coll. 1996-04, Lebanon Valley Coll., 1996-04, Boston U., 2004-. Avocations: woodworking, music, water sports. Office: Box 249 Lawrence MA 01842

**WEAVER, PHILIP G.,** tire company executive; BS, Bowling Green State U.; degree advanced mgmt. internat. sr. mgr. program, Harvard Bus. Sch. Cert. CPA. Principal, sr. mgr. Ernst & Young; tire divsn. contr. Cooper Tire & Rubber, 1990—94; v.p. Cooper Tire & Rubber Co., Tire Divsn., 1994—98; v.p., CFO Cooper Tire & Rubber Co., Findlay, Ohio, 1998—. Mem.: Blanchard Valley Health Assn., Blanchard Valley Reg. Health Ctr., Am. Inst. of CPAs, Ohio Soc. of CPAs, Toledo Chpt. Fin. Exec. Inst. Office: Cooper Tire & Rubber Co 701 Lima Ave Findlay OH 45840

**WEAVER, REG (REGINALD WEAVER),** educational association administrator; b. Danville, Ill. BS, Ill. State U.; MS, Roosevelt U., Chgo. Teacher Danville High Sch., Danville, Ill.; local Nat. Edn. Assoc. (NEA) pres. Harvey, Ill., 1967—71; pres. Ill Edn. Assoc. 1981—87; mem. NEA exec. com., 1989—95; v.p. NEA, 1996—2002, pres., 2002—. Mem. exec. bd. Nat. Coun. for Accreditation of Tchr. Edn.; chair IEA Political Action Com. for Edn. (IPACE); appointed to Ill. Commn. for Improvement of Elementary and Secondary Edn., Ill. Project for Sch. Reform Adv. Coun., Ill. Literacy Coun., Task Force on At-Risk Youth; mem. Ill. State Bd. of Edn. Blue Ribbon Comm. on Improvement of Tchg. as a Profession. Named One of the Outstanding Men of America; named one of Most Influential Black Americans, Ebony mag., 2006; recipient Ebony Mag. Influential Black Educators award, Ill. Edn. Assoc. Human Relations award, Wall of Fame, Danville High Sch. Mem.: Nat. Parent Tchr. Assn. (hon.). Office: NEA 1201 16th St NW Washington DC 20036*

**WEAVER, RICHARD L., II,** writer, educator; b. Hanover, NH, Dec. 5, 1941; s. Richard L. and Florence B. (Grow) W.; m. Andrea A. Willis; children: Richard Scott, Jacquelynn Michelle, Anthony Keith, Joanna Corinne. AB, U. Mich., 1964, MA, 1965; PhD, Ind. U., 1969. Asst. prof. U. Mass., 1968-74; assoc. prof. speech communication Bowling Green State U., 1974-79, prof., 1979-96, dir., basic speech communication course, 1974-96. Vis. prof. U. Hawaii-Manoa, 1981-82, Bond U., Queensland, Australia, 1990, St. Albans, Melbourne, Australia, 1990, Western Inst., Perth, Australia, 1990. Author: (with Saundra Hybels) Speech/Communication, 1974, 2d edit., 1979, Speech/Communication: A Reader, 1975, 2d edit., 1979, Speech/Communication: A Student Manual, 1976, 2d edit., 1979, Understanding Interpersonal Communication, 1978, 2d edit., 1981, 3d edit., 1984, 4th edit., 1987, 5th edit., 1990, 6th edit., 1993, 7th edit., 1996, (with Raymond K. Tucker, Cynthia Berryman-Fink) Research in Speech Communication, 1981, Foundations of Speech Communication: Perspectives of a Discipline, 1982, Speech Communication Skills, 1982, Understanding Public Communication, 1983, Understanding Business Communication, 1985, Understanding Speech Communication Skills, 1985, Readings in Speech Communication, 1985, (with Saundra Hybels) Communicating Effectively, 1986, 2d edit., 1989, 3d edit., 1992, 4th edit., 1995, 5th edit., 1998, 6th edit., 2001, 7th edit., 2004, 8th edit., 2007, Skills for Communicating Effectively, 1985, 2d edit., 1988, 3d edit., 1991, 4th edit., 1993, rev. edit., 1995, (with Howard W. Cotrell) Innovative Instructional Strategies, 1987, 2d edit., 1988, 3d edit., 1989, 4th edit., 1990, 5th edit., 1992, 6th edit., 1993, (with Curt Bechler) Listen to Win: A Guide to Effective Listening, 1994, Study Guide to Accompany Communicating Effectively, 1995, 2d edit., 1998, Essentials of Public Speaking, 1996, 2d edit., 2001, (with Edgar E. Willis) How to be Funny on Purpose: Creating and Consuming Humor, 2005. Mem. emeritus Nat. Comm. Assn., Cert. States Speech Assn., Ohio Speech Assn. Home and Office: 9583 Woodleigh Ct Perrysburg OH 43551-2669 Office Phone: 419-874-2124. Personal E-mail: Richard@Weaverworks.net. Business E-Mail: weaverii@sbcglobal.net.

**WEAVER, ROBERT COOPER,** small business owner, volunteer; b. Talladega, Alabama, Dec. 29, 1927; s. William Kiser and Roberta (Cooper) Weaver. BA, Howard Coll., 1949. Pres. Wood Weaver, Inc., Talladega, Ala., 1950—. Prodr.: (series of 53 radio programs for Talladega C.C.) Let's Do More in '54, 1954; filmed: (movie) Youth Recreation in Talladega, 1958; prodr.: (singing the Lord's Prayer) by deaf and blind children, 1983—; author hundreds of graphic Sunday sch. lessons for deaf children; dir.: (Sunday night worship svc. for deaf children), 1991—; coord. (deaf and blind students singing with voice and sign language) Talladega Super Speedway and Nat. TV program, The Deaf Shall Hear, —, designed (USS Talladega Monument) Talladega County Courthouse, 2002. Organized world's first Fellowship of Christian Athletics Chpt. for the Deaf Ala. Sch. for the Deaf, 1981; organizer City Basketball League, Talladega, Ala., 1953; chmn. Turkey Festival Parade, Talladega, 1953; organizer $1 season tickets, increasing attendance by thousands per season Municipal Pool, Talladega, Ala., 1954; organizer Kiwi Baseball League, Talladega, Ala., 1960, Athletic Club Basketball League, Talladega, Ala., 1961, Ala. Sch. for the Deaf Boys Basketball League, 1970; mem. libr. bd., Talladega, Ala., 1972—75; organizer Flag Tag Football League, Talladega, Ala.; organized Ala. State Table Tennis Tournament; organized Sunday morning devotional programs AIDB Lunchroom workers, Talladega, Ala.; organizer Little League Baseball, Talladega, Ala., 1953; music leader area Ch. revivals, Ala.; dir. Cmty. Ch. for the Deaf, Ala., 1971—76; established, directed Helen Keller Sch. of Ala. Sunday Sch., 1976—85; established sixty-second-sermons ministries writing and distr. leaflets to Sunday workers and jails; dir. AIDB's Hawkins Chapel, Talladega, Ala., 1985—88; mem. First Bapt. Ch., Talladega, Ala.; bd. mem., treas. Greater Talladega C of C., Ala.; bd. mem. North Talladega County United Way, Ala., North Talladega County Assn. for Retarded Citizens, Ala., 2004—. Recipient Talladega Citizen of the Yr. Notable Svc. Award, C. of C., 1955, first Lotus Award, Ala., 1982, Outstanding Good Neighbor in Am., Good Neighbor Search in N.Y., Newsweek Mag., 1990, Civitan Svc. Award, 1963, Ala. Recreation Soc. Lay Award, 1965, Alablind Award, Alumni and Workers Assn., 1970, Ala. Assn. for Deaf Award, 1981, Ala. Inst. for the Deaf and Blind dormitory named Robert C. Weaver Cottage, 1983, Alablind Award, Alumni and Workers Association, 1989, first AIDB Robert C. Weaver Vol. Award, 1995, Ala. Assn. for Deaf Award, 1997, Outstanding Talladegans of the Centuries 1834-2000 Award, 2000, many others awards. Mem.: Ala. Assn. for Deaf (Ala. Royal Amb. chair 2003), Talladega Jaycees (chmn. horse show 1952, orginated newsboy appreciation day 1953), Talladega Kiwanis Club. Achievements include invention of electronic Weaver board game for blind children, 1965; development of campus radio sta. at the Ala. Sch. for the Blind to aid blind students at wrestling matches, 1967; reading aids for pre-school deaf children, 1980; attracted more than 15,000 boy scouts from southeastern states to walk the Odum Scout Trail at Cheaha Mountain; design of trail medal and color brochure to promote the Odum Scout Trail. Office: Wood Weaver Inc 112 Ct Square E Talladega AL 35160 Office Phone: 256-362-4741. Personal E-mail: weaver52@bellsouth.net.

**WEAVER, ROBIN GEOFFREY,** lawyer, educator; b. Columbus, Ohio, Aug. 19, 1948; BA, Ohio State U., 1970; JD, U. Mich., 1973. Bar: Ohio 1974, U.S. Dist. Ct. (no. dist.) Ohio 1974, U.S. Ct. Appeals (6th cir.) 1980, U.S. Ct. Appeals (3d cir.) 1998, U.S. Ct. Appeals (2d, 7th, and 11th cirs.) 2002, U.S. Supreme Ct., 2002, U.S. Dist. Ct. (so. dist.) Ohio 2004. Assoc. Squire, Sanders & Dempsey, Cleve., 1973-83, ptnr., 1983—; mem. faculty Nat. Inst. for Trial Adv. Northwestern U., Chgo., 1983—. Mem. Ohio Supreme Ct. Bd. of Commrs. on Grievances and Discipline, chair, 1974-99, master commr., 2002-. With U.S. Army, 1974. Fellow Am. Coll. Trial Lawyers, Internat. Soc. Barristers; mem. Cleve. Bar Assn. (pres. 2002-03); mem. ABA, Ohio Bar Assn., Cleve. Assn. Trial Attys. (life), 8th Appellate Jud. Conf., Am. Inns of Ct. (master bencher Cleve. chpt.). Office: Squire Sanders & Dempsey 4900 Key Tower Cleveland OH 44114 Office Phone: 216-479-8500.

**WEAVER, RUSSELL,** music educator; MusB, U. Iowa, 1985. Dir. bands Osceola County Schs. for Arts, Kissimmee, Fla., 2002—. Pres. Cyberwinds Music Com., Kissimmee. Composer: Kissimmee Blues, Mommy Got a Day Gig, Wound It Out. Nominee Grammy award, 1990; named Disney Am. Tchr. Honoree, Hollywood, Calif., 1999. Mem.: IAJE, FBA, Music Educators Nat. Conf. Democrat. Avocation: building electric vehicles. Office: Osceola County Sch Arts 3151 N Orange Blossom Tr Kissimmee FL 34744

**WEAVER, SIGOURNEY (SUSAN ALEXANDRA WEAVER),** actress; b. NYC, Oct. 8, 1949; d. Sylvester (Pat) Weaver and Elizabeth Inglish; m. Jim Simpson, Oct. 1, 1984; 1 child, Charlotte. BA in English, Stanford U., 1971; MA in Drama, Yale U., 1974. Actress: (theatre) including Watergate Classics, 1973, The Frogs, 1974 The Nature and Purpose of the Universe, 1974, Daryl and Carol and Kenny and Jenny, The Constant Wife, 1975, Titanic, 1976, Das Lusitania Songspiel (also co-writer), 1976, Marco Polo Sings a Song, 1977, A Flea in Her Ear, 1978, Conjuring an Event, 1978, Beyond Therapy, 1981, As You Like It, 1981, Hurlyburly, 1984-85, Sex and Longing, 1996, The Merchant of Venice, 1986, The Guys, 2002, The Mercy Seat, 2002, Mrs. Farnsworth, 2004, (films) Annie Hall, 1977, Madman, 1978, Alien, 1979, Eyewitness, 1981, The Year of Living Dangerously, 1982, Deal of the Century, 1983, Ghostbusters, 1984, Une femme ou deux, 1985, Aliens, 1986 (Acad. Award nomination for best actress, 1987), Half Moon Street, 1986, Gorillas in the Mist, 1988 (Acad. Award nomination for best actress, 1989, Golden Globe for best actress - drama, 1989), Working Girl, 1988 (Acad. Award nomination for best supporting actress, 1989, Golden Globe for best supporting actress in a motion picture, 1989), Ghostbusters II, 1989, 1492: Conquest of Paradise, 1992, Dave, 1993, Death and the Maiden, 1994, Jeffrey, 1995, Copycat, 1995, Snow White: A Tale of Terror, 1997, The Ice Storm, 1997 (BAFTA Film Award for best supporting actress, 1998), A Map of the World, 1999, Galaxy Quest, 1999, Airframe, 1999, Company Man, 2000, Speak Truth to Power, 2000, Heartbreakers, 2001, Big Bad Love (voice), 2001, Tadpole, 2002, The Guys, 2002, Holes, 2003, The Village, 2004, Imaginary Heroes, 2004, (TV series) Somerset, 1976, (TV miniseries) The Best of Families, 1977, (TV movies) 3 by Cheever: The Sorrows of Gin, 1979, 3 by Cheever: O Youth and Beauty!, 1979; co-prodr., actress: (films) Alien 3, 1992, Alien: Resurrection, 1997. Recipient Star on the Walk of Fame, 1999, Lifetime Achievement award, Chicago Internat. Film Festival, 2001. Office: William Morris Agy One William Morris Pl Beverly Hills CA 90212

**WEAVER, TERRY L.,** special education educator, writer; s. Amos B. and Esther L. Weaver; m. Kay I. Isbell, June 20, 1981; children: Carol Lee, Patricia M., John Andrew. BS, Fla. Atlantic U., 1972, MEd, 1973; PhD, Vanderbilt U., 1984. Tchr. Miami (Fla.) Dade Bd. Pub. Instrn., 1973—79; asst. prof. spl. edn. Carson Newman Coll., Jefferson City, Tenn., 1983—92; assoc. prof. spl. edn. Union U., Jackson, Tenn., 1992—. Author: (textbook) Teaching Mathematics to All Children, 2002, 2nd edit., 2006. Co-chair conf. planning Harrison Coun. for Children with Behavior and Learning Problems & West Tenn. Healthcare Found., Jackson, 1993—2005. Mem.: Coun. for Learning Disabilities. Presbyterian. Avocations: gardening, board games, video games. Office: Union University 1050 Union University Dr Jackson TN 38305 Office Phone: 731-661-5388. Office Fax: 731-661-5063. Business E-Mail: tweaver@uu.edu.

**WEAVER, THOMAS HAROLD,** health facility administrator; b. Asheville, N.C., July 21, 1943; s. Thomas Harold and Evelyn (Morris) W.; m. Marsha Va Fossen, Dec. 17, 1982; 1 child, Sallie Jayne. BA, Va. Mil. Inst., 1964; MEd, U. Ga., 1970; MAHA, George Washington U., 1973. Vol. EMS, various locations, 1965-94; mgmt. analyst VA Med. Ctr., Martinez, Calif., 1972-74; health planner VA Ctrl. Hdqs., Washington, 1974-76, sr. health sys. specialist, 1976-79; asst. dir. VA Med. Ctr., Lexington, Ky., 1979, COO, assoc. dir. Ft. Howard, Md., 1980-82, sr. exec. sys. specialist Durham, N.C., 1982-85, COO, assoc. med. dir. Pitts., 1985-89, CEO, med. ctr. dir. Martinsburg, W.Va., 1989-94, CEO, dir. Bay Pines, Fla., 1994—. V.p., bd. dirs. Berkeley County Emergency Ambulance Authority, Martinsburg, 1989—94; pres., chmn. bd. Bedington Vol. Fire and Rescue Dept., 1989—93; disting. vis. lectr. W.Va. U., 1992—94; adj. prof. U. Tampa, 1996—98; instr. dept. emergency mgmt. St. Petersburg Coll., 1997—2002. Contbr. articles to profl. jours., chpt. to book. Emergency med. svcs. instr. various locations, 1967—98, W.Va., 1990—94; bd. dirs. Pinellas County EMS MEd. Control Bd., 1995—2001, Hurricanes and Health Care Consortium, 1995—98; mem. Pinellas County Disaster Adv. Com., 1996—2002; incident comdr. Bay Pines Hazmat Decon Team, 1997—2002; chair hosp. terrorism task force Fla. Dept. Health, 2000—01; bd. dirs. Hurricanes and Health Care Consortium, 2001—02. Named Preceptor of Yr. Xavier U., 2002; recipient Nat. Cmty. Svc. award, Sec. Vet. Affairs, Washington, 1975, cert. of merit, Geico Pub. Svc., Washington, 1985, Spl. Act Commendation award, DVA and County Commn. for outstanding actions during cmty. disaster, 1993, John. J. Stuvdevent Partnership award, 1998, Fla. Sch.-to-Work Gold award, 1998, award, Nat. Assn. State Dirs. of Vocat. Edn., 1999, Outstanding Achievement award, Fla. State Emergency Response Commn., 2001. Fellow Am. Coll. Healthcare Execs. (Fed. Exec. of Yr. W.Va. chpt. 1994); mem. Nat. Registry EMTs. Home: 840 Scoggin Rd Tallahassee FL 32303-4655

**WEAVER, TIMOTHY ALLAN,** lawyer; b. Elkhart, Ind., Nov. 30, 1948; s. Arthur and Joan Lucile (Yoder) W.; m. Catherine Anne Power, Nov. 23, 1974; children: Daniel Timothy, Christopher Matthew, David Colwell. AB, Brown U., 1971; JD, U. Ill. 1974. Bar: Ill. 1974, U.S. Wis. 1999, U.S. Dist. Ct. (no. dist.) Ill. 1975, U.S. Ct. Appeals (7th cir.) 1975, U.S. Dist. Ct. (no. dist. trial bar) Ill. 1982, U.S. Dist. Ct. (ea. dist.) Wis. 1999. Asst. pub. defender Cook County Pub. Defender, Chgo., 1974-75; trial atty. Chgo. Transit Authority, 1975-78; assoc. Philip E. Howard Ltd., Chgo., 1978, Pretzel & Stouffer, Chartered, Chgo., 1978-82, ptnr., 1982—. Editor: Medical Malpractice, 1989, 92, 96; contbr. chpts. to books. Mem. ABA, Ill. State Bar Assn., Ill. Assn. Def. Trial Counsel, State Bar of Wis., Civil Trial Counsel of Wis., The Lawyers Club of Chgo. Office: Pretzel & Stouffer Chartered One S Wacker Dr #2500 Chicago IL 60606 Office Phone: 312-578-7416. E-mail: tweaver@pretzel-stouffer.com.

**WEAVER, WILLIAM CHARLES,** manufacturing executive; b. Nov. 10, 1941; s. Curtis D. and Mary (Yahres) W.; m. Karla Lee Kottas, June 13, 1964; children: Michael, Kelli. BS in Edn., Indiana U. of Pa., 1963; postgrad. in acctg., Tex. Christian U., 1964-65. CPA, Pa. With Price Waterhouse & Co., Pitts., 1965-73, audit mgr., 1970-73; corp. contr. Kennametal Inc., Latrobe, Pa., 1973-78, v.p., contr., 1978-83, v.p., treas., 1983-86, v.p., CFO, 1987-89; sr. v.p., CFO Oak Industries, Inc., Waltham, Mass., 1990-95; ret., 1995. Bd. dirs. Gemini Precision Products; chmn. bd. Weaver Enterprises, Inc., 1996—. Pres. Mountain View Parent Tchrs. Orgn., 1976—77; bd. dirs. East High Acres Civic Assn., 1976—77; treas. Greater Latrobe Hockey Club, 1982—87; chmn. bd. dirs., mem. adv. coun. Jr. Achievement, Latrobe, 1982—85; chmn. bd. trustees Latrobe United Way, 1988—89; trustee Hampton United Presbyn. Ch., 1972—73. 1st lt. U.S. Army, 1963—65. Mem.: Fin. Execs. Inst., Palmetto Dunes Club Inc. (pres. 1998—2001). E-mail: kbweaver@hargray.com.

**WEAVER, WILLIAM CLAIR, JR., (MIKE WEAVER),** human resources development executive; b. Ind., Pa., Apr. 11, 1936; s. William Clair and Zaida (Bley) W.; m. Janet Marcelle Boyd, Sept. 18, 1963 (div. 1978); 1 child, William Michael; m. Donna June Hubbuch, Feb. 10, 1984. B Aero Engring., Rensselaer Poly. Inst., 1958; MBA, Washington U., St. Louis, 1971; postgrad., Rutgers U.; grad., Armed Forces Indsl. Coll. Registered profl. engr. Engr. aerodynamics N.Am. Aviation, LA, 1959-60; engr. flight test ops. Boeing/Vertol, Phila., 1963-66; engr. flight test project Lockhead Electronics, Plainfield, NJ, 1966—69; project engr. advanced systems, sr. staff engr. Emerson Electric Co., St. Louis, 1969—72; pres. Achievement Assocs., Inc., St. Louis, 1972—. Founder, charter mem. Catalyst, 1978—; faculty Leadership Mgmt., Inc.; spkr. in field. Author: Winning Selling, 1983; contbr. articles to profl. jours. Active on Boy Scouts Am. Founder, Brainerd, Mo., 1974. Capt. USAF, 1960-63, USAFR. Mem. AIAA, NSPE, Cato Inst., Am. Soc. Tng. and Devel., Am. Soc. Bus. and Mgmt. Cons., Am. Ordnance Soc., Assn. MBA Execs., Air Force Assn., Am. Helicopter Soc., Acacia Frat., St. Louis C.

of C., Mensa, Mo. Athletic Club, Beta Gamma Sigma. Republican. Lutheran. Avocations: photography, music, sports. Home and Office: 1016 Evergreen Rd Yardley PA 19067-1018 Office Phone: 215-428-3400. Personal E-mail: acacia@aol.com.

**WEAVER, WILLIAM SCHILDECKER,** retired electric power industry executive; b. Pitts., Jan. 15, 1944; s. Charles Henry and Louise (Schildecker) W.; m. Janet Kae Jones, Mar. 7, 1981. BA, Hamilton Coll., 1965; JD, U. Mich., 1968. Bar: Wash. 1968. Assoc. Perkins Coie, Seattle, 1968-74, ptnr., 1975-91; exec. v.p., CFO Puget Sound Power & Light Co., Bellevue, Wash., 1991-97; vice chmn., chmn. unregulated subs. Puget Sound Energy, 1997, pres., COO, 1997, pres., CEO 1998—2002, chmn., 2001—02, ret. Bd. dirs. Wash. Rsch. Coun., Seattle, 1991-97, chmn., 1995-97; trustee Seattle Repertory Theatre, 1992-95, 99-2000, chmn., 2000-02, Corp. Coun. Arts, 1995-2002, Pacific Sci. Ctr., 1997-2002; bd. dirs. Edison Electric Inst., 1998-2002. Mem. ABA, Wash. State Bar Assn., Seattle Yacht Club, Flounder Bay Yacht Club.

**WEAVER, WILL(IAM WELLER),** language educator, writer; b. 1950; Farmer, Park Rapids, Minn., 1977-81; with Bemidji (Minn.) State U., part-time writing instr., 1979-81, assoc. prof., 1981-90, prof. English 1990—. Author: Red Earth, White Earth, 1986, A Gravestone Made of Wheat, 1989, Striking Out, 1993; contbr. articles to profl. publs. Office: Bemidji State U Dept English Bemidji MN 56601

**WEAVER-STROH, JOANNE MATEER,** education educator, consultant; b. May 21, 1930; d. Kenneth Hall and Jean (Weakley) Mateer; children: Karen, Mark, Laurie. BS in Edn., U. Pa., 1952, elem. and secondary prin. cert., 1979; MS in Psychology Reading, Temple U., 1968. Tchr. Paoli (Pa.) Sch., 1952-53, Somerville Sch., Ridgewood, NJ, 1953-55, Bryn Mawr (Pa.) Sch., 1955-57, Erdenheim Sch., Springfield, Pa., 1957-58; reading specialist Abington (Pa.) Sch. Dist., 1966-67, curriculum specialist, 1967-73, coord. human rels. programs, 1973-80; prin. Rydal Elem. Sch., Abington, 1980-88, Willow Hill Elem. Sch., 1988-96; ret., 1996. Cons., tchr. Marywood Coll., Scranton, Pa., 1972—; coord. drug and alcohol abuse program Abington Sch. Dist., 1989-96; cons. Conflict Resolution, 1996—. Chmn. Abington Human Rels. Adv. Coun., 1973-88; chmn. Cmty. Rels. Com. Abington Twp., 1978—; mem. Ea. Montgomery County Human Rels. Adv. Coun., 1981-83, 2006—; chmn. No Place for Hate project Abington Twp., 2003—; mediator Abington Twp.; leader Stephen Ministry program Abington Presbyn. Ch.; mem. ctr. internat. leadership and comm. bd. advisors Pa. State U., Abington, 2006—. Named Citizen of the Week Times Chronicle Newspaper, 1976; recipient award Four Chaplains Temple U., 1979, Disting. Citizens award Roslyn Jr. C. of C., 1981, Citizens for Progress Humanitarian award, 1982, Cmty. award Abington YMCA, 1987, Dr. Martin Luther King Jr. award Abington Twp., 1989, East Montgomery County/Pa. State Human Rels. Intergroup award, 2000, Citizens That Care award Abington Cmty. Taskforce, 2003, Disting. Cmty. Svc. award Intersvc. Clubs of Glenside, 2003. Mem. ASCD, NASEP, Internat. Coop. Learning Assn., Pa. Assn. Elem. Prins., Phi Delta Kappa, Delta Kappa Gamma. Republican. Home: 109 Durham Ct Maple Glen PA 19002-2854 Personal E-mail: rwstroh@att.net.

**WEBB, ANTHONY ALLAN,** banker, director; b. Lincoln, Nebr., May 24, 1943; s. Robert McGraw and Ruth Irene (Good) W.; m. Micheline Tourville, July 10, 1971; children— Annie, Christian BA, U. Colo., 1965; B.Internat. Mgmt., Am. Grad. Sch. Internat. Mgmt., 1970. Various positions Royal Bank Can., Montreal and London, 1970-77, assoc. mgr. Toronto, Ont., Canada, 1977-80, v.p., 1980-83, sr. v.p. merchant banking, 1983-84, dir. gen. Geneva, 1984-88, sr. v.p. personal fin. svcs. Montreal, 1988-93; chmn. Royal Bank Can. Suisse, Royal Bank Can., Channel Islands; pres., CEO Royal Trust, Toronto, 1993-99; chair The Exec. Com., 2000—. Served to lt. comdr. USNR, 1965-69 Home: 90 Binscarth Rd Toronto ON Canada M4W 1Y4 E-mail: tonywebb@rogers.com.

**WEBB, CARL B.,** banker; BA, W. Tex. State U., 1972; attended, Tex. Tech. U., Masters Bus.; grad., Southern Methodist U., 1981. Corp. banking divn. InterFirst Bank, Dallas; v.p., dir. Gerald Ford's First United Bank Group, 1983; pres., COO First Nat. Bank, Lubbock, Tex., 1983-88, First Gibraltar Bank, 1988-93, First Nationwide Bank, 1994-97, Ca. Federal Bank, 1997—. Office: 135 State Bancorp I Sansome St Lubbock TX 79401

**WEBB, CHARLES FRANKLIN,** computer engineer; b. Oklahoma City, Okla. Feb. 18, 1960; s. Leland and Geneva Webb; m. Jennifer Jane Herrala, Dec. 1, 1984; children: Anastasia Grace, Evangeline Jean, Isaac Barnabas, Joel Micah, Martha Abigail. BS in Computer & Sys. Engring., Rensselaer Poly. Inst., Troy, N.Y., 1978—82, M of Computer & Sys. Engring., 1982—83. Processor performance analysis IBM Corp., Poughkeepsie, NY, 1983—87, mainframe processor design, 1987—2000, disting. engr., 2000—03, ibm fellow, 2003—. Asst. scoutmaster Boy Scout Troop 95, Fishkill, NY, 2005; elder Valley Bible Fellowship Ch., LaGrangeville, NY, 2001. Recipient award, IBM Corp., 1999, 2000, 2002. Mem.: IEEE. Mem. Christian Ch. Achievements include patents for 58 Patents Related To Processor And Computer System Design. Avocations: piano, tuba. Office Phone: 845-435-6367. Business E-Mail: cfw@us.ibm.com.

**WEBB, CHARLES HAIZLIP, JR.,** retired university dean; b. Dallas, Feb. 14, 1933; s. Charles Haizlip and Marion (Gilker) W.; m. Kenda McGibbon, June 21, 1958; children: Mark, Kent, Malcolm, Charles Haizlip III. AB, MMus, So. Meth. U., 1955; DMus, Ind. U., 1964; DMus (hon.), Anderson Coll., 1979. Asst. to dean Sch. Music, So. Meth. U., 1957-58; mem. faculty Sch. Music, Ind. U., 1960-97, dean, 1973-97. Disting. prof., 1997—. Mem. Nat. Rec. Preservation Found., 2002—. Dir. Indpls. Symphony Orch., 1967-81; guest condr. chorus and orch. festivals throughout U.S.; duo-pianist with Wallace Hornibrook in U.S. and Australian tour, 1973; organist First Meth. Ch., Bloomington, 1961-, mem. hymnal revision com. Meth. Ch.; mem. jury Chopin competition; mem. jury internat. piano competitions in Munich, Budapest, South Africa, Paris, Chile, Warsaw, Bolzano, London, Cologne, Japan, Israel; mem. adv. bd. Classical Insites. Chmn. adv. bd. Internat. Music Festivals, Inc.; mem. Ind. Arts Commn., 1975-83, U.S.-USSR Commn. on Music Performance Edn., Am. Coun. Learned Socs./USSR Ministry of Culture; mem. adv. panel The Music Found.; mem. recommendation bd. Avery Fisher Prize Program; bd. dirs. Busoni Found.; mem. bd. advisors Van Cliburn Internat. Piano Competition; mem. nat. adv. bd. Am. Guild Organists; trustee Indpls. Symphony Orch.; mem. Nat. Recording Preservation Found., 2002; mem. adv. com. on cultural diplomacy U.S. Dept. State, 2004. With U.S. Army, 1955-57. Decorated D.S.M.; recipient Disting. Alumni award So. Meth. U., 1980, Sagamore of Wabash Gov. award, 1987, 89, 97, Thomas Hart Benton medal Ind. U., 1987, Disting. Alumni award Highland Park High Sch., Dallas, 1989, Disting Alumni award, Indiana U., 2005, Ind. Gov. award for arts, 1989, Rocking Chair award, Ind. U., 1997, Sterling Patron award Mu Phi Epsilon Internat., 1989, Ind. Gen. Assembly House Resolution # 39 for meritorious svc., 1997, Pres.'s award Ind. U., 2000; subject of tribute in U.S. Congl. Record, 1997; Rockefeller scholar Bellagio Study Ctr., 1997; named Ind. Living award, 2004, named to Cong. Com. to Advise the Sec. of State on Cultural Diplomacy, 2004; Paul Harris fellow, Rotary Internat., 1997. Mem. Ind. Acad., Century Assn. of N.Y., Pi Kappa Lambda, Phi Mu Alpha, Phi Delta Theta. Home: 648 S Woodcrest Dr Bloomington IN 47401-5417

**WEBB, CHARLES RICHARD,** retired university president; b. Berkeley, Calif., Oct. 4, 1919; s. Charles Richard and Adele (McDaniel) W.; m. Andrée Bonno; 1 child, Charles Richard III. AB, U. Calif., Berkeley, 1942, MA, 1944, Harvard U., 1947, PhD, 1949. Faculty San Diego State Coll., 1949-64, prof., 1958-64, chmn. dept. history, 1956-58; dean acad. affairs Stanislaus State Coll., Turlock, Calif., 1964-66; prof. history San Diego State Coll., 1966-70; pres. Eastern Conn. State U., Willimantic, 1970-88; ret., 1988; former acad. dean acad. planning Calif. State Colls., 1966-69, former dep. state coll. dean acad. planning. Author: Workbook in Western Civilization, 2 vols, 1959, Western Civilization vol. 1 (with Schaefer); vol. 2 (with Palm), 1958, (with

Crosby) The Past as Prologue, 2 vols, 1973; contbr. articles to profl. jours. Mem. pers. com. Santa Rosa Symphony Assn., New Eng. Program, Windham Meml. Comty. Hosp., Sea Rsch. Found.; mem. Commn. on Conn.'s Future. With USNR, 1941-45. Mem. AAUP, Am. Hist. Assn., Am. Fedn. Musicians, Nat. Pks. and Conservation, Sonoma Land Trust, Sierra Club, Nature Conservancy, New Eng. Hist. Assn., Assn. Calif. State Coll. Profs. (v.p. 1958-60), Save the Redwoods League, Conn. Employees Assn., Am. Assn. State Colls. and Univs., Phi Alpha Theta, Kappa Delta Pi, Omicron Delta Pi, Alpha Delta Phi. Clubs: University (San Diego), Commonwealth of Calif., Willimantic Country, Saddle Club, Santa Rosa, Montecito Heights Health & Racquet Club, Santa Rosa. Home: 6495 Timber Springs Dr Santa Rosa CA 95409-5900

**WEBB, DAN K.,** lawyer; b. Bushnell, Ill., Sept. 5, 1945; s. Keith L. and Phyllis I. (Clow) W.; student Western Ill. U., 1963-66; J.D., Loyola U., 1970; m. Laura A. Buscemi, Mar. 15, 1973; children: Jeffrey, Maggie, Michael, Melanie, Meagan. Bar: Ill. 1970, U.S. Dist. Ct. Ill. (no. dist.), U.S. Ct.Appeals (6th-8th Cir., Fed. Cir.), U.S. Supreme Ct. Chief spl. prosecutions divsn. U.S. Atty.'s Office, Chgo., 1970-76; ptnr., Cummins, Decker & Webb, Chgo., 1976-79; dir., Ill. Dept. Law Enforcement, Chgo., 1979-80; ptnr. Pierce, Webb, Lydon & Griffin, Chgo., 1980-81; US atty. (no. dist.)Il, US Dept. Justice, Chgo., 1981-85; ptnr. Winston & Strawn LLP, Chgo., 1985—, chmn., 2006- head litigation dept., mem. exec. com.; Iran-Contra spl. trial counsel; instr. John Marshall Law Sch., 1975—, Loyola U. Sch. Law, 1980—. Vice chmn. Met. Fair and Expn. Authority, 1978—81; bd. advisers Mercy Hosp. and Med. Ctr.; mem. Chgo. Council on Arson. Contbr. articles to profl. jours. Recipient spl. commendation award US Dept. Justice, 1975; named 1 of 10 Outstanding Young Chicagoans, Chgo. Jaycees, 1979. Mem. ABA, Ill. Bar Assn., Chgo. Bar Assn., Fed. Bar Assn., Legal Club Chgo., Execs. Club Chgo., Nat. Inst. of Trial Advocacy, 1979-. Republican. Office: Winston & Strawn LLP 35 W Wacker Dr Ste 4200 Chicago IL 60601-9703 Office Phone: 312-558-5856. Office Fax: 312-558-5700. E-mail: dwebb@winston.com.*

**WEBB, DARRELL,** retail executive; MBA, Portland State U., 1980. Group v.p. procurement The Kroger Co.; pres. Quality Food Ctr., Inc., 1999—2002, Fred Meyer, Inc., 2002—06; chmn., pres., CEO Jo-Ann Stores, Inc., Hudson, Ohio, 2006—. Office: Jo-Ann Stores Inc 5555 Darrow Rd Hudson OH 44236-4011 Office Phone: 330-656-2600. Office Fax: 330-463-6675.*

**WEBB, DARRYL WILLARD,** systems engineer; s. La Verne Willard and Jeraldine Marie Webb; m. Christina Denise Kowalski, Aug. 27, 1971; children: Shannon J., Meagan C. AA in Liberal Arts, Fullerton Coll., Calif., 1973; BA in Bus. Ops. Rsch., Calif. State U., Fullerton, 1974. Life cycle cost analyst Northrop Corp., Anaheim, Calif., 1975—79; exec. advisor Rockwell Internat., Anaheim, 1979—86; prin. investigator ACS, Inc., Tustin, Calif., 1986—91; project mgr. Boeing Co., Huntington Beach, Calif., 1991—2000; tech. dir. Econ Inc., Huntington Beach, 2000—01; mgr. we. region Price Sys., Inc., El Segundo, Calif., 2001—03; sr. engring. specialist Aerospace Corp., El Segundo, 2003—. Mem. adv. bd. Cost Credibility Team NASA, Marshall Space Flight Ctr., Ala., 2002; presenter in field. Contbr. articles to profl. publs. Cpl. USMC, 1968—70. Vietnam. Mem.: Internat. Soc. Parametric Analysts (pres. So. Calif. chpt. 1981—83, bd. dirs. 1986—87, tech. dir. So. Calif. chpt. 1980, Parametrician of Yr. 1984, Freiman award 2003), Phi Tau Sigma (hon. Student Mentor award 1996). Avocations: collecting historical photography, music, research in technology. Office: The Aerospace Corp 2350 E El Segundo Blvd El Segundo CA 90245 Office Fax: 310-336-5581. Business E-Mail: darryl.w.webb@aero.org.

**WEBB, DONALD ARTHUR,** minister; b. Wales, May 4, 1926; came to U.S., 1958; s. Arthur and Emily W.; m. Renee Mowbray, May 18, 1946; children— Cheryl, Marian, Christopher, Alison, Ian. Student, Queen's Coll., Cambridge U., Eng., 1944-45; BA, Ohio Wesleyan U., 1960; MDiv, Methodist Theol. Sch. in Ohio, 1963; PhD, Drew U., 1966; postdoctoral, Lincoln Coll., Oxford U., Eng., 1969, 72; LLD, Centenary Coll. La., 1991. Ordained to ministry Methodist Ch., 1960. Insp. Brit. Social Services, 1953-58; pastor various chs. Ohio and N.J., 1958-68; dean admissions, asst. prof. theology and lit. Meth. Theol. Sch. in Ohio, 1968-75; admissions', 1975-77; pres. Centenary Coll. La., Shreveport, 1977-91; sr. pastor First United Meth. Ch., Shreveport, 1991-92, scholar-in-residence, 1992—. Author: The Flame and Dusty Miller, 1970, We Hold These Truths, 1960; author: Dostoevsky and Christian Agnosticism, 1971, Deep Calls to Deep, 1998, The Best Year Yet, 2004. With Brit. Royal Navy, 1945-53. Mem. Shreveport C. of C. (bd. dirs. 1978-80). Home: 5709 Lakefront Dr Shreveport LA 71119-3913 Office: First United Meth Ch Head of Tex Shreveport LA 71165-1567 Office Phone: 318-636-0630.

**WEBB, EMILY,** retired plant morphologist; b. Charleston, S.C., Apr. 10, 1924; d. Malcolm Syfan and Emily Kirk (Moore) W.; m. John James Rosemond, Apr. 23, 1942 (div. 1953); 1 child, John Kirk; m. Julius Goldberg, Sept. 9, 1954; children: Michael, Judith. Student, Coll. Charleston, 1951—54; AB in Liberal Arts and Scis. with honors, U. Ill., Chgo., 1968, MS in Biol. Scis., 1972, PhD in Biol. Scis., 1985. Undergrad. fellow in bacteriology Med. Coll. S.C., Charleston, 1952-54; teaching asst. U. Ill., Chgo., 1969-72, 77-84, rsch. asst., 1977; teaching fellow W.Va. U., Morgantown, 1974, instr. 1974-75. Rsch. in N.Am. bot. needlework art, 1986—. Author: Studies in Several North American Species of Ophioglossum, 1986; translator Nat. Transl. Ctr., Chgo., 1976; contbr. articles to profl. jours. James scholar U. Ill., 1968-69. Mem. DAR, ACLU. Democrat. Episcopalian. Avocations: gardening, writing, money management. Home and Office: 1356 Mandel Ave Westchester IL 60154-3433

**WEBB, JACK M.,** lawyer; b. Monroe, La., Feb. 23, 1936; s. Sam L. and Lillian Etta (McCowen) W.; m. Diane Adele Waterman, Aug. 22, 1964; children: Julia Lillian Pogue, Kathryn Joy, Samuel Logan. BS in Geology, Centenary Coll. La., 1957; JD, Tulane U., 1960; student, JFK Sch. Govt. Harvard U., 1999. Bar: La. 1960, Tex. 1962. Atty. Standard Oil Co. Tex., Houston, 1961-66; staff atty. Trunkline Gas Co., Houston, 1966-71; sr. atty. M.W. Kellogg Co., Houston, 1971-73; sec., asst. gen. counsel Gulf Resources & Chem. Corp., Houston, 1973-78, v.p. govt. rels., adminstrv. asst. to chmn. bd., 1978-82; pres. Jack M. Webb & Assocs., 1983—; U.S. spl. amb. to Bolivia, 1985, to Finland, 1986, to Haiti, 1991, to Angola, 1992, to Ghana, 1993; hon. consul of Ghana, 1995—. Bd. dirs. Bradmark, Inc., Am. Meridian Ins. Co., Scotia Pacific Holding Co., Veri Med Rsch. Corp., Crystal Fuels, Inc. Bd. dirs. U.S. Peace Corps, 1985-86, Nat. Park Found., 1986-92, Boy Scouts Am., 1975—. Capt. U.S. Army, 1960-61. Mem. Tex. Bar Assn., La. Bar Assn. Methodist. Home: 3434 Locke Ln Houston TX 77027-4139 Office Phone: 281-586-7166. E-mail: jackw@jackwebb.com

**WEBB, JOHN GIBBON, III,** lawyer; b. Flint, Mich., June 1, 1944; s. John Gibbon Jr. and Martha W.; m. Fain Murphey, July 6, 1968; children: Jennifer Horn, Philip, Andrew Aidan, John Matthew. AB, Davidson Coll., 1966; JD, Vanderbilt U., 1970. Bar: N.Y. 1971, N.J. 1981. Assoc. Curtis, Mallet-Prevost, Colt & Mosle, N.Y.C., 1970—80; gen. counsel, v.p., sec. J.M. Huber Corp., Edison, NJ, 1980—95; pvt. bus. law practice Mt. Olive, NJ, 1996—. Episcopalian. Office: Ste 125 500 International Dr N Budd Lake NJ 07828 Office Phone: 973-426-8435. Personal E-mail: webbgc@aol.com.

**WEBB, JULIA JONES,** elementary school educator, minister; b. Portsmouth, Va., Apr. 3, 1962; d. William Edward Jones Jr. and Fannie Ford Jones; m. Alexander Maurice Webb Sr., Nov. 17, 1990; children: Brittany Alexandria, Alexander Maurice II. BA in Early Childhood Edn., Norfolk State U., 1988; postgrad., Va. Union U., 2004—. Lic. early edn. Va. Educator Chesapeake (Va.) Pub. Schs., 1988—, chmn. grade level II Southwestern Elem., 2005—. Assoc. minister First Bapt. Ch. Gilmerton, Chesapeake, 1999—2002, New Hope Bapt. Ch., Chesapeake, 2002—05, Grove Bapt. Ch., Portsmouth, Va., 2005—. USAA All-Am. scholar, Norfolk State U., 1989. Mem.: Va. Edn. Assn. (del. 1990—91), Chesapeake Tchr. Forum. Democrat.

**WEBB, KARRIE,** professional golfer; b. Ayr, Queensland, Australia, Dec. 21, 1974; Profl. golfer, 1994—; mem. LPGA Tour, 1996—; mem. Australian Team Women's World Cup of Golf, 2005. Named Rookie of Yr., Women Profl. Golfers' European Tour, 1995, Rolex Rookie of Yr., LPGA, 1996, Rolex Player of Yr., 1999, 2000, Outstanding Women's Golf Performer of Yr., ESPN Espy awards, 1997, 2001, Female Player of Yr., Golf Writers Assn. Am., 2000, Queensland Sportswomen of Yr., 2000—02, 2001, 2002; recipient Vare Trophy, LPGA, 1997, 1999, 2000, Crowne Plaza Achievement award, 2000. Achievements include winning LPGA Tour events including the Weetabix Women's Brit. Open, 1995, 97, 2002, Healthsouth Inaugural, 1996, Sprint Titleholders Championship, 1996, SAFECO Classic, 1996, 1997, ITT LPGA Tour Championship, 1996, Susan G. Koman Internat., 1997, Australian Ladies Masters, 1998, 99, 2000; winner, LPGA Tour events including the City of Hope Myrtle Beach Classic, 1998, Wegmans Rochester Internat., 1999, Mercury Titleholders Championship, 1999, Standard Register PING, 1999, The Office Depot, 1999, 2000; winner, LPGA Tour events including the du Maurier Classic, 1999, Nabisco Championship, 2000, Oldsmobile Classic, 2000, LPGA Takefuji Classic, 2000, AFLAC Champions presented by Southern Living, 2000, US Women's Open, 2000, 01; winner, LPGA Tour events including the McDonald's LPGA Championship presented by AIG, 2001, Tyco/ADT Championship, 2001, Wegmans Rochester LPGA, 2002, John Q. Hammons Hotel Classic, 2003, Kellogg-Keebler Classic, 2004, Kraft Nabisco Championship, 2006, Michelob Ultra Open, 2006, Evian Masters, 2006; winner, international events including the AAMI Women's Australian Open, 2002, ANZ Ladies Masters on the Robe di Kappa Ladies European Tour, 2005; inducted into World Golf Hall of Fame, 2005; first LPGA player to achieve the Super Career Grand Slam by winning all 5 majors available in her career, 2002. Avocations: reading, basketball, fishing. Office: c/o LPGA 100 Internat Golf Dr Daytona Beach FL 32124-1092*

**WEBB, LAMAR THAXTER,** architect; b. Hapeville, Ga., Sept. 13, 1928; s. Eugene Garnette and Sara Ethel (Moore) W.; m. Bettye Jayne Jackson, Dec. 6, 1957; children: Mark Maynard, Robin Lynn. BBA in Fin., U. Ga., 1950; BS, Ga. Inst. Tech., 1959, BArch, 1960. Reg. arch. Ga., Fla., Tenn. Intern architect Abreu and Robeson, Inc., Brunswick, Ga., 1960-66; architect, pres. Webb & Baldwin, Inc., St. Simons Island, Ga., 1966-72; pres., owner Lamar T. Webb, Arch., Inc., St. Simons Island, 1972—. 1st lt. USAF, 1953—55. Mem. AIA (State bd. dirs. 1985-91, v.p. Golden Isles chpt. 1988-89, pres. 1989-90), Am. Soc. Interior Designers, Am. Soc. Landscape Architects (affiliate), Audubon Soc., Nat. Hort. Soc., Humane Soc. (local bd. dirs. 1985-87), Smithsonian Assocs., Coastal Alliance for Arts, Nat. Trust for Hist. Preservation, Ga. Trust for Hist. Preservation, Coastal Ga. Hist. Assn., Met. Mus. Art, Golden Isles Gourmet Club (bd. dirs.) Chien de Rotessieurs, G.I. Chap. Avocations: cooking, drawing, painting, travel. Home: 121 Runnymede Saint Simons Island GA 31522 Office: 13 Retreat Pl Saint Simons Island GA 31522 Home: Willow Creek 614 Brice Station Rd Silver Creek GA 30173 Office Phone: 912-638-8621. Personal E-mail: ltwarch@hotmail.com.

**WEBB, LUCY JANE,** actress, film producer, consultant; d. Phillip Carlen and Marcia Jane Webb; m. Kevin Pollak, Dec. 19, 1995. BA, U. Tenn.; student, New Sch. Social Rsch. Lydon Baines Johnson intern Joe Evans Congressman, Tenn.; Congl. intern Albert Gore, Jr. Congressman, Tenn.; pres. Calm Down Prodns., Inc., LA; prodr. Warner Bros. TV, CBS. V.p. spl. events Women in Film, LA. Actor: (TV series) Private Benjamin, Laughtrax, Not Necessarily the News; exec. prodr.: FX TV, 2005; prodr.: (plays) All Grown Up and No Place to Go, (Broadcaster Film Critic awards), 1999; exec. prodr.: (Crystal/Lucy Awards) Women in Film, 2004—05. Chmn. AIDS charity Angel Women at Risk. Recipient ACE award, Cable ACE Assn., 1985, 1986, 1987, 1988, 1990. Mem.: Beverly Hills Country Club. Democrat. Roman Catholic. Avocations: piano, antiques, travel, films. Office Phone: 323-650-4027.

**WEBB, MARK RUSSELL,** music educator; b. Lansing, Mich., May 12, 1953; s. Russell Nathan and Vadah Ann Webb; m. Susan Joan Hanna, May 27, 1978; children: Natalie Lauren, Ashley Victoria. MusB, U. Mich., 1975, MusM, 1976. Cert. music tchr. K-12 Mich. Vocal music tchr. Kentwood Pub. Schs., Kentwood, Mich., 1976—95; choral coord., dir. internat. choir Blue Lake Fine Arts Camp, Twin Lake, Mich.; dir. coll. chorus Aquina Coll., Grand Rapids, Mich.; dir. chancel choir Mayflower Congregational Ch., Grand Rapids, Mich.; dir. choral activities East Grand Rapids Pub. Schs., East Grand Rapids. Named Tchr. of Yr., Mich. Sch. Vocal Music Assn., 2003, Arts Educator of Yr., ArtServe of Mich., 2003. Mem.: Mich. Sch. Vocal Music Assn. (pres. 1999—2005). Avocations: reading, music arranging. Home: 2851 Oakwood Dr SE Grand Rapids MI 49506 Office: E Grand Rapids HS 2211 Lake Dr SE Grand Rapids MI 49506 Office Phone: 616-235-7555 X5135. Office Fax: 616-235-7592. E-mail: mwebb@egrps.org.

**WEBB, MARTY FOX,** principal; b. Des Moines, July 15, 1942; d. Joseph John and Jean (Way) Fox; m. Andrew H. Rudolph, Aug. 17, 1963 (div. Jan. 1988); children: Kristen Ann, Kevin Andrew; m. Eugene J. Webb, Nov. 23, 1991. BS, U. Mich., 1964; MEd, Houston Bapt. U., 1982; EdD, U. San Francisco, 1993. Cert. adminstr., Tex., elem. and spl. edn. educator, Mich., Tex. Tchr. spl. edn. Hawthorn Ctr., Northville, Mich., 1964-70; tchr. Bellaire (Tex.) Sch. for Children, 1977-80; prin. Corpus Christi Sch., Houston, 1980-97; founder, head of sch. The Monarch fich. Houston, 1997—, 3prin. In field. Bd. dirs. DeBusk Found. Recipient Elem. Sch. Recognition award U.S. Dept. Edn., 1989-90, Blue Ribbon Sch. award, 1990, Outstanding Doctoral Student award, 1994. Mem. ASCD, U. Mich. Alumni Assn. Avocations: reading, fly fishing, camping, hiking, bodybuilding. Home: 3531 Sun Valley Dr Houston TX 77025-4148 Office: The Monarch Sch 1231 Wirt Rd Houston TX 77055-6852 Office Phone: 713-479-0800. Business E-Mail: mwebb@monarchschool.org.

**WEBB, MARY CHRISTINE,** reading recovery educator, in-class reading specialist; b. Ames, Iowa, Jan. 3, 1947; d. Howard Darrell and Lorena Faye (North) Webb; m. Harlen DuWayne Groe, Dec. 29, 1989 (div. Oct. 1997). BS in Elem. Edn., Iowa State U., 1969, MS in Emotional Disabilities, 1980, MEd in Learning Disabilities, 1986. Cert. tchr. K-9, learning disabilities, behavioral disabilities, multicategorical, Iowa; cert. in reading endorsement, Iowa, 2001; lic. brain gym instr. cons. 2006. 1st grade tchr. Holy Spirit Sch., Carroll, Iowa, 1970; severe behavior disabilities tchr. Area Edn. Agy 7, Waterloo, Iowa, 1979-85; tchg. and rsch. assistantship Iowa State U., Ames, 1985-86; multicategorical 3-8 self contained with integration tchr. Madrid Elem. and Jr. H.S., 1986-87; behavior disability self contained with integration tchr. Des Moines Pub. Schs., 1987-88, resource rm. tchr., 1988-95, multicategorical self contained with integration tchr., 1995-99, reading recovery tchr., behavior interventionist, 1999-2000, reading recovery tchr., title reading tchr., 2000—02, reading recovery tchr., reading specialist, 2002—. Lic. brain gym cons., 2006—. Active People to People Spl. Edn. Del. to Mainland China, 1993. Mem.: NEA, ASCD, Iowa State Edn. Assn., Des Moines Edn. Assn. Office: King Acad Math and Sci 1849 Forest Ave Des Moines IA 50314-1336

**WEBB, MAYNARD G., JR.,** retired Internet company executive; BA, Fla. Atlantic U. With Thomas Chan, figgie Internat., IBM; dir. info. tech. Quantum Corp., 1991—95; v.p., CIO Bay Networks Inc., 1995—98; sr. v.p., CIO Gateway, Inc., 1998—99; pres. eBay Techs. Ebay Inc., San Jose, Calif., 1999—2002, COO, 2002—06. Bd. dir. Hyperion, 2006—.*

**WEBB, O. GLENN,** retired farm supplies company executive; b. 1936; married BS, U. Ill., 1957; PhD, So. Ill. U., 1973. With Growmark, Inc., Bloomington, Ill., 1966—2000, sec., 1968-72, v.p., 1972-80, pres.,

**WEBB, ORVILLE LYNN,** retired physician, pharmacologist, educator; b. Tulsa, Okla., Aug. 29, 1931; s. Rufus Aclen and Berla Ophelia (Caudle) W.; m. Joan (Liebenheim), June 1, 1954 (div. Jan. 1980); children: Kathryn Gilbert, Benjamin; m. Jeanne P. (Heath), Aug. 24, 1991. BS, Okla. State U., 1953; MS, U. Okla., 1961; PhD in Pharmacology, U. Mo., 1966, MD, 1968. Diplomate Nat. Bd. Med. Examiners, Am. Bd. Family Practice; cert. med. examiner, 1999. Rsch. assoc. in pharmacology U. Okla., 1959—61; rsch. fellow NIH, 1962—66; instr. pharmacology U. Mo., Columbia, 1966—68, asst. prof., 1968—69; intern U. Mo. Med. Ctr., 1968—69; family practice New Castle, Ind., 1969—89; med. dir. VA Clinic, Lawton, Okla., 1989—94, Comanche County Hosp., Lawton, Okla., 1994—98; pvt. practice medicine Lawton, Okla., 1998—2002; owner Comanche County Med. Clinic, Lawton, Okla., 1998—2002, Okla. Med. Clinic, Lawton, 1999—2003; ret. 2003. Clin. assoc. prof. family medicine U. Okla. Coll. Medicine, 1989—; adj. assoc. prof. pharmacology U. Okla. Coll. Medicine, 1989—; mem. U. Okla. Medicine Admissions Bd., 1995-98; mem. staff Henry County Meml. Hosp., New Castle, Ind. 1969-89; guest prof. pharmacy and pharmacology Butler U. Coll. Pharmacy, Indpls., 1970-75; owner, dir. Carthage Clinic, 1975-89; clin. assoc. prof. family medicine Ind. U. Coll. Medicine, 1986-89; county physician, jail med. dir. Henry County, Ind., 1976-89. Author: (with Blissitt, Stanaszek, Lea, and Febiger) Clinical Pharmacy Practice, 1972; contbr. numerous articles to profl. journals. Bd. dir. Lawton Philharm., 1990-95. Recipient Cert. of Merit in Pharmacol. and Clin. Med. Rsch., 1970, Med. Student Rsch. Essay Award Am. Acad. Neurology, 1968. Fellow Am. Acad. Family Physicians, Am. Coll. Physician Exec.; mem. AMA (ann. award recognition 1975-2001), AAAS, Ind. State Med. Assn., Am. Coll. Sports Medicine, Am. Coll. Occupl. and Environ. Medicine, N.Y. Acad. Sci., Am. Soc. Contemporary Medicine and Surgery, Okla. State Med. Assn., Festival Chamber Music Soc. (bd. dirs. Indpls. 1981-87), Nat. Fraternity Eagle Scouts, Mensa, Columbia Club, Skyline Club, Country Club, Kiwanis, Elks, Sigma Xi, Phi Sigma. Achievements include research in harmful effects of anabolic steroids on athletes; cholesterol and other lipids. Home: 85 Quail Creek Dr NW Lawton OK 73507-9026 Personal E-mail: olynnwebb@earthlink.net.

**WEBB, OTIS D.,** retired underwriter; b. Moticello, Ky., Aug. 4, 1937; s. Ova H. and Margaret E. Webb; m. Rita K. Webb, Aug. 13, 1984; m. Patty P. Phillips (div.); children: Terri L. Hendon, Richard A., Michael D., Christa L. Cons. mgr. Met Life, Louisville, 1958—72; sales mgr. Star Furniture TV and Appliance, Owensboro, Ky., 1972—83; regional mgr. Zee Med., Sheperedville, Ky., 1983—89; sales cons. Met Life, Owensboro, 1989—2000; ret., 2000; owner,operator Webb 1st Aid Safety Supply, 2003—. Instr. Life Underwriter Tng. Coun., Wash., DC, 1990—99; pres. Life Underwriters Assn., Owensboro, Ky., 1968—70, Owensboro, 1992—94. Mem. Young Dem., 1959—64; conf. bd. mem. St. Vincent DePaul, Owensboro, 2005—06. Mem.: Fraternal Order of Moose, Fraternal Order of Eagles. Democrat. Cath. Avocations: fishing, hunting, golf. Home: 3810 Broadleaf Ct Owensboro KY 42301 Office: Webb First Aid and Safety 3810 Broadleaf Ct Owensboro KY 42301 Office Phone: 270-684-2605.

**WEBB, PAUL,** physiologist, educator, researcher, consultant; b. Cleve., Dec. 2, 1923; s. Monte F. and Barbara (Webb) Bourjaily; m. Eileen Whalen, Mar. 13, 1948; children: Shaun P., Paul S. Womacks. BA, U. Va., 1943, MD, 1946; MS in Physiol., U. Wash., 1951. Asst. prof. physiology U. Okla. Sch. Medicine, Oklahoma City, 1952—54; chief environ. sect. Aeromed. Lab., Wright-Patterson AFB, Ohio, 1954-58; prin. assoc. Webb Assocs., Yellow Springs, Ohio, 1959-82; vis. scientist INSERM, Paris, 1983; vis. prof. U. Limburg, Maastricht, The Netherlands, 1986, U. Uppsala, Sweden, 1988-89; clin. prof. bioengring. Wright State U., Dayton, 2005—. Cons. aerospace and undersea medicine, energy balance and thermal physiology, Yellow Springs, 1980—. Author: Human Calorimeters, 1985; contbr. articles to profl. jours. Village councilman Village of Yellow Springs, Ohio, 1969-75; mem. Air Force Scientific Adv. Bd., Washington, 1984-88. Recipient Ely award Human Factors Soc., 1972. Fellow Aerospace Med. Assn. (Aerospace Indsl. Life Scis. Assn. award 1969), Am. Inst. Med. and Biol. Engring.; mem. Am. Physiol. Soc., Am. Soc. for Clin. Nutrition, Undersea Med. Soc. (oceaneering internat. award 1979, pres. 1980-81). Home and Office: 370 Orton Rd Yellow Springs OH 45387-1321 Business E-Mail: paul.webb@wright.edu.

**WEBB, RICHARD C.,** engineering company executive; b. Omaha, Sept. 2, 1915; m. Virginia; 1 son. BSE.E., U. Denver, 1937, DSc (hon.), 1996; MSE.E., Purdue U., 1944, PhD, 1951; DSc (hon.). U. Denver, 1996. Registered profl. engr., Colo. Traffic engr. Mountain States Telephone and Telegraph Co., Denver, 1937-39; research engr. RCA Labs. Div., Princeton, N.J., 1945-53; pres., founder, tech. dir. Colo. Research Corp. (subs. Carrier Corp.), Syracuse, N.Y., 1956-61; pres., founder. tech. dir. Colo. Instruments, Inc., Broomfield, Colo., 1961-71; pres., gen. mgr. Colo. Instruments div. Mohawk Data Scis. Corp., Utica, N.Y.C., 1971-73; pres. Webb Engring. Co. (name changed to Data Ray Corp.), Boulder, Colo., 1973-85. Vis. lectr. U. Colo., 1962-82; prof. elec. engring. U. Denver, 1953-56, Iowa State Coll., 1950 Author: Tele-Visionaries: The People Behind the Inventin of Television, 2005; contbr. articles pub. to profl. jours. Recipient Disting. Engring. Alumnus award Purdue U., 1970, Profl. Achievement award U. Denver Alumni Assn., 1983, Outstanding Elec. Engr. award Purdue U., 1992. Fellow IEEE; mem. Soc. Motion Picture and TV Engrs., Acoustical Soc. Am., Instr. Aerospace Scis., Am. Ordnance Assn., Western Electronics Mfrs. Assn. (past v.p., dir.), Sigma Xi, Tau Beta Pi, Eta Kappa Nu. Achievements include patents in field. Home: PO Box 3078 Estes Park CO 80517 3078

**WEBB, RICHARD STEPHEN,** manufacturing executive; b. Nottingham, Eng., Aug. 3, 1944; came to U.S., 1988; s. Sydney and Kathleen Florence (Day) W.; m. Pamela Anne Fowlds, Sept. 3, 1966 (dec. July 1976); children: Jane, Simon, Elizabeth; m. Anne Hessel, Aug. 19, 1978 (div. 1997); children: Clare, Penelope; m. Cynthia Draper, Mar. 1, 2003. BSc, U. Sheffield, Eng., 1966, PhD, 1970. Chartered scientist UK, 2005. Rsch. scientist U. Sheffield, 1966-69; tech. asst. C.E. Ramsden & Co. Ltd., Stoke-on-Trent, Eng., 1969-74; mktg. exec. Magnesium Elektron Ltd., Manchester, Eng., 1974-80, mktg. mgr., 1980-84; bus. devel. mgr. Alcan Aluminium, Mont. Can., 1984-88; bus. mgr. Alanx Products Inc., Newark, Del., 1988-91, pres., 1992-95, Lanxide Coated Products divsn. Lanxide Performance Materials, Newark, Del., 1995-97; dir. sales and mktg. ESL Electro-Sci., King of Prussia, Pa., 1997—. Chem. Ind. Mfg. Alliance, 1993-95. Contbr. articles to profl. jours. Fellow: Inst. Materials, Minerals, Mining (U.K.); mem.: Am. Chem. Soc., Am. Ceramic Soc. Avocations: marathon and road running. Office: ESL ElectroSci 416 E Church Rd King Of Prussia PA 19406-2625 E-mail: rwebb@electroscience.com.

**WEBB, ROBERT W., JR.,** lawyer; b. Thomasville, Ga., Mar. 16, 1950; BA magna cum laude, Vanderbilt Univ., 1972; JD, Univ. Va. 1975. Bar: Ga. 1975. Assoc. Troutman Sanders LLP, Atlanta, 1975—80, ptnr., 1981—, mng. ptnr., 1992—, and mem. exec. com. Mem.: ABA, State Bar Ga., Atlanta Bar Assn., Phi Beta Kappa. Office: Troutman Sanders LLP One Logan Sq Ste 5200 600 Peachtree St NE Atlanta GA 30308-2216 Office Phone: 404-885-3240. Office Fax: 404-962-6716. Business E-mail: robert.webb@troutmansanders.com.

**WEBB, THEODORE STRATTON, JR.,** aerospace scientist, consultant; b. Oklahoma City, Mar. 4, 1930; s. Theodore S. and Helen (Klabzuba) W.; m. Cuba Evans, Sept. 2, 1952; children: Theodore S. III, Kelly Elizabeth. BS in Physics, Okla. U., 1951; PhD in Physics and Math., Calif. Inst. Tech., 1955. Engr. Ft. Worth div. Gen. Dynamics, 1955-62, program mgr., 1962-69, dir. aero. tech., 1969-75, v.p. rsch. and engring., 1975-80, v.p. F-16 programs, 1980-89; pvt. practice cons. Ft. Worth, 1989—. Mem. engring. adv. bd. U. Okla., Norman, 1983-87; mem. aerospace coun. Soc. Automotive Engrs., 1975-81. Bd. mem. Engring. Found. U. Tex., Austin, 1975-81, Found. for Sci. and Engring. So. Meth. U., Dallas, 1974-81, Tarrant County Day Care Assn.,

Ft. Worth, 1975-80, 89-96; All Saints Episcopal Hosp., 1989-2003, Goodwill Industries of Tarrant Country, 1989-96. Mem. AAAS, Am. Phys. Soc., Rivercrest Country Club. Office: 6100 Southwest Blvd Ste 250 Fort Worth TX 76109-6902 Home: 3705 Briarhaven Rd Fort Worth TX 76109-3245 E-mail: ted.webb@nationwide.net.

**WEBB, THOMAS IRWIN, JR.,** lawyer, director; b. Toledo, Sept. 16, 1948; s. Thomas Irwin and Marcia Davis (Winters) W.; m. Polly S. DeWitt, Oct. 11, 1986; 1 child, Elisabeth Hurst. BA, Williams Coll., 1970; postgrad., Boston U., 1970—71; JD, Case Western Res. U., 1973. Bar: Ohio, Mich. Assoc. Shumaker, Loop & Kendrick, Toledo, 1973—79, ptnr., 1979—, chmn. corp. law dept., 1992—94, 1994mgmt. com., 1994—99. Dir. Calphalon Corp., 1990-98, Yark Automotive Group, Inc. Coun. mem Village of Ottawa Hills, Ohio, 1979-85, adviser Ohio Securities, 1979-85, Village of Ottawa Hills, 1999—; bd. dirs. Kiwanis Found. Toledo, 1982-2002, Toledo Area Regional Transit Authority, 1989-91, Arts Commn. Greater Toledo, 1993-2003, exec. com., 1994-99, v.p., 1994-96, pres., 1996-97; bd. dirs. Jr. Achievement of Northwestern Ohio Inc., 1992-2005, Lourdes Coll. Found., 1995-2001, Toledo Orch. Assn., 1999—, Med. Coll. Ohio, 2001-05, Lourdes Coll., 2001—, Maumee Valley Country Day Sch., 2005—. Mem. ABA, Ohio Bar Assn. (corp. law com. 1989—), Toledo Bar Assn., Mich. Bar Assn., Northwestern Ohio Alumni Assn. of Williams Coll. (pres. 1974-83), Toledo-Rowing Found. (trustee 1985-2001), Toledo Area C. of C. (trustee 1991-98, exec. com. 1993-98, fin. com. 1993—), Order of Coif, Crystal Downs Country Club, Toledo Country Club, The Toledo Club (trustee 1984-90, pres. 1987-90), Williams Club NY, Crystal Lake Yacht Club. Republican. Episcopalian. Office: Shumaker Loop & Kendrick 1000 Jackson St Toledo OH 43624-1573 Office Phone: 419-321-1237, 231-352-7542. Business E-Mail: twebb@slk-law.com.

**WEBB, THOMAS J.,** utilities executive; b. Alexandria, Va., Oct. 3, 1952; m. Donna; 3 children. BA in Fin. with honors, George Mason U.; MBA. Various fin. mgmt. positions Ford Motor Co. and subs.; controller Electronics divsn., Large Front-Wheel Drive Vehicle Ctr.; CFO Visteon Corp.; chief fin. info. officer Ford Motor Co.; exec. v.p., CFO Kellogg Co., Battle Creek, Mich., 2000—02, CMS Energy, Dearborn, Mich., 2002—. Bd. dirs. Conix, Can., Hall Climate Control, Korea, Halla Electronics, Korea, Samcor, South Africa, Yan Feng, China, Toledo (Ohio) Molding and Die, Climate Sys., India, others. Office: CMS Energy 1 Energy Plaza Dr Jackson MI 49201-2357

**WEBB, TROY HOOKER,** education educator; adopted s. Farren and Louise Webb; m. Tina Blocker, May 18, 1998. EdD, Fielding Grad. U., Santa Barbara, Calif., 2003. Tchr. pub. sch. Farmington (N.Mex.) Mcpl. Schs., 1998—2003; prof. tchr. edn. Ft. Lewis Coll., Durango, Colo., 2003—. Cons. and lectr. in field, Ignacio, Colo., 2003—. Contbr. articles to profl. publs. Voting mem. Youthtracks, Ignacio, 2003. With U.S. Army, 1988—92. Recipient Red Apple Tchg. award, Red Apple Com., 1998—2002. Mem.: Nat. Coun. for the Social Studies. Independent. Office: Ft Lewis Coll 1000 Rim Dr Durango CO 81301 Office Phone: 970-247-7223.

**WEBB, WATTS RANKIN,** surgeon; b. Columbia, Ky., Sept. 8, 1922; s. Frank Elbert and Susie Josephine (Rankin) W.; m. Frances Luella Cooke, Aug. 19, 1944; children: Michael Andrew, Paul Alan, Harvey Elbert, Gordon Lewis. BA, U. Miss., 1942; MD, Johns Hopkins U., 1945. Diplomate Am. Bd. Surgery, Am. Bd. Thoracic Surgery, Am. Bd. Surg. Critical Care. Intern Barnes Hosp., St. Louis, 1945-46; resident in surgery VA Hosp., Biloxi, Miss., 1946-48; resident in gen. and thoracic surgery Barnes Hosp., 1948-52; chief surgeon Miss. State Sanatorium, 1952-63; instr. surgery U. Miss., 1955-56, asst. prof. surgery, 1956-58, prof., 1958-63; prof., chmn. div. thoracic and cardiovascular surgery U. Tex. Southwestern Med. Sch., Dallas, 1964-70; prof., chmn. dept. surgery SUNY Upstate Med. Center, Syracuse, 1970-77; prof. surgery Tulane U., New Orleans, 1977-93, La. State U., New Orleans, 1993—; chmn. dept. Tulane U., New Orleans, 1977-89. Author: Pulmonary Problems in Surgery, 1974, Surgery in Acute Coronary Problems, 1974, Aneurysms, 1983, Cardiovascular Emergencies, 1986, Atlas of Pulmonary Resections, 1988, (with others) Surgical Management for Chest Injuries, Vol. VII, 1990; editorial bd.: Annals of Thoracic Surgery, 1968-79, Surg. Rounds, 1978-82, Surgery Clinics, 1980-82, Microcirculation, 1983-84, Brit. Jour. Surgery, 1981-89; contbr. over 450 articles to profl. jours. Recipient award Hadassah, 1965, Knockers Soc. Outstanding Tchr. award SUNY Upstate Med. Ctr., 1972, Owl Club Clin. Tchr. of Yr. award Tulane U. Med. Sch., 1978, 86, 88-93, Gloria P. Walsh award for best tchr. in Med. Sch., 1992, Aesculapian Tchr. of Yr. award La. State U., 1995, 96. Fellow ACS, Am. Coll. Chest Physicians; mem. AMA, Am. Assn. Thoracic Surgery, Am. Coll. Cardiology, Am. Fedn. Clin. Research, Am. Heart Assn. (Silver medal 1963), Am. Physiol. Soc., So. Surg. Assn., Am. Thoracic Soc., Halsted Soc., La. Med. Soc., Orleans Parish Med. Soc., New Orleans Surg. Soc., Societe International de Chirurgie, Soc. Cryobiology, Soc. Thoracic Surgeons, Soc. Univ. Surgeons, Southeastern Surg. Congress, So. Med. Assn., So. Soc. Clin. Research, So. Surg. Assn. (Shipley medal 1961), So. Thoracic Soc., So. Thoracic Surg. Assn., Surg. Assn. La., Surg. Biology Club II, Internat. Soc. Heart Transplantation, Gulf Coast Vascular Soc., Sigma Xi, Alpha Omega Alpha, Pi Kappa Pi, Beta Beta Beta, Alpha Epsilon Delta. Methodist. Home: 364 Windermere Blvd Alexandria LA 71303 Office: VHA Alexandria Shreveport Hwy Alexandria LA 71306-9004 Office Phone: 318-542-1812. Personal E-mail: wattsrwebb@yahoo.com.

**WEBB, WELLINGTON EDWARD,** political organization administrator, former mayor; b. Chgo., Feb. 17, 1941; m. Wilma J. Webb; 4 children. BA in Edn., Colo. State Coll., 1964; MA in Edn., U. No. Colo., 1971. Tchr., 1964-76; mem. Colo. Ho. of Reps., 1973—77; regional dir. HEW, 1977-81; exec. dir., Dept. Regulatory agencies State of Colo., 1981-87; auditor City of Denver, 1987-91, mayor, 1991—2003; vice chair Democratic Nat. Com., 2004—. V.p Nat. Conf. Dem. Mayors; bd. dir. Nat. League Cities, mem. adv. bd., Brookings Inst. Ctr. Urban and Met. Policy; mem. Nat. Infrastructure Assurance Coun.; bd. dirs. Cenveo, Inc., Maximus Corp.; founder Webb Group Internat. Cons., 2003. Pres. U.S. Conf. of Mayors, 1993—2003, Nat. Conf. Black Mayors, 2000—. Named One of Top 25 Mayors in Nation, Newsweek, 1996, Chevalier of the Legion of Honor, Country of France, 1999; recipient Nat. Wildlife Fedn. Achievement award, 1999, Govt. Leadership in the Arts award, Ams. for the Arts, 2001, Bridge Builders award, Disting. Pub. Svc. award, US Conf. of Mayors, 2003. Office Phone: 303-893-9322. E-mail: wew@webbgroupintl.com.

**WEBB, WILLIAM LOYD, JR.,** retired military officer; b. Mineral Wells, Tex., Sept. 30, 1925; s. William Loyd and Francis (Mayer) W.; m. Muriel Emma Hinson, Dec. 27, 1947; children: George Sidney, William Loyd III, Lucinda Adrienne, Alicia Muriel. Student, Tex. A & M Coll., 1942-44; BS, U.S. Mil. Acad., 1947; MA, U. Pa., 1958. Commd. 2d lt. U.S. Army, 1947, advanced through grades to maj. gen., 1974; co. comdr. Korea, 1950, Ft. Riley, Kans., 1951-52, Germany, 1953-54; assoc. prof. English U.S. Mil. Acad. West Point, N.Y., 1958-61; regimental comdr., dep. comdt. of cadets U.S. Mil. Acad., 1969-71; squadron comdr. 14th Armored Cavalry Germany, 1963-64; mem. faculty U.S Army War Coll., 1965-68; comdr. support command 1st Inf. Div. mut. assistance command Vietnam, 1968—69; dep. comdg. gen. Ft. Ord, Calif., 1971-73; ops. officer 8th Army, U.S. Forces Korea, 1973-75; sr. mem. UN Command Mil. Armistice Commn., 1975; comdr. 1st Armored Div., U.S. Army Europe W.Ger., 1975-78; dep. comdg. gen. V Corps, U.S. Army Europe W. Ger., 1978; asst. dep. chief of staff for personnel Dept Army Washington, 1978-82. Decorated D.S.M., Legion of Merit with oak leaf cluster, D.F.C., Bronze Star medal with oak leaf cluster, Air medal with 5 oak leaf clusters, Army Commendation medal with 2 oak leaf clusters, Purple Heart. Mem. Assn. U.S. Army, Armor Assn. Anglican. Office: 10148 Hillington Ct Vienna VA 22182-2908

**WEBB, WILLIAM TIMOTHY,** mobile communications professional; b. Walton-on-Thames, England, May 4, 1967; s. Christopher David and Genebeth Carol W.; m. Alison Margaret Porter, June 17, 1995; children: Katherine, Hannah. B of Engring., U. Southampton, 1989, PhD, 1992; MBA, Southamp-

ton Mgmt. Sch., 1997. Chartered engr. Tech. dir. Multiple Access Technologies, Southampton, England, 1990—94; prin. cons. Smith System Engring., Guildford, England, 1994—98; dir. strategy Motorola, Schaumburg, Ill., 1998—2001; mng. cons. PA Cons., 2001—03; head R & D Ofcom, England, 2004. Mem. innovation awards judging panel Wall St. Jour.; vis. prof. U. Surrey, England, 2003—. Author: Modern Quadrature Amplitude Modultion, 1994, Introduction to Wireless Local Loop, 1998, Understanding Cellular Radio, 1998, The Complete Wireless Communications Professional, 1999, Single and Multi-Carrier QAM, 2000, Narrowband and Broadband Wireless Local Loop, 2000, The Future of Wireless Communications, 2001; contbr. articles to profl. jours. Fellow: Royal Acad. Engring., Inst. for Elec. Engrs. (v.p. 2004—); mem.: IEEE (sr.). Office Phone: 44 20 7981 3770. Business E-Mail: william.webb@ofcom.org.uk.

**WEBB, WILLIAM YERICK,** lawyer; b. Mont Estoril, Portugal, Apr. 13, 1935; came to U.S., 1939; s. Leslie A. and Laura E. (Detrich) W.; m. Jeannette L. Richardson, June 20, 1959; children: Elizabeth T., Douglas L., Philip N. AB, Dartmouth Coll., 1956; JD cum laude, U. Mich., 1961. Bar: Pa. 1961, U.S. Dist. Ct. (ea. dist.) Pa. 1961. Assoc. Ballard, Spahr, Andrews & Ingersoll, Phila., 1961-69, ptnr., 1969—2000; v.p., gen. counsel, sec. Phila. Phillies, 2000—. Adj. prof. law Widener U. Law Sch., 1989; adj. prof. sports law Villanova Law Sch.; sec., dir. AMR Internat. Inc. and subs., 1971-81; gen. counsel Opera Co. Phila., 1975-81. Asst. editor U. Mich. Law Rev. Bd. dirs., sec., counsel Children's Country Week Assn., 1978-85; bd. dirs., chmn. Schuylkill Ctr. Environ. Edn., 1989-95; pres., bd. dirs. Radnor A Better Chance, Inc., 1982-88; chmn., bd. dirs. History Ctr. in Phila., 1996. Lt. (j.g.) USNR, 1956-58. Mem. Sports Law Assn. (bd. dirs. 1984—, past pres.), Lake Paupac Club Greentown, Pa., (bd. dirs. 1990—, pres.), Applebrook Golf Club. Episcopalian. Office: The Phillies One Citizens Bank Way Philadelphia PA 19148-5249

**WEBBER, ADAM BROOKS,** science educator; b. Chapel Hill, N.C., Dec. 20, 1962; s. Howard Rodney and Helen Margaret Webber; m. Kelly Shawn Autrey, Dec. 27, 1984; children: Fern Athena, Fox Pythagoras. BA, Dartmouth Coll., 1984; PhD, MS, Cornell U., 1993. Design engr. True BASIC, Inc., Hanover, NH, 1985—88; asst. prof. Western Ill. U., Macomb, Ill., 1993—97, U. Wis.-Milw., 1998—2000, assoc. scientist; assoc. prof. Monmouth (Ill.) Coll., 2005—. Prin. investigator NSF-funded projects at U. Wis.-Milw. and Western Ill. U., 1997—2004. Author: (textbook) Programming Languages: A Practical Introduction, Fluent Pascal: the Pascal Trainer Laboratory Guide, Formal Language: A Practical Introduction. Organist, composer Open Prairie United Ch. of Christ, Princeton, Ill., 2003—. Grantee, NSF, 2000—04, 1997—2000. Mem.: Songwriters Guild of Am., Assn. for Computing Machinery, Upsilon Pi Epsilon. Avocation: Karate. Home: 316 Park Ave W Princeton IL 61356 Office Phone: 309-457-2200. Personal E-mail: adam@webber-labs.com. E-mail: awebber@monm.edu.

**WEBBER, CARL MADDRA,** lawyer; b. Champaign, Ill., May 23, 1944; s. Charles Maddra and Lucille Ethelyn (Rankin) W.; children: Wendy Elizabeth, Christopher Maddra, Alexandra Sandeen. BS, Northwestern U., 1966; JD, U. Ill., 1973. Bar: Ill. 1974, U.S. Dist. Ct. (cen. dist.) Ill. 1974, U.S. Ct. Appeals (7th cir.) 1979. Pres. Webber & Thies PC, Urbana, Ill., 1974—. Adj. prof. Coll. Commerce U. Ill., 1987-90. Contbr. articles to profl. jours. Active Champaign County Jail Cts. Tech. Adv. Com., 1978-79, Downtown Devel. & Redevel. Commn., Urbana, 1978-79, U. Ill. Pres. Coun., 1984—; pres. Downtown Urbana Promotion Com., 1981-82; bd. dirs. Prairielands Coun. Boy Scouts Am., 1974—, v.p., 1979-82, pres., 1997-99; bd. dirs. U. Ill. Libr. Friends Bd., v.p., 1984-86, pres., 1986-88; bd. visitors U. Ill. Coll. Law, 1980—. Lt. USN, 1966-70. Recipient Appreciation award City of Urbana, 1980. Fellow Am. Bar Found., Ill. Bar Found.; mem. ABA, Urbana C. of C. (dir. 1978-81, 87-89, chmn. bd. 1989-90), Champaign County Bar Assn. (bd. dirs. 1980-83, pres. 1981-82), Ill. Bar Assn. (family law sect. coun. 1978-79, real estate sect. coun. 1983-87, co-chmn. contract drafting com. 1984-88), Rotary (dir. local club 1980-82). Home: 1910 Woodfield Rd Champaign IL 61822 Office: Webber & Thies PC 202 Lincoln Square PO Box 189 Urbana IL 61801 Office Phone: 217-367-1126.

**WEBBER, CHRIS, III, (MAYCE EDWARD CHRISTOPHER WEBBER),** professional basketball player; b. Detroit, Mar. 1, 1973; s. Mayce and Doris Webber. Student, U. Mich., 1991—93. Drafted Orlando Magic, Fla., 1993; forward Golden State Warriors, San Francisco, 1993—94, Washington Bullets, 1994—98, Sacramento Kings, 1998—2005, Philadelphia 76ers, 2005—. Founder Timeout Found. Named Nat. H.S. Player of Yr., 1990—91, Mr. Basketball, State of Mich., 1991, Coca-Cola Classic NBA Player of Yr., 1994, Brut Bullets Player of Yr., 1994—95; named to NBA All-Rookie 1st team, 1994. Achievements include being drafted 1st round Orlando Magic, 1993. Avocation: collecting signed historical documents of prominent African-Am. Office: 3601 S Broad St Philadelphia PA 19148*

**WEBBER, DIANA L.,** management consultant executive, engineering educator; b. Sacramento, May 12, 1960; d. Ralph and Mary P. (Chace) Van Tuyl. BS, Tex. A&M U., Coll. Sta., Tex., 1980—83; M in Computer Systems Mgmt., Creighton U., Omaha, Nebr., 1984—87; PhD, George Mason U., Fairfax, Va., 1997—2001. Aerospace engr. USAF, Crystal City, Va., 1978—2001, Scitor Corp., Chantilly, Va., 1995—2001; adj. prof. George Mason U., Fairfax, Va., 2001—; sr. assoc. Booz Allen Hamilton, McLean, Va., 2001—. Mem. adv. bd., assoc. editor: Booz Allen Tech. Jour.; contbr. articles to profl. jours. Capt. USAF, 1978—94, Pentagon. Mem.: ACM, IEEE Computer Soc. Democrat. Achievements include research in The Variation Point Model. Avocations: walking, reading, swimming. Office: Booz Allen Hamilton 8283 Greensboro Dr Mc Lean VA 20191 Office Phone: 703-902-4062. Personal E-mail: drwebber@comcast.net. Business E-Mail: webber_diana@bah.com.

**WEBBER, JOHN BENTLEY,** orthopedic surgeon; b. Morristown, NJ, Jan. 27, 1941; s. George Bentley and Gladys (Moody) W.; m. Mary Christina Thometz, Feb. 25, 1978; children: John Bentley, Edward Alan BA, Lehigh U., 1962; MD, Temple U., 1966. Intern Rochester Gen. Hosp., NY, 1966-67; resident Temple U. Med. Ctr., Phila., 1967-70; Stelrling Bunnell fellow in hand surgery Pacific Med. Ctr., San Francisco, 1971; assoc. prof. orthopedic surgery and rehab. Hahnemann Med. Coll. and Hosp., Phila., 1973—, chief sect. on hand surgery, 1973—; attending surgeon St. Christopher's Hosp. for Children, Phila., 1996—. Cons. in hand surgery Mcpl. Med. Svcs., Phila. 1973-87, USPHS, Phila., 1973-76, burn ctr. St. Agnes Med. Ctr., Phila., 1973—, Phila. unit Shriners' Hosp. for Crippled Children, 1979-95. Served to maj. USAF, 1971-73. Fellow ACS (Pa. com. on trauma), Am. Acad. Orthopedic Surgeons; mem. AMA, Am. Soc. for Surgery of Hand, Bunnell Hand Club (pres. 1978-80), Assn. for Acad. Surgery, Eastern Orthopedic Soc., Pa. Med. Soc., Phila. Orthopedic Soc., Phila. Hand Soc. (pres. 1987-89), Phila. County Med. Soc., Phila. Coll. Physicians, Meigs Med. Assn., Rotary, Union Leauge, Riverside Yacht Club (fleet surgeon), Phila. Country Club, Delaware Valley Ducks Unltd. (chmn. 1983-88), U.S. Coast Guard (cert. master). Republican. Congregationalist. Home: 1139 Rock Creek Rd Gladwyne PA 19035-1439 Personal E-mail: handweb@aol.com.

**WEBBER, JOHN CHARLES,** composer, music educator; b. London, May 4, 1949; DMA, Cath. U. of Am., Washington 1979; MA, Ind. U. of Pa., 1976; FTCL, Trinity Coll. of Music, London, 1975, LTCL, 1973; Diploma, Konservatorium, Cologne, Germany, 1975. Owner Webber Music, Kalamazoo, 1980—; music dir. Portsmouth New Music Orch., Portsmouth, England, 1995—2000, Ithaca Cmty. Orch., Ithaca, NY, 2001—05. Part-time instr. Western Mich. U., Kalamazoo, 2006, Ithaca Music Acad., 2001—03; part-time lectr. U. of Southampton, 1996—97, Kingston Coll., Portsmouth, 1996—98; part-time instr. The Crowden Sch., Berkeley, Calif., 1985—88. Composer: (9 symphonies, concertos, chamber music, other) John Webber Collected Works. Musician Royal Marines Band Svc., 1963—72, Eng. Mem.: Broadcast Music Inc. (assoc.). Office: Webber Music PO Box 20535 Kalamazoo MI 49019 E-mail: jcw@webbermusic.com.

**WEBBER, PAMELA D.,** information technology executive; Sr. mgr. applications devel. eCommerce Arrow Electronics, Inc., Melville, NY. Mem.: The Computer Tech. Industry Assn. (bd. mem. electronics industry data exch. leadership 2003—). Office: Arrow Electronics 50 Marcus Dr Melville NY 11747

**WEBBER, RICHARD JOHN,** lawyer; b. Mpls., July 27, 1948; s. Richard John and Mary Lee (Moore) W.; m. Susan Barbara Listerman, Jan. 8, 1972; children: Hillary, Joanna. BA, Princeton U., 1970; JD, U. Mich., 1973. Bar: D.C. Ct. Appeals 1974, U.S. Ct. Appeals (9th and D.C. cirs.) 1980, U.S. Dist. Ct. D.C. 1980, U.S. Claims Ct. 1974, U.S. Supreme Ct. 1980. Law clk. U.S. Ct. Claims, Washington, 1973-75; trial atty. U.S. Dept. Justice, Washington, 1975-80; assoc. Arent, Fox et al, Washington, 1980-85, ptnr., 1985—. Mem. ABA (chmn. fed. contract claims and remedies com. sect. pub. contract law 1986-91), Fed. Bar Assn. (chmn. govt. contracts sect. 1992-94, 1994-96, chmn. ADR sect. 2002-03). Office: Arent Fox Washington Sq 1050 Connecticut Ave NW Ste 500 Washington DC 20036-5303 Office Phone: 202-857-6254. E-mail: webberr@arentfox.com.

**WEBBER, ROSS ARKELL,** management educator; b. New Rochelle, NY, July 18, 1934; s. Richard and Muriel (Arkels) W.; m. Mary Louise Foradora, Sept. 29, 1956; children: Sarah Ruth, Judith Mary, Gregory Ross, Jennifer Louise, Stephen Andrew. BSE, Princeton U., 1956; PhD, Columbia U., 1966; MS (hon.), U. Pa., 1972. Indsl. engr. Eastman Kodak Co., Rochester, NY, 1959-61; instr. Columbia U., N.Y.C., 1961-64; lectr. Wharton Sch. U. Pa., Phila., 1964-65, asst. prof., 1965-70, assoc. prof., 1970-76, prof., 1976-2000, chmn. dept. mgmt., 1992-95, prof. emeritus, 2000—; v.p. U. Pa., Phila., 1981-86. Dir. Wharton-Industry Exec. Program, U. Pa., 1966-68, chmn. Wharton Internat. Bus. com., 1968-69, coord. Orgn. Behavior and Mgmt. Group, 1968-75, asst. dept. chmn., PhD com., 1972-75, coord. Orgnl. and Mgmt. Component, Advanced Mgmt. Program in Health Care Adminstrn., 1973-74, mem. Univ. Coun., 1975-77, adv. com. Pub. Mgmt. Unit, The Wharton Sch., 1977-81, chmn. Grad. Admissions com.; mem. editl. bd. The Wharton Mag. Author: Organizational Behavior and the Practice of Management, 1968, 5th rev. edit., 1987; Spanish lang. edit., 1982, Culture and Management: Text and Reading in Comparative Management, 1969, Management: Basic Elements of Managing Organizations, 1979, 3rd rev. edit., 1984, Polish lang. edit., 1984, Management Pragmatics: Readings and Cases on Managing Organizations, 1979, Time is Money!: The Key to Managerial Success, 1980, Japanese lang. edit. 1983, Swedish edit. 1983, Spanish lang. edit., 1985, Portugese lang. edit., 1989, To Be a Manager, 1981, A Guide to Getting Things Done, 1984, Becoming a Courageous Manager: Overcoming Career Problems of New Managers, 1991, Breaking Your Time Barriers: Becoming a More Effective Strategic Time Manager, 1992; contbr. over 55 articles to profl. jours. Past mem. bd. dirs. United Way Southeastern Pa.; coach youth athletics, fund raiser for ch., religious educator. Lt. (j.g.) USN, 1956-59. Avocations: painting, tennis, skiing. Office: U Pa Wharton Sch 2000 Steinberg Hall Philadelphia PA 19104 Office Phone: 215-898-9368. Business E-Mail: webber@wharton.upenn.edu.

**WEBER, ALBAN,** professional society administrator, lawyer; b. Chgo., Jan. 29, 1915; s. Joseph A. and Anna (von Plachecki) W.; m. Margaret Kenny, Dec. 29, 1951; children: Alban III, Peggy Ann, Gloria, Brian. AB, Harvard U., 1935, JD, 1937; MA, Northwestern U., 1962; LLM, John Marshall Law sch., 1967. Bar: Ill. 1938, U.S. Supreme Ct. 1946, Mich. 1985, Fla. 1997. Ptnr. Weber & Weber, 1937-41; gen. counsel Fgn. Liquidation Commn., State Dept., 1946; trust officer Lake Shore Nat. Bank, Chgo., 1952-55; univ. counsel Northwestern U., Evanston, Ill., 1955-70; pres. Fedn. Ind. Ill. Colls. and Univs., Evanston, 1970-85; of counsel Schuyler, Roche & Zwirner, Evanston, 1984-94; pres. Benjamin Franklin Fund, Inc., 1965-75, Northwestern U. Press, Inc., 1961-65; chmn. State Assn. Execs. Coun., 1981. Pres. N.E. Ill. coun. Boy Scouts Am., 1970-71, dist. chmn. Gulfstream coun., 1994-95; alderman City of Chgo., 1947-51. Comdr. USNR, 1941-45, rear adm., 1969-75. Recipient Silver Beaver award Boy Scouts Am., 1946, Meritorious Svc. award Loyola U., 1978, Edn. for Freedom award Roosevelt U., 1984. Mem. Nat. Assn. Coll. and Univ. Attys. (pres. 1962), Harvard Law Soc. Ill. (pres. 1984), Navy League (pres. Evanston coun. 1967-70), Univ. Risk Mgmt. Assn. (pres. 1965), Naval Order U.S. (nat. comdr. 1970-72), Harvard Club, Port St. Lucie Rotary Club, Chgo. Yacht Club, White Lake Yacht Club, Kiwanis (lt. gov., pres. Port St. Lucie club), St. Lucie River Power Squadron (comdr.), Anchor Line Yacht Club (commodore). Home: 761 Alliance Dr #233 Virginia Beach VA 23454

**WEBER, ALFONS,** physicist; b. Dortmund, Germany, Oct. 8, 1927; s. Alexander and Ilona W.; m. Jeannine K. Weber, Oct. 8, 1955; children: Karl, Louise, Paul. PhD, Ill. Inst. Tech., 1956. Instr. physics Ill. Inst. Tech., Chgo., 1953-56; from asst. prof. physics to prof. Fordham U., Bronx, NY, 1957-81, prof. physics and chemistry, 1976-81, chmn. dept. physics, 1964-70; rsch. physicist Nat. Inst. Stds. and Tech., Gaithersburg, Md., 1977-98, acting chief molecular spectroscopy divsn., 1980-81, chief molecular physics divsn., 1982-95, sr. scientist physics lab., 1995-98, scientist emeritus, 1999—; program mgr. condensed matter physics divsn., materials rsch NSF, 1998—2001, program dir. exptl. phys. chemistry, chemistry divsn., 2001—04. With chem scis. divsn. U.S. Dept. Energy, 1991-92, chem. divsn. NSF, 1992-95. Editor: Raman Spectroscopy of Gases and Liquids, 1979; Structure and Dynamics of Weakly Bound Molecular Complexes, 1987, Spectroscopy of the Earth's Atmosphere and Interstellar Medium, 1992; former mem. editl. bd. Jour. of Raman Spectroscopy, Jour. Chem. and Phys. Reference Data. V.p. Union Free Dist. # 1 Sch. Bd., Eastchester, N.Y., 1970-73. Postdoctoral fellow NRC Can., U. Toronto, 1956-57. Fellow AAAS, Am. Phys. Soc. (councillor 1987-91); mem. Coblentz Soc., Soc. Applied Spectroscopy, Am. Chem. Soc. Office: Nat Inst Stds & Tech Gaithersburg MD 20899 Business E-Mail: aweber@nist.gov.

**WEBER, ARNOLD L.,** lawyer; b. Little Cedar, Iowa, Oct. 4, 1926; divorced; children: Katherine Weber Hickle, Thomas, Margaret Weber Robertson. PhB magna cum laude, Marquette U., 1949; MA, Harvard U., 1950; JD, George Washington U., 1954, LLM, 1956. Bar: D.C. 1954, Md. 1961, Calif. 1962, U.S. Dist. Ct. D.C. 1954, (no. dist.) Calif. 1962, (cen. dist.) Calif. 1992, U.S. Ct. Claims 1960, U.S. Tax Ct. 1965, U.S. Ct. Appeals (D.C. cir.) 1954, (9th cir.) 1962, (fed. cir.) 1991, U.S. Supreme Ct. 1959. Lawyer Housing and Home Fin., Washington, 1954; pvt. practice Washington, 1954-55; lawyer Tariff Commn., Washington, 1954-55, FCC, Washington, 1955-56, IRS, Washington, 1956-61; assoc. Brobeck, Phleger & Harrison, San Francisco, 1961-64; sr. gen. atty. So. Pacific Transp., San Francisco, 1964-84; western tax counsel Santa Fe Pacific Corp., San Francisco, 1985-88; pvt. practice San Francisco, 1988—. With USNR, 1944-54, PTO. Mem. ABA, Olympic Club, Bar Assn. San Francisco, State Bar of Calif. Office: PO Box 638 San Francisco CA 94104-0638

**WEBER, ARNOLD ROBERT,** academic administrator; b. N.Y.C., Sept. 20, 1929; s. Jack and Lena (Smith) W.; m. Edna M. Files, Feb. 7, 1954; children: David, Paul, Robert. BA, U. Ill., 1951; MA, MIT, 1958, PhD in Econs., 1958; DHL (hon.), U. Notre Dame, 2005, U. Ill., 2005, Northwestern U., 2005, Loyola U., 2005, Ripon Coll., 2005, U. Colo., 2005. Instr., then asst. prof. econs. MIT, 1955-58; faculty U. Chgo. Grad. Sch. Bus., 1958-69, prof. indsl. relations, 1963-69; asst. sec. for manpower Dept. Labor, 1969-70; exec. dir. Cost of Living Council; also spl. asst. to Pres. Nixon, 1971; Gladys C. and Isidore Brown prof. urban and labor econs. U. Chgo., 1971-73; former provost Carnegie-Mellon U.; dean Carnegie-Mellon U. (Grad. Sch. Indsl. Adminstrn.), prof. labor econs. and pub. policy, 1973-80; pres. U. Colo., Boulder, 1980-85, Northwestern U., Evanston, Ill., 1985-95, chancellor, 1995-98, pres. emeritus, 1998—. Cons. union, mgmt. and govt. agys., 1960—; cons. Dept. Labor, 1965; mem. Pres.'s Adv. Com. Labor Mgmt. Policy, 1964, Orgn. Econ. Coop. and Devel., 1987; vice chmn. Sec. Labor Task Force Improving Employment Svcs., 1965; chmn. rsch. adv. com. U.S. Employment Svc., 1966; assoc. dir. OMB Exec. Office of Pres., 1970—71; chmn. Presdl. R.R. Emergency Bd., 1982; trustee Com. for Econ. Devel., Nat. Multiple Sclerosis Soc.; bd. dirs. Diamond Cluster Inc.; asst. sec. manpower U.S. Dept. Labor, 1969—70. Contbr. articles to profl. jours. Laureate, Lincoln

Acad. Ill.; Ford Found. Faculty Rsch. fellow, 1964-65. Mem. Am. Acad. Arts and Scis., Indsl. Rels. Rsch. Assn., Nat. Acad. Pub. Adminstrn., Comml. Club Chgo. (pres., civic com. 1995-2000), Econ. Club Chgo. (pres. 1995-97), Phi Beta Kappa. Jewish. Office: Northwestern U Office of Pres Emeritus 555 Clark St 209 Evanston IL 60208-0805 E-mail: arnold-weber@nwu.edu.

**WEBER, BRADLEY R.,** music educator; b. Creighton, Nebr., Oct. 13, 1954; s. Marvin R. and Virginia A. Weber; m. Deb K. Thieman; children: Melissa Woockman, Megan, Micaela. BFA in Edn., Wayne State Coll., Wayne, Nebr., 1977; MA in Edn., U. Wyo., Laramie, Wyo., 1992. Percussionist Sioux City Mcpl. Concert Band, Sioux City, Iowa, 1975—77; instr. instrumental music Emerson-Hubbard (Nebr.) H.S., 1977—86, Wayne (Nebr.) H.S., 1986—. Mem. staff summer music camp Wayne (Nebr.) State Coll., 1976—; adj. faculty, 1984—. Musician: Sioux City (Iowa) Mcpl. Concert Band, 1975—87, Laramie (Wyo.) Mcpl. Concert Band, 1984—87, Columbus (Nebr.) Jazz Orch., 2003—; dir.: Nebr. Masonic All-Star Marching Band, 1999—. Named Educator of Yr., Wayne Area C. of C., 1999; named to Nat. Honor Soc., Wayne H.S., 1992; recipient Achievement In Edn. award, Wayne Area Optimist Club, 2004. Mem.: NEA, Nebr. Music Educators Assn. (chmn. band affairs 1992—94, mem. dist. nominating com. 1983, Participation Recognition award 2005, 2006), Music Educators Nat. Conf., Nebr. State Bandmasters Assn. (sec. 1985—87, mem. spl. marching band com. 1990—91, class B rep. 1992—93, chmn. membership 1999—2002, Marching Excellence Merit cert. 1999, scholar 1986), Wayne Edn. Assn., Phi Delta Psi, Phi Beta Mu, Kappa Kappa Psi, Phi Delta Kappa. Home: 2314 Highview Drive Wayne NE 68787 Office: Wayne High School 611 W 7th Wayne NE 68787 Office Phone: 402-375-3150. Office Fax: 402-375-5251. Personal E-mail: bweber1310@msn.com. Business E-mail: brweber1@wayneschools.org.

**WEBER, BRUCE,** photographer, filmmaker; b. Greensburg, Penn., Mar. 29, 1946; Studied, NYU, New School for Soc. Rsch., NYC, Princeton. Photographer Calvin Klein underware campaign, Ralph Lauren, Abercrombie & Fitch; owner Weberbilt clothing line. Prodr.: (films) Broken Noses, 1987, The Beauty Brothers, Parts I-IV, 1987, Beauty Brothers, 1987, Let's Get Lost, 1989, Backyard Movie, 1991, Gentle Giants, 1994, The Teddy Boys Of The Edwardian Draper Society, 1995, Chop Suey, 2001, A Letter to True, 2004; author: Bruce Weber, 1983, O Rio De Janeiro, 1986, The Andy Book, 1987, Let's Get Lost: A Film Journal, 1988, Bruce Weber, 1988, Sam, 1990, Bear Pond, 1991, Bruce Weber, 1991, Hotel Room with a View, 1992, No Valet Parking, 1994, Gentle Giants, 1994, A House is not a Home, 1994, Branded Youth, 1997, The Chop Suey Club, 1999, Shufly, 2000, Heel to Heal, 2004; dir.: (music videos) Chris Isaak, Pet Shop Boys. Recipient Eugenia Sheppard award for Excellence in Fashion Journalism, Coun. of Fashion Designers of Am., 2006.*

**WEBER, BRUCE EDWARD,** art historian; b. Bklyn., Dec. 29, 1951; s. Harry and Sylvia Weber; m. Joanne Pagano. PhD, CUNY, 1985. Curator U. Ky. Art Mus., Lexington, 1979—81; curator of collections Morton Mus. Art, West Palm Beach, Fla., 1981—88; dir. rsch. and exhbns. Berry-Hill Galleries, N.Y.C., 1990—. Faculty NYU, N.Y.C., 1999—. Author: Paintings of New York, 1800-1950, 2005, (exhbn. catalog) Homage to the Square: Picturing, Washington Square, 1890-1960, Heart of the Matter: The Still Lifes of Marsden Hartley, (poetry) Poetic Justice, 2004. Fellow Smithsonian fellow, Smithsonian Instn., Washington, 1977. Mem.: Assn. Am. Mus.

**WEBER, CARL,** publishing executive, retail bookstore executive, writer; b. Queens, 1966; married; 3 children. MBA in Mktg., Univ. Va. Former bus. teacher, NYC; book retailer Black Facts I, Bklyn., Black Facts II, Queens, Horizon Books, Newark; pres., founder, editl. dir. Urban Books LLC (subs. Kensington Publishing), Long Island, 2002—; founder, owner Urban Knowledge bookstore (and five other locations), Balt., 2005—; pres. Q-Boro Books (acquired by Urban Books), 2006—. Author: (novels) Lookin' for Luv, 2001, Married Men, 2001, Baby Momma Drama, 2003, Player Haters, 2004, The Preacher's Son (debuted No. 1 Essence Bestseller list), So You Call Yourself a Man, 2005. Named Blackboard Bookseller of Yr., 2000. Office: Urban Books 74 Andrews Ave Wyandanch NY 11798 Office Phone: 631-643-6828.*

**WEBER, DONALD FRANK,** obstetrician, gynecologist; b. Minot, ND, May 15, 1956; s. Sebastian and Loretta Mae Weber; m. Kathleen Ann Weeks, Apr. 21, 1979; children: Christine Marie, Brian Joseph, Eric James. BS, U. ND, 1978, MD, 1982. Diplomate Am. Bd. Ob-Gyn. Resident Mt. Sinai Med. Ctr., U. Wis. Sch. Medicine, 1982—86; obstetrician-gynecologist Luther-Midelfort, Eau Claire, Wis., 1986—; chair, credentials com. Luther Hosp., Eau Claire, 1996—. Clin. asst. prof. U. Wis. Sch. Medicine, 1987—; chief of staff Luther Hosp., Eau Claire, 1994—96. Bd. dirs. Big Bros. Big Sisters of the Chippewa Valley, Eau Claire, Wis., 1994—2002, Perinatal Found., Madison, Wis., 2001—, Barron Meml. Med. Ctr., Wis., 1999—2002. Recipient Meritorius Svc., State Med. Soc. Wis., 2001, WAPC Appreciation award, Wis. Assn. for Perinatal Care, 1992, 2003. Fellow: Am. Coll. Ob-Gyn. (vice chair Wis. sect. 2001—05, chair Wis. sect. 2005—); mem.: AMA, Wis. Assn. for Perinatal Care (treas., pres. 1996—98), Am. Inst. Ultrasound in Medicine, Golf and Country Club (bd. dirs. 2002—03). Avocations: golf, ice hockey, history, travel. Office: LutherMidelfort 1400 Bellinger St Eau Claire WI 54702-1510 Office Phone: 715-838-6100. E-mail: weber.donald@mayo.edu.

**WEBER, EUGEN,** historian, educator, writer; b. Bucharest, Romania, Apr. 24, 1925; arrived in U.S., 1955; s. Emanuel and Sonia (Garrett) Weber; m. Jacqueline Brument-Roth, June 12, 1950. Student, Inst. d'études politiques, Paris, 1948-49, 51-52; BA, Emmanuel Coll., 1950; MA, Emmanuel Coll., Cambridge U., 1954, M.Litt., 1956; D of Humanities, Occidental Coll., L.A., 2006. History supr. Emmanuel Coll., 1953—54; lectr. U. Alta., 1954—55; asst. prof. U. Iowa, 1955—56; from asst. prof. history to prof. UCLA, 1956—84, Joan Palevsky prof. modern European history, 1984—, chmn. dept., 1965—08, dir. study center U. Calif., France, 1968—70; dean social scis. UCLA, 1976—77, dean Coll. Letters and Scis., 1977—82. Frum Meml. lectr. Toronto U., 1999; Ford faculty lectr. Stanford U., 1965; Patten lectr. Ind. U., 1981; vis. prof. Collège de France, Paris, 1983; dir. d'études Ecole des hautes études, Paris, 1984—85; Christian Gauss lectr. Princeton U., 1990. Author: Nationalist Revival in France, 1959, The Western Tradition, 1959, Paths to the Present, 1960, Action Française, 1962, Satan Franc-Maçon, 1964, Varieties of Fascism, 1964; author: (with H. Rogger) The European Right, 1965; author: A Modern History of Europe, 1971, Europe Since 1715, 1972, Peasants into Frenchmen, 1976 (Commonwealth prize Calif., 1977), La Fin des Terroirs, 1983 (Prix de la Société des gens de lettres, 1984), France Fin-de-siècle, 1986 (Commonwealth prize Calif., 1987), The Western Tradition (WGBH/PBS TV Series), 1989, My France, 1990, Movements, Currents, Trends, 1991, The Hollow Years, 1994, La France des années trente, 1995, Prix M. Baumont, 1995, Prix Etats-Unis/France, 1995, Prix de l'Academie des Jeux Floraux, 1997, Apocalypses, 1999; adv. editor: Jour. Contemporary History, 1966—2005, French History, 1985—, French Cultural Studies, 1990—, Am. Scholar, 1992—98, Nuova Storia Contemporanea, 1999—. Capt. Brit. Army, 1943—47. Decorated Ordre Nat. des Palmes Académiques, France; recipient Luckman Disting. Tchg. award, UCLA Alumnae Assn., 1992; fellow, Fulbright Found., 1952, Rsch. fellow, 1963—64, sr. fellow, Am. Coun. Learned Soc., 1962, Guggenheim fellow, 1963—64, sr. fellow, NEH, 1973—74, 1982—83; grantee, Social Sci. Rsch. Coun., 1959—61; Fulbright fellow, 1982—83; Fellow: Am. Philos. Soc., Am. Acad. Arts and Scis., Netherlands Inst. Advanced Studies, Assn. Française de Sci. Politique; mem.: Soc. French Hist. Studies, Soc. d'histoire moderne, Am. Hist. Assn. (scholarly distinguished award 1999), Phi Beta Kappa (hon.; senator 1988—2000, Ralph Waldo Emerson prize 1977). Office: UCLA Dept History Los Angeles CA 90095-1473

**WEBER, FREDRIC ALAN,** lawyer; b. Paterson, NJ, July 31, 1948; s. Frederick Edward and Alida (Hessels) W.; m. Mary Elizabeth Cook, June 18, 1983. BA in History, Rice U., 1970; JD, Yale U., 1976. Bar: Tex. 1976, U.S. Dist. Ct. (so. dist.) Tex. Assoc. Fulbright & Jaworski LLP, Houston, 1976-80, participating assoc., 1980-83, prin., 1983—, and head, public fin. and adminstrn. dept. Dir. Houston Symphony Soc., 1993—, v.p. devel., 2001-03,

sr. v.p. devel., 2005-. Mem. ABA, Am. Coll. Bond Counsel (treas. 2003-04, v.p. 2004—), Nat. Assn. Bond Lawyers (bd. dirs. 1988-89, treas. 1989-90, pres.-elect 1991, pres. 1991-92), Houston Bar Assn. Office: Fulbright & Jaworski LLP 1301 McKinney St Ste 5100 Houston TX 77010-3095 Office Phone: 713-651-5151. Office Fax: 713-651-5246. Business E-mail: fweber@fulbright.com.

**WEBER, GEORGE,** oncology and pharmacology educator, researcher; b. Budapest, Hungary, Mar. 29; came to U.S., 1959; s. Salamon and Hajnalka (Arvai) W.; m. Catherine Elizabeth Forrest, June 30, 1958; children: Elizabeth Dolly Arvai, Julie Vibert Wallace, Jefferson James. BA, Queen's U., 1950, MD, 1952; MD (hon.), U. Chieti, Italy, 1979, Med. Faculty, Budapest, 1982, U. Leipzig, Fed. Republic of Germany, 1987, Tokushima U., Japan, 1988; degree, Kagawa U., Japan, 1992. Rsch. assoc. Montreal Cancer Inst., 1953-59; prof. pharmacology Ind. U. Sch. Medicine, Indpls., 1959—; dir. Lab for Exptl. Oncology Sch. Medicine, Ind. U., Indpls., 1974—; Milan Panič prof. oncology Ind. U., Indpls., 1994—, Wellcome prof., 1995—; prof. Lab. for Exptl. Oncology Sch. Medicine, Ind. U., Indpls., 1974-90, disting. prof. Lab. for Exptl. Oncology, 1990—. Chmn. study sect. USPHS, Washington, 1976-78; sci. adv. com. Am. Cancer Soc., N.Y.C., 1972-76, 94—. Damon Runyon Fund, N.Y.C., 1971-76; mem. U.S. Nat. Com., Internat. Union Against Cancer, Washington, 1974-80, 90-94, NAS, Washington, 1974-80, 90-94, U.S. Army Med. Rsch. and Breast Cancer Rsch. Program, 1996-97; prof. Brit. cancer campaign U. Oxford, Oxford, Eng., 2001; vis. prof. U. Bologna, Italy, 2001-02, 03-06. Editor: Advances in Enzyme Regulation, Vols. 1-47, 1962—; assoc. editor Jour. Cancer Rsch., 1969—80, 1982—89. Recipient Alecce Prize for cancer rsch. Tiberine Acad., Rome, 1971, Best Prof. award Student AMA, Indpls., 1966, 68, G.F. Gallanti prize for enzymology Internat. Soc. Clin. Chemists, 1984, Outstanding Investigator award Nat. Cancer Inst., NIH, 1986-94, Semmelweis medal & diploma Budapest, Hungary, 2001, medal Gastroenterological Soc., Aliga, Hungary, 2001, Prestigious External Award Recognition Ind. U., Indpls., Ind., 2002. Mem. Am. Soc. for Pharmacology and Exptl. Therapeutics, Am. Assn. Cancer Rsch. (G.H.A. Clowes award 1982), Russian Acad. Sci. (hon.), Hungarian Cancer Soc. (hon.), Hungarian Acad. Scis. (hon.), Acad. Scis. Bologna (Italy) (hon.). Home: 7307 Lakeside Dr Indianapolis IN 46278-1618 Office: Ind U Sch Medicine Lab Exptl Oncology 699 West Dr Indianapolis IN 46202-5119 Office Phone: 317-274-7921.

**WEBER, GEORGE RICHARD,** financial and internet marketing executive, writer; b. The Dalles, Oreg., Feb. 7, 1929; s. Richard Merle and Maud (Winchell) W.; m. Nadine Hanson, Oct. 12, 1957; children: Elizabeth Ann Weber Katooli, Karen Louise Weber Zaro, Linda Marie. BS, Oreg. State U., 1950; MBA, U. Oreg., 1962. CPA, Oreg. Sr. trainee U.S. Nat. Bank of Portland (Oreg.), 1950-51; jr. acct. Ben Musa, CPA, The Dalles, Oreg., 1954; tax and audit asst. Price Waterhouse, Portland, 1955-59; sr. acct. Burton M. Smith, CPA, Portland, 1959-62; pvt. practice Portland, 1962-99; assoc. World Mktg. Alliance, 1996-99, Waterman and Assocs., 2000—01, Allstate Fin. Svcs., 2001—03, Legacy for Life, 2004—, Extras Casting, 2005—. Lectr. acctg. Portland State Coll.; expert witness fin. and tax matters. Author: Small Business Long-term Finance, 1962, A History of the Coroner and Medical Examiner Offices, 1963, CPA Litigation Services References, 1991, Letters to a Friend, 1995; contbr. to profl. publs. and poetry jours. Sec.-treas. Nat. Hood Kiwanis Camp, Inc., 1965; exec. counselor SBA; mem. fin. com., powerlifting team U.S. Powerlifting Fedn., 1984, amb. People to People, China, 1987. Arty. officer AUS, 1951-53. Decorated Bronze Star. Mem. AICPA, Internat. Platform Assn., Oreg. Hist. Soc., Oreg. City Traditional Jazz Soc., Order of the Holy Cross Jerusalem, Order St. Stephen the Martyr, Order St. Gregory the Illuminator, Knightly Assn. St. George the Martyr, World Literary Acad., Portland C.S. Lewis Soc., Beta Alpha Psi, Pi Kappa Alpha. Clubs: Kiwanis, Portland Track, City (Portland); Multnomah Athletic; Sunrise Toastmasters. Republican. Lutheran. Home and Office: 3715 NE Alberta Ct Portland OR 97211-8144 Office Phone: 503-288-3328. E-mail: grweber@earthlink.net. *My basic beliefs are in faith, family and freedom through limited government and personal responsibility, with personal responsibility including development and use of capabilities.*

**WEBER, GLORIA RICHIE,** retired minister, retired state legislator; married; 4 children. BA, Washington U., St. Louis; MA, MDiv, Eden Theol. Sem., Webster Groves, Mo. Ordained to ministry Evang. Luth. Ch. Am., 1974. Family life educator Luth. Family and Children's Svcs. Mo.; mem. Mo. Ho. of Reps., 1993-94. Mo. state organizer, dir. comm. Mainstream Voters C.A.R.E., 1995. Editor: Interfaith Voices for Peace and Justice, 1996—2000. Exec. dir. Older Women's League, 1990—95. Named Woman of the Yr., Variety Club, 1978, Woman of Worth, Older Women's League, 1993; recipient Woman of Achievement award, St. Louis Globe-Dem., 1977, Unselfish Cmty. Svc. award, St. Louis Sentinel Newspaper, 1985, Faith in Action award, Luth. Svcs. St. Louis, 1994. Mem.: Older Wiser Luths. in Svc. (devotion leader), Assn. Lutheran Older Adults (mem. nat. bd. 2004—), N.Am. Interfaith Network (bd. dirs. 1993—2003), Phi Beta Kappa. Democrat. Personal E-mail: gloriaweber9@aol.com.

**WEBER, HANNO,** architect; b. Barranquilla, Colombia, Sept. 24, 1937; arrived in US, 1952; s. Hans and Ester (Oks) Weber. BA magna cum laude, Princeton U., 1959, MArch, 1961. Registered arch., Ill., Fla., Mo., Pa., NJ, Va. Urban designer, rsch. assoc. Guayana project MIT and Harvard U., Caracas, Venezuela, 1961-63; project arch. Paul Schweikher Assocs., Pitts., 1963-67; asst. prof. architecture Princeton U., NJ, 1967-73; assoc. prof. Washington U., St. Louis, 1973-80; sr. design arch., studio head, assoc. Skidmore, Owings & Merrill, Chgo., 1980-83; prin. Hanno Weber & Assocs., Chgo., 1984—. Vis. lectr. Escuela Nacional de Arquitectura Universidad Nacional de Mex., 1975; rsch. assoc. Rsch. Ctr. Urban and Environ. Planning, Princeton; project dir. Cmty. Design Workshop Washington U. Sch. Architecture, St. Louis, 1973—78; prof. architecture U. Wis. Milw., 1993—. Contbr. articles to profl. jours. Mem. Pres.'s Commn. Edn. Women Princeton U., 1968—69. Finalist, Okla. City Meml. Internat. Design Competition, 1997, Green Homes for Chgo. Design Competition, 2000; recipient 1st prize winner, Flagler Dr. Waterfront Master Plan Design Competition, West Palm Beach, Fla., 1984, Mcpl. Ctr. Design Competition, Leesburg, Va., 1987, Chgo. AIA Disting. Bldg. award Citation of Merit, 1987, Urban Design award Mcpl. Govt. Ctr., Leesburg, AIA, 1992; fellow, NEH, 1970, Graham Found., 1973. Mem.: Nat. Coun. Arch. Registration Bds., Phi Beta Kappa. Office: Hanno Weber & Assocs 11 E Adams St # 702 Chicago IL 60603-6301 Office Phone: 312-922-5589. Business E-mail: weber@hannoweber.com.

**WEBER, HANS JÜRGEN,** physics professor; b. Berlin, May 3, 1939; came to U.S., 1966; naturalized, 1993; s. Hans Gustav Wilhelm and Hedwig Bertha Elisabeth (Angermann) W.; m. Edith E. Enzian, Aug. 19, 1966; 1 child, Chris H. MS in Math., U. Frankfurt, Fed. Republic Germany, 1961, PhD in Physics, 1965. Postdoctoral rsch. assoc. U. Frankfurt, 1965-66, Duke U., Durham, NC, 1966-67, U. Va., Charlottesville, 1968; asst. prof. physics, 1968-71, assoc. prof., 1971-77, prof., 1977—2003. Vis. scientist U. Mainz, Fed. Republic Germany, 1972, 77, 91, U. Paris-Sud, Orsay, France, 1979; vis. prof. U. Lyon, France, 1978. Co-author: Mathematical Methods for Physicists, 1995, 2001, 2005, Essentials of Math Methods for Physicists, 2003; contbr. to Physics Reports, Springer Tracts, Phys. Letters, Phys. Rev. Rsch. grantee NSF, 1971-95. Mem. Am. Phys. Soc., Am. Assn. Physics Tchrs., Sigma Xi. Lutheran. Achievements include development of a nuclear force (NN interaction) from quark models and a possible connection between quantum chromodynamics and meson dynamics; research on isobars in nuclei. Office: U Va Inst Nuclear and Particle Physics Mccormick Rd Charlottesville VA 22904-0001 Business E-mail: hw@virginia.edu.

**WEBER, HERMAN JACOB,** district judge; b. Lima, Ohio, May 20, 1927; s. Herman Jacob and Ada Minola (Esterly) W.; m. Barbara L. Rice, May 22, 1948; children: Clayton, Deborah. BA, Otterbein Coll., 1949; JD summa cum laude, Ohio State U., 1951. Bar: Ohio 1952, U.S. Dist. Ct. (so. dist.) Ohio 1954. Ptnr. Weber & Hogue, Fairborn, Ohio, 1952-61; judge Fairborn Mayor's Ct., 1956-58; acting judge Fairborn Mcpl. Ct., 1958-60; judge Greene County Common Pleas Ct., Xenia, Ohio, 1961-82, Ohio Ct. Appeals

(2d dist.), Dayton, 1982-85, U.S. Dist. Ct. (so. dist.) Ohio, Cin., 1985—2002, sr. judge, 2002—. Chmn. Sixth Cir. Dist. Judges Conf., 1988, Ohio Jud. Conf., Columbus, 1980-82; pres. Ohio Common Pleas Judges Assn., Columbus, 1975. Vice-mayor City of Fairborn, 1955-57, council mem., 1955-59. Served with USNR, 1945-46. Office: US Dist Ct 801 100 E 5th St Cincinnati OH 45202-3905

**WEBER, IDELLE,** artist, art educator; b. Chgo., Mar. 12, 1932; d. J. Earl and Min (Wallach) Feinberg; m. Julian L. Weber, Apr. 17, 1957; children: Jonathan Todd, Suzanne. BA, UCLA, 1954, MA, 1955. Adj. assoc. prof. art, grad. div. NYU, 1974-88; assoc. prof. Carpenter Ctr. Harvard U., 1988-91; prof. Nat. Acad., 2004-2006. Exhibited one-woman shows: Bertha Schaefer Gallery, N.Y.C., 1963, 64, Hundred Acres Gallery, N.Y.C., 1973, 75, 77, Chatham Coll., Pitts., 1979, O.K. Harris Gallery, N.Y.C., 1979, 82, Ruth Siegel Gallery, N.Y.C., 1984, 85, 87, Antony Ralph Gallery, N.Y.C., 1989, Arts Club of Chgo., 1986, Homart, Houston, 1987, Barbara Fendrick Gallery, Washington, 1987, Jean Albano Gallery, Chgo., 1994, Victorian Coll. of Arts, Melbourne, U., Australia, 1995, Contemporary Arts Forum, San Francisco, 1995, Nassau Mus. Art, 2004, Ferregut Tower Gallery, N.Y., 2005; group shows: Pa. Acad. Fine Arts, San Antonio Mus., Larry Aldrich Ctr. for Contemporary Arts, Ridgefield, Conn., 1981, Mus. Modern Art, N.Y.C., 1956, Guggeheim Mus., N.Y.C., 1964, Wadsworth Atheneum, Hartford, Conn., 1964, 66, Darnstadt (W.Ger.) Mus., Yale U. Mus., New Haven, 1975, Va. Mus., Richmond, Nat. Collection Fine Art, Washington, Butler Inst., Youngstown, Ohio, Fendrick Gallery, Washington, 1978, 85, Nat. Acad. 2002, 05, 06, Danforth Mus., Framington, Mass, 1980, San Francisco Mus. Art, 1985-86, Contemporary Art Ctr., New Orleans, 1986, Indpls. Mus. Art, 1986, Graham Modern Mus., N.Y.C., 1986, Ft. Wayne Mus. Art, 1988, Carpenter Ctr. Harvard U., 1988, Met. Mus. Art, N.Y.C., 2001, U. Va. Art Mus., 2002, Gracie Mansion, Chelsea, N.Y.C., 2002, Nat. Acad. Design Mus., 2003, Neuberger Mus. Art, 2004, Nat. Acad., 2004, Ferregut Tower Gallery, Southampton, N.Y., 2005; represented permanent collections: Nat. Collection Fine Art, Va. Mus., Sydney and Francis Lewis Found., Richmond, Yale U. Art Gallery, Albright Knox Gallery, Buffalo, Worcester (Mass.) Art Mus., Rochester (N.Y.) U. Mus., McNay Art Inst., N.Y. Pub. Library, Met. Mus. Art, N.Y.C., Pacific Bell, Calif., Bklyn Mus., Albright-Knox Gallery, Buffalo, Nelson -Atkins Mus. Art, Kansas City, Mo., Met. Mus. Art, Art Inst. Chgo., Kranert, U. Ill., Urbana, Whitney Mus. Art, Nat. Acad. and Sch. Fine Arts. Recognized in various publs. including: Arts Mag., 1979, 82, 84, 86, Photo Realism (L. Meisel), 1980, San Antonio Mus. Catalogue (L. Nochlin), 1981, Art in Am. (E. Lubell), Am. Women Artists (C.S. Rubenstein), 1982, Wall St. Jour., 1985, Christian Sci. Monitor, 1985, 86, Art in America, 1986, Washington Post, 1986, Chgo. Tribune, 1986, Washington Post, 1986, 87, Art Examiner, 1986; subject of work: American Realist Painting, 1945-1980 (John L. Ward), 1989; Scholastic Arts mag. scholar, 1950. Mem. Coll. Art Assn., Women's Caucus for Art, Artists Equity, Nat. Acad.

**WEBER, JANICE ANN,** library director, grant writer; b. Baytown, Tex., Aug. 28, 1952; d. James Thelmer Jr. and Doris Geraldine (Bush) Foster; m. Louis Haldane Weber, Feb. 1, 1983. BS, Tex. Women's U., Denton, 1982, MLS, 1985. Libr. dir. Dimmit County Libr., Carrilo Springs, Tex., 1985-86, Val Verde County Libr., Del Rio, Tex., 1986-89, Laredo (Tex.) Pub. Libr., 1989—. Sec., bd. dirs. Literary Vol. of Am., Laredo, 1989-95, bd. dirs. Webb County Heritage Found., Laredo, 1990-94; chmn. Webb County Hist. Commn., 1989-94; mem. Tuesday Music & Lit., Laredo, 1997—. Grantee numerous orgns., 1990—. Mem. Nonprofit Mgmt. Assn., Tex. Libr. Assn., Tex. Mcpl. Libr. Dirs. Assn. Avocations: gourmet cooking, weaving. Office: Laredo Pub Libr 1120 E Calton Rd Laredo TX 78041-7328

**WEBER, JOHN WALTER,** insurance company executive; b. Rochester, N.Y., Jan. 10, 1959; s. Donald J. and Patricia M. (Mangon) W. BS, U. Conn., 1984. Claims supr. Hartford Ins. Group, Southington, Conn., 1986-90; regional claims mgr. Housing Authority Risk Retention Group, Cheshire, Conn., 1990—. Contbr. articles to tech. publs. Mem. U. Conn. Alumni Assn. Avocations: running, reading, softball, cooking. E-mail: jweber6@charter.net.

**WEBER, JONATHAN,** editor, journalist, educator; BA in Philosophy, Wesleyan U.; postgrad., Columbia U. Reporter The Times, San Francisco, N.Y.C.; Paris corr. Electronic News, MIS Week; founding sr. editor World Link; columnist, tech. editor L.A. Times, 1989—97; founding editor-in-chief The Industry Std., 1997—2001; T. Anthony Pollner disting. prof. U. Mont. Sch. Journalism, Missoula, 2002; exec. editor internat. rsch. OTA Off the Record Rsch., San Francisco. Recipient First Pl. award in bus. category, AP News Exec. Coun. in Calif./Nev., 1993.

**WEBER, KENNETH J.,** hotel executive; b. 1946; With Arthur Young & Co., N.Y.C., 1968-71, ITT-Grinnell Corp., Providence, 1971-73, Farmbest Foods Internat., Jacksonville, 1973-74; regional contr. Marriott Corp., Washington, 1974-76, group contr., 1976-77, divsn. contr., 1977-79, pres., CEO Farrell's Ice Cream divsn., 1983-86; exec. v.p., CFO Isaly Co., Pitts., 1979-80; v.p., contr. Country Kitchens Internat. divsn. Carlson Cos., Inc., Mpls., 1980-81; sr. v.p. Poppin Fresh Restaurant divsn. Pillsbury Co., Mpls., 1981-83; sr. v.p., corp. contr. Red Lion Hotels Corp., Vancouver, Wash., 1987-92; sr. v.p., CFO Omni Hotels Corp., Hampton, N.H., 1992—; also v.p., treas. Omni Ctr. Corp., Richmond, Va.

**WEBER, KLAUS,** finance educator; PhD, U. Mich., Ann Arbor, 2003. Asst. prof. Kellogg Sch. Northwestern U., Evanston, Ill., 2003—. Office: Northwestern Univ Kellogg Sch 2001 Sheridan Rd Evanston IL 60208-2001 Office Phone: 847-491-2201.

**WEBER, LISA M.,** insurance company executive; BA in Psych., SUNY, Stony Brook. With Painewebber, 1988—98; sr. v.p. human resources MetLife, Inc., NYC, 1998—2003; sr. v.p., 1999, exec. v.p., 1999—2001, sr. exec. v.p., chief adminstrv. officer, 2001—04, pres. individual bus., 2004—. Bd. dirs. New Eng. Fin., Gt. Am. Fin., Reinsurance Grp. of Am.; bd. dirs. benefits com. MetLife, Inc.; mem. social responsibility com. MetLife Found. Bd. Mem.: Phi Beta Kappa. Office: MetLife Inc 200 Park Ave New York NY 10166*

**WEBER, MARK,** clothing company executive; With Phillips-Van Heusen, NYC, 1972—2006, sr. v.p., gen. merchandise mgr., exec. v.p. merchandising, 1995—98, pres., COO, 1998—2005, CEO, 2005—06.

**WEBER, MARK W.,** librarian, dean; BS, U. Wis., 1968, MLS, 1972; MA in History and Edn., Colgate U., 1970. Dir. pub. svcs. Clifford Libr. and Learning Resources U. Evansville, 1975—79; tchr. reference and rsch., 1976—79; archives asst. Case Western Reserve U., 1979—80; tchr. labor history Cleve. State U., 1983; pub. svcs. / outreach libr. Cuyahoga CC, 1981—85, tchr. labor history and collective bargaining, 1984—88, asst. personnel dir. / EEOC officer, 1985—88; tchr. labor. mgmt. Ind. U., 1990; asst. univ. libr. for personnel U. Cin., 1988—91; dir. staff svcs. Kent State U. Librs., 1991—2000, dean librs. and media svc., 2001—. Contbr. articles to profl. jours. Founding bd. mem. Ethical Soc. of Cleve. Mem.: ALA, Assn. of Jewish Librs., Greater Cleve. Labor History Soc., Jewish Secular Cmty. Office: Kent State U Librs and Media Svcs PO Box 5190 Kent OH 44242-0001 Office Phone: 330-672-2962. E-mail: markw@lms.kent.edu.*

**WEBER, MATTHEW GEORGE,** lawyer; s. Robert H. and Helena K. Weber; m. Ann Ralston Weber, Aug. 31, 1996; children: Caroline, Lindsey, Thomas. BA magna cum laude, The Colo. Coll., 1982—85; JD, Northwestern U. Sch. Law, 1985—88. Bar: U.S. Dist. Ct., Dist. of Colo., D.C. Ct. Appeals 1988, U.S. Dist. Ct., DC 1989, Colo. Supreme Ct. 1989, U.S. C. Appeals D.C. Circuit 1989, U.S. Supreme Ct. 1992, U.S. Ct. Appeals, 10th Circuit 1995. Assoc. atty. Dow, Lohnes & Albertson, Washington, 1988—90, Baker & Hostetler, Washington, 1991—94, Hoskin, Farina, Aldrich & Kampf, P.C., Grand Junction, Colo., 1994—99, sharehold. 1999—2003; atty. Holland & Hart, LLP, Denver, 2004—. Chair of law day com. Mesa County Bar Assn., Grand Junction, 2002. Author: (68 den. u. l. rev. 57) Media Liability for the Publication of Advertising: When to Kill the Messenger; contbr. (ABA book)

Managed Care Litigation. Bd. dirs. Mesa County Chpt. of ARC, Grand Junction, Colo., 1995—96; bd. trustees Mesa County Pub. Libr. Dist., Grand Junction, 1999—2003. Mem.: ABA, Am. Health Lawyers Assn., Denver Bar Assn. Office: Holland & Hart LLP 555 17th St Ste 3200 Denver CO 80202 Office Phone: 303-295-8565.

**WEBER, PAULA M.,** lawyer; b. Washington, Pa., June 6, 1959; BA magna cum laude, Colgate Univ. 1981; JD with high honors, George Washington Univ., 1985. Bar: Calif. 1985. Ptnr., comm. Employment & Labor practice Pillsbury Winthrop Shaw Pittman, San Francisco. Mem.: Phi Beta Kappa, Order of the Coif. Office: Pillsbury Winthrop Shaw Pittman 50 Fremont St San Francisco CA 94105 Office Phone: 415-983-7488. Office Fax: 415-983-1200. Business E-mail: paula.weber@pillsburylaw.com.

**WEBER, RAY EVERETT,** engineering executive, consultant; b. Kenton, Ohio, Dec. 11, 1946; s. Mervin Clarence and Phylis Jean Weber; m. Carolyn Antinoro, Aug. 16, 1980; children: David Charles, Stephen Ray. BS in Physics, Ohio State U., 1973. Lic. real estate agt. N.Y., 1992-1997. Project engr. Erie Lackawanna R.R., Hoboken, NJ, 1974—75; nuclear engring. adminstr. ASME, N.Y.C., 1975—78; cognizant engr. Burns & Roe Inc., Oradell, NJ, 1978—80; supervising engr. Impell Corp., Melville, NY, 1980—88; pres. Webtor Inc., Northport, NY, 1988—; owner Weber Real Estate, Northport, NY, 1978—. Pres. Forest Ventures Inc., Northport, N.Y., 1987—. Author: Nuclear Codes/Standards. With USN, 1966—70. Mem.: ASME (nuclear subcom.), Marco Island Yacht Club, Northport Yacht Club, Am. Legion. Avocations: boating, fishing, skiing, golf. Office: Forest Ventures Inc 115 Soundview Ter Northport NY 11768-1231 Office Phone: 516-885-8059. Personal E-mail: rweber3@optonline.net.

**WEBER, ROBERT A.,** surgeon; b. Cleve., Mar. 31, 1962; s. Robert Alan Weber Sr. and Julia Elizabeth Weber; m. Patricia Lynn Weber, June 22, 1985; children: Elizabeth Brooke, Rebekah Lynn, Robert Alan Weber, III, David Michael, Rebekah Lynn, Elizabeth Brooke, Robert Alan III, David Michael. BSE, U. Pa., Phila., 1984; MD, Tex. A&M U., 1988. Lic. physician Tex., 1989, diplomate Am. Bd. of Plastic Surgery, 1998, added qualification in hand surgery Am. Bd. Of Plastic Surgery, 1999. Chief sect. of hand surgery Scott & White Hosp., Temple, Tex., 1994—; vis. prof. of hand surgery Tartu U., Estonia, 2002—03. Assoc. prof. of surgery Tex. A&M Coll. of Medicine, College Station, 1999—; plastic surgery residency program dir. Scott & White Hosp., Temple, Tex., 2004—. Author: (textbook chapt.) Nerve Lacerations: Repair of Acute Injuries; contbr. articles to profl. jours. Elder Temple Bible Ch., Tex., 1999—2006; pres. Jerome H. Smith, MD Found., Temple, Tex., 1989—2006. Recipient Sr. award, Plastic Surgery Ednl. Found., 1999. Mem.: Assn. of Acad. Chairmen of Plastic Surgery, Am. Assn. of Plastic Surgeons, Am. Soc. of Plastic Surgery, Am. Soc. for Surgery of the Hand. Achievements include first to establish the specialty of hand surgery in Estonia. Avocation: Bible study. Office: Scott & White Hosp 2401 S 31st St Temple TX 76508 Office Phone: 254-724-4263. Office Fax: 254-724-0315. Business E-Mail: rweber@swmail.sw.org.

**WEBER, ROBERT CARL,** lawyer; b. Chester, Pa., Dec. 18, 1950; s. Robert Francis and Lucille (Nobili) W.; m. Linda Brediger, June 30, 1972; children: Robert F., Mary Therese, David P., Joseph T. BA cum laude, Yale U., 1972; JD, Duke U., 1976. Bar: Ohio 1976, U.S. Dist. ct. (no. dist.) Ohio 1976, U.S. Ct. Claims 1980, U.S. Ct. Appeals (6th cir.) 1981, U.S. Ct. Appeals (5th cir.) 1995. Assoc. Jones, Day, Reavis & Pogue (now Jones Day), Cleve., 1976—83, ptnr., 1983—2006; sr. v.p., legal and regulatory affairs IBM Corp, Armonk, NY, 2006—. Bd. dirs. United Way Svcs. of Cleve., 1992-2002. Fellow Am. Coll. Trial Lawyers, Internat. Acad. Trial Lawyers; mem. Ohio Bar Assn., Am. Law Inst., Product Liability Adv. Coun., Cleve. Bar Assn. (chmn. jud. selection com. 1985-86, trustee 1990-93, pres.-elect 1994-95, pres. 1995-96), Jud. Conf. for 8th Jud. Dist. Ohio (life), Order of Coif. Roman Catholic. Office: Jones Day North Point 901 Lakeside Ave E Cleveland OH 44114-1190 Business E-Mail: rcweber@us.ibm.com.

**WEBER, ROBERT MAXWELL,** cartoonist; b. LA, Apr. 22, 1924; p. Milton and Edith (Huston) W.; m. Marilyn Baum, Oct. 11, 1953 (div.); children—Peter, Lee; m. Debora Graves, Dec. 24, 1988. Student, Pratt Inst., 1945-48, Art Students League, 1948-50. Fashion illustrator, 1949-54; artist New Yorker mag., 1962—; work commd. by IBM, N.Y. Telephone, Am. Airlines, Mobil, Blue Cross/Blue Shield, U.S. Healthcare, Goodyear Co., J.C. Penney Co., Air Canada, Swissair, others; contbr. cartoons to nat. mags. Served with USCGR, 1942-45. Office: New Yorker 4 Times Sq New York NY 10036-6522

**WEBER, ROCHELLE IRENE,** editor, writer; b. Chgo., Jan. 9, 1951; adopted d. William Hale and Frances Irene (Peterson) Johnson; m. Timothy John Weber, May 27, 1972 (div. Mar. 17, 1983); 1 child, Christine Renee; 1 child, Elizabeth Anne Johnson. BA, Columbia Coll., 1988. Pres. RIW Comm., Rantoul, Ill., 1992—; mng. editor Inara Press, Battle Ground, Wash., 2005—. Coord. editl. bd. Oestara Pub., Key Biscayne, Fla., 2005—. Author: (novel) Rock Bound, (song) It's Not My Fault (Gold Medal, Spl. Recognition, Nat. Veteran's Creative Arts Competition, 2005), (article) Bulimia (Inclusion in Hair Trigger, Columbia Coll. Student Anthology, 1988); singer: (performance) God Bless My SUV (Silver Medal, Vocal Solo Comedy, Nat. Veteran's Creative Arts Competition, 2004), (performance in chorus) Oklahoma (Gold Medal Group, Broadway, Nat. Veteran's Creative Arts Competition, 2003), Seasons of Love (Gold Medal Group, Broadway, Nat. Veteran's Creative Arts Competition, 2002). Vol. VA Med. Ctr., Chgo., 2001—02, Ronald McDonald Ho. Nr. Children's Meml. Hosp., Chgo., 1998—2003, VA Med. Ctr., Danville, Ill., 2003—06; sec. bd. trustees Overeaters Anonymous Intergroup, Chgo., 1987—89; sec. Overeaters Anonymous Intergroup No. Ill., Waukegan, 1986—87. Hosp. corpsman USN, 1971—73. Mem.: Am. Mensa. Avocations: reading, writing, needlepoint, singing, acting. Home: 1532 Hobson Drive Apt 9 Rantoul IL 61866-1322 Office: RIW Communications 1532 Hobson Drive Apt 9 Rantoul IL 61866-1322 Office Phone: 217-531-9779. Personal E-mail: riweber@mchsi.com. E-mail: riwcom@mchsi.com.

**WEBER, SHARALYN,** graphics designer; BA in Speech Commn., Old Dominion U., 1992. Graphic designer Old Dominion U., Norfolk, Va.; artist Brandon Advt., Myrtle Beach, SC; comm. specialist Roadway Services, Inc., Akron, The Hampton Co., Akron; graphic artist Internat. Bus. Machines Corp., Akron. Recipient ADDY, 1996, ADDY Citation of Excellence, Coastal Advt. and Mktg. Professionals, 1996, 1996, Award of Distinction, The Communicator Awards, 2004, Award of Excellence, Communicator Awards, 2004, Gold, MarCom Creative Awards, 2005. Mem.: Sigma Soc., Mensa, Omicron Delta Kappa.

**WEBER, STEPHEN LEWIS,** academic administrator; b. Boston, Mar. 17, 1942; s. Lewis F. and Catherine (Warns) W.; m. Susan M. Keim, June 27, 1965; children: Richard, Matthew. BA, Bowling Green State U., 1964; postgrad., U. Colo., 1964-66; PhD, U. Notre Dame, 1969; EdD (hon.), Capital Normal U., China, 1994. Asst. prof. philosophy U Maine, Orono, 1969—74, assoc. prof., 1974—79, asst. to pres., 1976-79; dean arts and scis. Fairfield U., Conn., 1979-84; v.p. acad. affairs St. Cloud State U., Minn., 1984-88; pres. SUNY Oswego, 1988—96; interim provost SUNY Albany, 1995-96; pres. San Diego State U., 1996—. Contbr. numerous articles on philosophy and acad. adminstrn. to profl. jours. Mentor Commn. on Internat. Edn. and Commn. on Govtl. Rels.; bd. dirs. The Peres Ctr. for Peace, San Diego Found.; bd. dirs. San Diego Regional Econ. Devel. Corp.; mem. internat. adv. bd. Found. for the Children of the Californias. Named Outstanding Humanities Tchr., U. Maine, 1975. Mem. Am. Philos. Assn., Am. Assn. Higher Edn. Democrat. Avocations: art, woodworking, swimming, boating. Office: San Diego State Univ Office Pres 5500 Campanile Dr San Diego CA 92182-8000 E-mail: presidents.office@sdsu.edu.

**WEBER, STEPHEN VANCE,** physics researcher; b. Wooster, Ohio, Oct. 31, 1951; s. Dale Sarge and Lucy June (Smith) W.; m. Marie Christensen (dec. 2005), June 21, 1980; children: Erik, Kristina. AB in Physics, Princeton U.,

1973; MA in Astronomy, U. Calif., Berkeley, 1974, PhD, 1978. Rsch. fellow Calif. Inst. Tech., Pasadena, 1978-80; asst. prof. Dartmouth Coll., Hanover, NH, 1980-82; rsch. scientist, physicist Lawrence Livermore Nat. Lab., Livermore, Calif., 1982—. Contbr. articles to profl. jours. Mem. Am. Astronomical Soc., Am. Physical Soc. (excellence in plasma physics award 1995). Achievements include investigations of Rayleigh-Taylor instability and implosions in inertial confinement fusion. Office: Lawrence Livermore Nat Lab MS L16 PO Box 808 Livermore CA 94551-0808 Business E-mail: svweber@llnl.gov.

**WEBER, SUSAN A.,** lawyer; b. 1958; BA, Drake U., 1984; JD, MBA, SUNY, Buffalo, 1989. Bar: Pa. 1990, D.C. 1992, Ill. 1993, U.S. Ct. Appeals (4th cir.) 1990, U.S. Ct. Appeals (3d cir.) 1991, U.S. Ct. Appeals (7th cir.) 1992. Clk. to Justice Byron White U.S. Supreme Ct.; clk. to Judge James Sprouse U.S. Ct. Appeals (4th cir.); with Sidley Austin Brown & Wood, Chgo., 1993—, ptnr., 1997—. Office: Sidley Austin Brown and Wood One Bank Plz 10 S Dearborn St Chicago IL 60603

**WEBER, THOMAS WILLIAM,** chemical engineering professor; b. Orange, N.J., July 15, 1930; s. William A. and Dorothy (Negus) W.; m. Marianne S. Hartmann, June 4, 1966; children: Anne Louise, William Alois B.Chem. Engring., Cornell U., 1953, PhD, 1963; MS in Chem. Engring., Newark Coll. Engring., 1958. Registered profl. engr., N.Y. Chem. engr. econs. and planning Esso Research & Engring., Linden, NJ, 1955-58; instr. Cornell U., 1961-62; asst. prof. SUNY-Buffalo, 1963-66, assoc. prof. chem. engring., 1966-82, prof., 1982-2000, assoc. chmn. dept., 1980-82, chmn. dept., 1982-89, acting chmn., 1996-97, prof. emeritus, 2000—. Author: An Introduction to Process Dynamics and Control, 1973 Named Prof. of Yr., Tau Kappa Chi, 1965; recipient Chancellor's award for excellence in teaching, 1981, Tchr. of Yr. award Tau Beta Pi, 1982 Fellow AIChE (chmn. western N.Y. sect. 1969-70, Profl. Achievement award western N.Y. sect. 1978), Am. Soc. Engring. Edn. (chmn. instrumentation divsn. 1975-77, chmn. St. Lawrence sect. 1979-80, 92-94, chmn. divsn. experimentation and lab.-oriented studies 1985-86, chmn. Zone I 1999-2001, Outstanding Zone Campus Rep. award 1988, AT&T Found. award 1987-88); mem. Tech. Socs. Coun. Niagara Frontier (sec. 1973-75, pres. 1975-76, treas. 1978-2004), Swedish Club of Buffalo (pres. 1974-76), U.S. Masters Swimming Club, Sigma Xi, Phi Kappa Phi, Tau Beta Pi, Theta Xi. Presbyterian. Home: 52 Autumnview Rd Buffalo NY 14221-1602 Business E-mail: twweber@eng.buffalo.edu.

**WEBER, W. DAVID,** music educator; b. Forest City, N.C., Aug. 1, 1946; s. Wallace Monroe and Leona Jane Weber; m. Linda Joy Weber, Aug. 10, 1974; 1 child, Heidi Joy. MusB, U. Cin., 1968, MusM, 1969; MusD, U. Mo., 1988. Dir. choral and band R.S. Ctrl. H.S., Rutherfordton, NC, 1969—72; prof. voice Friends U., Wichita, Kans., 1973—; dir. music Opera Music Theater Dept., 1988—, head Dept. Voice, 1997—. Musician: Wichita (Kans.) Symphony Orch. Dir. music Pleasant Valley United Meth. Ch., Wichita, 1976—. Named one of Outstanding Young Men Am., 1976. Mem.: Am. Choral Dirs. Assn., Music Educators Nat. Conf., Am. Mus. Tchrs. Singing (nat. bd. dirs. 1994—99, regional pres. 1994—97), Rotary (Svc. Above Self award 1998). Meth. Office: Friends Univ 2100 University Wichita KS 67204

**WEBER, WILLIAM RANDOLPH,** lawyer; b. Columbia, Ohio, Dec. 3, 1952; s. William Harry and Marie Antoinette (Fehlig) W.; m. Sondra Jean Gust, Aug. 12, 1972; children: Ashley Elizabeth, William Matthew, Stacey Pauline. BA cum laude, Vanderbilt U., 1974; JD, St. Louis U., 1977. Bar: Mo. 1977, Ill. 1978, U.S. Dist. Ct. (ea. dist.) Mo. 1978, U.S. Ct. Appeals (8th cir.) 1978. Ptnr. Thompson Coburn, St. Louis, 1977-99, Hazelwood & Weber LLC, St. Charles, Mo., 1999—. Chmn. adv. bd. U.S. Bank N.A.; mem. staff St. Louis U. Law Jour., 1975-76. Spl. counsel City of St. Peters, 1998—; counsellor St. Charles County, 1985—87; v.p. bd. govs. Truman State U., 1986—87; chmn. Boone Trails Dist. St. Louis Area Coun. Boy Scouts Am., 2000—03; chmn. St. Charles County Rep. Com., 1978—84; mem. Mo. State Rep. Com., Jefferson City, 1978—86; regional panel White House Fellowship Commn, 1988—92; vice-chmn. St. Charles County Transit Authority, 1992—2000; chmn. bd. advisors Salvation Army, St. Charles, 1980—83; bd. gov. Truman State U., 1981—87; bd. dir. St. Charles C. of C., 1984—98, pres., 1997; chmn. bd. dir. March of Dimes Birth Defects Found., St. Louis. Named Ky. Col., State of Ky., 1990; recipient Dist. award of Merit, Boy Scouts Am., Silver Beaver award, Bronze Pelican award, Disting. Cmty. Svc. award, St. Charles Jaycees, 1984, State of Mo. Econ. Devel. Leadership award, 1994, Citizen of Yr. award, St. Charles C. of C., 2003, 2003. Mem. ABA (ho. of dels. 1987-89), Am. Soc. Hosp. Attys., Mo. Bar Assn. (rep. young lawyers sect. 1982-88), St. Charles County Bar Assn. (pres. 1984), Ill. Bar Assn., Eagle Scout Assn., Equestrian Order of Holy Sepulchre of Jerusalem (knight). Roman Catholic. Office: Hazelwood & Weber LLC 200 N Third St Saint Charles MO 63301 E-mail: wweber@hazelwoodweber.com.

**WEBER, WILLIAM WESLEY,** accountant; b. Columbus, Ohio, Dec. 2, 1951; s. Richard Dick and Donna Marie (Inboden) W.; m. Kay Ruth Swope, Feb. 14, 1976; children: Kristen Marie, Richard Stewart. BS, Ohio State U., 1973; MBA, Baldwin-Wallace Coll., 1983. CPA, Tex.; cert. internal auditor, cert. fraud examiner, cert. info. tech. prof. Staff acct. Arthur Andersen, Cin., 1973-74; staff auditor Federated Dept. Stores, Cin., 1974-75, Diamond Shamrock, Cleve., 1975-77, sr. auditor, 1977-83, audit supr. San Antonio, 1983-97; acctg. mgr. Ultramar Diamond Shamrock, San Antonio, 1997-2000, bus. process specialist, 2000-01, mgr. fin. sys., 2001—04, Valero Energy Corp., 2002—04; mgr. info. sys. Governance, 2004—. Treas. Holy Trinity Presbyn. Ch., San Antonio, 1986-95. Mem. AICPA, Assn. Cert. Fraud Examiners, Inst. Internal Auditors (adj. faculty 1988-97, internat. seminars com. 1996-97), Tex. Soc. CPAs. Avocations: reading, watching auto racing. Home: 14307 Rowe Dr San Antonio TX 78247-3122 Office: Valero PO Box 696000 San Antonio TX 78269-6000 Business E-Mail: bil.w.weber@valero.com.

**WEBLEY, WILMORE CHRISTOPHER,** microbiologist, researcher; b. Bellas Gate, Jamaica, Jan. 1, 1972; s. Clifford Webley and Kathleen Henry-Webley. Postgrad., U. Mass., 1998—2003, M in microbiology, 2000; PhD in microbiology (pathagenic bacteriology and immunology), U. Mass. 2003; BS in med. tech., Northern Caribbean U., Jamaica, 1994. Cert. med. technologist Ministry of Health, Jamaica. Assoc. instr. No. Caribbean U., Mandeville, Jamaica, 1994—98; grad. rsch. asst. U. Mass., Amherst, 2000—03, asst. prof. microbiology, 2003—. Contbr. articles various profl. jours. Co-founder Adventist Christians Together to Serve, Amherst, 2001. Fulbright scholar, 1998—2000. Mem.: AAAS, Am. Soc. for Apheresis, N.Y. Acad. Scis., Am. Soc. Microbiologists, Nat. Geog. Soc. 7th Day Adventist. Achievements include research in new entry pathway for chlamydia. Avocations: travel, cricket, mountain sight seeing. Office: U Mass Morrill IVN Rm 203 Amherst MA 01003 E-mail: wilmore@microbio.umass.edu.

**WEBRE, SEPTIME,** ballet company artistic director, choreographer; b. New Orleans, Dec. 7, 1961; s. Alfred L. and Juanita (Chisholm) Webre. BA, U. Tex., 1984. Dancer Merce Cunningham Dance Co., N.Y.C., 1991, Am. Repertory Ballet/Princeton (N.J.) Ballet, 1987—99, choreographer, 1988—99, artistic dir., 1993-99, The Washington Ballet, 1999—. Freelance choreographer with Les Grands Ballets Canadienne, 1988—, Pacific N.W. Ballet, 1988—, Sacramento Ballet, 1988—, N.C. Dance Theatre, 1988—, Columbia City Ballet, 1988—, Ballet Austin, 1988—, Dayton Ballet, 1988—, Eglevsky Ballet, 1988—, The Aspen Ballet, the Carslife Project, 1988—, others, 1988—; guest master tchr. various ballet cos., 1990—. Former mem. exec. bd. Young Dems. Am., Austin. Choreographic fellow, N.J. Coun. on Arts, 1992. Roman Catholic. Office: The Washington Ballet 3515 Wisconsin Ave NW Washington DC 20016-3085

**WEBSTER, CATHERINE T.,** telecommunications industry executive; B in Econs., NJ City U. CPA. With Bell Atlantic NJ, 1978, dir. fin. planning and analysis for Telecom/Network, 1993; asst. v.p. fin. planning Corp. Fin. Grp. Bell Atlantic, 1996; v.p. fin. Network Svcs. and Wholesale Markets Verizon Comm., v.p. fin., sr. v.p. investor rels., 2005—. Office: Verizon Comm 140 West St New York NY 10007*

**WEBSTER, CHRISTOPHER R.,** chemist, physicist, research scientist; b. Anglesey, Wales, Mar. 3, 1953; arrived in U.S., 1979; s. Donald McLeod Webster, Pamela Lilian Webster; m. Julie C. Webster; children: Genevieve, Philip, Jeffrey Foster, John Foster. BSc with honors, Reading U., Eng., 1974; PhD, Bristol U. Eng., 1977. Sr. rsch. scientist Jet Propulsion Lab., Pasadena, Calif., 1981—. Contbr. articles to profl. jours. Office: Jet Propulsion Lab 4800 Oak Grove Dr Pasadena CA 91109 Business E-Mail: Chris.R.Webster@jpl.nasa.gov.

**WEBSTER, CHRISTOPHER WHITE,** foreign service officer; b. Boston, Oct. 30, 1953; s. Henry deForest and Marion (Havas) W. BA cum laude, Amherst Coll., 1975; MA, Johns Hopkins U., 1977. Asst. comml. attache Am. Embassy, Buenos Aires, 1977-79; econ. comml. officer Georgetown, Guyana, 1979-81; desk officer for Jamaica and Guyana, 1982—84; econ. officer Office of Energy, Washington, 1984-86, fin. and devel. officer Lisbon, Portugal, 1986—89, econ. sect. chief Algiers, Algeria, 1989—92; dep. dir. Office of Pakistan, Afghanistan and Bangladesh Affairs, Washington, 1992—95; dep. chief of mission Khartoum, Sudan and Addis Ababa, Ethiopia, 1995-96; chief, developed Country Trade Divsn., Washington, 1996-98; dep. dir. Office of Ctrl. Am. and Panamanian Affairs, Washington, 1998-00, dep. chief of mission Dhaka, Bangladesh, 2000—03, Oslo, 2003—06; dir. Office of Devel. Fin., Washington, 2006—. Recipient Superior Honor award Dept. State, 1983, 91, 98-2000. E-mail: websterc@state.gov.

**WEBSTER, DAVID ARTHUR,** retired life insurance company executive; b. Downs, Ill., July 20, 1937; s. Harold Sanford and Carmen Mildred (Moore) W.; m. Anna Elizabeth Prosch, June 10, 1956; children: David Elizabeth Anna, Arthur Lee, William Harold. BS, U. Ill., 1960. Actuarial asst. Mass. Mut. Life Ins. Co., Springfield, 1960-64; cons. actuary George Stennes & Assocs., Mpls., 1964-68; v.p., actuary Piedmont Life Ins. Co., Atlanta, 1968-72, Pacific Fidelity Life Ins. Co., Los Angeles, 1972-74; v.p., chief actuary U.S. Life Corp., N.Y.C., 1974-76, exec. v.p., 1976-78, dir. 1976-78; pres., dir. Beneficial Pension Svcs, BPS Agy., Inc.; v.p., treas., dir. Beneficial Assurance Co., 1978-82; asst. sec., dir. Beneficial Computer Svcs., Inc.; treas. Tel-Assurance Corp.; exec. v.p., dir. Beneficial Standard Life, 1978-82; pres., dir. U.S. Life Ins. Co. of Calif., 1982-84, Western World Fin. Group Inc., 1984-86; exec. v.p., COO R.W. Durham and Co., 1987-99. Fellow Soc. Actuaries. Home: 1150 Ladera Ln Paso Robles CA 93446 E-mail: SLODavidPaso@aol.com.

**WEBSTER, DAVID MACPHERSON,** lawyer; b. Chgo., June 22, 1950; s. Robert Fielden and Julia Orendorff (Macphers) Webster; m. Lucia Maxwell Blair, Oct. 3, 1987; 1 child, Jessie Maxwell. BA in History magna cum laude with honors, Williams Coll., 1972; JD, U. Va., 1975; DD (hon.), Seabury-Western Theol. Sem., 2000. Bar: Ill. 1975. Assoc. Winston & Strawn, Chgo., 1975-81, ptnr., 1981-87; White House fellow Washington, 1987-88; spl. asst. to dir. FBI, Washington, 1988-89; asst. gen. counsel for multilateral negotiations U.S. Arms Control and Disarmament Agy., Washington, 1989—94; v.p., gen. counsel A.T. Kearney, Inc., Chgo., 1994—2002; of counsel Butler Rubin Saltarelli & Boyd, Chgo., 2002—03; sr. v.p., gen. counsel Hawaiian Airlines, Honolulu, 2003—05; v.p., gen. counsel, sec. DeVry Inc., Oakbrook Terrace, Ill., 2005—. Mem. adv. com. Ill. Bus. Corp. Ill. Sec. of State, Chgo., 1982—87. Bd. dirs. Ill. Soc. Prevention Blindness, Chgo., 1980—87, 1997—2004, pres. 1999—2001; trustee Village of Winnetka, Ill., 2003—; bd. dirs. Better Govt. Assn., Chgo., 1997—99; trustee Episc. Charities and Profl. Svcs., Chgo., 1980—87; bd. dirs. WBEZ Alliance, Inc., Chgo., 1996—2004; chair bd. trustees Seabury-Western Theol. Sem., Evanston, Ill., 1993—96, trustee, 1988—96, 2002—05. Mem.: Manuscript Soc., Ill. State Hist. Soc. (life), White House Fellows Assn., Abraham Lincoln Assn., Phi Beta Kappa (mem. exec. com. Chgo. chpt. 1996—98). Episcopalian. Avocations: history, writing. Home: 596 Arbor Vitae Rd Winnetka IL 60093-2302 Personal E-mail: davidmwebster@comcast.net. Business E-Mail: dwebset@derry.com.

**WEBSTER, ERNEST WESLEY,** musician, educator; b. Mt. Vernon, Ill., Oct. 30, 1932; s. Melvin Harold and Nora Mae (Wimberley) Webster; m. Arlene Waite (div. 1972); m. Judith Ann Hichman (dec. 1995); children: Elizabeth Ann Webster Kennedy, Victoria Christina; m. Lindsey Carvalho Campos, Oct. 4, 2003. Diploma in ch./conducting, Moody Bible Inst., Chgo., 1953; student, Northwestern Schs., Mpls., 1953—54; diploma in music edn. and piano, U. Ariz., 1957. Owner Webster Sch. Music, Ft. Lauderdale, 1957—. Instr. Barry U. Mem.: Accordion Tchrs. Guild Internat. (v.p.), Fla. State Music Tchrs. Assn. (pres. dist. 6). Home: 105 Lake Emerald Dr #112 Fort Lauderdale FL 33309 Office: Webster Sch Music 3058 N Federal Hwy Fort Lauderdale FL 33304 Office Phone: 954-537-5309.

**WEBSTER, GORDON VISSCHER, JR.,** minister; b. Huntington, N.Y., Oct. 2, 1947; s. Gordon Visscher and Marion Beatrice W.; m. Gloria Marie Farwagi, May 31, 1975; children: David Gordon (dec.), Daniel Farwagi, Diana Alexandra. AB, Hamilton Coll., 1969; postgrad., St. Andrews Div. Sch., 1970-71, McCormick Theol. Sem., 1982-87; MDiv, Union Theol. Sem., 1973. Ordained to ministry Presbyn. Ch. (USA), 1973. Staff assoc. Met. Ch. Bd., Syracuse, NY, 1973-75; assoc. pastor 1st Presbyn. Ch., 1975-83; missionary Mid. East Coun. of Chs., Limassol, Cyprus, 1983-84; missionary-in-residence Presbyn. Ch. (USA), Stony Point Center, NY, 1984-86; interim pastor 1st Presbyn. Ch., Oneida, 1988-89, United Presbyn. Ch., Cortland, 1989-91; pastor Ogden Presbyn. Ch., Spencerport, 1991-2001, Downtown United Presbyn. Ch., Rochester, 2001—. Exec. dir. Am. Coalition Mid. East Dialogue, Jamesville, N.Y., 1986-88, Common Good Planning Ctr. of Rochester Area Cmty. Found., 1998-2001; v.p. Greater Rochester Cmty. Chs., 1992-93, pres., 1994-97, exec. term, 2002—; chair Interfaith Forum Greater Rochester, 1995, 99; pres. Interfaith Alliance Rochester, 1998-99; mem. Mayor's Stewardship Coun. Comprehensive Planning, City of Rochester, 1996—; mem. Mayor's Commn. on Race and Ethnicity, 2000-05; bd. dirs. Odyssey Humanity, 2006—, Ctr. for Interfaith Study and Dialogue, 2005—; Presbyn. Commr. to Gen. Assembly of Nat. Coun. of Chs. of Christ in USA, 2000—; mem. Nat.Strategy Team for Let Justice Roll 2005—, Martin Luther King Jr. Commn. of Monroe County, 1995-2000; mem. pub. policy commn. N.Y. State Cmty. Chs. 1996-99; mem. Presbytery Genesee Valley, 1991—, trustee, 2003-06; commr. PC (USA) Gen Assembly, 2004; leader workshops on Mid. East, 1983-89; moderator Syracuse Mid. East Dialogue Group, 1981-83; mem. gen. coun. Presbytery of Utica, 1988-89. Gen. coun. Cayuga-Syracuse Presbytery, 1975-83; nat. bd. mem. Am. Friends of Neve Shalom Wahat al Salam, 2004—; presbyn. commr. Gen. Assembly Presbyn. Ch., 2004. Grantee George Gund Found., 1987, Presbyn. Women's Opportunity Giving, 1987, Joan and Harold Feinbloom Supporting Found. of the Rochester Area Cmty. Found., 1998-2002. Mem. Witherspoon Soc. (steering com. 1974-76), Presbyn. Peace Fellowship (bd. advisors, nat. com. 1972-83). Democrat. Office: Downtown United Presbyn Ch 121 N Fitzhugh St Rochester NY 14614 Office Phone: 585-325-4000. E-mail: regvw@aol.com.

**WEBSTER, HAROLD FRANK,** physicist; b. Buffalo, June 25, 1919; s. Stephen and Florence Kathryn (Frank) W.; m. Helen Voorhis, Sept. 15, 1951; children: Sue Helen, Kenneth Harold, Jean Phyllis. BA magna cum laude, U. Buffalo, 1941, MA, 1944; PhD, Cornell U., 1953. Staff mem. Radiation Lab. MIT, Cambridge, 1943-45; rsch. assoc. Rsch. Lab. GE, Schenectady, N.Y., 1951-85, cons. R&D Ctr., 1985-90; ret. Contbg. author: Packaging of Power Semiconductor Devices, 1986, Advances in Electronics, Vol. 17, 1962; patentee in field. U.S. del. to XIII Gen. Assembly of Internat. Sci. Radio Union, London, 1960. Mem. IEEE (WRG Baker award 1958), Am. Phys. Soc., Phi Beta Kappa, Sigma Xi. Achievements include discovering vortex instability in electron sheet beams, deriving current/voltage characteristics of thermionic diodes from space charge distribution, measuring dependence of thermionic emission and wetting on crystal face of metal crystals in cesium vapor. Home: 77 St Stephens Ln W Scotia NY 12302-4229 Personal E-mail: hvhweb@verizon.net.

**WEBSTER, HENRY DE FOREST,** neuroscientist; b. NYC, Apr. 22, 1927; s. Leslie Tillotson and Emily (deForest) W.; m. Marion Havas, June 12, 1951; children: Christopher, Henry, Sally, David, Steven. AB cum laude, Amherst Coll., 1948; MD, Harvard U., 1952. Intern Boston City Hosp., 1952-53, resident, 1953-54; resident in neurology Mass. Gen. Hosp., 1954-56, rsch. fellow in neuropathology, 1956-59, prin. investigator NIH rsch. grants, electron micros. studies peripheral neuropathy, 1959-69, mem. staffs; instr. neurology Harvard Med. Sch., Boston, 1959-63, assoc. in neurology, 1963-66, asst. prof. neuropathology, 1966; assoc. prof. neurology U. Miami Sch. Medicine, Fla., 1966-69, prof., 1969; chief sect. cellular neuropathology Nat. Inst. Neurol. Diseases and Stroke, Bethesda, Md., 1969-97; chief Lab. Exptl. Neuropathology, 1984-97; scientist emeritus NIH, 1997—; mem. staff Newton-Wellesley Hosp. Disting. scientist, lectr. dept. anatomy Tulane U. Sch. Medicine, 1973; Royal Coll. lectr. Can. Assn. Neuropathologists, 1982; Saul Korey lectr. Am. Assn. Neuropathologists, 1992; chmn. Winter Conf. on Brain Rsch., 1985-86; head neuropathology del. to visit China in 1990, Citizen Amb. Program, People to People Internat.; exec. com. rsch. group on neuromuscular disease World Fedn. Neurology, 1986-93. Author: (with A. Peters and S.L. Palay) The Fine Structure of the Nervous System, 1970, 3rd edit., 1991, Cellular Neuroscience: Projects and Images, 2006; contbr. sci. articles to profl. jours. Recipient Superior Svc. award USPHS, 1977, A. von Humboldt award Germany, 1985, Sci. award Peripheral Neuropathy Assn., 1994; named hon. prof. Norman Bethune U. of Med. Scis., Chanchun, China, 1991. Mem. Am. Assn. Neuropathologists (v.p. 1976-77, pres. 1978-79, Weil award 1960, Meritorious Contbns. to Neuropathology award 2001), Internat. Soc. Neuropathology (hon., councillor 1976-80, v.p. 1980-84, exec. com. 1980-84, 86-94, pres. 1986-90), Internat. Congress Neuropathology (sec. gen. VIII 1978), Peripheral Nerve Study Group (exec. com. 1975-93, chmn. 1977 meeting), Japanese Soc. Neuropathology (hon.), Am. Neurol. Assn., Am. Acad. Neurology, Royal Soc. Medicine, Am. Soc. Cell Biology, Soc. Neurosci., Rotary Internat., Ausable Club (exec. com. 1964-67). Office: NIH Rm 5B-16 Bldg 10 MSC 1400 Bethesda MD 20892-1400 Office Phone: 301-496-4747. Business E-Mail: websterh@ninds.nih.gov.

**WEBSTER, JAMES RANDOLPH, JR.,** physician; b. Chgo., Aug. 25, 1931; s. James Randolph and Ruth Marian (Burtis) W.; m. Joan Burchfield, Dec. 28, 1954; children: Susan, Donovan, John. BS, U. Chgo.-Northwestern U., 1953; MD, MS, Northwestern U., 1956. Diplomate: Am. Bd. Internal Medicine (sub bd. pulmonary disease and geriatrics). Intern Phila. Gen. Hosp., 1956-57; resident in medicine Northwestern U., 1957-60, NIH fellow in pulmonary disease, 1962-64; chief medicine Northwestern Meml. Hosp., Chgo., 1976—88; prof. medicine Northwestern U. Med. Sch., 1977—, chief gen. med. sect. dept. medicine, 1987-88; chief exec. officer Northwestern Med. Group Practice, 1978-88; dir. Buehler Ctr. on Aging Northwestern U. Med. Ctr., 1988-2000. Chief staff Northwestern Meml. Hosp., 1988-90; pres. Chgo. Bd. Health, 2002—, Inst. Medicine, Chgo., Ill., 2002-04, exec. dir., 2004—; chair Ill. Ad Hoc Com. to Defend Health Care. Contbr. chpts. to books, articles to med. jours. Capt. U.S. Army, 1960-62. Recipient Outstanding Clin. tchr. award Northwestern U. Med. Sch., 1974, 77, 84, 86, Alumni Merit award Northwestern U., 1979, Henry P. Russe-Inst. of Medicine award for exemplary compassion in health care, 1997, Aeschulapian award as Physician of Yr., Anti Defamation League, 1998. Master: ACP (gov. for Ill. 1988—92, chair sub-com. on aging 1993, Clayppole award 1994); mem.: Ill. Geriatrics Soc. (pres. 1992—94), Am. Geriatrics Soc., Alpha Omega Alpha. Office: Inst Medicine Chgo Ste 525 332 S Michigan Ave Chicago IL 60604 Home: PO Box 274 Lakeside MI 49116 Office Phone: 312-563-0040. Business E-Mail: j-webster@northwestern.edu. *Life should best be measured not by how long you live, but how well you function.*

**WEBSTER, JEFFREY LEON,** graphic designer; b. Idaho Falls, Idaho, Nov. 23, 1941; s. Leon A. and Marjory M. (McAllister) W.; student Sch. Associated Arts, St. Paul, 1962; m. Judith Kess, Apr. 17, 1965; children: Eric J., Marjorie P. Sci. illustrator Mayo Clinic, Rochester, Minn., 1963-66; layout artist Brown & Bigelow, St. Paul, 1966; graphic designer U. Minn., Mpls., 1966-67, U. Calgary (Alta., Can.), 1967-68; sr. artist Control Data Corp., St. Paul, 1968-70; mem. Idaho State U. Meml. Lectureship Com.; graphic designer Idaho State U., 1970-78; owner, operator studio, Harmony, Minn.; mktg. and advt. cons. to 45 regional and nat. firms, 1978—. Mem. Idaho Civic Symphony Bd. Chairperson rub. rels. Unitarian Ch. Rochester, 1991—; bd. dirs. Gift of Life Transplant House, Rochester, Minn. 1996, Rochester Orch. and Chorale, 1996. Recipient Profl. citation Libr. Congress, 1976; 1st Pl. Best Trucking ad, Overdrive Mag., 1990. Mem. Sierra Club (nat. agrl. com. 2003--). Artist dup. ednl. exhibits. Home and Office: RR 1 Harmony MN 55939-9801

**WEBSTER, JOHN CROSBY BROWN,** minister, educator; b. NYC, July 14, 1935; s. Leslie Tillotson and Emily Johnston (deForest) Webster; m. Ellen Low Purdy (div.); children: Elizabeth Low Webster Shillington, Marilyn White; m. Penelope Stearns, Jan. 3, 1988. BA, Amherst Coll., Mass., 1957; MDiv, Union Theol. Sem., NYC, 1960; MA, Lucknow U., India, 1962; PhD, U. Pa., Phila., 1971. Ordained minister Presbyn. Ch. Supply pastor La Bagh Meth. Ch., Lucknow, 1960—62; lectr. Baring Union Christian Coll., Batata, India, 1963—68, 1971—76; dir. Christian Inst. Sikh Studies, Batata, 1971—76; asst. prof., prof. United Theol. Coll., Bangalore, India, 1977—81; vis. prof. Pitts. Theol. Sem., 1981—83; pastor Crossroads Presbyn. Ch., Waterford, Conn., 1984—91; diaconal worker in India Presbyn. Ch. USA, Louisville, 1994—2001; ret., 2001. Lectr. in ecumenics Union Theol. Sem., 1985—; vice moderator Presbytery So. New England, Presbyn. Ch. (USA), 2003—04, moderator, 2004-05. Editor: The Study of History and Cullege History Teaching, 1965, History for College Students, 1966, History and Contemporary India, 1971, Popular Religion in the Punjab Today, 1974; author: The Christian Community and Change in Nineteenth Century North India, 1976, An Introduction to History, 1977, 2d edit., 1981, The Nirankari Sikhs, 1979, The Dalit Christians: A History, 1992, 2d edit., 1994, Hindi edit., 2004, The Pastor to Dalits, 1995, Studying History, 1997, Religion and Dalit Liberation: An Examination of Perspectives, 1999, 2d edit., 2002; co-author: From Role to Identity: Dalit Christian in Transition, 1997; co-editor: Local Dalit Christian History, 2002; editor: Bangalore Theol. Forum, 1977—81, Dalit Internat. Newsletter, 1996—. Bd. dirs. Drop-In Learning Ctr., New London, Conn., 1985—91, pres., 1990—91; bd. dirs. Habitat for Humanity Southeastern Conn., 1986—92, Union Theol. Sem., 1989—; mem. Waterford Housing Partnership, 1990—93; bd. dirs. Southeastern Conn. AIDS Project/Alliance for Living, New London, 1993—98, Opportunities Industrialization Ctr. New London County, 2004—; bd. mgrs. Am. Bapt. Hist. Soc., Valley Forge, Pa., 2005—. Recipient Human Rights award, Dalit Liberation Edn. Trust, Chennai, India, 1997; travel grantee, Am. Coun. Learned Socs., NEH, 1981. Mem.: Assn. Profs. Mission (v.p. 1991—92, pres. 1992—93), Assn. Presbyterians in Cross-Cultural Mission (pres. 1984—94). Democrat. Avocations: tennis, hiking.

**WEBSTER, JOHN GOODWIN,** biomedical engineering educator, researcher; b. Plainfield, NJ, May 27, 1932; s. Franklin Folger and Emily Sykes (Boody) W.; m. Nancy Egan, Dec. 27, 1954; children: Paul, Robin, Mark, Lark BEE, Cornell U., 1953; MSEE, U. Rochester, 1965, PhD, 1967. Engr. North American Aviation, Downey, Calif., 1954-55; engr. Boeing Airplane Co., Seattle, 1955-59. Academic Inst.; Melbourne, Fla., 1959-61; staff engr. Mitre Corp., Bedford, Mass., 1961-62, IBM Corp., Kingston, NY, 1962-63; asst. prof. elec. engring. U. Wis. Madison, 1967-70, assoc. prof. elec. engring., 1970-73, prof. elec. and computer engring., 1973-99, prof. biomed. engring., 1999—2001, prof. emeritus biomed. engring., 2001—. Author: (with others) Medicine and Clinical Engineering, 1977, Sensors and Signal Conditioning, 1991, 2d edit., 2001, Analog Signal Processing, 1999; editor: Medical Instrumentation: Application and Design, 3d edit., 1998, Clinical Engineering: Principles and Practices, 1979, Design of Microcomputer-Based Medical Instrumentation, 1981, Therapeutic Medical Devices: Application

and Design, 1982; Electronic Devices for Rehabilitation, 1985; Interfacing Sensors to the IBM-PC, 1988, Encyclopedia of Medical Devices and Instrumentation, 2d edit., 2006, Tactile Sensors for Robotics and Medicine, 1988, Electrical Impedance Tomography, 1990, Teaching Design in Electrical Engineering, 1990, Prevention of Pressure Sores, 1991, Design of Cardiac Pacemakers, 1995, Design of Pulse Oximeters, 1997, The Measurement Instrumentation, and Sensors Handbook, 1999, Encyclopedia of Electrical and Electronics Engineering, 1999, Mechanical Variables Measurement, 2000, Minimally Invasive Medical Technology, 2001, Electrical Measurement, Signal Processing and Displays, 2004, Bioinstrumentation, 2004. Recipient Rsch. Career Devel. award NIH, 1971-76; NIH fellow, 1963-67; recipient Western Electric Fund award Am. Soc. Engring. Edn., 1978, Best Reference Work award, 1999, Theo C. Pilkington Outstanding Educator award, 1994. Fellow IEEE (3d Millennium medal 2000, IEEE-EMBS Career achievement award 2001), Am. Inst. Med. and Biol. Engring., Inst. Physics, Instrument Soc. Am. (Donald P. Eckman Edn. award 1974), Assn. for Advancement Med. Instrumentation (Found. Laufman-Greatbatch prize 1996). Democrat. Unitarian Universalist. Office: Univ Wis Dept Biomed Engring 1550 Engineering Dr Madison WI 53706-1609 Office Phone: 608-263-1574. Business E-Mail: webster@engr.wisc.edu.

**WEBSTER, KIM S.,** music educator; b. Effingham, Ill., Jan. 9, 1960; d. Wayne and Arlene Niehaus; m. Michael Webster, Feb. 22, 1992. MusB, Eastern Ill. U., 1982. Band dir. AC Ctr. CUSD, Ashland CUSD, Ashland, 1982—. Band rep, dist. pres. Ill. Music Educators Assn., Dist. 4, Ill., 2001—05. Mem.: IMEA, Ill. Music Educators Assn. (dist. pres. 2006—), Music Educators Nat. Conf., Cass County Fair. Republican. Cath. Home: 420 S East Virginia IL 62691 Office Phone: 217-476-3313. E-mail: frecklesrusty1@yahoo.com.

**WEBSTER, LARRY RUSSELL,** artist; b. Arlington, Mass., Mar. 18, 1930; s. James Burpee and Ethel (Hughes) W.; m. Rosemary Siekman, June 13, 1953; children: Wendy Lyn, Ricky Stewart, Holly Jean. B.F.A., Mass. Coll. Art, 1952; MS, Boston U., 1953. Package designer Union Bag & Paper Co., N.Y.C., 1953-54; art dir. graphic designer, v.p., dir. Thomas Todd Co., Boston, 1956-78; asst. prof. design Mass. Coll. Art, 1964-66. Paintings in permanent collections including, DeCordova Mus., Lincoln, Mass., Grand Rapids (Mich.) Art Mus., Springfield (Mo.) Art Mus., Davenport (Iowa) Municipal Gallery, Colby Coll. Art Mus., Waterville, Maine, Peabody Mus. Salem, Mass.; work represented in The Best of Watercolor 2, 1997. Served with U.S. Army, 1954-56. Recipient Silver medal Am. Watercolor Soc., 1968. 72; recipient C.F.S. award, 1963, Ed Whitney award, 1973, High winds medal, 1983, Rhinehold award, 1967, Ranger Fund Purchase prize, 1965, Adolph and Clara Obrig prize in watercolor NAD, 1970, gold medal Allied Artists Am., 1971, Washington Sch. Art award, 1977, Lena Newcastle award, 1978, Colo. Watermedia award, 1978, Golden award Rocky Mountain Nat. Watermedia Exhbn., 1979, Lorraine Fetzer Meml. award, 2d prize N.Am. Open Competition, 1990. Mem. NAD (assoc. 1974-91, academician, 1991-), Soc. Printers Boston (past mem. council), Am. Watercolor Soc. (Dolphin fellow 1981), Boston Watercolor Soc. (pres. 1974-75), Guild of Boston Artists.

**WEBSTER, LESLEY DANIELS,** bank executive; married; 2 children. PhD in Econs., Stanford U. Asst. prof. Wash. U., 1977-83; with Chase Securities, 1983—90; mng. dir., head arbitrage trading group Union Bank Switzerland, N,Y.C., 1990-94; exec. v.p. market risk mgmt. Chase Manhattan Corp. (now JPMorganChase), N,Y.C., 1994—. Bd. dirs. United Way of N.Y.C., chair Women United in Philanthropy for N.Y.C. Named one of 25 Women to Watch, US Banker Mag., 2003. Mem.: Securities Industry Assn. (risk mgmt. com.). Office: Chase Manhattan Corp 270 Park Ave Fl 12 New York NY 10017-2036

**WEBSTER, LESLIE TILLOTSON, JR.,** pharmacologist, educator; b. N.Y.C., N.Y., Mar. 31, 1926; s. Leslie Tillotson and Emily (de Forest) W.; m. Alice Katharine Holland, June 24, 1955; children: Katharine White, Susan Holland Webster Van Drie, Leslie Tillotson III, Romi Anne. BA, Amherst Coll., 1947, Sc.D. (hon.), 1982; student, Union Coll., 1944; MD, Harvard U., 1948. Diplomate: Am. Bd. Internal Medicine. Rotating intern Cleve. City Hosp., 1948-49, jr. asst. resident in medicine, 1949-50; asst. resident medicine Bellevue Hosp., N.Y.C., 1952-53; research fellow medicine Harvard and Boston City Hosp. Thorndike Meml. Lab., 1953-55; from demonstrator to instr. medicine Sch. of Medicine Western Res. U., 1955-60; research assoc. to sr. instr. biochemistry Case Western Res. U. Sch. Medicine, 1957—60, asst. prof. medicine, 1960-70, asst. prof. biochemistry, 1960-65, asst. prof. pharmacology, 1965-67, asso. prof., 1967-70, prof. pharmacology, 1976-92, chmn. pharmacology dept., 1976-91, prof. medicine, 1980-86, prof. emeritus pharmacology dept., 1992—; rsch. prof. pediat., divsn. pediat. pharmacology and critical care Rainbow Babies and Children's Hosp., Case Western Res. U. Sch. Medicine, 1992—. Prof., chmn. pharmacology dept. Northwestern U. Med. and Dental Sch., 1970—76; dir. med. scientist tng. program Case Western Res. U. Sch. Medicine, 1979—92; mem. gastroenterology nutritional tng. grants com. NIAMD, NIH, 1965—69; mem. sci. working group on schistosomiasis WHO, 1977—83, chmn. subsect. on chemotherapy biochemistry, 1977—83; mem. exec. com. Gt. Neglected Diseases Network, Rockefeller Found., 1978—86; mem. cellular and molecular basis of disease rev. com. NIGMS, NIH, 1984—88; cons. World Bank, Laos, 2003. Contbr. articles to sci. jour. Served to lt. med. corps. USNR, 1950-52. Russell M. Wilder fellow Nat. Vitamin Found., 1956-59; Sr. USPHS Research fellow, 1959-61; USPHS Rsch. Career Devel. awardee, 1961-69; Macy faculty scholar, 1980-81. Mem. ACP (life), Central Soc. Clin. Rsch. Coalition (emeritus), Am. Soc. Clin. Investigation, Am. Soc. Biochemistry and Molecular Biology (emeritus), Assn. Med. Sch. Pharmacology (emeritus), Am. Soc. Pharmacology and Expd. Therapeutics (emeritus), Alpha Omega Alpha (hon.). Home: 12546 Cedar Rd No 4 Cleveland Heights OH 44106-3294 Office: Univ Hosps of Cleve Rainbow Babies and Childrens Hosp 2074 Abington Rd Cleveland OH 44106-2602 Office Phone: 216-844-3310.

**WEBSTER, MURRAY ALEXANDER, JR.,** sociologist, educator; b. Manila, Philippines, Dec. 10, 1941; s. M.A. and Patricia (Morse) W. AB, Stanford U., 1963, MA, 1966, PhD, 1968. Asst. prof. social sci. Johns Hopkins U., Balt., 1968-74, assoc. prof., 1974-76; prof. sociology, adj. prof. psychology U. S.C., Columbia, 1976-86; vis. prof. sociology Stanford U., 1981-82, 85, 88-89; sr. lectr. San Jose State U., 1987-89; dir. sociology program NSF, 1989-91,99-2000; prof. sociology U. N.C., Charlotte, 1993—. Author (with Barbara Sobieszek): Soruces of Self-Evaluation, 1974; author: Actions and Actors, 1975; author: (with Martha Foschi) Status Generalization: New Theory and Research, 1988; mem. editl. bd. Am. Jour. Sociology, 1976—79, Social Psychology Quar., 1977—80, 1993—, Social Sci. Rsch., 1975—. Recipient First Citizens Bank Scholars award, 2003; NIH fellow, 1966-68; grantee NSF, Nat. Inst. Edn. Mem. N.Y. Acad. Scis., Am. Sociol. Soc., Am. Sociol. Assn. Office: Univ NC Dept Sociology Charlotte NC 28223 Office Phone: 704-687-4079. Business E-Mail: mawebste@email.uncc.edu.

**WEBSTER, NORMAN ERIC,** journalist, foundation administrator; b. Summerside, P.E.I., Can., June 4, 1941; s. Eric and Elizabeth (Paterson) W.; m. Pat Roop, 1966; children: David, Andrew, Derek, Gillian, Hilary. BA, Bishop's U., Que., Can.; MA, St. John's Coll., Oxford, Eng. Corr. Globe and Mail, Que. and Ottawa, Ont., Canada; editor Globe Mag., Toronto, Ont.; corr. Globe and Mail, Peking, China, 1969-71, columnist Ont. affairs Toronto, European corr. London, editor-in-chief Toronto, 1983-89, Montreal (Que.) Gazette, 1989-93; pres. R. Howard Webster Found., Montreal, 1993—. Chancellor U. P.E.I., 1996-2005; chmn. North-South Inst., Ottawa, 1998-2000; bd. dirs. Internat. Press Inst., Vienna, Montreal Children's Hosp. Found., McGill U. Health Ctr. Found., Asia Pacific Found. Can., Commonwealth Journalists Assn., Can. Inst. for Advanced Rsch., Bishop's U., Michener Found. Recipient Nat. Newspaper award for Peking corr., 1971, for editl. writing, 1988; Rhodes scholar; mem. Order of Can. Office: R Howard Webster Found Ste 2912 1155 Rene Levesque Blvd W Montreal PQ Canada H3B 2L5 Office Phone: 514-866-2424.

**WEBSTER, OWEN WRIGHT,** chemist; b. Devils Lake, N.D., Mar. 25, 1929; s. Daniel Milton and Maude May (Wright) W.; m. Lillian Brostek; children: Ellen, Anne, John, James, Mary. BS in Chemistry, N.D. U., 1951, DSc (hon.), 1986; PhD in Chemistry, Pa. State U., 1955. Research chemist E.I. Du Pont de Nemours, Wilmington, Del., 1955-74, group leader, 1974-79, research supr., 1979-84, research leader, 1984-95, Du Pont fellow, 1986-95; ret., 1995. Adj. prof. dept. chemistry U. Ala., 2003. Patentee in field; contbr. articles to profl. jours. Recipient Chem. Pioneer award Am. Inst. Chemists, 1995. Fellow AAAS, Am. Chem. Soc. (chmn. Del. sect. 1975-76, Excellence in Resch. award 1987, Applied Polymer Sci. award 1993); mem. Sigma Xi. Republican. Roman Catholic. Avocations: chess, bridge, golf. Home: 318 S Village Ln Chadds Ford PA 19317-7319 Personal E-mail: owwebster@aol.com.

**WEBSTER, PETER DAVID,** judge; b. Framingham, Mass., Feb. 12, 1949; s. Waldo John and Helen Anne (Borovek) W.; m. Michele Page Hernandez, Jan. 13, 1989; 1 stepchild, Alana Perryman. BS, Georgetown U., 1971; JD, Duke U., 1974; LLM, U. Va., 1995. Bar: Fla. 1974, U.S. Dist. Ct. (mid. dist.) Fla. 1975, U.S. Ct. Appeals (5th cir.) 1975, U.S. Dist. Ct. (so. dist.) Fla. 1977, U.S. Dist. Ct. (no. dist.) Fla. 1978, U.S. Supreme Ct. 1978, U.S. Ct. Appeals (11th cir.) 1981. Law clk. U.S. Dist. Judge, Jacksonville, Fla., 1974-75; assoc. Bedell, Bedell, Dittmar, Smith & Zehmer, Jacksonville, 1975-78; ptnr. Bedell, Bedell, Dittmar & Zehmer, Jacksonville, 1978-85; cir. judge State Fla., Jacksonville, 1986-91; judge Dist. Ct. of Appeal, First Dist., State of Fla., Tallahassee, 1991—. Master of bench Chester Bedell Am. Inn of Ct., 1988-91, Tallahassee Am. Inn Ct., 1992-2003, pres. 1999-2000; chmn. com. on standard jury instrns. in civil cases, chmn. court reporter cert. planning com.; mem. com. on trial ct. info. sys.; com. on confidentiality of records of jud. br. Fla. Supreme Ct.; adj. prof. Fla. Coastal Sch. Law, 1997—. Contbg. author: Sanctions: Rule 11 and Other Powers, 1986, Florida Criminal Rules and Practice Manual, 1990. Bd. dirs. Jacksonville Area Legal Aid, Inc., 1978-82, River Region Human Svcs., inc., Jacksonville, 1986-88; mem. adv. bd. P.A.C.E. Ctr. for Girls, Inc., Jacksonville, 1986-91; com. mem. Shawnee dist. North Fla. coun. Boy Scouts Am., 1974-78; mem. delinquency task force Mayor's Commn. on Children and Youth, City of Jacksonville, 1988-91; officer, mem. exec. bd. Suwanee River Area coun. Boy Scouts, 1991-96. Mem. Am. Judicature Soc. (bd. dirs. 2000—), Fla. Conf. Appellate Judges, Jacksonville Bar Assn., Tallahassee Bar Assn., Phi Beta Kappa, Phi Alpha Theta, Phi Eta Sigma. Office: 1st Dist Ct Appeal 301 Martin Luther King Blvd Tallahassee FL 32399-1850 Office Phone: 850-487-1000.

**WEBSTER, ROBERT BYRON,** lawyer; b. Mar. 9, 1932; s. Don B. and Glennie E. (Cole) Webster; children: Anne Elizabeth, Allison Dee, Peter Hey, James Byron. BA, U. Mich., Ann Arbor, 1955, JD, 1957. Bar: Mich. 1958, U.S. Dist. Ct. (ea. dist.) Mich., 1958, U.S. Dist. Ct. (west. dist.) Mich. 1972, U.S. Ct. Appeals (6th cir.) 1958, U.S. Supreme Ct. 1972. Law clk. U.S. Dist. Ct., 1957-59; assoc., ptnr. Hill, Lewis, Adams, Goodrich & Tait, 1959-73; judge Cir. Ct., Oakland County, 1973—82; chief judge, 1977; ptnr. Hill Lewis PC, 1982—95; chmn. Clark Hill PLC, 1995—2002; shareholder Cox, Hodgman & Giarmarco, PC, Troy, Mich., 2003—. Chmn. Supreme Ct. Com. to Revise Ct Rules, 1975-78; mem. Mich. Ct. Rule Adv. Com., 1984; chair, State Bar Appellate Task Force, 1993; trustee, chmn. Horizon Health Systems, 1983-2002; co-chair Legis. Commn. on Cts. in 21st Century, 1990. Chmn. Oakland Rep. Com., 1970-71, commr. Nat. Commn. on Uniform State Laws, 1995—; chmn. State Officers Compensation Commn., 1998-2002; trustee Family and Children Svcs. Oakland County, 1976-84; mem. Oakland Cmty. Mental Health Bd. 1971-73; trustee Henry Ford Health Sys., 1995-2002; co-chair jud. qualifications com. State Bar, 1990—. With USAF, 1951-53. Fellow Am. Bar Found. (life), State Bar Mich. Found. (life), Am. Coll. Trial Lawyers; mem. ABA (mem. ho. dels. 1990-2004), Am. Law Inst., Fed. Bar Assn., State Bar Mich. (commr. 1982-90, v.p. 1987-88, pres. elect 1988-89, pres. 1989-90), Oakland Bar Assn. Republican. Office: 101 W Big Beaver Rd 10th Fl Troy MI 48084-5280 Office Phone: 248-457-7050. Business E-Mail: rwebster@chglaw.com. E-mail: rbwebster@ameritech.net.

**WEBSTER, ROBERT G.,** virologist, educator; b. Balclutha, New Zealand, July 5, 1932; BSc, Otago U., New Zealand, 1955, MSc, 1957; PhD, Australian Nat. U., Canberra, 1962. Virologist New Zealand Dept. Agr., 1958—59; postdoctoral fellow (Fulbright scholar) dept. epidemiology U. Mich. Sch. Pub. Health, Ann Arbor, Mich., 1962—63; rsch. fellow dept. microbiology Australian Nat. U., John Curtain Med. Sch., Canberra, 1964—66, fellow dept. microbiology, 1966—67; assoc. prof. dept. microbiology U. Tenn. Med. Units, Memphis, 1968—69, 1969—74; prof. dept. microbiology U. Tenn. Ctr. for Health Sciences, Memphis, 1974—75, 1975—78, prof. dept. microbiology and immunology, 1978—85; Rose Marie Thomas chair dept. virology and molecular biology St. Jude Children's Rsch. Hosp., Memphis, 1988—. Assoc. mem. lab. immunology St. Jude Children's Rsch. Hosp., Memphis, 1968—69, mem. labs. virology and immunology, 1969—74, 1974—75, mem. divsn. virology, 1975—78, mem. dept. virology and molecular biology, 1978—85, 1985—88; Fogarty internat. sr. fellow Nat. Inst. for Med. Rsch., Med. Rsch. Coun., London, 1978—79. Contbr. articles to sci. jours. Named a Rsch. Leader within Sci. Am. 50, 2005; recipient Bristol-Meyers Squibb award, 2002, Disting. Biotechnologist of the Yr. award, New Zealand Biotechnology Assn., 2006. Fellow: Royal Soc. Medicine, Royal Soc. London, Royal Soc., New Zealand (hon.); mem.: AAAS, Am. Soc. for Virology, Am. Soc. for Microbiology, NAS. Achievements include research in emergence and control of influenza; viral immunology; discovery of link between human and avian influenza viruses. Office: St Jude Children's Rsch Hosp 332 N Lauderdale St Memphis TN 38105-2794 Office Phone: 901-495-3400. E-mail: robert.webster@stjude.org.*

**WEBSTER, ROBERT KENLY,** lawyer; b. NYC, May 16, 1933; s. Francis Kenly and Mary Louise (Rathbone) W. m. Sally Irene Stratton, Apr. 16, 1960; children: Timothy Kenly, Kimberly Anne. AB, Princeton U., 1955; LLB, U. Va., 1960. Assoc. Cadwalader, Wickersham & Taft, N,Y.C., 1960-65; asst. U.S. atty. Dept. of Justice, Washington, 1965-68; prin. dep. asst. counsel Dept. of Army, Washington, 1968-73; ptnr. Kennedy & Webster, Washington, 1973-81, Shaw, Pittman, Potts & Trowbridge, Washington, 1981-98; sole practice Washington, 1999—. Spl. investigator Iran FMS program Sec. of Def., Washington, 1977; advisor conflict of interest issues Watergate defendants Dept. Justice, Washington, 1977. Gen. counsel Princeton (N.J.) Project 55, Inc., 1989—. Lt. j.g. USN, 1955—57. Mem. ABA, ATLA, Fed. Bar Assn., Met. Club. Avocations: pottery, reading, travel, tennis.

**WEBSTER, ROBERT LEE,** accounting educator, researcher; b. Little Rock, Oct. 4, 1946; s. Daniel and Mildred LaNette (Patshall) W.; m. Mary Katherine Fiske, Aug. 26, 1967; children: Elizabeth Ashley, Jessica Lee. BA, Ouachita Bapt. U., 1968; MBA, Syracuse U., 1975; MS, L.I. U., 1986; DBA, La. Tech. U., 1993. Cert. govt. fin. mgr. Commd. 2d lt. U.S. Army, 1968, advanced through grades to lt. col., 1985; dep. contr. U.S. Army Electronics R&D Command, Adelphi, Md., 1975-80; chief of ops., comms. security NATO, Mons, Belgium, 1980-83; asst. prof. acctg. and fin. U.S. Mil. Acad., West Point, N.Y., 1983-86; prof. mil. sci. Henderson State U., Arkadelphia, Ark., 1986-88; ret. U.S. Army, 1988; asst. prof. acctg. Henderson State U., 1988-91, chair dept. acctg., econs. and bus. edn., 1991-93; chair dept. acctg. Ouachita Bapt. U., Arkadelphia, 1993—, George Young chair bus., 1995—. Bd. dirs. Hospitality Care Ctr., Arkadelphia, 1992-93; speaker in field. Editor Jour. Bus. & Behavioral Scis., 1995; author articles. Recipient Dean's award for acad. achievement, L.I. U., 1986; Army scholar, Syracuse U., 1974—75, Exch. Educator to Republic of Kazakhstan, 1994—95. Mem. Nat. Social Sci. Assn. (bd. govs. 1992—, Outstanding Conf. Paper award 1992), Am. Acctg. Assn. (chmn. Southwest region 2006—), Assn. of Govt. Accts., Beta Gamma Sigma, Sigma Beta Delta. Avocations: coin collecting/numismatics, exercise. Home: 724 Colonial Dr Bryant AR 72022 Office: Ouachita Bapt U PO Box 3689 Arkadelphia AR 71998 Office Phone: 870-245-5254. Business E-Mail: websterb@obu.edu.

**WEBSTER, RONALD B.,** lawyer; b. Cle Elum, Wash., June 11, 1942; s. Burnette O. and Lucille (Beck) W.; m. M. Gail Skinner, June 26, 1971; children: Noel, Michelle. BA, U. Wash., 1964; JD, Gonzaga U., 1969. Bar:

Wash., U.S. Dist. Ct. (ea. and we. dists.) Wash., U.S. Ct. Appeals (9th cir.). Dep. pros. atty. Cowlitz County, Kelso, Wash., 1970-73; ptnr. Hickman, Webster, Ensley & Carpenter, Colfax, Wash., 1973-90, Hickman, Webster & Moulton, 1990-92, Hickman & Webster, P.S., 1992-95. Mem. Whitman County Bd. Mental Health, Pullman, Wash., 1973-83; chmn. civil svc. commn. Whitman County Sheriffs Office, Colfax, 1973—; pres. Colfax and Cmty. Fund, 1973-74; pres. Whitman Cmty. Concerts, 1990-93; mem. ch. coun. Peace Luth. Ch., 1996-98; chmn. bd. dirs. Whitman County Libr., 1997—, chmn. bd. trustees, 1998—. Named Rotarian of Yr., 1998, Paul Harris fellow, 1998. Mem. Whitman County Bar Assn. (pres. 1981-82), Wash. State Bar Assn. (inter profl. com. 1986-89—, disciplinary com. 1986-97). Clubs: Colfax Golf and Country. Lodges: Rotary (pres. Colfax club 1983-84). Home: 1801 N Oak St Colfax WA 99111-9705 Office: Webster & Frey PLLC 105 W Island St Colfax WA 99111

**WEBSTER, SHARON B.,** economist; b. Wildwood, Fla., Aug. 23, 1937; d. James McWilliams and Marion (Hallbrook) Boen. BA in Polit. sci., Econ. and Psychology, U. Fla., 1959; vis. doctoral fellow, Princeton U., 1964—65; PhD, U. Va., 1965. Asst. prof. No. Mich. U., Marquette, 1962—64, U. Md., 1964—66, Hollins Coll., Roanoke, Va., 1966—71; prof. Fed. Exec. Inst., Charlottesville, Va., 1971—72; mgr. internat. program Dept. Treasury, Washington, 1972—74; economist Econ., Stats. and Coop. Svc. U.S. Dept. Agr., Washington, 1974—79; mem. Presdl. Commn. for Exec. Exch., 1979—80; dir. internat. econ. Occidental Petroleum Corp., L.A., 1980—83; investment banker, account exec. Johnston, Lemon and Co., Inc., Washington, 1983—88; fin. cons. Shearson Lehman Hutton, Washington, 1988—. Mem. adv. bd. Pres.'s Caribbean Basin Initiative, 1982; chmn. bd. dirs. NATA, Inc.; bd. dirs. Genta, Inc., NABE; pres., CEO A.A. Global; bd. advisors Sintal Comm. USA, Inc., Internat. Trade Coun.; bd. advisors Patterson Sch. Diplomacy and Internat. Commerce U. Ky.; bd. advisors Consumer Health and Svcs. Am., Inc. Contbr. articles to profl. jours. Recipient Presdl. award Pvt. Sector Iniatve, 1982; NDEA fellow. Mem.: AAUP, Assn. Polit. Risk Analysts, Washington Soc. Money Mgrs., Soc. Internat. Devel., Internat. Studies Assn., Nat. Assn. Bus. Economists, Am. Polit. Sci. Assn., Am. Assn. Agrl. Economists, Internat. Assn. Energy Economists, Internat. Policy Inst. (v.p. 1977—), Fed. Exec. Inst. Alumni Assn., Pres.'s Exec. Exch. Assn., Nat. Coun. Career Women, Internat. Club, Army Navy Club, Capital Spkrs. Club. Home: The Winthrop # 602 1727 Massachusetts Ave NW Washington DC 20036-2153 Office: AA Global 9039 Furrow Ave Ellicott City MD 21042-1841

**WEBSTER, STEPHEN BURTIS,** dermatologist, educator; b. Chgo., Dec. 3, 1935; s. James Randolph Webster and Ruth Marion (Burtis) Holmes; m. Katherine Griffith Webster, Apr. 4, 1959; children: David Randolph, Margaret Elizabeth, James Lucian. BS, Northwestern U., 1957, MD, 1960. Diplomate Am. Bd. Dermatology (bd. dirs. 1992—, v.p. 1997-98, pres.). Intern Colo. Gen. Hosp., Denver, 1960-61; resident Walter Reed Gen. Hosp., Washington, 1962-65; staff physician Henry Ford Hosp., Detroit, 1969-71, Gundersen Lutheran Med. Ctr., La Crosse, 1971—; assoc. clin. prof. U. Wis., Madison, 1976—; clin. prof. U. Minn., Mpls., 1978—. Lt. col. U.S. Army, 1962-69. Fellow Am. Acad. Dermatology (sec.-treas. 1985-88, pres. 1991); mem. AMA, Am. Dermatol. Assn. (pres. 1996-97), Am. Bd. Dermatology (v.p. 1997-98, pres. 1999-2000, assoc. exec. dir. 2001—), Wis. Med. Soc., La Crosse County Med. Soc., Soc. Investigative Dermatology, Alpha Omega Alpha. Republican. Congregationalist. Avocations: bagpipes, model trains. Home: N2062 Wedgewood Dr E La Crosse WI 54601-7175 Office: Gundersen Clinic Ltd 1836 South Ave La Crosse WI 54601-5494 Business E-Mail: sbwebste@gundluth.org.

**WEBSTER, SUSAN,** lawyer; b. Hartford, Conn., Dec. 21, 1956; BA, Wesleyan U., 1977; JD, Fordham U., 1984. Bar: N.Y. 1985. Ptnr., corp. Cravath, Swaine & Moore, N.Y.C. Mem. ABA, N.Y. State Bar Assn., Assn. of Bar of City of N.Y. Office: Cravath Swaine & Moore Worldwide Plz 825 8th Ave Fl 38 New York NY 10019-7475 Office Phone: 212-474-1660. Office Fax: 212-474-3700. Business E-Mail: swebster@cravath.com.

**WEBSTER, THOMAS GLENN,** psychiatrist, educator; b. Topeka, Jan. 23, 1924; s. Guy Welland and Iva Amanda (Keefover) W.; m. Mary Tupper Dooly, June 27, 1948; children: Warnie Louise, Guy Weyman, David Michael AB, Ft. Hays State Coll., 1946; MD, Wayne State U., 1949. Intern Los Angeles County Gen. Hosp., Calif., 1949-50; resident in psychiatry Mass. Mental Health Ctr., Boston, 1953-55, resident in child psychiatry, 1955-56, James Jackson Putnam Children's Ctr., Boston, 1956-58; dir. presch. program for retarded children Greater Boston, 1958-62; coordinator 3d yr. med. student psychiatry clerkship Harvard U. Med. Sch.-Mass. Mental Health Ctr., Boston, 1960-63; practice medicine specializing in psychiatry Boston, 1953-62, Bethesda, Md., 1963-72, Washington, 1972—; tng. specialist psychiatry, then chief continuing edn. br. NIMH, Bethesda, Md., 1963-72; prof. psychiatry George Washington U., Washington, 1972-86, chmn. dept. psychiatry and behavioral scis., 1972-75, prof. emeritus, 1986-96. Vis. prof. Harvard U. Med. Sch., 1980-83, McLean Hosp., 1980-86; U.S.-Poland exchange health scientist, 1981 Pres. Woodhaven Citizens Assn. Served with AUS, 1943-46; as sr. asst. surgeon USPHS, 1951-53 Fellow Am. Coll. Psychiatrists, Am. Coll. Psychoanalysts; mem. Assn. Acad. Psychiatry (pres. 1976-78), Group Advancement Psychiatry Home: 8506 Woodhaven Blvd Bethesda MD 20817-3117

**WEBSTER, WILLIAM G., JR.,** career military officer; b. Baton Rouge, La., July 3, 1951; BS, U.S. Mil. Acad., 1974. Commd. 2d lt. U.S. Army, 1974, advanced through grades to brig. gen., tank co. comdr. Fort Polk, La., 1974—78, ops. and plans officer Seventh Army Combined Arms Tng. Ctr., 1979—82, ops. officer 3-64 Armor, 3d Inf. Divsn. Germany, 1979—82, asst. G-3 and brigade ops. officer 24th Inf. Divsn. Ft. Stewart, Ga., 1984—87, joint staff War Plans Divsn. Washington, 1988—91, comdr. 3d bn., 77th armor in 4th inf. divsn., 1991-93; sr. armor observer contr. Cobra Team Nat. Tng. Ctr., Ft. Irwin, Calif., 1993-94; comdr. 1st brigade 1st cavalry divsn. Ft. Hood, 1995-97; asst. divsn. comdr. 3d Inf. Divsn., Ft. Stewart, Ga., 1997-98; comdr. Ft. Irwin and Nat. Tng. Ctr., 1998—2000; deployed Ops. Desert Thunder U.S. Army, 1998, Army's dir. tng. Office Dep. Chief of Staff G-3, 2000—01, dep. J-3 U.S. Ctrl. Command Operation Enduring Freedom Afghanistan, 2001—02, dep. comdg. gen. for ops. Third U.S. Army, Combined Forces Land Component Command, Operation Iraqi Freedom Kuwait, 2002—03, Iraq, 2002—03, comdg. gen. 3d Inf. Divsn. Ft. Stewart and Hunter Army Airfield, 2003—. Decorated Legion of Merit with 4 oak leaf clusters, Air Assault badge, Parachutist badge, Def. Superior Svc. medal, Armed Forces Expeditionary medal, Legion recipient Bronze Star. Office: 3d Infantry Divsn Ste 204 42 Wayne Pl Fort Stewart GA 31314

**WEBSTER, WILLIAM HEDGCOCK,** lawyer, former CIA director; b. St. Louis, Mar. 6, 1924; s. Thomas M. and Katherine (Hedgcock) W.; m. Drusilla Lane, May 5, 1950 (dec. 1984); children: Drusilla Lane Busch, William Hedgcock, Katherine Hagee Roessle; m. Lynda Clugston, Oct. 20, 1990. AB Amherst Coll., 1947, LLD, 1975; JD, Washington U., 1949, LLD, 1978; LLD (hon.), William Wood Coll., 1978, DePauw U., 1978, Drury Coll., Columbia Coll., U. Dayton, U. Notre Dame, Center Coll., Dickinson Coll., U. Miami, DePaul U., Am. U., John Jay Coll., Westminster Coll., Georgetown U., Rockhurst Coll., Pepperdine U. Bar: Mo. 1949, D.C. 1981. With Armstrong, Teasdale, Kramer and Vaughan (and predecessors), St. Louis, 1949-50, 52-59, 61-70; U.S. atty. U.S. Dist. Ct. (ea. dist) Mo., 1960-61, judge, 1971-73, U.S. Ct. Appeals (8th cir.), 1973-78; dir. FBI, 1978-87, CIA, 1987-91; sr. ptnr. Milbank, Tweed, Hadley & McCloy LLP, Washington, 1991—. Mem. Mo. Bd. Law Examiners, 1964-69, mem. adv. com. on criminal rules, 1971-78, mem. ct. adminstrs. com., 1975-78; bd. dirs. Anhauser-Busch Cos., Maritz Inc., Pinkertons Inc., T.L.C. Beatrice Internat. Holdings Inc., Nextwave, Inc., Regulatory DataCorp Internat.; mem., advisory bd., Dilligence LLC; chmn. Pub. Co. Acctg. Oversight Bd., 2002 Trustee Washington U., 1974—; bd. dirs. Atlantic Coun., Nat. Legal Ctr. for Pub. Interest, Nat. Symphony Assn., Coun. on Fgn. Rels.; bd. dirs. Big Bros. Am., 1966, hon. bd. dirs., 1978—. Lt. USNR, 1943-46, 50-52. Recipient Disting. Alumnus award Washington U., 1977, Stein award Fordham U., Law award U. Va., Theodore Roosevelt award for

Excellence in Pub. Svc., Internat. Platform Assn., 1983, Jefferson award for the Greatest Pub. Svc. by an Elected or Appointed Official, 1984, Freedoms Found. Nat. Svc. medal, 1985, Disting. Intelligence medal, 1991, Presdl. medal of Freedom, 1991, Nat. Security medal, 1991, Silver Buffalo award Boy Scouts Am., Disting. Svc. award, Am. Legion, Justice award, Am. Judicature Soc., 2001, Am. Bar Assn. medal, 2002; named Father of Yr., 1986, Man of Yr., St. Louis Globe Dem., 1980. Fellow Am. Bar Found.; mem. ABA (chmn. sect. on corp. banking and bus. law 1977-78), FBA, Mo. Bar Assn., St. Louis Bar Assn., Am. Law Inst. (mem. coun. 1978—), Wash. U. Alumni Fedn. (pres. 1956-57), Rotary, St. Louis Country Club, Noonday Club (St. Louis), Met. Club, Chevy Chase Club, Alfalfa Club, St. Alban's Tennis Club, Order of Coif, Psi Upsilon, Delta Sigma Rho, Phi Delta Phi. Office: Milbank Tweed Hadly Mccloy Llp 1850 K St Nw Washington DC 20006-2213 E-mail: wwebster@milbank.com.

**WECHSLER, ARNOLD,** obstetrician, gynecologist; b. N.Y.C., June 10, 1923; s. David and Eva (Kirsch) W.; m. Marlene Esta Jurnovoy, Sept. 11, 1955 (div. Sept. 1986); children: Diane, Paul, Stewart. Grad., Rutgers U.; DO, Phila. Coll. Osteo. Medicine, 1952. Diplomate Am. Bd. Osteo. Obstetricians and Gynecologists; lic. physician, Pa., N.Y., Fla. Intern Hosps. of Phila. Coll. Osteo. Medicine, 1952-53, resident in ob-gyn. and gen. surgery, 1953-56; lectr. in ob-gyn. Nursing Sch. Phila. Coll. Osteo. Medicine; founder, mem. staff Tri County Hosp., Delaware County, Pa., from 1960, chief staff, 1960-62, chief dept. ob-gyn. surgery, 1960-77, dir. med. edn., 1968-71; attending and cons. in ob-gyn. surgery Met. Hosp., Phila., 1956-60, 71-75; chief dept. ob-gyn. Humana Hosp.-South Broward, Hollywood, Fla., 1980-84; cons. and attending in gynecol. surgery Drs. Hosp. of Hollywood, 1982-86. Insp. for intern and resident tng. programs Bur. Hosps. of Am. Osteo. Assn., 1965-66; founder, med. dir. Women's Med. Svcs., 1973-77, Nutrients Inc., Phila., 1977-79, Supplements Inc., Phila., 1979-80, Alternative Lifestyle Ctr., Fla., 1983-86; founder, dir. A.W. Profl. Consultants, Inc.; cons. Practice Mgmt. Group, Med Temps Plus, Plantation, Fla.; provider ambulatory gyn. surgery for multiple gyn ctrs. in Dade, Broward and Palm Beach Counties, Fla. Author: Dr. Wechsler's New You Diet, 1978. Staff Sgt. Signal Corps, USAF, 1942-46, PTO, Japan. Fellow Am. Coll. Osteo. Obstetricians and Gynecologists, Internat. Coll. Applied Nutrition; mem. AMA, Am. Osteo. Assn., Pa. Osteo. Med. Assn., Philadelphia County Osteo. Soc., Fla. Osteo. Med. Assn., Fla. Med. Soc., Fla. Ob-Gyn. Soc., Broward County Osteo. Med. Assn., Am. Soc. Bariatric Physicians, Assn. Maternal and Child Welfare, Internat. Acad. Preventive Medicine, Inst. Food Technologists, Coun. for Responsible Nutrition, Internat. Coll. Gynecologic Laparoscopists, Assn. Reproductive Health Profls. Avocations: photography, sculpture, woodworking. Home: 10419 NW 2nd St Coral Springs FL 33071-7334 Office Phone: 954-981-9045. Personal E-mail: wechslea@bellsouth.net.

**WECHSLER, DANIEL STEVEN,** medical educator; s. Morris Herschel and Ann Wechsler; m. Stephanie Burns, Aug. 21, 1994; children: Caroline Susannah, Julie Rebecca. AB, Harvard U., Cambridge, Mass., 1982; MD, McGill U., Montreal, 1987; PhD, McGill U., 1987. Diplomate Am. Bd. Pediat. Assoc. prof. U. Mich. Med. Sch., Ann Arbor, 1994—. Dir. pediat. hematology-oncology fellowship tng. program U. Mich., 2000—. Mem.: Am. Soc. Pediatric Hematoloy-Oncology (tng. com. 2003—06). Achievements include research in chromosomal translocations in infant leukemia. Home: 1604 Brooklyn Ave Ann Arbor MI 48104 Office: U Mich 1500 E Medical Ctr Dr CCGC 4312 Ann Arbor MI 48109-0936 Office Phone: 734-936-8875. Office Fax: 734-647-9654. E-mail: dwechsl@umich.edu.

**WECHSLER, GIL,** lighting designer; b. N.Y.C., Feb. 5, 1942; s. Arnold J. and Miriam (Steinberg) W. Student, Rensselaer Poly. Inst., Troy, N.Y., 1958—61; BS, NYU, N.Y.C., 1964; MFA, Yale U., New Haven, 1967. Lighting designer Harkness Ballet, N.Y.C., 1967—69, Pa. Ballet, Phila., 1969—70, Stratford Shakespeare Festival, Ont., Canada, 1969—78, 1997—2004, Guthrie Theatre, Mpls., 1971, Lyric Opera, Chgo., 1972—76, Met. Opera, N.Y.C., 1976—96, Equus, Stratford Shakespeare Festival, 1997, Macbeth, Stratford Festival, 2004, Coriolanus, Stratford Festival, 2006. Tchr. NYU, Rensselaer Poly. Inst., 1998; guest lectr. Teatro Colon, Buenos Aires, 1985, Yale U., 1980, Broadway Lighting Designers, 1994—98; guest lighting designer Am. Ballet Theatre, N.Y.C., 1980, Paris Opera, 1983, Chatelet Theatre, Paris, 1991; dean's adv. coun. Rensselaer Poly. Inst. Cons. editor Opera Quar., 1983-90. Recipient Emmy award nominations, Illuminating Engring. Soc., United Scenic Artists. Avocations: collecting ocean liner memorabilia, gardening, kayaking. Home: 1 Lincoln Plz New York NY 10023-7129 E-mail: gillights@aol.com.

**WECHSLER, JESSICA See JOSELL, JESSICA**

**WECHSLER, MARY HEYRMAN,** lawyer; b. Green Bay, Wis., Jan. 8, 1948; d. Donald Hubert and Helen (Polcyn) Heyrman; m. Roger Wechsler, Aug. 1971 (div. 1977); 1 child, Risa Heyrman; m. David Jay Sellinger, Aug. 15, 1981; 1 stepchild, Kirk Benjamin; 1 child, Michael Paul. Student, U. Chgo., 1966-67, 68-69; BA, U. Wash., 1971; JD cum laude, U. Puget Sound, 1979. Bar: Wash. 1979. Assoc. Law Offices Ann Johnson, Seattle, 1979-81; ptnr. Johnson, Wechsler, Thompson, Seattle, 1981-83; pvt. practice Seattle, 1984-87; ptnr. Mussehl, Rosenberg et al, Seattle, 1987-88, Wechsler, Becker LLP, Seattle, 1988—. Mem. Bd. Ct. Edn., 1998—2006, sec., 2003—05, vice chair, 2006; bd. dirs. U. Wash. Law Sch. Child Advocacy Clinic, 1996—99; mem. Wash. State Commn. on Jud. Selection, 1995—96, Wash. State Commn. on Domestic Rels., 1996—97, 1999—2004; chair edn. com. Access to Justice Bd., 1996—99, mem. pub. trust and confidence com., 2000—05; mem. Jud. Coll. Bd. Trustees, 2005—; moderator Wash. State Summit on Jud. Independence and Jud. Selection, 2005; presenter in field. Author: Family Law in Washington, 1987, rev. edit., 1988, Marriage and Separation, Divorce and Your Rights, 1994; contbr. articles to legal publs. Mem. Wash. State Ethics Adv. Com., 1992-95; bd. dirs. Seattle LWV, 1991-92. Named Super Lawyer, Wash. Law and Politics, 2000—06; named one of Seattle's Top Lawyer's, Seattle Mag., 2003, 2004, 2005, 2006. Fellow Am. Acad. Matrimonial Lawyers (Wash. state chpt., sec.-treas. 1996, v.p. 1997-98, pres. 1999-2000, nat. arbitration com. 1999-2000, nat. interdisciplinary com. 1999-2000, nat. admissions procedure com. 2000-02, nat. long range planning com. 2003-05, chair 2003—, nat. bylaws com. 2005, nat. budget com. 2004-06); mem. ABA (chmn. membership Wash. state 1987-88), Wash. State Bar Assn. (exec. com. family law sect 1985-91, chair family law sect. 1988-89), profl. devel. com. 2002-03, media project com. 2001, ct. improvement com. 1998-2000, legs. com. 1991-96, Outstanding Atty. of Yr. family law sect. 1988, comms. com. 1997-98, disciplinary hearing officer 1998—), Wash. Women Lawyers, King County Bar Assn. (legis. com. 1985-2000, vice-chair 1990-91, chair family law sect. 1986-87, chair domestic violence com. 1986-87, trustee 1988-90, policy planning com. 1991-92, 2d v.p. 1992-93, 1st v.p. 1993-94, pres. 1994-95, long-range planning com. 1998-99, awards com. 1997-99, nominations com. 2003, co-chair Bench-Bar Conf. 2003, Outstanding Atty. award 1999), Nat. Conf. of Bar Pres., King County Bar Found. (trustee 1997-2000), Am. Judicature Soc. (v.p. Washington chpt. 2000-03, pres. 2003—). Office: Wechsler Becker LLP Ste 4550 701 5th Ave Seattle WA 98104-7097 Office Phone: 206-624-4900. Business E-Mail: mhwechsler@wechslerbecker.com.

**WECHSLER, SERGIO,** automotive executive, consultant; b. Rio de Janeiro, Aug. 10, 1944; arrived in US, 1965; s. Michael and Gertrud (Putziger) W.; children: Mark, Andrew. Student, Mackenzie U., 1962, Kettering U., 1967; MBA in Internat. Bus., NYU, 1974; PhD in Internat. Bus., Kennedy-Western U., 1996. Quality supr. GM do Brasil, Sao Paulo, 1963-65; quality control supt., 1967-70; quality control mgr. Gillette Corp., Berlin, 1970-71; project mgr. GM, N.Y.C. 1971-76; plant mgr. GM de Portugal, Lisbon, 1976-79; project mgr. Adam Opel AG, Russelheim, Fed. Republic of Germany, 1979-81; quality dir. GM, Linden, NJ, 1981-85, dir. ops. and quality control Warren, Mich., 1985-93, mgr. internat. programs, 1985-95, program mgr. Cadillac Luxury Car divsn. Flint, Mich., 1995-96. Pres., CEO Marswex Global Enterprises, Palm Harbor, Fla., 1982—, Hudson Plaza, 1984-99; chmn. Auto Exchange Club, Clearwater, Fla., 1997-2001, MSX Internat., Detroit, 1996-99, v.p. German ops., 1999-2001. V.p. Temple Beth

Jacob, Pontiac, Mich., 1986, pres. 1987—89. Mem. Am. Soc. Quality Control (cert. quality engr. 1992), Radio Club. Republican. Avocations: amateur radio, travel, auto restoration. Personal E-mail: marswex@aol.com.

**WECHSLER, STEVEN L,** virologist, researcher; s. Milton and Ola Wechsler; m. Elizabeth Anne Wechsler, May 19, 1974; children: Adrianna, Robert, Matthew, Michelle. BS, CCNY, 1970; PhD, U.N.C, Chapel Hill, 1975. Post doctoral fellow Harvard Med. Sch., Boston, 1975—80; asst. prof. Gamble Inst. of Med. Rsch., Cin., 1980—86; prof. Cedars Sinai Med. Ctr., Los Angeles, Calif., 1986—2001, U. Calif., Irvine, 2001—. Contbr. over 100 rsch. papers. Grants, NIH, 1981—. Achievements include 5 patents related to Herpes simplex virus vaccines; 2 patents on use of herpes simplex virus as an expression vector. Home: Univ of Calif Irvine 101 The City Drive Bldg 55 Romm 226 Orange CA 92868 Office Phone: 714-456-7362. E-mail: wechsler@uci.edu.

**WECHTER, CLARI ANN,** manufacturing executive; b. Chgo., June 1, 1953; d. Norman Robert and Harriet Beverly (Golub) W.; m. Gordon Jay Siegel, Feb. 10, 1980; 1 child, Alix Jessica. BA, U. Ariz., 1975; BE, Loyola U., Chgo., 1977. Cert. tchr., Ill. Saleswoman, v.p. sales Federated Paint Mfg. Co., Chgo., 1979—. Republican. Jewish. Avocation: travel. Home: 25 E Cedar St Chicago IL 60611-1109 Office: Federated Paint and Pioneer Powder Mfg Co 1521 N 31st Ave Melrose Park IL 60160 Office Phone: 708-345-4848 x622.

**WECHTER, IRA MARTIN,** tax specialist, financial planner; b. Bkyn., June 26, 1947; s. Nathan Harris and Mollie (Bauer) W.; m. Myrna Ellen Rosenbaum, Dec. 22, 1968; 1 child, Megan Jill. BA, CCNY, 1969; MPA, Bernard Baruch Coll., 1973. CFP; cert. practitioner of taxation; accredited tax advisor; registered investment advisor; lic. gen. securities prin.; enrolled to practice before IRS; lic. gen. securities prin., life, health and disability ins., N.J., N.Y. Dir. adminstrv. svcs. N.Y.C. Dept. City Planning, 1971-77; dep. asst. budget dir. N.Y., N.Y.C. Office Mgmt. and Budget, 1977-81; dep. commr. N.Y.C. Dept. Environ. Protection, 1981-84; pres. Wechter Fin. Svcs., Inc., Parsippany, NJ, 1984—. Mem. Community Bd. No. 1 S.I., 1973-76, 1st v.p., 1976-77; treas. S.I. Coun. on Arts, 1974-75. Recipient Outstanding Citizenship award Borough Pres. of S.I., 1977. Mem. Nat. Assn. Enrolled Agts., Inst. Cert. Fin. Planners, Nat. Assn. Tax Practitioners, Nat. Soc. Tax Preparers, Nat. Soc. Pub. Accts. Republican. Jewish. Avocations: stamp collecting/philately, organ. Office: Wechter Fin Svcs Inc 1719 State Rt 10 Ste 310 Parsippany NJ 07054-4507 also: 1719 Route 10 Ste 224 Parsippany NJ 07054-4507 Office Phone: 973-605-1448. Business E-Mail: wfs@wechterfinancial.com.

**WECK FARRAG, KRISTIN W.,** bank executive; b. Elgin, Ill., Nov. 5, 1959; d. John Francis and Florence Elaine (Ebel) W.; married Nov. 6, 2004. BBA, Augustana Coll., Rock Island, Ill., 1981. Lic. real estate broker, Ill., life/health ins. producer; registered securities rep. (series 7 and series 24); registered uniform investment advisor series 65. Intern with investment banking group First Chgo. Bank, London, 1980; intern Prudential-Bache Co., Ft. Lauderdale, Fla., 1981; residential appraiser Fox Valley Appraisal Counselors, Ltd., West Dundee, Ill., 1982-84; asst. real estate loan officer First Nat. Bank, Barrington, Ill., 1982-84; savs. and loan field examiner III Office of Thrift Supervision, Chgo., 1984-90; mng. agt. Resolution Trust Corp., Elk Grove Village, Ill., 1990-91; pres., treas., bd. dirs. Cardunal Savs. Bank, West Dundee, Ill., 1991—; dir. Prairie State Bank, Marengo, Ill., 1998—2002. Project Bus. cons. Jr. Achievement, 1992-96; literacy tutor Vols. of Am., 1998-99; dist. chmn. Found. Ednl. Excellence, 2003-04. Recipient Outstanding Achievement award Fed. Home Loan Bank Bd., 1985, Leading Us In Commerce and Industry award for fin. svcs., 1998, Sam Walton Bus. Cmty. Leader award, 1999. Mem. Nat. Assn. Securities Dealers (registered rep., registered prin.), Rotary Club Dundee Twp. (pres. 2001-02, Rotarian of Yr. 1997-98, Disting. Pres. 2002). Republican. Lutheran. Avocations: scuba diving, golf, walking, reading. Home: PO Box 930 Dundee IL 60118-0930 Office: Cardunal Savings Bank PO Box 839 Dundee IL 60118-0839 Personal E-mail: kweck@cardunal.net.

**WEDDING, CHARLES RANDOLPH,** architect; b. St. Petersburg, Fla., Nov. 16, 1934; s. Charles Reid and L. Marion (Whitaker) W.; m. Audrey Whitsel, Aug. 18, 1956 (div. Apr. 1979); children: Daryl L., Douglas R., Dorian B.; m. Vonnie Sue Hayes, June 22, 1984 (dec. 1991); stepchildren: Stephanie W., Brian E.; m. June A. Free, Mar. 31, 1993; stepchildren: Gregory, Kristine. BArch, U. Fla., 1957. Registered arch., Fla., Ga., N.C., S.C., Del., Va., Tex., Ill., Ind., Kans., La., Mo., Okla., Tenn. Arch. in tng. Harvard & Jolly AIA, St. Petersburg, 1957-60; arch., prin., pres. Wedding & Assocs., St. Petersburg, 1960—. Mayor City of St. Petersburg, 1973-75; past chmn. Pinellas County Com. of 100, Bldg. Dept. Survey Team, City of St. Petersburg; trustee All Children's Hosp., 1968-70; sect. leader St. Petersburg United Fund, 1965-70; mem. city coun. Action Team for Pier Redevel., 1967-68; mem. exec. com. Goals for City of St. Petersburg, 1970-72; den leader Webelos, Boy Scouts Am., 1971-72; chmn., trustee Canterbury Sch. YMCA, 1968-72; mem. adv. com. Tomlinson Vocat. Sch., 1969-79; past trustee Mus. Fine Arts; past bd. dirs. Neighborly Ctr., Jr. Achievement Pinellas County; chair Downtown Partnership, 2001—. Served to 1st lt. U.S. Army, 1958-60. Fellow AIA (5 Silver Spike awards, Merit of Honor, Medal of Honor); mem. Am. Soc. Landscape Archs., St. Petersburg Assn. Archs. (past pres.), Fla. Assn. Archs. (8 Merit Design awards), St. Petersburg Yacht Club, Suncoasters Club. Republican. Episcopalian. Avocations: sailing, hunting, golf, tennis. Home: 6900 10th Ave N Saint Petersburg FL 33710-6152 Office: Wedding/Stephenson/Ibargüen Archs Inc 300 1st Ave S Saint Petersburg FL 33701-4209 Office Phone: 727-821-6610. Business E-Mail: randy@weddingarchitects.com.

**WEDDINGTON, SARAH RAGLE,** lawyer, educator; b. Abilene, Tex., Feb. 5, 1945; d. Herbert Doyle and Lena Catherine Ragle. BS magna cum laude, McMurry Coll., 1965, PhD (hon.), 1979; JD, U. Tex., 1967; PhD (hon.), Hamilton Coll., 1979, Southwestern U., 1989, Austin Coll., 1993, Nova Southeastern U., 1999; PhD in Human Letters (hon.), Fitchburg State Coll., 2004. Bar: Tex. 1967, D.C. 1979, U.S. Dist. Ct. (we., no. and ea. dists.) Tex., U.S. Ct. Appeals (5th cir.), U.S. Supreme Ct. Pvt. practice law, Austin, 1967-77; gen. counsel Dept. Agr., Washington, 1977-78; spl. asst. to U.S. pres. Washington, 1978—79; asst. to U.S. pres., 1979—81; chmn. Interdepartmental Task Force on Women, 1978-81; mem. Pres.'s Commn. on Exec. Exchange, 1981; Carl Hatch prof. law and pub. adminstrn. U. N.Mex., Albuquerque, 1982-83; pvt. practice law Austin, Tex., 1985—; dir. Tex. Office State-Fed. Rels., Austin, Washington, 1983-85. Vis. prof. govt. Wheaton Coll., Norton, Mass., 1981-83; sr. lectr. Tex. Woman's U., Denton, 1981-90, 93, U. Tex., Austin, 1986-1989, adj. assoc. prof. 1989-2001, adj. prof. 2001-. Author: A Question of Choice, 1992; contbr. articles to various mags.; contbg. editor Glamour mag., 1981-83. Mem. Tex. Ho. of Reps., 1973-77; named hon. chair San Francisco Bar Assn. Breast Cancer Hotline/Network, 2001, named hon. chair am. benefit for Breast Cancer Rsch. Ctr., Austin, 2002, named lecture showcase presenter Nat. Assn. Campus Activities, 2003. Named Lectr. of Yr., Nat. Assn. Coll. Activities, 1990, Tex. Woman of Century, Tex. Women's C. of C., 1999, Face of Century, San Antonio Express News, 1999, 2000, Outstanding Alumnus, McMurry U., 2004, Nat. Pub. Health Hero, U. Calif., Berkeley, 2005; named one of Most Influential Lawyers of the 20th Century, Tex. Lawyer, 2000; recipient Woman of Yr. award, Tex. Women's Polit. Caucus, 1973, Outstanding Young Am. Leaders, Time Mag., 1979, Leadership award, Ladies Home Jour., 1980, spl. recognition, Esquire mag., 1984, Elizabeth (Betty) Boyer award, Equity Action League, 1992, Woman Who Dares award, Nat. Coun. Jewish Women, 1993, Woman of Distinction award, Nat. Conf. for Coll. Women Student Leaders, 1993, Colby award for Pub. Svc., Sigma Kappa, 1996, Hummingbird award, Leadership Am., 1996, Tallest Texan award, Houston Chronicle, 2000, Speaking Out for Justice award, AAUW Legal Advocacy Fund, 2001, AAUW Ednl. Found., 2001, Ally award, Possible Woman Leadership Conf., 2001, Sarah Weddington Leadership Conf. named in her honor, Tex. Woman's U., 2001. Mem. Tex. Bar Assn. Office: The Weddington Ctr 709 W 14th St Austin TX 78701-1707 Business E-Mail: sw@weddingtoncenter.com.

**WEDDLE, LAURA MILDRED THOMAS,** retired language educator; b. Keene, Ky., June 28, 1933; d. John Wesley and Elizabeth (Munson) Thomas; m. Leo Franklin Weddle, June 15, 1955; children: Laura Lynn, Leo Jeffrey. BA, Georgetown Coll., 1955; MA, U. Ky., 1959, Morehead State U., 1977, MA, 1986. Asst. prof. Campbellsville (Ky.) Coll., 1961—65, U. Ky. C.C., Somerset, 1965—66, assoc. prof. Prestonsburg, 1966—72, prof., 1972—94; ret. Adv. bd. Nat. Coun. Staff Devel., Washington, 1975—90, David (Ky.) Alternative Sch., 1980—90. Author short stories. Dir. Children's Theater, Prestonsburg, 1970—75; mem. Prestonsburg City Coun., 1973—74. Mem.: Penwomen Am. Avocations: reading, antiques, travel, swimming.

**WEDEL-COWGILL, MILLIE REDMOND,** secondary school educator, performing arts educator, communications educator, education educator; b. Harrisburg, Pa., Aug. 18, 1939; d. Clair L. and Florence (Heiges) Aungst; m. T.S. Redmond, 1956 (div. 1967); children: T.S. Redmond II; m. Frederick L. Wedel, Jr., 1974 (div. 1986); m. Paul R. Cowgill, May 19, 2001. BA, Alaska Meth. U., 1966; MEd, U. Alaska, Anchorage, 1972; postgrad. in comm., Stanford U., Calif., 1975-76. Lic. third class broadcasting, FCC. Profl. actress Charming Models & Models Guild of Phila., 1954-61; asst. dir. devel. in charge pub. rels. Alaska Meth. U., Anchorage, 1966, part-time lectr., 1966, 73; comm. tchr. Anchorage Sch. Dist., 1967-96; owner Wedel Prodns., Anchorage, 1976-86; cons. comms., media and edn., owner Cowgill Cons., 2003—. Pub. rels. staff Alaska Purchase Centennial Exhibit, U.S. Dept. Commerce, 1967; writer gubernatorial campaign, 1971; instr. Chapman Coll., 1990-93; adj. instr. U. Alaska, Anchorage, 1972, 77-79, 89-2001; cons. Cook Inlet Native Assn., 1978, No. Inst., 1979; judge Ark. Press Women's Writing Contest, 1990-91; sec. exec. bd. Alaska Dept. Edn. Profl. Tchg. Practices Commn., 1993-94. Bd. dirs Sta KAKM, Alaska Pub. TV, membership chmn., 1978-80, nat. lay rep. to Pub. Broadcasting Svc. and Nat. Assn. Pub. TV Stas., 1979; bd. dirs. Ednl. Telecom. Consortium for Alaska, 1979, Mid-Hillside Cmty. Coun., Municipality of Anchorage, 1979-80, 83-88, Hillside East Cmty. Coun., 1984-88, pres., 1984-85; rsch. writer, legal asst. Vinson & Elkins, Houston, 1981; v.p., bd. dirs. Inlet View ASD Cmty. Sch., 1994-95, pres., 1995-97; Valley Forge Freedoms Found., Murdoch Scholarships; bd. dirs. Rev. Richard Gay Trust, Alaska and Pa., 1992-2000. Recipient awards for newspapers, lit. mags.; award Nat. Scholastic Press Assn., 1981, 82, 83, 84; Alaska Coun. Econs., 1982, Merits award Alaska Dept. Edn., 1982-93, Legis. commendation State of Alaska, nat. lay del. 1980), Indsl. TV Assn. (San Francisco and Houston 1975-81), Alaska Press Club (chmn. high sch. journalism workshops, 1968-69, 73, awards for sch. newspapers 1972, 74, 77), Alaska Fedn. Press Women (dir. 1978-86, 94-95, pres. 1995-96, h.s. journalism competition youth projects dir., award for brochures 1978, chair youth writing contest 1994-95), World Affairs Coun., Chugach Electric (chair 1990, nomination com. for bd. dirs. 1988-90), Hood Coll. Alaska Alumni Assn., Stanford U. Alumni Club (Alaska pres. 1982-84, 90-92, 99-2000, v.p. 1998-99), Rotary Club of Naples (photographer and asst. program chair 2003), Imperial Golf Course Country Club, Club at Pelican Bay, Naples (Fla.) Philharm. League, Naples Players Theatre Guild, Pelican Bay Women's League, Naples Fla. U. Pa. Club, English Speaking Union. Presbyterian. Home: PO Box 111489 Anchorage AK 99511-1489 Office: Cowgill Cons PO Box 770662 Naples FL 34107-0662

**WEDEPOHL, LEONHARD MARTIN,** electrical engineering educator; b. Pretoria, South Africa, Jan. 26, 1933; s. Martin Willie and Liselotte B.M. (Franz) W.; m. Sylvia A.L. St. Jean; children: Martin, Graham. BSc in Engring., Rand U., 1953; PhD, U. Manchester, Eng., 1957. Registered profl. engr., BC. Planning engr. Escom, Johannesburg, 1957-61; mgr. L.M. Ericson, Pretoria, South Africa, 1961-62; sect. leader Reyrolle, Newcastle, England, 1962-64; prof., head dept. Manchester U., 1964-74; dean engring. U. Man., Winnipeg, Canada, 1974-79; dean applied sci. U. BC, Vancouver, Canada, 1979-85, prof. elec. engring., 1985-97, prof. emeritus, 1998—, dean applied sci. emeritus, 1998—. Mem. Sci. Rsch. Coun., London, 1968-74; dir. Man. Hydro, Winnipeg, 1975-79, BC Hydro, Vancouver, 1980-84, BC Sci. Coun., 1982-84; cons. Horizon Robotics, Saskatoon, 1986; chmn. implementation team Sci. Place, Can., 1985; cons. CEPEL, Rio de Janeiro; adv. Man. High Voltage DC Rsch. Ctr.; tech. advisor RTDS Techs., Inc., Winnipeg, 1994—; head protection devel. Rolls Royce Indsl. Power Group, 1995-96; adj. prof. U. Man., 2002-; co-chair Knowledge Cluster, Okanagan Partnership, Kelowna, Can., 2004-; bd. dirs. Okanagan Partnership; co-chair faculty engring. adv. com. UBC-O. Contbr. articles to sci. jours.; patentee in field. Named Hon. Citizen, City of Winnipeg, 1979. Fellow Instn. Elec. Engrs. (premium 1967), Engring. Inst. Can.; mem. Assn. Profl. Engrs. BC. Avocations: music, cross country skiing, hiking. Office: 1511 Chardonnay Pl Westbank BC Canada V4T 2P9 Business E-Mail: wedepohl@shaw.ca.

**WEDGE, CAROLE C.,** architectural firm executive; B in Environ. Design, U. Colo., 1981; student, Alliance Francaise, 1982; BArch, Boston Archtl. Ctr., 1990. With J. & W. Seligman & Co., 1983—86; joined Sheple Bulfinch Richardson & Abbott, Boston, 1986, assoc., 1996, sr. assoc., 1996, prin., 2000, pres., 2004—. Lectr. in field. Mem.: ALA, AIA, Soc. Coll. and Univ. Planners, Assn. Coll. and Rsch. Librs. Office: Shepley Bulfinch Richardson & Abbott 40 Broad St Boston MA 02109-4306

**WEDGE, CHRIS,** animation director, studio executive; b. 1958; Grad., SUNY, Purchase, 1981; MA, Ohio State U. Stop-motion animator; with MAGI/SynthaVision; v.p. creative devel., founder Blue Sky, Ossining, N.Y. Animator: (films) Tron, 1992, Joe's Apt., 1996, Alien Resurrection, 1997, Bunny, 1998 (Best Animation Oscar award 1999); actor, dir.: (films) Ice Age, 2002, Robots, 2005, Ice Age: The Meltdown, 2006; creator: (films) The Daymaker, Tuber's Two Step, Balloon Guy. Office: c/o Jayson Enguist Blue Sky Studios Inc 44 S Broadway 17th Fl White Plains NY 10601 also: Blue Sky Prodns 100 Executive Blvd Ossining NY 10562-2557 Fax: (914) 259-6505. E-mail: christ@blueskystudios.com.*

**WEDGE, ERIC,** archbishop; b. Fort Wayne, Ind., Jan. 27, 1968; m. Kate Wedge; 1 child, Ava Catherine. Garduate, Wichita St. Univ. Profl. baseball player Boston Red Sox, 1991—92, 1994, Colo. Rockies, 1993; mgr. AAA Buffalo Bison, 2000—03, Cleve. Indians, 2003—. Vol. First Energy Grand Slam Summer Reading Literacy Program, Feed the Need at Cleve. St. Augustine Church, Ronald McDonald House. Office: Cleveland Indians Jacobs Field 2401 Ontario St Cleveland OH 44115-4003*

**WEDGE, MICHAEL T.,** wholesale distribution executive; With BJ's Wholesale Club, Inc., Natick, Mass., 1988—, exec. v.p. club ops., 1997—2002, pres., CEO, 2002—. Office: BJs Wholesale Club Inc 1 Mercer Rd Natick MA 01760-2400 Fax: 508-651-6114.*

**WEDGEWORTH, ANN,** actress; b. Abilene, Tex., Jan. 21, 1935; m. Rip Torn (div.); 1 child, Danae; m. Ernest Martin; 1 child, Dianna. Attended, U. Tex.; BA in Drama, So. Methodist U. Actor: (Broadway debut) Make A Million, 1958, (Broadway appearances) Chapter Two (Tony award), Thieves, Blues for Mr. Charlie, The Last Analysis, (off-Broadway appearances) Line, Chaparal, The Crucible, Days and Nights of Beebee Fenstermaker, Ludlow Fair, The Honest to God Shnozzola, A Lie of the Mind, Elba, The Aunts, The Debutante's Ball, (premiers) In the Moonlight Smile at Pasadena Playhouse, Natural Affection in Pheonix, The Dream in Phila., (toured with nat. cos.) The Sign in Sidney Brustein's Window and Kennedy's Children, (appeared in TV series) Three's Company, The Edge of Night, Another World, Somerset, Filthy Rich, Evening Shade, (TV appearances) All That Glitters, The Equalizer, Roseanne, Bronk, Twilight Zone, Trapper John, M.D.; (TV films) The War Between the Tates, Right to Kill, Georgetown, Fight for Justice: The Nancy Conn Story, Bogie, A Stranger Waits; (films) Handle With Care (Nat. Soc. Film Critics award), Thieves, Bang the Drum Slowly, Scarecrow, Catamount Killing, Law and Disorder, One Summer Love, Dragon-Fly, Birch Intervals, Soggy Bottom, USA, No Small Affair, Sweet Dreams, The Mens Club, A Tiger's Tale, Made in Heaven, Far North, Miss Firecracker, Green Card, Steel Magnolias, Love and a 45, The Whole Wide World, The Hunter's

Moon, Hard Promises, Andy, My Science Project, The Hawk is Dying; TV host Evening at the Improv, A&E; actor: (play) Mother and Child, The Glass Menagerie. Address: 70 Riverside Dr Apt 6E New York NY 10024-5716

**WEDGWOOD, RUTH,** law educator, international affairs expert; b. NYC; d. Morris P. and Anne (Williams) Glushien; m. Josiah Francis Wedgwood; May 29, 1982; 1 child, Josiah Ruskin Wedgwood. BA magna cum laude, Harvard U., 1972; fellow, London Sch. Econs., 1972—73; JD, Yale U., 1976. Bar: D.C., N.Y., U.S. Supreme Ct. Law clk. to judge Henry Friendly U.S. Ct. Appeals (2d cir.), N.Y.C., 1976—77; law clk. to justice Harry Blackmun U.S. Supreme Ct., Washington, 1977—78; apl. asst. to asst. atty. gen. U.S. Dept. Justice, Washington, 1978—80; asst. U.S. atty. U.S. Dist. Ct. (so. dist.) N.Y., N.Y.C., 1980—86; prof. law Yale U., New Haven, 1986—2002, fellow Inst. for Social and Policy Studies, 1989—2002; fellow Berkeley Coll., Yale U., 1989—. Mem. Sec. of State's Adv. Com. Internat. Law, 1993—; sr. fellow for internat orgns. and law Coun. Fgn. Rels., 1994—2004; Charles Stockton prof. internat. law U.S. Naval War Coll., Newport, RI, 1998—99; mem. Hart-Rudman Commn. on Nat. Security in the 21st Century, Nat. Sec. Study Group, Dept. Def. Adv. Comm., 1999—2001; mem. acad. adv. com. to spl. rep. UN Sec.-Gen. for Children and Armed Conflict, 1999—2002; dir. studies Am. Soc. Internat. Law, 2000—03; guest scholar U.S. Inst. Peace, 2001—02; dir. studies Hague Acad. Internat. Law, 2001—02; elected U.S. mem. UN Human Rights Com., Geneva, 2002—; mem. Hist. Rev. Panel, adv. to dir. CIA, 2002—; mem. Def. Policy Bd., advisor to U.S. Sec. Def., 2002—; prof. du Droit internat. U. Paris I (Sorbonne), 2004; Berlin Prize fellow Am. Acad., 2006. Exec. editor Yale Law Jour., 1975-76; author: The Revolutionary Martyrdom of Jonathan Robbins, 1990, The Use of Force in International Affairs, 1992, American National Interest and the United Nations, 1996, Toward an International Criminal Court?, 1999, After Dayton: Lessons of the Bosnian Peace Process, 1999; mem. bd. editors Yale Jour. Law and Humanities, 1988-98, Am. Jour. Internat. Law, 1998-, World Policy Jour. (New Sch. Social Rsch.), 2001—, Am. Interest, 2005—, The Nat. Interest, 2005—, adv. coun.; contbr. articles to profl jours. and popular publs. including N.Y. Times, Washington Post, Christian Sci. Monitor, Internat. Herald Tribune, Wall St. Jour., Washington Times, Fin. Times, L.A. Times, Die Zeit, Fgn. Affairs, Fgn. Policy, Nat. Interest, Time mag.; commentator for CNN, PBS, Fox, Nat. Pub. Radio, MSNBC, BBC, Lehrer News Hour, PBS. Prin. rapporteur U.S. Atty. Gen.'s Guidelines on FBI Undercover Ops., Informant Use and Racketeering and Gen. Crime Investigations, 1980; bd. dirs. Lawyers Com. for Human Rights, N.Y.C., 1988-94; mem. policy adv. com. UN Assn. U.S.A., 1998-2003; bd. dirs. Freedom House, 2003-, UN Watch, 2004—. Recipient Israel Peres prize, 1976, Disting. Contbn. to Internat. Law award N.Y. State Bar Assn., 2000; Ford Found. Rsch. grantee; Rockefeller Found. fellow; Am. Acad. Berlin prize fellow, 2006. Mem. ABA (standing com. on law and nat. security 2002—, coun. Internat. Law sect. 2003—), Am. Law Inst., Am. Soc. Internat. Law (exec. com. 1995-98, v.p. 2005—), Internat. Law Assn. (v.p. 1994—, program chmn. Am. br. 1992), Assn. Am. Law Sch. (chmn. sect. internat. law 1995-96), Assn. Bar City N.Y. (chmn. arms control and internat. security affairs com. 1989-92, chmn. internat. affairs coun. 1992-95, exec. com. 1995-99), Union Internationale des Avocats, U.S.A. (chpt. bd. govs. 1993-98), Women in Internat. Security (bd. dirs. 2006—), Ctr. for Global Prosperity (bd. dirs. 2006—), Coun. on Fgn. Rels., Internat. Inst. for Strategic Studies, Elizabethan Club, Mory's Assn., Yale Club (N.Y.C.). Office: Johns Hopkins Sch Advanced Internat Studies 1619 Massachusetts Ave NW Washington DC 20036 Office Phone: 202-663-5666 Business E-Mail: rwedgwood@jhu.edu. *Notable cases include: U.S. vs. Kostadinov, involving a Bulgarian spy traded for 25 East Bloc detainees; U.S. vs. Kampiles, involving government employee who gave satellite secrets to the Soviet Union; U.S. vs. Gold, Orosz, Egerhazi and Kompar, involving a million dollar racketeering/landlord arson ring in N.Y.C. that defrauded Lloyd's of London Sasse Syndicate; U.S. vs. Kazemzadeh and DeVelasco, involving pub. corruption in N.Y.C. Health and Hospitals Corporation and the fed. WIC program.*

**WEDLAKE, PHILIP RUSSELL, JR.,** school system administrator; b. San Francisco, Aug. 1, 1945; s. Philip R. and Agnes L. Wedlake; children: Jeremy Michael, Dawn M. BA, Biola U., 1968; MA in ednl. curriculum, Cal. Poly, 1973, MA in ednl. Supr., 1978; EdD, Brigham Young U., 1983. Resource tchr. Santa Maria Bonita Sch. Dist., Santa Maria, Calif., 1971—81; prin. Parkview Sch., Taft City Sch. Dist., Taft, Calif., 1981—86; coord. assessment Turlock Unified Sch. Dist., Turlock, Calif., 1986—98; asst. supr. Los Banos Unified Sch. Dist., Los Banos, Calif., 1998—2002; supr. assessment Ceres Unified Sch. Dist., Ceres, Calif., 2002—. Bd. admin. Assn. Calif. Sch., Calif., 1981—; pres. Calif. Cooperative Projects Dir., Calif., 1991—92. Bd. mem. United Way, Merced, Calif., 1999—2002. SP4 U.S. Army, 1968—70, Korea. Named Curriculum Administrator of Yr., ACSA- Region 9, 2002. Mem.: Assn. Calif. Sch. Admin., Assn. Supervision and Curriculum Devel. Republican. Avocations: reading, camping. Home: 1360 Shady Ln # 615 Turlock CA 95382 Office: Ceres Unified Sch Dist 2503 Lawrence St Ceres CA 95307 Office Phone: 209-538-0164. Business E-Mail: pwedlake@ceres.k12.ca.us.

**WEDNER, H. JAMES,** physician, researcher; b. Pitts., May 12, 1941; s. Benjamin Mayer and Lucille Ruth (Jacobs) W.; m. Maureen Patricia Martin, June 18, 1978; children: Bryna Kimberly, Jason Oliver. BS, Cornell U., 1963; MD, Cornell Med. Coll., 1967. Intern Barnes Hosp., St. Louis, 1967—68; resident internal medicine Washington U. Med. Sch., St. Louis, 1970—71, fellow allergy and immunology, 1971—73; lt. comdr. USPHS, Govenor's Island, NY, 1968—70; prof. medicine Washington U. Med. Sch., St. Louis, 1990—, dir. tng. program allergy and immunology, 1986—95, 2001—, chief clin. allergy and immunology, 1988—, med. dir. The Asthma and Allergy Ctr., 2000—, acting chief Divsn. Allergy and Clin. Immunology, 2001—02, chief, 2002—. vis. prof. Am. Coll. of Allergy and Immunology, Little Rock, 1991, U. Buffalo Med. Sch., 1999; William Pierson vis. prof. Ea. Va. Med. Sch., 2003; prin. investigator psychosocial aspects of asthma, St. Louis Asthma Study Unit; chmn. steering com. Nat. Coop. Inner City Asthma Study; prin. investigator Fungal Allergies Innercity Homes. Editor: Allergy: Theory and Practice, 1984, 2d rev. edit., 1991; mem. editl. bd. Jour. Immunology, 1980-82, Jour. Allergy and Clin. Immunology, 1991-96; assoc. editor Anaphylaxis and Drug Allergy Current Allergy Reports, 2000—; sect. editor Anaplylaxis and Drug Allergy, Current Allergy and Asthma Reports Fellow Am. Acad. Allergy Asthma Immunology; mem. Internat. Soc. Immunopharmacology, Am. Coll. Allergy Asthma Immunology, Am. Assn. Immunology, Clin. Immunology Soc., European Acad. Allergology and Clin. Immunology. Achievements include initial description of Parthenium hysterophruis allergy; research on asthma and the psychosocial aspects of asthma, molecular characterization of plant and fungal allergens and the role of fungi in asthma. Office: Washington U Med Sch Campus Box 8122 660 S Euclid Ave Saint Louis MO 63110-1010 Office Phone: 314-454-7937. Personal E-Mail: wednerj@att.net. Business E-Mail: jwedner@im.wustl.edu.

**WEE, CHRISTINE DIJOS,** elementary school educator; b. Honolulu, Jan. 8, 1968; d. Cosme Dayne and Victoria Amparo Dijos; m. Phillip Ying Kin Wee, July 15, 2000; children: Deanna Rae Patacsil, Logan Wayne. BEd, U. Hawaii, Manoa, 1991. Cert. tchr. Hawaii, prof. diploma in elem. edn. Univ. Hawaii, 1992. Kindergarten tchr. Island Paradise Sch., Honolulu, 1992—93, Pauoa Elem. Sch., Honolulu, 1993—94, choral dir., 1997—2005, 6th grade tchr., 1994—2002, 5th grade tchr., 2003—04, 3d grade tchr., 2004—; spl. edn. summer sch. aide Wailupe Valley Elem. Sch., Honolulu; Challenger Ctr.-trained educator, NASA program Barber's Point Elem. Sch., Kapolei, Hawaii, 1996—2002. Regional conf. del. Sch.-to-Work, Honolulu, 1998; cadre mem. Roosevelt Complex Writing Inst., Honolulu, 1999, student svcs. coord., 2002—03; mem. music action rsch. team Hawaii State Dept. Edn., 1999—2001. Mem. coun. Sch. Cmty.-Based Mgmt. Coun., Pauoa Elem. Sch., 2001—03; vol., chmn. Honolulu Dist. Choral Festival, 1994—2002, 2005; mem. ch. choir; asst. dir. Sweet Adelines Internat.; bd. mem. Pauoa Elem. Sch. PTA, 1996—97, 2005—06. Mem.: Hawaii Orff-Schulwerk Assn., Am. Choral Dirs. Assn., Hawaii State Tchrs. Assn. (union rep. 1995—96, 2000—01), Hawaii Music Educators Assn. (3d v.p. 2000—02, chmn. 2001—02), Delta

Kappa Gamma. Avocations: walking, collecting keychains and unicorns, singing. Home: 823 9th Ave Honolulu HI 96816 Office: Pauoa Elem Sch 2301 Pauoa Rd Honolulu HI 96813 E-mail: tiniwee86@hawaii.rr.com.

**WEED, EDWARD REILLY,** marketing executive; b. Chgo., Jan. 25, 1940; s. Cornelius Cahill and Adelaide E. (Reilly) W.; m. Lawrie Irving Bowes, Feb. 2, 1969. Student, Fordham U., 1959-61, Loyola U., 1961-62. Account exec. Leo Burnett Co., Chgo., 1961-71; pres., corp. officer GDC Ad Inc., Miami, Fla., 1971-74; v.p., account supr D'Arcy Mac Manus & Masius, Chgo., 1975; group v.p. mktg. Hart Schaffner & Marx (Hartmarx), Chgo.; pres. Hart Svcs., Inc., 1975-82; v.p mktg. Tishman, 1983-86; exec. v.p. Hannah Marine, 1986-87; exec. v.p., dir. U.S. Auction, 1988-92; v.p. mktg. Telemedia, 1992-95; mng. dir. Brochure Assocs./The Consultancy, Lake Geneva, Wis., 1996—. Dir. First Nat. Bank So. Miami; seminar instr. Grad. Sch. Notre Dame U., South Bend, Ind.; guest faculty Loyola U., Chgo., Fla. Internat. U. Author, publisher: Genealogical Family History, editor manuscript reviewer: several books; contbr. articles to profl. jours. Trustee Latin Sch. Found., 1976—, The Admiral, 1999—; bd. dirs. North Ave. Day Nursery, 1969-73, Santa for Poor, 1975-87, Off-the-Street Club, 1982-87, Chgo. Boys' and Girls' Clubs, 1983-87, Map Inc., 1988-98, Geneva Lake Conservancy, 1994—; adv. bd. Fiduciary Mgmt. Assocs., 1998-2006. With Ill. N.G. Recipient Chi Ad Club award. Mem.: Casino Club, Lake Geneva Country Club. Republican. Roman Catholic. Office: The Consultancy 3638 Snake Rd Lake Geneva WI 53147

**WEED, ROGER OREN,** rehabilitation services professional, educator; b. Bend, Oreg., Feb. 2, 1944; s. Chester Elbert and Ruth Marie (Urie) W.; m. Paula J. Keller. BS in Sociology, U. Oreg., 1967, MS in Rehab. Counseling, 1969; PhD in Rehab. Counseling, U. Ga., 1986. Cert. rehab. counselor; cert. disability mgmt. specialist; lic. profl. counselor; cert. case mgr., cert. life care planner. Vocat. rehab. counselor State of Alaska, Anchorage, 1969-71; instr. U. Alaska, Anchorage, 1970-76; counselor Langdon Psychiat. Clinic, Anchorage, 1971-74; from asst. dir. to exec. dir. Hope Cottages, Anchorage, 1974-79; owner Profl. Resources Group, Anchorage, 1978-80; mng. ptnr. Collins, Weed & Assocs., 1980-84; assoc. dir. Ctr. for Rehab. Tech. Ga. Tech. U., Atlanta, 1986-87; catastrophic injury rehab. Weed & Assocs., Atlanta, 1984—; from asst. prof. to prof. Ga. State U., Atlanta, 1987—. Adj. faculty Ga. Inst. Tech.; courtesy faculty U. Fla., 1996—. Co-author: Vocational Expert Handbook, 1986, Transferable Work Skills, 1988, Life Care Planning: Spinal Cord Injured, 1989, 2d edit. 1994, Life Care Planning: Head Injured, 1994, Life Care Planning for the Amputee, 1992, Rehab Cons. Handbook, 1994, rev. edit., 2001; editor: Life Care Planning and Case Mgmt. Handbook, 1999 (rev., 2004); assoc. editor Jour. Lifecare Planning, 2002—; mem. editl. bd. Jour. of Pvt. Sector Rehab., 1986—, Jour. Forensic Vocational Analysis; contbr. articles to profl. jour. Bd. dirs. Found. for Life Care Planning Rsch. Recipient Gov.'s award Gov.'s Com. on Employment, Alaska, 1982, Goldpan Svc. award Gov.'s Com. on Employment, Alaska, 1978, Profl. Svc. award Am. Rehab. Counselors Assn., 1993. Fellow Nat. Rehab. Assn. (chmn. legis. com., bd. dir. met. Atlanta chpt. 1987-89, pres. Pacific region 1983-85, Pres.'s award Pacific region 1986), Internat. Assn. Rehab. Profls. (chmn. resh. and tng. com. 1988-93, pres. 1994-95, named Educator of Yr. 1991, 97, Lifetime Achievement award 2004), Internat. Life Care Planning (Ann. Conf. Lifetime Achievement award 2005, Disting. Prof. award 2006), Nat. Brain Injury Assn., Pvt. Rehab. Suppliers Ga., Rehab. Engring. Soc. N.Am., Anchorage Amateur Radio Club Republican. Methodist. Avocations: sailing, skiing, bicycling, flying, computers. Office: Ga State U Coll Edn Dept Counseling/Psychol Svc 9th Fl Atlanta GA 30303

**WEEDIN, JAMES FRANK,** biology professor, researcher; b. San Antonio, Tex., Dec. 17, 1949; m. Teresa Faye Johnson, Dec. 30, 1972. BA, San Antonio Coll., Tex., 1969; BA, U. Tex., Austin, 1975; MS, Sul Ross State U., Alpine, Tex., 1976. Prof. C.C. of Aurora, Colo., 1981—, sci. divsn. chair, 1985—93. Bot. cons. Tex. Natural Areas Survey, Austin, 1976—77. Author: (book) Cacti of the Trans-Pecos and Adjacent Areas (SW Book award Border Regional Libr. Assn., 2005), A Field Guide to the Cacti of Texas, (profl. papers) American Jour. Botany, Southwestern Naturalist, Annals of the Mo. Botanical Gardens. Mem. nursing adv. bd. Pickens Tech. Ctr., Aurora, 1982—2006. Named Faculty of Yr., C.C. of Aurora, 1990; recipient Excellence award, U. Tex. Nat. Inst. Staff and Orgnl. Devel., 1991, Master Tchr. award, U. Tex. Nat. Inst. Staff and Faculty Devel., 1991; grantee, U. Tex.-Austin, 1971, Chihuahuan Desert Rsch. Inst., 1975, Cmty. Colls. Colo., 1985. Mem.: Cactus and Succulent Soc. Am. (assoc.), Southwestern Assn. Naturalists (assoc.), Western Interior Paleontol. Soc. (assoc.), Colo. Cactus and Succulent Soc. (assoc.; v.p. 1988—89). Avocations: hiking, camping, photography, travel. Home: 1189 Norfolk St Aurora CO 80011 Office: Cmty Coll of Aurora 16000 E CentreTech Pkwy Aurora CO 80011 Office Phone: 303-361-7398. Office Fax: 303-361-7374. Personal E-Mail: weedin@comcast.net. Business E-Mail: jim.weedin@ccaurora.edu

**WEEKLEY, FREDERICK CLAY, JR.,** lawyer; b. San Antonio, Aug. 29, 1939; s. F. Clay and Topsy (Stevens) W.; m. Lynda Freeman; children: Amber Lee Carothers, Caroline Lee. BBA, Baylor U., 1962, JD, 1963; LLM, NYU, 1969. Bar: Tex. 1963. Ptnr. Bracewell & Patterson, Houston, 1974-90; atty. Bank One, Tex., N.A., 1990-98; ptnr. Shannon, Gracey, Ratliff & Miller, LLP, Ft. Worth, 1999—. Mem. coun. real property, probate and trust law sect., State Bar of Tex., 1987-90; mem. adminstrv. coun. trust divsn. Tex. Bankers Assn., 1992-95, chmn. legis. com., 1992-95. Mem. Commn. Probate Law Examiners, Tex. Bd. Legal Specialization, 1978-82. Fellow Am. Coll. Trust and Estate Counsel. Home: 1821 Mossy Oak St Arlington TX 76012-5619 Office: 777 Main St Fort Worth TX 76102 Business E-Mail: fweekley@shannongracey.com.

**WEEKLEY, JUDY LIDDINGTON,** special education educator; b. Tacoma, Wash., Dec. 18, 1956; d. William Raymond and Shirley Charlotte Liddington; m. John Weekley, June 27, 1980 (dec. Feb. 1996). BA, Southeastern La. U., 1978, MEd, 1984. Tchr. Jefferson Parish Pub. Sch. Sys., Harvey, La., 1978—2002, Individual Edn. plan specialist, 2002—; instr., lectr. Our Lady Holy Cross Coll., New Orleans, 1992—. Presenter in field; cons. in field. Dir. area games, coach Spl. Olympics, La., 1978—92. Recipient Excellence in Tchg. award, C. of C., 1988, 1990, Spl. Edn. Tchr. of Yr., 1999; grantee, Jefferson Parish Pub. Sch. Sys., 1990, 1995. Mem.: Coun. Exceptional Children (Tchr. of Yr. La. 2001), Phi Delta Kappa (bd. dirs. 1992—2003, editor 1992—2003). Methodist. Avocations: gardening, cooking, music, dance, computer and video creations. Home: 3817 Lake Providence Dr Harvey LA 70058 Office Phone: 504-349-8668. Personal E-Mail: judyweek@aol.com.

**WEEKS, ALBERT LOREN,** writer, educator, journalist; b. Highland Park, Mich., Mar. 28, 1923; s. Albert Loren and Vera Grace (Jarvis) W. Student, U. Mich., 1942-43; MA, U. Chgo., 1949; PhD, Columbia U., 1965; cert., Russian Inst., 1960. Reporter Chgo. City News Bur., 1946; polit. analyst U.S. Dept. State, 1950-53, Free Europe Com., Inc., 1953-56; editorial asst. Newsweek mag., 1957-58; Russian tech. glossary compiler McGraw-Hill Book Co., 1960-61; prof. continuing edn. NYU, 1959-89. Lectr. U.S. diplomatic history and soviet govt. Columbia U., 1951-52; mem. adv. coun. Nat. Strategy Info. Ctr., 1979-89; instr. Ringling Sch. Art and Design, 1991—; pub. spkr. S.W. Fla. Host: A Week's View of Red Press, Sta. WNBC, 1965-68; series Myths That Rule America, NBC-TV, 1979-82; author: Reading American History, 1963, The First Bolshevik: A Political Biography of Peter Tkachev, 1968, The Other Side of Coexistence: An Analysis of Russian Foreign Policy, 1970, Andrei Sakharov and The Soviet Dissidents, 1975, The Troubled Detente, 1976, Solzhenitsyn's One Day in the Life of Ivan Denisovich, 1976, Myths That Rule America, 1980, War and Peace: Soviet Russia Speaks, 1983; editor/compiler Brassey's Soviet and Communist Quotations, 1987, The Soviet Nomenklatura, 1987-1991, Stalin's Other War: Soviet Grand Strategy 1939-1941, 2002, Russia's Life-Saver: Lend-Lease Aid to the USSR in World War II; internat. affairs editor Def. Sci. mag., 1982-85; columnist Def. Report, 1982-90; contbr. articles to N.Y. Times, New Republic, New Leader, Annals, Russian, Slavic revs., Christian Sci. Monitor,

Problems of Communism, Survey, Mil. Intelligence, Strategic Rev., World War II mag., Air Univ. Rev., L.A. Times, Washington Times, Orbis, Global Affairs, Panorama, Sarasota Herald-Tribune, Bradenton Herald, Defense and Diplomacy, Am. Intelligence Jour., USA Today, Rossiiskiye Vesti, Vechernii Vladimir, CityTempo mag., Modern Age mag. Home: 4884 Kestral Park Cir Sarasota FL 34231-3369 E-mail: aweeks1@compuserve.com.

**WEEKS, ARTHUR ANDREW,** lawyer, educator; b. Hanceville, Ala., Dec. 2, 1914; s. A.A. and Anna S. (Seibert) W.; m. Carol P. Weeks; children: John David, Carol Christine, Nancy Anna. AB, Samford U., 1936; LL.B., JD, U. Ala., 1939; LL.M., Duke U., 1950; LL.D. (hon.), Widener U., 1980. Bar: Ala. 1939, Tenn. 1948. Sole practice, Birmingham, Ala., 1939-41, 1946-47, 1954-61; dean, prof. law Cumberland U. Sch. Law, 1947-54; dean, prof. Samford U., 1961-72, prof. law, 1972-74; Cumberland Sch. Law, Samford U., 1984—, Del. Sch. Law of Widener U., Wilmington, 1974-82, dean, 1974-80, interim dean, 1982-83, dean emeritus, prof., 1983—; ret. Served to capt. AUS, 1941-46. Mem. ABA, Tenn. Bar Assn., Ala. Bar Assn., Birmingham Bar Assn., Del. Bar Assn. (assoc.), Phi Alpha Delta, Phi Kappa Phi, Delta Theta Phi Home: 400 University Park Dr Apt 445 Birmingham AL 35209-6482

**WEEKS, CLIFFORD MYERS,** musician, academic administrator; b. N.Y.C., Apr. 15, 1938; s. Vernal C. and Adeline (Campbell) W.; m. Ethel Lynn Fleming, Oct. 26, 1963 (dec. 1982); children: Clifford M. Jr., Michele Lynn. Diploma in Arranging and Composition, Berklee Coll. Music, 1962; MusB magna cum laude, Boston Conservatory Music, 1963, MusM, 1975; cert. in edn. administrn., Boston State Coll., 1977. Cert. secondary sch. administr. and tchr. music, Mass. Tchr. music Boston Pub. Schs., 1964-74, condr. All-City Stage Band, 1972-79, administrv. asst. to asst. supt., 1974-75, coordinator instrumental music, 1975-79, asst. prin., 1979, administrv. asst. to asst. supt., 1979-96, acting community supt., 1983, cluster coord., 1996-2001, exec. asst. supt. office, 2001—03; ret., 2003. Arranger, composer, trombonist, 1963—; condr. Boston Coll. Jazz and Stage Band, Chestnut Hill, Mass., 1976-78. Composer Tryptych for tuba and piano, 1971, (oratorio) The King-Life and Teachings of Dr. Martin Luther King Jr., 1976; composer, arranger various jazz compositions, 1975. Mem. Medford (Mass.) Jaycees, 1975-76; adv. bd. Roxbury (Mass.) Boys and Girls Club, 1970—, Berklee Coll. Music, Boston, 1972. Recipient Mayor's Parkman Club award, 1999, Suskind Young at Art award Wang Ctr. Boston Theatres, 2001. Mem. Boston Assn. Sch. Adminstrs. and Suprs. (adminstrs. union 1997—), Boston Tchrs. Union, Black Educators Alliance Mass. (treas. 1972-76, award 1976), ASCAP, Adminstrv. Assts. Assn. (chmn. local chpt. 1982—), Assn. for Supervision and Curriculum Devel., Omega Psi Phi. Methodist.

**WEEKS, DAVID FRANK,** foundation administrator; b. Salt Lake City, Sept. 9, 1926; s. Frank Harold and Myrtle June (Larsen) W.; m. Betty Alice Tellin, Aug. 14, 1949; children: David Rice, Clayton Frank. Student, So. Meth. U., 1945, U. Tex., 1946; BS (Union Pacific Carl Raymond Gray scholar), U. Idaho, 1949; HHD (hon.), U. Louisville, 1993. Pres. Assoc. Students U. Idaho, 1948-49; announcer Sta. KBIO, Burley, Idaho, 1949; legor. Nat. Found. for Infantile Paralysis, Boise, 1949-53, asst. to nat. dir. fund raising N.Y.C., 1953-57; asst. nat. dir. March of Dimes, N.Y.C., 1957-59; account exec. Kersting, Brown & Co., N.Y.C., 1959-61; exec. dir. Rsch. to Prevent Blindness, Inc., N.Y.C., 1961-70, exec. v.p., 1970-83, pres., 1983-99, chmn. bd. dirs., 1999—; pres., trustee RPB Endowment Fund Inc., N.Y.C., 1988—2002; mem. borough coun. Borough of Ho-Ho-Kus, NJ, 1966-68, mayor, 1968-75; consumer rep. subcom. ophthalmic prostheses HEW, 1976-79; chmn., trustee RPB Endowment Fund, Inc., NYC, 2002—. Cons. Bur. Med. Devices, FDA, 1977-80; mem. nat. adv. eye coun. NIH, HHS, 1985-90. Mem. Ho-Ho-Kus Planning Bd., 1962-65, chmn., 1965; mem. Zoning Bd., 1975-85, Bergen County (N.J.) Ethics Bd., 1977-82; founder, pres. Ho-Ho-Kus Republican Club, 1983-86. Served with USN, 1944-46. Recipient Bronze Palm Eagle Scout award Boy Scouts Am., 1941, Disting. Pub. Svc. award Am. Acad. Ophthalmology and Otolaryngology, 1976, cert. of recognition Johns Hopkins U. Schs. Medicine, Hygiene and Pub. Health, 1984, Nat. Vision Rsch. Leadership award Assn. U. Profs. Ophthalmology, 1989, Disting. Svc. award Johns Hopkins Med. Instns.-Wilmer Ophthal. Inst., 1989, Disting. Svc. award Am. Acad. Ophthalmology, 1995; named Ky. col., 1969, U. of Idaho Alumni Hall of Fame award, 1992. Mem. Assn. Rsch. in Vision and Ophthalmology (hon.), Pan Am. Ophthalmol. Assn. (assoc.), Am. Soc. Assn. Execs., Internat. Assn. Eye Rsch., Bergen County Mayors Assn. (pres. 1975-77), Assn. U. Profs. Ophthalmology (hon.), Met. Club. Home: 4058 NW Northcliff Bend OR 97701-8248 Office: Rsch Prevent Blindness 645 Madison Ave New York NY 10022-1010

**WEEKS, GERALD,** psychologist, educator; b. Morehead City, NC, Nov. 20, 1948; s. Marion G. and Ada (Willis) W. BA in Philosophy and Psychology, East Carolina U., 1971, MA in Gen. Psychology, 1973; PhD in Clin. Psychology, Ga. State U., 1979. Diplomate Am. Bd. Profl. Psychology (pres. 1987-88, bd. dirs. 1982-87), Am. Bd. Family Psychology, Am. Bd. Sexology; cert. marital and family therapist; lic. practicing psychologist, Nev., Pa. Intern in family therapy Harlem Valley Psychiat. Ctr., Wingdale, NY, 1978-79; assoc. prof. psychology U. N.C., Wilmington, 1979-85; dir. tng. Penn Coun. for Relationships, 1985—; clin. asst. prof. psychology Sch. Medicine U. Pa., Phila., 1985-87, clin. assoc. prof., 1988-98; chair, prof. dept. counseling U. Nev.-Las Vegas, 1999—. Pvt. practice Carolina Ob-gyn. Ctr., Wilmington, 1980-85. Author: Paradoxical Therapy, 1982, Treating Couples: The Intersystem Model of the Marriage Council of Philadelphia, 1989, Promoting Change through Paradoxical Therapy, 1991, Paradoxical Psychotherapy: Theory and Practice with Individuals, Couples, and Families, 1982; co-author: (with L. L'Abate) Family Therapy: Basic Concepts and Terms, 1985, (with L. L'Abate) Integrating Sex and Marital Therapy: A Clinicians Guide, 1987, Erectile Dysfunction, 2000, (with N. Gambescia) Couples in Treatment, 1992, rev. edit., 2001, Integrative Solutions: Treating Common Problems in Couple's Therapy, 1995, (with Hof and Trent) Focused Genograms: Intergenerational Assessment of Individuals, Couples and Families, 1999, (with Demaria & Ltof) Hypoactive Sexual Desire, 2002, Treating Infidelity, 2004, (with Gambescia and Jenkins) Handbook of Family Therapy, 2003, (with Odell and Methuen) If Only I Had Known: Common Mistakes in Couples Therapy, 2004; contbr. articles to profl. jours. Fellow Am. Assn. Marital and Family Therapy (clin. mem., nat. adv. bd., approved supr.); mem. APA, Acad. Family Psychology, Interpersonal and Social Skills Assn. (founding mem.), Acad. Psychologists in Marital, Sex, and Family Therapy. Office: U Nev Dept Counseling PO Box 453045 4505 S Maryland Pky Las Vegas NV 89154-3045 Office Phone: 702-895-1392. Business E-Mail: gerald.weeks@unlv.edu.

**WEEKS, JANET HEALY,** retired supreme court justice; b. Quincy, Mass., Oct. 19, 1932; d. John Francis and Sheila Josephine (Jackson) Healy; m. George Weeks, Aug. 29, 1959; children: Susan, George. AB in chemistry, Emmanuel Coll., Boston, 1954; JD, Boston Coll., 1958; LLD (hon.), U. Guam, 1984. Bar: Mass. 1958, Guam 1972. Trial atty. U.S. Dept. Justice, Washington, 1958-60, Trapp & Gayle, Agana, Guam, 1971-73; ptnr. Trapp, Gayle, Teker, Weeks & Freidman, Agana, 1973-75; judge Superior Ct. Guam, Agana, 1975-96; assoc. justice Guam Supreme Ct., Guam, 1996-99, retired assoc. justice Guam, 1999. Chmn. task force crts., prosecution and def. Terr. Crime Commn., 1973-76; mem. Terr. Crime Commn. Bd., 1975-76, Guam Law Revision Commn., 1981—; rep. Nat. Conf. State Trial Judges, 1982. Mem. Cath. Sch. Bd. Guam, 1973. Mem. ABA, Nat. Assn. Women Judges (charter), Am. Judges Assn., Fed. Bar Assn. (chpt. sec. 1974), Guam Bar Assn., Internat. Club (Guam). Office: 120 W Obrien Dr Hagatna GU 96910-5174

**WEEKS, JOHN ROBERT,** geographer, social studies educator; b. Sacramento, June 1, 1944; s. Robert Louis and Thelma Hope (Evans) W.; m. Deanna Jean Hosea, May 16, 1965; children: John Robert, Gregory, Jennifer. AB, U. Calif., Berkeley, 1966, MA, 1969, PhD, 1972. Asst. prof. sociology Mich. State U., East Lansing, 1971-74, San Diego State U., 1974-78, assoc. prof., 1978-81, prof., 1981-92, prof. geography, 1992—, chmn. dept., 1978-85; adminstrv. dir. Internat. Population Ctr., 1985—; clin. prof. family & preventive medicine U. Calif. Sch. Medicine, San Diego, 1998—. Vis. rsch. demographer U. Calif., Berkeley, 1972; cons. Allied Home Health Assn.,

1978-80, Area Agy. on Aging, San Diego, 1979-81, Los Angeles Regional Family Planning Coun., 1986—, East County Econ. Devel. Coun., 1986—, UN Food and Agrl. Orgn., 2002—. Author: Teenage Marriages, 1976, Population, 9th edit., 2005, Aging, 1984, Demography of Islamic Nations, 1988, High Fertility Among Indochinese Refuges, 1989, Demographic Dynamics of the U.S.-Mex. Border, 1992. Grantee USPHS, 1983-84, 87-88, 88-89, 90—, U.S. Administrn. on Aging, 1979-80, U.S. Bur. of Census, 1988-89, Andrew W. Mellon Found., 1998-2001, NSF, 2001—, NICHD, 2004—; trainee USPHS, 1967-71. Mem. Population Assn. Am., Am. Sociol. Assn., Internat. Union for Sci. Study Population, Am. Assn. Geographers. Democrat. Office: San Diego State U Dept Geography San Diego CA 92182 Office Phone: 619-594-8040. E-mail: john.weeks@sdsu.edu.

**WEEKS, LEE,** hotel executive; Exec. mgr. Ritz-Carlton, Naples, Fla.; v.p. resort ops. Grand Wailea (Hawaii) Resort & Spa; v.p. ops. Atlantis Resort and Casino, Nassau, Bahamas; gen. mgr. LaPlaya Beach Resort, Naples, Fla.; pres., owner Coral Beach, Naples; pres., COO Coral Beach Hotels, Naples. Office: 9180 Galleria Ct Ste 600 Naples FL 34109-4385

**WEEKS, MARTA JOAN,** retired priest; b. Buenos Aires, May 24, 1930; arrived in U.S., 1932; d. Frederick Albert and Anne (Newman) Sutton; m. Lewis Austin Weeks, Aug. 17, 1951; children: Kermit Austin, Leslie Anne. BA in Polit. Sci., Stanford U., 1951; MDiv, Episcopal Theol. Sem. S.W., 1991; LHD (hon.), U. Utah, 2005; DDiv (hon.), Episcop. Theol. Sem. of the S.W., 2006. Ordained priest Episcopal Ch., 1992. Legal libr., sec. Mene Grande Oil Co., Caracas, Venezuela, 1948; English tchr. Centro-Venezolano Americano, Caracas, 1948; sec. Household Fin. Corp., Salt Lake City, 1951; legal sec. McKelvey & McKelvey Attys., Durango, Colo., 1952; sec., dir. Weeks Air Mus., Miami, Fla., 1985—2001; chaplain Jackson Meml. Hosp., 1992-93; interim asst. St. James Episcopal Ch., Salt Lake City, 1994-95; assisting priest St. Andrew's Episcopal Ch., Miami, Fla., 1999—2002; priest-at-large Episcopal Diocese of S.E. Fla., 2002—04. Trustee Beloit Coll., Wis., 1980—82, U. Miami, 1983—88, 1995—, Bishop Gray Inns, Lake Worth and Davenport, Fla., 1992—2002; advisor Ctr. for Sexuality and Religion, 1997—; mem. adv. coun. U. Utah, 1998—; dir. S.E. Fla. Episcopal Found., 2002—05. Mem.: Am. Soc. Order St. John of Jerusalem. Address: 7350 SW 162nd St Miami FL 33157-3820 Personal E-mail: msweeks@attglobal.net.

**WEEKS, PATSY ANN LANDRY,** librarian, educator; b. Luling, Tex., Mar. 3, 1930; d. Lee and Mattie Wood (Callihan) Landry; m. Arnett S. Weeks, Dec. 2, 1950; children: Patsy Kate, Nancy Ann, Janie Marie. BS, Southwest Tex. State U., 1951; MLS, Tex. Woman's U., 1979. Tchr. art, reading, math. Grandview Ind. Sch. Dist., Tex., 1950—52; tchr. phys. edn. Beaumont Ind. Sch. Dist., Tex., 1953; tchr. art, coll. algebra Cisco Jr. Coll., Tex., 1957—58; tchr. remedial reading Taylor County Schs., Tuscola, Tex., 1965—66, Anson Ind. Sch. Dist., Tex., 1971—73; libr. Bangs Ind. Sch. Dist., Tex., 1973—79, learning resources coord., 1979—90; dir. Heart of Tex. Ctr. for the Rev. and Exam. of Children's and Young Adults' Lit., 1988—2001; cons. Heart of Tex. Lit. Ctr., 2001—03. Bd. dirs. Anson Pub. Libr., Tex., 1971—72, Brownwood Pub. Libr., 2003—; mem. adv. com. Edn. Svc. Ctr., 1978—83; coord. Reading is Fundamental Program, 1978—83; counsilor Children's Round Table, 1993—; cons. Heart of Tex. Lit. Ctr., 2000—03, dir. projects, 2003—. Exhibitions include oil paintings, pastels various Tex. Fairs (1st prize, 1952, 1960), Gary Air Force Base, San Marcos, 1952. Named Coming Home Queen, Howard Payne U., 2006. Mem.: ALA, Tex. Assn. Sch. Libr. Adminstrs., Teenage Libr. Assn. Tex. (chmn. audio-visual award com. 1984), Tex. Assn. Improvement Reading, Tex. Assn. Sch. Librs. (media prodns. award com. 1985—86), Tex. Libr. Assn. (mem. intellectual freedom and profl. responsibility com. 1979—81, mem. Tex. Bluebonnet award com. 1982—85, chair adv. com. 1987, chair children's round table 1987, sec. young adult round table 1991—92, publs. com. 1991—, round table coun. 1993—95), Intellectual Freedom Round Table, Am. Assn. Sch. Librs., Young Adult Libr. Svcs. Assn. (outstanding books for coll.bound-fine arts com., publ.'s liaison com.), Assn. Libr. Svc. to Children (Caldecott award com. 1986, Grosset and Dunlap Group award selection com. 1988, nominating com. 1989, chair 1989—91, Newbery award com. 1999, Disting. Svc. award com. 2002—, Disting. Svc. award com. chair 2003—, cons. priority gorup III profl. devel.), Tex. State Tchr. Assn. (life), Bangs Profl. Women's Club (treas. 1974—76), Delta Kappa Gamma, Beta Phi Mu, Alpha Chi, Kappa Pi, Phi Delta Kappa. Bapt. Office: Howard Payne Univ Sta Walker Memorial Library Heart of Tex Ctr Brownwood TX 76801 Office Phone: 325-649-8606. Business E-Mail: pweeks@hptux.edu.

**WEEKS, ROBERT ANDREW,** materials science researcher, educator; b. Birmingham, Ala., Aug. 23, 1924; s. William Andrew and Annie Bell (Hammond) W.; m. Jane Sutherland, Mar. 20, 1948; children: Kevin Dale, Robin Dee, Loren Hammond, Kerry Andrew. BS, Birmingham-So. Coll., 1947; MS, U. Tenn., 1951; PhD, Brown U., 1966. Sr. physicist Union Carbide Corp., Oak Ridge, Tenn., 1951-84; rsch. prof. material sci. Vanderbilt U., 1984-99, prof. emeritus, 1999—. Disting. vis. prof. Am. U. in Cairo, 1970-71; invited prof. Ecole Poly. Fed. de Lausanne, Switzerland, 1981; vis. prof. Cath. U., Leuven, Belgium, 1983; cons. numerous pvt. corps. and fed. agys.; prin. investigator lunar materials, 1968-74; co-prin. investigator expdn. Western desert of Egypt to desert glass site, 1981; CEO Oak Ridge Cons., 1993—. Co-editor: Effects of Modes of Formation on Structure of Glass, 1985, 88, Editing the Refereed Scientific Journal, 1994; assoc. editor Jour. Geophys. Rsch., 1968-74; editor Jour. Noncrystalline Solids, 1988-98; conf. editor Jour. Non-Crystalline Solids, 1998-2000; contbr. numerous articles to profl. jours. Served with U.S. Army, 1943-46. Union Carbide fellow, 1964; Fulbright lectr., 1980, Rsch. fellow Reading U., 1971, USIA Am. participant Egypt, India, Nepal and Sri Lanka, 1986. Fellow Am. Ceramic Soc. (symposium hon. chmn. 2004, 06, R. A. Weeks Symposium named in his honor, Honolulu 1991, 2004, George W. Morey award 1998, Sir Neville Mott award 2006); mem. AAAS, Am. Phys. Soc., Sigma Xi. Avocation: photography. Home and Office: 509 Shannondale Way Maryville TN 37803 Personal E-mail: e1e2e4@aol.com.

**WEEKS, ROSS LEONARD, JR.,** museum executive; b. Jamestown, NY, Sept. 11, 1936; s. Ross Leonard and Cecile Forbes (Carrie) W.; m. Patricia Ann Earley, June 10, 1961 (div.); children: Susan Woodall, Ross Leonard III, William Andrew, David James. AB, Colgate U., 1958; MS, George Washington U., 1971; cert., Fed. Exec. Inst., 1988. Reporter Jamestown (Va.) Post-Jour., 1958-60, Richmond (Va.) News Leader, 1960-65; dir. pub. info. Coll. William and Mary, Williamsburg, Va., 1965-71, asst. to exec. v.p., 1971-74, asst. to pres., dir. univ. comms., 1974-81; exec. dir. Jamestown-Yorktown Found., 1981-91, Hist. Crab Orchard Mus., Inc., Tazewell, Va., 1992—2002; ret., 2002; pres. Blue Ridge Concepts, Ltd., 1999—. Editor William and Mary Alumni Gazette, 1966-81; author: Virginia's Tazewell County: A Last Great Place, 2000; editor: 'Cause I'm Colored-The Black Heritage of Tazewell County, 2001; columnist: Clinch Valley News, 1998-2004. Chmn. Williamsburg-James City Bicentennial, 1975-77; treas. Coalfield Regional Tourism Devel. Authority S.W. Va., 1993-97; Va. S.W. Blue Ridge Highlands, Inc., 1993-97, v.p., 1996-97, pres., 1997-99; sec., treas. Frontier Culture Found., 1982-86; exec. dir. Va. Independence Bicentennial Commn., 1981-83; trustee coun. Thirteen Original States, 1982-87; chair Tazewell County Tourism Devel. Commn., 1993-97; mem. regional grant panel Va. Com. on the Arts, 1998—; mem. Gov.'s Va. History Initiative, 1995-2002; mem. parish coun., parish adminstr. Tazewell-Buchanan Cath Ch., 2003—; sec. Va. Textile Mus., Inc., 2005-. Mem. Am. Assn. Mus. (mus. assessment coms. 1988—), Am. Assn. State and Local History, Masons, Rotary (Paul Harris fellow 1987), Clan Ross Assn., SAR (pres. Clinch Mountain Militia chpt. 2001-03), Sigma Delta Chi, Kappa Delta Rho (Ordo Honora 1986). Avocations: travel, landscaping, antiques, history. Home: 205 View Hill Tazewell VA 24651 Personal E-mail: ross@4sw.us.

**WEEKS, STEVEN WILEY,** lawyer; b. Topeka, Mar. 7, 1950; s. Glen Wiley and Grace Aileen (West) W.; m. Lee Nordgren, Aug. 1, 1974 (div. 1985); 1 child, Kirstin Nordgren. BS summa cum laude, Washburn U., 1972; JD cum laude, Harvard U., 1977. Bar: Ohio. Project leader Nat. Sanitation Found.,

Ann Arbor, Mich., 1972; engr. Kans. Dept. Health and Environ., Topeka, 1972-74; ptnr. Taft, Stettinius & Hollister, Cin., 1977—. Dir. The Myers Y. Cooper Co., Cin.; adj. faculty Chase Coll. Law, 1987-88. Mem. adv. com. prosecuting atty., Hamilton County, Cin., 1992; mem. Hamilton County Rep. Ctrl. Com., 1994-2006. Mem. Ohio State Bar Assn., Cin. Bar Assn. Republican. Methodist. Avocations: computers, golf. Home: 3560 Traskwood Cir Cincinnati OH 45208

**WEEKS, THEODORE R.,** history professor; BA, U. Colo., 1980, MA, 1984, PhD, 1992. Asst. prof. So. Ill. U., Carbondale, Ill., 1993—97, assoc. prof., 1997—. Assoc. editor: Kritika: Explorations in Russian and Eurasian History, 1999—; author: Nation and State in Late Imperial Russia, 1996, From Assimilation to Antisemitism: The Jewish Question in Poland, 1850-1914, 2006. Office: So Ill Univ History Dept MC 4519 1000 Faner Dr Rm 3374 Carbondale IL 62901 Office Phone: 618-453-7874.

**WEEKS, WILFORD FRANK,** retired geophysics educator, glaciologist; b. Champaign, Ill., Jan. 8, 1929; married; 3 children. BS, U. Ill., 1951, MS, 1953; PhD in Geology, U. Chgo., 1956. Geologist mineral deposits br. U.S. Geol. Survey, 1952-55; glaciologist USAF Cambridge Research Ctr., 1955-57; asst. prof. Washington U., St. Louis, 1957-62; adj. math. earth scis. Dartmouth Coll., Hanover, NH, 1962-85; glaciologist Cold Regions Rsch. and Engring. Lab., Hanover, 1962-89; chief scientist Alaska Synthetic Aperture Radar Facility, Fairbanks, 1986-93; prof. geophysics Geophys. Inst. U. Alaska, Fairbanks, 1986-96. Cons. in field, 1996—; vis. prof. Inst. Low Temperature Sci. Hokkaido U., Sapporo, Japan, 1973; chair Arctic marine sci. USN Postgrad. Sch., Monterey, Calif., 1978-79; mem. earth sys. sci. com. NASA, Washington, 1984-87; advisor U.S. Arctic Rsch. Commn., divsn. polar programs NSF, Washington, 1987-88; chmn. NAS Com. on Cooperation with Russia in Ice Mechanics, 1991-92; mem. environ. task force MEDEA Cons. Group, 1992-2002. Capt. USAF, 1955-57. Recipient Emil Usibelli Prize for Rsch., 1996, U. Ill. Dept. Geology Alumni Achievment award, 1999. Fellow Arctic Inst. N.Am., Am. Geophys. Union; mem. NAE, Internat. Glaciological Soc. (v.p. 1969-72, pres. 1973-75, Seligman Crystal award 1989), Am. Polar Soc. (hon.). Avocation: contrabassist. Home and Office: 6533 SW 34th Ave Portland OR 97239-1077 Office Phone: 503-244-1695. E-mail: w-f-weeks@comcast.net.

**WEEKS, WILLIAM RAWLE, JR.,** oil industry executive; b. Denver, Oct. 23, 1920; s. William Rawle Sr. and Besse Elizabeth (Griffith) W.; m. June Suzanne Stephens, Jan. 22, 1944 (div. 1980); children: Stephen R., Tacy A. Weeks Hahn. BA, Stanford U., 1943. With book prodn. divsn. Stanford U. Press, 1948-49; advt. exec. Palo Alto, Calif., 1949-50; with CIA, 1951—; gen. ptnr. Weeks, Brewer & Assocs., 1971; CEO Fort Collins Consol. Royalties, Inc., Cheyenne, Wyo., 1983—. Author: Knock and Wait Awhile, 1957 (Edgar Allan Poe award 1958, Commonwealth award 1958). Nat. press and media advance man Muskie Vice Presdl. Campaign, 1968. 2nd lt. U.S. Army, 1943-46. Mem. Nat. Press Club, Denver Petroleum Club. Avocations: flying, skiing, golf, hiking.

**WEEMS, CARRIE MAE,** photographer; BA, Calif. Inst. Arts, Valencia, 1981; MFA, U. Calif., San Diego, 1984; postgrad., U. Calif., Berkeley, 1984-87. Asst. prof. Hampshire Coll., Amherst, Mass., 1987-91, Calif. Coll. Arts and Crafts, Oakland, 1991-95; artist, prof. Harvard U., 1995—. Vis. prof. Hunter Coll., N.Y., 1988-89, Williams Coll., 2000, Harvard U., 2001. One-person shows include Inst. Contemporary Art, 1991, Trustman Gallery, Simmons Coll., Boston, 1991, The New Mus. Contemporary Art, N.Y., 1991, Matrix Gallery, Wadsworth Atheneum, Hartford, Conn., 1991, Albright Coll., Reading, Pa., 1991, Greenville County Mus. Art, S.C., 1992, San Francisco Art Inst., 1992, Linda Cathcart Gallery, Santa Monica, Calif., 1993, Rhonda Hoffman Gallery, Chgo., 1993, New Langton Arts, San Francisco, 1993, Hood Mus. Art, Dartmouth Coll., N.H., 1994, Mus. Modern Art, N.Y., 1995, The Bunting Inst., 1996, Contemporary Arts Mus., Houston, 1996, Everson Art Mus., Syracuse, N.Y., 1998, High Mus. Art, Atlanta, 2000, Internat. Ctr. Photography N.Y., 2000, Parrish Art Mus., 2001; group shows include Reframing the Family Artists Space, 1991, Whitney Mus. Am. Art, 1991, Mus. Modern Art, 1992, Randy Alexander, 1992, Artists of Conscience: 16 Years of Social and Polit. Commentary, Alt. Mus. N.Y., 1991-92, Through the Kitchen Door, NAME, 1991-92, Disclosing the Myth of Family, Art Inst. Chgo., The Betty Rymer Gallery, Chgo., 1992, The Theater of Refusal: Black Art and the Mainstream Criticism (traveling), 1993-94, States of Loss: Migration, Displacement, Colonialism and Power, Jersey City Mus., N.J., 1993-94, Gesture and Pose, Mus. Modern Art, N.Y., 1994, Bad Girls, Part 1, New Mus. Contemporary Art, N.Y., 1994, Who's Looking at the Family? Barbican Art Gallery, London, 1994, Equal Rights and Justice, High Mus. Art and Nat. Black Arts Fest, Atlanta, 1994, Imaging Families: Images and Voices, Smithsonian Instn., 1994-95, Black Male, Representations of Masculinity in Contemporary Am. Art, Whitney Mus. Am. Art, N.Y., 1994-95, Embedded Metaphor, Ringling Mus. Art, Sarasota, 1996, Alternate Cultures, Johannesberg Biennial, Africa, 1997, Changing Spaces, Detroit Inst. Art, 1998, Bearing Witness, Polk Mus. Art, 1998, Art Worlds in Dialog, Mus. Ludwig, Cologne, Germany, 1999, Paradise Now, Exit Art, N.Y., 2000, Collection in Context, Studio Mus. Harlem, N.Y., 2001. Office: PPOW Gallery 555 W 25th St New York NY 10001-5542

**WEEMS, HELEN RACHEL,** music educator, musician; b. Morgantown, W.Va., Dec. 12, 1962; d. David Burnola and Charys (Ford) Weems; m. Robert Raymond Provine, June 8, 1996. BA, Sch. of the Ozarks, Point Lookout, Mo., 1986; MM, Peabody Conservatory of Music, Balt., 1991; MA, U. Md. Baltimore County, 1996. Cert. piano tchr. Music Tchrs. Nat. Assn., 2004. Radio host Sta. KSOZ, Point Lookout, 1985-86, Sta. WJHU, Balt., 1994-96; freelance pianist, tchr., singer, 1975—. Balinese dancer UMBC Gamelan, Balt., 1993—96; coord. Harper's Glen Watch, Columbia, 1998—; Choir dir. St. Luke's Episcopal Ch., Brookeville, Md., 1997—. Neighborhood improvement grantee, Gov.'s Office of Crime Control and Prevention, 1999—2002. Mem.: Greater Columbia Music Tchrs. Assn. (v.p. 1997—2000, pres. 2005—), Howard County Music Tchrs. Assn. (pres. 1999—2003, concert mgr. 2002—06). Democrat. Episcopalian. Avocations: running, gardening. Office: Helen R Weems Piano Studio 5473 Green Dory Ln Columbia MD 21044-1912

**WEEMS, KERRY N.,** federal agency administrator; PhB, N.Mex. State U., B in Mgmt.; MBA, U. N.Mex., 1981. Staff mem. Senate Appropriations Com.; dir. divsn. budget policy U.S. Dept. Health and Human Svcs., Washington, chief budget planning br., program analyst Office of Budget, program and budget analyst, acting asst. sec. for budget, tech. and fin., 2003—. Office: US Dept Health and Human Svcs Office Budget Tech and Fin 200 Independence Ave SW Washington DC 20201

**WEEMS, LORI K.,** lawyer; b. Lubbock, Tex., Sept. 26, 1968; BA, Baylor Univ., 1990, JD summa cum laude, 1994. Bar: Fla. 1996. Law clerk U.S. Ct. Appeals, 5th Cir., Fla., 1994—96; ptnr. Holland & Knight, Miami, 1996—. Recipient Lynn Futch Most Productive Young Lawyer, Fla. Bar, 2003, Vol. Atty. of Yr., Lawyers for Children Am., 2004. Mem.: Dade County Bar Assn., ABA (bd. gov. 2002—). Office: Holland & Knight LLP Suite 3000 701 Brickell Ave Miami FL 33131

**WEEN, MARTIN M.,** lawyer; b. Bklyn., Aug. 31, 1946; BA in English cum laude, SUNY, Buffalo, 1967; JD, NYU, 1971. Bar: NY 1971, US Dist. Ct. So. Dist. NY, US Dist. Ct. Ea. Dist. NY, US Dist. Ct. No. Dist. NY. Ptnr. Wilson, Elser, Moskowitz, Edelman & Dicker LLP, NYC. Mem.: ABA (tort & ins. practice sect.), NY State Bar Assn. (corp., banking & bus. law sections). Office: Wilson Elser Moskowitz Edelman & Dicker LLP 150 E 42nd St 23rd Fl New York NY 10017-5639 Office Phone: 212-490-3000 ext. 2290. Office Fax: 212-490-3038. Business E-Mail: weenm@wemed.com.

**WEERACKODY, VIJITHA,** electrical engineer, researcher; PhD, U. Pa., Phila., 1984—89. Mem. tech. staff Bell Laboratories, Lucent Technologies, Murray Hill, NJ, 1990—2001; pres. PetaNetworks, N.Y.C., 2002—05; sr.

profl. staff Johns Hopkins U./APL, Laurel, Md., 2005—. Cons. TLVentures, Wayne, Pa., 2004—; adj. assoc. prof. U. Pa., Phila., 2004—. Achievements include patents for About 25 US Patents on Wireless/Communication Systems. Office: Johns Hopkins Univ/APL 11100 Johns Hopkins Rd Laurel MD 20723 Personal E-mail: vijitha@ieee.org. Business E-mail: vijitha.weerackody@jhuapl.edu.

**WEERASINGHE, RENU M.,** quality assurance professional; b. Karawanella, Sri Lanka; arrived in U.S., 1992; d. Upasena and Kusuma Attanayake; m. Denzil Weerasinghe; children: Dillon, Shanali. MD, Inst. Medicine and Pharmacy, Bucharest, Romania, 1985; MPH, U. Rochester, 2002. House officer Base Hosp., Wathupitiwela, Sri Lanka, 1985—86, med. officer Avissawella, Sri Lanka, 1986—90; sr. med. officer Nat. Hosp., Colombo, Sri Lanka, 1990—92; internal auditer/study coord. Rochester (N.Y.) Clin. Rsch., 1996—2000, dir. quality assurance and regulatory affairs, 2000—03; internal monitor Rsch. Dynamics Consulting Group, Rochester, 2003—. V.p. Overseas Qualified Med. Grads. Assn., Colombo, 1988—2000. Student scholar, Assn. Tchrs. in Preventive Medicine, 2001. Mem.: Sri Lanka Med. Coun., Assn. Clin. Rsch. Profls. Avocations: travel, reading, gardening. Office: 49 Redwood Dr Penfield NY 14526-1941

**WEERTMAN, JOHANNES,** materials science educator; b. Fairfield, Ala., May 11, 1925; s. Roelof and Christina (van Vlaardingen) W.; m. Julia Ann Randall, Feb. 10, 1950; children: Julia Ann, Bruce Randall. Student, Pa. State Coll., 1943-44; BS, Carnegie Inst. Tech. (now Carnegie Mellon U.), 1948, DSc, 1951; postgrad., Ecole Normale Superieure, Paris, 1951-52. Solid State physicist U.S. Naval Rsch. Lab., Washington, 1952-58, cons., 1960-67; sci. liaison officer U.S. Office Naval Rsch., Am. Embassy, London, 1958-59; faculty Northwestern U., Evanston, Ill., 1959—, prof. materials sci. dept., 1961-68, chmn. dept., 1964-68, prof. geol. scis. dept., 1963—, Walter P. Murphy prof. materials sci. and engring. emeritus, 1999—. Vis. prof. geophysics Calif. Inst. Tech., 1964, Scott Polar Rsch. Inst., Cambridge (Eng.) U., 1970-71, Swiss Fed. Inst. Reactor Rsch., 1986; cons. Cold Regions Rsch. and Engring. Lab., U.S. Army, 1960-75, Oak Ridge (Tenn.) Nat. Lab., 1963-67, Los Alamos (N.Mex.) Sci. Lab., 1967—; co-editor materials sci. books MacMillan Co., 1962-76. Author: Dislocation Based Fracture Mechanics, 1996, (with Julia Weertman) Elementary Dislocation Theory, 1964, 2d edit., 1992; mem. editorial bd. Metal. Trans., 1967-75, Jour. Glaciology, 1972—; assoc. editor Jour. Geophys. Rsch., 1973-75, 2000-01; contbr. articles to profl. jours. With USMC, 1943-46. Honored with naming of Weertman Island in Antarctica.; Fulbright fellow, 1951-52; recipient Acta Metallurgica gold medal, 1980; Guggenheim fellow, 1970-71 Fellow Am. Acad. Arts and Scis., Am. Soc. Metals, Am. Phys. Soc., Geol. Soc. Am., Am. Geophys. Union (Horton award 1972, AIME Mathewson Gold medal 1977); mem. AAAS, NAE, Am. Inst. Physics, Internat. Glaciol. Soc. (Seligman Crystal award 1983), Arctic Inst., Am. Quaternary Assn., Explorers Club, Fulbright Assn., Sigma Xi, Tau Beta Pi, Phi Kappa Phi, Alpha Sigma Mu, Pi Mu Epsilon. Home: 834 Lincoln St Evanston IL 60201-2405 Office: Northwestern U Materials Sci Dept Evanston IL 60208-0001 Office Phone: 847-491-3197. Business E-mail: j-weertman2@northwestern.edu.

**WEERTMAN, JULIA RANDALL,** materials engineering educator; b. Muskegon, Mich., Feb. 10, 1926; BS in Physics, Carnegie-Mellon U., 1946, MS in Physics, 1947, DSc in Physics, 1951. Physicist U.S. Naval Rsch. Lab., Washington, 1952-58; vis. asst. prof. dept. materials sci. and engring. Northwestern U., Evanston, Ill., 1972-73, asst. prof., 1973-78, from asst. prof. to assoc. prof., 1973-82, prof., 1982-99, Walter P. Murphy prof., 1989, chmn. dept., 1987-92, vis. to dean grad. studies and rsch. Tech. Inst., 1973-76, Walter P. Murphy prof. emeritus, 1999—. Mem. various NRC coms. and panels. Co-author: Elementary Dislocation Theory, 1964, 1992, also pub. in French, Japanese and Polish; contbr. numerous articles to profl. jours. Mem. Evanston Environ. Control Bd., 1972-79. Recipient Creativity award NSF, 1981, 86; Guggenheim Found. fellow, 1986-87; named Robert Mehl lectr. Inst. of Metals, 2005. Fellow Am. Soc. Metals Internat. (Gold medal 2005), Minerals, Metals and Materials Soc. (leadership award 1997); mem. NAE, Am. Acad. Arts and Scis., Am. Phys. Soc., Materials Rsch. Soc. (Von Hippel award 2003), Soc. Women Engrs. (Disting. Engring. Educator award 1989, Achievement award 1991). Home: 834 Lincoln St Evanston IL 60201-2405 Office: Northwestern U Dept Material Sci & Engring 2220 Campus Dr Evanston IL 60208-0876 Office Phone: 847-491-5353. Business E-mail: jrweertman@northwestern.edu.

**WEERTS, RICHARD KENNETH,** music educator; b. Peoria, Ill., Oct. 7, 1928; s. Gerhard Nicholas and Ellen Marie (Lindeburg) W. BS, U. Ill., 1951; MA, Columbia U., 1956, EdD, 1960; MA, N.E. Mo. State U., 1973. Tchr. Lyndhurst (N.J.) Pub. Schs., 1956-57; dir. instrumental music Scotch Plains (N.J.) Pub. Schs., 1957-61; prof. music Truman State U., Kirksville, 1961—, chair dept. music, 1994—. Author: Handbook for Woodwinds, 1965, Developing Individual Skills for the High School Band, 1969, How to Develop and Maintain a Successful Woodwind Section, 1972, Original Manuscript Music, 1973, Handbook of Rehearsal Techniques for Band, 1976; numerous papers and monographs; nat. bd. editors The Quarterly, jour. of Ctr. for Rsch. in Music Learning and Teaching, 1989. Dir. music First United Meth. Ch., Kirksville, 1970—. Served with U.S. Army, 1951-55. Mem. Coun. for Rsch. in Music Edn., Nat. Assn. Coll. Wind and Percussion Instrs. (nat. exec. sec./treas. 1971—, editor jour 1968—), Music Educators Nat. Conf., Phi Delta Kappa. Office: NACWPI Truman State U Divsn Fine Arts Kirksville MO 63501

**WEESE, BENJAMIN HORACE,** architect; b. Evanston, Ill., June 4, 1929; s. Harry Ernest and Marjorie (Mohr) W.; m. Cynthia Rogers, July 5, 1963; children: Daniel Peter, Catharine Mohr. B.Arch., Harvard U., 1951, M.Arch., 1957; cert., Ecole des Beaux Arts, Fontainebleau, France, 1956. Assoc., Harry Weese & Assocs. Architects, Chgo., 1957 771 prin. Weese Langley Weese Chgo., 1977—. Co-founder, pres. Chgo. Arch. Found.; Glessner House, Chgo., 1966— Trustee Graham Found. for Advanced Studies in Fine Arts, 1988—, pres. 1995-99; mem. Commn. Chgo. Landmarks, 1998—. Fellow AIA; mem. Nat. Council Archtl. Registration Bds. Home: 2133 N Hudson Ave Chicago IL 60614-4522 Office: Weese Langley Weese Ltd 9 W Hubbard St Chicago IL 60610-4630 E-mail: bweese@wlwltd.com.

**WEESE, CYNTHIA ROGERS,** architect, educator; b. Des Moines, June 23, 1940; d. Gilbert Taylor and Catharine (Wingard) Rogers; m. Benjamin H. Weese, July 5, 1963; children: Daniel Peter, Catharine Mohr. BSA.S., Washington U., St. Louis, 1962; B.Arch., Washington U., 1965. Registered architect, Ill. Pvt. practice architecture, Chgo., 1965-72, 74-77; draftsperson, designer Harry Weese & Assocs., Chgo., 1972-74; prin. Weese Langley Weese Ltd., Chgo., 1977—; design critic Ball State U., Muncie, Ind., 1966-72; Trustee Graham Found. for Advanced Studies in Fine Arts, 1988—; dean sch. architecture Washington U., St. Louis, 1993—. Bd. regents Am. Architecture Found., 1990-93; bd. mem. Landmarks Commn. St. Louis.; mem. Mayor's Task Force Downtown Now, St. Louis, 1997—. Recipient Alpha Rho Chi award Washington U., 1965, Met. Chgo. YWCA Outstanding Achievement award, 1990. Mem. AIA (bd. dirs. Chgo. chpt. 1980-83, v.p. 1983-85, 1st v.p. 1986-87, pres. 1987-88, regional dir. 1990-92, Disting. Bldg. awards 1977, 81-83, 86, 91, 95, Interior Architecture award 1981, 90, 92, nat. v.p. 1993, chmn. urban design task force St. Louis 2004 1997—), AIA/ACSA Coun. on Archtl. Rsch. (chair 1991-92), AIA Found. (pres. Chgo. chpt. 1988-89), Soc. Archtl. Historians (bd. dirs. 1992-94), Chgo. Women in Architecture, Chgo. Network, Nat. Inst. Archtl. Edn. (bd. dirs. 1988-90), Chgo. Archtl. Club (pres. 1988-89), Washington U. Sch. Architecture Alumni (nat. coun. 1988-93), Lambda Alpha. Clubs: Arts, Chgo. Archtl. Found. Office: Washington U Sch Architecture PO Box 1079 Saint Louis MO 63188-1079

**WEESE, JOHN AUGUSTUS,** mechanical engineer, educator; b. Topeka, July 24, 1933; s. Ray Edward and Margaret Maureen (Richmond) Weese; m. Betty Kay Dietrich, June 5, 1955; children: Carol Ann, Katherine Lynn. BSME, Kans. State U., 1955; MS, Cornell U., 1958, PhD, 1959. Asst. prof.

USAF Acad., Colo., 1960-62; assoc. prof. mech. engring. U. Denver, 1963-67, prof., 1967-74, chmn. mech. sci. and environ. engring., 1968-70, dean engring., 1970-74, Old Dominion U., Norfolk, Va., 1974-83; dir. mech. engring. and applied mechanics NSF, Washington, 1983-85, dir. mechanics structures and materials engring., 1985-86; prof. mech. engring. Tex. A&M U., College Station, 1986—2005, head dept. engring. tech., 1986-97, coord. accreditation, regents prof., 1997—2005, interim head mech. engring. dept., 2001—03, prof. emeritus, 2005—. Structural dynamics engr. Boeing Co., Wichita, Kans., 1959—60, rsch. specialist, 1962—63; rsch. engr. Martin-Marietta Corp., Denver, 1963; bd. dirs. ABET, Inc., 1994—98, 2002—. Co-author: (book) Mechanics of Materials, 4th edit., 1985; contbr. articles to profl. jours. Fellow: ASME (ad hoc visitor 1977—83, Ben C. Sparks medal 1994), Am. Soc. Engring. Edn. (projects bd. engring. rsch. coun. 1982—85, chmn. publs. com. 1983—86, exec. com. 1984—90, chmn. engring. rsch. coun. 1988—90, v.p. pub. affairs 1995—97, pres.-elect 1998—99, pres. 1999—2000, Outstanding Educator mechanics divsn. 1989, Frederick J. Berger award 1997, W. Leighton Collins award 2004, Presdl. Disting Svc. award 2005). Republican. Congregationalist. Avocations: fishing, photography. Home: 9300 Lake Forest Ct South College Station TX 77845-8763 Office: Tex A&M U Dept Mech Engring College Station TX 77843-3123 Office Phone: 979-845-2302. Business E-mail: jweese@tamu.edu.

**WEETER, JOHN MONTGOMERY,** plastic surgeon; b. Louisville, Aug. 8, 1945; s. Anne (Brunton) and John Calvin Weeter; m. Linda Kaye Locklar, Sept. 4, 1970; children: Christina Lynn, Leslie Anne, Ashley Denise Weeter O'Hara, Katherine Alexis Sailor. BA, Vanderbilt U., Nashville, 1967; MD, U. Ky., Lexington, 1971. Diplomate Am. Bd. of Plastic Surgery, 1971, cert. advanced edn. cosmetic surgery Am. Soc. Aesthetic Surgery. Resident gen. surgery Med. U. S.C., Charleston, 1971—75; fellow plastic and reconstructive surgery St. Francis Meml. Hosp., San Francisco, 1975—78; clin. dir. burn unit Kosair Children's Hosp., Louisville, 1980—2003; asst. clin. prof. Divsn. Plastic Surgery U. Louisville, 1980—; pvt. practice/ ptnr. Assocs. in Plastic Surgery, Louisville, 1978—. Vol. plastic surgeon Interplast, Guayaquil and Portoviejo, Ecuador, 1990—; vis. prof. Children's Hosp., La Plata, Argentina, 1994; vol. plastic surgeon Children's Aid Mission Internat., Coban, Guatemala. Author (prodr., actor): (med. ednl. film) Initial Assessment and Management of Burns; author: (textbook chpt.) Thermal, Electrical, Chemical Injuries. Recipient Disting. Citizen award, Mayor of Louisville, 1985, VIP Vol. award, Sister Cities of Louisville, 1995. Fellow: ACS; mem.: Am. Burn Assn., Am. Cleft Lip/Craniofacial Assn., Am. Soc. Aesthetic Surgery, Am. Soc. Plastic Surgeons. Avocations: tennis, sailing, growing orchids. Office: Associates in Plastic Surgery PLLC 4001 Kresge Way #220 Louisville KY 40207 E-mail: jmweeter@hotmail.com.

**WEFALD, JON,** academic administrator; b. Nov. 24, 1937; s. Olav and Walma (Ovrum) W.; m. Ruth Ann; children— Skipp, Andy. BA, Pacific Lutheran U., Tacoma, 1959; MA, Wash. State U., Pullman, 1961; PhD, U. Mich., Ann Arbor, 1965. Teaching asst. Wash. State U., Pullman, 1959—61; teaching fellow U. Mich., Ann Arbor, 1961—64; assoc. prof. history Gustavus Adolphus Coll., St. Peter, Minn., 1965—70; commr. agr. State of Minn., St. Paul, 1971—77; pres. Southwest State U., Marshall, Minn., 1977—82; chancellor Minn. State Univ. System, St. Paul, 1982—86; pres. Kans. State U., Manhattan, 1986—. Author: A Voice of Protest: Norwegians in American Politics 1890-1917, 1971. Mem. Mid-Am. Internat. Agri-Trade Council (pres. 1974-75), Midwest Assn. State Depts. of Agr. (sec.treas. 1976-77), U.S. Dept. Agr. Joint Council on Food and Agrl. Scis. Office: Kans State U Office of Pres 110 Anderson Hall Manhattan KS 66506-0100 E-mail: pres@ksu.edu.*

**WEG, JOHN GERARD,** physician; b. N.Y.C., Feb. 16, 1934; s. Leonard and Pauline M. (Kanzleiter) W.; m. Mary Loretta Flynn, June 2, 1956; children: Diane Marie, Kathryn Mary, Carol Ann, Loretta Louise, Veronica Susanne, Michelle Celeste. BA cum laude, Coll. Holy Cross, Worcester, Mass., 1955; MD, N.Y. Med. Coll., 1959. Diplomate: Am. Bd. Internal Medicine. Commd. 2nd lt. USAF, 1958, advanced through grades to capt., 1967; intern Walter Reed Gen. Hosp., Washington, 1959-60; resident, then chief resident in internal medicine Wilford Hall USAF Hosp., Lackland AFB, Tex., 1960-64, chief pulmonary sect., 1964-66, chief inhalation sect., 1964-66, chief pulmonary and infectious disease service, 1966-67; resigned, 1967; clin. dir. pulmonary disease div. Jefferson Davis Hosp., Houston, 1967-71; from asst. prof. to assoc. prof. medicine Baylor U. Coll. Medicine, Houston, 1967-71; assoc. prof. medicine U. Mich. Med. Sch. Univ. Hosp., Ann Arbor, 1971-74, prof., 1974—2001, prof. emeritus, 2001—. Physician-in-charge pulmonary divsn., 1971-81, physician-in-charge pulmonary and critical care med. divsn., 1981-85, co-chair intstl. review bd., 2004—; cons. Ann Arbor VA, 1971—, Wayne County Gen. Hosps., 1971-84; mem. adv. bd. Washtenaw County Health Dept., 1971-84; mem. respiratory and nervous sys. panel, anesthesiology sect. Nat. Ctr. Devices and Radiol. Health, FDA, 1983—, chmn., 1985-88. Contbr. med. jours., reviewer, mem. editorial bds. Decorated Air Force Commendation medal; travelling fellow Nat. Tb and Respiratory Disease Assn., 1971; recipient Aesculpaius award Tex. Med. Assn., 1971 Master ACP (chmn. Mich. program com. 1974); fellow Am. Coll. Chest Physicians (chmn. bd. govs. 1976-79, gov. Mich. 1975-79, chmn. membership com. 1976-79, prof.-in-residence 1972—, chmn. critical care coun. 1982-85, chmn. ethics com. 1998, master fellow, 2002, master FCCP, 2002, master), Am. Coll. Chest Physicians and Internat. Acad. Chest Physicians (master, exec. council 1976-82, pres. 1980-81); mem. AAAS, Am. Fedn. Clin. Rsch., AMA, Am. Thoracic Soc. (sec.-treas. 1974-76), Am. Assn. Inhalation Therapy, Air Force Soc. Internists and Allied Specialists, Soc. Med. Consultants to Armed Forces, Internat. Union Against Tb, Mich. Thoracic Soc. (pres. 1976-78), Mich. Lung Assn. (dir. Bruce Douglas award 1981), Am. Lung Assn., Rsch. Club U. Mich., Assn. Advancement Med. Instrumentation, Central Soc. Clin. Rsch., Am. Bd. Internal Medicine (subsplty. com. on pulmonary disase 1980-86, critical care medicine com. 1983-87, critical care medicine policy com. 1986-87), N.Y. Med. Coll. Alumni Assn. (medal of honor 1990), Alpha Omega Alpha. Home: 3060 Exmoor Rd Ann Arbor MI 48104-4132 Office: B I H 245 Box 0026 1500 E Medical Center Dr Ann Arbor MI 48109-0005 Office Phone: 734-763-2540. Business E-mail: jweg@umich.edu.

**WEGELIN, JACOB ANDREAS,** statistician; b. Eugene, Oreg., Dec. 14, 1954; s. Christof Andreas and Caroline (Locke) W. BA, BS, U. Wash., 1986, MS, 1989, PhD, 2001. With Shiloh Youth Revival Ctrs., Inc., Oreg., Wash., Calif., Ariz., Alaska, 1971-76, Eugene Hotel, 1976-78; deckhand fishing industry, Alaska, 1978-79; tech. writer, editor IBM Corp., San Jose, Calif. and, N.Y., Poughkeepsie, N.Y., 1985-86; cook, deckhand, bull cook Alaska Boat Co., Wards Cove Packing Co., 1991-93; instr. MathSoft, Seattle, 1995; statistician U. Wash., Seattle, 1996—2002, U. Calif., Davis, 2002—. Recipient Pres.'s medal U. Wash., 1986; NSF fellow, 1986-89. Mem. Am. Statis. Assn., Phi Beta Kappa. Office: U Calif Dept Epidemiology/Preventive Medicine I Shields Ave TB-168 Davis CA 95616-8638

**WEGENER, MARK DOUGLAS,** lawyer; b. Nov. 1, 1948; BA cum laude, Cen. Coll., Pella, Iowa, 1970; JD, Rutgers U., 1973. Assoc. Howrey & Simon, Washington, 1973-79; ptnr., mem. exec. com. Howrey LLP, Washington, 1979—, chmn. global litigation practice group. Office: Howrey LLP 1299 Pennsylvania Ave NW Washington DC 20004-2400

**WEGENER, PETER PAUL,** engineering educator, writer; b. Berlin, Aug. 29, 1917; came to U.S., 1946; naturalized, 1953. m. Annette Schleiermacher, Aug. 14, 1961; children: Paul, Christopher, Philip. Dr rer. nat., U. Berlin, 1943; MA (priv.), Yale U., 1960; Dr. Ing. (h.c.), U. Karlsruhe, Germany, 1979. Researcher supersonic wind tunnels, Kochel, Germany, 1943-45; researcher gasdynamics, hypersonic wind tunnels U.S. Naval Ordnance Lab., 1946-53, Jet Propulsion Lab. Calif. Inst. Tech., 1953-60; prof. applied sci. Yale U., New Haven, 1960-72, Harold Hodgkinson prof. engring. and applied sci., 1972—, chmn. dept. engring. applied sci., 1966-71, prof. emeritus, 1987— Sr. Am. scientist Humboldt Found., 1979 Author: (books) The Peenemünde Wind Tunnels: A Memoir, 1996, What Makes Airplanes Fly?, 1997; researcher and contbr. articles on hypersonics, condensation

metastable state, chem. kinetics, flow systems real gases, bubbles to profl. jours. Inst. Advanced Study Berlin fellow, 1986. Fellow Am. Phys. Soc., Conn. Acad. Sci. & Engring. (charter). Home: 29 Montgomery Pkwy Branford CT 06405-5128

**WEGERSON, EDWARD J.,** lawyer; b. Chgo. Heights, Ill., Mar. 25, 1953; s. Edward Louis and Eileen W. Wegerson; m. Mary D. Simonett, July 19, 1980; children: Paul Edward, Sarah Maria. BA, U. Minn., Duluth, 1975; JD, U. Minn., Mpls., 1978. Assoc. Fryberger Buchanan, Duluth, 1978—81, Weise & Cox. Ltd., Mpls., 1981—83, Lindquist & Vennum, Mpls., 1983—87, ptnr., 1987—. Recipient Disting. Alumni award, U. Minn. Duluth Dept. Econs., 2001. Office: Lindquist & Vennum LLP 80 S 8th St Minneapolis MN 55402 Office Phone: 612-371-3549. Office Fax: 612-371-3707. Business E-Mail: ewegerson@lindquist.com.

**WEGGE, LEON LOUIS FRANÇOIS,** retired economics educator; b. Breendonk, Antwerp, Belgium, June 9, 1933; came to U.S., 1959; s. Petrus Maria and Alberta (De Maeyer) W.; m. Beate Maria Teipel, Nov. 22, 1962; children: Simone, Robert, Elizabeth. B in Thomistical Philosophy, cath. U. Louvain, Belgium, 1957, Licentiate in Econ. Sci., 1958; PhD in Indsl. Econs., MIT, 1963. Assoc. lectr. U. New S. Wales, Kensington, Australia, 1963-66; prof. econs. U. Calif., Davis, 1966-94, retired, 1994. Vis. prof. U. Bonn, Fed. Republic Germany, 1980-81. Assoc. editor Jour. Internat. Econs., 1971-84; contbr. articles to profl. jours. Rsch. fellow Ctr. for Ops. Rsch. and Econometrics, 1972-73, fellow The Netherlands Inst. for Advanced Study, 1987-88. Mem. Econometric Soc., Am. Statistical Assn. Roman Catholic. Home: 26320 County Rd # 98 Davis CA 95616

**WEGMAN, COLLEEN,** food service executive; m. O'Donnell Chris Wegman; 2 children. Grad., U. Colo., 1994; MBA, Simon Sch., U. Rochester, 2000. With Wegmans Food Markets, Inc., Rochester, 1991—, various positions, including store mgr. to dir., e-commerce, 1991—2002, sr. v.p., merchandising, 2002—05, pres., 2005—. Developed Wegmans' Nature's Marketplace depts. Named one of Rochester's Influential Women, Rochester Bus. Jour., 2005. Avocation: skiing. Office: Wegmans Food Markets Inc 1500 Brooks Ave Rochester NY 14624*

**WEGMAN, DANIEL R.,** food service executive; m. Stency Wegman; children: Colleen, Nicole. BA in Economics, with honors, Harvard U., 1969. Joined Wegman's Food Markets, Rochester, NY, 1969, pres., 1976—2005, CEO, 2005—. Chmn. bd. govs. Uniform Code Coun. Named Supermarket Impresario, Self Mag., 1998; recipient Friend of Extension award, Cornell Cooperative Extension, 1997. Mem.: Food Mktg. Inst. (chmn. 1999—2001). Office: Wegmans Food Markets 1500 Brooks Ave Rochester NY 14624*

**WEGMAN, HAROLD HUGH,** management consultant; b. Cin., June 29, 1916; s. Clarence H. and Lillian (de Tellem) W.; m. Ruth Ellen Volk, May 1, 1937; children— Susan Ruth (Mrs. Michael Manning), Sally Ann (Mrs. Jerry Fine). BBA, U. Cin., 1941; MBA, Xavier U., 1954. Band leader, studio mgr. Rudolph Wurlitzer Co., 1946-50; Tng. supr., then asst. to v.p. Gruen Watch Co., 1950-55; personnel dir., asst. to pres. Bavarian Brewing Co., Covington, Ky., 1955-59; dir. indsl. relations, asst. to pres. Howard Paper Co., Dayton, Ohio, 1959-62; v.p., gen. mgr. Elano Corp., Xenia, Ohio, 1962-64; v.p., dir. indsl. relations Champion Papers Inc., Hamilton, Ohio, 1964-67; v.p. U.S. Plywood Champion Papers, Inc., 1967-71, Champion Internat., 1971-72; pres. PEP Group, 1972—; dir. Mgmt. Center, Sacred Heart U., 1974—. Contbr. articles to profl. publs. Trustee Foreman Found., 1965-71. Served to lt. (j.g.) USNR, 1944-46. Mem. Am. Soc. Personnel Administrs. (bd. dirs. 1969—, treas. 1970), Am. Soc. for Tng. and Devel., NAM, Am. Paper Inst., Am. Mgmt. Assn., Conn. songwriters assn., Lambda Chi Alpha. Personal E-mail: halwegman@aol.com.

**WEGMAN, WILLIAM GEORGE,** artist; b. Holyoke, Mass., Dec. 2, 1943; s. George W. and Eleanor (Vezina) W. BFA in Painting, Mass. Coll. Art, 1965; MFA, U. Ill., 1967. One-man shows include Gallerie Sonnabend, Paris, 1971, Pomona Coll. Art Gallery, 1971, Sonnabend Gallery, N.Y.C., 1972, 77, Galerie Ernst, Hanover, Ger., 1972, Situation, London, 1972, Konrad Fischer Gallery, 1972, 75, 79, Courtney Sale Gallery, 1972, Tex. Gallery, Houston, 1973, 75, 79, L.A. County Mus. of Art, Calif., 1973, 112 Greene St., N.Y.C., 1974, Mayor Gallery, London, 1975, Galleria Alessandra Castelli, Milan, 1975, The Kitchen, N.Y., 1976, Bruna Soletti Gallery, Milan, 1977, 82, Rosamund Felsen Gallery, 1978, Holly Solomon Gallery, N.Y.C., 1979, 80, 82, 84, 86, 88, 90, 92, Arnolfini Gallery, Eng., 1979, U. Wis., Milw., 1979, U. Colo. Art Galleries, Boulder, 1980, Marianne Deson Gallery, Chgo., 1980, Vivianne Esders Gallery, Paris, 1981, Magnuson Lee Gallery, Boston, 1981, Robert Hull Fleming Mus., Burlington, Vt., 1981, Locus Solus, Genoa, Italy, 1982, Dart Gallery, Chgo., 1982, Fraenkel Gallery, San Francisco, 1982, 88, 90, 92, 93, James Corcoran Gallery, Los Angeles, 1982, 90, Nancy Drysdale Gallery, Washington, 1982, 87, 94, Walker Art Ctr, Mpls., 1982, Ft. Worth Art Mus., Tex., 1982, De Cordova & Dana Mus. & Park, Mass., 1982, Southeastern Ctr. for Contemporary Art, Winston-Salem, N.C., 1982, The Contemporary Arts Ctr., Ohio, 1982, Newport Harbor Mus., Calif., 1982, Inst. Contemporary Arts at Va. Mus., Richmond, 1983, Fine Arts Gallery, U. Mass., Amherst, 1983, Tex. Gallery, Houston, 1983, 86, Greenville County Mus. Art, 1984, Lowe Mus. Art, Miami, Fla, 1985, Cleve. Mus. Art, 1986, Honolulu Acad. Arts, 1987, Mass. Coll. Art, Boston, 1987, U. San Diego, La Jolla, Calif., 1988, Pace MacGill Gallery, N.Y., 1988, 90, 92, 93, San Francisco Mus. Modern Art, Calif., 1988, Galerie Durand-Dessert, Paris, 1989, Budoin Lebon, Paris, 1989, Maison de la Culture et de la Communication de Saint Etienne, France, 1989, Linda Cathcart Gallery, L.A., 1990, 92, 94, The Taft Mus., Cin., 1990, The Butler Inst., Ohio, 1990, Sperone Westwater Gallery, N.Y., 1992, Kunstmuseum, Lucerne, Switzerland, 1990, ICA, London, 1990, fitzelijk Mus., The Netherlands, 1990, Frankfurt Kunstverein, Germany, 1990, Pompidou Ctr., Paris, 1990, ICA, Boston, 1990, Ringling Mus., Fla., 1990, Whitney Mus., N.Y., Contemporary Arts Mus., Tex., 1990, Neuberger Mus., SUNY, 1991, Galerie Andreas Binder, Germany, 1992, Athenaeum Music & Arts Library, Calif., 1992, Lisa Sette Gallery, Phoenix, 1994, Greg Kucera Gallery, Seattle, 1994, George Eastman House: Internat. Mus. Photography and Film, 1995, Aspen Art Mus., ACC Galerie, Weimar, Germany, 1995, Pace Wildenstein, L.A., 1995, Anderson Gallery, Pitts., 1995, Pace/MacGill Gallery, N.Y., 1995, Tex. Gallery, Houston, 1995, Jay Gorney Gallery, N.Y., 1996, Galleri Larsen, Stockholm, 1996, Ehlers Caudill Gallery, Chgo., 1996, Gallery Art Point, Tokyo, 1997, Isetan Mus. Art, Tokyo, 1997, Saks 5th Ave., N.Y.C., 1998, Geral Peters Gallery, Dallas, 1998, Mass. Coll. Art, Boston, 1999, SOMA Gallery, La Jolla, Calif., 1999, ACC Gallery Weimar, Germany, 1999, Birmingham (Ala.) Mus. Art, 1999, Durant-Dessert Gallery, Paris, 1999, Springfield (Mass.) Mus., 1999; others; exhibited in group shows at Walker Art Ctr., Mpls., 1968, N.J. State Mus., Trenton, 1968, Detroit Inst. Art, 1969, Mus. Contemporary Art, Chgo., 1969, 77, Allen Meml. Mus., 1970, L.A. County Mus., Calif., 1971, Pasadena Art Mus., 1972, Contemporary Arts Mus., Houston, 1972, Whitney Mus. Am. Art, N.Y.C., 1973, 81, 89, Sonnabend Gallery, N.Y.C., 1974, Milw. Art Ctr., 1975, Sarah Lawrence Coll. Gallery, 1975, Phila. Mus. Art, 1976, San Francisco Mus. Modern Art, 1976, U. Calif.-Berkeley Art Mus., 1976, U. Chgo., 1976, Ringling Mus. Art, Sarasota, Fla., 1977, Walker Art Gallery, Eng., 1978, Holly Solomon Gallery, N.Y.C., 1978, 82, 87, Mus. Fine Arts, Houston, 1978, Aspen Ctr. Visual Arts, 1979, Santa Barbara Mus. Art, 1979, Mus. Modern Art, N.Y.C., 1980, 82, 83, Sidney Janis Gallery, 1981, Art Inst. Chgo., 1981, 82, Young Hoffman Gallery, Chgo., 1983, Inst. Contemporary Art, Boston, 1983, Castelli Graphics, N.Y.C., 1983, Queens Mus., N.Y., 1986, James Madison U., Harrison, Va, 1987, Fay Gold Gallery, Atlanta, 1988, Hudson River Mus., 1989, Volcano Arts Ctr., 1989, Pace/MacGill, N.Y.C., 1990, The History of Travel, The Taft Museum, Cin., The Butler Inst. Youngstown, Ohio, 1990, William Wegman: Paintings, Drawings, Photographs, Videotapes, Kunstmuseum, Luzern, Stedelijk Museum, Amsterdam, Frankfurt Kunstverein Frankfurt, Centre Nat. d'Art et de Culture Georges Pompidou, Paris, Inst. of Contemporary Art, London, Inst. of Contemporary Arts, Boston, Contemporary Arts Mus., Houston, J.M. Ringling Mus., Sarasota, Whitney Mus., of American Art, N.Y., 1990-92, Outdoor Photographs, Neuberger Mus., State U. of N.Y. at Purchase, 1991, William Wegman:

L'oeuvre photographique, 1969-76, Fonds Regional d'Art Contemporary, Limousin, France, 1991, New Polaroids, Holly Solomon Gallery, N.Y.C., Early Black and White Photographs, Pace/MacGill Gallery, N.Y.C., New Paintings, Sperone Westwater Gallery, N.Y.C., 1992, Turner/Krull Galleries, L.A., 1993, Calif. Ctr. Arts, Escondido, 1994, Drawing Space, N.Y., 1995, Found. Cartier pour l'art Contemporain, Paris, 1996, Lance Fung Gallery, N.Y., 1997, Huntington Beach (Calif.) Art Ctr., 1998, Art: Concept, Paris, 1999, many others; contbr. articles to profl. jours.; videography: Reel 1, 1970-72, Reel 2, 1972, Reel 3, 1972-73, Reel 4, 1973-74, Reel 5, 1975, Reel 6, 1975-76, Reel 7, 1976-77, Reel 8, 1997-98, Reel 9, 1999, Spit Sandwich, 1970, Gray Hairs, 1974-75, World History, 1976, Man Ray, Man Ray, 1978, Accident, 1979, How to Draw, 1983, The World of Photography, 1985, Blue Monday Music Video, 1988, Alive From Off Center, 1988, Sesame Street Videos, 1989, 92, 93, 94, 95, 96, 97, 98, 99; film: Dog Baseball, 1986, The Hardly Boys in Hardly Gold, 1995; publications: Man's Best Friend, 1982, Everyday Problems, 1984, William Wegman: Paintings, Drawings, Photographs, Videotapes, 1990, Cinderella, 1993, Little Red Riding Hood, 1993, ABC, 1994, 1, 2, 3, 1995, Triangle, Circle, Square, 1995, Mother Goose, 1996, Farm Days, 1997, Puppies, 1997, My Town, 1998, What Do You Do?, 1999, Pup, 1999, Fay, 1999, William Wegman, Orange Co Mus Art, Newport Beach, Calif, 2000, Pillbury & Peters Gallery, Washington, DC, 2000, Grant Selwyn Fine Art, Calif, 2003, David Adamson Gallery, Wash DC, 2003, Sperone Westwater, NY, 2003, Pace-Macgaill Gallery, NY, 2003, many others; represented in numerous pub. collections including Kunstaus, Zurich, Mpls. Inst. Art, Mus. Fine Art, Houston, Bklyn. Mus., L.A. County Mus. Art, Mus. Fine Art, Houston, St. Louis Mus. Modern Art, Walker Art Ctr., Mpls., Whitney Mus. Am. Art, N.Y., Albright-Knox Gallery, Buffalo, Austrlian Nat. Gallery, Canberra, others; exhibited in numerous film and video festivals. Recipient Creative Artists Pub. Svc. award, 1979; Guggenheim Found. fellow, 1975, 86, Nat. Endowment for the Arts grantee, 1976, 82.

**WEGNER, GARY ALAN,** astronomer; b. Seattle, Dec. 26, 1944; s. Herbert Edward and Melba Jean (Gardner) W.; m. Cynthia Kay Goodfellow, June 25, 1966; children: Josef, Kurt, Christina, Peter-Jürgen, Emma. Student, Wash. State U., Pullman, 1963-65; BS, U. Ariz., 1967; PhD, U. Wash., Seattle, 1971. Fulbright fellow Mount Stromlo Obs., Camberra, A.C.T., 1971-72; departmental demonstrator in astrophysics Oxford U., England, 1972-75; sr. sci. rsch. officer South African Astron. Obs., Capetown, Republic of South Africa, 1975-78; Annie J. Cannon fellow U. Del., Newark, 1978-79; asst. prof. Pa. State U., State College, 1979-82; asst. prof. to assoc. prof. physics and astronomy Dartmouth Coll., Hanover, NH, 1982-88, Margaret Anne and Edward Leede Disting. prof. physics and astronomy, 1988—; dir. Mich.-Dartmouth-MIT Obs., 1991-99. Vis. astronomer Cornell U., 1992; vis. fellow St. Catherine's Coll., Oxford, 2002. Editor: White Dwarfs, 1989; contbr. articles to jours. in field. Keeley fellow Wadham Coll., Oxford, 1992-93, vis. fellow in astrophysics Oxford U., 1992-93; vis. prof. Astron. Inst. Ruhr U. Bochum, Germany, 1993-94; recipient rsch. prize The Alexander von Humboldt Found., Germany, 1993-94, numerous grants NSF, NASA. Mem. Am. Astron. Soc., Internat. Union. Luthran. Office: Dartmouth Coll Dept Physics & Astronomy Wilder Lab Hanover NH 03755 Business E-Mail: gary.wegner@dartmouth.edu.

**WEGNER, JUDITH WELCH,** lawyer, educator, dean; b. Hartford, Conn., Feb. 14, 1950; d. John Raymond and Ruth (Thulen) Welch; m. Warren W. Wegner, Oct. 13, 1972. BA with honors, U. Wis., 1972; JD, UCLA, 1976. Bar: Calif. 1976, D.C. 1977, N.C. 1988, U.S. Supreme Ct. 1980, U.S. Ct. Appeals. Law clk. to Judge Warren Ferguson, U.S. Dist. Ct. for So. Dist. Calif., L.A., 1976-77; atty. Office Legal Counsel and Land & Natural Resources Divsn. U.S. Dept. Justice, Washington, 1977-79; spl. asst. to sec. U.S. Dept. Edn., Washington, 1979-80; vis. assoc. prof. U. Iowa Coll. Law, Iowa City, 1981; asst. prof. U. N.C. Sch. Law, Chapel Hill, 1981-84, assoc. prof., 1984-88, prof., 1988—, assoc. dean, 1986-88, dean, 1989-99; sr. scholar Carnegie Found. for Advancement of Tchg., 1999—2001; chmn. faculty U. N.C. 2003—. Spkr. in field. Chief comment editor UCLA Law Rev., 1975-76; contbr. articles to legal publs. Mem. ABA (chmn. planning com. African Law Sch. Initiative 1994, co-chmn. planning com. 1994 mid-yr. deans meeting sect. on legal edn. and admission to bar), N.C. Assn. Women Attys. (Gweneth Davis award 1989), N.C. State Bar Assn., Assn. Am. Law Schs. (mem. exec. com. sect. on law & edn. 1985-88, mem. exec. com. sect. on local govt. law 1989-92, mem. accreditation com. 1986-88, chmn. 1989-91, program chmn. 1992 ann. meeting, program chmn. 1994 ann. meeting, mem. exec. com. 1992-96, pres. 1995), Soc. Am. Law Tchrs., Nat. League Cities (coun.-mentor program 1989-91), Women's Internat. Forum, Order of Coif (nat. exec. com. 1989-91), Phi Beta Kappa. Democrat. Office: U of NC Sch Law Van Hecke Wettach Hall Campus Box 3380 Chapel Hill NC 27599-3380 Office Phone: 919-962-4113. Business E-Mail: judith_wegner@unc.edu.

**WEGNER, LUCY SIEFERT,** information specialist; b. Santa Monica, Calif., Dec. 11, 1953; MLS, MBA, UCLA, 1987; MA, Calif. State U., Northridge, 1980. Dir. Ctr. for Scholarly Tech. U. So. Calif., 1993-97, head strategic planning coord., 1998—99; dir. libr. Rand Corp., 2000—. Mem. Spl. Librs. Assn. Democrat. Avocations: travel, music.

**WEH, ALLEN EDWARD,** aviation executive; b. Salem, Oreg., Nov. 17, 1942; s. Edward and Harriet Ann (Hicklin) W.; m. Rebecca Ann Roberton, July 5, 1968; children: Deborah Susan, Ashley Elizabeth, Brian Roberton. BS, U. N.Mex., 1966, MA, 1973. Asst. to chief adminstrv. officer Bank N.Mex., Albuquerque, 1973; pres. N.Mex. Airways, Inc., Albuquerque, 1974; dep. dir. N.Mex. Indochina Refugee Program, Santa Fe, 1975-76; dir. pub. affairs UNC Mining & Milling Co., Albuquerque, 1977-79; pres., CEO, CSI Aviation Svcs., Inc., Albuquerque, 1979—. Bd. dirs. N.Mex. Symphony Orgh., Albuquerque Conv. and Visitors Bur., 1982; mem. Albuquerque Police Advisory Bd., 1977-78; co-chmn. fin. com. Rep. Heather Wilson (Rep.-N.Mex.) Re-Election Campaign, 1999-2004; mem. state fin. com. G.W. Bush for Pres.; co-chmn. N.Mex. Victory, 2000; chmn. N.Mex. Rep. Party, 2004—; mem. nat. adv. bd. U. N.Mex. Anderson Sch. Bus.; elected del. GOP Nat. Conv., 2000, 04; chmn. Nat. Com. for Employer Support of the Guard and Res., 2002-03. Capt. USMC, 1966-71, Vietnam; Col. USMCR, 1971-97, active duty, 1990-91, Persian Gulf, 1992-93, Somalia, 2003-04, Iraq. Decorated Silver Star, Legion of Merit, Bronze Star with V device, Purple Heart with two gold stars, Meritorious Svc. medal with gold star, five Air medals. Mem. Marine Corps Res. Officers Assn. (life, bd. dirs. 1973, 86), Res. Officers Assn. U.S. (life), SCV (life), N.Mex. Retail Assn. (chmn. 1999-2000). Episcopalian. Office: CSI Aviation Svcs Inc 3700 Rio Grande Blvd NW Albuquerque NM 87107-2876 Office Phone: 505-761-9000.

**WEHMEIER, KAI FREDERICK,** philosopher, educator; b. Summit, N.J., Mar. 15, 1968; s. Friedel Heinrich Gustav Paul and Marlis Wehmeier; m. Elisabeth Giehl, Aug. 5, 2002; m. Katja Ramberg, June 5, 1992 (div. July 24, 2002); 1 child, Anna Sara Marie. MA, U. Calif., Berkeley, Calif., 1992; degree, Westfälische Wilhelms-U., Münster, Germany, 1996; MA, Ruhr-U. Bochum, Germany, 1999. Asst. prof. logic and philosophy of sci. U. Calif., Irvine, Calif., 2002—04, assoc. prof. logic and philosophy of sci., 2004—. Office: Logic and Philosophy of Science UC Irvine 3151 Social Science Plaza A Irvine CA 92697 Office Phone: 949-824-7792.

**WEHN, KAREN SWANEY,** education educator, consultant; b. Chillicotne, Ohio, Mar. 1, 1950; d. Glenn Warren and Joyce Wood Swaney; m. David Carl Wehn, Apr. 8, 1989; 1 child, Glenn Ian Taylor. BA, Ohio State Univ., Columbus, Ohio, 1980; MS, Kent State Univ., Kent, Ohio, 1986. Cert. Profl. Geologist 1996. Rsch. asst. Ohio State Univ., Columbus, Ohio, 1976—92; project geologist Conestoga Rover 3 Assoc., Niagara Falls, NY, 1992—97, Golder Assoc., Niagara Falls, NY, 1997—; lectr. Buffalo State Coll., Buffalo, 1997—; asst. prof. Erie CC, Buffalo, 2000—. Rschr., Antarctica, 1980—85; pres. Buffalo Assn. of profl. Geologists, Buffalo, 1997—98. Contbr. articles pub. to profl. jour. Yale leader Warrens Corners United Meth. Ch., 2004—05. Grantee travel to Australia, Nat. Sci. Found., 1982, travel and work in Nigeria, Earth Watch, 1990—91. Mem.: Air and Waste Mgmt. Assn. (bd. mem.). Meth. Business E-Mail: wehnks@bscmail.buffalostate.edu.

**WEHR, MATTHEW,** music educator; b. Allentown, Pa., Sept. 7, 1980; s. Mark and Julie Wehr. BA in Music Edn., Lebanon Valley Coll., Annville, Pa., 2002, Assoc. organist First Presbyn. Ch., Allentown, Pa., 2003—; music tchr. No. Lehigh Sch. Dist., Slatington, Pa., 2002—06, So. Lehigh Sch. Dist., Center Valley, Pa., 2006—. Sec. No. Lehigh Edn. Assn., Slatington, 2002. Mem.: Am. Guild Organists. Presbyterian. Avocations: travel, golf, theater. Home: 2209 W Walnut St Allentown PA 18104 Office: Southern Lehigh High Sch 5800 Main St Center Valley PA 18034 Office Phone: 610-282-1421.

**WEHR, WILLIAM JAMES,** judge; b. Covington, Ky., July 13, 1950; s. Robert F. and Margaret O. (Schmaeling) W.; m. Nancy Jean Harrison, Dec. 29, 1971; children: Laura Beth, Lindsay Ann. BA, U. Ky., 1972; JD, No. Ky. U., 1976. Bar: Ky. 1976, U.S. Dist. Ct. (ea. dist.) Ky., 1976, U.S. Supreme Ct. 1980. Assoc. Kaufman, Johnson and Blau, Newport, Ky., 1976-77; ptnr. Twehues, Verst & Wehr, Newport, 1978-88; asst. county atty. Campbell County, Newport, 1978-88; judge Campbell County Cir. Ct. Divsn. I, Newport, 1988—2004, chief regional cir. judge No. Ky. region, 1996—2004, chief sr. status judge, 2004—. Guest lectr. Chase Coll. Law, 1981-90, adj. faculty, 1991—. Bd. dirs. Sr. Citizens No. Ky., Inc., Covington, 1980-87, pres., 1984-85; bd. dirs. Hosea House Soup Kitchen, 1992-2003. Served with USCGR, 1968-74. Recipient Disting. Prosecutor award Citizens for Decency Through Law, Inc., 1981. Mem.: No. Ky. Bar Assn. (pres. 1984), Ky. Bar Assn. (ho. of dels. 1985—88), Elks. Roman Catholic. Office: Chef Sr Status Judge 57 Memory Ln Fort Thomas KY 41075-1035 Business E-Mail: williamwehr@kycourts.net.

**WEHRING, BERNARD WILLIAM,** nuclear engineering educator; b. Monroe, Mich., Aug. 3, 1937; s. Bernard Albert and Alma Christina (Graf) W.; m. Margaret Mary Robinson, Sept. 5, 1959; children: Mary Ann, James, Susan, Barbara. BSE. in Physics, U. Mich., 1959, BSE. in Math, 1959; MS in Physics, U. Ill., 1961, PhD in Nuclear Engring, 1966. Asst. prof. nuc. engring. U. Ill., Urbana, 1966-70, assoc. prof., 1970-77, prof., 1977-84, asst. dean engring., 1981-82; prof. nuc. engring. N.C. State U., Raleigh, 1984-89; dir. nuc. reactor program NC State U., Raleigh, 1988-84; prof. mech. engring. U. Tex., Austin, 1989-2000, dir. Nuc. Engring. Tchg. Lab., 1989-2000; adj. prof. nuc. engring. NC State U., Raleigh, 2000—. Cons. Argonne and Los Alamos nat. labs.; mem. crosssect. evaluation working group Brookhaven Nat. Lab. Contbr. sects. to books, articles to profl. publs. AEC fellow, 1963-65; NSF grantee, 1968— Fellow Am. Nuc. Soc.; mem. Am. Nuclear Soc. (standards com.), Am. Phys. Soc. Achievements include contributing in the generation of basic nuc. data and develop. of new instruments and exptl. techniques. Home: 516 Westbrook Dr Raleigh NC 27615-7321 Business E-Mail: bwwehrin@eos.ncsu.edu.

**WEHRLE, LEROY SNYDER,** economist, educator; b. St. Louis, Feb. 5, 1932; s. Fred Joseph and Eleanor (Snyder) W.; m. JoAnn Griffith, Aug. 29, 1959; children— Chandra Lee, Lon Joseph. BS, Washington U., St. Louis, 1953; MA in Econs, Yale, 1956, PhD with honors, 1959. Asst. instr. Yale, 1958-59; with econ. sect. AID mission to Laos, 1960-61; sr. staff economist President's Council Econ. Advisers, 1961-62; spl. econ. adviser to U.S. Ambassador Unger, Vientiane, 1962; dep. dir. AID mission to Laos, 1963-64; asst. dir. AID mission, also econ. counsellor to U.S. ambassador, Saigon, 1964-67; assoc. dir. AID Mission, Saigon, 1964-67; dept. asst. adminstr. Vietnam, AID, Dept. State, 1967-68; univ. fellow Harvard, 1968-69; sr. fellow Brookings Instn., 1969-70; dir. Ill. Inst. for Social Policy, Springfield, 1970-72; aide to Lt. Gov. Paul Simon, 1972; prof. economics Sangamon State U., 1972-88; founding ptnr., chief exec. officer Health Econs. and Mkt. Analysis Inc., Springfield, 1987-94; pres. Healthcare Cost Analysis, Inc., 1994—. Chmn. bd. Tie Collar, Ltd. Mem. spl. study group Alliance Progress, 1962; mem. Rockefeller Latin Am. Mission, 1969; chmn. study team world food and nutrition study Nat. Acad. Sci., 1976-77. Served with AUS, 1953-55. Recipient William A. Jump meml. award, 1966 Home and Office: 2001 S Bates Ave Springfield IL 62704-3304 Office Phone: 217-203-7781. Personal E-mail: wehrle@springnet1.com.

**WEHRMANN, PAUL ALAN,** lawyer; s. Ralph Frederick and Dorothy Mary Wehrmann; m. Tracy Elizabeth McCartor, May 22, 1999; children: Anna Fair, Joseph Alan, Audrey Rose. BA magna cum laude, So. Meth. U., Dallas, 1987, JD, 1990. Bar: Tex. 1990. Summer assoc. Baker & McKenzie, Dallas, 1988—89; Sydney, NSW, Australia, 1989, Vinson & Elkins L.L.P., Dallas, 1989, assoc., 1990—93, Washington, 1992—93, Cassell & Stone, L.L.P., Dallas, 1993—98, Haynes and Boone, L.L.P., Austin, Tex., 1998—99, Dallas, 1999—2000, sr. counsel Richardson, Tex., 2000—03; pvt. practice Dallas, 2003—04; ptnr. Wood & Sartain, LLP, Dallas, 2003—. Contbr. articles to newspapers. Asst. gen. counsel Dallas Internet Soc., 2002; mem. Metroplex Tech. Bus. Coun. Internat. Com., Dallas, 2002—03; bd. mem., treas., sec. Texchange Dallas, 2002—06; bd. mem., treas., gen. counsel Twelve Hills Nature Ctr., Dallas, 2004—05; bd. mem., sec., gen. counsel Video Assn. Dallas, 2001—06. Recipient Am. Jurisprudence award, The Lawyers Coop. Pub. Co., 1988, Kilgore & Kilgore award, So. Meth. U. Sch. Law, 1988, Barfield-Hunsucker award, 1990; scholar, Nat. Merit Scholarship Corp., 1984; Pres. scholar, So. Meth. U., 1984—87, univ. scholar, 1984—87, Hatton W. Sumners scholar, Hatton W. Sumners Found., 1987—90. Mem.: ABA (assoc.), State Bar Tex. (licentiate), Travis County Bar Assn. (assoc.), Dallas Bar Assn. (assoc.), Coll. State Bar Tex. (assoc.), Phi Beta Kappa, Mensa (assoc.). Roman Catholic. Avocations: travel, writing, cooking, hockey. Home: 1821 Timbergrove Cir Dallas TX 75208 Office: Wood & Sartain LLP 12655 N Central Expressway Dallas TX 75243 Office Phone: 972-759-3817.

**WEHRWEIN, AUSTIN CARL,** freelance/self-employed reporter; b. Austin, Tex., Jan. 12, 1916; s. George S. and Anna (Ruby) W.; m. Judith Oakes, 1950; children: Sven Austin, Paul, Peter, Joanna Judith. AB, U. Wis., 1937; LL.B., Columbia U., 1940; student, London Sch. Econs., 1948. Reporter Washington Bur., UP, 1941-43, 46-48; information specialist E.C.A., London, Copenhagen, Oslo, Stockholm, 1948-51; financial writer Milw. Jour., 1951-53; staff corr. Time, Inc., Chgo., 1953-55; reporter Chgo. Sun-Times, 1955-56, fin. editor, 1956-57; chief Chgo. bur. N.Y. Times, 1957-66; editorial writer Mpls. Star, 1966-82. Editor The Observer, 1984-87. Served with USAAF, 1943-45; mem. staff Stars and Stripes 1945-46, Shanghai, China. Recipient Pulitzer prize for internat. reporting, 1953; Disting. Journalism award U. Wis., 1963; cert. of merit ABA Gavel competition, 1968, 80; Gavel award, 1969, 71 Home and Office: 2309 Carter Ave Saint Paul MN 55108-1640 E-mail: wehr2309@msn.com.

**WEI, BENJAMIN MIN,** engineering educator; b. Hebei, China, Aug. 11, 1930; s. Fu Shun and Yuan Qing (Zhang) W.; m. Diana Yun Dee; 1 child: Victor Mark. BSME, Chung Cheng Inst. Tech., 1953; MSME, Concordia U., 1970; PhD, Pa. State U., 1981. Mech. engr. Ordnance Corps Arsenal, Taipei, Taiwan, 1953-59; tchr. Wenshan High Sch., Taipei, 1960-61; teaching asst. New Brunswick (Can.) U., 1962-64; supr. Domtar Constrn. Materials Co., Can., 1964-66; computer programmer McGill U., Can., 1966-67, Montreal (Can.) U., 1967-68; tchr. Pierrefond Comprehensive High sch., Que., 1970-73; prof. Norfolk (Va.) State U., 1974—. Hon. prof., cons. Taiyuan U. Polytech. Contbr. articles to profl. jours. Mem. Statistical Quality Control of China. Home: 1152 Janaf Pl Norfolk VA 23502-2631

**WEI, BING,** mathematics professor; s. Baiying Wei and Huiqin Luo; m. Lanzhen Song, Apr. 13, 1984; 1 child, Wei. BS, Huazhong Normal U., Wuhan, China, 1982, MS, 1986; PhD, Tech. U. Berlin, 1992. Lectr. Huazhong Normal U., Wuhan, China, 1986—89; assoc. prof. Inst. Sys. Sci., Academia Sinica, Beijing, 1996—2001; prof. Inst. of Sys. Sci., Academia Sinica, 2001—; asst. prof. U. Miss., University, 2002—. Fellow, Croucher Found. of Hong Kong, 2000; grantee, Natural Sci. Found. of China, 1998—2003, Nat. Edn. Com. of China, 1993—96. Office: U Mississippi 310 Hume University MS 38677 Office Phone: 662-915-1250. Business E-Mail: bwei@olemiss.edu.

**WEI, DONG,** technologist; s. Dachang Wei and Youchun Yan; m. Yuhong Zhai Zhai, Oct. 5, 1993; children: Brian Myles, Brandon McKinley. MSEE, BSEE, U. of Idaho, 1988—94, MS in physics, 1988—94. Design engr. Morrison-Knusen Co, Boise, Idaho, 1993—94; software engr. ACS Infosystems, Boise, Idaho, 1994—95; design engr. Hewlett Packard Co. Roseville, Calif., 1995—98, engr./scientist 1998—2003, master, 2003—04; disting. technologist Hewlett Packard Co., Roseville, Calif., 2004—. Bd. dirs., v.p. Unified EFI Forum, Wash., 2005—. Recipient Intel Achievements award, Intel, 2001, 1st Pl., Uniforum, 1995, 2nd Pl., HIMSS, 1995, 1st Pl., Windows World, 1995. Mem.: IEEE (sr.). Achievements include design of platform architecture of the Intel Itanium processor-based HP integrity servers; patents pending for computer systems; first to remove PC-AT legacy in server designs based on Intel processors; development of computer platform interfaces with operating systems. Personal E-mail: dong.wei@ieee.org.

**WEI, JAMES,** chemical engineering professor, academic dean; b. Macao, China, Aug. 14, 1930; came to U.S., 1949, naturalized, 1960; s. Hsiang-chen and Nuen (Kwok) W.; m. Virginia Hong, Nov. 4, 1956; children: Alexander, Christina, Natasha, Randolph (dec.). BS in Chem. Engring. Ga. Inst. Tech., 1952; MS, MIT, 1954, ScD, 1955; grad. Advanced Mgmt. Program Harvard, 1969. From rsch. engr. to rsch. assoc. Mobil Oil, Paulsboro, NJ, 1956-62, sr. scientist Princeton, NJ, 1963-68, mgr. corp. planning N.Y.C., 1969-70; Allan P. Colburn prof. U. Del., Newark, 1971-77; Sherman Fairchild distinguished scholar Calif. Inst. Tech., 1977; Warren K. Lewis prof. MIT, Cambridge, 1977-91, head dept. chem. engring., 1977-88; Pomeroy and Betty Smith prof. chem. engring. Princeton (N.J.) U., 1991—, dean Sch. Engring. and Applied Sci., 1991—2002. Vis. prof. Princeton, 1962-63, Calif. Inst. Tech., 1965; cons. Mobil Oil Corp.; cons. com. on motor-vehicle emissions Nat. Acad. Sci., 1972-74, 79-80; mem. sci. adv. bd. EPA, 1976-79; mem. Presdl. Pvt. Sector Survey Task Force on Dept. Energy, 1982-83. Bd. editors Chem. Tech, 1971-80, Chem. Engring. Communications, 1972—; cons. editor chem. engring. series, McGraw-Hill, 1964—; editor-in-chief: Advances in Chemical Engineering, 1980; Contbr. papers, monographs to profl. lit., The Structure of Chemical Processing Industries, 1979. Trustee Am. U. Beirut, 1998—, Smith Coll., 1999—. Recipient Am. Acad. Achievement Golden Plate award, 1966. Mem. AIChE (dir. 1970-72, Inst. lectr. 1968, Profl. Progress award 1970, Walker award 1980, Lewis award 1985, v.p. 1987, pres. 1988, Founders award 1990), Am. Chem. Soc. (award in petroleum chemistry 1966), Nat. Acad. Engring. (nominating com. 1981, 96, peer com. 1980-82, membership com. 1983-85, Draper award com. 1995-97, chair chem. engring. sect. 1998-99), AAAS, Am. Acad. Arts and Scis., Academica Sinica of Taiwan, Sigma Xi. Home: 571 Lake Dr Princeton NJ 08540 Office: Princeton U Engring Quadrangle Princeton NJ 08544-5263 E-mail: jameswei@princeton.edu.

**WEI, RONGHUA,** research scientist; s. Zhengqi Wei and Fuying Wang; m. Guihua Tao; 1 child, Ron. PhD, Colo. State U., 1990. Rsch. assoc. Space Sci. and Tech. Ctr., Beijing, 1981—85; sr. scientist Colo. State U., Fort Collins, Colo., 1990—93, Hughes Rsch. Labs., Malibu, Calif., 1993—2000; staff scientist S.W. Rsch. Inst., San Antonio, 2001—. Mem. various conf. coms. Contbr. chapters to books, over 70 articles to profl. jours. Recipient Malcolm R. Currie Innovation award, Hughes Electronics Corp, 1997. Achievements include patents for method and apparatus for testing parts and materials in a controlled environment such as an atomic oxygen atmosphere; method of plasma ion deposition of diamondlike carbon coatings; method and apparatus for plasma processing a workpiece in an enveloping plasma; method of in-situ displacement/stress control in electroplating; method of plasma assisted diamond polishing; method and apparatus for large-scale diamond polishing; method for depositing coatings on the interior surfaces of tubular walls; method and apparatus of plasma enhanced coaxial magnetron for sputter-coating interior surfaces. Office: Southwest Research Institute 6220 Culebra Road San Antonio TX Office Phone: 210-522-5204. Office Fax: 210-522-6220. Business E-Mail: rwei@swri.org.

**WEI, XIANGDONG,** physicist, researcher; s. Bo and Jinzhi Wei. BS in Astrophysics, Peking U., Beijing, 1982; MS in Physics, Syracuse U., NY, 1992, PhD, 1988. From tchg. asst. to rsch. assoc. Syracuse U., 1988—98; asst. physicist Brookhaven Nat. Lab., Upton, NY, 1998—2000, assoc. physicist, 2000—03, physicist, 2003—. Presenter in field. Contbr. articles to profl. jours. Mem.: Am. Phys. Soc. Achievements include development of highly polarized frozen-sipn HD targets for both nuc. physics and inertial-confinement-fusion experiments; design of utilizing the polarized HD target sys. for nuc. physics measurements; research in spin-lattice relaxation time of HD-hydrogen deuteride. Office: Brookhaven Nat Lab 20 Pennsylvania Ave Upton NY 11973 Office Phone: 631-344-8012.

**WEI, XINZHOU,** engineering educator; b. China; PhD, CUNY, N.Y., 2002. Lectr. CUNY, Coll. Tech., Bklyn., 2002—03; asst. prof., 2003—. Program com. Internat. Symposium on Knowledge Comm. and Conf., Orlando, Fla., 2006—; session chair The 8th World Multi-Conf. on Systemics, Cybernetics and Informatics, Orlando, 2004; Asian Am. high edn. coun. Asian Rsch. Inst., NYC, 2004—; info. tech. com. CUNY Coll. Tech., Bklyn., 2003—; reviewer IEE Jour. of Network. Security, 2006—. Recipient Sue Rosenberg Zalk Student Rsch. and Travel award, CUNY, 2002, Best Paper award, 6th World Multi-Conf. Systemics, Cybernetics and Informatics, 2002, 8th World Multi-Conf. Systemics, Cybernetics and Informatics, 2004, 2d prize, Chinese Nat. Higher Edn. Com., 1991; grantee Perkins grantee, N.Y. State, 2006—, PSC-CUNY grantee, Rsch. Found. of the CUNY, 2006—, 2005—06, 2004—05. Mem.: Internat. Soc. of Systemics, Cybernetics and Informatics, Asian Rsch. Inst. (ny 2004—06), IEEE. Office: City University of New York / CityTech Dept of Electrical Eng 300 Jay Street Brooklyn NY 11201

**WEI, YING,** chemist; b. Harbin, China, Aug. 29, 1952; d. Wen-Jia Wei and Su-Zhen Xu; m. Jian-Ming Jiang, Jan. 28, 1981 (div. Feb. 1997); 1 child, Mike Jiang. BS in Chemistry, Hei Long Jiang U., China, 1982; MS, Rennes I U., France, 1984, PhD, 1986. Postdoc. fellow A&M U., College Station, Tex., 1989—90, Lamar U., Beaumont, Tex., 1990—91; IT corp. lab. supr. IT Corp., Cosby, Tex., 1991—95; city lab. mgr. City of Houston/Water Prodn., 1996—. Contbr. articles to profl. jour. Mem.: Am. Water Works Assn. Home: 3414 Almond Creek Dr Houston TX 77059 Office: City of Houston 2300 Federal Rd Houston TX 77015 E-mail: ying.wei@cityofhouston.com.

**WEI, YINGHONG,** finance educator; b. Nan Chang, China, Apr. 3, 1969; d. Zhijin Wei and Dahua Wu; m. Ardeshir Owrang, Mar. 6, 2004; 1 child, Mariam Boshen Wei Owrang. B, East China Jiaotong U., Nan Chang, 1990; M, City U. of Hong Kong, 1999; PhD, U. NC, Chapel Hill, 2005. Cert. acct., Ministry of Pers. and Fin., People's Republic of China. Asst. acct. Rlwy. Ministry of China, Beijing, 1990—92; asst. acct. cost mgmt. Fin. and Acctg. Dept., Gold Peak (China) Electronic Ltd., Hui Zhou, 1992—93; acting gen. mgr., chief acct. Desay Chemical-Light Corp., Hui Zhou, 1993—95; auditor Stephen Liu & Co., Hong Kong, 1995—97; with Okla. State U., 2005—. V.p. edn. Toastmasters Club, Chapel Hill, 2003. Recipient 1st pl. club level, area level and divsn. level, 3d pl. state level, Toastmasters Club, 2003, winner doctoral dissertation award competition, Inst. for the Study of Bus. Markets, Pa. State U., 2004; scholar, City U. of Hong Kong, 1997—99, Chinese U. of Hong Kong, 1999—2000, U. N.C. Chapel Hill, 2000—04; Dissertation fellow, Kauffman Found., 2004—05. Mem.: Assn. Consumer Rsch., Product Devel. and Mgmt. Assn., Acad. Mgmt., Am. Mktg. Assn. ((Sheth) Found. Vis. Scholars Travel grantee 2004). Avocations: swimming, table tennis, travel, music, reading.

**WEI, YUCHUAN,** mathematician, electrical engineer, physicist, researcher; b. Jiaozuo, Henan, China, Sept. 1, 1966; s. Bangfu and Cuilan (Liu) W. BS, Lanzhou U., 1988; MS, Chinese Acad. Sci., Beijing, 1994; PhD, Beijing U of Sci. and Tech., 1998. Asst. prof. Gansu Univ. of Industry, Lanzhou, 1988-91; lectr. dept. physics Beijing Univ. Sci. and Tech., 1994—; postdoctoral fellow dept. elec. engring. Beijing U. Aeronautics and Astronautics, 1999—. Internat. advisor for Internat. Conf. on Math. Modelling of Nonlinear Systems, India Inst. Tech., Khakagpur; vis. scholar Inst. Applied Maths., Italy,

2000—. Contbr. articles to profl. jours. Office: Beijing U Sci & Tech Dept Physics Beijing 100083 China also: Inst Applied Math CNR Via P Castellino 111 80131 Napoli Italy Fax: 39-081-5608288.

**WEIANT, ELIZABETH ABBOTT,** retired biology professor; b. New Britain, Conn., July 4, 1913; d. William Armstrong and Flora (Abbott) W. BS, MS, Tufts U., 1943; MA, Radcliffe Coll., 1952; EdD, Boston U., 1970. Instr. biology Tufts Coll., Medford, Mass., 1943-56, asst. prof., 1957-61; asst. prof. biology Simmons Coll., Boston, 1961-71, assoc. prof., 1972-79, chmn. dept., 1977-79, ret., 1979; corr. Evening Citizen, Laconia, N.H., 1987-98, Franklin-Tilton Telegram, Franklin, N.H., 1990-2000. Rschr. OSRD, USPHS, NSF, 1943-61; sr. rsch. fellow Max-Planck Inst., Seewiesen, Fed. Republic Germany, 1958; physiologist for product validation Cordis Corp., Miami, Fla., 1970 Contbr. articles to profl. jours. Active Hist. Dist. Commn., Sanbornton, NH, 1979-83; sec., Sanbornton Conservation Commn., 1979-83, Trustees of Trust Fund, Sanbornton, 1985-96; bd. dirs., sec. NH affiliate Am. Heart Assn., Manchester, 1981-85; bd. dirs., com. mem. Franklin, NH, Regional Hosp., 1984-91; pres. Sanbornton Hist. Soc., 1980-82; publicity chmn. Friends NH Music Festival; alumna trustee Tufts U., 1974-81, trustee emeritus, 1981. Recipient Disting. Svc. award Tufts U., 1970, Tower award Westbrook Coll., Portland, Maine, 1974, Woman of Yr. award Tilton-Northfield Bus. and Profl. Women, 1980, Heart of Gold award Am. Heart Assn., 1986, award for Pub. Svc. Belknap County Pomona Grange, 1990, Gov.'s Outstanding Vol. award, 1992. Mem.: Am. Inst. Biol. Scis., Grange, Sigma Xi (sec. Tufts U. chpt. 1947—59). Republican. Home: PO Box 11 Sanbornton NH 03269-0011

**WEICHER, JOHN CHARLES,** economist, research director; b. Chgo., Mar. 8, 1938; s. John Jr. and Ruth Agnes (Waits) W.; m. Alice Jean Landt, Sept. 30, 1972; children: John Victor, Stephany Jean Ruth. AB, U. Mich., 1959; PhD, U. Chgo., 1968. Acting asst. prof. U. Calif., Irvine, 1965-67; assoc. and asst. prof. econs. Ohio State U., Columbus, 1967-77; with div. policy rsch. OEO, Washington, 1972-73; dir. div. econ. policy HUD, Washington, 1973-74, dep. asst. sec. econ. affairs, 1975-77, asst. sec. policy devel. and rsch., 1989—93, asst. sec. housing, commr. FHA, 2001—05; dir. econs. and fin. markets program Urban Inst., Washington, 1977-81; F.K. Weyerhaeuser scholar in pub. policy Am. Enterprise Inst, Washington, 1981-87; assoc. dir. econ. policy Office Mgmt. and Budget, Washington, 1987-89; dir. urban polity studies Hudson Inst., Washington, 1993—2001, dir. Ctr. Housing and Fin. Markets, 2005—. Author: Urban Renewal: Federal Program for Local Problems, 1972, Housing: Federal Policies and Programs, 1980, Maintaining the Safety Net, 1984; contbr. articles to profl. jours. Mem. Am. Econ. Assn., Am. Real Estate and Urban Econs. Assn. (pres. 1982, George Bloom award career achievement, 1993). Republican. Presbyterian. Avocation: sports. Office: Hudson Inst 1015 15th St NW Washington DC 20005 Office Phone: 202-974-2420. Office Fax: 202-974-2410. Business E-Mail: john@hudson.org.

**WEICK, CYNTHIA WAGNER,** business educator; b. Lincoln, Nebr., Jan. 29, 1957; d. Richard and Gloria Jean (Larsen) W. PhD, The Wharton Sch. U. of Pa, Phila., PA, 1982—86; MS, The Ohio State U., Columbus, OH, 1979—80, BS, 1975-79. Prof. of bus. administrn. U. of the Pacific, Stockton, Calif., 1990—; corp. planner Pioneer Hi-Bred, Internat., Des Moines, Iowa, 1987—90; cons. United Nat. Devel. Program, Manhattan, NY, 1984—85; rsch. scientist Battelle Columbus Laboratories, Columbus, Ohio, 1980—82. Contbr. articles on mgmt. of tech. to profl. jours. Dean's fellow Wharton Sch. U. Pa., 1983-84. Mem. AAAS. Avocations: art, philosophy, kayaking. Office: Univ of the Pacific 3601 Pacific Avenue Stockton CA 95211 Office Phone: 209-946-2631. Business E-Mail: cwagner@uop.edu.

**WEICKERT, WANDA OPAL,** child welfare and attendance counselor, psychotherapist, educator; b. North Hills, Calif., Apr. 10, 1941; d. Frank W and Opal M Weickert. BS in Phys. Edn., Kans. State Coll., 1959—63, MS in Phys. Edn., 1963—66; MA in Marriage and Family Therapy, Phillips Grad. Inst., 1983—85; Pupil Personnel Services Credential, Calif. Luth. Coll., 1987—89. Marriage Family Child Therapist Bd. of Behavioral Sciences-California, 1991; Teaching Credential Kans., 1963, Calif. 1969. Health phys. edn. tchr. Circle HS, Towanda, Kans., 1963—69; phys. edn. tchr. Nightingale Mid. Sch., LA, 1969—73; coach & phys. edn. tchr. Reseda Sr. HS, LA, 1973—81; career edn., coach, tchr. Kennedy Sr. HS, LA, 1981—89; child welfare & attendance counselor LA Unified Sch. Dist., 1989—; marriage family child therapist Self Employed, LA, 1991—; dist. counselor LA Unified Schs., 1994—2001. Coord. cheerleaders, kayettes and pep club Circle HS, Towanda, Kans., 1963—69; dir. camp waterfront Young Women's Christian Assn., Wichita, Kans.; counselor San Fernando Valley Mental Health Clinic, Van Nuys, Calif., 1985—88; drug prevention program dir. Kennedy HS, LA, 1987—89; counselor Valley Cmty. Clinic, North Hollywood, Calif., 1989—92; adv. bd. Sch. Attendance Rev. Bd. LAUSD, LA, 1991—2001; coach 1st pl. gymnast fl. exercise, city championships LA Unified Schs., 1976, coach 3d pl. volleyball team city championships, 79, coach 3d pl. gymnast all-around events, city championships, 80, crisis team leader, 1996—2001. Choreographer (drill team performance) LA Coliseum, 1977, Hollywood Christmas Parades, 1984—86, (1st pl. band and drill team championships) LA Unified Schs., 1978. Vol. Girl Scouts, LA, 1994—95; contbr. Civitan, Burbank, Calif.; presidents club contbr. Pitts. State U., Kans. Recipient Commendation for 32 years Pub. Sch. Svc., Mayor Jim Hahn, LA, 2001. Mem.: Calif. Assn. of Marriage and Family Therapists, Calif. Teachers Assn., Delta Psi Kappa (life), Alpha Sigma Alpha (life). Avocations: quilting, gardening, camping, swimming, walking. Office Phone: 818-893-2756. Personal E-mail: res1fosk@verizon.net.

**WEIDA, JOHNNY A.,** career military officer; BS, USAF Acad., 1978; MPA, Golden Gate Univ., 1987; M in nat. security & strategic studies, Naval War Coll., 1993. Commd. 2d lt. USAF, advanced through grades to brig. gen., 2003; pilot training, instr. pilot, flight examiner Williams AFB, Ariz., 1978—83; F-16 student pilot MacDill AFB, Fla., 1983—84; F-16 pilot 35th Tactical Fighter Squadron, Kunsan Air Base, Republic of Korea, 1984—85; F-16 instr. pilot & flight examiner 33rd Tactical Fighter Squadron, Shaw AFB, SC, 1985—88; Thunderbird pilot & ops. officer Nellis AFB, Nev., 1988—91; comdr. Cadet Squadron 27 USAF Acad., Colorado Springs, Colo., 1991—92; exec. officer, comdr. 20th Ops. Support Squadron Shaw AFB, SC, 1992—95; comdr. 12th Ops. group, Randolph AFB, Tex., 1995—97; dep. asst. chief of staff U.S. Forces Korea, Yongsan Army Garrison, Republic of Korea, 1997—99; chief combat forces dir. USAF HQ, Washington, 1999—2000; comdr. 388th Fighter Wing, Hill AFB, Utah, 2000—01, Squadron Officer Coll., Maxwell AFB, Ala., 2001—03; comdt. of cadets & comdr. 34th training wing USAF Acad., Colorado Springs, Colo., 2003—. Decorated Def. Superior Svc. medal, Legion of Merit with oak leaf cluster, Disting. Flying Cross, Air Force Meritorious Svc. medal with 4 oak leaf clusters, Air Force Commendation medal, Air Force Achievement medal. Office: Commandant of Cadets U S A F Academy CO 80840

**WEIDEMANN, CELIA JEAN,** social sciences educator, management consultant, financial consultant; b. Denver, Dec. 6, 1942; d. John Clement and Hazel (Van Tuyl) Kirlin; m. Wesley Clark Weidemann, July 1, 1972; 1 child, Stephanie Jean. BS, Iowa State U., 1964; MS, U. Wis., Madison, 1970, PhD, 1973; post grad., U. So. Calif., 1983. Advisor UN FAO, Ibadan, Nigeria, 1973—77; ind. rschr. Asia and Near East, 1977—78; program coord., asst. prof., rsch. assoc. U. Wis., Madison, Wis., 1979—81; chief inst. and human resources US AID, Washington, 1982—85; team leader, cons. Sumatra, Indonesia, 1984; dir. fed. econ. program Midwest Rsch. Inst., Washington, 1985—86; founder, pres. emeritus Weidemann Assoc., Arlington, Va., 1986—2000; pres. Weidemann Found., Arlington, Va., 2000—. Cons. U.S. Congress, Aspen Inst., Ford Found., World Bank, Egypt, Nigeria, Gambia, Pakistan, Indonesia, AID, Thailand, Jamaica, Panama, Philippines, Sierra Leone, Kenya, Jordon, Poland, India, Egypt, Russia, Finnish Internat. Devel. Agy., Namibia, pvt. client Estonia, Latvia, Russia, Japan, Internat. Ctr. Rsch. on Women, Zaire, UN FAO, Ghana, Internat. Statis. Inst., The Netherlands, Global Exch., 1986-87, Asian Devel. Bank, Mongolia, Nepal, Vietnam, Bangladesh, Indonesia, Philippines; bd. visitors Sch. Human Ecology, U. Wis., 2002—; bd. dirs. Cmty. Counseling and Edn. Ctr, Santa Barbara, Calif.;

peer reviewer NRC, NAS Author: (book) Planning Home Economics Curriculum for Social and Econ. Develop., Agrl. Ext. for Women Farmers in Africa, 1990, Fin. Services for Women, 1992, Egyptian Women and Micro.: The Invisible Entrepreneurs, 1992, Small Enterprise Development in Poland: Does Gender Matter?, 1994, Micro. and Gender in India, 1995, Supporting Women's Livelihoods: Micro Fin. That Works for the Majority, 2002; contbr. chapters to books and articles to profl. journals. Bd. dirs. Cmty. Counseling Ctr., Santa Barbara, Calif., 2004—. Am. Home Econ. Assn. Fellow, 1969-73; grantee Ford Found., 1987-89. Mem. Soc. Internat. Devel., Am. Sociol. Assn., Assn. for Women in Devel. (pres. 1989, founder, bd. dirs.), Women in Devel. (steering com.), Coalition for Women's Econ. Devel. and Global Equality, Internat. Devel. Conf. (bd. dirs., exec. com.), Internat. Platform Assn., Pi Lambda Theta, Omicron Nu. Avocations: mountain trekking, piano and pipe organ, canoeing, photography, poetry. Office: Weidemann Found 749 Westwood Drive Santa Barbara CA 93109 Office Phone: 805-965-2902. Personal E-mail: jweidemann@aol.com.

**WEIDENAAR, BRADLEY WILLIAM,** literature and language educator; b. Amsterdam, The Netherlands, Jan. 5, 1971; s. Harry John Weidenaar and Grace Ann Weidnaar; m. Kari Kay Dekkers, June 15, 2005; children: Elliot James, Alexander William, Quinn Nicole. BA, Dordt Coll., 1994; MA, Vitorbo U., 1998. Tchr. English Marshalltown High Sch., Iowa, 1994—, head English dept., 2002—06. Home: 608 Fremont Marshalltown IA 50158 Office: Marshalltown High Sch 1602 S 2d Ave Marshalltown IA 50158

**WEIDENAAR, DENNIS JAY,** retired economics professor; b. Grand Rapids, Mich., Oct. 4, 1936; s. John and Jennie (Beukema) W.; m. Kristin Andrews, July 14, 1943; children: Kaarin Jaye, John Andrews. AB, Calvin Coll., Grand Rapids, 1958; MA, U. Chgo., 1961; PhD, Purdue U., 1969. Asst. prof. econs. Purdue U., West Lafayette, Ind., 1966-72, assoc. prof., 1972-77, prof., 1977-83; interim dean Krannert Sch. of Mgmt., West Lafayette, 1983-84, assoc. dean, 1984-99; dean Krannert Grad. Sch. Mgmt., West Lafayette, 1990-99, prof. econs., 1999—. Cons. TRW, B.F. Goodrich, Ea. Panhandle; bd. dirs. Lafayette Ins. Co. Author: Economics. Contbr. articles to profl. jours. Bd. dirs. Ind. Coun. on Econ. Edn., Lafayette, 1974-83. Recipient The Leavey Awd for Excellence in Pvt. Enterprise Edn., Freedom's Found., Valley Forge, 1983, Distinguished Service Awd., Joint Council on Econ. Edn., N.Y., 1986, Golden Key Nat. Honor Soc., 1985. Mem. Rotary, Delta Sigma Pi, Beta Gamma Sigma (bd. dirs.), Phi Delta Kappa. Presbyterian. Home: 217 Rosebank Ln West Lafayette IN 47906-8614

**WEIDENBACH, MARY E.,** music educator; b. Miller, S.D., Nov. 11, 1949; d. Gordon LeRoy and Olive Hildred (Cellan) Parker; m. John H. Weidenbach, Jan. 1, 1971; children: Christina Myers, Justin, Jessica. BS in Music Edn., U. SD. 1972. Music tchr. Highmore (S.D.) Sch. Dist., 1972—76, Holy Family Cath. Sch., Mitchell, SD, 1977—80. Armour (S.D.) Sch., 1986—. Organist United Ch. of Christ, Parkston, SD, 1976—86, Armour, 1986—2006, United Meth. Ch., Highmore, 1972—76; mem. 14th Army Band, Mitchell, SD. With U.S. Nat. Guard, 1974—77. Mem.: ACDA, S.D. Music Educators Assn. (30-Yr. Tchg. award 2006). Home: PO Box 215 Armour SD 57313

**WEIDENBAUM, MURRAY LEW,** economist, educator; b. Bronx, N.Y., Feb. 10, 1927; s. David and Rose (Warshaw) Weidenbaum; m. Phyllis Green, June 13, 1954; children: Susan, James, Laurie. BBA, CCNY, 1948; MA, Columbia U., 1949; MPA, Princeton U., 1954, PhD, 1958; LLD, Baruch Coll., 1981, U. Evansville, 1983, McKendree Coll., 1993. Fiscal economist Bur. Budget, Washington, 1949—57; corp. economist Boeing Co., Seattle, 1958—62; sr. economist Stanford Rsch. Inst., Palo Alto, Calif., 1962—63; mem. faculty Washington U., St. Louis, 1964—, prof., chmn. dept. econs., 1966—69, Mallinckrodt prof., 1971—, dir. Ctr. for Study Am. Bus., 1974—81, Washington U., St. Louis, 1982—95; chmn. Ctr. for Study Am. Bus. Washington U., St. Louis, 1995—2000; asst. sec. econ. policy US Dept. Treasury, Washington, 1969—71; chmn. Coun. of Econ. Advisors The White House, Washington, 1981—82; hon. chmn. Weidenbaum Ctr. on the Economy, Govt. and Pub. Policy, St. Louis, 2001—. Chmn. rsch. adv. com. St. Louis Regional Indsl. Devel. Corp., 1965—69; exec. sec. Pres.'s Com. on Econ. Impact of Def. and Disarmament, 1964; mem. U.S. Fin. Investment Adv. Panel, 1970—72; cons. various firms and instns.; chmn. U.S. Commn. to Rev. the Trade Deficit, 1999—2000. Author: Federal Budgeting, 1964, Modern Public Sector, 1969, Economics of Peacetime Defense, 1974, Economic Impact of the Vietnam War, 1967, Government-Mandated Price Increases, 1975, The Future of Business Regulation, 1980, Rendezvous With Reality: The American Economy After Reagan, 1988, Rendezvous With Reality: The American Economy After Reagan, paperback edit., 1990, Business, Government, and the Public, 1990, Small Wars, Big Defense, 1992, The Bamboo Network, 1996, Business and Government in the Global Marketplace, 2004, One-Armed Economist, 2004, Advising Reagan: Making Economic Policy, 1981-82, 2005; mem. editl. bd.: Publius, 1971—2004, Jour. Econ. Issues, 1972—75, Challenge, 1974—81, 1983—, Business and the Contemporary World, 1997—2000. With U.S. Army, 1945. Named Banbury fellow, Princeton U., 1952—54; named to Free Market Hall of Fame, 1983; recipient Alexander Hamilton medal, U.S. Dept. Treasury, 1971, Disting. Writer award, Georgetown U., award for disting. tchg., Freedoms Found., 1980, award for best book in econs., Assn. Am. Pubs., 1993. Fellow: Assn. for Pvt. Enterprise Edn. (Adam Smith award 1986), City Coll. Alumni Assn. (Townsend Harris medal 1969), Soc. Tech. Comm., Nat. Assn. Bus. Economists, Cosmos. Office: Washington Univ Weidenbaum Ctr 1 Brookings Dr Saint Louis MO 63130-4899 Office Phone: 314-935-5662.

**WEIDENFELD, EDWARD LEE,** lawyer; b. Akron, Ohio, July 15, 1943; s. Sam and Beatrice (Cooper) W.; m. Sheila Rabb, Aug. 11, 1968; children: Nicholas, Daniel. BS, U. Wis., 1965; JD, Columbia U., 1968. Bar: NY 1968, admitted to pr. practice: US Supreme Ct, 1972, bar: DC 1973. Pvt. practice, NYC, 1969-71, 73-82, Washington, 1982—. Spl. cons. N.Y.C. Dept. Bldgs., 1967; counsel, dir. energy staff Com. on Interior and Insular Affairs, U.S. Ho. of Reps., 1971—73; mem. faculty Am. Law Inst.-ABA CLE Programs; mem. Internat. Del. to Observe Philippine Election, 1986, Internat. Del. to Observe Republic Korea Election, 1987, Pakistan Election, 1988, Chilean Election, 1989, Albanian Election, 1997; mem. D.C. Bar Task Force on the Omnibus Trusts and Estates Amendment Act of 2000, 1999—2001; lectr. to profl. groups. Editor in chief Atomic Energy Law Jour., 1975-76; contbg. author: Generations: Planning Your Legacy, 1999. Mem. Pres.'s Commn. on White House Fellowships, 1977; nat. chmn. Lawyers for Reagan/Bush, 1980; chief counsel Reagan/Bush Campaign, 1980; chmn. Reagan/Bush '84 Legal Adv. Bd., 1984; mem. D.C. Rep. Com., 1984-92, vice chmn., 1984-88; mem. Coun. Adminstrv. Conf. of U.S., 1981-92, sr. fellow, 1992-95; overseer dept. def. regional ctrs.; sec. Salvation Army Adv. Bd.; trustee Danny Kaye and Sylvia Fine Kaye Found.; vice chmn. bd. visitors Nat. Def. U. Named one of 75 Best Lawyers in Washington, Washingtonian mag., 2002; recipient medal of Peter the Great, Russian Fedn., 2000. Mem. ABA, D.C. Bar Assn., Am. Law Inst. (life), Assn. Bar City N.Y., Met. Club (bd. govs., Washington). Office: 888 17th St NW Washington DC 20006 Office Phone: 202-785-2143. Business E-Mail: edward@weidenfeldlaw.com.

**WEIDENFELD, SHEILA RABB,** television producer, writer; b. Cambridge, Mass., Sept. 7, 1943; d. Maxwell M. and Ruth (Cryden) Rabb; m. Edward L. Weidenfeld, Aug. 11, 1968; children: Nicholas Rabb, Daniel Rabb. BA, Brandeis U., 1965. Assoc. prodr. Metromedia, Inc., Sta. WNEW-TV, N.Y.C., 1965-68; talent coord. That Show with Joan Rivers, NBC, N.Y.C., 1968-71; coord. NBC network game programs, N.Y.C., 1968-71; prodr. Metromedia, Inc., Sta. WTTG-TV, Washington, 1971-73; creator/prodr. Take It From Here, NBC (WBC-TV), Washington, 1973-74; press sec. to first lady Betty Ford, spl. asst. to Pres. Gerald R. Ford, 1974-77; mem. Pres.'s Adv. Commn. on Hist. Preservation, 1977-81; TV prodr., moderator On the Record, NBC-TV, Sta. WRC-TV, Washington, 1978-79; pres. D.C. Prodns., Ltd., 1978; prodr., host Your Personal Decorator, 1987; mem. Sec. State's Adv. Commn. on Fgn. Svc. Inst., 1972-74; founding mem. Project Censured Panel of Judges, 1976—. Bd. dirs. First Star. Author: First Lady's Lady, 1979. Mem. U.S. Holocaust Meml. Coun., 1987-97; corporator Dana Hall Sch., Wellesley, Mass.; bd. dirs. Wolf Trap Found., Women's Campaign Fund,

1978-79; bd. dirs. D.C. Contemporary Dance Theatre, 1986-88, D.C. Rep. Ctrl. Com., 1984—, D.C. Preservation League, 1987-90; chmn. C&O Canal Nat. Hist. Park Commn., 1988—; bd. dirs. Am. Univ. Rome, 1988—96, Friends of the Scuola San Rocco, 2002—. Recipient awards for outstanding achievement in the media AAUW, 1973, 74, Silver Screen award A Campaign to Remember for the U.S. Holocaust Meml. Coun., 1989, Bronze medal Internat. Film and Video Festival N.Y., 1990; named hon. consul gen. of Republic of San Marino to Washington; knighted by Order of St. Agatha, Republic of San Marino, 1986. Mem. NATAS (Emmy award 1972), Washington Press Club, Am. Newspaper Women's Club, Am. Women in Radio and TV, Cosmos Club, Consular Corps, Sigma Delta Chi. Home: 3059 Q St NW Washington DC 20007-3081 E-mail: Sheila.Weidenfeld@verizon.net.

**WEIDENKOPF, THOMAS W.,** human resources specialist; b. 1959; married; 2 children. BA, Cornell U. Various human resources positions Pepsi-Cola, Pizza Hut; mgr. orgn. and staffing GE, 1981—83; dir. global staffing and devel. Honeywell Internat., Inc., 1995—97; v.p. human resources Honeywell Aerospace, 1999—2002; sr. v.p. human resources and comm. Honeywell Internat., Inc., Morristown, NJ, 2002—. Office: Honeywell Internat 101 Columbia Rd Morristown NJ 07962

**WEIDENTHAL, MAURICE DAVID (BUD WEIDENTHAL),** academic administrator, journalist; b. Cleve., Nov. 26, 1925; s. William and Evelyn (Kolinsky) W.; m. Grace Schwartz, Apr. 14, 1957; 1 child, Susan Elizabeth Weidenthal Saltzman. BA, U. Mich., 1950. Mem. staff Cleve. Press, 1950-81, editl. writer, 1950-51, asst. city editor, 1956-58, edn. editor, 1958-81; v.p. pub. affairs Cuyahoga C.C. Dist., Cleve., 1981-88; dir. Urban Colls. Project, Wash., 1989—. Editor The Urban Report, Cleve., 1989-2005. Mem. pub. affairs com. Greater Cleve. Growth Assn., 1981-88; mem. bd. advisors Coun. for Advancement and Support of Edn., 1981-88, Nat. Coun. Mktg. and Pub. Rels., 1981—; alt. bd. dirs. St. Vincent Quadrangle, 1983-88; trustee Hebrew Free Loan Assn., 1975-86. With AUS, 1944-45. Decorated Air medal. Mem. Edn. Writers Assn., Soc. Profl. Journalists, (bd. dirs. 1996-2003), Cleve. City Club (bd. dirs. 1969-76), Cleve. Press Club. Home: 25858 Fairmount Blvd Cleveland OH 44122-2214 Office: 4250 Richmond Rd Cleveland OH 44122-6104 Personal E-mail: u2w@adelphia.net. Business E-Mail: bud.weidenthal@tri-c.edu.

**WEIDMAN, DAVID N.,** chemicals executive; BSChE, Brigham Young Univ., 1978; MBA, Univ. Mich., 1980. Positions with Am. Cyanamid, 1980—87; mng. dir. Cyanamid Nordiska, Stockholm, 1987—89; v.p., gen. mgr. Cyanamid Canada, 1989—90; v.p., gen. mgr. fibers div. Am. Cyanamid, 1990—94; v.p., gen. mgr. performance additives Allied Signal, 1994—95, pres., gen. mgr. fluorine products, 1995—98, pres. performance polymers & mem. corp. exec. council, 1998—2000; CEO Celanese Chemicals, 2000—02; COO Celanese AG, 2002—04, vice-chmn. bd. mgmt., 2003—04; pres., CEO Celanese Corp., Dallas, 2004—. Bd. mem. Am. Chemistry Council. Mem. Nat. Adv. Council Marriott Sch. Mgmt. Mem.: Soc. Chem. Industry (hon. treas.). Office: Celanese Corp 1601 W LBJ Freeway Dallas TX 75234*

**WEIDMAN, JEFFREY,** librarian; b. NYC, Feb. 17, 1945; s. Jerome and Elizabeth Ann (Payne) W. AB, Hamilton Coll., 1967; MA in Art History, Ind. U., 1969, PhD in Art History, 1981, MLS, 1982. Advt. trainee Masius, Wynne-Williams, Ltd., London, summer 1964; researcher libr./art dept. Hamilton Coll., Clinton, N.Y., 1966-67; circulation, reference and res. asst. Law/Undergrad. Librs. Cornell U., Ithaca, N.Y., 1969-71; teaching and rsch. asst. art dept. Ind. U., Bloomington, 1967-68, assoc. instr., reader art dept., 1972-74, 76, libr. asst. microforms dept., 1976-79; evening supr. acad. svcs. Ind. Cen. U. Indpls., 1979-80; art libr. Oberlin (Ohio) Coll. 1983—97. Project dir. Ohio Artists Project, Oberlin, 1991-97; chmn. ARLIS/NA's Wittenborn Com., 1990; cons. and presenter in field Co-editor: The First College Bowl Question Book, 1961; author essays in field, (exhbn. catalogue) William Rimmer: A Yankee Michelangelo, 1985. Pres. Spectrum, Oberlin, 1990-91, program chmn. 1989-90; mem. online governing bd. Dictionary Art, Grove Art, 2004—; art historian adv. Kansas City Save Outdoor Sculpture, 1999-2000; curator Harley Terra Candella Archive of Mail Art and Artistamps Clarence Ward Art Libr. Oberlin Coll., 1993-1997. Samuel H. Kress fellow Ind. U., Bloomington, 1974-75. Mem. Acad. Libr. Assn. of Ohio, Art Librs. Soc. N.Am. (recipient Gerd Muehsam award 1983), Coll. Art Assn., Midwest Art History Assn. Art Librs. Soc. N.Am., Assn. Historians of Am. Art, Catalogue Raisonne Scholars Assn., Coll. Art Assn. Avocation: philosophy. Home: 4319 Adams St Kansas City KS 66103-3410 Office: Spencer Art Reference Libr The Nelson-Atkins Mus Art Kansas City MO 64111 Office Phone: 816-751-1215. Business E-Mail: jweidman@nelson-atkins.org.

**WEIDMAN, JOHN CARL, II,** education and sociology educator, consultant; b. Ephrata, Pa., Oct. 3, 1945; s. John Carl and Mary Elizabeth (Grube) W.; m. Carla Sue Fassnacht, Aug. 20, 1967; children: Jonathan Scott, Rebecca Mary. AB in Sociology cum laude, Princeton U., 1967; AM, U. Chgo., 1968, PhD, 1974. Acting asst. prof. edn. U. Minn., Mpls., 1970-74, asst. prof. edn., sociology and Am. studies, 1974-77; sr. rsch. assoc. Bur. Social Sci. Rsch., Inc., Washington, 1977-78; assoc. prof. edn. and sociology U. Pitts., 1979-86, prof. edn. and sociology, 1986—, chmn. dept. adminstrv. and policy studies, 1986-93, dir. Inst. for Internat. Studies in Edn., 2004—. Cons. Nat. Ctr. Adminstrv. Justice, Youthwork, Inc., Upper Midwest Tri-Racial Gen. Assistance Ctr., Acad. for Ednl. Devel., Asian Devel. Bank, Indonesia, Laos, Kyrgyz Republic, Mongolia, German Acad. Exch. Svc., Mongolia, Germa-Belgium, Mongolia, Uzbekistan, CRA Internat., Saudi Arabia; UNESCO chair higher edn. rsch. Maseno U. Coll., Kenya, 1993. Author: Rsch. monographs; mem. editl. bd. Rev. of Higher Edn., 1984-88, Am. Ednl. Rsch. Jour., 1991-92, 96-98; co-author: Research on Higher Education in Developing Countries: Suggested Agendas and Research Strategies, 1991, Implementing a Faculty Assessment System: A Case Study at the University of Pittsburgh-USA, 1994, Higher Education Costs and Tuition, 1996, Higher Education in Korea: Tradition and Adaptation, 2000, Socialization of Graduate and Professional Students: A Perilous Passage?, 2001, Finance Higher Education, 2001; asst. editor Comparative Edn. Rev., 2003—; cons. editor Jour. Higher Edn., 1989—; contbr. chpts. to books, articles to profl. jours. Bd. dirs. Sch. Vol. Assn. Pitts., 1982-90, pres., 1984-87. Grantee U.S. Office Edn., 1971-73, Spencer Found., 1973-76, Nat. Inst. Edn., 1976-79, NEH, 1985-86, Asian Devel. Bank, Laos, 1995-96, Mongolia, 1997-2000, 2005, Indonesia, 2001, Krygyz Republic, 2003; Fulbright scholar U. Augsburg, Germany, 1986-87. Mem. Am. Ednl. Rsch. Assn. (sec. postsecondary divsn. 1987-89), Am. Sociol. Assn., Assn. Study of Higher Edn., Comparative and Internat. Edn. Soc., Sigma Psi, Phi Delta Kappa. Office: U Pitts 5910 Posvar Hall 230 S Bouquet St Pittsburgh PA 15260

**WEIDMAN, SHEILA,** marketing professional; b. Bradenton, Fla., July 11, 1961; BS in sci., Journalism and Comm., U. Fla., 1983. Mgr. comm. ASHRAE, 1983—88; mgr. corp. comm. Georgia-Pacific Corp., 1988—90, dir. external comm. and corp. advt., 1990—98, dir., spl. asst. to chmn. and CEO, 1998—2000, sr. dir. corp. mktg. and sales excellence, 2000—01, v.p. corp. mktg., 2001—02, v.p. corp. comm. and mktg. Atlanta, 2002—. Com. mem. Am. Heart Assn., Atlanta Hist. Soc.; mem. Leadership Atlanta, Class of 2004. Recipient Women of Achievement awards, YWCA, 1995. Mem. Atlanta Sports Coun. Mem. (chmn. mktg. com.), Atlanta CMO Roundtable, CMO Group of N.Am., Ga. Press Assn., Ga. State CMO Roundtable, Met. Atlanta C. of C. (vice chair chmn.'s campaign 2003), Mktg. Leadership Coun. (vice chair chmn.'s campaign 2004), Pub. Rels. Soc. Am., Sales and Mktg. Execs., Atlanta Press Club. Office: Georgia-Pacific Corp 133 Peachtree St NE Atlanta GA 30303

**WEIDMANN, K. TIMOTHY,** not-for-profit fundraiser, writer; b. Bronxville, NY, May 28, 1950; s. Carl Frederick and Kathryn Henrietta Weidmann; m. Deborah Ann Emanuel, Sept. 18, 1976; children: Sarah, Seth, Grace. Francise AB, Harvard Coll., Cambridge, MA, 1972, MDiv, Yale Div. Sch., New Haven, CT, 1980—80. Mktg. rep. IBM, White Plains, NY, 1972—80; assoc. dir. Yale U., New Haven, 1983—87; assoc. v.p. Northwestern U., Evanston, Ill., 1987—2001; sr. cons. Marts & Lundy, Inc., Lyndhurst, NJ, 2001—. V.p. devel. ALS Les Turner Found., Chicago, Ill., 1990—95; chair of devel. com.

Vt. Studio Ctr., Johnson, Vt., 2001—. Co-author: Lives and Legacies: An Encyclopedia of People Who Changed the World, 1999; contbr. articles to mags. Sr. warden St. John's Ch., New Haven, 1986—87; vestry mem. St. Mark's Ch., Evanston, Ill., 1990—92. Recipient Scholarship, Harvard Club of Westchester, 1968; fellow fellowship, Roothbert Fund, 1977-80, Leopold Schepp Found., 1977-80, Vt. Studio Ctr., 2000. Fellow: Timothy Dwight Coll., Yale (residential fellow 1985—87); mem.: Am. Healthcare Profls., Am. Fundraising Profls., Coun. on Aid and Support of Edn. Episcopalian. Achievements include built infrastructure for corporate philanthropy at Yale; built infrastructure for grateful patient philanthrophy as basis of fundraising at Northwestern University Medical School. Avocations: reading, squash, travel, poetry. Home: 9018 Sleeping Bear Rd Skokie IL 60076 Personal E-mail: tweidmann@lumc.edu.

**WEIDNER, DONALD J.,** dean, law educator; BS, Fordham U., 1966; JD, U. Tex., Austin, 1969. Bar: SC, U.S. Tax Ct., U.S. Dist. Cts. for No. Dist. Ohio and Dist. SC, Supreme Ct. U.S. Assoc. Willkie Farr & Gallagher, New York, NY, 1969—70; Bigelow Fellow U. Chgo. Law Sch., 1970—71; asst. prof. U. SC Sch. Law, 1971—74; assoc. prof. Cleveland State U., 1974—76, Fla. State U. Coll. Law, 1976—78, prof., 1978—, assoc. dean, 1984—85, dean, 1991—97, interim dean, 1998—2000; dean, 2000—. Vis. prof. U. Tex. Sch. Law, 1978, U. N.Mex, 1979, Stanford Law Sch., 1981, U. NC Sch. Law, 1991; prof in residence Ruden McClosky Smith Schuster & Russell, PA, 1997; reporter Uniform Partnership Act (1994) Nat. Conf. Commrs. on Uniform State Laws, 1987—94. Co-author: Real Estate: Taxation and Bankruptcy, 1979, General and Limited Liability Partnerships Under the Revised Uniform Partnership Act, 1996, The Revised Uniform Partnership Act, 1998, 1999, 2000, 2001, 2002, 2003, 2004. Order of Coif. Mem.: Am. Law Inst., Assoc. Am. Law Schs. (mem. Membership Review (Accreditation) Com. 2001—03), Fla. Supreme Ct. Hist. Soc. (Bd. Trustees), Fla. Supreme Ct. Commn. on Professionalism. Office: Coll Law Fla State U Rotunda Rm R201 Tallahassee FL 32306-1601 Office Phone: 850-644-3071. Office Fax: 850-644-5487. E-mail: dweidner@law.fsu.edu.

**WEIDNER, EDWARD WILLIAM,** academic administrator, political scientist; b. Mpls., July 7, 1921; s. Peter Clifford and Lillian (Halbe) W.; m. Jean Elizabeth Blomquist, Mar. 23, 1944 (dec. Apr., 1997); children: Nancy Louise, Gary Richard (dec.), Karen, William; m. Marjorie M. Fermanich, June 6, 1998. BA magna cum laude, U. Minn., 1942, MA, 1943, PhD, 1946; postgrad., U. Wis., 1943-45; LHD (hon.), U. No. Mich. U., 1969; PhD (hon.), Linköping U., Sweden, 1975. Staff mem. Nat. Mcpl. League, 1944, research assoc., 1944-45; cons. govts. div. U.S. Bur. Census, 1945, statistician Washington, 1946; lectr. U. Wis., Madison, 1945; instr. U. Minn., Mpls., 1945-47, asst. prof., 1947-49, asst. dir. research in inter-govtl. relations, 1946-53; asst. prof. UCLA, 1949-50; faculty Mich. State U., East Lansing, 1950-62, from assoc. prof., dir. govtl. research bur., to prof. polit. sci., 1952-62, chmn. polit. sci. dept., 1952-57; coordinator, chief adviser Vietnam Project, 1955-57; dir. Inst. Research on Overseas Programs, 1957-61; sr. scholar E.W. Ctr., 1961—62, vice chancellor, 1962—65; prof. polit. sci., dir. ctr. for devel. change U. Ky., Lexington, 1965-67; chancellor U. Wis., Green Bay, 1966-86, prof. polit. sci., 1966-89, chancellor emeritus, prof. emeritus, 1989—, dir. Cofrin Arboretum, 1986-89. Planning dir. Weidner Ctr. for the Performing Arts, 1987-93; bd. dirs. Univ. Bank, Green Bay; cons. Fgn. Ops. Adminstrn., Vietnam, 1954-55, Baltimore County (Md.) Reorgn. Commn., 1953-54, Ford Found., Pakistan, 1956, Nat. Assn. Fgn. Student Advisers, 1959-60, Pres.'s Task Force Fgn. Econ. Assistance, 1961, Dept. State, 1962-63, AID, 1964-65, Lees Coll., 1971-72, Green Bay Bot. Garden, 1997-98; mem. Gov. Mich. Commn. Inter-Govtl. Rels., 1954-55. Author: (with William Anderson) American Government, 1951, State and Local Government, 1951, (with others) The International Programs of American Universities, 1958, Intergovernmental Relations as Seen by Public Officials, 1960, (with William Anderson, Clara Penniman) Government for the Fifty States, 1960, The World Role of Universities, 1962, Technical Assistance in Public Administration Overseas, 1964; editor: Development Administration in Asia, 1970. Mem. Wis. Gov.'s Commn. on UN, 1975-81; trustee Prairie Sch., 1969-91, mem. adv. bd., 1991—; bd. dirs. Inst. for Shipboard Edn., 1976-89; mem. Lab. Ornithology, Cornell U., bd. dirs. 1989-98; chmn. adv. bd. Lakeland chpt. ARC, 1981-84; mem. N.Am. adv. group UN Environ. Programme, 1983-90; bd. advisers Nature Conservancy Wis., 1984-91; bd. dirs. Heritage Hill Found., 1987-92, 95-97, pres. 1991-92; bd. dirs. Assn. Am. Colls., 1978-80, Brown County, Family Svc. Assn., 1988-93; chmn. Brown County Cultural Coun., 1991-94; mem. nat. coun. ASPA, 1947-50; mem. internat. coun. UN 4-U, 1974-80; bd. dirs. Am. Coun. on Edn., 1971-74, sec. bd., 1971-72; mem. nat. coun. Am. Polit. Assn., 1950-52. Recipient Outstanding Achievement award U. Minn., 1975. Mem. Wis. Soc. Ornithology, Wilderness Soc., World Wildlife Fund, Interfaith Alliance, Common Cause, Nature Conservancy, Audubon Soc., Am. Birding Assn., Green Bay Area C of C. (bd. dirs. 1970-74), Mcpl. Clks. Edn. Found. (bd. dirs. 1980-97), Phi Beta Kappa, Pi Sigma Alpha. Home: 1656 Twin Lakes Cir Green Bay WI 54311-4207 E-mail: osggg@netnet.net.

**WEIDNER, MARK,** environment research executive; b. 1952; MS in Analytical Chemistry, Purdue U., 1976. With Mich. State U., East Lansing, 1976-78; instr. Finnigan Corp., San Jose, Calif., 1978-80; sr. chemist Metro Lab., Seattle, 1980-85; now pres., treas. Analytical Resources, Inc., Seattle, 1985—. Office: Analytical Resources Inc 4611 S 134th Pl #100 Tukwila WA 98168-3212

**WEIER, CARLTON TIMOTHY,** retired mathematics professor; b. Mt. Clemens, Mich., Nov. 5, 1949; s. George A. and Loretta M. Weier; m. Diana Hardy Weier, Mar. 24, 1975; children: Melissa Marie, Marc Timothy. MA, Ctrl. Mich. U., 1985. Continuing tchg. cert. Mich., 1971. Tchr. Reese (Mich.) Pub. Schs., 1971—99; adj. math. instr. Delta Coll., University Center, Mich., 1986—88; adj. math. instructor Saginaw Valley State U., University Center, Mich., 1999—99, math. lectr., 1999—2003; adj. math. instr. North Ctrl. Mich. Coll., Petoskey, 2003—. Bd. reference hearing officer Mich. Edn. Assn., East Lansing, 1999—2003; standing tech. adv. com. Mich. Dept. Edn., Lansing, 2000—03. Rd. adv. bd. Blumfield Twsp, Reese, 1995—2003. Recipient Mary H. Anderson Outstanding Adj. award, Saginaw Valley State U., 1998. Methodist. Avocations: fly fishing, camping. Personal E-mail: ctweier@aol.com.

**WEIERSTALL, RICHARD PAUL,** retired pharmaceutical chemist; b. Jersey City, N.J., Nov. 5, 1942; s. William August and Emily (Haughey) W.; m. Gail Janet Thomsen, Aug. 17, 1968; children: Eric, Kurt, Karen. BS, Rutgers U., 1966, MS, 1969; PhD, U. Calif., San Francisco, 1973. Unit head drug metabolism Sandoz Pharm., East Hanover, N.J., 1973-74; dir. tech. svc. Banner Gelatin Products, Chatsworth, Calif., 1974-76; v.p. tech. svc. Banner Gelatin Prod., Chatsworth, Calif., 1976-81; dir. pharm. sci. Ayerst Labs Inc., Rouses Point, N.Y., 1981-87; asst. v.p. Wyeth Ayerst Rsch., Rouses Point, 1987-95, asst. v.p. quality assurance, 1995-99; ret., 1999. Mem. Am. Assn. Pharm. Sci., Am. Pharm. Assn. Home: 7 Stewart St Rouses Point NY 12979-1511 E-mail: rweiers@northnet.org.

**WEIGEL, DENNIS PHILIP,** orthopedic surgeon; b. Wells, Minn., July 29, 1969; s. Micheal H. and Joyce L. Weigel; m. Karin Joan Weigel, Aug. 30, 1997; children: Sydney S., Kaylee M., McKenzie K., Chelsey D. BA, Ctrl. U. Iowa, 1991; MD, U. Iowa, Iowa City, 1995. Cert. Am. Bd. Orthop. Surgery. Resident dept. orthop. U. Iowa, Iowa City, 1996—2000; orthop. surgeon Alexandria (Minn.) Orthop. Assocs., 2000—. Chief of surgery Douglas County Hosp., Alexandria, 2005—06. Contbr. articles to profl. jours. Maj. USAR, 1995—2006. Recipient W.R Ingram award, U. Iowa Coll. Medicine, 1993, McClintock award, 1993. Fellow: Am. Assn. Orthop. Surgeons; mem.: Minn. Orthop. Soc., Mid-Am. Orthop. Assn., Am. Assn. Hip and Knee Surgeons, Alpha Omega Alpha. Office: Alexandria Orthop Assocs 1500 Irving St Alexandria MN 56308 Office Fax: 320-762-1935.

**WEIGEL, GEORGE SHILLOW, JR.,** theologian; b. Balt. m. Joan Balcombe; children: Gwyneth, Monica, Stephen. BA, St. Mary's Seminary, Balt., 1973; MA, U. St. Michael's Coll., Toronto, Can., 1975. Asst. prof. theology

from asst. to dean of studies St. Thomas Sem. Sch. of Theology, Kenmore, 1975-77; scholar-in-residence World Without War Coun. Greater Seattle, 1977-84; founding pres. James Madison Found., 1986-89; pres. Ethics and Pub. Policy Ctr., Washington, 1989—96, sr. fellow, 1996—. Author: Tranquillitas Ordinis: The Present Failure & Future Promise of American Catholic Thought on War & Peace, 1987, American Interests, American Purpose: Moral Reasoning & US Foreign Policy, 1989, Catholicism and the Renewal of American Democracy, 1989, Freedom and its Discontents, 1991, The Final Revolution: The Resistance Church and the Collapse of Communism, 1992, Idealism Without Illusions: US Foreign Policy in the Nineties, 1994, Soul of the World, 1996, Witness to Hope: The Biography of Pope John Paul II, 1999, The Truth of Catholicism, 2001, The Courage to Be Catholic, 2002, Letters to A Young Catholic, 2004, The Cube and the Cathedral, 2005, God's Choice: Pope Benedict XVI and the Future of the Catholic Church, 2005; co-author (with James Turner Johnson): Just War and the Gulf War, 1991; co-editor (with Robert Royal): Building the Free Society, 1993; columnist Catholic Northwest Progress, 1993—, mem. editl. bd. First Things. Recipient papal cross Pro Ecclesia et Pontifice; fellow Woodrow Wilson Internat. Ctr. for Scholars, 1984—85. Fellow: Ethics & Pub. Policy Ctr. (sr.). Office: Ethics and Pub Policy Ctr 1015 15th St NW Washington DC 20005-2605 Office Phone: 202-682-1200.

**WEIGEL, KENNETH GEORGE,** lawyer; b. Neptune, N.J., Aug. 28, 1954; s. Hugo Karl and Dolores May (Ambrose) W. BA, U. Mich., 1976; JD, George Washington U., 1979. Bar: D.C. 1979. Assoc. Barnes, Richardson & Colburn, Washington, 1979-83, Bayh, Tabbert & Capehart, Washington, 1983-85, Morgan, Lewis & Bockius, Washington, 1985-89; ptnr. Webster & Sheffield, Washington, 1989-1990, Baker & Hostetler, Washington, 1991—93, Kirkland & Ellis, 1993—2002; ptnr., co-chmn., internat. trade and regulatory group Alston & Bird LLP, Washington, 2002—. Mem. ABA (chmn. customs law com., internat. law and practice sect. 1988-91). Office: Alston & Bird LLP 10th fl 601 Pennsylvania Ave Washington DC 20004-2601 Office Phone: 202-756-3431. Office Fax: 202-756-3333. Business E-Mail: kweigel@alston.com.

**WEIGEL, OLLIE J.,** dentist, former mayor; b. Guthrie County, Iowa, Sept. 29, 1922; s. Verne Noble and Ethel Rebecca (Johnson) W.; m. Mary Kathryn Finnegan, June 3, 1944 (dec. Sept. 1999); children: John, Marilyn, Larry, Susan. DDS, U. Iowa, 1951. Practice dentistry, Ankeny, 1951-94; mayor City of Ankeny, 1974-93. Mem. Metro Planning Orgn., 1995-2000; bd. dirs. Neveln Resource Ctr., 1995-2000. Mem. Ankeny Bd. Adjustment, 1953-58, Ankeny Planning and Zoning Commn.,' 1953-65, Ankeny City Coun., 1966-73, Des Moines Area C.C. Found. Bd., 1993—, mem. emeritus; mem. Des Moines Area Metro Forum, 1985-93, found. bd. On With Life, 1994-2000; life mem. Ankeny Indsl. Devel. Corp.; bd. dirs. Ankeny Cmty. Dist. Sch. Found.; mem. adv. bd. dirs. Brenton Bank of Ankeny, 1994-2000; mem. Polk County Aviation Authority, 2001-2003. 1st lt. USAAF, 1943-45, ETO. Named to Mayors Hall of Fame, 1993—96; recipient Person of Vision award, Ankeny Indsl. Devel. Corp. (1st recipient), 2001. Mem. ADA (life), Iowa Dental Assn. (life), Des Moines Dist. Dental Assn., Ankeny C. of C. (charter mem., life, pres. 1953, 70, Outstanding Citizen 1976, 93), Mid Iowa Assn. Local Govts. (chmn. 1983), League of Iowa Municipalities (pres. 1976-77), Ctrl. Iowa Regional Govts. (pres. 1978), Am. Legion (life), Republican. Methodist. Avocation: fishing. Home and Office: 2506 NW 4th St Ankeny IA 50021-1002

**WEIGEL, PAUL HENRY,** biochemistry educator educator, researcher, consultant; b. N.Y.C., Aug. 11, 1946; s. Helmut and Jeanne Weigel; m. Nancy Shulman, June 15, 1968 (div. Dec. 1987); 1 child, Dana J.; m. Janet Oka, May 17, 1992 BA in Chemistry, Cornell U., 1968; MS in Biochemistry, Johns Hopkins U., Balt., 1969, PhD in Biochemistry, 1975. NIH postdoctoral fellow Johns Hopkins U., Balt., 1975-78; asst. prof. U. Tex. Med. Br., Galveston, Tex., 1978-82, assoc. prof., 1982—87, prof. biochemistry and cell biology, 1987-94, vice chmn. dept. human biol. chemistry and genetics, 1990-93, acting chmn. dept. human biology, chemistry and genetics, 1992-93; prof., chmn. dept. biochemistry and molecular biology U. Okla. Health Scis. Ctr., Oklahoma City, 1994—, George Lynn Cross rsch. prof., 2004—; co-founder Hyalose LLC, 2000—. Mem. NIH Pathobiochemistry Study Sect., Washington, 1985-87; cons. Teltech, Mpls., 1985—, Hyalose LLC 2000—. Contbr. articles to profl. jours. Treas. Bayou Chateau Neighborhood Assn., Dickinson, Tex., 1981-83, v.p. 1983-84, pres., 1984-86. With U.S. Army, 1969-71. Grantee NIH, 1979—; Office Naval Rsch., 1983-87, Tex. Biotech., 1989-94, Okla. Ctr. Advancement Sci. and Tech., 2000-03; recipient Disting. Tchr. award U. Tex. Med. Br., 1989, Disting. Rsch. award, 1989. Mem.: Internat. Soc. for Hyaluronan Sci. (founding mem. 2004, sec. 2004—), Soc. for Glycobiology (mem. nominations com. 2004—), Assn. Med. and Grad. Depts. Biochemistry (webmaster 2002—06, bd. dirs. 2002—, pres.-elect 2006), Am. Soc. Biochemistry and Molecular Biology (mem. pub. affairs adv. com. 2000—03), Am. Soc. Cell Biology, Am. Chem. Soc. Democrat. Lutheran. Achievements include 16 patents in field. Avocations: racquetball, baseball card collecting, poetry, camping. Home: 817 Hollowdale Edmond OK 73003-3022 Office: U Okla Health Scis Ctr Dept Biochem & Mol Biology Bmsb Rm 860 Oklahoma City OK 73190-0001 Office Phone: 405-271-2227. Business E-Mail: paul-weigel@ouhsc.edu.

**WEIGEL, RUSSELL H.,** headmaster; BA, Bowdoin Coll.; MA, George Washington U., 1967; PhD, U. Colorado. Prof. of psychology Amherst Coll., Amherst, Mass., 1975—95, former dean of students; head of sch. Loomis Chaffee Sch., Windsor, Conn., 1995—; pres. The Loomis Inst., Windsor, Conn., 1995—. Co-author: (jour. articles) Ecological Beliefs and Behaviors: Assessment and Change, Race Relations on Prime Time Television Reconsidered: Patterns of Continuity and Change. Office: Loomis Chaffee Sch 4 Batchelder Rd Windsor CT 06095

**WEIGELE, RICHARD SAYRE,** police officer; b. Passaic, NJ, Oct. 5, 1949; s. Louis Charles and Marjorie (Sayre) W. BA, Hope Coll., Holland, Mich., 1972; MPA, Kean Coll. N.J., Union, 1989. Police officer Summit (N.J.) Police Dept., 1973-80; mobile intensive care paramedic Overlook Hosp., Summit, 1977—2006; first response teg. coord. Union County Police acad., Scotch Plains, NJ, 1980—2005; police sgt., 911 mcpl. coord. Mountainside Police Dept., NJ, 1980—, commandt. Emergency Svcs. Unit NJ, 1998—2003. Paramedic preceptor Overlook Hosp., 1980-2003, pre-hosp. trauma life support instr., 1993—, pediatric prehosp. emergency care instr., 1995—; CPR instr. Am. Heart Assn., Summit, 1978; police instr. Union County Police Acad., 1980—; EMS text reviewer Brady Publishing, 1996. Officer Summit First Aid Squad, 1975-80; vol. Overlook Hosp., 1974-81; mem. Liberty Corner First Aid Squad, 1993-98; instr. ARC, Somerville, N.J., 1992-98. With N.J. Army NG, 1972-78. Recipient Award of Merit N.J. State Police Benevolent Assn., 1974, Award of recognition, Union County Police Acad., 1990. Mem. Nat. Assn. EMT/Paramedics (charter), N.J. Police Honor Legion, Internat. Police Assn. (reception officer 1989—, NDC rep. 1999-, pres. 2002-), Mountainside Police Benevolent Assn. (Police Officer of the Yr. 1986), Pi Alpha Alpha. Ref. Ch. of Am. Avocations: skiing, biking, computers, community service. Home: 268 Crabtree Ct Basking Ridge NJ 07920-3154 Office: Mountainside Police Dept 1385 Route 22 Mountainside NJ 07092-2699

**WEIGEND, GUIDO GUSTAV,** geographer, educator; b. Zeltweg, Austria, Jan. 2, 1920; came to U.S., 1939, naturalized, 1943; s. Gustav F. and Paula (Sorgo) W.; m. Areta Kelble, June 26, 1947 (dec. 1993); children: Nina, Cynthia, Kenneth. BS, U. Chgo., 1942, MS, 1946, PhD, 1949. With OSS, 1943-45; with mil. intelligence U.S. War Dept., 1946; instr. geography U. Ill., Chgo., 1946-47; instr. then asst. prof. geography Beloit Coll., 1947-49; asst. prof. geography Rutgers U., 1949-51; assoc. prof., 1951-57, prof., 1957-76, acting dept. chmn., 1951-52, chmn. dept., 1953-67, assoc. dean, 1972-76; dean Coll. Liberal Arts, Prof. geography Ariz. State U., Tempe, 1976-84, prof. geography, 1976-89; ret., 1989. Fulbright lectr. U. Barcelona, 1960-61; vis. prof. geography Columbia U., 1963-67, NYU, 1967, U. Colo., summer 1968, U. Hawaii, summer 1969; liaison rep. Rutgers U. to UN, 1950-52; invited by Chinese Acad. Scis. to visit minority areas in Chinese Cent. Asia, 1988; mem. U.S. nat. com. Internat. Geog. Union, 1951-58, 61-65; chmn. Conf. on Polit.

and Social Geography, 1968-69 Author articles, monographs, bulls. for profl. jours.; contbr.: (4th edit.) A Geography of Europe, 1977; geog. editor-in-chief: Odyssey World Atlas, 1966. Bd. adjustment Franklin Twp., N.J., 1959; mem. Highland Park (N.J.) Bd. Edn., 1973-75, v.p., 1975; mem. Ariz. Coun. on Humanities and Pub. Policy, 1976-80; vice chmn. Phoenix Com. on Fgn. Rels., 1976-79, chmn., 1979-81; mem. exec. com. Fedn. Pub. Programs in Humanities, 1977-82; bd. dirs. Coun. Colls. Arts and Scis., 1980-83; commr. N. Cen. Assn. Colls. and Schs., 1976-80, bd. dirs. commn. on instns. of higher edn., 1980-83. Research fellow Office Naval Research, 1952-55, Rutgers Research Council, 1970-71; grantee Social Sci. Research Council, 1956, Ford Found., 1966, Am. Philos. Soc., 1970-71, German Acad. Exchange Service, 1984; Fulbright travel grantee Netherlands 1970-71. Mem. Assn. Am. Geographers (chmn. N.Y. Met. divsn. 1955-56, editl. bd. 1955-59, mem. coun. 1965-66, chmn. N.Y.-N.J. divsn. 1965-66), Am. Geog. Soc., Phoenix Chamber Mus. Soc. (bd. dirs. 1995-2003, pres. 2000-03), Sigma Xi (pres. Ariz. State U. chpt. 1989-91). Home: 2094 E Golf Ave Tempe AZ 85282-4046 Office: Ariz State U Dept Geography Tempe AZ 85287

**WEIGER, JOHN GEORGE,** foreign language educator; b. Dresden, Germany, Feb. 6, 1933; came to U.S., 1938, naturalized, 1945; s. Willy and Elisabeth (Prinz) W.; m. Leslie Lawrence Carpenter, Dec. 28, 1955; children: Robert Boyden, Mark Owen, Heidi Elaine. BA, Middlebury Coll., 1955; MA, U. Colo., 1957; PhD (NDEA fellow), Ind. U., 1966. Instr. U. Colo., Boulder, 1955-57, Lawrence Coll., Appleton, Wis., 1957-58; instr. Romance langs. U. Vt., Burlington, 1958-62, asst. prof., 1964-67, assoc. prof., 1967-73, prof., 1973-98, prof. emeritus, 1998—, vice chmn. Romance lang. dept., 1964-68, chmn., 1994-98, asst. dean Coll. Arts and Scis., 1968-69, assoc. dean, 1969-71, dean, 1971-76; instnl. rep. for Rhodes scholarships, Danforth fellowships, Turrell Fund scholarships, 1971-76; program chmn. George Aiken lecture series, 1975; vis. lectr. U. Bologna, 1978, 87, U. Venice, Italy, 1987, U. Valencia, Spain, 1987; Cervantes lectr. Fordham U., 1990. Cons. Eirik Borve, Inc., 1979-80. Author: Introduction to the Youthful Deeds of the Cid, 1969, The Valencian Dramatists of Spain's Golden Age, 1976, Cristobal de Virues, 1978, Hacia la Comedia, 1978, The Individuated Self: Cervantes and the Emergence of the Individual, 1979, The Substance of Cervantes, 1985, In the Margins of Cervantes, 1988; editor: Las Hazañas del Cid, 1981, La Infelice Marcela, 1985; mem. editl. bd.: Bull. of Comediantes, 1978-2000; editl. bd.: Hispania, 1993-01; contbr. articles to profl. jours., also chpts. to books. U. Vt. Faculty Research fellow, 1967, 83, 86; Am. Council Learned Socs. grantee, 1978; U. Vt. Univ. scholar for the humanities, 1985-86. Mem. MLA (chmn. comedia sect. 1970-71), Renaissance Soc. Am., Am. Assn. Tchrs. Spanish and Portuguese (chmn. com. hon. mems. and fellows 1984), The Comediantes, Internat. Assn. Hispanists, Cervantes Soc. Am., Phi Beta Kappa, Phi Sigma Iota, Phi Eta Sigma (hon.). Home: 63 Woodbine Rd Shelburne VT 05482-6702 E-mail: jweiger@adelphia.net.

**WEIGERT, ANDREW JOSEPH,** sociology educator; b. NYC, Apr. 8, 1934; s. Andrew Joseph and Marie Teresa (Kollmer) W.; m. Kathleen Rose Maas, Aug. 31, 1967; children: Karen Rose, Sheila Marie. BA, St. Louis U., 1958, PhL, 1959, MA, 1960; BTh, Woodstock (Md.) Coll., 1964; PhD, U. Minn., 1968. NIMH trainee U. Minn., Mpls., 1965-67; asst. prof. sociology U. Notre Dame, Ind., 1968-72, assoc. prof. Ind., 1972-76, prof. Ind., 1976—, chmn. dept. Ind., 1980-84, 88-89. Vis. assoc. prof. Yale U., New Haven, 1973-74. Co-author: Family Socialization, 1974, Interpretive Sociology, 1978, Society and Identity, 1986; author: Everyday Life, 1981, Social Psychology, 1983, Life and Society, 1983, Mixed Emotions, 1991, Self, Interaction, and Natural Environment, 1997, Religious and Secular Views on Endtime, 2004; adv. editor various sociology jours.; contbr. articles to profl. jours., chpts. to books. Recipient tchg. awards, 1999, 2002, 05; NSF grantee, 1969. Avocation: woodlot and prairie management. Office: U Notre Dame Dept Sociology Notre Dame IN 46556 Office Phone: 574-631-7408. Business E-Mail: aweigert@nd.edu.

**WEIGHT, DOUG,** professional hockey player; b. Warren, Mich., Jan. 21, 1971; Student, Lake Superior State Coll., Mich. Center NY Rangers, 1990-93, Edmonton Oilers, 1993—2001, St. Louis Blues, 2001—06, 2006—, Carolina Hurricanes, 2006. Mem. U.S. Olympic Hockey Team, Nagano, Japan, 1998, Salt Lake City, 2002, Team U.S.A., World Cup of Hockey, 1996, 2004. Named to NHL All-Star Game, 1996, 1998, 2001, 2003. Achievements include being a member of World Cup Champion Team USA, 1996; being a member of Stanley Cup Champion Carolina Hurricanes, 2006. Office: St Louis Blues Savvis Ctr 1401 Clark Ave Saint Louis MO 63101-2709*

**WEIGLE, PEGGY,** information technology executive; BA in philosophy cum laude, U. Mass. V.p. N. Am. sales Arbor Software, 1996; v.p. worldwide field operations Hyperion (merged with Arbor Software), v.p., gen. mgr. performance mgmt. divsn.; CEO Perfecto Tech. (now Sanctum, Inc.), 1999—. Chmn. application sub-com. BENS Silicon Valley Cyber Security Working Group; mem. tech. sub-com. Silicon Valley Blue Ribbon Task Force on Aviation Security and Tech. Named one of 50 Most Powerful Women in Networking, Network World mag., 2003.

**WEIGNER, BRENT JAMES,** secondary school educator; b. Pratt, Kans., Aug. 19, 1949; s. Doyle Dean and Elizabeth (Hanger) W.; m. Sue Ellen Weber Hume, Mar. 30, 1985; children: Russell John Hume, Scott William Hume. BA, U. No. Colo., 1972; MEd, U. Wyo., 1977, PhD, 1984. Cert. Nat. Bd. for Profl. Tchg. Stds. Counselor, coach Olympia Sport Village, Upson, Wis., 1968; dir. youth sports F.E. Warren AFB, Cheyenne, 1973—74; instr. geography Laramie County Comm. Coll., Cheyenne, 1974-75; tchr. social sci. McCormick Jr. HS, Cheyenne, 1975—, Laramie County Sch. Dist. 1, Cheyenne, 1975—; head social studies dept. McCormick Jr. HS, 1987-99, 2001—02; curriculum adv. com. Laramie County Sch. Dist. No. 1, 1988-89. Lectr. ednl. methods U. Wyo., 1989, clin. faculty, 1992-94; nat. chmn. Jr. Olympic cross-country com. AAU, Indpls., 1980-81; pres. Wyo. Athletic Congress, 1981-87; tchr. cons. Nat. Geog. Soc. Geography Inst., 1991, North Pole Marathon cons. Global Expdns. 2002-03; South Pole marathon cons. and guide Adventure Network Internat., 2001-02; alt. cert. assessor Wyo. State Dept. Edn., 2001-02; cons. Adventure Network Internat., 1999-02; cons. North Pole marathon, Polar Running Adventures, 2003-04, Arctic Watch, 2004—; presenter, cons. in field. Fgn. exch. student U. Munich, 1971-72; head coach Cheyenne Track Club, 1976—, pres., 1980; race dir. Wyo. Marathon, 1978—; deacon 1st Christian Ch., Cheyenne, 1987-90, elder, 1991-93; rep. candidate gen. election Wyo. Legis., 1991; bd. dirs. United Med. Ctr. of Wyo. Found., 1995—, Cheyenne Boys and Girls Club, 1999-2005; keynote spkr., Okla. Marathon, 2002. Named Wyoming State bd. edn. Disting. Educator, Wyo. U.S. West Outstanding Tchr., 1989, Wyo. Coun. for the Social Studies K-8 Tchr. of Yr., 1994-95, Jr. High Coach of Yr., Wyo. Coaches Assn., 1996, Vol. of Yr., office Youth Alternatives, 2000; fellow Taft Found., 1976, Earthwatch-Hearst fellow, Punta Allen, Mex., summer 1987, Christa McAuliffe fellow, 1991-92, Wyo. Christa Mcauliffe Fellowship Selection Com., 1994, 95, 01; Fulbright grantee, Israel, summer 1984; Fulbright scholar Ghana and Senegal, 1990; People-to-People Internat. Ambassador to Vietnam, 1993; recipient Masons of Wyo. Disting. Tchr. award 1994. Mem. NEA, Nat. Network for Ednl. Renewal, Nat. Coun. Social Studies, Nat. Coun. Geog. Edn., Dominican Rep. Nat. Coun. for Geog. Edn. (Cram scholarship 1992), Wyo. Geog. Alliance (steering com., Amazon Workshop Fellowship 1998), Cheyenne Tchrs. Edn. Assn. (govtl. rels. com., instrn. and profl. devel. com.), U. No. Colo. Alumni Assn., Cheyenne C. of C., Wyo. Heritage Soc., Wyo. Edn. Assn. (World Book Ency. classroom rsch. project cons. 1976—, accountability task force 1989-90), Fulbright Alumni Assn. (life), U. Wyo. Alumni Assn. (life), Cheyenne Sunrise, Lions (bd. dirs. Cheyenne 1987, pres. 1995-96, 1st v.p. 1993-94, Melvin Jones Fellowship 1995), Phi Delta Kappa (life, bd. dirs. Cheyenne 1989—, v.p., edn. award for rsch. 1990, pres. 1992-93, ednl. found. rep. 1993-94, area 4-D coord. 1994-95, Gerald Read Internat. Seminar scholar 1994; mem. outstanding doctoral dissertation com. 1994, 96), Phi Delta Kappa (Ed. award 2000). Achievements include first to run ultramarathon races on all seven continents, 1999; South Pole Ultramarathon champion, 2002; sr. men's nat. snowshoe champion, 2003, 05; North Pole Ultramarathon champion, 2003; first person in the world to run ultramarathons at both the North Pole, 2003, and the South

Pole, 2002. Home: 402 W 31st St Cheyenne WY 82001-2527 Office: McCormick Jr HS 6000 Education Dr Cheyenne WY 82009-3991 Office Phone: 307-771-2650. Personal E-mail: runwyo@msn.com.

**WEIHAUPT, JOHN GEORGE,** geophysics educator, academic administrator; b. La Crosse, Wis., Mar. 5, 1930; s. John George and Gladys Mae (Ash) W.; m. Audrey Mae Reis, Jan. 28, 1961. Student, St. Norbert Coll., De Pere, Wis., 1948-49; BS, U. Wis., 1952, MS, 1953, U. Wis.-Milw., 1971; PhD, U. Wis., 1973. Exploration geologist Am. Smelting & Refining Co., Nfld., 1953, Anaconda Co., Chile, S.Am., 1956-57; seismologist United Geophys. Corp., 1958; geophysicist Arctic Inst. N.Am., Antarctica, 1958-60, Geophys. and Polar Research Center, U. Wis., Antarctica, 1960-63; dir. participating Coll. and Univ. program, chmn. dept. phys. and biol. sci. U.S. Armed Forces Inst., Dept. Def., 1963-73; assoc. dean for acad. affairs Sch. Sci., Ind. U.-Purdue U., Indpls., 1973-78, prof. geology, 1973-78; asst. dean (Grad. Sch., prof. geoscis. Purdue U.), 1975-78; prof. geology, assoc. acad. v.p., dean grad. studies and research, U. San Jose (Calif.) State U., 1978-82; vice chancellor for acad. affairs U. Colo., Denver, 1982-86, prof. geoscis., 1987—. Sci. cons., mem. sci. adv. bd. Holt Reinhart and Winston, Inc., 1967—; sci. editor, cons. McGraw-Hill Co., 1966—; hon. lectr. U. Wis. 1963-73; geol. cons., 1968—; editorial cons. John Wiley & Sons, 1968; editorial adv. bd. Dushkin Pub. Group, 1971— Author: Exploration of the Oceans: An Introduction to Oceanography; mem. editorial bd. Internat. Jour. Interdisciplinary Cycle Research, Leiden; co-discoverer USARP Mountain Range (Arctic Inst. Mountain Range), in Victoria Land, Antarctica, 1960; discoverer Wilkes Land Meteorite Crater, Antarctic. Mem. Capital Community Citizens Assn.; mem. Madison Transp. Study Com., Found. for Internat. Energy Research and Tng.; U.S. com. for UN Univ.; mem. sci. council Internat. Center for Interdisciplinary Cycle Research; mem. Internat. Awareness and Leadership Council; mem. governing bd. Moss Landing Marine Labs.; bd. dirs. San Jose State U. Found. Served as 1st lt. AUS, 1953-55, Korea. Mt. Weihaupt in Antarctica named for him, 1966; recipient Madisonian medal for outstanding community service, 1973; Outstanding Cote Meml. award, 1974; Antarctic medal, 1968 Fellow Geol. Soc. Am., Explorers Club; mem. Antarctican Soc., Nat. Sci. Tchrs. Assn., Am. Geophys. Union, Internat. Council Corr. Edu., Soc. Am. Mil. Engrs., Wis. Alumni Assn., Soc. Study Biol. Rhythms, Internat. Soc. for Chronobiology, Marine Tech. Soc., AAAS, Univ. Indsl. Adv. Council, Am. Council on Edn., Expdn. Polaire France (hon.), Found. for Study Cycles, Assn. Am. Geographers, Nat. Council Univ. Research Administrs., Soc. Research Administrs., Man-Environ. Communication Center, Internat. Union Geol. Scis., Internat. Geog. Union, Internat. Soc. Study Time, Community Council Pub. TV, Internat. Platform Assn., Ind., Midwest assns. grad. schs., Western Assn. Grad. Schs., Council Grad. Schs. in U.S., Wis. Alumni Assn. of San Francisco, Kiwanis, Carmel Racquet Club (Rinconada), The Ridge at Hiwan (Evergreen, Colo., pres. 1991-93). Achievements include discovery of the Wilkes Land Anomaly and of the USARP Mt. Range in Victoria Land, both in Antarctica; also credited with revision of the discovery date of Antarctic continent by 3 centuries. Home: 30296 Snowbird Ln Evergreen CO 80439-9469 Office: U Colo Campus Box 172 PO Box 173364 Denver CO 80217-3364

**WEIHRICH, HEINZ,** management educator; b. Germany; came to US, 1959; s. Paul and Anna Weihrich; m. Ursula Weihrich, Aug. 3, 1963. BS, UCLA, 1966, MBA, 1967, PhD, 1973; Dr. (hon.), San Martin de Porres U., Peru, 2000. Assoc. Grad. Sch. Mgmt. UCLA, 1968-73; from asst. to assoc. prof. Ariz. State U., Tempe, 1973-80; prof. global mgmt. and behavioral sci. U. San Francisco, 1980—. Vis. China Europe Internat. Bus. Sch., Shanghai, Grad. Sch. Bus. Administrsn., Switzerland, Peking U., Beijing; global mgmt. cons. in field; vis. prof. U. Applied Sci., Ludwigshafen, Germany. Author: Administración una perspectiva global, 1988 (best seller), Administração Fundamentos da Teoriae da Cienca, Primeiro Volume, 1986, Administração Organização Planejamento e Controle, Segundo Volume, 1987, Administracão Recursos Humanos: Desenvolvimento de Administradores, Terceiro Volume, 1; author: (with Harold Koontz and Cyril O'Donnell) Management, 1980, Japanese, Chinese and Indonesian edits., 1984, Singapore edit., 1985, Indonesian edit., 1986, Philippines edit., Bengali edit., 1989, Taiwan edit., 1985; author: (with Harold Koontz) 9th edit., 1988, Singapore edit., 1988, Chinese edit., 1989, Spanish edit., 1990 (best-seller Spanish speaking world), Korean edit., 1990, Pengurusan (Malaysian) edit., 1991, Czech edit., 1993, Hungarian edit., 1992; author: (with Harold Koontz and Cyril O'Donnell) Management: A Book of Readings, 1980, Essentials of Management, 1982, Taiwan, Philippines, Chinese and India edits., 1986, with Harold Koontz and Cyril O'Donnell: 6th edit., 2004, Chinese edit., Administracion Moderna, 1986; author: (with Harold Koontz) Management: A Global Perspective, 1993, Spanish edit., 1993 (best-seller Spanish speaking world), Chinese, 1998, Singapore edit., 1993, Croatian edit., 1995, Measuring Managers--A Double-Barreled Approach, 1981, Manajamen, Jilid 1, 1987, Manajamen, Jilid 2, 1986, Elementos de Administracion, 1983, with Harold Koontz: 6th edit., 2002, Management Excellence--Productivity through MBO, 1985, Japanese edit., 1990, Greek edit., Produttivita con L' Italian edit., 1987, Administracion, 1985, Management Basiswissen, 1986, Excelencia Administrativa (Mex.), 1987, Chinese edit., 1997, Management: A Global Perspective, internat. edit., 1993, 1993, Administración: Una Perspectiva Global, 1994, 12th edit., 2005 (best seller), Korean edit., 1996, 2006, Croatian edit., 1996, Czech edit., 1996, Elementos de Administracion - Enfoque International, Exta Edicion, 2002; author: (with George Odiorne and Jack Mendleson) Executive Skills: A Management by Objectives Approach, 1980, with George Odiorne and Jack Mendleson: 6th edit., 2002; author: (with Harold Koontz and A. Ramachandra Aryasri) Principles of Management, 2004; editor (with Jack Mendleson): Management: An MBO Approach, 1978; contbr. articles to profl. jour. Grantee Am. Mgmt. Assn., 1970. Fellow Internat. Acad. Mgmt., mem. Acad. Mgmt., Assn. Mgmt. Excellence (trustee 1995-97), Axtil. Bus. Simulation Exptl. Learning, Acad. Internat. Bus., Beta Gamma Sigma, Sigma Iota Epsilon. Roman Catholic. Office: U San Francisco 2130 Fulton St San Francisco CA 94117-1080 Personal E-mail: weihrich_h@gmail.com.

**WEIJER, CHARLES,** medical educator, researcher; b. Edmonton, Canada, May 26, 1964; s. Jan and Dorothy Lillian Weijer; life ptnr. Anthony Belardo, Apr. 28, 1970. BSc in Medicine, U. Alta., 1985, MD, 1988; BA with hons., McGill U., 1993, MSc, 1995, PhD, 1997. Asst. prof. of medicine U. of Toronto, Toronto, Ont., Canada, 1996—98; asst. prof. of bioethics Dalhousie U., Halifax, N.S., Canada, 1998—2001, assoc. prof. bioethics, medicine, and surgery, 2001—05; chmn. tier i in bioethics U. We. Ont., London, Ont., Canada 2005—, assoc. prof. philosophy and medicine, 2005—. Vis. fellow Clare Hall, Cambridge, England 2003—04; vis. scholar U. Cambridge, 2003—04; cons. in field. Mem. editl. bd. Bioethics, IRB: Ethics and Human Research; contbr. articles to profl. jours. Recipient Excellence in Med. Rsch. AWARD, Dalhousie Med. Rsch. Found., 2002; fellow, Med. Rsch. Coun. Can., 1993—97; grantee, Can. Insts. Health Rsch., 1998—2001, 1998—2003, 2001—04, 2003—05, 2004—; scholar, Dalhousie U., 1998—2003. Fellow: Royal Coll. Physicians and Surgeons Can., The Hastings Ctr. Office: University of Western Ontario Talbot College London ON Canada N6A 3K7 Office Phone: 519-661-3453. Office Fax: 519-661-3922.

**WEIKEL, MALCOLM KEITH,** healthcare company executive; b. Shamokin, Pa., Mar. 9, 1938; s. Malcolm J. and Marian Eleanor (Faust) Weikel; m. Barbara Joan Davis, Dec. 17, 1960; children: Richard, Kristen. BSc, Phila. Coll. Pharmacy and Sci., 1960; MSc, U. Wis., 1962, PhD, 1966. Mgr. Roche Labs., 1966—70; commr. health svcs. HEW, Washington, 1970—77; v.p. mem. Med. Internat., 1978—82; pres., CEO, 1982—84; exec. v.p., COO, Manor Healthcare Corp., Silver Spring, Md., 1984—86; exec. v.p. Health Care & Retirement Corp., 1988—98, sr. exec. v.p., COO, 1988—98, sr. exec. v.p., 1998—. Recipient Sec.'s Spl. citation, HEW, 1975, 1977. Mem. Health Care Assn. (v.p. 1990—, chmn. multifacility group 1990—93). Office: Health Care & Retirement Corp PO Box 10086 Toledo OH 43699-0086

**WEIKSNER, SANDRA S.,** lawyer; b. Washington, Nov. 9, 1945; d. Donald B. and Dick (Cutter) Smiley; m. George B. Weiksner, Aug. 19, 1969; children: Michael, Nicholas. BA in Psychology, Stanford (Calif.) U., 1966, JD, 1969. Tchg. fellow Stanford U., 1969-70; assoc. Cleary, Gottlieb, Steen & Hamilton, N.Y.C., 1970-77, ptnr., 1978—2003, sr. counsel, 2004—. Vis. lectr. Yale Law Sch., 1991-92. Bd. dirs. N.Y. Law Sch.; mem. Union Theol. Sem. Fellow Am. Bar Found., Am. Coll. Trusts and Estates Counsel, Internat. Acad. Estate and Trust Law; mem. Assn. Bar City of N.Y. Democrat. Unitarian Universalist. Home: 164 E 81st St New York NY 10028-1804 Office: Cleary Gottlieb Steen & Hamilton 1 Liberty Plz Fl 43 New York NY 10006-1404

**WEIL, ANDREW THOMAS,** physician, educator; b. Phila., June 8, 1942; s. Daniel Pythias and Jenny (Silverstein) Weil. BA, Harvard U., 1964, MD, 1968. Intern Mt. Zion Hosp. Med. Ctr., San Francisco, 1968-69; assoc. Harvard Bot. Mus., Cambridge, Mass., 1971-84; fellow Inst. Current World Affairs, NYC, 1971-75; lectr. U. Ariz., Tucson, 1983—, dir. program in integrative medicine, clin. prof. medicine, 1996—. Author: Natural Mind, 1972, Marriage of the Sun and Moon, 1980, From Chocolate to Morphine, 1983, Health and Healing, 1984, Natural Health, Natural Medicine, 1990, Spontaneous Healing, 1995, 8 Weeks to Optimum Health, 1997, Eating Well for Optimum Health, 2000, The Healthy Kitchen, 2002, Healthy Aging: A Lifelong Guide to Your Physical and Spritual Well-Being, 2005, (newsletter) Self-Healing, (website) drweil.com. Served to lt. USPHS, 1969-70. Fellow Linnean Soc. London; mem. Am. Acad. Achievement, Sigma Xi. Democrat. Buddhist. Avocations: gardening, backpacking. Home: 6700 S X9 Ranch Rd Vail AZ 85641-6202 Office: Ariz Health Scis Ctr PO Box 245153 Tucson AZ 85724-5153 Office Phone: 520-647-7865. Personal E-mail: nancy@x9ranch.com.

**WEIL, D(ONALD) WALLACE,** business administration educator; b. Cleve., July 20, 1923; s. Laurence J. and Carol S. (Wallace) W.; m. Jane A. Bittel, Dec. 29, 1947; children— John Wallace, Charles Andrew, Margaret Jane, Carol Wyn. BA, Oberlin Coll., 1947; JD, Willamette U., 1950. Pres. James Foundry Corp., Fort Atkinson, Wis., 1960-70; faculty bus. adminstrn. U. Wis., Eau Claire, 1971-74, chmn. dept. bus. adminstrn., 1974-77, prof., 1985—2003, ret., prof. emeritus, 2003—; pres. Diversified Industries, Inc., St. Louis, 1977-81, UHI Corp., Los Angeles, 1981-85. Dir. U.H.I. Corp. Diversified Industries, Inc., St. Louis, Sales Investments, Mgmt. Inc., Elmwood, Wis., Jane B. Inc., Eau Claire Served with AUS, 1942-45. Mem. Am. Security Council, Nat. Council Small Bus. Mgmt. Devel., Phi Kappa Phi, Beta Gamma Sigma. Republican. Congregationalist. Home: 1530 Canfield St Eau Claire WI 54701-4018 Office: U Wis-Eau Claire Dept Bus Adminstrn Eau Claire WI 54701

**WEIL, EDWARD DAVID,** chemist, researcher, consultant, educator; b. Phila., June 13, 1928; s. Irving E. and Minna M. (Stainbrook) W.; m. Barbara Joy Hummel, Sept. 11, 1952; children: David L., Claudia E. BS in Chemistry, U. Pa., 1950; PhD in Organic Chemistry, U. Ill., 1953; MBA, Pace U., 1982. Chemist, supr. Hooker Chem. Co., Niagara Falls, NY, 1950-65; supr., sr. scientist Stauffer Chem. Co., Dobbs Ferry, NY, 1965-86; ind. cons., patent agt., propr. Intertech. Svcs., 1986—; dir. exploratory rsch. Adelphi Rsch. Ctr., Garden City, 1986-87; rsch. prof. Poly U., Bklyn., 1987—; IP fellow U. Akron Rsch. Found., 2006—. Contbr. articles to Kirk-Othmer Ency., Ency. Polymer Sci., Rsch. Mgmt., others. Recipient IR-100 award Indsl. Rsch. Mag. Mem. Am. Chem. Soc. (chmn. profl. rels. com. N.Y. sect. 1980-95), Assn. Cons. Chemists and Chem. Engrs., Sigma Xi. Achievements include more than 220 patents for commercial flame retardants, processes, agricultural chemicals, others. Home: 850 Sumner Pkwy Apt 301 Copley OH 44321 Office Phone: 330-664-1075. E-mail: eweil@poly.edu.

**WEIL, FRANK A.,** investment banker, lawyer; b. Bedford, N.Y., Feb. 14, 1931; s. Sylvan and Ruth Alice (Norman) W.; m. Denie Sandison, Feb. 10, 1951; children: Deborah Weil Harrington, Amanda, Sandison, William. AB cum laude, Harvard U., 1953, LL.B., 1956. Bar: N.Y. 1956. Practiced in N.Y.C., 1957-60; gen. partner Loeb, Rhoades & Co., N.Y.C., 1960-71; pres. Abacus Fund, Inc., 1968-72; chief fin. officer, dir. Paine, Webber, Jackson & Curtis, N.Y.C., 1972-77; asst. sec. industry and trade Dept. Commerce, Washington, 1977-79; partner firm, bd. chmn., Ginsburg, Feldman, Weil & Bress, Washington, 1979-83, Wald, Harkrader & Ross, Washington, 1983-85; chmn., chief exec. officer, dir., Abacus and Assocs., Inc., 1985—; chmn. bd. SyVox Corp., Exxel/Atmos, Inc. Dir. Geico, Dorr-Oliver, Inc., Stamford, Conn., 1968-77, Hamburg Savs. Bank, N.Y.C., 1975-77, J.B. Lippincott Co., Phila., 1975-77, Govt. Research Corp., 1975-77, 79-85; dir., pres. Norman Found., 1953-77, 79, 92, chmn. bd. trustee, Ednl. Alliance. Trustee Tchrs. Coll., Columbia U., 1976-79, Montefiore Hosp., 1960-77; trustee, vice chmn. No. Westchester Hosp., 1971-77; past vice chmn. bd. govs. Atlantic Inst. Internat. Affairs; past pres. Ednl. Alliance, trustee, 1957-77; trustee, sec. Fedn. Jewish Philanthropies, N.Y.C., 1965-77; trustee, chmn. Harvey Sch., 1969-76; trustee Hurricane Island Outward Bound Sch., 1974—, Washington Opera, 1984-85, Asia Soc., 1993—; bd. dirs., pres., vice chmn., Hickrill Found., Inc., 1953-77, 79—; chmn. bd. dirs. Coun. Excellence in Govt., 1984—, chmn., 1988-93, Am. Assembly, 1992—, Smithsonian Inst., 1994—, chmn., 1997—; mem. vis. com. Kennedy Sch. Govt., Harvard U., chmn., 1998—; chmn. tax com., mem. N.Y. State Econ. Devel. Bd., 1975-77, mem. Appleseed Found. bd., 1995—; chmn., mem. N.Y. State Bd. Equalization and Assessment, 1976-77; adv. bd. Sch. Advanced Internat. Studies, Johns Hopkins U., 1979-88; mem. N.Y. State Council on Fiscal and Econ. Priorities, 1985-89, N.Y. Coun. Fgn. Rels.; mem. N.Y. State Adv. Commn. on Liability Ins., 1986. Mem. Century Assn., Harvard Club, River Club, Met. Club. Home: 1516 28th St NW Washington DC 20007-3058 Office: Abacus & Assocs Inc 147 E 48th St # 3fl New York NY 10017-1223 Office Phone: 212-230-9801. Business E-Mail: fweil2@abacusny.com.

**WEIL, IRWIN,** literature and language professor; b. Cin., Apr. 16, 1928, s. Sidney and Florence (Levy) W.; m. Vivian Weil, Dec. 27, 1950; children: Martin, Alice, Daniel. AB, U. Chgo., 1948, MA, 1951; PhD, Harvard U., 1960. Sr. social sci. research analyst Library of Congress, 1951-54; teaching fellow Harvard U., 1956-58; mem. faculty Brandeis U., 1958-65; mem. faculty dept. Slavic langs. and lit. Northwestern U., Evanston, Ill., 1966—, chmn. dept., 1976-82. Vis. prof. U. Moscow, Soviet Acad. Scis.; set up series of internat. symposia between Am. scholars and USSR Acad. Scis.; founder 1st Soviet-Am. TV Student Competition in Lit., 1988-89; active in establishment of American Studies Ctr. Humanities U., Moscow, Russia. Author books and articles pub. in field, pub. in U.S.A. and Russia. Recipient Pushkin Internat. gold medal for outstanding teaching and research, 1984, Outstanding Teaching award Northwestern U. Alumni Assn., 1987, Tempo All-Professor Team, Humanities, Chicago Tribune, 1993; Ford Found. fellow, 1954-55. Mem. Am. Assn. Tchrs. Slavic and East European Langs. (exec. sec. 1962-68, Excellence in Teaching award 1993), Am. Coun. Tchrs. Russian (v.p. 1975-79, pres. 1980-84), Internat. Assn. Profs. Russian (founding U.S. mem.). Jewish. Achievements incude establishing TV competition on American and Russian literature between several high schoolers. Office: Northwestern U Slavic Dept Evanston IL 60208-0001 Office Phone: 847-491-8254. Business E-Mail: i-weil@northwestern.edu. *As a scholar and teacher trying hard to develop mutual understanding and cultural exchange with the USSR, I have discovered how important and fruitful it is to apply the normal standards of friendly discourse with people from an entirely different country and historical background.*

**WEIL, JEFFREY GEORGE,** lawyer; b. Allentown, Pa., Apr. 28, 1951; s. Russel G.E. and Irene Marie (Kozlowski) W.; children: Michael, Stephen, Brooke, Lauren, Kristen. AB, Princeton U., 1973; JD, Harvard U., 1976. Bar: Pa. 1976, U.S. Dist. Ct. (ea. dist.) Pa. 1976, U.S. C. Appeals (3d cir.) 1976, U.S. Supreme Ct., 1988. Assoc. Dechert, Phila., 1976—84, ptnr., 1984—, chmn. firm hiring com., 1987—89, mem. firm exec. com., 1990—94. Chmn. com. United Way Southeastern Pa., Phila., 1982-85, trustee, 1983-89, funding policy com., 1987-90; participant Cmty. Leadership Seminar Program, Phila.; 1986; bd. dirs. Hawk Mountain Sanctuary, 1993-99, chmn. bd. dirs., 2000-05; bd. dirs. Pa. Wildlife Fedn., 1996-99. Mem. ABA (vice-chmn. adminstrn. law com. on pub. advs. and pub. representation 1985-88, antitrust sect. pvt. litig.

subcom. 1991-2002), Pa. Bar Assn., Phila. Bar Assn. (fed. cts. com. 1985—), Princeton U. Alumni Schs. Com., Phila. Athenaeum, Princeton Club Phila. Avocations: fly fishing, reading. Home: 195 Shelbourne Ln Phoenixville PA 19460-5710 Office: Cira Centre 2929 Arch St Philadelphia PA 19104-2808 Office Phone: 215-994-2538, 215-994-2538. Business E-Mail: jeffrey.weil@dechert.com.

**WEIL, JOHN WILLIAM,** technology management consultant; b. N.Y.C., Feb. 3, 1928; s. Frank Leopold and Henrietta Amelia (Simons) W.; m. Joan Leatrice Landis, June 15, 1950; children— Nancy Ellen, Linda Jill. BS, MIT, 1948; PhD, Cornell U. 1953. Various positions in nuclear reactors and computers Gen. Electric Co. (various locations), 1953-70; v.p. advanced systems and tech. Honeywell Info. Systems, Inc., Waltham, Mass., 1970-74; v.p., chief tech. officer Bendix Corp., Southfield, Mich., 1974-77, v.p., chief tech. officer, 1977-83; v.p. advanced tech. and engring. Allied Corp., Southfield, 1983; pres. Modular Bio Systems, Inc., 1983-85, Weil Assocs., Inc., Bloomfield Hills, Mich., 1985-97. Founder Met. Detroit Sci. and Engring. Coalition, 1977, sec., 1977-80, pres., 1980-82; chmn. Mich. Biotech. Inst., 1981-85, trustee, 1985-92; mem. Army Sci. Bd., 1982-84. Contbr. articles to prof. jours. AEC fellow, 1950-51 Home and Office: 218 Guilford Rd Bloomfield Hills MI 48304-2737 Personal E-mail: johnww@weilhome.com.

**WEIL, LEONARD,** banker; b. 1922; married With U.S. Dept. State, Vienna, Austria, 1946; with Union Bank, Los Angeles, 1946-62; pres., CEO Mfrs. Bank, Los Angeles, 1962-86, pres. emeritus, 1986—. Adj. asst. prof. fin. Anderson Grad. Sch. Mgmt., UCLA; Trustee UCLA Found.; bd. visitors UCLA Grad. Sch. Mgmt.; past pres. Town Hall; bd. dirs. Braille Inst. Served with U.S. Army, 1943-45 Mem. Calif. Bankers Assn. (bd. dirs., past pres.), Am. Mgmt. Assn., Am. Econs. Assn., Am. Bankers Assn. (past dir.). Office: PO Box 571150 Tarzana CA 91357-1150 Address: 4501 La Barca Pl Tarzana CA 91356-5029 Office Phone: 818-344-3183.

**WEIL, LOUIS ARTHUR, III,** retired newspaper publishing executive; b. Grand Rapids, Mich., Mar. 14, 1941; s. Louis Arthur, Jr. and Kathryn (Halligan) W.; m. Mary Elizabeth Buckingham, Sept. 7, 1963 (div. June 1977); children: Scott Arthur, Christopher Davison, Timothy Buckingham; m. Daryl Hopkins Goss, Jan. 26, 1980. BA in English, Ind. U., 1963; DHL (hon.), Mercy Coll., Grand Valley State U. Various positions Times Herald, Port Huron, Mich., 1966-68; personnel dir., pub. Journal and Courier, Lafayette, Ind., 1968-73; gen. mgr., pub. Gannett Westchester Rockland Newspapers, White Plains, N.Y., 1973-74, pres., gen. mgr., 1974-77, pres., pub., 1977-79; v.p. devel. Gannett Co., Inc., N.Y.C., 1979-83, sr. v.p. planning and devel., 1982-86; chmn., pub. Gannett Westchester Rockland Newspapers, White Plains, 1984-86; pres. The Detroit News, 1986-89, pub., 1987-89; U.S. pub. Time Mag., 1989-91; pub., chief exec. officer, pres. v.p. Ariz. Republic, Phoenix Gazette, Ariz. Bus. Gazette, 1991-96; chmn., pres., CEO Central Newspapers, Inc., Phoenix, 1996-2000. Bd. dirs. Ctrl. Newspapers, Inc., Prudential. Trustee Garvin Sch. Internat. Mgmt. Thunderbird; campaign chmn. Valley of the Sun United Way, 1992; past chmn. Greater Phoenix Leadership; past pres. bd. trustees Phoenix Art Mus. With USN. Office: 15974 N 77th St #102 Scottsdale AZ 85260

**WEIL, LYNNE AMY,** communications executive, writer; b. Santa Monica, Calif., Apr. 29, 1963; d. Robert Harry and Miriam Ruth Weil; m. Nils Johan Axel Bruzelius, Aug. 10, 2002; 1 child, Emilie Anna Bruzelius. BA in Comm., U. Calif., L.A., 1985; M in Pub. Policy, Princeton U., 2001. Freelance fgn. corr. Nat. Pub. Radio, Monitor Radio, Marketplace pub. radio, BBC, various others, Bonn, Germany, 1993—96; prodr., reporter Radio Deutsche Welle, Cologne, 1991—92; European corr. Cath. News Svc., Rome, 1996—99; reporter UPI, L.A., 1986—88; prodr., reporter Calif. Pub. Radio Network, Long Beach, 1988—91; press sec. Senate Fgn. Rels. Com., Washington, 2001—03; comm. dir. Ho. Internat. Rels. Com. Dem. staff, 2003—. Cons. Woodrow Wilson Sch., Princeton U., NJ, 2003. Contbr. articles to profl. jours. Recipient Coll. journalism award with stipend, Pub. Interest Radio and TV Soc., 1985; scholar, Woodrow Wilson Sch., Princeton U., 2000—01; Congl. fellow, Am. Polit. Sci. Assn., 1999—2000. Mem.: Fgn. Corr. Assn. Germany (pres. 1995—96, v.p. 1994—95), Women in Internat. Security. Avocations: skiing, tennis, various musical instruments. Office Phone: 202-225-6735.

**WEIL, MAX HARRY,** internist, cardiologist, educator, medical researcher; b. Baden, Switzerland, Feb. 9, 1927; arrived in U.S., 1937, naturalized, 1944; s. Marcel and Gretl (Winter) Weil; children: Susan Margot, Carol Juliet. AB, U. Mich., 1948; MD, SUNY, N.Y.C., 1952; PhD, U. Minn., 1957; DSc (hon.), SUNY Downstate Med. Ctr., 2004. Diplomate Am. Bd. Internal Medicine and Critical Care Medicine, Nat. Bd. Med. Examiners. Intern in internal medicine U. Cin. Med. Ctr., 1952-53; resident U. Minn. Hosps., Heart Hosp., VA Hosp., Mpls., 1953-55; rsch. fellow U. Minn., Mpls., 1955-56; sr. fellow Nat. Heart Inst., Mayo Clinic, Rochester, Minn., 1956-57; chief cardiology City of Hope Med. Ctr., Duarte, Calif., 1957-59; asst. clin. prof. U. So. Calif. Sch. Medicine, LA, 1957-59, asst. prof., 1959-63, assoc. prof., 1963-71, clin. prof., 1971-81; chmn. L.A. Com. on Emergency Med. Svcs., 1968-73; prof., chmn. Dept. Medicine, chief divsn. cardiology Chgo. Med. Sch. U. Health Scis., North Chgo., 1981-91, disting. univ. prof., 1992-94, disting. univ. prof. emeritus Weil Inst. Critical Care Medicine, 1994—, 1994—. Adj. prof. medicine Northwestern U. Med. Sch., Chgo., 1992—; prof. clin. med. bioengring. U. So. Calif., L.A., 1972-91, adj. prof. medicine, 1981-94, clin. prof. anesthesiology, 1995—, rsch. prof. surgery, 1996—; disting. univ. prof. Inst. Critical Care Medicine, Rancho Mirage, Calif., 1995—. Sect. editor Archives Internal Medicine, 1983-86, JAMA, 1969-72, guest editor Am. Jour. Cardiology, 1982, Critical Care Medicine, 1985; mem. editl. bd. Am. Jour. Medicine, 1971-79, Chest, 1980-95, Jour. Circulatory Shock, 1979-92, Clin. Engring. Newsletter, 1980—, Methods of Info. in Medicine, 1977-91, Jour. Clin. Illness, 1986—, Clin. Intensive Care, 1989—; mem. editl. adv. bd. Emergency Medicine, 1978—, Issues in Health Care Tech., 1983-86; assoc. editor Critical Care Medicine, 1973-74, mem. editl. bd., 1973-91, 94-96, sr. editor, 1997; editor-in-chief Acute Care, 1983-90, Jour. Cardiovasc. Pharmacol. Theories, 2003—; contbr. over 1100 articles to profl. jours.; patentee in field. Pres. Temple Brotherhood, Wilshire Blvd. Temple, L.A., 1967-68; bd. dirs. Hollywood Presbyn. Med. Ctr., 1976-81, L.A. chpt. Met. Am. Heart Assn., 1962-67, Chgo. chpt. Met. Am. Heart Assn., 1982-88; active City Health and Med. Welfare Commn., Rancho Mirage, 2002—. With U.S. Army, 1946-47. Recipient prize in internal medicine SUNY, 1952, Alumni medallion SUNY, 1984; Disting. Svc. award Soc. Critical Care Medicine, 1984; numerous rsch. grants, 1956—; named Disting. Alumni Lectr., 1967, Oscar Schwindetzky Meml. Lectr. Internat. Anesthesia Rsch. Soc., 1978; recipient Lawrence R. Medoff award Chgo. Med. Sch., 1987, Morris L. Parker Rsch. award, 1989, Mission of Mercy award Israeli Nat. Emergency Svcs., 2001; Lilly scholar, 1988-89. Master ACP; fellow Am. Coll. Cardiology (chmn. emergency cardiac care com. 1974-82), master, fellow Am. Coll. Chest Physicians, Am. Coll. Clin. Pharmacology, Am. Coll. Critical Care Medicine (Disting. Investigator award 1990, 96, A.S. Laerdal Lifetime Achievement award 2000, Lifetime Achievement award 2001), Am. Heart Assn. (coun. circulation, coun. basic sci., coun. cardiopulmonary and critical care, coun. clin. cardiology, Dickinson W. Richards Meml. lectureship 1998, Emergency Cardiac Care Lifetime Achievement award 2000), Vet. Emergency Critical Care Soc. (Knowles Meml. lectr. 2002), NY Acad. Sci., Chgo. Soc. Internal Medicine; mem. AMA (sect. editor jour. 1969-72), IEEE, L.A. County Med. Assn., Am. Physiol. Soc. Am. Soc. Pharmacology and Exptl. Therapeutics, Am. Trauma Soc. (founding mem.), Assn. Computing Machinery, Assn. Am. Med. Colls., Ctrl. Soc. Rsch. Chgo. Cardiol. Group (sec.-treas. 1986-87, chmn. 1988-90), Chgo. Soc. Internal Medicine, Lake County Heart Assn. (bd. govs. 1984-86), Intensive Care Soc. U.K., L.A. Soc. Internal Medicine, Soc. Exptl. Biology and Medicine, Western Soc. Clin. Rsch., Fedn. Am. Socs. Exptl. Biology, Am. Soc. Parenteral and Enteral Nutrition, Nat. Acad. Practice (disting. practitioner), Skull and Dagger, Sigma Xi, Alpha Omega Alpha. Jewish. Avocations: swimming, tennis, photography, philosophy-economics. Office: Chgo Med Sch U Health Scis Weil Inst Critical Care Medicine 35100 Bob Hope Dr Rancho Mirage CA 92270 Office Phone: 760-778-4911. Business E-Mail: weilm@911research.org.

**WEIL, PETER HENRY,** lawyer; b. NYC, Nov. 20, 1933; s. Frank L. and Henrietta Amelia Weil; m. Helen Fay Kolodkin, Dec. 18, 1960; children: Karen L., Frank L. BA cum laude, Princeton U., 1954; LLB cum laude, Harvard U., 1957. Bar: N.Y. 1957, U.S. Dist. Ct. (so. and ea. dists.) N.Y. 1972. Assoc. Weil, Gotshal & Manges, N.Y.C., 1958-62; from assoc. to ptnr. Kaye Scholer, N.Y.C., 1962-95; ret., 1995. Lectr. SMU Inst. Comml. Financing, 1985—94, Banking Law Inst., 1987—89. Author: Asset Based Lending: An Introductory Guide to Secured Financing, P.L.I., 1989, 3d edit., 1996. Former chmn. N.Y. bd. overseers, former bd. govs. Hebrew Union Coll., Jewish Inst. Religion, Cin., N.Y.C., L.A., Jerusalem. With U.S. Army, 1957—58. Recipient U.S. Nat. Sr. Champions Ringwood Golden Master Volleyball Team award, 1983. Mem.: ABA, Assn. Bar of City of N.Y. (mem. banking law com. 1975—78). Personal E-Mail: phweil@aol.com.

**WEIL, RANDOLPH ALLEN,** engineering executive; b. Champaign, Ill., Nov. 23, 1951; s. Nicholas Andrew and Audrey Florence W.; m. Susan Kay Rostad, Feb. 26, 1977; children: Alexandra, Aaron. BS in Econs., U. Ill., Chgo., 1973; MBA, U. Calif., Berkeley, 1974. Gen. sales mgr. Cummins Engring. Co., Downers Grove, Ill., 1975-83; gen. mgr. ops. Sub of Cummins Engine. Co., Chgo., 1983-85; v.p., gen. mgr. Global Parts, Inc. (sub.co. of The Budd Co.), Dallas, 1985—87; dir. distbn. ops. Square D Co., Florence, Ky., 1988-92; v.p. logistics AT&T Network Systems, Morristown, NJ, 1992-94; v.p. svc. logistics NCR Corp., Dayton, Ohio, 1994—2000; pres., COO IHS Engring., 2001—03; exec. v.p. IHS Group, 2003—04; pres., CEO Weil Operations West, LLC, 2004—; pres. Highlands Ranch Parks and Rec. Found., 2005—; dir. comm. St. Mary's Acad. Parents, 2005—; dir. Power Kure, Inc., 2005—. Dir. Jr. Achievement, Dayton, 1996—99, Boy Scouts Am., Columbus, 1978—80. Mem. Am. Prodn. & Inventory Control Soc., Coun. Logistics Mgrs. Avocations: bicycling, swimming, opera, remodelling, gardening. Office Phone: 303-425-3255. Personal E-Mail: raweil@att.net.

**WEIL, REX,** artist, art critic; BA, Northwestern U.; JD, U. Cin. Dir. art program for handicapped children; instr., contemporary art & theories of art Corcoran Coll. Art & Design, Washington. Art critic, contbg. editor ARTnews mag.; new art examiner The Wall Street Jour., Washington City Paper. Art critic, contbg. editor ARTnews mag. Founder Corcoran Summer Art and Writing Inst.; founding mem., Corcoran Mentorship Program Corcoran Coll. Art & Design. Office: ARTnews 48 W 38th St New York NY 10018 Office Phone: 212-398-1690. Office Fax: 212-819-0394.

**WEIL, ROLF ALFRED,** economist, retired university president; b. Pforzheim, Germany, Oct. 29, 1921; arrived in U.S., 1936, naturalized, 1944; s. Henry and Lina (Landauer) W.; m. Leni Metzger, Nov. 3, 1945; children: Susan Linda, Ronald Alan. BA, U. Chgo., 1942, PhD, 1950; D Hebrew Letters, Coll. Jewish Studies, 1967; DHL, Loyola U., 1970, Bowling Green State U., Ohio, 1986; LHD, Roosevelt U., 1988. Rsch. asst. Cowles Commn. for Rsch. in Econs., 1942-44; rsch. analyst Ill. Dept. Revenue, 1944-46; mem. faculty Roosevelt U., Chgo., 1946—; prof. fin. and econs., also chmn. dept. fin., 1954-65, dean Coll. Bus. Adminstrn., 1957-64, acting pres., 1965-66, pres., 1966-88, pres. emeritus, 1988—. Past pres. Selfhelp Home for the Aged, Chgo. Author: Through these Portals-from Immigrant to College President, 1991; contbr. articles on fin. to profl. jours. Bd. dirs. trustees Roosevelt U., Selfhelp of Chgo., Inc. Mem. Am. Econ. Assn., Cliff Dwellers Club. Office Phone: 312-341-4330. Personal E-Mail: rolfleniweil@aol.com. Business E-Mail: rweil@roosevelt.edu.

**WEIL, ROMAN LEE,** finance educator; b. Montgomery, Ala., May 22, 1940; s. Roman L. and Charlotte (Alexander) W.; children: Alexis Cherie, Charles Alexander Roman, Lacey Lorraine. BA, Yale U., 1962; MS in Indsl. Adminstrn, Carnegie-Mellon U., 1965, PhD in Econs., 1966. CPA, CMA, Ill. From instr. to prof. U. Chgo., 1965-93, Sigmund E. Edelstone prof. acctg., 1993-97, V. Duane Rath prof. acctg., 1997—, dir. Dir.'s Coll., 1998—; dir. Chgo./Stanford/Wharton Dirs. Consortium, 2002—; Mills B. Lane prof. indsl. mgmt. Ga. Inst. Tech., 1974-76; mem. acctg. com. replacement cost implementation SEC, 1976-77. Bd. dirs. NY Life Ins Mainstay VP Funds, chmn. audit com.; prof. acctg. Stanford (Calif.) U., 1984, 2004, prof. econs., 1985, prof. law, 1990-96; prof. acctg. and law NYU Sch. Law, 1985; mem. adv. coun. Fin. Acctg. Stds., 1989-94; mem. task force on consolidations Fin. Acctg. Stds. Bd., 1984-89, mem. task force on discounting, 1989-99, mem. task force on fin. instruments, 1994-98, mem. adv. coun., 1989-94; dir. Dir.'s Coll., 1999—; co-founder Chgo./Stanford/Wharton Dir.'s Consortium, 2002-. Author: Fundamentals of Accounting, 1975, Financial Accounting, 10th edit., 2002, Accounting: The Language of Business, 10th edit., 1994, Inflation Accounting, 1976, Replacement Cost Accounting, 1976, Managerial Accounting, 1979, 7th edit., 2000, Litigation Svcs. Handbook, 3d edit., 2001, Litigation Services Report Writing, 2003; editor: Handbook of Modern Accounting, 1977, 3d edit., 1983, Handbook of Cost Accounting, 1980, Handbook of Cost Management, 2005, Acctg. Rev., 1974-79, Fin. Analysts Jour., 1980-88. NSF grantee, 1967-81 Mem. AICPA, Ill. Soc. CPAs, Am. Econ. Assn., Inst. Mgmt. Scis., Nat. Assn. Accts. (cert. mgmt. acct.), Am. Acctg. Assn., Inst. Managerial Acctg., Assembly Am. Collegiate Schs. Bus. (acctg. accreditation com. 1987-88), Oenonomy Soc. (co-chmn.). Home: #306 600 N Kingsbury St Chicago IL 60610 Office: U Chgo Grad Sch Bus 1101 E 58th St Chicago IL 60637-1511 E-mail: roman.weil@gsb.uchicago.edu.

**WEIL, THOMAS ALEXANDER,** retired electronics engineer; b. N.Y.C., Jan. 22, 1930; s. Frank Leopold and Henrietta Amelia (Simons) W.; m. Dianne Isaacs; children: Deborah, Elizabeth, Alexander. BSEE, MIT, 1951. Engr. modulator sect. Raytheon Co., Watertown, Mass., 1951-55, sect. mgr. transmitters, 1955-69, dept. mgr. transmitters, 1969-77, staff scientist equipment devel. labs., 1972-95, lab. mgr. radar systems, 1977-79, lab. mgr. advanced devel., 1979-80, program mgr. oil shale program, 1980-84, sr. sci., 1985—95, ret., 1995. Cons. in field. Contbr. 3 chpts. to books, over 40 articles to profl. jours. Recipient Excellence in Tech. award Raytheon co., 1990; Raytheon Co. fellow, 1989. Fellow IEEE (tech. papers com. Modulator Symposia, Microwave Tube Symposia, Germeshausen award 1994). Universalist-Unitarian. Avocations: classical music, photography, mountain climbing, cosmology. Home: 14 Lanark Rd Wellesley MA 02481-3029 Personal E-mail: taweil@aol.com. *Evolution and survival of the fittest have left mankind aggressive and prone to make war. Peace depends on finding how to overcome this heritage. Shouldn't we be working on how to resteer mankind's instincts?.*

**WEIL, THOMAS P.,** retired health services consultant; b. Mount Vernon, N.Y., Oct. 2, 1932; s. H.M. and Alice (Franc) W.; m. Janet Whalen, Feb. 13, 1965. BA, Union Coll., 1954; MPH, Yale U., 1958; PhD, U. Mich., 1964. S.S. Goldwater fellow Mount Sinai Med. Ctr., N.Y.C., 1957-58; assoc. cons. J.G. Steinle Assocs., Garden City, NY, 1958-61; asst. prof. UCLA, 1962-65; assoc. dir. Touro Infirmary, New Orleans, 1964-66; prof., dir. U. Mo., 1966—71; v.p. E.D. Rosenfeld Assocs., N.Y.C., 1971-75; pres. Bedford Health Assocs. Inc., N.Y., N.Y.C., 1975-2000; ret. Chmn. Health Edn. & Applied Rsch. Found., Washington, 1981-83; bd. dirs. Albany (N.Y.) Med. Ctr., Inc., 1974-77; cons. to numerous hosps., med. schs., health related orgs., 1958-2000. Contbr. articles profl. jours. Named vis. prof. W.K. Kellogg Found., Sydney, Australia, 1969; recipient svc. award Am. Assn. Healthcare Cons., 1982; Weil Disting. Prof. in Health Svcs. Mgmt., U. Mo., 1991-2001. Fellow APHA (emeritus), Am. Assn. Healthcare Cons. (emeritus), Am. Coll. Healthcare Execs. (emeritus). Jewish. Avocations: Appaloosa and Quarter Horses, Pointers. Office Phone: 828-252-1616. Personal E-mail: Tpweil@aol.com.

**WEILAND, ANDREW J.,** orthopaedic surgeon; MD, Wake Forest U., 1968. Diplomate Am. Bd. Orthop. Surgery (pres. 1998-99). Resident in gen. surgery U. Mich., Ann Arbor, 1969-70; resident in orthop. surgery Johns Hopkins Hosp., Balt., 1972-75; attending orthopedist Hosp. for Spl. Surgery, NYC; prof. surgery (orthop. and plastic) Cornell U. Med. Coll., Ithaca, NY, 1990—. Contbr. over 250 articles to profl. jours.; editl. bd. Jour. Bone and Joint Surgery, Jour. Hand Surgery, Internat. Jour. Microsurgery. Recipient Kappa Delta award for outstanding rsch., 1986, 91, Joseph Boyes award 43rd Ann. Meeting of Am. Soc. Surgery of the Hand, 1988; ASIF fellow in internal fixation of fractures, Switzerland, 1974, Christine Kleinert Hand fellow, 1975; ABC Traveling Fellow, 1981. Mem. Am. Orthop. Assn. (pres. 1998-99), Am. Soc. Reconstructive Microsurgery (pres. 1991), Am. Soc. for Surgery of the Hand (pres. 1995), Am. Acad. Orthopedic Surgeons (treas. 2000-) Achievements include research in dupuytren's contractures, upper extremity joint replacement and free vascularized bone grafts. Office: Hospital for Special Surgery 535 E 70th St New York NY 10021-4898 Office Phone: 212-606-1575. Office Fax: 212-535-0426. Business E-Mail: weilanda@hss.edu.

**WEILAND, JULIETTE MARIE,** public relations executive, freelance photographer, writer; b. St. Cloud, Minn., Oct. 5, 1944; d. Raymond Henry and Marie Julie (Fradette) Peterson; m. James Edward Weiland, Sept. 18, 1965; children: James Edward Jr., Timothy Paul, Kristin Juliette, Stephanie Marie. BS, U. Minn., Duluth, 1967; student, U. Calif., Berkeley, 1978-83, Silvermine Sch. Art, New Canaan, Conn., 1987, Am. Mgmt. Assn., 1993. Cert. English tchr. Tchr. English Anoka Hennepin Sch. Dist., Coon Rapids, Minn., 1968-71, tutor ESL Anoka, Minn., 1971-73, Cherry Creek Sch. Dist., Englewood, Colo., 1975-76; pvt. tutor ESL Bethel, Conn., 1976-78; ptnr., owner, author Pamphleteers & Co., Wilton, Conn., 1986-96; pub. rels. dir. Nursing & Home Care, Wilton, Conn., 1988-95; owner Breathe Easy Environ. Assocs., Wilton, Conn., 1991-96. Freelance writer, Acton, Mass., 1982—84; newspaper columnist on politics, govt. issues, 1987—89; newspaper columnist on pub. rels. issues for small bus., 2000—. Author: (short story) Somewhere There's A Child Waiting For Me, 1984; co-editor Wilton Voter, Wilton LWV, 1994-95; photographer various newspapers, mags.; contbr. articles to profl. jours.; contbr. columns to newspapers Co-chair Open Door Soc. for Adoptive Parents, Acton, 1980-83; pub. rels. dir. LWV Conn., Hamden, 1986-88, comm. cons., 1988-89; publicity dir. Crop Walk for Hungry, Wilton, 1987-88; active Graffiti Task Force, Norwalk, 1998-99. Recipient Apex award, 2002—06, Communicator award, 2003, Marcom Creative Awards, Gold prize, 2006. Mem. Pub. Rels. Soc. Am. (treas. 1998, v.p. 1999, chmn. job bank 1997-2000, pres. 2000, nominating chmn. 2001-02, chmn. hospitality com. 2003-05, publicity chair 2004-06, revenue devel. com. chair 2006), Internat. Freelance Photographers Orgn., Nat. Fedn. Press Women, Fairfield County Pub. Rels. Assn., Conn. Press Club (pres. 2000-02, 3rd prize external ann. report for non-profits 1990, 2d prize 1991, 3d prize news photo 1991), Healthcare Pub. Rels. and Mktg. Soc. Greater NY, Wilton C. of C. Democrat. Roman Catholic. Avocation: photography. Office: Juliette Weiland & Co 25 River Rd #7207 Wilton CT 06897-1930 Office Phone: 203-834-1359. Business E-Mail: jmw@jweilandcompany.com. E-mail: jweiland@optonline.net.

**WEILAND, SCOTT RICHARD,** singer; b. Santa Cruz, Calif., Oct. 28, 1967; m. Mary Forsberg, 2000 (div. 2003); children: Noah, Lucy Olivia. Founder, lead singer Mighty Joe Young (later renamed Stone Temple Pilots), 1987; lead singer Stone Temple Pilots, 1992—, Velvet Revolver, 2003—; founder Softdrive Records, 2003. Singer: (albums) (with Stone Temple Pilots) Core, 1992, Purple, 1994, Tiny Music...Songs From the Vatican Gift Shop, 1996, No. 4, 1999, Shangri-La Dee Da, 2001, Thank You, 2003, (solo) 12 Bar Blues, 1998, (with Velvet Revolver) Contraband, 2004; co-prodr.: (albums) Break Your Silence, Cinder, 2003. Office: RCA Records 1540 Broadway New York NY 10036

**WEILBAECHER, KATHERINE,** oncologist; b. Balt., May 22, 1965; married; children: Julia, Ellie, Erik. BA magna cum laude, Harvard U., Cambridge, 1987; MD with honors, Stanford Sch. Medicine, Palo Alto, Calif., 1992. Diplomate Am. Bd. Internal Medicine, Am. Bd. Med. Oncology, lic. physician Mo. Intern Stanford U. Hosp., Palo Alto, 1992—93, resident in internal medicine, 1993—94; fellow med. oncology Dana Farber Cancer Inst., Boston, 1994—98; instr. medicine Harvard Med. Sch., Boston, 1998—2000; asst. prof. pathology and immunology Washington U., St. Louis, 2000—03, asst. prof. medicine divsn. oncology, molecular oncology, 2000—; asst. prof. medicine and cell biology and physiology Washington U. Sch. Medicine, St. Louis, 2003—. Reviewer in field. Contbr. articles to profl. jours. Recipient House Staff Clinical Tchg. award, Stanford Med. Sch., 1994; grantee, NIH, 1998—, Mallinckrodt Jr. Found., 2001—04; Biomed. grant, Washington U./Pfizer, 2003—05. Mem.: Am. Assn. Cancer Rsch., Am. Soc. Clinical Oncology, Am. Soc. Bone and Mineral Rsch. Achievements include patents for methods of treating, preventing and inhibiting cancer metastasis and tumor formation. Office: Washington Univ 660 S Euclid Ave Box 8069 Saint Louis MO 63110

**WEILER, EDWARD J.,** federal agency administrator; b. Chgo., 1949; PhD, Northwestern U., 1976. Staff scientist, chief ultraviolet/visible and gravitational astrophysics NASA, 1979, chief scientist Hobble Space Telescope, 1979—96, dir. origins program, 1996—98, assoc. adminstr. space sci., 1998—2004; dir. NASA/Goddard Space Flight Ctr., Greenbelt, Md., 2004—. Office: NASA Goodard Space Flight Ctr Code 100 Greenbelt Rd Greenbelt MD 20771

**WEILER, JEFFRY LOUIS,** lawyer; b. N.Y.C., Dec. 31, 1942; s. Kurt and Elaine (Kabb) W.; m. Susan Karen Goodman, June 8, 1964; children: Philip K., June M. BS, Miami U., Oxford, Ohio, 1964; JD, Cleve. State U., 1970. Bar: Ohio 1970, Fla. 1981; CPA, Ohio 1968; bd. cert. specialist in estate planning trust and probate law, Ohio; bd. cert. tax specialist, Fla., 1983—. Acct. Meaden & Moore, CPAs, Cleve., 1964-65; IRS agt. U.S. Dept. Treasury, Cleve., 1965-70; assoc. Ulmer & Berne, Cleve., 1970-71; ptnr. Benesch, Friedlander, Coplan & Aronoff, LLP, Cleve., 1971—. Adj. assoc. prof. Cleve.-Marshall Coll. Law, Cleve. State U., 1980-87. Contbr. to profl. pubs. Fellow Am. Coll. Trust and Estate Counsel; mem. ABA (sect. taxation, estate and gift tax subcom.), Ohio State Bar Assn. (coun. estate planning trust and probate law sect. 1999—), Cleve. Estate Planning Inst. (chmn. 1980), Cleve. Tax Inst. (chmn. 1983), Cleve. Bar Assn. (treas. 1993-96, trustee 1988-91), Tax Club of Cleve. (sec. 1996-97, v.p. 1997-99, pres. 1999-2000). Avocations: photography, sailboat racing. Office: Benesch Friedlander Coplan & Aronoff LLP 2300 BP Tower 200 Public Sq Cleveland OH 44114-2378 Home: 451 Muirfield Dr Highland Heights OH 44143 Office Phone: 216-363-4551. Business E-Mail: jweiler@bfca.com.

**WEILER, RORY THOMAS,** lawyer; b. Evergreen Park, Ill., Nov. 3, 1953; s. Erving Thomas and Elaine Helen (Elliott) W.; m. Susan Jean Cucich, June 26, 1976; children: Timothy Elliott, Melissa Jean. BS, No. Ill. U., 1975; JD, John Marshall Law Sch., 1979. Bar: Ill. 1979, U.S. Dist. Ct. (no. dist.) Ill. 1979. Assoc. Melvin E. Dunn, Ltd., Elburn, Ill., 1979-82; ptnr. Rory T. Weiler, P.C., Elburn, 1982-89, Weiler & Noble, P.C., Batavia, Ill., 1989—2006, Weiler & Lengle, P.C., Geneva, Ill., 2006—. Pres. Bulldog Booster Club, Batavia, 1996-97; alderman City of Batavia, 1985-95; telethon host, fundraiser Aurora (Ill.) Easter Seals, 1983-96. Recipient Family Law award Leading Ill. Attys., 1996, Leonard C. McAndrew's award, ISBA, 2005. Mem. Ill. State Bar Assn. (mem. family law sect. coun. 2002—, mem. assembly), Kane County Bar Assn. (chmn. cts. facilities 1991-94, family law com. 1983—, chmn. 1997-99, 2005-, Pro Bono award 2001). Republican. Roman Catholic. Avocations: skiing, golf, reading. Office: Weiler & Lengle PC 425 Williamsburg Ave Geneva Ill 60134-1091 Office Phone: 630-262-1270. Business E-Mail: rweiler@foxvalleylawyers.net.

**WEIL-GARRIS BRANDT, KATHLEEN (KATHLEEN BRANDT),** art historian; b. Surrey, Eng. d. Kurt Hermann and Charlotte (Garris) Weil; m. Werner Brandt (dec. 1983). BA with honors, Vassar Coll., Poughkeepsie, N.Y., 1956; postgrad., U. Bonn, Germany, 1956-57; MA, Radcliffe U., 1958; PhD, Harvard, 1966; MA, Oxford U., 1998. Asst. prof. NYU, N.Y.C., 1963-67, assoc. prof., 1967-72, prof., 1973—; asst. prof. NYU Inst. Fine Arts, N.Y.C., 1966-67, assoc. prof., 1967-72, prof., 1973—; vis. prof. Harvard U., Cambridge, Mass., 1980; editor in chief The Art Bulletin, N.Y.C., 1977-81; Slade prof. Oxford U., 1998. Cons. on Renaissance art Vatican Mus., 1987—; vis. fellow Bibliotheca Hertziana (Max-Planck Inst.) Rome. Author: Leonardo and Central Italian Art, 1974, Problems In Cinquecento Sculpture, 1977; author: (with J. d'Amico) The Renaissance Cardinal's Ideal Palace, 1981, (with C. d'Acidini, J. Draper, N. Penny) Giovinezza di Michelangelo, 1999-2000; editor: Michelangelo: la Cappella Sistina: documentazione e interpretazione, vol. III, 1996; contbr. articles to profl. jours. Mem. Am. com. Medici Archive Project, 1996—; bd. dirs. Raccolta Vinciana, 1997—. Decorated officer Order of Merit (Italy); recipient Rsch. award Humboldt Found., 1985, Disting. Tchg. award Lindback Found., 1967, Golden Dozen Tchr. award NYU, 1993, Alumni Great Tchr. award, 1996; Guggenheim fellow, 1976; grantee Henkel Found., 1987, Samuel H. Kress Found., 1999. Mem. Coll. Art Assn. (bd. dirs. 1973-74, 77-81), Renaissance Soc. Am. (editl. bd. 1992—), Soc. Archtl. Historians, Friends of the Frances Lehman Loeb Art Ctr. (bd. mem. 2005—), N.Y. Acad. Scis., Phi Beta Kappa (v.p. NYU chpt. 1979-81). Avocations: art films, conservation, music, dance. Office: NYU Inst Fine Arts 1 E 78th St New York NY 10021-0119 Business E-Mail: kathleen.brandt@nyu.edu.

**WEILL, GEORGES GUSTAVE,** mathematics professor; b. Strasbourg, France, Apr. 9, 1926; arrived in US 1956; s. Edmond and Germaine (Falck) W. Student, Ecole Polytechnic, Paris, 1950; E.N.S., Telecom., Paris, 1952; Licence de Mathematiques, U. Paris, France, 1954, D.Sc. in Physics, 1955; PhD in Math, U. Calif. at Los Angeles, 1960. Research scientist Compagnie Generale de Telegraphie Sans Fil, France, 1952-56; rsch. fellow dept. elec. engring. Calif. Inst. Tech., Pasadena, 1956-59; tchg. assoc. math. UCLA, 1959-60; rsch. fellow math. Harvard, 1960-62; lectr., rsch. assoc. Yale, 1962-64; vis. assoc. prof. Belfer Grad. Sch. Sci., Yeshiva U., 1964-65; assoc. prof. math. Poly. U., Bklyn., 1964-65, prof., 1966-95, prof. math. emeritus, 1995—. Adj. prof. math. Cooper Union, N.Y.C. Mem. Am. Math. Soc., Societe Mathematique de France, IEEE (sr. mem.), Sigma Xi, Pi Mu Epsilon. Office: Polytechnic Univ 333 Jay St Brooklyn NY 11201-2990

**WEILL, HANS,** medical educator; b. Berlin, Aug. 31, 1933; came to U.S., 1939; s. Kurt and Gerda (Philipp) W.; m. Kathleen Burton, Apr. 3, 1958; children: Judith, Leslie, David. BS, Tulane U., 1955, MD, 1958. Diplomate: Am. Bd. Internal Medicine. Intern Mt. Sinai Hosp., N.Y.C., 1958-59; resident Tulane Med. Unit, Charity Hosp. La., New Orleans, 1959-60, chief resident, 1961-62, sr. vis. physician, 1972—; NIH research fellow dept. medicine and pulmonary lab. Sch. Medicine Tulane U., New Orleans, 1960-61, instr. medicine, 1962-64, asst. prof. medicine, 1964-67, assoc. prof., 1967-71, prof. medicine, 1971—, Schlieder Found. prof. pulmonary medicine, 1985-97; chief Environ. Medicine sect. Tulane Med. Center, 1980-96; dir. univ. Ctr. for Bioenviron. Rsch., 1989-93; dir. interdisciplinary research group in occupational lung diseases Nat. Heart, Lung and Blood Inst., 1972-92, mem. nat. adv. council, 1986-90, chmn. pulmonary disease adv. com., 1982-84; active staff Tulane Med. Center Hosp., 1976—; program dir. Nat. Inst. for Environ. Health Sci., 1992-96. Cons. pulmonary diseases Touro Infirmary, New Orleans, 1962—; cons. NIH, Nat. Inst. Occupational Safety and Health, Occupational Safety and Health Adminstrn., USN, NAS, EPA; lectr., participant workshops and confs. profl. groups in U.S., France, Can., U.K.; dir. Nat. Inst. Environ. Health Scis Superfund. Basic Rsch. Program, 1992-96. Mem. editorial bd. Am. Rev. of Respiratory Disease, 1980-85, CHEST, 1987-91; editor Respiratory Diseases Digest, 1981; guest editor Byssinosis conf. supplement, CHEST, 1981. Fellow Am. Acad. Allergy, Royal Soc. Medicine, ACP; mem. Am. Thoracic Soc. (pres. 1976), Am. Lung Assn. (bd. dirs. 1975-78), New Orleans Acad. Internal Medicine (sec., treas. 1973-75), Am. Coll. Chest Physicians (gov. for La. 1970-75), Am. Fedn. Clin. Research, So. Soc. Clin. Investigation, N.Y. Acad. Scis., Brit. Thoracic Assn., Internat. Epidemiol. Assn., Am. Heart Assn. (task force on environment and cardiovascular system 1978), Brit. Thoracic Soc., Phi Beta Kappa, Alpha Omega Alpha. Home and Office: 755 Hearthstone Dr Basalt CO 81621-8205 Personal E-mail: hweill@earthlink.net.

**WEILL, SANFORD I. (SANDY WEILL),** former diversified financial services company executive; b. Bklyn., Mar. 16, 1933; s. Max and Etta (Kalika) W.; m. Joan Mosher, June 20, 1955; children: Marc P., Jessica M. Bibliowicz. BA, Cornell U., 1955, student Grad. Sch. Bus. and Pub. Adminstrn., 1954-55. Chmn. bd., CEP Carter, Berlind & Weill (name changed to CBWL-Hayden, Stone, Inc. 1970, to Hayden Stone, Inc. 1972, to Shearson Hayden Stone 1974, to Shearson Loeb Rhoades), NYC, 1960-84, dir., chmn. exec. com., 1981-83, pres., 1983-85, Am. Express Co., 1983—85, chmn., CEO Fireman's Fund Ins. Co. subs., 1984-85; chmn., CEO Am. Express Ins. Services., Inc., 1984—85; chmn., pres., CEO Comml. Credit Co., Balt., 1986—88; chmn., CEO Primerica Corp., NYC, 1988—93, pres., 1988—92; chmn. Primerica Holdings Inc., NYC; chmn., CEO Travelers Group, NYC, 1986—98; CEO Citigroup, Inc., NYC, 1998—2003, chmn., 1998—2006, chmn. emeritus, 2006—. Bd. dirs. Citigroup, Inc., 1986-2006, AT&T Corp., 1998-2002, I. Du Pont Nemours & Co., 1998-2001, United Technologies Corp., 1999-2003, Fed. Res. Bank N.Y., 2001-; vice chmn. adv. council The Johnson Grad. Sch. of Mgmt.; former Acad. of Fin. Co-author (with Judah S. Kraushaar): The Real Deal: My Life in Business and Philanthropy, 2006. Mem. bd. overseers Joan and Sanford I. Weill Med. Coll. and Grad. Sch. Med. Scis. of Cornell U. (formerly Cornell Med. Coll.), 1982-, chmn., 1996-; chmn. bd. trustees Carnegie Hall, N.Y.C., 1991-; trustee N.Y. Presbyn. Hosp.; bd. overseers Meml. Sloan-Kettering Cancer Ctr.; bd. dirs. Balt. Symphony Orch.; bd. gov. NY Hosp.; mem. adv. coun. Cornell Univ. Johnson Grad. Sch. Mgmt.; mem. US Treasury Dept. Working Group on Child Care. Named one of the halls in honor of at Carnegie Hall, CEO of the Yr., Chief Exec. mag., 2002; named one of Top 25 Managers of Yr., BusinessWeek, 2001, 50 Most Generous Philanthropists, 2005, 400 Richest Americans, Forbes, 2006; named to Acad. of Achievement, Washington, D.C., 1997; recipient NY State Gov.'s Art award, 1997. Mem. N.Y. Soc. Security Analysts Clubs: Cornell (N.Y.C.), Century Country (Purchase, N.Y.), Harmonie (N.Y.C.); chmn. Nat. Acad. Found. Office: Citigroup Inc 399 Park Ave New York NY 10022-4614 also: Citigroup Inc 153 E 53rd St New York NY 10043-0001*

**WEIMER, JOHN L.,** state supreme court justice; b. Thibodaux, La., Oct. 2, 1954; m. Penny Hymel; 3 children. BS (with honors), Nicholls State U., 1976; JD, La. State U., 1980. Pvt. practice law, 1980—95; judge 17th Judicial Dist. Ct., 1995—98, 1st Cir. Ct. of Appeal, Dist. 1, Divsn. B, 1998—2001; assoc. justice La. Supreme Ct., 2001—. Adj. prof. law Nicholls State U., 1982—97; regional co-chmn. Citizens' Summit for Justice Reform, 1997. Mem. Thibodaux Vol. Fire Dept., Rotary Club, Nicholls State U. Alumni Bd., Thibodaux Chamber of Commerce, Houma-Terrebonne Chamber of Commerce, Assumption Chamber of Commerce; established Lafourche Parish Student Govt. Day Program. Recipient Crimefighter's Outstanding Jurist award, Outstanding Just. award, Victims & Citizens Against Crime. Mem.: Lafourche Parish Bar Assn., La. State Bar Assn. (delegate). Achievements include development of Lafourche Parish Drug Treatment Court. Office: La Supreme Ct 400 Royal St New Orleans LA 70130*

**WEIMER, ROBERT JAY,** geology educator, energy consultant, civic leader; b. Glendo, Wyo., Sept. 4, 1926; s. John L. and Helen (Mowrey) W.; m. Ruth Carol Adams, Sept. 12, 1948; children: Robert Thomas, Loren Edward (dec.), Paul Christner, Carl Scott. BA, U Wyo., 1948, MA, 1949; PhD, Stanford U., 1953. Geologist Union Oil Co. Calif., 1949-54; cons. geologist U.S. and fgn. petroleum exploration, 1954—; prof. geology Colo. Sch. Mines, 1957-83, prof. emeritus, 1983—; Getty prof. geology, 1978-83; vis. prof. U. Colo., 1961, U. Calgary, Can., 1970, Inst. Tech., Bandung, Indonesia, 1975. Fulbright lectr. U. Adelaide, South Australia, 1967; disting. lectr. and continuing edn. lectr. Am. Assn. Petroleum Geologists, Soc. Expl. Geophysicists; ednl. cons. to petroleum cos., 1964—; mem. energy rsch. adv. bd. Dept. Energy, 1985-90, Bd. on Mineral and Energy Resources, Nat. Rsch. Coun., 1988. Editor: Guide to Geology of Colorado, 1960, Symposium on Cretaceous Rocks of Colorado and Adjacent Area, 1959, Denver Earthquakes, 1968, Fossil Fuel Exploration, 1974, Studies in Colorado Field Geology, 1976, Petroleum System, Denver Basin, 1996. Trustee Colo. Sch. Mines Research Found., 1967-70; pres. Rockland Found., 1982-83; bd. dirs. Foothills Art Ctr., 1997-2002. With

USNR, 1944-46. Recipient Disting. Alumnus award U. Wyo., 1982, Mines medal Colo. Sch. Mines, 1984, Brown medal, 1990, Parker medal Am. Inst. Profl. Geologists, 1986, Exemplary Alumni award U. Wyo., 1994, ISEM Hedberg award, 2001, Hall of Fame award IPAMS, Legendary Geoscientist award, 2006, Carla Coleman Conservation award, 2005. Fellow Geol. Soc. Am. (chmn. Rocky Mountain sect. 1966-67, Sloss award 2003), AAAS; mem. Am. Assn. Petroleum Geologists (hon. pres. 1992, Sidney Powers medal 1983, Dist. Educator award 1996), Soc. for Sedimentary Geology (hon., sec.-treas. 1966-67, v.p. 1971, pres. 1972, Twenhofel medal 1995), Colo. Sci. Soc. (hon., pres. 1981), Rocky Mountain Assn. Geologists (hon., pres. 1969, found. bd. 1976-86, Scientist of Yr. 1982, Legend award 2003), Nigerian Mining and Geoscis. Soc. (hon.), Can. Soc. Petroleum Geologists (hon.), Wyo. Geol. Assn. (hon.), Colo. Sch. Mines Alumni Assn. (hon., Coolbaugh award 1996), Am. Geol. Inst. Found. (sec., treas. 1984-88, Legendary Geosci. award 2006-), Geol. Soc. Am. Found. (bd. dirs. 1999-04), Nat. Acad. Engring. (ch. sec. 11 1999), Northwoodside Inc. Land Conservancy Found. (v.p. 1995-96, pres. 1997—, Carla Coleman Conservation award 2005), Mt. Vernon Country Club (Golden, bd. dirs. 1956-59, 81-84, pres. 1983-84). Home: RR 3 25853 Mt Vernon Rd Golden CO 80401-9699 Business E-Mail: rweimer@mines.edu.

**WEIMER, THOMAS R. (R. THOMAS WEIMER),** federal agency administrator; BS, ME, Harvey Mudd Coll., Claremont, Calif., 1972; MEE, U. Wash., Seattle, 1976. Subcom. staff dir., com. on sci. US Ho. of Reps; legis. dir. Nat. Lab. Affairs, Office of Fed. Govt. Relations U. Calif.; chief of staff to sec. US Dept. Interior, 1989—93, prin. dep. asst. sec. water & sci., 2001—04, acting asst. sec. water & sci., 2004—05, asst. sec. policy mgmt. & budget, 2005—. Office: US Dept Interior Rm 5113 1849 C St NW Washington DC 20240 Office Phone: 202-208-1927. Business E-Mail: tom_weimer@ios.doi.gov.

**WEIN, ALAN JEROME,** urologist, educator, researcher; b. Newark, Dec. 15, 1941; s. Isadore R. and Jeanette Frances (Abrams) Wein. AB cum laude, Princeton U., 1962; MD, U. Pa., 1966; PhD (hon.), U. Patras, Greece, 2005. Diplomate Am. Bd. Urology (trustee emeritus). Intern mixed surgery Hosp. U. Pa., Phila., 1966-67, resident surgery, 1967-68; resident urology U. Pa., Phila., 1969-72, fellow Harrison Dept. Surg. Rsch. Urology Sch. Medicine, 1968-69, asst. instr. surgery Sch. Medicine, 1967-68, asst. instr. urology, 1969-71, instr., 1971-72, asst. prof., 1974-76, assoc. prof., 1976-83, prof., 1983—, asst. chief urology, 1974-79, dir. Urodynamic Evaluation Ctr. 1974—, chmn. div. urology, 1981—, chief urology 1981—. Dir. resident edn. com. div. urology Sch. Medicine U. Pa., 1976—, coord. program urologics oncology, 1976—; chief urology VA Hosp., Phila., 1974-82, attending urologist, 1982-96; asst. surgeon Children's Hosp. Phila., 1974—; cons. CDC Coun. Incontinence, 1990—; assoc. surgeon Pa. Hosp., Phila., 1977—; attending urologist Grad. Hosp., Phila., 1980-97. Author: (with D.M. Barrett) Controversies in Neuro-Urology, 1984, Voiding Function and Dysfunction: A Logical and Practical Approach, 1988, 2d edit., 1995, (with A.R. Mundy and T.P. Stephenson) Urodynamics: Principles, Practice and Application, 1984, 2d edit., 1994, (with P.M. Hanno) A Clinical Manual of Urology, 1987, 2d edit., 1994, (with Hanno, Staskin and Krane) Interstitial Cystitis, 1990, Common Problems in Urology: Comon Problems in Infertility and Impotence, 1990, (with Abrams) The Overactive Bladder: A Widespread and Treatable Concition, 1998, (with Abrams and Khourys) Incontinence, 1999, (with Flanigan and Resnick) Objectives for Urologic Residency Education, 2001, (with Walship, REtika, Vaughan) Campbell's Urology, 8th edit., 2002, others; editl. bd. asst. Urol. Survey, 1978-81; editl. bd. cons. Investigative Urology, 1978-81; mem. editl. bd. World Jour. Urology, 1982—, Am. Urol. Assn. Update series, 1983—, Urol. Survey, 1987—, Internat. Jour. Impotence Rsch.: Basic and Clin. Studies, 1989-99, Urology, 1991—; ad hoc reviewer Cancer, 1985—; cons. editor Sexuality and Disability, 1985—; asst. editor Jour. Urology, 1980-89, ad hoc reviewer clin. sect., 1989—, editl. bd. investigative sect., 1989—; assoc. editor Neurourlogy and Urodynamics, 1982—; contbr. over 600 articles and abstracts to profl. jours. chpts. to 21 books. Mem. coun. urology Nat. Kidney Found., Inc.; mem lectrs. bur. Am. Cancer Soc., 1984—; mem. adv. panel Nat. Assn. for Incontinence, 1987—; mem. adv. bd. Simon Found., 1987—; mem. med. adv. bd. Institial Cystitis Assn., 1987—; chmn. bladder health coun. Am. Found. Urologic Disease, 1990-95; trustee Am. Bd. Urology, 1990-96. Maj. MC, U.S. Army, 1972-74. Grantee VA, 1974-79, 79, 81, 81-84, 82-85, 85-88, 88-92, Eaton Labs., 1975-76, 78-80, McCabe Rsch. Fund, 1975-82, 87-88, Merrell Nat. Labs., 1979-82, 1980-82, Nat. Kidney Found., 1980-81, NIH, 1980-83, 83-88, 84-87, 87—, Roche Labs., 1981, Smith Kline and French Labs., 1982, 86-88, Eli Lilly Labs., 1986-88, 91, Found. Interstitial Cystitis, 1986-87, 87-88, Sterling Drug Co., 1991; recipient F. Brantley Scott award Am. Found. for Urologic Disease, 1996, Hugh Hampton Young award, 1997, AUA Disting. Svc. award, 2000, AUA Disting. Contbn. award, 2001, Legion of Honor Gold Medallion award Chapel of Four Chaplains, VAlley Forge, Pa., 2001. Fellow ACS; mem. AAAS, AMA (cons. com. drug evaluation 1977-90), Am. Acad. Clin. Neurophysiology, Am. Assn. Surgery of Trauma, Am. Assn. Clin. Urologists, Am. Assn. Genito-Urinary Surgeons, Am. Surg. Assn., Am. Soc. Pharmacology and Exptl. Therapeutics, Am. Soc. Andrology, Am. Soc. Clin. Oncology, Am. Urol. Assn. (chmn. practical cases urology 1982—, rsch. com. 1985—, editl. com. mid-Atlantic sect. 1988—, pub. rels. adv. bd. 1998—, Disting. Svc. award 2000), Assn. Acad. Surgery, Can. Urol. Assn., Clin. Soc. Genito-Urinary Surgeons, Ea. Coop. Oncologic Group, Endourol. Soc., Internat. Continence Soc., Nat. Assn. VA Physicians, N.Y. Acad. Scis., Coll. Physicians Phila., John Morgan Soc., Pa. Med. Assn., Pa. Oncologic Soc., Phila. Acad. Surgery, Phila. County Med. Soc., Phila. Profl. Standards Rev. Orgn., Phila. Urologic Soc. (pres. 1990-91), Ravdin-Rhoads Surg. Soc., Urol. Assn. Pa., Radiation Therapy Oncology Group (genitourinary working com. 1980—), Royal Soc. Medicine. Soc. Internat. d'Urologie, Soc. Basic Urologic Rsch., Soc. Sex Therapy and Rsch., Soc. Govt. Svc. Urologists, Soc. Pelvic Surgeons, Soc. Univ. Surgeons, Soc. Univ. Urologists (counselor 1996—, pres. 1999-2000), Soc. Urologic Oncology, Univ. Urologic Forum, Urodynamics Soc. (exec. com. 1980—, Lifetime Achievement award 1996), Urologic Rsch. Soc., Urologist's Corr. Club, Sigma Xi. Home: 1224 Mirabeau Ln Gladwyne PA 19035-1048 Office: Hosp U Pa 9 Penn Tower 34th and Civic Center Blvd Philadelphia PA 19104-4206 Office Phone: 215-662-6755. Business E-Mail: alanwein@uphs.upenn.edu.

**WEINBACH, ARTHUR FREDERIC,** computer company executive; b. Waterbury, Conn., May 3, 1943; s. Max and Winifred (Eckstein) Weinbach; m. Joanne Kaplan, Nov. 20, 1970; children: Michael Scott, Jonathan David. BS in Econs., U. Pa., 1965, MS in Acctg., 1966. CPA. With Touche Ross & Co., N.Y.C., 1966—75, prtnr. Stamford, Conn., 1976—79; from v.p. to pres. Automatic Data Processing, Inc., Roseland, 1980—84, CEO, 1996—2006, chmn., 1998—. Bd. dirs. Schering-Plough Corp., First Data Corp., N.J. Inst. Tech., N.J. Seeds. Bd. dirs. Boys Hope, 1991—2003, Overlook Hosp. Found., 1991—98, Metro N.J. U. Pa. Club, 1993—99, United Way of Tri-State, 1998—2004. Jewish. Office: ADP Inc 1 ADP Blvd Roseland NJ 07068-1786*

**WEINBERG, ADAM D.,** museum director; b. NYC, Dec. 10, 1954; s. James Lionel and Edith (Zickerman) Weinberg; m. Lorraine Ferguson; children: Zoé, Kira. BA, Brandeis U., 1977; MFA, SUNY, Buffalo, 1981. Dir. edn., asst. curator Walker Art Ctr., Mpls., 1981-88; dir., equitable ctr. Whitney Mus. Am. Art, NYC, 1988-90; artistic and program dir. Am. Ctr., Paris, 1990—92; sr. curator, curator of permanent collection Whitney Mus. Am. Art, NYC, 1993—99, mus. dir., 2003—; dir. Addison Gallery of American Art, Andover, Mass., 1999—2003. Author: (catalog) On the Line: The New Color Photojournalism, 1986, (book & catalog) Vanishing Presence, 1989, (exhbn. catalogs) Aldo Crommelynck: Master Prints with Am. Artists, 1989, Contingent Realms, 1990. Trustee Whitney Mus. Am. Art, Alice Pratt Brown Dir. Mem.: Coll. Art Assn., Am. Assn. Mus. Office: Whitney Mus Am Art 945 Madison Ave New York NY 10021 Business E-Mail: director@whitney.org.

**WEINBERG, DAVID B.,** investor; b. Chgo., Feb. 19, 1952; s. Judd A. and Marjorie (Gottlieb) W.; m. Linne Ellen Mesirow, July 6, 1980. AB cum laude, Harvard U., 1974; JD, Georgetown U., 1977. Bar: Ill. 1977, U.S. Dist. Ct. (no. dist.) Ill. 1977, U.S. Ct. Appeals (7th cir.) 1978. Law clerk to Hon. William

G. Clark Supreme Ct. Ill., 1977-79; assoc. Lord, Bissell & Brook, Chgo., 1979-84, ptnr., 1985-89, Mayer, Brown & Platt, Chgo., 1989-96; chmn., CEO Judd Enterprises, Inc., Chgo., 1996—; pres. Digital BandWidth LLC, Chgo., 1996—. Ill. Supreme Ct. com. Profl. Responsibility, Chgo., 1984-94, chmn. subcom. lawyers certification. Chmn. bd. trustees Ravinia Festival Assn., Highland Park, Ill., 1998—2001; vice chmn. bd. trustees Northwestern U., 1999—. Mem. Chgo. Club, Econ. Club Chgo., Lake Shore Country Club, Arts Club Chgo., Comml. Club Chgo. Civic Com. Office: Judd Enterprises Bank One Plz 21 S Clark St Ste 3140 Chicago IL 60603-2090

**WEINBERG, EUGENE DAVID,** microbiologist, educator; b. Chgo., Mar. 4, 1922; s. Philip and Lenore (Bergman) W.; m. Frances Murl Izen, Sept. 5, 1949; children— Barbara Ann, Marjorie Jean, Geoffrey Alan, Michael Benjamin. BS, U. Chgo., 1942, MA, 1948, PhD, 1950. Instr. dept. microbiology Ind. U., Bloomington, 1950-53, asst. prof., 1953-57, asso. prof., 1957-61, prof., 1961—, head microbiology sect., med. sci. program, 1978—92. Mem. sci. adv. bd., chair publs. Iron Disorders Inst., 1998—. Served with AUS, 1942-45. Mem.: Am. Soc. Microbiology. Office: Ind U Biology Dept Jordan Hall Bloomington IN 47405 Fax: 812-855-6705. Office Phone: 812-336-5556. Business E-Mail: eweinber@indiana.edu.

**WEINBERG, GERHARD LUDWIG,** history professor; b. Hannover, Germany, Jan. 1, 1928; came to U.S., 1940, naturalized, 1949; s. Max Bendix and Kate Sarah (Gruenebaum) W.; m. Janet Kabler White, Apr. 29, 1989. BA, N.Y. State Coll. Tchrs., Albany, 1948; MA, U. Chgo., 1949, PhD, 1951; LHD honoris causa, SUNY, Albany, 1989; PhD (hon.), U. Hannover, 2001. Research analyst War Documentation project Columbia U., 1951-54; vis. lectr. history U. Chgo., 1954-55, U. Ky., Lexington, 1955-56; dir. project microfilming captured German documents Am. Hist. Assn., 1956-57; asst. prof. U. Ky., 1957-59; mem. faculty U. Mich., Ann Arbor, 1959-74, prof. history, 1963-74, chmn. dept., 1972-73; William Rand Kenan, Jr. prof. history U. N.C., Chapel Hill, 1974-99, prof. emeritus, 1999—, acting chmn. dept., 1989-90. Vis. prof. Bonn U., 1983, USAF Acad., 1990-91; Shapiro sr. scholar-in-residence U.S. Holocaust Meml. Mus., 2001-02; bd. dirs. World War II Studies Assn., 1968—; cons. in field. Author: Guide to Captured German Documents, 1952, Germany and the Soviet Union, 1939-41, 1954, 1972, The Foreign Policy of Hitler's Germany, 1933-36, 1970, The Foreign Policy of Hitler's Germany, 1937-39, 1980, World in the Balance: Behind the Scenes of World II, 1981, A World at Arms: A Global History of World War II, 1994, 2005, Germany, Hitler and World War II, 1995, Visions of Victory, The Hopes of Eight World War II Leaders, 2005, Hitler's Foreign Poljcy 1933-1939: The Road to World War II, 2005; co-author: Soviet Partisans in World War II, 1964; editor: Hitlers zweites Buch, 1961, 95, Transformation of a Continent, 1975, Hitler's Second Book, 2003; bd. editors Jour. Modern History, 1970-72, Central European History, 1970-72, Kansas Humanities Series, 1987—, Internat. History Rev., 1990-2000, Jour. Intelligence History, 2001—. Chmn. Ann Arbor Dem. Com., 1961-63; mem. Mich. Dem. Ctrl. Com., 1963-67; mem. adv. com. on the air force history program Sec. of Air Force, 1987-90; mem. adv. com. army history program Sec. Army, 1996-2003, chmn., 1998-2003; mem. dept. defence Hist. Records Declassification Adv. Panel, 1996-2002; chmn. hist. adv. panel to interagy. working group on Nazi War Crimes and Imperial Japanese Records Disclosure, 1999—. With AUS, 1946-47. Fellow Social Sci. Research Council, 1962-63; fellow Am. Council Learned Socs., 1965-66; fellow Guggenheim Found., 1971-72; fellow Nat. Endowment Humanities, 1978-79 Mem. Am. Hist. Assn. (George Louis Beer prize 1971, 95, v.p. rsch. 1982-84), So. Hist. Assn. (chmn. European sect. 1989), Conf. Group for Ctrl. European History (chmn. 1982), Coordinating Com. Women in Hist. Profession, German Studies Assn. (exec. com. 1989-92, Halverson prize 1981, v.p. 1994-96, pres. 1996-98), World War II Studies Assn., Am. Acad. Arts and Scis., Phi Beta Kappa. Jewish. Home: 1416 Mount Willing Rd Efland NC 27243-9646 E-mail: gweinber@email.unc.edu.

**WEINBERG, H. BARBARA,** art historian, educator, curator; b. NYC, Jan. 23, 1942; d. Max and Evelyn Kallman; m. Michael B. Weinberg, Aug. 30, 1964. AB, Barnard Coll., 1962; MA, Columbia U., NYC, 1964, PhD, 1972. Prof. art history Queens Coll. Grad. Sch., CUNY, 1957—94; curator Am. paintings sculpture Met. Mus. Art., NYC, 1990—98; Alice Pratt Brown curator Am. paintings sculpture Met. Mus. Art, NYC, 1998—. Author: The Decorative Work of John La Farge, 1977, The American Pupils of Jean-Léon Gérome, 1984, The Lure of Paris: Nineteenth-Century American Painters and Their French Teachers, 1991, Thomas Eakins and the Metropolitan Museum of Art, 1994, co-author: American Impressionism and Realism: The Painting of Modern Life, 1885-1915, 1994, American Drawings and Watercolors in The Metropolitan Museum of Art: John Singer Sargent, 2000, John Singer Sargent in The Metropolitan Museum Art, 2000, Childe Hassam, American Impressionist, 2004, Americans in Paris, 1860-1900, 2006; mem. editl. bd. Am. Art Jour., 1984—. Mem.: Phi Beta Kappa. Office: Met Mus Art 1000 5th Ave New York NY 10028-0198 Office Phone: 212-879-5500.

**WEINBERG, HERSCHEL MAYER,** lawyer; b. Bklyn., Oct. 13, 1927; s. Jacob and Gertrude (Wernick) W. BA, Bklyn. Coll., 1948; LL.B., Harvard U., Cambridge, Mass., 1952. Bar: N.Y. 1952. Atty. firm Payne & Steingarten, N.Y.C., 1952-57, Jacobs, Persinger & Parker, N.Y.C., 1957-61; partner firm Rubin, Rubin, Weinberg, & Di Paola, N.Y.C., 1961-78, Weinberg Tauber & Pressman, 1979-90; pvt. practice N.Y.C., 1990—. Served with AUS, 1946-47. Mem. Assn. of Bar of City of N.Y., N.Y. State Bar Assn. Clubs: Harvard (N.Y.C.). Home: 50 Sutton Pl S New York NY 10022-4167

**WEINBERG, HUBERT,** plastic surgeon; b. Clermont-Ferrant, France, Feb. 2, 1950; came to U.S., 1955; s. Paul and Esther Weinberg; m. Rita Weinberg, June 24, 1974; children: Deborah, Nevin, Michael, Jennifer, Lauren. Anne, BA, Yeshiva U. 1971, MD, Cornell U., 1975. Diplomate Am. Bd. Plastic Surgery. Intern, resident Mt. Sinai Hosp.; instr. Mt. Sinai Med. Ctr. N.Y.C., 1982-84, assoc. prof., 1984-97, prof., 1998-2000; clin. prof., 2000—; assoc. attending physician Mt. Sinai Med. Ctr., N.Y.C., 1984-97, dir. microsurgery rsch. dept., 1982-2000, attending physician, 1998—, Westchester Med. Ctr., Valhalla, N.Y., 2000—. Adj. prof. N.Y. Med. Coll., 2000— Author: (with others) Musculoskeletal Oncology, 1992; contbr. articles to profl. jours. including Current Surgery, Plastic Reconstrn. Surgery, and Jour. Reconstructive Microsurgery; Recipient 2d pl. award Plastic Surgery Ednl. Found., 1983. Fellow ACS, N.Y. Acad. Scis. (1st prize awards 1987, 93); mem. Am. Soc. Plastic and Reconstructive Surgeons, Am. Assn. Plastic Surgeons. Avocations: computer graphics, gardening, landscaping. Office: Westchester Med Ctr Burn Ctr Macy Pavilion Valhalla NY 10595 E-mail: weinbh01@doc.mssm.edu.

**WEINBERG, IGOR,** clinical psychologist, researcher; b. Moscow, June 7, 1973; s. Yakov and Raia Weinberg. BA, Bar-Ilan U., Ramat-Gan, Israel, 1994, MA in Clin. Psychology, 2000, PhD in Clin. Psychology, 2005. Coinvestigator Geha Mental Health Ctr., Petah-Tiqva, Israel, 1999—. Rsch. cons. Mental Health Dept., IDF, Tel-Hashomer, Israel, 2003—. Contbr. articles and revs. to profl. jours. Lt. Tel-Hashomer, 1994—97, Israel. Named winner all-Moscow contest in math., 1985; fellow, McLean Hosp., Harvard Med. Sch., 2003—. Office Phone: 617-855-3163. E-mail: iweinberg@mclean.harvard.edu.

**WEINBERG, JEFFREY J.,** lawyer; b. NYC, Aug. 27, 1948; s. Arnold Mitchell and Lucile (Barton) W.; m. Bonnie J. Sandhaus, Aug. 23, 1970; children: Seth, Andrew. BA, SUNY, Stony Brook, 1969; JD, Georgetown U. 1973. Bar: N.Y., U.S. Dist. Ct. (so. and ea. dists.). Assoc. Weil, Gotshal & Manges, N.Y.C., 1973-81, ptnr., 1981—. Acting judge Village of Roslyn Estates. Author: Sales of Troubled Business, 1991, 92, 93, 94. Former trustee Village of Roslyn Estate. Mem.: Friars Club. Avocation: sailing. Office: Weil Gotshal & Manges 767 5th Ave Fl Conc1 New York NY 10153-0119

**WEINBERG, JOHN LEE,** federal judge; b. Chgo., Apr. 24, 1941; s. Louis Jr. and Jane Kitz (Lee) W.; m. Sarah Kibbee, July 6, 1963; children: Ruth, Leo. BA, Swarthmore Coll., 1962; JD, U. Chgo., 1965. Bar: Ill. 1966,

Wash. 1967, U.S. Dist. Ct. (we. dist.) Wash. 1967, U.S. Ct. Appeals (9th cir.) 1967. Law clk. to Hon. Henry L. Burman Ill. Appellate Ct., Chgo., 1965-66; law clk. to Hon. Walter V. Schaefer Ill. Supreme Ct., Chgo., 1966; law clk. to Hon. William T. Beeks U.S. Dist. Ct. Wash., Seattle, 1967-68; atty. Perkins Coie Law Firm, Seattle, 1968-73; magistrate judge U.S. Dist. Ct.; U.S. Magistrate judge Seattle, 1973—2003; ret., 2003; recalled, 2003—. Author: Federal Bail and Detention Handbook, 1988. Mem. ABA, Am. Judicature Soc., Wash. State Bar Assn., Seattle-King County Bar Assn., Fed. Magistrate Judges Assn. (nat. pres. 1982-83). Avocations: sports and physical fitness activities, bridge. Office: US Magistrate Judge 12th Fl United States Courthouse 700 Stewart St Seattle WA 98101 Office Phone: 206-370-8910.

**WEINBERG, JOHN SIDNEY,** investment banker; m. Amy Marie Shepherd, Mar. 3, 1984. BA in History, Princeton U., 1979; MBA, Harvard U. Mgmt. trainee Knight-Ridder Newspapers, Miami; assoc. corp. fin. dept. Goldman, Sachs & Co., 1983, co-head of investment banking services, 1997—2001; mem. mgmt. com. The Goldman Sachs Group, Inc., 2002—, co-head global investment banking, 2002—, vice chmn. NYC, 2006—. Bd. dirs. Steppingstone Found.; trustee NY-Presbyterian Hosp., 2000—. Office: The Goldman Sachs Group Inc 85 Broad St New York NY 10004*

**WEINBERG, LEONARD BURTON,** political scientist; b. NYC, Nov. 10, 1939; s. Max R. and Rose (Levin) W.; m. Ellen Bach, Aug. 23, 1966 (div.); 1 son, David; m. Sinikka Palomaki, June 4, 1986. BA, Syracuse U., 1961, PhD, 1967; MA, U. Chgo., 1963. Instr. polit. sci. U. Wis., Milw., 1966-67; asst. prof. polit. sci. U. Nev., Reno, 1967-71, assoc. prof., 1971-78, prof., 1978—, chmn. dept., 1979-82. Vis. prof. U. Florence, Italy, 1992. Author: Comparing Public Policies, 1977, After Mussolini, 1979, The Rise and Fall of Italian Terrorism, 1987, Introduction to Political Terrorism, 1989; editor: Political Parties and Terrorist Groups, 1992, Revival of Right-Wing Extremism in the 1990s, 1996, Political Violence and the Democratic Experience. 2000; co-editor: Encounters with the Radical Right, 1992, The Transformation of Italian Communism, 1994, Revival of Right-Wing Extremism in the 1990s, 1997, The Emergence of a Euro-American Radical, 1998. Recipient Fulbright Rsch. award, 1984; Italian Govt. Borsa di Studio, 1965-66; Fulbright grantee, 1965-66, Harry F. Guggenheim grantee, 1995-96. Mem. Am. Polit. Sci. Assn., Internat. Polit. Sci. Assn. (political sociology com.), Conf. Group on Italian Politics of Am. Polit. Sci. Assn., Phi Kappa Phi. Jewish. Office: U Nev Dept Polit Sci Reno NV 89557-0001 Business E-Mail: weinbrl@unr.nevada.edu.

**WEINBERG, LILA SHAFFER,** editor, writer; d. Sam and Blanche (Hyman) Shaffer; m. Arthur Weinberg, Jan. 25, 1953; children: Hedy, Anita, Wendy Clare. Editor Ziff-Davis Pub. Co., 1944—53; assoc. chief manuscript editor jours. U. Chgo. Press, 1966—80, sr. manuscript editor books, 1980—98; mem. faculty Sch. for New Learning DePaul U., Chgo., 1973—89. Vis. faculty continuing edn. programs U. Chgo., 1984-92. Author: (with A. Weinberg) The Muckrakers, 1961 (selected for White House Library 1963), Verdicts Out of Court, 1963, Instead of Violence, 1963, Passport to Utopia, 1968, Some Dissenting Voices, 1970, Clarence Darrow: A Sentimental Rebel, 1980; contbr. articles and revs. to various publs. Bd. dirs. Hillel Found. U. Chgo., 1988-96. Recipient Friends of Lit. award Chgo. Found. Lit., 1980, Social Justice award Darrow Community Ctr., 1980, Disting. Body of Work award Friends of Midwest Authors, 1987, John Peter Altgeld Freedom of Speech award, 2001. Mem. Soc. Midland Authors (dir. 1977-83, pres. 1983-85, Best Midwest Biography award 1980), ACLU, Clarence Darrow Commemorative Com., YIVO, Authors' League, Work in Progress. Home: 5421 S Cornell Ave Chicago IL 60615-5646

**WEINBERG, LORETTA,** state legislator; b. NYC, Feb. 6, 1935; d. Murray Isaacs and Raya Hamilton; m. Irwin S. Weinberg, July 25, 1960 (dec. Feb. 1999); children: Daniel J., Francine S. BA, UCLA, 1956. Former aide NJ Assemblyman D. Bennett Mazur, Trenton; mem. NJ Assembly, Trenton, 1992—, NJ State Senate, 2005—. Mem. Teaneck Coun., 1990-94. Recipient Legis. Leadership award No. NJ Chiropractic Assn., 1992, Woman of Achievement award Bus. and Profl. Women's Club of East Bergen, 1993, Carrie Chapman Catt award No. NJ NOW, 1997, Ethical Recognition award Ethical Culture Soc. of Bergen County, 1998, Barbara Boggs Sigmund award, Women's Polit. Caucus, 2004, Legis. Recognition, Consumers for Civil Justice; named Citizen of Yr. NJ Jewish War Vets., Legislator of Yr., NJ State Nurse's Assn., 2000; named Women in Govt., Good Housekeeping, 2005. Mem. Nat. Coun. Jewish Women (life mem., Hannah G. Solomon award 1995, Disting. Achievement award Women's Commn.). Democrat. Jewish. Office: State of NJ 545 Cedar Ln Teaneck NJ 07666-1740 Office Phone: 201-928-0100. Business E-Mail: senweinberg@njleg.org.

**WEINBERG, LOUISE,** law educator, writer; b. N.Y.C. m. Steven Weinberg; 1 child, Elizabeth. AB summa cum laude, Cornell U.; JD, Harvard U., 1969, LLM, 1974. Bar: Mass. Sr. law clk. Hon. Chas. E. Wyzanski, Jr., Boston, 1971-72; assoc. in law Bingham, Dana & Gould, Boston, 1969-72; teaching fellow Harvard Law Sch., Boston, 1972-74; lectr. law Brandeis U., Waltham, Mass., 1974; assoc. prof. law Suffolk U., Boston, 1974-76, prof., 1977-80; vis. assoc. prof. law Stanford U., Palo Alto, Calif., 1976-77; vis. prof. law Sch. Law, U. Tex., Austin, 1979, prof. law, 1980-84, Thompson prof. law, 1984-90, Andrews and Kurth prof. law, 1990-92, Fulbright and Jaworski regents rsch. prof., 1991-92, Angus G. Wynne, Sr. prof., 1992-97, Fondren chair faculty excellence, 1995—, Eugene R. Smith Centennial rsch. prof. law, 1993-97, holder William B. Bates chair, 1997—. Vis. scholar Hebrew U., Jerusalem, 1989; Forum fellow World Econ. Forum, Davos, Switzerland, 1995—; pub. spkr., lectr. in field. Author: Federal Courts: Judicial Federalism and Judicial Power, 1994, and ann. supplements; co-author: Conflict of Laws, 1990, 2d edit., 2002; contbr. chpts. to books, articles to profl. jours. Bd. dirs. Ballet Austin, 1986-00, Austin Coun. on Hgn. Affairs, 1985—, Austin Civil War Round Table, 1998—. Recipient Disting. Educator award Tex. Exes Assn., 1996. Mem.: Supreme Ct. Hist. Soc., Am. Constn. Soc., Maritime Law Assn., Tex. Asian C. of C., Assn. Am. Law Schs. (chair sect. on conflict laws 1991—93, chair sect. on fed. cts. 2003—04, acting chair 2004—05, chair sect. admiralty 2005—06), The Philos. Soc. Tex., Am. Law Inst. (consultative com. complex litigation 1989—93, consultative com. enterprise liability 1990—95, adv. group fed. judicial code revision project 1996—2001, mems.' consultative group, intellectual property 2004—), internat. jurisdiction and judgments 2004—, aggregate litigation), Phi Kappa Phi, Phi Beta Kappa. Office: U Tex Sch Law 727 Dean Keeton St Austin TX 78705-3224 Business E-Mail: lweinberg@law.utexas.edu. Personal philosophy: The right thing is usually also the humane and liberal thing.

**WEINBERG, MAX,** musician; b. So. Orange, NJ, Apr. 13, 1951; m. Becky Weinberg, 1978; children: Ali, Jay. Owner record label and prodn. co. Hard Ticket Entertainment; drummer with Bruce Springsteen's E Street Band, 1974—89; music dir. band The Max Weinberg Seven and performer in various late night comedy sketches on TV series Late Night with Conan O'Brien NBC TV, 1993—. Musician: (albums) The Max Weinberg Seven, 2000; author: The Big Beat: Conversations with Rock's Great Drummers; prodr.: (CD collection) Max Weinberg: Let There Be Drums; actor: (films) Get Well Soon, 2001. Office: c/o NBC TV Network Late Night with Conan OBrien 30 Rockefeller Plz New York NY 10112

**WEINBERG, MILTON, JR.,** retired cardiovascular and thoracic surgeon; b. Sumter, S.C., Aug. 8, 1924; s. Milton and Ethel (Harper) W.; m. Joan Ehrenstrom, Nov. 24, 1950; children: Caryl, Susan, Amy. Student, Duke U., 1941-43, MD, 1947. Diplomate Am. Bd. Surgery, Am. Bd. Thoracic Surgery. Attending surgeon Rush Presbyn.-St. Luke's Med. Ctr., Chgo., 1957-90, emeritus attending, 1990—; attending surgeon Cook County Hosp., Chgo., 1956-80, Luth. Gen. Hosp., Park Ridge, Ill., 1986—, mem. governing coun., 1996—2001; assoc. prof. Rush Med. Coll., Chgo., 1969-78, prof. surgery, 1978-90, emeritus prof., 1990—; clin. prof. U. Chgo., 1990-99, 1997-79; presenter movies at mtgs. ACS. Mem. editorial bd. Annals of Thoracic Surgery, 1968-79; contbr. articles to profl. jours., chpts. to surg. textbooks.

Trustee The Presbyn. Home, Evanston, Ill., 1984—; bd. dirs. Chgo. Symphony Orch., 1985-95; advocate Charitable Found. Bd., 1996-2002. Maj. U.S. Army, 1951-53. Decorated Bronze Star. Fellow ACS, Am. Coll. Chest Physicians, Am. Coll. Cardiology; mem. Am. Assn. Thoracic Surgery, Soc. Thoracic Surgeons, Soc. Vascular Surgery, Internat. Cardiovascular Soc., Ctrl. Surg. Soc. Avocations: fly fishing, fly rod building. Home: 983 Kirkhill Ln Lake Forest IL 60045-4209 E-mail: mw983@yahoo.com.

**WEINBERG, PETER AMORY**, investment banker; s. Sidney J. Weinberg Jr.; m. Deborah Beth Lindenauer, June 1, 1986; 3 children. BA, Claremont McKenna Coll., 1979; MBA, Harvard U., 1983. With Morgan Stanley, 1983—88, Goldman Sachs Internat., 1988—2005, ptnr., 1992, co-head global investment banking divsn. London, co-head partnership com., CEO; co-founder Perella Weinberg Partners, NYC, 2006—. Non-exec. dir. BAE Systems plc, 2005—. Trustee Brunswick Sch., Greenwich, Conn., Deerfield Acad., Mass., Kravis Leadership Inst., Claremont McKenna Coll., King's Academy, Virginia. Office: Perella Weinberg Partners LP 767 Fifth Ave New York NY 10153*

**WEINBERG, RICHARD ALAN**, psychologist, educator; b. Chgo., Jan. 28, 1943; s. Meyer and Mollie I. (Soell) W.; m. Gail E. Blumberg, Aug. 25, 1964; children: Eric, Brett. BS, U. Wis., 1964; MAT, Northwestern U., 1965; PhD, U. Minn., 1968. Lic. psychologist, Minn. Asst. prof. Tchrs. Coll., Columbia U., N.Y.C., 1968-70; prof. ednl. psychology and child psychology U. Minn., Mpls., 1970—; Birkmaier professorship, 1994-97, U. disting. tchg. prof., 1999—. Former dir. Inst. Child Devel.; former chair adv. coun. Children, Youth, and Family, chair steering com. U. Minn. Pres.'s Initiative on Children, Youth, and Family Consortium; cons. EPA; reviewer Office of Edn., NSF, NRC; guest speaker TV and radio shows. Author: (with A. Boehm) The Classroom Observer: Developing Observation Skills in Early Childhood Settings, 1997, (with Scarr and Levine) Understanding Development, 1986; former assoc. editor Contemporary Psychology; former editor: Applied Developmental Science. Bd. dirs. Children's Mus. Minn.; past pres. Am. Assn. State Psychol. Bds.; trustee Am. Assn. State Psychol. Bds. Found.; liaison Nat. Register Health Care Providers in Psychology. Grantee Bush Found., NSF, NIH. Fellow APA, Am. Psychol. Soc.; mem. Soc. Rsch. in Child Devel. (former chair pub. policy coun., chair fin. comm.), Behavior Genetics Assn., Am. Psychol. Soc. (bd. dirs.), NCAA Championship Cabinet, Phi Beta Kappa, Phi Kappa Phi. Office: U Minn 180 Child Devel 51 E River Rd Minneapolis MN 55455-0365 Business E-Mail: weinb002@umn.edu.

**WEINBERG, ROBERT ALLAN**, biochemist, educator; b. Pitts., Nov. 11, 1942; s. Fritz E. and Lore (Reichhardt) Weinberg; m. Amy Schulman Weinberg, Nov. 19, 1976; children: Aron, Leah Rosa. S.B., MIT, 1964, Ph.D, 1969; PhD (hon.), Northwestern U., 1984. Instr. Stillman Coll., Tuscaloosa, Ala., 1965—66; research fellow Weizmann Inst., Rehovoth, Israel, 1969—70; Salk Inst., LaJolla, Calif., 1970—72; from asst. prof. to assoc. prof. dept. biology & ctr. cancer rsch. MIT, Cambridge, 1973—82, prof. biology, 1982—, Daniel K. Ludwig prof. for cancer rsch., 1997—. Mem. Whitehead Inst., Cambridge, 1982—; rsch. prof. Amer. Cancer Soc., 1985; elected mem. Inst. of Medicine, 2000; mem. adv. bd. GM Cancer Rsch. Found. Author: (books) Racing to the Beginning of the Road: The Search for the Origin of Cancer, 1996, One Renegade Cell: How Cancer Begins, 1998, One Renegade Cell: The Quest for the Origin of Cancer, Vol. 3; contr. articles articles to profl. jours. Named Scientist of Yr., Discover mag., 1982; recipient Bristol Myers award, 1984, Brown-Hazen award NY State Dept. Health, 1984, Sloan prize, GM Cancer Rsch. Found., 1987, Rsch. Recognition award, Samuel Roberts Noble Found., 1990, Gairdner Found. Internat. award, 1992, Harvey Prize, Technion, 1994, G.H.A. Clowes Meml. award, 1996, Nat. Medal of Sci., 1997, Wolf Prize in Medicine, Wolf Found., 2004. Fellow: Am. Acad. of Arts & Sciences; mem.: NAS (sci. award 1984). Avocations: genealogy, house building. Office: Whitehead Inst 9 Cambridge Ctr Cambridge MA 02142-1479 Office Phone: 617-258-5159. Fax: 617-258-5213. E-mail: Weinberg@wi.mit.edu.*

**WEINBERG, STEVEN**, physics professor; b. NYC, May 3, 1933; s. Fred and Eva (Israel) Weinberg; m. Louise Goldwasser, July 6, 1954; 1 child, Elizabeth. BA, Cornell U., 1954; postgrad., Copenhagen Inst. Theoretical Physics, 1954—55; PhD, Princeton U., 1957; AM (hon.), Harvard U., 1973; ScD (hon.), Knox Coll., 1978, U. Chgo., 1978, U. Rochester, 1979, Yale U., 1979, CUNY, 1980, Clark U., 1982, Dartmouth Coll., 1984, Columbia U., 1990, U. Salamanca, 1992, U. Padua, 1992, Bates Coll., 2002, McGill U., 2003, U. Waterloo, 2004, D (hon.), U. Barcelona, 1996; PhD (hon.), Weizmann Inst., 1985; DLitt (hon.), Washington Coll., 1985. Rsch. assoc., instr. Columbia U., 1957-59; rsch. physicist Lawrence Radiation Lab., Berkeley, Calif., 1959-60; mem. faculty U. Calif., Berkeley, 1960-69; prof. physics, 1964-69; vis. prof. MIT, 1967-69, prof. physics, 1969-73; Higgins prof. physics Harvard U., 1973-83; sr. scientist Smithsonian Astrophys. Lab., 1973-83; Josey prof. sci. U. Tex., Austin, 1982—; sr. cons. Smithsonian Astrophys. Obs., 1983—. Cons. Inst. Def. Analyses, Washington, 1960—73, ACDA, 1973; Sloan fellow, 1961—65; chair in physics Coll. de France, 1971; mem. Pres.'s Com. on Nat. Medal of Sci., 1979—82, Coun. of Scholars, Libr. of Congress, 1983—85; sr. adv. La Jolla Inst.; mem. Com. on Internat. Security and Arms Control, NRC, 1981, Bd. on Physics & Astronomy, 1989—90; adv. coun. Tex. Superconducting Supercollider High Energy Rsch. Facility, 1987; Loeb lectr. in physics Harvard U., 1966—67, Morris Loeb vis. prof. physics, 1983—; Richtmeyer lectr., 1974; Scott lectr. Cavendish Lab., 1975; Silliman lectr. Yale U., 1977; Lauritsen Meml. lectr. Calif. Inst. Tech., 1979; Bethe lectr. Cornell U., 1979; de Shalit lectr. Weizmann Inst., 1979; Cherwell-Simon lectr. Oxford U., 1983; Bampton lectr. Columbia U., 1983; Einstein lectr. Israel Acad. Arts and Scis., 1984; Hilldale lectr. U. Wis., 1985; Clark lectr. U. Tex., Dallas, 1986; Dirac lectr. U. Cambridge, 1986; Klein lectr. U. Stockholm, 1989; Brittin lectr. U. Colo., 1994; Sackler lectr. U. Copenhagen, 1994; Gibbs lectr. Am. Math. Soc., 1996; Bochner lectr. Rice U., 1997; Sanchez lectr. Tex. A&M Internat. U., 1998; Witherspoon lectr. Washington U., 2001; Hamilton lectr. Royal Irish Acad. 2005; Messenger lectr. Cornell U., 2007; mem. Supercollider Sci. Policy Com., 1989—93; bd. dirs. Fedn. Am. Scientists. Author: Principles and Application of the General Theory of Relativity, 1972, The First Three Minutes: A Modern View of the Origin of the Universe, 1977, The Discovery of Subatomic Particles, 1982, revised edit., 2003; author: (with R. Feynman) Elementary Particles and the Laws of Physics; author: Dreams of a Final Theory, 1992, The Quantum Theory of Fields - Vol. I: Foundations, 1995, Modern Applications, Vol. II, 1996, Supersymmetry, Vol. III, 2000, Facing Up: Science and Its Cultural Adversaries, 2001, Glory and Terror: The Growing Nuclear Danger, 2004; rsch. and publs. on elementary particles, quantum field theory, cosmology, coeditor monographs on math. physics Cambridge U. Press, mem. adv. bd. Issues in Sci. and Tech., 1984—87, mem. sci. book bom. Sloan Found., 1985—91, editl. bd. Jour. Math. Physics, 1986—88, mem. bd. editors Daedalus, 1990—, Jour. Math. Physics, 1998—, mem. bd. assoc. editors Nuc. Physics B, —. Bd. advisors Santa Barbara Inst. Theoretical Physics, 1983—86; bd. overseers SSC Accelerator, 1984—86; bd. dirs. Headliners Found., 1993—. Recipient J. Robert Oppenheimer Meml. prize, 1973, Dannie Heineman prize in math. physics, 1977, Am. Inst. Physics U.S. Steel Found. sci. writing award, 1977, Nobel prize in Physics, 1979, Elliott Cresson medal, Franklin Inst., 1979, Madison medal, Princeton U., 1991, Nat. medal of Sci., NSF, 1991, Andrew Gemant prize, Am. Inst. Physics, 1997, Piazzi prize, Govts. Sicily and Palermo, 1998, Lewis Thomas prize, Rockefeller U., 1999. Mem.: NAS, Tex. Inst. Letters, Philos. Soc. Tex., Royal Soc. London, Am. Philos. Soc. (Benjamin Franklin medal 2004), Coun. Fgn. Rels., Internat. Astron. Union, Am. Phys. Soc., Am. Acad. Arts and Scis., Cambridge Sci. Soc., Headliners Club, Saturday Club (Boston), Tuscan Club (Austin), Phi Beta Kappa. Business E-Mail: weinberg@physics.utexas.edu.

**WEINBERG, SYLVAN LEE**, cardiologist, educator, editor, writer; b. Nashville, June 14, 1923; s. Abraham J. and Beatrice (Kottler) W.; m. Joan Hutzler, Jan. 29, 1956; children: Andrew Lee, Leslie. BS, Northwestern U., 1945, MD, 1948. From intern to resident, fellow Michael Reese Hosp., Chgo., 1947—51; attending physician Good Samaritan Hosp., Dayton, Ohio, 1953—99, chief of cardiology, 1966—99, founding dir. coronary care unit,

1967—99; clin. prof. medicine Wright State U., Dayton, 1975—; dir. med. edn. Dayton Heart Hosp., 2000—. Former panelist Med. Affairs, nat. TV; pres. Weinberg Marcus Cardiomed. Group, Inc., 1970-99; pres. Arts & Comms. Internat., Inc., 1995—. Author: An Epitaph for Merlin and Perhaps for Medicine, 1983, The Golden Age of Medical Science and the Dark Age of Health Care Delivery, 2000; founding editor Dayton Medicine, 1980—, Heart & Lung, 1972-87, The American Heart Hosp. Jour., 2002—; contr. articles to profl. jours. Capt. U.S. Army, 1951-53, Korea. Recipient Army Commendation medal, Richard A. DeWall MD award for excellence in cardiology, Am. Heart Assn., 2001, Outstanding Pub. Svc. award, Ohio State Senate, 1980. Fellow ACP (Ohio Laureate award 1997), Am. Coll. Cardiology (editor in chief jour. ACCEL 1985-2000, pres. 1993-94), Am. Coll. Chest Physicians (pres. 1984); mem. Montgomery County Med. Soc. (pres. 1980). Avocations: writing, travel, golf. Home: 4555 Southern Blvd Dayton OH 45429-1118 Office: Dayton Heart Hosp 707 S Edwin Moses Blvd Dayton OH 45408 Personal E-mail: slwjal@aol.com

**WEINBERG, WALTER S.**, lawyer; b. Chgo., Sept. 12, 1956; BA, U. Chgo., 1978; JD cum laude, Northwestern U., 1981. Bar: Ill. 1981. Ptnr., Chmn. Corp. Group Katten Muchin Rosenman LLP, Chgo. Mem.: Nat. Assn. of Small Bus. Investment Co. Office: Katten Muchin Rosenman LLP 525 W Monroe St Chicago IL 60661 Office Phone: 312-902-5405. Office Fax: 312-577-8771. Business E-Mail: walter.weinberg@kattenlaw.com.

**WEINBERG, WILLIAM HENRY**, chemical engineer, physicist, educator; b. Columbia, SC, Dec. 5, 1944; s. Ulrich Vivian and Ruth Ann (Duncan) W. BS, U. S.C., 1966; PhD in Chem. Engring. U. Calif., Berkeley, 1970; NATO postdoctoral fellow in phys. chemistry, Cambridge U., Eng., 1971. Asst. prof. chem. engring. Calif. Inst. Tech., 1972-74, assoc. prof., 1974-77, prof. chem. engring. and chem. physics, 1977-89, Chevron disting. prof. chem. engring. and chem. physics, 1981-86; prof. chem. engring. and chemistry U. Calif., Santa Barbara, 1989—, assoc. dean Coll. Engring., 1992-96; chief tech. officer Symyx Techs., Santa Clara, Calif., 1996—. Vis. prof. chemistry Harvard U., 1980, U. Pitts., 1987-88, Oxford U., 1991; Alexander von Humboldt Found. fellow U. Munich, 1982; cons. E.I. DuPont Co. Author: (with Van Hove and Chan) Low-Energy Electron Diffraction, 1986; editor 4 books in field; mem. editl. bd. Jour. Applications Surface Sci., 1977-85, Handbook Surfaces and Interfaces, 1978-80, Surface Sci. Reports, 1980—, gen. editor, 1992—, Applied Surface Sci., 1985—, Langmuir, 1990-96, Surface Sci., 1992—, Jour. Combinatorial Chemistry, 1998—; contr. articles to profl. jours., chpts. to books. Recipient Giuseppe Parravano award Mich. Catalysis Soc., 1989, Disting. Teaching award Coll. of Engring., U. Calif. Santa Barbara, 1989; fellow NSF, 1966-69, Alfred P. Sloan Found., 1976-78, Camille and Henry Dreyfus Found., 1976-81. Fellow AAAS, Am. Phys. Soc. (Nottingham prize 1972), Am. Vacuum Soc.; mem. AIChE (Colburn award 1981), Am. Chem. Soc. (LaMer award 1973, Kendall award 1991, Arthur W. Adamson award 1995), N.Am. Catalysis Soc., Nat. Acad. Engring., Phi Beta Kappa. Office: Symyx Technologies 3100 Central Expy Santa Clara CA 95051-0801 Office Phone: 408-764-2000. Business E-Mail: hweinberg@symyx.com.

**WEINBERG-APTEKAR, DORIS MAE**, psychotherapist, school psychologist, hypnotherapist; b. Bronx, NY; d. Jack Weinberg and Mildred Rosofsky; m. Seymour Aptekar, May 31, 1985; children: Liandra Heather Aptekar, Jordanne Arielle Weinstein. BA, Boston U., 1965; MS, Queens Coll., 1975; PhD, Fordham U., 1987. Cert. sch. psychologist, tchr. advanced hypnotherapist, lic. mental health counselor. Elem. tchr., spl. edn. tchr., NYC, 1961—74; sch. psychologist Amityville Union Free Sch. Dist., NY, 1975—2003, Nassau County Bd. Coop. Edn. Sys., 1977—78; pvt. practice Roslyn Estates, NY, 1975—. Pre-sch. cons. Manchester Recreation Ctr., Vt., 2003—; cons. South Shore Health Ctr., Freeport, NY, 2004—, Willow Rd. Sch., Franklin Sq., NY, 2006, Vincent Smith Sch., Pt. Washington, NY, 2006—; evaluator, counselor Quality Evaluations, Rego Pk., NY, 2005—. Mem. Planned Parenthood, NOW. Recipient Svc. award, NYC Works Cmty. Workshop, 1989. Mem.: NE Psychol. Assn., NY Psychol. Assn. Avocations: tennis, travel, reading. Home: Roslyn Estates 30 The Hemlocks Roslyn NY 11576 also: 633 McNamara Rd Dorset VT 05251 Personal E-mail: doctordma@msn.com.*

**WEINBERGER, ADRIENNE**, artist, art appraiser; b. Washington, Apr. 28, 1948; d. Samuel Aaron and Marta (Barta) W.; m. Edward Herschel Egelman, Mar. 21, 1980; children: Serge Maurice, Liana Dora. BA, Goucher Coll., 1970; MEd, Johns Hopkins U., 1973; MA, Northwestern U., 1974; postgrad., Sch. of Mus. of Fine Arts, 1979-82. Lectr. Art Inst. Chgo., 1973-75; lectr., docent trainer Mus. of Fine Arts, Boston, 1978-82; mus. educator Yale Ctr. Brit. Art, Yale Art Gallery, New Haven, 1984-86; instr., coord. alumni coll. Albertus Magnus Coll., New Haven, 1987-89; instr. Mpls. C.C., 1989-94; propr. Studio 95, Edina, Minn., 1995-99, Charlottesville, Va., 1999—. Panelist New England Regional Confs., Am. Assn. Muss., Mass., Conn., 1976-77; workshop leader New Haven Green Found., New Haven 350 Com., 1987-88; pres. Cmty. Art Fund., 2000—. Author: illustrator: New Haven Coloring Book, 1987, CulchaMan Visits New York City, 1988, CulchaMan Visits Washinton, D.C., 1988. Participant Edina Futures Forum, 1990; dir. Edina-Woodhill Assn., 1997—98; active State Affirmative Action Commn., 1996—98; del. chair, mem. nominating com. Dem. State Conv., St. Paul, 1994, del., chair Rochester, 1996, St. Cloud, 1998, del. Norfolk, 2000, Roanoke, 2004; active Dem. State Exec. Com., 1997—99; sec. Dem.-Farmer Labor Party, Edina, Eden Prairie, 1990—94, chair, 1994—96, treas. 3d Congl. Dist., 1996—99; active Dem. State Cen. Com., 1994—99, Albemarle County Dem. Com., 2005; adv. bd. gifted edn. svcs. Edina Pub. Schs., 1993—96; bd. dirs. Consortium for Advancement of Arts, 2001—03, Leadership Charlottesville, 2002—, Northwestern U. Alumni Club, 2003—, Northwestern U. Club Va. Recipient Juror's award Berkshire Mus., Pittsfield, Mass., 1981, New Haven Brush & Palette Club, 1985, Edina Art Ctr., 1991. Mem. Am. Soc. Appraisers (accredited sr. appraiser; sec. Twin Cities chpt. 1997-99, pres. Richmond chpt. 2000-01, 3d v.p. Richmond chpt. 2001-03), Charlottesville C. of C. (Amb. Corps. 2000, legis. action com. 2000—2006, legal action com. 2000-2006), U. Va. Art Mus.(vol. bd. 2003-), Leadership Charlottesville Alumni Assn. (bd. dirs. 2006—), Northwestern U. Alumni Club Va. (bd. dirs. 2003—), Alumni Assn. Avocations: travel, reading, politics. Office: Studio 95 3100 Waverly Dr Charlottesville VA 22901-9576 Office Phone: 434-297-0694. Business E-Mail: studio95@guanotronic.com.

**WEINBERGER, ALAN DAVID**, lawyer, business executive; b. Washington, July 31, 1945; s. Theodore George and Shirley Sunshine (Gross) W.; m. Lauren Myra Kaminski, Dec. 2, 1979; children: Mark Henry, Benjamin Charles. BA, NYU, 1967, JD, 1970; LLM, Harvard U., 1973. Bar: N.Y. 1971, D.C. 1978, U.S. Supreme Ct. 1980. Assoc. White & Case, N.Y.C., 1970-72; founding law prof. Vt. Law Sch., South Royalton, 1973-75; atty. SEC and Fed. Home Loan Bank Bd., Washington, 1977-81; founder, chmn. bd. dirs., CEO The ASCII Group Inc., Washington, 1984—; founder, chmn. bd. dirs. Tech. Net, Inc., Bethesda, Md., 1995. Adv. bd. Ashton Tate Inc., Torrance, Calif., 1986-87; sponsor, agt. All Union Fgn. Trade Acad., Acad. Nat. Economy of USSR in U.S.A., 1988-90; chmn. U.S. adv. bd. Moscow State U. of Commerce, 1992—; chmn. govt. affairs com. Computer Tech. Industry. Author: White Paper to Reform Business Education in Russia, 1996; law rev. editor NYU Sch. Law, 1970. Named one of Top 25 Most Influential Execs. in Computer Industry, Computer Reseller News, 1988; recipient CEO of Yr. award Cyber Chanels, 1999; named eInnovator of Yr. Cyber Channels Assn., 2000. Mem. Nat. Orgn. on Disability (CEO coun.), D.C. Bar Assn., Order of Coif, Kenwood Country Club. Avocation: tennis. Office: ASCII Group Inc 7101 Wisconsin Ave Bethesda MD 20814-4871 Business E-Mail: aw@ascii.com.

**WEINBERGER, ARNOLD**, retired electrical engineer; b. Bardejov, Czechoslovakia, Oct. 23, 1924; came to U.S., 1939; s. Henry C. and Bina (Shapira) W.; widowed; children: Paul I., Ronda B., Keith A. BSEE, CCNY, 1950. Engr. Nat. Bur. Standards, Washington, 1950-60; rsch. staff mem. IBM, Yorktown Heights, N.Y., 1960-66, engr., Poughkeepsie, N.Y., 1966-91, ret.,

1991. Contbr. articles on computer arithmetic, logic, large-scale integration, system organization, memories, design automation. Patentee in field. With U.S. Army, 1944-46, ETO. Fellow IEEE (Outstanding sect. award 1981). Avocation: ping pong/table tennis.

**WEINBERGER, DANIEL R.**, psychiatrist, neurologist; b. NYC, May 24, 1947; married; 1 child. BA, Johns Hopkins U., 1969; MD, U. Pa., 1973. Diplomate Am. Bd. Psychiatry and Neurology. Intern L.A. County-Harbor Gen. Hosp., Torrance, Calif., 1973-74; grad. fellow in medicine UCLA Sch. Medicine, 1973-74; clin. fellow in psychiatry Harvard U., 1974-77; resident in psychiatry Mass. Mental Health Ctr., Boston, 1974-76, chief resident, 1976-77; assoc. in medicine, divsn. psychiatry Peter Bent Brigham Hosp., Boston, 1974-76; asst. clin. prof. psychiatry George Washington U., Washington, 1978-81, assoc. clin. prof., 1982, assoc. clin. prof. neurology and psychiatry, 1984; resident in neurology George Washington U. Med. Ctr., Washington, 1980-83; dir. rsch. ward adult psychiatry br., intermural rsch. program NIMH, Washington, 1977-78, staff psychiatrist, 1977-81; head clin. neuropsychiatry and neurobehavior unit NIMH/St. Elizabeth's Hosp., Washington, 1981-82, chief sect., 1983-86, chief clin. brain disorders br., 1986—; dir. movement disorder, dementia clinic, experimental therapeutics br. Nat. Inst. Neurol. Diseases and Stroke, Washington, 1983-86; dir. behavioral neurology svc. St. Elizabeth's Hosp., Washington, 1983-88. Part-time gen. practice Bridgewater Med. Ctr., East Bridgewater, Mass., 1974-76; emergency rm. physician Cardinal Cushing Gen. Hosp., Brockton, Mass., 1974-77; examiner Am. Bd. Psychiatry and Neurology; part-time gen. practice psychiatry and neurology, Washington, 1978—; scientists promotion review com. NIMH, 1984-87; elected to coun. Assembly of Scientists NIMH/Nat. Inst. Neurological Disease and Stroke, 1985-88; Roerig vis. prof. U. N.Mex., 1990, U. Mich., 1992; adv. bd. Alzheimer Disease Found., 1990—, Adams Super Ctr. Brain Studies, Tel Aviv, 1993—; Neal Mysell lectr. Harvard Med. Sch., 1993; steering com. in vivo NMR Ctr., NIH, 1993—. Mem. editorial bd. Biol. Psychiatry, 1986—, Internat. Jour. Schizophrenia Rsch., 1987—, Jour. Neuropsychiatry and Clin. Neurosci., 1987—, Psychiatry, 1987—, Progress in Neuropsychiatry and Psychopharmacology, 1989—, Jour. Clin. Brain Imaging, 1989—, Psychiatry Research: Neuroimaging, 1990—, Jour. Psychiatry and Neurosci., 1990—, Neuropsychopharmacology, 1991—, Development and Psychopathology, 1991—, Harvard Review of Psychiatry, 1992—; contbr. articles to profl. jours.; patentee in field. Capt. USPHS, 1977-86. Recipient Morton Prince award Am. Psychopathol. Assn., 1984, Judith B. Silver award Nat. Alliance for Mentally Ill, 1985, Arthur S. Flemming award Washington Jaycees, 1986, Established Investigator award NARSAD, 1990, Lieber award, 1993, Dean award Am. Coll. Psychiatrists, 1994. Fellow Am. Coll. Neuropsychopharmacology (Joel Elkes internat. award 1989); mem. AMA, AAAS, Am. Psychiat. Assn. (Found. Fund prize for rsch. 1991), Am. Acad. Neurology (sci. program com. 1993—), Am. Neuropsychiatric Assn., Soc. Biol. Psychiatry (A.E. Benett Found. award clin. science 1981), Behavioral Neurology Soc., Soc. Neurosci. (pub. lectr. 20th ann. meeting 1990), Washington Neurology Soc., Washington Psychiat. Soc., Phi Beta Kappa, Alpha Omega Alpha, Inst. Medicine. Office: NIMH Clinical Brain Disorders Branch 10 Center Dr Rm 4S235 Bldg 10 Bethesda MD 20892-1379

**WEINBERGER, ELIOT**, literary essayist, poet, translator; b. NYC, 1949; Author: Works on Paper, 1986, Nineteen Ways of Looking at Wang Wei: How a Chinese Poem is Translated, 1987, Outside Stories, 1992, What I Heard About Iraq, 2005, What Happened Here: Bush Chronicles, 2005 (finalist Nat. Book Critics Circle prize), (essays) Written Reaction: Poetics, Politics, Polemics 1979-1995, 1996, Karmic Traces, 2000, 9/12: New York After, 2003; co-author (with Vija Celmins): Stars, 2005; editor (tranlator): Octavio Paz' Collected Poems, 1987; editor: (translator) Vicente Huidobro's Altazor, 1988 (MLA Scaglione Translation award), American Poetry Since 1950: Innovators and Outsiders, 1993 (Bestseller in Mexico), Jorge Luis Borges's Selected Non-Fictions, 1999 (Nat. Book Critic's Cir. prize for criticism, TLS Internat. Book of Yr.), Bei Dao's Unlock, 2000; editor: The New Directions Anthology of Classical Chinese Poetry, 2003, World Beat, 2006. Bd. mem. Mexican Cultural Inst., U.S./Mex. Fund for Culture, Iowa Internat. Writers Program, Berlin Internat. Lit. Festival. Recipient PEN's first Gregory Kolovakos award for work promoting Hispanic lit. in US, 1992, Order of the Aztec Eagle (first Am. lit. writer to receive award), Govt. of Mexico, 2000. Office: New Directions Pub 80 Eighth Ave New York NY 10011

**WEINBERGER, FRANK**, information management consultant; b. Chgo., Sept. 18, 1926; s. Rudolph and Elaine (Kellner) W.; m. Beatrice Natalie Fixler, June 27, 1953; children: Alan J., Bruce I. BSEE, Ill. Inst. Tech., Chgo., 1951; MBA, Northwestern U., 1959; DBA, U.S. Internat. U., San Diego, 1996. Registered profl. engr., Ill, Calif. Engr. Admiral Corp., Chgo., 1951-53; sr. engr. Cook Rsch., Chgo., 1953-59; mem. tech. staff Rockwell Internat., Downey, Calif., 1959-80, info. systems advisor, 1980-95; info. mgmt. cons., 1995—. Pres. Temple Israel, Long Beach, Calif., 1985-87, bd. dirs. 1973-85. With USN, 1944-46. Mem. Assn. for Computer Machinery. Democrat. Jewish. Avocation: microcomputers. Home and Office: 3231 Yellowtail Dr Los Alamitos CA 90720-5253 E-mail: weinberger@covad.net. *Don't ask "what can I do?" Instead, survey the needs, prepare the information, and give your best recommendation.*

**WEINBERGER, HAROLD PAUL**, lawyer; b. NYC, Mar. 12, 1947; s. Fred and Elaine (Schonfeld) W.; m. Toby Ann Strassman, Dec. 15, 1968; children: James David, Karen Ellen. BA, CCNY, 1967; JD, Columbia U., 1970. Bar: N.Y. 1971, U.S. Dist. Cts. (so., ea., and no. dists.) N.Y. 1972, U.S. Ct. Appeals (2d cir.) 1972. Law clk. to presiding justice U.S. Ct. Appeals (2d cir.), N.Y.C., 1970-71; assoc. Kramer Levin Naftalis Frankel LLP, N.Y.C., 1971-77, ptnr., 1978—; lectr. in law Columbia U. Sch. Law, N.Y.C., 2005—. Recipient John Ordronaux prize Columbia U. Law Sch., 1970. Mem. ABA (intellectual property law sect. 1999—), Assn. Bar City N.Y. (com. fed. legislation 1975-78, com. on products liability 1983-86, mem. com. on trademarks and unfair competition 1995-97). Democrat. Jewish. Home: 336 Central Park W New York NY 10025-7111 Office: Kramer Levin Naftalis & Frankel LLP 1177 Ave of the Americas New York NY NY 10036 Office Phone: 212-715-9132. E-mail: hweinberger@kramerlevin.com.

**WEINBERGER, MARK ALAN**, corporate financial executive, former federal agency administrator; b. 1961; m. Nancy Weinberger; children: Rachel, Noah, Sean, Benjamin. Grad., Emory U.; MBA, Case We. Res., 1987; LLM in Taxation, Georgetown U., 1987. Chief tax & budget counsel to Senator John Danforth US Senate, 1993—96; co-founder, ptnr. Washington Counsel, P.C. (merged with Ernst & Young), 1996—2000; dir. U.S. nat. tax practice Ernst & Young LLP, 2000—02; dep. vice chmn., tax services The Americas, 2002—; asst. sec. for tax policy US Dept. Treasury, Washington, 2001—02. Chief of staff, counsel Pres. Bipartisan Commn. on Entitlement and Tax Reform; sr. advisor Kemp Commn.; commr. Nat. Commn. on Retirement Policy; mem. Social Security Adv. Bd., 2000—01. Office: Ernst & Young LLP 5 Times Sq 14th Fl New York NY 10036*

**WEINBERGER, MILES M.**, pediatrician, educator; b. McKeesport, Pa., June 28, 1938; divorced; 4 children; m. Leslie Kramer, Aug. 22, 1992. AB, U. Pitts., 1960, MD, 1965. Diplomate Am. Bd. Pediatrics, Am. Bd. Allergy and Immunology, Am. Bd. Pediatric Pulmonology. Intern U. Calif. Med. Ctr., San Francisco, 1965-66, pediatric resident, 1966-67; research assoc NIH, Bethesda, Md., 1967-69; allergy and pulmonary fellow U. Colo., Denver, 1969-71; staff Ross Valley Med. Clinic, Greenbrae, Calif., 1971-73; clin. pharmacology fellow U. Colo., Denver, 1973-75; divsn. dir. U. Iowa, Iowa City, 1975—. Cons. D.C.Hosp. for Sick Children, 1967-69, allergy and immunology Family Practice Program, Sonoma County Community Hosp., U. Calif. Sch. Medicine, 1972-73; clin. instr. pediatrics Georgetown U. Sch. Medicine, Washington, 1967-69; staff pediatrician part-time West Side Neighborhood Health Ctr., Denver, 1970-71; pediatric sr. staff mem. Nat.Jewish Hosp. and Research Ctr., 1970-75; clin. asst. U. Colo. Med.Ctr., 1974-75; assoc. prof. pediatrics, chmn. pediatric allergy and pulmonary div. U. Iowa Coll. Medicine, 1975-80, assoc. prof. pharmacology, 1975-79, dir. Cystic Fibrosis Ctr., 1977—, prof. pediatrics, 1980—, dir. pediatric allergy and pulmonary div., 1975—. Author: Managing Asthma, 1990; contbr. numerous articles to profl. jours., chpts. to books, also audio-visual materials, commentaries, pub. letters and presentations in field Recipient Clemens von Pirquet award Am. Coll. Allergy, 1974; grantee NIH, 1980-85, Cystic Fibrosis Ctr., Pharm. Mfrs. Assn. Fellow Am. Acad. Pediatrics (allergy sect. 1972, sect. on clin. pharmacology and therapeutics 1978, diseases of chest 1978); mem. Am. Acad. Allergy, Am. Soc. Clin. Pharmacology and Therapeutics, Soc. for Pediatric Rsch., Am. Thoracic Soc. (pres. Iowa Thoracic Soc. 1992-93), Camp Superkids of Iowa (adv. bd. 1981—), Am. Lung Assn. (pediatric pulmonbary ctr. task force com. 1984-86). Office: U Iowa Dept Pediatrics Iowa City IA 52242 Office Phone: 319-356-3485. Business E-Mail: miles-weinberger@uiowa.edu.

**WEINBERGER, MYRON HILMAR,** medical educator; b. Cin., Sept. 21, 1937; s. Samuel and Helen Eleanor (Price) W.; m. Myrna M. Rosenberg, June 12, 1960; children: Howard David, Steven Neal, Debra Ellen. BS, Ind. U., Bloomington, 1959, MD, 1963. Intern Ind. U. Med. Ctr., Indpls., 1963-64, resident in internal medicine, 1964-66, asst. prof. medicine, 1969-73, assoc. prof., 1973-76, prof., 1976—, dir. Hypertension Research Ctr., 1981—; USPHS trainee in endocrinology and metabolism Stanford U. Med. Ctr., Calif., 1966-68, USPHS spl. fellow in hypertension Calif., 1968-69. Contbr. articles to profl. jours. Recipient Tigerstedt award Am. Soc. Hypertension, 1996, Page-Bradley Lifetime Achievement award Am. Heart Assn. Coun. for High Blood Pressure Rsch., 1999. Fellow ACP, Am. Coll. Cardiology, Am. Coll. Nutrition, Am. Soc. for Clin. Pharmacology and Therapeutics; mem. AAAS, Am. Fedn. Clin. Research, AMA, Am. Heart Assn. (lifetime achievement award coun. for high blood pressure rsch. 1999), Am. Soc. Nephrology, Internat. Soc. Nephrology, Central Soc. Clin. Research, Endocrine Soc., Internat. Soc. Hypertension, Soc. for Exptl. Biology and Medicine Home: 135 Bow Ln Indianapolis IN 46220-1023 Office: Ind U Hypertension Research Ctr 541 Clinical Dr Indianapolis IN 46202-5233 Office Phone: 317-274-8153. Business E-Mail: mweinbe@iupui.edu.

**WEINBERGER, STEVEN,** lawyer, educator; b. Bklyn., Apr. 13, 1953; s. Robert Ira and Elaine (Lichtenthal) W.; m. Maureen Susan Horan, Oct. 15, 1978 (div. 1998); children: John William, Matthew Lawrence; m. Maria DiBenedetto, Sept. 26, 1998. BA, SUNY, Binghamton, 1974; JD, U. Miami, 1977; MS, Hartford Grad. Ctr., 1989. Bar: N.Y. 1978, Conn. 1987, U.S. Dist. Ct. (no. dist.) N.Y. 1981, U.S. Dist. Ct. Conn. 1990. Legis. atty. N.Y. City Council, 1977-78; asst. atty. Westchester County, White Plains, N.Y., 1978-79; sr. asst. atty. Broome County, Binghamton, N.Y., 1979-81, dep. personnel officer, 1981-82; from labor rels. specialist to chief employee svcs. bur. State of Conn., Hartford, 1982-95, dir. retirement and benefit svcs. divsn., 1995—2004; exec. dir. United Faculty Fla., Tallahassee, 2004—. Adj. prof. Teikyo Post U., Waterbury, Conn., 1984-04, Albertus Magnus Coll., New Haven, 2000-04. Democrat. Jewish. Office: United Faculty Fla 118 N Monroe St Tallahassee FL 32301 Office Phone: 850-224-8220. Business E-Mail: steven.weinberger@floridaea.org.

**WEINBLATT, ALAN S.,** psychologist; s. Marvin and Roslyn Weinblatt; m. Lisa DeLoria, Oct. 13, 1972; 1 child, Ananda Cohen. BA in Elem. Edn., CUNY, Queens, 1976; MS in Spl. Edn., CUNY, 1979, Profl. Diploma in Sch. Psychology, 1984; PsyD, Yeshiva U., Bronx, 1993. Lic. psychologist Dept. of Edn., N.Y., 1994, cert. sch. psychologist N.Y. Dept. Edn., 1984, NASP, 1984, lic. N.Y.C. Bd. of Edn., 1984, spl. edn. tchr. N.Y.C. Bd. of Edn., 1979, elem. edn. tchr. N.Y. State Dept. of Edn., 1976. Sr. psychologist Little Meadows Early CHildhood Ctr., Fresh Meadows, NY, 1986—; psychologist in pvt. practice Little Neck, NY, 1995—. Cons. psychologist Little Meadows at the Samuel Field YMHA, Little Neck, NY, 1995—; asst. prof. of edn. and psychology, dir. of the grad. program in spl. edn. Touro Coll., Grad. Sch. of Edn. and Psychology, N.Y.C., 1995—2000; spl. edn. tchr. Pub. Sch. 134Q, Hollis, NY, 1978—79; sch. psychologist Lowell Sch., Fresh Meadows, NY; spl. edn. tchr. Hillside Jr. H.S., Floral Park, NY, 1980—83, Queens Children's Psychiat. Ctr., NY. Mem.: APA (assoc.). Achievements include research in Maternal style and mediational practices under varying mother-child interactive conditions. Office: Alan S Weinblatt PsyD 255-17 Northern Blvd Ste B1 Little Neck NY 11362 Office Phone: 718-279-4808.

**WEINBLATT, CHARLES SAMUEL,** retired academic administrator; b. Toledo, Dec. 23, 1952; s. Morris and Clara (Volk) W.; m. Frances Barbara Auslander, Aug. 12, 1973; children: Brian J., Lauren M. BA, U. Toledo, 1974. Cert. edn. and tng. counselor, Ohio. Psychiat. counselor St. Vincent Hosp., Toledo, 1974-77; vocat., rehab. counselor Goodwill Industries, Toledo, 1977-85; employment cons., pvt. practice Toledo, 1985—; tng. counselor UAW Chrysler, Perrysburg, Ohio, 1987; dir. divsn. devel. and leadership U. Toledo, 1988—. Employment svcs. cons. Employers' Assn. Toledo, 1985-90; outplacement cons. Toledo Pub. Schs., 1986; spkr. in field of labor and mgmt. rels., employee involvement. Author: Job Seeking Skills for Students, 1987. Mem. Toledo Vision Com., 1989-90. Recipient Quality Improvement award Chrysler, 1987, cert. Am. Inst. Banking, 1989. Mem. ASTD, Ohio Continuing Higher Edn. Assn., Toledo Area Human Resource Assoc., World Future Soc. Jewish. Avocations: music, sports, gardening, writing, astronomy. Home: 5118 Brenden Way Sylvania OH 43560-2223 Personal E-mail: cswl@sev.org. Business E-Mail: charles.weinblatt@utoledo.edu.

**WEINBRENNER, GEORGE RYAN,** aeronautical engineer; b. June 10, 1917; s. George Penbrook and Helen Mercedes (Ryan) W.; m. Billie Marjorie Elwood, May 2, 1955. BS, MIT, 1940, MS, 1941; AMP, Harvard U., 1966; ScD (hon.), Mapua Inst. Tech., Manila, 1994. Commd. 2d lt. USAAF, 1939, advanced through grades to col., 1949; def. attaché Am. Embassy, Prague, Czech Republic, 1958—61; dep. chief staff intelligence Air Force Sys. Command, Washington, 1962—68; comdr. fgn. tech. divsn. USAF, Wright-Patterson AFB, Ohio, 1968—74, comdr. Brooks AFB, Tex., 1974—75; ret., 1975; exec. v.p. B.C. Wills & Co., Inc., Reno, 1975—84; chmn. bd. Hispano-Technica S.A. Inc., San Antonio, 1977—. Lectr. Sch. Aerospace Medicine Brooks AFB, Tex., 1975-84; adv. dir. Plaza Nat. Bank, San Antonio; cons. Def. Dept., 1981, Dept. Air Force, 1975-84. Decorated D.S.M., Legion of Merit, Bronze Star, Air medal, Purple Heart, Ordre Nat. du Merite, Medaille de la Resistance, Croix de Guerre (France). Fellow AIAA (assoc.); mem. World Affairs Coun., Air Force Assn. (exec. sec. Tex. 1976-84), Assn. Former Intelligence Officers (nat. dir.), Air Force Hist. Found. (dir.), U.S. Strategic Inst., Nat. Mil. Intelligence Assn., Tex. Aerospace & Nat. Def. Tech. Devel. Coun., Am. Astron. Soc., Aerospace Ednl. Foun. (trustee), Disabled Am. Vets. (life), Mil. Order World Wars, Am. Legion, Assn. Old Crows, Army-Navy Club (Washington), Kappa Sigma. Roman Catholic. Office: AFA Texas 8406 Cadmus San Antonio TX 78214-3001 Business E-Mail: afatexas@member.afa.org.

**WEINBROT, HOWARD DAVID,** language educator; b. Bklyn., May 14, 1936; s. William and Rose (Shapiro) W. BA, Antioch Coll., Yellow Springs, Ohio, 1958; MA with honors (Woodrow Wilson fellow 1959, grad. fellow 1959-63), U. Chgo., 1959, PhD, 1963. Tchg. fellow U. Chgo., 1962-63; instr. English Yale U., 1963-66; asst. prof., then assoc. prof. U. Calif., Riverside, 1966-69; mem. faculty U. Wis., Madison, 1969—, prof. English, 1972-84; Ricardo Quintana prof., 1984-87, Vilas prof., 1987—. Andrew Mellon vis. prof. Inst. Advanced Studies, Princeton, N.J., 1993-94. Author: The Formal Strain, 1969, Augustus Caesar in Augustan England, 1978, Alexander Pope and the Traditions of Formal Verse Satire, 1982, Essays on 18th-Century Satire, 1988, Britannia's Issue, 1993, Aspects of Samuel Johnson, 2005, Menippean Satire Reconsidered, 2005; also numerous articles, revs.; editor: New Aspects of Lexicography, 1972, Northrop Frye and 18th Century Studies; co-editor: The 18th Century: A Current Bibliography for 1973, 1975, Poetry in English, An Anthology, 1987, Eighteenth-Century Contexts, 2001. NEH fellow, 1975-76; Guggenheim fellow, 1988-89. Mem. Am. Soc. 18th Century Studies (mem. editl. bd. 1977-80, exec. com. 96-99)), Internat. Soc. 18th Century Studies UCLA (planning com. 2003), Johnsonians, Johnson Soc. (sec.-treas. 1970-75, v.p. 2000-01, pres. 2002-03), Midwest Am. Soc. Eighteenth Century Studies, Eighteenth Century Scottish Studies, Inst. Adv.

Study (vis. 2002). Home: 1505 Wood Ln Madison WI 53705-1456 Office: U Wis English Dept 600 N Park St Madison WI 53706-1403 Office Phone: 608-263-3819. Business E-Mail: weinbrot@wisc.edu.

**WEINER, ALLEN S.,** law educator; b. 1963; AB in Social Studies, magna cum laude, Harvard U., 1985; JD, Stanford U., 1989. Law clk. to Judge John Steadman US Ct. Appeals DC Cir., 1989—90; atty.-adviser Office of Legal Adviser, US Dept. State, 1990—96, Office Internat. Claims and Investment Disputes, 1990—92, Office Inter-Am. Affairs, 1992—95, Office Politico-Mil. Affairs, 1995—96; attaché US Embassy, The Hague, Netherlands, 1996—98, counselor for legal affairs, 1998—2001; rsch. fellow TMC Asser Inst., The Hague, 2002—03; Warren Christopher prof. of practice of internat. law and diplomacy Stanford Law Sch. & Stanford Inst. Internat. Studies, 2003—. Vis. lectr. faculty law U. Amsterdam, 2001, 02, U. Leiden, 2002; mem. adv. com. Amsterdam-Nyenrode Law Sch., 2001—03. Office: Stanford Law Sch Crown Quadrangle 559 Nathan Abbott Way Stanford CA 94305-8610 Office Phone: 650-724-4818. Business E-Mail: aweiner@stanford.edu.

**WEINER, ANDREW JAY,** lawyer; b. Hartford, Conn., Dec. 19, 1950; m. Debra Lewin, May 29, 1977; children: Joshua Isaac, Hannah Leah. BA, Yale Coll., 1972; JD, Harvard U., 1976. Bar: N.Y. 1977. Planner N.Y.C. Dept. City Planning, 1972-73; assoc. Shcarman & Sterling, N.Y.C., 1976-84; ptnr. Gordon Hurwitz Butowsky Weitzen Shalov & Wein, N.Y.C., 1984-89, Morrison & Foerster LLP, N.Y.C., 1990—. Office: Morrison & Foerster LLP 1290 Avenue Of The Americas Fl 40 New York NY 10104-0050 Office Fax: 212-468-7900. Business E-Mail: aweiner@mofo.com.

**WEINER, ANNE LEE,** social worker; b. Chelsea-Malden, Mass., Nov. 2, 1932; d. Nathan and Edith E. (Sigel) Varnick; m. Paul J. Weiner, Jan. 25, 1959; children: Berdine R., Ronald M. Diploma in med. sec., Chandler Sch. for Women, 1952; AA in Social Work, Middelsex C.C., 1974; BSW, Salem Coll., 1987. Med. sec. New Eng. Med. - Boston U. Hosp., Boston, 1952-1960; social worker Lynn-Union Hosp., Lynn, Mass., 1968-1982; home care social worker Mass. Elder Care, Peabody, 1982-1987; dir. Dept. Social Work Logan Homes, Wingate Homes, Hill Haven Homes, Mass., 1987-99. Mem. region bd. Hadassah steering com. social work, Hadassah Boston and Fla. Atlantic region; pres. Chessed, 2003—06; active Hist. Soc. Peabody; organizer social work support groups North Shore, Mass., 2003—04. Personal E-mail: lighthouse@bellsouth.net.

**WEINER, ANTHONY DAVID,** congressman; b. Bklyn., Sept. 4, 1964; BA, SUNY, Plattsburgh, 1985. Budget dir., press-fgn. affairs asst., dist. office liaison Staff of US Rep. Charles E. Schumer from NY, 1985—91; mem. City Coun. from Dist. 48, NYC, 1991-98, mem. pub. safety, consumer affairs, transp. coms., chmn. subcommittee crime in pub. housing; mem. US Congress from 9th NY dist., 1999—, mem. judiciary com., mem. transp. and infrastructure com. Bd. dirs. Bklyn. Bd. Boys Town Jerusalem, Shaare Zedek Hosp., Israel. Named Legislator of Yr., Jewish Cmty. Coun. Rockaway Peninsula, 2002, Friend of the Nat. Pks., Nat. Pks. Conservation Assn., 2003; recipient Breaking the Silence award, Rachel's Children Reclamation Found., 2003, Friends of RESOLVE award, RESOLVE (Nat. Infertility Assn.), 2003. Democrat. Jewish. Office: US Ho Reps 1122 Longworth Ho Office Bldg Washington DC 20515-3209 Office Phone: 202-225-6616.*

**WEINER, BRUCE BARNET,** psychologist; b. Glen Cove, NY, Sept. 27, 1955; s. Howard and Deborah Weiner; m. Betsy Weiner, Aug. 12, 1979; children: Joshua, Daniel. BA in Psychology, Farleigh Dickenson U., 1979; MEd, U. Cin., 1981. Cert. sch. psychologist N.Y., 1980. Sch. psychologist, chair com. spl. edn. Berlin Ctrl. Sch. Dist., NY, 1981—; co-founder and co dir. Berkshire Inst. for Growth and Devel., Williamstown, Mass., 2000—. Adj. prof. Coll. of St. Rose, Troy, NY, 2005, Sage Colls., Troy, 2006—. Bd. mem. Acad. for Character Edn., Troy, 2001—06, Bleeding Disorders Assn. NE NY, Albany, 2005—06. Mem.: NY Assn. Sch. Psychologists, Nat. Assn. Sch. Psychologists. Achievements include development of Character Education: A Discipline Program that Works, presented Academy for Character Education Conferences and Summer Institutes, Sage Colleges, Troy New York, 2003, 04, 05; Using Magic within the Practice of School Psychology, presented New York Association of School Psychologists Conference, 1999; Using School Records to Understand Children's Disabilities, presented New York State Bar Association Disability Attorney's Conference, Albany, 1996, 98; Support for Children with Disabilities in Rural Settings, presented National Association on Mental Retardation Conference, San Diego, 1998; Using Magic with Children with ADHD, presented National Association of School Psychologists Conference, Boston, 1989. Avocations: rhythm and blues drummer, scuba diving, kayaking, sailing, magic. Home: 260 Whitman Rd Williamstown MA 01267 Office Phone: 518-658-2515.

**WEINER, CARL DORIAN,** historian; b. NYC, Mar. 26, 1934; s. Alexander and Ann (Goodson) Weiner; m. Ruth Ann Feinglass, Sept. 6, 1959; children: Nicholas, Kevin, Daniel. BA, Queens Coll., 1955; postgrad., U. Wis., 1958-61; MA, Columbia U., 1959. Instr. U. Pitts., 1961-62; mem. faculty Carleton Coll., Northfield, Minn., 1964—2004, chmn. dept. history, 1974-77, 95-98, prof., 1982—2002, William H. Laird prof. history and the liberal arts, 2002—04, prof. emeritus, 2004. With U.S. Army, 1957. Recipient 2d Century award, Carleton Coll., 1968; Bush grantee, 1983—84. Jewish. Home: 403 Laurel Ave Saint Paul MN 55102-2015 Office Phone: 507-646-4209. E-mail: cweiner@carleton.edu.

**WEINER, CHARLES,** historian, educator; b. Bklyn., Aug. 11, 1931; s. Louis and Minnie (Florman) W.; m. Shirley Marks (div. 1976); 1 child, Susan; m. JoAnn Hughes, 1993. BS, Case Inst. Tech., 1960, MA, 1963, PhD, 1965. Asst. editor Tooling and Production mag., Cleve., 1958-60, asso. editor, 1961; editor The Explorer, Cleve. Museum of Natural History, 1960-62; dir. Project on History of Recent Physics in the U.S., Am. Inst. Physics, N.Y.C., 1964-65, Center for History of Physics, 1965-74; prof. history of sci. and tech. Mass. Inst. Tech., 1974—79, dir. oral history program, 1975—86, prof. emeritus, 1996—. Vis. prof. U. Calif., Berkeley, 2001, Regents lectr., 03. Co-editor: The Legacy of George Ellery Hale, 1972, Robert Oppenheimer: Letters and Recollections, 1980; editor: Exploring the History of Nuclear Physics, 1972, History of 20th Century Physics, 1977; mem. editorial council: Bull. of Atomic Scientists, 1984-98. Mem. com. social orgn. sci. Social Sci. Research Council, 1968-71; adv. com. to Library of Congress on Nat. Union Catalog of Manuscript Collections, 1965-71; mem. editorial adv. bd. Joseph Henry Papers, Smithsonian Instn., 1968-86; com. on history of recent biochemistry and molecular biology Am. Acad. Arts and Scis., 1968-80, project dir. com. history contemporary physics, 1966-74; mem. adv. bd. Center for the Study of Consumer Movement, Consumers Union; mem. humanities adv. bd. Sta. WGBH, Boston, 1978-79; mem. adv. bd. Sci. in Am. Life, Smithsonian Inst., 1990-94; cons. Pres. Adv. Com. Human Radiation Experiments, 1994-95. Served with U.S. Army, 1951-53. Recipient Disting. Service citation Am. Assn. Physics Tchrs., 1974; Case fellow, 1961-64; Guggenheim fellow, 1970-71; NSF grantee, 1965, 68, 70, 73, 75, 77, 81, Nat. Endowment Humanities grantee, 1976, 77, 81, 86. Fellow AAAS (council 1969-75, com. on meetings 1969-72), History of Sci. Soc. (council 1968-70, chmn. Met. N.Y. Sect. 1969-70), Soc. for History of Tech. (adv. council 1977-79). Office: 56 Main St Yarmouth Port MA 02675

**WEINER, CLAIRE MURIEL,** freelance writer; b. Bronx, N.Y., Dec. 18, 1951; d. David and Norma (Berry) W. BA, U. Miami, Coral Gables, Fla., 1973; MA, U. Md., 1980. Pub. rels. specialist Hialeah Recreation Div., Hialeah, Fla., 1974-77; freelance writer North Miami Beach, 1977-78, Germantown, Md., 1989—; Montgomery County, Md., 1981—. Govt. affairs liaison for new ednl. data base co. being formed, Montgomery County, 1982—; acting comm. dir. Ednl. Info. Svcs., 1996—. Contbr. articles to local newspapers; contbr. travel articles to profl. jours, mags. Active membership com. newsletter Greater Miami Jewish Fedn., 1974-77; charter mem. Women for Today chpt. B'nai B'rith Women, Washington, 1985-89. Named Hon.

Citizen of Historic Williamsburg. Life fellow Am. Biog. Inst. Rsch. Assn.; World Lit. Acad.; mem. NAFE, Internat. Platform Assn., Nat. Trust for Hist. Preservation. Jewish. Home: 18828 Sky Blue Cir Germantown MD 20874-5398

**WEINER, EARL DAVID,** lawyer; b. Balt., Aug. 21, 1939; s. Jacob Joseph and Sophia Gertrude (Rachanow) W.; m. Gina Helen Priestley Ingoglia, Mar. 30, 1962; children: Melissa Danis Balmain, John Barlow. AB, Dickinson Coll., 1960; LL.B., Yale U., 1968. Bar: NY 1969. Assoc. Sullivan & Cromwell, N.Y.C., 1968-76, ptnr., 1976—. Adj. prof. Rutgers U. Sch. Law, 1987-88; bd. dirs. Solvay Techs. Inc., Hedwin Corp., The Acting Co., vice-chmn., 1992-2003, chmn., 2003—. Gov. Bklyn. Heights Assn., 1980-87, pres., 1985-87, adv. com., 1987—; gov. The Heights Casino, 1979-84, pres., 1981-84; trustee Bklyn. Bot. Garden, 1985—, chmn. 1998—; trustee Green-Wood Cemetery, 1986—, Bklyn. Hosp. Ctr., 1998—; bd. advisors Dickinson Coll., Carlisle, Fla., 1986-90, chmn., 1988-90, trustee, 1988-2002, vice chmn., 1998-2002; mem. adv. com. East Rock Inst., 1988-; bd. visitors U. Md. Ctr. for Environ. Sci., 2002—; bd. trustees Theatre Devel. Fund, 2005—. Lt. USN, 1961-65. Fellow Fgn. Policy Assn. (sr.); mem. ABA, N.Y. State Bar Assn., Assn. Bar City N.Y. Office: Sullivan & Cromwell 125 Broad St Fl 28 New York NY 10004-2489

**WEINER, EDWARD,** civil engineer, federal agency administrator; b. Bklyn., Mar. 31, 1941; s. Abe C. and Elsie (Botwinick) W.; m. Joanne Jessen, Sept. 9, 1967 Idiv. Mar. 1988); children: Jennifer Lynn, Michael Andrew; m. Janis Lynn Wolford, Oct. 7, 1995. BA, BCE, NYU, 1963; MS in Civil Engring., Purdue U., 1964; MPA, U. So. Calif., 1978. Registered profl. engr. Hwy. rsch. engr. Bur. of Pub. Rds., then Fed. Hwy. Administrn., Washington, 1964—70; mgr. urban analysis program Office Sec. Transp., Washington, 1970—77, sr. policy analyst, 1978—2001, mobility and infrastructure team leader, 2001—. Sec. Task Force on Pub. Transp., Transp. Rsch. Bd., 1971-72, mem. Com. on Travel Behavior and Values, Oct. 1973—; group 1 coun., transp. sys. planning and adminstrn., 1984-90; mem. com. Intergovernmental Rels. and Policy Process, Telecom. and Travel Behavior; guest lectr. George Washington U., U. Va., Portland State U., U. Wis.; U.S. rep. internat. working groups on urban travel and sustainability. Co-editor: Emerging Transportation Planning Methods, 1978; author, co-author: Urban Transportation Planning in the U.S., 1987, revised edit., 1999, National Transportation System Initiative, 1999; (monographs) Role of Taxicabs in Urban Transportation, 1974, Glossary of Urban Public Transportation Terms, 1978, Modal Split, 1966; co-editor Internat. Assn. for Travel Behavior newsletter, 1985-88; contbr. over 80 articles to profl. jours. and books; mem. editl. adv. bd. Transp., 1978-80, 92-2000. Asst. troop leader Girl Scouts Am., Silver Spring, Md., 1981—82; v.p. Unitarian Universalist Ch. of Silver Spring, 1984—, pres., 1985—86, v.p., 1998—99. Edn. for Public Mgmt. fellow U.S. Dept. Transp., 1978; recipient Bronze medal Dept. Transp., 1981, Spl. Achievement award, 1990, 95, 98, 99, 2000. Mem. ASCE, Transp. Rsch. Bd. Home: 16615 Harbour Town Dr Silver Spring MD 20905-4082 Office: US Dept Transp P-40 400 7th St SW Washington DC 20590-0001 Business E-mail: ed.weiner@dot.gov.

**WEINER, FERNE,** psychologist; b. N.Y.C., June 14, 1928; d. Irving Kapp and Peggy (Finkelstein) Hessberg; m. Howard Weiner, July 20, 1948; children: Irving Kenneth, Laurie. BA, Skidmore Coll., 1965; MA, Sarah Lawrence Coll., 1971; PhD, U. Hawaii, 1975. Lic. psychologist, Calif., Hawaii. Asst. prof. West Oahu Coll. U. Hawaii, Honolulu, 1975—77; staff psychologist Cmty. Guidance Clinic, Manchester, Conn., 1978—83; chief cons. psychologist Consultation and Evaluation Ctr., Meriden, Conn., 1984—85; psychologist cons. Disability Determination Svcs., Hartford, Conn., 1986—87, Honolulu, 1988—; police psychologist Honolulu Police Dept., 1988. Pvt. practice, Greenwich, Conn., 1983-87, Honolulu, 1988—; cons. Adopt-A-Sch. Project, Honolulu, 1991-94; interviewer, therapist Sexual Abuse Treatment Team, Manchester, 1979-83; cons., trainer Conn. schs., day care, ch. groups, 1979-87. Contbr. articles to profl. jours. Active Disaster Assistance Mgmt. Team, Hawaii, 1994-95; v.p., sec. Queens Court at Kapiolani Bd., Honolulu, 1992-95; admissions rep. Hawaii Sarah Lawrence Coll., Honolulu, 1970-80; cons. to adoptees search Orphan Voyage, Conn., 1980-87; mentor Girl Scout Coun. Am., Oahu, 1993-94. Mem. Am. Psychol. Assn. (clin. psychotherapy and neuropsychology divsn.), Hawaii Psychol. Assn., Nat. Registry Health Svcs. Providers, Outrigger Canoe Club, Shiley Sports Club. Democrat. Jewish. Avocations: aerobics, interior design, property renovation, gourmet cooking, travel. Personal E-mail: wferne1@san.rr.com.

**WEINER, GERALD ARNE,** stockbroker; b. Chgo., Dec. 20, 1941; s. Irwin S. and Lilyan (Stock) W.; m. Barbara I. Allen, June 18, 1967; children: Rachel Anne, Sara Naomi. BSS, Loyola U., Chgo., 1964; student, U. Vienna, 1962-63; MS, Georgetown U., 1966; postgrad., Ind. U., 1966-72, S.E. Asian Areas Cert., 1967. Pacification specialist AID, Laos, 1967; instr. polit. sci. Loyola U., Chgo., 1970-72; asst. v.p. A.G. Becker & Co., Chgo., 1973-78; sr. v.p. Oppenheimer & Co., Chgo., 1978-83, J. David Securities, Inc., Chgo., 1983-84, Morgan Stanley, Chgo., 1984—. Exec. edn. for securities industry Wharton Sch. Bus. U. Pa., 1988-90. Trustee Highland Park Police Pension Fund, 1991-2004. Mucia fellow, 1969. Mem. Midwest Bonsai Soc., Equinox Club. Republican. Jewish. Office: Morgan Stanley 70 W Madison St Ste 300 Chicago IL 60602-4278 Office Phone: 312-827-6634. Business E-Mail: gerald.weiner@morganstanley.com.

**WEINER, HOWARD MARC,** physician; b. Feb. 25, 1946; BSc, Marietta Coll., 1967; MD, U. Cin., 1971; MPH, Med. Coll. Wis., 1994. Diplomate Am.Bd. Allergy, Asthma and Immunology, Am. Bd. Preventive Medicine/Occupl. Medicine, Am. Bd. Ind. Med. Examiners. Intern medicine Temple U. Hosp., Phila., 1971—72, resident internal medicine, 1972—74; fellow allergy and clin. immunology Hosp. U. Pa., Phila., 1974—76; pres., physician Allergy & Asthma Assoc. West Boca, Boca Raton, Fla., 1988—; pres., med. dir. Med. Assessment Inst. Inc., Boca Raton, Fla., 1997—. Chmn. ethics com. Palm Beach County Med. Soc., West Palm Beach, Fla., 1994-97; bd. dirs. Primus Physicians Svcs., Inc., So. Fla. Mem. Omicron Delta Kappa Soc., Pi Kappa Epsilon. Office: 9980 Central Park Blvd N Boca Raton FL 33428-1762 Office Phone: 561-451-0200.

**WEINER, I. DAVID,** nephrologist; b. Orlando, Fla. s. Richard and Louise Weiner; m. Evangeline M. Weiner; children: AJ, Alison. MD, Vanderbilt U., 1984. Cert. nephrology Am. Bd. Internal Medicine, 2000, internal medicine Am. Bd. Internal Medicine, 1987. Asst. prof. medicine U. Fla. Coll. Medicine, Gainesville, 1990—96, assoc. prof. medicine and physiology, 1996—2005, prof. medicine and physiology 2005—. Asst. editor: Am. Jour. Physiology-Renal Physiology, 2001—06; contbr. articles to profl. jours. Mem. Dept. Vets. Affairs Merit Rev. Bd. in Nephrology, Washington, 2001—03, chairperson, 2003—05. Recipient Clinician Scientist award, Am. Heart Assn., 1990, Am. Soc. Nephrology Young Investigator award, Nat. Kidney Found., 1993, Exemplary Tchr. award U. Fla. Coll. Medicine, 2003. Achievements include research in mechanisms by which the gaseous molecule ammonia functions as an autocrine signaling molecule in renal physiology; identification of mechanisms of bicarbonate and chloride transport in the collecting duct; role of Rh glycoproteins in mammalian health and disease; mechanisms by which ammonia functions as an intrarenal signaling molecule; mechanisms and regulation of proton, bicarbonate, chloride and potassium trnasport in the collecting duct; discovery of method to measure intracellular pH in single renal collecting duct cells. Office: University of Florida PO Box 100224 Gainesville FL 32610 Office Phone: 352-273-5358.

**WEINER, IRVING BERNARD,** psychologist; b. Grand Rapids, Mich., Aug. 16, 1933; s. Jacob H. and Mollie Jean (Laevin) W.; m. Frances Shair, June 9, 1963; children: Jeremy Harris, Seth Howard. BA, U. Mich., Ann Arbor, 1955, MA, 1957, PhD, 1959. Diplomate Am. Bd. Profl. Psychology. From instr. to prof. psychiatry and pediat. U. Rochester, NY, 1959-72; head divsn. psychology U. Rochester Med. Center, 1968-72; prof. psychology, chmn. dept. Case Western Res. U., 1972-77, dean grad. studies, 1976-79; vice chancellor for acad. affairs U. Denver, 1979-83, prof. psychology, 1979-85; v.p. for acad. affairs Fairleigh Dickinson U., Teaneck, NJ, 1985-89, prof.

psychology, 1985-89; prof. psychiatry U. South Fla., Tampa, 1989—. Adv. editor John Wiley & Sons, 1967-93, 99—, Lawrence Erlbaum Assocs., 1993-99; psychology edn. rev. com. NIMH, 1977-81. Author: Psychodiagnosis in Schizophrenia, 1966, Psychological Disturbance in Adolescence, 1970, rev. edit., 1992, Rorschach Handbook, 1971, Child Development, 1972, Principles of Psychotherapy, 1975, rev. edit., 1998, Development of the Child, 1978, Child and Adolescent Psychopathology, 1982, Rorschach Assessment of Children and Adolescents, 1982, rev. edit., 1995, Adolescence, 1985, rev. edit., 1995, Handbook of Forensic Psychology, 1987, rev. edit., 2006, Principles of Rorschach Interpretation, 1998, rev. edit., 2003, Handbook of Psychology, 2003; editor: Readings in Child Development, 1972, Clinical Methods in Psychology, 1976, 83, Adult Psychopathology Case Studies, 2004, Jour. Personality Assessment, 1985-93, Rorschachiana, 1989-96; mem. editl. bd. Profl. Psychology, 1971-76, Jour. Adolescent Health Care, 1979-87, Children and Youth Svcs. Rev., 1979-91, Jour. Pediat. Psychology, 1981-87, Devel. and Behavioral Pediat., 1985-96, Studi Rorschachiani, 1985—, European Jour. Psychol. Assessment, 1985—, Jour. Adolescent Rsch. 1986-91, Jour. Personality Disorders, 1986-92, Psychol. Assessment, 1994—2003, Jour. Personality Assessment, 2003—, Assessment, 2004—, Jour. Child Custody, 2005—. Recipient Disting. Profl. Achievement award Genesee Psychol. Assn., 1974 Fellow APA, Am. Psychol. Soc., Acad. Clin. Psychology, Acad. Forensic Psychology, Acad. of Assessment Psychology (Lifetime Achievement awrd 2001); mem. Assn. Advancement Psychology, Soc. Personality Assessment (pres. 1976-78, 2005—, Disting. Contbn. award 1983), Assn. Internship Ctrs. (exec. com. 1971-76), Soc.·Rsch. in Adolescence, Soc. for Rsch. in Child and Adolescent Psychopathology, Soc. for Exploration Psychotherapy Integration, Soc. Pediat. Psychology, Am. Psychol. Law Soc., Internat. Rorschach Soc. (pres. 1999-2005), Phi Beta Kappa, Sigma Xi, Phi Kappa Phi. Home and Office: 13716 Halliford Dr Tampa FL 33624-6903 Office Phone: 813-961-8032. Business E-Mail: iweiner@health.usf.edu.

**WEINER, JEROME HARRIS,** mechanical engineering educator; b. NYC, Apr. 5, 1923; s. Barnet and Dora (Muchar) W.; m. Florence Mensch, June 24, 1950; children: Jonathan David, Eric Daniel. B. Mech. Engring., Cooper Union U., 1943; A.M., Columbia U., 1946, PhD, 1952. Mem. faculty Columbia U., N.Y.C., 1952-68, prof. mech. engring., 1960-68, acting chmn. dept., 1961-62; L. Herbert Ballou Univ. prof. Brown U., Providence, 1968-93; L. Herbert Ballou Univ. prof. emeritus, 1993—. Author: (with B.A. Boley) Theory of Thermal Stresses, 1960, Statistical Mechanics of Elasticity, 1983. Fulbright research scholar Rome, Italy, 1958-59, Haifa, Israel, 1965- 66; Guggenheim fellow, 1965-66 Mem. Am. Phys. Soc., Am. Math. Soc., ASME Home: 24 Taber Ave Providence RI 02906-4113 Office: Brown U 79 Waterman St Providence RI 02912-9079 Business E-Mail: jerome_weiner@brown.edu.

**WEINER, KAREN COLBY (KAREN LYNN COLBY),** psychologist, lawyer; b. Oak Park, Ill., Oct. 28, 1943; d. Leonard L. and Mildred Irene (Berman) Colby; m. J. Laevin Weiner, July 26, 1964; children: Joel Laevin, Doren Robin, Anthony Justin. BA, Mich. State U., East Lansing, 1964; JD, U. Detroit, 1977, MA, 1986, PhD, 1988. Bar: Mich. 1977, D.C. 1978. Speech therapist Oak Park Sch. Dist., 1965-68; law clk. justice G. Mennen Williams Mich. Supreme Ct., Lansing, 1977-79; assoc. Dickinson, Wright, Moon, Van Dusen & Freeman, Detroit, 1979-83; intern in psychology Detroit Psychiat. Inst., 1986-88; psychologist Northland Clinic, Southfield, Mich., 1987-88; postdoctoral intern Wyandotte (Mich.) Hosp. and Health Ctr., 1988-90; psychologist Counseling Assocs., Southfield, 1988—2004, dir. psychol. svcs., quality assurance coord., 1991-99; bd. dirs. Mich. Psychoanalytic Inst. Found., 2004—. Hearing panelist Atty. Discipline Bd., Detroit, 1982-95; hearing referee Mich. Civil Rights Commn., Detroit, 1983-91; mem. Mich. Bd. Psychology, 1999—, vice chair, 2004—; adj. prof. U. Detroit Mercy, 2001-03; ethics com. Internat. Coaching Fedn., 2003—; adj. prof. Inst. Life Coach Tng., 2004—. Author: The Little Book of Ethics for Coaches, 2004; contbr. articles to profl. jours. Adv. bd. Mich. chpt. Anti-Defamation League, 1981-90. Fellow Mich. Psychol. Assn. (mem. ethics com. 1992—2000, chmn. legis. com. 1993, chmn. ethics com. 1997-99); mem. APA, Internat. Coaching Fedn. (ethics and stds. com.), Mich. Soc. for Psychoanalytic Psychology (pres. 1995-97, sec. 1991-92, treas. 1992-94), Women Lawyers Assn. Mich. (pres. 1981-82, pres. Found. 1982-83), Mich. Bar Assn. (chmn. spl. com. for expansion under represented groups in law 1980-83). Jewish. Home: 2501 Long Lake Rd West Bloomfield MI 48323 Office: 29260 Franklin Rd Ste 115 Southfield MI 48034-1144 Office Phone: 248-353-1020. Personal E-mail: drkcw@comcast.net.

**WEINER, KENNETH BRIAN,** lawyer; b. N.Y.C., Oct. 13, 1954; s. Irwin I. and Elayne B. (Biffer) W.; m. Sandra Hong, Apr. 30, 2000; 1 child: Quinton. BSCE, Case Western Res. U., 1976; JD summa cum laude, N.Y. Law Sch., 1986. Bar: N.Y. 1986, Washington 1997; registered profl. engr., N.J. Quality control engr. Cosmic Constrn. Co., Newport News, Va., 1976-77; project engr., geotech. engr. Mueser Rutledge Cons. Engrs., N.Y.C., 1977-86; assoc. Olwine, Connelly, Chase, O'Donnel & Weyner, N.Y.C., 1986-91, Ballard Spahr Andrews & Ingersoll LLP, Washington, 1992, Reid & Priest LLP, Washington, 1992-95, ptnr., 1996-98, Thelen Reid & Priest LLP, Washington, 1998—. Contbr. articles to profl. jours. Mem. Aircraft Owners and Pilots Assn. Avocation: flying. Office: Thelen Reid & Priest LLP 701 Eighth St NW Washington DC 20001-3721 Office Phone: 202-508-4347. Business E-Mail: kweiner@thelenreid.com.

**WEINER, LAWRENCE,** lawyer; b. Phila., Aug. 20, 1942; s. Robert A. and Goldie Weiner; m. Jane M. Coulthard, Feb. 28, 1976; 1 child, Kimberly. BS in Econs., U. Pa., 1964, JD, 1967. Bar: Pa. 1967, U.S. Dist. Ct. (ea. dist.) Pa. 1967, Fla. 1970, U.S. Dist. Ct. (so. dist.) Fla. 1976, U.S. Ct. Appeals (5th cir.) 1976, U.S. Tax Ct. 1984. Assoc., ptnr. Blank, Rome, Klaus & Comisky, Phila., 1967-71, 1975-77; ptnr. Weiner & Weisenfeld, P.A., Miami Beach, Fla., 1971-73, Pettigrew & Bailey, Miami, Fla., 1973-75; pres. Lawrence Weiner P.A., Miami, 1977-83; ptnr. Spieler, Weiner & Spieler, P.A., Miami, 1983-89, Weiner & Cummings, P.A., Miami, 1989-94, Weiner, Cummings & Vittoria, Miami, 1994—. Lectr. Wharton Sch. U. Pa., Phila., 1968-70; instr. bus. law and acctg. Community Coll. Phila., 1967-70; lectr. estate planning various non-lawyer groups, Miami, 1972—. Mem. Fla. Bar (liaison non-lawyers groups 1980-87), Pa. Bar Assn., Phila. Bar Assn., Dade County Bar Assn. (chmn. ins. com. 1977-78, probate law com. 1992-2002). Democrat. Jewish. Office: Weiner Cummings & Vittoria 1428 Brickell Ave Ste 400 Miami FL 33131-3436 Office Phone: 305-371-7800. E-mail: lweiner@wcvlaw.com.

**WEINER, LAWRENCE CHARLES,** artist; b. Bronx, NY, Feb. 10, 1942; One-man shows include Hirshhorn Mus. and Sculpture Garden, Washington, 1990, San Francisco Mus. Modern Art, 1992, Walker Art Ctr., Mpls., 1994, Städtische Galerie Chemnitz, Germany, 1994, Phila. Mus. Art, 1994, Radio Düsseldorf, Germany, 1994, Leo Castelli Gallery, NY, 1994, NY Pub. libr., 1995, Mus. Ludwig Köln, 1995, Mus. Boijmans Van Beuningen, Rotterdam, 1996, The Lawrence Weiner Poster Archive, Kunsthalle Nüurnberg, 1998, Yvon Lambert Gallery, Paris, 2003, Galleri Susanne Ottesen, Copenhagen, 2003, The Wrong Gallery, 2004, Cristina Guerra Contemp. Art, 2004, Mus. Tamayo Arte Contemp., 2004, Davis Mus. Cult. Ctr., 2004, Mai 36 Gallery, 2004, Yvon Lambert Gallery, 2004, Gallery Rose Marie, 2004, Marian Goodman Gallery NYC, 2005, Regen Projects, LA, 2005, Lisson Gallery, London, 2005, others; exhibited in group shows Mus. Modern Art, NY, 1970, Art Inst. Chgo., 1974, Tate Gallery, London, 1982, Mus. Contemporary Art, LA, 1983, Deutsche Guggenheim, Berlin, 2000, Kunstmuseum Rolfsburg, 2000, Reyjkavik Arts Festival, 2005; represented in permanent collections Mus. Modern Art, N.Y., Guggenheim Mus., NY, Van Abbe Mus., Eindhoven, The Netherlands, Staatliches Mus.Mönchengladbach, Germany, Ctr. Georges Pompidou, Paris, Nat. Gallery Australia, Canberra, others. Recipient Arthur Köpcke prize, Copenhagen, 1991, Wolfgang Hahn prize, 1995, Skowhegan medal for painting, 1999; fellow Nat. Endowment Arts, 1976, 83; John Simon Guggenheim fellow, 1994. Home: 297 W 4th St New York NY 10014-2207

**WEINER, LESLIE PHILIP,** neurology educator, researcher; b. Bklyn., Mar. 17, 1936; s. Paul Larry and Sarah (Paris) W.; m. Judith Marilyn Hoffman, Dec. 26, 1959; children: Patrice, Allison, Matthew, Jonathan. BA, Wilkes Coll., 1957; MD, U. Cin., 1961. Diplomate Am. Bd. Psychiatry and Neurology. Intern in medicine SUNY, Syracuse, 1961-62; resident in neurology Johns Hopkins Hosp., Balt., 1962-65, fellow, 1967-69; resident Balt. City Hosp., 1962-63; fellow in virology Slow Virus Lab., Nat. Inst. Neurol and Communicative Disorders-Stroke, NIH, Balt., 1969; asst. prof. neurology Johns Hopkins U., 1969-72, assoc. prof., 1972-75; prof. neurology and microbiology U. So. Calif. Sch. Medicine, L.A., 1975—, chmn. dept. neurology, 1979—2003, Richard Angus Grant Sr. chair in neurology, 1987—; Chief neurologist U. So. Calif. Univ. Hosp., 1991-96, mem. bd. govs.; chief neurologist L.A. county-U. So. Calif. Med. Ctr., 1979-94.; chmn. U. So. Calif. Gen. Clin. Res. Ctr., 1994-95; mem. neurosci. tng. study sect. NIH, 1990-93; mem. sci. adv. bd. Hereditary Disease Found., 1992—, chmn., 1994-96; mem. programs rsch. adv. com. Nat. Multiple Sclerosis Soc., 2000—; cons. in field. Assoc. editor: Neurobase, 1994-95, Neuronet; mem. editl. bd. Infectious and Geographic Neurol., 1994—; editor: Neural Stem Cells Methods and Protocols; assoc. editor: Neurobase; contbr. chpts. to books; contbr. over 140 articles to profl. jours. Bd. dirs. Starbright Found., L.A., 1991—99. Capt. M.C. U.S. Army, 1965—67. Grantee, Conrad Hilton Found., 1995—97, Kenneth Norris Found., 1995—, NIH, 1990—, Race to Erase MS Nancy Davis Ctrs. Without Walls, 2000—, McDonald Found., Oxnard Found., Gogian Found., Heron Found. Fellow: Am. Acad. Neurology; mem.: AAAS, Nat. MS Soc. (mem. adv. com. rsch. program 2000—, grant 2000—), Coalition Advancement Med. Rsch., Assn. Univ. Profs. Neurology, L.A. Acad. Medicine, Johns Hopkins U. Soc. Scholars, Soc. Neurosci., Am. Neurology Assn., Am. Health Assistance Found., Alpha Omega Alpha. Democrat. Jewish. Avocations: collecting books, concerts, plays. Office: RMR 506 2025 Zonal Ave Los Angeles CA 90089 Office Phone: 323-442-3020. Office Fax: 323-442-5500. Business E-Mail: lweiner@usc.edu.

**WEINER, LYNN YVETTE,** history professor, academic administrator; b. Detroit, Feb. 8, 1951; d. Charles Mendel and Audrey (Allen) W.; m. Thomas Glenn Moher, May 5, 1974; children: Andrew Allen, Jeffrey Stephen. AB, U. Mich., 1972; MA, Boston U., 1975, PhD, 1981. Rsch. assoc. Jane Addams papers project U. Ill., Chgo., 1983-84; vis. asst. prof. Northwestern U., Evanston, Ill., 1990-91; instr., lectr. history Roosevelt U. Chgo., 1985-90, assoc. prof., 1991-97, assoc. dean Arts and Scis., 1993—2001, prof., 1997—, dean Arts and Scis., 2001—, interim provost and exec. v.p., 2003—04. Exec. dir. Coordinating Com. on Women in Hist. Profession/Conf. Group on Women's History, 1989-91. Author: From Working Girl to Working Mother: The Female Labor Force in the U.S., 1820-1980, 1985 (nominated for Pulitzer prize 1985); also articles and book revs. Fellow NEH, 1988. Mem. Am. Hist. Assn., Orgn. Am. Historians (Binkley-Stephenson prize 1995), Am. Studies Assn., LWV, NOW. Democrat. Jewish. Home: 527 Clinton Ave Oak Park IL 60304-1110 Office: Roosevelt U 430 S Michigan Ave Chicago IL 60605-1394 Office Phone: 312-341-3670. Business E-Mail: lweiner@roosevelt.edu.

**WEINER, MARK GORDON,** medical educator; s. Michael and Karen Weiner; m. Meredith Weiner; children: Robin, Julie. MD, U. Pa. Sch. Medicine, 1992. Diplomate Am. Bd. of Internal Medicine, PA, 2005. Asst. prof. medicine U. Pa. Sch. Medicine, Phila., 1997—. Office: Univ Pa Sch Medicine 423 Guardian Dr Rm 1116 Philadelphia PA 19104 Business E-Mail: mweiner@mail.med.upenn.edu.

**WEINER, MAX,** psychology professor; b. Hartford, Conn., May 7, 1926; s. Harry Sam and Gertrude (Cohen) W.; m. Gloria Sall, Feb. 24, 1960; children: William Ronald, Jennifer Sharon. BA, U. Conn., 1950; MA, Trinity Coll., 1953; PhD, Yale U., 1957. Sci. tchr. Meriden (Conn.) Pub. Schs., 1952-55; guidance dir. White Plains (N.Y.) Pub. Schs., 1956-59; assoc. prof. Bklyn. Coll., CUNY, 1959-68; prof. Grad. Sch. CUNY, 1968-81, acting univ. dean, tchr. edn., 1973-74, exec. officer PhD program edn. psychology, 1970-76, dir. Ctr. for Advanced Study Edn., 1970-78, acting dean rsch. Grad. Sch., 1978-79; dean edn. Fordham U., N.Y.C., 1981-93, prof. ednl. psychology, 1981-97, prof. and dean emeritus, 1997—. Cons. psychologist SUNY Health Sci. Ctr., Bklyn., 1967-89; mem. nat. commni. on excellence in edn. adminstrn. Univ. Coun. for Edn. Adminstrn., 1985-87; mem. nat. adv. commni. Coll. Bd. Equity 2000, 1993-2000. Contbr. articles to profl. jours. Treas. N.Y. Alliance for Pub. Schs., N.Y.C., 1987-93; mem. Mayor's Commni. on Spl. Edn., N.Y.C., 1984-85; bd. dirs. Arthritis Found., Atlanta, 1974-76; trustee Beth El Synagogue, New Rochelle, N.Y., 1985-2001, La Scuola, N.Y., 1986-2003; bd. visitors Scranton U. Sch. Edn., 1992-2002. Fellow, Japan Soc. Promotion Scis., 1978. Fellow APA, Am. Psychol. Soc., N.Y. Acad. Scis.; mem. ACA (life), AAAS, Arthritis Health Professions Assn. (pres. 1974-75), Am. Ednl. Rsch. Assn., Assn. Colls. and Schs. Edn. in State Univs. and Land Grant Colls. and Affiliated Pvt. Univs. (mem. exec. com. 1986-89, 92-93), Assn. for Measurement and Evaluation in Guidance (senator 1966-72, sec. 1973-75), Nat. Coun. Measurement in Edn., Westchester Assn. Hebrew Schs. (pres. 1982-84), Sigma Xi, Phi Delta Kappa, Kappa Delta Pi. Office: Fordham U Grad Sch Edn Neparan Rd Tarrytown NY 10591 Personal E-mail: maxglow22@aol.com.

**WEINER, PERRIE M.,** lawyer; b. Beverly Hills, Calif., 1961; BA summa cum laude, UCLA, 1982; JD, Loyola Law Sch., 1985. Bar: Calif. 1988. Judicial extern Judge Ralph J. Geffen, US Dist. Ct. ctrl. dist. Calif., 1985; law clk. Judge John R. Kronenberg, US Dist. Ct. ctrl. dist. Calif., 1986—87; atty. Brobeck, Phleger & Harrison, 1988—2002; ptnr., internat. co-chmn. Securities Litigation practice group DLA Piper Rudnick Gray Cary, LA, 2002—. Named a So. Calif. Super Lawyer, Los Angeles mag., 2005, 2006; named one of Calif. Top Mega-Rainmakers, LA Daily Jour., 2004; recipient, 2005. Mem.: Beverly Hills Bar Assn., LA County Bar Assn., Phi Beta Kappa. Office: DLA Piper Rudnick Gray Cary 4th Fl 1999 Ave of the Stars Los Angeles CA 90067-6022 Office Phone: 310-595-3024. Office Fax: 310-595-3324. Business E-Mail: perrie.weiner@dlapiper.com.

**WEINER, PETER H.,** lawyer; b. NYC, July 10, 1944; BA, Harvard U., 1966; MSc, London Sch. Econs., 1967; LLB, Yale U., 1970. Bar: Calif. 1971. Ptnr. Paul, Hastings, Janofsky & Walker LLP, San Francisco, 1997—, chmn. environ. practice group. Mem. Phi Beta Kappa.

**WEINER, RICHARD,** public relations executive; b. Bklyn., May 10, 1927; s. George M. and Sally (Kosover) W.; m. Florence Chaiken, Dec. 9, 1956; children: Jessica Weiner Lampert, Stephanie Weiner Iosbaker. BS, U. Wis., 1949, MS, 1950. Pres. Creative Radio Assocs., Madison, Wis., 1951-52, Weiner-Morton Assocs., Madison, 1952-53; sr. v.p. Ruder & Finn, Inc., N.Y.C., 1953-68; pres. Richard Weiner, Inc., N.Y.C., 1968-86; pres. N.Y. divsn. Porter/Novelli, N.Y.C., 1987-88; sr. counselor, 1988—. Author: Professional's Guide to Public Relations, 1968, News Bureaus in the U.S., 1970, Syndicated Columnists, 1972, Professional's Guide to Publicity, 1979, Military Publications, 1979, College Alumni Publications, 1980, Investment Newsletters, 1981, Webster's New World Dictionary of Media and Communications, 1996, The Skinny About Best Boy: Dollies, Green Rooms, Leads and other Media Lingo, 2006. Bd. dirs. Shake-A-Leg Miami, Fla. Fellow Pub. Rels. Soc. Am. (accredited counselor, Silver Anvil award 1965, 84, 86, 87, John Hill award 1984, Gold Anvil award 1990). Jewish. Office Phone: 305-865-3262. E-mail: rweiner522@aol.com. *The essence of life is growth, adaptation, change. I hope to continue to succeed in living vigorously.*

**WEINER, RICHARD DAVID,** psychiatrist, researcher; b. N.Y.C., Nov. 25, 1945; BS, MIT, 1967; M of Systems Engring., U. Pa., 1969; MD, PhD, Duke U., 1973. Diplomate Am. Bd. Psychiatry and Neurology. Prof. psychiatry Duke U. Med. Ctr., Durham, NC, 1997—; dir. electroconvulsive therapy program, 1991—; chief, mental health svc. line VA Med. Ctr., Durham, 1993—. Office: Duke U Med Ctr PO Box 3309 Durham NC 27702-3309

**WEINER, ROBERT NEIL,** lawyer; b. San Antonio, May 20, 1952; s. Arthur and Sheila (Freedman) W.; m. Cheryl Toubin, May 29, 1977; children: Courtney, Lindsay. AB summa cum laude, Princeton U., 1974; JD, Yale U., 1977. Bar: D.C. 1979, U.S. Supreme Ct. 1983, N.Y. 1993. Law clk. to presiding judge U.S. Ct. Appeals, 1977—78; law clk. to presiding justice U.S. Supreme Ct., Washington, 1978—79; from assoc. to ptnr. Arnold & Porter, Washington, 1979—97; sr. counsel to Counsel to the President of the United States Washington, 1997—98; ptnr., chair litig. practice group Arnold & Porter, Washington, 1998—. Adj. prof. Georgetown U. Law Ctr., Washington, 1984-86; lectr. Univ. Va. Law Sch., 1994; assoc. ind. counsel, 1987; chmn. hearing com. D.C. Bd. Profl. Responsibility. Recipient Servant of Justice award, Legal Aid Soc., William Reece Smith Jr. award, Nat. Assn. Pro Bono Profls. Mem. ABA, D.C. Bar Assn. (co-chmn. ct., lawyers and adminstrn. of justice 1987-90, chmn. coun. on sects. 1989-90, bd. govs. 1990-92, gen. counsel 1992-94, pres 1995-96), Am. Law Inst., Lawyers' Commn. on Civil Rights (bd. advisers), Am Bar Found., D.C. Bar Found. (pres.), Phi Beta Kappa. Home: 4248 50th St Washington DC 20016 Office: Arnold & Porter 555 12th St NW Washington DC 20004-1206 Office Phone: 202-942-5855. Office Fax: 202-942-5999. Business E-Mail: robert.weiner@aporter.com.

**WEINER, ROBERT STEPHEN,** federal agency administrator; b. Paterson, N.J., Apr. 3, 1947; s. Jess Joseph Weiner and Dorothea Violet (Slavin) Tabor. BA, Oberlin Coll., 1969; MA, U. Mass., 1974. Student coord. Hampshire County, dir. telephone bank Kennedy for U.S. Senate, Amherst, Mass., 1970; dir. nat. voter registration Young Dems. Am., Washington, 1971-72; dir. voter registration, media dir. get out the vote Dem. Nat. Com., Washington, 1972; legis. asst. Congressman Edward Koch, Washington, 1974-75; staff dir. subcom. health and long-term care U.S. Ho. of Reps., Washington, 1975-76, staff dir. com. aging, 1976-80; sr. assoc. Mgmt. Recruiters Internat., Springfield, Mass., 1981-83; dir. Robert Weiner Assocs., Amherst, 1983-86; media dir., press sec. com. narcotics U.S. Ho. of Reps., Washington, 1987-90, press sec./comms. dir. com. on govt. ops., 1990-95; dir. comm. Ho. Judiciary com. Minority and Cong. John Conyers Jr., 1995; dir. pub. affairs White House Drug Policy Office, Washington; pres. Robert Weiner Assocs., Pub. Affairs and Issues, 2002—. Dir. gen. press rm. Dem. Nat. Conv., Atlanta, 1988, N.Y.C., 1992, Chgo., 1996, L.A., 2000, Boston, 2004; cons. Carter-Mondale Transition, Washington, 1976-77, Congressman Claude Pepper, Washington, 1975-89. Represented in permanent exhbns. Nat. Mus. Am. History, Smithsonian Instn., Washington; contbr. numerous articles to profl. jours. Dem. nominee for U.S. Congress, Mass., 1986; chmn. Road Runners Am. Nat. 10 Mile Championship, Amherst, 1984; vice chmn. Dem. Town Com., Amherst, 1984-87; legis. chmn. Pioneer Valley Gray Panthers, Amherst, 1981-87; nat campaign aide Kennedy for Pres., Washington, 1980. Named Communicator of Yr., Washington Crime News Svcs., 1988, 89, 90; 2d place U.S. Nat. Masters Track Championship, 1994, 97, 2003, 2004. Mem. Nat. Dem. Club (bd. govs. 2002—), Sugarloaf Mountain Athletic Club (pres. 1984-86), White House Athletic Ctr. (exec. bd. 1995-2001), Potomac Valley Track Club, Capitol Hill Runners (pres. 1991—). Avocations: running, attending performing arts, hiking. Home: 1104 Sanford Ln Accokeek MD 20607-2324 Office: PO Box 28271 1750 Pennsylvania Ave NW Washington DC 20038-8271 Office Phone: 202-329-1700.

**WEINER, SANFORD ALAN,** lawyer; b. Houston, Aug. 21, 1946; s. Abe I. and Zelda C. (Caplan) Weiner; m. Leslie Eve Grenadier, Aug. 16, 1970; children: Edward, David, Evan, Rebecca. BA, U. Tex., 1968; JD, Harvard U., 1971. Bar: Tex. 1971. Ptnr. Vinson & Elkins, Ltd. Liability Partnership, Houston, 1971—. Pres. Am. Coll. Real Estate Lawyers, 2003. Mem. Houston Bar Assn., Tex. Bar Assn., Houston Real Estate Lawyers Council, Anglo-Am. Real Property Inst. Jewish. Office: Vinson & Elkins LLP 1001 Fannin St Ste 2300 Houston TX 77002-6760 Office Phone: 713-758-2558. Business E-Mail: sweiner@velaw.com.

**WEINER, STEPHEN ARTHUR,** lawyer; b. Bklyn., Nov. 20, 1933; s. Joseph Lee W. and Ruth Lessall (Weiner); m. Mina Rieur, Sept. 1, 1958; children: Karen, James. BA summa cum laude, Harvard U., 1954; JD cum laude, Yale U., 1957. Bar: N.Y. 1958, U.S. Supreme Ct. 1963. Assoc. Winthrop, Stimson, Putnam & Roberts, N.Y.C., 1958-65, ptnr., 1968—2000, vice chmn. mgmt. com., 1984-97; acting prof. law U. Calif., Berkeley, 1965-68; ptnr. Pillsbury Winthrop LLP, N.Y.C., 2001, sr. counsel, 2002—04, Pillsbury Winthrop Shaw Pittman LLP, N.Y.C., 2005—. Arbitrator NASD Dispute Resolution, 2002—; mem. com. on character and fitness 1st dept. appellate divsn. N.Y. Supreme Ct., 1998—, spl. master, 1999—; mem. N.Y. State Jud. Inst. on Professionalism in the Law, 1999—; adj. prof. law Bklyn. Law Sch., 2003—. Contbr. articles to legal publs.; comment editor Yale Law Jour., 1956—57. Fellow Am. Coll. Trial Lawyers, Am. Bar Found., N.Y. Bar Found.; mem. Assn. of Bar of City of N.Y. (chmn. recruitment of lawyers com., chmn. com. on Stimson medal), Fed. Bar Coun. (chmn. com. on 2d cir. cts., trustee), Order of Coif, Phi Beta Kappa. Home: 190 Harbor Rd Sands Point NY 11050-2636 Office: Pillsbury Winthrop Shaw Pittman LLP 1540 Broadway New York NY 10036 Office Phone: 212-858-1749. Business E-Mail: stephen.weiner@pillsburylaw.com.

**WEINER, STEPHEN MARK,** lawyer; b. Boston, Mar. 20, 1943; s. Meyer and Esther (Lowenstein) W.; m. Roslyn G. Weiner, Dec. 19, 1967 (div. 1992); children: Jeremiah, Ben, Miriam, Isaac. AB magna cum laude, Harvard U., 1964; LLB, Yale U., 1968. Bar: Mass. 1968. Teaching fellow Boston Coll. Law Sch., Chestnut Hill, Mass., 1968-69; assoc. Goodwin, Proctor & Hoar, Boston, 1969-71; spl. asst. to Gov. Francis W. Sargent Commonwealth of Mass., Boston, 1971-74; chmn. Mass. Rate Setting Commn., Boston, 1972-78; assoc. prof. Boston U. Sch. Law, 1978-81, adj. prof. law, 1993—94, dir. Ctr. for Law and Health Scis.; adj. prof. law Yale Law Sch., 1994—95, Suffolk U. Sch. Law, 1997—; mem. Goulston & Storrs, Boston, 1981-90, Mintz, Levin, Cohn, Ferris, Glovsky and Popeo, PC, Boston, 1990—, ptnr., chmn., Health Care Sect. Mem. editl. bd. New Eng. Jour. Human Svcs., 1979-81; adv. bd. Hosp. Risk Mgmt., 1979-83; contbr. articles to profl. jours. Legal adv. com. AIDS Action Coun., Washington; dir., treas. AIDS Action Com., Mass., 1989—97; bd. dirs. GLAD, Inc., 1999—2000, Boston Film Video Found., 1986—2003; del. Mass. Easter Seal Soc.; trustee Beth Israel Hosp., Boston, 1979—95, Spaulding Rehab. Hosp., Boston, 1979—95, Corp. Ptnrs. Healthcare Sys., Inc., Boston, 1994—2001, Boston Ballet, treas., 2001—05; overseer Boston Lyric Opera; dir. New Eng. Conservatory Lab. Charter Sch. Found.; trustee Huntington Theater Co., Boston; pres. Health-Wall Found., 2003; mem. govt. task force to evaluate Mass. Determination of Need Program, 1979—80; profl. adv. coun. Mass. Dept. Elder Affairs, 1979—81; Mass. atty. gen. Mass. Adv. Com. on Health Care and Tobacco Control. Mem.: Mass. Bar Assn., Nat. Health Lawyers Assn., ABA, Boston Bar Assn., Phi Beta Kappa. Office: Mintz Levin Cohn Ferris Glovsky and Popeo PC 1 Financial Ctr Boston MA 02111-2657 Office Phone: 617-348-1757. Office Fax: 617-542-2241. Business E-Mail: sweiner@mintz.com.

**WEINER, TIMOTHY EMLYN,** newspaper journalist; b. June 20, 1956; s. Herbert and Dora B. Weiner. BA, Columbia U., 1978, MS in Journalism, 1979. Reporter, freelance writer, N.Y.C., 1979-81; reporter Kansas City (Mo.) Times, 1981-82, Phila. Inquirer, 1982-93, N.Y. Times, Washington, Mexico City, NYC, 1993—. Author: Blank Check: The Pentagon's Black Budget, 1990; co-author: Betrayal: The Story of Aldrich Ames, an American Spy. Recipient Pulitzer prize (with others) Kansas City Times, 1982, for nat. reporting, Phila. Inquirer, 1988. Office: New York Times 229 W 43d St New York NY 10036 Office Phone: 212-556-1234. Office Fax: 212-556-7614.

**WEINER, WALTER HERMAN,** bank executive, lawyer; b. Bklyn., Aug. 29, 1930; s. Harry and Sylvia (Freifeld) W.; m. Nina Ester Avidar, Oct. 11, 1966; children: Thomas Field, Jon Michael. BA, U. Mich., 1952, JD, 1953. Bar: N.Y. 1953. Sr. ptnr. Kronish, Lieb, Weiner & Hellman, N.Y.C., 1965-79; chmn. exec. com., CEO Republic N.Y. Corp., 1980-81, pres., CEO, 1981-83, chmn. bd., CEO, 1983—; chmn. exec. com., CEO Republic Nat. Bank of N.Y., 1980-82, pres., CEO, 1981-86, chmn. bd., CEO, 1986-99, also bd. dirs.; pres. WHW Mgmt. Corp., N.Y.C. Bd. dirs. Republic N.Y. Corp., Republic Nat. Bank of N.Y. Assoc. editor U. Mich. Law Rev. Bd. dirs. Interant. Sephardic Edn. Found.; mem. N.Y. Holocaust Meml. Commn.; bd. visitors U.

Mich. Law Sch. Recipient Humanitarian award NAACP, 1987, Human Rels. award Accts., Bankers, Factors and Fin. divsn. Am. Jewish Com., 1988, Man of Yr. award Bklyn. Sch. for Spl. Children, 1988, Good Scout award Greater N.Y. Couns./Boy Scouts Am., 1994, Jewish Theol. Sem.'s Louis Marshall award, 1994, numerous others. Mem. ABA, N.Y. State Bar Assn., Assn. of Bar of City of N.Y. Office: WHW Management Corp Ste 1401 477 Madison Ave New York NY 10022-5836

WEINER, WENDY L(OU), elementary school educator, writer; b. Milw., Jan. 2, 1961; d. Kenneth J. and Jessie M. Weiner. AA, U. Wis. Washington County, West Bend; BS, MS, U. Wis., U. Wis., Milw., 1993; prin. lic., Marian Coll. Cert. nat. cert. early childhood edn. Nat. Bd. Profl. Tchg. Standards, tchr. Wis. Tchr. Milw. Pub. Schs. Contbr. articles to profl. jours. Mem. Milw. Pub. Mus. Tchr. Adv. Coun., TV and Tech. Com., Vision and Tech. Com., Learning Mag.'s Student Best Adv. Coun. Recipient Presdl. Award in Sci. Tchg. Excellence, AT&T Recognition in Sci. Tchg. Excellence, Wis. Aerospace Educator of Yr., Milw. Tchr. of Yr., Grad. Last Decade award U. Wis. Milw. Alumni Assn., Warner Cable-Tchg. Creativity with Cable award, Excellence in Sci. Tchg. award. Wis. Elem. Sci. Tchrs. Assn., Nat. Urban Tech. in Edn. award Coun. Great City Schs., Sen. Herb Kohl Tchr. Achievement award, Ameritech-Wis. Bell Gold Tchr. Recognition award, Presdl. award for elem. sci. tchg. excellence; grantee Greater Mil. Edn. Trust, Wis. Space Grant Consortium/NASA, NSF. Mem. PTA, Wis. Aerospace Edn. Assn. (instr. mag. adviser, Sam's Club Tchr. of Yr.), YMCA-Young Astronauts, Nat. Arbor Day Assn., NSTA, Wis. Elem. Tchrs. Assn., Milw. Kindergarten Assn., Wis. Secondary Sci. Assn., Wis. Assn. Sch. Adminstrs., Milw. Reading Assn., Midwest Devel. Corp., Assn. Presdl. Awardees in Sci., Soc. for Elem. Presdl. Awardees, Coun. Elem. Sci. Internat., Civil Air Patrol (sr. officer). Avocations: crafts, walking. Office: Parkview Sch 10825 W Villard Milwaukee WI 53225 Personal E-mail: wlw23@prodigy.net.

WEINER, WILLIAM P., law educator; b. Three Rivers, Mich., May 14, 1947; s. Leonard J. and Jane E. (Pauli) W.; m. Paula R. Latovick, Aug. 17, 1985; children: Jeffrey, Robert. BA, Kalamazoo Coll., Mich., 1969; JD, MA, U. Mich., Ann Arbor, 1972; LLM, Cambridge U., Eng., 1985. Bar: Mich. 1972, U.S. Dist. Ct. (we. dist.) Mich. 1972. Assoc. Howard & Howard, Kalamazoo, 1972-73; staff atty. Pros. Attys. Appellate Svc., Lansing, Mich., 1973-74; prof. law Thomas M. Cooley Law Sch., Lansing, 1975—. Mem. appellate rev. of sentencing com. Mich. Supreme Ct., 1980s, rules of criminal procedure com., 1980s. Co-author: Michigan's Basic Law of Arms to Search and Seizure, 1979, Handbook of Michigan Criminal Law and Procedure, 1980, International Environmental Law, 1993. Bd. dirs., chair Boarshead Theater, Lansing, 1987-94; bd. dirs. Greater Lansing Symphony Orch., 1995—. Fellow Mich. State Bar Found.; mem. State Bar of Mich. (criminal jury instrns. com. 1989-94), Am. Soc. Internat. Law, Ingham County Bar Assn. (bd. dirs., sec. 1987-90). Office: Thomas M Cooley Law Sch 300 S Capitol Ave Lansing MI 48933-1503 Office Phone: 517-371-5140 x2804. Business E-Mail: weinerw@cooley.edu.

WEINER-HEUSCHKEL, SYDELL, theater educator; b. N.Y.C., Feb. 18, 1947; d. Milton A. and Janet (Kay) Horowitz; children: Jason, Emily; m. Rex Heuschkel, Sept. 3, 1992. BA, SUNY, Binghamton, 1968; MA, Calif. State U., L.A., 1974; postgrad., Yale U., 1968-70; PhD, NYU, 1986; MS, Calif. State U., Dominguez Hills, 1996. Lic. marriage and family therapist. Prof. theater arts, chmn. dept., dir. honors program Calif. State U. Dominguez Hills, Carson, 1984—. Guest lectr. Calif. Inst. Arts, 1988. Appeared in play Vikings, Grove Shakespeare Festival, 1988; dir. Plaza Suite, Brea (Calif.) Civic Theatre, 1982, Gypsy, Carson Civic Light Opera, 1990, Same Time Next Year, Muckehthaler, 1987, Slow Dance on the Killing Ground, Alternative Repertory Theatre, 1989; co-author: School and Community Theater Problems: A Handbook for Survival, 1978, (software) Public Speaking, 1991; contbr. Am. Jour. Psychotherapy, 1997, Jour. Clin. Psychology, 1998. Yale U. fellow, 1969; recipient Lyle Gibson Disting. award, 1989. Mem. Screen Actors Guild, Am. Fedn. TV and Radio Artists, Calif. State U. Women's Coun. (treas. 1989-91), Phi Kappa Phi. Office Phone: 310-243-3534. Business E-Mail: sweiner@csudh.edu.

WEINFURTER, DANIEL JOSEPH, business services executive; b. Milw., Apr. 16, 1957; s. Joseph Thomas and Betty E. (Stanton) W.; m. Martha Kay Brennan, May 14, 1983; children: Amy Jordan, Andrea Taylor. BSBA, Marquette U., 1979, MBA, 1984; postgrad., George Washington U., 1984-85. Account rep. Gen. Electric Info. Svcs., Milw., 1979-81, sr. account rep., 1982-84, project mgr. Rockville, Md., 1984-86; acting regional sales mgr. Gen. Electric Corp., Morristown, N.J., 1986, dist. sales mgr. Bensonville, Ill., 1986-87; regional sales mgr. Intelogic Trace, Inc., Schaumburg, Ill., 1987-89, area sales mgr., 1989; dir. bus. devel. Alternative Resources Corp., Lincolnshire, Ill., 1989-90, v.p. ops., 1990-93; pres. Alternative Resources Corp. Ventures, Lincolnshire, Ill., 1993—; CEO and founder Parson Group, Chgo., 1995—2002; CEO Capital H Group, Chgo., 2003—. Ad-hoc com. Riverwoods (Ill.) Village Coun., 1990—; mem. YMCA. Named number 1 of INC 500, INC Mag., 2000. Democrat. Avocations: running, raquetball, bicycling, golf, reading. Home: 201 Cumberland Ave Kenilworth IL 60043-1169 Office: Capital H Group 225 W Washington St Chicago IL 60606

WEINGAND, DARLENE ERNA, librarian, educator; b. Oak Park, Ill., Aug. 13, 1937; d. Edward Emil and Erna (Heidenway) W.; m. Wayne Anthony Weston, Sept. 7, 1957 (div. June 1976); children: Kathleen Mary, Lynda Anne, Judith Diane, Barbara Jeanne; m. James Elberling, May 1977 (div. 1980); m. Roger Paul Couture, Apr. 7, 1984. BA in History and English, Elmhurst Coll., 1972; MALS, Rosary Coll., 1973; PhD in Adult Edn./Libr. Sci., U. Minn., 1980. Asst. prof. U. Wis., Madison, 1981-86, assoc. prof., 1986-92, prof., 1992-99, prof. emerita, 1999—, SLIS acting dir., 1991, summer 86, SLIS asst. dir., 1990-94, adminstr. SLIS Continuing Edn. Svcs., 1981-99; adj. prof. and mem. affiliate grad. faculty. U. Hawaii Manoa, Manoa, 1999—2006. Cons. in mktg., continuing edn., libr. futures, info, issues, and mgmt., 1980—; invited mentor Snowbird Leadership Inst., 1990, 92; vis. fellow Curtin U. Tech. Perth, Australia, 1990; Fulbright lectr. U. Iceland, 1988; lectr. 2d World Conf. on Continuing Edn. for Info. and Info. Sci., Barcelona, 1993, Internat. Fedn. Libr. Assn. Author: Customer Svc. Excellence: A Concise Guide for Librarians, 1997, Future Driven Library Marketing, 1998, Marketing/Planning Library and Information Services, 1999, 4th edit., 2001, Administration of the Small Public Library, 4th edit., 2001, Budgeting and the political Process in Libraries, Simulation Games, 1992 (with others), Connections: Literacy and Cultural Heritage: Lessons from Iceland, 1990, Managing Today's Public Library: Blueprint for Change, 1994, author (with others) Continuing Professional Education and Internat. Fed. of Libr. Assoc.: Past, Present, and a Vision for the Future, 1992; contbr. articles to profl. jours. Recipient excellence award Nat. Univ. Continuing Edn. Assn., 1989, Econ. and Cmty. Devel. award, 1989, outanding achievement in audio applications award Internat. Teleconferencing Assn., 1991, LITA/Libr. Hi-Tech award, 1996, disting. alumna award Dominican U., 1998; Russia project fellow Assn. Libr. and Info. Sci., 1994. Mem. ALA, AAUW, Wis. Assn. for Adult and Continuing Edn., Beta Phi Mu. E-mail: weingand@lava.net.

WEINGART, ROBERT PAUL, financial consultant; b. East Orange, NJ, Oct. 3, 1937; s. Paul Edward and Loretta Madeline (Heagney) W.; m. Susan Beresford Lyman, July 22, 1967 (div.); children: Nicole, Melinda, Deborah, Lindsey. BA in Sci., U. Notre Dame, 1959, BSME, 1960; MBA, U. Mich. 1970. Lic. securities rep.; cert. investment specialist; registered fin. planner, fin. cons. Sales engr. New Departure Hyatt (Divsn. GMC), Sandusky, Ohio, 1960-70; dist. mgr. Xerox Corp., Pasadena, Calif., 1970-73; fin. cons. Grosse Point Farms, Mich., 1973—. Chmn. U.S. Navy Recruiting Dist. Assistance Coun. for State of Mich. Contbr. articles to profl. jours. Mem. St. Alan's Parish Coun., Troy, Mich., 1997-98; precinct del., candidate Mich. Rep. Party, Troy. Comdr. USNR, 1962-94. Mem. USN Inst., Assn. Naval Aviation, Internat. Assn. Fin. Planning, Internat. Assn. Registered Fin. Cons., Knight Sovereign Mil. Order of Temple of Internat. Jerusalem. Republican. Roman Catholic. Avocations: golf, reading. Home: 2020 Somerset Blvd Apt 106 Troy MI 48084-3902 Office: 21 Kercheval Ave Ste 270 Grosse Pointe Farms MI 48236-3633 Office Phone: 313-885-2700.

WEINGARTEN, JOSEPH LEONARD, aerospace engineer; b. N.Y.C., June 5, 1944; s. Herman H. and Irene Jane (Binzer); m. Cindy L. Carter; 1 child, Toby stepchildren: Mark Carter, Jill Supancik. B Mech. Engring., NYU, 1966; postgrad., Air War Coll., 1976. Chief engr. Air Transportability Test Loading Agy. Wright-Patterson AFB, Wright-Patterson AFB, Ohio, 1972-74; project engr. dept. engring. USAF, Wright-Patterson AFB, 1966-72, sr. project engr. dept. engring., 1974-76, planning and project engr. dept. engring., 1976-81, chief mgmt. ops. dept. engring., 1981-83, sr. tech. planner dept. engring., 1983-92; tech. asst. DCS Engring. and Tech. Mgmt. Air Force Material Command, Wright-Patterson AFB, 1992-93; founder, CEO Huffman Wright Inst., 1993-98; cons. Main Net Inc., Urbana, Ohio, 1997—2002; exec. dir. MAC Reseller Assn., 2002—; pres. Weingarten & Winburn, LLC, Inc., 2005—. CEO Weingarten Gallery, Dayton, Ohio, 1967—; pres., v.p., sec., treas., bd. dirs. Ohio Designer Craftsmen, Columbus; sec. Ohio Designer Craftsmen Enterprise, Columbus, 1982-90; chmn. continuing edn. design dept. Affiliate Socs. Coun., Dayton, 1971-74, chmn. edn. coord. com. Kettering Inst., Wright State U., 1974-76, chmn. scientist and engr. awards panel, 1990-91, mem., 1992-94; scholar adv. Gerson Lehrman Group, 2006. Contbr. articles on systems engring. to Aeronautical Sys. divsn. Mech. Engring. Jour. (1st place award nat. contest 1970), Procs. 4th Intersoc. Conf. on Transp., Air Force Sys. Command, USAF Spl. Purpose Report, Gems and Minerals, Friends Jour. USAF Mus., Ceramics Monthly, The Crafts Report, Macintosh Software. Scoutmaster Troop 81, Boy Scouts Am., Kettering, Ohio, 1985—91, com. mem., 1991—93, dist. chmn. Wright Bros. Dist., 2000—04, dist. chmn. Sequoia Dist. Miami Valley Coun., 1991—93, asst. coun. commr., 1993—2000, exec. bd. Miami Valley Coun., 2004—; pres. Friends of Montessori Sch., South Dayton, Ohio, 1978—94. Capt. USAF, 1967—71. Recipient Disting. Eagle award Boy Scouts Am., 1992, Silver Beaver award Boy Scouts Am., 1995, Pinnacle award Dayton Region Micronage, Inc., 1999; named as one of 5 bus. execs. of yr. Miami Valley Bus. Advisor/Cox Pub., 1998. Mem. AIAA (sr. mem., air transport systems tech. com. 1976-78, 80-82, Lawrence Sperry award 1977), ASME (sr. mem.), Am. Nat. Standards Inst. (materials handling 5 com. 1968-70), Soc. Automotive Engrs. (aircraft ground support equiment com. 1969-75). Achievements include 11 patents for expendable air cargo pallet, mail container, collapsible air cargo container, process for reinforcing extruded articles, process for large scale extrusions, air flotation cargo handling system, integral aircraft barrier net, load distributive cargo platform, laminated plastic packaging material, computer printer paper support, and investment casting mold base; developments include 3g cargo restraint criteria used worldwide on aircraft/spacecraft/shuttles, rope extraction system for C-5A, system for large scale structural plastics extruxions, advanced planning documents for Air Force, report in new type of DOD procurement system; other achievements include the design and creation of jewelry sold in museums and retail stores. Personal E-mail: mrmac@aol.com.

WEINGARTEN, MARC, lawyer; b. Phila., Mar. 24, 1950; BS, U. Pa., 1971; JD, Georgetown U., 1974. Bar: NY 1975. Ptnr., corp. dept. Schultz Roth & Zabel LLP, NYC, mem. exec. com. Case & notes editor Georgetown Law Rev., 1973—74. Mem.: Assn. of Bar of City of NY (corp. law com. 1984—87, 1989—92, spl. com. on mergers, acquisitions and corp. control contests 1995—2001), ABA (Bus Law Sect, com. on long range issues affecting bus. law practice 1991—99), NY State Bar Assn. Office: Schulte Roth & Zabel LLP 919 Third Ave New York NY 10022-3902 Office Phone: 212-756-2280. Office Fax: 212-593-5955. Business E-Mail: marc.weingarten@srz.com.

WEINGARTEN, REID H., lawyer; b. Newark, Mar. 9, 1950; divorced; 1 child, Ross. BS, Cornell U., 1971; cert., Hague Acad. Internat. Law, The Netherlands, 1974; JD, Dickinson Law Sch., 1975. Bar: Pa. 1975, DC 1981, US Ct. Appeals 4th, 5th, 11th, and DC Circuits 1981. Dep. dist. atty. Dauphin County, Harrisburg, Pa., 1975-77; trial atty. Pub. Integrity Sect. US Dept. Justice, Washington, 1977-87; joined Steptoe & Johnson, Washington, 1987, now ptnr., head white collar def. group. Instr. FBI, Washington, 1978—; adj. prof. law. Georgetown U. Law Ctr. Co-founder See Forever Found., 1995—; bd. dirs., 1995—, chair, 1997—2003. Named one of 75 Best Lawyers in Washington, Washingtonian survey mag., 2002. Fellow Am. Coll. Trial Lawyers; mem. ABA (mem. com. criminal justice sect. 1996-97, chair white collar crime com. 1992-94), Fed. Bar Assn. (Young Fed. Lawyer Award 1984), DC Bar Assn. Office: Steptoe & Johnson 1330 Connecticut Ave NW Washington DC 20036 Office Phone: 202-429-6238. Office Fax: 202-429-3902. Business E-Mail: rweingarten@steptoe.com.

WEINGARTEN, RHONDA (RANDI WEINGARTEN), labor union administrator, lawyer; b. NYC, Dec. 18, 1957; d. Gabriel and Edith (Appelbaum) W. BS, Cornell U., 1980; JD cum laude, Benjamin N. Cardozo Sch. Law, 1983. Bar: N.Y. 1984, U.S. Dist. Ct. (so. and ea. dists.) N.Y. 1984. Legis. asst. Labor Com. N.Y. State Senate, Albany, 1979-80; assoc. Stroock, Stroock and Lavan, NYC, 1983-86; counsel to pres. United Fedn. Tchrs., NYC, 1986—98; tchr. Clara Barton HS, Brooklyn, 1991—97; asst. sec. United Fedn. Teachers, NYC, 1995, treas., 1997, pres., 1998—; v.p. Am. Fedn. Teachers. Bd. dirs. N.Y. State United Teachers; adj. instr. Cardozo Sch. Law, N.Y.C., 1986; mem. Mayor Bloomberg's transition com., N.Y.C., 2001. Mediator Bklyn. Mediation Ctr. Victim Services Agy., 1981-82 (outstanding achievement award, 1981); mem. N.Y. Com. Safety and Health, 1986, Park Slope Safe Homes Project, 1984—, Dem. Nat. Com.; bd. dirs. Justice Resource Ctr., Coun. for Unity, N.Y. Com. on Occupational Safety and Health, N.Y. Region Anti-Defamation League, United Way Greater N.Y. Internat. Rescue Com. Mem. ABA (labor and employment sect.), N.Y. State Bar Assn., Women's Bar Assn., Council N.Y. Law Assocs., Cardozo Sch. Law Alumni Assn. (treas., bd. dirs. 1983—). Democrat. Jewish. Avocations: gardening, running, music, theater. Office: United Fedn Tchrs 52 Broadway New York NY 10004

WEINGARTNER, H(ANS) MARTIN, finance education, b. Heidelberg, Germany, Apr. 4, 1929; came to U.S., 1939, naturalized, 1944; s. Jacob and Grete Weingartner; m. Joyce Trellis, June 12, 1955; children— Steven M., Susan C. De La Paz, Eric H., Kenneth L. AB, SB, U. Chgo., 1950, AM, 1951; MS, Carnegie Mellon U., 1956, PhD, 1962. Economist Dept. Commerce, 1951-53; instr. Grad. Sch. Indsl. Adminstrn., Carnegie Mellon U., 1956-57; instr., then asst. prof. Grad. Sch. Bus., U. Chgo., 1957-63; assoc. prof. fin. Alfred P. Sloan Sch. Mgmt., Mass. Inst. Tech., 1963-66; prof. Grad. Sch. Mgmt., U. Rochester, N.Y., 1966-77; Brownlee O. Currey prof. fin. Owen Grad. Sch. Mgmt., Vanderbilt U., Nashville, 1977-98, Brownlee O. Carrey Prof. of Fin., emeritus, 1998—; dir. Computer Consoles, Inc., 1974-89. Cons. to industry. Author: Mathematical Programming and the Analysis of Capital Budgeting Problems, 3d edit, 1974, (with George Benston and Dan Horsky) An Empirical Study of Mortgage Redlining, 1978; also articles.; Deptl. editor: Mgmt. Sci., 1967-73. Served with AUS, 1953-54. Mellon fellow, 1954-55; Ford Found. fellow, 1955-56, recipient first prize Dissertation Competition, 1963. Fellow: Inst. for Ops. Rsch. and the Mgmt. Scis.; mem.: Coun. Sci. Soc. Pres. (alumni mem.), Inst. Mgmt. Scis. (v.p. fin. 1978—84, pres. 1985—86), Harbor Island Yacht Club (bd. mem. 2005—), Beta Gamma Sigma. Home: 1616 Ash Valley Dr Nashville TN 37215-4202 Office: Vanderbilt U Owen Grad Sch Mgmt 401 21st Ave S Nashville TN 37203

WEINGARTNER, RUDOLPH HERBERT, philosophy educator; b. Heidelberg, Germany, Feb. 12, 1927; came to U.S., 1939, naturalized, 1944; s. Jacob and Grete (Kahn) W.; m. Fannia Goldberg-Rudkowski, Dec. 28, 1952 (dec. Nov. 4, 1994); children: Mark H., Eleanor C.; m. Regitze E.G. Winkelhorn Hamburger, June 13, 1997. AB, Columbia U., 1950, MA, 1953, PhD, 1959. Fellow Inst. Philos. Rsch., San Francisco, 1953—55; instr. philosophy Columbia U., 1955—59; from asst. prof. to prof., chmn. dept. philosophy San Francisco State Coll., 1959—68; prof. philosophy Vassar Coll., Poughkeepsie, 1968—74, chmn. dept., 1968—74, Taylor prof. philosophy, 1973—74, dean Coll. Arts and Scis.; prof. philosophy Northwestern U., Evanston, Ill., 1974—87; provost U. Pitts. 1987—89, prof. philosophy, 1987—94, chmn. dept. philosophy, 1991—93. Author: Experience and Culture: The Philosophy of Georg Simmel, 1962, The Unity of the Platonic Dialogue: The Cratylus, The Protagoras, The Parmenides, 1973, Undergradu-

ate Education: Goals and Means, 1992 (Frederick W. Ness book award 1993), Fitting Form to Function: A Primer on the Organization of Academic Institutions, 1996, The Moral Dimensions of Academic Administration, 1999, Mostly About Me: A Path Through Different Worlds, 2003; editor: (with Joseph Katz) Philosophy in the West, 1965; exhibited sculptures in Mendelson Gallery, 1992, 94, UP Gallery, 1992, Assoc. Artists Pitts. Gallery, 2000, Internat. Images Gallery, 2002-03; contbr. articles to profl. jours. Bd. dirs. Chamber Music Chgo., 1982—87, pres., 1986—87; mem. bd. advisors Pitts. Symphony, 1991—2000, bd. dirs., chmn. artistic com., mem. exec. com., 2000—05. Social Sci. Rsch. Coun. fellow, 1958—59, Guggenheim fellow, 1965—66, Am. Coun. Learned Socs. fellow, 1971—72, residency, Rockefeller Found. Study and Conf. Ctr. in Bellagio, 1994. Mem. Am. Philos. Assn., Assn. Am. Colls. (bd. dirs. 1985-89, task force on gen. edn. 1985-88, editl. bd. liberal edn. jours. 1986-94), Assoc. Artists Pitts. (artist), Phi Beta Kappa. Home: 5448 Northumberland St Pittsburgh PA 15217-1129 E-mail: rudywein@pitt.edu.

WEINGER, STEVEN MURRAY, lawyer; b. Chgo., Feb. 7, 1954; s. Murray and Joan (Taxay) W.; children: Blake, Paige, Haley. BA, Hampshire Coll., 1975; JD, U. Chgo., 1978. Bar: Fla. 1979, Ill. 1979, U.S. Dist. Ct. (so. dist.) Fla. 1979, U.S. Ct. Appeals (5th cir.) 1980, U.S. Ct. Appeals (11th cir.) 1981, U.S. Supreme Ct. 1982, U.S. Dist. Ct. (mid. dist.) Fla. 1989. Mem. faculty U. Miami Sch. Law, Coral Gables, Fla., 1978-79; ptnr. Kurzban, Kurzban & Weinger, P.A., Miami, Fla., 1979—. Bd. dirs. Sunrise Cmty. for Mentally Retarded, Miami, United Cerebral Palsy Tallahassee, Inc., Palmer-Trinity Sch., Miami, GobleStage, Inc., 1999—. Recipient Chmn.'s award Sunrise Cmty. for Mentally Retarded, 1987; honoree United Cerebral Palsy in South Fla., 1995, Fla. Assn. Rehab. Facilities, 1996, United Cerebral Palsy Assn., 1997. Mem. ABA, Assn. Trial Lawyers Am., Fla. Assn. Trial Lawyers. Office: Kurzban Kurzban & Weinger 2650 SW 27th Ave Fl 2D Miami FL 33133-3003 E-mail: swmiami@aol.com.

WEINGROW, HOWARD LOUIS, finance company executive; b. NYC, Dec. 6, 1922; s. Nathan and Anna (Mintzes) W.; m. Muriel Corrine Franzblau, Nov. 24, 1946; children: Terry Vaccaro, Caron Abby Haim. DHL (hon.), Hofstra U., 2004. Owner Legion Fluorescent Corp., N.Y.C., 1946-56; ptnr. Hechler & Weingrow, Inc., N.Y.C., 1956-58, Hechler, Lifton & Weingrow, Inc., N.Y.C., 1958-78; exec. v.p. Tanscontinental Investing Corp., N.Y.C., 1960-67, pres., 1967-70; prin. Lifton & Weingrow, N.Y.C., 1958—; co-chmn. Marcade Group, Inc., N.Y.C., 1986-91, bd. dirs., 1986-93; pres. Medis Techs., Ltd. (MDTL), 1992—, Stanoff Corp., 1980—, Wesak Internat., 1992-94, dep. chmn., 1992—94; chmn. Wesak Chrysler, 1992-94; pres. Medis Techs. Ltd., 1992—2006, Cell Kinetics, 2006—. Bd. dirs. Preferred Health Care, N.Y.C., Four Winds Inc., N.Y.C., Medis-El, Medis Techs. Ltd., Xilas Med., Inc.; founder Ctr. for Chilhood Asthma Schneider Children's Hosp., 2002, Weingrow Family Pediatric Urology Lab., L.I. Jewish Hosp., 1989, The Howard L. and Muriel Weingrow Collection of Avant-Garde Art and Lit., Hofstra U., 1972; chmn. Vision Telemedia, Inc., 1995-98; founder endowed scholarship program Hofstra U., 2005., Treas. Dem. Nat. Com., Washington, 1970-72; mem. bd. govs. Hofstra U. Law Sch., 1977-79; dep. fin. chmn. Pres. Carter, Washington, 1976, 80; trustee Hofstra U., Hempstead, N.Y., 1973-76, James S. Brady Presdl. Found., 1982, Children's Med. Fund, L.I. Jewish Children's Hosp., Lake Success, N.Y., 1986—, Am. Jewish Congress, 1988-96; treas. Nassau County Mus. Fine Arts, 1988—, North Shore, L.I. Jewish Hosp. Sys., 1999—; advisor to Pres. Lyndon Johnson, OEO, Washington; fin. advisor to the Govt. of Grenada and Office of Prime Minister Gairy, 1977-79. Decorated DFC, Air medal, 2 bronze, 2 silver clusters; recipient Presdl. medal, Hofstra U., 1985. Office: Stanoff Corp 805 3rd Ave Fl 15 New York NY 10022-7513 Office Phone: 212-935-8484. Business E-Mail: hweingrow@medistechnologies.com.

WEINHOLD, LINDA LILLIAN, psychologist, researcher; b. Reading, Pa., Nov. 9, 1948; d. Aaron Zerbe Weinhold and Nancy Louise (Spotts) Weikel; m. Jack Wayne Prisk, Jan. 21, 1967 (div. 1969). Lic. practical nurse, AVTS, 1970; BS, Penn State U., 1975; MS, C.W. Post Ctr., 1982; PhD, Fordham U., 1986. LPN; cert. profl. counselor. Instr., asst. prof. Gettysburg (Pa.) Coll., 1985-86; post doc. fellow John Hopkins U., Balt., 1986-88; staff fellow NIH NIDA Addiction Rsch. Ctr., Balt., 1988-93; cons. NIH NIDA Medications Devel., Rockville, Md., 1993-94; soc. sci. program coord. Med. Ctr. NIDA Rsch., Washington, 1994-95; cons. The Clin. Cons. Group Antech, Inc., Balt., 1995; substance abuse counselor Hope Village, Inc., Washington, 1996—. Various presentations. Mem. Am. Psychological Assn., Phi Kappa Phi, Sigma Xi. Democrat. Avocations: singing, dance, painting, photography, reading. Home: 2611 Bowen Rd SE Apt 203 Washington DC 20020-6623 Office: Hope Village Inc 2840 Langston Pl SE Washington DC 20020-3241

WEINKAUF, MARY LOUISE STANLEY, retired clergywoman, educator; b. Eau Claire, Wis., Sept. 22, 1938; d. Joseph Michael and Marie Barbara (Holzinger) Stanley; m. Alan D. Weinkauf, Oct. 12, 1962 (dec. Nov. 2000); children: Stephen, Xanti. BA, Wis. State U., 1961; MA, U. Tenn., 1962, PhD, 1966; MDiv, Luth. Sch. Theology, Chgo., 1993. Grad. asst., instr. U. Tenn. 1961-66; asst. prof. English Adrian Coll., 1966-69; prof., head dept. English Dakota Wesleyan U., Mitchell, SD, 1969-89; instr. Columbia Coll., 1989-91. Pastor Calvary Evang. Luth. Ch., Siloa Luth. Ch., Ontonagon Faith, White Pine, Mich., Gowrie, Iowa. Author: Hard-Boiled Heretic, 1994, Sermons in Science Fiction, 1994, Murder Most Poetic, 1996. Trustee The Ednl. Found., 1986-90; bd. dirs. Ontonagon County Habitat for Humanity, 1995-97, Lakeland Area Food Pantry, 2000—; mem. bd. Luth. Campus Ministry for Wis. and Upper Mich., 1996—2002, Fortune Lake Bible Camp, 2003-04. Mem. AAUW (divsn. pres. 1978-80), Nat. Coun. Tchrs. English, S.D. Coun. Tchrs. English, Sci. Fiction Rsch. Assn., Popular Culture Assn., Milton Soc., S.D. Poetry Soc. (pres. 1982-83), Delta Kappa Gamma (pres. loc. chpt.), mem. state bd. 1972-89, state v.p. 1979-83, state pres. 1983-85), Sigma Tau Delta, Pi Kappa Delta, Phi Kappa Phi. E-mail: woodwork@nnex.net.

WEINKAUF, WILLIAM CARL, communications executive; b. Fond du Lac, Wis., Apr. 7, 1934; s. Carl Alfred and Erma Gertrude (Lueck) Weinkauf; m. Carole Jean Hill, May 3, 1958 (div.); children: Carl William, Mary Gretchen, Donald Hill; m. Jean Boyne Hawks, Sept. 10, 1988. BA, Ripon Coll., 1955; postgrad., U. Wis., 1954, 57-58. Dir. Wis. Ctrl. Lumber Co., 1959-63; with Carlton Films, Beloit, Wis., 1965-68; founder, pres. IMCO, Inc., Green Lake, Wis., 1968—, IMCO Pub. Co., Green Lake. Bd. dirs. Peterson Sys., Inc.; co-founder, chmn. Affluence Unlimited, Inc., Dallas, 1986; founder, pres. Weinkauf Techs., LLC, Dallas, 1996. Chmn. coun. Cub Scouts Am., 1968—69; mem. exec. com. County Reps., 1970—71; trustee United Ch. Christ, Green Lake, 1965—66, deacon Dallas, 1989—93, chmn. bd. deacons, 1992—93. Mem.: Nat. Sch. Supply and Equipment Assn. (bd. dirs. 1986—87), Nat. Audio Visual Assn. (chmn. legis. com. Wis. 1975—), Heroes of '76, U.S. Res. Officers Assn. (chpt. pres. 1966—70), Scotish Rite (32 deg.), Order Ea. Star (worthy patron Dallas 2001—), Sojourners, Masons (32d degree), Sigma Nu. Office: 2215 Commerce St Dallas TX 75201-4345

WEINKE, CHRIS, professional football player; b. St. Paul, Minn., July 31, 1972; Attended, Fla. State Univ. Quarterback Carolina Panthers, 2001—; winner Heisman Trophy. Achievements include ranking second in NFL history for passing yards as a rookie. Office: Carolina Panthers 800 S Mint St Charlotte NC 28202

WEINKOPF, FRIEDRICH J., lawyer; b. Bautsch, Germany, Feb. 17, 1930; Referandar, U. Marburg, Germany, 1954; LLM, U. Pa., 1958; JD, Chgo.-Kent Coll. Law, 1967. Bar: Ill. 1967. Sr. counsel Baker & McKenzie, Chgo. Office: Baker & McKenzie 1 Prudential Plz 130 E Randolph St Fl 3600 Chicago IL 60601-6315

WEINMAN, CONNIE GERMANN, banker, lawyer; b. Celina, Ohio, Jan. 2, 1943; d. Elmer John and Berniece (Buck) Germann; m. George C. Weinman; children: Matthew, Jeffrey. BS, Capital U., 1965; JD, Hamline U.,

1977. V.p. Nat. City Bank, Mpls., 1978—. Bd. dirs. Fairview, Mpls., Wheatridge, Colo., Chgo., Riverside Med. Ctr., Mpls.; mem. CORE Commn., state govt. reform. Mem. Minn. Women's Econ. Round Table. Republican. Lutheran.

**WEINMAN, DARYL GAIL,** lawyer; b. North Tarrytown, N.Y., Dec. 22, 1967; d. Lawrence S. Weinman and Serena Negrin Michelson; m. Donald Paul Morehart, July 19, 1997; children: Nathan Daniel Morehart, Benjamin Jake Morehart. BA, Colgate U., 1988; JD, N.Y. Law Sch., 1993. Bar: Tex. 1994, U.S. Dist. Ct. (we. dist.) Tex. 1994, U.S. Ct. Appeals (5th cir.) 1995, U.S. Supreme Ct. 1997, bd. cert. family law: 2000. Pvt. practice, Austin, Tex., 1994—2000; ptnr. Morehart and Weinman, Austin, 2000—. Vol. Sidelines, Austin, 1999—; mem. Jewish Cmty. Ctr., Austin, 1998—; local coord. Stepmothers Internat., Austin, 1999—; founding fellow Travis Bar Found. Mem.: Tex. Acad. Family Specialists, Dist. 9A Grievance Com., Pro Bono Coll. State Bar, Coll. State Bar of Tex., State Bar Tex., Travis County Bar. Democrat. Jewish. Avocations: quilting, travel, children's activities. Office: Morehart and Weinman 316 W 12th St Ste 602 Austin TX 78701 Office Phone: 512-472-4040. Personal E-mail: darylesq@aol.com.

**WEINMAN, GLENN ALAN,** lawyer; b. NYC, Dec. 9, 1955; s. Seymour and Iris Rhoda (Bergman) W. BA in Polit. Sci., UCLA, 1978; JD, U. So. Calif., 1981. Bar: Calif. 1981. Assoc. counsel Mitsui Mfrs. Bank, LA, 1981-83; assoc. McKenna, Conner & Cuneo, LA, 1983-85, Stroock, Stroock & Lavan, LA, 1985-87; sr. counsel Buchalter, Nemer, Fields & Younger, LA, 1987-91; ptnr. Keck, Mahin & Cate, LA, 1991-93; sr. v.p., gen. counsel Western Internat. Media Corp., LA, 1993-96; v.p. gen. counsel and human resources, sec. Guess?, Inc., LA, 1996-2000; chief adminstrv. officer Competitive Knowledge, Inc., 2000; v.p., gen. counsel, sec. Luminent, Inc., Chatsworth, Calif., 2000-01; exec. v.p., COO Insolvency Svcs. Group, Woodland Hills, Calif., 2001—03; v.p., gen. counsel, sec. Inter-Con Security Sys., Inc., Pasadena, Calif., 2003—05. Mem. ABA (corp. banking and bus. law sect., com. on savs. instns., com. on banking law corp. counsel sect.), Calif. Bar Assn. (bus. law sect., com. fin. instns. 1989-91, com. consumer svcs. 1991-94), LA County Bar Assn. (corp. legal depts. sect., bus. and corps. law sect., subcom. on fin. instns.), Calif. Fashion Assn. (exec. bd. 1997-2000), Am. Apparel Mfrs. Assn. (govt. rels. com. 1997-2000), Legion Lex, U. So. Calif. Law Alumni Assn., Phi Alpha Delta. Avocation: tennis. Office Phone: 818-512-8100. Personal E-mail: gaweinman@aol.com.

**WEINMAN, HOWARD MARK,** lawyer; b. N.Y.C., May 6, 1947; s. Joseph and Kate (Dorn) Weinman; m. Pamela Eve Brodie, Jan. 6, 1980; children: David Lewis, Nathaniel Saul. BA magna cum laude, Columbia U., 1969; MPP, Harvard U., 1973, JD cum laude, 1973; LLM with highest hons. in Taxation, George Washington U., 1981. Bar: D.C. 1973. Assoc. Fried, Frank, Harris, Shriver & Kampelman, Washington and N.Y.C., 1973—78; legis. atty. Joint Com. on Taxation U.S. Congress, Washington, 1978—80; assoc. Sachs, Greenebaum & Tayler, Washington, 1980—82, Crowell & Moring LLP, Washington, 1982—84, ptnr., 1984—. Adj. prof. internat. tax Georgetown U. Law Ctr., Washington, 1988—89. Contbr. articles to profl. jours. Mem.: ABA (taxation sect.), Phi Beta Kappa. Jewish. Home: 5404 Center St Chevy Chase MD 20815-7101 Office: Crowell & Moring LLP 1001 Pennsylvania Ave NW Fl 10 Washington DC 20004-2595

**WEINMANN, ERIC,** retired lawyer; b. Teplice, Czech Republic, July 29, 1913; came to U.S., 1942; s. Ing Edmund and Josefine (Taussig) W.; m. Camilla Behn, May 4, 1946 (div. 1953); children: Edward Marvin, Gail Greenwood; m. Mary Ethel de Limur Carothers, Dec. 21, 1974. Diploma, Handelshochschule, Berlin, 1935; MA, Columbia U. 1943, JD, 1957; LLM, Georgetown U., 1963. Bar: N.Y. 1957, D.C. 1958, U.S. Supreme Ct. 1963. Assoc. counsel Legal and Monetary Subcom. Ho. of Reps., Washington, 1957—60; atty. SEC, Washington, 1960—63; asst. dep., counsel SBA, Washington, 1963—89; ret., 1989. Contbr. articles to profl. jours. Trustee emeritus Folger Shakespeare Libr., Washington, 1985. Mem. Met. Club City of Washington Home: 3244 Nebraska Ave NW Washington DC 20016-2704 Personal E-mail: maryeweinmann@aol.com.

**WEINMANN, ROBERT LEWIS,** neurologist; b. Newark, Aug. 21, 1935; s. Isadore and Etta (Silverman) Weinmann; m. Diana Weinmann, Dec. 13, 1980 (dec. Dec. 1989); children: Paul, Chris, Dana, Paige. BA, Yale U., 1957; MD, Stanford U., 1962. Diplomate Am. Bd. EEG and Neurophysiology (v.p.), Am. Acad. Pain Mgmt., Am. Bd. Forensic Medicine. Intern Pacific Presbyn. Med. Ctr., San Francisco, 1962-63; resident in neurology Stanford (Calif.) U. Hosp., 1963-66, chief resident, 1965-66; pvt. practice San Jose, Calif., 1969—. Former clin. instr. neurology Stanford U. Chmn. editl. bd. Clin. EEG Jour., mem. editl. bd. Clin. Evoked Potentials Jour.; contbr. articles to various publs. Capt. M.C. U.S. Army, 1966—68. Recipient award, State of R.I., Santa Clara County Med. Soc., Calif. State Assembly, U.S. Congress, other orgns.; fellow, U. Paris, 1957—58. Fellow: Am. Coll. Forensic Medicine; mem.: Union Am. Physicians and Dentists (pres. 1990—, bd. dirs. 1972—, pres. Calif. fedn. 1990—). Avocations: softball, tennis, music, theater, martial arts. Office: Union Am Physicians & Dentists 1330 Broadway Ste 730 Oakland CA 94612-2589 Office Phone: 510-839-0193, 408-292-0802. Personal E-mail: uapdhq@aol.com.

**WEINRAUCH, HARRY,** physician; b. Vienna, Oct. 27, 1928; arrived in U.S., 1940; s. Nathan and Cele Beile Weinrauch; m. Roslyn Weinrauch; 3 children. BA, NYU, 1950; MD, SUNY, Bklyn., 1954. Diplomate Am. Bd. Internal Medicine. Assoc. attending physician Mt. Sinai Hosp., 1964—; asst. clin. prof. Mt. Sinai Med. Coll., 1981—. Capt. USAF, 1955—57. Avocation: stamps. Office: 1049 Park Ave New York NY 10028 Office Phone: 212-348-0222.

**WEINREB, LLOYD LOBELL,** law educator; b. NYC, Oct. 9, 1936; s. Victor and Ernestine (Lobell) Weinreb; m. Ruth Plaut, May 5, 1963; children: Jennifer, Elizabeth, Nicholas. BA in History, Dartmouth Coll., 1957; BA in Philosophy, Politics, and Economics, U. Oxford, 1959, MA in Philosophy, Politics, and Economics, 1963; LLB, Harvard U., 1962. Bar: NY 1963, Mass. 1969. Atty. US Dept. Justice, Washington, 1964—65; asst. prof. law Harvard Law Sch., Cambridge, Mass., 1965—68, prof., 1968—, Dane prof., 1993—. Author: Denial of Justice, 1977, The Law of Criminal Investigation, 1982, Natural Law and Justice, 1987, Oedipus at Fenway Park: What Rights Are and Why There Are Any, 1994, Criminal Process, 1998, 2004, Criminal Law: Cases, Comments, Questions, 2003, Leading Constitutional Cases on Criminal Justice, 2003, 2004, Legal Reason, 2005; co-author (with James D. Whaley): The Field Guide to Law Enforcement, 2003. Office: Harvard Law Sch 1563 Massachusetts Ave Cambridge MA 02138 Office Phone: 617-495-3191. Office Fax: 617-496-4865. Business E-mail: weinreb@law.harvard.edu.

**WEINREB, MICHAEL PHILIP,** physicist; b. Lakewood, NJ, Feb. 2, 1939; s. Sol and Lillian (Bolotsky) W.; m. Alice Kogan, Aug. 28, 1966; children: Jenya, Elizabeth. BA, U. Pa., 1960; MA, Brandeis U., 1963, PhD, 1966. Physicist NASA, Cambridge, Mass., 1965-70, U.S. Dept. Transp., Cambridge, 1970, Nat. Oceanic and Atmospheric Adminstrn., Washington, 1970—2004, Gen. Dynamics Advanced Info. Sys., Washington, 2004—. Adj. prof. math. Am. U., Washington, 1984-85. Contbr. articles to profl. jours. Recipient Gold medal U.S. Dept. of Commerce, 1998, Bronze medal, 1994, 2003. Mem. Am. Meteorol. Soc., Am. Geophys. Union, Phi Beta Kappa. Avocation: music. Business E-mail: michael.weinreb@noaa.gov.

**WEINREB, TZVI HERSH,** religious organization administrator, rabbi; m. Chavi Taub, 1965; 3 children. MA in pyschology, New Sch.for Social Rsch.; PhD, U. Md., 1970. Asst. supervisor psychological services Prince George's County Public Schools; chief psychologist Potomac Found. Mental Health; private practice, psychotherapy; rabbi Congregation Shomrei Emunah, Balt., 1989—2002; exec. v.p. Orthodox Union, 2002—. V.p Rabbinical Coun. Am.; rabbinic liaison N. Am. Network Orthodox Mental Heath Professionals; mem.

ethics com. Veterans Admin. Hosp.; mem. rabbinic cabinet United Jewish Communities. Office: Orthodox Union 11 Broadway New York NY 10004 Office Phone: 212-563-4000. Office Fax: 212-564-9058.

**WEINREICH, GABRIEL,** physicist, minister, educator; b. Vilnius, Lithuania, Feb. 12, 1928; came to U.S., 1941, naturalized, 1949; s. Max and Regina (Szabad) W.; m. Alisa Lourié, Apr. 19, 1951 (dec. 1970); m. Gerane Siemering Benamou, Oct. 23, 1971; children: Catherine, Marc, Daniel, Rebecca, Natalie. AB, Columbia U., 1948, MA, 1949, PhD, 1954. Ordained priest Episcopal Ch., 1986. Mem. staff Bell Telephone Labs., Murray Hill, NJ, 1953-60; mem. faculty U. Mich., Ann Arbor, 1960—, prof. physics, 1964-95; prof. emeritus, 1995—; Collegiate prof. U. Mich., 1974-76. Adj. min. St. Clare's Episcopal ch., Ann Arbor, 1985-90; rector St. Stephen's Episcopal Ch., Hamburg, Mich., 1993-96. Author: Solids: Elementary Theory for Advanced Students, 1965, Fundamental Thermodynamics, 1968, Notes for General Physics, 1972, Geometrical Vectors, 1998, Confessions of a Jewish Priest: From Secular Jewish War Refugee to Physicist and Episcopal Clergyman, 2005; editor: Mechanics of Musical Instruments, 1995. Recipient Disting. Teaching award U. Mich., 1968, Klopsteg award Am. Assn. Physics Tchrs., 1992, Internat. medal French Acoustical Soc., 1992, Hutchins Gold medal for lifetime achievement in mus. acoustics, 2002. Fellow Acoustical Soc. Am. (assoc. editor Jour. 1987-89). Home: 2116 Silver Maples Dr Chelsea MI 48118-1189 Business E-mail: weinreic@umich.edu.

**WEINREICH, GADI,** lawyer; b. Tel Aviv, Apr. 25, 1962; BA magna cum laude, Brown U., 1983; JD cum laude, Harvard U., 1987; LLM, Cambridge U., 1992. Bar: Mass. 1987, DC 1988. Ptnr. Shaw Pittman LLP, Washington; ptnr., health care practice group Sonnenschein Nath & Rosenthal LLP, Washington, 2003—. Mem. The Shakespeare Theatre Lawyers Com. Mem.: ABA (health law sect.), Gerson Lehrman Law Coun., DC Bar Assn. (health law sect.), Health Care Compliance Assn., Am. Health Lawyers Assn. Office: Sonnenschein Nath & Rosenthal LLP Ste 600, E Tower 1301 K St NW Washington DC 20015 Office Phone: 202-408-9166. Office Fax: 202-408-6399. Business E-mail: gweinreich@sonnenschein.com.

**WEINRICH, BRIAN ERWIN,** mathematician, computer scientist; b. Passaic, N.J., Jan. 8, 1952; s. Erwin H. and Ann E. (Gall) Weinrich. BS, Pa. State U., 1974, MA, 1978; MS, Shippensburg U., Pa., 1983; postgrad. in computer engring., U. Fla., 2002—. Mathematician U.S. Dept. Agr., Agrl. Rsch. Svc., University Park, Pa., 1974-80; instr. math and computer sci. Shippensburg U., 1980-84; assoc. prof. maths. and computer sci. California U. of Pa., 1984-97, assoc. prof. emeritus of mathematics and computer scis., 1997—. Cons. in field; mem. Wall St. Jour. Panel, 1990—; devel. articulation agreements in Malaysia California U. of Pa., 1992—2001; vis. sc. lectr. in computer sci. Inti Coll., Subang Jaya, Malaysia 1993—2001; cons. in math., sys. and database programming, 1981—2002. Author (with A. S. Rogowski): (book) Water Movement and Quality on Strip-Mined Lands: A Compilation of Computer Programs, 1984; author: (with others) Surface Mining, 1990; contbr. articles to profl. jours. Mem. mission bd. Calvary Bapt. Ch., State College, Pa., 1975—80; visitation team Prince St. United Brethren Ch., Shippensburg, 1982—84; Bible study leader, asst. Sunday sch. tchr. Libr. Bapt. Ch., 1986—92; workshop leader, follow-up trainer Gator Christian Life, Cypress Ch., 2002—. Fellow, U. Fla., 2002—; grantee, U.S. Dept. Age, 1982—89. Mem.: Assn. Computing Machinery, Am. Biog. Inst. (bd. advisors 1989—), Computer Soc. of IEEE. Republican. Home: 1001 SW 16th Ave Apt 67 Gainesville FL 32601 Office: U Fla Dept Computer and Info Sci and Engring PO Box 116120 Gainesville FL 32611 Office Phone: 352-392-1200. Personal E-mail: brianew@cise.ufl.edu.

**WEINROTH, LOIS L.,** lawyer; b. NYC, 1941; AB cum laude, Barnard Coll., 1963; LLB cum laude, Columbia U., 1968. Bar: N.Y. 1968. Ptnr., N.Y.C. Office: Orthodox ptnr., structured fin. practice area Stroock & Stroock & Lavan LLP, N.Y.C. Office: Stroock & Stroock & Lavan LLP 180 Maiden Ln New York NY 10038-4982 Office Phone: 212-806-5868. Office Fax: 212-806-6006. Business E-mail: lweinroth@stroock.com.

**WEINSCHEL, ALAN JAY,** lawyer; b. Bklyn., Feb. 9, 1946; m. Barbara Ellen Schure, Aug. 20, 1967; children: Lawrence, Adam, Naomi. BA. Bklyn. Coll., 1967; JD, NYU, 1969. Bar: N.Y. 1970, U.S. Dist. Ct. (so. and ea. dists.) N.Y. 1973, U.S. Ct. Appeals (2d cir.) 1979, U.S. Ct. Appeals (9th cir.) 1986, U.S. Ct. Appeals (3d cir.) 1993, U.S. Ct. Appeals (7th cir.) 1996. Assoc. Breed, Abbott & Morgan, N.Y.C., 1969-74, Weil, Gotshal & Manges, N.Y.C., 1974-78, ptnr., 1978—. Lectr. Practising Law Inst., Ohio Legal Ctr., Am. Mgmt. Assn., Law Jour. Seminars, Law and Bus. Seminars, Glasser Legalworks, Insight Seminars, Mfrs.' Alliance. Author: Antitrust Intellectual Property Handbook, 2000. Trustee N.Y. Inst. Tech., Old Westbury, N.Y., 1969-76, Temple Sinai, Roslyn, N.Y., 1981-87, 89-95. Capt. U.S. Army res., 1969-74. Mem. ABA (editl. bd. Antitrust Devels. 1981-87), N.Y. State Bar Assn. (chmn. antitrust sect. 1993-95), Assn. Bar of City of N.Y. Office: Weil Gotshal & Manges 767 5th Ave New York NY 10153-0119 Office Phone: 212-310-8550.

**WEINSHEIMER, WILLIAM CYRUS,** lawyer; b. Chgo., Jan. 12, 1941; s. Alfred John and Coress (Searing) W.; m. Roberta Limarzi, June 5, 1965; children: William C. Jr., Kurt R., Robert L. BBA in Mktg., U. Notre Dame, 1962; JD, Northwestern U., 1965. Bar: Ill. 1965, U.S. Dist. Ct. (no. dist.) Ill. 1967, U.S. Tax Ct. 1968. Ptnr. Foley and Lardner LLP, Chgo., 2001—, co-chmn. estates & trusts practice group Sinai Hosp.—. Lectr. continuing legal edn. programs; mem. estate planning adv. coun. Northwestern U. Author: (with others) The New Generation Skipping Tax; Analysis, Planning & Drafting, 1987; Drafting Wills and Trust Agreements, 1990; contbr. articles to profl. jours. Bd. dirs. The Ragdale Found., Lake Forest, Ill., 1987-93, Lawyers for Creative Arts, 1973-90, Winnetka United Way, 1989-92; pres. Family Svc. Winnetka-Northfield, Inc., 1978-79. Capt. U.S. Army, 1965-67. Fellow Am. Coll. Trust and Estate Coun. (bus. planning com. 1993-2002, internat. estate planning com., 1997-99, chair Ill. chpt. 1989-92, editor Actec Notes 1991-92, bd. regents 1992-96, chair edit. bd. 1993-96), chair Promotion Com., 2004-; mem. ABA (vice chmn. con. on generation-skipping tax 1988-92), Ill. Bar Assn., Chgo. Bar Assn. (chmn. probate practice com. 1989), Chgo. Bar Found. (bd. dirs. 1992—), Ill. Bar Found. (bd. dirs. 1985-91), Lawyer Club, Econ. Club, Mid-Day Club, Skokie Country Club, Notre Dame Club Chgo. (bd. govs. 1984-90). Roman Catholic. Avocations: golf, visual arts, performing. Office: Foley and Lardner LLP 321 N Clark St Ste 2800 Chicago IL 60610 Office Phone: 312-832-4590. Business E-mail: wweinsheimer@foley.com.

**WEINSHENKER, NAOMI JOYCE,** clinical psychiatrist, educator, researcher; b. Ridgewood, NJ, Mar. 28, 1961; d. Theodore and Anne Betty (Jaffe) W. BA summa cum laude, Yale U., 1983; MD, U. Pa., 1989. Diplomate Am. Bd. Psychiatry and Neurology. Rotating intern Overlook Hosp., Summit, N.J., 1989-90; resident in adult psychiatry Mass. Mental Health Ctr., Harvard U. Med. Sch., Boston, 1990-92, fellow in child and adolescent psychiatry, 1992-93, Boston Childrens Hosp., Harvard Med. Sch., 1993—94; staff psychiatrist Choate Health Systems, Woburn, Mass., 1994-96; asst. prof. clin. psychiatry U. Medicine and Dentistry of N.J., Newark, 1996-2000; asst. prof. clin. psychiatry Sch. Medicine NYU, 2000—06; pvt. practice psychiatry, 2006—; freelance medical reporting News12, Norwalk, Conn., 2006—. Staff psychiatrist Univ. Behavioral HealthCare, Newark, 1996—97; asst.dir. Univ.Hosp. Psychiat. Outpatient Ctr., 1998—2000; mem. faculty NYU Child Study Ctr., 2000—06; cons. child outpatient svcs Tri-City Mental Health and Retardation Ctr., Inc., Medford, Mass., 1996; dir., young adult inpatient program Tisch Hosp., 2000—04. Contbr. articles to profl. jours.; editl. asst. Emergency Medicine mag., 1983-84. Vol. psychiatry unit, coord. Phila. Adult Spl. Olympics, 1985. Mem. Am. Psychiat. Assn., Am. Acad. Child/Adolescent Psychiatry, N.J. Psychiat. Assn. (Essex County rep. Tri-County chpt. 1997-98, treas. 1998-99, sec. 1999-00, v.p. 2000-2001, pres-elect 2001-02), N.Y. Coun. Child/Adolescent Psychiatry, Phi Beta Kappa,

Sigma Xi. Democrat. Jewish. Avocations: theater, nutrition, vegetarianism, weightlifting, aerobics. Personal E-mail: nami_weinshenker@yahoo.com. Business E-mail: naomi.weinshenker@nyumc.org.

**WEINSHILBOUM, RICHARD M.,** pharmacologist, educator, biomedical researcher; b. Eldorado, Kans., Mar. 31, 1940; s. Robert Saul and Rose Lazer Weinshilboum; m. Lily Shuling, June 4, 1965; children: Rebecca Y., David H. BA, U. Kans., 1962; MD, U. Kans., Kansas City, 1967; LLD (hon.), New Eng. U., 1995. Cert. bd. cert. in internal medicine, bd. cert. in clin. pharmacology. Rsch. assoc. NIMH, Bethesda, Md., 1969—71; resident in internal medicine Mass. Gen. Hosp., Boston, 1967—69, 1971—72; asst. to assoc. prof. pharmacology and medicine Mayo Med. Sch., Mayo Clinic, Rochester, Minn., 1972—79, prof. molecular pharmacology and expti. therapeutics and medicine, 1979—. Contbr. articles to profl. jours. Burroughs-Wellcome in Clin. Pharmacology scholar, 1981—86. Mem.: Catecholamine Club (Julius Axelrod award 2003), Am. Soc. Pharmacology and Expti. Therapeutics (Harry Gold award 2003), Am. Soc. Clin. Pharmacology and Therapeutics (Rawls-Palmer award 1979, Oscar B. Hunter award 1998). Jewish. Achievements include major contributions to the fields of pharmacogenetics and pharmacogenomics of drug metabolism. Avocation: tennis. Office: Mayo Clinic 200 First St SW Rochester MN 55905 Office Phone: 507-284-2790.

**WEINSTEIN, ALI ANNE,** psychologist, researcher; b. Takoma Park, Md., June 19, 1977; d. Lyle and Aviva Fox Berlin; m. Jeffrey Michael Weinstein, Jan. 15, 2006. BS, Lafayette Coll., Easton, PA, 1999; MA, U. Md., College Park, 2001; postgrad., Uniformed Services U., Bethesda, Md., 2001—. Grad. fellow Uniformed Services U., Bethesda, 2001—. Fellow Henry M. Jackson fellow, Henry M. Jackson Found., 2006—. Mem.: APA (assoc.; co-chair student cen. 2005—06). Independent. Jewish. Achievements include research in exercise withdrawal. Avocation: volleyball. Office Phone: 301-295-3522. Business E-mail: aberlin@usuhs.mil.

**WEINSTEIN, ALLEN,** archivist; b. NYC, Sept. 1, 1937; s. Samuel and Sarah (Popkoff) W.; m. Adrienne Dominguez, June 14, 1995; children: Andrew Samuel, David Meier. BA, CCNY; MA, Yale U., PhD, 1967. Prof. history Smith Coll., Northampton, Mass., 1966-81; editl. staff The Washington Post, 1981; exec. editor, The Washington Quarterly Georgetown Ctr. for Strategic and Internat. Studies, Washington, 1981—83; prof. Georgetown U., Washington, 1981—84; pres. Ctr. for the Study of Democratic Institutions, Santa Barbara, 1984; editor The Ctr. Magazine, 1984; prof. history Boston U., 1985-89; founder, pres. The Ctr. for Democracy, Washington, 1985—2003; sr. adviser for democratic institutions and dir. Internat. Found. for Elections Sys., Washington, 2003—; archivist of the US Nat. Archives & Records Admin., 2005—. Author: Prelude to Populism:Origins of the Silver Issue, 1970, Freedom and Crisis: An American History, 1974, Perjury: The Hiss-Chambers Case, 1978 (NISC award 1978), new edit., 1998, Between the Wars: American Foreign Policy From Versailles to Pearl Harbor, 1978; co-author: The Haunted Wood: Soviet Espionage in America-The Stalin Era, 1999, The Story of America, 2002; editor: American Negro Slavery, 1968, 3d edit., 1981, Harry S Truman and the American Commitment to Israel, 1981. Exec. dir. The Democracy Program, Washington, 1982-83; acting pres. Nat. Endowment for Democracy, Washington, 1983-84; chmn. edn. com. U.S. Inst. Peace, Washington, 1986-2001; mem. U.S. Observer del., Feb., 1986 Philippines election, co-author report; vice chmn. U.S. del. UNESCO World Conf. on Culture, 1982, UNESCO/IPDC meeting, 1983; chmn. Internat. IMPAC/Dublin Lit. award, 1996-2003. Recipient Meade prize in history CCNY, 1960, Egleston prize Yale U., 1967, Binkley-Stephenson prize Orgn. Am. Historians, 1968, UN Peace medal, 1986, Coun. of Europe Silver medal, 1990, 96; Fulbright lectr., Australia, 1968, 71; Commonwealth Fund lectr. U.S. History, U. London, 1981; Fourth of July Orator Fanueil Hall, Boston, 1987. Fellow Woodrow Wilson Ctr., NEH; mem. Soc. Am. Historians, Cosmos Club. Democrat. Jewish. From 1982-84 directed the rsch. study which led to the creation of the Nat. Endowment for Democracy (NED). Office: Nat Archives & Records Adminstrn 8601 Adelphi Rd Rm 4200 College Park MD 20740

**WEINSTEIN, ANDREW H.,** lawyer; b. Pitts., Oct. 5, 1943; s. Adolph J. and Meta I. (Schwarz) W.; m. Susan Balber, Aug. 11, 1968; children: Jodi L., Toby M., Jamie M. BSBA, Duquesne U., 1965; JD, U. Pitts., 1968; LLM in Taxation, NYU, 1969. Bar: Pa. 1969, U.S. Tax Ct. 1969, Fla. 1970, U.S. Dist. Ct. (so. dist.) Fla., U.S. Ct. Fed. Claims. Trial atty. IRS, L.A., 1969-70, Miami, Fla., 1970-73; ptnr. Glass, Schultz, Weinstein & Moss, Coral Gables, Fla., 1973-80, Holland & Knight, Miami, 1980—. Contbr. articles to profl. jours. Bd. dirs. Zool. Soc. Fla., Red Cross. Fellow Am. Coll. Tax Counsel, Am. Coll. Trusts and Estates Counsel; mem. ABA (tax sect., bd. cert. tax law), ARC, Fla. Bar., Best Lawyers in Am. Avocations: golf, travel. Office: Holland & Knight 701 Brickell Ave Ste 3000 Miami FL 33131-2898 Office Phone: 305-789-7755. Business E-mail: andrew.weinstein@hklaw.com.

**WEINSTEIN, BOB (ROBERT WEINSTEIN),** film company executive; b. Queens, NY, Oct. 18, 1954; s. Max and Miriam (Postel) Weinstein; m. Annie Clayton, Apr. 29, 2000. Student, SUNY, Fredonia, 1971—73. Co-founder, co-chmn. (with Harvey Weinstein) Miramax Films Corp., NYC, 1979—2005; co-founder (with Harvey Weinstein) The Weinstein Co., 2005—. Prodr. (films) Playing for Keeps (also dir.), 1986, Gandahar, 1988, Mimic, 1997, Reindeer Games, 2000; exec. prodr. (films) Hardware, 1990, Strike It Rich, 1990, The Pope Must Die, 1991, Into the West, 1992, Benefit of the Doubt, 1993, Map of the Human Heart, 1993, The Night We Never Met, 1993, True Romance, 1993, Hour of the Pig, 1993, Mother's Boys, 1994, Road Killers, 1994, Prêt-à-Porter, 1994, The Englishman Who Went Up a Hill But Came Down a Mountain, 1995, Things to Do in Denver When You're Dead, 1995, Smoke, 1995, The Crossing Guard, 1995, A Month by the Lake, 1995, The Journey of August King, 1995, Blue in the Face, 1995, Beautiful Girls, 1996, Flirting with Disaster, 1996, The Pallbearer, 1996, Emma, 1996, I Love You, I Love You Not, 1996, The Crow: City of Angels, 1996, The English Patient, 1996, Scream, 1996, Sono pazzo di Iris Blond, 1996, Nightwatch, 1997, Addicted to Love, 1997, Robinson Crusoe, 1997, Mononoke-hime, 1997, Air Bud, 1997, Cop Land, 1997, Wings of the Dove, 1997, Good Will Hunting, 1997, Scream 2, 1997, Jackie Brown, 1997, Wishful Thinking, 1997, A Price Above Rubies, 1998, Phantoms, 1998, Senseless, 1998, Wide Awake, 1998, Ride, 1998, Velvet Goldmine, 1998, The Mighty, 1998, 54, 1998, Heaven, 1998, Rounders, 1998, Talk of Angels, 1998, The Faculty, 1998, Shakespeare in Love, 1998, Playing by Heart, 1998, She's All That, 1999, Guinevere, 1999, My Life So Far, 1999, Teaching Mrs. Tingle, 1999, Outside Providence, 1999, In Too Deep, 1999, Mansfield Park, 1999, Holy Smoke, 1999, Music of the Heart, 1999, Cider House Rules, 1999, Allied Forces, 1999, Down to You, 2000, Committed, 2000, The Crow: Salvation, 2000, Scream 3, 2000, Love's Labour's Lost, 2000, Takedown, 2000, The Yards, 2000, Boys and Girls, 2000, Scary Movie, 2000, Highlander: Endgame, 2000, Backstage, 2000, Malèna, 2000, Bounce, 2000, Chocolat, Dracula 2000, 2000, Spy Kids, 2001, Texas Rangers, 2001, Daddy and Them, 2001, Scary Movie 2, 2001, The Others, 2001, Shu shan zheng zhuan, 2001, Jay and Silent Bob Strike Back, 2001, Lord of the Rings: The Fellowship of the Ring, 2001, Shipping News, 2001, Kate & Leopold, 2001, Only the Strong Survive, 2002, Full Frontal, 2002, Spy Kids 2: Island of Lost Dreams, 2002, Below, 2002, Equilibrium, 2002, Waking Up in Reno, 2002, Lord of the Rings: The Two Towers, 2002, Gangs of New York, 2002, Chicago, 2002, Confessions of a Dangerous Mind, 2002, Spy Kids 3-D: Game Over, 2003, The Human Stain, 2003, Duplex, 2003, Kill Bill: Vol. 1, 2003, Scary Movie 3, 2003, Bad Santa, 2003, Lord of the Rings: The Return of the King, 2003, Cold Mountain, 2003, Ella Enchanted, 2004, Kill Bill: Vol. 2, 2004, Fahrenheit 9/11, 2004, Finding Neverland, 2004, Shall We Dance, 2004, The Aviator, 2004, Cursed, 2005, Sin City, 2005, The Adventures of Sharkboy and Lavagirl 3-D, 2005, The Great Raid, 2005, The Brothers Grimm, 2005, Proof, 2005, Derailed, 2005, Scary Movie 4, 2006, Pulse, 2006, others; co-exec. prodr. (films) Scandal, 1989, The Lemon Sisters, 1990, The Big Man, 1990, Dust Devil, 1992, Pulp Fiction, 1994, Victory, 1995, Jane Eyre, 1996, She's So Lovely, 1997, Halloween H20: 20 Years Later, 1998, B. Monkey, 1998, Halloween:

Resurrection, 2002; prodr. (TV series) The Real Magees, 1973, Wasteland, 1999, Clerks, 2000, Project Greenlight, 2001, Glory Days, 2002, Tokyo Pig, 2002. Named one of 50 Most Powerful People in Hollywood, Premiere mag., 2004—06.*

**WEINSTEIN, DAVID,** lawyer, educator; b. Phila., Feb. 6, 1926; s. Harry and Bertha (Berman) Weinstein; m. Florine S. Dutkin, May 18, 1952; children: Lee M., Norman J., Debra E. BS in Edn., U. Pa., 1949, MS, 1953, postgrad., 1953-55; JD, Temple U., 1959. Bar: Pa. 1960, U.S. Dist. Ct. (ea. dist.) Pa. 1960, U.S. Ct. Appeals (3d cir.) 1961; cert. tchr., ednl. adminstr. Pa. Tchr. Phila. Sch. Dist., 1952-60; legal adviser Phila. Dept. Revenue, 1960-62; pvt. practice Phila., 1962-89; ptnr. Weinstein, Goss, Katenstein, Schleifer & Eisenberg, Phila., 1989—. Prof. Coll. Boca Raton, Fla., 1989—, Lynn U., Boca Raton, 1989—2004. Mem. Temple U. Law Rev., 1958—59. Active Boynton Beach (Fla.) Edn. Adv. Com., 1993, 1996, 2005. With USAAC, 1944—45, 1st lt. U.S. Army, 1950—52. Mem.: Phila. Bar Assn. (mem. edn. com. 1982—84), Fed. Bar Assn. (fed. jud. com. Phila. 1988—89), Masons, Kappa Phi Kappa, Phi Delta Kappa. Avocations: writing, golf, tennis, bridge, woodworking. Home: 2 Northwoods Ln Boynton Beach FL 33436-7404 Office: 2001 Market St Philadelphia PA 19103-7044

**WEINSTEIN, EDWARD MICHAEL,** architect, consultant; b. Bklyn., May 5, 1947; s. Hyman and Freda (Rochkes) W.; m. Melanie Jane Ross, June 22, 1969; children: Valerie, David. BS, CCNY, 1969. Registered architect; lic., NJ; NY. Jr. architect N.Y.C. Dept. Ports and Terminals, 1970-72, architect, 1972-75, sr. urban designer, 1975-80, dir. waterfront devel., 1980-84, asst. commr., 1984-87; pres. EMW Assocs., Hastings-On-Hudson, NY, 1984—; ptnr. The Hastings Design Group, Hastings-On-Hudson, 1987—2001; prin. Edward M. Weinstein, Planning and Architecture, 2001—02, Edward M. Weinstein, Architecture and Planning, P.C., 2002—. Adv. bd. Metro Marine Express Ltd., N.Y.C., 1989-91. Active Planning Bd., Hastings-on-Hudson, 1990-2000, Waterfront Ctr.; trustee Greenburgh Hebrew Ctr., Dobbs Ferry, N.Y., 1986-89, 92—; v.p. N.Y. Port Promotion Assn., N.Y.C., 1984-87; adv. com. on waterfront devel. N.Y. State Assembly; chair Village of Hastings-on-Hudson Waterfront Revitalization Com., 1999—. Recipient Gold Key award House Plan Assn., 1969. Mem. AIA, Am. Assn. Port Authority, N.Y. Soc. Architects, The Waterfront Ctr., CCNY Alumni Assn., Bklyn. Tech. H.S. Alumni Assn. (life), Am. Inst. of Cert. Planners, Mcpl. Art Soc. Democrat. Jewish. Avocations: tennis, art. Office: EMW Architecture and Planning PC 14 Spring St Hastings On Hudson NY 10706 Office Phone: 914-478-0800, 914-478-0800. Business E-Mail: edward@emweinsteinpc.com.

**WEINSTEIN, HARRIS,** lawyer; b. Providence, May 10, 1935; s. Joseph and Gertrude (Rusitzky) W.; m. Rosa Grunberg, June 3, 1956; children: Teme Ring, Joshua, Jacob. BS in Math., MIT, 1956, MS in Math., 1958; LLB, Columbia U., 1961. Bar: D.C. 1962. Law clk. to Judge William H. Hastie U.S. Ct. Appeals (3d cir.), Phila., 1961-62; with Covington & Burling, Washington, 1962-67, 69-90, 1993—; chief counsel Office of Thrift Supervision U.S. Dept. of Treasury, Washington, 1990-92; asst. to solicitor gen. U.S. Dept. Justice, 1967-69. Pub. mem. Adminstrv. Conf. of U.S., 1982-90; lectr. U. Va. Law Sch., 1996; mgmt. com. Undiscovered Mgrs., LLC, 1998-2001. V.p. Jewish Social Svc. Agy., 1995—98; mem. MIT Corp., 1989—95; bd. dirs. Jewish Cmty. Rels. Coun. Greater Washington, 2004—. Mem. Nat. Press Club. Home: 7717 Georgetown Pike Mc Lean VA 22102-1411 Office: Covington & Burling 1201 Pennsylvania Ave NW Washington DC 20004

**WEINSTEIN, HARVEY,** film company executive, film producer; b. Queens, NY, Mar. 19, 1952; s. Max and Miriam (Postel) Weinstein; m. Eva Chilton, 1987 (div. 2004); 3 children. Student, SUNY, Buffalo, 1969—73. With Harvey & Corkey Presents, Buffalo, 1973—79; co-founder, co-chmn. (with Bob Weinstein) Miramax Films Corp., N.Y.C., 1979—2005; co-founder (with Bob Weinstein) The Weinstein Co., 2005—. Bd. dirs. Six Flags Inc., 2005—. Dir. (films) Playing for Keeps (also writer), 1986, The Gnome's Great Adventure, 1987, Gandaharm, 1988; prodr. (films) The Burning, 1981, Deep End, 1985, Playing for Keeps, 1986, Shakespeare in Love, 1998 (Academy award best picture, 1998, Golden Globe award best picture, 1998, Golden Satellite award best picture, 1998, BAFTA award best picture, 1999), Malena, 2000, Gangs of New York, 2002; exec. prodr. (films) including Hardware, 1990, Strike It Rich, 1990, The Pope Must Die, 1991, Benefit of the Doubt, 1993, Map of the Human Heart, 1993, The Night We Never Met, 1993, The Hour of the Pig, 1993, Mother's Boys, 1994, The Road Killers, 1994, Pret-a-Porter, 1994, The Englishman Who Went Up a Hill But Came Down a Mountain, 1995, Things to Do in Denver When You're Dead, 1995, Smoke, 1995, The Crossing Guard, 1995, A Month by the Lake, 1995, Blue in the Face, 1995, Beautiful Girls, 1996, Flirting With Disaster, 1996, The Pallbearer, 1996, Emma, 1996, I Love You, I Love You Not, 1996, The Crow: City of Angels, 1996, The English Patient, 1996, Nightwatch, 1997, Addicted to Love, 1997, Robinson Crusoe, 1997, Air Bud, 1997, Cop Land, 1997, The Wings of the Dove, 1997, Good Will Hunting, 1997, Scream 2, 1997, Jackie Brown, 1997, Wishful Thinking, 1997, The Prophecy II, 1998, A Price Above Rubies, 1998, Phantoms, 1998, Senseless, 1998, Wide Awake, 1998, Ride, 1998, Velvet Goldmine, 1998, The Mighty, 1998, 54, 1998, Heaven, 1998, Rounders, 1998, Talk of Angels, 1998, The Faculty, 1998, She's All That, 1999, Teaching Mrs. Tingle, 1999, Mansfield Park, 1999, Music of the Heart, 1999, The Cider House Rules, 1999, Down to You, 2000, The Crow: The Salvation, 2000, Scream 3, 2000, Love's Labour's Lost, 2000, Reindeer Games, 2000, Scary Movie, 2000, Highlander: Endgame, 2000, Bounce, 2000, Chocolat, 2000, Dracula, 2000, Spy Kids, 2001, Texas Rangers, 2001, Daddy and Them, 2001, Scary Movie 2, 2001, The Others, 2001, Jay and Silent Bob Strike Back, 2001, The Lord of the Rings: The Fellowship of the Ring, 2001, Iris, 2001, The Shipping News, 2001, Kate & Leopold, 2001, Spy Kids 2: Island of Lost Dreams, 2002, Waking Up in Reno, 2002, The Lord of the Rings: The Two Towers, 2002, Chicago, 2002, Confessions of a Dangerous Mind, 2002, Spy Kids 3-D: Game Over, 2003, The Human Stain, 2003, Duplex, 2003, Kill Bill: Vol. 1, 2003, Scary Movie 3, 2003, Bad Santa, 2003, The Lord of the Rings: The Return of the King, 2003, Cold Mountain, 2003, Ella Enchanted, 2004, The Aviator, 2004, Cursed, 2005, Sin City, 2005, The Adventures of Sharkboy and Lavagirl 3-D, 2005, The Great Raid, 2005, The Brothers Grimm, 2005, Proof, 2005, Derailed, 2005, Scary Movie 4, 2006, Pulse, 2006, others; co-exec. prodr. (films) including Scandal, 1989, The Lemon Sisters, 1990, Into the West, 1992, Pulp Fiction, 1994, Restoration, 1995, Jane Eyre, 1996, Scream, 1996, She's So Lovely, 1997, Mimic, 1997, Imposter, 2002; exec. prodr. (TV series) Clerks, 2000, Project Greenlight, 2001, Glory Days, 2002, Tokyo Pig, 2002; recipient BAFTA Britannia award (with Bob Weinstein, 1996, IFP Gotham Lifetime Achievement award (with Bob Weinstein), 1997. Named Comdr., Order of British Empire, 2004; named one of 50 Most Powerful People in Hollywood, Premiere mag., 2004—06.*

**WEINSTEIN, HERBERT,** chemical engineer, educator; b. Bklyn., Mar. 10, 1933; s. Abraham and Pauline (Feldman) W.; m. Judith Cooper, Apr. 6, 1957; children: Michael Howard, Edward Marc, Ellen Rachel. B.Engring. in Chem. Engring, Coll. City N.Y., 1955; MS in Chem. Engring, Purdue U., 1957; PhD, Case Inst. Tech., 1963. Staff mem. Los Alamos Sci. Lab., 1956-58; research engr. NASA Lewis Research Center, Cleve., 1959-63; asst. prof. chem. engring. Ill. Inst. Tech., 1963-66, assoc. prof., 1966-72, prof., 1972-77; dir. Center for Biomed. Engring., 1973-77; prof. CUNY, 1977—2005, Herbert G. Kayser prof. of chem. engring., 1987—2003, dep. exec. officer PhD program, 2003—05, prof. emeritus, 2005—. Vis. rsch. assoc., mem. Rsch. Inst. Michael Reese Hosp. and Med. Ctr., Chgo., 1965-77; vis. prof. mech. engring. Technion-Israel Inst. Tech., 1972-73; vis. prof. biomed. engring. Rush Med. Coll., Chgo., 1973-76; summer prof. Exxon Rsch. and Engring. Co., annually, 1981-92; Lady Davis vis. prof. Technion-Israel Inst. Tech., 1985; cons. to industry, rsch. labs. Mem.: Am. Inst. Chem. Engrs., Sigma Xi. Achievements include research publs. and patents on fluidization, chem. reactor engring., fluid mechanics, biomed. engring. Office: CUNY Dept Chem Engring New York NY 10031 Business E-Mail: hweinst@att.net, hweinst@ccny.cuny.edu.

**WEINSTEIN, I. BERNARD,** oncologist, director, geneticist, educator; b. Madison, Wis., Sept. 9, 1930; married, 1952; 3 children. BS, U. Wis., 1952, MD, 1955, DSc (hon.), 1992. Nat. Cancer Inst. spl. rsch. fellow bacteriology/immunology Harvard Med. Sch./MIT, Boston, 1959-61; career scientist Health Rsch. Coun., City of N.Y., 1961-72; assoc. vis. physician Francis Delafield Hosp., 1961-66; from asst. attending physician to assoc. attending physician Presbyn. Hosp., 1967-81, attending physician, 1981—; from asst. to assoc. prof. medicine Columbia U. Coll. Phys. and Surg., N.Y.C., 1978-90; prof. medicine Columbia U., N.Y.C., 1973—, prof. pub. health, 1978—, prof. genetics and devel., 1990—, Frode Jensen prof. medicine, 1990—, dir. comprehensive cancer ctr., 1985-96. Advisor Lung Cancer Segment, Carcinogenesis Program, Nat. Cancer Inst., 1971-74, Chem. and Molecular Biol. Segment, 1973-76; mem. interdisciplinary comm. program Smithsonian Inst., 1971-74, Pharmacology B Study Sect., NIH, 1971-75, numerous sci. and adv. coms. Nat. Cancer Inst., Am. Cancer Soc., 1976-88; advisor Roswell Park Meml. Inst., Buffalo, Brookhaven Nat. Lab., Divsn. Cancer Cause and Prevention, Nat. Cancer Inst., Coun. on Analysis and Projects, Am. Cancer Soc., Internat. Agy. for Rsch. on Cancer, WHO, Lyon, France; Nakasone vis. prof., Tokyo, 1987; GM Cancer Rsch. Found. vis. prof. Internat. Agy. Rsch. Cancer, Lyon, 1988; mem. adv. coun. Nat. Inst. Environ. Health Scis., 1995—; chmn. Bristol-Myers Squibb Cancer Awards, 1993-96; mem. adv. coun., GM Cancer Rsch. Found. Assoc. editor Cancer Rsch., 1973-76, 86-95, Jour. Environ. Pathology and Toxicology, 1977-84, Jour. Cellular Physiology, 1982-89, Oncogene, 1989-99, Clin. Cancer Rsch., 1998—. Named Louise Weissberger lectr., U. Rochester, 1981, Mary Ann Swetland lectr., Case Western Res. U., 1983, Daniel Laszlo Meml. lectr., Montefiore Med. Ctr., 1983, Samuel Kuna Disting. lectr., Rutgers U., 1985, Ester Langer lectr., U. Chgo., 1989, Harris Meml. lectr., MIT, 1989, Rufus Cole lectr., 1997, travel fellow, Europcan Molecular Biology Orgn., 1970—71; recipient Meltzer medal, 1964, Clowes award, Am. Assn. Cancer Rsch., 1987, Silvio O. Conte award, Environ. Health Inst., 1990, Nakahara award, 1996, Anthony Dipple Carcinogenesis award, 2000, Disting. Achievement award, Am. Soc. Preventive Oncology, 2001, Am. Assn. Cancer Rsch./Am. Cancer Soc. award, 2001, Charles Heidelberger award, 2004. Mem.: AAAS (coun. del. 1985—88), N.Y. Acad. Sci., Am. Soc. Clin. Investigation, Internat. Soc. Quantum Biology, Am. Soc. Microbiology, Am. Assn. Physicians, Am. Acad. Arts and Scis., Inst. Medicine/Nat. Acad. Sci., Am. Assn. Cancer Rsch. (pres. 1990—91). Achievements include research in cellular and molecular aspects of carcinogenesis, environmental carcinogenesis, molecular epidemiology, cancer prevention. Office: Cancer Ctr Columbia Univ 701 W 168th St New York NY 10032-2704 Office Phone: 212-305-6921. Business E-Mail: ibw1@columbia.edu.

**WEINSTEIN, JACK BERTRAND,** federal judge; b. Wichita, Kans., Aug. 10, 1921; s. Harry Louis and Bessie Helen (Brodach) W.; m. Evelyn Horowitz, Oct. 10, 1946; children: Seth George, Michael David, Howard Lewis. BA, Bklyn. Coll., 1943; LLB, Columbia U., 1948, LLD (hon.), 2004, Yeshiva U., Albany U., Hofstra U., L.I. U., Yale U., NYU. Bar: N.Y. 1949. Assoc. Columbia Law Sch., 1948-49; law clk. N.Y. Ct. Appeals Judge Stanly H. Fuld, 1949-50; ptnr. William Rosenfeld, N.Y.C., 1950-52; mem. faculty Columbia Law Sch., 1952-67, prof. law, 1956-67, adj. prof., 1967-97; U.S. judge (Eastern Dist. N.Y.), 1967-93, chief judge, 1980-88; sr. judge Ea. Dist. N.Y., 1993—. Vis. prof. U. Tex., 1957, U. Colo., 1961, Harvard U., 1982, Georgetown U., 1991, Bklyn. Law Sch., 1988-97, others; counsel N.Y. Joint Legis. Com. Motor Vehicle Problems, 1952-54, State Sen. Seymour Halpern, 1952-54; reporter adv. com. practice and procedure N.Y. State Temp. Commn. Cts., 1955-58; adv. com. practice N.Y. Judicial Conf., 1963-66; adv. com. rules of evidence U.S. Jud. Conf., 1965-75, mem. com. jurisdiction, 1969-75, mem., 1983-86; mem. 2d Cir. Jud. Coun., 1982-88, U.S. Jud. Conf., 1983-86, others in past. Author: (with Morgan and Maquire) Cases and Materials on Evidence, 4th edit, 1965, (with Maguire, Chadbourne and Mansfield, 5th edit.), 1971, 6th edit., 1975, (with Mansfield, Abrams and Berger), 9th edit., 1997, (with Rosenberg) Cases and Materials on Civil Procedure, 1961, rev. edit, (with Smit), 1971, (with Smit, Rosenberg and Korn), 1976, (with Korn and Miller) New York Civil Procedure, 9 vols., rev. edit, 1966, Manual of New York Civil Procedure, 1967, Basic Problems of State and Federal Evidence, 1976, (with Berger) Weinstein's Evidence, 7 vols., 1967, rev. edit., 1993, Revising Rule Making Procedures, 1977, A New York Constitution Meeting Today's Needs and Tomorrow's Challenges, 1967, Disaster, A Legal Allegory, 1988, (with Greenawalt) Readings for Seminar on Equality and Law, 1979, (with Murphy) Readings for Seminar in Individual Rights in a Mass Society, 1990-91, (with Berger) Readings for Seminar in Science and Law, (with Feinberg) Mass Torts, 1992, 94, Individual Justice in Mass Litigation, 1995. Chmn. N.Y. Dem. adv. com. on Constl. Conv., 1955; bd. dirs. N.Y. Civil Liberties Union, 1956-62, Cardozo Sch. Law, Conf. on Jewish Social Studies, 1980-88; nat. adv. bd. Am. Jewish Congress, 1960-67, CARE, 1985-90, Fedn. Jewish Philanthropies, 1985-94; chmn. lay bd. Riverside Hosp. Adolescent Drug Users, 1954-55. Lt. USNR, 1943-46. Mem. ABA, N.Y. State Bar Assn., Assn. of Bar of City of N.Y., Nassau County Bar Assn., Am. Law Inst., Soc. Pub. Tchrs. Law (Eng.), Am. Acad. Arts and Scis. Jewish. Office: US Dist Ct US Courthouse 225 Cadman Plz E Brooklyn NY 11201-1818

**WEINSTEIN, JAY A.,** social sciences educator, researcher; b. Chgo., Feb. 23, 1942; s. Lawrence E. and Jacqueline L. (Caplan) W.; m. Diana S. Staffin, Sept. 16, 1961; m. Marilyn L. Schwartz, Nov. 25, 1972; children— Liza, Bennett. AB, U. Ill., 1963, PhD, 1971. MA, Washington U., St. Louis, 1965. Teaching fellow U. Ill. Urbana, 1963-64; teaching asst. McGill U., Montreal, Que., Canada, 1966-68; instr. Sir George Williams U., Montreal, Que., Canada, 1967-68; lectr. Simon Fraser U., Vancouver, B.C., Canada, 1968; asst. prof. North Central Coll., Naperville, Ill., 1970-71, U. Iowa, 1973-77; prof. social sci. Ga. Inst. Tech., Atlanta, 1977-86; head dept. sociology Eastern Mich. U., 1986-90, 2004—, faculty rsch. fellow, 1990-91; grantee ednl. devel. project USIA-Soros Found., Albania, 1992—; dir. Applied Rsch. Unit, 1996—. Cons. World Bank Study Social and Econ. Vulnerability in Albania, 1997, World Bank Study on Closing the Vulnerability Gap, Albania, 1997—98; project dir. Ea. Mich.-U-Ypsilanti Cmty. Outreach Partnership Ctr.; cons. pvt. and pub. agencies; rschr. in field. Author: Madras: An Analysis of Urban Ecological Structure in India, 1974, Demographic Transition and Social Change, 1976, Sociology-Technology: Foundations of Postacademic Social Science, 1982, The Grammar of Social Relations: The Major Essays of Louis Schneider, 1984; editor: Paradox and Society, 1986; (with Vinod Tewari and V.L.S. Prakash Rao) Indian Cities: Ecological Perspectives, Social and Cultural Change: Social Science for a Dynamic World, 1997, 2005, The Holocaust: A Sociological Analysis, 1997, Demography: The Science of Population, 2000; Studies in Comparative International Development, 1978-88; mem. editorial bd. Social Development Issues, 1977-85; specialized contbr. Calcutta Mcpl. Gazette, 1979—; editor: Social and Cultural Change, 1974-75; editor Mich. Soc. Rev., 1997-2003, Jour. Applied Sociology, 2004—, editl. reviewer Jour. Asian Studies, Social Devel. Issues, Tech. and Culture, Am. Sociologist, Technol. Forecasting and Social Change; contbr. chpts. to book, articles to profl. jours. Recipient Charles Horton Cooley award for outstanding contbns. to sociology in Mich., 1998, Alex Boros award, 2005; Fulbright prof. Ahmedabad, India, 1975-76, Hyderabad, India, 1981-82; grantee Soc. Tech. Found., 1981-82, World Order Studies Course, 1994-97, State of Mich. Rsch. Excellence Fund; Steinberg fellow, 1967. Mem. Am. Sociol. Assn. (pres. 2002-03), Soc. for Applied Sociology (v.p. 1998-99, chair sociol. practice sect., 2004-05), mem. exec. bd. 2004, 2002-03), Mich. Sociol. Assn. (pres. 1988-89, v.p. 1994-95), Sigma Xi. Jewish. Office: Eastern Mich U Sociology Dept Ypsilanti MI 48197 Office Phone: 734-487-0012. E-mail: weinst@aol.com, jay.weinstein@emich.edu.

**WEINSTEIN, JOYCE,** artist; b. June 7, 1931; d. Sidney and Rose (Bier) W.; m. Stanley Boxer, Nov. 28, 1952. Student, CCNY, 1948-50, Art Students League, 1948-52. Exec. coord. Women in Arts Found., Inc., 1975-79, 81-82, coord. bd., 1983-87. One-person shows include Perdalma Gallery, N.Y.C., 1953-56, L.I. U., Bklyn., 1969, U. Calif.-Santa Cruz, 1969, T. Bortolazzo Gallery, Santa Barbara, Calif., 1972, Dorsky Gallery, N.Y.C., 1972, 74, Galerie Ariadne, N.Y.C., 1975, Gloria Cortella Gallery, N.Y.C., 1976, Meredith Long Contemporary Gallery, N.Y.C., 1978, 79, 88-90, Martin Gerard Gallery, Edmonton, Alta., Can., 1981, 82, 84, Galerie Wentzel, Cologne, Fed. Republic of Germany, 1982, 87, Haber Theodore Gallery, N.Y.C., 1983, 95, Gallery One, Toronto, Ont. Can., 1983, 2002, Paul Kuhn Gallery, Calgary, 1985, Eva Cohn Gallery, Highland Park, Ill., 1985, Meredith Long & Co., Houston, 1988, 90, Alena Adlung Gallery, N.Y.C., 1989, Flanders Contemporary Art, Mpls., 1999, 2005, Harmon-Meek Gallery, Naples, Fla., 2000, Gallery One, Toronto, 2002, Flanders Contemporary Art, Mpls., 2005; exhibited in group shows at Marlborough Gallery, N.Y.C., 1968, Bula Mus. Art, Calcutta, India, 1970, Phoenix Gallery, N.Y.C., 1988, Provident Nat. Bank, 1988, Alena Adlung Gallery, 1989, 90, Edmonton Art Mus., 1975, 77, 83, 85, 89, Rose Fried Gallery, N.Y.C., 1970, Hudson River Mus., 1971, Dorsky Gallery, 1972, 94, Suffolk Mus., Stony Brook, N.Y., 1972, N.Y. Cultural Ctr., 1973, Stamford (Conn.) Mus., 1973, Landmark Gallery, N.Y.C., 1974, Women's Interart Ctr., N.Y.C., 1974, 75, 78, New Sch. Social Rsch., N.Y.C., 1975, Bklyn. Mus., 1975, Galerie Ariadne, 1975, Mus. of Modern Art, N.Y.C., 1981, The Queens Mus. N.Y., 1984, The Centre de Creacio Contemporania, Barcelona, Spain, 1987, Fairleigh Dickinson U., Hackensack, N.J., 1976, Gloria Cortella, Inc., 1976, Northeastern U., Boston, 1977, Lehigh (Pa.) U., 1977, Meredith Long Contemporary Gallery, 1977, 78, 79, 80, Galerie Wentzel, 1981-85, Martin Gerard Gallery, 1981-84, Gallery One, 1983, 84, Haber Theodore Gallery, 1982-85, Jerald Melberg Gallery, Charlotte, N.C., 1984, Richard Green Gallery, N.Y.C., 1986, Rosel Art Fair, Basel Switzerland, 1986, Meredith Long & Co., 1988-90, Broome St. Gallery, N.Y.C., 1991, 97, Andre Zarre Gallery, N.Y.C., 1990, Cork Gallery, N.Y.C., 1990, Chgo. Internat. Art Exbn., 1990, Queens Coll. N.Y.C., 1991, Miami Art Fair, 1993, Bklyn. Botanic Gardens, 1994, Dorothy Blau Gallery, Bay Harbor Islands, Fla., 1997-98, Harmon-Meek Gallery, Naples, Fla., 1998-99, Flanders Contemporary Art, Mpls., 1999, 2005, Hubert Gallery, N.Y.C., 2003; represented in permanent collections: Pa. Acad. Fine Arts, N.J. State Mus., Ciba-Geigy Corp., New Sch. Social Rsch., Bula Mus. Art, U. Calif., Mus. Modern Art, N.Y.C., McMullen Gallery, Edmonton, Ga., De Spisset Mus., U. Santa Clara, Edmonton Art Gallery Mus., The Hines Collection, Boston, others; represented by Flanders Contemporary Art, Mpls., Gallery One, Toronto, Yellow Bird Gallery, Newburg, NY, Amy Simon Fine Art, Westport, Conn. Recipient Lambert Fund award Pa. Acad. Fine Arts, 1955, Susan B. Anthony award NOW, 1983. Home: 46 Fox Hill Rd Ancramdale NY 12503-5311 Office Phone: 518-329-0614. Personal E-mail: weinsteinjoyce@aol.com.

**WEINSTEIN, MARTA,** packaging services company executive; V.p. ops. Logo Co.; co-founder iLogistix (formerly Logistix), Fremont, Calif., 1984—, exec. v.p., v.p. ops., co-chairwoman, 1998—99, CEO, 2001—.

**WEINSTEIN, MARTIN,** aerospace transportation executive, manufacturing executive, materials scientist; b. Mar. 3, 1936; s. Benjamin and Dora (Lemo) W.; m. Sandra Rebecca Yaffie, June 5, 1961; children: Hilary Ann, Sarah Elizabeth, Joshua Aaron. BS in Metals Engring., Rensselaer Poly. Inst., 1957; MS, MIT, 1960, PhD, 1961. Mgr. materials sci. Tycolabs., Waltham, Mass., 1961-69; tech. dir. turbine support divsn. Chromalloy Am. Corp., San Antonio, 1968-71, v.p., asst. gen. mgr., 1971-74, pres., 1975-79, Chromalloy Compressor Techs., San Antonio, 1979-82; group pres. Chromalloy Gas Turbine, San Antonio, 1982-86, chmn., CEO N.Y.C., 1986—; vice chmn., exec. officer SEQUA Corp., N.Y.C., 2004—05, vice chmn., CEO, 2005—. Supervisory mng. dir. Turbine Support Europe, Tilburg, Netherlands, 1975—; bd. dirs. Turbine Support Thailand, Bankok, Chromalloy U.K., Nottingham, Eng., Internat. Coating Co., Tokyo, Japan, Chromalloy, France, Malichaud Orleans, France. Patentee diffusion coating of jet engine materials; contbr. articles to profl. jours. Bd. dirs. Jewish Fedn., 1981-85, Chamber Players of San Antonio, 1979-83, NCCJ, 1982-85, Sequa Corp., N.Y.C., 1999—, vice chmn., exec. officer, 2004; mem. vis. com. dept. metallurgy and materials sci. MIT, 1992-2001. Recipient Turner Meml. award Electrochem. Soc., 1963, Achievement award NASA, 1963; Am. Iron and Steel Inst. fellow, 1960. Mem. Am. Soc. Metals, Am. Inst. Metall. Engrs., N.Y. Acad. Sci., Sigma Xi. Home: 111 Sheffield San Antonio TX 78213-2626 Office: Chromalloy Gas Turbine Corp 200 Park Ave New York NY 10166-0005 Office Phone: 212-986-5500. Business E-Mail: mweinstein@sequa.com. E-mail: mw@chronalloy.com.

**WEINSTEIN, MARY HELEN,** musician, educator; b. Phoenix, Nov. 20, 1953; d. Marvin Seymour and Joan Haykin Weinstein; 1 child, Forrest Dylan Connor. MusB, Eastman Sch. Music, Rochester, NY, 1976; MusM, Eastman Sch. Music, 1977; tchg. credentials, nat. U., San Jose, Calif., 1993. Violin II, rank 2-4 The Galilee Orch., Tiberias, Israel, 1977—78; instr. music Western State Coll., Gunnison, Colo., 1978—79; violin I, rank 5 San Jose Symphony Orch., 1979—96; tchr. music Cmty. Sch. Music and Arts, Mountain View, Calif., 1998—. Freelance violinist, 1979—; violist New Millenium Quartet, Calif., 2005—; tchr. music Summit Charter HS, Redwood City, Calif., 2006—. Mem.: Music Tchrs. Assn. Calif., Am. Fedn. Musicians. Avocation: making beaded jewelry. E-mail: mhw440@yahoo.com.

**WEINSTEIN, MICHAEL ALAN,** political science professor; b. Bklyn., Aug. 24, 1942; s. Aaron and Grace (Sosin) W.; m. Deena Schneiweiss, May 31, 1964. BA summa cum laude, NYU, 1964; MA in Polit. Sci., Case Western Res. U., 1965, PhD, 1967. Asst. prof. polit. sci. Case Western Res. U., summer 1967, Va. Poly. Inst., 1967-68; asst. prof. Purdue U., 1968-70, assoc. prof., 1970-72, prof., 1972—; Milward Simpson disting. prof. polit. sci. U. Wyo., 1979. Author: (with Deena Weinstein) Living Sociology, 1974, The Polarity of Mexican Thought, 1976, The Tragic Sense of Political Life, 1977, Meaning and Appreciation, 1978, The Structure of Human Life, 1979, The Wilderness and the City, 1982, Unity and Variety in the Philosophy of Samuel Alexander, 1984, Finite Perfection, 1985, Culture Critique: Fernand Dumont and New Quebec Sociology, 1985, (with Helmut Loiskandl and Deena Weinstein) Georg Simmel's Scopenhauer and Nietzsche, 1986; (with Deena Weinstein) Deconstruction as Cultural History/The Cultural History of Deconstruction, 1990, La Deconstruction un Jeu Symbolique, 1990, (with Deena Weinstein) Georg Simmel: Sociological Flâmeur/Bricoleur, 1991, Photographic Realism as a Moral Practice, 1992, (with Deena Weinstein) Postmodern(ized) Simmel, 1993, (with Arthur Kroker) Data Trash: The Theory of the Virtual Class, 1994, Culture/Flesh: Explorations of Postcivilized Modernity, 1995, Peter Viereckl Reconciliation and Beyond, 1997, East/West: Globalizing Civilization, 2000, (with Deena Weinstein) Hail to the Shrub: Mediating the President, 2002, The Power of Silence and the Limits of Discourse at Oliver Wendell Holmes's Breakfast Table, 2005, The Imaginative Prose of Oliver Wendell Holmes, 2006; artist in residence Columbia Coll., 2002; mem. editl. bd. Humanitas, Social Philosophy Rsch. Book Series. Recipient Best Paper prize Midwest Polit. Sci. Assn., 1969; Guggenheim fellow, 1974-75; Rockefeller Found. humanities fellow, 1976; fellow Center Humanistic Studies, Purdue U., 1981, Lily Endowment Tchg. grant, 2001. Mem. Phi Beta Kappa. Home: 800 Princess Dr West Lafayette IN 47906-2038 Office: Dept Polit Sci Purdue U West Lafayette IN 47907 *And which is worse, to be arbitrary or to be contradictory? I have attempted to be the most consistent rationalist of all by refusing to harmonize what is irreconcilable in the name of reason.*

**WEINSTEIN, MICHAEL P.,** marine scientist, administrator; s. Jack and Beatrice Weinstein; m. Yael Sisso, Dec. 22, 1991; children: Heather Ann Campbell, Lee Thomas. BA, Hofstra U., 1966; MS, Rutgers U., 1969; PhD, Fla. State U., 1975. Pres. TEVA Environ. Associates, Millburn, 1984—96; pres., CEO NJ. Marine Sciences Consortium, Fort Hancock, 1996—. Author: Concepts and Controversies in Tidal Marsh Ecology, 2000 (Governor's Tourism Award, 2004); contbr. more than 150 to profl. jours., chapters to books. Mem. working group, bd. dirs. Nat. Transp. Rsch. Bd., Nat. Acads., Washington, 2003—04. Grantee, various fed. and state agys., 1970—. Office Phone: 732-872-1300 ext. 21.

**WEINSTEIN, MILTON CHARLES,** decision scientist, educator; b. Brookline, Mass., July 14, 1949; s. William and Ethel (Rosenbloom) W.; m. Rhonda Kruger, June 14, 1970; children: Jeffrey William, Daniel Jay. AB, AM, Harvard U., 1970, MPP, 1972, PhD, 1973. Asst. prof. John F. Kennedy Sch. Govt., Harvard U., Cambridge, Mass., 1973-76, assoc. prof., 1976-80;

prof. policy and decision scis. Harvard Sch. Pub. Health, Boston, 1980-86, Henry J. Kaiser prof. health policy and mgmt., 1986—; prof. medicine Harvard Med. Sch., Boston, 1992—; v.p. Innovus Rsch. Inc., Medford, Mass., 1998—. Adj. prof. cmty. and family medicine Dartmouth Med. Sch., Hanover, N.H., 1981-87; vis. lectr. Intermountain Health Care, Salt Lake City, 1997—; cons. U.S. Office Tech. Assessment, 1979-87, HHS, 1979—, VA, 1984-88, EPA, 1983—, New Eng. Med. Ctr., 1986-87, Intermountain Health Care, 1987—; mem. adult treatment panel Nat. Cholesterol Edn. Program, NIH; co-chair Panel on Cost-Effectiveness in Health and Medicine, USPHS, 1993-96. Author: Clinical Decision Analysis, 1980, Hypertension: A Policy Perspective, 1976, Cost-Effectiveness in Health and Medicine, 1996, Decision Making in Health and Medicine, 2001; mem. editl. bd. Med. Decision Making, 1981-94, Jour. Environ. Econs. and Mgmt., 1986-88, Jour. Clin. Oncology, 1996-99; assoc. editor Med. Decision Making, 1994-2001. NSF fellow, 1972. Mem. Inst. Medicine of NAS (com. on priorities new vaccine devel., com. to evaluate the NIH artificial heart program), Soc. Med. Decision Making (trustee 1980-82, pres. 1984-85), Internat. Health Econs. Assn., Internat. Soc. Pharmacoens. and Outcomes Rsch., Am. Med. Joggers Assn., US Speedskating (bd. dirs. 1996-00), Phi Beta Kappa.

**WEINSTEIN, PHILIP MERRILL,** lawyer; b. Providence, Nov. 12, 1942; s. Sidney and Isabelle W.; m. Nancy F. Freedman; children: Benjamin, Noah. BS, Boston U., 1965; JD, Howard U., 1968. Bar: Mass., R.I., U.S. Dist. Ct. Mass., U.S. Dist. Ct. R.I. Ptnr. Decof, Weinstein & Mandell, Providence, 1972-80; sole practice Providence, 1980-87; ptnr. Weinstein & Doren, Providence; pvt. practice. Mem. bd. trustees Gordon Sch., Providence, 1985—, Cmty. Prep Sch., Providence, 1999—; past pres. Temple Beth David. Fellow (life) RI Bar Found.; mem. ABA, Assn. Trial Lawyers Am., RI Trial Lawyers Assn, Mass. Bar Assn. (mem. exec. com., ho. of delegates, 1985-), RI Bar Assn. (mem. ho. of delegates, 1972-, mem. exec. com., v.p.), Phi Sigma Delta. Avocations: sports, flute, cooking. Office: Law Office Philip M Weinstein One Providence Washington Plz Providence RI 02903-7104 Office Phone: 401-521-3500. E-mail: pweinst@aol.com.

**WEINSTEIN, ROY,** physics professor; b. N.Y.C., Apr. 21, 1927; s. Harry and Lillian (Ehrenberg) W.; m. Janet E. Spiller, Mar. 26, 1954 (dec. 1995); children: Lee Davis, Sara Lynn; m. Gail A. Birdsell, July 26, 1996. BS, MIT, 1951, PhD, 1954, ScD (hon.), Lycoming Coll., 1981. Rsch. asst. Mass. Inst. Tech., 1951-54, asst. prof., 1956-59, Brandeis U., Waltham, Mass., 1954-56; assoc. prof. Northeastern U., Boston, 1960-63, prof. physics, 1963-82, exec. officer, chmn. grad. div. of physics dept., 1967-69, chmn. physics dept., 1974-81; spokesman MAC Detector Stanford U., 1981-82; dean Coll. Natural Scis. and Math. U. Houston, 1982-88; prof. physics, 1982—; dir. Inst. Beam Particle Dynamics U. Houston, 1985-95; assoc. dir., spokesman Tex. Ctr. for Superconductivity, 1987-89. Vis. scholar and physicist Stanford (Calif.) U., 1966-67, 81-82; bd. dirs. Perception Tech., Inc., Winchester, Mass., Omniwave Inc., Gloucester, Mass., Wincom Inc., Woburn, Mass.; cons. Vislidyne Inc., Burlington, Mass., Houston Area Rsch. Ctr., Stanford U., Hodotector Inc., Houston, Park Square Engring., Marietta, Ga., Harvard U., Cambridge, Mass., Cambridge Electron Accelerator, mem. adv. com., 1967-69; adv. com. and portfolio evaluation com. Houston Venture Ptnrs., 1990-99; chmn. bd. dirs. Xytron Corp., 1986-91; dir., mem. exec. com. Houston Area Rsch. Ctr., 1984-87; chmn. organizing com. Internat. Conf. on Meson Spectroscopy, 1974, chmn. program com., 1977, mem. organizing com., 1980; chmn. mgmt. group Tex. Accelerator Ctr., Woodlands, 1985-90; chmn. Tex. High Energy Physicists, 1989-91; keynote spkr. MIT Alumni series, 1988; permanent mem. exec. com. Large Vol. Detector (Underground Neutrino Telescope, Italy), 1988—; organizer session High Temperature Superconducting Magnets 3d and 4th World Congress on Superconductivity, Munich, 1993, Orlando, 1994. Author: Atomic Physics, 1964, Nuclear Physics, 1964, Interactions of Radiation and Matter, 1964; editor: Nuclear Reactor Theory, 1964, Nuclear Materials, 1964; editor procs.: 5th Internat. Conf. on Mesons, 1977; contbr. over 200 articles to profl. jours. Active Lexington (Mass.) Town Meeting, 1973-84; vice chmn. Lexington Coun. on Aging, 1977-83. With USNR, 1945-46. Recipient Founders award World Congress Superconductivity, 1988, Materials/Devices award Internat. Superconductivity Technology Ctr., Japan, and Materials Rsch. Soc., U.S., 1995, High Current award, 1997, Excellence award for great achievements in the field of bulk superconducting materials Internat. Program Com. Processing and Applications of Large Superconducting Rare Earth Grains Worshop, 1999, NSF Rsch. awards, 1961-96, Tex. Rsch. award, 1986-87, 90—, U.S. Dept. Energy award 1974, 77, 87-97, NASA award, 1990-98, 2004—, ARO award, 1994—, Elec. Power Rsch. Inst. award, 1990-95, Welch Found. award, 1997—, Nat. Cancer Inst. award, 2000—; NSF fellow Bohr Inst., Copenhagen, 1959-60, Stanford U. 1969-70, Guggenheim fellow Harvard U., 1970-71. Fellow Am. Phys. Soc. (organizer session SSC and High Energy Physics 1984); mem. Am. Assn. Physics Tchrs., Masons, Sigma Xi, Phi Kappa Phi (chpt. pres. 1977-79, Nat. Triennial Disting. Scholar prize 1980-83), Pi Lambda Phi (pres. Theta chpt. 1949-50). Unitarian Universalist. Achievements include measurement of fine structure of positronium; first measurement of rho meson coupling to gamma rays, of phi meson decay to two muons; early observation of break down in SU3 symmetry; demonstration of electron-muon universality, discovery of non-applicability of Lorentz contraction to length measured by a single observer; disproof of splitting of A2 meson; independent discovery of upsilon meson (bottom quark); achievement of highest magnetic field for any permanent magnet, in YBa2Cu307, 10.1 Tesla; achievement of highest current density in textured superconductor, 0.8 megA/cm2; development of MILD pinning centers for high temperature superconductors. Home: 4368 Fiesta Ln Houston TX 77004-6603 Office: U Houston IBPD 632 SR1 Houston TX 77204-5005 Office Phone: 713-743-3608. Business E-Mail: weinstein@uh.edu.

**WEINSTEIN, SIDNEY,** retired university program director; b. NYC, July 1, 1920; s. Jacob and Yetta W.; m. Celia Kahn, June 6, 1943 (dec.); children: Risa, Jeri; m. Florence Landau, June 21, 1988. BA, Bklyn. Coll., 1951; MA, Columbia U., 1955; DPA, Indsl. Coll. Armed Forces, 1964. Contract adminstr. U.S. Corps Engrs., 1941-43; mgmt. analyst Dept. Army, N.Y.C., 1946-55; dir. data processing procurement GSA, 1956-68, dep. asst. commr. automated data mgmt. services Washington, 1968-72, asst. commr. automated data and telecommunications, 1972-75; exec. dir. Assn. Computing Machinery, N.Y.C., 1975-85; assoc. dir. affiliates program Ctr. Research Info. Systems, Leonard N. Stern. Sch. Bus. NYU, 1985-99, ret., 1999. Cons. to chmn. U.S. CSC. Served with USAF, 1943-46. Recipient Exceptional service award, U.S. Govt., 1975. Mem. ABA (arbitrator 1989—), Coun. Engring. and Sci. Soc. Execs. (dir.), N.Y. Soc. Assn. Execs., Assn. Indsl. Coll. Armed Forces, Assn. Fed. Execs. Inst., Assn. Computing Machinery, Soc. Info. Mgmt. Home: 360 E 72nd St New York NY 10021-4753 Personal E-Mail: s_weinstein@msn.com.

**WEINSTEIN, SIDNEY,** neuropsychologist; b. Apr. 27, 1922; s. Celia (Schneider) W.; children: Curt, Karen, Laura; m. Margaret Carla Diamond, July 28, 1968; children: Ethan, Ari. BS, CCNY, 1949; MA in Exptl. Psychology, NYU, 1950, PhD in Physiol. Psychology, 1952. Lic. psychologist, N.Y., Conn. Dir. neuropsychol. lab., rsch. assoc. prof. Albert Einstein Coll. Medicine, N.Y.C., 1958-66, rsch. asst. prof. dept. neurology, 1958-60, rsch. assoc. prof. neurology, 1960-66; rsch. assoc. neuropsychology Bronx Mcpl. Hosp. Ctr., 1958-66; pres. NeuroCommunication Rsch. Labs., Inc., Danbury, Conn., 1974-77, CEO, 1977—. Vis. asst. prof. NYU, 1958-64, adj. clin. prof. dept. neurology, 1975—; vis. assoc. prof. Yeshiva U., 1960-67; adj. prof. CUNY, 1966—; lectr. Mt. Sinai Sch. Medicine, 1966—; prof. dept. pediat. N.Y. Med. Coll., N.Y.C., 1967-80, prof., dir. neuropsychol. lab. N.Y. Med. Coll.-Flower and Fifth Ave. Hosps., 1967-73. Author: (with others) Somatosensory Changes After Penetrating Brain Wounds in Man, 1960; The Neuropsychology of Alcohol Ingestion, 1970; editor-in-chief Internat. Jour. Neuroscience; editor Neuroscience Monographs; contbr. articles to profl. jours. Mem. bd. dirs. Neuropsychol. Rsch. Found., Danbury 1974—. Decorated knight of honor and merit Imperial Order St. John Jerusalem Ecumenical. Mem. AAAS, APA (pres. divsn. physiol. and comparative psychology 1963), Internat. Coun. Psychologists; mem. AAUP, Eastern Psychol. Assn., Soc. Cosmetic Chemists, Am. Acad. Neurology, Psychonomic

---

Soc., Acad. Aphasia (bd. govs. 1966-70), Internat. Neuropsychol. Soc. (bd. govs. 1980-82), Soc. Rsch. Child Devel., Assn. Am. Med. Colls., European Brain and Behavior Soc. (charter), Soc. Neuroscience (charter), Soc. Psychophysiol. Rsch., Internat. Soc. Bioengineering and Skin, Dermal Clin. Evaluation Soc. (charter), Conn. Psychol. Assn., N.Y. Acad. Scis., N.Y. State Psychol. Assn. (mem. divsn. exec. com. 1965-68), N.Y. Brain Function Group (charter, scribe 1964), Sigma Xi, Psi Chi. Address: 2300 Cherry Laurel Ln Chapel Hill NC 27516-8306

**WEINSTEIN, STANLEY,** Buddhist studies educator; b. Bklyn., Nov. 13, 1929; s. Louis Arthur and Ruth (Appleson) W.; m. Lucie Ruth Krebs, Sept. 23, 1951; 1 son, David Eli. BA, Komazawa U., Tokyo, 1954-58; MA, U. Tokyo, 1960; PhD, Harvard U., 1966; MAH (hon.), Yale U., 1974. Lectr. Sch. Oriental and African Studies, London, 1962-68; assoc. prof. Buddhist studies Yale U., New Haven, 1968-74, prof., 1974—, prof. emeritus, 2003—, chmn. coun. East Asian studies, 1982-85. Author: Buddhism under T'ang, 1987. Served with U.S. Army, 1952-54. Ford Found. fgn. area fellow, 1958-62; NEH sr. fellow, 1974-75 Mem. Am. Oriental Soc., Assn. Asian Studies Home: 270 Ridgewood Ave Hamden CT 06517-1426 Business E-Mail: stanley.weinstein@yale.edu.

**WEINSTEIN, STEPHEN BRANT,** communications executive, researcher, writer; b. NYC, Nov. 25, 1938; s. Max S. and Evelyn A. (Brandt) W.; m. Judith Louise Benham, June 10, 1961; children: Brant M., Anna M. SB, MIT, 1960; MS, U. Mich., 1962; PhD, U. Calif. at Berkeley, 1966. Mem. tech. staff Philips Rsch. Labs., Eindhoven, The Netherlands, 1967-68, Bell Labs., Holmdel, N.J., 1968-79; v.p. tech. strategy Am. Express Co., N.Y.C., 1979-84; exec. dir. subscriber systems rsch. Bellcore, Morristown, N.J., 1984-93; fellow, mgr. comm. tech. rsch. C&C Rsch. Lab., NEC USA, Inc., 1994—2001; pres. Comm. Theory & Tech. Cons., 2002—. Editor-in-chief KICS Jour. Comms. and Networks, 1999-2001; adj. prof. Columbia U., 2002—. Author: Getting the Picture: A Guide to CATV and the New Electronic Media, 1986, The Multimedia Internet, 2005; co-author: Data Communication Principles, 1992; contbr. articles to profl. jours.; patentee in field. Recipient Basic Rsch. award, Eduard Rhein Found., 2006. Fellow IEEE (div. III dir. 2002-03, chmn. Press 1979-82, Centennial medal 1984), IEEE Comms. Soc. (pres. 1996-97, v.p. tech. affairs 1994-95, dir. publs. 1990-93, chief info. officer 2006—, editor-in-chief Comms. mag. 1984-89). Avocations: skiing, digital photography. Home and Office: 150 Woodland Ave Summit NJ 07901-2029 Personal E-Mail: s.weinstein@ieee.org.

**WEINSTEIN, STEVEN D.,** lawyer; b. Phila, May 3, 1946; s. Leon and Elizabeth (Evantash) W.; m. Karin Elkis, Feb. 16, 1986. BA, Rutgers U., 1968, JD, 1975. Bar: NJ 1975, Pa. 1975, US Dist. Ct. 1975, US Dist. Ct. (ea. dist.) Pa. 1975, US Supreme Ct. 1979, US Ct. Appeals (3d cir.) 1981, US Ct. Claims 1986, US Dist. Ct. (NJ) (mediator). Assoc. Lewis Katz P.C., Cherry Hill, NJ, 1975-78; pvt. practice law Collingswood, NJ, 1978-84; ptnr. Blank Rome LLP, Cherry Hill, 1984—. Counsel Camden County, NJ, 1982—84. Trustee Camden County Coll., Blackwood, NJ, 1983, West Jersey Hosp. Found., Camden, 1984-96, chmn. 1989-91, Rowan Coll., NJ, 1990-96, chmn. 1992-94, trustee devel. fund. bd., 1989-90; mem. N.J. Bus. Higher Edn. Forum; mem. cmty. impact bd. United Way of Camden County, 2004—; bd. dir. N.J. Alliance for Action, Inst. Effective Governance, Washington, D.C. Mem.: NJ County Counsels Assn. (pres. 1983), Haddonfield Bd. Edn. (v.p. 2002—), Camden County Bar Assn., Israel-Am. Affiliates (South Jersey chpt.), Ben Gurion U. of the Negev (chair 1998—2002), NJ Higher Edn. Alliance (chair), NJ Governing Bd. Assn. (sec. 1993—94, vice-chair 1996). Democrat. Jewish. Office: Blank Rome LLP Woodland Falls Corporate Park 210 Lake Dr E Ste 200 Cherry Hill NJ 08002-1163 Office Phone: 856-779-3601. Business E-Mail: weinstein@blankrome.com.

**WEINSTEIN-BACAL, STUART ALLEN,** lawyer, educator; b. Stuttgart, Germany, May 23, 1948; s. Marvin Stuart and Mae (Beal) W.; m. Holly Laurette Thompson, Aug. 7, 1982; children: Rachel Lee, Maximillian II, Sarah Nicole. BA, U. Va., 1970, MEd, 1973; JD cum laude, U. Miami, 1979. Bar: D.C. 1979, Va. 1981, V.I. 1985, P.R. 1988. Tchr., pvt. tutor various schs., Conn., Fla., Costa Rica, 1973-76; mem. prof. staff Merchant Marine and Fisheries Com. U.S. Ho. of Reps., Washington, 1978; assoc. Cameron, Hornbostel & Adelman, Washington, 1979-80, Burch, Kerns & Klimek, PC, Washington, 1980-81; staff atty. C.A.C.I., Washington, 1982-83; sr. assoc. Dudley, Dudley & Topper, St. Thomas, U.S. Virgin Islands, 1984-85; v.p., gen. counsel Redondo Construction Corp., San Juan, PR, 1985-89; founder Indiano, Williams & Weinstein-Bacal, San Juan, PR, 1989-2000; owner Weinstein-Bacal & Miller, P.S.C., Old San Juan, PR, 2000—. Contbr. articles to profl. jours. Capt. USAR, 1970-85. Mem. ABA, Am. Arbitration Assn. (pres., Caribbean region adv. coun. 1988—, arbitrator 1989—), Res. Officers Assn., Colegio de Abogados de P.R., U. Va. Alumni Assn., Nature Conservancy, Sovereign Order of the Oak (knight comdr.), Rotary Club of San Juan (bd. dirs. 1991-95), Middlebury Tennis Club, Bankers Club P.R., Loudoun Golf & Country Club, Phi Alpha Delta. Avocations: sailing, golf, tennis, riding, gourmet cooking. Home: Villas Del Mar E # 7D Carolina PR 00979 also: Mallory Chase Farm 35919 Turkey Roost Rd Middleburg VA 20117-3401 Office: Gonzalez Padin Bldg-Penthouse 154 Rafael Cordero St Plz Armas Old San Juan PR 00901 Office Phone: 787-977-2550. Personal E-mail: swb@hotmail.com. Business E-Mail: swb@w-bmlaw.com.

**WEINSTOCK, GEORGE DAVID,** financial services company executive; b. Vienna, Jan. 31, 1937; came to U.S., 1940; s. Paul and Ernestine Esther (Stark) W.; m. Lorna Smith, July 17, 1965; children: Pamela Ellen, Andrea Joan. AB, Columbia U., 1958, BSEE, 1959, MS, 1962; cert., Coll. for Fin. Planning, Denver, 1985. cert. fin. planner. Sr. engr. ITT, Nutley, N.J., 1959-61; sr. mem. tech. staff RCA, N.Y.C., 1961-65; project dir. Computer Scis. Co., Paramus, N.J., 1965-69; v.p., dir., sec. Ultimacc Systems, Inc., Maywood, N.J., 1969-78; v.p. Satnick Devel. Group, Hoboken, N.J., 1978-84; sr. v.p. Knitwaves, Inc., Moonachie, N.J., 1984-85; chmn. bd. Bancroft Group, Inc., Paramus, 1985-88; pres. Atrium Adv. Group, Inc., Paramus, 1990—. Mem. faculty Fairleigh Dickinson U., Baruch Coll., Coll. Fin. Planning. Author: System 360/DOS Operation, 1971, Multi-Taxation of Retirement Plans, 1991, Retirement Planning and Employee Benefits, 1992, Solving the Pre-59 1/2 Distribution Ten Percent Penalty Tax, 1992. Com. mem. United Jewish Cmty. Bergen County, 1988; pres. N.J. Estate Planning Coun., 1993-95, trustee, 1995—. Mem. IEEE, Inst. for CFPs, Nat. Assn. Accts. Jewish. Home and Office: Atrium Adv Group Inc 6th Fl 400 Kelby St Fort Lee NJ 07024 Personal E-Mail: georgelorn@aol.com.

**WEINSTOCK, HAROLD,** lawyer; b. Stamford, Conn., Nov. 30, 1925; s. Elias and Sarah (Singer) W.; m. Barbara Lans, Aug. 27, 1950; children—Nathaniel, Michael, Philip. BS magna cum laude, N.Y. U., 1947; JD, Harvard, 1950. Bar: Conn. bar 1950, Ill. bar 1950, Calif. bar 1958. Atty. SEC, Washington, 1950-52, IRS, 1952-56; tax atty. Hunt Foods & Industries, Inc., Los Angeles, 1956-58; pvt. practice Beverly Hills, Calif., 1958-71, Los Angeles, 1971—; mem. Weinstock, Manion, Reisman, Shore & Neumann (and predecessor firms), 1958—. Lectr. extension divsn., estate planning courses U. Calif., LA, 1969-86; estate planning and vacation courses Calif. Continuing Edn. of the Bar, 1960-87. Author: Planning An Estate, 4th edit., 2002; contbr. articles to profl. publs. Nat. trustee Union Am. Hebrew Congregations, 1976-79; trustee Jewish Cmty. Found., L.A., 1993-99; adv. bd. Estate Planning Inst. UCLA Law Sch., 1979-92, NYU Inst. on Fed. Taxation, 1986-95. Mem. ABA, Calif. Bar Assn., Beverly Hills Bar Assn. (chmn. probate and trusts com. 1967-68), LA Bar Assn., Beverly Hills Estate Planning Council (pres. 1968-69), Estate Counselors Forum of LA (pres. 1963-64) Jewish (pres. temple 1974-76). Office: Weinstock Manion 1875 Century Park E Fl 15 Los Angeles CA 90067-2501

**WEINSTOCK, LEONARD,** lawyer; b. Bklyn., Aug. 18, 1935; s. Samuel Morris and Evelyn (Reiser) W.; m. Rita Lee Itkowitz, May 25, 1963; children: Gregg Douglas, Valerie Lisa, Tara Diane. BS, Bklyn. Coll., 1956; JD, St. John's U., Bklyn., 1959. Bar: N.Y. 1961, U.S. Supreme Ct. 1964, U.S. Ct. Appeals (2d cir.) 1963, U.S. Dist. Ct. (ea. and so. dists.) N.Y. 1963, U.S. Tax Ct. 1963. Assoc. Bernard Helfenstein law practice, Bklyn., 1962-63; supr. All

---

State Ins. Co., Bklyn., 1963-64; atty. Hertz Corp., N.Y.C., 1964-65; ptnr. Nicholas & Weinstock, Flushing, NY, 1965-68; v.p., ptnr. Garbarini & Scher, P.C., N.Y.C., 1968—. Lectr. Practicing Law Inst., N.Y.C., 1975—; arbitrator Nassau County Dist. Ct., Mineola, N.Y., 1979—, U.S. Dist. Ct. (ea. dist.) N.Y. 1986—; mem. Med. Malpractice Mediation Panel, Mineola, 1978—. Legal counsel Massapequa Soccer Club, N.Y., 1981—; county committeeman Dem. Party, Massapequa Park, N.Y., 1979—. With U.S. Army, 1959-62. Mem. ABA, N.Y. State Bar Assn., Nassau County Bar Assn. (mem. med. jurisprudence ins. com. 1978), N.Y. Trial Lawyers Assn. Avocations: stamp collecting/philately, softball, racquetball. Home: 38 Barstow Rd Great Neck NY 11021-2218 Office: Garbarini and Scher PC 432 Park Ave S New York NY 10016-8013 Office Phone: 212-689-1113.

**WEINSTOCK, ROBERT,** physics professor; b. Phila., Feb. 2, 1919; s. Morris and Lillian (Hirsch) W.; m. Elizabeth Winch Brownell, Apr. 22, 1950; children: Frank Morse, Robert B. Weinstock-Collins. AB, U. Pa., 1940; PhD, Stanford U., 1943. Instr. physics Stanford U., Calif., 1943—44, instr. math., 1946—50, acting asst. prof. math., 1950—54; rsch. assoc. radar countermeasures Radio Rsch. Lab. Harvard U., Cambridge, Mass., 1944—45; asst. prof. U. Notre Dame, Ind., 1954—58, assoc. prof. math., 1958—59; vis. assoc. prof. math. Oberlin Coll., Ohio, 1959—60, assoc. prof., 1960—66, prof. physics, 1966—83, emeritus prof., from 1983. Author: Calculus of Variations, 1952; contbr. numerous tech. articles to profl. jours. Fellow AAAS, Ohio Acad. Sci.; mem. ACLU, Am. Assn. Physics Tchrs., Am. Phys. Soc., History of Sci. Soc., Brit. Soc. for the History of Sci., Sigma Xi. Avocations: concert going, reading. Home: Oberlin, Ohio. Died 2006.

**WEINSTOCK, ROSE,** artist; b. N.Y.C., July 12, 1931; d. Jack and Dorothy (Rosenthal) Himoff; m. Seymour Weinstock, June 25, 1953 (dec.); children: Martin, Amy, Ronald. BA, Wellesley Coll., 1953. Artist, N.Y.C. Mem. N.Y. com. Friends of Art, 1984. One-woman shows include Art Upstairs Gallery, East Williston, N.Y., 1987, Oakeside-Bloomfield Cultural Ctr., Bloomfield, N.J., 1990, Pen and Brush Club, Inc., N.Y.C., 1995, 1999, Arts Club Washington, 2001, Interchurch Ctr., N.Y.C., 2002, Blue Mountain Gallery, 2004, Port Washington Libr., NY, 2006, exhibitions include Guild Hall, East Hampton, N.Y., 1990, Nat. Acad. Design, N.Y.C., 1990, Port Washington Pub. Libr., 1991, Bowery Gallery, N.Y.C., 1991, Benjamin Rosenthal Libr., Flushing, N.Y., 1991, Wright Gallery, Kennebunkport, Maine, 1992, Salmagundi Club, N.Y.C., 1992, Washington and Lee Univ. Gallery, Lexington, Va., 1993, Great Neck Libr., N.Y., 1993, Heckscher Mus., Huntington, N.Y., 1993, Union Gallery, Stony Brook, N.Y., 1994, Greater Lafayette Mus. Art, Ind., 1996, Eleftherias Pk. Art Ctr., Athens, Greece, 1996, Nat. Acad. Design, N.Y.C., 1996, Sheldon Swope Mus. Art, Terre Haute, Ind., 1997, C.W. Post Coll., Brookville, N.Y., 1998, Longview Art Mus., Tex., 1998, N.J. Ctr. for Visual Arts, Summit, 1999, 2000, The Flinn Gallery, Greenwich, Conn., 2001. Recipient Gladys Svc. award, Heckscher Mus., 1985, 1990, Medal of Honor Audrey Hope Shirk Meml. award, Nat. Assn. Women Artists, 1991, Beatrice Jackson Meml. award, 1995, Medal of Honor, 2003, Elizabeth Stanton Blake Meml. award, 2003, William Meyerowitz Meml. award, Salmagundi Club N.Y.C., 1997, Salmagundi Club award, Nat. Arts Club, N.Y.C., 1997, Curator's Choice award, Phoenix Gallery, N.Y.C., 1998, Peoples' Choice award, Cahterine Lorillard Wolfe Art Club, N.Y.C., 2001; fellow, Tyrone Guthrie Ctr., Ireland, 1999, Vt. Studio Ctr., 1998, 2000, 2001, 2003, 2004, 2005, 2006. Mem.: Cahterine Lorillard Wolfe Arts Club, Artist's Equity, Audubon Artists, Nat. Assn. Women Artists. Home: 35 East 75th St #7C New York NY 10021 Mailing: Blue Mountain Gallery 530 W 25th St 4th Fl New York NY 10001 Office Phone: 212-439-0187. Business E-Mail: roseweinstock@alum.wellesley.edu.

**WEINSTOCK, WALTER WOLFE,** systems engineer; b. Phila., Aug. 18, 1925; s. Abraham and Jeanne (Feldman) W.; m. Doris Alpert, Sept. 21, 1946; children— Steven Eric, Bruce Alan. BSE.E., U.Pa., 1946, MSE.E., 1954, PhD, 1964. Design engr. Philco, 1946-49; with RCA Corp., 1949-87; prin. scientist RCA Corp. (Missile and Surface Radar div.), Moorestown, N.J., 1979-87; cons., 1987—. Mem. planning and steering adv. group Surface Ship Security Panel, Dept. Navy, 1979-82 Contbg. author: Modern Radar, 1965, Practical Phased Array Antenna Systems, 1991; contbr. articles to profl. jours. Recipient David Sarnoff award for Outstanding Achievement in Enrging. RCA, 1972 Fellow IEEE (Pioneer Recognition award 2004); mem. Tau Beta Pi, Eta Kappa Nu, Sigma Tau, Pi Mu Epsilon. Achievements include patents in field. Home: 6 Beryl Rd Cheltenham PA 19012-1206 E-mail: walt1925@earthlink.net.

**WEINSTOCK RAD, KATHERYN LOUISE,** music educator; d. Henry Robert and Jeanallan Joyce Weinstock; m. Jalal Rad, Aug. 23, 1993; 1 child, Jason Shyaan Rad. Aux. music study, U. Birmingham, England, 1983—84, U. Keele, Staffordshire/Newcastle, 1983—84; MusB, U. Tulsa, 1985, MusM, 1988. Cert. Okla. Tchr. Cert. State of Okla., 1988. Cellist Signature Symphony Okla. Sinfonia, Tulsa, 1982—, Tulsa (Okla.) Philharm., 1982—; adj. cello instr. Northeastern State U, Tahlequah, Okla., 1988—90; music tchr. Tulsa Pub. Sch., 1989—96; dir. of strings, tchr. Broken Arrow (Okla.) Pub. Sch., 1996—99; music curriculum coord. Tulsa Pub. Sch., 1999—2002; music coord. Tulsa Cmty. Music Sch., 2003; adj. cello instr. Performing Arts Ctr. Edn. Tulsa C.C., 2000—; fine arts coord. Cent. High Sch. Acad. Arts, 2003—. Mem. bd. fine arts task force Tulsa Pub. Sch., 1996—; adv. Barthelmes Conservatory, 2000—02; bd. mem. Chamber Music Tulsa(Okla.), 2001—; performer cellist Tulsa Philharmonic, Tulsa Signature Symphony, Okla. City Philharmnic; prin. cellist Light Opera Orchestra of Okla.; performer has performed with many classical, pop/rock, jazz and blues artists, including a live performance on NPR. Grandstand, judge Vet. Day Parade, Tulsa, 1999—2002; mem. Tulsa Now Task Force - Mayor Bill Fortune, 2002—; fundraiser raised over one half million dollars music programs Tulsa Pub. Schs. Recipient Tchr. Touching Tomorrow Award, Tulsa Pub. Sch., 1996, Superior Civilian Svc. Award, Dept. of the U.S. Army, 1999—2000; grantee VH-1 save the Music Grant, VH-1, 2001, U.S. Dept. Edn., 2002, music study at Internat. Music Workshops in Graz, Austria, Found. for Tchrs., 2004. Mem.: Hyetchka, Am. Federation of Musicians. Avocations: playing cello in variety of genres, cooking, exercise. Home: 630 Pioneer Rd Sapulpa OK 74066 Office: Tulsa Central HS Acad Fine Arts 3101 W Edison Tulsa OK 74127 Office Phone: 918-833-8492. Business E-Mail: radka@tulsaschools.org.

**WEINTRAUB, JOSEPH BARTON,** publishing executive; b. Phila., Dec. 2, 1945; s. George and Edith (Lubner) W.; m. Denise Waters, June 14, 1974. BA, U. Pitts., 1966; MA, U. Chgo., 1967, PhD, 1973. Assoc. faculty U. Ind., Gary, Ind., 1970-74; mktg. specialist journalism div. U. Chgo. Press, 1974-75, sr. copywriter journalism div., 1975-78; periodical specialist ABA, Chgo., 1978-80, mktg. mgr., 1980-92, dir. publ. planning, 1992-97, dir. book publ., 1997-99; mgr. dir. mktg. U. Chgo. Press, 1999—. Writer You, 2000; contbr. essays, translations, plays, poems, short fiction to lit. revs. and small press anthologies. Recipient award Literary awards, Ill. Art Coun., 1984-2004, Barrington Art Coun. Mem. Phi Beta Kappa. Avocations: writing, language study, running. Office: U Chgo Press 1427 E 60th Street Chicago IL 60637-5418

**WEINTRAUB, NEAL L.,** medical educator, cardiologist; Student, Tulane u., 1977-80, MD, 1984. Diplomate Am. Bd. Internal Medicine, Am. Bd. Cardiovasc. Diseases. Resident Emory U., Atlanta, 1984-86, U. Ill., Urbana-Champaign, 1986-87, clin. instr. medicine Coll. Medicine, 1987-88, asst. clin. prof. medicine Coll. Medicine, 1988-90; staff physician VA Med. Ctr., Danville, Ill., 1987-90, St. Louis, 1990-91; asst. prof. medicine St. Medicine St. Louis U., 1990-95, postdoctoral fellow clin. pharmacology, 1992-94; asst. cardiology divsn. U. Iowa Coll. Medicine, Iowa City, 1995-97, assoc. prof. cardiology, 1997—. Contbr. articles to profl. jours. Recipient Travel award Am. Coll. Cardiology/Bristol-Myers Squibb, 1994, Clinician Scientist award Am. Heart Assn., 1996. Mem. Alpha Omega Alpha. Achievements include research in vascular biology and physiology and lipid biochemistry. Office: U Iowa Coll Medicine CV Div Dept Internal Medicine 200 Hawkins Dr Iowa City IA 52242-1009

**WEINTRAUB, RUSSELL JAY,** lawyer, educator; b. N.Y.C., Dec. 20, 1929; s. Harry and Alice (Lieberman) W.; m. Zelda Kresshover, Sept. 6, 1953; children: Sharon Hope, Harry David, Steven Ross. BA, NYU, 1950; JD, Harvard U., 1953. Bar: N.Y. 1955, Iowa 1961, Tex. 1980. Tchg. fellow Harvard U. Law Sch., 1955-57; asst. prof. law U. Iowa, 1957-61, prof., 1961-65, U. Tex., 1965—, Marrs McLean prof. law, 1970-80, Bryant Smith chmn., 1980-82, John B. Connally chmn., 1982-98, Powell chmn., 1998—2003, emeritus, 2004—. Vis. prof. law U. Mich., 1965, UCLA, 1967, U. Calif., Berkeley, 1973-74, Bklyn. Law Sch., 1990, 95, Inst. Internat. Comparative Law, Paris, 1975, Florence, Italy, 1997, Barcelona, 1999, 2002, London, 2000, U. Houston, 1979-80, Inst. Internat. and Comparative Law, Oxford, Eng., 1982-83, 86-87, 92, 2003, Dublin, Ireland, 1991, La. State U., Aix-en-Provence, France, 1993, Tulane U., Spetses, Greece, 1998, Australian Nat. U., 2001; Ronald Graveson Meml. lectr. King's Coll., London, 2000; lectr. Hague Acad. Internat. Law, 1984; cons. U.S. Dept. State, 1995-2000, European Union Parliament, 2005; cons. in field. Author: International Litigation and Arbitration, 1994, 5th rev. edit., 2006, ann. supplement; (with Eugene Scoles) Cases and Materials on the Conflict of Laws, 1967, 2d rev. edit., 1972, supplement, 1978, Commentary on the Conflict of Laws, 1971, 5th rev. edit., 2006, ann. supplement; (with Hamilton and Rau) Cases and Materials on Contracts, 1984, 2d rev. edit., 1992; (with Hay and Borchers) Cases and Materials on the Conflict of Laws, 12th rev. edit., 2004, annual supplement; contbr. articles to profl. jours. Trustee U. Iowa Sch. Religion, 1960-65. With U.S. Army, 1953-55. Recipient Disting. Prof. award U. Tex. Sch. Law, 1977, Teaching Excellence award, 1979, cert. of meritorious service Am. Bar Assn., 1977, cert. of meritorious service Tex. Bar Assn., 1978, Best Tchr. award U. Houston, 1980, Carl Fulda award scholarship in internat. law, 1993. Mem. Am. Law Inst., Am. Bar Found. (life), Tex. Bar Found. (life), Scribes. Jewish. Office: U Tex Sch Law 727 E Dean Keeton Austin TX 78705-3224 Office Phone: 512-232-1370. E-mail: rweintraub@law.utexas.edu. *The only true happiness lies in useful work done to the best of your ability.*

**WEINTRAUB, SIDNEY,** economist, educator; b. NYC, May 18, 1922; s. Reuben and Anna Weintraub; m. Gladys Katz, Aug. 11, 1946; children: Jeffrey, Marcia Weintraub Plunkett, Deborah Weintraub Chilewich. BBA, CCNY, 1943; B, MA in Journalism, U. Mo., 1948; MA in Econs., Yale U., 1958; PhD in Econs., U. Mo., 1966. Commd. fgn. svc. officer Dept. State, 1949, dep. asst. sec. of state for internat. fin. and devel. Washington, 1969-74; asst. adminstr. for interagy. devel. coordination AID, 1974-75, exec. dir. interagy. devel. coordination com., 1974-75; ret., 1975; sr. fellow Brookings Instn., Washington, 1978-79; Dean Rusk prof. Lyndon B. Johnson Sch. Pub. Affairs, U. Tex., Austin, 1976-96, prof. emeritus, 1996, also co-dir. Program for U.S.-Mex. Policy Studies; William E. Simon chair in polit. economy Ctr. Strategic and Internat. Studies, 1993—. Disting. vis. scholar Ctr. for Strategic and Internat. Studies, Washington, 1990. Author: Free Trade with Mexico, 1984, A Marriage of Convenience: Relations Between Mexico and The United States, 1990, NAFTA: What Comes Next, 1994, NAFTA at Three: A Progress Report, 1997, Financial Decision-Making in Mexico: To Bet a Nation, 2000, Commentaries on International Political Economy: Constructive Irreverence, 2004, NAFTA's Impact on North America: The First Decade, 2004; contbr. articles to profl. jours. Served with U.S. Army, 1943-46. Recipient Disting. Career Svc. award AID, 1975 Mem.: Am. Econ. Assn., Am. Fgn. Service Assn., Coun. on Fgn. Rels., Cosmos (Washington). Office: Ctr Strategic and Internat Studies 1800 K St NW Washington DC 20006-2202 Home: Apt 2E 3900B Watson Pl NW Washington DC 20016 Personal E-mail: sxw1@erols.com. Business E-Mail: sweintraub@csis.org. E-mail: sidney.weintraub@csis.org *Once having been thrust into the Second World War, my main intellectual interest has been in foreign affairs. I had concluded, as President Kennedy did later, that domestic issues can hurt but misplaced foreign policy can kill. My drive has been to understand what motivates nations, what stimulates people within different nations, what is the U.S. national interest, and to become as expert as my talents would allow about such crucial issues as domestic security, international economic interaction, social mobility, and human development generally. This remains my ambition.*

**WEINTRAUB, STANLEY,** arts and humanities educator, writer; b. Phila., Apr. 17, 1929; s. Ben and Ray (Segal) W.; m. Rodelle Horwitz, June 6, 1954; children: Mark, David, Erica. BS, West Chester State Coll., Pa., 1949; MA, Temple U., 1951; PhD, Pa. State U., 1956. Instr. Pa. State U., University Park, 1953-59, asst. prof., 1959-62, asso. prof., 1962-65, prof. English, 1965-70, research prof., 1970-86, Evan Pugh prof. Arts and Humanities, 1986-99, Evan Pugh prof. Emeritus, 2000—; dir. Inst. for Arts and Humanistic Studies, 1970-90. Vis. prof. U. Calif. at Los Angeles, 1963, U. Hawaii, 1973, U. Malaya, 1977, Nat. U. Singapore, 1982 Author: Private Shaw and Public Shaw, 1963, The War in the Wards, 1964, Reggie, 1965, The Art of William Golding, 1965, Beardlsey, 1967, The Last Great Cause, The Intellectuals and the Spanish Civil War, 1968, Evolution of a Revolt; Early Postwar Writings of T.E. Lawrence, 1968, The Literary Criticism of Oscar Wilde, 1968, Journey to Heartbreak, 1971, Whistler: A Biography, 1974, Lawrence of Arabia: the Literary Impulse, 1975, Four Rossettis, A Victorian Biography, 1977, Aubrey Beardsley: Imp of the Perverse, 1976, The London Yankees: Portraits of American Writers and Artists in England, 1894-1914, 1979, The Unexpected Shaw. Biographical Approaches to G.B. Shaw and His Work, 1982, A Stillness Heard Round the World: The End of the Great War, 1985, Victoria. An Intimate Biography, 1987, Long Day's Journey into War: December 7, 1941, 1991, Bernard Shaw: A Guide to Research, 1992, Disraeli: A Biography, 1993, The Last Great Victory-The End of World War II, July/August 1945, 1995, Shaw's People. Victoria to Churchill, 1996, Uncrowned King: The Life of Prince Albert, 1997, MacArthur's War: Korea and the Undoing of an American Hero, 2000, The Importance of Being Edward. King in Waiting, 1841-1901, 2000, Silent Night. The Remarkable 1914 Christmas Truce, 2001, Charlotte and Lionel: A Rothschild Love Story, 2003, General Washington's Christmas Farewell; A Mount Vernon Homecoming, 1783, 2003, Iron Tears; America's Battle for Freedom, Britain's Quagmire: 1775-1783, 2005; editor: An Unfinished Novel by Bernard Shaw, 1958, C.P. Snow: A Spectrum, 1963, The Yellow Book: Quintessence of the Nineties, 1964, The Savoy: Nineties Experiment, 1966, The Court Theatre, 1966, Biography and Truth, 1967, Evolution of a Revolt: Early Postwar Writings of T.E. Lawrence, 1968, The Literary Criticism of Oscar Wilde, 1968, Shaw: An Autobiography 1856-1898, 1969, Shaw: An Autobiography, The Playwright Years, 1898-1950, 1970, Bernard Shaw's Nondramatic Literary Criticism, 1972, Directions in Literary Criticism, 1973, Saint Joan Fifty Years After: 1923/24-1973/74, 1973, The Portable Bernard Shaw, 1977, (with Anne Wright) Heartbreak House. A Facsimile of the Revised Typescript, 1979, (with Richard Aldington) The Portable Oscar Wilde, 1981, Modern British Dramatists, 1900-1945, 1982, The Playwright and the Pirate. Bernard Shaw and Frank Harris: A Correspondence, 1982, British Dramatists Since World War II, 1983, Bernard Shaw, the Diaries, 1885-1897, 1986, Bernard Shaw on the London Art Scene, 1885-1950, 1989, (with Rodelle Weintraub) Dear Young Friend. The Letters of American Presidents to Children, 2000, also editor Comparative Literature Studies, 1987-92, Shaw, The Ann. of Bernard Shaw Studies, 1956-89. Pres. Jewish Community Council of Bellefonte (Pa.) State Coll., 1966-67. Served to 1st lt. AUS, 1951-53, Korea. Decorated Bronze Star medal.; Guggenheim fellow, 1968-69; recipient Disting. Humanist award Pa. Humanities Council, 1985 Mem. The Authors' Guild, PEN. Home: 4 Winterfield Ct Newark DE 19711-2957 Office Phone: 302-235-2859. Personal E-mail: sqw4@comcast.net. *I subscribe to Bernard Shaw's declaration in the Preface to Man and Superman that "This is the true joy in life, the being used for a purpose recognized by yourself as a mighty one; the being thoroughly worn out before you are thrown on the scrap heap; the being a force of Nature instead of a feverish selfish little clod of ailments and grievances complaining that the world will not devote itself to making you happy.".*

**WEINTZ, JACOB FREDERICK, JR.,** retired investment banker; b. NYC, June 27, 1926; s. Jacob Frederick and Grace (Cortelyou) W.; m. Elisabeth Hamlin Brewer, Nov. 26, 1955; children: Elizabeth Weintz Cerf, Polly Weintz Sanna, Eric Cortelyou, Karl Frederick. Student, Norwich U., 1943—44, D (hon.) in Fin. Mgmt., 2001; BA, Stanford U., 1948; MBA, Harvard U., 1951.

Salesman Vick Chem. Co., NYC, 1948-49; assoc. buying dept. Goldman, Sachs & Co., NYC, 1951-54, assoc. new bus. dept., 1954-65, ptnr., 1965-84; ltd. ptnr. Goldman, Sachs Group L.P., 1984—99; ret., 1999; with BCRS Assocs. LLC, NYC. Pres., chmn. bd. dirs. Stonebridge Condominium Assn., Snowmass Village, Colo., 1978-85; trustee Pace U., 1981-97, Norwich U., Stanford U., 1985-95, Sierra Club Found., 1984-90, 92—98; trustee Harbor Lights Found., N.Y.C., Nat. Lighthouse Mus., S.I.; leadership coun., Harvard Sch. Pub. Health, Pace U. Fin. and Audit and Investment com., 1997-, bd. vis., Stanford Inst. Internat. Studies; vice chmn. bd. dirs. Guiding Eyes for Blind, 1984-93; bd. dir. The Forum World Affairs, Stamford, Conn., 1988-94; pres. Harvard U. Bus. Sch. Alumni Assn., 1988-90; former del. Coun. Governing Bds., Albany, N.Y.; chmn. bd. dirs. N.Y. Young Rep. Club, 1957-58; mem. exec. com. Greenwich Rep. Town Com., Conn., 1962-69, The Task Force on Def. Spending, The Economy and the Nation's Security, BENS-ED Commn. on Fundamental Def. Mgmt. Issues, 1991-92; mem. Stanford in Washington Coun. With USAAF, 1944-45. Recipient La Medaille de la Ville de Paris, 1990, Stanford Gold Spike award, 1992. Mem. Ambs. Round Table (Stamford), Bond Club (N.Y.), Newcomen Soc. N.Am., Down Town Assn., Harvard Club (NYC), Riverside Yacht Club, Flying Scot Sailing Assn. (pres. 1968-69), Theta Chi. Republican. Episcopalian. Home: Harbor Lights 43 Jones Park Dr Riverside CT 06878-2205 Office: BCRS Assocs LLC 100 Wall St New York NY 10005 Office Phone: 212-440-0849. Business E-Mail: fweintz@mkllp.com, fweintz@bcrsllc.com.

**WEIR, ALEXANDER, JR.,** chemical engineer, consultant; b. Crossett, Ark., Dec. 19, 1922; s. Alexander and Mary Eloise (Field) W.; m. Florence Forschner, Dec. 28, 1946; children: Alexander III, Carol Jean, Bruce Richard BSChemE, U. Ark., 1943; MChemE, Poly Inst. Bklyn., 1946; PhD, U. Mich., 1954; cert., U. So. Calif. Grad. Sch. Bus. Administrn., 1968. Chem. engr. Am. Cyanamid Co., Stamford Rsch. Labs., 1943-47; with U. Mich., 1948-58; rsch. assoc., project supr. Engring. Rsch. Inst., U. Mich., 1948-57; lectr. chem. and metall. engring. dept. U. Mich., 1954-56, asst. prof., 1956-58; cons. Ramo-Woolridge Corp., L.A., 1956-57; mem. tech. staff, sect. head, asst. mgr. Ramo-Wooldridge Corp., L.A., 1957-60, incharge Atlas Missile Captive test program, 1956-60; tech. adv. to pres. Northrop Corp., Beverly Hills, Calif., 1960-70; prin. scientist for air quality So. Calif. Edison Co., L.A., 1970-76, mgr. chem. rsch. R & D, 1976-86, chief rsch. scientist, 1986-88; utility cons. Playa Del Rey, Calif., 1988—. Rep. Am. Rocket Soc. to Detroit Nuc. Coun., 1954-57; chmn. session on chem. reactions Nuc. Sci. and Engring. Congress, Cleve., 1955; U.S. del. AGARD (NATO) Combustion Colloquium, Liege, Belgium, 1955; Western U.S. rep. task force on environ. R & D goals Electric Rsch. Coun., 1971; electric utility advisor Electric Power Rsch. Inst., 1974-78, 84-87; industry advisor dept. chemistry and biochemistry Calif. State U., L.A., 1981-88. Author: Two and Three Dimensional Flow of Air through Square-Edged Sonic Orifices, 1954; (with R.B. Morrison and T.C. Anderson) Notes on Combustion, 1955, also some 60 tech. papers; inventor acid rain prevention device used in 5 states. Sea scout leader, Greenwich, Conn., 1944-48, Marina del Rey, Calif., 1965-70; bd. govs., past pres. Civic Union Playa del Rey, chmn. sch., police and fire, nominating, civil def., army liaison coms.; mem. Senate, Westchester YMCA, chmn. Dads sponsoring com., active fundraising; chmn. nominating com. Paseo del Rey Sch. PTA, 1961; mem. L.A. Mayors Cmty. Adv. Com.; asst. chmn. advancement com., merit badge dean Cantinella dist. L.A. Area coun. Boy Scouts Am. Recipient Nat. Rsch. Coun. Flue Gas Desulfurization Industrials Scale Reliability award NAS, 1975, Power Environ. Achievement award EPA, 1980, Excellence in Sulfur Dioxide Control award EPA, 1985; named Arkansas Traveler by Gov. Bill Clinton, 1989. Mem.: AIChE, Am. Geophys. Union, Navy League U.S. (v.p. Palos Verdes peninsula coun. 1961—62), NY Acad. Scis., Sci. Rsch. Soc. Am., Am. Chem. Soc., U.S. Power Squadron (navigator), St. Andrew Soc. So. Calif. (hon. capt. of fleet 1997, mem. bd. govs., chair scholarship com.), Clan Buchanan Soc. Am., Ark. Soc. Children of Am. Revolution (past pres.), Betty Washington Lewis Soc. Children of Am. Revolution (past pres.), Clan MacFarlane Soc., Clan Chattan of the US, Clan Farquharson Assn., Clan Macnachtan Assn., Santa Monica Yacht Club (lifetime hon. cannoneer, chief of protocol, vice chmn. marina mgmt. com.), Sigma Xi, Phi Kappa Phi, Phi Lambda Upsilon, Alpha Chi Sigma, Lambda Chi Alpha. Office: 8229 Billowvista Dr Playa Del Rey CA 90293-7807

**WEIR, ANNE,** writer; b. Boston, Feb. 9, 1942; d. John Weir and Martha (Kingman) Perry; children: Emily Weir, Sarah Noel, Katherine Joy. BA, Swarthmore Coll., Pa., 1964; MEd, U. Maine, 1984. Cert. elem. and secondary edn. tchr. Editor: Marlowe: Being In the Life of the Mind, 1996, A Book of Certainties, 1998, The Color Book, 1998, Marlowe, corrected and augmented, 1999, Christopher's Journey, Acts & Scenes, News, The Bird's Eye, 1996-2000, A Native Woman poems, 1999, American City, 2000, A Codebook for the Plays, 2000, Waking, An Academic Celebration, 2001, A Teacher's Holiday, "Streamlines" A Study in Bibliography, New Songs, 2001, The Reincarnation of Love, 2002, Literary Picture Notebooks, And in Aftertimes, 2003, Songs for the 20th Century, 2004, Summer Poems, Notes and Notice, 2005. Office: Writing Press PO Box 10364 Portland ME 04104-0364

**WEIR, BONNIE E.,** reliability engineer; d. Gene W. and Ruth Spear; m. David A. Weir, June 24, 1989; children: Janelle Marie, Elise Noelle, Timothy Gene, Isaiah Richard. BA in Physics, Swarthmore Coll., 1988; PhD, Stevens Inst. Tech., Hoboken, NJ, 1994. Mem. tech. staff AT&T Bell Labs., Murray Hill, NJ, 1988—96, Bell Labs., Lucent Techs., Murray Hill, 1996—2002; sr. mem. tech. staff Agere Sys., Allentown, Pa., 2002—. Trustee Geneva Coll., Beaver Falls, Pa., 1995—99. Mem.: IEEE. Achievements include patents related to detection of dielectric breakdown in semiconductor devices. Office: Agere Sys 555 Union Blvd Allentown PA 18109 Office Phone: 610-712-2042. E-mail: bew@agere.com.

**WEIR, BRYCE KEITH ALEXANDER,** neurosurgeon, neurologist, educator; b. Edinburgh, Scotland, Apr. 29, 1936, arrived in U.S., 1992; s. Ernest John and Marion Weir; m. Mary Lou Lauber, Apr. 25, 1976; children: Leanora, Glyncora, Brocke. BSc, McGill U., Montreal, Que., Can., 1958, MD, CM, 1960, MSc, 1963. Diplomate Am. Bd. Neurol. Surgery, Nat. Bd. Med. Examiners. Intern Montreal Gen. Hosp., 1960-61; resident in neurosurgery Neurological Inst., Montreal, 1962-64, 65-66, NY Neurol. Inst., NYC, 1964—65; neurosurgeon U. Alta., Edmonton, Can., 1967-92, dir. div. neurosurgery, 1982-86, Walter Anderson prof., chmn. dept. surgery, 1986-92; surgeon-in-chief U. Alta. Hosps., 1986-92; Maurice Goldblatt prof. surgery and neurology U. Chgo., 1992—2002, dir. Brain Rsch. Inst., 1993—2001, interim dean biol. scis. divsn. and Pritzker Sch. Medicine, v.p. med. affairs, 2001—02. Past pres. V Internat. Symposium on Cerebral Vasospasm; mem. neurology A study sect. NIH, 1991—93; invited speaker at over 135 profl. meetings; vis. prof. over 68 univs., including Yale U., Cornell U., Columbia U., Duke U., U. Toronto, U. Calif., San Francisco; lectr. in field. Author: Aneurysms Affecting the Nervous System, 1987, Subarachnoid Hemorrhage-Causes and Cures, 1998, Cerebral Vasospasm, 2001; co-editor: Primer on Cerebrovascular Diseases, 1997, Stroke: Pathophysiology, Diagnosis and Management, 4th edit., 2004; mem. editl. bd. Jour. Neurosurgery, chmn. bd, 1993—94, mem. editl. bd. Neurosurgery Quar., Jour. Cerebrovascular Disease, Neurosurgery; contbr. over 275 articles to profl. jours. Named Officer of the Order of Can., 1995. Fellow: ACS, Royal Coll. Surgeons Can., Royal Coll. Surgeons Edinburgh (hon.); mem.: Can. Neurosurg. Soc. (Inaugural Lifetime Achievement award 2006), Interurban Neurosurg. Soc. (chmn.), Nat. Acad. Scis., Inst. Medicine, Japan Neurosurg. Soc. (hon.), Soc. Neurol. Surgeons (Grass gold medal 1992), Am. Acad. Neurol. Surgeons, James. IV Assn. Surgeons, Am. Surg. Assn. Achievements include rsch. in cerebral vasospasm and the surgical management of intracranial aneurysms. Home: 1262 Saturna Dr Parksville BC V9P 2X6 Canada

**WEIR, DAME GILLIAN CONSTANCE,** musician; b. Martinborough, New Zealand, Jan. 17, 1941; d. Cecil Alexander and Clarice M. Foy (Bignell) W. Grad., Royal Coll. Music, London, 1965; Mus D (hon.), U. Victoria of Wellington, New Zealand, 1983; DLitt (hon.), Huddersfield U., 1997; Mus D (hon.), Hull U., 1999, Exeter U., 2001; Doctorate (hon.), U. Ctrl. Eng., 2001; Mus D (hon.), Leicester Univ., 2003; MusD (hon.), U. Aberdeen, Scotland,

2004. Artist-in-residence numerous univs. including Yale U, Washington U., St. Louis, U. Western Australia, Johns Hopkins U., 2005, others; vis. lectr. Royal No. Coll. Music, Manchester, Eng., 1974-89; vis. organ Royal Acad. Music, London, 1997-98; Prince Consort prof. Royal Coll. of Music, London, 1999—; spkr. BBC programs on music and performance; subject of Melvyn Bragg's TV documentary South Bank Show, 2000; apptd. Disting Artist-in-residence Peabody Inst., John Hopkins U., Balt., 2005. Concert appearances with leading Brit. Orchs. and Boston Orch., Seattle Orch., Australian ABC Orch., Wurttemberg Chamber and other fgn. orch.; appeared in major internat. festivals including Edinburgh, Flanders, Aldeburgh, Bath, Proms, Europalia; appeared at concert halls including Royal Festival Hall, Royal Albert Hall, Lincoln Ctr., NY, Sydney Opera House; numerous radio and TV appearances in Brit. and world-wide including Royal Festival Hall Jubilee; organ cons.; adjudicator internat. competitions; contbr. The Messiaen Companion, 1995; contbr. articles to profl. jour.; recs. include complete organ works of Olivier Messiaen, others; TV documentary film on career, 1982, BBC TV programs The King of Instruments, 1989. Decorated comdr., dame comdr. Order Brit. Empire; recipient Turnovsky award 1985, Evening Std. award for outstanding solo performance, 1998-99, Lifetime Achievement award The Link Found., London, 2005; winner 1st prize St. Albans Internat. Organ Competition, 1964. Fellow Royal Coll. Organists (hon., mem. coun. 1977—, mem. exec. 1981-85, pres. 1994-96, 1st Woman pres.), Royal Can. Coll. Organists (hon.), Royal Coll. Music (London); mem. Royal Acad. Music (hon.), Inc. Soc. Musicians (1st woman pres. 1992-93), Albert Schweitzer Assn. (Silver medal 1998). Office: care Karen McFarlane Artists 2385 Fenwood Rd Cleveland OH 44118-3803 Office Phone: 216-397-3345. Personal E-mail: gillianweir@gillianweir.com.

**WEIR, MIKE,** professional golfer; b. Sarnia, Ontario, May 12, 1970; m. Bricia Weir; children: Elle Marisa, Lili. BS, Brigham Young U., 1993. Winner Air Canada Championships, 1999, WGC-Am. Express Championships, 2000, The Tour Championships, 2001, Bob Hope Chrysler Classic, 2003, Nissan Open, 2003, Masters Tournament, 2003, Nissan Open, 2004. Mem. Presidents Cup team, 2000, 03. Recipient The Canadian Press Male Athlete of Yr., 2000, 2001, 2003. Avocations: hockey, skiing, fly fishing. Office: c/o PGA Tour 112 PGA Tour Blvd Ponte Vedra Beach FL 32082

**WEIR, PETER LINDSAY,** film director; b. Sydney, Australia, Aug. 21, 1944; s. Lindsay Weir and Peggy Barnsley; m. Wendy Stites, 1966; 2 children. Educated, Scots Coll., Sydney, Vaucluse Boys H.S., Sydney U. Worked in real estate until 1965; worked as stagehand in TV, Sydney, 1967; dir. film sequences in variety show, 1968; dir. amateur univ. revs., 1967-69; dir. for Film Australia, 1969-73; made own short films, 1969-73, ind. feature film producer, dir. and writer, 1973—. Films include: Cars That Ate Paris, 1973, Picnic at Hanging Rock, 1975, The Last Wave, 1977, The Plumber (TV), 1978, Gallipoli, 1980 (Australian Film Inst. award for best dir., 1981), The Year of Living Dangerously, 1982, Witness, 1985, The Mosquito Coast, 1986, Dead Poets Society, 1989, Green Card, 1990, Fearless, 1993, The Truman Show, 1997 (David Lean award for best dir.), BAFTA, 1999, London Critics Circle Film award for best dir., 1999), Master and Commander: The Far Side of the World, 2003. Raymond Longford Award, Australian Film Inst., 1990, Douglas Sirk Award, 1998. Mem. Australia A.M. Office: Creative Artists Agy care John Ptak 9830 Wilshire Blvd Beverly Hills CA 90212-1804

**WEIR, ROBERT H.,** lawyer; b. Dec. 7, 1922; s. Abraham and Beatrice (Stern) W.; m. Ruth Hirsch, July 2, 1954 (dec. Nov. 1965); children: Nicole F., Daniella F.; m. Sylvia T. Frias. Bar: Mass. 1948, Washington 1952, Calif. 1957. Spl. asst. to atty. gen. U.S. Dept. Justice, Seattle, 1953—56; pvt. practice San Jose and Palo Alto, Calif., 1957—. Instr. taxation of real estate U. Calif. at San Jose and San Francisco; lectr. U. So. Calif. Tax Inst.; CEO Villa Tita Group, 1974—2001; spkr. on taxation at ann. meetings Nat. Assn. Real Estate Bds., 1958—60. Author: Advantages in Taxes, 1960; tax columnist: Rural Realtor, 1959—; author: Taxes Working for You, 1966, How to Make the Most of Depreciation Write Off; contbr. articles to profl. jours. Bd. dirs. San Jose Light Opera Assn., Inc.; mem. prison com. Am. Friends Svc. Com. With U.S. Army, 1942—45. Mem.: ABA, Am. Judicature Soc., State Bar Calif., Santa Clara County Bar Assn. Address: 1200 California St Apt 20B San Francisco CA 94109 Office Phone: 650-248-5262.

**WEIR, SONJA ANN,** artist; b. Hazleton, Pa., Oct. 12, 1934; d. Stephen and Anna (Prehatny) Tatusko; m. Richard Clayton Weir, Jan. 14, 1956; children: Robert, Carl, Donna, Lisa, and Nancy. Studied with Mary Ellen Silkotch, 1963—83; student, Art Students League, N.Y.C., 1985—87. Artist Knickerbocker Toy Co., Middlesex, NJ, 1980; represented by Agora Gallery, Soho, NY, 1999. Tchr. adult art edn. in Jointure, NJ., 2001-03; guest spkr. career day Bridgewater H.S., 1993-94. One-woman shows include Johnson & Johnson, Piscataway, N.J., 1992, Stillman, N.J., 2003 (Meml. award), Somerset County Libr., Bridgewater, N.J., 1992—94, Manville (N.J.) Pub. Libr., 1994—99, exhibited in group shows at Raritan Valley Art Assn., 1982—83, 1995, 1998 (Best in Show award, 1983, 2d prize, 1995, 1st pl. for oil, 1998), Ariel Gallery, N.Y.C., 1991, Am. Artists Profl. League, 1991, 1994, Barren Art Ctr., Woodbridge, N.J., 1993, Agora Gallery, N.Y.C., 1995—99, 2001, Somerset County Libr., 1998—99, Am. Artists Profl. League, 1999, Atrium Gallery, Morristown, N.J., 2001, Somerset County Cultural and Heritage Gallery, 2003, Johnson & Johnson, Stillman, N.J., 2003, Children's Specialized Hosp., N.J., 2003, Barrons Art Ctr., Woodbridge, N.J., 2003, Art Extraordinaire, Bernardsville, N.J., 2004, N.J. Soc. Watercolor Show, 2004 (award of excellence, 2004), Amsterdam Whitney Gallery, N.Y.C., 2005, Taiwan Ctr., Flushing, NY, 2006, Lamington Ch., Bedminster, NJ, 2006, Represented in permanent collections N.W.B. Bank of South Bound Brook, N.J., Summit Bank; featured in Artis Apectrum mag., vol. 11/6, 1999, Star Ledger, 2000; Star Ledger, 2003, Chronicle, Bound Brook, N.J., 2003. Judge Essex Watercolor Soc. Recipient Peter Matulavage award Salmagundi Club, Meml. award Am. Artists Profl. League, NYC, annual Lighument Meml. award Salmagundi Club, 2003; Sr. Artist Exhbn. Citation award, Bd. of Chosen Freeholders in Somerset County, NJ, 2005. Fellow: Nat. Am. Artists Profl. League (v.p. N.J. chpt. 1988—91, publicity com. 1988—91, show chmn. 1989—91, pres. N.J. chpt. 1992—95, editor newsletter 1992—99, nat. exec. bd. 1998—2000, show chmn. 2001—04, nat. pres. 2001—05); mem.: Am. Artists Profl. League (nat. pres. 2001—05), Miniature Art Soc. Fla., Nat. Miniature Assn. (assoc.), Raritan Valley Arts Assn. (pres. 1982—84), Nat. Mus. Women in the Arts. Home: 25 Madison St South Bound Brook NJ 08880-1244

**WEIR, W. THOMAS,** lawyer; b. Abilene, Tex. BA in Econ., Univ. Tex., 1970, JD, 1973; LLM in Tax., NYU, 1977. Bar: Tex. 1973, cert.: Tax Law, Tex. Bd. Legal Specialization. Ptnr. Akin Gump Strauss Hauer & Feld LLP, 1985—, now ptnr.-in-charge San Antonio, head tax practice group and mem. mgmt. com. San Antonio. Mem.: ABA, Internat. Bar Assn., State Bar of Tex. (former chmn., partnership and real estate tax com., sect. of taxation). Office: Akin Gump Strauss Hauer & Feld LLP ste 1500 300 Convent St San Antonio TX 78205-3732 Office Phone: 210-281-7227. Office Fax: 210-224-2035. Business E-Mail: tweir@akingump.com.

**WEIS, CHARLIE,** college football coach; b. Trenton, NJ, Mar. 30, 1956; m. Maura Weis; 2 children. BA speech, drama, Notre Dame Univ., 1978; MA education, South Carolina Univ., 1989. Asst. coach Boonton High School, NJ, 1979, Morristown High School, NJ, 1980—84; grad. asst., defensive backs coach South Carolina U., 1985, 1986, defensive ends coach, 1987, asst. recruiting coord., 1988; head coach Franklin Township High School, 1989; def. asst., asst. special teams coach NY Giants, 1990, running backs coach, 1991—92; tight ends coach New England Patriots, 1993—94, running backs coach, 1995, wide receivers coach, 1996, NY Jets, 1997, offensive coord., wide receivers coach, 1998—99; offensive coord., running backs coach New England Patriots, 2000, offensive coord., quarterbacks coach, 2001—02, offensive coord., 2003—05; head coach Notre Dame U., South Bend, Ind., 2005—. Achievements include being a member of Super Bowl Champion New York Giants, 1990, New England Patriots, 2000, 2003, 2004. Office: C112 Joyce Center Notre Dame IN 46556*

**WEIS, JOSEPH FRANCIS, JR.,** federal judge; b. Pitts., Mar. 12, 1923; s. Joseph Francis and Mary (Flaherty) Weis; m. Margaret Horne Weis, Dec. 27, 1958; children: Maureen, Joseph Francis, Christine. BA, Duquesne U., 1947; JD, U. Pitts., 1950; LLD (hon.), Dickinson Coll., 1989. Bar: Pa. 1950. Pvt. practice, Pitts., 1950—68; judge Ct. Common Pleas, Allegheny County, Pa., 1968—70, U.S. Dist. Ct. (we. dist.), Pa., 1970—73, U.S. Ct. Appeals (3d cir.), Pitts., 1973—88, sr. judge, 1988—. Lectr. trial procedures, 1965—; adj. prof. law U. Pitts., 1986—; chmn. Fed. Cts. Study Com., Jud. Conf. Com. on Expt. to Videotape Trial Procs. within the 3rd Cir., Internat. Jud. Conf. on Joint Am.-Can. Appellate Judges Conf., Toronto, 1986, London, 85; futurist subcom. bicentennial com. Ct. Common Pleas, Allegheny County, Pa., 1988; participant programs legal medicine, Rome, London; mem. Am.-Can. Legal Exch., 1987; apptd. by Chief Justice Rehnquist U.S. Jud. Conf., Com. on Internat. Jud. Rels., 1998—2004; com. on adminstrn. bankruptcy sys., subcom. on jud. improvements Jud. Conf. U.S., 1983—87, chmn. civil rules com., 1986—87, chmn. standing com. rules of practice and procedure, 1988. Contbr. articles to profl. jours. Active Mental Health and Mental Retardation Bd., Allegheny County, 1970—73, Leukemia Soc., 1970—73, Disabled Am. Vets., Cath. War Vets, Mil. Order of the World Wars; trustee Forbes Hosp. Sys., Pitts., 1969—74; bd. adminstrn. Cath. Diocese Pitts., 1971—83. Capt. U.S. Army, 1943—48. Decorated Bronze Star, Purple Heart with oak leaf cluster; recipient St. Thomas More award, 1971, Phillip Amram award, 1991, Edward J. Devitt Disting. Svc. to Justice award, 1993, History Makers award, 1997. Fellow: Am. Bar Found., Internat. Acad. Trial Lawyers (hon.); mem.: ABA (chmn. appellate judges' conf. 1981—83), Inst. Jud. Adminstrn., Am. Judicature Soc., Acad. Trial Lawyers Allegheny County (past pres.), Allegheny Bar Assn. (past v.p.), Pa. Bar Assn., 4th Armored Divsn. Assn., Am. Legion, Knights of Malta, KC. Office: US Ct Appeals 513 US PO & Courthouse 7th Ave & Grant St Pittsburgh PA 15219*

**WEIS, JUDITH SHULMAN,** biology professor; b. N.Y.C., May 29, 1941; d. Saul B. and Pearl (Cooper) Shulman; m. Peddrick Weis; children: Jennifer, Eric. BA, Cornell U., 1962; MS, NYU, 1964, PhD, 1967. Lectr. CUNY, 1964-67; asst. prof. Rutgers U., Newark, 1967-71, assoc. prof., 1971-76, prof., 1976—. Congl. sci. fellow U.S. Senate, Washington, 1983—84; mem. grant rev. panel NSF, Washington, 1976—82, program dir., 1988—90; mem. rev. panel EPA, 1984—92; mem. NOAA Nat. Sea Grant Rev. Panel, 1997—; vis. scientist EPA Lab., Gulf Breeze, Fla., 1992. Mem. marine bd. NAS, 1991—94. Grantee NOAA, 1977—, N.J. EPA Rsch., 1978-79, 81-83, N.J. Marine Scis. Consortium Rsch., 1987—; NSF fellow, 1962-64, U.S. Geol. Survey, 1996—, NSF, 1998—. Mem.: NOW (pres. Essex County 1972), AAAS (chair biology sect. 1999), Assn. Women in Sci. (councilor 2002—05), Ecol. Soc. Am., Estuarine Rsch. Fedn., Soc. Environ. Toxicology and Chemistry (bd. dirs. 1990—93), Am. Inst. Biol. Scis. (bd. dirs. 1986—88, 1989—91, 1997—99, pres.-elect 2000—01, pres. 2001), Sierra Club (bd. dirs. N.J. chpt. 1986—88). Avocations: choral singing, swimming, light opera. Office: Rutgers U Dept Biol Scis Newark NJ 07102 Business E-mail: jweis@andromeda.rutgers.edu.

**WEIS, MARGARET EDITH,** writer, editor; b. Independence, Mo., Mar. 16, 1948; d. George Edward and Francis Irene (Reed) W.; m. Robert William Baldwin, Aug. 22, 1970 (div. 1981); children: David William (dec.), Elizabeth Lynn; m. Donald Bayne Stewart Perrin, 1996 (div. 2003). BA in Creative Writing, U. Mo., 1966-70. Proofreader Herald Pub. House, Independence, Mo., 1970-73, advt. dir., 1973-82; dir. ind. Independence Press, 1977-82; editor TSR Inc, Lake Geneva, Wis., 1982-86. Freelance writer; owner Sovereign Press, Williams Bay, Wis., margaretweis.com, Margaret Weis Prodns., Ltd. Author: (short story) The Test of the Twins, 1984, (books) The Endless Catacombs, 1984, Tower of Midnight Dreams, 1984, (with Tracy Hickman) The Dragonlance Chronicles, Vols. 1-3, 1984, 85, Dragonlance Legends, Vols. 1-3, 1985, 86, The Darksword Trilogy, Vols. 1-3, 1987, (with Roger Moore) Riddle of The Griffon, 1985, (under Margaret Baldwin) The Boys Who Saved The Children, 1982, Kisses of Death, 1983, (with Pat O'Brien) Wanted: Frank and Jesse James, The Real Story, 1981, (with Janet Pack) Children of The Holocaust, 1986, My First Thanksgiving, 1983, (with Gary Pack) Computer Graphics, 1984, Robots and Robotics, 1984, (short story) The Thirty Nine Buttons, 1987, (novella) (with Tracy Hickman) The Legacy, 1987, Wanna Bet?, 1987; editor: The Art of Dungeons and Dragons, 1985, Leaves of the Inn of the Last Home, 1987, The Art of Dragonlance, 1987, Dragonlance Tales, vol. 1, 2, 3, 1987, (with Tracy Hickman) The Rose of the Prophet, 1989, (with Tracy Hickman) Death's Gate, vol. 1, 1990, vols. 2, 3, 4, 5, 6, 7, Star of the Guardian, vol. 1, The Lost King, 1990, King's Test vol. 2, 1991, King's Sacrifice Vol. 3, 1991, Ghost Legion Vol. 4, 1991, Dragons of Summer Flame, 1996, (with Don Perrin), Doom Brigade, 1997, Mag Force 7 novels, 3 vols., The Soulforge, 1998, Brothers in Arms, 1999, (with Tracy Hickman) Starshield, Vols. 1-3, 1997, Legacy of the Darksword, 1997, War of Souls, 3 vols., 2000; editor: Kender, Gully Dwarves and Gnomes, 1989, Love and War, 1991, Reign of Istar, 1993, Dragons of War, 1996, Dragons of Chaos, 1997, Relics and Omens, 1998, Sovereign Stone Role-Playing Games, 1999, Sovereign Stone novels, (with Tracy Hickman) vol. 1, Well of Darkness, 2000, vol. 2, Guardians of the Lost, 2001, Journey Into the Void, vol. 3, 2003, Mistress of Dragons, 2003, Draconian Measures, 2000, Dragon's Son, 2004, Ashes and Amber, 2004, Master of Dragons, 2005, Ashes and Iron, 2005, (with Tracy Hickman) The Lost Chronicles, vol. 1 Dragons of the Dwarven Depths. Named to Writer's Hall of Fame, 2002, Adventure Gaming Hall of Fame, 2002; recipient Origins award, 2001. Avocations: role-playing games, flyball, agility. Office Phone: 262-248-2419.

**WEIS, ROBERT FREEMAN,** supermarket company executive; b. Sunbury, Pa. m. Patricia Ross; children: Jennifer, Colleen, Jonathan. Grad., Mercersburg Acad., 1937; BA, Yale U., 1941. With Weis Markets, Sunbury, Pa., 1946—, v.p., treas., bd. dirs., treas., 1995—, chmn. bd. dirs., 2002—. Chair steering com. capital campaign Susquehanna U., Selinsgrove, Pa., past vice chmn. bd. trustees; past pres. bd. trustees Sunbury Cmty. Hosp., trustee; bd. dirs. Lown Cardiovascular Rsch. Found., Brookline, Mass. Past pres. Sunbury C. of C.; past chmn. bd. dirs. First Nat. Trust Bank Sunbury, emeritus dir.; past dir. Susquehanna Bancshares; treas. Sunbury chpt. United Jewish Appeal. Office: Weis Markets Inc 1000 S 2d St PO Box 471 Sunbury PA 17801-0471

**WEISBACH, DAVID A,** law educator; b. 1963; BS in math., U. Mich., Ann Arbor, 1985; MS in math., Wolfson Coll., Oxford U.En, Eng., 1986; JD, Harvard Law Sch., Cambridge, Mass., 1989. Bar: Ill. 1989, DC 1990. Jud. clk. to Hon. Joel M. Flaum US Ct. Appeals, 7th Cir., Chgo., 1989—90; assoc. Miller & Chevalier, Washington, 1990—92; atty. advisor Office of Tax Legis. Counsel, Washington, 1992—95; assoc. tax legis. counsel Office Tax Policy US Dept. Treasury, Washington, 1995—96; assoc. prof. Georgetown U. Law Ctr., Washington, 1996—98, U. Chgo. Law Sch. 1998—2000, prof., 2000—, dir. Olin Program Law and Econ., 2001—. Trustee Am. Inst. Tax Policy, Washington, 2003—. John M. Olin Fellow in Law and Econ., John M. Olin Found. Office: U Chgo Law Sch 1111 E 60th St Chicago IL 60637 Office Phone: 773-702-3342. E-mail: d-weisbach@uchicago.edu.

**WEISBERG, BARBARA,** writer, editor; b. Phila., Apr. 3, 1946; d. Samuel Weisberg and Miriam (Rosenbach) Weisberg-Kind; m. David Black, June 20, 1996; stepchildren: Susannah Black, Tobiah Black. BA, U. Pa., 1968; MPhil, Yale U., 1972; MFA, Brkpn. Coll., 1992. Prodr. writer Harcourt Brace Jovanovich, N.Y.C., 1973-77; writer WNET/Thirteen, N.Y.C., 1977-80; assoc. dir. TV devel. Scholastic, N.Y.C., 1980-83; dir. TV devel. Consumer Reports, Mt. Vernon, N.Y., 1983-87; writer, prodr., editor N.Y.C., 1987—. Co-creator (TV series) Charles in Charge, 1984; author: (children's books) Susan B. Anthony, 1989, Coronado's Golden Quest, 1993, Knights and Castles, 1994, (nonfiction) Talking to the Dead, Kate and Maggie Fox and the Rise of Spiritualism, 2004, paperback, 2005. Mem. Hadassah, 1970—, NOW, 1970—, Planned Parenthood, 1985—. Recipient fellowship Yale U., 1971, MacArthur scholarship in poetry Bklyn. Coll., 1991, Wallace fellow for creative artists and writers Am. Antiquarian Soc., 1998, D. Scott Rogo award for Parapsychol. Lit., Parapsychology Found., 1998. Mem. Writers Guild of Am. East, Am. Antiquarian Soc., Authors Guild, Phi Beta Kappa. Democrat. Jewish.

**WEISBERG, DAVID CHARLES,** lawyer; b. N.Y.C., June 25, 1938; s. Leonard Joseph and Rae M. (Kimberg) W.; m. Linda Gail Kerman, Aug. 27, 1975; children: Leonard Jay, Karen M. BA, U. Mich., 1958; LLB, Harvard U., 1961. Bar: N.Y. 1962, U.S. Dist. Ct. (so. and ea. dists.) N.Y. 1965, U.S. Supreme Ct. 1970. Assoc. Dreyer & Traub, Bklyn., 1962, Lee Franklin, Mineola, NY, 1962-65; pvt. practice, Patchogue, NY, 1965-67, 77-80; ptnr. Bass & Weisberg, Patchogue, 1967-77, Davidow, Davidow, Russo & Weisberg, Patchogue, 1981-82, Davidow, Davidow, Weisberg & Wismann, Patchogue, 1982-87, Davidow, Davidow & Wismann, Patchogue, 1988-92, Weisberg & Wismann, Patchogue, 1992-98; propr. The Lawyer's Equalizer, 2000—. Assoc. justice and justice Village of Patchogue, 1968-70, village atty., 1970-85; spl. asst. dist. atty. Suffolk County, Patchogue, 1970-85; assoc. estate tax atty., appraiser N.Y. State Dept. Taxation and Fin., Hauppauge, N.Y., 1975-85; lectr. estate tax Suffolk County Acad. Law, 1976-84, negligence law, 1994; cons. in field. Law chmn. Suffolk County Dem. Com., N.Y., 1975-85; bd. dirs. Temple Beth El of Patchogue. With USAR, 1961-62. Mem. ATLA, N.Y. State Bar Assn., Suffolk County Bar Assn., Nassau-Suffolk Trial Lawyers Sect., Lions (pres. Medford 1978-79, 2d v.p. 1984-85). Avocations: bicycling, skiing. Office Phone: 631-476-6752. Personal E-mail: dcw608@yahoo.com. Business E-Mail: dcw@lawyersequalizer.com.

**WEISBERG, DAVID STEVEN,** healthcare consultant; s. Harry and Rena Weisberg; children: Maya Tubwon, Heather Tubwon. BA magna cum laude, Dartmouth Coll., 1969. Registered sanitarian Minn. Prin. lab. tech. U. Minn., Mpls., 1969—80, asst. scientist, 1980—91; assoc. rschr. U. Wis., River Falls, 1991—93; environ. health inspector City of St. Paul, 1994—2000, environ. health specialist, 2000—. Contbr. articles to profl. jours. Treas. Bicking for City Coun., Mpls., 2005. Recipient Marcus Heiman award, Dartmouth Coll., 1968. Mem.: Minn. Environ. Health Assn. (mem. legis. com. 2000—), Nat. Environ. Health Assn. (registered environ. health specialist). Home: 2425 Franklin Ave E Minneapolis MN 55406 Office: City of St Paul Office License Inspection & Environ Prot 8 E 4th St Ste 200 Saint Paul MN 55101

**WEISBERG, HERBERT FRANK,** political science professor; b. Mpls., Dec. 8, 1941; s. Nathan R. and Jean (Schlessinger) W.; m. Judith Ann Robinson, Dec. 16, 1979; 1 child, Bryan Bowen. BA, U. Minn., 1963; PhD, U. Mich., 1968. Asst. prof. polit. sci. U. Mich., Ann Arbor, 1967-73, assoc. prof. polit. sci., 1973-74, Ohio State U., Columbus, 1974-77, prof. polit. sci., 1977—, chmn. Dept. Polit. Sci., 2005—. Author: Central Tendency and Variation, 1992, The Total Survey Error Approach, 2005; co-author: Theory Building and Data Analysis, 1984, Controversies in Voting Behavior, 2001, Survey Research Polling and Data Analysis, 1996, Classics in Congressional Politics, 1999; editor: Political Science: Science of Politics, 1985, Democracy's Feast: Elections in America, 1995; co-editor Am. Jour. Polit. Sci., 1979-82, Great Theatre: The American Congress in the 1990's, 1998, Reelection 1996: How Americans Voted, 1999, Models of Voting in Presidential Elections, 2004. Mem.: Am. Polit. Sci. Assn. (program chmn. 1983), Midwest Polit. Sci. Assn. (pres. 2001—02), Phi Kappa Phi, Pi Sigma Alpha, Phi Beta Kappa. Home: 742 Gatehouse Ln Columbus OH 43235-1732 Office: Ohio State U Dept Polic Sci 2140 Derby Hall 154 N Oval Mall Columbus OH 43210-1330

**WEISBERG, LEONARD R.,** retired engineering executive, researcher; b. N.Y.C., Oct. 17, 1929; s. Emanuel E. and Esther (Raynes) W.; m. Frances Simon, Mar. 23, 1980; children: Glenna Weisberg Andersen, Orren Weisberg Falk, Frances Weisberg Brookner. BA magna cum laude, Clark U., 1950; MA, Columbia U., 1952. Rsch. asst. Watson Labs. IBM, N.Y.C., 1953-55; with RCA Labs., Princeton, NJ, 1955-71, mem. tech. staff, 1955-66, head rsch. group, 1966-69, dir. semicondr. device rsch. lab., 1969-71; dir. materials rsch. lab. Itek Corp., Lexington, Mass., 1972-74, v.p., dir. ctrl. rsch. lab., 1974-75; dir. electronics tech U.S. Dept. Def., Washington, 1975-79; v.p. rsch. and engring. Honeywell Inc., Mpls., 1980-94, ret., 1994. Mem. adv. group on electron devices U.S. Dept. Def., 1981-99; bd. dirs. TimeLab Corp. Contbr. articles to profl. jours. Recipient award for initiating VHSIC program U.S. Dept. Def., 1979. Fellow IEEE; mem. Am. Phys. Soc., Sigma Xi. Home: 1250 S Washington St # 202 Alexandria VA 22314-4455 Office Phone: 703-549-8151. Personal E-mail: LenW5678@aol.com.

**WEISBERG, LYNNE WILLING,** psychiatrist, consultant; b. N.Y.C., Apr. 11, 1948; d. Stanley S. and Pearl R. Willing. BA, Barnard Coll., 1969; PhD, U. Mich., 1972; MD, SUNY, Downstate, 1978. Diplomate Am. Bd. Psychiatry and Neurology, Am. Bd. Adolescent Psychiatry. Intern NYU Med. Ctr., 1978-79; resident in adult psychiatry Mt. Sinai Hosp., N.Y.C., 1979-81; fellow in child psychiatry Columbia Med. Ctr., 1981-83; staff psychiatrist Fair Oaks Hosp., Summit, N.J., 1983-85, asst. dir. child and adolescent psychiatry, 1985-88, assoc. dir. child and adolescent psychiatry, 1988-92; dir. child and adolescent outpatient psychiat. svcs. Psychiat. Assocs. N.J. at Fair Oaks Hosp., Summit, 1992—; pvt. practice Morris County, N.J., 1993—. Cons. Bonnie Brae Sch., Millington, N.J., 1984-92. Author: When Acting Out Isn't Acting, 1991. Horace Rackham Prize fellow, 1972. Mem. AMA, Med. Soc. N.J., Am. Soc. Clin. Psychopharmacology. Office: 135 Columbia Tpke Ste 201 Florham Park NJ 07932-2104 Office Phone: 908-850-7141.

**WEISBERG, MORRIS L.,** retired lawyer; b. Phila., June 7, 1921; s. Alexander and Hilda (Lichtenstein) W.; m. Mildred Norma Lubich, July 7, 1948; children— Richard, James, John BA, U. Pa., 1943, LL.B., 1947; MA, Yale U., 1944. Bar: Pa. 1950, U.S. Dist. Ct. (ea. dist.) Pa. 1950, U.S. Supreme Ct. 1962. Bigelow teaching fellow U. Chgo. Law Sch., 1947-48, Raymond grad. fellow, 1948-49; Gowen fellow U. Pa. Law Sch., Phila., 1948-49; ptnr. Harry Norman Ball, Phila., 1950-56; assoc. Blank, Rome, Comisky & McCauley, and predecessor, Phila., 1956-60, ptnr., 1960-93. Permanent mem. Jud. Conf. 3d Cir. Fellow Am. Bar Found.; mem. Order of Coif, Phi Beta Kappa Assocs. Office: Blank Rome 1 Logan Sq Fl 3 Philadelphia PA 19103-6998

**WEISBERG, ROBERT,** law educator; b. 1946; BA in English, magna cum laude, CCNY, 1966; PhD in English Lit., Harvard U., 1971; JD, Stanford U., 1979. Bar: Calif. 1980. Teaching fellow Harvard U., 1967—69; asst. prof. English Skidmore Coll., 1970—76; instr. English Great Meadow State Penitentiary, Comstock, NY, 1974—76; law clk. to Hon. J. Skelly Wright US Ct. Appeals DC Cir., 1979—80; law clk. to Hon. Potter Stewart US Supreme Ct., 1980—81; mem. faculty Stanford Law Sch., 1981—, prof. law, 1986—, Edwin E. Huddleson, Jr. prof. law, 1996—, assoc. dean academic affairs, 1987—89, academic coord., 1994—99; affiliated faculty mem. Program in Modern Thought and Lit. Stanford U., 1991—; vice-provost faculty relations, 1994—99, spl. asst. to provost for faculty recruitment and retention, 1999—. Consulting atty. NAACP Legal Def. & Edn. Fund, Inc., 1981—86, Calif. Appellate Project, 1986—. Co-author (with Guyora Binder): Literary Criticisms of Law, 2000; co-editor (with Binder and John Kaplan): Criminal Law: Cases and Materials, 2004. Office: Stanford Law Sch Crown Quadrangle 559 Nathan Abbott Way Stanford CA 94305-8610 Office Phone: 650-723-0612. Business E-Mail: weisberg@stanford.edu.

**WEISBERG, RUTH,** artist; Laurea in Painting and Printmaking, Acad. di Belle Arti, Perugia, Italy, 1962; BA, U. Mich., 1963, MA, 1965. Lectr., demonstrator, juror, curator U. Mich., 1987, 88, U. Hawaii, Honolulu, 1988, Pa. Acad., Phila., 1987, Queens Coll., N.Y.C., 1987, CCNY, 1987, U. Iowa, 1978, 87, U. N.D., Grand Forks, 1987, Fresno (Calif.) Arts Ctr. and Mus., Carnegie Mellon U., Pitts., 1986, 87, U. Tenn., Knoxville, 1986, U. Calif., Santa Cruz, 1985, U. Washington, Seattle, U. Kans., Lawrence, Skirball Mus. Hebrew Union Coll., Los Angeles, Calif. Inst. Arts, Valencia, Otis Art Inst., Los Angeles, Mass. Coll. Art, Boston, Norwegian Graphic Artists' Assn., Oslo, Coll. Art Assn. Conf., Detroit, many others; current chairperson art dept., U. So. Calif. Solo and two-person exhibitions include: Pollack Gallery, Toronto, 1969, 71, Richard Nash Gallery, Seattle, 1971, 72, 74, Seaberg Isthmus Gallery, Chgo., 1972, Mepl. Art Gallery, Oslo, 1972, Triad Gallery, Los Angeles, 1974, Norwegian Graphic Arts Assn., Oslo, 1976, Palos Verdes (Calif.) Art Gallery, 1976, El Camino Coll., Los Angeles, 1977, Oglethorpe U., Atlanta, 1978, Peppers Art Gallery, U. Redlands (Calif.) 1980, Kellas Gallery, Lawrence, Kans., 1979-81, M. Shore and Sons, Santa Barbara, Calif.,

1981, U. Richmond, Va., 1985, U. Tenn., Knoxville, 1986, Sierra Nev. Mus. Arts Reno, 1987, The Alice Simsar Gallery, Ann Arbor, Mich., 1968, 69, 72, 74, 77, 88, Associated Am. Artists, N.Y.C., 1987, Jack Rutberg Fine Arts, Los Angeles, 1983, 85, 88; group exhibitions include: Chgo. Art Inst., 1978, E.B. Crocker Art Mus., 1978-80, Contemporary Arts Ctr., New Orleans, 1980, Pratt Graphic Ctr., N.Y.C., 1978-80, U. Art Mus., U. N.M., 1981, Loyola Marymount U., Los Angeles, 1982, Kenkeleba House, N.Y.C, 1984, The Design Ctr., Los Angeles, 1984, Palos Verdes Art Ctr., 1984, Gallery in the Plaza, Security Pacific Bank, Las Angeles, 1985, Thomas Ctr. Gallery, Gainesville, Fla., Associated Am. Artists, N.Y.C., 1987, many others; works published in The Survey Exhibition Catalogues, 1968-88; permanent collections include: The Achenback Found. for Graphic Arts, Fine Arts Mus., San Francisco, Ariz. State U. Mus., Tempe, The Art Inst. Chgo., The Dance Collection, Lincoln Ctr., N.Y.C., Detroit Inst. Arts, Grunwald Found. for Graphic Arts, Los Angeles, Calif. Inst. Arts, France, Paris, Los Angeles County Mus. Art, The Jewish Mus. N.Y.C, The Nat. Gallery, Washington, The Nat. Musl Women in the Arts, many others; contbr. articles to profl. jours. Mem.: L.A. Printmaking Soc., L.A. Artists Equity (adv. bd.), Tamarind Inst., Coll. Art Assn. (past pres., co-chair studio sessions, nat. adv. bd.). Office: Sch Fine Arts U S Calif Watt Hall 104 Los Angeles CA 90089-0001

**WEISBERGER, BARBARA,** artistic director, advisor, educator; b. Bklyn., Feb. 28, 1926; d. Herman and Sally (Goldstein) Linshes; m. Sol Spiller, Sept. 3, 1945 (div. 1948); m. Ernest Weisberger, Nov. 15, 1949; children: Wendy, Steven. BS in Edn., Psychology, Pa. State U., 1945; L.H.D. (hon.), Swarthmore Coll., 1970; D.F.A. (hon.), Temple U., 1973, Kings Coll., 1978, Villanova U., 1978, U. New England, 1996. Founder, dir., Wilkes-Barre (Pa.) Ballet Theater, 1953-63; founder, dir. Pa. Ballet, Phila., 1962-82, Carlisle (Pa.) Project, 1984—96; artistic advisor Peabody Dance, Balt., 2001—. Vice chmn. dance panel Nat. Endowment for the Arts, Washington, 1975-79. Performed with Met. Opera Ballet, N.Y.C., 1937, 38, Mary Binney Montgomery Co., Phila., 1940-42, ballet mistress, choreographer, Ballet Co. of Phila. Lyric Opera, 1961-62; choreographic works include Italian Concerto, Bach, Symphonic Variations, Franck; also operas for, Phila. Lyric Opera Co. Named Disting. Dau. of Pa., 1972, Disting. Alumna, Pa. State U., 1972; recipient 46th ann. Gimbel Phila. award, 1978. Mem. Psi Chi. Home and Office: 571 Charles Ave Kingston PA 18704-4711 Office Phone: 570-287-8349.

**WEISBERGER, JOSEPH ROBERT,** retired state supreme court justice; b. Providence, Aug. 3, 1920; s. Samuel Joseph and Ann Elizabeth (Meighan) W.; m. Sylvia Blanche Pigeon, June 9, 1951; children: Joseph Robert, Paula Ann, Judith Marie. AB, Brown U., 1942; JD, Harvard U., 1949; LLD (hon.), R.I. Coll., Suffolk U., Mt. St. Joseph Coll.; DCL (hon.), Providence Coll.; DHL (hon.), Bryant Coll.; LLD (hon.), Roger Williams Coll., 1992; LLD (hon.), Brown U., 1992, Constantine U., 1997; LLD, So. New England Sch. Law, 1998; DHL (hon.), Salve Regina U., 2001. Bar: Mass. 1949, R.I. 1950. With Quinn & Quinn, Providence, 1951-56; solicitor Glocester, RI, 1953-56; judge Superior Ct. R.I., Providence, 1956-72; presiding justice R.I. Superior Ct., Providence, 1972-78; justice R.I. Supreme Ct., Providence, 1978—, chief justice, 1993—2001; ret., 2001; vol. mediator, 2001—. Adj. prof. U. Nev., 1986—; mem. faculty Nat. Jud. Coll.; vis. lectr. Providence Coll., Suffolk Law Sch., Roger Williams Coll.; chmn. New Eng. Regional Conf. Trial Judges, 1962, 63, 65, New Eng. Regional Commn. Disordered Offender, 1968-71, R.I. Com. Adoption on Rules Criminal Procedure, 1968-72, R.I Adv. Com. Corrections, 1973; bd. dirs. Nat. Ctr. for State Cts., 1975-81; chmn. bd. dirs., bd. overseers Roger Williams U.; chmn. bd. dirs. Roger Williams U. Sch. Law Chmn. editl. bd. Judges Jour., 1973-75. Pres. R.I. Health Facilities Planning Coun., 1967-70; chmn. Gov. R.I. Coun. Mental Health, 1968-73; moderator Town of East Providence, 1954-56; mem. R.I. Senate, 1953-56, minority leader, 1955-56; vice chmn. bd. trustee R.I. Hosp., hon. trustee, 2006—, 1968-92, St. Joseph's Hosp., trustee, 1962—. Lt. comdr. USNR, 1941-46. Named to R.I. Hall of Fame; recipient Erwin Griswold award, Nat. Jud. Coll., 1989; Paul Harris fellow, Rotary Internat. Fellow Am. Bar Found.; mem. ABA (ho. of dels., task force on criminal justice stds. 1977-79, exec. com. appellate judges' conf. 1979-95, nat. conf. state trial judges 1977-78, exec. com. appellate judges conf. 1979—, vice chmn., 1983-85, chmn., 1985-86), KC, R.I. Bar Assn., Am. Judges Assn. (gov.), Inst. Jud. Adminstrn., Am. Judicature Soc. (Herbert Harley award 1990), Am. Law Inst., Order of St. Gregory (knight comdr. with star 1989, Goodrich award for Svc. 1995), Phi Beta Kappa (past pres. Alpha chpt. Brown U.). Home: 60 Winthrop St Riverside RI 02915-2624 Office: RI Supreme Ct 250 Benefit St Ste 7 Providence RI 02903-2724 Office Phone: 401-433-0081. *My professional life for the last 48 years has been occupied with judicial duties. I have been blessed with the opportunity to meet ever changing challenges and to attempt to solve a myriad of problems. These opportunities have been rewarding and absorbing. I consider judicial work to be a great privilege.*

**WEISBERG-SAMUELS, JANET S.,** psychologist; b. N.Y.C., Mar. 21, 1940; d. Morris and Vivian (Wank) Weisberg; m. Richard Samuels, Jan. 16, 1983; children: Debra Samuels, David Samuels. BBA, CCNY, 1960; MS, CUNY, 1967; PhD, Yeshiva U., 1984. Lic. psychologist, cert. sch. psychologist N.Y. Psychologist, adminstr. Bklyn. Jewish Hosp., 1969—75, Beth Israel Hosp., N.Y.C., 1975—87; dir. edn. Interfaith Med. Ctr., Bklyn., 1987—; pvt. practice psychology, N.Y.C., 1985—. Cons. Westchester Jewish Comm. Svcs., 2000—; team leader N.Y. State Dept. Mental Hygiene, N.Y.C., 1977; cons. N.Y.C. Bd. Edn., 1977, Parent-Child Consultation Ctr., 1980—; program dir. Brotherhood Synagogue, N.Y.C., 1968—75, dir. edn. and tng., 1987—, dept. psychiatry Interfaith Med. Ctr. Pres. singles divsn. Park Ave. Synagogue, N.Y.C., 1980—83; bd. dirs. Couples Club, 1986—, pres., 1988—90. Mem.: APA, Manhattan Psychol. Assn. (exec. bd. 1993—, pres.-elect 1997—98), Ea. Psychol. Assn., N.Y. State Psychol. Assn. (chair internship dirs. 2003—06). Avocations: opera, museums, ballet. Office: 160 E 89th St Apt 1B New York NY 10128-2306 Office Phone: 212-410-4391.

**WEISBLATT, BARBARA ANN,** secondary school educator; b. New Brunswick, N.J., Mar. 21, 1958; d. Stanley Herman and Clara Armel Friedelbaum; m. Alan Joel Weisblatt, Dec. 27, 1992. BA in French/Spanish, Rutgers U., 1979, MAT in French, 1986, supr. cert., 1991. Cert. French, Spanish tchr. K-12 N.J. Tchr. Somerville (N.J.) H.S., 1980—; supr. Somerville Pub. Schs., 1993—94. Mem. Holocaust H.S. and Dist. Coms., Somerville, 1995—, Mid. States Steering Com., Somerville, 2000—02, H.S. Renaissance Com., Somerville, 2000—, H.S. Quality Coun., Somerville, 2002—. Author: (test) French Placement Test for Middle School Students, 1995. Mem. Hebrew HS bd. edn. Temple Sholom, Bridgewater, NJ, 1995—. Recipient Tchr. Recognition award, Gov. State of N.J., 2001; NEH grantee, Figaro Inst., 1991. Mem.: NEA, Assn. for Supervision and Curriculum Devel., Fgn. Lang. Educators N.J., Am. Assn. Tchrs. French, Somerville Edn. Assn., N.J. Edn. Assn. Avocations: reading, photography, travel, exercise. Home: 85 Perrine Pike Hillsborough NJ 08844 Office: Somerville HS 222 Davenport St Somerville NJ 08876 Office Phone: 908-218-4157.

**WEISBROD, BURTON ALLEN,** economist, educator; b. Chgo., Feb. 13, 1931; s. Leon H. and Idelle C. (Chernoff) W.; m. Shirley Lindsay, Dec. 23, 1951; children: Glen, Linda. BS, U. Ill., 1951; MA in Econs Northwestern U., 1952, PhD, 1958. Lectr. econs. Northwestern U., Evanston, Ill., 1954-55; instr. econs. Carleton Coll., Minn., 1955-57, Washington U., St. Louis, 1957-58, asst. prof. econs., 1958-62, assoc. prof. econs., 1962-64; vis. assoc. prof. Princeton (N.J.) U., 1962-63; sr. staff mem. Council of Econ. Advs., Pres. U.S. 1963-64; assoc. prof. dept. econs. U. Wis., Madison, 1964-66, prof., 1966-91, Evjue-Bascom prof. econs., 1985—91; dir. Ctr. for Urban Affairs and Policy Rsch. Northwestern U., Evanston, Ill., 1990-95, John Evans prof. econs., 1990—. Vis. prof. SUNY, Binghamton, 1972; sr. Fulbright lectr. U. Autonoma de Madrid, summer, 1970; vis. prof. Yale U., 1972; Ziskind vis. prof. Brandeis U., 1982-83; vis. scholar, Brotman fellow J.F. Kennedy Sch., Harvard U., 1982-83; tchg. fellow Australian Nat. U., 1986; mem. rsch. adv. com. Econ. Devel. Adminstrn., U.S. Dept. Commerce, 1967-69; mem. adv. com. Commn. on Pvt. Philanthropy and Pub. Needs, 1973-75; cons. various fed. and state govt. agys., 1964—; also IBM, Econ.

Coun. Can., 1969, 71, 76, 78; mem. bd. econ. advs. Public Interest Econs. Ctr., 1973-86; mem. adv. com. med. care and med. econs. to 3d Nat. Cancer Survey, 1969-71; U.S. del. UN World Population Conf., Belgrade, Yugoslavia, 1965; bd. dirs. Nat. Bur. Econ. Rsch., Inc., 1979-90; vis. scholar Phi Beta Kappa Soc., 1998-99; mem. nat. rsch. resources coun. NIH, 1999-03; mem. panel on nonmarket activity NRC, 2002-04; chair com. on philanthropy and the nonprofit sector Social Sci. Rsch. Coun., 2002-04; mem. IRS stats income divsn. Users Adv. Group, 2004-. Author: Economics of Public Health, 1961, External Benefits of Public Education, 1964, (with W. Lee Hansen) Benefits, Costs, and Finance of Public Higher Education, 1969, (with Ralph L. Andreano) American Health Policy, 1974, The Voluntary Nonprofit Sector: An Economic Analysis, 1978, (with Joel F. Handler and Neil K. Komesar) Public Interest Law: An Economic and Institutional Analysis, 1978; contbg. author: (with others) Disease and Economic Development: The Case of Parasitic Diseases in St. Lucia, West Indies, 1974, Economics and Medical Research, 1983, The Nonprofit Economy, 1988; editor (with James Worthy) The Urban Crisis, 1997; author, editor: To Profit or Not to Profit, 1998; contbr. nearly 200 articles on econs. of edn., program evaluation, health care and econs. of pvt. non-profit sector to profl. jours.; mem. editl. bd.: Jour. Human Resources, 1966-86, Internat. Jour. Social Econs, 1972—, Jour. Public Econs, 1971-87, Pub. Fin. Rev., 1990—, Nonprofit and Voluntary Sector Quar., 1997—; assoc. editor: Public Fin. Quar, 1972-87. Guggenheim fellow, 1969-70; Ford Faculty fellow, 1971-72; Sr. research fellow Brookdale Inst., Jerusalem, 1978—; recipient Disting. Lifetime Rsch. award Assn. Rsch. Nonprofit Orgns. and Voluntary Assns., 1997; co-recipient Carl Taube award Disting. Rsch., APHA, 1992. Fellow AAAS; mem. Am. Econ. Assn. (exec. com. 1975-77, com. status of assn. jours. 1973-74, chmn. budget com. 1977), Midwest Econs. Assn. (pres. 1980-81), Nat. Acad. Scis. Inst. Medicine, Public Choice Soc., Internat. Inst. Public Finance, AAUP (exec. com. Washington U. chpt. 1961-62). Office: Northwestern U Econs Dept 2003 Sheridan Rd Evanston IL 60208-0826 Business E-Mail: b-weisbrod@northwestern.edu.

**WEISBROD, CARL,** lawyer, public official; b. NYC, Oct. 5, 1944; s. Walter and Hilda (Pelzer) W.; m. Jody Adams, Jan. 21, 1979; 1 child, William. BS, Cornell U., 1965; JD, NYU, 1968. Bar: N.Y., 1968; U.S. Dist. Ct. (so. dist.) N.Y., 1969. Asst. commr. N.Y.C. Housing Dept., 1970-72; counsel, chief exec. officer Wildcat Svc. Corp., N.Y.C., 1972-77; gen. counsel Manpower Demonstration Rsch. Corp., N.Y.C., 1977-78; dir. Mayor's Office of Midtown Enforcement, N.Y.C., 1978-84; exec. dir. City Vol. Corps, N.Y.C., 1984-86, N.Y.C. Planning Commn., 1986-87; pres. 42d St. Devel. Project, N.Y.C., 1987-90; pres., chief exec. officer N.Y.C. Econ. Devel. Corp., 1990-94; pres. Alliance for Downtown N.Y., 1995—2005, Trinity Real Estate, N.Y.C., 2005—; dir. Sept. 11 Fund, 2001—. Chmn. N.Y.C. Loft Bd., 1982-84; chmn. Wildcat Svc. Corp., 2002-. Contbr. articles to profl. jours. Trustee The Ford Found., 1996-, NYU Downtown Hosp., 1999-2005; dir. Tarragon Realty Advisors, Inc., Lower Manhattan Devel. Corp., Convention Ctr. Devel. Corp. Office: Trinity Real Estate 74 Trinity Pl New York NY 10006 Office Phone: 212-602-0814. Business E-Mail: cweisbrod@trinitywallstreet.org.

**WEISBROD, JOHN,** former professional sports team executive; b. Syosset, N.Y., Oct. 8, 1968; Degree, Harvard U. Exec. v.p., dir. hockey ops., alt. gov. Albany (N.Y.) River Rats, 1993—97; v.p., gen. mgr. Orlando (Fla.) Solar Bears, 1997—2000; COO Orlando (Fla.) Magic, 2000—04, gen. mgr., 2004—05. Mem. Nat. Championship Hockey Team, 1989. Recipient Donald Angier trophy, Harvard U.

**WEISBROD, KEN (JOSEPH LOUIS WEISBROD),** marketing professional; b. Los Angeles, July 31, 1957; s. Louis Isadore and Dolores Joan (Adamczyk) W.; m. Kary Lin Shirley, Jan. 25, 1992 (div. Apr. 2004); children: Katherine Irene, Benjamin Joseph. Cert., Gemological Inst. Am, 1988. Jewelry designer House of Time Jewelers, Granada Hills, Calif., 1968-79; pres. Ken Weisbrod Prodns., Inc., Chatsworth, Calif., 1979-85; v.p. The Ramolap Co., Chatsworth, 1985—. Dir. prodn. Katherine's of Broadway Market, Chatsworth, 1987-, The Sch. of the Arts, 2003-. Designer jewelry for numerous art exhibits, 1969-75. Mem. Advt. Prodn. Assn. L.A., Greater L.A. Zoo Assn., Advertising Prodn. Assn. L.A. Republican. Roman Catholic. Office: Sch of the Arts PO Box 4778 Chatsworth CA 91313-4778 Personal E-mail: weischats3@aol.com.

**WEISBROT, DEBORAH MARCIA,** psychiatrist; BA (hons.), Cornell U. Coll. of Arts and Scis., 1975; MD, SUNY, 1979. Cert. diplomate adult, child and adolescent psychiatry 1991. Unit chief, long term treatment unit program Dept. Psychiatry Albert Einstein Coll. of Medicine, Bronx, 1986—91, assoc. dir. residency tng., 1988—91; child, adolescent and adult psychiatry pvt. practice, N.Y.C. and Long Island, 1986—98; dir. child and adolescent outpatient svcs. Univ. Hosp., 1998—. Dir. child and adolescent outpatient svcs. Univ. Hosp. Author multiple jour. articles on mood and anxiety disorders in chi. Mem.: Greater L.I. Psychiat. Soc. (bd. dirs.), Acad. Child and Adolescent Psychiatry, Am. Psychiatric. Office: Divsn Child and Adolescent Psychiatry Putnam Hall S Campus SUNY Stony Brook NY 11790-8794 Office Phone: 631-632-8840.

**WEISBUCH, ROBERT ALAN,** academic administrator; b. Rochester, NY, Nov. 22, 1946; s. Irving Arthur and Ferne (Paull) W.; m. Candy Jaye Cooper, Aug. 27, 1994; 1 child, Gabriel; children from previous marriages: Michael, Sarah, Max. BA magna cum laude, Wesleyan U., Middletown, Conn., 1968; MPhil in English, Yale U., 1970, PhD in English, 1972. Asst. prof. English U. Mich., Ann Arbor, 1972-76, assoc. prof., 1976-85, prof., 1985—, assoc. chmn. dept. English, 1981-84, chmn., 1987-94, assoc. v.p. rsch., assoc. dean faculty programs Rackham Sch. Grad. Studies, 1994-95, assoc. v.p. rsch., 1994-95, interim dean Grad. Sch., 1995-96; pres. The Woodrow Wilson Nat. Fellowship Found., 1997—2005; dir. Mellon Fellowships Humanistic Studies, 1998—2005; pres. Drew U., Madison, NJ, 2005—. Author: Emily Dickinson's Poetry, 1975, Atlantic Double-Cross, 1986; co-editor Dickinson and Audience, 1995. Am. Coun. Learned Socs. fellow, 1976-77, Rackham fellow, U. Mich., 1983; recipient Amoco teaching award U. Mich., 1986 Mem. Phi Beta Kappa. Office: Drew U Office of Pres 36 Madison Ave Madison NJ 07940 Office Phone: 973-408-3100. E-mail: rweisbuc@drew.edu.

**WEISBURGER, ELIZABETH KREISER,** retired chemist; b. Greenlane, Pa., Apr. 9, 1924; d. Raymond Samuel and Amy Elizabeth (Snavely) Kreiser; m. John H. Weisburger, Apr. 7, 1947 (div. May 1974); children: William Raymond, Diane Susan, Andrew John. BS, Lebanon Valley Coll., 1944, DSc (hon.), 1989; PhD, U. Cin., 1947, DSc (hon.), 1981. Rsch. assoc. U. Cin., 1947-49; col. USPHS, 1951-89; postdoctoral fellow Nat. Cancer Inst., Bethesda, Md., 1949-51, chemist, 1951-73, chief carcinogen metabolism and toxicology br., 1972-75, chief Lab. Carcinogen Metabolism, 1975-81, asst. dir. chem. carcinogenesis, 1981-89, ret. Cons. in field; lectr. Found. for Advanced Edn. in Scis., Bethesda, 1980-95; adj. prof. Am. U., Washington, 1982-83. Asst. editor-in-chief Jour. Nat. Cancer Inst., 1971-87; mem. editl. adv. bd. Chem. Health and Safety, 1994-99, Jour. Applied Toxicology, 1996—; contbr. articles to profl. jours. Trustee Lebanon Valley Coll., 1979—; pres. bd. trustees, 1985—89. Recipient Meritorious Svc. medal USPHS, 1973, Disting. Svc. medal, 1985; Hillebrand prize Chem. Soc. Washington, 1981, Charles Gordon award, 1999. Fellow AAAS (nominating com. 1978-81); mem. Am. Chem. Soc. (Garvan medal 1981, Tillmanns-Skolnick award divsn. chem. health and safety 2001), Am. Assn. Cancer Rsch., Soc. Toxicology, Am. Soc. Biochem. and Molecular Biology, Royal Soc. Chemistry, Am. Conf. Govtl. Indsl. Hygienists (Herbert Stokinger award 1996, William Wagner award 2003), Grad. Women in Sci. (hon.), Iota Sigma Pi. Lutheran. Office Phone: 301-309-0078.

**WEISBURGER, JOHN HANS,** medical researcher; b. Stuttgart, Germany, Sept. 15, 1921; came to U.S., 1943, naturalized, 1944; s. William and David (Barth) W.; children: William, Diane, Andrew. AB, U. Cin., 1947, MS, 1948, PhD, 1949; MD (hon.), U. Umeå, Sweden, 1980. Officer USPHS, 1950-72; mem. staff Nat. Cancer Inst., NIH, Bethesda, Md., 1950-61, head carcinogen screening sect., 1961-72; dir. bioassay segment, Carcinogenesis Programs Nat. Cancer Inst., Bethesda, Md., 1971-72; v.p. rsch. Am. Health Found.,

Valhalla, NY, 1972-87; dir. Naylor Dana Inst. for Disease Prevention, Valhalla, 1972—87; rsch. prof. pathology N.Y. Med. Coll., Valhalla, 1974—; pres. Weisburger Assocs., North White Plains, NY, 1987—. Mem. biochemistry and nutrition study sect. NIH, 1957—58; mem. interdepartmental panel on carcinogens FDA, USDA, USPHS, 1962—71; chmn. carcinogenesis subcom. Nat. Large Bowel Cancer Project, 1972—75; mem. expert panel on nitrites and nitrosamines USDA, 1973—77; mem. Nat. Cancer Inst. Clearinghouse on Environ. Carcinogens, 1976—78; co-chmn. organizing com. US-Japan Coop. Workshop on GI Tract Cancer, 1979; chmn. sci. rev. panel NJ State Commn. Cancer Rsch., 1988—90; co-chmn. internat. symposium on health effects of tea, NY, 1991; chmn. nutrition and cancer sect. 3d Anticarcinogenesis & antimutagenesis conf., Italy, 1991; chmn. study sect. NIH-Nat. Cancer Inst., Bethesda, Md., 1991; rsch. fellow Japanese Found. for Promotion of Cancer Rsch. Nat. Cancer Ctr. Rsch. Inst., Tokyo, 1992; adv. com. rev. RDA Food & Nutrition Bd. NAS, 1993; lectr. numerous lectures in field; chmn. numerous confs. national & internat. Assoc. editor Jour. Nat. Cancer Inst., 1960-62, Xenobiotica, 1971—2004, Archives of Toxicology, 1977-87, Internat. Jour. Toxicology, 1982-2002, Preventive Medicine, 1988-2004; mem. internat. editl. adv. bd. Food and Chem. Toxicology, 1967—2004; assoc. editor Cancer Rsch., 1969-80, mem. cover editl. bd., 1987-99; mem. editl. bd. Chemico-Biol. Interactions, 1969-88, Carcinogenesis, 1979-87, Inst. Sci. Info. Atlas of Sci., 1987-89, Cancer Epidemiology Biomarkers Prevention, 1991-98, Cancer Detection Prevention, 1994-2004; mem. guest editl. bd. Japanese Jour. Cancer Rsch., 1987—; hon. editor Protective Effects of Tea on Human Health, 2006; contbr. articles to profl. jours. With U.S. Army, 1944—46, Italy, Austria, ret. col. USPHS. Decorated D.S.M.; recipient Meritorious Svc. medal USPHS HEW, 1970, Outstanding Service award Westchester div. Am. Cancer Soc., 1984, Meyer and Anna Prentis award Mich. Cancer Ctr., 1987; named one of 1000 most cited scientists, ISI List, 1981. Leadership plaque N.J. State Commn. Cancer Rsch., 1990. Fellow N.Y. Acad. Scis., Am. Coll. Nutrition; mem. Am. Assn. Cancer Rsch. (hon. mem., rep. to European Assn. Cancer Rsch. 1985-89), Am. Chem. Soc. (hon. com. environ. improvement 1992-94, chmn. tech. chemistry and health 31st Middle Atlantic regional meeting 1997, chmn. symposium tea and health, N.Y., 2003), Am. Gastroent. Assn., Am. Soc. Biochem. Molecular Biologists, Am. Soc. Preventive Oncology (founding mem., bd. dirs. 1983-90, Disting. Svc. award 1990), Biochem. Soc. (London, emeritus), Environ. Mutagen Soc., European Assn. Cancer Rsch. (coun. 1985-90), Japan Cancer Assn. (hon. life), Soc. Exptl. Biol. Medicine, Soc. Toxicology (chmn. bd. publs. 1968-71, councilor 1972-74, amb. toxicology Mid-Atlantic divsn. 1990, hon. mem. 1995, Award of Merit 1981), Westchester Chem. Soc. (Disting. Scientist 1996), Sigma Xi, Alpha Chi Sigma (pres. Washington profl. chpt. 1967-68), Phi Lambda Upsilon. Achievements include rsch. in lifestyle and chronic disease prevention, relevant mechanisms, and medical care cost reduction. Home: 4 Whitewood Rd White Plains NY 10603-1137 Personal E-mail: johnweisburger@aol.com. *In my lifetime a revolutionary change occurred in our knowledge of the causes and the mechanisms involved in the major premature killing diseases—heart disease, hypertension, stroke, many forms of cancer. These key advances stemmed from the partnership between the federal government, public-supported societies and academic institutions that encourage health research. The impact of these diseases can be reduced in virtually all countries of the world provided their political bodies can agree that peaceful endeavors and cooperation in fostering better health for their people can be made a high priority goal. Medical science now can implement successful prevention efforts. I am glad I have lived through this period and have played a role in this development.*

**WEISEL, MICHAEL LLOYD,** lawyer, educator; m. Deborah Lamm Weisel, June 6, 1987; children: Avery Christiana, Schuyler McFall. BS in Bus. Mgmt. and History, Guilford Coll., 1977; JD, Campbell U., 1980; postgrad., Duke U. 2002—; MA in History, N.C. State U., 2003. Bar: N.C. 1980; lic. securities arbitrator Nat. Assn. Securities Dealers, 1998, securities license Series 7, 24 Nat. Assn. Securities Dealers. V.p. equity Wells Fargo Bank, NA, Washington, 1988—90; v.p., portfolio mgr. Kemper Fin. Svcs., Chgo. 1990—95; atty. Allen & Pinnix, Raleigh, 1996—2003, Taylor, Penry, Rash & Riemann PLLC, Raleigh, 2003—06; gen. counsel to spkr. pro tempore N.C. Ho. Reps., NC, 2006—. Bd. mem. NC State Banking Commn., Raleigh, 1993—97; trustee N.C. Tchrs. and State Employees' Retirement Systems, Raleigh, 1993—95, N.C. Local Govt. Employees' Retirement Sys., Raleigh, 1993—95; chair Fgn. Trade Zone #93, Raleigh, 1997—; sec. N.C. R.R. Co., 1999—2004, N.C. Devel. Fin. Corp., 2000—; bd. dirs. Local bd. mem. US SSS, NC, 2003—; commn. mem. Legislative Sch. Capital Constrn. Study Commn., Raleigh, 1993—95; bd. mem.,vice chair fin. com. N.C. Bd. Cmty. Colls., Raleigh, 1997—2000; com. mem. NC Legislative Fin. Institutions Com., Raleigh, 1998—99; chair Wake County Smart Start, Inc., NC, 1997—; elected chair Wake County Dem. Party, NC, 1999—2003; mem. N.C. Dem. Party State Exec. Com., 1997—; candidate Office N.C. State Treas., 1995—96. Named one of Outstanding Young Man of Am., Nat. Jaycees; fellow, Inst. Polit. Leadership; History Departmental fellow, Duke U., 2002—, Summer Seminar in Mil. History fellow, West Point Mil. Acad., 2004. Mem.: Penn Club NY, Union League Club Chgo., Phi Alpha Theta. Office: Taylor Penry Rash & Riemann PLLC Ste 319 510 Glenwood Ave Raleigh NC 27603 Office Phone: 919-833-9449.

**WEISEL, THOMAS W.,** investment company executive; Founder, chmn. & CEO Montgomery Securities, San Francisco, 1978—98, Thomas Weisel Partners, San Francisco, 1999—. Co-author (with Lance Armstrong & Richard Bryant): Capital Instincts: Life As an Entrepreneur, Financier & Athlete, 2003. Trustee Mus. Modern Art, N.Y.C., San Francisco. Office: Thomas Weisel Ptnrs 1 Montgomery St San Francisco CA 94104

**WEISENBURGER, PETER DOMINIC,** theater educator, director; b. Buffalo, Oct. 18, 1971; s. Paul Francis and Mary Catherine Weisenburger; m. Merritt Susan Minnemeyer, Sept. 9, 2000; 1 child, Elijah Paul. BA in Theater Arts & Broadcasting TV, Buffalo State Coll., 1991, 96; MFA in Acting, Bklyn Coll., 1997—99. Cert. SAFD unarmed combat NY, 1999. Art educator various theaters, Seattle, 2000—03; drama dept. head, dir., prodr. Monte Vista Christian Sch., Watsonville, Calif., 2003—. Pvt. acting coach, Monterey, Calif., 2004—. Dir.: R & J MBR Theater; composer (film soundtrack) One Particular Person, singer/songwriter Band 'me 'n' Pete (Nominee Best Original Rock Band, Buffalo, 1996); actor: (theater) Holes Seattle Children's Theater, Macbeth, Seattle Shakespeare Company, Raised in Captivity, Spare Change, The Castle, Myriad Arts Prodns., Bus Stop, Angels in America Part 1, Caucasian Chalk Circle (Best Ensemble Cast award, ACTF Competition, 1995). Eucharistic min. Mother of Divine Grace, Buffalo, 1989—91. Mem.: Actor's Equity Assn. Democrat-Npl. Roman Catholic. Avocations: travel, reading.

**WEISENBURGER, THEODORE MAURICE,** retired judge, poet, educator; b. Tuttle, N.D., May 12, 1930; s. John and Emily (Rosenau) W.; children: Sam, Jennifer, Emily, Todd, Daniel, Dwight, Holly, Michael, Paul, Peter; m. Maylyne Chu, Sept. 19, 1985; 1 child, Irene. BA, U. N.D., 1952, LLB, 1956, JD, 1969; BFT, Am. Grad Sch. Internat. Mgmt., Phoenix, 1957. Bar: N.D. 1963, U.S. Dist. Ct. N.D. 1963. County judge, tchr. Bensen County, Minnewaukan, ND, 1968-75, Walsh County, Grafton, ND, 1975-87; trial judge Devils Lake Sioux, Ft. Totten, ND, 1968-84, Turtle Mountain Chippewa, Belcourt, ND, 1974-87; U.S. magistrate U.S. Dist. Ct., Minnewaukan, 1972-75; Justice of the Peace pro tem Maricopa County, Ariz., 1988-92; instr. Rio Salado C.C., 1992—. Tchr. in Ethiopia, 1958-59. Author: Poetry and Other Poems, 1991. 1st lt. U.S. Army, 1952-54. Recipient Humanitarian award U.S. Cath. Conf., 1978, 82, Right to Know award Sigma Delta Chi, 1980, Spirit of Am. award U.S. Conf. Bishops, 1982. Home: 4353 E Libby St Phoenix AZ 85032-1732 Office Phone: 602-992-0492. Personal E-mail: tweisenburger@cox.net.

**WEISER, DENNIS CHARLES,** writer, philosopher; b. Phila., Apr. 4, 1951; s. Richard Charles Weiser and Edith Gertrude Stevens; m. Helen Elizabeth Lewandowski, Dec. 7, 1991; children: Saundra Marie Schnoebelen, Kathryn Joan Thomas, Barbara Lynn Damron. BA in Liberal Arts, Westminster Coll., 1978; MA in Philosophy, U. Kans., 1991. Bus. humorist, journalist Kans. City

Bus. Jour., Mo., 1984—85; philosophy tchr. Johnson Country CC, Mo., 1988—96, Avila CC, 1988—96, Met. CC, 1988—96, Kans. City Kans. CC, 1988—96; journalist Pitch Weekly, Kansas City, 1998. Author: (novel) Allegory, 2004, Crash Dummies, 2005; poet: is/2, 2005, Nature: New & Selected Poems, 2006, Exceptional Poems, 2006, The Third Awakening, 2006. Nominee fellowship, Rockefeller Found., 1973; recipient Samuel Robins prize in Religion, Robins Found., Westminster Coll., 1977, Prose Fiction First prize, Chgo. Printers Row Book Fair, 2004. Mem.: Writers Place, TallGrass Writers Guild, Soc. Social and Polit. Philosophy, Ctrl. States Philos. Assn., Am. Philos. Assn. Personal E-mail: reversed.thunder@yahoo.com.

**WEISER, RALPH RAPHAEL,** oil industry executive; b. N.Y.C., May 25, 1925; children: Jane, Jeffrey. BA, NYU, 1947; JSD, Harvard U., 1950. Bar: N.Y. 1950. Ptnr. Lotterman & Weiser, Esq., N.Y.C., 1955-64; pres. Dragor Shipping Inc., N.Y.C., 1964-65; chmn. Nat. Equipment Rental, N.Y.C., 1965-67; exec. v.p. Am. Export Industries, N.Y.C., 1967-69; pvt. practice investment, 1970-84; chmn. World Fuel Svc. Corp. (NYSE-INT), Miami, Fla., 1984—. Office: World Fuel Services Corp 9800 NW 41st St Ste 400 Miami FL 33178

**WEISER, SHERWOOD MANUEL,** hotel and corporation executive, lawyer; b. Cleve., Mar. 9, 1931; s. Aaron A. and Helen (Scheiner) W.; m. Judith A. Zirkin, July 31, 1955; children: Douglas J., Warren P., Michele A. BS, Ohio State U., 1952; LLB, Case Western Res. U., 1955. Bar: Ohio 1955. Ptnr. Weiser & Weiser, Attys., Cleve., 1955-65, Weiser & Lefton, Attys., Cleve., 1965-69; chmn., chief exec. officer TCC, Miami, Fla., 1970—. Bd. dirs. Mellon United Bank, Miami, Interstate Hotels, Watsco. Trustee Fla. Internat. U. Found., Miami, 1984-94, U. Miami, 1988—, New World Symphony, Miami, 1987—; trustee, chmn. bd. Ransom-Everglades Sch., Miami, 1974-84; co-chmn. bd. advisors Coconut Grove Playhouse, 1986-90; chmn. Performing Arts Ctr. Found., 1994—. Mem. Cleve. Bar Assn. Soc. of Benchers, Order of Coif. Jewish. Avocations: tennis, sailing, art. Office: The Continental Companies LLC 3250 Mary St Miami FL 33133-5232 Office Phone: 305-445-4220. E-mail: weiser@tcchotels.com.

**WEISERT, KENT ALBERT FREDERICK,** lawyer; b. Passaic, N.J., Sept. 9, 1949; s. Frederick William and Waleska Anna Sophia (Bischoff) W.; m. Deborah Jean Searing, Mar. 12, 1983; 1 child, Christianna Lillian. BA magna cum laude, Rutgers U., 1971, JD, 1974. Bar: N.J. 1974, U.S. Dist. Ct. N.J. 1974, U.S. Tax Ct. 1975, U.S. Ct. Appeals (3d cir.) 1978, U.S. Supreme Ct. 1987. Adminstrv. asst. trust dept. Howard Savs. Bank, Newark, 1973-74; ptnr. Schwartz, Tobia & Stanziale, Montclair, NJ, 1975—2001; pvt. practice law Bloomfield, NJ, 2001—. Arbitrator U.S. Dist. Ct., Newark, 1985—. Contbr. chpt. to book New Jersey Transaction Guide, 1987. Pres. ch. coun. Holy Trinity Luth. Ch., Nutley, N.J., 1982-83; session mem., elder Watchung Presbyn. Ch., Bloomfield, N.J.; mem. Greater N.J. Estate Planning Coun.; trustee, v.p. Oakeside Bloomfield Cultural Ctr. Mem. N.J. State Bar Assn., Essex County Bar Assn., Rutgers Law Sch. Alumni Assn., Nat. Trust Hist. Preservation, N.J. Hist. Soc., Phi Beta Kappa, Phi Alpha Theta, Pi Delta Epsilon. Republican. Presbyterian. Avocations: classical music, antiques, tennis, historical preservation, military and general history. Home and Office: Kent AF Weisert Esq 51 Fairway Bloomfield NJ 07003 Office Phone: 973-338-5533.

**WEISFELDT, MYRON LEE,** cardiologist, educator; b. Milw., Apr. 25, 1940; s. Simon Charles and Sophia (Price) W.; m. Linda Nan Zaremski, Dec. 29, 1963; children: Ellyn Joy, Lisa Janel, Sara Michelle Student, Northwester U., 1958-60; BA, Johns Hopkins U., 1962, MD, 1965. Intern and resident Columbia-Presbyn. Med. Ctr., N.Y.C., 1965-67; fellow in cardiology Mass. Gen. Hosp., Boston, 1970-72; asst. prof. medicine Johns Hopkins U., Balt., 1972-78, prof. medicine, 1978-91, Robert L. Levy prof. cardiology, 1979-91; Samuel Bard prof. medicine, chair dept. Columbia-Presbyn. Med. Ctr., N.Y.C., 1991—2001; William Osler prof. medicine, dir. dept. medicine Johns Hopkins Med. Sch., 2001—; physician in chief Johns Hopkins Hosp., 2001. Dir. cardiology Johns Hopkins Med. Inst., Balt., 1975-91, Peter Belfer Lab. for Johns Hopkins, Ischemic Heart Disease Spl. Ctr. Rsch., 1977-91; nat. pres. Am. Heart Assn., 1989-90; cardiology adv. com. Nat. Heart, Lung and Blood Inst., 1986-90, chmn., 1988-90; mem. adv. coun. Nat. Inst. on Aging, 1999-2002; study chair resuscitation outcomes consortium Nat. Heart Lung and Blood Inst., 2004—. Editor: The Aging Heart, 1980; editorial bd. Jour. Clin. Investigation, 1984-88, Circulation, 1980-86, 88—2004, Jour. Am. Coll. Cardiology, 1987-93; Jour. Molecular and Cellular Cardiology, 1975-80, 86-89; Circulation Rsch., 1988-94. With USPHS, 1967—69. NIH grantee, 1977-91; recipient Golden Heart award Am. Heart Assn., 1998, Harrick award, 2004. Fellow AAAS, ACP (Phillips award in clin. medicine 2006), Am. Coll. Cardiology; mem. Assn. Univ. Cardiologists, Am. Soc. Clin. Investigation, Assn. Am. Physicians, Assn. Prof. Medicine, Inst. of Medicine, Phi Beta Kappa, Alpha Omega Alpha, Interurban Clin. Club. Jewish. Office: Johns Hopkins Medicine 1830 E Monument St Ste 9026 Baltimore MD 21287 Home: 1002 Rolandvue Ave Baltimore MD 21204 Office Phone: 410-955-6642. Business E-Mail: mlw5@jhmi.edu.

**WEISGAL, JEANNE NANCY,** writer; b. Balt. Oct. 24, 1925; d. Hirsh and Freddy (Mesirow) de LaViez; m. Fred Weisgal, June 15, 1948; children: Margit B., Lawrence D., Samuel J., Aran K., Rebecca E. Student, U. Minn., 1946—47, Natanya, Jerusalem, 1969-70; BS, U. Md., 1948. Tchr. Balt. Pub. Schs., 1948-49; tchr. drama Chizuk Amuno Synagogue, Balt., 1950-51; exec. sec. Md. branch ACLU, Balt., 1954-63; owner That Handbag Place, Balt., 1967-69, Gypsy Ladies Boutique, Jerusalem, 1975-80; columnist Jerusalem Post, 1982-84; pvt. practice writing Jerusalem-Balt., 1984—. Cons. theater Profl. Frats. United Jewish Appeal, Balt., 1953-67; cons. Goliath Bar-Restaurant, Jerusalem, 1975. Author: (cookbooks) Entertaining in Jerusalem, 1985, Dinner for Eight, 1996. Publ. adv. Dem. Com., Balt., 1952-66; vol. Israel Def. Forces, Jerusalem, 1973-74. Avocation: antique quilts. Home and Office: 4401 Roland Ave Unit 612 Baltimore MD 21210-2795 Office Phone: 410-243-1823.

**WEISGALL, JONATHAN MICHAEL,** lawyer; b. Balt., Mar. 17, 1949; s. Hugo David and Nathalie (Shulman) W.; m. Ruth Macdonald, June 3, 1979; children: Alison, Andrew, Benjamin. BA, Columbia Coll., 1970; JD, Stanford U., 1973. Bar: D.C. 1974, N.Y. 1974, U.S. Supreme Ct. 1982, Marshall Islands 1983. Law clk. to judge U.S. Ct. Appeals (9th cir.), San Francisco, 1973-74; assoc. Covington & Burling, Washington, 1974-79; from assoc. to ptnr. Ginsburg, Feldman, Weil & Bress, Washington, 1983-99; pvt. practice Washington, 1983-99; v.p. Legis. and Regulatory Affairs MidAmerican Energy Holdings Co., 1995—. Adj. prof. Georgetown U. Law Ctr. Author: Operation Crossroads: The Atomic Tests at Bikini Atoll, 1994; exec. prodr. documentary film Radio Bikini. Chmn. bd. dirs. Ctr. for Energy Efficiency and Renewable Techs.; trustee Arena Stage, Washington; bd. dirs. Meet the Composer, Geothermal Resources Coun. Mem. Geothermal Energy Assn. (past v.p., bd. dirs., pres.), Geothermal Resources Coun. (bd. dirs.), Phi Beta Kappa. Jewish. Home: 5309 Edgemoor Ln Bethesda MD 20814-1323 Office: Ste 300 1200 New Hampshire Ave NW Washington DC 20036-6812 Office Phone: 202-828-1378. Personal E-mail: jmweisgall@midamerican.com.

**WEISKOPF, WANDA,** mezzo soprano, writer, poet; b. Jefferson City, Mo., Aug. 2, 1921; d. Elmer and Stella Jane (Buster) Connell; m. Herbert Weiskopf (dec.); children: Douglas McK., Marta Jane. Student, L.A. Conservatory, 1950—55. Pvt. voice tchr., Portland, Oreg., 1970—80. Activities dir., editor Skylines Portland Ctr., 1970—85; adjudicator Met. Opera Auditions, Seattle, 1990. Singer: (Operas) Portland Cathedral and St. Michael's, 1970—85, appeared in maj. opera houses, leading roles in Mo., Calif., Oreg., Italy, San Remo; author: All Is Not Winter, 1976, On the Wings of Song, 1995, Listen To The River, 2001. Organizer meml. concert Am. Heart Assn., Portland, 1971; active Dem. Party, Burbank, Calif., 1990. With U.S. Army, 1942. Mem.: Nat. Assn. Tchrs. Singing, Nat. Writers Assn. (sec. LA chpt. 1989—2005). Democrat. Avocation: walking. Home: 1207 N Cordova St #105 Burbank CA 91505-2218

**WEISMAN, ERIC,** music company executive; With Premier Artists Svcs., 1985, Bassin Distbr., 1985—90, Alliance Entertainment Corp., Minnetonka, Minn., 1990, pres., CEO, 1997—2003; CEO Musicland Holding Corp. 2003—05, advisor, 2005—. Office: Musicland Holding Corp 10400 Yellow Circle Dr Minnetonka MN 55343

**WEISMAN, GARY ANDREW,** biochemist; b. Bklyn., June 18, 1951; s. Joseph Herman and Elaine (Melman) W.; m. Sandra Kay Hille, Aug. 4, 1979; children: Laura Joanne, Pamela Michelle, Veronica Evelyn. BS, Polytechnic U., 1972; postgrad., U. Bordeaux, France, 1972-74; PhD, U. Nebr., 1980. Postdoctoral rsch. assoc. Cornell U., N.Y.C., 1980-85; asst. prof. U. Mo., Columbia, 1985-92, assoc. prof., 1992-98, prof., 1998—. Spl. reviewer NIH, mem. ODCS Study Section; reviewer NSF, Am. Jour. Physiology, Jour. Biol. Chemistry, Molec. Pharmacology, Euro. Jour. Pharmacol. GLIA; editl. bd. Purinergic Signalling. Contbr. articles to profl. jours. Grantee USDA, 1987—; NIH, 1988—; CF Found., 1994-2000, Am. Diabetes, 1995-2002, Am. Heart Assn. 1994-. Mem. AAAS, Am. Chem. Soc., Am. Soc. Biochem. and Molecular Biology, Am. Diabetes Assn., Am. Heart Assn., NY Acad. Scis., Soc. for Neurosci., Am. Soc. Nutr. Scis., Am. Soc. Pharmacol. and Exptl. Therapeut. Home: 1804 University Ave Columbia MO 65201-6004 Office: U Mo Dept Biochemistry 540E Life Scis Ctr Columbia MO 65211-7310 Business E-Mail: weismang@missouri.edu.

**WEISMAN, JOEL,** retired engineering educator; b. NYC, July 15, 1928; s. Abraham and Ethel (Marcus) W.; m. Bernice Newman, Feb. 6, 1955; 1 child, Jay (dec.) B.Ch.E., CCNY, 1948; MS, Columbia U., 1949; PhD, U. Pitts. 1968. Registered profl. engr., N.Y. Plant engr. Etched Products, NYC, 1950-51; from jr. engr. to assoc. engr. Brookhaven Nat. Lab., Upton, NY, 1951-54; from engr. to fellow engr. Westinghouse Nuclear Energy Systems, Pitts., 1954-59, from fellow engr. to mgr. thermal and hydraulic analysis 1960-68; sr. engr. Nuclear Devel. Assocs., White Plains, NY, 1959-60; assoc. prof. nuclear engring. U. Cin., 1968-72, prof. nuclear engring., 1972-96, dir. nuclear engring. program, 1977-86, dir. lab. basic and applied nuclear research, 1984-94, prof. emeritus nuclear engring., 1996—. Co-author: Thermal Analysis of Pressurized Water Reactors, 1970, 2d edit., 1979, Chinese edit., 1981, 3rd edit., 1996, Introduction to Optimization Theory, 1973, Modern Power Plant Engineering, 1985; editor: Elements of Nuclear Reactor Design, 1977, Chinese edit., 1982, 2d edit., 1983; contbr. tech. articles to profl. jours.; patentee in field. Mem. Cin. Environ. Adv. Council, 1976-78; mem. Cin. Asian Art Soc., 1977—, v.p., 1980-82, pres., 1982-84; mem. exec. bd. Air Pollution League Greater Cin., 1980-90. Sr. NATO fellow, Winfrith Lab., U.K. Atomic Energy Authority, 1972; sr. fellow Argonne Nat. Lab., Ill., 1982; NSF research grantee, 1974-78, 82-85, 86-89; recipient Dean's award U. Cin. Coll. Engring., 1987. Fellow Am. Nuclear Soc. (v.p. Pitts. sect. 1957-58, mem. exec. com. thermal-hydraulics div. 1989-92); mem. Am. Inst. Chem. Engrs., Sigma Xi Democrat. Jewish. Avocation: Japanese art. Office: U Cin Dept Mech Ind & Nuclear Engr Cincinnati OH 45221-0001

**WEISMAN, LORENZO DAVID,** investment banker; b. Guatemala, Central America, Apr. 22, 1945; arrived in US, 1957. s. Eduardo and Suzanne (Loeb) Weisman; m. Danielle Maysonnave, June 22, 1971; children: Melissa Anne, Alexia Maria, Thomas Alexander. BA in History and Lit. cum laude (hon.), Harvard U., 1966; postgrad., Conservatoire Nat. D'Art Dramatique, Paris, 1966—71; MBA in Fin., Columbia U., 1973. V.p. Dillon, Read, and Co., Inc., N.Y.C., 1977—80; sr. v.p., 1980—82, mng. dir. London, 1982—84; pres., CEO Dillon Read, Ltd., London, 1984—93; head Internat. Dillon, Read, and Co., Inc., N.Y.C., 1993—97; head L.Am. corp. fin. UBS Warburg, N.Y.C., 1997—2001; co-founder, mng. mem. Hill St. Capital, LLC, N.Y.C., 2002—. Com. univ. resources Harvard U., 1991, mem. adv. com. David Rockefeller Ctr. for L.Am. studies, 1995—; mem. bd. overseers Columbia Bus. Sch., 1992. Co-chmn., trustee French Inst./Alliance Français, N.Y.C., 1995. Mem.: Harvard Club (NYC), Travelers Club (Paris), Knickerbocker Club (NYC), NY Yacht Club. Office Phone: 212-326-2601. E-mail: lweisman@hillstreetcap.com.

**WEISMAN, RICHARD SCOTT,** lawyer; b. NYC, Nov. 3, 1956; s. Harold and Sarah (Delaney) Weisman. AB, Harvard Coll., 1978, JD, 1982. Bar: N.Y. 1983. Spl. asst. Senator Daniel Patrick Moynihan, Washington, 1978-79; assoc. Cahill Gordon & Reindel, N.Y.C., 1982-84, Sidley & Austin, N.Y.C., 1984-87, Winthrop Stimson Putnam & Roberts, N.Y.C., 1987-90; atty. Richard S. Weisman, Esq., N.Y.C. and Westchester, N.Y., 1990-91, Beller & Keller, N.Y.C., 1992-95; mng. ptnr. Weisman & Calderon LLP, Mt. Vernon, N.Y., 1996—. Mem.: Bronx County Bar Assn. (bd. dirs.), Westchester County Bar Assn., Nat. Guardianship Assn., Mt. Vernon Bar Assn., N.Y. State Trial Lawyers Assn., N.Y. State Bar Assn. Office: Weisman & Calderon LLP 6 Gramatan Ave Ste 206 Mount Vernon NY 10550-3209 Office Phone: 914-668-8900. E-mail: weismanr@erols.com.

**WEISMAN, STEVEN ROGER,** newspaper editor; b. L.A., Nov. 10, 1946; s. Joseph Harris and Etta Gladys (Sugarman) W.; m. Elisabeth Bumiller, Oct. 23, 1983; children: Madeleine Elisabeth, Theodore Joseph. BA, Yale, 1968. Reporter N.Y. Times, N.Y.C., 1968—, City Hall bur. chief, 1976-78, Albany bur. chief, 1978, White House corr., 1979-81, sr. White House corr., 1981-85, New Delhi bur. chief, 1985-88, Tokyo bur. chief, 1989-92, dep. fgn. editor, 1992-95, mem. editl. bd., 1995—2002, chief diplomatic corr., Washington bur., 2002—. Bd. dirs. Yale Alumni Publs., New Haven, Conn., 1983—. Author: The Great Tax Wars, 2002 (Sidney Hillman book award, 2003). Recipient award Silurian Soc., N.Y.C., 1975, Edward Weintal Prize, 2004. Jewish. Office: NY Times Washington Bur 7th Fl 1627 I St Washington DC 20006 Home: 5212 Falmouth Rd Bethesda MD 20816-2913 Office Phone: 202-862-0353. Office Fax: 202-862-0340. E-mail: weisman@nytimes.com.*

**WEISMANN, DONALD LEROY,** artist, educator, filmmaker, writer; b. Milw., Oct. 12, 1914; s. Friedrich Othello and Stela Priscilla (Custer) W.; m. M. Virginia Stant; children: Anne Wilder, Christopher Thomas. BS, U. Wis., 1935; PhM, U. Wis., Madison, 1940; PhD, Ohio State U., 1950. Asst. prof. art Ill. State U., Normal, 1940-42, 47-48, Wayne U., Detroit, 1949-51; prof., head dept. art U. Ky., Lexington, 1951-54; prof., chmn. dept. art U. Tex., Austin, 1954-58, Univ. prof. arts, 1959-81, prof. emeritus, 1981—. Cons. Ford Found., N.Y.C., 1958, 66, U.S. Nat. Com. UNESCO, 1953, Rockefeller Found., 1956, Nat. Council Arts., 1966-72; spl. cons. USIS, Forence, Italy, 1961-62 Author: Language and Visual Form, 1968, Visual Arts as Human Experience, 1970, Duncan Phyfe & Drum, 1984, Follow the Bus with the Greek License Plates, 1981, Frank Reaugh, Painter to the Longhorns, 1985, The Stuff of Stories, 1999, Artifacts, Fictions and Memory, 2001, An American Fugue, 2002, Jelly Is Where You Find It, 2006; contbr. articles, poems, stories and revs. to profl. jours.; painter, collagist one-man shows, Cushman Gallery, Houston, Nye Gallery, Dallas, Petite Gallery, NYC, Art Mus. U. N. Mex., group shows, Bocour Gallery, NYC, Chgo. Art Inst., Dallas Mus. Fine Arts, Rockefeller Ctr., NYC, Vanucci Gallery, Pistoia, Italy, Villa Monte Carlo Chapala, Jalisco, Mexico; film-maker numerous productions. Served to lt. (j.g.) USN, 1942-45, PTO Recipient Letter of Commendation Pres. U.S., 1972; honoree for book Some Folks Went West, 12th Ann. Writers Conf., Austin, 1960; grantee U. Tex. Rsch. Inst., Italy, Eng., 1961-62, 71, Pub. Broadcast Corp., 1970, 72; named fine arts scholar Harvard U., 1941 Mem. Nat. Humanities Faculty Home: 4513 Edgemont Dr Austin TX 78731-5223 Office: Am Studies U Tex Austin TX 78712

**WEISMANTEL, GREGORY NELSON,** management consultant, computer company executive; b. Houston, Sept. 8, 1940; s. Leo Joseph and Ellen Elizabeth (Zudis) W.; m. Marilyn Ann Fanger, June 18, 1966; children: Guy Gregory, Christopher Gregory, Andrea Rose. BA in English, U. Notre Dame, 1962; MBA in Internat. Bus., Loyola U., Chgo., 1979. With mgmt. staff Gen. Foods Corp., White Plains, NY, 1966-80; pres., chief exec. officer Manor House Foods, Inc., Addison, Ill., 1980-82, Weismantel & Assocs., Downers Grove, Ill., 1982-84; v.p. perishable div. Profl. Marketers, Inc., Lombard, Ill., 1984-86, group v.p. sales and mktg. services, dir. corp. strategy, 1986-87; v.p. mng. prin. CPG Industry, Louis A. Allen Assoc. Inc., Palo Alto, Calif., 1987-88; pres., chief exec. officer The Vista Tech. Group, Ltd., St. Charles, Ill., 1989-2000, chmn. bd., 2001—02; pres. Epic Global Technol., 2002—.

**WEISMILLER, ELEANOR KOVACS,** library director; b. Perth Amboy, NJ, Aug. 12, 1942; d. Louis T and Ethel D Kovacs; m. David L Weismiller (dec.); children: Chris, David. BA, Duquesne U., 1964; tchg. cert., Wash. Montessori Inst., 1967. Cert. Notary Public State of Calif. Tchr. Montessori Child Develop., West Covina, Calif., 1978—80; sch. libr. Rowland Unified Sch. Dist., Rowland Hts., Calif., 1981—87; libr. asst. County of Los Angeles Pub. Libr., 1987—96, cmty. libr. mgr. Whittier, Calif., 1996—. Founding mem. Friends of the Sorensen Libr., Whittier, Calif., 1989—. Mem. West Whittier Cmty. Coun., Population Stabilization, Washington. Avocation: art. Office: Sorensen Libr 11405 E Rose Hedge Dr Whittier CA 90606 Office Phone: 562-695-3979.

**WEISS, ALLAN JOSEPH,** transport company executive, lawyer; b. Boston, Nov. 1, 1932; s. Mark and Eve S. (Kane) Weiss; m. Sherrill Roecker, Feb. 18, 1973 (dec. Jan. 2004); children: Stephanie Eve, Mark Allan. BS, U.S. Mcht. Marine Acad., 1955; JD, Cornell U., 1961. Bar: N.Y. 1961, D.C. 1962, Calif. 1965, U.S. Supreme Ct. 1965. Trial atty. admiralty and shipping U.S. Dept. Justice, 1961-67, chief trial atty. admiralty office San Francisco, 1967-74; Pacific counsel Sea-Land Service, Inc., Oakland, Calif., 1974-76, dep. gen. counsel, 1977-78, gen. counsel, 1978-82, sr. v.p., 1979-82; assoc. gen. counsel Sea-Land Industries, 1979-82; pres. Freights Unltd., Inc., 1982—; gen. counsel Toledo, Peoria & Western Rwy., 1991-96. Adj. prof. law McGeorge Sch. Law, 1974-76 Served with U.S. Navy, 1956-57. Mem. Fed. Bar Assn., Calif. Bar Assn., D.C. Bar Assn., Maritime Law Assn., Maritime Law Assn. U.S., Cornell U. Law Assn., Kings Point Alumni Assn. Home: 89 Loft Dr Martinsville NJ 08836-2246 Office: Freights Unlimited Inc 89 Loft Dr Martinsville NJ 08836-2246 Office Phone: 732-627-5007. Business E-Mail: freights@optonline.net.

**WEISS, ALVIN HARVEY,** chemical engineer, educator, research scientist, consultant; b. Phila., Apr. 28, 1928; s. Louis and Helen F. (Wilinsky) W.; children: Linda S., Louis B.; m. Devorah Schwartz, June 10, 1979. BSChemE, U. Pa., 1949, PhD in Phys. Chemistry, 1965; MSChemE, Newark Coll. Engring., 1955. Registered profl. engr., Mass., Del. Chem. engr. Fiber Chem. Corp., Cliffwood, NJ, 1949-51, Colgate-Palmolive Co., Jersey City, 1953-55, Houdry Process and Chem. Co., Linwood, Pa., 1956-63; rsch. assoc., lectr. U. Pa., Phila., 1963-66; prof. chem. engring. Worcester (Mass.) Poly. Inst., 1966-94, prof. emeritus, 1994—. Vis. prof. Northeastern U., Boston, 2000—01; NASA-ASEE summer faculty fellow Stanford U. Ames Rsch. Ctr., 1967—68; affiliate scientist Worcester Found. Exptl. Biology, 1972—74; Fulbright-Hays sr. faculty fellow to dept. chem. engring. Ben-Gurion U. of Negev, Beersheva, Israel, 1973—74, vis. prof. chem. engring., 1974; U.S. coord. U.S.-USSR Coop. Sci. Program in Chem. Catalysis, Topic IV, 1973—76, prin. investigator (with M.M. Sakharov), 1976—78; prin. investigator (with K.I. Ione) U.S.-USSR Coop. Sci. Program in Chem. Catalysis, Topic III, 1978—80; Fulbright-Hays vis. lectr. dept. chem. engring. Mid. East Tech. U., Ankara, Turkey, 1974, vis. prof., 91; vis. rsch. scientist dept. organic chemistry Weizmann Inst., Rehovoth, Israel, 1974; vis. lectr. Inst. Isotopes and Ctrl. Inst. Chemistry, Hungarian Acad. Scis., Budapest, 1976; vis. prof. Inst. Cultural Rels. and Inst. Isotopes, Hungarian Acad. Scis., 1978, 80; UNIDO chief tech. advisor to Petrochem Complex of Bahia Blanca, Argentina, 80; sr. rsch. fellow chem. sys. lab. Army Chem. Ctr., Md., 1981; UNIDO expert in chem. process devel. Rsch. Inst. for Chem. Industry, Beijing, 1982; UNIDO expert in catalysis to YARPET Petrochem. Complex, Yarimca, Turkey, 1986—87; bd. dirs. U.S. com. for sci. coop. with Vietnam; vis. scient. Nat. Ctr. for Sci. Rsch., Hanoi Inst. of Indsl. Chemistry, Ho Chi Minh City, 1986; vis. prof., vis. scientist Ctr. for Advanced Microgravity Materials Processing, Northeastern U., Boston, 2000—02. Translator: (with M. Delleo, G. Dembinski and J. Happel) Catalysis by Non-Metals (O.V. Krylov), 1970; author (autobiography): Chemistry, Engineering and Other Stories, 1994; contbr. articles to profl. jours.; patentee in field. With U.S. Army, 1951-53. Recipient Sci. Achievement award Worcester Engring. Soc., 1984; Rsch. grantee NSF, PRF, NASA, DOD, DOE, EPA Fellow AIChE (rsch. com. 1968-80, symposia chmn. 1973-84); mem. AAUP, Catalysis Soc. (bd. dirs., sec. 1968-88), Catalysis Soc. New Eng. (founding pres. 1967-68, bd. dirs. 1968—), Am. Chem. Soc. (New Eng. petroleum divsn. rep. 1970-88, session chmn. 1973—), German Assn. for Chemische Apparatwesen Personal E-mail: ahweiss@yahoo.com.

**WEISS, ANTHONY A.,** computer company executive; Positions through sr. v.p. sales, distribution & support CompUSA, Dallas, 1988—98, exec. v.p. bus. solutions, 1998—2001, exec. v.p., GMM, 2001—03, COO, then CompUSA Stores, 2003—06, pres., CEO, 2006. Office: CompUSA 14951 Dallas Pkwy Dallas TX 75254*

**WEISS, ARMAND BERL,** economist, association management executive; b. Richmond, Va., Apr. 2, 1931; s. Maurice Herbert and Henrietta (Shapiro) W.; m. Judith Bernstein, May 18, 1957; children: Jo Ann Michele, Rhett Louis. BS in Econs., Wharton Sch. Fin., U. Pa., 1953, MBA, 1954; DBA, George Washington U., 1971. Cert. assn. exec. Officer USN, 1954—65; spl. asst. to auditor gen. Dept. Navy, 1964—65; sr. economist Ctr. for Naval Analyses, Arlington, Va., 1965—68; project dir. Logistics Mgmt. Inst., Washington, 1966—74; dir. sys. integration Fed. Energy Adminstrn., Washington, 1974—76; sr. economist Nat. Commn. Supplies and Shortages, 1976—77; tech. asst. to v.p. Sys. Planning Corp., 1977—78; chmn. bd., pres., CEO Assns. Internat. Inc., 1978—; chmn. bd. dirs., CFO Rail Digital Corp., 1988—91; v.p., treas. Tech. Frontiers, Inc., 1978—80; sr. v.p. Weiss Pub. Co., Inc., Richmond, 1960—. V.p. Condo News Internat., Inc., 1981; v.p. bd. dirs. Leaders Digest Inc., 1987—88; sec., bd. dirs. Mgmt. Svcs. Internat. Inc., 1987—88, 1989—90; vis. lectr. George Washington U., 1971; assoc. prof. George Mason U., 1984; treas. Dranesville (Va.) Dist. Dem. Com., 1989—93, 2003—06, Fairfax County (Va.) Dist. Dem. Com., 1992—94; assisted Pres. Clinton, v.p. Gore transition at White Ho., 1993—; pres. Washington Mgmt. and Bus. Assn., 1993—; chmn. US del., session chmn. NATO Symposium on Cost-Benefit Analysis, The Hague, Netherlands, 1969, NATO Conf. on Operational Rsch. in Indsl. Sys., St. Louis, 1970; pres. Nat. Coun. Assns. Policy Scis., 1971—77; chmn. adv. group Def. Econ. Adv. Coun. Dept. Def., 1970—74; resident assoc. Smithsonian Instn., 1973—; expert cons. Dept. State, GAO; undercover agt. FBI, 3 yrs.; del. conf. UN, 2004. Co-editor: Systems Analysis for Social Problems, 1970, The Relevance of Economic Analysis to Decision Making in the Department of Defense, 1972, Toward More Effective Public Programs: The Role of Analysis and Evaluation, 1975; editor: Cost-Effectiveness Newsletter, 1966-70, Operations Rsch./Systems Analysis Today, 1971-73, Operation Rsch./Mgmt. Sci. Today, 1974-87, Feedback, 1969-93, Condo World, 1981, The Democrat, 1997-2000; assoc. editor Ops. Rsch., 1971-75; pub. IEEE Scanner, 1983-89, Spl. and Individual Needs Tech. (SAINT) Newsletter, 1987-88, Jour. Parametrics, 1984-88. Del. Pres.'s Mid-Century White House Conf. on Children and Youth, 1950; scoutmaster Japan, U.S.; leader World Jamborees, France, Can., U.S., 1945-61; Eagle scout, 1947; U.S. del. Internat. Conf. on Ops. Rsch., Dublin, Ireland, 1972; organizing com. Internat. Cost-Effectiveness Symposium, Washington, 1970; spkr. Internat. Conf. Inst. Mgmt. Scis., Tel Aviv, 1973, del., Mexico City, 1967; mem. bus. com. Nat. Symphony Orch., 1968-70, Washington Performing Arts Soc., 1974-88; bus. mgr. Nat. Lyric Opera Co., 1983—, Internat. Assn. Med. Sci. Educators, 1997-98, Data Adminstrv. Mgmt. Assns. Nat. Capital, 1992-2001, Potomac Pedalers Touring Club, 1990-2001, Am. Friends of London Sch. Econs., 1988-97; mem. mktg. com. Fairfax Symphony Orch., 1984-91; bd. dirs. McLean (Va.) Orch., 1992-94; exec. com. Mid Atlantic coun. Union Am. Hebrew Congregations, 1970-79,

treas., 1974-79, mem. nat. MUM com., 1974-79; mem. dist. com. Boy Scouts Am., 1972-75; bd. dirs. Nat. Coun. Career Women, 1975-79; pres. Jewish temple, 1970-72; adminstr. Daniel Heumann Fund for Spinal Cord Rsch., 2000-; treas. Quest for the Cure, 2000-; mem. Coalition for Advancement of Med. Rsch., 2002-; del. UN Sci. Conf., 2004; mem. adv. bd. U. Pa. Mid. Atlantic Region, 2003- Named Hero of Hope, Rutgers U. Rally for Cure, 2004; recipient Silver medal 50-yard free style and half mile swimming meet, No. Va. Sr. Olympics, 1990, Gold, 2 Silver, 3 Bronze medals, 2001. Fellow AAAS, Washington Acad. Scis. (gov. 1981-92, v.p. 1987-88, pres.-elect 1989-90, pres. 1990-91, past pres. 1991-92), Va. Acad. Scis., Nat. Assn. Acad. Sci. (del. 1991-93), Ops. Rsch. Soc. Am. (chmn. meetings com. 1969-71, chmn. cost-effectiveness sect. 1969-70), Washington Ops. Rsch./Mgmt. Sci. Coun. (editor newsletter 1969-93, sec. 1971-72, pres. 1973-74, trustee 1975-77, bus. mgr. 1976-93, Moving Spirit award 1994), Internat. Inst. Strategic Studies (London), Am. Soc. Assn. Execs. (membership com. 1981-82, assn. mgmt. co. sect. coun. 1995-98, cert.), Inst. Ops. Rsch. and Mgmt. Scis., Am. Econ. Assn., Wharton Grad. Sch. Alumni Assn. (exec. com. 1970-73), Nat. Eagle Scout Assn., VFW, Am. Legion, Navy League U.S., Greater Washington Soc. Assn. Execs. (new ventures com. 1995-97), Alumni Assn. George Washington U. (governing bd. 1974-82, chmn. univ. publs. com. 1976-78, Alumni Svc. award 1980), Alumni Assn. George Washington U. Sch. Govt. and Bus. Adminstrn. (exec. v.p. 1977-78, pres. 1978-79), George Washington U. Doctoral Assn. (sr. v.p. 1968-69), Wharton Sch. Washington (sec. 1967-69, pres. 1969-70, exec. dir. 1987-2001, Joseph Wharton award 1991, Lifetime Svc. award 2000). Home: 6516 Truman Ln Falls Church VA 22043-1821 Office Phone: 703-237-1104. Personal E-mail: aiboss@aol.com.

**WEISS, ARNOLD HANS,** lawyer; b. Nurnberg, Germany, July 25, 1924; m. Artemis Lychos, May 5, 1956; children: Daniel L., Andrew A. BA, U. Wis., 1951, JD, 1952. Bar: Wis. 1953, DC 1958. Atty. advisor Office Gen. Counsel US Treasury, 1953-60; atty. Inter Am. Devel. Bank, 1960-61, dep. gen. counsel, 1961-70, gen. counsel, 1970-77; ptnr. Arent, Fox, Kintner, Plotkin & Kahn, Washington, 1977-90; cons. Chevy Chase, Md., 1991; sec., gen. counsel Emerging Markets Corp., Washington, 1992—2002, sr. advisor, 2004—. With US Army, 1942-47; served to lt. col. JAGC USAR, 1948-62. Decorated Bronze Star Mem.: ABA, Inter-Am. Bar Assn., Am. Soc. Internat. Law, Columbia Country Club (Chevy Chase, Md.), Army and Navy Club (Washington), Univ. Club D.C. Office: Emerging Markets Corp 2001 Pennsylvania Ave NW # 1100 Washington DC 20006-1850

**WEISS, BARBARA G.,** artist; b. Phila., Mar. 14, 1917; d. Carl Jacob Greenspan, Nellie Ellen Moyed; m. Victor Hugo Jr., May 6, 1942 (div. Dec. 1945); m. John Weiss, Nov. 10, 1946; children: Warren P., Willard Eric. Student, Calif. Art Ctr., Los Angeles, 1962—64. Owner, creator Balema Hugo Studio, Phila., 1942—49; interior designer L.A., 1953—63. Organizer workshops Charles Reid and other Artists of note, Thousand Oaks, 1994—99; creator gallery City of Thousand Oaks Civic Arts Plaza, 1996; creator mo. art show Umbrella Artists, Westlake Village, 1997—. Represented in permanent collections, L.A., Tucson, San Francisco, Paris, Rome; dir.(show): (art) The Gallery/Barnsdal Mcpl. Art Gallery, 1993—95, Heritage Gallery/Ventura County Adminstrn. Bldg., 1994—96; Exhibited in group shows at Viva Gallery, Los Angeles, 1996—97, collections, Still life, Corina/M. & Mme René BoeuF (Chagal collectors), À Cap Martin Morning on Santarini, Anne Murphy (Collects Calif. Arts), geometrics, Dr. Francoise Farneti, Rome, Le Lac, Pamela Peterson Galley Dir., Rythmns, À LeMarché, Le Petit Pont, Mme Monique Salvie, Tuscon, Ar. Social chmn. San Fernando Valley for John F. Kennedy campaign, Pierre Salinger Senatorial Campaign; pres. Westlake Village Art Guild, Calif., 1994—96, program dir., 1993—2001; art show dir. Caruso Holdings Ltd., Westlake Village, Calabasas, Calif., 1997—. Recipient 1st prize, Westlake Village Art Guild, 1996, Best of Show, Dr. Winefrid Higgins, Judge, U. Calif./San Diego, 1998, 1st prize, Westlake Village Art Guild, 2000. Mem.: Valley Watercolor Soc. Home: 31756 Bedfordhurst Ct Westlake Village CA 91361

**WEISS, BOB (ROBERT WILLIAM WEISS),** former professional basketball coach; b. Easton, Pa., May 7, 1942; m. Tracy Pritchard. BA, Pennsylvania State U., University Park, PA, 1965. Player Phila. 76er's, 1965-67, Seattle SuperSonics, 1967-68, Milwaukee Bucks, 1968, Chgo. Bulls, 1969-74, Buffalo Braves, 1974-76, Washington Bullets, 1976-77; asst. coach San Diego Clippers, 1977-79, Dallas Mavericks, 1980-86; head coach San Antonio Spurs, 1986-88; asst. coach Orlando Magic, 1989-90; head coach Atlanta Hawks, 1990-93, LA Clippers, 1993—94; asst. coach Seattle SuperSonics, 1994—2005, head coach, 2005—06.

**WEISS, BROCK LANDON,** physics professor; b. Allentown, Pa., Aug. 22, 1965; s. Larry and Cheryl Weiss. BS in Physics, Pa. State U., University Park, 1989, MS in Applied Physics, 1994, PhD in Materials, 1999. Postdoctoral scholar U of P.R., San Juan, 2000—2001; asst. prof. of physics Sonoma State U., Rohnert Park, Calif., 2001—03, Pa. State U., Altoona, 2003—. Vol. Nittany Beagle Rescue, State College, Pa., 2005—06. Achievements include research in Field emission from wide band gap semiconductor thin films. Office: Pa State U 3000 Ivyside Park Altoona PA 16601 Office Phone: 814-949-5303. Business E-Mail: blw8@psu.edu.

**WEISS, CARL,** aerospace company executive; b. Bklyn., Dec. 6, 1938; s. Morris Harold and Sonia B. (Botwinick) W.; m. Judith Fellner, Jan. 27, 1963; children: Daniel Oren, Jonathan Michael. BBA, CUNY, 1961, MBA, 1968; postgrad., Harvard U., Boston, 1970. CPA, NY. Acct. Joseph Warren & Co., NYC, 1965-68; asst. contr. Fisher Radio Corp., LI, NY, 1968-69; sr. v.p. Deutsch Relays, Inc., East Northport, NY, 1969-83; owner, exec. v.p. Logical Solutions, Inc., Melville, NY, 1983-92; owner, pres., COO G&H Tech., Inc., Camarillo, Calif., 1992—. Bd. dirs. Deutsch Dagan, Inc. With U.S. Army, 1961-67. Mem. AICPA (future issues com. 1985-88); NY Soc. CPA. Office: G & H Tech Inc 750 W Ventura Blvd Camarillo CA 93010-8382

**WEISS, CAROL JULIET,** psychiatrist; b. N.Y.C., Mar. 5, 1957; d. Eugene and Rose (Schwartz) Weiss. BA, Wesleyan U., 1977; MD, Johns Hopkins U., 1983. Diplomate Am. Bd. Psychiatry and Neurology. Intern N.Y. Hosp., N.Y.C., 1983—84; resident Payne Whitney Clinic, N.Y. Hosp., N.Y.C., 1984—87; asst. psychiatrist Payne Whitney Clinic - N.Y. Hosp., N.Y.C., 1983—87; clin. fellow Cornell U., N.Y.C., 1987—89, instr. and clin. affiliate in psychiatry and pub. health, 1989—91, clin. assoc. prof. in psychiatry and pub. health N.Y.C., 1992—; pvt. practice N.Y.C., 1987—. Cons. in field. Contbr. articles to profl. jours., chpts. to books. Mem. Am. Psychiat. Assn., Am. Soc. Addiction Medicine, Phi Beta Kappa. Office: 1044 Madison Ave New York NY 10021-0138 Office Phone: 212-988-1209.

**WEISS, CHARLES, JR.,** educator; b. San Francisco, Dec. 20, 1937; s. Charles and Dorothy (Wilkes) W.; m. Edith Gayle Brown, July 24, 1969; children: Jed Ariel, Tamara Ginger. BA summa cum laude, Harvard U., 1959, PhD, 1965. Post-doctoral fellow U. Calif., Berkeley, 1967-69; chemist Lawrence Berkeley Lab., U. Calif., Berkeley, 1969; staff scientist IBM Watson Lab., Columbia U., N.Y.C., 1969-71; sci. and tech. advisor World Bank, Washington, 1971-86; internat. Tech. Mgmt. and Fin., 1987-91, Innovation Ptnrs., 1987-91; pres. Global Tech. Mgmt., 1991—. Lectr. U. Pa., Phila., 1986-90; vis. lectr. Woodrow Wilson Sch., Princeton U., 1989-94; professorial lectr. Sch. Advanced Internat. Studies, Johns Hopkins U., 1994-97; disting. prof. Sch. Fgn. Svc., Georgetown U., 1997—, chair sci., tech. and internat. affairs, 1997—2006; corp. bd. mem. Vols. in Tech. Assistance, Arlington, Va., 1974-85; mem. U.S. Nat. Climate Adv. Com., Washington, 1978-81, Coun. of Fgn. Rels., 1985—. Editor: Mobilizing Technology for World Development, 1979, Technology, Finance and Development, 1984, Choice and Management of Technology, 1987; contbr. articles to profl. jours. Land use chmn. Bannockburn Cmty. Assn., 1990-94. Capt. U.S. Army, 1965-67. Fellow NSF, 1959-62, NIH, 1962-65, Woodrow Wilson Found. (hon.). Fellow AAAS; mem. Internat. Engr. Chem. Socs. for Devel. (exec. officer biotic exploration fund 1995-2006), Am. Chem. Soc., Soc. Internat. Devel., Georgetown U. Faculty Senate, US State Dept. Adv. Com. on

Internat. Comm. and Info. Policy, Phi Beta Kappa. Avocation: ethnographic art and music. Office: Sch Fgn Svc Georgetown Univ 37th & O Sts NW Washington DC 20057-0001 E-mail: weissc@georgetown.edu.

**WEISS, CHARLES ANDREW,** lawyer; b. Perryville, Mo., Jan. 24, 1942; s. Wallace Francis and Iola Francis Weiss; m. Marie Suzanne Desloge, June 10, 1972; children: Christopher, Robert, Julie, Anne. BJ with highest honors, U. Mo., 1964, AB with hons. in History, 1965; JD cum laude, Notre Dame U., 1968. Bar: Mo. 1968, U.S. Dist. Ct. (ea. dist.) Mo. 1968, U.S. Ct. Appeals (8th cir.) 1968, U.S. Supreme Ct. 1972, U.S. Ct. Appeals (9th cir.) 1974, U.S. Ct. Appeals (2d cir.) 1977, U.S. Ct. Appeals (1st cir.) 1987, U.S. Ct. Appeals (5th cir.) 1992, U.S. Ct. Appeals (fed. cir.) 2003, U.S. Ct. Appeals (7th cir.) 2003. Law clk. to chief judge U.S. Ct. Appeals (8th cir.), 1968; ptnr. Bryan Cave LLP, St. Louis, 1969—. Lectr. St. Louis U. Law Sch., 1970-73; chmn. Legal Aid Mo. Statewide, Inc., 2003—; Supr. Red Cross Water Safety Program, Perry County, Mo., 1962-64; dir. Neighborhood Youth Corps., Perry County, 1965-66; pres. Perry County Young Dems. Club, 1965-67; committeeman Boy Scouts Am., 1982-86; mem. St. Louis Met. Sewer Dist. Civil Svc. Commn., 1999—; bd. dirs. United Way of Greater St. Louis, 1988-90. Fellow Am. Coll. Trial Lawyers; mem. ABA (ho. of dels. 1986-02, 04-, bd. govs. 2006-), Met. Bar Assn. St. Louis (pres. 1984-85), Mo. Bar Assn. (bd. govs. 1985, v.p. 1994-95, pres.-elect 1995-96, pres. 1996-97), St. Louis Bar Found. (pres. 1983), Mo. Lawyers Trust Account Found. (pres. 1992), Mo. Athletic Club (St. Louis), The Riverlands Assn., Inc. (pres. 1991-93), Jefferson Nat. Parks Assn. (chmn. 1993-00), Notre Dame Club St. Louis (dir.), Notre Dame Law Assn. (dir., pres. 1997—). Roman Catholic. Office: Bryan Cave 211 N Broadway, Ste 3600 Saint Louis MO 63102-2733 Office Phone: 314-259-2215. Business E-Mail: cweiss@bryancave.com.

**WEISS, CHRISTOPHER JOHN,** lawyer; b. Oswego, NY, Sept. 1, 1952; s. Robert Leo and Flora Elizabeth Weiss; children: Allison Ardis, Natalie Elizabeth, Christine Corinne, Kathryn Creigh. BS, Fla. State U., 1970, JD, 1977. Bar: Fla. 1977, U.S. Dist. Ct. (mid. and so. dists.) Fla. 1977, U.S. Supreme Ct. Ptnr. Holland and Knight (and predecessor firm), Orlando, Fla., 1977—. Lectr., author various constrn. litigation issues, 1977—. Mem. Orlando Rep. Com., 1975—. Mem. Fla. Bar, Orange County Bar Assn. (constrn. com. 1987—), Am. Arbitration Assn. (nat. panelist 1982—), Assoc. Gen. Contractors, Assoc. Builders and Contractors, Constrn. Fin. Mgrs. Assn. Avocations: reading, travel. Office: Holland & Knight PO Box 1526 Orlando FL 32802-1526 Office Phone: 407-244-1110. Business E-Mail: cweiss@hklaw.com.

**WEISS, DANIEL EDWIN,** minister, educator; b. Kenosha, Wis., June 9, 1937; s. Edwin and Ruth J. (Stromquist) Weiss; m. Rachel A. Johnson, Aug. 9, 1958 (div. 2004); children: Daniel E. Jr., Kristen R.; m. Barbara A. Williams, Oct. 30, 2004. BA, Wheaton Coll., 1959, MA, 1962; MDiv, Gordon Conwell Theol. Sem., South Hamilton, Mass., 1962; PhD, Mich. State U., 1964; DD (hon.), Judson Coll., 1976, Franklin Coll., 1990; DHL (hon.), Ottawa (Kans.) U., 1997; STD (hon.), Linfield Coll., 2000. Ordained to ministry Am. Bapt. Ch., 1962. Prof. ministry Gordon Div. Sch., Wenham, Mass., 1964—69; v.p. Gordon Coll., 1969—73; pres. Eastern Coll., St. Davids, Pa., 1973—81, Eastern Bapt. Theol. Sem., Phila., 1973—81; exec. v.p. Pace U., N.Y.C., 1981—83; exec. dir. Am. Bapt. Bd. Edn. and Publ., Valley Forge, Pa., 1983—88; gen. sec. Am. Bapt. Chs. U.S.A., 1988—2000. Mem. ctrl. com. World Coun. Chs., Geneva, 1989—98; mem. gen. bd. Nat. Coun. Chs., N.Y.C., 1989—2000; mem. gen. coun. Bapt. World Alliance, Washington, 1985—2000. Home: 4401 Gulf Shore Blvd N #1506 Naples FL 34103

**WEISS, DANIEL H.,** academic administrator, former dean; m. Sandra Jarva; children: Teddy, Joel. BA, George Washington U., 1979; MA, Johns Hopkins U., 1982, PhD, 1992; MBA, Yale U., 1985. With Booz, Allen & Hamilton; chair Art Hist. Dept. Johns Hopkins U., Balt., 1998—2001, dean faculty, 2001—02, dean Zanvyl Krieger Sch. Arts and Scis., 2002—05; pres. Lafayette Coll., Easton, Pa., 2005—. Bd. mem. Walter Art Mus., John Hopkins, Shriver Hall Concert Series; trustee Park School, Baltimore. Office: Lafayette Coll 316 Markle Hall Easton PA 18042 Office Phone: 610-330-5200.

**WEISS, DAVID I.,** real estate company executive, lawyer, writer; s. Kurt George and Phyllis Lee Weiss; m. Lynn Alice Epstein, Apr. 5, 1987; 1 child, Alexander Jacob. BS in Fin., U. Fla., 1983; JD, Nova Southeastern U., 1986. Bar: State Fla. Bar Assn. 1986 (so., mid. and no. dists.) 1987, U.S. Tax Ct. 1988, U.S. Ct. Appeals (11th cir.) 1988, U.S. Supreme Ct. 1990. Law clk. to Hon. Joe Eaton U.S. Dist. Ct. (so. dist.) Fla., 1986—87; ptnr. Herzfeld & Rubin, Miami, Fla., 1988—95; CEO Am. Coastal Corp., Plantation, Fla., 1995—; v.p. gen. counsel Nat. Gen. Corp., Ft. Lauderdale, Fla., 1997—; pres. Hawks Landing, Plantation, 1997—; CEO Design Safety Corp., Plantation, 2000—; ptnr. SouthStar Storage LLC, Boca Raton, Fla., 2001—, Security Storage, Delray Beach, Fla., 2003—; pres. Bluewater Groves, Inc., Ft. Pierce, Fla., 2003—; mng. mem. RPS Properties, LLC, Plantation. Mem. bd. editors U.S. Dist. Ct. So. Dist. Digest, Miami, 1987; CEO Organon Wireless, Inc., Ft. Lauderdale, 2000—; mng. mem. Royal Palm Square Properties, Inc., Coral Springs, Plantation, Fla., 2005—. Author: (children's book) When I Was A Duck, 2004; co-author: (law review article) On the Differences Between Blood and Red Ink: Economic Loss Rule (Outstanding Law Review Article, Product Liablity Jour., 1996), Conflicts of Interest under ERISA (Outstanding Law Review Article, West Pub., 1986). Bd. dirs. youth tennis program City of Plantation, 2001—; bd. dirs. Soref Jewish Cmty. Ctr. Mem.: Fla. Bar Assn. (YLD bd. govs. 1994), Dade County Bar Assn., Broward County Bar Assn., Fed. Bar Assn., Nat. Leukemia and Lymphoma Soc. (bd. reps. 2004—05, bd. trustees 2004—05), Leukemia and Lymphoma Soc. (nat. del. 2004, South Fla. bd. dirs. 2004—). Democrat. Achievements include patents in field of food, service, technology and medical testing include US patent #6, 230, 021 (lid closure mechanism); #6, 207, 100 (lid closure mechanism); #D469, 693 (lid closure design); #D468, 206 (lid closure design); #6, 273, 111 (retractable water protective device); patents pending for wireless interaction, meta and collection system-PageJump (TM); lid closure mechanisms (24 pending); 30 international patents awarded on lid closure design and utility patents. Avocations: swimming, running, tennis, weight training. Office: Bluewater Groves 151 N Nob Hill Rd Ste 233 Fort Lauderdale FL 33324 Office Phone: 954-472-4000 303. Business E-Mail: bluewatergroves@aol.com.

**WEISS, DONALD S.,** real estate developer; b. St. Petersburg, Fla., Aug. 18, 1947; s. Jonas Weiss and Miriam Kahan; m. Anne M. Weiss, Feb. 1978 (div. Jan. 1991); children: Laurie Blumstein, Melissa, Jason. BSBA, U. Fla., 1969. Lic. real estate broker N.Y. Asst. portfolio mgr. Chase Manhattan Bank, N.Y.C., 1969—70; office space leasing salesperson Williams & Co., N.Y.C., 1971—74, Sylvan Lawrence & Co., N.Y.C., 1974—78; pvt. real estate investor N.Y.C., 1978—; developer, creator Sugar Hill Art Ctr., N.Y.C., 2001—. Dir. Com. for a New Am., Com. for Rational Housing Laws and Econ. Devel. in N.Y.C. and N.Y. State. Exhibited in group shows. With U.S. Army, 1969—73. Avocations: skiing, bridge, photography. Home: 243-07 73 Ave Douglaston NY 11362 Office: 555 W 151 St #26 New York NY 10031

**WEISS, EARLE BURTON,** physician; b. Waltham, Mass., Nov. 23, 1932; s. Murray E. and Ruth R. (Pill) W.; m. Ruth Lithwick, Dec. 1, 1963; children: Ilana, Joshua. BS with honors, Northeastern U., 1955; MS, MIT, 1957; MD, Albert Einstein Coll. Medicine, 1961. Intern King's County Hosp., Bklyn., 1961—62; resident Boston City Hosp., 1962—64, Nat. Heart Inst. fellow, 1964—66; sr. rsch. assoc. Tufts Lung Sta., 1964—71; founder/first dir. respiratory ICU, sr. attending physician pulmonary & med. svc. Boston City Hosp., 1964—71, dir. Pulmonary Physiology Lab., 1966—71; assoc. chief of medicine Tufts Med. Svc., 1969—71; dir. divsn. respiratory diseases St. Vincent Hosp., Worcester, Mass., 1971—89, also acting med. dir., 1985—87; prof. medicine U. Mass. Med. Sch., 1977—; sr. pulmonary rsch. scientist, dept. anesthesia Mass. Gen. Hosp., Brigham and Womens Hosp., Boston, 1989—. Cons. medical devices adv. panel FDA, 1975-77; cons. in physiology Norfolk County Sanitorium, 1966-69; lectr. medicine Tufts Med. Sch., 1978-; assoc.

prof. life scis. Worcester (Mass.) Poly. Inst., 1976—; vis. prof. Faculty of Medicine, dept. of anesthesia Harvard Med. Sch., 1990-2002, vis. prof. U. Guadalajara, Mexico, 1973, 77, prof. extraordinario faculty medicine, 1977, 82; med. dir. Found. Rsch. in Bronchial Asthma and Related Diseases, 1980—; Tb cons. Commonwealth of Mass., 1972-89; dir. regional inpatient Tb and outpatient Tb clinic, Worcester County, 1972-89 Author: Bronchial Asthma, 1976, 2d edit., 1985, 3d edit., 1993, Status Asthmaticus, 1978; contbr. (with artist Frank H. Netter) Ciba Collection: The Respiratory System Anatomy of Lung and Asthma Sections and Clinical Symposia Bronchial Asthma, Acute Respiratory Failure in COPD, 1969; contbr. over 90 articles to profl. jours., abstracts, audio tapes and book chpts. Capt. USAFR, 1965-70. Named one of Am.'s Top Physicians, 2003—; recipient 1st Dr. J. McKeever Meml. award for outstanding med. educator, 1970, The Acad. Honor Soc., Tchg. and Patient Care award, Boston City Hosp. (I-III), 1971. Fellow ACP, Am. Coll. Chest Physicians, Royal Coll. Physicians; mem. AAAS, AMA, Mass. Thoracic Soc. (pres. 1976-78, Chadwick medal for meritorious contbn. in Respiratory Diseases 1990), Am. Thoracic Soc. (co-founder clin. assembly, rep. councilor 1979-82, founder, chmn. med. devices com. 1972-79, rep. ANSI med. tech. adv. bd. 1973-75, med. edn. com. 1972-74), Am. Assn. Clin. Scientists, Am. Soc. Internal Medicine, Soc. Free Radical Rsch., N.Y. Acad. Scis., Interasthma, Sigma Xi. Achievements include introduction and pioneering use of controlled mechanical ventilation in acute respiratory failure of chronic lung disease, arterial blood gas profiles in status asthma, "cross-over" point in status-severe asthma, recording of breath sounds, the theory of the role of calcium and oxygen toxic products in causing asthma and airways reactivity 1979, percutaneous lung biopsy for diagnosis of respiratory infections, effect thyroid hormones upon cerebral cortex maturation and first isolation of alpha-hydroxy acid oxidase; establishment student research fellowship at Albert Einstein College of Medicine. Home: 57 South St Natick MA 01760-5526 Office: Brigham and Womens Hosp Dept Anesthesia Rsch L Boston MA 02115 Personal E-mail: drwe@comcast.net. Business E-Mail: eweiss@bics.bwh.harvard.edu.

**WEISS, GEORGE HERBERT,** mathematician, consultant; b. N.Y.C., Feb. 19, 1930; s. Morris and Violet (Mayer) W.; m. Delia Esther Orgel, Dec. 20, 1961; children: Miriam Judith, Alan Keith, Daniel Jonathan. BA, Columbia U., 1951; MA, U. Md., 1953, PhD, 1958. Physicist USN, White Oak, Md., 1951-61; asst. prof. U. Md., College Park, 1959-63; fellow Rockefeller U., N.Y.C., 1963-64, Weizmann Inst., Rehovot, Israel, 1958-59; mathematician NIH, Bethesda, Md., 1964—. Cons. GM, IBM, GE. Author: Lattice Dynamics in the Harmonic Approximation, 1963, 2d edit., 1971, The Master Equation in Chemical Physics, 1977, Contemporary Problems in Statistical Physics, 1994, Aspects and Applications of the Random Walk, 1994, Introduction to Crystallographic Statistics, 1995. With U.S. Army, 1954-56. Recipient Disting. Svc. in Math. award Washington Acad. Sci., 1967, Disting. Svc. award NIH, 1970. Avocations: photography, music, chess, stamp collecting/philately. Office: NIH Bethesda MD 20892 Business E-Mail: weissgh@mail.nih.gov.

**WEISS, GERHARD HANS,** German language educator; b. Berlin, Aug. 6, 1926; came to U.S., 1946; s. Curt Erich and Gertrud (Grothus) W.; m. Janet Marilyn Smith, Dec. 27, 1953; children: John Martin, Susan Elizabeth Weiss Spencer, James David. BA, Washington U., St. Louis, 1950, MA, 1952; PhD, U. Wis., 1956. Prof. German U. Minn., Mpls., 1956—98, assoc. dean, 1967—71, 1979, chmn. dept. German, 1987-95, prof. emeritus, 1998—, interim dir. Ctr. Austrian Studies, 1999-2001. Mem. German-Am. Textbook Commn., Braunschweig, Fed. Republic Germany, 1985-88. Author: Begegnung mit Deutschland, 1970; editor: Unterrichtspraxis, 1975-80, Minn. Monographs in the Humanities, 1964-70; contbr. articles to profl. jours. Served to lt. col. USAR, 1946-75. Recipient Cross Merit, Fed. Republic Germany, 1982, Austrian Cross of Honor 1st Class Sci. and Arts, Republic of Austria, 2004. Mem. MLA, Am. Assn. Tchrs. German (pres. 1982-83, cert. of merit 1981, Disting. German Educator award 1991, elected hon. mem. 1995), German Studies Assn. (v.p. 1997-98, pres. 1999-00), Am. Coun. Tchg. Fgn. Langs. (Nelson Brooks award 1987). Methodist. Home: 4101 Abbott Ave S Minneapolis MN 55410-1004 Business E-Mail: weiss∅∅3@umn.edu.

**WEISS, GERSON,** endocrinologist, educator; b. N.Y.C., Aug. 1, 1939; s. Samuel and Lillian (Wolpe) Weiss; m. Linda Gordon, Dec. 24, 1959; children: Jonathan, David, Michele, Andrew. BA, NYU, 1960, MD, 1964. Diplomate Am. Bd. Ob-Gyn. Intern, fellow dept. medicine Johns Hopkins Sch. Medicine, 1964-65; resident ob-gyn NYU Med. Ctr., 1964-69; rsch. fellow physiology U. Pitts. Sch. Medicine, 1971-73; asst. prof. ob-gyn NYU Med. Ctr., 1971-76, assoc. prof., 1976-80, prof., 1980-85; dir. reproductive endocrinology NYU Med. Center, 1975-85; prof. ob-gyn U. Med. and Dentistry NJ-NJ Med. Sch., 1986—, chmn. dept., 1986—; dir. divsn. reproductive endocrinology Hackensack U. Med. Ctr., NJ, 1996—2002. Rep. Am. Bd. Med. Spltys. Mem. editl. bd.: Fertility and Sterility Jour., 1986—93, Gyn.-Ob. Investigation; contbr. scientific papers to profl. jours. Served to maj. MC U.S. Army, 1969—71. Rsch. grantee, NIH, 1975—, United Cerebral Palsy Found., 1977—83, Mellon Found., 1982—85; Rsch. fellow, John Polachek Found. Mem.: ACOG, Soc. Study Reprodn., N.Y. Gynecol. Soc. (pres. 1989—90), N.Y. Obstet. Soc. (pres. 1990—91), Soc. Gynecol. Investigation (pres. 2005—06), Endocrine Soc., Am. Bd. Ob-Gyn. (mem. divsn. reproductive endocrinology 1985—90, mem. ob-gyn. residency rev. com. 1995—2000, bd. dirs., treas. 1997—98, pres. 1999—2002, chmn. 2002—06, pres. bd. dirs. 1999—2002), Am. Gyn.-Ob. Soc., Alpha Omega Alpha, Sigma Xi, Phi Beta Kappa. Home: 185 West End Ave Apt 7MN New York NY 10023 Office: UMDNJ NJ Med Sch Dept Ob-Gyn 185 S Orange Ave Newark NJ 07103-2757 Business E-Mail: weissge@umdnj.edu.

**WEISS, HARVEY,** artist, educator; b. N.Y.C., Apr. 10, 1922; s. Louis and Bertha (Weiss) W.; m. Miriam Schlein, 1955 (div. 1983); children: Elizabeth Sarah, John Mark; m. Margaret I. McKinnickinick, 1981. Student, NYU, 1939-40, U. Mo., 1940-41; pvt. studien with Jose DeCreeft, 1946-47, Ossip Zadkine, Paris, 1950-51. Owner Weiss Assocs., 1948-49, 51, 52, S.R. Leon Co., 1954-56; freelance sculptor and writer, 1956—; assoc. prof. Adelphi U., 1976—, prof., 1982—. With U.S. Army, World War II. Mem. AAUP, Authors Guild, Sculptors Guild (pres. 1968-70), Westport Coun. on the Arts, Nat. Acad., Nat. Sculpture Soc. Democrat. Jewish. Avocations: tennis, sailing. Home and Office: 42 Maple Ln Westport CT 06880

**WEISS, HOLLY ANNE,** music educator, singer; b. Camden, N.J., Dec. 23, 1950; d. Nicholas John Weiss and Dorothy Lora Sloan; m. Ernest Libby Whitehouse, June 26, 1996. BS in Music Edn. summa cum laude, West Chester U., 1973; Master of Music, Northwestern U., 1974. Cert. tchr. music K-12 Pa., N.J. Instr. Northeastern Bible Coll., Essex Fells, NJ, 1974—79, choir dir. and tour dir., 1975—76; instr. Utica Coll., N.Y., 1990—2001; pvt. practice vocal studio N.Y.C., 1974—96, NJ, 1974—96, New Hartford, NY, 1996—. Singer: (Operas) The Opening, 2003, A Game of Chance, 2005, Salvatore Rosa, Carmen, Don Giovanni, Il Trovatore, Madame Butterfly, La Boheme, (oratorio) Elijah, Festival Te Deum, Requiem, La Nativité, Requiem, Christmas Oratorio, La Fiesta de la Posada, Magnificat, (oratorio radio broadcast) Gloria, (oratorio) Magnificat, 1993, Messiah, 1995, 1996; singer: (appearances include) Everson Mus., 1999, Munson Williams Proctor Inst., 1999, 2003, Utica Symphony, 2001, numerous others; accompanist: for students in studio and performance, resident soloist: First Presbyn. and Trinity Ch., 1980—85, Temple Emanu-El, 1980—85; singer: (TV) State of the Arts, 1983. Active Post Polio Support Group, 1989—; contributor Compassion Internat.; chair Trinity Covenant Ch., Livingston, 1990—96; chair 2d svc. task force First United Meth. Ch., New Hartford, 1997—98. Mem.: Nat. Assn. Tchrs. of Singing, B-Sharp Musical Club, Phi Beta Kappa. Avocations: gardening, art, reading, cooking, lay speaking. Office: Holly Weiss Vocal Studios 43 South Hills Dr New Hartford NY 13413

**WEISS, JAMES LLOYD,** cardiology educator; b. Chgo., Jan. 15, 1941; s. Edward Huhner and Ruth (Wingerhoff) W.; m. Susan Forscher Weiss. July 23, 1967; children: Ethan James, Lisa Fleur. BA, Harvard Coll., 1963; MD, Yale U., 1968. Intern, resident U. Mich. Hosp., Ann Arbor, 1968-70; staff fellow NIH, Bethesda, Md., 1970-72; resident medicine Johns Hopkins Hosp., Balt.,

1972-73, fellow cardiology, 1973-75, dir. Heart Station, 1976—, asst. prof. Medicine, 1975-81, assoc. prof. Medicine, 1981-90, prof. Medicine, Cariology, 1990—, Michael J. Cudahy prof. of cardiology, 1992—, assoc. dean admissions and acad. affairs, 1999—, dir. cardiology fellowship and tng. program, 1999—. Mem. editl. bd.: Johns Hopkins Med. Letter, 1991—, Jour. Am. Coll. Cardiology, 1995—; contbr. 120 articles to profl. jours. Recipient Harvard Book prize, 1959. Fellow Am. Coll. Cardiology, AHA Coun. on Circulation; mem. Harvard Club N.Y.C., Ctr. Club. Office: Cardiology Divsn Johns Hopkins Hosp 600 N Wolfe St Baltimore MD 21287-0005 Office Phone: 410-955-6834. E-mail: jlweiss@jhmi.edu.

**WEISS, JAMES MICHAEL,** financial analyst, portfolio manager; b. Chgo., July 20, 1946; s. Harold Cornelius and Elizabeth Josephine (Jesse) W.; m. Kathleen Jane Postorino, July 18, 1970; children: Elizabeth, Ann, Jane, William. BA, Marquette U., 1968; MBA, U. Pa., 1972. CFA; chartered investment counselor. Credit analyst Provident Nat. Bank, Phila., 1972; ptnr., portfolio mgr. Stein Roe & Farnham Investment Counsel, Chgo., 1972—87, 1st v.p., prin., sr. portfolio mgr., 1987—90, sr. v.p., prin., sr. portfolio mgr., 1991—92; exec. v.p., sr. portfolio mgr. IDS Adv. Group, Inc., Mpls., 1993—95; pres., chief investment officer IDS Equity Advisors, 1995; sr. v.p., dep. chief investment officer Equities, State St. Rsch. & Mgmt. Co., Boston, 1995—97, exec. v.p., mem. mgmt. com., dep. head of equities, 1998—99, exec. v.p. mem. mgmt. com., chief invest. officer, bd. dirs., 1999—2002; pres. Weiss Capital Mgmt., Inc., 2002—. Bd. dirs. Tropp & Co., Chgo.; v.p. Stein Roe Cash Reserves Fund, Chgo., 1982-87; mem. investment com. Pro Mutual Group, Boston, Mass., 2004—. Author: (with others) Handbook of Cash Flow and Treasury Management, 1987; contbr. articles to profl. jours. Commr. Glenview (Ill.) Zoning Bd., 1978-80; trustee Glenview Village Bd. Trustees, 1980-86; chmn. Marquette U. Exec. Senate, Chgo., 1984-87; active Glenview Bus. Area Redevel. Com., 1990-93; bus. adv. coun. Elmhurst (Ill.) Coll., 1986-93; founding bd. dirs. Glenview Edn. Found., 1990-93; bd. trustees Fenn Sch., Concord, Mass., 1996-2002, Fenn Sch. investment com., 1996—; co-chmn. Fenn Sch. Capital Campaign, 1997-2000; bd. dirs. Gaining Ground, Concord, 2003—. With U.S. Army, 1968-70. Recipient Cert. Merit Village of Glenview, 1987. Mem.: Investment Counsel Assn., CFA Inst., Boston Analysts Soc., Marquette U. Alumni Assn. (nat. bd. dirs. 1989—91, liberal arts bd. 2000—05, Nat. Svc. award 1995), Indian River Country Club (Vero Beach, Fla.), Boston Coll. Club, Wedgewook Pines Club (Stow, Mass.), North Shore Country Club (Glenview, Ill.). Avocations: golf, travel, writing. Office: Weiss Capital Mgmt PO Box 1128 Concord MA 01742-1128 Home: 13 Wright Farm Rd Concord MA 01742-1528 Office Phone: 978-505-5435. E-mail: jweiss6@earthlink.net.

**WEISS, JERRY KENNETH,** sales executive, consultant, marketing professional; BA, State U. Ohio, Toledo, 1968; MA, State U. Ohio, 1968; postgrad., NYU, 1976—80. Sales and mktg. rep. Panasonic Corp., 1968—70; v.p. mktg. Danville Industries, 1970—79; sales and mktg. mgr. Sharp Electronics, 1980—82; dir. nat. sales Mattel Corp., 1982—84; sr. ptnr. The CE Group, Inc., 1984—2004. Bd. dirs. CE2, Inc., Cedarhurst. Author: (audio cassette/cd) Sales Directions. Fundraiser Westchester Reform Temple, Scarsdale, NY, 1998—2003. Scholar, State U. Ohio. Fellow: Sigma Alpha Mu (sec.), Acad. Mktg. Sci. (founding assoc.); mem.: Phi Beta Kappa, Phi Alpha Theta. Avocations: motorcycling, auto racing, white-water rafting. Office: The CE Group. Avocations: motorcycling, auto racing, white-water rafting. Personal E-mail: jerryweiss6@aol.com.

**WEISS, JOANNE MARION,** writer; b. Wayne, N.J., Mar. 16, 1960; d. Henry Daniel and Florence Frances (Zaratkiewicz) W. BA, Bennington Coll., 1982; MA, U. Cambridge, Eng., 1988. Prodn. mgr. The Suburban News, N.J., 1982-83; gardener Artistic Landscaping, N.J., 1983; case mgr. Mid-Bergan Mental Health Ctr., N.J., 1985-86. Founder Isis Farm Writers, 1995—, Cambridge Actors, 1988—. Author: dir. play The Gift, 1987, 88; author: (plays) Catherine the Queen, 1997, Mother America, 1998; contbr. 4 poems to Tears in the Fence, 2002. Translator Solidarity, Poland, 1983; co-leader Vols. for Peace, 1986; mem., worker Pregnancy Adv. Svc., Cambridge, 1991-92. Recipient scholarship Inst. for Brit. and Irish Studies, Trinity Coll., Dublin, 1985, Chancellor's medal for poetry U. Cambridge, Eng., 1988, grants for Edinburgh, Sir John Gielgud, 1988, grant Judith Wilson Fund, U. Cambridge, Eng., 1988. Mem. N.H. Carriage Horse Assn., Dramatists Guild, Am. Horse Show Assn. Avocations: horse training, farming.

**WEISS, JOHN ROBERT,** lawyer; b. Chgo., May 7, 1961; s. Robert Gordon and Elizabeth Jean (Malecki) W.; m. Elizabeth Anne Zur, Dec. 5, 1987. BA, Northwestern U., 1982, JD, 1985. Bar: Ill. 1985, U.S. Dist. Ct. (no. dist.) Ill. 1985, U.S. Dist. Ct. (ctrl. dist.) Ill., 1997, U.S. Ct. Appeals (7th cir.) 1987, U.S. Ct. Appeals (8th cir.), 1999, U.S. Supreme Ct. 1989. Assoc. Chapman & Cutler, Chgo., 1985; ptnr. Katten Muchin Rosenman, Chgo. Tchr. Chgo. Coalition for Law-Related Edn., 1985—; atty. Chgo. Vol. Legal Services, 1985—. Mem. ABA, 7th Cir. Bar Assn., Am. Judicature Soc., Ill. Bar Assn., Am. Bankruptcy Inst., Turnaround Mgmt. Assn. Roman Catholic. Avocations: golf, tennis, billiards. Office: Katten Muchin Rosenman LLP 525 West Monroe St Chicago IL 60661 Office Fax: 312-577-4733. Business E-Mail: john.weiss@kattenlaw.com.

**WEISS, JONATHAN ARTHUR,** lawyer; b. May 1, 1939; s. Paul and Victoria Brodkin Weiss. BA, Yale U., New Haven, Conn., 1960, LLB, 1963; student, U. Chgo. Law Sch., 1960—61. Bar: NY 1967, DC 1994, Vet.'s Ct. (2d and 3d cirs.), U.S. Supreme Ct. 1967. Mng. atty. Neighborhood Legal Svcs., Washington, 1964-66, Mobilization for Youth Legal Svcs., N.Y.C., 1969-71; with Ctr. on Welfare Law, Columbia U. Law Sch., N.Y.C., 1967-69; dir. Legal Svcs. for Elderly, N.Y.C., 1971—. Lectr. Hebrew U., Jerusalem, 1966; vis. prof. Tex. So. U. Law Sch., Houston, 1971; adj. prof. Yeshiva U. Cardozo Law Sch., NYC, 1983—85. Co-author, editor: The Law and the Elderly, 1976; co-author: Right and Wrong a Philosophical Dialogue Between Father and Son, 1968; contbr. numerous articles and revs. to law and philos. jours and to epigrs in US and Italy. Truth and Russians in hands of novels Bd. dirs. Disability Legal Def. Fund, World Trust Fund Inc. Named Pro Bona Lawyer of Yr., N.Y. County Bar Assn.; recipient Disting. Scholar medal, Hofstra U., 1972; Fulbright scholar, 1966, archived at U. Ind. Libr., Indpls. Fellow: ABA (adv. coun. ethics 2000 com., Centennial com.), Am. Bar Found.; mem.: NY County Bar Assn. (Public Service award), NY State Bar (internat. sect. human rights), Native Am. Bar Assn. Democrat. Office: Legal Svcs for Elderly 130 W 42d St New York NY 10036 Office Phone: 212-391-0120.

**WEISS, JOSEPH JOEL,** consulting company executive; b. Newark, July 27, 1931; s. Harry H. and Belle (Sass) W.; m. Leah Kneller, Apr. 10, 1954 (div. 1961); children: Sara, Daniel; m. Carol Lynn Seegott, Sept. 29, 1967; children: Laura, John. BSBA, Rutgers U., 1953, MBA, 1958. Dist. mgr. N.J. Bell Telephone Co., 1955-61; asst. comptroller ITT P.R. Telephone Co., San Juan, 1964-68; sr. cons. N.Y.C., 1968-71; v.p. data services Rio De Janeiro, 1971-74; dir. ops. N.Y.C., 1975-80; v.p. Control Data Corp., Rio De Janeiro, 1974-75; exec. v.p., chief adminstrv. officer Burger King Corp., Miami, 1980-89; chief oper. officer Goode, Olcott, Knight & Assocs., Coral Gables, Fla., 1989-90; pres. Contraband Detection Internat., Miami, Fla., 1990-92; sr. v.p. Seegott Inc., Streetsboro, Ohio, 1992—. Bd. dirs. Sta. WPB-TV. Pres. Civic Betterment Assn., Franklin Twp., N.J., 1961; trustee U. Miami Citizens Bd., 1987—; bd. dirs. Boy Scouts Am., 1982—. Recipient Strategic Planning Achievement award Boy Scouts Am., 1985. Mem. Hist. Soc. Fla. (bd. dirs. 1986—). Clubs: Fisher Island. Republican. Presbyterian. Avocations: painting, tennis. Home: 6682 Brookside Woods Ct Se Ada MI 49301-8219

**WEISS, KENNETH ANDREW,** lawyer, educator; b. New Orleans, Jan. 16, 1951; s. Irving and Julia (Mayer) Weiss. BA, Tulane U., 1972, JD with honors, 1975; LLM in Taxation with highest honors, George Washington U., 1981. Bar: La. 1975, DC 1976. Editl. writer, Washington Com. The Times-Picayune, New Orleans and Washington, 1973-79; news editor Congl. Quarterly, Washington, 1979-81; mng. editor Reporters Com. for Freedom of the Press, Washington, 1981-82; assoc. McGlinchey Stafford, New Orleans, 1982-84, dir., 1984—. Prof. Tulane U. Law Sch., New Orleans, 1987—, La. State U. Law Sch., 2000—; mem. trust code com. La. Law Inst., Baton

Rouge, 1993—, mem. successions and donations com., 1996—; mem. planning com. Tulane Tax Inst., 1996—; chair Tulane U. Law Sch. Ann. Estate Planning Seminar, 1995—2001, Tulane U. Estate Planning Inst., 2002—; dean's adv. coun. Tulane Law Sch., 2003—. Co-author: Bankers' Guide to Establishing, Managing and Operating Common Trust Funds, 1986, Business Uses of Life Insurance, 1986, Executive Compensation, 1990; assoc. editor Tulane Law Rev., 1974-75, mem. bd. adv. editors, 1992—; contbr. articles to profl. jours. Bd. dirs. Longue Vue House and Gardens Adv. Corp., 1993-95, bd. dirs. Longue Vue Found., 1995—2003; trustee Greater New Orleans Ednl. TV Found., Sta. WYES-TV, 1994-98; bd. dirs. So. Repertory Theatre, 1996-2001, pres., 1998-99; bd. advisors Project Lazarus, 1996-2000, pres. 1997-99; mem. profl. adv. com., Jewish Endowment Found., 1982—; mem. planned gifts adv. com. Tulane U., 1989—; active Met. Area Com. Leadership Forum, New Orleans, 1983; fellow Inst. Politics Loyola U., New Orleans, 1989-90; mem. devel. com. Greater New Orleans Found., 1995—. bd. dirs., Innocence Project New Orleans, 2002-05, treas., 2002-04. Recipient Addy award for polit. advt., 1989, awards for investigative reporting; Phi Delta Phi scholar, 1972-73. Fellow Am. Coll. Trust and Estate Counsel; mem. La. State Bar Assn. (taxation sect., bd. cert. tax atty., bd. cert. estate planning and adminstrn. specialist), New Orleans Bar Assn. (chair taxation law com. 2003), Nat. Coun. Planned Giving (greater New Orleans chpt.), New Orleans Estate Planning Coun., Order of the Coif. Republican. Jewish. Office Phone: 504-596-2751.

**WEISS, LAWRENCE N.,** lawyer; b. N.Y.C., Aug. 9, 1942; s. Joseph and Martha (Guggenheimer) W.; m. Osnat Gad. BA, CCNY, 1963; LLB summa cum laude, Columbia U., 1966. Bar: N.Y. 1966, U.S. Ct. Appeals (2d cir.) 1967, U.S. Dist. Ct. (so. and ea. dists) N.Y. 1968, U.S. Supreme Ct. 1971, U.S. Ct. Appeals (3d cir.) 1968, U.S. Ct. Appeals (6th cir.) 1980, U.S. Tax Ct. 1977. Assoc. Kaye, Scholer, Fierman, Hays & Handler, N.Y.C., 1966-67, 67-73; law clk. to judge N.Y. Ct. Appeals, Albany and N.Y.C., 1967; assoc. Botein, Hays, Sklar & Herzberg, N.Y.C., 1973-76, Weisman, Celler, Spett, Modlin & Wertheimer, N.Y.C., 1976, ptnr., 1977-79, counsel, 1979-81; prin. Lawrence N. Weiss, P.C., N.Y.C., 1981—, Pantaleoni & Weiss, N.Y.C., 1993—2003. Arbitrator Civil Ct., N.Y.C., 1985—; mediator U.S. Dist. Ct. (ea. dist.) N.Y. and N.Y. Supreme Ct. Mem. N.Y. County Lawyers Assn. (arbitrator joint com. fee disputes), Assn. Bar of City of N.Y. (com. on legal edn. and admission to bar, arbitrator joint com. fee disputes), N.Y. State Bar Assn. (chair com. CLE, com. on fed. judiciary, spl. com. on copyright, vice chair com. on UN, subcom. internat. cts., litig. sect., judiciary com.). Avocation: shakespearean theatre. Home: 107 E 37th St New York NY 10016-3065 E-mail: larry@lweiss.net.

**WEISS, LEONARD,** mathematician, consultant; b. N.Y.C., Mar. 14, 1934; s. Max and Sadie (Albert) W.; m. Sandra Joyce Raynes, June 15, 1958; children: Madelyn, Eugene. B.E.E., CCNY, 1956; MS, Columbia U., 1959; PhD, Johns Hopkins U., 1962. Lectr. CCNY, 1956-59; staff scientist Research Inst. for Advanced Studies, Balt., 1962-64; asst. prof. Brown U., Providence, 1964-66, assoc. prof., 1966-68; prof. U. Md., College Park, 1968-78; legis. asst. to Senator John Glenn of Ohio, 1976-77; cons. Naval Research Lab., Washington, 1970-77; staff dir. Senate Subcom. on Energy, Nuclear Proliferation and Govt. Processes, 1977-86, Senate Com. Govtl. Affairs., 1987-99; cons. Lawrence Livermore Nat. Lab., 1999—. Editor: Ordinary Differential Equations, 1972; contbr. articles to profl. jours. and mags.; author legislation on nuclear proliferation, energy, health and safety, govt. orgn., and govt. mgmt. Alfred P. Sloan research fellow, 1966-68, IEEE Congl. fellow, 1976, Stennis Congl. fellow, 1997. Home and Office: 11701 Auth Ln Silver Spring MD 20902-1644 Office Phone: 301-593-1699.

**WEISS, LISA ANN,** lawyer; b. Chgo., Dec. 6, 1958; d. Benjamin B. and Suzanne (Harris) W. BA, Yale U., 1980; JD, Columbia U., 1983. Bar: N.Y. 1984. Assoc. Stroock Stroock & Lavan, NYC, 1983-86, Rosenman & Colin, NYC, 1986-92, ptnr., 1992—2000; dep. gen. counsel Sony Music, 2000—01, gen. counsel, 2001—05, Sony BMG, 2005—06; ptnr. Morrison & Foerster LLP, NYC, 2006—. Bd. dirs. Lightspeed Audio Labs., 2006—. Mem. NYC Bar Assn. (corp. law com. 1992-95). Office: Morrison & Foerster LLP 1290 Ave of the Americas New York NY 10104-0050 Office Phone: 212-468-8003.

**WEISS, LYN DENISE,** physician; b. Bethpage, N.Y., Apr. 13, 1959; d. Eugene and Lois Zanger; m. Jay M. Weiss, Apr. 7, 1984; children: Ari, Helene, Stefan, Richard. BA, U. Va., 1981; MD, SUNY, Bklyn., 1985. Diplomate Am. Bd. Electrodiagnostic Medicine, Nat. Bd. Med. Examiners, Am. Bd. Phys. Medicine and Rehab. Resident Dept. Phys. Medicine & Rehab. Nassau U. Med. Ctr., East Meadow, NY, 1985—89; attending physician Dept. Phys. Medicine & Rehab. Nassau U. Med. Ctr., 1989—94, dir. Electrodiagnostic Medicine Dept. Phys. Medicine Rehab., 1991—; dir. residency tng. Dept. Phys. Medicine & Rehab. Nassau U. Med. Ctr., 1993—; acting chmn. Dept. Phys. Medicine & Rehab. Nassau U. Med. Ctr., 1994—96; chmn. Dept. Phys. Medicine & Rehab. Nassau U. Med. Ctr., 1996—. Bd. dirs. Ctr. for Rehab. Rsch. Tech., Massapequa, N.Y., 1996—. Author: Cumulative Trauma Disorders, 1997, Skin Care Triad, 2000, Easy EMG, 2004.

**WEISS, LYNNE S.,** pediatrician, educator; MD, Hahnemann Med. Coll., Phila., 1974. Diplomate Pediatrics Am. Bd. Pediatrics, 1979, Pediatric Nephrology Am. Bd. Pediatrics, 1982. Intern in Pediatrics Michael Reese Hosp., Chgo., 1974—75, resident in Pediatrics, 1975—77, fellow in Nephrology (pediatric), 1977—79; physician, chief divsn. pediat. nephrology & hypertension UMDNJ-Robert Wood Johnson Med. Sch., New Brunswick, NJ, 1985—. Prof. Pediatrics Robert Wood Johnson Univ. Hosp., New Brunswick, NJ, 1987—, dir. Pediatric Nephrology, 1987—. Office: UMDNJ-Robert Wood Johnson Med Sch Pediatric Nephrology and Hupertension 98 French St 2221 New Brunswick NJ 08901 Office Phone: 732-235-7880.

**WEISS, MARCIA J.,** lawyer, educator; b. N.Y.C., 1944; BA, U. Wis., 1966; MA, George Washington U., 1971; JD, Duquesne U., 1981. Translator French, Spanish and Italian U.S. Govt., Washington, 1966—69, World Bank, 1969—73, Rockwell Internat., Pitts., 1975-77; jud. law clk. Ct. Common Pleas, Allegheny County, Pa., 1981-83, Pa. Commonwealth Ct., 1983-84; prof. law Point Park U., Pitts., 1985—. Vis. assoc. Ctr. for Med. Ethics, Pitts., 1992-93; panel presenter, 2004-05. Freelance writer Salem Press, Pasadena, Calif., 1992—; reviewer Proteus: A Jour. of Ideas, 1994—; contbr. articles to profl. jours. Newsletter editor Ladies Hosp. Aid Soc. We. Pa., Pitts., 1996—, bd. dirs., 1997—, v.p. pub. rels., 1998—, exec. v.p., 1999-2001, pres., 2001-03; v.p. Hadassah Greater Pitts., 2003—, cert. leadership trainer, 2004, advocacy specialist, 2004, pres., 2005—; mem. ethics com. U. Pitts. Med. Ctr., 2003—; mem. instl. rev. bd. U. Pitts. Med. Ctr., 2003—; vice chair U. Pitts. Israel Heritage Com., 2006—. Named Vol. of Yr., United Jewish Fedn., 2003; recipient Nat. Leadership award, Hadassah, 2004; fellow, NEH, 1986, 1989. Mem. Am. Soc. Bioethics and Humanities, Hastings Ctr., Am. Soc. Law, Medicine and Ethics, Assn. for Practical and Profl. Ethics, Federalist Soc. Office: Point Park Univ Dept Humanities 201 Wood St Pittsburgh PA 15222-1984

**WEISS, MARIANNA SHRENGER,** psychotherapist; b. Pakrac, Croatia, Dec. 10, 1941; arrived in U.S., 1951; d. Edoardo and Vanda Schrenger Weiss; 1 child, Jacob Solomon. BA, MA, U. Calif., Berkeley, 1966; MS, Calif. State U., Hayward, 1985. Lic. marriage, family, and child counselor Bd. of Behavioral Scis., Calif. Workshop leader, hotline response worker Rape Crisis Ctr., Richmond, Calif., 1987—89; coord., group facilitator, newsletter editor and contbr. Tikvah, Holocaust survivors self-help group, San Francisco and Berkeley, 1989—94; therapist Family and Children's Svcs. of Contra Costa County, Walnut Creek and Richmond, Calif., 1989—93; therapist, dir. svcs. to Holocaust survivors Family Svc. of Silicon Valley, Los Gatos, Calif., 1999—2001; therapist Ctr. for Cmty. Counseling, Eugene, Oreg., 2002—; leader chronic illness workshop PeaceHealth Med. Ctr., Eugene, 2003—. Actor: (residential theater). Office: CCC 1465 Coburg Rd Eugene OR 97401

**WEISS, MARK ANSCHEL,** lawyer; b. NYC, June 20, 1937; s. George and Ida (Galin) W.; m. Joan Roth, June 8, 1958; children: Rebecca, Sarabeth, Jonathan, Deborah. AB, Columbia U., 1958; LLB magna cum laude, Harvard U., 1961. Bar: N.Y. 1961, D.C. 1962, U.S. Supreme Ct. 1965. Assoc. Covington & Burling, Washington, 1961-66, 69-70, ptnr., 1970—; spl. asst. to Under Sec. Treasury Dept. Washington, 1966-68; spl. asst. to sec., 1968-69. Mem. editl. adv. bd. Electronic Banking Law and Commerce Report. Mem. ABA, D.C. Bar, Fed. Bar Assn. (banking law com.). Office: Covington & Burling 1201 Pennsylvania Ave NW Washington DC 20004-2401 Office Phone: 202-662-5308. Business E-mail: mweiss@cov.com.

**WEISS, MARTIN HARVEY,** neurosurgeon, educator; b. Newark, Feb. 2, 1939; s. Max and Rae W.; m. R. Debora Rosenthal, Aug. 20, 1961; children: Brad, Jessica, Elisabeth. AB magna cum laude, Dartmouth Coll., 1960, BMS, 1961; MD, Cornell U., 1963. Diplomate Am. Bd. Neurol. Surgery (bd. dirs. 1983-89, vice chmn. 1987-88, chmn. 1988-89). Intern Univ. Hosps., Cleve., 1963-64, resident in neurosurgery, 1966-70; sr. instr. to asst. prof. neurosurgery Case Western Res. U., 1970-73; assoc. prof. neurosurgery U. So. Calif., 1973-76, prof., 1976-78, prof., chmn. dept., 1978—2004, Martin H. Weiss chair in neurol. surgery, 1997—. Chmn. neurology B study sect. NIH; mem. residency rev. com. for neurosurg. Accreditation Commn. for Grad. Med. Edn., 1989—, vice chmn., 1991—93, chmn., 1993—95, mem. appeals coun. in neurosurg., 1995—; vis. prof. U. Mich, 1987; vis. prof. Med. Sch. Harvard U., 1988; vis. prof. U. Wash., 1988, U. Calif., San Francisco, 1994—, U. Oreg., 1995, Tufts U., 1996, U. Melbourne, 1996, U. Sydney, 1996, U. Erlangen/Nurnberg, 1999, U. Oregon, 1999, U. Tex., 2004, U. Oreg., 2004, Stanford U., 2005; vis. prof., Bronson Ray lectr. Cornell U., 2005—06; Afrox traveling prof. South African Congress Neurol. Surgeons, 1989; hon. guest Royal Coll. Physicians Endocrine Sect., London, 2001; lectr. in field. Author: Pituitary Diseases, 1980; editor-in-chief Clin. Neurosurgery, 1980-83; assoc. editor Bull. L.A. Neurol. Socs., 1976-81, Jour. Clin. Neurosci., 1981—; mem. editl. bd. Neurosurgery, 1979-84, Neurol. Rsch., 1980—, Jour. Neurosurgery, 1987—, chmn., 1995—, assoc. editor, 1996—. Served to capt. USAR, 1964—66, assoc. in gen. surgery USAH, USMA, 1964—66, West Point, NY. Spl. fellow in neurosurgery NIH, 1969-70; recipient Jamieson medal Australasian Neurosurg. Soc., 1996. Mem. ACS (adv. coun. neurosurgery 1985-88), Soc. Neurol. Surgeons (v.p. 1999, pres.-elect 2000—, pres. 2001-02), Neurosurg. Soc. Am., Am. Acad. Neurol. Surgery (exec. com. 1988-89, v.p. 1992-93, Kurze Lect. 2005, Cushing medal 2005), Rsch. Soc. Neurol. Surgeons, Am. Assn. Neurol. Surgeons (bd. dirs. 1988-91, sec. 1994-97, pres.-elect 1998-99, pres. 1999-00, past pres. 2000-01, Cushing Medalist, 2005), Congress Neurol. Surgeons (v.p. 1982-83), Western Neurosurg. Soc. (Cloward medal 2006), Neurosurg. Forum, So. Calif. Neurosurg. Soc. (pres. 1983-84), Neurosurgeon Rsch. & Edn. Found. (chmn., exec. com. 2004-), Phi Beta Kappa, Alpha Omega Alpha. Home: 357 Georgian Rd La Canada Flintridge CA 91011-3520 Office: 1200 N State St Los Angeles CA 90033-1029 Office Phone: 323-226-7421. Business E-mail: weiss@usc.edu.

**WEISS, MELVYN I.,** lawyer; b. NYC, Aug. 1, 1935; s. Joseph and Jean Weiss; m. Barbara Joan Kaplan, Dec. 27, 1958; children: Gary Michael, Stephen Andrew, Leslie Caryn. BBA, CCNY, 1957; JD, NYU, 1959. Bar: NY 1960, US Dist. Ct. (so. dist.) NY, US Dist. Ct. (ea. dist.) NY, US Ct. Appeals (2d, 3rd, 4th, 5th, 6th, 8th, 9th and 10th cirs.) 1975, US Supreme Ct. 1976. Assoc. Strasser, Spiegelberg, Fried & Frank, NYC, 1959-61, Galef & Jacobs, NYC, 1962-65; founding ptnr. Milberg Weiss Bershad & Schulman LLP, 1966—, La., 1966. Lectr. panelist univs., bar groups, CLE orgns.; vice chair bd. Drum Major Inst.; bd. dirs. ActiVote, Washington, NYU Sch. Law, Lawyer's Com. for Civil Rights Under Law; hon. prof. U. Argentine, Buenos Aires. Contbr. articles to profl. jours. Founder Melvyn and Barbara Weiss Pub. Interest Student Loan Repayment Found., NYU; mem. exec. com. Israel Policy Forum; internat. chmn. Hatikvah Project; former bd. mem. Am. Jewish Congress, Salzburg Seminar. Named 1 of 13 Attys. in Am. Who Stand Out from the Crowd, Nat. Law. Jour., 2003; named one of Most Influential Leaders in Bus., Crain's NY, 2002; named to Top 100 Most Influential People in Acctg., Accounting Today, 2001, 2002, 2003, 2004; recipient Gotham and Humanitarian award, Anti Defamation League, 1976, Outstanding Alumni Assn. Achievement award, 1982, Arthur T. Vanderbilt medal, NYU Law Sch., 1993, Proskauer award, United Jewish Appeal, 1997. Fellow Am. Coll. Trial Lawyers, NY Bar Found.; mem. ABA, B'nai B'rith (Human Rels. award Anti Defamation League 1976), CCNY Alumni Assn. (Oustanding Alumni award 1982), NYU Sch. Law (trustee, Vanderbilt medal 1993), Glen Oaks Golf and Country Club, Boca Rio Golf Club. Office: Milberg Weiss Bershad & Schulman LLP Ste 4900 1 Pennsylvania Plz New York NY 10119-0165 Office Phone: 212-594-5300. Office Fax: 212-868-1229. Business E-mail: mweiss@milbergweiss.com.

**WEISS, MICHAEL ALLEN,** retired retail executive; b. N.Y.C., Apr. 21, 1941; s. Robert and Estelle (Kirchner) W.; m. Arlene Markman, Dec. 25, 1962; children: Eloise Kyle, Katherine Jane. BA, Syracuse U., 1962. Buyer Abraham & Straus, Bklyn., 1965-72, Casual Corner, Enfield, Conn., 1972-74; merchandiser Apparel Industries, N.Y.C., 1974-81; pres., CEO Limited Express, Columbus, Ohio, 1981-93; vice chmn. The Limited, Inc., Columbus, 1993—2004. Bd. dirs. Chicos, FAS, Inc., 2005—. Bd. dirs. United Way of Franklin County, ARC. Mem. Winding Hollow Country Club, Capitol Club, New Albany Country Club.*

**WEISS, MITCH,** journalist; Corr. AP, Ohio, 1986—98; state editor Block News Alliance (The Blade and The Pitts. Post-Gazette), 1998—. Recipient Pulitzer Prize for investigative reporting, 2004, medal winner, Investigative Reporters and Editors Inc., 2004. Office: The Blade 541 N Superior St Toledo OH 43660

**WEISS, MITCHELL JOSEPH,** librarian; b. Chgo., Nov. 12, 1942; s. Harry Edward and Gertrude Plotkin Weiss. ScB in Biology with high honors, Brown U., 1964; PhD in Zoology, U. Mich., 1970; MLS, Rutgers U., 1988. NIH postdoctoral rsch. fellow U. Wash., Seattle, 1970—73; postdoctoral instr. in zoology U. Iowa, Iowa City, 1973—74; asst. prof. biology Rutgers U., New Brunswick, NJ, 1974—81, vis. asst. prof., 1981—82, guest investigator, 1982—2000; sci. writer New Brunswick, 2001—02; reference libr., digital/global access libr. coord. Fairleigh Dickinson U., Teaneck, NJ, 2002—. Cons. Oriel Corp., Stamford, Conn., 1983, Knoll Pharm. Co., Mt. Olive, NJ, 1999—2000. Contbr. articles to sci. jours. Grad. fellow, NSF, 1964—69, rsch. grantee, 1976—78. Mem.: Internat. Assn. Meiobenthologists, Am. Microscopical Soc. Achievements include research in structure and development of insect brain centers at microscopic and ultrastructural levels; biology of phylum Gastrotricha, with current emphasis on sexuality, life cycles and systematics of freshwater gastrotrichs. Avocations: classical music, swimming. Office: Fairleigh Dickinson U 1000 River Rd T-WL1-01 Teaneck NJ 07666 Office Phone: 201-692-2139. E-mail: mjweiss@fdu.edu.

**WEISS, MORRY,** greeting card company executive; b. Czechoslovakia, 1940; m. Judith Stone. Grad., Wayne State U. Salesman, field mgr. Am. Greetings Corp., Cleve., 1961-66, advt. mgr., 1966-68, v.p., 1969-73, group v.p. mktg. and sales, 1973-78, pres., 1978—2003, COO Cleve., 1978—87, bd. dir., chief exec. officer, 1987—2003, chmn., 1992—. Office: Am Greetings Corp 1 American Rd Cleveland OH 44144-2301*

**WEISS, MYRNA GRACE,** management consultant; b. NYC, June 22, 1939; d. Herman and Blanche Ziegler; m. Arthur H. Weiss; children: Debra Anne Huddleston, Louise Esther Pennington. BA, Barnard Coll., 1958; MA, Hunter Coll., 1968; MPA, NYU, 1978; cert. in Mktg., U. Pa. Tchr., N.Y.C. and Vallejo, Calif., 1959-68; dir. admissions Columbia Prep. Sch., N.Y.C., 1969-72; dir. PREP counselling NYU, N.Y.C., 1973-74; dept. head Hewitt Sch., N.Y.C., 1974-79; mgr. Met. Ins. Co., N.Y.C., 1979-84; mktg. exec. Rothschild, Inc., NYC, 1985—; pres. First Mktg. Capital Group Ltd., N.Y.C., 1985—; mng. dir. Wrap Co. Internat. N.V., 1992-97; advisor Lared Group, N.Y.C., 1987-97; CEO, pres. bd. dirs. Ibnet, 1999—2002. Advisor Gov.'s Hwy. Safety Svc., N.Y.C., 1985-88; pres. Fin. Women's Assn. N.Y., 1984-85. Bd. dirs. 92nd Y, N.Y.C., 1972—90, ARC, N.Y.C., 1989—96, 1997—, asst. treas. 1993—96, 1997—. Mem. Internat. Women's Forum (bd.

**WEISS, PAUL RICHARD,** plastic surgeon; b. Bklyn., July 4, 1942; s. Murray and Belle (Edelman) W.; m. Linda Wayne, Aug. 23, 1964; children: Fredda Susan, Jonathan Michael. BS, Tufts U., 1964; MD, Tulane U., 1969. Diplomate Am. Bd. Plastic Surgery, 1977, Am. Bd. Surgery, 1975. Intern Bronx Muni Hosp Ctr, NY, 1969—70, resident surgery, 1970—72, Montefiore Hosp. Med. Ctr., NY, 1972—74 resident surgery, 1974—76; attending plastic surgeon Montefiore Med. Ctr., NY, 1976—, Albert Einstein Coll. Med. Hosp., NY, 1976—, Beth Abraham Hosp., NY, 1976—, Jewish Home & Hosp., NY, 1976—, Beth Israel Med. Ctr., NY, 1986—; clin. prof. plastic surgery Albert Einstein Coll. Medicine, Bronx, NY, 1994—. Adv. bd. FOJP Medical Malpractice, NYC, 1988—. Fellow ACS (Bronx chpt., pres. 1995-96); Am. Soc. Plastic Surgeons, Am. Assn. Plastic Surgeons, Am. Soc. Aesthetic Plastic Surgery, Med. Soc. Plastic Surgeons (pres. 1992-93), Montefiore Med. Ctr. Staff Alumni Assn. (pres. 1994-97), Am. Assn. Hand Surgery, Northeastern Soc. Plastic Surgeons, Harry Benjamin Soc. Jewish. Avocations: landscape gardening, vintage automobiles, stamp collecting/philately, collecting and restoring antique furniture. Home: 11 Ross Rd Scarsdale NY 10583-4425 Office: 1049 5th Ave Ste 2D New York NY 10028-0115 Office Phone: 212-861-8000. Office Fax: 212-861-8376. Personal E-mail: pweissmd@verizon.net.

**WEISS, RENÉE KAROL,** editor, musician; b. Allentown, Pa., Sept. 11, 1923; d. Abraham S. and Elizabeth (Levitt) Karol; m. Theodore Weiss. BA, Bard Coll., 1951; student, Conn. Sch. Dance; studied violin with, Sascha Jacobinoff, Boris Koutzen, Emile Hauser, Ivan Galamian. Mem. Miami U. Symphony Orch., 1941, N.C. State Symphony, 1942-45, Oxford U. Symphony, Opera Orchs., Eng., 1953-54, Woodstock String Quartet, 1956-60, Bard Coll. Chamber Ensemble, 1950-66, Hudson Valley Philharmonic, 1960-66, Hudson Valley String Quartet, 1965, Princeton Chamber Orch., 1980-93; orchestral, chamber work, 1966—. Participant Theodore and Renée Weiss poetry writing workshops Princeton U., 1985, Hofstra Coll., 1985, modern poetry workshop Cooper Union, 1988, Princeton Adult Edn.; tchr. modern dance to children Bard Coll., Kindergarten Tivoli, NY Pub. Sch., 1955-58 Author: (children's books) To Win A Race, 1966, A Paper Zoo, 1968 (best books for children N.Y. Times, Book World 1968, N.J. Author's award 1968, 70, 88), The Bird From the Sea, 1970, Biography: David Schubert: Works and Days, 1984; co-editor, mgr. Quar. Rev. Lit., 1945-2005; author: (with Theodore Weiss) The Always Present Present, 2005; author of poems. Mem.: PEN (Nora Magid Lifetime Achievement award with Theodore Weiss 1997). Office: Q R L Poetry Series Princeton U 185 Nassau St Princeton NJ 08544-4914 Office Phone: 609-759-3366. Business E-Mail: qrl@princeton.edu.

**WEISS, RICHARD A.,** state official; b. Africa; m. Jan Weiss; 3 children. Grad. in liberal arts, Baylor U. Adminstr. Office of Budget, Dept. Fin. and Adminstrn., Little Rock, dep. dir., dir., 1994-97; CFO, State of Ark., Little Rock, 1994—; dir. Ark. Dept. Fin. and Adminstrn., Little Rock, 2001—. Office: Fin and Adminstrn Dept PO Box 3278 Little Rock AR 72203-3278 Office Phone: 501-682-2242. E-mail: richard.weiss@dfa.state.ar.us.

**WEISS, RICK,** reporter; married; 1 child. BS in Biology, Cornell U., 1974; M in Journalism, U. Calif. Berkeley, 1985. Lic. med. technologist various hosp. labs., 1974—84; biology and biomedicine writer Sci. News Mag., Wash.; staff writer Health Mag., San Francisco; sci. and med. reporter health sect. Wash. Post, 1993—96, sci. and med. reporter nat. news desk, 1996—. Contbg. writer: NY Times, L.A. Times, Science, Discover. Recipient Sci. Journalism award, AAAS, 2000, Sci. in Soc. Journalism award, Nat. Assn. Science Writers, Inc., 2002, Victor Cohn Prize for Excellence in Medical Science Reporting, 2005. Office: Wash Post 1150 15th St NW Washington DC 20071-0070 Office Phone: 202-334-5514. Business E-Mail: weissr@washpost.com.*

**WEISS, ROBERT EDWARD,** urologist, educator; b. Manchester, Conn., Sept. 17, 1959; BS magna cum laude, Brown U., 1981; MD, NYU, 1985. Intern Mt. Sinai Med. Ctr., N.Y.C., 1985-86, resident surgery, 1986-87, resident urology, 1987-91; fellow urol. surgery Meml. Sloan-Kettering Cancer Ctr., N.Y.C., 1991-94; assoc. prof. urology R.W. Johnson Hosp. Med. Ctr., New Brunswick, NJ, 1994—. Fellow ACS; mem. Am. Urol. Assn., Soc. Urologic Oncology, Soc. Surg. Oncology, N.Y. Urol. Assn., N.Y. Urol. Assn., Soc. of Basic Urologic Rsch. Office: RW Johnson Med Ctr 1 RW Johnson Pl CN-19 New Brunswick NJ 08903 Office Phone: 732-235-7776.

**WEISS, ROBERT FRANCIS,** retired academic administrator, religious organization administrator, consultant; b. St. Louis, Aug. 27, 1924; s. Frank L.G. and Helen M. (Beck) Weiss. BA, St. Louis U., 1951, Ph.L., MA, St. Louis U., 1953, S.T.L., 1961; PhD, U. Minn., 1964. Joined Soc. of Jesus, 1946; ordained priest Roman Catholic Ch., 1959; tchr. Rockhurst H.S., Kansas City, Mo., 1953—56; adminstrv. asst. to pres. St. Louis U., 1961—62; asst. dean Rockhurst Coll., Kansas City, Mo., 1964—66, dean, v.p., asst. prof. edn., 1966—72, pres., 1977—88, St. Louis U. HS, 1973—77, interim pres., 1992; asst. higher edn. and continuing formation Mo. Province S.J., St. Louis, 1989—92, treas., 1992—2003, asst. higher edn. and continuing formation, 1997—2005, asst. to treas., 2003—05, del. higher edn., 2005—. Mem. Commn. on Govtl. rels. Am. Coun. Edn., 1985—87; bd. dirs. Kansas City Regional Coun. for Higher Edn., 1987—88, Boys Hope Girls Hope, 1977—. Contbr. chapters to books, articles to profl. jours. Trustee St. Louis U., 1973—87, 1991—2003, Loyola U., New Orleans, 1973—82, 1985—88, United Student Aid Funds, Inc., 1977—94, U. San Francisco, 1987—99, Marymount Coll., Salina, Kans., 1986—88, St. Louis U. H.S., 1989—99, 2003—, Fontbonne Coll., St. Louis, 1973—77, Sacred Heart Program, Radio and TV Apostolate, St. Louis, 1990—96, pres., 1992—96, bd. mem., 2000—05; bd. dirs. Creighton U., Omaha, 1981—97, Our Little Haven, St. Louis, 1992—, St. Elizabeth Acad., St. Louis, 1997—2004, DeSmet Jesuit HS, 2003—, Loyola Acad., St. Louis, 2003—, chmn. bd. mems., 2005—; bd. dirs. St. John's Coll., Belize City, Belize, 2003—; bd. trustees St. Louis (Mo.) Archdiocesan Fund, 2006—; bd. regents Conception Sem. Coll., Mo., 2004—. 1st sgt. U.S. Army, 1943—46. Decorated Bronze Star. Mem.: Am. Assn. for Higher Edn., Vets. Assn. Rainbow divsn. (nat. chaplain 1976—84, 1988—90, pres.-elect 1990—91, pres. 1991—92, assoc. nat. chaplain 1992—, found. pres. 2003—05), Alpha Phi Omega, Alpha Sigma Nu. Office: Mo Province SJ 4511 W Pine Blvd Saint Louis MO 63108-2109 Office Phone: 314-361-7765. Business E-Mail: rweiss@jesuits-mis.org. *The only way for me to look at life is in the light of faith, which I consider one of God's greatest gifts. Life for me is an opportunity to serve God and as many of my neighbors as I can. I am basically an optimist. There is so much beauty around us, so many good people, so many marvels to behold— that I thank the Lord for giving me the ability to know and experience this life and to look forward to eternal life with God, the Source of all life. Any success I have had I attribute to taking advantage of the opportunities that God has put in my path.*

**WEISS, ROBERT JEROME,** psychiatrist, educator; b. West New York, N.J., Dec. 9, 1917; s. Harry and Dora (Samuels) W.; m. Minnie Thompson Moore, Apr. 21, 1945; children— Scott Tillman, James Woodrow, Elizabeth Thompson. Student, Johns Hopkins, 1937; AB, George Washington U., 1947; MD, Columbia, 1951; MA (hon.), Dartmouth, 1964. Intern Columbia Univ. Bellevue Hosp., 1951, asst. resident medicine, 1953; resident psychiatry N.Y. Psychiat. Inst., 1954-56; asst. attending Vanderbilt Clinic, 1957-58, Presbyn. Hosp., N.Y.C., 1958-59; chief psychiatry Mary Hitchcock Meml. Hosp., 1959-70; career tchr. trainee Nat. Inst. Mental Health, 1956-58; tchr., research Columbia Coll. Phys. and Surg., 1956-59; prof. psychiatry, founder dept. psychiatry, chmn. dept. Dartmouth Med. Sch., 1959-70; psychiatrist Beth Israel Hosp., 1958-90; attending physician Presbyn. Hosp., 1975-85, cons., 1985—. Vis. prof. cmty. medicine Harvard Med. Sch., 1970-75, assoc. dir. cmty. health, 1970-75, assoc. dean health care planning; prof. psychiatry and social medicine Columbia Coll. Physicians and Surgeons, 1975-86, also dir.

Ctrs. for Cmty. Health, 1975-86; De Lamar prof. pub. health practice, dean Columbia U. Sch. Pub. Health, 1980-86, dean and De Lamar prof. of pub. health practice, prof. psychiatry, prof. social medicine, prof. emeritus, 1986—, dean emeritus, 1996—; vis. prof. cmty. medicine U. N.Mex. Med. Sch., 1986-89; adj. prof. arts and sci. U. Maine, Orono, 1997—; cons. Nat. Ctr. for Health Svcs. Rsch., 1975-86, NIMH, 1977-86; chmn. psychiatry tng. com. NIMH, 1967-68, mem. coord. panel, 1965-67, ad hoc com. interdisciplinary tng. program, 1966, mem. agenda com., 1966; cons. AT&T, 1990-92; chmn. bd. Academica, 1992, Employee Managed Care Corp., 1994-96; prin. Weiss, Baldacci & Fletcher; mem. com. trade treaties State Senate, 2004—. Co-editor: Columbia U. Coll. Physicians and Surgeons Complete Home Medical Guide, 1986, editor emeritus 2d and 3d edits., 1989; contbr. articles to profl. jours., chpts. to books. Founder dept. psychiatry Dartmouth Med. Sch., 1959. Served to maj. AUS, 1941-46. Recipient Bi-Centennial medal Columbia Coll. Phys. and Surg., 1967. Fellow Am. Psychiat. Assn. (life); mem. Am. Assn. Chmn. Depts. Psychiatry (pres. 1979-80). Achievements include first telemedicine 2-way transmission between medical centers; demonstrated social supports reduce disability due to mental illness; research in special health care delivery, health care preventive psychiatry. Home: 10 Cromwell Dr Orono ME 04473-3639 Personal E-mail: rjw4007@verizon.net.

**WEISS, ROBERT M.,** urologist, educator; b. NYC, Jan. 13, 1936; s. David and Laura W.; m. Ilana Shemer, May 20, 1973; children: Erik Daniel, Dana Alexandra. BS magna cum laude, Franklin and Marshall Coll., Lancaster, Pa., 1957; MD, SUNY, Bklyn., 1960; MA (hon.), Yale U., 1976. Diplomate: Am. Bd. Urology, Nat. Bd. Med. Examiners. Intern Cornell Med. Divsn., Bellevue Hosp., N.Y.C., 1960-61; resident in gen. surgery Beth Israel Hosp., N.Y.C., 1961-62; resident in urology Squier Urol. Clinic, Presbyn. Hosp., N.Y.C., 1963-64, 65-67; vis. fellow Columbia U. Coll. Physicians and Surgeons, N.Y.C., 1961 65, adj. assoc. prof. pharmacology, 1975-77, adj. prof. pharmacology, 1977—; mem. faculty Yale U. Med. Sch., New Haven, 1967—, prof. urology, 1976-88, prof., chief sect. of urology, 1988—, interim chmn. dept. surgery, 1999-2001; attending urology Yale-New Haven Hosp., New Haven, 1967-88, head sect. of urology, 1988—, interim chief dept. surgery, 1999—2001, pres. med. staff, 2004—06. Cons. West Haven VA Hosp., Waterbury (Conn.) Hosp. Contbr. articles to profl. jours. Trustee Am. Bd. Urology, 1998-2004. With USAR, 1962-63. Fellow ACS, Am. Acad. Pediat.; mem. AAAS, Am. Assn. Genito-Urinary Surgeons, Am. Surg. Assn., Am. Physiol. Soc., Soc. Gen. Physiologists, Assn. Univ. Urologists, Soc. Pediatric Urology, Am. Urol. Assn., Clin. Soc. Genito-Urinary Surgeons, New Eng. Surg. Soc., Phi Beta Kappa, Sigma Xi. Office: Yale U Sch Medicine Dept Urology PO Box 208041 New Haven CT 06520-8041 Office Phone: 203-785-2815. Business E-Mail: robert.weiss@yale.edu.

**WEISS, ROBERT MICHAEL,** dentist; b. Bklyn., June 5, 1940; s. Henry and Rena (Bluth) W.; m. Irene Marilyn Sternick, June 30, 1962; children: Lori Ann, Julie Lynn, Karen Michelle. Trustees scholar, L.I. U., 1958-61; DDS, NYU, 1965; postdoctoral cert., LD Pankey Inst. for Advanced Dental Edn. 1979. Pvt. practice dentistry, Avon, Conn., 1967—; pres. Avon Dental Group, P.C., 1972—; clin. prof. Coll. Dentistry U. Conn., 2000—. Nat. cons. Conn. Gen. Ins. Co. for ins. coverage for Gen. Electric Co., 1980—; advisor dental assisting program Briarwood Coll.; cons. CNA Ins. Co., 1988—; mem. mentorship program U. Conn. Coll. Dentistry; bd. dirs. Sentinel Bank; mentor program U. Conn. Coll. Dentistry. Chmn. Children's Dental Health Week, Hartford County, Conn., 1971; chmn. Jewish Adult Edn., West Hartford, Conn., 1986-87; trustee Temple Beth Israel, 1983—. Served to capt. USAF, 1965-67. Fellow Acad. Gen. Dentistry, Am. Acad. Gen. Dentistry, Pierre Fauchand Acad. (hon.); mem. ADA, Am. Soc. Preventive Dentistry (pres. Conn. chpt.), Acad. Osseointegration, Internat. Congress Oral Implantologists, Hartford Dental Soc. (exec. com. 1993—, chmn. centennial yr. 1994, 100th anniversary 1996-97), Conn. State Dental Assn. (ho. of dels. 1992—), Chronic Fatigue Immune Dysfunction Syndrome (Conn. bd. dirs. 1992—), So. New Eng. Assn. Practice Adminstrn., Starnard Beach Assn. (pres. 1984-86), Avon Jr. C. of C. (pres. 1971-72), Masons, Alpha Omega, Sigma Alpha Mu. Home: 13 Alpine Meadow Ln Avon CT 06001-3935 Office: Avon Dental Group 20 W Avon Rd Ste 2 Avon CT 06001-3540

**WEISS, ROBERT ORR,** speech educator; b. Kalamazoo, Apr. 8, 1926; s. Nicholas John and Ruth (Orr) W.; m. Ann Lenore Lawson, Sept. 16, 1951; children: Elizabeth Ann, John Lawson, James Robert, Virginia Lenore. BA, Albion Coll., 1948; MA, Northwestern U., 1949, PhD, 1954. Instr. speech Wayne State U., Detroit, 1949-51; instr. pub. speaking Northwestern U., Evanston, Ill., 1954-55; mem. faculty DePauw U., Greencastle, Ind., 1955—2002, H.B. Gough prof. speech, 1965-97, head comm. arts and scis., 1963-78, 85-86, 93. Author: Public Argument, 1995; editor: Speaker and Gavel, 1968-75, Speaking Across the Curriculum, 1990—; co-editor: Current Criticism, 1971; contbr. articles to profl. jours. Served with AUS, 1945-46. Recipient Fred C. Tucker Disting. Career award, 1995, Lifetime award, Nat. Ednl. Debate Assn., 1997, Presdl. citation Nat. Communication Assn., 1999. Mem. AAUP (pres. DePauw U. chpt. 1961-62), Nat. Communication Assn. (legis. assembly 1966-68), Am. Forensic Assn. (sec.-treas. 1958-59), Cntl. States Communication Assn., Phi Beta Kappa, Delta Sigma Rho-Tau Kappa Alpha (nat. pres. 1981-83, pres. 1983-85), Sigma Nu. Home: 210 W Poplar St Greencastle IN 46135-2638 Office Phone: 765-658-4490. Business E-Mail: robertweiss@depauw.edu.

**WEISS, RONALD L.,** lab administrator; MD, Creighton U.; MBA, U. Utah. Cert. in anatomic and clin. pathology, microbiology and hematology. Chief med. officer, dir. labs. ARUP Labs., Salt Lake City, 1993—2002, sr. v.p., dir., bus. devel., 2002—03, pres., COO, 2003—; prof., pathology U. Utah Sch. Medicine, Salt Lake City. Office: ARUP Labs 500 Chipeta Way Salt Lake City UT 84108

**WEISS, RONALD PHILLIP,** lawyer; b. Springfield, Mass., Apr. 28, 1947; s. Kermit Paul and Fay Roslyn (Robinovitz) W.; m. Janet Faye Landon, June 15, 1969; children: Emily, Katherine. BA, Dartmouth Coll., 1968; JD, U. Pa., 1972. Bar: Mass. 1972, U.S. Dist. Ct. Mass. 1975, U.S. Tax Ct. 1979, U.S. Ct. Appeals (1st cir.) 2000. Assoc Bulkley, Richardson and Gelinas, Springfield, Mass., 1972-78; prtnr. Bulkley, Richardson and Gelinas, LLP, Springfield, 1978—. Pres. Estate Planning Coun. Hampden County, 1979-81; trustee Mass. Continuing Legal Edn. Inc., 1978-81. Author: (with others) Drafting Wills and Trusts in Massachusetts, 1990, 92, 94; editor: (with others) Massachusetts Corporate Tax Manual, 1986. Trustee Springfield Symphony Orch., 1986—, v.p., 1988—89, pres., 1989—91, chmn., 1991—94; mem. bd. advisors U. Mass. Family Bus. Ctr., 1992—; mem. adv. panel Hanson Initiative for Lang. and Literacy, MGH Inst. Health Professions, 2001—; counsel Cmty. Found. of Western Mass.; appropriations com. Town of Longmeadow, Mass., 1990—96, chmn., 1991—92, 1995—96; trustee Jewish Fedn. Greater Springfield, 1986—90. Mem. ABA, Mass. Bar Assn. (chmn. taxation sect. 1978-81, bd. dels. 1979-81), Mass. Bar Found., Hampden County Bar Assn., Rotary. Office: Bulkley Richardson and Gelinas LLP 1500 Main St Ste 2700 Springfield MA 01115-5507 Office Phone: 413-272-6259.

**WEISS, SAMUEL ABRAHAM,** psychologist, psychoanalyst; b. N.Y.C. m. Alice Langer, May 20, 1958; children: Benjamin 2., Naomi E., Susan J. BA, Yeshiva U., 1944; MA, NYU, 1948, PhD, 1957. Diplomate in clin. psychology, Am. Bd. Profl. Psychology. Intern Bellevue Psychiat. Hosp., N.Y.C., 1955—56; assoc. rsch. scientist NYU Med. Ctr., N.Y.C., 1956—59, rsch. scientist 1959—68, assoc. dir. amputee psychology rsch., 1958—66; assoc. prof. psychology Yeshiva U., N.Y.C., 1961—71, psychol. cons. Stern. Coll. for Women, 1960—71; psychologist, psychotherapist, psychoanalyst in pvt. practice N.Y.C., 1972. Cons. N.Y. State Div. Vocat. Rehab., 1958-73. Contbr. articles to profl. jours. Fellow AAAS (Rosette award 1991), APA (editl. cons. rehab. psychology 1972-80), Am. Psychol. Soc. Jewish. Achievements include new research on medical factors in phantom limb pain and rehabilitation. Home: 80-40 Lefferts Blvd Kew Gardens NY 11415-1723 Office: 7 Park Ave Apt 66 New York NY 10016-4356 Office Phone: 212-686-8324.

**WEISS, SCOTT ALAN,** commercial real estate consultant; s. Stuart Rollin Weiss and Sandy Carol Courson, Dan Christopher Courson; m. Corey Elizabeth Weilbacher, June 17, 2000. BA in Journalism, La. State U., 1997; JD, South Tex. U., 2003; grad. cert., Cornell U. Cert. comml. investment mem. Jud. law clk. 4th Ct. Appeals, Tex.; atty. Daw & Ray, PC. Editor: Constrn. Law Jour., 2002, South Tex. Law Review. Scholar, HBAI Constrn. Law Sect.; Blask Fed. fellow award for fed. interns. Mem.: Currents Internat. Trade Law (mng. editor 2002), South Tex. Law Rev. (asst. editor 2001—02). Avocations: running, reading. Office Phone: 713-266-3121. E-mail: scottalanweiss@yahoo.com.

**WEISS, SHIRLEY F.,** retired urban and regional planner, economist, educator; b. NYC, Feb. 26, 1921; d. Max and Vera (Hendel) Friedlander; m. Charles M. Weiss, June 7, 1942. BA, Rutgers U., 1942; postgrad., Johns Hopkins U., 1949-50; M in Regional Planning, U. NC, 1958; PhD, Duke U., 1973. Assoc. research dir. Ctr. for Urban and Regional Studies U. N.C., Chapel Hill, 1957-91, lectr. in planning, 1958-62, assoc. prof., 1962-73, prof., 1973-91, prof. emerita, 1991—; joint creator-sponsor Charles and Shirley Weiss Urban Livability Program, U. N.C., Chapel Hill, 1992—; research assoc. Inst. for Research in Social Sci., U. N.C., 1957-73; research prof. U. N.C., Chapel Hill, 1973-91, acting dir. women's studies program Coll. Arts and Scis., 1985, faculty marshal, 1988-91. Grad. edn. advancement bd. U. NC, Chapel Hill, 2001—. tech. com. Water Resources Rsch. Inst., 1976-79; adv. com. on housing for 1980 census Dept. Commerce, 1976-81; cons. Urban Inst., Washington, 1977-80; rev. panel Exptl. Housing Allowance Program, HUD, 1977-80; adv. bd. on built environ. Nat. Acad. Scis.-NRC, 1981-83, program coordinating com. fed. constrn. coun. of adv. bd. on built environ., 1982-83; mem. Planning Accreditation Bd., Site Visitation Pool, Am. Inst. Cert. Planners and Assn. Collegiate Schs. Planning, 1985—; discipline screening com. Fulbright Scholar awards in Architecture and City Planning, Coun. for Internat. Exchange of Scholars, 1985-88; N.Mex. adv. bd. Enterprise Found., Santa Fe, 1997-2002; governing bd. Acad. Freedom Fund, AAUP, 1997-2000. Author: The Central Business District in Transition: Methodological Approaches to CBD Analysis and Forecasting Future Space Requirements, 1957, New Town Development in the United States: Experiment in Private Entrepreneurship, 1973; co-author: A Probabilistic Model for Residential Growth, 1964, Residential Developer Decisions: A Focused View of the Urban Growth Process, 1966, New Communities U.S.A., 1976; co-author, co-editor: New Community Development: Planning Process, Implementation and Emerging Social Concerns, vols. 1, 2, 1971, City Centers in Transition, 1976, New Communities Research Series, 1976-77; mem. editl. bd.: Jour. Am. Inst. Planners, 1963-68, Rev. of Regional Studies, 1969-74, 82-92, Internat. Regional Sci. Rev., 1975-81. Trustee Friends of Libr., U. N.C., Chapel Hill, 1988-94, Santa Fe Chamber Music Festival, adv. coun., 1990-91, 97-98, trustee, 1991-97, 98-2004, trustee emerita, 2004-; bd. dirs. Triangle Opera, 1986-89, 91-2002, Chamber Orch. of the Triangle, 1997-2005, hon. life mem., 2005-. Recipient Cornelia Phillips Spencer Bell award U. NC, Chapel Hill, 1996, Disting. Alumni award Alumni Assn. Dept. City and Regional Planning, U. NC, Chapel Hill, 1996, Mary Turner Lane award Assn. Women Faculty, 1994, (with Charles M. Weiss) Gifford Phillips award Santa Fe Chamber Music Festival, 2000, Disting. Alumni and Alumnus award U. NC, Chapel Hill, 2003; Adelaide M. Zagoren fellow Douglass Coll., Rutgers U., 1994. Emeritus fellow Urban Land Inst. (sr. fellow, exec. group, cmty. devel. coun. 1978—); mem. Am. Inst. Planners (sec., treas. southeast chpt. 1957-59, v.p. 1960-61), Am. Inst. Cert. Planners, Am. Planning Assn., Am. Econ. Assn., So. Regional Sci. Assn. (pres. 1977-78), Regional Sci. Assn. (councillor 1971-74, v.p. 1976-77), Nat. Assn. Housing and Redevelopment Ofcls., Interamerican Planning Soc., Internat. Fedn. Housing and Planning, Town and Country Planning Assn., Internat. Urban Devel. Assn., Econ. History Assn., Am. Real Estate and Urban Econs. Assn. (regional membership chmn. 1976-82, 84-85, dir. 1977-80), AAUP (chpt. pres. 1976-77, pres. N.C. Conf. 1978-79, mem. nat. coun. 1983-86, William S. Tacey award Assembly of State Confs.), Douglass Soc., Order of Valkyries, Phi Beta Kappa. Home: 750 Weaver Dairy Rd # 2114 Chapel Hill NC 27514-1483

**WEISS, SIMONA,** retired paralegal; d. Leon and Rose Weiss; m. Morton B. Elliot, Apr. 14, 1951 (div. May 10, 1972); children: Russell Wayne Elliot, Linda Beth Elliot-Morris. BA cum laude, Fairligh Dickinson U., 1974; postgrad., Columbia U., 1968—70; grad. in Pub. Adminstrn., NYU, 1974—76; postgrad., William Patterson U., 2001—03. Cert. paralegal Upsala Coll. N.J., 1980. Paralegal adminstr. Witco Chem. Corp., N.Y.C., 1980—81; paralegal supr. Pitney, Hardin, Kipp & Szuch, Morristown, NJ, 1982—82; real estate paralegal Willkie Farr & Gallagher, N.Y.C., 1983—84; real estate and corp. paralegal Robinson Silverman Pearce Aronsohn & Berman, N.Y.C., 1984—90; real estate paralegal Freddie Mac, New York, NY, 1991—91; legal asst. Gen. Investment Sect. Legal Dept. The Prudential Ins. Co. of Am., Newark, 1992—94; comml. real estate paralegal Cleary, Gottlieb, Steen & Hamilton, N.Y.C., 1994—96; real estate and corp. paralegal Hannoch Weisman, Roseland, NJ, 1996—98; comml. real estate paralegal Unilever Bestfoods, Englewood Cliffs, NJ, 1998—2002. Chmn. Haworth (N.J.) Parks & Playgrounds Com., 1972—78; county com. mcpl. chmn. Haworth (N.J.) Rep. Orgn., 1973—79; candidate Non-Partisan Bergen County (N.J.) Charter Study Commn., 1973—74; primary candidate Bergen County (N.J.) Bd. of Chosen Freeholders, 1977—77; fin. and corr. sec. Temple Beth El, Closter, NJ, 1968—72; program and publicity chmn. 1st Bergen County Women's Ctr., Teaneck, NJ, 1972—74; v.p. fund raising Haworth (N.J.) Home and Sch. Assn., 1967—69. Recipient Mayor's Cert., Borough of Haworth, 1979; scholar, Fairleigh Dickinson U., 1971—74. Mem.: Legal Asst. Mgmt. Assn., Nat. Paralegal Assn., Phi Omega Epsilon. Independent. Avocations: theater, movies, opera, ballet, reading. Personal E-mail: simona_wei@msn.com.

**WEISS, STEPHEN J.,** lawyer; b. NYC, Sept. 12, 1938; s. Morris and Frances (Dinkin) W.; m. Madeline Adler, Aug. 12, 1962; children: Lynn H. Andrew, Valerie Elizabeth, Bradley Lawrence. BS, Queens Coll., 1959; LL.B., Cornell U., 1962; LL.M., Georgetown U., 1966. Bar: N.Y. 1963, D.C. 1966, U.S. Supreme Ct. 1975. Atty. SEC, Washington, 1962-65; assoc. firm Arent Fox Kintner Plotkin & Kahn, Washington, 1965-70, ptnr., 1971-94, Holland & Knight LLP, Washington, 1994—. Lectr. securities, corp. law, dirs. and officers liability and ins. Am. Law Inst., ABA, Fed. Bar Assn., Practicing Law Inst., Bur. Nat. Affairs, Exec. Enterprises, Aspen Law & Bus. Orgn. Mgmt., Inc., Inst. for Internat. Rsch., Profl. Liability Underwriting Soc.; mem. adv. bd. Securities Regulation and Law Report, Bur. Nat. Affairs, 1989—. Author: Regulation D-A Practical Guide, 1994, Navigating the D&O Maze: A Handbook for Purchasers of Directors and Officers Liability Insurance, 1997, Navigating the EPLI Maze: A Handbook for Purchasers of Employment Practices Liability Insurance, 1998; dirs. and officers liability ins. columnist Dirs. & Bds. mag., 1998—; contbr. articles to profl. jours. Mem. nat. com. Cornell Law Sch. Fund, 1987-88. Named to Best Lawyers in Am. Mem. ABA (fed. regulation securities com. 1970—, chmn. Rule 10b-5 subcom. 1976-78, chmn. civil liabilities subcom. 1978-81, chmn. com. fgn. corrupt practices legislation 1976-77, Guiding Principles Task Force bus. ins. com. 1994-95, devels. in bus. financing com. 1982—), Fed. Bar Assn. (chmn. securities law comm. 1968-70, exec. coun. of securities law com. 1971—, chmn. coun. on financing and taxation 1971-72, chmn. publs. bd. 1977-78, nat. coun. 1972-80, Leadership commendation 1973, Disting. Svc. award), Cornell Law Club Washington (pres. 1971-79). Office: Holland & Knight LLP 2099 Pennsylvania Ave NW Washington DC 20006 Office Phone: 202-457-5920. Business E-Mail: steve.weiss@hklaw.com.

**WEISS, STEVEN GARY,** physician; b. Gary, Ind., June 28, 1949; s. Morris Eugene and Edith (Wolinsky) W.; m. Irene Cohn, May 14, 1977; children: Leah Rose, Julia Inger, Mara Emily, Max martin. BA, Ind. U., 1971, MD, 1974. Intern Highland Gen. Hosp., Oakland, Calif., 1974; resident Mt. Zion Hosp. and Med. Ctr., San Francisco, 1977; fellow U. Chgo., 1982; Assoc. prof. U. South Fla. Coll. Medicine, Tampa, 1984—; physician pvt. practice, Clearwater, Fla., 1984—. Chief of med. staff Mease Hosps., Dunedin, Fla., 1991-92. Trustee Mease Health Care, 1991-94. Fellow Am. Acad. Allergy/Immunology, Am. Coll. Allergy.

**WEISS, SUSAN,** newspaper editor; Mng. editor Life Section, USA Today, Arlington, Va. Office: USA Today 7950 Jones Branch Dr Mc Lean VA 22108-0001

**WEISS, WALTER STANLEY,** lawyer; b. Newark, Mar. 12, 1929; s. Jack and Mollie (Orkin) W.; m. Misty M. Moore; children from previous marriage: Jack Stephen, Andrew Scott. AB, Rutgers U., 1949, JD, 1952. Bar: D.C. 1952, N.J. 1956, Calif. 1961. Trial atty. IRS, Phila., Los Angeles, 1957-62; asst. U.S. atty., chief tax div. Los Angeles, 1962-63; ptnr. firm Goodson & Hannam, Los Angeles, 1963-67; mng. ptnr. firm Long & Levit, Los Angeles, 1967-79; ptnr. firm Greenberg & Glusker, Los Angeles, 1979-81, Rosenfeld, Meyer and Susman, Beverly Hills, Calif., 1981-93; prin. Law Office of Walter S. Weiss, L.A., 1993—. Judge pro tem L.A. and Santa Monica (Calif.) Mcpl. Cts., 1994—. Contbr. articles to legal jours. Served to capt. JAGC USAF, 1953-56. Named Arbitrator Nat. Assn. Securities Dealers, 1974 Fellow Am. Coll. Trial Lawyers; mem. ABA, Los Angeles County Bar Assn., Beverly Hills Bar Assn. Home: 12349 Ridge Cir Los Angeles CA 90049-1183 Office: 12400 Wilshire Blvd Ste 1300 Los Angeles CA 90025-1055 Office Phone: 310-207-6679. E-mail: waltersweiss@yahoo.com.

**WEISS, ZEV,** corporate financial executive; s. Morry Weiss. With Am. Greetings Corp., Cleve., 1992—, exec. dir., Nat. Accounts, 1997—2000, v.p., Strategic Business Unit Division, 2000—01, sr. v.p., 2001—, CEO, 2001—. Office: American Greeting Corp 1 American Rd Cleveland OH 44144-2398

**WEISSBACH, HERBERT,** biochemist, researcher; b. N.Y.C., Mar. 16, 1932; s. Louis and Vivian (Ruhalter) W.; m. Renee Kohl, Dec. 27, 1953; children— Lawrence, Nancy, Marjorie, Robert BS, CUNY, 1953; MS, George Washington U., 1955, PhD, 1957. Chemist Nat. Heart Inst., Bethesda, Md., 1953-68; acting chief NIH, Bethesda, 1968-69; assoc. dir. Roche Inst. Molecular Biology, Nutley, NJ, 1969-83, dir., 1983-96; v.p. Hoffmann-La Roche, Nutley, 1983-96; disting. rsch. prof. dir. ctr. for molecular biology and biotech. Fla. Atlantic U., Boca Raton, 1997—. Adj. prof. George Washington U., 1964-69, Columbia U., 1969-85, U. Medicine and Dentistry N.J., Newark, 1981-93, Princeton U., 1984-85. Editor: Molecular Mechanisms of Protein Biosynthesis, 1977, Archives of Biochemistry and Biophysics; contbr. articles to profl. jours. Recipient Superior Svc. award HEW, 1968, Enzyme award Am. Chem. Soc., 1970, Disting. Alumni award George Washington U., 1994. Mem. Am. Chem. Soc., Am. Soc. Biol. Chemists, Am. Soc. Pharmacology and Exptl. Therapeutics, Am. Soc. Microbiology, Nat. Acad. Scis., AAAS Home: 8008 Desmond Dr Boynton Beach FL 33437-5011 Office: Fla Atlantic U 777 Glades Rd Boca Raton FL 33431-6424 E-mail: herbweissbach@aol.com.

**WEISSBARD, SAMUEL HELD,** lawyer; b. N.Y.C., Mar. 3, 1947; children: Andrew Joshua, David S. BA, Case Western Res. U., 1967; JD with highest honors, George Washington U., 1970. Bar: D.C. 1970, U.S. Supreme Ct. 1974, Calif. 1998. Assoc. Fried, Frank, Harris, Shriver & Kampelman, 1970-73, Arent, Fox, Kintner, Plotkin & Kahn, 1973-78; prin. Weissbard & Fields, P.C., 1978-83; shareholder, v.p. Wilkes, Artis, Hedrick & Lane, Washington, 1983-86; ptnr. Foley & Lardner, Washington, 1986-97, L.A., 1997-98, co-chair creditors' rights workout and bankruptcy group Washington, 1992-95; sr. counsel Cox, Castle & Nicholson, L.L.P., Newport Beach, Calif., 1998—2001; exec. v.p., gen. counsel Makar Properties, LLC, Newport Beach, 2001—. Editor in chief George Washington U. Law Rev., 1969-70. Bd. dirs. Luther Rice Soc., George Washington U., 1985-87, Atlanta Coll. Art, 1993, Nat. Learning Ctr., 1993-96, Georgetown Arts Commn. and gen. counsel 1995-96; Chmn. steering com. of Lawyer's Alliance for Nat. Learning Ctr. and Capital Children's Mus., 1989-90; mem. steering com. DC/NLC Don't Drop Out Campaign, 1992,93, bd. dirs., 1994-96; devel. com. Shelter for the Homeless, 1998-99. Recipient John Bell Larner medal, 1970. Mem. ABA, D.C. Bar, Calif. Bar Assn., Orange County Bar Assn., Georgetown Bus. and Profl. Assn. (bd. dirs. 1993-96, sec., gen. counsel 1993-96), Orange County Bus. Assn. (legis. com. 1998-99), Order of Coif. Office: Makar Properties LLC 4100 MacArthur Blvd Ste 200 Newport Beach CA 92660-2063 E-mail: sweissbard@makarproperties.com.

**WEISS-CORNWELL, AMY,** interior designer; b. Mpls., Dec. 8, 1950; d. August Carl and Margaret Amelia (Wittman) Weiss; m. Dan Cornwell, July 31, 1995; 1 child, Emma Cornwell. AA in Home Econs., Cerritos Coll.; student, Long Beach State U., Santa Ana Jr. Coll. Asst. to interior designer Bobbi Hart at Pati Pfahler Designs, Canoga Pk., Calif., 1974-75; interior designer B.A. Interiors, Fullerton, Calif., 1976-78, Birns Co., Rancho Mirage, Calif., 1978-79; staff interior designer Assoc. Design Studios, Costa Mesa, Calif., 1979-81; interior designer Carole Eichen Interiors, Fullerton, 1981, Sears, Roebuck and Co., Alhambra, Calif., 1982-84; sr. corp. designer, mgr. design studio Barratt Am., Irvine, Calif., 1984-88; owner, retail designer Amy Weiss Designs, Coronado, Calif., 1988—; office, yacht designer, 1997—. Designer in residence San Diego Design Ctr., 1990—92; participant Pacific Design Ctr.; Designer on Call program, 1994—95. Prin. works include interior designs for residences, yachts; comml. interiors including lobbies and offices. Mem. Am. Soc. Interior Designers (Globe-Guilders steering com. 1989-92, chmn. Christmas party, co-chmn. Christmas on Prado 1989, 89, designer for ASID showcase house 1992, 93), Bldg. Industry Assn. (sales and mktg. coun. awards com. 1993, mem. sales and mktg. coun. 1986-88, mem. home builders coun. 1994, 2d place M.A.M.E. award 1987, 1st place M.A.M.E. award 1986, 2d place S.A.M. award 1987), Building Industry Assn. Remodeler's Coun., Nat. Kitchen and Bath Assn., Coronado C. of C., Coronado Cays Yacht Club. Office: Amy Weiss Designs 1123 Marysville Ave Chula Vista CA 91913 Office Phone: 619-216-6002. Personal E-mail: amyweissdesigns@cox.net.

**WEISSENBURGER, DAVID ALLEN,** psychologist, educator, consultant; b. Anchorage, Sept. 7, 1953; s. Kenneth Albert and Dolores Jean Weissenburger; m. Barbara Jean Lyon, Nov. 28, 1998 (div. Apr. 2005); m. Jan Elizabeth Stone, Aug. 20, 1977 (div. Sept. 15, 1997); children: Jon Eric, Caryn Ann. AA, Sauk Valley Coll., 1973; BS, Western Ill. U., 1975; MA, Stephen F. Austin State U., 1979; PhD, Tex. Woman's U., 1994. Lic. psychol. assoc. Tex. State Bd. Examiners of Psychologists, 1980; cert. comprehensive diagnosis and evaluation - psychology Tex., 1980, qualified mental retardation profl. Tex., 1980. Unit dir., psychologist Tex. Dept. MHMR, Denton, 1976—87; dir. mental retardation svcs. Denton County MHMR Ctr., 1987—88; v.p. assessment and rsch. Behavioral Scis. Rsch. Press, Dallas, 1991—94; assoc. prof. U. Ctrl. Tex., Killeen, 1994—99, Tarleton State U., Killeen, 1999—2005, Stephenville, Tex., 2005—05, prof., 2005—. Gen. ptnr. Weiss-Lyon Assocs., Copperas Cove, Tex., 1997—2004; faculty senate pres. Tarleton State U., Stephenville, Tex., 2002—03; v.p. West Tex. region Tex. Coun. Faculty Senates, Austin, 2002—04, pres.-elect, 2004—05, pres., 2005—. Author: (psychological test) Weiss-Lyon Scale. Mem. Ctrl. Tex. Coop. Workshop Coun., Killeen, 2001—02; asst. scoutmaster Boy Scouts, Roanoke, Tex., 1989—95; dir., past pres., v.p. Families in Crisis, Inc., Killeen, 1997—2005; mem. Texan Club - Tarleton State U., Stephenville, 2000—; pres. Student Govt. Assn. - Sauk Valley Coll., Dixon, Ill., 1972—73. Fellow Sr. fellow, Tex. Higher Edn. Coordinating Bd., 2002; scholar, State of Ill., 1971—75. Mem.: APA, Nat. Assn. Sch. Psychologists, Southwestern Psychol. Assn.; Assn. Psychol. Sci., Optimist Club, Phi Theta Kappa, Psi Chi. Personal E-mail: dweissenburger@earthlink.net.

**WEISSKOPF, BERNARD,** pediatrician, child behavior, development and genetics specialist, educator; b. Berlin, Dec. 11, 1929; came to U.S., 1939, naturalized, 1944; s. Benjamin and Bertha (Loew) W.; m. Penelope Allderdice, Dec. 26, 1965; children: Matthew David, Stephen Daniel. BA, Syracuse U., 1951; MD, U. Leiden, Netherlands, 1958. Diplomate Am. Bd. Med. Mgmt. Intern Meadowbrook Hosp., East Meadow, N.Y., 1958-59, resident, 1959-60, Johns Hopkins Hosp., Balt., 1962-64; fellow child psychiatry Johns Hopkins U. Sch. Medicine, Balt., 1962-64; asst. prof. pediatrics U. Ill. Coll. Medicine, Chgo., 1964-66; faculty U. Louisville, 1966—, prof. pediatrics, 1970-2000, emeritus prof. pediat., 2000—, assoc. in psychiatry, pathology and ob-gyn., 1966-2000, dir. Child Evaluation Ctr., 1966-2000. Chmn. Gov.'s Adv. Com. Early Childhood, Gov.'s Council on Early Childhood, Ky.,

1986-88. Contbr. articles to profl. jours. Trustee Jewish Hosp., Louisville, 1974-77. Served to capt. USAF, 1960-62. Fellow Am. Acad. Pediatrics, Am. Assn. Mental Deficiency; mem. Am. Soc. Human Genetics, So. Soc. Pediatric Rsch., Am. Soc. Law and Medicine, Am. Coll. Physician Execs. Home: 6409 Deep Creek Dr Prospect KY 40059-9422 Office: Weisskopf Ctr Evaluation Children 571 S Floyd St Ste 100 Louisville KY 40202-3828 E-mail: bernweisul@aol.com.*

**WEISSMAN, ALLAN M.,** medical researcher; BS in biochemistry, SUNY, Stony Brook, 1977; MD, Albert Einstein Coll. Medicine, 1981. Resident in internal medicine Washington U.; postdoctoral fellow Cell Biology and Metabolism Br. Nat. Inst. Child Health & Human Devel., NIH, 1984; ind. investigator Nat. Cancer Inst., 1989; chief Regulation of Protein Functions Lab. Ctr. Cancer Rsch., Nat. Cancer Inst., 2001—03, acting chief Regulation of Cell Growth Lab.; Regulation of Protein Synthesis Lab. and Regulation of Cell Growth Lab. merged to form Lab. Protein Dynamics and Signaling, 2003, chief, 2003—. Mem.: Assn. Am. Physicians, Am. Soc. Clin. Investigation, Alpha Omega Alpha. Office: Lab Protein Dynamics and Signaling Nat Cancer Inst Frederick PO Box B Bldg 560 Rm 22-103 Frederick MD 21702-1201 Office Phone: 301-846-1222. Office Fax: 301-846-1666. E-mail: amw@nih.gov.

**WEISSMAN, BARRY LEIGH,** lawyer; b. Los Angeles, May 30, 1948; s. Sidney and Eleanor (Siegel) W.; m. Beverly Jean Blumenfeld, Sept. 12, 1982. BA, U. Calif.-Davis, 1970; JD, U. Santa Clara, 1973. Bar: Calif. Supreme Ct. 1973, U.S. Dist. Ct. (cen. dist.) Calif. 1976, U.S. Supreme Ct. 1977, U.S. Ct. Appeals (D.C. cir.) 1978, N.Y. Ct. Appeals 1992. Sole practice law, Beverly Hills, Calif., 1974-82; ptnr. Valentini, Fini, Ferrara, Gallavotti & Weissman, Brentwood, Calif., 1982-85; mng. ptnr. L.A. office Kroll & Tract, 1985-87; ptnr. Knapp, Petersen & Clarke, L.A., 1989-93; ptnr. Graham & James, L.A., Calif., 1994-2000, ptnr. Squire Sanders & Dempsey, L.A., Calif., ptnr. Alschuler Grossman Stein & Kahan, LLP, ptnr. Sonnenschein Nath & Rosenthal, LLP; judge pro tem L.A. Mcpl. Ct., 1975-1979; arbitrator Am. Arbitration Assn.; examiner State Bar Calif., 1976-80; mem. adv. commn malpractice ins., Calif. State Senate. Named a 2005 Southern Calif. Super-Lawyer, Law & Politics. Mem. ABA (mem. spl. com. on prepaid legal services, co-chmn. editorial bd. gen. practice sect.'s publs.), Beverly Hills Bar Assn., Century City Bar Assn. (bd. govs., chmn., editor Century City Bar Jour.), Beverly Hills C. of C. (co-chmn. legal justice com.), Calif. State Bar (chmn. standing com. ins. law, Bus. Law Sect.), Nat. Assn. Ins. Commissioners, Colorado River Assn., Western Los Angeles Regional C. of C. (dir., chmn. com. on energy prodn. and conservation). Office: Sonnenschein Nath & Rosenthal LLP Ste 1500 601 S Figueroa St Los Angeles CA 90017 Office Phone: 213-892-5098. Office Fax: 213-623-9924. E-mail: bweissman@sonnenschein.com.*

**WEISSMAN, DAVID L.,** lawyer; b. NYC, Jan. 12, 1965; BA with honors, George Washington U., 1987; JD, Hofstra U., 1990; LLM, NYU, 1993. Bar: NY 1991, US Dist. Ct. So. Dist. NY 1991, US Dist. Ct. Ea. Dist. NY 1991. With Richards & O'Neil LLP, Seyfarth Shaw Fairweather & Geraldson; ptnr. Reed Smith LLP, NYC, 1999—, practice group head employment law & labor law group, 1999—. Mem.: Indsl. Rels. Rsch. Assn. (LI chpt.). Office: Reed Smith LLP 599 Lexington Ave 29th Fl New York NY 10022 Office Phone: 212-521-5466. Office Fax: 212-521-5450. Business E-Mail: dweissman@reedsmith.com.

**WEISSMAN, IRVING L.,** medical researcher; b. Great Falls, Mont., Oct. 21, 1939; married, 1961; 4 children. BS, Mont. State Coll., 1960, DSc (hon.), 1992; MD, Stanford U., 1965. NIH fellow dept. radiology Stanford U., 1965—67, rsch. assoc., 1967—68, from asst. prof. to assoc. prof. dept. pathology, 1969—81; prof. pathology Stanford U. Sch. Medicine, 1981—, Karel & Avice Beekhuis Prof. Cancer Biology, 1987—, prof. devel. biology, 1989—, dir., Inst. of Stem Cell Biology and Regenerative Medicine, 2003—, prof. by courtesy, neurosurgery, prof. by courtesy, biol. sciences. Sr. Dernham fellow Calif. divsn. Am. Cancer Soc., 1969—73; mem. immunobiology study sect. NIH, 1976—80; mem. founding scientific adv. bd. Amgen, 1981—89, DNAX, 1981—92; James McGinnis Meml. lectr. Duke U., 1982; mem. sci. rev. bd. Howard Hughes Med. Inst., 1986; George Feigen Meml. lectr. Stanford U., 1987; Albert Coons Meml. lectr. Harvard U., 1987; Jane Stahlman lectr. Vanderbilt U., 1987; mem. sci. adv. com. Irvington House Inst., 1987; 5th Ann. vis. prof. cancer biology U. Tex. Health Sci. Ctr., 1987; R. E. Smith lectr. U. Tex. Sys. Cancer Ctr., 1988; co-founder SyStemix, Inc., 1988, bd. dirs., 1988—97; mem. founding scientific adv. bd. T-Cell Scis. (now Avant, Inc.), 1988—92; Chauncey D. Leake lectr. U. Calif., 1989; Harvey lectr. Rockefeller U., 1989; Rose Litman lectr., 90; disting. lectr. Western Soc. Clin. Investment, 1990; chmn. US-Japan Immunology Bd., 1992—94; chmn. sci. adv. com. McLaughlin Rsch. Inst., 1992—, trustee, 1992—; bd. govs. Project Inform, 1995—; co-founder StemCells, 1996—, mem. bd. dirs.; co-founder Celltrans (now Cellerant), 2001—; chair scientific adv. bd. Cellerant; spkr. in field. Contbr. articles to profl. publications. Named One of Top 100 Alumni, Mont. State U., 1993, Mont. Conservationist of Yr., Mont. Land Reliance, 1994; recipient Faculty Rsch. award, Nat. Am. Cancer Soc., 1974—78, Basic Cell Rsch. award, Am. Assn. Cytopathology, Pasarow Award for cancer rsch., 1989, Kaiser Award for Excellence in Preclinical Teaching, Outstanding Investigator Award, NIH, E. Donnall Thomas Award, Am. Soc. Hematology, deVillers Award for Outstanding Achievements in Leukemia Rsch., Leukemia Soc. Am., J. Allyn Taylor Internat. Prize in Medicine, Bass Award, Soc. Neurological Surgeons, Calif. Scientist of Yr., 2002, Elliott Proctor Joslin medal, Am. Diabetes Assn., 2003, Van Bekkum Stem Cell Award, 2003, Disting. Scientist Award, Am. Assn. Cancer Inst., 2003, Alan Cranston Awardee, Alliance for Aging Rsch., 2004, Rabbi Shai Shacknai Mem. Prize in Immunology and Cancer Rsch., Lautenberg Ctr. for Gen. and Tumor Immunology, 2004, medal for Disting. Contributions to Biomedical Rsch., NY Acad. Medicine, 2004; scholar, Josiah Macy Found., 1974—75. Fellow: AAAS; mem.: IOM, NAS (steering com. NIOM AIDS panel 1985—86, chair, Panel on Sci. & Med. Aspects of Human Reproductive Cloning, Jessie Stevenson Kovalenko Medal 2004), Inst. Immunology, Am. Assn. Cancer Rsch., Am. Soc. Microbiology, Am. Assn. Pathologists, Am. Assn. Univ. Pathologists, Am. Assn. Immunologists (pres. 1994—95), Am. Acad. Arts and Scis. Achievements include research in phylogeny and developmental biology of cells that make up blood-forming and immune systems; first to isolate, in mice and in man, the blood-forming stem cell; knowledge expected to lead to improved treatment of people with myeloma, lymphoma and breast cancer. Avocations: football, ballet, fly fishing. Office: Stanford U Sch Medicine Dept Pathology B257 Beckman Ctr Stanford CA 94305-5323 E-mail: irv@stanford.edu.*

**WEISSMAN, JACK (GEORGE ANDERSON),** retired editor; b. Chgo., June 6, 1921; s. Ben and Ida (Meyerson) W.; m. Bernice Platt, Nov. 13, 1949; children: Bruce, David, Ellen Weissman Montgomery. BA in Edn., Northwestern U., Evanston, Ill., 1943, MS in Journalism, 1944. Asst. editor Bankers Monthly, Chgo., 1944-45; mng. editor Practical Knowledge, Chgo., 1945-50; with pub. relations dept. Roosevelt U., Chgo., 1947-50; editor Opportunity Mag., Chgo., 1950-89, ret. Author: Make Money at Home, 1963, How to Make Correct Decisions, 1964, Money Making Businesses You Can Start for $500 Or Less, 1965, Making It Big Selling, 1987. Served to cpl. USAAF, 1945-46 Mem. Sigma Delta Chi, Phi Delta Kappa. Jewish. Personal E-mail: jacknbernice@access4less.net.

**WEISSMAN, MICHAEL LEWIS,** lawyer; b. Chgo., Sept. 11, 1934; s. Maurice and Sue (Goldberg) Weissman; m. Joanne Sherwin, Dec. 19, 1961; children: Mark Douglas, Greg Steven, Scott Adam, Brett Anthony. Student White scholar, U. Chgo., 1951-52; BS in Econs, Northwestern U., 1954; MBA in Acctg., U. Pa., 1956; JD, Harvard U., 1958; postgrad. Fulbright scholar, U. Sydney, Australia, 1958-59; postgrad., Harvard Acad. Internat. Law, 1959. Bar: D.C. 1958, Ill. 1959. Asst. prof. bus. law Roosevelt U., Chgo., 1959-61; pvt. practice Chgo., 1959-61; mem. firm Aaron, Aaron, Schimberg & Hess, 1969-73; sr. ptnr. Boorstein & Weissman, 1978-82, Weissman, Smoley & Solow, 1982-88, Foley & Lardner, 1988-92, McBride Baker & Coles, Chgo., 1992—2001; exec. v.p., gen. counsel Bridgeview Bank Group, Chgo.,

2001—04; of counsel Holland & Knight LLC, 2001—. Asst. prof. Roosevelt U., 1960—62; lectr. Lake Forest (Ill.) Coll., 1979—80; chmn. Banking Group, Union League Club Chgo.; panelist Risk Mgmt. Assn., Banking Law Inst., Midwest Fin. Conf., Greater O'Hare Assn., Miss. Law Inst., Bank Lending Inst., Chgo. Assn. Commerce and Industry, State of Art Seminars, Infocast Inc., SBA, Fed. Res. Bank Chgo., Lenders Ednl. Inst., Bank Adminstrn. Inst. Found., Lender's Forum, Clarion Legal; Fulbright sr. specialist Sch. Bus. Adminstrn., Turiba, Latvia, 2006; adj. prof. law John Marshall Law Sch., 2001—02, 2006—. Author: (book) Lender Liability, 1988, Commercial Loan Documentation and Secured Lending, 1990, How to Avoid Career-Ending Mistakes in Commercial Lending, 1996, The Lender's Edge, 1997; mem. editl. bd.: Commercial Damages, 1985—; contbr. articles to profl. jours. Mem. adv. bd. Affective Disorders Clinic, U. Ill. Med. Sch., 1979—81; instr. mentor program Risk Mgmt. Assn. Scholar, Fulbright Found., 1958—59, 2006; White scholar, U. Chgo., 1951—52. Mem.: ABA, Robert Morris Assn., Comml. Fin. Assn. Ednl. Found. (adv. bd.), Turnaround Mgmt. Assn. (steering com. Chgo. chpt.), Harvard Law Soc. Ill., 2005, Comml. Fin. Attys. (bd. dirs.), Ill. Inst. CLE (bd. dirs. 1989—2000, chmn. 2001—02), Ill. Bankers Assn. (mem. com. bank counsel 1987—88, vice chmn. 1988—89), Chgo. Bar Assn., Ill. Bar Assn., Beta Alpha Psi. Home: 2067 Old Briar Rd Highland Park IL 60035-4245 Office: Holland & Knight LLP 131 S Dearborn St 30th Fl Chicago IL 60603-5506 Office Phone: 312-715-5767. Business E-Mail: michael.weissman@hklaw.com.

**WEISSMAN, MORRIS,** printing company executive; b. 1942; Grad., NYU, 1962. Assoc. Demou Morris Levin & Shein, 1965-70; mng. dir. Gen. Mortgage Investments, 1971; pres. Midwest, 1973-86; vice chmn. U.S. Banknote; chmn., chief exec. Am. Banknote Co. and Am. Banknote Holographics. Trustee UN Bus. Coun.

**WEISSMAN, MYRNA M.,** epidemiologist, researcher, medical educator; PhD in Chronic Disease Epidemiology, Yale U., 1974. Prof. psychiatry and epidemiology Yale U.; prof. epidemiology and psychiatry Coll. Physicians and Surgeons, Columbia U., N.Y.C. Chief divsn. clin. and genetic epidemiology N.Y. Psychiat. Inst., N.Y.C. NY Psychiatric Inst Columbia U 1051 Riverside Dr Unit 24 New York NY 10032 Office Phone: 212-534-5880. Business E-Mail: mmw3@columbia.edu.

**WEISSMAN, WALTER,** artist, photographer; b. Bklyn., Dec. 9, 1946; s. Samuel Weissman and Estelle Berkowitz; m. Eunice Golden. AA, Kingsborough C.C., 1967; BA, Bklyn. Coll., 1970; MA in Fine Arts, Hunter Coll., 1975. Pres., owner Weissman Photo Graphics Studio, Inc., NYC, 1988—; photo-journalist Globe Photos, 1994—2000, Star Max, Inc., 2000—. Pres. Found. Cmty. Artists, NYC, 1980—84. Author, editor, pub. (of an anti-catalog artists meeting for cultural change), 1979. Avocations: gardening, swimming, running. Home and Studio: 463 West St B-332 New York NY 10014 E-mail: wweissmanphoto@nyc.rr.com.

**WEISSMAN, WILLIAM R.,** lawyer; b. NYC, Aug. 16, 1940; s. Emanuel and Gertrude (Halpern) W.; m. Barbra Phylis Gershman; 1 child, Adam; stepchildren: Eric, Jace, Julie Greenman. BA, Columbia U., 1962, JD cum laude, 1965. Bar: N.Y. 1965, D.C. 1969, U.S. Dist. Ct. (no. dist.) Tex. 1965, U.S. Dist. Ct. (so. and ea. dists.) N.Y. 1977, U.S. Ct. Appeals (D.C. dir.) 1969, U.S. Ct. Appeals (9th cir.) 1973, U.S. Ct. Apeals (2d and 3d cirs.) 1974, U.S. Ct. Appeals (10th cir.) 1979, U.S. Ct. Appeals (11th cir.) 1981, U.S. Supreme Ct. 1968. News dir., progrm dir. WKCR-FM, N.Y.C., 1960-62; law clk. U.S. dist. judge, Dallas, 1965-66; trial atty. antitrust divsn. Dept. Justice, Washington, 1966-69; spl. asst. U.S. atty. Washington, 1967; assoc. Wald, Harkrader & Ross, Washington, 1969-72, ptnr., 1973-85, Piper & Marbury LLP, Washington, 1986-99, Piper Rudnick LLP, Washington, 2000—04, DLA Piper US LLP, Washington, 2005—. Instr. D.C. Bar continuing legal edn. program Georgetown U. Law Sch., Washington, 1980-89; environ. regulation course Exec. Enterprises, Inc., 1985-95. Mem. editl. bd. Jour. Environ. Regulation, 1991-95, Environ. Regulation & Permitting, 1995-2000. Mem. Arlington (Va.) County Tenant-Landlord Commn., 1973—77, chmn., 1975—77; parliamentarian Arlington County Dem. Com., 1971—75. Mem.: ASTM (E-50 com. environ. assessment 1996—, rec. sec. 1998—99, vice chmn. 2000—), ABA, Columbia U. Club Washington (bd. dirs. 1987—93). Jewish. Home: 3802 Lakeview Ter Falls Church VA 22041-1313 Office: DLA Piper US LLP 1200 19th St NW Fl 7 Washington DC 20036-2430 Office Phone: 202-861-3878. Business E-Mail: william.weissman@dlapiper.com.

**WEISSMANN, ANDREW,** lawyer, former prosecutor; b. NYC, Mar. 17, 1958; BA in history, Princeton U., 1980; JD, Columbia U. Law Sch., 1984. Law clk. to Hon. Eugene Nickerson US Dist. Ct. (Ea. Dist.) NY, 1984—85; atty. Cleary Gottlieb Steen & Hamilton LLP, NYC; asst. US atty. (ea. dist.) NY, chief criminal divsn. US Dept. Justice, Bklyn., 2000—03; ptnr. Jenner & Block LLP, NYC, 2006—. Dep. dir. Enron Task Force, US Dept. Justice, 2002—04, dir., 2004—05. Office: Jenner & Block LLP 919 Third Ave New York NY 10022*

**WEISSMANN, CHARLES,** molecular biologist, educator; b. 1931; MD, PhD, U. Zurich, Switzerland; D honoris causa, U. Verona, Italy, 1992, U. Ghent, Belgium, 1994, Swiss Fed. Inst. Tech., Zurich, 1998, U. Zurich, 2000, U. St. Andrews, 2000, Ecole Polytech. Fed. Lausanne, 2001. Prof., dir. Inst. Molecular Biology, U. Zurich, 1967-99; pres. Swiss Soc. for Cell and Molecular Biology; chmn. sci. bd. Biogen, 1984-86; pres. Ernst Hadorn-Stiftung, Zurich, 1986—; chmn. dept. Scripps Rsch. Inst., Fla., 2004—. Bd. dirs. F. Hoffmann-LaRoche Ltd., Basel, 1988—2001; mem. sci. adv. bd. ZMB, Heidelberg, 1988—2001, Roche Inst. Molecular Biology, Nutley, NJ, 1993—95, Osaka Biosci. Inst., Japan, 1994—2000, Roche Molecular Sys., Alameda, Calif., 1994—98, Swiss Inst. for Cancer Rsch., Lausanne, 1994—98; mem. sci. coun. Swiss Nat. Fund, 1989—94, Internat. Human Frontiers Rsch. Program, 1994—98; mem. internat. sci. adv. bd. The Netherlands Cancer Inst., Amsterdam; bd. govs. Tel Aviv U., 1997—2004; chmn. European Com. Group on Bovine Spongiform Encephalopathy, 1996; Samuel Rudin disting. vis. prof. Columbia U., N.Y.C., 1999; vis. prof. Imperial Coll., London, 2001—04. Assoc. editor Molecular Medicine, 1994-03; mem. editl. bd. Procs. Royal Soc. Decorated fgn. mem. Order for Merit for Sci. and Art (Germany); Hon. Sr. fellow Inst. Neurology, U. Coll., London; recipient Ruzicka prize in chemistry, 1996, Otto Warburg prize, 1980, H.P. Heineken prize, 1982, Sir. H. Krebs medal, 1974, Marcel Benoist prize, Bern, 1970, Scheele medal, Uppsala, 1982, Krebspreis Schweizerische Krebsliga, 1987, Jung prize for medicine, Hamburg, 1988, Gabor medal Royal Soc., London, 1993, Robert Koch medal, Bonn, 1995, Danta lectureship award FEBS, 1998, Charles Leopold Mayer prize French Acad. Sci., 1996, Royal Soc. Glaxo Wellcome prize, 1996, August Wilhelm von Hofmann Denkmünze, 1997, Klaus Joachim Zülch prize, 1997, Max Delbrück medal, Berlin, 1997, Wilhelm Exner medal, Vienna, 1997, Disting. Svc. award, Miami, 1998, Mendel medal Genetical Soc., London, 1998, Koetser prize, Zurich, 2001, Friedrich-Bauer prize for med. rsch., Munich, 2001, Warren Alpert Found. prize, Boston, 2004, Fifth Ann. Dart/NYU Biotech. award, NY, 2006. Fellow: Am. Acad. Microbiology; mem.: NAS (fgn. assoc.), Acad. Med. Scis. (London chpt.), Berlin-Brandenburgischen Acad. Sci. (extraordinary), Nordheim-Westfälischen Acad. Sci. (corr.), Human Genome Orgn., Academia Europaea, Weizmann Inst. Sci. (bd. govs. 1985—), Royal Soc. (fgn.), Deutsche Akademie Naturforscher Leopoldina, Swiss Acad. Med. Sci., Am. Acad. Arts and Scis., European Molecular Biology Orgn. Office: Scripps Fla 5353 Parkside Dr RF-2 Jupiter FL 33458 Home: Apt 603E 100 Sunrise Ave Palm Beach FL 33480 Office Phone: 442078373611, Ext. 4441, 561-799-8910, 561-799-8895. Office Fax: 442076762180, 561-799-8960. Business E-Mail: charlesw@scripps.edu.

**WEISSMANN, GERALD,** internist, researcher, educator, editor, writer; b. Vienna, Aug. 7, 1930; came to U.S., 1938; s. Adolf and Greta (Lustbader) W.; m. Ann Raphael, Apr. 1, 1951; children: Lisa, Andrew. BA with honors, Columbia U., N.Y.C., 1950; MD, NYU, 1954. Diplomate Am. Bd. Internal Medicine. Intern Mt. Sinai Hosp., N.Y.C., 1954-55, asst. resident medicine 1957-58; chief resident medicine Bellevue Hosp., N.Y.C., 1959-60; fellow

depts. biochemistry and medicine Arthritis and Rheumatism Fedn., NYU, 1958-59; rsch. asst. dept. medicine NYU Sch. Medicine, 1959-60, instr. medicine, 1959-62, asst. prof., 1962-65, assoc. prof., 1966-70, prof., 1970—, dir. div. cell biology, 1969-73, dir. div. rheumatology of dept. medicine, 1973-2000; dir. Ctr. Biotech. Studies, 2000—. USPHS spl. rsch. fellow dept. biophysics Strangeways Lab., Cambridge, Eng., 1960-61; sr. investigator Arthritis and Rheumatism Found., N.Y.C., 1961-65; career rsch. scientist Health Rsch. Coun. N.Y.C., 1966-71; instr. physiology Marine Biol. Lab., Woods Hole, Mass., 1973-77, investigator, 1970—, trustee, 1993—; vis. investigator ARC Inst. Animal Physiology, Babraham, Eng., 1964-69, Centre de Physiologie et d'Immunologie Cellulaires, Hosp. St. Antoine, Paris, 1973-74, William Harvey Rsch. Inst., London, 1987; mem. postdoctoral fellowships rev. com. Pfizer Internat., N.Y.C., 1983-89; mem. scholarship selection com. Pew Scholars in Biomed. Scis., New Haven, 1984-94; lectr. Johns Hopkins U., 1976, 89, Med. Coll. Ga., Augusta, 1980, Med. Coll. Pa., 1988, William Harvey Rsch. Inst., London, 1987, others; nat. adv. bd. Ellison Med. Found., 1997—. Author: The Woods Hole Cantata, 1995, They All Laughed at Christopher Columbus, 1987, The Doctor With Two Heads, 1990, The Doctor Dilemma, 1992, Democracy and DNA, 1996, Darwin's Audubon, 1998, The Year of the Genome, 2001; editor-in-chief Inflammation, 1975-01, Advances in Inflammation Rsch., 1979—, MD Mag., 1989-94, The FASEB Jour., 2005-; mem. editl. bd. Clin. Immunology and Immunopathology, 1972-88, Advances in Prostaglandin, Thromboxane and Leukotriene Rsch., 1975—, Am. Jour. Medicine, 1976-88, Tissue Reactions, 1979, Immunopharmacology, 1982; contbr. over 300 articles to profl. jours. Capt. M.C., U.S. Army, 1955-57. Recipient Allesandro Robecchi prize Internat. League Against Rheumatism, 1972, Marine Biol. Lab. award, 1974, 1979, U. Bologna medal, 1978, Lila Gruber Cancer Rsch. award Am. Acad. Dermatology, 1979, Solomon A. Berson Med. Alumni Achievement award NYU, 1980, Merit award NIH, 1987, Centennial award Marine Biol. Lab., 1988, C.M. Plotz award N.Y. Arthritis Found., 1993, Paul Klemperer award N.Y. Acad. Medicine, 1997, others; Guggenheim Found. fellow, N.Y.C., 1973-74. Fellow AAAS; mem. Am. Coll. Rheumatology (pres. 1982-83, Disting. Investigator award 1992, master 1996), Am. Fedn. Clin. Rsch., Soc. Exptl. Biology and Medicine, Am. Soc. Pharmacology and Exptl. Therapeutics, Am. Soc. Exptl. Pathology, Assn. Am. Immunologists, Am. Soc. Cell Biology, Am. Soc. Clin. Investigation, Am. Soc. Biol. Chemistry and Molecular Biology, Assn. Am. Physicians, Harvey Soc. of N.Y. (pres. 1981-82), Interurban Clin. Club, PEN Am. Ctr., Phi Beta Kappa, Alpha Omega Alpha, fgn. mem. Accademia Nazionale dei Lincei (Rome) Avocation: tennis. Office: NYU Med Ctr Dept Medicine BCD686 550 1st Ave New York NY 10016-6402

**WEISSMANN, HEIDI SEITELBLUM,** radiologist, educator; b. NYC, Feb. 4, 1951; d. Louis and June (Joseph) Seitel Bloom; m. Murray H. Weissmann, June 16, 1973; 1 dau. Lauren Erica BS in Chemistry magna cum laude, Bklyn. Coll., CUNY, 1970; MD, Mt. Sinai Sch. Medicine, N.Y.C., 1974. Diplomate Nat. Bd. Med. Examiners. Intern Montefiore Med. Ctr. Bronx, N.Y., 1974-75, resident in diagnostic radiology N.Y., 1975-78; fellow in computerized transaxial tomography and ultrasonography N.Y. Hosp.-Cornell U. Med. Ctr., N.Y.C., N.Y., 1978-79; instr. in radiology and nuclear medicine Albert Einstein Coll. Medicine, Montefiore Med. Ctr., Bronx, N.Y., 1979-80; asst. prof. radiology and nuclear medicine Albert Einstein Coll. Medicine and Montefiore Med. Ctr., Bronx, N.Y., 1980-84, assoc. prof. nuclear medicine 1984-94, assoc. prof. radiology, 1986-94; dir. Ctr. for Women, Medicine and Healthcare, Washington, 1994—. Adj. attending physician Montefiore Med. Ctr., 1979-87; chmn. Nuclear Medicine Grand Rounds: Greater N.Y., 1980-87; physician coord. Nuclear Medicine Technologist In-Service Tng. Program, 1982-86; cons. NIH, 1984-86, NIH Diagnostic Radiology, 1985-86 Assoc. editor Nuclear Medicine Ann., 5 vols., 1979-84, editor 5 vols., 1985—; contbr. chpts. to books, articles to jours.; editor Jour. Sci. and Engring. Ethics, 1994—; reviewer Jour. of Radiology, 1981—, mem. editl. adv. bd., 1985-86, assoc. editor, 1986—; reviewer Jour. of Nuclear Medicine, 1981—, Am. Jour. of Roentgenology, 1986—, Gastroenterology, 1986—, Western Jour. of Medicine, 1985—; contbr. audiovisual programs and films Recipient Saul Horowitz, Jr., Meml. award (Disting. Alumnus award), Mt. Sinai Sch. Medicine, 1980, Pres.' award, Am. Roentgen Ray Soc., 1979, Berta Rubinstein, M.D., Resident award, 1978, Cavallo award for moral courage, 1993, others. Mem. Radiol. Soc. N.Am. (mem. subcom. for nuclear medicine of program com., 1981, 82, 83, chmn. 1984, 85, 86), Soc. Nuclear Medicine (trustee 1983-87, 88—, sec.-treas. Correlative Imaging Council 1979-82, exec. bd. 1982-84, pres. 1984-86, exec. bd. 1986—, mem. acad. council 1980—, task force on interrelationship between nuclear medicine and nuclear magnetic resonance 1983-85, gov. Greater N.Y. chpt. 1983-85, treas., 1985-86, 86-87, 2d ann. Tetalman award of Edn. and Research Found. 1982, mem., vice chmn. coms. and subcoms.), Soc. Gastrointestinal Radiologists, Am. Inst. Ultrasound in Medicine, N.Y. Acad. Scis., Assoc. Alumni Mt. Sinai Med. Ctr., Nuclear Radiology Club (chmn. 1983—). Phi Beta Kappa. Home and Office: 14 Powder Hill Rd Saddle River NJ 07458-3215

**WEISSTEIN, ULRICH WERNER,** English literature educator; b. Breslau, Germany, Nov. 14, 1925; came to U.S., 1950, naturalized, 1959; s. Rudolf and Berta (Wende) W.; m. Elisabeth Rieckh; children: Cristina, Cecily, Eric Wolfgang, Anton Edward. Student, Goethe-Universität, Frankfurt, 1947-50, 51-52, U. Iowa, 1950-51; MA, Ind. U., 1953, PhD, 1954; Doctorate (hon.), U. Lund, Sweden, 1993. Instr. Lehigh U., Bethlehem, Pa., 1954—58, asst. prof., 1958; asst. prof. English and comparative lit. Ind. U., Bloomington, 1959-62, assoc. prof., 1962-66, prof. German and comparative lit., 1986—90, chmn. comparative lit. program, 1985-89; dir. Ind. U.-Purdue U. Studienprogramm U. Hamburg, 1981-82. Vis. prof. U. Wis., summer 1966, Middlebury Sch. German, summer 1970, U. Hamburg (Germany), spring 1971, spring 1982, U. Vienna, 1976, Stanford U., 1979, Graz U., Austria, 1985, 95, 96, U. Bologna, Italy, 1991, U. Antwerp, Belgium, 1992, U. Salzburg, 1997; external examiner comparative lit. U. Hong Kong, 1974-76. Author: Heinrich Mann, 1962, The Essence of Opera, 1964, Max Frisch, 1967, Einführung in die Vergleichende Literaturwissenschaft, 1968, English version: Comparative Literature and Literary Theory, 1973; Spanish version: Introduccion a la Literatura Comparada, 1975, Chinese version, 1987, Japanese version, 1976, Korean version, 1979; Forschungsbericht zur Vergleichenden Literaturwissenschaft, 1968-1977, 1981, Links und links gesellt sich nicht: Gesammelte Aufsätze zum Werk Heinrich Manns und Bertolt Brechts, 1985; editor: Literatur und Bildende Kunst: Ein Handbuch zur Theorie und Praxis eines komparatistischen Grenzgebiets, 1992, Selected Essays on Opera 1960-1996, 2006; editor German sect. Twayne World Authors series, 1984-86, Yearbook of Comparative and General Literature, 1960-90, Oper Im Brennpunkt, 2001-, Expressionism as an International Literary Phenomenon, 1973; co-editor: Literature and the Other Arts, 1981, Texte und Kontexte: Festschrift für Norbert Fuerst, 1973, Intertextuality: German Literature and Visual Art from the Renaissance to the Twentieth Century, 1993, Musico-Poetics Today: Calvin S. Brown in Memoriam, 2000; translator: The Grotesque in Art and Literature (W. Kayser), 1963 Recipient Grosses goldenes Ehrenzeichen des Landes Steiermark, 1996; Guggenheim fellow, 1974-75; MLA grantee, 1958-59. Mem.: Gesellschaft der Freunde der Oper in Graz (pres. 1991—97, hon. pres. 2003—), Coun. Internat. Exchange Scholars (area com. for West Germany and Austria 1983—85), Internat. Comparative Lit. Assn. (exec. coun. 1979—85, sec. 1985—89). Home: Baiernstrasse 54/IV 8020 Graz Austria

**WEISWASSER, STEPHEN,** electronics executive; b. Detroit, Nov. 21, 1940; BA, Wayne State U.; postgrad., Johns Hopkins U.; JD magna cum laude, Harvard U. Ptnr. Wilmer, Cutler & Pickering; sr. v.p. Capital Cities/ABC, Inc.; pres., CEO Americast, 1995-98; ptnr. Covington & Burling, Washington, 1998-99; exec. v.p., gen. counsel Gemstar Internat. Group Ltd., Pasadena, Calif., 1999—, also bd. dirs. Woodrow Wilson Nat. fellow Johns Hopkins U. Office Fax: 626-792-0257.

**WEISZ, PAUL B(URG),** physicist, researcher, chemical engineer; b. Pilsen, Czechoslovakia, July 2, 1919; naturalized, 1946; s. Alexander and Amalia (Sulc) Weisz; m. Rhoda A.M. Burg, Sept. 4, 1943; children: Ingrid B., P. Randall. Student, Tech. U. Berlin, 0193—1939; BS, Auburn U., 1940; ScD,

Swiss Fed. Inst. Tech., Zurich, 1965, ScD (hon.), 1980. Research physicist Bartol Research Found., Swarthmore, Pa., 1940—46, Mobil Oil Corp. (formerly Socony Mobil Oil Corp.), 1958—61, sr. scientist, 1961—69, mgr. process research sect., 1967—69; mgr. Central Research Lab. Mobil Research & Devel. Corp., Princeton, NJ, 1969—82, sr. scientist and sci. adv., 1982—84; Disting. prof. chem. and bio-engring. sci. U. Pa., 1984—90, prof. emeritus, 1990—. Adj. prof. Pa. State U., 1992—; cons. rsch. and tech. strategy; vis. prof. Princeton U., 1974—76, mem. adv. coun. dept. chem. engring., 1973—78; mem. adv. and resource coun. Princeton U. Sch. Engring., 1974—78; chmn. ctr. policy bd. Ctr. for Catalytic Sci. and Tech., U. Del., 1977—81; mem. energy rsch. adv. bd. U.S. Dept. Energy, 1985—90. Editor: Advances in Catalysis, 1956—93; editl. bd. Jour. Catalysis, 1962—83, Chem. Engring. Comms., 1972—78, Heterogeneous Chem. Revs., 1993—96, monthly columnist Sci. of the Possible, Chemtech, 1980—83, contbr. 180 articles to sci. jours., holder 92 patents. Recipient ann. award, Catalysis Club Phila., 1973, Lavoisier medal, Chem. Soc. France, 1983, Perkin medal, Soc. Chem. Industries, US Nat. medal of Tech., 1992. Fellow: NAE, AIChE (R.H. Wilhelm award 1978), Am. Inst. Chemists (Chem. Pioneer award 1974), Am. Phys. Soc.; mem.: N.Y. Acad. Scis., Am. Chem. Soc. (sci. award South Jersey sect. 1963, E.V. Murphree award 1972, 1977, Chemistry of Contemporary Tech. Problems award 1986, Carothers award 1987), Nassau Club (Princeton). Mem. Soc. Of Friends. Fax: 814-237-3202. E-mail: pweisz@aol.com, pbweisz@mailaps.org.

**WEISZ, RACHEL,** actress; b. London, Mar. 7, 1971; 1 child. BA, U. Cambridge, England. Motion picture and T.V. actress. Actor (films) Death Machine, 1995, Stealing Beauty, 1996, Chain Reaction, 1996, Going All the Way, 1997, Amy Foster, 1997, Land Girls, 1998, I Want You, 1998, Swept From the Sea, 1998, The Mummy, 1999, Sunshine, 1999, Beautiful Creatures, 2001, Enemy at the Gates, 2001, The Mummy Returns, 2001, About a Boy, 2002, The Shape of Things, 2003 (also prod.), Confidence, 2003, Runaway Jury, 2003, She Died on Canvas, 2003, Envy, 2004, Constantine, 2005, The Constant Gardener, 2005 (Best Performance by an Actress in a Supporting Role in a Motion Picture, Hollywood Fgn. Press Assn. (Golden Globe award), 2006, Outstanding Performance by a Female Actor in a Supporting Role, Screen Actors Guild award, 2006, Performance by an Actress in a Supporting Role, Acad. Motion Picture Arts & Sciences, 2006); (TV films) Scarlet and Black, 1993, My Summer with Des, 1998; (plays) Design For Living, 1994, Last Summer, 1999, The Shape of Things, 2001. Office: c/o Creative Artists Agency 9830 Wilshire Blvd Beverly Hills CA 90212

**WEITBERG, ALAN BARRY,** physician, researcher; b. Phila., Mar. 2, 1950; s. Sidney and Esther Weitberg; m. Katherine Raphaela Bick, Sept. 6, 1975 (div. Apr. 1993); children: Allison Ross, Seth Raphael. AB, Cornell U., Ithaca, NY, 1972; MD, Univ. Medicine and Dentistry NJ, Newark, 1976; MEd (hon.), Brown U., Providence, 1992. Lic. MD RI, 1978, Mass., 1982, cert. Nat. Bd. Med. Examiners, 1977, Internal Medicine, 1980, Med. Oncology, 1987, Hematology, 1988. Resident and chief resident in medicine Roger Williams Med. Ctr. and Brown Med. Sch., Providence, 1976—80; hematology fellow Mass. Gen. Hosp. and Harvard U., Boston, 1980—82; instr. med. sch. Harvard Med. Sch., Boston, 1982—85; chief divsn. hematology, oncology Brown Med. Sch. and Roger Williams Med. Ctr., Providence, 1985—91; prof. and chmn., dept. medicine Roger Williams Med. Ctr. and Boston U. Sch. Medicine, Providence, 1991—. Dir. divsn. med. oncology Brown U., 1988—; prof. medicine Boston U. Sch. Medicine, 1988—; bd. trustees Roger Williams Med. Ctr., 2002—04. Author: Cancer of the Lung, 2002; contbr. more than 75 sci. papers to profl. jours., chapters to books, articles to over 60 profl. jours. Critical care, med. appraisal, med. audit, med. rec. Roger Williams Hosp., 1979—80, infection control, nutritional support, patient care/greivence, 1979—80, intern selection, clin. competence com., 1985—, chmn. cancer com., 1986—99, chmn. credentials com., 1987—91, transfusion com., 1988—92, physician's adv. com., 1989—, exec. com., 1991—, strategic planning com., 1992—, joint conf. com., 1992—, quality improvement steering coun., 1992—, oncology task force, 1995—, pres., med. assoc., 1996—, bd. trustees, 2002—, Univ. Med. Group, 1999—, exec. com. bd., 2001—; chmn. admissions com. for an integrated med. residency program Brown U., 1990—; com. sectional chiefs Boston U., 1997—. Nominee Ernesta Nuti Internat. prize for Cancer Rsch., Rome, 1992; named to Mu Eplison Delta Hon. Soc., Cornell U., 1971, Watts Scholarship Soc., Cornell Univ., 1971; recipient Dean Charles L. Brown award, Univ. Medicine and Dentistry NJ, 1976, Tchr. of Yr. award, Brown U. Sch. Medicine, 1992, Eminent Scientist award, Internat. Rsch. Promotion Coun., Physician's Recognition award with commendation, AMA, 2005; Arts and Sci. Dean's scholar, Cornell U., 1969, over 30 rsch. grants from various colls. and univs. Fellow: ACP (exec. coun. RI chpt. 1992—); mem.: AMA (Physicians Recognition award 2005—), AAAS, Cancer Trials Support Unit, Assn. Acad. Med. Ctr., Clin. Oncology Group, Am. Soc. Hematology, Assn. Am. Med. Coll., Leukemia Soc. Am. (bd. dirs. 1989—), Am. Bd. Internal Medicine (recertification com. 1993—), Am. Soc. Cancer Rsch. (chmn. carcinogenesis sect. 1987—, state legis. com. 1992—), Am. Soc. Clin. Oncology (chmn. lung cancer sect. 1987—), Am. Cancer Soc. (chmn. nominating com. 1992, instl. rsch. grant rev. study sect. 1992—), Am. Fedn. for Clin. Rsch. (chmn. hematology sect. 1993—), Internat. Soc. Free Radical Rsch., Sigma Xi. Avocations: painting, opera, running, reading. Office: Roger Williams Med Ctr Dept Medicine 825 Chalkstone Ave Providence RI 02908 Office Phone: 401-456-2070.

**WEITHORN, STANLEY STEPHEN,** lawyer; b. NYC, Aug. 28, 1924; s. Louis W. and Florence O. (Mandel) W.; m. Corinne J. Breslow, Dec. 26, 1949 (dec. 1987); children: Lois Ann, Michael J.; m. Muriel Casper, Sept. 9, 1990; 1 stepchild, Corey Casper. BSBA, Hofstra U., 1947; JD, NYU Law Sch., 1954, LLM in Taxation, 1956. Bar: N.Y. 1955. Assoc. firm Olwine, Connelly, Chase O'Donnell & Weyher, N.Y.C., 1956—61; ptnr. firm Lewis, McDonald & Varian, N.Y.C., 1961—62; pvt. practice N.Y.C., 1962—63, 1967—68; ptnr. firm Wormser, Koch, Keily & Alessandroni, N.Y.C., 1963—66; sr. ptnr. firm Baer, Marks & Upham (successor to Upham, Meeker & Weithorn), N.Y.C., 1968—88, Epstein, Becker & Green, N.Y.C., 1988—89; sr. counsel Reid & Priest, N.Y.C., 1989—94, Morrison & Foerster, Palo Alto, Calif., 1994—96, Fennemore Craig, Phoenix, 1996—2000, Roberts & Holland, N.Y.C. & Scottsdale, 1996—. Spl. prof. law Hofstra U., 1974-78; adj. prof. law U. Miami, Fla., 1975-79; mem. adv. coun. U. Miami Law Ctr. Ann. Inst. Estate Planning, 1974-80; coordinator fed. budget and tax policy course nat. policy studies program New Sch. Social Rsch., N.Y.C., 1975; mem. fund raising mgmt. adv. com. Grad. Sch. Mgmt. and Urban professions, New Sch. for Social Rsch., N.Y.C., 1977-84; mem. adv. com. N.Y. U. Inst. on Fed. Taxation, 1980-90; program chmn. Practicing Law Inst. confs., N.Y.C., 1962-78, N.Y. Law Jour. confs., 1980, NYU Inst. on Fed. Taxation confs., 1955-88; tax coms. Pres's. Coun. on Environ. Quality, 1970; lectr. fed. taxation to univ. insts., non-profit org. confs., profl. bus. meetings. Author: Penalty Taxes on Accumulated Earnings and Personal Holding Companies, 1963, Tax Techniques for Foundations and Other Exempt Organizations, 7 vols, 1964, The Accumulated Earnings Tax, 1966; Contbg. editor, mem. adv. bd.: Tax Mgmt, 1959-68; feature columnist: Nat. Law Jour, 1978-79; Contbr. articles to profl. jours. Co-chmn. Port Washington-Manhasset (N.Y.) unit New Dem. Coalition, 1968-69; tax adviser nat. fin. com. McGovern for Pres., 1971-72, mem. N.Y. fin. com., 1971-72; bd. dirs., exec. com. Equal Employment Coun. Inc., N.Y.C., 1968-71; bd. dirs., sec. New Priorities Edn. Fund, 1969-70; bd. dirs., exec. com., sec., co-chmn., pres. Fund for New Priorities in Am., 1969-2004; bd. dirs., treas. Cow Bay Manpower Devel. Corp., Port Washington, 1969-71; bd. dirs., chmn. exec. com., pres. L.I. Pub. Affairs Coun., 1973-78; bd. dirs., pres. Mental Health Assn. Nassau County, N.Y., 1980-85, Herman and Amelia Ehrmann Found., 1977-95; pres. Weithorn and Ehrmann Families Found., 1995—. Am. Soc. Technion, 1992-2000, Social Venture Ptnrs. Ariz., 2003—; bd. dirs. Jewish Family and Children's Svcs., San Francisco; mem. legacy com. United Cerebral Palsy, N.Y.C., 1975-90; bd. dirs. Cmty. Action for Legal Svcs., 1976-78, Frederick and Amelia Schimper Found., 1977-94, Florence Weithorn Warner Found., N.Y.C., 1967-72, N.Y. Reform Synagogues, 1973-78, Nat. Coalition for Children's Justice, 1980-90, Am. Inst. for Philanthropic Studies, L.A. and N.Y.C., 1981-92, Nat. Health Coun., 1984-92, Laurent and Alberta Gerschel

Found., 1986-96, Interns for Peace, Am.-Israeli Civil Liberties Coalition, 1987-95, Inst. Am. Values, 1987-91, Fund for Human Dignity, 1989-90, Found. Fund, 1986-92, L.I. Cmty. Found., 1989-93, Cancer Prevention Rsch. Inst., 1989-96, Green Seal, 1989-92, New Israel Fund, 1996-2002, Albert L. Schultz Jewish Cmty. Ctr., 1996-2000, Nat. Ctr. Law & Social Justice, 1996—, Am. Jewish World Svc., 2001-, Internat. Edn. and Rsch. Network, 2002, Heller Family Found., 1994-, Rouhana Family Found., 1990-, Scottsdale Cultural Coun., 2000-, Ariz. State U. Found., 1996-2004, Am. Com. for Weizmann Inst. Sci., 2000-, Piper Fund Proteus Found, 2000-; mem. Emergency Task Force on Juvenile Delinquency Prevention, 1976-79; mem. adv. panel N.Y. chpt. Am. Jewish Com., 1978-80; mem. com. on deferred giving Fedn. Jewish Philanthropies N.Y., 1978-86; mem. legal and tax panel United Jewish Appeal/Fedn. Jewish Philanthropies, N.Y., 1986-91; nat. chair Planned Giving Program, Am. Assocs. Ben-Gurion U. Negev, 1992-2000, mem. exec. com. N.W. region; mem. com. tax policy Nat. Assembly Vol. Health, Social Welfare Orgns. Inc., N.Y.C., 1961-73; mem. com. bequests and legacies Nat. Jewish Hosp., Denver, 1965-78; mem. estate planning com. ARC of Greater N.Y., 1970-98; mem. leadership coun. United Jewish Appeal, N.Y.C., 1966-70; mem. adv. coun., project on ch., state and taxation NCCJ, 1980-85; mem. legacy adv. coun. Am. Jewish Congress, N.Y.C., 1968-72; mem. Internat. Coun. on Environ. Law, 1982-92; mem. Pres.'s adv. com. ACLU Found., 1983-2000; chmn. Uptown Tax Discussion Group, 1957-69, Exempt Orgns. Discussion Group, 1973-79, Fresh Meadows Civic Assn., 1961-63; mem. legal activities policy bd. Tax Analysts, 1974—. Served with AUS, 1943-46, ETO. Recipient Allard K. Lowenstein Meml. award Am. Jewish Congress, 1988; honoree Mental Health Assn. Nassau County, N.Y., 1991, Ariz. Citizen Action, 2000, Am. Com. for Weizmann Inst. Sci., 2002, Nat. Gay and Lesbian Task Force, 2003 Fellow Am. Coll. Tax Counsel, Am. Coll. Trust and Estate Counsel; mem. ABA (chmn. subcom. exempt orgns. 1965-69, subcom. charitable contbns. 1971-75), N.Y. State Bar Assn. (exec. com. 1967-69), Assn. of Bar of City of N.Y., Internat. Acad. Estate and Trust Law (exec. coun. 1974-78, 90-96), Univ. Club, Knickerbocker Yacht Club (bd. dirs. 1986-88). Jewish (trustee synagogue 1970-74). Home (Winter): 10440 E Happy Valley Rd #435 Scottsdale AZ 85255 Office: Roberts & Holland LLP 825 8th Ave 37th Fl New York NY 10019 also: 8655 E Via de Ventura G200 Scottsdale AZ 85258 Home (Summer): 150 Central Parks #1610 New York NY 10019-1566 E-mail: sweithorn@rhtax.com. *No one truly is an altruist. We all attempt to do what most fulfills us. For some this motivates apparently selfish behavior; for others it is quite the opposite. However, why we act as we do affects only the actor whereas what we do affects society. Look to the deed, not to the doer; good deeds make for a better world.*

**WEITZ, HOWARD HY,** cardiologist, educator; b. Phila., July 6, 1952; s. Thelma and Arnold Weitz; m. Barbara Malett, May 3, 1987; children: Aaron Richard, Benjamin Isaac, Hannah Sarah. BS, Muhlenberg Coll., Pa., 1974, DS (hon.), 2003; MD, Jefferson Med. Coll., Phila., 1978. Diplomate Am. Bd. Internal Medicine, 1981, cert. Cardiovascular Diseases Am. Bd. Internal Medicine, 1985. Dir. divsn. cardiology Jefferson Med. Coll., Phila., 1995—98, prof. medicine, 2005—, sr. vice-chmn., dept. of medicine, 2005—; co-dir. Jefferson Heart Inst., Phila., 1998—; commr. Fed. Medicaid Commn., Washington, 2005—. Author: Medical Management of the Surgical Patient, 1992 (NBI Healthcare Found. Humanism in Medicine Faculty award, 1998), 2d edit., 1998, Peripheral Vascular Disorders, 2004. Fellow: Am. Coll. of Cardiology, ACP. Office: Jefferson Heart Inst 925 Chestnut St Philadelphia PA 19027 Office Phone: 215-955-4194. Business E-mail: howard.weitz@jefferson.edu.

**WEITZ, JOHN JEROME, JR.,** city planner; b. Mobile, Ala., Aug. 19, 1961; s. John J. and Marcheta (Knight) W.; m. Patricia L. Weitz, Oct. 20, 1990; 1 child, John Jerome III. AA, Oxford Coll. of Emory Univ., 1981; BA, Emory U., Atlanta, 1983; M City Planning, Ga. Inst. Tech., Atlanta, 1985; D Philosophy Urban Studies, Portland (Oreg.) State U., 1998. Cert. planner. Planner technician City of Roswell, Ga., 1985-87; planner II Fulton County Dept. Planning and Econ. Devel., Atlanta, 1987-88; zoning adminstr. Albany-Dougherty Planning Commn., Albany, Ga., 1988-89; sr. planner Ga. Mountains Regional Devel. Ctr., Gainesville, 1989-94; urban growth mgmt. specialist State of Oreg., Salem, 1994-97; cons. Benkendorf Assocs., Portland, 1994-96; planning divsn. mgr. Cowlitz Coun, Kelso, Wash., 1997-99; planning dir. City of Roswell, 1999-2000; pres. Jerry Weitz & Assocs., Inc., Alpharetta, 2001—; adj. asst. prof. pub. adminstrn. Kennesaw (Ga.) State U., 2001; asst. prof. pub. adminstrn. Troy U., Atlanta, 2001—04. Exec. com. Ga. Planning Assn., Atlanta, 1993—94, v.p. legislative affairs, 2000—03, pres.-elect, 2002—03, pres., 2003—05; adj. faculty city and regional planning program Ga. Inst. of Tech., 2003—04. Author: Sprawl Busting: State Programs to Guide Growth, 1999, Jobs-Housing Balance, 2003; co-author: Smart Growth Audits, 2002. Coun. mem. City of Gillsville, Ga., 1994; mem. design rev. bd. City of Beaverton, Oreg., 1997-99. Recipient Outstanding Achievement award Alpharetta Jaycees, 1986. Mem. Am. Planning Assn., Urban Affairs Assn., Internat. City/County Mgmt. Assn., Assn. Collegiate Schs. Planning, Ga. Planning Assn. (disting. profl. achievement in planning award 2000), ASPA, Am. Inst. for Cert. Planners. Avocations: fishing, camping, golf. Home: 1225 Rucker Rd Alpharetta GA 30004 Personal E-mail: jerryweitz@aol.com.

**WEITZEL, GINGER M.,** entrepreneur, critical care nurse; b. Richland, Wash., Dec. 28, 1952; d. Carl Benton and Margaret Allee White; m. Gregory L. Weitzel, Aug. 28, 1978; children: Skylar Benjamin, Spencer Cameron. AA, Pima CC, Tucson, 1976; student, U. Ariz., 1971—73, U. Denver, 1995—98. RN, cert. ACLS. Nat. sales support mgr. Valleyrab, Boulder, Colo., 1984—90; exec. sales mgr. 3M, St. Paul, 1990—98; sales mgr. Am. Telecare, St. Paul, 1998—99; nurse emergency dept. Exempla Health Care, Wheat Ridge, Colo., 2000—02; pvt. practice Arvada, Colo., 2002—. Nat. acct. mgr. Sims-Deltec, St. Paul, 1994—96. Mem.: Legal Nurse Cons., Emergency Nurses Assn. Democrat. Methodist. Avocations: gardening, walking, reading, politics. Home: 5975 Braun Way Arvada CO 80004 Office: Weitzel and Assoc 5975 Braun Way Arvada CO 80004

**WEITZEL, JOHN PATTERSON,** lawyer; b. Pitts., Aug. 24, 1923; s. Albert Philip and Elizabeth (Patterson) W.; m. Elisabeth Swan, Mar. 20, 1965; children: Mary Middleton, Paul Patterson. AB, Yale U., 1946; LL.B., Harvard U., 1949. Bar: Mass. 1949, U.S. Supreme Ct. 1960. Assoc. Herrick, Smith, Donald, Farley & Ketchum (now Herrick & Smith), Boston, 1949-53, ptnr., 1961-86, Palmer & Dodge, Boston, 1986-93, of counsel, 1993—2005; spl. asst. to asst. sec. treasury, 1953-55; asst. to under sec. treas, 1955-56; asst. gen. counsel Treasury Dept., 1956-59; dep. to sec. treasury, 1959-60, asst. sec. treasury, 1960-61; U.S. exec. dir. World Bank, 1960-61; of counsel Edwards, Angell, Palmer & Dodge, 2005—. Mem. planning bd. NSC, 1959-61; cons. to sec. def., 1973. Mem. Mass. Council Arts and Humanities, 1966-71; overseer, dir. sec. Boys and Girls Clubs, Boston; mem. corp. Mass. Gen. Hosp., Boston Mus. Sci.; trustee Roxbury Latin Sch. Served with USAAF, 1943-45. Mem. Am.; Boston bar assns., Am. Law Inst. Clubs: Harvard (Boston), Union Boat (Boston). Home: 45 Devon Rd Chestnut Hill MA 02467-1851 Office: Edwards Angell Palmer & Dodge 111 Huntington Ave Boston MA 02199-7613

**WEITZEL, JOHN QUINN,** bishop; b. Chgo., May 10, 1928; s. Carl Joseph and Patricia (Quinn) W. BA, Maryknoll Sem., NY, 1951, M of Religious Edn. 1953; PMD, Harvard U. Ordained priest Roman Cath. Ch., 1955. With ednl. devel. Cath. Fgn. Mission Soc. of Am., Maryknoll, 1955—63, nat. dir. vocations for Maryknoll, dir. devel. dept. and info. services, 1963—72, mem. gen. coun., 1972—78; asst. parish priest Cath. Ch., Western Samoa, 1979—81, pastor, vicar gen., 1981—86; consecrated bishop, 1986; bishop Diocese of Samoa-Pago Pago, 1986—. Roman Catholic. Office: Diocese Samoa-Pago Pago PO Box 596 Pago Pago AS 96799-3594 E-mail: QUINN@samoatelco.com.

**WEITZEL, MARK P.,** lawyer; b. 1954; AB with distinction, Stanford U., 1976; MBA, JD, UCLA, 1980. Bar: Calif. 1980, lic.: US Tax Ct., registered: Law Soc. of Eng. & Wales (fng. lawyer). Ptnr. Thelen Reid & Priest LLP, San

Francisco, mem. partnership coun. Mem. UCLA Law Rev., 1979—80. Mem.: Order of Coif, Beta Gamma Sigma. Office: Thelen Reid & Priest LLP 101 Second St Ste 1800 San Francisco CA 94105-3601 Office Phone: 415-369-7007. Office Fax: 415-371-1211. Business E-mail: mweitzel@thelenreid.com.

**WEITZEL, WILLIAM CONRAD, JR.,** lawyer; b. Washington, Feb. 6, 1935; s. William Conrad and Pauline Lillian (Keeton) W.; m. Loretta LeVeck, Mar. 10, 1978; children: William Conrad III, Richard S., Sarah L., Andrew K. AB, Harvard U., 1956, LLB, 1959; postgrad., MIT, 1974. Bar: D.C. 1961. Law clk., chief judge U.S. Cts. Md., Balt., 1959-60; asst. U.S. atty., Washington, 1961-66; atty. Texaco, Inc., White Plains, N.Y., 1966-73, assoc. gen. counsel, 1973-76, gen. counsel, 1977-82, v.p., gen. counsel, 1982-84, sr. v.p., gen. counsel, 1984-90; pres. Texaco Philanthropic Found., Inc., 1980-90; ptnr. Cummings & Lockwood, Stamford, Conn., 1991—, bus. clients dept., 1991-94. Trustee, Ctr. Am. Internat. Law Trustee Southwestern Legal Found., Forman Sch. With USN, 1960-61. Mem. ABA, Am. Law Inst., Conn. Bar Assn., D.C. Bar Assn., Assn. Gen. Counsel (v.p., bd. dirs. 1988-90), Westchester-Fairfield Corp. Counsel Assn. (pres. 1981, chmn., chief legal officers com. 1982-90), Am. Petroleum Inst. (gen. com. on law, chmn. 1983-84), Darien (Conn.) Country Club, Harvard Club (dir. Harvard Alumni Assn. for Conn. 1990-93, pres. Fairfield County club 1987—). Republican. Episcopalian. Office: Cummings & Lockwood 4 Stamford Plz PO Box 120 Stamford CT 06904-0120

**WEITZEL, WILLIAM DAVID,** psychiatrist; b. Detroit, Sept. 16, 1942; s. William Howard and Mary Ann (Burgaster) Weitzel; m. Joan Carol Heiser, June 8, 1968; children: Erica Marie, Jennifer Joan, Sarah Elizabeth. BS cum laude, Xavier U., 1964; MD, St. Louis U., 1968; postgrad. alcohol studies Rutgers U., 1970; tng. family therapy, The Washington Sch. Psychiatry, 1971—72. Diplomate Am. Bd. Psychiatry and Neurology, Am. Bd. Forensic Psychiatry. Intern William Beaumont Gen. Hosp., El Paso, Tex., 1968—69; psychiat. resident Walter Reed Gen. Hosp., 1969—72; chief dept. psychiatry and neurology Moncrief Army Hosp., Columbia, SC, 1972—74; asst. prof. psychiatry and dir. Hosp. Inpatient Psychiatry Svc. Coll. Medicine, U. Ky., Lexington, 1974—78, assoc. prof. psychiatry, 1979, assoc. clin. prof. psychiatry, 1980—88, clin. prof. psychiatry, 1988—. Lectr. Coll. Law, 1977—82; supervising and cons. psychiatrist William S. Hall Psychiat. Inst., Columbia, 1973—74; psychiat. cons. Commn. on Ministry Episcopal Diocese of Lexington, 1975—87, Clin. Rsch. Ctr. Project, Ky. Bur. Health Svcs., Homestead Nursing Ctr., Lexington, 1978—88. Contbr. numerous articles to profl. jours. Mem. Ky. Gov.'s Task Force on Welfare Reform, 1978—79, Ky. Commn. on Corrections and Cmty. Svc., 1992—96. Maj. MC AUS, 1968—74. Fellow: AAAS, Am. Psychiat. Assn. (disting. life) (pres. Ky. dist. br. 1979—80, co-author task force report on involuntary outpatient commitment 1987), Am. Coll. Psychiatrists; mem.: Am. Acad. Psychiatry and the Law, Group for Advancement of Psychiatry. Office: Ste 128 1725 Harrodsburg Rd Lexington KY 40504-3628 Office Phone: 859-277-5419. Personal E-mail: wweitzel@pol.net.

**WEITZMAN, ARTHUR JOSHUA,** language educator; b. Newark, Sept. 13, 1933; s. Louis I. and Cecele W.; m. Catherine Ezell, Aug. 8, 1982; children: Peter A., Anne E. BA, U. Chgo., 1956, MA, 1957; PhD, NYU, 1964. Instr. English, Bklyn. Coll., 1960-63; asst. prof. Temple U., Phila., 1963-69; assoc. prof. Northeastern U., Boston, 1969-72, prof., 1972—2002, prof. emeritus, 2002—; mem. faculty Brookline (Mass.) Adult and Cmty. Edn., 2003—, Cambridge (Mass.) Ctr. Adult Edn., 2003—; lectr. Sarasota Inst. of Lifetime Learning, 2006—. Editor: Letters Writ by a Turkish Spy (G.P. Marana), 1970; founder, co-editor: The Scriblerian, 1968—2004; co-editor: Milton and the Romantics, 1980-81; contbr.: revs. and articles to profl. jours. and newspapers including Los Angeles Times, Boston Globe, Miami Herald NEH fellow, 1972-73; Mellon fellow, 1976; research grantee Temple U.; research grantee Northeastern U. Mem.: MLA. Na. Assn. Scholars, Am. Soc. 18th Century Studies. Jewish. Home: 4 Bellis Ct Cambridge MA 02140-3240 E-mail: ajwajwajw@hotmail.com.

**WEITZNER, HAROLD,** mathematics professor; b. Boston, May 19, 1933; s. Morris and Alice Savitz W.; m. Lois S. Friedlander, June 12, 1962; children: Daniel J., Henry D. AB, U. Calif., Berkeley, 1954; AM, Harvard U., 1955, PhD, 1958. Assoc. rsch. scientist Courant Inst. NYU, N.Y.C., 1959-60, rsch. scientist, 1960-62, asst. prof., 1962-65, assoc. prof., 1965-69, prof., 1969—; assoc. dir. Magneto-Fluids div. Courant Inst. NYU, N.Y.C., 1988—, dir., 1973-79, 84-88; chmn. Math. Dept. Courant Inst. NYU, N.Y.C., 1989-91. Cons. Oak Ridge Nat. Labs., Oak Ridge, Tenn., 1980—, mem. fusion energy divsn. adv. com., 2005-; mem. magnetic fusion adv. com. U.S. Dept. Energy, 1986-89, fusion energy adv. com., 1991-93; mem. adv. com. Gen. Atomics Corp., 1994-96. Contbr. articles to sci. jours. Fellow Am. Phys. Soc.; mem. Univ. Fusion Assn. (exec. com. 1993-96). Home: 10 Cedar Ave Larchmont NY 10538-4121 Office: NYU Courant Inst 251 Mercer St New York NY 10012-1110

**WEITZNER, STEVE,** publishing executive; BA, York Coll., CUNY; MA, SUNY, Stony Brook. With Hearst Bus. Communications, CMP Media, LLC, Manhasset, NY, 1984—, various positions, editor to pres., electronics group, exec. v.p., COO, 2002—05, pres., CEO, 2005—. Office: CMP Media LLC 600 Community Drive Manhasset NY 11030 Office Phone: 516-562-5000.*

**WEIXELMAN, JOSEPH OWEN,** history professor; b. Manhattan, Kans., Dec. 11, 1957; s. Donald Bernard and Diane Gayle Weixelman; m. Jessica Ryan Burke, Jan. 1, 1979 (div. Aug. 19, 1983); 1 child, Shawn Thomas; m. Cathy Fisher, Oct. 8, 1983 (div. July 17, 1989); 1 child, Christopher George; m. Chris Tee Kuhlmann, Sept. 2, 1990; 1 child, James Husayn; 1 child, Kel Anthony. BA in Anthropology, U. Colo., 1981; MA in History, Mont. State U., 1992; PhD in History, U. N.Mex., 2004. Tchr. social studies Sept. Sch., Boulder, Colo., 1982—88; tchr. social studies and english Western Wyo. H.S., Jackson, Wyo., 1989—90; tchr. social studies Durango (Colo.) H.S., 1992—96; guest lectr. Ea. Mich. U., Ypsilanti, 2000—01; instr. U. N.Mex, Albuquerque, 2002—. Interpretive ranger Mesa Verde (Colo.) Nat. Pk., 1993—, Yellowstone (Wyo.) Nat. Pk., 1999—2000, cultural resource asst., 1998—98; interpretive ranger Petroglyph Nat. Monument, Albuquerque, 1997. John F. Kennedy History fellowship, U. N.Mex., 2000, Senator Joseph M. Montoya History fellowship, 2001. Mem.: Colo. Hist. Soc., Nat. Coun. Pub. History, Am. Hist. Assn., We. History Assn. Bahá'Í. Avocations: travel, photography, hiking, backpacking. Home: 1828 Blume NE Albuquerque NM 87112-3106 Office: Dept of History UNM 1104 Mesa Vista Hall Albuquerque NM 87131-1181 Office Phone: 505-277-6232. Personal E-mail: jweix@aol.com.

**WEIXLMANN, JOSEPH NORMAN, JR.,** language educator, academic administrator; b. Buffalo, Dec. 16, 1946; s. Joseph Norman and Mary C. (Degenhart) W.; m. Sharron Pollack, Mar. 14, 1982; children: Seth Jacob, Adira Jenna, Benjamin Ari. AB, Canisius Coll., 1968; MA, Kans. State U., 1970, PhD, 1973. Instr. U. Okla., Norman, 1973-74; asst. prof. Tex. Tech U., Lubbock, 1974-76; from asst. prof. to prof. Ind. State U., Terre Haute, 1976—2001, assoc. dean, 1987-92, acting dean, 1992-94, dean, 1994—2001; prof. St. Louis U., 2001—, dean, 2001—02, provost, 2002—. Author: John Barth, 1976, American Short-Fiction Criticism, 1982; co-editor: Black American Prose Theory, 1984, Belief vs. Theory in Black American Literary Criticism, 1986, Black Feminist Criticism, 1988, Studies in Black Am. Lit. Ann., 1984-88; editor African Am. Rev., 1976-2004; contbg. editor High Plains Lit. Rev., 1987-2002; adv. editor Langston Hughes Rev., 1982—. Fellow NDEA, 1970-72, NEH, 1980; Nat. Endowment for Arts grantee, 1988-95. Mem. MLA (exec. com. divsn. Black Am. Lit. and Culture 1985-2004), Coll. Lang. Assn., Langston Hughes Soc., Zora Neale Hurston Soc., Coun. Lit. Mags. and Presses (grantee 1977-96, Editor's grantee 1986), Coun. Editors Learned Jours. (Disting. Editor award, 2005). Office: Saint Louis U DuBourg Hall #106 Saint Louis MO 63103 Home: 6344 Wydown Blvd Saint Louis MO 63105-2213 Office Phone: 314-977-3718. Business E-mail: weixlmj@slu.edu.

**WEJCMAN, LINDA**, retired state legislator; b. Dec. 1939; m. Jim. Student, Iowa State U. Minn. State rep. Dist. 61B, 1991—2000, ret., 2000. Home: 3203 5th Ave S Minneapolis MN 55408-3248

**WELBORN, CARYL BARTELMAN**, lawyer; b. Phila., Jan. 29, 1951; d. Raymond C. and Helen Ann Bartelman; m. Lucien Ruby, Apr. 11, 1987. AB, Stanford U., 1972; JD, UCLA, 1976. Bar: Ill. 1976, Calif. 1978. Assoc. Isham Lincoln & Beale, Chgo., 1976—78; from assoc. to ptnr. Morrison & Foerster, San Francisco and L.A., 1978—95; prin. Law Office of Caryl Welborn, 1995—2004; ptnr. DLA Piper Rudnick Gray Cary US LLP, San Francisco, 2004—. Lectr. real property law. Named Best Lawyers in America. Mem. ABA (chmn. com. on partnerships, real property sect. 1989-93), Am. Coll. Real Estate Lawyers (bd. govs. 1994-2002, pres. 2001), Anglo-Am. Real Property Inst. Office: DLA Piper Rudnick Gray Cary US LLP Ste 800 153 Townsend St San Francisco CA 94105-2150 Office Phone: 415-659-7100. Business E-Mail: caryl.welborn@dlapiper.com.

**WELBORN, REICH LEE**, lawyer; b. Winston-Salem, N.C., Nov. 1, 1945; s. Bishop M. and Hazel (Weatherman) W.; m. Martha Huffstetler, Aug. 27, 1966; children: Judson Allen, Spencer Brooks. AB, U. N.C., 1968, JD with honors, 1971. Bar: N.C. 1971. Assoc. Moore & Van Allen, PLLC and predecessor Powe Porter & Alphin, P.A., Durham, NC, 1971-76; ptnr. Moore & Van Allen and predecessor Powe Porter & Alphin, P.A., Durham, NC, 1976—. V.p. Family Counseling Svc., Durham, 1978-79; bd. trustees N.C. Sch. Sci. & Math., 2002—. Recipient Order of Long Leaf Pine award Gov. of N.C., 1981, Spl. Citation, 1983. Mem. ABA, N.C. Bar Assn., Durham County Bar Assn. (pres. 1989-90), N.C. State Bar, Croasdaile Club (pres. 1989-90), Sertoma (pres. Durham chpt. 1987-88), N.C. Jaycees (pres. 1981-82), Durham C. of C. (bd. dirs. 1992-93). Home: 7 Lanecrest Pl Durham NC 27705-1854 Office: Moore & Van Allen PLLC PO Box 13706 Research Triangle Park NC 27709-4658 Office Phone: 919-286-8000. Business E-Mail: welbornr@mvalaw.com.

**WELBURN, EDWARD T.**, automotive executive; b. Phila, Dec. 14, 1950; BA, Howard U., 1972. Assoc. designer GM Advanced Design Studios, 1972, Buick Exterior Studio, 1973, Oldsmobile Exterior Studio, 1975—85, chief designer, 1989—98; with Saturn global design GM, Rüsselsheim, Germany, 1996—98; dir. GM Corp. Brand Ctr., Warren, Mich., 1998—2001; exec. dir. design body-on-frame architectures GM, 2002, v.p. design N. Am., 2003—05, v.p. global design, 2005—. Designer Indianapolis 500 Pace Car, 1985. Recipient The Best Concept Truck, N. Am. Internat. Auto Show, 2003, Best Concept Car, Autoweek, 1995, Award of Design Excellence, Indsl. Designers Soc. Am., 1988.

**WELCH, ASHLEY JAMES**, engineering educator; b. Ft. Worth, May 3, 1933; married, 1952; 3 children. BS, Tex. Tech U., 1955; MS, So. Meth. U., 1959; PhD in Elec. Engring., Rice U., 1964. Cert. profl. engr., Tex. Aerophys. engr. Gen. Dynamics, Ft. Worth, 1957-60; instr. elec. engring. Rice U., 1960-64; asst. prof. elec. engr. U. Tex., Austin, 1964—70, dir. engring. computer facility, 1964—68, 1995—96, assoc. prof. elec. engr., 1970—75, prof. elec. engr. and biomedical engr., 1971—, Marion E. Forsman Centennial prof. engring., 1985—, faculty advisor undergraduate biomedical engring. students, 2002—03. Chmn. Gordon Conf. in Lasers in Medicine and Biology, Am. Soc. Lasers in Med. Surgery Annual Meeting; bd. dirs. Am. Soc. Lasers in Med. Surgery, 1989—92, 1999—2002. Editor, author Optical-Thermal Response of Laser-Irradiated Tissue; contbr. more than 500 articles to profl. jours. Lt. U.S. Army, 1955—56. Recipient Best Dissertation award, Rice U., 1964, Hocott award, U. Tex., 2004. Fellow: IEEE, Am. Inst. for Med. and Biol. Engring., Am. Soc. Lasers in Surgery and Medicine (W.B. Mark award 2002); mem.: Internat. Soc. Optical Engring. (chmn. sessions). Achievements include research in laser-tissue interaction, application of lasers in medicine; patents in field. Office: U Tex at Austin Dept Biomedical Engring Austin TX 78712 Home: 10821 Pointe View Austin TX 78738 Office Phone: 512-471-1453. Business E-Mail: welch@mail.utexas.edu.

**WELCH, C. DAVID**, assistant secretary of state, former ambassador; b. Munich, 1953; m. Gretchen Gerwe; children: Emma, Molly, Hannah. BA, Georgetown U., 1975; MA, Tufts U., 1977; student, London Sch. Econs., 1973—74. With Office of State. for Security Assistance, Sci. and Tech. 1977—79; polit. officer US Embassy, Islamabad, Pakistan, 1979—81, officer responsible for Syria Washington, 1981—82, officer responsible for Lebanon, 1982—83, chief polit. sect. Damascus, Syria, 1984—86, polit. officer Amman, Jordan, 1986—88; mem. staff Nat. Security Coun. at White House, Washington, 1989—91; exec. asst. to under sec. polit. affairs US Dept. State, Washington, 1991—92; chargé d'affaires US Embassy, Riyadh, Saudi Arabia, 1992—94, dep. chief of mission, 1992—95; prin. dep. asst. sec. of state Bur. Near Ea. Affairs US Dept. State, Washington, 1996—97, asst. sec. for internat. orgn. affairs, 1998—2001, U.S. amb. to Egypt Cairo, 2001—05, asst. sec. Bur. Near Eastern Affairs Washington, 2005—. Mem.: Am. Fgn. Svc. Assn., Coun. Fgn. Rels. Office: US Dept State Harry S Truman Bldg 2201 C St NW Rm 6242 Washington DC 20520 Office Phone: 202-647-7209.

**WELCH, CHARLES EDGAR, JR.**, retired English language educator, writer; b. Phila., July 20, 1918; s. Charles Edgar and Eva Dudley (Morris) W.; widower. BS in Edn., West Chester U., 1947; MA in Early Am. History, U. Pa., 1948, PhD in Folklore, 1970; cert. in 20th Century poetry, Oxford (Eng.) U., 1948. Cert. tchr., Pa. Lectr. English, Phila. Coll. Pharmacy and Sci., 1947-50, asst. prof., 1951-60, assoc. prof., 1960-69, prof., 1969-77, emeritus prof., 1977—, chmn. dept. langs. and social scis., 1950-77. Adj. prof. ESL, Temple U., Phila., 1977-96; part-owner Trevose Summer Theater, 1950-52; contbr., cons. Ledger Syndicate, 1950-70; actor, asst. stage mgr. New Angola (Pa.) Summer Theater, 1955; program dir. Folk Fair, Nationalities Svc. Ctr., Phila., 1955-75; contbr. to humanities program Thomas Jefferson U.; writer Milestones, Phila.; a host You and Your Health, Sta. WFIL-TV, 1958-70; folklorist for documentary on Phila. Mummers Parade Look Who's Having Fun, 1986. Author: Oh! Dem Golden Slippers: A History of the Philadelphia Mummers Parade, 1970, revised, 1993, (with A. Osol): A Sesquicentennial of Service 1821-1971 of the Philadelphia College of Pharmacy and Science; contbr. articles and book revs. to profl. jours., newspapers and mags. Stage mgr. fund raising program, fund raiser Erlanger Theater, Phila., Internat. House, Phila. Mem. Acad. Natural Scis., Pa. Hist. Soc., Pa. Acad. Arts, Nat. Mus. Women in Arts (charter). Republican. Avocation: writing. Home: 2423 Pine St Philadelphia PA 19103-6416

**WELCH, CLAUDE (CLAUDE RAYMOND WELCH)**, theology studies educator; b. Genoa City, Wis., Mar. 10, 1922; s. Virgil Cleon and Deone West (Grenelle) W.; m. Eloise Janette Turner, May 31, 1942 (div. 1970); children— Eric, Thomas, Claudia; m. Theodosia Montigel Blewett, Oct. 5, 1970 (dec. 1978); m. Joy Neuman, Oct. 30, 1982 (dec. 2005). BA summa cum laude, Upper Iowa U., 1942; postgrad., Garrett Theol. Sem., 1942-43; BD cum laude, Yale U., 1945, PhD, 1950; DD (hon.), Ch. Div. Sch. of Pacific, 1972, Jesuit Sch. Theology, 1982; LHD (hon.), U. Judaism, 1976. Ordained to ministry Meth. Ch., 1947. Instr. religion Princeton (N.J.) U., 1947-50, asst. prof., 1950-51, vis. prof., 1962; asst. prof. theology Yale U. Div. Sch., New Haven, 1951-54, assoc. prof., 1954-60; Berg prof. religious thought, chmn. dept. U. Pa., Phila., 1960-71, assoc. dean Coll. Arts and Scis., 1964-68, acting chmn. dept. philosophy, 1965-66; prof. hist. theology Grad. Theol. Union, Berkeley, Calif., 1971—, dean, 1971-87, pres., 1972-82. Vis. prof. Garrett Theol. Sem., 1951, Pacific Sch. Religion, 1958, Hartford Sem. Found., 1958-59, Princeton Theol. Sem., 1962-63, U. Va., 1987; Fulbright sr. lectr. U. Mainz, Germany, 1968; Sprunt lectr. Union Theol. Sem., Richmond, Va., 1958; Willson lectr. Southwestern U., Georgetown, Tex., 1994; dir. study of grad. edn. in religion Am. Coun. Learned Socs., 1969-71; del. World Conf. on Faith and Order, 1963. Author: In This Name: the Doctrine of the Trinity in Contemporary Theology, 1952, (with John Dillenberger) Protestant Christianity, interpreted through its Development, 1954, 2d rev. edit., 1988, The Reality of the Church, 1958, Graduate Education in Religion: A Critical Appraisal, 1971, Religion in the Undergraduate Curriculum, 1972, Protestant Thought in the 19th Century, vol. 1, 1799-1870, 1972, vol. 2, 1870-1914, 1985; Editor, translator: God and Incarnation in Mid-19th Century German

Theology (Thomasius, Dorner and Biedermann), 1965; Contbr. to publs. in field. Recipient decennial prize Bross Found., 1970; Guggenheim fellow, 1976; NEH research fellow, 1984, Fulbright research fellow, 1956-57. Mem. Am. Acad. Religion (pres. 1969-70), Coun. of Socs. for Study of Religion (chmn. 1969-74, 85-90), Soc. for Values in Higher Edn. (pres. 1967-71), Am. Soc. Ch. History, Am. Theol. Soc., Phi Beta Kappa. Methodist. Home: 123 Fairlawn Dr Berkeley CA 94708-2107 E-mail: claudew2@juno.com.

**WELCH, DAVID WILLIAM**, lawyer; b. St. Louis, Feb. 26, 1941; s. Claude LeRoy Welch and Mary Eleanor (Peggs) Welch; m. Candace Lee Capages, June 5, 1971; children: Joseph Peggs, Heather Elizabeth, Katherine Laura. BSBA, Washington U., St. Louis, 1963; JD, U. Tulsa, 1971. Bar: Okla. 1972, Mo. 1973, U.S. Dist. Ct. (we. dist) Mo. 1973, U.S. Dist. Ct. (ea. dist.) Mo. 1974, U.S. Ct. Appeals (8th cir.) 1977, U.S. Ct. Appeals (7th cir.) 1991. Contract adminstr. McDonnell Aircraft Corp., St. Louis, 1965-66; bus. analyst Dun & Bradstreet Inc., Los Angeles, 1967-68; atty. U.S. Dept. Labor, Washington, 1972-73; ptnr. Moller Talent, Kuelthau & Welch, St. Louis, 1973-88, Lashly & Baer, St. Louis, 1988-96, Armstrong Teasdale LLP, St. Louis, 1996—. Author: (handbook) Missouri Employment Law, 1988; contbr. book chpts. Missouri Bar Employer-Employee Law, 1985, 87, 89, 92, 94, Missouri Discrimination Law, 1999; co-editor: Occupational Safety and Health Law, 1996. Mem. City of Creve Coeur Ethics Commn., 1987-88, Planning and Zoning Commn., 1988-96; bd. dirs. Camp Wyman, Eureka, Mo., 1982—, sec., 1987-88, 2nd v.p. 1988-89, 1st v.p. 1990-92, pres., 1992-94. Mem. ABA, Fed. Bar Assn., Mo. Bar Assn., Okla. Bar Assn., St. Louis Bar Assn., Kiwanis (bd. dirs. St. Louis 1979—, sec. 1982-83, 93-94, 2003-04, v.p. 1983-84, 88-90, 92-93, 2003-04, Man of Yr. award 1985). Democrat. Mem. Christian Ch. (Disciples Of Christ). Avocations: travel, music. Office: Armstrong Teasdale 1 Metropolitan Sq Ste 2600 Saint Louis MO 63102-2740

**WELCH, EDWARD P.**, lawyer; b. Columbus, Ohio, Mar. 12, 1950; s. Charles E. and Charma L. (Overbeck) W.; m. Noreen R. Welch, Sept. 8, 1973. BS in Bus. Administrn., Georgetown U., 1972; JD, Villanova U., 1976. Bar: Del. 1976, U.S. Dist. Ct. Del. 1977, U.S. Ct. Appeals (3d cir.) 1981, U.S. Supreme Ct. 1981, N.Y. 1982, U.S. Ct. Appeals (fed. cir.) 1985, (5th cir.) 1992. Law clk. Del Ct. Chancery, Wilmington, 1976-77; assoc. Prickett, Ward, Burt & Sanders, Wilmington, 1977-79, Skadden, Arps, Slate, Meagher & Flom, Wilmington, 1979-84, ptnr., 1984—. Mem. com. charged with drafting evidence code Del., com. charged with drafting dir. liability legis., Wilmington 1977-78, Ct. Chancery Rules Com., Wilmington, 1990—. Author: Folk, Ward & Welch: Folk on the Delaware General Corporation Law, 1988, 3d edit., 1998; co-editor: Folk On The Delaware General Corporation Law Fundamentals, 1993. Bd. dirs. United Cerebral Palsy of Del., Wilmington, 1977-87, The Mary Campbell Ctr., 1987—; co-chmn. United Cerebral Palsy's Camp Manito, Wilmington, 1982-83; trustee The Tatnall Sch., Wilmington, 1992-95. Recipient Community Svc. award United Cerebral Palsy of Del., Wilmington, 1981. Mem. Del. Bar Assn. (coun. corp. law, Young Lawyers award 1986), Corp. Law Coun. Office: One Rodney Sq PO Box 636 Wilmington DE 19899-0636 Business E-Mail: ewezeth@skadden.com.

**WELCH, ERIC D.**, electrical engineer, consultant; b. Rochester, Mich., Mar. 15, 1970; s. George D. and Susan M. Welch; m. Krista M. Hebeisen, Feb. 10, 2006. MusB, Mich. State U., East Lansing, 1993; student, Mich. Technol. U., Houghton, 2004—. Lic. master electrician Mich., elec. contractor Mich. Owner, operator Dexter Electric Systems, Lansing and Houghton, Mich., 1999—; elec. engring. cons. Technisource/Smiths Aerospace, Hancock, Mich., 2005—. Recipient Academic Excellence award, Coll. Engring., Mich. Technol. U., 2004—05. Mem.: IEEE (corr.; chair Mich. Technol. U. chpt. 2005—), Internat. Brotherhood Elec. Workers (assoc.), Mensa (assoc.). Buddhist. Home: 401 W Douglass Ave Houghton MI 49931 Home Fax: 906-482-1706. Personal E-mail: dexterelectric@sbcglobal.net.

**WELCH, GERALD THOMAS**, lawyer, electrical engineer; b. Detroit, Aug. 2, 1949; s. Gerald John and Mary Eileen (Metty) W.; m. Lucia Ann Urso, Sept. 10, 1972; children: Gerald J., Anthony M., David T., Lucia M. BEE, U. Notre Dame, 1971; MBA magna cum laude, U. Utah, 1974; JD, U. Toledo, 1979. Bar: Ohio 1980, Tex. 1981, NY 1990, U.S. Patent Office 1981, US Dist. Ct. (Tex. dist.), U.S. Ct. Appeals (Fed. cir.) 1982. Assoc. John C. Purdue Co., L.P.A., Toledo, 1978-80; atty. Exxon Prodn. Research, Houston, 1980-81; legal counsel Owens-Ill., Toledo, 1981-85; v.p., gen. counsel, sec. M&SD Corp., Lyndhurst, NJ, 1985—88; dir., licensing & tech. devel. Eastman Kodak Co., 1988-91; ptnr., Intellectual Property, Telecom. & Emerging Tech., Tech. Law practices Patton Boggs LLP, Dallas, dep. chmn., Intellectual Property dept., mem. mgmt. com., office mng. ptnr. V.p. Welmet Inc., Flemington, N.J. Served to capt. USAF, avionics engring. & JAG, 1971-77. Life fellow, Dallas Bar Found.; mem. ABA, Tex. Bar Assn., NY State Bar Assn., Dallas Bar Assn., Am. Intellectual Property Law Assn. (chmn. Mgmt. of IP Assets com. 2001-03), Am. Corp. Counsel Assn., Licensing Exec. Soc. Roman Catholic. Avocations: golf, tennis. Office: Patton Boggs LLP Suite 3000 2001 Ross Ave Dallas TX 75201-8001 Office Phone: 214-758-6610. Office Fax: 214-758-1550. Business E-Mail: gwelch@pattonboggs.com.

**WELCH, JACK HAMILL**, retired internist; b. Columbus, Ohio, July 14, 1915; s. John Orr and Evelyn (Bigger) Welch; m. Mary Elaine Childs, Apr. 25, 1943 (div. 1976); children: David, Pamela, Michael; m. Alice Elizabeth Welch, May 6, 1978. BA, Ohio State U., 1936; MD, Duke U., 1940. Diplomate Am. Bd. Internal Medicine, Nat. Bd. Med. Examiners. From intern to resident Henry Ford Hosp., Detroit, 1940-42, 46-48; pvt. practice internal medicine Columbus, 1948-50, Hollywood, Calif., 1950-52, San Fernando Valley, 1952-83; ret., 1983. Instr. medicine White Meml. Hosp. Loma Linda Sch. Medicine, L.A., 1954—56; moderator Nat. Issues Forum, 1985—91, participant, 1992—94; active supporter Calif. Proposition 186 Universal Health Care, Fresno, 1994. Author: Battalion Surgeon WWII, 1996. Mem. Visions of Cmty., 1984—94, chair, 1990—92; initiator Peace and Justice com. United Ch. of Christ, Fresno, 1990—97; co-founder, bd. dirs Fresno Ctr. for Non Violence, 1992—, Black.White Dialogue Group, Fresno, 1997—. With M.C. U.S. Army, 1942—45, ETO. Decorated Bronze Star; fellow, Ctrl. Calif. Inst., prog. pub. policy rsch. found., Fresno, 2003. Mem.: ACP, AMA, Fgn. Policy Assn., Physicians for Social Responsibility (No. dels. 1987—88). Democrat. Avocations: singing, writing, walking, tv, golf. Home: 6432 N Dolores Ave Fresno CA 93711

**WELCH, JASPER ARTHUR, JR.**, security company executive, consultant; b. Baton Rouge, Jan. 5, 1931; s. Jasper Arthur and Oramay Ballinger (Young) W.; m. Frances Carroll Wright, Mar. 28, 1953 (div. Nov. 1984); children: Jasper Arthur III, Carroll Welch Pawlikowski, Brent Ballinger; m. Jane Ann Alford Tudor, Dec. 31, 1985. BS in Physics, La. State U., 1952; MA in Physics, U. Calif., Berkeley, 1954, PhD in Physics, 1958. Commd. officer 2d lt. USAF, 1952, advanced through grades to maj. gen., 1975; chief analyst Hdqs. USAF, Washington, 1969—71; chief strategic analysis Office Sec. Def., Washington, 1971—74; chief strategic concepts Hdqs. USAF, 1974—75, asst. chief staff for analysis, 1975—79; coord. def. policy NSC, 1979—81; asst. dept. chief staff Hdqs. USAF, 1981—83; ret., 1983; tech. cons. Jasper Welch Assocs., Santa Fe, 1983—. Bd. dirs. Sci. Applications Internat. Corp., San Diego; mem. tech. adv. coun. Sikorsky Aircraft, Stratford, Conn., 1984—2005; mem. adv. coun. NASA, Washington, 1985-89; chmn. mil. adv. panel to dir. CIA, Washington, 1986-98; mem. nat. security panel U. Calif., 2000—. Author: Atomic Theory of Gas Dynamics, 1965; contbr. articles to sci. jours., including Phys. Rev., Strategic Rev. Youth dir. St. Matthews Epis. Ch., Pacific Palisades, Calif., 1969-74, St. Andrews Epis. Ch., Arlington, 1965-68; mem. found. bd. Santa Fe Chamber Music Festival 1998—2004. Decorated D.S.M. with oak leaf cluster, Legion of merit with two oak leaf clusters. Mem. NAE (found. bd. 1999—2005), Am. Geophys. Union, Am. Phys. Soc., Coun. on Fgn. Rels. Avocations: music, theater, gardening, hiking, racing sailboats. Office: Sci Applications Internat Corp 2129 Foothills Rd Santa Fe NM 87505

**WELCH, JOE BEN**, academic administrator; b. Amite County, Miss., May 18, 1940; s. H.A. Joe and Mildred Pill (Bean) W.; m. Dorothy Louise Rostron, June 2, 1962; children: Wendi Jo Welch Sands, Robin Clare Welch Peveto, Sandra Tres Welch Dobbs, Roxana Merry Welch Blackwell. BS, La. Tech. U., 1963; MEd, Lamar U., 1967; EdD, McNeese State U., 1974. Instr. math., sci. Clinton (La.) High Sch., 1963-64; instr. math. Port Neches (Tex.) Groves H.S., 1964-67; acting head math. and sci. dept. Trinity Christian Coll., Baton Rouge, 1967-68; head math. and sci. dept. Mid-City Bapt. Jr. Coll., New Orleans, 1968-69; instr. math. Orange (Tex.) Extension Ctr., Lamar U., 1969-70, dir., 1970-75; dean Lamar U. Ctr.-Orange, 1975-81, provost, 1981-83, pres., 1983-89. Middle Ga. Coll., Cochran, 1989-98; chancellor River Parishes C.C., Sorrento, La., 1998—. Adv. bd. dirs. Bleckley Meml. Hosp., 1989—. Recipient Grateful Appreciation award West Orange-Cove Consol. Sch. Dist., 1976-82, Outstanding and Dedicated Svc. award ARC, Orange, 1985; named Citizen of Yr. C. of C., Orange, 1985. Mem. Am. Assn. Community and Jr. Colls., Cochran (Ga.) Bleckley C. of C., Macon City Club (bd. dirs. 1991—), Phi Delta Kappa. Baptist. Office: River Parishs Cmty Coll PO Box 310 Sorrento LA 70778-0310

**WELCH, JOHN DANA**, retired urologist; b. Canton, Ill., Mar. 14, 1938; m. Myrna Lee Loring, Dec. 23, 1962; children: Timothy Lance, Christina Dawn. BS, U. Ill., 1960, MD, 1963. Diplomate Am. Bd. Urology, Nat. Bd. Med. Examiners, Fla. Bd. Med. Examiners. Rotating intern Tampa (Fla.) Gen. Hosp., 1963-64, resident in urology, 1964-68; pvt. practice, Sarasota, Fla., 1970-98. Bd. dirs. Bay Area Renal Stone Ctr., 1986-98; chief surgery HCA Doctors Hosp., 1981, chief of staff, 1983, trustee, 1988-91. Bd. dirs. Asolo Ctr. for Performing Arts, 1982-95, 2003—, sec., 1989-90, v.p., 1990-93, pres., 1993-94; pres., founder Sarasota Film Festival, 1998—. Maj. USAF, 1968-70; mem. Fla. Film and Entertainment Adv. Coun., 2002—. Mem. AMA, Fla. Med. Assn., Sarasota County Med. Soc., Am. Urological Assn. (SE sect.), Fla. Urological Soc. (pres. 1986), Am. Lithotripsy Soc. Home and Office: 650 Mourning Dove Dr Sarasota FL 34236-1926 E-mail: SRQDOC@aol.com.

**WELCH, JOHN KIRTLAND**, nuclear energy industry executive; b. Waltham, Mass., Mar. 8, 1950; s. Raymond Vencent and Justine Louise (Fairbank) W.; m. Michele Anne Mules, June 10, 1972; children: Nicole Kristen, Alison Corrinne. BA in Aero. Engring., U.S. Nav. Acad., 1972; MS in Aeronautics, Naval Postgrad. Sch., 1973; MBA in Fin., Loyola Coll., Balt., 1984. Registered profl. engr., Md. Commd. ens. USN, 1972, advanced through grades to lt., resigned, 1979; systems engr. Gen. Electric Co., Evendale, Ohio, 1979-80; div. dir. Gen. Physics Corp., Columbia, Md., 1980-84; ops. ctr. mgr. Advanced Tech., Inc., Reston, Va., 1984; various positions to exec. v.p. marine sys. group Gen. Dynamics Corp., 1989—2005; pres., CEO USEC Inc., 2005—. Lt. USNR, 1979—. Mem. ASME (chmn. plant engring. com. 1980—), Am. Soc. Naval Engrs. Avocations: swimming, photography, sailing. Office: USEC Inc 6903 Rockledge Dr Bethesda MD 20817*

**WELCH, JUDY ANN**, language educator; b. Miami Beach, Fla. Nov. 16, 1965; d. Albert and Frances Blue Swain; m. Albert P. Welch, Dec. 18, 1999; children: Dominique, Brittany. BA in English, Spelman Coll., Atlanta, 1987; MS in English Edn., Nova Southeastern U., Fort Lauderdale, Fla., 2001, EdD, 2004. English tchr. Miami-Dade County Pub. Schs., Fla., 1989—2001; lang. arts tchr. Palm Beach Sch. Dist., Boca Raton, Fla., 2001—03; adj. prof., English Lynn U., Boca Raton, Fla., 2001—; mem. English faculty Miami Dade Coll., 2003—; adj. prof., English Broward Cmty. Coll., Boca Raton, Fla., 2001—. Mem. Hopewell Baptist Missionary Ch., Pompano, Fla., 2001—. Mem.: Zeta Phi Beta. Democrat. Baptist. Avocations: singing, dance, poetry. Office: 11380 NW 27th Ave Miami FL 33167 Home: 3060 Palm Trace Landings Dr Apt 209 Davie FL 33314-1889 Office Phone: 561-237-7012. Business E-Mail: jwelch@aiufl.edu. E-mail: professorjawelch@aol.com.

**WELCH, LLOYD RICHARD**, electrical engineer, educator, communications engineer, consultant; b. Detroit, Sept. 28, 1927; s. Richard C. and Helen (Felt) W.; m. Irene Althea Main, Sept. 12, 1953; children: Pamela Irene Towery, Melinda Ann, Diana Lia Worthington. BS in Math., U. Ill., 1951; PhD in Math., Calif. Inst. Tech., 1958. Mathematician NASA-Jet Propulsion Lab., Pasadena, Calif., 1956-59; staff mathematician Inst. Def. Analyses, Princeton, NJ, 1959-65; prof. elec. engring. U. So. Calif., L.A., 1965-99, prof. emeritus, 1999—. Cons. in field of elec. comms Contbr. articles to profl. jours. Served with USN, 1945-49, 51-52 Fellow IEEE (Shannon award Info. Theory Soc. of IEEE 2003); mem. Nat. Acad. Engring., Am. Math. Soc., Math. Assn. Am., Phi Beta Kappa, Sigma Xi, Phi Kappa Phi, Pi Mu Epsilon, Eta Kappa Nu Office: U So Calif Elec Engring Bldg 500A Los Angeles CA 90089-0001 E-mail: lloydwelch@earthlink.net.

**WELCH, LOUISE BANNER**, retired minister; b. McKinney, Tex., Aug. 6, 1926; d. Beverley Barrett and Ella Lorraine (Bost) Banner; m. John Calvin Goodloe Sr. (div.); children: John Goodloe Jr., Mary Louise Dykes; m. Edgar Welch (dec.). MA in Econs., Western Ill. U., Macomb, 1971; MA in Polit. Sci., Tex. A&M U., College Station, 1979; MA in Theol. Study, So. Meth. U., Dallas, 1982. Minister United Meth. Ch., Ladonia, Tex., 1979-89, Ladonia-Pecan Gap, Tex., 1989-99; ret., 1999. Author: Luke's Twelve Eyewitnessess, 2002, Rightly Dividing the Gospel of Luke, 2003, Decoding Luke, 2005, Luke Knew Isaiah's E.L.S., 2006. Avocation: structural analysis of Gospel of Luke. Home: 2509 Rolling Hills Dr Greenville TX 75402-6814 Personal E-mail: welch@bible-luke.com. E-mail: louise.b.welch@worldnet.att.net.

**WELCH, LYNNE BRODIE**, nursing school dean; b. Norwalk, Conn., Oct. 19, 1941; d. John and Jeannette Brodie; m. C. William Welch, Aug. 1965 (div. Dec. 1980); children: John, Andrew. BS, U. Conn., 1963; MSN, Cath. U. Am., 1968; EdD, Columbia U., 1979. From staff nurse to instr. Sch. of Nursing Stamford (Conn.) Hosp., 1963-65; staff nurse, instr. Children's Hosp. Ctr., Washington, 1965-66; staff nurse CCU Washington Hosp. Ctr., 1966-67; staff nurse ICU/CCU Danbury (Conn.) Hosp., 1968-69; asst. prof. Western Conn. State U., Danbury, 1970-79; assoc. prof., chairperson Pace U., Pleasantville, N.Y., 1979-82; prof., dean Sch. Nursing So. Conn. State U., New Haven, 1982-86; prof., dean Coll. of Nursing and Allied Health U. Tex., El Paso, 1986-89; statewide dir. S.C. Area Health Edn. Consortium Med. U. of S.C., Charleston, 1989-91; prof., dean Sch. of Nursing Marshall U., Huntington, W.Va., 1991—98, dean Coll. of Health Professions, 1998—. Mem. joint bd. Kellogg Community Partnership, Morgantown, W.Va., 1991—; mem. bd. W.Va. Ptnrs. of the Americas, Charleston, 1992—; chairperson W.Va. Health Care Planning Commn. Task Force, Charleston, 1992—. Editor: Women in Higher Education: Changes and Challenges, 1990, Minority Women in Higher Education, 1992, Roles of Nursing Faculty in Higher Education, 1992, Strategies for Promoting Pluralism in Education and the Work Place, 1997. Mem. Leadership Tri State, Ashland, Ky., 1992, Leadership W.Va., 1993, Leadership El Paso, Class 10, 1988. Mem. ANA, Nat. League for Nursing, Am. Assn. Acad. Adminstrs. (state commr. 1979-92), Sigma Theta Tau, Phi Kappa Phi. Republican. Presbyterian. Avocations: gardening, cooking, travel. Home: 3200 Orchard Dr Huntington WV 25701-9534 Office: Marshall U Pritchard Hall 426 1 John Marshall Dr Huntington WV 25755-0003

**WELCH, LYNNE G.**, language and music educator; b. Long Beach, Calif., Dec. 13; d. Wallace M. Welch and Beth May Gardiner; children: Samuel Meadd, Thaddeus Cates. BA, Calif. State U., 1964, MA, 1970. ESL tchr. State of Calif., 2003—04; English tchr. Garden Grove Unit, Calif.; journalist Mass Media Sch. Dist.; English tchr. Compton Unit Sch. Dist. Recreational asst. Long Beach, Calif. 1997—99. Named Outstanding Tchr., Compton Unified Sch. Dist., 1995, 1996; named to Wall of Tolerance (signed by Rosa Parks); recipient Outstanding Tchr., Compton Unified Sch. Dist., 1996. Mem.: Coda Internat., Emotions Anonymous, Alanon Internat. Meth. Home: 11420 E 216th ST Lakewood CA 90715

**WELCH, MARTHA GRACE**, physician, researcher; b. Buffalo, June 21, 1944; d. Thomas Harris and Jane Elizabeth (Todd) W.; m. Anthony H. Horan, July 11, 1970 (div. May 1985); 1 child, Thomas Bramwell Welch Horan. BA, N.Y.U., 1966; MD, Columbia U., 1971. Diplomate Am. Bd. Psychiatry and

Neurology. Intern Greenwich (Conn.) Hosp. Assn., 1971-72; resident Albert Einstein Coll. Med., Bronx, N.Y., 1972-74, fellow, 1974-77, instr., 1977-79; dir., founder The Mothering Ctr., Greenwich, 1978—; asst. clin. prof. psychiatry Columbia U., N.Y.C., 1997—. Author: Holding Time, 1989, (with others) Autistic Children, 1983; contbr. articles to profl. jours. Pres. alumni coun. Columbia U. Coll. Physicians and Surgeons, 2001-2002 Recipient Alumni Achievement award Middlebury (Vt.) Coll., 1995. Mem. Am. Psychiat. Assn., Internat. Soc. for Devel. Psychobiology, Soc. for Neuroscience. Avocations: reading, skiing, tennis, sewing, biking, music. Office: 15 E 91st St New York NY 10128-0648 Office Phone: 212-369-8566.

**WELCH, MARTHA LYNN,** environmentalist, educator; d. Margaret Melvina Sandifer and Richard Charles O'Connell; m. John Tyler Welch II, Aug. 28, 1987. BA in Environ. Studies, U. N.C., Wilmington, N.C., 1983; MS in Edn., Old Dominion U., 1996; EdD, Fla. Internat. U., 2004. Asst. edn., exhibits coord. N.C. Aquarium, Ft. Fisher, 1984—86; owner, operator Manatee Tours, Inc., Islamorada, Fla., 1990—93; marine edn. specialist Coll. William and Mary, Va. Inst. Marine Sci., Gloucester Point, 1996—97; field leader, instr. Audubon Fla., Miami, 1999—2003; dir. edn. Fla. Flora and Fauna, Inc., Hutchinson island, 1999—. Cons. Sch. Dist. Palm Beach County, Fla., 2002—. Author: Mandy the Manatee Saves the Day; contbr. articles to profl. jours. Mem.: ASCD, NSTA (assoc.), Fla. Assn. Sci. Tchrs., Nat. Marine Edn. Assn. (assoc.), Nat. Audubon Soc., Fla. Marine Sci. Edn. Assn., Phi Kappa Phi. Avocations: travel, snorkeling, boating. Home and Office: 137 Queens Rd Hutchinson Island FL 34949 Office Phone: 561-951-9313. Personal E-mail: jwelch261@sprintpcs.com.

**WELCH, MARTIN E., III,** investor, retail executive; b. Detroit, June 25, 1948; m. Anne Welch; children: Michele, James, Mary Beth, Brian. BS in Acctg., U. Detroit Mercy, 1970, MBA, 1973. Audit mgr Arthur Young & Co., Detroit, 1970-77; dir. mktg. acctg. Fruehauf divsn. Fruehauf Corp., Detroit, 1977-82; mgr. corp. acctg. Chrysler Corp., Highland Park, Mich., 1982-83, asst. contrr., 1983-86, gen. auditor, 1987-88, asst. treas., 1988-91; CFO Chrysler Can., Windsor, Ont., 1986-87; sr. v.p., CFO Federal-Mogul corp., Southfield, Mich., 1991-95; exec. v.p., CFO Kmart Corp. Troy, Mich., 1995—2001; bus. advisor, dir. York Mgmt. Svcs., Somerset, NJ, 2002—; exec. v.p., CFO Oxford Automotive, Inc., Troy, Mich., 2003—04, United Rentals, Inc., Greenwich, Conn., 2005—. Mem. nat. adv. bd. JP Morgan Bank, 1997—2000; bd. dirs. No. Group Retail, Ltd. Bd. dirs. U. Detroit-Mercy. Mem.: Fin. Execs. Internat. E-mail: martywelch@yahoo.com.

**WELCH, MICHAEL JOHN,** chemistry educator, researcher; b. Stoke-on-Trent, Staffordshire, Eng., June 28, 1939; came to U.S., 1965; s. Arthur John W. and Mary (Welch); m. Stephanie Louise Conocchiolli, Apr. 22, 1967 (div. 1979); children: Colin, Lesley. BA, Cambridge U., Eng., 1961; MA, Cambridge U., 1964; PhD, London U., 1965. Asst. prof. radiation chemistry in radiology Washington U. Sch. Medicine, St. Louis, 1967-70, assoc. prof., 1970-74, assoc. prof. dept. chemistry, 1971-75, prof. dept. chemistry, 1978—, prof. radiology, 1991—, prof. molecular biology and pharmacology, 1993—; prof. biomed. engring. program Washington U., St. Louis, 1996; co-dir. Mallinckrodt Inst. Dir. radiol. scis. dept. Washington U., 1990—; mem. diagnostic radiology study sect. NIH, 1986-89, chmn., 1989-91; mem. scit. adv. com. Whitaker Found., 1995-2003. Author: Introduction to the Tracer Methods, 1972; editor: Radiopharmaceuticals and Other Compounds Labeled with Shortlived Radionuclides, 1977; assoc. editor Jour. Nuclear Medicine, 1989—2003; contbr. chpts. to books, more than 400 articles to profl. jours. Recipient Georg Charles de Hevesy Nuclear Medicine Pioneer award, 1992; scholar St. Catharine Coll. Cambridge U., 1958-61. Mem. Soc. Nuclear Medicine (trustee, pres. 1984, Paul C. Aebersold award 1980, de Hevesy Nuclear Pioneer award 1992), Radiopharm. Sci. Coun. (pres. 1980-81), Am. Chem. Soc. (St. Louis award 1988, award for nuclear chemistry 1990, Mid-West award 1991), Chem. Soc. London, Radiation Rsch. Soc., Inst. of Medicine, Sigma Xi Office: Washington U Sch Medicine Edward Mallinckrodt Inst Radiology 510 S Kingshighway Blvd Box 8225 Saint Louis MO 63110-1016 E-mail: welchm@mir.wustl.edu.

**WELCH, MICHAEL R.,** sociologist, educator; b. Ogdensburg, NY, Feb. 8, 1947; s. Carlton Curtis Welch and Eleanor (Clary) Caruso; m. Helena Rose Kleist, Jan. 29, 1966; children: Kristen Reynolds, Michael Jr., Scott, Brian. BA, LeMoyne Coll., 1972; MA, U. N.C., 1975, PhD, 1980. Asst. prof. Fla. Atlantic U., Boca Raton, 1976—80, U. Cin., 1980—81; full prof. U. Notre Dame, 2006—. Contbr. articles to profl. jours. Mem.: Am. Soc. Criminology, Am. Sociol. Assn., Alpha Kappa Delta, Pi Gamma Mu. Roman Catholic. Office: Univ Notre Dame Sociology Dept 810 Flanner Hall Notre Dame IN 46556

**WELCH, MORGAN E.,** lawyer; b. Joplin, Mo., May 25, 1950; s. Morgan and Virginia Welch; m. Cheryl Welch, Oct. 23, 1982; children: Rick Martin, Ashley. BS, Westminster Coll., 1972; JD, U. Ark., 1975. Bar: Ark. 1975, U.S. Dist. Ct. (ea. dist. Ark.) 1975, U.S. Dist. Ct. (we. dist. Ark.) 1975, U.S. Ct. Appeals (8th cir.) 1984, U.S. Supreme Ct. 1990, U.S. Air Force Ct. Mil. Rev., U.S. Army Ct. Mil. Rev., Armed Forces Ct. Appeals. Jr. ptnr. Patterson and Welch, North Little Rock, Ark., 1976—80; owner Morgan Welch PA, North Little Rock, 1980—89; ptnr. Hurley Whitwell Shephard & Welch, North Little Rock, 1989—90, Welch & Adcock, Little Rock, 1990—95; owner Morgan Welch PA, Little Rock, 1995—2000; ptnr. Eubanks, Welch, Baker, Schulze, Little Rock, 2000—03; sr. ptnr. Welch and Kitchens LLC, Little Rock, 2003—. Counsel Ark. Legis., Little Rock, 1975—76. Pres. North Little Rock Jaycees, 1978—79; sec. North Pulaski County Bar Assn., North Little Rock, 1979—80; mem. 8th cir. Ark. Ho. Dels., 1994—96. Recipient Roxanne Wilson Trial Adv. award, 1997. Mem.: ATLA (bd. govs.), ABA, Am. Inns Ct. Found. (Master of Bench), Ark. Trial Lawyers Assn. (pres. 1991, Outstanding Trial Lawyer award 1990, President's award 2005). Democrat. Methodist. Office: One Riverfront Pl Ste 413 North Little Rock AR 72114 Office Phone: 501-978-3030.

**WELCH, OLIVER WENDELL,** retired pharmaceutical executive; b. Jacksonville, Tex., Jan. 9, 1930; s. Jackson Andrew and Annie Laura (Trapp) W.; m. Wanda Virginia Urrey, Nov. 14, 1948. BA, Tex. Tech U., 1952; MA, Columbia U., 1958. Pharm. rep., supr. mktg. rsch., manpower devel. Warner Lambert Co., Morris Plains, N.J., 1962-72; mgr. corp. devel. Boehringer Mannheim Corp., N.Y.C., 1972-75; v.p. Biomed. Data Co., N.Y.C., 1975-77; assoc. dir., dep. dir. regulatory affairs Sterling Winthrop Inc., N.Y.C., 1977-94; ret., 1994. Cons. Sanofi Winthrop, Inc., N.Y.C., 1995. Mem. Regulatory Affairs Profls. Soc., Drug Info. Assn., Order St. John of Jerusalem. Republican. Episcopalian. Avocations: music, travel, theater. *Pursue excellence. Pay attention to detail. Expect a positive result.*

**WELCH, PHILIP BURLAND,** electronics and office products company executive; b. Portland, Maine, Nov. 15, 1931; s. Philip Gerald Welch and Clara Jenny (Berry) Hawxwell; m. Sheila Mae Preston, May 19, 1960 (dec.); children: Jahna Holly Welch Roth, Victoria Preston Welch Rothlubber; m. Aloma Gale Baskin, Sept. 14, 2005. Student, Berklee Coll., 1955—58. Profl. trumpeter, arranger, composer, NYC, 1958—65; dist. sales mgr. Rheem Mfg. Co., Phila., 1965—66, regional sales mgr., 1966—70; nat. sales mgr. Akai Am. Ltd., Anaheim, Calif., 1970-73, BSR, USA, Blauvelt, NY, 1973-76; nat. sales and mktg. mgr. Philips High Fidelity Labs., Ft. Wayne, Ind., 1976-79; dir. mktg. Pioneer Electronics, Moonachie, NJ, 1979-82; pres. Schneider N.Am. Ltd., Dayton, NJ, 1982-83; v.p. Lyons & Assocs., Indpls., 1986-88; pres. Nat. Electric Mktg. Co., Jacksonville, Fla., 1975-88, Hemisphere Enterprises Corp., Jacksonville, 1988-91, Phil Welch Enterprises, Jacksonville, 1989-99, ret., 1999. Cons. ContraTech Corp., Portland, Oreg., 1986-87, Kukje Internat., NYC, 1986, FCI Inc., NJ, 1985, Multiform Products, Inc., Jacksonville, 1989-90, gen. mgr., v.p., 1990-96; pres. Atlantic Office Sources, Inc., Jacksonville, 1996-99, comdr. Am. Legion Post 372, Jacksonville, 2003, 04. Contbr. articles to profl. jours. With USAF, 1950—54. Named Man of Decade Audio/Video Cons. USA, 2000. Man of Yr. Soc. Audio Cons., 1974. Republican. Avocations: flying, golf. Home and Office: 12821 Julington Forest Dr W Jacksonville FL 32258-3454 Office Phone: 904-608-6073. Personal E-mail: philwelch@bellsouth.net.

**WELCH, RAQUEL,** actress; b. Chgo., Sept. 5, 1940; d. Arm and Josepha (Hall) Tejada; m. James Westley Welch, May 8, 1959 (div.); children: Damon, Tahnee; m. Patrick Curtis (div.); m. Andre Weinfeld, July 1980 (div.). Actress: (films) including Fantastic Voyage, 1966, One Million B.C, 1967, The Biggest Bundle of Them All, 1968, Fathom, 1967, The Queens, 1967, 100 Rifles, 1969, Magic Christian, 1970, Bedazzled, 1971, Fuzz, 1972, Bluebeard, 1972, Hannie Caulder, 1972, Kansas City Bomber, 1972, Myra Breckinridge, 1970, The Last of Sheila, 1973, The Three Musketeers, 1974 (Golden Globe award for best actress), The Wild Party, 1975, The Four Musketeers, 1975, Mother, Jugs and Speed, 1976, Crossed Swords, 1978, L'Animal, 1979, Chairman of the Board, 1998, (TV movies) The Legend of Walks Far Woman, 1982, Right to Die, 1987, Scandal in a Small Town, 1988, Trouble in Paradise, 1989, Torch Song, 1993, Naked Gun 33 1/3, 1993, Folle d'elle, 1998; (Broadway debut) Woman of the Year, 1982; star Victor/Victoria (on Broadway), 1997; (TV series) Central Park West, 1995; author: The Raquel Welch Total Beauty and Fitness Program, 1984.*

**WELCH, RICHARD LEROY,** personal improvement company executive; b. Lincoln, Nebr., Oct. 15, 1939; s. Raymond Nathanial and Helen Lila (Ludwig) W.; m. Donna Lee Gysegem, Nov. 3, 1991; children: Terri L. Flowerday, Julie A. Kuhl; 1 stepchild, Shannon Panzo. Student, U. Nebr.; PhD (hon.), Devonshire U., Eng., 2000. Agt. Gurantee Mut. Life, Lincoln, Nebr., 1960-61; agt., mgr. Mut. of Omaha, 1962-68; gen. agt. Loyal Protective Life, Omaha, 1969-70; mgr. Mut. Benefit Life, Dallas, 1971-73; br. mgr. Great West Life, San Jose, Calif., 1973-74; pres. Internat. Speedreading Inst., Phoenix, 1975-80; CEO, founder Educom, Inc./Subliminal Dynamics, Dynamic Brain Mgmt., Centennial, Colo., 1980—. Mem. adv. bd. Great West Life, San Jose, 1973; pres. bd. dirs. Internat. Speedreading Inst., Phoenix, 1975-80, Subliminal Dynamics, Inc., San Jose, 1980-93, Educom, Inc., Aurora, 1993—; scientist, spkr., author, educator in field. Author: Brain Management, 1996. Inductee Lincoln H.S. Athletic Hall of Fame, 2000. Mem. Shriners, Masons (32d degree). Democrat. Avocations: sports, music, travel. Office: DBA Subliminal Dynamics Brain Mgmt 2553 North Carson St Ste 5885 Carson City NV 89706 Fax: 775-883-2384. E-mail: subdyn@subdyn.com.

**WELCH, ROBERT BENNETT,** retired music educator, retired conductor; b. Fleming, Ky., Feb. 20, 1935; s. Thomas Earl and Malinda Welch; m. Joyce Ann Broome, June 3, 1958; children: Robert Keith, David Bennett. BA, Morehead State U., Ky., 1963, MA, 1967; D in Musical Arts, U. Ky., Lexington, 1984. Cert. tchr. Ky., Va. Band dir. Letcher County Schs., Neon, Ky., 1957—58, Norton Schs., Va., 1958—63; band dir., orch. dir. Ea. HS, Louisville, 1963—67; condr. Louisville Youth Orch., 1964—68; band dir. We. Carolina U., 1968—79; condr., artistic dir. Asheville Symphony Orch., NC, 1977—81; head divsn. fine arts Limestine Coll., Gaffney, SC, 1979—84; dean Coll. Arts Valdosta State Coll., Ga., 1984—2000. Dir. Jekyll Island Musical Theater, Jekyll Island, Ga., 1987—95, Artsouth, Valdosta, 1989—95; condr., founder Valdosta Symphony Orch., 1989—93; guest condr. over 300 occasions in US & Europe. Mgr. Arts Rsch.Programs in Europe & US, 1980—84; mem. Arts Com., Cullowhee, NC, 1970—74; pres. Arts Assn. Gaffney, 1980—84; v.p. Lowndes Valdosta Arts Soc., 1985—95. Home: 1060 Arbor Creek Dr Roswell GA 30076 Personal E-mail: robertbwelch@bellsouth.net.

**WELCH, ROBERT BOND,** ophthalmologist, educator; b. Balt., May 24, 1927; s. Robert S.G. and Sally (Bond) W.; m. Elizabeth Truslow, May 30, 1953. AB, Princeton U., N.J., 1949; MD, Johns Hopkins U., Balt., 1953. Diplomate: Am. Bd. Ophthalmology. Intern in internal medicine Duke U. Hosp., 1953-54; resident in ophthalmology Wilmer Inst., Johns Hopkins U., 1954-57, chief resident in ophthalmology, 1959, co-dir. retina service, 1959-84, dir. retina service, 1984-85; retinal cons. in ophthalmology Walter Reed Army Hosp., 1961—2003, Bethesda Naval Hosp, 1976-99; assoc. prof. ophthalmology Johns Hopkins U.; chmn. dept. ophthalmology Greater Balt. Med. Ctr., 1985-91. Author: (with others) The Wilmer Institute 1925-1975, 1976; author: The Wilmer Opthalmological Institute 1925-2000, 2000; editor Transactions Am. Ophthal. Soc., 1984-91; mem. editorial staff Retina mag., 1980-86. Served with USNR, 1945-47. Recipient Disting. Alumnus award, Johns Hopkins U., 2001, Superior Civilian Svc. award, U.S. Army, 2004, Robert Bond Welch professorship in opthalmology, Johns Hopkins Medicine and Wilmer Eye Inst., 2006, Julia A. Haller award, 2006. Mem. Am. Ophthal. Soc. (v.p. 1992-93, pres. 1993-94, editor 1984-90), Retina Soc. (pres. 1981-83), Pan. Pacific Surg. Assn. (v.p. 1972-80), Md. Soc. Eye Physicians and Surgeons (pres. 1963-64), Md. Club, Elkridge Club, South River Club. Democrat. Episcopalian. Home: 4409 Atwick Rd Baltimore MD 21210-2811 Office: 86 State Cir Annapolis MD 21401-1906

**WELCH, RONNIE SCOTT,** health facility administrator; b. San Diego, Oct. 1, 1959; s. Marvin and Evelyn Welch. Student, Brigham Young U., 1987—88; cert. in Bus. Adminstrn., Long Beach City Coll., 1994, AA in Bus. Adminstrn. with honors, 1994, AA in Social Scis. with honors, 1995, cert. in Gen. Bus., 2002; BA in Econ., Calif. State U., Long Beach, 2001, cert. in Entrepruership, 2002; cert. in Profl. Fiduciary Mgmt. for Conservators, Calif. State U., Fullerton, 2002; postgrad., Coll. Fin. Planning, Greenwood Village, Colo., 2001—; AA in Acctg. with high honors, Long Beach City Coll., 2003, cert. in Acctg., 2003. Cert. residential care facility for elderly adminstr., IRS enrolled agt., accredited bus. acct., accredited tax advisor, accredited tax preparer, registered fin. cons., cert. retirement counselor, retirement adminstr., bus. mgr. Adminstr., CEO, CFO Cerritos Manor, Inc., Long Beach, Calif., 1977—. Recipient Mayor's Cert. of Award for contbns. to elderly, City of Signal Hill, Calif., 1993. Mem.: Nat. Assn. Tax Profls., Nat. Soc. Accts., Internat. Assn. Registered Fin. Cons., Fin. Planning Assn., Am. Fin. Assn., Am. Tax Assn., Am. Acctg. Assn., Inst. Internal Auditors, Inst. Mgmt. Accts., Golden Key, Omicron Delta Epsilon (mem. Tau chpt.). Avocations: reading, writing, jogging, walking. Office: Cerritos Manor Inc 1046 East Fourth St Long Beach CA 90802-1634 mail: rscottwelch@cs.com.

**WELCH, ROSS MAYNARD,** plant physiologist, educator; b. Lancaster, Calif., May 8, 1943; s. Lloyd C. and Theda W. (Slane) W.; m. Jill Susanne Varley, Aug. 22, 1965; children: Renell Cherie, Brent Ross BS, Calif. Poly. U., 1966; MS, U. Calif., Davis, 1969, PhD, 1971. Plant physiologist Agrl. Rsch. Svc. USDA, Ithaca, NY, 1971—; rsch. assoc. Cornell U., Ithaca, 1971—75, asst. prof. plant nutrition, 1975—81, assoc. prof. plant nutrition, 1981—87, prof., 1987—, co-organizer food sys. for improved health program Coll. Agr. and Life Scis., 1990—2000. Disting. vis. scientist Murdoch U., Perth, Australia, 1980-81; vis. disting. scholar and lectr. U. Adelaide, Australia, 1991—. Editor: Crops as Sources of Nutrients for Humans, 1984; co-editor: Micronutrients in Agriculture, 2d edit., 1989; contbr. over 185 rsch. articles and 55 rev. articles to profl. jours. Recipient Outstanding Scientist of Yr. award, USDA Agrl. Rsch. Svc., 2003. Fellow: Soil Sci. Soc. Am., Am. Soc. Agronomy (rsch. award N.E. br. 1992); mem.: AAAS, Am. Soc. Agronomy, Corp. Sci. Soc. Am., Am. Soc. Plant Physiologists, Masons (master 1984—85), Sigma Xi. Republican. Mem. United Ch. of Christ. Achievements include discovery that nickel is an essential element for all higher plants; discovery that zinc plays a role in maintaining the integrity of root-cell plasma membranes. E-mial. Home: 24 Hickory Cir Ithaca NY 14850-9673 Office: US Plant Soil & Nutrition Lab Tower Rd Ithaca NY 14853 Business E-mail: rmw1@cornell.edu.

**WELCH, STANTON,** performing company executive; b. Melbourne, Australia, Oct. 15, 1969; s. Garth Welch and Marilyn Jones. Studied at, San Francisco Ballet Sch. Dancer to soloist Australian Ballet, 1989, resident choreographer, 1995—2003; artistic dir. Houston Ballet, 2003—. Artistic assoc. Ballet Met, Columbus, Ohio. Choreographer (ballets) Maninyas, San Francisco Ballet, 1996, Taiko, 1999, Tutu, 2003, Falling, 2005, Plowbeard, Birmingham Royal Ballet, 1999, Ønsket, Royal Danish Ballet, 1998, Ander, 1999, Indigo, Houston Ballet, 1999, Bruiser, 2000, Tales of Texas, 2004, Blindness, 2004, Bolero, 2004, Nosotros, 2005, Clear, Am. Ballet Theatre, 2001, Evolution, BalletMet, Don Quixote, A Dance in the Garden of Mirth, 2000, Green, Moscow Dance Theatre, 2000, OPUS X, 2001; created

commissions for many of the world's best companies including American Ballet Theater, Houston Ballet, San Francisco Ballet, Royal Danish Ballet, Australian Ballet et al. Avocations: country music, country and western dancing. Office: Houston Ballet 1921 W Bell St Houston TX 77019*

**WELCH, W(ALTER) SCOTT, III,** lawyer; b. Jackson, Miss., Sept. 7, 1939; s. Walter Scott Jr. and Velma Lou (Hines) W.; m. Hermine McBee Copeland, Nov. 5, 1960 (div. Sept. 1981); children: Hermine, Walt; m. Mary Anne Kendrick, Dec. 6, 1981; children: Dennis, Kasi. BA cum laude, U. of South, 1961; LLB with distinction, U. Miss., 1964. Bar: Miss. 1964, U.S. Dist. Ct. (no. dist.) Miss. 1964, U.S. Dist. Ct. (so. dist.) Miss. 1967, U.S. Ct. Appeals 1968, U.S. Supreme Ct., 1970. Assoc. Welch, Gibbes & Graves, Attys., Laurel, Miss., 1964; chmn. litigation dept. Butler, Snow, O'Mara, Stevens & Cannada, Jackson, 2002—05, ptnr., 1967—2006; shareholder Baker, Donelson, Bearman, Caldwell & Berkowitz, PC, 2006—. Capt. USAF, 1964-67. Fellow Am. Coll. Trial Lawyers, Am. Bar Found., Found. Am. Bd. Trial Advs. (trustee 1999-2002, pres. 2001), Miss. Bar Found.; mem. ABA (ho. of del. 1994—, standing com. on public info. 1998-2000, 03-06, state del., nominating com. 2000-06, faculty tips trial acad., 2003, bd. govs. 2006—), Am. Bd. Trial Advs. (nat. dir. 1992—, local pres. 1987, v.p. 1999, pres.-elect 2000, nat. pres. 2001), Internat. Assn. Def. Counsel (faculty def. counsel trial acad. 1997), Miss. Def. Lawyers (past bd. dirs.), Miss. State Bar Assn. (commr. 1989-95, exec. com. 1991-92, pres.-elect 1993-94, pres. 1994-95, disting. svc. award 2004), Hinds County Bar Assn. (pres. 1979-80, Best Lawyers in Am.). Home: 6223 Waterford Dr Jackson MS 39211-2910 Office: PO Box 14167 Jackson MS 39236-4167 Office Phone: 601-351-2440. Business E-mail: swelch@bakerdonelson.com.

**WELD, BILL (WILLIAM FLOYD WELD),** lawyer, former governor; b. Smithtown, N.Y., July 31, 1945; s. David and Mary Blake (Nichols) W.; m. Susan Roosevelt (div. 2002), June 7, 1975; children: David Minot, Ethel Derby, Mary Blake, Quentin Roosevelt, Frances Wylie; m. Leslie Marshall, June 14, 2003 AB summa cum laude, Harvard U., 1966, JD cum laude, 1970; diploma with distinction, Oxford U., Eng., 1967. Bar: Mass. 1970. Law clk. to Hon. R.A. Cutter, Supreme Jud. Ct. Mass., 1970-71; ptnr. firm Hill & Barlow, Boston, 1971-81; assoc. minority counsel U.S. Ho. of Reps. Judiciary Com. Impeachment Inquiry, Washington, 1973-74; U.S. atty. (Dist. Mass.) US Dept. Justice, Boston, 1981-86, asst. atty. gen., criminal divsn. Washington, 1986-88; sr. ptnr. Hale & Dorr, Boston, Washington, 1988-90; gov. Commonwealth of Mass., Boston, 1991—97; ptnr. McDermott, Will & Emery LLP, N.Y.C. and Boston, 1997—2005; CEO Decker Coll., Louisville, 2005; prin. Leeds Weld & Co., NYC, 2000—06. Author: Mackerel by Moonlight, 1988, Big Ugly, 1999, Stillwater, 2002; actor: (films) Traffic, 2000. Republican nominee for atty. gen., Mass., 1978. Republican.*

**WELD, JONATHAN MINOT,** lawyer; b. Greenwich, Conn., Feb. 25, 1941; s. Alfred White and Sally (Duggan) W.; m. Jane Paige, June 19, 1965; children: Elizabeth, Eric. AB in History cum laude, Harvard U., 1963; JD, Cornell U., 1967. Bar: NY 1967, U.S. Ct. Appeals (2d cir.) 1969, U.S. Dist. Ct. (ea. and so. dists.) NY 1970. Assoc. Shearman & Sterling, NYC, 1967-75, ptnr., 1976—2004, London, 1982-85, of counsel, 2005—. Bd. dirs. Bank of N.S. Internat.; chmn., bd. dirs. The Evergreens, Bklyn. Hosp. Bd. dirs. St. Ann's Sch., Bklyn. Bot. Garden, NY Presbyn. Healthcare Sys.; former bd. dirs. Bklyn. Home for Children, Harvard Coll. Fund, Winant and Clayton Vols. Mem.: ABA, NY State Bar Assn. Office: 599 Lexington Ave Fl C2 New York NY 10022-6030 Office Phone: 212-848-8075. Business E-mail: jweld@shearman.com

**WELDER, RACHAEL MAE,** mathematician, educator; d. Larry and Mary Hatzenbuhler; m. Sean Welder, May 26, 2001. MS in Math., U. ND, 2003; postgrad., Mont. State U., 2003—. Cert. secondary edn. tchr. ND. Grad. tchg. asst. U. ND, Grand Forks, 2001—03; grad. tchg. asst., instr. Mont. State U., Bozeman, 2003—. Activist People for the Ethical Treatment of Animals, Bozeman, 2000—06. Scholar, ND U. Sys., 1997—2001, US Achievement Acad., 2000, AAUW. Mem.: Am. Math. Soc. Democrat. Achievements include research in prerequisite knowledge for learning of algebra. Avocations: volunteering at local animal shelter, travel, reading. Office: Mont State Univ Dept Math PO Box 172400 Bozeman MT 59717-2400

**WELDON, CHARLES JAUVERN,** actor; b. Wetumka, Okla., June 1, 1940; s. Roosevelt and Beatrice (Jennings) W.; m. Debbi Morgan, 1979 (div.) 1984; children: Charles Jr., Barbara Rae, Nick Alonzo. Actor, dir. Negro Ensemble Co., N.Y.C., 1970-94; pres. Alumni of Negro Ensemble Co., N.Y.C., 1995-97. Featured in films Malcolm X, Stir Crazy, 1981, Fast Walking, A Woman Called Moses, 1978, The River Niger, Serpico, Rooster Cogburn, Drop Squad, Love Bazarr; (TVappearances) NY Undercover, Another World, LA Law, Law and Order, The Atlanta Child Murders, Hill St. Blues, Roots: The Next Generation, 1979, Another Woman's Child, All My Children, Sanford and Son, Kojak, Police Story, Streets of San Francisco, DA's Investigator; (Broadway/NY theatre) The River Niger, 1972, Big Time Buck White, Salaam Huey Salaam, Little Tommy Parker, Jonquil, Raisin in the Sun, Colored Peoples Time, The Great Macdaddy, The Brownsville Raid, Perry's Mission, Pillhill, Fences, Birdie Blue, 2005, Seven Guitars, 2006; (regional theatre) King Lear, Canterbury Tales, Fences, Two Trains Running, Ma Rainey's Black Bottom, Coming of the Hurricane, Much Ado About Nothing, King Henry VI Part 1, Saint Joan, Born a Unicorn, Are You Now...Or Have You Ever Been?, Soldier's Play, The Secret Place, Hair, Taming of the Shrew.*

**WELDON, CURT (WAYNE CURTIS WELDON),** congressman; b. Marcus Hook, Pa., July 22, 1947; m. Mary Gallagher; children: Karen, Kristin, Kimberly, Curt, Andrew. BA in Humanities, West Chester U., 1969; AAS in Fire Sci., Del. County CC, Media, Pa., 1972; state instrn. cert. Cheyney State Coll.; postgraduate student, Cabrini Coll., Temple U., St. Joseph's U. Lic. tchr. Pa. Tchr. to head tchr. Walnut St. Sch., Darby-Colwyn-William Penn Sch. Dist., Pa., 1972-76; dir. tng. and manpower devel. CIGNA (INA Corpn.), Del. County, 1976-87; mayor Marcus Hook, Pa., 1977-81; mem. Coun., Del. County, 1981-87, vice-chmn. to chmn., 1984-87; mem. US Congress from 7th Pa. dist., 1987—, mem. sci. com., vice chmn. armed svcs. com., chmn. tactical air and land forces subcommittee. Asst. dir. Elem. Secondary Edn. Act Title I Prog., 1972-76; environ. specialist Project KARE, 1972-76; chmn. R&D Ho. Nat. Security Com. Readiness; mem. Com. on Sci. Energy and Environ. Tech.; co-chmn. Congl. Fire Svcs. Caucus, Globe Ocean Protection Task Force, Congl. Missile Def. Caucus, US-FSU Energy Caucus. Named Man of Yr. Chester Bus. and Profl. Assn., Most Effective Freshman Legislator Am. Security Coun., Citizen of Yr. Del. County C. of C., Clean Air Champion Sierra Club, Man of Yr. Internat. Soc. Fire Protection Engrs., 1988, Taxpayers Hero Citizen's Against Government Waste; recipient Outstanding Govt. Leadership award Nat. Recycling Coalition, Fed. Legis. award Pa. Dirs. Assn. Cmty. Action Agencies, Spirit of Enterprise award US C. of C., Golden Bulldog Watchdogs of Treasury award. Republican. Office: US Ho Reps 2466 Rayburn Ho Office Bldg Washington DC 20515-0001 Office Phone: 202-225-2011.*

**WELDON, DAVID JOSEPH, JR.,** congressman, physician; b. Amityville, N.Y., Aug. 31, 1953; s. David Joseph and Anna Weldon; m. Nancy Sourbeck, Aug. 18, 1979; children: Kathryn, David. BS, SUNY, Stony Brook, 1978; MD, SUNY, Buffalo, 1981. Intern Letterman Army Med. Ctr., 1981-82, resident in internal medicine, 1982-84; pvt. practice, Melbourne Internal Medical Assoc., 1987—94; mem. U.S. Congress from 15th Fla. dist., Washington, 1995—; mem. appropriations com. Fellow ACP; mem. AMA, Fla. Med. Assn Republican. Office: US Ho of Reps 2347 Rayburn Ho Office Bldg Washington DC 20515-0915

**WELDON, IRENE ELIZABETH,** music educator; b. Portland, Oreg., Mar. 20, 1953; d. Herbert Weldon Butt and Olive Naylor; children: Alicia Marie Bowers, Rachel Kathleen Bowers. BA, So. Oreg. U., 1988; MS in Tchg. Music, Portland State U., 1998. Organist, choir dir. Laurelhurst Presbyn. Ch., Portland, 1998—2000; piano tchr. Chordination Piano Sch., Lake Oswego,

Oreg., 1999—2004; cantor Grace Meml. Episcopal Ch., Portland, 2000—05; voice instr. Warner Pacific Coll., Portland, 2002—. Singer (recital performer, ch. soloist); singer: (mem.) Trinity Chamber Singers, Portland Baroque Chorus, Portland Symphonic Choir, Bach Cantata Choir; singer: (solo engagements include) Vivaldi's Gloria with Portland Symphonic Choir, Purcell's Dido and Aeneas with Portland Baroque Orch., Handel's Israel in Egypt with Trinity Consort. Mem.: Oreg. Music Tchrs. Assn. (assoc.), Nat. Assn. Tchrs. of Singing (assoc.). Democrat. Episcopalian. Avocations: hiking, travel, gardening, theater, cooking.

**WELDON, JEFFREY ALAN,** lawyer; b. Billings, Mont., May 6, 1963; s. Richard Allen and Monica (Michaud) Weldon; m. Leslie Helen Boileau, July 7, 1990; 2 children. BA, U. Mont., 1986, MPA, 1994, JD, 1996. State senator, Mont., 1993-97; assoc. atty. Moulton Bellingham, Longo & Mather, P.C., Billings, Mont., 1997-2000; chief legal counsel Office of Pub. Instrn., State of Mont., Helena, 2000—03; legal counsel, human resources dir. Billings Pub. Schs., 2003—04; assoc. atty. Felt, Martin, Frazier, Jacobs & Rapkoch, PC, Billings, 2005—. Office Phone: 406-248-7646. E-mail: jweldon@feltmartinlaw.com.

**WELDON, THEODORE TEFFT, JR.,** manufacturing executive; b. Evanston, Ill., July 19, 1932; s. Theodore Tefft and Dorothe Galbraith (Stover) Weldon; m. Barbara Ann Eskilson, Aug. 17, 1957; children: Lisa Courtney Weldon LeFevre, Theodore Tefft III, Margaret Helen Weldon Wickstrom. BA, Dartmouth Coll., 1954. Retail store salesman Sears Roebuck & Co., Gary, Ind., 1954-58, retail advt. mgr. Kankakee, Ill., 1958-62, sales mgr. Craftsman Chgo., 1962-69, advt. mgr. Craftsman, 1969-70, mktg. mgr. tires, 1970-81, sr. buyer sporting goods, 1981-82, nat. gen. catalog mgr., 1982-86; dir. home TV shopping Sears/QVC, Chgo., 1986-92. Cons. Drake, Beam, Morin, Inc., Chgo., 1992-94, Focus Media, Inc., L.A., 1993-96, Std. Mktg. Corp., Naperville, Ill., 1993-98, King World Direct, L.A., 1993-97, Guthy-Renker, Las Vegas, 1997-98, Sears Roebuck and Co., 1997-2000, Ovation Group, Atlanta, 1997-2003, Home Depot, 1997-98, Kmart, 1997-98, Walmart, 1997-98, Pearle Vision, 1998, 3M, 1998, Tyee, Portland, Oreg., 1998-2000, Target Stores, 1998, Panasonic 1997-2000; v.p. mktg. Link Tools Internat., USA, 1998-2006, Content = Commerce Inc., 2001-03, pres. Weldon & Weldon, 1990-2005, pres. Weldon et Fille, 1996-, pres. Weldon & Son, 1998-. Mem. Jr. Achievemnt. Chgo., 1966-68; rep. Winnetka (Ill.) Village Caucus, 1972-74; advisor Children's Theatre of Winnetka, 1972—; pres. Sunset Improvement Assn., Winnetka, 1975—. Avocations: travel, theater, swimming, bicycling, golf. Home and Office: 426 Sunset Rd Winnetka IL 60093-4232

**WELDON, THÉRÈSE HEMLER,** secondary school educator, art educator; b. Washington; d. Edward Francis and Kaye Hemler; children: Samantha, Benjamin. BS, Kutztown U., Pa., 1971, MEd, 1973. Tchr. art Chesterfield (Va.) County Schs., 1974—. Illustrator: Me, Too, 1990. Mem.: NEA, Nat. Art Edn. Assn. Home: 1200 Salisbury Dr Midlothian VA 23113 Office: Matoaca High School 17700 Longhouse Ln Chesterfield VA 23838-6000

**WELDON, VIRGINIA V.,** retired food products executive, retired pediatrician; b. Toronto, Sept. 8, 1935; arrived in US, 1937; d. John Edward and Carolyn Edith (Swift) Vernal; children: Ann Weldon Doyle, Susan Weldon Erlinger. AB cum laude, Smith Coll., 1957; MD, SUNY-Buffalo, 1962; LHD (hon.), Rush U., 1985. Diplomate Am. Bd. Pediatrics, Am. Bd. Pediatric Endocrinology and Metabolism, Nat. Bd. Med. Examiners (bd. dirs. 1987-89). Intern Johns Hopkins Hosp., Balt., 1962-63, resident in pediatrics, 1963-64; fellow pediatric endocrinology Johns Hopkins U., Balt., 1964-67, instr. pediatrics, 1967-68; from instr. to assoc. prof. Washington U., St. Louis, 1968—79, prof., 1979-89, v.p. Med. Ctr., 1980-89, dep. vice chancellor med. affairs, 1983-89, dir. Ctr. Study Am. Bus., 1998-99; v.p. sci. affairs Monsanto Co., St. Louis, 1989, v.p. pub. policy, 1989-93, sr. v.p. pub. policy, 1993-98. Mem. gen. clin. rsch. ctrs. adv. com. NIH, Bethesda, Md., 1976—80, mem. rsch. resources adv. coun., 1980—84; advisor, dir. Monsanto Co., 1989—98. Contbr. articles to sci. jours. Mem. risk assessment mgmt. commn. EPA, 1992—97; commn. St. Louis Zool. Pk., 1983—92; mem. Pres.'s Com. Advisors Sci. and Tech., 1994—2000; trustee Calif. Inst. Tech., 1996—, Whitaker Found., 1997—99, St. Louis Sci. Ctr.; bd. dirs., vice chmn., chmn. St. Louis Symphony Orch., 1993—2005, hon. trustee, 2005—; bd. dirs. United Way Greater St. Louis, 1978—90, St. Louis Regional Health Care Corp., 1995—04; mem. adv. com. on agrl. biotech. USDA, 2000—01. Fellow: AAAS, Am. Acad. Pediat.; mem.: St. Louis Med. Soc., Soc. Pediat. Rsch., Endocrine Soc., Am. Pediat. Soc., Assn. Am. Med. Colls. (disting. svc. mem., del., chmn. coun. acad. socs. 1984—85, chmn. assembly 1985—86), Nat. Acads. (nat. assoc.), Inst. Medicine, Equestrian Order of Holy Sepulchre, Alpha Omega Alpha, Sigma Xi. Roman Catholic. Home: 242 Carlyle Lake Dr Saint Louis MO 63141-7544

**WELDON, WILLIAM C.,** pharmaceutical executive; b. Bklyn., Nov. 26, 1948; m. Barbara Weldon; 2 children. BS in biology, Quinnipiac U., 1971. With sales and mktg. McNeil Pharm. Johnson & Johnson, 1971—82; mgr. ICOM Regional Develop. Ctr., 1982—84; v.p. mng. dir. Korea Mcneal Ltd., 1984—86; mng. dir. Ortho-Cilag Pharm., 1986—89; v.p. sales mktg. Janssen Pharm., 1989—92; pres. Ethicon Endo-Surgery, 1992, group chmn., 1995, chmn., pharm. group, 1998; vice-chmn., bd. dirs. Johnson & Johnson, New Brunswick, NJ, 2001—02, chmn., 2002—, CEO, 2002—. Mem. Bus. Coun., Bus. Roundtable; bd. dirs., exec. com. mem., chmn. Pharm. Rsch. and Manufacturers of Am.; bd. mem. JP Morgan Chase; chmn. Pharm. Rsch. and Mfr., 2005—. Serves Liberty Sci. Center Chmn.'s Adv. Coun.; mem. Sullivan Commn. on Diversity in the Healthcare Workforce; trustee Quinnipiac Univ. Avocation: basketball. Office: Johnson & Johnson 1 Johnson & Johnson Plaza New Brunswick NJ 08933

**WELDON, WILLIAM FORREST,** electrical and mechanical engineer, educator; b. San Marcos, Tex., Jan. 12, 1945; s. Forrest Jackson and Rubie Mae (Wilson) W.; m. Morey Shepard McGonigle, July 28, 1968; children: William Embree, Seth Forrest. BS in Engring. Sci., Trinity U., San Antonio, 1967; MME, U. Tex., Austin, 1970. Registered prof. engr. Tex. Engr. Cameron Iron Works, Houston, 1967-68; project engr. Glastron Boat Co., Austin, Tex., 1970-72; chief engr. Nalle Plastics Co., Austin, 1972-73; rsch. engr. U. Tex., Austin, 1973-77, dir. Ctr. Electromechanics, 1977-85, dir. Ctr. Electromechanics, 1985-93, prof., 1985-2000, Josey Centennial prof. in energy resources, 1992-2000, Josey Centennial prof. emeritus, 2000—. Mem. permanent com. Symposium on Electromagnetic Launch Tech., Naval Rsch. Adv. Com., 1992-97, 2001-05, vice-chmn. 1995-98; cons. numerous cos. and govts., 1973—; chief scientist Office Naval Rsch.-Europe, 1998-99; tech. dir. Office Naval Rsch. Internat. Field Office, 1998-99. Contbr. articles to profl. jours. Bd. dirs Water Control and Improvement Dist. No. 10, Travis County, Tex., 1984—97. Recipient Peter Mark medal Electromagnetic Launch Symposium, 1986, IR 100 award Indsl. Rsch. mag., 1983, Navy Superior Pub. Svc. award, 1998, 99. Fellow ASME; mem. IEEE (sr.), NSPE. Achievements include patents in field. Personal E-mail: weldon@ctesc.net.

**WELEBER, RICHARD GORDON,** ophthalmologist, geneticist, medical educator, researcher; s. Frederick Joseph and Carolyn Ruth Weleber; m. Barbara Carolyn Berry, Apr. 6, 1968; children: Misha Gordon, Sasha Kristin. BS, Oreg. State U, Corvallis, Oreg., 1959—63; MD, Oreg. Health & Sci. U, Portland, Oreg., 1963—67; Rotating Internship, Mary Fletcher Hosp., U of Vt., Burlington, VT, 1967—68; fellowship in Genetics, Oreg. Health & Sci. U, Portland, Oreg., 1971—72, residency in Ophthalmology, 1972—75; fellowship in Genetics, U of Colo. Med. Ctr., Denver, Colo., 1975—76. Diplomate Am. Bd. of Ophthalmology, 1976, Diplomate, Clinical Genetics Am. Bd. of Med. Genetics, 1981, Founding Fellow Am. Coll. of Med. Genetics, 1993. Instr. in ophthalmology Oreg. Health & Sci. U, Portland, Oreg., 1976—82, assoc. prof. of ophthalmology and molecular and med. genetics, 1982—88, prof. of ophthalmology and molecular and med. genetics, 1988—. Dir. of visual electrophys. svc. Oreg. Health & Sci. U, Portland, Oreg., 1976—, dir. Oreg. retinal degeneration ctr., 1984—, dir. of cataract services, 1978—2002, dir., ophthalmic genetics svc., 1976—. Author 130 peer-rev. jour. articles, 27 book chapt., 115 sci. abstracts. Mem. sci. adv. bd.

Found. Fighting Blindness. Maj. US Army MC, 1968—71, Germany. Recipient Francheschetti Award and Lecture, Internat. Soc. for Genetic Eye Disease, 2001. Mem.: Internat. Soc. for Clin. Electrophys. of Vision (assoc.), sec. for the am., dir. of edn. 1998—2002). Avocations: classical music, sports, reading. Office: Casey Eye Inst 3375 SW Terwilliger Blvd Portland OR 97239-4197

**WELGE, DONALD EDWARD,** food manufacturing executive; b. St. Louis, July 11, 1935; s. William H. and Rudelle (Fritze) W.; m. Mary Alice Childers, Aug. 4, 1962; children: Robert, Tom. BS, La. State U., 1957. With Gilster-Mary Lee Corp., Chester, Ill., 1957—, pres. gen. mgr., 1965—. Dir. Buena Vista Bank of Chester; pres. Buena Vista Bankcorp. Former chmn. St. John's Luth. Bd. Edn. 1st lt. Transp. Corp, U.S. Army, 1958-63. Named So. Ill. Bus. Leader of Yr. So. Ill. U., 1988. Mem. Perryville C. of C. (pres. 1989), Chester, Ill. C. of C. (past pres.), Alpha Zeta, Phi Kappa Phi. Republican. Lutheran. Home: 5 Knollwood Dr Chester IL 62233-1416 Office: Gilster Mary Lee Co PO Box 227 Chester IL 62233-0227

**WELGE, JACK HERMAN, JR.,** lawyer; b. Austin, Tex., Sept. 12, 1951; s. Jack Herman and Regina Victoria (Hunger) W.; m. Frances Ava Roddy Avent, Dec. 23, 1977; children: Kirsten Frances Page Welge, Kathleen Ava Regina Welge. BA, U. Tex., 1974; JD, St. Mary's U., 1977. Bar: Tex. 1977, U.S. Dist. Ct. (ea. dist.) Tex. 1979, U.S. Dist. Ct. (no. dist.) Tex. 1982, U.S. Ct. Appeals (5th cir.) 1983, U.S. Supreme Ct., 1984; cert. family law Tex. Bd. Legal Specialization 1984. Asst. dist. atty. Gregg County Criminal Dist. Atty., Longview, Tex., 1978-79; assoc. Law Office of G. Brockett Irwin, Longview, 1979-81; judge Mcpl. Ct. of Record, Longview, 1979-81; ptnr. Adams & Sheppard, Longview, 1981-83; pvt. practice, 1983—; mediation practice, 2005—. Of counsel East Tex. Assn. for Abused Families, Longview, 1985-90. Co-chair profl. divsn. Gregg County United Way, 1996—97; mem. bail bond bd. Gregg County, Tex., 2006—; mem. vestry Trinity Episcopal Ch., Longview, 1993—96, 2001—04; bd. directors Longview Cmty. Theater, 1979—82, East Tex. Coun. on Alcoholism and Drug Abuse, Longview, 1981—83, East Tex. Assn. for Abused Families, Longview, 1983—85, Longview Mus. and Arts Ctr., 1991—94; bd. directors adv. com. Salvation Army, 1991—, chmn., 1997; mem. sch. bd. Trinity Sch. of Tex., 2001—04. Mem.: Tex. Acad. Family Law Specialists, Gregg County Bar Assn. (pres. 1983), N.E. Tex. Bar Assn., State Bar of Tex. (pro bono coll., contested custody case panel, protective case panel, Gregg County lawyers pro bono project, Outstanding Contbn. award 1990, Disting. Svc. award 1993, Outstanding Pro Bono Atty. 1994, Disting. Svc. award 1995, Outstanding Pro Bono Atty. 1997), East Tex. Knife and Fork Club (pres. 1983—84), Rotary (pres. Longview Club 1987—88, Paul Harris fellow 1982, 27 Yrs. Perfect Attendance 2003, IFFR fellowship 2006—), Shriners, Scottish Rite (25 yr. pin), Mason, Delta Upsilon (Tex. chpt. found. bd. 1974—78), Delta Theta Phi (dean 1977, Bickett Senate). Office: 413-415 S Green St PO Box 3624 Longview TX 75606-3624 Office Phone: 903-753-5683. Personal E-mail: welgjhjr@hotmail.com.

**WELINSKY, HOWARD STEVEN,** film distribution executive; b. Hollywood, Calif., Dec. 14, 1949; s. Jack and Molly (Peskin) W. BA in Polit. Sci., UCLA, 1972. Sales analyst Warner Bros. Distbn. Corp., Burbank, Calif., 1973-78, dir. br. ops., 1979-84, v.p. br. ops., 1984-88, v.p. adminstrn., 1988—. Chmn. Culver City (Calif.) Human Svcs. and Pks. Commn., 1974-80; bd. dirs. L.A. met. br. Jewish Fedn. Coun., 1989—; active Calif. Dem. State Com., 1975—, L.A. County Dem. Cen. Com., 1990—. Mem. First Entertainment Credit Union (bd. dirs. 1989—), UCLA Alumni Assn. (v.p. 1989—). Office: Warner Bros Distbn Corp 4000 Warner Blvd Burbank CA 91522-0002

**WELIVER, EVELYN RUTH,** academic librarian; b. Meadville, Pa., June 30, 1944; d. H.D.L. and Phyllis A. (Irons) VanBockern; m. E. Delmer Weliver, Sept. 6, 1964; children: Phyllis, Wraight. BS, Cen. Mich. U., 1977, MA, 1981. High sch. librarian St. Francis High Sch., Traverse City, Mich., 1978-79; jr., sr. high sch. librarian Benzie Cen., Benzonia, Mich., 1979-81; acad. librarian Interlochen (Mich.) Ctr. for the Arts, 1984—. Mem. adv. bd. Regional Ednl. Media Ctr., Traverse City, 1978-81, 84—. Mem. Am. Library Assn., Mich. Assn. Media in Edn. (chairperson region 2 and 3, 1988-89). Avocations: walking, travel.

**WELK, RICHARD ANDREW,** plastic surgeon; b. Aug. 9, 1956; BS, U. Mich., 1977, MD, 1981. Diplomate Am. Bd. Surgery, Am. Bd. Plastic Surgery. Resident gen. surgery, Grand Rapids, Mich., 1981-86; resident plastic surgery U. Calif., Irvine, 1986-88; plastic surgeon pvt. practice, Kirkland, Wash., 1988-91, Polyclinic, Seattle, 1991—. Mem. Am. Soc. Plastic & Reconstructive Surgery, Am. Soc. Aesthetic Plastic Surgery, Wash. State Med. Assn., Wash. Soc. Plastic Surgeons (pres. 1995-96). Office: Polyclinic 1145 Broadway Seattle WA 98122-4299 Office Phone: 206-860-2317.

**WELK, THOMAS JOHN,** lawyer; b. Hoven, S.D., Aug. 12, 1950; s. Al John and Monica Rose (Coyle) W.; m. Genevieve T. Welk, 1975; children: Colleen, David, Kathleen. BS in Econs. with honors, U. S.D., 1972, MBA, JD, 1975. Bar: S.D. 1975, U.S. Dist. Ct. S.D. 1967, U.S. Ct. Appeals (8th cir.) 1977, U.S. Ct. Appeals (9th cir.) 1987, U.S. Tax Ct. 1981, U.S. Supreme Ct. 1981; bd. cert. civil advocacy Nat. Bd. Trial Advocacy 1995. Asst. atty. gen. State of S.D., Pierre, 1975-79, dep. atty. gen., 1979; ptnr. Boyce, Greenfield, Pashby & Welk, LLP (formerly Boyce, Murphy, McDowell & Greenfield) Sioux Falls, SD, 1979—. Mem. ABA (mem. adminstrv. law, antitrust sect.), SD Bar Assn. (chmn., numerous comms., pres. 2004-05), Am. Bd. Trial Advs., Internat. Assn. Def. Counsel, SD Def. Lawyers Assn. (past pres., leadership award Def. Rsch. Inst.), Westward House Country Club (pres.). Republican. Roman Catholic. Avocations: golf, hunting, travel. Office: Boyce Greenfield, Pashby & Welk LLP 101 N Phillips Ave Ste 600 PO Box 5015 Sioux Falls SD 57117-5015 Office Phone: 605-336-2424. Office Fax: 605-334-0618. Business E-Mail: tjwelk@bgpw.com.

**WELKER, JAMES ANTHONY,** physician; b. Pitts., Oct. 27, 1969; s. James Edward and Janet Rachael Welker. BS, Ohio No. U., 1991; DO, Phila. Coll. Osteo. Medicine, 1995. Diplomate Am. Bd. Internal Medicine, cert. physician investigator. Intern U. Medicine and Dentistry N.J., Stafford, 1995-96; resident in internal medicine Washington Hosp., 1996-99; dir. hospitalist sect. Harbor Hosp. Ctr., Balt., 1999—2004; dir. hospitalist residency Franklin Square Hosp., Balt., 2004—, dir. Clin. Trial Rsch. Ctr., 2004—; asst. prof. medicine U. Md. Sch. Medicine. Cons., software developer Med. Info. Sys.; founding ptnr. real estate investment co.; prin. investigator multi-instnl. clin. trials; mem. faculty Med. Sch., U. Md., 2005—; expert witness in med. malpractice; spkr. in field. Contbr. articles to profl. jours. Vol. physician Mobile Med. Care, Rockville, 1997-99; ref. for peer-reviewed jours. Recipient numerous honors and awards. Roman Catholic. Avocations: exercising, outdoors. Office: Franklin Sq Hosp 9000 Franklin Sq Dr Baltimore MD 21237 Office Phone: 443-777-7706. Personal E-mail: jimwelker@hotmail.com.

**WELKOWITZ, WALTER,** biomedical engineer, educator; b. Bklyn., Aug. 3, 1926; s. Samuel and Shirley (Rosenblum) W.; m. Joan Horowitz, June 17, 1951; children: David, Lawrence, Julie. BS, The Cooper Union, N.Y.C., 1948; MS, U. Ill., 1949, PhD, 1954. Prof. engr., N.J. Rsch. assoc. U. Ill., Urbana, 1948-54, Columbia U., N.Y.C., 1954-55; asst. to pres., gen. mgr. Gulton Industries, Inc., Metuchen, NJ, 1955-64; prof., chmn. elec. engring Rutgers U., Piscataway, NJ, 1964-86, prof. biomed. engring., 1986—, chmn. biomedical engring., 1986-90. Cons. Gulton Industries, Metuchen, N.J., 1964-74. Author: Engineering Hemodynamics: Application to Cardiac Assist Devices, 1977, 2d edit., 1987; co-author: Biomedical Instruments: Theory and Design, 1976, 2d edit., 1992; author numerous chpts. in books; contbr. more than 100 articles to profl. jours. With U.S. Navy, 1944-46. Rutgers U. Rsch. Coun. fellow, 1974-75; recipient Centennial medal IEEE, 1984, Excellence in Rsch. award Rutgers Bd. Trustees, 1985, IEEE Career Achievement award Soc. Engring. Med. Biology, 1991; Llewellyn Thomas vis. prof. U. Toronto, Can., 1989. Fellow IEEE (engring. in medicine and biol. soc. career achievement

award 1991), N.Y. Acad. Medicine, Am. Inst. of Medicine and Biol. Engring. Achievements include 26 patents for Electron Tube, Ultrasonic Flowmeter, Ultrasonic Transducer, Piezoelectric Heart Assist Apparatus, Method and Apparatus for Non-Invasive Monitoring Dynamic Cardiac Performance, and others. Home: PO Box 2289 Lenox MA 01240-5289 Office: Rutgers U Biomed Engring PO Box 909 Piscataway NJ 08855-0909 Office Phone: 413-637-8267. Personal E-mail: wwelkowitz@msn.com.

**WELL, IRWIN,** language educator; b. Cin., Apr. 16, 1928; s. Sidney and Florence (Levy) Well; m. Vivian Max, Dec. 27, 1950; children: Martin, Alice, Daniel. BA, U. Chgo., 1948, MA, 1951; PhD, Harvard U., 1960; D (hon.), Nevsky Inst., Petersburg, Russia, 1999. Tchg. fellow Harvard U., Cambridge, Mass., 1955-58; asst. prof. Brandeis U., Waltham, Mass., 1958-65; assoc. prof. Northwestern U., Evanston, Ill., 1966-70, prof. Russian, Russian Lit., 1970—. Pres., bd. dirs. Am. Coun. Tchrs. Russian, Washington, 1967—. Author: numerous books in field; contbr. articles to scholarly jours. Recipient Pushkin medal, Internat. Assn. Russian Profs. Jewish. Avocations: music, singing. Office: Northwestern U Slavic Dept Evanston IL 60208-2163 Office Phone: 847-491-8254. Business E-Mail: i-weil@northwestern.edu.

**WELLBERG, EDWARD LOUIS, JR.,** insurance company executive; b. Eagle Pass, Tex., June 5, 1945; s. Edward L. Wellberg and Nell L. (Kownslar) Walker; children: Elizabeth, Ashley, Jennifer; m. Yvonne Hill, Feb. 4, 1989. Student, St. Mary's U., San Antonio, 1978. CLU, Life Underwriters Tng. Coun. Fellow. Sales agt. Washington Nat. Ins. Co., San Antonio, 1969-82; ptnr. Mazur Bennett Wellberg Assocs., San Antonio, 1982-91; mktg. exec. Wellberg Assocs., San Antonio, 1991—. Bd. dirs. Tex. State Ins. Bd. Adv. Coun., Austin, 1988-94. Contbr. articles to profl. jours. Mem. Am. Soc. CLU's, Tex. Assn. Ins. and Fin. Advisors (bd. dirs. 1983-86, 92-93, pres. 1996, state nat. com. 1997-2000), Tex. Life Underwriters Polit. Action Com. (vice chmn. 1981-83, 88-90, chmn. 1990-92, state nat. committeeman 1997-2000), San Antonio Assn. Ins. and Fin. Advisors (pres. 1982). Home: 1746 Santa Fe Trail San Antonio TX 78232 Office: 14400 Northbrook Dr Ste 200 San Antonio TX 78232-5038 Office Phone: 210-490-1188. Personal E-mail: ed@wellberg.net.

**WELLBORN, CHARLES IVEY,** information technology consultant; b. Houston, Dec. 9, 1941; s. Fred W. and Emily R. (Gladu) W.; m. JD McCausland, Aug. 14, 1965; children: Westly O., Kerry S. Phillips. BA in Econs., U. N.Mex., 1963, JD, 1966; LLM, NYU, 1972. Bar: N.Mex. 1966, U.S. Dist. Ct. N.Mex. 1966. Assoc. Neal & Matkins, Carlsbad, N.Mex., 1966-68, Robinson & Stevens, Albuquerque, 1969-71; ptnr. Schlenker, Parker, Payne & Wellborn, Albuquerque, 1971-76, Parker & Wellborn, Albuquerque, 1976-82, Modrall, Sperling, Roehl, Harris & Sisk, Albuquerque, 1982-95; pres., CEO Sci. & Tech. Corp. at U. N.Mex., Albuquerque, 1995-2000; pres. Wellborn Strategies LLC, Albuquerque, 2000—06. Chmn. N.Mex. Tax Rsch. Inst., 2002—06, N.Mex. Small Bus. Investment Corp., 2003—06. Vice chair U. N.Mex. Found., Inc., 1990—94; mem. Econ. Forum, 1986—2002, chmn., 1995—96; mem. City-County Unification Charter Commn., 2002—03; bd. dirs. N.Mex. Assn. Commerce and Industry, 2003—, N.Mex. Cmty. Capital, 2005—, N.Mex. Symphony Orch., 1988—91, U. N.Mex. Anderson Schs. Mgmt. Found., 1989—94, N.Mex. First, 1989—93, 2000—04, Accion N.Mex., 1995—97, Outpost Performance Space, 2000—04; private equity investment adv. com. N.Mex. State Investment Coun., 1991—98; mem. Govs. Prayer Breakfast Com., 1991—2002, chair, 2000—02; bd. dirs. Next Generation Economy Inc., 2002—, Sci. and Tech. Corp. at U. N.Mex., 2000—. Sgt. USAF, 1968—69, Korea. Mem.: ABA (ho. of dels. 1984—91), State Bar N.Mex. (pres. 1982—83), N.Mex. Bar Found. (pres. 1980—82), Albuquerque Bar Assn. (pres. 1977—78). Democrat. Roman Catholic. Office: Wellborn Strategies LLC 3819 La Hacienda Dr NE Albuquerque NM 87110-6115 Office Phone: 505-238-7890. E-mail: chuckwellborn@gmail.com.

**WELLBORN, MICHAEL,** county official; b. Carmel, Calif., Feb. 9, 1956; s. William C. and JoAnn Wellborn; m. Susan S. Wellborn; children: Scott, Heather. BS, U. Calif., Berkeley, Calif., 1978. Asst. mgr. Holubar Mktg., Phoenix, 1978—84; land use planner County Orange, Santa Ana, Calif., 1984—, mgr. water resources, 2000—02, zoning adminstrator, 2004—. Pres. bd. Calif. Watershed Network, 2004—; bd. dirs. Watershed Mgmt. Coun., Boise, Idaho, 2004—; co-chmn. land use com. Calif. Watershed Coun. Office: 300 N Flower St 3rd Fl Santa Ana CA 92703 Office Phone: 714-932-8689. Business E-Mail: michael@watershednetwork.org.

**WELLEIN, MARSHA DIANE AKAU,** military educator, director; d. George Herbert and Trude (Michelson) Akau; m. Daniel Navarro Atoigue; 1 child, Daniel Hokule'a; m. Lawrence Theodore Wellein (dec.); children: Geoffrey Michael, Nicholas Patrick. BA, U. Hawaii, 1966, tchg. cert., 1971; MEd, U. Guam, 1974; postgrad. in ednl. leadership, Argosy U., 2005. Instr. Hawaii Job Corps Ctr., 1969—71; tchr. spl. edn., reading, lang. arts, adults, pre-kindergarten to HS, U. Guam, 1972—80; reading specialist Waipahu Intermediate; instr. (full and part time) Leeward CC, U. Hawaii, 1981—85, instr. reading, 1983—85; full time guidance counselor US Army, Ft. Shafter Edn. Ctr., 1983—85, Larson Barracks, Germany, 1985—86, Dept. Army, Schofield Barracks, 1990; edn. svcs. officer, dir. Multinat. Force and Observers, North Camp, El Gorah, Sinai, Egypt, 1987—90; edn. svcs. officer Dept. Army, Soto Cano Air Base, Honduras, 1991—93, Ft. Kobbe, Panama, 1991—93; edn. svcs. specialist Dept. Army, Kuwait and Saudi Arabia (Desert Storm), 1993, Schofield Barracks Edn. Ctr. 25th Infantry, Hawaii, 1994—96, Camp Zama Edn. Ctr., Japan, 1996—98, 8th Army, Republic of Korea, 1998—99, Dept. Army, Ft. Shafter, 2000—01; dir. edn. and libr. svcs. US Army South, 1999—2000; svcs. and test control officer USAR, Honolulu, 2006—. Author: (juvenile hardback novel) The Endless Summer, An Adventure Story of Guam, 1976; editor: Kalihi Kids Can Communicate, 1976. Bd. mem. Internat. Reading Assn., 1972—80, pres. 1980; mem. Oahu Com. Children and Youth, Honolulu, 1969. Named Outstanding Edn. Svcs. Officer, Dir. Edn., USAR, 2003; recipient Multinat. Force and Observers medal, US State Dept., 1987—89, Achievement medal civilian svc., Kuwait, 1993, Japan, 1997, Comdr.'s award civilian svc., 1986, 1987, 1988, 1998, Cold War cert., Camp Zama, Japan, 1998, Equal Opportunity award, 1998, Unsung Heroes award, Dir. Army Edn., Hdqrs., Washington, 2005, Lamp Lighters award, USAR, 2005. Mem.: Coun. Coll. and Mil. Educators, Am. Assn. Adult and Continuing Edn. Avocations: travel, reading, theater. Home: 95-086 Waihonu Pl Mililani HI 96789 Office: HQ G1 US Army Res APIX-PE 1557 Pass St Honolulu HI 96819-2135 Office Phone: 988-984-8727. Office Fax: 808-438-1379. Personal E-mail: welleinmd@hotmail.com.

**WELLEN, ROBERT HOWARD,** lawyer; b. Jersey City, Aug. 19, 1946; s. Abraham Louis and Helen Rose (Krieger) W.; m. Anita Fass, June 16, 1968; children: Elizabeth, Judith Maria. BA, Yale Coll., 1968; JD, Yale U., 1971; LLM in Taxation, Georgetown U., 1975. Bar: Conn. 1971, D.C. 1972, Colo. 1982. Assoc. Fulbright & Jaworski, Washington, 1975-76, participating assoc., 1976-79, ptnr., 1979-93, Ivins, Phillips & Barker, Washington, 1993—. Adj. prof. law Georgetown U. Law Ctr., 1982-85. Contbr. articles to legal publs. Served to lt. JAGC, USNR, 1971-75. Mem. ABA (past asst. sec., past chmn. com. on corp. tax, sect. taxation, past supr. editor sect. taxation newsletter, vice chair law devel. com. on corp. tax), Fed. Bar Assn. (coun. taxation), Phi Beta Kappa. Jewish. Office: Ivins Phillips & Barker 1700 Pennsylvania Ave NW Ste 600 Washington DC 20006-4723 Office Phone: 202-662-3401. E-mail: rwellen@ipbtax.com.

**WELLER, CECIL EDDIE, JR.,** history professor; b. Tuscaloosa, Ala., Mar. 3, 1961; s. Cecil Eddie and Sarah Powell Weller; m. Lanetta Lyn Hollis, June 14, 1986; 1 child, Cecil Trey III. BA, Tex. Christian U., 1983, MA, 1986, PhD, 1994. Prof. history San Jacinto Coll. South, Houston, 1989—, dir. honors program, 1996—2005. Chmn. Gulf Coast Intercollegiate Honors Coun., Houston, 2001—02; co-chmn. 2-year coll. com. Nat. Collegiate Honors Coun., Ames, Iowa, 2004—06. Editor: (history reader) Our Legacy: Articles and Documents in American History, 1993; author: (biography) Joe T. Robinson: Always a Loyal Democrat, 1998; contbr. chapters to books. Chmn. Forest Bend Home Owners Assn., Friendswood, Tex., 1995—97;

deacon, Sunday sch. tchr.; ch. coun. Nassau Bay Bapt. Ch., Houston, 1989—. Recipient Ottis Locke Tchg. award, East Tex. Hist. Assn., 1994, NISOD Excellence award, Nat. Inst. of Staff and Orgnl. Devel., U. Tex., 1995, Mary Jon and J.P. Bryan Excellence in Edn. award, Tex. State Hist. Assn., 2003. Mem.: Southwestern Social Sciences Assn. (exec. coun. 2003—05, exec. com. 2005—), Southwestern Hist. Assn. (v.p., program chmn. 2001—04, pres. 2004—05), So. Hist. Assn., Tex. State Hist. Assn., Am. Hist. Assn., Phi Beta Kappa, Phi Alpha Theta. Home: 907 Timber Cove Dr Taylor Lake Village TX 77586 Office: San Jacinto Coll South 13735 Beamer Rd Houston TX 77089 Office Phone: 281-484-1900 3505. Office Fax: 281-929-4693. Personal E-mail: eddie.weller@sjcd.edu.

**WELLER, ELIZABETH BOGHOSSIAN,** child and adolescent psychiatrist; b. Aug. 7, 1949; m. Ronald A. Weller, Feb. 18, 1978; children: Andrew, Christine. BS, Am. U., Beirut, Lebanon, 1971, MD, 1975. Lic. psychiatrist, Lebanon, Mo., Ohio, Pa. Intern Barnes Hosp./Washington U., St. Louis, 1975-78; fellow U. Kans. Med. Ctr., Kansas City, 1978-79; asst. prof. psychiatry U. Kans. Med. Sch., Kansas City, 1979-85; chief child/adolescent psychiatry Ohio State U., Columbus, 1985-94, assoc. chair dept. psychiatry, 1994-96; prof. psychiatry and pediat. U. Pa., 1996—, chmn. dept. psychiatry child and adolescent psychiatry, 1996-99, vice chmn. dept. psychiatry, prof. psychiatry/pediatrics, 1996—. Fred Allen chair dept. psychiatry Children's Hosp. of Phila., med. dir. Child Guidance Ctr., 1996-99; pres. Am. Bd. Psychiatry and Neurology, 2004. Co-author: Psychiatric Disorders in Child/Adolescent, 1990, Current Perspectives on Major Depressive Disorders in Children, 1984, Children's Interview for Psychiatric Syndromes, 1999; Fellow APA, Am. Acad. Child/Adolescent Psychiatry; mem. AMA, ACP, World Fedn. for Mental Health, Soc. Biol. Psychiatry, Am. Bd. Psychiatry and Neurology (pres. 2004). Office: 3440 Market St Philadelphia PA 19104-4399 Office Phone: 215-590-7573. Business E-Mail: weller@email.chop.edu.

**WELLER, GERALD C.,** congressman; b. Streator, Ill., July 7, 1957; s. LaVern and Marilyn Weller; m. Zury Rios Sosa. Degree in Agriculture, U. Ill., 1979. Aide to U.S. Congerssman Tom Corcoran, 1977-78; aide to U.S. Sec. of Agriculture John R. Block, 1981-85; active family farm, 1985-88; mem. Ill. Ho. of Reps., 1987—93, U.S. Congress from 11th Ill. dist., 1995—; asst. majority whip; mem. ways and means com., 1996—; mem. Internat. Relations Com., 2003—. Rep. House Republican steering com.; mem. Newt Gingrich's policy com.; exec. com. NRCC, House Banking Com., House Veterans Affairs Com., House Transp. and Infrastructure Com. Mem. 1st Christian Ch. of Morris, Ill. Mem. Nat. Republican Legis. Assn. (nominated Legislator of Yr.). Republican. Office: US Ho Reps 1210 Longworth Ho Office Bldg Washington DC 20515-1311*

**WELLER, MARTHA RIHERD,** physics and astronomy professor, consultant; b. Charleston, SC, Oct. 20, 1952; d. Paul Markey and Martha Carroll Riherd; m. Robert Allen Weller, June 21, 1975; children: Rachel Weller Deaton, Robert Samuel, Rebecca Shelley. BA in Physics, Rice U., 1973; PhD in Physics, Calif. Inst. Tech., 1979. Rsch. physicist Naval Rsch. Lab., Washington, 1979—80; rsch. staff physicist rsch. assoc. Yale U., New Haven, 1980—87; asst. prof. physics Mid. Tenn. State U., Murfreesboro, Tenn., 1988—93, assoc. prof. physics, astronomy, 1993—98, prof. of physics, astronomy, 1998—. Com. mem. Brentwood 2020, Tenn., 1998—98; pres. Edmondson Elem. PTO, Brentwood, Tenn., 1995—96, Centennial H.S. Parent Tchr. Student Orgn., Franklin, Tenn., 1998—99; sch. bd. rep. Williamson County Bd. of Edn., Franklin, Tenn., 2002—. Mem.: Tenn. Acad. of Sci. (physics and astronomy editl. bd. 1991—, exec. bd. mem. 1995—97), Sigma Xi, Am. Assn. of Physics Tchrs., Am. Phys. Soc. Office: Mid Tenn State Univ PO Box 403 Murfreesboro TN 37132 Office Phone: 615-898-2792. Office Fax: 615-898-5303. E-mail: mweller@mtsu.edu.

**WELLER, MILTON WEBSTER,** wetland ecologist, educator; b. St. Louis, May 23, 1929; m. Doris Laverne Leach; 1 child, Mitchel Wayne. AA, Harris Jr. Coll., 1949; BA, U. Mo., 1951, MS, 1954, PhD, 1956. Instr. dept zoology U. Mo., Columbia, 1956-57; asst. prof. zoology Iowa State U., Ames, 1957-61, assoc. prof., 1961-67; asst.-in-charge wildlife and fish, 1967-74; prof., head fish and wildlife U. Minn., St. Paul, 1974-82; prof., Kleberg chair wildlife Tex. A&M U., College Station, 1982-94, prof. emeritus, 1995—. Dir. Nat. Audubon Soc., N.Y.C., 1987-92; mem. Environ. Steering Com., Tex. Utilities, Dallas, 1990-99; assoc. editor Wetlands, Ann Arbor, Mich., 1988-92. Editor: Waterfowl in Winter, 1988; author: Wetland Birds, 1999; Freshwater Marshes, 1994, 3rd edit.; contbr. chpts. to Wetland Creation & Restoration, 1989, Habitat Use By Breeding Waterfowl, 1992; contbr. articles to profl. jours. Recipient Lifetime Achievement award Soc. Wetland Sci., 1996, Aldo Leopold Meml. award The Wildlife Soc., 1997. Fellow AAAS, Am. Ornithologist Union. Achievements include rsch. in wetland dynamics in relation to wildlife populations and regional biodiversity, wetland restoration and creation, waterbird ecology and management. Office Phone: 830-257-1048.

**WELLER, PHILIP DOUGLAS,** lawyer; b. Richmond, Ind., May 5, 1948; s. Lawrence E. and Barbara Jean (Hughes) W.; m. Kathryn Jean Deucker, Apr. 3, 1971; 1 child, Leigh Rachel. Student, Ohio U., 1966-67; BS, Bowling Green State U., 1970; JD, Bates Coll. Law, 1975. Bar: Tex. 1975. Assoc. Vinson & Elkins, Houston, 1975-79, ptnr. Houston, Dallas, N.Y.C., 1980—, Baker, Brown, Sharman, Wise & Stephens, Houston, 1979-80. Speechwriter. Mem. ABA, ACMA, AARPI, ICSC, ULI, Am. Coll. Real Estate Lawyers, Tex. Bar Assn., Houston Bar Assn., Dallas Bar Assn., D.C. Bar Assn., Assn. Bar City N.Y. Office: 2300 First City Tower 1001 Fannin St Houston TX 77002-6760 Office Phone: 713-758-2242. Business E-Mail: pweller@velaw.com.

**WELLER, ROBERT N(ORMAN),** hotel executive; b. Harrisburg, Pa., Feb. 1, 1939; s. Charles Walter and Martha Ann (MacPherson) W.; m. Nancy M, Wood, June 21, 1975, (children); m. Wendi Elizabeth, Terric Lynn, Nikki Ann. BS, Cornell U., 1969. Mgr. Hall's Motor Transit Co., Harrisburg, 1961-65; market rsch. analyst Carrolls Devel. Corp., Syracuse, NY, 1970-72; asst. to pres. Econo-Travel Motor Hotel Corp., Norfolk, Va., 1972-74, dir. franchise sales, 1975, pres., dir., 1976-84, Econo-Travel Devel. Corp., Norfolk, 1977-84; pres. Internat. Data Bank Ltd., 1985-86; pres., dir. Econo Lodges of Am., 1986-90; group pres., exec. v.p. Choice Hotels Internat., Silver Spring, Md., 1990-91; with Hospitality Ventures, Virginia Beach, Va., 1991—93; pres. Super 8 Motels, Inc. divsn. Hospitality Franchise Systems, Parsippany, NJ, 1993—2001; group pres. hotel divsn. Cendant Corp., Parsippany, 2001—. Served in USMC, 1957-60. Home: 3027 Lynndale Rd Virginia Beach VA 23452-6233 Office: Cendant Hotel Group Inc One Sylvan Way Parsippany NJ 07054 Business E-Mail: bob.weller@cendant.com.

**WELLER, ROBERT STEPHEN,** anesthesiologist; b. Syracuse, NY, Feb. 1, 1955; s. Elizabeth W Stein and Ralph N Weller; m. Elizabeth A McGowan, Nov. 30, 1991; children: Erin E Power, Jeffrey M McGowan, Kevin P McGowan. MD summa cum laude, Northwestern U., Chgo., 1979. Asst. prof. of anesthesiology U. of Conn. Sch. of Medicine, Farmington, Conn., 1984—91, assoc. prof. of anesthesiology, 1991—97, Wake Forest U. Sch. of Medicine, Winston-Salem, NC, 1997—. Residency program dir. U. of Conn. Anesthesiology Dept., Farmington, Conn., 1986—96; cons. in anesthesiology Am. Bd. Anesthesiologists, 1984. Named Outstanding Tchr., Residents in Anesthesiology, 2001; recipient LB Arey award, Northwestern U. Sch. of Medicine, 1977, FK Rawson award, 1979, David Little award, Hartford Hosp. Anesthesiology Program, 1983. Mem.: Internat. Anesthesia Rsch. Soc., Am. Soc. of Regional Anesthesia and Pain Medicine, Am. Soc. of Anesthesiologists. Office: Wake Forest University School of Med Medical Center Blvd Winston Salem NC 27157 Office Phone: 336-716-7150. Personal E-mail: rweller@triad.rr.com. E-mail: rweller@wfubmc.edu.

**WELLER, SOL WILLIAM,** chemical engineering professor; b. Detroit, July 27, 1918; s. Ira and Bessie (Wieselthier) W.; m. Miriam Damick, June 11, 1943; children: Judith, Susan, Robert, Ira BS, Wayne State U., 1938; PhD, U. Chgo., 1941. Asst. chief coal hydrogenation U.S. Bur. Mines, Pitts., 1945-50;

head fundamental rsch. Houdry Process Corp., Linwood, Pa., 1950-58; mgr. propulsion rsch. Ford Aeronutronic Co., Newport Beach, Calif., 1958-61; dir. chem. lab. and materials rsch. lab. Philco-Ford Co., Newport Beach, 1961-65; prof. chem. engring. SUNY-Buffalo, 1965—; emeritus, 1989; C.C. Furnas prof. SUNY-Buffalo, 1983—. Vis. fellow Oxford U., 1989. Author numerous sci. papers, book chpts., ency. entries Fulbright lectr. Madrid, 1975, Istanbul, 1980; recipient Chancellor's Tchg. award SUNY, 1973. Mem. ASTM (founder com. D32 on catalysts), Am. Chem. Soc. (chmn. Orange County sect. 1964, H.H. Storch award 1981, E.V. Murphree award 1982, Schoellkopf medal 1984). Achievements include patents in field. Office: SUNY Buffalo 305 Furnas Hall Buffalo NY 14260-4200

**WELLER, THOMAS HUCKLE,** physician, retired medical educator; b. Ann Arbor, Mich., June 15, 1915; s. Carl V. and Elsie A. (Huckle) Weller; m. Kathleen R. Fahey, Aug. 18, 1945; children: Peter Fahey, Nancy Kathleen, Robert Andrew, Janet Louise. AB, U. Mich., 1936; MS, 1937, LL.D. (hon.), 1956; MD, Harvard, 1940; Sc.D., Gustavus Adolphus U., 1975, U. Mass., 1985; L.H.D., Lowell U., 1977. Diplomate Am. Bd. Pediatrics. Teaching fellow bacteriology Harvard Med. Sch., 1940—41, research fellow tropical medicine, pediatrics, 1947—48, instr. comparative pathology, tropical medicine, 1948—49, asst. prof. tropical pub. health Sch. Pub. Health, 1949—50, assoc. prof., 1950—54, Richard Pearson Strong prof. tropical pub. health, 1954—85, prof. emeritus, 1985—, head dept., 1954—81; intern bacteriology and pathology Children's Hosp., Boston, 1941, intern medicine, 1942, asst. resident medicine, 1946, asst. dir. research div. infectious diseases, 1949—55; mem. commn. parasitic diseases Armed Forces Epidemiol. Bd., 1953—72, dir., 1953—59. Contbr. articles to sci. jours. Maj. M.C. U.S. Army, 1942—46. Named Stern Symposium honoree, 1972; recipient Mead Johnson award for devel. tissue culture procedures in study virus diseases, Am. Acad. Pediats., 1953, Kimble Methodology award, 1954, Nobel Prize in physiology and medicine, 1954, George Ledlie prize, 1963, Weinstein Cerebral Palsy award, 1973, Bristol award, Infectious Diseases Soc. Am., 1980, Gold medal and diploma of honor, U. Costa Rica, 1984, First Sci. Achievement award, VZV Rsch. Found., 1993, Walter Reed medal, Am. Soc. Tropical Medicine, 1996. Fellow: Am. Acad. Arts and Scis., Royal Soc. Tropical Medicine and Hygiene (hon.); mem.: NAS Inst. Medicine, Am. Soc. Tropical Medicine and Hygiene, Assn. Am. Physicians, Am. Pediat. Soc., Am. Epidemiol. Soc., Harvey Soc., NAS, AMA, Alpha Omega Alpha, Sigma Xi, Phi Beta Kappa.*

**WELLES, JUDITH,** public affairs executive; b. N.Y.C., Jan. 15, 1946; d. John and Millicent (Richman) Welles; m. Alan M. Bekelman, 1966 (div. 1994); children: David Bekelman, Justin Bekelman; m. Timothy P. Shank, Apr. 18, 1998; 1 child, Jenica Shank. BA, Vassar Coll., 1963. Speechwriter, editor U.S. Dept. Interior, Washington, 1965-66; asst. to dir. VISTA, Washington, 1967-70; speechwriter to sec. HHS, Washington, 1971-76, mgr. pub. affairs, 1977-86; dir. comm. and pub. affairs Pension Benefit Guaranty Corp., Washington, 1987-2000; worklife editor, sr. reporter PlanetGov.com, Fairfax, Va., 2000—. Commr. County Health Planning Commn., Md., 1986-88. Recipient 1st place ann. report competition Fin. World, 1991, 92. Mem. Nat. Assn. Govt. Communicators (Gold Screen award 1992, award of Excellence 1994). Office: PlanetGov.com 14155 Newbrook Dr Chantilly VA 20151-2224 E-mail: Jwelles@planetgov.com.

**WELLFORD, HILL B., JR.,** lawyer; b. Tulsa, Apr. 30, 1942; BA, Davidson Coll., 1964; JD, U. N.C., 1967. Bar: Va. 1968. Ptnr., adminstrv. head, litig., labor group Hunton and Williams LLP, Richmond, Va. Lectr. in law. Fellow Am. Bar Found., Va. Law Found.; mem. ABA, Va. Bar Assn. (chmn. com. labor rels. and employment law 1977-87); Richmond Bar Assn., Phi Delta Phi. Office: Hunton & Williams Riverfront Plz East Tower 951 E Byrd St Richmond VA 23219-1535 Office Phone: 804-788-8518. Business E-Mail: hwellford@hunton.com.

**WELLIN, KEITH SEARS,** investment banker; b. Grand Rapids, Mich., Aug. 13, 1926; s. Elmer G. and Ruth (Chamberlin) W.; m. Carol D. Woodhouse, Sept. 5, 1951 (dec. 1970), m. Wendy C.H. Lane, Nov. 15, 2002; children: Cynthia Wellin Plum, Peter, Marjorie Wellin King. BA, Hamilton Coll., 1950; MBA, Harvard U., 1952. With E.F. Hutton & Co., Inc., Chgo., 1952-71, regional v.p., dir., 1962-66, pres. N.Y.C., 1967-71, vice chmn., 1970-71; sr. v.p., treas., dir. Reynolds Securities Inc., 1971-74, pres., dir., 1974-78; exec. v.p., dir. Dean Witter Reynolds Org., from 1978; chmn. Dean Witter Reynolds Inter-Capital, from 1978; former vice chmn. Dean Witter Reynolds Inc. Chmn. bd. Moorco Internat., Houston; former gov., mem. exec. com. Assn. Stock Exchange Firms; mem. governing council Securities Industry Assn. Mem. investment com., trustee Hamilton Coll. Served to 2d lt., inf. AUS, 1945-47. Mem.: Knickerbocker (N.Y.C.); Clove Valley Rod and Gun (La Grangeville, N.Y.); Round Hill (Greenwich, Conn.); River Club. Home (Summer): Seaside Farm PO Box 335 Friendship ME 04547-0335 Office: c/o Dean Witter Reynolds 1345 Avenue Of The Americas New York NY 10105-0302 Home: John's Island 161 Coquille Way Vero Beach FL 32963

**WELLING, KATHRYN MARIE,** editor; b. Ft. Wayne, Ind., Feb. 4, 1952; d. Arthur Russell Sr. and Genevieve (Disser) W.; m. Donald Robert Boyle, Oct. 21, 1978; children: Brian Joseph, Thomas Arthur. BS in Journalism, Northwestern U., 1974. Copy reader Dow Jones News Retrieval, N.Y.C., 1974-75; copy reader, reporter AP-Dow Jones, N.Y.C., 1975-76; copy editor Wall Street Jour., N.Y.C., 1976; reporter Barron's, N.Y.C., 1976-81, asst. to editor, 1981, mng. editor, 1982-92, assoc. editor, 1992—99; ltd. ptnr. Weeden & Co. L.P., Greenwich, Conn., 1999—; prin. Welling@Weeden, Greenwich, 1999—. Columnist Welling's Acute Observations, Traders Mag. Online. Charter mem. Northwestern U. Coun. of One Hundred. Avocations: sailing, skiing. Office: Weeden & Co LP 145 Mason St Greenwich CT 06830 Office Phone: 203-861-7643. Business E-Mail: welling@weedenco.com.

**WELLINGHOFF, JON,** commissioner; BS, U. Nev., 1971; MS, Howard U., 1972; JD, Antioch Coll., 1975. Dep. dist. atty. consumer fraud divisn. Washoe County, Nev., 1976—77; asst. majority staff counsel consumer com., commerce com. U.S. Senate, 1978; staff atty. energy and product info. divisn. FTC, 1978—79; adimstrv. asst. Pub. Utilities Commn., Nev., consumer advocate Nev., staff counsel Nev.; mng. prin. and regulatory atty. Efficiency Engergy Systems, Inc.; commr. Fed. Energy Regulatory Commn, Washington, 2006—. Ptnr. Beckley Singleton. Office: Fed Energy Regulatory Commn 888 First St NE Washington DC 20426 Office Phone: 702-474-2629. Office Fax: 202-208-0064.*

**WELLINGTON, CAROL STRONG,** law librarian; b. Altadena, Calif., Jan. 30, 1948; d. Edward Walters and Elizabeth (Leonards) Strong; m. David Heath Wellington, May 27, 1978; one child, Edward Heath BA, Lake Forest Coll., Ill., 1969; MLS, Simmons Coll., 1974. Libr. Hill & Barlow, Boston, 1973—88, Peabody and Arnold, LLP, Boston, 1988—2002, Day, Berry, and Howard, LLP, Boston, 2002—. Mem.: Soc. of Competitive Intelligence Profls., Law Librs. of New England, Spl. Librs. Assn., Assn. Boston Law Librs. (v.p. 1979—80, pres. 1980—81), Am. Assn. Law Librs. Office: Day Berry & Howard LLP One International Pl Boston MA 02110 Office Phone: 617-345-4807. Business E-Mail: cswellington@dbh.com.

**WELLINGTON, HARRY HILLEL,** lawyer, educator; b. New Haven, Aug. 13, 1926; s. Alex M. and Jean (Ripps) W.; m. Sheila Wacks, June 22, 1952; children: John, Thomas. AB, U. Pa., 1947; LLB, Harvard U., 1952; MA (hon.), Yale U., 1960; LL.D, N.Y Law Sch. Bar: D.C. 1952. Law clk. to U.S. Judge Magruder, 1953-54, Supreme Ct. Justice Frankfurter, 1955-56; asst. prof. law Stanford U., 1954-56; mem. faculty Yale U., 1956—, prof. law, 1960—, Edward J. Phelps prof. law, 1967-83, dean Law Sch., 1975-85, Sterling prof. law, 1983-92, Sterling prof. emeritus law, 1992—, Harry H. Wellington prof. lectr., 1995—; pres., dean, prof. law N.Y. Law Sch., N.Y.C., 1992-2000, dean emeritus, prof., 2000—. Ford fellow London Sch. Econs., 1965; Guggenheim fellow; sr. fellow Brookings Instn., 1968-71; Rockefeller Found. fellow Bellagio Study and Conf. Ctr., 1984; faculty mem. Salzburg Seminar in Am. Studies 1985; John M. Harlan disting. vis. prof. N.Y. Law

Sch., 1985-86; review person ITT-SEC; moderator Asbestos-Wellington Group; cons. domestic and fgn. govtl. agys.; trustee N.Y. Law Sch.; bd. govs. Yale U. Press; mem. jud. panel, exec. com. Ctr. Public Resources Legal Program; Harry H. Wellington lectr., 1999—. Author: with Harold Shepherd) Contracts and Contract Remedies, 1957, Labor and the Legal Process, 1968, (with Clyde Summers) Labor Law, 1968, 2d edit., 1983, (with Ralph Winter) The Unions and the Cities, 1971, Interpreting the Constitution, 1990; contbr. articles to profl. jours. Mem. ABA, Bar Assn. Conn., Am. Law Inst., Am. Arbitration Assn., Am. Acad. Arts and Scis., Common Cause (nat governing bd.). Office: NY Law Sch 57 Worth St New York NY 10013-2959 also: Yale U Sch Law New Haven CT 06520

**WELLINGTON, RALPH GLENN,** lawyer; b. Three Rivers, Mich., June 18, 1946; s. Cleon G. and Gladys M. (Cole) W.; m. Margaret Brennan; children: Ralph Glenn II, Jeffrey Scott, Tyler Cahill. BA, Kalamazoo Coll., 1968; JD, U. Mich., 1970. Bar: Pa. 1971, U.S. Dist. Ct. (ea. dist.) Pa. 1971, U.S. Dist. Ct. (mid. dist.) Pa. 1976, U.S. Ct Appeals (3d cir.) 1978, U.S. Ct. Appeals (6th cir.) 1985, U.S. Supreme Ct. 1987. Atty. Schnader Harrison Segal & Lewis, Phila., chmn., 1998—. Frequent lectr. on litigation and ethics in U.S.A. and abroad. Contbr. articles to profl. jours. Trustee Kalamazoo Coll., 1992-2006, vice-chmn.; bd. dirs. Mann Ctr. for Performing Arts, Phila. C. of C. and CEO Coun Fellow Am. Coll. Trial Lawyers, Internat. Acad. Trial Lawyers; mem. ABA, Nat. Assn. R.R. Trial Counsel, Aviation Ins. Assn., Phila. Bar Assn. (chair profl. responsibility com. 1988), Phila. Cricket Club. Lutheran. Avocations: squash, golf, jazz piano. Home: 604 W Hartwell Ln Philadelphia PA 19118-4114 Office: Schnader Harrison Segal & Lewis 1600 Market St Ste 3600 Philadelphia PA 19103-7287 Office Phone: 215-751-2488. E-mail: rwellington@schnader.com.

**WELLINGTON, WILLIAM GEORGE,** entomologist, ecologist, educator; b. Vancouver, BC, Can., Aug. 16, 1920; s. George and Lilly (Rae) W.; m. Margret Ellen Reiss, Sept. 22, 1959; children: Katherine Jean, Stephen Ross. BA, U. B.C., 1941; MA, U. Toronto, 1945, PhD, 1947. Meteorol. officer Can. Meteorol. Svc., Toronto, 1942-45; rsch. entomologist Can. Dept. Agr., Sault Sainte Marie, Ont., 1946-51; head bioclimatology sect. Can. Dept. Forestry, Sault Sainte Marie, Ont., Victoria, B.C., 1951-67, prin. scientist Victoria, 1964-68; prof. ecology U. Toronto, Toronto, 1968-70; dir. Inst. Animal Resource Ecology, U. B.C., Vancouver, 1973-79, prof. plant sci. and resource ecology, 1970-86, hon. prof. dept. plant sci., 1986—, prof. emeritus, 1986—; Killam sr. rsch. fellow U. B.C., 1980-81. Inaugural lectr. C.E. Atwood Meml. Seminar Series, Dept. Zoology, U. Toronto, 1993; vis. prof. NC State U., 1972, 75, 81, San Diego State U., 1975, Laval U., 1981, U. Calgary, 1983, Simon Fraser U., 1987. Contbr. articles to profl. jours. Fellow Entomol. Soc. Can. (pres. 1976-78, Gold medal 1968), Royal Soc. Can., Explorers Club; mem. Am. Meteorol. Soc. (award 1969), Entomol. Soc. Am. (C. J. Woodworth award 1979), Japanese Soc. Population Ecology, Entomol. Soc. Ont., Am. Philatelic Soc. Club. Anglican. Home: 1010 W 42d Ave # 305 Vancouver BC Canada V6M 2A8 Office: U BC Faculty Land and Food Sys Vancouver BC Canada V6T 1W5

**WELLISCH, DAVID,** Internet company executive; b. Ecuador; arrived in US, 1990; B in Econ., Polit. Sci, Brown Univ., 1992; MBA, Harvard Univ. Joined AOL, 2001, dir. advanced svcs., exec. dir. strategic devel., Web Properties Group; v.p., gen. mgr. AOL Latino, Va., 2003—. Bd. adv. Hispanic Caucus of State Legislators. Named one of 50 Most Important Hispanics in Tech., Bus., Hispanic Engineer and Info. Tech. mag., 2005. Office: AOL Latino 22000 AOL Way Sterling VA 20166 Office Phone: 703-265-0602. Business E-Mail: dwellish01@aol.com.*

**WELLISZ, STANISLAW,** economics professor; b. Warsaw, Mar. 28, 1925; came to U.S., 1941; s. Leopold and Jadwiga (Landau) W.; m. Anna Blaszkiewicz; children: Tadeusz, Krzysztof BA magna cum laude, Harvard Coll., 1946, MA, 1949; postgrad., U. Cambridge, England, 1949-52; PhD, Harvard U., 1953; D (hon.), Warsaw U., 1998. Asst. prof. U. Chgo., 1957-60, assoc. prof., 1960-63; prof. Columbia U., N.Y.C., 1964-94, Kathryn and Shelby Cullom Davis prof. econs. & internat. affairs, 1994—. Vis. prof. Warsaw U., 1989-97; adv. Polish Ministry Fin., 1989-91. Author: The Economics of the Soviet Bloc, 1964; co-author: The Political Economy of Growth, 1993; co-editor: Stabilization in Poland, 1993. NSF fellow, 1975, 82; named officer Polish Order Merit, Govt. Poland, 1997. Office Phone: 212-854-8033. Business E-Mail: SW11@columbia.edu.

**WELLIVER, WARREN DEE,** lawyer, retired judge; b. Butler, Mo., Feb. 24, 1920; s. Carl Winfield and Burdee Marie (Wolfe) W.; m. Ruth Rose Galey, Dec. 25, 1942; children: Gale Dee (Mrs. William B. Stone), Carla Camile (Mrs. Dayton Stone), Christy Marie. BA, U. Mo., 1945; JD, U. Mo., 1948. Bar: Mo. 1948. Asst. pros. atty. Boone County, Columbia, 1948-54; sr. ptnr. Welliver, Atkinson and Eng, Columbia, 1960-79; tchr. law Law Sch. U. Mo., 1948-49; mem. Mo. Senate, 1977-79; justice Supreme Ct. Mo., Jefferson City, 1979-89. Mem. Gov. Mo. Adv. Coun. Alcoholism and Drug Abuse, chmn. drug coun., 1970-72; chmn. Task Force Revision Mo. Drug Laws, 1970-71; liaison mem. coun. Nat. Inst. Alcoholism and Alcohol Abuse, 1973-76; mem. Cen. Regional Adv. Coun. Comprehensive Psychiat. Svcs., 1990-92. Bd. dirs. Nat. Assn. Mental Health 1970-76, regional v.p., 1973-76; pres. Mo. Assn. Mental Health, 1968-69, Stephens Coll. Assocs., 1965-79; pres. Friends of Libr., U. Mo., 1976, bd. dirs., 1979-92; chmn. Dem. Com., 1954-64; hon. fellow Harry S. Truman Libr. Inst., 1979—; bd. dirs. Supreme Ct. Hist. Soc., 1982—; vice chair adv. bd. U. Mo. Multiple Sclerosis Inst., 1992—; bd. curators Stephen's Coll., 1980-92. With USNR, 1941-45. Recipient Disting. Alumni medal and award U. Mo., 1994. Fellow Am. Coll. Trial Lawyers, Am. Bar Found., Mo. Bar Found.; mem. ABA, Mo. Bar Assn. (pres. 1967-68), Boone County Bar Assn. (pres. 1970), Am Judicature Soc. Am I(-gion (past comdr.), Multiple Sclerosis Soc. (Gateway chpt. bd. dirs. 1986-92), Order of Coif, Country Club of Mo., Columbia Country Club (past pres.). Home: 3430 Woodrail Ter Columbia MO 65203-0926

**WELLMAN, BARCLAY ORMES,** furniture company executive; b. Jamestown, N.Y., May 13, 1936; s. Albert Austin and Leona (Greenlund) W.; m. Diane Taylor, July 2, 1960; children: Barclay Ormes Jr., Taylor A., Alexandra C. BA, Dartmouth Coll., 1959; grad., U.S. Army War Coll., 1982. Interior designer Wellman Bros., Inc., Jamestown, 1963-64, treas., 1964—, pres., 1978—. Trustee Lakeview Cemetery Assn., Jamestown, 1978—; Sheldon Found., Jamestown, 1981—. Maj. gen. U.S. Army, ret. Mem. Am. Soc. Interior Designers (v.p. 1972-74), Am. Appraisers Assn., Am. Legion, Res. Officers Assn., Sr. Army Res. Comdrs. Assn., Sportsmens Club, Moon Brook Country Club, Naples (Fla.) Yacht Club, Delta Kappa Epsilon. Republican. Presbyterian. Avocation: fishing. Home: 1235 Prendergast Ave Jamestown NY 14701-3146 Office: Wellman Bros Inc 130 S Main St Jamestown NY 14701-6623

**WELLMAN, CARL PIERCE,** philosophy educator; b. Lynn, Mass., Sept. 3, 1926; s. Frank and Carolyn (Heath) Wellman; m. Farnell Parsons, June 20, 1953; children: Timothy, Philip, Lesley, Christopher. BA, U. Ariz., 1949; MA, Harvard U., 1951, PhD, 1954; postgrad. U. Cambridge, Eng., 1951-52. Instr. Lawrence U., Appleton, Wis., 1953-57, asst. prof., 1957-62, assoc. prof., 1962-66, prof., chmn. dept. philosophy, 1966-68; prof. philosophy Washington U., St. Louis, 1968-88, Hortense and Tobias Lewin Disting. prof. humanities, 1988-99, Hortense and Tobias Lewin Disting. prof. emeritus, 1999—. Mem. rev. panel rsch. grants NEH, 1968—71. Author: The Language of Ethics, 1961, Challenge and Response: Justification in Ethics, 1971, Morals and Ethics, 1975, Welfare Rights, 1982, A Theory of Rights, 1985, Real Rights, 1995, An Approach to Rights, 1997, The Proliferation of Rights, 1999, Medical Law and Moral Rights, 2005. Recipient Uhrig Distinguished Teaching award Lawrence U., 1968; Am. Council Learned Socs. fellow, 1965-66; NEH sr. fellow, 1972-73; Nat. Humanities Center fellow, 1982-83 Mem.: Internat. Assn. for Philosophy Law and Social Philosophy (hon. pres.), Am. Philos. Assn. Home: 625 S Skinker Blvd # 902 Saint Louis MO 63105-2340 E-mail: cpwellma@artsci.wustl.edu.

**WELLMAN, ROBERT JONATHAN,** medical educator; b. Riverside, Calif., Mar. 1, 1945; s. Harvey Wellman and Ethel Feinstein; m. Mary Margaret Haunss, Aug. 17, 1969. BA with honors, UCLA, 1965; MS, LI U, 1973; PhD, U. Conn., Storrs, 1982. Cert. psychologist, health service provider Mass., 1974, addictions specialist Am. Acad. Healthcare Providers in the Addictive Disorders, 1990. Ednl. rsch. cons. Brentwood Pub. Schs., NY, 1968—69, sch. psychologist, 1969—70, Bd. Coop. Ednl. Svcs., Riverhead, NY, 1968—69, Smithtown Pub. Schs., NY, 1970—72; counselor, adj. asst. prof. counseling LI U. - C. W. Post Campus, Brookville, NY, 1972—74; psychologist Pvt. Practice, Charlton, Mass., 1974—92; sr. psychologist Hubbard Human Svcs. Ctr., Webster, Mass., 1974—82; dir. adolescent & family svcs. Marathon of RI, Providence, 1988—89; clin. dir. outpatient svcs. Attleboro Area Youth & Family Svcs., Mass., 1989—92; asst. prof. psychology Framingham State Coll., Mass., 1993—95; asst. prof. behavioral scis. Fitchburg State Coll., Mass., 1995—2000, assoc. prof. behavioral scis., 2000—05, prof. behavioral scis., 2005—; adj. assoc. prof. family medicine and cmty. health U. Mass. Med. Sch., Worcester, Mass., 2004—05, adj. prof. family medicine and cmty. health, 2005—. Founding editor, family psychologist APA Divsn. Family Psychology, Washington, 1984—89, member-at-large, bd. dirs., 1988—91, president-elect, 1992—93, pres., 1993—94, past pres., 1994—95. Contbr. articles various profl. jours. Recipient Faculty award for Rsch., Fitchburg State Coll. Found., 2006. Mem.: APA, Am. Acad. Healthcare Providers in the Addictive Disorders, Ea. Psychol. Assn., Assn. Psychol. Sci., Soc. Rsch. on Nicotine & Tobacco. Office: Fitchburg State Coll 160 Pearl St Fitchburg MA 01420-2697 Office Phone: 978-665-3708. Business E-Mail: rwellman@fsc.edu.

**WELLNER, MARCEL NAHUM,** research scientist, educator; b. Antwerp, Belgium, Feb. 8, 1930; came to U.S., 1949; s. Jules and Lucie (Rapoport) W.; m. Magdeleine Misselyn, Apr. 7, 1961; children: Pierre, Lucie. BS, MIT, 1952; PhD, Princeton U., 1958. Instr. Brandeis U., Waltham, Mass., 1957-59; mem. Inst. Advanced Study, Princeton, NJ, 1959-60; rsch. assoc. Ind. U., Bloomington, 1960-63; vis. scientist Atomic Energy Rsch. Establishment, Harwell, England, 1963-64; from asst. prof. to prof. Syracuse (N.Y.) U., 1964-95, prof. emeritus, 1995—; sr. rsch. scientist SUNY, Syracuse, 1995—. Author gen. physics textbook; contbr. numerous articles on quantum field theory, fractals and excitable media to profl. jours. Mem. Am. Phys. Soc. Office Phone: 315-464-8018.

**WELLON, ROBERT G.,** lawyer; b. Port Jervis, NY, Apr. 18, 1948; s. Frank Lewis and Alice (Stevens) W.; m. Jan Montgomery, Aug. 12, 1972; children: Robert F., Alice Wynn. AB, Emory U., 1970; JD, Stetson Coll. Law, 1974. Assoc. Turner, Turner & Turner, Atlanta, 1974-78; ptnr. Ridley, Wellon, Schwieger & Brazier, Atlanta, 1978-86; of counsel Wilson, Strickland & Benson, Atlanta, 1987—2000; pvt. practice Atlanta, 2000—. Adj. prof. Atlanta Law Sch., 1981—94; adj. prof. law Emory U. Sch. of Law, 1995—. Gov.'s task force chmn. Atlanta 2000, 1978; exec. com., treas., 2nd v.p. Atlanta Easter Seals Soc., 1983-88; rep. Neighborhood Planning Unit, 1981-83; adminstrv. bd. Northside United Meth. Ch., 1996-99, Stephen min.; active Atlanta Sports Coun. with USAR, 1970-76. Named Super Lawyer Atlanta Mag., 2004, 05, 06. Master: Charles Longstreet Weltner Family Law Inn of Ct. (founding pres. 1997—2000); fellow: Am. Bar Found.; mem.: Lawyers Found. of Ga., Atlanta Bar Found. (bd. dirs. 1996—), Am. Judicature Soc., Atlanta Bar Assn. (bd. dirs. 1978—88, pres. 1986—87), Atlanta continuing legal edn. bd. trustees 1994—97, del. to ho. of dels. 1999—2005, Charles E. Watkins Svc. award 1995, Disting. Svc. award 2005), State Bar of Ga. (professionalism com. 1994—), Fla. Bar, Atlanta Found. for Psycho-analysis, Inc. (bd. dirs. 1994—, exec. com. 1997—), Old War Horse Lawyers Club, Lawyers Club Atlanta. Methodist. Office: Ste 1900 Promenade II 1230 Peachtree St NE Atlanta GA 30309 Office Phone: 404-942-3505. E-mail: rgwlaw@earthlink.net.

**WELLS, ALAN HILARY,** biomedical researcher; b. N.Y.C., Dec. 15, 1958; AB, Brown U., 1979; D Med. Sci., Karolonska Inst., Stockholm, 1982; postdoctoral studies, Brown U., 1981—. Assoc. prof. Okayama (Japan) U. Med. Sch., 1983-84; postdoctoral fellow U. Calif., San Francisco, 1984-86; asst. prof. U. Ala., Birmingham, 1986—. Contbr. articles to profl. jours. Recipient ICRETT award Union Internat. Against Cancer, Geneva, 1980. Mem. AAAS, N.Y. Acad. Scis., Sigma Chi, Phi Beta Kappa, N.Y. Acad. Scis. Jewish. Avocations: hiking, skiing, reading, travel. Home: Brown Univ Med Program Box G Providence RI 02912-0001

**WELLS, ANNIE,** photographer; b. 1954; B in Sci. Writing, U. Calif., Santa Cruz; postgrad., San Francisco State U. Past photographer Herald Jour., Logan, Utah, Greeley (Colo.) Tribune, Associated Press, San Francisco; photographer Press Dem., Santa Rosa, Calif., 1989—97, L.A. Times, 1997—. Photographer (permanent collections) Nat. Mus. Women Arts, Washington. Recipient Pulitzer Prize spot news photography, 1997. Office: LA Times 202 West First St Los Angeles CA 90012 E-mail: annie.wells@latimes.com.

**WELLS, ARTHUR STANTON,** retired manufacturing executive; b. Kingsport, Tenn., Jan. 8, 1931; s. Arthur Stanton and Blanche Welch (Duncan) W.; m. Ellen N. Blackburn, June 15, 1957; children: Arthur S., Thomas B., Emily B., Richard R. BS, Yale U., 1953; MBA, Harvard U., 1957. Fin. analyst Eastman Kodak Co., Kingsport, Tenn., 1957-65; mgr. profit analysis Xerox Corp., Rochester, NY, 1966-68, asst. treas. Stamford, Conn., 1969-76, treas., 1976-79; v.p. fin. Barnes Group Inc., Bristol, Conn., 1979-86, exec. v.p. fin., 1987-93, pres., CEO, 1994-96, also dir. Phares Nash Engring. Co., Trumbull, Conn., 1995—98. Trustee, treas. Wilton (Conn.) Libr. Assn., 1972-78; trustee Lincoln Acad., Newcastle, Maine, 2002—; bd. dirs. New Eng. Opera Assn., 1972-78; assoc. bd. dirs. Conn. Bank and Trust Co., Hartford, 1984-90; chmn. bd. trustees, exec. com Conn. Pub. Expenditure Coun., Inc., 1990-93. With USAR, 1953-55. Mem. Fin. Execs. Inst. Episcopalian. Republican. Avocations: art, fishing. Home: 4 CCIA Rd South Bristol ME 04568-4710 E-mail: wellses@midcoast.com.

**WELLS, BRADLEY W.,** foundation administrator; BA in polit. sci., Calif. State U., Long Beach, 1983. Positions at Calif. State U., Fullerton, 1983—86, dir. budget planning and adminstrn., 1986—89; joined Chancellor's Office Calif. State U. System, Long Beach, 1989, sr. fin. analyst, dir. info. and analysis, 1993—95, named exec. asst. to vice chancellor, CFO, 1995, asst. vice chancellor fin. services; assoc. dir. program analysis and planning J. Paul Getty Trust, LA, 1998—99, named v.p. fin. 2001, now v.p. fin. and adminstrn. Office: J Paul Getty Trust 1200 Getty Ctr Dr Los Angeles CA 90049-1679 Office Phone: 310-440-7300.*

**WELLS, CAROL MCCONNELL,** genealogist, retired archivist; b. Phila., Feb. 21, 1918; d. William Hugh McConnell and Edith Mary Lower; m. Tom Henderson Wells, Dec. 31, 1943; children: Lucy, Sarah, Tom, Christopher, Julia, Peter. BA, Pa. State Coll., 1939; MA, Northwestern State U., Natchitoches, La., 1973. Archivist Northwestern State U., Natchitoches, La., 1974-88; editor So. Studies, Natchitoches, 1982-88. Spkr. in field. Author: Williamson County, Tennessee: A Genealogical Abstract of the County Court Minutes, 1800-1804, 1987, 88, Davidson County, Tennessee, County Court Minutes 1783-1792, 1990, Davidson County, Tennessee, County Court Minutes, 1792-1799, 1991, Davidson County, Tennessee, County Court Minutes 1799-1803, 1991, Genealogical Abstracts of Edgefield, SC, Equity Court Records, 2002, Edgefield County, South Carolina, Probate Records, Boxes 1-3, 2004, many others Mem. Natchitoches Hist. Found., 1994—. Lt. (j.g.) USNR, 1944. Named Woman of Yr. C. of C., 1975; recipient Clio award Phi Alpha Theta, 1988. Mem. DAR, PEO Sisterhood, Phi Mu, Phi Beta Kappa, Phi Kappa Phi. Republican. Anglican Catholic. Avocation: gardening. Home: 607 Williams Ave Natchitoches LA 71457 Personal E-mail: carolwells@cp-tel.net.

**WELLS, CHARLES,** sculptor, printmaker; b. NYC, Dec. 24, 1935; m. Diana Wells. Student, George Sch., Newton, Pa., Amherst Coll.; apprentice, Leonard Baskin, 1961—64. With Am. Sch., Rome, 1964—65. Represented in permanent collections Nat. Mus. Am. Art, Washington, Nat. Portrait Gallery,

Libr. Congress, Whitney Mus., NYC, MIT, NAD, NYC, James A. Michener Art Mus., exhibitions include Bucks County Coun. for Arts, Doylestown, Pa., 1985, Prince St. Gallery, 2003, La Salle Univ. Art Mus., 2004, Printworks Gallery, Chgo., exhibited in group shows at Bklyn. Mus. Art, Whitney Mus., Spoleto Festival, Italy, Macedonian Mus. of Modern Art, Thessaloniki, Greece, Amsterdam Concertgebouw, Corcoran Gallery. Recipient Prix de Rome, 1964, 3 gold medals, NAD Annual. Fellow: Am. Acad., Rome; mem.: NAD (academician 1994—). Home: Box 222 Washington Crossing PA 18977

**WELLS, CHARLES TALLEY,** state supreme court justice; b. Orlando, Fla., Mar. 4, 1939; BA, U. of Florida, 1961, JD, 1964. Bar: Fla. 1965, U.S. Dist. Ct. (mid. dist.) Fla., U.S. Ct. Appeals (5th and 11th cirs.) 1966, U.S. Supreme Ct. 1969, U.S. Dist. Ct., U.S. Dist. Ct. (so. dist.) Fla. 1976, U.S. Ct. of Claims 1990. Trial atty. U.S. dept justice, Washington, 1969; pvt. practice Maguire, Voohris and Wells, PA, Orlando, Fla., 1965—68, 1970—75, Wells, Gattis, Hollowes & Carpenter, PA, Orlando, Fla., 1976—94; justice Fla. Supreme Ct., Tallahassee, 1994—, chief justice, 2000—02. Active in Orange County Legal Aid Soc., 1968—94; mem. bd. trustees, 1988—89; bd. directors Conference of Chief Justices; mem. Federal Judicial Conference Standing Com. on Rules of Practice & Procedure. Former mem. bd. directors Orlando Area Chamber of Commerce, Orlando Jaycees, Orange County YMCA. Served in U.S. Army. Fellow: Am. Bar Foundation; mem.: Tallahassee Bar Assn., ABA, Fla. Bar (bd. governors), Orange County Bar Assn. (pres. 1989—90). Methodist. Office: Fla Supreme Ct 500 S Duval St Tallahassee FL 32399-1925*

**WELLS, CHRISTOPHER LINDELL,** art educator, football coach, baseball coach; b. Springfield, Ill., Oct. 21, 1968; s. Nathaniel Hawthorne and Linda Crawford Wells; m. Angela Kristin Skelton Wells, Nov. 11, 1995; children: Kristin Elise Bloyd, Kathleen Grace Bloyd, Nicholas James, Daniel Luke. BA, Olivet Nazarene U., Bourbonnais, Ill., 1991, MA, 1993. Graphic artist Olivet Nazarene U., Bourbonnais, Ill., 1991—93; tchr. art Cuba Sch. Dist, 1993—96, Cuba Unified Sch. Dist. #140, Eureka, Ill., 1996—. Head baseball coach Cuba Sch. Dist., 1993—96, asst. football coach, 1993—96, Cuba Unified Sch. Dist #140, Eureka, 1996—2001, asst. baseball coach, 1996—2001, head football coach, 2001—04. Mem.: NEA, Nat. Arts Edn. Assn., Ill. Edn. Assn. Republican. Evangelical. Avocations: art, football, skiing, baseball, church activities. Home: 105 Walnut Cir Eureka IL 61530 Office: Eureka HS 200 W Cruger Ave Eureka IL 61530-1323

**WELLS, CHRISTOPHER M.,** lawyer; b. Honiton, England, Oct. 21, 1957; BA, Kalamazoo Coll., 1978; JD, Univ. Mich., 1981. Bar: NY 1982. Ptnr., head Global Investment Funds practice Coudert Bros. LLP, NYC. Contbr. articles to profl. jours. Mem.: Phi Beta Kappa. Office: Coudert Bros LLP 1114 Ave of the Americas New York NY 10036 Office Phone: 212-626-4925. Office Fax: 212-626-4120. Business E-Mail: wellsc@coudert.com.

**WELLS, DAMON,** investment company executive; b. Houston, May 20, 1937; s. Damon and Margaret Corinne (Howze) W. BA magna cum laude, Yale U., 1958; BA, Oxford U., 1964, MA, 1968; PhD, Rice U., 1968. Owner, CEO Damon Wells Interests, Houston, 1958—; pres. Damon Wells Found., Houston, 1993—. Author: Stephen Douglas: The Last Years, 1857-61, 1971 (Tex. Writer's Roundup prize, 1971), paperback edit., 1990. Bd. dirs. Child Guidance Ctr. of Houston, 1970-73; trustee Christ Ch. Cathedral Endowment Fund, 1970-73, 84-88, chmn., 1987-88; trustee Kinkaid Sch., 1972-86, Camp Allen retreat of Episc. Diocese of Tex., 1976-78, Kinkaid Sch. Endowment Fund, 1981-86, Churchill Grave Trust, 2002—, Winston Churchill Found. U.S., 2003—; hon. friend of Somerville Coll., Oxford U., 1988—, mem. sr. common rm. Pembroke Coll., Oxford U., 1972-; founding bd. dirs. Brit. Inst. US, 1979-80; pres.'s coun. Tex. A&M U., 1983-89; hon. dir. Stephen A. Douglas Assn., 1975—; mem. chancellors ct. Oxford U., 2006—. Named Hon. Comdr. Most Excellent Order of Brit. Empire by Her Majesty Queen Elizabeth II, 1991, Outstanding Alumnus Yr. by Kinkaid Sch., 1994; fellow Jonathan Edwards Coll. (assoc.), Yale U., 1982—, Sterling fellow Yale U., 2000—, hon. fellow Pembroke Coll., Oxford U., 1984—. Mem. English-Speaking Union (nat. dir. 1970-72, v.p. Houston br. 1966-73), Coun. Fgn. Rels., Houston Country Club, Houston Club, Yale Club (N.Y.C.), United Oxford and Cambridge U. Club (London), Cosmos Club (Washington), Buck's Club (London), Coronado Club (Houston), Little Ship Club (London). Phi Beta Kappa, Pi Sigma Alpha. Anglican. Home: 5555 Del Monte Dr Houston TX 77056-4100 Office: 2001 Kirby Dr Ste 806 Houston TX 77019-6088

**WELLS, DAVID LEE,** professional baseball player; b. Torrance, Calif., May 20, 1963; Grad. high sch., San Diego. Pitcher Toronto Blue Jays, 1987—92, 1999—2001, Detroit Tigers, 1993-95, Cin. Reds, 1995, Balt. Orioles, 1996, N.Y. Yankees, 1997-98, 2002—03, Chgo. White Sox, 2001, Boston Red Sox, 2005—06, San Diego Padres, 2004—05, 2006—. Named Am. League All-Star Team, 1995, 98, 2000; Perfect game thrown May 17th, 1999; mem. World Series champion Toronto Blue Jays, 1992, N.Y. Yankees, 1998. Office: c/o San Diego Padres PO Box 2000 San Diego CA 92112-2000*

**WELLS, DEWEY WALLACE,** lawyer; b. Raleigh, N.C., Oct. 14, 1929; s. B.C. and Alma (Blanchard) W.; m. Ann D. Wells, Aug 25, 1951; children: Robert, Betty, Daniel, Brady, Jeff. AA, Mars Hill Coll., 1950; BS, Wake Forest U., 1952, JD, 1954. Bar: N.C. 1954, U.S. Dist. Ct. (ea. dist.) N.C. 1960, U.S. Ct. Appeals (4th cir.) 1961, U.S. Dist. Ct. (mid. and we. dist.) N.C. 1985. Exec. sec. N.C. Jud. Council, Raleigh, 1954-55; ptnr. LeRoy, Wells, Shaw, Hornthal & Riley, Elizabeth City, NC, 1958-85, Womble, Carlyle, Sandridge & Rice, PLLC, Winston Salem, NC, 1985—. Judge Superior Ct., 1st Jud. Dist. N.C., 1974. Trustee N.C. Natural Heritage Trust, 1990—, chmn. 1996-2003. 1st lt. USAR, 1954-58. Fellow Am. Coll. Trial Lawyers; mem. N.C. Bar Assn. (pres. 1980-81). Republican. Baptist. Home: 1890 Pilot Ridge Rd Blowing Rock NC 28605-8917 Office: Womble Carlyle Sandridge & Rice 1 W 4th St Winston Salem NC 27102-0084

**WELLS, GLADYSANN,** library director; BA in English, Greensboro Coll., NC, 1970; MLS, SUNY, Albany, 1972. Libr. Empire State Coll., 1972—73; legis. reference libr. N.Y. State Libr., Albany, 1973—78; with Senate Rsch. Svc., 1975—80; libr. Senate Libr., 1978—80; adminstr. N.Y. State Libr., 1980—95; interim dir. N.Y. State Libr. Rsch. Libr., 1995—97; state libr. Ariz. State Libr., 1997—. Editor several books on the economy of the northeast; contbr. articles to profl. jours. Avocations: horseback riding, cross country skiing, hiking, snow shoeing. Office: Ariz State Libr 1700 W Washington Ste 200 Phoenix AZ 85007-2896

**WELLS, HUEY THOMAS, JR.,** lawyer; b. Gadsden, Ala., Mar. 22, 1950; s. Huey Thomas Sr. and Ruth (Allison) W.; m. Jan McKenzie, Dec. 29, 1972; children: Lynlee, Trey. BA with honors, U. Ala., 1972, JD, 1975. Bar: Ala. 1975, U.S. Dist. Ct. (no. dist.) Ala. 1975, U.S. Ct. Appeals (D.C. and 5th cirs.) 1977, U.S. Supreme Ct. 1984, U.S. Ct. Appeals (11th cir.) 1982. Assoc. Cabaniss, Johnston, Gardner, Dumas & O'Neal, Birmingham, Ala., 1977-82, ptnr., 1983-84; Maynard, Cooper & Gale P.C., 1984—. Chmn. adv. com. on civil justice reform U.S. Dist. (no. dist.) Ala., 1991-95. Legal co-chmn. championship Profl. Golf Assn., Birmingham, 1984, legal chmn., 1990; legal chmn. U.S. Amateur Golf Championship, Birmingham, 1986. Served to capt. USAF, 1975-77. Mem. ABA (standing com. profl. disciple 1985-88, standing com. on environ. law 1988-94, chmn. environ. litigation com. of litigation sect. 1988-91, chmn. ho. of dels. 2002-04, Ala. state del. 1992-2001—, mem. coun. litigation sect. 1992-95, chair litigation sect. 1999-2000), Birmingham Bar Assn. (law day com., grievance com., divsn. dir. litigation sect. 1991-92), Ala. Bar Assn. (jud. liaison). Roman Catholic. Avocations: golf, softball, reading. Office: Maynard Cooper & Gale PC 2400 AmSouth/Harbart Plz 1901 6th Ave N Ste 2400 Birmingham AL 35203-4604 Office Phone: 205-254-1062. Business E-Mail: twells@maynardcooper.com.

**WELLS, JAMES H.,** plastic surgeon; m. Karen Wells; children: Sara, Gregory. MD, U. Tex., 1966. Cert. Am. Bd. Plastic Surgery, 1978. Med. staff St. Mary's Med. Ctr., Long Beach, Calif., Los Alamitos Hosp., Hoag Prsbyn.

Hosp., Newport Beach Hosp., Comm. Hosp., Long Beach; resident, gen. and plastic surgery Ochsner Found. Hosp., New Orleans, U. Va. med. Ctr., Charlottesville, Va.; currently pvt. practice Long Beach. Mem.: Am. Soc. Plastic Surgeons (pres. 2002—). Office: 2880 Atlantic Ave Ste 290 Long Beach CA 90806

**WELLS, JAMES M., III,** bank executive; b. 1946; Student, U. N.C.; Rutgers U., U. Colo. Mgmt. trainee United Va. Bankshares, 1968-71, corporate adminstrv. officer, sec., 1971; br. officer, mgr. United Va. Bankshares/State-Planters, 1971-74; v.p. and treas. United Va. Mortgage Corp., 1974-79; pres., CEO United Va. Leasing Corp., 1974-79; exec. v.p. United Va. Bank, Norfolk, Va., 1979-83, pres. Ea. region, 1983-85, exec. v.p. corporate banking, 1985-86, exec. v.p. banking group, 1986-88; pres., CEO Crestar Fin Corp, Richmond, Va., 1988—2000; vice chmn. SunTrust Banks Inc., Atlanta, 2000—04, pres., COO, 2004—. Office: SunTrust Banks Inc 303 Peachtree St NE Atlanta GA 30308 Mailing: SunTrust Banks Inc PO Box 4418 Atlanta GA 30308-4418*

**WELLS, JERRY,** protective services official; b. Hodgenville, Ky., Dec. 1950; s. Lawrence and Margaret Wells. BA in History, Western Ky. U., 1973; postgrad., So. Police Inst., Louisville, 1987; MS in Criminal Justice Adminstrn., Ea. Ky. U., 1990; grad., FBI Nat. Acad., Quantico, Va., 1998. Cert. police officer, police mgmt. instr. Ky. Audio visual technician, police dispatcher Western Ky. U., Bowling Green, 1972-74, police officer, detective, sgt., 1975-76; police officer City of Bowling Green, 1976-83, police sgt., 1983-87, police capt., 1987-94, sector comdr., capt., 1994-99, capt. profl. stds. unit, 2000—02, maj., dep. chief support svcs. divsn., 2002—03, lt. col., dep. chief support svcs., 2003—. Part-time tchr. police related topics; legal mgmt. rschr. Mem., grad. Leadership Bowling Green, 1989. Mem.: FBI Nat. Acad. Assocs., Ky. Assn. Chiefs Police, Internat. Assn. Chiefs Police, Fraternal Order Police (treas. 1981—84, Svc. award 1979, 1981), Coll. Law Enforcement Alumni Assn., Leadership Bowling Green Alumni Assn., Eastern Ky. U. Alumni Assn., So. Police Inst. Alumni Assn., Western Ky. U. Alumni Assn. Republican. Baptist. Avocations: reading, bowling, golf, travel, historical research. Home: PO Box 684 Bowling Green KY 42102-0684 Office: Bowling Green Police Dept 911 Kentucky St Bowling Green KY 42101-2105 Office Phone: 270-393-4511. Business E-Mail: jerry.wells@bgky.org.

**WELLS, JOHN CALHOUN,** physics professor; b. Tampa, Fla., May 12, 1941; s. John Calhoun and Ethel Bernice (Hitchcock) W.; m. Marilee Winifred Mays, Dec. 21, 1963; children: Sarah Kathleen, John Bryan. BS, Fla. State U., 1961; PhD, Johns Hopkins U., 1968. Postdoctoral researcher U.S. Naval Ordnance Lab., Silver Spring, Md., 1968-70; asst. prof. Tenn. Tech. U., Cookeville, 1970-75, assoc. prof., 1975-80, prof. physics, 1980—. Adj. rsch. scientist nuclear physics Oak Ridge (Tenn.) Nat. Lab., 1976—2001. Mem.: Tenn. Acad. Scis., Am. Phys. Soc., Sigma Xi. Avocation: music. Office: Tenn Tech U Dept Physics Cookeville TN 38505-0001 Office Phone: 931-372-3482. Business E-Mail: jwells@tntech.edu.

**WELLS, JOHN MARCUM,** producer, writer; b. Alexandria, Va., May 28, 1956; s. Llewellyn Wallace Jr and Marjorie Elizabeth (Risberg) Wells; m. Belinda Casas, Dec. 30, 1978 (div.); m. Marilyn Wells; 2 children. BFA in Drama, Carnegie-Mellon U., 1979; MFA in Cinema, U. So. Calif., 1982. Founder, artistic dir. Pitts. New Playwrights Festival, 1978-79; asst. to v.p. mktg. Paramount Pictures Corp., 1981-82; theatrical producer various plays, Los Angeles, 1982-85; producer, writer Warner Bros. TV, Los Angeles, 1987, co-exec. producer, writer, 1988, 89, 90; producer New World Pictures, Los Angeles, 1986-87; suprg. producer, creater Roughhouse, Los Angeles, 1988. Prodr.(writer): (plays) Balm In Gilead, She Also Dances, Battery, Judgement, Ground Zero, Steaming, Femme Fatale, Tanzi, (writer, dir.): (TV series) China Beach (George Foster Peabody award, 3 Writers Guild of Am. Nominations, 6 Emmy nominations); exec. prodr.: Angel Street, 1992, Jonny Zero, 2005, The Evidence, 2006—, (writer, dir.) ER, 1994—2006, (writer) Trinity, 1998—99, The West Wing, 1999—2006, Third Watch, 1999—2005, Citizen Baines, 2001; exec. prodr. (writer): (TV series) Presidio Med, 2002—03; exec. prodr.(writer): (TV series) Smith, 2006; prodr.(writer): (films) Nice Girls Don't Explode, Interview With A Vampire, A Time To Kill, Wired, White Oleander, 2002, The Good Thief, 2002, A Home at the End of the World, 2004, Duma, 2005, Doom, 2005; exec. prodr.: The Grey Zone, 2001, One Hour Photo, 2002, Far from Heaven, 2002, Party Monster, 2003, The Company, 2003, A Dirty Shame, 2004, The Notorious Bettie Page, 2005, Infamous, 2006. Assoc. producer nat. Dem. fundraising events, L.A., 1984, Carnegie-Mellon U. Endowment Drive, Pitts., 1986; mem. exed. adv. coun. U. So. Calif. Sch. Cinema and TV. Recipient Los Angeles Drama Critics Circle award, 1982, Los Angeles Weekly award, Drama-Logue mag. award, 1985, Writers Guild Am. award, 1989, Humanitas award, 1989, Peabody award, 1990, Golden Globe award, 1990; grantee Triseme Corp., 1982. Mem.: NATAS, Carnegie-Mellon U. West Coast Alumni Assn. (bd. dirs. 1982—, pres. 1986—90), Writers Guild Am. (pres. Writers Guild Am. West 1999). Democrat. Episcopalian. Office: 4000 Warner Blvd # 2 Burbank CA 91522-0001*

**WELLS, JULIA ELIZABETH See DAME ANDREWS, JULIE**

**WELLS, KENNETH BROOKS,** medical educator, researcher; Prof. psychiatry & biobehavioral scis. UCLA Semel Inst. & Hosp. and Sch. of Medicine; sr. scientist RAND; prin. investigator UCLA/RAND Ctr. for Rsch. Quality in Managed Care. Co-author: Caring for Depression, 1996, Beating Depression: The Journey to Hope, 2002. Recipient Young Investigator Award, Disting. Investigator Award, Acad. Health. Mem.: Am. Psychiatric Assn. (Sr. Health Svc. Rsch. Award), NAS, Inst. Medicine (chair Neuroscience and Behavioral Health Bd.). Address: 1776 Main St Santa Monica CA 90401-3208 Office: UCLA Health Svcs Rsch Ctr 10920 Wilshire Blvd, Ste 300 Los Angeles CA 90024-6505 Office Phone: 310-794-3725. E-mail: kenneth_wells@rand.org.

**WELLS, KIMBERLY K.,** not-for-profit organization executive; BA in Psychology, MA in Counseling Psychology. Dir. youth svcs., dir. program svcs., assoc. exec. dir. Home Sweet Home Mission, 1987—97; exec. dir. Corp. Alliance to End Prtnr. Violence, 1997—. Mem. Workplace Com. Nat. Task Force to End Sexual and Domestic Violence Against Women; chair Promotion Com., State of Ill.; mem. Gov.'s Commn. on Status of Women in Ill. Violence Reduction Group, Ill. Corp. Citizenship Initiative; mem. steering com. Ill. Family Violence Coordinating Coun.; mem. 11th Jud. Cir. Family Violence Coordinating Coun. Planning Com.; co-chair McLean County Domestic Violence Task Force Youth and Children Work Group; treas., bd. dirs. Ill. Ctr. for Violence Prevention; grad. Leadership Am. Am. Issues Forum, 1999; guest lectr. Ill. State U., Heartland C.C. Office: 2416 E Washington St Ste E Bloomington IN 61704-4472

**WELLS, KITTY (ELLEN MURIEL DEASON),** musician; b. Nashville, Aug. 30, 1919; d. Charles Cary and Myrtle Bell (Street) Deason; m. Johnnie Robert Wright, Oct. 30, 1937; children: Ruby Jean Wright Taylor, Bobby Wright, Carol Sue Wright-Sturdivant. Grad. high sch. Country music singer; sang gospel in chs. as a child; formed group Deacon Sisters, performed on radio, early 30's; with Johnny and Jack and the Tenn. Mountain Boys, late 1930's-early 1940's, regular on Grand Ole Opry, from 1952, had own family TV show, late 1960's-early 1970's, now with Johnny Wright, Bobby Wright and the Tennessee Mountain Boys; songs include: Gathering Flowers for the Master's Bouquet, How Far is Heaven, Release Me, It Wasn't God Who Made Honky Tonk Angels, Making Believe, Thank You For the Roses; albums include Kitty Wells & Roy Drusky, Vol. 1 & 2, Back to Back Patsy Kline, 1995, (with Red Foley, Webb Pierce, others) Duets, 1995; author: Kitty Wells Cookbook. Bd. dirs. Nashville Meml. Hosp. Recipient award as number 1 female singer Cashbox Mag., 1953-62, Billboard 1954-65, award of yr. for top female country vocalist Record World mag. 1965, award for highest artistic achievement in rec. arts 1964, various awards Downbeat Mag., award as all-time queen of country music Music Bus. Mag. 1964, Woman of Yr. award 1974, Pioneer award Acad. Country Music 1985, Living Legend award

Music City news 1991, voted nation's number one Country Female Artist for 14 consecutive years; named Top Female Artist of Decade, Record World Mag. 1974; named to Country Music Hall of Fame 1976. Mem. Country Music Assn., Nat. Assn. Rec. Arts and Scis. (Govs. award for Outstanding Achievement in Recording Industry, 1981, Grammy Lifetime Achievement award, 1991). Mem. Ch. of Christ. Achievements include being the first woman to hit No. 1 on the country charts with "It Wasn't God Who Made Honky Tonk Angels.".

**WELLS, LESLEY,** federal judge; b. Muskegon, Mich., Oct. 6, 1937; d. James Franklin and Inez Simpson Wells; m. Charles F. Clarke, Nov. 13, 1998; children: Lauren Elizabeth, Caryn Alison, Anne Kristin, Thomas Eliot. BA, Chatham Coll., 1959; JD cum laude, Cleve. State U., 1974. Bar: Ohio 1975, US Dist. Ct. (no. dist.) Ohio 1975, US Supreme Ct. 1989. Pvt. practice, Cleve., 1975; ptnr. Brooks & Moffet, Cleve., 1975—78; dir., atty. ABAR Litigation Ctr., Cleve., 1979—80; assoc. Schneider, Smeltz, Huston & Ranney, Cleve., 1980—83; judge Ct. Common Pleas, Cleve., 1983—94, U.S. Dist. Ct. (no. dist.) Ohio 6th Cir., Cleve., 1994—. Adj. prof. law and urban policy Cleve. State U., 1980-83, 90-93. Editor, author: Litigation Manual, 1980. Past pres. Cleve. Legal Aid Soc.; legal chmn. Nat. Women's Polit. Caucus, 1981-82; chmn. Gov.'s Task Force on Family Violence, Ohio, 1983-87; mem. biomed. ethics com. Case Western Res. U. Med. Sch., 1985-94; mem. NW Ordinance US Constn. Commn., Ohio, 1986-88; master William K. Thomas Inn of Ct., 1989—, counselor, 1993, pres., 1998-99; trustee Rosemary Ctr., 1986-92, Miami U., 1989-92, Urban League Cleve., 1989-90, Chatham Coll., 1989-94. Recipient Superior Jud. award Supreme Ct. Ohio, 1983, J. Irwin award Womenspace, Ohio, 1984, award Womens City Club, 1985, Disting. Alumna award Chatham Coll., 1988, Alumni Civic Achievement award Cleve. State U., 1992, Golden Gavel award Ohio Judges Assn., 1994, Outstanding Alumni award Cleve. Marshall Law Alumni Assn., 1994, Greater Cleve. Achievement award YWCA, 1995. Mem. ABA (coun. litigation sect. 1996-99), Am. Law Inst., Ohio State Bar Assn., Ohio Womens Bar Assn., Cleve. Bar Assn. (Merit Svc. award 1983), Cuyahoga County Bar Assn., Nat. Assn. Women Judges, Philos. Club Cleve. Office: 328 US Court House 201 Superior Ave Cleveland OH 44114-1234 Office Phone: 216-615-4480. Business E-Mail: lesley_wells@ohnd.uscourts.gov.

**WELLS, LINTON, II,** federal agency administrator; b. Luanda, Angola, Apr. 7, 1946; s. Linton and Helen Fay (Gillis) W.; m. Linda Marie Motta; children: Linton III, Frank. BS in Physics and Oceanography, U.S. Naval Acad., 1967; MSE in Math. Scis., PhD in Internat. Rels., Johns Hopkins U., 1975; student, Boueikeushusho (Japanese Nat. Def. Coll.), Tokyo. Commd. ensign USN, 1967; commdr. USS Joseph Strauss, 1984-86, Destroyer Squadron 21, 1989-91; advanced through grades to capt. USN, 1994, ret. 1994; asst. to under sec. for policy US Dept. Def., Washington, 1991-93, dep. to under sec. def. policy, 1993-98, dep. under sec. def. policy support, 1998, prin. dep. asst. sec. def. networks & info. integration, 1998—, acting asst. sec. def. networks & info. integration, chief info. officer, 2004—05. Co-author: Japanese Cruisers of the Pacific War, 1997. Decorated Def. Superior Svc. medal, Legion of Merit (2), others; recipient Def. Disting. Pub. Svc. medal, C.N.G. Hendrix award for excellence in oceanography, 1967, Arleigh Burke Leadership award, 1975, Silver medal prize essay contest Naval Inst., 1985. Mem. Army and Navy Club, U.S. Naval Inst., Soc. Physics Students, Explorers Club, Tau Beta Pi (hon.). Avocations: flying, scuba diving, reading, travel. Office: Prin Dep Asst Sec Def N11 6000 The Pentagon Rm 3e172 Washington DC 20301-6000

**WELLS, LLOYD ALLAN,** psychiatrist, educator; b. Providence, Mar. 4, 1948; s. Lloyd Alvin and Elizabeth Hunter Wells; m. Denise Marie Coutu, Dec. 15, 1973; children: Aynslee, Llyd, Ethan. BA, Harvard Coll., 8, 1968; PhD, U. Rochester, 1973, MD with distinction, 1974. Diplomate Am. Bd. Psychiatry and Neurology. Cons. Mayo Clinic, Rochester, Minn., 1974—2001, assoc. prof., 1983—, sect. head, 1980—91, vice-chmn. edn., 1999—, chair divsn. child and adolescent psychiatry and psychology, 2001—. Contbr. articles to profl. jours. Active Olmsted County Task Force on Family Violence, Rochester, Minn., 1982—83, Olmsted County Task Force on Guidelines for Hospitalization, Rochester, Minn., 1989. Named Tchr. of Yr., Assn. for Acad. Psychiatry, 1998; named to Tchg. Hall of Fame, Mayo Graduate Sch. Medicine, 1987; recipient Fisher award, Internat. Hibernation Soc., 1969, Writing award, Perspectives in Biology and Medicine, 1976; fellow Falk fellow, Am. Psychiatric Assn., 1976—77, Laughlin fellow, Am. Coll. Psychiatrists, 1977. Fellow: Am. Psychiat. Assn. (psychiat. nursing com. 1977—80); mem.: Am. Acad. Child and Adolescent Psychiatry (com. on substance abuse 1988—93), Am. Assn. for the History of Medicine (Harvey Osler award 1972), Am. Assn. Dirs. of Psychiatry Residency Training Pprograms (child and adolescent caucus), Soc. Profs. of Child and Adolescent Psychiatry (edn. chmn. 2003—), Assn. for the Advancement of Philosophy and Psychiatry, Am. Acad. Psychoanalysis (managed care com., edn. com. 1998—2002), Am. Soc. Adolescent Psychiatry (coun. on fellowships, treas., dir. ednl. resources 1990—94), Am. Bd. Psychiatry and Neurology, Inc. (assoc. examiner), Acad. Psychosomatic Medicine (ednl. dir. 1983), Minn. Psychiat. Soc. (nominating com. 1979, ethics com. 1989), Sigma Xi. Home: 623 8th Ave SW Rochester MN 55902 Office: Mayo Clinic Rochester MN 55905 Office Phone: 507-284-2933. Business E-Mail: wells.lloyd@mayo.edu.

**WELLS, MARY ELIZABETH THOMPSON,** deacon, director, chaplain, director; b. Dallas, Oct. 9, 1950; d. Owen Perry and Ruth Marie Thompson; children: Tadd Whitney, Britony Ruth. BA in Sociology, Syracuse U., 1958; MA in Child Devel., Tufts U., 1964, MEd in Counseling Psychology, 1974; MA in Theology, St. Vincent de Paul Regional Sem., 2005. Ordained min. Diocese of Southeast Fla., 2002. Asst. dir. pub. rels. Inst. Crippled and Disabled, N.Y.C., 1958-59; head tchr. Eliot-Pearson Children's Sch., Tufts U., Medford, Mass., 1964-66; psychotherapist Mental Health Ctr. Greater Cape Ann, Gloucester, Mass. 1964-09, deacon, chaplain, spiritual dir. St. Paul's Episcopal Ch., Delray Beach, Fla., 1999—, dir. Diocesan Sch. S.E. Fla., 2003—. Mem.: APA, Spiritual Dirs. Internat., Assn. Profl. Chaplains, Assn. Clin. Pastoral Educators, Am. Orthopsychiatric Assn. Home: 1183 Canoe Point Delray Beach Delray Beach FL 33444 Office: Saint Pauls Episcopal Ch 188 S Swinton Ave Delray Beach FL 33444-3698

**WELLS, MARY JULIA,** psychologist; b. Arlington, Va., Nov. 23, 1958; d. John Murrell and Rollene Sumner Wells; m. Michael Tracy Poegl, May 26, 1996; stepchildren: Nicole Lee Poegl, Christopher Michael Poegl. BS, Va. Commonwealth U., 1980; MPhil, George Wash. U., 1988, PhD, 1990. Lic. clin. psychologist Va., 1991. Psychology assoc. Wash. Pain and Rehab Ctr., Wash., DC, 1988—90; asst. prof. Med. Coll. Va., Richmond, Va., 1990—93; clin. psychologist Inst. Chronic Pain Mgmt., Richmond, 1993—96, pvt. practice, Richmond, 1996—2000, Sheltering Arm Hosp., Richmond, 2000—. Contbr. chapters to books. Pres. Richmond Acad. Clin. Psychologists, Richmond, Va., 1995—96, mem. chair, 2002—04, pres., 2005; anti racism trainer Unitarian, Universalist Assn., Richmond, Va., 1999. Mem.: Am. Psychological Assn., Va. Psychological Assn., Richmond Acad. Clin. Psychologists. Democrat. Unitarian. Avocations: music, dogs. Office: Sheltering Arms Physical Rehab Hosp 8254 Atlee Rd Mechanicsville VA 23116 Office Phone: 804-723-3275. Business E-Mail: mwells@shelteringarms.com.

**WELLS, MELISSA FOELSCH,** ambassador; b. Tallinn, Estonia, Nov. 18, 1932; emigrated to U.S., 1936, naturalized, 1941; d. Kuno Georg and Miliza (Korjus) Foelsch; m. Alfred Washburn Wells, 1960; children: Christopher, Gregory. BS in Fgn. Service, Georgetown U., 1956. Fgn. svc. officer Dept. State, Washington, 1958-61, consular officer Trinidad, 1961-64; econ. officer mission OECD, Paris, 1964-66; econ. officer London, 1966-71; internat. economist, 1971-73; dep. dir. maj. export projects Dept. Commerce, 1973-75; commnl. counselor Brazil, 1975-76; amb. to Guinea-Bissau and Cape Verde Dept. of State, 1976-77; U.S. rep. ECOSOC, UN, N.Y.C., 1977-79; resident rep. UNDP, Kampala, Uganda, 1979-81; dir. IMPACT program Geneva, 1982-86; amb. to Mozambique, 1987-90; amb. to Zaire, Kinshasa, 1991-93; under-sec. gen. for adminstrn. and mgmt. UN, N.Y., 1993-94; consul gen. Sao

Paulo, Brazil, 1995-97; amb. to Republic of Estonia Dept. of State, 1998—2001. Bd. dirs. U.S.-Baltic Found. Mem. Am. Fgn. Service Assn., Am. Acad. Diplomacy. Office: Casa Wells Plz Leoncio Bento 7 38830 Agulo Gomera Canary Islands Spain

**WELLS, NINA MITCHELL,** state official; b. 1950; m. Theodore V. Wells; 2 children. BA, Newton Coll. of Sacred Heart, 1973; JD, Suffolk U. Atty. Bell Comms. Rsch., 1985; dir. div. rate counsel NJ Pub. Advocate; dir. minority student program and fin. aid Rutgers U. Sch. Law, asst. dean, 1996—97; v.p. pub. affairs Schering-Plough Corp., Kenilworth, NJ, 1998—2004; sec. of state State of NJ, Trenton, 2006—. Pres. Schering-Plough Found. Recipient Garden State Bar Assn. award, 2005. Democrat. Office: Office Sec of State PO Box 300 Trenton NJ 08625 Office Phone: 609-984-1900. Office Fax: 609-292-9897. E-mail: feedback@sos.state.nj.us.*

**WELLS, NORMAN, JR.,** metal products executive; BS metallurgy, indsl. engring., U. Wash., 1971; MBA, Gonzaga U., 1980. With Castech Aluminum Group Inc., Akron, Ohio, 2006—. Office: Castech Aluminum Group Inc 753 W Waterloo Rd Akron OH 44314-1525

**WELLS, PETER SCOVILLE,** retired marketing professional; b. N.Y.C., Apr. 25, 1938; s. Jonathan Godfrey and Eleanore Shannon (Scoville) Wells; m. Patricia Ann Trent, Dec. 8, 1973; 1 child from previous marriage, Peter Scoville. Asst. to contr. Laird & Co., N.Y.C., 1961-63; asst. to ptnr. charge ops. Goldman Sachs, N.Y.C., 1963-64; mgr. new bus. dept. B.J. Herkimer Co., N.Y.C., 1964-67; divisional policy and procedures adminstr. Paine, Webber, Jackson & Curtis, Inc., N.Y.C., 1967-70, asst. to exec. cashier, 1970-73, asst. v.p., mgr. employment svcs., adminstr. equal employment opportunity, 1973 80; pers. officer, exec. recruiter N.Y. Stock Exch., N.Y.C., 1980-86, mgr. employment; sr. v.p. Wesley Brown & Bartle, 1986-87; sr. v.p., dir. Alliance Mktg., Inc., 1987; ptnr. Richards & Wells, 1988-90, Brookman Assocs., Inc., 1990—2000; ret., 2000. With U.S. Army, 1958—66. Mem.: SAR, Vet. Corps Arty., L'Ordre Militaire, KT, Order of Lafayette, Mil. Order Loyal Legion, Knights of Malta (knight comdr.), Phi Kappa Psi. Home: 449 E 78th St New York NY 10021-1649

**WELLS, RAYMOND O'NEIL, JR.,** mathematics professor, researcher; b. Dallas, June 12, 1940; s. Raymond O. and Hazel (Rand) W.; m. Rena Schwarze, Aug. 1, 1963; children: Richard Andrew, René Michael. BA, Rice U., 1962; MS, NYU, 1964, PhD, 1965. Asst. prof. math. Rice U., Houston, 1965-69, assoc. prof., 1969-74, prof. math., 1974-2000, prof. edn., 1993-2000; chmn. dept. math., 1976-79; chmn. dept. math. Rice U., Houston, 1994-98, dir. sch. math. project, 1987-2000, dir. computational math. lab., 1990-2000, prof. math emeritus, 2000—, asst. to pres., 2000-01; v.p. external affairs, prof. math. Internat. U., Bremen, 2001—05, disting. prof. math., 2005—. Vis. asst. prof. Brandeis U., Waltham, Mass., 1967-68; vis. prof. U. Göttingen, Germany, 1974-75, U. Colo., Boulder, 1983-84, U. Bremen, Germany, 1995-96, Internat. U. Bremen, 1998-2001; adj. prof. cmty. medicine Baylor Coll. Medicine, 1994-2000; active Inst. for Advanced Study, Princeton, N.J., 1970-71, 79-80; exch. visitor NAS, Sofia, Bulgaria, 1984; planning com. Internat. U., Bremen, 1997-99. Author: Differential Analysis on Complex Manifolds, 1973, Mathematics in Civilization, 1973, Twister Geometry and Field Theory, 1990, Wavelet Analysis: The Scaleable Structure of Information, 1998; editor: Mathematical Heritage of Herman Weyl, 1989, (book series) Expositions in Mathematics, 1988—2003, The Founding of International University Bremen: Perspectives for the Twenty First Century, 2003; contbr. numerous articles to sci. jours. Pres. Stages Repertory Theater, Houston, 1989-90; sec. bd. dirs. IUB Found. Am., Inc., 2004— Recipient Alexander von Humboldt Sr. U.S. Scientist award U. Göttingen, 1974-75; Fulbright fellow, 1968, Guggenheim fellow, 1974. Fellow AAAS (coun. 1989—); mem. Am. Math. Soc. (coun., editor 1978-88), Cosmos Club Washington, Carl Schutz Soc. (pres.) Home: Lüder-von-Bentheim Str 12 28209 Bremen Germany Office: Internat Univ Bremen PO Box 750561 28725 Bremen Germany Office Phone: 49 421 200 4321. Business E-Mail: wells@iu-bremen.de.

**WELLS, REBECCA,** writer; b. Alexandria, La. married. Student, Naropa Inst., Boulder, Colo. Founder Performing Artists for Nuclear Disarmament, Seattle. Author: (plays) Splittin' Hairs (nominee, Showtime's Excellence in Am. Theater), Gloria Duplex, (novels) Divine Secrets of the Ya-Ya Sisterhood, 1996 (Adult trade Abby award, 1999, #1 NY Times bestseller), Little Altars Everywhere, 1998 (Western States Book award, NY Times bestseller), Ya-Yas in Bloom, 2005 (NY Times bestseller). Roman Catholic. Mailing: c/o HarperCollins 10 E 53rd St New York NY 10022

**WELLS, RICHARD A.,** manufacturing executive; BSBA, U. Wis., Madison, 1960; cert. in data processing, U. Wis., Milw. CPA, Wis. With Kohler (Wis.) Co.; sr. v.p. fin., CFO, 1979-1999, also mem. exec. com., pension investment com., bd. dirs. Office: Kohler Co 444 Highland Dr Kohler WI 53044-1500

**WELLS, ROBERT ALFRED,** lawyer; b. Louisiana, Mo., Dec. 1, 1942; s. Harry Armstrong and Irene Jacobson W.; m. Binney Kitchel, Dec. 21, 1968; children: Hylah, Theodore. BA with honors, DePauw U., 1964; JD cum laude, U. Mich., 1967. Bar: N.Y. 1968, N.H. 1971, Mo. 1981, US Tax Ct. 1973, U.S. Supreme Ct. 1976, U.S. Mil. Ct. Appeals 1978. Assoc. Dewey, Ballantine, Bushby, Palmer & Wood, N.Y.C., 1967-68, McLane, Graf, Raulerson & Middleton, Manchester, N.H., 1971—. Trustee Heritage Heights/Homewood, 1994—2001, Soc. for Protection of N.H. Forests, 1988—96, sec., 1995—96; trustee, treas. Children's Trust Fund; dir. pres. Office Pub. Guardian; dir. v.p. Concord Cmty. Music Sch., 1995—2001; advance studies program chair adv. com. St. Paul's Sch.; active St. Andrew's Episc. Ch., Hopkinton, N.H., 1971—, vestry mem., 1974—77, warden, 1979—85; trustee Protestant Episc. Ch. of N.H., 1983 ; bd. dirs. Am. Lung Assn. of N.H., pres., 1980—81, sec., 1990—2002; bd. dirs. Am. Lung Assn., 1982—94, exec. com., 1987—2002, v.p., 1990; mem. Town of Hopkinton Planning Bd., 1977—79, Town of Hopkinton Budget Com., 1992—2005; co-chmn. Hopkinton Master Plan Revision Com., 1986—88; chmn. State Adv. Com. to the U.S. Civil Rights Commn., 1985—89; bd. dirs. Pat's Peak Ednl. Found., Inc., 1982—87, Youth Soccer Assn. Lt. USN, 1968—70. Mem. Am Coll. Trust and Estate Counsel, N.H. Bar Assn. (chmn. elderly legal devel. Program 1978-81, continuing legal edn. program 1981—, fee dispute resolution com. 1986-88), Internat. Assn. Fin. Planners (edn. com. 1985—90), Phi Beta Kappa. Episcopalian. Office: PO Box 326 Manchester NH 03105-0326

**WELLS, ROGER STANLEY,** software engineer; b. Seattle, Apr. 13, 1949; s. Stanley A. and Margaret W. BA, Whitman Coll., 1971; postgrad., U. Tex., Austin, 1973—74; BS, Oreg. State U., 1977. Software evaluation engr. Tektronix, Beaverton, Oreg., 1979—83; computer engr. Aramco, Dhahran, Saudi Arabia, 1983—84; software engr. Conrac Corp., Clackamas, Oreg., 1984—85, Duarte, Calif., 1985; software analyst Lundy Fin. Systems, San Dimas, Calif., 1986—89; pvt. practice Seattle, 1989—92; sr. project engr. Illuminet, Olympia, Wash., 1993—2000; mgr. configuration New Edge Networks, Vancouver, Wash., 2000—01; tech. advisor E-corps Wash. Svc. Corps, 2002—04; software builder Volt Tech. Resources, 2004—05; computer process specialist Boeing, 2005—. Adv. to chair Cascadia N.Am. Sci. Fiction Conf., 2003—05; mem. Exec. of Yr. com. Illuminet, Olympia, 1998—99. Bd. dirs. Lydia Whitney Found., Collinsville, Conn., Found. for Preservation Sci. Fiction and Fantasy Memorabilia, Salem, Oreg.; co-founder, bd. dirs., pres. Oreg. Sci. Fiction Conv., 1979-81; vol. Americorps, Yakima, Wash., 2002-03, Pasco, Wash., 2003-04, ARC, 2004—. Mem. IEEE, Am. Philatelic Soc., Nat. Assn. Parliamentarians, Am. Inst. Parliamentarians (chpt. v.p. 1996-97, pres. 1997-98), Fantasy Amateur Press Assn., N.W. Sci. Fiction Soc., Mensa, Assn. Computing Machinery, L.A. Sci. Fantasy Soc., Melbourne (Australia) Sci. Fiction Club, Toastmasters Internat. (club pres. 1980, v.p. edn. 1994-95, area gov. 1994-95, dist. 32 parliamentarian 1996-99). Internat. Platform Assn. (2d place Monologue contest 1997, conv. com. 1998-99, bd. govs. 1999-2000)

Achievements include design of software program to transfer billing records for regional telephone companies. Avocations: travel, public speaking, science fiction, stamp collecting/philately. Home: PO Box 69254 Seatac WA 98168-9254 Office: PMB 178 15031 Military Rd S Ste B Seatac WA 98188 Personal E-mail: rswells@acm.org.

**WELLS, ROGER W.,** lawyer; b. Sioux Falls, S.D., May 7, 1957; BSBA summa cum laude, Creighton U., 1979, JD summa cum laude, 1981. Bar: Nebr. 1981, U.S. Dist. Ct. Nebr. 1981, U.S. Tax Ct. 1981. And gen. counsel ConAgra Foods Inc., Omaha, 2002—; head, mergers and acquisitions McGrath, North, Mullin & Kratz, Omaha, 1981—. Mem. editl. staff: Creighton U. Law Rev., 1980—81. Mem.: ABA (mem. corp., banking and bus. sect., mem. taxation sect., mem. internat. law sect.), Omaha Bar Assn., Nebr. Bar Assn., Beta Gamma Sigma. Office: McGrath North Mullin and Kratz PC Ste 3700 1st Nat Tower 1601 Dodge St Omaha NE 68102 Office Phone: 402-341-3070. Business E-Mail: rwells@mnmk.com.

**WELLS, ROSS R.,** secondary school educator, writer; b. Lockhart, Tex., Aug. 26, 1949; s. Ross Roberts and Evelyn Jewell Wells; m. Linda Williams Wells, Oct. 25, 1975; children: Terence, Chelsea. BA, Tex. Tech. U., Lubbock, 1972, MA, 1982. Artistic dir. Lockhart Cmty. Theatre, Tex., 1981—87; dir. theatre Brookstone Sch., Columbus, Ga., 1987—95; dir. pub. rels. Keystone Sch., San Antonio; dir. debate/speech Holmes H.S., San Antonio, 2001—04; dir. theatre Devine H.S., Tex., 2004—06; owner, operator Wells Comm., San Antonio, 2001—. Author: (novels) eXplZion!, 2002, Red T-Bird, 2006, (plays) Of Strange Voices and Watermelon Men, 2006. Dir. region 1 Tex. Cmty. Edn., Lockhart, 1984, pres.-elect, 1986; Key Club sponsor cmty. svc. Keystone Sch., San Antonio, 1998 2001; bd. mcm. Key Club Bexar Kiwanis Club, San Antonio, 2001. Recipient Outstanding Video Prodn. award, Tex. Tech. Film/Video Fest, 1980, Pres. award, Bexar Kiwanis Club, 2001. Mem.: Nat. Ednl. Theatre Assn., Tex. Ednl. Theatre Assn. Avocations: photography, entertainment memorabilia. Home: 26 Campden Cir San Antonio TX 78218

**WELLS, SAMUEL ALONZO, JR.,** surgeon, educator; b. Cuthbert, Ga., Mar. 16, 1936; s. Samuel Alonzo and Martha Steele W.; m. Barbara Anne Atwood, Feb. 13, 1964; children: Sarah, Susan. Student, Emory U., 1954—57, MD, 1961. Intern Johns Hopkins Hosp., Balt., 1961—62, resident in internal medicine, 1962—63; asst. resident in surgery Barnes Hosp., St. Louis, 1963—64; resident in surgery Duke U., Durham, NC, 1966—70; guest investigator dept. tumor biology Karolinska Inst., Stockholm, 1967—68; asst. prof. surgery Duke U., Durham, NC, 1970—72, assoc. prof., 1972—76, prof., 1976—81; clin. assoc. surgery br. Nat. Cancer Inst., NIH, Bethesda, Md., 1964—66, sr. investigator surgery br., 1970—72, cons. surgery br., 1975—; prof., chmn. dept. surgery Washington U., St. Louis, 1981—98; dir. ACS, Chgo., 1998—99; group chair, prin. investigator ACS Oncology Group, Chgo., 1998—2005. Dir. Duke U. Clin. Rsch. Ctr., 1978—81; mem. Residency Rev. Com. Surgery, 1987—93, chmn., 1991—93; mem. bd. regents ACS, 1989—98, vice chmn. bd. regents, 1999—; prof. surgery Duke U. Sch. Medicine, 2001—. Mem. editl. bd.: Annals of Surgery, 1975—93, Surgery, 1975—93, Jour. Surg. Rsch., 1981—93, editor in chief: World Jour. Surgery, 1983—92, Current Problems in Surgery, 1989—. Pres. GM Cancer Rsch. Found., 1996—. Lt. comdr. USPHS, 1964—66. Fellow: AAAS; mem.: ACS, Soc. Internationale de Chirurgie (pres. 2001), Soc. Surg. Oncology (pres. 1993—94), Halsted Soc. (pres. 1987), Nat. Cancer Adv. Bd., Inst. Medicine of NAS, Am. Soc. Clin. Investigation, Soc. Clin. Surgery (treas. 1980—86, v.p. 1986—88, pres. 1988—90), Soc. Univ. Surgeons (exec. coun. 1976—78), Am. Surg. Assn. (mem. coun. 1986—91, pres. 1995—96, recorder, Sci. Achievement medallion 2004), Am. Bd. Surgery (exec. com. 1986—89, vice chmn. 1987—88, chmn. 1988—89), Alpha Omega Alpha. Office: Dept Surgery Box 3285 Duke U Sch Medicine Durham NC 27710 Office Phone: 919-201-0310. Business E-Mail: wells029@mc.duke.edu. E-mail: wells029@gmail.com.

**WELLS, STEVEN WAYNE,** lawyer; b. Ft. Walton Beach, Fla., Sept. 8, 1960; s. H. Wayne and Shirley A. W.; m. Lisa Stieler, May 20, 1983; Robert, James, Jessica. BA in Comm., Mich. State U., 1982; JD with distinction, Detroit Coll. of Law, 1985. Bar: Mich. Asst. prosecutor Oakland County, Pontiac, Mich., 1985-88; mng. ptnr. Schnelz, Bondy & Wells, PC, Troy, Mich., 1988-93; shareholder, mng. ptnr. Cross Wrock, PC, Detroit, 1993-99; prin. shareholder Schnelz Wells P.C., Birmingham, Mich., 1999—. Lectr., presenter in field. Contbr. articles to State Bar Jour. Pres. Bloomfield Village Bd. Fellow Mich. Bar Assn.; ABA, ATLA, Detroit Bar Assn., Mich. Trial Lawyers Assn., Nat. Dist. Attys. Assn. Avocations: golf, tennis, coaching youth baseball, soccer. Office: 280 N Old Woodward Ste 250 Birmingham MI 48009 Office Phone: 248-258-7074. E-mail: swells@swlawpc.com.

**WELLS, THEODORE V., JR.,** lawyer; b. Washington, Apr. 28, 1950; BA, Holy Cross, 1972; MBA, Harvard U., 1976; JD, Harvard Law Sch., 1976. Bar: N.J. 1977; Washington, DC 2001; NY, 2001. Law clk. to Hon. John J Gibbons U.S. Ct. Appeals (3rd cir.), 1976-77; ptnr. Lowenstein, Sandler, Kohl, Fisher & Boylan P.C., Roseland, NJ, Paul, Weiss, Rifkind, Wharton & Garrison LLP, NYC. Mem. adj. faculty trade regulation Sch. Law, Seton Hall U., 1980-81; mem. faculty trial advocacy Practicing Law Inst., 1982—; mem. lawyers adv. com. U.S. Ct. Appeals (3rd cir.), 1982-85, 88—; former mem., bd. dirs. CIT Corp.; co-chair White Collar Criminal Sec. Nat. Assoc. Criminal Defense Lawyers; gen. counsel N.J. Dem. Party; tchg. team mem. Harvard Law Sch. Trial Advocacy Workshop; fel. Am. Trial Lawyers Assn. Bd. trustees Coll. Holy Cross, 1977—, Newark Mus., 1979-82, N.J. Performing Arts Ctr., NAACP Legal Defense Fund; bd. dirs. Essex County Urban League, 1979-88; N.J. co-chairperson United Negro Coll. Fund; gen. counsel, NJ NAACP. Named one of 75 Best Lawyers in Washington, Washingtonian survey mag., 2002, named to Am.'s Top Black Lawyers, Black Enterprise mag., 2003. Mem. ABA (antitrust law sect., state antitrust law subcom. 1980—), Assn. Criminal Def. Lawyers (trustee 1984—), N.J. State Bar Assn. (antitrust law com. 1980—) Office: Paul, Weiss, Rifkind, Wharton & Garrison LLP 1285 Avenue of the Americas New York NY 10019-6064 Office Phone: 212-373-3089. E-mail: twells@paulweiss.com.

**WELLS, THOMAS B.,** federal judge; b. Akron, OH, July 2, 1945; BS, Miami U., 1967; JD, Emory U., 1973; LLM, NYU, 1978. Atty. Graham & Wells, Vidalia, Ga., 1973—77; city atty. City of Vidalia, Ga., 1975—77; county atty. Toombs County, Ga., 1975—77; atty. Hurt, Richardson, Garner, Todd & Cadenhead, Atlanta, 1978—81, Shearer & Wells, Atlanta, 1981—86; judge U.S. Tax Ct., Washington, 1986—97, 1997—2000, 2004—, chief judge, 1997, 2000—04. With USNR, 1967—70. Recipient Disting. Alumnus award, Emory Law Alumni, 2001. Mem. ABA. Office: US Tax Ct 400 2nd St NW Washington DC 20217-0002

**WELLS, TULLOS,** lawyer; b. Urbana, Ill., Apr. 11, 1949; m. Carri Baker Wells; 1 child, McKensie Lynd. BA, U. Tex., Austin, 1971; JD, U. Tex. Sch. Law, 1974. Bar: Tex. 1974, admitted to practice: US Ct. Appeals (DC Cir.), US Ct. Appeals (5th Cir.) 1981, US Ct. Appeals (11th Cir.) 1981, US Dist. Ct. (No. Dist.) Tex. 1980, US Dist. Ct. (So. Dist.) Tex. 1980, US Dist. Ct. (We. Dist.) Tex. 1980, cert.: Tex. Bd. Legal Specialization (in labor and employment law). Ptnr. Wells, Pinckney & McHugh; mng. ptnr. Bracewell & Giuliani, San Antonio, 1999—; outside gen. counsel San Antonio Spurs, 1995—. Spkr. in field. Bd. dirs. Spurs Found.; bd. trustees, exec. com. United Way of San Antonio; bd. dir. Greater Kelly Devel. Corp., 1995—2000; chmn. bd. Greater San Antonio C. of C., 1995, former chmn., govt. affairs coun., former chmn., mil. affairs coun.; bd. dir. Tex. Assn. of Atlantic Coun. of US, San Antonio Econ. Devel. Found.; bd. dir. Tex. Bus. Hall of Fame; bd. gov. Cancer Therapy & Rsch. Ctr.; chmn. bd. Austin-San Antonio Inter-Municipal Commuter Rail Dist. Named one of Top 50 Lawyers Ctrl. and West Tex. Region Super Lawyers, Tex. Super Lawyer, 2003, 2004, 2005. Mem.: State Bar Tex. Avocation: sailing. Office: Bracewell & Giuliani 800 One Alamo Ctr 106 S St Mary's St San Antonio TX 78205-3603 Office Phone: 210-299-3525. Office Fax: 210-299-0126. E-mail: tullos.wells@bracewellgiuliani.com.*

**WELLS, WYATT CLINTON,** historian; b. Nashville, June 18, 1964; s. Charles Edmon and Ann Harwell Wells; m. Barbara Jean Gilbert, Aug. 11, 2001; children: Wyatt Clinton children: Charles Edmon. BA, Vanderbilt U., 1986; MA, U. N.C., 1988, PhD, 1992. Instr. U. N.C.-Chapel Hill, 1992—93; asst. editor Andrew Jackson Papers, Knoxville, Tenn., 1993—96; Newcomen fellow Harvard U. Bus. Sch., Boston, 1996—97; prof. history Auburn U., Montgomery, Ala., 1997—. Author: (book) Economist in an Uncertain World: Arthur F. Burns and the Federal Reserve, 1970-1978, 1994, Antitrust and the Formation of the Postwar World, 2002, American Capitalism, 1945-2000, 2003; editor: (edited papers) Papers of Andrew Jackson, Volume 6, 1825-1828, 2002. Fellow, Fulbright Found., 2001-2002. Republican. Episcopalian. Office: Univ Montgomery Dept History PO Box 244023 Montgomery AL 36124-4023 Office Phone: 334-244-3363.

**WELLS-HENDERSON, RONALD JOHN,** investment counselor; b. Jan. 28, 1934; s. William Noel and Sylvia Mary (Gowen) W-H.; m. Kathleen Louise McDonnell, Sept. 14, 1957; children: Anne, John. BA, U. Wash., 1955; MBA, Northwestern U., 1957. CFA. Security analyst Continental Bank, Chgo., 1957—59; fin. analyst Boeing Co., Seattle; trust investment mgr. Seattle Trust, 1970—80; prin. KAS Investment Cons., Seattle, 1980—. Contbr. articles to profl. jours. Mem. Seattle Art Mus., Bellevue Art Mus., 1957—; treas. Civil Affairs Assn., 1975—79; curator-treas. Seattle King County Mil. History Soc., 1978—80. Lt. col. USAR, 1955—83. Named Gazzam Found. scholar, 1952—55. Mem.: Washington Water Trails Assn., CFA Inst. (charter holder), Seattle Soc. Fin. Analysts. Episcopalian. Home: 13005 SE 46th St Bellevue WA 98006-2042 Office: KAS Investment Cons PO Box 5617 Bellevue WA 98006-0117 Office Phone: 425-641-7645. Personal E-mail: ronw-h@prodigy.net.

**WELNA, CECILIA,** retired mathematics professor, dean; b. New Britain, Conn., July 15, 1927; d. Joseph and Sophie (Roman) Welna. BS, St. Joseph Coll., 1949; MA, U. Conn., 1952, PhD, 1960. Instr. Mt. St. Joseph Acad., 1949-50; asst. instr. U. Conn., 1950-55; instr. U. Mass., Amherst, 1955-56; prof., chmn. dept. math. and physics U. Hartford, 1956—82; dean Coll. Edn., Nursing and Health Professions, 1982—93, prof. math., 1993—. Mem.: Math. Assn. Am., Nat. Council Tchrs. Math., Assn. Tchrs. Math. Conn., Sigma Xi. Personal E-mail: seawell31@aol.com.

**WELNAK, LLOWELL A.,** retired lawyer; b. Milw., July 19, 1926; s. Albert George Welnak and Wilhelmina Helena Struck; children: Ann Harvey, Peter. BA, Marquette U., 1948, LLB, 1960. Claim mgr. Md. Casualty Co., Phila., 1950—63, Ctrl. Mut., Van Wert, Ohio, 1963—73; v.p., gen. counsel Peerless Ins. Co., Keene, NH, 1973—88; ret., 1988. Active YMCA. Mem.: Lions.

**WELSCH, KEVIN EUGENE,** music educator; b. Oxford, Nebr., Sept. 25, 1953; s. Robert Eugene and Marian May Welsch; m. Lori Ann Tobaben, May 17, 1978; children: Hillary May, Jeremy Robert, Kristin Ann. BA in Mus. Edn., Kearney State Coll., Nebr., 1975. Cert. tchr. Nebr. Dept. Edn., 1975. Instr. music Elwood Pub. Schs., Elwood, 1976—78, Orleans Pub. Schs., 1979—81, Leigh Cmty. Schs., 1981—. Past pres. Leigh Cmty. Club, 1991—93; sec. Club 91 Golf Course, 1995—2005, St. John's Luth. Ch., 1986—88. Avocations: music, golf, travel, crafts. Home: 233 Beech St Leigh NE 68643 Office: Leigh Cmty Schs 310 Short St Leigh NE 68643 Office Phone: 402-487-2228.

**WELSCH, ROBERT LOUIS,** anthropologist, curator; b. St. Louis, May 19, 1950; s. Russell Louis and Carmen Celia Welsch; m. Sarah Leslie Leslie, Oct. 15, 1988. BA, Northwestern U., 1972; MA, U. of Wash., 1976, PhD, 1982. Adj. curator of anthropology The Field Mus., Chgo., 1984—. Vis. prof. anthropology Dartmouth Coll., Hanover, NH, 1994—. Author: An American Anthropologist in Melanesia, 1998. Recipient Morton H. Fried prize, Am. Anthrop. Assn., 1992, Antiquity prize, Antiquity Jour., 1998; fellow Sylvan C. Coleman and Pamela Coleman Meml. Fund fellowship, Met. Mus. of Art, 2001; grantee, Fulbright Found., 1977—79, NSF, 1977—79, Fulbright Found., 1985—87, NSF, 1989—90, NEH, 1993—94, NSF, 1993—94, Mus. Planning grant, Nat. Endowment for the Humanities, 1999—2001, NSF, 2000—01. Mem.: Pacific Arts Assn. (treas. 1999—2001, spl. publs. editor 2001—). Office: Dartmouth Coll Dept Anthropology 6047 Silsby Hall Hanover NH 03755

**WELSCH, ROY ELMER,** statistician, educator; b. Kansas City, Mo., July 31, 1943; AB, Princeton U., 1965; MS, Stanford U., 1966, PhD in math., 1969. Asst. prof. ops. rsch. Sloan Sch. Mgmt. Mass. Inst. Tech., Cambridge, Mass., 1969-73, assoc. prof., 1973-79, prof. mgmt. sci. and stats. and engring. systems, 1979—, dir. statistics ctr., 1981—89. Sr. rsch. assoc. Nat. Bur. Econ. Rsch., 1973—79. Assoc. editor: Jour. Am. Statist. Assn. Fellow Am. Statis. Assn., Inst. Math. Statis. Office: MIT Dept Mgmt & Stats 77 Massachusetts Ave Bldg E53-383 Cambridge MA 02139-4307 Fax: 617-258-7579. E-mail: rwelsch@mit.edu.

**WELSER, WILLIAM, III,** military officer; B in Biology, U. Buffalo, 1971; grad., Squadron Officer Sch., 1977, Air Command and Staff Coll., 1980; M in Pers. Mgmt., Webster U., 1981; grad., Armed Forces Staff Coll., 1982, Nat. War Coll., 1988; exec. devel. program, U. N.H., 1994. Commd. 2d lt. USAF, 1971, advanced through grades to maj. gen., 1998; F-4 br. chief, job control duty officer 8th Tactical Fighter Wing, Ubon Royal Thai AFB, Thailand, 1973-74; C-141 pilot, crew control. 20th Mil. Airlift Squadron, Charleston AFB, S.C., 1975-79; instr. pilot, asst. chief pilot 6th Mil. Airlift Squadron Airlift Wing, McGuire AFB, N.J., 1982-83; chief airlift mgmt., chief vis. wing current ops. 438th Mil. Airlift Wing, McGuire AFB, 1983-85; ops. officer, comdr. 6th Mil. Airlift Squadron, McGuire AFB, 1985-87; spl. asst. for gen. and flag officer matters Office of Dir., Joint Staff, Washington, 1988-90; vice comdr. 443d Airlift Wing, Altus AFB, Okla., 1990-92; comdr. 436th Airlift Wing, Dover AFB, Del., 1992-94; vice comdr. Tanker Air Lift Control Ctr., Hdqs. Air Mobility Command, Scott AFB, Ill., 1994-95, comdr., 1995-97, Air Mobility Warfare Ctr., Ft. Dix, N.J., 1997-99; dir. ops. HQ Air Edn. and Tng. Command, Randolph AFB, Tex., 1999—. Decorated Def. Superior Svc. medal, Legion of Merit with oak leaf cluster, Meritorious Svc. medal with 2 oak leaf clusters.

**WELSER-MÖST, FRANZ,** conductor, music director; b. Linz, Austria, Aug. 16, 1960; LHD (hon.), Case Western Reserve U., 2003. Chief condr. Sinfonieorkester Norrköping, Sweden, 1986-91, Stadtorchester Winterthur, Switzerland, 1987-90; condr. St. Louis Symphony Orch., 1989; music dir. London Philharm., 1990—96, Zurich Opera, 1995—2002, prin. condr., 2002—05, gen. music dir., 2005—; music dir. The Cleve. Orch., 2002—. Guest condr. Berlin Philharmonic, Cleveland Orch. Youth Orch., Vienna Philharm., Bavarian Radio Symphony Orch., Gustav Mahler Youth Orch. Conducting debut Salzburg Festival, Austria, 1985; Am. debut St. Louis, 1989; appearances include Vienna biennial, Lucerne Festival, Carnegie Hall. Recipient Outstanding Achievement award, Western Law Ctr. for Disability Rights, 1995, Gramophone award, 1996, Condr. of Yr. award, Musical Am. Internat. Directory of Performing Arts, 2003, Silver medal of Export of Upper Austria, 2003. Mem.: Vienna Singverein (hon.). Office: Severance Hall 11001 Euclid Ave Cleveland OH 44106*

**WELSH, SIR ALFRED JOHN,** lawyer, investment advisor; b. Louisville, May 10, 1947; s. Elvin Alfred and Carol (Kleymeyer) W.; m. Lee Mitchell, Aug. 1, 1970; children: Charles Kleymeyer, Kathryn Thomas. BA, Centre Coll., 1969; JD, U. Ky., 1972; LLM in Internat. Law cum laude, U. Brussels, 1973. Bar: Ky. 1972, U.S. Dist. Ct. (we. and ea. dists.) Ky. 1972, U.S. Ct. Appeals (6th cir.) 1972, U.S. Supreme Ct. Asst. atty. Ky. Atty. Gen. Office, Frankfort, 1973-74; legis. counsel to congressman Ho. of Reps., Washington, 1974-77; mng. ptnr. Adams, Hayward and Welsh, Louisville, 1977—, Boone Welsh and Hayward Internat. Law. Hon. counsel of Belgium, 1983—; econ. devel. advisor Kingdom of Belgium; mem. Ky. Econ. Adv. Coun., 1991-94; pres. Transcontinental Trading Cos., Ltd.; del. North African Mideast Econ. Summit Conf., Morocco, 1994; bd. dirs. Intervention Resources Ctr., Inc.; presenter in field. Bd. dirs. Greater Louisville Swim Found., 1983-94, exec. com., 1994—; bd. dirs. Melody Lake Ranch Inc.; bd. dirs. Louisville com. Coun. Fgn. Rels., 1981—, also pres.; chmn. Louisville Com. on Fgn. Rels.; bd. dirs. Am. Com. on Fgn. Rels.; bd. dirs. Jefferson County Alcohol and Drug Abuse Found., Louisville, 1986-98, Internat. Resolve, Louisville Internat. Cultural Ctr.; mem. econ. task force of Ky. Legis. Agts.; mem. Louisville Meml. Auditorium Commn., Am. Com. Fgn. Rels.; mem. Union Internat des Avocats. Decorated knight Order of the Crown (Belgium). Mem. ABA (internat. law sect., commn. on impairment, com. on substance abuse), ATLA, Va. Bar Assn., Ky. Bar Assn. (bd. dirs. 1981-82, pres. young lawyers divsn. 1981-82), Ky. Acad. Trial Lawyers, Am. Judicature Soc., Louisville C. of C., Am. Ctr. Fgn. Rels. (chmn. Louisville com. on fgn. rels.), Am. Com. on Fgn. Rels. (exec. com.). Democrat. Presbyterian. Avocations: swimming, water polo, soccer. Office: Barristers Hall 1009 S 4th St Louisville KY 40203-3207 Office Phone: 502-584-8583. Personal E-mail: bwbh@earthlink.net.

**WELSH, CAROLINE MASTIN,** curator, art historian; b. St. Louis, Nov. 30, 1948; d. Charles O'Fallon and Georgann Logsdon Mastin; m. Peter Corbett Welsh, Sept. 8, 1970; 1 child, James Munson Corbett. Degree cum laude, Kent Sch., 1966; AB in Art History, Wellesley Coll., Mass., 1970. Editl. asst. Smithsonian Jour. History, 1969; coord. exhibits Travelling Exbn. Svc. Smithsonian Instn., 1971—72; guest curator Albany (N.Y.) Inst. History and Art, 1975—76; dir. exhibits Marketechs Exhibit Design and Prodn., Inc., York, Pa., 1976—86; prin., owner The Welsh Group, Camp Hill, Pa., 1984—88; from cons. curator to chief curator The Adirondack Mus., Blue Mountain Lake, NY, 1986—92, chief curator, 1992—, dir. ops., 1994—, acting dir. pubs., 2002—. Adv. bd. Adirondack Pk. Centennial Project WCFE Pub. TV, 1991—92; advisor film WMHT Ednl. Telecomms., 1993—95; mem. com. visual arts Hamilton Coll., 2002—; bd. dirs. Lake Placid Winter Olympic Mus., Lake Placid Ctr. Arts. Fellow, Smithsonian Instn., 1970—71. Mem.: Am. Assn. Mus. (peer reviewer mus. assessment program 2002—), The Soc. Preservation Am. Modernists (bd. dirs. 1994—), The Century Assn. Home: 34 Second St Tupper Lake NY 12986 Office: The Adirondack Museum Rte 28/30 Blue Mountain Lake NY 12812 Office Phone: 518-352-7311.

**WELSH, DIANE M.,** federal judge; BA in Polit. Sci. magna cum laude, Villanova U., 1976, JD, 1979. Bar: Pa. 1979, U.S. Dist. Ct. (ea. dist.) Pa. 1981, U.S. Ct. Appeals (3rd cir.) 1984, U.S. Supreme Ct. 1985. Legal counsel Pa. Senate Judiciary Com., 1980-81; dep. dist. atty. Bucks County Dist. Atty.'s Office, Pa., 1981-84; ptnr. Gold-Bikin Welsh & Assocs., 1984-94; magistrate judge U.S. Dist. Ct. (ea. dist.) Pa., Phila., 1994—. Spkr. in field. Contbr. articles to legal jours. Trustee Manor Jr. Coll., 1981-83, Norristown State Hosp., 1987-90. Mem. ABA, Fed. Bar Assn., Fed. Magistrate Judge Assn., Nat. Assn. Women Judges, Pa. Bar Assn., Montgomery County Bar Assn., Phila. Bar Assn., Brehon Law Soc. Office: US Courthouse 3029 US Courthouse 601 Market St Philadelphia PA 19106-1713

**WELSH, DONALD EMORY,** publisher; b. Youngstown, Ohio, Oct. 6, 1943; s. Edward Francis and Clevelle Rose W.; m. Elizabeth Bourne Floyd, June 25, 1966; children: Leah Bourne, Emory Philip. AB, Columbia U., 1965; JD, Cleveland Marshall Sch. Law, 1969. Bar: Ohio 1969. Trust devel. officer Cleve. Trust Co., 1968-70; advt. sales rep. Fortune mag., Time, Inc., N.Y.C., 1970-75; advt. dir. Rolling Stone mag., N.Y.C., 1975-77, v.p., assoc. pub., 1977-78; pub. Outside mag., N.Y.C., 1978-82; pub. Muppet mag. and pres. Lorimar Pub. Group (formerly Telepictures Publs., Inc.), 1982-87; pres. Welsh Pub. Group, Inc., 1987-94; exec. v.p. Marvel Comics Group, N.Y.C., 1994-96; chmn. Group XXVII Comms., N.Y.C., 1997-2000; pres. pub. group Digital Convergence Inc., N.Y.C., 2000-2001; chmn. Budget Living Commn., N.Y.C., 2001—05; pub. Outside's Go Mag., NYC, 2005—. Global adv. Outward Bound, U.S.A.; bd. dirs. Cousteau Soc.; former bd. dirs. Big Apple Circus, B.P.A. Consumer Mags. Mem. ABA, Mag. Pubs. Assn. (past bd. dirs.), Century Assn., Sharon Country Club (Conn.), Ocean Reef Club (Fla.), Brook Club (N.Y.C.). Home: 501 E 79th St New York NY 10021-0735 Office: Outside Mag 420 Lexington Ave New York NY 10170 E-mail: DonaldEWelsh@aol.com.

**WELSH, DOROTHY DELL,** columnist, writer; d. Roland Fields and Martha Gladys (Sheppard) Butler; m. James Robert Welsh, June 26, 1965; children: Pamela Jeanne(dec.), James Michael, Julie Marie. BA, U. Okla., 1957, MA, 1964; postgrad., U. Tex., Austin, 1983-84, U. Tex., San Antonio, 1984. Newspaper reporter summer intern Pryor Jeffersonian, Okla., 1952—55; tchr. English and journalism Classen HS, Oklahoma City, 1957-61, Henderson Jr. HS, Nev., 1961-62, Desert HS, Edwards, Calif., 1965-66; dir. publs. Amarillo (Tex.), HS, 1962-64; tchr. English Palmdale HS, Calif., 1964-65; lectr. English San Antonio Coll., 1979-88; tchg. assoc. U. Tex., San Antonio, 1986-91; reporter Swimming World mag., Sedona, Ariz., 1980—2000; freelance writer, 1992—. Lectr. journalism John Brown U., 1992. Author: The Butlers of Oklahoma, 1957, A Good Man is Hard to Find, 1961, To Seattle for a Bone Marrow Transplant, 1982, Fact, Fiction and Poetic License, 1995, The Butlers: A Newspaper Family, 2002; editor: Crescent News, 1974—80, 1983—86, The Swimmer's Ear, 1983—84, Off the Blocks, 1985—86; contbr. articles to profl. jours. Bd. dirs., publicity chmn. S. Tex. Swimming Assn., Austin, 1982—84; mem. info. com. Tex. Swimming Assn., Dallas, 1983—84; v.p. Mayes County Geneal. Soc., Okla., 2002; mem. Mayes County Hist. Soc., Okla., Rogers County Hist. Soc., Okla., Okla. Hist. Soc. Recipient citation superior work journalism, U. Interscholastic League, Austin, 1964, Svc. award, San Antonio Aquatic Club, 1983, Outstanding Svc. award, U.S. Swimming/Phillips 66, 1989, Pres.'s award, Okla. Press Assn., 2003. Mem.: DAR, MLA, Clan Grant Soc. U.S., Okla. Anthrop. Soc., Journalism Edn. Assn., Soc. Profl. Journalists, Indian Women's Pochohontas Club, U. Okla. Assn., Tulsa Archeol. Soc., Okla. Geneal. Soc., Elks, Pryor (Okla.) Red Hat Soc., First Families Okla., Gamma Phi Beta (charter officer 1992—94, pres. San Antonio 1972—73, 1987—88, v.p. 1973—74, Svc. award 1977, Internat. Merit Roll 1986). Baptist. Office Phone: 405-872-7172. Business E-Mail: jrwddw39@okplus.net.

**WELSH, H. RONALD,** lawyer; b. Orange, N.J., Jan. 9, 1950; s. Harry A. and Faye L. (Neal) W.; children: Austin, Ben. BS, Northwestern U., 1972; JD, U. Tex., 1975. Bar: Tex. 1975, U.S. Dist. Ct. (so. dist.) Tex. 1989, U.S. Ct. Appeals (5th and 11th cirs.) 1981; cert. in civil trial law and personal injury trial law Tex. Bd. Legal Specialization. Ptnr. Vinson & Elkins, Houston, 1982—2003, Cunningham, Welsh, Darlow, Zook & Chapoton, LLP, Houston, 2004—. Fellow Am. Coll. Trial Lawyers, Am. Bd. Trial Advs., Tex. Bar Found., Houston Bar Found. Office: Cunningham Welsh Darlow Zook & Chapoton LLP Ste 1700 600 Travis St Houston TX 77002 Office Phone: 713-255-5500. Business E-Mail: rwelsh@cdzc.com.

**WELSH, JOHN BERESFORD, JR.,** retired lawyer; b. Seattle, Feb. 16, 1940; s. John B. and Rowena Morgan (Custer) W Student, U. Hawaii, 1960, Georgetown U., 1960; BA, U. Wash., 1962; LLB, 1965. Bar: Wash. 1965. Staff counsel Joint Com. on Govtl. Cooperation, 1965-66; asst. atty gen. Dept. Labor and Industries, 1966-67; atty. Legis Counsel; acting as counsel Pub. Health Com., Labor Com., Pub. Employees Collective Bargaining Com., Com. on State Instns. and Youth Devel., State of Wash., 1967-73; sr. counsel Wash. Ho. of Reps., Ho. Com. on Social and Health Svcs., Olympia, WA, 1973-86; atty., spkr. Ho. of Reps., 1973; counsel Ho. Com. Human Svcs., 1987-91, 93-95, Ho. Com. on Health Care, 1987—2003, ret., 2003. Counsel Ho. Com. on Trade and Econ. Devel., 1995-98, Joint Select Com. on Oral Health, 1996, legal cons. Gov.'s Planning Commn. Vocat. Rehab., 1968, Gov.'s Commn. on Youth Involvement, 1969; envoy from Gov. Wash. to investiture of Prince of Wales, London, 1969, nat. Nat. Conf. State Legislatures, Denver, 1977, New Orleans, 1977; fac. Coun. Licensure, Enforcement and Regulation, San Francisco, 1984, Orlando, Fla., 1985, Denver, 1986, Kansas City, Mo., 1987, Washington, 1988, Indpls., 1989, Seattle, 1990, Ft. Lauderdale, Fla., 1991, Albuquerque, 1992, Boston, 1994, San Antonio, 1995, Norfolk, 1997; suggested state legis. com. Coun. of State Govts., 1988-95; subcom. scope and agenda, 1988-95, steering com., 1986-90, legis. issues com., 1986-88 Vol. Hampton Rds. U.S. Naval Mus., gov's. state medal merit com., 1986-2003 Recipient Gov.'s award for excellence in state health care policy, 2002, Spkr. of House award for dedicated pub. svc., 2002, Sec. of State award for pub. svc. to state legislature and people of state of Wash., 2003, Sec. of Health award for creating meaningful health policy change, 2003. Mem. Assn. Washington Gens., French Soc. SAR, Nat. Soc. SAR, Wash. Bar Assn., Soc. des Amis du Musee de l'Armee, Paris, Alliance Francaise, English Speaking Union, Soc. Napoleonienne (pres.), Sons Union Vets. Civil War, Custer Battlefield Hist. and Mus. Assn., Colonial Williamsburg Found. (profl. Rochambeau charter actor), Jamestown-Yorktown Found., Napoleonic Alliance (bd. dirs., exec. v.p. 2002—), World Affairs Coun., Friends of Old Ft. Stevens (bd. dirs.), Friends of Willie and Joe, Northwest Hist. Assn. (pres. 2003) Personal E-mail: jbwelsh@comcast.net.

**WELSH, JOHN FRANCIS,** retired advertising executive; b. New Haven, May 19, 1916; s. Pierce Jerome and Irene (Kennedy) W.; m. Margaret Burke, Sept. 18, 1947; children: Peter Burke, Diana Margaret. BA, Yale U., 1937. With Warwick & Legler, Inc., N.Y.C., 1946-81; exec. v.p., mgmt. supr., mem. mgmt. com.; vice chmn. Warwick, Welsh & Miller, Inc., 1973-81. Served with AUS, 1941-45. Decorated Bronze Star, Croix de Guerre (France). Mem.: Tokeneke (Darien). Home: 3372 Meadow Ridge Redding CT 06896

**WELSH, KELLY RAYMOND,** lawyer, investment company executive; b. Chgo., July 6, 1952; s. Raymond J. and Mary Jane (Kelly) W.; m. Ellen S. Alberding, June 28, 1985; children: Katherine A., Julia S. AB cum laude, Harvard U., 1974; MA, Sussex U., Eng., 1975; JD magna cum laude, Harvard U., 1978. Assoc. Mayer, Brown & Platt, Chgo., 1979-85, ptnr., 1985-89; corp. counsel City of Chgo., 1989-93; v.p., assoc. gen. counsel Ameritech Corp., Chgo., 1993-96, exec. v.p., gen. counsel, 1996—2001, Northern Trust Corp., Chgo., 2001—. Chmn. Met. Pier and Exposition Authority, Chgo., 1994—. Mem. ABA, Chgo. Bar Assn., Chgo. Coun. Lawyers, Chgo. Coun. Fgn. Rels. (mem. Chgo. com.), Legal Club Chgo. Office: Northern Trust Corp 50 S LaSalle Chicago IL 60675

**WELSH, MICHAEL JAMES,** medical educator, biophysicist, educator; b. Marshalltown, Iowa, Dec. 22, 1948; Student, Loras Coll., 1967-69; BS, U. Iowa, 1970, MD, 1974. Intern and resident internal medicine U. Iowa Coll. Medicine, Iowa City, 1974-77; clin. fellow internal medicine U. Calif. San Francisco, 1977-78; rsch. fellow cardiovasc. rsch. unit U. Calif. San Francisco, 1978-79; rsch. fellow physiology and cell biology U. Tex., Houston, 1979-80; asst. prof. medicine U. Iowa Coll. Medicine, Iowa City, 1981-84, assoc. prof. medicine, 1984-87, prof. medicine, 1987—; prof. physiology and biophysics, 1989—. Cons. VA Hosp., Iowa City, 1981—; investigator Howard Hughes Med. Inst., U. Iowa., Iowa City, 1989—. Contbr. chpts. to books and numerous articles to profl. jours. Recipient Doris F. Tulcin Cystic Fibrosis Rsch. award, 1992, Paul di Sant-Agnese Disting. Sci. Achievement award, 1993. Mem. Am. Fedn. for Clin. Rsch., Am. Physiol. Soc., Am. Thoracic Soc. (J. Burns Amberson award 1994), Iowa Thoracic Soc. Office: Howard Hughes Med Inst 500 EMRB Univ Iowa Coll Medicine Iowa City IA 52242

**WELSH, PETER CORBETT,** museum director, historian; b. Washington, Aug. 28, 1926; s. Arthur Brinkley and Susan Jane (Putney) W.; m. Catherine Beatrice Allen, Nov. 27, 1951 (div. 1969); children— Susan Jane, Peter Corbett; m. Caroline Levert Mastin, Sept. 8, 1970; 1 child, James Munson Corbett. BA, Mt. Union Coll., Alliance, Ohio, 1950; postgrad., U. Va., 1950-51; MA (Hagley fellow), U. Del., 1956. Research asst., fellowship coordinator Eleutherian Mills-Hagley Found., Wilmington, Del., 1956-59; assoc. curator dept. civil history Mus. History and Tech., Smithsonian Instn., 1959-61; curator Growth U.S., 1962-64, curator dept. civil history, 1964-69, asst. dir. gen. mus. of instn., 1969-70, dir. Office Mus. Programs, 1970-71; dir. N.Y. State Hist. Assn., Cooperstown, 1971-74; vis. prof. Cooperstown Grad. Program, N.Y. State Hist. Assn.; dir. Cooperstown Grad. Program, 1971-74; dir. spl. projects N.Y. State Mus., Albany, 1975-76; dir. Bur. Hist., Pa. Hist. and Mus. Commn., 1976-84; pres. The Welsh Group, 1984-86; curator The Adirondack Mus., Blue Mountain Lake, N.Y., 1986-88, sr. historian, 1988-89; mus. cons., lectr., 1989—. Adj. prof. SUNY; cons. FDR Mus. and Little White House, Warm Springs, Ga., 1968-72; trustee Landon Sch., Bethesda, Md., 1964-70; bd. dirs., mem. exec. com. Ctr. for Conservation of Hist. Art and Artifacts, 1979-83; bd. dirs. Lake Placid Ctr. for the Arts, 1992-96; mem. publs. adv. com. The Adirondack Mus., 2002—. Author: Tanning in the United States: A Brief History, 1964, American Folk Art: The Art and Spirit of the People, 1967, Track and Road: The American Trotting Horse, 1820-1990, 1968, The Art of Enterprise: A Pennsylvania Tradition, 1983, Jacks, Jobbers and Kings: Logging the Adirondacks, 1850-1950, 1996; contbr. articles to profl. publs.; editor Smithsonian Jour. History, 1967-70. Served to 1st lt. AUS, 1951-54. Mem. Am. Hist. Assn., Am. Studies Assn., Am. Assn. Mus., N.Y. State Assn. Mus. (council 1971-75), Am. Assn. State and Local History (publ. com.), Soc. History of Tech., Sigma Nu. Clubs: Country of Harrisburg. Democrat. Roman Catholic. Office: 34 Second St Tupper Lake NY 12986-2011

**WELSH, WILLIAM DANIEL,** geriatric medicine family practice physician; b. Balt., May 18, 1950; s. Joseph Leo and Bessie Mary (Tangires) W.; m. Loraine Lynn Barkhaus, July 11, 1985; children: Sean William, Ryan Daniel. Student, Johns Hopkins U., 1971; BS in Biology cum laude, Fairleigh Dickinson U., 1972; DO, Coll. Osteo. Medicine-Surgery, Des Moines, 1975. Diplomate Nat. Bd. Osteo. Physicians; cert. ATLS; approved supr. physician assts. Osteopathic Med. Bd. Calif.; radiography and fluoroscopy x-ray supr., operator Calif. Intern Martin Place Hosp., Madison Heights, Mich., 1975-76, resident in internal medicine, 1976-77; pvt. practice Detroit, 1977-79; pvt. practice, Whittier, Calif., 1979—. Instr. ACLS, L.A., 1980-92; bd. dirs. Whittier Hosp. Med. Ctr., 1981, vice chief staff, 1982-84, med. dir. family asthma forum, 1979-88, med. dir. Summit Place alcohol treatment program, 1983-88; med. dir. Mirada Hills Rehab. Hosp., La Mirada, Calif., 1980-88; former clin. preceptor Coll. Osteo. Med. Pacific, Pomona, Calif.; clin. assoc. prof. internal medicine; mem. dept. family practice, physician rev. com. Friendly Hills Regional Med. Ctr., La Habra, Calif., 1994-97; mem. staff Presbyn. Intercmty. Hosp., Whittier, Whittier Hosp. Med. Ctr., chmn. by laws com. 1999-2001, mem. exec. com. 1999-2001; med. dir. Royal Ct. Convalescent Hosp.; spkr. in field. Participant Calif. Beach Clean Up Day, 1996, Med. Mission, Mex. Recipient Physician Recognition award AMA, 1991, 95, 96, Commn. of Merit Rep. Nat. Com., 1995. Mem. Am. Osteo. Assn., Am. Coll. Osteo. Family Physicians, Osteo. Physicians and Surgeons Calif., Am. Coll. Osteopathic Family Practitioners (bd. cert. family practice 1991, geriatrics 2000). Republican. Roman Catholic. Avocations: boating, skiing, reading, tennis. Home: 16871 Marina Bay Dr Huntington Beach CA 92649-2913 Office Phone: 562-945-9333. Home Fax: 562-592-2259. Personal E-mail: wdwelsh@socal.rr.com, wdwelshd@socal.rr.com.

**WELSHANS, MERLE TALMADGE,** management consultant; b. Murphysboro, Ill., June 17, 1918; s. Arthur Isaac and Martha Ellen (Blair) W.; m. Mary Katherine Whitenbaugh, June 2, 1942; children: Elizabeth Margaret Van Steenbergh, Arthur Edmund, Janice Ann. BEd, So. Ill. U., 1940; MA, Washington U., St. Louis, 1947, PhD, 1951. Asst. v.p. Merc. Mortgage Co. Olney, Ill., 1940; exec. officer, dept. bus. adminstrn. George Washington U., 1950-54; prof. fin. Grad. Sch. Bus. Adminstrn., Washington U., 1954-69; v.p. fin. Union Electric Co., St. Louis, 1969-83; mgmt. cons., 1983—. Dir. Hotchkis & Wiley Funds, Deaconess Found. Author: (with R.W. Melicher) Finance, 9th edit., 1992; editor Fin. Newsletter, 1965-69. Capt. U.S. Army, 1942-45. Decorated Bronze Star medal. Mem. Fin. Mgmt. Assn. (dir.), Am. Econ. Assn., Am. Fin. Assn., Fin. Analysts Assn. Nat. U.S. Army (trustee), Beta Gamma Sigma, others. Methodist. Address: 14360 Ladue Rd Chesterfield MO 63017-2524 Office Phone: 314-469-6066. Personal E-mail: mwelshans@worldnet.att.net.

**WELSHIMER, MARK J.,** lawyer; b. Canton, Ohio, 1951; AB, Harvard U., 1973, JD, 1976. Bar: NY 1977. Assoc. Sullivan & Cromwell, NYC, ptnr., 1983—, and coord. asset-based fin. practice area. Mem.: ABA. Office: Sullivan & Cromwell 125 Broad St Fl 28 New York NY 10004-2489 Office Phone: 212-558-4000. Office Fax: 212-558-3588. Business E-Mail: welshimerm@sullcrom.com.

**WELSOME, EILEEN,** journalist, writer; b. NYC, Mar. 12, 1951; d. Richard H. and Jane M. (Garity) Welsome; m. James R. Martin, Aug. 3, 1983. BJ with honors, U. Tex., 1980. Reporter Beaumont (Tex.) Enterprise, 1980—82, San Antonio Light, 1982—83, San Antonio Express-News, 1983—86, Albuquerque Tribune, 1987—94, Westword Newspaper, Denver, 2000—01. Author: The Plutonium Files, 1999 (PEN/Martha Albrand award for first nonfiction, 2000). Recipient Clarion award, 1989, News Reporting award, Nat. Headliners, 1989, John Hancock award, 1991, Mng. Editors Pub. Svc. award, AP, 1991, 1994, Roy Howard award, 1994, James Aronson award, 1994, Gold Medal award, Investigative Reporters and Editors, 1994, Sigma Delta Chi award, 1994, Investigative Reporting award, Nat. Headliners, 1994, Selden Ring award, 1994, Heywood Broun award, 1994, George Polk award, 1994, Sidney Hillman Found. award, 1994, Pulitzer Prize for nat. reporting, 1994, PEN/West Lit. award for rsch. nonfiction, PEN, 2000; John S. Knight fellow, Stanford U., 1991—92.

**WELT, PHILIP STANLEY,** lawyer, consultant; b. Freeport, NY, July 5, 1959; s. Morris and Rose (Offenberg) W.; m. Karen Teresa Gault, May 22, 1994. BBA summa cum laude, Hofstra U., 1983; MBA, Columbia U., 1988; JD cum laude, NYU, 1995. Bar: NJ 1995, NY 1995; US Dist. Ct. NJ 1995, US Dist. Ct. (so. and ea. dists.) NY 1996, US Ct. Appeals (2d cir.) 1997, US Ct. Appeals Armed Forces 2000, US Supreme Ct. 1999; CPA, NY. Sr. mgr. Deloitte & Touche, N.Y.C., 1983-92; assoc. Reboul MacMurray Hewitt Maynard & Kristol, N.Y.C., 1993, Davis Polk & Wardwell, N.Y.C., 1994, 1996-2001; jud. clk. U.S. Dist. Ct. N.J., Newark, 1995-96; special asst. dist. atty. Kings Co., NY, 1999—2001; asst. gen. counsel Am. Internat. Group, Inc., 2001—04; v.p., sr. counsel W.R. Berkley Corp., Greenwich, Conn., 2004—. Bd. dirs., treas. Pub. Interest Law Found., N.Y.C., 1993-94; guest spkr. Boy Scouts Am., Nassau County, 1984-91, Nat. Assn. Accts., N.Y./N.J., 1988-92, others. Sr. editor Columbia Jour. World Bus., 1986-88; sr. exec. editor Am. Survey Am. Law, 1993-95; contbr. articles to profl. jours. Vol. income tax asst. Dept. Treasury, IRS, N.Y.C., 1981-87; vol. Variety-The Children's Charity, N.Y.C., 1985-87; advisor Friends of Jon Kaiman, Nassau County, 1995. Provost's scholar Hofstra U., 1981-83, Deloitt & Touche fellow Columbia U., 1986-88; recipient Appreciation cert. Dept. Treasury, IRS, 1981-87, Variety, 1985-87, Bovenaan Outstanding Cmty. Svc. award Hofstra U., 1983, Orison S. Marden Moot Ct. Advocacy award NYU Sch. Law, 1993, Seymore A. Levy meml. award, 1995. Mem. ABA, AICPA, N.Y. State Bar Assn., N.Y. State Soc. CPAs, Beta Alpha Psi, Beta Gamma Sigma. Avocations: golf, rock climbing, photography, stamp collecting/philately, amateur radio. Home: 157 Mountain Wood Rd Stamford CT 06903-2107 Office: W R Berkley Corp 475 Steamboat Rd Greenwich CT 06830 Office Phone: 212-629-3000. Business E-Mail: pwelt@wrberkley.com.

**WELTER, PAULA JOY,** singer, songwriter; b. Chgo., July 1, 1951; d. Paul Anthony and Patricia Ann Welter; m. Paul R. McManus, 1971 (div. 1979); 1 child, Noah B. McManus; m. Stephen F. Baltzell, Dec. 20, 1981 (div. 1991). AS in Photography, City Coll. of San Francisco, 1976; postgrad., Occidental Coll., LA, 1969—71. Cert. shorthand reporter Calif., lic. Ct. Reporters of Calif./Dept. Consumer Affairs. Sales/mktg. profl. Camellia Color Corp., Sacramento, 1980—82; customer svc. rep. Fed. Express, Sacramento, 1982—85; freelance deposition reporter Calif., 1999—; ind. singer, songwriter, 1993—; admin. asst. Shriners Hosp. for Children, Calif.; mem. com. staff Calif. State Assembly, Sacramento. Songwriter, performer: CD Morning Light, 1995, Still Hidden Places, 2005. Avocations: photography, bicycling, fabric arts, watercolor. Office: Starry Sky Music PO Box 19672 Sacramento CA 95619-0672 E-mail: paulajoy@paulajoywelter.com.

**WELTER, WILLIAM MICHAEL,** marketing and advertising executive; b. Evanston, Ill., Nov. 18, 1946; s. Roy Michael and Frances (DeShields) W.; m. Pamela Bassett, June 11, 1971; children: Barclay, Robert Michael. BS, Mo. Valley Coll., 1966. Account exec. Leo Burnett Co., Inc., Chgo., 1966-74; v.p., account supr. Needham Harper Worldwide, Chgo., 1974-80; v.p. mktg. Wendy's Internat., Inc., Dublin, Ohio, 1981, sr. v.p. mktg., 1981-84, exec. v.p., 1984-87; owner, chief exec. officer Haunty & Welter Advt. Agy., Worthington, Ohio, 1987-91; sr. exec. v.p. mktg. Rax Restaurants Inc., Dublin, 1992; sr. v.p. mktg. Metromedia Steakhouses, Inc., Dayton, 1992-93; sr. v.p. mktg. Metromedia Co. Dayton, 1993-95; exec. v.p., chief mktg. officer Heartland Foods Inc., Dublin, Ohio, 1995-96; exec. v.p. brand mgmt. Late Nite Magic, Inc., Las Vegas, Nev., 1996—99; pres., CEO W.M. Welter & Assocs., Las Vegas, 1996—; pres. Wings West LLC, Las Vegas, 1999—, Buffalo Wild Wings, Inc., Las Vegas, 2001—. Founder Santa's Silent Helpers, Columbus, Ohio, 1985 Mem. Advt. Fedn. Las Vegas, Spanish Trail Country Club. Avocations: golf, fishing. Home: 1517 Angelberry St Las Vegas NV 89117-1372 Office: Ste 103 8064 W Sahara Las Vegas NV 89117 Fax: 702 360-8379. Office Phone: 702-304-9292. E-mail: buffalodad@hotmail.com.

**WELTERS, ANTHONY,** health services executive; BA in Econs., Manhattanville Coll.; JD, NYU. Atty. SEC; exec. asst. to Sen. Jacob Javits; sr.-level positions Amtrak and US Dept. Transp.; chmn. bd., pres., CEO Americhoice (subs. of UnitedHealth Grp.), 1989—. Bd. trustees Healthcare Leadership Coun.; vice chmn. bd. Morehouse Sch. Medicine; mem. bd. NYU Law Sch., Wolf Trap Found. Recipient Horatio Alger award, 1998. Office: Americhoice 8045 Leesburg Pike Ste 650 Vienna VA 22182*

**WELTMAN, DAVID LEE,** lawyer; b. Springfield, Mass., Jan. 12, 1933; s. Sol Walter and Esther (Zicklind) W. m This Handmaker, Sept. 2, 1956 (dec. June 2005); children: John, Elizabeth, Herman, Sally. AB, Yale U., 1954; LLB, Harvard U., 1957; DHL (hon.), Newbury Coll., 2002. Bar: Mass. 1957. Assoc. Mintz, Levin & Cohn, Boston, 1957-60; v.p. Ansonia Mills, Inc., Taunton, Mass., 1960-63; assoc. Foley, Hoag & Eliot, Boston, 1963-67, ptnr., 1967—. Sec., clk. Charles River Assocs., Boston, 1965-97, Brigham Med. Group Found., 1972—2001, Siemens-Nixdorf Info. Systems, Burlington, Mass., 1979-94, Am. Brush Co., Clairmont, N.H., 1982-92. Chmn. leadership devel. coun. Jewish Fedn. and Welfare Funds, 1966-68; trustee New Eng. Med. Ctr., Boston, 1970-82, Combined Jewish Philanthropies, Boston, 1970—, Hebrew Coll., Boston, 1995-2002; chmn. Newbury Coll., Boston, 1972-2002, chmn. Lown Cardiovasc. Rsch. Found., 2004-; incorporator Mus. Sci., Boston, 1972-92. Boston U. Med. Ctr., 1965-96; pres. Beaver Country Day Sch., Chestnut Hill, Mass., 1975-80, Jewish Cmty. Ctr., Brookline and Newton, 1968-71; bd. overseers South Shore Hosp. Found., Weymouth, Mass., 1990—. Recipient Young Leadership award Combined Jewish Philanthropies, 1968, Class of 1954 award Yale U., 1989, Founders Day award Beaver Country Day Sch., 1991. Mem. ABA, Boston Bar Assn., Nat. Health Lawyers Assn., Cohasset Golf Club, Cohasset Yacht Club, Plantation Golf and Country Club. Avocations: tennis, sailing, golf. Home: 90 Gammons Rd Cohasset MA 02025-1406 Office: Foley Hoag LLP 155 Seaport Blvd Boston MA 02210

**WELTMAN, EDWARD S.,** lawyer; AB cum laude, Brandeis Univ., 1972; JD, Washington Univ., 1975. Bar: NY 1976. Sr. ptnr. Schneck Weltman & Hashmall LLP, NYC; ptnr., litig. dept. Goodwin Procter LLP, NYC, chair, products liability group, mem., exec. com. Comment topics editor Wash. Univ. Law Quarterly. Mem.: Nat. Judicial Coll., Internat. Assn. Def. Counsel. Office: Goodwin Procter LLP 599 Lexington Ave New York NY 10022 Office Phone: 212-459-7420. Office Fax: 212-355-3333. Business E-Mail: eweltman@goodwinprocter.com.

**WELTON, SHARON MARIE,** food service executive; b. Waterbury, Conn., Nov. 18, 1943; d. George Galvin Touponse and Catherine Marie Coon; m. Allen Richard Welton (div.); children: Catherine Welton-Pando, Douglas Allen Sr. AAS, Mattatuck Cmty. Coll., 1988; BS, U. Conn., 1996. Cert. dietary mgr. Nat. Dietary Managers Assn., 1992, instr. for Serv-Safe Course Nat. Restaurant Assn., 2002, food protection profl. 1996. Legal sec. Membrino/Fitzgerald, Waterbury, Conn., 1963—64; asst. mgr. Judy's Deli, Southbury, Conn., 1980—84; prin./mgr. Feasts by Sharon, Conn., 1981—2001; intern- affirmative action office Southbury Training Sch., Conn., 1995, supvr. food svc. Conn., 1984—. Cons./trainer State of Conn., 1990—, State of Conn. Nutritional Work Group, 1999—2003, Southbury Training Sch., 1992—. Polit. action com. mem. Dietary Managers Assn., 1993—95; mem./leader Girl Scouts, Watertown, Conn., 1951—61, 1977—81; com. mem. Christmas Town Festival, Bethlehem, 1999. Recipient State Achievement award, Dietary Managers Assn., 1994—95. Mem.: Dietary Managers Assn. (legis. coord. 1992—98, 2003—, pres. 1994—95). Republican. Roman Cath. Avocations: sewing, swimming, wine tasting, interior decorating, aerobics. Home: 143 Pine Hill Rd 22B Thomaston CT 06787 Office: Southbury Training Sch Rte 172 Southbury CT 06488 Office Phone: 203-586-2193.

**WELTY, INGA ANN,** mathematics educator; b. Olean, N.Y., Apr. 18, 1975; d. Bernard James and Kathy Jean Wenke; m. Lawrence James Welty; children: Kayla Ray, Karly Jean, Mia Ann, Mallory Renee. AS, Jamestown C.C., Olean, N.Y., 1995; BSc in Math., St. Bonaventure U., N.Y., 1997, MS in Advanced Instrnl. Processes, 2002. Cert. tchr. N.Y., 2002. Tchr. math. H.S. Portville Ctrl. Sch., NY, 1998—, coach jr. varsity girls basketball, 2001—06. Instr. religious edn. Sacred Heart Ch., Portville, 2002—06. Mem.: Nat. Coun. Tchrs. Math. Home: 43 Temple Street Portville NY 14770 Office: Portville Central School 500 Elm Street Portville NY 14770 Office Phone: 716-933-6000.

**WELTY, JOHN DONALD,** academic administrator; b. Amboy, Ill., Aug. 24, 1944; s. John Donald and Doris (Donnelly) W.; m. Sharon Welty; children: Anne, Elisabeth, Bryan, Darren, Heather. BS, Western Ill. U., 1965; MA, Mich. State U., 1967; Ed.D., Ind. U., 1974. Asst. v.p. for student affairs SW State U., Marshall, Minn., 1973-74; dir. residences SUNY-Albany, 1974-77, assoc. dean for student affairs, 1977-80; v.p. for student and univ. affairs Indiana U. of Pa., 1980-84, pres., 1984-91; Calif. State U., Fresno, 1991—. Lectr. in field. Contbr. articles to profl. jours. Chair Am. Assn. State Colls. and Univs., Western Assn. Schs. and Colls. Recipient Chancellor's award SUNY, 1977, Chief Exec. Leadership award Coun. for Advancement and Support of Edn., 1999, John Templeton Found. award for leadership in student character devel., 1999. Mem. Fresno Bus. Coun., Fresno Econ. Devel. Commn., Sunnyside Country Club. Lodges: Rotary. Roman Catholic. Office: Calif State U 5241 S Maple Ave Fresno CA 93725-9739 Business E-Mail: johnw@csufresno.edu.

**WELTZ, MARTIN DAVID,** hematologist; b. Phila., Jan. 18, 1948; children: Michael, Adam. BS in Biology, Bklyn. Coll., 1969; DO, Kans. City U. Medicine Biosci., 1973; MBA, Johns Hopkins U., 2002, MPH, 2003. Diplomate Nat. Bd. Med. Examiners for Osteo. Physicians and Surgeons, Am. Bd. Internal Medicine, (subspecialty of med. oncology, subspecialty of hematology, subspecialty hospice and palliative medicine). Commd. 2d lt. USMC, 1973, advanced through grades to lt. col., 1981; intern Walter Reed Army Med. Ctr., Washington, 1973-74, resident, 1974-76, fellow hematology and med. oncology sect., 1976-79, attending physician dept. internal medicine, 1979-81, staff hematologist, med. oncologist, dir. med. edn., 1979-80, chief divsn. head Clin. Cancer Chemo-Pharmacology Rsch. Lab., 1979-80, asst. chief, dir. clin. pharmacy hematology-med. oncology, 1980-81; resigned USMC, 1981; pvt. practice, sr. v.p., founder Hematology-Oncology Cons., Greenbelt. Md., 1983—, v.p., sec., 1986—; pres. med.-dental staff Laurel Regional Hosp., 1993-99; chmn. dept. internal medicine Washington Adventist Hosp., 1997-2001. V.p., sec., 1986—; attending med. staff AMI Drs. Hosp., Prince George's County, Lanham, Md., 1983, Washington Adventist Hosp., Takoma Park, Md., 1983—, sec.-treas. dept. internal medicine, 1991-94, asst. chmn., 1994-97; asst. chief hematology/med. oncology Prince Georges Hosp. Ctr., 1986—; staff Laurel Regional Hosp., 1983—, chmn. hematology-med. oncology, 1989-1998, med. dir. Hospice in Prince George's County, 1989—, chmn. dept. internal medicine, 1989-92, chmn. tumor bd., 1989—, chmn. employees ann. benefit med.-dental staff, 1990-2000, chmn. med. exec. com., 1993-2000, pres. med. and dental staff, 1993-99, trustee, 1993-99; bd. dirs. Dimensions Corp., Landover, Md., sec.-treas. bd. dirs., 1990-99; pres. Med. Dental Staff laurel Regional Hosp., 1993-99; vice chmn. Dept. Internal Medicine, Washington Adventist Hosp., 1994-96; chmn. Dimensions Health Care Network PHO, 1994-99; med. dir. Hospice in Prince Georges County, 1990-98, Hospice of the Chesapeake, 1999-; bd. dirs. Universal Health Care Network, Medi-Cen of Md.; bd. dirs., found. chmn. med. exec. com., pres. med.-dental staff Laurel Regional Hosp., 1993—; bd. dirs. Dimensions Healthcare Network, Dimensions Health Care Corp. Medi-Cen of Md. and Universal Healthcare Corp., Cancer Care, Inc.; chmn., founder tumor bd. Laurel Regional Hosp. and Washington Adventist Hosp., 1988—; chmn. transfusion com. Washington Adventist Hosp., 1990—; sec. Laurel Hosp. Found., 2000-05. Contbr. articles to profl. jours. Bd. dirs. Am. Cancer Soc., Prince George's County, 1981—; med. advisor cansurmount program Am. Cancer Soc., Montgomery County, Md., 1982-90; ring dir. Ea. Regional Karate Tournament, Montgomery Coll., Rockville, Md., 1987—; mem. advisor Md. Blood Ctr., 1987-88; mem. med. adv. bd. Hospice Prince George's County, Largo, Md., 1991-99, active archtl. and design com., capital campaign com., bldg. com., 1992—; mem. com. Parent Fund and Centurion Campaign; bd. dirs. Found. Laurel Regional Hosp., 1993—, others. Fellow ACP, Acad. Medicine N.J.; mem. AMA, Am. Soc. Internal Medicine, Am. Soc. Clin. Oncology, Am. Soc. Hematology, Acad. Hospice and Polliative Medicine, Am. Coll. Clin. Pharmacology, Am. Coll. Osteo. Internists, Am. Soc. Clin. Oncologists, Am. Coll. Physician Execs., Am. Soc. Clin. Pharmacology and Therapeutics, Am. Soc. Contemporary Medicine and Surgery, Am. Fedn. for Clin. Rsch., Royal Soc. Medicine (London), Md. Osteo. Assn., Oncology Soc, N.J. N.J. Soc. Internal Medicine, N.Y Aca.l 9c.h., N.Y. Oncology Soc., Md. Soc. Clin. Oncology, George Washington U. Parent Assn., Luther Rice Soc., Johns Hopkins Alumni Assn. Office: Greenway Center Dr Greenbelt MD 20770 Personal E-mail: martinweitz@aol.com. Business E-Mail: martinweitz@jhsph.com.

**WELU, JAMES A.,** art museum director; b. Dubuque, Iowa, Dec. 15, 1943; s. Andrew L. and Anna E. (Riley) W. BA, Loras Coll., 1966; MA, U. Notre Dame, 1967, MFA, 1968; PhD, Boston U., 1977. Instr. St. Mary-of-the-Woods (Ind.) Coll., 1968-70; asst. curator Worcester Art Mus., Mass., 1974-76, assoc. curator Mass., 1976-80, instr. Mass., 1977-78, 80-81, chief curator Mass., 1980-86, dir. Mass., 1986—. Instr. Clark U., Worcester, 1980. Panelist Mass. Coun. on Arts and Humanities, Boston, 1981-82, 90, Utilization of Mus. Resources Nat. Endowment for the Arts, 1988; trustee Williamstown Regional Art Conservation Lab., Mass., 1981-86; mem. panel Utilization Mus. Resources, NEA, 1988. Boston U. grantee, 1973, NEA Mus.' Profl. grantee, 1976-81; Samuel H. Kress Found. fellow, 1973; recipient Netherland-Am. Found. award Netherland Found., 1973, Disting. Alumni award Boston U. Grad. Sch., 1986. Mem.: Historians Netherlandish Art, New Mus. Assn., Am. Assn. Mus. (accreditation commr. 2000—). Coll. Art Assn. Am., Am. Fedn. Arts, Assn. Art Mus. Dirs. (v.p. 1998—99, pres. 1999—2000, trustee 2000—01). Home: 10 Massachusetts Ave Worcester MA 01609-1649 Office: Worcester Art Mus 55 Salisbury St Worcester MA 01609-3196

**WELZ, REBECCA BEALL,** sculptor, educator; d. Carl John Welz and Jerry Beall Hatcher; m. Toshitada Sakai, July 10, 1999. BA, Empire State Coll., N.Y.C., 1995. Adj. prof. with cert. of continuing employment Pratt Inst., Bklyn., 1998—; vis. instr. Parsons Sch. of Design, N.Y.C., 1997—98; vis. artist Vt. Studio Ctr., Johnson, 2001. One-woman shows include Landmark Gallery, NYC, 1979, Bernice Steinbaum Gallery, 1985, Grace Borgenicht Gallery, 1989, 1991, 1994, June Kelly Gallery, 1997, 2000, 2002, 2005, Butters Gallery, 2001, 2003, Gallery 555, Oakland, Calif., 2004, exhibited in group shows at Boston City Hall, 1973, Auction 393, NYC, 1976, Landmark Gallery, 1982, Grace Borgenicht Gallery, 1987, World Trade Ctr., 1989, Coll. New Rochelle, NY, 1992, Rosa Esman Gallery, NYC, 1992, Rockville Arts Pl., Md., 1993, Va. Ctr. Craft Arts, Richmond, 1993, Adam Baumgold Gallery, NYC, 1995, Sotheby's, 1996, Pratt Inst., Bklyn., 1998, Rutgers U., NJ, 2001, Delaware Valley Arts Ctr., Narrowsburg, NY, 2003, Sculpturesite Gallery, San Francisco, 2005, others, Represented in permanent collections Goldman Sachs, NYC, Merck, NJ, Prudential Life Ins. Corp., NYC, Cortec Corp., Sidney Lewis, Richmond, Va., William Kaufman Orgn., NYC, Credit Lyonnais, Warburg Pincus, Mound, Cotton, Wollan, Windmueller Fine Arts, Scarsdale, NY, Cleary, Gottlieg, Steen & Hamilton, NYC, AXA Corp., Pfizer. Recipient Faculty Devel. award, Pratt Inst., 2002, 2006; fellow, N.Y. Exptl. Glass Workshop (now Urban Glass), 1992; grantee, Pollock-Krasner Found., 1987, 1992, E.D. Found., 1990, 1995. Mem.: Assn. Women Indsl. Designers (founder 1991, pres. 1991—).

**WEMPLE, ERIK C.,** editor-in-chief; b. Schenectady, NY, 1965; Washington corr. Inside.com, CableWorld mag.; sr. editor & polit. columnist Washington City Paper, Washington, editor-in-chief, 2002—. Office: Village Voice 36 Cooper Sq New York NY 10003*

**WEMPNER, GERALD ARTHUR,** engineering educator; b. Waupun, Wis. s. Paul Christian and Thekla Nelda (Jung) W.; m. Lorraine Bischel, Sept. 6, 1952 (div. Apr. 1983); children: Susan K., Paul J. BS, U. Wis., 1952, MS, 1953; PhD, U. Ill., 1957. Instr. U. Ill., Urbana, 1953-57, asst. prof., 1957-59; assoc. prof. U. Ariz., Tucson, 1959-62; prof. U. Ala., Huntsville, 1964-73, Ga. Inst. Tech., Atlanta, 1973-91, prof. emeritus, 1991—. Vis. prof. U. Calif., Berkeley, 1962-63. Author: Mechanics of Solids, 1973; co-author: Mechanics of Deformable Bodies, 1961, Mechanics of Solids, 1995, Mechanics of Solids and Shells, 2003; contbr. articles to profl. jours. With U.S. Army, 1946—48. NSF fellow, Stanford (Calif.) U., 1963-64, Sr. fellow Alexander von Humboldt Found., Germany, 1973, Killam fellow U. Calgary, Can., 1983. Fellow ASME (asssoc. editor 1976-83), Am. Acad. Mechanics. Avocations: art, sculpture, photography, woodwork. Home and Office: 3397 Hidden Acres Dr Doraville GA 30340-4445

**WEN, GEORGE WALTER SUN,** editor; b. Seattle, Jan. 22, 1948; s. Herbert Jack Hsiu-rui and Rena Sun (Hsing-fang) Wen. BA magna cum laude, Dartmouth Coll., 1970; BA hon., Cambridge U., Eng., 1973; postgrad., Harvard U., 1970—71; MA, Cambridge U., Eng., 1976; Licence-ès-Lettres, Univ. Paris-VII, 1979; MS in Journalism, Columbia U., 1986. Sr. lectr. Inst. d'Etudes Politiques de Paris, Paris, 1982—85; sr. editor Attenzione Mag., N.Y., 1986; editor N.Y. Mag., N.Y., 1987; mng. editor Henry Holt and Co., N.Y., 1990—. Trustee, bd. trustees Hemophilia Assn. of N.Y., 2002—. Yaddo residency, Saratoga Springs, NY, 2001, Reynolds scholar, 1972—73. Mem.: Phi Kappa Phi, Phi Beta Kappa. Office: Flatiron Bldg 175 Fifth Ave New York NY 10010

**WEN, GEYI,** applied physics professor; b. Pingjiang, Hunan, China, Dec. 28, 1962; s. Zhiwu and Meiran Li Wen; m. Jun Yuan Wen, Jan. 22, 1988; 1 child, Lan. BS, Xidian U., Xian, China, 1982, MS, 1984, PhD, 1987. Lectr. S.E. U., Nanjing, China, 1988-90; assoc. prof. U. Electronic Sci. and Tech. China, Chengdu, 1990-92, prof., 1993—. Vis. rschr. U. Calif., Berkeley, 1992-93j; vice chmn. Inst. Applied Physics, U. Electronic Sci. and Tech. China, 1996-97, chmn., 1997—; vis. prof. U. Waterloo, Can., 1998; EM rschr. Rsch. in Motion, Can., 1998—. Author: Modern Methods for Electromagnetic Computation, 1996, Advances in Electormagnetic Theory, 1999; contbr. articles to profl. jours. Recipient Talent through Century award Sichuan Province, Chengdu, China, 1994, Sci. and Tech. Progress award China Soc. Sci. and Tech., 1996, Talent through Century award Nat. Edn. Com., Beijing, 1996. Mem. IEEE (editl. bd. IEEE Transactions on Microwave Theory & Techniques 1992—), China Soc. Computational Physics (mem. couns. 1992—), China Inst. Electronics (editl. bd. Jour. Electromagnetic Waves 1997—). Avocations: ping pong/table tennis, chinese chess. Office: Rsch in Motion 295 Phillip St Waterloo ON Canada N2L 3W8 E-mail: gwen@rim.net.

**WEN, QUAN,** economics professor, researcher; BS in Math., Jilin U., China, 1985; MA in Econ., U. Western Ontario, Can., 1987, PhD in Econ., 1991. Asst. prof. econs. U. Windsor, Ont., Canada, 1991—95, assoc. prof. econs., 1995—2001, Vanderbilt U., Nashville, 2001—04, prof. econs., 2005—. Office: Dept Econs Vanderbilt U 2301 Vanderbilt Pl Nashville TN 37235-1819 Office Phone: 615-322-0174. Office Fax: 615-343-8495. Business E-Mail: quan.wen@vanderbilt.edu.

**WEN, SHEREE,** computer company executive; BS in Physics, Natural Tsiug Hua U, Taiwan; PhD, U. Calif., Berkeley, 1979. Rsch. divsn. staff IBM, 1979-81, dept. mgr. Materials, Characterization and Analysis, 1981-84, program mgr. Tech., 1984-86, sr. mgr of Optics 1986, prog. mgr., tech. asst. to sr. v.p.; pres. WenLab USA Inc., N.Y.C. Patentee in field; Contbr. articles to profl. jours. Recipient John E. Dom Achievement award Am. Soc. for Metal, 1978, Outstanding tech. Achievement award, IBM, 1986, invention Achievement award, IBM, 1987; The Robert Lansing Hardy gold Metal The Metals, Materials & Minerals Soc. (TMS-AIME); the AIME as the most promising young Materials Scientist in Am., 1979 Mem. TMS-AIME's Process Monitor & Control Com. (chmn.), Materials Design & Mfg. Divsn. Award Com.; Indsl. Liaison for U. Calif. at Berkeley's ctr. for Materials. Office: Wen Technology Corp 22 Saw Mill River Rd Ste 5 Hawthorne NY 10532-1549 Fax: 914-376-7092.

**WEN, SHIH-LIANG,** mathematics professor; came to U.S., 1959; s. S.W. and C.F. (Hsiao) W.; m. Liang Tao; children: Dennis, Andy, Jue, Nannan. BS, Nat. Taiwan U., Taipei, 1956; MS, U. Utah, 1961; PhD, Purdue U., 1968. Assoc. research engr. The Boeing Co., Seattle, 1961-63; with dept. math. Ohio U., Athens, 1968—, successively asst. prof., assoc. prof. and prof., chmn. dept. math., 1993-95. Rsch. analyst Applied Math Rsch, Lab, USAF Wright-Patterson AFB, Ohio, summer, 1972; vis. rsch. scientist Courant Inst. Math. Scis. NYU, 1978-79; hon. prof. Jiangxi U., People's Republic of China, 1985; disting. vis. prof. Lanzhou U., People's Republic of China, 1989. Mem. Am. Math. Soc., Soc. for Indsl. and Applied Math., Math. Assn. Am. Avocations: fishing, bridge, music. Office: Ohio Univ Dept Math Athens OH 45701 E-mail: wen@math.ohiou.edu.

**WENDEBORN, RICHARD DONALD,** retired manufacturing executive; b. Winnipeg, Man., Can. came to U.S., 1950; naturalized, 1988; s. Curtis and Rose (Lysecki) W.; m. Dorothy Ann Munn, Aug. 24, 1957; children: Margaret Gayle, Beverley Jane, Stephen Richard, Peter Donald, Ann Elizabeth. Diploma, Colo. Sch. Mines, 1952; grad. advanced mgmt. program, Harvard U., 1974. With Can. Ingersoll-Rand Co., Montreal, 1952—, gen. mgr., v.p., dir., 1968, pres., 1969-74, chmn. bd., 1976—; exec. v.p. Ingersoll-Rand Co., Woodcliff Lake, NJ, 1976-89; ret., 1989. Mem. Can Govt. Oil and Gas Tech. Exch. Program with former USSR, 1972—, Minerals and Metals Mission to China, 1972—. Mem. Resource Fund Colo. Sch. Mines; past pres., dir. Town and River Civic Assn. Mem. Machinery and Equipment Mfrs. Assn. Can. (bd. dirs. 1974—, past chmn.), Royal Palm Yacht Club (commodore 1994), Internat. Order of Blue Gavel (past Commodore's Club, past pres. Royal Palm br. dist. 8), Useppa Island Club, Tau Beta Pi. Home: 12998 Beacon Cove Ln Fort Myers FL 33919-3802 Personal E-mail: dickandda@aol.com.

**WENDEL, CHARLES ALLEN,** lawyer; b. Lockport, N.Y., Aug. 13, 1942; s. Harold Henry and Doris Lillian (Gardner) W.; m. Helen W. Roberts, June 23, 1973; children: William Charles, Jonathan David. BChem Engring., Rensselaer Poly Inst., 1964; JD, Am. U., 1968. Bar: N.Y. 1969, Va. 1971, D.C. 1980, U.S. Ct. Appeals (fed. and 4th cirs.), U.S. Dist. Ct. (ea. and we. dists.) Va., U.S. Supreme Ct. Patent examiner U.S. Patent and Trademark Office, Washington, 1964—66; patent trainee Union Carbide Corp., Washington, 1966—68, patent atty. N.Y.C., 1968—70; assoc., then ptnr. Stevens, Davis, Miller & Mosher, Arlington, Va., 1970—83; ptnr. firm Wegner & Bretschneider, Washington, 1983—85; assoc. solicitor U.S. Patent and Trademark Office, 1985—88; assoc. Lyon & Lyon, Washington, 1988—90; founding ptnr. Parkhurst & Wendel, Alexandria, Va., 1995—2005, Steptoe & Johnson, LLP, 2005—06, Oblon, Spivak, McClelland, Maier & Nuestadt P.C.,

2006—. Contbr. articles to profl. jours. Mem. Va. State Bar (patent trademark copyright sect., chmn. 1977-78), Am. Intellectual Patent Law Assn., Patent Lawyers Club Washington (prs. 1982-83), Delta Theta Phi. Republican. Office Phone: 703-412-6044.

**WENDEL, JOAN AUDREY,** music educator; b. N.Y.C., Dec. 1, 1931; d. Adam and Edna Sophia Wohlfart; m. Ralph Aurol Wendel, July 21, 1962 (dec. May 1998); 1 child, Tracy Lynn. BA summa cum laude, Dowling Coll., 1969; MA, Adelphi U., 1971. Cert. elem. tchr., N.Y. Sec. A.C. Edwards Ins., Sayville, NY, 1950-53; office mgr. John V. Potter Ins., East Islip, NY, 1953-59, Pilger Agy., Patchogue, NY, 1959-66; tchr. Connetquot CSD of Islip, Bohemia, NY, 1969-91; pvt. music tchr. Bohemia, 1979—; music dir. Christ Luth. Ch., Cape Coral, Fla., 1996—, Sounds of Fla., Cape Coral, 1999—2003. Mem. Music Tchrs. Nat. Assn., Music Educators Nat. Conf., Assn. Luth. Ch. Musicians, Ft Myers Music Tchrs. Assn. (v.p. 1999), Order Eastern Star (worthy matron 1964, assoc. grand marshal 1973, grand musician 1987). Republican. Lutheran. Avocations: walking, golf, music, reading. Home: 2218 SE 10th Ter Cape Coral FL 33990-6217 Office: Christ Luth Ch 2911 Del Prado Blvd S Cape Coral FL 33904-7297

**WENDEL, JOHN FREDRIC,** lawyer, consultant; b. Newark, Nov. 8, 1936; s. John J. and Margaret D. (Mortimer) W.; m. Barbara Vaughn Smith, Dec. 17, 1960 (dec. July 1978); children: David I., Stephen F.; m. Carlene M. Arnoldini, 1 child, Carlene Margaret. BA, U. Fla., 1958; JD, Stetson U., 1963. Bar: Fla. 1963, U.S. Dist. Ct (so. and mid. dists.) 1964, U.S. Ct. Appeals (5th, 9th, and 11th cirs.) 1964, U.S. Supreme Ct. 1968. Chmn. Wendel & Chritton Chartered and predecessor firms, Lakeland, Fla., 1965—. Town atty. Town of St. Leo, Fla., 1964-78, town judge, 1968; mcpl. judge Lakeland, Fla., 1966; county atty. Citrus County, Fla., 1976-81; of counsel, Whyte and Hirschboeck, Milw., 1989-90, gen. counsel and spl. counsel to various profl. baseball leagues, 1969-1998; vis. prof. law, dir. Nat. Sports Law Inst., Marquette U. Law Sch., Milw., 1989-90; adj. prof. law Marquette U. Law Sch., Milw., 1990-91, adj. prof. Stetson U. Coll. Law, 1992-93; adj. faculty mem. Fla. So. Coll., Lakeland, 1963-65; faculty mem. St. Leo Coll., 1963-73; del. 2d Internat. Conf. Ptnrs. for Alliance for Progress; mem. Fla. Columbia Alliance Coms. and Subco.; gen. counsel Sun 'n Fun Fly-In, Inc., 1998—. Mem. editorial bd. Sports Law and Fin., 1992-98. Assoc. mem. counsel Fla. Sports Adv. Coun. Served to 1st lt. USMC, 1957-59. Named one of Lakeland's Five Outstanding Young Men, Jaycees, 1967. Mem. Am. Arbitration Assn. (arbitrator alternative dispute resolution to settle sports disputes), Sports Lawyers Assn. (pres. 1986-93, sec., v.p., bd. dirs. 1974—, pres. and dir. emeritus, Award of Excellence 1993), The Fla. Bar (exec. coun. entertainment, arts and sports law sect.), Lakeland Bar Assn., Fla. Assn. County Attys. (pres. 1981), Nat. Assn. of Profl. Baseball Leagues, Inc. (gen. counsel 1971-82), Lakeland Yacht and Country Club, KC. Republican. Roman Catholic. Office: Wendel & Chritton Chartered 325 E Lemon St Ste 351 Lakeland FL 33801 Office Phone: 863-603-7730. E-mail: jwendel@wendelchritton.com

**WENDEL, RICHARD FREDERICK,** economist, educator, consultant; b. Chgo., Apr. 29, 1930; s. Elmer Carl and Victoria Matilda (Jeffery) W.; m. Leslie Jane Travis, June 15, 1957; children: John Travis, Andrew Stewart. AB, Augustana Coll., 1951; MBA, U. Pa., 1957, PhD (fellow 1962-64), 1966. Asst. to pres. Flexonics Corp., Maywood, Ill., 1957-59; sales rep., product mgr. Kordite div. Nat. Distillers Corp., Macedon, N.Y., 1959-62; instr. Wharton Sch., U. Pa., 1964-65; asst. prof. mktg. Grad. Sch. Bus. Adminstrn., Washington U., St. Louis, 1965-69; asso. prof. U. Conn., 1969-74, prof., 1974-90, prof. emeritus, 1990. Mem. U.S. Census Field Adv. Commn., 1967-69; mem. acad. adv. commn. Bur. Labor Stats., U.S. Bur. Census Survey of Consumer Expenditures, 1971-76; mem. Conn. Export Devel. Council, Dept. Commerce, 1972-76; dir. Neon Software Inc. Author: (with M.L. Bell) Economic Importance of Highway Advertising, 1966; (with W. Gorman) Selling: Preparation. Persuasion. Strategy., 1983, 88; editor: Readings in Marketing, 1973-74, 75-76, 77-78, 78-79, 79-80, 80-81, (with C.L. Lapp) Add to Your Selling Know-How, 1968; editorial staff: jour. Mktg., 1965-74. Bd. dirs. Roper Center. Served with USAF, 1951-55. Center for Real Estate and Urban Econs. grantee, 1969-70 Mem. Am. Mktg. Assn., N.Y. Acad. Scis. Republican. Episcopalian. Home: 106 S Queen St Chestertown MD 21620-1522 Office Phone: 410-778-7185.

**WENDELSTEDT, HARRY HUNTER, JR.,** umpire; b. Balt., July 27, 1938; m. Cheryl Maher, Nov. 2, 1970; children: Harry III, Amy. Student, Essex Community Coll.; BS in Edn., U. Md. Profl. baseball umpire, 1962—; with minor leagues, Ga.-Fla., 1962, (Northwest), 1963, Tex., 1964, (Internat.), 1965, maj. leagues (Nat.), 1966-98; umpire All-Star Game, 1968, 76, 83, 92, Nat. League championship series, 1970, 72, 77, 80, 82, 84, 88, 90, 96, World Series, 1973, 80, 86, 91, 95; umpire supr. Nat. Baseball League, 1999—. Owner, operator Harry Wendelstedt Umpire Sch. Named Top Umpire in Maj. League Baseball Md. Profl. Baseball Players Assn., 1975, Best Umpire in Nat. League Chgo. Tribune, 1982, Best Ball and Strike Umpire Sports Illustrated, 1982, Major League Umpire of Yr., 1992, Fla. Diamond Club, 1993. Mem. Major League Umpires Assn. (4 term past pres.) Address: care Wendelstedt Sch for Umpires 88 S Saint Andrews Dr Ormond Beach FL 32174-3857

**WENDER, IRA TENSARD,** lawyer; b. Pitts., Jan. 5, 1927; s. Louis and Luba (Kibrick) W.; m. Phyllis M.Bellows, June 24, 1966; children: Justin B., Sarah T; children by previous marriage: Theodore M., Abigail A., John B. Swarthmore Coll., 1942-45; JD, U. Chgo., 1948; LLM, NYU, 1951. Atty. Lord, Day and Lord, N.Y.C., 1950-52, 54-59; asst. dir. internat. program in tax. Harvard U. Law Sch., 1952-54; lectr. N.Y. U. Sch. Law, N.Y.C., 1954-59; ptnr. Baker and McKenzie, Chgo., 1959-61; founding ptnr. N.Y.C. office, 1961-71; sr. ptnr. Wender, Murase & White, 1971-82; of counsel, 1982-86; chmn. C. Brewer and Co., Ltd., Honolulu, 1969-75; pres., CEO A. G. Becker Paribas Inc., 1978-82; chmn., CEO Sussex Securities Inc., 1983-85; of counsel Patterson, Belknap, Webb & Tyler, N.Y.C., 1986-87, ptnr, 1988-93; of counsel, 1994—. Chmn. Perry Ellis Internat., Inc., N.Y.C., 1994; bd. dirs. REFAC Corp., N.Y.C., Dime Bancorp, N.Y.C.; bd. mgrs. Swarthmore Coll, 1978-89; pres., bd. mgrs. PARC Vendome Condominium, 1990-94; trustee Putnet (Vt.) Sch., 1985-92, 93—, vice chmn., 1998—; trustee Brearley Sch., N.Y.C., 1980-85. Author: (with E.R. Barlow) Foreign Investment and Taxation, 1995. Dir., treas. Fountain House, Inc., N.Y., 1998—; dir. Am. Near East Refug ad, Washington; mem. Coun. on Fgn. Rels. Mem. ABA, N.Y. State Bar Assn., Assn. of Bar of City of N.Y. Home: 115 E 67th St New York NY 10021-5951 Office: Patterson Belknap Webb & Tyler LLP Ste 2200 1133 Avenue Of The Americas New York NY 10036-6731*

**WENDER, PAUL ANTHONY,** chemistry professor; BS, Wilkes Coll., 1969; PhD, Yale U., 1973; PhD (hon.), Wilkes U., 1993. Asst. prof., assoc. prof. Harvard U., 1974-81; prof. chemistry Stanford U., 1981—; Bergstrom prof. chemistry, 1994—. Cons. Eli Lilly & Co., 1980—, lectr. Am. Chem. Soc. Recipient ICI Am. Chem. award Stuart Pharm., merit award NIH, Pfizer rsch. award, 1995. Fellow AAAS; mem. Am. Chem. Soc. (Arthur C. Cope Sholan award 1990, Guenther award, award for creative work in synthetic chemistry 1998). Office: Stanford U Mudd Bldg Rm 390 Mail Code 5080 Stanford CA 94305

**WENDER, PHYLLIS BELLOWS,** literary agent; m. Ira Tensard Wender; children: Justin Bellows, Sarah Tensard. BA, Wells Coll., 1956. Publicity dir. Grove Press, NYC, Dell Pub. Co., NYC; theatrical agt. Artists Agy. Inc., NYC; agt. Wender & Assocs., NYC; prin., agt. ptnr. Rosenstone/Wender, NYC. Bd. dir Just Women Inc., Bklyn., 1982, mem. adv. com., 1983-87; bd. dir. Fortune Soc., N.Y.C., 1977-80; trustee Wells Coll., Aurora, N.Y., 1980-90. Mem. Women's Media Group (dir. 1988-90), Cosmopolitan Club. Office: Rosenstone Wender 38 East 29th St 10th Flr New York NY 10016 Personal E-mail: pbwender@aol.com

**WENDEROFF, ALAN J.,** psychologist, educator; b. Bklyn., Apr. 23, 1952; s. Morton L. and Joan Wenderoff; m. Avril C. Clemendor, Nov. 1, 1955; children: Abby L., Joshua D., Alexander P. BA, SUNY, Stony Brook; PhD,

Walden U., 1998. Lic. psychologist N.Y., sch. psychologist N.Y. Psychologist SteppingStone Day Sch., Kew Garden Hills, NY, 1993—2003, North Shore-LIJ Ctr. for Autism, Bethpage, NY, 2003—05, Rothman Therapeutic Svcs., Plainview, NY, 2005—. Asst. prof. Hofstra U. Sch. Edn., Hempstead, NY, 2000—06. Mem.: NASP. Home: 181 Pearsall Dr 1E Mount Vernon NY 10552 Office: Rothman Therapeutic Services 45 Executive Plaza Plainview NY Office Phone: 516-576-2166. Personal E-mail: awenderoff@optonline.net. Business E-mail: alanw@rothmantherapy.com.

**WENDLANDT, GARY E.,** insurance company executive; BS in applied math., computer sci., Wash. U., Mo. Various positions Mass. Mutual Life Ins. Co., 1972—92, exec. v.p., chief investment officer, 1992—99; chmn., CEO New York Life Investment Mgmt. LLC; exec. v.p., exec. mgmt. com. New York Life Ins. Co., 1999—. Fellow: Soc. of Actuaries; mem.: Am. Acad. of Actuaries. Office: NY Life Ins Co 51 Madison Ave New York NY 10010

**WENDLINGER, ROBERT MATTHEW,** communications and memory consultant; b. N.Y.C., 1922; s. Harry and Rose (Pollock) W.; m. Dalis Peralta, 1955 (div. 1973); children: David, Marcella, Marta; m. Joan Hays Cole, June 23, 1984. Student, U. Calif., Berkeley, 1942—43, Columbia U., 1947—52. Editor script Radio Free Europe, N.Y.C., 1950—52; assoc. editor Ind. Film Jour., N.Y.C., 1953—57; gen. mgr. Kermit Rolland and Assocs., Princeton, NJ, 1957—59; exec. asst. in charge editl. svcs. United Hosp. Fund of N.Y., N.Y.C., 1959—60; editl. assoc. in pub. rels. N.Y. Life Ins. Co., N.Y.C., 1960—65; mgr. info. sect. Com. for Air and Water Conservation Am. Petroleum Inst., N.Y.C., 1965—66; with Bank of Am. NT & SA, San Francisco, 1967—78, adminstrv. officer, 1967—70, asst. v.p. comm., 1970—78; pres. Comm. Cons. and Svcs., Berkeley, Calif., 1978—82; pub. rels. Nestle Corp., White Plains, NY, 1983—84; pres. Proust Press, Oakland, Calif., 1994—. Mem. grad. faculty St. Mary's Coll., Moraga, Calif., 1975-78; mem. Astron Corp. Author: (with James M. Reid, Jr.) Effective Letters: A Program in Self-Instruction, 1964, 3d edit., 1978, Japanese edit., 1996, The Memory Triggering Book: Using Your Memories to Enhance Your Life and Your Relationships, 1995; contbr.: Everybody Wins: TA Applied to Organizations, 1973, Affirmative Action for Women, 1973, McGraw-Hill Ency. Professional Management, 1978. Fellow Am. Bus. Comm. Assn.; mem. Indsl. Comm. Coun. (past pres.). Office Phone: 510-845-5551.

**WENDORF, RICHARD HAROLD,** library director, educator; b. Cedar Rapids, Mar. 17, 1948; s. Harold Albert and Jeanne Ellen (Hamblin) W.; m. Barbara Hilderman, 1970 (div. 1983); m. Diana Thanet French, 1984 (div. 1995); children: Reed Thanet Wendorf-French, Carolyn Thanet Wendorf-French; m. Elizabeth Morse, 1997. BA, Williams Coll., 1970; PhB, U. Oxford, Eng., 1972; MA, Princeton U., 1974, PhD, 1976. From asst. prof. English to assoc. prof. English Northwestern U., Evanston, Ill., 1976-86, assoc. dean, 1984-88, prof. English and art history, 1986-89; libr. dir. Houghton Libr., Harvard U., Cambridge, Mass., 1989-97; Stanford Calderwood dir. and libr. Boston Athenaeum, 1997—. Sr. lectr. fine arts Harvard U., 1990-97, acting libr. Fine Arts Libr., 1991-92; lectr. Phi Beta Kappa Assocs., 1992-96; dir. NEH summer seminars for coll. tchrs. Northwestern U., 1987, Harvard U., 1990, 92, 96, Boston Athenaeum, 2002, 04; Robert Sterling Clark vis. prof. art history Williams Coll., 1993; bd. mgrs. Lewis Walpole Libr., 2005-. Author: William Collins and Eighteenth-Century English Poetry 1981, The Elements of Life: Biography and Portrait Painting in Stuart and Georgian England, 1990, paperback edit., 1991, Sir Joshua Reynolds: The Painter in Society, 1996, The Scholar-Librarian, 2005, After Sir Joshua, 2005; editor: Articulate Images: The Sister Arts from Hogarth to Tennyson, 1983, Rare Book and Manuscript Libraries in the Twenty-First Century, 1993, (with Charles Ryskamp) The Works of William Collins, 1979; contbr. essays in field; mem. editl. bd. Studies in 18th Century Culture, 1985-89, Word and Image, 1992-2000, Yale edit. Writings of Samuel Johnson, Old-Time New Eng., 1996-99. Trustee Mus. Fine Arts, Boston. Rsch. grantee Folger Shakespeare Libr., Washington, 1976, Am. Philos. Soc., Phila., 1977, 82, Henry E. Huntington Libr., 1979, 2003, Yale Ctr. for Brit. Art, 1983, Brit. Acad., 2003; jr. rsch. fellow Am. Coun. Learned Socs., 1978-79; summer stipend NEH, 1979; sr. rsch. fellow Am. Coun. Learned Socs., 1981-82; NEH rsch. fellow Newberry Libr., Chgo., 1988-89; fellow John Simon Guggenheim Meml. Found., 1989-90. Mem.: Mass. Hist. Soc, The Johnsonians (chmn. 1994—95, 1997—98), Nat. Com. on Stds. in Arts, Colonial Soc. Mass., Soc. Brit. Art Historians, Coll. Art Assn., Am. Soc. 18th Century Studies (pres. Midwest regional soc. 1986, Annibel Jenkins Biography prize 1998), Am. Antiquarian Soc., Keats-Shelley Assn. Am. (bd. dirs. 1993—98), Signet Soc. (assoc.), U. Club (NY), Union Club Boston, Cambridge Sci. Club, Saturday Club, Grolier Club, Phi Beta Kappa (sec. Boston Chgo. 1984—87, nominating com. 1999—2002). Office: Boston Athenaeum 10 1/2 Beacon St Boston MA 02108-3777

**WENDT, CHARLES WILLIAM,** soil scientist, educator; b. Plainview, Tex., July 12, 1931; s. Charles Gottlieb and Winnie Mae (Bean) W.; m. Clara Anne Diller, Oct. 15, 1955; children: Charles Diller, John William, Elaine Anne, Cynthia Lynne. BS in Agronomy, Tex. A&M U., 1951, PhD in Soil Physics, 1966; MS in Agronomy, Tex. Tech U., 1957. Research asst. Tex. Tech Coll., 1953-55, instr. agronomy, 1957-61, asst. prof., 1961-63; research asst. soil physics Tex. A&M U., 1963-65, research assoc., 1965-66; asst. prof. Tex. A&M U. (Agrl. Research and Extension Center), Lubbock, 1966-69, assoc. prof., 1969-74, prof., 1974-91, prof. emeritus, 1991—. Cons. cotton prodn. Ministry of Agr. Sudan, summer 1960; cons. Irrigation Assn., 1977-81, Office of Tech. and Assessment, 1982, S.E. Consortium for Internat. Devel., 1989, Rhone Poulenc Agrl. Co., 1992-93; prin. backstop scientist U.S. AID West African Rsch. Program on Soil-Plant0Water Mgmt., 1982-91; chmn. agrl. sect. Southwestern and Rocky Mountain divsn. AAAS, 1982-83. Contbr. articles to profl. jours., chpt. to book. Del. Lubbock County Rep. Conv., 1978; elder Westminster Presbyn. Ch.; Tex. rep. to Great Plains Coun. 1 com. on evapotranspiration; bd. dirs. Presbyn. Ctr., Inc., 1999—, The South Plains Food Bank, 1999—, bd. dirs. farm, orchard and garden divsn., 2002- . 1st lt. U.S. Army, 1951-53. Named Outstanding Researcher High Plains Research Found., 1982; recipient Superior Achievement award for rsch., soil and crop scis. dept. Tex. A&M Univ., 1987, Vice Chancellors award in excellence as mem. TROPSOILS Rsch. team Tex. A&M U., 1996; grantee industry and water dists. Dept. Interior, U.S. AID, EPA. Mem. Soil Sci. Soc. Am., Am. Soc. Agronomy, Optimist Club (1st v.p., bd. dirs. 2001-2004). Home: 4518 22nd St Lubbock TX 79407-2515 Office: Texas Agrl Expt Station RR 3 Lubbock TX 79403-9803 E-mail: absendt@aol.com, absendt@cox.net.

**WENDT, DAVID ALLEN,** literature and language educator; b. Havana, Ill., Nov. 13, 1959; s. William Clarence and Elinor Marie (Yetter) W. AA, Spoon River Coll., 1980; BS, So. Ill. U., 1982; postgrad., Western Ill. U., 1983-84, EdS, 1998; MA, U. Iowa, 1996. Cert. tchr., Iowa. Grad. asst., speech coach Western Ill. U., Macomb, 1983-84; tchr. in speech and English Burlington (Iowa) Community High Sch., 1984-89; tchr. in speech, English and drama Keokuk (Iowa) High Sch., 1989—. Summer fellow Northwestern U., 1997; convention co-chair Iowa Coun. Tchrs. English and Lang. Arts, 1998, 99; Am. Jewish Labor fellow, summer, 1999. Contbr. articles, poems to profl. publs. Sponsor Civil War re-enactment, Keokuk; bd. dirs. Planned Parenthood, Keokuk; coord. Summer Children's Theatre, Burlington, 1985-86; dramaturgist Great River Players Theatre, Keokuk, 1990; active ISEA State Com. on Minority Affairs, 1992-94, Keokuk Fine Arts Coun., 1993—; state pres. Fedn. of Iowa Speech Orgns., 1993-95; bd. dirs. Gt. River Players, 2005—Recipient Outstanding Speech Coach award Iowa Am. Legion, 1988; named to Outstanding Young Men in Am., 1989. Mem. Nat. Comm. Assn. (mem. ednl. policies bd. 2003—, Oberle award 2000), Iowa Human Rels. Assn., Nat. Forensic League (mem. com. local diet 1984—, Nat. Champion Coach award 1989), Iowa Comm. Assn. (state pres. 2000-2002), Southeast Iowa Speech Coaches (pres. 2003-2004), Spoon River Coll. Alumni Assn., Iowa Forensic League (state com. 1992—, Outstanding Speech Coach award 1988), So. Ill. U. Alumni Assn., Iowa State Edn. Assn. (state com. on minority affairs 1992—), S.E. Iowa Tchrs. of English, Iowa Comm. Assn. (pres. 2000-02), Iowa H.S. Speech Assn. (mem. all-state festival com. 2004). Avocations:

travel, writing, softball, volleyball. Home: 2806 Windsor Hts Keokuk IA 52632-2550 Office: Keokuk High Sch 2285 Middle Rd Keokuk IA 52632-2834 Office Phone: 319-524-2542. Business E-Mail: dwendt@keokuk.k12.ia.us.

**WENDT, E. ALLAN,** international affairs consultant; b. Chgo., Nov. 8, 1935; s. John Arthur Frederic and Dorothy S. BA magna cum laude, Yale U., 1957; Cert. in Politics, Inst. d'Etudes Politques, 1958; MPA, Harvard U., 1967. Econ. comml. officer Am. Embassy, Saigon, Vietnam, 1967-71; fin. officer U.S. Mission to European Cmtys., Brussels, 1971-74; State Dept. fellow Coun. on Fgn. Rels., N.Y.C., 1974-75; dir. Office Internat. Commodities Dept. State, Washington, 1975-79; counselor for econ. and comml. affairs Am. Embassy, Cairo, 1979-81; dep. asst. sec. of state for internat. energy and resources policy Dept. State, 1981-86, sr. rep. for strategic tech. policy, 1987-92, with rank of amb., 1988-92, U.S. amb. to Republic of Slovenia Ljubljana, 1993-95, spl. rep. Internat. Donor Activities in Kosovo, 1998-2000; internat. affairs cons., 2000—. Councillor Atlantic Coun. of U.S.; mem. Coun. Fgn. Rels. Washington Inst. Fgn. Affairs.; mem. adv. bd Nat Youth Leadership Forum; bd. dir Assn. Dip Tng. and Studies. Contbr. articles to profl. jours., radio stas. and newspapers. Recipient award for heroism Dept. State, 1968, Presdl. Meritorious Svc. award, 1986, Superior Honor award Dept. State, 1992. Episcopalian.

**WENDT, GEORGE ROBERT,** actor; b. Chgo., Oct. 17, 1948; m. Bernadette Birkette; children: Joshua, Andrew, Hilary, Joe, Daniel. BA in Econs., Rockhurst Coll., 1971. Mem. Second City comedy troupe, Chgo., 1974-81. Actor: (feature films) My Bodyguard, 1980, Somewhere in Time, 1980, Airplane II: The Sequel, 1982, Jeckyl & Hyde: Together Again, 1982, The Women in Red, 1984, Thief of Hearts, 1984, No Small Affair, 1983, Fletch, 1985, House, 1986, Plain Clothes, 1988, Guilt by Suspicion, 1991, Forever Young, 1992, Man of the House, 1995, The Lovemaster, 1997, Rupert's Land, 1998, Outside Providence, 1999, Pooch and the Pauper, 1999, Lakeboat, 2000, Teddy Bears' Picnic, 2002, My Dinner with Jimi, 2003, King of the Ants, 2003, The Life Coach, 2005, Kids in America, 2005, (TV films) Alien Avengers, 1996, Star Truckers, 1997, Price of Heaven, 1997, Alice in Wonderland, 1999, My Beautiful Son, 2001, Robertson's Greatest Hits, 2001, (TV series) Cheers, 1982-1993, The George Wendt Show, 1995, The Naked Truth, 1995, Sabrina, the Teenage Witch, 2001-02, House of Dreams, 2004-; appeared in various commls.: guest-star: (TV series) Alice, Soap, Taxi, Hart to Hart, The American Dream, Seinfeld, Wings, St. Elsewhere, Spin City, The Simpsons, The Larry Sanders Show, Madigan Men, 2000, Becker, 2002, Frasier, 2002, The Jamie Kennedy Experiment, 2002; appeared on stage with the Second City comedy troupe, also Wild Men, 1993.*

**WENDT, RICHARD L.,** manufacturing executive; b. 1931; From mgr. of frame factory to mgr. ops. Caradco; CEO Jeld-Wen Inc., Klamath Falls, Oreg., 1960—2003, chmn., 2003—. Address: Jeld Wen Inc PO Box 1329 Klamath Falls OR 97601-0268 Office: Jen Weld Inc 401 Harbor Isles Blvd Klamath Falls OR 97601*

**WENDT, THOMAS,** finance company executive; CPA, Wis. Auditor Coopers & Lybrand, Milw., 1973-75; supr. Conley, McDonald, Sprague & Co., Milw., 1975-80; CFO E. Cen./Select Sires, Waupun, Wis., 1981—, also rec. sec., bd. dirs. Bd. dirs. Moravian Homes Inc., Mueller Apts., Inc., Marquardt Meml. Manor, Inc., Watertown, Wis., sec., treas. bd. dirs., 1986—; bd. dirs. Hus Apts., Inc., sec.-treas., 1993—. Mem. Marquardt Found., 1988—; bd. dirs. Zinsendorf Hall, 1989—, sec., treas., 1989—, forward campaign chmn.; 1988; pres. bd. trustees Watertown Moravian Ch., 1981-84, bd. elders, 1990-93, ch. sec., 2000-03; adv. bd. Western Dist. Synod, Wis., 1982, 86, 90, 96; bd. dirs. Moravian Homes of Sturgeon Bay, 1991—; bd. dirs. Hus Apts., Inc., 1993—, sec., treas., 1993—. Mem. AICPA, Wis. Inst. CPAs, Milw. Art Mus., Beaver Dam Lions Club (bd. dirs. 2005—). Office: E Central/Select Sires PO Box 191 Waupun WI 53963-0191

**WENDT, VERNON EARL,** internist, cardiologist; b. Cleve., Mar. 26, 1931; s. Raymond C. and Esther L. (Naujoks) W.; m. Hildegarde Caroline Moeller, Aug. 14, 1953; children: David, Frederick, Kathryn, Elizabeth, Doralyn, James, Vernon Earl, Jr. BS in Zoology and Chemistry cum laude, Baldwin-Wallace Coll., 1952; MD, Columbia U., 1956. Diplomate Am. Bd. Internal Medicine. Intern Detroit Receiving Hosp., 1956—57, resident, 1959—62; USPHS postdoctoral fellow in cardiology Wayne State U. Sch. of Medicine, Detroit, 1962—65, from instr. to asst. prof. medicine, 1961—65; dir. rsch. Blodgett Meml. Med. Ctr., Grand Rapids, Mich., 1965—67; pvt. practice internal medicine and cardiology Grand Rapids, 1967—2000. Capt. M.C., USAF, 1957-59. Fellow: ACP, Coun. on Geriatric Cardiology, Am. Coll. Angiology, Am. Coll. Cardiology; mem.: AMA, Mich. State Med. Soc., Mich. Health Coun. (trustee 1998—), Am. Acad. Anti-Aging Medicine, Kent County Med. Soc., Mich. Soc. Internal Medicine. (pres. 1991—92), Am. Lung Assn. Mich. (pres. 1978—80), Am. Heart Assn. Mich. (trustee 1973—93, pres. 1987—88). Lutheran. Avocations: golf, gardening, walking. Home and Office: 1620 Andover Rd SE Grand Rapids MI 49506 Business E-Mail: vhwendt@comcast.net.

**WENDZEL, ROBERT LEROY,** political science professor; b. May 28, 1938; married; 3 children. BA in Polit. Sci. magna cum laude, Kalamazoo Coll., 1960; PhD in Polit. Sci., U. Fla., 1965. Assoc. prof. polit. sci. U. Maine, Orono, 1977-81, 82-83; prof. internat. affairs U.S. Air War Coll., Maxwell AFB, Ala., 1981-82, prof. internat. politics, 1986-87, ednl. advisor to the Commandant, 1987-2000, prof. internat. security studies, 2002—06; asst. dean arts and scis., prof. polit. sci., coord. internat. affairs program U. Maine, 1984-86; Paschal P. Vacca prof. liberal arts U. Montevallo, Ala., 2001; Merrill prof. polit. sci. Utah State U., Logan, 2001. Internat. affairs com., U. Maine, 1970-86, budget adv. com., 1983-86, coord. internat. affairs program, 1984-86. Author: International Relations: A Policymaker Focus, Thai edit., 1989, Relacoes Internacionais, 1985, International Politics: Policymakers and Policymaking, 1981, International Relations: A Policymaker Focus, 1977, 2d edit., 1980; co-author: America's Foreign Policy in a Changing World, 1994, Defending America's Security, 1988, 2d edit., 1990, To Preserve the Republic: The Foreign Policy of the United States, 1985, Games Nations Play, 9th edit., 1996; contbr. articles to profl. jours. Mem. Phi Beta Kappa. Home: 160 Old Field Dr Montgomery AL 36117-3938 Personal E-mail: blw052838@aol.com.

**WENEGRAT, SAUL S.,** art association administrator; b. Jersey City, Mar. 28, 1933; s. John and Tillie (Freeman) W. BA, Rutgers U., 1960; PhD, Harvard U., 1965; cert., London U., 1975. Dir. art program Port Authority of N.Y. & N.J., N.Y.C., 1962-95; prof. grad. divsn. Fashion Inst. Tech., N.Y.C., 1987-95; v.p. Forums Internat., 1995—; cons. arts advisor Voorsanger and Assocs., Archs., 2001—04. Pub. art panelist N.J. State Com. Arts, Trenton, 1985-95, Conn. State Com. Arts, Hartford, 1988, N.Y.C. Cultural Affairs, 1980-88, Met. Transit Authority, N.Y., 1994-95. Editor: Art for the Public, 1985. Capt. USAF, 1953-57. Recipient Doris Freedman award Mayor of N.Y.C., 1984, Merit cert. Mcpl. Art Soc., 1980, 85; Carnegie fellow, 1960, Fels fellow, 1960. Mem. Nat. Assn. Corp. Art Adminstrn. (chmn. bd. 1985-95), Internat. Art Advisors, Am. Assn. Museums, Harvard Club. Avocations: bridge, walking, museums. Home: 2 Beekman Pl New York NY 10022-8058

**WENER, BRIAN D.,** psychologist; s. Martin M. and Rachel Wener; m. Rachel Kurshan, May 22, 1994; 1 child, Sara. BA in Psychology with honors, Carleton U., 1971; MA in Psychology, SUNY, Plattsburgh, 1975; D of Psychology, Ctrl. Mich. U., 1982. Lic. psychologist NH, 1983. Mass., 1995, cert. sch. psychologist NH, 1981. Clin. psychologist Riverbend Counseling, Concord, NH, 1983—87; psychologist II Philbrook Ctr., 1975—78; clin. psychologist pvt. practice, Portsmouth, 1987—; sch. psychologist Hampton Schs., 2000—06. Cons., evaluator NH Medicaid Disability Unit, Concord, 1993—. Fellow: NH Psychol. Assn. (bd. dirs. 1992—94); mem.: APA, NH Assn. Sch. Psychologists. Avocations: photography, guitar. Office: 118 Maplewood Ave Portsmouth NH 03801 Office Phone: 603-431-1294.

**WENG, DANIELLA,** pharmacist, researcher; d. Kwok Soo and Zhao Quin Young. BS in Pharmacy, L.I. U., 1998, MS in Pharmaceutics, 2002. Intern in pharmacy N.Y. Hosp.-Cornell Med. Ctr., N.Y.C., 1996—97; clin. pharmacy extern Meml. Sloan-Kettering Cancer Ctr., N.Y.C., 1997; intern in pharmacy Vis. Nurse Svc. N.Y., N.Y.C., 1998—99; rsch. project L.I. U., Bklyn., 1999—2002; pharmacist Kingsbrook Jewish Med. Ctr., Bklyn., 2001, Woodhull Med. Ctr., Bklyn., 2001—. Pharmacy Alumni scholar, Arnold & Marie Schwartz Coll. Of Pharmacy, 1993—98. Mem.: Am. Pharm. Assn., Am. Assn. Pharm. Scientists. Achievements include research in pharmacokinetics of acyclovir in rabbit estimated via microdialysis sampling after IV-bolus and iontophoretic administration. Avocations: hiking, ice skating, dance, reading, travel. Personal E-mail: daniella_weng@yahoo.com. E-mail: daniellaweng@aol.com.

**WENG, GEORGE JUENG-CIOUS,** engineering educator; b. Oct. 8, 1944; s. Wan-Chung and Kuang-chieh (Hsieh) Weng; m. Jackie Li; children: Shawn, Cidney, Zoe;children from previous marriage: Bruce, Joyce. BS, Taiwan U., 1967; MPhil, Yale U., 1971, PhD, 1974. Rsch. fellow Delft U. Tech., Netherlands, 1973—74; postdoctoral fellow Yale U., UCLA, 1974—76; sr. rsch. engr. GM Rsch. Lab., Warren, Mich., 1976—77; asst. prof. mech. and aerospace engring. Rutgers U., New Brunswick, NJ, 1977—80, assoc. prof., 1980—84, prof., 1984—92, disting. prof., 1992—, grad. dir., 1995—98. Contbr. more than 150 articles to profl. jours.; editor Acta Mechanica, 1985—, tech. editor Jour. Engring. Materials and Tech., trans. ASME, 1992—97, mem. editl. bd. Internat. Jour. Plasticity, 1985—, Acta Mechanica Solida Sinica, 1997—, JSME Internat. Jour., 1997—2002, Mechanics and Materials in Design, 2004—, Mechanics of Advanced Materials and Structures, 2004—. NSF grantee, 1978—. Fellow ASME, Am. Acad. Mechanics. Achievements include work in mechanics of materials, micromechanics of composite materials, shape-memory alloys, ferroelectric ceramics, nano-grained materials. Home: 65 Sycamore Way Warren NJ 07059 Office: Sch Engring Rutgers U New Brunswick NJ 08903 Office Phone: 732-445-2223. Business E-mail: weng@jove.rutgers.edu.

**WENG, WEN-KAI,** oncologist, medical researcher; b. Taipei, China, Dec. 11, 1962; arrived in U.S., 1990; s. Hua-Min and Lee (Chu) W. MD, Chung-Shan Med. & Dental Coll., Taichung, China, 1988; PhD, U. Minn., 1996. Rsch. asst. U. Minn., Mpls., 1990-96; resident in internal medicine U. Tex./Houston Med. Sch., 1996-99; fellow in oncology Stanford U., Calif., 1999—2002, clin. instr. oncology Calif., 2002—. Ad hoc reviewer Blood-Jour. Am. Soc. Hematology, 1996. Dir. acad. com. Minn. Chinese Soc. Biomed. Sci., Mpls., 1993-96; cons. Minn. Chinese Student Assn., Mpls., 1993-96. With Rep. of China Army, 1988-90. Recipient fellowship U. Minn. Grad. Sch., 1995-96, rsch. fellowship Lymphoma Rsch. Found., 2002-04, Nat. Rsch. Svc. award NIH, 1994-95. Mem. Chinese Med. Assn., Am. Soc. Hematology, Am. Assn. Cancer Rsch., Sigma Xi (Charles and Dorothy Andrew Bird award 1996). Avocations: wildlife photography, birding, rock climbing, computers. Office: Stanford Division Of Oncology 875 Blake Wilbur Dr Palo Alto CA 94304-2205 Office Phone: 650-723-7621.

**WENGER, JAMES L.,** education educator; b. Horton, Kans., Aug. 4, 1944; s. Donald and Edith Wenger; m. Phyllis C. Newton, June 2, 1973; children: Scott, Stacy. BSE, Emporia State Univ., Emporia, Kans., 1967, MS, 1972. Cert. DP/CIS Vocational Kans. State Bd. Edn., 2006. Dir. data processing North Ctrl. Kans. Tech. Coll., Beloit, Kans., 1970—76; instr. Emporia State Univ., Kans., 1976—79, asst. prof., 1979—2004, assoc. prof., 2004—. Contbr. articles pub. to profl. jour. Recipient Svc. award, Emporia State U., 1989, Pres. Equity award, 1997, 2003, Tchg. award, 2005, Disting. Rsch. award, Allied Academies, 2003; grantee Microsoft grant, Microsoft, 1997. Mem.: Kans. Nat. Edn. Assn., Nat. Edn. Assn., Assn. Info. Sys., Assn. Info. Tech. Profls., Mid Am. Assn. for Computers in Edn. (pres. 1982—83, bd. dirs 1983—85, sec. 1985—). Beta Gamma Sigma. Luthern. Avocations: golf, fishing. Office: Emporia state Univ 1200 Commercial St Emporia KS 66801 Office Phone: 620-341-5488. Business E-Mail: jwenger@emporia.edu.

**WENGER, JOHN CHILDS,** retired mathematics educator, labor union administrator; b. NYC, Jan. 13, 1941; s. Samuel and Frieda (Smigrod) Wenger; m. Sally Caplan, June 16, 1963; children: Susan, Karen. BS, U. Mich., 1963; MS, U. Chgo., 1966; PhD, Ill. Inst. Tech., 1979. Computer programmer Western Electric, Chgo., 1966-68; from instr. to prof. City Colls. Chgo., 1968—2002; grievance chmn. Cook County Coll. Tchr. Union, Chgo., 1986—2002; ret., 2002. Editor: Sci. Insights, 2002—06. Jewish. Avocation: tennis.

**WENGER, LARRY BRUCE,** law librarian, educator; b. Everett, Wash., Dec. 21, 1941; s. Lester Edwin Wenger and Selma Marie (Norberg) W. Saterstrom; m. Marilyn Diane Watt, June 26, 1965; children: Bruce Daniel, Kathleen Marie. BA, U. Wash., 1964, JD, 1967; MLS, Simmons Coll., 1969. Reference libr. Sch. Law Harvard U., Cambridge, Mass., 1967-69; asst. law libr. SUNY, Buffalo, 1969-71, law libr., assoc. prof. law, 1971-76; law libr., prof. law U. Va., Charlottesville, 1976—. Cons. to law librs.; bd. dirs. Nat. Ctr. for Preservation Law. Editor: Marine Affairs Bibliography. Mem. Am. Assn. Law Librs., Internat. Assn. Law Librs. (pres. 1995-2001), Bibliog. Soc., Bibliog. Soc. Am. Home: 2630 Meriwether Dr Charlottesville VA 22901-9513 Office: U Va Law Libr 580 Massie Rd Charlottesville VA 22903-1739

**WENGER, NANETTE KASS,** cardiologist, researcher, educator; b. N.Y.C., Sept. 3, 1930; d. Aaron Zelig and Edith (Malkin) Kass; m. Julius Wenger; children: Deborah, Judith, Beth. BA summa cum laude, Hunter Coll., 1951; MD, Harvard U., 1954. Intern Mt. Sinai Hosp., N.Y.C., 1954—55, chief resident in cardiology, 1956—57; sr. resident in medicine Grady Meml. Hosp., Atlanta, 1958; fellow in cardiology Sch. Medicine, Emory U., 1958—59; instr. medicine Schs. Medicine and Dentistry, Emory U., Atlanta, 1959—62, assoc. in medicine, 1962—64, asst. prof. cardiology, 1964—68, assoc. prof., 1968—71, prof., 1971—; mem. med. staff Crawford W. Long Hosp., Atlanta, 1977— Dir. Cardiac clinics Grady Meml. Hosp., 1960—; chief cardiology, 1998—; cons. cardiology VA Med. Ctr., Atlanta, 1988—; participant numerous profl. symposiums and confs.; mem. cardiovas. and renal drugs adv. com. U.S. FDA, 1978-82; co-chair nat. plan for cardiac rehab. com. Div. Vocat. Rehab., Social and Rehab. Svcs., HEW, 1973-90; mem. Internat. Task Force for Prevention of Coronary Heart Disease, 1989—; founding fellow Soc. Geriatric Cardiology, 1986, bd. dirs., 1987—, pres., 1994-95. Mem. editl. bd. various profl. publs. including Cardiac Rehab. Quar., 1974-79, Primary Care, 1975-79, Internat. Jour. Sports Cardiology, 1983—, Med. Month, 1983-84, Jour. Cardiovasc. and Pulmonary Medicine, 1983—, Geriatric Cardiology, 1986—, Nutrition, Metabolism and Cardiovasc. Disease, 1989—; reviewer publs. including Am. Jour. Medicine, 1972—, Am. Jour. Cardiology, 1979—, Am. Heart Jour., 1975—, European Heart Jour., 1983—; editor Am. Jour. Geriatric Cardiology, 1992—. Active Ga. affiliate Am. Heart Assn., 1960—, chair Heart Sunday program, 1968-69, program chair Fulton County Heart Unit, 1969-71, bd. dirs., 1969-79, 80-82, pres., 1977-78; fellow coun. clin. cardiology, Am. Heart Assn., 1970, chair rehab. com., 1972-75, chair artherosclerosis task force, 1973-74, program v.p., 1975-76, pres., 1977-78, bd. dirs., 1975-79, mem./past mem. numerous other coms.; mem. med. adv. and cardiovasc. health coms. Butler St. YMCA, 1980-82. Recipient Myrtle Wreath award Atlanta Hadassah, 1967, award of Achievement, Nat. Ctr. for Vol. Action, 1978, Bronze Disting. Svc. medallion Ga. affiliate Am. Heart Assn., 1970-71, Silver Disting. Svc. medallion, 1978, Gold Disting. Svc. medallion, 1979, Disting. Achievement award, Sci. Coun. Am. Heart Assn. and Women in Cardiol. Mentoring award, 1999, Juha P. Kokko award for Excellence in Cardiovascular Lecturing and Edu., Dept. Med. Housestaff, Emory Univ. Sch. Med., 1999-2000, Emory Williams Disting. Tchg. award, 2004, Evangeline Papageorge Alumni Tchg. award, 2004, Shining Star award Atlanta Women in Law and Medicine, 2000, R. Bruce Logue award for Excellence in Medicine, Am. Heart Assn., 2001, Gold Heart award, 2004; Disting. Fellow Soc. Geriatric Cardiology, 2002; honoree Women of Yr. issue Time Mag., 1990; named Joseph B. Martin award Am. Coll. Sports Medicine, 2001. Fellow ACP (James D. Bruce Meml. award 2000), Am. Coll. Cardiology (gov. for Ga. 1983-86, trustee 1987-89, various coms.); mem. AMA, WHO (expert adv. panel on cardiovasc. disease 1989—).

**WENGER, SCOTT ANDREW,** orthopedist, surgeon; b. Winter Park, Fla., Nov. 25, 1971; s. Thomas James and Katherine Wenger; m. Virginia Elliott, June 22, 1996; children: Luke Andrew, Adam Scott. BA in Bus. Adminstrn., So. Meth. U., 1994, BSc in Biology, 1994; MD, U. Tex. Southwestern Med. Sch., 1998. Lic. physician Tex. State Bd. of Med. Examiners, 2003, Med. Bd. Calif., 2003. Intern gen. surgery U. Tex. Southwestern Med. Ctr., Dallas, 1998—99, resident orthop. surgery, 1999—2003; sports medicine fellow Kerlan-Jobe Orthop. Clinic, L.A., 2003—04; orthopaedic surgeon Coll. Sta. (Tex.) Orthopaedics, 2004—. Mem.: AMA, Tex. Orthop. Assn., Tex. Med. Assn., Brazos-Robertson County Med. Soc., Am. Orthop. Soc. Sports Medicine, Am. Acad. Orthop. Surgeons, Arthroscopy Assn. N.Am. (assoc.), Alpha Omega Alpha. Office: College Station Orthopaedics 1602 Rock Prairie Road STE #460 College Station TX 77845 Office Phone: 979-696-3344.

**WENGER, SHARON LOUISE,** cytogeneticist, researcher, educator; b. Washington, Sept. 25, 1949; d. William Fred and Lois Helen (Compton) W.; m. George E. Fromlak Jr., Jan. 10, 1976; children: Nicholas Edward, Holly Louise, Andrea Lee. BA in Biology, Thiel Coll., 1971; MS in Human Genetics, U. Pitts., 1973, PhD in Human Genetics, 1976. Cert. in clin. cytogenetics Am. Bd. Med. Genetics. Asst. prof. U. Pitts. Sch. Med., 1980-89, assoc. prof., 1989—97; prof. pathology W. Va. U., 1997—. Contbr. articles to profl. jours. Mem. Am. Soc. Human Genetics, Am. Coll. Med. Genetics, Assn. Genetic Technologists, Assn. Molecular Pathology, Am. Soc. Hematology. Achievements include research of sister chromatid exchange and fragile sites, chromosome syndromes and mechanism of tissue limited mosaicism. Home: 50 Crescent Heights Morgantown WV 26505 Office: W Va U Dept Pathology PO Box 9203 Morgantown WV 26506-9203 Office Phone: 304-293-3212.

**WENGLER, MARGUERITE MARIE,** counseling administrator; b. Kokomo, Ind., Nov. 18, 1943; d. Eugene Ferdinand and Flavia Marie (Marullo) Scalzo; m. James Burton Wengler, Oct. 4,1969; children: James Eugene, Dale Douglas, Lauren Christine. BS in Edn., Hofstra U., 1964; MA in Moderate Spl. Needs Edn., Assumption Coll., 1991. Cert. elem. tchr. N.Y., Mass., spl. needs tchr. Mass. Spl. needs dir. Montessori Primary and Upper Schs., Lexington, Mass.; spl. edn. tchr. Lincoln-Sudbury Pub. Schs., Sudbury, Mass., 1987-88; from assoc. lectr. to sr. lectr. Program Advanced Lng. Curry Coll., Milton, Mass., 1993—; outreach dir., 1997-98. Dir. Learning Success Helpline, Acton, Mass., 1984—; profl. devel. provider towards tchr. cert. Dept. of Edn. state of Mass. Author: 60 Minutes to Much Higher Grades, coll. edit., 1995, 60 Minutes to Much Higher Grades, H.S. edit., 1997; contbg. author A Closer Look, 1995; mng. editor Shared Visions of Teaching and Learning, 1997-2001. Del. People to People/Citizen Amb., China, 1994; dir., founder A Friend in Need, Acton, Mass., 1990-96, bd. dirs. Recipient Grant to Friend in Need, United Way, 1991—94, Cmty. Chest, 1993. Mem. AAUP, Learning Disabilities Network. Office: Program Advancement Lng Curry Coll Blue Hill Ave Milton MA 02186-2302 Office Phone: 617-333-2169. Personal E-mail: learningsuccess@yahoo.com.

**WENGLOWSKI, GARY MARTIN,** economist; b. Rochester, NY, Sept. 2, 1942; s. Henry Bernard and Isabelle (Franc) W.; m. Joyce Richards, Oct. 3, 1964; children: Gary Martin, Catherine Jean. BS in Econs., U. Pa., 1964, MA, 1965. PhD in Econs., 1967. With Goldman Sachs & Co., N.Y.C., 1967—, v.p., dir. econ. rsch., 1972-78, ptnr., 1978-86, ltd. ptnr., 1986-99; ret. ptnr., 1999—. Chmn. vis. com. econ. dept. U. Pa., 1985-98; adj. prof. Baruch Coll., 1998-02. Author: Industry Profit Forecasting, 1972, Industry Profit Forecasting—Progress Report, 1975. Trustee CARE Found., 1991—, Haystack Mountain Sch., 1993-2002. Named Best Economist on Wall St., Ann. Instnl. Investor Mag. Polls, 1976-86; NDEA fellow, 1965, 67. Fellow Nat. Assn. Bus. Economists; mem. Am. Econ. Assn., Deer Isle Yacht Club (vice commodore 1993-94, commodore 1994-2000). Home: 32 Partridge Ridge Rd Katonah NY 10536-3500

**WENGLOWSKI, JOYCE,** painter; b. Rochester, N.Y., Sept. 2, 1943; d. Harwin E. and Martha A. (Weit) Richards; m. Gary M. Wenglowski, Sept. 2, 1942; children: Gary M., Jr., Catherine J. Student, Rochester Inst. of Technology, 1961-63; BFA cum laude, Manhattanville Coll., 1980. Owner Joyce Wenglowski Gallery, Blue Hill, Maine, 1996-99; tchr. Artists Roster-Westchester Arts Coun., White Plains, 1995-2004; tchr., designer art program Waterview Hills Nursing Ctr., Purdy's, N.Y., 1999-99; tchr. painting, YMHA-YWHA, Pleasantville, N.Y., 1990-92; guest spkr. New Castle Pks. and Recreation, Chappaqua, N.Y.; tchr. artist-in-residence New Rochelle Day Nursery, 2000-01, vis. artist, Empire State Partnership, Westchester Magnet Acad., 2005.; spkr. in field. One-woman shows include The Joyce Wenglowski Gallery, Blue Hill, Maine, 1996-99, Deer Isle (Maine) Artists Assn., Maine, 1993, 98, Landmark Gallery, Stamford, Conn., 1996, Island Fishermen's Wives Hardship Fund, Deer Isle, 1995, CARE, Pound Ridge, N.Y., 1993, The Annex., N.Y.C., 2002, Northern Westchester Hosp., 2000—, Katonah Mus. of Art, 2002; exhibited in group shows at The Katonah Mus. of Art studio tour, 2000, Paramount Ctr. for the Arts, Peekskill, N.Y., 1999, Westchester Arts Coun., White Plains, N.Y., 1999, 2000, 03, 04, 05, Mus. Gallery, White Plains, 1999, The Gallery at Macy Pavilion, Valhalla, N.Y., 1998, The Walter Meade Gallery, Roxbury, N.Y., 1997, Manhattanville Coll., Purchase, N.Y., 1997, Neiman Marcus, Westchester Art Coun., White Plains, N.Y., 1996, Silvermine Galleries, New Canaan, Conn. 1989, Manhattanville Artists Guild, N.Y.C., 1994, Faber Birren Nat. Color Award Exhibit, Stamford, Conn., 1997, The Studio, Armonk, N.Y., 1999, 2000, 01, 02, 03, 05, 06, The Katonah Mus. Art, 2002, G. Watson Gallery, Stonington, Maine, 2001-06, The Hammond Mus. North Salem, N.Y., 2004, others; featured interview WFAS Radio, White Plains, 1999; represented in pvt. and corp. collectors, U.S. and Eng.; contbr. articles to profl. jours. Recipient Making a Difference award Westchester Arts Coun., 1993, Alumni Disting. in the Arts award Manhattanville Coll., 1991, Mixed Media award Stamford Conn., 1996, Katonah Mus. Artists' Assn., 2001; named NYNEX Patent Trader Vol. of Month, Westchester, 1992. Mem. Katonah Mus. Artsts Assn. (adv. bd. 1995—, pres. 2002-03, The Studio adv. bd., 2002—), Deer Isle Artists Assn. (adv. bd. 1993-97), Exhibiting Artists Ltd. (pres. 1982-83).

**WENGROVITZ, JUDITH,** artist, educator; b. Bklyn., Jan. 3, 1931; d. Harry and Hilda (Seigal) Kanarick; m. Seymour Wengrovitz, Feb. 23, 1952; children: Michael, Phillip, David BA Art Edn., Hunter Coll., 1952. Layout artist and copywriter Woodward & Lothrop, Washington, 1952—55; art dir., instr. Judy Wengrovitz Sch. Art, Springfield, Va., 1962—2006. One-woman shows include Art League-Torpedo Factory, Alexandria, 1981, 88, 97, George Mason U., Arlington, Va., 1984, Gallery West, Alexandria, 1986, City Gallery, Washington, 1989, U.S. Too Studio, Fairfax, Va., 1990, NIH, Bethesda, Md., 1992, 98, Washington Tech. Pk., JSC of No. Va., 2003, Mason Dist. Govt. Ctr., 2005; exhibited in group shows at Capricorn Gallery, 1995-96, Art League-Torpedo Factory, Alexandria, 1986-2006, Fairfax County Coun. Arts, 1987-2002, Springfield Art Guild, 1987-2005, Nat. League Pen Women (award 2004), Miniature Soc. Internat. Exhibit, 1991-2004, Mid-Atlantic Watercolor Exhibit (award 2006), So. Watercolor Soc., others; permanent collections include Allen Corp., Alexandria, Edward Bennett Williams, Wash., McGuire, Woods, Battle & Boothe, Mitre Corp., Falls Church, Va., Texaco, Harrison, N.Y., NIH Clin. Ctr. Galleries, others Recipient Equal Merit award, Art League at Torpedo Factory, 2004. Mem. Potomac Valley Watercolor Assn. (pres. 1978), Va. Watercolor Soc. (pres. 1987-88, Best in Show award 1986), Art Guild Springfield and Vienna (Va.), Nat. League Am. Pen Women (pres. 1974-76, Excellence award 2004), Springfield Art Guild (pres. 1997-98)

**WENIG, CINDY L.,** lawyer; b. Queens, NY, Mar. 26, 1966; AB summa cum laude, Princeton U., 1988; JD, Columbia U., 1991. Bar: NY 1992. Ptnr., Real Estate Practice Group Chadbourne & Parke LLP, NYC. Adv. bd. Stewart Title Guaranty Co., Profl. Women's Alliance of NYC. Harlan Fiske Stone Scholar. Mem.: Real Estate Bd. NY, Women Exec. in Real Estate (WX) (sec.), Nat. Assn. Women Bus. Owners. Office: Chadbourne & Parke LLP 30 Rockefeller Plz New York NY 10112 Office Phone: 202-408-1188. Office Fax: 212-541-5369. Business E-Mail: cwenig@chadbourne.com.

**WENIG, DEVIN NORSE,** communications executive; b. Brooklyn, Oct. 20, 1966; BA, Union Coll., 1988; JD, Columbia U. Sch. Law. Mergers and acquisitions atty. Cravath, Swaine and Moore; corp. counsel Reuters N. Am. Reuters, 1993, various sr. mgmt. roles, including mng. dir. mktg. Reuters Info., sr. v.p. bus. devel., exec. v.p. mktg., Reuters Am., pres., Investment Banking Services London, 2001—03, pres. Reuters Info., 2001, pres. customer segments, 2003—06, COO, 2006—. Chmn. Nastech Pharmaceutical Co., 1991—99, bd. dirs., 1999—, Instinet. Named a Forty Under Forty, Crain's NY Bus., 2005. Office: Reuters 3 Times Sq New York NY 10036*

**WENIGER-PHELPS, NANCY ANN,** media specialist, photographer; b. Kingman, Kans., Sept. 4, 1948; d. Watson and Reva Jo (Schlup) W. BA in Phys. Edn., Ottawa U., Kans., 1970; MA in LS, U. Denver, 1980. Cert. K-12 media specialist, secondary phys. edn. tchr., Ariz. Phys. edn. tchr. Grand Junction Sch. Dist., Colo., 1970—73; instr. mgr. World Book Ency., 1973—74; personal sec. Younger Bail Bond Svc., Grand Junction, 1974—76; media specialist K-12, phys. edn. tchr. Kingman Unified Sch. Dist., Kans., 1976—78, Ovid Sch. Dist., Colo., 1980—82, Sargeant Sch. Dist., Monte Vista, Colo., 1982—84, Antonito Sch. Dist., Ovid, 1984—85; photographer's asst. Bill Westenberg Photography, Alamosa, Colo., 1985—86; sch. media specialist Window Rick Unified Sch. Dist., Ariz., 1986—96. Profl. photographer; trainer adult and student storytellers; head dist. libr. computer program. Author: Photographic Uses in the Library; exhibited in group shows Gallup (N.Mex.) Gallery, 1989, Window Rock Elem. Sch., 1989, Sunflower Shop, Wichita, Kans. 1989-90, 96-98, also Alamosa, Colo., 1985-87, 1st Nat. Bank, Kingman (Kans.), Fernley (Nev.) Phys. Therapy, 1993, Greatest Little Art Show in Reno, Nev., 2003, Moms Arts and Crafts Show, Reno, Nev., 2003; photo consignment Trout Creek Nursery, Trucker, Calif., 2003—. Mem.: Alpha Delta Kappa. Home and Office: 5255 Tyrone Rd Reno NV 89502

**WENK, BRIDGET KELLY,** music educator, musician; b. Houston, Oct. 6, 1953; d. Marion Anthony and Frances Clawson Kelly; children: Amy Marie Lewis, Angela Lynn, Sarah Elizabeth Bodley, Timothy James. MusB summa cum laude, U. Houston, 1995. Dir. music and liturgy St. Augustine Cath. Ch., Houston, 1976—90; dir. liturgical music St. Mary's Sem., Houston, 1991—. Mem. adj. faculty U. St. Thomas, Houston, 2001—; workshop presenter Archdiocese of Galveston-Houston, 1995—, various chs., Tex., 1995—, organist, recitalist, Tex., 1972—. Commn. mem., chair music subcom., apptd. by archbishop Archdiocesan Liturgical Commn., Houston, 2004—; com. mem, apptd. by archbishop Ongoing Formation of Priests' Com., Houston, 2002—; co-founder, current music dir. St. Mary's Men's Choir. Mem.: Am. Choral Dirs. Assn., Am. Guild Organists, Nat. Assn. Pastoral Musicians (sec. 2005), St. Mary's Book Club, Pi Kappa Lambda. Liberal. Roman Catholic. Avocations: travel, books, films. Office: St Mary's Sem 9845 Memorial Dr Houston TX 77024 Office Phone: 713-686-4345.

**WENK, EDWARD, JR.,** civil engineer, educator, writer, policy analyst; b. Balt., Jan. 24, 1920; s. Edward and Lillie (Heller) Wenk; m. Carolyn Frances Lyford, Dec. 27, 1941 (dec.); children: Lawrence Shelley, Robin Edward Alexander, Terry Allan(dec.). BE, Johns Hopkins U., 1940, DEng, 1950; MSc, Harvard U., 1947; DSc (hon.), U. R.I., 1968; LHD (hon.), Johns Hopkins U., 1989. Registered profl. engr. Head structures div. USN David Taylor Model Basin, Washington, 1942-56; chmn. dept. engring. mechanics S.W. Research Inst., San Antonio, 1956-59; sr. specialist sci. and tech. Legis. Reference Service, Library of Congress, Washington, 1959-61, chief sci. policy research div., 1964-66; tech. asst. to U.S. President's sci. adviser and exec. sec. Fed. Council for Sci. and Tech., White House, Washington, 1961-64; exec. sec. Nat. Council on Marine Resources and Engring. Devel., Exec. Office of Pres., Washington, 1966-70; prof. engring. and pub. affairs U. Wash., Seattle, 1970-83, prof. emeritus, 1983—, dir. program in social mgmt. tech., 1973-79; tech. advisor to gov. State of Wash., 1993-96. Nat. Adv. Com. on Oceans and Atmosphere, 1972-73; vice chmn. U.S. Congress Tech. Assessment Adv. Coun., 1973-79; adviser Congress, GAO, NSF, EPA, NOAA, White House, UN Secretariat, Wash. State, Alaska, U.K., Australia, Sweden, The Philippines, Alaska Oil Spill Commn., 1989, Wash. State Marine Oversight Bd., 1992, pub. interest groups, 1997, US Dept. Transportation; vis. scholar Woodrow Wilson Internat. Ctr. for Scholars, 1970-72, Harvard U., 1976, Woods Hole Oceanographic Instn., 1976, U. Sussex, 1977, Bellagio Ctr., Rockefeller Found., 1977, 90; lectr., cons. in field. Author: The Politics of the Oceans, 1972, Margins for Survival, 1979, Tradeoffs-Imperatives of Choice in a High-Tech World, 1986, Making Waves—Engineering, Politics and the Social Management of Technology, 1995, The Double Helix: Technology and Democracy in the American Future, 1999, Normal Risks: Coping with Mother Nature, Human Nature and Technology's Unintended Consequences, 2006; editor Exptl. Mechs. Jour., 1954-56, Engring. Mechs. Jour., 1958-60; mem. editl. bd. Tech. Forecasting. Tech. in Soc.; contbr. articles to profl. jours.; designer Aluminaut submarine. Bd. dirs. Human Interaction Rsch. Inst., 1980-90, Smithsonian Sci. Info. Exch., 1977-82, URS Corp., 1973-88; mem. Interfaith Alliance. Ensign USNR, 1944-45. Recipient Navy Meritorious Civilian Svc. award, 1946, authors prize Gov. Wash., 1974, ann. prize Edn. Press Assn., 1997; named Disting. Alumnus Johns Hopkins U., 1979, Tchr. of Yr., Wash. State Engrs., 1980, Tchr. of Yr., Students in Pub. Adminstrn., 1986, Disting. Alumnus, Balt. Poly. Inst., 1991; Ford Found. grantee, 1970; Rockefeller Found. Bellagio fellow, 1976, 90; in Stockenburg Inst. Wash. U., 1988; Regents lectr. U. Calif., Berkeley, 1989, Woodrow Wilson award Johns Hopkins U., 2004. Fellow ASME (exec., Ralph Coats Roe medal 1999), AAAS; mem. ASCE, NSPE, LWV, Soc. Exptl. Stress Analysis (past pres. and William M. Murray lectr.), Internat. Assn. Impact Assessment (pres. 1981-82), NAE (chmn. com. on pub. policy 1970-75), Nat. Acad. Pub. Adminstrn., Am. Soc. for Pub. Adminstrn. (chmn. com. on sci. and tech. in govt. 1974-78), Assembly Engring. and Marine Bd. NRC, Nat. Oceanography Assn. (v.p. pub. affairs 1970-72), Cousteau Soc. (chmn. adv. bd. 1975-97), USA Club of Rome (bd. dirs. 1997-98), Explorers Club, Sigma Xi, Tau Beta Pi, Chi Epsilon. Home: 900 University St # 13G Seattle WA 98101 Business E-Mail: future@u.washington.edu. *Each of us has the opportunity, indeed responsibility, to contribute to the human experience and to enrich the lives of future generations. In a world of change, cultural diversity and uncertainty, we must be ourselves and not merely slaves of conventional thought. We must act on the basis of what we believe to be right rather than only from the desire to be loved.*

**WENK, MICHAEL SCOTT,** regulatory administrator; b. Livingston, NJ, Jan. 16, 1973; s. Robert Theodore and Georgia Irene Wenk; m. Cynde Lynn Hisel, Oct. 27, 1999; children: Andrew, Lauren. BS in Human Ecology, Rutgers U., New Brunswick, NJ, 1995; MS in Environ. Sci., NJ Inst. Tech., Newark, 2003; MBA, U. Md., College Park, 2006. Mgr. regulatory affairs Selig Industries, Atlanta, 1997—99, EKA Chems. Inc., Marietta, Ga., 1999—. Spkr. in field. The European Union's Eco-Management and Audit Scheme, 2005; contbr. articles to profl. jours. Mem.: Nat. Registry Environ. Profs. Office: EKA Chems Inc 1775 West Oak Commons Ct Marietta GA 30062

**WENNER, CHARLES RODERICK,** lawyer; b. New Haven, Jan. 10, 1947; s. Charles Bellew and Joan Rhoda (Morrison) Wenner; m. Jovita C. Vergara, June 11, 1999; children: Abigail Jessica, Charles Roderick Jr. BA, Boston Coll., 1969; JD, U. Conn., 1973. Bar: Conn. 1974, DC 1977. Law clk. Conn. Superior Ct., Hartford, 1973—74; staff atty. SEC, Washington, 1974—76, spl. counsel to chmn., 1976—77; assoc. Fulbright & Jaworski, 1977—81, ptnr., 1981—2005; of counsel Arnold & Porter LLP, 2005—. Lectr. law U. Conn. Sch. Law, 1973—74. Trustee United Meth. Ch.,

Arlington, Va., 1993—95, 1997—98; counselor Gospel Mission Washington, 1991—. Recipient Am. Hist. award, DAR, 1969. Mem.: ABA, DC Bar Assn. Methodist. Avocation: running. Home: 1808 South Lynn St Arlington VA 22202 Office: Arnold & Porter LLP 555 Twelfth St Washington DC 20004 Office Phone: 202-942-6974. Office Fax: 202-942-5999. Business E-Mail: charles.wenner@aporter.com.

**WENNER, DEBBY LINN,** mezzo soprano, educator; b. Cumberland, Md., Nov. 9, 1953; d. Raymond Calvin and Beatrice Linn Wenner; adopted children: Timothy Alan, Lois Linn. BS in Music, Frostburg State U., 1975; postgrad., W.Va. U., 1976, Cath. U. Am., 1977; MusM, George Washington U., 1984. Pvt. voice instr., Alexandria, Va., 1975—; vocal instr. George Washington U., Washington, 1979—84, Foxes Music, Falls Church, Va., 1980—85, Olde Towne (Va.) Music, 1981—86; theory tutor Mary Baldwin Coll., 1984; voice/opera instr. St. Mary's (Md.) Coll., 1985—90; adj. prof. voice and pedagogy George Mason U., Fairfax, Va., 2000—. Alto soloist Rodef Shalom Temple, Falls Church, 1980—, Ch. of the Annunciation, Washington, 1995—; alto soloist, sect. leader Foundry United Meth., Washington, 1980—95. Singer: (world premiere) Carnegie Hall; soloist: Tidewater Music Festival, 1985—90, recitalist: Kennedy Ctr. Terr. Theater, Nat. Portrait Gallery. Vol., fundraiser Challenger Little League, Springfield, Va., 1992—; vol., coord. Eddies Club for Disabled Children, Springfield, 1993—. Recipient Washington Post/Maude Steward awards, Met. Opera Coun., N.Y.C., 1987, Study award, 1987, Outstanding Alumni award, Frostburg State U., 1992. Mem.: Associated Bal. Royal Schs. Musicians, Nat. Assn. Tchrs. Singing, Spina Bifida Assn. Democrat. Avocations: neuroscience, poetry, interior decorating, jazz, baseball. Home: 6524 Fairland St Alexandria VA 22312 Office: George Mason Univ Music Dept 4400 University Dr Fairfax VA 22030 E-mail: metdeb@att.net.

**WENNER, GENE CHARLES,** arts management executive; b. Catasauqua, Pa., Dec. 21, 1931; s. Clinton G. and Bertha (Taggert) W.; m. Carole Brunner, Aug. 15, 1953; children: Robert Larren, Laurel E. Wenner Carsell BS in Music, West Chester StateColl., Pa., 1953; M.Ed. in Music, Pa. State U., 1954. Tchr. music Phila. pub. schs., 1945-55, 56-60; assoc. prof. Kutztown (Pa.) State Coll., 1960-66; dir. coll. choir, 1960-66; fine arts & music Pa. Dept. Edn., 1966-69, U.S. Office Edn., 1969-71; asst. dir. arts in edn. program John D. Rockefeller 3d Fund, 1971-78; arts edn. coordinator Office Commr., U.S. Office Edn., 1978-79; pres. Am. Music Conf., Wilmette, Ill., 1979-81; v.p. for programs Nat. Found. Advancement in Arts, Miami, Fla., 1983-87; pres. Arts and Edn. Cons., Inc., Reston, Va., 1987-91; sr. cons. Bus. & Industry for Arts Edn., 1990-91; exec. dir. Charlotte (N.C.) Community Sch. for the Arts, 1991-96; pres. Arts & Edn. Cons., Inc., Pittsfield, Mass., 1996—. Fund raising cons. Nat. Pub. Radio, Nat. Music Found., Mohawk Theater Capital Campaign, Goldman Meml. Band, Jacob's Pillow, Berkshire C.C. Non-Profit mgmt. Counsel, Mass. Coll. Liberal Arts; mus. dir. Allentown (Pa.) Mcpl. Oper, 1962-63, Allentown Civic Little Theatre, 1964, Little Theatre Alexandria, Va., 1971; dir. Hershey (Pa.) Little Theatre, 1967-68, Hershey Community Chorus, 1967-69 Composer: I'll Never Forget You, 1968, Chorale of Dedication, 1974, Great Things God Hath Done, 1986, In My Father's House, 1986; original music and script Adventures in the Arts, Hershey, 1968; also original TV music, I Am the Way, 1985, When You Remember, 1985; author papers, reports in field. Served with AUS, 1955-56. Named Best Mus. Dir. Little Theatre Alexandria Mem. Music Educators Nat. Conf., Network Performing and Visual Arts Schs. Clubs: Masons. Home and Office: 112 Doreen St Pittsfield MA 01201 Office Phone: 413-499-5311. Personal E-mail: gwenner@berkshire.rr.com.

**WENNER, JANN SIMON,** editor, publisher; b. NYC, Jan. 7, 1946; s. Edward and Ruth N. (Simmons) Wenner; m. Jane Ellen Schindelhim, July 1, 1968 (separated 1995); children: Alexander Jann, Theodore Simon, Edward Augustus. Student, U. Calif.-Berkeley, 1964—66. Co-founding editor, pub. Rolling Stone mag., NYC, 1967—; editor, pub. Record, NYC, 1981—86, Look mag., NYC, 1979, Men's Jour., 1992—; editor in chief Outside Mag., San Francisco, 1977—79, US Mag., NYC, 1985—, Men's Jour., 1992—; pub. Family Life, 1993—95; editor in chief Wenner Media Inc., 1993—; founder Cease Fire Inc., 1995—. Vice chmn. Rock & Roll Hall of Fame. Author: Lennon Remembers, 1971, Garcia, 1972; actor: (films) Perfect, 1985, Jerry Maguire, 1996, Almost Famous, 2000, Breakfast with Hunter, 2003. Bd. dirs. Robinhood Found. Recipient Disting. Achievement award, U. So. Calif. Sch. Journalism and Alumni Assn., 1976, Nat. Mag. award, 1970, 1977, 1986, 1987, 1988, 1989, Lifetime Achievement award, Rock and Roll Hall of Fame, 2004. Mem.: Am. Soc. Mag. Editors. Achievements include youngest editor to be inducted into the American Society of Mag. Editors Hall of Fame, 1997. Office: Rolling Stone Wenner Media Inc 1290 Avenue Of The Americas Fl 2 New York NY 10104-0295*

**WENNER, STEVEN MARC,** orthopedist, surgeon; b. NYC, Sept. 30, 1949; s. Harry Eugene and Estelle Bergida Wenner; m. Nadine Mont Porcelan, June 25, 1972; children: Jeremy David, Andrea Gail. MD, Jefferson Med. Coll., Pa., 1974; BA, Yale Coll., 1970. Diplomate Am. Bd. Orthop. Surgery. Chief divsn. orthop. surgery Baystate Med. Ctr., Springfield, Mass., 1980—; chief sect. hand surgery Shriners Hosp. for Children, Springfield, 1980—; orthop. hand surgeon New Eng. Orthop. Surgeons, Springfield, 1980—. Trustee Baystate Health, Inc., Springfield, Mass., 2002—; bd. dirs. Health New Eng., Springfield, Mass. Fellow: Am. Soc. for Surgery of the Hand, Am. Acad. Orthop. Surgery. Office: New Eng Orthop Surgeons 300 Birnie Ave Ste 201 Springfield MA 01107-1107 Home: 30 Academy Dr Longmeadow MA 01106 Office Phone: 413-785-4666. Office Fax: 413-788-5772.

**WENNERGREN, DAVID M.,** civilian military employee; b. Camp Hill, Pa. m. Sandra Wennergren; children: Heather, Kaelyn, Skylar. BA in comm./pub. rels., Mansfield State U.; M in pub. sector fin. mgmt., U. Md. Positions in Office of Dep. Chief Naval Ops., 1985—92, head plans and policy branch, shore installation mgmt. divsn.; dep. chief info. officer enterprise integration and security dept. Navy, 1998—2002, chief info. officer, 2002—. Named one of Premier 100 IT Leaders, Computerworld, 2005; recipient Superior Civilian Svc. Award, Dept. Navy, Meritorious Civilian Svc. Award, Exceptional Civilian Svc. Award, Office of Sec. Def.; Sec. Navy. Civilian Fellowship in fin. mgmt. Office: Dept Navy Rm 4B463 1200 Navy Pentagon Washington DC 20350-1200 Office Phone: 703-602-1800. E-mail: david.wennergren@navy.mil.*

**WENNERSTROM, ARTHUR JOHN,** aeronautical engineer; b. N.Y.C., Jan. 11, 1935; s. Albert Eugene and Adele (Trebus) W.; m. Bonita Gay Westenberg, Sept. 6, 1969 (div. Jan. 1980); children: Bjorn Erik, Erika Lindsay; m. Vicki Lynn Merrick, Feb. 17, 1990. BS in Mech. Engrng., Duke U., 1956; MS in Aero. Engrng., MIT, 1958; DSc of Tech., Swiss Fedn. Inst. Tech., Zurich, 1965. Sr. engr. Aircraft Armaments, Inc., Cockeysville, Md., 1958-59; rsch. engr. Sulzer Bros., Ltd., Winterthur, Switzerland, 1960-62; project engr. No. Rsch. and Engring. Corp., Cambridge, Mass., 1965-67; rsch. leader Air Force Aerospace Rsch. Lab., Dayton, Ohio, 1967-75, Air Force Aero Propulsion Lab., Dayton, 1975-91; dir. NATO Adv. Group for Aerospace R & D, Paris, 1991-94; engring. cons. Hillsborough, NC, 1994-95, Hot Springs Village, Ark., 1995—2003, Henderson, Nv., 2003—. Mem. tech. adv. com., von Karman Inst. for Fluid Dynamics, Rhode-St-Genese, Belgium, 1988-94, bd. dirs.; lectr. in field. Contbr. articles to profl. jours. 1st lt., USAF, 1962-65. Recipient Cliff Garrett Turbo Machinery award Soc. Automotive Engrs., 1986; named Fed. Profl. Employee of Yr. Dayton C of C, 1975; fellow Air Force Wright Aeronautical Labs., 1987; named Hon. Prof., Inst. Engring. Thermophysics, Chinese Acad. Scis. and Beijing U. Aeronautics and Astronautics, 1994. Fellow AIAA (assoc. editor 1980-82, Air Breathing Propulsion award 1979), ASME (chmn. turbomachinery com. gas turbine divsn. 1973-75, mem. exec. com. 1977-82, chmn. 1980-81, program chmn. internat. gas turbine conf. 1976, Beijing internat. gas turbine symposium 1985, mem. nat. nominating com. 1985-87, mem. TOPC bd. on rsch. 1985-88, mem.-at-large energy conversion group 1986-88, mem. bd. com. 1989-91, editor Jour. Engring. for Gas Turbines and Power 1983-88, chmn. bd. editors 1989-91, founder, editor Jour. Turbomachinery 1986-88, mem. internat. adv. com. 1995-96, R. Tom Sawyer award 1993). Achievements include introduc-

tion of wide-chord integrally-bladed fan, introduction of swept blading into mil. aircraft turbine engines; 5 patents in field. Home and Office: 363 Marlin Cove Rd Henderson NV 89012-4829 Office phone: 702-837-1344. E-mail: wennco1@cox.net.

**WENRICH, JOHN WILLIAM,** college president; b. York, Pa., June 8, 1937; s. Ralph Chester and Helen Louise (McCollam) W.; m. Linda Larsen, June 23, 1961 (dec. Sept. 1966); 1 child, Thomas Allen; m. Martha Gail Lofberg, Sept. 1, 1967; 1 child, Margaret Ann AB, Princeton U., 1959; MA, U. Mich., 1961, PhD, 1968. Fgn. service officer Dept. State, Washington, 1962-65; rep. Internat. Devel. Found., N.Y.C., 1965-66; project dir. U. Mich., Ann Arbor, 1966-69; asst. to pres. Coll. San Mateo, Calif., 1969-71; v.p. Ferris State U., Big Rapids, Mich., 1971-75, pres., 1984-88; Canada Coll., Redwood City, Calif., 1975-79, Santa Ana Coll., Calif., 1979-84; chancellor San Diego C.C. Dist., 1988-90, Dallas (Tex.) C.C., 1990—2003, chancellor emeritus, 2003—. Co-author: Leadership in Administration of Technical and Vocational Education, 1974, Administration of Vocational Education. Recipient Meritorious Service medal Dept. State, 1966; Hinsdale scholar Sch. Edn. U. Mich., 1968 Avocations: bridge, tennis, travel. Home: 3504 Springbrook St Dallas TX 75205-4337 Office: 4343 North Hwy 67 Mesquite TX 75150-2095 Office Phone: 972-860-7494. E-mail: bwenrich@dcccd.edu.

**WENSINGER, ARTHUR STEVENS,** literature and language professor, writer, translator; b. Grosse Pointe, Mich., Mar. 9, 1926; s. Carl Franklin and Suzanne (Stevens) W. Grad., Phillips Acad. Andover, 1944; BA, Dartmouth Coll., 1948; MA, U. Mich., 1951, PhD, 1958; postgrad., U. Munich, 1948, postgrad., 1950—51, U. Innsbruck, 1953—54. Instr., asst. prof., assoc. prof. Wesleyan U., Middletown, Conn., 1955-68, prof. German and humanities, 1968-93, Marcus Taft prof. German and humanities, 1977-93, prof. emeritus, 1994—, chmn. dept. German lang. and lit., 1971-93, also sr. tutor Coll. Letters; pres. Friends of Davison Art Ctr.; co-editor Higganum Hill Books, 2003—. Mem. selection com. German Acad. Exch. Svc., 1980-92. Author: Hogarth on High Life, 1970, Plays by Arthur Schnitzler, 1982-1983, 1995; translator, editor (with W. Gropius): The Theater of the Bauhaus, 1961, rev. edit., 1996, translator, editor: The Letters and Journals of Paula Modersohn-Becker, 1983, 2d edit., 1990, Querelle: The Film Book, 1983, Franz Kafka: Pictures of a Life, 1984; translator: Marlene Dietrich: Portraits, 1984, Shabbat (Peter Stefan Jungk), 1985, Hanna Schygulla and R.W. Fassbinder, 1986, Kaethe Kollwitz: The Work in Color, 1988, Niklas Frank, In the Shadow of the Reich, 1991, (plays) Arthur Schnitzler; co-translator: Kafka: The Sons, 1989, Günter Grass, Two States-One Nation?, 1990; editor: Stone Island (Peter S. Boynton), 1973; co-editor: Hesse's Siddhartha, 1962; continuing editor: Correspondence of Norman Douglas, 1868-1952, exhbn. and symposium catalog articles on Norman Douglas, continuing translator: plays of Schnitzler, contbr.: Columbia U. Database CD-ROM for quotations, aphorisms, 1995—, contbr. (DVD): Munich 1948/2005, 2005; contbr. articles to profl. jours. Wesleyan Ctr. for Humanities fellow, 1974, Reynolds fellow, 1950-51, Fulbright fellow, 1954-55, Danforth fellow, 1959, Ford Found. fellow, 1970-71; Inter Nations grantee, 1978, 82, NEH rsch. grantee, 1993. Mem. MLA, Am. Assn. Tchrs. German, Heinrich von Kleist Gesellschaft, Internat. Brecht Soc., Kafka Soc. Am., Auden Soc., Soc. Preservation New Eng. Antiquities, Conn. Acad. Arts and Scis., Yale Libr. Assocs., Haddam, Conn. Land Trust, Grosse Ile Nature and Land Conservancy, Phi Beta Kappa, Phi Kappa Phi, Delta Tau Delta. Home: Candlewood Farm 95 Jacoby Rd Higganum CT 06441-4225 Office: Wesleyan U Fisk Hall Middletown CT 06459-6082 Office Phone: 860-685-3357. Business E-Mail: awensinger@wesleyan.edu.

**WENSITS, DAVID L.,** aerospace transportation executive; b. Sept. 19, 1947; AAS in Aviation Maintenance, Purdue U., 1968, BS in Indsl. Supervision, 1970. Supportability mgr. Rolls-Royce Corp., Indpls., 1970—. With U.S. Army, 1971-73. Recipient Aerospace Maintenance award AIAA, 1996. Office: Rolls-Royce Corp, SPEED Code S27C PO Box 420 Indianapolis IN 46206-0420 Office Phone: 317-230-4949. E-mail: david.l.wensits@rolls-royce.com, davewensits@comcast.net.

**WENSKI, THOMAS GERARD,** bishop; b. West Palm Beach, Fla., Oct. 18, 1950; s. Chester Stephen and Louise Mary (Zawacki) W. AA, St. John Vianney Sem., Miami, Fla., 1970; BA, St. Vincent De Paul Sem., Boynton Beach, Fla., 1972, MDiv, 1975; MA, Fordham U. Ordained priest Roman Cath. Ch., 1976. Assoc. pastor Corpus Christi Cath. Ch., Miami, 1976-79; assoc. dir. Haitian Cath. Ctr., Miami, 1979-84, dir., 1984-98; pastor Notre Dame d'Haiti Roman Cath. Ch., Miami, 1984-98, aux. bishop, 1997—2004; bishop Diocese of Orlando, Fla., 2004—. Episcopal vicar to cultural groups, Miami, 1990-2003; dir. Cath. Charities Archdiocese Miami, 1996-2003; former chmn. migration com. US Conf. Cath. Bishops, chair Devel. and World Peace Internat. Policy Com., 2005. Office: Diocese of Orlando PO Box 1800 Orlando FL 32802 Office Phone: 407-246-4815.

**WENSYEL, MARY KATHLEEN,** elementary school educator; b. Weston, W.Va., June 15, 1948; d. Charles Fredrick Rowgh and Sara Theresa Dunn; m. John Robert Wensyel, Oct. 14, 1978; 1 child, Patrick Matthew. BA, Univ. Pitts, Pa., 1973; M in Reading, W. Va. Univ., Morgantown, 1976. Tchr. Upshur County Sch., Buckanon, W.Va., 1973—75; title/reading specialist Marshall County sch., Moundsville, 1975—2005, literacy facilitator, 2005—. Historian Alpha Delta Kappa. Moundsville, 2004—. Recipient Tchr. of the Yr., McNinch elem. Mem.: W. Va. Dept. of Edn., W.Va. Reading Assn. Avocations: quilting, reading. Home: 40 Raven Ave Wheeling WV 26003 Office: Marshall County Sch Moundsville WV 26041

**WENTWORTH, DENNIS LADD,** historic sites and parks administrator; b. Rochester, NH, Jan. 14, 1950; s. Arnold Howard Wentworth and Cora Rachel Downs; m. Ann Elizabeth Kennedy, Dec. 24, 1973; children: Rachel Ann, Margaret Kennedy, Trevor Downs. BA in Anthropology, Beloit Coll., 1972; MA in Anthropology, SUNY, Albany, 1988. Historic site asst. NY State Parks Bur. Hist. Sites, Waterford, 1975—96, archaeologist, 1976—87, collection mgr., 1988—90; regional hist. reservation supr. NY State Parks Saratoga Coastal Region, Saratoga Springs, 1987, NY State Parks Taconic Region, Staatsburg, 1992—95, 2005—, dir. regional ops., 1995—2003. Contbr. articles to profl. jours. Elder Pleasant Plains Presbyn. Ch., Staatsburg, 1990—92; mem. Hist. Hyde Park (NY) Corridor Commn., 2000—; bd. dirs. Lyndhurst Property Coun., 2005—; elder, deacon 1st United Presbyn. Ch., Troy, NY, 1982—90; elder 1st Presbyn. Ch., Poughkeepsie, NY, 1992—. Recipient Black Belt, World Tae Kwon Do Assn., 1998. Mem.: Hudson River Heritage (pres. 1994—95), Mid-Atlantic Assn. Museums. Avocations: gardening, music, hiking, walking, antiques. Home: 137 E Market St Rhinebeck NY 12572 Office: NY State Parks Staatsburg NY 12580 Personal E-Mail: dennislw@frontiernet.net. Business E-Mail: dennis.wentworth@oprhp.state.ny.us.

**WENTWORTH, DIANA VON WELANETZ,** author; b. L.A., Mar. 4, 1941; d. Eugene and Marguerite (Rufi) Webb; m. Frederic Paul von Welanetz, Nov. 2, 1963 (dec. Mar. 19, 1989); 1 child, Lexi Welanetz Bursin; m. Theodore S. Wentworth, Dec. 9, 1989; stepchildren: ChristinaWentworth Coyne, Kathryn Allison Wentworth Purdy. Student, UCLA, 1958-60. Ptnr. von Welanetz Cooking Workshop, L.A., 1968-85; host TV series New Way Gourmet, 1983-86; founder Inside Edge Found. Edn., Calif., 1985-93. Spkr. in field. Author: The Pleasure of Your Company, 1976 (Cookbook of Yr.), With Love from Your Kitchen, 1976, The Art of Buffet Entertaining, 1978, The Von Welanetz Guide to Ethnic Ingredients, 1983, L.A. Cuisine, 1985, Celebrations, 1985, Chicken Soup for the Soul Cookbook, 1995, Send Me Someone, 2001, Chicken Soup to Inspire The Body and Soul, 2003. Treas. Louise L. Hay Found., Carson, Calif., 1988—; advisor Women of Vision, Calif., 1995—. Mem. Internat. Food, Wine & Travel Writers Assn., Angels of Arts/Orange County Performing Arts Ctr., Ctr. Club, Confrérie de La Chaîne des Rôtisseurs, N. Am. Travel Journalists Assn. Avocations: painting, art, travel, design. Office: 4631 Teller Ave Ste 100 Newport Beach CA 92660-8105 E-mail: diana@dianawentworth.com.

**WENTWORTH, EARL JEFFREY,** lawyer, realtor, state legislator; b. San Antonio, Nov. 20, 1940; s. Earl and Margaret Wentworth; m. Karla Whitsitt; children: Jason, Matthew. BA, Tex. A&M U., 1962; JD, Tex. Tech. U., 1972. Bar: Tex. 1971, DC 1972. Staff mem. U.S. Congressman Bob Price; pvt. practice law San Antonio; mem. Tex. Ho. of Reps., 1988-92, Tex. Senate, 1993—. County commr. Bexar County, 1977-82; bd. regents Tex. State U. Sys., 1987-88. Spl. agt. U.S. Army Counterintelligence Corps, 1962—65. Republican. Office: PO Box 12068 Austin TX 78711-2068 also: Ste 925 1250 NE Loop 410 San Antonio TX 78209-1500 Office Phone: 210-826-7800. Personal E-mail: ejeffrey@swbell.net. Business E-Mail: jeff.wentworth@senate.state.tx.us.

**WENTWORTH, JACK ROBERTS,** business educator, consultant; b. Elgin, Ill., June 11, 1928; s. William Franklin and Elizabeth (Roberts) W.; m. Rosemary Ann Pawlak, May 30, 1956; children: William, Barbara Student, Carleton Coll., 1946-48; BS, Ind. U., 1950, MBA, 1954, DBA, 1959. Coord. displays Cadillac divsn., Gen. Motors Corp., Detroit, 1954-56; asst. prof. bus., assoc. dir. research Sch. of Bus. Ind. U., Bloomington, 1957-60, assoc. prof., dir. rsch., 1960-70, prof., 1970-93, chmn. MBA program, 1970-76, chmn. dept., faculty rep. NCAA, 1978-85, dean Sch. of Bus., 1984-93, Arthur M. Weimer prof., 1993-97, Arthur M. Weimer prof. emeritus, 1997—. Mktg. cons., Bloomington, 1960—; bd. dirs. Kimball Internat., Jasper, Ind. Editor: (monograph) Marketing Horizons, 1965; exec. editor Bus. Horizons, 1960-70 Served to 1st lt. USAF, 1950-53 Recipient Teaching award MBA Assn., 1973, 78, 81, 84, 85, Svc. award Assn. for Bus. and Econ. Rsch., 1983; Disting. Alumni Svc. award Ind. U., 1999. Mem. Am. Mktg. Assn. (v.p. 1971-73), Grad. Mgmt. Admissions Coun. (chmn. bd. trustees 1977-81), Univ. Club, Masons, Beta Gamma Sigma (pres. Alpha of Ind. chpt. 1971-72, bd. govs. 1986-98, nat. pres. 1994-96). Republican. Methodist. Avocations: travel, bicycling, magic, model railroading, sports. Office: Indiana Univ Kelley Sch Bus Bloomington IN 47405 E-mail: lurojack@yahoo.com.

**WENTWORTH, LAVERNE WELLBORN,** university program coordinator; b. Bryan, Tex., July 26, 1929; d. Charles Floyd and Ethel Berneice (Swanzy) Wellborn; m. Thomas Richard Wentworth (wid. 1986); children: Jason Charles, Rance Richard, Paige Lynn Wentworth Honkerkamp. BA, Baylor U., 1949, MA in Am. Civilization, 1951; postgrad., State Tchrs. U. N.J., Southwestern State Tchrs. U., San Marcus, Tex., U. Ky. Sch. tchr. Tex. and N.J., 1949—58; tchr. JFK White House Paper on Youth, 1963; comm. edn. instr. Georgetown (Ky.) Coll., 1988—90; elderhostel program coord. U. Ky., Lexington, 1992—2001; Boyce Sch. instr. So. Bapt. Theol. Seminary, Lexington, 1990; pers. dept. Cardinel Hill Rehab. Hosp., Lexington, 1987-93. Tchg. cons. U.S. Steel Co., Trenton, N.J., 1957; cons., instr. Interdenominational Young People Confs., Pocono Plateau, Pa., 1958-87; field supr. U.S. Dept. Commerce, Bur. of Census, Washington, 1970-88; guest lectr. Georgetown (Ky.) Coll. Author: (books) Manifest Destiny in Walt Whitman's Prose, 1954, Tryst, 1959 Pres. Princeton Theol. Sem. Wives, 1956-57, Rotary Anne, W.Va., 1982-83; mem. Scott County Women's Club, Georgetown, 1987-93; mem. by-laws com. Ky. Bapt. Fellowship, 2004—. Recipient Ship of State award W.Va. State of Sec., 1983. Mem. AAUW (pres. 1987-90), Scott County Hist. Soc. (program chmn. 2001-03), Georgetown Coll. Woman's Assn. (life), Faith Bapt. Ch. of Georgetown (tchr., chmn. by-laws 1998—2006), Ky. Bapt. Fellowship (by-laws com. 2004—).

**WENTWORTH, LYNN A.,** telecommunications industry executive; BSBA, Babson Coll.; MS in Taxation, Bentley Coll.; MBA Ga. State U. Various positions with numerous depts. including handling tax, strategic planning, investor rels. and fin. integration Bellsouth Corp., 1985—2003, v.p., treas. Atlanta, 2003—. Tutor C.W. Hill Elem. Sch., Atlanta. Mem.: AICPA, Ga. Soc. CPA's.

**WENTWORTH, MURRAY JACKSON,** artist, educator; b. Boston, Jan. 18, 1927; s. Harold Squires and Mary Louise (Murray) W.; m. Elaine Magnuson, June 16, 1953; 1 child, Janet Louise. Diploma, Art Inst. Boston, 1950. Advt. artist Agy. Art Svcs., Boston, 1950-58; instr. Art Inst. Boston, 1958-78; artist, instr. Norwell, Mass., 1968—. Group shows, Allied Artists Am., 1980, 82 (Silver medal 1980), Allied Art Am., 1982 (Obrig prize 1982), Am. Watercolor Soc., 1980 (Dolphin fellow 1980), Rocky Mount Nat. Exhibition, 1982 (Grumbacher award 1982). Cpl. U.S. Army, 1945-47. Recipient Hudson Valley Art Assn. award, 1991, Whitney Meml. award, 1996, Guild Boston Artists award, 1992, Watercolor award Acad. Artists' Assn., 1997, Daler Rowney award, 1998, Hudson Valley Art Assn. Watercolor award, 1998. Mem. NAD (Pike Meml. award 1986, award of merit 1997), Allied Artists Am. (Mina Mora Meml. award for watercolor 1997), Am. Watercolor Soc., New Eng. Watercolor Soc. (Grumbacher gold medal 1989). Office Phone: 607-432-6322.

**WENTWORTH, THEODORE SUMNER,** lawyer; b. Bklyn., July 18, 1938; s. Theodore Sumner and Alice Ruth (Wortmann) W.; m. Sharon Linelle Arkush, 1965 (dec. 1987); children: Christina Linn, Kathryn Allison; m. Diana Webb von Welanetz, 1989; 1 stepchild, Lexi von Welanetz. AA, Am. River Coll., 1958; JD, U. Calif., Hastings, 1962. Bar: Calif. 1963, U.S. Dist. Ct. (no. and cent. dists.) Calif., U.S. Ct. Appeals (9th cir.), U.S. Supreme Ct.; diplomate Nat. Bd. Trial Advocacy; cert. trial lawyer Calif. State Bar. Assoc. Adams, Hunt & Martin, Santa Ana, Calif., 1963-66; ptnr. Hunt, Liljestrom & Wentworth, Santa Ana, 1967-77; pres. Solabs Corp.; chmn. bd., exec. v.p. Plant Warehouse, Inc., Hawaii, 1974-82; ptnr. Law Offices of Wentworth, Paoli & Purdy, Newport Beach & Temecula, Calif.; judge pro tem Superior Ct. Attys. Panel Harbor Mcpl. Ct.; owner, CEO Home Guardens, Inc., Murrietta, Calif., 2000—05. Owner Eagles Ridge Ranch, Temecula, 1977-2003. Author: Build a Better Spouse Trap, 2002. Pres., bd. dirs. Santa Ana-Tustin Cmty. Chest, 1972; v.p., trustee South Orange County United Way, 1973-75; pres. Orange County Fedn. Funds, 1972-73; bd. dirs. Orange County Mental Health Assn. Mem. ABA, Am. Bd. Trial Advs., State Bar Calif., Orange County Bar Assn. (dir. 1972-76), Calif. Trial Lawyers Assn. (bd. govs. 1968-70), Orange County Trial Lawyers Assn. (pres. 1967-68), Bahia Corinthian Yacht Club (founder). Achievements include research in vaidika principles, natural law, quantum physics and mechanics. Office: 4631 Teller Ave Ste 100 Newport Beach CA 92660-8105 also: 41530 Enterprise Cir S Temecula CA 92590-4816 Office Phone: 949-752-7711. Personal E-mail: oclawfirm@aol.com.

**WENTZ, PETER (PETER LEWIS KINGSTON WENTZ III),** musician; b. Wilmette, Ill., June 5, 1979; Student, DePaul U. Bassist, vocalist & lyricist Fall Out Boy, 2001—; owner Clandestine Industries, Decaydence Records. Author: The Boy With the Thorn in His Side, 2005; musician: (albums) Fall Out Boy's Evening Out with Your Girl, 2002, Take This to Your Grave, 2003, From Under the Cork Tree, 2005, (songs) Sugar, We're Going Down, 2003 (MTV2 award, MTV Video Music Awards, 2005), Dance, Dance, 2005 (Choice Music Single, Choice Rock Track, Teen Choice Awards, 2006, Viewer's Choice award, MTV Video Music Awards, 2006); actor: (films) Bedussey, 2005. Recipient Choice Music Rock Group award, Teen Choice Awards, 2006. Office: Fall Out Boy Box 219 1187 Wilmette Ave Wilmette IL 60091*

**WENTZ, SIDNEY FREDERICK,** insurance business executive, foundation administrator; b. Dallas, Mar. 27, 1932; s. Howard Beck and Emmy Lou (Cawthon) W.; m. Barbara Strait, Sept. 9, 1961; children: Eric, Jennifer, Robin. AB, Princeton U., 1954; LLB, Harvard U., 1960. Bar: N.Y. 1961. Atty. White & Case, N.Y.C., 1960-65, Western Electric Co., 1965-66, AT&T Corp., 1966-67; with Crum & Forster Inc., Morristown, N.J., 1967—, v.p., gen. counsel, 1967-71, sr. v.p., gen. counsel, 1971-72, exec. v.p., 1972, pres., 1972-87, chmn. bd., 1987-88, chmn. exec. com., 1988-90, also bd. dirs.; chmn. bd. Robert Wood Johnson Found., Princeton, N.J., 1989-99. Trustee Morristown Meml. Hosp., 1974-96, Drew U., 1991—. Served to lt. (j.g.) USNR, 1954-57. Mem. Morris County Golf Club, Sakonnet (R.I.) Golf Club, Baltusrol Golf Club, Jupiter Hills (Fla.) Golf Club, Loblolly Pines (Fla.) Golf Club, Carnegie Abby Golf Club (R.I.).

**WENTZ, WILLIAM HENRY, JR.,** aerospace engineer, educator; b. Wichita, Kans., Dec. 18, 1933; BS in Mech. Engring. cum laude, Wichita State U., 1955, MS in Aeronautical Engring., 1961; PhD in Engring. Mechanics, U. Kans., 1969. Lic. profl. engr., Kans. Liaison engr. Beech Aircraft, 1952-53; propulsion engr. Boeing Co., Wichita, Kans., 1955; instr. mech. engring. Wichita State U., 1957-58; aerodynamicist Boeing Co., Wichita, 1958-63; from asst. prof. to assoc. prof. aeronautical engring. Wichita State U., 1963-75, prof. aeronautical engring., 1975-83, Gates-Learjet prof. aeronautical engring., 1983-86, disting. prof. aerospace engring., 1986-98, dir. Ctr. Basic and Applied Rsch. Inst. Aviation Rsch., 1986-89, exec. dir. Nat. Inst. Aviation Rsch., 1988-97; sr. fellow Nat. Inst. Aviation Rsch., 1997-98; disting. prof. emeritus aerospace engring., exec. dir. emer. Nat. Inst. Aviation Rsch., 1999; ret. Dir. rsch. projects Boeing Co., 1960, 61, NASA, 1964-66, 66-68, 70-71, 71-83, 86-87, 86-88, 82-87, Dept. of Def., 1986-88, Kans. Tech. Enterprise Corp., 1988-96, FAA, 1986-96. Contbr. articles to profl. jours. With USAF, 1955-57. Recipient Disting. Engr. Svc. award Wichita State U., 1999, Kans. Aviation Honors award Gov. Bill Graves, 1999; Sci. Faculty fellow NSF, 1967-68. Fellow AIAA (assoc., past chmn. Wichita sect., Outstanding advisor student chpt. 1964, 65, 70, Gen. Aviation award 1981, Engr. of Yr. award Wichita sect. 1992, Engr. of Yr. award Region V 1991-92; mem. Soc. Automotive Engrs. (Ralph R. Teeter award 1973), Sigma Gamma Tau, Tau Beta Pi.

**WENTZEL, JUDITH ANN,** retired librarian; b. West Reading, Pa., Sept. 15, 1947; d. Quentin Roosevelt and Dorothy Evelyn (Little) Keath; m. Michael Bruce Wentzel, June 26, 1971; 1 child, Eric Michael. BA in Libr. Sci., Millersville (Pa.) State Coll, 1969; MA in Libr. Sci., Kutztown (Pa.) State U., 1973. Libr. Reading (Pa.) Sch. Dist., 1969-75, Wyomissing (Pa.) Area Sch. Dist., 1981—2004, ret., 2004. Mem. Pa. Sch. Librs. Assn., Wyomissing Area Fdn. Assn (treas, 1987—). Republican. Lutheran. Avocations: reading, crafts, sports. Home: 36 Buckingham Dr Reading PA 19610-3101

**WENTZEL, PAUL H., JR.,** state agency administrator; b. 1949; m. Kathy Wentzel; 1 child, Kathy. BA in polit. sci., MA in polit. sci.. East Stroudsburg U. Rsch. analyst House Bus. and Commerce Com.; exec. asst. Pa. Dept. Banking, 1981—. Office: 333 Market St 16th fl Harrisburg PA 17101-2290 Office Phone: 717-787-2112.

**WENTZLAFF, SISTER MARIBETH FAYE,** nun, director; b. Huron, S.D., Jan. 16, 1966; d. Robert Joseph and Marivonne Faye Wentzlaff. BA, Mt. Marty Coll., Yankton, S.D., 1988; MA, St. Mary's U., Winona, Minn., 2001. Cert. Spiritual Direction Sacred Heart Monastery, 2005, joined Benedictine Sisters from Sacred Heart Monastery. Tchr./campus min. O'Gorman H.S., Sioux Falls, SD, 1990—96; dir. campus ministry Mt. Marty Coll., Yankton, SD, 1996—, dir. residence life/dir. campus ministry, 2004—. V.p. Women and Children's Ctr/Shelter, Yankton, 2001—05; mem. Avera St. Benedict's Hosp., Parkston, SD, 2004—. Mem.: Assn. Benedictine Campus Ministers (assoc.; exec. dir. 2002—05). Roman Catholic. Avocations: fishing, playing cards, reading, travel. Home: 1005 West 8th St Yankton SD 57078 Office: Mount Marty College 1105 West 8th St Yankton SD 57078 Office Phone: 605-668-1392. Business E-Mail: mwentzlaff@mtmc.edu.

**WENYI, BI,** science educator; s. Manping Bi and Min Jiao; m. Jihua Zhang, June 21, 1954; 1 child, Jing Bi. PhD, Nova Southeastern U., Ft.t Lauderdale, Fla., 2001. Prof. Miami Dade Coll., Miami, 1998—2004; asst. prof. Cheyney U. of Pa., Cheyney, 2004—. Prof. Am. Internat. U., Ft. Lauderdale, 2000—03. Mem.: IEEE. Office: Cheyney U of Pa 1837 University Cir Cheyney PA 19319 Office Phone: 610-399-2612. E-mail: wbi@cheyney.edu.

**WENZEL, JAMES ANDREW,** religious studies educator; b. Wakefield, Mass., Apr. 1, 1930; s. William Lawrence Wenzel and Gertrude Frances McFadden. PhB in Philosophy, Villanova U., Pa., 1953; ThM in Theology, Wash. Theol. Union, Silver Spring, Md., 1989; MA in Religious Studies, Emmanuel Coll., Boston, Mass., 1973; D of Ministry, Cath. U. of Am., Washington, D.C., 1993. Assoc. pastor St. Augustine Parish, Andover, Mass., 1958—68, pastor Lawrence, Mass., 1968—74, St. Nicholas of Tolentine Parish, Jamaica, NY, 1974—79, St. Mary Immaculate Conception Parish, Lawrence, 1979—86; faculty Wash. Theol. Union, Silver Springs, Md., 1986—95; retreat dir. Order of St. Augustine, San Gimignano, Italy, 1995—99; coord. of ednl. and spiritual programs Ctr. of Augustinian Study and Legacy at Merrimack Coll., North Andover, Mass., 1999—2005; dir. of the ctr. for augustinian study and legacy Merrimack Coll., North Andover, Mass., 2006—. Mem. bd. of dirs. Mary Immaculate Restorative Ctr., Lawrence, 2000—. Mem. Augustinian Vol., Villanova, Pa., 2002—06. Order Of St. Augustine. Mem: St Ambrose Friary 196 Elm St Andover MA 01810-1638 Office: Merrimack Coll 315 Turnpike St North Andover MA 01845 Office Phone: 978-837-5219. Home Fax: 978-475-8485; Office Fax: 978-837-5069. Personal E-mail: jwenzelosa@aol.com. E-mail: james.wenzel@merrimack.edu.

**WENZEL, LOREN ALVIN,** finance educator; b. Dec. 12, 1945; s. Alvin Karl Gustav and Lois LaVonne (Kuechenmeister) W.; children: Lisa Anne (Wenzel) Szumilas, Karl Louis, Sara Kirsten Wenzel; m. Nylah Onalee. DBA, U. Memphis, 1990. Asst. prof. acctg. Wichita (Kans.) State U., 1987-88; prof. acctg. Mankato (Minn.) State U., 1988-98, U. Md. European Divsn., Heidelberg, Germany, 1996-97, Buena Vista U., Storm Lake, Iowa, 1998-99, Austin Peay State U., Clarksville, Tenn., 1999-2000; prof. and head divsn. accountancy and legal environment Marshall U., 2000—; Elizabeth McDowell Lewis endowed chair Lewis Coll. Bus., 2000—05, prof., 2005—, Bharatiya Vidya Bhavan, Bangalore, India, 2005—. Founder, pres. W.Va. Coun. Educators, 2003—05. Contbr. articles to profl. pubs. Named W.Va. Outstanding Acctg. Educator of Yr., W.Va Soc CPAs 2004. Office: Marshall U Lewis Coll Bus Div Acctancy/Legal Environ One John Marshall Dr Huntington WV 25545 Office Phone: 304-696-2660. Business E-Mail: wenzel@marshall.edu.

**WEPRIN, BRADLEY,** neurosurgeon; b. Chgo. m. Rebecca Weprin; 2 children. BA in Biology, Washington U., St. Louis, 1988; MD with honors, U. Tex. Southwestern Med. Sch., 1992. Diplomate Am. Bd. Neurol. Surgery, Nat. Bd. Med. Examiners, lic. physician Minn., Ala., Tex. Intern in gen. surgery U. Minn. Hosps. and Clinics, Mpls., 1992, resident in neurol. surgery, 1992—97; fellow in pediat. neurosurgery U. Ala. Birmingham-Children's Hosp. of Ala., 1998—99; asst. prof. neurol. surgery U. Tex. Southwestern Med. Sch., Dallas, 1999—. Attending neurosurgeon Children's Med. Ctr. Dallas, Med. City Dallas Hosp., Tex. Scottish Rite Hosp. for Children; presenter in field. Mem.: AMA, Joint Sect. Pediat. Neurosurgery, Alpha Omega Alpha. Office: Children's Med Ctr-Neurosurgery 1935 Motor St Dallas TX 75235

**WERB, ZENA,** cell biologist, educator; BSc in Biochemistry, U. Toronto, 1966; PhD in Cell Biology, Rockefeller U., 1971. Postdoctoral fellow in protein chemistry Strangeways Rsch. Lab., Cambridge, Eng., 1971-73, rsch. scientist, 1973-75; vis. asst. prof. medicine Dartmouth Med. Sch., Hanover, N.H., 1975-76; asst. prof. radiobiology and radiology U. Calif., San Francisco, 1976-80, asst. prof. anatomy, 1979-80, assoc. prof. anatomy and radiology, 1980-83, prof. anatomy, 1983—. Vis. prof. Sir William Dunn Sch. Pathology, U. Oxford, Eng., 1985-86. Mem. editl. bd. Jour. Cell Biology, 1982-85, Am. Jour. Physiology, 1982-87, Neoplasia, 1999—, Jour. Cell Scis., 1999—; adv. editor Jour. Exptl. medicine, 1985—; bd. reviewing editors Sci., 1990—; assoc. editor Matrix Biology, 1999—; contbr. numerous articles to profl. jours. Recipient Excellence in Sci. award Am. Soc. Exptl. Biology, 1996, Women's Excellence in Scis. award Fdn. Am. Socs. Exptl. Biology, 1996; U. Toronto scholar, 1963-66; John Simon Gugenheim Found. fellow, 1985-86, other grants and awards. Mem. AAAS, ASCB, ASIP, ASBMB, ISMB. Office: U Calif Dept Anatomy HSW 1320 513 Parnassus Ave San Francisco CA 94143-0001

**WERBA, GABRIEL,** public relations consultant; b. Paris, Feb. 28, 1930; came to U.S., 1941; s. Aron and Dina (Lewin) W.; m. Barrie Celia Sakolsky, June 1, 1952; children: Dean Steffen, Annmarie Alexandra Bragdon. BA in Journalism, U. Tex., 1948; postgrad., NYU Grad. Sch. Bus., 1948-49, NYU Sch. Law, 1961-62. Account exec. Harold C. Meyers & Co., N.Y.C., 1959-61; dir. pub. rels. and advt. Yardney Electric Corp., N.Y.C., 1961-63, 57-59; sr. assoc. Shiefman & Assocs., Detroit, 1963-66; account exec. Merrill Lynch, Detroit, 1966-70; exec. v.p. Shiefman Werba & Assocs., Detroit, 1970-73; sr. v.p., exec. v.p., pres., chief oper. officer Anthony M. Franco, Inc., Detroit, 1973-88; pres., chief exec. officer The Werba Group, Inc. and Gabriel Werba and Assocs., Inc., Detroit, 1988-94; prin. Durocher, Dixson, Werba, L.L.C., Detroit, 1994—2003; pres. Gabriel Werba & Assoc. LLC, Farmington Hills, Mich., 2004—. Bd. dirs. Erudite Corp., Detroit. Contbr. articles to profl. jours. Bd. dirs. Oakland Citizens League, Detroit, 1970-93, Detroit Symphony Orch. Hall, 1985—, Detroit Chamber Winds, 1985-91, The Common Ground Sanctuary, Mich., 1989—, 2d vice chmn., Bloomfield Hills, 2000—; bd. dirs. The Attic Theatre, Detroit, 1989-93, The Children's Ctr., Detroit; mem. strategic planning com., chmn. comm. com., bd. dirs., 1989-95, 1996-2002, 03-05, adv. bd., 1995-96, 2002-03; bd. dirs. NATAS, Detroit, 1993-98, The Jewish Cmty. Coun. Met. Detroit, 1989-95, 2004—, Margaret W. Montgomery Hosp., 1993-95, adv. bd. 1988-93; bd. dirs. Lawrence P. Doss Found., 2002—, 1st vice-chmn., 2002—; mem. comm. Detroit Inst. Arts, 1986-92, exhibits com., 1990-2001. Named to, PRSA-Detroit Hall of Fame, 2001. Mem. Nat. Investor Rels. Inst. (past dir., pres. Detroit chpt., spkr., panelist), Pub. Rels. Soc. Am. (bd. dirs. Detroit chpt. 1988-94, pres. 1992-93, past treas. Detroit Counselors' sect. past co-chmn. nat. sect. coun., past nat. chmn. fin. sect., spkr., panelist), Fin. Analysts Soc. Detroit (past chmn. pub. info. com.), Am. Mensa (bd. dirs. 1975-91, 2003-05, nat. chmn. 1979-83), Internat. Mensa (bd. dirs. 1979-83, 85-93). Avocations: art collecting, concerts, theater. Home: 21920 River Ridge Tr Farmington IIills MI 48335 Office: Gabriel Werba & Assoc LLC 21920 River Ridge Tr Farmington MI 48335 Office Phone: 248-478-1281. E-mail: gabewerba@sbcglobal.net.

**WERBITT, WARREN,** gastroenterologist, educator; b. Phila., Jan. 29, 1939; s. Saull Boris and Pearl (Weiner) W.; m. Drue Natalie Engman Werbitt, Aug. 30, 1964; children: Julie Michele, Jeffrey Brian. BS in Pharmacy, Temple U., 1960; D in Osteopathy, U. Osteo. Med. and Health Sci., Des Moines, 1966; MD, Drexel U. Coll. Med., 1973. Diplomate Am. Osteo. Bd. Internal Medicine, also sub-splty. bd. Gastroenterology; diplomate Am. Bd. Internal Medicine, also sub-splty. bd. Gastroenterology. Intern Doctor's Hosp., Columbus, Ohio, 1966-67, resident in internal medicine, 1967-68, Kennedy Meml. Hosps., Cherry Hill, NJ, 1968-69, Mercy Cath. Med. Ctr., Phila., 1969-70, Drexel U. Coll. Medicine, Phila., 1971—72, fellow in gastroenterology, 1970-71, 72-74, instr., 1973—, attending physician and cons. in gastroenterology, 1977-94; instr. Phila. Coll. Osteo. Medicine, Phila., 1973-75, chmn. divsn. gastroenterology, 1975-77; clin. assoc. prof. medicine U. Medicine and Dentistry, NJ, 1977—; attending physician and cons. in gastroenterology Vet. Adminstrn. Hosp., Phila., 1972-75; chmn. Div. Gastroenterology, Dept. Medicine Phila. Coll. Osteopathic Medicine, 1975-77; chmn. Dept. Medicine Kennedy Meml. Hosp. U. Med. Ctr., Cherry Hill, 1979-81, chmn. subsect. Gastroenterology, 1979-87. Contbg. editor The N.J. Jour. for Ostepathic Physicians and Surgeons, 1980—; mem. scientific adv. com. Phila. chpt. Nat. Found. Ileitis & Colitis, Inc., 1982—; contbr. articles to profl. jours. Recipient Profl. Svc. award Med. Soc. N.J., 1991. Fellow Am. Coll. Physicians, Am. Coll. Gastroenterology, Acad. Med. N.J., Am. Gastroent. Assn.; mem. AMA, Am. Soc. Gastrointestinal Endoscopy, Am. Soc. Parenteral and Enteric Nutrition, Am. Inst. Ultrasound in Medicine, Am. Assn. Gynecologic Laparoscopists, Phila. Gastrointestinal Rsch. Forum, State Med. Soc. N.J., Camden County Med. Soc., N.J. Endoscopic Soc., Del. Valley Soc. for Gastrointestinal Endoscopy, South Jersey Gastroenterological Soc., Am. Osteopathic Assn., N.J. Soc. Osteopathic Physicians and Surgeons, Am. Coll. Osteopathic Internists, Camden County Osteopathic Assn., Am. Cancer Soc. (bd. dirs. N.J. chpt.), Crohn's and Colitis Found. Am. Inc. (Phila. and Del.), Pres.'s Circle Am. U., N.Y. Acad. Scis., John Sherman Myers Soc., Med. Club Phila., Lambda Omicron Gamma. Avocations: golf, running, music, reading, american history. Office: Profl Gastroenterology Assn 1939 Route 70 E Ste 250 Cherry Hill NJ 08003-4507 Office Phone: 856-429-4433. Personal E-mail: progastro@comcast.net.

**WERCHNIAK, ANDREW EUGENE,** dermatologist, educator; s. Wolodymyr and Anna Werchniak; m. Jeanine Courchesne Courchesne, Jan. 7, 1994; children: Andrew Morris, Anne, Alexander, Ethan, Elias, Kiernan. BS, U. Md., 1993; MD, U. Va., 2000. Diplomate Am. Acad. Dermatology, 2004. Internship internal medicine Dartmouth, Lebanon, NH, 2000—01, resident dermatology, 2001—04; instr. dermatology Harvard Med. Sch., Boston, 2004—. Clin. scholar, Brigham and Women's Hosp., 2004—. Fellow: Am. Acad. Dermatology; mem.: AMA. Office: Brigham Dermatology Associates 221 Longwood Ave Boston MA 02115 Office Phone: 617-732-4918.

**WERDEGAR, KATHRYN MICKLE,** state supreme court justice; b. San Francisco; d. Benjamin Christie and Kathryn Marie (Clark) Mickle; m. David Werdegar; children: Maurice Clark, Matthew Mickle. Student, Wellesley Coll., 1954—55; AB with honors, U. Calif., Berkeley, 1957; JD with highest distinction, George Washington U., 1962; JD, U. Calif., Berkeley, 1990. Bar: Calif. 1964, U.S. Dist. Ct. (no. dist.) Calif. 1964, U.S. Ct. Appeals (9th cir.) 1964, Calif. Supreme Ct. 1964. Legal asst. civil rights divsn. U.S. Dept. Justice, Washington, 1962—63; rsch. atty., author Calif. State Study Commn. on Mental Retardation, 1963—64; assoc. U. Calif. Ctr. for Study of Law and Soc., Berkeley, 1965—67; sr. cons. State Dept. Mental Health, 1967—68; cons., author Calif. Coll. Trial Judges, 1968—71; dir. criminal law divsn. Calif. Continuing Edn. of Bar, 1971—78; assoc. dean acad. and student affairs, assoc. prof. Sch. Law, U. San Francisco, 1978—81; sr. staff atty. Calif. 1st Dist. Ct. Appeal, 1981—85, Calif. Supreme Ct., 1985—91; assoc. justice Calif. 1st Dist. Ct. Appeal, 1991—94, Calif. Supreme Ct., San Francisco, 1994—. Regents' lectr. U. Calif., Berkeley, 2000. Author: Benchbook Misdemeanor Procedure, 1971, Misdemeanor Procedure Benchbook rev., 1975, Misdemeanor Procedure Benchbook, 1983; contbr. California Continuing Education of the Bar books; editor: California Criminal Law Practice series, Discovery, 1975, California Uninsured Motorist Practice, 1973, I California Civil Procedure Before Trial, 1977. Recipient 5 Am. Jurisprudence awards 1960—62, Charles Glover award, George Washington U., 1962, J. William Fulbright award for disting. pub. svc., George Washington U. Law Sch. Alumni Assn., 1996, Excellence in Achievement award, Calif. Alumni Assn., 1996, Roger J. Traynor Appellate Justice of Yr. award, 1996, Justice of Yr. award, Consumer Attys. of Calif., 1998, Citation award, Boalt Hall Sch. Law U. Calif., Berkeley, 2002. Mem.: Am. Law Inst., Nev./Calif. Women Judges Assn., Calif. Judges Assn., Nat. Assn. Women Judges, Calif. Supreme Ct. Hist. Soc. (bd. dir.), Order of the Coif. Office: Calif Supreme Court 350 McAllister St San Francisco CA 94102-4797 Office Phone: 415-865-7032.

**WERDER, RICHARD I., JR.,** lawyer; b. White Plains, NY, 1951; BA magna cum laude, Canisius Coll., 1979; JD, Univ. Mich., 1982. Bar: Ohio 1984, NY 2003. Law clk. to Hon. Harry T. Edwards US Ct. Appeals, (DC Cir.), 1982; law clk. to Justice Byron White US Supreme Ct., 1983; assoc. Jones Day, NYC, 1984—89, ptnr., co-chmn. technology issues practice; ptnr. Quinn Emanuel Urquhart Oliver & Hedges LLP, NYC, 2006—. Editor-in-chief Law Rev., 1982. Mem.: ABA, NY Stat Bar Assn., Cleve. Bar Assn., Ohio State Bar Assn., Fed. Liability Adv. Coun., Order of Coif. Office: Quinn Emanuel Urquhart Oliver & Hedges LLP 51 Madison Ave 22nd Fl New York NY 10010 E-mail: rickwerder@quinnemanuel.com.*

**WERESH, THELMA FAYE,** sculptor; b. Baca County, Colo., Mar. 15, 1919; d. William Lee Cotton and Myrtle Mae (Quiet) Cotton-Winston; m. Andrew Anthony Weresh, Jan. 28, 1939; children: Charlotte Maria, Catherine Ann. BA, Coll. St. Mary, 1967. Art tchr. Ralston (Nebr.) Pub. Schs., 1967-73, Father Flanagan's Boys Home, Boys Town, Nebr., 1973-75. Bd. dirs. Alliance of Arts Coun., Lincoln, Nebr., 1975; chmn. Visual Arts Commn., Leadwood, Colo., 1990-91. One person exhibn. includes Ariel Gallery, N.Y., 1991; featured in Artist's Profile KRMA TV, 1995. Recipient SOHO Internat. 1st Place, 1990, 1st Place United Coun., 1990, 2nd Place, 1991, 1st Place George

Lewis, 1991, 1st Place Southwest Art, 1992, 1st Place Women Artists, 1992, Spl. award Mus. N.W., 1992, First Annual Hall of Fame award Revue mag., 1996. Mem. Allied Artists Am., Loveland (Colo.) Sculpture Group. Home: 2009 Lakewood Dr Loveland CO 80538-3423

**WERFELMAN, WILLIAM HERMAN, JR.,** public relations executive; b. Bridgeport, Conn., July 11, 1953; s. William H. and Helen D. (Rainier) W.; m. Patricia Aileen Maytrott, Aug. 28, 1977; children: Lauren Aileen, Juliana Aileen. BA in English, St. Bonaventure U., 1975; postgrad., Georgetown U., 1975—76. Staff writer Post-Telegram newspapers, Bridgeport, 1976—79; product publicity specialist Dictaphone Corp., Rye, NY, 1979—81; supr. press rels. GE, Fairfield, Conn., 1981—84; mgr. corp. pub. rels. Olin Corp., Stamford, Conn., 1984—90, dir. pub. rels./comm., 1990—94; v.p. external comms. Home Ins. Co., N.Y.C., 1994—95; v.p. media rels. N.Y. Life Ins. Co., N.Y.C., 1995—2003; first v.p. N.Y Life Ins. Co., N.Y.C., 2003—. Mem., chmn. Zoning Bd. Appeals, Redding, Conn., 1977-89, 92-99; party recruitment chmn. Rep. Town Com., Redding, 1976-90. Recipient Fin. World Bronze award for ann. report, 1992. Mem. Internat. Assn. Bus. Communicators (Best Pub. Rels. results 1982), Pub. Rels. Soc. Am., Nat. Assn. Investors (Best Ann Report 1988, 90). Republican. Roman Catholic. Avocations: writing, investments. Home: 195 Gallows Hill Rd Redding CT 06896-1423 Office: NY Life Ins Co Rm 516 51 Madison Ave New York NY 10010-1603

**WERKEMA, MARK ANDREW,** pilot; writer; BA, Malone Coll., Canton, Ohio, 1987. Freelance writer, 1987—; airline pilot, 1999—. Author: (fiction) On Fulcrum's Wings, 2000, (children's book) The Flight Before Christmas, 2004. With Mich. Air N.G., 1985—90.

**WERKING, RICHARD HUME,** librarian, historian, academic administrator; b. Charleston, S.C., Sept. 29, 1943; s. F. Woody and Mary S. (Prissinger) W. BA, U. Evansville, 1966; MA in Am. History, U. Wis., 1967, PhD in Am. History, 1973; MA in Librarianship, U. Chgo., 1975. Instr. history Northland Coll., Ashland, Wis., 1967-68; pers. staffing specialist U.S. Civil Svc. Commn., Indpls., 1968-69; reference libr. Lawrence U., Appleton, Wis., 1975-77; head reference dept., asst./acting libr. dir. U. Miss., Oxford, 1977-81, asst. prof. history, 1977-81; assoc. libr. dir., asst. prof. history Trinity U., San Antonio, Tex., 1981-83, libr. dir., assoc. prof. history, 1983-91; libr. dir., assoc. dean, prof. history U.S. Naval Acad., Annapolis, Md., 1991—. Author: The Master Architects: Building the U.S. Foreign Service, 1977. With Ind. Nat. Guard, 1961—65, with U.S. Army, 1962. Sparks fellow Phi Kappa Phi, 1966, postdoctoral fellow Coun. on Libr. Resources, 1974. Mem. ALA (chmn. coll. librs. sect. 1987-88), Soc. Historians of Am. Fgn. Rels. Office: US Naval Acad Nimitz Libr 589 Mcnair Rd Annapolis MD 21402-1323 Business E-Mail: rwerking@usna.edu.

**WERKMAN, SIDNEY LEE,** psychiatrist, educator; b. Washington, May 3, 1927; AB, Williams Coll., 1948; MD, Cornell U., 1952. Diplomate Am. Bd. Psychiatry and Neurology. Am. Bd. Child Psychiatry. Intern U. Va. Hosp., Charlottesville; resident in psychiatry Yale U., 1953-55, St. Elizabeth's Hosp., Washington, 1955-56; assoc. prof. psychiatry George Washington U., Washington, 1960-69; prof. U. Colo. Sch. Medicine, Denver, 1969-87; dir. div. adolescent psychiatry Children's Hosp. of Washington, 1965-69; clin. prof. Georgetown U. Sch. Medicine, Washington, 1989—; psychiatrist Capital Area Permanente Med. Group, Washington, 1990—. Cons. grants NIMH, Washington, 1982—, guest rschr., 1984—85. Author: The Role of Psychiatry in Medical Education, 1966, Only a Little Time: A Chronicle of Dying, 1972, Bringing Up Children Overseas, 1977 Bd. dirs. Med. U. So. Africa, Performing Arts Soc., Nat. Mus. Arts, Young Concert Artists Assn., Washington Concert Operas. Master sgt. U.S. Army. Fellow, Commonwealth Fund, Florence, Italy, 1963—64, NEH, 1979. Mem. Am. Psychiat. Assn., Am. Acad. Child Psychiatry, Group for Advancement Psychiatry, Am. Orthopsychiat. Assn. (bd. dirs. 1970-73), Colo. Psychiat. Soc. Office: 3636 16th St NW Ste AG29 Washington DC 20010-8138 Office Phone: 202-483-4637.

**WERLICH, DAVID PATRICK,** history professor; b. Mpls., Nov. 2, 1941; s. Eugene Gordon and Mary Ellen (Doran) W.; m. Sandra Cecilia Januszewski, Dec. 28, 1960; children: David A., Thomas G., Susan E. BA, U. Minn., 1963, MA, 1967, PhD, 1968. Lectr. history U. Minn., Mpls., 1966-67; asst. prof. history So. Ill. U., Carbondale, 1968-78, assoc. prof., 1978-84, prof., 1984—2003, chmn. dept. history, 1988—2000; vis. prof., 2003—. Author: Peru: A Short History, 1978, Research Tools for Latin American Historians, 1980, Admiral of the Amazon, 1990. Recipient Delta award Friends of Morris Libr., So. Ill. U., 1991. Mem. Conf. of L.Am. History, Midwest Assn. for L.Am. Studies. Office: Southern Illinois Univ Dept of History Carbondale IL 62901-4519 Office Phone: 618-453-4391. E-mail: elmaximo@siu.edu.

**WERLIN, LAWRENCE B.,** obstetrician, gynecologist, endocrinologist; b. Albany, N.Y., 1948; s. Esther (Caplan) W.; m. Sally Rosso, Dec. 24, 1970; children: Rachel, Evan, Emma. BA, Boston U., 1970; MD, Mt. Sinai Sch. Medicine, N.Y.C., 1976. Diplomate Am. Bd. Ob-Gyn. Intern Harbor Gen. Hosp., Torrance, Calif., 1976-77, resident in ob-gyn., 1977-80; fellow in reproductive endocrinology NIH, Bethesda, Md., 1980-82; mem. staff Hoag Meml. Hosp., Newport Beach, Calif. Nat. Reproductive Medicine fellow, 1980-82. Mem. AAAS, Am. Soc. Reproductive Medicine, Soc. for Assisted Reproductive Tech., Pacific Coast Fertility Soc. Office: Coastal Fertility Med Ctr 4900 Barranca Pky Ste 103 Irvine CA 92604-8603 E-mail: werlmd@coastalfertility.com.

**WERLLA, VANESSA LYNN,** psychiatrist; b. Houston, Tex., Sept. 23, 1953; d. Charles Julius Werlla, Jr. and Virginia Bushnell Werlla; m. Richard Billings Noulles, July 7, 1979, children: Rebekah Lynn Noulles, Sarah Elizabeth Noulles, Mary Katherine Noulles. BA with Honors in Biology, U. of Tex. at Austin, 1971—74; MD, U. Okla. Coll. of Medicine, 1976—80. Diplomate Am. Bd. Psychiatry & Neurology, 1989. Chmn. dept. psychiatry St. John Med. Ctr., Tulsa, 1992—2002; med. dir. behavioral health Cmty. Care HMO, Tulsa, 1993—2002; clin. asst. prof., dept. psychiatry U. Okla. Coll. Medicine, 1994—; psychiatric med. reviewer Blue Cross/Blue Shield of Okla., Oklahoma City, 1996—; med. cons. Family Children's Svcs., Tulsa, 2002—05; pvt. practice Tulsa, 2004—. Mem. nat. cmty. mental health adv. bd. Eli Lilly Pharm., 2003—; nat. spkr. Forest Pharm., 2003—, Astra Zeneca Pharm., 2003—. Mem. Nat. Rep. Congl. Com., 2004; bd. mem. Tulsa Mental Health Assn. Bd., Tulsa, 2005—. Recipient Ronald Regan Gold Medal award, 2004; Michael DeBakey fellowship, Baylor Coll. Medicine, Houston, 1971—72. Mem.: AMA, Tex. Med. Assn., Okla. Med. Assn., APA, Tex. Execs. (life), Alpha Lambda Delta. Republican. Protestant. Avocations: painting, piano. Office: 2626 E 21st St Ste 6 Tulsa OK 74114 Office Phone: 918-712-7488.

**WERMAN, DAVID SANFORD,** psychiatrist, psychoanalyst; b. NYC, Jan. 1, 1922; s. Morris and Blanche (Heftel) W.; m. Marjolijn R. de Jager, Oct. 25, 1958 (div. 1975); children: Daniel A., Ba, Queens Coll., 1942; postgrad., Columbia U., 1946-47; MD, Cert. d'Etudes Medicales, U. Lausanne, Switzerland, 1952. Diplomate Am. Bd. Obstetrics and Gynecology, Am. Bd. Psychiatry and Neurology. Intern Beth Israel Hosp., N.Y.C., 1953-54, resident NYC, 1954-57, Montefiore Hosp., Bronx, NY, 1964-67; pvt. practice specializing in ob-gyn. NYC, 1957-64; faculty acad. psychiatry U. NC, Chapel Hill, 1967-76, assoc. prof., instr. psychoanalytic tng. program, 1974—; prof. psychiatry Duke U. Med. Ctr., Durham, NC, 1976—, supervising and tng. analyst psychoanalytic tng. program, 1981-97, Honored prof. psychiatry, 1990—, emeritus, 1992—, supervising and tng. analyst emeritus, 1997—. Cons. Durham VA Hosp. Author: The Practice of Supportive Psychotherapy, 1984. Contbr. chpts. to books, articles to profl. jours. With AUS, 1943-45 Named Outstanding Tchr. psychiatry U. N.C., 1975, honored tchr. psychiatry Duke U., 1978, hon. prof., 1990. Fellow ACS, Am. Psychiat. Assn., Am. Coll. Psychoanalysts, others Home and Office: 1225 Park Ave New York NY 10128 Office Phone: 212-722-0744. Home Fax: 212-722-0744. Personal E-mail: davidwerman@aol.com.

**WERMAN, THOMAS EHRLICH,** record producer; b. Newton, Mass., Mar. 2, 1945; s. Lester and Ruth (Ehrlich) W.; m. Susan Lynne Gould, Aug. 25, 1968; children: Julia Gould, Nina Eve, Daniel Lester. BA, Columbia U. 1967, MBA, 1969. Asst. account exec. Grey Advt., N.Y.C., 1969-70; asst. to dir. Epic Records Artistes and Repertoire, 1972-73; dir. talent acquisition Epic Records, 1973-76, staff producer, 1976-80; v.p., exec. producer CBS Records, Inc., L.A., 1980-81; v.p. Elektra Records, 1981-82; pres. Julia's Music Inc., L.A., 1981—; v.p. artists and repertoire EMI-Capitol Entertainment Properties, L.A., 1997-98; owner, operator Stonover Farm Bed and Breakfast, Lenox, Mass., 2001—. Bd. trustees Berkshire Music Sch. Recipient N.Y.C. Civilian Commendation award for heroism, 1968, 14 platinum records awards Rec. Industry Assn. Am., 1977—, 10 Gold Record awards, 1977—. Mem.: Lenox C. of C. (bd. dirs. 2005), Country Club of Pittsfield. Democrat. Jewish. Office Phone: 413-637-9100. E-mail: werm1000@aol.com.

**WERMUTH, PAUL CHARLES,** retired language educator; b. Phila., Oct. 28, 1925; s. Paul C. and Susan (Manga) W.; m. Barbara Ethel Braun, Aug. 26, 1951; children— Geoffrey Paul, Paul Charles, Alan John, Stephen Mark. AB, MA, Boston U., 1951; PhD, Pa. State U., 1955. Instr. Clarkson Coll. Potsdam, N.Y., 1951-52; part-time instr., grad. asst. Pa. State U., 1952-55; asst. prof. Coll. William and Mary, 1955-57; mem. faculty Central Conn. State Coll., New Britain, 1957-68, asso. prof. English, 1966-68; prof. English Northeastern U., 1968-90, prof. emeritus, 1990—, chmn. dept., 1968-75. Vis. prof. Middlebury Coll., 1963-64 Author: Modern Essays on Writing and Style, 2d edit, 1969, Essays in English, 1967, Bayard Taylor, 1974, Selected Letters of Bayard Taylor, 1997, also articles. Served with USAAF, 1943-46. Danforth summer study grantee, 1961 Mem. Modern Lang. Assn., AAUP. Mensa. Home: 73 Mostyn St Swampscott MA 01907-1616 Office: English Dept Northeastern Univ Boston MA 02115 E-mail: pwermuth@comcast.net.

**WERNER, BETTY ANN,** academic administrator; b. Kingman, Kans., Nov. 25, 1941; d. Marvin Louis and Mildred Werner. BS in Elem. Edn., Kans. Neumann U., Wichita, 1963; MS in Edn. and Counseling, St. Francis U., Ft. Wayne, Ind., 1970; cert. in applied theology, Grad. Tehol. Union, Berkeley, Calif., 1999. Cert. elem. adminstr. Tchr., grades 1,2,3,5 St. Rose Sch., Great Bend, Kans., 1963—69; asst. prin., tchr. grades 3,5,6 Holy Trinity Sch., Westminster, Colo., 1969—76; prin., tchr. grades 3-6 St. John Sch., Hoising-ton, Kans., 1976—79; prin., tchr. Inst. of So. Plains, Hammond, Okla., 1979—80; prin. St. Mary Sch., Walsenburg, Colo., 1981—90; pres. Great Bend Kans. Dominican Sisters, Great Bend, Kans., 1990—98; tchr. grade 5 Goodnight Elem., Pueblo, Colo., 1999—2001; supr., dir. pastoral life Diocese of Pueblo, Pueblo, Colo., 2001—05. Guitarist, song leader St. Mary's Parish, Walsenburg, Colo., 1981—90; vol. Ecumenical Ch. Drug Alcohol Ctr., Denver, 1983—84, Ecumerical Ch. Shut Ins Program, West-minster, Colo., 1982—90. Wilderness hiking counselor for disadvantaged children Ch. Women United, Denver, 1983; probation counselor Jefferson County Court, Denver, 1985. Mem.: Delta Kappa Gamma. Roman Catholic. Avocations: hiking, guitar, calligraphy, playing cards, visiting friends. Home: 1702 Claremont Pueblo CO 81004 Office: Diocese of Pueblo 1001 N Grand Ave Pueblo CO 81003 Office Phone: 719-544-9861 X 114. E-mail: bwerner@dioceseofpueblo.com.

**WERNER, CLARENCE L.,** transportation executive; b. 1937; Asst. mgr. Larson Grain Co., Omaha, 1958-61; with Bus. Motor Express, Inc., Omaha, 1961-62; founder Werner Enterprises, Inc., Omaha, 1956-82, pres., 1982-84, chmn. bd. dirs., CEO, 1984—. Office: Werner Enterprises Inc 14507 Frontier Rd PO Box 45308 Omaha NE 68145-0308*

**WERNER, DAVID A.,** paper company executive; BS, MBA, U. So. Calif. CPA. With Peat, Marwick, Mitchell & Co., 1974-78; various mgmt. positions Lear Siegler's Telecomms. divsns./subsidiaries, Anaheim, Calif., 1978-86, v.p. fin. and adminstrn., 1986-90; v.p., CFO Microdot Components Group, 1990-94; exec. v.p., dir. Kaynar Technologies Inc. (formerly Microdot Components), Orange, Calif., 1994-99; exec. v.p., CFO Day Runner, Irvine, 1999—. Office: 101 Oneil RD Sidney NY 13838-1055

**WERNER, DONNA,** philosopher, educator; d. George Edward and Vesta Jean Sammons; 1 child, Matthew. BA in Bus. Adminstrn. and Acctg., U. Mo., 1986; MA in Philosophy, So. Ill. U. at Edwardsville, 1995; PhD, St. Louis U., 2004. Acct./auditor McDonnell Douglas Corp., St. Louis, 1986—92; adj. faculty St. Louis U., St. Louis, 1993—2002, program coord. St. Louis, Mo., 1998—2002; asst. prof., philosophy St Louis C.C., Meramec, St Louis, Mo., 2002—05, assoc. prof. philosophy, 2005—. Co-editor (with John Kavanaugh SJ): What's Ethics Got to Do with It?. Fellow Grad. Tchg. Assistantship, St. Louis U. Grad. Sch., 1993-1998. Mem.: NACRA, C.C. Humanities Assn., Am. Assn. of Philosophy Tchrs., Soc. for Ethics Across Curriculum, Assn. for Practical and Profl. Ethics, Am. Philos. Assn. E-mail: dwerner@stlcc.edu.

**WERNER, JUDITH,** not-for-profit developer, literature educator; b. N.Y.C., Oct. 26, 1941; d. Aaron T. Gerber and Lillian Seldin; divorced; children: Elizabeth, Joseph. AB, Barnard Coll., 1962; postgrad., Columbia U., 1963. Asst. editor Am. Artist mag., N.Y.C., 1968—69, Van Nostrand Reinhold, N.Y.C., 1970—76; grants and gifts mgr. Habitat for Humanity, N.Y.C., 1993—; poetry hr. Caring Cmty., N.Y.C., 1996—; sr. editor Rattapallax mag., N.Y.C., 1999—2002. Recipient numerous awards, Lyric mag. Avocations: astrology, tarot reading. Home: 24 Joralemon St Brooklyn NY 11201 Office: Habitat for Humanity NYC 334 Furman St Brooklyn NY 11201

**WERNER, KAREN ELAINE,** music educator; b. Mexico, Mo., July 14, 1953; d. Leroy Herbert and Myrtle Marie Sperry; children: Kristina, Angela. BS Music Edn., SW Mo. State U., 1975; MA Music History, U. Mo., 1980. Cert. music tchr. Mo. Tchr. music Niangua Pub. Schs., Mo., 1975—76; dir. choirs Ava Jr. and Sr. H.S., Mo., 1977—81; dir. choir Rolla Pub. Schs., Mo., 1981—84; head choral dept. McEvoy Music, San Diego, 1984—89; tchr. music La Jolla Elem., Calif., 1989—94; assoc. prof., dir. singers Moberly Area C.C., Mo., 1994—. Dir. music La Jolla Children's Theater Workshop, 1990—94; leader music workshop Choral Condrs. Guild, San Diego, 1991—94; clinician, adjudicator area h.s. music contests and festivals, 1994—; vis. instr. Christ Ch. U. Coll., Canterbury, Kent, England, 1999; presenter Global Edn. Conf., Kansas City, 2001. Bd. dirs. Moberly Area Coun. of Arts, 1997—2002; music dir. Palisades Presbyn. Ch., San Diego, 1991—94. Recipient Tchg. Excellence award, Gov. Mo., 2003, Alfred & Hazel Parrish award, 2005. Mem.: Mo. C.C. Assn. (chair salary com.), Am. Choral Dirs. Assn. (chair state repertoire and stds. 1999—2003), Mo. Music Depts. and Schs. Music (bd. dirs. 2001—04), Music Educator's Nat. Conf. (dist. choral v.p. 1981—84). Methodist. Avocations: running, gardening, travel. Office: Moberly Area Cmty Coll 101 College Ave Moberly MO 65270 Office Phone: 660-263-4110 ext. 357. Business E-Mail: karenw@macc.edu.

**WERNER, LAWRENCE H.,** editor; BA in Journalism, Mich. State U., 1969. Reporter Courier-Jour., 1969—78; asst. features editor (Louisville) Courier-Jour., 1978—79; bus. editor Grand Rapids (Mich.) Press, 1979; consumer reporter Detroit Free Press, 1979—81; mng. editor features and sports Buffalo Courier-Express, 1981—82; features editor Dallas Times Herald, 1982—83; asst. mng. editor bus. Star Tribune, Mpls., 1983—95; reader involvement editor, 1995—. Mem.: Soc. Am. Bus. Editors and Writers (past pres.). Avocations: coaching youth soccer, travel, reading. Office: Star Tribune 425 Portland Ave Minneapolis MN 55488-0002 E-mail: werner@startribune.com.

**WERNER, LEO C.,** music educator, consultant; s. Michael and Sally Ann Werner; m. Melissa Kim Werner, Dec. 9, 1990; children: Mitchell, Alicia. B in Music Edn., M in Music Edn., Ariz. State U., Tempe. Cert. Nat. Bd. Profl. Tchg. Stds. Dir. bands Mountain Pointe H.S., Phoenix, 1990—, chair performing arts, 1990—. Dir. Lionhearts Marching Band, Phoenix, 1990—2006; dir. wind ensemble Mountain Pointe H.S., 1990—2006. Mem.: Music Educators Nat. Conf. Avocation: culinary arts. Office: Mountain Point HS 4201 E Knox Rd Phoenix AZ 85044 Office Phone: 480-759-6111. Office Fax: 480-759-8458. E-mail: l.werner.mtp@tuhsd.k12.az.us.

**WERNER, PATRICE (PATRICIA ANN WERNER),** academic administrator; b. Jersey City, May 31, 1937; d. Louis and Ella Blanche (Smith) W. BA in French, Caldwell Coll., 1966; MA in French, McGill U., 1970; PhD in French, NYU, 1976; postgrad. Inst. Ednl. Mgmt., Harvard U., 1991. Joined Dominican Sisters of Caldwell, 1954. Sch. tchr. Archdiocesan Sch. Systems, N.J., Ala., 1954-62; tchr. French, Latin Jersey City, Caldwell, NJ, 1962-72; instr. French Caldwell (NJ) Coll., 1973-76, dir. continuing edn., 1976-79, chair dept. fgn. langs., assoc. prof. French, 1979-85, acad. dean, prof. French, 1985-94, pres., 1994—. Trustee Caldwell Coll.; mem. corp., trustee Providence Coll.; mem. Dominican Higher Edn. Coun.; mem. Pres.' Coun. liaison com. to NJ Higher Edn. Partnership for Sustainability. Named Salute to Policy Makers award, Exec. Women NJ, 2006, Outstanding Woman in Am. History, DAR Maj. Joseph Bloomfield Chpt.; recipient Woman of Achievement award, N. N.J. Coun. of Boy Scouts of Am., 1999, The Archbishop T.E. McCarrick award for Disting. Svc. to the Ch., 2000, Cmty. Woman of Achievement, West Caldwell Hist. Soc. and West Essex Women's Club, 2000, Caldwell Cup, Excellence in Edn. award, N. Essex C. of C. Found., 2003; scholar AATF Summer Grant. Mem.: Assn. Gov. Bds. of Univs. and Colls., N.J. C. of C., Assn. Cath. Colls. and Univs., Nat. Assn. Ind. Colls. and Univs. (bd. dirs., sec. bd. dirs., com. policy analysis and pub. rels.), Coun. Ind. Colls. (bd. dirs., pub. info. com.), Ind. Coll. Fund. N.J. (trustee, vice chmn. exec. com.), Assn. Ind. Colls. and Univs. in N.J. (chmn. bd. dirs.). Avocations: tennis, reading, avid sports fan, travel. Office: Caldwell Coll 9 Ryerson Ave Caldwell NJ 07006-6195 Office Phone: 973-618-3217. Business E-Mail: spwerner@caldwell.edu.

**WERNER, ROBERT L.,** lawyer, consultant; b. NYC, Feb. 28, 1913; s. Abraham L. and Elsa (Ludwig) W.; m. Raye Davies, Oct. 13, 1945; children: William, John. AB, Yale U., 1933; LLB, Harvard U., 1936. Bar: N.Y. 1936, U.S. Supreme Ct. 1936, also various fed. cts. and adminstrv. agys. 1936. Spl. asst. to U.S. atty. So. Dist. N.Y., 1936, asst. U.S. atty, 1937-40, confidential asst., 1940-42; dep. asst. atty. gen. U.S. Dept. Justice, Washington, 1946-47; spl. asst. to atty. gen. U.S., 1946-47; mem. law dept. RCA, N.Y.C., 1947, v.p., gen. atty., 1951-62, exec. v.p., gen. atty., 1962-66, exec. v.p., gen. counsel, 1966-78, dir., 1963-79, cons., 1978-83. Mem. adv. bd. Internat. and Comparative Law Ctr. Southwestern Legal Found., Dallas, 1966—, treas., 1970-72, vice chmn., 1972-73, chmn. advisory bd., 1974-76, found. trustee 1976-88, hon. trustee 1988—; lectr. Conf. Bd., Practising Law Inst., others; mem. nat. adv. council corp. law depts. Practising Law Inst., 1974-78; cons. on restrictive bus. practices U.S. council Internat. C. of C., 1973-78; N.Y. Lawyers' Com. for Civil Rights under Law, 1972-78. Trustee Ithaca Coll., N.Y., 1968-88, hon. trustee, 1988—, chmn. bd., 1978-79; trustee Salisbury (Conn.) Sch., 1975-77, N.Y. Chiropractic Coll., 1986-89; bd. dirs. Midtown Arts Common at St. Peter's Ch., 1983-89. Capt. U.S. Army, 1942-44; to lt. col. USAAF, 1944-46, ETO. Recipient Disting. Service award Ithaca Coll. 1988. Fellow Am. Bar Found.; mem. Internat., Fed., Am., N.Y. State, City N.Y., FCC bar assns., IEEE (sr.), Am. Legion, Harvard Law Sch. Assn., Assn. Gen. Counsel (emeritus), U.S. Naval Inst., Internat. Law Assn. (Am. br.), Nat. Legal Aid and Defender Assn., Am. Judicature Soc., New-comen Soc., N.Y. County Lawyers' Assn., Am. Soc. Internat. Law, Yale Club, Harvard Club N.Y., Army and Navy Club (Washington), Coral Beach Club (Bermuda). Home: 116 E 68th St New York NY 10021-5955

**WERNER, ROBERT WILLIAM,** federal agency administrator; b. Feb. 20, 1959; married; 3 children. Bachelor's degree, Amherst Coll.; master's degree, Columbia U.; JD, NYU. Law clk. to assoc. justices Lewis F. Powell, Jr. and Anthony M. Kennedy; officer Phoenix Home Life Mutual Ins. Co. (now The Phoenix Cos.); ptnr. Bingham Dana LLP (now Bingham McCutchen); assoc. atty. gen. State of Conn.; fed. prosecutor U.S. Atty.'s Office; head gaming regulatory agy.; with office legal counsel US Dept. Justice, Washington; asst. gen. counsel for enforcement and intelligence US Dept. Treasury, Washington, counselor to gen. counsel, dir. Office Fgn. Assets Control, 2004—06, dir. Fin. Crimes Enforcement Network, 2006—. Office: US Dept Treasury Fin Crimes Enforcement Network 1500 Pennsylvania Ave NW Washington DC 20220*

**WERNER, SAMUEL ALFRED,** physicist, educator; b. Elgin, Ill., Jan. 5, 1937; s. Charles August and Frances Agnes (Tasch) W.; m. Laura Louise Reed, Sept. 1, 1961; 1 dau., Catherine Louise. AB, Dartmouth Coll., 1959, MS, 1961; PhD, U. Mich., 1965. Staff scientist physics dept. Ford Motor Co., Dearborn, Mich., 1964-75; adj. prof. nuclear engring. U. Mich., Ann Arbor, 1968-75; prof. physics U. Mo., Columbia, 1975-2000, chmn. physics dept., 1981-83, Millsap Disting. prof., 1986—, Curator's prof., 1992—, prof. emeritus, 2000—; scientific cons.physics lab. Nat. Inst. Standards Tech., Gaithersburg, Md., 2000—. Vis. scientist A.B. Atomenergi, Studsvik, Sweden, 1970, Institut Laue-Langevin, Grenoble, France, 1977, Argonne Nat. Lab., Oak Ridge Nat. Lab., Brookhaven Nat. Lab.; cons. Argonne Nat. Lab., 1968—, mem. solid scis. div. rev. com., 1972-77, chmn. spl. com. Intense Pulsed Neutron Source, 1978-82; cons. Nat. Acad. Scis., 1977, 83; vis. scientist Nat. Bur. Stds, 1983-84; vis. scientist Nat. Inst. Stds. and Tech., 1996—, chmn. com. on assessment of physics lab., 1992-95. Contbr. numerous articles to profl. jours. Grantee NSF; fellow Swedish Rsch. Coun.; recipient outstanding alumni award U. Mich., 1980, Chancellor's award for Outstanding Rsch. U. Mo., 1980, Presdl. Rsch. award U. Mo., 1973. Fellow Am. Phys. Soc.; mem. Sigma Xi Home: 7302 Augustine Way Gaithersburg MD 20879-4587 Office: Reactor Bldg 235 NIST Mail Stop 8461 Gaithersburg MD 20899 Office Fax: 301-926-1604. Personal E-mail: slwerner@starpower.net.

**WERNER, STUART LLOYD,** computer services company executive; b. NYC, June 2, 1932; s. Leroy Louis and Frances Werner; m. Davideen Price, Jan. 6, 1990; children by previous marriage: Joan Leslie, Susan Lyn, Richard Wayne. BArch, Rensselaer Poly. Inst., 1954. Ptnr. in charge architecture Werner-Dyer & Assocs., Washington, 1959-68; v.p. Rentex Corp., Phila., 1968-70; pres. Werner & Assocs., Inc., Washington, 1970-81; v.p. spl. projects ARA Svcs., Inc.; v.p. ARA, 1981-83; pres. Werner & Monk, Inc., 1983-90, STN, Inc., 1981-99, chmn. Falls Church, Va., 2000—. Author: FilePro Developer's Reference, 4th edit., 2002; contbr. articles to tech. jours. Bd. dirs. Watergate South, 1984-90, Washington Opera Soc., Friends of the Corcoran Gallery, Washington, Hampton West Condo, 2001—, Fla. Grand Opera Guild; mem. Econ. Devel. Coun., City of Aventura, Fla., 2002. With AUS, 1955-57. Mem. AIA, Am. Inst. Indsl. Engrs., Marinette Yacht Club, Masons, Tau Beta Pi. Democrat. Office Fax: 305-933-7028.

**WERNER, TOM,** television producer, professional baseball team executive; b. NJ, Apr. 12, 1950; m. Jill Werner; children: Teddy, Carolyn, Amanda. BA, Harvard Univ., 1971. With ABC Television, Inc., 1972-82; co-owner Carsey-Werner Co., Studio City, Calif., 1982—; chmn. San Diego Padres, 1991-94; co-owner Boston Red Sox baseball club, 2002—. Mem. bd. dirs. Old Globe Theatre, Sharp Hospital. Prodr.(co-exec): (TV series) Oh, Madeline, 1983—84, A Different World, 1987—93, Chicken Soup, 1989, Grand, 1990, Davis Rules, 1991, You Bet Your Life, 1992, Frannie's Turn, 1992, Grace Under Fire, 1993—98, She TV, 1994, Cosby, 1996—2000; exec. prodr.: The Cosby Show, 1984 (Emmy award. Outstanding Comedy Series, 1985); (TV films) Roseanne, 1988—97; (TV series) Cybill, 1995—98, 3rd Rock from the Sun, Cosby, 1996—2001, Townies, 1996, Damon, 1998, God, the Devil and Bob, 2000, Normal, Ohio, 2000—01, Grounded for Life, 2001—05, You Don't Know Jack, 2001, The Downer Channel, 2001, That '80s Show, 2002, Whoopi, 2003—04, The Tracy Morgan Show, 2003—04, Game Over, 2004, Good Girls Don't..., 2004; exec. prodr.: (TV series) The Scholar, 2005; exec. prodr.: (TV films) The Cosby Show: A Look Back, 2002, These Guys, 2003, Grand Union, 2006, Happy Hour, 2006; prodr.: (TV films) The Mayor of Oyster Bay, 2002. Office: Carsey Werner Prodns 4024 Radford Ave Bldg 3 Studio City CA 91604-2101*

**WERNER-JACOBSEN, EMMY ELISABETH,** developmental psychologist; b. Eltville, Germany, May 26, 1929; came to U.S., 1952, naturalized, 1962; d. Peter Josef and Liesel (Kunz) W. BS, Johannes Gutenberg U., Germany, 1950; MA, U. Nebr., 1952, PhD, 1955; postgrad., U. Calif., Berkeley, 1953-54. Research asso. Inst. Child Welfare, U. Minn., 1956-59; vis. scientist NIH, 1959-62; asst. prof. to prof. human devel., rsch. child psychologist U. Calif., Davis, 1962-94, rsch. prof., 1995—. Sr. author: The Children of Kauai, 1971, Kauai's Children Come of Age, 1977; author: Cross-Cultural Child Development: A View from the Planet Earth, 1979, Vulnerable, but Invincible, 1982, 3d edit., 1998, Child Care: Kith, Kin and Hired Hands, 1984, Overcoming the Odds, 1992, Pioneer Children on the Journey West, 1995, Reluctant Witnesses: Children's Voices From the Civil War, 1998, Through the Eyes of Innocents: Children Witness World War II, 2000, Unschuldige Zeugen, 2001, Journeys From Childhood to Mid Life: Risk, Resilience and Recovery, 2001, A Conspiracy of Decency: The Rescue of the Danish Jews in World War II, 2002, In Pursuit of Liberty, 2006; contbr. articles to profl. jours. Recipient Disting. Contbn. to Child Devel. award, Soc. Rsch. Child Devel., 1999, Dolly Madison Presdl. award for outstanding lifelong contbns. to devel. and wellbeing of children and families, Zero to Three, 1999, Arnold Gesell award, German Soc. Pediat., 2001, award for disting. career contbns. to sci. study of lifespan devel., Soc. for Study of Human Devel., 2005. Fellow: Assn. Psychol. Scis., Soc. Rsch. Child Devel., German Acad. Social Pediats. (hon.). Business E-Mail: eewerner@ucdavis.edu.

**WERNICK, JOEL,** health facility administrator; BBA, U. Ark, Fayetteville; MHA, Xavier U., Cin. V.p. ops. Baptist Reg. Health Svcs., Pensacola, Fla., 1982—88; pres. CEO Phoebe Putney Meml. Hosp., Albany, Ga., 1988—. Bd. dir. Voluntary Hosp. Am. (VHA) Health Found., Inc., Ga., 2003—. Ga. Alliance Cmty. Hosp.; chmn. Med. Resource Network. Mem. S.W. Ga. Alliance for Progress. Recipient Discovery Health Channel Med. Honors, 2004. Fellow: Am. Coll. Healthcare Exec. Office: Phoebe Putney Meml Hosp 417 Third Ave Albany GA 31701 Office Phone: 229-312-1000. Business E-Mail: jwernick@ppmh.org.*

**WERNICK, RICHARD FRANK,** composer, educator, conductor; b. Boston, Jan. 16, 1934; s. Louis and Irene (Prince) W.; m. Beatrice Messina, July 15, 1956; children: Lewis, Adam, Peter (dec.). BA, Brandeis U., 1955; MA, Mills Coll., 1957. Instr. music U. Buffalo, 1964-65; asst. profl. music, dir. univ. symphony U. Chgo., 1965-68; conductor Pa. Contemporary Players, 1968-93; prof. music U. Pa., 1968-96, prof. emeritus, 1996—. Co-founder Community Youth Orch. of Delaware County; cons. Contemporary Music, The Phil. Orch., 1983-89, spl. cons. to the music dir., 1989-93; bd. dirs. Theodore Presser Co. Music dir. Royal Winnipeg Ballet Can., 1957-58; composer: Haiku of Basho, 1967, A Prayer for Jerusalem, 1971 (Naumburg award 1975), Moonsongs from the Japanese, 1972, Kaddish Requiem, 1973, String Quartet 2, 1973, Songs of Remembrance, 1974, Visions of Terror and Wonder, 1976 (Pulitzer prize 1977), Contemplations of the Tenth Muse, Book I, 1976, Book II, 1978, Introits and Canons, 1977, A Poison Tree, 1979, Concerto for Cello and Ten Players, 1980, In Praise of Zephyrus, 1981, Piano Sonata: Reflections of a Dark Light, 1982, Sonata for cello and piano: Portraits of Antiquity, 1982, The Oracle of Shimon bar Yochai, 1983, Concerto for Violin and Orch. 1983-84 (Friedheim 1st prize 1986); Oracle II for soprano, oboe and piano, 1985, Concerto for Viola and Orch., 1985-86, Musica Ptolemeica brass quintet, 1987, Symphony #1, 1988, String Quartet #3, 1988, Concerto for Piano and Orch. (Friedheim award 1992), 1989-90, Fragments of Prophecy, 1990, String Quartet #4, 1991 (Friedheim 1st prize 1991), Concerto for Saxophone Quartet and Orch., 1991, Cello Concerto #2, 1992, Symphony #2, 1993, ...and a time for peace, 1994, String Quartet #5, 1995, Cassation-Music Tom Jefferson Knew, 1995, Trio for violin, cello, piano, 1996, Da'ase for solo guitar, 1996, Games of Menoretti for solo bassoon, 1997, Sonata for violin and piano, 1997, Duettino for violin and oboe, 1997, String Quartet 6, 1998, Musica da Camerata, 1999, Telino's Acrobats, (for solo bass clarinet), 1999, Piano Sonata # 2, 2000, The Name of the Game, 2000, Duo for cello and piano, 2001, Quintet for Horn & String Quartet, 2002, Suite for Unaccom-panied Cello, 2003, Sextet (for string quartet, double bass, piano), 2003, Double Duo for 2 pianos, 2 cellos, 2004, A Song for Phil, 2004, Woodwind Quintet, 2005, Tristam Redux for guitar and percussion, 2006. Recipient music award Nat. Inst. Arts and Letters, 1976, Nat. Endowment Arts grantee, 1975, 79, 82; Fellow Ford Found., 1962-64, Guggenheim Found., 1976. Mem. ASCAP. Democrat. E-mail: rfwernick@aol.com.

**WERONSKI, PAWEL,** physicist, researcher; MSc in Physics, A. Mick-iewicz U., Poznan, Poland, 1989; PhD in Chemistry, Polish Acad. Scis., Krakow, Poland, 2000. Assoc. prof. Inst. Catalysis and Surface Chemistry Polish Acad. Scis., 2000; postdoctoral assoc. Chem. Engring. Dept. Yale U., New Haven, 2001—03; postdoctoral assoc. Los Alamos Nat. Lab., N.Mex., 2005—. Recipient Disting. Ph.D. Thesis award, Inst. Catalysis and Surface Chemistry, Polish Acad. Scis., 2000, Outstanding Oral Presentation in Bioscis. award, Los Alamos Nat. Lab., 2005; grantee, Polish Ministry Sci. Rsch. and Info. Tech., 2004. Achievements include research in monte carlo and molecular dynamics computer simulations in chemical physics, colloid and protein adsorption, self-assembling nanostructures, cellular membranes and nucleic acids, artificial life. Office: Los Alamos Nat Lab Ms-B284 Los Alamos NM 87544 Office Phone: 505-667-9956. Business E-Mail: pawel@lanl.gov.

**WERRONEN, BETSY WARREN,** political organization administrator; BA in Polit. Sci., Newton Coll. Sacred Heart, 1965. Legis. asst. to Sen. Thruston B. Morton, 1966-68; exec. asst. to Sen. Edward W. Brooke, 1968-75; dir. legis. nuclear energy and taxes Edison Electric Inst., 1979-81, chief lobbyist on nuclear power issues, 1979-81; dep. asst. sec. of state for legis. affairs Dept. of State, Washington, 1981-85, prin. dep. asst. sec. of state for legis. affairs, 1987-89; prin. dep. asst. sec. for congl., intergovtl., pub. affairs Dept. of Energy, Washington, 1985-86; founder, pres. Warren and Co., 1989—; fin. chmn. Rep. Com. DC Rep. Party, Washington, 1998-2000, chmn. Rep. Com., 2000—. Mem. nat. steering com., congl. steering com. Women for Bush/Quayle, 1992; co-chair Ward 2, 1996-98; alternate del. Rep. Nat. Conv., 1996, del., 2000, 04. Apptd. U.S. election observer, El Salvador, 1988; bd. dirs. Fgn. Student Coun., 1993-97. Mem. League of Rep. Women (1st v.p. 1997-99, pres. 1999-2000). Office: DC Rep Party 1275 K St, NW, Ste 102 Washington DC 20005 Office Phone: 202-289-8005.

**WERTELECKI, WLADIMIR,** pediatrician, educator; s. Eugene and Anna Wertelecki; m. Susan J. Paquette, Dec. 12, 1980. MD, U. Buenos Aires, Argentina, 1961; D (hon.), Mohyla U., Kyiv, Ukraine, 2003. Prof. med. genetics U. South Ala., Mobile, Ala., 1974—, chmn., 1974—. Dir. ala. birth defects surveillance, Mobile, Ala., 1995—; dir. birth defects surveillance Ukraine OMNI-Net, Kyiv, 1999—. Author: International Birth Defects Information System; Pandora's Word Box; mem. editl. bd.: Jour. Pediat. and Neonatology, 2005—. Sr. surgeon USPS, 1968—70. Recipient Humanitarian award, Ala. Assn. Retarded Citizens, 1990, Humanitarian of Yr. award, Mobile Ala. Assn. Retarded Citizens, 1996. Fellow: Am. Coll. Med. Genetics, Am. Pediat. Soc., Am. Assn. Pediat.; mem.: Ukranian Acad. Scis. (corr.), Argentina Acad. Scis. (corr.). Office: University of South Alabama 307 University Blvd HSB Suite 1400 Mobile AL 36688 Office Phone: 251-460-7505. Office Fax: 251-461-1591. Business E-Mail: wwertele@usouthal.edu.

**WERTHAMER, NATHAN RICHARD,** physicist; b. Milw., Feb. 9, 1935; BA, Harvard Coll., 1956; PhD in physics, U. Calif., 1961. Rsch. assoc. U. Calif., San Diego, 1961-62; mem. tech. staff Bell Labs, 1962-75; mem. corp. planning dept. AT&T, 1975-76; chmn. N.Y. State Energy Rsch. and Devel. Authority, 1976-78; sr. advisor sci. and tech. dept. Exxon Corp., 1978-83; exec. dir. Becton Dickinson Devel. Corp., 1983-89; exec. officer Am. Phys. Soc., 1990-93; mgmt. cons. Chelsea Technols, 1993—. Fellow AAAS, Am. Phys. Soc. Office: Chelsea Techs 43 W 16th St Apt 7D New York NY 10011-6321 Business E-Mail: chelseatechnologies@nyc.rr.com.

**WERTHAN, JEFFREY MICHAEL,** lawyer; b. NYC, Sept. 28, 1954; s. Fred and Evelyn (Rabinowitz) W.; m. Susan Elizabeth Miller, Aug. 27, 1978; children: David E., Benjamin J. Student, The Juilliard Sch., N.Y.C., 1972-74; BA, Tufts U., 1976; JD, Boston U., 1979. Bar: D.C. 1979, N.Y. 1980, U.S. Ct. Appeals (1st, 6th and 9th cirs.). Staff atty. Fed. Home Loan Bank Bd./FSLIC, Washington, 1979—80, spl. asst. atty., 1981, sr. atty., 1981-83; assoc. Silver, Freedman & Taff, L.L.P., Washington, 1983-85, ptnr., 1986—2001, Katten

Muchin Rosenman LLP, Washington, 2001—. Mem. ABA (banking com. 1990—), Metro Baseball Umpires Assn. Avocations: music, baseball, golf. Office Phone: 202-625-3500. Office Fax: 202-339-8281. Business E-Mail: jeff.werthan@kattenlaw.com.

**WERTHEIM, MARY DANIELLE,** educational coordinator; b. N.Y.C. d. Daniel Leo and Helen Loretta (Sudimick) Conroy; m. Stanley Claude Wertheim, Mar. 9, 1963. BA in English with honors, CCNY, 1960, MA, 1979. Coord. English and lang. arts Horace Mann Lower Sch., Riverdale, NY, 1969—. Pvt. investor Wertheim Trust, N.Y.C., 1985—; pres. winner's cir. Horace Mann Investment Club, Riverdale, 1989—. Founder, advisor Horace Mann Lower Sch. Drama Svc. Group, Riverdale, 1980—; active Rep. nat. Com., 1980—. Mem.: ASCD, Nat. Assn. Investors Corp., The Internat. Netsuke Soc. (sec. N.Y. chapter), Priory Scholars, Am. Firm, Mensa, The Grolier Club. Avocations: desk top publishing, manuscript collecting. Home: 180 Cabrini Blvd # 57 New York NY 10033-1138 Office: Horace Mann Lower Sch 4440 Tibbett Ave Bronx NY 10471-3416 E-mail: herbieboo@aol.com.

**WERTHEIM, MITZI MALLINA,** information technology executive; b. N.Y.C. d. Rudolf and Myrtle B. (McGraw) Mallina; m. Ronald P. Wertheim, Feb. 25, 1965 (div. July 1988); children: Carter, Tiana. BA, U. Mich., 1960. Asst. dir. div. research Peace Corps, Washington, 1961-66; sr. program officer Cafritz Found., Washington, 1970-76; dep. undersec. navy, 1977-81; with Fed. Sector Div. IBM, 1981-94; v.p. enterprise solutions SRA Corp., 1994-98, CNA Corp., 1998—. Woodrow Wilson vis. fellow, 1979, 80; founder, dir. The Energy Consensus, 2005—. Bd. dirs. Nat. Coalition Sci. and Tech., 1983—86; mem. vis. com. MIT, 1983—89; bd. dirs. Youth Policy Inst., 1986—91, VITA, 2001—, Cebrowski Inst., Naval Post Grad. Sch.; founder MIT Seminar XXI, 1985—. Recipient Federally Employed Women award Def. Dept., 1980; Disting. Pub. Svc. medal Navy Dept., 1981; fellow Maxwell Sch. Syracuse U., 1996-97. Mem.: Naval Studies Bd., Coun. on Fgn. Rels. Episcopalian. Home: 3113 38th St NW Washington DC 20016-3726

**WERTHEIM, RAM D.,** lawyer; b. Tel Aviv, May 15, 1954; BA cum laude, City U., 1979; JD magna cum laude, Georgetown U., 1982. Bar: NY 1983. Atty. Simpson, Thacher & Bartlett, NYC; gen. counsel, chief adminstrn. officer CapMAC Holdings, Inc.; co-head structured fin. divsn. MBIA, Inc., Armonk, NY, 1998—2000, gen. counsel, 2000—. Alt. mem. legal, regulatory, acctg., and tax. com. Am. Securitization Forum. Editor: Georgetown Law Jour., 1981—82. Office: MBIA Inc 113 King St Armonk NY 10504 Office Phone: 914-765-3945. Office Fax: 914-765-3163. E-mail: ram.wertheim@mbia.com.

**WERTHEIM, ROBERT HALLEY,** national security consultant; b. Carlsbad, N.Mex., Nov. 9, 1922; s. Joseph and Emma (Vorenberg) W.; m. Barbara Louise Selig, Dec. 26, 1946; children: Joseph Howard, David Andrew. Student, N.Mex. Mil. Inst., 1940-42; BS, U.S. Naval Acad., 1945; MS in Physics, M.I.T., 1954; postgrad., Harvard U., 1969. Commd. ensign U.S. Navy, 1945, advanced through grades to rear adm., 1972; assigned Spl. Projects Office, Washington, 1956-61, Naval Ordnance Test Sta., China Lake, 1961-62, Office Sec. Def., Washington, 1962-65; head Missile br. Strategic Systems Project Office, Washington, 1965-67, dep. tech. dir., 1967-68, tech. dir., 1968-77, dir., 1977-80; v.p. Lockheed Corp., 1981-88; cons. nat. def., 1988—. Emeritus mem. Draper Lab., Inc.; mem. U. Calif. Pres. Adv. Coun.; mem. sci. adv. group Dept. Def., Dept. Energy, U.S. Strategic Command; mem. nat. security adv. Lawrence Livermore Nat. Lab. Decorated D.S.M. with cluster, Legion of Merit, Navy Commendation medal, Joint Svc. Commendation medal; recipient Rear Adm. William S. Parsons award Navy League U.S., 1971, Chmn. Joint Chiefs of Staff Disting. Pub. Svc. award, 1996, Sec. of Def. medal for outstanding pub. svc., 1996, Disting. Grad. award U.S. Naval Acad., 2005; named to Hall of Fame NMMI, 1987. Fellow AIAA, Calif. Coun. Sci. Tech.; mem. Am. Soc. Naval Engrs. (hon. mem., Gold medal 1972), Nat. Acad. Engring., U.S. Naval Inst., Bernardo Heights Country Club, Sigma Xi, Tau Beta Pi. Home: 17705 Devereux Rd San Diego CA 92128-2014 Office: Sci Applications Internat Corp 16701 W Berardo Dr MS RB-2 San Diego CA 92127-3608 E-mail: rhwertheim@aol.com.

**WERTHEIM, SALLY HARRIS,** director, academic administrator, dean, education educator, consultant; b. Cleve., Nov. 1, 1931; d. Arthur I. and Anne (Manheim) Harris; m. Stanley E. Wertheim, Aug. 6, 1950; children: Kathryn, Susan B., Carole J. BS, Flora Stone Mather Coll., 1953; MA, Case Western Res. U., 1967, PhD, 1970. Cert. elem. and secondary edn. tchr. Ohio. Social worker U. Hosps., Cleve., 1953-54; tchr. Fairmount Temple Religious Sch., Cleve., 1957-72; mem. faculty John Carroll U., Cleve., 1969—, chair dept. edn., 1979—86, dean Grad. Sch., 1986—99, dir. planning and assessment, 1999—2004, interim dean Coll. Arts and Scis., 2004—05, cons. Office of Acad. V.P., 2005—, interim dir. Career Ctr., 2005—06. Cons. in field; cons. Jennings Found., Cleve.; chmn. sch. com. Cleve. Commn. on Higher Edn., 1987-99. Contbr. articles to profl. jours. Sec. Cuyahoga County Mental Health Bd., Cleve., 1978—82; pres. Montefiore Home, Cleve., 1987—90; bd. dirs. Mt. Sinai Med. Ctr., Cleve., 1984—93, Cleve. Edn. Fund, 1992—94; chair edn. com. Cleve. Found. Commn. on Poverty, 1988—93, Cleve. Cmty. Bldg. Initiative, 1993—95, United Way Svcs., 1994—2001; trustee Mt. Sinai Health Care Found., 1998, Gerson Found., 1998, Miller Found., 1998, Begun Found., 2001, Mandel Found., 2001; pres. Jewish Family Svc. Assn., Cleve., 1974—77; v.p. Jewish Cmty. Fedn., 1988—91, pres., 1994—97, trustee, 1975, life trustee, 1997—. Named One of 100 Most Influential Women, Cleve. mag., 1983, One of 29 Most Influential Women, Cleve. Mag., 1997; recipient award John Carroll U., Curtis Miles award for cmty. svc., 1997; grantee Jennings Found., 1984-87, Cleve. and Gund Found., 1987-90, Lilly Found., 1988; S.H. Wertheim scholarship and dean. excellence award established John Carroll U., 1997. Mem. Am. Assn. Colls. for Tchrs. Edn. (bd. dirs. 1982-85), Ohio Assn. Colls. for Tchrs. Edn. (pres. 1981-83), Coun. of Grad. Schs. Avocations: flower arranging, travel, antiques. Office: John Carroll Univ Office of Acad VP Cleveland OH 44118 Business E-Mail: werthoim@jcu.edu

**WERTHEIMER, ANDREW B.,** library and information scientist, educator; s. Albert and Marcia Wertheimer; m. Noriko Asato, Oct. 4, 1997; 1 child, Shunpei Joey Asato. BA, U. Wis., Eau Claire, 1993; PhD, U. Wis., Madison, 2003; MS in Libr. and Info. Sci., U. Bloomington, 1995. Pub. svcs. libr., head of acquisitions Spertus Inst. of Jewish Studies, Chgo. Jewish Archives, Chgo., 1996—97; libr. Woodman Astron. Libr., U. Wis., Madison, 1997—99; asst. prof., libr. Lincoln Librs. U. Nebr., 1999—2001; adj. prof. San Jose State U., Calif.; asst. prof. Libr. and Info. Sci. Program, Info. and Computer Scis. Dept. U. Hawaii at Manoa, Honolulu, 2003—. Mem. adv. bd. Japanese Cultural Ctr. of Hawaii-Resource Ctr., Honolulu, 2003—; cons. Kawasaki Reading Rm. for Japanese Studies, Lincoln, Nebr., 1999—2003; hist. cons. KDN Films/ Nebr. Ednl. Telecomm. Author: (monograph) Public Libraries Behind Barbed Wire: Japanese American Libraries in America's Concentration Camps, 1942-1946; editor: Library History Research in America: Essays Commemorating the Fiftieth Anniversary of the American Library Association — Library History Round Table; mem. editl. bd. Libr. History jour., London, 2005—. Faculty advisor Amnesty Internat. Student Chpt., Honolulu, 2004; sec. Friends of Manoa Pub. Libr., Honolulu, 2004. Mem.: ALA (chair Libr. History Round Table 2005—06), Assn. Libr. and Info. Sci. Edn. (convener hist. rsch. spl. interest group 2001—02), Japan Soc. Libr. and Info. Sci., Soc. Am. Archivists, Soc. for History of Authorship, Reading and Pub. Assn. Hawaii Archivists (vice chair, bd. dirs. 2004), Am. Libr. Association-Library History Round Table, Beta Phi Mu (faculty advisor Xi chpt. 2005). Avocations: poetry, Japanese-American history, human rights, photography. Office: Info and Computer Scis Dept 317 Post Bldg 1680 East-W est Rd Honolulu HI 96822 Office Phone: 808-956-3494. Office Fax: 808-956-3548. E-mail: wertheim@hawaii.edu.

**WERTHEIMER, FREDRIC MICHAEL,** professional society administrator; b. Bklyn., Jan. 9, 1939; s. Irving Wertheimer and Mildred (Klein) Van Brink; m. Linda Cozby, June 15, 1969. BA, U. Mich., 1959; LL.B., Harvard U., 1962. Bar: N.Y. bar 1963, D.C. bar 1971. Atty. SEC, 1963-66; legis. counsel Congressman Silvio Conte, 1967-68; counsel House Small Bus.

Com., 1969-70; lobbyist, legis. dir., v.p. Common Cause, Washington, 1971-81, pres., 1981-95; news polit. analyst CBS News, Washington, 1996; pres. Democracy 21, 1997—. Fellow Press Politics and Policy Ctr. Harvard U., 1996; J. Skelly Wright fellow, vis. lectr. Yale Law Sch., 1997; polit. analyst ABC News, 1999-2000. Author: Common Cause Manual on Money and Politics. With U.S. Army, 1962-63. Fellow Inst. Politics Harvard U., 1972. Jewish. Home: 3502 Macomb St NW Washington DC 20016-3162

**WERTHEIMER, MARILYN LOU,** librarian, educator; b. Pueblo, Colo. Dec. 1, 1928; d. Louis Robert and Alice Erdine Schuman; m. Y. Ernest Satow, Jan. 4, 1953 (div. Oct. 1958); m. Michael M. Wertheimer, Sept. 12, 1970; stepchildren: Karen Anne, Mark David, John Benjamin. BA, Stanford U., 1950; MA, Columbia U., 1953; postgrad., U. Calif., Berkeley, 1961—62; MLS, U. Calif., L.A., 1967. Sec., proofreader various publ. firms, N.Y.C., 1953—56; sec. Rockefeller Bros. Fund, 1956—57; personal staff, sec. Nelson A. Rockefeller, 1957—58; sec. Gen. Dynamics Corp., San Diego, 1959—64; cataloguer U. Calif., 1965—68; reference libr. U. Colo., Boulder, 1968—93, prof. honors sem., 1972—91, prof. emeritus, 1993—. Mem. libr. del. U.S. Exch. China, 1985, U.S. Exch. U.S.S.R., 1988; cons. Archives of History Am. Psychology, Akron, Ohio, 1980. Co-author: Sources of Information in the Social Sciences, 1986; co-editor: History of Psychology: A Guide, 1979; one-woman shows include Boulder (Colo.) Pub. Libr., 2004, Sun Microsystems, Broomfield, Colo., 2004, Norlin Libr. U. Colo., Boulder, 2005, Classical Acad., Colorado Springs, Colo., 2005. Mem. del. vis. Tibet, Boulder-Lhasa Sister Cities Program, 1988; vol. Christian Sci. Ch., 1986—; bd. dirs. U. Club, U. Colo., Boulder, 1976—79. Recipient First prize, Internat. Libr. Photography, Owings Mills, Md., 1999—2000. Mem.: ALA. Democrat. Home: 546 Geneva Ave Boulder CO 80302 Office: Norlin Libr U Colo Campus Box 184 Boulder CO 80309-0184 Business E-Mail: wertheim@colorado.edu

**WERTHEIMER-SEXTON, WILLA RENEE,** clinical psychologist; b. Chgo., May 10, 1964; d. William Ralph and Faye Ruth Wertheimer; m. Peter Patrick Sexton, Aug. 15, 1990; children: Maitiú Daibhid, Liam Dainéal. BA Psychology, DePaul U., Chgo., 1987; PsychoID, Ill. Sch. Profl. Psychology, 1996. Cert. Clin. Pschologist Ill. Dept. Profl. Regulation. Intern Forest Hosp., Des Plaines, Ill., 1992—93; postdoctoral intern North Shore Counseling and Consulting, 1993—94; ind. contractor, therapist Bannockburn, Ill., 1994—98; pres. Advocacy Counseling Ctr., Woodstock, Ill., 1998—. Affiliated staff psychologist Centegra Meml. Hosp., 1998—. Mem. adv. bd. McHenry County Head Start, Woodstock, Ill., 2001—; vol. presenter Head Start, Woodstock, 2001—; vol. teen group leader (family relationships) Woodstock H.S., 2003; numerous free workshops to various groups McHenry County, Ill. Mem.: APA. Jewish. Avocations: art, reading, spiritual development. Office: Advocacy Counseling Ctr 115 E South St Woodstock IL 60098 Office Phone: 815-243-6789. Office Fax: 815-334-0312. E-mail: dr.willa@sbc.global.net.

**WERTIME, TIMOTHY RAY,** music educator; b. Chambersburg, Pa., Apr. 10, 1954; s. Rudolf Milton and Phyllis Jane (Carrington) Wertime. BA, Wittenberg U., 1976, M of Sacred Music, 1985. Cert. music/elem. tchr. Ohio Dept. Edn., water safety instr. Red Cross, 1990. Dir. youth choir Covenant Presbyn. Ch., 1975—76; substitute tchr. Springfield City Schs., Ohio, 1977—92, Clark County Schs., Springfield, 1977—92; organist Northminster Presbyn. Ch., Springfield, 1977—92; tchr. Wertime's Keyboard Studio, Greencastle, Pa., 1995—; organist/choirmaster St. John's Evang. Luth. Ch., Mercersburg, Pa., 1995—. Author: (rsch. project) English Liturgical Music of the Sixteenth Century, 1984; composer: (music anthem) Magnificat-Song of Mary, 1984. Singer Mercersburg Area Cmty. Chorus; deacon Northminster Presbyn. Ch., 1990. Fellowship of Christian Athletes, Wittenberg U., 1975—76. Mem.: Am. Guild Organists, Royal Sch. Ch. Music Eng., Music Educators Nat. Conf., Phi Delta Kappa. Republican. Presbyterian. Avocations: walking, hiking, music, exercise, camping. Home and office: Wertime's Keyboard Studio 441 Leitersburg Rd Greencastle PA 17225

**WERTS, MERRILL HARMON,** retired management consultant; b. Smith County, Kans., Nov. 17, 1922; s. Mack Allen and Ruth Martha (Badger) Werts; m. Dorothy Wilson, Mar. 22, 1946 (dec. Jan. 15, 2003); children: Stephen M., Riley J., Todd J., Kelly M. BS, Kans. State U., 1947; MS, Cornell U., 1948. Beef sales mgr. John Morrell & Co., Topeka, Memphis, 1948-53; dir. mktg. Kans. Dept. Agr., Topeka, 1953-55; sec.-treas. Falley's Markets, Inc., Topeka, 1955-58; v.p. S.W. State Bank, Topeka, 1958-65; pres. First Nat. Bank, Junction City, Kans., 1965-78; pvt. practice mgmt. cons. Junction City, 1978-98; ret., 1998. Pres. Junction City CC, 1975—76. Mem. adv. com. U.S. Comptroller Currency, 1971—72; mem. Topeka Bd. Edn., 1957—61, Kans. Bank Mgmt. Commn., 1967—71, Kans. Pub. Employees Rels. Bd., 1989—94, Kans. Commn. Future Health Care, 1991—94; trustee Kans. State U. Found., 1958—2001, Kans. Synod Presbyn. Westminster Found., 1965—72, Kans. Pub. Policy Inst., 1999—99; pres. Junction City Indsl. Devel., Inc., 1966—72, Junction City-Geary County United Fund, 1967—68; chmn. Kans. WWII Commemoration Com., 1995—96, Kans. Commn. Vets. Affairs, 1995—98, Geary County Pub. Bldg. Commn., 1996—99; civilian aide Sec. Army for Kans., 1991—95; pres., bd. govs. Ft. Riley Ctrl. Kansas chpt. AUSA, 1994—95; mem. Kans. Senate, 1978—88; bd. dirs. Kans. Hist. Soc., 1989—97. 1st lt. inf. U.S. Army, 1943—46. Decorated Bronze Star, Purple Heart; named Outstanding State legis., Am. Legis. Exch. Coun., 1988; named to Inf. Officer Candidate Hall of Fame, 1981. Mem.: DAV, VFW, Kans. Livestock Assn., Kans. Farm Bur., Kans. Bankers Assn., Kans. U.S. Army (bd. govs., Gen. Creighton W. Abrams medal 1997), Kans. State U. Alumni Assn. (pres. 1957), Junction City Country Club (past pres.), Kansas (dist. gov. 1973—74), Am. Legion, Masons, Jesters, Shriners, Sigma Phi Epsilon. Republican. Presbyterian. Address: 1228 Miller Dr Junction City KS 66441-3312

**WERTSMAN, VLADIMIR FILIP,** librarian, writer, library and information scientist, translator; b. Secureni, Romania, Apr. 6, 1929, came to U.S., 1967; s. Filip and Anna Wertsman. LLM summa cum laude, U. A.I. Cuza, Romania, 1953; MLS, Columbia U., 1969. Judge lower and appellate cts., Romania, 1953-67; examiner stock certs. 1st Nat. City Bank, N.Y.C., 1967-68; reference libr. sci. div. Bklyn. Pub. Libr., N.Y.C., 1969-74, sr. libr. Canarsie br., 1974-77, sr. libr. Greenpoint br., 1977-80, sr. libr. Leonard br., 1980-82; sr. libr., Slavic and Romanian specialist Donell Ctr. N.Y. Pub. Libr., 1982-86; sr. libr. Learner's Adv. and Job Info. Ctr., 1987-93. Author, editor: The Romanians in America, 1748-1974, 1974, The Ukrainians in America, 1608-1975, 1976, The Russians in America, 1727-1970, 1977, The Armenians in America, 1618-1976, 1978, The Romanians in America and Canada, 1980, Librarian's Companion: A Handbook of Thousands of Facts and Figures on Libraries/Librarians, 1987, 2d edit., 1996, Career Opportunities for Bilinguals and Multilinguals: A Directory of Resources in Education, Employment and Business, 1991, 2d eidt., 1994, What's Cooking in Multicultural America, 1996, New York: The City in Over 500 Memorable Quotations From American & Foreign Sources, 1996, paperback edit., 1999, Romanians in the United States and Canada: A Guide to Ancestry and Heritage Research, 2002, Directory of Ethnic and Multicultural Publishers, Distributors and Resource Organizations, 3d edit., 1995, 4th edit., 1999, 5th edit., 2003; co-author: Ukrainains in Canada and United States, 1981, Free Voices in Russian Literature, 1950s-1980s, 1986; editl. cons. Harvard Ency. Am. Ethnic Groups, 1980; contbr. Books, Libraries and Information in Slavic and East European Studies, 1986, Immigrant Labor Press in North America, 1840s-1970s, 1987, Through American Eyes, 1989, Ency. of N.Y.C., 1995; mem. adv. bd., contbr.: Gale Ency. Multicultural Am., 1995, 99; contbr. articles, book revs. to profl. jours. Recipient Disting. Lit. Achievement award Am. Soc. Writers, 1977, Cert. of Merit, Yeshiva U., 1981, Spl. Recognition award Pub. Libr. Assn. Am., 1990. Mem. ALA (chair multilingual libr. materials and svcs. com. 1976-88, chair pub. and multicultural material com. of Emie Round Table Ala. 1989—, ethnic and multicultural info. exchange roundtable, spl. merit award 1988, David Cohen Emiert Multicultural award 2003), Am. Assn. Advancement of Slavic Studies, Am. Romanian Acad. Arts and Scis., Delta Tau Kappa. Avocations: chess playing, travel, stamp collecting/philately, dance. Personal E-mail: vvladimirw@aol.com. *America is by its very nature of historical formation and development a multiethnic, multicultural and*

*multilingual society. And if variety is the spice of life then American ethno-linguistic and cultural mosaique is the spice of our society. America's pluralism is also a microcosm of the entire world its citizens representing virtually all continents.*

**WERTZ, FREDERICK,** psychologist, educator; b. NYC, Sept. 9, 1951; m. Joan Wertz; children: Frederik Joseph, Hannah Rose. PhD, Duquesne U., Pitts., 1982. Lic. psychologist NY. Prof., chmn. Fordham U., Bronx, NY, 1985—. Editor: Jour. Phenomenological Psychology, 1992—. Named Prof. of Yr., Grad. Student Assn. Fordham U., 2006; recipient Walter Bingham award, Beloit Coll., 1969, Disting. Tchg. award, Fordham U., 2005. Mem.: APA (pres. divsn. humanistic psychology 1994, pres. divsn. theoretical and philos. psychology 1998—99). Achievements include research in phenomenological psychology, theoretical and empirical psychology. Office: Fordham Univ Southern Blvd Bronx NY 10458 Office Phone: 7188173775. Office Fax: 71881738785. Business E-Mail: wertz@fordham.edu.

**WERTZ, JOHN ALAN,** retired secondary school educator; b. Mpls., May 28, 1945; s. John Edward and Florence (Carlson) Wertz; m. Margaret M. Schlangen, 1993. BS, Hamline U., 1967; MS, St. Cloud State Coll., 1973; postgrad., George Washington U., 1985. Cert. St. Cloud Area Leadership Program. Tchr. social sci. St. Cloud Cmty. Schs., St. Cloud, Minn., 1967—2002; ret. 2002. Trainer, field rep. New Games Found., San Francisco, 1980—83; tchr., coach mock trial team Apollo HS, 1987—2000. Mem. affirmative action com. St. Cloud Cmty. Schs., 1975—78; mem. site coun. Apollo HS, 1994—96, co-chair site coun., 1995—96; chair St. Cloud Human Rights Commn., 1979—83; advisor Ctrl. Minn. Sexual Assault Ctr., 1981—83; bd. dirs. St. Cloud Area Tenants Assn., 1975—77, St. Cloud Area Spl. Olympics, 1982—83, United Way St. Cloud Area, 1996—2001, Minn. Edn. Assn., Great River Roundtable, 1997—2003, sec., 1997—98; mem. Edn. Minn. Transition Bd., 1998—99, Edn. Minn. Governing Bd., 1999—2002, St. Cloud Area Disabilities Coun., 1995—, pres., 2002—04; bd. dirs. St. Cloud Area Family YMCA, 2001—, bd. sec., 2002—03, pres., 2003—05; counselor Sr. Corps Ret. Execs., 2002—, treas., 2004—05; candidate Minn. State Legislature, 2000, 2002; mem. com. social action Minn. Synod Luth. Ch., 1971—74; chair social action com. Salem Luth. Ch. Coun., St. Cloud, 1974—76; mem. steering com. Create Cmty., 2004—. Recipient Merit award, St. Cloud Area Coun. Handicapped, 1976, Disting. Vol. award, YMCA USA, Minn. Alliance, 2004. Mem.: NEA, Am. Hist. Soc. Germans from Russia, St. Cloud Edn. Assn. (chair govtl. rels. coun. 1978—83, 1988—96), Edn. Minn., St. Cloud Area C. of C. (edn. divsn. 1992—97, vice-chmn. Pre K-12 com. 1993—94, chair edn. recognition com. 1994—96, mem. Thayer Youth Leadership steering com. 1995—97). Avocations: theater, travel. Home: 816 Rilla Rd Saint Cloud MN 56303-1037

**WERTZ, KENNETH DEAN,** real estate company officer; b. Oklahoma City, July 14, 1946; s. Walter K. and Kathryn L. (Moore) W.; children: Adam Troy, Kirsten Paige. BS in Acctg., Okla. State U., 1968, MS in Acctg. and Econs., 1969; JD, U. San Francisco, 1978. CPA, Okla., Calif; lic. real estate broker, Okla. Sr. acct. Deloitte, Haskins & Sells, San Francisco, 1969-70, 71-75; v.p. acquisitions, mng. dir. Landsing Corp., Menlo Park, Calif., 1975-86; pres. Detrick Salsberry Mgmt Inc., Tulsa, 1987-88; v.p. asset mgmt. Corporex Co., Cin., 1989-90; exec. v.p. real estate Brunner Cos., Dayton, Ohio, 1990-92; pres. Pillar Real Estate Advisors, Dayton, 1992—. Lt. col. Med. Svc. corps U.S. Army, 1968-84. Decorated Army Commendation medal with three oak leaf clusters, Meritorious Svc. medal. Mem. AICPA, Okla. Soc. CPAs, Calif. Soc. CPAs, Nat. Assn. Securities Dealers (fin. prin., registered sales rep.). Republican. Methodist. Avocations: bicycling, snow and water skiing, racquetball, camping, fishing. Home: 835 Huntersknoll Ln Cincinnati OH 45230-4343 Office: Pillar Real Estate Advisors 5335 Far Hills Ave Ste 318 Dayton OH 45429-2317 Office Phone: 937-434-4250. Personal E-mail: kdu@okclighthouse.com.

**WERTZ, VIRGINIA LORYMA,** retired librarian; b. Washington, Aug. 21, 1933; d. Melvin Moore and Ruth Belle (Johnson) W. AA, Am. U., Washington, 1958; BA, Am. U., 1961; MSLS, Cath. U., Washington, 1983. Clk. C and P Telephone Co., Washington, 1951—62; libr. Washington D.C. Pub. Libr. Sys., 1962—93; ret., 1993. Mem.: Order Ea. Star. Democrat. Episcopalian. Avocations: writing, theater, films. Home: 5332 41st St NW Washington DC 20015-1904

**WESBERRY, JAMES PICKETT, JR.,** anti-corruption specialist, management consultant; b. Columbia, SC, Sept. 22, 1934; s. James P. and Ruby L. (Perry) W.; m. Lea Esdras Casteneda, June 13, 1975; children: Jonathan Jesse, Perry Latimer, Ruby Lee Nilda; children by previous marriage: James Pickett III, Elisa Marie, Lillian Sue, Paul Armand. BBA, Ga. State U., 1955; LLD (hon.), Atlanta Law Sch., 1967; MPA, Am. U., 1983. CPA, Ga.; cert. internal auditor, fraud examiner, govt. fin. mgr., fin. svcs. auditor. Page U.S. Ho. Reps., 1949-51; acct., mgmt. cons. Atlanta, 1956-67; v.p. fin. and adminstrn. Computer Tech. South, Atlanta, 1969-70; sr. cons. Inst. Pub. Adminstrn., NYC, 1967-69, 70-76; cons. to comptr. gen. Peru, 1970-74, Ecuador, 1974-78; adv., prof. Latin Am. Inst. Auditing Scis. Peruvian and Ecuadorean Sch. Govtl. Auditing, 1971-78; dir. sys., stds. and procedures Days of Inns Am., Inc., 1979-80; chief auditor OAS, Washington, 1980-82; cons. World Bank, 1982-83; prin. advisor acctg. and auditing pub. sector Latin Am. and Caribean Region, 1994-97; dir. America's accountability/anti-corruption project Casals & Assocs., Alexandria, Va., 1997—2001, dir. accountability audit, anti-corruption project Project -ATLATL-Mex., 2001—03; dir. anti-corruption project si Se Puede, Mgmt. Sys. Internat., Quito, Ecuador, 2003—06, dir. anti-corruption projects L.Am., 2006—. Founder, pres. Accountability 21, 1998—2003; advisor to pres. of Latin Am. Orgn. of Supreme Audit Instn., 1993—2000; sr. adv. to comptr. gen. U.S., 1983—85; dir. internat. ops. Price Waterhouse, 1985—88; sr. fin. advisor USAID, 1998—93, prin., CEO Inst. Pub. Adminstrn., 1993—94, trustee; dir. N.Y. Bur. Mcpl. Rsch., 1993—94; mem. panel of experts in acctg. and auditing UN, 1972—82; adj. prof. Am. U., Washington, 1981—85; founding dir. Internat. Consortium Govtl. Fin. Mgmt., 1977—88, 1994—97, pres., 1984—87; cons., tchr. all Spanish-speaking We. Hemisphere nations Brazil, Haiti, Jamaica, The Netherlands Antilles, Guyana, Peoples Republic China, The Philippines, Can., U.S. Co-author: UN Handbook on Government Auditing for Developing Countries; editor: Latin American Manual of Professional Auditing in the Public Sector, Spanish Lang. newsletter Pistas de Auditoria, 1985-92; mem. editl. bd. Pub. Budgeting and Fin. Mgmt., 1982-92, The Govt. Accts. Jour.; contbr. articles to profl. jours. Mem. Ga. Senate, 1962-67, Fulton County Dem. Exec. Com., 1962-66. Decorated Order of Merit (Peru), 1972, Comptr. Gen. Venezuela, 1998; recipient Outstanding Career Achievement award USAID, 1993, Most Meritorious Accountant of the Americas award Interamerican Accounting Assn., 2003. Mem. AICPA (hon. life, chmn. interam. com. 1988-95), Interam. Acctg. Assn. (cert. assoc., bd. dirs. 1989-95, chmn. pub. sector com. 1989-91, 2000-2001, exec. com. 1994-95, Vet. Acct. Am. award 1987, Lifetime Acct. of Am. 1995, Most Meritorious Acct. 2003), Am. Acctg. Assn., Assn. Govt. Accts. (Authors award 1981-82, 89-90, chmn. internat. affairs com. 1987-82, 89-91), Inst. Internal Auditors (v.p. Latin Am. 1978-79, internat. rels. com. 1977-82, 84-88, regional dir. Latin Am. 1986-88, chpt. bd. govs. 1981-87, v.p. 1982-84, pres. 1984-85, vice chmn. internat. membership com. 1989-90, chpt. Disting. Svc. award 1987, Bradford Cadmus Meml. award internat. engr. 1989, Outstanding Author's award 1990), Honduras CPA Soc. (Hon. award 1990), Jr. Chamber Internat. (life senator); Quito (Ecuador) Inst. Internal Auditors (life bd. dirs.), U.S. Pub. Accts. (hon.), Lima Jr. C. of C. (hon.), Pinchicha (Ecuador) Coll. Pub. Accts. (hon.), Ecuador Fedn. Pub. Accts. (hon.), Baptist. Home: PO Box 17-22-20297 Cumbaya Quito Ecuador Office: Mgmt Sys Internat 600 Water St SW Washington DC 20024 Personal E-mail: jwesberry@aol.com.

**WESBURY, STUART ARNOLD, JR.,** health science association administrator, educator; b. Phila., Dec. 13, 1933; s. Stuart Arnold and Jennie (Glazewska) W.; m. June Carol Davis, Feb. 23, 1957; children: Brian, Brent, Bruce, Bradford. BS, Temple U., 1955; MHA, U. Mich., 1960; PhD, U. Fla., 1972. Capt. USPHS, 1955, served as adminstrv. officer, hosp. and clinic pharmacist, resigned, 1958; adminstrv. asst. Del. Hosp., 1960-61; asst. adminstr. Bronson Meth. Hosp., 1961-66; assoc. dir., asst. prof. U. Fla. Tchg. Hosp., 1966-67, dir. assoc. prof., 1967-69; v.p. Computer Mgmt. Corp., Gainesville, Fla., 1969-72; dir. grad. studies in health svcs. mgmt. U. Mo., Columbia, 1972-78; pres. Am. Coll. Healthcare Execs., Chgo., 1979-91; sr. v.p. TriBrook Group, Inc., Westmont, Ill., 1992-94; prof. Sch. of Health Adminstrn. and Policy Ariz. State U., Tempe, 1994-2000, dir., exec. edn. programs Coll. Bus., 1996-2000, prof. emeritus, 2000—. Chmn. bd. trustees, trustee emeritus Blood Sys., Inc., Scottsdale, Ariz. Co-author: Why We Spend Too Much on Health Care; numerous articles to profl. jours. Bd. dirs. Health Task, Inc., Atlanta, Boys Clubs, Gainesville, Heartland Inst.; chmn. bd. dirs. Mid-Am. chpt. ARC, 1988-91, DuPage County Dist., 1984-87; active Boy Scouts Am.; chmn. adminstrv. bd. Meth. Ch.; trustee Nat. Blood Found.; Rep. Congl. candidate Dist. 13, Ill. Named to Health Care Hall of Fame, 2005, Gallery of Success, Temple U.; recipient Award of Honor. Fellow Am. Coll. Health Care Adminstrs. (hon.), Am. Coll. Healthcare Execs. (Silver Medal award 1991); mem. APHA, Am. Hosp. Assn., Hosp. Mgmt. Sys. Soc., Assn. Univ. Programs in Health Adminstrn. (chmn. 1977-78), Am. Assn. Healthcare Cons. (hon.), Rotary (past pres.). Home and Office: 950 Willow Valley Lakes Dr H-312 Willow Street PA 17584 Business E-Mail: stu.wesbury@asu.edu.

**WESCHCKE, CARL LLEWELLYN,** publishing executive; BS, Babson Coll., 1951. Pres., publisher Llewellyn Worldwide Ltd., St. Paul, 1957—. Mem. Pub. Roundtable Minn. Office: Llewellyn Worldwide 2143 Wooddale Dr Saint Paul MN 55125-2989

**WESCOTT, JOSEPH WARREN, II,** academic administrator, education educator; b. Wilmington, N.C., July 19, 1959; s. James Warren and Delores (Pridgen) Wescott; m. Lisa Ann Blanton (div. Oct. 2002); children: Rachael, Joseph, Rose. BA, Wake Forest U., 1981, MA, 2000; MS, N.C. State U., 1998, EdD, 2005. Officer U.S. Army, Columbia, SC, 1984—87, U.S. Army Res., Garner, NC, 1987—94; dir. alt. learning ctr. Beulaville Mid. Sch., NC, 1988; bus. mgr. Associated Ins. Agy., Wallace, NC, 1989—96; dir. grants and spl. projects Duplin County Hist. Assn., Rose Hill, NC, 1998—2000; coll. instr. James Sprunt C.C., Kenansville, NC, 1999—2001; fed. rels. analyst Duke U., Durham, NC, 2001—05. Assoc. AAU Coun. on Fed. Rels., Washington, 2002—03; U. rep. The Sci. Coalition, Washington, 2001—03; com. mem. Edn. Adv. Com. and Ind. Agts., Raleigh, NC, 1998—2002. Editor: 1870 Fed. Census: The African Am. Population in Duplin County, 2000; author (contbr.): Ency. of N.C., 2005. Lay pastor Town Creek Christian Ch., Winabow, NC, 1990—; bd. dirs. Duplin County 250th Celebration, Kenansville, NC, 2000, Duplin County Hist. Found., 2005. Cap. U.S. Army, 1984—87, S.C. Rsch. grant, N.C. State U., 1998—2000, full fellowship, Wake Forest U., Winston-Salem, N.C., 1982—84. Mem. Phi Alpha Theta, Phi Kappa Phi. Pentecostal. Avocations: reading, gardening, travel, public speaking. Home: 676 Wescott Rd SE Bolivia NC 28422-8562 Office: U NC Gen Adminstrn NCSAA Chapel Hill NC 27515 Business E-Mail: history@post.com.

**WESCOTT, SETH,** Olympic athlete; b. Durham, NC, June 28, 1976; US Olympian Snowboarder Winter Olympics, 2006; owner The Rack Restaurant, Kingfield, Maine. Achievements include Winning Snowboard Cross World Championships, 2004-2005; finishing second X Games Snowboard Cross Championship, 2005; Gold Medal in Snowboard Cross, Winter Olympics, 2006. Office: The Rack Restaurant Sugarloaf Mountain A Kingfield ME 04947*

**WESCOTT, WILLIAM BURNHAM,** oral maxillofacial pathologist, educator; b. Pendleton, Oreg., Nov. 10, 1922; s. Merton Girard and Josephine (Creasey) W.; m. Barbara L., Dec. 31, 1944 (dec. June 12, 1969); children: William Douglas, Diane Elizabeth; m. Gloria Greer-Collins, Aug. 28, 1989. DMD, U. Oreg., Portland, 1951, MS, 1962. Asst. prof. to assoc. dean admin. U. Oreg. Dental Sch., Portland, 1953-72; co-dir. oral disease rsch. VA, Houston, 1972-75; dir. dental edn. ctr. L.A., 1980-85; acting dir. Reg. Med. Edn. Ctr., Birmingham, Ala., 1978-80; chief dental svc. Dept. of Veteran's Affairs, San Francisco, 1985-94; clin. prof. U. Calif., San Francisco, 1994—; cons. Northern System of Clinics Dept. Vets. Affairs, 1994—. Dental surgeon, Oreg. Air N.G., Portland, 1954-68; cons. Madigan Army Med. Ctr., Ft. Lewis, W. Va., 1971-74, VA Med. Ctrs., No. Calif., 1985—; oral pathology Duke U. Med. Sch., 1977-79; cons. U. Med. Ctr., Fresno, 1998—; bd. dirs. Enloe Hosp. Head and Neck Malignancy Tumor. Contbr. 80 articles to profl. jours. and several chpts. to profl. books; 4 chpts. to books. Dist. chmn. Boys Scouts Am., Portland, 1965-67; dir. Am. Cancer Soc., Portland, 1964-67; comdr. Veterans Foreign Wars Post 5731, Gridley, Calif., 1994-95, comdr., 1996-98; chmn. Mil. Vets Ct. of Honor Meml., No. Calif., 1997—. With Oreg. N.G., 1938-40; with U.S. Army, 1940-42; lt. col. USAF, 1942-68. Decorated DFC with oak leaf cluster USAF, Oreg. N.G. Merit Svc. Medal, Portland, Fedn. des Anciens Combattants Français medal. Fellow Am. Acad. Oral and Maxillofacial Pathology, Mil. Officers Assn. Am. (sec. 2000—), Omicron Kappa Upsilon, Sigma Xi. Avocations: woodworking, fishing. Home: 437 Justeson Ave Gridley CA 95948-9434 Office: U Calif Sch Dentistry S 512 San Francisco 3rd & Parnassus San Francisco CA 94143-0424 Office Phone: 415-476-4866. Business E-Mail: wesco83@sbcglobal.net.

**WESEL, RICHARD D.,** education educator, researcher; s. Joseph Henry and Luada Elaine Wesel; m. Ellen Rana Kayata, July 8, 1995; children: Kevin E., Andrew R., Emily E. BS, MS in Elec. Engring., MIT, Cambridge, 1989; PhD in Elec. Engring., Stanford U., 1996. Rschr. AT&T Bell Labs., Los Alamitos, Calif., 1989—91; prof. U. Calif., LA, 1996—; vice chair undergraduate affairs UCLA, 2004—. Mem. Legislative Assembly of the UCLA Academic Senate, LA, 1997—2001; chair UCLA Electric Engring. Ann. Rsch. Rev., LA, 2002; serving UCLA Sch. Engring. Faculty Exec. Com., LA, 2000—, UCLA Electric Engring. Dept. Non-Tenure Rev. Com., LA, 2005. Author: (research publications) Reduced-State Representations for Trellis Codes Using Constellation Symmetry, (research publication) Selective Avoidance of Cycles in Irregular LDPC Code Construction, Superposition Turbo-TCM for Multi-Rate Broadcast, Efficient Computation of Trellis Code Generating Functions, Universal Trellis Codes for diagonally Layered Space-Time Systems; assoc. editor IEEE Transactions on Comms., 1999—. Recipient CAREER award, NSF, 1998, Rsch. in Info. and Telecom. award, Okawa Found., 1999, TRW Excellence in Tchg. award, UCLA Sch. of Engring. and Applied Sci., 2000; fellow PhD, AT&T Found., 1990; Nat. Merit Scholar, Nat. Merit Scholarship Corp. Mem.: IEEE, Sigma Xi, Etta Kappa Nu, Tau Beta Pi (chpt. pres. 1987—88). Achievements include patents for Transmission System Using Code Designed for Transmission with Periodic Interleaving; System and Method for I/Q Trellis Coded Modulation; Adaptive Frequency Dependent Compensation for Telephone; Adaptive Frequency Dependent Compensation for Telephone Channels; Echo Protection Tone Detection and Regeneration for Digital Transmission of Facsimile Calls. Office: UCLA 7440-D Boelter Hall Los Angeles CA 90095 Office Phone: 310-267-2150.

**WESELAK, ANNA MARIE SCHMIDT,** educational association administrator, media consultant; b. Aurora, Ill., Oct. 28, 1949; d. John Joseph and Anna Florence (Sandor) Schmidt; m. Kevin John Weselak, May 20, 1972; children: Timothy Charles, Thomas John, Kristin Marie. BS, No. Ill. U., 1971, MS, 1974. Cert. early childhood edn. tchr., elem. edn. tchr. First grade tchr. Sch. Dist. 131, Aurora, 1971-75; kindergarten tchr. Pioneer Child Care Ctr., Lombard, Ill., 1987-92; sales and mktg. mgr. Minuteman Press, Addison, Ill.; owner, cons. Weselak & Assocs., 1994—; cons. Pearson Skylight, 1996—; sch. collaborative design team cons. The Ball Found., 1999—2000. Graphic media cons. Minuteman Press, Addison, Ill., 1991—; bd. dirs. DuPage regional unit Chgo. Assn. for Edn. Young Children; chmn. parent-child fair for Wk. of Young Child, 1988-89; program chmn., 1989-91, full conf. chmn., 1991-92. Pres. Lombard PTA Coun., 1987-89, 5th dist. Gen. Fedn. Women's Clubs Ill., 1988-90, Lombard Newcomers, 1976-77, Lombard Svc. League, 1981-83; grand marshall Lombard Lilac Parade, 1993. Recipient 10 Yr. Svc. award No. Ill. U. Alumni Assn., 1980, Ill. State Bd. Edn. Those Who Excel award of merit, 1992-93; named gift AAUW, 1985, one of Outstanding Young Women Am., 1983, Lombard Woman Yr., 1989. Mem. Ill. PTA (bd. mgrs., dist. 32 dir. 1988-91, chair leadership tng. 1991-93, v.p. dist. dirs. 1993—),

---

state conv. chmn. 1992, 93, Book of Recognition award 1990, hon. life mem.), Nat. PTA (hon. life mem., pres. elect 2003-05, pres. 2005-7), Ill. Fedn. Women's Clubs (chair budget and fin. 1990-92, editor Ill. Clubwoman mag. 1991—), Sigma Lambda Sigma (pres. 1970). Roman Catholic. Avocations: crafts, needlecrafts, sewing. Office: Nat PTA Ste 1300 541 N Fairbanks Ct Chicago IL 60611-3396

**WESELY, EDWIN JOSEPH,** lawyer; b. NYC, May 16, 1929; s. Joseph and Elizabeth (Bellas) W.; children: Marissa Celeste, Adrienne Lee; m. Marcy Brownson, Sept. 23, 1992. Ed., Deep Springs Coll., 1945-47; AB, Cornell U., 1949; JD, Columbia U., 1954. Bar: N.Y. 1954, D.C. 1985, U.S. Supreme Ct. 1960, others. Law clk. to judge U.S. Dist. Ct. (so. dist.) N.Y., 1954-55; asst. U.S. atty. So. Dist. N.Y., 1955-57; assoc. Winthrop, Stimson, Putnam & Roberts, N.Y.C., 1957-63, ptnr., 1964-2000; sr. counsel Pillsbury Winthrop LLP, NYC, 2001—05, Pillsbury Winthrop Shaw Pittman LLP, NYC, 2005—. Spl. master numerous cases; chmn. spl. com. on effective discovery in civil cases U.S. Dist. Ct. (ea. dist.) NY, 1982-84, com. on civil caseflow, 1985-88, com. on civil litigation, 1988-2002, chmn. emeritus, 2002—, civil justice reform adv. group, 1990-95; com. on pretrial phase civil cases Jud. Coun. 2d Cir., 1984-86, standing com. on improvement civil litigation, 1986-89; ex-officio Civil Justice Reform Act adv. group U.S. Dist. Ct. (so. dist.) NY; pres. CARE, 1986-89, chmn., 1978-86, 89-90, internat. bd. dirs., 1981-90, pres., 1987-90; bd. dirs. Internat. Rescue Com.; bd. dirs., exec. com. Internat. Ctr. in NY, 1990—, chmn., 1998-2003, chmn. emeritus, 2003-. Trustee Deep Springs Coll., 1991-2000; vice-chair, chmn. 1998-2000. Decorated Order of Civil Merit (Republic of Korea); recipient World Humanitarian award Fgn. Press Assn., 1988, Commendation Bd. Judges U.S. Dist. Ct. (ea. dist.) N.Y., 1993, Deep Springs Medal, Deep Springs Coll., 2003. Fellow Am. Coll. Trial Lawyers; mem. ABA (spl. adv. com. on internat. activities 1990-93, litigation sect. chmn. com. on discovery 1977-78, spl. com. study discovery abuse 1977-82, chmn. task force on liaison with internat. profl. assns. on matters of mutual concern 1989-93, Civil Justice Reform Act task force 1991-93, task force on the state of the justice sys. 1993-95, fed. initiatives task force 1995-98, co-chmn. task force on fed. and local rules 1997-98), UN Assn. U.S.A. (bd. dirs. 1991-2004), Assn. of Bar of City of N.Y. (com. chmn., organized demonstration observation panel), Coun. on Fgn. Rels. Office: Pillsbury Winthrop Shaw Pittman LLP 1540 Broadway New York NY 10036-4039 Office Phone: 212-858-1712. Business E-Mail: edwin.wesely@pillsburylaw.com.

**WESELY, MARISSA CELESTE,** lawyer; b. NYC, Apr. 25, 1955; d. Edwin Joseph and Yolanda Teresa (Pyles) W.; m. Frederick Hamerman; 1 child, Emma Elizabeth Wesely Allen. BA magna cum laude, Williams Coll., 1976; JD cum laude, Harvard U., 1980. Bar: N.Y. 1981. Assoc. Simpson Thacher & Bartlett, NYC, 1980-82, 84-88, London, 1982-84, ptnr., 1989—. Lectr., cons. Harvard Inst. Internat. Devel., Beijing, 1981, Jakarta, Indonesia, 1982; guest lectr. Yale Law Sch., New Haven, 1991; spkr. Am. Conf. Inst., Practicing Law Inst., Bankers Assn. for Fgn. Trade, N.Y. State Bar Assn. confs., 1993—. Bd. dirs. City Lore, NYC; capital campaign com. Lawyers Alliance NY; legal adv. Legal Momentum. Mem.: Internat. Bar Assn., N.Y. State Bar Assn., N.Y.C. Bar Assn., Phi Beta Kappa. Office: Simpson Thacher & Bartlett LLP 425 Lexington Ave Fl 20 New York NY 10017-3954 Office Phone: 212-455-7173. Office Fax: 212-455-2502. Business E-Mail: mwesely@stblaw.com.

**WESEMAN, VICKI LYNNE,** elementary school educator; b. Hastings, Nebr., Oct. 29, 1954; d. Virgil John and Vera Lillie (Berg) Kennedy; m. Creighton Lee Weseman, May 28, 1988 (div. Oct. 1999); 1 child, Jason K. BS, U. Nebr., 1977, MA, 1988. Cert. elem. tchr. Nebr., profl. tchr. Nebr. Elem. tchr. Hanover Elem. Sch., Glenvil, Nebr., 1977—2003, Lincoln Elem. Sch., Grand Isle., Nebr., 2003—. Pres. Adams County Edn. Assn., Hastings, Nebr., 1996—97; team leader stds. Adams County Schs., Hastings, 2000—01. Oregon Trail rodeo pageant coord. Adams County Agrl. Soc., Hastings, 1992—. Named Miss Rodeo, Nebr., 1977, Com. Person of Yr., Oregon Trail Rodeo, Hastings, 1999. Mem.: Nebr. Edn. Assn. (mem. selection com. 2000), Women's Profl. Rodeo Assn., Alpha Delta Kappa. Democrat. Lutheran. Avocation: barrel racing in rodeo. Office: Lincoln Elem 805 Beal St Grand Island NE 68801

**WESLER, KEN,** performing arts company executive; b. Phila., Apr. 3, 1964; s. Irwin Harvey and Marcia Elaine (Trilling) W.; m. Deborah Lee Rader, Nov. 2, 1986; children: Alexander, Samantha. BA, Temple U., 1994. Prodn. mgr. The Wilma Theatre, Phila., 1983-89; gen. mgr. Gretna Prodns., Inc., Mt. Gretna, Pa., 1989, 90, Walnut St. Theatre, Phila., 1989-95; CEO The Grand Opera House, Wilmington, 1995—. Guest lectr. Cabrini Coll., Phila., 1988, Temple U., Phila., 1988—1995, Springfield Coll. Mem.: Downtown Visions. Office: The Grand Opera House 818 N Market St Wilmington DE 19801-3011 Office Phone: 302-658-7897. Personal E-mail: kwesler2000@yahoo.com.

**WESLEY, ERIC,** sculptor, artist; b. LA, 1973; BA, UCLA. One-man shows include Camper, China Art Objects Galleries, LA, 1999, 2000, Two Story Clocktower, CalTech, Pasadena, Calif., 2001, Meyer Riegger Galerie, Karlsruhe, 2002, Metro Pictures, NY, 2002, Galleria Franco Noero, Turin, 2002, Art Basel, 2003, Pico Youth Ctr., China Art Objects Galleries, LA, 2004, exhibited in group shows, Brent Petersen Gallery, LA, 1998, I-Candy, Rosamund Felsen Gallery, Santa Monica, Calif., 1998, LA Edge Festival, 1999, Young & Dumb, ACME, LA, 2000, Drive: Power, Progress, Desire, Govett Brewster Art Gallery, New Plymouth, New Zealand 2001, Circles 3: Silver Lake Crossings, Zentrum Fur Kunst and Mediatechnologie, Karlsruhe, Germany, 2001, Purloined, Artists Space, NY, 2001, Snapshot: New Art From LA, UCLA Hammer Mus., 2001, Mus. Contemporary Art, Miami, 2001, Santa Monica Mus. Art, 2001, Freestyle, Studio Mus., Harlem, NY, 2001, Drive By: Nine Artists from LA, Reynolds Gallery, Va., 2002, Adios Pendejos, Oficina Para Proyectos de Arte, Guadalajara, Mex., 2003, New Space! New Show!, Galleria Franco Noero, Italy, 2003, More Boots = Many Routes, Transmission Gallery, Glasgow, Scotland, 2003, Fade (1990-2003), Craft & Folk Art Mus., Luckman Gallery, LA, 2004, Whitney Biennial, Whitney Mus. Am. Art, 2004. Mailing: c/o Whitney Museum American Art 945 Madison Ave New York NY 10021

**WESLEY, GLEN,** professional hockey player; b. Red Deer, Alta., Can., Oct. 2, 1968; m. Barb Wesley; children: Amanda, Josh, Matthew. Defenseman Boston Bruins, 1987—94, Hartford Whalers, 1994—97, Carolina Hurricanes, 1997—2003, 2003—, Toronto Maple Leafs, 2003. Player NHL All-Star Game, 1989. Achievements include being a member of Stanley Cup Champion Carolina Hurricanes, 2006. Office: Carolina Hurricanes RBC Ctr 1400 Edwards Mill Rd Raleigh NC 27607*

**WESLEY, JOHN E.,** photographer, educator; b. Seattle, Aug. 6, 1944; s. Jerome B. and Carol J. Ellingson; 1 child, Alisa N. BA, Minn. State U., 1967. Prof. photography, art Bellevue C.C., Wash., 1972—2004, prof. emeritus, 2005. Founding ptnr. Photoprintworks Gallery, Seattle, 1975—79. One-man shows include Libr. Gallery Bellevue (Wash.) C.C., 1983, Oreg. Gallery Mus. Art, U. Oreg., Eugene, Oreg., 1984, Seattle (Wash.) Art Mus., 1985, Edn. Access Channel 28, Bellevue, Wash., 1986, Arts and Humanities Divsn. Retreat, 1987, Cable Cmty. TV Channel 34, Eugene, Oreg., 1987, Libr. Gallery, Bellevue, Wash., 1990, Pacific Luth. U., Tacoma, Wash., 1994, exhibited in group shows at Libr. Gallery (Wash.) Bellevue C.C., 1990, 1991, Video 911 Gallery, Seattle, Wash., 1991, Green River C.C., Auburn, Wash., 1992, Bellevue (Wash.) C.C., 1994, many others, Represented in permanent collections Seattle Arts Commn., Wash. Arts Commn., Wash. State Arts Commn. Mem.: Kirkland Art Ctr., N.W. Soc. Photog. Gallery, Inc. (treas. 1985—88). Avocations: music, jazz. Business E-Mail: jwesley@bcc.ctc.edu.

**WESLEY, JOHN MERCER,** artist; b. LA, Nov. 25, 1928; s. Ner Wesley and Elsa Marie (Patzwaldt) W.; m. Hannah Allen Green, Dec. 18, 1971; children: Christine Alice, Ner. Student, Los Angeles City Coll., UCLA, 1947-50. One-man shows include, Robert Elkon Gallery, N.Y.C., 1963-80, 84, Premio Internat., Instituto Torcuato di Tella, Buenos Aires, 1967,

---

Documenta 5, Kassel, 1972, Carl Solway Gallery, Cin., 1972, 85, 89, Galerie Rudolf Zwirner, Cologne, 1973, Rush Rhees Gallery, U. Rochester, 1974, PS 1, N.Y.C., 1978, Reinhard Onnasch Ausstellungen, Berlin, 1982-83, 101 Spring St. Gallery, N.Y.C., 1987, fiction/non fiction, N.Y.C., 1990, 91, Chinati Found., Marfa, Tex., 1990, 98, Daniel Weinberg Gallery, Santa Monica, Calif., 1992, 98, Portikus, Frankfurt, 1993, Stedelijk Mus., Amsterdam, 1993, Kunstverein, Ludwigsburg, Germany, 1993, daad-Galerie, Berlin, 1993, Galerie Rolf Ricke, Cologne, 1994, José Freire Gallery, N.Y.C., 1994, Jessica Fredericks Gallery, N.Y.C., 1996, 98, 99, 2000, 01, 02, 03, Galerie Haus Schneider, Karlsruhe, Germany, 1996, Danese Gallery, N.Y.C., 1998, P.S.1 Contemporary Art Ctr., N.Y.C., 2000-01, Sert Gallery, Harvard U., 2001, Gagosian Gallery, London, 2001, Daniel Weinberg Gallery, L.A., 2002, 04; group exhbns. include, Whitney Mus., 1968, 69, 76, Indpls. Mus., 1976, Royal Academy, London, 1991, Mus. Contemporary Art, L.A., 1992-93, Mus. Beaux Arts, Montreal, 1992-93, Deichtorhallen, Hamburg, 1997, Kunsthaus, Zürich, 1997; represented in permanent collections Albright-Knox Mus., Buffalo, Mus. Modern Art, N.Y.C., U. Tex., Austin, Mpls. Soc. Fine Arts., Chinati Found., Marfa, Tex., Rose Art Gallery, Brandeis U., Waltham, Mass., U. Kentucky, Lexington, Kunstmuseum, Basel, Switzerland, Dayton (Ohio) Mus. Art, Portland (Oreg.) Art Mus., Whitney Mus., Stedelijk Mus., Speed Mus., Louisville, Ky. Guggenheim fellow, 1976; grantee Nat. Endowment Arts, 1989. Address: 27 Washington Sq N New York NY 10011

**WESLEY, NICOLE LEIGH,** dancer, choreographer; b. Lake Charles, La., Feb. 26, 1971; d. Cynthia Wesley Reynolds and John Douglas Wesley, Terri Wesley (Stepmother); m. Dustin Earl Downs, Dec. 20, 2006. BFA, U. Tex., Austin, 1994; MFA, Tex. Woman's U., Denton, 2003. Asst. prof. dance Spelman Coll., Atlanta, 2004—. Guest artist/guest lectr. Zoetic Dance Ensemble, Atlanta, 2006—; adj. prof. dance Tex. State U., San Marcos, Tex., 2003—04. Rehearsal dir. (choreographic work) Approximations (Nat. Coll. Dance Festival, 2006), (dance) Marionette and Her Five Strings (Am. Coll. Dance Festival/South Ctrl., 2006), Exodus and the Blues (Modern Atlanta Dance Festival, 2005). Animal rights activist ASPCA, Ga., 2004—06; donor Aids Services Austin, Austin, 1994—2004. Recipient Outstanding Dancer award, Tex. Woman's U., 2001—02, Outstanding Tchg. award, 2002—03, cert. Artistic Merit, 2003; grantee, Spelman Coll., 2004. Mem.: Phi Kappa Phi (Honor Soc. Membership 2003). Achievements include research in Laban Movement analysis within a writing curriculum to encourage a greater understanding of authorship through kinesthetic intelligence and learning at Spelman College. Office: Spelman College 350 Spelman Lane SW Atlanta GA 30314 Office Phone: 404-270-5474. Personal E-mail: nwesley@spelman.edu.

**WESLEY, NORMAN H.,** metal products executive; b. 1949; BA, MBA, U. Utah, 1973. With Crown Zellerbach Corp., San Francisco, 1973—83; pres., CEO, Fortune Brands Home & Office ACCO World Corp., Wheeling, Ill., 1983—99; pres. & COO Fortune Brands, Inc., Lincolnshire, Ill., 1999, chmn & CEO, 1999—. Office: Fortune Brands Inc 300 Tower Pkwy Lincolnshire IL 60069-3640*

**WESLEY, RICHARD C.,** federal judge; b. Canandaigua, NY, Aug. 1, 1949; s. Charles and Beatrice W.; m. Kathryn Rice; 2 children. BA summa cum laude, SUNY, Albany, 1971; JD, Cornell U., 1974. Bar: N.Y. 1975. Assoc. Harris, Beach & Wilcox, 1974-76, Welch, Streb & Porter, 1976-77; ptnr. Streb, Porter, Meyer & Wesley, 1977—87; asst. counsel to minority NY State Assembly, 1979—82; justice Supreme Ct. 7th Jud. Dist., 1987—94; supervising judge Criminal Cts. 7th Jud. Dist., 1991; judge appellate div. Supreme Ct. 4th Dept., 1994—96; assoc. judge NY Ct. Appeals, Albany, 1997—2003; judge US Ct. Appeals, (2nd cir.), New York, NY, 2003—. Creator Felony Screening Program, 1993; lectr. in field; bd. trustees Ctr. Dispute Resolution, Pre-Trial Svcs. Corp. Editor: Cornell Law Rev. Asst. counsel to Assembly Rep. leader James L. Emery, 1979-1982; assemblyman N.Y. State 136th Assembly Dist., 1982-84, 84-86; chair Livingston County Alcohol and Drug Abuse Prevention Coun.; bd. trustees United Ch. Livonia, Chances and Changes, Charles Settlement House; bd. dirs. Myers' Found.; driver Livonia Vol. Ambulance. Named Legislator of Yr., Livingston-Wyoming Assn. Retarded Citizens, 1988; recipient Disting. SUNY Alumni award SUNY Alumni Assn., 1997. Fellow N.Y. State Bar Found.; mem. Livingston County Bar Assn. (sec.), Supreme Ct. Justices Assn. (pres. 7th jud. dist.). Office: 1702 US Courthouse 40 Centre St New York NY 10007-1561*

**WESLEY, RUBY LAVERNE,** nursing educator, administrator, researcher; b. Detroit, Nov. 25, 1949; d. David Williams and Leatrice (Gragg) Williams; 1 child, Nathaniel Rogers Wesley III. Diploma, Providence Hosp. Sch. Nursing, Southfield, Mich., 1971; BS in Nursing, Wayne State U., Detroit, 1974, MEd, 1977; PhD, U. Md., Balt., 1987. Clin. instr. U. Tenn. Sch. Nursing, 1978-79; community health nursing instr. U. Md., Balt., 1984-85; assoc. prof. Bowie State U., 1985-89; asst. dean Coppin State Coll., Balt., 1989-90; asst. prof. Wayne State U., 1991—; nurse researcher Rehab. Inst. Mich., 1992, dir. nursing practice Detroit, 1992-93, dir. nursing, 1993-96; asst. v.p. med./surg. rehab. nursing Sinai Hosp., Detroit, 1996—98; chief oper. officer Detroit Inst. for Children, 1998—99; pres., CEO Big Bros/Big Sisters of Metro Detroit, 2000—02; v.p. programs Detroit Urban League, 2002—03; exec. dir. Wayne County Patient Care Mgmt. Sys., 2003—06; assoc. chief nurse educator VA Med. Ctr., Washington, 2006—. Henry C. Welcome fellow, 1986-87; Nat. Inst. Disability and Rehab. rsch. fellow, 1991-92. Office: Washington VA Med Ctr 50 Irving St NW Upper Marlboro MD 20774 Office Phone: 202-745-8486. E-mail: drrwesley@hotmail.com.

**WESLING, DONALD TRUMAN,** English literature educator; b. Buffalo, May 6, 1939; s. Truman Albert and Helene Marguerite (Bullinger) W.; m. Judith Elaine Dulinawka, July 28, 1961; children: Benjamin, Molly, Natasha. BA, Harvard U., 1960, PhD, 1965; BA, Cambridge U., Eng., 1962. Asst. prof. U. Calif. at San Diego, La Jolla, 1965-67, assoc. prof., 1970-80, prof. 1981—. Lectr. U. Essex, Colchester, Eng., 1967-70. Author: Wordsworth and Landscape, 1970, Chances of Rhyme, 1981, The New Poetries, 1985, The Scissors of Meter, 1996, (with T. Slawek) Literary Voice, 1995, Bakhtin and the Social Moorings of Poetry, 2003. Office: U Calif Lit # 0410 La Jolla CA 92093 Business E-Mail: dwesling@ucsd.edu.

**WESSE, DAVID JOSEPH,** higher education administrator, consultant; b. Chgo., May 5, 1951; s. Herman Theodore and Lorraine Joan (Holland) W.; m. Deborah Lynn Smith, IN, 1975; children: Jason David, Eric Joseph. AA, South Suburban Coll., 1971; postgrad., Purdue U., 1977-72; BEd, Ill. State U., 1973; MS, Loyola U., Chgo., 1983. Cert. mgr. adminstrn. Administr. Reuben H. Donnelley Corp., Chgo., 1974-76; adminstrv. mgr. Loyola U., Chgo., 1976-79, Joint Commn. on Accreditation of Healthcare Orgns., Oakbrook Terrace, Ill., 1979-81; adminstrv. dir., asst. sec. Northwestern U., Evanston, Ill., 1981-97; higher edn. cons. KPMG Peat Marwick, LLP, Chgo., 1997-2000; exec. dir. U. Houston, 2000; prin. Joslyn Assocs., Alexandria, La., 2000—; asst. v.p. U. North Fla., 2000—03; vice chancellor fin. and adminstrv. svcs. La. State U., Alexandria, 2003—; pres. Alexandria (La.) Student Housing Corp., 2004—05, The Oaks Found. Alexandria, 2005—. Seminar leader Nat. Assn. Coll. Aux. Svcs., 1998. Contbr. numerous articles to profl. publs. Pres., bd. dirs. Riverdale (Ill.) Libr. Dist., 1975, Riverdale Youth Commn., 1975; bd. dirs. Better Bus. Bur. Chgo. and No. Ill., 1991-97, Adminstrv. Mgmt. Soc. Found., 1998—. Recipient Svc. Recognition award Riverdale Libr. Dist., 1975, Excellence in Journalism award Nat. Assn. Coll. Aux. Svcs., 1989. Mem. Adminstrv. Mgmt. Soc. (bd. dirs. Chgo. chpt. 1983-88, pres. 1986-87, bd. regents 1986-88), Acad. Adminstrv. Mgmt. (bd. regents 1992-94), Profl. Office Mgmt. Assn. Chgo. (bd. dirs. 1992-93, sec. 1993-95, pres. 1995), Nat. Mgmt. Assn. (pres. 1995), Nat. Assn. Coll. and Univ. Bus. Officers (com. mem. 1986-87, 89-90, cost reduction awards 1986-88, 90, 92), Midwest Higher Edn. Commn. (com. mem. 1996-97), Assn. Coll. Adminstrn. Profls. (seminar leader 1995, 98, 99), Chgo. Area Bus. and Support Svc. Adminstrs. (founder 1988), Big Ten Bus. and Support Svc. Adminstrs. (founder 1992), Kiwanis Internat.(v.p. 2005-06), Ctrl. La. C. of

C., U. North Fla. Adminstrv. and Profl. Assn. (pres. 2002-03), Phi Theta Kappa, Lambda Epsilon. Lutheran. Office: 8216 Tom Bowman Dr N Alexandria LA 71302-9307 Office Phone: 318-473-6409. Business E-Mail: dwesse@lsua.edu.

**WESSEL, FREDERICK WARNER,** artist, educator; b. NY, June 14, 1946; s. Frederick W., Sr. Wessel and Augustina Jean Wesssel; m. Lee-Ann G. Chellis, Aug. 3, 1974; children: Brett Peter, Kerri Ann. BFA, Syracuse U., 1968; MFA, U. Mass., 1976. Prof. Hartford Art Sch., Conn., 1976—. One-man shows include Evansville Mus. of Art, Represented in permanent collections Mus. Modern Art, NY, Phila., Mus. Art, Pa., Libr. of Congress, DeCordova and Dana Mus. Art, others. Mem.: Tempera Soc. Avocation: travel. Home: 4 Edgewood Ter Northampton MA 01060 Office: Hartford Art Sch Univ of Hartford 200 Bloomfield Ave West Hartford CT 06117 Office Phone: 413-586-0708.

**WESSEL, GREGORY JAMES,** music educator; b. Iowa City, Iowa, Dec. 17, 1967; s. Carl Irving and Donna Mae Wessel; m. Angela Leigh Shaffer, Aug. 1, 1992; children: Allison, Madeline, Donovan, Jonathan. MusB, U. Northern Iowa, 1990. Vocal music dir. Hubbard-Radcliffe Cmty. Sch., Hubbard, Iowa, 1991—. Adult ch. choir dir. Zion United Ch. of Christ, Hubbard, Iowa, 1992—; mentor tchr. Iowa Dept. Edn., Iowa, 2004—. Coun. mem. Hubbard City Coun., Hubbard, Iowa, 2001—03; dir. cmty. Christmas cantata Hubbard Cmty Chorus, Hubbard, Iowa, 1991. Avocations: travel, antiques, movies. Office: Hubbard Radcliffe Cmty Sch 200 E Chestnut Hubbard IA 50122 Office Phone: 641-864-2211. Office Fax: 641-864-2422. E-mail: gwessel@po-1.hubbard.k12.iu.us.

**WESSEL, HENRY,** photographer; b. Teaneck, NJ, July 28, 1942; s. Henry and Jennie (Cincotta) W.; children by previous marriage: Nicholas, Rider. BA, Pa. State U., 1966; M.F.A., SUNY, Buffalo, 1972. Propr., mgr. comml. photog. studio, State Coll., Pa., 1966-68; cinematographer for documentary film Dept. HEW, 1967; instr. dept. art Pa. State U., Phila., 1967-69; prof. dept. photography San Francisco Art Inst., 1973-98, chmn. grad. program photography, 1977-78, chmn. dept. photography, 1987-93; asst. prof. San Francisco State U., 1974-75; vis. lectr. photography various colls. and art schs., 1967-81; propr., dir. Photographic Resources, Point Richmond, Calif., 1977—. Vis. artist Mills Coll., 1987-88; resident faculty, San Francisco Art Inst. One-man show at Mus. Modern Art, NYC, 1973, Visual Studies Workshop, Rochester, NY, 1977, Fraenkel Gallery, San Francisco, 1981, 89, 92, Gallery Min, Tokyo, 1987, Gallery Ram, Santa Monica, Calif., 1996, Mus. Contemporary Art, LA, 1998, Rena Bransten Gallery, San Francisco, 2000, 02, Gallery Luisotti, Santa Monica, Calif., 2002, Palm Springs Art Mus., Calif., 2005, others; represented in permanent collections, Mus. Modern Art, NYC, Phila. Mus. Art, Boston Mus. Fine Arts, Library of Congress, Am. Arts Documentation Center, Exeter, Eng., Nat. Gallery of Can., Ottawa, Tokyo Met. Mus. Photography, Japan, Seattle Art Mus., Wash., Oakland Mus., Calif., Met. Mus. Art, NYC, Denver Art Mus., Colo. Australian Nat. Gallery, Canberra, Art Inst. Chgo., Ill., Charles Cowles Gallery, NYC, Robert Mann Gallery, NYC, others; author: Henry Wessel, 1987, House Pictures, 1992, Night Walk, 2000, Odd Photos, 2002, Five Books, 2006 Guggenheim fellow, 1971, 78; Nat. Endowment Arts fellow, 1975, 77, 78 Home: PO Box 70475 Richmond CA 94807-0475*

**WESSEL, MORRIS ARTHUR,** retired pediatrician; b. Providence, Nov. 1, 1917; s. Morris Jacob and Bessie (Bloom) Wessel; m. Irmgard Rosenzweig, June 1, 1952; children: David, Bruce, Paul, Lois. BA, Johns Hopkins U., 1939; MD, Yale U., 1943. Diplomate Am. Bd. Pediat. Intern Babies Hosp., NYC, 1943-44; fellow in pediat. Mayo Found., Rochester, Minn., 1947-48; rooming-in fellow in pediat. Yale U. Sch. Medicine, 1948-51; asst. dir. pediatric outpatient clinic Yale-New Haven Hosp., 1951-52, dir. pediatric outpatient clinic, 1952-57; staff pediatrician, collaboration project Yale U. Sch. Medicine, 1957-62, instr. pediat., 1950-53, clin. asst. prof., 1963—71, clin. assoc. prof., 1961-75, clin. prof., 1975-97; ret., 1997. Bd. dirs. Clifford Beers Child Guidance Clinic, New Haven, 1950—55, cons. pediatrician, 1967—; bd. dirs. Women's Health Svc., New Haven, 1992—97, Child Welfare League, NYC, 1979—91. Author: Parents Book on Raising a Healthy Child, 1987. Maj. U.S. Army, 1944—47, ETO. Mem.: New Haven County Med. Soc., Conn. Med. Soc., Soc. Adolescent Medicine, Am. Acad. Pediatrics (Practitioner Rsch. award 1994, C. Anderson Aldrich award 1997). Office: Clifford Beers Clinic 93 Edwards St New Haven CT 06515 Fax: 203-387-1927. E-mail: morriswessel@comcast.net.

**WESSELINK, DAVID DUWAYNE,** finance company executive; b. Webster City, Iowa, Sept. 5, 1942; s. William David and Lavina C. (Haahr) W.; m. Linda R. DeWitt, Dec. 27, 1971; children: Catherine, Bill. BA in Bus., Ctrl. Coll., 1964; MBA, Mich. State U., 1970. Tchr. Peace Corps, Turkey, 1964-66, Karabuk Koleji, Turkey, 1967-68, Robert Koleji, Turkey, 1969-70; rsch. analyst Household Fin. Corp., Chgo., 1971-73, asst. dir. rsch., 1973-77, asst. treas. Prospect Heights, Ill., 1977, v.p., dir. rsch., 1977-82, group v.p., CFO, 1982-86, v.p., CFO, 1986—; v.p., treas. Household Internat., Prospect Heights, 1988-93; sr. v.p., CFO Advanta Corp., 1993-98; exec. v.p., CFO Metris Cos., Saint Louis Park, Minn., 1998-2000, vice chmn., 2000—02, chmn., CEO, 2002—. Bd. dirs. CFC Internat., Chicago Heights, Ill., Am. Fin. Svcs. Assn., Saxon Capital Corp., Glen Allen, Va.; mem. U.S. regional bd. Mastercard Internat., 2003—. Bd. dirs. Ctrl. Coll., Pella, Iowa, 1990—. Mem.: Fin. Execs. Inst., Econ. Club Chgo. E-mail: david.wesselink@metriscompanies.com.

**WESSELMANN, GLENN ALLEN,** retired health facility administrator; b. Cleve., Mar. 21, 1932; s. Roy Arthur and Dorothy (Oakes) W.; m. Genevieve De Witt, Sept. 6, 1958; children: Debbie, Scott, Janet. AB, Dartmouth, 1954; MBA with distinction, Cornell U., 1959. Research aide Cornell U., Ithaca, NY, 1958-59; adminstrv. resident Meml. Hosp., N.Y.C., 1957-58, adminstrv. asst., 1959-61, asst. adminstr., 1961-65, asst. v.p., 1965-68; v.p. for adminstrn. Meml. Hosp. for Cancer and Allied Diseases, N.Y.C., 1968-79 · · · · ; chief operating officer St. John Hosp., Detroit, 1979-84; pres., CEO St. John Health System, 1984-95, vice chmn., 1995-97; chmn., pres., CEO St. John Hosp. & Med. Ctr., 1984-94, ret., 1995. Mem. bus. adv. bd. City of Detroit, 1991-95, chmn., 1993-94; mem. exec. com. Greater Detroit Area Health Coun.; bd. dirs. Caymich Ins. Co. Ltd., Mich. Health Care Alliance, SelectCare, Detroit Econ. Growth Corp. Trustee Sisters of St. Joseph Health System 1981-94, Sisters of St. Joseph Health Svc., 1983-95, St. John Hosp. and Med. Ctr., 1979-95, St. John Health System, 1984-95, The Oxford Inst., 1984-95, Eastwood Clinics, 1992-95; pres. Providence Ch. Corp., Hilton Head Island, S.C., chmn. ch. fin. ocm., corp. pres. session; mem. bus. adv. bd.! City of Detroit, 1991-95, chmn. 1993-94. Served with MC AUS, 1955-57. Fellow ACHE; mem. Am. Hosp. Assn., Internat. Hosp. Fedn., Mich. Hosp. Assn. (trustee, chmn. 1994-95, mem. exec. com.), Assn. Am. Med. Colls. (Coth rep.), Am. Cancer Soc. (regional adv. bd. 1994-95), Med. Group Mgmt. Assn., Soc. Health Service Adminstrs., Sigma Phi Epsilon. Home: 63 Big Woods Dr Hilton Head Island SC 29926-2604 Personal E-mail: glengen@hargray.com.

**WESSELS, BRUCE W.,** materials scientist, educator, department chairman; b. NYC, Oct. 18, 1946; m. Beverly T. Wessels; children: David, Kirsten. BS in Metallurgy and Materials Sci., U. Pa., 1968; PhD in Materials Sci., MIT, 1973. Tech. staff GE R&D Ctr., 1972-77, acting br. mgr., 1976; from asst. prof. to assoc. prof. Northwestern U., Evanston, Ill., 1977-83, prof. materials sci. and engring., 1984—, prof. elec. and computer engring., 1987—, Walter P. Murphy prof., 1984—, dept. chair elec. engring. and computer sci., 2005—. Vis. sci. Argonne Nat. Lab., 1978; mem. program com. Trans. Supernat. Superlattices, Microdevices and Microstructures, 1987. Editor 5 books including (with G.Y. Chin) Advances in Electronic Materials, 1986; mem. editl. bd. Jour. Electronic Materials, 1982-88, 98—; contbr. articles to profl. jours.; patentee in field. Fellow ASM, Am. Phys. Soc., AIME (bd. trustees 1996-97); mem. TMS, The Minerals, Metals and Materials Soc. (chmn. electronic materials com. 1987-89, conf. program chmn. 1986-87, key reader Trans. of AIME 1985-92, bd. dirs. 1993-98, vice-chmn. exec. coun. electronic, magnetic and photonic materials divsn. 1991-92, chmn. 1993-95, v.p.

---

1995, pres. 1996), Electrochem. Soc. Materials Rsch. Soc. (symposium organizer 1993, 95), Optical Soc. Am., Electroceramics (internat. program com. 2000-05), Sigma Xi, Tau Beta Pi. Office: Materials Science-Engring Northwestern U 2220 Campus Dr Evanston IL 60208-3108 E-mail: b-wessels@northwestern.edu.

**WESSELS-MCCOY, DENISE WENDY,** pre-school administrator, consultant; b. Windsor, NY, Aug. 18, 1955; d. Bess Marie Urbani and David Wilfred Wessels; children: Joseph J. McCoy, Ryan D. McCoy. BA in Child Devel., San Jose State U., 1977; MS, Nova Southeastern U., 1990, postgrad., 2002—. Owner Learning Tree Pre Sch., Santa Cruz, Calif., 1980—89; instr. U. Calif., Santa Cruz, 1989—91; child devel. program supr. Child Devel. Inc., Campbell, Calif., 1992—99; instr. Monterey Peninsula Coll., Monterey, Calif., 1996—2002, Cabrillo Coll., Aptos, Calif., 1999—2002, Ctrl. Sierra ROP, Placerville, Calif., 2005—; Calif. State U., Sacramento, 2005—. Cons. Pathways Cons., Placerville, Calif., 2002—; county coord. ACT Against Violence, Santa Cruz, Calif., 2000—; presenter in field. Active Human Rights Roundtable, Placerville, Calif., 2004—05; bd. dirs. Calif. Assn. for the Edn. of Young Children, Sacramento, 2000—04. Recipient Cert. of Appreciation, Santa Cruz County Children and Families Commn., 2002, Cabrillo Coll. ECE and Ctrl. Coast Assn. Edn. Young Children, 2002. Mem.: Nat. Assn. for the Edn. Young Children (sect. pres. 2002—04, acad. validator 1994—2005). Avocation: travel. Home: 1640 Pheasant Run Placerville CA 95667 Personal E-mail: travelerdenise@comcast.net.

**WESSEN, DOUGLAS JOHN,** psychologist; b. Rapid City, S.D., Aug. 9, 1956; s. Donald Everett and Cynthia (Phillips) Wessen; life ptnr. Shelly Eidsness. BS, James Madison U., 1978, MEd, 1986, EdS, 1987. Tchr., spl. edn. We. State Hosp., Staunton, Va., 1979, Grafton Sch., Berryville, Va., 1979—81; tchr., spl. edn., group leader Dooley Sch., Richmond, Va., 1981—83; grad. asst. James Madison U., Harrisonburg, Va., 1983—85, tchg. asst., 1985—87; intern sch. psychologist Harrisonburg City Schs., 1987—88; sch. psychologist Southeast Regional Resources Ctr., Juneau, Alaska, 1988—89. Elem. counselor Juneau Sch. Dist., 1989—94, sch. psychologist, 1994—; glacier guide Northstar Trekking, 1998—. Pres. Alaska Sch. Psychologist Assn., 2000—01; exec. officer Juneau Mountain Rescue; team leader spl. teams Capital City Fire/Rescue Dept., Juneau, 1997—; coach Harborview Hoppers, Juneau, 1999—2002; asst. coach Juneau Jumpers, World Champion Jump Rope Team, 1996—97; bd. dirs. Critical Incident Stress Mgmt. Team, Juneau, Southeast Alaska Guidance Assn., Juneau, 1994—99. Recipient Cert. of Appreciation, Nat. Assn. Sch. Psychologist, 2003, Meritorious Pub. Svc. award, U.S. Coast Guard, 1999. Mem.: Mountain Rescue Assn., Critical Incidence Stress Found., Nat. Assn. Sch. Psychologists, Am. Alpine Club. Independent. Avocations: photography, softball, mountaineering, sea kayaking. Home: 300 W 9th St Juneau AK 99801 Office: Juneau Sch Dist 10014 Crazy Horse Dr Juneau AK 99801 Office Phone: 907-523-1760. Office Fax: 907-523-1769. Business E-Mail: douglas_wessen@jsd.k12.ak.us.

**WESSLER, MELVIN DEAN,** farmer, rancher; b. Dodge City, Kans., Feb. 11, 1932; s. Oscar Lewis and Clara (Reiss) W.; m. Laura Ethel Arbuthnot, Aug. 23, 1951; children: Monty Dean, Charla Cay, Virgil Lewis. Grad. high sch. Farmer, rancher, Springfield, Colo., 1950—. Dir., sec. bd. Springfield Co-op. Sales Co., 1964-80, pres. bd., 1980—; pres. Arkansas Valley Co-op Coun., SE Colo. Area, 1965-87, Colo. Co-op Coun., 1969-72, v.p. 1974, sec. 1980-86; cmty. com. chmn. Baca County, Agr. Stablzn. and Conservation Svc., Springfield, 1961-73, 79—, vice chmn. Baca County Com., 1980-90; mem. spl. com. on grain mktg. Far-Mar-Co; mem. com. for PROMARK, Hutchinson, Kans., 1978. Mem. adv. bd. Denver Bapt. Bible Coll., 1984-89; chmn. bd. dirs. Springfield Cemetery Bd., 1985—; apptd. spl. com. Farmland Industries spl. project Tomorrow, 1987—. Recipient The Colo. Cooperator award Colo. Coop. Coun., 1990. Mem. Colo. Cattlemen's Assn., Colo. Wheat Growers Assn., Southeast Farm Bus. Assn. (bd. dirs. 1991-95), Big Rock Grange (treas. 1964-76, master 1976-82), Southwest Kans. Farm Bus. Assn. (dir. 1996—, pres. 1999-2001). Address: 18363 County Road Pp Springfield CO 81073 Personal E-mail: wesslerfarms@lcommic.com.

**WESSLER, SUSAN R.,** biologist, educator; b. NYC, 1953; BS in Biology, SUNY, Stony Brook, 1974; PhD, Cornell U., 1980. Postdoctoral fellow Am. Cancer Soc. Carnegie Inst. Dept. Embryology, Washington, 1980—82; asst. prof. botany U. Ga., 1983, prof. botany and genetics, 1992—, disting. rsch. prof., 1994—. Editl. bd. Current Opinions in Plant Biology, Proceedings of NAS, assoc. editor Genetics; co-author (with M. Gerald Neuffer and Edward H. Coe): The Mutants of Maize. Mem.: NAS (coun. mem.). Office: The Wessler Lab Univ Ga Dept Plant Biology 4505 Miller Plant Sciences Bldg Athens GA 30609 Office Phone: 706-542-1857. Office Fax: 706-542-1805. E-mail: sue@plantbio.uga.edu.

**WESSLING, GREGORY JAY,** retail executive; b. Chgo., Dec. 11, 1951; s. Robert J. and Doris (Tosch) W.; m. Mary Anne Richmond, Nov. 16, 1974; children: Douglas A., James R., Robert E. BBA, U. N.C., 1974; postgrad., Wake Forest U. Sch. Bus., 1974-76, MBA, 1987. Store mgr. Lowe's Co., Inc., Winston-Salem, NC, 1973-76, mktg. mgr. North Wilkesboro, NC, 1976—, dir. merchandising, 1978-80, v.p. merchandising, 1980-96, sr. v.p., gen. merchandise mgr., 1996—99, sr. v.p. store ops., so. divsn., 1999—2004; prin. A&G Assocs. & Ptnrs., LLC, 2005—; chmn., CEO HouseRaising, Inc., 2005. Bd. dirs. DJR Corp., Winston-Salem; mem. alumni coun., bd. visitors Babcock Grad. Sch. Mgmt., Wake Forest U. Mem. Home Ctr. Leadership Council. Republican. Methodist. Avocations: skiing, water-skiing. Personal E-mail: team1agw@hotmail.com.

**WESSLING, ROBERT BRUCE,** retired lawyer; b. Chgo., Oct. 8, 1937; s. Robert Euans and Marguerite (Rickert) W.; m. Judith Ann Hanson, Aug. 26, 1961; children: Katherine, Jennifer, Carolyn. BA, DePauw U., 1959; JD, U. Mich., 1962. Bar: U.S. Ct. Appeals (9th cir.) 1965. Assoc. Latham & Watkins, L.A., 1962-70, ptnr., 1970-94; ret., 1995. Bd. govs. Fin. Lawyers Conf., Los Angeles, 1974-2000. Mem. World Affairs Coun., L.A., Town Hall, L.A.; trustee DePauw U. Mem. ABA, Los Angeles Bar Assn., Phi Beta Kappa, Phi Delta Phi, Phi Eta Sigma, Order of Coif. Democrat. Methodist. Avocations: tennis, travel. Personal E-mail: bbwessling@aol.com.

**WESSON, KENNETH ALAN,** educational consultant; b. Oakland, Calif., Aug. 5, 1948; s. Oliver and Dorothy Mae Wesson; m. Victoria Vilay Lim, Sept. 29, 2000; children: Tyler Keanly, Adam Shai, Aaron Kenneth. MA, San Jose State U., 1972. Cert. tchr. Calif., 1972. Ind. ednl. cons. in neurosci., spkr. in field, San Jose, Calif. Spkr. in field. Author: What All Educators Should Know About the Human Brain, Where is God in the Brain, Memory and the Brain, Early Brain Development and Learning, Brain Basics, What Recent Brain Research Tells Us About Learning, The Neuropsychology of Prejudice. Mem.: AAAS, NSTA (Shell Sci. scholar 2002), ASCD, Am. Assn. Coll. Adminstrs., United Profs. Calif., Western Psychol. Assn., Nat. Kindergarten Alliance (founding mem.), Nat. Assn. Black Psychologists (founding mem.), Soc. Neurosci., Orgn. Human Brain Mapping, Nat. Coun. Tchrs. Math., Am. Math. Assn., Internat. Soc. Infant Studies, Tobacco Edn. and Rsch. Oversight Com., Justice Sys. Bd. Santa Clara County, Mental Health Bd. Santa Clara County, Tchr. Credentialing Task Force, Nat. Sch. Bds. Assn. D-Conservative. Achievements include research in cognitive neuroscience. Avocation: travel. Home: 1497 Elsman Ct San Jose CA 95120 Office Phone: 408-323-1498, 408-323-1498. Personal E-mail: kenawesson@aol.com.

**WEST, ALFRED PAUL, JR.,** financial services executive; b. Brooksville, Fla., Dec. 7, 1942; s. Alfred Paul Sr. and Jane (Coogler) W.; m. Loralee Smith, June 16, 1964; children: Angela Paige, Alfred Paul III, Andrew Palmer. B in Aerospace Engring., Ga. Inst. Tech., 1964; MBA, U. Pa., 1967, postgrad., 1967-68. Chmn., chief exec. officer SEI Investments, Wayne, Pa., 1968—, pres., 1978. Bd. dirs. All-Star Forum, Phila., 1983—, Paoli Meml. Hosp., 1990—, grad. exec. bd. Wharton Sch. of Bus., 1983—; chmn. bd. dirs. Wharton's SEI Ctr. for Advanced Studies in Mgmt., 1989—; bd. dirs. World

---

Affairs Council, Phila., 1985-89, mem. exec. com., 1989, chmn. adv. com., 1989—. Named one of Forbes' Richest Americans, 2006. Republican. Presbyterian. Avocations: skiing, golf, photography. Office: SEI Corp PO Box 1100 Oaks PA 19456-1100*

**WEST, A(RNOLD) SUMNER,** chemical engineer; b. Phila., Jan. 12, 1922; s. Arnold and Mary (Sumner) W.; m. Beverly Helen Lehman, Oct. 5, 1946; children: Barbara Ann, Richard Sumner. BSChemE, U. Pa., 1943; MS, Pa. State U., 1946. With Rohm and Haas Co., Phila., 1946—87, rsch. engr., 1946—62, rsch. supr., 1962—72, mgr. rsch. dept., 1972—77, sr. tech. specialist govt. and regulatory affairs, 1978—87; owner, prin. A.S. West Assocs., Huntingdon Valley, Pa., 1987—. Cons. dept. chem. engring. U. Pa., 1952-72; mem. indsl. and profl. adv. com. Coll. Engring., Pa. State U., 1978-84, chmn. chem. engring. divsn., 1980-81, chmn. com., 1982-83. Editor: AIChE Safety and Health News, 1996—. Mem. Lower Moreland Twp. (Montgomery County) Authority, 1970, sec., 1971—; vice-chmn. bd. dirs. Chemical Heritage Found., 1984-92; pres. United Engring. Trustees, 1986-87. Fellow Am. Inst. Chem. Engrs. (dir. 1964-66, treas. 1973-75, v.p. 1976, pres. 1977); mem. Engrs. Joint Council (dir. 1976-79), Am. Assn. Engring. Socs. (vice chmn. public affairs council 1981, chmn. council 1982-83), Am. Chem. Soc., Nat. Soc. Profl. Engrs., Soc. Automotive Engrs., Water Environ. Fedn. Clubs: The Valley (Huntingdon Valley). Home and Office: 3896 Sidney Rd Huntingdon Valley PA 19006-2347 Office Phone: 215-938-7181. Personal E-mail: aswest@worldnet.att.net.

**WEST, BARRY J.,** telecommunications industry executive; With British Telecom, Dir., value-added svcs.; dir., corp. mktg. Cellnet (subsidiary of British Telecom); exec. v.p. Nextel Comm., Inc., Reston, Va., 1996—, chief tech. officer, 2005—. Office: Nextel Comm Inc 2001 Edmund Halley Dr Reston VA 20191 Office Phone: 703-433-4000.*

**WEST, BETSY,** broadcast executive; m. Oren Jacoby. Grad., Brown U.; MS, Syracuse U. Reporter WHEN Radio, Syracuse, N.Y., 1974; writer, editor ABC Radio, 1975; writer ABC News World News Tonight, Chgo., 1978-82; sr. prodr. ABC News Nightline, 1983-89; sr. broadcast prodr. ABC News Turning Point, 1989-98; exec. prodr. ABC News; v.p. primetime news CBS, N.Y.C., 1998—2004. Recepient 19 Emmy awards, Christopher award, duPont-Columbia award. Mem. Phi Beta Kappa (trustee).

**WEST, BOB,** pharmaceutical executive; b. Ellenville, N.Y., Mar. 7, 1931; s. Harry and Elsie May Wicentowsky; m. Betty Parker, May 9, 1957 (div.); children: Debra Ellen, Elizabeth Ann, Sharon Lynn; m. Jacqueline Cutler, Jan. 3, 1982. BS, Union U., 1952; MS, Purdue U., 1954, PhD, 1956; postgrad. mgmt. seminar, U. Chgo., 1972. Pres., dir. research Food, Drug, Chem. Svcs., Stamford, Conn., 1975—; pres., dir. research Bob West Assocs., Inc., Stamford, 1975—. Pres. Drug Info. Assn., Phila., 1974-75; sci. adv. bd. Fountain Pharms., Inc., Largo, Fla., 1993—; Dovetail Techs., Inc., College Park, Md., 1996—, Phytopede, Inc., Sarasota, Fla., 1999—. Mem. editl. bd. Drug Info. Assn. Jour., Phila., 1977-85; contbr. articles to profl. jours. Mem. ASPET, Soc. Toxicology, Acad. Pharm. Scis., Assn. Rsch. Dirs., Drug Info. Assn., Assn. Univ. Tech. Mgrs. Home and Office: Food Drug Chem Svcs 7925 Meadow Rush Loop Sarasota FL 34238-4319 Office Phone: 941-925-8958. Personal E-mail: bjwest2@verizon.net.

**WEST, CATHERINE G.,** retail executive; b. Sept. 6, 1959; BA, Lynchburg Coll. With People's Express Airline, 1981—85; v.p. credit card ops. Chevy Chase Bank FSB, 1985—91; sr. v.p. card mem. svcs. to exec. v.p. mktg. svcs. First USA Bank, 1991—2000; sr. v.p. U.S. consumer risk ops. Capital One, 2000—04, pres. U.S. card bus., 2004—06; exec. v.p., COO JC Penney Co., Inc., 2006—. Office: JC Penney Co Inc 6501 Legacy Dr Plano TX 75024-3698 Office Phone: 972-431-1000. Office Fax: 972-431-9140.*

**WEST, CHARLES CONVERSE,** retired theologian; b. Plainfield, N.J., Feb. 3, 1921; s. George Parsons and Florence (Farish) W.; m. Ruth Floy Carson, Sept. 6, 1944; children: Russell Arthur, Walter Lawrence, Glenn Andrew. BA, Columbia U., 1942; B.D., Union Theol. Sem., N.Y.C., 1945; PhD, Yale U., 1955. Ordained to ministry Presbyterian Ch. U.S.A., 1946; missionary, fraternal worker Bd. Fgn. Missions Presbyn. Ch. U.S.A., 1946-56; instr., chaplain Cheeloo U., Hangchow, China, 1948-49; instr. Nanking Theol. Sem., 1949-50; indsl. mission work Gossner Mission, Mainz-Kastel, Germany, 1950-51; lectr. Kirchliche Hochschule, Berlin, 1951-53; lectr. Hartford Sem. Found., 1955-56; asso. dir. Ecumenical Inst., Bossey, Switzerland under World Council Chs., 1956-61; chargé de cours U. Geneva, 1956-61; instr. Peking Nat. U., 1948; assoc. prof. Christian ethics Princeton Theol. Sem., 1961-63, Stephen Colwell prof. Christian ethics, 1963-91, prof. emeritus, 1991—, acad. dean, 1979-84. Mem. Commn. to Form Statement Faith U.P. Ch. U.S.A., 1961-67, chmn. internat. affairs com., 1963-66; Chmn. U.S. Com. for Christian Peace Conf., 1965-72; chmn. working com. Dept. Studies in Mission, Evangelism World Council Chs., 1967-68; member Commn. on Internat. Affairs, Nat. Council Chs., 1968-73 Author: Communism and the Theologians, 1958, Outside the Camp, 1959, Ethics, Violence and Revolution, 1969, The Power to be Human, 1971, Perspective on South Africa, 1985, Power, Truth and Community in Modern Culture, 1999, Storm Front, 2003; editor: The Sufficiency of God, Essays in Honor of Dr. W.A. Visser't Hooft, 1963; assoc. editor: Religion in Eastern Europe, 1985—; translator: J. Hamel-A Christian in East Germany, 1960. Mem. Am. Soc. Christian Ethics (v.p. 1972-73, pres. 1973-74), Am. Theol. Soc. (v.p. 1982-83, pres. 1983-84), Presbytery N.Y.C., Ams. for Dem. Action., Christians Associated for Rels. with Eastern Europe (pres. 1988-92). Presbyterian. Home: 9 Hedge Row Rd Princeton NJ 08540-5047 Office: Princeton Theological Seminary CN821 Princeton NJ 08542

**WEST, CLARK DARWIN,** pediatric nephrologist, educator; b. Jamestown, NY, July 4, 1918; s. Clark Darwin and Frances Isabel (Blanchard) W.; m. Ruthann Asbury, Apr. 12, 1944 (div.); children: Charles Michael, John Clark, Lucy Frances; m. Dolores Lachman, Mar. 1, 1986. AB, Coll. of Wooster, 1940; MD, U. Mich., 1943. Intern Univ. Hosp., Ann Arbor, Mich., 1943-44, resident in pediatrics, 1944-46; fellow in pediatrics Children's Hosp. Research Found., Cin., 1948-49, research asso., 1951-89, asso. dir., 1963-89, dir. div. immunology and nephrology, 1958-89; with cardiopulmonary lab. chest service Bellevue Hosp., N.Y.C., 1949-51; attending pediatrician Children's Hosp., 1951-89; asst. prof. pediatrics U. Cin., 1951-55, asso. prof., 1955-62, prof., 1962-89. Mem. coms. NIH, 1965-69, 1972-73 Mem. editorial bd.: Jour. Pediatrics, 1960-79, Kidney Internat., 1977-89, Clin. Nephrology, 1989-96; contbr. articles to profl. jours. Served to capt. M.C., AUS, 1946-47. Decorated Army commendation medal; recipient recognition award Cin. Pediat. Soc., 1980, Mitchell Rubin award, 1986, Henry L. Barnett award, 1995, Daniel Drake medal, 1996. Mem. Am. J. Peters award, 1996. Mem. Soc. Pediatric Research (sec.-treas. 1958-62, pres. 1963-64), Am. Pediatric Soc., Am. Soc. Pediatric Nephrologists (pres. 1973-74), Am. Physiol. Soc., Am. Assn. Immunologists, Am. Soc. Nephrology, Internat. Pediatric Nephrology Assn., Sigma Xi, Alpha Omega Alpha. Achievements include research on immuno-pathogenesis and treatment of glomerulonephritides and in the complement system. Home: 11688 Aristocrat Dr Harrison OH 45030-9753 Office: Children's Hosp Med Ctr Cincinnati OH 45229 Office Phone: 513-636-4531. Personal E-mail: CWest_2865@fuse.net

**WEST, CORNEL RONALD,** humanities educator, writer; b. Tulsa, June 2, 1953; s. Clifton L. W.; 1 child from previous marriage, Clifton; m. Elleni Gebre Amlak. BA, Harvard U., 1973; PhD, Princeton U., 1980. Prof. religion Union Theol. Sem., NY, 1977-84, 87-88, Yale U. Divinity Sch., New Haven, 1984-87; prof. religion, dir. Afro-Am. Studies Princeton U., 1988-94, Class of 1943 Univ. prof. of religion, 2002—; prof. Afro-Am. studies, philosophy of religion Harvard U., Cambridge, Mass., 1994—99, Alphonse Fletcher jr. prof., 1999—2002. Am. corr. Le Monde Diplomatique; vis. prof. U. Paris; DuBois fellow Harvard U., 1994-99. Author: Black Theology and Marxist Thought, 1979, Prophesy Deliverance! An Afro-American Revolutionary Christianity, 1982, Prophetic Fragments, 1988, The American Evasion of Philosophy: A Genealogy of Pragmatism, 1989, Breaking Bread: Insurgent

Black Intellectual Life, 1991, The Ethical Dimensions of Marxist Thought, 1991, Race Matters, 1993, Beyond Eurocentrism and Multiculturalism, Vol. I: Prophetic Thought in Postmodern Times. Vol. II: Prophetic Reflections: Notes on Race and Power in America, 1993, Keeping Faith: Philosophy and Race in America, 1994, (with Paula Giddings) Regarding Malcolm X, 1994, (with Michael Lerner) Jews and Blacks: Let the Healing Begin, 1995, (with Michael Lerner) Jews and Blacks: A Dialogue on Race, religion, and Culture in America, 1996, (with Henry Louis Gates Jr.) The Future of the Race, 1996, Restoring Hope: Conversations on the Future of Black America, 1998, (with Roberto Unger) The Future of American Progressivism, 1998, (with Sylvia Ann Hewlett) The War Against Parents, 1998, The Cornel West Reader, 1999, (with Henry Louis Gates Jr.) The African American Century: How Black Americans Have Shaped Our Century, 2000, Democracy Matters: Winning the Fight Against Imperialism, 2004; co-prodr. (with Derek "D.O.A." Allen, Clifton West & Mike Daily) album, Sketches of my Culture, 2001. Named one of 100 Most Influential Black Americans, Ebony mag., 2006; recipient Literary Lion award, NY Pub. Libr., 1993. Office: Princeton U Dept Religion Hall 208 Marx Hall Princeton NJ 08544-1066 Office Phone: 609-258-4302. E-mail: kappiah@princeton.edu.*

**WEST, DANA ERIC,** mathematician, educator; b. Williamsport, Pa., Oct. 3, 1967; s. Richard West and Lula Mae Fair, Richard Fair (Stepfather) and Ann West (Stepmother); m. Cheri West; children: Shaelyn, Kalleigh. Bachelors, Pa. State U., 1990; Masters, Wilkes U., 1996. Cert. secondary edn. tchr. Pa., 1990. Tchr. 8th grade math. Pleasant Valley Mid. Sch., Brodheadsville, Pa., 1990—. Head dept. math. Pleasant Valley Mid. Sch., Brodheadsville, Pa., 1996—. Maj. U.S. Army, 1989—2005. Decorated Army Commendation medals U.S. Army. Meritorious Svc. medal; recipient R.O.T.C. scholarship, 1985. Mem.: Nat. Educators Assn. Office: Pleasant Valley Mid Sch Rt 115 Brodheadsville PA 18322 Office Phone: 570-402-1000.

**WEST, DANIEL CHARLES,** dentist; b. Trenton, N.J., July 23, 1955; s. Harry E. and Alma R. (Washburn) W.; m. Deborah L. Scott, May 28, 1977; children: Elizabeth, Colin Jeffrey, Aaron Samuel. BS, Ea. Nazarene Coll., 1977; DMD, U. Pitts., 1982; M, Acad. Gen. Dentistry, 2003. Min. youth music South Hills Ch. of the Nazarene, Bethel Park, Pa., 1977-82; pvt. practice Terre Hill, Pa., 1982-95; prin., owner New Holland (Pa.) Dental Care, 1995—. Mem. Internat. Gen. Bd. Ch. of Nazarene, Kansas City, Mo., 1989—2002, lay mem. dist. adv. bd. Phila. dist., Frazer, Pa., 1985—, coord. work and witness program, 1988—90, dir. compassionate ministries, 1990—; bd. dirs. Mission Am.; dir. Phila. Dist. IMPACT, 1982—89, 2001—; trustee Ea. Nazarene Coll., Wollaston, Mass., 1984—, mem. exec. com., chmn. dept. fin., chmn. bd. dirs., 2002—; mem. clin. faculty U Pa. Sch. Dental Medicine, Med. U. Ukraine, Kiev, Pediat. Med. U., Moscow; mem. Mission Am. Bd., 1997—. Contbr. articles to jours. Bd. dirs. Garden Spot Village Retirement Cmty., 1996—97; interim min. music Fairview Village Ch. of Nazarene, 2001—02; mng. ptnr. CIS Partnership for Ministry, 1998—2002; chmn. bd. trustees Eastern Nazarene Coll., 2002—, mem. found. bd., 2004—. Lt. USPHS, 1982—85. Recipient Alumni Achievement award, Eastern Nazarene Coll., 1996, Citation for Exceptional Achievement, Pa. Ho. Reps., 2004. Master Am. Acad. Gen. Dentistry; mem. ADA (Cert. Recognition for Internat. Svc. in a Fgn. County 1996), Am. Acad. Cosmetic Dentistry, Pa. Dental Assn., Lancaster County Dental Soc. Republican. Home: 1442 Hay Field Dr East Earl PA 17519-9685 Office: 650 E Main St New Holland PA 17557-1410 Office Phone: 717-354-3200. Business E-Mail: info@drdanwest.com. *The greatest joy I have is in serving others through ministry in the church, my dental practice, and especially in my home.*

**WEST, DANIEL JONES, JR.,** health care consultant, educator; b. Coaldale, Pa., Sept. 19, 1949; s. Daniel J. and Mildred Elizabeth (Kreiger) West; m. Linda Jean Werdt, Sep. 18, 1971; children: Jeffrey Bryan, Christopher Jones, Danielle K. BS cum laude, Pa. State U., 1971, EdM summa cum laude, 1972; postgraduate studies, Montgomery Cmty. Coll., 1973, Rutgers U., 1974; PhD summa cum laude in Counseling Psych., Pa. State U., 1982. Adminstr. Good Samaritan Hosp., Pottsville, Pa., 1975-78, asst. v.p. ambulatory svcs., 1978-83; adminstr MEDIQ, Inc. Scranton State Hosp., Pa., 1983-85; pres., CEO HTC Consulting Grp., Inc., Gouldsboro, Pa., 1985-; adj. prof. to asst. prof. Grad. Sch. Health Adminstrn. U. Scranton, 1983-93, chmn., assoc. prof., 1990, chmn., prof. Instr. Pa. State U., Schuylkill Haven, 1973-83, Univ. Park. 1974-75; adj. bd. dirs. Healthcare Mgmt. Forum of Northeastern Pa., 1997—; vice chmn. ABHM cert. com., 1997—; adv. bd., NRCI Hereditary Cancer Prog., 1997—; mem. Cmty. Med. Ctr. CPS planning com., 2000—; bd. mem., Behavioral Health Rsch. Inst., 1998—; mem. N.E. Regional Cancer Inst., edn. and support com., ann. workplan, 2001—; adv. panel, Pa. Med. Soc., 2002—; prof. Wilkes Coll., 1986; CEO Medi-Group, Inc., Penn Health Care, Inc., A.I.R., Inc., Med. Lab., Inc., Lackawanna Med. Grp., P.C., Scranton, 1986-91; stockholder, ptnr. Penn Health Care, Inc., 1987-1990, Health Care Support Svcs., Scranton, 1983-1990; stockholder, bd. dirs. N.E. Women's Diagnostic Ctr., Scranton, 1989-1990; regional dir. ops. HCP Consulting Grp., Inc., Willow Grove, Pa., 1990-95; moderator First Ann. Conf. on Drug and Alcohol Abuse, Bedford, Pa., 1977; mem. adv. com. to rehab. counseling progs. Pa. State U., 1983-93; numerous positions State Bd. of Medicine, Commonwealth of Pa., 1991-95; mem. departmental rev. bd. for rsch. U. Scranton, 1991—; me. Scranton Temple residency prog. instnl. rev. bd. Mercy Hosp., 1991—. mem. Fedn. of State Med. Bd. of US, Inc., 1994-96, mem. editl. adv. bd., 1984-85, voting del. from Pa. for osteopathic bd.; bd. dirs. comm. com. Midwest Regional Med. Bd., 1994-95; mem. task force on health care Econ. Devel. Coun. N.E. Pa., 1994-95; vis. prof. Trnava U., Slovakia, 1997—; assoc. prof., 1998-1999, full prof., 1999—; vis. prof. U. Matej Bel, Slovakia, 1997-1998; bd. dirs. Robert Charles Zaloga Found.; spkr. in field. Author manuals on mgmt. and health care; contbr. articles to profl. jours. Chmn. planning and implementation coun. Schuylkill County Gov.'s Coun. on Drug and Alcohol Abuse, State of Pa., 1973-74; mem. Drug Adv. Task Force, 1973-74, Task Force Child and Family Resource Devel. Prog., Schuylkill County, 1973-74, Criminal Justice Sys. Task Force, Schuylkill County, 1975-76; mem. adv. bd. Holy Family Home Health Care Agcy., Schuylkill County, 1977-78, chmn. bd. edn. com., 1977-78; bd. dirs. St. David's Sch. Schuylkill and Carbon Counties, 1976-79, Health Sys. Agy., N.E. Pa., 1977-80; mem. instnl. rev. bd. Cmty. Med. Ctr., 1986-96; bd. dirs. Scranton Counseling Ctr., 1990—, mem. long range planning com. and pers. com.; bd. dirs. Telespond Sr. Svcs., Inc., 1991-1996; mem. Diocesan health care com. Diocese of Scranton, 1992-93; mem. steering com. Citizen Advocacy Ctr., AARP Health Advocacy Svcs., 1992-95; bd. dirs., v.p. Citizen Advocacy Ctr., Arlington, Va., 1994-95; mem. ad hoc com. on children health United Way, 1995-96. Recipient Rsch. award Am. Ednl. Rsch. Assn., 1983, Svc. and Leadership award Schuylkill County Drug and Alcohol Exec. Commn., 1982, Dedication and Leadership award Gov.'s Coun. Drug and Alcohol Abuse Prog. Adv. Task Force, 1978; Fellow Accrediting Commn. Edn. for Health Svcs. Adminstrn., 1994-95, Regents award, 1997. Fellow Am. Acad. Adminstrs. (editl. com. 1993—, diplomate award 1995), Internat. Acad. Behavioral Medicine, Counseling and Psychotherapy, Inc., Am. Coll. Healthcare Execs. (regents adv. bd. Pa. Area B 1995—, regents award 1997), Fedn. State Med. Bds. US, Inc. (editl. com. 1994-95), Coll. Osteo. Healthcare Execs. (editl. com. 1991-1998), Am. Coll. Med. Practice Execs., Am. Coll. Health Care Adminstr., Assn. Mental Health Adminstrs. (cert., editl. com. 1992—, mem. fellowship rev. com.); mem. APHA, AAAS, AAUP, Nat. Rehab. Assn., Nat. Rehab. Adminstrn. Assn., Am. Hosp. Assn., Med. Grp. Mgmt. Assn., Acad. Memg., Assn. Univ. Progs. in Health Adminstrn., NY Acad. Scis., Nat. Assn. Healthcare Consultants, Am. Soc. Tng. and Devel., Acad. Health Svcs. Rsch. and Health Policy, Strategic Mgmt. Soc., Nat. Coun. Cmty. Behavioral Healthcare, Cmty. Hosp. Med. Edn. Alliance, Hosp. Assn. Pa., Pa. Rehab. Assn., Pa. Med. Grp. Mgmt. Assn., Phi Kappa Phi, Iota Alpha Delta. Office: Dept Health Adminstrn and Human Resources U Scranton 415 McGurrin Hall Scranton PA 18510-4523 E-Mail: westd1@scranton.edu.*

**WEST, DOYLE THOMAS,** retired music educator; b. Smithfield, Utah, May 10, 1932; s. Preston Dangerfield West and Eliza Genevieve Mecham; m. Ardyth Mae Hansen, July 13, 1962; children: MaryLynne Pope, Barbara Ann Livacich, David Hansen, Roger Hansen, Paul Hansen. BS, Utah State U., 1954. Cert. tchr. Utah, Calif. Jr. HS choral music tchr. Tooele Sch. Dist., Utah,

1954—58; asst. Brigham Young U., Provo, Utah, 1961—62; HS choral music tchr. San Lorenzo Unified Sch. Dist., Calif., 1962—92, dist. music chmn., supr.; ret., 1992. Pvt. voice tchr. 1958—2006. Prodr., music dir.: Temple Hill Pageant, 1964—2004, music dir.: annual Handel's Messiah, 1977—2006. Missionary to Cape Town, South Africa LDS Ch., 1958—60. Named Outstanding Tchr. of Yr., San Lorenzo H.S., 1963, Dist. Tchr. of Month, San Lorenzo Unified Sch. Dist., 1992. Mem.: NEA (life), Am. Choral Dirs. Assn. (life), Calif. Music Educator Assn. (life), Choral Music Nat. Assn. (life), Music Educators Nat. Conf. (life). Republican. Mem. Lds Ch. Home: 19535 Eagle St Castro Valley Ca 94546

**WEST, ERIC M.,** mathematician, educator; b. Houston; BA, Bethany Coll., Lindsborg, Kans.; MA, PhD, U. Kans., Lawrence. Asst. prof. math. Benedictine Coll., Atchison, Kans., 2001—. Mem.: Math. Assn. Am., Am. Math. Soc. Avocation: music.

**WEST, GAIL BERRY,** lawyer; b. Cin. d. Theodore Moody and Johnnie Mae (Newton) B.; m. Togo D. West, Jr., June 18, 1966; children: Tiffany Berry, Hilary Carter. BA magna cum laude, Fisk U., 1964; MA, U. Cin., 1965; JD, Howard U., 1968. Bar: D.C. 1969, U.S. Supreme Ct. 1978. Staff atty. IBM, 1969-76; spl. asst. to sec. HUD, 1977-78; staff asst. to spl. asst. to Pres., Washington, 1978-80; dep. asst. sec. for manpower res. affairs installations Dept. Air Force, 1980-81; atty. AT&T, Washington, 1983-84; exec. dir. govt. affairs Bell Comm. Rsch. Inc., Washington, 1985—2003; dir. govt. rels. Armstrong World Industries, Inc., Washington, 1995—2003, cons., 2003—. Mem. exec. com. ARC, Washington, 1974-85; bd. dirs. Family and Child Svcs., Washington, 1974-87; trustee Corcoran Gallery Art, 1983-2000, Arena Stage, 1992-99, Decatur House, 1994—, WETA, 1995-2001, Fisher House Found., Inc.; bd. dirs. Meridian House, 1994-2000; mem. D.C. Commn. Fine Arts, 2003-; mem. cathedral chpt. Nat. Cathedral; bd. dirs. Nat. Mus. of Am. History, Smithsonian, 2005-. Ford Found. fellow, 1965-68. Mem. ABA, D.C. Bar Assn., Unified Bar D.C. Democrat. Episcopalian. Home: 4934 Rockwood Pkwy NW Washington DC 20016-3211

**WEST, GEOFFREY B.,** theoretical physicist, physics professor; b. England; BA in Physics, Cambridge U., 1961; PhD in Physics, Stanford U., 1966. Faculty Stanford U., 1970; high energy particle physics grp. leader Los Alamos Nat. Lab., N.Mex., 1974, high energy physicist, 1982—; prof. biology U. N.Mex, Albuquerque, 1999—; disting. prof. Santa Fe Inst., 2003—, pres., 2005—. Sr. lab. fellow Los Alamos Nat. Lab., 2003. Named one of 100 Most Influential People, Time Mag., 2006. Fellow: Am. Phys. Soc. Office: Los Alamos Nat Lab PO Box 1663 Los Alamos NM 87545*

**WEST, GLENN D.,** lawyer; b. Mineral Wells, Tex., Jan. 29, 1953; BA, Tarleton State U., 1975; JD, Tex. Tech U., 1978. Bar: Tex. 1978, NY, DC, England, Wales. Mng. ptnr. corp. acquisitions Weil, Gotshal & Manges LLP, Dallas, mem. mgmt. com. Articles and topics editor Tex. Tech Law Rev., 1978. Mem. State Bar Tex., Order of Coif, Phi Delta Phi. Office: Weil Gotshal & Menges LLP 200 Crescent Ct Ste 300 Dallas TX 75201 Office Phone: 214-746-7780. Office Fax: 214-746-7777. Business E-Mail: gdwest@weil.com.

**WEST, GREGORY ALAN,** physician; b. Houston, Aug. 1, 1950; s. Wayne Garland and Frankie Onalita (Russell) W.; m. Catherine Ann Sharp, June 18, 1976 (div. Oct. 1980); 1 child, Benjamin M.; m. Linda French Lucas, Apr. 13, 1985 (div. 1994); children: Robert, Scott; m. Cynthia Lee Swainston, Apr. 30, 1997. BA, Austin Coll., 1972; PhD, U. Louisville, 1980, MD, 1982; MDiv, Louisville Presbyn. Theol. Sem., 1981. Diplomate Am. Bd. Pediat., 1987, Am. Bd. Emergency Medicine, 1990, 99, with additional cert. in pediat. emergency medicine, 1997. EMT Louisville Emergency Med. Svc., 1977-79; intern in pediatrics U. Louisville Affiliated Hosps., 1982-83, resident in pediatrics, 1983-85; staff physician emergency dept. St. Anthony Hosp., Louisville, 1985-86, King's Daus. Hosp., Madison, Ind., 1985-95, med. dir. emergency med. svcs., 1989-91; staff physician emergency dept. Tri-County Cmty. Hosp., La Grange, Ky., 1991-92, Hardin County Meml. Hosp., Elizabethtown, Ky., 1995-99, Harrison County Hosp., Corydon, Ind., 2000—03, Russell Co. Hosp., Ky., 2003—05, Ohio County Hosp. Hartford, Ky., 2005—. Contbr. articles to profl. jours. Recipient pediatric radiology award and chmn.'s achievement award U. Louisville Affiliated Hosps. Fellow Am. Acad. Emergency Medicine, Am. Acad. Pediatrics; mem. Omicron Delta Kappa. Episcopalian. Avocations: tae kwon do karate, scuba diving, travel.

**WEST, JAMES C., JR.,** lawyer; b. White Sulphur Springs, W.Va., Mar. 15, 1932; LLB, W.Va. U., 1959. Law clk. to. Hon. Herbert S. Boreman, Judge of 4th Cir. Ct. Appeals, 1958—59; atty. Clifford, Jones & Williams, Clarksburg, W.Va., 1960—89, West & Jones (formerly Clifford, Jones & Williams), Clarksburg, W.Va., 1989—. Fellow: Am. Bd. Trial Advs., Am. Coll. Trial Lawyers; mem.: ABA, W. Va. Bar Assn. (pres. 2003), Assn. Trial Lawyers Am., W.Va. Trial Lawyers Assn. (pres. 1971), Harrison County Bar Assn., W.Va. State Bar (bd. govs. 1975 1978), Phi Delta Phi. Office: West and Jones PO Box 2348 360 Washington Ave Clarksburg WV 26301

**WEST, JAMES HAROLD,** finance company executive; b. San Diego, Oct. 11, 1926; s. Robert Reed and Clara Leona (Moses) W.; m. Norma Jean, 1953 (div.); 1 son, Timothy James; m. Jerel Lynn Smith, Nov. 16, 1976; 1 child, James Nelson. BS, U. So. Calif., 1949. CPA, Calif. Ptnr. McCracken & Co., San Diego, 1950-61; mgr. Ernst & Ernst, San Diego, 1961-64; ptnr. West Turnquist & Schmitt, San Diego, 1964—97, West, Rhode & Roberts, 1997—. Bd. govs. ARC, Washington, 1981-87; pres., bd. dirs. Combined Arts and Edn. Coun., San Diego, 1980-83; pres. Francis Parker Sch., 1988-90; bd. dirs. San Diego Hosp. Assn., 1981-95, 97—, San Diegans Inc., 1989-92, Mus. Photographic Arts, 1990-92; trustee Calif. Western Sch. Law, 1985-2004; mem. bd. advisors U. So. Calif. Sch. Acctg., 1985-97; treas. San Diego Nat. Sports Tng. Found., 1988-92; mem. acctg. exec. bd. U. San Diego, 1992—. With AUS, 1945-46, PTO. Mem. AICPAs, Calif. Soc. CPAs (bd. dirs. 1963-64), Univ. Club (San Diego), Capital Hill Club (Washington), Masons. Republican. Home: 3311 Lucinda St San Diego CA 92106-2931 also: 3104 4th Ave San Diego CA 92163-5803 Personal E-mail: westcphs@aol.com.

**WEST, JAMES JOSEPH,** lawyer; b. Tarentum, Pa., Nov. 26, 1945; s. Samuel Elwood and Rose (McIntyre) W.; m. Kathleen Geslak, Aug. 19, 1967; children: Joseph Allen, Yvonne Michelle, KaiLynn Ann. BS in Econs., St. Vincent Coll., 1967; JD, Duquesne U., 1970. Bar: Pa. 1971, U.S. Dist. Ct. (we. dist.) Pa. 1971, U.S. Ct. Appeals (3d cir.) 1971, U.S. Dist. Ct. (mid. dist.) Pa., 1980. Law clk. to presiding justice US Dist. Ct., Pa., 1970-74; asst. U.S. atty. chief appellate sect. U.S. Atty.'s Office, Pitts., 1974-79; dep. dir. criminal law Pa. Atty. Gen.'s Office, Harrisburg, 1979-82; 1st asst. U.S. atty. US Dist. Ct. (mid. dist.) Pa., Harrisburg, 1982-84, U.S. atty., 1984-93; assoc Sprague & Sprague, Phila., 1993-95; pvt. practice Harrisburg, Pa., 1995—. Mem. Nat. Environ. Enforcement Coun. Recipient Outstanding Performance award U.S. Dept. Justice, 1974-78, Commendation Gov. of Pa., 1981. Mem. Pa. Bar Assn., Allegheny County Bar Assn., Dauphin County Bar Assn. Republican. Roman Catholic. Home: 1222 Cardinal Way Rd Hummelstown PA 17036-8548 Office: James West 105 N Front St Harrisburg PA 17101-1483 Office Phone: 717-233-5051. Personal E-mail: jwestlaw@aol.com. Business E-Mail: jwest@jwestlaw.com.

**WEST, JASON BROSSARD,** education educator, consultant; b. Salt Lake City, Utah; PhD, U. Ga., 2002. Postdoctoral fellow U. Minn., St. Paul, 2002—04; rsch. assoc. U. Utah, 2004—05, rsch. assoc. prof., 2006—. Sci. and tech. cons., Salt Lake City, 2005—. Postdoctoral fellowship, U. Minn., 2002—04, grant, NSF, 2000—02, Dissertation completion award, U. Ga., 2000—01. Mem.: AAAS, Ecol. Soc. of Am., Am. Geophys. Union. Office: Dept of Biology U of Utah 257 South 1400 East Salt Lake City UT 84112 Office Phone: 801-581-6517.

**WEST, JERRY ALAN,** professional basketball team executive; b. Chelyan, W.Va., May 28, 1938; s. Howard Stewart and Cecil Sue (Creasey) West; m. Martha Jane Kane, May 1960 (div. 1977); children: David, Michael, Mark; m.

Karen Christine Bua, May 28, 1978; 1 child, Ryan. BS, W.Va. U., 1960; LHD (hon.), W.Va. Wesleyan Coll., W. Va. U., 2006. Mem. L.A. Lakers, NBA, 1960—74, coach, 1976—79, spl. cons., 1979—82, gen. mgr., 1982—94, exec. v.p. basketball ops., 1994—2000; pres. basketball ops. Memphis Grizzlies, 2002—; mem. first team Nat. Basketball Assn. All-Star Team, 1962—67, mem. second team, 1968—69. Mem. NBA champion L.A. Lakers, 1972. Author (with William Libby): Mr. Clutch: The Jerry West Story, 1969. Named capt., U.S. Olympic Basketball Team, 1960, Most Valuable Player NBA Playoff, 1969, All-Star Game Most Valuable Player, 1972, NBA Exec. of Yr., Sporting News, 1994—95, NBA Exec. of the Year, 1995, 2004; named to Naismith Meml. Basketball Hall of Fame, 1979, NBA Hall of Fame, 1980, NBA 35th Anniversary All-Time Team, 1980. Office: Memphis Grizzlies 191 Beale St Memphis TN 38103-3715

**WEST, JESSE MICHAEL,** pediatric neuropsychologist; b. Anderson, SC, Nov. 30, 1961; s. Ernest Calvin and Patricia (Byrd) West. BA, Clemson U., 1984; PhD, U. Oslo, Norway, 1994. Neuropsychologist Sunnaus Hosp., Oslo, 1994—96, Carolinas Hosp. Sys., Florence, SC, 1996—2000, U. SC, Florence, 2000—02; neuropsychologist, clin. instr. Med. U. of SC, Florence, 2002—05; neuropsychologist Carolina Neurobehavioral Assn., Florence, 2000—05. Medicaid adv. bd. Dept. of Health, State of SC, Columbia, SC, 2002—03; psychological cons. Lighthouse Care Ctrs., Conway, SC, 2002—05. Contbr. articles European Jour. of Pediat.Surgery. Mem. City Coun., Hoyre Party, Oslo, 1996. Mem.: SC Psychological Assn., Am. Psychological Assn. Office: Carolina Neurobehavioral Assoc 1504 Heritage Ln Florence SC 29505 Office Phone: 843-413-0303. Office Fax: 843-413-0340. E-mail: westbyrd@aol.com.

**WEST, JOHN BURNARD,** physiologist, educator; b. Adelaide, Australia, Dec. 27, 1928; came to U.S., 1969; s. Esmond Frank and Meta Pauline (Spehr) W.; m. Penelope Hall Banks, Oct. 28, 1967; children: Robert Burnard, Joanna Ruth. MB, BChir, Adelaide U., 1951, MD, 1958, DSc, 1980; PhD, London U., 1960; DSc (hon.), U. Barcelona, Spain, 1987, U. Ferrara, Italy, 2004; U. Athens, 2006. Resident Royal Adelaide Hosp., 1952, Hammersmith Hosp., London, 1953-55; physiologist Sir Edmund Hillary's Himalayan Expdn., 1960-61; dir. respiratory rsch. group Postgrad. Med. Sch., London, 1962-67, reader medicine, 1968; prof. medicine and physiology U. Calif., San Diego, 1969—. Leader Am. Med. Rsch. Expdn. to Mt. Everest, 1981; U.S. organizer China-U.S. Conf. on respiratory failure, Nanjing, 1986; mem. life scis. adv. com. NASA, 1985-88, task force sci. uses of space sta., 1984-87, aerospace med. adv. com., 1988-89, chmn. sci. verification com. Spacelab SLS-1, 1983-92, commn. on respiratory physiol. Internat. Union Physiol. Scis., 1985—, commn. on clin. physiol., 1991—, commn. gravitation physiol., 1986—, study sect. NIH, chmn., 1973-75; prin. investigator Spacelabs SLS 1, 2, LMS, Neurolab, 1983—; co-investigator European Spacelabs, D2, Euromir, 1987—; external examiner Nat. U. Singpore, 1995; Wiltshire lectr., London, 1971, Schwidetzky lectr., 1975, Fleischner lectr., 1977, Robertson lectr. Adelaide U., 1978, I.J. Flance lectr. Washington U., 1978, W.A. Smith lectr. Med. Coll. SC, 1982, S. Kronheim lectr. Undersea Med. Soc., 1984, McClement lectr. NYU, 1996. Author: Ventilation/Blood Flow and Gas Exchange, 1965, Respiratory Physiology-The Essentials, 1974, Translations in Respiratory Physiology, 1975, Pulmonary Pathophysiology-The Essentials, 1977, Translations in Respiratory Physiology, 1977, Bioengineering Aspects of the Lung, 1977, Regional Differences in the Lung, 1977, Pulmonary Gas Exchange (2 vols.), 1980, High Altitude Physiology, 1981, High Altitude and Man, 1984, Everest-The Testing Place, 1985, Best and Taylor's Physiological Basis of Medical Practice, 1985, 91, Study Guide for Best and Taylor, 1985, High Altitude Medicine and Physiology, 1989, The Lung: Scientific Foundations, 1991, 2d edit., 1997, Lung Injury, 1992, Respiratory Physiology: People and Ideas, 1996, High Life: A History of High Altitude Physiology and Medicine, 1998; founder, editor-in-chief High Altitude Medicine and Biology, 2000-. Recipient Ernest Jung prize for medicine, Hamburg, 1977, Presdl. citation Am. Coll. Chest Physicians, 1977, Kaiser Tchg. award 1980; scholar Macy Found., 1974; Jeffries Med. Rsch. award AIAA, 1992. Fellow Royal Coll. Physicians (London), Royal Australasian Coll. Physicians, Royal Geog. Soc. (London), AAAS (med. sci. nominating com. 1987-93, coun. del. sect. med. scis.), Am. Inst. for Med. and Biol. Engring. (founding fellow 1992), Am. Heart Assn. (G.C. Griffith lectr. 1978, D.W. Richards lectr. 1980), Internat. Soc. for Mountain Medicine (pres. 1991-94), Am. Acad. Arts and Scis.; mem. NAS (com. space biology and medicine 1986-90, subcom. on space biology 1984-85, com. advanced space tech. 1992-94, panel on small spacecraft tech. 1994), Am. Assn. Thoracic Surgery (hon.), Nat. Bd. Med. Examiners (physiology test com. 1973-76), Am. Physiol. Soc. (pres. 1984-85, coun. 1981-86, chmn. sect. on history of physiology 1984-92, hist. pubs. adv. com., Reynolds prize for history 1987, Ray Daggs award 1998, Guyton Tchg. award 2002, Julius H. Comroe lectr. 2003), Inst. of Medicine of NAS, Am. Soc. Clin. Investigation, Physiol. Soc. Gt. Britain, Am. Thoracic Soc. (Edward Livingston Trudeau medal 2002), Assn. Am. Physicians, Western Assn. Physicians, Russian Acad. Sci. (elected fgn. mem.), Explorers Club, Fleischner Soc. (pres. 1985), Harveian Soc. (London), Royal Instn. Gt. Britain, Royal Soc. Medicine (London), Hurlingham Club (London), La Jolla Beach & Tennis Club. Home: 9626 Blackgold Rd La Jolla CA 92037-1110 Office: U Calif San Diego Sch Medicine 0623 Dept Medicine La Jolla CA 92093 Business E-Mail: jwest@ucsd.edu.

**WEST, JOHN THOMAS,** retired surgeon; b. Live Oak, Fla., June 23, 1924; s. James Whitaker and Lelah Eulalia (Moore) W.; m. Ruth Marita Blakely, June 18, 1948; children: Phyllis Ann, Rebecca Ruth, James Carl, Jeffrey Moore, Paul Blakely. BS, U. Mich., 1946; MD, Vanderbilt U., 1951. Diplomate Am. Bd. Surgery. Commd. officer USPHS, 1951, advanced through grades to capt., 1963; rotating intern USPHS Hosp., Seattle, 1951—52; chief surgery USPHS Alaska Native Hosp., Anchorage, 1957—60, resident gen. surgery. 1954—57; chief surgery USPHS Hosp., Seattle, 1963—69, USPHS Indian Hosp., Phoenix, 1969—71; sr. investigator surg. br. Nat. Cancer Inst. USPHS, Bethesda, Md., 1960—63, ret. Nat. Cancer Inst., 1971; clin. asst. prof. U. Wash., Seattle, 1964—68; clin. assoc. prof. Tex. Tech U., Lubbock, 1974—77; pvt. practice La Grange, Ga., 1971—74, 1977—94; ret., 1994. Mem. active staff West Ga. Med. Ctr., La Grange, 1971-74, 77-94. Bd. dirs. Ga. divsn. Am. Cancer Soc., 1972-77, 77-92. Recipient Meritorious Svc. medal USPHS, 1968. Fellow ACS, Soc. Surg. Oncology. Presbyterian. Achievements include report of facilitation of major hepatic resection by an innovation in the surgical exposure of the liver. Home: 134 Hickory Ln Lagrange GA 30240-8622 Personal E-mail: rvtom@mindspring.com.

**WEST, JOSEPH D.,** lawyer; b. Ashland, Pa., Apr. 18, 1949; BCE, Villanova U., 1971; JD, George Washington U., 1977. Bar: Va. 1977, D.C. 1977. Sr. ptnr. Arnold & Porter, Washington, 1993—. Mem. Order of Coif. Office: Arnold & Porter 555 12th St NW Washington DC 20004-1206 E-mail: Joseph_West@aporter.com.

**WEST, KANYE,** rap artist; b. Atlanta; s. Ray and Donda West. Founder G.O.O.D. (Getting Out Our Dreams) Music, 2004—. Prodr.: songs for various artists including Jay Z, Ludacris and Alicia Keys; singer: (albums) The College Dropout, 2004 (Grammy award for Best Rap Album, 2005), Late Registration, 2005 (Grammy award for Best Rap Album, 2006), (songs) Jesus Walks, 2004 (Best Male Video, MTV Video Music awards, 2005), Grammy award for Best Rap Song, 2005), Diamonds from Sierra Leone, 2005 (Grammy award for Best Rap Song, 2006), Gold Digger, 2005 (Grammy award for Best Rap Solo Performance, 2006, Soul Train Music award for Best Rap Video, 2006, 2 BET award for Best Duet & Video of Yr., 2006); composer (for Alicia Keys) You Don't Know My Name, 2003 (Grammy award for Best R&B Song, 2005). Named Male New Artist of Yr., Billboard Music Awards, 2004, Best New R&B/Hip-Hop Artist of Yr., 2004, R&B/Hip-Hop Prodr. of Yr., 2004, Rap Artist of Yr., 2004; named one of Time Mag. 100 Most Influential People, 2005, The 10 Most Fascinating People of 2005, Barbara Walters Special; recipient Artist Achievement award, Billboard Music Awards, 2005, Vibe award, best rapper, 2005, 3 Grammy Awards, 2005, Image award for Outstanding New Artist, NAACP, 2005, 3 Grammy

Awards, 2006, Best Hip Hop Entertainer, Internat. Reggae & World Music Awards, 2006. Office: Roc A Fella Records 825 8th Ave 19th Floor New York NY 10019-7416 also: GOOD Music 550 Madison Ave New York NY 10022*

**WEST, KARRIE L.,** school psychologist; d. Craig A. West and Mary A. d'Avignon. BA with honors, Calif. State U., 1998; MA, Gallaudet U., 1999, PsyS, 2001. Sch. psychologist Kings County Office Edn., Harford, Calif., 2001—02, Padaro Valley Unified Sch. Dist., Watsonville, Calif., 2002—. Mem.: Nat. Assn. Sch. Psychologists, Golden Key. Avocation: Am. sign language. Office: 294 Green Valley Rd Watsonville CA 95076 Office Phone: 831-786-2130.

**WEST, KEITH,** physicist; b. Jackson, Miss., Dec. 16, 1966; s. Charles and Charlene West; m. Kathy Little, Dec. 16, 2000; 1 adopted child, Sergey. PhD, U. Tex. at Dallas, Richardson, Tex., 1996. Head, phys. scis. program Yavneh Acad. Dallas, 1996—98; vis. asst. prof. physics Angelo State U., 1998—99; asst. prof. physics Tex. A&M U., Commerce, 1999—. Deacon 1st Bapt. Ch., Commerce, 2003—. Grantee, Tex. Space Grant Consortium, 2005—06. Avocations: writing, Aikido, bicycling. Office: Texas A&M Univ Commerce Dept Physics Commerce TX 75429 Office Phone: 903-886-5488.

**WEST, KENNETH IRWIN,** automotive executive; b. Aza Kuwae, Okinawa, Japan, July 1, 1966; (parents Am. citizens); s. Jackie Eugene and Ritsuko Maki West. Diploma in small engine repair, Foley-Belsaw Inst., Kansas City, Mo., 1983; A in Bus. and Auto/Diesel Tech., U. Northwestern Ohio, 1985; diploma in computer repair, Internat. Corr. Sch., 1991. Cert. automotive svc. excellence Bur. Automotive Repair. Gen. mgr. Great Bear Auto Ctr., Huntington Beach, Calif., 1987—. Avocations: building models, computer programming, computer graphics, multiplayer online gaming, building high performance street cars.

**WEST, LEE ROY,** federal judge; b. Clayton, Okla., Nov. 26, 1929; s. Calvin and Nicie (Hill) W.; m. MaryAnn Ellis, Aug. 29, 1952; children: Kimberly Ellis, Jennifer Lee. BA, U. Okla., 1952, JD, 1956; LL.M. (Ford Found. fellow), Harvard U., 1963. Bar: Okla. 1956. Individual practice law, Ada, Okla., 1956-61, 63-65; faculty U. Okla. Coll. Law, 1961-62; Ford Found. fellow in law teaching Harvard U., Cambridge, Mass., 1962-63; judge 22d Jud. Dist. Okla., Ada, 1965-73; mem. CAB, Washington, 1973-78, acting chmn., 1977; practice law Tulsa, 1978-79; spl. justice Okla. Supreme Ct., 1965; judge U.S. Dist Ct. (we. dist.) Okla., 1979-94; sr. judge U.S. Dist. Ct. (we. dist.), Okla., 1994—. Editor: Okla. Law Rev. Served to capt. USMC, 1952-54. Named to Field Trial Hall of Fame, 2005; recipient Humanitarian award Nat. Conf. Cmty. and Justice, 2000, Jud. Excellence award Okla. Bar Assn., 2000, E.T. Dunlap medal and Lectureship award, 2006, Constn. Day award Rogers State U., 2006. Mem. U. Okla. Alumni Assn. (dir.), Phi Delta Phi (pres. 1956), Phi Eta Sigma, Order of Coif. Home: 6500 E Danforth Rd Edmond OK 73034-7601 Office: US Dist Ct 3001 US Courthouse 200 NW 4th St Oklahoma City OK 73102-3027 Office Phone: 405-609-5140.

**WEST, MACDONALD,** real estate executive; b. Bournemouth, Eng., July 15, 1943; arrived in U.S., 1968; s. Joseph Stanley and Maisie Siswick W.; m. Charlotte Denise Duvall, Nov. 1, 1980. Diploma, London U. Coll. Estate Mgmt., 1968; MBA, Columbia U., 1970. Trainee surveyor Navy Works Dept., Admiralty, London, 1960—64; sr. assoc. Robinson & Roods, London, 1965—68; dir. cost control Nat. Liberty Corp., Valley Forge, Pa., 1970—71; v.p., dir. Philipsborn Cos., Coral Gables, Fla., 1972—76, Allen Morris Co., Miami, Fla., 1976—89; sr. v.p., COO Allen Morris Constrn. Co., 1978—89, also sr. v.p. asset mgmt. divsn.; pres. Miami Lakes Devel., Inc., Fla., 1989—91; exec. v.p. Graham Cos., Miami Lakes, 1989—91; pres., CEO Macdonald West Co., Miami, 1991—; mng. dir. Allen Morris Co., 2000—02. Deacon U. Bapt. Ch., Coral Gables, 1977—. Fellow Royal Instn. Chartered Surveyors; mem. Counselors Real Estate (pres. 1995), Nat. Assn. Realtors, Am. Arbitration Assn., Realtors Comml. Alliance (chair 2000, 2004-2006), Nat. Assn. Indsl. and Office Parks, Indsl. Assn. Dade County, Realtors Comml. Alliance Greater Miami (pres. 2000), Builders Assn. South Fla. (pres. 1996), Nat. Assn. Home Builders, Ocean Reef Club, Rotary (Miami). Republican. Home: 5325 Orduna Dr Coral Gables FL 33146-2640 Office: 1172 S Dixie Hwy Ste 600 Miami FL 33146-2918 Office Phone: 305-667-2100.

**WEST, MARC,** information technology executive; B in Computer sci., Univ. of Md.; M in Human Resource Mgmt., Golden State Univ., San Francisco. Various positions Quick & Reilly, Move.com, Oracle and Mobil Oil; sr. v.p. and global chief info. officer Electronic Arts, Redwood City, Calif., 2000—04; sr. v.p. & chief info. officer H&R Block, Kansas City, Mo., 2004—. Named one of Premier 100 IT Leaders, Computerworld, 2006. Office: SVP & CIO H&R Block Inc 4400 Main St Kansas City MO 64111*

**WEST, MARK D.,** law educator; BA magna cum laude, Rhodes Coll.; JD with honors, Columbia U. Law clk. for Hon. Eugene H. Nickerson US Dist. Ct. (ea. dist.) NY; atty. Paul, Weiss, Rifkind, Wharton & Garrison, NYC; Nippon Life Prof. Law, dir. Japanese Legal Studies Prog. & Ctr. for Internat. and Comparative Law U. Mich. Law Sch., Ann Arbor. Tchr. U. Toyko, Kyoto U. Fulbright Rsch. Scholar, Abe Fellow. Fellow: Japan Soc. for Promotion of Sci. Office: U Mich Law Sch 935 Legal Research 625 S State St Ann Arbor MI 48109-1215 Office Phone: 734-647-4041. Office Fax: 734-763-8309. E-mail: markwest@umich.edu.

**WEST, MARK OTTO,** psychology professor; b. Omaha, Nebr., Jan. 16, 1948; s. Otto Cornelius and Cathryn Ann West; m. Carol Anne Christian, Aug. 12, 1984; children: Tivoli Anne, Heidi Cathryn, Whitney Caroline, Dane Mark, Skye Shannon, Dallas Kristin, Robert Edward. BS, U. of Calif., 1976; PhD, Wake Forest U., 1982. Postdoctoral rsch. assoc. U. of Tex. Southwestern Med. Sch., Dallas, 1982—86; prof. of psychology Rutgers U., New Brunswick, NJ, 1986—. Ad hoc reviewer NIH, Bethesda, Md., 1990 . Contbr. rsch. articles to sci. jours.; edtl. reviewer: manuscripts for jours. With U.S. Army, 1968—69, Vietnam. Grantee, NSF, 1987—90, Nat. Inst. on Drug Abuse, 1987—92, 1990—93, 1992—97, 1993—97, 1997—2001, 2001—05. Mem.: Soc. for Neurosci. Achievements include discovery of functional reorganization of brain connections in basal ganglia in Parkinson's disease; First described somatotopic arrangement (functional organization) of the striatum in the basal ganglia of the rat brain; discovery of electrical activity in rat hippocampus correlated with updating (working) memory and activity in mesolimbic dopamine system correlated with relapse to cocaine abuse. Avocations: running, swimming, bicycling. Office: Rutgers U Busch Campus 152 Frelinghuysen Rd Piscataway NJ 08854 Business E-Mail: markwest@rci.rutgers.edu.

**WEST, MICHAEL ALAN,** retired hospital administrator; b. Waseca, Minn., Aug. 4, 1938; s. Ralph Leland and Elizabeth Mary (Brann) W.; m. Mary Thissen, Jan. 21, 1961; children: Anne, Nancy, Douglas. BA, U. Minn., 1961, MHA, 1963. Sales corr. Physicians and Hosps. Supply Co., Mpls., 1959-60; adminstrv. resident R.I. Hosp., Providence, 1962-63, adminstrv. asst., 1963-65, asst. dir., 1965-68; exec. asst. dir. Med. Center U. Mo., Columbia, 1968-70, assoc. dir., 1970-74, asst. prof. community health and med. practice, 1968-74; v.p. for adminstrn. Luth. Gen. Hosp., Park Ridge, Ill., 1974-80, exec. v.p., 1980-84; pres., CEO Akron Gen. Med. Ctr., Ohio, 1984-97, Akron Gen. Health Sys., 1997—2002. Bd. dirs. Vol. Hosps. Am. Inc.; chair VHA-Ctrl., Inc. Bd. dirs. Great Trails Coun. Boy Scouts Am. Mem. Am. Coll. Healthcare Execs., Akron Regional Hosp. Assn. (chmn.), Portage Country Club, Akron City Club, Catawba Island Club, Noreaster Club. Home: 495 Woodbury Dr Akron OH 44333-2780

**WEST, MICHAEL D.,** cloning and stem cell research company executive; BS, Rensselaer Polytechnic Inst., 1976; MS in Biology, Andrew U., 1982; PhD, Baylor Coll. Medicine, 1989. Organized and managed rsch. between Geron and academic collaborators James Thomson and John Gearhart that led to the first isolation of human embryonic stem and human embryonic germ cells, 1995—98; founder, dir., v.p. Gernon Corp., Menlo Park, Calif.,

1990—98; CEO Advanced Cell Tech., Inc., Worcester, Mass., 1998—2005, chmn., 1998—, pres., chief scientific officer, 2005—. Adj. prof., bioengineering U. Calif. Berkeley. Extensive academic and business experience in age-related degenerative disease, telomerase molecular biology, and human embryonic stem cells research and development. Office: Advanced Cell Technology Inc 381 Plantation St Biotech V Worcester MA 01605 also: Advanced Cell Technology Inc 1201 Harbor Bay Pkwy Ste 120 Alameda CA 94502 Office Phone: 508-756-1212. Office Fax: 508-756-4468.*

**WEST, MICHAEL G.,** electric power industry executive; BS in Electronic Engring.; BS in Math., Oreg. State U.; MSEE, U. Ill. Integrated cir. designer Floating Point Sys., 1982—86; integrated cir. design engr. Bipolar Integrated Tech., 1986—87; chief scientist, sr. engr. In Focus Sys., 1988—96; co-founder, v.p. tech. Pixelworks, Inc., Tualatin, Oreg., 1997—, fellow, 2003—. Office: Pixelworks Inc Ste 300 8100 SW Nyberg Rd Tualatin OR 97062

**WEST, MILDRED MARIE,** art educator; b. Mill Creek, Okla., July 7, 1934; d. Minor Hubert and Audrey Eunice (Baker) Hughes; m. Joe Dean West, Dec. 18, 1954; children: Michael, Jared, Adam; stepchildren: Sue, Carla. BS Home Econs., East Ctrl. U., Ada, Okla., 1982. Cert. K-12 art edn., Okla., 6-12 home econs., Okla. Presenter in field of art edn. Columnist Ada Evening News, 1987-92; paintings exhibited Legis. Art Show, Oklahoma City, 1984-92. Chair women's com. Farm Bur., 2002—; chmn. Farm Bur. Womens Commn., 2005—06, v.p.; past pres. Ada Artists, Allied Arts. Mem. AAUW (past pres.), Ada Artists Assn. (art show com.), Allied Arts Tanti Study Club (past pres.), Magic Brush Art Guild, Holdenville Soc. Painters and Sculptors, Beta Sigma Phi. Democrat. Member Church of Christ. Avocations: walking, aerobics, gourmet cooking, travel. Studio: 6121 County Rd 3610 Ada OK 74820-2149

**WEST, NATALIE ELSA,** lawyer; b. Greenwich, Conn., Mar. 11, 1947; AB, Smith Coll., 1968; JD, U. Calif., Berkeley, 1973. Bar: Calif. 1974. Counsel Calif. Fair Polit. Practices Commn., Sacramento, 1975-79; city atty. City of Berkeley, Calif., 1980-85, City of Novato, Calif., 1985-92, City of Brentwood, Calif., 1994-99; gen. counsel Livermore-Amador Valley Water Mgmt. Agy., 1996—2001; shareholder McDonough, Holland & Allen, Oakland, Calif., 1991—. Lectr. law U. Calif., Berkeley, 2000-01. Pres. city attys. dept. League of Calif. Cities, 1986-87, bd. dirs., 1995-97. Mem. State Bar Calif., Alameda County Bar Assn.

**WEST, NORMAN ELLSWORTH,** artist; b. Exeter, N.H., May 16, 1952; s. Norman Ellsworth and Alice Marie West. BS, Plymouth State Coll., 1976; BFA, Maine Coll. of Art, 1980. Leader color workshops regional schs.; York County, 1981—; artist in residence Holmes Acad., Plymouth, N.H., 1989-91; set designer Shenanigans Prodns., Portland, Boston, 1993-96; tchr. Heartwood Coll. of Art, Kennebunk, Maine, 1994—. Dir. Heartwood Coll. Art Gallery, 2002. One person shows include West Kuhn Gallery, Cape Neddick, Maine, 1988, Van Ward Gallery, Ogunquit, Maine, 1994, 98; group shows include Currier Gallery, Manchester, N.H., 1988, 89, Barn Gallery, Ogunquit, 1988, Mast Core Galleries, Kennebunkport, Maine, 1988, 89, Ogunquit Art Assn., 1988—, Maine Coast Artists, Rockport, Maine, 1989, 90. Bd. dirs. Shellfish Commn., Ogunquit, Maine, 1996—; clam warden Town of Ogunquit, 1997-99. Mem. Ogunquit Art Assn. (curator invited sculptor's exhibit 1996—), Ogunquit Arts Collaborative (v.p. 2000—), Ogunquit Rotary Club. Home: PO Box 1560 Ogunquit ME 03907

**WEST, PAUL NODEN,** writer, playwright; b. Eckington, Derbyshire, Eng., Feb. 23, 1930; arrived in US, 1961, naturalized, 1971; s. Alfred Massick and Mildred (Noden) W. Student, Oxford U., 1950-53; MA, Columbia U., 1953. Asst. prof. English Meml. U. Nfld., Canada, 1957-58, assoc. prof., 1958-60; faculty Pa. State U., Pa., 1962-95, prof. English and comparative lit. Pa., 1968-95; prof. emeritus, 1995—. Crawshaw prof. Colgate U., 1972; Melvin Hill disting. vis. prof. Hobart and William Smith Coll., 1973; vis. English prof. Cornell U., 1986; disting. writer in residence Wichita State U., 1982; vis. prof. English Brown U., 1992; fiction judge Creative Artists Pub. Svc. Program, NYC, 1974, 81; writer-in-residence U Ariz., 1984; judge Katherine Ann Porter Prize for Fiction, 1984, Artists Found. Author: Byron and the Spoiler's Art, 1960, rev. edit., 1990, I Said the Sparrow, 1963, The Snow Leopard, 1965, Tenement of Clay, 1965, The Wine of Absurdity, 1966, Alley Jaggers, 1967, libretta for opera, 1968, I'm Expecting to Live Quite Soon, 1970, Words for a Deaf Daughter, 1970, Caliban's Filibuster, 1972, Colonel Mint, 1973, Gala, 1976, The Very Rich Hours of Count von Stauffenberg, 1980, Out of My Depths: A Swimmer in the Universe, 1983, Rat Man of Paris, 1986, theatrical version, 1987, Sheer Fiction, 1987, The Universe and Other Fiction, 1988, The Place in Flowers Where Pollen Rests, 1988, Lord Byron's Doctor, 1989, Portable People, The Women of Whitechapel and Jack the Ripper, 1991, Sheer Fiction: II, 1991, James Ensor, 1991, Love's Mansion, 1992, Tenement of Clay, 2d edit., 1993, Sheer Fiction, III, 1994, A Stroke of Genius, 1995, The Tent of Orange Mist, 1995 (memoir) My Mother's Music, 1996, My Father's War, 2005; (novel) Sporting with Amaryllis, 1996, Terrestrials, 1997, Life With Swan, 1999, O.K.: The Corral, The Earps, and Doc Holliday, 2000, The Dry Danube: A Hitler Forgery, 2000, The Secret Lives of Words, 2000, A Fifth of November, 2001, Master Class, 2001, Oxford Days, 2002, Cheops: A Cupboard for the Sun, 2002, (play) Any Old How, 2002, (radio play) The Sacrifice, 1955, The Immensity of the Here and Now, 2003, Sheer Fiction IV, 2004, Samuel Beckett: Born Astride A Grave, 2004, My Father's War, 2005, Tea with Osiris, 2005; contbr. Washington Post and NY Times, 1962—, Harper's Mag., Paris Rev., Yale Rev., Parnassus, Agni, Conjunctions, War, Literature and the Arts, First Intensity, Tin Roof; translator Les Romanesques by Rostand, 1954 fiction judge NY Found. for the Arts, Nat. Book award, 1990. Served RAF, 1954—57. Decorated chevalier de l'Ordre des Arts et des Lettres (France); recipient Aga Khan Fiction prize, 1973, Hazlett Meml. award for Excellence in Arts (lit.), 1981, Lit. award Am. Acad. and Inst. Arts and Letters, 1985, Pushcart prize 1987, 91, 2003, The Best Am. Essays award 1990, Outstanding Achievement medal Pa. State U., 1991, Grand Prix Halperine Kaminsky award, 1992, Lannan Fiction award, 1993, Tchg. award Northeastern Assn. Grad. Sch., 1994, Art of Fact prize SUNY, 2000; named Lit. Lion NY Pub. Libr., 1987; Guggenheim fellow, 1963; NEA Creative Writing fellow, 1979, 84; nominated for Médicis, Femina and Meilleur Livre Etranger prizes, France, 1991, Lannan Lit. Videos 35, Nat. Book Critics award for fiction, 1996; named to Honor Roll The Yr. in Fiction, DLB Yearbook, 1996, Conf. on works of West, U. of Tours, France, 2003; manuscript collection at Pattee Libr., Pa. State U. Office: Elaine Markson Agy 44 Greenwich Ave Fl 3 New York NY 10011-8389 *The unexamined life may not be worth having, but the examined life is endurable only to an open mind, through which life holistically flows, keeping that mind as incomplete as our knowledge of the universe itself.*

**WEST, RALPH LELAND,** veterinarian; b. Grand Rapids, Minn., Apr. 23, 1915; s. Ralph Leland and Elsie (Wardall) W.; m. Mary Elizabeth Brann, June 14, 1937; children: Michael Alan, Janet Lee West Friedrich, Thomas James. DVM, Iowa State U., 1936; MS, Purdue U., 1972. Pvt. practice, Waseca, Minn., 1936-42, 46-70; grad. asst. Sch. Vet. Medicine Purdue U., West Lafayette, Ind., 1970-72; asst. dir. sci. activities Am. Vet. Med. Assn., Schaumburg, Ill., 1972-77, dir. sci. activities, 1977-84. Contbr. articles to jours. in field. Mem. Pk. Bd., Waseca, 1948-50, Youth Commn., 1948-52; mem., chmn. Waseca Hosp. Bd., 1954-64; trustee Sunny Acres Village Inc., Denver, 1988-95. Maj. U.S. Army, 1942-46, ETO. Recipient Stange award Iowa State U., 1988 AMVA (award 1990), Am. Assn. Ret. Vets. (dir. 1987-90), Am. Vet. History Soc., Colo. Vet. Med. Assn., Minn. Vet. Med. Assn., Iowa State U. Vet. Alumni Assn., Phi Zeta. Republican. Avocations: reading, tv sports, stock market. Home: 1719 E Bijou St Apt 611 Colorado Springs CO 80909-5751 Personal E-mail: WDrwest1@aol.com.

**WEST, REXFORD LEON,** retired bank executive; b. Syracuse, N.Y., Feb. 18, 1938; s. Rexford A. and Nina (Crysler) W.; m. Elaine, Julie, Gregory, Kristen AAS, Auburn C.C., N.Y., 1957; BS magna cum laude, Syracuse U., N.Y., 1972; Advanced Mgmt. Program, Harvard Bus. Sch., Boston, 1984. Accountant Marine Midland Bank, Syracuse, NY, 1959-67, v.p., asst. treas.,

1967-72; v.p., contr. Marine Midland Services Corp., Buffalo, 1972-76; v.p. ops. divsn. Marine Midland Bank, N.A., Buffalo, 1976-77, sr. v.p., sr. ops. officer, 1977-79, exec. v.p., sr. ops. officer, 1979-85, divsn. exec. ops., 1985-87, sector exec. ops. and fin. mgmt., 1987-90, sr. exec. v.p. corp. engring., 1990-92; exec. v.p. adminstrv. svc. Fleet Bank, Melville, NY, 1992-94; exec. v.p. loan servicing Fleet Mortgage Group, Columbia, SC, 1994-96; ret., 1996. Served with U.S. Army, 1957-61

**WEST, ROBERT GRADY,** lawyer; b. Dallas, Aug. 13, 1947; s. Robert Sorrells and Thelma Grady W.; m. Marsha Lee Riegert, June 5, 1971; children: Kathryn Lee, Laura Elaine. BA, Midwestern State U., 1969; JD, U. Tex., 1972. Bar: Tex. 1972, U.S. Dist. Ct. (no. dist.) Tex. 1975, U.S. Ct. Appeals (5th cir.) 1976, U.S. Dist. Ct. (ea. dist.) Tex. 1992. Assoc. McGown, Godfrey, Decker, McMackin, Shipman & McClane, Ft. Worth, 1972-77, ptnr., 1977-88, Decker, McMackin & McClane, Ft. Worth, 1988-90, Decker, Jones, McMackin, McClane, Hall & Bates, Ft. Worth, 1990-93; assoc. Michener, Larimore, Swindle, Whitaker, et al, Ft. Worth, 1993-98, ptnr., 1999-2000, Whitaker, Chalk, Swindle & Sawyer, 2000—. Contbr. articles to profl. jours. Bd. regents Midwestern State U., Wichita Falls, Tex., 1992-98; dir. Grace Found., Dallas, 1990-92, Hist. Camp Bowie, Inc., Ft. Worth, 2002-; mem. Tex. Ctr. Legal Ethics and Professionalism, 1994—, Leadership Ft. Worth, 1984; elder, trustee Presbyn. Ch. Mem. ABA, Am. Assn. Profl. Landmen, State Bar Tex., Tarrant County Bar Assn. (mem. real estate sect. 2001-02, 04-, spkr. CLE seminars). Avocations: travel, musical theatre, walking, volunteering. Office: Whitaker Chalk Swindle & Sawyer 3500 City Ctr Tower II 301 Commerce St Fort Worth TX 76102-4186 E-mail: rwest@whitakerchalk.com.

**WEST, ROBERT MACLELLAN,** science educator, consultant; b. Appleton, Wis., Sept. 1, 1942; s. Clarence John and Elizabeth Ophelia (Moore) West; m. Jean Sydow, June 19, 1965; 1 child, Christopher. BA, Lawrence Coll., 1963; SM, U. Chgo., 1964, PhD, 1968. Rsch. assoc. Princeton (N.J.) U., 1968-69; asst. prof. Adelphi U., Garden City, NY, 1969-74; curator geology Milw. Pub. Mus., 1974-83; dir. Carnegie Mus. Natural History, Pitts., 1983-87, Cranbrook Inst. Sci., Bloomfield Hills, Mich., 1987-91; prin. RMW Sci. Action, Washington, 1992-95; pres. Informal Sci., Inc., Washington, 1993-98, Informal Learning Experiences, Inc., Washington, 1999—. Adj. prof. U. Wis., Milw., 1974—83. Contbr. articles to profl. jours. Bd. dirs. Friends New Zoo, Pitts., 1984—87; treas. E. Mich. Environ. Action Coun., Birmingham, 1987—92. Named Man of the Yr. in Sci., Vectors Pitts., 1988; recipient Arnold Guyot prize, Nat. Geographic Soc., 1982; NSF fellow, 1965—68, NSF Rsch. grantee, 1970—82, Nat. Geographic Soc. Rsch. grantee, 1973, 1976, 1977, 1979, 1980, 1982. Mem.: Visitor Study Assn. (bd. dirs. 2005—), Am. Assn. Mus., Mus. Group, Paleontology Soc., Geol. Soc. Am., Soc. Vertebrate Paleontology, Nat. Ctr. Sci. Edn. (bd. dirs. 1984—88, 1992—), Rotary. Avocations: nature, history, sports. Office: Informal Learning Experiences Inc PO Box 42328 Washington DC 20015-0928 Office Phone: 202-362-5823. Business E-Mail: ile@informallearning.com.

**WEST, ROYCE,** lawyer, state legislator; b. Sept. 26, 1952; BA, MA, U. Tex., Arlington; JD, U. Houston. Sr. ptnr. Law Firm of West & Gooden, P.C.; mem. Tex. Senate, 1993—, mem. com. of the whole on legis. and congl. redistricting; mem. com. fin., health and human svs., jurisprudence; chmn. subcom. higher edn.; vice chmn. edn. Named one of 25 Most Powerful People in Tex. Politics, Tex. Monthly Mag., Ten Best Legislators in Tex., two-time hon. mention, Key Players of 2005 Legislature, Movers and Shakers list, AP. Democrat. Address: 5787 S Hampton Rd Ste 385 Dallas TX 75232-6331 Office: PO Box 12068 Austin TX 78711-2068 Office Phone: 214-467-0123.

**WEST, STEPHEN ALLAN,** lawyer; b. Salt Lake City, Mar. 23, 1935; s. Allan Morrell and Ferne (Page) W.; m. Martha Sears, Mar. 21, 1960; children: Stephen Allan, Jr., Page, Adam. JD, U. Utah, 1961, BS in Philosophy, 1962. Law clk. to judge U.S. Dist. Ct., Utah, 1961-62; assoc. Marr, Wilkins & Cannon, Salt Lake City, 1962-65, ptnr., 1965-67; atty. Jennings, Strouss, Salmon & Trask, Washington, 1967-68, Marriott Corp., Washington, 1968-71, asst. gen. counsel, 1971-74, v.p. and assoc. gen. counsel, 1974-87, v.p. and dep. gen. counsel, 1987-93; sr. v.p., gen. counsel Marriott Internat., Inc., Washington, 1993-94; pres. Tex. San Antonio mission Ch. of Jesus Christ of Latter-day Saints, 1995-98, Gen. Authority, 1998—2005. Bd. dirs. Interfaith Conf. Met. Washington, 1989-93, vice chmn., 1992-93; mem. exec. bd. Christa McAuliffe Inst. Task Force of Nat. Found. for Improvement Edn. Mem. ABA (exec. coun. young lawyers sect. 1964-65), Utah Bar Assn. (exec. com. young lawyers sect. 1962-67), D.C. Bar Assn., Utah Profl. Rels. Com., U. Utah Alumni Assn. (Disting. Alumni award 1971), Skull and Bones, Owl and Key, Phi Delta Phi, Sigma Chi. Office: 1117 Fox Farm Rd Logan UT 84321

**WEST, STEPHEN KINGSBURY,** lawyer, director; b. Pittsfield, Mass., Sept. 28, 1928; s. William Bradford and Ruth (Osteyee) W.; m. Ann Wick, Apr. 30, 1955; children: Timothy Wick, Lucy West Engebretson, Todd Kingsbury, Daniel Wick. BA, Yale U., 1950; LL.B., Harvard U., 1953. Assoc. Sullivan & Cromwell, N.Y.C., 1957-64, ptnr., 1964-97, of counsel, 1997—. Bd. dirs. Pioneer Mut. Fund, Boston, Swiss Helvetin Fund, Inc. Trustee Morven Mus. and Garden, Princeton, NJ, Hancock (Mass.) Shaker Village; dir. Atlantic Salmon Fedn. Served to lst lt. inf. U.S. Army, 1953—5. Mem.: N.Y. State Bar Assn., Assn. Bar City N.Y. Office: Sullivan & Cromwell 125 Broad St Fl 28 New York NY 10004-2489

**WEST, SUSAN R.,** elementary school educator, consultant; b. Herkimer, N.Y., Feb. 22, 1957; d. Robert E. and Dorothy H. West. AS, Herkimer County C.C., Herkimer, N.Y., 1977; BS in Elem. Edn., SUNY, Oneonta, 1979; MS in Elem. Edn., 1983. Cert. early childhood generalist. Tchr. grades 3 and 4 Annunciation Regional Sch., Ilion, NY, tchr. 1st grade Herkimer Ctrl. Sch. Chair, bd. dirs. Mohawk Regional Tchr. Ctr., Herkimer. Mem.: N.Y. State Reading Assn., Mohawk Valley Reading Assn. (bd. dirs. 1995—). Avocations: reading, cross stitch. Home: 5478 State Rt 28 Newport NY 13416

**WEST, SYLVIA WANDELL,** small business owner, director, educator, researcher; b. Harrisburg, Pa., Dec. 26, 1937; d. John George Wient and Kathleen Hill Wandell; m. Henry Earl Seidmeyer, Sept. 18, 1994; m. Jack Dennis West, Aug. 30, 1958 (div. June 15, 1971); children: Todd Conner, Jill Conner, Gary Conner, Susan Conner, Blake Conner. BFA, Tex. Christian U., 1961, MLA, 1988, MS, 1991, PhD, 1993. Tutor The Tutoring Rm., Ft. Worth, 1962—2005; founding dir. Lollypop Sch., 1964—67, Hill Sch., 1974—84; owner, dir. West Acad., 1984—. Rschr., presenter in field. Mem. Hill Sch., Ft. Worth, 1982—83. Achievements include research in Academic Achievement with Failure Avoidant Students. Avocations: swimming, reading, writing curriculum, cooking, interior remodeling. Home: 3821Arundel Ave Fort Worth TX 76109 Office: West Acad 3825 McCart Ave Fort Worth TX 76110 Office Phone: 817-924-3535. Home Fax: 817-926-3399; Office Fax: 817-926-3399. E-mail: drsylviawest@yahoo.com.

**WEST, TERESA L. (TERRI WEST),** semiconductor company executive; BA in journalism, Univ. North Tex., 1982. Student intern Tex. Instruments Inc., 1978, former mgr. media rels., former v.p. and mgr. strategic comm., currently sr. v.p. comm. and investor rels. Dallas. Dir. Dallas Pub. Broadcasting System affiliate, KERA-TV; mem. Nat. Investor Rels. Inst. and Conf. Bd.; founding mem. Women of TI Fund; v.p. Tex. Instruments Found.; chair comm. com. (during renewal of US-Japan Semiconductor Trade Arrangement) Semiconductor Industry Assn., 1992, 96. Chancellor's leadership coun. U. North Tex. Office: Tex Instruments Inc 12500 TI Blvd Dallas TX 75243 Office Phone: 972-995-2011, 972-995-4360.

**WEST, THOMAS S.,** lawyer; b. 1951; BA, St. Lawrence U., 1974; JD, Union U., Albany Law Sch., 1977. Bar: NY 1978. Law clk. to Hon. Edmund I. Shea NY Supreme Ct., 1977—78; ptnr. LeBoeuf, Lamb, Greene & MacRae LLP, Albany, NY, chmn. Environ. Practice Group, 1992—96, chmn. litig. dept. Mem.: NY State Bar Assn. (chmn., legis. com. 1984—89, chmn., civil litig. com. 1989—93), ABA - Natural Resources Sect. Office: LeBoeuf Lamb Greene & MacRae LLP 99 Washington Ave Ste 2020 Albany NY 12210-2820 Office Phone: 518-626-9307. Office Fax: 518-626-9010. Business E-Mail: twest@llgm.com.

**WEST, TOGO DENNIS, JR.,** lawyer, retired cabinet member; b. Winston-Salem, NC, June 21, 1942; s. Togo Dennis and Evelyn (Carter) W.; m. Gail Estelle Berry, June 18, 1966; children: Tiffany Berry, Hilary Carter. BSEE, Howard U., 1965, JD cum laude, 1968; LLD (hon.), Winston-Salem U., 1996, Gannon U., 1998. Bar: D.C. 1968, N.Y. 1969, U.S. Ct. Mil. Appeals 1969, U.S. Supreme Ct. 1978, U.S. Ct. Claims 1981. Elec. engr. Duquesne Light and Power Co., 1965; patent researcher Sughrue, Rothwell, Mion, Zinn and McPeak, 1966-67; legal intern U.S. EEOC, 1967; law clk. firm Covington & Burling, Washington, 1967-68, summer assoc., 1968, assoc., 1973-75, 76-77, 2000—05; law clk. to Judge Tyler U.S. Dist. Ct. for So. Dist. N.Y., 1968-69; assoc. dep. atty. gen. U.S. Dept. Justice, Washington, 1975-76; gen. counsel Dept. Navy, Washington, 1977-79; spl. asst. to sec. and dep. sec. Dept. Def., Washington, 1979-80, gen. counsel, 1980-81; mng. prinr. Patterson, Belknap, Webb & Tyler, Washington, 1981-90; sr. v.p. govt. rels. Northrop Corp., Washington, 1990-93; sec. of Army Washington, 1993-98; chair Panama Canal Com., 1997; sec. U.S. Dept. of Veterans Affairs, Washington, 1998—2000; of coun. Covington & Burling, 2000—04; pres., CEO Joint Ctr. Polit. & Econ. Studies, 2004—06; with TLI Leadership Group, Washington, 2006—. Adj. prof. Duke U. Sch. Law, 1980-81; bd. cons. Riggs Nat. Bank, Washington, 1990-93; bd. dirs. Krispy Kreme Doughnuts, Inc., Bowater, Inc., Washington Hosp. Ctr.; mem. coun. trustees AUSA; chmn. bd. trustees Mitretek Sys., Inc., 2001—. Mng. editor: Howard Law Jour, 1968. Commr. D.C. Law Rev. Comm., 1982-89, chmn., 1985-89; mem. Nat. Council of Friends of John F. Kennedy Ctr. for Performing Arts, 1984-91, treas., 1987-91; bd. govs. Antioch U. Sch. Law, 1983-87, vice chmn., 1986-87; bd. visitors Wake Forest U. Sch. Law, 1991-94; chmn. Greater Washington Bd. Trade, legis. bur., 1987-89, bd. dirs., 1987-93, mem. exec. com. 1987-92; mem. fed. legis. com., 1990-93; chmn. Kennedy Ctr. Community and Friends Bd., 1991-2001; mem. Washington Lawyers' Com. Civil Rights Under Law, 1987-93, D.C. Com. on Pub. Edn., 1988-93, chmn., 1990-91; trustee The Aerospace Corp., 1983-90, Ctr. for Strategic and Internat. Studies, 1987-90, Nat. Lawyers Com. for Civil Rights Under Law, 1987-93, Inst. for Def. Analyses, 1989-91, Protestant Episcopal Cathedral Found., 1989-95, Shakespeare Theatre at The Folger, 1990-93, N.C. Sch. Arts, 1990-2002, Aerospace Edn. Found. of Air Force Assn., 1991-93; bd. dirs. D.C. Law Students in Ct. Program, 1986-92, World Affairs Coun., 1991-93, 2000—, Atlantic Coun., 1991-93, 2000—; mem. fin. com. Episcopal Diocese of Washington, 1989—90, mem. standing coun., 1990-92; sr. warden St John's Ch., Lafayette Sq.; mem. Coun. Fgn. Rels., 1996—; chmn. trustee coun. YMCA Metro. Wash., 1990-92; mem. nat. adv. coun. UN Assn. USA, 1991-93; D.C. Ct. Appeals Admissions Com., 1990-93; pres. Nat. Capital Area Coun. Boy Scouts Am.; chmn. Greater Washington Bd. of Trade; bd. trustees Assn. of U.S. Army, 2001—. Served to capt. Judge Adv. Gen. Corps U.S. Army, 1969-73. Decorated Legion of Merit, Meritorious Svc. medal; recipient Disting. Pub. Svc. medal Dept. Def., 1981, 88, Disting. Eagle Scout award Boy Scouts Am., 1995, Svc. to Howard U. award, 1965, Medal of Merit, Brazil, Disting. Civil Svc. medal, 1998, Dept. Vet. Affairs, 2000, Silver Buffalo award, 2000, Silver Beaver award, 2003; named one of Most Influential Black Americans, Ebony mag., 2006. Mem. ABA, Nat. Bar Assn., Washington Coun. Lawyers (dir. 1973-75), Sigma Pi Phi, Phi Alpha Delta, Omega Psi Psi, Alpha Phi Omega. Clubs: Metropolitan, University (Washington). Office: TLI Leadership Group 888 17th St NW Ste 302 Washington DC 20006 Business E-Mail: twest@tlileaders.com.

**WEST, W. RICHARD,** museum director; b. San Bernardino, Calif., Jan. 6, 1943; s. W. Richard Sr. and Maribelle (McCrea) W.; m. Mary Beth Braden, June 29, 1968; children: Amy Elizabeth, Benjamin Braden. BA magna cum laude in Am. History, U. Redlands, 1965; AM in Am. History, Harvard U., 1968; JD, Stanford U., 1971; LHD (hon.), Bacone Coll., 1992, Ottawa U., 1994, U. Okla., 1995. Bar: Calif., D.C., U.S. Ct. Appeals (8th cir.), U.S. Supreme Ct. Clk. to Hon. Benjamin C. Duniway U.S. Ct. Appeals (9th cir.), 1971-72; assoc. Fried, Frank, Harris, Shriver & Jacobson, Washington, 1973-79, ptnr., 1979-88; dir. direct support component Am. Indian Lawyer Tng. Program, Inc., 1976-77; ptnr. Gover, Stetson Williams & West P.C., Albuquerque, 1988-90; founding dir. Smithsonian Instn's Nat. Mus. Am. Indian, Washington, 1990—. Treas. Am. Indian Lawyer Tng. Program, Inc., 1973—; adj. prof. Indian law Stanford U., 1977. Mem. edit. bd. Am. Indian Historian, 1969-71; note editor Stanford Law Review, 1970-71; contbr. articles to profl. jours. Coord., treas. Native Am. Coun. Regents Inst. Am. Indian Arts, 1975-80; bd. visitors Stanford Law Sch., 1978-81; trustee Phelps Stokes Fund, 1981-87, Bush Found., 1991—, Bacone Coll., 1986-89, chmn., 1988-89, Morning Star Found., 1987-93, U. Redlands, 1991—, alumni bd., 1987-89, Ednl. Found. Am., 1993-96; bd. dirs. Amerindian Circle, Inc., 1981-88, Nat. Indian Justice Ctr., 1982-89; cultural edn. com. Smithsonian Inst., 1987-90; nat. support com. Native Am. Rights Fund, 1990—; adv. com. Winslow Found., 1991—; hon. coun. Wings Am., 1993—; mem. Environ. Def. Fund, bd. trustees, 1986—. Recipient Career Achievement award U. Redlands, 1987, Disting. Svc. award, 1992, award Appreciation and Recognition, Cheyenne and Arapaho Tribes Okla., 1990, Spirit of the People award Okla. Inst. Indian Heritage, 1990; named (with another) Amb. of Yr. Red Earth Indian Ctr. Okla., 1993. Mem. Am. Indian Bar Assn. (charter pres. 1976-77). Mem. Cheyenne and Arapaho Tribes Okla. Office: Nat Mus of Am Indian 470 Lenfant Plz SW Ste 7102 Washington DC 20024-2124

**WEST, WALTER MATTHEW,** military officer; b. High Point, NC, Oct. 3, 1981; s. Leslie Ray and Brenda Denise West. Sgt. USMC, Newport, RI, 2004—05, Columbia, SC, 2005—. Sgt. USMC, 29 Palms, Calif., 2000—04. Decorated Navy and Marine Corps Achievement Medal with V for Valor in Combat. Mem.: Semper Fi Soc. Conservative. Church Of God. Achievements include Led 32 Marines in Operation Iraqi Freedom 1; Led 68 Marines in Operation Iraqi Freedom 2.

**WEST, WILLIAM ROBERT,** history professor; b. Woodbury, NJ, Feb. 4, 1947; s. William Robert Sr. and Genevieve Jane (Cooper) West; m. Rhonda Gaye Foster, Apr. 4, 1981; children: Shaun Cooper Foster West, Ryan William Foster West. BA, Ky. Wesleyan Coll., 1970; MA, Western Ky. U., 1973; postgrad., U. Louisville, U. Shanghai, U. Denver, U. Wash., others. Ky. secondary cert. life. Tchr. Daviess County Pub. Schs., Owensboro, 1971-86; prof. history Ky. Cmty. Tech. Coll. Sys., 1984—; faculty senate coun. rep. univ. studies, coun. mem., 1994—97, elected faculty rep., bd. regents, 2003—06. Parent rep. local sch. based coun. Mem. Leadership Owensboro Class of 1988, Leadership Ky. Class of 1997; exec. dir. Owensboro Sister Cities Program, 1990—; mem. state mgmt. team Ky. Sister Cities, 1991—; internat. rep. Shawnee Trails Coun. Boy Scouts Am. Recipient cert. of merit Ky. Ednl. TV-Ashland Oil Found., 1982, Internat. Scout award Boy Scouts Am., 2002, award City of Olomouc, Czech Republic, 2004; rsch. scholar Lyndhurst Found., 1984, scholar Japan Endowment at U. Wash., 1983, N.E. Asia Coun. of Assn. for Asian Studies, 1983; travel grantee U.S.-Japan Found., 1983. Mem. Am. Assn. Individual Investors, Nat. Geographic Soc., Nat. Trust Historic Preservation, Hon. Order Ky. Cols., U.S.-China Peoples Friendship Assn. (nat. bd. dirs. 1997-2001), UN Assn. U.S.A., Ky. C.C. Humanities Assn., The So. Hist. Assn. (European history sect.), others. Democrat. Unitarian Universalist. Avocations: reading, travel. Home: 5829 Jack Hinton Rd Philpot KY 42366-9641 Office: Owensboro Cmty and Tech Coll 4800 New Hartford Rd Owensboro KY 42303-1800 Office Phone: 270-686-4644. Business E-Mail: bill.west@ketcs.edu.

**WESTBERRY, ANITA PARRISH,** education educator; b. Clewiston, Fla., Oct. 5, 1946; d. Virgil Ennis and Onetta Armour Parrish; m. Lawrence Ray Westberry, Sr., Nov. 5, 1966; children: Danita Westberry Thomas, Lawrence Ray Jr. AA, Edison Cmty., Fort Myers, Fla., 1978; BS, Nova S.E. U., Fort Lauderdale, Fla., 1988; MEd, Tenn. State U., Nashville, 1999. Elem. tchr. Glades County Schs., Moore Haven, Fla., 1988—89, Hendry County Schs., LaBelle, Fla., 1989—97; ESL tchr. Franklin County Schs., Winchester, Tenn., 1997—98, Rutherford County Schs., Murfreesboro, Tenn., 1998—2004; instr.

U. Phoenix, Nashville, 2002—, online instr.; instr. Western Internat. U., Phoenix, 2004—; online instr. Axia Coll., Western Internat. U. Rep. S.W. Fla. Tchr. Edn. Ctr., Fort Myers, 1995—97. Named Leader of Yr., 4-H, 1980. Church Of Christ. Avocations: reading, travel. Home: 256 White Oak Dr Manchester TN 37355 Office Phone: 931-570-4140. Personal E-mail: 2awestberry@charter.net. Business E-Mail: purplenannie@netzero.net.

**WESTBERRY, JOSEPH RYAN,** music educator, director; s. James Riley Westberry Jr. and Nancy Jane Westberry; m. Wendy Marie Bennis, July 10, 1999; 1 child, Ella Grace. MusB, Furman U., Greenville, SC, 1998; MusM in Edn., U. SC., Columbia, 2003. Instrumental music educator Divsn. of Tchr. Quality, SC, 1998. Asst. dir. bands Effingham County H.S., Springfield, Ga., 1998—2001; grad. asst., Carolina bands U. SC., Columbia, 2001—03; dir. bands Cyril B. Busbee Mid. Sch., Cayce, SC, 2003—04, Aiken Mid. Sch., SC, 2004—. Dean of students Furman U. Summer Music Camp, Greenville, SC, 2001—05. Musician Palmetto Concert Band, Columbia, 2001. Recipient Tchr. of Yr., Aiken Mid. Sch., 2004—05. Mem.: Aiken County Band Dirs. Assn. (assoc.; pres 2005), SC Band Dirs. Assn. (assoc.), SC Music Educators Assn. (assoc.), Music Educators Nat. Conf. (assoc.). Office Phone: 803-641-2570.

**WESTBERRY, PAULA I.,** nursing administrator; b. Worcester, Mass., Aug. 7, 1954; d. Richard R. and Patricia I. (Gilbert) Wood; m. Chuck Westberry, 2005; children: Laura, Andrew, Brian. Diploma summa cum laude, David Hale Fanning Schs., 1974; BS in Computer Sci. summa cum laude, Clark U., 1986; AAS summa cum laude, SUNY, Albany, 1988; BSN, Barry U., 1996, MSN summa cum laude, 1998; PhD summa cum laude, Columbus U., 1999. Cert. nursing adminstrn. advanced. ANA, dir. nurses Nat. Assn. Dirs. Nursing Adminstrn./Long Term Care, nursing adminstrn. cert. legal nurse cons. Head nurse Seven Hills Adolescent Program, Worcester, 1985-88; coord. utilization rev. Worcester County Hosp., 1988-90, 45th St. Mental Health Ctr., West Palm Beach, Fla.; nurse mgr. N.Medico Neurol. Rehab. Ctr. of Palm Beach (Fla.), 1990-91; dir. nurses Edgewater Pointe Estates, Boca Raton, Fla., 1991-93; DON Emparity Care, Boca Raton, 1993-96; owner Traditional Home Health Svcs., Inc., Lake Worth, Fla., 1996-99; nurse mgr. Genesis Eldercare Network, Laconia, N.H., 1998-99; DON Hollywood Hills Nursing Home, 1999-2001; adminstr. Physician's Choice Home Health Svcs., 2001—03, Total Home Health Inc., Sebring, Fla., 2006—; v.p. clin. ops. Home Care Solutions Group, Ft. Lauderdale, 2003—06. Mem. content expert panel ANCC Nurse Adminstrn., 2002—. Trustee Fla. Nurse Found., 2003—06, v.p., 2003—06. Mem.: ANA, Nat. Assn. Dir. Nursing Adminstrn. (chairperson home health coun., cert.), Fla. Nurses Assn. (Quality and Unity in Nursing coun. mem., dist. XI bd. mem.), Fla. Orgn. Nursing Execs., Sigma Theta Tau. Republican. Office Phone: 863-381-1958. Personal E-mail: docpaula54@yahoo.com. Business E-Mail: pwood@homecaresolutionsgroup.com.

**WESTBERRY, ROBERT KENT,** lawyer; b. Marion, Ky., July 21, 1955; s. B.M. and Nancy Elizabeth (Kent) W.; m. Leslie Gail Fitzhill, Sept. 24, 1988. AB, Centre Coll., 1977; JD, Salmon P. Chase Coll., 1981. Bar: Ky. 1981, U.S. Dist. Ct. (we. dist.) Ky. 1982, U.S. Ct. Appeals (6th cir.) 1982, U.S. Supreme Ct. Assoc. Westberry and Roberts, Marion, 1981; asst. U.S. atty. U.S. Dist. Ct. (we. dist.) Ky., Louisville, 1981-87; assoc. Greenebaum, Doll & McDonald, Louisville, 1987-89, Landrum and Shouse, Louisville, 1989—. Moderator, lectr. Comprehensive Crime Criminal Act Seminar, 1985, Prosecution of Criminal RICO Action, 1986. Vice chmn. Jefferson County Rep. Party. Louisville, 1988—. Mem. Ky. Bar Assn. (chmn. younger lawyers sect., pres. 2004). Episcopalian. Office: Landrum and Shouse Ste 1900 220 W Main St Louisville KY 40202

**WESTBIE, BARBARA JANE,** retired graphics designer; b. Little Rock, Nov. 3, 1946; d. Freeman Bryant Davis and Virginia Lee Thompson; children: Suzanne Michelle, Derrek Christopher. Grad. in graphic design, U. Calif., Davis, 1992; student, Miramar Coll., San Diego, 1976, Chabot Coll., Hayward, Calif., 1974. Exec. dir. Ambiance, Danville, Calif., 1980—84; dir. Lake Gallery, Tahoe City, Calif., 1985—87; art cons. Reed Gallery, Tahoe City, 1988—90; ret., 1990. Art dir., creative cons. Associated Students Re-Entry Ctr. Chico State U., Calif., 2001—03. Inventor Fat Fuzzy/Iknonotronic Family, 1981, artist (poster/logo) Project Mana Fundraising Event, 1988, (brochure/media kit) Chocolate Festival, 1989. Vol. crisis intervention counselor CIS/Tahoe Women's Svcs., Kings Beach, 1989—91; lead counselor Emotions Anonymous 12-Step Program, North Lake Tahoe Area, 1990—93; vol. pk. svc. Washoe Lake State Pk., Carson City, Nev., 1993—94; coord. new vols. ARC, Chico, 2000—01, vol. Butte County, 2000—, Emergency Animal Rescue Svcs., 2002—. Named Vol. of Yr., Tahoe Women's Svcs., 1989; recipient Disting. Svc. award, CIS/Tahoe Women's Svcs., 1989—90. Mem.: Smithsonian Instn. (assoc.). Protestant. Avocations: skiing, reading, gardening, writing, painting.

**WESTBROOK, BRIAN,** professional football player; b. Washington, DC, Sept. 2, 1979; BS in Mgmt. Info Sys., Villanova Univ., 2001, studied towards MBA, 2002. RB Phila. Eagles, 2002—. Organizer Variety Club, Phila.; host of Charity and Celebrity Weekend Police Athletic League Phila. Named to Pro-Bowl, NFL, 2004. Achievements include having jersey retired by Villanova Univ., 10/22/05. Office: Phila Eagles 1621 Franklin Mills Cir Philadelphia PA 19154*

**WESTBROOK, CLINTON HOWARD,** retired military petty officer, retired protective services official; b. Bklyn., Mar. 1, 1919; s. Alfred and Daisy (Gamble) Westbrook; m. Catherine Veronica Wetzel, Dec. 13, 1942 (dec. June 24, 2006); children: James Howard, Cathy Ann, John Alfred(dec.), Clinton Howard Jr., Robert Vincent(dec.). Enlisted USN, 1940, served on USS Maddux and USS Arizona, 1940—41, served on 23 campaigns in Atlantic and Pacific, 1941—45, served on USS Taylor, 1942—46; discharged to active reserve USNR, 1947; recalled to active duty USN, 1950—52, ret. chief petty officer, 1967; security patrol So. Pacific Railroad, San Francisco, 1946; with Parcel Post, NYC, 1947; field engr., 1952—56; dir. emergency/civil def. County of Seminole, Fla., 1967—74; vet. svcs. officer Seminole County, 1967—84; ret., 1984. Hon. chmn. Golden Age Games, Sanford, 2003; vol. cmty. resource lectr. Seminole County Schs., Meml. Day Parade, Sanford, Fla., 2003, 2004, 2005, 2006, parade marshall, 2004. Decorated Purple Heart; named State Vet. Svc. Officer of Yr. outstanding svc., Seminole County Commr., 1969—84; recipient Order of the Eagle Feather plaque, numerous unit awards and citations, Presdl. Unit award. Mem.: DAV (life), Pearl Harbor Survivors Assn. (life), Tin Can Sailor Assn. (life), USS Ariz. Reunion Assn. (life; bd. dirs. 1999—2002, v.p. 2003, v.p.-elect 2005). Democrat. Roman Catholic. Achievements include being a survivor of the USS Arizona during the Pearl Harbor attack in 1941. Avocations: stamp collecting/philately, coin collecting/numismatics, photography, volunteering. Home: Lakeview Ter Bldg C Unit 2 283 Raintree Dr Altoona FL 32702-9604

**WESTBROOK, DON ARLEN,** minister; b. Clinton, N.C., June 2, 1941; s. Ennis and Geneva (Gainey) W.; m. Carrol Ann Holder, Sept. 15, 1963; children: Felisha Ann, Neal Vance. Student, Logos Bible Coll./Grad. Sch., 1989. Ordained to ministry Full Gospel Fellowship Chs. and Mins. Internat., 1965. Pastor Bethel Christian Ctr., Durham, N.C., 1969—. V.p. Full Gospel Fellowship Chs. and Mins. Internat., Dallas, 1982—; missionary to India, Nicaragua and Haiti, 1990; leader Durham In Prayer, 1999—. Chmn. Concerned Citizens for Moral Govt., Durham, 1989. Home: 5311 Emeraldwood Dr Durham NC 27705-7170 Office: Bethel Christian Ctr 3518 Rose Of Sharon Rd Durham NC 27712-3306

**WESTBROOK, GARY WAYNE,** music educator, consultant; b. Burlington, N.C., June 29, 1966; s. Betty Biggs Smith. MusB, East Carolina U., 1989; MusM, U. N.C., 1996, DPhil Music Edn., 2002. Dir. bands So. Nash High Sch., Spring Hope, NC, 1989—90, Blenheim Mid. Sch., Blenheim, SC, 1990—92, South Florence High Sch., Florence, 1992—95; dir. athletic bands and percussion studies Concord Coll., Athens, W.Va., 2001—03; asst. prof. music, asst. dir. bands La. Tech. U., Ruston, 2003—. Percussionist Florence

Symphony Orch., Florence, 1990—94; instr./arranger percussion Liberty High Sch., Bedford, 1995—; drummer Necessary Jazz Combo, Tazewell, 2000—; dir. corps ops. and program coord. Carolina Gold Sr. Drum and Bugle Corps, Raleigh, NC, 2001—; Member, Pit Section Leader Bridgemen Drum and Bugle Corps, Bayonne, NJ, 1986—87; adj. instr. percussion Pfeiffer U., Meisenheimer, 1999—2001, Concord Coll., 1999—2001. Contbr. articles to profl. jours. Mem.: Music Educators Nat. Conf., Music Tchrs. Nat. Assn., Percussive Arts Soc., Internat. Assn. Jazz Edn. Pentecostal. Avocations: hiking, bicycling, swimming, basketball. Office: Concord Coll Department of Music Athens WV 24712 Office Phone: 304-384-6041. Personal E-mail: Blwinkl@stargate.net.

**WESTBROOK, JACK HALL,** metallurgist, consultant; b. Troy, N.Y., Aug. 19, 1924; s. Russell Tippett and Grace Hall (Wager) W.; m. Elizabeth Kirkland, Sept. 20, 1947 (dec.); children: Nicholas, Kathryn, Melissa, Kirkland, Daniel; m. Jeanette (Sylvan) Hughson, July 26, 2003. B in Metall. Engring., Rensselaer Poly. Inst., 1944, M in Metall. Engring., 1947; ScD, MIT, 1949. Registered profl. engr., N.Y. Mem. staff Gen. Electric Corp., Schenectady, NY, 1949—71, mgr. materials info. svcs., 1971-82, cons. engring. and mfg., 1982-85; pres., prin., cons. Sci-Tech Knowledge Sys., Scotia, NY, 1985-91, Brookline Techs., Ballston Spa, NY, 1991—. Trustee Engring. Info. Inc., N.Y.C., 1977-80, chmn. indsl. data comm., mem. exec. com. Codata, 1988-94; cons. in field. Editor: Intermetallic Compounds, 1967, 21 other books; co-editor: Intermetallic Compounds: Principles and Practice, Vols. 1 and 2, 1994, Vol. 3, 2002; mem. editl. adv. bd. CRC Handbook of Chemistry and Physics, 1994-97; author of more than 170 publs., 100 book reviews, and 6 patents. Mem. zoning bd. Town of Ballston, N.Y., 1966-72; bd. edn. Ballston Spa Sch. Dist., 1970-76. With USN, 1944-46. Recipient Turner award Electrochem. Soc., 1957, Hofmann prize Lead Devel. Assn., 1971, Rensselaer Poly. Inst. Outstanding Career award, 1988; NAS traveling fellow to USSR, 1971. Fellow AAAS, Am. Ceramic Soc., Am. Soc. Metals (Campbell lectr. 1976, Jeffries lectr. 1979, Sauveur award 2001), Am. Inst. Chemists, Inst. Physics U.K.; mem. ASTM (Templin award 1959), AIME (New Eng. Regional Conf. award 1963), Inst. Materials (U.K.), Nat. Acad. Engring. Avocations: old house restoration, history of science and technology. Home and Office: 5 Brookline Rd Ballston Spa NY 12020-3523 Office Phone: 518-885-8840. Personal E-mail: jhwestbrook@earthlink.net.

**WESTBROOK, JAMES EDWIN,** law educator; b. Camden, Ark., Sept. 7, 1934; s. Loy Edwin and Helen Lucille (Bethea) W.; m. Elizabeth Kay Farris, Dec. 23, 1956; children: William Michael, Robert Bruce, Matthew David. BA with high honors, Hendrix Coll., 1956; JD with distinction, Duke U., 1959; LLM, Georgetown U., 1965. Bar: Ark. 1959, Okla. 1977, Mo. 1982. Assoc. Mehaffy, Smith & Williams, Little Rock, 1959-62; asst. counsel, subcom. of U.S. Senate Jud. Com., Washington, 1963; legis. asst. U.S. Senate, Washington, 1963-65; asst. prof. law U. Mo., Columbia, 1965-68, asst. dean, 1966-68, assoc. prof., 1968-70, prof., 1970-76, 80—, James S. Rollins prof. law, 1974-76, 80—, Earl F. Nelson prof. law, 1982-99, emeritus prof., 1999—, interim dean, 1981-82; dean U. Okla. Coll. Law, Norman, 1976-80. George Allen vis. prof. law, U. Richmond, 1987; vis. prof. law Duke U., 1988, Washington U., St. Louis, 1996, 2001; reporter Mid-Am. Assembly on Role of State in Urban Crisis, 1970; dir. Summer Internship Program in Local Govt., 1968; cons. various Mo. cities on drafting home-rule charters; mem. Gov.'s Adv. Coun. on Local Govt. Law, 1967-68, Fed. Practice Com. U.S. Dist. Ct. (we. dist.) Mo., 1986-90; chmn. Columbia Charter Revision Commn., 1973-74; mem. spl. com. labor relations Mo. Dept. Labor and Indsl. Rels., 1975; mem., chmn. subcom. on domestic violence Task Force on Gender and Justice, Mo. Jud. Conf., 1990-93; mem. com. to rev. govtl. structure of Boone County, Mo., 1991. Author: (with L. Riskin) Dispute Resolution and Lawyers, 1987, supplement, 1993, 3d edit., 2005, (with L. Riskin, C. Guthrie, T. Heintz, J. Robbennolt and R. Reuben); contbr. articles to profl. jours. Chair search com. for chancellor U. Mo., Columbia, 1992, chair search com. for provost, 1998; mem. fin. com. Roman Cath. Diocese of Jefferson City, 2003—; mem. investment com. Mem. ABA, Nat. Acad. Arbitrators, Assn. Am. Law Schs. (chmn. local govt. law material task coun. 1972), Ctrl. States Law Sch. Assn. (pres. 1982-83), Mo. Bar Assn. (vice chmn. labor law com. 1986-87, chmn. 1987-88, Spurgeon Smithton award 1995), Order of Coif, Blue Key, Alpha Chi. Roman Catholic. Home: 3609 S Woods Edge Rd Columbia MO 65203-6606 Office: U Mo Sch Law Columbia MO 65211-0001 Office Phone: 573-882-6540.

**WESTBROOK, JAY LAWRENCE,** law educator; b. Morristown, NJ, Dec. 11, 1943; s. Joel W. and Elaine Frances (Summers) W.; m. Pauline June Travis, Feb. 15, 1969; 1 child, Joel Mastin. BA in Polit. Sci./Philosophy, U. Tex., 1965, JD, 1968. Bar: Tex. 1968, D.C. 1969, U.S. Ct. Appeals (D.C. cir.) 1969, U.S. Supreme Ct. 1976, U.S. Ct. Appeals (4th cir.) 1978, U.S. Ct. Appeals (2d cir.) 1979. Assoc. Surrey & Morse (name now Jones, Day, Reavis, Pogue), Washington, 1969-74; ptnr. Surrey & Morse (name now Jones, Day, Reavis, Pogue, Surrey & Morse), Washington, 1974-80; mem. law faculty U. Tex., Austin, 1980—, Benno C. Schmidt Chair Bus. Law, 1991—. Vis. prof. U. London, 1990, Harvard Law Sch., 1991-92; advisor Tex. Internat. Law Jour., 1985-91; reporter Am. Law Inst. Transnat. Insolvency Project, 1994-2000; co-leader U.S. delegation to UN Commn. on Internat. Trade Law Working Group on Model Law Internat. Insolvency, 1995-97, 99; sr. advisor Nat. Bankruptcy Rev. Com., 1997; mem. State Dept. Adv. Com. on Pvt. Internat. Law, 1997-2000; vis. scholar Humboldt U., Berlin, 2002. Co-author: As We Forgive Our Debtors: Bankruptcy and Consumer Credit in America, 1989 (Silver Gavel award ABA 1989), The Law of Debtors and Creditors: Text, Cases and Problems, 5th edit., 2005, Teacher's Manual, The Law of Debtors and Creditors, 4th edit., 2001, The Fragile Middle Class: Americans in Debt, 2000(Ann. Writing award Am. Coll. Consumer Fin. Svcs. Lawyers); contbr. articles to profl. jours. Grantee U. Tex. Law Sch. Found., 1982, U. Rsch. Inst., 1982-83, NSF, 1983-86, Polity Rsch. Inst., Lyndon Johnson Sch. Pub. Affairs, 1984, Tex. Bar Found., 1985, Nat. Inst. Child Health and Human Devel., 1986, Nat. Conf. Bankruptcy Judges, 1991, 93, Am. Coll. Banker, 2004. Mem. ABA (bus. bankruptcy com., vice chair internat. bankruptcy subcom. 1999—, Meyer rsch. grant 1986), Am. Law Inst., Am. Coll. Bankruptcy, Nat. Bankruptcy Conf., State Bar Tex. (governing coun. internat. sect. 1987-89), Internat. Insolvency Inst. (bd. dirs. 2000—), Internat. Acad. Comml. and Consumer Law, Order of Coif. Office: U Tex Sch Law 727 E Dean Keeton St Austin TX 78705-3224

**WESTBROOK, REEVES C.,** lawyer; b. Aug. 21, 1949; BA magna cum laude, Vanderbilt U., 1971; JD, Yale U., 1974. Bar: DC 1975. Ptnr. Covington & Burling, Washington, coord., Tax Practice Group. Mem.: Internat. Bar Assn. Office: Covington & Burling 1201 Pennsylvania Ave NW Washington DC 20004-2401 Office Phone: 202-662-5150. Office Fax: 202-662-6291. Business E-Mail: rwestbrook@cov.com.

**WESTBY, TIMOTHY SCOTT,** lawyer, researcher; b. Fargo, N.D., Apr. 16, 1957; s. Joseph Arlo and Dorothy Mae (Nye) W.; m. Ann Amoroso Westby, June 16, 2001. SBChemE, MIT, 1979; PhDChemE, U. Tex., 1984; JD, U. Houston, 1994. Bar: Tex. 1994 (s.c. dist.) Tex., U.S. Patent and Trademark Office, U.S. Ct. Appeals (fed. cir., 5th cir.). Researcher Energy Lab., MIT, Cambridge, 1976-79; rsch. asst. U. Tex., Austin, 1979-84, teaching asst., 1981-83; assoc. rsch. engr. Shell Devel. Co., Houston, 1984-87, rsch. engr., 1987-91, sr. rsch. engr., 1991-94; assoc. Conley, Rose & Tayon, P.C., Houston, 1994—2002; shareholder, dir. Conley Rose, PC, Houston, 2002—. Mem. adv. com. Ohio Combustion Rsch., Columbus, 1985-90, Pa. Coal Rsch. Coop., University Station, 1986-89; adj. prof. chemistry Rice U., 1998—; spl. asst. atty. gen. State of ND, 2005-. Contbr. articles to profl. jours.; patentee method for in situ coal drilling, patentee coal blends having improved ash viscosity. Campaigner United Way, Houston, 1989-91. Scholar MIT, 1975-79; fellow U.S. dept. Energy, 1979-82, Getty Oil Co., 1983-84. Mem. ABA, AIChE, ASTM (com. D-5 1989-94), ASME (advisor rsch. com. on corrosion and deposits from flue gases 1988—), N.Am. Catalysis Soc., Southwestern Catalysis Soc., Am. Intellectual Property Law Assn., Fed. Cir. Bar Assn., Bar Assn. 5th Fed. Cir., State Bar of Tex., Houston Bar Assn., Houston Intellectual Property Law Assn., Coll. of State Bar of Tex., Porsche Club Am.

(bd. dirs., treas. 2001–). Avocations: golf, sailing, skiing, auto racing. Office: Conley Rose 600 Travis Ste 7100 Houston TX 77002-2912 Office Phone: 713-238-8000. Business E-Mail: twestby@conleyrose.com.

**WESTCOTT, BRIAN JOHN,** manufacturing executive; b. Rexford, N.Y., June 19, 1957; s. John Campbell and Norma (Cornell) W.; m. Andrea Belrose, Apr. 23, 1988; children: Sarah Katharine, Paul Brian. BS, Lehigh U., 1979; MS, Stanford U., 1980, PhD, 1981. Engr. Combustion Engring., Windsor, Conn., 1980-81; rsch. engr. Gen. Electric Corp. Rsch., Niskayuna, NY, 1981-83; rsch. fellow Stanford (Calif.) Grad. Sch. Bus., 1987-88; mgr. Gen. Electric Corp. Mgmt., Bridgeport, Conn., 1988-89; prin. A.T. Kearney Tech. Inc., Redwood City, Calif., 1989–; CEO Westt, Inc., Menlo Park, Calif., 1990–2005, eInnovate, Menlo Park, Calif., 1999–. Author: (with others) Paradox and Transformation, 1988; contbr. articles to profl. jours.; inventor, patentee in field. Mem. Menlo Park Vitality Task Force, 1993-94; mem. Lehigh U. Leadership Coun., 2002–. Recipient Tech 500 award Westt, Inc., 1996, 97, 98, Inc. 500 award, 1997, Silicon Valley Tech fast 50 award, 1997, 98, San Francisco and San Jose award for top 100 fastest growing pvt. cos.; co. named among Top 50 Fastest Growing Pvt. Cos. in San Francisco and San Jose, 2001; postdoctoral rsch. fellow Stanford U. Grad. Sch. Bus., 1987, 88; rsch. fellow Electric Power Rsch., Stanford, 1983-87. Mem. ASME. Avocations: sports, politics. Office: eInnovate 325 Sharon Park Dr # 321 Menlo Park CA 94025 Personal E-mail: westcottbj@yahoo.com.

**WESTCOTT, JOHN MCMAHON, JR.,** lawyer; b. NYC, Aug. 1, 1944; s. John M. Sr. and Mary Sabin (Pitkin) W.; m. Suzanne Hillard Laporte, June 27, 1970; children: Valerie, John M. III, Jeffrey. BA cum laude, Yale U., 1966; JD, Harvard U., 1969. Bar: Mass. 1969. Assoc. Hale and Dorr, Boston, 1969-75, jr. ptnr., 1975-79, sr. ptnr., 1979–2004, asst. mng. ptnr., 1980–2004; asst. mng. ptnr. & mem. Corp. dept. Wilmer Cutler Pickering Hale & Dorr, Boston, 2004–. Gen. ptnr. Hale and Dorr Capital Mgmt. LLC, Boston, 1988–. Mem. corp. Winsor Sch., Boston, 1986–, clk., trustee, 1989–. Served with USAR, 1969-75. Named a Mass. Super Lawyer, Boston Mag., 2004. Mem. Brookline Country Club, Union Boat Club, Somerset Club. Republican. Episcopal. Office: Wilmer Cutler Pickering Hale and Dorr 60 State St Boston MA 02109-1816 Office Phone: 617-526-6061. Office Fax: 617-526-5000. Business E-Mail: john.westcott@wilmerhale.com.

**WESTEN, BRODIE CURTIS, JR., (CURT WESTEN),** lawyer; b. Champaign, Ill., Nov. 10, 1960; s. Brodie Curtis and Sarah Jane (Mullen) W.; m. Sue Lynn Heubner, Nov. 21, 1987. BS, Western Ill. U., 1982, MBA, 1983; JD, U. Calif., Berkeley, 1986. Bar: Ill. 1986. Fin. analyst Nat. Credit Union Adminstrn., Washington, 1983; atty. Lord, Bissell & Brook, Chgo., 1986–92; asst. gen. counsel, asst. sec. QualMed (merged with Health Net to form Health Systems Internat. Inc. in 1994), 1992–93, v.p. adminstrn., 1993–94, sr. v.p., gen. counsel, sec., 1994–95, Health Systems Internat. Inc. (merged with Found. Health Corp. to become Found. Health Sytems Inc. in 1997), 1995–97, Found. Health Systems Inc. (changed named to Health Net Inc. in 2000), 1997–2000, Health Net Inc., Woodland Hills, Calif., 2000–. Mem. Colo. Commn. on Coop. Health Care Agreements, 1994–96. Bd. trustees The Children's Burn Found., Sherman Oaks, Calif. Mem. ABA, Ill. Bar Assn., Chgo. Bar Assn. Avocation: golf. Office: Health Net Life Insurance Co 21281 Burbank Blvd Woodland Hills CA 91367-6607

**WESTER, R. GLEN,** music educator, director; b. Wichita Falls, Tex., Oct. 7, 1938; s. George Olus and Minnie Mae Wester; m. Theresa Lois Ward, Nov. 27, 1968; children: Suzanne, Karen, George. MusB in edn., Midwestern State U., Wichita Falls, Tex., 1961; MusM in edn., U. of North Tex., Denton, 1968. Cert. piano and voice (nat.) Nat. Music Tchrs. Assn. Instr. music Southeastern Christian Coll., Winchester, Ky., 1971—72, Vernon (Tex.) Regional Jr. Coll., 1972—74; choral dir. Springlake - Earth HS, Earth, Tex., 1975—76, Leander (Tex.) HS, 1976—80, La Marque (Tex.) HS, 1980—82; instr. music San Jacinto Coll., Pasadena, Tex., 1982—. Judge Nat. Piano Guild, 1985–2002. Bd. dir. Comty. Concerts, Vernon, Tex., 1973—75. With USN, 1961—65. Named one of Most Prominent Music Tchers. in Tex., 1983; named to Hall of Fame, Nat. Piano Guild. Mem.: Nat. Assn. of Tchrs. of Singing (sec. 1986—), Pasadena Music Teachers (v.p. 1984—, Tchr. of the Yr. 1993), Nat. Music Tchrs. (v.p. 1982—). Avocations: bicycling, gardening. Home: 4201 Kelvin Deer Park TX 77536

**WESTERBERG, ARTHUR WILLIAM,** retired chemical engineering professor; b. St. Paul, Oct. 9, 1938; s. Kenneth Waldorf and Marjorie Claire (Darling) W.; m. Barbara Ann Dyson, July 14, 1963; children: Kenneth (dec.), Karl. BS, U. Minn., 1960; MS, Princeton U., 1961; PhD, Imperial Coll., London, 1964. Pres. Farm Engring. Sales Inc., Savage, Minn., 1964-65; sr. analyst Control Data Corp., San Diego, 1965-67; asst. prof., assoc. prof., prof. U. Fla., Gainesville, Fla., 1967-76; prof. chem. engring. Carnegie-Mellon U., Pitts., 1976—2004, chmn. dept., 1980-83, Swearingen prof., 1982—2004, dir. Design Research Ctr., 1978-80, univ. prof., 1992—; dir. Engring. Design Rsch. Ctr., 1986-89. Co-author: Process Flowsheeting, 1979, Systematic Methods of Chemical Process Design, 1997. Recipient Murphree award Am. Chem. Soc., 1997, Steven J. Fenves Sys. Engring. award Carnegie Mellon, 1998, Engring. Disting. Prof. award, 2002, Robert E. Doherty Edn. award, 2003. Fellow AIChE (lectr. 1989, Computers and Sys. Tech. divsn. award 1983, Walker award 1987, McAfee award 1990, Founders Outstanding Contbns. Chem. Engring. award 1995); mem. NAE, Am. Soc. Engring. Edn. (chem. engring. divsn. lectr. 1981, GE Sr. Rsch. award 1999, Computer Aides Chem. Engring. and Edn. Excellence in Chem. Engring. Edn. award 2003). Home: 5564 Beacon St Pittsburgh PA 15217-1972 Business E-Mail: a.westerberg@cmu.edu.

**WESTERBERG, KERMIT BERNDT,** librarian; b. Aurora, Ill., Apr. 2, 1946; s. Wesley Magnus and Lorraine Jeanette (Larson) Westerberg. BA, Oberlin Coll., 1968; MA in Religion, Yale U., 1970; MLS, U. Minn., 1977. Libr. asst., dept. supr. Uppsala U. Library, Sweden, 1977-81; libr. archivist, instr. Swedish Swedish Immigration Rsch. Ctr., Augustana Coll., Rock Island, Ill., 1981-92; monographs libr. Yale Div. Sch. Library, New Haven, 1992-95; mgr. cataloging, collection devel. officer Thomson-Gale, Primary Source Microfilm, Woodbridge, 1996—. Grant projects reviewer NEH, Washington, 1985—99; free-lance translator Swedish to English, Upsalla, Sweden, 1971—74, 1978—81. Co-translator: From Sweden to America, 1976; translator: Swedish Exodus, 1979; translator, assoc. editor: On the Left in America, 1999; contbr. articles and essays to profl. publs. Recipient award of commendation, Concordia Hist. Inst., 1985; Hooker fellow, Yale U., 1970. Mem.: Spl. Librs. Assn., Soc. Am. Archivists, Midwest Archives Conf., Swedish-Am. Hist. Soc. (bd. dirs. 1989–92, 1996—2002, bibliography project co-editor 1982—83). Episcopalian. Avocations: books, music, photography, tennis, travel. Home: 1077 Whitney Ave Hamden CT 06517-3449 Office: Thomson-Gale Primary Source Microfilm 12 Lunar Dr Woodbridge CT 06525 Office Phone: 203-397-2600 ext. 3112.

**WESTERBERG, LARS,** automotive safety systems company executive; b. 1948; MBSS, Royal Instl Tech. Stockholm, 1972; MBA, U. Stockholm, 1978. With ASEA (now ABB), 1972; various positions Esab AB, welding machine co.; pres. N.Am. subs. Esab AB welding machine co., 1984-87, pres., CEO, 1991—94, Granges AB, aluminum and plastics, 1994—99, Autoliv Inc., Stockholm, 1999—. Office: Autoliv Inc World Trade Ctr Klarabergsviadukten 70 SE-10724 Stockholm Sweden Office Phone: 468 587 20620. Business E-Mail: lars.westerberg@autoliv.com.

**WESTERFIELD, CAROLYN ELIZABETH HESS,** urban planner; b. New Haven, May 3, 1933; d. Orvan Walter and Carol Woodruff (Maurer) Hess; m. Holt Bradford Westerfield, Dec. 17, 1960; children: Pamela Bradford Bingham, Leland Avery. BA, Wellesley Coll., 1954; postgrad., Yale U., 1954-55, M of City Planning, 1959. Planner, office mgr. Tech. Planning Assocs., New Haven, 1955-57, 61-62; assoc. planner City Plan Dept., New Haven, Conn., 1956-59; planner, editor State of Conn. Devel. Commn., 1959-61; cons., 1962—; prin. planner South Cent. Conn. Planning Region, 1979-87; asst. plan dir. Town of Fairfield (Conn.), 1987; planning and zoning adminstr. Town of

North Branford (Conn.), 1987-89. Devel. pvt. programs New Haven Hosp.-Boston City Hosp., 1952-54; lectr. city planning U. New Haven, 1988-2003. Mem. alumni bd. Yale U. Sch. Architecture, 1964-76, 85-96, pres., 1993-95; bd. dirs. alumni orgns. Prospect Hill Sch., New Haven, St. Thomas Day Sch.; class officer Wellesley Coll.; mem. Econ. Devel. Commn. Consortium, Hamden, Conn., mem. design rev. com.; clk. Ethics Commn. Mem. Am. Planning Assn., Am. Inst. Cert. Planners, Conn. Women in Planning and Devel., Alliance for Architecture (steering com. 1995–), New Haven Colony Hist. Soc., Jr. League New Haven (various exec. position), Watch Hill Improvement Soc. (pres. 1971-73), Conn. Child Welfare Assn., Yale U. Women's Orgn. (pres. 1979-81). Avocations: music, arts, sports, cultural exchange. Home and Office: 29 Old Orchard Rd North Haven CT 06473

**WESTERFIELD, HOLT BRADFORD,** retired political scientist; b. Rome, Mar. 7, 1928; s. Ray Bert and Mary Beatrice (Putney) W.; m. Carolyn Elizabeth Hess, Dec. 17, 1960; children: Pamela Bradford, Leland Avery. Grad., Choate Sch., 1944; BA, Yale U., 1947; MA, Harvard U., 1951, PhD, 1952. Instr. govt. Harvard U., 1952-56; asst. prof. polit. sci. U. Chgo., 1956-57; mem. faculty Yale U., 1957—, prof. polit. sci., 1965-2000, chmn. dept., 1970-72, Damon Wells prof. internat. studies, 1985-2000; prof. emeritus, 2000—; rsch. assoc. Washington Center Fgn. Policy Research, Johns Hopkins Sch. Advanced Internat. Studies, 1965-66. Vis. prof. Wesleyan U., Middletown, Conn., 1967, 71; bd. visitors U.S. Joint Mil. Intelligence Coll., Washington, 1998—. Author: Foreign Policy and Party Politics: Pearl Harbor to Korea, 1955, The Instruments of America's Foreign Policy, 1963; editor: Inside CIA's Private World: Declassified Articles from the Agency's Internal Journal, 1955-92, 1995. Sheldon traveling fellow Harvard, 1951-52; Henry L. Stimson fellow Yale, 1962, 73; sr. Fulbright-Hays scholar, 1973; hon. vis. fellow Australian Nat. U., 1973. Mem. Am. Polit. Sci. Assn. (Congl. fellow 1953-54), Internat. Polit. Sci. Assn., Internat. Studies Assn.

**WESTERFIELD, PUTNEY,** management consulting executive; b. New Haven, Feb. 9, 1930; s. Ray Bert and Mary Beatrice (Putney) W.; m. Anne Montgomery, Apr. 17, 1954; children: Bradford, Geoffrey, Clare. Grad., Choate Sch., 1942-47; BA, Yale, 1951. Co-founder, v.p. Careers, Inc., NYC, 1950-52; mgr. S.E. Asia Swen Publs., Inc., Manila, Philippines, 1952; mem. joint adv. commn. Korea, 1953-54; polit. officer Am. embassy, Saigon, Vietnam, 1955-57; asst. to pub. Time mag., NYC, 1957-59, asst. circulation dir., 1959-61, circulation dir., 1961-66, asst. pub., 1966-68, Life mag., NYC, 1968; pub. Fortune mag., NYC, 1969-73; pres. Chase World Info. Corp., NYC, 1973-75; v.p. Boyden Assocs. Internat., San Francisco, 1976-80, sr. v.p., western mgr., 1980-84, pres., chief exec. officer NYC, 1984-90, San Francisco, 1984—90, mng. dir. NYC, San Francisco, 1990—2005. Bd. dirs. Urban League, N.Y.C., 1969-71, Children's Village, 1968-71, Mediterranean Sch. Found., 1969-71, Nat. Boys Club, 1970-73, U.S. -S. Africa Leaders Exch. Program, 1971-03, Bus. Coun. Internat. Understanding, 1974-76, Yale-China Assn., 1975-78, East Meets West Found., 1991—; trustee Choate Sch., Wallingford, Conn., 1967-76, Westover Sch., Middlebury, Conn., 1975-79, Watch Hill Chapel Soc., 1963-77, Assn. Yale Alumni, 1972-75, 80-83. Mem. Burlingame Country Club, Pacific Union Club, Bohemian Club. Home and Office: 10 Greenview Ln Hillsborough CA 94010-6424 E-mail: putneyw@pacbell.net.

**WESTERFIELD, RANDOLPH W.,** finance educator, former dean; BA in econs., UCLA, 1963, MA in econs., 1965, PhD in fin., 1968. Asst. prof. fin. The Wharton Sch., U. Pa., Phila., 1968-73, assoc. prof. fin., 1973-81, sr. rsch. assoc., Rodney L. White Ctr. Fin. Rsch., 1977-88, prof. fin., 1981-88, chair fin. dept., 1986-88; Charles B. Thornton prof. fin., bus. econs. chair U So. Calif. Sch. Bus. Adminstrn., L.A., 1988-93; dean, Robert R. Dockson chair in bus. adminstrn. Marshall Sch. Bus., U. So. Calif., L.A., 1993–2004. Bd. dirs. William Lyon Homes, 2000-, Health Mgmt. Assocs. Inc., 2000-, Nicholas Applegate Growth Equity Fund; vis. prof. fin. U. Nova de Lisbon, Portugal, 1981, Stanford U., Palo Alto, Calif., 1981-82, Claremont (Calif.) Grad. Sch., 1983; mem. trust com. Continental Bank, Phila., 1979-88; mem. pension rsch. coun., The Wharton Sch., 1979-88; mem. editl. adv. bd. John Wiley & Sons (Asia) Pte Ltd., 1996; mem. authors adv. coun., Times Mirror-Irwin Co., 1987-97; chmn. Consortium for Grad. Study in Mgmt., 1997; past cons. AT&T, Mobil Oil, UN, U.S. Depts. Labor and Justice. Co-author: (with Stephen A. Ross, Jeffrey Jaffe) Corporate Finance, 1988, 90, 93, 96 (including Can., Australian and internat. edits.), (with Stephen A. Ross, Bradford D. Jordan) Fundamentals of Corporate Finance, 1992, 93, 95, 97 (including South African, Can., Australian, Chinese, Dutch and Spanish edits.), (with Stephen A. Ross, Bradford D. Jordan) Essentials of Corporate Finance, 1996; author monographs; contbr. chpts. to books, numerous articles to profl. jours. and conf. procs.; assoc. editor Fin. Rev., 1985-92. Mem. Nat. Assoc. Corp. Bds. (mem. bd. L.A. chpt. 1996). Office: Marshall Sch Bus Adminstrn U So Calif Hoffman Hall 800 701 Exposition Blvd Los Angeles CA 90089-0001

**WESTERGAARD, GEORGE HENRY,** secondary school educator; b. Sumas, Wash., Aug. 4, 1942; s. Henry C. and Mary T. Westergaard; m. Donna M. Westergaard, June 20, 1964; 1 child, Kristen. BA in Edn., Ctrl. Wash. State Coll., 1964; MS in Interdisciplinary Studies, U. Oreg., 1969; DA in History, Carnegie Mellon U., 1976. Cert. secondary edn. tchr., Wash. Tchr. social studies and English Woodrow Wilson Jr. H.S., Yakima, Wash., 1964-67, Cal Young Jr. H.S., Eugene, Oreg., 1967-73; mem. staff, asst. rsch. historian Carnegie Mellon U., Pitts., 1971-73; tchr. social studies, counselor Thomas Jefferson Jr. H.S., Eugene, 1973-83; tchr. govt., econs., global studies, and psychology South Eugene H.S., 1983-88, tchr. social scis., chair social studies dept., 1988-94, tchr. advanced placement govt. and politics, 1994-99; tchr. advanced placement psychology, comp. govt., politics, U.S. history Sammamish H.S., Bellevue, Wash., 1999—. Cons. AP Govt. and Politics workshops, 1990—; adj. prof. edn. U. Oreg., summer 1991; mem. social studies task force State of Oreg., 1997-99; nat. reader, question leader AP Gov. and Politics; adj. prof. Pacific Luth. U., 2001-05; editor, writer govt. and politics curricula and texts; chmn. program devel. Sammamish H.S. 2002-05 Mem. budget rev. com. Bellevue Sch. Dist. Fellow Ind. Study in the Humanities, 1986. Avocations: photography, fishing, hiking, boating. Home: 2323 167th Ave NE Bellevue WA 98008 Office: Sammamish HS Rm 510 100 140th Ave Bellevue WA 98005 Office Phone: 425-456-7676. Personal E-mail: westergg@comcast.net.

**WESTERGARD, SUE BENZEL,** elementary education educator; b. Apr. 17, 1954; BA, Whitworth Coll., 1976; M in Curriculum & Instrn., Nazarene Coll., 1993. Learning specialist Walla Walla (Wash.) Sch. Dist., 1976—. Office Phone: 509-527-3077. E-mail: swestergard@wwps.org.

**WESTERHOFF, JOHN HENRY, III,** clergyman, theology studies educator; b. Paterson, N.J., June 28, 1933; s. John Henry and Nona Celia (Walsh) W.; m. Alberta Louise Barnhart, Dec. 27, 1955 (div. 1991); children: Jill Louise, John Jeffrey, Beth Anne; m. Caroline Askew Hughes, Oct. 27, 1991. BS, Ursinus Coll., 1955; STB, Harvard U., 1958; EdD, Columbia U., 1974; DD, Ursinus Coll., 1990. Ordained to ministry United Ch. of Christ, 1958, Episcopal Ch., 1978; pastor Congl. Ch., Presque Isle, Maine, 1958-60, assoc. pastor Needham, Mass., 1960-64; pastor 1st Congl. Ch., Williamstown, Mass., 1964-66; edn. sec., editor Colloquy (United Ch. Bd. for Homeland Ministries), N.Y.C., 1966-73; Lentz lectr. Harvard U. Div. Sch., 1973-74; prof. Duke U. Div. Sch., Durham, NC, 1974-94; dir. Inst. Pastoral Studies, Atlanta, 1992–2003; interim rector St. Bartholomew Episcopal Ch., Atlanta, 1993-94; theologian in residence St. Lukes Episcopal Ch., Atlanta, 1994—2004; vis. prof. Gen. Theol. Sem., N.Y.C., 2004—; priest assoc., resident theologian St. Anne's Episc. Ch., Atlanta, 2005—. Author: Values for Tomorrows Children, 1970, A Colloquy on Christian Education, 1972, Generation to Generation, 1974, Tomorrow's Church, 1976, Will Our Children Have Faith?, 1976, McGuffey and His Readers, 1978, Who Are We?, 1978, Learning Through Liturgy, 1978, Inner Growth-Outer Change, 1979, The Church's Ministry in Higher Education, 1979, Liturgy and Learning Through the Life Cycle, 1980, Christian Believing, 1980, Bringing Up Children in The Christian Church, 1980, A Faithful Church, 1981, The Spiritual Life: Learning East and West, 1981, Building God's People, 1983, A Pilgrim People, 1984, Living the Faith Community, 1985, On the Threshold

of God's Future, 1986, Living Into Our Baptism, 1990, Schooling Christians, 1992, The Spiritual Life: Foundation for Preaching and Teaching, 1994; A People Called Episcopalians, 1995, Holy Baptism: A Guide for Parents and Godparents, 1996, Grateful and Generous Hearts, 1997, To Love and to Cherich Till Death Do Us Part, 1998, Sensing Beauty, 1998, A Pilgrim People, 1999, Will Our Children Have Faith?, 2000, Living Faithfully as a Prayer Book People, 2005; editor: Religious Edn, 1979-89. Mem. Assn. Profs. and Researchers in Religious Edn. Religious Edn. Assn. Democrat. Episcopalian. Personal E-mail: johnwest33@bellsouth.net.

**WESTERHOUT, GART,** retired astronomer; b. The Hague, The Netherlands, June 15, 1927; arrived in U.S., 1962, naturalized, 1969; s. Gerrit and Magdalena (Foppe) W.; m. Judith Mary Monaghan, Nov. 14, 1956; children: Magda C., Gart T., Brigit M., Julian C. Drs., Leiden U., Netherlands, 1954, PhD, 1958. Asst. Leiden U. Observatory, 1952-56, sci. officer, 1956-59, chief sci. officer, 1959-62; prof., dir. astronomy U. Md., 1962-73, chmn. div. math. and phys. scis. and engring., 1972-73, prof. astronomy, 1973-77; sci. dir. U.S. Naval Observatory, Washington, 1977-93; vis. astronomer Max Planck Inst. Radio Astronomy, Bonn, Germany, 1973-74, mem. adv. bd., 1976-79. Mem. astronomy adv. bd. NSF, 1963-67; vice chmn. divsn. phys. sci. NRC, 1969-73; mem. com. on radio frequencies, 1971-92; trustee Assoc. Univs. Inc., 1971-74; mem. Inter Union Commn. on Allocation of Frequencies, 1974-82; mem. sci. coun. Stellar Data Ctr., Strasbourg, France, 1978-84, chmn., 1981; chmn. working group on astrometry, astronomy survey com. NAS, 1979-81; mem. adv. bd. Haystack-N.E. Radio Obs. Consortium, 1974-77; mem. Arecibo adv. bd. Nat. Astronomy and Ionosphere Ctr., 1977-80, chmn., 1979-80; mem. U.S. nat. com. CODATA, 1985-91. Contbr. on radio astronomy, spiral structure of our Galaxy and astrometry to profl. jours. Recipient citation for teaching excellence Washington Acad. Scis., 1972; U.S. Sr. Scientist award Alexander von Humboldt Stiftung, Ger., 1973; NATO fellow, 1959. Mem. Internat. Astron. Union (chmn. working group on astron. data 1985-91), Internat. Sci. Radio Union (pres. commn. on radio astronomy 1975-78), Am. Astron. Soc. (councillor 1975-78, v.p. 1985-87), Royal Astron. Soc. Roman Catholic.

**WESTERMAN, LIANE MARIE,** research scientist executive; b. Long Branch, NJ, June 20, 1949; d. Charles Wilson and Edith Doris (Johnson) Case; m. S. Thomas Westerman; children: David Aaron, Charles Paul. BA in Psychology, Monmouth U., West Long Branch, N.J., 1972; MA in Teaching, Coll. of N.J., 1979. Cert. tchr. of handicapped, N.J. Supvr. spl. edn., dir. afternoon program S.E.A.R.C.H., Ocean, NJ, 1972-74; tchr. spl. edn. Jackson (N.J.) Twp. Sch. System, 1974-79; exec. dir. Otologic Edn., Inc., Shrewsbury, NJ, 1980-88; dir. clin. rsch. Nat. Patent Analytical Systems, Inc., Roslyn Heights, NY, 1983-86, v.p. rsch., 1986-88; pres. Westerman Rsch. Assocs., Inc., Shrewsbury, NJ, 1988—. Participant numerous convs., profl. organs. and spl. interest groups, U.S.A., Israel and The Netherlands, 1974—; software devel. expert to knowledge engr. for Visual Perceptual System, 1984—; v.p. Otologic Edn., Inc., Shrewsbury, 1988—. Co-contbr. articles and chpts. to profl. publs.; U.S. and Can. patentee computer-aided drug-abuse detection. Fundraiser Am. Heart Assn., 1991; bd. dirs. Women's Coun. for Leon Hess Cancer Ctr. at Monmouth Med. Ctr., 2003—; active MADD; activist Nat. Audubon Soc. Mem. Am. Acad. Otolaryngology, Head and Neck Surgery (assoc.), Internat. Regulatory Affairs Profls. Soc., Nat. Graphic Soc., Assn. Clin. Pharmacologists, Regulatory Affairs Profls. Soc., Monmouth County Assn. Children with Learning Disabilities, Psi Chi, Sigma Xi. Avocations: travel, classical music, creative writing. Office: Westerman Rsch Assocs Inc 170 Ave at the Common Ste 6 Shrewsbury NJ 07702-4003

**WESTERMANN, EDWARD BURTON,** military officer, analyst, educator; b. Temple, Tex., Nov. 18, 1961; s. Francis X. and Suzann Westermann; m. Brigitte Angelika Engel, Dec. 16, 1991; children: Sarah E, Marie-Louise. BS, USAF Acad., 1984; MA in European History, Fla. State U., 1992; MA, Sch. Advanced Airpower Studies, Maxwell AFB, 1997; PhD in European History, U. N.C., 2000. Helicopter Pilot USAF, 1985. Commd. 2d lt. USAF, 1984, advanced through grades to col.; exch. instr. pilot with German air force Hubschraubertransportgeschwader 64, Ahlhorn, Germany, 1988—91; asst. prof. history U.S. Air Force Acad., Colorado Springs, 1992—95; strategy devel. officer Hdqs. European Command, Stuttgart, Germany, 2000—02; prof. comparative mil. theory Sch. Advance Air and Space Studies, Maxwell AFB, Ala., 2002—; sr. mil. prof. USAF Acad., 2006—. Author: (historical work) Hitler's Police Battalions: Enforcing Racial War in the East, Flak: German Anti-Aircraft Defenses, 1918-1945. Decorated Ehrenkreuz der Bundeswehr in Bronze Fed. Rep. Germany; recipient John L. Snell prize, 1998, League of WWI Aviation Historians Nat. award, 1999; fellow, German Academic Exch. Svc., U. Calif. Berkeley, 1993, Fulbright fellow, U.S. Govt., 1994—95, U.S. Holocaust Meml. Mus., 1999, German Academic Exch. Svc., 1999, 2003—04. Mem.: Soc. Mil. History (Mancado prize 2002), Am. Hist. Assn., German Studies Assn., Daedalians (life), Phi Alpha Theta. Independent. Roman Catholic. Office: Dept Mil Strategic Studies USAF Acad U S A F Academy CO 80840 Home: 4158 Douglass Way U S A F Academy CO 80840 Office Phone: 719-333-9169. Home Fax: 334-953-3015. Personal E-mail: bawebw4@aol.com. Business E-Mail: edward.westermann@usafa.af.mil.

**WESTERMEIER, JOHN THOMAS, JR.,** lawyer, educator; b. West Point, N.Y., Sept. 14, 1941; s. John Thomas and Louise (Melick) W.; m. Joddie Lynn Stephens, Feb. 8, 1964 (div. Dec. 1966); 1 child, Blake Lynn; m. Cynthia Ann Heins, Aug. 23, 1980. BS, U.S. Mil. Acad., 1963; MBA, George Washington U., 1969, LLM, 1978; JD, Am. U., 1974; cert. in data processing, Inst. for Cert. of Computer Profls., 1978. Bar: Va. 1974, D.C. 1975, U.S. Supreme Ct. 1978, Md. 1982, U.S. Dist. Ct. D.C. 1982, U.S. Dist. Ct. (ea. dist.) Va. 1983, U.S. Dist. Ct., Md. 1987, U. S. Claims Ct. 1990. Commd. 2d lt. U.S. Army, 1963, advanced through grades to maj. Vietnam, 1966, 70, resigned, 1974; assoc. Arent, Fox, Kintner, Plotkin & Kahn, Washington, 1974-79; ptnr. Alsuann, Westermeier & Goldberg P.C., Washington, 1980-89, Fenwick & West, Washington, 1989—. Adj. prof. law Am. U., Washington, 1985-86; instr. continuing legal edn. Georgetown U. Law Ctr., Washington, 1987—; mem. bd. advisors Computer Negotiations, Orlando, Fla., 1982—, Computer Law Strategist, N.Y.C., 1985—, Computer Law Reporter, Washington, 1990—; mem. Va. Gov.'s Coun. Info. Mgmt., 1987-91. Author and editor: Data Processing and the Law, 1981, Computer Law Case Materials, 1986; articles editor Am. U. Law Rev., 1973; legal editor Information Strategy: The Executive's Jour., 1984—, bd. advisors, 1984—; contbr. over 80 articles to profl. jours. Bd. advisors No. Va. Hotline, Arlington, 1975-78; del. Va. Rep. Conv., Virginia Beach, 1985, Richmond, 1990-93. Decorated 2 Bronze Stars, Vietnamese Cross of Gallantry; recipient Disting. Information Scis. award Data Processing Mgmt. Assn., Chgo., 1987 Fellow Am. Bar Found.; mem. ABA (chmn. com. of professionalism and malpractice of computer specialists computer law divsn. 1978—), D.C. Bar Assn. (instr. continuing legal edn., steering com. computer law sect. 1986-92, co-chmn. 1989), Data Processing Mgmt. Assn. Washington (pres. 1982), D.C. Computer Law Forum (bd. dirs. 1984), Phi Alpha Delta. Clubs: West Point Soc. (Washington) (bd. govs., sec. 1974-82). Republican. Episcopalian. Avocations: tennis, golf, swimming, writing. Office: DLA Piper 1775 Wiehle Ave Suite 400 Reston VA 20190-5159*

**WESTERMEYER, JOSEPH JOHN,** psychiatrist; b. Chgo., Apr. 8, 1937; m. Rachel Moga; children: Michelle, Joseph; 5 foster children. Student, U. Notre Dame and St. Thomas Coll., 1955-57; BS in Biology and Chemistry, U. Minn., 1959, MD, 1961, MA in Anthropology, 1969, MPH, PhD, 1970. Diplomate Am. Bd. Psychiatry and Neurology, Am. Bd. Family Practice. Rotating intern St. Paul-Ramsey Hosp., 1961-62; gen. practice medicine Payne Ave. Med. Clinic, St. Paul, 1962-65; dep. chief chmn. pub. health AID, Laos, 1965-67; resident in psychiatry U. Minn., Mpls., 1967-70, instr., 1970-71, asst. prof., 1971-74, assoc. prof., 1974-78, prof. psychiatry, 1978—, prof., chair, 1989, adj. prof. anthropology, 1979—89, 1993—, adj. prof. psychology, 1979—89, mem. student edn. dept. psychiatry, 1976-82; mem. psychiatry staff, outpatient psychiat. practice U. Minn. Hosps. and Clinics, Mpls., 1970-89; prof., chmn. dept. psychiatry and behavioral sci. Okla. U. Med. Ctr., Oklahoma City, 1989—92; founder, dir. acute in-patient service U. Minn. Hosps. and Clinics, Mpls., 1970-72, founder, dir. day hosp., 1971-73, cons. primary care clinic, 1970-83, founder, dir. outpatient clinic for refugees from S.E. Asia, 1977—89, founder, dir. program for alcohol and drug dependence, 1982—89, founder, dir. internat. clinic dept. psychiatry, 1984—89; chief psychiatry, dir. mental health Mpls. VA Med. Ctr., 1993—. Mem. ad hoc com. on Indochinese refugees Minn. Dept. Pub. Welfare, 1980-82; cons. methadone program Minn. VA Hosp., 1977-84, dept. psychiatry Mpls. VA Hosp., 1978-85; mem. case devel. com. for computer-based exam. Nat. Bd. Med. Examiners, 1983-88; mem. com. on mental and behavioral assessment and disorder in pilots FAA and AMA, 1984-85; chmn., co-editor devel. of a teaching manual on drug/alcohol dependence WHO, 1982-85, chmn., co-editor task force and report on methadone treatment in opiate dependence, 1982-85, research cons. internat. collaborative study of drug dependence intervention and treatment in primary health care, 1982-85; sec. Group for Advancement of psychiatry, 1999-2005, co-chair addiction psychiatry cert. Am. Bd. Psychiatry and Neurology, 2003-, Spl. Polulation Com. Health Svc Rsch VA, 2005-; cons. in field; vis. prof. various colls.; lectr. in field. Author: A Primer on Chemical Dependency: A Clinical Guide to Alcohol and Drug Problems, 1976, Poppies, Pipes and People: A Study of Opium and Its Use in Laos, 1983, (with C. Williams) Refugees Mental Health Issues in Resettlement Countries, 1986, A Clinical Guide to Drug and Alcohol Problems, 1986; (with A. Arif) A Manual for Substance Abuse Education, 1988, An Update on Methadone, 1988; The Psychiatric Care of Migrants, 1989; editor: Anthropology and Mental Health, 1976; co-editor: (with E. Foulks, R. Wintrob and A. Favazza) Transcultural Psychiatry, 1977, (with R. weiss and D. Ziedonis) Comorbid Affective Disorder and Substance Abuse, Johns Hopkins Press, 2003; contbr. revs. and articles to profl. jours., chpts. to books; mem. editorial bd. Am. Jour. Drug and Alcohol Abuse, 1973—, Jour. Operational Psychiatry, 1977-86, Am. Jour. Pub. Health, 1980-83, 83-87, Advances in Alcohol and Substance Abuse, 1980—, Alcoholism: Clin. and Exptl. Research, 1980-86, Alcohol and Research World, 1981—; social sci. editor Substance Abuse Newsletter, 1979-83; rev. reader Am. Jour. Psychiatry, 1978—, Transcultural Psychiat. Revs., 1980-84, Archives Gen. Psychiatry, 1981—, White Cloud Jour., 1981—, Jour. Nervous and Mental Disease, 1977—, Current Anthropology, 1979, 83, 85, Culture, Medicine and Psychiatry, 1979-80, various others. Recipient Meritorious Service award U.S. All, 1967; Ginzburg fellow Group for Advancement of Psychiatry, 1969-70, NIH summer fellow Grad. Session in Epidemiology, U. Minn. Continuation Ctr., 1970, 72, 78; research grantee Office Internat. Programs, U. Minn., 1974-75, 78, 81, NIMH, 1973-74, 80-81, 82-84, Nat. Inst. Alcohol Abuse and Alcoholism, 1974-77, 78-79, Grad. Sch. U. Minn., 1977-78, Office Drug Abuse Prevention, U. Minn., 1977-78, Minn. Med. Found., 1974-75, 81, 82-83, Nat. Inst. Drug Abuse, 1977-78, 83-85, State Minn., 1979-80, Ctr. Urban and Regional Affairs, U. Minn., 1982-83, career tchr. grantee Alcohol, Drug Abuse and Mental Health Adminstrn., HEW, 1973-75, Biomed. research support grantee U. Minn. Med. Sch., 1977-78, Minn. Med. Found., 1977, tng. grantee Office Alcohol and Other Drug Abuse Programming, U. Minn., 1979-83, Indochinese Health Professionals, 1979-81, Archie; recipient numerous other research grants. Fellow Am. Anthropol. Assn., Am. Acad. Family Practice, Am. Psychiat. Assn. (com. on drug abuse 1985—); mem. World Psychiat. Assn. (transcultural sect.), Am. Soc. Social Psychiatry, Soc. Med. Anthropology, Assn. Med. Educators and Researchers in Substance Abuse (award for disting. contributions to the field 1987), AAAS, Assn. Behavioral Sci. and Med. Edn., Assn. Acad. Psychiatrists, Am. Pub. Health Assn., Research Soc. on Alcoholism, World Psychiat. Assn. (sect. on transcultural psychiatry, Soc. for Study of Psychiatry and Culture (steering com. 1979—, secretariat 1984-85), Am. Med. Soc. on Alcoholism (state chmn. 1979—), Am. Acad. Psychiatrists in Alcoholism and Addictions, Soc. Traumatic Stress Studies, Minn. Psychiat. Assn. (mem. chem. dependency subcom. 1979—85, mem. Minn. mental health interdisciplinary interest group rep. 1980-85, pres. 1984-86), Minn. State Med. Assn. (resource group on alcoholism and other chem. dependencies 1976-81), Alpha Omega Alpha. Home: 1935 Summit Ave Saint Paul MN 55105-1430 Office Phone: 612-725-2037. Business E-Mail: joseph.westermeyer@med.va.gov, weste010@umn.edu.

**WESTERN, KARL AUGUST,** physician, epidemiologist; b. Trenton, N.J., July 6, 1940; s. August Earl and Lillian Theresa (Murphy) W.; m. Aileen Martin Worthington, May 2, 1964; children: Ann Western Bittman, Mark August. AB, Georgetown U., 1961, MD, 1965; diploma of tropical pub. health, London Sch. Tropical Medicine & Hygiene, 1972. Intern Bellevue Hosp.-Cornell Meml.-Sloan Kettering Joint Program, N.Y.C., 1965-66, resident, 1966-67; medical epidemiologist Ctr. Disease Control, Atlanta, 1967-70; resident supr. infectious diseases L.A. County-USC Med. Ctr., 1971-72; med. epidemiologist Va. State Health Dept., Richmond, 1972-74; dept. head Pan Am. Health Orgn., Washington, 1975-79; asst. dir., dir. Office of Global Affairs, NIAID, Bethesda, Md., 1979—. Med. dir. USPHS, 1967-97. Recipient Okeke award U. London, 1972, Meritorious Service award, 1970, Commendation award 1983, Outstand. Service award, 1987, USPHS. Mem. AMA, Am. Soc. Tropical Medicine and Hygiene (editor Tropical Med. news, 1987-99), Am. Pub. Health Assn. (sec. epidemiology sect. 1973-78), Nat. Coun. Internat. Health (chair annual meeting 1986). Republican. Roman Catholic. Home: 6436 31st St NW Washington DC 20015-2342 Office: Nat Inst Allergy Infectious Diseases/NIH 9000 Rockville Pike Bethesda MD 20892-6613

**WESTERVELT, JAMES JOSEPH,** retired insurance company executive; b. Bklyn., July 8, 1946; s. Cornealius V. and Regina Elizabeth (May) W.; m. Sue Jane Brubaker, Aug. 5, 1972; children: Kevin K., Natalie M. BBA, Manhattan Coll., 1967. Mgr. auditing Peat, Marwick & Mitchell, N.Y.C., 1967-78; dir. auditing City Investing, N.Y.C., 1978-81; asst. v.p., asst. contr. The Hartford Financial Svcs. Group, Inc., Conn., 1981-89, v.p., group contr. Conn., 1989-94; sr. v.p., group contr. Hartford, Conn., 1994—2001; group contr. Hartford Fin. Svc. Group, 1998-99; sr. v.p., CFO Himco, 1999—2001; sr. v.p. Hartford Fin. Svc., Inc.; ret., 2002—. With U.S. Army, 1968-69. Mem. AICPA, Hawaii Soc. CPAs, Conn. Soc. CPAs, Am. Ins. Assn. Roman Catholic. Avocations: skiing, wine tasting, tennis, chess, electronics.

**WESTFALL, CONSTANCE COURTNEY,** lawyer; b. Plainview, Tex., Nov. 29, 1960; d. M.H. and Carolyn Courtney; m. Monte Jay Westfall, Jan. 3, 1998; children: William, John. BS, U. Tex., 1982, JD, 1985. Bar: Tex., U.S. Dist. Ct. (we. and no. dists.) Tex., U.S. Dist. Ct. (we. and ea. dists.) Ark., U.S. Dist. Ct. (we. dist.) Okla., U.S. Ct. Appeals (5th and 8th cirs.) Tex. Com. clk. Natural Resources Com., Tex. Ho. of Rep., 1979; legis. staff to hon. Buck Florence Tex. Ho. of Rep., 1980-82; law clk. to hon. Jerre Williams U.S. Ct. Appeals (5th cir.), 1985-86; assoc. Thompson & Knight, Dallas, 1986-92, Brown McCarroll, Dallas, 1992-94; ptnr. Hutcheson & Grundy, Dallas, 1994-98, Strasburger & Price, Dallas, 1998—. Contbr. articles to profl. jours. Moderator So. Meth. U. Sch. Law Environ. Career Seminar, 1989-2000. Mem.: ABA, State Bar Coll., State Bar Tex. (mem. law sch. com. 1988—97, chmn. outreach com. environ. sect. 1989—92, chmn. law sch. com. 1997—2003, chmn. environ. and natural resources sect. 2003—04, mem. sect. coord. com. 2004—06). Office: Strasburger & Price 901 Main St Ste 4300 Dallas TX 75202-3724

**WESTFALL, DAVID,** lawyer, educator; b. Columbia, Mo., Apr. 16, 1927; s. Wilhelmus David A. and Ruth (Rollins) W.; children: Elizabeth Stewart, William Beatty, Thomas Curwen, Katharine Putnam. AB, U. Mo., 1947; LLB magna cum laude, Harvard U., 1950. Bar: Ill. 1950, Mass. 1956. Assoc. Bell, Boyd, Marshall & Lloyd, Chgo., 1950-55; asst. prof. law Harvard Law Sch., 1955-58, prof., 1958—, John H. Watson Jr. prof. law 1980—83, John L. Gray prof., 1983—, Carl F. Schipper Jr. prof., 1996—. Author: Estate Planning Cases and Text, 1985, Every Woman's Guide to Financial Planning, 1984, Family Law, 1993; co-author: Estate Planning Law and Taxation, 4th edit., 2001; co-editor: Readings in Federal Taxation, 1983. Served as 1st lt. JAGC, AUS, 1951-53. Fellow Am. Coll. Trust and Estate Counsel (council 1977—). Mem. ABA, Mass. Bar Assn., Am. Law Inst., Phi Beta Kappa, Phi Delta Theta. Office: 1525 Massachusetts Ave Cambridge MA 02138-2903 Office Phone: 617-495-4630. Business E-Mail: dwestfal@law.harvard.edu.

**WESTFALL, MARGARET V.,** science educator; d. Alan K. Williams and Barbara H. Martin, James F. Martin (Stepfather) and Peggie Williams (Stepmother); m. David D. Westfall, Sept. 3, 1957; children: Allison B., Daniel M. BA, Colo. Coll., Colorado Springs, 1978; PhD, Loyola U., Maywood, Ill., 1988. Rsch. asst. prof. U. of Mich., Ann Arbor, 1998—2000, asst. prof., 2000—. Mem.: Biophysical Soc. Office: U Mich 1150 W Medical Center Dr Ann Arbor MI 48109 Office Phone: 734-615-8911.

**WESTFALL, MORRIS,** farmer, retired state legislator; b. Apr. 5, 1939; s. Raymond Earl and Ethel Faye (Neill) W.; m. Sharon Kay Douglas, Dec. 19, 1964; children: Craig Lin, Christi Dawn. BS, U. Mo., 1962. Mem. Mo. Ho. of Reps., Jefferson City, 1971-81; minority whip, 1977—80; asst. minority floor leader, 1981; mem. Mo. Senate from 28th dist., Jefferson City, 1994—2002; chmn. Senate Majority Caucus, 2001—02; operator livestock farm Halfway, Mo. State exec. dir. agrl. stabilization conservation svc. USDA, Mo., 1981-93. Mem. U. Mo. Alumni Assn., Saddle Club.

**WESTFALL, TERRI LEE,** kindergarten educator; d. Lee Roger and Louise Kathleen Krout; m. Bryan Matthew Westfall, Dec. 16; 1 child, Nolan Matthew. BS in Edn., Messiah Coll., Grantham, Pa., 1998; MEd in Tchg. and Curriculum, Pa. State U., Harrisburg. Day camp dir. YMCA, Littlestown, Pa., 1998; tchr. Fairfield Area Sch. Dist., Pa., 1998—. Mem.: Delta Kappa Gamma (corr. sec. 2002—). Lutheran. Avocations: exercise, scrapbooks. Office: Fairfield Area Sch Dist 4842 Fairfield Rd Fairfield PA 17320

**WESTFIELD, FRED MEINHARD,** economics professor; b. Essen, Germany, Nov. 7, 1926; came to U.S., 1940; s. Dietrich and Grete (Stern) W.; m. Joyce A. Horwitz Nochlin, Nov. 15, 1968; stepchildren: Steven Nochlin, Keith Nochlin. BA magna cum laude, Vanderbilt U., 1950; PhD in Indsl. Econs., MIT, 1957. Teaching asst., instr. MIT, Cambridge, 1952-53; lectr. Northwestern U., Evanston, Ill., 1953-57, asst. prof., 1957-60, assoc. prof., 1960-65; prof. econs. Vanderbilt U., Nashville, 1965-98, mem. faculty coun. Coll. Arts and Sci., 1974-76, mem. faculty senate, 1979-82, 94-95, dir. undergrad. studies dept. econs. and bus. adminstrn., 1984-87, mem. grad. faculty coun., 1991, prof. econs. emeritus, 1998—. Vis. prof. U. Colo., summers 1973-74; condr. seminars, lectr., participant univs. and rsch. orgns.; Fulbright sr. lectr. U. Nac. del Sur, Argentina, 1986; cons. Coun. Econ. Advisers, Exec. Office Pres., 1968, World Bank and Water and Power Devel. Authority, Pakistan, 1970-72, World Bank and East African Power and Light Co., Kenya, 1975, NSF, 1975, FTC, 1976-78, World Bank, UN Devel. Program and Econ. Planning Bd. South Korea, 1975-76; expert witness Tenn. Pub. Svc. Commn., 1980-89, Consumer Advocate Tenn. Atty. Gen., 1994; also others. Mem. editl. bd. Utilities Policy, 1990—2002, mem. bd. editors So. Econ. Jour., 1973—75, editl. referee Am. Econ. Rev., Jour. Polit. Economy, Econometrica, So. Econ. Jour., Econ. Inquiry; contbr. articles and book revs. to profl. jours. With U.S. Army, 1945—46. Fellow Gen. Edn. Bd., MIT, Ford Found., 1958-59. Mem. Am. Econ. Assn., Econometric Soc. (program com. 1967, chmn. conf. sessions), So. Econ. Assn. (v.p. 1976-77, chmn. conf. sessions), Phi Beta Kappa. Home: 1097 Lynnwood Blvd Nashville TN 37215-4540

**WESTFIELD, MARGARET ANN HOYERT,** architect; b. Cheverly, Md., July 31, 1959; d. Robert Scott and Frances K. Hoyert; m. Michael Matthew Westfield, Sept. 3, 1983; children: Marina Michelle, Emily Elizabeth. BArch, U. Md., 1982; MA Preservation Studies, Boston U., 1985. Registered Pa., 1986, N.J., 1988. Ptnr. Westfield Architects & Preservation Cons., Haddon Heights, NJ, 1988—; historic architect State of N.J., Trenton, 1998—2000. Adj. lectr. Drew U., Madison, NJ, 1999—; adj. prof. Burlington County Coll., Pemberton, NJ, 2000—. Mem.: Haddon Heights Hist. Soc. (pres. 1999—2001), Assn. Preservation Tech. (chair Delaware Valley chpt. 1996—2000), Preservation N.J. (dir. 2001). Office: Westfield Architects 425 White Horse Pike Haddon Heights NJ 08035-1706

**WESTHAUSER, KARL E.,** historian; b. N.Y.C., July 27, 1961; s. Karl Edwin and Margaret Marie Westhauser. BA, Cornell U., 1983; MA, Brown U., 1985, PhD, 1994. Prof. history Ala. State U., Montgomery, Ala., 1993—. Editor: Creating Community, 2005; mem. editl. bd.: Jour. African.-Am. Studies, 2005—. Docent Montgomery (Ala.) Mus. Fine Arts, 1996—2001. Mem.: So. Conf. African-American Studies, Am. Hist. Assn., Montgomery (Ala.) County Hist. Soc. Office: Campus Box 25 Alabama State U 915 S Jackson St Montgomery AL 36101

**WESTHEIMER, FRANK HENRY,** chemist, educator; b. Balt., Jan. 15, 1912; s. Henry Ferdinand and Carrie (Burgunder) Westheimer; m. Jeanne Friedmann, Aug. 31, 1937; children: Ruth Susan, Ellen. AB, Dartmouth Coll., 1932, ScD (hon.), 1961; MA, Harvard U., 1933, PhD, 1935; ScD (hon.), U. Chgo., 1973, U. Cin., 1976; ScD (hon.), Tufts U., 1978, U. N.C., 1983, Bard Coll., 1983, Weizmann Inst., 1987; ScD (hon.), U. Ill., Chgo., 1988. Rsch. assoc. U. Chgo., 1936—37, instr. 1937—41, asst. prof., 1941—44, assoc. prof., 1944—48, prof. chemistry, 1948—53; vis. prof. Harvard U., 1953—54, prof. chemistry, 1954—82, sr. prof., 1982—83, prof. emeritus, 1983—, chmn. dept., 1959—62; Overseas fellow Churchill Coll., U. Cambridge, England, 1962—63. Mem. Pres.'s Sci. Adv. Com., 1967—70; rsch. supr. Explosives Rsch. Lab., Nat. Def. Rsch. Com, 1944—45; presenter in field. Mem. editl. bd.: Jour. Chem. Physics, 1942—44, 1952—54, 1960—69; contbr. articles to profl. jours. Recipient Naval Ordnance Development award, 1946, Army-Navy cert. of appreciation, 1946, James Flack Norris award in phys.-organic chemistry, 1970, Willard Gibbs medal, 1970, Theodore W. Richards medal, 1976, Richard Kokes award, 1980, Charles Frederick Chandler medal, 1980, Rosenstiel award, 1981, Nichols medal, 1982, Robert A. Welch award, 1982, Cope award, 1982, Ingold medal, 1983, Nat. Medal of Sci., 1986, Paracelsus medal, 1988, Priestley medal, 1988, Repligen award, 1992, Nakanishi award, 1997, Westheimer medal, Harvard U. Dept. Chemistry, 2003; fellow, Columbia U. NRC, 1935—36, Guggenheim Found., 1942—43, Fulbright-Hays Found., 1974, Japan Soc. Promotion of Sci., 1982; Exchange fellow, NAS, China, 1982. Mem.: Royal Soc., Am. Acad. Arts and Scis. (sec. 1985—90), Am. Philos. Soc. (council 1981—84), Nat. Acad. Sci. (council 1971—75, 1976—79, chmn. com. survey chemistry 1964—65, award in chem. scis. 1980). Home: 3 Berkeley St Cambridge MA 02138-3409 E-mail: westheimer@chmistry.harvard.edu.

**WESTHEIMER, GERALD,** optometrist, educator; b. Berlin, May 13, 1924; naturalized, 1944, came to U.S., 1951; s. Isaak and Ilse (Cohn) W. Optometry diploma, Sydney Tech. Coll., Australia, 1943, fellowship diploma, 1950; BSc, U. Sydney, 1947; PhD, Ohio State U., 1953; DSc (hon.), U. NSW, Australia, 1988; ScD (hon.), SUNY, 1990; MD (hon.), U. Tubingen, 2005. Practice optometry, Sydney, 1945-51; research fellow Ohio State U., 1951-53; prof. physiol. optics U. Houston, 1953-54; asst. prof., then assoc. prof. physiol. optics Ohio State U., 1954-60; postdoctoral fellow neurophysiology Marine Biol. Lab., Woods Hole, Mass., 1957; vis. researcher Physiol. Lab., U. Cambridge, Eng., 1958-59; mem. faculty U. Calif. at Berkeley, 1960—, prof. physiol. optics, 1963-68, chmn. group physiol. optics, 1964-67, prof. physiology, 1968-89, prof. neurobiology, 1989—, head div. neurobiology, 1987-92; adj. prof. Rockefeller U., N.Y., 1992—. Sackler lectr. Tel Aviv U. Med. Sch., 1988, D.O. Hebb lectr. McGill U., 1991, Grass Found. lectr. U. Ill., 1991, Wertheimer lectr. U. Frankfort on the Main, 1998; mem. com. vision NRC, 1957-72; mem. visual scis. study sect. NIH, 1966-70, chmn. visual scis. B study sect., 1977-79; mem. vision, research and tng. com. Nat. Eye Inst., NIH, 1970-74, chmn. bd. sci. counselors, 1981-83; mem. exec. council com. vision NAS-NRC, 1969-72; mem. communicative scis. cluster Pres.'s Biomed. Rsch. Panel, 1975. Author rsch. papers; editor: Vision Rsch., 1972-79; editl. bd. Investigative Ophthalmology, 1973-77, Exptl. Brain Rsch., 1973-89, Optics Letters, 1977-78, Spatial Vision, 1985—, Ophthalmic and Physiological Optics, 1985—, Vision Rsch., 1985-92, Jour. of Physiology, 1987-94. Recipient Von Sallman prize Columbia U., 1986; Prentice medal Am. Acad. Optometry, 1986, Bicentennial medal Australian Optometric Assn., 1988. Fellow AAAS, Royal Soc. London (Ferrier lectr. 1992, editl. bd. procs. 1990-96, 2000—), Am. Acad. Arts and Scis., Optical Soc. Am. (Tillyer medal 1978, assoc. editor jour. 1980-83), Am. Acad. Optometry; mem. Royal Soc. New So. Wales, Soc. Neurosci., Assn. Rsch. in Vision and Ophthalmology

(Proctor medal 1979), Internat. Brain Rsch. Orgn., Physiol. Soc. Gt. Britain, Sigma Xi. Home: 582 Santa Barbara Rd Berkeley CA 94707-1746 Office Phone: 510-642-4828. E-mail: gwestheimer@berkeley.edu.

**WESTIN, DAVID LAWRENCE,** broadcast executive, lawyer; b. Flint, Mich., Dec. 19, 1952; s. Lawrence Rae and Mary Louise (Holman) W.; m. Victoria Peters; children: Victoria, Elizabeth, Matthew. BA, U. Mich., 1974, JD, 1977. Bar: D.C. 1979. Law clk. U.S. Ct. Appeals (2d cir.), N.Y.C., 1977-78, U.S. Supreme Ct., Washington, 1979; assoc. Wilmer, Cutler & Pickering, Washington, 1979-84, ptnr., 1985-91; sr. v.p., gen. counsel Capital Cities/ABC, Inc., N.Y.C., 1991-93; pres. of prodn. ABC TV Network, N.Y.C., 1993-94, pres., 1994-97, pres. of news, 1997—. Lectr. Harvard U. Law Sch., Cambridge, Mass., 1986; adj. prof. Georgetown U. Law Ctr., Washington, 1989-91. Bd. dirs. Lincoln Ctr. Film. Soc., 1994—, Am. Arbitration Assn., 1991—. Mem.: Chevy Chase (Md.). Democrat. Presbyterian. Office: ABC TV Network 47 W 66th St Fl 5 New York NY 10023-6201*

**WESTLAKE, E. J.,** performing arts educator; d. Curtis Edison Westlake and Joy Louise Hauser; life ptnr. Claudia Rene Wier; 1 child, Travis Ross. B. U. Minn., Mpls., 1985; PhD, U. Wis., Madison, 1997. Co-found. Stark Raving Theatre, Portland, Oreg., mng. dir., 1988—92; asst. prof. U. Mich., Ann Arbor, 2001—. Vis. asst. prof. Auburn U., Ala., 1999—2000, Bowling Green State U., Bowling Green, Ohio, 2000—01. Author: (book) Our Land is Made of Courage and Glory, (play) A.E.: The Disappearance and Death of Amelia Earhart (Oreg. Book Award, 1992). Mem. Soc. Of Friends. Office: U Mich Dept Theatre 1226 Murfin Ave Ann Arbor MI 48109 Home Fax: 206-222-2361; Office Fax: 206-222-2361. Personal E-mail: jewestla@umich.edu.

**WESTLAKE, MERLE T., JR.,** architect; BArch, Carnegie Inst. Tech.; MArch and Urban Design, Cranbrook Acad. of Art. Author: Josiah Fox (1763-1847), 2001; contbr. articles to Pa. Mag. of History and Biography, to Am. Neptune, numerous arch. jours. Fellow: AIA; mem.: NAD (academician 1994—).

**WESTLEY, JOHN RICHARD,** economist; b. Fairmont, Minn., Feb. 25, 1939; s. Richard and Margaret (Kindschi) W.; m. Sidney Kathryn Bohanna, Mar. 26, 1966(div. Sept. 1977); children: Elizabeth Laura, Karen Margaret, Marian Bohanna; m. Joan Nancy Ehrlich, Apr. 12, 1980; 1 child, Katherine Matthea. BA in Philosophy, Yale U., 1961; MA in Econs., Columbia U., 1966; PhD in Econs., Am. Univ., 1983. Internat. economist U.S. Dept. Treasury, Washington, 1966-69; loan officer U.S. AID, Addis Ababa, Ethiopia, 1970-72, economist Nairobi, Kenya, 1973-75, Washington, 1976-78, program officer New Delhi, 1979-84, dir. mission to Bangladesh Dhaka, 1985-87, assoc. asst. adminstr. bur. Africa Washington, 1987-90, dir. mission to Kenya Nairobi, 1990-94; dir. Mission to Egypt US AID, Cairo, 1994-98; v.p. Internat. Fund Agrl. Devel., Rome, 1998—2002; adj. assoc. prof. econs. John Cabot U., Rome, 2002—. Author: Agriculture and Equitable Growth, 1986. With U.S. Army, 1961-64. Mem. Am. Econ. Assn., Phi Beta Kappa. Presbyterian. Office: John Cabot Univ Via Della Lungara 233 00165 Rome Italy E-mail: jwestle@tin.it.

**WESTLUND, MARIBETH,** secondary school educator; b. Chgo., Apr. 29, 1961; d. Francis Joseph and Catherine Marie Balda. BS, Ill. State U., 1983; MEd, DePaul U., 1993. Cert. ednl. adminstr., tchr. Ill. Tchr. Our Lady of Knock Cath. Sch., Calumet City, Ill., 1985—86; dept. chair of social studies, tchr. Schaumburg H.S., Schaumburg High School, Ill., 1986—. Bd. dirs. N.W. Ctr. Against Sexual Assault. Nominee Golden Apple Educator Nominee, Golden Apple Found., 2002. Mem.: AAUW, NOW, Nat. Coun. Social Studies. Avocations: travel, hiking, bicycling, tennis. Office: Schaumburg HS 1100 W Schaumburg Rd Schaumburg IL 60194 Personal E-mail: mbwestlund@yahoo.com. E-mail: mwestlund@d211.org.

**WESTMAN, BARBARA,** artist; b. Boston, Apr. 3, 1929; d. Frederick Waldemar Westman and Eleanor (Proctor) Furminger; m. Arthur Coleman Danto, Feb. 15, 1980. AB in Art History, Goucher Coll., 1950; postgrad., Malschule Die Form, Munich, 1953-56, Boston Mus. Fine Arts Sch., 1957-60, 60-61. Tchr. painting Boston Mus. Fine Arts Sch., 1963-67; tchr. art Beaver Country Day Sch., Brookline, Mass., 1963-65; draftsman, designer Peabody Mus., Harvard U., Cambridge, Mass., 1967-77; staff artist Harvard U. Gazette, Cambridge, Mass., 1977-80; freelance artist N.Y.C. 1980—; cover artist New Yorker Mag., 1983—. Author, artist: The Bean and the Scene: Drawings of Boston and Cambridge, 1969, The Beard and the Braid: Drawings of Cambridge by Barbara Westman with Her Own Observations, 1970; (with others) A Boston Picture Book, 1974; author, artist: A Beacon Hill Christmas, 1976, Anna's Magic Broom, 1977, Drawings for I Like the Music, 1987 (Reading Rainbow prize, named Harper Trophy Book), Drawings for My Perfect Neighborhood, 1990, The Day Before Christmas, A Story of Charlotte and Emilio, 1990, Dancing Dogs, 1991; represented in permanent collections Boston Mus. Fine Arts, Boston Pub. Libr., Harvard's Peabody Mus., Busch-Reisinger Mus., Boston Athenaeum, Listasafn Reykjavikur, Reykjavik, Iceland, Bergen Kunstmuseum, Hafnarborg (Iceland) Inst. Culture and Fine Arts, others. Ruth Sturdivant scholar Boston Mus. Fine Arts Sch., 1961, Boston (Mass.) Mus. Fine Arts, 2003. Mem.: Denman Waldo Ross Soc. Home and Office: 420 Riverside Dr Apt 1C New York NY 10025-7751 Office Phone: 212-666-3588.

**WESTMAN, CARL EDWARD,** lawyer; b. Youngstown, Ohio, Dec. 12, 1943; s. Carl H. and Mary Lillis (Powell) W.; m. Carolyn J., July 17, 1965; children: C. Forrest, Stephanie A. BBA, Sam Houston State U., 1966; JD, U. Miami, 1969, LLM in Taxation, 1972. Bar: Fla. 1969. Ptnr. Frost & Jacobs, 1983-93, Roetzel & Andress, 1993-98; adminstrv. ptnr. Steel, Hector & Davis, Naples, Fla., 1999—2004, Cohen & Grigsby, 2004—. Active S.W. Fla. coun. Boy Scouts Am. Eagle Bd. of Rev., 1987—; chmn. planned giving com. Audubon of Fla. for S.W. Fla.; trustee David Lawrence Found. for Mental Health, Inc., 1976-86, chmn., 1985-86; trustee Pikeville Coll., 1993-2005, trustee, 1991, chmn. NCH Healthcare Sys. Inc., 2005—, chmn. profl. capabilities com. physician credentialing, 1998—; trustee, chmn. Naples Cmty. Hosp., 2001; past pres. bd. trustees, elder Moorings Presbyn. Ch. Master lic. capt. USCG. Mem. Fla. Bar Assn., Collier County Bar Assn., Estate Planning Coun., Marco Island Yacht Club, Marco Island Marina Asso (pres.). Home: 1952 Crayton Rd Naples FL 34102-5070 Office: Collier Place I 3003 Tamiami Trail N Ste 3003 Naples FL 34103-2718 Office Phone: 239-430-1800. E-mail: cwestman@cohenlaw.com.

**WESTMAN, CRAIG ELLERY,** academic administrator; s. Franklin A. and Virginia Westman Vickers; m. Lee Ann Elliott Westman, Aug. 14, 1993; children: Madeleine Lee, Erica Grace, Jillian Grace, Paige Martha. BA, Fla. Atlantic U., 1988, MA, 1990; PhD, Fla. State U., 1997. Asst. registrar Fla. State U., Tallahassee, 1993—98; registrar Ferris State U., Big Rapids, Mich., 1998—2000, assoc. dean enrollment svcs., 2000—. Cons. enrollment mgmt. Ferris State U., Big Rapids, Mich., 2003—06. Author: AACRAO's Guide to Basic Enrollment Management, 2005, Gamers Go To College, 2006. V.p.bd. trustees Woodbridge Group, Big Rapids, Mich., 2000—06. Recipient Distinquished Staff award, Ferris State U., 2004. Office: Ferris State U 1201 South State St Ste 201 Big Rapids MI 49307 Office Phone: 231-591-2797. Business E-Mail: westmanc@ferris.edu.

**WESTMAN, JACK CONRAD,** child psychiatrist, educator; b. Cadillac, Mich., Oct. 28, 1927; s. Conrad A. and Alice (Pedersen) W.; m. Nancy K. Baehre, July 17, 1953; children—Daniel P., John C., Eric C. MD, U. Mich., 1952. Diplomate Am. Bd. Psychiatry and Neurology. Intern Duke Hosp., Durham, NC, 1952-53; resident U. Mich. Med. Ctr., 1955-59; dir. outpatient svcs. Children's Psychiat. Hosp., Ann Arbor, Mich., 1961-65; assoc. prof. U. Mich. Med. Sch., 1964-65; coord. diagnostic and treatment unit Waisman Ctr., U. Wis., Madison, 1966-74, prof. psychiatry, 1965-96, prof. emeritus, 1997—. Cons. Joint Commn. on Mental Health of Children, 1967-69, Madison Pub. Schs., 1965-74, Children's Treatment Ctr., Mendota Mental Health Inst., 1965-69 Author: Individual Differences in Children, 1973, Child Advocacy, 1979, Handbook of Learning Disabilities, 1990, Who Speaks for the Children?, 1991, Licensing Parents, 1994, Born to Belong, 1997, Parenthood in America, 2001; editor Child Psychiatry and Human Devel., 1984-99; contbr. articles to profl. jours. Vice-pres. Big Bros. of Dane County, 1970-73; v.p. Wis. Assn. Mental Health, 1968-72; co-chmn. Project Understanding, 1968-75; pres. Wis. Cares, 1998—. With USNR, 1953-55. Fellow Am. Psychiat. Assn., Am. Coll. Psychiatrists, Am. Acad. Child and Adolescent Psychiatry, Am. Orthopsychiat. Assn. (bd. dirs. 1973-76); mem. Am. Assn. Psychiat. Svcs. for Children (pres. 1978-80), Multidisciplinary Acad. Clin. Edn. (pres. 1992-98). Home: 1234 Dartmouth Rd Madison WI 53705-2214 E-mail: jwestman@facstaff.wisc.edu.

**WESTMAN, JUDITH ANN,** clinical geneticist, dean; b. Columbus, Ohio, Nov. 7, 1957; d. Paul Marshall and Anna Marie (Stahly) Whetstone; m. David Arthur Westman, Apr. 12, 1980; children: Matthew, Joel, Rachel, Deborah. BA, Ohio No. U., 1978; MD, Ohio State U., 1981, MS, 1987. Diplomate Am. Bd. Pediatrics, Am. Bd. Med. Genetics. Resident in pediatrics Children's Hosp. Ohio State U., Columbus, 1981-84, chief resident, 1984-85, fellow clin. genetics, 1985-87, clin. asst. prof., 1987-95, clin. assoc. prof., 1995—, assoc. dean admissions and student affairs, 1996-99, assoc. dean student and med. edn., 1999—2005, assoc. dean med. edn. adminstrn., 2005—. Chair admissions com. Ohio State U. Coll. Medicine, 1990-96. Author: Medical Genetics for the Modern Clinician, 2005; contbr. articles to profl. jours. Mem. adv. bd. Coll. Arts and Scis., Ohio No. U., Ada, 1988-97, trustee, 1997—; trustee Malone Coll., Canton, Ohio, 1988-94. Grantee FDA, 1987, NCI, 2001. Fellow Am. Acad. Pediatrics, Am. Soc. Human Genetics. Republican. Mem. Ch. of God (Anderson). Avocations: music, church activities. Office: 155 Meiling Hall 370 W 9th Ave Columbus OH 43210-1238

**WESTMAN, STEVEN RONALD,** rabbi; b. Chgo., Sept. 16, 1945; s. Kurt S. and Hilda (Schmoller) W.; m. Sherri, Nov. 30, 1980; children: Rachel Dara, Emily Nicole, Molly Sarah Levin. BA, U. Ill., 1967; B of Hebrew Letters, Hebrew Union Coll., 1969, MA in Hebrew Letters, 1972, DDiv., 1997. Ordained rabbi, 1972. Asst. rabbi Congregation Rodeph Shalom, Phila., 1972-75; rabbi Temple Israel, Stroudsburg, Pa., 1975-83, Temple Beth Torah, Wellington, Fla., 1983-95, Temple Beth El Israel, Ft. Pierce, Fla., 1995-00, Temple Beth El, West Palm Beach, 2000—. Mem. Commn. for Jewish Edn., West Palm Beach, Fla., 1990-94; del. dirs. Jewish Cmty. Day Sch., West Palm Beach, 1988-91, Jewish Cmty. Ctr., 1987-89; pres. Palm BEach County Bd. Rabbis, 1989-92. Bd. dirs. Palms West Hosp., Loxahatchee, Fla., 1986-91, Pocono Hosp., East Stroudsburg, Pa., 1979-83; found. bd. dirs. Hospice of Monroe County, East Stroudsburg, 1978-83; bd. dirs. Palm Beach Liturgical Culture Soc., West Palm Beach, 1986-95. Recipient Tower of David award State of Israel Bonds, 1988, Leadership award Jewish Fedn. of Palm Beach County, 1985. Mem. Cen. Conf. of Am. Rabbis, Rotary. Home: 5170 Foxhall Dr S West Palm Beach FL 33417 Office: Temple Beth El 2815 N Flagler Dr West Palm Beach FL 33407 E-mail: rabbiwestman@bellsouth.net. *The theme and spirit of my rabbinate are found in the words of Pirkey Avot, the ethics of the Fathers: "Be of the disciples of Aaron, loving peace and pursuing peace, loving your fellow creatures and bringing them close to the Torah." (Avot 1:12).*

**WESTMORE, MICHAEL GEORGE,** make-up artist, writer; b. Hollywood, Calif., Mar. 22, 1938; s. Montague George and Edith Adeline Westmore; m. Marion Christine Bergeson, Dec. 4, 1965; children: Michael George, Michele, McKenzie. BA, U. Calif., Santa Barbara, 1961. Apprentice make-up artist Universal City Studios, Universal City, Calif., 1961-63, staff make-up artist, 1964, asst. head dept. make-up lab., 1965-71; freelance make-up artist various studios, Hollywood, Calif., 1971-87; make-up supr. and designer Paramount Studios, Hollywood, 1987—2005. Instr. theatre arts dept. Los Angeles Valley Coll., 1966—71; pres. Cosmetic Control Ctrs., Inc., 1971—76, Hollywood Magic Cosmetics, 1985—87; rsch. cons., lectr. therapeutic cosmetics for med. assns. Author: The Art of Theatrical Make-Up for Stage and Screen, 1971; contbr. chapters to books; co-author: Star Trek Makeup FX Journal, Star Trek-Aliens & Artifacts; make-up artist TV spls. Eleanor and Franklin (Emmy award NATAS, 1976), Why Me? (Emmy award, 1984), Three Wishes of Billy Grier (Emmy award, 1985), Star Trek (Emmy award, 1988, 1992, 1993, 1995, 1996, Emmy nomination, 2005), Amazing Stories (Emmy award, 1987), make-up artist films 2010 (Acad. award nomination, 1985), Mask (Acad. award, 1986), Clan of the Cave Bear (Acad. award nomination, 1987), Star Trek First Contact (Acad. award nomination, 1996); contbr. articles to Make-Up Artists mag. Served with AUS, 1956. Nominee Emmy, 1973, 1976; recipient Best Spl. Effects Make-up on TV for Geppetto award, Hollywood Make-up Artists Guild, 2001, Emmy, 1977, 1985, 1987, 1990, 1992, 1993, 1995, 1996, 1997, 1998, 1999, 2001, 2002, 2003, 2004, 2005, Three Emmys, 1978, Two Emmys, 1986, 1988, 1989, 1991, 1994, 2000. Mem.: Archive of Am. TV, Internat. Alliance Theatrical Stage Employees, Knights of the Vine, Soc. Make-up Artists, Vikings of Scandia, Lambda Chi Alpha (life Order of Achievement award). Address: 4616 Balboa Blvd Encino CA 91316-4105

**WESTMORELAND, ANDREW,** academic administrator; m. Jeanna Westmoreland; 1 child, Riely. Grad., Ouachita Baptist U., 1979; MA in Polit. Sci., U. Ark., Fayetteville; PhD in Higher Edn. Adminstrn., U. Ark., Little Rock. With Ouachita Baptist U., 1979—2006, prof. polit. sci. and edn., exec. v.p., v.p. acad. affairs, pres., 1998—2006, Samford U., Birmingham, Ala., 2006—. Cons., evaluator Higher Learning Commn. Author: Leading by Design, 2005. Office: Samford U 800 Lakeshore Dr Birmingham AL 35229*

**WESTMORELAND, LYNN A.,** congressman; b. Atlanta, Ga., Apr. 2, 1950; m. Joan Eskew; children: Heather Smith, Marcy, Trae. Attended, Ga. State Univ. Mem. Ga. Ho. Reps., Atlanta, 1992—2004, US Congress from 8th Ga. dist., 2005—, mem. Govt. Reform com., Small Bus. com., transp. and Infrastructure com. Mem. Fayette (Ga.) Bd. Realtors, Nat. Bd. Realtors. Mem.: Midwest Ga. Homebuilders Assn. Republican. Baptist. Office: US Ho Reps 1118 Longworth Ho Office Bldg Washington DC 20515-1008 Office Phone: 202 225 5901. Office Fax: 202-225-2515.

**WESTMORELAND, PRESTON,** radio personality; b. CT, 1947; m. Nancy Westmoreland, 1972. Talk show host KTAR-AM 620, Phoenix, 1978—2004; real estate agt. Russ Lyon Realty, Carefree, Ariz., 2004—. Co-prodr.: (films) Stay Alive: A Guide to Survival in the Desert Southwest. Radio reporter USMC. Named one of 100 Most Important Radio Talk Show Hosts in Am., Talkers mag., 1998—2004; recipient Marconi Radio award for Large Market Personality of Yr., Nat. Assn. Broadcasters, 2003. Avocation: aviation. Office: Russ Lyon Realty Co Carefree 34305 N Scottsdale Rd Scottsdale AZ 85262 Office Phone: 480-488-2400, 480-488-2400. Office Fax: 480-488-9530.*

**WESTNEY, GLORIA ELAINE,** medical educator; d. Adrian T. and Lizette I. Westney; m. Perry V. Hughes, Sept. 26, 1958. MD, U. Louisville, Ky., 1986; MS, Morehouse Sch. of Medicine, Atlanta, Ga., 2005. Diplomate Am. Bd. of Internal Medicine, 2000. Asst. prof. of medicine Morehouse Sch. of Medicine, Atlanta, 1996—. Fellow: Am. Coll. of Chest Physicians; mem.: Am. Thoracic Soc. Office: Morehouse Sch of Medicine 720 Westview Dr SW Atlanta GA 30310 Office Phone: 404-616-9538.

**WESTOFF, CHARLES FRANCIS,** demographer, educator; b. N.Y.C., July 23, 1927; s. Frank Barnett and Evelyn (Bales) Westoff; m. Joan P. Uszynski, Sept. 11, 1948 (div. Jan. 1969); children: David, Carol; m. Leslie Aldridge, Aug. 1969 (div. Feb. 1993); m. Jane DeLung, May 1997. AB, Syracuse U., 1949, MA, 1950; PhD, U. Pa., 1953. Instr. sociology U. Pa., 1950—52; rsch. assoc. Milbank Meml. Fund, N.Y.C., 1952—55; rsch. assoc. Office Population Rsch. Princeton (NJ) U., 1955—62; Maurice P. During '22 prof. demographic studies and sociology, 1962—99, prof. emeritus, 1999—, sr. rsch. demographer, 1999—, chmn. dept. sociology, 1965—70, assoc. dir. Office Population Rsch., 1962—75, dir., 1975—92; assoc. prof. sociology N.Y.U., also chmn. dept. sociology Washington Sq. Coll., 1959—62; vis. sr. fellow East-West Population Inst., Honolulu, 1979—81; Disting. vis. prof. Am. U., Cairo, 1979; mem. vis. com. Harvard-MIT Joint Ctr. for Urban Studies, 1980—83. Exec. dir. Commn. Population Growth and Am. Future,

1970—72; mem. adv. com. on population stats. U.S. Bur. Census, 1973—79; chmn. Nat. Com. for Rsch. on 1980 Census, 1981—88; bd. dirs. Alan Guttmacher Inst., 1977—88, 1989—; sr. tech. advisor Demographic Health Surveys, 1984—; bd. dirs. Population Resource Ctr., 1985—, Population Ref. Bur., 1988—94, Population Commns. Internat., 1992—98; com. on population NAS, 1983—88. Co-author: Family Growth in Metropolitan America, 1961, The Third Child, 1963, College Women and Fertility Values, 1967, The Later Years of Childbearing, 1970, From Now to Zero, 1971, Reproduction in the United States, 1965, 1971, Toward the End of Growth: Population in America, 1973, The Contraceptive Revolution, 1976, Demographic Dynamics in America, 1977, Mass Media and Reproductive Behavior in Africa, 1997, Unmet Need at the End of the Century, 2002, Reproductive Preferences in Developing Countries at the Turn of the Century, 2002, Trends in Marriage and Early Childbearing in Developing Countries, 2006, Recent Trends in Contraception and Abortion in Twelve Countries, 2005, The Stall in the Fertility Transition in Kenya, 2006; contbr. articles on demography and sociology to profl. jours. Recipient Irene Taeuber award for Outstanding Rsch. Contbns., 1995. Fellow: Am. Acad. Arts and Scis.; mem.: Internat. Union Sci. Study Population, Population Assn. Am. (bd. dirs. 1960—62, 1968—70, 1st v.p. 1972—73, pres. 1974—75), Planned Parenthood Fedn. Am. (dir. 1978—81), Inst. Medicine-NAS. Home: 1 Highland Rd Princeton NJ 08540 Office: Princeton U Wallace Hall Princeton NJ 08544 Business E-Mail: westoff@princeton.edu.

**WESTON, ARTHUR WALTER,** chemist, consultant, retired chemicals executive; b. Smith Falls, Ont., Can., Feb. 13, 1914; came to U.S., 1935, naturalized, 1952; s. Herbert W. and Alice M. (Houghton) W.; m. V. Dawn Thompson, Sept. 10, 1940; children: Roger L., Randall K., Cynthia B. BA, Queen's U., Kingston, Ont., 1934, MA, 1935; PhD, Northwestern U., 1938. Postdoctoral fellow Northwestern U. Evanston, Ill., 1938-40; with Abbott Labs., North Chgo., Ill., 1940-79, dir. rsch. and devel., 1959-61, v.p. rsch. and devel., 1961-68, dir. company, 1959-68, v.p. sci. affairs, 1968-77, v.p. corp. licensing, 1977-79; v.p., dir. San-Abbott, Japan, 1976-79; cons. Abbott Labs., North Chgo., Ill., 1979-85; pres. Arthur W. Weston & Assocs., Lake Forest, Ill., 1979—. Contbr. chapters to books, articles to profl. jours. Mem. Office Sci. Rsch. and Devel., War Manpower Commn., 1942-45; mem. exec. com. indsl. chemistry, div. chemistry and chem. tech. NRC, 1961-65; mem. indsl. panel on sci. and tech. NSF, 1974-80; mem. ad hoc com. chem. agts. Dept. Def., 1961-65. Mem. Rsch. Dirs. Assn. Chgo. (pres. 1965-66), Am. Chem. Soc. (trustee Chgo. 1965-2004, dir. Chgo. sect. 1952-59, nat. com. contbn. assocs 1967-72), Dirs. Indsl. Rsch., Indsl. Rsch. Inst. (bd. dirs. 1970-73), Phi Beta Kappa, Sigma Xi, Phi Lambda Upsilon. Achievements include patents in field. Home and Office: 349 Hilldale Pl Lake Forest IL 60045-3031 Personal E-mail: awweston@aol.com.

**WESTON, DAWN THOMPSON,** artist, researcher; b. Joliet, Ill., Apr. 15, 1919; d. Cyril C. and Vivian Grace Thompson; m. Arthur Walter Weston, Sept. 10, 1940; children: Roger Lance, Randall Kent, Cynthia Brooke. Student, Penn Hall Jr. Coll., Chambersburg, Pa., 1937-38; BS, Northwestern U., 1942; student, Art Inst. Chgo., 1954, Pestalozzi-Froebel, Chgo., 1955; postgrad., Northwestern U., 1960—61; student, Phila. Inst. for Achievement Human Potential, 1963; postgrad., U. Ill., 1964; MA in Ednl. Adminstrn., Northwestern U., 1970. Cert. tchr./adminstr. Ill. Therapist USN Hosp., Great Lakes, Ill., 1940—45; tchr. Holy Child and Waukegan (Ill.) High Schs., 1946—54, Lake Forest (Ill.) H.S., 1966—69; elem. and jr. high art dir. Lake Bluff (Ill.) Schs., 1954—58; pioneer ednl. dir. Grove Sch. for Brain-Injured, Lake Forest, 1958—66, life mem., treas. corp., chmn. bd., 1982—. Ind. rschr., lectr. on shifting visual imagery due to trauma, 1982—99; rschr. on uneven growth, 1969—. One-woman shows include Evanston Woman's Club, Northwestern U., Deerpath Gallery, Lake Forest, The Hein Co., Waukegan, numerous group shows, 1939—76, Represented in permanent collections ARC, Victory Meml. Hosp., Waukegan, Sierra Assocs., Chgo., numerous pvt. collections U.S., Can., Japan, Africa, works include:, Poisonous Plants of Midwest set of etchings for Country Gentleman mag., 1956, Clouds mural, 1981. Mem. 1st found. bd. for srs. in Lake Forest, 1999; chair Grove Sch. Inc., 1996—; chmn. July 4th parade 100th Anniversary Child-Serve Greater Chgo., 1994; mem. Presdl. Gold Chain, Trinity Coll., 1979; mem. alumni bd. leadership com. Northwestern U., 2003; del. ann. conf. Meth. Ch., 1982—90; lay leader Grace United Meth. Ch., Lake Bluff, 1990—93. Named Citizen of Yr., Grove Sch., 1978, rm. at sch. named in her honor, 1982; scholar, Penn Hall Jr. Coll., 1937—38. Mem.: Deerpath Art League (bd. dirs.), Penn Hall Alumni Assn. (class pres. 1938—40), Art Inst. Chgo., Pi Lambda Theta. Home and Office: 349 E Hilldale Pl Lake Forest IL 60045-3031

**WESTON, FRANCINE EVANS,** secondary school educator; b. Mt. Vernon, NY, Oct. 8, 1946; d. John Joseph and Frances (Fantino) Pisaniello. *Dr. Weston voiced her gratitude to her maternal grandfather by dedicating "Beautifully Old" to him in 1984. She fondly acknowledges here: The paternal grandparents who allowed her to spend what seemed like hours happily, though cacophonously, "playing" their piano, the various aunts who took her to Radio City, Horn-N-Hardart and for wheelbarrow rides, the godparents who took her to the rodeo, and especially the maternal grandmother for whom she picked raspberries, who typed her first essay contest entry (three times), and who was the only person who could make "You're just like your father," sound like a compliment.* BA, Hunter Coll., 1968; MA, Lehman Coll., 1973; cert., Am. Acad. Dramatic Arts, NYC, 1976; PhD, NYU, 1991. Cert. elem., secondary tchr., NY. Tchr. Yonkers Bd. Edn., NY, 1968—; aquatic dir. Woodlane Day Camp, Irvington-on-Hudson, NY, 1967-70, Yonkers Jewish Community Ctr., NY, 1971-75. Creative drama tchr. John Burroughs Jr. HS, Yonkers, 1971-77; stage lighting designer Iona Summer Theatre Festival, New Rochelle, NY, 1980-81, Yonkers Male Glee Club, 1981-89, Roosevelt HS, 1980-97; freelance, 1998—; rsch. specialist Scholarship Locating Svc., 1992-94, Yonkers Civil Def. Police Aux., 1994—; master electrician NYU Summer Mus. Theatre, 1979-80; appointed program developer for Cadet Acad. of Police & Fire Scis. Pub. Safety Magnet, Roosevelt HS, 2001, program dir., 2004-. *Although an explosion at school on 3/10/97 changed Dr. Weston's life forever by substantially impairing her hearing, she resumed her professional life as an outstanding educator and active member of Yonkers' volunteer citizenry. Fortified with hearing aids and 300 hours of speechreading exercises, she stalwartly returned to the classroom and to the auxiliary police. Her volunteer responsibilities are restructured to administrative duties, but her contribution and value to the Yonkers Public School System remains unchanged. Never a clockwatcher, she continues to provide expert instruction, emotional support, tutorial help, guidance and inspiration as a Teacher/Program Director and activities sponsor.* Actress in numerous comty. theater plays including A Touch of the Poet, 1979; dir. stage prodns. including I Remember Mama, 1973, The Man Who Came to Dinner, 1975; author: A Descriptive Comparison of Computerized Stage Lighting Memory Systems With Non-Computerized Systems, 1991, (short stories) A Hat for Louise, 1984, Old Memories: Beautiful and Otherwise, 1984; lit. editor: (story and poetry collection) Beautifully Old, 1984; editor: Command Post Dispatch quar., 1997—. Mem. Yonkers Civil Def. Police Aux., 1994—, adminstrv. asst. to commanding officer, 1996—, capt. adminstrn., 2002—, capt., 2002—, steering com. chairperson Roosevelt H.S.-Middle States Assn. of Schs. and Colls. Self-Evaluation, 1985—88. Named Tchr. of Excellence, NY State English Coun., 1990, 95, 2000; recipient Monetary award for Teaching Excellence, Carter-Wallace Products, 1992; President's Call to Svc. award, Lifetime (4,000 hour) award, USA Freedom Corps, 2005; named to Arnd Tchrs. Honor Roll, 1992. Republican. Roman Catholic. Avocations: swimming, theater. Office: Roosevelt High Sch Tuckahoe Rd Yonkers NY 10710

**WESTON, SIR JOHN (SIR PHILIP JOHN WESTON),** company non-executive director, retired diplomat; b. Apr. 13, 1938; s. Philip George and Edith Alice Bray (Ansell) W.; m. Margaret Sally Ehlers, 1967; 3 children. Grad. with 1st class honors, Worcester Coll., Oxford (Eng.) U.; student Chinese lang., Hong Kong, 1964-66, Peking, China, 1967-68. Joined diplomatic svc. Govt. of Gt. Britain, 1962, served Fgn. Office, 1962-63, 69-71, with Treasure Ctr. for Adminstrv. Studies, 1964, permanent rep. to EEC Brussels, 1972-74, asst. pvt. sec. to sec. state fgn. affairs and commonwealth affairs, 1974-76, counsellor, head EEC presidency secretariat Fgn. and

Commonwealth Office, 1976-77, counsellor Brit. Embassy Washington, 1978-81, head def. dept. Fgn. and Commonwealth Office, 1981-84, asst. under-sec. state Fgn. and Commonwealth Office, 1984-85, min. Brit. Embassy Paris, 1985-88, dep. sec. to cabinet Cabinet Office, 1988-89, dep. under-sec. state def. Fgn. and Commonwealth Office, 1989-90, polit. dir. Fgn. and Commonwealth Office, 1990-92, amb., permanent rep. to NATO, also accredited to Western European Union Brussels, 1992-95; U.K. amb. to UN, U.K. permanent rep. UN Security Coun., N.Y.C., 1995-98. Non-exec. dir. Brit. Telecom, 1998-2002, Rolls-Royce plc, 1998-2004, Hakluyt & Co. Ltd., 2001—; vis. fellow Old Souls Coll., Oxford (Eng.) U., 1977-78; hon. fellow Worcester Coll., Oxford, 2003. Chmn. governing body Sherborne Sch., 2001-04; trustee Nat. Portrait Gallery; Am. assoc. Royal Acad., 1999-2004; bd. govs. Ditchley Found., 2000-04; mem. coun. Internat. Inst. Strategic Studies, 2001—; hon. pres. Cmty. Found. Network, 1999—. Served Royal Marines, 1956-58. Decorated knight comdr. St. Michael and St. George (Eng.); Order of Merit with star (Fed. Republic Germany). Address: 13 Denbigh Gardens Richmond Surrey TW10 6EN England

**WESTON, JOHN FREDERICK,** business educator, consultant; b. Ft. Wayne, Ind., Feb. 6, 1916; s. David Thomas and Bertha W.; children: Kenneth F., Byron L., Ellen J. BA, U. Chgo., 1937, MBA, 1943, PhD, 1948. Instr. U. Chgo. Sch. Bus., 1940-42, asst. prof., 1947-48; prof. The Anderson Sch. UCLA, 1949—, Cordner prof. The Anderson Sch., 1981-94, prof. emeritus recalled The Anderson Sch., 1986—; dir. rsch. program in competition and bus. policy, 1969—, dir. Ctr. for Managerial Econs. and Pub. Policy, 1983-86. Econ. cons. to pres. Am. Bankers Assn., 1945-46; disting. lecture series U. Okla., 1967, U. Utah, 1972, Miss. State U., 1972, Miami State U., 1975. Author: Scope and Methodology of Finance, 1966, International Managerial Finance, 1972, Impact of Large Firms on U.S. Economy, 1973, Financial Theory and Corporate Policy, 1979, 2d edit., 1983, 3d edit., 1988, Mergers, Restructuring and Corporate Control, 1990, Takeovers, Restructuring and Corporate Governance, 3d edit., 2000, Managerial Finance, 9th edit, 1992; assoc. editor: Jour. of Finance, 1948-55; mem. editorial bd., 1957-59; editorial bd. Bus. Econs., Jour. Fin. Rsch., Managerial and Decision Econs.; manuscript referee Am. Econ. Rev., Rev. of Econs. and Statistics, Engring. Economist, Bus. Econs., Fin. Mgmt. Bd. dirs. Bunker Hill Fund. Served with Ordnance Dept. AUS, 1943-45. Recipient Abramson Scroll award Bus. Econs., 1989-94; McKinsey Found. grantee, 1965-68; GE grantee, 1967; Ford Found. Faculty Rsch. fellow, 1961-62. Fellow Nat. Assn. Bus. Economists; mem. Am. Finance Assn. (pres. 1966, advd. bd. 1967-71), Am. Econ. Assn., Western Econ. Assn. (pres. 1962), Econometric Soc., Am. Statis. Assn., Royal Econ. Soc., Fin. Analysts Soc., Fin. Mgmt. Assn. (pres. 1979-80) Home and Office: UCLA 258 Tavistock Ave Los Angeles CA 90049-3229 Office Phone: 310-472-5110. Business E-mail: jweston@anderson.ucla.edu.

**WESTON, MICHAEL C.,** retired lawyer; b. Asheville, N.C., Aug. 13, 1938; m. Mary Ann Damme; two children. AB in English, Brown U., 1960; JD, U. Mich., 1963. Bar: Mich. 1964, Ill. 1973. Assoc. Clark Hill, Detroit, 1963-68; from sec. to pres. orgal. and consultium. Econ. Devel. Corp. of Greater Detroit, 1969-73; chief staff atty. Northwestern U., Evanston, Ill., 1973-81, v.p. legal affairs, 1981-89; v.p. and gen. counsel, 1990-2001; sr. cons. Acad. Search, Inc., 2004—. Lectr. minority bus. devel. Inst. Continuing Legal Edn., conflicts of interest Nat. Coun. Univ. Rsch. Adminstrs. Contbr. articles to profl. jours. Chmn. Univ. Gallery Com., 1982-85; bd. dirs. Northwestern U. Press. Mem. ABA (sec. taxation, com. on exempt orgns., ho. of dels., lectr. Inst. on Minority Bus. Devel.), Chgo. Coun. Lawyers, Nat. Assn. Coll. and Univ. Attys. (lectr. fed. tax matters, outside activities faculty mems. univ.-cmty. rels., med. risk mgmt., bd. dirs. 1985-88, 92-97, pres. 1995-96). E-mail: m-weston@northwestern.edu.

**WESTON, ROGER LANCE,** banker; b. Waukegan, Ill., Mar. 2, 1943; s. Arthur Walter and Vivian Dawn Weston; children: Cynthia Page, Kent Andrew, Arthur Eladio, Rebecca Dawn, Alice Sinclair, Elliot Churchill, Evan Walter, Spencer Lance. BS, MacMurray Coll., 1965; MBA, Washington U., St. Louis, 1967. Investment adviser Harris Trust & Savs. Bank, Chgo., 1967-69; sr. investment counselor Security Suprs., Chgo., 1969-70; gen. ptnr. Sierra Capital Group, Chgo., 1970-85; exec. v.p., treas., chief fin. officer Telemed Corp., Hoffman Estates, Ill., 1971-79; vice chmn. Bank Lincolnwood, Ill., 1979-85; pres., CEO, GSC Enterprises, Lincolnwood, 1979-85; chmn. bd. dirs., pres., CEO, GreatBanc, Inc., Lisle, Ill., 1986—. Mem. Barrington Hills (Ill.) Zoning Bd. Appeals, 1987-2003, com. Asian art Art Inst. Chgo., 1987; mem. nat. coun. John M. Olin Sch. Bus., Washington U. Mem. Washington U. Eliot Soc. (Chgo. nat. com., chmn. membership com. 1996-92), Univ. Club. Republican. Presbyterian. Office: Great Banc Inc 1 N Wacker Dr Ste 4075 Chicago IL 60606

**WESTON, SAUNDRA OLIVIA (SAUNDRA LAIDLAW),** quality assurance professional, minister; b. Loiret, France, Sept. 23, 1954; arrived in U.S., 1957; d. Cleophus Hamiter, Olivia Hamiter; m. Michael LaRay Laidlaw, Nov. 22, 2001. AAS, Milw. Tech. Coll., 1996; B in Elective Studies, St. Cloud State U., 2002. Ordained pastor Abundant Life Ch., 1999, Ordained to ministry Evangelist Ch., 1992. Data entry operator Blue Cross & Blue Shield United Wis., Milw., 1987, acctg. technician, 1987—89, microcomputer technician, 1989—93, microcomputer project analyst II, 1993—96, sys. adminstr., 1996—99; software programmer EMR Innovations, St. Cloud, Minn., 1999—2001, quality assurance analyst, 2001—. Cons., Milw., 1992—99. Author: (book) One That Got Away, 2002. V.p. Overcomers Internat., St. Cloud, 2002; pastor Temple Faith Ch., St. Cloud, 2000—. Finalist State Amb., Milw. Area Tech. Coll., 1996; recipient Lamp of Knowledge, 1996. Pentecostal. Avocation: travel. Office Phone: 320-252-0234. Home Fax: 320-354-0026. E-mail: slaidlaw@tds.net.

**WESTON, W. GALEN, SR., (GALEN WESTON),** diversified financial services company executive; b. Eng., Oct. 29, 1940; s. Willard Garfield Weston and Reta L. Howard; m. Hilary Frayne, 1966; 2 children. BA, U. Western Ont., LLD (hon.). Chmn. bd. Wittington Investments, Ltd., George Weston Ltd., Toronto, Ont., Can., Holt, Renfrew & Co. Ltd., Loblaw Cos. Ltd., Selfridges & Co., Weston Foods Ltd. Bd. dirs. Fortnum and Mason PLC (U.K.); bd. dirs. Assoc. Brit. Foods PLC (U.K.), Brown Thomas Group Ltd. (Ireland). Hon. trustee The Upper Can. Coll. Found.; mem. internat. adv. bd. Columbia U. Officer Order of Can. Mem. Windsor Club (Fla.), Deepdale Golf Club (NY). Office: George Weston Limited 22 St Clair Ave E Ste 2001 Toronto ON Canada M4T 2S3 Office Phone: 416-922-2500.

**WESTPHAL, CAROL JEAN,** media specialist; d. John Gerald and Florine Theresa Sapienza; m. Robert Michael Westphal, Aug. 11, 1979; 1 child, Christina Marie. BA in English, Iona Coll., 1976; MS in Spl. Edn., Coll. of New Rochelle, NY, 1979; MS in Libr. and Info. Sci., LI U., 2000. Montessori lic. St. Nicholas Tng. Ctr. Montessori tchr. New Rochelle Acad., 1976—87; 2d grade tchr. Christ the King, Yonkers, NY, 1987—88, computer tchr., 1988—96; libr. media specialist Ralph Waldo Emerson Mid. Sch., Yonkers, 1996—. Coun. mem. Yonkers Sch. Libr. Sys., 2003—. Grantee, Laura Bush Found., 2004. Mem.: ALA, Westchester Libr. Assn., Sch. Libr. Media Specialists of Southea. NY. Home: 2 E High St Valhalla NY 10595 Office: Ralph Waldo Emerson Mid Sch 160 Bolmer Ave Yonkers NY 10703 Office Phone: 914-376-8300 ext 254. Fax: 914-421-1825. E-mail: cwestphal@emerson.ypschools.org.

**WESTPHAL, JOSEPH W.,** former academic administrator; m. Linda Westphal; 4 children. PhD in Polit. Sci., Univ. Mo.; BA, Adelphi Univ. Head political sci. dept. Okla. State Univ.; prof.; spl. asst. Dept. Interior; exec. dir. Congressional Sunbelt Caucus, 1988—95; sr. policy adv. US Environment Protection Agency; asst. sec. US Army, 1998—2001, acting sec., 2001; sr. ptnr. Patton Boggs, Washington, 2001—02; chancellor Univ. Maine Sys., 2002—06. Served House Com.; adj. prof. Georgetown Univ. Contbr. articles to jours. Acting sec. U.S. Army, asst. sec. U.S. Army, 1998. Decorated Disting. Civilian Svc. Dept. Army. Mem.: Patton Boggs, LLP (sr.), Wash. Law Firm (sr.).*

**WESTPHAL, PAUL**, professional basketball coach; b. Torrance, Calif., Nov. 30, 1950; m. Cindy Westphal; children: Victoria, Michael Paul. Degree in phys. edn., U. So. Calif., 1972. Player Boston Celtics, 1972-75, Phoenix Suns, 1975-80, 83-84, Seattle Supersonics, 1980-81, NY Knicks, 1981-83; coach SW Coll., Phoenix, 1985-86, Grand Canyon Coll., 1986-88; asst. coach Phoenix Suns, 1988-92, head coach, 1992—95; coach high sch., 1995—98; head coach Seattle Supersonics. Named All-Star 5 times, Comeback Player of Yr.; uniform number retired by Suns, 1989.

**WESTPHALEN, OLAV**, artist, sculptor; b. Hamburg, Germany, 1963; arrived in NY, 1997; MA in Design, Fachhochschule fur Gestaltung, Hamburg, Germany, 1990; MFA in Visual Arts, U. Calif. San Diego, 1993. Exhibited in group shows, ACME Gallery, Santa Monica, Calif., 1996, Kunstverein Kassel, Germany, 1997, Yerba Buena Ctr. Arts, 1997, Apex Art, NY, 1999, End Papers, Neuberger Mus. Art, NY, 2000, Fido, Hunter Coll. Gallery, NY, 2000, Greater NY: New Art in NY Now, P.S. 1 Contemporary Art Ctr., Long Island City, NY, 2000, Out of Bounds, Luckman Gallery, Calif. State U., LA, 2001, Tele, Kunsthalle Wien, Austria, 2001, After Effect, Centre d'Art Neuchatel, Switzerland, 2001, Whitney Biennial, Whitney Mus. Am. Art, NY, 2004, one-man shows include, Swiss Inst., NY, 2001, Mus. Liljewalchs, IASPIS, Stockholm, 2001, Michael Neff Gallery, Frankfurt, 2002, Maccarone Inc, NY, 2002, Sculpture Ctr., NY, 2003, Galerie Georges-Philippe & Nathalie Vallois, Paris, 2004. Mailing: c/o Maccarone Inc 45 Canal St New York NY 10002

**WESTRA, JAMES R.**, lawyer; b. Cleve., June 3, 1951; m. Jean Westra; children: Christian, Alexander, Nicholas. AB, Harvard Coll., 1973; JD, Boston U. Law Sch., 1977. Bar: Mass. 1978. With Hutchins, Wheeler & Dittmar, 1977—2002; ptnr. Weil, Gotshal & Manges, LLP, Boston, 2002—. Overseer Boston Symphony Orchestra; bd. chmn. CAST, Inc.; bd. dir. Rescue Mission; chmn. bd. appeals Wenham, Mass. Mem.: ABA. Office: Weil Gotshal & Manges 100 Federal St Fl 34 Boston MA 02110 Office Phone: 617-772-8377. Office Fax: 617-772-8333. Business E-Mail: james.westra@weil.com.

**WESTRA, MITZI SUE**, music educator; b. Sioux Falls, S.D., Apr. 16, 1964; d. Marlin Duane Westra and Myrna Rae Hughes; m. Frank Felice, Nov. 12, 1993. BA, Augustana Coll., 1986; MusM, U. Minn., 1992, D of Mus. Arts, 1995. Adj. faculty Lamar U., Beaumont, Tex., 1996—98; pvt. voice tchr. Indpls., 1998—; adj. faculty Wabash Coll., Crawfordsville, Ind., 1998—2004; assoc. faculty U. Indpls., 1998—. Performing artist: CD For the Family, 2004. Choir dir. St. Andrew's Presbyn. Ch., Beaumont, Tex., 1996—98; contract singer 2d Presbyn. Ch., Indpls., 1998—. Mem.: Nat. Assn. Tchrs. of Singing, Coll. Music Soc. Avocations: hiking, reading, horseback riding. Home: 2040 Landmark Dr # 809 Indianapolis IN 46260 Office: Univ Indpls 1400 E Hanna Indianapolis IN 46227 Office Phone: 317-409-7654. E-mail: mitziwestra@yahoo.com.

**WESTREICH, BENZION JOSEPH**, lawyer; b. NYC, June 2, 1952; s. Osias and Gerda (Gerwitz) W.; m. Joyce M. Mayer, Sept. 13, 1978; children: Jonathan Michael, Daniel Stephan, Zachary Mark. BS summa cum laude, CUNY, 1974, postgrad., 1974-75; JD, Columbia U., 1978. Bar: N.Y. 1979, U.S. Dist. Ct. (ea. and so. dists.) N.Y., Calif. 1988. Assoc. Shearman & Sterling, NYC, 1978-86, ptnr., 1987-88, LA, 1988—; Katten Muchin Zavis Rosenman, LA. Stone decide Columbia U., 1977, 78. Mem. Phi Beta Kappa. Office: Katten Muchin Zavis Rosenman Ste 2600 2029 Century Park E Los Angeles CA 90067 Office Phone: 310-788-4409, 310-712-8228. E-mail: benny.westreich@kmzr.com.

**WESTREICH, NEIL P.**, lawyer; b. NYC, Mar. 7, 1950; BA with honors, Cambridge Univ., 1974; JD magna cum laude, Harvard Univ., 1977. Bar: England and Wales 1975, NY 1979. Atty., London, 1978—79; assoc. Cravath Swaine & Moore LLP, NYC, 1979—85, ptnr., corp., 1985—. Mem.: Bar Assn. City NY, NY State Bar Assn., ABA. Office: Cravath Swaine & Moore LLP Worldwide Plz 825 Eighth Ave New York NY 10019-7475 Office Phone: 212-474-1518. Office Fax: 212 474 3700. Business E-Mail: nwestreich@cravath.com.

**WESTRICH, GEOFFREY HOWARD**, orthopaedic surgery; b. South Orange, NJ, May 26, 1964; BS in Engring. (with honors), Tufts U., 1986; MD, Tufts U. Sch. Medicine, 1990. Cert. Orthopaedic Surgery, NY. Intern, gen. surgery North Shore-Cornell U. Program, Manhasset, NY 1990-91; resident, orthop. surgery Hosp. for Spl. Surgery-NY Hosp. Cornell Med. Ctr., NY, 1991—95; orthop. trauma fellowship AO fellowship Inselpital, Bern, Switzerland, 1995; hip/knee fellowship, adult reconstruction Hosp. Spl. Surgery, NY, asst. scientist NY, 1996—; asst. attending, orthop. surgery NY, 1996—2002, assoc. attending, orthop. surgery NY, 2002—; asst. prof., orthop. surgery NY Presbyterian Weill Cornell Med. Ctr., NY, 2001—02, assoc. attending, orthop. surgery NY, 2002—; asst. prof., orthop. surgery Weill Med. Coll. Cornell U., 1999, assoc. prof. clin. orthop. surgery. Mem. Orthop. Trauma Soc. Contbr. articles to profl. jours. Named one of Medical Marvels, New York Mag., 2006; recipient Resident's award, NY Acad. Medicine, 1994, Resident award paper, Smith & Nephew Richards, Inc., 1995, Fellow award paper, Eastern Orthop. Assn., 1996, Hip Soc. Recipient, Orthop. Rsch. and Edn. Found., 1998. Mem.: NY County Med. Soc., Am. Acad. Orthop. Surgeons, AMA, Alpha Omega Alpha. Avocations: boating, fishing, skiing, tennis, calligraphy. Address: Hosp for Spl Surgery 535 E 70th St New York NY 10021-4872 Office: Affiliated Physician Offices 176-60 Union Turnpike Fresh Meadows NY 11366 Address: NY Presbyterian Weill Cornell Med Ctr 525 E 68th St Starr 2 New York NY 10021 Office Phone: 212-606-1510. Office Fax: 212-639-9266.*

**WESTROPE, MARTHA RANDOLPH**, psychologist, consultant; b. Gaffney, S.C., May 19, 1922; d. Gordon Robert and Hannah (Brown) W.; 1 adopted child, Ashley Randolph. BS, Winthrop Coll., 1942; MA, U. N.C., 1944; PhD, State U. of Iowa, Iowa City, 1952. Lic. psychologist, S.C. Pvt. practice, Greenville, S.C., 1960—; part-time pvt. practice, 1987-96; part-time staff mem. Spartanburg (S.C.) Mental Health Clinic, 1971-73, Greenville Mental Health Ctr., 1974-85, Patrick B. Harris Psychiat. Hosp., Anderson, S.C., 1985-87; med. cons. S.C. Vocat. Rehab. Dept., Greenville, 1987-91, part-time med. cons., 1993-99. Cons. S.C. Parole Bd. for Psychol. Evaluation, S.C. Dept. Corrections, 1983-87. Mem. Am. Psychol. Assn., Southeastern Psychol. Assn., S.C. Psychol. Assn., Am. Assn. for Advancement of Psychology, Greenville County Mental Health Assn., Am. Group Psychotherapy Assn., Coun. for the Nat. Register of Health Svc. Providers in Psychology. Democrat. Presbyterian. Avocations: wildlife preservation, fine arts, doll collecting, stamp collecting/philately. Home: 11 Darien Way Greenville SC 29615-3236

**WESTWATER, EDGEWORTH RUPERT**, physicist; b. Denver, Oct. 29, 1937; s. Edgeworth Clark and Lola Maud Westwater; m. Geraldine Lucille Perna, May 14, 1994. BA, Western State Coll. of Colo., Gunnison, 1955; MS, U. of Colo., 1962, PhD, 1970. Physicist U. S. Dept. of Commerce Boulder Labs., Boulder, Colo., 1960—95, CIRES, U. of Colo./NOAA, Boulder, Colo., 1995—. Named Remote Sensing Lectr., Am. Meteorol. Soc., 1997; recipient 15th Vilho Vaisala award, World Meteorol. Orgn., 2001. Fellow: IEEE Geosci. and Remote Sensing Soc. (assoc. editor, Disting. Achievement award 2003); mem.: Am. Geophys. Union, Math. Assn. of Am., Am. Meteorol. Soc., Internat. Union of Radio Sci. (corr.; commn. f chmn. 1999—2002). D-Conservative. Avocations: Italian language, Russian language, weightlifting. Office: CIRES University of Colorado/NOAA 325 Broadway R/PSD4 Boulder CO 80305 Office Phone: 303-497-6527.

**WESTWOOD, ALBERT RONALD CLIFTON**, management consultant, researcher; b. Birmingham, Eng., June 9, 1932; came to U.S., 1958, naturalized, 1974; s. Albert Sydney and Ena Emily (Clifton) W.; m. Jean Mavis Bullock, 1956; children: Abigail, Andrea. BSc with honors, U. Birmingham, 1953, PhD in Phys. Metallurgy, 1956, DSc in Materials Sci., 1968. Chartered engr. and physicist, U.K. Tech. officer research dept., metals

div. Imperial Chem. Industries, Birmingham, 1956—58, successively scientist, sr. scientist, assoc. dir., head materials sci. dept., dep. dir., 1958—74; dir. Martin Marietta Labs., Balt., 1974—84, corp. dir. R & D 1984—87; v.p. R & D Martin Marietta Corp., Bethesda, Md., 1987—90, v.p. sci., 1990, v.p. rsch. and tech., 1990—93; v.p. rsch. and exploratory tech. Sandia Nat. Labs. divsn. Lockheed Martin Corp., Albuquerque, 1993—96; v.p. emeritus Sandia Nat. Labs., 2002—; chmn., chief exec. Cen. Lab. of Rsch. Couns., England, 1998—2000; internat. cons. R. and D. Mgmt. Mem. numerous govt. and univ. adv. coms. including Office Sci. and Tech. Policy, NASA, NRC, NAS, NAE, NSF, Nat. Inst. Stds. and Tech., U. Md., U. Fla., MIT, Ga. Inst. Tech., Coun. on Competetiveness; bd. dir. Martin Marietta Energy Systems, Assn. Ind. Rsch. and Tech. Orgns. U.K., U.S. Civilian R&D Found.; mem. European rsch. coun. informatics and math. resources bd. Brit. Nat. Space Sci. Ctr.; mem. R&D coun. European Spallation Source; mem. coun. Found. Tech. Innovation and Tech. U.K.; lectr. in field. Contbr. over 100 articles to profl. jours. Chmn. Md. Humanities Coun., N.Mex. Humanities Coun., N.Mex. Symphony Orch.; bd. dirs Santa Fe Opera; adv. com. Sci. and Tech. Corp., U. N.Mex. Recipient Disting. Young Scientist award Md. Acad. Scis., 1966, Centennial award U. Md., 1994, Beilby gold medal Royal Inst. Chemistry, 1970, J. Herbert Holloman award Acta Metallurgica, 1996, Tewksbury lectr. U. Melbourne, 1974, Wenk lectr. Johns Hopkins U., 1995. Fellow AAAS (chmn. indsl. sci. sect.), Am. Soc. Metals Internat. (Burgess lectr. 1984, Campbell meml. lectr. 1987, disting. lectr. materials and soc. 1995, medal for advancement sci. 2006), Inst. of Physics, Inst. of Materials, The Minerals, Metals and Materials Soc. (dir., fin. officer, pres. 1990, Krumb lectr. 1988, leadership award 1992); mem. NRC (chmn. com. engring. and tech. sys. 1992-97), ASME (disting. lectr. 1989), NAE (elected), Royal Swedish Acad. Engring. Scis. (elected), Russian Acad. Engring. (elected), Royal Acad. Engring. (elected, U.K.), Md. Acad. Scis. (coun.), Md. Inst. Metals (pres.), Indsl. Rsch. Inst. (bd. dirs., pres. 1989-90). Home: 13539 Canada Del Oso Pl NE Albuquerque NM 87111-8045 Personal E-mail: arwestwood@aol.com.

**WESTWOOD, JAMES NICHOLSON**, lawyer; b. Portland, Oreg., Dec. 3, 1944; s. Frederick Alton and Catherine (Nicholson) W.; m. Janet Sue Butler, Feb. 23, 1980; children: Laura, David. BA, Portland State U., 1967; JD, Columbia U., 1974. Bar: Oreg. 1974, U.S. Dist. Ct. Oreg. 1974, U.S. Ct. Appeals (9th cir.) 1978, U.S. Supreme Ct. 1981, U.S. Ct. Appeals (fed. cir.) 1984, U.S. Ct. Appeals (D.C. cir.) 1997. Assoc. Miller, Anderson, Nash, Yerke & Wiener, Portland, 1974-76, 78-81; asst. to pres. Portland State U., 1976-78; ptnr. Miller, Nash, Wiener, Hager & Carlsen, Portland, 1981-99, Stoel Rives LLP, Portland, 1999—. Recipient Disting. Svc. award Portland State U. Found., 1984, Outstanding Alumni award Portland State U., 1992. Mem. ABA (chmn. forest resources com. 1987-89), Oreg. Bar Assn. (chmn. appellate practice sect. 1996-97, chmn. constnl. law sect. 2005—), Am. Acad. Appellate Lawyers, Univ. Club (bd. govs. 1994), City Club (pres. 1991-92), Park Blocks Found. (pres. 1999—). Republican. Unitarian Universalist. Home: 3121 NE Thompson St Portland OR 97212-4908 Office: Stoel Rives LLP 900 SW 5th Ave Ste 2600 Portland OR 97204-1268 Office Phone: 503-294-9187. Business E-Mail: jnwestwood@stoel.com.

**WESTWOOD, MELVIN NEIL**, horticulturist, pomologist; b. Hiawatha, Utah, Mar. 25, 1923; s. Neil and Ida (Blake) W.; m. Wanda Mae Shields, Oct. 12, 1946; children: Rose Dawn, Nancy Gwen, Robert Melvin, Kathryn Mae. Student, U. Utah, 1948-50; BS in Pomology, Utah State U., 1952; PhD in Pomology, Wash. State U., 1956. Field botanist Utah State U., Logan, 1951-52, supt. Howell Field Sta., 1952-53; rsch. asst. State Coll. Wash., 1953-55; assoc. prof. Oreg. State U., Corvallis, 1960-67, prof., 1967-80, prof. emeritus, 1986—; rsch. dir. Nat. Clonal Germplasm Repository, Corvallis, 1980-83, nat. tech. advisor, 1983-86. Author: Deciduous Fruit and Nut Production, 1976, Temperate-Zone Pomology: Physiology and Culture, 1978, 3d edit., 1993, Contract Military Air Transport: From the Ground Up, 1995, Pear Varieties and Species, 1996, the Foods of Lewis and Clark, 2005; author: (with others) Cherry Nutrition, 1966, Pear Rootstocks, 1987, Management and Utilization of Plant Germplasm, 1988, Maintenance and Storage: Clonal Germplasm, 1989, Genetic Resources of Malus, 1991; contbr. articles to profl. jours. With U.S. Air Transport Command, 1943-45, USAAF, 1946-47. Grantee NSF, 1966; recipient Hartman Cup award Oreg. Hort. Soc., 1989, Earl Price Excellence in Rsch. award Oreg. State U., 1983. Fellow Am. Soc. Hort. Sci. (bd. dirs. 1974-75, chmn. com. environ. quality 1971, adv. coun. 1974-79, mem. pomology sect. 1967-74, publs. com. 1971-74, pres. Western region 1974, Joseph Harvey Gourley award for Pomology 1958, 77, Stark award for Pomology 1969, 77, Outstanding Rschr. award 1986); mem. AAAS, Am. Soc. Plant Physiologists, Am. Pomological Soc. (mem. adv. bd. 1970-75, mem. exec. bd. 1980-84, Paul Howe Shepard award 1968, 82, Wilder medal 1980), UN Assn. USA, Ams. United for Separation of Ch. and State, Amnesty Internat., Phi Kappa Phi, Gamma Sigma Delta. Baptist. Achievements include patent for Autumn Blaze ornamental pear; research on Pyrus (pear), Malus (apple) and Prunus (plum, cherry, peach) and on the physiology of rootstock genera. Office: Oreg State U Dept Horticulture Corvallis OR 97331

**WETENHALL, JOHN**, museum director; b. June 1, 1957; s. Jack Wetenhall and Jane (Rinaud) Keating; m. Tanya Williams, Aug. 28, 2004. AB cum laude, Dartmouth Coll., 1979; MA, Williams Coll., Williamstown, Mass., 1982, Stanford U., 1985, PhD, 1988; MBA, Vanderbilt U., 1999. Fellow Smithsonian Instn., Washington, 1986-87, 88-89; lectr. Santa Clara (Calif.) U., 1985, U. Minn., Mpls., 1988; curator painting and sculpture Birmingham (Ala.) Mus. Art, 1989-95; dir. Checkwood Mus. Art, Nashville, 1995-2001; exec. dir. John and Mable Ringling Mus. Art, Sarasota, Fla., 2001—. Founder Thomas Art Projects, Birmingham, 1992-95, Carell Woodland Sculpture Trail, Nashville, 1996-99; cons. Vietnam Women's Meml. Project, Washington, 1988-89, U. So. Calif. Pub. Art Program, 1991. Author: (with Karal Ann Marling) Iwo Jima: Monuments, Memories and the American Hero, 1991, (with David Cass) (catalogue) Italian Paintings, 1850-1910, 1982; editor: (catalogue) Splendors of the American West, 1990; contbr. articles to profl. jours.; appearance in Am. Masters: Alexander Calder, PBS, 1998. Chair Livelier City Ctr. com. Oreg. New Birmingham, 1994—95, chair cultural dist. forum, 1992—94; nat. register peers, design excellence program Gen. Svcs. Adminstrn., 1998—; chair Nashville Rotary Adopt-A House Program; mem. Leadership Manatee, 2002, Leadership Fla., 2003; bd. Sarasota Conv. and Visitors Bur., 2006—. Recipient Award of Excellence Tenn. Assn. Mus., 1996, 2001, Gold and Silver medals for ednl. programming Southeastern Mus. Conf., 1999; B. Gerald Cantor fellow, 1986, Nat. Endowment for the Arts grantee, 1991, Lyndon Baines Johnson Found. Moody Travel grantee, 1986, John F. Kennedy Libr. Found. grantee, 1986, Inst. Mus. and Libr. Svcs. grantee. Mem. Am. Tchrs. Assn. of the Martial Arts (sensei), Rotary (Paul Harris fellow), Kiwanis, Sarasota C. of C. (bd. dirs 2005—), Beta Gamma Sigma, Assn. Art Mus. Dirs. Avocations: white water kayaking, flying, aiki ju jitsu (blackbelt). Office: Ringling Mus of Art 5401 Bay Shore Rd Sarasota FL 34243 Business E-mail: jwetenhall@ringling.org.

**WETHERBY, IVOR LOIS**, retired librarian; b. Louisville, May 22, 1924; d. Luther Silas and Clara Morris (Hite) W.; m. Herbert Charles Howard, July 4, 1947; children: Ivor Jane, Elizabeth Wetherby, John Allen, Luther Hite, Ann Dell. AB, Ky. Wesleyan Coll., 1944; MS in Library Sci., Fla. State U. 1965; SEd, Fla. Atlantic U., 1984; EdD Fla. Internat. U., 1992. Various clerical and secretarial positions, 1944-50; tchr. Our Lady of Mercy Acad., Louisville, 1963-64; librarian Palm Beach Jr. Coll., Lake Worth, Fla., 1966-78; head librarian Sebring (Fla.) Pub. Library, 1978; health scis. reference librarian Miami (Fla.)-Dade CC, Med. Ctr. Campus, 1978-87; librarian med. library Moncrief Army Cmty. Hosp., Ft. Jackson, S.C., 1987-89; ref. libr. Fla. Internat. U., 1992, ret., 1992. Active New Life Alliance Ch., West Palm Beach, Fla., Pleasant Grove Bapt. Ch., Louisville. Mem. DAR, Palm Beach County Geneal. Soc., Daus. of Founders and Patriots of Am., Nat. Soc. Colonial Dames XVII Century, Holland Soc. NY, Huguenot Soc., Nat. Soc. Daus. Union 1861-65. Home: 615 Laurel Lake Dr Apt A224 Columbus NC 28722

**WETHERELL, ALBERT A.**, secondary school educator; b. Queens, NY; s. Albert M. and Hedwig D. Wetherell. BA, St. John's U., Queens, 1965, PhD 1979; MA, Fordham U., 1967. Tchr. NYC Bd. Edn., 1962—2004. Recipient Bunzel award, United Fed. Tchrs., 1992, Achievement award, Am. Fedn. Tchrs., 2005. Mem.: Polish Inst. Arts and Sci., Am. Hist. Assn., Queens Hist. Soc., Phi Alpha Theta, Phi Delta Kappa. Avocation: historical research.

**WETHERELL, DAVID S.**, communications executive; b. OH Wesleyan U. Chmn., sec. CMGI Inc., Waltham, Mass., 1986—2006, CEO, 1986—2002, pres., 1986—2001. Office: 425 Medford St Charlestown MA 02129-1408

**WETHERELL, THOMAS KENT**, academic administrator; b. Daytona Beach, Fla., Dec. 22, 1945; m. Virginia B. Wetherell; children: Kent, Blakely, Page. BS in Social Studies, Fla. State U., 1967, MS in Social Studies, 1968, PhD in Adminstrn., 1974. Pres. Wetherell Enterprises, Inc.; dir. housing and adminstrn., asst. v.p., asst. dean housing U. Ctrl. Fla.; assoc. dean Bethune-Cookman Coll.; exec. asst. to pres. to dean of instrn. Daytona Beach CC, v.p., provost acad. and univ. transfer programs, dist. v.p., planning and devel.; pres. First Am. Mortgage and Investments, Inc., Tallahassee CC, 1975, Fla. State U., Tallahassee, 2003—. Mem. Fla. Ho. of Reps., 1980-92, spkr. 1990-92, chair appropriations com., 1989-90, chair appropriations edn. com., 1986-88, chair higher edn. com., 1984-86, majority fl. leader, 1982-84, chair Volusia county legis. delegation, 1981-83, 86-87. Bd. dirs. Econ. Devel. Coun., ARC, Canaveral Nat. Seashore Park, Southern Scholarship Found., United Way. Mem. Tallahassee C. of C. (bd. dirs.), Lions, Kiwanis, Blue Lodge, Shriners, Bahia Temple. Office: Office of Pres Fla State U 211 Westcott Bldg Tallahassee FL 32306-1470 Office Phone: 850-644-1085. Office Fax: 850-644-9936.*

**WETHERILL, EIKINS**, lawyer, investment company executive; b. Phila., Oct. 3, 1919; s. A. Hecksher and Edwina (Brunner) W. LL.B., U. Pa., 1948. Practiced in, Phila., 1948-55, Norristown, 1955-98; assoc. firm Evans, Bayard & Frick, 1948-50; ptnr. Reilly, Hepburn, Earle & Wetherill, 1950-55; firm Henderson, Wetherill, O'Hey & Horsey, 1955-98; pres. Phila. Stock Exchange, Inc., 1965-81. Bd. dirs. Germantown Savs. Bank; fin. commentator CBS-TV News, 1966-68; chmn. bd. Sta. WHYY-TV, 1970-76, dir., 1976-90; dir. 1st Pa. Corp., 1st Pa. Bank, solicitor to lt. gov. Pa., 1951-55, asst. U.S. atty. gen., 1953-55, treas., Montgomery County, 1956-59; pres. Montgomery County Bd. Commrs., 1960-63; chmn. Pa. Securities Commn., 1963-65; commr. Delaware Valley Regional Planning Commn., 1965—, chmn., 1968-69, 70-71, 78-79. Former bd. dirs. Greater Phila. Partnership; chmn. Phila. Drama Guild, 1975-80, dir., 1980-87; trustee Davis and Elkins Coll., 1973-91, G.H. Montgomery County Open Space, 1994—. Served to capt., cav. Signal Corps, OSS, AUS, 1941-45. Mem. ABA, Phila. Bar Assn., Delta Psi. Clubs: Phila. (Phila.), Racquet (Phila.). Episcopalian.

**WETHERILL-SMITH, LINDA MARIE**, music educator, musician, performing arts association administrator; b. Milw., Mar. 2, 1950; d. Albert Edward Christensen and Elsa Dorothea Etterman; m. Joseph David Smith, July 7, 2000. MusB, U. Rochester, 1972, performers cert., 1971; MusM, SUNY, Stony Brook, 1991. 1st flutist solo and ensemble Chamber Artists Garbarino of La Scala, Milan, 1973—76; solo and 1st flutist Frankfurt Radio Symphony Orch., 1975—76, IRCAM, Ensemble Intercontemporain, Paris, 1976—80; internat. soloist freelance, U.S.I.S. and McCann Artists, Ltd., London, 1973—; prof. music major TURKish univs., Istanbul, 1987—90; cultural amb. U.S. Info. Svc., Washington, 1985—; prof. music Adelphi U., Garden City, NY, 1994—; solo flutist Aspelete, 2006—, Salzburg Mozarteam, 2006—, Orch. of Our Time, N.Y.C., 2006—. Judge Internat. Competition, Salzburg, Austria, 2004—; solo performer, lectr. Internat. Soc. Cont. Music, Miami, 2004; performances and master classes in Argentina and Brazil; cons. various internat. programs, 1973—. Editor: L.I. Flute Notes, 1994—; editor, performer (solo CD) Sound and Repercussion, Far Amazon, 2000 (Amazon award, 2003), (book and CD) International Anthology of Solos for Alto and Bass Flutes, 2005; contbr. articles and interviews to profl. jours. Pres., founder Muzarte, Phila., N.Y.C., 1987—. Grantee, NY State Coun. for the Arts, 1997—2005. Mem.: L.I. Flute Club (bd. dirs., adv. bd. 1994—2005), Sigma Alpha Iota. Achievements include first woman to perform publicly for mixed audiences in Saudi Arabia in 1986; first American flute soloist to perform and teach in Hunan province of China in 2002. Avocations: travel, political diplomacy, world cultures. Home: 38 W 74th Ave Apt 3C New York NY 10023 Office: Adelphi U South Ave Garden City NY 11530 Office Phone: 917-861-4528. E-mail: muzarte@msn.com, muzarte@lindawetherill.com.

**WETHINGTON, CHARLES T., JR.**, academic administrator; AB, Ea. Ky. U., 1956; postgrad., Syracuse U., 1958-59; MA, U. Ky., 1962, PhD, 1965. Instr. ednl. psychology U. Ky., Lexington, 1965-66; dir. Maysville (Ky.) C.C., 1967-71; asst. v.p. c.c. system U. Ky., Lexington, 1971-81, v.p. c.c. system, 1981-82, chancellor c.c. system, 1982-88, chancellor c.c. system and univ. rels., 1988-89, interim pres., 1989-90, pres., 1990—2001, pres. emeritus, 2001—. Chmn. legis. com. State Dirs. Community and Jr. Colls., 1983-85, chmn. nat. coun., 1985-86; commn. on colls. So. Assn. Schs. and Colls., 1978-84, vice chmn. exec. commn., 1984, trustee, 1986-89; mem. So. Regional Edn. Bd., 1988-2000, mem. exec. com., 1989-93, vice-chmn., 1991-93; pres. Southeastern Conf., 1993-95, chair exec. com. NCAA, 1999-2001. Bd. dirs. Bluegrass State Skills Corp., 1984-91, vice-chmn. bd. dirs., 1986-87; bd. visitors C.C. Air Force, 1986-90; jud. nominating commn. 22nd Jud. Dist., Fayette County, Ky., 1988-91, So. Growth Policies Bd., 1990-2000; bd. dirs. NCAA Found., 1999—; active Bus.-Higher Edn. Forum, 1999-2001. With security svc. USAF, 1957-61. Home: 2926 Four Pines Dr Lexington KY 40502 Office: U Ky 5-52 Wm T Young Libr Lexington KY 40506-0456 E-mail: cwething@email.uky.edu.

**WETLE, TERRIE FOX**, gerontologist, educator, dean; b. Bremerton, Wash., Nov. 7, 1946; d. Gerald Lee and Elinor Myrle (Martindale) Todd; m. Richard W. Besdine, July 2, 1981; children: Sarah, Molly. BS in Psychology, Portland State U., 1968, MS in Psychology, 1971, PhD of Urban Studies, 1976. Assoc. prof. Portland (Oreg.) State U., 1976-78; social policy analyst Dept. Health, Edn. and Welfare, Washington, 1978-79; asst. prof. Yale U., New Haven, 1979-81, Harvard U., Boston, 1981-88; dir. Braceland Ctr., Hartford, Conn., 1988-95; assoc. prof. U. Conn. Health Ctr., Farmington, 1989—95; dep. dir. Nat. Inst. Aging, NIH, Bethesda, Md., 1995-2000; assoc. dean medicine, prof. cmty. health Brown U. Med. Sch., Providence, 2000—. Bd. dirs. Armed Forces Retirement Home, Washington. Editor: Older Veterans, 1984, Handbook of Geriatric Care, 1982; contbr. articles to profl. jours. Pres. Alzheimer's Assn. Greater Hartford, 1993-95; apptd. Alzheimer's Coalition Conn., 1991-95. Fellow: Gerontol. Soc. Am. (chair com.); mem.: APHA (del., governing coun.), Am. Soc. Aging. Office: Brown U Sch Medicine 97 Waterman St G-A2 Providence RI 02912

**WETMORE, KEITH CHIDESTER**, lawyer; b. Valparaiso, Ind., Oct. 17, 1956; s. Leonard Leander and Dorisann (Chidester) W. BA, Northwestern U., 1977; JD magna cum laude, U. Mich., 1980. Bar: Calif. 1981, U.S. Dist. Ct. (no. dist.) Calif. 1981. Law clk. to Hon. J. Edward Lumbard U.S. Ct. Appeals (2d cir.), 1980-81; assoc. Steinhart & Falconer, San Francisco, 1981-82, Morrison & Foerster LLP, San Francisco, 1982-86, ptnr., 1986—, chmn. NYC, 2000—. Articles editor U. Mich. Law Rev. 1980-81. Mem. ABA, Calif. Bar Assn., Bay Area Lawyers for Individual Freedom, San Francisco Bar Assn. Methodist. Office: Morrison & Foerster LLP 1290 Ave Americas New York NY 10104 Business E-Mail: kwetmore@mofo.com.*

**WETSCH, JOHN ROBERT**, information scientist; b. Dickinson, ND, Aug. 27, 1959; s. Joseph John (dec.) and Florence Mae (Edwards) W.; m. Laura Jean Johnson, Aug. 29, 1981; children: Julie Elizabeth, Katherine Anne, John Michael, Joseph Harold. BS, Excelsior Coll., Albany, 1984; MA, Antioch U., 1989; PhD, Nova Southeastern U., 1994; BS, U. N.D., 2001; M in Astronomy, U. Western Sydney, 2002; grad. in Theology, Australian Cath. U. Radiation physics instr. Grand Forks (N.D.) Clinic, 1983-85; sr. programmer PRC, Inc., Cavalier Air Force Sta., ND, 1987-91, PARCS project-SAFEGUARD sys.; pres. Dakota Sci. Inc., Langdon, ND, 1988-95; instr. U. N.D.-Lake Region,

Devils Lake, 1988-91; systems adminstr. U.S. Courts Nat. Fine Ctr., Raleigh, NC, 1991-94; project leader U.S. Postal Svc., Raleigh Integrated Bus. Sys. Solution Ctr., 1994—2001, program mgmt. info. tech. enabling portfolio, 2001—03; sr. tech. fellow Litton/PRC, 1997—2002; tech. fellow Northrop Grumman Info. Tech., 2002—06, sys. engr., 2004—06; program mgr. NC Window of Info. on Student Edn. NC Dept. Pub. Instrn., 2006—. Cons. on Wave Obs./N.D. Proposal, Gov.'s Office, Bismarck, 1991; founder, developer Dakota Sci., Inc., Langdon, 1988-95; instr. divsn. continuing edn. Wake Tech. C.C., 1993-99; adj. faculty computer info. systems N.C. Wesleyan Coll., 1997—; adj. faculty N.C. State U., 1999-2000, Capella U., Mpls., 2006—, U. Phoenix, 1998-2001. Author: Distributed UNIX System Administration, 1998; (with others) COMPUTE!'s 2nd Book of Amiga, 1988; contbr. articles to COMPUTE! Jour. of Progressive Computing, 1987, other profl. jours. Program coord. Lake Region Outreach, U. N.D., Cavalier Air Force Sta., 1988—91; mem. bd. alumni trustees USNY-Regents Coll., Albany, 1995—2000, v.p., 1996—97, pres., 1997—2000, ex-officio mem. bd. overseers, 1997; pres. Zeta Rho chpt. Pi Kappa Alpha, Grand Forks, 1981; pres. Alumni Assn. Excelsior Coll., 1999—2001; ex-officio voting Excelsior Coll. Bd. Trustees, 1999—2001, bd. trustees, 2001—. Decorated knight comdr. Order of St. Gregory the Great (Vatican); named Larimore-Mathews scholar, U. N.D., Grand Forks, 1978, N.D. Acad. Sci. scholar, 1978, SMITS scholar, N.D. Acad. Sci., 1990; recipient Westinghouse Sci. Talent Search award, 1978, Nova Southeastern U. Leadership award, Internat. Alumni Assn., 1998. Mem.: Dakota Astron. Soc. (pres. 1987—91, co-founder), Assn. for Computing Machinery. Roman Catholic. Achievements include rsch. in missile simulation; microcomputer short range weather forecasting algorithm, study in astronomy and culture, astronomy information systems, large scale sys. integration to govt. info. sys. Office: 301 N Wilmington St Raleigh NC 27601 Business E-Mail: drwetsch@msn.com.

**WETSCH, LAURA JOHNSON,** lawyer; b. Fargo, N.D., Nov. 18, 1959; d. Ronald Lee Johnson and Jacqualene Lee (Goudie) Johnson Trefz; m. John Robert Wetsch, Aug. 29, 1981; children: Julie Elizabeth, Katherine Anne, John Michael. Joseph Harold. AA, Bismarck (N.D.) State Coll., 1980; BA, U. N.D., 1982, JD, 1985. Bar: N.D. 1985, N.C. 1992. Law clk. to Hon. Patrick A. Conmy, U.S. Dist. Ct. for N.D., Bismarck, 1985-88; pvt. practice, Langdon, ND, 1988-91; assoc. Jordan Price Wall Gray Jones & Carlton, PLLC, Raleigh, NC, 1992-99; dir., v.p. legal affairs Hytec Cons., Inc., Cary, NC, 1999—2003; of counsel Joyce L. Davis & Assocs., Raleigh, 1999—2006; ptnr. Winslow & Wetsch, LLP, Raleigh, 2006—. Instr. bus. and criminal law U. N.D.-Lake Region, Cavalier, 1990-91; instr. paralegal studies Ctrl. Carolina C.C., Sanford, N.C., 1991-92; instr. bus. law Wake Tech. C.C., Raleigh, 1992-93. Author, editor (pamphlet) Crime Survivors Handbook, 1996; editor N.D. Women Lawyers Assn. Newsletter, 1990-91; contbr. articles to profl. jours. Vol. mediator and arbitrator Burleigh County Housing Authority, Bismarck, 1986-88; concessions co-chmn. Sanderson H.S. Band Boosters, 1996-2000; curbside cons. in employment law, N.C. Ctr. for Nonprofits, 1998. Mem. Nat. Employment Lawyers Assn., N.C. Bar Assn. (citizen edn. com. young lawyers divsn. 1994-96, chmn. membership svcs. com. young lawyers divsn. 1996-97), N.C. Acad. Trial Lawyers, Wake County Bar Assn. (fee arbitration com. 2001—). Democrat. Roman Catholic. Office: 416 Morson St Raleigh NC 27601 Office Phone: 919-834-6534. E-mail: lwetsch@winslow-wetsch.com.

**WETSEL, WILLIAM DAVID,** literature educator; b. Sweetwater, Tex., May 28, 1949; s. W.B. Wetsel and Elizabeth Heriot Evans. BA with highest honors, U. Tex., 1971; MDiv, U. Chgo., 1989; PhD, Brandeis U., 1978. Vis. prof. U. Stuttgart (Germany), 2005, U. Paris IV, Sorbonne, 2006. Author: Scripture and the Rest: Pascal's Pensées in the Exegetical Tradition of Port-Royal, 1983, Pascal and Disbelief: Catechesis and Conversion in the Pensées, 1995; editor: N.Am. Soc. Seventeenth Century French Literature Tempe Acta, 6. vol., 2003, Pascal Translation Project. Faculty co-ordinator Gay and Lesbian Student Caucus Ariz. State U. Recipient Acad. Palms award, French Govt., 2005; fellow, Fulbright Found., 1971—72, Woodrow Wilson Found., 1972; grantee, Am. Coun. of Learned Societies, 1979; Andrew Mellon fellow, U. Pitts., 1980—81, Fulbright scholar, U. Paris, 1982—83. Mem.: N.Am. Soc. for Seventeenth-Century French Lit. (pres. 2000—02), Phi Beta Kappa. Democrat. Episcopalian. Achievements include research in French 17-th century studies, Cajun French language, gay studies in France. Avocations: religious art, minority languages. Home: 3508 N Pueblo Way Scottsdale AZ 85251 Office: Arizona State U Dept Langs Tempe AZ 85287-0202 Office Phone: 480-994-8942. Personal E-mail: wdwetsel@aol.com.

**WETTER, VIRGINIA FORWOOD PATE,** broadcast executive; b. Havre De Grace, Md., Aug. 10, 1919; BA, Coll. William and Mary, 1940, D (hon.) of Pub.Svc., 2006, PhD (hon.) in Pub. Svc., 2006. Pub. rels. Std. Oil Co. of Pa., 1940, Irwin and Leighton Contractor, 1941; pres. gen. mgr. WASA and WHDG radio Havre de Grace, MD, 1960—85; pres. Multiview Cable Co. (later Comcast), 1965—80; chmn. bd. Chesapeake Broadcasting Corp., 1985—. Trustee Harford CC Bd. of Trustees, 1959—69, chmn., 1966—69; pres. Md. Assn. Bds. of Edn., 1963—64, Md. Dist. of Columbia Del. Broadcaster's Assn., 1965—66; mem. Harford County Bd. Edn., 1959—69, pres., 1966—69; mem. radio code bd. Nat. Assn. of Broadcasters, 1966—71; libr. bd. Broadcast Pioneers, 1980—2004; pres. Multiview Cable Co., 1966—82. Dir. Harford County Heart Assn. and Cancer Soc., Susquehanna Coun. of Girl Scouts; county chmn. Pres.'s Com. to Promote Employment of Physically Handicapped; plans bd. United Way; dir. Blood Bank of Md.; vol. Harford Meml. Hosp. Aux.; chmn. ann. fund drive Coll. William and Mary, 1985; endowment assn. trustee, pres.'s coun.; vestry St. John's Episcopal Ch., chair 150th anniversary celebration, co-chair bldg. com. Recipient Alumni Medallion award, Coll. William and Mary, 1969, Am. Broadcast Pioneer award, Broadcasters' Found., 2001, Disting. Svc. to Broadcasting award, Broadcast Pioneers of Washington Area, 2001. Mem.: Am. Women in Radio and Television (life; nat. pres. 1970—71, Bd. Dirs. award 1991, Radio Leadership award 2000), Md. Congress of Parents and Tchrs (life), Delta Kappa Gamma (hon.). Home: 1000 Chesapeake Dr Havre De Grace MD 21078 Personal E-mail: vwetter@aol.com.

**WETTERAU, MARK S.,** food products/distributor executive; m. Virginia Wetterau; children: Stephen, Elizabeth, Olivia. BA, Westminster Coll. With Wetterau Inc., 1980—92; pres., CEO Shop 'n Stop Warehouse Foods, 1988—90; pres. retail & ind. group Wetterau Inc., 1990—91, pres., COO, 1991—92; co-founder, ptnr. Wetterau Assoc., 1992—; pres., CEO Quality Beverage, 1992—98; chmn., CEO, pres. Golden State Foods (of Wetterau Assoc.), Irvine, Calif., 1998—. Chmn. GSF found.; bd. mem. Second Harvest Food Bank of Orange County. Office: Golden State Foods Ste 1100 18301 Von Karman Ave Irvine CA 92612*

**WETZEL, BETTY PREAT,** writer; b. Roundup, Mont., Nov. 7, 1915; d. Alfred William and Rachel Preat (Johnston) Eiselein; m. Winston Warren Wetzel, June 5, 1940; children: Susan Hinman, Kurt, Gretchen Grafin von Rittberg, Rebecca. BA in Journalism, U. Mont., 1937. Columnist, reporter Roundup (Mont.) Rec.-Tribune, 1938-46; sec. SEATO Cholera Rsch. Lab. and Hosp., Dacca, Bangladesh, 1965-67; adminstrv. asst. to v.p. Wellesley (Mass.) U., 1969-73; dir. pub. rels. Oxfam-Am., Boston, 1973-77; book rev. editor Mont. Mag., Helena, 1989-91. Author: The Making of a Montanan, 1986, Missoula, The Town and The People, 1988, After You, Mark Twain, 1990; co-author: Older Women in the Outdoors, 1996. Bd. dirs. Flathead Lake Biol. Sta., Bigfork, Mont., 1980-86. Democrat. Avocations: mountain hiking, tennis, reading, politics. Home: 189 Pierce Ln PO Box 693 Bigfork MT 59911-0693 Personal E-mail: bwetzel@digisys.net.

**WETZEL, HEINZ,** foreign language educator; b. Ziesar, Germany, May 11, 1935; immigrated to Can., 1965; s. Ernst and Katharina (Jentzsch) W.; m. Marianne Dummin, Mar. 19, 1957; children: Andreas, Suzanne, Claudia. Staatsexamen, Free Univ., Berlin, 1960; Dr. phil., U. Göttingen, Fed. Republic Germany, 1967. Asst. prof. German dept. Queen's U., Kingston, Canada, 1965-69; assoc. prof., grad. sec. German dept. U. Toronto, 1969-72, prof. German dept., 1972—2000, prof. emeritus, 2000—, chmn. German

dept., 1984-89. Vis. prof. U. Calif., San Diego, 1973, Technische U. Braunschweig, Germany, 1973, Humboldt U. Berlin, 1995, 97, 99. Author: Konkordanz zu den Dichtungen Georg Trakls, 1971, Klang und Bild in den Dichtungen Georg Trakls, 2d edit., 1972, Banale Vitalitaet und laehmendes Erkennen, Drei vergleichende Studien zu T.S. Eliots, The Waste Land, 1974; editor: Seminar: A Journal of Germanic Studies, 1980-85; contbr. 50 articles on German and comparative lit. to profl. jours. Fellowships and grants from Social Scis. and Humanities Rsch. Coun. of Can. Mem. MLA of Am., Can. Assn. Univ. Tchrs. German.

**WETZEL, KARL JOSEPH,** physics professor, dean; b. Waynesboro, Va., May 29, 1937; s. Mark Ernest and Margaret K. (Jungbluth) W.; m. Barbara Carol Damutz, Aug. 3, 1968; children: Sebastian P., Christopher M. BS in Physics, Georgetown U., 1959; MS in Physics, Yale U., 1960, PhD in Physics, 1965. Physicist Nat. Bur. Standards, Washington, 1959; postdoctoral fellow Inst. Nuclear Physics, Darmstadt, Germany, 1965-67, Argonne (Ill.) Nat. Lab., 1967-69; asst. prof. physics U. Portland, Oreg., 1969-72, assoc. prof. Oreg., 1972-80, prof. Oreg., 1980-2000, prof. emeritus Oreg., 2001—, chmn. sci. dept. Oreg., 1980-86, dean Grad. Sch. Oreg., 1987-98. Cons. in field; adj. prof. State of Oreg. Dept. Continuing Edn., Portland, 1976-96. Contbr. articles to profl. publs. Bd. dirs. Friendly House Ctr., Portland, 1979-82, Choral Arts Ensemble, Portland, 1988-95, 98—. NSF fellow, 1965, 76-77; recipient Pres.' award Oreg. Mus. Sci. and Industry, 1972, Outstanding Advisor award Am. Coll. Test/Nat. Academic Advising Assn., 1984. Mem. Am. Phys. Soc., AAUP. Achievements include first to describe experiments using germanium detectors with neutron-capture gamma-ray spectroscopy; first measurement of Delbrück effect in photon scattering. Office: U Portland 5000 N Willamette Blvd Portland OR 97203-5743

**WEVERS, JOHN WILLIAM,** retired Semitic languages educator; b. Baldwin, Wis., June 4, 1919; emigrated to Can., 1951; s. Bernard and Wilemina (Te Grootenhuis) W.; m. Grace Della Brondsema, May 22, 1942; children: Robert Dick, John William, Harold George, James Merritt. AB, Calvin Coll., Grand Rapids, Mich., 1940; ThB, Calvin Sem., 1943; ThD, Princeton Theol. Sem., 1945; DD (hon.), Knox Coll., Toronto, 1973; DHC (hon.), Leiden U., 1985. Lectr., then asst. prof. O.T. and Semitic langs. Princeton Theol. Sem., 1946-51; mem. faculty U. Toronto, Ont., Canada, 1951—, prof. Near Eastern studies Ont., 1963—, prof. emeritus Ont., 1984—, grad. chmn. Ont., 1972-75, chmn. dept. Ont., 1975-80. Chmn. adminstrv. council Presbyn. Ch. Can., 1960-65 Author: Commentary on the Book of Ezekiel, 1969, Septuaginta Vetus Testamentum Graecum: Genesis, 1974, Deuteronomium, 1977, Numeri, 1981, Leviticus, 1986, Exodus, 1991; also text histories, 1974, 78, 83, 86, 92, Notes on the Greek Text of Exodus, 1990, Genesis, 1993, Deuteronomy, 1995, Leviticus, 1997, Numbers, 1998. Bd. govs. Ctrl. Hosp., Toronto, 1963-96, chmn., 1967-80; chmn. Hosp. Coun. Met. Toronto, 1974-75; bd. govs. Ont. Hosp. Assn., 1974-84, pres., 1978-79. Recipient Queen's Jubilee medal, 1978. Fellow Royal Soc. Can.; mem. Oriental Club Toronto, Internat. Orgn. Septuagint and Cognate Studies (pres. 1972-80, hon. pres. 1989—), Can. Bibl. Studies (hon. life), Akademie Wissenschaften Goettingen (corr.), Arts and Letters Club (Toronto). Home: 116 Briar Hill Ave Toronto ON Canada M4R 1H9 E-mail: j.wevers@utoronto.ca.

**WEXELBAUM, MICHAEL,** lawyer; b. Bklyn., Aug. 12, 1946; s. Joseph and Beatrice (Skurnick) W.; m. Cynthia Debra Schorr, Apr. 15, 1973 (dec. 1984); children: Joshua David, Stephanie Faye; m. Joan Brenda Math, Aug. 21, 1994; stepchildren: Jonathan David Kaye, Matthew Lawrence Kaye, Julie Dana Kaye. BA in Econs., Bucknell U., 1968; JD, NYU, 1971. Bar: N.Y. 1972, U.S. Dist. Ct. (so. and ea. dists.) N.Y. 1973, U.S. Dist. Ct. (ea. dist.) Wis. 1998. Assoc. Sherman; Citron & Karasik, P.C., N.Y.C., 1972-80, ptnr., head litigation dept., 1980-2001; ptnr. litigation dept. Snow Becker Krauss P.C., N.Y.C., 2001—, co-chair litigation dept., 2003—. Arbitrator Nat. Arbitration Forum, 1999—. Arbitrator Am. Arbitration Assn. and Gen. Arbitration Coun. of Textile and Apparel Industries, N.Y.C., 1982—. Named a N.Y. Super Lawyer, 2006. Mem. Bankruptcy Lawyers Bar Assn., Lawyers Assn. Textile and Apparel Industries (bd. govs.), Am. Arbitration Assn. (arbitrator), Nat. Arbitration Forum (arbitrator), Assn. Comml. Fin. Attys. Democratic. Jewish. Avocations: tennis, skiing, biking, theater. Home: 85 Norrans Ridge Dr Ridgefield CT 06877-4237 Office: Snow Becker Krauss PC 605 Third Ave New York NY 10158-0125 Office Phone: 212-455-0486. Office Fax: 212-455-0455. Personal E-mail: jmwex@hotmail.com. Business E-Mail: mwexelbaum@sbklaw.com.

**WEXLER, ALLAN,** architect, educator; BFA, R.I. Sch. Design, 1971, BArch, 1972; MArch, Pratt Inst, 1976. Asst. prof. Sch. Arch. N.J. Inst. Tech., 1974—83; mem. faculty environ. design Parsons Sch. Design, 1983—94; assoc. adjunct Arch. Pratt Inst., 1999—; arch., designer Ronald Feldman Fine Arts, N.Y.C. Mem. faculty Brown U. Sch. Art, 1986, Temple U. Tyler Coll. Art, 1989, Cooper Union Sch. Fine Arts, 1989; artist-in-residency U. Calif., San Diego, 1991; vis. prof. R.I. Sch. Design, Sch. Arch., 1992, Hochschule der Kunste, Berlin, 1994; vis. critic in sculpture SUNY, Purchase, 1993. One-man shows include Albright Coll., Freedman Gallery, Reading, Pa., 1985, Brown U., List Art Ctr., Providence, 1985, Ronald Feldman Fine Arts, N.Y.C., 1985, 1988, 1990, 1992, 1994, 1998, Temple U. Gallery, Phila., 1986, McIntosh/Drysdale Gallery, Washington, 1986, The Jewish Mus., N.Y.C., 1988, Univ. Gallery, U. Mass., Amherst, 1989, Inst. Contemporary Art, U. Pa., 1989, Horace Richter Gallery, Old Jaffa, Israel, 1990, San Diego Mus. Contemporary Art, La Jolla, Calif., 1991, U. Gallery, U. Mass. Amherst, 1991, The Forum Gallery, St. Louis, 1991, De Cordova Mus. and Sculpture Park, Lincoln, Mass., 1992, Karl Ernst Osthaus Mus., Hagen, Germany, 1993, Hochschule der Kunste, Berlin, 1994, Three Rivers Art Festival, Pitts., 1995, Md. Inst. Coll. Art, Balt., 1996, Parsons Sch. Design, Dept. Arch. and Environ. Design, 1997, Stadtgalerie Saarbricken, Germany, 1997, Gallery Joe, Phila., 1997, Atlanta Coll. Art Gallery and City Gallery at Chastain, Atlanta, 1999, Stephen Wirtz Gallery, San Francisco, 2000, Forum for Contemporary Art, St. Louis, 2000, San Francisco Mus. Modern Art, 2001, Ronald Feldman Fine Arts, NYU, 2002, Parrish Art Mus., Southampton, N.Y., 2002, exhibited in group shows at Arlene Bujese Gallery, East Hampton, N.Y., 1995, N.J. Ctr. Arts, Summit, 1995, Davis Mus. and Cultural Ctr., Wellesley (Mass.) Coll., 1996, Calif. Ctr. Arts. Mus., Escondido, 1996, Gallery Joe, Chgo., 1997, Union Brauerei/Dortmunder U. Germany, 1998, White Box, N.Y., 1999, Aldrich Mus. Contemporary Art, Ridgefield, Conn. 2000, 2002, Wave Hill Glyndor Gallery, Bronx, N.Y., 2000, Apex Art, N.Y.C., 2001, Westfalisches Landesmuseum, Munster, Germany, 2001, Hallwalls Contemporary Arts Ctr., Buffalo, N.Y., 2001, Yeshiva U., N.Y.C., 2002, Wilhelm-Hack Mus. and Kunstverein Ludwigshafen, Germany, 2002, Denver Art Mus., 2002, Karl Ernst Osthaus-Mus., Hagen, Germany, 2002, Ronald Feldman Fine Arts, N.Y.C., 2002, Mus. Contemporary Arts, Chgo., 2002, numerous others, commns. include, Vera List, Greenwich, Conn., 1990, Parson's Sch. Design, 1993, ARTWALK, 1995, others, NYC Bd. Edn., 1999, Schneider Vineyard, 2000—, Expo 2000, Hannover, Germany, 2000, Met. Transp. Authority, NYC, 2001—, Hudson River Park, 2002—. Recipient First prize The City as a Significant Environment Competition, Milano and Casabella Mag., 1972, First prize Birch Burdette Long Competition, Archtl. League, 1975, Bessie award 40 Under 40, Interiors Mag., 1986, Sponsored Project award N.Y. State Coun. on Arts, 1989, Chrysler award for design innovation, 1997, George Nelson Design award, Interiors mag., 1999; fellow, N.Y. Found. Arts, 1985, 1990; grantee, Archtl. League, 1975. Office: 305 W 20th St New York NY 10011

**WEXLER, ANNE,** government relations and public affairs consultant; b. NYC, Feb. 10, 1930; d. Leon R. and Edith R. (Rau) Levy; m. Joseph Duffey, Sept. 17, 1974; children by previous marriage: David Wexler, Daniel Wexler. BA, Skidmore Coll., 1951, LLD (hon.), 1978; DSc in Bus. (hon.), Bryant Coll., 1978. Assoc. pub. Rolling Stone mag., 1974-76; personnel adviser Carter-Mondale transition planning group, 1976-77; dep. undersec. regional affairs Dept. Commerce, 1977-78; asst. to Pres. of U.S., Washington, 1978-81; pres. Wexler and Assocs., Washington, 1981-82; govt. relations and pub. affairs cons., chmn. Wexler, Reynolds, Harrison & Schule, Inc., Washington, 1981-90; vice chmn. Hill and Knowlton PA Worldwide, Wash-

ington, 1990-92; chmn. The Wexler Group, 1992—. Bd. dirs. Methanex, Dreyfus Index Funds, Wilshire Mut. Funds, Dreyfus Family of Funds. Bd. dirs. Washington Econ. Club, WETA. Decorated officer Order of Australia; named Outstanding Alumna Skidmore Coll., 1972, recipient most disting. alumni award, 1984, Bryce Harlow award, 1989. Mem. Coun. on Fgn. Rels., Nat. Women's Forum. Jewish. Office: Wexler Group 1317 F St NW Ste 600 Washington DC 20004-1157

**WEXLER, HASKELL,** film producer; b. Chgo., 1922; s. Simon Wexler; m. Nancy Ashenhurst (div.); two children; m. Marian Witt (div.); 1 son, Mark; m. Rita Taggart. Edn. documentaries, Chgo., for eleven years; cinematographer films: The Hoodlum Priest, The Best Man, America America, The Loved One, In the Heat of the Night, Who's Afraid of Virginia Woolf? (Acad. award), The Thomas Crown Affair, American Graffiti, One Flew Over the Cuckoo's Nest, Introduction to the Enemy, Bound for Glory (Acad. award), Coming Home, Colors, Three Fugitives, 1988, Blaze, 1989, Lookin' to Get Out, Matewan, Other People's Money, The Babe, Mulholland Falls, 1995, Rich Man's Wife, 1995, (with others) Days of Heaven, (with others) Rolling Stones-IMAX, The Secret of Roan Inish, Canadian Bacon, Limbo, 1999, HBO 61—, 2001, Silver City, 2004; writer, dir., photographer: Medium Cool, 1969; wrote and directed Latino, 1985; feature documentary Bus Riders Union, Five Days in March, From Wharf Rats to Lords of the Docks, Who Needs Sleep?. Received star on Hollywood's Walk of Fame, 1996. Mem. Acad. Motion Picture Arts and Scis. (bd. govs. cinematographers br.). Personal E-mail: perigol@aol.com.

**WEXLER, HERBERT IRA,** retail company executive; b. Newark, Sept. 6, 1916; s. Irving and Jeanette (Lesser) W.; m. Elaine L. Ellis, Oct. 10, 1948; children: Susan, Peter, Toni. Student, Rutgers U., 1939-41; student Advanced Mgmt. Program, Harvard U., 1956. From stock boy to asst. buyer L. Bamberger & Co., 1935-47; from buyer appliances to sr. v.p., exec. com., dir. R.H. Macy & Co., N.Y.C., 1947-73; pres., CEO, chmn. bd. dirs. Marcade Group Inc., N.Y.C., 1973-86, cons., bd. dirs., 1987-97. Vice chmn. Greater N.Y. coun. Boy Scouts Am.; organizer, fundraiser Yale Grace New Haven Hosp.; mem. Gov. Harriman's Com. to Investigate Fraud and Misrepresentation in Consumer Products; mem. adv. coun. to bd. trustees Greens Farms Acad., Westport, Conn.; gen. chmn. State of Israel Bond Drive, 1980, testimonial, 1978; gen. chmn. N.Y. Cmty. Svc. Soc.; chmn. N.Y. sect. for fundraising Denver Jewish Hosp; dir. Children's Blood Found. N.Y. Hosp. Capt. U.S. Army, 1941—46. Named Key Man of Yr. Am. Jewish Com. and B'nai B'rith, 1957; named B'nai B'rith Man of Yr., 1976; recipient Disting. Service award Am. Jewish Com. and Anti-Defamation League, 1960, Award of Honor Fedn. Jewish Philanthropies of N.Y., 1961, Scroll of Honor United Jewish Appeal of Greater N.Y., 1964, Man of Yr. award Conn. Digestive Disease Soc., 1973 Mem.: Birchwood Country Club, Harvard Club. Home: Greenfield Hunt 49 Palmer Brg Fairfield CT 06430-7830

**WEXLER, LEONARD HOWARD,** pediatric oncologist; b. Bklyn., Nov. 21, 1961; s. Theodore and Florence Wexler; m. Beth Sue Brown, 1999. BA, Boston U.; MD, Boston U. Sch. Medicine, 1985. Cert. Pediatrics, Pediatric Hematology-Oncology. Intern, pediatrics Albert Einstein/Montefiore, Bronx, NY, 1985—88, resident, pediatrics, 1985—88; fellow, pediatric hematology and oncology NIH-Nat. Cancer Inst., Bethesda, Md., 1988—92, sr. clin. investigator, pediatric branch, 1992—96; dir. clin. services Babies & Children's Hosp., NYC, 1996—99; assoc. mem. dept. pediatrics Meml. Sloan-Kettering Cancer Ctr, NY, 1999—; asst. prof. pediatrics Uniformed Services Univ. of the Health Sciences; assoc. prof. pediatrics, divsn. pediatric oncology Columbia U., NY, 1996—99; assoc. prof. pediatrics Weill Med. Coll.-Cornell U., NY, 1999. Co-chair of internat. study to evaluate the effectiveness of chemotherapy for the treatment of children with osteosarcoma; co-investigator clin. trial that evaluates a novel combination of chemotherapy agents & radiotherapy techniques for the treatment of children with rhabdomyosarcoma, Meml. Sloan-Kettering. Med. editl. adv. bd. Libby Shriver Sarcoma Initiative. Named one of Medical Marvels, New York Mag., 2006. Office: Meml Sloan Kettering Cancer Ctr 1275 York Ave New York NY 10021 Office Phone: 212-639-7990. Business E-Mail: wexlerl@mskcc.org.*

**WEXLER, PATRICIA SUSAN,** dermatologist, surgeon; b. 1951; MD, U. Libre de Bruxelles, Belgium, 1979. Cert. Am. Bd. Internal Medicine 1983, Am. Bd. Dermatology 1986. Intern Beth Israel Med. Ctr., NY, 1979—80, resident internal medicine NY, 1980—82, fellowship infectious disease NY, 1982—83, attending physician NY, Mt. Sinai Hosp., NY; private practice Wexler Dermatology, Manhattan, NY. Tchr. Beth Israel Med. Ctr. Dermatology Surgery Clinic; asst. clin. prof. Albert Einstein Sch. Medicine, Bronx, NY; cons. in the develop. of several skin care and make-up lines. Author medical rsch. publs. Recipient Am. Acad. Cosmetic Surgery award for Excellence in Cosmetic Surgery. Fellow: Am. Soc. Dermatologic Surgery. Office: 145 E 32nd St 7th Fl New York NY 10016-6055 Office Phone: 212-684-2626.

**WEXLER, PETER JOHN,** artist, photographer, theater designer; b. NYC, Oct. 31, 1936; s. David and Berda (Sarnoff) W.; m. Constance Ann Ross, Nov. 30, 1962. BS in Design, U. Mich., 1958; student, Yale Sch. Drama, 1958. Designs include White House stage, 1961, War and Peace, 1964, The White Devil, 1965, A Joyful Noise, 1966, The Happy Time, 1967, In the Matter of J. Robert Oppenheimer, 1968, Merv Griffin TV show, 1965, Terra Nova, 1979 (L.A. Dramalogue Critics award); prin. designer, Center Theatre Group, L.A., 1967-70, designer, N.Y. Philharmonic Promenades, 1965-78; play and film The Trial of the Catonsville 9, 1971-72; Leonard Bernstein's Mass, L.A., 1973, N.Y. Philharmonic Rug Concerts, 1973-77, Les Troyens, Met. Opera Co., 1973, Le Prophète, Met. Opera Co., 1977, Un Ballo in Maschera, Met. Opera Co., 1980, Theatre Space Prodns., Pitts. Pub. Theatre, 1975-77; designer team for Frank O. Gehry & Assocs., redesign Hollywood Bowl; designer: Albert Herring, Savonlinna Opera Festival, Finland, 1981; centennial prodn. Les Troyens, Met. Opera, 1983, also dir. Cold Storage, Ariz. Theatre Co., 1978, Terra Nova, Pitts. Public Theatre, 1981; producer, Dallas Symphony Orch.'s Star Fest 80; producer Rocky Mountain Music Festival, Denver Symphony Orch., 1983-84, Star Spangled Banner, Permanent Exhibition U.S. Nat. Emblem, Smithsonian Instn., Washington, 1982; producer, design exhbn. Am. Anthem, LTV Ctr., Dallas/Smithsonian Instn., 1985; designer, broker exhbn. Liberties with Liberty, Trammell Crow Co./Mus. Am. Folk Art, 1985; designer Horizons '86, N.Y. Philharmonic, 1986; co-producer, designer video, exhbn. and space Albany Urban Cultural Park, Albany, N.Y., 1986; producer, dir. Pletka, multimedia theatre piece for orch., Dallas Symphony Orch., 1987; programmer, interior designer Trans-Hudson Ferry for the Port Authority of N.Y. and N.J., 1987-88; producer The Search for Life, Smithsonian Inst., 1987; producer Mstislav Rostropovich 60th Anniv. Gala Concert, Nat. Symphony Orch., Kennedy Ctr., Washington, 1987, Navy 87, Navy 89, USN multi-media orchestral prodn., Washington, 1987; founder, producer, artistic dir. Spring Creek Music Festival, Garland, Tex. Dallas Ft. Worth Metroplex, 1992-94; dir. Lost in the Stars, A.C.O., Carnegie Hall, 1989; visual cons. Lifetime Med. (cable TV), 1989-90; design cons. Reebok River Stage - Radio City Music Hall Prodns, 1989; program designer Mega-Mall, Oxford Devel. Co., Pitts., 1990; designer Unfinished Stories, 1994; prodr. *TV) A Salute to Slava, Kennedy Ctr., Washington, 1994; cons. (TV net) Music in America Nat. Symphony Orch., Washington, 1997; creator Boston Pops Environment, 1995-97; cons. Boston Symphony Hall Sys. Update Plan, 1995-98; design cons. ABC News-Good Morning Am., 20/20, World News Tonight, 1997-98; cons. Nat. Underground Railroad Freedom Ctr., 1998; cons., devel. new material Nextstage Entertainment Corp., 1999-2000; cons. image and I.D. program Shubert Ticketing Svs. Telecharge, 1999; author, designer, photographer "The Remarkable Adventures of Texas and Bubba in Venice", 2003; designer scenery and projections The Talk Cure, Mark Taper Forum, 2004; one-man exhbn. U.S. Equities, Chgo., 2006—; cons. in field. Project leader Outdoor Performance Facility, Met. Opera Co., N.Y. Philharmonic Symphony, Dept. Cultural Affairs City of N.Y., 1980-2004; cons. Temp. Quarters Project San Francisco Ballet, 1994. Recipient Internat. Theatre Inst. competition award ANTA, 1965, most imaginative use of scene design award Saturday Rev., 1965, Drama Desk-Joseph Maharam award for The Happy Time as best designer of mus., 1968, L.A. Drama Critics Circle award, 1971, Bard award for Excellence in Architecture & Urban Design, 1996. Address: 277 W End Ave New York NY 10023-2604 Office Phone: 212-877-9494. E-mail: peterwexler@mindspring.com.

**WEXLER, ROBERT,** academic administrator; m. Hannah Wexler. BA summa cum laude, UCLA, MA, PhD, UCLA; MBA, Baruch Coll. Ordained rabbi Jewish Theol. Seminary. Lectr. Near Eastern Studies Princeton U.; prof. U. Judaism, LA, 1978—. Colen Disting. Lectr. in Bible, pres., 1992—. Mem. Israel Democracy Inst. (exec. com. bd. mem.), World Coun.of Synagogues (exec. com. mem.), Am. Jewish Com. (exec. com. mem.). Office: U Judaism 15600 Mulholland Dr Los Angeles CA 90077-1599 E-mail: rwexler@uj.edu.

**WEXLER, ROBERT,** congressman; b. Queens, Jan. 2, 1961; m. Laurie Wexler; children: Rachel, Zachary, Hannah. BA in Polit. Scis., U. Fla., 1982; JD, George Washington U. Law Sch., 1985. Mem. Fla. State Senate, 1990-96, U.S. Congress from 19th Fla. dist., 1997—; mem. internat. rels. com., judiciary com. Recipient Senatorial Leadership award Fla. Prosecutor's Assn.; named Legis. of the Year Palm Beach Police Benevolent Assn., Top Environ. Senator Fla. Leagues Conservation Voters, 1996. Democrat. Office: Ho Rep 213 Cannon Ho Office Bldg Washington DC 20515-0919

**WEXLER, SANDRA M.,** artist, medical illustrator; b. NYC, Dec. 17, 1945; d. Irving and Sophie Engel; children: Jason, David. AA, Fashion Inst. Tech., 1965. Cert. medical asst. Balt., 1996. CMA Johns Hopkins Hosp., Lutherville, Md., 1996—97; CMA, clin. coord. Drs. Stanley Klatsky & Adam Basner, Balt., 1997—2000; CMA Dr. Eve Bruce, Lutherville, 2001—03, Dr. Seth Goldberg, Rockville, Md., 2004—. Exhibitions include Am. Inst. Architects Gallery, Sch. 33, Katzenstein Gallery, Slayton House Gallery, Women's Resource Ctr, Greater Balt. Med. Ctr., Gormley Gallery, Coll. Notre Dame, one-woman shows include Shainberg Gallery, Gallerie Elan, 2005, Represented in permanent collections The Art Resource, Balt., Susan Perrin Fine Art Balt., limited edit. greeting cards, Balt. Mus. Art Shop, Corporate Collections, Bloomingdales, NYC, Hyatt Regency, Balt., The Hammers Co., Greenbelt, Md., Wharton, Levin, Ehrmantraut, Klein & Nash, Bethesda, Md., Edward Friedman, CPA, Balt., Signature Mgmt., Balt., Levindale Hebrew Geriatric Ctr. & Hosp., Balt., Ampersand Inc., Reiserstown, Md., Penan & Scott, P.A., Rockville, Md., Martin, Junghans, Snyder & Bernstein, Balt., TCAG, Rockville, Potts & Potts, P.A., Balt., Royal Ins. Co., Balt., Cooper Wingard, Balt., Wiley, Rein & Fielding LLC, DC, Art Forms Gallery, Red Bank, NJ, A. Lee Dellon, MD, Balt., Arles Mgmt., Inc., NY, Gallerie Elan, Bethesda, Ellicott City, Md. Vol. surg. holding area Sinai Hosp., Balt., 1993—2000. Fellow, Vt. Studio Colony, 1990. Jewish. Avocations: art, reading, travel, cooking, photography.

**WEXNER, ABIGAIL,** apparel executive; m. Leslie H. Wexner. Dir. Ltd. Brands, Inc., Columbus, Ohio, 1997—. Past chair governing com. Columbus Found.; chair Ctr. for Child and Family Advocacy; mem. bd. trustees Children's Hosp., Inc, The Columbus Acad., The Wexner Ctr. Found.; founder, chair Columbus Coalition Against Family Violence. Named one of Top 200 Collectors, ARTnews Mag., 2004. Avocation: Collector of Modern and Contemporary Art; British Sporting Pictures. Office: Ltd Brands Inc Three Limited Pky PO Box 16000 Columbus OH 43216

**WEXNER, LESLIE HERBERT,** retail executive; b. Dayton, Ohio, 1937; BSBA, Ohio State U., 1959, HHD (hon.), 1986; LLD (hon.), Hofstra U., 1987; LHD (hon.), Brandeis U., 1990; PhD (hon.), Jewish Theol. Sem. Founder, pres., chmn. bd. The Limited, Inc., fashion chain, Columbus, 1963—. Dir., mem. exec. com. Banc One Corp., Sotheby's Holdings Inc., vis. com. Grad. Sch. Design Harvard U.; mem. mus. adminstrn. adv. coun. Ohio State U.; chmn. Retail Industry Trade Action Coalition. Bd. dirs. Columbus Urban League, 1982-84, Hebrew Immigrant Aid Soc., NYC, 1982—; co-chmn. Internat. United Jewish Appeal Com.; nat. vice chmn., treas. United Jewish Appeal; bd. dirs., mem. exec. com. Am. Jewish Joint Distbn. Com., Inc.; trustee Columbus Jewish Fedn., 1972, Columbus Jewish Found., Aspen Inst., Ohio State U., Columbus Capital Corp. for Civic Improvement; former trustee Columbus Mus. Art, Columbus Symphony Orch., Whitney Mus. Am. Art, Capitol South Community Urban Redevel. Corp.; former mem. Governing Com. Columbus Found.; founding mem., first chair The Ohio State U. Found; exec. com. Am. Israel Pub. Affairs Com. Decorated cavaliere Republic of Italy; named Man of Yr., Am. Mktg. Assn., 1974; named one of Top 200 Collectors, ARTnews Mag., 2004. Mem. Young Presidents Orgn., Sigma Alpha Mu. Clubs: B'nai B'rith; fellow Am. Acad. Arts & Sciences Achievements include being named one of world's richest people and 400 richest Americans, Forbes Mag. Avocation: Collector of Modern and Contemporary Art; British Sporting Pictures. Office: Limited Inc PO Box 16000 3 Limited Pkwy Columbus OH 43230-1450*

**WEYAND, CORNELIA M.,** medical educator; Prof., medicine and immunology Mayo Med. and Grad. Sch., Rochester, Minn., 1990—2003; prof. medicine Emory U., Atlanta, 2004—. Office: Emory Univ 101 Woodruff Cir #1003 Atlanta GA 30322 Office Phone: 404-727-7310.

**WEYDT, PATRICK ROMAN PHILIPP,** neuroscientist; s. Harald and Sigrun Weydt; m. Anke Witting, July 16, 2005, MD, Freie Universität, Berlin, 1997. Sr. fellow U. Wash., Seattle, 2002—, vis. scholar. Chief sci. officer Dox Med. and Sci. Cons., Munich. Rsch. Devel. grant, Muscular Dystrophy Assn., 2005—, Leopoldina fellowship, German Acad. of Sciences Leopoldina, 2000—02. Mem.: German Soc. for Neurosci., World Fedn. of Neurology Motor Neuron Disease Rsch. Group, Soc. for Neuroscience.

**WEYER, DIANNE SUE,** health facility administrator; b. Anchorage, Aug. 15, 1954; d. Vernon H. and Myrtle M. Larson; m. Merlin D. Weyer; 1 child, Alison. BSW magna cum laude, Augustana Coll., Sioux Falls, S.D., 1976; MPA, U.S.D., Vermillion, 1989. LCSW 1996. Program dir. Threshold, Sioux Falls, SD, 1976—78; policy analyst S.D Divsn. Law Enforcement Assistance, Pierre, SD; coord. youth projects Mountain Plains Youth Svcs. Coalition, Pierre, 1980—82; social worker S.D. Dept. Social Svcs., Pierre, 1983—85; child and adolescent program specialist S.D. Divsn. Mental Health, Pierre, 1985—96; mgr. Social Svcs. St. Mary's Healthcare Ctr., Pierre, 1996—2000, dir. outreach, 2002—. Social work adv. bd., adj. faculty Augustana Coll., Sioux Falls, 1977—79; interagy. coord. coun., state bd. mem. S.D. Dept. Edn., Pierre, 1989—96; state rep. for children and youth Nat. Assn. State Mental Health Program Dirs., Washington, 1985—96; chair S.D. Interagy. Coordination Network Coun., Pierre, 1991—96; social work adv. bd. Presentation Coll., Aberdeen, SD; adj. faculty Capital U., Pierre, 2000—06; exec. bd., past pres. S.D. Social Work Leaders in Health Care, Sioux Falls, 1999—2001. Healthcare com. Pierre C of C, 1999—2003; tchr., confirmation guide Luth. Meml. Ch., Pierre, 1985—2001; bd. dirs. Missouri Shores Resource Ctr., Pierre, 1980—82; exec. bd. Healthy Cmtys./Healthy Youth, Pierre, 1999—. Recipient Spl. Recognition award, Capitol Area Counseling Svc., 2001, S.D. Family-Based Svcs. Assn., 1994, Outstanding Svc. award, S.D. Corrections Assn., 1990; grantee S.D. CASSP-Local Infrastructure Demonstration, Ctr. Mental Health Svcs., 1993—96, Rural Mental Health Demonstration, NIH, 1987—89, HHS Adminstrn., Children, Youth and Family Svcs., 1987—90. Mem.: NASW, S.D. Alliance for the Mentally Ill, S.D. Social Work Leadership in Healthcare (sec., v.p., pres. 1998—2001, Spl. Recognition award 1996), Nat. Social Work Leadership in Healthcare, Optimist Club (sec. bd. dirs. 2006). Home: 1217 Hilgers Dr Pierre SD 57501 Office: St Mary's Healthcare Ctr 801 E Sioux Pierre SD 57501 Personal E-mail: mdweyer@pic.midco.net. Business E-mail: diannewweyer@catholichealth.net.

**WEYERHAEUSER, GEORGE H., JR.,** paper manufacturing company executive; b. w; B in Philosophy/Maths., Yale U., 1976; MS, MIT, 1986. Tech. forester, contract logger adminstr., sawmill supr. Weyerhaeuser Co., Dierks, Ark., 1978-80, v.p., mill mgr. Containerboard Valliant, Okla., 1981-90, v.p. mfg. pulp & paper bus. Federal Way, 1990-93, pres., CEO Can. divsn., 1993-98, sr. v.p. technology, 1998—. Office: Weyerhaeuser Co 33663 Weyerhaeuser Way S PO Box 9777 Federal Way WA 98063-9777*

**WEYERS, LARRY LEE,** energy executive; b. Nebr. BA, Doane Coll., 1967; MS, Columbia U., 1971; MBA, Harvard U., 1975. Registered profl. engr. With Babcock & Wilcox, 1971—73, Commonwealth Edison, 1975—84; mgmt. cons. Towers Perrin, 1984—85; dir. fuel svc. WPS Resources Corp., Green Bay, 1985—89, asst. v.p. energy supply, 1989—92, v.p. energy supply, 1992—94, v.p. power supply & engring., 1994—95, sr. v.p. power supply & engring., 1995, pres., COO, 1995—97, bd. dir., 1996—, pres., CEO, 1997, chmn., pres., CEO, 1998—. Bd. dir. WS Packaging Corp., Wis. Pub. Svc. Corp., 1996—; bd. mem. Edison Elec. Inst., Am. Gas Assn., 2004, Assn. Edison Illuminating Cos., 2003. Bd. mem. Bellin Health, Green Bay Packers, Wis. Manufacturers & Comm., Competitive Wis., UTECH Ventures, Utility Bus. Edn. Coalition. Office: WPS Resources Corp PO Box 19001 Green Bay WI 54307-9001

**WEYMAN, STEVEN ALOYSIUS,** retired military officer; b. Fort Thomas, Ky., May 31, 1957; s. Edward Joseph Weyman and Carol Jean (Steffen) Jackson; m. Kathleen Anne Bradford, June 2, 1990; 1 child, Jennifer Elizabeth. BS in Math., No. Ky. U., 1978; MS in Comm. Sys. Tech., Naval Postgrad. Sch., 1988. Commd. 2d lt. U.S. Army, 1978, advanced through grades to lt. col., 1995; bn. signal officer 8th Engr. Bn., 1st Cav. Divsn., Ft. Hood, Tex., 1979-81, 2nd M.I. Bn., Pirmasens, Germany, 1982-85; co. comdr. B Co., 307th M.I. Bn., Ludwigsburg, Germany, 1985-86; signal combat devel. project officer Combined Arms Command, Ft. Leavenworth, Kans., 1988-91; student U.S. Army Command Gen. Staff Coll., Ft. Leavenworth, 1991-92; bn. exec. officer 123rd Signal Bn., 3rd Inf. Divsn., Kitzingen, Germany, 1992-94; asst. divsn. signal officer 3rd Inf. Divsn., Wuerzburg, Germany, 1994-95; operational readiness evaluation team chief 5th U.S. Army (West), Ft. Lewis, Wash., 1995-97; def. info. sys. network deployed program mgmt. chief Def. Info. Sys. Agy., Arlington, Va., 1997-2000, ret., 2000; student Armed Forces Staff Coll., Norfolk, Va., 1998; tech. acct. mgr. Intel Online Svcs., 2000—01; teleport installation program mgr., prin. engr. Arrowhead Global Solutions Inc., 2001—03; network sys. lead engr. Mitre Corp., 2003—. Decorated Legion of Merit. Mem. U.S. Signal Corps Assn. (Bronze Order of Mercury 1995), Armed Forces Comm. Electronics Assn. Avocations: computers, travel, reading, sports. E-mail: steve@weyman.net, sweyman@mitre.org.

**WEYMAN, TODD D.,** art appraiser; BA, Conn. Coll.; MA in Art Hist., Williams Coll. Curatorial asst. British Arts Ctr., Yale Univ., New Haven; head, acquisitions Johnson Art Mus., Cornell Univ., Ithaca, NY; now v.p., dir., print, drawings dept. Swann Gallery, NYC. Appraiser Antiques Roadshow, WGBH-PBS, 1997—. Office: Swann Galleries 104 E 25th St New York NY 10010 Office Phone: 212-254-4710 Ext. 32. Office Fax: 212-979-1017. Business E-Mail: tweyman@swanngalleries.com.

**WEYMOUTH, ELIZABETH (LALLY) GRAHAM,** editor, columnist; children: Katharine, Pamela Bass. BA in Am. History and Lit. with honors, Harvard U. Reporter The Boston Globe, 1965—66, freelance writer, reporter, 1966—76; with Bedford Stuyvesant Restoration Corp. Senator Robert Kennedy, 1968—69; freelance journalist, contbg. editor numerous publs. including NY Times Mag., Esquire, Atlantic Monthly, Parade, LA Times, New York, 1977—83; contbg. editor LA Times, 1983—86, Washington Post, 1987—92; sr. editor, spl. diplomatic corr. Newsweek Mag., 1992—. Interviewer Washington Post, 1986—; mem. Coun. Fgn. Rels. Author: America in 1876: The Way We Were, 1976; editor, compiler Thomas Jefferson: The Man, His World, His Influence, 1973. Mem. Coun. Foreign Relations; mem. adv. com. Ctr. Strategic and Internat. Studies.

**WEYRAUCH, KRISTIE LYNN,** music educator, director; b. Kenosha, Wis., Aug. 23, 1974; d. Jeffrey Paul Weyrauch and Marilyn Elizabeth Pinzger, Thomas Pinzger (Stepfather). BFA in Music Edn., U. Wis., 1997. Tchr. music Franklin Pk. and Tice Elementaries, Fort Myers, Fla., 1997—98; band dir. Kenosha Unified Schs. Kenosha, Wis., 1998—2002, Mahone Mid. Sch., Kenosha, 2002—. Musician: Kenosha Pops Concert Band, WSMA Tchrs Convention, 2005, Racine Concert band, 2004—. Bd. dirs. Kenosha (Wis.) Pops Concert Band, 2005. Recipient John Philip Sousa Band award, Mary D. Bradford H.S., 1992; scholar, U. Wis., 1992—97. Mem.: U. Wis. Milw. Alumni Assn., Nat. Flute Assn., Nat. Band Dirs. Assn., Wis. State Music Assn. Office Phone: 262-605-8127. Personal E-mail: kweyrauch@wi.rr.com. Business E-Mail: kweyrauc@kusd.edu.

**WEYRAUCH, WALTER OTTO,** law educator; b. Lindau, Germany, Aug. 27, 1919; came to U.S., 1952; s. Hans Ernst Winand and Meta Margarete (Lönholdt) W.; m. Jill Carolyn White, Mar. 17, 1973; children from previous marriages: Kurt Roman (dec.), Corinne Harriet Irene, Bettina Elaine (dec.). Student, U. Freiburg, 1937, U. Frankfurt Main, Germany, 1940-43, Dr. iur, 1951; LL.B., Georgetown U., 1955; LL.M., Harvard, 1956; J.S.D., Yale, 1962; Golden Dr. diploma (hon.), U. Frankfurt Main, 2001. Referandar, Frankfurt, Germany, 1943-48; atty. German cts. U.S. Ct. Appeals, Allied High Commn., Frankfurt, 1949-52; expert on trade regulations, visit in U.S. under auspices Dept. State, 1950; Harvard U. Dumbarton Oaks Library and Collection, Washington, 1953-55; asst. in instrn. Law Sch., Yale, 1956-57; assoc. prof. law U. Fla., Gainesville, 1957-60, prof., 1960-89, Clarence J. TeSelle prof. law, 1989-94, Stephen C. O'Connell chair, 1994—, disting. prof. law, 1998—; hon. prof. law Johann Wolfgang Goethe U., Franfurt Main, 1980—. Vis. cons. U. Calif. at Berkeley, Space Scis. Lab., 1965-66; vis. prof. law Rutgers U., 1968; vis. prof. polit. sci. U. Calif. at Berkeley, 1968-69; vis. prof. law U. Frankfurt, 1975; cons. Commn. of Experts on Problems of Succession of the Hague Conf. on Pvt. Internat. Law, U.S. Dept. State, 1968-71; Rockefeller Found. fellow, Europe, 1958-59; Richard G. Huber disting. lectr. Law Sch. Boston Coll., 1999. Author: The Personality of Lawyers, 1964, Zum Gesellschaftsbild des Juristen, 1970, Hierarchie der Ausbildungsstätten, Rechtsstudium und Recht in den Vereinigten Staaten, 1976, Gestapo V-Leute: Tatsachen und Theorie des Geheimdienstes, 1989, 2nd edit., 1992; author: (with Sanford N. Katz) American Family Law in Transition, 1983; author: (with Katz and Frances E. Olsen) Cases and Materials on Family Law: Legal Concepts and Changing Human Relationships, 1994; author: Das Recht der Roma und Sinti: Ein Beispiel autonomer Rechtsschöpfung, 2002; author, editor: Gypsy Law: Romani Legal Traditions and Culture, 2001; contbr. Mem. Law and Soc. Assn., Internat. Soc. on Family Law, Assn. Am. Law Schs. (chmn. com. studies beyond 1st degree in law 1965-67), Order of Coif. Home: 2713 SW 5th Pl Gainesville FL 32607-3113 Office: U Fla Coll Law Gainesville FL 32611 Office Phone: 352-273-0662. Business E-Mail: weyrauch@law.ufl.edu.

**WEYRICH, PAUL MICHAEL,** think-tank executive; b. Racine, Wis., Oct. 7, 1942; s. Ignatius A. and Virginia M. (Wickstrom) W.; m. Joyce Anne Smigun, July 6, 1963; children: Dawn, Peter, Diana, Stephen, Andrew. AA, U. Wis., 1962. Ordained deacon Melkite Greek Eparchy, 1990. News dir., announcer, program dir. WLIP, WAXO-FM, Kenosha, Wis., 1960-63; reporter Milw. Sentinel, 1963-64; polit. reporter, newscaster CBS, Milw., 1964-65; news dir. Sta. KQXI, Denver, 1966; press sec. to Sen. Gordon Allott US Senate, Washington, 1967-73, spl. asst. to Sen. Carl T. Curtis, 1973-77; founder, pres. Heritage Found., 1973-74; nat. chmn. Free Congress PAC, Coalitions for Am., 1987—, BOD, Amtrak, 1987-93; pres. Free Congress Rsch. & Ednl. Found., 1977—2002, chmn., CEO, 2002—; pres. Krieble Inst., 1989—96. Nat. editor Transport Central, 1968-71; treas. Coun. Nat. Policy, 1981-92, pres. America's Voice, 1991-97; bd. dirs. All News Radio WEEI, Boston, 1984-90, Krieble Inst. Russia; nat. chmn. Com. for Effective State Govt.; chmn. bd. Yorktownuniversity.com, 1999—. Author: The Role of Rails series, 1964; pub. Polit. Report, 1975-89, The New Electric Rwy. Jour. 1988-96, Spotlight on Congress, 1989-93; host (daily talk show) Direct Line, 1993-98; co-host The New Electric Rwy. Jour., 1994-96, Ways & Means, 1994—. Recipient Youth of Yr. award Racine Optimist Club, 1960, Excellence in Reporting citation Milw. Common Council, 1964, Documentary of Yr. award for Wis. TV, 1965, Crystal Ball award for predicting outcome 1996 presdl. election Washington Post, 1996, Thomas Jefferson award for servant leadership Coun. Nat. Policy, 1997. Mem. Ctrl. Electric Railroaders Assn. Internat. Policy Forum (chmn. 1983-84); former mem. HUD Adv. Commn. on Regulatory Barriers to Affordable Housing. Greek Catholic. Home: 12615

Lake Normandy Ln Fairfax VA 22030-7262 Office: Free Congress Found 717 2nd St NE Washington DC 20002-4368 Office Phone: 703-815-1086. Business E-Mail: paulwey@freecongress.org.

**WHALE, ARTHUR RICHARD,** retired lawyer; b. Detroit, Oct. 28, 1923; s. Arthur B. and Orpha Louella (Doak) W.; m. Roberta Lou Donaldson, Oct. 29, 1949; children: Richard Donaldson, Linda Jean. BSChemE, Northwestern U., 1945; LLB, George Washington U., 1956. Bar: D.C. 1957, Mich. 1957, Ind. 1977, U.S. Patent and Trademark Office 1957. Chem. engr. Ansul Chem. Co., Marinette, Wis., 1946-47, Parke, Davis & Co., Detroit, 1947-50, writer med. lit., 1950-52; chem. engr. Bur. Ships, U.S. Dept. Navy, Washington, 1952-55, dep. sect. head, indsl. gas sect., 1954-55; patent engr. Swift & Co., Washington, 1955-56; patent atty. Upjohn Co., Kalamazoo, 1956-65; asst. mgr. organic chems. sect. patent dept. Dow Chem. Co., Midland, Mich., 1965-66, mgr., 1967-73, mng. counsel, 1973-75; asst. sec., gen. patent counsel Eli Lilly & Co., Indpls., 1975-86; of counsel Miller, Morriss, & Pappas, Lansing, Mich., 1986-89, Baker & Daniels, Indpls., 1987—2003; ret., 2003. Bd. dirs. Wyckoff Chem. Co., South Haven, Mich., 1985-99; lectr. Practicing Law Inst., John Marshall Law Sch. Contbr. articles to profl. jours. Pres. Nat. Inventors Hall of Fame Found., 1987-79; bd. dirs. Holcomb Rsch. Inst., Indpls., 1982-86. Served to lt. (j.g.) USNR, 1943-46. Mem. State Bar Mich. (chmn. patent trademark copyright sect. 1967-69), D.C. Bar Assn., Midland County Bar Assn. (pres. 1974-75), Am. Bar Assn. (mem. patent trademark copyright sect.), Assn. Corp. Patent Counsel, Nat. Coun. Patent Law Assns. (chmn. 1979-80), Am. Intellectual Property Law Assn. (pres. 1974-75), Ashlar Lodge, Masons, Shriners. Republican. Presbyterian. Avocation: golf. Office: Baker & Daniels Ste 2700 300 N Meridian St Indianapolis IN 46204-1782 Office Phone: 239-262-8561. Business E-Mail: arwhale@bakerd.com.

**WHALEN, CHARLES WILLIAM, JR.,** writer, retail executive, congressman, educator; b. Dayton, Ohio, July 31, 1920; s. Charles William and Colette (Kelleher) W.; m. Mary Barbara Gleason, Dec. 27, 1958; children— Charles E., Daniel D., Edward J., Joseph M., Anne E., Mary B. BS, U. Dayton, 1942, HHD (hon.), 1980; MBA, Harvard U., 1946; postgrad., Ohio State U., 1959-60; LLD, Central State U., Ohio, 1966. Vice pres. Dayton Dress Co., 1946-52; faculty U. Dayton, 1952-66; mem. 90th-95th Congresses 3d Dist. Ohio; pres. New Directions, Washington, 1978-79; fellow Woodrow Wilson Internat. Center for Scholars, 1980; adj. prof. Sch. Internat. Service, Am. U., 1981. Mem. Ohio Ho. of Reps., 1954-60, Ohio Senate, 1960-66; mem. Internat. Vol. Svcs., Inc., 1985-95; v.p. Washington Inst. Fgn. Affairs, 1982-98; mem. U. Dayton adv. bd. Ctr. for Internat. Studies, 1990-96; bd. dirs. Harvard Bus. Sch., Washington, 1982-84, 91-94. 1st lt. AUS, 1943-46. Recipient Disting. Alumnus award U. Dayton Alumni Assn., 1975, Alumni Lifetime Achievement award U. Dayton Sch. Bus. Adminstrn., 2001. Mem.: Dayton Bicycle Club, Kenwood Country Club, Capitol Hill Club. Roman Catholic.

**WHALEN, JOHN PHILIP,** retired academic administrator, priest, lawyer; b. Troy, N.Y., Jan. 4, 1928; s. Philip Joseph and Mary Catherine (Doyle) W. BA summa cum laude, St. Mary's Sem. and Univ., Balt., 1949; STL, Cath. U., 1953, MA, 1954, STD summa cum laude, 1965; JD, George Washington U., 1976; postgrad., Johns Hopkins U., 1959-60, U. Md., College Park, 1958-59, Fordham U., 1953-54; LHD (hon.), Marymount U., 1987. Ordained priest Roman Cath. Ch., 1953. Instr. Mater Christi Sem., Albany, 1953-58; asst. prof. Mt. St. Mary's Coll., Emmitsburg, Md., 1959-61; assoc. prof. Cath. U. Am., Washington, 1961-67, acting pres., 1968-69; pastor St. Mary's Ch., Oneonta, NY, 1970-72; pres. Consortium of Univs. of Washington area, 1972-88; mng. editor New Cath. Ency., 1963-67; pres., editor-in-chief Corpus Publs., 1967-94, ret., 1994. Cons. 12 colls. and univs.; founder, chmn. Univ. Support Svcs., Inc., 1986-94, pres., CEO, founder; cons. student loans, capital access trust, capital loans to colls., 1999-2000; founder, prin. Power Systems, Inc.; founder Whalen Holdings, LLC; founder prin. Full Measure, LLC, Whalen Holdings, LLC, JMJ Whalen Found., Inc., Vinegar Hill Assoc. LLC, 2005; bd. dirs. U.S. Fund for Improvement Postsecondary Edn., 1988-91 Mem. editl. bd. Law and Edn.; weekly columnist Evangelist, Albany; contbr. to Nat. Geog. mag.; contbr. articles to ednl. and theol. jours. Pres. Univ. Extension Ednl. Corp., 1974—94; mem. Fed. City Coun., 1982—, Coun. for Ct. Excellence, 1984—90; chmn. Ctr. Advanced Studies of the Ams., 1984—90; bd. dirs. Sta. WETA-TV, 1968—69, Washington Ctr. for Met. Studies, 1968—69, Cath. U. Am., 1968—69, Nat. Shrine of Immaculate Conception, 1968—69, Dumbarton Coll., 1970—72, Trinity Coll., 1969—72, St. Mary's Coll., South Bend, Ind., 1970—74, St. Anselm's, 1979—85, Mt. Vernon Coll., 1982—84, CBR Found., 2001—. Met. Bd. Trade, Washington, 1975—90, sec bd. dirs., 1983—85. Named Man of the Yr., 1984; recipient Disting. Alumnus award George Washington U., 1988. Mem. Nat. Cath. Edn. Assn., Cath. Theol. Soc. Am. (dir. 1966-68), Higher Edn. Group Washington (pres. 1974-75), Tired Hands Club (pres. 1982-84), Cosmos Club (Washington), City Club, Rotary. Office: 1614 Parham Rd Silver Spring MD 20903-2256 Personal E-mail: jwhalen@erols.com.

**WHALEN, JOHN SYDNEY,** management consultant; b. Moncton, NB, Can., Sept. 26, 1934; s. Harry Edward and Maude (Bourgeois) W.; m. Margaret Joan Carruthers, May 3, 1958; children: Bradley Graham, Elizabeth Ann. Grad., Can. Inst. Chartered Accts., 1959. Chartered acct. Coopers & Lybrand (formerly McDonald, Currie & Co.), St. John, N.B., 1954-63; with Kaiser Services, Oakland, Calif., 1963-75, telecommunications mgr., 1966-69, asst. controller, 1969-70, controller, 1970-74; mgr. corp. acctg. Kaiser Industries Corp., Oakland, 1975; controller Kaiser Engrs., Inc., Oakland, 1975-76, v.p. fin. and adminstrn., 1976-82; mgmt. cons., owner Whalen & Assocs., Inc., Alamo, Calif., 1983—. Pres. Round Hill Holdings, Inc., 1993-99. Mem. Commonwealth Club, Rancho Cañada Golf Club. Home: PO Box 709 Alamo CA 94507-0709 Office Phone: 925-820-3506. Personal E-mail: sydwhalen@aol.com.

**WHALEN, LUCILLE,** retired academic administrator; b. L.A., July 26, 1925; d. Edward Cleveland and Mary Lucille (Perrault) W. BA in English, Immaculate Heart Coll., Los Angeles, 1949; MSLS, Catholic U. Am., 1955; DLS, Columbia U., 1965. Tchr. elem. and secondary parochial schs., L.A., Calif., 1945—52; tchr., libr. Conaty Meml. H.S., L.A., 1950—52; reference/serials librarian, instr. in library sci. Immaculate Heart Coll., 1955-58; dean Immaculate Heart Coll. (Sch. Library Sci.), 1958-60, 65-70; assoc. dean, prof. Library Sci., Albany, 1971-78, 84-87, prof. Sch. Info. Sci. and Policy, 1979-87; dean grad. programs, libr. Immaculate Heart Coll. Ctr., Los Angeles, 1987-90; ref. libr. (part-time) Glendale Community Coll., 1990—. Dir. U.S. Office Edn. Instn. Author, editor (with others): Reference Services in Archives, 1986; author: Human Rights: A Reference Handbook, 1989; author: (with Nina Redman) Human Rights: A Reference Handbook, 2d edit., 1998. Mem. ACLU, Common Cause, Amnesty Internat. Democrat. Roman Catholic. Home: 320 S Gramercy Pl Apt 101 Los Angeles CA 90020-4542 Office: Glendale CC 1500 N Verdugo Rd Glendale CA 91208-2809 Personal E-mail: lucillew213@sbcglobal.net.

**WHALEN, STEPHEN R.,** education educator; PhD, U. Maine, Orono, 1999. Adj. prof. Castleton State Coll., Vt., 2001—.

**WHALEN, THOMAS EARL,** psychology professor; b. Toledo, June 26, 1938; s. T. Mylo and Alice E. (Tallman) W.; m. Carolyn Margaret Lapham, Dec. 24, 1960; children: Jennifer Susan, Holly Elizabeth. BA, UCLA, 1960; MA, San Diego State U., 1967; PhD, U. Conn., 1970. Cert. secondary tchr., Calif. Secondary tchr. San Diego City Schs., 1964-68; rsch. assoc. Southwest Regional Lab., Inglewood, Calif., 1969; prof. Calif. State U. Hayward, 1970—2000, chair ednl. psychology dept., 1977-79, asst., assoc. dean sch. edn., 1987—89, 1995—99, prof. emeritus, 1997. Rsch. con. Evaluation Assocs., San Francisco Bay Area Schs., 1971-88, Lawrence Livermore (Calif.) Nat. Lab., 1982-83. Author: (test book) Ten Steps to Behavioral Research, 1989; contbr. articles to profl. jours. Lt. USN, 1960—63. U.S. Office of Edn. fellow U. Conn., 1968-70, post doctoral scholar Am. Edn. Rsch. Assn., U. Iowa, 1972. Mem. Am. Ednl. Rsch. Assn., APA, Calif. Ednl.

Rsch. Assn. (bd. dirs. 1982-84), Bay Area Coun. on Measurement and Evaluation in Edn. (pres. 1976-77), United Profs. of Calif. (exec. bd. Calif. State U. Hayward 1975-76). Avocations: golf, travel, computers. Home: 325 Conway Dr Danville CA 94526-5511

**WHALEN, THOMAS VINCENT,** pediatric surgeon; b. Woonsocket, R.I., June 17, 1952; s. Thomas Vincent and Ethel (Chamberlin) Whalen; m. Elaine Therese Whalen, June 5, 1976; children: Daniel Michael, Patrick Charles, Kevin Thomas. AB, Boston U., 1973, MD, 1976; M Med. Mgmt., Carnegie Mellon U., 1999. Diplomate Am. Bd. Gen. Surgery, Am. Bd. Pediat. Surgery, Am. Bd. Surg. Critical Care. Intern Boston U. Med. Ctr., 1976-77; resident Naval Med. Ctr., Portsmouth, Va., 1978-82; fellow in pediatric surgery Children's Hosp. of L.A., 1982-84; commd. ensign USN, 1977, advanced through grades to capt., 1991, resigned, 1989; head divsn. pediat. surgery Robert Wood Johnson Med. Ctr., Camden, N.J., 1989—. Mem. gen. and plastic surgery devices adv. panel FDA, Rockville, Md., 1989-99. Contbr. articles to profl. jours., chpt. to book. Capt. USNR, 1989—. Fellow ACS, Am. Acad. Pediats.; mem. AMA (alt. del.). Roman Catholic. Office: 3 Cooper Plz Rm 411 Camden NJ 08103-1438 E-mail: Whalen@umdnj.edu.

**WHALEN, WAYNE W.,** lawyer; b. Savanna, Ill, Aug. 22, 1939; s. Leo R. and Esther M. (Yackley) W.; m. Paula Wolff, Apr. 22, 1970; children: Amanda, Clementine, Antonia, Nathaniel, Daniel. BS, U.S. Air Force Acad., 1961; JD, Northwestern U., 1967. Bar: Ill. 1967, US Ct. Appeals (7th cir.) 1968, US Supreme Ct. 1972. Commd. 1st lt. USAF, 1961, ret., 1964; assoc. Mayer, Brown & Platt, Chgo., 1967-74, ptnr., 1974, Skadden, Arps, Slate, Meagher & Flom LLP, Chgo., 1984—. Bd. dir. Van Kampen Funds, Oak Brook, Ill, Abraham Lincoln Pres. Libr., Springfield, Ill. Author: Annotated Illinois Constitution, 1972. Del. 6th Ill. Constitutional Conv., 1969-70, chmn. style drafting and submission com. Named Outstanding Young Lawyer, Chgo. Bar Found., 1970. Mem. Chgo. Club. Office: Skadden Arps 2 N La Salle St Ste 2200 Chicago IL 60602-3963

**WHALEY, CHARLES HENRY, IV,** communications company executive; b. Elmhurst, N.Y., Jan. 15, 1958; s. Charles Henry III and Edna Mae (Squires) W.; m. Jeanette Marie Smith, Sept. 26, 1987. AAS in Electrical Tech., Queensborough Community Coll., Bayside, N.Y., 1979. Testing engr. GTE/Telenet, Mount Laurel, NJ, 1979-81; field service engr. Gen. Dynamics Communications Co., St. Louis, 1981-82; ops. engr. United Techs. Communications Co., Pine Brook, NJ, 1982-84; sr. ops. engr. N.Y.C., 1984-85, ops. supr., 1985-86; project mgr. Telex Computer Products, N.Y.C., 1986; pres. Pertel Comms. of N.E., Hartford, Conn., 1990—, Metrocom Tech. Svcs., N.Y.C., 1997—. Democrat. Presbyn. Avocations: computers, classic automobiles, music, US history. Office: 350 Fifth Ave New York NY 10018 also: Pertel Comm of NE Inc 14th Fl 100 Pearl St Hartford CT 06103 Office Phone: 212-760-1339. E-mail: cwhaley@pertelne.com.

**WHALEY, FRANK,** actor; b. Syracuse, N.Y., July 20, 1963; m. Heather Bucha. Film appearances include: Ironweed, 1987, Field of Dreams, 1989, Little Monsters, 1989, Born on the Fourth of July, 1989, The Freshman, 1990, JFK, 1991, The Doors, 1991, Career Opportunities, 1991, Back in the U.S.S.R., 1992, A Midnight Clear, 1992, Hoffa, 1992, Swing Kids, 1993, Pulp Fiction, 1994, Swimming With Sharks, 1995, Homage, 1995, Cafe Society, 1995, The Winner, 1996, Broken Arrow, 1996, Retroactive, 1997, Went to Coney Island on a Mission from God: Be Back by Five, 1998, Curtain Call, 1999, Glam, 2001, Pursuit of Happiness, 2001, Chelsea Walls, 2001, A Good Night to Die, 2003, World Trade Center, 2006; TV movies include: Unconquered, 1989, Flying Blind, 1990, To Dance with the White Dog, 1993, Fatal Deception: Mrs. Lee Harvey Oswald, 1993, Dead Man's Gun, 1997, The Wall, 1998, When Trumpets Fade, 1998, Shake, Rattle and Roll: An American Love Story, 1999, Bad News Mr. Swanson, 2001, Sun Gods, 2002, Detective, 2005, Mrs. Harris, 2005, Where There's a Will, 2006; stage appearances include: Tigers Wild, 1986, The Years, 1993. Office: ICM 8942 Wilshire Blvd Beverly Hills CA 90211-1934*

**WHALEY, GARWOOD,** music company executive; Diploma, Juilliard Sch., 1965; Mus M, Cath. U. Am., 1971, D of Musical Arts, 1977. Pres., founder Meredith Music Pub., 1979—. Condr. emeritus Bishop Ireton Symphonic Wind Ensemble, Alexadria, Va.; adj. prof. music Catholic Univ. of Am.; curriculum coord. instrumental music Diocese of Arlington SCh., Va. Editor (chief): Music for Percussion, Inc., author 22 method books; contbr. articles pub. to profl. jour. Recipient Outstanding Secondary Educators of Am. award, Nat. Band's Assn., Outstanding Nat. Cath. Bandmaster, Citation of Excellence, Nat. Fedn. Interscholastic Music Assn., Outstanding Music Educator award, John Philip Sousa Found., Legion of Honor. Mem.: Am. Bandmasters Assn. (assoc.), Kappa Delta Pi. Mailing: PO Box 344 Galesville MD 20765 Office Phone: 410-867-0074. E-mail: garwoodw@comcast.net.

**WHALEY, JOHN A.,** management consultant; b. Bryan, Tex., June 14, 1950; s. Wilburn Holloway Whaley and Sadie J. Franklin-Whaley; m. Adrianne K. Thompson, June 15, 1971; children: Matthew A., Monica Dawn(dec.), Jeremy O. Student, Western Gov. U., Utah, U. Nev., Reno. Advt. account exec. The Record Courier, Gardnerville, Nev., 1977—82; advt. dir. Sparks Tribune / Big Nickel, Sparks, 1982—84; retail advt. dir. Tahoe Daily Tribune, South Lake Tahoe, Calif., 1984—85; dir. sales & mktg. Laughlin Associates, Inc., Carson City, Nev., 1986—90; advt. account exec. Fox TV, KAME TV, Reno, 1990—91; mgmt. analyst iv State of Nev., Carson City, 1991—. Bd. chmn. Morris Sheppard, Inc., Nev.; v.p., CEO A Class Act, Inc., Nev.; pres., CEO SP Jones, Inc, Nev. Author: (childrens novel) The InvestiGators. Deacon First So. Bapt. Ch., Minden, Nev., 1985—92. With U.S. Army, 1969—71, Vietnam. Decorated Nat. Def. Svc. medal U.S. Army, Vietnam Svc. medal. Mem.: MENSA (life). Independent. Avocations: writing, bicycling, running, travel, swimming. Home: 926 Ridgefield Dr Carson City NV 89706 Office: NV Div Health Care Financing & Policy 1100 E William St Carson City NV 89701 Personal E-mail: johnawhaley@sbcglobal.net.

**WHALEY, ROBERT HAMILTON,** judge; m. Lucinda Schilling Whaley; 3 children. BA, Princeton U., 1965; JD, Emory U., 1968. Litigator Land and natural resources divsn. Dept. Justice, 1969-71; asst. U.S. atty. U.S. Dist. Wash. (ea. dist.), 1971-72; assoc. Winston & Cashatt, Spokane, Wash., 1972-76, ptnr., 1976—; judge Spokane County Superior Ct., 1992-95, U.S. Dist. Ct. (ea. dist.) Wash., Spokane, 1995—. Office: US Dist Ct Ea Dist Wash PO Box 283 920 Riverside Ave W Spokane WA 99210

**WHALEY, ROGER GLENN,** music educator; s. R. Glenn and Joan K. Whaley; m. Melanie J. Seela, July 19, 1986; children: Erika children: Mark. BS, ND State U., 1982; MS, So. Oreg. U., 1994. Cert. K-12 music tchr. Minn., ND, SD. Band dir. Beach (ND) Pub. Schs., 1982—87, Williams Mid. Sch., Sturgis, SD, 1987—89, Larimore (ND) Pub. Schs., 1989—93, Grandview Mid. Sch., Mound, Minn., 1993—. Cons. MakeMusic!, Eden Prairie, Minn., 2005—. Named Exceptional Tchr., Tech. Info. Edn. Svcs., 2004. Mem.: Edn. Minn., Music Educators Nat. Conf. Lutheran. Avocations: computers, photography writing golf. Office: Westonka Pub Schs 1881 Commerce Blvd Mound MN 55364 Office Phone: 952-491-8338. Personal E-mail: roger@rogerwhaley.com.

**WHALEY, ROSS SAMUEL,** environmentalist, educator; b. Detroit, Nov. 7, 1937; s. Lyle John and Margaret Nielson (Semple) W.; m. Beverly Mae Heemstra, June 14, 1958; children: Heather Jean, Susan Lesli, Lindsay John. BS, U. Mich., 1959, PhD, 1969; MS, Colo. State U., 1961. Asst. prof., assoc. prof., prof. Utah State U., Logan, 1965—70, dept. head, 1967—70; assoc. dean Colo. State U., Ft. Collins, 1970—73; dept. head U. Mass., Amherst, 1973—76, dean, 1976—78; dir. econ. research USDA Forest Service, Washington, 1978—84; pres. SUNY Coll. Environ. Scis. and Forestry, Syracuse, 1984—2000, 2000—; chair Adirondack Park Agy., 2003—. Cons. UN FAO, Rome, 1983-84, UN, Budapest, Hungary, 1974, U.S. Peace Corps., South Am., 1972, Geddes, Brecher, Qualls & Cunningham, Denver, 1971-72; chmn. Adirondack Pk. Agy. Contbr. articles to profl. jours. Bd. dirs.

Glynwood Ctr., Paul Smith's Coll.; trustee Paul Smiths Coll. Fellow Soc. Am. Foresters (pres. 1991). Mem. Christian Ref. Ch. Avocations: reading, swimming, hiking, fly fishing, cross country skiing.

**WHALEY, STORM HAMMOND,** retired federal agency administrator; b. Sulphur Springs, Ark., Mar. 15, 1916; s. Storm Onus and Mabel Etta (Prater) W.; m. Jane Florence Bucy, Oct. 6, 1935; children: Carroll Jean Whaley Anderson, Ann Marie Whaley Adams, Rebecca Glenn Whaley Dyess. BA, John Brown U., 1935; LL.D. (hon.), 1959; postgrad., Am. U. Law Sch., 1954; D.Sc. hon., U. Ark. for Med. Scis., 1983. Mgr. Sta. KUOA, Siloam Springs, Ark., 1935-53, Sta. KGER, Long Beach, 1948-53, KOME, Tulsa, 1951-53; asst. to Congressman J.W. Trimble, 1953-54; asst. to pres. U. Ark., 1954-59, acting pres., 1959-60, v.p. health scis., 1960-70; assoc. dir. communications NIH, Bethesda, Md., 1970-92; ret., 1992. Mem. U.S. del. World Health Assembly, 1962-64; nat. adv. health coun. USPHS, 1963-66; chmn. ad hoc com. Report to Pres. and Congress Regional Med. Programs, 1967; mem. U.S. Sr. Exec. Service, 1979 Author: They Call It, 1951. Del. Democratic Nat. Conv., 1940, 44, 48, 52. Recipient Superior Service award HEW, 1974, SES Performance award, 1982, Superior Service award USPHS, 1987; named Outstanding Alumnus, John Brown U., 2001. Fellow AAAS; mem. Broadcast Pioneers, Ark. Broadcasters Assn. (life), NIH Alumni Assn., Masons (33d deg.), Omicron Delta Kappa, Lambda Chi Alpha. Home and Office: 849 Coast Blvd CN105 La Jolla CA 92037 E-mail: swhaley@san.rr.com.

**WHALIN, ROBERT W.,** physicist; B in Physics, U. Ky.; M in Physics, U. Ill.; PhD of Phys. Oceanography, Tex. A&M U. Registered Profl. Engr. Tech. dir. U.S Army Corps Engr. Coastal Engring. Rsch. Ctr., Fort Belvoir, Va., 1982—85, U.S. Army Engr. Waterways Experiment Sta., Vicksburg, Miss., 1985—92, dir., 1992—98, Army Rsch. Lab., Adelphi, Md., 1998—. Adj. prof. Miss. State U., Tex. A&M U., U. Miss.; mem. external rsch. adv. com. Miss. State U.; engring. adv. coun. mem. U. Fla.; rsch. adv. com. for Army High Performance Computing Rsch. Ctr. U. Minn.; adv. bd. mem. Dept. Civil Engring. U. New Orleans. Contbr. numerous articles to profl. jours. Mem.: ASCE, Sr. Exec. Assn., Army Engr. Assn., Soc. Am. Mil. Engrs., Tsunami Soc., Permanent Internat. Assn. Navigation Congresses, Am. Soc. Engring. Edn., Sigma Xi, Phi Kappa Phi, Phi Eta Sigma.

**WHALIN, W. TERRY,** writer, editor; b. Huntington, W.Va., Aug. 12, 1953; s. Wallace Eugene and Rose Terry (Estill) W.; children: Jonathan David, Timothy Benjamin; m. Christine Elizabeth Johnson, May 3, 1995. BA, Ind. U., 1975; cert., Multnomah Sch. of Bible, 1977; MA, U. Tex., Arlington, 1984. Linguist Wycliffe Bible Translators, Huntington Beach, Calif., 1975-85, mng. editor In Other Words, 1985-93; assoc. editor Decision mag. Billy Graham Evangelistic Assn., Mpls., 1993-94; CEO, pres. Whalin & Assocs., Colorado Springs, Colo., 1994—. Instr. Inst. of Children's Lit., 1997—. Author: When I Grow Up, 1992, Never Too Busy, 1993, A Strange Place to Sing, 1994, Chuck Colson, 1994, Today's Heroes Series, 1994, The Brave But Gentle Shepherd, 1996, Samuel Morris, Heroes of the Faith series, 1997, Sojourner Truth Heroes of the Faith Series, 1997, Luis Palau, Men of Faith Series, 1996, Billy Sunday, Young Reader's Christian Libr., 1996, John Perkins, 1996, Today's Heroes Series, 1996, Luis Palau, Young Reader's Christian Libr., 1998, Pocket Prayer Companion series: Prayers for My Son, Prayers for My Daughter, Prayers for My Wife, Prayers for My Husband, 1999, Lighthouse Psalms, 1999, Love Psalms, 1999, Billy Graham, Men of Faith Series, 2000; co-author: One Bright Shining Path, 1993, Ayacucho Para Cristo, 1995, Bottom-Line Faith, Ten Characteristics of Committed Christians, 1995, Let the Walls Fall Down, 1996, The World at Your Door, 1997, Better Men on the Path to Purity, 1998, The Book of Prayers: A Man's Guide to Reaching God, 1998, Sharing God with Others, 1998, Lessons from the Pit, 1999, Money for Life, 1999; ghostwriter (books): Seeking Christ, 1994, Freedom From Addiction, 1996, Pathway to His Prescence, 2000; contbr. articles to profl. publs. and mags. Treas. Evangelical Press Assn., Earlysville, Va., 1992-94. Mem. Evangelical Press Assn., Am. Soc. Journalists and Authors, Soc. Children's Book Writers and Ilustrators. Republican.

**WHAM, DAVID BUFFINGTON,** secondary school educator; b. Evanston, Ill., May 25, 1937; s. Benjamin and Virginia (Buffington) W.; m. Joan Field Wilber, Mar. 9, 1968 (div. May, 1972); children: Benjamin, Rachel. AB cum laude, Harvard U., 1959; MA, So. Ill. U., Carbondale, 1967. Instr. U. Wyo., Powell, 1963-65, So. Ill. U., Carbondale, 1965-67; legis. asst. U.S. Congress, Washington, 1969-78; freelance writer Chgo., 1980-89; tchr. Chgo. Pub. Schs., 1994—. Speechwriter Adlai Stevenson for Gov. campaign, 1986, Dawn Netsch for Gov. campaign, 1994. Author: My Farewell to Bohemia, 1968, The Comic Genuflection, 1984, A Wave of Bright Boys, 1994. With U.S. Army, 1959-62. Recipient fiction award Columbia Pacific U., 1994. Mem. Harvard Club Chgo. (interviewer 1984—), Spee Club Harvard, Hasty Pudding Club Harvard. Democrat. Episcopalian. Home: 860 Hinman Ave # 724 Evanston IL 60202 Office: 125 S Clark St Chicago IL 60603-5200

**WHANG, SUKOO JACK,** pathologist, microbiologist; b. Seoul, South Korea, Feb. 3, 1934; arrived in U.S., 1963, naturalized; m. Chung A. Park, Nov. 30, 1963; children: Selena, Stephanie, John. BS, Oreg. State U., 1957; MS, UCLA, 1960, PhD, 1963; MD, Korea U., Seoul, 1972. Diplomate Am. Bd. Tropical Medicine, Am. Bd. Forensic Medicine, Am. Bd. Pathology, Am. Bd. Med. Microbiology. Intern Good Samaritan Hosp., Dayton, Ohio, 1973—74; resident White Meml. Med. Ctr., L.A., 1974—77, clin. pathologist, 1977—87; mem. infection control com., 1977—87, dir. Sch. Med. Tech., 1977—87; dep. med. examiner L.A. County Coroner's Dept., L.A., 1991—2000. Recipient Physician's Recognition award, AMA, 1980—. Fellow: ACP, Coll. Am. Pathologists (Pathology Continuing Med. Edn. award 1984—), Am. Coll. Forensic Medicine, Am. Coll. Tropical Medicine, Am. Soc. Clin. Pathologists. Republican. Seventh Day Adventist. Avocations: swimming, reading. Home: 1325 Via Del Rey South Pasadena CA 91030

**WHARTON, DANNY CARROLL,** zoo biologist; b. Ontario, Oreg., Mar. 13, 1947; s. Carroll Curtis and Norma (Gragg) W.; m. Marilyn Christine Hoyt, Sept. 22, 1973; children: Amanda, Catherine, Margaret, Arcadio. BA in Psychology, Coll. Idaho, 1969; MA in Internat. Adminstrn., Sch. for Internat. Tng., 1975; PhD in Biology, Fordham U., 1990. Rsch. assoc. Foresta Inst., Carson City, Nev., 1973-74; curatorial asst. Woodland Park Zool. Garden, Seattle, 1974-79; asst. curator N.Y. Zool. Soc./The Wildlife Conservation Soc., Bronx, 1979-85; assoc. curator N.Y. Zool. Soc., Bronx, 1985-89, curator, 1989—; dir. Ctrl. Pk. Wildlife Ctr., N.Y.C., 1994—; adjunct sci. faculty Columbia U. Chmn. Internat. Advisors Internat. Snow Leopard Trust, Seattle, 1986; mem. US-USSR Environ. Agreement of U.S. Fish and Wildlife Svc., 1983. Contbr. articles to profl. jours.; editor Jour. Zoo Biology, 1996-98, exec. editor, 1998—. Vol. U.S. Peace Corps., Ecuador, 1969-71. Fulbright scholar, U. Münster, Fed. Republic Germany, 1976-77. Fellow Am. Assn. Zool. Parks and Aquariums (chmn. gorilla species survival plan 1992—, chmn. snow leopard species survival plan 1986—, co-chmn. marsupial and monotre,e taxon adv. group 1990-94; mem. Soc. for Conservation Biology, Internat. Union for Conservation of Nature/Species Survival Commn. (mem. captive breeding specialist group); Office: Wildlife Conservation Soc Ctrl Park Wildlife Ctr 830 5th Ave New York NY 10021-7001 Business E-Mail: dwharton@wcs.org.

**WHARTON, JOHN MICHAEL,** lawyer; b. Ames, Iowa, June 16, 1944; s. Michael M. and M. Myrna (Petersen) W.; m. Pamela M. Rafdal, June 28, 1986; children: Lisa Elaine, Kimberly. BS, Iowa State U., 1967; JD, Drake U., 1970. Bar: Iowa 1970, Fla. 1972, U.S. Dist. Ct. (no. and so. dists.) Iowa 1974, U.S. Ct. Appeals (8th cir.) 1975, U.S. Ct. Mil. Appeals 1971. With Peddicord, Wharton, Spencer & Hook, LLP, Des Moines, 1974—. Mem. Iowa Bd. Law Examiners, Des Moines, 1983-90. Capt. JAGD, USAF, 1970-74. Recipient Disting. Svc. award Phi Alpha Delta, 1970. Mem. Iowa State Bar Assn., Iowa Acad. Trial Lawyers, Lawyer-Pilots Bar Assn., Def. Rsch. Inst., Iowa Def. Counsel Assn., Assn. Trial Lawyers Am., Des Moines Golf and Country Club. Republican. Lutheran. Office: Peddicord Wharton Spencer & Hook LLP 405 6th Ave Ste 700 Des Moines IA 50309-2415 Office Phone: 515-243-2100.

**WHARTON, LENNARD,** engineering company executive; b. Boston, Dec. 10, 1933; s. Nathaniel Philip and Deeda (Levine) W.; m. Judith R. Gordon, Dec. 26, 1957; children: Ruth, Rebecca, Nathaniel. BS in Chem. Engring. MIT, 1955; BA, MA, Cambridge U., 1957; A.M., Harvard U.; A.M. (NSF fellow 1957-60), 1960, PhD (Jr. fellow Soc. of Fellows 1960-63), 1963. Registered profl. engr., N.J., Ill. Prof. dept. chemistry U. Chgo., 1963-80; v.p. engring. ITE Imperial Corp., 1972-73; v.p. tech. Studebaker-Worthington, Barrington, Ill., 1978-79, McGraw Edison Co., Rolling Meadows, Ill., 1979-80, v.p. engring. and tech. Worthington group Mountainside, NJ, 1980-85; corp. v.p. tech. Material Research Corp., Pearl River, NY, 1985-87; v.p. Packer Engring. Inc., Naperville, Ill., 1987-95, chmn. bd., 1994-95; pres. Evidentia Engring. Inc., Short Hills, NJ, 1995—. Sloan fellow, 1964-66; named Outstanding Young Man of Chgo. Chgo. Jr. Assn. Commerce and Industry, 1968 Mem. IEEE (sr.), Nat. Fire Protection Assn., Am. Inst. Chem. Engrs. Office: 10 Park Pl Short Hills NJ 07078-2826

**WHARTON, MARGARET AGNES,** artist; b. Portsmouth, Va.; 1943; BS, U. Md., 1965; MFA, Sch. of Art Inst. Chgo., 1975. Vis. artist Sch. of Art Inst. of Chgo., 1978, 89, 90, Columbia Coll., Chgo., 1994. One women shows include Phyllis Kind Gallery, Chgo., 1976, 80, 85, 88, 91, N.Y.C., l977, 78, 79, 81, 83, 87, 90, Mus. Contemporary Art, Chgo, 1981-82, Laguna Gloria Art Mus., Austin, Tex., 1981-82, Zolla/Lieberman Gallery, Inc., Chgo., 1992, 94, Evanston Art Ctr., 1995, Rockford (Ill.) Coll., 2000, Jean Albano Gallery, Chgo., 1996, 97, 2000; exhibited in group shows at The Cinn. Art Mus., 1988-90, U. Wis. Art Mus., Milw., 1991, The Chgo. Cultural Ctr., 1992, Rockford (Ill.) Art Mus., 1994, and numerous others; represented in permanent collections Am. Med. Assn., Art Inst. of Chgo., Dallas Mus., Seattle Art Mus., State Ill. Collection, Whitney Mus. Am. Art, and others; commns. include Mus. of Contemporary Art, Chgo., 1985, Chgo. Pub. Libr., West Lawn Branch, Chgo., 1986. Founding mem. Artemesia Cooperative Gallery, Chgo., Ill. Recipient NEA grant 1979, 88, 93, Ill. Art Coun. grantee, 1999; recipient Visual Arts award, 1984. Home: 2147 S Halsted St Chicago IL 60608-4532

**WHARTON, PENELOPE LEE (PENNY WHARTON),** music educator; b. Tucson, May 24, 1954; d. Russell Arnold and Beverley Joyce Stuve; m. Gary Steven Wharton, Aug. 12, 1989; children: Sabrina Jo, Cody Ian. MusB in Edn., Pacific U., Forest Grove, Oreg., 1976. Cert. tchr. Supt. Pub. Instrn. Wash. State, 1979. Dir. H.S. choir First Congl. Ch., Forest Grove, Oreg., 1975—76; tchr. music Bandon Sch. Dist., 1976—79; music specialist Evergreen Pub. Schools, Vancouver, 1979—. Dir. children's choir Image All-Star Choir, Vancouver, Wash., 1999—, Vancouver Heights United Meth. Ch., program dir. children's summer program, 2004—; children's recorder club Image Elem., 2004—; coord. ctrl. choral festival Evergreen Sch. Dist., 2005—06; co-dir. cmty. benefit concerts. Lyricist: songs The Scientific Method Rap. Mem.: Evergreen Edn. Assn., United Meth. Women. Methodist. Avocations: singing, crafts, reading, movies, camping. Office: Evergreen Pub Sch #114 13501 NE 28th St Vancouver WA 98682 Office Phone: 360-604-4000. E-mail: pwharton@egreen.wednet.edu. *In my 30 years of teaching music, I have influenced at least 8 children, now adults, to become music teachers. It is very rewarding to know that I am directly responsible for children being actively involved with music.*

**WHARTON, RALPH NATHANIEL,** psychiatrist, educator; b. Boston, June 15, 1932; s. Nathaniel Philip and Deeda (Levine) W.; children: Naida, Philip, Laura. AB cum laude, Harvard U., 1953; MD, Columbia U., 1957, degree in psychoanalysis, 1970. Cert. Neurology and Psychiatry 1969. Intern Cornell divsn. Bellevue Hosp., N.Y.C., NY, 1957—58; resident Columbia-Presbyn. Med. Ctr., 1961—64; pvt. practice psychiatry/pharm., 1964—; assoc. psychiatry Coll. Physicians and Surgeons, 1964—69, asst. prof. clin. psychiatry, 1969—72, assoc. prof., 1972—83, prof., 1984—; sr. rsch. psychiatrist N.Y. State Psychiat. Inst., 1964—70; assoc. attending psychiatry Columbia-Presbyn. Hosp., NY, 1970—80, attending psychiatrist, 1980—; sr. cons. supr. psychiatric svc NY Presbyteriuan Hosp. Ex-officio mem. bd. trustees Columbia-Presbyn. Med. Ctr., pres. soc. practitioners, 1980—82, attending, 1984—; exec. dir. Wharton Fund for Brain Rsch.; med. dir. Black Sea project Macalester Coll., 1994—98; co-dir. Reiner for Behaviour and Psychosomatic Rsch. and Tchg. Columbia U. Med. Ctr., 2004—; exec. dir. Wharton Fund Brain Rsch., 1993—. Author: Landmark Papers, Lithium Carbonate for Affective Disorders, 1966; contbr. Mood Anxiety chapters, Merritt's Textbook of Neurology, 2005, AARP chapter, Art of Aging, 2006, numerous papers, publs. in profl. jours. and chpts. to books. Mem. alumni coun. Coll. Physicians and Surgeons, Columbia U., 2001—. Served to Capt. M.C., U.S. Army, 1958-60, US Army Hosp. Orleans, France, 1960-61 Capt. med. corp U.S. Army, 1958—60. Named one of Best Drs., NY Mag. Fellow: Am. Coll. Psychoanalysts (pres. 1996, bd. dirs. 1996—), N.Y. Acad. Medicine, Am. Psychiat. Assn. (life Hon. Life fellow 2002); mem.: AMA, Internat. Assn. Study of Pain (founder), Royal Soc. Medicine, Soc. Practitioners (exec. com. 1990—), Harmonie Club, Harvard Club (class agent 1953—), Salon de Virtuosi (founding bd. mem. 1991—, treas. 1991—), Lotos Club. Avocations: skiing, sailing, literature. Office: Columbia-Presbyn Med Ctr Atchley Pavilion Ste 209 161 Ft Washington Ave New York NY 10032-3713 also: 1070 Park Ave Ste 1D New York NY 10128-1000 Office Phone: 212-860-2666. Business E-Mail: rnw1@columbia.edu.

**WHATLEY, JOE RAMON, JR.,** lawyer; b. Selma, Ala., June 14, 1953; AB cum laude, Harvard U., 1975; JD, U. Ala. Sch. Law, Tuscaloosa, 1978. Bar: Ala. 1978, Tex. 1997. Law clk. to Hon. Frank H. McFadden No. Dist. Ct. Ala., 1978—79; previously ptnr. with Cooper, Mitch, Crawford, Kukendall & Whatley, Birmingham, Ala.; ptnr. Whatley Drake LLC, Birmingham, Ala., 1998—. Mem.: Assn. Trial Lawyers of Am., Ala. Trial Lawyers Assn., Ala. State Bar (labor & employment sect. 1990—91, past pres.), ABA (labor & employment sect., litig. sect.). Office: Whatley Drake LLC 2323 2nd Ave N Birmingham AL 35203-2605 Office Phone: 205-328-9576. Office Fax: 205-328-9669. E-mail: jwhatley@whatleydrake.com.

**WHATLEY, MARK A.,** education educator; s. Richard and Diane Salsitz. PhD, U. of Ky., Lexington, KY. Prof. U. Sys. of Ga., Atlanta, 1998—. Office Phone: 229-293-6320. E-mail: drwhatley@hotmail.com.

**WHATMORE, GEORGE BERNARD,** research scientist, writer, internist; b. Seattle, Aug. 31, 1917; s. Harry Joseph and Delia (Frolich) Whatmore; m. Frances Maxwell Beatty, May 28, 1942; children: Pamela Frances, David Blake, Nancy Janice. BS, U. Wash., 1940, MS, 1941, PhD U. Chgo., 1946, MD, 1948. Intern King County Hosp., Seattle, 1948—49, resident, 1949—50, Lab. Clin. Physiology, Chgo., 1950—51; pvt. practice and rsch. in internal medicine, clin. neurophysiology, functional disorders Seattle, 1951—. Mem. staff Virginia Mason Hosp., Seattle, 1951—, Swedish Hosp., Seattle, 1951—, Med.-Dental Bldg. Hosp., Seattle, 1951—, Eastern State Hosp., Medical Lake, Wash., 1955—58; prin. investigator Pacific N.W. Rsch. Found. and Inst., Seattle, 1966—. Author (with Daniel R. Kohli): Dysponesis: A Neurophysiologic Factor in Functional Disorders, 1968, The Physiopathology and Treatment of Functional Disorders, 1974; author: A Scientist Looks at Christianity, A Probability Analysis, 1992, 2d edit., 1995, A Scientist Looks at Religion, Based on Evidence Plus Logic, 3d edit., 2002, 4th edit., 2003, De-contaminating The New Testament, Based on Lessons Learned from The Galileo Scandal, 2004; contbr. articles to profl. jours. Recipient Ginsburg award, U. Chgo., 1946; Univ. fellow, 1941—45, Rawson fellow, 1945—46, Sheldon fellow, 1945—46. Mem.: AMA, AAAS (life), Western Acad. Beaux Arts, King County Med. Soc., Wash. State Med. Assn., Assn. for Applied Psychophysiology and Biofeedback, Acad. Psychosomatic Medicine, Behavior Therapy and Rsch. Soc., Biofeedback Rsch. Soc., Internat. Stress and Tension Control Assn., Am. Physicians Soc. for Physiologic Tension Control, N.Y. Acad. Sci., Sigma Xi. Home and Office: 10524 SE 27th Dr Bellevue WA 98004-7231 Office Phone: 425-454-7273.

**WHAYNE, THOMAS FRENCH, JR.,** cardiologist, educator; b. Ft. Leavenworth, Kans., Aug. 25, 1937; s. Thomas French and Mary Lutenia (Porter) W.; m. Eugenia McDonald Ingram, June 22, 1963; children: Thomas French III, James Givens, Katherine Ingram. AB in Chemistry, U. Pa., 1959, MD,

1963; PhD in Biochemistry, U. Calif., San Francisco, 1970. Intern in medicine The N.Y. Hosp., 1963-64, resident in medicine, 1964-66; fellow in cardiovascular disease Cardiovascular Rsch. Inst., San Francisco, 1966-69, U. Toronto, Ontario, Can., 1969-70; asst. prof. medicine Ohio State U., Columbus, 1970-72; assoc. prof. medicine U. Okla., Oklahoma City, 1972-77; clin. prof. medicine U. Ky., Lexington, 1977-98, prof. medicine cardiovascular medicine, 1998—. Assoc. mem. Okla. Med. Rsch. Found., 1972-77; staff cardiologist Lexington Clinic, 1977-98. Contbr. over 100 articles to profl. jours. and abstracts, 6 articles in Spanish, over 50 internat. presentations in Spanish lang. Named Man of Yr., Okla. Heart Assn., 1975—76. Fellow: ACP, Internat. Coll. Angiology, Coll. Physicians of Phila., Am. Heart Assn., Am. Coll. Cardiology. Presbyterian. Avocations: Spanish language, golf, scuba diving, photography. Office: Divsn Cardiovascular Medicine 326 Wethington Bldg 900 S Limestone Lexington KY 40536-0200 Office Phone: 859-323-5479. Business E-mail: twhayn0@uky.edu.

**WHEALEY, LOIS DEIMEL,** humanities scholar; b. N.Y.C., June 20, 1932; d. Edgar Bertram Deimel and Lois Elizabeth (Hatch) Washburn; m. Robert Howard Whealey, July 2, 1954; children: Richard William, David John, Alice Ann. BA in History, Stanford U., 1951; MA in Edn., U. Mich., 1955; MA in Polit. Sci., Ohio U., 1975. Tchr. 5th grade Swayne Sch., Owyhee, Nev., 1952-53; tchr. 7th grade Ft. Knox (Ky.) Dependent's Sch., 1955-56; tchr. adult basic edn. USAF, Oxford, 1956-57; tchr. 6th grade Amerman Sch., Northville, Mich., 1957-58; tchr. 8th grade English, social studies Slauson Jr. High Sch., Ann Arbor, Mich., 1958-59; adminstrv. asst. humanities conf. Ohio U., Athens, 1974-76, 83. Part-time instr. Ohio U., Athens, 1966-68, 75, VISTA with Rural Action, 1996-98. Contbr. articles to profl. jours. Mem. Athens County Regional Planning Commn., 1974—78, treas., 1976—78; mem. Ohio coord. com. Internat. Women's Yr., 1977; v.p. Black Diamond Girl Scout Coun., 1980—86; chair New Day for Equal Rights Amendment, 1982; mem. Athens City Bd. Edn., 1984—90, v.p., 1984, pres., 1985; mem. Tri-County Vocat. Sch. Bd., Nelsonville, Ohio, 1984—90, v.p., 1988—89; mem. adv. com. Ohio River Valley Water Sanitation Commn., 1986—95; Ohio outreach liaison Nat. Town Meeting for Sustainable Am., 1999; bd. dirs. Ohio Environ. Coun., 1984—90, sec., 1986—90; bd. dirs. Ohio Alliance for Environ., 1994—98, v.p., 1998; bd. dirs. Organize Ohio, 1999—, bd. pres., 2001—; bd. dirs. Ohio Women, Inc., 1995—, sec., 1997—; bd. dirs. Unitarian Universalist Svc. Com., 2001—03, Ohio Meadville Dist. Unitarian-Universalist Assn., 1975—81; co-chair nat. vol. network Unitarian Universalist Svc. Com., 2003—05. Recipient Unsung Unitarian Universalist award Ohio-Meadville Dist. Unitarian Universalist Assn., 1984, Thanks badge Black Diamond Girl Scout Coun., 1986, How-to award Ednl. Press Assn. Am., 1990, Donna Chen Women's Equity award Ohio U., 1994, Cmty. Svc. award Athens County Cmty. Svcs. Coun., 1998, award for an individual contbn. over a lifetime Ohio Alliance for Environment, 2002; named Woman of Achievement, Black Diamond Girl Scout Coun., 1987, Peacemaker Appalachian Peace and Justice Network, 1998, Outstanding Feminist, Athens Herstory Celebration, 2002. Mem. AAUW (pres. Athens br. 1969-70, 89-90, 93-2001, AAUW/Ohio bd. 1995-2004), LWV (pres. 1975-77), Phi Lambda Theta, Phi Kappa Phi. Democrat. Avocations: classical music, genealogy. Home: 14 Oak St Athens OH 45701-2605

**WHEALY, MICHAEL THOMAS,** data processing executive, lawyer; b. Sioux Falls, S.D., Apr. 29, 1952; s. Donald Stuart and Elaine Helen Whealy; m. Brenda L. Whealy, May 18, 1974; children: Andrew, Michael. BSChemE with highest honors, S.D. Sch. Mines & Tech., 1974; JD cum laude, Harvard U., 1977. Bar: Mass. 1977, Nebr. 1981, Ga. 1988. Asst. to gen. counsel Dept. Army, Washington, 1977-81; from assoc. to ptnr. Kutak Rock, Omaha, 1981-91; staff atty. First Data Corp., Omaha and Atlanta, 1991-97, gen. counsel, sec. Atlanta, 1998—, exec. v.p., chief adminstrv. officer, 1998—. Lt. col. USAR, 1974-96. Avocations: hunting, fishing, hiking. Office: 6200 S Quebec St Greenwood Village CO 80111 E-mail: mike.whealy@firstdatacorp.com.

**WHEAR, J. KEVIN,** information technology executive; b. Omaha, June 16, 1964; s. John Anthony and Kathyan Jean Whear; m. Joy Lois Bixler; children: Justin, Lindsey, Caleb, Sara, Abigail, Zachary, Ethan, Mercy, Jubilee. BChemE, U. Tulsa, 1986. Cert. quality engr. Process engr. Texaco Chem. Co., Port Arthur, Tex., 1986—88, W.R. Grace, Owensboro, Ky., 1988—90, tech. mgr., 1990—93, dir. quality, 1993—95; dir. tech. Daramic, Inc., Owensboro, 1995—2003, v.p. tech., 2003—. Contbr. articles to profl. jours. Elder Presbyn. Ch., Owensboro, 1986—. Achievements include patents in field. Avocations: running, reading. Office: Daramic LLC 5525 US 60 E Owensboro KY 42301

**WHEAT, MYRON WILLIAM, JR.,** cardiothoracic surgeon; b. Sapulpa, Okla., Mar. 24, 1924; s. Myron William and Mary Lee (Hudiburg) W.; m. Erlene Adele Plank, June 12, 1949 (div. June 1970); children: Penelope Louise, Myron William III, Pamela Lynn, Douglas Plank; m. Carol Ann Karmgard, June 18, 1970 (div. Apr. 1996); 1 child, Christopher West. AB, Washington U., St. Louis, 1949; MD cum laude, Washington U., 1951. Diplomate Am. Bd. Surgery, Am. Bd. Thoracic Surgery. Instr., clin. fellow Washington U., St. Louis, 1956—58; asst. prof. surgery U. Fla., Gainesville, 1958—65, prof. surgery, 1965—72; dir. profl. svcs., chief clin. physician U. Fla. Shands Tchg. Hosp., Gainesville, 1968—72; prof. surgery, dir. thoracic and cardiothoracic surgery U. Louisville Sch. Medicine, 1972—75, clin. prof. surgery, 1975—; cardiothoracic surgeon Cardiac Surg. Assocs., P.A., St. Petersburg, Fla., 1975—91; cons. thoracic surgery Bay Pine VA Hosp., St. Petersburg, 1994—; clin. prof. surgery U. So. Fla. Sch. Medicine, Tampa, 1995—; cardiothoracic surgeon Cardiac Surg. Assocs., P.A., Clearwater, Fla., 1991—. Clin. prof. surgery U. South Fla., 1995—; cons. Bay Pines VA Hosp. St. Petersburg, 1991—; mem. Am. Bd. Thoracic Surgery, 1969-75 Author (with others) 18 books; mem. editl. bd. Am. Heart Jour., 1971; contbr. over 100 articles to profl. jours.; developed drug therapy for acute dissecting aneurysms of the aorta 1st lt. USAF, 1943-46, ETO Named First Howard W. Lillenthal Meml. lectr. Mt. Sinai Hosp., 1963; recipient DFC Air medal, Presdl. Citation Fellow ACS (gov.), Am. Coll. Cardiology (chmn. bd. govs. 1968-69); mem. Am. Surg. Assn., Am. Assn. Thoracic Surgery (sec. 1972-78), So. Surg. Assn., So. Thoracic Surg. Assn., Soc. Thoracic Surgeons, Soc. Thoracic Surgeons Gr. Britain and Ireland, Alpha Omega Alpha Republican. Home and Office: PO Box 136 Largo FL 33779-0136 Office Phone: 727-446-4637. Personal E-mail: myronwheat@msn.com.

**WHEAT, SHEREE RENEE,** elementary school educator; d. Jesse Robert and Irene Louise Pinkerton; children: Harold Christopher, Stephen Patrick, Brittany Alyce. BSc in Social Scis., Secondary Edn., U. Tenn., 1980; M in Ednl. Leadership, Tenn. Tech. U., 2002. Cert. Elem. Edn. Tchr. U. Tenn., Knoxville, 1982, in English Edn. U. Tenn., Knoxville, 1983, U. Tenn., Knoxville, 2001, Ednl. Specialist Tenn. Tech. U., 2003. Tchr. Chattanooga Pub. Schs., 1990—94, elem. adv. com. mem.; sci., math., lang. arts tchr. Hamilton County Schs., Chattanooga, 1996—, sci. coord.; flight dir. rep. Chattanooga pub. schs. U. Tenn., 1994—96. Workshop attendee in field, 1992—2003. Vol. homeless tutoring program. NEH fellowship, Trinity Coll., 1996, U. Va., Charlottesville, 2000, Tenn. Space grant, Tenn. Tchrs. Assn., Vanderbilt U., 2000. Mem.: Internat. Reading Assn., Assn. Supervision and Curriculum Devel., Tenn. Sci. Tchrs. Assn. (3d dist. exec. com. sci. rep., exec. bd. mem.), Nat. Sci. Tchrs. Assn., Chattanooga Edn. Assn., Tenn. Edn. Assn., Phi Lambda Theta, Alpha Kappa Alpha. Avocations: reading, writing, acting, singing, computers.

**WHEATLAND, RICHARD, II,** fiduciary services executive, museum executive; b. Boston, Nov. 25, 1923; s. Stephen and Dorothy (Parker) W.; m. Cynthia McAdoo, Feb. 13, 1954; 1 child, Sarah Wheatland Fisher. AB, Harvard U., 1944, postgrad., 1946-47; JD, Columbia U. 1949. Various positions with Marshall Plan adminstrn. Office Spl. Rep. in Europe, Dept. State, Paris, 1950-53; v.p. N.Y. Airways, N.Y.C., 1953-68; pres. Acadia Mgmt. Co., Inc., Boston, 1968-93, chmn., 1993—. Bd. dirs., v.p. Pingree Assocs., Bangor, Maine. Mem. Mayor's Com. Inst. Leaders for Youth, N.Y.C., 1963-66; mem. corp. New Eng. Forestry Found.; mem., former chmn. Fund for Preservation of Wild Life and Natural Areas, Boston, 1980-92, bd. dirs. 1980-91; trustee Penobscot Marine Mus., Searsport, Maine, 1968-90,

hon. trustee, 1990—,; bd. dirs. Friends of Pub. Garden, Boston, 1972-89, 90-96, 97—, Beacon Hill Civic Assn., Boston, 1985-89, Boston Natural Areas Fund, 1987—, asst. treas., 1993-94, treas. 1994-96, bd. dirs. 1997, acting chair, 1997—; treas. Frank Hatch for Gov. com., Boston, 1977-78; chmn., bd. trustees & overseers Peabody Essex Mus. (formerly Peabody Mus. of Salem) Salem, Mass., 1992—, trustee, 1972-92, pres., 1983-92. Lt. (j.g.) USN, 1943-46, PTO. Mem. Am. Assn. Mus. (bd. dirs. trustee com. 1976-86, govt. affairs com. 1985-89), Mus. Trustee Assn. (founder, bd. dirs. 1986—, sec. 1986-92), City Club Corp. (former bd. mgrs., former treas.). Avocations: jogging, sailing, travel.

**WHEATLEY, CHARLES HENRY, III,** information technology executive; b. Balt., Aug. 11, 1932; s. Charles Henry Jr. and Rebecca W. (Cloud) Wheatley; m. Charlotte Beryl Davis, June 11, 1955; children: Charles H. IV, Craig A., Cheryl L.W. Wilhelm. BA in Polit. Sci. (hon.), Western Md. Coll., 1954; JD (hon.), U. Md., 1959. Bar: Md. 1960, DC 1981, US Supreme Ct. 1964. Tchr. Carroll County Pub. Sch., Westminster, Md., 1955-56; officer, missiles, judge adv. U.S. Army, 1957-62; law clk. assoc. judge William R. Horney Md. Ct. Appeals, Annapolis, 1959-60; pvt. practice Md. and Washington, 1960—; mem. Md. Ho. of Del., Annapolis, Md., 1962-66; pres., COO, advisor corp. rels., dir. Cell Works, Inc., Balt., 1997—2002. SOI Assoc., real estate, ins. exec. AID Realty & Ins. Co., Balt., 1960—; adj. coll. instr. Western Md. Coll., Westminster, 1963-65, Villa Julie Coll., 1980-86, Balt. C.C., 1966-72, Caroll C.C., 2002—; chmn. bd., CEO Regional Mfg. Inst., Balt., 1993-96; nat. del. White House Conf. on Small Bus., Washington, 1985; pres. Fish Am., Inc., 1990—, Replex, Inc., 1986—, Life, Inc., 1994—; spkr. in field. Contbr., editor: (weekly newspaper) Maryland Teacher, 1974-77; guest News Makers program WJZ-TV, 1985; contbr. articles to profl. jours. Md. del. Md. State Constitutional Conv., Annapolis, 1967-68; councilman Balt. City Coun., 1971-74; trustee Baltimore County Gen. Howp., 1963-65. 1st lt. Missile Brigade, JAG US Army, 1957-62. Received Cell Works Co. Computerworld-Smithsonian Science Innovation laureate award, 1999. Mem.: Md. State Tchrs. Assn. (exec. sec. 1974—77), Supreme Ct. Bar, Dist. Columbia Bar Assn., Md. State Bar Assn., Md. Commn. Mfg. Competitiveness, Order of Coif, Pi Gamma Mu. Methodist. Avocations: education, music, writing, photography, health. Office: 707 Wheatley Dr Westminster MD 21157 Office Phone: 410-876-5052. E-mail: lifeinc@earthlink.net.

**WHEATLEY, DEBORAH A.,** music educator; b. Mt. Clemens, Mich., Oct. 28, 1954; d. Ernest William Wheatley and Joanne Smith. AA with honors, Miami-Dade CC, 1975; BA magna cum laude, U. Ctrl. Fla., 1978; grad., US Army Element Sch. Music, 1984. Music instr. Lecanto (Fla.) Primary, 1978—81; band dir. Lecanto Mid. Sch., 1981—83, fine arts tchr., 1986—96, band dir., 1996—; with signal corps band U.S. Army Elem. Sch. Music, Ft. Gordon, Ga., 1984; summer duty U.S. Army, 1986—92. With Signal Corps Band U.S. Army, 1984—86. Recipient U.S. Army Commendation medal, 1986. Republican. Avocations: running, promoting healthy lifestyle to middle school students. Home: 1801 Silverwood St Inverness FL 34453 Office: Lecanto Mid Sch 3800 W Educational Path Lecanto FL 34461 Office Phone: 352-746-2050. E-mail: debwheat@mailstation.com.

**WHEATLEY, MELVIN ERNEST, JR.,** retired bishop; b. Lewisville, Pa., May 7, 1915; s. Melvin Ernest and Gertrude Elizabeth (Mitchell) W.; m. Lucile Elizabeth Maris, June 15, 1939; children: Paul Melvin, James Maris, John Sherwood (dec.). AB magna cum laude, Am. U., 1936, DD, 1958; BD summa cum laude, Drew U., 1939; DD, U. of Pacific, 1948. Ordained to ministry Meth. Ch., 1939. Pastor area Meth. ch., Lincoln, Del., 1939-41; assoc. pastor First Meth. Ch., Fresno, Calif., 1941-43; pastor Centenary Meth. Ch., Modesto, Calif., 1943-46, Cen. Meth. Ch., Stockton, Calif., 1946-54, Westwood Meth. Ch., L.A., 1954-72; bishop Denver Area, 1972-84; ret., 1984. Instr. philosophy Modesto Jr. Coll., 1944; summer session instr. Hebrew-Christian heritage U. of Pacific; instr. Homiletics U. So. Calif., So. Calif. Sch. Theology, Claremont; lectr. St. Luke's Lectures, Houston, 1966; mem. Bd. of Ch. and Soc., Commn. on Status and Role of Women, United Meth. Ch., 1976-84; condr. European Christian Heritage tour, 1961, Alaska and Hawaii Missions, 1952, 54, Israel in behalf of Stockton Jewish Congregation, 1951. Author: Going His Way, 1957, Our Man and the Church, 1968, The Power of Worship, 1970, Family Ministries Manual, 1970, Christmas Is for Celebrating, 1977; contbr. articles to profl. jours. Chmn. Community Rels. Conf. So. Calif., 1966-69; pres. So. Calif.-Ariz. Conf. Bd. Edn., 1960-68; hon. trustee Iliff Sch. Theology; hon. dir., active mem. Parents and Friends of Lesbians and Gays, 1980—. Recipient Disting. Alumnus award Am. U., 1979, Ball award Meth. Fedn. Social Action, 1984, Prophetic Leadership award The Consultation on Homosexuality, Tolerance and Roman Cath. Theology, 1985, Human Rights award Universal Fellowship of Met. Community Congregations, 1985, award for social justice Calif.-Pacific Meth. Fedn. for Social Action, 2000, Lifetime Achievement award Denver Parents, Families and Friends of Lesbians and Gays, 2000, Outstanding Svc. award Parents Reconciling Network, 2000, Hilton award Nat. Pa. Reconciling Network, 2004. Home: 859 Ronda Mendoza Unit A Laguna Woods CA 92637-5940

**WHEATLEY, RANDALL,** theater educator, theater director, playwright; b. Anchorage, Apr. 24, 1954; s. Andy Clarence and Betty Florence Wheatley; m. Liana E. Welker, Apr. 20, 1991; children: Quentin, Chloe. EdB, Tex. State U., San Marcos, 1977; MFA in Directing, U. Nebr., Lincoln, 1995. Artistic dir. AAA Theatre, Austin, Tex., 1984—90; playwright in residence Capitol City Play Ho., Austin, 1988—90; artistic dir. Permian Playhouse, Odessa, Tex., 1996—98; prof. Lamar U., Beaumont, Tex., 2001—. Author: (plays) Along for the Ride, Billy's Last Broadcast (Best New Play of the Yr., 1989). Democrat. Unity. Avocations: bicycling, travel, theater. Home: 5250 Bristol Dr Beaumont TX 77707 Office: Lamar U PO Box 10044 Beaumont TX 77710 Office Phone: 409-880-8154. Business E-Mail: wheatleyrl@hal.lamar.edu.

**WHEATLEY, SEAGAL V.,** lawyer, legal association administrator; b. Houston, May 24, 1935; s. Seagal V.and Hilda (Guess) W.; m. Wanda Jean Wheatley, Dec. 15, 1978; children: Jill Wilder, Julie. BA in Govt., North Tex. U., 1957; JD, U. Tex., 1960. Bar: Tex. 1960. Ptnr. Beckman, Standard, Wood & Vance, San Antonio, 1960-69; atty. U.S. Dept. of Justice, Tex., 1969-71; pres. Oppenheimer, Rosenberg, Kelleher & Wheatley Inc., San Antonio, 1971—97; ptnr., litig. practice Jenkens & Gilchrist, San Antonio, 1997—. Adj. prof. U. Tex. Sch. of Law, Austin, 1985, 86, 89. Contbr. articles to profl. jours. Del. Rep. Nat. Conv., Miami, Fla., 1968; chmn. Bexar City Reps., San Antonio, 1968. Fellow Tex. Bar Found.; mem. ABA, Assn. Trial Lawyers Am., Tex. Bar Assn., San Antonio Bar Assn., Fed. Bar Assn., 5th Cir. Bar Assn. (past pres.), Internat. Soc. of Barristers. Avocations: golf, tennis. Office: Jenkens & Gilchrist Ste 900 Weston Ctr 112 E Pecan St San Antonio TX 78205-1533 Office Phone: 210-246-5635. Office Fax: 210-246-5999. Business E-Mail: swheatley@jenkens.com.

**WHEATON, DOUGLAS B.,** city manager, lawyer; b. Milw., July 21, 1972; s. Frank and Doreen Wheaton. BS in criminal justice, Carroll Coll., 1994; JD, Marquette U. Law Sch., 1998; MA in polit. sci., Marquette U. Grad. Sch., 1999; attended program of inst. for law, Harvard Law Sch., 2000. Bar: Wis. 1998, US Ct. of Appeals, 7th Circuit, US Dist. Ct., Ea. Dist. Wis., US Dist. Ct., Western Dist. Wis. Jud. intern Milw. County Circuit Ct., 1996; Congl. intern US Congress, Wash., 1996; atty. Bailey Law Office, LLC, Milw., 1999; legis. asst. Wis. State Senate, Madison, 1999—2002; govt. affairs dir. Wis. Realtors Assn., Madison, 2002—05; dir. city devel. City of Franklin, Wis., 2005—. Mem. bd. visitors Ave Maria Sch. of Law, Ann Arbor, Mich., 2000—. Mem. Internat. Econ. Devel. Coun., Internat. Coun. Shopping Ctrs. Recipient CALI Excellence for the Future award, Ctr. for Computer Assisted Legal Instr., 1997, Outstanding Svc. award, Kenosha Realtors Assn., 2003, 2004. Mem.: Southeastern Chamber United in Bus., Wis. Econ. Devel. Assn., Nat. Assn. Office and Indsl. Properties, Acad. Polit. Sci., Milw. Bar Assn., Seventh Cir. Bar Assn., Marquette U. Alumni Assn., Am. Enterprise Inst., Am. Polit. Sci. Assn. Achievements include first law student to complete graduate studies at Marquette University Aspin Center for Government, Washington DC, 1996. Avocations: travel, reading. Office: Franklin City Hall 9229 W Loomis Rd Franklin WI 53132 Office Phone: 414-425-4024. Business E-Mail: dwheaton@franklinwi.gov.

**WHEATON, M. GENE,** investigator, consultant; b. Pawnee, Okla., May 19, 1935; s. Bert Albert Wheaton and Ruth Savannah Bartlett; m. Theresa Joyce Bryant, Nov. 23, 1956 (dec. June 2004); children: Gary B., Denise M., Anita L. BS in Law Enforcement, U. Nebr., Omaha, 1969; MA in Pub. Adminstrn., Webster U., 1975. Cert. polygraph examiner U.S. Army Polygraph Sch., Farsi linguist Def. Lang. Inst., bd. cert. police comdr. Internat. Assn. Chiefs of Police. Police officer Tulsa (Okla.) Police Dept., 1957—58; spl. agt. Office Spl. Investigations USAF, 1958—66; spl. agt. Criminal Investigations Divsn. U.S. Army, 1966—75; dep. dir. Pub. Safety Dept., Kish Island, Iran, 1976—77; exec. asst. to v.p. Rockwell Internat., Tehran, Iran, 1977—79; v.p. Nat. Airlines, Calif., 1985—86. Police/counter-terrorism advisor to Shah of Iran, 1971—73, 1975—79; mem. adv. bd. Nat. Security Inst., Framingham, Mass., 1986—93; cons. in field, 1986—. Mem. exec. bd. Homeowners Assn., Winchester, Calif., 2000. Sgt. USMC, 1953—56, chief warrant officer U.S. Army, 1966—75. Decorated Bronze star U.S. Army, Vietnam, Legion of Merit U.S. Army, Iran, Meritorious Svc. medal U.S. Army. Mem.: VFW (life; former vice comdr.), CID Agts. Assn., Alpha Kappa Delta. Avocations: swimming, shooting, exercising.

**WHEATON, MARILYN,** musician; b. Warren, Ohio, Feb. 1, 1933; d. Russell and Donabelle Irene Donehue; m. Warren Randall Wheaton, June 20, 1953; 1 child, Janean Renee Vaupel-Wilson. BS in Music Edn. cum laude, Kent State U., 1955. Cert. Yamaha music instr. Pvt. piano and organ tchr., Ohio and Ariz., 1950—; profl. pianist, organist, accompanist, 1946—; elem. music supr. Austintown Pub. Schs., Youngstown, Ohio, 1955-61. Founder, dir. Potter's Clay Christian singing group, Phoenix, 1981-85; choir dir., organist, pianist at various chs., Ohio and Ariz., 1942—; rep. for elem. music texts and programs Mahoning County Schs., Youngstown, 1959-60; tchr., organizer student trips to numerous concerts; tchr., dir. choirs and soloists for dist. and state competitions, 1955—. Composer (poems to music) Seven Last Words of Christ, also anthems, introits, reponses; arranges music for beginning and handicapped students. Dir., accompanist Terry's Variety Show, Austintown, 1951, Potter's Clay, 1980-85; pianist at various sr. citizens' groups Kent State U. and Youngstown U. scholar, 1951-55. Mem. Music Tchrs. Nat. Assn., Delta Omicron (life, charter mem., pres. Delta Upsilon chpt.). Avocations: travel, camping, reading, walking, piano recitals. Home and Office: 3245 W Yucca St Phoenix AZ 85029-4133

**WHEDON, GEORGE DONALD,** medical association administrator, researcher; b. Geneva, N.Y., July 4, 1915; s. George Dunton and Elizabeth (Crockett) W.; m. Margaret Brunssen, May 12, 1942 (div. Sept. 1982); children: Karen Anne, David Marshall. AB, Hobart Coll., 1936, ScD (hon.), 1967; MD, U. Rochester, 1941, ScD (hon.), 1978. Diplomate Am. Bd. Internal Medicine, Am. Bd. Nutrition. Intern in medicine Mary Imogene Bassett Hosp., Cooperstown, NY, 1941-42; asst. in medicine U. Rochester Sch. Medicine; also asst. resident physician strong Meml. Hosp., Rochester, 1942-44; instr. medicine Cornell U. Med. Coll., 1944-50, asst. prof. medicine, 1950-52; chief metabolic diseases br. Nat. Inst. Arthritis, Diabetes, Digestive and Kidney Diseases, NIH, Bethesda, Md., 1952-65, asst. dir., 1956-62, dir., 1962-81, sr. assoc. adv., 1981-82; sr. assoc., dir. conf. program Kroc Found., Santa Ynez, Calif., 1982-84; adj. prof. medicine (endocrinology) UCLA Sch. Medicine, 1982-84; dir. med. rsch. programs Shriners Hosps. for Crippled Children, Tampa, 1984-91. Mem. subcom. on calcium, com. dietary allowances Food and Nutrition Bd., NRC, 1959-64; cons. to office manned space flight NASA, 1963-78, chmn. Am. Inst. Biol. Scis. med. program adv. panel to. 1971-75, chmn. NASA life scis. com., 1974-78, mem. space program adv. coun., NASA, 1974-78; cons. on endocrinology and metabolism adv. com. Bur. Drugs, FDA, 1977-82; mem. subcommn. on gravitational biology Com. on Space Rsch., Internat. Union Physiol. Scis., 1979-85; mem. rsch. adv. bd. Shriners Hosps., 1981-84; mem. subcom. spacecraft maximum allowable concentrations, com. toxicology, bd. on environ. studies and toxicology Commn. on Life Scis. NRC, 1989-99; cons. in medicine Wadsworth Gen. Hosp. VA Ctr., L.A., 1982-84; mem. U.S. Del. of U.S.-Japan Coop. Med. Sci. Program, 1984-93; mem. Internat. Soc. Gravitational and Space Physiol., 1991—. Mem. editorial bd. Jour. Clin. Endocrinology and Metabolism, 1960-67; adv. editor Calcified Tissue Rsch., 1967-76; contbr. articles to profl. publs. Mem. med. alumni coun. Sch. Medicine, mem. trustees' coun. U. Rochester, 1971-76, vice chmn. trustees' coun., 1973-74, chmn. 1974-75; trustee Dermatology Found., 1978-82; bd. dirs. Osteogenesis Imperfecta Found., 1991-97, med. adv. coun., 1993-96. Recipient Superior Svc. award USPHS, 1967, Alumni citation U. Rochester, 1971, Alumni citation Hobart Coll., 1986, Hobart Medal of Excellence, 1998, Exceptional Sci. Achievement medal NASA, 1974, NASA award of Merit, 1996. Fellow Royal Soc. Medicine; mem. AAAS, Am. Fedn. Med. Rsch., Assn. Am. Physicians, Aerospace Med. Assn. (Arnold D. Tuttle Meml. award 1978), Internat. Bone and Mineral Soc., Md. Acad. Scis. (sci. coun. 1964-70, 81-82), Endocrine Soc. (Robert H. Williams Disting. Leadership award in endocrinology 1982, Ayerst award 1974), Am. Physiol. Soc., Am. Inst. Nutrition, Am. Acad. Orthopaedic Surgeons (hon.), Am. Soc. Bone and Mineral Rsch., Orthopaedic Rsch. Soc., Am. Soc. Gravitational/Space Biology (Founders award 1994), Internat. Soc. Gravitational Physiology, Theta Delta Chi. Episcopalian. Home: 1290 Gulf Blvd #1802 Clearwater Beach FL 33767 Office Phone: 727-577-8694.

**WHEDON, RALPH GIBBS,** manufacturing executive; b. Elizabeth, N.J., Aug. 10, 1949; s. Ralph Gibbs and Jane (MacMaster) W.; m. Lorna Jean Neebe, June 3, 1972; children: Deborah, David. Student, Clarkson Coll., 1968-70; BS, St. Lawrence U., 1972; student, Rensselaer Polytech. Inst., 1978; MBA, De Paul U., 1985. CPA, Ohio. Credit rep. Internat. Harvester Credit Corp., Albany, NY, 1972-75, ops. supr., 1975-79; mgr. export ops. Internat. Harvester Co., Chgo., 1979-86; treas. Pettibone Corp., Des Plaines, Ill., 1986-91; mgr. cash resources Bailey Controls Co., Wickliffe, Ohio, 1991-95, acting dir. treas., 1992-95, mgr. adminstrn., 1993-95; dir. MIS HMI Industries, Cleve., 1995-97; project mgr. Unum Am., Portland, Maine, 1997-98; mgr. Unum Provident, 1998—2003; CFO ProActivHealth, 2000—; info. sys. audit mgr. U. Maine System, 2004—. Sec. Tube Form, 1995-97; sec. Bliss Mgg., 1995-97; sec. Newton Falls Holding Co., 1995-97. Bd. dirs. Naperville (Ill.) Cmty. Chorus, 1985-87; trop leader Boy scouts Am., Naperville, 1985-91; mem. adv. coun. United Way, 1993-95; mem. adv. coun. Cleve. Treas. Club, 1992-97, bd. dirs., 1994-96; pres. Brightwood Lakes Assn., 1996-97; treas. S.J.E.C. Found., 1996-97. Episcopalian. Avocations: sailing, flying. also: 7 Fairwind Way Ellsworth ME 04605-2935 Home: 15 S Spring St Box 137 Stillwater ME 04489-0137

**WHEELAN, BELLE S.,** educational association administrator; 1 child, Reginald. BA in Psychology and Sociology, Trinity U.; MA in Devel./Ednl. Psychology, La. State U.; D in Ednl. Adminstrn., U. Tex., 1984. Asst. prof. psychology, dir. devel. edn. air. acad. support svcs. San Antonio Coll., 1974—87; dean student svcs. Thomas Nelson C.C., Hampton, Va., 1987—89; provost Tidewater C.C., Portsmouth, Va., 1989—92; pres. Ctrl. Va. C.C. 1992, No. Va. C.C., 1998—2001; sec. of edn. Commonwealth of Va. Richmond, 2002—05; pres. Commn. on Colls. So. Assn. for Colls. and Schs., Decatur, Ga., 2005—. Mem. Am. Coll. Testing Bd., Nat. Commn. on NAEP 12th Grade Assessment and Reporting, 2003—. Recipient Outstanding Alumnus award, Trinity U., 2002, Strong Men and Women award, 2003. Mem.: Nat. Coun. on Black Am. Affairs (pres. roundtable). Office: Commn on Colls So Assn Colls and Schs 1866 Southern Lane Decatur GA 30033 Office Phone: 404-679-4512. Business E-Mail: belle.whelan@sacscoc.org.

**WHEELAN, R(ICHELIEU) E(DWARD),** lawyer; b. NYC, July 10, 1945; s. Richard Fairfax and Margaret (Murray) Wheelan. BS, Springfield (Mass.) Coll., 1967; MS, Iona Coll., 1977; JD, Pace U., 1981. Bar: N.Y. 1982, Minn. 1983, Colo. 1989, Tex. 1990. U.S. Dist. Ct. (no dist.) Calif. 1982, (so. dist.) Tex. 1991, U.S. Internat. Trade 1982, U.S. Ct. Appeals (2d cir.) 1982, (9th cir.) 1983, (5th cir.) 1993, U.S. Supreme Ct. 1994, U.S. Tax Ct. 1998, U.S. Dist. Ct. (no. dist.) Tex. 2003, U.S. Dist. Ct. (ea. dist.) Tex. 2004; bd. cert. in criminal law. Lt. of detectives White Plains (N.Y.) Police Dept., 1967-81; area counsel IBM, Armonk, NY, 1981-89; gen. counsel Kroll Assocs. (Asia), Hong Kong, 1989-91; pvt. practice, Houston, 1991—. Abogado consultor Mex. Consulate. Mem.: ABA (mem. sentencing guidelines com.), Tex. Assn.

Criminal Def. Lawyers, Pro Bono Coll. State Bar Tex., New York County Lawyers Assn., N.Y. State Bar Assn., Coll. of State Bar Tex., Nat. Assn. Criminal Def. Lawyers (life; mem. death penalty com., Champion adv. bd.). Office: 440 Louisiana St Houston TX 77002-1639 Office Phone: 713-225-1300. E-mail: defensecounsel@houston.rr.com.

**WHEELDON, CHRISTOPHER,** dancer, choreographer; b. Yeovil, Somerset, England, 1973; s. Peter and Judy Wheeldon. Student, West Coker Ballet Sch., Somerset, Royal Ballet Sch., London, 1981-89, student higher sch., 1989-91. Dancer Royal Ballet, 1991-93; dancer-corps de ballet NYC Ballet, 1993—98, soloist, 1998—2001, resident choreographer, 2001—. Early roles include Fritz in The Nutcracker, Royal Ballet, Covent Garden, 1984; choreographer The Syncopated Clock, Royal Ballet Sch., 1984, more recently Le Voyage, Royal Ballet, 1995, Danses Bohémiennes, NYC Ballet, 1995 (Mae L. Wien award for Young Choreographer 1995), Souvenir, Royal Ballet, 1996, A Midsummer Night's Dream, Colo. Ballet, 1996, Diversions, Royal Ballet Sch., 1996; choreographer Ctr. Stage (film), 2000, Variations Serieuses, 2001, Polyphonia, 2001, Sweet Smell of Success, 2002, Tryst, 2002, Morphoses, 2002, Carousel, 2002, Carnival of the Animals, 2003, Liturgy, 2003. Recipient Gold Medal for dance (original choreography), Prix de Lausanne, 1991, Nat. Dance award, best choreography (classical), London Critics' Cir., 2004, Dance Mag. award, 2005, Martin E. Segal award, Lincoln Ctr., Am. Choreography award, Olivier award. Office: c/o NYC Ballet 20 Lincoln Center Plz New York NY 10023-6913*

**WHEELER, ALBIN GRAY,** retired military officer, retail executive, educator; b. Huntington, W.Va., Mar. 16, 1935; s. Harvey Gray and Hattie Benson (Weddle) W.; m. Beatrice Thomas, May 17, 1958; children: Dianne, Michelle, Patrice. BA, Marshall U., 1958; MBA, Pepperdine U., 1975; student, Army War Coll., 1976, Harvard U., 1990; DHI (hon.), Marshall U., 2004. Enlisted U.S. Army, 1952, commd. 2d lt., 1959, advanced through grades to maj. gen., 1982; comdr. divsn. spt. command, chief of staff 1st Inf. Divsn., Ft. Riley, Kans., 1978-80; CEO Army AF Exch. Svc.-Europe/Middle East, Munich, 1981-83; comdr. 2d Spt. Command, VII U.S. Corps, Germany, 1983-85; pres. Indsl. Coll. Armed Forces, Washington, 1985-89; CEO Army and Air Force Exch. Svc., Dallas, 1991-93; ret. U.S. Army, 1993; exec. dir. Arent Fox, Washington, 1993-96. Exec. com. Soc. Yeager Scholars, Marshall U. Decorated Def. and Army D.S.M., Bronze Star with two oak leaf clusters, Legion of Merit with two oak leaf clusters; inducted into Army Quartermaster Hall of Fame, 1999. Mem. Marshall U. Alumni Assn. (disting. alumnus 1983). Personal E-mail: albin10@earthlink.net.

**WHEELER, BURTON M.,** language educator, dean; b. Mullins, S.C., Mar. 12, 1927; s. Paul and Elizabeth (Cleveland) W.; m. Jacquelyn Mulkey, Aug. 20, 1950; children— Paul, Geoffrey, Kristin AB, U. S.C., 1948, MA, 1951; PhD, Harvard U., 1961. Teaching fellow Harvard U., Cambridge, Mass., 1953-56; mem. faculty Washington U., St. Louis, 1956-96, prof., 1974-96; prof. emeritus, 1996—; dean Coll. Arts and Scis. Washington U., St. Louis, 1966-78, interim dean univ. librs., 1988-89. Cons., panelist Danforth Found., St. Louis, 1958-82; mem. GPEP panel Assn. Am. Med. Colls., Washington, 1981-84; cons.-evaluator North Cen. Assn., Chgo. Author: Close to Me, But Far Away, 2001; contbr. articles to profl. jours. Mem. spkrs. bur. Alzheimers Assn. Eli Lilly Found. fellow, 1965-66 Mem. Alzheimer's Assn., Phi Beta Kappa (senator 1992-2004, chmn. qualifications com., chmn. com. on chpts.). Business E-Mail: bwheeler@artsci.wustl.edu.

**WHEELER, CATHY JO,** federal agency administrator; b. Birmingham, Ala., Feb. 14, 1954; d. Charles Edwin and Hazel Josephine Wheeler; m. David Arthur Tate, 1994. BA, U. Montevallo, 1975; postgrad., U. Ala., 1982—84. With Social Security Adminstrn., Birmingham, 1975—, sr. employment devel. specialist, 1983-85, mgr. tech. tng. dept., 1985-91, mgmt. analyst, 1991—2000, staff advisor to asst. regional commr. Process Ctr. Ops., 2000-01, tng. mgmt specialist, 2001—. V.p. Fed. Women's Program, Birmingham, 1984—85; treas., charter mem. Federally Employed Women, Birmingham, 1984—88. Mem. Art Alumni Adv. Bd., 1997—2001, v.p., 1998—2000; bd. dirs. U. Montevallo Found., 2002—, sec. found. bd., 2005—. Mem.: ASTD (treas. 1987—88, pres. elect 1989, pres. 1990, asst. regional dir. 1991—92), Ala. Designer-Craftsmen, Soc. Govt. Meeting Planners (v.p. 1989—90, sec. 1990—91), U. Montevallo Nat. Alumni Assn. (bd. dirs. 1991—94, v.p. fin. 1994—98, pres.-elect 1998—2000, pres. 2000—02, parliamentarian 2002—04), Riverchase Women's Club, Jaycees (v.p. mgmt. devel. Hoover Ala. chpt. 1988—89), Chi Omega Alumni Assn. (treas. 1991, advisor 1991—2000). Avocations: photography, reading, travel. Home: 4001 Fairchase Ln Birmingham AL 35244-1300 Office: Social Security Adminstrn 2001 12th Ave N Birmingham AL 35285 Personal E-mail: cathyjowheeler@bellsouth.net.

**WHEELER, CHRIS D.,** investment company executive; Degree in applied physics with honors, Calif. Inst. Tech., 1978; MBA, Harvard U., 1980. Various positions including group mng. ptnr. Trammell Crow Residential, 1982-98; sr. v.p. strategic initiatives Gables Residential Trust, Atlanta, 1998-99, pres., CEO, 1999—. Office: Gables Residential Trust 2859 Paces Ferry Rd SE Ste 1450 Atlanta GA 30339-5716

**WHEELER, DANIEL SCOTT,** management executive, editor; b. Richmond, Virginia, Apr. 23, 1947; s. Arthur Bruce Jr. and Lavinia (Akers) W.; m. Kathy E. (Wheeler); children: Matthew, Beth Marie, Jennifer Lynne, Brandy, and Jennifer Ann. Attended, Va. Commonwealth U., 1966-69, Butler U., 1981, Ind. U., 1984-85. Spl. agt. Northwestern Mut. Life, Richmond, 1969-71; enlisted U.S. Navy, 1971, resigned, 1979; editor Am. Legion Mag., Indpls., 1979-85, pub., editor-in-chief, 1985-95; exec. dir. The Am. Legion, Indpls., 1995—; pub., editor in chief The Am. Legion Mag., Indpls., 2003—. Bd. dir. HPC/PM Direct. Pres. Citizen's Flag Alliance, Inc. Mem. Am. Legion, Mensa. Republican. Avocation: painting. Home: 4518 Fairhope Dr Indianapolis IN 46237-2951 Office: Am Legion PO Box 1055 Indianapolis IN 46206-1055

**WHEELER, DAVID LAURIE,** university dean; b. Saginaw, Mich., July 30, 1934; s. Clayton Final and Blanche Beatrice (Hunt) W.; m. Jane Louise Manchester, Sept. 6, 1958; children: Elizabeth, Anne. AB, U. Mich., 1956, AM, 1958, PhD, 1962. Asst. dean student service Ill. State U., Normal, 1967-68, assoc. dean, 1968-69, assoc. dean grad. sch., 1969-72; dean grad. sch. West Tex. State U., Canyon, 1972-79, Ball State U., Muncie, Ind., 1979-96, dean emeritus, 1996—. Cons. McGraw-Hill Pub. Co., N.Y.C., Van Nostrand Reinhold Pub. Co., N.Y.C. Editor: The Human Habitat: Contemporary Readings, 1971. Woodrow Wilson fellow, 1961; recipient Commdrs. Pub. Svc. award Dept. of Army, 1996. Mem. Assn. Am. Geographers, Nat. Coun. Univ. Rsch. Adminstrs., Western History Assn., Tex. State Hist. Assn., U.S. Army War Coll. Found., Rotary, Sigma Xi, Phi Kappa Phi, Kappa Sigma. Republican. Presbyterian. Personal E-mail: wheeler2@onlinecol.com.

**WHEELER, DOUGLAS PAUL,** conservationist, state agency administrator, lawyer; b. Bklyn., Jan. 10, 1942; s. Robert S. and Lottie (Neubauer) W.; m. Heather A. Campbell, Aug. 28, 1965; children— Clay Campbell, Christopher Campbell. AB in Govt. with honors, Hamilton Coll., Clinton, N.Y., 1963; LLB, Duke U., 1966. Bar: N.C. 1966, D.C. 1999. Assoc. Levine, Goodman & Murchison, Charlotte, NC, 1966-69; legis. atty. to asst. legis. counsel U.S. Dept. Interior, Washington, 1969-72, dep. asst. sec. Fish and Wildlife and Pks., 1972-77; exec. v.p. Nat. Trust for Hist. Preservation, Washington, 1977-80; pres. Am. Farmland Trust, Washington, 1980-85, now life mem.; exec. dir. Sierra Club, San Francisco, 1985-86; v.p. Conservation Found., Washington, 1986-88, exec. v.p. 1989-91; sec. for resources State of Calif., 1991-99; ptnr. Hogan & Hartson LLP, Washington, 1999—. Vis. lectr. Duke U. Sch. Law; mem. Trust and Econ. Adv. Coun.; U.S. Trade Rep. Honlife mem. bd. visitors Duke U. Sch. of Law; chair bd. visitors Bren Sch. Environ. Mgmt., U. Calif., Santa Barbara; candidate N.C. Ho. of Reps., 1968; mem. D.C. Rep. Ctrl. Com., 1984-85; chmn. Am. Farmland Trust; mem. adv. coun. The Conservation Fund; mem. biodiversity conservation working group N.Am. Commn. for Environ. Cooperation; chmn. adv. bd. Nat. Park Sys.;

trustee Colo. Conservation Trust; mem. coun. Yosemite Fund. Lt. JAGC, USNR, 1969-75. Recipient commendation U.S. Dept. Interior, 1976, Achievement award, 1980, Conservation award Gulf Oil Corp., 1985, Charles S. Murphy award for pub. svc, 1995, Presdl. award for sustainable devel., 1996, Nat. Conservation Leadership award The Conservation Fund, 1997. Mem. ABA, D.C. Bar Assn., N.C. Bar Assn., Sierra Club (life), Am. Farmland Trust (life). Episcopalian. Home: 4541 45th St NW Washington DC 20016-4473 Business E-Mail: dpwheeler@hhlaw.com.

**WHEELER, EDWARD,** engineering educator; b. Milan, Tenn., Feb. 16, 1959; s. Wylie and Marie Wheeler; m. Ellen Glasco, June 26, 1982; 1 child, Abigail. BS in Engring. Tech., U. Tenn., Martin, 1980; MBA, U. Tenn., 1982; MS in Indsl. and Sys. Engring., U. Memphis, 1987. Assoc. prof. dept. engring. U. Tenn., Martin, 1980—. Editor: (textbook supplement) Study Guide for Engineering Economic Analysis, 2004. Mem.: Am. Soc. Engring. Edn. (chmn. engring. economy divsn. 2002—03). Home: 2019 Chickadee Dr Milan TN 38358 Office: U Tenn Martin 101 Johnson EPS Bldg Martin TN 38238

**WHEELER, EDWARD NORWOOD,** chemical consultant; b. Yancey, Tex., Oct. 11, 1927; s. Wilber Basel and Clara Clementine (Stafford) W.; m. Luella Jean Brossette, Nov. 21, 1950; children: Gordon A., Sterling R., Darrell S. Charlotte, Murray H. BS, Tex. A&I U., 1947, BSChemE, 1949; MA, U. Tex. 1951, PhD, 1953. Rsch. chemist Celanese Chem. Co., Corpus Christi, 1953-55, group leader, 1955-62, section mgr., 1962-67, dir. rsch., 1967-72, dir. devel., 1972-74, planning dir. N.Y.C., 1974-75, dir. rsch. devel. planning, 1975-76, v.p. rsch. devel. planning, 1976-79, v.p. rsch. & devel. Dallas, 1979-83; cons. and expert witness White and Case, Hong Kong and N.Y.C., 1986-91. Contbr. articles to profl. jours. Treas. Dallas Bethlehem Ctr., 1985-89; hon. life mcm., adv. coun. U. Tex. Coll. Natural Sci. Found.; bd. trustees Tex. A&M U.-Kingsville Found., 1994-98; pres. North Tex. Conf. Coun. on Fin. and Adminstrn., United Meth. Ch., 1992-96. Recipient Disting. Alumnus award Tex. A&I U., Kingsville, 1981. Mem. Am. Chem. Soc., Indsl. Rsch. Inst., Synthetic Organic Chem. Mfrs. Assn. (bd. govs. 1977-81), Littlefield Soc. U. Tex. Methodist. Achievements include patents in field. Avocations: gardening, genealogy, cooking. Home and Office: 9238 Moss Haven Dr Dallas TX 75231-1412

**WHEELER, ELTON SAMUEL,** financial executive; b. Salinas, Calif., Oct. 25, 1943; s. Luther Elton and Naomi E. (Beatty) W.; m. Moretha Jean Miller, June 17, 1995; children: Pamela Kathleen, Leslie Elizabeth-Anne, Deborah Suzanne, Jonathan Samuel. BS, Calif. State U., 1966. CPA, Calif. Acct. Pricewaterhouse Coopers, Oakland, Calif., 1967-70, Adams Properties, Inc., San Francisco, 1970-71, treas., 1972-75, v.p., CFO, 1976-77, Adams Capital Mgmt. Co., San Francisco, 1977-79, pres., CEO, 1979-87; pres., CEO, bd. dirs. Calif. Real Estate Investment Trust, 1980-88, Franklin Select Real Estate Income Trust, 1989-2000, Franklin Advantage Real Estate Income Trust, 1990-96; owner E. Samuel Wheeler, CPA, 1992—. Chair audit com. Mother Lode Bank, Sonora, Calif., 2004—, bd. dirs. Bd. trustees Sierra Repertory Theatre, 2006—. With USMCR, 1966-72. Mem. Nat. Assn. Real Estate Investment Trusts, Inc. (sec., treas., bd. govs. 1984-89), Am. Inst. CPAs, Calif. Soc. CPAs, United Way of Tuolumne-Calaveras Counties (pres., dir., treas. 1989-98), Rotary (Sonora, Calif., pres. 1994-95), Rotary Internat. (dist. 5220 dir. 1998-99, asst. gov. 2000-2001, dist. conf. chair 2001-2002, youth exch. officer 2005—). Home: 16399 Crestridge Ave Sonora CA 95370-8752 Office: PO Box 3718 Sonora CA 95370-3718 Business E-Mail: swheeler@samwheelercpa.com

**WHEELER, GEORGE CHARLES, JR.,** materials and processes engineer; b. Balt., Oct. 9, 1943; s. George Charles and Julia Elizabeth (Watrous) W.; m. Dorothy W. Whittemore, Sept. 13, 1947; children: Scott, Craig, Mark, Matthew, Tracy, Bruce; m. Clare Frances Weiner, Jan. 21, 1978. BS in Metall. Engring., Lehigh U., 1944. Various engring. and supervisory positions GE, Mass. and N.Y., 1944-62; mgr. materials, welding and nondestructive test engring. Knolls Atomic Power Lab., G.E., Schenectady, NY, 1962-68; mgr. nondestructive testing G.E. Power Sys., Schenectady, NY, 1968-85; pres., CEO Wheeler Nondestructive Testing, Inc., Schenectady, 1985-95, Materials and Processes Cons., Schenectady, 1995—; mgr. tech. svcs. Am. Soc. for Nondestructive Testing, Columbus, Ohio, 1993-94. Cons. UN, NYC, 1985-98, IAEA, Vienna, Austria, 1985-98, ASNT, 1997—, others; guest lectr. Rensselaer Poly. Inst., Troy, NY, Union Coll., Schenectady, 1978-87; mem. math. sci. and tech. com. Schenectady County CC, 1978-85, adj. prof., 1987-97; US del. Internat. Stds. Orgn., com. TC 135/SC7 NDT Pers. Qualification, 1987-97, convenor working group #2, ISO-9712; mem. ASNT Cert. Mgmt. Bd., 1994-98, chmn. 1976-80, 86-89. Author: Guide to Personnel Cert., 1990, rev. edit., 2003, Guide to Developing Certification Exams, 1992, co-author revised edit., 2005; Level II Study Guide: Radiographic Testing, 1998, Level II Study Guide: Ultrasonic Testing, 1999; contbg. editor JMaterials Evaluation, Jour. of ASNT; tech. editor Nondestructive Testing Handbook, 3d edit., vol. 3. Fellow Am. Soc. Nondestructive Testing (hon. life mem., bd. dirs. 1976-85, pres. 1983-84, chmn. 1984-85, chmn. cert. com. 1976-80, 86-89, Gold medal); mem. ASTM (com. internat. stds., com. nondestructive testing), NRA (life), Am. Soc. Metals (life), Nature Conservancy (life), Adirondack Mountain Club, Adirondack Forty-Sixers, Trout Unlimited (life) Achievements include pioneering personnel qualifications and certifications for nondestructive testing work worldwide for ASTM and ASNT. Avocations: mountain climbing, flying, firearms, photography, cross country skiing, golf, fishing. Personal E-mail: geocharles@aol.com.

**WHEELER, GERALDINE HARTSHORN,** historian, writer; b. Pomona, Calif., Feb. 5, 1919; d. Albion True and Beatrice Osa (Barnes) Hartshorn; m. Lloyd Franklyn Wheeler, Dec. 2, 1938 (dec. Mar. 1996); children: Russell Lloyd, Robert Gerald. AA, Santa Barbara, Calif.) C.C., 1950's. Co-owner Atheling's, Santa Barbara, Calif., 1971-76, Pomona, 1976-90; chmn. bd. trustees Atheling Heritage Trust, Claremont, Calif. 1991—. Pub., editor mag. Atheling's, 1974—75, newsletter Grand Priory of America Order of St. Lazarus, 1974—86; editor: St. Margaret's Jour., 1975—; author: (essays) A World Full in 1891, 1975—, President John Adams - A Profile, 1975—, Ralph Waldo Emerson—A Profile, 1975, The Many Masks of Communism, 1975, A Tale of St. Nicholas, 1995, Post Cards and Postal Cards, 1996, Pocahontas Kinships, 1996. Vol. PTA, Fontana and Santa Barbara, 1945-60; mem. various coms. and choir First Congl. Ch., Santa Barbara, 1952-72; leader Cub Scouts Am., Santa Barbara 1953-56; grey lady unit chmn. Santa Barbara chpt.-ARC, 1958-62; women's project bd. v.p., activities chmn., active various coms. Santa Barbara Hist. Soc., 1960-74; exec. sec. 1960 Nixon for Pres. Campaign, Santa Barbara, 1960; mem. spkrs. bur. Nixon for Gov. Campaign, Santa Barbara, 1962; mem. Rep. state ctrl. com. State of Calif., 1962-64; blitz chmn. Rockefeller for Pres. Campaign, Santa Barbara, 1964; coord. vol. svcs. Office of Civil Def., City of Santa Barbara, 1965-76; coord. tv series on earthquakes Sta. KEYT, Office of Civil Def., Santa Barbara, 1968; bd. dirs. Calif. Ctrl. Coast Area, U.S.O., 1968-76, treas. bd., 1970-76; supporter Vis. Nurses and Hospice Assn., 1994—; others. Decorated Dame of Grace, Mil. and Hospitaller Order of St. Lazarus of Jerusalem, Cert. of Merit, 1973, The Alan Weaver Hazelton award; recipient Cert. of Merit, Santa Barbara Jr. Coll., 1954-55, Medal of Appreciation SAR, 1972, Cert. of Award Nat. Soc. Daus. of Founders and Patriots of Am., 1977. Mem. Acad. Polit. Sci., Calif. Hist. Soc., New Eng. Hist. and Geneal. Soc., The Pomona Ebell (pres. 1998-2000), Wilson Ctr. Assocs., Smithsonian Assocs., Nat. Trust for Hist. Preservation, Am. Farmland Trust, Nat. Woman's History Mus., Nat. Arbor Day Found., Pomona Valley Hist. Soc., La Verne Hist. Soc., La Salle County Hist. Soc., Nat. Wildlife Fedn., Colonial Williamsburg Found., The Postcard Soc. (founder), Musicians Club Pomona Valley, Shakespeare Club Pomona Valley, Nat. Soc. DAR (past regent chpts.), Calif. Huguenot Soc., Nat. Soc. Dames Am. (orgn. pres. chpt. XX), Nat. Soc. Daus. Colonial Wars (state officer), Nat. Soc. Women Desc. Ancient and Honorable Artillery Co. (past nat. chaplain and state officer), Soc. Mayflower Desc. (past colony gov.), Nat. Soc. Dames of the Ct. of Honor, Nat. Soc. New Eng. Women, Hereditary Order Desc. Colonial Govs. (past nat. officer), Soc. Desc. Most Noble Order of the Garter, Ams. Armorial Ancestry, Ams. Royal Descent, Colonial Order

of the Crown, The Plantagenet Soc., Nat. Soc. Magna Charta Dames, Order of the Crown of Charlemagne in USA, Nat. Soc. Ams. Royal Descent, Nat. Soc. Desc. Early Quakers (founding nat. clk.), Nat. Guild St. Margaret of Scotland (founder), Nat. Gavel Club, Mt. Vernon Ladies' Assn., Order of the Merovingian Dynasty. Republican. Avocations: book collecting, reading, genealogy, classical music, needlecrafts. Home: 1047 E Baseline Rd Claremont CA 91711-1577

**WHEELER, GRACE R.,** retired market researcher; b. Phila., May 17, 1927; d. Norman F.S. Russell and Ella Dewees Eisenbrey; m. Philip Price Sharples, Oct. 9, 1954 (div.); children: Martha Sharples Daniels, Grace Sharples Cooke, Russell Price Sharples; m. Alexander Bowman Wheeler, Aug. 16, 1980 (dec.). BA, Bennington Coll., 1948; MBA, Temple U., 1968. Rsch. analyst ARCO, Phila., 1948-51, Alderson & Sessions, Phila., 1951-54; owner Gen. Rsch. Assn., Bryn Mawr, Pa., 1974-88; ret., 1988. Contbr. (sch. history): ...better than riches..., 1989; author, editor exhibit catalog, 1982. Adv. bd., Academy Genesis II, Phila., 1980—; founder Gladwyne (Pa.) Montessori Sch., 1960; mem. William Penn Charter Sch. Bd., 1973-2005, emeritus, 2005—, head of bd., 1975-85; mem. bd., Darby Creek Valley Assn., Drexel Hill, Pa., 1998—. Republican. Mem. Soc. Of Friends. Avocations: land stewardship, gardening. Home: 3824 Darby Rd Bryn Mawr PA 19010

**WHEELER, HEWITT BROWNELL,** surgeon, educator; b. Louisville, July 21, 1929; s. Arville and Lois (Vance) W.; m. Elizabeth Jane Maxwell, July 21, 1956; children: Stephen, Elizabeth, Jane, Mary. Student, Vanderbilt U., 1945-48; MD, Harvard U., 1952. Diplomate Am. Bd. Surgery (bd. dirs. 1984-90). Cushing fellow Harvard Med. Sch., Boston, 1953, Peters fellow, 1956, research fellow, 1959-60, instr. surgery, 1961-64, clin. assoc. surgery, 1964-67, asst. clin. prof. surgery, 1967 70, assoc. prof. surgery, 1970-71; asst. in surgery Peter Bent Brigham Hosp., Boston, 1959-60, jr. assoc. surgery, 1961-64, assoc. surgery, 1964-69, sr. assoc. surgery, 1969-71; asst. chief surgery Roxbury VA Hosp., Boston, 1961-62, chief surgery, 1962-71, chief of staff, 1968-71; cons. surgery U. Mass. Med. Sch., Worcester, 1966-71; prof., chmn. dept. surgery U. Mass. Med. Sch. at Worcester, 1971-98, Harry M. Haidak disting. prof. surgery, 1985-98, prof. emeritus, 1998—; chief staff U. Mass. Hosp., 1974-76, surgeon-in-chief, 1976-96; exec. dir. Ctr. for Advanced Clin. Tech., 1995—; affiliate prof. biomed. engring. Worcester Poly. Inst., 1974—; lectr. surgery Harvard Med. Sch., 1974-96; chief surgery St. Vincent Hosp., Worcester, 1971-75. Cons. Meml. Hosp., Worcester City Hosp., 1970-96, Worcester Hahnemann Hosp., 1974-94, Peter Bent Brigham Hosp., 1973-96; chmn. surg. research program com. VA, Washington, 1965-67, nat. participant surg. cons., 1965-69, chmn. ad hoc adv. com. surgery, 1969-71. Pres. Mass. Compassionate Care Coalition, 2000—; trustee Ctrl. Mass. Health Care Found., 1975—77, Worcester Found. for Biomed. Rsch., 1996—, Hospice Ctrl. Mass. Inc.; 1997—2000, U. Mass. Meml. Found., 1998—, Boston Med. Libr., 1996—. 1st lt. M.C. AUS, 1953—55. Mem. ACS (bd. govs. 1984-90, coun. Mass. chpt. 1973-76, pres. 1980), AAAS, AMA, Am. Surg. Assn., Soc. Univ. Surgeons, Internat. Cardiovascular Soc., New Eng. Surg. Soc. (treas. 1977-84, v.p. 1986-87, pres. 1989-91), Boston Surg. Soc. (pres. 1995-96), Worcester Surg. Soc. (pres. 1973-75), Transplantation Soc., Mass. Med. Soc. (100th Shattuck lectr. 1990; lifetime achievement award 2005), Worcester Dist. Med. Soc. (sec. 1996-99, v.p. 1999-00, pres. 2000-01), New Eng. Vascular Soc. (v.p. 1985-86, pres. 1988-89). Achievements include rsch. in exptl. transplantation, blood vessel surgery, method to detect blood clots, improving end-of-life care. Home: 52 Cloyster Rd South Portland ME 04106-5110 E-mail: bwheele1@maine.rr.com.

**WHEELER, JAMES DONLAN,** chemistry professor; b. St. Louis, July 19, 1923; s. John Ingraham and Nan (Donlan) Wheeler. MS, St. Louis U., 1952, PhL, 1948, STL, 1956; PhD, U. Mo., 1965. Instr. chemistry St. Louis U. H.S., 1950—51; prof. chemistry Rockhurst U., Kans. City, Mo., 1956—. Author: (Book) Chemistry Problem Solving, 1979. Mem. Am. Chem. Soc. (chmn. local sect. 1968), AAAS, NSTA, Soc. Coll. Sci. Tchrs., Rho Chi, Phi Lambda Upsilon Roman Catholic. Avocations: exercise physiology, weightlifting. Home: 5138 Tracy Ave Kansas City MO 64110-2516 Office: Rockhurst U 1100 Rockhurst Rd Kansas City MO 64110-2508 Office Phone: 816-501-4068. Business E-Mail: James.Wheeler@rockhurst.edu.

**WHEELER, JANE FRANCES,** protective services official; b. McAlester, Okla. Dir. Consumer Protection, Oklahoma City, 1984—. Office: Consumer Protection Atty Gen 313 NE 21st St Oklahoma City OK 73105

**WHEELER, JOHN ARCHIBALD,** physicist, educator; b. Jacksonville, Fla., July 9, 1911; s. Joseph Lewis and Mabel (Archibald) Wheeler; m. Janette Hegner, June 10, 1935; children: Isabel Letitia Wheeler Ufford, James English, Alison Christie Wheeler Lahnston. PhD, Johns Hopkins U., 1933; ScD (hon.), Western Res. U., 1958, U. N.C., 1959. U. Pa., 1968, Middlebury Coll., 1969, Rutgers U., 1969, Yeshiva U., 1973, Yale U., 1974; PhD (hon.), U. Uppsala, 1975; ScD (hon.), U. Md., 1977, Gustavus Adolphus U., 1981, Cath. U. Am., 1982, U. Newcastle-upon-Tyne, 1983, Princeton U., 1986, U. Conn., 1989, U. Maine, 1992, Tufts U., 1992; LLD (hon.), Johns Hopkins U., 1977; LittD (hon.), Drexel U., 1987. NRC fellow, N.Y., Copenhagen, 1933—35; from asst. prof. to assoc. prof. physics U. N.C., 1935—38; asst. prof. physics Princeton U., 1938—42, assoc. prof., 1945—47, prof., 1947—76, Joseph Henry prof. physics, 1966—76, Joseph Henry prof. physics emeritus, 1976—; prof. physics and dir. Ctr. for Theoretical Physics, U. Tex., Austin, 1976—86; Ashbel Smith prof. U. Tex., Austin, 1979—86, Blumberg prof., 1981—86, Smith and Blumberg prof. emeritus, 1986—. Cons. and physicist on atomic energy projects Princeton U. 1939—42, U. Chgo., 1942, E.I. duPont de Nemours & C, Wilmington, Del., Richland, Wash., 1943—45, Los Alamos, 1950—53; dir. Project Matterhorn (H-bomb) Princeton U., 1951—53; Guggenheim fellow, Paris and Copenhagen, 1949—50; summer lectr. U. Mich., U. Chgo., Columbia U; Lorentz prof. U. Leiden, 1956; Fulbright prof. Kyoto U., 1962; vis. fellow Clare Coll., Cambridge U., 1964, Ritchie lectr. Edinburgh, 1958; vis. prof. U. Calif.-Berkeley, 1960; Battelle prof. U. Wash., 1975; I.I. Rabi vis. prof. Columbia U., 1983; sci. advisor U.S. Senate del. to 3d ann. conf. NATO Parliamentarians, Paris, 1957; mem. adv. com. Oak Ridge Nat. Lab., 1957—65, U. Calif., Los Alamos and Livermore, 1972—77; v.p. Internat. Union Physics, 1951—54; chmn. joint com. on history of theoretical physics in 20th century Am. Phys. Soc. and Am. Philos. Soc., 1960—72; sci. adv. bd. USAF, 1961—62; chmn. Dept. Def. Advanced Rsch. Projects Agy. Project 137 (now Project Jason), 1958; mem. U.S. Gen. Adv. Com. Arms Control and Disarmament, 1969—72, 1974—77. Author: Geometrodynamics, 1962; author: (with others) Gravitation Theory and Gravitational Collapse, 1965; author: Spacetime Physics, 1966; author: (with E. Taylor) Spacetime Physics, 2d edit., 1992; author: (in German) Einstein's Vision, 1968; author: (with C.W. Misner and K.S. Thorne) Gravitation, 1973; author: (with M. Rees and R. Ruffini) Black Holes, Gravitation Waves and Cosmology, 1974; author: Frontiers of Time, 1979, A Journey into Gravity and Spacetime, 1990, At Home in the Universe, 1994; author: (with I. Ciufolini) Gravitation and Inertia, 1995; author: also translations, 1991—92; author: (with Kenneth Ford) Geons, Black Holes and Quantum Foam: A Life in Physics, 1998; editor (with W. Zurek): Quantum Theory and Measurement, 1983; contbr. 375 articles to phys. jours. Trustee Battelle Meml. Inst., 1959—89, S.W. Rsch. Inst., San Antonio, 1977—92, Unitarian Ch., 1965. Recipient A. Cressy Morrison prize for work on nuc. physics, N.Y. Acad. Scis., 1947, Albert Einstein prize, Strauss Found., 1965, Enrico Fermi award, AEC, 1968, Franklin medal, Franklin Inst., 1969, Nat. medal of Sci., 1971, Herzfeld award, 1975, Outstanding Grad. Tchg. award, U. Tex., 1981, Niels Bohr Internat. Gold medal, 1982, Oersted medal, Am. Assn. Physics Tchrs., 1983, J. Robert Oppenheimer Meml. prize, 1984, Matteucci medal, Nat. Acad. Sci. Rome, Soc. of the Forty, 1994, Wolf prize in physics, Wolf Found., Israel, 1997. Fellow: AAAS (dir. 1965—68), Am. Phys. Soc. (pres. 1966, Einstein prize 2003); mem.: NAS, Royal Danish Acad. Scis., Royal Soc. (London), Accademia Nazionale dei Lincei, Internat. Union Physics (v.p. 1951—54), L'Academie Internationale de Philosophie des Sciences 1987—90), Tex. Philos. Soc., Royal Acad. Sci. (Uppsala, Sweden), Philos. Soc. of Tex., Am. Philos. Soc. (councillor 1963—66, v.p. 1971—73, councillor 1976—79, Franklin medal 1989), Am. Acad. Arts and Scis., Internat. Astron. Union, Am. Math. Soc., Princeton Club (N.Y.C.), Century

Assn. (N.Y.C.), Sigma Xi, Phi Beta Kappa. Unitarian Universalist. Office: Princeton U Dept Physics Princeton NJ 08544-0001 Business E-Mail: jawheeler@pupgc.princeton.edu. *We will first understand how simple the universe is when we recognize how strange it is.*

**WHEELER, JOHN CRAIG,** astrophysicist, writer; b. Glendale, Calif., Apr. 5, 1943; s. G. L. and Peggy Wheeler; m. Hsueh Lie, Oct. 29, 1967; children: Diek Winters, J. Robinson. BS in Physics, MIT, 1965; PhD in Physics, U. Colo., 1969. Asst. prof. astronomy Harvard U., Cambridge, Mass., 1971-74; assoc. prof. U. Tex., Austin, 1974-80, prof., 1980—, Samuel T. and Fern Yanagisawa Regents prof. astronomy, 1985—, chmn. astronomy dept., 1986-90. Vis. fellow Joint Inst. Lab. Astrophysics, Boulder, 1978—79, Japan Soc. Promotion Sci., 1983; 1st vis. prof. Assn. Univs. Rsch. Astronomy, 1990; vis. sr. scientist Inst. Theoretical Physics U. Calif., Santa Barbara, 1997; gen. mem. Aspen (Colo.) Ctr. Physics; mem. exec. com. Tex. Symposium Relativistic Astrophysics; mem. com. origin and evolution life NRC Space Studies Bd., 2002—05, mem., 2002—06. Author: The Krone Experiment, 1986, Cosmic Catastrophes, 2000; editor: Accretion Disks in Compact Stellar Systems, 1993, Supernovae, 1990, Disk Instabilities in Close Binary Systems, 1999, Proceedings of the 20th Texas Symposium on Relativistic Astrophysics, Cosmic Explosions in Three Dimensions. Recipient award, U. Tex., 1984, 1986, 1999, Pres.'s Assocs. Tchg. Excellence award, 1999; Fulbright fellow, Italy, 1991, Dads Assn. Centennial Tchg. fellow, U. Tex., 1999. Mem.: Am. Phys. Soc., Acad. Disting. Tchrs., Internat. Astron. Union, Am. Astron. Soc. (v.p. 1999—2002, pres. 2006—), Sigma Xi. Avocations: running, writing, reading. Office: U Tex Dept Astronomy Austin TX 78712

**WHEELER, JOHN OLIVER,** geologist; b. Mussoorie, India, Dec. 19, 1924; s. Edward Oliver and Dorothea Sophie (Danielsen) W.; m. Nora Jean Hughes, May 17, 1952; children: Kathleen Anna Wheeler Hunter, Jennifer Margaret Wheeler Crompton. BASc in Geol. Engring., U. BC, 1947, DSc (hon.), 2000; PhD in Geology, Columbia U., 1956. Geologist Geol. Survey Can., Ottawa, Ont., 1951-61, Vancouver, B.C., 1961-65, rsch. scientist, 1965-70, rsch. mgr. Ottawa, 1970—, chief regional and econ. geology divsn., 1970-73, dep. dir. gen., 1973-79; rsch. scientist Geol. Survey Can. (Cordilleran divsn.), 1979-90, rsch. scientist emeritus, 1990—. Gen. editor: Geology of Canada, 8 vols., 1989-98; compiler of regional geol. maps of we. Can., Can. and no. N.Am. and Greenland; contbr. articles to profl. jours.; chpts. to books. Recipient Queen's Silver Jubilee medal, 1977, Can. 125 medal, 1994, Earth Sci. Sector and Dept. awards Nat. Resources Can., 1996, Spl. award of BC-Yukon Chamber of Mines for outstanding contbn. to Can. Cordilleran geology, 2000, Massey medal Royal Can. Geog. Soc., 2002, hon. fellow 2003. Fellow Royal Soc. Can. (Geol. Assn. Can. (pres. 1970-71, Logan medal 1983, Disting. fellow 1996), Geol. Soc. Am. (councillor 1971-74), Can. Geosci. Coun. (pres. 1981), mem. Can. Inst. Mining and Metallurgy, Can. Geol. Found. (pres. 1974-79), Can. Alpine Club, Am. Alpine Club. Anglican. E-mail: njwheeler@shaw.ca.

**WHEELER, JOHN S., JR.,** urologist; s. John S. Wheeler Sr. and Virginia S. Wheeler; m. Michele A. Marganski, June 4, 1977; children: Nicholas, Anne. BA, Dartmouth Coll., 1972; MD, Georgetown U., 1977. Lic. physician Ill., cert. Mass. Resident gen. surgery Boston Med. Ctr., 1977—79, resident urology 1979—82; faculty Loyola U. Med. Ctr., Maywood, Ill., 1983—; staff urologist Hines VA Hosp., 1983—, RML Hosp., Hinsdale, 2001—. Cons. in field. Contbr. articles to profl. jours., chapters to books. Fellow, Boston U. Med. Ctr., 1982—83. Mem.: Am. Paraplegia Soc. (rsch. com. 1984—), Am. Coll. Surgeons, Am. Urological Assn., Alpha Omega Alpha. Roman Catholic. Avocations: golf, skiing. Office: Loyola U Med Ctr Dept Urology 2160 S First Ave Maywood IL 60153 Office Phone: 708-216-4076. Business E-Mail: jwheeler@lumc.edu.

**WHEELER, JOHN WATSON,** lawyer; b. Murfreesboro, Tenn., Sept. 11, 1938; s. James William and Grace (Fann) W.; m. Dorothy Anita Pressgrove, Aug. 5, 1959; children: Jeffrey William, John Harold. BS in Journalism, U. Tenn., 1960, JD, 1968. Bar: Tenn. 1968, U.S. Dist. Ct. (ea. dist.) Tenn. 1968, U.S. Dist. Ct. (mid dist.) Tenn. 1968, U.S. Dist. Ct. (we. dist.) Tenn. 1968, U.S. Supreme Ct. 1974, U.S. Ct. Appeals (6th cir.) 1975. Editor The Covington (Tenn.) Leader, 1963-65; adminstrv. asst. to lab. dir. UT-AEC Rsch. Lab., Oak Ridge, Tenn., 1965-68; assoc. Hodges, Doughty & Carson, Knoxville, Tenn., 1968-72, prtnr., 1972—2005, of counsel, 2005—. Mem. commn. to study Appellate Cts. in Tenn.; chair U.S. magistrate merit selection panel, U.S. Dist. Ct. (ea. dist.) Tenn., 1991, 2002, 03, mem. bankruptcy judge merit selection panel, 1992-94; chmn. hist. soc., U.S. Dist. Ct. (ea. dist.) Tenn. 1993-2004. Mem. organizing com. Tenn. Supreme Ct. Hist. Soc. Lt. U.S. Army, 1961-63, capt. Res. Fellow Am. Bar Found. (life, Tenn. chair 1999—), Tenn. Bar Found. (life); mem. ABA (ho. of dels. 1986-2000), Tenn. Bar Assn. (pres. 1989-90, bd. govs. 1981-91), Nat. Conf. Bar Pres., Am. Inns. of Ct. (master of bench, emeritus), Internat. Assn. Def. Counsel, So. Conf. Bar Pres., 6th Cir. Jud. Conf. (life), Fox Den Country Club (bd. dirs. 2001-04). Republican. Lutheran. Avocations: golf, travel. Home: 12009 N Fox Den Dr Knoxville TN 37922-2540 Office: Hodges Doughty & Carson PO Box 869 Knoxville TN 37901-0869 Office Phone: 865-546-9611. Business E-Mail: jwheeler@hdclaw.com.

**WHEELER, KARLA,** education educator; d. Kristine and George Bloechl; m. Robert Wheeler, May 11, 1996. BA in Art History, U. Wis., Milw., 1998, MA in Pub. History, 2001; postgrad., U. Wis., Madison, 2006—. Curatorial asst. Waukesha County Mus., Wis., 1998—2000, dir. of pub. edn., 2000—02; curator of edn. Logan Mus. of Anthropology, Beloit, Wis., 2002—; asst. prof. Beloit Coll., Wis., 2002—. Grad. student rep. UW-Milw., Dept. of History, 2001. Mem.: Nat. Coun. for History Edn., Mus. Edn. Roundtable, Nat. Coun. on Pub. History, Assn. of Midwest Museums, Am. Assn. of Museums, Nat. Vocat. and Tech. Honor Soc. (life). Avocation: travel. Office: Beloit College 700 College St Beloit WI 53511 Office Phone: 608-363-2678. E-mail: wheelerk@beloit.edu.

**WHEELER, KATHERINE WELLS,** retired state legislator; b. St. Louis, Feb. 8, 1940; d. Benjamin Harris and Katherine (Gladney) Wells; m. Douglas Lanphier Wheeler, June 13, 1964; children: Katherine Gladney, Lucille Lanphier BA, Smith Coll., 1961; MA, Washington U., St. Louis, 1966. Founder auction N.H. Pub. TV, Durham, 1973-76; pub. mem. N.H. Pub. Broadcasting Coun., Durham, 1975-80; founding mem. bd. govs. N.H. Pub. TV, 1980-88; elected N.H. Ho. of Reps., Concord, 1988, 90, 92,94; mem. N.H. Senate, 1996—98, 1998—2000, 2000—02, chmn. health & human svcs. com. Coord. internat. visitors program N.J. Coun. World Affairs, 1981-95. Bd. dirs. Planned Parenthood No. New England, 1989-95, Gt. Bay Svcs., Newington, N.H., 1989-97, Behavioral Health and Devel. Svcs Strafford County, Inc., 1991—; vice chairperson Strafford County Legis. Del., 1993-94; active Commn. on Health, Human Svcs. and Elderly Affairs N.H. Ho. of Reps., Concord, 1988-96; bd. dirs. N.H. Pub. Health Assn., 1996—, pres., 2003—; bd. dirs. NAMI N.H., 2002—, NARAL N.H. Found., 1998—. Named Woman of Yr., Union Leader Newspaper, 1984, Citizen of Yr., Homemakers of Strafford County, 1990, N.H. sect. NASW, 1993, Legislator of Yr., N.H. Nurses Assn., 1996, N.H. Acad. Pediat., 1996; recipient Elizabeth Campbell Outstanding Pub. TV Vol. award Nat. Friends Pub. Broadcasting, 1984, Meritorious Svc. award N.H. Women's Lobby, 1992, Dist. Contbn. award N.H. Psychol. Orgn., Inc., 1994, Cert. of Achievement for Outstanding Legis. Leadership N.H. Citizen Action, 1994; Fleming fellow Leadership Inst., Ctr. for Policy Alternatives, Washington, 1997-98. Mem. AAUW, LWV, Am. Assn. Ret. Persons, Order of Women Legislators, N.H. Smith Coll. Club (v.p. 1974-76, pres. 1976-78, v.p. Class of 1961, 1991-96), N.H. Assn. Social Workers (Legislator of Yr. 1993), N.H. Psychol. Orgn. Inc. (Disting. Contbn. award 1994). Democrat. Mem. United Ch. of Christ. Home and Office: 27 Mill Rd Durham NH 03824-3006

**WHEELER, M. CASS,** health science association administrator; b. Texas; BA in advertising, U. Texas, Austin, 1963. Stockbroker NY Stock Exch. firm, Dallas, 1969—73; with Am. Heart Assn., Austin, Tex., 1973—82, COO Dallas, 1982, sr. v.p., field ops., 1996, CEO, 1997—. Guest lecturer Harvard U. Sch. of Bus. & Pub. Health, U. Texas Sch. of Mgmt., Dallas, U. Texas

---

Lyndon B. Johnson Sch. of Pub. Affairs, Austin; former bd. chmn. Nat. Health Coun.; bd. mem. Partnership for Prevention, Research! Am., Nat. Ctr. for Tobacco-Free Kids, Nat. Assembly of Health and Human Service Organizations; advisory bd. mem. Discovery Health Media, Inc.; mem. Citizens Advisory Council for the Campaign for Med. Rsch.; former mem. President's Commn. on Improving Econ. Opportunity in Communities Dependent on Tobacco Production While Protecting Pub. Health. Avocations: running, skiing, bicycling. Office: Am Heart Assn 7272 Greenville Ave Dallas TX 75231-5129*

**WHEELER, MALCOLM EDWARD,** lawyer, educator; b. Berkeley, Calif., Nov. 29, 1944; s. Malcolm Ross and Frances Dolores (Kane) W.; m. Donna Marie Stambaugh, July 25, 1981; children: Jessica Ross, M. Connor. SB, MIT, 1966; JD, Stanford U., 1969. Bar: Calif. 1970, Colo. 1992, U.S. Dist Ct (cen. dist.) Calif. 1970, U.S. Ct. Appeals (9th cir.) 1970, U.S. Ct. Appeals (10th cir.) 1973, U.S. Dist. Ct. (no., so., ea. and cen. dists.) Calif. 1975, U.S. Ct. Appeals (11th cir.) 1987, U.S. Ct. Appeals (D.C. cir.) 1987, U.S. Supreme Ct. 1976, U.S. Ct. Appeals (3d cir.) 1989, (4th cir.) 1992, (8th cir.) 1993, (5th cir.) 1995, (Fed. cir.) 1998. Assoc. Howard, Prim, Smith, Rice & Downs, San Francisco, 1969-71; assoc. prof. law U. Kans., Lawrence, 1971-74; assoc. Hughes Hubbard & Reed, Los Angeles, 1974-77, ptnr., 1977-81, 83-85, cons., 1981-83; ptnr. Skadden, Arps, Slate, Meagher & Flom, Los Angeles, 1985-91; dir. Parcel, Mauro, Hultin & Spaanstra P.C., Denver, 1991-98, Wheeler Trigg & Kennedy, P.C., Denver, 1998—. Vis. prof. U. Iowa, 1978, prof., 1979; prof. U. Kans., Lawrence, 1981-83; chief counsel U.S. Senate Select Com. to Study Law Enforcement Undercover Activities, Washington, 1982-83. Mem. editl. bd. Jour. Products Liability, 1984-90, Fed. Litigation Guide Reporter, 1986-90; contbr. articles to profl. jours. Fellow Am. Coll. Trial Lawyers; mem. ABA, Calif. Bar Assn., Colo. Bar Assn., Am. Law Inst. Home: 100 Humboldt St Denver CO 80218-3932 Office Phone: 303-292-2525. E-mail: wheeler@wtklaw.com.

**WHEELER, MARGARET JANE,** actress, soprano, voice educator; b. Apr. 16, 1925; d. William Henry and Ruth Bond Wheeler. BA in Voice, George Peabody Coll. (now Vanderbilt U.), Nashville, 1947; grad. study in voice and opera with L. Vaida, St. Louis Inst. Music, 1950; grad. study with Oren Brown, 1976—77; studied voice, Franco Iglesias, Aida Favia Artsay, Thomas Houser, Thomas Cultice, Willard Young, Julia Drobner, Anthony Frisell, 1960—90; acting study, Stella Adler Studio, 1964—65, David LeGrant Sudio, 1965—69; MA in Voice Performance, Hunter Coll., NYC, 1976. Louis Nicholas voice tchr. Peabody Coll., 1943—47; tchr. Army Dependents Sch., La Rochelle, France, 1955—56; tchr. music Rockland County Pub. Schs., NY, Westchester County Pub. Schs.; tchr.music L.I. Pub. Schs., St. Louis Pub. Schs.; asst. prof. music dept. Millersville State Coll., Pa. Dir. adult choir Asbury Meth. Ch., Croton-on-Hudson, NY; dir. Cmty. Chorus, Croton-on-Hudson, NY; dir. choirs Evang. Ch., Overland, Mo.; voice tchr. Bronx Conservatory of Music, NY, 1990—; tchr. sr. citizen singing classes Co-op City, 2001—04; voice tchr. Bronx Music Ho., Bennett Conservatory of Music, Croton-on-Hudson; tchr. continuing edn. opera appreciation Briarcliff Manor, N.Y.C., White Plains. Performer: (classical and light opera) Brunswick Summer Playhouse, 1961, Lake George Opera Co., 1965, Pitts. Civic Light Opera Co., 1967, Phila. Grand Opera Co., 1971, Assoc. Concert Artists, 1972, 1973, Sycamore Performing Arts Festival, 1973, (classical and light opera conduted by Thoma Cultice) The Medium, 1975, (classical and light opera) Staten Island Opera Co., 1976, (sacred music) Peabody Coll., 1947, Park Ave. Meth. Ch., 1960, St. Matthew's Luth. Ch., 1980, North Yonkers Cmty. Ch., 1985—94; soloist: sacred music Park Ave. Meth. Ch., 1961—67, Christian Sci. Ch., 1968—72, 1974—75, Cmty. Synagogue, 1968—72, soloist: First Westminster Presbyn. Ch., 1976, St. Paul's Episcopal Ch., 1976—77; performer: (showcases) Gunda Morden, 1960, Opera Club of Am., 1960, Messina Opera Co., 1960; soloist and recitalist: Bronx Conservatory of Music, 1970—90, Grad. Recital Hunter Coll. Playhouse, 1976, Westchester Conservatory Music, 1977, Faculty Recitals Millersville (Pa.) Coll., 1977—78, Stewart Smith Singers Concert, 1985, North Yonkers Cmty. Ch., 1985—94, Warner Libr., 1986, Bennett Conservatory, 1986, Westchester CC, 1991; soloist and recitalist Westchester CC, 1994; soloist and recitalist: Sigma Alpha Iota Am. Musicales, 1999—2002; performer: Met. Opera Extra Chorus, 1962, Schola Cantorum NY, 1962—70, Camerata Singers, 1970; dir.: Children's Wing Croton Shakespeare Festival; performer: (musical theater) The Sound of Music, 1971, (multimedia) A Weapon Most Unusual!, 2005. Mem. delegation music tchrs. People to People, China, 1988, Hong Kong, 1988. Mem.: Nat. Assn. Tchrs Singing, Am. Guild Musical Artists, Actor's Equity, Sigma Alpha Iota. Home: 786 Sleepy Hollow Rd Briarcliff Manor NY 10510-2525

**WHEELER, MARK ANDREW, SR.,** lawyer; b. Pitts., Feb. 14, 1963; s. Andrew Mate Wheeler and Anna Ruth (Whitfield) W.; m. Valentina, Sept. 19, 2004; children: Mark Andrew Jr., Lauren Anna, Layne Allison, Livia Arden, Olga Piper. BA in Philosophy, Hampden-Sydney Coll., 1985; JD, W.Va. U., 1991. Bar: Pa. 1992, U.S. Dist. Ct. (we. dist.) Pa. 1993; ordained to ministry Lighthouse Ch., 1997. Staff litigator W.Va. U. Coll. Law Legal Clinic, Morgantown, 1991-92; jud. clk. Mahoning County, Youngstown, Ohio, 1991-92; pvt. practice Reynoldsville, Pa., 1993—, Clarion, Pa., 1994—. Legal cons. S.T. & E., Inc. Punxsutawney, Pa., 1993—; Jefferson County Gun Owners Assn., Brookville, Pa., 1994—, Crimestoppers of Jefferson County, Brookville, 1993-94, Five Star Homes, Inc., 1995-97, Bemberg Cons., Inc., 1994—. Bd. dirs. Reynoldsville Area Indsl. Bd., 1993-96; mem. exec. dist. com. Boy Scouts Am., Dubois, Pa., 1993—; bd. dirs. Reynoldsville Pub. Libr. Assn., 1993-96; mem. Dubois Christian and Missionary Alliance Ch., mem. choir, 1995—. Mem. ABA, ATLA, Internat. Platform Assn., Pa. Bar Assn. (young lawyers divsn., chair zone 7), Am. Ctr. for Law and Justice, Pa. Trial Lawyers Assn., Pa. Assn. Notaries, Jefferson County Bar Assn., Western Pa. Trial Lawyers Assn., Clarion County Bar Assn., Nat. Eagle Scout Assn. Republican. Avocations: songwriting, public speaking, home renovation, car restoration. Office: PO Box 176 512 Main St Reynoldsville PA 15851-1335 also: PO Box 770 Clarion PA 16214-0770 Office Phone: 814-653-2000. E-mail: markwheelerlaw@netzero.com.

**WHEELER, OTIS BULLARD,** retired language educator, retired director; b. Mansfield, Ark., Feb. 1, 1921; s. Clarence Charles and Georgia Elizabeth (Bullard) W.; m. Doris Louise Alexander, Jan. 17, 1943; children: Ann Carolyn, Ross Charles; m. Anne Carol Loveland, Mar. 23, 1991. BA, U. Okla., 1942; MA, U. Tex., 1947; PhD, U. Minn., 1951. Mem. faculty La. State U., Baton Rouge, 1952—, prof. English, 1965-81, prof. emeritus, 1981—, chmn. dept., 1974, asst. dean grad. sch., 1962-67, vice chancellor for acad. affairs, 1974-80, acting chancellor, 1981. Fulbright-Hayes lectr. U. Innsbruck, Austria, 1968-69 Author: The Literary Career of Maurice Thompson, 1965; photographer: (with R.W. Heck) Religious Architecture in Louisiana, 1995, (with Anne C. Loveland) From Meetinghouse to Megachurch, 2003. Served with U.S. Army, 1942-46, 51-52. Decorated Bronze Star medal. Mem. Phi Kappa Phi, Omicron Delta Kappa. Democrat. Methodist. Home: 657 Highland Oaks Dr Baton Rouge LA 70810-5348

**WHEELER, RAYMOND LOUIS,** lawyer; b. Ft. Sill, Okla., Feb. 10, 1945; s. Raymond Louis and Dorothy Marie (Hutcherson) W.; m. Priscilla Wheeler, July 1, 1966 (div. 1982); children: Jennifer, Hilary; m. Cynthia Lee Jackson, July 14, 1984 (div. 1994); children: Matthew Raymond, Madeline Elizabeth; m. Freddie Kay Park, June 10, 1995. BA, U. Tex., 1967; JD, Harvard U., 1970. Bar: Calif. 1972, U.S. Dist. Ct. (no., cen., ea., so. dists.) Calif., U.S. Ct. Appeals (9th cir., 7th cir.), U.S. Ct. Appeals (7th cir.) U.S. Supreme Ct. Law clk. to hon. Irving L. Goldberg U.S. Ct. Appeals (5th cir.) 1970-71; assoc. Morrison & Foerster, San Francisco, 1971-76, ptnr., 1976-90, Palo Alto, Calif., 1990—, labor & employment dept. coord. Chmn. labor and employment law dept. Morrison & Foerster, San Francisco, 1984-88, 92—; lectr. labor and EEO law. Exec. editor Harvard Law Rev., 1969-70; editor in chief The Developing Labor Law; mem. nat. adv. bd. Berkeley Jour. Employment and Labor Law, 1980—; contbr. articles to law jours. Fellow Coll. Labor and Employment Lawyers; mem. ABA (chmn. com. on law devel. under labor

---

rels. act 1990-93, coun. mem. sect. labor and employment 1994-02). Republican. Office: Morrison & Foerster LLP 755 Page Mill Rd Palo Alto CA 94304-1018 Office Phone: 650-813-5656. Office Fax: 650-494-0792. Business E-Mail: rwheeler@mofo.com.

**WHEELER, R(ICHARD) KENNETH,** lawyer, educator; b. Washington, July 25, 1934; s. Nathaniel Dudley and Ruth Lee (Matthews) W.; m. Christine Kandris, Jan. 11, 1990; children by previous marriage: Jennifer L., Ruth E. BA, Emory and Henry Coll., U. Richmond, 1957; LLB, U. Richmond, 1964. Bar: Va. 1963, D.C. 1977, U.S. Tax Ct. 1978. Assoc., then ptnr. Hunton, Williams, Gay, Powell & Gibson and successor firms, Richmond, 1963-88; sr. ptnr. Kane, Wheeler, Fenderson & Jeffries, Richmond, 1988-90; counsel Durrette, Irvin, Lemons & Fenderson, P.C., Richmond, 1990-94; sr. ptnr. Wallace, Harris & Wheeler, Richmond, 1994-95. Adj. prof. law T.C. Williams Sch. Law, U. Richmond, 1966, 83, bd. dirs., 1977-79; adj. prof. law U. Commonwealth U., 1970; lectr. trial practice U. Va., 1981-82, 85, 87; arbitrator Am. Arbitration Assn. Served to capt. USMCR, 1957-61. Williams scholar U. Richmond, 1961-63. Mem. Am. Law Inst., Va. State Bar (chmn. com. liaison with law schs. 1977-78, chmn. com. legal edn. and admission to bar 1978-80, spcl. com. on professionalism 1987-88), Web Soc., McNeill Law Soc., Marine Corps League (life), Rector's Club (U. Richmond, life), Pi Sigma Alpha, Phi Delta Phi, Omicron Delta Kappa (hon.).

**WHEELER, RURIC E.,** mathematics professor; b. Clarkson, Ky., Nov. 30, 1923; s. Mark H. and Mary (Sullivan) Wheeler; m. Joyce Ray, May 31, 1946; children: Eddy Ray, Paul Warren. AB, We. Ky. U., 1947; MS, U. Ky., 1948, PhD, 1952. Instr. math. U. Ky., Lexington, 1948—52; asst. prof. stats. Fla. State U., 1952—53; assoc. prof. math. Samford U., 1953—55, prof., head math. dept., 1955—65, chmn. natural scis. divsn., 1965—67, asst. to dean, 1967—68; dean Howard Coll. Arts and Scis., 1968—70, v.p. acad. affairs, 1970—87, univ. prof., 1987—94, rsch. prof., 1994—. Cons. in field; dir. NSF Inst., 1961, Ala. Vis. Scientist Program, 1962—67. Author: Modern Math., 1966, 12th edit., 2005, Fundamental Concepts of Math, 1968, 2d edit., 1976, Modern Math for Business, 1969, 4th edit., 1986, A Programmed Study of Number Systems, 1972, Finite Mathematics, 1974, 3d edit., 1985, Intuitive Geometry, 1975, Introducion a los Conjuntos Numericos, 1976, Mathematics, an Everyday Language, 1979, Student Activities Manual, Elementary Mathematics, 1984, Mathematicas un Lenguaje Cotidiano, 1982, Activities Manual for Elementary School Teachers, 1988, Modern Mathematics for Elementary School Teachers, 1994, Finite Mathematics (A Problem Solving Approach), 1991, College Mathematics (a Graphing Calculator Approach), 1996, Brief Calculus (a Graphing Calculator Approach), 1996, Chinese Translation of Brief Calculus, 1997, (novels) All Because of Polly, 2002, Modern Mathematics: Fundamentals and Concepts, 2005, Modern Mathematics for Elementary Educators, 2005. Mem. Birmingham Manpower Area Planning Coun., 1972—75; trustee Gorgas Found., 1968—94, chmn., 1988—92; mem. Jefferson County Ednl. Consortium, 1981—93, pres., 1986—90; mem. Com. to Upgrade Jefferson County Schs., 1982—86; deacon Bapt. Ch. So. Conf. Deans Faculties and Acad. V.P. (pres. 1982), Am. Conf. Acad. Deans, Am. Assn. Univ. Adminstrs. (exec. com. Ala. sect. 1972—74, v.p. 1974—76, pres. 1976—77), Assn. Ala. Coll. Adminstrs. (exec. com. 1976—80, pres. 1978—79), Am. Assn. Higher Edn., Ala. Acad. Sci. (pres. 1967—69), Assn. So. Bapt. Colls. and Schs. (sec. 1973, v.p. 1974, pres. 1975, deans sect.), Assn. Math. Tchrs. Ala. (pres. 1963), Nat. Coun. Tchrs. Math., Am. Math. Assn. (chmn. SE sect. 1966—67, vis. lecture program 1989—93), Am. Math. Soc., Am. Math. Edn. Assn., Rotary (pres. of Vestavia rotary club 1983—84). Home: 1347 Badham Dr Birmingham AL 35216-2939 Office Phone: 205-726-2389. Business E-Mail: rewheele@samford.edu.

**WHEELER, SIDNEY EARL,** education educator, consultant; s. Sidney John and Lillian Ruth (Joiner) Wheeler; children: Barton E., Scott M. BS, U.S. Naval Acad., Annapolis, Md., 1962; MS, George Washington U., Washington, D.C., 1969, Naval Postgrad. Sch., Monterey, Calif., 1974; PhD, U. Fla., Gainesville, 1985; MAS, Embry Riddle Aeor. U., Daytona Beach, Fla., 2004. Cert. project mgmt. profl. Asst. prof. U. Fla., Gainesville, 1980—87; prof. Embry Riddle Aero. U., 1988—. Prin. Wheeler & Assoc., Green Cove Springs, Fla., 1983—, WND Cons., Orange Park, Fla., 1996—. Officer, pilot, surface warfare officer USN, 1957—85. Decorated various mil. awards USN. Mem.: Am. Soc. for Quality, Am. Mgmt. Assn., Project Mgmt. Inst. Avocations: fishing, shooting. E-mail: wheels63@comcast.net.

**WHEELER, STEPHEN ANTHONY,** biology educator; b. Falls Church, Va., Oct. 3, 1978; s. Laurence P. and Susie A. Wheeler. BA in Biol. Scis., U. Chgo., 2000; MS in Bio Defense, George Mason U., Fairfax, Va., 2005. Biology, chemistry tchr. Falls Ch. H.S., Va., 2000—03; asst. jr. varsity baseball coach St. Albans Sch., Washington, 2004, head jr. varsity baseball coach, 2005—, biology tchr., 2003—. Nat. honor soc. sponsor Falls Ch. H.S., 2001—03, h.s. sports announcer (voice of the jaguars), 2001—04. Mem.: Delta Kappa Epsilon (life). Office: St Albans Sch 3001 Wisconsin Ave Washington DC 20016 Office Phone: 202-537-6473. E-mail: swheeler@cathedral.org.

**WHEELER, STEPHEN FREDERICK,** legal administrator; BA in Polit. Sci., Mt. Union Coll., Alliance, Ohio, 1968; MS in Adminstrn. of Justice, Am. U., 1974. Probation officer 19th Dist. Juvenile and Domestic Rels. Ct. Prince William County, Manassas, Va., 1972-75; ct. systems planner Office of Jud. Planning Ky. Jud. Coun., Frankfort, 1975-76; co-dir. Ky. pretrial svcs. Adminstrv. Office of Cts. Ky. Ct. of Justice, Frankfort, 1976-81; ct. adminstr. Jud. Dist. 27A, Gastonia, N.C., 1982-87, Colorado Springs (Colo.) Mcpl. Ct., 1987—2005; ret. Ct. systems cons. Nat. Criminal Justice Collaborative, Sea Island, Ga., 1981-85. E-mail: stvwhlr@cs.com.

**WHEELER, STEVE DEREAL,** neurologist; b. Chgo., Sept. 15, 1951; s. Clarence and Tommie L. (Andrews) W.; m. Debra B. Buckingham; children: Winter N., Ryan S., Gabrielle S. Student, Mich. State U., 1970-73; MD, Dartmouth Coll., 1976. Diplomate Am. Bd. Psychiatry and Neurology, Nat. Bd. Med. Examiners; lic. Mich., Ohio, Fla. Intern Thomas Jefferson U., Phila., 1976-77; emergency physician River Dist. Hosp. Emergency Cons., Inc., St. Clair, Mich., 1977-78; fellow Dartmouth Med. Sch., 1978; resident U. Miami, Fla., 1978-81; fellow Washington U., St. Louis, 1981-82; instr. in neurology Med. Coll. Pa., Phila., 1982-83; electroencephalograph reader, attending neurologist VA Med. Ctr., Phila., 1982-83; asst. neurologist, attending neurologist Muscle Clinic U. Hosps. Cleve., 1983-86; electromyographer Rainbow Babies and Children's Hosp., U. Hosps. Cleve., 1983-86; chief neuromuscular diseases divsn., asst. prof. neurology Case Western Res. U., Cleve., 1983-86, co-dir. muscle disease ctr. and lab., 1985-86; clin. assoc. prof. of neurology U. Miami, 1987-89; pvt. practice Miami, 1987—; dir., co-founder Ryan Wheeler Headache Treatment Ctr., Miami, 2001—. Lectr. Myasthenia Gravis Found., Vermillion, Ohio, 1984, Cleve., 1983—86; vol. assoc. prof. U. Miami Sch., 1992—97, 2004—, vis. lectr., 1993—2001; chief headache divsn. Neurologic Ctr. for South Fla.; neurology cons. Low Back Pain Team U. Hosps. Cleve., 1984—86; mem. quality assurance com. Coral Reef Hosp., Miami, 1987—88; cons. dir. planning Bapt. Headache Clinic Bapt. Hosp., Miami, 1993—95; mem. adminstrv. com. Deering Hosp. Pain Mgmt. Ctr., Miami, 1993—94; mem. sleep diagnostic ctr. com. Bapt. Hosp., 1990—92, 1994—98, advisor to headache support group, 1995—; lectr. in field; co-founder, dir. Ryan Wheeler Headache Treatment Ctr. Author: (chpt.) Intensive Care For Neurological Trauma and Disease, 1982, (chpt.) Migraine and the Primary Headaches, 2002; mem. editl. bd.: Headache, 2001—02, ad hoc reviewer; 2000—02, Cephalalgia, 1999—, Jour. Nat. Med. Assn., 2001—, contbr. chpt.: Miscellaneous Primary Headache, 2004. Named Internat. Man Yr., 1991-92; recipient Celebration Excellence Black Achiever award Family Christian Retail Assn. Am., 1992. Fellow Royal Soc. Medicine, Am. Acad. Neurology; mem. ACP, Am. Headache Soc., So. Med. Assn. (chmn. psychiatry and neurology sect. 2000-02), Nat. Headache Found., Internat. Headache Soc., Fla. Med. Assn., Fla. Soc. Neurology, Fla. Soc. Internal Medicine, N.Y. Acad. Scis., Muscular Disease Soc. Northeastern Ohio (trustee 1984-86), Dade County Med. Assn., So. Pain Soc., Internat. Assn. Study of Pain, Dartmouth Club Greater Miami, Am. Coun. for Headache Edn.

Achievements include research in plasmapheresis in treatment of acute Guillain-Barre Syndrome; repeat neuroimaging in headache when first study normal, migraine with cluster features, hemicrania continua migraine-associated gluten sensitivity. Office: Ryan Wheeler Headache Treatment Ctr 5975 Sunset Drive Ste 501 Miami FL 33143 Office Phone: 305-661-2022.

**WHEELER, SUSIE WEEMS,** retired school system administrator; b. Cassville, Ga., Feb. 24, 1917; d. Percy Weems and Cora (Smith) Weems-Canty; m. Dan W. Wheeler Sr., June 7, 1941; 1 child, Dan Jr. BS, Fort Valley (Ga.) State U., 1945; MEd, Atlanta U., 1947, EdD, 1978; postgrad., U. Ky., 1959-60; EdS, U. Ga., 1977. Tchr. Bartow County Schs., Cartersville (Ga.) City Schs., 1938-44, Jeanes supr., 1946-58; supr., curriculum dir. Paulding Sch. Sys.-Stephens Sch., Calhoun City, 1958-64; summer sch. tchr. Atlanta U., 1961-63; curriculum dir. Bartow County Schs., 1963-79; ret., 1979. Pres., co-owner Wheeler-Morris Svc. Ctr., 1990—; mem. Ga. Commn. on Student Fin., 1985-95. Coord. Noble Hill-Wheeler Meml. Ctr. Project, 1983—. Recipient Oscar W. Canty Cmty. Svc. award, 1991, Woman in History award Fedn. Bus. and Profl. Women, 1995, New Frontiers Cmty. Svc. award, 1997, Outstanding Achievement for Preserving Georgia Hist., 2000, Life Achievement award Etowah Valley Hist. Soc., 2005; recognized for dedicated svc. on behalf of Bartow County Citizens Comm. Clarence Brown, 2003; named one of Women of Excellence, Star of the Past Bartow Women at Work, 2003. Mem. AAUW (v.p. membership 1989-91, Ga. Achievement award 1993, Edn. Found. award Cartersville-Bartow br.), Ga. Assn. Curriculum and Supervision (pres.-elect 1973-74, pres. 1974-75, Johnnye V. Cox award 1975), Delta Sigma Theta (pres. Rome alumnae chpt. 1978-80, mem. nat. bd. 1984, planning com. 1988—, Dynamic Delta award 1967, 78, Grand Chpt. cert. recognition 2002, recognition 50 plus years, Cartersville Rotary Club (Jean Harris award, 2004), Delta Sigma Theta Sorority, Inc., 2002), Ga. Jeanes Assn. (pres. 1968-70), Delta Kappa Gamma. Home: 105 Fite St Cartersville GA 30120-3410

**WHEELER, THOMAS CRAIG,** federal judge; b. Chgo., Mar. 18, 1948; married; 2 children. BA, Gettysburg Coll., 1970; JD, Georgetown U., 1973. Bar: DC, US Dist. Ct. DC, US Ct. Appeals 4th, 10th, DC, and Fed. Circuits, US Ct. Fed. Claims, US Supreme Ct. Ptnr. DLA Piper Rudnick Gray Cary (formerly Piper & Marbury), Washington, 1995—2005; judge US Ct. Fed. Claims, Washington, 2005—. Mem.: DC Bar Assn., Nat. Def. Indsl. Assn., Boards of Contract Appeals Bar Assn., ABA (pub. contract law sect., litig. sect.). Avocations: skiing, photography, writing, softball, hiking. Office: US Ct Fed Claims 717 Madison Pl NW Washington DC 20005*

**WHEELER, THOMAS EDGAR,** private equity executive; b. Redlands, Calif., Apr. 5, 1946; s. Charles Taylor and Martha (Edgar) W.; married; children: Nicole Fraser, Maxwell. BS, Ohio State U., 1968. Asst. dir. Ohio State U. Alumni Assn., Columbus, 1968-69; v.p. Grocery Mfrs. Am., Inc., Washington, 1969-76; exec. v.p. Nat. Cable TV Assn., Washington, 1976-79, pres., CEO, 1979-85, NABU: The Home Computer Network, 1985-86; chmn., CEO, NuCable Resources Corp., Washington, 1986-94; pres., CEO, Cellular Telecom. Industry Assn., Washington, 1992—2003; pres. Shiloh Group, LLC, 2003—; ptnr. Core Capital Ptnrs., 2004—. Author: Leadership Lessons from the Civil War, 1999. Bd. trustees John F. Kennedy Ctr. for Performing Arts; bd. dirs. Pub. Broadcasting Svc., Earthlink, Telephia, InPhonic; pres. Found. for Nat. Archives. Democrat. Office: Core Capital 901 15th St NW Ste 950 Washington DC 20005

**WHEELER, WARD CHRISTOPHER,** curator; b. NYC, Dec. 12, 1963; BA, Yale U., New Haven, 1985; PhD, Harvard U., Cambridge, Mass., 1988. Curator invertebrates Am. Mus. Natural History, NYC, 1989—. Contbr. more than 100 articles to profl. publs.; author books in field. Office: Am Mus Natural History-IZ Central Park West 79th St New York NY 10024-5192 Office Phone: 212-769-5754. Business E-Mail: wheeler@amnh.org.

**WHEELER, WILLIAM J.,** insurance company executive; AB, Wabash Coll., 1983; MBA, Harvard Univ. Sr. v.p. Donaldson Lufkin Jenrette, MetLife, Inc.; NYC, 1997—2003, exec. v.p., CFO, 2003—. Bd. dir. LIMRA. Trustee Wabash Coll. Mem.: Phi Beta Kappa. Office: MetLife Inc 200 Park Ave New York NY 10166*

**WHEELER, W(ILLIAM) SCOTT,** composer, conductor, music educator; b. Washington, Feb. 24, 1952; s. Malcolm Frederick and Aurora Dorothy (Anas) W.; m. Christen Struthers Frothingham, Jan. 5, 1985; children: Margaret Lee, Catherine Elizabeth. BA, Amherst Coll., 1973; MFA, Brandeis U., 1978, PhD, 1984. Artistic dir. Dinosaur Annex Music Ensemble, Boston, 1975—; dir. Cambridge (Mass.) Chorale, 1976-78; tchr. music, condr. Emerson Coll., Boston, 1978—. Composer (choral) A Babe is Born, 1979, (chamber) Winter Hills, 1987 (Somerville Arts Coun. commn.), (symphony) Northern Lights, 1987 (Koussevitzky commn.), (operas) The Construction of Boston (libretto by Kenneth Koch), 1989, Democracy, 2004, (choral) The Angle of the Sun, 1994 (Nat. Endowment for the Arts). Guggenheim fellow, 1988-89. Mem. Am. Music Ctr., ASCAP. Episcopalian. Home: 6 Sunset Ave North Reading MA 01864-1427 Office: Emerson Coll Div Performing Arts 120 Boylston St Boston MA 02116-4624 Office Phone: 617-824-8385. Business E-Mail: scott_wheeler@emerson.edu.

**WHEELER, WILMOT FITCH, JR.,** diversified manufacturing company executive; b. Southport, Conn., June 5, 1923; s. Wilmot Fitch and Hulda Day (Chapman) W.; m. Barbara Rutherford, Sept. 30, 1944 (dec. Sept. 1971); children: Wilmot Fitch III, James Alexander, John R. (dec.), Susan; m. Nonnye Landers, Dec. 20, 1973; children: Tracy Lynne, Alexa Margaret. BA, Yale U., 1945; postgrad., NYU, 1947-48; LLD honoris causa, Sacred Heart U., 1999. Staff engr. Stevenson, Jordan & Harrison, Inc. (mgmt. cons.), 1946-51; with Am. Chain & Cable Co., Inc., N.Y.C., 1951-76, pres., chmn., CEO, 1966-76; chmn., dir. Jelliff Corp., Southport, Conn., 1976—; prin. Case & Co, Inc. (mgmt cons.) 1977-83; trustee Dollar Dry Dock Savs. Bank, 1974-83, chmn., CEO, 1982-83; chmn., trustee, CEO Dollar Dry Dock Savs. Bank, 1983-84. Vice chmn., chmn., bd. dirs., CEO Manhattan Nat. Bank, 1986-90; v.p. William T. Morris Found., 1976—; bd. dirs. Am. Mut. Liability Ins. Co., 1969-89, Am. Policyholders Ins. Co., 1969-89, Am. Dist. Telegraph Co., 1968-88, Bristol Co. of Can. Ltd., 1955-76, Brit. Wire Products Ltd. (Eng.), 1955-76, Cables Automotrices, S.A. (Mexico), 1955-76, Dominion Chain Co. Ltd., 1955-76, FATA, SpA (Italy), 1975-76, Hersey Products Corp., 1976-86, Instrumentos Bristol, S.A. (Mexico), 1955-76, Manhattan Life Ins. Co., 1972-93, Arthur G. McKee & Co., 1972-79, Parsons Controls Ltd., 1955-76, People's Bank, 1988-98, People's Mut. Holdings, 1975-98, Pratt-Read Corp., 1978-85, Pujol y Tarrago S.A. (Spain), 1969-85, Sormir Petroleum, Inc., 1994-98, Union Ctrl. Life Ins. Co., 1990-93, Wilmot F. Wheeler Found., 1944—. Trustee Am. Farm Sch., 1981-93, Bridgeport Hosp., 1977-94, U. Bridgeport, 1978-88. With AUS, 1943-46. Decorated Bronze Star. Mem. Yale Club (N.Y.C.), Country Club Fairfield. Episcopalian. Home: PO Box 429 Southport CT 06490-0429 Office: Jelliff Corp PO Box 758 354 Pequot Ave Southport CT 06490-1369

**WHEELEY, NANCY JANINE,** librarian; b. Steubenville, Ohio, July 22, 1944; d. B. Otto and Kathleen Marie (Wilson) W. BA, Muskingum Coll., 1966; MLS, U. Pitts., 1967. Spl. projects libr. Miss. U. for Women, Columbus, 1967—. Mem. Lowndes County (Miss.) Rep. Exec. Com., Columbus Arts Coun. Guild, 1996—. Mem. AAUW, Am. Bus. Women's Assn. (pres. 2002-), Miss. Libr. Assn., Pilot Internat. Baptist. Avocations: Columbus pilgrimage, choral groups, politics. Office: Fant Meml Libr W-1625 Columbus MS 39701

**WHEELOCK, DOUGLAS H.,** astronaut, military officer; b. Binghamton, N.Y., May 5, 1960; s. Olin and Margaret Wheelock; m. Cathleen Hollen; 1 child. BS in Applied Sciences and Engring., U.S. Mil. Acad., West Point, N.Y., 1983; MS in Aerospace Engring, Ga. Inst. Tech., 1992. Commd 2d lt. U.S. Army, West Point, NY, 1983; student Army Aviation Schs., Ft. Rucker, Ala., 1983—84; from combat sect. leader, platoon leader, co. exec. officer, battalion ops. officer and comdr. officer Pacific Theater, Air Cavalry Troop,

9th U.S. Cavalry; advanced weapons rsch. and devel. engr. Aviation Directorate of Combat Developments, Fort Rucker, Ala.; mem. class 104 U.S. Naval Test Pilot Sch.; from exptl. test pilot to divsn. chief for fixed wing testing of airborne signal and imagery intelligence systems. U.S. Army Aviation Tech. Test Ctr., 1997—98; astronaut NASA Johnson Space Ctr., Houston, 1998—; support engr. for 5 space missions, lead engr. for 2 NASA 2000—. Crew support astronaut Internat. Space Station Expedition 2, 2001, Internat. Space Station Expedition 4, 2001—02; spacecraft communicator (CAPCOM) Mission Control Ctr., Houston, 2002; lead CAPCOM Internat. Space Station Expedition 8; NASA's dir. ops. Gagarin Cosmonaut Tng. Ctr., Star City, Russia, 2005; mission specialist STS-120 Mission to Internat. Space Station, 2006. Named Outstanding Spokesman for Freedom, VFW, 1990, Disting. Grad., U.S. Army Initial Entry Flight Tng. Course, 1984; recipient Gamble award, U.S. Naval Test Pilot Sch., 1995, Group Acheivement award, NASA, 1997, NASA Group Achievement awards: Global Positioning System, 1997, Russian Liaison Support Team, 2001, NASA Superior Accomplishment award, 2002, 2004. Mem.: Army Aviation Assn. Am., Assn. U.S. Army, Soc. Am. Military Engineers, Soc. Exptl. Test Pilots. Avocations: baseball, flying, coaching youth sports, hiking, sports. Office: Astronaut Office/CB Johnson Space Ctr Houston TX 77058*

**WHEELOCK, KEITH WARD,** retired investment company executive, educator; b. Phila., Oct. 17, 1933; s. Ward and Margot Trevor (Williams) W.; m. Susan Bowen Kimball, June 15, 1956 (div. Nov. 1975); children: Helen Fraser, James Voorhees; m. Bente Lorentzen Ott, July 1978 (div. June 1988); m. Georgia Whidden, May 17, 1997. BA, Yale U., 1955; MA, U. Pa., 1957; MS, MIT, 1972. Fgn. svc. officer Dept. State, Washington, 1960-69; dir. programs and policy divsn. N.Y.C. Housing and Devel. Adminstrn., 1970-71; devel. officer Moody's Investors Svc., Inc., N.Y.C., 1972-74, v.p. internat. ops., 1974-75, exec. v.p., 1975-76; pres. The Fantus Co., Millburn, N.J., 1976-83; mem. Sr. Dun & Bradstreet Mgmt. Group, 1979-83; prin. Wheelock Cons., 1983-88; project dir. Mng. Growth in N.J., 1986-90; assoc. prof. Raritan Valley C.C., 1992—. Rsch. asst. Fgn. Policy Rsch. Inst., U. Pa. Author: Nasser's New Egypt, A Critical Analysis, 1960, New Jersey Growth Management, 1989. Mem. Montgomery (N.J.) Twp. Com., 1986-88; pres. adv. coun. Eisenhower Exch. Fellowship. Sloan fellow MIT, 1972. Home: 325 Mountain View Rd Skillman NJ 08558-2412 E-mail: kwheelock@rcn.com.

**WHEELOCK, PAM,** financial executive; BA in History, Coll. St. Catherine; MA in Applied Econs., Marquette U. Exec. budget officer Minn. Dept. Fin., 1988—92; budget dir. City of St. Paul, 1992—94; dep. mayor, 1994—96, dir. dept. planning and econ. devel., 1996—99; commr. Minn. Dept. Fin., 1999—2002; sr. v.p., CFO Minn. Sports and Entertainment, 2002—. Office: Minn Wild 317 Washington St Saint Paul MN 55102

**WHEELON, ALBERT DEWELL,** physicist; b. Moline, Ill., Jan. 18, 1929; s. Orville Albert and Alice Geltz (Dewell) W.; m. Nancy Helen Hermanson, Feb. 28, 1953 (dec. May 1980); children: Elizabeth Anne, Cynthia Helen; m. Cicely J. Evans, Feb. 4, 1984. BSc, Stanford U., 1949; PhD, MIT, 1952. Tchg. fellow, then rsch. assoc. physics MIT, Boston, 1949-52; with Douglas Aircraft Co., 1952-53, Ramo-Wooldridge Corp., 1953-62; dep. dir. sci. and tech. CIA, Washington, 1962-66; with Hughes Aircraft Co., L.A., 1966-88, chmn., CEO, 1987-88. Vis. prof. MIT, 1989; mem. Def. Sci. Bd., 1968-76; mem. Pres.'s Fgn. Intelligence, 1983-88; mem. Presdl. Commn. on Space Shuttle Challenger Accident, 1986; trustee Aerospace Corp., 1990-93, Calif. Inst. Tech., 1985-, Rand Corp., 1993-2001. Author Electromagnetic Scintillation: Vol. 1 and 2, 2001, 03; contbr. 36 papers on radiowave propagation and guidance systems. Recipient R.V. Jones Intelligence award, 1994. Fellow IEEE, AIAA (Von Karman medal 1986, Goddard Astronautics award 1997), Am. Phys. Soc.; mem. NAE, Sigma Chi. Episcopalian. Independent. Address: 181 Sheffield Dr Montecito CA 93108-2242

**WHELAN, JAMES ROBERT,** investor, import/export company executive; b. Buffalo, July 27, 1933; s. Robert and Margaret (Southard) Whelan; m. Isabel Margarita Gomez, 2004; children from previous marriage: Robert J., Heather Elizabeth. Student U. Buffalo, 1951-53, U. R.I., 1955-57; BA, Fla. Internat. U., 1974. Staff corr. UPI, Buffalo, 1952—53, bur. mgr. Providence, 1955—57, divsn. news editor Boston, 1957—58, Latin Am. corr. Buenos Aires, 1958—61, country mgr. Caracas, Venezuela, 1961—66, divsn. mgr San Juan, PR, 1966, divsn. mgr., 1968; regional dir. corp. rels., then v.p. ops. ITT World Directories, San Juan, 1968—70; Latin Am. corr. Scripps-Howard Newspaper Alliance, Washington, 1970-71; mng. editor Miami (Fla.) News, 1971-73; free-lance writer, 1973-74; pres., editor, pub. Hialeah (Fla.) Pub. Co., 1975-77; v.p., editl. dir. Panax Corp., Washington, 1977-80; v.p., editor Sacramento Union, 1980-82; editor, pub. Washington Times, 1982-84; mng. dir. CBN News, 1985-86; pres. Capital Comm. Internat., 1986—; regional dir. PTC-internet, 1986—2001; editor-in-chief Conservative Digest, 1988-89; vice chmn. Inter-Am. Found., Arlington, Va., 1991-94; external affairs advisor Inter-Am. Investment Corp., 1992-93; dir. strategic planning Cocetel Holding, Santiago, Chile, 1993-94; pres. Minera Silver Standard S.A., 1994—, Silver Std. Resources, Mexico, 1995—2000, advisor to bd., 2001—04, advisor to pres., 2004—. Freelance writer; guest lectr. Boston U., U. Miami, Ctrl. U., Venezuela, Cath. U., Washington, Andrès Bello U., Chile, U. Chile, U. Tex., Austin, U. Concepcion, Chile, U. Santiago; guest prof. U. Fla., 1973; adj. prof. U. Md., 1992—93; vis. prof. Polit. Sci. Inst. U. Chile, 1993—95; assoc. prof. Finis Terrae U., 1993—; scholar World Assn. Internat. Studies Stanford U., 1999—; adj. scholar Inst. World Politics, Washington, 2003—. Author: Through the American Looking Glass; Central America's Crisis, 1980, Allende: Death of a Marxist Dream, 1981, Catastrophe in the Caribbean: The Failure of America's Human Rights Policy in Central America, 1984, The Soviet Assault on America's Southern Flank, 1988, Out of the Ashes: Life, Death and Transfiguration of Democracy in Chile, 1833-1988, 1989, Hunters in the Sky, 1991, Desde las Cenizas: Vida, Muerte y Transfiguracion de la Democracia en Chile, 1833-1988, 1993, 2nd edit., 1995. Del dir. Christian Community Service Agy., Miami, 1973, Hialeah-Miami Springs (Fla.) C. of C., 1976-77, Wolf Trap Found., 1984-87; bd. dirs. Nat. Council for Better Edn.; chmn. print media div. United Way campaign, Sacramento, 1981; bd. govs. Council on Nat. Policy, Washington, 1981-87; del. Commn. of Californias, 1981; chmn. Council for Inter-Am. Security Ednl. Inst., 1986-90; mem. spl. task force on pub. safety Greater Washington Bd. Trade; mem. Nat. Commn. on Free and Responsible Media, 1983-84; bd. dir. Nat. Bus. Consortium for Gifted and Talented Children, 1985-87; bd. govs. Internat. Policy Forum, 1985—; mem. Presdl. Bd. Fgn. Scholarships (Fulbright Commn.), 1986-92, exec. planning com., 1987-92. With Signal Corps U.S. Army, 1953-55. Nieman fellow Harvard U., 1966-67; recipient citation of excellence Overseas Press Club, 1971, Unity award Lincoln U., 1976, Golden Press award Am. Legion Aux., 1977, Freedom award Valley Forge Found., 1981, Bernardo O'Higgins award Chilean Govt., 1990, presented at Chilean Embassy by Amb. Octavio Errazuriz. Mem.: Instituto O'Higginiano de Chile, Harvard Club (N.Y.C.), Cosmos Club, Georgetown Club. Office Phone: (56-2) 246-3061. E-mail: jamesrwhelan@hotmail.com.

**WHELAN, JOHN JOSEPH,** education educator; b. Cleve., May 2, 1942; s. Thomas Patrick and Margaret Mary (Geddes) W; children: Sean Joseph, Thomas Gordon. BA, John Carroll U., 1965; MS, Case Western Res. U., 1970. Cert. K-8 tchr., elem. prin., Ohio. Tchr. 7th, 8th and 12th grades St. Francis Schs., Cleve., 1965-67; tchr. 6th grade Prospect Elem. Sch., East Cleveland, Ohio, 1967-69; prin. Chambers Elem. Sch., East Cleveland, 1969-90; fellow in urban edn., asst. prof. edn. John Carroll U., University Heights, Ohio, 1991—. Instr. John Carroll U., 1987, 88; apptd. peer reviewer and adv. office Ednl. Rsch. and Improvement, 1988; panelist Chpt. 1 Nat. Program Unusually Successful Programs the Serve Disadvantaged Youth, 1988; mem. review panel Am. Educators since a Nation at Risk, 1988; mem. Whitman Award panel 1989-90, urban concersn com. Ohio Assn. Elem. Sch. Adminstrs., 1990; adv. bd. John Carroll Profl. Devel. Ctr. for Adminstrs. and Tchrs., 1990, Greater Cleved. Mental Devel. Ctr., 1991; ednl. cons. Scholarship-in-Escrow, Cleve. 1990-91; mem. parental involvement task force Cleve. Summit on Edn., 1990; spk. numerous confs. and events including Goshen (Ind.) H.S., IRA Plains Conf., S.D., Ontario Sch. Dist.,

Oreg. NAESD, San Francisco, Minn. Sch. Bds. Assn., 1990, Parent Tng. Inst., 1990, Pa. Sch. Bds. Assn., 1990, Met. Sch. Dist., 1990, Warrick County Sch. Corp., 1991, Minn. Elem. Prin. Assn., 1991, Ill. Renewal Inst., Saratoga Springs, N.Y., 1991, Ednl. Commn. States Nat. Forum, Denver, 1991, U. Calif., Santa Cruz., 1991, Big Springs Sch. Dist., Pa., 1991, Nat. Assn. Elem. Sch. Prins., 1992, Nat. Prins. Meeting, San Diego, 1994, Archdiocese of Denver, N.D. Reading Assn., Reading Assn. of Ireland, Dublin, Bottineau Pub. Schs. in N.D., Baldwin Coll., Cleve., NAESP, Orlando, San Diego; sr. cons. Natl. Sch. Conf. Inst./Learning 24/7, Phoenix, 2003. Bd. trustees John Carroll U.; life mem. Ohio PTA. Named Nat. Disting. Prin. Ohio, U.S. Dept. Edn., 1988-89; recipient Educator's award United Black Fund, Cleve., 1987, Ednl. Excellence award Urban League Greater Cleve., 1987, Recognition award Rotary Club Cleve., 1987. Mem. NAESP (Nat. Disting. Prin. award 1988), ASCD, Nat. Assn. for Schs. Excellence, John Carroll U. Alumni Assn. (pres. Cleve. 1992, recipient Alumni medal 1986), Phi Delta Kappa (v.p. 1986-87). Roman Catholic. Avocations: skiing, golf, jogging. Home: 344 E 276th St Euclid OH 44132-1304 Office: John Carroll U Dept Edn 20700 N Park Blvd Dept Edn University Heights OH 44118-4581

**WHELAN, JOHN WILLIAM,** law educator; b. Cleve., Apr. 23, 1922; s. Walter Edmund and Stacia Miriam Whelan; m. Maryrose Shields, May 29, 1947; children: Moira Ann Whelan Dykstra, Thomas M. AB, John Carroll U., 1943; JD, Georgetown U., 1948. Assoc. prof. law Columbus U., Washington, 1948-50; asst. prof. U. Va., Charlottesville, 1955-56; assoc. prof. U. Wis., Madison, 1956-59; prof. Georgetown U., Washington, 1959-67, U. Calif., Davis, 1967-75, Hastings Coll. Law U. Calif., San Francisco, 1975-91, prof. emeritus, 1991—. Mem. atomic energy com. Bd. Contract Appeals, 1965—73; cons. to atty. gen. Trust Ter. Pacific Island, 1976—78, adminstrn. law judge constrn. contracts, 1984—86; hearing examiner Medi Cal Fiscal Intermediary Contract, 1979—82; vis. prof. Nihon U. Coll. Law, Tokyo, 1989; cons. to govt. contracts to Govt. of Poland, 92. Author (with R. S. Pasley): (book) Federal Government Contracts, 1975; author: (with K. H. York) Insurance, 1983, 2d edit., 1988, Federal Government Contracts, 1985, 2d edit., 2002; author: (with James F. Nagle) Supplement, 1989; author: Understanding Government Contracts, 1994; author: (with K. H. York, Leo Martinez) Insurance, 4th edit., 2001; editor: Yearbook of Procurement Articles, 1965—90; mem. editl. bd. Pub. Procurement Law Rev., 1991—; contbr. articles to profl. jours. Served with U.S. Army, 1943—45, with JAG U.S. Army, 1950—55, ret., 1982. Decorated Bronze Star; Ford Found. grantee, 1958—59, 1963—64, 1970. Mem.: ABA, Fed. Cir. Bar Assn., Bds. Contract Appeals Bar Assn., Nat. Contract Mgmt. Assn., DC Bar Assn., Fed. Bar Assn. Home: 306 Bristol Pl Mill Valley CA 94941-4005 Office: U Calif Hastings Coll Law 200 Mcallister St San Francisco CA 94102-4707 Personal E-mail: jww4037@msn.com.

**WHELAN, JOSEPH L.,** neurologist; b. Chisholm, Minn., Aug. 13, 1917; s. James Gorman and Johanna (Quilty) W.; m. Gloria Ann Howard, June 12, 1948; children: Joe, Jennifer. Student, Hibbing Jr. Coll., 1935-38; BS, U. Minn., 1940, MB, 1942, MD, 1943. Diplomate Am. Bd. Psychiatry and Neurology. Intern Detroit Receiving Hosp., 1942-43; fellow neurology U. Pa. Hosp., Phila., 1946-47; resident neurology U. Minn. Hosps., Mpls., 1947-49; chief neurology svc. VA Hosp., Mpls., 1949; spl. fellow electroencephalography Mayo Clinic, Rochester, Minn., 1951; practice medicine specializing in neurology Detroit, 1949-73, Petoskey and Gaylord, Mich., 1973-87; asst. prof. Wayne State U., 1957-63. Chief neurology svcs. Grace Hosp., St. John's Hosp., Bon Secour Hosp., Detroit; cons. neurologist No. Mich. Hosps., Charlevoix Area Hosp.; instr. Med. Sch. U. Minn., 1949; cons. USPHS, Detroit Bd. Edn. Contbr. articles to profl. jours. Founder, mem. ad hoc Com. to Force Lawyers Out of Govt. Fellow Am. Acad. Neurology (treas. 1955-57), Am. Electroencephalography Soc.; mem. AMA, AAAS, Assn. Rsch. Nervous and Mental Diseases, Soc. Clin. Neurologists, Mich. Neurol. Assn. (sec.-treas. 1967-76, Disting. Physician award 1988), Mich. Med. Soc., No. Mich. Med. Soc., Grosse Pointe (Mich.) Club. Address: 9797 N Twin Lake Rd NE Mancelona MI 49659-9203

**WHELAN, RICHARD J.,** retired academic administrator; b. Emmett, Kans., June 23, 1931; s. Richard Joseph and Margaret Alma (Cox) W.; m. Carol Ann King, Nov. 21, 1959; children— Mark Richard, Cheryl Lynne BA, Washburn U., 1955; Ed.D., U. Kans., 1966. Dir. edn. Menninger Clinic, Topeka, 1959-62; dir. edn. children's rehab. unit U. Kans. Med. Ctr., Kansas City, Kans., 1966—2000; prof. spl. edn. and pediatrics, chmn. dept. spl. edn. U. Kans., Lawrence, 1966-72, 78-80, 83-88, assoc. dean grad. studies and outreach, 1988-94, Ralph L. Smith disting. prof. child devel., 1968—2000, dean sch. edn., 1992-94, prof. emeritus, 2000—; div. dir. U.S. Office Edn., Washington, 1972-74; cons. Blue Valley Sch. Dist., Overland Park, Kans., 2000—; complaint investigator Kans. Bd. of Edn., 2000—. Cons. colls. and univs., state and fed. agys.; chmn. policy bd. Evaluation Tng., Kalamazoo, 1975-81 Author, editor: Promising Practices..., 1983, Emotional and Behavioral Disorders, 1998; cons. editor Ednl. Research Ency., 1982; contbr. articles to profl. jours., chpts. to books Chmn. adv. bd. Kans. Bd. Edn., Topeka, 1982-92; mem. adv. bd. Shawnee Mission Sch. Dist., Kans., 1984-92; mem. Gov.'s Task Force on Early Childhood, 1984-92; hearing officer various sch. dists. Kans. Bd. Edn., Bur. Indian Affairs; mediator and trainer Kans. Supreme Ct Mem. Soc. for Learning Disabilities (pres. 1980-81), Council for Exceptional Children, Assn. for Persons with Severe Handicaps (bd. dirs. 1975-79), Kans. Council for Exceptional Children (pres. 1963-64, Service award 1978, award for excellence 2000), Phi Kappa Phi Avocations: reading, music, golf, flying. Home: 7400 West 148th St Overland Park KS 66223 E-mail: rwhelan@kumc.edu.

**WHELAN, ROGER MICHAEL,** lawyer, educator; b. Montclair, N.J., Nov. 12, 1936; s. John Leslie and Helen Louise (Callahan) W.; m. Rosemary Bogdan, Aug. 26, 1961; children: Helen, Theresa, John, James, Kathleen (dec.), Julie, Jennifer. AB cum laude, Georgetown U., 1959, JD, 1962. Bar: DC 1962, US Dist. Ct. DC 1962, US Ct. Appeals (DC cir.) 1962, US Supreme Ct. 1968. Assoc. Fried, Rogers & Ritz, Washington, 1961—66; ptnr. Doctor & Whelan, Washington, 1967—72; judge U.S. Bankruptcy Ct., Washington, 1972—83; sr. mem. Verner, Liipfert, Bernhard, McPherson & Hand, Chartered, Washington, 1984—89; ptnr., sr. counsel Shaw, Pittman, Potts & Trowbridge, Washington, 1989—2000; outside counsel to several Washington & Md. law firms, 2000—; resident scholar Am. Bankruptcy Inst., 2004. Dir. Lincoln Ctr. for Legal Studies, Arlington, Va., 1974-84; disting. lectr. Columbus Sch. Law, Cath. U. Am., Washington, 1975—; bd. govs. Conf. on Consumer Fin. Law, 1995-2005; resident scholar Am. Bankruptcy Inst., 2004. Sec. local campaign com., Alexandria, Va., 1984; trustee YMCAA, Silver Spring, Md., 1972-74. Recipient award DC Cir. Jud. Conf., 1984. Fellow: Am. Coll. Bankruptcy (bd. regents 1989—95, bd. dirs. 1995—2002); mem.: FBA (chmn. bankruptcy subcom. 1988, exec. com. 1993—96, pres. 1999—2000), Assn. Former Bankruptcy Judges (sec.-treas. 1996—), Am. Bankruptcy Inst. (bd. dirs. 1991—97, chmn. legis. com. 1991—99, exec. com. 1993—95, apptd. resident scholar 2004), Walter Chandler Inn of Ct. (master emeritus 1990—). Republican. Roman Catholic. Avocations: fishing, hunting, boating. Home: 17908 Ednor View Ter Ashton MD 20861-9757 Office Phone: 301-260-7707. Personal E-mail: rmwhelan@comcast.net.

**WHELAN, STEPHEN THOMAS, JR.,** lawyer; b. Phila., July 28, 1947; s. Stephen Thomas and Virginia King (Ball) W.; m. Elizabeth Ann Murphy, Apr. 3, 1971; children: Christine B. Whelan. BA magna cum laude, Princeton U., 1968; JD, Harvard U., 1971. Bar: N.Y. 1972, U.S. Dist. Ct. (so. dist.) N.Y. 1975. Assoc. Mudge Rose Guthrie & Alexander, NYC, 1971-75, Thacher Proffitt & Wood, NYC, 1975-77; ptnr. Thacher Proffitt & Wood LLP, NYC, 1978—, exec. com., 1982—88, 2003—05, chmn. corp. dept., 1992-97; lectr. politics dept. Princeton U., 1999—. Author: New York's Uniform Commercial Code Article 2A, 1994, The ABCs of the UCC: Article 2A (Leases), 1997, The ABCs of the UCC: Amended Article 2A, 2005; contbr. articles to profl. jours. Bd. dir. Atlantic Legal Found., 1997—; active N.Y. County Rep. Com., 1985—; active Princeton U. Alumni Coun., 1993—; trustee The Cloister Inn of Princeton U., 1996—; mem. adv. coun. James Madison program, 2000-. Fellow Am. Coll. Investment Counsel; mem. ABA (chmn. subcom. on leasing 1994-04), N.Y. State Bar Assn., Equipment Leasing Assn. Am. (fed. govt.

rels. com. 1992-97, legal com. 1995-97), S.R. (bd. dir. NY 1979—). Roman Catholic. Avocations: road racing, secondary school students mentor, golf. Office Phone: 212-912-7654. Business E-Mail: SWhelan@tpw.com.

**WHELAN, SUSAN,** former Canadian government official; b. Windsor, Ont., Can., May 5, 1963; d. Elizabeth and Eugene Whelan. Degree in commerce, U. Windsor, B in Laws, 1988; JD, U. Detroit. Bar: Ont. 1990. Assoc. Yuffy, Roberts, Goldstein, Manzocco, Windsor, 1988-93; M.P. for Essex-Windsor House of Commons, 1993—2004, parliamentary sec. to Min. Nat. Revenue, 1993-96, mem. standing com. pub. accouts, 1994-96, assoc. mem. standing com. on fin., 1994-96, vice chair fin. com., 1996-97, mem. justice subcom. on draft regulations on firearms, 1996-97, mem. subcom. on rev. of spl. import measures act, 1996, chair industry com., 1997—2002, min. internal cooperation, 2002—03. Former dir. Essex Region Conservation Found., Alzheimer Soc. Windsor and Essex County. Named "Hon. Susan E. Whelan", Minister for Internat. Coop., 2002. Mem. Law Soc. Upper Can., Can. Bar Assn., Essex County Law Assn.

**WHELAN, WILLIAM J., III,** lawyer; b. NYC, Apr. 29, 1959; BA with distinction, Univ. Va., 1980; JD cum laude, Fordham Univ., 1983. Bar: NY 1984. Law clk., Hon. William H. Timbers US Ct. of Appeals, 2nd Cir.; assoc. Cravath Swaine & Moore LLP, NYC, 1984—90, sr. atty., 1990—98, ptnr., corp., 1998—. Mng. editor Fordham Law Rev. Mem.: ABA, Assn. Bar City NY (securities regulation com.). Office: Cravath Swaine & Moore LLP Worldwide Plz 825 Eighth Ave New York NY 10019-7475 Office Phone: 212-474-1644. Office Fax: 212-474-3700. Business E-Mail: wwhelan@cravath.com.

**WHELCHEL, BUTCH E.,** agricultural studies educator; b. Pawhuska, Okla., Feb. 21, 1949; s. Arvel Elton and Ida Mae Whelchel; m. Lynnette Jane Shipley, July 26, 1975; children: Bo Hunter, Jed Leo. BS in Agrl. Edn., Okla. State U., 1971. Tchr. Jennings (Kans.) HS, 1971—75, Pratt (Kans.) HS, 1975—76, Jetmore (Kans.) HS, 1976—80, Kensington (Kans.) HS, 1988—; pvt. practice Deway, Okla., 1988—. Coach meats team Future Farmers Am., 1988—, coach entomology teams, 1988—. Mem.: Kans. Assn. Agr. Educators (mem. state agr. edn. inservice 1998—). Avocation: hunting. Office: RR 1 Box 14 Gaylord KS 67638-9731

**WHELCHEL, SANDRA JANE,** writer; b. Denver, May 31, 1944; d. Ralph Earl and Janette Isabelle (March) Everitt; m. Andrew Jackson Whelchel, June 27, 1965; children: Andrew Jackson, Anita Earlyn. BA in Elem. Edn., U. No. Colo., 1966; postgrad., Pepperdine Coll., 1971, UCLA, 1971. Elem. tchr. Douglas County Schs., Castle Rock, Colo., 1966-68, El Monte (Calif.) schs., 1968-72; br. libr. Douglas County Librs., Parker, Colo., 1973-78; zone writer Denver Post, 1979-81; reporter The Express newspapers, Castle Rock, 1979-81; history columnist Parker Trail newspapers, 1985-93; columnist Authorship Mag., 1991—; Gothic Jour., 1994; writing tchr. Aurora Parks and Recreation, 1985-91; writing instr. Arapahoe C.C., 1991-2000; exec. dir. Nat. Writers Assn., 1991—. Lectr. on writing and history Durango Writer's Workshop, 1996-97, Estes Park Writer's Retreat, 1996-97, Pikes Peak Writer's Workshop, 1997, Sinipee Writer's Workshop, 1998, Oasis for Seniors, 2000, Denver Women's Press Club, 1999, Rocky Mountain Gold Conf., 1999, Colo. Writers Fellowship, 2000, Colo. Ind. Publishers, 2000; spkr. Internat. Olympiad of Mind, Paris, 2000, Art Cafe, 2003; motivational spkr. various Optomist groups in Denver area; hist. tours, Parker, Colo. Editor Authorship mag., 1992-98; lit. agent NWLA, 1996-99; contbr. short stories and articles to various publs. including: The Writer, Writer's Open Forum, Writer's Jour., Reunions, Fresno Bee, Ancestry Newsletter, Calif. Horse Rev., Jack and Jill, Child Life, Children's Digest, Peak to Peak mag.; author (non-fiction books): Your Air Force Academy, 1982, A Guide to the U.S. Air Force Acad., 1990, Parker, Colorado: A Folk History, 1990, The Beginning Writer's Writing Book, 1996, A Folk History of Parker and Hilltop, 1996; co-author: The Writer's Office, 1998, Writing for Beginners, 2006, The Register, 1989, (coloring books) A Day at the Cave, 1985, A Day in Blue, 1984, Pro Rodeo Hall of Champions and Museum of the American Cowboy, 1985, Pikes Peak Country, 1986, Mile High Denver, 1987, (novel) Hide & Seek, 2006; contbr. chpts. to books Mem.: Nat. Writers Assn. (pres. 1990, 1991, 2003—04), Colo. Author's League (awards com. 1999—2000, who's who com. 2001), Parker Area Hist. Soc. (pres. 1987—89), Nat. Writer's Club (treas. Denver Metro chpt. 1985—86, v.p. membership 1987, sec. 1990, bd. dirs., pres. 1990—91, v.p. programs 1992, v.p. membership 2002, bd. dirs., pres. 2003). Office Phone: 303-841-0246. *Personal philosophy: Tenacity and perseverance are keys to success. Optimism and self-belief open the door. The goals achieved through these elements are the most thrilling and savory.*

**WHELDEN, CRAIG B.,** retired army officer; b. Ind., Oct. 8, 1951; m. Karen Lusk; children: Scott, Holly. BA, Purdue U.; MA, Webster U. Commd. 2d lt. U.S. Army, 1973, advanced through grades to maj. gen.; comdr. 98th area Support Group, Wuerzburg, Germany, 1994-95; chief of staff 3d Inf. Divsn., 1995-96; dep. dir. for ops. Nat. Mil. Command Ctr., Pentagon, Washington, 1996-98; comdg. gen. Cmty. and Family Support Ctr., Alexandria, Va., 1998—2000; dep. comdr. U.S. Army Pacific, Ft. Shafter, Hawaii, 2000—04; ret.; ind. sales assoc. Pre-Paid Legal Svcs., Inc., Celebration, Fla. Bd. mem. World Trade Ctr.-Orlando, Army's Morale, Welfare and Recreation Exec. Com. Decorated Legion of Merit, Army Commendation medal, others. Home and Office: 1250 Celebration Ave Celebration FL 34747

**WHELESS, JAMES WARREN,** neurologist; b. Glens Falls, NY, Apr. 18, 1956; s. True and Adelphine Ada (Bump) Wheless; m. Annette Carolyn Hyland, Apr. 7, 1984; children: Catherine Elizabeth, Margaret Caroline. BS, U. Okla., Oklahoma City, 1978, MD, 1982. Diplomate Am. Bd. Pediatrics, Am. Bd. Psychiatry and Neurology, Am. Bd. Clin. Neurophysiology. Intern, then pediatric resident U. Okla.-Tulsa Med. Coll., 1982-85; fellow in child neurology Northwestern U., Chgo., 1985-88; fellow in clin. neurophysiology/epilepsy Med. Coll. Ga., Augusta, 1988-89; asst. prof. neurology and pediatrics U. Tex., Houston, 1989-95, dir. epilepsy monitoring unit, 1989—2005, assoc. prof. neurology and pediatrics, 1995-2000, prof. neurology and pediats., 2000—05; dir. pediat. epilepsy sect., head clin. EEG, dir., co-founder Tex. Comprehensive Epilepsy Program, 1998—2005; prof. neurology and pediat., chief pediat. neurology, LeBonheur chair in pediatric neurology U. Tenn. Health Sci. Ctr., 2005—. Dir. LeBonheur Comprehensive Epilepsy Program; dir. Neurosci. Inst. LeBonheur Children's Med. Ctr.; clin. chief,dir. pediat. neurology St. Jude Children's Rsch. Hosp., Memphis. Contbr. articles to profl. jours., chapters to books; mem. editl. bd. Jour. Child Neurology, Formulary. Camp physician Kamp Kleidoscope, Livingston, Tex., 1995—2005; exec. bd. internat. epilepsy consortium Nat. Tuberous Sclerosis Assn., mem. profl. bd.; Citizens United Rsch. Epilepsy. Pres.'s Fund grantee, U. Tex., Houston, 1990, Children's Miracle Network Telethon grantee, Hermann Children's Hosp., Rsch. grantee, NIH. Fellow: Child Neurology Soc., Am. Acad. Neurology; mem.: AMA, Epilepsy Assn. Houston/Gulf Coast (chmn. profl. adv. bd. 1992—94), Am. Acad. Pediat., Am. Epilepsy Soc. Avocations: running, camping, writing, travel, reading. Office: UTHSC Pediatric Neurology 777 Washington Ave P250 Memphis TN 38105 Office Phone: 901-287-5207. Business E-Mail: jwheless@utmem.edu.

**WHELIHAN, ALAN STUART,** real estate developer, automotive executive; b. Phila., Sept. 17, 1932; s. John Franklin and Dorothy Dodge W.; m. Joan Murrell, June 20, 1959; children: Pamela, Deborah, Linda, Jacqueline. BS in Engring., Princeton U., 1954; MBA, U. Pa., 1960. Elect. engr. Philco Corp., Phila., 1954-55; product line mgr. govt. and indsl. divsn. RCA, Camden, NJ, 1959-65; gen. mgr. Chem. Micromilling Co., Pensauken, NJ, 1965-66; mgmt. cons. Peat Marwick Mitchell & Co., Washington, NJ, 1966-72; asst. commr. Fed. Supply Svc., Arlington, Va., 1973-79; dir. planning and coordination U.S. Metric Bd., Arlington, Va., 1979-82; dir. metric program U.S. Dept. Commerce, Washington, 1983-94; pres. VAW, LLC, Frederick, Md., 1994—, W Properties, L.L.C., Frederick, 1994. Dir. Am. Nat. Stds. Inst., 1973-75, Am. Nat. Metric Coun., Washington, 1990-92; consumer adv. coun. Underwriters Labs., 1974—; adv. coun. Alcoa Eastalco Works, 2002-2006. Lt. Comdr. USNR, 1955-57. Mem. IEEE (life), Soc. Automotive Engrs. (metric adv. bd.

1990—), Congl. Country Club. Republican. Avocation: collecting antique automobiles. Office: W Properties LLC Stanford Indsl Park 4975 Winchester Blvd Frederick MD 21703-7400 Home: PO Box 221 Adamstown MD 21710-0221

**WHELPLEY, DENNIS PORTER,** lawyer; b. Mpls., Feb. 16, 1951; s. John Olsen and Harriet Marie (Porter) W.; m. Patricia Jan Adamy, Nov. 27, 1976; children: Heather Nicolle, Christopher Eric. BA, U. Minn., 1973, JD magna cum laude, 1976. Bar: Minn. 1976. Assoc. Oppenheimer Wolff & Donnelly, St. Paul, 1976-83, ptnr., 1983—. Mem. Order of Coif (Minn. chpt.), Phi Beta Kappa (Alpha of Minn. chpt.), Psi Upsilon (Mu chpt.), Dellwood Hills Golf & Country Club. Avocations: golf, tennis, squash, bridge. Home: 49 Locust St Mahtomedi MN 55115-1542 Office: Oppenheimer Wolff & Donnelly 45 S 7th St Ste 3300 Minneapolis MN 55402-1614 Office Phone: 612-607-7397. Business E-Mail: dwhelpley@oppenheimer.com.

**WHELTLE, MARGARET MAIE,** retired secondary school educator; b. Balt., Oct. 19, 1934; d. Albert F. and Ruth (Morse) Wheltle. BA, Mt. St. Agnes Coll., Balt., Md., 1956; JD, U. Md., 1959; postgrad., Loyola Evening Coll. Balt., 1960—61, Cath. U. Am., Wash., DC, 1967—69; STM, St. Mary's Sem. and U. Balt., 1972. Bar: Md. 1959, U.S. Supreme Ct. 1969. Assoc. Harley Wheltle Victor & Rosser, Balt., 1959—64; asst. to pres., dir. devel. TV prodn. coord. Mt. St. Agnes Coll., Balt., 1964—67; coord. religious edn. St. Agnes Roman Cath. Congregation, Inc., Balt., 1971—74; lectr. theology Mount de Sales Acad., Balt., 1978—85, chair religion dept., 1979—85, trustee, 1979—82, ret., 1986. Instr., dir. theology dept. and bus. law dept. Harmony Hill H.S., Watertown, SD, 1969—70; lectr. St. Martin's Home for Aged, 1975; mem. spkrs. bur. Howard County Right to Life, Birthright of Md., Archdiocese of Balt. Pres. nat. alumnae Mt. St. Agnes Coll., 1961—65, mem. pres.'s coun., 1961—67; pres. Corban Corp., 1986—89; vice-chair Birthright of Md., 1975—76; co-founder, bd. chair St. Martin's Home for Aged Ladies Aux., 1973—76, bd. dirs.; adv. St. Martin's Home for Aged, 1977—80, Little Sisters of Poor, 1977—80, mem. Jeanne Jugan Assn. 2003—06; mem. pub. rels. com. Archdiocese of Balt., 1975—76; v.p. parish coun. St. Mark Roman Cath. Ch., Catonsville, Md., 1986—87, pres. parish coun., 1987—88; mem. west county regional coun. Archdiocese of Balt., 1986—90; liaison Bd. Christian Formation, 1987—90; mem. sch. bd., chairperson devel. com. Resurrection-St. Paul Sch., 2001—04; sodality prefect St. William of York, Balt., 1965—67, mem. parish planning team for total Christian edn., 1971, mem. total parish edn. com., 1975—76, instr. adult edn., 1976, mem. nat. catechism directory com., 1977. Recipient Cert. of Appreciation, Archdiocese Balt., 1981, Mount de Sales Acad., 1982. Mem.: Order of Malta. Home and Office: 2823 Country Ln Ellicott City MD 21042-2566

**WHERRY, ROBERT ALLEN, JR.,** federal judge, lawyer; b. Langley Field, Va., Apr. 7, 1944; s. Robert Allen and Lorene Fletcher (Ivy) W.; m. Leslie Anne Ross, June 23, 1943; children: Richard Washburn, Marsha Ivy. Student, Ohio State U., 1962-63; BS, U. Colo., 1966, JD, 1969; LLM in Taxation, NYU, 1972. Bar: Colo. 1969, U.S. Dist. ct. (fed. dist.) 1969, U.S. Tax Ct. 1973, U.S. Ct. Appeals (10th cir.) 1976, U.S. Ct. Claims, 1978, U.S. Ct. Appeals (fed. cir.) 1991, U.S. Supreme Ct. 1992. Constrn. laborer EBY Constrn. Co., Denver, 1965; acct. CF&I Steele, Pueblo, Colo., 1966; jr. acct. Ernst & Ernst, Denver, 1967-69; tax analyst Colo. Atty. Gen. Office (Inheritance Tax Divsn.), Denver, 1972; atty. Lentz, Evans & King P.C., Denver, 1973—; judge US Tax Ct., Wash., 2003—. Spkr. continuing edn. U. Denver, Tulane U. Tax Inst., Colo. Soc. CPA's, Englewood, 1984—; corr. State Tax Notes, Tax Analysts, Arlington, Va., 1991—. Tax coun. Colo. Assn. Commerce & Industry, 1987—; mem. Colo. Dept. Revenue Adv. Com., 1989-82, 89-90, Denver Mayor's Tax Com., Denver, 1992-93. With U.S. Army, 1970-71. Fellow Am. Coll. Tax Counsel (regent); mem. ABA (former chmn. administrv. practice com. tax sect.), Colo. Bar Assn. (tax sect., chmn. 1981-82), Greater Denver Tax Counsel (chmn. 1986.) Republican. Methodist. Avocations: bridge, chess. Office: US Tax Ct 400 Second St NW Washington DC 20217

**WHETSELL, PAUL W.,** hotel executive; Grad.. Davidson Coll. Various positions to v.p. Quality Inns; v.p. devel. Lincoln Hotels, Dallas; founder, chmn., pres., CEO CapStar Hotel Co., Washington, 1987—; chmn. & CEO MeriStar Hotels & Resorts, Inc., MeriStar Hospitality Corp, Washington, D.C. Bd. dirs. Cystic Fibrosis Found. of Nat. Capitol Area; bd. govs. Marriott Hospitality H.S. NAREIT. Office: Meristar Hospitality Corp #800 4501 Fairfax DR Arlington VA 22203-1656 Fax: 202-295-2230.

**WHETSTONE, JONI LEE,** music educator; b. Cumberland, Md., July 25, 1955; d. John Moyer and Eleanor Mae Shambach; 1 child, Leanna Lynn. MusB in Edn., Lee U., 1977; MusM, Ind. U. Pa., 1982. Instr. vocal music Everett (Pa.) Area Jr. Sr. H.S., 1983—. Lectr. music Pa. State U., Altoona, Pa., 1986—; instr. vocal music Everett (Pa.) Christian Academy, 1977—78, 1980—83; dir. music First Evang. Luth. Ch., Altoona, 1987—89. Named Claes Nobel Educator Distinction, Nat. Soc. H.S. Scholars, 2004. Mem.: NEA, Pa. State Educators Assn., Am. Choral Dirs. Assn., Pa. Music Educators Assn., Music Educators Nat. Conf. Republican. Home: PO Box 1495 Altoona PA 16603 Office: Everett Area Jr Sr High Sch 1 Renaissance Cir Everett PA 15537-1406 Office Phone: 814-652-9114 1302. Business E-Mail: jwhetstone@everett.k12.pa.us.

**WHETTEN, JOHN D.,** food products executive; b. Chgo., June 8, 1940; s. Lester and Kate (Allred) Whetten; m. Becky Pearse; children: Carma, Rebecca, Mary Coza. BS, Brigham Young U., 1965; MBA, U. Calif., Berkeley, 1967. Advt. and mktg. mgr. The Clorox Corp., Oakland, Calif., 1967-79; pres. CEO Challenge Dairy Products, Inc., Dublin, Calif., 1982—; CEO DairyAmerica, Inc., Dublin, Calif., 1995-98. U.S. rep. Internat. Dairy Mktg. and Promotion Ann. Meeting, 1996. Co-chair U.S. Butter Task Force, 1990—97; bd. dirs. Epidermolysis Bullosa Med. Rsch. Found., 1991—, U.S. Dairy Export Coun., 1995—98; mem. nat. steering com. Brigham Young U. Sch. Mgmt., 1992—95; mem. nat. adv. coun. Utah Valley State Coll., 2001—. Recipient Disting. Svc. award, Brigham Young U. Sch. Mgmt., 2005. Mem.: Western Assn. Milk Mktg. Coop. (bd. dirs. 1992—2002, sec. 1994—2002), Barbecue Industry Assn. (dir. 1974—79, pres. 1977—78), Dairy Mktg. Coop. Fedn. (pres. 1992—), Dairy Export Incentive Program Coalition (pres. 1994—), Am. Dairy Products Inst. (bd. dirs. 1982—, mem. hof. life dir. 1999—), Am. Butter Inst. (bd. dirs. 1982—, v.p. 1995—99, pres. 1999—2001, Pres.'s Disting. Svc. award 1991). Office: Challenge Dairy Products Inc 11875 Dublin Blvd Ste B230 Dublin CA 94568-2818 E-mail: john@challengedairy.com.

**WHETTEN, LAWRENCE L.,** international relations educator; b. Provo, Utah, June 12, 1932; s. Lester B. and Kate (Allred) W.; m. Gabriele Indra, Oct. 28, 1974 (dec. May 1985). BA, Brigham U., 1954, MA, 1955; PhD with honors, NYU, 1963. Sr. polit. analyst Hdqrs. USAFE, Wiesbaden, Fed. Republic Germany, 1963-70; resident dir. grad. program in internat. relations U. So. Calif., Munich, Fed. Republic Germany, 1971-78, dir. studies USC/SIR grad. program in Germany, 1978-86; Erich Voegelin Gast prof. Munich U., 1987-88; lectr. Boston U., 1988—; lectr. Profl. Assoc. Ctr. Def. and Strategic Studies S.W. Mo. State U., Springfield, 1991—. Cons. Fgn. Policy Inst., Phila. 1969-71, 76-79, R & D Assocs., Munich, 1977; prof. Hochschule für Politik, Munich U.; adj. prof., profl. assoc. Ctr. for Def. and Strategic Studies, S.W. Mo. State U., 1991—. Author: Germany's Ostpolitik, 1971, Contemporary American Foreign Policy, 1974, The Canal War: Four Power Conflict, 1974, Germany East and West, 1981. Author, editor: Present State Communist Internationalism, 1983, The Interaction of Political Reforms Within the East Block, 1989. Served to capt. USAF, 1960-63 Penfield fellow NYU, 1957-59; grantee Ford Found., 1970, Royal Inst. Internat. Affairs, London, 1970, Thyssen Found., Cologne, Germany, 1974-82, 89, Volkswagen Found., 1982-85 Mem. Am. Acad. Polit. and Social Scis., Internat. Inst. Strategic Studies, Am. Assn. Advancement of Soviet Studies, Gesellschaft für Auslandskunde, German Am. Assn. Home: Widenmayerstrasse 41 80538 Munich Germany

**WHETZEL, JULIE ANNE,** special education educator; b. Alexandria, Va., June 28, 1971; d. John Wesley Kennedy and Patricia Jean Burns; m. Karl Edward Whetzel, June 6, 1998. BS, James Madison U., 1993; MEd, N.C. State U., 2004. Human resources asst. Va. Tech., Blacksburg, 1998—99, testing coord., 1999; project dir. N.C. State U., Raleigh, 1999—2004; tchr. spl. edn. Wake County Schs., 2004—. Comm. dir. N.C. Sch.-Age Care Coalition Governing Bd., Raleigh, 2002—04. Editor: (newsletter) The Link, 2002—04, SAC in the Know, 2003. Tutor Comm. in Schs., Raleigh, 2003—04. Mem.: ASCD, Internat. Reading Assn., Coun. Exceptional Children, Delta Gamma (advisor 2003). Republican. Avocations: reading, hiking, travel, cooking. Home: 5401 Royal Train Dr Raleigh NC 27604 Office: Combs Elem Sch 2001 Lorimer Rd Raleigh NC 27606

**WHICHARD, WILLIS PADGETT,** lawyer, educator, retired judge; b. Durham, N.C., May 24, 1940; s. Willis Guilford and Beulah (Padgett) W.; m. Leona Irene Paschal, June 4, 1961; children: Jennifer Diane, Ida Gilbert. AB, U. N.C., 1962, JD, 1965; LLM, U. Va., 1984, SJD, 1994. Bar: N.C. 1965. Law clk. N.C. Supreme Ct., Raleigh, 1965-66; ptnr. Powe, Porter, Alphin & Whichard, Durham, 1966-80; assoc. judge N.C. Ct. Appeals, Raleigh, 1980-86; assoc. justice N.C. Supreme Ct., Raleigh, 1986-98; dean, prof. law Campbell U., 1999—2006. Instr. grad. sch. bus. adminstrn. Duke U., 1978; vis. lectr. U. N.C. Sch. Law, 1986-98. Contbr. articles to profl. jours. Rep. N.C. Ho. of Reps., Raleigh, 1970-74; senator N.C. Senate, 1974-80, chair numerous coms. and commns.; N.C. legis. rsch. commn., 1971-73, 75-77, land policy coun., 1975-79; bd. dirs. Sr. Citizens Coordinating Coun., 1972-74; chair local crusade Am. Cancer Soc., 1977, state crusade chair, 1980, chair pub. issues com., 1980-84; pres., bd. chmn. Downtown Durham Devel. Corp., 1980-84; bd. dirs. Durham County chpt. ARC, 1971-79; Durham county campaign dir. March of Dimes, 1968, 69, chmn., 1969-74, bd. dirs. Triangle chpt., 1974-79; bd. advisors Duke Hosp., 1982-85, U. N.C. Sch. Pub. Health, 1985-96, U. N.C. Sch. Social Work, 1989—; bd. visitors N.C. Ctrl. U. Sch. Law, 1987—; mem. law sch. dean search com. U. N.C., 1978-79, 88-89, self-study com., 1985-86; pres. N.C. Inst. Justice, 1984-94; bd. dirs. N.C. Ctr. Crime and Punishment, 1984-94. Staff sgt. N.C. Army NG, 1966-72. Recipient Disting. Service award Durham Jaycees, 1971, Outstanding Legis. award N.C. Acad. Trial Lawyers, 1975, Outstanding Youth Svc. award N.C. Juvenile Correctional Assn., 1975, named Citizen of Yr. Eno Valley Civitan Club, Durham, 1982, Faith Active in Pub. Life award N.C. Coun. of Churches, 1983, Outstanding Appellate Judge award N.C. Acad. Trial Lawyers, 1983; named to Durham H.S. Hall of Fame, 1987. Mem. ABA, N.C. Bar Assn. (v.p. 1983-84, 2001-02), Durham County Bar Assn., U. N.C. Law Alumni Assn. (pres. 1978-79, bd. dirs. 1979-82), Nat. Guard Assn. (judge adv. 1972-73, legis. coun. 1974-76), Order of Golden Fleece, Order of Grail, Order of Old Well, Amphoterothen Soc., Order of Coif, Phi Alpha Theta, Phi Kappa Alpha, Durham-Chapel Hill Torch Club (pres. 1984-85), Watauga Club (Raleigh, pres. 1994-95). Democrat. Baptist. Home: 84402 Winslow Chapel Hill NC 27517 Office: Wiggins Sch Law Campbell Univ PO Box 158 Buies Creek NC 27506-0158 Personal E-mail: wpwhichard@earthlink.net.

**WHICKER, AMY MARIE,** computer science professor; b. Greenville, SC, Jan. 7, 1977; d. Glenn Ross and Cathy Pate; m. R. Eric Whicker, May 15, 2004. BS in Acctg., Clemson U., SC, 1999; BS in Computer Sci. and Math., Francis Marion U., Florence, SC, 2003; ME in Computer Sci. and Engring., U. SC, Columbia, 2005. Graduate tchg. asst., computer sci. and engring. U. SC, Columbia, 2003—05; asst. prof. computer sci. Francis Marion U., Florence, 2005—. Recipient Outstanding Tchg. Asst. award, u. SC, 2005.

**WHIDDON, THOMAS E.,** retail executive; BS in Acctg. magna cum laude, U. Ala., 1974. Tax ptnr. KPMG Peat Marwick, Tampa, Fla.; various positions to v.p. and treas. Eckerd Corp.; sr. v.p., treas. Zale Corp., 1994-95, sr. v.p., CFO, 1995-96; exec. v.p., CFO, Lowe's Cos., Inc., North Wilkesboro, N.C., 1996-2000, exec. v.p. logistics and tech., 2000—. Office: Lowe's Cos Inc PO Box 1111 North Wilkesboro NC 28659-1111

**WHIFFEN, JAMES DOUGLASS,** surgeon, educator; b. N.Y.C., Jan. 16, 1931; s. John Phillips and Lorna Elizabeth (Douglass) W.; child from a previous marriage, Gregory James; m. Sally Vilas Runge, Aug. 21, 1993. BS, U. Wis., 1952, MD, 1956. Diplomate: Am. Bd. Surgery. Intern Ohio State U. Hosp., 1955-56; resident U. Wis. Hosp., 1956-57, 59-61; instr. dept. surgery U. Wis. Med. Sch., 1962-64, asst. prof., 1964-67, assoc. prof., 1967-71, prof., 1971-96, vice chmn. dept., 1970-72, acting chmn., 1972-74; asst. dean Med. Sch., 1975-96; prof. emeritus U. Wis. Med. Sch., 1996—; mem. exam. council State of Wis. Emergency Med. Services, 1974-77. Bd. dirs. Wis. Heart Assn. Served to lt. comdr. USNR, 1957-59. John and Mary R. Markle scholar in acad. medicine, also; Research Career Devel. award NIH, 1965-75 Fellow A.C.S., Am. Soc. Artificial Internal Organs. Clubs: Maple Bluff Country. Achievements include research publs. on biomaterials, thrombo-resistant surfaces and the physiology of heart-lung bypass procedures. Home: 17 Cambridge Ct Madison WI 53704-5906 Office: 600 Highland Ave Madison WI 53792-0001 E-mail: jwhiffen@wisc.edu.

**WHIGHAM, MARK ANTHONY,** computer scientist; b. Mobile, Ala., Jan. 14, 1959; s. Tommie Lee Sr. and Callie Mae (Molette) W. BS in Computer Sci., Ala. A&M U., 1983, MS in Computer Sci., 1990; postgrad., Ala. A&M Univ., 1995—. Computer programmer U.S. Army Corps of Engrs., Huntsville, Ala., 1985-88; programmer analyst, coord. acad. computing Ala. A&M U., Normal, Ala., 1988-89; programmer analyst II, DEC systems coord., instr. part-time computer sci. dept., 1989-91; systems engr. Advanced Bus. Cons. Inc.-La. div. Dow Chem. Co., 1991-93; owner Whigham's Computer Cons., 1990—; sys. engr. DOW Chem. Co.-USA La. Divsn., Plaquemine, La., 1991-93; instr. computer info. system Calhoun C.C., Decatur, Ala., 1993-97; network specialist/cons. Ala. A&M U., Normal, 1994—; computer info. sys. instr. Calhoun C.C., Decatur, Ala., 1994—; mgmt. info. sys. dir., CIO J.F. Drake Tech. Coll., Huntsville, Ala., 1997-98; software engr. Colsa Corp., Huntsville, Ala., 1998—99; dir. info. tech. Lane Coll., 1999—2000; instr. computer sci. Lawson State CC, 2000—. Instr. computer sci. dept. Ala. A&M U., 1989-91; network specialist, cons. Ala. A&M U., Normal, 1994—. Active Huntsville Interdenominational Ministerial Fellowship, Huntsville, 1984. Mem. Nat. Assn. Sys. Programmers, Ala. Coun. for Computer Edn., Assn. for Computing Machinery, Huntsville Jaycees, Nat. Soc. Black Engrs., Assn. Info. Tech. Profls., So. Poetry Assn., Nat. Arts Soc., Internat. Black Writers and Artists Assn., Optimists, U.S. Chess Fedn. (cert. chess coach), Future Bus. Leaders of Am.-Phi Beta Lambda, Sigma Tau Epsilon, Alpha Phi Omega. Baptist. Avocations: chess, skating, reading, playing piano. Office: Lawson State CC 3060 Wilson Rd Birmingham AL 35209-1542 Home: Apt 202 917 Valley Ridge Dr Birmingham AL 35209-1542 Office Phone: 205-929-2023. Business E-Mail: mwhigham@cougar.ls.cc.al, mwhigham@lawsonstate.edu.

**WHILDEN, ROBERT HARRAL, JR.,** lawyer; b. Houston, May 20, 1935; s. Robert Harral and Elizabeth (Hoyt) W.; m. Mary Preston, Aug. 24, 1957; children: Elizabeth, Margaret, Robert III. BA, U. Tex., 1957, LL.B., 1960. Bar: Tex. Ptnr. Vinson & Elkins, Houston, 1960—2000, mem. mgmt. com.; sr. v.p., gen. counsel, sec. BMC Software Inc., 2000—. Bd. dirs. Baker Assn., Houston Bar Assn. Home: 5718 Indian Trl Houston TX 77057-1305 Office: BMC Software 2101 City W Blvd Houston TX 77042 Office Phone: 713-918-8800. E-mail: bob_whilden@bmc.com.

**WHINERY, MICHAEL ALBERT,** physician; b. Watsford, Eng., June 30, 1951; s. Leo Howard and Doris Eileene W. and Alma Piper; m. Tatijana Dunnebier, 1976 (dec. Jan. 1981); m. Judy Renee Wright, Apr. 30, 1982; children: Rhiannon Daire Eileene, Terron Rae Lee. BS, Okla. U., 1976; D of Osteopathy, Okla. State U., 1980. Diplomate Am. Bd. Family Practice. Intern Hillcrest Health Ctr., Oklahoma City, 1980-81; with McLoud Clinic, McLoud, Okla., 1981-98; staff physician Okla. Vets. Ctr., Claremore, 2000—. House physician McLoud Nursing Ctr., 1988—; med. examiner Pottawatomie County Health, McLoud, 1983—. Author: Poetic Voices of America, 1991; composer lyrics and music at Stella Gospel Rec. Studio, 2000, A Soldier Last Prayer. Mem. Presdl. Order Merit Nat. Repub. Senatorial Com'l., Washington, 1991, Presdl. Task Force, 1983—, Senatorial Commn. Repub. Senatorial

Inner Circle, Washington, 1991; mem. U.S. Congrl. Adv. Bd., 1993. Served with USMC, Vietnam era. Recipient Acknowledgement of Outstanding Contbn. in Clin. Rsch. award SANDOZ Labs., 1992, Rep. Presdl. Legion of Merit, 1994, Rep. Majority medal, U.S. Senate, 1997, Rep. Task Force medal of merit, 1997. Mem. Am. Legion, C. of C., Jr. C. of C., U.S. Senatorial Club (preferred mem.), U.S. Congressional Act Bd. (state advisor 1990-91). Baptist. Avocations: fishing, music, composing songs, poetry and writing lyrics. Office: PO Box 2745 3001 W Bluestarr Claremore OK 74018-2745 Office Phone: 918-342-5432. Business E-Mail: mwhinery@odva.state.ok.us.

**WHINES, ANTHONY LORING,** automotive executive; b. Altus, Okla., Sept. 19, 1941; s. William A. and Edna Lee (Allen) H.; m. Nancy Campbell, Sept. 19, 1959 (div. 1962); children: William, Todd; m. Jo Ann Willoughby, June 22, 1963; children: Donna, Larry, Teresa, Toni, Michael. BSChemE, U. Okla., 1967; MSChemE, Okla. State U., 1969; PhDME, U. Tex., 1973. Registered profl. engr., Tex. Asst. prof. chem. engring. Ga. Inst. Tech., Atlanta, 1973-75; asst. to assoc. prof. chem. engring. Colo. Sch. Mines, Golden, 1975-80; prof. chem. engring., head dept. U. Wyo., Laramie, 1980-83; assoc. dean engring. rsch. Okla. State U., Stillwater, 1983-87; prof. chem. engring., dean engring. U. Mo.-Columbia, 1987-93; v.p. Honda of Am., Mfg., Inc., Marysville, Ohio, 1993-97; sr. v.p. Honda of Am., Mfg. Inc., Marysville, Ohio, 1997; v.p. mfg. Navistar Internat. Corp., Springfield, Ohio, 1998, group v.p. engring. and mfg. ops., 1999; dean coll. engring. U. Iowa, Iowa City, 1999—2000. Site visitor NSF, 1988-90; mem. Mo. Corp. for Sci. & Tech., 1991—; mem. rev. panel on air quality Internat. Energy Agy., 1991; mem. rev. panel Laser, 1990; mem., lead reviewer Lumcon, 1994. Co-author: Mass Transfer Fundamentals and Applications, 1984, Mass Transfer Solutions Manual, 1985, Indoor Air, Quality and Control, 1988; contbr. articles to profl. jours. Mem. Okla. Coun. Sci. and Tech. Rsch. Task Force, 1984, Regional Commerce and Growth Assn., St. Louis, 1988—; assoc. mem. Columbia Regional Econ. Devel., Inc., 1989- ; mem. Columbia Area Regional Econ. Devel., Inc., 1989—. Mem. NSPE, ASHRAE (com. on sorption 1988—), Nat. Inst. for Engring. Mgmt. and Systems (bd. govs. 1990—), Am. Inst. Chem. Engrs. (sec. separations div. 1991), Mo. Soc. Profl. Engrs., Am. Soc. Engring. Edn., Avocations: hunting, fishing, handball, basketball.

**WHINSTON, ARTHUR LEWIS,** lawyer; b. NYC, Feb. 5, 1925; s. Charles Nathaniel and Charlotte (Nalen) W.; m. Melicent Ames Kingsbury, Mar. 19, 1949; children: Ann Kingsbury, James Pierce, Melicent Ames, Louise Ellen, Patricia Kingsbury. B.C.E., Cornell U., 1945; MSE., Princeton U., 1947; JD, N.Y. U., 1957. Bar: N.Y. 1957, Oreg. 1964, U.S. Supreme Ct 1966, U.S. Patent Office 1958, U.S. Ct. Appeals (fed. cir.) 1959; registered profl. engr., N.Y., Oreg. Engr. Chas. N. & Selig Whinston, N.Y.C., 1947-50; lectr. Coll. City N.Y., 1950-51; structures engr. Republic Aviation Corp., Farmingdale, NY, 1951-57; patent lawyer Arthur, Dry & Kalish, 1957-64, Klarquist Sparkman, LLP, 1964—; chmn. Oreg. Bar com. on patent, trademark and copyright law, 1968-69, 77-78, mem. com. unauthorized practice law, 1970-73, chmn., 1972-73, com. on profl. responsibility, 1973-75. Served as ensign, C.E.C., USNR, 1945-46. Recipient Fuertes medal Cornell U. Sch. Civil Engring., 1945 Mem. ABA, Oreg. Bar Assn., N.Y. Bar Assn., Multnomah County Bar Assn., Am. Intellectual Property Law Assn., N.Y. Intellectual Property Law Assn., Oreg. Patent Law Assn. (pres. 1977-78), Profl. Engrs. Oreg. (past state regis. chmn.), Sigma Xi, Chi Epsilon, Phi Kappa Phi. Clubs: Multnomah Athletic. Republican. Home: 3824 SW 50th Ave Portland OR 97221-2112 Office: One World Trade Ctr Ste 1600 Portland OR 97204

**WHIPPLE, DEAN,** federal judge; b. 1938; BS, Drury Coll., 1961; postgrad., U. Tulsa, 1961-62; JD, postgrad., U. Mo., Kansas City, 1965. Pvt. practice, Lebanon, Mo., 1965-75; cir. judge div. II 26th Jud. Cir. Mo., 1975-87; judge US Dist. Ct. (we. dist.) Mo., Kansas City, 1987-2000, chief judge, 2000—. Prosecuting atty. Laclede County, Mo., 1967-71. With Mo. N.G., 1956-61; USAR, 1961-66. Mem. Mo. Bar Assn. (mem. pub. info. com. 1971-72, mem. judiciary com. 1971-72, mem. bd. govs. 1975-87, mem. exec. com. 1983-84, 86-87, mem. planning com. for ann. meeting 1985, 87, chmn. 1986, mem. selection com. for Lon Hocker award 1986), Mo. Trial Judges Assn., 26th Jud. Bar Assn., Laclede County Bar Assn. (pres. 1968-69, 72-73), Kansas City Met. Bar Assn., Kansas City Inn of Ct. (instr. 1988-93), Mo. Hist. Soc., Phi Delta Phi. Office: US Courthouse 400 E 9th St Kansas City MO 64106-2607

**WHIPPLE, HARRY M.,** newspaper publishing executive; b. Tulsa, June 30, 1947; children: Garth, Erin. Student, Ind. U., 1965-68, U. Evansville, 1965-68, Ark Poly. Coll., 1965-68. Gen. mgr. Mt. Vernon (Ind.) Pub. Co., 1972-75; pub. Pioneer Newspapers (formerly Scripps League Newspapers), Monongahela, Pa., 1975-77; advt. dir. Rockford (Ill.) Morning Star and Register Republic, 1977-81; pres., pub. Valley News Dispatch, The Herald, North Hills News Record, Tarentum, Pa., 1981-84; v.p., regional mgr. Midwest Gannett Media Sales/Gannett Nat. Sales, Chgo., 1984-87; pres. TNI Ptnrs., Tucson, 1987-92; pres., pub. The Cincinnati Enquirer, 1992—2003; ret. The Cin. Enquirer, 2003—. Co-chair adv. bd. Nat. Underground R.R. Freedom Ctr. Mem. Greater Cin. C. of C. (chmn. bd. trustees). Home: 5640 Windridge Court Cincinnati OH 45243

**WHIPPLE, JUDITH ROY,** retired editor; b. N.Y.C., May 14, 1935; d. Edwin Paul and Elizabeth (Levis) Roy; m. William Whipple, Oct. 26, 1963. AB, Mount Holyoke Coll., 1957. Head libr. Am. Sch. Lima (Peru), S.A., 1957-59; asst. editor children's books G.P. Putnam's Sons, N.Y.C., 1959-62; assoc. editor W.W. Norton & Co., Inc., N.Y.C., 1962-68; editor Four Winds Press, 1968-75; editor-in-chief Scholastic Gen. Book Divsn., 1975-77; pub. Four Winds Press subs. Scholastic Inc., N.Y.C., 1977-82; pub.; v.p. Macmillan Pub. Co., N.Y.C., 1982-89, exec. editor, 1989-94; editl. dir. Cavendish Children's Books, Tarrytown, NY, 1994—2002, ret. 2002. Mem.: PEN, Children's Book Coun. (pres. 1977, bd. dirs. 1970—79), Women's Nat. Book Assn., Soc. Children's Book Writers and Illustrators. Avocations: gardening, swimming, piano, travel. Personal E-mail: jrwhipple@stny.rr.com.

**WHIPPLE, KENNETH,** utilities executive; b. 1934; BS, MIT, 1958. With Ford Motor Co., Dearborn, Mich., 1958—, systems mgr. Ford Credit, 1966-69, mgr. mgmt. svcs. dept. fin. staff, 1969-71, systems analysis mgr. fin. staff, 1971-74, asst. contnr. internat. fin. staff, 1974-75, v.p. fin. Ford Credit, 1975-77, exec. v.p. Ford Credit, 1977-80, pres. Ford Credit, 1980-84, v.p. corp. strategy, 1984-86; v.p. chmn. Ford of Europe, 1986-88; exec. v.p., pres. Ford Fin. Svcs. Group, Dearborn, 1988—99; chmn. bd., CEO CMS Energy, Dearborn, Mich., 2002—04; chmn. CME Energy, Dearborn, Mich., 2004—. Office: CMS Energy 1 Energy Plaza Drive Jackson MI 49201*

**WHIPPLE, WILLIAM, JR.,** government policy consultant, writer; b. Sinclare, La., Feb. 4, 1909; s. William and Genevieve (Randolph) W.; m. Dixie Ancrum, Mar. 30, 1935 (dec. Oct. 1955); children: Anne Calhoun, William III, Claire Randolph; m. Renée Pauline Exiga, July 21, 1956 (div. May 1974); 1 child, Philip; m. Frances Edith Cheek, June 1, 1974 (dec. July 1983); m. Alice Terry Goodloe, Dec. 1, 1984. BS, U.S. Mil. Acad., 1930; BA, Oxford (Eng.) U., 1933, MA, 1937; Civil Engr., Princeton U., 1936. Registered profl. engr., N.J. Commd. 2d lt. Corps Engrs., U.S. Army, 1930, advanced through grades to brig. gen., ret., 1960; chief engr. N.Y. World's Fair Corp., Flushing Meadow, N.Y., 1960-64; pvt. practice cons. engr. N.Y.C., 1964-65; dir. Water Resources Rsch. Inst. Rutgers U., New Brunswick, N.J., 1965-79, rsch. prof. Coastal and Environ. Inst., 1979-81; asst. dir. divsn. water resources Dept. Environ. Protection, Trenton, N.J., 1981-89, coord. nonpoint source control program divsn. water resource, 1989-90; prin. Greeley Polhemus Group, Chester, Pa., 1990-2000; pvt. practice cons. Princeton, N.J., 1999—. Author: New Perspectives on Water Supply, 1994, Comprehensive Water Planning and Regulation, 1996, Water Resource: A New Era for Coordination, 1998; contbr. articles to publs. on water resources. Chmn. Flood Control Com., Princeton, N.J., 1975-81; adv. coun., Revision of N.J.'s Water Supply Master Plan, 2001. Recipient Trustees award N.J. inst. Tech., 1985, govt. award Water Resource Assn. of Delaware River Basin, 1987, Toulmin award for best articles Mil. Engr., 1975, Formal Commendation from Pres. of U.S., 1971. Fellow AAAS, ASCE (life, chmn. urban water resources rsch. coun. 1973-75, Lifetime Achievement award Inst. Environ-

ment and Water Resources 2001), Soc. Am. Mil. Engrs. (life), Am. Water Resources Assn. (pres. 1993, Icko Iben award 1978, William Ackerman medal 1989, Boggess award; mem. Am. Acad. Environ. Engrs. (diplomate), Univs. Coun. on Water Resources (chmn. 1976-78), Sigma Xi. Avocation: history and biography. Home and Office: 2 Hedge Row Rd Princeton NJ 08540-5055

**WHIPPLE, WILLIAM PERRY,** foundation administrator; b. Cedar Rapids, Iowa, Nov. 1, 1913; s. Robert Milo and Jeanette (Fry) W.; m. Gayle Schroeder, Sept. 18, 1937; children: John William, Robert Milo. BA, Coe Coll., 1935, PhD (hon.), 1996. Prin. Whipple Ins. Agy., Cedar Rapids, 1935-57; pres. Whipple and Winterberg, Cedar Rapids, 1957-71; chmn. Frank B. Hall of Iowa, Inc., Cedar Rapids, 1971-74; pres. Hall Found., Inc., Cedar Rapids, 1974-95, also bd. dirs.; chair Hall-Perrine Found., Cedar Rapids, 1995—. Exec. in residence Colo. State U., Fort Collins, 1973; bd. dirs. Fire Mark Cir. of Ams., Chamblee, Ga., Interocean Reins. Corp., Cedar Rapids, 1st Fed. Savs. and Loan, Cedar Rapids, Nissen Corp., Cedar Rapids, 1966-72, Banks of Iowa, Inc., Des Moines, 1982-85. Trustee Cedar Rapids Pub. Library, Coe Coll., chmn.; hon. bd. dirs. Methwick Manor, Cedar Rapids, Linn County ARC, Greater Cedar Rapids Found. Recipient Outstanding Layman award YMCA, Cedar Rapids, 1986, Alumni Achievement award, Coe Coll., 1990, Founders Day award Coe Coll., 2001, First Community Svc. award, Cedar Rapids Rotary, 1993. Mem. Rotary (Paul Harris fellow 1987), Elks. Presbyterian. Avocations: signvierist, stamp collecting/philately. Home: 1224 13th St NW Cedar Rapids IA 52405-2404 Office: Hall-Perrine Found 115 3d St SE Cedar Rapids IA 52401-1222

**WHIPPLE, WOODROW THOMAS,** artist, educator; b. Brattleboro, Vt., June 5, 1944; s. Howard Woodrow Whipple and Anna Mastelar; m. Tina Sue Huggins, Dec. 31, 1992 (div. Apr. 24, 1996); m. Evelyn Crowley, May 9, 1967 (div. June 29, 1988); 1 child, Lori Michelle Pate. Student, Columbus Sch. of Art, 1963—65. Graphic artist Dept. of Def., Ft. Benning, Ga., 1971—74; gallery owner, art instr. Le Gallerie, Columbus, Ga., 1974—78; visual info. specialist Dept. of Def., Ft. Benning, Ga., 1978—95; art instr., graphic designer, cons. Visual Imagery Prodns., Columbus, Ga., 1995—99; instr. graphic arts Ga. Dept. of Corrections, Pulaski State Prison, Hawkinsville, 1999—; owner, founder BackYard Woodys Grill-N-Sauces, Bonaire, Ga., 2000—. Author (illustrator): Wing Ding Party Book; painting, Gunboat Chattahoochee (Purchase award for Ga. Bicentential Top 10 Ga. Artist, 1975), Savannah Pier (Purchase award for permanent exhbn. collection in the Bradley Mus. of Art, 1975), exhibit, CISM XXIV Internation Shooting Championships Norway (Outstanding Contibution, 1985). Mem.: Ga. Correctional Edn. Assn., Lower Chattahoochee Archaeol. Soc. (pres. 1985—86), Middle Ga. Culinary Assn., Am. Culinary Fedn. (sgt. at arms 2005—06), Sports Car Club of Am. (regional exec. 1966—67), U.S. Power Squardon (comdr. 1987—88), Columbus Artist Guild. Republican. Episcopalian. Avocations: fine art, photography, cooking, travel. Home: 110 Chipper St Bonaire GA 31005 Office: Ga Dept of Corrections PSP Rte 2 Upper River Rd Hawkinsville GA 31036 Personal E-mail: gdcwhip@cox.net.

**WHIPPS, EDWARD FRANKLIN,** lawyer; b. Columbus, Ohio, Dec. 17, 1936; s. Rusk Henry and Agnes Lucille (Green) W.; children: Edward Scott, Rusk Huot, Sylvia Louise, Rudyard Christian. BA, Ohio Wesleyan U., 1958; JD, Ohio State U., 1961. Bar: Ohio 1961, U.S. Dist. Ct. (so. dist.) Ohio 1962, U.S. Dist. Ct. (no. dist.) Ohio 1964, U.S. Ct. Claims 1963, U.S. Supreme Ct. 1963, Miss. 1965, U.S. Ct. Appeals (6th cir.) 1980. Assoc. George, Greek, King & McMahon, Columbus, 1961-66; ptnr. George, Greek, King, McMahon & McConnaughey, Columbus, 1966-79, McConnaughey, Stradley, Mone & Moul, Columbus, 1979-81, Thompson, Hine & Flory, Columbus, 1981-93; prin. Edward F. Whipps & Assocs., Columbus, 1993-94, 2000—; ptnr. Whipps & Wistner, Columbus, 1995-99. Founder, trustee Creative Living, Inc., 1969—; trustee, v.p. Unverferth House, Inc., 1989; trustee Eagle Scholarship Trust. Host: (TV) Upper Arlington Plain Talk, 1979-82, Bridging Disability, 1981-82, Lawyers on Call, 1982—, U.A. Today, 1982-86, The Ohio Wesleyan Experience, 1984—. Mem. Ohio Bd. Psychology, 1992—, pres. 2001-02; active Upper Arlington (Ohio) Bd. Edn., 1971-80, pres. 1978-79; bd. alumni dirs. Ohio Wesleyan U., 1975-79; trustee Walden Ravines Assn., 1992-96, pres. 1993-96. Mem. ABA, Columbus Bar Assn., Ohio State Bar Assn., Am. Trial Lawyers Am., Ohio Acad. Trial Lawyers, Franklin County Trial Lawyers Assn., Am. Judicature Soc., Columbus Bar Found., Ohio Bd. Pscyhology, Columbus C. of C., Upper Arlington Area C. of C. (trustee 1978—), Lawyers Club, Barrister Club, Columbus Athletic Club, Nat. Football Found. & Hall of Fame, Columbus Touchdown Club, Downtown Quarterback Club, Ohio State U. Faculty (Columbus) Club, Ohio State U. Golf Club, Highlands Golf Club (dir. 2001—), Delta Tau Delta (nat. v.p. 1976-78). Republican. Home: 51 Highland Ct Pataskala OH 43062-8910 Office: Edward F Whipps & Assocs 500 S Front St Columbus OH 43215-7619 Office Phone: 614-461-6006. E-mail: efwhipp@aol.com. *Personal philosophy: Commitment to personal growth, the development of interpersonal relationships, the rule of law and a firm belief in the unique value of every individual in a holographic universe are the primary factors seen in my approach to life.*

**WHISENHUNT, DONALD WAYNE,** historian, educator, dean; b. Meadow, Tex., May 16, 1938; s. William Alexander Whisenhunt and Beulah (Johnson) King; m. Betsy Ann Baker, Aug. 27, 1960; children: Donald Wayne Jr., William Benton. BA, McMurry Coll., 1960; MA, Tex. Tech U., 1962, PhD, 1966. Tchr. Elida (N.Mex.) High Sch., 1961-63; from asst. to assoc. prof. history Murray (Ky.) State U., 1966-69; assoc. prof., chmn. dept. Thiel Coll., Greenville, Pa., 1969-73; Dean Sch. Liberal Arts and Scis., Ea. N.Mex. U., Portales, 1973-77; v.p. acad. affairs U. Tex., Tyler, 1977-83; v.p., provost Wayne (Nebr.) State Coll., 1983-91, interim pres., 1985; prof. history, chmn. dept. Western Wash. U., Bellingham, 1991—. Fulbright lectr. Peoples Republic of China, 1995, Republic of Korea, 1994, Belarus, 2004. Author: Environment and American Experience, 1974. Depression in the Southwest, 1979, Chronological History of Texas, vol. 1, 1982, Vol.2, 1987, Texas Sesquicentennial Celebration, 1984; editor: Encyclopedia USA, 1988—, Poetry of the People: Poems to the President, 1929-1945, 1996, Tent Show: Arthur Names and His Famous Players, 2000, It Seems to Me: Selected Letters of Eleanor Roosevelt, 2001. Democrat. Methodist. Home: PO Box 1032 Murray KY 42071-1032 Business E-Mail: donw@wwu.edu.

**WHISENHUNT, WILLIAM BENTON,** history professor; b. Murray, Ky., Oct. 29, 1968; s. Donald Wayne, Sr. and Betsy Ann (Baker) Whisenhunt; m. Michele Diane Zographos, May 30, 1992; children: Meredith Jane, Matthew Benton. BA History, Cornell Univ., Mt. Vernon, Iowa, 1990; MA History, Univ. Nebr., Omaha, 1992; PhD History, Univ. Ill., Chgo., 1997. Tchg. asst. Univ. Nebr., Omaha, 1991—92, Univ. Ill., Chgo., 1992—95; adj. instr. Coll. Lake County, Grayslake, 1993—97, Coll. DuPage, Glen Ellyn, 1992—97, asst. prof., 1997—99, assoc. prof., 1999—2003, prof., 2003—. Textbook reviewer Prentice Hall, 1999—. Author: In Search of Legality, 2001; contbr. articles pub. to profl. jour. Mem. Sycamore Hist. Soc., 2003—. Recipient Commitment to Svc. award, Coll. DuPage, 1999. Mem.: Am. Assn. Advancement of Slavic Studies (com. on edn. 2003—03), Am. Hist. Assn. Office: Coll DuPage 425 Fawell Blvd Glen Ellyn IL 60137

**WHISENNAND, CYNTHIA SIMMONS,** librarian; b. Dallas, Oct. 29, 1956; d. Mickey Thorne Simmons and Diane Katherine (Gale) Neel; m. Dietrich P. Whisennand, June 28, 1980; 1 child, Matthew William. BA, So. Meth U., 1979; MLS, North Tex. State U., 1985; DD, Pathways Sem., 2005. Cert. tchr. Tex. Tchr. Dallas Ind. Sch. Dist., 1979—83; libr. Irving (Tex.) Ind. Sch. Dist., 1985—. Mem. dist. com. Mustang Dist. Cir. 10 coun. Boy Scouts Am., Dallas, 1980—; Solar Sys. amb., 2004—; deacon Christian Ch. Lt. col., comdr. Irving Composite Squadron CAP Aux. USAF. Recipient Dist. award of Merit, Boy Scouts Am., 1983, Wood badge, 1986, Silver Beaver award, 1991. Mem.: ALA, Tex. Assn. Profl. Educators, Am. Assn. Sch. Llbrs., Tex. Libr. Assn., Alpha Phi Omega. Republican. Mem. Disciples Of Christ. Avocations: Judo, photography, music, shooting, computers. Office: MacArthur HS 3700 N MacArthur Blvd Irving TX 75061 Office Phone: 972-261-2192. E-mail: cswhiz@whisennand.net.

**WHISLER, JAMES STEVEN,** mining executive, lawyer, rancher; b. Centerville, Iowa, Nov. 23, 1954; s. James Thomas and Betty Lou (Clark) W.; m. Ardyce Dawn Christensen, Jan. 20, 1979; children: James Kyle, Kristen Elyse. BS, U. Colo., Boulder, 1975; JD, U. Denver, 1978; MS, Colo. Sch. Mines, 1984, DSc (hon.), 2001; AMP, Harvard Bus. Sch., 1998. Bar: Colo. 1978; CPA, Ariz. Assoc. gen. counsel, sec. We. Nuc., Inc., Denver, 1979—81; exploration counsel Phelps Dodge Corp., N.Y.C., 1981—85, legal and adminstrv. mgr. Phoenix, 1985—87, v.p., gen. counsel, 1987—88, sr. v.p., gen. counsel, 1988—91, pres., COO, 1997—99, chmn., pres., CEO, 2000—03, chmn., CEO, 2003—; pres. Phelps Dodge Mining Co., 1991—98. Bd. dirs. Am. West Holdings Corp., 2001—05, Phelps Dodge Corp., Burlington No. Santa Fe Corp., U.S. Airways Group, Inc., Copper Devel. Assn., Internat. Copper Assn., Nat. Mining Assn.; mem. Bus. Coun. Mem.: AIME, AICPA, Nat. Cowboy and Western Heritage Mus., Mining and Metall. Soc. Am., Colo. Bar Assn., Soc. Mining Engrs., Mont. Cattlemen's Assn. Links Club. Office: Phelps Dodge Corp One N Central Ave Phoenix AZ 85004-2306 E-mail: jswhisler@phelpsdodge.com.

**WHISLER, JOE B.,** lawyer; b. Nevada, Mo., May 31, 1947; BA, Ctrl. Meth. Coll., 1969; JD, So. Meth. Univ., Dallas, 1972. Mem., atty. Cooling & Herbers PC, Kans. City, Mo. Bd. of editors: Jour. of Air Law and Commerce, 1971—72. Mem.: ABA, Lawyers Assn. of Kans. City (pres., jr. sect. 1977—78), Kans. City Met. Bar Assn., Bar Assn. of Met. St. Louis, Barristers, Mo. Bar (pres.-elect 2003, pres. 2004), Phi Alpha Delta. Office: Cooling & Herbers PC 2400 City Ctr Sq 1100 Main St Kansas City MO 64105

**WHISNAND, REX JAMES,** association housing executive; b. Van Nuys, Calif., Jan. 2, 1948; s. Harold Theodore Whisnand and Laura Fay Brigham Whisnand; m. Cathy Ladeane Bennett, Apr. 1, 1978; 1 child, Bryce James. BS in Agrl. Bus. Mgmt., Calif. Poly State U., 1970; BSBA, Calif. State U., Sacramento, 1976; MPA in Housing Adminstrn., U. San Francisco, 1985; grad., U.S. Naval Submarine Sch., 1972; postgrad., Inst. for Orgn. Mgmt.; EdD in Orgn. and Leadership, U. San Francisco, 2000. Generalist W & W Hardware Store, Orcutt, Calif., 1964—70; state park ranger Calif. Dept. Parks and Recreation, Lompoc and Sacramento, 1969—75; exec. asst. Constrn. Industry Legis. Coun., Sacramento, 1974—75; dir. assn. svcs. Bldg. Industry Assn. Superior Calif., Sacramento, 1976—79; exec. v.p. West Bay divsn. Bldg. Industry Assn. No. Calif., Redwood City, 1980—84; exec. v.p. Bldg. Industry Assn., Tacoma/Pierce County, 1984—86; supr. Lumberjack Store, Lodi, Calif., 1988—90; exec. v.p. Rental Housing Owners Assn. of So. Alameda County, Hayward, Calif., 1990—96; field ops. supv., crew leader census 2000, Am. Housing Survey, 1997—98, crew leader, 2000; field rep. Westat survey U.S. Pub. Health Svc., 2000—; exec. dir. Housing Conservation and Devel. Corp., San Francisco, 2002—05; exec. v.p. Calaveras County Assn. Realtors, Angels Camp, Calif., 2005—. Com. mem. Calif. Bldg. Industry Assn., Sacramento, 1976-84; mem. exec. officers coun., local govt. com. Calif. Apt. Assn., 1991-96; mem. Alameda County Housing Rsch. Adv. Bd., Hayward, 1990-93; adj. faculty U. San Francisco; guest svc. rep. Oakland Athletics, 1997-05; columnist Calaveras Enterprise, 2006 Editor Pierce County Builder, 1984-86 (Assn. Achievement award Nat. Assn. Home Builders 1984-85), Superior California Builder Mag., 1978-80. Active 20-30 Club Internat. #1, Sacramento, 1976-80, officer, 1981-82; mem. South Sacramento Area Cmty. Planning Adv. Bd., 1978-79; grad. Pleasanton Leadership, 1995; chmn. Coastside Coalition for Safe Hwys., Half Moon Bay, 1983-84; bd. congregations Family Emergency Shelter Coalition Alameda County, 1995-96; active Pleasanton Gen. Plan Econ./Fiscal Growth Com., 1994-96, Bay Area Indsl. Edn. Coun., 1995-96, Hayward Coalition for Youth, 1995-96, San Francisco Coun. Cmty. Housing Orgns., 2002-05; mem. San Francisco Planning and Urban Rsch. Assn.-Homeless Taskforce, Housing Com., 2002-04, Non-Profit Housing Assn. No. Calif., 2002-05, Pleasanton Housing Commn., 2003-06, Pleasanton Housing Authority, 2003-06; officer Half Moon Bay C. of C., 1982-84; cert. basketball coach Nat. Youth Sports Assn., 1994-97. With USNR, 1970-76, U.S. Army, N.G., 1990-92. Named Outstanding Young Man in Am., Jr. C. of C., Foster City, Calif, 1983. Mem. Internat. Assn. Bus. Communicators (pres. Sacramento chpt. 1979, pres. Peninsula chpt. 1981), Am. Soc. Assn. Execs. (cert.), No. Calif. Soc. Assn. Execs. (bd. dirs. 1994-97, com. chmn. 1993-95), Pleasanton C. of C. (econ. devel. com. 1990-96), Wash. State Home Builders Assn. (pres. exec. officers coun. 1985), We. Conf. Assn. Execs. (com. 1995-96), Hayward C. of C. (govt. rels. coun. 1990-95), Calif. Vocat. Indsl. Clubs Am. (bd. dirs. 1977-80), Calif. Polytech. Alumni Assn., San Francisco Comprehensive Ho. (affordable strategy com. 2002-04), Calaveras County Assn. Realtors (exec. v.p. 2005-06), Calif. Assn. Realtors (exec. officer coun. 2006—, govt. affairs dir. 2006—), Alpha Gamma Rho (charter, com. chair 1969-99). Episcopalian. Avocations: dog breeding, genealogy. Home: 2332 Buffalo Way Copperopolis CA 95228-9572

**WHISNANT, JACK PAGE,** neurologist; b. Little Rock, Oct. 26, 1924; s. John Clifton and Zula I. (Page) W.; m. Patricia Anne Rimmey, May 12, 1944; children: Elizabeth Anne, John David, James Michael. BS, U. Ark., 1948, MD, 1951; MS, U. Minn., 1955. Intern Balt. City Hosp., 1951-52; resident in medicine and neurology Mayo Grad. Sch. Medicine, Rochester, Minn., 1952-55, instr. neurology, 1956-60, asst. prof., 1960-64, asso. prof., 1964-69, prof., 1969—; Meyer prof. neurosci. Mayo Med. Sch.; chmn. dept. neurology Mayo Clinic, Mayo Med. Sch., Mayo Grad. Sch. Medicine, 1971-81; chmn. dept. health scis. research Mayo Clinic and Mayo Med. Sch., 1987-93. Cons. neurology Mayo Clinic, 1955-96, head sect. neurology, 1963-71; dir. Mayo Cerebrovascular Clin. Rsch. Ctr., 1975-96. Contbr. articles on neurology and cerebrovascular disease to med. jours. Trustee YMCA, Rochester, pres. 1977. With USAAF, 1942-45. Decorated Air medal. NIH grantee, 1959-96. Fellow Am. Heart Assn., Am. Acad. Neurology (pres. 1993-95); mem. AMA, Am. Neurol. Assn. (pres. 1981-82), Am. Bd. Psychiatry and Neurology (bd. dirs. 1983-90, pres. 1989), Zumbro Valley Med. Soc., Minn. Med. Assn., Minn. Soc. Neurol. Scin., Ctrl. Soc. Neurol. Rsch. (pres. 1961), Alumni Assn. Mayo Found. Presbyterian. Office: Mayo Found Dept Health Scis Rsch 201 1st St SW Rochester MN 55905-0001 Home: 211 2nd St NW Apt 716 Rochester MN 55901-2813 Business E-Mail: whisnant@mayo.edu.

**WHISNANT, STEPHEN LABRON,** music educator; b. Shelby, NC, Sept. 15, 1970; s. Harvey Labron and Johnnie Rebecca Whisnant; m. Sherry Lynn French, Dec. 3, 1994; children: Allison Nichole, Rebecca Ann. MusB, Mars Hill Coll., 1994. Band dir. West Columbus H.S., Cerro Gordo, NC, 1995—97; band dir., orch. dir. Loris H.S., SC, 1998—. Mem.: Music Educators Nat. Conf. Home: 4004 Mullins St Loris SC 29569 Office: Loris High Sch 301 Loris Lions Rd Loris SC 29569 Office Phone: 843-756-7455. Personal E-mail: whizzy@sccoast.net. E-mail: swhisna@lh.hcs.k12.sc.us.

**WHITACRE, EDWARD E., JR.,** telecommunications company executive; b. Ennis, Texas, Nov. 4, 1941; m. Linda Whitacre; 2 children. BS in Indsl. Engring., Tex. Tech U., 1964. With Southwestern Bell Tel. Co., 1963-85, various positions in opers. dept., Kans. divsn. Topeka, 1982-85; group pres. Southwestern Bell Corp., 1985-86, v.p. revenues and pub. affairs, vice-chmn., CFO St. Louis, 1986-88, pres., COO, 1988-89; chmn., CEO SBC Communications (now AT&T, Inc.), San Antonio, 1990—. Mem. adv. coun. Nat. Security Telecomm.; bd. dirs. Anheuser Busch, Inc., May Dept. Stores, 1989—2004, Burlington No. Santa Fe, Inc., Emerson Electric Co., 1990—2004. Pres. Boy Scouts Am., 1999—2000; campaign chmn. United Way, San Antonio, 1998; mem. gov. bus. coun. State of Tex.; chmn. bd. regents Tex. Coun. U. Health Sci., Lubbock, Tex., 1992—98; bd. govs. S.W. Found. Bio Med. Rsch. Recipient Internat. Citizen of Yr. award World Affairs Coun. San Antonio, 1997; Spirit of Achievement award Nat. Jewish Med. and Rsch. Ctr., 1998; Freeman award San Antonio C. of C., 1997; named to Tex. Bus. Hall of Fame, 1997. Presbyterian. Avocations: golf, hunting, cooking, reading. Office: AT&T Inc 175 E Houston St San Antonio TX 78205-2255 Office Phone: 210-821-4105.*

**WHITAKER, BRUCE EZELL,** college president; b. Cleveland County, NC, June 27, 1921; s. Oveda E. and Fay A. Whitaker; m. Esther Adams, Aug. 22, 1947; children: Barry Eugene, Garry Bruce. BA, Wake Forest U., 1944;

BD, So. Bapt. Theol. Sem., 1947, ThM, 1948, PhD, 1950; postgrad., George Peabody Coll., 1952; DL, Wake Forest U., 1987. Ordained to ministry Bapt. Ch., 1945; pastor Smithfield, Ky., 1945-49; instr. sociology and philosophy Ind. U., 1947-50; prof. religion Cumberland U., Lebanon, Tenn., 1950-51, Belmont Coll., Nashville, 1951-52; prof. sociology, asst. to pres. Shorter Coll., Rome, Ga., 1952-53; asso. pastor, minister edn. Atlanta, 1953-54; state sec., student dept. Bapt. State Conv., NC, 1954-57; pres. Chowan Coll., Murfreesboro, NC, 1957-89, pres. emeritus, 1989—. Mem. adv. com. to Nat. Higher Edn., 1962-66; to N.C. Commn. Higher Edn. Facilities, 1964—; pres. N.C. Conf. Social Svc., 1965-67, Assn. Governing Bds., 1973-82, Assn. So. Baptist Colls. and Schs., 1967-68, Assn. Eastern N.C. Colls., 1968-69; bd. dirs. Regional Edn. Lab. for Carolinas and Va. Pres. bd. trustees N.C. Found. Church-Related Colls., 1970-74; bd. dirs., v.p. Nat. Coun. Ind. Jr. Colls., 1974-75, pres., 1975-76; mem. adv. coun. presidents Assn. Southern Ind. Colls. and Univs. (dir. 1976-82, Leadership Recognition award 1989), Nat. Assn. Ind. Colls. and Univs. (dir. 1977-78, 81-85), Am. Assn. Higher Edn., Am. Coun. Edn. (bd. dirs. 1985-89), Internat. Platform Assn., Omicron Delta Kappa. Clubs: Capital City (Raleigh, N.C.), Rotary (chmn. dist. student exchange com. 1969-72, Paul Harris fellow); Optimist; Beechwood Country (Ahoskie, N.C.); Harbor (Norfolk, Va.). Office: 2430 Springmoor Cir Raleigh NC 27615 Personal E-mail: bwhitaker10@nc.rr.com.

**WHITAKER, ELIZABETH D.,** lawyer; b. Washington, Feb. 20, 1953; BA in Anthropology magna cum laude, Wheaton Coll., 1979; JD cum laude, So. Meth. U., Dallas, 1980. Bar: Tex. 1980. Co-mng. ptnr. Bracewell & Giuliani, LLP, Dallas. With Carrington, Coleman, Sloman & Blumenthal LLP, 1980—81, 1982—99, Dallas County Dist. Atty. Office, 1981—82; exec. com., bd. dirs. Com. for Qualified Judiciary, 2000, 01; exec. com. So. Meth. U. Sch. Law, 1998—, Inst. Tech. Law; barrister Patrick Higginbotham Inns of Ct., 2004—; trustee Ctr. Am Internat. Law; spkr. in field. Contbr. articles to profl. law jours. Commr. State of Tex. Lottery Commn., 2000—03; mem. United Way, Women's Initiative, 2002; bd. dirs. Cmtys. in Schs., 2004—; Grammen Chiapas Initiative, 2004—. Recipient The Innovator award, Profiles in Leadership, 2004. Fellow: Am. Bar Found. (founder), Dallas Bar Found., Tex. Bar Found.; mem.: Am. Law Inst., Order of Coif, Coll. of State Bar Tex., State Bar Tex. (chair continuing legal edn. com. 1996—97, bd. dirs 1996—99, chair bd. dirs. 1998—99, pres.-elect 2002—03, pres. 2003—04). Republican. Office: Bracewell & Patterson LLP 500 N Akard St Ste 4000 Dallas TX 75201-3387 Office Phone: 214-758-1000. Business E-mail: betsywhitaker@hotmail.com.    E-mail: betsy.whitaker@bracewellgiuliani.com.

**WHITAKER, EWEN ADAIR,** retired astronomer; b. London, Eng., June 22, 1922; arrived in US, 1958; s. George Frederick and Gladys Emily (Johnstone) Whitaker; m. Beryl Joyce Horswell, June 22, 1946; children: Malcolm John, Graham David, Fiona Carolyn. Higher Nat. Cert. in Mech. Engring., Woolwich Polytechnic, Eng., 1944. Spectrographer Siemens Bros. & Co. Ltd., London, 1940—49; asst. exptl. officer Royal Greenwich Obs., London, 1949—58; rsch. assoc. U. Chicago, Yerkes Obs., Williams Bay, Wis., 1958—60; assoc. rsch scientist U. Arizona, Lunar & Planetary Lab., Tucson, 1960—87; retired, 1987. Cons. Air Force Chart & Info. Ctr., St. Louis, 1958—72; co-experimenter NASA Ranger Lunar Missions, 1963—66; team mem. NASA Lunar Surveyor TV, 1965—68, NASA Apollo Orbital Sci. Photog. Team, 1970—73. Author: Mapping & Naming the Moon, 1999, The University of Arizona's Lunar & Planetary Laboratory - Its Founding & Early Years, 1985; co-author: Orthographic Atlas of the Moon, 1960—61, Photographic Lunar Atlas, 1960, Rectified Lunar Atlas, 1963, Consolidated Lunar Atlas, 1967. Recipient Goodacre Gold Medal & Gift, British Astron. Assoc., 1982. Fellow: Royal Astron. Soc.; mem.: Internat. Astron. Union, Natl. Assoc. of Watch & Clock Collectors. Achievements include first to be able to produce differential bi-spectral imagery of moon; use of coronagraphic techniques to stars; discovery of orbital inclination and eccentricity of Uranus' satellite Miranda; chose impact location for Ranger 7, NASA's first successful moonshot; discovery of landing location of Surveyor 3 on the moon to which Apollo 12 was later targeted; received international approval for choosing two separate groups of 7 craters in the lunar farside Apollo basin to receive the names of the deceased Challenger and Columbia Space Shuttle astronauts; asteroid 7948 named Whitaker for contributions to NASA lunar programs and lunar science, Internat. Astron. Union. Avocation: clock repair and restoration. Home: 4332 E 6th St Tucson AZ 85711

**WHITAKER, FOREST,** actor, film producer, director; b. Longview, Tex., July 15, 1961; m. Keisha Nash, May 4, 1996; children: Sonnet, True Isabella 1 stepchild, Autumn; 1 child, Ocean Alexander. Attended, U. So. Calif. Pres. Spirit Dance Entertainment. Stage appearances (London) Swan, Romeo and Juliet, Hamlet, Ring Around the Moon, Craig's Wife, Whose Life Is It Anyway?, The Greeks; other stage appearances include Patchwork Shakespeare, Beggar's Opera, Jesus Christ Superstar; TV appearances include Amazing Stories, Hill Street Blues, Cagney and Lacey, Trapper John, M.D., The Fall Guy, Different Strokes, Feast of All Saints, 2001, The Twilight Zone, 2002; TV movies Hands of a Stranger, 1987, Criminal Justice, 1990, Last Light, 1993, Rebound: The Legend of Earl "The Great" Manigault, 1996, The Split, 1998, Witness Protection, 1999, Light It Up, 1999, Ghost Dog, 1999, Four Dogs Playing Poker, 1999, Deacons for Defense, 2003; mini-series North & South, 1985, North and South Book II, 1986; TV series The Shield, 2006-; films: Fast Times at Ridgemont High, 1982, Vision Quest, 1985, The Color of Money, 1986, Platoon, 1986, Stakeout, 1987, Good Morning, Vietnam, 1987, Bloodsport, 1988, Bird, 1988 (best actor Cannes Festival 1988), Johnny Handsome, 1989, Downtown, 1990, (also co-prodr.) Rage in Harlem, 1991 (also co-prodr.), Article 99, 1992, Diary of a Hit Man, 1992, Consenting Adults, 1992, Body Snatchers, 1993, The Crying Game, 1993, Blown Away, 1994, Jason's Lyric, 1994, Prêt-à-Porter, 1994, Species, 1995, Smoke, 1995, Phenomenon, 1996, The Split, 1997, Battlefield Earth, 2000, Four Dogs Playing Poker, 2000, Green Dragon, 2001, The Fourth Angel, 2001, Panic Room, 2002, Phone Booth, 2002, Jiminy Glick in La La Wood, 2004, Mary, 2005, A Little Trip to Heaven, 2005, American Gun, 2005, Even Money, 2006, The Marsh, 2006, The Last King of Scotland, 2006, (voice) Everyone's Hero, 2006; dir.: (films) Strapped (Toronto Film Festival award for best new dir.), Waiting to Exhale, 1995, Hope Floats, 1998; exec. prodr.: (TV films) Black Jaq, 1998, (TV miniseries) Feast of All Saints, 2001, (films) First Daughter (also dir.), 2004; co-exec. prodr. (TV films) Door to Door, 2002; prodr. (films) Chasing Papi, 2003. Office: care DGA 7920 W Sunset Blvd Los Angeles CA 90046-3300*

**WHITAKER, G(EORGE) WARREN,** lawyer; b. N.Y.C., Oct. 13, 1950; s. George Warren Jr. and Stella S. (Stann) W.; m. Marian Kramer, Sept. 15, 1982; children: Alexander Stuart, Emily Kate. BA, Rutgers U., 1972; JD, Columbia U., 1976. Bar: N.J. 1976, N.Y. 1977, U.S. Tax Ct. 1991. Assoc. Davidson, Dawson, N.Y.C., 1977-80, Curtis, Mallet, N.Y.C., 1980-83; sr. atty. Breed, Abbott, N.Y.C., 1983-91; assoc. Chadbourne & Parke, N.Y.C., 1991-94; sr. atty. Jones, Day, Reavis & Pogue, N.Y.C., 1994-96; ptnr. Law Offices James E. Hughes Jr., N.Y.C., 1996-98, Hughes and Whitaker, N.Y.C., 1998—2001, Day, Berry & Howard LLP, N.Y.C., 2002—. Counsel Pelham (N.Y.) Art Ctr., 1995-2001; bd. dirs. Shakespeare's Globe, USA; mem. banker lawyer adv. com. N.Y. Philharmonic, 2003—; counsel, bd. dirs. Picture Ho. Regional Theater, 2005—. Fellow N.Y. Bar Found.; mem. ABA (vice chair internat. estate planning com. 1996—), Soc. Trust and Estate Practioners (chmn. N.Y. chpt. 1998—), N.Y. State Bar Assn. (chair internat. estate

---

planning com. 1996-98, 1st dist. rep. 1999-2001, treas. 2001-02, sec. 2002-03, chair-elect 2003—04, chair 2004-05), N.Y.C. Bar Assn. (estate tax com. 1996—). Republican. Avocations: bicycling, book collecting. Home: 514 Esplanade Pelham NY 10803-2400 Office: Day, Berry & Howard Fl 28 875 3d Ave New York NY 10022 Office Phone: 212-829-3602. E-mail: gwwhitaker@dbh.com.

**WHITAKER, GILBERT RILEY, JR.,** economics professor, academic administrator, business economist; b. Oklahoma City, Oct. 8, 1931; s. Gilbert Riley and Melodese (Kilpatrick) W.; m. Ruth Pauline Tonn, Dec. 18, 1953; children: Kathleen, David Edward, Thomas Gilbert. BA, Rice U., 1953; postgrad., So. Methodist U., 1956-57; MS in Econs., U. Wis., Madison, 1958, PhD in Econs. (Ford Found. dissertation fellow), 1961. Instr., Sch. of Bus. Northwestern U., 1960-61, asst. prof. bus. econs., Sch. of Bus., 1961-64, assoc. prof., Sch. of Bus., 1964-66, rsch. assoc. Transp. Center, Sch. of Bus., 1962-66; assoc. prof. Washington U., St. Louis, 1966-67, prof., 1967-76, adj. prof. econs., 1968-76, assoc. dean Sch. Bus. Adminstrn., 1969-76; dean, prof. bus. econs. M.J. Neeley Sch. Bus., Tex. Christian U., 1976-79; dean U. Mich., 1979-90; prof. Sch. Bus. Adminstrn. U. Mich., 1979-97; provost, v.p. acad. affairs U. Mich., Ann Arbor, 1990-93, provost, exec. v.p. acad. affairs, 1993-95; sr. advisor Andrew W. Mellon Found., 1996—2004; dean Jesse Jones Grad. Sch. Mgmt. Rice U., Houston, 1997—2005, prof. bus. econs., 1997—. Dir. Am. Assembly of Collegiate Schs. of Bus., 1984-91, v.p., pres.-elect, 1988-89, pres., 1989-90, dir. Washington campus, 1980-89, chmn., 1985-88; bd. dirs. Westlake Chem.Co.; sr. economist banking and currency com. U.S. Ho. of Reps., 1964; mem. Grad. Mgmt. Admissions Coun., 1972-75, chmn., 1974-75; bd. dirs. Washtenaw County United Way, 1990-96. Author: (with Marshall Colberg and Dascomb Forbush) Business Economics, 6th edit., 1981; (with Roger Chisholm) Forecasting Methods, 1971. Bd. trustees, sec.-treas. JSTOR, 1995-2002. With USN, 1953-56. Mem.: Am. Econ. Assn., Ft. Worth Boat Club. Office: Rice U Jesse Jones Grad Sch of Mgmt PO Box 2932 Houston TX 77252-2932 Business E-mail: grwhit@rice.edu.

**WHITAKER, JOEL,** publishing executive, public official; b. Indpls., May 27, 1942; s. Quincy Myers and Sigur Elizabeth (Moore) W.; m. Donna Kay, Apr. 27, 1986. BS in Bus. Journalism, Ind. U., 1964, MA in Journalism, 1971; JD, Temple U., 1979. Reporter St. Petersburg (Fla.) Times, 1964, copy editor, 1966-68, Wall St. Journal, N.Y.C., 1968-73; bus. news editor Phila. Evening and Sunday Bull., 1973-78; law clk. Fellheimer, Krakower & Eiclen, Phila., 1978—79; mng. editor Bank Letter, N.Y.C., 1979-80; editor, pres. Whitaker Newsletters Inc., Silver Spring, Md., 1980—. Chmn. Fanwood Planning Bd., 1981-85; trustee Fanwood cmty. Found. 1998-2004; mem. Downtown Redevel. Commn., Fanwood, 1983-85; mem. Union County (N.J.) local adv. commn. on alcoholism and drug abuse, 1993-97, chmn., 1994-95, vice chmn. 1997; councilman Borough of Fanwood, 1998-2003, coun. pres., 2000-03. Mem. Newsletter Publishers Assn. (bd. dirs. 1983-92, found. trustee 1986—, treas. 1989-93, found. treas. 2005-06), Soc. Profl. Journalists (treas. N.J. profl. chpt. 1997-2005), Nat. Press Club (Washington), Rotary (bd. dirs. Fanwood-Scotch Plains club 1996-98), Army and Navy Club (Washington). Republican. Roman Catholic. Office: Whitaker Newsletters Inc 14305 Shoreham Dr Silver Spring MD 20905-4481 Office Phone: 301-384-1573. Personal E-mail: joelwhitaker@verizon.net.

**WHITAKER, JOHN KING,** retired economics professor; b. Burnley, Lancashire, Eng., Jan. 30, 1933; arrived in US, 1967; s. Ben and Mary Whitaker; m. Sally Bell Cross, Aug. 24, 1957; children: Ann Elizabeth, Jane Claire, David John. BA in Econs., U. Manchester, 1956; AM, Johns Hopkins U., 1957; PhD, Cambridge U., 1962. Lectr. U. Bristol, England, 1960-66, prof., 1966-69; vis. prof. U. Va., Charlottesville, 1967-68, prof. econs., 1969-86, chmn. dept. econs., 1979-82, Paul Goodloe McIntire prof. econs., 1986-92, Georgia Bankard prof. econs., 1992—2003, Georgia Bankard prof. econs. emeritus, 2003—. Author: The Early Economic Writings of Alfred Marshall, 1867-1890, 2 vols., 1975, The Correspondence of Alfred Marshall, Economist, 3 vols., 1996. Mem. Am. Econ. Assn., Royal Econ. Soc., History of Econs. Soc. Office: 1615 Yorktown Dr Charlottesville VA 22901-3046

**WHITAKER, LINTON ANDIN,** plastic surgeon; b. Navasota, Tex., Nov. 16, 1936; s. Ira Andin and Lena Rivers (Stedman) W.; m. Renata Grasmanis, Dec. 20, 1963; children: Derek Andin (dec.), Ingrid Marlena, Brandon Andrew. BA, U. Tex., 1958; MD, Tulane U., 1962. Diplomate Am. Bd. Surgery, Am. Bd. Plastic Surgery. Founder, dir. ctr. human appearance U. Pa. Med. Ctr., Phila., 1988—; resident in gen. surgery Dartmouth Affiliated Hosps., Hanover, NH, 1965-69; resident in plastic surgery U. Pa. Hosp., Phila., 1969-71; chief plastic surgery Grad. Hosp., 1971-77, U. Pa. Hosp., Phila., 1987—2005, attending surgeon, 1971—; chief plastic surgery Children's Hosp. Phila., 1981—2001, attending surgeon, 1971—; v.p. med. staff Children's Hosp., Phila., 1992-94, pres. med. staff, 1994-96; attending physician VA Hosp., 1971—, Phila. Gen. Hosp., 1971—. assoc. in plastic surgery Sch. Medicine, U. Pa., Phila., 1971-73, asst. prof. in plastic surgery, 1973-76, assoc. prof., 1976-81, prof., 1981—; founder, dir. ctr. human appearance U. Pa. Med. Ctr., Phila., 1988—. Vis. prof. South Australia Craniofacial Unit, Adelaide, Australia and New Zealand, 1981, U. Hawaii, 1983, Brown U., Providence, 1983, Mass. Gen. Hosp., Boston, 1984, U. Utah, Salt Lake City, 1984, U. B.C., Vancouver, 1986, U. Pitts., 1988, U. Calif., San Diego, 1992, Ohio Valley Soc. for Plastic and Reconstructive Surgery, 1992, N.Y. U., 1994; Curts vis. prof. Dartmouth U. Med. Ctr., Hanover, N.H., 1990, Kazanjian vis. prof. Mass. Gen. Hosp., Boston, 1990; First Seiichi Ohmori Meml. lectr. All Asiatic Congress on Aesthetic Surgery, Tokyo, 1988; vis. speaker Inst. Cosmotology and Inst. Stomatology, Moskow, Russia, 1985, vis. prof. Seoul Nat. U. and vis. speaker Korean Soc. for Plastic Surgeons, 1994; hon. vis. spkr. Chinese Plastic Surgery Soc., Beijing, 1996; lectr., speaker at univs., assns. in field. Co-author: Atlas of Cranio-maxillofacial Surgery, 1982, Aesthetic Surgery of the Facial Skelton, 1992; editor (with P. Randall): Symposium on the Reconstruction of Jaw Deformity, Clinics in Plastic Surgery, 1987, 1991; co-editor: Yearbook of Plastic and Reconstructive Surgery, 1980—97; assoc. editor: Seminars in Complementary Medicine, 2001—, mem. editl. bd.: Jour. Cutaneous Aging and Cosmetic Dermatology, 1988—; contbr. articles to profl. jours. Capt. M.C., U.S. Army, 1963-65. Foederer fellow Foederer Fund for Excellence, 1985-88; NIH grantee, 1976-79, 81-87, 82-85, 89, Plastic Surgery Edn. Found. Rsch. grantee, 1980-82; recipient James IV Surg. Traveller award, 1979. Fellow ACS, Am. Soc. Ophthalmic Plastic and Reconstructive Surgery (hon.); mem. AMA, Am. Assn. Plastic Surgeons (mem. program com. 1988, chmn. 1989, Rsch. grantee 1984-85), Am. Surg. Assn., Am. Alpine Workshop in Plastic Surgery (founding mem.), Am. Cleft Palate Assn. (chmn. com. classification craniofacial anomalies 1976-80, mem. program com. for 1978 mtg. 1977, mem. long-range planning com. 1980, mem. coun. 1981-84, mem. internat. rels. com. 1981-83), Am. Cleft Palate Ednl. Found. (bd. dirs. 1975-84, chmn. rsch. com. 1975-78, chmn. instl. courses 1980-81), Am. Soc. Aesthetic Plastic Surgery, Am. Soc. Craniofacial Surgery (mem. coun. 1992—), Am. Soc. Maxillofacial Surgeons (Spl. Honors 2003, bd. dirs. 2003—), Am. Soc. Plastic and Reconstructive Surgeons, mem. plastic surgery speakers bur. 1977—), Am. Soc. Plastic and Reconstructive Surgeons Ednl. Found. (chmn. ednl. assessment com., maxillofacial truama and craniofacial anomalies 1975-78, mem. clin. symposia com. 1978-82, chmn. clin. symposia com. 1981-82), Internat. Cleft Palate and Related Craniofacial Anomalies Soc., Internat. Soc. Aesthetic Surgery, Internat. Soc. Craniofacial Surgeons (founding mem., organizer, mem. exec. com. 1987—, sec and treas. 1993-95, pres. 1995-97), Phila. Med. Soc., Phila. Acad. Surgery, Coll. Physicians Phila., Assn. Acad. Surgery, Northeastern Soc. Plastic Surgery (chmn. program com. 1987, mem. programcom. 1988), Plastic Surgery Rsch. Coun., John Morgan Soc., Robert H. Ivy Soc., The Columbian Soc. Plastic, Maxillofacial and Hand Surgery (hon.), Academia Medica Lombarda (Italy, hon.), Sociedad Jamie Planas de Cirugia Plastica (Spain, hon.), Mt. Kenya Safari Club (hon.), Japan Soc. Craniomaxillofacial Surgeons (hon.), Asian Pacific Cranofacial Assn., Japan Soc. Plastic and Reconstructive Surgery (hon.), Phila. Club, Merion Cricket Club, Confrerie des chevaliers du

---

Tastevin, Grand Senechat. Avocations: mountain climbing, skiing, wines. Office: U Pa Med Ctr 10 Penn Tower 3400 Spruce St Philadelphia PA 19104-4206 Office Phone: 215-662-2048. Business E-Mail: linton.whitaker@uphs.upenn.edu.

**WHITAKER, MARK THEIS,** editor; b. Lower Merion, Pa., Sept. 7, 1957; s. Cleophus Sylvester and Jeanne (Theis) W.; m. Alexis Lynn Gelber, May 5, 1985; children: Rachel Eva, Matthew Edward. BA summa cum laude, Harvard U., 1979; postgrad., Oxford (Eng.) U., 1979-81; LLD (hon.), Wheaton Coll. Assoc. editor Newsweek mag., NYC, 1981-83, gen. editor, 1983, sr. writer, 1984-86, sr. editor, bus. editor, 1987-91, asst. mng. editor, 1991-95, mng. editor, 1996-98, corp. editor, editor NYC, 1998—2006; v.p.; editor in chief new ventures Washingtonpost Newsweek Interactive Co., LLC Washington Post Co., 2006—. Bd. dir. Literacy Partners, NYC. Marshall scholar Brit. Marshall Fund, Oxford U., 1979-81. Mem. Nat. Assn. Black Journalists, Am. Soc. Mag. Editors (bd. dirs., 1999-, pres., 2004-2006), Coun. on Fgn. Rels., Century Assn., Phi Beta Kappa. Achievements include first African-American editor of a newsweekly; Newsweek won two National Magazine Awards for General Excellence during his tenure as editor.*

**WHITAKER, MARY JANE,** retired elementary school educator; b. Port Clinton, Ohio, Mar. 14, 1947; d. Walter Anthony and Mary Louise (Horak) Kania; m. Ralph Maxwell Whitaker, Dec. 4, 1970; children: Shelly A., Christy L., Mark P. BS in Edn., Bowling Green State U., Ohio, 1969; MEd in Reading, U. Toledo, 1989. Tchr. Rising Sun (Ohio) Elem., 1969, Carroll Elem., Oak Harbor, Ohio, 1969—70, R.C. Waters Elem., Oak Harbor, 1970—75, 1985—2005, Rocky Ridge (Ohio) Elem., 1976—85; ret., 2005. Mem. Oak Harbor (Ohio) Athletic Boosters, Oak Harbor (Ohio) Music Boosters; sec. St. Boniface Sch. Bd., Oak Harbor; chmn. celebrations Oak Harbor (Ohio) Bicentennial Com., 2000—03. Mem.: NEA, Ohio Edn. Assn., Delta Kappa Gamma. Roman Catholic. Home: 14424 W True Rd Oak Harbor OH 43449

**WHITAKER, MATTHEW GEORGE,** prosecutor; JD, MBA, U. Iowa, 1995. Corp. counsel SUPERVALU; atty. Briggs & Morgan, Finley Alt Smith, Des Moines; US atty. (so. dist.) Iowa US Dept. Justice, Des Moines, 2004—. Office: US Courthouse Annex Ste 286 110 E Ct Ave Des Moines IA 50309*

**WHITAKER, MICAL ROZIER,** theater director, educator; b. Metter, Ga., Feb. 10, 1941; s. Ellis and Alma Mical Whitaker; m. Georgenia Lyons Whitaker, Sept. 1, 1978 (div. June 0, 1991); 1 child, Mical Anthony. BFA, NC A&T State U., Greensboro, 1989. Founder and dir. East River Players, New York, NY, 1964—76; prodr. Ossie Davis and Ruby Dee Story Hour, New York, NY, 1975—77; asst. prof. Ga. So. U., Statesboro, Ga., 1981—. Cons. Children's TV Productions Sesame St., 1969; artistic dir. Richard Allen Ctr. Culture and Art, 1978—82; writer and dir. Teleprompter Cable TV, New York, NY, 1971; founder and coord. Lincoln Ctr. St. Theatre Festivals, New York, NY, 1979—81. Dir.: (festival) Words from the Renaissance, (birthday pageant) A Place of Sunshine, (tragedy) Othello, (ceremony) The Audelco Awards, (historical drama) The Drinking Gourd, (tragi-comedy) The Real Queen of Hearts Ain't Even Pretty, (fables for children) Story Theatre, (comedy) I'm Not Rappaport, The Last Night at Ballyhoo, The Foreigner, Purile Victorious, (musical) Tambourines to Glory, Before the Flood, Everyman and Roach, The Fantasticks; (plays) A Glance From God, To Be Young, Gifted and Black, Shades of Harlem, Eyes, One More Sunday, Black Nativity, Home, On the Brink of the Mountaintop, Ceremonies in Dark Old Men, High on People, The Importance of Being Earnest, St. Louis Woman, Boochie, From the Mississippi Delta, Spunk, Maricella de la Luz, Long Day's Journey into Night, Stairs to the Roof, Jitney; actor: As You Like It; dir.: (dramas) Agamemnon, The Miracle Worker, The Biko Inquest, In Splendid Error, Who's Afraid of Virginia Woolf, The Piano Lesson, The Amen Corner, Johnny Moonbeam and the Silver Arrow, A Christmas Carol; actor: (plays) Everyman and Roach, Merlin, The Bloodknot, Ma Rainey's Black Bottom, The Piano Lesson, I'm Not Rappaport, Twelfth Night, The Cherry Orchard. Recipient Dir. Musical, Audelco Awards, 1975, Emmy, Seattle Chpt., 1979-1980, G.S.C. Masquers award, G.S.C., 1982, Jefferson citation Directing, Kuumba Theatre, 1979, Spl. award St. Theatre, NYC, 1973, Renaissance and Cultural Devel. award, Black Image Awards, 2000, YMCA Little Theatre Award Set Design, YMCA, 1963, AUDELCO award St. Theatre, AUDELCO, 1977, AUDELCO award Directing, 1979; fellow Nat. Endowment Humanities fellowship, Duke U., 1991, Fulbright-Hays and U.S. Dept. Edn. fellowship, Ga. Consortium, 1992. Mem.: NAACP. Achievements include founding of Candler County Cultural Center committee. Avocations: travel, reading, home decorating, theater. Home: 515 Washington Street Metter GA 30439 Office: Georgia Southern University Po 8091 Statesboro GA 30460 E-mail: mrwhit@gasou.edu.

**WHITAKER, SCOTT,** former federal agency administrator, lobbyist; m. Michelle Whitaker; 2 children. B in Polit. Sci., Palm Beach Atlantic Coll.; M in Govt., Johns Hopkins U. Legis. asst. Senate Asst. Majority Leader Don Nickles, 1994—97, policy adviser, 1997—2001; asst. sec. for legislation US Dept. HHS, Washington, 2001—03, chief of staff, 2003—05; exec. v.p. Biotechnology Industry Org., Wash., DC, 2005—. Republican. Office: Biotech Industry Org 1225 Eye St NW Suite 400 Washington DC 20005

**WHITAKER, SUSANNE KANIS,** veterinary medical librarian; b. Clinton, Mass., Sept. 10, 1947; AB in Biology, Clark U., 1969; MS in Library Sci., Case Western Res. U., 1970. Regional reference librarian Yale Med. Library, New Haven, 1970-72; med. librarian Hartford Hosp., Conn., 1972-77; asst. librarian Cornell U., Ithaca, NY, 1977-78; vet. med. librarian Coll. Vet. Medicine, Cornell U., 1978-98; vet. pub. svcs. libr., 1998—. Mem. Med. Libr. Assn. (vet. med. librs. sect. 1983-84, chmn. 1984-85, chmn. pub. rels. com. 2000—), Med. Libr. Assn. (Upstate NY and Ont. chpt.), Acad. Health Info. Profls. (disting. mem.), Am. Vet. Med. History Soc. (sec.-treas. 2004—). Home: 23 Wedgewood Dr Ithaca NY 14850-1064 Office: Cornell U Coll Vet Medicine Flower-Sprecher Libr Ithaca NY 14853-6401 Office Phone: 607-253-3499. Business E-Mail: skw2@cornell.edu.

**WHITAKER, THOMAS BURTON,** agricultural engineer, educator; b. Asheville, N.C., May 16, 1939; BS, N.C. State U., 1962, MS, 1964; PhD in Agrl. Engring., Ohio State U., 1967. From asst. prof. to assoc. prof. N.C. State U., 1967-86, prof. biol. and agrl. engring., 1976—. Agrl. engr. USDA, 1967—. Recipient Golden Peanut Rsch. award Nat. Peanut Coun., 1980. Mem. Am. Soc. Agrl. Engrs., Am. Peanut Rsch. and Edn. Soc. (Bailey award 1976), Sigma Xi. Office: Dept Biol and Agrl Engring 124 Weaver Hall PO Box 7625 Raleigh NC 27695-0001

**WHITAKER, THOMAS O'HARA,** theater educator, theater director; s. Thomas Russell and Dorothy Whitaker. BA, Oberlin Coll., Ohio, 1975; MFA, Carnegie-Mellon U., Pitts., 1983. Instr. acting Carnegie-Mellon U., Coll. Fine Arts, 1982—83; instr. SW Mo. State U., Springfield, 1983—84; asst. prof. Ind. State U., Terre Haute, 1984—87, U. Tex., Austin, 1987—92, U. Calif., Santa Barbara, 1992—96, assoc. prof., 1996—. Cons. dir., tchr. Conn. Humanities Coun., Hartford, 1980—81; cons. Ctr. Theatre Techniques Edn. Stratford, 1980—81, Comprehensive Arts Program, New Haven, 1980—81; guest artist Oberlin Theater Inst., 1987; tenured dir. Tex. Shakespeare Festival, Kilgore, 1989—; cons. Beijing Inst. World Theater and Film, 2005—; guest prof. Nanjing U., China, 2006—. Actor(musician): (theater/puppet) Young Woman's Sorrow, Man is Man, Loot, The Misanthrope, Advice to the Players, Love's Labor's Lost; actor: King Lear; dir.: Tartuffe, Taming of the Shrew; actor: Heartbreak House, (theatre/puppet) Grey Lady Cantata; dir.: (theater) The Bourgeois Gentleman, Two Gentlemen of Verona; dir.: As You Like It; actor: Henry IV, part 1; dir.: Big Love, Arms and the Man, The Merchant of Venice, Life's a Dream, Cyrano de Bergerac, bobrauschenbergamerica; actor: (film) The Meadow's Green; (theater) Revel's World of Shakespeare; actor: The Marilyn Project, The Forced Marriage; dir.: Time Play, Misalliance, Fool for Love, Buried Child.

Recipient Boettcher award Directing, Carnegie-Mellon U., 1983; grantee, Conn. Humanities Coun., 1980; scholar, Carnegie-Mellon U., 1982—83. Mem.: Phi Beta Kappa. Office Phone: 805-893-7646.

**WHITAKER, THOMAS PATRICK,** lawyer; b. Washington, Sept. 22, 1944; s. Thomas J. and Mary K. (Finn) W.; m. Donna Mae Brenish, Feb. 16, 1974; children: Laura, Kevin. BA, George Washington U., 1966, MPA, 1973, JD, 1979; postgrad., Naval War Coll., 1984. Bar: Va. 1979. Staff asst. Adminstrn. Office of U.S. Cts., Washington, 1972-73, analyst, 1975-77; cons. Planning Research Corp., McLean, Va., 1973-75; program analyst Social Security Adminstrn., Falls Church, Va., 1982—; congrl. aide Rep. Abercrombie, 2005. Served to lt. (j.g.) USNR, 1966-71, Vietnam, capt. with Res. 1983-97. Asst. U.S. Naval Attache, Egypt, 1988, Malaysia, 1992. Home: 9817 Days Farm Dr Vienna VA 22182-7306 Office Phone: 703-605-8292. Personal E-mail: twhitake@hotmail.com.

**WHITAKER, THOMAS RUSSELL,** English literature educator; b. Marquette, Mich., Aug. 7, 1925; s. Joe Russell and Sarah Genevieve (Houk) W.; m. Dorothy Vera Barnes, June 17, 1950 (dec. Dec. 1995); children: Thomas O'Hara, Sarah Mae, Mary Beth, Gwendolyn Anne; m. Joan Bower Horwitt, Oct. 4, 1997 (div. Sept. 2002); m. Lillian Ann Traub, Jul. 26, 2003. BA summa cum laude, Oberlin Coll., 1949; MA, Yale U., 1950, PhD, 1953. Instr. English Oberlin (Ohio) Coll., 1952-55, asst. prof., 1955-59, assoc. prof., 1959-63, prof., 1963-64; tchr. lit. Goddard Coll., Plainfield, Vt., 1964-66; prof. English U. Iowa, Iowa City, 1966-75, Yale U., New Haven, Conn., 1975-95, prof. theater studies, 1986-95, chmn. dept. English, 1979-85, Frederick W. Hilles prof. English, 1989-95; Frederick W. Hilles prof. emeritus English, 1995—. Author: Swan and Shadow: Yeats's Dialogue with History, 1964, 2d edit. with new preface, 1989, William Carlos Williams, 1968, rev. edit., 1989, Fields of Play in Modern Drama, 1977, Tom Stoppard, 1983, augmented edit., 1984, Mirrors of Our Playing. Paradigms and Presences in Modern Drama, 1999; editor: Twentieth Century Interpretations of the Playboy of the Western World, 1969, Teaching in New Haven: The Common Challenge, 1991; editor Iowa Rev., 1974-77; chmn. editorial bd. On Common Ground, 1993—; author, narrator video script: Excellence in Teaching: Agenda for Partnership, 1997; writer, advisor Yale-New Haven Tchrs. Inst. Nat. Demonstration Project, 1998-02, Yale Nat. Initiative, 2002—. Served with C.E. U.S. Army, 1944-46. Recipient Harbison award for gifted teaching Danforth Found., 1972, Seton Elm and Ivy award, City of New Haven and Yale U., 2005; fellow, Am. Council Learned Socs., 1969—70, NEH-Huntington, 1981. Mem. MLA. Home: 38 Wilford Rd Branford CT 06405-5321

**WHITBREAD, THOMAS BACON,** language educator, writer; b. Bronxville, N.Y., Aug. 22, 1931; s. Thomas Francis and Caroline Nancy (Bacon) W. BA, Amherst Coll., 1952; A.M., Harvard U., 1953, PhD, 1959. Instr. English, U. Tex. at Austin, 1959-62, asst. prof., 1962-65, asso. prof., 1965-71, prof., 1971—. Vis. assoc. prof. Rice U., 1969-70; mem. lit. adv. panel Tex. Commn. on Arts and Humanities, 1972-76 Author (poetry): Four Infinitives, 1964, Whomp and Moonshiver, 1982; contbg. author: Prize Stories, 1962, The O. Henry Awards, 1962; editor: Seven Contemporary Authors, 1966. Recipient third Aga Khan prize for fiction Paris Rev., 1960, Lit. Anthology Program award Nat. Endowment for Arts, 1968, Outstanding Freshman Tchr. award Phi Eta Sigma, 1972-73 Mem. AAUP, Tex. Inst. Letters (Poetry award 1965, 83), Nat., Am. amateur press assns., Phi Beta Kappa. Democrat. Home: 1014 E 38th St Austin TX 78705-1835 Office: U Tex Dept English 1 Univ Station B5000 Austin TX 78712 Business E-Mail: whitbread@mail.utexas.edu.

**WHITBURN, GERALD,** insurance company executive; b. Wakefield, Mich., July 12, 1944; s. Donald and Ruby E. (Nichols) W.; m. Charmaine M. Heise, May 3, 1969; children: Bree, Luke. BS, U. Wis., Oshkosh, 1966; MA, U. Wis., Madison, 1968; postgrad., Harvard U., 1988, 00, U. Pa., 1997. Aide Gov. Warren P. Knowles, Wis., 1966-69; personal asst. USN sec. John H. Chafee, Washington, 1969-72; automobile dealer, real estate developer Merrill, Wis., 1973-80; exec. asst. to Senator Robert W. Kasten U.S. Senate, Washington, 1981-87; dep. sec. Wis. Dept. Adminstrn., Madison, 1987-89; sec. Wis. Dept. Industry, Labor and Human Rels., Madison, 1989-91, Wis. Dept. Health and Social Svcs., Madison, 1991-95; sec. exec. office of health and human svcs. Commonwealth of Mass., Boston, 1995-96; chmn., pres., CEO Ch. Mut. Ins. Co., Merrill, Wis., 1996—; dir. Property Casualty Insurers Assn. of Am., Wis. Mfrs. and Commerce, Wis. Ctr. Academically Talented Youth. Mem. U.S. Labor Sec.'s Commn. on Achieving Necessary Skills, Washington, 1990-92. Contbr. articles to newspapers. Del. Rep. Nat. Conv., 1988, 92, 2004. Recipient Disting. Alumni award U. Wis., Oshkosh, 1991. Office: Ch Mut Ins Co 300 Schuster Ln Merrill WI 54452 Home: 827 Parcher St Wausau WI 54403

**WHITBURN, MERRILL DUANE,** English literature educator; b. Mpls., Apr. 29, 1938; s. George and Marie Ellen (Carlstedt) W.; m. Diane Robertson, June 15, 1960; children: Stephen, Mark, Elizabeth. AB, U. Mich., 1960, AM, 1968; PhD, U. Iowa, 1973. With Western Electric Co., N.Y.C. and Indpls., 1965-67; asst. prof. Tex. A&M U., College Station, 1973-77, assoc. prof., 1977-79; assoc. prof. English Rensselaer Poly. Inst., Troy, NY, 1979-83, prof., 1983-89, Louis Ellsworth Laffin prof., 1989—, chmn. dept., 1979-85, 89; rsch. fellow Yale U. Divinity Sch., New Haven, 2003; Rensselaer Poly. Inst. Exch. prof. humanities and social sci. SUNY-Albany U., 2005. Co-owner Pride and Prejudice Books, Ballston Lake, N.Y., 1985—. Author: Rhetorical Scope and Performance: The Example of Technical Communication, 2000; co-author: (booklet) Guide for Departments of English, 1985; contbr. articles to profl. publs. Recipient Disting. Svc. award Tex. A&M U., 1976, Disting. Teaching award, 1979, Jay R. Gould award for excellence in tchg. tech. comm. Soc. Tech. Comm., 1995, Trustee's Outstanding Tchr. award Rensselaer Poly. Inst., 2002; grantee Fund for the Improvement of Postsecondary Edn., 1983. Mem. Nat. Coun. Tchrs. English (best article in tech. writing award 1981), Coun. for Programs in Tech. and Sci. Communication.

**WHITCOMB, JAMES HALL,** geophysicist, foundation administrator; b. Sterling, Colo., Dec. 10, 1940; s. Clay Thane and Julia Melvina Whitcomb; m. Sandra Lynn McMurdo, July 13, 1965 (div. 1978); m. Teresa R. Idoni, Feb. 3, 1989; children: Lisa Michelle, Marisa Giulia, Sabina Maria. Geophysics engring. degree, Colo. Sch. of Mines, 1962; MS in Oceanography, Geophysics, Oreg. State U., 1964; PhD in Geophysics, Calif. Inst. Tech., 1973. Grad. rsch. asst. dept. oceanography Oreg. State U., Corvallis, 1962-64; geophysicist Ctr. Astrogeology U.S. Geol. Survey, Flagstaff, Ariz., 1964-66; Fulbright-Hayes program rsch. fellow Seismol. Inst. U. Uppsala, Sweden, 1966-67; grad. rsch. asst. seismol. lab. Calif. Inst. Tech., Pasadena, 1967-73, sr. rsch. fellow seismol. lab., 1973-79; assoc. prof. attendant rank dept. geol. scis. U. Colo., Boulder, 1979-82, fellow Coop. Inst. Rsch. in Environ. Scis., 1979-84; v.p. technical applications and mktg. ISTAC, Inc., Pasadena, 1984-88; program dir. seismology NSF, Washington, 1989-99, acting dep. divsn. dir., 1999—2002, asst. head, 2002—. Expert witness U.S. Ho. Reps. Com. on Sci. and Tech., 1977; mem. geodynamics rev. bd. Jet Propulsion Lab., 1980-82, com. on geodesy Nat. Acad. Scis., 1982-85; pres. Boulder Systems, Inc., Pasadena, 1987-88. Recipient Outstanding Achievement award U.S. Geol. Survey, 1964, Dir.'s award for mgmt. excellence NSF, 1995, 2003; scholar State of Colo., 1958-62, Mobil Oil Co., 1960; fellow Sweden-Am. Found., 1966. Mem. AAAS, Am. Geophysical Union, Seismol. Soc. Am., Soc. Exploration Geophysicists (scholar 1963), Tau Beta Pi, Phi Kappa Phi, Sigma Xi. Office: Nat Sci Found Geosciences 4201 Wilson Blvd Arlington VA 22230-0002

**WHITCOMB, JAMES STUART,** videographer, photographer, production company executive; b. Buffalo, May 7, 1957; s. C. Stuart and Helen Nancy (O'Reilly) W. BA in Journalism/Broadcasting, SUNY, Buffalo, 1983. Cert. master herbalist, iridologist. Pres., owner Ad Astra Prodns., Williamsville, NY, 1987—; co-owner, videographer, photographer STB Prodns., Williamsville, 1989—; owner legal books and computer software co. JSW Pub., Williamsville, 1997—. Videographer, editor nature/stress reduction Videos A Celebration of the Four Seasons, 1991, Autumn on Cape Cod and Martha's Vineyard, 1993, Gardens, Blossoms & Blooms, 1994, A Walk Through St.

Francis Woods, 1994, Nantucket Noel: Christmas on Nantucket, 1994, Reflections: Nature's Watercolors, 1995, Autumn in Vermont, 1995, A Day On the Farm, 1995, Window Shopping, 1995, Singalong with your Old Favorites, 1997, A Celebration of the Four Seasons II: Seasons of the Seashore, 1997, Kids and Animals, 1998; videographer, writer promotion video Internat. Modeling and Talent Assn., 1990; videographer numerous prodns. for modelling, fashion, and spl. interest, owner, Jim's Project's Inc. Supporter St. Joseph's Indian Sch., Chamberlain, S.D, supporter Interlink Resources, Taraz, Kazakhstan. Mem. People for Ethical Treatment of Animals, Wilderness Soc., Am. Hiking Soc., Nat. Audubon Soc., Farm Sanctuary, Best Friends Animal Sanctuary, Assn. for Rsch. and Enlightenment, Adirondack Mountain Club. Achievements include first to Started a small non-profit organization called Jim's Project's Inc. to help the children in Kazakhstan, and in Hong Kong and China, and to bring a better life to the orphan children. Avocations: skiing, hiking. Home: 71 Rinewalt St Williamsville NY 14221-5736 Office: Ad Astra and STB Prodns PO Box 1725 Williamsville NY 14231-1725 Office Phone: 716-626-5319.

**WHITCOMB, KAY,** artist; b. Arlington, Mass., May 20, 1921; d. Herbert Hartwell Whitcomb and Mildred Parker Carr; divorced; children: Richard Y., Deborah N. Degree (hon.), RI Sch. Design, Cambridge Sch. Art, 1941. Enamel artist, craftsperson, Rockport, Mass. Guest curator Laguna Beach (Calif.) Musuem of Art, 1976; creator enamel courses, instr. La Jolla Museum, 1956-59; founder Enamel Guild West, 1976. Editor Cloisonné Collectors, 1980—; exhibitions include Boston Pub. Libr., 1999, Lexington (Mass.) Soc. Arts and Crafts, 1999, YAW Gallery, Birmingham, Mich., 1998 SOFA, N.Y.C., Chgo., SNAG Conf. Artemis Gallery, Richmond, Va., 2001 (award), Gallery 21, San Diego, 2002 (award), Mus. Contemporary Enamel Spain Mus., Salou, Spain, 2003 (2d prize), Internat. Enamel Festival, Republic of Ga., 2004, others; design appeared on cover of Better Homes and Gardens Needlepoint; exhbns. include Bead Internat. 2000, Ohio, Three Rivers Arts Festival 2000, Pitts., Laguna Beach Mus. Art, San Diego Mus. Art, Allied Craftsmen, Everson Mus., Art of Enamel Limoges, France, 1975 (award 1978), Syracuse, N.Y., La Jolla Mus. Art, Art in Embassy, Singapore, Knowles Gallery, La Jolla, Artspace, Atlanta, Soc. Arts and Crafts, Boston, Internat. Cloisonné, Tokyo, others; comms. include Hotel de Ville, Belgium, U. Hosp., San Diego, Dubai United Arab Emirates Internat. Airport, Niles Coll., Chgo., Basilica Sacred Heart. Recipient Young Ams. award Am. Crafts Coun., 1950, Decorative Arts, Wichita, 1962, Internat. Biennale Email, 1978, Prix du Syndicat d'Initiative, Limoges, Internat. Shippo, Tokyo, 1981, 85, 94, Quilt Design award San Diego Hist. Soc. Bicentennial Gift to City, 1976, Modern Liturgy Bene award, 1989, Grand prize Internat. Cloisonné, 1994, ArtsBoston award, 1997, DAR award, Mass., 2004, DAR Congress award, 2004. Mem. Enamel Guild (bd. dirs.), Enamel Guild North East, Enamel Guild West (founder, 1st pres. 1976-78), San Diego Art Guild (chmn. 1968-69, bd. dirs. 1967-65), Allied Craftsmen of San Diego, So. Calif. Designer Craftsmen, Soc. N.Am. Goldsmiths (Conf. Exhbn. prize 2001). Home: 115 South St Rockport MA 01966-2352

**WHITCOMB, RICHARD TRAVIS,** aeronautical consultant; b. Evanston, Ill., Feb. 21, 1921; s. Kenneth Frederick and Gladys (Travis) Whitcomb. BS in Aero. Engring., Worcester Poly. Inst., 1943, DEng (hon.), 1956; DSc (hon.), Old Dominion U., 1985. Aero. rsch. scientist Langley Rsch. Ctr. NASA, Hampton, Va., 1943—58, head transonic aerodynamics br., 1958—80, disting. rsch. assoc., 1980—85; pvt. practice aero. cons. Hampton, 1980—90. Patentee aero. equipment. Named to Nat. Inventors Hall of Fame, 2003; recipient Collier Trophy, Nat. Aero. Assn., 1955, Nat. Medal for Sci., Office of the Pres. U.S., 1973, Wright Bros. trophy, Nat. Aero. Assn., 1974, award in Aero. Engring., NAS, 2000. Fellow: AIAA (hon. Reed award 1969, Daniel Guggenheim medal 2002); mem.: NAE. Avocations: music, reading, exercise.

**WHITE, ALAN FREDERICK,** academic administrator; b. Evansville, Ind., Dec. 17, 1937; s. Hubert Ruben and Nota Lizzee (Culver) W.; m. Patricia Lynn Townsend, Nov. 7, 1959; children: Gregory Townsend, Samuel Townsend. AB, Miami U., Oxford, Ohio, 1963; MS, MIT, 1971. Dir. U. Hawaii Ctr. Crosscultural Tng. and Rsch., Hilo, 1967-70, exec. asst. to pres. Honolulu, 1971-73; Alfred P. Sloan fellow MIT, Cambridge, 1970-71, assoc. dir. exec. edn., 1973-78, dir. exec. edn., 1978-85, assoc. dean for exec. edn., 1985-95, sr. assoc. dean, COO, sr. lectr., 1991; vis. prof. Hong Kong U. Cons. AT&T, Brit. Petroleum, Alcoa Young Pres. Orgn.; bd. dirs. Certified Coaches Internat. Consortium for Exec. Edn. Rsch.; bd. advisors The StartupAvenue.com, Toffler Assoc., Lingnan U., China, The Internat. Fin. Corp.; mem. Internat. Mgmt. Devel., 1985—; vis. prof. Hong Kong U., 2006. Contbr. articles to profl. jours. Recipient Gordon Y. Billard award for Disting. Svc. to MIT, 2005. Mem. Consortium of Univ. Dirs. of Exec. Edn., Japan Mgmt. Inst. (adv. bd.), Mgmt. Scis. for Health (bd. dirs.). Avocations: painting, tennis, swimming, golf, gardening. Home: 13 Pickman Dr Bedford MA 01730-1009 Office Phone: 617-253-7189.

**WHITE, ALICE ELIZABETH,** physicist, researcher; b. Glen Ridge, N.J., Apr. 5, 1954; d. Alan David and Elizabeth Joyce (Jones) W.; m. Donald Paul Monroe, Oct. 13, 1990; children: Ellen Elizabeth White Monroe, Janet Clare White Monroe. BA in Physics, Middlebury (Vt.) Coll., 1976; MA in Physics, Harvard U., 1978, PhD in Physics, 1982. Postdoctoral mem. tech. staff AT&T Bell Labs., Murray Hill, N.J., 1982-84, mem. tech. staff, 1984-88; dir. Bell Labs Lucent Technologies, Murray Hill, N.J., 1988—. Contbr. over 100 articles to profl. pubs.; patentee in field. Recipient Alumni Achievement award Middlebury Coll., 1994; Bell Labs. fellow, 2001. Fellow Am. Phys. Soc. (Maria Goeppert-Mayer award 1991); mem. IEEE, Optical Soc. of Am., Phi Beta Kappa.

**WHITE, ALICE VIRGINIA,** academic administrator; b. Wichita, Kans., June 30, 1946; d. Harry Houston White and Margaret V. Milligan. BA in Spanish and with honors in Russian, U. Kans., 1967; MS in Counseling, Ft. Hays State U., 1973; PhD in Journalism, U. Tex., 1991. Tchr. Russian and Spanish Ingalls Sch. Dist., Kansas City, Mo., 1967-72; instr. Dodge City (Kans.) C.C., 1972-73, 84; tchr. Arrowhead West, Inc., 1984-85; asst. dir. Ctr. for Bus. & Industry Dodge City C.C., Kans., 1984-85, dir. community rels. and resource devel., 1985-87; co-founder, treas. Breitenbach Farms, Inc., Dodge City, Kans., 1970-79, pres., 1979-85; asst. to dean for devel. Coll. Comm., U. Tex., Austin 1990-93, asst. instr. journalism, 1988-90, lectr. pub. rels., 1992; asst. coord. Shots Across Tex. coord. Tex. Dept. Health, Austin, 1993-95, coord. spl. health initiatives, 1995-96; mgr. Tex. Vol. Health Corps, 1996—2002; liaison Tex. Alliance for Healthy Communities, 1999—2002; program dir. Tex. Higher Edn. Coordinating bd. Coll. for Texans Campaign, 2002—04; dir. pub. rels. Tex. Tech U. System, 2005—06; liaison, cmty. coll. rels. Tex. Tech. U., 2006—. Media judge Headliners Found., Austin, 1989, Tex. Hosp. Assn., 1990, 91; dir. job placement Kans. Elks Tng. Ctr. for Handicapped, 1984-85; mgr. dental office, 1973-83; bd. dirs. Dispute Resolution Ctr., 1992-93; adv. bd. N.E. Caregivers of Austin, 2002-04; mem. chancellor's coun. Tex. Tech. U. Sys., 2005—. Treas. Ford County Hist. Soc., 1972—77, Ofcl. Bicentennial Com. Ford County, 1975—77; lifetime mem. Leadership Kans. Alumni, 1986—; active Leadership Austin, 1990—91; mem. Leadership Tex., 1999; co-founder Leadership Dodge, 1987, Tex. Leadership Inst. Lower Colo. River Authority, 1999—2004; founder Walk-a-Dog project Williamson County SPCA, Austin State Sch., 1991—92; media judge Tex. PTA, 1992, Tex. Med. Assn., 1994; mem. chancellors coun. U. Tex. Sys.; mem. endowment com. United Way Capital Area, 1994; mem. Ready Teddy, the Emergency Med. Svcs. Bear-A-Medic Mascot, 1994—2001, Wiley the Crab mascot Coll. for Texans Campaign, 2005, Gov.'s Blue Ribbon Selection Com. for Tex. vol. awards, 1998, 1999; mem. Vols. of Yr. selection com. Tex. Commn. on Volunteerism and Cmty. Svcs., 2000—03; mem. Gov.'s Unified State Planning/Cmty. Svc. Com., 1997, 1998; 2d v.p. Pub. Health Mus. of Tex., 1999—2002, bd. dirs., 2003—04; treas. Pet Helpers, Inc., 2000—04; mem. Animal Trustees of Austin's Vol. Spotlight, 2000; mem. selection com. for Tex. vol. awards Tex. Dept. Human Svcs., 2001; hon. life. laboratorian Tex. Dept. Health, 2000—; 5th grade mentor Gullett Elem. Sch., 2001—03; mem. founding adv. bd. Women's Giving Network, 2003—04; Goodwill Amb. to Turkey, Interfaith Dialog, 2006.

Recipient Most Creative Vol. Project award Tex. Mental Health and Mental Retardation, 1992, Athena winner Women's C. of C., 1987, Kans. PRIDE honoree, 1988; U. Tex. fellow, 1987-89; named of one of 100 Best-Managed Farms in U.S., Farm Futures Mag., 1983; named endowments at Austin Cmty. Found., Wichita (Kans.) Cmty. Found., Arthur E. and Cornelia Scroggins Found., Dodge City, Kans. Fellow: Tex. Pub. Health Assn.; mem.: AAUW (treas. 1977—78, pres. Kans. 1979—81, gift honoree 1973, 1981, 1991), Austin C. of C., Women in Comm. (liaison to student chpt. 1989—91), Tex. Health Found. (life), Nat. Assn. Individual Investors (life), Tex. Pub. Rels. Soc. (bd. dirs. 1993), Pub. Rels. Soc. Am. (mentor, profl. advisor U. Tex. 1987—93), Tex. Tech. Alumni Assn., Tex. Exes Alumni Assn. (life), Austin-Travis County Humane Soc. (life), U. Kans. Alumni Assn. (nat. bd. dirs. 1977—82), U. Tex. Pres.'s Assocs., U. Tex. Littlefield Soc., U. Kans. Chancellor's Club, Waterloo Benevolent Soc. of United Way Capital Area, Lone Star Cir. (State Employee Charitable Campaign 2001—02, 2004—05, 2005—06), Leave a Legacy Tex. Style, KLRU Pub. TV Prodrs. Cir., Phi Kappa Phi, Phi Beta Kappa (treas. Austin Alumni Assn. 2001—02), Chi Omega Alumae of Austin, Chi Omega. Home: 403 Topeka Lubbock TX 79416-4906 Office: Tex Tech U MS 42022 Lubbock TX 79409 Office Phone: 806-742-4719. Business E-Mail: Alice.White@ttu.edu.

**WHITE, ANN MARIE,** medical educator; b. Rochester, N.Y., Dec. 3, 1969; d. Domenick and Beatrice H. White; m. David Robert Mowry; 2 children. BS with honors, Cornell U., 1992; MA, Columbia U. Tchrs. Coll., 1993; EdD, Harvard U., 2002. Rsch. asst. Cornell U. Ithaca, NY, 1991—92, Tchrs. Coll. Columbia U., N.Y.C., 1992—93, Harvard U., Cambridge, Mass., 1993—95; data analyst Wellesley Coll., 1993—99; rsch. assoc. Harvard Grad. Sch. Edn., 1998—2001; sr. instr., dir. dept. psychiatry U. Rochester Med. Ctr., NY, 2004—. Rsch. cons. in field Follow, U.S. Senate, Washington, 2002—03, NIH. Bethesda, Md., 2003—04. Mem.: Soc. Rsch. Child Devel. (student rep. to policy com. 1997—99). Roman Catholic. Office: U Rochester Med Ctr 300 Crittenden Blvd Rochester NY

**WHITE, AUGUSTUS AARON, III,** orthopaedic surgeon; b. Memphis, June 4, 1936; s. Augustus Aaron and Vivian (Dandridge) W.; m. Anita Ottemo; children: Alissa Alexandra, Atina Andrea, Annica Akila. AB in Psychology cum laude (high honors), Brown U., 1957; MD, Stanford U., 1961; PhD, Karolinska Inst., Sweden, 1969; Advanced Mgmt. Program, Harvard U., 1984; DHL (hon.), U. New Haven, 1987; DMS (hon.), Brown U., 1997; DS (hon.), So. Conn. State U., 2000. Diplomate Nat. Bd. Examiners, Am. Bd. Orthopaedic Surgery. Intern U. Mich. Hosp., Ann Arbor, 1961-62; asst. resident in gen. surgery Presbyn. Med. Center, San Francisco, 1962-63; asst. resident in orthopaedic surgery Yale Med. Center, New Haven, 1963-65, sr. instr., resident orthopaedic surgery, 1965-66; asst. prof. orthopaedic surgery Yale Med. Sch., 1969-72, assoc. prof., 1972-76, prof., 1977-78, dir. biomech. rsch. dept. orthopaedics, 1970-78; prof. orthopaedic surgery Harvard Med. Sch., 1978—; orthopaedic surgeon-in-chief Beth Israel Deaconess Med. Ctr., Boston, 1978-92, orthopaedic surgeon-in-chief emeritus, 1996—2001; sr. assoc. orthopaedic surgery Children's Hosp. Med. Ctr., Boston, 1979-89; assoc. in orthopaedic surgery Brigham & Women's Hosp., Boston, 1980-89; cons. div. surgery Sidney Farber Cancer Inst., Boston, 1980—; Ellen and Melvin Gordon prof. of med. edn., prof. orthopaedic surgery Harvard Med. Sch., 2002. Rschr. biomechanics lab. Beth Israel Deaconess Med. Ctr.; chair sci. adv. bd., dir. OrthoLogic, Inc., Phoenix; sci. adv. bd. Am. Shared Hosp. Svcs., San Francisco; chair sci. adv. bd.; bd. dirs. Zimmer Holding, Inc.; cons. orthop. surgery West Haven (Conn.) VA Hosp., 1970—78, Hill Health Ctr., New Haven, 1970—78; chief orthop. surgery Conn. Health Care Plan, 1976—78; adv. coun. Nat. Inst. Arthritis, Metabolism and Digestive Disease, NIH, 1979—82; mem. admissions com. Yale Med. Sch., 1970—72; presenter, moderator Symposium on Cervical Myelopathy, San Francisco, 1987; chmn. grant rev. com. NIH, 1985; founding mem., bd. overseers Brown U. Sch. Medicine, 1996—99; bd. overseers WGBH Radio/TV, Boston, 1996—98, trustee, 1998—; Alfred R. Shands Jr. lectr. Am. Orthop. Assn., 2001; Pres. guest lectr. Scoliosis Rsch. Soc., 2001; chair com. culturally competence care Harvard Med. Sch., 2002; hon. staff orthopaedics Beth Israel Deaconess Med. Ctr., 2005; mem. adv. coun. biology and medicine Brown U., 2005; mem. adv. coun. Nat. Ctr. for Minority Health and Health Disparities, NIH, 2001—06. Author: Clinical Biomechanics of the Spine, 1978, 2d edit., 1990, (with M. Panjabi) Biomechanics in the Musculoskeletal System, 2001, Symposium on Idiopathic Low Back Pain, 1982, Your Aching Back-A Doctor's Guide to Relief, 1983, rev. edit., 1990, translated in German, 1992; guest editor Clin. Orthop. and Related Rsch., 1999; contbr. articles to profl. jours., chpts. to books. Trustee Brown U., Providence, 1971-76, bd. fellows, 1981-92, fellow emeritus, 1992—, chmn. corp. com. on minority affairs, 1981-86, chmn. corp. com. on med. edn., 1989-96, chmn. vis. com. on diversity; trustee Northfield Mt. Hermon Sch., Northfield, Mass., 1976-81; bd. dirs. The Partnership, Boston, 1984—. Capt. AUS, 1966-68. Decorated Bronze Star medal; named one of 10 Outstanding Young Men U.S. Jr. C. of C., 1969, Selected for Exceptional Black Scientist poster series CIBA-GEIGY Corp., 1992; recipient Martin Luther King, Jr. Med. Achievement award, 1972, Kappa Delta award, nat. prize for outstanding rsch. in orthopaedics field, 1975; nat. award for spinal rsch. Eastern Orthopaedic Assn., 1980, Disting. Service award Northfield Mt. Hermon Sch. Alumni Assn., 1983; William Rogers award Associated Alumni Brown U., 1984, Outstanding Achievement award Delta Upsilon, 1986, Brown Bear award Brown Alumni Assn., Lifetime Achievement award Beth Israel Deaconess Med. Ctr., 2005, Candle in the Dark in Medicine award Morehouse Coll., 2006, J.E. Wallace Sterling Lifetime Achievement award Stanford Med. Sch., 2006; Am.-Brit.-Canadian Travelling fellow Am. Orthopaedic Assn., 1975; Ann. Spine Symposium named in his honor Beth Israel Deaconess Med. Ctr., 2004. Fellow Am. Acad. Orthopaedic Surgeons (chmn. diversity com. 1997—, Diversity award 2006), Scoliosis Rsch. Soc.; mem. The Acad. Harvard Med. Sch., Orthopaedic Rsch. Soc., Cervical Spine Rsch. Soc., Internat. Soc. for Study Lumbar Spine, Internat. Soc. Orthopaedic Surgery and Traumatology, Nat. Med. Assn. (Orthopaedic Scholar award 1994), Cervical Spine Rsch. Soc. (pres. 1980), N.Am. Spine Soc., Acad. Orthopaedic Soc. (co-chmn. com. on diversity), Clin. Orthopaedic Soc. (Nix Ethics award 2002), J. Robert Gladden Orthopaedic Soc. (founding pres. 2000-03), Fedn. of Spine Assns. (pres. 1998), Sigma Xi, Sigma Pi Phi, Delta Upsilon (pres. Brown U. chpt. 1956, Charles Evan Hughes award for advancement of justice 2006, Augustus White award for excellence in medicine established 2006). Business E-Mail: augustus_white@hms.harvard.edu.

**WHITE, BARRY BENNETT,** lawyer; b. Boston, Feb. 13, 1943; s. Harold and Rosalyn (Schneider) W.; m. Eleanor Greenberg; children: Joshua S., Adam J., Benjamin D. AB magna cum laude, Harvard U., 1964, JD magna cum laude, 1967. Bar: Mass. 1967, U.S. Dist. Ct. Mass. 1967, U.S. Ct. Appeals (1st cir.) 1967. Assoc. Foley Hoag & Eliot, Boston, 1969—74, chmn. exec. com., 1987—91, mng. ptnr, 1991—92, 1993—2001, sec., 1992—93, ptnr., 1975—. Chmn. Lex Mundi, 1994; bd. dirs. Edgewater Tech., Inc., 2005—. Editor Harvard Law Rev., 1965-67. Sec., gen. counsel, exec. com. Greater Boston C. of C., 1998—, Initiative for Competitive Inner City, 1995—; bd. dirs. and exec. com. Mass. Assn. Mental Health, 1985—, Vol. Lawyers Project, 1987-93, Support Ctr. of Mass., 1988-95; mem. Jewish Family and Children's Svcs., Boston, 1979-87; bd. visitors Boston U. Grad. Sch. Dentistry, 1981—; bd. overseers Jewish Cmty. Rels. Coun., 1988-92; chmn. com. for Clinton/Gore New Eng. Lawyers, 1992-96; chmn. Tsongas for Pres. Com., 1991-98; co-chair Mass. Lawyers for Kerry for Pres., 2004; bd. dirs. Edgewater Tech., Inc., 2005—. With USPHS, 1967-69. Mem. ABA, Mass. Bar Assn., Boston Bar Assn., Internat. Bar Assn., Am. Acad. Hosp. Attys., Am. Hosp. Assn. (adj. task force on health planning 1982-84, contbg. editor hosp. law manual 1981-84), Harvard Club Boston, Badminton and Tennis Club. Democrat. Office: Foley Hoag LLP 155 Seaport Blvd Boston MA 02210 Office Phone: 617-832-1000. E-mail: bbwhite@foleyhoag.com.

**WHITE, BENJAMIN TAYLOR,** lawyer; b. Atlanta, Nov. 10, 1946; s. Edward Street and Jane Shannon (Taylor) W.; m. Ramona Taylor, Aug. 14, 1971; 1 child, Alexander Taylor. AB with honors, U. N.C., 1969; JD cum laude, Harvard U., 1973. Bar: Ga. 1973. Assoc. Alston & Bird LLP, Atlanta,

1973-79, ptnr., 1979—, and group leader, exempt orgns. group. Trustee The Taft Sch., Watertown, Conn., 1978-81, Woodruff Arts Ctr., Atlanta, 1983—; pres., founder Ga. Vol. Lawyers for the Arts, 1979-82; chmn. Lee Harper and Dancers, Atlanta, 1979-83; pres. Alliance Theatre Co., Atlanta, 1985—. Fellow Am. Coll. Probate Counselors; mem. ABA, State Bar of Ga. (chmn. fiduciary law sect. 1986—), Atlanta Bar Assn., Internat. Bar Assn., Atlanta Tax Forum, Atlanta Estate Planning Council, Harvard Law Sch. Assn. Ga. (pres. 1981-82). Home: 3315 Valley Rd NW Atlanta GA 30305-1150 Office: Alston & Bird 1 Atlantic Ctr 1201 W Peachtree St NW Atlanta GA 30309-3424 Office Phone: 404-881-7488. Office Fax: 404-881-7777. Business E-Mail: bwhite@alston.com.

**WHITE, BERTRAM MILTON,** chemicals executive; b. Boston, Nov. 17, 1923; s. Samuel Louis and Jennie Anne (Cohen) W.; m. Bernice Hannah Ginns; children: Mark Alan, Leland Jeffrey. BS, Lowell Inst. Tech., Cambridge, Mass., 1943. Product mgr. Philipps Bros. Chems. Inc., Holbrook, Mass., 1952-65, Sobin Chems. Inc., South Boston, 1965-69; pres. Solvent Chems. Co., Inc., Malden, Mass., 1969-73; v.p. I.C.C. Chems. Inc., NYC, 1973—80; sr. v.p. Asoma Chems. Inc., Boston, 1980-83, Laporte Chems. USA, Hackensack, N.J., 1983-84; pres. Gen. Plastics and Chems. Co., Natick, Mass., 1984-91, GFI Chems. Inc., Sudbury, Mass., 1991-93; vice chmn. E & F King & Co. Inc., Norwood, Mass., 1994—96; cons. Holtrachem Inc., 1997—2000. Bd. dirs. Sudexco N.V., Brussels, Recochem Inc., Montreal, Que., Can.; cons. Holtrachem Group, Natick, 1996-2000, Lithium Co., LLC, White Plains, NY, 1997-2000, BMW Chems. Inc., 1998—, Salvage.com, Houston, 2000-01; pres. BMW Chems., Inc., Natick, Mass. Served with Corps of Engring. U.S Army, 1943-46, ETO. Decorated Purple Heart. Mem. Drug Chem. and Allied Trades Assn., New Eng. Chemists Club, N.Y.C. Chemists Club, Salesmen's Assn. of Am. Chem. Industry. Jewish. Avocations: tennis, golf, boating. Office Phone: 508-650-5800. Office Fax: 508-651-0294. Personal E-Mail: bmwchem@aol.com.

**WHITE, BETTY,** actress, comedienne; b. Oak Park, Ill., Jan. 17, 1922; m. Dick Barker 1945 (div. 1945), m. Lane Allen 1947 (div. 1949), m. Allen Ludden, 1963 (dec. 1981). Student pub. schs., Beverly Hills, Calif. Appearances on radio shows This Is Your FBI, Blondie, The Great Gildersleeve; actress: (TV series) including Hollywood on Television, The Betty White Show, 1952-54, Life With Elizabeth, 1953-55, A Date With The Angels, 1957-58, The Pet Set, 1971, Mary Tyler Moore Show, 1974-77, The Betty White Show, 1977, Mama's Family, 1983-86, The Golden Girls, 1985-92 (Emmy award for best actress 1986), Another World, 1988, The Golden Palace, 1992-93, Maybe This Time, 1995, (TV films) With This Ring, 1978, The Best Place to Be, 1979, Before and After, 1979, Eunice, 1982, Chance of a Lifetime, 1991, The Story of Santa Claus, 1996, A Weekend in the Country, 1996, The Retrievers, 2001, Annie's Point, 2005, (films) Advise and Consent, 1962, Dennis the Menace 2, 1998, Hard Rain, 1998, The Story of Us, 1999, Bringing Down the House, 2003, The Third Wish, 2004; guest appearances include Petticoat Junction, 1969, The Odd Couple, 1972, Fame, 1983, St. Elsewhere, 1985, Who's the Boss, 1985, Matlock, 1987, Empty Nest, 1989, 92, Carol & Company, 1990, Nurses, 1991, Diagnosis Murder, 1994, The Naked Truth, 1995, Suddenly Susan, 1996, (voice) King of the Hill, 1999, 2002, Ally McBeal, 1999, (voice) The Simpsons, 2000, Yes, Dear, 2002, Providence, 2002, That 70s Show, 2002, 03, Everwood, 2003, 04, The Practice, 2004, My Wife and Kids, 2004, Malcolm in the Middle, 2004, (voice) Father of the Pride, 2004, Boston Legal, 2005; frequent celebrity guest on numerous game shows including Hollywood Squares, Match Game; summer stock appearances Guys and Dolls, Take Me Along, The King and I, Who Was That Lady?, Critic's Choice, Bells are Ringing; author (book) Betty White's Pet-Lovers: How Pets Take Care of Us, 1987, Here We Go Again: My Life in Television, 1995; contbr. to forward(book) The Irrepressible Toy Dog, Dr. Fisher's Life on the Ark: Green Alligators, Bushman and Other "Hare Raising" Tales from America's Most Popular Zoo and Around the World, 2004, (preface) The Pets are Wonderful Family Album. Mem. Morris Animal Found., 1976—; zoo commr. Greater LA Zoo, 1998—. Recipient Emmy award NATAS, 1975, 76, 86; LA Area Emmy award, 1952, Living Legacy award, Women's Internat. Ctr., 1988, star on the Hollywood Walk of Fame; inducted into TV Hall of Fame, 1995; named Amb. to the Animals, Greater LA Zoo, 2006. Mem. AFTRA, Am. Humane Assn., Greater LA Zoo Assn. (dir.). Office: c/o William Morris Agy Betty Fanning 151 S El Camino Dr Beverly Hills CA 90212-2704*

**WHITE, BEVERLY JANE,** cytogeneticist; b. Seattle, Oct. 9, 1938; Grad., U. Wash., 1959, MD, 1963. Diplomate Nat. Bd. Med. Examiners, Am. Bd. Pediatrics, Am. Bd. Med. Genetics; lic physician and surgeon, Wash., N.J., Calif. Rsch. trainee dept. anatomy Sch. Medicine U. Wash., Seattle, 1960-62, pediatric resident dept. pediatrics, 1967-69; rotating intern Phila. Gen. Hosp., 1963-64; rsch. fellow med. ob-gyn. unit Cardiovascular Rsch. Inst. U. Calif. Med. Ctr., San Francisco, 1964-65; staff fellow lab. biomed. scis. Nat. Inst. Child Health and Human Devel. NIH, Bethesda, Md., 1965-67, sr. staff fellow, attending physician lab. exptl. pathology Nat. Inst. Arthritis, Metabolism and Digestive Diseases, 1969-74, acting chief sect. cytogenetics, 1975-76, rsch. med. officer, attending physician sect. cytogenetics lab. cellular biology and genetics, 1974-86, dir. cytogenetics unit, interinstitute med. genetics program clin. ctr., 1987-95; dir. cytogenetics Corning Clin. Labs., Teterboro, NJ, 1995-96; assoc. med. dir. cytogenetics Nichols Inst.-Quest Diagnostics, San Juan Capistrano, Calif., 1996-97, med. dir. cytogenetics 1998—2000, med. dir. genetics divsn., 2000—02, med. dir. cytogenetics and genetic counseling, 2002—. Vis. scientist dept. pediat. divsn. genetics U. Wash. Sch. Medicine, 1983-84; intramural cons. NIH, 1975-95; cons. to assoc. editor Jour. Nat. Cancer Inst., 1976; cons. dept. ob-gyn. Naval Hosp., Bethesda, 1988-89; lectr. presenter in field. Recipient Mosby Book award, 1963, Women of Excellence award U. Wash. and Seattle Profl. chpt. Women in Comm., 1959, Reuben award Am. Soc. for Study Sterility, 1963. Fellow Am. Coll. Med. Genetics (founding), Am. Acad. Pediatrics; mem. AMA. Am. Soc. Human Genetics, Assn. Genetic Technologists (program com. 1989). Home: 14 Toulon Laguna Niguel CA 92677 Office: Nichols Inst Quest Diagnostics Inc Dept Cytogenetics San Juan Capistrano CA 92690-6130 Office Phone: 949-728-4301. E-mail: bjwsur@aol.com.

**WHITE, BRETT,** real estate company executive; Sales trainee, indsl. salesperson CB Richard Ellis, L.A., 1984—91, sales mgr., 1991—2001, mng. dir. Newport Beach, 1991—2001, regional mgr. L.A., 1991—2001, pres. brokerage, 1991—2001, then The Ams., 1991—2001, pres., 2001—, also bd. dirs., mem. exec. com. Office: CB Richard Ellis 34th Fl 865 S Figueroa St Los Angeles CA 90017

**WHITE, BURTON LEONARD,** retired educational psychologist, writer, consultant; b. Boston, June 27, 1929; s. Jack J. and Evelyn S. W.; m. Janet Hodgson-White; children— Laura, Emily, David, Daniel. BSM.E., Tufts Coll., 1949; BA, Brandeis U., 1956, MA, 1957; PhD, Brandeis U., 1960. Research assoc. Brandeis U., 1960-62, M.I.T., 1962-65; sr. research assoc. Harvard Grad. Sch. Edn., 1965-78; head Center Parent Edn., Newton, Mass., 1978-99, ret., 1999. Author: books including Human Infants, 1971, Experience and Environment, Vol. I, 1973, Vol. II, 1978, The First Three Years of Life, 1975, latest edit. 1995, The Origins of Competence, 1979, Educating the Infant and Toddler, 1988, Raising A Happy, Unspoiled Child, 1994, The New First Three Years of Life, 1995; contbr. articles to profl. jours. Served with AUS, 1951-53. Home: 115 Pine Ridge Rd Newton MA 02468-1616

**WHITE, C. VANESSA,** director; d. Robert Lee White and Doris Jean Redd White Foster, Herbert Randolph Foster (Stepfather). BS, No. Ill. U., DeKalb, 1978; M in Theol. Studies, Cath. Theol. Union, Chgo., 1990, D in Ministry, 2005. Cert. master catechist Xavier U. La., 1991. Child life specialist Michael Reese Hosp., Chgo., 1979—85; dir. Claretian vols. and lay missionaries Claretian Missionaries, Chgo., 1986—94; dir. retreat program and staff Christian Brother's LaSalle Manor Retreat Ctr., Plano, Ill., 1994—97; dir. Augustus Tolton scholar's program Cath. Theol. Union, Chgo, 1998—. Faculty Inst. for Black Cath. Studies Xavier U., New Orleans; bd. dirs. US Conf. Cath. Bishops Commn. on Certification and Accreditation, Washington; adv. bd. Fullerton Cenacle Retreat Ctr., Chgo. Editor: Songs of Our Hearts

and Meditations of Our Souls; contbr. documentary film, articles to profl. jours. Active Secular Franciscan Order, Chgo., 1985—2006. Recipient Fr. Augustus Tolton Archdiocesan award, Archdiocese of Chgo., 1998. Mem.: Cath. Theol. Union Alumni Assn., Nat. Assn. for Lay Ministry, Knights of Peter Claver - Ladies Aux. (Sr. Thea Bowman award 1992, Adele Stadeker Svc. award 2003). Independent. Roman Catholic. Office: Catholic Theological Union 5401 S Cornell Chicago IL 60615 Office Phone: 773-753-7478. Business E-Mail: tolton@ctu.edu.

**WHITE, CALVIN JOHN,** zoo executive, zoological association executive, financial manager; b. Twillingate, Nfld., Can., Feb. 28, 1948; s. Harold and Meta Blanche (Abbott) W.; m. Lorna Joan Maclachlan; children: Chelsea Elizabeth, Evan Alexander. B in Commerce, U. Toronto, Ont., Can., 1971. Fin. analyst Can. GE Co. Ltd., Toronto, 1971-72, Ford Motor Co. Can., Oakville, Ont., 1972-74; sr. fin. analyst Municipality of Met. Toronto, 1974-77, asst. dir. budget and ops. analysis, 1977-81, dir. budget analysis and internal control, 1981-86; CEO Toronto Zoo, 1986—. Bd. dirs. Borealis Hydro Elec. Holdings Inc., Can. Assn. Zoos and Aquariums, Ctr. for Endangered Reptiles, 1989-91, Rouge Pk. Alliance, Toronto Chongqing Assn., Can. Mus. Assn., pres. Pres. Tourism Toronto, 2005—. Fellow Am. Zoo and Aquarium Assn.; mem. Am. Assn. Zoo Keepers, Inst. Pub. Adminstrn. Can. (bd. dirs. 1989-91), Toronto Zoo Found. (bd. dirs. 1991—, CEO 1994—), World Conservation Union, World Zoo Orgn., Toronto Sportmen's Assn., Mensa. Office: Toronto Zoo 361A Old Finch Ave Scarborough ON Canada M1B 5K7 Office Phone: cwhite@torontozoo.ca, 416-392-5909.

**WHITE, CAROL SIMPSON,** mathematics professor; b. Glens Falls, NY, Oct. 15, 1942; d. Kenneth Alfred and Claire Tripp Simpson; m. Donald George White, Jr., Oct. 23, 1942; children: Donald George White, III, Constance Tripp Callahan, Christopher Crandall Matt, Ann Michele Mc-Carter. BS in Math. Edn., U. Vt., Burlington, 1964; MEd in Math. Jacksonville U., Fla., 1985. Cert. math. tchr. State Edn. Dept. NY, 1967. Tchr. Bristol Union, Vt., The Weeks Sch., Vergennes, Vt., 1966, St. Johnsville Ctrl., NY, 1967—68, Fonda-Fultonville Ctrl. Sch., NY, 1970—76, Broach Sch., Jacksonville, Fla., 1976—77, Jacksonville Country Day Sch., 1976—77, Terry Parker HS, 1977—83; homebound tchr. State Vt., Addison Co. 1966—67; prof. Fla. CC, 1982—91, 1997—98; instr. Cumberland U., Lebanon, Tenn., 1991—97; adj. prof. U. N. Fla., Tallahassee CC, 1997, NOVA SE, Tallahassee, 1997; asst. prof. Flagler Coll., St. Augustine, Fla., 1999—2006. Tutor pvt., Fla., 1991—; presenter in field. Proofreader (textbook) Mathematics All Around (Thomas L. Pirnot). Vol. Boys & Girls Club, Smyrna, Tenn., 1997; missions com. First Christian Ch., St. Augustine, 1999—2002, Oceanside Christian Ch., Atlantic Beach, Fla., 2003—05; ch. treas. First Christian Ch., St. Augustine, 1999—2002; pregnancy counselor St. Gerard Campus, St. Augustine, 2004—06. Mem.: Am. Math. Assn. of Two-Yr. Colls. Avocations: walking, cooking, reading, gardening.

**WHITE, CAROLYN LOUISE,** music educator; b. LaCrosse, Wis., Sept. 5, 1939; d. Julius Elmer and Nora Marie Forde; m. Ronald Glenn White, Aug. 18, 1962; children: Elizabeth, Sara, Andrea. BA, Luther Coll., 1961. Tchr. Madison (Wis.) Pub. Schs., 1961-67; piano tchr. pvt. lessons, Madison, 1965—; substitute tchr. Verona Area Schs., Wis., 1970—85. Dir. music camp Bethel Horizons, Madison; sec., pres. Fitchrona EMS, Verona, 1978—83; accompanist children's choir Bethel Luth. Ch., Madison, Wis. Mem.: Verona Area Performing Arts Series (pres. 1998—2003), Madison Symphony Orch., Madison Symphony Orch. League (pres. 2000), Madison Area Piano Tchrs. Assn. (pres. 1992), Attic Angel Assn., Madison Civics Club (pres. 1998). Achievements include development of Verona Area Performing Arts Series. Avocations: gardening, travel, reading. Home: 6871 Sunset Dr Verona WI 53593

**WHITE, CECIL RAY,** librarian, consultant; b. Hammond, Ind., Oct. 15, 1937; s. Cecil Valentine and Vesta Ivern (Bradley) W.; m. Frances Ann Gee, Dec. 23, 1960 (div. 1987); children: Timothy Wayne, Stephen Patrick. BS in Edn., So. Ill. U., 1959; postgrad., Syracuse U., 1961; MDiv, Southwestern Bapt. Sem., 1969; MLS, No. Tex. State U., 1970, PhD, 1984. Libr. Herrin (Ill.) H.S., 1964-66; acting reference libr. Southwestern Sem., Ft. Worth, 1968-70, asst. libr., 1970-80; head libr. Golden Gate Bapt. Sem., Mill Valley, Calif., 1980-88, West Oahu Coll. Pearl City, Hawaii, 1988-89; dir. spl. projects North State Coop. Libr. System, Yreka, Calif., 1989-90; dir. libr. St. Patrick's Sem., Menlo Park, Calif., 1990—. Library cons. Hist. Commn., So. Bapt. Conv., Nashville, 1983-84, Internat. Bapt. Sem., Prague, Czech Republic, 1996; mem. Thesaurus Com., 1974-84; adv. bd. Cath. Periodical and Lit. Index, 1995—, chair, 1999—. Bd. dirs. Hope and Help Ctr., 1986-88, vice chmn., 1987-88. With USAF, 1960-64. Lilly Found. grantee Am. Theol. Assn., 1969. Mem. ALA, Am. Theol. Libr. Assn. (coord. cons. svc. 1973-78, program planning com. 1985-88, chmn. 1986-88), Nat. Assn. Profs. Hebrew (archivist 1985—), Assn. Coll. and Rsch. Librs., Cath. Libr. Assn. (mem. exec. bd. 1999-2005), Phi Kappa Phi, Beta Phi Mu. Democrat. Baptist. Home: 229 Rome Place Hayward CA 94544 Office: St Patricks Sem 320 Middlefield Rd Menlo Park CA 94025-3563 Office Phone: 650-321-5655. E-mail: cecilrwhite@hotmail.com, stpats@ix.netcom.com. *Personal philosophy: Except for the gift of life and faith, the best gift that has been given to me, and which I can give, is the unique gift of oneself in friendship. No one else can give it, and it cannot be bought at any price.*

**WHITE, CHARLES FRANKLIN,** music educator; b. Lakeland, Fla., Apr. 30, 1978; s. Charles Franklin and Fran White. MusB, Fla. So. Coll., Lakeland, 2000. Cert. tchr. Fla., 2000. Tchr. Hillsborough Co. Sch. Dist., Tampa, Fla., 2000—. Democrat-Npl. Catholic. Avocations: singing, piano. Office Phone: 813-744-8018. Personal E-Mail: chasewhitesings@aol.com.

**WHITE, CHARLES R.,** former mayor; b. Boston; m. Maria White; 4 children. Grad., Riverside CC. Mayor City of Moreno Valley, 1997. Mem. Moreno Valley City Coun., 1996—; mem. So. Calif. Assn. Govt., Regional Coun., Transp. & Comm. Policy Com., Magnetic Levitation Task Force, Growth Visioning Com.; bd. Riverside Transit Agency; mem., chmn. March Joint Powers Commn., 1999, vice chmn., 2001, chmn., 02. Served Planning Commr., Redevelopment Project Area Com., Traffic Safety Adv. Com., Disaster Preparedness Com., Mayor's Drug Task Force; treasurer Friends Moreno Valley Sr. Ctr.; mem. Moreno Valley Elks Lodge; vice comdr. Moreno Valley VFW Post; jr. deacon Moreno Valley Masonic Lodge; pres. Sunnymead Little League; v.p. Sunnymead PTA; co-founder Moreno Valley Youth Fedn. Served USAR. Mem.: Idylwild Am. Legion Post (life). Office: 14177 Frederick St PO Box 88005 Moreno Valley CA 92552

**WHITE, CHARLES SIDNEY JOHN,** retired humanities educator; b. New Richmond, Wis., Sept. 25, 1929; s. Ferne Rosemary Holt. BA in English with honors, U. Wis., 1951; MA magna cum laude, U. de las Am. Mexico City Coll., 1957; MA, U. Chgo., 1962, PhD with distinction, 1964; diploma in Buddhist Studies, U. Hyderabad, India, 2006. Staff pub. rels. and advt. Wallace Supplies Mfg. Co., Chgo., 1957—61; asst. prof. Indian studies U. Wis., Wis., 1965—66; asst. prof. religious thought U Pa., 1966—71; assoc. prof. philosophy and religion Am. U., Wash., 1971—78, prof. philosophy and religion, 1978—94, prof. emeritus philosophy and religion, 1995—, dir. Asia Ctr. Sch. Internat. Svc., 1976—78, chmn. dept. philosophy and religion, 1984—87, 1988—94. Vis. lectr. history of religions Princeton (N.J.) U., 1968; vis. prof. world religions Lakehead U., Thunder Bay, Ont., Canada, 1974—88; vis. prof. Wesley Seminary, 1985, 86; lectr. in field; vis. prof. Hindu studies faculty theology Oxford U., England, 2002, mem. program adv. com., 06. Author: The Caurāsī Pad of Srī Hit Harivaṃś, 1977, Ramakrishna's Americans, 1979, The Adyar Library, The Institute for Vaisnava Studies and The American University Microfilm Collection of Vaisnava Literature, 2001, Teaching Sarāṇāgati: A Dialogue with HH Sri Sathguru Swami Gnanananda Sarasvathi, 2002, Catalogue of Vaisnava Literature, 2004, The Garden of Loneliness, Jay Shankar Prasad's Tears, 2006, Roses from the Desert of my Heart, A Book of Poetry, 2006; co-author: The Religious Quest, 1983, 2d edit., 1985, Joseph Campbell: Transformations of Myth Through Time, 1990; contbr. chapters to books, articles to profl. jours. With USN, 1951—55. Fellow, Hindi-Urdu U., Chgo., 1961—64, Am. Inst. Indian Studies, India,

1964, 1968, 1974, 1978, 1995; grantee, Smithsonian Instn., India, 1982—83. Mem.: Am. Inst. Indian Studies (exec. com. 1988—90). Office Phone: 202-885-2925. Business E-Mail: philrel@american.edu.

**WHITE, CHRISTINE A.,** internist, oncologist, pharmaceutical executive; BA in Biology, U. Chgo., MD. Cert. Internal Medicine, Med. Oncology. With Scripps Meml. Hospitals, San Diego, 1984—94, med. dir. oncology rsch., 1990—94, chair, dept. medicine, 1994; dir., clin. oncology rsch. Sidney Kimmel Cancer Ctr., San Diego, 1994—96; several sr. positions, most recently served as sr. v.p., global med. affairs Biogen Idec, Cambridge, Mass. 1996—2005. Bd. dir. Pharmacyclics, Inc., Sunnyvale, Calif., 2006—, Arena Pharm., Inc., San Diego, 2006—. Mem. editl. bd. Cancer Biotherapy and Radiopharmaceutical, Expert Review of Anti-Cancer Therapy, Journal of Immunotherapy, and several others; contbr. articles to profl. jours. Office: Pharmacyclics Inc 995 E Argues Ave Sunnyvale CA 94085*

**WHITE, CHRISTOPHER HERRICK,** artist, art educator, critic; b. Clifton Forge, Va., May 22, 1951; d. Edward Thomas White and Nancy Beirne Miles; m. Andrea May Barnet, Sept. 17, 2003; 1 child, Philippa Parsons. AB, Harvard U., Cambridge, Mass., 1973. Artist, NYC, 1975—; asst. prof. Pratt Inst., Bklyn., 1997—; instr., lectr. Met. Mus., NYC, 2004—. Bd. mem., trustee Alliance for Young Artists and Writers, NYC, 2002—. Recipient Louis Comfort Tiffany award for painting, Tiffany Found., 1979. Mem.: Century Assn. Avocations: historic preservation, flying.

**WHITE, CHRISTOPHER TODD,** language educator, anthropologist; b. Columbia, Mo., Dec. 7, 1965; s. Eric B. and Barbara K. White. BA, U. Nebr., Lincoln, 1990; MA, U. Mo., Kansas City, 1994, U. Nev., Las Vegas, 1998; PhD, U. So. Calif., L.A., 2005. Adj. lectr. Rockhurst Coll., Kansas City, Mo., 1994—95; editl. asst. BkMk Press, Kansas City, 1993—95; adj. lectr. English U. Mo., Kansas City, 1993—95; acad. advisor Ednl. Talent Search, Las Vegas, Nev., 1995—96; asst. prof./lectr. U. Nev., Las Vegas, 1996—98; instr. Glendale C.C., Calif., 1998—2003; tchr., rsch. asst. dept. anthropology U. So. Calif., L.A., 1998—2005; asst. prof. anthropology SUNY, Brockport, NY, 2005—. Dir. Homosexual Info. Ctr., L.A., 2001—, ONE Inst. and Archives, L.A., 2001—02. Editor: San Dieguito and La Jolla: Collected Papers of Claude N. Warren and Colleagues, 2006; asst. editor Before Stonewall: Activists for Gay and Lesbian Rights in Historical Context, 2002; editor: U. Nev.-Las Vegas Jour. Anthropology, 1995—2005; contbr. articles to profl. jours.; editl. adv. bd. Collegiate Press, 2002, referee Popular Culture Rev.; columnist: Orange County/Long Beach Blade Mag., 2006—. Recipient Patricia Roccio Award in Anthropology, U. Nev.-Las Vegas, 1997, Dissertation Fellowship award, U. So. Calif., 2005; scholar Hal Call Mattachine scholar, Inst. for Study of Human Resources, 2000—01. Mem.: Assn. for Psychol. Anthropology, Homosexual Info. Ctr. (sec.-treas. 2001—), Southwestern Anthropol. Assn., Soc. of Lesbian and Gay Anthropologists (sec.-treas. 1998—), Soc. of Linguistic Anthropology, Am. Anthropol. Assn., Am. Fedn. Tchrs. Democrat. Avocations: camping, book collecting, piano, running, bicycling. Home: 4622 Charmion Ln Encino CA 91316 Office: SUNY Dept Anthropology 350 New Campus Dr Brockport NY 14420 Office Phone: 818-292-0048.

**WHITE, CLARA JO,** small business owner, consultant; b. County Cherokee, Tex., June 26; d. William and Elmira Walker; m. Jeff White; children: Anita, Jackie, Mona Lisa, Jeris, Gina. Diploma, Ft. Worth Bus. Coll., Tex., 1947, IGAS Congress Inst. Tng., Chgo., 1979; AA in Social Sci., Riverside City Coll., 1986; Master Diploma with honor Social Sci., World Acad. Letters, Am. Biog. Inst., NC, 2004. Cert. graphoanalyst 1977, mus. docent 1977, cert. graphoanalyst Internat. Graphoanalysis Soc., Inc., Chgo., 1977, diploma IGAS Congress Inst. Training, 1979, cert. mgmt. supr. devel. U. Calif., Riverside, 1986, counseling skills U. Riverside, 1990. Owner, pres. White Handwriting Analysis Svc., Riverside, Calif., 1982—. Instr. Internat. Congress and Resident Inst., Internat. Graphoanalysis Soc., 1989, discussion group leader, 882; analyzed handwriting Lady Margaret Beaufort, 1992, Mary Queen of Scots, 1994, Hillary Rodham Clinton, 1994, Pres. Bill Clinton, 1997, Georgia O'Keeffe, 1999, presidents George Washington, Abraham Lincoln, John F. Kennedy, 2000; participant 24th Internat. Congress on Arts and Comm. Oxford U., England, 1997; dir. gen. Internat. Biog. Ctr., Cambridge, 2002; cons. graphoanalysis, Riverside, Calif., 1977—; presenter and spkr. in field. Editor (asst. editor): Reflections, 1986; author: numerous poems; presenter (edn. symposium) ABI/IBC World Forum, Oxford U., Eng., 2006. Mem. children's conf. planning com. Riverside Mental Health Assn. 1981—; v.p. Heritage Ho. Mus., Riverside, Calif., 1981—, co-pres., 1985—86, pres; historian Riverside Juvenile Hall Aux., 1984—, pres., 1987—; mem. U.S. Olympic Com., 1984; bd. dir. Riverside Mus. Assoc., 1985—87, vol., 1985—88, aux. historian, 1984—, pres., 1987—88. Recipient Cert. of Appreciation Riverside County Probation Dept., 1986, County Riverside Suprs., 1988, Riverside Mental Health, 1990; award F.H. Butterfield Sch., 1980, Golden Poet award The Homer Honor Soc., 1987, 90, cert. appreciation Nat. Law Enforcement Officers Meml. Fund, 1990, cert. appreciation Nat. Vol. of Yr., recipient cmty. svc. cert. Riverside City Coll., 1982; named to Hall of Fame, Riverside Juvenile Hall Aux., 1984; recipient First pl. writing-poetry Am. Biog. Rsch. Assn., 1991, trophy Outstanding Svc. to Cmty. Sta. KQLH-FM, Trophy pl. Vol. Ctr. of Riverside, 1991, trophy and Individual Svc. award Riverside County Juvenile Hall of Fame, 1990-91, cert. Recognition Riverside County Probation Dept., 1991, Calif. Legis.-State Assembly, 1991, So. Calif. Chpt. IGAS, 1990-91, Riverside County Bd. Suprs. and Riverside County Probation Dept., 1993, 26th Children's Conf. Com., 1999; Participation award 21st Internat. Congress Arts and Comm., Scotland, 1994, Lisbon, Portugal, 1999, Internat. Gold Medal of Honor for disting. participation ABI/IBC 26th Congress On Arts and Comm., Lisbon, Portugal, 1999, Graphoanalyst of Yr. award So. Calif. chpt. Graphoanalysts, 2000, Disting. Svc. award City of Riverside, 2004, Order of Ambassadors Sovereign award ABI/IBC Inaugural World Forum, 2006. Master: Internat. Graphoanalysis Soc. (life; 2d then 1st v.p. so. Calif. chpt. 1984, Merit cert. 1981, Pres. Excellence award 1982, 1983, 1984, Pres. Merit citation 1988, Achievement cert. 1995); mem.: NAFE, YWCA, AAUW, DAV Aux. (life), Nat. Mus. Women in Arts, World War II Meml. Soc. (charter mem.), Smithsonian Assocs., Nat. Geographic Soc., Met. Mus. Assocs., Calif. Probation, Parole, and Corrections Assn. (cert. of tng. 1995), Top Cops Nat. Assn. Police Orgns., The Rsch. Coun. of Scripps Clinic and Rsch. Found., Riverside C. of C., U.S. Olympic Soc. (U.S. Olympic Team, U.S. Olympic Com. Sixth Ring charter mem. 2004, Replica Bronze medal 2004), Women's Networking Club (Riverside chpt.), Confederation of Chivalry (life; grand coun., dame officer). Avocations: sewing, music, collecting antiques, dance, exercise. Home and Office: 7965 Helena Ave Riverside CA 92504-3513

**WHITE, DALE ANDREW,** journalist; b. Jacksonville, Fla., Feb. 17, 1958; s. John Andrew and Jeannelle Corinne White. B in Journalism, U. Fla., 1983. Reporter UPI, Miami, Fla., 1980, Orlando (Fla.) Sentinel Star, 1981; corr. Fla. Times-Union, Gainesville, 1982; reporter, columnist, editl. writer, editor Sarasota Herald-Tribune, Fla., 1983—. Contbr. short stories to profl. publs. Recipient Chmn.'s award N.Y. Times, 1987, 2004, 3d place Editorial Writing award Fla. Soc. Newspaper Editors, 1993, 1st place Ind. Reporter Media award Fla. Sch. Bds. Assn., 1996. Office: PO Box 1695 Bradenton FL 34206-1695

**WHITE, DANIKA ELAINE,** music educator; b. Waimea, Hawaii, Nov. 8, 1970; d. Stephen Eveleth White and Christine Alyss Kirkpatrick. MusB, Ctrl. Meth. Coll., 1988—93; MusM, U. of Ark., 1995—97. Cert. in K-12 music edn. Dept. Elem. and Secondary Edn., Mo., 1993. K-12 music instr. Verona R-VII Schs., Mo., 1993—95; grad. assist. U. of Ark., 1995—97; k-12 music instr. Verona R-VII Schs., 1997—98; dir. of bands Lathrop R-II Schs., Mo., 1998—2002, Maryville R-II Schs., Mo., 2002—06, Monett R-I Schs., Mo. Clinician NW Mo. State U. - Summer Music Camps, 2002—05; flute judge Mo. Bandmasters Assn., 2003—; h.s. band v.p. NW Mo. Dist. #1-Mo. Music Educators Assn., Maryville, 2004—06. Recipient Pi Kappa Lambda, Academic Frat., U. of Ark., 1997, Omicron Delta Kappa, Nat. Leadership Frat., Ctrl. Meth. Coll., 1992, Outstanding Young Women of Am., 1991; scholar Grad. Assistantship, U. of Ark., 1995—97. Mem.: Music Educators Nat.

Conf., Nat. Bandmasters Assn., Mo. Bandmaster Assn., Mo. Music Educators Assn., Mo. Women Band Dirs. Assn. (pres. 2004—06, pres.-elect N.W. Dist. 1). Avocations: reading, flute, gardening, home improvement. Office: Monett R I Schs 1 David Sippy Dr Monett MO 65708 Business E-Mail: dwhite@monett.k12.mo.us.

**WHITE, DAPHNE MILBANK,** writer; b. Vancouver, Can., Apr. 12, 1927; d. Robbins Milbank and Mary Lightfoot; m. Barrie M. White Jr., Sept. 13, 1947 (div. 1966); children: Deborah, Pamela, Ellen, Barrie. BA in Polit. Sci., Smith Coll., 1948; MS in Pub. Affairs, Am. U., 1979; postgrad., George Washington U., 1979—82. Co-mgr. four small bus., 1947—51; br. chief Am. U., Cultural Info. Analysis Ctr., Washington, 1967—68; voters svc. sr. staff specialist League of Women Voters Edn. Fund, Washington, 1969—72; comm. dir. Pub. Affairs Coun., Washington, 1973—74; writer, editor, paralegal, Office Gen. Coun. Nat. Oceanic and Atmospheric Adminstrn., Washington, 1975—78, writer, editor regulations. devel. analyst Nat. Marine Fisheries Svc., 1979—90, program analyst, Ctr. Ocean Analysis and Prediction Monterey, Calif., 1990—92, program analyst, Monterey Bay Nat. Marine Sanctuary, 1992—93; ret., 1993. Contbr. articles to profl. jours. Enumerator and reviewer Census, 1960; bd. dirs. Youth Citizenship Fund, 1970—72; bd. dirs. Memton Fund, Inc., 1981—95, pres., 1989—94; vol. guide Monterey Bay Aquarium, 1993—97; mem. adv. coun. subcom. Monterey Bay Nat. Marine Sanctuary, 1994—; bd. dirs. LWV Monterey Peninsula, 1994—97, Girl Scouts Am. Mem.: LWV, Elkhorn Slough Found., Nonprofit Devel. Ctr., U.N. Assn., Fgn. Policy Assn., Marine Mammal Ctr., Save Our Shores, Cmty. Found., Friends Long Marine Lab, Coyote Point Mus., Monterey History and Art Assn., Environ. Defense, Ocean Conservancy.

**WHITE, DAVID CALVIN,** electrical engineer, educator, energy executive, consultant; b. Sunnyside, Wash., Feb. 18, 1922; s. David Calvin Sr. and Leafie Eloise (Scott) W.; m. Glorianna Guilii, July 30, 1949 (dec. Dec. 1965); 1 child, Julie Anne White Coman (dec.); m. Margot Ann Fuller, June 4, 1966; 1 child, Constance Anne. BS, Stanford U., 1946, MS, 1947, PhD, 1949. Registered profl. engr. Elec. engr. Kaiser Industries, Vancouver, Wash., 1941-42, 43-45; assoc. prof. elec. engring. U. Fla., Gainesville, 1949-52; asst. prof. elec. engring. MIT, Cambridge, 1952-54, assoc. prof., 1954-58, prof., 1958-62, Ford prof. engring., 1962-92, dir. energy lab., 1972-89, Ford prof. engring. emeritus, 1992—. Pres., dir. Energy Conversion, Inc., 1961-64; cons. Gulf Oil, 1976-84, Johnson Controls, 1980-98; sr. advisor and vis. prof. Birla Inst., India, 1968-70; mem. coun. U. Benin, Nigeria, 1972; trustee Lowell Tech. Inst., Mass., 1972-74; mem. corp. Woods Hole Oceanographic Inst., Mass., 1977-84; mem. research coordinating panel Gas Research Inst., Chgo., 1977-85; chmn. adv. council Electric Power Research Inst., Palo Alto, Calif., 1984-86, mem., 1980-87. Author: (with others) Electromechanical Energy Conversion, 1959 Commr. Electric Light Plant, Concord, Mass., 1959-64, Kalmia Woods Water Dist., Concord, 1960-63 Named hon. prof. Instituto Politecnico Nacional, Mex., 1961 Fellow IEEE; mem. Nat. Acad. Engring., Am. Acad. Arts and Scis., Am. Soc. Engring. Edn. (George Westinghouse award 1961), Country Club Boca Raton, Phi Beta Kappa, Sigma Xi, Tau Beta Pi, Eta Kappa Nu. Republican. Avocations: golf, boating. Home: 23401 Water Cir Boca Raton FL 33486 Office: MIT 77 Massachusetts Ave Rm E40-473 Cambridge MA 02139-4307 Personal E-mail: dcmfwhite@aol.com.

**WHITE, DAVID HYWEL,** physics professor, researcher; b. Cardiff, Wales, June 4, 1931; arrived in US, 1959, naturalized, 1966; s. William Richard and Bessie (Morgan) W.; m. Frances Mary Shearman, July 23, 1954; children: Richard Gerwyn, Christopher David. BS, U. Wales, 1953; PhD, Birmingham U., 1956. Asst. lectr. Birmingham U., 1958-59; asst. prof. U. Pa., 1961-64; assoc. prof. Cornell U., Ithaca, NY, 1964-69, prof., 1969-78; sr. physicist, head exptl. facilities div. Isabelle Project, Brookhaven Nat. Lab., Upton, L.I., NY, 1978-86; group leader nuclear and particle physics rsch. P divsn. Los Alamos (N.Mex.) Nat. Lab., 1986-88, lab. fellow, 1998—. Cons., 1967-69, 76-78, 99—. Author: Elementary Electronics, 1967; Editor: Scintillation Counters, 1966. NSF sr. postdoctoral fellow, 1970; JSPS fellow, 1981 Fellow Am. Phys. Soc. Home: 913 Calle Vistoso Santa Fe NM 87501-1031 Personal E-mail: hywelwhite@comcast.net.

**WHITE, DAVID L.,** electronics executive; b. Kansas City, Mo., Apr. 20, 1955; s. Joseph D. and Barbara H. (Gosling) W.; m. Nicole J. Davis, Dec. 18, 1976; children: Christina L., Jennifer M., Trisha D. BS in Physics, Brigham Young U., 1977; MBA, U. Wash., 1979. Applications cons. Burroughs Corp., Seattle, 1978-79; mgr. fin. planning Digital Equipment Corp., Colo. Springs, Colo., 1979-84; corp. controller Zehntel Inc., Walnut Creek, Calif., 1984-89; v.p., corp. controller Conner Peripherals, Inc., San Jose, Calif., 1989; pres., CEO Candescent Tech.; sr. v.p., CFO Asyst Tech.; exec. v.p., CFO Sanmina-SCI Corp., San Jose, Calif., 2004—. Advisor Boy Scouts Am., 1979-92. Named to All Am. Swimming Team, NCAA, 1975. Mem. Fin. Execs. Inst., Am. Prodn. and Inventory Control Soc. Republican. LDS Ch. Avocations: swimming, racquetball. Office: Sanmina SCI Corp 2700 N First St San Jose CA 95134*

**WHITE, DAVID R.,** healthcare company executive; Grad., Univ. Tenn.; M healthcare adminstrn., Trinity Univ., San Antonio. Regional v.p. Republic Health Corp.; exec. v.p., COO Cmty. Health Systems Inc.; pres. Atlantic group HCA/Columbia, 1994—98; pres., CEO LifeTrust, 1998—2000; nonexec. chmn. IASIS Healthcare, Franklin, Tenn., 1999—2000, CEO, 2000—04, pres., 2001—04, chmn., CEO, 2004—. Bd. dir. Am. Fedn. Hospitals. Office: IASIS Healthcare Corp Bldg E 113 Seaboard Ln Franklin TN 37067*

**WHITE, DAWN MARIE,** elementary school educator; b. Providence, Oct. 1, 1961; d. Edgar George and Linda Joan Hamel; m. Steven Ralph White, June 19, 1982; children: Brandon John Michael, Karlyca Lee-Anne, Steven Ralph Edgar George. BS in Edn magna cum laude, R.I. Coll., Providence, 2000 Profl. tchr. elem. edn, R.I. Dept. Elem. and Secondary Edn., 2000, advanced religious cert. Diocese of Providence, 2001. Dietary aide Zambarano Meml. Hosp., Wallum Lake, RI, 1981—84; waitress Levesques Restaurant, Pascoag, 1990—91; bus monitor Burrillville Sch. Dept., Harrisville, 1991—94; prop. Pennies Consignment Store, Pascoag, 1993—94; tchr. aide and substitute tchr. Father Holland Elem. Sch., 1994—2000; tchr. grade 3 Greater Woonsocket Cath. Regional Sch. Sys., 2000—. Mem. prin. search com. Wiliam Callahan Sch., Harrisville, 1992; sch. coord. CAT testing Diocese of Providence, 2001—; revisor sci. and social studies curriculum com. Greater Woonsocket Cath. Regional Sch. Sys., 2003—. Sr. vol. resource instr. U.S. Army Reserve Family Readiness Program, Washington, 2001—; vol. Operation Stand Down for Homeless Veterans, Woonsocket, 1993—94; asst. den leader Boy Scouts Am., Pascoag, 1990—92; master trainer family team bldg. U.S. Army Cmty. and Family Support Command, Alexandria, Va., 1995—; family support command. U.S. Army Reserves 94th Regional Support Command, Devens, Mass., 1996—2000; catechist St. Joseph Roman Cath. Ch., Pascoag, RI, 1993—2000. Carr scholar, Feinstein Sch. of Edn. and Human Devel., 1999—2000, Gilda R. Martone 38 Endowment scholar, 1999—2000, Phyllis Moorman Salk scholar, 1999—2000. Mem.: Nat. Cath. Ednl. Assn., Pi Epsilon Rho, Kappa Delta (life). Roman Catholic. Avocations: camping, travel, boating, foreign currency collecting.

**WHITE, DEBORAH O.,** forensic psychologist; d. Earle William White and Mildred Ottilie Schleinkofer; m. Gary Scott Spenik, Sept. 17, 1988; children: Katherine Mary, Andrew Nicholas William. BA, Trinity Coll., Conn., 1987; MSW, U. Md., 1994; PhD in Clin. Psychology, Alliant U., 1999. Lic. psychologist Va., 2002, Mass. Bd. Psychology, 2005. Grad. asst. Dept. Mental Health Psychology, Calif. Med. Facility, Vacaville, Calif., 1997—98, pre-doctoral internship tng. coord., 1997—2001, pre-doctoral intern, 1998—99, staff psychologist, 2000; pvt. practice Portsmouth, Va., 2003—05; instr. psychiatry dept. Harvard Med. Sch., Boston, 2005—; forensic evaluator Erich Lindemann Mental Health Ctr., Boston, 2005—. Vestry Christ Episcopal Ch., Alameda, Calif., 1999—2001; lay pastoral care com. St. Thomas Episcopal Ch., Chesapeake, Va., 2002—05; lay minister St. Stephen's Episcopal Ch., Cohasset, Mass., 2005—. Mem.: Soc. Personality Assesment, APA. Democrat. Episcopal.

Avocations: running, writing. Home: 14 Bayberry Ln Cohasset MA 02225 Office: Erich Lindemann Mental Health Ctr 25 Staniford St Boston MA 02225 Office Phone: 617-626-8642. E-mail: forensicpsychsvc@aol.com.

**WHITE, DIANE O'DONNELL,** retired librarian; b. Petersburg, Alaska, Dec. 4, 1944; d. John James O'Donnell, Vera Gertrude O'Donnell; m. Max A. White. BA in German Lang. and Lit., U.Oregon, 1967, MLS, 1970; media specialist, Western Oreg. State U., 1989. Cert. tchr. grades K-12. Serials cataloger U. Oreg., Eugene, 1970—75; adult svcs. libr. Kern County Libr., Bakersfield, Calif., 1986—87; coord. Oregon Index Oreg. State Libr., Salem, 1987—88; media specialist Harrisburg (Oreg.) Elem. Sch., 1989—92; reference libr. Albany (Oreg.) Pub. Libr., 1992—96, supervising libr. 1997—2000, libr. dir., 2001—02, ret., 2002. Mem.: Oreg. Libr. Assn., Greater Albany Rotary, Alpha Lambda Delta, Phi Beta Kappa. Presbyterian. Avocations: jogging, singing, dance, animal rights. Office: Albany Pub Libr 1390 Waverly Dr SE Albany OR 97321

**WHITE, DONALD HARVEY,** retired physics professor; b. Berkeley, Calif., Apr. 30, 1931; s. Harvey Elliott and Adeline White; m. Beverly Evalina Jones, Aug. 8, 1953; children: Jeri, Brett, Holly, Scott, Erin. AB, U. Calif., Berkeley, 1953; PhD, Cornell U., 1960. Rsch. physicist Lawrence Livermore (Calif.) Nat. Lab., 1960-71, cons., 1971-90; prof. physics Western Oreg. U., Monmouth, 1971-95; ret. Vis. rsch. scientist Inst. Laue-Langevin, Grenoble, France, 1977-78, 84-85, 91-92. Author: (with others) Physics, an Experimental Science, 1968, Physics and Music, 1980. Pres. Monmouth-Independence Cmty. Arts, 1983. DuPont scholar, 1958; Minna-Heineman Found. fellow, Hannover, Germany, 1977. Mem. Am. Phys. Soc., Oreg. Acad. Sci. (pres. 1979-80), Phi Kappa Phi (pres. West Oreg. chpt. 1989-90) Democrat. Presbyterian. Home: 1450 SW Bridlewood Dr #13 Dallas OR 97338 Office Phone: 503-623-5470.

**WHITE, DOUGLAS JAMES, JR.,** lawyer; b. NYC, Mar. 20, 1934; s. Douglas James and Margaret (Stillman) W.; m. Denise Beale, May 28, 1960; children: Brian Douglas, James Roderick. BA, U. Oreg., 1955; LLB, Willamette U., 1958. Bar: Oreg. 1958. Law clk. to assoc. justice Oreg. Supreme Ct., Salem, 1958-59; assoc. Schwabe, Williamson & Wyatt (formerly known as Mautz, Souther, Spaulding, Kinsey & Williamson), Portland, Oreg., 1959-69; shareholder, gen. ptnr. Schwabe, Williamson & Wyatt, P.C. (formerly known as Schwabe, Williamson, Wyatt, Moore & Roberts), Portland, Oreg., 1969-79, sr. ptnr., 1979-93; shareholder, 1994-98; of counsel, 1999—. Trustee Jesuit H.S. Beaverton, 1991-94; bd. dirs. St. Vincent de Paul Child Devel. Ctr., Portland, 1979-90, Portland Coun., Soc. St. Vincent de Paul, 1989-92, Portland House of Umoja, 1995—, Friends Sat. Acad., 2006—; bd. dirs., officer Maryville Nursing Home, Beaverton, 1993-99, St. Vincent de Paul Conf. of St. Thomas More, Portland, 1966—, Friends of Saturday Acad., Portland, 2006—; adv. bd. Saturday Acad., Portland, 1982-2005. Mem.: Oreg. State Bar Assn. (real estate and land use sect. exec. com. 1984—85), Flyfisher Club Oreg., Multnomah Athletic Club. Republican. Roman Catholic. Avocations: fly fishing, bridge, walking, travel, hiking. Home: 6725 SW Preslynn Dr Portland OR 97225-2668 Office: Schwabe Williamson & Wyatt 1211 SW 5th Ave Ste 1800 Portland OR 97204-3713 Office Phone: 503-222-9981.

**WHITE, DOUGLAS RICHIE,** anthropology educator; b. Mpls., Mar. 13, 1942; s. Asher Abbott and Margaret McQuestin (Richie) W.; m. Jayne Chamberlain (div. Feb. 1971); m. Lilyan Amdur Brudner, Mar. 21, 1971; 1 child, Scott Douglas. BA, U. Minn., 1964, MA, 1967, PhD, 1969. Asst. prof. U. Pitts., 1967-72, assoc. prof., 1972-76, U. Calif., Irvine, 1976-79, prof., 1979—. Dep. dir. Lang. Attitudes Rsch. Project, Dublin, 1971—73; vis. prof. U. Tex., Austin, 1974—75, Ecole des Hautes Etudes en Sci. Sociales, Paris, 1999—2002, Inst. Nat. d'Etudes Démographique, 2000; chmn. Linkages: World Devel. Res. Coun., Md., 1986—, pres., Md., 1986—90. Co-editor: Research Methods in Social Networks, 1989, Anthropology of Urban Environments, 1972, Kinship, Networks and Exchange, 1998; founder, gen. editor World Cultures Jour., 1985-90; author sci. software packages; editor Structure and Dynamics Jour.; contbr. articles to profl. jours. Recipient Sr. Disting. U.S. Scientist award, Alexander von Humboldt Stiftung, Bonn, Germany, 1989—91, Bourse de Haute Niveau award, Ministry Rsch. and Tech., Paris, 1992; fellow, Ctr. for Advanced Studies, Western Behavioral Sci. Inst., La Jolla, Calif., 1981—84. Mem. Social Sci. Computing Assn. (pres. elect 1991, pres. 1992), Santa Fe Inst. (mem. working groups 1999, 2000, 2001, external faculty 2004+). Democrat. Home: 8633 Via Mallorca Unit C La Jolla CA 92037 Office: U Calif School Social Sci Irvine CA 92697-0001 Office Phone: 949-824-5893.

**WHITE, EDITH REYNOLDS,** librarian; b. Passaic, N.J., Nov. 4, 1923; d. Earl Charlton and Haila (Holtgen) Reynolds; m. Forrest Prettyman White, Sept. 14, 1946; children: Forrest R., Ann Holland, Elizabeth Barrett, Mark Wallace. AB, Vassar Coll., 1944; Libr. Cert., Old Dominion U., 1966. Libr. Norfolk (Va.) Acad., 1961-83, Larchmont United Meth. Ch., Norfolk, 1983—. Writer book revs. Norfolk Virginian Pilot, 1984—; story teller Norfolk area, 1984—. Pres., bd. dirs. Friends Town-N-Down, Norfolk, 1986-87; founder, bd. dirs. Friends of Women's Studies at Old Dominion U., 1986-90, pres., 1988; bd. dirs. Feldman Chamber Music Soc., 1990-97; vol. tchr. of great books course Meadowbrook Sch., 1986-97; mem. adminstrv. bd. Larchmont United Meth. Ch., Norfolk, 1986-90, Sunday Sch. tchr., 1960—, libr. chmn., 1985—; bd. dirs. Va. Symphony Orch., 1951-86; sponsor Lit. Festival, Old Dominion U., 1995—, mem. adv. bd. Coll. Arts and Letters. Mem. AAUW (bd. dirs. 1954-02, pres. 1970-72), Va. Libr. Assn. (sec. sch. libr. sect. 1972-74), World Future Soc., Norfolk Story League (1st place nat. story contest 1989, hon. mem. 1991), LWV, Internat. Assn. Torch Clubs (bd. dirs., pres. 1987-88), Tidewater Artists (Best in Show award 1991), Va. Poetry Soc. (winner 1991). Democrat. Methodist. Avocations: watercolor painting, tennis, storytelling, teaching. Home: 7320 Glenroie Ave #8D Norfolk VA 23505-3152

**WHITE, EDMUND VALENTINE,** writer; b. Cin., Jan. 13, 1940; s. Edmund Valentine and Delilah (Teddlie) W. BA, U. Mich., 1962. Writer Time-Life Books, N.Y.C., 1962-70; sr. editor Saturday Rev., N.Y.C., 1972-73; exec. dir. N.Y. Inst. for Humanities, N.Y.C., 1982-83; asst. prof. writing seminars John Hopkins U., Balt., 1977-79; adj. prof. Columbia U. Sch. Arts, N.Y.C., 1981-83. Prof. Brown U., Providence, 1990-92. Novelist: Forgetting Elena, 1973, Nocturnes for the King of Naples, 1978, A Boy's Own Story, 1982, Caracole, 1985, The Darker Proof, 1987, The Beautiful Room is Empty, 1988, Skinned Alive, 1995, The Farewell Symphony, 1997; author: States of Desire, 1980, The Faber Book of Gay Short Fiction, 1991, Genet: A Biography, 1993, The Burning Library, 1994, Our Paris, 1994, The Flaneur (Writer and the City), 2001, Arts and Letters, 2004, (autobiography) My Lives, 2006. Named Ingram Merrill fellow, 1978, Guggenheim fellow, 1983; recipient Chevalier de l'ordre des arts et lettres, 1993, Nat. Book Critics Circle award, 1994. Mailing: Author Mai l- Ecco Press HarperCollins Publishers 10 E 53rd St New York NY 10022*

**WHITE, EDMUND WILLIAM,** chemical engineer; b. Phila., July 8, 1920; s. Edmund Brittin and Grace Salome (Faunce) W.; m. Kathrine Nathalie Cadwallader, Apr. 24, 1948; children: Christine Louise, William Cadwallader, Thomas Edmund, James Christopher. BA, Columbia Coll., 1940; BS, Columbia Sch. Engring., 1941, MChemE, 1942; PhD, Lehigh U., 1952. Jr. chemist Westvaco Chlorine Products Corp., South Charleston, W.Va., 1942-44; chem. engr. C.L. Mantell, N.Y.C., 1946-47, Diamond Alkali Co., Painesville, Ohio, 1947-49; grad. asst. Lehigh U., Bethlehem, Pa., 1949-51; sr. chemist Cities Svc. R & D Co., various cities, NJ, 1951-59, 1964—65, Athabasca Inc., Edmonton, Alberta, Canada, 1960-64; project mgr. U.S. Dept. Navy, Washington, 1965-66; rsch. chem. engr. Naval Surface Warfare Ctr., Annapolis, Md., 1966-95; cons. ret. 1995. Cons. in field; mem. U.S. del. to ISO TC 28 mtgs. in Budapest, 1990, Phila., 1992, Paris, 1994; mem. Quadripartite Navies group on Fuels, Lubricants and Allied Products, mem. U.S. del., Ottawa, Can., 1989, Camberra, Australia, 1991 and co-chair mtg., 1993; presenter in field Contbr. articles to profl. jours. Treas., v.p., pres. sch. PTAs, Silver Spring, Md., 1968-79; den father, mem. troop com. Boy Scouts Am.,

Silver Spring, 1966-75. Ensign USN, 1944-46. Fellow ASTM (chair task force, sect. subcom., com. 1967—, mem. award of merit com. 1996-98, mem. coord. com. on Flash Point 1989-99, Award of Merit 1990, Scroll of Honor 1993, Award of Excellence 1999, Lowrie B. Sargent Jr. award 2003, George V. Dysoff award, 2005), mem. AIChE (50 Yr. award), Am. Chem. Soc. (50 Yr. award), Potomac Curling Club (bd. dirs., pres. 1982-84), Internat. Assn. for Stability and Handling of Liquid Fuels (hon. mem., mem. steering com. 1985-95, Hon. Membership award 1999), Sigma Xi. Republican. Achievements include 4 patents and 2 Canadian patents; research in consensus standardization, fuel stability testing, fuel stability, synthetic fuels, separation processes, wax oxidation, mixing and chlorine-caustic electrolytic cell. Home: 908 Crest Park Dr Silver Spring MD 20903-1307

**WHITE, EDWARD ALFRED,** lawyer; b. Elizabeth, N.J., Nov. 23, 1934; BS in Indsl. Engring., U. Mich., 1957, JD, 1963. Bar: Fla. 1963, U.S. Ct. Appeals (5th cir.) 1971, U.S. Ct. Appeals (11th cir.) 1981, U.S. Supreme Ct. 1976. Assoc. Jennings, Watts, Clarke & Hamilton, Jacksonville, Fla., 1963-66, ptnr., 1966-69, Wayman & White, Jacksonville, Fla., 1969-72; pvt. practice Jacksonville, Fla., 1972—. Mem. aviation law com. Fla. Bar, 1972-94, chmn., 1979-81, bd. govs., 1984-88, admiralty com., 1984—, chmn., 1990-91, chmn. pub. relations com., 1986-88, exec. coun. trial lawyers sect., 1986-91, chmn. admiralty cert. com., 1995-97. Fellow Am. Bar Found.; mem. ABA (vice chmn. admiralty law com. 1995—), Fla. Bar Assn. (bd. cert. civil trial lawyer, bd. cert. admiralty lawyer), Jacksonville Bar Assn. (chmn. legal ethics com. 1975-76, bd. govs. 1976-78, pres. 1979-80), Assn. Trial Lawyers Am. (sustaining mem. 1984—), Acad. Fla. Trial Lawyers (diplomate), Fla. Coun. Bar Assn. Pres.'s, Lawyer-Pilots Bar Assn., Am. Judicature Soc., Maritime Law Assn. (proctor in admiralty), Southeastern Admiralty Law Inst. (bd. dirs. 1982-84, chmn., pres. 1994), Am. Bd. Trial Advocates (city of Jacksonville Mpl. code enforcement bd., 2006—). Home: 1959 Largo Rd Jacksonville FL 32207-3926 Office: 901 Blackstone Bldg 233 E Bay St Jacksonville FL 32202-3452 Fax: 904-356-6508. Office Phone: 904-356-6500.

**WHITE, EDWARD ALLEN,** electronics executive; b. Jan. 1, 1928; s. Joseph and Bessie (Allen) W.; m. Joan Dixon, Dec. 22, 1949 (div. Aug. 1978); children: Leslie Ann; m. Nancy Rhoads, Oct. 6, 1979. BS, Tufts U., 1947. Vice chmn. White Electronic Designs Corp., Phoenix, 1951—. Pres. Ariz. Digital Corp., Phoenix, 1975—91, Interactive Digital Corp., Phoenix, 1992—. Patentee in field. Bd. dirs. Gov.'s Coun. Children, Youth and Families, Phoenix, 1982-84, Planned Parenthood Fedn. Am., 1984-88; pres., bd. dirs. Planned Parenthood Ctrl. and No. Ariz., 1984-88; trustee Internat. House, N.Y.C., 1973-75, Tufts U., 1973-83. Recipient Horatio Alger award, 1962. Mem.: World Pres.'s Orgn., Paradise Valley Country Club, Tau Beta Pi. Home: 5786 N Echo Canyon Cir Phoenix AZ 85018-1242 Office: White Electronic Designs Corp 3601 E University Dr Phoenix AZ 85034-7254 Office Phone: 602-437-1520 x111. Business E-Mail: ewhite@whiteedc.com.

**WHITE, EMILY,** epidemiologist, researcher; b. Trenton, N.J., Sept. 11, 1946; d. Max and Celia (Lev) Lewin; m. Richard B. White, May 29, 1970; 1 child, Rebecca L. Milliman. SBc Applied Math., Brown U., Providence, 1968; MS Bio stats., U. Wash., Seattle, 1979, PhD Epidemiology, 1982. Prof. epidemiology U. Wash., Seattle, 1982—. Assoc. dean Sch. Pub. Health U. Wash., Seattle, 2006—; mem. staff Fred Hutchinson Cancer Ctr., Seattle, 1983—. Author: (textbook) Principles of Exposure Measurement in Epidemiology; contbr. articles sci. articles to profl. jours. Grantee, Nat. Cancer Inst. and others, 1985—. Office: University of Washington Box 357230 Seattle WA 98195-7230 E-mail: ewhite@fhcrc.org.

**WHITE, EMMET, JR.,** retirement community administrator; b. Newark, Oct. 18, 1946; s. Emmet, Sr. and June (Howlett) White; m. Betty Orr, June 7, 1970; children: Benjamin, Suzanne, George. BA, Lafayette Coll., 1968; JD, Coll. William and Mary, 1971. Bar: Hawaii 1972; nursing home adminstr., Hawaii. Law ptnr. Mau and White, AAL, Honolulu, 1975-83, White and Tom, AAL, Honolulu, 1983-95; pres., CEO Arcadia Retirement Residence, Honolulu, 1996—. Trustee Ctrl. Union Ch., Honolulu, 1980-84, chmn. 1983-84, moderator, 1987, also deacon; mem. Health Planning Coun. Honolulu. Col. USAR, 1968-94. Mem.: Nat. Com. Employer Support of Guard and Res. (ombudsman), Hawaii Long Term Care Assn. (chmn. 2001—03), Hawaii Bar Assn. Avocation: physical activities. Office: Arcadia Retirement Residence 1434 Punahou St Honolulu HI 96822-4754 Office Phone: 808-983-1823. E-mail: ewhite@arcadia-hi.org.

**WHITE, EUGENE VADEN,** retired pharmacist; b. Cape Charles, Va., Aug. 13, 1924; s. Paul Randolph and Louise (Townsend) W.; m. Laura Juanita LaFontaine, Aug. 28, 1948; children: Lynda Sue, Patricia Louise. BS in Pharmacy, Med. Coll. Va., 1950; PharM (hon.), Phila. Coll. Pharmacy and Sci., 1966; DSc (hon.), Shenandoah U., 2001. Pharmacist McKim & Huffman Drug Store, Luray, Va., 1950, Miller's Drug Store, Winchester, 1950-53; pharmacist, ptnr. Shiner's Drug Store, Front Royal, 1953-56; pharmacist, owner Eugene V. White, Pharmacist, P.C., Berryville, 1956-98; ret. 1998. Sturmer lectr. Phila. Coll. Pharmacy and Sci., 1979; Lubin vis. prof. U. Tenn. Sch. Pharmacy, Memphis, 1974; mem. bd. visitors Sch. Pharmacy, U. Pitts., 1969. Author: The Office-Based Family Pharmacist, 1978; created first office practice in community pharmacy, 1960, developed patient medication profile record, 1960. 2d lt. USAAC, 1943-45. Recipient Nat. Leadership award Phi Lambda Sigma, 1979, Outstanding Pharmacy Alumnus award Med. Coll. Va. Sch. Pharmacy Alumni Assn., 1989; Eugene V. White scholarship named in his honor Shenandoah U. Sch. Pharmacy, 1996, Eugene V. White Disting. Lecture Series established by Delta Xi chpt. Kappa Psi Pharm. Fraternity, Shenandoah U. Sch. Pharmacy, 1998. Fellow Am. Coll. Apothecaries (J. Leon Lascoff award 1973); mem. Am. Pharm. Assn. (Daniel B. Smith award 1965, Remington Honor medal 1978), Va. Pharm. Assn. (Pharmacist of Yr. award 1966, Outstanding Pharmacist award 1992). Methodist. Avocations: reading, woodworking, computers. Personal E mail: evwhite@visalllink.com.

**WHITE, FRED B., III,** lawyer; b. Somerville, NJ, 1947; BA, Wheaton Coll., 1969; JD with honors, George Washington U. Nat. Law Ctr., 1972. Bar: NJ 1972, DC 1972, Mass. 1976, Del. 1983, NY 1990. Co-head, banking/savings and loans mergers and acquisitions Skadden, Arps, Slate, Meagher & Flom LLP, NYC. Office: Skadden Arps Slate Meagher & Flom LLP 4 Times Sq New York NY 10036 Office Phone: 212-735-2144. Office Fax: 917-777-2144. Business E-Mail: fwhite@skadden.com.

**WHITE, FREDERICK ANDREW,** retired physics professor, retired physicist; b. Detroit, Mar. 11, 1918; s. Andrew Bracken and Mildred (Witzel) W.; m. Dorothy Janet Sibley, Nov. 7, 1942 (dec.); children: Wendell William, Lawrence Sibley, Eric Sibley, Roger Randolph (dec.). BS, Wayne State U., Detroit, 1940; MS, U. Mich., 1941; postgrad., U. Rochester, N.Y., 1941-43; PhD, U. Wis., 1959. Insp. U.S. Army Ordnance, Rochester, 1941—43; rsch. asst. Manhattan project U. Rochester, 1943—45, grad. instr. rsch. Manhattan project, 1946; rsch. asst., rsch. assoc., cons. physicist Knolls Atomic Power Lab. GE, Schenectady, NY, 1947—62; adj. prof. nuc. sci. Rensselaer Poly. Inst., Troy, NY, 1961—62, prof. nuc. engring. and environ. engring., adj. liaison scientist, 1962—81, prof. emeritus, 1981—96; ret., 1996. Cons. NASA, 1965-80; organist and assoc. physicist, vis. and liaison scientist Rochester Gas and Electric Co., 1978-96; adj. prof. physics SUNY Albany, 1986-88 Author: American Industrial Research Laboratories, 1961, Mass Spectrometry in Science and Technology, 1968, Our Acoustic Environment, 1975, Mass Spectrometry: Applications in Science and Engineering, 1986 Mem. AIAA, IEEE, Optical Soc. Am., Am. Guild Organists Achievements include developing mass spectrometric instrumentation and its uses in measurements relating to nuclear and atomic physics; co-discoverer last naturally-occurring stable isotope. Home: 2456 Hilltop Rd Niskayuna NY 12309-2405 Personal E-mail: whitef@taconic.net. E-mail: fwhite@nycap.rr.com.

**WHITE, GARY RICHARD,** electrical engineer; b. Detroit, Nov. 15, 1962; s. Thomas Richard and Davene (Reynolds) White. BSEE, Wayne State U., 1986; MSIS/MBA, Hawaii Pacific U., 2006. Electronics engr. U.S. Army

Info. Sys. Engring. Command, Ft. Belvoir, Va., 1987-88, Ft. Shafter, Hawaii, 1988-92; elec. worker U.S. Navy Pub. Works Ctr., Pearl Harbor, Hawaii, 1992-96, plant operator, 1996—. Mem. IEEE, NRA, NSPE, Assn. Computing Machinery, Am. Assn. Individual Investors, Am. Mgmt. Assn. Avocations: weightlifting, bicycling, computers, music, movies. Office: PO Box 19055 Honolulu HI 96817-8055 Office Phone: 808-474-2202.

**WHITE, GEORGE COOKE,** theater director, foundation administrator; b. New London, Conn., Aug. 16, 1935; s. Nelson Cooke and Aida (Rovetti) W.; m. Elizabeth Conant Darling, July 5, 1958; children: George Conant, Caleb Ensign, Juliette Darling. Student, U. Paris, 1956; BA, Yale U., 1957, MFA, 1961; student, Shakespeare Inst., 1959; ArtsD (hon.), Conn. Coll., 1994. Stage mgr. Imperial Japanese Azumakabuki Co., 1955; asst. mgr. Internat. Ballet Festival, Nervi, Italy, 1955; prodn. coordinator Talent Assos., 1961-63; adminstrv. v.p. score prodns. Paramount Pictures, 1963-65; founder, pres. Eugene O'Neill Meml. Theater Found., 1965—2000; adviser, dir. Theatre One, Conn. Coll. Women, 1967-70; exec. dir. The Johnny Mercer Found., 1999; regional theater cons. Nat. Ednl. TV Network; guest lectr. Wagner Coll., 1970; acting dir. Hunter Coll. Hunter Arts, 1972-73; chmn. Florence Acad. Art, 2004—. Adj. prof. U. NC; prof. theater adminstrn. program Yale U., 1978-91; co-chmn. Yale Drama Sch.; mem. exec. com. Theatre Libr. Assn., 1967; bd. govs. Am. Playwrights Theatre; mem. bd. ANTA, 1967-68; mem. Mayor NYC's Theatre Adv. Com.; advisory bd. Internat. Theatre Inst.; panel mem. Exptl. Theatre; US State Dept. cultural exchange grantee to Australia; guest adminstr. Australian Nat. Playwrights Conf., 1973; US del. Internat. Theatre Inst. Congress, Moscow, 1973; mem. Conn. Commmn. on Arts, 1978-93, mem. exec. com., 1979-83, vice chair, 1992-93; co-founder Caribbean-US Theatre Exchange; dir. Actors Theatre St. Paul, 1979, 80, 82, 83, 86, Hartman Repertory Theatre, 1980; guest dir. Chinese Theater Assn., Beijing, 1984, 87, Hedgerow Theatre, 1986; mem. nominating com. Antoinette Perry Awards, 1984-86, 88, 94-96, 98-2002, adminstrv. com. Am. Theater Wing, 1997; dir. Anna Christie Beijing Cen. Dramatic Theater, 1984, 87; bd. dirs. New London Day. Appeared in TV series Citizen Soldier, 1959-61; appeared in off-Broadway prodn. John Brown's Body. Trustee Goodspeed Opera House, 1966-68, Nat. Theatre Conf., 1973—, Eastern Conn. Symphony, Dance Arts Coun., Conn. Opera Assn., Conn. Pub. TV, 1973-83, Mitchell Coll., 1994—, Arts & Bus. Coun., 1994—, Arts Internat., 2001, 02, Boston Conservatory, 2000-; trustee Conn. Edn. Telecommunications Corp., 1973-83, chmn., 1982; mem. planning bd. Op. Rescue; bd. dirs. Rehearsal Club, Centre for Inter-Am. Rels., Theater of Latin Am., Manhattan Theatre Club, 1970-80, Met. Opera Guild; Performance mag.; exec. com. Yale Drama Alumni, 1963-73; mem. Yale Alumni Bd.; bd. overseers drama dept. Brandeis U.; adv. bd. Am. Musical Theatre Program, Hartford Conservatory, Bd. Arts & Bus. Coun., Brandeis Creative Arts Award Jury, Theater and New Music Theatre Works Panel, NEA; mem. Waterford (Conn.) Rep. Town Meeting, 1975-77, 2001—; presdl. appointment to Nat. Coun. NEA, 1992; mem. Nat. Coun. Arts, 1992-97; trustee Arts Internat.; bd. dirs. Day Pub. Co., RKO Pictures, American Acad. Dramatic Arts; bd. mem. Boston Conservatory; mem. Coast Guard Auxillary, watch q.m. US Coast Guard Barque Eagle. Served with AUS, 1957-59; Flotilla Cmdr., US Coast Auxillary, 1998-99. Named Officer first class, Royal Swedish Order of Polar Star; recipient spl. citation, New England Theatre Conf., 1968, 1998, Margo Jones award, 1968, Pub. Svc. award, New London County Bar Assn., 1975, Disting. Citizen's award, Town of Waterford, 1976, Distin. Svc. award, Conn. mag., 1981, Contbns. to State award, 1981, Lifetime Contbn. to Theatre award, Am. Theater Assn., 1989, Contbn. to Conn. Arts award, Quinnipiac Coll., 1989, Medal of Arts, Russian Federation, Chevalier des artes et des lettres (France), 1983, gold medal, Cairo Internat. Experimental Theater Festival, Cavalieri, Order of St. Maurice and Lazarus; grantee Internat. Communications Agy. cultural exch. grantee to People's Republic of China, 1980. Fellow Royal Soc. Arts, Coll. of Am. Theatre; mem. Chinese Theatre Assn. (hon.). Clubs: Century; Cosmos (Washington); Thames (New London); White's Point Yacht. Office: 234 W 44th St New York NY 10036 Home: Whites Point 22 New Shore New York NY 10036 Office Phone: 212-382-2790, 860-439-0667. Personal E-mail: whitebg@att.net.

**WHITE, GEORGE EDWARD,** law educator, lawyer; b. Northampton, Mass., Mar. 19, 1941; s. George LeRoy and Frances Dorothy (McCafferty) W.; m. Susan Valre Davis, Dec. 31, 1966; children: Alexandra V., Elisabeth McC. BA, Amherst Coll., 1963; MA, Yale U., 1964, PhD, 1967; JD, Harvard U., 1970. Bar: D.C. 1970. Va. 1975. U.S. Supreme Ct. 1973. Vis. scholar Am. Bar Found., 1970—71; law clk. to Chief Justice Warren U.S. Supreme Ct., 1971—72; asst. prof. law U. Va., 1972—74, assoc. prof., 1974—77, prof., 1977—86, John B. Minor prof. law and history, 1987—2003, disting. univ. prof., John B. Minor prof. law and history, 1992—2003, David and Mary Harrison disting. prof. law, 2003—. Vis. prof. Marshall-Wythe Law Sch. spring 1988, N.Y. Law Sch., fall 1988; acad. visitor London Sch. Econs. and Polit. Sci., 2005 Author: The American Judicial Tradition, 1976, 2nd edit., 1988, Tort Law in America: An Intellectual History, 1980 (Gavel award ABA, 1981), 2nd edit., 2003, Earl Warren: A Public Life, 1982 (Gavel award ABA, 1983), The Marshall Court and Cultural Change, 1988, 2nd edit., 1991 (James Willard Hurst prize, 1990), Justice Oliver Wendell Holmes: Law and the Inner Self, 1993 (Gavel award ABA, 1994, Scribes award, 1994, Littleton-Griswold prize, 1994, Triennial Order of the Coif award, 1996), Intervention and Detachment: Essays in Legal History and Jurisprudence, 1994, Creating the National Pastime: Baseball Transforms Itself, 1903-1953, 1996, The Constitution and the New Deal, 2000, Alger Hiss's Looking-Glass Wars, 2004, others; editor: Studies in Legal History, 1980—86, Delegate in Law, 1986—97. Mem. AAAS, Am. Law Inst., Am. Soc. Legal History (bd. dirs. 1978-81), Soc. Am. Historians. Office: Law Sch U Va 580 Massie Rd Charlottesville VA 22903-1789 Business E-mail: gew@virginia.edu.

**WHITE, GILBERT CASE, II,** internist, hematologist; b. Durham, NC, Nov. 19, 1944; s. Finley Tomlinson and Jane Dinsmoor White; m. Judy Camp Atkins White; children: Ingle Tomlinson, Mason Carpenter, Andrew Eliot. BA, U. NC, 1966, MD, 1971. Diplomate Am. Bd. Internal Medicine. Intern then resident Georgetown U., Washington, 1971—73; from resident to prof. U. NC, Chapel Hill, 1973—2004; dir. Blood Rsch. Inst. Blood Ctr. Wis., Milw., 2004—; assoc. dean Med. Coll. Wis., Milw., 2003—. Office Phone: 414-937-3866.

**WHITE, GILBERT F. (GILBERT FOWLER WHITE),** geographer, educator; b. Chgo., Nov. 26, 1911; s. Arthur E. and Mary (Guthrie) W.; m. Anne Elizabeth Underwood, Apr. 28, 1944; children: William D., Mary, Frances; m. Claire Sheridan, July 18, 2003. BS, U. Chgo., 1932, SM, 1934, PhD, 1942; LLD (hon.), Hamilton Coll., 1951; ScD (hon.), Haverford Coll., 1955; LLD (hon.), Swarthmore Coll., Earlham Coll., Mich. State U., Northland Coll.; degree (hon.), U. Ariz., 2002; LLD (hon.), Augustana Coll., 2003. Geographer Miss. Valley Com. of P.W.A., 1934, Nat. Resources Bd., 1934-35; sec. land and water com. Nat. Resources Com. and Nat. Resources Planning Bd., 1935-40; with Exec. Office Pres., Bur. Budget, 1941-42; asst. exec. sec. Am. Friends Service Com., 1945-46; relief adminstr. in France, 1942-43; interned Baden-Baden, 1943-44; sec. Am. Relief for India, 1945-46; pres. Haverford Coll., 1946-55; prof. geography U. Chgo., 1956-69; prof. geography, dir. Inst. Behavioral Sci., U. Colo., 1970-78, Gustavson disting. prof. emeritus, 1979—; dir. Natural Hazards Info. Ctr., 1978-84, 92-94; exec. editor Environment mag., 1983-93. Vis. prof. Oxford U., 1962-63; cons. Investigations Lower Mekong Basin, 1961-62, 70; U.S. mem. UNESCO adv. com. on arid zone research, 1954-55; mem. mission Am. Vol. Agys. Relief Germany, 1946; vice chmn. Pres.'s Water Resources Policy Commn., 1950; mem. com. natural resources Hoover Commn., 1948; chmn. UN Panel Integrated River Basin Devel., 1956-57; chmn. Task Force Fed. Flood Control Policy, 1965-66; sci. adv. to adminstr. UN Devel. Program, 1966-71; chmn. adv. bd. Energy Policy Project, 1972-74; chmn. Am. Friends Service Com., 1963-69; chmn. com. on man and environment IGU, 1969-76; chmn. steering com. High Sch. Geography com., 1964-70; mem. Tech. Assessment Adv. Council, 1974-76; chmn. environ. studies bd. NRC, 1975-77; pres. Sci. Com. on Problems of Environment, 1976-82; chmn. bd. Resources for Future, 1973-79; co-chmn. U.S.-Egypt Joint Consultative Com. on Sci. and Tech., 1981-86; mem. adv. group on greenhouse gases World

Meteorol. Orgn., Internat. Council of Scientific Unions, UN Environ. Program., 1986-90; chmn. tech. rev. com. Nev. Nuclear Waste Project, 1987-93; mem. adv. group on water UN Environ. Program, 1989-93, working group for Action Plan for Aral Sea Basin, USSR, 1990-93; chmn. nat. rev. com. Status U.S. Floodplain Mgmt., 1989; bd. dirs. Am. Soc. Flood Plain Mgrs. Found., 1996—. Author: Human Adjustment to Floods, 1942, Science and Future of Arid Lands, 1960, Social and Economic Aspects of Natural Resources, 1962, Choice of Adjustment to Floods, 1964, Strategies of American Water Management, 1969; co-author: Drawers of Water, 1972, Assessment of Research on Natural Hazards, 1975, Flood Hazard in the United States, 1975, The Environment as Hazard, 1978, Water and Life: Water Management and Environmental Policy, 2003; editor: Natural Hazards: Local, National and Global, 1974, Environmental Aspects of Complex River Development, 1977; co-editor: Environmental Issues, 1977, The World Environment, 1972-1982, 1982, Environmental Effects of Nuclear War, 1983, Water for Life, 2003. Reicpient Daly medal Am. Geog. Soc., 1971, Eben award Am. Water Resources Assn., 1972, Caulfield medal, 1989, Alumni medal U. Chgo., 1979, Outstanding Achievement award Nat. Coun. for Geog. Edn., 1981, Sasakawa UN Evniron. prize, 1985, Tyler prize, 1987, Laureat d'Honneur award Internat. Geog. Union, 1988, Vautrin Lud Internat. Geog. prize, 1992, Hubbard medal Nat. Geog. Soc., 1994, Volvo Environment prize, 1995. Mem. AAAS, NAS (commn. on natural resources 1973-80, chmn. 1977-80, chmn. com. on water 1964-68, chmn. com. on sustainable water supplies of Middle East 1996-99, Environ. award 1980, Pub. Welfare medal 2000), Assn. Am. Geographers (pres. 1962, Outstanding Achievement award 1955, 74, Anderson medal 1986, US Nat. Medal Sci 2000, Lifetime Achievement award 2002), Internat. Coun. Sci. Unions (steering com. on study of environ. consequences of nuclear war 1983-87, adv. com. on environ. 1990-96), Internat. Water Resources Assn. (Millenium award 2000), Russian Geog. Soc. (hon.), Royal Geog. Soc. (hon.), Am. Am. State Flood Plain Mgrs. (nat. flood forum 2004—), Russian Acad. Scis. (fgn.), Am. Philos. Soc., Cosmos Club (Washington, award 1993), Sigma Xi. Mem. Soc. Friends. Home: 624 Pearl St Apt 302 Boulder CO 80302-5072 Business E-mail: gilbert.white@colorado.edu.

**WHITE, GORDON ELIOT,** historian; b. Glen Ridge, NJ, Oct. 25, 1933; s. Maurice Brewster and Sarah Fullilove (Gordon) W.; m. Nancy Johnson, 1955 (div. 1957); m. Mary Joan Briggs, Aug. 6, 1960 (dec. Nov. 1987); children: Sarah Elizabeth and Gordon O'Neal Brewster (twins), David McIntyre; m. Francis C. Barrineau, 1989 (div. 1996); m. Angela Tyler, Mar. 27, 1999. BA, Cornell U., 1955; MS in Journalism, Columbia U., 1957. Lic. master mariner USCG; lic. pilot FAA. Stringer Nassau Daily Rev.-Star, Rockville Centre, L.I., NY, 1948-50, Freeport (N.Y.) Leader, 1949-50; sports writer Morris County (N.J.) Citizen, 1950-51; stringer Ithaca (N.Y.) Evening News, 1951-55; photo editor, editl. writer Cornell Daily Sun, 1951-55; copy editor Am. Banker, N.Y.C., 1958; Washington corr. Chgo. Am., 1958-61; chief Washington bur. Deseret News, Salt Lake City, 1961-88. Also corr. in Europe, U.S. and Antarctic for WJR, Detroit; KSL-KSL-TV, Salt Lake City, also KGMB, Honolulu; free lance writer with U.S. Navy, Army and Air Force, 1959; cons. Nat. Air and Space Mus.; auto racing, mil. aviation electronics historian. Author: Offenhauser, the Legendary American Racing Engine and the Men Who Built It, 1996, The Indianapolis Racing Cars of Frank Kurtis, 1940-1963, 2000, Kurtis-Kraft: Masterworks of Speed & Style, 2001, Lost Race Tracks, 2003, The Marvelous Mechanical Designs of Harry A. Miller, 2004, Ab and Marvin Jenkins and the Mormon Meteors, 2006. Advisor auto racing Nat. Mus. Am. History, Smithsonian Instn., 1989—; curator Miller-Offenhauser Archive of historic race engine blueprints. Recipient Raymond Clapper Meml. award White House Corrs. Assn., 1978; award for excellence in reporting Exec. Dept. and White House; Roy W. Howard award for outstanding pub. svc. by a newspaper corr., 1979; award for disting. investigative reporting Investigative Reporters and Editors, 1980, Reser-Tuthill award for writing on history of automobile racing, Indpls., 1985. Mem. Nat. Press Club (Washington, Excellence in Reporting award 1979), Sigma Delta Chi (1st prize for newsphoto, 1954, Nat. award 1979), Pi Kappa Phi, Pi Delta Epsilon Episcopalian. Home and Office: PO Box 129 Hardyville VA 23070 Office Phone: 804-776-7947. Personal E-mail: gewhite@crosslink.net.

**WHITE, GREGORY A.,** prosecutor; b. Nov. 1949; BA in Criminal Justice and Police Adminstrn., Kent State U., 1973; JD magna cum laude, Cleveland Marshall Coll., 1976. Atty. Wilcox and White Law Firm, 1977—84; law dir. City of Elyria, 1979; prosecutor Lorain County, Ohio, 1981—2002; US atty. (no. dist.) Ohio US Dept. Justice, 2003—. With USMC, Vietnam. Office: US Attys Office 801 W Superior Ave Ste 400 Cleveland OH 44113-1852*

**WHITE, GRETCHEN NANCE,** education educator, writer; d. Virginia Lee Nance; m. Ronald Craig White (dec.); children: Lorenzo De'Warren, David Lee, Mark Du'Pree, Paul Keith, Anthony O'Lunte, Michelle Ja'Nesse Jefferson. Diploma in child daycare, ICS, Pa., 1995; diploma in mgmt. in health care, Calif. Coll. of Health Scis., 1998, diploma in bus. comm., 2001. Cert. ordination Tex., 2001, Tex. Notary Pub. Commn. Pvt. duty nurses asst. Meth. Hosp., Houston, 1984—87; vocat. coord. Richmond (Tex.) State Sch., 1988—. Founder, pres. White's Internat. Scholarship, Inc. (nat. scholarship Tex., 2001—. Author: (book) It's Vision Time, 2000, The Four F''s/Faith, Fear, Failure, Forgiveness, 2000, A Nation on the Rise to Be Educated or Not to Be Educated, 2003. Host bible study chat group, vol. Read-A-Thon; sponsor free hot meal program for low-income housing project area, 2004—; pastor A Nation on the Rise Youth/Teen Ministry Explosion. Grantee, Wal-mart Super Ctr., 2004. Avocations: cooking, reading, health glider, sports. Office: Whites Internat Scholarship Inc PO Box 1283 Rosenberg TX 77471 Office Phone: 281-846-8558. Business E-mail: gretchen.white@dads.state.tx.us.

**WHITE, H. KATHERINE,** lawyer; b. Salina, Kans., May 21, 1945; BS, MIT, 1967; JD, Rutgers U., 1975. Bar: Calif. 1975, NJ 1982. Joined Sealed Air Corp., Saddle Brook, NJ, 1982, v.p., gen. counsel, sec., 1998—. Mem.: NJ Corp. Counsel Assn. (dir. 1994—96), Am. Corp. Counsel Assn., Am. Soc. Corp. Secretaries, State Bar Calif., NJ State Bar Assn., ABA. Office: Sealed Air Corp Pk 80 E Saddle Brook NJ 07663-5291

**WHITE, HAROLD JACK,** pathologist; b. Bklyn., Jan. 4, 1920; s. Abraham and Jennie (Warshawsky) W.; m. Lucette Darby, July 19, 1962; children: Elizabeth, Darby, Matthew, Esther. BS, Harvard U., 1941; MD, U. Geneva, 1952. Diplomate Am. Bd. Pathology. Intern, resident in pathology Yale U. Sch. Medicine, New Haven, 1953-58, fellow, 1957-58; assoc. pathologist Brigham and Women's Hosp., Boston, 1962-66; chief lab. svc. VA Hosp., West Roxbury, Mass., 1962-66, Little Rock, 1966-80; sr. scientist, acting head biomed. sci. dept. GM Rsch. Labs., Warren, Mich., 1980-85, cons., 1985—. Prof. pathology, microbiology U. Ark. Med. Sch., Little Rock, 1966—; vis. scientist dept. comparative medicine, MIT, Cambridge, 1988—. Contbr. over 100 articles, abstracts in pathology, microbiology, immunology, toxicology, biomedicine to profl. jours. 1st lt. USAAF, 1942-46. Fellow Coll. Am. Pathologists, Internat. Coll. Pathology. Home: 24 Bass Rocks Rd Gloucester MA 01930-3276 Office: 35 Main St Gloucester MA 01930-5730 Office Phone: 978-281-3531. E-mail: hjwriverrun@aol.com.

**WHITE, HARRY EDWARD, JR.,** lawyer; b. Menominee, Mich., Apr. 26, 1939; s. Harry Edward and Verena Charlotte (Leisen) W.; m. Mary P.A. Sheaffer, June 7, 1980. BS in Fgn. Svc., Georgetown U., Washington, 1961; LLB, Columbia U., 1964. Bar: N.Y. 1965, U.S. Supreme Ct. 1970, U.S. Dist. Ct. (so. dist.) N.Y. 1979, U.S. Tax Ct. 1980. Assoc. Milbank, Tweed, Hadley & McCloy, N.Y.C., 1964-65, 67-73, ptnr., 1974—2004, cons. ptnr., 2004—. Contbr. chpts. to books, articles to legal jours. Served with M.I., U.S. Army, 1965-66, Vietnam. Decorated Bronze Star. Mem. ABA, Internat. Bar Assn., N.Y. State Bar Assn. (chmn. taxation com. internat. law practice sect. 1987-90, co-chmn. exempt orgns. com. tax sect. 1987-88), Internat. Law Assn., ssn. Bar City N.Y., Internat. Fiscal Assns., The Players. Republican. Roman Catholic. Home: 333 E 55th St New York NY 10022-8316 Office: Milbank Tweed Hadley & McCloy 1 Chase Manhattan Plz Fl 47 New York NY 10005-1413 Office Phone: 212-530-5092. E-mail: hwhite@milbank.com.

**WHITE, HELENE NITA,** federal judge; b. Jackson Heights, NY, Dec. 2, 1954; d. Frank William and Ruth (Gruber) White. AB, Columbia U., 1978; JD, U. Pa., 1978. Bar: Pa. 1979, Mich. 1979. Law clk. to justice Mich. Supreme Ct., Southfield, 1978—80; judge Common Pleas Ct., Detroit, 1981, 36th Dist Ct., Detroit, 1981—83, Wayne Cir. Ct., Detroit, 1983—92, Mich. Ct. Appeals, Detroit, 1992—. Bd. dirs., chmn. bylaws com. Met. Detroit YWCA, 1986—87, Coalition Temporary Shelter, 1986—, chmn. nominating com., 1988—; program com. bus. and profl. dist. Jewish Welfare Fedn., 1987—; bd. advisors Sojourner Found., 1988, Detroit Women's Forum, 1988—. Mem.: ABA, Women Lawyers Assn. Mich., Nat. Assn. Women Judges (chmn. publicity 1984, membership com. 1985—), Detroit Bar Assn., Pa. Bar Assn. Jewish.

**WHITE, HENRY F., JR.,** legal association administrator, retired military officer; BS, U.S. Naval Acad.; grad., Fordham U., 1976. Pres. Inst. Internat. Container Lessoers; mem. adv. com. on comml. ops. customs and border protection U.S. Dept. Homeland Security; mem. Hill, Betts & Nash, LLP; dep. commr. transp. NYC; counsel to Mayor; mng. mem. Barger & Wolen LLP; exec. dir. ABA. Rear admiral, vice comdr., U.S. Fleet Forces Command USNR. Office: ABA 321 N Clark St Chicago IL 60610-4714 Office Phone: 312-988-5000. Office Fax: 312-988-6281.*

**WHITE, HENRY J.,** engineering educator, consultant; b. NYC, Nov. 20, 1965; s. Henry and Dolores White; m. Yuxie P. White, Dec. 26, 1998; children: Hillary X., Francis H. BS, Poly. U., Bklyn., 1987; MS, U. Tenn., 1992; PhD, Stony Brook U., 1999. Registered profl. engr., NY. Metall. technician Lucius Pitkin Inc., NYC, 1985—87, LI Testing Lab., North Babylon, NY, 1986—87; metallurgist ABB Lummus Global, Bloomfield, NJ, 1987—90; materials engr. Misonix Inc., Farmingdale, NY, 1993—94; mgr. heat treating opns. Skyo Industries Inc., Deer Park, NY, 1994—2000; profl. Stony Brook (NY) U., 2000—. Cons. NSF, Arlington, Va., 2000—, Air Force Office Sci. Rsch., Arlington, 2005—; ABET program evaluator Metall. Soc., Warrendale, Pa., 2002—, profl. registration com., 2003—, faculty fellow. Fellow, Am. Soc. for Engring. Edn./NASA, 2001; grantee, NSF, 2004. Mem.: Assn. Iron and Steel Tech., Metall. Soc., Materials Rsch. Soc., Am. Soc. Engring. Edn., Am. Soc. Materials Internat. (chmn. LI chpt. 2002—03, bd. dirs. metro NY/NJ chpt. 2003—, vice chmn. metro NY/NJ chpt. 2006—, Quality Performance Program award 2002, 2003), Soc. Mfg. Engrs. Achievements include patents for densification of thermal spray coatings. Home: 6 Raspberry Ln Nesconset NY 11767 Office: Stony Brook Univ Dept Materials Sci Stony Brook NY 11794-2275 Personal E-mail: hwhite@notes.cc.sunysb.edu.

**WHITE, HERBERT SPENCER,** library and information scientist, educator, dean; b. Vienna, Sept. 5, 1927; came to U.S., 1938, naturalized, 1944; s. Leon and Ernestine (Lichteneger) Hochweis; m. Mary Virginia Ebner, Feb. 19, 1953 (dec.); 1 son, Jerome; m. Nancy J. Cornell, May 1, 2002. BS in Chemistry, CCNY, 1949; MSLS, Syracuse U., 1950; PhD in Humane Letters (hon.), Ind. U., 2003. Intern Libr. of Congress, Washington, 1950, mem. tech. info. divsn., 1950-53; tech. libr. AEC, Oak Ridge, Tenn., 1953-54; organizer, mgr. corp. libr. Chance Vought Aircraft, Dallas, 1954-59; mgr. engring. libr. IBM Corp., Kingston, N.Y., 1959-62, mgr. tech. info. ctr. Poughkeepsie, N.Y., 1962-64; exec. dir. NASA Sci. and Tech. Info. Facility, College Park, Md., 1964-68; v.p. info. mgmt. Leasco Systems & Rsch. Corp., Bethesda, Md., 1968-70; sr. v.p. Inst. Sci. Info., Phila., 1970-74, corp. dir., 1971-74; pres. Stechert-Macmillan, Inc., Pennsaucken, N.J., 1974-75; prof., dir. Rsch. Ctr. Grad. Libr. Sch. Ind. U., Bloomington, 1975-80, dean Sch. Libr. and Info. Scis., 1980-90, disting. prof., 1991-95; prof. emeritus, 1995—. Adj. prof. U. Ariz. Sch. Libr. Scis., 1995—; vis. prof. Alberta, San Jose State, Hawaii; cons., lectr. Author: Librarianship Quo Vadis?, 2000, others; contbr. articles to profl. publs.; columnist Libr. Jour. Mem. Pres.'s Adv. Com. for Adminstrn. Title II-B Higher Edn. Act, 1965-68, Libr. Rsch. Planning Com. for 1980s, U.S. Dept. Edn., v.p. Green Valley Cmty. Coordinating Coun., 1997—; grant reviewer Inst. Mus. and Librs., 1998—. Spl. honoree, U. of Essen (Germany) Conf., 1992. Fellow Spl. Libraries Assn. (pres. 1969-70, J.C. Dana award 1985, Hall of Fame 1994); mem. ALA (councillor 1988-92, planning com. 1989-91, Dewey medal 1987), Am. Soc. Info. Sci. (pres. 1973-74, W. Davis award 1977, award of merit 1981, named Pioneer, 1987), Assn. Libr. and Info. Sci. Edn. (chmn. govtl. rels. com. 1980-88), Am. Fedn. Info. Processing Svcs. (dir. 1972-78), Federation Internationale de Documentation (Netherlands, bd. dir. 1976-78, treas. 1978-82), Soc. for Scholarly Pub. (bd. dirs. 1981-82), Assn. Rsch. Libraries (com. on libr. edn 1983-85), Coun. Libr. Resources (rsch. priorities task force 1984-88, Ind. Libr. Lifetime Achievement award 1990), Beta Phi Mu (Svc. award 1995). Address: 5950 N Fountains Ave #7102 Tucson AZ 85704-7863

**WHITE, HOWARD D.,** information science educator; b. 1936; PhD, U. Calif., Berkeley, 1974. Joined, Coll. of Information Sci. and Tech. Drexel U. Phila., 1974, prof. libr. sci., disting. prof., 1998—2002, prof. emeritus, 2002—. Co-author (with Marcia Bates and Patrick Wilson): For Information Specialists: Interpretations of Reference and Bibliographic Work, 1992; author: Brief Tests of Collection Strength, 1995; contbr. articles to profl. publs. Recipient award of merit, Am. Soc. Info. Sci. and Tech., 2004, Price medal, Internat. Soc. Scientometrics and Informetrics, 2005. Office: Drexel U Coll Info Sci & Tech Rush Bldg 13 33rd and Market St Philadelphia PA 19104 Office Phone: 215-895-2481. Office Fax: 215-895-2494. Business E-Mail: whitehd@drexel.edu.

**WHITE, JACK (JOHN ANTHONY GILLIS),** musician, producer; b. Detroit, July 9, 1975; m. Meg White, Sept. 21, 1996 (div. Mar. 24, 2000); m. Karen Elson, June 1, 2005; 1 child, Scarlett. Former drummer Goober and the Peas, The Go, The Upholsterers, Jack White and The Bricks; singer, guitarist The White Stripes, 1999, De Stijl, 2000, Party of Special Things to Do, 2000, White Blood Cells, 2001, Maximum, 2002, Elephant, 2003 (Grammy award for best alt. music album, 2003, Grammy award for best rock song, 2003), Get Behind Me Satan, 2005; actor, composer (films) Cold Mountain, 2003; actor: (films) Coffee and Cigarettes, 2003; prodr.: (albums) Lack of Communication, 2001, Do Rabbits Wonder?, 2003; prodr., guitarist, singer (Loretta Lynn album) Van Lear Rose, 2004 (Grammy award for best country album, 2004). Office: Press Here Publicity 138 W 25th St New York NY 10001

**WHITE, JAMES, JR.,** psychiatric, mental health nurse, consultant; b. Muskogee, Okla., Nov. 24, 1944; s. James Sr. and Mary Bd. (Brassfield) W.; children: Stacie R., Stephen W. BA, Northeastern State U., 1969; MS, Pittsburg State U., 1972, BSN, 1982; PhD, Columbia Pacific U., 1984. Diplomate Am. Bd. Forensic Examiners, Soc. for Study of Neuronal Regulation; CSW, advance register nurse practitioner, cert. rehab. counselor, cert./lic. psychologist, nationally bd. cert. counselor. Exec. dir. Sanilac County Mental Health, Sandusky, Mich., 1975-78, Crawford County Mental Health, Pittsburg, 1978-80; psychologist Psychol. and Ednl. Svcs., Pittsburg, 1982—84; psychiatric practitioner Family Counseling and Resource Ctr., Joplin, 1983-86; pvt. practice Joplin, 1986-88; med. sociologist Mich. Health Ctr., Detroit, 1988-91; psychiatric practitioner Wayne County Sheriff and Sinai Hosp. Psychiatry, Detroit, 1990—; clin. coord. Detroit Health Care for Homeless, 1991—. Chmn. recipient right com. Lafayette Clinic, Detroit, 1991—, coun. mem., 1990—. Lt. U.S. Army, 1969-82. Mem. ANA for Nurses in Advanced Practice, Am. Psychiatric Nurses Assn., Am. Acad. Nurse Practitioners (Mich. State Rep. 1991—), Am. Bd. Med. Psychotherapists (cert., clin. assoc.), Coun. Psychiatric and Mental Health Nursing, Am. Acad. Pain Mgmt. Avocations: biking, swimming, boating. Home: 42029 Utah Dr Sterling Heights MI 48313-2965 Office: Inst for Inner Resource 75 W Square Lake Rd Troy MI 48098-2929 E-mail: info@expertsinmind.com.

**WHITE, JAMES BOYD,** law educator; b. Boston, July 28, 1938; s. Benjamin Vroom and Charlotte Green (Conover) W.; m. Mary Louise Fitch, Jan. 1, 1978; children: Emma Lillian, Henry Alfred; children by previous marriage: Catherine Conover, John Southworth White. AB, Amherst Coll., 1960; AM, Harvard U., 1961, LLB, 1964. Assoc. Foley, Hoag & Eliot, Boston, 1964-67; asst. prof. law U. Colo., 1967-69, assoc. prof., 1969-73, prof.,

1973-75; prof. law U. Chgo., 1975-83; Hart Wright prof. law and English U. Mich., Ann Arbor, 1984—. Vis. assoc. prof. Stanford U., 1972 Author: The Legal Imagination, 1973, (with Scarboro) Constitutional Criminal Procedure, 1976, When Words Lose Their Meaning, 1981, Heracles' Bow, 1985, Justice as Translation, 1990, "This Book of Starres", 1994, Acts of Hope, 1994, From Expectation to Experience, 1999, How Should We Talk About Religion?, 2006, The Edge of Meaning, 2001, Living Speech, 2006. Sinclair Kennedy Traveling fellow, 1964-65; Nat. Endowment for Humanities fellow, 1979-80, 92; Guggenheim fellow, 1993; vis. scholar Phi Beta Kappa, 1997-98. Mem. AAAS, Am. Law Inst. Office: U Mich Law Sch 1035 Legal Research 625 S State St Ann Arbor MI 48109-1215 Office Phone: 743-936-2989. Business E-Mail: jbwhite@umich.edu.

**WHITE, JAMES D.,** food products executive; m. Lisa White; children: Krista, Jasmine. BS, U. Mo.; MBA, Fontbonne Coll. Various positions Coca-Cola Co., Nestle Purina Petcare, 1987—2002; sr. v.p. bus. devel. Gillette Co., 2002—05; sr. v.p. corp. brands Safeway, Inc., Pleasanton, Calif., 2005—. Bd. dirs. Keane, Inc. Mem.: Nat. Black MBA Assn., Alpha Phi Alpha. Office: Safeway Inc 5918 Stoneridge Mall Rd Pleasanton CA 94588-3229 Office Phone: 925-467-3000. Office Fax: 925-467-3321.*

**WHITE, JAMES EDWARD, III,** historian, educator; b. Kinston, N.C., Apr. 24, 1949; s. James E. White Jr. and Nina (Gilgo) White; m. Nancy Brinson, Aug. 4, 1973; children: James E. White IV, M. Jason, Jerry L. AA, Louisburg Coll., 1969; AB, U. N.C. Chapel Hill, 1971; MEd, E. Carolina U., 1978, EdS, 1985. Cert. tchr. N.C., prin. N.C., supt. N.C. Tchr. Pamlico Jr. H.S., Bayboro, NC, 1972—75; Arapahoe Elem. Sch., Arapahoe, NC, 1975—80; prin. Tyrrell Elem. Sch., Columbia, NC, 1980—85; Bridgeton Elem. Sch., Bridgeton, NC, 1986—93; tchr. West Craven H.S., Vanceboro, NC, 1993—2002, Pamlico C.C., Grantsboro, NC, 2002—. Author: Gilgoes of Portsmouth Island, 1979, Whichcotes of Maryland, 1982, Craven County Honor Roll 1861, 1980. Recipient Outstanding Young Men Am., Jaycees, 1981. Mem.: New Bern Hist. Soc., Colonial Historians, Assn. So. Historians, Masonic Lodge St. John #3. Episcopalian. Avocations: history, Civil War reenacting. Home: 405 W Wilson Creek Dr New Bern NC 28562 Office Phone: 252-249-1851. E-mail: jewhite3@earthlink.net.

**WHITE, JAMES PATRICK,** law educator; b. Iowa City, Sept. 29, 1931; s. Raymond Patrick and Besse (Kanak) W.; m. Anna R. Seim, July 2, 1964. BA, U. Iowa, 1953, JD, 1956; LLM, George Washington U., 1959; LLD (hon.), U. Pacific, 1984, John Marshall Law Sch., 1989, Weidner U., 1989, Campbell U., 1993; Jur D (hon.), Whittier Coll., 1992; LLD (hon.), Campbell U., 1993, Southwestern U., 1995, Quinnipiac U., 1995, Calif. Western Law Sch., 1997; LLD, Roger Williams U., 1999, New England Sch. of Law, 2001, Seattle U., 2001, We. New Eng. Coll., 2002; LHD (hon.), Barry U., 2005. Bar: Iowa 1956, D.C. 1959, U.S. Supreme Ct. 1959. Teaching fellow George Washington U. Law Sch., 1958-59; asst. prof. U. N.D. Law Sch., Grand Forks, 1959-62, asso. prof., acting dean, 1962-63, prof., asst. dean, 1963-67; dir. agrl. law rsch. program, prof. law Ind. U. Law Sch., Indpls., 1967—2002, also dir. urban legal studies program, 1971-74, prof. emeritus, 2002—; dean acad. devel. and planning, spl. asst. to chancellor Ind. U., Indpls., 1974-83. Mem. for N.D., Commn. on Uniform State Laws, 1961-66; cons. legal edn. ABA, 1974-2001, cons. emeritus, 2001—. Contbr. papers to tech. lit. Trustee Butler U., John Marshall Law Sch., Atlanta, Indpls. Mus. Art. Capt. JAGC, 1st lt. USAF, 1956—58. Recipient Thomas More award, St. Mary's U., 1965, Sagamore of the Wabash award, State of Ind.; Carnegie postdoctoral fellow, U. Mich. Ctr. for Study Higher Edn., 1964—65. Fellow: Soc. for Advanced Legal Studies (Eng.) (chair Fulbright com. awards in law 1989—92), Indpls. Bar Found. (disting. fellow), Am. Bar Found. (life); mem.: ABA (Kutak award medal 2001), Indpls. Bar Assn., Am. Law Inst. (life), Iowa Bar Assn., Ind. Bar Assn., Woodstock Club (Indpls.), Order of Coif. Roman Catholic. Home: 7707 N Meridian St Indianapolis IN 46260-3651 Office: Ind U 530 W New York St Indianapolis IN 46202-3225 Office Phone: 317-278-9690. Business E-Mail: jwhite@iupui.edu.

**WHITE, JAMES RICHARD,** lawyer; b. McKinney, Tex., Jan. 22, 1948; s. James Ray and Maxine (Brown) White; children: Nicole Olivia, Mandi Leigh, James Derek. BBA, So. Meth. U., 1969, MBA, 1970, JD, 1973, LLM, 1977. Bar: Tex. 1973, US Tax Ct. 1975, US Supreme Ct. 1989, US Ct. Appeals (5th cir.) 1989; cert. Comml. Real Estate Law Tex. Bd. Legal Specialization. Assoc. Elliot, Meer, Vetner, Denton & Bates, Dallas, 1973-74, Atwell, Cain & Davenport, Dallas, 1974-75; atty. Sabine Corp., Dallas, 1975-77; assoc. Brice & Barron, Dallas, 1977-79; ptnr. Millard & Olson, Dallas, 1979-82, Johnson & Swanson, Dallas, 1982-83, Winstead, Sechrest & Minick P.C., Dallas, 1983—, hiring ptnr., 1987-2001, exec. com., 2000-01. Mem. staff Southwestern Law Jour., Dallas, 1971-73; mem. So. Meth. U. Moot Ct. Bd., Order Barristers, Dallas, 1972-73; prof. North Lake Coll., Dallas, 1985; bd. dirs. Tex. Assn. Young Lawyers, Austin, 1980-82; sec. bd. dirs. Dallas Assn. Young Lawyers, 1976-80. Contbr. articles to profl. jours. Chmn. bd. dir. Tex. Lawyers Credit Union, Austin, 1980-82; pres. North Tex. Premier Soccer Assn., Dallas, 1979-81; v.p. Lake Highlands Soccer Assn., 1995-96, pres., 1996—; North Tex. State Soccer Assn., Volunteer of the Year, 2003; mem. regional mobility task force Real Estate Coun., City of Dallas, 1991-92, mem. downtown revitalization com., 1995-97; mem. Dallas Indsl. Devel. Bd., 1992-93, Dallas Higher Edn. Authority Bd., 1994-96; spkr.'s bur. and accreditation divsn. World Cup USA '94; mem. exec. coun. Recreational Interleague Assn. Dallas, 2002—; pres. Storm Soccer Club, 2003-05; founding mem. Premiere Acad. League, 2004—. Named a Texas Super Lawyer, 2003—; named Vol. of the Yr., North Tex. State Soccer Assn., 2003; named to Best Lawyers in Am., 2003—. Mem. ABA (mem. title ins. and survey, mortgage loan origination and structure com., mortgage financing and opinion, non-traditional comml. real estate fin. coms.), Tex. Bar Assn. (cert. 1973, mem. mortgage loan opinion com.), Tex. Coll. Real Estate Attys., Coll. State Bar Tex., Storm Soccer Club (pres. 2003-05). Methodist. Avocations: soccer, golf, skiing, racquetball. Home: 8003 Hundley Ct Dallas TX 75231-1728 Office: Winstead Sechrest & Minick 5400 Renaissance Tower 1201 Elm St Ste 5400 Dallas TX 75270-2199 Office Phone: 214-745-5126. Business E-Mail: jrwhite@winstead.com.

**WHITE, JAN TUTTLE,** information technology executive; b. Bridgeport, Conn., Nov. 5, 1943; d. Michael and Jennie Agnes (Leko) Soltis; m. David Dustin Tuttle, Oct. 7, 1972 (div. Apr. 1988); m. Benjamin Winthrop White, May 6, 1989. BS in Math., Bates Coll., Lewiston, Maine, 1965; MBA in Mktg. and Ops. Rsch., Columbia U. N.Y.C., 1967. Cert. comml. real estate broker, Mass. With corp. staff IBM Corp., Armonk, NY, 1966, sys. engr. N.Y.C., 1967-69, mktg. rep. to Harvard U., corp. staff., sys. engr., Harvard U. account mgr. Cambridge, Mass., 1969-72; asst. to dir. info. processing svcs. MIT, Cambridge, Mass., 1972-75; mng. dir. Tuttle Family Trust, Cambridge, Mass., 1975-81; VAX product mktg. mgr., sr. product mgr. Digital Equipment Corp., Marlborough, Mass., 1981-86, artificial intelligence market devel. mgr., 1986-87, fin. sys. group market devel. mgr., 1987-90, market devel. mgr. banking/investments group, 1990; program mgr. MIT Internat. Fin. Svc. Rsch. Ctr., Hudson; med. sys. mgr. Beth Israel Deaconess Med. Ctr., Boston, 1990—; in field: sponsor Harvard Host Family Program Appeared in Disney channel documentary film Silver Men, 1987, Boston Mus. Sci. introductory film for opening of Mugar Omni Theatre, 1987; contbr. (books) An Olde Concord Christmas, 1980, Boston Symphony Orch. Cookbook, 1983, Boston Cooks, 1991 Chmn. Concord Coun. Boston Symphony Orch., assoc. assn. vols., supporter Tanglewood scholarship programs, capt. Centennial Major Gifts campaign; active guild bd. Opera Co. Boston, co-chmn. auditions com.; patron Fledrmaus Ball; life mem., chmn. Emerson Hosp. Aux.; treasure vol. mgmt. rev. com. Women's Ednl. and Indsl. Union; edn. com. chmn. Ladies Assn.; life mem., bd. Concord Antiquarian Mus., nominating com. edn. long-range planning com., chmn. edn. com., costumes and textiles com., exhibit designer An Old Concorde Christmas, established; family meml. fund; bd. adv. Sci. Mus. Exhibit Collaborative, Garden Club Concord, Boston Mus. Sci.; life mem. Mus. Fine Arts, Boston, patron Friends Music; life mem. Nat. Trust for Scotland, Friends Loch Lomond, Friends Beth Israel Med. Ctr, Harvard Neighbors; mem. fin. com. Trinitarian Congl. Ch.; trustee, life mem. Women's Ednl. and Indsl. Union; bd. dirs., life mem.

Hannah Duston Garrison House Assn.; life mem. Friends New Eng. Deaconess Hosp., Boston, Friends Beth Israel Deaconess Med. Ctr., Boston; mem. Isabella Stewart Gardner Mus.; invitational alumni Hurricane Island (Maine) Outward Bound Sch., Thompson Island Bound (Boston Harbour) Sch., mem. adv. bd., 1987-90, underwriter Silver Anniversary video 1987; water safety instr., sr. life saving instr., First Aid instr. Red Cross Nat. Aquatic Sch., 1964 Recipient numerous industry achievement awards, 10th Anniversary Cert. Appreciation VAX Sys. Spl. Interest Group U.S. chpt. Digital Equipment Corp. User Soc.; nominated White House fellow, 1971; honoree Nat. Women's Day, 1987 Mem. Am. Mass. Artificial Intelligence, Inst. for Mgmt. Scis., Ops. Rsch. Soc. Am., MIT Faculty Club, Harwich Hist. Assn. (life), Stratford Hist. Soc. (life), Cambridge Hist. Soc., Bates Coll. Class 1965 (sec., treas., reunion chmn., com. chmn. 25th reunion major gifts), Columbia U. Grad. Sch. Bus. Alumni Assn. (nat. chmn. membership, bd. dirs.), Mass. Hort. Soc., Conn. Soc. Genealogists, Nat. Assn. Underwater Instrs. (cert. scuba diver), Columbia Bus. Club Boston (founding dir., bd. dirs.), Columbia U. Club New Eng. (founding dir.), Columbia Club N.Y., Concord Country Club, Harvard Club (Boston, N.Y.C.), Harvard U. Art Mus., Harvard Faculty Club, Stone Horse Yacht Club, Women's City Club (com. membership), Royal Scottish Automobile Club, North Atlantic Yacht Racing Union, So. Mass. Yacht Racing Assn., Arnold Arboretum Harvard U., Housatonic Boat Club Republican. Avocations: the arts, sports, horticulture, environmental preservation, genealogy.

**WHITE, JEFFREY D.,** federal agency administrator; BS in applied engring. and physics, Cornell U., 1979; MD, Howard U., 1984. Resident in internal medicine Washington Hosp. Ctr., Washington, fellow in oncology, fellow in hematology; joined Metabolism Br. Nat. Cancer Inst., 1990, dir. Clin. Trials and Clin. Care Program, Metabolism Br.; oncology cons. to NIH Nat. Ctr. for Complementary and Alternative Medicine, 1995—98; dir. Office of Cancer Complementary and Alternative Medicine Nat. Cancer Inst., 1998—. Office: Office Cancer Complementary and Alternative Medicine Nat Cancer Inst 6116 Executive Blvd Ste 609 MSC 8339 Bethesda MD 20892

**WHITE, JEFFREY GEORGE,** healthcare consultant; b. Lawrence, Mass., Apr. 16, 1944; s. Alfred James and Ruth Virginia (Maylum) W.; children: Jennifer L., Tracy E. AB in Econs., Bowdoin Coll., 1966; MBA, U. N.H. 1985. Asst. pers. dir., then asst. administr. Maine Med. Ctr., Portland, 1967-71; asst. administr. Regional Meml. Hosp., Brunswick, Maine, 1971, adminstr., 1971-74; assoc. dir. Elizabeth Ann Seton Hosp., Waterville, 1974-75; assoc. adminstr. Mid-Maine Med. Ctr., 1975-79, v.p. ops., 1979-83; asst. dir. Wentworth-Douglass Hosp., Dover, NH, 1983-85; exec. v.p. Frisbie Meml. Hosp., Rochester, NH, 1985-89, pres., 1989-92; sr. cons., prin. Helms & Co., Inc., Concord, NH, 1992—. Interim pres., CEO New London (NH) Hosp. 2002-03; preceptor dept. health mgmt. and policy U. NH, Durham, 1985-92, adj. asst. prof., 1991-93, asst. prof., 1991-93, dean's leadership coun. sch. health human svcs., 1998—; bd. dirs. Riverwoods at Exeter, 2000-2003. Vol. pub. TV sta.; bd. dirs. Greater Seacoast United Way, 1991-94, chmn. comty. campaign, 1993; pres. Greater Rochester C. of C., 1990. Fellow Am. Coll. Healthcare Execs. (past regent for N.H.); mem. N.H. Hosp. Assn. (trustee emeritus). Republican. Avocations: walking, skiing, reading, travel. Home: Rivermoor Landing 21 125 Main St Newmarket NH 03857 Office: Helms & Co Inc 1 Pillsbury St Concord NH 03301-3556 Office Phone: 603-225-6633. E-mail: jwhite@helmsco.com.

**WHITE, JEFFREY MUNROE,** lawyer; b. Lewiston, Maine, Jan. 16, 1948; BS in Applied Physics magna cum laude, Tufts U., 1970; JD, Boston Coll., 1975. Bar: Maine 1975, U.S. Ct. Appeals (1st cir.) 1979. Semiconductor engr. Fairchild Semiconductor, 1970—72; ptnr., head litig. group and antitrust and trade regulation group Pierce, Atwood, Portland, Maine, 1975—. Lectr., contbr. to profl. publs. on antitrust, litig., and intellectual property topics. Chmn. Cape Elizabeth Sch. Study Com., 1990-91. Mem. ABA (antitrust, intellectual property and litig. sects.), N.E. Bar Assn. (dir. 1982-85), Maine Bar Found., Maine State Bar Assn. (co-chmn. com. CLE 1981-83), Maine Trial Lawyers Assn., Cumberland County Bar Assn. Office: Pierce Atwood Monument Sq Portland ME 04101 Office Phone: 207-791-1100. E-mail: jwhite@pierceatwood.com.

**WHITE, JENNIFER PHELPS,** counselor; b. Palo Alto, Calif., Aug. 31, 1943; d. Delmer Frank and Luella Elizabeth (McHugh) Phelps; m. Charles Evan White, Oct. 29, 1965; children: George Kevin, Colleen Elizabeth. AA in Liberal Arts, Foothill Jr. Coll., 1964; BA in Sociology & Anthropology, U. N.Mex., 1967, MPA, 1987. Lic. profl. mental health counselor N.Mex. Counseling and Therapy Bd. Sales clk. Barron Park Pharmacy, Palo Alto, 1960-64; caseworker State of N.Mex., Albuquerque, 1968-70; info. sys. coord. City of Albuquerque, 1971-75; rsch. specialist Pub. Interest Rsch. Group, 1976-77; interviewer Sandia Market Rsch., 1980-81; acad. adviser, counselor U. N.Mex., 1981-88; rehab. specialist Intracorps, 1988-89; dir. career svcs. ctr. YWCA, 1989-96; athletic advisor U. N.Mex., Albuquerque, 1996—. Mem. women in transition Planning Commn. State of N.Mex., Albuquerque, 1990—; mem. career guidance project adv. com. Commn. on Status of Women, Albuquerque, 1993-95; employment com. Genesis Project, Albuquerque, 1989-91; mem. steering com. United Staff U. N.Mex., 1996—, staff coun., 2000—. Chair women's affirmative action com. City of Albuquerque, 1976-82; mem. steering com. Choice Pac, Albuquerque, 1984—; mem. Human Rights Coalition, 1995—. Named Outstanding N.Mex. Women, Office of Gov., State of N.Mex., 1994; recipient Grassroots Accomplishment award Nat. Coun. Negro Women, Las Mujeres de Lulac, 1994, Human Rights award City of Albuquerque, 1995. Mem. NOW (mem. Albuquerque and N.Mex. chpts., bd. dirs., pres., coord. 1975—, lobbyist N.Mex. State Legislature 1978-87), Nat. Abortion Rights Action League/Right to Choose (bd. dirs. 1980-93), Career Devel. Assn., Women Work! Nat. Network (Svc. awards 1994-95), Women's Housing Coalition (bd. dirs., pres., v.p. 1989—, project change bd. dirs. 1996—). Democrat. Avocations: political activist, pre-columbian anthropology, sewing. Home: 416 Montclaire Dr SE Albuquerque NM 8/100-2630 Office. Univ NMex Athletic Dept Main Campus Albuquerque NM 87131-0001

**WHITE, JESSE,** state official; b. Alton, Ill., 1934; BS, Ala. State U. 1957. With Chgo. Cubs; tchr., adminstr. Chgo. Pub. Sch. Sys.; mem. Ill. Gen. Assembly, Springfield, 1972—74, 1976—92, chmn. com. on human svcs., mem. edn. com., mem. select com. on children and aging; recorder of deeds Cook County, Chgo., 1992—98; sec. of state State of Ill., Springfield, 1999—. Founder Jesse White Tumbling Team, 1959; Dem. committeeman 27th Ward, Chgo., 1996—; libr. State of Ill. State Libr.; archivist State of Ill.; mem. Ill. N.G. With USAF. Recipient Archbishop Richard Chenevix Trench award, 1999; Inductee Southwestern Athletic Conf. Hall of Fame, 1995, Chgo. Pub. League Basketball Coaches Assn. Hall of Fame, 1995, Ala. State U. Sports Hall of Fame, 1999; named one of 100 Most Influential Black Americans, Ebony mag., 2006. Democrat. Office: Office Sec of State 213 State Capitol Springfield IL 62706 Office Phone: 217-782-2201. Office Fax: 217-785-0358. E-mail: jessewhite@ilsos.net.

**WHITE, JESSICA BAILEY,** biology professor; d. Jeffrey Barnes and Karen Lee White; m. Benjamin Whalen LaPointe, Oct. 7, 2006. BA, Hollins U., Roanoke, Va., 2000; Masters, Va. Commonwealth U., Richmond, 2003. Adj. faculty Va. Commonwealth U., Richmond, 2003—04; faculty John Tyler C.C., Chester, Va., 2004—. Co-chair Phi Theta Kappa, Chester, Va., 2006—. Mem.: Human Anatomy and Physiology Soc. D-Liberal. Achievements include development of assessment techniques for all biology classes at John Tyler Community College. Avocations: running, travel, horseback riding. Office: John Tyler CC 13101 Jefferson Davis Hwy Chester VA 23831 Office Phone: 804-706-5069.

**WHITE, JILL CAROLYN,** lawyer; b. Santa Barbara, Calif., Mar. 20, 1934; d. Douglas Cameron and Gladys Louise (Ashley) W.; m. Walter Otto Weyrauch, Mar. 17, 1973. BA, Occidental Coll., L.A., 1955; JD, U. Calif., Berkeley, 1974. Bar: Fla. 1974, Calif. 1975, U.S. Supreme Ct. Staff mem. U.S. Dept. State, Am. Embassy, Rio de Janeiro, 1956-58; with psychol. rsch. units Inst. Human Devel., Inst. Personality Assessment and Rsch., U. Calif.,

Berkeley, 1961-68; adj. prof. criminal justice program U. Fla., Gainesville, Fla., 1976-78; pvt. practice immigration and nationality law, Gainesville, 1976—2002. Contbr. articles to profl. jours. Mem.: Fla. Bar (immigration and nationality law cert. com. 1994—99, chmn. cert. com. 1997—98, cert. in immigration and nationality law 1995—), Bar Assn. 8th Jud. Cir. Fla., Am. Immigration Lawyers Assn. (bd. dirs. Ctrl. Fla. chpt. 1985—94, 1995—96, 1997—2000, chmn. Ctrl. Fla. chpt. 1988—89, co-chmn. so. regional liaison com. 1990—92, nat. bd. dirs. 1988—89), Altrusa. Democrat. Office Phone: 352-380-9122. Personal E-mail: jwhite49@earthlink.net.

**WHITE, JOHN, JR.,** lawyer; b. St. Louis, Oct. 20, 1943; s. John Aaron and Helen Inez (Stewart) W.; children: Dorian, Cameron, Lauren, John Aaron III. B.A., U. Nev., 1965; J.D., George Washington U., 1968. Bar: D.C. 1969, Nev. 1969, U.S. Dist. Ct. (D.C. dist.) 1969, U.S. Supreme Ct. 1979. Atty. City Atty.'s Office, Reno, 1969-74; sole practice Reno, 1974-78; ptnr. White Law Chartered, Reno, 1978—; adj. prof. in nationality Old Coll. Nev. Sch. of Law, 1986-87; lectr. computers and law Nev. State Bar Conv., 1986. Co-author: Nevada Civil Practice Manual, 1986-88. Mem. Gov.'s Commn. on Status of People, 1975-78; founder Family Ch. Jesus. Served with USMCR, 1961-68. Mem. ABA, Nev. State Bar Assn., D.C. Bar Assn., Am. Bankruptcy Inst., Washoe County Bar Assn., Reno Host Lions (past pres.). Pioneer in litigating early cases against Dow Corning and Dow Chemical involving silicone breast implants. Republican. Office: White Law Chartered 335 W 1st St Reno NV 89503-5344 Office Fax: 775-322-1228. E-mail: john@whitelawchartered.com.

**WHITE, JOHN ARNOLD,** physics professor, research scientist; b. Chgo., Jan. 30, 1933; s. Maxwell Richard and Dorothy Edith (Arnold) W.; m. Rebecca Anne Cotten, June 20, 1964; children: Lauren, Thomas, Julia. BA. Oberlin Coll., 1954; MS, Yale U., 1955, PhD, 1959. Instr. physics Yale U. 1958-59, Harvard U., 1959-62; research assoc. Yale U., 1962-63; research physicist Nat. Bur. Standards, Washington, 1963-64; research assoc. U. Md., College Park, 1965-66; assoc. prof. Am. U., Washington, 1966-68, prof., 1968-97, prof. emeritus, 1997—. Cons. Nat. Bur. Standards, 1965-72; mem. tech. staff Bell Telephone Labs., summers 1954, 60-62; vis. scientist MIT, fall 1972, Nat. Bur. Standards, Washington, summer 1981; vis. prof. Inst. for Phys. Sci. and Tech., U. Md., College Park, fall 1993. Author sci. papers on atomic structure and fluorescence, magnetism, lasers, speed of light, thermodynamic fluctuations, critical point phenomena, extended renormalization group theory of fluids. Recipient (with Zoltan Bay) Boyden Premium Franklin Inst., Phila., 1980; honor scholar, 1950-54; Noyes Clark fellow, 1954-57; NSF fellow, 1957-58; grantee NSF, 1966, 67, 69, 71; grantee Office Naval Research, 1973, 74; Am. Soc. Engring. Edn. faculty fellow Naval Research Lab., Washington, summer 1985; Dept. Energy Office Basic Energy Scis. grantee, 1986, 88, 90. Fellow Am. Phys. Soc.; mem. AAUP, Washington Philos. Soc., Phi Beta Kappa, Sigma Xi. Home: 7107 Fairfax Rd Bethesda MD 20814-1234 Office: Am U Dept Physics Washington DC 20016-8058 E-mail: jwhite@american.edu.

**WHITE, JOHN AUSTIN, JR.,** engineering educator, academic administrator; b. Portland, Ark., Dec. 5, 1939; s. John Austin and Ella Mae (McDermott) W.; m. Mary Elizabeth Quarles, Apr. 13, 1963; children: Kimberly Elizabeth White Brakmann, John Austin III. BS in Indsl. Engring., U. Ark., 1962; MS in Indsl. Engring., Va. Poly. Inst., 1966; PhD, Ohio State U., 1970; PhD (hon.), Cath. U. of Leuven, Belgium, 1985, George Washington U., 1991. Registered profl. engr., Va. Indsl. engr. Tenn. Eastman Co., Kingsport, 1961-63, Ethyl Corp., Baton Rouge, 1965; tchg. assoc. Ohio State U., Columbus, 1966-70; instr. Va. Poly. Inst. and State U., Blacksburg, 1963-66, asst. prof., 1970-72, assoc. prof., 1972-75, Ga. Inst. Tech., Atlanta, 1975-77, prof., 1977-84, Regents' prof., 1984-97, Gwaltney prof., 1988-97, dean engring., 1991-97; disting. prof. indsl. engring., chancellor U. Ark., Fayetteville, 1997—. Asst. dir. engring. NSF, 1988-90, acting dir., 1990-91; founder, chmn. SysteCon Inc., Duluth, Ga., 1977-84; exec. cons. Coopers & Lybrand, N.Y.C., 1984-93; mem. mfg. studies bd. NRC, Washington, 1986-88; bd. dirs. Russell Corp., Eastman Chem. Co., Motorola Corp., Logility Inc., J.B. Hunt Transport, Inc., Nat. Sci. Bd., Malcolm Baldrige Nat Quality Award Found.; chair coun. presidents Southeastern U. Rsch. Assn.; pres. Nat. Consortium for Grad. Degrees for Minorities in Engring. and Sci., Inc., 1993-95; bd. dirs. Nat. Collegiate Athletic Assn.; mem. exec. com. NCAA, 2003—; apptd. U.S. del. to the Internat. Steering Com. of the Intelligent Mfg. System, 1995-97; mem. Nat. Sci. Bd., 1994—; pres. S.E. Conf., 2002—. Co-author: Facility Layout and Location: An Analytical Approach, 1974 (Book of Yr. award Inst. Indsl. Engrs. 1974), 2d edit., 1991, Analysis of Queueing Systems, 1975, Principles of Engineering Economic Analysis, 4th edit., 1998, Capital Investment Decision Analysis for Management and Engineering, 1980, 3d edit., 2003, Facilities Planning, 1984 (Book of Yr. award Inst. Indsl. Engrs. 1984), 2d edit., 1996; editor: Production Handbook, 1987; co-editor: Progress in Materials Handling and Logistics, Vol. 1, 1989; also numerous articles to profl. jours., chpts. to books and handbooks in field, conf. procs. Recipient Outstanding Tchr. award Ga. Inst. Tech., 1982, Disting. Alumnus award Ohio State U. Coll. Engring., 1984, Disting. Indsl. Engring. alumnus award Va. Polytech. Inst. and State U., 1993, Reed-Apple award Material Handling Edn. Found., 1985, Disting. Svc. award NSF, 1991, Rodney D. Chipp Meml. award Soc. Women Engrs., 1994. Fellow Am. Inst. Indsl. Engrs. (pres. 1983-84, facilities planning and design award 1980, outstanding indsl. engr. award region III 1974, region IV 1984, Albert G. Holzman disting. educator award 1988, outstanding pub. award 1988, David F. Baker disting. rsch. award 1990, Frank and Lillian Gilbreth award 1994), Am. Assn. Engring. Socs. (bd. govs., chmn. 1986, Kenneth Andrew Roe award 1989); mem. Nat. Acad. Engring., Am. Acad. Indsl. Engring., Am. Soc. Engring. Edn. (Donald E. Marlowe award 1994), Internat. Material Mgmt. Soc. (material mgr. of yr. 1989), Soc. Mfg. Engrs. (mfg. educator award 1990), Nat. Soc. Profl. Engrs. Inst. for Ops. Rsch. and the Mgmt. Scis. (hon.), Golden Key, Sigma Xi, Alpha Pi Mu, Omicron Delta Kappa, Phi Kappa Phi, Tau Beta Pi, Omega Rho. Baptist. Avocations: reading, golf, writing. Office: Chancellor U Ark Office of the Chancellor 425 Administration Bldg Fayetteville AR 72701

**WHITE, JOHN DAVID,** composer, musician; b. Rochester, Minn., Nov. 28, 1931; s. Leslie David and Millie (Solum) W.; m. Marjorie Manuel, Dec. 27, 1952; children: Jeffrey Alan, Michele Kay, David Eliot. BA magna cum laude, U. Minn., 1953; MA, U. Rochester, 1954, PhD, 1960, performance cert., 1960. Mem. faculty Kent (Ohio) State U., 1956-58, 60-63, 65-73, prof. music, assoc. dean Grad. Sch., 1967-73; asst. prof. U. Mich., 1963-65; dean Sch. Music, Ithaca (N.Y.) Coll., 1973-74; vis. prof. U. Wis., 1975-78; chmn. music dept. Whitman Coll., 1978-80; prof. U. Fla., 1980-97, prof. emeritus, 1997—; prof. U. Innsbruck, 1994; disst. chair U. Vienna, 2003—04. Prin. cellist Eastman Philharmonia, 1959, Akron Symphony Orch., 1969-73; cellist Fla. Baroque Ensemble, 1980-97, Fla. Arts Trio, 1986-93; dir. Fla. Musica Nova, 1991-97; author: (with A. Cohen) Anthology of Music for Analysis, 1965, Understanding and Enjoying Music, 1968 (pub. in Japanese 1978), Music in Western Culture, 1972, The Analysis of Music, 1976, 2d edit., 1984, Comprehensive Musical Analysis, 1994, Theories of Musical Texture in Western History, 1995, New Music of the Nordic Countries, 2002; editor: Music and Man; editl. bd. Jour. for Musicological Research, Jour. Music Theory Pedagogy; contbr. articles to profl. jours.; Composer: Symphony No. 2, 1960, Blake Songs, 1961; Divertimento for Flute, Violin and Viola, 1961; opera The Legend of Sleepy Hollow, 1962; Three Choruses From Goethe's Faust, 1965, Three Joyce Songs, 1966, Ode to Darkness, 1967, Cantos of the Year, 1969; (for clarinet and piano) Variations, 1971, Whitman Music, 1970, Three Madrigals, 1971, Russian Songs for Voices and Winds, 1972, Prayer (Solzhenytsin), 1973, String Quartet 1, 1975, Variations, 1976, Suite, 2001; Ode on the Morning of Christ's Nativity (Donne), 1977, Music for Oriana, 1978, Pied Beauty, 1980; (for cello and piano) Sonata, 1981, Zodiac, 1981, Music for violin and piano, 1982, The Soft Voice, 1983, Concerto for Flute and Wind Ensemble, 1983, Dialogues, 1984, Sonata, 2001, Symphony for Wind Band (3rd Symphony), 1985, Concerto da Camera, 1985, Symphony for a Saint (4th Symphony), 1986, Music for Cello and Percussion, 1988, Songs of the Shulamite, 1989, Mirrors, 1990, But God's Own Descent (5th

Symphony), 1991, Music of the Open Road, 1993, Daylight and Moonlight, 1993, O Sing to the Lord a New Song, 1993, Illusions for Three, 1994, Tryptich, 1994, Ars Poetica, 1995, Colors of Earth and Sky (6th Symphony), 1995, Summer Storm Madrigals, 1996, Time and the Water, 1996, O Sing to the Lord a New Song, 1997, Maria Laudata, 1998, God's Own Descent, 1998, The Song of Ruth, 1999, Symbolic Interaction for Orchestra, 1999; Suite for Harpsichord, 1999, The Heavens are Telling, 1999, Flower Songs, 2000, Concerto, 2000, Sonata da Camera for Piano, 2001, Music for 2 Cellos, 2002, Pindar Hymns for Choir and Orch., 2003, Olympiad for Chorus, Brass, Percussion and Piano, 2004, The Canonical Hours for Chorus, 2005, Music for Victims of our Earth, 2005, Echoes and Airs for Soprano, Viola and Piano, Mass for Chorus, 2006, Alone and not Alone, 2006; recs. on Advent, Mark, Capstone, Cygnus and Opus One Labels. With AUS, 1954-56. Recipient Benjamin award, 1960, award Nat. Fedn. Music Clubs, 1962, internat. composition award U. Wis.-Oriana Trio, 1979, composition award Am. Choral Dirs. Assn., 1984; grantee NEA; Fulbright rsch. fellow, 1995-96; Fulbright Disting. Lectr., 2003-04. Fellow Am. Scandinavian Found., 1997; mem. ASCAP (awards 1965—), Soc. Composers, Inc. (nat. coun. 1987-89, 93-96), Soc. Music Theory, Pi Kappa Lambda, Delta Omicron (nat. patron), Phi Mu Alpha, Phi Beta Delta. Home: 10599 N Osceola Dr Westminster CO 80031 Personal E-mail: jwhite48@earthlink.net.

**WHITE, JOHN JOSEPH, III,** lawyer; b. Darby, Pa., Nov. 23, 1948; s. John J. Jr. and Mary (Lafferty) W.; m. Catherine M Staley, Dec. 9, 1983. BS, U. Scranton, 1970; MPA, Marywood U., 1977; JD, Loyola U., New Orleans, 1983. Bar: Pa. 1983, U.S. Dist. Ct. (ea. dist.) Pa. 1983, N.J. 1984, U.S. Ct. Appeals (3d cir.) 1983, U.S. Dist. Ct. N.J. 1984, U.S. Tax Ct. 1984, D.C. 1985, U.S. Supreme Ct. 1987. Exec. dir. Scranton Theatre Libre, Inc., Pa., 1973—77; publ. Libre Press Inc., Scranton, 1977—83; pvt. practice Phila. 1983—. Founder, publ. Metro Mag., 1977—83; pres. eMercury, Inc., Lansdowne, Pa., 1987—; N.Am. agt. Palacky U. Med. Sch., Olomouc, Czech Republic, 1995—2001. Founder, Scranton Pub. Theatre, 1976; exec. dir. Scranton Theatre Libre, Inc., 1973. Capt. USAF, 1970—73, lt. col. Res., 1973—99, col. ANG 1999—2000, ret., 2000. Mem.: ABA, N.G. Assn., Phila. Bar Assn., Nat. Acad. Elder Law Attys., Mil. Order of Fga. Wars, Air Force Assn. (chpt. pres. 1975—), Phi Delta Phi Internat. Legal Frat. Democrat. Roman Catholic. Avocations: jogging, art collecting. Office Phone: 215-732-2000. Personal E-mail: lawfirmusa@aol.com.

**WHITE, JOHN MICHAEL,** chemistry professor; b. Danville, Ill., Nov. 26, 1938; married, 1960; 3 children. BS, Harding Coll., 1960; MS, U. Ill., 1962, PhD in chemistry, 1966. From asst. to assoc. prof. chemistry U. Tex., Austin, 1966—76, prof., Hackerman prof. chemistry, 1985—2000, Robert A. Welch chair chemistry, dir. Materials Chem. Ctr., 2001—. Dir. Inst. Interfacial Catalysis Pacific N.W. Nat. Lab., 2005—. Mem.: Am. Phys. Soc., Am. Chem. Soc. Achievements include research in surface and materials chemistry. Office: Univ Tex Dept Chemistry Welch Hall 3-310 Austin TX 78712 Business E-Mail: jmwhite@mail.utexas.edu.

**WHITE, JOHN PATRICK,** lawyer; b. Boston, Oct. 14, 1946; s. John Marion and Margaret Patricia (Gannon) W.; m. Gemma Mary Flattly, Feb. 9, 1980; 1 son, John Myles. BS in Chem. Engring., Columbia U., 1968, MA in Biochemistry, 1971, MPh in Molecular Biology, 1975; JD, Fordham U., 1977. Bar: NY 1978, US dist. ct. (ea. and so. dists.) NY 1978, US Ct. Customs and Patent Appeals 1979, US Ct. Appeals (Fed. cir.) 1982, US Supreme Ct. 2006. Legis. dir. Cmty. Coun. Greater N.Y., 1971-77; assoc. Cooper, Dunham, Clark, Griffin & Moran, N.Y.C., 1977-81, ptnr., 1981-88, Cooper & Dunham, LLP, N.Y.C., 1988—. Owner Shallow Brook Farm, Stillwater, N.J.; breeder Reg Angus Cattle, Ringneck Pheasants and Carriage Horses; dir. OSI Pharm., Inc., BioTech. Gen. Corp.; instr. Practicing Law Inst. Contbr. articles to sci. and legal jours. Democratic dist. leader, 1975-81; vice chmn. Dem. Com. N.Y. County, 1977-81; jud. del. 1st jud. dept., 1975, 76, 77, 79; administr. screening panel 2d Mcpl. Ct. Dist.; pub. mem. Columbia U. Recombinant DNA Biosafety Com. Columbia U. faculty fellow, 1969-71; NIH grantee, 1969-71. Mem. ABA, Am. Chem. Soc., Am. Intellectual Property Law Assn., NY Intellectual Property Law Assn., Assn. Bar City NY, Fed. Bar Coun. (com. patents), Club. Columbia of NYC, Four In Hand Club, Newton (NJ) Country Club, NY Coaching Club. Office: Cooper & Dunham LLP Ste 2200 1185 Avenue Of The Americas New York NY 10036-2615 Office Phone: 212-278-0421. Business E-Mail: jwhite@cooperdunham.com.

**WHITE, JOHN POSTON,** architect, educator; b. Anson, Tex., Feb. 21, 1933; s. Victor Philemon and Lucy Alice (Baker) W. B.Arch., U. Tex., 1957; M.Arch., U. Nebr., 1973. Registered architect, Tex. Architect Peters & Fields, AIA, Odessa, Tex., 1962-72; draftsman Bahr Vermeer Haecker, Lincoln, Nebr., 1972-73; asst. prof. Tex. Tech. U., Lubbock, 1973-77, assoc. prof. architecture, 1977-87; prin. White Assocs., AIA Architects, Lubbock, 1975—; prof. architecture Tex. Tech. U., 1987—. Project supr. Hist. Am. Bldgs. Survey, summers 1974-99. Served with USAF, 1957-61. Mem. AIA, Tex. Soc. Architects (chmn. hist. resources com. 1984), AIA (treas. Lubbock chpt. 1985, bd. dirs. 1987—), Lubbock Heritage Soc. (bd. dirs. 1987—), Tau Sigma Delta, Delta Chi (chpt. adviser 1982—, treas exec. bd., 1993-2000, v.p., 2000-2001, pres., 2002-2004). Democrat. Methodist. Home: 2813 24th St Lubbock TX 79410-1635

**WHITE, JOHN VINCENT,** surgeon, consultant; b. Chgo., May 7, 1952; BS, Northwestern U., 1974; MD, Columbia U., 1978. Diplomate Am. Bd. Surgery. Instr. surgery Columbia U., N.Y.C., 1982-83; asst. prof. surgery Temple U., Phila., 1984-88, assoc. prof. surgery, 1988-94, prof. surgery, 1994-99; chmn. dept. surgery Luth. Gen. Hosp., Park Ridge, Ill., 1999—. Adj. sr. fellow Sch. Health Econs. U. Pa., Phila., 1994—; tech. cons. Boston Scientific Corp., Natick, Mass., 1995—; surg. cons. Dept. of Health N.Y. State, 1993; surg. tech. cons. Congl. Office of Tech. Assessment, Washington, 1995; laser tech. cons. Office of Naval Rsch., Washington, 1993-97. Editor: Hemodilution in Patient Care, 1989, Alternatives to Open Vascular Surgery, 1995, Surgical Clinics of North America, 1998; founding editor: Jour. Laparoendoscopic Surgery, 1990. Recipient Samuel D. Gross award Phila. Acad. Surgery, 1992. Mem. Am. Soc. Laser Medicine and Surgery, Soc. Univ. Surgeons (mem. found. bd. dirs. 1994-98), Del. Valley Vascular Soc. (pres. 1995—), Soc. Vascular Surgery (mem. com. outcomes analysis 1994—), Alpha Omega Alpha. Office: Lutheran Gen Hosp 1775 Dempster St Park Ridge IL 60068-1173 Office Phone: 847-723-7200. Office Fax: 847-696-3394. Business E-Mail: john.white-md@advocatehealth.com.

**WHITE, JOHN W.,** federal agency administrator, lawyer; b. Washington, Dec. 2, 1947; BS cum laude, U. Va., 1970; JD magna cum laude, NYU, 1973. Bar: NY 1974. Law clk. to hon. John J Gibbons US Ct. Appeals, (3rd cir.); assoc. Cravath Swaine & Moore LLP, NYC, 1975—80, ptnr., corp. fin. governance, 1980—2006; dir. divsn. corp. fin. SEC, Washington, 2006—. Mem. NYSE Legal Adv. Com.; vice chmn. Securities Regulation Inst.; mem. advisory group Pub. Co. Acctg. Oversight Bd., 2006. Mng. editor NYU Law Rev. Office: SEC 100 F St NE Washington DC 20549*

**WHITE, JOHN WESLEY, JR.,** retired academic administrator; b. Nashville, Oct. 20, 1933; s. John W. and Ernestine (Engle) W.; m. Martha Ellen Bragg, June 24, 1956; children: Marcus Wesley, Michelle Suzanne. Student, Martin Jr. Coll., 1952-54; BA, Vanderbilt U., 1956, BD, 1959; MA, George Peabody Coll., 1966, PhD, 1968; LHD, U. Nebr., 1983; LLD, Kwansai Gakuin U., Japan, 1991. Dean admissions, dir. student affairs Martin Coll., 1960-65; asst. to acad. v.p. George Peabody Coll., 1965-67; assoc. dean for humanities Oklahoma City U., 1968-70, dean Coll. Arts and Scis., 1970-77, assoc. prof. English, 1968-73, prof., 1973-77; pres. Nebr. Wesleyan U., 1977-97, chancellor 1997-98, pres. emeritus, 1998—. Cons. in field; chmn. Nebr. Ednl. Temecom. Commn., 1996-97. Past pres. U. Senate, United Meth. Ch.; bd. dirs. Cooper Found. Eli Lilly Sr. Scholar Vanderbilt U., 1959. Mem. Nat. Assn. Ind. Colls. and Univs. (bd. dirs. 1989-93, 95-97), Lincoln C of C. (bd. dirs. 1990-93). Rotary (pres. West Oklahoma City 1976), Kappa Delta Pi, Phi Kappa Phi, Alpha Mu Gamma, Blue Key. *Two principles have been paramount in my life: One, related to the attitude toward myself, is that we can help to shape life, not simply endure it. We are "creative" creatures,*

*not just "surviving" creatures. The second principle, related to the attitude toward others, is that communication is essential to coexistence; and only as we make a real effort to hear what is meant, rather than simply what is said or written, are we able to communicate effectively.*

**WHITE, JOSEPH CHARLES,** manufacturing and retailing company executive; b. Toronto, Ont., Can., Aug. 14, 1922; s. Joseph Cleveland and Edith Parker (Johnson) W.; m. G. Evelyn Vipond, July 15, 1944; children— Ronald, Richard, JoAnne. Chartered acct., Queens U., Kingston, Ont.; B.Commerce, U. Toronto. Vice-pres., dir. Agnew-Surpass, Inc., Brantford, Ont., Can., 1964-78; v.p., dir. Genesco Can., Inc., Cambridge, Ont., Can., 1978-82, exec. v.p., dir., 1982-87, pres., gen. mgr. retail op., 1986-87. Dir., v.p Genesco Group Inc.; dir. Genesco Fin. Ltd.; pres. Brantford Art Gallery, 1994-95, Brantford Probus Club, 1995-96. Chmn. Ross MacDonald Found., Brantford, Ont., 1983-86; pres. YMCA, Brantford, 1968-69; chmn. Brant County Post-Secondary Edn. Corp., Brantford, 1973-76. Served with Royal Can. Air Force, 1943-45 Mem. Ont. Inst. Chartered Accts., Can. Council Distbn. (pres. 1972-73), Brant County C. of C. (treas. 1966-68) Mem. United Ch. of Can. Avocations: skiing, tennis. Office: Genesco Can Inc 401 Fountain St Cambridge ON Canada N3H 4V5 Home: 40 Museum Drive Unit 420 Orillia ON L3V 7T9 Canada Office Phone: 705-326-7098.

**WHITE, JOY MIEKO,** retired communications executive; b. Yokohama, Japan, May 1, 1951; came to U.S., 1951; d. Frank Deforest and Wanda Mieko Mellen; m. George William White, June 5, 1948; 1 child, Karen. BA Comm., Calif. State U., Fullerton, 1974, student, 1977, Orange Coast C.C., 1981, Golden West C.C., 1990. Cert. secondary tchr., Calif.; cert. tchr. Coast C.C.s Dist. Secondary tchr. Anaheim Union H.S. Dist., Calif., 1977—80; tech. writer Pertec Computer Corp., Irvine, Calif., 1980—81; supr. large sys. disvn. Burroughs, Mission Viejo, Calif., 1981—83; mgr. Lockheed disvn. CalComp, Anaheim, 1983—86; owner, pres. Communicator's Connection, Irvine, 1986—90; pres. Info Team, Inc., 1989—2004; ret., 2004. Adj. faculty, coord. tech. comm. program Golden West Coll., Huntington Beach, Calif., 1987-90; instr. U. Calif., Irvine, 1987-89, Calif. State U., Fullerton, 1988-91; sec. Santa Ana Dist. chpt. U.S. SBA Assn. for Minority-Owned Bus., 1991-96; presenter in field Active Performing Arts, Costa Mesa, 1986— Fellow Soc. Tech. Comm. (assoc., internat. assoc., sr., Orange County chpt. 1987, Mem. of Yr.); mem. NAFE, Soc. Profl. Journalists, Women in Comm. (pres. Orange County Profl. chpt. 1989-90), Nat. Assn. Women Bus. Owners, Rembrandts Wine Club (Yorba Linda), Girl Scouts U.S. (life, active 1994—, troop leader 1995-2003) Republican. Avocations: writing short stories, needlecrafts, camping, fishing. Home: 3531 Brentridge Dr Corona CA 92881-8445 Business E-Mail: infoteam@comcast.com. E-mail: joywhitemk@comcast.com.

**WHITE, JOYCE LOUISE,** librarian; b. Phila., June 7, 1927; d. George William and Louisa (Adams) W. BA, U. Pa., 1949; MLS, Drexel U., 1963; MA in Religion, Episc. Sem. S.W., 1978. Head libr. Penniman Libr. Edn. U. Pa., Phila., 1960-76; archivist St. Francis Boys' Home, Salina, Kans., 1982-84; libr. Brown Mackie Coll., Salina, 1983-86; libr., dir. St. Thomas Theol. Sem., Denver, 1995-96; libr., dir. Archbishop Vehr Theol. Libr. Archdiocese of Denver, 1995-96. Author: Biographical and Historial Yarnall Library, 1979, Colorado Episcopal Clergy in the 19th Century: A Biographical Register, 2003; asst. editor: Women Religious History Sources, 1983; contbr. articles to profl. jours. and chpts. to books. Vol. libr. St. John's Cath., Denver, 1993—. Mem. Ch. and Synagogue Libr. Assn. (life, founding, pres. 1969-70, exec. sec. 1970-72, exec. bd. 1967-76, ann. conf. chair 1996). Avocations: gardening, cats, church libraries. Office: 1350 Washington St Denver CO 80203-2008

**WHITE, JUNE MILLER,** mathematics professor, educational consultant; b. East Bernstead, Ky., June 13, 1938; d. James Fulton and Ida Mae (Hansel) Miller; m. Richard Allen White, Aug. 27, 1960; children: Jennifer Lynn, Richard Allen Jr. BS with high honors, Denison U., 1960; MA, U. Rochester, 1969; PhD, Bryn Mawr Coll., 1980. Engring. asst. AT&T, Kansas City, Mo., 1960-61; math. tchr. William Chrisman H.S., Independence Pub. Schs., Independence, Mo., 1961-62, Brighton (N.Y.) H.S., 1962-69, Conestoga H.S. Tredyffrin-Easttown Pub. Schs., Berwyn, Pa., 1970-72; chair math. dept. Hill Top Prep. Sch., Rosemont, Pa., 1972-76, curriculum coord., 1976-81; instr. math. St. Petersburg Jr. Coll., Clearwater, Fla., 1982-84, dir. math. program, 1984—2002, prof. math. edn., 2002—. Presenter in field. Author: A Collection of Mathematics Applications for College Students, 1989; editor SPECTRUM, 1983-95; contbr. articles to profl. jours. Elder Northwood Presbyn. Ch., Clearwater, 1986-90; chmn. blood drive ARC, King of Prussia, Pa., 1973-74; chmn. citizens adv. com. Upper Merion Pub. Schs., King of Prussia, 1975-76. Mem. Am. Math. Assn. of Two Yr. Colls., Math. Assn. Am. (v.p. Fla. and Caribbean sect. 1988-91, sec. 1994-99, pres.-elect 1999, pres. 2000), Nat. Coun. Tchrs. Math., Fla. Assn. Cmty. Colls., Rsch. Coun. for Diagnostic and Prescriptive Math., Pinellas County Assn. for Children and Adults with Learning Disabilities (bd. dirs. 1987-88), Phi Beta Kappa. Avocations: camping, sailing, travel. Home: 4951 Bacopa Ln S Unit 103 Saint Petersburg FL 33715-2617 Office Phone: 727-791-2567. Business E-Mail: whitejune@spcollege.edu.

**WHITE, KAREN RUTH JONES,** information systems executive; b. Ft. Meade, Md., Oct. 8, 1953; d. Frank L. Jones and Inge H. Lesser; m. M. Timothy Heath, Apr. 23, 1973 (div. Aug. 1976); m. Carl W. White, May 30, 1993 AS Electronic Data Processing, N.H. Tech. Inst., Concord, 1977; BS MIS high honors, Northeastern U., Boston, 1984, MS Info. Sys., 1997. Prof. Project Mgmt. Inst., 2001. Programmer Chubb Life Ins. Co., Concord, NH, 1977—79, Retailers Electronics Account Processing, Woburn, Mass. 1979—82; sr. programmer, analyst N.H. Ins. Group, Manchester, 1982—84; prin. sys. analyst Wang Labs., Inc., Lowell, Mass., 1984—89; project mgr. TASC, Inc., Reading, Mass., 1989—2000; dir. consulting svcs. PM Solutions, Havertown, Pa., 2000—. Bd. dirs Brandywyne Common Assn., Derry, N.H., 1991-94; mem. St. Paul's Sch. Advanced Studies Program Alumni Assn., Concord With U.S. Army Res., 1974-84 Decorated Army Commendation medal, 1980 Mem.: NAFE, IEEE (program chair 5th reengring. forum 1996, exec. adv. bd. 1996—99, dep. conf. chair 6th reengring. forum 1998, computer soc., tech. com. in software engring.), Project Mgmt. Inst. (Mass. Bay chpt. program dir. 1992—93, project chair 1994—96, dir. sem. seminars/symposium 1996—98, adv. group 1999—2000, ethics rev. com. 2000—02, awards rev. com. 2001—03, chair ethics rev. com. 2003—06, ethics stds. rev. com. 2004—, chairperson ethics stds. implementation planning com. 2006, bd. dirs. Found.), Sigma Epsilon Rho. Home: 50 Merrill Rd Weare NH 03281-4708 Office: PM Solutions 50 Merrill Rd Weare NH 03281-4708 Business E-Mail: kwhite@pmsolutions.com.

**WHITE, KATE,** editor-in-chief; m. Brad Holbrooke; 2 children. BA, Union Coll. Editor Child mag., 1988—89; editor-in-chief Working Woman mag., NYC, 1989—91, McCall's mag., NYC, 1991—94, Redbook, NYC, 1994—98, Cosmopolitan mag., NYC, 1998—. Author: Why Good Girls Don't Get Ahead and Gutsy Girls Do, 1995, (novels) If Looks Could Kill, 2002, A Body to Die For, 2003, 'Til Death Do Us Part, 2004, Over Her Dead Body, 2005. Recipient Matrix award, Women in Comms., 2003. Office: Cosmopolitan Hearst Magazines 224 W 57th St New York NY 10019-3299 also: Sandra Dijkstra Lit Agy 1237 Camino Del Mar Del Mar CA 92014 Office Phone: 212-649-3561. Office Fax: 212-397-7581.*

**WHITE, KATHERINE E.,** law educator; BSE elec. engring. and computer sci., Princeton U., 1988; JD, U. Wash., 1991; LLM in Intellectual Property, George Washington U., 1996. Bar: Mich. 1996, U.S. Supreme Ct, U.S. Ct. Appeals (fed. cir.), U.S. Ct. Appeals Armed Forces, U.S. Army Ct. Mil. Rev., U.S. Patent and Trademark Office, Wash. 1992. Intellectual property counsel U.S. Army Corps Engrs., Washington, 1992—95; jud. law clk. for Hon. Randall Rader U.S. Ct. Appeals (fed. cir.), 1995—96; assoc. prof. Wayne State U. Law Sch., Detroit, 1996—. Adj. prof. George Washington U. Law Ctr., Washington, 1994—96; regent U. Mich., Ann Arbor, 1999—; mem. patent pub. adv. com. U.S. Patent and Trademark Office, 2000—02. Actor: Intellectual Property Litigation, Pretrial Practice Guide, 1999; co-author (with

Eric Dobrusin): Intellectual Property Litigation, Pretrial Practice Guide, 1999; contbr. articles to profl. publs. CPT JAG U.S. Army, 1992—95, maj. JAG USAR, 1995—. Recipient Fulbright Sr. Scholar award, Max-Planck Inst. for Fgn. Internat. Patent, Copyright and Competition Law, 1999—2000; grantee, Max-Planck-Inst. for Fgn. Internat. Patent, Copyright and Competition Law, 2000; scholar, ROTC, Washington Law Found., 1988—91; Shaw fellow, 1994—96, White House Fellow, special coun. to the sec. of agr., 2001—02. Mem.: AAUP, ABA, Wolverine Bar Assn., Wash. State Bar Assn., Nat. Bar Assn., Mich. Patent Lawyer's Assn., Am. Intellectual Property Law Assn., Am. Assn. Law Schs., State Bar Mich. (mem. coun. intellectual property law sec., co-chmn. student liaison com., co-chmn. com. pattent issues in legislation), Princeton Club Mich. Office: Wayne U Law Sch 471 W Palmer Detroit MI 48202

**WHITE, KATHY JEAN,** educator; b. Findlay, Ohio, Oct. 27, 1955; d. Clyde Arthur and Annabel Thomas; children: Ryan, Jason, Tyler. BS in Edn., Bowling Green State U., 1977; M, U. Toledo, 1992. Lic. in adminstrn. U. Dayton, 2005. Tchr. Riverdale Local Schools, Wharton, Ohio, 1978—83, Whitmer Mich. Sch., Toledo, 1987—91, Christ the King Sch., Toledo, 1993—. Mem.: ASCD. Cath. Avocations: reading, gardening, sports. Office: Christ the King Sch 4100 Harvest Lane Toledo OH 43623

**WHITE, KEITH BRANDON (BABE),** music company executive, songwriter, actor, producer, author; b. Detroit, Sept. 27, 1975; s. John Delbert and Emma Jean White. Student. U. Mich., 1993—97. Sales exec. Clear Channel Broadcasting Inc. (WJLB FM 98), Detroit, 2000; adminstr. Alpha Data Svcs., Inc., Detroit, 2000, Sylvan Edn. Solutions, Detroit, 2003—05; tchr. Evans Solutions Inc., Detroit, 2003—03, Carter, Reddy & Assoc., Inc., Detroit, 2004—05; pres., CEO Fonosynthesis, Inc./Fono Records/Main Chord Music (ASCAP), Detroit, 2001—; mortgage loan officer HomeLoan USA, Detroit, 2005—. Mem.: NAACP, Prepaid Legal Svcs., Inc. Avocations: reading, theater, travel.

**WHITE, KERR LACHLAN,** retired physician, foundation administrator; b. Winnipeg, Man., Can., Jan. 23, 1917; s. John Alexander and Ruth Cecelia (Preston) Stevenson; m. Isabel Anne Pennefather, Nov. 26, 1943; children: Susan Isabel, Margot Edith. BA with honors (Oliver Gold medal), McGill U., 1940, MD, CM, 1949; DM (hon.), U. Leuven, 1978; postgrad., London Sch. Hygiene and Tropical Medicine, 1960; DSc (hon.), McMaster U., 1983. Intern, resident in medicine Mary Hitchcock Meml. Hosp., Hanover, NH, 1949—52; Hosmer fellow McGill U. and Royal Victoria Hosp., Montreal, Que., Canada, 1952—53; asst. prof. medicine U. N.C. Sch. Medicine, Chapel Hill, 1953—57, assoc. prof. medicine and preventive medicine, 1957—62; Commonwealth advanced fellow Med. Rsch. Coun., Social Medicine Rsch. unit London Hosp., 1959—60; chmn., prof. epidemiology and community medicine U. Vt., Burlington, 1962—64; prof. Sch. Hygiene and Pub. Health Johns Hopkins U., Balt., 1965—76, chmn. dept. health care orgn., 1965—72; dir. Inst. Health Care Studies United Hosp. Fund N.Y., 1977—78; dep. dir. health scis. Rockefeller Found., N.Y.C., 1978—97, ret., 1997. Chmn. U.S. Nat. Com. Vital and Health Stats., 1975—79; mem. health adv. panel Office of Tech. Assessment, U.S. Congress, 1975—82; cons. Nat. Ctr. Health Stats., 1967—83, WHO, 1967—. Editor: Manual for Examination of Patients, 1960, Medical Care Research, 1965, Health Care: An International Study, 1976, Epidemiology as a Fundamental Science, 1976, Task of Medicine, 1988, Healing the Schism, 1991; mem. editl. bd.: Med. Care, 1962—73, Inquiry, 1967—79, Internat. Jour. Epidemiology, 1971—81, Internat. Jour. Health Svcs., 1971—; contbr. chapters to books, articles to profl. jours. Trustee Case-Western Res. U., 1974—79; bd. dirs. Found. for Child Devel. 1969—80. With Can. Army, 1942—45. Recipient Pew Primary Care Achievement award, 1995, Baxter Found. award, 1996, Wood award for lifetime contbns. to primary care rsch., 1999. Fellow: APHA (gov. coun. 1964—68, 1971—73, coun. med. care sect. 1962—65), NAS (Inst. Medicine coun. 1974—76, chmn. membership com. 1975—77), ACP, AAAS, Am. Heart Assn., Am. Acad. Preventive Medicine, Royal Soc. Medicine (hon.); mem.: AMA, Kerr L. White Inst. Health Svcs. Rsch. (hon. dir. 1995—), Internat. Epidemiol. Assn. (hon.; life, pres. 1974—71), Am. Pub. Health Assn. 74—71, 1974—77, coun. 1971—81), Am. Hosp. Assn. (adv. coun. ednl. and rsch. trust 1965—68), Assn. Tchrs. Preventive Medicine (coun. 1963—68), Century Club (N.Y.C.), Cosmos Club (Washington), Alpha Omega Alpha, Sigma Xi. Office Phone: 434-972-2499. Business E-Mail: klw2j@virginia.edu.

**WHITE, KEVIN J.,** education educator, consultant; s. Sandra G. Weigel-White and Jason C. White. BS in Philosophy, SUNY Brockport, 1998; MA in Am. studies, SUNY Buffalo, 2000, PhD candidate, 2000—06. Lectr. SUNY, 1999—2001, Brockport, 1999—2002, instr. Oswego, 2003—, academic planning counselor, 2002—; assoc. mgr. Pinewoods Cmty. Farming Inc, Gowanda, NY, 1999—. Chair Native Am. Indian Edn. Assn. of N.Y., Oneida, 2004—; bd. dirs. N.Y. Folklore Soc., Schenectady, NY, 2005—, Native Am. Cultural Ctr., Rochester, NY, 1996—98; region vi representative Am. Indian Sci. & Engring. Soc., Albuquerque, 1997—98. Author: (student resource handbook) Timeline of Native American History, (ori student resource handbook) The Ever Changing Indian, (conf. jour. proceedings) Imagery that Evolves Out of the Fur Trade Era Indian. Mem. N.Y. Folklore Soc., Schenectady, 2005—; chair Native Am. Indian Edn. Assn. of NY, Oneida, 2004—06. With U.S. Army, 1991—93. Recipient Writing Intensive Candidate, Monroe C.C., 1995, Honory Inductee, Chi Alpha Epsilon, 2004; fellow Tchg. Assistantship, SUNY Buffalo, 1998—2000, Grad. Assistantship, 2000—02. Mem.: No. Consortium of Native Studies Programs (assoc.), I-81 Ctrl. Consortium of NY (assoc.), Native Am. Indian Edn. Assn. of NY (assoc.; chair 2004—06), Am. Studies Assn. (assoc.), Native Am. Student Assn. SUNY Brockport (assoc.; exec. 1996—98), U. of Rochester AISES Chpt. (assoc.; exec. and co-founder 1996—98), Am. Studies Assn. (assoc.; exec. 1998—2002), Coun. of Ongwehonweh Grad. Students (assoc.; exec. 2000—02). Avocations: native american education, iroquois white corn project, reading, writing. Home: 214 Liberty St Oswego NY 13126 Office: SUNY Oswego 110 Mahar Hall Oswego NY 13126 Office Phone: 315-312-2645. Home Fax: 315-207-0471; Office Fax: 315-312-5676. Personal E-Mail: kwhite33@verizon.net. Business E-Mail: kwhite3@oswego.edu.

**WHITE, LAWRENCE EDWARD,** treasurer, financial executive; b. Pitts., Mar. 5, 1950; s. Edward A. and Dolores C. (Cole) W.; m. Marjorie Claire Ertle, July 29, 1972; children: Matthew E., Christopher L. BS in Chem. Engring., Carnegie-Mellon U., 1972, MS in Indsl. Adminstrn. with distinction, 1976. Product devel. engr. Eastman Kodak Co., Rochester, 1972-74; fin. analyst, supr. Ford Motor Co., Dearborn, Mich., 1976-82; mgr. fin. analysis Lone Star Techs., Dallas, 1982-85, mgr. corp. acctg., 1985-87; dir. fin. analysis and planning, corp. treas. TGI Friday's Inc., Dallas, 1987-89; v.p., treas. Metromedia Steakhouses, Inc., Dayton, Ohio, 1989—. Active YMCA Youth Orgns., local ch. fin. com. Mem. Assn. for Corp. Growth., Fin. Execs. Inst., Carnegie-Mellon Univ. Alumni Assn. Republican. Methodist. Office: Metromedia Steakhouses Inc PO Box 578 Dayton OH 45401-0578 Home: 6 Missionary Ln Brentwood TN 37027

**WHITE, LAWRENCE J.,** economics professor; b. NYC, June 1, 1943; s. Martin H. and Florence M. (Meiman) W. AB, Harvard U., 1964, PhD, 1969; MS in Econs., London Sch. Econs., 1965. Econ. adviser Harvard Devel. Adv. Svc., Pakistan and Indonesia, 1969-70; asst. prof. econs. Princeton U., NJ, 1970-76; mem. faculty Stern Sch. Bus., NYU, 1976—, prof. econs., 1979—, chmn. dept., 1990-95, dep. chmn. dept., 2005—; sr. staff economist U.S. Coun. Econ. Advisers, 1978-79; dir. econ. policy office, antitrust div. Dept. Justice, Washington, 1982-83. Mem. Fed. Home Loan Bank Bd., 1986-89; cons. in field. Author: The Automobile Industry Since 1945, 1971, Industrial Concentration and Economic Power in Pakistan, 1974, Reforming Regulation: Processes and Problems, 1981, The Regulation: Processes and Problems, 1981, The Regulation of Air Pollutant Emissions from Motor Vehicles, 1982, The Public Library in the 1980s: The Problems of Choice, 1983, International Trade in Ocean Shipping Services: The U.S. and the World, 1988, The S&L Debacle: Public Policy Lessons for Bank and Thrift Regulation, 1991; editor or co-editor: The Deregulation of the Banking and Securities Industries, 1979, Mergers and Acquisitions: Current Problems in Perspective, 1982, Technology and the Regulation of Financial Markets: Securities, Futures and Banking, 1986, Private Antitrust Litigation: New Evidence, New Learning, 1988, The Antitrust Revolution, 1989, Bank Management and Regulation, 1992, Structural Change in Banking, 1993, The Antitrust Revolution: The Role of Economics, 2d edit., 1994, The Antitrust Revolution: Economics, Competition, and Policy, 3d edit., 1999, 4th edit., 2004; N.Am. editor Jour. Indsl. Econs., 1984-87, 90-95; co-editor Rev. of Indsl. Orgn., 2003-04, gen. editor, 2004-. NSF fellow, 1965—69. Mem. Am. Econ. Assn., Western Econ. Assn. Internat. (bd. mem., treas. 2006—), Phi Beta Kappa. Office: NYU Stern Sch Bus 44 W 4th St New York NY 10012-1126 Office Phone: 212-998-0880. Business E-Mail: lwhite@stern.nyu.edu.

**WHITE, LILLIAS,** actress; Appeared in Broadway plays Titanic, Cats, Once on This Island, Dreamgirls, Rock 'n' Roll: The First 5000 Years, Barnum, How to Succeed in Business..., The Life (Tony award 1997), Chicago, 2006; (off-Broadway) Waiting for Godot, The Princess and The Black-eyed Pea, Antigone Africanus, Romance in Hard Times (Obie award); (nat. and internat. tour) Ain't Misbehavin', The Wiz, Tintypes, Dreamgirls (Drama-Logue award), Purlie, 2005, South Pacific, 2005; (TV series) Sesame Street (Emmy award), Law & Order, NYPD Blue; (film) (voice) Hercules; concert appearance include Carnegie Hall, Lincoln Ctr., The White House. Office: Don Buchwald & Assocs 10 E 44th St Fl 2 New York NY 10017-3654*

**WHITE, LINDA DIANE,** lawyer; b. NYC, Apr. 1, 1952; d. Bernard and Elaine (Simons) Schwartz; m. Thomas M. White, Aug. 16, 1975; 1 child, Alexandra Nicole. AB, U. Pa., 1973; JD, Northwestern U., 1976. Bar: Ill. 1976. Assoc. Walsh, Case, Coale & Brown, Chgo., 1976-77, Greenberger & Kaufmann (merged into Katten, Muchin), Chgo., 1977-82, ptnr., 1982-85, Sonnenschein Nath & Rosenthal LLP, Chgo., 1985—. Mem. trustees coun. Penn Women; mem. Samuel Zell and Robert Lurie Real Estate Ctr., Wharton Sch., U. Pa. Mem.: ABA (mem. real property fin. com., mem. comml. leasing com., mem. real property, probate and trust law sect. 1987—), Practicing Law Inst. (chmn. program negotiating comml. leases 1995—99, mem. real estate law adv. com.), Chgo. Bar Assn., Ill. Bar Assn. Office: Sonnenschein Nath & Rosenthal LLP 7800 Sears Tower 233 S Wacker Dr Ste 7800 Chicago IL 60606-6491 Office Phone: 312-876-8950. Business E-Mail: lwhite@sonnenschein.com.

**WHITE, LINDA LEE LOCY,** secondary educator; b. Detroit, Sept. 12, 1943; d. John Lorenzo and Vivian Bethia (Greenlee) Locy. BA, Western Mich. U., 1965; MA in Speech Comm., San Francisco State U., 1982. Cert. secondary tchr., Calif. English tchr. Hillside Jr. H.S., Kalamazoo, 1965-67, Sinaloa Jr. H.S., Novato, Calif., 1975-83; mentor tchr. Novato Unified Sch. Dist., 1993-96, program overseer-at-large student tutorial, 1997—99, English tchr., Journalism tchr., 1968—73, 1983—93. Bd. dirs. Hear Me & Co., San Francisco, 1997-98, Bay Area Women's Resource Ctr., San Francisco, 1977-78; grief counselor Marin Cmty. Counseling, San Rafael, 1991—; active Internat. Women's Conf., Nairobi, Kenya, 1985. Tech. grant Calif. State Dept. of Edn., 1987; learning fellowship Buck Inst. for Edn., 1997. Avocations: hiking, reading, golf.

**WHITE, LINDA MARIE,** former fraternal organization administrator; b. Cleve., Apr. 21, 1942; BA, Clark Coll., 1963; MA, U. Chgo., 1969. Mgmt analyst HHS, Washington; social security adminstr. Chgo.; area dir. Chgo. East Dist. Office. Bd. dirs. United Negro Coll. Fund. Named one of Most Influential Black Americans, Ebony mag., 2006. Mem.: NAACP (life), Alpha Kappa Alpha Sorority (supreme basileus, internat. pres. 2002—06). Office: Alpha Kappa Alpha Sorority, Inc 5656 S Stony Island Ave Chicago IL 60637*

**WHITE, LONNIE JOE,** retired history educator; b. Knox City, Tex., Feb. 12, 1931; s. John Alexander and Fannie Coates White; m. Nancy Louella Evans, June 23, 1951; children: John Evans, Brenda Jo White Holman. BA in History, W. Tex. State Coll., 1950; MA in History, Tex. Tech. Coll., 1955; PhD in History, U. Tex., Austin, 1961. Tchg. asst. history U. Tex., Austin, 1957—61; prof. history Memphis State Univ. (now U. Memphis), 1961—89; prof. emeritus U. Memphis, 1989—. Editl. adv. bd. Jour. of the West, Manhattan, Kans., 1963—88; assoc. edit. Military History of Texas and the Southwest, Austin, Tex., 1977—88. Author: Politics on the Southwestern Frontier: Arkansas Territory, 1819-1836, 1964, Panthers to Arrowheads: The 36th (Texas-Oklahoma) Division in World War I, 1984, The 90th Division in World War I: The Texas-Oklahoma Draft Division in the Great War, 1996; co-author: Hostiles and Horse Soldiers: Indian Battles and Campaigns in the West, 1972; co-editor: By Sea to San Francisco, 1849-50: The Journal of Dr. James Morison, 1977, 2nd edit., 2000; editor: Old Mobeetie, 1877-1885: Texas Panhandle News Items from the Dodge City Times, 1967, The Miles Expedition of 1874-1875: An Eyewitness Account of the Red River War, 1971, Chronicle of a Congressional Journey: The Doolittle Committee in the Southwest, 1865, 1975; contbr. more than 45 articles to profl. jour., book reviews over 97 pub. to prof. jour. Sgt. U.S. Army, 1951—53. Grantee Rsch. Grant, Am. Philos. Soc., 1963. Mem.: So. Hist. Assn., Am. Hist. Assn. Republican. Baptist. Avocations: history, writing, travel, flying, genealogy.

**WHITE, LORAY BETTY,** TV talk show host, writer, television producer, director, vocalist, actress; b. Houston, Nov. 27, 1934; d. Harold White and Joyce Mae (Jenkins) Mills; m. Sammy Davis Jr., 1957 (div. 1958); 1 child, Deborah R. DeHart. Student, UCLA extension, 1948-50, 90-91, Nichiren Shoshu Acad., 1988-92; AA in Bus., Sawyer Bus. Sch., 1970; study divsn. mem. dept. L.A., Calif. Study Group of Japan, 1970-86. Editor, entertainment writer L.A. Community New, 1970-81; exec. sec. guest rels. KNBC Prodns., Burbank, Calif., 1969-75; security specialist Xerox X10 Think Tank, L.A., 1975-80; exec. asst. Ralph Powell & Assocs., L.A., 1980-82; pres., owner, producer LBW & Assocs. Pub. Rels., L.A., 1980—; owner, producer, writer, host TV prodn. co, Pub, Pub, Rels, L.A. 1987—, Dir, producer L.B.W. Prodn. "Yesterday, Today, Tomorrow, L.A., 1981-2005; with CBS news dept./Bogey's Corner, The Vol. Brigade Corps, KCBS News, 1999. Actor: (films) Ten Commandments, 1956; singer: (films) The Jazz Review, 1960—65; headline singer Radio City Music Hall, N.Y.C., 1961, Can Can Cafe Concert in Mex., 1967—75, feature singer Hilton Hotel Mex., featured singer Hotel Maria Isabel, Acapulco, Disneyland, Calif.; singer: TV, 1981—2005, (Broadway plays) Joy Ride; appearances in the following (endorsements) Budweiser Beer, Old Gold Cigarettes, Salem Cigarettes, TV commls. including Cheer, Puffs Tissue, Coca Cola, Buffern, others, entertainment editor (newspaper) L.A. Community News, 1970—73, writer (column) Balance News, 1980—82. Vol. ARC, 1995, L.B.W. & Assocs., Ltd. Ann. Prodn. of Mother and Daughter of the Yr. Tribute, 1999, United Peace and Cultural Exch. Dinner and Awards Show, 1999; exec. prodr. The Fifth L.B.W. and Assocs. Internat. Ann. Achievement Awards Show, 1999. The Sixth L.B.W. and Assocs. Internat. Ann. Achievement Awards Show, 2000; mem. Habitat for Humanity Internat. Nat. Com. Preserve Soc. Sec. and Medicare, 1998-99, Nat. Black Network Assn., AARP, So. Calif. Com. Sr. Citizens, re-elect Scott Wildmen Rep. campaign; mem. resident adv. bd. Burbank Housing Authority, HUD, 2000—; mem. Com. to Reelect Ted McConkey to Burbank City Coun., 1999; bd. dir. Chamblee Found. of Calif., 1998-; apptd. area coord. San Fernando Valley area, Myohoji Temple of Nichiren Shoshu, West Hollywood, Calif., 2004-. Recipient Cert. of Honor, ARC, 1984, Internat. Orgn. Soka Gakkai Internat. of Japan, Cmty. Vols. of Am. award, 1994, Mother and Daughter of Yr. Tribute, 2000-01, 6th Internat. Achievement award L.B.W. and Assocs.; named Performer of Yr. Cardella Demillo, 1976-77. Mem. ARC (planning, mktg., prodn. event com. 1995), UCLA Alumni Assn., Lupus Found. Am. (So. Calif. chpt.), Nat. Fedn. Blind, Myohoji-Hokkeko Internat. (USA chpt., 2002, attendee Tozon Internat., participant 750th Anniv. of Nichiren Shoshu Head Temple Taisekiji, Japan), Libr. of Congress Assn. (charter). Buddhist. Avocations: singing, acting, tv writing and producing. Office: 818-955-7728. Personal E-mail: blwjoyce@aol.com. Accepting challenges in life is a choice. The choice is always yours. I've chosen never to give up-to always give my best. To constantly keep a growing and open mind. To remember to strengthen and reinforce the quality of my integrity no matter what. Be a winner to yourself.

**WHITE, LOWELL ELMOND, JR.,** retired medical educator; b. Tacoma, Wash., Jan. 16, 1928; s. Lowell E. and Hazel (Conley) W.; m. Margie Mae Lamb, June 21, 1947; children: Henry, Leanna White Maynes, Inger-Britt White Peterson. BS in Pharm., U. Wash., 1951, MD, 1953. Diplomate Am. Bd. Neurol. Surgery. Intern N.C. Meml. Hosp., Chapel Hill, 1953-54; resident neurosurgery, asst. to instr. U. Wash., 1954-60, asst. prof., 1960-64, assoc. prof., 1964-70; asso. dean U. Wash. Sch. Medicine, 1965-68; prof., chief divsn. neurol. surgery U. Fla., 1970-72; prof. U. South Ala., 1972-94, chmn. divsn. neurosci., 1972-77, ret., 1994. Adj. prof. Ala. Sch. Math. and Sci., 1993-94; chmn. nat. adv. com. Animal Resources NIH, 1966-70; cons. rsch. facilities and resources NIH; cons. divsn. hosp. and med. facilities USPHS; cons. grants adminstrn. policy U.S. Dept. HEW. Contbr. articles profl. jours. Bd. dirs. Mobile County Emergency Med. Svcs. Coun., 1973-82, Epilepsy chpt. Mobile, 1973-89, Mobile cpt. Myasthenia Gravis Found. Am., 1974-90, Mobile, Ala. Mental Health Assn., 1979-89, Spl. Edn. Action Com., 1985-97, pres. 1996; vol. Homeland Security Med. Res.Corps and ARC, 2005. With USN, 1946—47, with USNR, 1948—66. Guggenheim fellow, 1958-59 Mem. AMA, Am. Assn. Neurol. Surgeons, Am. Assn. Neuropathologists, Am. Acad. Neurol. Surgeons, Soc. for Neurosci., Assn. Am. Med. Colls., Am. Assn. Anatomists, Rsch. Soc. Neurol. Surgeons, Neurosurg. Soc. Ala. (pres. 1975), Am. Physicians Poetry Assn., Odyssey U. South Ala., Soc. for Arts in Healthcare, Snohomish County Med. Soc., Sigma Xi. Home: 11009 E Villa Monte Dr Mukilteo WA 98275-4881

**WHITE, LUCETTE DARBY,** painter, sculptor; b. Sprinfield, Ill., Nov. 22, 1931; d. William Edson and Maurine McVicar Darby; married, July 19, 1962; children: Elizabeth, Darby, Matthew, Esther. At, Newcomb Coll., New Orleans, La., 1950—51, U. Ark., Fayetteville, 1951—53, Sarasota Sch. Art, Fla., Inst Contemporary Art, Boston, Ark. Arts Ctr., Little Rock, studied with Helen Terry Marshall, Russellville, Ark., Edwin Brewer, Little Rock, James Valone, Ark. Arts Ctr., Hilton Leech, Sarasota, Fla., George Demetrios, Boston. Bd. trustees Ark. Arts Ctr., Little Rock, 1972—76; mem. acquisition com. Cape Ann Mus., Gloucester, Mass., 1988—90; bd. trustees Montserrat Sch. Art, Beverly, Mass., 2000. Prin. works include Black Light, Storm Fantasy, one-woman shows include U. Ark. Med. Sch., Little Rock, 1959, Lakewood Ho. Gallery, North Little Rock, 1966, ML Gallery Fine Arts, N.Y.C., 1976, La. Tech. U., Ruston, 1976, Judi Rotenberg Gallery, Boston, 1990, Endicott Coll., Beverly, Mass.1990, Turnbridge (Vt.) Pub. Libr., 1995, Mercury Gallery, Boston, 1996, 1998, Rockport, Mass, 2002, Hill Country Arts Found., Ingram, Tex., 1997, Granite Shore Gallery, Rockport, 2000, 2001, exhibitions include 62d Ann. Exhibit Allied Artists in Am., N.Y.C., 1975, 63d Ann. Exhibit Allied Artists in Am., 1976, Nat. Acad. Design 153d Ann. Exhbn., 1978, Judi Rotenberg Gallery, Boston, 1987, 1991, 1992, DeCordova & Dana Mus., Lincoln, Mass., 1988—90, Boston - "90, 1990, West End Gallery, Gloucester, Mass., 1997, Acacia Galleriy, 1998, 2000, Cape Ann Mus., 1999, Mercury Gallery, Boston, 2000, 2002, 2003, 2004, U.S. Artist Am. Fine Art Exhibit, Phila., 2002, Represented in permanent collections Bank Am., Little Rock, First Nat. Bank, Harrison, Ark., Nat. Old Line Ins. Co., Little Rock, St. Vincent Infirmary, William J. Clinton Presdl. Libr. Mem.: Nat. Acad. Design (assoc.), Allied Artists Am. (assoc.). Democrat. Avocations: swimming, hiking, outdoor painting. Home: 24 Bass Rocks Rd Gloucester MA 01930

**WHITE, LUCIE E.,** law educator; b. NC, June 13, 1949; BA, Radcliffe Coll., 1972; grad. studies in comparative lit., Yale U., 1972—74; JD, Harvard U., 1981. Bar: DC 1981, NC 1982, Calif. 1987. Law clk. to Judge James McMillen US Dist. Ct. We. Dist. NC, Charlotte, 1981—82; staff atty. Legal Services of So. Piedmont, Charlotte, 1982—84; supervising atty. U. NC, 1984—86; asst. prof. UCLA, 1986—89, acting prof., 1989—90, prof., 1990—95; prof. law Harvard Law Sch., Cambridge, Mass., 1995—, Louis A. Horvitz Prof. Law, 1998—. Office: Harvard Law Sch 1563 Massachusetts Ave Cambridge MA 02138 Office Phone: 617-496-3358. Office Fax: 617-495-4299. Business E-Mail: lwhite@law.harvard.edu.

**WHITE, LYNN H.,** psychology professor, researcher; d. Robert D. and Shirley White; m. Andrew R. Milner, May 11, 1996; children: Burgess A Milner, Triolus R. MA Physiol. Psychology, McGill U., Montreal, Quebec, Canada, 1990—93; PhD Physiol. Psychology, McGill U., Montreal, Quebec, Can., 1997; BA Applied Psychology, Bishop's U., Lennoxville, Quebec, Can., 1990. Asst. prof. psychology So. Utah U., Cedar City, 1997—2003, instl. rev. bd. dir., 2000—06, assoc. profes. psychology, 2003—, dir. undergraduate rsch. 2006—; liaison officer Coun. on Undergraduate Rsch., Washington, 2002—03. Dir. behavioral neuroscience lab So. Utah U., Cedar City, 1998—, dir. psychology undergraduate rsch. lab, 1999—. Com. mem. Human Rights Com. Danville Svcs., Cedar City, 1999; vice chair Iron Parke Corp., Cedar City, Utah, 1997—2002. Mem.: Rocky Mountain Psychol. Assn. (assoc.), Alpha Chi (hon.; Utah beta faculty sponsor 1998—, region vii v.p. 2002—04, region vii pres. 2004—06). Avocations: fossil collecting, camping, hiking. Office: Southern Utah Univ 351 West University Blvd Cedar City UT 84720 Office Phone: 435-586-7913. Office Fax: 435-865-8289. Business E-Mail: white_l@suu.edu.

**WHITE, MARILYN DOMAS,** information science educator; b. Franklin, La., Aug. 16, 1940; d. George Julian and Mamie Domas; m. Roger Stuart White, Aug. 31, 1968; 1 child, Joshua Stuart. BA, Our Lady of the Lake Coll., San Antonio, 1962; MS, U. Wis., 1963; PhD, U. Ill., 1971. Dir. Commerce Libr. U. Wis., Madison, 1963-65; head Social Sci./Bus. Libr. So. Ill. U., Edwardsville, 1965-67; cons. So. Ill. /U./US AID Adv. Team, South Vietnam, 1967; asst. prof. SUNY, Buffalo, 1972-74; lectr., vis. asst. prof. U. Md., College Park, 1976-77, asst. prof. info sci., 1977-82, assoc. prof. info. sci., 1982—. Cons. USIA, Washington and abroad, 1977—83, Inst. for Def. Analyses, Bowie, Md., Supercomputing Rsch Ctr., 1990—91, Am. Health Care Assn., Washington, 1990—92, Am. Coun. on Edn., 1995, U.S. Bur. of Census, 2003—04. Contbr. articles to profl. jours. including Libr. Quar., Libr. & Info. Sci. Rsch., Jour. Documentation, Jour. Am. Soc. for Info. Science. James Lyman Whitney grantee ALA, 1983, Spl. Libr. Assn. rsch. grantee, 1993-94, Coun. Libr. Resources grantee, 1995-96, Info. Sci. Abstracts grantee, 1997-98. Mem. Am. Soc. for Info. Sci., Spl. Libr. Assn. Office: U Md Coll Info Studies Hornbake 4117F South Wing College Park MD 20742-0001 Office Phone: 301-405-2047. Business E-Mail: whitemd@umd.edu.

**WHITE, MARTHA VETTER,** allergist, immunologist; b. Richmond, Va., Oct. 23, 1951; d. Robert Joseph and Miriam Ernestine (Thomas) Vetter; m. Frederick Joseph Kozub, Oct. 11, 1975 (div. June 1982); m. John Irving White, Feb. 18, 1984; children: Josh, Christie. Student, Vanderbilt U., Nashville, 1969-71; BA, U. Richmond, 1973; MD, Va. Commonwealth U., Richmond, 1978. Cert. m. Bd. Pediatrics, Am. Bd. Allergy and Immunology. Pediatric intern and resident Va. Commonwealth U., Richmond, 1978-81; locum tenans Pub. Health, Richmond, Va., 1981-82; fellow Allergy and Immunology U. Southern Calif., L.A., 1983-84, Georgetown U., 1983-84; sr. staff fellow Food and Drug Adminstrn., Bethesda, Md., 1984-85; NSRA fellow Nat. Inst. Allergy and Infectious Diseases, Bethesda, Md., 1985-88; sr. staff fellow, 1988-93; rsch. dir. Inst. for Asthma and Allergy, Wheaton, Md., 1993—. Cons. Sandoz Pharms., Marion Merrell Dow, Glaxo, Boehringer Ingleheim, Ciba-Geigy, Miles Generict; rsch Glaxo, Abbott, Pfizer, Marion Merrell Dow, Miles, Rhône Poulenc Rhoen, Sanofi, Adams, Astra, Merck, Neurbiol. Techs., 3M, Zeneca, Wyeth, Smith-Kline Beecham; bd. dirs. Allery & Asthma Network/Mothers of Asthmatics, 1987—; med. editor MA Report, 1986—; assoc. editor Allergy, Asthma and Immunology Guide, 1989-90. Contbr. numerous scientific papers, abstracts, chpts. and reviews in field. Recipient Norwich Eaton Rsch. award, 1987; Merrell Dow scholar in allergy, 1989; Geigy fellow, 1984. Mem.: Soc. Prin. Investigators (pres. 2002—03), Am. Thoracic Soc., Am. Coll. Allergy and Immunology, Adm. Acad. Allergy and Immunology, Am. Acad. Pediat., Am. Assn. Immunologists, Gamma Sigma Epsilon, Psi Chi, Beta Beta Beta. Office: Inst Asthma and Allergy 11002 Veirs Mill Rd # 414 Wheaton MD 20902 Office Phone: 301-962-5800.

**WHITE, MARTIN CHRISTOPHER,** academic administrator; b. Anderson, S.C., Oct. 16, 1943; s. Jesse Martin and Christine Freida (Powell) W.; m. Linda Ann Fleming, July 31, 1965; children: Martin Lynn, Andrew Christopher. AB, Mercer U., 1965; MDiv, So. Bapt. Theol. Sem., 1968; PhD, Emory U., 1972. Prof. Elon Coll. (N.C.), 1972-76, dean acad. affairs, 1976-82, v.p. for acad. and student affairs, 1982-86; pres. Gardner-Webb U., Boiling Springs, NC, 1986—2002, Chowan U., Murfreesboro, NC, 2002—. Cons. So. Assn. Colls. and Schs., Atlanta, 1982—. Contbr. articles in field. Bd. dirs. United Way, Shelby, N.C., 1987. Woodrow Wilson fellow, 1971. Mem. Soc. Bibl. Lit., Nat. Assn. Bapt. Profs. of Religion, N.C. Ind. Coll. Assn., Alpha Chi, Omicron Delta Kappa. Lodges: Rotary (bd. dirs. Burlington, N.C. chpt. 1986). Democrat. Baptist. Avocations: golf, tennis, music, travel. Home: 100 Jones Dr Murfreesboro NC 27855-1800 Office: One University Dr Murfreesboro NC 27855 Office Phone: 252-398-6221. E-mail: whitec@chowan.edu.

**WHITE, MARY JO,** lawyer, former prosecutor; b. Kansas City, Mo., Dec. 27, 1947; d. Carl and Ruth King Monk; m. John W. White, Jan. 24, 1970. BA, Coll. William and Mary, 1970; MA in Psychology, New Sch. for Social Rsch., 1971; JD, Columbia U., 1974. Bar: NY 1975. Law clk. to Hon. Marvin E. Frankel US Dist. Ct. (So. dist.) NY, 1975—76; assoc. Debevoise & Plimpton LLP, 1976—78, litig. ptnr., 1983—90, ptnr., chair of litig., 2002—; asst. U.S. atty., chief appellate atty. criminal divsn. (So. dist.) NY US Dept. Justice, 1978—81; instr. in profl. responsibility and ethics Columbia Law Sch., 1981—; chief asst., acting U.S. atty. (ea. dist.) NY US Dept. Justice, Bklyn., 1990—93, U.S. atty. (So. dist.) NY Manhattan, 1993—2002. Chair Atty. Gen. Janet Reno's Adv. Com. of U.S. Attys., 1993—94. Recipient "Magnificent 7" award, Bus. & Profl. Women USA, Law Enforcement Person of the Year award, Soc. of Profl. Investigators, Human Relations Award, Anti-Defamation League Lawyer's Div., 1996, Edward Weinfeld award for disting. conthn. to Admin. of Justice, N.Y. County Lawyers' Assn., 1998, Nat. Law Jour. 2002 list of Top Women Litigators, John P. O'Neill Pillar of Justice award, Respect for Law Alliance, 2002, Sandra Day O'Connor award for Distinction in Public Svc., 2002, dir. of FBI's Jefferson Cup award for contbn. to Rule of Law in the fight against terrorism and crime, 2002, George H. W. Bush award for excellence in counter-terrorism and the Agency Seal Medallion, CIA, 2002, Women of Power and Influence award, NOW. Fellow: Am. Coll. Trial Lawyers; mem.: ABA, N.Y. State Bar Assn., Assn. Bar City of N.Y. Achievements include First women to serve as U.S Atty. for So. Dist. of N.Y; first chairperson of Atty. Gen. Janet Reno's Advisory Com.of U.S. Attys. Office: Debevoise & Plimpton LLP 919 Third Ave 46t Fl New York NY 10022 Business E-Mail: mjwhite@debevoise.com.

**WHITE, MEG (MEGAN MARTHA WHITE),** musician, vocalist; b. Grosse Pointe, Mich., Dec. 10, 1974; m. John Gillis, 1996 (div. 2000). Drummer, vocalist The White Stripes, 1997—; toured with Pavement and Sleater-Kinney, 1999, 2000. Performer: (albums) The White Stripes, 1999, De Stijl, 2000, White Blood Cells, 2001, Maximum, 2002, Elephant, 2003, Get Behind Me Satan, 2005; actor: (films) Coffee and Cigarettes, 2003, Cold Mountain, 2003. Office: Monotone Inc 150 S Rodeo Dr # 200 Beverly Hills CA 90212-2408

**WHITE, MICHAEL DENNIS,** food products executive; b. Norwood, Mass., Jan. 11, 1952; s. Thomas Michael and Sally (Davenport) W.; m. Susan Lee Burns, June 30, 1972; children: Larissa, Paul, Jennifer. BA, Boston Coll., Newton, Mass., 1974; cert. of proficiency, Leningrad (USSR) State U., 1974; MA in Internat. Rels., Johns Hopkins U., 1976. CPA, Mass. Cons. Arthur Andersen & Co., Mgmt. Info. Cons. Div., Washington, Boston, 1976-80, mgr., 1980-81; cons. Bain & Co., Boston, 1981-84, mgr., 1984-86; v.p. planning, devel. Avon Products, N.Y.C., 1986-87, v.p. retail devel., 1987-88; sr. v.p., gen. mgr. internat. Parfums Stern Inc. (subs. Avon Products), N.Y.C., 1988-90; v.p. planning Frito-Lay Inc., Plano, Tex., 1990—91, sr. v.p. fin. CFO; exec. v.p., CFO PepsiCo, Intern. Snack div.; sr. v.p., CFO PepsiCo Foods Co., 1996—98, PepsiCo, Inc., 1998—2000; pres., CEO Frito-Lay, Europe/Africa/Middle East division, 2000—03; chmn., CEO PepsiCo International, 2003—; vice chmn. PepsiCo, Inc., 2006—. Active Tri-State United Way, N.Y.C.; v.p. Westport (Conn.)-Weston United Way, 1988-90. Office: PepsiCo Inc 700 Anderson Hill Rd Purchase NY 10577*

**WHITE, MILDRED VIRGINIA,** secondary school educator, retired counseling administrator; d. Stanis Augustus and Elsie Emma Watkins; m. Richard Clarence White, Jan. 1, 1949; children: Michael Kenneth, Valerie Clarissa. BSc, Tuskegee Inst., 1948; MA, Atlanta U., 1965. Cert. counseling Ala., 1965. H.S. health and phys. edn. tchr. Macon County Tng. Sch./Macon County Bd. Edn., Tuskegee, Ala., 1950—65; career counselor for adult students Manpower Tng. Act/Labor Dept. Fed. Govt., Tuskegee, Ala., 1965—66; guidance dir. /job developer H.S. equivalency program OEO, Tuskegee, 1966—67, 1968—69; program dir. for rsch. and demonstrational program Adult Edn. Rsch. Program HEW, Tuskegee, 1967—68; career devel. specialist for head start teachers Head Start Supplementary Program for Tchrs., Tuskegee, 1970—71; world history instr. for headstart tchrs. Tuskegee Inst. Fed. Govt., 1971—72; h.s. guidance counselor Deborah Cannon Wolfe H.S./Macon County Bd. Edn., Shorter, Ala., 1972—81; coord. health program Tuskegee Inst. Health, Edn. and Welfare, 1984; career coord. Explorer Pk., Tuskegee, 1994—95. Cons. Adult Edn. State Workshop for Tchrs., Tuskegee, 1970—70; coun. mem. for tng. program Tng. and Preparation for Employment, Montgomery, Ala., 1970—72; dir. Consortium Minorities in Engring., 1984—86; mem. state retirement com. representing Macon County State Retirement and Membership Com./Ala. Tchrs. Assn., Tuskegee, 1995—97. Co-author Handbook for Counselors for Disadvantaged Adults, 1956. Den mother Macon County Cub Scout Pack, Tuskegee Inst., 1962—64; rsch. coord. Tuskegee Inst./HEW, 1974; explorer career coord. Explorer Post of Tuskegee, 1995—95; neighborhood chmn. United Way, Tuskegee, 1998—2003. Fellow, Tuskegee Inst., 1944, Kellogg Found./Tuskegee Inst. Resource Devel. Ctr., Ohio State U., Columbus, 1969. Mem.: NEA, Ret. Tchrs Assn., Ala. Edni. Assn., Macon County Ret. Tchrs. Assn. (v.p. 1992—94, pres. 1994—96), Tuskegee Optimist Mrs. Club (pres. 1997—98), Delta Sigma Theta (life; founder, dir. Delteen youth club 1984—91, pres. 1990—91). Home: 903 N Marable Dr Tuskegee AL 36083 Personal E-mail: mildredgreta@aol.com.

**WHITE, MILES D.,** pharmaceutical executive; b. Minneapolis, MN; BS in Mech. Engring., Stanford U., MBA. Mgmt. cons. McKinsey & Co.; with Abbott Labs., 1984—, v.p. diagnostic sys. and ops., 1993-94, sr. v.p. diagnostic ops., 1994-98, exec. v.p., dir., 1998-99, CEO, chmn., 1999—. Bd. trustee Field Mus., Chicago, Northwestern U., Joffrey Ballet, Chicago, Culture Ednl. Found.; dep. chmn. Fed. Reserve Bank of Chgo.; mem. Stanford Grad. Sch. of Bus. Adv. Coun., Stanford Adv. Coun. on Interdisciplinary Biosciences. Mem.: Econ. Club of Chgo., Executives' Club of Chgo. (chmn.). Office: Abbott Labs 100 Abbott Park Rd Abbott Park IL 60064-6400*

**WHITE, MORTON GABRIEL,** philosopher, writer, historian, retired educator; b. NYC, Apr. 29, 1917; s. Robert and Esther (Levine) Weisberger; m. Lucia Perry, Aug. 29, 1940 (dec.); children: Nicholas Perry, Stephen Daniel; m. Helen Starobin, June 30, 1997. BS, CCNY, 1936; LL.H.D. CUNY, 1975; A.M., Columbia U., 1938, PhD, 1942. Instr. philosophy Columbia U., 1942—46; instr. physics CCNY, 1942—43; asst. prof. philosophy U. Pa., 1946—48, Harvard U., 1948—50, assoc. prof., 1950—53, prof., 1953—70, chmn. dept., 1954—57, acting chmn. dept., 1964—67. Inst. Advanced Study, 1970—87; prof. emeritus, 1987—; ret. 1987. Guggenheim research fellow, 1950-51; vis. prof. Tokyo U., 1952, 60, 66, U. Oslo, 1977-78; Nessima lectr. Doshisha U., Kyoto, 1985, CUNY, 1968-69, Rutgers U., 1987-88, 88-89 Keio U., Tokyo, 2002-03; mem. Inst. Advanced Study, 1953-54, 62-63, 67-68, 68-69. Author: The Origin of Dewey's Instrumentalism, 1943, Social Thought in America, 1949, The Age of Analysis, 1955, Toward Reunion in Philosophy, 1956, Religion, Politics and the Higher Learning, 1959, (with Lucia White) The Intellectual Versus the City, 1962; Editor: (with Arthur M. Schlesinger, Jr.) Paths of American Thought, 1963, Foundations of Historical Knowledge, 1965, Science and Sentiment in America, 1972, Documents in the History of American Philosophy, 1972, Pragmatism and the American Mind, 1973, The Philosophy of the American Revolution, 1978, What Is and What Ought to Be

Done, 1981, (with Lucia White) Journeys to the Japanese, 1952-79, 1986, Philosophy, The Federalist and the Constitution, 1987, The Question of Free Will, 1993, A Philosopher's Story, 1999, A Philosophy of Culture, 2002, From a Philosophical Point of View, 2005. Fellow Center Advanced Study Behavioral Scis., 1959-60; fellow Am. Council Learned Socs., 1962-63 Mem. Am. Acad. Arts and Scis., Am. Antiquarian Soc., Am. Philos. Soc. Office: Inst for Advanced Study Princeton NJ 08540

**WHITE, NICHOLAS JOHN,** musician, director, composer; b. London, Aug. 9, 1967; s. Ronald John and Andre Bernice White; 1 child, Samuel Dempsey. MA, Cambridge U., 1986—89. Organ scholar Clare Coll., Cambridge, England, 1986—89; dir. of choral music McMurry U., Abilene, Tex., 1992—94; asst. organist and choirmaster Wash. Nat. Cathedral, Washington, 1994—98; music dir. Woodley Ensemble, Washington, 1997—2000; dir. of music St. Michael's Ch., NYC, 1998—2005; music dir. Tiffany Consort, NYC, 2003. Composer: (choral work) Magnificat, 1997, Full Freedom, 2002, Alleluia! Puer Natus Est Nobis, 2003, In Sure and Certain Hope, 2006; musician: (cd recording) The Amsterdam Bach, 1999, O Magnum Mysterium, 2004. Bd. mem. St. Wilfrid's Club, NYC, 2001—04. Mem.: Am. Guild of Organists (advtg. dir. 1998—2005, exec. bd. mem. 1998—2003), Assn. of Anglican Musicians, Royal Coll. of Organists (assoc.), St. Wilfrid's Club. Ch. Of England. Avocations: musical theatre, travel. Home: 4701 Pine St D-12 Philadelphia PA 19143 Personal E-mail: nicholaswhite@earthlink.net.

**WHITE, NICHOLAS L,** law educator; b. 1925; AB, Ohio Wesleyan U., 1950; JD, U. Cin., 1956. Bar: Ohio 1956, Ind. 1971, Tenn. 1978. Assoc. Taft, Stettinius & Hollister, Cin., 1956-65, ptnr., 1965-70; asst. dean adminstrn. Ind. U., Bloomington, 1970-73, prof. law, 1970-77, assoc. dean, 1974-77; dean, prof. law Memphis State U., 1977-84; prof. law Humphreys Law Sch. U. Memphis, 1985—. Vis. prof. McGeorge Sch. of Law, Sacramento, Calif., 1984-85; cons. EPA Water Quality Divsn., 1974-77, Nat. Commn. Water Quality, 1975. Served with USMC, 1943-46. Mem. Phi Beta Kappa, Order of Coif, Omicron Delta Kappa. Office: Rm 227 Humphreys Law Sch U Memphis Memphis TN 38152 Office Phone: 901-678-4259. Business E-Mail: nlwhite@memphis.edu.

**WHITE, PAMELA JANICE,** lawyer; b. Elizabeth, NJ, July 13, 1952; d. Emmet Talmadge and June (Howlett) W. BA, Mary Washington Coll., 1974; JD, Washington and Lee U., 1977. Bar: Md. 1977, U.S. Dist. Ct. Md. 1978, D.C. 1979, U.S. Dist. Ct. D.C. 1979, U.S. Ct. Appeals (4th cir.) 1979, U.S. Ct. Appeals (D.C. cir.) 1981, U.S. Ct. Claims 1981, U.S. Ct. Appeals (2d cir.) 1983, N.Y. 1983, U.S. Dist. Ct. (so. dist.) N.Y. 1983, U.S. Ct. Appeals (9th cir.) 1998, U.S. Supreme Ct. 1981. Assoc. Ober, Grimes & Shriver, Balt., 1977-84; prin. Ober, Kaler, Grimes & Shriver PC, Balt., 1985—. Chair Employment Group, 1994—; mem. bd. law examiners, 1986-94, select com. on Gender Equality, 1989-2000, chair, 1997-99, judiciary pub. trust and confidence com., 2001-05, spl. com. on ethics 2002-04, jud. campaign conduct com., 2005—; mem. fed. dist. ct. adv. group Civil Justice Reform Act, 1990; exec. com. Am. Inst. Continuing Profl. Edn. Lawyers, 2000-02, vol. faculty; adv. bd. Md. Mediation and Conflict Resolution Ctr., 2001-02; equal justice coun. Legal Aid Bur. 2000-06. Note and comment editor Washington and Lee Law Rev. 1976-77, Washington and Lee Law Council 1983-87, pres. 1991-92. Mem. Fed. Ct. Bicentennial Com., 1988-90; vol. Profl. Gov.'s Drug-Free Workplace Initiative, 1990-93; bd. trustees Washington and Lee U., 1995-2004; trustee Balt. Hist. Soc., 2002—. Recipient Leadership in Law award Md. Daily Record, 2001, Exemplary Svc. award Legal Aid Bur. 2002, Outstanding Pro Bono Cert., 2004; named Disting. Alumna, Washington and Lee U., 1994, Mary Washington Coll., 2001; named among Md. Top 100 Women, 2000, 04. Fellow Am. Bar Found., Md. Bar Found. (award for excellence 1996, bd. dirs. 2000-); mem. ABA (chair tort and ins. practice employer/employee rels. com. 1999-2000, del. 2000-02), Am. Arbitration Assn. (arbitrator, mediator employment and comml., large complex case panels), Balt. Bar Found. (bd. dirs. 2003—), Fed. Bar Assn., Md. State Bar Assn. (coun. legal edn. sect. 1987-96, chmn. 1992-93, labor sect. coun. 1992-96, professionalism com. 1991—, chmn. 1994-97, bd. govs. 1993-95, 1998 2003, exec. com. 1994-95, 99-01, pres. 2001-02, immediate past pres. 2002-03, task force on professionalism chair 1996-97), D.C. Bar Assn., Balt. City Bar Assn. (exec. coun. 1995-96, 1997-98), Md. Legal Svcs. Corp. (bd. mem. 2006-), U. Md. Washington Alumni Assn. (bd. mem. 2006-), Women's Bar Assn., Md. (treas. 1986-87, v.p. 1987-88, pres.-elect 1988-89, pres. 1989-90, bd. dirs. 1984-86, Rita C. Davidson award 2000), Md. Assn. Def. Counsel, Pro Bono Resource Ctr. (exec. com. 2000-02, bd. trustees 2002-03, Leaders of Equal Justice award 2002), Order of Coif, Phi Beta Kappa (hon. alumni), Omicron Delta Kappa (hon. alumni). Presbyterian. Avocation: baseball. Office: Ober Kaler Grimes & Shriver PC 120 E Baltimore St Ste 800 Baltimore MD 21202-1643 Office Phone: 410-347-7323. Business E-Mail: pjwhite@ober.com.

**WHITE, PAMELA JO,** elementary school educator; b. Lynchburg, Va., June 20, 1943; d. Robert E. and Josephine T. (Patterson) W. BA in Art and Elem. Edn., Lynchburg Coll., 1968, MA in Teaching, 1969; postgrad., U. Va., Kent State U. Elem. tchr. Baltimore County Pub. Schs., Towson, Md., Bedford County Pub. Schs., Bedford, Va., Appomattox County Pub. Schs., Appomattox, Va.; ret., 1990. Recipient Outstanding Vol. award 4-H Club, Cystic Fibrosis Found. Mem. Am. Fedn. Tchrs., Nat. Trust for Hist. Preservation, Smithsonian Assocs., Kappa Delta Pi, Delta Kappa Gamma, Beta Sigma Phi.

**WHITE, PATRICIA DENISE,** dean, law educator; b. Syracuse, NY, July 8, 1949; d. Theodore C. and Kathleen (Cowles) Denise; m. Nicholas P. White, Feb. 20, 1971 (div. 1997); children: Olivia Lawrence, Alexander Cowles; m. James W. Nickel, Sept. 15, 2005. BA, U. Mich., 1971, MA, JD, 1974. Bar: D.C. 1975, Mich. 1988, Utah 1995. Assoc. Steptoe & Johnson, Washington, 1975-76; vis. asst. prof. Coll. of Law U. Toledo, 1976-77; assoc. Caplin & Drysdale, Washington, 1977-79; asst. prof. Law Ctr. Georgetown U., 1979-84, assoc. prof. Law Ctr., 1985-88; vis. scholar U. Mich., Ann Arbor, 1988-94; assoc. prof. U. Utah, Salt Lake City, 1994-98; counsel Parsons, Behle and Latimer, Salt Lake City, 1995—98; dean, prof. Ariz. State U. Coll. Law, 1999—. Counsel Bodman, Longley and Dahling, Detroit, Ann Arbor, 1990-95. Contbr. articles to profl. jours. Fellow: Am. Coll. Tax Coun. Office: Ariz State Sandra Day O'Connor U Coll Law McAllister & Orange Sts PO Box 877906 Tempe AZ 85287-7906 Office Phone: 480-965-6188. Office Fax: 480-965-6125. Business E-Mail: patricia.white@asu.edu.

**WHITE, PATRICIA MARIE,** psychology professor, researcher; d. Robert Amos and Margaret Agnes White; m. William Tate Troyer, Aug. 17, 1997; 1 child, Dylan Jon Troyer. BA, Stanford U., 1981, BS, 1986; PhD, UCLA, 2001. Asst. prof. U. Oreg., Eugene, 2001—. Recipient Michael Goldstein Disting. Dissertation award, UCLA, 2001. Mem.: APA, Assn. Behavioral and Cognitive Therapies, Soc. Psychophysiological Rsch. Achievements include research in ERP, P50 suppression. Office: U Oregon 1227 University of Oregon Eugene OR 97403-1227 Office Phone: 541-346-3942. Home Fax: 541-346-4911; Office Fax: 541-346-4911. Personal E-mail: troyer@uoregon.edu. Business E-Mail: pmwhite@uoregon.edu.

**WHITE, PATRICK E.,** academic administrator; m. Chris White; children: Katie, Molly, Paddy. Grad. with honors, U. Chgo., 1971; MA, U. Iowa, PhD in English and Am. Lit. Tchr. Westmar Coll., 1976—85; chair Dept. Language and Lit. Pfieffer Coll., 1985—88; assoc. dean faculty St. Mary's Coll., Notre Dame, Ind., 1988—2002, v.p., dean faculty, 2002—06, co-founder Ctr. for Academic Innovation; pres. Wabash Coll., Crawfordsville, Ind., 2006—. Office: Wabash Coll Office of Pres PO Box 352 Crawfordsville IN 47933 Office Phone: 765-361-6221. Office Fax: 765-361-6461. E-mail: president@wabash.edu.*

**WHITE, RALPH PAUL,** automotive executive, consultant; b. Watertown, Mass., Aug. 1, 1926; s. Irving William and Margaret Sarah (McRobert) W.; m. Shirley Irene Christie, Nov. 22, 1947; children: Karin Ann, Eric John. BS in Indsl. Engring., Columbia U., 1951; postgrad., Yale U., 1958-59. Instr. engring. mechanics U. Conn., Torrington, 1956-57; mgr. data processing. B.F.

Goodrich Co., Shelton, Conn., 1956—61; ptnr. mgmt. cons. Bavier, Bulger & Goodyear, New Haven, 1961-66; v.p. Davidson Rubber Co., Dover, NH, 1966-69, pres., 1969-80; group v.p. parent co. Ex-Cell-O, Troy, Mich., 1980-83; pres. Troy (N.H.) Mills Inc., 1983-86, chief exec. officer, 1983-89, chmn., 1987-89. Bd. dirs. J.A. Wright Co., Keene, NH, J.D. Cahill Co., Hampton, NH, Exeter Trust Co., D.G. O'Brien Co., Seabrook, NH. Mem. N.H. Indsl. Devel. Authority, 1972-80, 85-88, Pease Devel. Authority, State of N.H., 1990-93, N.H. Bus. Fin. Authority, 1992-2004; exec. bd. Whittemore Sch. Bus., U. N.H. Durham, 1984-2002. Mem. Am. Inst. Indsl. Engrs., Soc. Automotive Engrs., N.H. Bus. and Industry Assn. (bd. dirs. 1970-80, pres. 1972-73, vice chmn. 1984-86), Abenaqui Country Club, Rye Beach Club, Coral Beach Club. Republican. Roman Catholic. Avocations: skiing, golf. Home: 25 Worthey Rd Apt 3312 Durham NH 03824 Personal E-mail: rpw99@aol.com.

**WHITE, RAYMOND LESLIE,** geneticist; b. Orlando, Fla., Oct. 23, 1943; s. Lawrence and Marjorie White; m. Joan Palmer Distin, June 1, 1968; children: Juliette, Jeremy. BS in Microbiology, U. Oreg., 1965; PhD in Microbiology, MIT, 1971; postdoctoral studies, Stanford. Rsch. assoc., instr. MIT, Cambridge, 1971-72; postdoctoral fellow Sch. Medicine Stanford (Calif.), U., 1972-75; asst. prof. Dept. Microbiology U. Mass. Sch. Medicine, Worcester, 1975-78, assoc. prof. Dept. Microbiology, 1978-80; investigator Howard Hughes Med. Inst. U. Utah Med. Ctr., 1980-94; assoc. prof. Dept. Cellular, Viral and Molecular Biology U. Utah Sch. Medicine, 1980-84, co-chmn. Dept. Human Genetics, 1984-94, prof. Dept. Oncological Scis., 1985—; prof. Dept. of Human Genetics U. Utah Sch. of Medicine, 1985—; chmn. Dept. Oncological Scis. U. Utah Sch. Medicine, 1994—, dir. Huntsman Cancer Inst., 1994—2000; chief sci. officer DNA Scis., Inc., Fremont, Calif., 2000—02; dir. Ernest Gallo Clinic & Rsch. Ctr. U. Calif. San Francisco (UCSF), Emeryville, Calif., 2002—, vice chair, prof. neurology, 2002—. Ad hoc mem. NIH Gen. Med. Sci. Inst. Coun., 1984, mem. NIH study sect., 1979-83. Consulting editor Jour. Clin. Investigation; subject area editor Genomics, 1987-90; contbr. articles to profl. jours. Woodrow Wilson fellow, 1965-66, NIH grad. fellow, 1966-71, Jane Coffins Childs Found. fellow, 1971-75; Nat. Cancer Inst. Cancer Ctr. Support grantee, 1995—; recipient Sword Hope award Am. Cancer Soc., 1995, Lewis S. Rosenstiel award Disting. Work Basic Med. Scis., Brandeis U., 1992, Rosenblatt award for excellence, 1993, Nat. Med. Rsch. award Nat. Health Coun., 1991, Friedrich von Recklinghausen award Nat. Neurofibromatosis Found., 1990, Charles S. Mott prize Gen. Motors Cancer Rsch. Found., 1990, Raymond Bourfine award, Paris, 2002. Mem. NAS, Am. Soc. Human Genetics (Allen Cancer Rsch. award 1989, assoc. editor Cancer Rsch.), Utah Acad. Scis., Inst. Medicine. Achievements include the development of a new technology for mapping and ultimately identifying human genes causing disease and the discovery of fundamental genes and genetic mechanisms important in the inherited and cellular pathways to cancer. Office: Ernest Gallo Clinic & Rsch Ctr Ste 200 5858 Horton St Emeryville CA 94608 Office Phone: 510-985-3102. Office Fax: 510-985-3101. E-mail: rayw@egcrc.net.*

**WHITE, RAYMOND PETRIE, JR.,** dentist, educator, dean; b. NYC, Feb. 13, 1937; s. Raymond Petrie and Mabel Sarah (Shutze) White; m. Betty Pritchett, Dec. 27, 1961; children: Karen Elizabeth, Michael Wood. Student, Washington and Lee U., 1955—58; DDS, Med. Coll. Va., 1962, PhD, 1967. Diplomate Am. Bd. Oral and Maxillofacial Surgery. Postdoctoral fellow anatomy Med. Coll. Va., Richmond, 1962—67, resident in oral surgery, 1964—67; asst. prof. U. Ky., Lexington, 1967—70, assoc. prof., 1970—71, chmn. dept. oral surgery, 1969—71; prof., asst. dean adminstrn. Va. Commonwealth U., Richmond, 1971—74; prof. Sch. Dentistry U. N.C., Chapel Hill, 1974—, Dalton L. McMichael disting. prof., 1993—, dean Sch. Dentistry, 1974—81, assoc. dean Sch. Medicine, Sch. Dentistry, 1981—92. Mem. staff U. N.C. Hosps., mem. exec. com., 1974—98, sec., 1977—78, assoc. chief staff, 1981—92; mem. adv. panel on dentistry U.S Pharmacopial Conv., 1985—; sr. program cons. The Robert Wood Johnson Found., 1982—90. Author (with E.R. Costich): Fundamentals of Oral Surgery, 1971; author: (with Bell and Proffit) Surgical Correction of Dentofacial Deformities, 1980; author: (with W.R. Proffit) Surgical Orthodontic Treatment, 1990; author: (with M.R. Tucker, B.C. Terry, J.E. Van Sickels) Rigid Fixations for Maxillofacial Surgery, 1991; co-editor: Internat. Jour. Adult Orthodontics and Orthodontic Surgery, 1985—2002; asst. editor: Jour. Oral and Maxillofacial Surgery, 1993—; author (with W.R. Profit, R.P. Jr., and D. Sarver): Contemporary Treatment of Dentofacial Deformity, 2002; contbr. sci. articles to profl. jours. Bd. dirs. Am. Fund for Dental Health, 1978—86, v.p., 1982—85. Recipient Disting. Svc. award, Am. Fund Dental Health, 1987, Dental Found. N.C., 1981, John C. Brauer award for acad. distinction, U. N.C. Alumni Assn., 2000, Daniel M. Laskin award, 2002, Rsch. Excellence award, Oral and Maxillofacial Surgery Found., 2003. Mem.: AAAS, ADA, N.C. Assn. Oral and Maxillofacial Surgeons, Am. Assn. Oral and Maxillofacial Surgeons (gen. chmn. sci. sessions com. 1974—76, chmn. strategic planning com. 1990—96, Outstanding Svc. award as committeeman 1976, William Gies award 2000, Disting. Svc. award 2003), Chalmers J. Lyons Acad. Oral Surgery, Inst. Medicine of NAS, Internat. Assn. Dental Rsch. (pres. Ky. sect. 1970), N.C. Dental Soc., Sigma Xi, Omicron Kappa Upsilon, Sigma Zeta, Alpha Sigma Chi, Delta Tau Delta, Psi Omega. Roman Catholic. Home: 1506 Velma Rd Chapel Hill NC 27514-7601 Office: U NC Sch Dentistry Dept Oral/Maxillofacial Surgery Chapel Hill NC 27599-7450 Office Phone: 919-966-1126. Business E-Mail: ray_white@dentistry.unc.edu.

**WHITE, REBECCA E.,** advocate; b. Washington, Nov. 17, 1945; d. Edward and Anna Pendleton White. BS, D.C. Tchrs. Coll., 1971; postgrad., Pepperdine U., Malibu, Calif., 1993, Calif. State U., L.A., 2003—04. Cert. tchr., D.C., Calif. Tchr. English D.C. Pub. Schs., Washington, 1971-73; paralegal specialist U.S. Dept. Justice, Washington, 1973-81; adminstr. U.S. Dept. Vet. Affairs VA Med. Ctr., L.A., 1982-89, 94-96, Sepulveda, Calif., 1992-94; patient/employee advocate U.S. Dept. Vet. Affairs, L.A., 1982-89, 92-96; tchr. English L.A. Unified Sch. Dist., 1989-91, children's advocate, 1989—2005; tchr. English Inglewood (Calif.) Unified Sch. Dist. 1996-97, children's advocate, 1996—98; tchr. spl. edn. Gladstone St. Elem. Sch., Azusa, Calif., 2003—04; freelance writer, 2005—; tchr. English Mpls. Pub. Schs., 2005—. Cmty. advocate Baldwin Hills Cmty., L.A., 1983—2004; children's advocate L.A. County Schs., 2005—; mem. L.A. World Affairs Coun., 1999-2004; mem. Nat. Campaign For Tolerance, 2006-. Mem. NEA, Calif. Tchrs. Assn. Avocations: writing, hiking, entertaining, reading. E-mail: rebecca.white@mpls.k12.minn.us.

**WHITE, REBECCA HANNER,** dean, law educator; BA, Ea. Ky. U.; JD, U. Ky. Judicial law clerk to Chief Judge George C. Edwards Sixth Cir. U.S. Ct. Appeals; atty. Dinsmore & Shohl, Cincinnati; prof. U. Ga. Sch. Law, 1989—, assoc. provost and assoc. v.p. academic affairs, interim dean, 2003—04, dean, 2004—, J. Alton Hosch Prof. Law. Co-author: Employment Discrimination, 2002, Cases and Materials on Employment Discrimination, 2003; editl. bd. The Labor Law Jour. Recipient Josiah Meigs award, 2000, John C. O'Byrne Award, Woman of Distinction award, State Bar Ga. Younger Lawyers Div., 2004. Office: U Ga Sch Law Athens GA 30602 Office Phone: 706-542-7140. Office Fax: 706-542-5556. E-mail: rhwhite@uga.edu.

**WHITE, RHEA AMELIA,** library and information scientist; b. Utica, NY, May 6, 1931; d. John Raymond and Rhea Jane (Parry) White. BA, Pa. State U., 1953; MLS, Pratt Inst., Bklyn., 1965; postgrad., SUNY, Stony Brook, 1990-92. Rsch. fellow Parapsychology Lab. Duke U., Durham, NC, 1954-58; editor Jour. Am. Soc. Psychical Rsch., N.Y.C., 1959-62, 84-00, editor-in-chief, 2001—; libr. dept. psychiatry Maimonides Med. Ctr., Bklyn., 1965-67; dir. info. Am. Soc. Psychical Rsch., N.Y.C., 1965-80; reference libr. East Meadow (N.Y.) Pub. Libr., 1965-95; founder, dir. Parapsychology Sources of Info. Ctr., Dix Hills, NY, 1981-90; editor Rsch. in Parapsychology, Metuchen, NJ, 1981-85, Theta, Durham, NC, 1981-86; founder, editor Parapsychology Abstracts Internat., Dix Hills, 1983-89, Exceptional Human Experience, Dix Hills, 1990—; founder, producer PsiLine Database, Dix Hills, 1983—; mng. editor Advances in Parapsychol. Rsch., N.Y.C., 1977; founder, dir. Exceptional Human Experience Network, New Bern, 1990-94, 95—; with Exceptional Human Experience News, 1994—2002. Rsch. fellow Menninger

Found., Topeka, 1963-65; abstractor Psychol. Abstracts, Washington, 1967-91; cons. Scarecrow Press, Metuchen, NJ, 1980-85; referee Jour. Parapsychology, Durham, 1981-85; chmn., keynote spkr. conf. on women and parapsychology Parapsychology Found., Dublin, Ireland, 1991; keynote speaker Acad. Religion and Psychical Rsch. Conf., 1992; founder, editor EHE News, Dix Hills, 1994, New Bern, 1995—; instr. exceptional human experience course Portland (Oreg.) State U., 1999. Author: Parapsychology: Sources of Information, 1973, Surveys in Parapsychology, 1975, Parapsychology: New Sources of Information, 1990; (with M. Murphy) The Psychic Side of Sports, 1978; parapsychology book reviewer Libr. Jour., NYC, 1974-86, Reprint Bull., 1974-79, (with Michael Murphy) In the Zone, 1995; regional editor European Jour. Parapsychology, 1975-90; mem. editl. bd. Advances in Parapsychol. Rsch., 1980-85, Archaeus, 1985-93, 3 books on key aspects of the transformative potential of non-ordinary exceptional hum. experiences; contbr. over 100 articles to profl. jours. Recipient Hans Peter Luhn award Am. Soc. Info. Sci., N.Y.C. chpt., 1965. Mem.: Assn. Near-Death Studies, Acad. Religion and Psychical Rsch. (mem. bd. 1982—84, publs. com. 1982—97), Parapsychological Assn. (mem. coun. 1958, 1962—63, 1982—85, pres. 1984, dir. 1986, Lifetime Outstanding Rsch. award 1992, conf. spkr. 1993), Ctr. for Psychology and Social Change, Soc. for Anthropology of Consciousness, Internat. Assn. Religion and Parapsychology, Internat. Soc. for Study Subtle Energies and Energy Medicine, Found for Shamanic Studies, Penn State Alumni Assn. Coll. Liberal Arts. Avocations: hiking, gardening, animals, reading, listening to music. Home and Office: 414 Rockledge Rd New Bern NC 28562-9553 Office Phone: 252-636-8734. Personal E-mail: ehenwhite@cox.net.

**WHITE, RICHARD DEAN,** art conservator; b. Longview, Tex., June 11, 1938; s. Melvin Wesley and Agnes Young White; m. Sherrill McAlister (div.); 1 child, Eric Dean; m. Susan Downing, Nov. 20, 2000. BA, La. State U., 1960, MA, 1962; MFA, U. Cin., 1969. Conservation asst. Phyllis Hudson, Conservator, New Orleans, Margaret Watherston Whitney Mus. Modern Art, NYC; pvt. practice conservator of paintings San Antonio, New Orleans, Mobile, Ala. Mem.: Am. Inst. Conservation (cert.). Home: 262 Jackson Dr Mobile AL 36609 Office: Po Box 40338 Mobile AL 36640

**WHITE, RICHARD EDMUND,** marketing executive; b. Reading, Pa., June 8, 1944; s. Carl Marshall and Miriam Elizabeth (Curry) W.; m. Kristen Margaret Lloyd, June 17, 1967; children: Ross, Peter, Andrew. BS in Econs., U. Pa., 1967; MBA with distinction, U. Mich., 1968. Gen. mgr. mktg. H. J. Heinz Co., Pitts., 1970-81; dir. mktg. Seven Up Co., St. Louis, 1981-83; v.p. mktg. & sales Herr Foods, Inc., Nottingham, Pa., 1984—. Bd. dirs. Conard-Pyle Co. Chmn. fin. com. Sewickley Borough Coun., Pa., 1977—81; pres. So. Chester County Devel. Found., Jennersville, Pa., 1988—94, So. Chester County YMCA, West Grove, Pa., 1988—93, bd. mgrs., 1988—93, Avon Grove United Way, 1988—93, pres., 1988—93; chmn. So. Chester County Med. Ctr., 1988—2001, bd. dirs., 1988—2001, Brandywine YMCA Assn.; chmn. bd. dirs. Jenners Pond, 2001—, Health and Welfare Found. So. Chester County, pres.; chmn. Health and Welfare Found. of So. Cheser County. Mem. Am. Mgmt. Assn. (mktg. coun.). Republican. Avocations: physical fitness, reading. Home: 7 Sullivan Chase Dr Avondale PA 19311-9347 Office: Herr Foods Inc PO Box 300 Nottingham PA 19362-0300 Business E-Mail: richard.white@herrs.com.

**WHITE, RICHARD LEE, JR.,** secondary school educator; b. Canton, Ill., July 18, 1951; s. Richard Lee and Beverly Jean White; m. Janice Arlene Hobbs, July 20, 1974; children: Benjamin Patrick, Anne Victoria. BA summa cum laude, Augustana Coll., 1973; MA, Ill. State U., 1982. Tchr. Pekin Cmty. H.S., Pekin, Ill., 1973—, dept. chmn., social studies, 1993—; adj. instr. U. of St. Francis, Joliet, Ill., 1982—98. Adv. bd. to investigate possible change in type of city govt., Pekin, Ill., 1994—95. Recipient Cavanaugh Prize, Master's Thesis in History, Ill. State U., 1982, Citation for Achievement in Edn., Pekin C. of C., 1993, Those Who Excel Award of Recognition, Ill. State Bd. of Edn., Springfield, 1996, Outstanding Contbr. to Pekin Cmty. H.S., 1997. Mem.: Christian Educators Assn. Internat., Phi Beta Kappa, Akron. Episcopalian. Avocations: reading, gardening, classic films. Home: 2503 Willow St Pekin IL 61554-2545 Office: Pekin Community High School Dist 303 1903 Court St Pekin IL 61554-5295 Office Phone: 309-347-4101 6268 Office Fax: 309-477-4377. Personal E-mail: whitehouse@insightbb.com. E-mail: rwhite@pekinhigh.net.

**WHITE, RICHARD THOMAS,** radiologist; b. Binghamton, N.Y., May 10, 1941; s. William Joseph and Winifred (Murphy) W.; 1 child by previous marriage, Kevin Michael; m. Rory Lynn Leyman. BS, SUNY, Binghamton, 1967; DO, Chgo. Coll. Osteo. Medicine, 1972. Intern Bi County Hosp., Warren, Mich.; staff radiologist Bi-County Hosp., 1977-79; resident Detroit Hosp., Children's Hosp., Detroit, 1973-76; fellow Johns Hopkins Hosp., Balt., 1976; asst. prof. radiology Mich. State U., East Lansing, 1980-84, cons. ultra-sound rsch., 1980-83, cons. nuclear magnetic rsch., 1982-83; asst. prof. radiology U. Tex., Houston, 1984-85, U. Ill., Chgo., 1985-88; chief radiology VA Med. Ctr., Bath, NY, 1988—; clin. prof. radiology U. Rochester (N.Y.) Sch. Medicine and Dentistry, 1989—. Cons. varsity sports, 1980-84, handicapped athletes Spl. Olympics, Washington, 1978-84, Detroit Red Wings hockey team, 1977-84; cons. in radiology St. James Hosp., Hornell, N.Y., 1989—. Med. dir. Mich. Spl. Olympics Ctrl. Mich. U., Mt. Pleasant, 1977-84; bd. dirs. Spl. Olympics, Mich., 1980-84, N.Y. Spl. Olympics, 1996-2000; med. advisor Amateur Hockey Assn. USA, Colorado Springs, Colo., 1980-84. With U.S. Army, 1960-66; lt. col. USAR, 1990-96, ret. Recipient Outstanding Contbn. award Spl. Olympics, 1980; named Team Physician U.S. Nat. Hockey Team, Mich. Amateur Hockey Assn., 1979, 81, 83. Mem. AMA, Am. Osteo. Assn., Am. Osteo. Coll. Radiology, Assn. Mil. Physicians and Surgeons, Am. Osteopath Assn., Radiol. Soc. N.Am., Am. Coll. Radiology, Am. Inst. Ultrasound in Medicine, Am. Acad. Sci., Soc. Med. Cons. to U.S. Armed Forces, Kiwanis, Am. Legion. Office: Office Phone: 607-664-4408.

**WHITE, RICK,** lawyer, former congressman; b. Nov. 6, 1953; BA in Govt. and French, Dartmouth Coll., 1975; postgrad., Pantheon-Sorbonne; JD, Georgetown U., 1980. Mem. 104th to 105th Congresses from 1st Wash. dist., 1995—98; mem. house commerce com.; ptnr. Perkins Coie LLP, Seattle, 1999—2001; pres., CEO TechNet, Palo Alto, Calif., 2001—05. Bd. dir. Motricity. Founder Congl. Internet Caucus, Books for Kids. Republican. Mailing: TechNet 2600 E Bayshore Rd Palo Alto CA 94303

**WHITE, ROBERT BROWN,** medical educator; b. Ennis, Tex., Jan. 5, 1921; s. Robert Brown and Willia Elizabeth (Latimer) W.; m. Jimmie Estelle Sims, Oct. 18, 1942; children: Robert B., Canelia White Layton, Margaret White Gilbert. BS, Tex. A & M Coll., 1941; MD, U. Tex., 1944; cert., Western New Eng. Psychoanalytic Inst., 1959. Intern Phila. (Pa.) Gen. Hosp., 1944-45; psychiat. residency John Sealy Hosp., Galveston, Tex., 1945-46, 48-49; psychiatry fellow Austen Riggs Ctr., Stockbridge, Mass., 1949-51, staff psychiatrist, 1951-62; assoc. prof. U. Tex. Med. Br., Galveston, 1962-67, prof., 1967—, Marie Gale prof. of psychiatry, 1981-93; prof. emeritus, 1993—; tng. analyst New Orleans (La.) Psychoanalytic Inst., 1966-76 Tng. analyst Houston-Galveston Psychoanalytic Inst., 1974-94; analyst emeritus, 1994—. Author: Elements of Psychopathology, 1975; contbr. chpts. to books and articles to profl. jours. Capt. U.S. Army, 1946-48. Recipient David Rapaport prize Western New Eng. Psychoanalytic Inst., New Haven, 1959; Ohio State award Ohio State Univ., 1976. Fellow Am. Psychiat. Assn., Am. Coll. Psychiatrists, Am. Coll. Psychoanalysts (bd. regents 1988-91); mem. Am. Psychoanalytic Assn., Alpha Omega Alpha. Democrat. Avocations: photography, carpentry. Home: 8523 Thackery St apt 7008 Dallas TX 75225-3960 Office: Univ Tex Med Br Galveston TX 77550

**WHITE, ROBERT EDWARD,** think-tank executive; b. Melrose, Mass., Sept. 21, 1926; s. Edward V. and Emily G. (McGuire) W.; m. MaryAnne Cahill, June 4, 1955; children: Christopher, Kevin, Claire, MaryLouise, Laura. BA, St. Michael's Coll., Winooski, Vt., 1952, DHL (hon.), 1978; MA, Tufts U., 1954; DHL (hon.), Simmons Coll., 1985. Joined Fgn. Svc., Dept. State; dir. Latin Am. Peace Corps, Washington, 1968-70; dep. chief mission Am. Embassy, Managua, Nicaragua, 1970-72, Bogota, Colombia, 1972-75;

dep. rep. Orgn. Am. States, Washington, 1975-77; US amb. to Paraguay US Dept. State, Asuncion, 1977-79, US amb. to El Salvador San Salvador, 1979-81; sr. assoc. Carnegie Endowment for Internat. Peace, Washington, 1981-83; prof. internat. rels. Simmons Coll., Boston, 1983-85; pres. Ctr. Internat. Policy, Washington, 1985—. Pres.'s spl. rep. Inter-Am. Conf. on Edn., Sci. and Culture, 1977-79. Contbr. numerous articles to Commonweal, Atlantic, N.Y. Times. With USN, 1944-46; PTO. Fulbright scholar U. Bristol, Eng., 1953. Mem. Fgn. Svc. Assn., Fund for Constl. Govt. (bd. dirs.), Cosmos Club. Office: Ctr for Internat Policy 1717 Massachusetts Ave NW Washington DC 20036-2102

**WHITE, ROBERT I.,** lawyer; b. Ventnor City, NJ, 1951; BA with honors, Haverford U., 1974; JD with honors, George Washington U., 1977. Bar: DC 1977, registered: US Ct. Appeals (5th cir.), US Ct. Appeals (8th cir.), US Ct. Appeals (10th cir.), US Ct. Appeals, (DC cir.). Atty., Office of Gen. Counsel Fed. Trade Commn., 1977—80; ptnr. Squire, Sanders & Dempsey LLP, Washington, chmn., Energy Practice Group. Mem.: Fed. Energy Bar Assn., ABA. Office: Squire Sanders & Dempsey LLP 1201 Pennsylvania Ave NW PO Box 407 Washington DC 20044-0407 Office Phone: 202-626-6285. Office Fax: 202-626-6780. Business E-Mail: rwhite@ssd.com.

**WHITE, ROBERT JAMES,** retired columnist; b. Mpls., Nov. 6, 1927; s. Robert Howard and Claire Lillian (Horner) W.; m. Adrienne Hoffman, Sept. 24, 1955; children: Claire, Pamela, Sarah. BS, U.S. Naval Acad., 1950. V.p. White Investment Co., Mpls., 1957-67; editl. writer Mpls. Tribune, 1967-73, assoc. editor, 1973-82; editor editl. pages Mpls. Star Tribune, 1982-93, columnist, 1993-95, contbg. columnist, 1996—. Recipient cert. of excellence Overseas Press Club, 1981. Mem. Coun. Fgn. Rels., Mpls. Club. Congregationalist. Home: Summit House 400 Groveland Ave #2212 Minneapolis MN 55403 E-mail: rjw823@aol.com.

**WHITE, ROBERT JOEL,** lawyer; b. Chgo., Nov. 1, 1946; s. Melvin and Margaret (Hoffman) W.; m. Gail Janet Edenson, June 29, 1969 (div. Dec. 1982); m. Penelope K. Bloch, Dec. 22, 1985. BS in Accountancy, U. Ill., 1968; JD, U. Mich., 1972. Bar: Calif. 1972, N.Y. 1985, U.S. Dist. Ct. (ctrl., ea., so. dists.) Calif. 1972, U.S. Ct. Appeals (9th cir.) 1978, U.S. Ct. Appeals (5th cir.) 1983, U.S. Ct. Appeals (6th cir.) 1984, U.S. Supreme Ct. 1977. Staff auditor Haskin & Sells, Chgo., 1968-69; assoc. O'Melveny & Myers, L.A., 1972-79, ptnr., 1980-2001, chair reorgn. and restructuring dept., 1986—; CEO O'Melvey Cons. LLC, 2001—. Vis. lectr. U. Mich. Law Sch., Ann Arbor, 1986; lectr. Profl. Edn. Sys., Inc., Dallas, 1987, L.A., 1987, 89, Phoenix, 1990, Practicing Law Inst., San Francisco and N.Y.C., 1989-93, 2001-, Southwestern Legal Found., Dallas, 1991, UCLA Bankruptcy Inst., 1993, UCLA, 1993; mem. L.A. Productivity Commn., 1993-96. Contbr. articles to profl. jours. Active Constl. Rights Found., 1980—; active Am. Cancer Soc., 1989—, mem. L.A. bd. dirs., 1995—, vice chair, partnership com., 2003-; chair chpt. 11 com. Nat. Bankruptcy Conf., 2004-. Fellow Am. Coll. Bankruptcy; mem. ABA (litig. sect., mem. comml. law and bankruptcy com. 1972—), L.A. County Bar Assn. (comml. law and bankruptcy sect., chmn. fed. cts. com. 1981-82, exec. com. 1982—), Assn. Bus. Trial Lawyers (bd. govs. 1983-85), Fin. Lawyers Conf. (bd. govs. 1986—, pres. 1990-91), Am. Bankruptcy Inst. Avocations: skiing, running, history. Office: O'Melveny & Myers 1999 Ave of Stars Los Angeles CA 90067-6035 Office Phone: 310-246-8485. Business E-Mail: rwhite@omm.com.

**WHITE, ROBERT LEE,** electrical engineer, educator; b. Plainfield, NJ, Feb. 14, 1927; s. Claude and Ruby Hemsworth Emerson (Levick) W.; m. Phyllis Lillian Arlt, June 14, 1952; children: Lauren A., Kimberly A., Christopher L., Matthew P. BA in Physics, Columbia U., 1949, MA, 1951, PhD, 1954. Assoc. head atomic physics dept. Hughes Rsch. Labs., Malibu, Calif., 1954-61; head magnetics dept. Gen. Tel. and Electronics Rsch. Lab., Palo Alto, Calif., 1961-63; prof. elec. engring., materials sci. and engring. Stanford U., Palo Alto, 1963, chmn. elec. engring. dept., 1981-86, William E. Ayer prof. elec. engring., 1985-88, prof. emeritus, 1988—; exec. dir. The Exploratorium, San Francisco, 1987-89; dir. Inst. for Electronics in Medicine, 1973-87, Stanford Ctr. for Rsch. on Info. Storage Materials, 1991—2003. Initial ltd. ptnr. Mayfield Fund, Mayfield II and Alpha II Fund, Rainbow Co-Investment Ptnrs., Halo Ptnrs.; vis. prof. Tokyo U., 1975, Nat. U. Singapore, 2002; Sony sabbatical chair, 1994; pres. Magarray Inc., 2005—; cons. in field. Author: (with K.A. Wickersheim) Magnetism and Magnetic Materials, 1965, Basic Quantum Mechanics, 1967; contbr. numerous articles to profl. jours. With USN, 1945-46. Fellow Guggenheim Oxford U., 1969-70, Canton Hosp., Swiss Fed. Inst. Tech., Zurich, 1977-78, Christensen fellow Oxford U., 1986, IEEE Magnetics Soc. Disting. lectr., 1998. Fellow IEEE, Am. Phys. Soc.; mem. Sigma Xi, Phi Beta Kappa. Home: 450 El Escarpado Stanford CA 94305-8431 Office: Stanford U Dept Material Sci Engr Stanford CA 94305 Business E-Mail: white@ee.stanford.edu.

**WHITE, ROBERT LESLIE GORDON, JR.,** aerospace transportation executive; b. Orange, NJ, Dec. 20, 1941; s. Robert L.G. and Gertrude Marie (Wilson) W.; m. Joan Adam, May 9, 1970; children: Robert L.G. III, Sonya Lynn. BS in Metallurgical Engring., Lafayette Coll., 1964. Sr. engr. Crucible Steel Co., 1964-68; various positions Curtiss-Wright Corp., Woodridge, NJ, 1968-76, plant mgr. nuclear facility, 1976-80, dir. gas turbine overhaul, 1980-83; v.p., gen. mgr. Curtiss-Wright/Marquette, Inc., Fountain Inn, SC, 1983-87; pres. GEC-Marconi Aerospace Inc., Whippany, NJ, 1987-94, Breeze-Eastern, Union, NJ, 1994-98; pres. aerospace products group Transtechnology Corp., Union, NJ, 1998—2003, pres., CEO, 2003—. Office: Transtechnology Corp 700 Liberty Ave Union NJ 07083-8198

**WHITE, ROBERT MARSHALL,** retired physicist, retired educator, retired government official, consultant; b. Reading, Pa., Oct. 2, 1938; s. Carl M. and Miriam E. White; m. Sara Tolles; children: Victoria, Jonathan. BS in Physics, MIT, 1960; PhD, Stanford U., 1964. Vis. scientist Osaka (Japan) U., 1963; NSF postdoctoral fellow U. Calif., Berkeley 1965-66; asst prof physics Stanford U., Palo Alto, Calif., 1966-70; NSF sr. postdoctoral fellow Cambridge U., England, 1970-71; mgr. solid state rsch. area XEROX PARC, 1971-78, mgr. storage tech., 1978-83, prin. scientist, 1983-84; v.p. rsch. and tech. Control Data Corp. Data Storage Products Group, Mpls., 1984-86; chief tech. officer, v.p. rsch. and engring. Control Data Corp., Mpls., 1986-89; v.p., dir. advanced computer techs. Microelectronics & Computer Tech. Corp., Austin, Tex., 1989-90; undersec. of commerce for tech. Dept. Commerce, Washington, 1990-93; prof., head dept. elec.l and computer engring. Carnegie Mellon U., Pitts., 1993-99, prof., dir. Data Storage Sys. Ctr., 1999—2004, prof. emeritus, 2004—; cons. prof. materials sci. & engring. Stanford U., 2004—. Vis. scientist Ecole Polytechnique, Paris, 1976-78, U. Pernambuco, Brazil, 1978, Max Planck Inst., Stuttgart, 1981; cons. prof. applied physics Stanford U., 1982-93; adj. prof. physics U. Minn., 1987-89; bd. dirs. Found. Nat. Medals Sci. and Tech., Silicon Graphics, STMicroelectronics, ENSCO; mem. sci. adv. bd. Data Storage Inst., Singapore, 2002—; mem. adv. bd. Pacific Enterprise Capital, LLC; mem. Nat. Adv. Com. on Semicondrs., 1990-92, Mfg. Forum, 1991, Nat. Critical Techs. Panel, 1990-91. Author: Quantum Theory of Magnetism, 1970 (Russian transl., 1972, Polish transl., 1979); Long Range Order in Solids, 1979 (Russian transl., 1982); Quantum Theory of Magnetism, 1983; Introduction to Magnetic Recording, 1985. Contbr. articles to profl. jours. Recipient Alexander von Humboldt prize, Fed. Republic of Germany, 1981. Fellow AAAS, IEEE (disting. lectr. Magnetics Soc., mem. editl. bd. SPECTRUM, IEEE Disting. Pub. Svc. award 1993), Am. Phys. Soc. (George E. Pake prize 2004); mem. NAE, NRC (mem. nat. materials adv. bd., chmn. com. magnetic materials 1984, material sci. and engring., vice chmn. IUPAP commn. on magnetism), Conf. Magnetism and Magnetic Materials (adv. com. 1976-78, 80-95, program com. 1973-75, chmn. 1981, chmn. Intermag. Conf. 1991), Internat. Conf. Magnetism (program chmn. 1985). Office: Carnegie Mellon U Elec & Computer Engring Dep Pittsburgh PA 15213-3890 Business E-Mail: white@ece.cmu.edu.

**WHITE, ROBERT MAYER,** meteorologist; b. Boston, Feb. 13, 1923; s. David and Mary (Winkeller) W.; m. Mavis Seagle, Apr. 18, 1948; children: Richard Harry, Edwina Janet. BA, Harvard, 1944; MS, Mass. Inst. Tech., 1949, Sc.D., 1950; D.Sc., L.I. U., 1976; D.Sc. (hon.), Rensselaer Poly. Inst.,

1977, U. Wis., Milw., 1978; ScD (hon.), U. Bridgeport, 1984, U. R.I., 1986, Clarkson U.; PhD (hon.), Johns Hopkins U., 1982, Drexel U., 1985, Ill. Inst. Tech., 1994. Project scientist Air Force Cambridge Research Center, 1950-58, chief meteorol. devel. lab., 1958-59; asso. dir. research dept. Travelers Ins. Co., 1959-60; pres. Travelers Research Center, Inc., 1960-63; chief U.S. Weather Bur., 1963-65; administr. Environ. Sci. Services Adminstrn., 1965-70, NOAA, 1970-77; pres. Joint Oceanographic Inst., Inc., 1977-79; chmn. Climate Research Bd., exec. officer Nat. Acad. Scis., 1977-79; Washington; administr. Nat. Research Council, 1979-80; pres. Univ. Corp. Atmospheric Research, 1980-83, Nat. Acad. Eng., 1983-95; Karl T. Compton lectr. MIT, Cambridge, 1995-96; sr. fellow Univ. Corp. Atmospheric Rsch., 1995—. Sr. fellow H. John Heinz III Ctr. for Sci., Econs. and Environment, 1996—2000; pres. Wash. Adv. Group, 1996—. Author: articles in field; mem. editl. bd.: Am. Soc. Engring. Edn. Jour. Bd. overseers Harvard U., 1977—79; mem. vis. com. Kennedy Sch. Govt., Harvard U.; bd. dirs. Resources for the Future, 1980—. Capt. USAF, World War II. Decorated Legion of Honor France; recipient Godfrey L. Cabot award, Aero Club Boston, 1966, Cleveland Abbe award, Am. Meteorol. Soc., 1969, Jesse L. Rosenberger medal, U. Chgo., 1971, Rockefeller Pub. Svc. award, 1974, David B. Stone award, New Eng. Aquarium, 1975, Neptune award, Am. Oceanic Orgn., 1977, Matthew Fontaine Maury award, Smithsonian Instn., 1976, Internat. Conservation award, Nat. Wildlife Fedn., 1976, Internat. Meteorol. Orgn. prize, 1980, Tyler prize for Environ. Achievement, U. Calif., 1992, Vannevar Bush award, Nat. Sci. Bd., 1998, Centenary medal, Australia, 2003, Milennium award, Australian Acad. Engring., 2003. Fellow: Am. Acad. Arts and Scis., Australian Acad. Tech. Scis. and Engring., Am. Geophys. Union, World Acad. Art and Scis., AAAS, UCAR (sr.), Am. Meteorol. Soc. (coun. 1965—67, 1977—, pres. 1980, Charles Franklin Brooks award1978); mem.: Royal Acad. Engring. (U.K.), Russian Acad. Engring., Royal Acad. Engring. (hon.), Engring. Acad. Japan (fgn. assoc.), Am. Philos. Soc., Finnish Acad. Tech. (fgn.), Nat. Action Coun. Minorities in Engring. Inc., Coun. Fgn. Rels., Marine Tech. Soc., NAE (coun. 1977, pres. 1983—95), Cosmos Club (Washington). Home: Somerset House II 5610 Wisconsin Ave Apt 1506 Bethesda MD 20815-4439 Office: 1275 K St NW Ste 1025 Washington DC 20005-4089 Office Phone: 202-682-0164. Business E-Mail: rmw@theadvisorygroup.com.

**WHITE, ROBERT STEPHEN,** retired physics professor; b. Ellsworth, Kans., Dec. 28, 1920; s. Byron F. and Sebina (Leighty) White; m. Freda Marie Bridgewater, Aug. 30, 1942; children: Nancy Lynn, Margaret Diane, John Stephen, David Bruce. AB, Southwestern Coll., 1942, DSc (hon.), 1971; MS, U. Ill., 1943; PhD, U. Calif., Berkeley, 1951. Physicist Lawrence Radiation Lab., Berkeley, Livermore, Calif., 1948-61; head dept. particles and fields Space Physics Lab. Aerospace Corp., El Segundo, Calif., 1962-67; physics prof. U. Calif., Riverside, 1967-92, prof. emeritus physics dept., rsch. physicist, 1992—; dir. Inst. Geophysics and Planetary Physics, 1967-92, chmn. dept. physics, 1970-73. Lectr. U. Calif., Berkeley, 1953—54, Berkeley, 1957—59. Author: Space Physics, 1970, Why Science?, 1998, Energy for the Public: The Case for Increased Nuclear Fission Energy, 2006; contbr. articles to profl. jours. Officer USNR, 1944—46. Grantee, NASA, NSF, USAF, numerous others; Sr. Postdoctoral fellow, NSF, 1961—62. Fellow: AAAS, Am. Phys. Soc. (mem. exec. com. 1972—74); mem.: AAUP, Am. Astron. Soc., Am. Geophys. Union. Home: 5225 Austin Rd Santa Barbara CA 93111-2905 Personal E-mail: stevewhite2@cox.net.

**WHITE, ROBERTA LEE,** financial analyst; b. Denver, Sept. 18, 1946; d. Harold Tindall and Araminta (Campbell) Bangs; m. Lewis Paul White, Jr., Jan. 23, 1973 (div. Sept. 1974). BA cum laude, Linfield Coll., 1976; postgrad., Lewis and Clark Coll. Lic. tax preparer, Oreg. Office mgr. Multnomah County Auditor, Portland, Oreg., 1977-81; rsch. asst. Dan Goldy and Assocs., Portland, 1981-83; regional asst. Vocat. Rehab., Eugene, Oreg., 1983-85; internal auditor Multnomah County, Portland, 1985-89; cons. Portland, 1989-91; fin. analyst City of Portland, 1991-93; comptr. Wordsmith Svc., Portland, 1993-97; fin. analyst City of Portland, 1997—. Mem. Com. for Implementation of the ADA, Portland, 1991—93. Treas. Mary Wendy Roberts for Sec. of State, Portland, 1992, Re-Elect Mary Wendy Roberts, Portland, 1990, Elect Hank Miggins Com., 1994; mem. Oreg. Women's Polit. Caucus, Portland, 1982-85, City Club, Portland, 1978-81. Democrat. Mem. Disciples Of Christ. Avocations: reading, hiking, opera, symphony, ballet. Home: 6685 W Burnside # 336 Portland OR 97210 Office: City of Portland Office of Mgmt/Fin Facil Svc Divsn Rm 1204 1120 SW 5th Ave Portland OR 97204-1912

**WHITE, RON,** comedian; b. Fritch, Tex., Dec. 18, 1956; Comedian Blue Collar Comedy Tour, 2000—03, 'Drunk in Public' Tour. Comedian (CDs) Drunk in Public, 2003, (films) Blue Collar Comedy Tour: The Movie, 2003, Blue Collar Comedy Tour Rides Again, 2004, (TV specials) Comedy Central Presents: Ron White, 2003, comedian, prodr. (videos) Ron White: They Call Me Tater Salad, 2004.*

**WHITE, RONALD JOSEPH,** biomedical researcher, physiologist, educator; b. Opelousas, La., Dec. 4, 1940; s. John Wesley and Alma Louise (LaSalle) White; m. Margaret Helen Launey, June 8, 1963; children: Joseph LaSalle, Angela Alma, Margaret Leslie. BS in Chemistry, U. S.W. La., 1963; PhD in Phys. Chemistry, U. Wis., 1968. NSF postdoctoral fellow in theoretical chemistry U. Oxford, England, 1967-68; rsch. assoc. Bell Tel. Labs., Murray Hill, NJ, 1968-70; from asst. prof. to assoc. prof. math. U. S.W. La., Lafayette, 1970—76, prof. math., dir. Univ. Honors Program, 1976—80; rsch. assoc. dept. physiology and biophysics U. Miss. Med. Ctr., Jackson, 1973-75; sr. scientist GE Co./Mgmt. and Tech. Svcs. Co., Washington and Houston, 1980-85; chief scientist Life/Biomed. Scis. and Applications Divsn. NASA, Washington, 1985—96; rsch. prof. physiology Uniformed Svcs. U. Health Scis., Bethesda, Md., 1985—96; prof. dept. otorhinolaryngology Baylor Coll. Medicine, Houston, 1996—2003; assoc. dir. Nat. Space Biomed. Rsch. Inst., 1997—2003; sr. fellow Univs. Space Rsch. Assn., Houston, 2003—, V.p. Ann. Gifted and Talented Students, La., 1977—80; pres. La. Collegiate Honors Coun., 1978—79. Editor (assoc. life scis.): Simulation, 1974—75; editor: (spl.) Medicine and Sci. in Sports and Exercise, 1996; contbr. numerous chpts. to books, papers to profl. jours. Recipient NASA traineeship, 1963—66, award, Am. Inst. Chemists, 1963, Disting. Prof. award, 1978, Med. Info. Processing Best Paper award, 15th ann. Hawaii Internat. Conf. on Systems Sci., 1982, Hon. Mem. award Soc. NASA Flight Surgeons, 1992, Exceptional Achievement medal, NASA, 1992; fellow, Woodrow Wilson Found., 1963. Mem.: Internat. Soc. Computational Biology, Internat. Acad. Astronautics (bd. trustees 1997—, chair life scis. 2001—, commr. space life scis. 2001—03, Luigi Napolitano Lit. award 1996), Am. Soc. Gravitational and Space Biology (charter mem.), Am. Phys. Soc., Aerospace Med. Assn., Sigma Xi (rsch. award 1976), Phi Kappa Phi. Home: 1303 Primrose Ln Seabrook TX 77586-4718 Office: USRA Divsn Space Life Scis 3600 Bay Area Blvd Houston TX 77058 Office Phone: 281-244-2025. Business E-Mail: white@dsls.usra.edu.

**WHITE, RONALD LEON,** financial management consultant; b. West York, Pa., July 14, 1930; s. Clarence William and Grace Elizabeth (Gingerich) W.; m. Estheranne Wieder, June 16, 1951; children: Bradford William, Clifford Allen, Erick David. BS in Econs, U. Pa., 1952, MBA, 1957. Cost analysis supr. Air Products & Chem. Corp., Allentown, Pa., 1957-60; cost control mgr. Mack Trucks, Inc., Allentown, 1960-64; mgmt. cons. Peat, Marwick, Mitchell & Co., Phila., 1964-66; mgr. profit planning Monroe, The Calculator Co. (divsn. Litton Industries), Orange, NJ, 1966-67, contr., 1967-68; v.p. fin. Bus. Sys. Group of Litton Industries, Beverly Hills, Calif., 1968-70; pres. Royal Typewriter Co. divsn., Hartford, Conn., 1970-73; exec. v.p., COO, treas., dir. Tenna Corp., Cleve., 1973-75, pres., dir. 1975-77; v.p. fin. Arby's, Inc., Youngstown, Ohio, 1978-79; exec. v.p., dir. Roxbury Am., Inc., 1979-81; v.p. fin., treas. Royal Crown Cos., Inc., Atlanta and Miami Beach, Fla., 1981-86, TDS Healthcare Sys. Corp., Atlanta, 1987-88; v.p. Corp. Fin. Assocs., Atlanta, 1988-90; prin. The Janelle Co., Atlanta, 1991—. Vice chmn. Ga. Mental Health, Mental Retardation, Substance Abuse Regional Bd. #6, 1994-2002, chmn. leadership coun., 1999-2000; v.p. and dir. Ga. Alliance for Mentally Ill, 1997-2003; instr. acctg. Wharton Sch. U. Pa., 1952-53, instr. industry, 1953-54. Deacon area United Ch. of Christ. Lt. USNR, 1954-57.

Mem. Am. Mgmt. Assn., Inst. Mgmt. Accts., Nat. Assn. Corp. Dirs., Fin. Execs. Internat., Acacia, Masons, Rotary. Office: The Janelle Co 2362 Kingsgate Ct Atlanta GA 30338-5931 Office Phone: 770-451-8763. Personal E-mail: rlwcfo@mindspring.com.

**WHITE, RONNIE L.,** state supreme court justice; b. St. Louis, Mo., May 31, 1953; m. Sylvia White. AA, St. Louis C.C., 1977; BA, St. Louis U., 1979; JD, U. Mo., Kansas City, 1983. Bar: Mo. Law intern Jackson County Prosecutors Office; legal asst. U.S. Def. Mapping Agy.; trial atty. Office of Pub. Defender; mem. Mo. Ho. of Reps., 1989-93; judge Mo. Ct. Appeals, 1994; spl. judge Mo. Supreme Ct., 1994-95, justice, 1994-95, assoc. justice, 1995—, chief justice, 2003—05. Adj. faculty Washington U. Sch. Law, 1997—. first African-Am. Supreme Ct. justice of Mo. Office: PO Box 150 Jefferson City MO 65102-0150*

**WHITE, ROY BERNARD,** performing arts association administrator; b. Cin. s. Maurice and Anna (Rudin) W.; m. Sally White, June 17, 1951; children: Maurice, Barbara Dee, Daniel Robert. BA, U. Cin., 1949. Sales staff Twentieth Century Fox Films, Cin.; pres. Mid-States Theatres; dir. Nat. Assn. Theatre Owners, nat. pres., exec. com., chmn. bd. Mem. film adv. panel Ohio Arts Coun.; bd. dirs. Will Rogers Meml. Fund, Found. Motion Picture Pioneers, Inc.; mem. media arts panel Nat. Endowment for Arts. Served with USAAF, 1944-45. Named Exhibitor of Year Internat. Film Importers and Distbrs. Am. Mem. Nat. Assn. Theater Owners (pres.), Am. Film Inst. (trustee 1972-75, exec. com. 1972-75, trustee emeritus), Fedn. Motion Picture Pioneers (v.p.), Masons, Queen City Racquet, Amberley Village (Ohio) Tennis Club (pres. 1972-73), Bankers Club, Quail Creek Country Club, Bay Colony Country Club, Bay Colony Golf Club, Morrings Country Club. Home: 1274 Waggle Way Naples FL 34108-1994 Personal E-mail: sallyw3140@aol.com

**WHITE, SARAH JOWILLIARD,** retired counselor; b. Oxford, N.C., Sept. 1, 1921; d. John Hiriam and Emma (Redfern) Isham; m. Hamilton B. Carson, Sept. 20, 1945 (div. 1968); 1 child, Lynne Denise. Student, Bennett Coll., 1939-42, Cornell U., 1979-82; BA, CCNY, 1973. Clk. N.Y. Dept. Law, N.Y.C., 1948—53; auditor U.S. Fed. Govt. Svc., N.Y.C., 1955—62; postal clk. U.S. Govt., Mt. Vernon, NY, 1963—66; prin. N.Y. State Dept. Labor, N.Y.C., 1966—88, ret., 1988; youth organizer N.Y. State Careerists Soc., Inc., N.Y.C., 1989—. Youth and employment counselor Women in Cmty. Svc., Nat. Coun. Negro Women, Manhattan sect., NYC, 1983—. Vol. Advanced Vocation Edn. Day, Albany, N.Y., 1988; vol., coord. Decade of the Youth, N.Y.C., 1989-90; corres. sec. Lower East Side United Neighbors, N.Y.C., 1989. Recipient Youth award, 1987, Recognition award, 1987, Internat. Assn. Pers. Employees Youth award, Plaque for Women in Cmty. Svcs., Outstanding Vol. Svc. award Gov. Mario Cuomo, 1994, Outstanding Vol. award, 1991-92, Outstanding Vol. award Women in Cmty. Svc., 1994, Cert. Appreciation, 1995, Appreciation award South Bronx Job Alumni chpt., 1995, Nat. Coun. Negro Women Recognition award, 1996; named one of N.Y.'s Finest Vols. Women in Cmty. Svcs. Mag., 1994, Woman on the Move, Cable TV, 1994, Outstanding Recognition award Women in Cmty. Svcs., 1996, Joint Action in Cmty. Svc. award, 1996, Nat. N.E. Regional award Women in Cmty. Svcs., 1997, Youth Recognition award Yale U., New Haven, 1997, award Joint Action in Cmty. Svc., 1997, N.E. Regional Pres. Vol. award, 1998, JAC Recognition award, 1998, Horthers Regional award, 1998, Nat. Coun. Negro Women Pres.'s award, 1998, 99, Cert., Women in Cmty. Svc. Northeast Regional Pres. award, 1998, Nat. Coun. Negro Women Pres. award, 1998, Joint Action Cmty. Svc. award, 1998, 99, Nat. Pres.'s award Women in Cmty. Svc., 1999, Samuel and May Rudin Cmty. Svc. award NYU, 1999. Mem.: NAFE, Internat. Assn. Pers. Employees, Nat. Coun. Negro Women (chairperson, Achievement award 1988—90, Cmty. Svc. award 2001, Legacy award 2002—05), Assn. U.S. Govt. Job Corps (Alumni Recognition award 1995), N.Y. Careerists Soc. (sec., Merit award 1988), Black Alumni CCNY (pub. rels. com., Outstanding award 1989). Democrat. 7th Day Sabbath Keeper House of God. Avocations: reading, writing, music.

**WHITE, SHANON KATHLEEN,** accountant, consultant; b. Hackensack, NJ, July 25, 1953; d. Patrick William Carr, Trudy McFarland; m. Chester Haines White, II; 1 child, Tiffany. Associate of Arts in Accounting, Community College of Aurora, Aurora, Colorado, 1982—84. Acct. Denver Cascade, Inc, Denver, 1984—86, MDC, Inc, Denver, 1986—86; owner Jacqueline, Too, Denver, 1986—86; contr. Michael's Constrn. Co., Kans. City, Kans., 1987—87; acctg. mgr., sys. mgr. Walton Constrn. Co, Inc, Kans. City, Mo., 1987—93; owner Profit Enhancement Profls., Olathe, Kans., 1993—98; acctg. mgr. Mark One Electric Co, Inc, Kans. City, Mo., 1998—99; owner Shanon White Cons., Kans. City, Mo., 1999—. Selection Com. Kans. City Fairness in Constrn. Bd., Kans. City, 1991—92; Bd. Pres. Greater Kans. City NAWIC Scholarship Found., Kans. City, 1992—95. Treas. Romanelli West Homes Assoc., Kans. City, 1999—2002. Mem.: Nat. Assn. of Women in Constrn. (pres. 1991—92), Greater Kansas City Timberline Users Group (organizer, local coord. 2001—). Avocation: Traveling, Dining, Reading. Office: Shanon White Consulting 10500 Meadow Ln Leawood KS 66206 Business E-Mail: scarrwhite@earthlink.net.

**WHITE, SHARON,** elementary school educator; b. Nov. 25, 1959; BS, So. Ill. U., 1981, MS, 1984; AA, Rend Lake Jr. Coll., 1978; EdS, Ea. Ill. U., 1993. Cert. elem. tchr., spl. edn. tchr., Ill. Tchr. Bluford (Ill.) Grade Sch., 1981-85; administr. Wayne City (Ill.) Unit 100, 1985—, tchr. Coord. sch. and community alcohol and drug program. Mem. adv. So. Cen. Spl. Olympics; co-dir. acteens leader vacation Bible sch. Wayne City First Bapt. Ch., 1989-90; mem. pers. com. Wayne City Youth Ctr.; mem. Wayne County Transition Com. Mem. NAFE, Delta Kappa Gamma, Pi Lambda Theta. Home: RR 2 Box 53A Cisne IL 62823-9527

**WHITE, SHAUN ROGER,** Olympic athlete, professional snowboarder, professional skateboarder; b. San Diego, Sept. 3, 1986; s. Kathy and Roger White. Profl. snowboarder Burton Snowboarding team, 1999—; skateboarder Tony Hawk Gigantic Skatepark Tour, 2002; profl. Skateboarder, 2003—; designer The White Collection. Snowboarder US Olympic Team, Torino, Italy, 2006. Actor: (films) The White Album, 2004. Named Sports-Choice Action Sports, Teen Choice Awards, 2006; recipient ESPY Award Best Action Sports Athlete, 2003, 2006, ESPY award Best US Olympian, 2006. Achievements include being the youngest snowboarder to win the US Open Slopestyle Championship, 2004; being the first athlete to compete in both Winter and Summer X Games, 2003; winning the gold medal at Winter X Games, Slopestyle, 2003-2006, Halfpipe, 2003, 2006; winning the gold metal at Summer X Games, Vert, 2005; winning all 5 Grand Prix Superpipes, 2005-2006; winning a gold metal at Torino Olympic Games, Men's Halfpipe, 2006. Office: c/o USSA Box 100 1500 Kearns Blvd Park City UT 84060*

**WHITE, SHELBY,** art association administrator; m. Leon Levy. BA, Mount Holyoke Coll.; MA, Columbia U. Chmn. Shelby White-Leon Levy Prog. for Archaeol. Publs., 1997—. Mem. Cultural Property Adv. Com., 2000. Named one of Top 200 Collectors, ARTnews Mag., 2004, 2006. Avocation: Collector of Antiquities. Office: Semitic Mus Harvard U 6 Divinity Ave Cambridge MA 02138 Office Phone: 617-495-9317. E-mail: info@whitelevy.org.*

**WHITE, STANLEY ARCHIBALD,** electrical engineer, researcher; b. Providence, Sept. 25, 1931; s. Clarence Archibald White and Lou Ella (Givens) Arford; m. Edia María Castán-Benítez, June 6, 1956; children: Dianne, Stanley Jr., Paul, John. BSEE, Purdue U., 1957, MSEE, 1959, PhD in Elec. and Aero. Engring. Scis., 1965. Registered profl. engr., Ind., Calif. Engr. Rockwell Internat., Anaheim, Calif., 1959-68, mgr., 1968-84, sr. scientist, 1984-90; pres. Signal Processing and Controls Engring. Corp. 1990—2000; pvt. practice San Clemente, Calif., 2000—. Lectr. in elec. engring. U. Calif., 1959-84, adj. prof., 1984-97; cons. and lectr. in field; bd. dirs. Asilomar Signals, Systems and Computers Conf. Corp., 1980-82. Contbr. chpts. to books; contbr. articles to encys. and profl. jours. With USAF, 1951-55. N.Am. Aviation Sci. Engring. fellow, 1963-65; recipient Disting. Lectr. award Nat. Electronics Conf., Chgo., 1973, Engr. of Yr. award Orange

County (Calif.) Engring. Coun., 1984, Engr. of Yr. award Rockwell Internat., 1985, Leonardo da Vinci Medallion, 1986, Sci. Achievement award, Disting. Engring. Alumnus award Purdue U., 1988, Meritorious Inventor's award Rockwell Internat. Corp., 1989, Outstanding Elec. Engr. award Purdue U., 1992, Boeing N.Am. Aviation Top Inventor award, 1998. Fellow AAAS (life), AIAA, IEEE (life; Centennial medal, Millenium medal, chair of ICASSP and ISCAS, Signal Processing Soc. disting. lect. and founding chmn. L.A. coun. chpt., Circuits and Sys. Soc. Tech. Achievement award 1996, Golden Jubilee medal 1999), Inst. for Advancement Engring., N.Y. Acad. Scis. (life); mem. VFW (life), Air Force Assn. (life), Am. Legion (life), Sigma Xi (life; founding pres. Orange County chpt., pres. 1988-00, 05—), Eta Kappa Nu (Paul K. Hudson disting. fellow, internat. dir. emeritus, Vladimir Karapetoff award 2005), Tau Beta Pi. Achievements include 82 US patents in field. Avocation: choral music. Office Phone: 949-498-5519. Business E-Mail: stan.white@ieee.org.

**WHITE, STEPHEN HALLEY,** biophysicist, educator; b. Wewoka, Okla., May 14, 1940; s. James Halley and Gertrude June (Wyatt) W.; m. Buff Ertl, Aug. 20, 1961 (div. 1982); children: Saill, Shell, Storn, Sharr, Skye, Sunde; m. Jackie Marie Dooley, Apr. 14, 1984. BS in Physics, U. Colo., 1963; MS in Physics, U. Wash., 1965, PhD in Physiology and Biophysics, 1969. USPHS postdoctoral fellow biochemistry U. Va., Charlottesville, 1971-72; asst. prof. physiology and biophysics U. Calif., Irvine, 1972-75, assoc. prof. physiology and biophysics, 1975-78, prof. physiology and biophysics, 1978—, vice chmn. physiology and biophysics, 1974-75, chmn. physiology and biophysics, 1977-89. Guest biophysicist Brookhaven Nat. Lab., Upton, L.I., N.Y., 1977-99; mem. NIH BBM study sect., 2005—. Contbr. numerous articles to profl. jours. Served to capt. USAR, 1969-71. Recipient Research Career Devel. award USPHS, 1975-80, Kaiser-Permanente Tchg. award, 1975, 92; fellow Biophysical Soc., 2002; grantee NIH, 1971—, NSF, 1971—. Mem. NSF (adv. panel for molecular biology 1982-85, mem. nat. steering com. advanced neutron source 1992-95), Internat. Union Pure and Applied Biophysics (U.S. nat. com. 1997—, chmn. 2000-04), Fedn. Am. Soc. for Exptl. Biology (bd. dirs. 1998-2002), Biophys. Soc. (chmn. membrane biophysics subgroup 1977-78, acting sec., treas. 1979-80, coun. 1981-84, exec. bd. 1981-83, program chmn. 1985, ann. meeting, sec. 1987-95, pres. 1996-97, Disting. Svc. award 1999), Am. Physiol. Soc. (editl. bd. 1981-93, membership com. 1985-86, publ. com. 1987-91), Assn. Chmn. Depts. Physiology (rep. to coun. acad. socs. 1981-82, councilor 1982-83, pres. 1986-87), Soc. Gen. Physiologists (treas. 1985-88), The Protein Soc. (electronic pub. coord. 1993—, NIH BBM study section 2005—). Avocations: skiing, cooking, travel. Office: U Calif Dept Physiology & Biophysics Med Sci I-D346 Irvine CA 92697-4560

**WHITE, TERRENCE HAROLD,** academic administrator, sociologist; b. Ottawa, Ont., Can., Mar. 31, 1943; s. William Harold and Shirley Margaret (Ballantine) W.; m. Susan Elizabeth Hornaday; children: Christine Susan, Julie Pamela. PhD, U. Toronto, 1972. Head dept. sociology and anthropology U. Windsor, Ont., Canada, 1973-75; prof., chmn. dept. sociology U. Alta., Edmonton, Canada, 1975-80, dean faculty of arts, 1980-88; pres. T.H. White Orgn. Rsch. Svcs. Ltd., Edmonton, 1975—, Brock U., St. Catharines, Ont., 1988-96, U. Calgary, Alta., 1996—2001, pres. emeritus, prof. bus., 2001—. Author: Power or Pawns: Boards of Directors, 1978, Human Resource Management, 1979; editor: Introduction to Work Science, 1981, QWL in Canada: Case Studies, 1982. Bd. dirs. Progressive Conservative Assn., Edmonton South, 1976-81, 1st v.p., 1981-85, pres., 1985-87; bd. dirs. Tri-Bach Festival Found., Edmonton, 1981-88, Alta. Ballet Co., 1985-88, Edmonton Conv. and Tourism Authority, Arch Enterprises, 1984-88, Niagara Symphony Soc., YMCA, St. Catharines, 1988-92; chair United Way Campaign St. Catharines, 1992, Fox Found., 1990-96, Can. Summer Games 2001 Bid Com.; bd. dirs. Edmonton Symphony Soc., v.p., 1986-88; bd. govs. U. Alta., 1984-88, Brock U., 1988-96, Ridley Coll., 1990—, Alta. Heritage Found. for Med. Rsch.; active Calgary R & D Authority, 1997; divsn. chair Calgary United Way Campaign, Calgary Econ. Devel. Authority, 1997-2000, McMahon Stadium Soc., Calgary Children's Initiative, Ctr. for Affordable Water and Sanitation; nat. bd. gov.'s Scouts Can., 2003- Recipient Can. 125 Commemorative medal Govt. of Can., Queen's Golden Jubilee medal. Mem. Calgary Petroleum Club, Ranchmen's Club, Rotary (pres. Edmonton South 1981-82), Delta Tau Kappa, Alpha Kappa Delta. Home: Box 68028 28 Crowfoot Terr NW Calgary AB Canada T3G 3N8 Office: U Calgary 2500 University Dr NW Calgary AB Canada T2N 1N4

**WHITE, TERRY EDWARD,** physician; b. Springfield, Mo., May 30, 1954; s. Roy Edward and Eselean (Moffis) W.; m. Susan Marie Peters, Aug. 16, 1981. BA, Drury Coll., 1976; MD, U. Mo., 1980. Diplomate Am. Bd. Physical Medicine and Rehab. Physician Lakeshore Hosp., Birmingham, Ala., 1983-86; clin. instr. U. Ala., Birmingham, 1984-86; physician Thomas Rehab., Asheville, NC, 1986-97, chief staff, 1994-97, vice-chief staff, 1992-94; physician Rehab. Solutions Western N.C., Asheville, 1998—; attending physician Mission Hosp., 1986—. Alternate Medicare State Carrier adv. com., Greensboro, N.C., 1993; bd. dirs. Nationwide Post Polio Support Group, Dallas, N.C., 1992-94; vice chmn. Western N.C. Health Care Provider Coun., 1995-96, chmn., 1996-97; mem. editl. adv. com. Stroke Rehabilitation. Author: A Patient's and Physician Guide to Late Effects of Polio, 1995; mem. editl. staff Stroke Rehabilitation-Patient Education Guide, 1995. Named Rehab. Physician Yr., N.C. Med. Soc., 1993. Fellow Am. Acad. Phys. Medicine and Rehab.; mem. N.C. Soc. Phys. Medicine and Rehab. (v.p. 1989-91, pres. 1991-93). Republican. Mem. Christian Ch. Avocations: gardening, woodwork, metal work, reading, music. Office: Rehab Solutions Western NC 4 Doctors Park Ste C Asheville NC 28801-4523 Office Phone: 828-283-9795. Personal E-mail: terrywhite@aol.com.

**WHITE, THOMAS EDWARD,** lawyer; b. N.Y.C., July 11, 1933; s. Thomas Aubrey and Gladys Mary (Piper) W.; m. Joan Carolyn Olsen, Dec. 2, 1967 (dec.); children: Charles Garret, Nancy Carolyn, Linda Marie, Penelope Lindsay, Elizabeth Ann. AB, Princeton U., 1955; LLB, Columbia U., 1960; BA summa cum laude, SUNY-Purchase Coll., 2002; student in Fine Arts, NYU, 2002—04. Bar: N.Y. 1961. Atty. Seward & Kissel, N.Y.C., 1960-69; gen. counsel Howmet Corp., N.Y.C., 1969-70; v.p., gen. counsel, sec. Howmedica, Inc., N.Y.C., 1970-74, sr. v.p., dir., 1974-83; pvt. practice N.Y.C., 1983-97. Ptnr. Westend Venture Ptnrs. (formerly Integrated Med. Venture Ptnrs.), N.Y.C., 1987-99; chmn. Shoreside Cons. Ltd., Miami, Fla., 1987-98. Mem. Mamaroneck Town Coun., 1971-75; mem. vestry Episcopalian Ch., 1987-90; mem. diocesan coun. Episcopal Ch. N.Y., 2001—. Served to 1st lt. U.S. Army, 1955-57. Mem.: Larchmont (N.Y.) Yacht; Princeton (N.Y.C.). Republican. Home: 260 Barnard Rd Larchmont NY 10538-1941

**WHITE, TIMOTHY PAUL,** brokerage house executive; b. Ft. Sill, Okla., Jan. 9, 1963; s. Paul R. and Lucille (Mattison) White; m. Susan Gertrude Foreman, Dec. 29, 1984; children: Jessica Lynn, Rebecca Anne, Kathleen Marie. BS in Fin., Pa. State U., 1985. Cert. fin. planner Colo. Assoc. planner, agt. Pa. Fin. Group, Harrisburg, Pa., 1988-92; mgr. mktg. and sales Meridian Securities, Inc., Reading, Pa., 1992-96; v.p. products and sales mgr. Core States Securities Corp., Reading, 1996-98; regional sales mgr. First Union Brokerage Svcs. Inc., 1998-2001; fin. advisor, sr. v.p. First Union Securities Inc., 2001—02; pres. Investors Ctrl. Comm. Inc.; mng. dir. Guidon, LLC 2001—; fin. advisor Wachovia Securities LLC, 2002—. Spkr. Nat. Mut. Fund Conf., 1995, Cmty. Bank Investment Program Symposium, 1996, Nat. Investment Products Conf., 1996. Author: Money Smart Records, 2002; contbg. editor: Bank Securities Jour.; contbr. articles to profl. jours. Program cons. Jr. Achievement, Lancaster, Pa., 1990-91; pres. Adamstown Recreation Bd., 1996. 1st lt. U.S. Army, 1985—88, with USAR, 1989—92. Decorated Commendation medal, Achievement medal; recipient George C. Marshal award, U.S. Army, 1985; scholar ROTC, 1980—84. Mem.: Fin. Planning Assn., Ctrl. Pa. Soc. Inst. CFP (bd. dirs. 1996—, pres. elect 1998, pres. 1999), U.S. Cav. Assn. (fundraising com. 1994—96), Inst. CFP. Republican. Lutheran. Avocations: military and political history, reading, gardening, woodworking. Office: Wachovia Securities LLC 12 E Market St York PA 17401 Office Phone: 717-852-5214. Business E-Mail: tim.white@wachovia.com.

**WHITE, TIMOTHY PETER,** academic administrator, physical education educator; b. Buenos Aires, July 9, 1949; came to U.S., 1957; s. Anthony Robert and Mary (Weston) W.; m. Nina Marie Kasper, Oct. 11, 1981; children: Randall Patrick, Timothy Anthony, Alexander John. Student, Diablo Valley Community Coll., 1966-67; BA magna cum laude, Fresno State U., 1970; MS, Calif. State U., Hayward, 1972; PhD, U. Calif., Berkeley, 1977. Asst. prof. phys. edn. U. Mich., Ann Arbor, 1978-82, assoc. prof., 1982-84, assoc. prof., chmn. dept. kinesiology, 1985-89; rsch. scientist Inst. Gerontology, 1986-91; prof., chmn. U. Mich., Ann Arbor, 1989-91; dept. chmn., prof. dept. human dynamics U. Calif., Berkeley, 1991—2000; provost, exec. v.p. Oreg. State Univ., 2000—04, interim pres., 2002—03; pres. Univ. Idaho, 2004—. Editor: (with others) Frontiers of Exercise Biology, 1983; contbr. articles to profl. jours. and chpts. to books on exercise and muscle. Fellow Am. Coll. Sports Medicine (trustee, v.p. 1991—, New Investigator award 1981), Am. Acad. Phys. Edn.; mem. AAAS, AAHPERD, Gerontol. Soc. Am., Am. Physiol. Soc., Sigma Xi, Phi Kappa Phi. Avocations: woodworking, nordic skiing, sailing, swimming, running. Office: University of Idaho Office of the President PO Box 443151 Moscow ID 83844-3151

**WHITE, TODD WILLIAM,** lawyer, educator; s. William Robert and Patricia Ann White; m. Tisa Lynn Lovett, Aug. 18, 1990; children: Mary Elizabeth, Abigail Ann. BA, U. Tex., 1987; JD, Tex. Tech U. Sch. Law, 1987—90. Bar: Tex. 1990, US Dist. Ct.: (no. dist.) Tex. 1991, (ea. dist.) Tex. 1996, US Ct. Appeals: (5th cir.) 1992, US Supreme Ct.: 1997. Assoc. Jones, Day, Reavis & Pogue, Dallas, 1990—95; pvt. practice Rockwall, Tex., 1995—. Assoc. prof. Collin County C.C., Plano, Tex., 2000—. Mem. Goals Rev. Com., Rockwall, Tex., 1991, North Ctrl. Tex. Regional Rev. Com., Arlington, Tex., 1996; mem., vice-chmn. Zoning Bd. of Adjustment, Rockwall, Tex., 1991—93; vice-chmn. Econ. Devel. Planning Com., Rockwall, Tex., 1992—93; chmn. Corridor Planning Taskforce, Rockwall, Tex., 1991—92, Rockwall County Reps., Rockwall, 1991—92, vol. legal coun., 1999—2004; coun. mem. City of Rockwall, 1993—98, mayor pro tem, 1996—97; chmn. Rockwall Housing Authority, Rockwall, Tex., 1999— Scholar, Helen Hodges Charitable Trust, 1989. Mem.: Tex. Tech U. Law Rev., Rockwall County Bar Assn., State Bar of Tex., KC, Order of the Coif, Phi Kappa Phi. Office: The White Law Firm 301 N San Jacinto Rockwall TX 75087 Office Phone: 972-771-8011. Office Fax: 972-771-8081. Business E-Mail: twhite@thewhitelawfirm.com.

**WHITE, TONY L.,** health and medical products executive; BA, We. Carolina U., 1969. Sales rep. Baxter Internat. Inc., 1970-74, dist. mgr., 1974-76, export mgr. Latin Am., 1976-82, v.p. AMPAC, pres. Travenol-Can., 1982-85, pres. Fenwal divsn., 1985-86, pres. scientific products, biomedical divsn., 1986, v.p. diagnostics Deerfield, Ill., 1986-92, exec. vp, 1992-95; chmn., pres., CEO Applera Corp., Norwalk, Conn., 1995—. With USAR, 1968-74. Office: Applera Corp 301 Merritt 7 PO Box 5435 Norwalk CT 06856-5435 Office Phone: 203-840-2000.

**WHITE, TYLER GOODRICH,** composer, conductor; b. Atlanta, Nov. 9, 1961; s. Edwin Chappell and Barbara Tyler White; m. Laura Garrigues Mooneyham, May 27, 1994; children: Caroline Barbara, Nicholas Garrick Chappell. AB Music. Univ. N.C., Chapel Hill, N.C., 1983; MFA Musical Composition, Cornell Univ., Ithaca, N.Y., 1986; guest student, Kobenhavns Univ., Copenhagen, Denmark, 1986—87; DMA, Cornell Univ., Ithaca, N.Y., 1991. Dir. orchestral activities, asst. prof. music Trinity Univ., San Antonio, 1989—94, Univ. Nebr., Lincoln, 1994—2000, dir. orchestral activities, assoc. prof. music, 2000—. Resident condr. Lincoln Symphony Orch., Nebr. 2000—; guest faculty (conducting) Ctrl. Conservatory of Music, Beijing, 2004. Composer: (symphony) Mystic Trumpeter (symphony no. 2), (opera) O Pioneers!, 1999, (concerto) Threnos for Cello and Orchestra, 1993. Recipient Best Prodn. award, Nat. Opera Assn., 1999, 2001, Prix Maurice Ravel, Conservatoire Am. De Fontainebleau and Mply. of Avon, France, 1988; Individual Artist fellowship, Nebr. Arts Coun., 2005. Mem.: Conductors Guild, Am. Music Ctr., Am. Soc. Composers, Authors, and Pub., Phi Beta Kappa. Episcopalian. Home: 6540 Rexford Dr Lincoln NE 68506 Office: Univ Nebr Lincoln Sch Music Westbrook Music Bldg 0100 Lincoln NE 68588 Office Phone: 402-472-7698.

**WHITE, W. CHRISTOPHER,** lawyer; b. Boston, Dec. 30, 1951; s. William George and Patricia Elizabeth (Brophy) W.; m. Anne Marie Cosgriff, Aug. 19, 1972; children: Jennifer, Andrew, Meghan. BA, U. Notre Dame, 1973; postgrad., London Sch. Econs., 1974; JD, U. Mich., 1977. Bar: N.Y. 1981, Mass 1978. Atty. Ryan & White, Springfield, Mass., 1977—78, Fred F. French Co., N.Y.C., 1978—80, Breed Abbot & Morgan, N.Y.C., 1980—87; ptnr. Breed, Abbott & Morgan, N.Y.C., 1984-87, Cadwalader Wickersham & Taft, N.Y.C., 1987—, chmn. Real Estate Dept. & mem. exec. com. Mem. Univ. Club. Office: Cadwalader Wickersham & Taft LLP 1 World Fin Ctr New York NY 10281 Office Phone: 212-504-6633. Office Fax: 212-504-6666. Business E-Mail: christopher.white@cwt.com.

**WHITE, WARREN JOHN,** education educator; b. Norton, Kans., Oct. 14, 1951; s. Warren Allen and Jean White; m. Candace Vlcek White, May 19, 1985; children: Tracy Lee Flynn, Elizabeth Jean, Melanie Grace. PhD, U.Kans., Lawrence, 1980. Coord. prevocational evaluation ctr. Shawnee Mission Schs., Kansas City, Kans., 1974—76; grad. tchg. asst. U. Kans., Lawrence, 1976—79; prof. Kans. State U., Manhattan, 1981—, dir. of assessment, coord. of tchr. edn., 1992—2004; spl. edn. tchr. Salina Pub. Schs., Salina, Kans. Spl. edn. hearing officer Kans. Dept. of Edn.; ombudsperson Kans. State U., Manhattan, 2003—; cons. numerous orgns., Kans., 1981—. Contbr. articles to profl. jours. Mem.: Coun. for Exceptional Children (pres. 1992—93). Avocations: hiking, reading, travel. Office: Kansas State Univ 312 Bluemont Hall Manhattan KS 66506 Office Phone: 785-532-6349.

**WHITE, WILL WALTER, III,** public relations consultant, writer; b. Glen Ridge, NJ, July 3, 1930; s. Will Walter and Miriam Chandler (Milburn) W.; m. Phyllis Marcia DuFlocq, Dec. 28, 1951 (div. 1971); children: Will Walter IV, Scott, Alan; m. Anne Elizabeth Levenson, Nov. 21, 1971 (div. 1992); children: Duncan, Christopher; stepchildren: Michael, Susan; m. Catherine Laur, Aug. 26, 1992. BA, Cornell U., 1952. Supr. Union Carbide Corp., N.Y.C., 1954-59; account exec. Ketchum, MacLeod & Grove, N.Y.C., 1959-62; sr. v.p. Wilson, Haight & Welch, Hartford, Conn., 1962-72; chmn., chief exec. officer Lowengard & Brotherhood, Hartford, 1972-83; pres., chief exec. officer Harland & Tine & White, Hartford, 1983-87; chmn. Donahue Inc., Hartford, 1987-89; ptnr. Laur White & White, Heathsville, Va., 1992—2000; owner Omega Cubed Press, 1996—. Exec. com. Conn. Dist. Export Council, 1979-88. Author: The Sunfish Book, 1983, 96; contbg. editor Mid-Gulf Sailing mag., 1994-95. Mem. exec. com. Hartford Stage Co., 1982-86; pres. Vis. Nurse Assn., Hartford, 1979; fin. chmn. Vis. Nurse and Home Care, Inc., Hartford and Waterbury, 1982-91; mem. pub. rels. com. Fairfield County Rep. Com., 1987-90; chmn. S.W. Fla. Regional Harbor Bd., 1995-2000. 1st lt. U.S. Army, 1952-54. Nat. champion Sunfish Racing Class, 1966, 68 Mem. Pub. Rels. Soc. Am. (accredited, chmn. investor rels. sect 1983, charter mem. Hall of Fame 1990), Bus. Profl. Advt. Assn. (cert. bus. communicator), Nat. Investor Rels. Inst., U.S. Sunfish Class Assn. (pres. 1985-88, charter mem. Hall of Fame 1991), Boaters Action and Info. League (exec. v.p. 1992-2000), Hist. Soc. Sarasota County (bd. dirs. 1995-2000). Address: 3220 S E Hansel Ave Arcadia FL 34266-3143

**WHITE, WILLIAM, III,** retail executive; BBA, Southwestern Meth. U., 1971. Ter. oper. mgr. Sears Roebuck and Co., 1988—89, nat. mktg. mgr. automotive, 1990—91, nat. mgr., product svc., 1991—93, regional v.p. southwest, 1993—99, sr. v.p., gen. mgr., automotive group, 1999—2003, exec. v.p., store ops., 2003—. Office: Sears Roebuck and Co 3333 Beverly Rd Hoffman Estates IL 60179

**WHITE, WILLIAM BLAINE,** geochemist, researcher; b. Huntingdon, Pa., Jan. 5, 1934; s. William Bruce and Eleanor Mae (Barr) W.; m. Elizabeth Loczi, Mar. 27, 1959; children: Nikki Elizabeth White Vezendi, William Brion (dec.). BS, Juniata Coll., 1954; PhD, Pa. State U., 1962. Rsch. assoc.

Mellon Inst., Pitts., 1954-58; asst. prof. Pa. State U., University Park, 1963-67, assoc. prof., 1967-72, prof. geochemistry, 1972—2002, emeritus prof., 2002—, chmn. grad. program in materials, 1990-93. Assoc. editor Am. Mineralogist, 1972-75, Materials Rsch. Bull., 1979-93, Jour. Am. Ceramic Soc., 1985-93, Water Resources Bull., 1992-93; editor earth scis. Nat. Speleological Soc. Bull., 1964-94; author: Geomorphology and Hydrology of Karst Terrains, 1988, (with Elizabeth L. White) Karst Hydrology: Concepts from the Mammoth Cave Area, 1989, (with Susan Barger) Daguerreotype: Nineteenth-Century Technology and Modern Science, 1991, (with David C. Culver) Encyclopedia of Caves, 2004; contbr. articles to profl. jours. Home: 4538 Miller Rd Petersburg PA 16669-2711 Office: Pa State U Materials Rsch Lab University Park PA 16802 Office Phone: 814-865-1152. Business E-Mail: wbw2@psu.edu.

**WHITE, WILLIAM FREDRICK,** lawyer; b. Elmhurst, Ill., Sept. 30, 1948; s. William Daniel and Carol Ruth (Laier) W.; m. Kathie Jean Nichols, May 27, 1979; children: Nicholas Roland, Andrew William. BA, U. Ill., 1970; JD, Antioch Sch. of Law, 1976. Bar: U.S. Ct. Appeals (D.C. cir.) 1976, Wis. 1982, U.S. Dist. Ct. (we. dist.) Wis. 1982, U.S. Dist. Ct. D.C. 1976, U.S. Ct. Claims 1978, U.S. Ct. Appeals (7th and 10th cirs.) 1982. With U.S. Dept. Labor, Washington, 1976; interim exec. dir. Common Cause, Washington, 1977; asst. counsel Nat. Treasury Employees Union, Washington, 1977-79, assoc. gen. counsel, 1979-81, dir. litigation, 1981-82; assoc. Michael, Best & Friedrich LLP, Madison, Wis., 1982-88, ptnr., chmn. assoc. devel. com., 1988-96, ptnr., 1988—, chair land and resources legal practice area, 1999—2002, mng. ptnr. Madison (Wis.) Office, 2002—. Bd. dirs. Med. Physics Pub. Co.; dir. Med. Physics Found., 1988—, sec., 1994—. Chmn. Pub. Health Commn., Madison, 1983-89; bd. dirs. exec. com. Dane County Mediation Program, Madison, 1983-90, Perinatal Found., Madison, 1984-96, Arthritis Found., Madison, 1984-92, Arthritis Found., Madison, 1986-92, chmn., 1991-92; bd. dirs. Dane County Natural Heritage Found., 1988-91, Veridian Found., 2005—; mem. Dane County Regional Airport Commn., 1991—, chmn. 1994—; chancellor Wis. Ann. Conf. United Meth. Ch., 1992—, gen. coun. Fin. and Adminstrn., 1991-2000, chmn. Legal Svcs. Com., 1992-96; bd. dirs. Downtown Madison Inc., sec. 1995-2001, chair transp. com.; mem. Dane County Transferrable Devel. Rights Task Force, Team Terrace Transp. Com., 1996-97, chair; bd. trustees Madison Mus. Contemporary Art, 1998—, dir., 2002—; co-chair Friends of Hudson Park, 1999—; Madison program chair Dane County Pub. Affairs Coun., 2000-02. Mem. ABA, D.C. Bar Assn., Med. Physics Found. (bd. dirs. 1987—), Dane County Bar Assn., State Bar Assn. (sec. Health Law sect.), Transp. Devel. Assn. (dir. 1999-2003, exec. com. 1999-2003). Democrat. United Methodist. Avocations: bicycling, skiing. Office: Michael Best & Friedrich LLP Ste 700 1 S Pinckney St Madison WI 53703-2892

**WHITE, WILLIAM H.,** mayor; married; 3 children. BS in Econs. magna cum laude, Harvard U., 1976; JD, U. Tex., 1979. Atty. Susaman Godfrey LLP, Houston, 1979—93; instr. antitrust law and voting rights U. Tex., Austin; dep. sec., COO Dept. Energy, Washington, 1993—95; chmn. Howe-Baker International., Tyler, Tex., 1997—2000; pres., CEO The Wedge Group, Houston, 1997—2003; mayor City of Houston, 2004—. Office: City Hall 901 Bagby St 3rd Fl Houston TX 77002 also: PO Box 1562 Houston TX 77251 Office Phone: 713-247-2200. E-mail: mayor@cityofhouston.net.*

**WHITE, WILLIAM NORTH,** retired chemistry professor; b. Walton, N.Y., Sept. 16, 1925; s. George Fitch and Frances (Peck) W.; m. Hilda R. Sauter, Sept. 8, 1951; children: Carla Ann, Eric Jeffrey. AB, Cornell U., 1950; MA, Harvard U., 1951. PhD, 1953. NRC postdoctoral fellow Calif. Inst. Tech., Pasadena, 1953-54; asst. prof. Ohio State U., Columbus, 1954-59, asso. prof., 1959-63; prof. chemistry U. Vt., Burlington, 1963-76, 77-95, prof. emeritus, 1995—, chmn. dept., 1963-70, acting chmn. dept., 1975-76; prof. chemistry U. Tex. at Arlington, 1976-77, chmn. dept., 1976-77; ret., 1995. NSF sr. postdoctoral fellow Brookhaven Nat. Lab., Upton, N.Y., 1963-64, Harvard U., 1965; vis. scholar Brandeis U., 1974-75; chmn. arrangements com. Nat. Organic Chemistry Symposium, 1965-67 Contbr. articles on organic chemistry profl. jours. Selectman Town of Shelburne, Vt., 1968-74, water commr., 1973-74, justice of the peace, 1981-, sewer commr., 1991-93, Natural Resources and Conservation com., 1970-74, 2004-; mem. Chittenden County Regional Planning Commn., 1983-91; mem. bd. suprs. Winooski (Vt.) Natural Resources Conservation Dist., 1999-2004. With AUS, 1943-46. Recipient Outstanding Forest Stewardship award Winooski Conservation Dist., 1997. Mem. Am. Chem. Soc. (chmn. Western Vt. sect. 1966-67), Royal Soc. Chemistry, New Eng. Assn. Chemistry Tchrs., AAAS, N.Y. Acad. Scis., Phi Beta Kappa, Sigma Xi, Phi Kappa Phi, Phi Lambda Upsilon. Home: 226 Pierson Dr Shelburne VT 05482 Business E-Mail: wnwhite@uvm.edu.

**WHITE, WILLIAM SAMUEL,** foundation executive; b. Cin., May 8, 1937; s. Nathaniel Ridgway and Mary White; m. Claire Mott, July 1, 1961; children: Tiffany, Ridgway Harding. BA, Dartmouth Coll., 1959, MBA, 1960; degree (hon.), GMI Engring. and Mgmt. Inst., 1996; LLD (hon.), Eastern Mich. U., 1975, U. Mich., 2006. With Barrett & Williams, N.Y.C., 1961-62; sr. assoc. Bruce Payne & Assos., N.Y.C., 1962-71; v.p. C. S. Mott Found., Flint, Mich., 1971-75, pres., 1976—, trustee, 1971—, also chmn. bd. dirs. Chmn. bd. dirs. U.S. Sugar Corp.; bd. dirs. Am. Water Works, 1999—2003. Mem. exec. com. Daycroft Sch., Greenwich, Conn., 1966-70; bd. dirs. Flint Area Conf., 1971-84, Coun. on Founds., 1985-90, Independent Sector, 1994-99, 2004—, Am. Friends Czech Republic, 1999-2004, European Found. Centre, 1994—, Civicus, 1995-2001; citizens adv. task force U. Mich., Flint, 1974-79; chmn. Coun. of Mich. Founds., 1979-81, Flint Area Focus Coun., 1988—, Afterschool Allstars, 2004-; mem. Pres.'s Task Force on Pvt. Sector Initiatives, 1982; trustee GMI Engring. and Mgmt. Inst., 1982-86, Network European Founds., 2000—, Madriaga Found., 2004—. With U.S. Army, 1960-62. Office: C S Mott Foundation 1200 Mott Foundation Bldg Flint MI 48502-1807

**WHITED, MARY ELIZABETH,** marketing professional; Marketing N.Y. Times Syndication Sales Corp. Office: NY Times Syndication Sales Corp 609 Greenwich St 6th Fl New York NY 10014 Office Phone: 212-499-3417. Office Fax: 212-499-3382. E-mail: whiteme@nytimes.com.

**WHITE-HAMMOND, GLORIA E.,** pastor, pediatrician, human rights advocate; m. Ray A. Hammond, 1973; children: Mariama, Adiya. BA in Biology, Boston U.; MD, Tufts U., 1976; MDiv, Harvard Divinity Sch., 1997; LHD (hon.), Tufts U., 2006. Pediatrician South End Cmty. Health Ctr., 1981—; co-pastor (with husband Rev. Ray A. Hammond, M.D.) Bethel AME Ch., Boston, 1997—. Medical missionary in several African countries including Botswana, Cote D'Ivoire and South Africa. Co-founder My Sister's Keeper, Sudan, 2002—; chair Million Voices for Darfur campaign; founder, cons. Do the Write Thing, 1994—; co-convener The Red Tent Group; co-chair Mass. Coalition to Save Darfur; trustee Brigham and Women's Hosp.; bd. overseers Tufts U. Coll. Cmty. and Public Svc.; bd. dirs. Am. Anti Slavery Group, Boston, Christian Solidarity Internat., Zurich. Recipient Humanitarian award, Boston Theological Inst., 2004, Liberating Vision award, Greater Boston Sect. Nat. Coun. Negro Women, 2004, Impact award, Am. Assn. Retired Persons, 2004, Exceptional Women award, Magic 106.7, 2006. Achievements include being involved in obtaining the freedom of 10,000 women and children in Southern Sudan who were enslaved during the two decades long civil war. Office: Bethel AME Church 215 forest Hills St Jamaica Plain MA 02130-3302*

**WHITEHEAD, DAVID BARRY,** lawyer; b. San Francisco, Oct. 14, 1946; s. Barry and Fritzi-Beth (Bowman) W.; m. René Dayan, May 26, 1990. AB in History, Stanford U., 1968, JD, 1971. Bar: Calif. 1972, U.S. Dist. Ct. (no. dist.) Calif. 1972, U.S. Ct. Appeals (9th cir.) 1972, U.S. Dist. Ct. (cen. dist.) Calif. 1974. Assoc. Cullinan Hancock Rothert & Burns, San Francisco, 1972-74, Cullinan Burns & Helmer, San Francisco, 1975-77, ptnr., 1977-78, Burns & Whitehead, San Francisco, 1979-85, Whitehead & Porter, San Francisco, 1986-97, Whitehead, Porter & Gordon LLP, San Francisco, 1998—. Bd. dirs. Rainbow Music, Inc., San Francisco, ITP, Inc., Sunnyvale, Calif.; founding dir. A. Lincoln High Sch. San Francisco, 1989—. Mem. San Francisco Rep. Steering Com., 1984—89; bd. dirs. Enterprise for High Sch.

Students, San Francisco, 1982—86; bd. dirs. San Francisco chpt. Easter Seal Soc., 1986—90; bd. dirs. Opera West Found., San Francisco, 1986, Traveler's Aid Soc., San Francisco, 1989—90, Hosp. de la Familia, 1995—2000, Gold Rush Trail Found., 1998, Calif. Hist. Soc. Found., 1998. Mem. ABA, Calif. Bar Assn., San Francisco Bar Assn., Calif. Scholarship Fedn. (life) Family Club San Francisco (bd. dirs. 1986-89, 93-95), World Trade Club, Abraham Lincoln High Sch. San Francisco Alumni Assn. (founding dir.). Roman Catholic. Avocations: writing, art, directing, singing. Home: 1896 Pacific Ave Apt 502 San Francisco CA 94109-2302 Office: Whitehead Porter LLP 220 Montgomery St Fl 18 San Francisco CA 94104-3402

**WHITEHEAD, EDGAR DOUGLAS,** urology educator; b. Galashiels, Scotland, Aug. 24, 1939; 1 child, Robin Stacey. BA, Vanderbilt U., 1961; MD, Ind. U., 1965; postgrad., U. London, 1972. Diplomate Am. Bd. Urology; med. lic. Ind., Ill., N.Y., Calif., N.J. Surgery intern Mount Sinai Hosp., N.Y.C., 1965-66; resident in surgery Presbyn.-St. Luke's Hosp., Chgo., 1966-67; resident in urology N.Y.U. Med. Ctr., 1969-73; clin. assoc. urology Mount Sinai Sch. Medicine, N.Y.C., 1973-77, sr. clin. instr. urology, 1977-80, asst. clin. prof. urology, 1980-92; pvt. practice, N.Y.C., 1973—; assoc. clin. prof. urology Mount Sinai Sch. Medicine, 1992-94, Albert Einstein Coll. of Medicine, 1994—; attending NYU Downtown Hosp. Assoc. attending Beth Israel Med. Ctr., N.Y.C.; advisor Impotence Anonymous & Jr., Diabetes Self-Mgmt., 1983-85, Jour. Urol. Nursing; med. adv. bd. Colostomy Soc., N.Y., Inc.; investigator Protocol 2560 (allays Alfuzosin study, 1998; cons. and speaker in field. Author: Viagra--The Wonder Drug for Peak Performance; editor: Current Operative Urology, 1975, 2d rev. edit., 1984, ann. edits. 1989-92, Mgmt. Impotence and Infertility, 1994, Sex Over Forty, 1990-2000, Atlas Surgical Techniques in Urology, 1997; mem. editl. bd. Female Patient, Med. Aspects of Human Sexuality; memcontbr. articles to profl. jours. Grantee U.S.P.H., Clin. Research Ctr. Fellow ACS, Clin. Soc. Am. Diabetes Assn., N.Y. Diabetes Affiliate; mem. AMA, AAAS, Am. Urol. Assn., Soc. Internat. Urology (diplomate), Sexual Medicine Soc. N.Am., Am. Assn. Clin. Urologists, N.Y. State Urol. Assn., Am. Acad. of Phalloplasty Surgeons (pres., bd. dirs.), Internat. Soc. for Artificial Organs, Am. So. Nephrology, Am. Assn. Sex Educators, Counselors and Therapists, Soc. for the Sci. Study of Sex, Soc. for Sex Therapy and Rsch., Sex Info. and Edn. Coun. of the U.S. Coalition on Sexuality and Disability, Am. Cancer Soc., Nat. Kidney Found., Am. Geriatric Soc., N.Y. Acad. Sci., N.Y. Acad. Medicine, N.Y. Urodynamic Soc., Internat. Continence Soc., Soc. Genitourinary Reconstructive Surgeons, Assn. Male Sexual Dysfunction (dir.), N.Y. Phalloplasty (dir.). Achievements include patents in field. Office: 330 E 38th St Ste 51B New York NY 10016 Office Phone: 212-879-3131. Business E-Mail: info@drwhitehead.com.

**WHITEHEAD, J. RENNIE,** science administrator, consultant; s. William and Beatrice Cora (Fenning) W.; m. Nesta Doone James, Nov. 1, 1944; children— Valerie Lesley (dec.), Michael James Rennie. B.Sc. in Physics, Manchester U., Lancashire, Eng., 1939; PhD in Phys. Chemistry, Cambridge U., Eng., 1949. Cert. profl. engr., Ont.; chartered engr., U.K. Sci. officer TRE (UK Radar), England, 1939-51; assoc. prof. McGill U., Montreal, P.Q., Canada, 1951-55; dir. research RCA Victor Co Ltd., Montreal, 1955-65; prin. sci. adviser Govt. of Can., Ottawa, Ont., 1965-75; sr. v.p. Philip A. Lapp Ltd., Ottawa, 1975-82; pvt. practice sci. cons. Ottawa, 1982-86. Author: Superregenerative Receivers, 1949. Bd. dirs. Found. for Internat. Tng., Toronto, 1976—86. Fellow Royal Soc. Can., Inst. Physics, Instn. Elec. Engrs., Can. Aeronautics and Space Inst., Can. Assn. for Club of Rome (chmn. 1976-81, editor and pub. newsletter and procs. 1987-99). Anglican. Avocations: automobiles, stamp collecting/philately, carpentry, computers. Home and Office: 1368 Chattaway Ave Ottawa ON Canada K1H 7S3 E-mail: drrennie@sympatico.ca.

**WHITEHEAD, JOHN CUNNINGHAM,** former bank executive; b. Evanston, Ill., Apr. 2, 1922; s. Eugene C. and Winifred W.; m. Helene E. Shannon, Sept. 28, 1946 (div. Dec. 1971); children: Anne Elizabeth, John Gregory; m. Jaan W. Chartener, Oct. 22, 1972 (div. 1986); 1 child, Sarah; m. Nancy Dickerson, 1989 (dec. 1997). BA, Haverford Coll., 1943; MBA, Harvard U., 1947; LLD (hon.), Pace. U., Rutgers U., Haverford Coll., Harvard U., Amherst Coll., Seton Hall U.; LLD, Bates Coll., 2004; Gen. Theological Seminary, Berea Coll. With Goldman, Sachs & Co., N.Y.C., 1947-84, ptnr. NYC, 1956-76, sr. ptnr. co-chmn., 1976-84; dep. sec. US Dept State, Washington, 1985-89; chmn. Fed. Res. Bank NY, NYC, 1996—2000, Lower Manhattan Devel. Corp., NYC, 2001—06. Trustee Haverford Coll.; past pres. bd. overseers Harvard U.; co-chmn. greater N.Y. coun. Boy Scouts Am.; past chmn. Internat. Rescue Com., UN Assn. U.S.A.; Andrew Mellon Found; chmn. Goldman Sachs Found., 1999-, World Trade Ctr. Meml. Found., 2005-, emeritus, Brookings Instn., Internat. House, Nat. Gallery of Art; dir. Nature Conservatory, East West Inst., Eisenhower Exchange Fellowship. With USNR, 1943—46. Mem. Coun. on Fgn. Rels., Links Club, Univ. Club.

**WHITEHEAD, JOHN WAYNE,** lawyer, educator, writer; b. Pulaski, Tenn., July 14, 1946; s. John M. and Alatha (Wiser) W.; m. Virginia Carolyn Nichols, Aug. 26, 1967; children: Jayson Reau, Jonathan Mathew, Elisabeth Anne, Joel Christofer, Joshua Benjamen. BA, U. Ark., 1969, JD, 1974. Bar: Ark. 1974, U.S. Dist. Ct. (ea. and we. dists.) Ark. 1974, U.S. Supreme Ct. 1977, U.S. Ct. Appeals (9th cir.) 1980, Va. 1981, U.S. Ct. Appeals (7th cir.) 1981, U.S. Ct. Appeals (4th and 5th cirs.) 1981. Spl. counsel Christian Legal Soc., Oak Park, Ill., 1977-78; assoc. Gibbs & Craze, Cleve., 1978-79; sole practice law Manassas, Va., 1979-82; pres. The Rutherford Inst., Charlottesville, Va., 1982—, also bd. dirs. Frequent lectr. colls., law schs.; past adj. prof. O.W. Coburn Sch. Law. Author: Schools on Fire, 1980, The New Tyranny, 1982, The Second American Revolution, 1982, The Stealing of America, 1983, The Freedom of Religious Expression in Public High Schools, 1983, The End of Man, 1986, An American Dream, 1987, The Rights of Religious Persons in Public Education, 1991, Home Education: Rights and Reasons, 1993, Religious Apartheid, 1994, Slaying Dragons, 1999, Grasping For the Wind, 2001, others; writer, dir.; (video series) Grasping for the Wind (Silver World medal N.Y. Film Festival), 1990-99; contbr. articles to profl. jours., chpts. to books. 1st lt. U.S. Army, 1969-71. Named Christian Leader of Yr. Christian World Affairs Conf., Washington, 1986; recipient Bus. and Profl. award Religious Heritage Am., 1990, Hungarian Freedom medal, Budapest, 1991. Mem. ABA, Ark. Bar Assn., Va. Bar Assn. Office: The Rutherford Inst PO Box 7482 Charlottesville VA 22906-7482 Office Phone: 434-978-3888. Business E-Mail: johnw@rutherford.org.

**WHITEHEAD, KENNETH DEAN,** writer, translator, retired federal agency administrator; b. Rupert, Idaho, Dec. 14, 1930; s. Clarence Christian and May Bell (Allen) W.; m. Margaret Mary O'Donohue, Aug. 2, 1958; children: Paul Daniel, Steven Francis, Matthew Patrick, David Joseph. BA in French, U. Utah, 1955; postgrad., U. Paris, 1956-57; cert. in Arabic and Middle East studies, Fgn. Service Inst., Beirut, 1962; LittD (hon.), Franciscan U., Steubenville, Oho, 2003. Instr. English U. Utah, Salt Lake City, 1955-56; fgn. service officer Dept. State, Rome, Beirut and Tripoli, Libya, 1957-65; chief Arabic service Voice of Am., Washington, 1965-67; dep. dir. fgn. currency program Smithsonian Instn., Washington, 1967-72; exec. v.p. Caths. United for Faith Inc., New Rochelle, NY, 1972-81; dir. Ctr for Internat. Edn. U.S. Dept. Edn., Washington, 1982-86, dep. asst. sec. for higher edn. programs, 1986-88, asst. sec. for postsecondary edn., 1988-89. Author: Respectable Killing: The New Abortion Imperative, 1972, Agenda for the Sexual Revolution, 1981, Catholic Colleges and Federal Funding, 1988, DOA: The Ambush of the Universal Catechism, 1993, Political Orphan? The Prolife Cause after 25 Years of Roe v. Wade, 1998, One, Holy, Catholic, and Apostolic: The Early Church Was the Catholic Church, 2000; co-author: The Pope, The Council and the Mass, 1981, rev. edit., 2006, Flawed Expectations: The Reception of the Catechism of the Catholic Church, 1996; sr. editor: World Almanac Book of Dates, 1982, Macmillan Concise Dictionary of World History, 1983; editor: Marriage and the Common Good, 2001, Pope John Paul II--Witness to Truth, 2001, The Catholic Imagination, 2003, Voices of the New Springtime, 2004, The Catholic Citizen: Debating the Issues of Justice, 2004; co-editor: The Battle for the Catholic Mind, 2001; translator 20 books from French, German, Italian, 1980—. Bd. dir. Notre Dame Inst. for Advanced Study, Arlington, Va., 1986-95, Philosophy Edn. Soc., 1995—,

Christas Magister Found., 1997-2001. Fulbright scholar U.S. Dept. State, 1956-57. Mem. Fellowship Cath. Scholars (bd. dir. 1990-2000, 04—), Brent Soc. Cath. Profls. (bd. dir. 1992-98), Cath. League for Religious and Civil Rights (bd. dir. 1992—), KC. Republican. Home: 809 Ridge Pl Falls Church VA 22046-3631 Office Phone: 703-538-5085. Fax: (703) 534-3015. E-mail: whiteheadz@msn.com.

**WHITEHEAD, LINDA SUE,** English, American history, and special education educator; b. Riverton, Wyo., May 22, 1953; d. Wayne Edmund Gotfredson and Julia Ann Davidson; m. Dan Frank Whitehead, Nov. 6, 1975; children: Rachel Ann Brooks, Jesse Linn, Jared Pierce, John Paul, Naomi Marie. BA, Brigham Young U., Provo, Utah, 1975; MA, Adams State Coll., Alamosa, Colo., 1998. Instr. Mancos Sch. Dist., Colo., 1994—. Chair accountability com. Mancos Re-6 Sch. Dist., 1992—93; pres. local women's orgn. LDS Ch., 1990—94. Mem.: Writer's Club (cofounder 1999—2006). Mem. Lds Ch. Achievements include design of Lesson Plan design chosen for Summer History Institute. Avocations: writing, reading, gardening, fishing, hiking. Office: Mancos School District 355 W Grand Mancos CO 81328 Office Phone: 970-533-7946. Personal E-mail: harleydvdsn@hotmail.com. E-mail: lwhitehead@mancosre6.edu.

**WHITEHEAD, MALCOLM T.,** research scientist; PhD, U. So. Miss., Hattiesburg, 2006. Instr. U. So. Miss., Hattiesburg, 2003—04; asst. prof. Northwestern State U., Natchitoches, La., 2004—. Office: Northwestern State University 305 Sam Sibley Dr Natchitoches LA 71497 Office Phone: 318-357-5133. E-mail: whiteheadm@nsula.edu.

**WHITEHEAD, MICHAEL ANTHONY,** chemistry professor; b. London, June 30, 1935; arrived in Can., 1962, naturalized, 2003; s. Francis Henry and Edith Downes (Rotherham) W.; 1 son, Christopher Mark. B.Sc. in Chemistry with honors, Queen Mary Coll., U. London, 1956, PhD, 1960, D.Sc., 1974. Asst. lectr. Queen Mary Coll., U. London, 1958-60; postdoctoral fellow U. Cin., 1960, asst. prof., 1961; asst. prof. theoretical chemistry McGill U., Montreal, Que., Canada, 1962-66, asso. prof., 1966-74, prof., 1974-99, prof. emeritus, 1999—. Vis. prof. U. Cambridge, Eng., 1971-72, U. Oxford, Eng., 1972-74; vis. professorial fellow Univ. Coll. Wales, Aberystwyth, 1980, U. Oxford, 1990-91; invited prof. U. Geneva, 1983-84; life guest prof. Nat. U. Def. Tech., Changsha, People's Republic of China; vis. Erskine fellow chemistry dept. U. Canterbury, Christchurch, N.Z., 2000, co-chair history and advanced in quantum chemistry 84th conf., Montreal, 2001; mem. Internat. Com. on Nuclear Quadrupole Resonance; co-chmn. 7th Internat. Symposium on Nuclear Quadrapole Resonance, Kingston, Ont., Can., 1983; convenor Can. and Internat. N.E. Symposium of Montreal, 2004; mem. Ctr. for Molecular Modelling, Concordia U., Montreal, 2005—; joint chmn. 1st Applied Pulp and Paper Molecular Modelling Symposium, 2005. Contbr. articles to profl. jours. Mem. parish coun. St. John the Evangelist; exec. coun. Can. Sci. and Christian Affiliation; chmn. Montreal Sch. Theology. Fellow Royal Chem. Soc., Chem. Inst. Can., Royal Soc. Arts; mem. Am. Chem. Soc., Am. Phys. Soc., James McGill Soc. (pres. 1993-95), Sigma Xi (pres. McGill chpt. 1971-72, 81-82, 92-95, 97-99, dir. Can. and internat. constituency group 2000—06, chair awards com. 2001—06, ad hoc mem. internat. com. 2001-05), Phi Lambda Upsilon. Anglican. Office: McGill U Dept Chemistry 801 Sherbrooke St W Montreal PQ Canada H3A 2K6 Office Phone: 514-398-6239. Business E-Mail: tony.whitehead@mcgill.ca. *My faith in God and belief in Christ.*

**WHITEHEAD, NEHEMIAH, III,** music educator; b. Ft. Hood, Tex., Nov. 8, 1955; s. Nehemiah and Robbie Mae Whitehead; m. Brenda Joice Morris, Oct. 17, 2003; children: Scotty Nehemiah, Earnest T. MusB, Tex. A&I, 1977. Cert. tchr. Tex., detention officer Tex. Band dir. Mabank (Tex.) Sch. Dist., 1977—80, Chilton (Tex.) Sch. Dist., 1981—84; tchr., detention officer Bell County Juvenile Detention, Belton, Tex., 1986—95; band dir. Dallas Sch. Dist., 1995—. Exec. bd. mem. Tex. Juvenile Detention Assn., 1990—95. Mem.: Tex. Music Educators Assn., Nat. Assn. Music Educators, NEA, Classroom Tchrs. Assn., Phi Mu Alpha, Kappa Kappa Psi. Democrat. Baptist. Avocations: saxophone, music, preaching gospel. Office Fax: 972-223-2343.

**WHITEHEAD, TANYA DIANNE GRUBBS,** psychologist, educator, research scientist; b. Scottsbuff, Nebr., June 23, 1953; d. William Elliott Grubbs and Esther Mary Cooper Grubbs; m. William Downing Whitehead, Aug. 12, 1971; children: Shana Alexandra, Thomas William, Bethany Rose. B in Psychology summa cum laude, Ottawa U., 1990; M in Clin. Psychology, Avila U., 1992; D in Psychology, U. Mo., 2001. Cert. specialist, developmental and handicapping conditions U. Kans. Sch. Medicine, 1993. Clin. instr. U. Kans. Sch. Medicine, Kansas City, 1987—96; rsch. prof. U. Mo., Kansas City, 1996—. Psychol. consulting burn unit, craniofacial team, spina bifida clinic, pediatric gastroenterology Sch. Medicine, U. Kans., Kansas City, 1987—96; state, regional and nat. advisor People First Self Advocacy Tng. Adults With Devel. Disabilities, 1997—2001; peer grant rev. facilitator and chair US Depts Health and Human Svcs., Corp. for Nat. Svc., Washington, 1999—; program evaluator, impact of asset bldg. on youth from disadvantaged circumstances Office of Cmty. Svc., US Dept. Health and Human Svs.; program evaluation: promoting higher edn. partnerships for global devel. US AID, Assn. Liaison Office for U. Cooperation in Devel., Cape Town, South Africa; dir. AmeriCorps VISTA Project in Self Advocacy, Statewide, Mo., 1998—2000; cons.: cmty. movement for urban progress cmty. devel. corp. Urban Core Cmty. Devel. Project, Kansas City, 2002—04; sr. program evaluator; assets for independence demonstration project, us hhs, office cmty. svcs. PeopleWorks, Inc., Washington, 2000—01. Author: (Self Determination Workshops) New Media Workshops for Adults with DD, (book) Exploring Self Advocacy from a Social Power Perspective, (film) Enslaved Minds: Final Barrier to Freedom and Justice; contbr. new media toolkit (Crystal Communicator Award, 2001); author: (disability accommodation guide) Exchange City Accommodation Guide. Fellow Ctr. for the City, U. Mo., 2004 2005; fellow, Studies in Cmty. Change, 2000. Mem. AMA (mem. commn. accreditation), AAUP, AAUW, LWV, APA, Assn. for the Advancement Ednl. Rsch. (bd. mem.), Am. Nurses Credentialing Ctr. (bd. Commn. on Accreditation). Office Phone: 913-488-7722. Business E-Mail: whiteheadt@umkc.edu.

**WHITEHEAD, WENDY LEE,** special education educator; b. Wabash, Ind., Mar. 1, 1955; d. John Francis and Virginia Mae (Ritzi) W. BS, Ball State U., 1977, MS, 1981; cert. in visually impaired edn., Ind. U., Ft. Wayne, 1987. Cert. spl. edn. tchr., Ind. Tchr. of primary severe disabilities Sharp Creek Elem. Sch., Met. Sch. Dist., Wabash, Ind., 1977—2004; tchr. life skills Bluffton Mid. Sch., 2004—. Active locla sch. dist. Assistive Tech. Team. Mem. Coun. for Exceptional Children (human rights com.). Republican. Roman Catholic. Avocations: reading, bowling, cross stitch. Office: Adams-Well Spl Svcs Co-op 925 Main St Bluffton IN 46714

**WHITEHILL, ANGELA ELIZABETH,** artistic director; b. Leeds, Yorkshire, Eng., Oct. 21, 1938; came to U.S., 1952, naturalized, 1995; d. Donald Paul and Audrey May (Clayforth) Warner; m. Norman James Whitehill, Jr., Dec. 23, 1959; children: Norman James III, Pamela Elizabeth; m. William Parker Noble, Dec. 27, 1998. Student, Arts Ednl. Sch., London, 1955-59. With corps de ballet Ballet Paris, 1958-59; dir. London Sch. Ballet, St. Thomas, V.I., 1960-63; asst. dir. Ocean County Ballet Co., Toms River, NJ 1965-68; founder, dir. Shore Ballet Sch., Toms River, 1968-76; artistic dir. Shore Ballet Co., Toms River, 1971-76; artist in residence Castleton State Coll., Rutland, Vt., 1977-79; founder, artistic dir. Burklyn Ballet Theatre, Johnson, Vt., 1977—2003, founding artistic dir., 2003—; dir. Ballet Umbrella, Dance Coun., Burklyn Designs, 2003—; artistic dir. Paradise Ballet Theatre, Key West, Fla., 2005—. Vis. prof. Colby Sawyer Coll., New London, N.H., 1978-79; resident designer Atlanta Ballet Co., 1982-83; designer, pub. relations N.J. Ballet Co., Orange, 1983-85; artistic dir. Vt. Ballet Theatre, Burlington, 1985-94; master tchr. 1st Congress Internat. de Ballet Classico Contemporaneo, Mex., 2000, Ft. Wayne Ballet, 2005, Regional Dance Am. SW Festival, 2006; interim artistic dir. Huntington Ballet Theatre, 2006. Choreographer Arensky Dances, 1983, A Deux, 1984, 4 Plus 2, 1986, Twins From A Time Gone By, 1987, Heart of the Island, 2002; co-author: Parent's

Book of Ballet, 1988, 2d edit., 2003, The Young Professional's Book of Ballet, 1990, The Dancer's Book of Ballet, 2000, Ballet Magic, The Burklyn Story, 2001, Nutcracker Backstage, 2004; dir. artistic advisor Paradise Ballet Theatre, Nutcracker Key West, 2005; costumer designer Grand Rapids Ballet Swan Lake Act III, 1984, Scottish Am. Ballet, La Sylphide, 1984, Legend of Ench. Bird, 1994, Burklyn Youth Ballet, 1999-05, Hansel & Gretel, Alice in Wonderland, Cinderella & The Flower Fairies, Little Mermaid, Beauty and the Beast, Aladdin, Huntington Ballet Theatre, Cinderella, 2005, Nutcracker Key West ACT II, 2005, Burklyn Youth Ballet, 2006. Dir. Vt. Ballet Theatre Found., Calledonia County, 1986-96. Recipient Francis Hopkins award Ocean County, N.J., 1976, Woman of Achievement award Vt. Woman, 1989, Author's award N.J. Inst. Tech., 1989. Mem. Vt. Council on the Arts, Regional Dance Am. Mem. Soc. Of Friends. Home: 218 Ocean Ave Island Heights NJ 08732 Home (Winter): PO Box 907 Island Heights NJ 08732-0907 Office: Dance Counsel PO Box 493 Johnson VT 05656-0493 Office Phone: 732-288-2660. Personal E-mail: awhitehill@aol.com. E-mail: awhitehill@comcast.net.

**WHITEHILL, MARY EVELYN,** artist, retired librarian; b. Newburgh, N.Y., Mar. 9, 1920; d. William Alexander and Carrie Evelyn Pope; m. W. Hugh Whitehill, July 10, 1943 (dec. Oct. 1972); children: David H., Walter J., Joan W. Roth, Brian T. BA, Wells Coll., 1941; MS, SUNY, Albany, 1966. Libr. Newburgh Bd. Edn., 1966-86. Sec. Middletown (N.Y.) Art Group, 1994-2006. One-woman shows include Intercounty Savs. Bank, New Paltz, N.Y., 1982, Beck Gallery, Hurley, N.Y., 1984, Pine Bush Art Assn., 1987—89, Putnam Valley Hosp., Carmel, N.Y., 1989, Interlude Gallery, Rhinebeck, N.Y., 1990, Unitarian Fellowship, Poughkeepsie, N.Y., 1998, Rock Tavern, N.Y., 2000, Howland Cultural Ctr., Beacon, N.Y. Invitationals, 2002—04, Plein Air Register of N.Y., 2005, Korpeles Mus., 2005, Mus. Hudson Highlands, 2006, Orange Invitational, SUNY, 2006, Represented in permanent collections Glen Ridge (N.J.) Country Club, Putnam Valley Hosp., Mt. St. Mary Coll., Newburgh, N.Y., numerous pvt. collections. Fellow: Salmagundi Club (N.Y.C.); mem.: Ridgefield Art Assn., Ridgewood Art Assn., Catskill Art Soc., N.E. Watercolor Soc. (sec. 1987—91, signature mem.), Pa. Watercolor Soc. (signature mem.), Kent Art Assn. (signature mem.). Presbyterian. Avocations: golf, gardening, music.

**WHITEHORN, CLARK ALLAN,** retired urologist; b. Chgo., Jan. 1, 1926; s. Rex Whitehorn and Pearl May Pollock; m. Virginia Brandt (dec.); m. Virginia Ida Gunn; children: Clark A.(dec.), Robert Brandt(dec.). Student, Johns Hopkins U., Balt., 1943—44; MD, U. Md., Balt., 1948. Lic. physician Fla., diplomate Am. Bd. Urology, Nat. Bd. Med. Examiners. Intern Detroit Receiving Hosp., 1948—49; asst. resident gen. surgery Md. Gen. Hosp., Balt., 1949—50; urology intern Johns Hopkins Hosp., Balt., 1950—51; urology resident Duke Hosp., Durham, NC, 1953—55; founder, chief of urology Gulf Coast Med. Ctr./Hosp., Panama City, Fla.; chief of staff, chief of surgery Bay Med.l Ctr./Hosp., Panama City; ret. Chmn. allocation com. Cmty. Svc. Found., 2006; comdr. U.S. Power Sqdn., Dist. 15, 1984; elder 1st Presbyn. Ch., 1984—2005; dir. Cmty. Svc. Found., 1990—. Capt. M.C. USAF, 1950—53. Fellow: Am. Coll. Urol. Surgeons; mem.: AMA, Fla. State Urol. Soc. (pres.), Bay Med. Soc. (pres.), Yacht Club. Avocations: gardening, golf, travel, reading.

**WHITEHORTON, THELMA,** educational administrator; b. Blyesville, Ark., Feb. 7, 1947; d. William Soloman and Corrine (Carrigans) White; m. Charles D. Horton, May 20, 1970 (div. 1991); children: Corrine Daniel Horton, Tiffany Louise, Charles William. Student, Fla. Internat. U.; BSW, Boise State U., 1975; D (hon.), World U.; student, St. Thomas U., 2006—. Team tchr. Dade County Pub. Schs., Parks and Recreation Coll., North Miami, 1979—80; lead tchr. gifted edn. Dade County Elem. Schs., Miami Dade C.C., Miami, 1980—; owner, dir. Hi School Day Care and Learning Ctr., Cutler Ridge, Fla., 1981—; reading tchr. Miami Dade CC, 1981—83. Lead tchr. gifted Naranja Elem. Sch.; owner Charisma, Fla.; tutor English, Perrine, Fla., 1982—; with Comet Lab, 1996-97; cons. WESTAT Rsch., Barr Industries, Perrine, 1981—, The Rand Co., Student Travel Svc. student placement; temp. Dade County Pub. Schs.; alternative edn. tchr. 5th grade Peskoe Elem. Sch.; advocate African-Am. voices; tchr. liberal arts Wardstone Coll.; adminstr. R.E.S.S. program for implementation of the Mex. Test/Archdiocese of Miami; creator of The Horton Chart for Math; pvt. tchr. tap dance. Author: Have Your Cake and Eat it Too, The Black C, Reciprocal Reading, African Curriculum Integration for Intermediate Education in the Classroom, Reciprocal Reading 1996-97, Epinions.com., Ms. T. Tuttle's 2nd Grade Class T.E.A.M., The Reading Quagmire: ERIC, Lessonpro, The Dream Catcher, 2004; contbr. papers to profl. jours. Active Boy Scouts Am., PTSA, ARC; mem. usher bd. Martin Meml. Meth. Ch.; st. capt. Neighborhood Crime Watch; advocate for Nat. Tchr. Cert., 1995-96; vol. The Horton Chart Eisenhower Nat. Clearinghouse; advocate African Am. Voices; children's advocate for Nat. Tchr. Cert., 1995-96; vol. The Horton Chart Eisenhower Nat. Clearinghouse; advocate African Am. Voices; children's advocate Idaho Gov.'s ADvocacy Program, Boise, 1974-76. Named Comet Lab. Tchr. of Yr., 1996; recipient Equity and Excellence award, Magnet Innovative Programs, Cmty. Svc. award, JESCA orgn. Mem. ACLU, The Exec. Female, Children's Advocates (pres. 1975-83), United Tchrs. Dade County, Alumni Assn. Boise State U., Inst. Children's Lit., Miami C. of C., Fla. Assn. for the Gifted, Kappa Delta Pi. Home: 15905 SW 105th Ct Miami FL 33157-1571 Office: 13990 SW 264th St Homestead FL 33032-7402 Personal E-mail: pug@bellso.net. E-mail: chinatown48@yahoo.com.

**WHITEHOUSE, DAVID BRYN,** museum director; b. Worksop, Notting-hamshire, Eng., Oct. 15, 1941; came to U.S., 1984; s. Brindley Charles and Alice Margaret (Dobson) W.; m. Ruth Delamain Ainger, 1963; children: Sarah, Susan, Peter; m. Elizabeth-Anne Ollemans, 1975; children: Julia, Simon, Nicola. BA, Cambridge U., 1963, MA, 1965, PhD, 1967. Dir. Brit. Inst. Afghan Studies, Kabul, Afghanistan, 1973-74, Brit. Sch., Rome, 1974-84; chief curator Corning Mus. Glass, NY, 1984-87, dep. dir., 1988-97, dir., 1992-99, exec. dir., 1999—. Dir. Sirat expdn. Brit. Inst. Persian Studies, Tehran, Iran, 1966-73. Author: (with Ruth Whitehouse) Archaeological Atlas of the World, 1975, (with David Andrews and John Osborne) Aspects of Medieval Lazio, 1982, (with Donald B. Harden and others) Glass of the Caesars, 1987, Glass of the Roman Empire, 1988, (with Richard Hodges) Mohammed, Charlemagne and the Origins of Europe, 1983, Glass: A Pocket Dictionary, 1993, English Cameo Glass, 1994, Roman Glass in The Corning Museum of Glass, Vol. 1, 1997, Vol. 2, 2001, Vol. 3, 2003, Excavations at ed-Dur (Umm al-Qaiwan, UAE), Vol. 1, The Glass Vessels, 1998, The Corning Museum of Glass, A Decade of Glass Collecting, 1990-1999, 2000, (with Stefano Carboni) Glass of the Sultans, 2001, Sasanian and Post-Sasanian Glass in the Corning Museum of Glass, 2005; contbr. numerous articles and revs. to profl. jours. Wainwright fellow, Oxford U., 1966—73. Fellow Soc. Antiquaries (London), Royal Geog. Soc., Pontificia Accademia Romana di Archeologia; mem. Accademia Fiorentina delle Arti del Disegno, Accademia di Archeologia, Lettere e Belle Arti di Napoli, Deutsches Archaologisches Inst., Internat. Assn. for the History of Glass (pres. 1991-95), Athenaeum Club (London). Office: Corning Mus of Glass 1 Mus Way Corning NY 14830-2253 Office Phone: 607-974-8424. Business E-Mail: whitehoudb@cmog.org.

**WHITEHOUSE, FRED WAITE,** endocrinologist, researcher; b. Chgo., May 6, 1926; s. Fred Trafton Waite and Grace Caroline (Peters) W.; m. Iris Jean Dawson, June 6, 1953; children: Martha, Amy, Sarah. Student, Northwestern U., 1943-45; BS, U. Ill., Chgo., 1947, MD, 1949. Diplomate Am. Bd. Internal Medicine; cert. endocrinology and metabolism. Intern, then resident Henry Ford Hosp., Detroit, 1949-53; staff physician, 1955—, chief divsn. metabolism, 1962-88, chief divsn. endocrinology and metabolism, 1988-95; divsn. head emeritus, 1995—; fellow Joslin Clinic, Boston, 1954-55. Cons. FDA, Washington, 1980—; mem. Coalition on Diabetes Edn. and Minority Health, 1989-91. Contbr. articles to profl. jours. Bd. dirs. Wheat Ridge Found., 1984-93. Lt. USNR, 1951-53. Master ACP; mem. NIH (nat. diabetes adv. bd. 1984-88), Am. Diabetes Assn. (pres. 1978-79, Banting medal 1979, Outstanding Clinician award 1989, Outstanding Physician Educators award 1994, Best award 1994), Detroit Med. Club (pres. 1976), Detroit Acad. Medicine (pres. 1991-92). Lutheran. Avocations: bicycling, gardening. Home:

1265 Blairmoor Ct Grosse Pointe Woods MI 48236-1230 Office: Henry Ford Hosp 3031 W Grand Blvd Ste 800 Detroit MI 48202 Office Phone: 313-916-2131. Office Fax: 313-916-8343. E-mail: fwhitehouse@comcast.net.

**WHITEHOUSE, JOHN HARLAN, JR.,** systems software consultant, diagnostician; b. Lakewood, Ohio, Sept. 12, 1951; s. John Harlan and Frances Elizabeth (Nation) W.; divorced; 1 child, John Harlan III. BA magna cum laude, Ohio Wesleyan U., 1973; postgrad., U. Chgo., 1974; MBA, Cleve. State U., 1976; PhD, Columbia Pacific U., San Rafael, Calif., 1988; postgrad., Vedic U. of Am., 1996—. Cert. computing profl.; cert. info. sys. auditor; cert. in Visual Basic. Programmer San Antonio Express-News, 1977; programming mgr. S.W. Info. Mgmt. Sys., San Antonio, 1977, Utility Data Corp., Houston, 1978; sr. data sys. auditor Nat. City Corp., Cleve., 1978-81; sys. programmer Std. Oil Co., Cleve., 1981-84; adv. sys. engr. IBM, Cleve., 1984-92; pres. Semiotica Corp., 1992—. Mem. exams. editl. coun. Inst. for Cert. Computer Profls., Des Plaines, 1990—, test deployment mgt., 1996-2001, dir. certification, 1999—. Author: CICS Problem Determination Workshop, 1990; co-author: ICCP Guidelines for Recertification, 1990, ICCP Official Study Guide, 1991-95; editor Clifton-Gaston Allen Light, 1994-2004; also numerous articles, columnist. Mem. Assn. for Computing Machinery (chmn. Greater Cleve. chpt. 1982-83, Svc. Recognition award 1984), Assn. of Inst. for Cert. Computer Profls. (regional dir. 1989-93, nominating com. 1991), Masons (dist. edn. officer 2001-02, dist. dep. Grand Master 2002-05), Philalethes Soc. (pres. Western Res. chpt. 2005-06), Phi Beta Kappa. Unitarian Universalist. Home: 22291 Berry Dr Rocky River OH 44116-2013 Office: Semiotica Corp Cleveland PMB 241 25935 Detroit Rd Westlake OH 44145-2449 Office Phone: 440-356-8738. Business E-Mail: sales@softwarecleveland.com.

**WHITEHURST, BROOKS MORRIS,** chemical engineer; b. Apr. 9, 1930; s. David Brooks and Bessie Ann (Lowry) W.; m. Carolyn Sue Boyer, July 4, 1951; children: Garnett, Anita, Robert. BS, Va. Poly. Inst. and State U., 1951. Registered profl. engr., N.C. Sr. process asst. Am. Enka Corp., Lowland, Tenn., 1951-56; sr. process devel. engr. Va.-Carolina Chem. Corp., Richmond, Va., 1956-63; project engr. Texaco Inc., Richmond, 1963-66; mgr. engring. svcs. Texasgulf, Inc., Aurora, NC, 1967-80, mgr. spl. projects, long range planning, 1980-81; pres. Whitehurst Assocs., Inc., New Bern, NC, 1981—. Instr., lectr., cons. alt. sources of energy comty. colls. and univs.; presenter paper Solar World Forum, Brighton, Eng., 1981. Co-chmn. NC state supt. task force on secondary edn., 1974—; mem. NC state adv. com. on trade and indsl. edn, 1971-77; chmn. Gov.'s Task Force Vols. in Workplace, 1981; chmn. State Adv. Coun. Career Edn., 1977—; gov.'s liaison for edn. and bus., 1978-79. Recipient commendation Pres. US, 1981 Mem. AIChE, Am. Inst. Chemists (cert., bd. dirs. 1980-84), NC Inst. Chemists (pres. 1975-77), Nat. Soc. Profl. Engrs., NC Soc. Profl. Engrs., Royal Soc. Chemistry. Achievements include patents and current work on biodegradable chelate systems, municipal yard waste disposal, micronutrients for agriculture, waste rubber recycling, conversion of industrial by-products containing manganese and phosphorous to useful non-toxic materials for use in agriculture for environmental clean-up; development of environmentally friendly products for forest fertilization and chelates for organic agriculture, and a process for purification of impure phosphoric acid. Home: 1983 Hoods Creek Rd New Bern NC 28562-9103 Office: PO Box 3335 New Bern NC 28564-3335

**WHITEHURST, GROVER JAY,** psychologist, educator, federal official; b. Washington, N.C., Sept. 28, 1944; s. Grover J. and Dixie (Daniel) W.; m. Janet E. Fischel, June 7, 1981; children: Owen E., Adam E. BA, East Carolina U., Greenville, 1966; MA, U. Ill., 1968, PhD. 1970. Lic. psychologist, N.Y. Asst. prof. SUNY, Stony Brook, 1970—74, assoc. prof., 1975—79, prof. psychology, 1981—2002, chair dept. psychology, 1998—2002; sr. lectr. U. N.S.W., Sydney, Australia, 1974—75; acad. v.p. Merrill-Palmer Inst., Detroit, 1979—81; dir. Inst. of Edn. Sciences, 2002—. Author: Child Behavior, 1977; editor Developmental Rev., 1981-2000; contbr. over 100 articles to profl. jours. Grantee NIH, 1985, Smith Richardson Found., 1990, Pew Charitable Trusts, 1992, U.S. Adminstrn. Children and Families, 1996, 2000. Fellow APA, Am. Assn. Profl. and Applied Psychology; Nat. Rsch. Coun. (commn. early childhood); Head Start, Nat. Adv. Bd. on Rsch. Avocation. sailing. Mailing: Dir Inst Educ Sciences US Dept Edu 555 New Jersey Ave NW Rm 600-D Washington DC 20208-5500 Office Phone: 202-219-1385. E-mail: grover.whitehurst@ed.gov.

**WHITEHURST, LUCINDA SNYDER,** school librarian; d. Wilma Jones and William Franklin Snyder; m. Mark Alexander Whitehurst, May 20, 1989; children: Megan Macye, Alexander William. BA, Coll. William and Mary, 1986; MS, U. Ill., 1987. Children's libr. DC Pub. Libr., 1987—89; young adult libr. County of Henrico Pub. Libr., Richmond, Va., 1989—92; lower sch. libr. St. Christopher's Sch., Richmond, 1992—. Adj. instr. continuing edn. U. Va., Richmond, 2001—. Contbr. articles and reviews to profl. jours.; editor: (newsletter) The Open Book. Mem. Friends of the Richmond Pub. Libr., 2000—07, State Networking Users Adv. Bd., Richmond, 2000—02; pres. Garfield F. Childs Meml. Fund, Richmond, 2003—04. Lois Wells Irwin fellow, U. Ill. Grad. Sch. Libr. and Info. Sci., 1986. Mem.: Va. Ednl. Media Assn., ALA (com. chair 2004—05). Office: St Christopher's Sch 711 St Christopher's Rd Richmond VA 23226

**WHITEHURST, MARY TARR,** artist, poet, writer; b. Norfolk, Va., Nov. 20, 1923; d. Henry Bennitt and Martha Ida Tarr; m. Jerry Rutter Whitehurst, Dec. 24, 1943; children: Henry Armistead, Jeffrey Tarr, Martha W. Bryant. Student, Coll. William & Mary, 1940-42, Wytheville C.C., 1968, Sullins Coll., 1976-80, Va. Western C.C., 1988. Docent Mus. Fine Arts, Roanoke, Va., 1973-75. Dir., endowing mem. Fine Arts Ctr. of New River Valley, Pulaski, Va., 1980-93; charter, endowing mem. Bristol Mus. Fine Arts, Va./Tenn., 1975-80; benefactor, mem. Arts Found. Radford U., Va., 1991—. One-woman shows include Mus. Fine Arts, Roanoke, Va., 1977, Emory & Henry Coll., Emory, Va., 1982, Radford U. Art Gallery, Va., 1991, Ashland Area Art Galery, Ky., 1993, Va. Polytech. Inst. & State U., Blacksburg, 1985—, New River C.C. Found., 1985—; Coll. William & Mary, Williamsburg, 1995; endowment Poly. Inst. & State U., Blacksburg, Va., 1998; author: (poetry) Silent As Birds, 1997. Endowing mem. Va. Polytech. Inst. & State U., Blacksburg, 1985—, New River C.C. Found., 1985—, Coll. William & Mary, Williamsburg, 1995; mem. Va. Polytech. Found., Blacksburg, Va. Recipient Clement Gueenberg award of distinction Mus. Fine Arts, Roanoke, 1976, Grumbacher Gold medal Soc. Water Color Artists, 1995; art dept. named in honor New River C.C., Dublin, Va., 1994. Mem. Catharine Lorillard Wolfe Art Club (Joyce Williams water color award 1985), Midwest Artists (assoc.) Water Color Soc., Blacksburg Regional Artists Assn., Allied Artists (assoc.), So. Water Color Soc. (two awards 1997, Blue Ribbon winner 2000). Avocations: travel abroad, art collection, history, philanthropy. Home: Painters Wood 2492 Forest Hill Dr Draper VA 24324-3224

**WHITEHURST, WILLIAM WILFRED, JR.,** management consultant; b. Balt., Mar. 4, 1937; s. William Wilfred and Elizabeth (Hogg) Whitehurst; m. Linda Joan Fisher, July 1, 1961; children: Catherine Elizabeth, William Wilfred III. BA, Princeton U., 1958; MS with distinction, Carnegie Inst. Tech., 1963. Mathematician Nat. Security Agy., Fort George G. Meade, Md., 1961—63; mgmt. cons. McKinsey & Co., Inc., Washington, 1963—66; ptnr. L.E. Peabody & Assocs., Washington, 1966—69, exec. v.p., dir. Lanham, Md., 1969—82, pres., dir., 1983—86; pres. W.W. Whitehurst & Assoc., Inc., Cockeysville, Md., 1986—. Contbr. Code of Fed. Regulations 49 C.F.R. Sect. 1157. Comdr. USNR, 1958—65. Recipient Diploma De Honor 14th Pan Am. Rwy. Congress. Mem.: CFA Inst., Washington Soc. Investment Analysts, Am. Rwy. Engring. Assn. Home and Office: 12421 Happy Hollow Rd Cockeysville Hunt Valley MD 21030-1711

**WHITEKER, ROY ARCHIE,** retired chemistry professor; b. Long Beach, Calif., Aug. 22, 1927; s. Ewing Harris and Mabel Mary (Williams) W.; m. Jean Fiske MacLean, June 3, 1960; 1 son, Scott MacLean. BS, UCLA, 1950, MS, 1952; PhD, Calif. Inst. Tech., 1956. Instr. chemistry M.I.T., 1955-57; asst. prof. Harvey Mudd Coll., Claremont, Calif., 1957-61, assoc. prof.,

1961-67, prof. chemistry, 1967-73; assoc. dir. fellowships Nat. Acad. Scis., Washington, 1967-68; dep. exec. sec. Com. on Internat. Exch. of Persons, Washington, 1971—72, exec. sec., 1972—75; dir. Coun. Internat. Exchange Scholar, 1975-76; prof. chemistry U. Pacific, Stockton, Calif., 1976-92, dean Coll. Pacific, 1976-89; ret., 1992. Bd. dirs. Stockton Symphony Assn., 1978-80; dir. cmty. adv. bd. Sta. KUOP, 1981-89; bd. dirs. Stockton Chorale, 1989-97; pres. U. of the Pacific Emeriti Soc., 1992-94, 2000-02. With USNR, 1945-46. Dow Chem. Co. fellow, 1953-54, DuPont Tchg. fellow, 1954-55, NSF Sci. Faculty fellow Royal Inst. Tech., Stockholm, Sweden, 1963-64 Mem. Am. Chem. Soc., Alpha Chi Sigma, Phi Beta Kappa, Phi Kappa Phi, Sigma Xi. Home: 3400 Wagner Hts Rd # 30 Stockton CA 95209 Business E-Mail: rwhiteker@pacific.edu.

**WHITELEY, BENJAMIN ROBERT,** retired insurance company executive; b. Des Moines, July 13, 1929; s. Hiram Everett and Martha Jane (Walker) W.; m. Elaine Marie Yunker, June 14, 1953; children: Stephen Robert, Benjamin Walker BS, Oreg. State U., 1951; MS, U. Mich., 1952; postgrad. advanced mgmt. program, Harvard U.; DHL (hon.), Pacific U., 2001. Clk. group dept. Standard Ins. Co., Portland, Oreg., 1956-59, asst. actuary group dept. then asst. actuary actuarial dept., 1959-63, asst. v.p., asst. actuary, 1963-64, asst. v.p., assoc. actuary, 1964-70, v.p. group ins. adminstrn., 1970-72, v.p. group ins. div., 1972-80, exec. v.p. group ins., 1980-81, exec. v.p., 1981-83, pres., CEO, 1983-92, chmn. bd. dirs., CEO, 1993-94, chmn. bd. dirs., 1994—98; ret., 2000. Bd. dir. The Greenbriar Cos., chmn. bd., 2004—. Past pres. Columbia Pacific coun. Boy Scouts Am.; past chmn. bd., trustee Pacific U., Forest Grove, Oreg.; past chmn. Oreg. Health Scis. Found., Oreg. Trail Coordinating Coun., Portland Opera Assn.; trustee Oreg. Cmty. Found., 1998—, chmn., 2004-06; campaign chair, bd. dir. United Way Portland, 1994. 1st. lt. USAF, 1952—55. Recipient Silver Beaver award Cascade Pacific coun. Boy Scouts Am., 1993, Harvey and Emiline Clark medal Pacific U., 1991, Alumni fellow award Oreg. State U., 1991, Aubrey R. Watzek award Lewis and Clark Coll., 1994, Lifetime Achievement award Bus. Youth Exch., Portland, Oreg., 1995. Fellow Soc. Actuaries; mem. Arlington Club (pres. 1991), Waverley Country Club, Multnomah Athletic Club. Republican. Methodist. Personal E-mail: eorbwhiteley@earthlink.net.

**WHITELEY, HENRY HOWARD,** religious studies educator, minister; b. Roswell, N.Mex., Oct. 31, 1928; s. Alford and Ruth Henrich Whiteley; m. Yvonna Margaret Cornell, Feb. 28, 1953; children: Emma Lachelle Whiteley Yoder, Lynn Howard. BS in Music Edn., John Brown U., Siloam Springs, Ark., 1961; postgrad., West Tex. State U., 1963. Tchr., band dir. K-12 Gravette Pub. Schs., Ark., 1960—62, Balko Pub. Schs., Okla., 1962—63; minister Big Spring, Tex., Galena, Kans., Hardesty, Okla., Logan, Okla., Baxter Springs, Kans.; prof. music, bibl. studies Apostolic Faith Bible Coll., Baxter Springs, 1965—68, 1984—88, 1995—, supt., 1977—78; pastor Pampa Chapel of Apostolic Faith, Tex., 1988—95. Founder, dir. Cantatas cmty. choir, 1965—70. Editor: Apostolic Faith Report, 1964—72. Dir. Ann. Nat. Ch. Camp, Laverne, Okla., 1973; pres. Historical Alliance, Pampa, 1990, sec. Baxter Springs, Kans., 1999—2000; dir. Ann. Youth Camp, Baxter Springs, 1965—69, 1996—2002, Ann. Nat. Ch. Camp, Baxter Springs, 1965—69, Ann. Youth Camp, Laverne, Okla., 1973—75; adv. bd. Salvation Army, Pampa, 1993—95; bd. dirs. Apostolic Faith Bible Coll., 1977—79. Cpl. U.S. Army, 1948—51. Trinity Apostolic Faith. Avocations: reading, music, travel. Mailing: 2353 Washington Baxter Springs KS 66713 Office Phone: 620-856-3283.

**WHITELO, VELMA HOLLAND,** special education educator; b. Memphis, Dec. 11; d. Willie Rogers and Lettie Sherrod Holland; 1 child, Valerie N. Jackson. BS, Lemoyne Owen Coll., 1973; MS in Edn., U. Memphis, 1986; student, Cumberland U., 1995. Spl. edn. tchr. Memphis City Sch., 1973—, homebound tchr., 1993—99. Coach Spl. Olympics, Memphis, 1978—; jr. deputy coord. Shelby County Sheriff Dept., 1983—; truant officer Memphis City Sch., 1993—99. Coord. Just Say No Club, 1985—99. Recipient United Way award, Nat. Children's Cancer Soc., Trust Officer of Year, Truancy Prevention Svc., Rotary award, Memphis Rotary Club, 1996; grantee Tchr. Initiative Grant, 1994. Mem.: Nat. Edn. Assn., Tenn. Edn. Assn., Memphis Edn. Assn., Delta Sigma Theta. Democrat. Baptist. Avocations: travel, dance.

**WHITEMAN, DOUGLAS E.,** publisher; b. Emporia, Kans., Mar. 4, 1961; s. Floyd E. and Phyllis E. (Troyer) W.; m. Susan R. Anderson, Sept. 14, 1985; 1 child, Aaron Anderson Douglas. BSBA, U. Kans., 1983. With Putnam Pub. Group, Denver and N.Y.C., 1983—, dir. trade sales and mktg., internat. sales mgr. N.Y.C., 1987—89, v.p. sales and mktg., 1989—94; sr. v.p., pub. Putnam and Grosset Book Group, N.Y.C., 1994—95, pres., pub., 1995—97; pres. Penguin Group (USA) Books for Young Readers, N.Y.C., 1997—; exec. v.p. Penguin Group, 1998—. Vice chmn., bd. dirs. Eric Carle Mus. of Picture Book Art, 2001—; bd. dirs. Children's Book Coun., 2004—. Mem.: Pub.'s Lunch Club N.Y.C. (pres. 2004—05). Methodist. Avocations: literature, tennis, fantasy baseball. Office: Penguin Group USA 345 Hudson St Fl 14 New York NY 10014-4592 Business E-Mail: doug.whiteman@us.penguingroup.com.

**WHITEMAN, JILL KAREN,** music educator; b. Circle, Mont., June 24, 1965; d. Floyd and Lorraine Jean Whiteman; m. Jerry Robert Losing, Nov. 28, 1992; children: Chandler John, Spencer James. BSc in Composite Music, Dickinson State U., N.D., 1987. Tchr. music Wing Sch., ND, 1987—90; tchr. asst. U. N.D., Grand Forks, 1990—91; tchr. music Baker Schs., Mont., 1991—. Vol. coach Baker AAU Swim Team, 2003—; vol. Baker Wrestling Club, 2004—. Mem.: Am. Choral Dirs. Assn., Mu Phi Epsilon. Achievements include development of HeartFelt Thanks Project, which distributes handmade Valentine's to Montana National Guard soldiers. Home: 907 S 2d St E Baker MT 59313

**WHITEMAN, JOSEPH DAVID,** retired lawyer, manufacturing company executive; b. Sioux Falls, S.D., Sept. 12, 1933; s. Samuel D. and Margaret (Wallace) W.; m. Mary Kelly, Dec. 29, 1962; children: Anne Margaret, Mary Ellen, Joseph David, Sarah Kelly, Jane. BA, U. Mich., 1955, JD, 1960. Bar: D.C. 1960, Ohio 1976. Assoc. Cox, Langford, Stoddard & Cutler, Washington, 1959-64; sec., gen. counsel Studebaker group Studebaker Worthington, Inc., N.Y.C., 1964-71; asst. gen. counsel United Telecommunications, Inc., Kansas City, Mo., 1971-74; v.p., gen. counsel, sec. Weatherhead Co., Cleve., 1974-77, Parker Hannifin Corp., Cleve., 1977-98; ret., 1998. Immediate past chmn. bd. dirs. St. Lukes Med. Ctr. Served as lt. USNR, 1955-57. Mem. ABA, Beta Theta Pi, Phi Delta Phi. Republican. Roman Catholic. Home and Office: 2508 Robinson Springs Rd Stowe VT 05672

**WHITEMAN, RICHARD FRANK,** architect; b. Mankato, Minn., Mar. 24, 1925; s. Lester Raymond and Mary Grace (Dawald) W.; m. Jean Frances Waite, June 20, 1948 (dec. May 1980); children: David, Sarah, Lynn, Ann, Carol, Frank, Marie, Steven; m. Mavis Patricia Knutsen, May 30, 1982. BArch, U. Minn., 1945; MArch, Harvard U., 1948. Registered architect, Minn. Designer Ellerbe Co., St. Paul, Minn., 1946; architect Thorshov and Cerny, Mpls., 1948-53; ptnr. Jyring and Whiteman, Hibbing, Minn., 1953-62; pres. AJWM Inc., Hibbing and Duluth, Minn., 1963-72, Architects Four, Duluth, 1972-83; owner Richard Whiteman, Duluth, 1983-95; sr. architect U. Minn., Duluth. Chmn. Architect Sect. Registration Bd., Minn., 1972-80. Prin. works include Washington Sch., Hibbing, 1957 (Minn. Soc. Architects Design award 1957), Whiteman Summer Home, Pengilly, Minn. (Minn. Soc. Architects Design award 1959), Bemidji State Coll. Phys. Edn. Bldg. (Minn. Soc. Architects Design award 1960), Whiteman Residence, Griggs Hall UMD, 1990. Pres. U. for Srs., 1993-94, 2000-01; chair Duluth Housing Authority, 2001-06, vice chair, 2006—. With UMD, 1943—45. Mem. Minn. Soc. Architects (pres. 1972), Northeast Minn. Architects (pres. 1962), Minn. Designer Selection Bd. (chmn. 1990). Clubs: Kitchi Gammi (Duluth). Lodges: Kiwanis. Democrat. Roman Catholic. Avocations: photography, fishing, cross country skiing, travel. Home: 3500 E 3rd St Duluth MN 55804-1812 E-mail: arch032425@aol.com.

**WHITEMAN, RICHARD MARK,** lawyer; b. Detroit; s. Wayne Donald and Margaret Rose (Marshick) Whiteman; m. Ellen Beth Rosenthal, Aug. 30, 1986; 1 child, Andrew. BA, Colgate U., 1970; JD, Wayne State U., 1982. Bar: Mich. Labor mgmt. relations examiner Nat. Labor Relations Bd., Detroit, 1973—84, atty., 1984—93, supr. atty., 1993—2002, dep. regional atty., 2002—. Mem.: State Bar Mich., Labor and Employment Law Section. Avocations: golf, jogging, tennis, travel, reading. Office: Nat Labor Relations Bd 477 Mich Ave Detroit MI 48226

**WHITENER, CAROLYN RAYE,** artist; b. Corpus Christi, Texas, Feb. 2, 1941; d. Rayburn N. and Alice G. Hamilton; m. Howard Dwain Whitener; children: Mark Dwain, Rynn Rayna. Student, U. Sci. and Arts Okla., 1981-85. Co-owner Honk'n'Holler's, Okla., 1962-75; owner Clynn's Designs, Okla. City, 1969—; co-owner W&W Cattle Ranch, Okla., 1973—; comml. artist, co-owner Colorvision, Inc., Okla. and Tex., 1979—. Cons. Tele-Weight, Buena Vista, Colo., 1985-92, Craig Versus Boren, 1972-76; comml. design cons. for one and two dimensional rendering drawings Rynn's Lawncare & Landscaping, Oklahoma City, 1997—; freelance designer staging and backdrops, N.Y., 1973-74; mem. adv. coun., Status of Okla. Woman, 2001—. Active Grady County Environ. Coalition, 1991—92; adv. mem. Gov.'s Okla. Commn. on Status of Women, 2000—. Recipient Outstanding Cmty. Svc. award, 1992, One Person Who Made a Difference LWVOK, 1997, Pres. Prestigious award Okla. State U., 1996, First Adv. award Okla. Commn. on Status of Women, 2001, Gov. Commendation award Gov. Frank Keating, 2001, State of Okla. Citation award Rep. Richard Phillips and Sen. Mike Fair, 2001; named Woman of Yr. Okla. City Coun. of Beta Sigma Phi, 1997-98. Mem. Okla. Assn. Family Cmty. and Edn., Grady County Ext. Homemakers, Oklahoma City Newcomer's Club, Beta Sigma Phi (Woman of Yr. award 1997-98, Outstanding Svc. award 1992, Evening Lions Homecoming Window Design awards, 1966-68), Chickesha Okla. H.S. Alumni Class (decorations com. 1989—). Democrat. Methodist. Avocations: art, sewing, cooking, travel. Home: 12324 St Lukes Ln Oklahoma City OK 73142 E-mail: CrWhitener@aol.com.

**WHITENER, WILLIAM GARNETT,** dancer, choreographer; b. Seattle, Aug. 17, 1951; s. Warren G. and Virginia Louise (Garnett) Whitener. Student, Cornish Sch. Allied Arts, Seattle, 1958-69. Dancer NYC Opera, 1969, Joffrey Ballet, NYC, 1969-77, Twyla Tharp Dance, NYC, 1978-87; asst. to choreographer Jerome Robbins for Robbins' Broadway, NYC, 1988; artistic dir. Les Ballets Jazz de Montréal, 1991-93, Royal Winnipeg Ballet, 1993-95, Kansas City Ballet, 1996—. Coord. dance dept. Concord Acad., Mass., 1988; vis. artist U. Wash., 1989—91; dance faculty mem. Harvard U. Summer Dance, 1989—90, NYU, 1985. Dancer (Broadway plays) Dancin', 1978, choreographer Princeton Ballet, Joffrey II, John Curry Ice Theatre, Ballet Hispanico of NY, Boston Ballet Internat. Choreography Competition, Tommy Tune, Martine Van Hamel/Kevin McKenzie, Ann Reinking, Seattle Repertory Theatre, Am. Ballroom Theatre, NYC, Hartford Ballet, Conn., On the Boards with Bill Irwin, PBS-TV Alive From Off Center, (Operas) A Little Night Music, Pacific Northwest Ballet, Rusalka, Seattle Opera, (Operas) Aida, dancer (films) Amadeus, Zelig, (TV films) The Catherine Wheel, Dance in America; performer: Garden of Earthly Delights, 1988. Bd. trustees Dance-USA, 2000—. Ford Found. scholar, 1963—64. Mem.: Am. Guild Musical Artists, Actor's Equity. Office: Kansas City Ballet 1601 Broadway Kansas City MO 64108-1207*

**WHITESCARVER, JACK EDWARD,** federal agency administrator; b. Palestine, Tex., May 16, 1937; s. A.B. and Elizabeth Lorraine (Kimball) W. BS, Sam Houston State U., 1959, MS, 1965; PhD, U. Medicine Dentistry NJ, 1974. Rsch. assoc. Harvard U. Sch. Pub. Health, Boston, 1976-77; grants assoc. NIH, Bethesda, Md., 1977-78; spl. ass't. to dir. NIH/NIAID, Bethesda, 1978-84; assoc. dean R&D Emory U. Sch. Medicine, Atlanta, 1984-86, asst. prof. pathology, 1985-88, assoc. dean, 1986-88; dep. dir. Office AIDS Rsch., NIH, Bethesda, 1988—99, acting dir., 1999—2002, dir., 2002—. Contbr. articles to Jour. Infectious Diseases, Jour. Investigative Dermatology, Tex. Reports Biol. Medicine. Fellow Albert Soiland Cancer Found., 1967-70; recipient Alumnus of Yr. U. Medicine and Dentistry NJ, 1991. Mem. Am. Acad. Allergy and Immunology, Am. Soc. for Microbiology, Infectious Diseases Soc. Am., Internat. AIDS Soc., Royal Soc. Medicine. Office. Office 301-496-0357. Office Fax: 301-496-3119.*

**WHITESELL, JOHN EDWIN,** retired motion picture company executive; b. DuBois, Pa., Feb. 23, 1938; s. Guy Roosevelt and Grace Ethlyn (Brisbin) W.; m. Amy H. Jacobs, June 12, 1960; 1 child, Scott Howard; m. Martha Kathlyn Hall, Sept. 3, 1975; m. Phyllis Doyle, May 8, 1993. BA, Pa. State U., 1962. Asst. mgr. non-theatrical div. Columbia Pictures Corp., N.Y.C., 1963-66; with Warner Bros., Inc., 1966—2003, nat. sales mgr. non-theatrical div. Burbank, Calif., 1968-75, v.p., 1975-76; v.p. internat. sales adminstrn. Warner Bros. Internat. TV Distbn., 1976-2001, cons., 2001—03, ret., 2003. Bd. dirs. Mastermedia Internat. Inc.; past bd. dirs. Found. for Entertainment Programming in Higher Edn.; mem. self-study com. Nat. Entertainment Conf., 1974-75. Served with USNR, 1956-58. Recipient Alumni Fellow award Pa. State U., 2001, Outstanding Alumnus award Pa. State U. DuBois Campus, 1995, Founders award Nat. Entertainment Conf., 1975. Mem. Nat. Audio-Visual Assn. (motion picture coun. 1973-76, exec. com. film coun. 1969-76, ednl. materials producers coun. 1970-76), Acad. TV Arts and Scis., Nat. Assn. Media Educators (adv. com. 1973-76)

**WHITESELL, PATRICK,** agent; Previously with Intertalent; agent United Talent Agy.; with Creative Artists Agy., 1995—2000, co-head motion picture talent dept., 2000—01; ptnr. Endeavor Agy., Beverly Hills, Calif., 2001—. Mem. Calif. Film Commn., 2006—. Named one of 50 Most Powerful People in Hollywood, Premiere mag., 2004—06.*

**WHITESELL, STEPHEN ERNEST,** parks director; BS in Environ. Resources, Calif. State U., Sacramento, 1973; M in Landscape Architecture, Harvard U., 1977. Landscape architect, planner Denver Svc. Ctr., Lakewood, Colo., 1977-80, Ind. Dunes Nat. Lakeshore, Porter, Ind., 1980-83; chief maintenance Apostle Islands Nat. Seashore, Bayfield, Wis., 1983-84; supt. Longfellow, John F. Kennedy, Frederick Law Olmsted Nat. Hist. Sites, Cambridge, Mass., 1984-87; supt. Sandy Hook Unit Gateway Nat. Recreation Area, Highlands, NJ, 1987—91; supt. Petroglyph Nat. Monument, San Antonio, 1991-95, San Antonio Missions Nat. Hist. Park, 1995—. Bd. dirs. Cultural Alliance of San Antonio Area Tourism Coun., City Year San Antonio. Recipient Award of Merit Boston Soc. Landscape Architects, 1985, U.S. Dept. Interior Superior Svc. Honor award, 1998. Mem. Rotary Club San Antonio, Los Compadres de San Antonio Missions (adv. bd.), San Antonio Tourism Coun. (bd. dirs.), Cultural Alliance San Antonio (City of Yr. San Antonio). Avocations: golf, fishing, gardening. Office: San Antonio Missions Nat Hist Park 2202 Roosevelt Ave San Antonio TX 78210-4919 Office Phone: 210-534-8833. Office Fax: 210-534-1106. Business E-Mail: steve_whitesell@nps.gov.

**WHITESIDE, CAROL GORDON,** foundation executive; b. Chgo., Dec. 15, 1942; d. Paul George and Helen Louise G.; m. John Gregory Whiteside, Aug. 15, 1964; children: Brian Paul, Derek James. BA, U. Calif., Davis, 1964. Pers. mgr. Emporium Capwell Co., Santa Rosa, 1964-67; pers. asst. Levi Strauss & Co., San Francisco, 1967-69; project leader Internat. Institute, San Francisco, 1983-88; with City Coun. Modesto, 1983-87; mayor City of Modesto, 1987-91; asst. sec. for intergovtl. rels. The Resources Agy., State of Calif., Sacramento, 1991-93; dir. intergovtl. affairs Gov.'s Office, Sacramento, 1993-97; pres. Great Valley Ctr., Modesto, Calif., 1997—. Trustee Modesto City Schs., 1979-83; nat. pres. Rep. Mayors and Local Ofcls., 1990; mem. Sierra Nev. Conservancy Bd., 2005-. Recipient Lifetime Achievement award League of Calif. Cities, 2002, Excellence in Pub. Svc. award, Fresno Bus. Coun., 2004; named Outstanding Woman of Yr. Women's Commn., Stanislaus County, Calif., 1988, Woman of Yr., 27th Assembly Dist., 1991; Toll fellow Coun. of State Govts., 1996, Champion of Am. Dream, Calif. State U., Stanislaus, 2002. Republican. Lutheran. Office: Great Valley Ctr 201 Needham St Modesto CA 95354-0903 E-mail: carol@greatvalley.org.

**WHITESIDE, CHARLES B., III,** investment company executive; b. Ft. Smith, Ark., Mar. 17, 1941; s. Charles B. Jr. and R. Evelyn cindy Whiteside; m. Catherine Ware, Jan. 29, 1966; children: Carrie H., Charles B. IV. BSBA, U. Ark., 1963. 1st v.p. Merrill Lynch & Co., Little Rock, 1965—. Trustee Ark. Children's Hosp., 1974—, chmn., treas., 1983—88; vice chmn. bd. dirs. Ark. Children's Hosp. Found., 1983—; trustee Ark. Children's Rsch. Inst. 1989—2000, chmn., 1990—; trustee, treas. Lyon Coll., Batesville, Ark., 1992—; bd. advisors U. Ark., Fayetteville, 2006. 1st lt. U.S. Army, 1963—65. Recipient Outstanding Vol. Fundraising award for State of Ark., Nat. Soc. Fund Raising Execs., 2000; Sr. Paul Harris fellow, Rotary. Mem.: Kappa Sigma Alumni Assn. (pres. bd. dirs. 1974—). Episcopalian. Avocations: hunting, fishing. Office: Merrill Lynch 2200 Rodney Parham Ste 300 Little Rock AR 72212 Office Phone: 501-312-7285.

**WHITESIDE, MEL L.,** information technology manager, educator, small business owner; s. Terry D. Whiteside and Sandra A. Smith; m. Kimberly C. Erickson, May 30, 1987; children: Brandon C., Lauren P., Michael C., Graham C. BS in Bus. Adminstrn., Tabor Coll., Wichita, Kans., 2001; MA in Career and Tech. Edn., Ball State U., Mincie, Ind., 2006. Civil designer MKEC Engring. Cons., Wichita, Kans., 1996—2000; lead instr., project mgr. Butler C.C., Andover, Kans., 2000—; prin., owner Whiteside Consulting, Wichita, 2000—. Cons. Whiteside Consulting, Wichita, Kans., 2000—06; mem. drafting standards com. Kans. State Bd. Edn., 2003—06; regional dir. coun. workforce edn. area IV State of Kans., 2005—06. Musician: (albums) The Path - Ave. G, Rich Mullins - Awesome God Tour, The Russians Love USA; book reviewer: Technical Drawing, 12th edit. Asst. coach girl's basketball Andover Recreation League, Kans., 2004—06, coach boy's baseball, 2006; mem. Hope Cmty. Ch., Andover, Kans., drummer, 1989—2006, tchr. Sunday sch., 2005—06; drummer Ctrl. Cmty. Ch., Wichita, 2005—06; v.p., sec. Hope In Transit, Bloomfield, N.Mex., 2004—06. Bd. dirs. Andover Pub. Libr. Nominee Godern Apple Tchr. of Yr., El Dorado C. of C., 2003; named New Faculty Mem. of Yr., Butler C.C., 2002, Outstanding Faculty Mem., Order of Purple, 2005; recipient Entrpreneurial Spirit award, Butler C.C., 2005. Mem.: Kans. Career and Tech. Educators Assn., Am. Design Drafting Assn., Kans. Inst. Tech. Edn. Avocations: softball, basketball, percussion. Office: Butler Community College 715 E 13th St N Andover KS 67002 Office Phone: 316-218-6135. Business E-Mail: mwhiteside@butlercc.edu.

**WHITESIDE, WILLIAM ANTHONY, JR.,** retired lawyer; b. Phila., Feb. 23, 1929; s. William Anthony and Ellen T. (Hensler) W.; m. Eileen Ann Ferrick, Feb. 27, 1954; children: William Anthony III, Michael P., Eileen A., Richard F., Christopher J., Mary P. BS, Notre Dame U., 1951; LLB, U. Pa., 1954. Bar: Pa. 1955. Assoc. Spinser, Satinsky, Gilliland & Packel, Phila., 1956—58, ptnr., 1958—61, Fox, Rothschild, O'Brien & Frankel, Phila. 1961—2001; ret., 2001. Past chmn. Police Athletic League, Phila.; trustee Am. Coll. Mgmt. and Tech., Dubrovnik, Croatia; chmn. emeritus bd. trustees, emeritus trustee, Rochester Inst. of Tech.; emeritus trustee C.C. Phila. Found.; trustee LaSalle Coll. H.S. Phila.; pres. adv. coun. U. Notre Dame; emeritus trustee Germantown Acad., past pres. 1st lt. USAF, 1954-56. Named Man of Yr., Notre Dame Club Phila., 1967. Mem.: ABA, Pa. Soc., Phila. Bar Assn., Pa. Bar Assn., Wissahickon Skating Club, Union League Club Phila. Republican. Roman Catholic. Home: 7808 Cobden Rd Glenside PA 19038-7256 also: 901 Gardens Plz Ocean City NJ 08226-4719 Office: Fox Rothschild LLP 2000 Market St Ste 10 Philadelphia PA 19103-3231 Office Phone: 215-299-2032.

**WHITESIDES, GEORGE MCCLELLAND,** chemistry professor; b. Louisville, Ky., Aug. 3, 1939; m. Barbara Breasted; children: George Thomas, Benjamin Haile. AB, Harvard U., 1960; PhD, Calif. Inst. Tech., 1964; D Honoris Causa (hon.), U. Twente, The Netherlands, 2001. Asst. prof. dept. chemistry MIT, Cambridge, 1963—69, assoc. prof., 1969—71, prof., 1971—75, Arthur C. Cope prof., 1975—80, Haslam and Dewey prof., 1980—82; prof. dept. chemistry Harvard U., Cambridge, 1982—86, Mallinckrodt prof., 1986—2004, Woodford L. and Ann A. Flowers U. prof., 2004—. Adv. position NRC, NSF, Dept. Def. Advanced Rsch. Projects Agy.; mem., chiar internat. sci. adv. bd. Genomics Rsch. Ctr., Academia Sinica. Recipient Pure Chemistry award, Am. Chem. Soc., 1975, Harrison Howe award, Rochester sect., 1979, Disting. Alumni award, Calif. Inst. Tech., 1980, Remsen award, 1983, Arthur C. Cope Scholar award, 1989, James Flack Norris award, 1994, Arthur C. Cope award, 1995, Def. Advanced Rsch. Projects Agy. award for Significant Technical Achievement, 1996, Madison Marshall award, Am. Chem. Soc., 1996, Nat. Medal of Sci., 1998, Disting. Chemist award, Sierra Nev. sect. Am. Chem. Soc., 1999, Wallac Oy Innovation award, Soc. Biomolecular Screening, 1999, Excellence award in Surface Sci., Surfaces Biomaterials Found., 1999, Von Hippel award, Material Rsch. Soc., 2000, World Tech. award for materials, World Tech. Network, 2001, Rschr. of Yr. award, Small Times Mag., 2002, Pitts. Analytical Chemistry award, Soc. Analytical Chemists of Pitts., 2003, Kyoto prize for advanced tech., Inamori Found., 2003, Paracelsus prize, Swiss Chem. Soc., 2004, Ralph and Helen Oesper award, Cin. sect. Am. Chem. Soc., 2004, Jacob Heskel Gabbay award in biotech. and medicine, 2004, Dickson Prize in Sci., 2005, Dan David Found. prize, 2005, Emanuel Merk Lect. prize, 2005, Linus Pauling medal, 2005, Welch award in Chemistry, 2005, Emanuel Merck Lecture prize, 2005, Linus Pauling Medal award, 2005, Welch award, 2005; Alfred P. Sloan fellow, 1968. Fellow: AAAS, Indian Nat. Sci. Acad., World Tech. Network, Chem. Rsch. Soc. India (hon.); mem.: NAE, NAS, Academia Sinica (chmn. internat. sci. adv. bd. Genomics Rsch. Ctr. 2006—), Royal Netherlands Acad. Arts and Scis., Materials Rsch. Soc. India (hon.), Am. Philos. Soc., Am. Acad. Arts and Scis. Office: Harvard U Dept of Chemistry 12 Oxford St Cambridge MA 02138-2902 Business E-Mail: gwhitesides@gmwgroup.harvard.edu.

**WHITESIDES, JOHN LINDSEY, JR.,** aerospace engineering educator, researcher; b. San Antonio, Feb. 27, 1943; s. John Lindsey and Florene Lyndelle (Wheelis) W.; m. Sheila LaVerne Beadle, May 30, 1964 (div. 1975); children: Lisa Diane, John Gregory; m. Andrea Martina Chavez Lewis, Mar. 26, 1994. BS in Aerospace Engring., U. Tex., 1965, PhD, 1968. Asst. prof. George Washington U., Hampton, Va., 1968-74, assoc. prof., 1974-80, prof., 1980—2005; assoc. dir. Joint Inst. for Advancement of Flight Scis., Hampton, 1986—2005. Contbr. articles to profl. jours. Mem. Sigma Series Lectures, Hampton, 1990-2000. Recipient disting. pub. svc. medal NASA, 1993, Malina medal Internat. Astronautical Fedn., 1995. Fellow AIAA (dir. 1987-93, nat. faculty advisor 1989, v.p. mem. svcs. 1999-2002, v.p. publs. 2006—); mem. Am. Soc. Engring. Edn., Soc. Engring. Sci. (organizing com. 1975, 76, 77), Tau Beta Pi, Phi Eta Sigma, Sigma Gamma Tau. Avocations: sports, art. Home: 218 Cheadle Loop Rd Seaford VA 23696-2428 Office: George Washington U-JIAFS 1 Old Oyster Point Rd Ste 200 Newport News VA 23602 Office Phone: 757-269-4949. Business E-Mail: jlw@gwu.edu.

**WHITE-THOMSON, IAN LEONARD,** retired mining executive; b. Halstead, Eng., May 3, 1936; came to U.S., 1969; s. Walter Norman and Leonore (Turney) W-T.; m. Barbara Montgomery, Nov. 24, 1971. BA with 1st class honors, New Coll., Oxford U., 1960, MA, 1969. Mgmt. trainee Borax Consol. Ltd., London, 1960-61, asst. to sales mgr., 1961-64, asst. to sales dir., 1964; comml. dir. Hardman & Holden Ltd., Manchester, Eng., 1965-67, joint mng. dir., 1967-69; v.p. mktg. dept. U.S. Borax Inc., Los Angeles, 1969-73, exec. v.p. mktg., 1973-88, pres., 1988-98, also dir., chmn., 1996-99; group exec. Pa. Glass Sand Corp., Ottawa Silica Co., U.S. Silica Co., 1985-87; exec. dir. L.A. Opera, 2000—01. Bd. dirs. Canpotex Ltd., chmn. bd., 1974-76. Bd. dirs. L.A. Master Chorale, Colburn Sch.; bd. dirs. Thornton Sch. U. So. Calif. With Brit. Army, 1954—56. Named Mfr. of Yr., Calif. Mfrs. Assn., 1997. Mem. Can. Potash Prodrs. Assn. (v.p. 1976-77, dir. 1972-77), Chem. Industry Coun. of Calif. (bd. dirs. 1982-85, chmn. 1984), Am. Mining Congress (bd. dirs. 1989), RTZ Borax and Minerals (bd. dirs. 1992, chief exec. 1995-99), Kerr-McGee Corp. (bd. dirs. 1999-2006), Calif. Club, Valley Hunt Club. Home: 1897 Braemar Rd Pasadena CA 91103-3712 Personal E-Mail: iwhitethom@aol.com.

**WHITE-WHITFIELD, LISA DENISE,** social worker; b. L.A., June 11, 1968; d. Charles L. White and Martha Staten; m. Ervin L. Whitfield, Apr. 25, 1992 (div. Oct. 1, 1995); 1 child, Alexis Ximara. BS in Bus. Adminstrn., Calif. State U., Long Beach, 1992; MPA, Calif. State U., Carson, 2006. Tchg. credential Calif. Bank teller Wells Fargo Bank, Lakewood, Calif., 1987—88; proof operator Bank of Am., Long Beach, 1988—89; spl. edn. tchrs. asst. Inglewood (Calif.) Unifield Sch. Dist., 1989—91; adminstrv. asst. Remax Realtors, Carson, 1991—92; substitute tchr. Compton (Calif.) Unified Sch. Dist., 1992—93; acctg. clk. United Airlines, El Segundo, Calif., 1993—94; social worker LA County Dept. Pub. Social Svcs., 1994—. Mentor Welfare-to-Work Career Mentor Program, El Monte, Calif., 2002—. Vol. March of Dimes, L.A., 1994—2000; vol., bd. mem. The Dance Connection Dance Acad., L.A., 2002; vol. Redeemer Christian Acad., L.A., 1999, West Angeles Ch. of God in Christ, L.A., 1996—2002. Scholar, Calif. Regional Purchasing Com., 1986. Mem.: ASPA, Dominguez Pub. Adminstrn. Assn., Assn. County Administrs., Calif. State U. Long Beach Alumni Assn., Phi Kappa Phi, Phi Alpha Alpha. Avocations: marathon running, social research, volunteering, travel, hiking. Office: Los Angeles County Dept Social Svcs 10728 S Central Ave Los Angeles CA 90059 E-mail: ldwmarathoner@yahoo.com.

**WHITFIELD, EDWARD (WAYNE WHITFIELD),** congressman; b. Hopkinsville, Ky., May 25, 1943; m. Constance Harriman; 1 child, Kate. BS in Bus., U. Ky., 1965; JD, U. Ky. Coll. of Law, 1969. Mem. Ky. Ho. of Reps., 1974-75; pvt. practice law, 1970-79; govt. affairs counsel Seaboard Sys. R.R. subs. CSX Corp., 1979-83, counsel to pres., 1983-85; v.p. state rels. CSX Corp., 1986-88, v.p. fed. r.r affairs, 1988-91; legal counsel to chmn. Interstate Commerce Commn., 1991-93; mem. US Congress from 1st Ky. dist., 1995—; mem. energy and commerce com. 1st lt. USAR. Republican. Office: US Ho Reps 301 Cannon Ho Office Bldg Washington DC 20515-1701

**WHITFIELD, FRED, JR.,** professional sports team executive; s. Fred Whitfield. B in Econs., Campbell U., Buies Creek, NC, 1980, MBA; JD, NC Ctrl. U. Sch. Law, Durham. Dir. Carolinas region Falk Assoc. Mgmt. Enterprises; dir. player devel. basketball divsn. Nike, dir. bus. and legal affairs Brand Jordan divsn., 2003—06; dir. player pers., asst. legal counsel Wash. Wizards, 2000—03; pres., COO Bobcats Sports & Entertainment, Charlotte, NC, 2006—. Founder, dir. Achievements Unlimited Basketball Sch., Greensboro, NC, 1985—. Office: Charlotte Bobcats 333 E Trade St Charlotte NC 28202*

**WHITFIELD, GRAHAM FRANK,** orthopedic surgeon; b. Cheam, Surrey, Eng., Feb. 8, 1942; arrived in U.S., 1969, naturalized, 1975; s. Reginald Frank and Marjorie Joyce W. BSc, King's Coll., U. London, 1963; PhD, Queen Mary Coll., U. London, 1969; MD, NY Med. Coll., 1976. Rsch. scientist Unilever Rsch. Lab., England, 1963-66; postdoctoral fellow dept. chemistry Temple U., 1969-71, instr., 1971-72, asst. prof., 1972-73; resident in surgery NY Med. Coll. Affiliated Hosps., NYC, 1976-78, resident in orthopedics, 1978-79, sr. resident in orthop. surgery, 1979-80, chief resident, 1980-81; attending orthop. surgeon Good Samaritan Hosp., West Palm Beach, Fla., 1981-87, JFK Med. Ctr., Lake Worth, Fla., 1981—, Palms Wellington Surg. Ctr., West Palm Beach, 1994-99, Wellington Regional Med. Ctr., West Palm Beach, 1996—, Bethesda Health City, Boynton Beach, Fla., 1996—, Palms West Hosp., Loxahatchee, Fla., 1997—2004, Columbia Hosp., West Palm Beach, 1997—2002. Instr. health professions divsn. Nova Southeastern U., North Miami, Fla., 1994-95, clin. asst. prof. dept. surgery, Coll. Osteo. Medicine, Nova Southeastern U., Ft. Lauderdale, Fla., 1995—. Author: (with Joseph Cohn and Louis Del Guercio) Critical Care Readings, 1981; editl. bd., contbg. editor Hosp. Physician, 1978-82; cons. editor Physician Asst. and Health Practitioner, 1979-82; orthop. cons. Conv. Reporter, 1980-82; assoc. editor-in-chief Critical Care Monitor, 1980-82; editl. bd. Complications in Orthopedics, 1986-96; practice panel cons. in orthop. surgery Complications in Surgery, 1982-96. Recipient N.Y. Med. Coll. Surg. Soc. award, 1976. Fellow: Internat. Coll. Surgeons; mem.: AMA, Fla. Orthop. Soc., So. Orthop. Assn., Royal Inst. Chemistry (Eng.), Palm Beach County Med. Soc., Fla. Med. Assn., Soc. the Four Arts, Rotary, Explorer's Club (N.Y.C.), Brit. Schs. and Univs. Club, Soc. Sons of St. George (N.Y.C.), Venerable Order Hospitalers of St. John of Jerusalem, Sigma Xi. Office: 2150 S Congress Ave West Palm Beach FL 33406-7604 Office Phone: 561-965-5200. Personal E-mail: gfw2150@aol.com.

**WHITFIELD, LYNN,** actress; b. Baton Rouge, May 6, 1953; d. Valerian and Jean (Butler) Smith; m. Vantile Whitfield (div.); m. Brian Gibson, July 4, 1990 (div. 1992); 1 child, Grace; m. Van Whitfield (div.). Student, Howard U. Actor: (films) Doctor Detroit, 1983, A Thin Line Between Love and Hate, 1996, Gone Fishin', 1997, Eve's Bayou, 1997, The Planet of Junior Brown, 1997, Stepmom, 1998, A Time for Dancing, 2000, Head of State, 2003, Madea's Family Reunion, 2006, (TV films) The Women of Brewster Place, 1989, (lead role) The Josephine Baker Story, 1991, Sophie and the Moonhanger, 1995, (Emmy award), Deep in My Heart, 1999, Dangerous Evidence: The Lori Jackson Story, 1999, Love Songs, 1999 (TV miniseries) The Wedding, 1998, A Girl Thing, 2001, (TV series) Equal Justice, The Cosby Mysteries, 1994, Lost in Oz, 2002. Recipient Image award for outstanding performance in a youth or children's series/spl., 1997, Image award for outstanding supporting actress in a drama series, 1998.*

**WHITFIELD, MARGARET DENNY,** retired music educator; b. Richmond, Va., Apr. 18, 1936; d. Theodore Marshall and Elizabeth Denny (Dixon) Whitfield; children: David Yong Kim, Susanne Elisabeth Nelson. MusB cum laude, Western Md. Coll., 1958; MusM, Eastman Sch. Music, 1964; student, Cornell U., Western Md. U., U. Tenn. Tchr. Meth. Bd. Missions, Okadagawa, Japan, 1958—61; instr. piano Hochstein Sch. Music, Rochester, NY, 1963—64; instr. piano Dept. Prep. Peabody Conservatory, Balt., 1964—65; orch. dir. Hanover (Pa.) Pub. Schs., 1968—70; dir. orch. Fairfax County (Va.) Pub. Schs., 1970—98. Ch. organist, 1957—58, 1963—; guest dir. orch. clinic James Madison U., Harrisonburg, Va., 1984, dir. H.S. orch. Carnegie Hall, N.Y.C., 1996. Piano concert soloist Western Md. Coll., 1957, Ithaca Coll. Orch., 1965; musician: Hanover (Pa.) Hall Nursing Home, 2003—04, various chs., 1960—61, Am. Cancer Soc., 2005. Vol. Eng. tchr., Japan, 1958—61; vol. driver Am. Cancer Soc., Falls Ch., 1999—; founder clothing shop Westminster (Md.) Meth. Ch., 1952; vol. Christian Witness Mission, Paducah, Ky., 1950, Christian Work Camp, Pharr, Tex., 1956, Seoul, Republic of Korea, 1959; missionary Meth. Bd. Missions and English Tchrs. Recipient Outstanding Intermediate Orch. award, Fairfax (Va.) Music Educators Assn., 1990, Citation award, Gov.'s Sch. of the Arts, 1993; scholar, Eastman Sch. Music, 1962—64. Mem.: Am. Guild Handbell Rings, Am. Guild Organists, Fairfax County (Va.) Ret. Educators Assn. Avocations: gardening, knitting, volunteering. Home: 7402 Monticello Ring Springfield VA 22150 Office: Westover Baptist Ch 1125 N Patrick Henry Dr Arlington VA 22205

**WHITFIELD, SIMON,** Olympic athlete; b. Kingston, Ont., Can., May 16, 1975; Can. Triathlon champion, Winnipeg, 1998—99, 2001; 1st place winner ITU World Cup, 2001; Bronze medallist Pan Am. Game, Winnipeg, 1999; competed and placed 10th (jr.) World Championships, Cancun, Mexico, 1995, competed and placed 9th Perth, Australia, 1997, competed and placed 7th Montreal, 1999, competed and placed 6th Edmonton, 2001; Gold medallist, flag bearer Can. Olympic Team Olympic Games, Sydney, Australia, 2000; Gold medallist Commonwealth Games, 2002. Spokesperson Multiple Sclerosis Soc., 2001. Named Triathlete of Yr., Triathlon Can., 2000, 11th Pl. Canadian Olympian, Athens, 2004; named to B.C. Sports Hall of Fame, 2001; recipient David Foster Olympic Achievement award. Office: c/o Michelle Comeau IMG Canada 175 Bloor St E Ste 400 S Tower Toronto ON Canada M4W 3RB

**WHITFORD, BRADLEY,** actor; b. Madison, Wis., Oct. 10, 1959; m. Jane Kaczmarek, Aug. 15, 1992; children: Frances, George, Mary. BA, Wesleyan U., 1981. Actor: (plays) Curse of the Starving Class, Three Days of Rain, Measure for Measure, Corionlanus; (Broadway plays) A Few Good Men, 1989—91; (films) Dead as a Doorman, 1986, Adventures in Babysitting, 1987, Revenge of the Nerds II, 1987, Vital Signs, 1990, Presumed Innocent, 1990, Young Guns II, 1990, Awakenings, 1990, Scent of a Woman, 1992, The

Silent Alarm, 1993, RoboCop 3, 1993, My Life, 1993, A Perfect World, 1993, Philadelphia, 1993, The Client, 1994, Cobb, 1994, Billy Madison, 1995, My Fellow Americans, 1996, The Spittin' Image, 1997, The People, 1997, Masterminds, 1997, Red Corner, 1997, Wildly Available, 1999, The Muse, 1999, Bicentennial Man, 1999, Kate & Leopold, 2001, The Sisterhood of the Traveling Pants, 2005, Little Manhattan, 2005; (TV films) C.A.T. Squad, 1986, The Betty Ford Story, 1987, Web of Deception, 1994, Nothing But the Truth, 1995, The Desperate Trail, 1995, In the Line of Duty: Blaze of Glory, 1997, Cloned, 1997, The Sky's on Fire, 1998, Behind the Mask, 1999, Fathers & Sons, 2005; (TV series) NYPD Blue, 1994, The West Wing, 1999—2006, Studio 60 on the Sunset Strip, 2006—. Co-founder Clothes Off Our Back Found. Office: Endeavor Agy 10th Fl 9601 Wilshire Blvd Beverly Hills CA 90212*

**WHITING, ALBERT NATHANIEL,** former university chancellor; b. Jersey City, July 3, 1917; s. Hezekiah Oliver and Hildegarde Freida (Lyons) W.; m. Charlotte Luck, June 10, 1950; 1 dau., Brooke Elizabeth. AB, Amherst Coll., 1938; student, Columbia, summer 1938, U. Pitts., 1938-39; MA in Sociology, Fisk U., 1941, L.H.D. (hon.), 1980; PhD in Sociology, Am. U., 1952; LL.D., Amherst Coll., 1968, Western Mich. U., 1974, Duke, 1974, Kyung Hee U., Seoul, Korea; L.H.D., N.C. Central U., 1983. Research and teaching asst. Fisk U., 1939-41; instr. sociology, dir. rural community study Bennett Coll., Greensboro, NC, 1941-43, 46-47; asst. prof. sociology Atlanta U., 1948-53; dean coll. prof. sociology Morris Brown Coll., Atlanta, 1953-57; asst. dean coll. Morgan State Coll., Balt., 1957-59, dean of college, 1960-67; pres. N.C. Central U., Durham, 1967-72, chancellor, 1972-83. Mem. bd. regents U. Md. Sys., 1988-95. Contbr. articles profl. jours. Bd. dirs. Am. Coun. Edn., Fdnl. Testing Svc ; bd. dirs., past pres. Assn. State Colls. and Univs.; v.p. Internat. Assn. Univ. Pres.; bd. dirs. Research Triangle (N.C.) Inst.; mem. Md. Higher Edn. Commn., 1995-98. 1st lt. AUS, 1943-46. Episcopalian. Home: 11253B Slalom Ln Columbia MD 21044-2810

**WHITING, ANTHONY,** executive search consultant; b. Saigon, Indochina, Nov. 6, 1951; s. Dinty Warmington and Lorraine (Yarborough) W. BA summa cum laude, Tulane U., 1973; MA with honors, Columbia U., 1974, MPhil, 1977, PhD, 1984. V.p. Columbia Consulting Group, N.Y.C., 1987-92; partner Johnson, Smith, and Knisely, N.Y.C., 1993-99; mng. dir. Illsley Bourbonnais, N.Y.C., 1999-2000; mng. ptnr. The Waterman Group, N.Y.C., 2000—. Vis. scholar Columbia U., 2001—03, Union Theol. Sem., 2006. Author: The Never Resting Mind: Wallace Stevens' Romantic Irony, 1996, Edward Thomas, 1996; contbg. author: Wallace Stevens: Comprehensive Research and Study Guide, 2003. Mem. Soc. of Mayflower Descendants, Order of Crown of Charlemagne, Baronial Order of Magna Carta, Soc. of the Cinn., Hereditary Order of Descendants of Colonial Govs., Soc. of Order of Founders and Patriots of Am., Soc. of Descendants of Colonial Clergy, Sons of Am. Revolution, Phi Beta Kappa. Office: 267 Fifth Ave New York NY 10016

**WHITING, BRIAN CHRISTOPHER,** hospitality consultant; b. Bronxville, N.Y., Aug. 14, 1969; s. William Gordon Whiting and Doris Edna (Chubb) Whiting Simmons. BA, U. R.I., 1990. Dir. The Ams. and Asia Pacific Commonwealth of Mass./Dept. Econ. Devel./Office Travel & Tourism, Boston, 1996—99; mgr./dir. internat. mktg. Europe and Mid. East Travel Industry Assn. Am., London, 1999—2000; travel and tourism practice leader, mgr. sports conv. and tourism PricewaterhouseCoopers LLP, N.Y.C., 2000—03; pres. & CEO Providence Warwick Conv. & Visitors Bur., Providence, 2003—. Chmn. bd. dirs. RI Festival of Trees; mem. RI Sports Commn., RI Transit and Urban Transp. Subcom.; mem. dean's adv. coun. U.R.I. Coll. Arts and Scis. Mem.: Destination Orgn. (bd. dirs. nat. coun.), Nat. Coun. Destination Orgns. (bd. dirs.), NY Soc. Assn. Execs., Internat. Assn. Conv. and Visitors Burs. Edn. Com. (mem. visitors bur. edn. com.), Am. Soc. Assn. Execs., Profl. Conv. Mgmt. Assn., Travel Industry Assn. Am., Skal Club Internat., Assn. Travel Mgmt. Execs., New Eng. Soc., The Downtown Assn., Bronxville Field Club, Racquet and Tennis Club, The Boston Athenaeum, Masons, Sigma Alpha Epsilon (pledge class pres. 1987—88). Republican. Avocations: travel, shooting, racquet sports. Office: Providence Warwick Conv & Visitors Bur One West Exchange St Providence RI 02903 Office Phone: 401-274-1636. Business E-Mail: bwhiting@goprovidence.com.

**WHITING, GORDON JAMES,** investment banker; b. Bronxville, N.Y., Nov. 17, 1965; s. William Gordon Whiting and Doris (Chubb) Whiting Simmons; m. Cornelia Conway Cabot, Aug. 30, 2003. BS, Cornell U., 1988; MBA, Columbia U., 1994. Sales and mktg. mgr. Epcot Ltd., Tsim Sha Tsui, Kowloon, Hong Kong, 1989-90; mng. dir. Stapenhurst Ltd., Victoria, Hong Kong, 1990-92; acquisitions assoc. W. P. Carey & Co. LLC, N.Y.C., 1993-94, 2d v.p., 1994-95, v.p., 1995-97, 1st v.p., 1997-98, sr. v.p., 1998-2000, dep. dir. of acquisitions, 1999—2003, exec. dir., 2000—; exec. v.p. and portfolio mgr. Corp. Property Assocs.: 14 Inc., N.Y.C., 1998-2000, pres. and portfolio mgr., 2000—. Bd. dir. Fed. Ret. Thrift Investment Bd.; mem. coun. Cornell U., 2002—. Local bd. mem. Selective Svc. Sys., Eagle Scout. Mem. Profl. Assn. Diving Instrs., Bronxville Field Club, Constant Spring Golf Club (Jamaica), Holland Lodge No. 8 F&AM, Leander Club (U.K.), The Camp Fire Club Am., Mashomack Preserve Club (Pine Plains, N.Y.), The Order of St. John, The Pilgrims, Hon. Order Ky. Cols., Racquet and Tennis Club, Royal Hong Kong Yacht Club, Sigma Chi. Republican. Episcopalian. Avocations: fly fishing, golf, scuba diving, skiing, squash. Home: 70 E 96th St Apt 11b New York NY 10128-0752 E-mail: gwhiting@angelogordon.com

**WHITING, HUGH RICHARD,** lawyer; b. East Chicago, Ind., Dec. 8, 1945; s. Harold C. and Nina (Hofstetter) W.; m. Sherry Ballast, July 2, 1965; 1 child, Kristin Anne. BA, U. Mich., 1967; JD, Ohio State U., 1974. Bar: Ohio 1974, Tex 1981 Salesman, adminstr. Proctor & Gamble, Cin. 1967-71; law clk. to Judge George Edwards U.S. Ct. Appeals (6th cir.) Ohio, Cin., 1974-75; assoc. Jones, Day, Reavis & Pogue, Cleve., 1975-81, ptnr., 1982—; mng. ptnr. Houston office Jones Day. Chmn. Firmwide Profl. Svcs. Com.; mem. civil justice reform act adv. com. No. Dist. Ohio Adv. Com., Cleve., 1990—; mem. Ohio State U. Coll. Law Nat. Coun., Columbus, 1984—; speaker, presenter on legal practice and practice mgmt. various confs. and seminars. Co-chmn. Gen. Bus. Campaign Cleve. Orch., 1992. Mem. ABA (litigation sect., sect. bus. law), Tex. Bar Assn., Cleve. Bar Assn., Mayfield Country Club, Order of Coif. Avocations: golf, travel, reading. Office: Jones Day Ste 3300 717 Texas Houston TX 77002-2712 Office Fax: 832-239-3600. Business E-Mail: hrwhiting@jonesday.com.

**WHITING, MARTHA COUNTEE,** retired secondary school educator; b. Marshall, Tex., Mar. 24, 1912; d. Thomas and Nannie Selena (Yates) Countee; m. Samuel Whiting, June 8, 1937; children: Jacqueline Bostic, Sammie Ellis, Nan Broussard, Tommye Casey, Martha Goddard. BA in Sci., Bishop Coll., 1934; M of Secondary Edn., Tex. So. U., 1959, postgraduate, 1962; postgrad., U. Colo., 1963. Tchr., sci., math Houston Ind. Sch. Dist., 1942-73; researcher, local history Houston, 1973—. Lectr. in field. Mem. exec. com. (life mem.) Houston YWCA, 1977; advisor Preservation 4th Ward, Houston, 1991—; trustee Antioch Missionary Bapt. Ch., Houston, 1977; instrumental in getting the Antioch Missionary Bapt. Ch. in Christ Inc. on the Nat. Register of Hist. Places, 1976; presented Queen Elizabeth II with miniature history of Antioch Missionary Bapt. Ch. in Christ, 1991; author nomination form for Tex. hist. marker Antioch Missionary Bapt. Ch. in Christ, 1994; presenter to Harris County Heritage Soc. of Jack Yates House, the only house built by a former slave to be maintain ed by a U.S. city, and chmn. Pathfinder presentation of achievements of 64 Negro pioneers in Harris County, 1966-1986. Named Woman Courage, Houston Radcliffe Club, 1985, Black Womens Hall Fame Mus. Africal Am. Life, Dallas, 1986; recipient Friend of the Soc. award Harris County Heritage Soc., 1994. Mem. Tex. Ret. Tchrs. Assn., Houston Mus. Fine Arts, Harris County Heritage Soc. (exec. com. 1984), Bluebonnet Garden Club (pres. 1968), Jack & Jill Am. (pres. Houston chpt. 1955-57), Smithsonian, Nationwide Trust for Historic Preservation. Avocations: writing, gardening, travel, sewing, singing. Home: 3446 Southmore Blvd Houston TX 77004-6349

**WHITING, RICHARD ALBERT,** lawyer; b. Cambridge, Mass., Dec. 2, 1922; s. Albert S. and Jessie (Coleman) W.; m. Marvelene Nash, Feb. 22, 1948 (div. 1984); children— Richard A. Jr., Stephen C., Jeffrey D., Gary S., Kimberly G.; m. Joanne Sherry, Oct. 14, 1984 AB, Dartmouth Coll., 1944; JD, Yale U., 1949. Bar: D.C. 1949. Assoc. Steptoe & Johnson, Washington, 1949-55, ptnr., 1956-86, of counsel, 1987—. Adj. prof. Vt. Law Sch., South Royalton, 1985-90; mem. exec. com. Yale Law Sch. Assn., New Haven, 1985-88; mem. adv. bd. The Antitrust Bull., N.Y.C., 1975-99. Contbr. articles to profl. jours. Trustee Colby-Sawyer Coll., 1987-97. 1st lt. U.S. Army, 1945-46. Mem. ABA (council mem. Antitrust Law sect. 1977-85, del. to Ho. Dels. 1982-83, chmn. 1984-85) Presbyterian. Home: PO Box 749 Grantham NH 03753-0749 Office: 1330 Connecticut Ave NW Washington DC 20036-1704 Office Phone: 202-429-8080. Business E-Mail: chopin03753@yahoo.com.

**WHITING, SUSAN DICKINSON,** media research company executive; b. Chgo., Aug. 1, 1956; BA in Econs. cum laude, Denison U., 1978. Mgmt. devel. program Nielsen Media Rsch., Dunedin, Fla., 1979-86, v.p. Nielsen Homevideo Index, 1986-87, mktg. mgr., 1987-93, sr. v.p., dir. mktg., 1993-97, gen. mgr. nat. svcs. & emerging markets, 1997—2001, pres., COO NYC, 2001—02, pres., CEO, 2002—. Mem. Cable Television Adminstrv. and Mktg. Assn., Women in Cable & Telecomm., Conn. Women's Forum (v.p.), N.Y. Radio and TV Rsch. Coun. (past pres.). Office: Nielsen Media Rsch Inc 770 Broadway New York NY 10003

**WHITINGTON, PETER FRANK,** pediatrics educator, pediatric hepatologist; b. Memphis, May 8, 1947; s. Frank Everett and Mary Lena (Hollingsworth) Whitington; m. Susan Maurine Hoagland, June 6, 1967; children: Helen Frances Josephic, Mary Louise, Katherine Daphne, Patrick M. BA in Econs., Tulane U., 1968; MD, U. Tenn., Memphis, 1971. Diplomate Am. Bd. Pediat., Am. Bd. Pediatric Gastroenterology. Resident in pediat., then chief resident U. Tenn. Ctr. for Health Scis., 1972—74, instr., 1975, asst. prof., 1978—81, assoc. prof., 1981—84, chief divsn. pediatric gastroenterology, 1978—84; rsch. fellow in gastroenterology Johns Hopkins Hosp., Balt., 1975—77; rsch. fellow in gastroenterologic dept. pediatrics U. Wis., Madison, 1977—78; assoc. prof. dept. pediat. U. Chgo. Pritzker Sch. Medicine, 1984—87, assoc. prof. depts. pediat. and medicine, 1987—92, prof., 1992—97; prof. pediat. Northwestern U. Med. Sch., 1997—, Sally Burnett Searle prof. pediat. and transplantation; dir. divsn. gastroenterology, hepatology & nutrition Children's Meml. Hosp., Chgo., 1997—, dir. organ transplantation, Siragusa Transplantation Ctr., 1997—; co-dir. Northwestern U. Affiliated Transplant Ctrs., 1997—. Chief gastroenterology LeBonheur Children's Med. Ctr., Memphis, 1978—84; numerous invited lectures and guest spkr. at profl. meetings, workshops, symposia, hosps., confs.; mem. pediatric transplantation com. United Network for Organ Sharing, Nat. Organ Procurement and Transplantation Network, 1992—94; reviewer numerous med. jours. including New Eng. Jour. Medicine, Gastroenterology, Hepatology, Jour. Pediat., Digestive Diseases and Scis., Pediat., Transplant. Editl. bd. Jour. Pediatric Gastroenterology and Nutrition, 1991—96, Liver Transplantation, 1994—, Pediatric Transplantation, 1997—, sect. editor Birth Defects Compendium, 1987—90, contbr. numerous articles and abstracts to med. jours. Mem. sci. adv. bd. Mid-South chpt. Nat. Found. for Ileitis and Colitis, Memphis, 1983—84; chmn. med. adv. com. Ill. chpt. Am. Liver Found., 1996—, mem., med. adv. bd. dirs., 1993—; med. dir. The Johnny Genna Found., Chgo., 1987—; bd. dirs. Parents for Crtl. H.S., Memphis, 1983—84, Liver/Organ Transplant Fund, Memphis, 1983—84. Recipient Cmty. Svc. award, NCCJ, Memphis, 1983; fellow postdoctoral rsch. NIH, 1977. Mem.: Am. Assn. Transplantation, N.A.m Soc. for Pediatric Gastroenterology and Nutrition, Soc. for Pediatric Rsch., Am. Gastroenterol. Assn., Gastroenterology Rsch. Group, Am. Assn. for Study of Liver Diseases. Avocations: making furniture, fly fishing. Home: 5490 S South Shore Dr Apt 8 Chicago IL 60615-5984 Office: Childrens Meml Hosp Box 57 2300 Childrens Plaza Chicago IL 60614-3394 Business E-Mail: p-whitington@northwestern.edu.

**WHITLEDGE, JOHN,** apparel designer; Grad. in Economics, Claremont McKenna Coll., 2002. Co-founder, designer (with Josia Lamberto-Egan, Sam Shipley, and Jeff Halmos) Trovata, 2002—, launched women's collection, 2005—. Recipient CFDA/Vogue Fashion Fund award. Office: Trovata 505 31st St Newport Beach CA 92663*

**WHITLEY, JOE D. (JOSEPH DALLY WHITLEY),** lawyer; b. Atlanta, Nov. 12, 1950; s. Thomas Youngie and Mary Jo (Dally) W.; m. Kathleen Pinion, Sept. 27, 1975; children: Lauren Jacqueline, Thomas McMillan. BA, U. Ga., 1972, JD, 1975. Bar: Ga. 1975, U.S. Supreme Ct. 1989. Assoc. Kelly, Denney, Pease & Allison, Columbus, Ga., 1975-78; asst. dist. atty. Chattahoochee Jud. Cir., Columbus, 1978-79; assoc. Hirsch, Beil & Partin, P.C., Columbus, 1979-81; U.S. atty. (mid. dist.) GA US Dept. Justice, Macon, 1981-87, dep. asst. atty. gen., criminal divsn. Washington, 1987-88, dep. assoc. atty. gen., 1988-89, acting assoc. atty. gen., 1989; ptnr. Smith, Gambrell & Russell, Atlanta, 1989-90; U.S. atty. (No. dist) GA US Dept. Justice, Atlanta, 1990-93; ptnr. Kilpatrick Stockton, Atlanta, 1993-97, Alston & Bird, Atlanta, 1997—2003, 2005—; gen. counsel US Dept. Homeland Security, Washington, 2003—05. Atty. gen.'s adv. com. Dept. Justice, Washington, 1982-85; chmn. organized crime and violent crime subcom. Atty. Gen.'s Adv. Com., 1990-93, mem. investigative subcom., chmn. white collar crime subcom., 1993-99; program chmn. Ga. Inst. of Continuing Legal Edn. programs; lectr. in field Treas. Muscogee County Young Reps., Columbus, 1979-80. Mem. ABA (mem. criminal justice sect. coun., vice-chmn. govt. affairs 2002-03), Ga. Bar Assn., Macon Bar Assn., Young Lawyers Club (pres. Columbus chpt. 1980-81), Lawyers Club of Atlanta. Republican. Presbyterian. Office Phone: 202-756-3189. Business E-Mail: joe.whitley@alston.com.

**WHITLEY, L. TRACEE,** lawyer; BA cum laude, Harvard U., 1988, MA Am. Govt., 1995; JD, Northeastern U., 1997. Bar: Mass. 1997, N.C. 1997. Dir., office chmn. Bingham McCutchen LLP, Boston, 2001—. Mem.: Ivy League Women's Silver Anniversary Soccer Team, 1998 (life), Harvard Varsity Club Hall Fame, 2003 (life). Office: Bingham McCutchen LLP 150 Federal St Boston MA 02110-1726 Office Phone: 617-951-8218. Office Fax: 617-951-8736. Business E-Mail: ltracee.whitley@bingham.com.

**WHITLEY, LENA FRANCES,** French educator; b. LaGrange, Ga., Oct. 27, 1962; d. John Hamilton and Lena Knight Whitley. BA in French, Psychology, Agnes Scott Coll., Decatur, Ga., 1984; MAT in French, Emory U., Atlanta, 1988. Cert. tchr. French Ga. French tchr. LaGrange Acad. Edn., LaGrange, 1986—87, Chambers County Bd. Edn., Valley, Ala., 1988—91; French, lang. arts tchr. Springwood Pub. Schs., Lanett, Ala., 1992—93; French tchr. The O'Neal Sch., Pinehurst, NC, 1993—94, Fulton County Bd. Edn., Atlanta, 1994—. Mem. Atlanta Hist. Soc.; vol. Margaret Mitchell House, Atlanta; mem. Thoreau Soc., Concord, Mass.; mem., vol. John F. Kennedy Mus., Boston. Mem.: NEA, PAGE, Am. Coun. on Tchg. Fgn. Langs., Ga. Edn. Assn., Am. Assn. Tchrs. French, Phi Beta Kappa. Democrat. Methodist. Avocations: reading, writing, theater, concerts. Home: 5212 Chastain Dr NE Atlanta GA Office: Autrey Mill Middle School 4110 Old Alabama Rd Alpharetta GA 30022

**WHITLEY, ROB,** medical educator, sociologist, researcher; b. Jersey, England, Aug. 3, 1972; arrived in US, 2005; BSc, U. Coll. London, 1995; MSc, London Sch. Hygiene and Tropical Medicine, 1998; PhD, King's Coll. London, 2003. Rsch. fellow McGill U., Montreal, Canada, 2003—05; asst. prof. Dartmouth Med. Sch., Hanover, NH, 2005—. Cons. U. W.I., Mona, Jamaica, 2005—, U. Addis Ababa, Ethiopia, 2004—. Office: Dartmouth Psychiatric Rsch Ctr Ste 202 2 Whipple Pl Lebanon NH 03766 Office Phone: 603-448-0263. Business E-Mail: rob.whitley@dartmouth.edu.

**WHITLOCK, CHARLES PRESTON,** former university dean; b. Highland Park, N.J., June 19, 1919; s. Frank Boudinot and Rosena Craig (Foster) W.; m. Patricia Hamilton Hoey, Mar. 10, 1960; children: Carol Foster, Adam Hoey, Susan Boudinot, Matthew Fitzsimmons, Beth Brewer. BA, Rutgers U., 1941; MA, Harvard U., 1947. Assoc. dir. Bur. Study Counsel Harvard U.,

1948-52, Allston Burr sr. tutor, 1952-58, lectr. social psychology, 1955-72, asst. to pres., 1958-70, assoc. dean of coll., 1970-72, dean of coll., 1972-76, assoc. dean faculty, 1976-82, master Dudley House, 1976-82. Dir. Cambridgeport Savs. Bank.; Mem. Mass. Higher Edn. Facilities Commn. Co-author: Harvard University Reading Films. Trustee Charity of Edward Hopkins, Lesley Coll.; bd. corporators New Eng. Deaconess Hosp.; treas. Annisquam Village Ch. Col. USAF. Decorated Silver Star, D.F.C., Air medal. Mem. Phi Beta Kappa. Home: 9 Barberry Heights Rd Gloucester MA 01930-1201 Office: Harvard U Cambridge MA 02138

**WHITLOCK, JOHN JOSEPH,** museum director; b. South Bend, Ind., Jan. 7, 1935; s. Joseph Mark and Helen Marcella (Cramer) Whitlock; m. Sue Ann Kirkman, June 10, 1956; children: Kelly Ann, Michele Lynn, Mark. BS in Art, Ball State U., 1957, MA in Art, 1963; EdD, Ind. U., 1971. Tchr. art Union City (Ind.) Pub. Schs., 1957-59; tchr. art, art dir. Madison (Ind.) City Schs., 1959-64; prof. art, dir. gallery Hanover (Ind.) Coll., 1964-69; dir. Burpee Art Mus., Rockford, Ill., 1970-72; prof. arts and humanities Elgin (Ill.) Community Coll., 1970-72; dir. Brooks Meml. Art Gallery, Memphis, 1972-78; prof. mus. studies Southwestern Coll., Memphis, 1973-78; adj. asst. prof. art and museology Memphis State U., 1976-78; dir. Univ. Mus., mem. grad. faculty So. Ill. U., Carbondale, 1978-2000, emeritus dir., 2000—, also dir. mus. studies, 1978-2000, adj. assoc. prof. anthropology, 1978-2000, adj. assoc. prof. polit. sci., 1988—, adj. assoc. prof. history, 1994—, dir. mus. studies, 1989—, mem. ROTC acad. avc. coun., 1988—, mem. president's coun., 1988-93, adj. assoc. prof. art Univ. Mus., 1978-99, vis. emeritus prof., 2000—; instr. art John A. Logan Coll., 2001—. Chmn. bd. Nat. Coal Mus., 1983-85; mem. Newsfront adv. bd. NC Broadcast News, Washington, 1982-85; sr. cons. Marine Mil. Acad. Mus., 1988—, mem. bd. advisors, 1991-97. Mem. Rockford Human Rels. Commn., 1971-72; mem. pres.'s coun. Southwestern Coll., 1973-78; vol. Carbondale Police Dept., 2000—, com. resources, forensics records and acad.; bd. dirs. Carbondale Crime Stoppers, 2000—, pres., 2006—; bd. dirs. DARE, 2000—, pres., 2006—; bd. dirs. Carbondale Fire and Police Commn., 2003—; univ. club bd. So. Ill. U., 2000—, univ. mus. amb., 2000—. Mem. Am. Assn. Mus., Internat. Coun. Mus., Midwest Assn. Mus., Assn. Art Mus. Dirs., Marine Corps League (commandant Shawnee detachment 1994-96, 99-2001, comdr. USCG Aux. 1994-95), Dept. Ill. Marine Corps League (trustee rank and file 1994-99, judge advocate 1999-2005), Semper Fi Soc. (faculty advisor So. Ill. U. 1995—). Office: So Ill U 605 W Walnut St Carbondale IL 62901-2615

**WHITLOCK, JOHN L.,** lawyer; b. New Orleans, Oct. 24, 1946; s. John Bert and Virginia Katherine (Marzolf) W.; m. Dorothy Florence Oeste, Sept. 13, 1969; children: Sarah Katherine, Thomas John. AB, Harvard U., 1968, JD, 1973. Bar: Mass. 1973, U.S. Dist. Ct. Mass. 1974, U.S. Ct. Appeals (1st cir.) 1975. Assoc. Herrick & Smith, Boston, 1973—80, ptnr., 1981—86, Edwards Angell Palmer & Dodge LLP, Boston, 1986—. Mem. ethics rules adv. com. Mass. Supreme Jud. Ct., 1996—, chair, 2006—. Bd. dirs., sec. Harvard-Radcliffe Collegiate Mus. Found., Inc., 1978—; treas. The Boston Cecilia, Inc., 1974-85, 98—, bd. dirs., 1974-86, 94—, pres. 1994-98. With U.S. Army, 1968-70. Mem. Boston Bar Assn. (coun. 1996-97). Lutheran. Avocation: singing. Office: Edwards Angell Palmer & Dodge LLP 111 Huntington Ave Boston MA 02199-7613 Office Phone: 617-239-0100. Business E-Mail: jwhitlock@eapdlaw.com.

**WHITLON, DONNA SUE,** neuroscientist, researcher; b. Flushing, N.Y., Oct. 24, 1952; d. Leonard E. and Eileen S. W.; m. Jack M. Rozental, Jan. 6, 1980; two children. BS, Mich. State U., 1974; PhD, U. Wis., 1979. Rsch. asst., NIH predoctoral trainee U. Wis. Dept. Biochemistry, Madison, 1974-79; biol. lab. scientist Manufactaras Arriol, Santo Domingo, Dominican Republic, 1980; high sch. sci. tchr. Carol Morgan Sch., Santo Domingo, Dominican Republic, 1981; postdoctoral fellow McArdle Lab. for Cancer Rsch. U. Wis., Madison, 1981-84, asst. scientist, 1985-91, assoc. scientist Waisman Cntr., 1991—. Contbr. articles to profl. jours. Mem. Assn. for Rsch. in Otolaryngology, Soc. for Neuroscience. Office: U Wis Rm 636 Waisman Ctr 1500 Highland Ave Madison WI 53705-2274

**WHITLOW, LILLIAN,** retired elementary school educator, poet; d. James Cooper and Clemmie McCowen; m. Leo Whitlow, July 1, 1951 (dec. Mar. 1989); children: Leo Perry, Leon Terry, Leona Marie. BA, Langston U., Okla., 1951; MA, Okla. U., 1957. H.s. music and English tchr. Okla. Pub. Schs., Hugo, 1951—56, Rural Paris Pub. Schs., Tex., 1960—66; h.s. music tchr. Grant Pub. Schs., Okla., 1966—70; tchr. music Portland Pub. Schs., Oreg., 1970—88; ret. Editor: KUUMBA, 1992—98; contbr. articles, poems to profl. jours. Vol. tutor Ockley Green Mid. Sch., Portland, 1996—98. Recipient John Jackson award, 2000, Woman of Excellence in Arts and Lit. award, Delta Sigma Theta, 1997, Plaque for outstanding contbn. to African Am. Lit., 1992. Mem.: Internat. Soc. Poets (Disting. Mem. plaque 1996), Portland Fedn. Women's Clubs (pres. 2000—), Maya Angelou Writers Guild (pres. 1997—), Multnomah Woman's Club, Portland Woman's Club (pres. 1998—), Alpha Kappa Alpha. Democrat. Roman Catholic. Avocations: walking, exercise, reading, sewing, writing. Home: 5714 NE 23d Ave Portland OR 97211 Personal E-Mail: lilwhi@msn.com.

**WHITLOW, STACEY MATAXIS,** language educator; b. Fort Beining, GA, Feb. 13, 1975; d. Theodore Christopher Mataxis, Kirby Jones Mataxis; m. Jeffrey Kenneth Whitlow. Master of Arts, North Dakota State University, Raleigh, North Carolina, 1999—2001; Bachelor of Arts, Universtity of North Carolina-Greensboro, Greensboro, NC, 1993—96. English Instructor Durham Technical Community College, Durham, NC, 2001—; High School English Teacher Pinecrest High School, Southern Pines, NC, 1996—99. Home: 6714 Lipscomb Dr Durham NC 27712-9289

**WHITMAN, CHRISTINA BROOKS,** law educator; b. 1947; BA, U. Mich., 1968, MA, 1970, JD, 1974. Law clk. to judge Harold Leventhal U.S. Ct. Appeals, Washington, 1974-75; law clk. to justice Powell U.S. Supreme Ct., Washington, 1975-76; asst. prof. U. Mich., Ann Arbor, 1976-79, assoc. prof., 1979-82, prof., 1982—, Francis A. Allen Collegiate Prof. Law. Contbr. articles to law jours. Office: U Mich Law Sch 338 Hutchins Hall 625 S State St Ann Arbor MI 48109-1215 Office Phone: 734-764-9535. Office Fax: 734-763-9375. E-mail: cwhitman@umich.edu.

**WHITMAN, CHRISTINE TODD,** former federal agency administrator, former governor; b. NYC, Sept. 26, 1946; d. Webster Bray and Eleanor Schley Todd; m. John Whitman, 1974; children: Kate, Taylor. BA in Govt., Wheaton Coll., 1968. Freeholder Somerset County, 1982—87; pres. NJ State Bd. Pub. Utilities, 1988—90; host radio talk show Sta. WKXW, Trenton, N.J.; gov. State of N.J., 1994-2001; adminstr. EPA, Washington, 2001—03. Chmn. Com. for an Affordable N.J.; bd. dirs. Texas Instruments Inc., 2003-, Millennium Challenge Corp., S.C. Johnson and Son, Inc., United Tech. Corp., 2003-, Chgo. Climate Exchange, Inc.; mem. steering com. Cancer Inst. NJ Leadership Coun.; co-chair Nat. Smart Growth Coun., Smart Growth Am.; mem. leadership coun. Rep. Pro-Choice Coalition, gov.'s bd. Oquirrh Inst., S&T presdl. and fed. adv. com. Appointments of Nat. Acads. Author: It's My Party Too: The Battle for the Heart of the GOP and the Future of America, 2005. Columnist newspapers. Bd. freeholders Somerset County, N.J., 1982-87; bd. pub. utilities, 1988-89; Rep. candidate for senator State of N.J., 1990; mem. Ctr. Civic Engagement and Volunteerism adv. bd. Raritan Cmty. Coll., UN sec-gen. adv. bd. Water and Sanitation. Republican. Achievements include first female governor in N.J.; delivered Republican response to President Clinton's 1995 State of the Union address.

**WHITMAN, DALE ALAN,** lawyer, educator; b. Charleston, W. Va., Feb. 18, 1939; m. Marjorie Miller; 8 children. Student, Ohio State U., 1956-59; BES, Brigham Young U., 1963; LLB, Duke U., 1966. Bar: Calif. 1967, Utah 1971. Assoc. O'Melveny & Myers, Los Angeles, 1966-67; asst prof., then assoc prof. sch. law U. N.C., Chapel Hill, 1967-70; vis. prof. law UCLA, 1970-71; dep. dir. Office Housing and Urban Affairs Fed. Home Loan Bank Bd., Washington, 1971-72; sr. program analyst FHA, HUD, Washington, 1972-73; prof. law Brigham Young U., 1973—78, 1992—98, U. Wash.,

1978—82; vis. prof. law U. Mo., Columbia, 1976; prof. law, dean U. Mo. Sch. Law, Columbia, 1982-88, prof., 1988—91, 1998—. Cons., lectr. in field; reporter Am. law Inst. Co-author: Cases and Materials on Real Estate Finance and Development, 1976, Real Estate Finance Law, 1979, 4th edit., 2001, Cases and Materials on Real Estate Transfer, Finance and Development, 1981, 7th edit., 2006, Land Transactions and Finance, 1983, 4d edit., 2004, The Law of Property, 1984, 3d edit., 2000, Contemporary Property, 1996, 2d edit., 2002, Restatement of Property (Mortgages), 1997; contbr. articles to profl. jours. Fellow Am. Bar Found.; mem. Am. Law Inst., Am. Coll. Real Estate Lawyers, Am. Coll. Mortgage Attys., Assn. Am. Law Schs. (pres. 2002). Office: Univ Mo 216 Hulston Hall Columbia MO 65211 Office Phone: 573-884-0946. Business E-Mail: whitmand@missouri.edu.

**WHITMAN, FARGO DEBORAH,** artist; b. Leesburg, Va., July 4, 1953; d. R. Fargo and Doreen (Kerr-Jarrett) W. BA, U. Va., 1975; MFA, Rutgers U., 1978, MA in Art Psychotherapy, 2004. Solo exhbns. include John Gibson Gallery, NYC, 1984, Whitney Mus. Am. Art, N.Y.C., 1985, John Weber Gallery, NYC, 1990; group exhbns. include Josh Baer Gallery, N.Y.C., 1991, The Bklyn. Mus., 1993, L.A. Film Festival, 2003, L.A. Gay and Lesbian Film Festival, 2004 (Grand Jury award for Best Documentary, 1994), Perth Internat. Film Fest., Australia, 2005; documentary A Fine State This Is. Recipient MacDowell Colony fellowship, 1986, 92, Corp. Yaddo fellow, 1993; Pollock-Krasner Found. grantee, 1990; grantee N.Y. Found., 1993. Home: 567 6th St Apt 8 Brooklyn NY 11215-3718 Office Phone: 718-499-5573. E-mail: fargowhi@yahoo.com.

**WHITMAN, GREGORY THEODORE,** neurologist; b. Lansdale, Pennsylvania, Oct. 16, 1966; s. Steven and Sheila Whitman. BA, Cornell Univ., Ithaca, NY, 1985—89; MD, Univ. of Conn., Farmington, 1990—94. Cert. in Neurology Am. Bd. of Psychiatry and Neurology, 2000. Medicine intern Boston City Hosp., Boston Univ., 1994—95, neurology resident, 1995—97, Tufts Univ., Boston, 1997—98; clin. instr. neurology Univ. Calif., Los Angeles, 1998—2000, asst. prof. of neurology Irvine, 2000—. Neurology residency program dir. Univ. of Calif., Irvine, 2002—. Co-author: (journal articles) Neurology, Archives of Neurology, Jour. of Neuroimaging, Stroke, Neurobiology of Aging. Mem.: Am. Acad. of Neurology. Office Phone: 714-456-2324.

**WHITMAN, MARGARET C. (MEG WHITMAN),** Internet company executive; b. LI, N.Y., Aug. 4, 1956; m. Griffith R. Harsh IV; children: Griff, Will. BA in Econs., Princeton U., 1977; MBA, Harvard U., 1979. Brand asst. Procter & Gamble, 1979—81; v.p. Bain & Co., 1982—89; v.p. mktg. & consumer products divsn. Walt Disney Co, Burbank, Calif., 1989—92; corp. v.p. strategic planning Stride Rite Corp., 1992—93, exec. v.p. Keds divsn., 1993—94, pres. Stride Rite Divsn., 1994—95; pres., CEO Florists' Transworld Delivery (FTD), 1995—97; gen. mgr. preschool divsn. Hasbro Inc., 1997—98; pres., CEO eBay, Inc., San Jose, Calif., 1998—. Bd. dirs. eBay, Inc., 1998—, Staples Inc., 1999, The Goldman Sachs Group Inc., 2001—02, Procter & Gamble Co., 2003, The Gap Inc., 2003—06, DreamWorks Animation SKG, Inc. Bd. trustees Princeton U. Named Number One on List of Best CEO's, Worth, 2002; named one of 25 Most Powerful Business Mgrs. (annually since 2000), Business Week, 25 Most Powerful People in Business, Fortune, 2004, Most Powerful Women in American Business, World's 100 Most Influential People, Time Mag., 2004, 2005, 100 Most Powerful Women, Forbes mag., 2005—06, 2006, 50 Women to Watch, Wall St. Journal, 2005. Avocation: fly fishing. Office: eBay Inc 2145 Hamilton Ave San Jose CA 95125*

**WHITMAN, MARINA VON NEUMANN,** economist, educator; b. N.Y.C., Mar. 6, 1935; d. John and Mariette (Kovesi) von Neumann; m. Robert Freeman Whitman, June 23, 1956; children: Malcolm Russell, Laura Mariette. BA summa cum laude, Radcliffe Coll., 1956; MA, Columbia U., 1959, PhD, 1962; LHD (hon.), Russell Sage Coll., 1972; LLD (hon.), Cedar Crest Coll., 1973, Hobart and William Smith Coll., 1973; LHD (hon.), U. Mass., 1975, N.Y. Poly. Inst., 1975; LLD (hon.), Coe Coll., 1975, Marietta Coll., 1976. Mem. faculty U. Pitts., 1962-79, prof. econs., 1971-73, disting. pub. svc. prof. econs., 1973-79, v.p., chief economist Gen. Motors Corp., N.Y.C., 1979-85, group v.p. pub. affairs, 1985-92; disting. vis. prof. bus. adminstrn., pub. policy U. Mich., Ann Arbor, 1992-94, prof. bus. adminstrn., pub. policy, 1994—. Mem. Trilateral Commn., 1973-84, 88-95; mem. Pres. Adv. Com. on Trade Policy and Negotiations, 1987-93; mem. tech. assessment adv. coun. U.S. Congress Office of Tech. Assessment, 1990-95; mem. Consultative Group on Internat. Econs. and Monetary Affairs, 1979—; mem. U.S. Price Commn., 1971-72, Coun. Econ. Advisers, Exec. Office of Pres., 1972-73. Author: Government Risk-Sharing in Foreign Investment, 1965, International and Interregional Payments Adjustment, 1967, Economic Goals and Policy Instruments, 1970, Reflections of Interdependence: Issues for Economic Theory and U.S. Policy, 1979, New World, New Rules: The Changing Role of the American Corporation, 1999; bd. editors: Am. Econ. Rev., 1974-77; mem. editl. bd. Fgn. Policy; contbr. articles to profl. jours. Trustee Nat. Bur. Econ. Rsch., 1993—, Princeton U., 1980-90, Inst. Advanced Study, 1999—; bd. dirs. Inst. for Internat. Econs., 1986—, Salzburg Seminar, 1994—, Eurasia Found., 1992-95; bd. overseers Harvard U., 1972-78, mem. vis. com. Kennedy Sch., 1992-98. Fellow Earhart Found., 1959-60, AAUW, 1960-61, NSF, 1968-70, Social Security Rsch. Coun.; recipient Columbia medal for excellence, 1973, George Washington award Am. Hungarian Found., 1975. Mem. Am. Econ. Assn. (exec. com. 1977-80), Am. Acad. Arts and Scis., Coun. Fgn. Rels. (dir. 1977-87), Phi Beta Kappa. Office: U Mich Gerald Ford Sch Pub Policy Joan and Sanford Weill Hall Rm 3228 Ann Arbor MI 48109-3091 Office Phone: 734-763-4173. Business E-Mail: marinaw@umich.edu.

**WHITMAN, MARLAND HAMILTON, JR.,** lawyer; b. Balt., Oct. 13, 1947; s. M. Hamilton and Josephine Lee (Chatard) W.; m. Susan Zimmerman, Mar. 21, 1976; children: Elizabeth Miles, Hannah Minor. AB, Princeton U., 1969; JD, U. Va., 1976. Bar: Md. 1976, U.S. Supreme Ct. 1982, U.S. Ct. Appeals (3d cir.) 1986, (4th cir.) 1979, U. S. Ct. Internat. Trade 1985, U.S. Dist. Ct. Md. 1977. From assoc. to ptnr. Ober, Kaler, Grimes & Shriver, Balt., 1976-98, shareholder, 1998—. Contbr. chpt. (book) Construction Litigation: Strategies and Techniques, 1990. Lt. USN, 1969-73. Mem. ABA, Maritime Law Assn. of U.S. (proctor 1977—), Md. State Bar Assn., Bar Assn. of Balt. City, Propeller Club of U.S. Pt. of Balt. Office: Ober Kaler Grimes & Shriver 120 E Baltimore St Baltimore MD 21202-1643 Office Phone: 410-347-7354.

**WHITMAN, MARTIN J.,** portfolio manager; b. NYC, Sept. 30, 1924; s. Irving and Dora (Cukier) W.; m. Lois M. Quick, Mar. 10, 1956; children: James Q., Barbara E., Thomas I. Chartered fin. analyst. Rsch. analyst, buyer Shearson Hammill & Co., N.Y.C., 1950—56; analyst William Rosenwald Co., N.Y.C., 1956—58; head rsch. Ladenburg, Thalmann & Co., N.Y.C., 1958—60; gen. ptnr. Gerstley Sunstein & Co., Phila., 1960—67; v.p., dir. Blair & Co., Inc., N.Y.C., 1967—68; pres., founder M.J. Whitman & Co. (now Inc.), N.Y.C., 1969—84; pres., CEO Equity Strategies Fund, Inc., N.Y.C., 1984—90; founder, chmn. Third Ave. Value Fund, Inc. (now Third Ave. Mgmt. LLC), N.Y.C., 1990—. CEO, Third Ave. Value Fund, 1990—95; dir. Nabors Industries, Inc.; past chmn. bd. Danielson Holding Corp.; Disting. Mgmt. Fellow in Fin. Yale U., New Haven, 1972—; mem. adj. bd. Yale Sch. Mgmt., New Haven, 1994—95; cons. disclosure study SEC, 1968; cons. Pres.'s Commn. on Accident at Three Mile Island, 1979; adj. prof. Sch. Bus. Columbia U., N.Y.C. 2001—; adj. prof. Whitman Sch., Syracuse U. Author: Value Investing: A Balanced Approach, 1999; co-author: The Aggressive Conservative Investor, 1979. new edit., 2005; contbr. articles to profl. publs. Chmn. 3d Ave. Fund, 1991. Served with USNR, 1942-46. Named in his hon. Martin J. Whitman Sch. of Mgmt., Syracuse Univ. named its bus. sch., 2003. Mem. N.Y. Soc. Security Analysts, Phila. Econ. Soc. Jewish. Home: 285 Central Park W New York NY 10024-3006 Office Phone: 212-888-5222. Business E-Mail: mwhitman@thirdave.com.

**WHITMAN, ROBERT VAN DUYNE,** civil engineer, educator; b. Pitts., Feb. 2, 1928; s. Edwin A. and Elsie (Van Duyne) W.; m. Elizabeth Cushman, June 19, 1954; children: Jill Martyne Whitman Marsee, Martha Allerton (dec.), Gweneth Giles Whitman Kaebnick. BS, Swarthmore Coll., 1948, DSc (hon.), 1990; SM, MIT, 1949, ScD, 1951. Faculty MIT, 1953—, prof. civil engring., 1963-93, head structural engring., 1970-74, head soil mechanics divsn., 1970-72; prof. emeritus, 1993—. Vis. scholar U. Cambridge, Eng., 1976-77; cons. to govt. and industry, 1953—; mem. adv. com. for nat. earthquake hazard reduction program Fed. Emergency Mgmt. Agy., 1991-94, mem. commn. engring. and tech. systems NRC, 1992-97. Author: (with T. W. Lambe) Soil Mechanics. Mem. Town Meeting Lexington, Mass., 1962-76, 85—, mem. permanent bldg. com., 1968-75, mem. bd. appeals, 1979-81, 84-2000. Lt. (j.g.) USNR, 1954-56. Recipient U.S. Scientist award Humboldt Found., 1984-90, H. Bolton Seed medal, 2006; Norwegian Geotech. Inst. Rsch. fellow, 1984. Mem. NAE, ASCE (Rsch. award 1962, Terzaghi Lecture 1981, Terzaghi award 1987, C. Martin Duke Lifeline Earthquake Engring. award 1992, James Croes medal 1994, H. Bolton Seed medal, 2006); Boston Soc. Civil Engrs. (Structural Sect. prize 1963, Desmond Fitzgerald medal 1973, Ralph W. Horne Fund award 1977); Internat. Soc. Soil Mechanics and Found. Engrs., Mex. Soc. Soil Mechanics (hon., Nabor Carrillo lectr. 2000), Earthquake Engring. Rsch. Inst. (dir. 1978-81, 84-88, v.p. 1979-81, pres. 1985-87, Disting. lectr. 1994, hon. 1997—). Achievements include research in soil mechanics, soil dynamics, earthquake engineering and earthquake loss estimation. Home: 1010 Waltham St # 557 Lexington MA 02421 Office: MIT Dept Civil & Environ Engring Cambridge MA 02139

**WHITMER, FREDERICK LEE,** lawyer; b. Terre Haute, Ind., Nov. 5, 1947; s. Lee Arthur and Ella (Diekhoff) W.; m. Valeri Cade; children: Caitlin Margaret, Meghan Connors, Christian Frederick. BA, Wabash Coll., 1969; JD, Columbia U., 1973. Bar: N.Y. 1975, U.S. Dist. Ct. (so. dist.) N.Y. 1975, N.J. 1976, U.S. Dist. Ct. N.J. 1976, U.S. Ct. Appeals (3d cir.) 1977, U.S. Ct. Appeals (fed. cir.) 1983, U.S. Ct. Appeals (2d cir.) 1987, U.S. Supreme Ct. 1988, U.S. Ct. Appeals (7th cir.) 1994. Assoc. Kaye, Scholer, Fierman, Hays & Handler, N.Y.C., 1973-76, Pitney Hardin and Kipp, Morristown, NJ, 1976—78; ptnr. Pitney Hardin LLP, Morristown, 1979—2004, Brown, Raysman, Millstein, Felder & Steiner, N.Y.C., 2004—. Mem. ABA, N.J. Bar Assn., Phi Beta Kappa. Republican. Episcopalian. Home: 190 Hurlbutt St Wilton CT 06897-2016 Office: Brown Raysman Millstein Felder & Steiner LLP 900 3d Ave New York NY 10022 Office Phone: 212-895-2593. Business E-Mail: fwhitmer@brownraysman.com.

**WHITMER, RICHARD E.,** insurance company executive; BS in Political Science, W. Mich. U., 1963; JD, U. Mich. Law School, 1965. Legislative counsel Gov. of Mich.; dir. Mich. Dept. of Commerce; sr. v.p., gen. counsel Blue Cross Blue Shield Mich., Detroit, 1977—87, pres., CEO, 1987—. Bd. mem. Greater Detroit Chamber of Commerce, Detroit Renaissance, United Way of Southeastern Mich., Detroit Economic Growth Corp.; chmn. New Detroit, 1991—93. Office: Blue Cross Blue Shield Mich 600 E Lafayette Blvd Detroit MI 48226-2927 Office Phone: 313-225-9000.

**WHITMORE, BRUCE G.,** lawyer; BA, Tufts U., 1966; JD, Harvard U., 1969. Bar: N.Y. 1970, Calif. 1973, Pa. 1979. Gen. atty. ARCO Transp. Co., 1985-86; assoc. gen. counsel corp. fin. ARCO, 1986-90; v.p., gen. counsel ARCO Chem. Co., 1990-94; sr. v.p., gen. counsel, corp. sec. Atlantic Richfield Co., L.A., 1995-2000. Mem. ABA.

**WHITMORE, DONALD CLARK,** retired engineer; b. Seattle, Sept. 15, 1932; s. Floyd Robinson and Lois Mildred (Clark) W.; m. Alice Elinor Winter, Jan. 8, 1955; children: Catherine Ruth, William Owen, Matthew Clark, Nancy Lynn, Peggy Ann, Stuart John. BS, U. Wash., 1955. Prin. engr. The Boeing Co., Seattle, 1955-87, ret., 1987. Developer, owner mobile home pk., Auburn, Wash., 1979—; vis. scholar Henry M. Jackson Sch. Internat. Studies, U. Wash., 2005—. Author: Towards Security, 1983, Characterization of the Nuclear Proliferation Threat, 1993, Rationale for Nuclear Disarmament, 1995. Activist for arms control, Auburn, Wash., 1962—; chmn. Seattle Coun. Orgns. for Internat. Affairs, 1973, Auburn Citizens for Scis., 1975; v.p. Boeing Employees Good Neighbor Fund, Seattle, 1977, Spl. Svc. award, 1977; pres. Abe Keller Peace Edn. Fund, 1998—, 2000—; pres., founder Third Millennium Found., 1993—; founder abolishnukes.com. Recipient Human Rights award, Seattle chpt. UN Assn., 2001. Avocations: hiking, travel, collecting. Home and Office: 16202 SE Lake Moneysmith Rd Auburn WA 98092-5274 Personal E-Mail: 3rdm@gte.net.

**WHITMORE, DOUGLAS MICHAEL,** physician; b. Cambridge, Mass., Oct. 30, 1947; s. Donald Herbert and Marcela (Klein) W.; m. Ana Maria Lopez. BS, MS in Physics, U. Ill., Champaign-Urbana, 1969; MS in Physics, Stanford U., 1970, PhD in Physics, 1975; MD, U. Miami, 1978. Diplomate Am. Bd. Internal Medicine, Am. Bd. Pulmonary Disease, Am. Bd. Critical Care Medicine, Am. Bd. Geriatric Medicine. Physician Holy Cross Hosp., Ft. Lauderdale, Fla., 1983—. Pres. med. staff Holy Cross Hosp., 1996-97, chief of medicine, 1995-98. Trustee Holy Cross Hosp., 1995-98. Fellow ACP, Am. Coll. Chest Physicians; mem. AMA, Caducean Med. Soc. (pres. 1996-97), Am. Thoracic Soc., Royal Soc. Medicine. Office: Med Complex West 1930 NE 47th St Ste 205 Fort Lauderdale FL 33308-7728

**WHITMORE, FRANK CLIFFORD, JR.,** retired geologist; b. Cambridge, Mass., Nov. 17, 1915; s. Frank Clifford and Marion Gertrude (Mason) W.; m. Martha Burling Kremers, June 24, 1939; children: Geoffrey, John, Katherine, Susan. BA, Amherst Coll., 1938; MS, Pa. State U., 1939; MA, Harvard U., 1941, PhD, 1942. Instr. geology R.I. State Coll., Kingston, 1942-44; geologist U.S. Geol. Survey, Washington, 1944-84, scientist emeritus, 1984—; mem. com. rsch. and exploration Nat. Geog. Soc., 1970-96, vice chmn., 1990-96, emeritus, 1997—; rsch. assoc. dept. paleibiology Smithsonian Instn., Washington, 1967—97; ret., 1997. Sci. cons. U.S. Army, Philippines, Japan, Korea, 1945-46; mem. adv. bd. Ctr. for Study of Early Man, U. Maine, Orono, 1985-90. Editor: Resources for 21st Century, 1982; contbr. articles to profl. jours. Bd. dirs. Prince Georges County Boys Clubs Md. 1954-56; mem. program com. Nat. Capital coun. Girl Scouts U.S.A., Washington, 1967-69; pres. Thornton Soc., Washington, 1977-84. Recipient medal of Freedom U.S. Army, 1946, spl. achievement award U.S. Geol. Survey, 1980, Meritorious Svc. award U.S. Dept. Interior, 1981, Arnold Guyot Meml. award Nat. Geog. Soc., 1993, Thomas Jefferson medal Va. Mus. Natural History, 2002; Tchg. fellow Harvard U., Cambridge, 1940-42. Fellow AAAS, Geol. Soc. Am.; mem. Soc. Vertebrate Paleontology (hon. life, exec. com. 1960-62), Midriver Club, Harvard Club. Democrat. Avocation: architecture. Home: 20 Woodmoor Dr Silver Spring MD 20901-2447

**WHITMORE, GEORGE MERLE, JR.,** management consulting company executive; b. Tarrytown, N.Y., Jan. 1, 1928; s. George Merle and Elizabeth Helen (Knodel) W.; m. Priscilla Elizabeth Norman, Mar. 30, 1963; children: Elizabeth Whitmore Lippincott, George Norman, Stephen Bradford. BE, Yale U., 1949; MBA, Harvard U., 1951. Test engr. Gen. Electric Co., Bridgeport, Conn., Erie, Pa., 1949; rsch. assoc. Harvard Bus. Sch., Boston, 1951-52; assoc. Cresap, McCormick and Paget Inc., N.Y.C., 1954-59, prin., 1959-61, ptnr., 1961-69, v.p., dir., 1969-79, mng. dir., CEO, 1979-81; mng. dir. Ayers, Whitmore & Co. Inc., N.Y.C., 1981-88, Ayers, Whitmore divsn. A.T. Kearney, Inc., N.Y.C., 1988-90, Whitmore & Co., Greenwich, Conn., 1990—. Bd. dirs. Carroll Enterprises, Inc., Worcester, Mass. Pres. N.E. Greenwich Assn. Inc., 2001—05; hon. trustee, former bd pres. Hackley Sch., Tarrytown; former trustee, chmn. bd. Greenwich Acad.; former trustee, treas. Salisbury (Conn.) Sch. With USAF, 1952—53. Mem. Inst. Mgmt. Cons. (founding mem.), Newcomen Soc., Stanwich Club (former dir.), Yale Club (N.Y.), Tau Beta Pi. Presbyterian. Home and Office: 7 Wyngate Rd Greenwich CT 06830-4032 E-mail: whitpen@aol.com.

**WHITMORE, MENANDRA M.,** librarian; b. Ancash, Peru; d. Rafael and Jacinta (Moreno) Mosquera; m. Jacob L. Whitmore III, Jan. 7, 1965; children: Jacqueline Grace, Michelle Jacinta. Degree in social work, U. Catolica del Peru, 1967; MLS, U. P.R., 1974. Catholic U. Am., Washington, 1984. Social worker Cornell U., Vicos, Peru, 1960-62, Servicio de Extension Agricola del Peru, 1962-63, Am. Friends Svc. Com., Mex. and Peru, 1963-65; libr. Colegio Maria Auxiliadora, P.R., 1971, Country Day Sch., San Jose, Costa Rica,

1974-76, Colegio San Ignacio, P.R., 1976-77; dir. libs. Am. Coll. P.R., 1977-80; libr. Lib. Gov. Printing Office, 1981-84; chief acquisitions sect., mgr. Hispanic employment program Pentagon Libr., Washington, 1984-99, chief tech. and stds. divsn., 1999—2002, acting dir., 2002—03, dir., 2003—. Author: (all pub. under name Menandra Mosquera) Bibliography on Hypsipyla, 1976, Bibliography of Forestry of Puerto Rico, 1984, Useful Trees of Tropical North America, 1998. Recipient commendation Dept. Def., 1987-98. Mem. ALA, Soc. for Acquisition Latin Am. Libr. Materials, Reforma (treas. Washington chpt. 1988, pres. 1989-91, 95-99, nat. ways and means chair 1991-92). Office Phone: 703-695-2006. Business E-Mail: mena.whitmore@hqda.army.mil.

**WHITNEY, BENSON K.,** ambassador; m. Mary Whitney; 4 children. BA magna cum laude, Vassar Coll.; JD, U. Minn. Atty. Popham, Halk, Schnobrich, Kaufman and Doty. Ltd.; mng. gen. ptnr. Gideon Hixon Fund; pres. Minn. Venture Capital Assn.; CEO Whitney Mgmt. Co.; U.S. amb. to Norway US Dept. State, Oslo, 2005—. Exec. dir., fin. chair Bush-Cheney '04 Rep. Nat. Com., Minn. Former trustee, dir., chmn., advisor numerous nonprofit orgns. including Guthrie Theater, Wilderness Inquiry, Minnesotans for Term Limits, Mpls. Acad., Persephone Fund, Headwaters Fund. Office: Am Embassy 5460 Oslo Pl Washington DC 20521*

**WHITNEY, CAROL MARIE,** securities trader; b. Torrington, Conn., Mar. 31, 1946; d. Charles Lester and Emily Mae (Orr) W. BA in French, Wells Coll., 1968; 5th yr. cert., So. Conn. State Coll., 1971; postgrad., N.Y. Inst. Fin., 1976; MS in Mgmt., Rensselaer Poly. Inst., 1992, MBA in Internat. Mgmt., 1997. Trainee/investment exec. Blyth-Eastman Dillon, Hartford, Conn., 1976-77; licensee ins. fixed, variable, life and health, various cos., 1977—; account exec./registered rep. Bache Halsey-Stuart Shields, Hartford, Danbury, Conn., 1977-81, Advest, Inc., Hartford, 1981-88; registered securities rep. West Hartford, Conn., 1988-91; internat. fin. con., investment analyst, pres. Ask My Assoc., Collinsville, Conn., 1988—; v.p. registered rep. E.T. Andrews & Co. Inc., Hartford, Conn., 1991-92; v.p. Conn. Fin. Network, 1991-92; v.p., registered prin. Buell Securities Corp., Wethersfield, Conn., 1992—; br. mgr. Torrington office, 1993-95. Sec. Internat. Assn. for Fin. Planning, Hartford, 1982-83, pub. rels. Conn. chpt., Hartford, 1983-85, ethics chairperson Conn. chpt., Hartford, 1985-86. Exhibited 5 paintings in State Cultural Mus., Karelia, Russia, 1999, 16 paintings in The Cultural Mus., Petrozavodsky, Russia, 2000; solo exhibit Cultural Mus., Petrozarodsk, Russia, 2000; prodr. (CD) Guennady Vavilov, 1999; author: Global Corporate Derivatives, 1997. Performing mem. Farmington Valley chpt. Sweet Adelines, Simsbury, Conn., 1976-82; founder, exec. dir. Lydia Whitney Found Inc.; exec. dir. for classical composers concert, The Bushnell, Hartford, 1998—. Named for Effective Speaking and Human Rels., Dale Carnegie, West Hartford, 1985. Mem. DAR, Internat. Platform Assn. (3rd prize Washington 1995 Katyn Forest, World Tour 1997 for 5 paintings, 1st prize 1997), World Affairs. Republican. Episcopalian. Avocations: international travel, cooking and baking, writing, russian language studies. Home: PO Box 462 Collinsville CT 06022-0462

**WHITNEY, CRAIG RICHARD,** journalist; b. Milford, Mass., Oct. 12, 1943; s. A. Gordon and Carol Alma (Kennison) W.; m. Heidi Witt, May 11, 1974; children: Alexandra Kennison, Stefan Robert. AB, Harvard, 1965. Reporter New York Times, Washington, 1965-66, N.Y.C., 1969-70, Saigon, Vietnam, 1971-72, Bonn, West Germany, 1973-77, Moscow, USSR, 1977-80, dep. fgn. editor, 1980-82, fgn. editor, 1982-83, asst. mng. editor, 1983-86, Washington Bur. chief, 1986-88, London bur. chief, 1988-92, European diplomatic corr., 1992-2000, asst. mng. editor, 2000—. Author: Spy Trader, 1993, All the Stops, 2003, The WMD Mirage, 2005. Served with USNR, 1966-69. Mem. Coun. Fgn. Rels., Harvard Club (N.Y.C.). Home: 1 Pierrepont St Brooklyn NY 11201-3302 Office: The NY Times 229 W 43rd St New York NY 10036-3959 Office Phone: 212-556-3909. E-mail: whitney@nytimes.com.

**WHITNEY, DANIEL LAWRENCE See LARRY THE CABLE GUY**

**WHITNEY, DAVID See MALICK, TERRENCE**

**WHITNEY, DOUGLAS EDGAR, SR.,** retired lawyer; b. Malden, Mass., May 1, 1939; s. Edgar Gordon and Jennie (Johnson) Whitney; m. Carol Annette Moore, July 31, 1965 (div. 1994); children: Douglas Jr., James A., Charles B.; m. Helleke Nieterink, May 11, 1996. BChem. Engring., Cornell U., 1962; JD, Columbia U., 1965. Bar: N.Y. 1965, Mass. 1970, Del. 1973, U.S. Dist. Ct. (so. dist.) N.Y. 1966, U.S. Dist. Ct. Mass. 1969, U.S. Dist. Ct. Del. 1973, U.S. Ct. Appeals (fed., 1st, 2d and 3d cirs.), U.S. Supreme Ct. 1972. Patent agt. Mobil Oil Corp., N.Y.C., 1963-65; assoc. Davis, Hoxie, Faithfull & Hapgood, N.Y.C., 1965-69; ptnr. Russell & Nields, Boston, 1969-72, Morris, Nichols, Arsht & Tunnell, Wilmington, Del., 1972—2004, ret., 2004. Bd. dirs. U.S. Orienteering Fedn., St. Louis, 1981-84, Tech. Properties, Inc., Ft. Worth, 1992-2000. Mem. ABA, Am. Intellectual Property Assn., Del. Bar Assn. Democrat. Congregationalist. Home: 10 Hickory Ln Chadds Ford PA 19317-9715 E-mail: dewsr@att.net.

**WHITNEY, EDWARD BONNER,** retired investment banker; b. Glen Cove, NY, June 6, 1945; s. Edward Farley and Millicent Bonner (Bowring) W.; m. Martha Congleton Howell, Aug. 17, 1974; children: William Howell, John Howell. BA, Harvard U., 1966, MBA, 1969. Systems engr. IBM, Cambridge, Mass., 1966-67; assoc. Dillon, Read & Co. Inc., N.Y.C., 1969-74, v.p., 1975-79, sr. v.p., 1980-83, mng. dir., 1984-97, also bd. dirs.; mng. dir. UBS Warburg, London, 1997—2002. Bd. dirs., IRRC Inst.; bd. dirs., 1st vice chmn. Am. Rivers. Mem. Harvard Club NYC E-mail: Nedwhitney@aol.com.

**WHITNEY, FRANK DEARMON,** federal judge, former prosecutor; b. Charlotte N.C., Nov. 22, 1959; s. A. Grant and Lillian (DeArmon) Whitney; m. Catherine Whitney; children: Anne Stone, Frances Hunter. BA, Wake Forest U., 1982; MBA, JD, U. N.C., 1987. Bar: N.C. 1987, D.C. 1988. Assoc. McKenna Conner Cuneo, Washington, 1987—90; law clk. to Hon. David B. Sentelle US Ct. Appeals (DC Cir.), 1988—89; asst. U.S. atty. (we. dist.) N.C. US Dept. Justice, Charlotte, 1990—2001; counsel Kilpatrick Stockton LLP, Charlotte, 2001—02; U.S. atty. (ea. dist.) N.C. US Dept. Justice, Raleigh, 2003—06; judge US Dist. Ct. (we. dist.) N.C., 2006—. Serves in USAR, 1982—. Presbyterian. Office: US Dist Ct Charles R Jonas Bldg 401 W Trade St Charlotte NC 28202*

**WHITNEY, JONATHAN B.,** lawyer; b. July 12, 1954; BA, Skidmore Coll., 1977; JD, Fordham Univ., 1981. Bar: NY 1982. Ptnr., leader NY Fin. dept. Pillsbury Winthrop Shaw Pittman, NYC. Mem.: ABA, Assn. Bar City of NY, Phi Beta Kappa. Office: Pillsbury Winthrop Shaw Pittman 1540 Broadway New York NY 10036 Office Phone: 212-858-1405. Office Fax: 212-858-1500. Business E-Mail: jonathan.whitney@pillsburylaw.com.

**WHITNEY, KENT R.E.,** securities trader; b. Chgo., Feb. 7, 1979; s. Kent R.N. and Arlene M. Whitney; m. Kiva R. Cosson, Mar. 21, 2004 (div. Apr. 18, 2006); 1 child, Kent E.E. Options market maker Chgo. Bd. Options Exchange, 1997—2000, COMEX, N.Y., 1999—2000; mem. Chgo. Bd. Trade, 2000—. Named Entrepreneur of Yr., Ernst & Young, 1997. Mem.: Plz. Club (life). Home: 233 East Wacker Dr Chicago IL 60601 Office: 141W Jackson Blvd Chicago IL Office Phone: 312-789-8172. Personal E-mail: krwoptions@yahoo.com.

**WHITNEY, PATRICK FOSTER,** design educator; b. Edmonton, Alta., Can., Sept. 5, 1951; came to US 1974; s. Gordon and Geraldine (Walker) W.; m. Cheryl Kent. BFA in Design with distinction, U. Alta., 1974; MFA in Design, Cranbrook Acad. Art, Bloomfield Hills, Mich., 1976. Designer RVI Corp., Chgo., 1976-79; chmn. Div. of Design Mpls. Coll. Art and Design, 1979-83; chmn. Inst. of Design, Ill. Inst. Tech. Chgo., 1983-87, dir., 1987—, Steelcase/Robert C. Pew Prof. Design. Lectr. in the field; mem., disting. advisor bd. Assn. Computing Machinery's Special Interest Group in Computer Human Interaction; chmn. US Conf. of Internat. Coun. on Graphic Design Assns., 1978; juror Presdl. Design Awards, 1995; mem. White House Council on Design; pres. Am. Ctr. for Design (ACD); principal investigator for a rsch. project called Global Companies in Local Markets. Editor Design in the Information Environment, 1984, Design Journal; author numerous published articles on design and communications. Mem. Am. Ctr. for Design (bd. dirs. 1984-86, v.p. 1986-90, pres. 1992-94), Arts Club. Office: Ill Inst Tech Inst Design 350 N LaSalle St Chicago IL 60610 Office Phone: 312-595-4900. Business E-Mail: whitney@id.iit.edu.

**WHITNEY, PHYLLIS AYAME,** author; b. Yokohama, Japan, Sept. 9, 1903; d. Charles J. and Lillian (Mandeville) W.; m. George A. Garner, July 2, 1925 (div. 1945); m. Lovell F. Jahnke, 1950 (dec. 1973). Grad., McKinley High Sch., Chgo., 1924. Instr. dancing, San Antonio, 1 yr; tchr. juvenile fiction writing Northwestern U., 1945; children's book editor Chgo. Sun, 1942-46, Phila. Inquirer, 1947, 48; instr. juvenile fiction writing N.Y.U., 1947-58; leader juvenile fiction workshop Writers Conf., U. Colo., 1952, 54, 56. Pres. exec. bd. 5th Ann. Writers Conf., Northwestern U., 1944. Author: A Place for Ann, 1941, A Star for Ginny, 1942, (vocat. fiction for teenage girls) A Window for Julie, 1943, (mystery novel for adults) Red Is for Murder, 1943, The Silver Inkwell, 1945, Willow Hill, 1947, Writing Juvenile Fiction, 1947, Ever After, 1948, Mystery of the Gulls, 1949, Linda's Homecoming, 1950, The Island of Dark Woods, 1951, Love Me, Love Me Not, 1952, Step to the Music, 1953, A Long Time Coming, 1954, Mystery of the Black Diamonds, 1954, The Quicksilver Pool, 1955, Mystery on the Isle of Skye, 1955, The Fire and The Gold (Jr. Lit. Guild), 1956, The Highest Dream (Jr. Lit. Guild), 1956, The Trembling Hills (Peoples Book Club), 1956, Skye Cameron, 1957, Mystery of the Green Cat (Jr. Lit. Guild), 1957, Secret of the Samurai Sword (Jr. Lit. Guild), 1958, The Moonflower, 1958, Creole Holiday, 1959, Thunder Heights, 1960, Blue Fire, 1961, Mystery of the Haunted Pool, 1961 (Edgar award Mystery Writers Am.), Secret of the Tiger's Eye, 1961, Window on the Square, 1962, Mystery of the Golden Horn, 1962, Seven Tears for Apollo, 1963, Mystery of the Hidden Hand, 1963 (Edgar award Mystery Writers Am. 1964), Black Amber, 1964, Secret of the Emerald Star, 1964, Sea Jade, 1965, Mystery of the Angry Idol, 1965, Columbella, 1966, Secret of the Spotted Shell, 1967, Mystery of the Strange Traveler, 1967, Silverhill, 1967, Hunter's Green, 1968, Secret of Goblin Glen, 1968, Mystery of the Crimson Ghost, 1969, Winter People, 1969, Secret of the Missing Footprint, 1970, Lost Island, 1970, The Vanishing Scarecrow, 1971, Listen for the Whisperer, 1971, Nobody Likes Trina, 1972, Snowfire, 1973, Mystery of the Scowling Boy, 1973, The Turquoise Mask, 1974, Spindrift, 1975, Secret of Haunted Mesa, 1975, The Golden Unicorn, 1976, Secret of the Stone Face, 1977, The Stone Bull, 1977, The Glass Flame, 1978, Domino, 1979, Poinciana, 1980, Vermilion, 1981, Guide to Fiction Writing, 1982, Emerald, 1983, Rainsong, 1984, Dream of Orchids, 1985, Flaming Tree, 1986, Silversword, 1987, Feather on the Moon, 1988, Rainbow in the Mist, 1989, The Singing Stones, 1990, Woman Without a Past, 1991, The Ebony Swan, 1992, Star Flight, 1993, Daughter of the Stars, 1994, Amethyst Dreams, 1997; sold first story to Chgo. Daily News; later wrote for pulp mags., became specialist in juvenile writing, now writing entirely in adult field. Spent first 15 years of life in Japan, China and P.I. (father in shipping and hotel bus.). Recipient Friends of Lit. award for contbns. to children's lit., 1974; Reynal and Hitchcock prize in Youth Today contest for book Willow Hill; Today's Woman award Coun. Cerebral Palsy Auxs., 1983, Agatha award Malice Domestic, 1990, Rita award Romance Writers Am., 1990, Lifetime award Romance Writers Am., 1990, Midland Authors award for a lifetime of literary achievement, 1995. Mem. Mystery Writers Am. (pres. 1975, Grandmaster award for lifetime achievement 1988), Am. Crime Writers League, Sisters in Crime, Authors League of Am., Authors Round Table (pres. 1943-44). Address: care McIntosh and Otis 353 Lexington Ave New York NY 10016-0941 *A learning period must be allowed for any talent. The accidental success is unfortunate because the person who achieves it doesn't really know how it happened. This does not mean that it ever becomes easy, even with learning. There is always work involved-long hours and dedication to that work-before a book is ready for publication. Any success demands a price, and the time and effort, and sometimes anguish a successful person gives to his work is that price. For me, the satisfactions have been worth it.*

**WHITNEY, RALPH ROYAL, JR.,** financial executive; b. Phila., Dec. 10, 1934; s. Ralph Royal and Florence Elizabeth (Whitney) W.; m. Fay Wadsworth, Apr. 4, 1959; children: Lynn Marie, Paula Sue, Brian Ralph. BA, U. Rochester, 1957, MBA, 1972. Spl. agt. Prudential Ins. Co., Rochester, NY, 1958-59, divisn. mgr., 1959-63; gen. agt. Nat. Life VT, Syracuse, 1963-64; contr. Wadsworth Mfg. Assocs. Inc., Syracuse, 1964-65, v.p., 1965-68, pres., 1968-71, Warren (Pa.) Components Corp., 1960-72; chmn. Hammond Kennedy Whitney & Co., N.Y.C., 1972—. Chmn. Reinhold Industries; chmn., CEO Grobet File Co.; bd. dirs. Baldwin Tech. Corp., First Tech., Ltd., Coast Composites Inc., MedTek Inc., Wyo. Bus. Coun., Relm Wireless Comms. Inc., 1st Internet Bank, Seneca Printing, Inc., Dura Automobile Sys. Inc., Maine Rubber Co. Trustee U. Rochester. Mem. N.Y. Yacht Club, Lotus Club (N.Y.C.), Century Club (Syracuse), Merion Cricket Club, Princeton Club. Episcopalian. Office Phone: 212-867-1010. E-mail: rrw@hkwinc.com.

**WHITNEY, RAY,** professional hockey player; b. Saskatchewan, Alta., Can., May 8, 1972; s. Floyd and Wendy Whitney Stick boy Edmonton Oilers, 1986-87, 87-88, player, 1997, Spokane Chiefs, 1988-91, 90-91, San Jose Sharks, 1991—97, Edmonton Oilers, 1997—98, Fla. Panthers, 1998—2001, Columbus Blue Jackets, 2001—03, Detroit Red Wings, 2003—04, Carolina Hurricanes, 2005—. Named most valuable player NHL, 1988-91, 90-91, Most Valuable Player All-Star Game IHL, 1992. Achievements include being a member of Stanley Cup Champion Carolina Hurricanes, 2006. Avocation: golf. Office: Carolina Hurricanes RBC Ctr 1400 Edwards Mill Rd Raleigh NC 27607-3624*

**WHITNEY, RICHARD BUCKNER,** lawyer; b. Corpus Christi, Tex., Mar. 1, 1948; s. Franklyn Loren and Betty Wolcott (Fish) Whitney; m. Chantal Marie Cindt, Aug. 10, 1972; children: Jennifer L, James R, Katherine E. BA in Polit. Sci., Union Coll., 1970; JD, Case Western Res. U., 1973. Bar: Ohio 1973, N.Y. 1998, US Ct Appeals (6th cir) 1974, US Ct Appeals (3d cir) 1987, US Dist Ct (so dist) NY 2000, U.S. Dist. Ct. (no. dist.) Ohio 1974. From assoc. to ptnr. Jones Day, Cleve., 1973—. Trustee Hospice of the We. Res. Mem.: Am Inns of Ct., Cleve. Bar Assn., Order of Coif. Home: 2750 Southington Rd Shaker Heights OH 44120-1603 Office: Jones Day 901 Lakeside Ave Cleveland OH 44114-1190 Business E-Mail: rbwhitney@jonesday.com.

**WHITNEY, RODGER FRANKLIN,** academic administrator; b. Dallas, Feb. 2, 1948; s. Roger Albert and Genevieve Mae (Mohr) W. Cert. higher studies, U. Lausanne, Switzerland, 1970; BA, So. Meth. U., 1971, M Liberal Arts, 1973; EdD, Harvard U., 1978. Dir. upperclass residences So. Meth. U., Dallas, 1971-73, mem. faculty, 1973-75; dir. Mohr Edn. Found., Dallas, 1975-77; dir. North Park East, Raymond D. Nasher Co., Dallas, 1977-79; dir. Stanford Housing Ctr., asst. dean student affairs Stanford (Calif.) U., 1979-91, exec. dir. housing, 1991—. Dir. Camp Grady Spruce, YMCA, Dallas, 1971-76, bd. dirs., 1976-80. Bd. dirs. Scientific Equip. Commons, Redwood City, Calif., 1989-91. Mem. Assn. Coll. and Univ. Housing Officers, Harvard Club San Francisco, Phi Beta Kappa. Avocations: swimming, travel, history, reading, music. Home: 861 Whitehall Ln Redwood City CA 94061-3685 Office: Stanford U Housing 565 Cowell Ln Stanford CA 94305-8512

**WHITNEY, WILLIAM ELLIOT, JR.,** advertising agency executive; b. Albany, N.Y., Feb. 22, 1933; s. William Elliot and Louise E. (Goldsmith) W.; m. Nancy B. Bivings, Mar. 1, 1958; children: Susan, James, Douglas. BA cum laude, Amherst Coll., 1954; MBA, Harvard U., 1956. Account exec. McCann-Erickson, N.Y.C., 1956-58, Marschalk Co., N.Y.C., 1958-60; v.p., then sr. v.p. Ogilvy & Mather, N.Y.C., 1960-80, sr. v.p., mng. dir. Chgo., 1980-85, exec. v.p., 1985-87, pres., 1987-89, chmn., 1990-91; cons. prin. Redirections, Inc., 1991-98. Lectr. U. Chgo. Grad. Sch. Bus., 1991-98. Bd. dirs.-v.p. Chgo. Coun. Boy Scouts Am., 1977-88—, off-the-St. Club, Chgo., 1979—, pres. 1988-89; bd. dirs. Hinsdale (Ill.) Cmty. House, 1981, King-Bruwaert House, 1988-2004; v.p. civic adv. bd. Hinsdale Hosp., 1989-93; bd. dirs. Exec. Svc. Corps of Chgo., 1996-2004, life dir., 2005—;

trustee Village of Hinsdale, 1993-97, pres., 1997-2001; bd. dirs. Hinsdale Area United Way, 2001-04. Mem. Econs. Club, Hinsdale Golf Club. Home: 736 S Park Ave Hinsdale IL 60521-4646

**WHITSEL, RICHARD HARRY,** retired biologist, entomologist; b. Denver, Feb. 23, 1931; s. Richard Elstun and Edith Muriel (Harry) W.; m. Laurie Pearson, May 25, 1997; children by previous marriages: Russell David, Robert Alan, Michael Dale, Steven Deane. BA, U. Calif., Berkeley, 1954; MA, San Jose State Coll., 1962. Sr. rsch. biologist San Mateo County Mosquito Abatement Dist., Burlingame, Calif., 1959—72; mgr. environ. program, chief watershed mgmt., chief planning, chief wetlands planning office Calif. Regional Water Quality Control Bd., Oakland, 1972—2000; ret. 2000. Trustee Alameda County Mosquito Abatement Dist., 1999-2001; mem. grad. faculty water resource mgmt. U. San Francisco, 1987-89. Served with Med. Svc. Corps, U.S. Army, 1954-56. Mem. Soc. Wetland Scientists, Entomol. Soc. Am., Calif. Alumni Assn., The Benjamin Ide Wheeler Soc., Nat. Parks and Conservation Assn. (life), Sierra Club. Democrat. Episcopalian. Home: 11552 Side Hill Cir Nevada City CA 95959 Personal E-mail: lwhitsel@sbcglobal.net.

**WHITSELL, JOHN CRAWFORD, II,** general surgeon; b. St. Joseph, Mo., Dec. 21, 1929; s. Ora Earl and Lorena (Spratt) W. AB, Grinnell Coll., 1950; MD, Washington U., St. Louis, 1954. Diplomate Am. Bd. Surgery, Am. Bd. Thoracic Surgery. From instr. to clin. prof. surgery Cornell U. Med. Ctr., N.Y.C., 1963—70; from asst. attending to attending in surgery N.Y. Hosp., N.Y.C., 1964—70; surg. dir. Rogosin Kidney Ctr. N.Y. Hosp.-Cornell Med. Ctr., N.Y.C., 1973—75; attending in surgery N.Y. Hosp., 1970—98, hon. attending surgeon, 2001—; clin. prof. surgery Cornell Med. Coll., 1970—98, clin. prof. surgery emeritus, 1998—. Surg. cons. Rogosin Kidney Ctr., 1975—, Chann (Conn.) Hosp., 1976-2001. Contbr. articles to profl. jours. Capt. USAF, 1961-63, Eng. Fellow ACS; mem. Transplantation Soc., N.Y. Surg. Soc., Am. Soc. Transplant Surgeons, N.Y. Soc. for Thoracic Surgery, Soc. Thoracic Surgeons, N.Y. Acad. Medicine, N.Y. Soc. Cardiovascular Surgery, Harvey Soc., Union Club of N.Y., Phi Beta Kappa. Avocations: golf, fishing, auto racing, antique cars. Personal E-mail: rmwhitsell@aol.com.

**WHITSETT, ELEANOR WATKINS,** musician, educator, composer; b. Kansas City, Mo., Dec. 9, 1931; d. Aura Clay and Bess Beck Watkins; m. Lowell Don Whitsett, Mar. 3, 1956; children: John Lowell, Jeffrey Clay. AB, Asbury Coll., Ky., 1952; MusM, U. Mo., Kansas City, 1972. Organist First Ch. of Nazarene, Kansas City, 1962—72; u. organist, adj. prof. of organ So. Nazarene U., Bethany, Okla., 1974—2001. Recitals and workshops Various Chs. and Colls., 1972—; assoc. Am. Guild of Organists, NY, 1982. Composer: (organ composition) In Dulci Jubilo (Commn. from Am. Guild of Organists, Region VII, 2003), At the Console, Progressive Communion, (music for organ and piano) Christmas Duets for Organ and Piano, Gospel Duos. V.p., edn. Okla. City Orch. League, 2000—01; v.p. Mu Phi Epsilon Alumni Chpt., Oklahoma City. Recipient Outstanding Hon. Alumnus, So. Nazarene U., 1982, Lifetime Achievement award, First Presbyn. Ch. Mem.: Okla. City Orch. League (life), Hymn Soc. of the US and Can. (life), Am. Soc. of Composers, Authors and Pubs., Mu Phi Epsilon (life). Avocations: travel, swimming, needlepoint. Home: 8101 N Bridgeport Ln Bethany OK 73008 Personal E-mail: ewhitsett@cox.net.

**WHITSETT, JEFFREY ALLEN,** pediatric educator; b. Cleve., May 19, 1947; s. William F. and Kathryn A. (Gilletly) W.; m. Dorinda Dew, May 3, 1975; children: Sarah, Anna, Margaret, David. BA, Colgate U., 1969; MD, Columbia U., 1973. Diplomate Am. Bd. Pediatrics, Am. Bd. Neonatology. Intern and resident Mt. Sinai Hosp., N.Y.C., 1973-76; fellow U. Cin. Children's Hosp., 1976-78, prof. pediatrics, pharmacology, cell biophysics, 1978—, dir. pulmonary biology, 1988—, chief neonatology, perinatal & pulmonary biol. sect. Contbr. articles to sci. publs.; patentee in field. Recipient E. Mead Johnson award Bristol-Meyers Co., 1988, NIH Merit award, William Cooper Procter award, Cin. Children's Hosp., Amerson Lecture award, Am. Thoracic Soc., Daniel Drake medal, U. Cin. Coll. Med.; Human Embryololgy Devel. and Study Sect. grantee NIH, 1987-91. Mem. Soc. for Pediatric Rsch. (coun. 1989-91), Am. Soc. Cell Biology, Am. Soc. Clin. Investigation, Inst. Medicine of NAS. Office: U Cin Childrens Hosp 231 Bethesda Ave Cincinnati OH 45229-2827 Office Phone: 513-636-4830. Office Fax: 513-636-7868. E-mail: jeff.whitsett@cchmc.org.*

**WHITSITT, BOB (ROBERT JAMES WHITSITT),** former professional football team executive; b. Madison, Wis., Jan. 10, 1956; s. Raymond Earl and Dolores June (Smith) W.; m. Jan Leslie Sundberg; children: Lillian Ashley, Sean James. BS, U. Wis., Stevens Point, 1977; MA, Ohio State U., 1978. Intern Ind. Pacers, Inpls., 1978, bus. tickets mgr., 1979, dir. bus. affairs and promotions, 1980, asst. gen. mgr., 1981-82; v.p. mktg. Kansas City Kings, 1982-84, v.p., asst. gen. mgr., 1984-85, Sacramento Kings, 1985-86; pres. Seattle Supersonics, 1986-97, Portland Trail Blazers, 1997—2003; pres. football ops. Seattle Seahawks, 1996—2005. Recipient Exec. of the Year, NBA, 1994. Mem. Nat. Basketball Assn. (alternate gov., mem. competition and rules com.). Lodges: Rotary. Republican. Lutheran. Avocations: skiing, jogging, reading, music.

**WHITSON, ELIZABETH TEMPLE,** graphics designer; b. Washington, D.C., Oct. 1, 1959; d. Norman Burkey Musselman, Elizabeth Temple (Henry) Musselman; m. William Stuart Whitson, Dec. 21, 1985; 1 child, Ian Alexander. BA, Va. Tech. U., 1982. Artist, office asst. Artisan Graphics, Alexandria, Va., 1983—84; graphic artist, office asst. Gestalt Assocs., Alexandria, 1984—86; graphic artist, sales rep., prodn. mgr. Gestalt Prodns., Herndon, Va., 1986—89, ImageMatrix, Inc., Falls Church, Va., 1989—91; graphic designer, publ. head CompuSlides, Vienna, Va., 1991—94, New Media Comms., Vienna, 1994—95; graphic designer, owner Port City Prodns., Inc., Alexandria, 1993—. Newsletter chmn.: Meeting House Coop. Pre-sch., 2000—; editor (illustrator): Highlights of the Alexandria Com., 1988. Mem. Brookville/Seminary Valley Civic Assn., Alexandria, 1988—2002; vol. Torpedo Factory Art Ctr.; active mem. The Alexandria Link Co.; com. vol. tchr., mem. Old Presbyn. Meeting House. Mem.: DAR (corr. sec. 1995—98, chmn. two coms. Mt. Vernon chpt.), The Old Presbyterian Meeting House (worship com. 1995—97, childcare com. 2000—03, childhood edn. com. 2003—04, Godly Play tchr. 2003—), Friends of Gunston Hall, The Alexandria Assembly, Nat. Soc. Colonial Dames of Am. (rec. sec. 1999—2002, directory chmn. 2002—, vice chmn. 2004—, Alexandria com.). Presbyterian. Avocations: remodeling, gardening, painting, illustration, piano. Home and Office: 1701 Sherwood Hall Ln Alexandria VA 22306 Office Phone: 703-718-0105. E-mail: sb.portcity23@verizon.net.

**WHITSON, JERRY E.,** lawyer; b. Alexandria, Va., June 15, 1955; BA in English cum laude, SUNY, Stony Brook, 1977; JD cum laude, Boston Univ., 1980. Bar: Va. 1980, NY 1991. Assoc. Hunton & Williams LLP, NYC, 1980—88, ptnr., global capital mkts, mergers, acquistions, 1988—. Exec. editor Boston Univ. Law Rev., 1980; mem.: ABA. Office: Hunton & Williams 53rd Fl 200 Park Ave New York NY 10166-0136 Office Phone: 212-309-1060. Office Fax: 212-309-1100. Business E-Mail: jwhitson@hunton.com.

**WHITT, GREGORY SIDNEY,** evolution educator; b. Detroit, June 13, 1938; s. Sidney Abram and Millicent (Ward) W.; m. Dixie Lee Blashey, Aug. 25, 1963, BS, Colo. State U., 1962, MS, 1965; PhD, Yale U., 1970. Asst. prof. zoology U. Ill., Urbana, 1969-72, assoc. prof. genetics and devel., 1972-77, prof., 1977-87, prof. ecology, ethology and evolution, 1987-2000, prof. animal biology, 2000—. Affiliate Ill. Natural History Survey, 1981—; mem. NIH study sect., 1975-76 Co-editor: Isozymes: Current Topics in Biological and Medical Research, 1977-87; editor: Isozyme Bull., 1978-81; mem. editl. bd. Biochem. Genetics, 1975—, Devel. Genetics, 1978-83, Jour. Molecular Evolution, 1979-2000, Molecular Biology and Evolution, 1983-93, Molecular Phylogenetics and Evolution, 1992-2000; contbr. articles to profl. jours.

Fellow AAAS; mem. Am. Soc. Microbiology, Soc. Protection Old Fishes, Archaeol. Inst. Am. Office: U Ill Dept Animal Biology 515 Morrill Hall 505 S Goodwin Ave Urbana IL 61801-3707 Home: 3108 Earle Ct Urbana IL 61802-7091

**WHITT, RICHARD ERNEST,** reporter; b. Greenup County, Ky., Dec. 15, 1944; s. Walter Charles and Irene (Hayes) W.; m. Terri Bellizzi; children: Hayes Chadwick, Emily Catherine, Christen Leigh McCollough. Student, Ashland Community Coll., Ky., 1966-68; BA in Journalism, U. Ky., 1970. Reporter Middlesboro (Ky.) Daily News, 1970-71; asst. state editor Waterloo (Iowa) Courier, 1971-72; city editor Kingsport (Tenn.) Times, 1972-76; No. Ky. bur. chief Courier-Jour., Louisville, 1977, Frankfort bur. chief, 1977-80, spl. projects reporter, 1980-89; investigative reporter Atlanta Jour. & Constn., 1989—. Served with USN, 1962-66. Decorated Air medal; recipient Pulitzer prize for coverage of Beverly Hills Supper Club fire, 1978; named Outstanding Ky. Journalist, 1978; recipient John Hancock award for excellence, 1983; named to U. Ky. Journalism Hall of Fame, 1995. Democrat. Office: Atlanta Jour & Constn 72 Marietta St NW Atlanta GA 30303-2804 Office Phone: 770-509-4079. E-mail: rwhitt@ajc.com, rewhitt@yahoo.com.

**WHITT, WARD,** science educator; b. Buffalo, Jan. 29, 1942; married, 1983; 2 children. AB, Dartmouth Coll., 1964; PhD in Ops. Rsch., Cornell U., 1969. Vis. asst. prof., dept. ops. rsch Stanford U., 1968-69; asst. prof. adminstrn. sci Yale U., Sch. Orgn. and Mgmt., 1969-73, assoc. prof. adminstrn. sci. and dept. stats., 1973-77; mem. tech. staff, ops. rsch. ctr. in rsch. area Bell Labs and AT&T Labs, Homdel, NJ, 1977—87, mem. tech. staff, Mat. Sciences Rsch. Ctr. Murray Hill, NJ, 1987—96; mem. rsch. AT&T Labs, Florham Park, NJ, 1996—2002; prof., dept. indsl. engring. and ops. rsch., Fu Found. Sch. Engring. and Applied Sci. Columbia U., NYC, 2002—. Cons. in field; lectr. in field; mem. AT&T Labs Fellowship Program Com., sharing in the Presdl. award for Excellence in Sci., Math. and Engring. Mentoring, 1998; Ray Fulkerson Lectr., Sch. of Ops. Rsch. and Indsl. Engring. Cornell U., 2000; co-founder, chief scientist SeatLink, 2004—; part-time cons. Avaya Labs Rsch., Basking Ridge, NJ, 2003—. Published over 275 articles related to: contact centers, queues, games and optimization, simulation, and communication networks; editl. bds. of Operations Research, Management Science, Mathematics of Operations Research, Journal of Applied Probability, Advances in Applied Probability, Queueing Systems, Stochastic Processes and their Applications, Journal of Discrete Event Dynamical Systems, Journal of the Operations research Soc. of Japan. NSF grant, 1971-73, rsch. grant, 1973-75; AT&T Fellow, 1997; recipient the first Marcel F. Neuts best paper award, 1998, Harold Lander prize, Can. Operational Rsch. Soc., 2001. Mem. NAE (mem. Sect. 8 Indsl., Mfg. and Ops. Sys. Engring. peer com. 1998-2000, chair, 2000), Inst. Math. Stats., Opns. Rsch. Soc. Am., Inst. for Ops. Rsch. and the Mgmt. Sciences (INFORMS)(mem. Applied Probability Soc.(mem. prize com., 1999-2001; recipient John von Neumann Theory prize, 2001, Inaugural INFORMS fellow, 2002, Frederick W. Lanchester prize, hon. mention, 1998, recipeint, 2003; Plenary spkr, INFORMS Telecommunications Conf., 1998, 2001). Achievements include 8 patents in field, 4 pending. Office: IOER Dept Columbia U 304 S W Mudd Bldg 500 W 120th St New York NY 10027-6699 Office Phone: 212-854-7255. Office Fax: 212-854-8103. Business E-Mail: ww2040@columbia.edu, wwhitt@seatlink.net.*

**WHITTAKER, BILL DOUGLAS,** minister; b. Bowling Green, Ky., June 14, 1943; s. Ewing A. and Lois (Jenkins) W.; m. Rebecca Kaye Howard, June 18, 1966; children: John, Karen, Mary. BA, Western Ky. U., 1965; MDiv, So. Bapt. Theol. Sem., Louisville, 1969, D of Ministry, 1974; MA, Union Coll., 2004. Ordained to ministry So. Bapt. Conv., 1964. Pastor 1st Bapt. Ch., Sturgis, Ky., 1969-76, Murray, Ky., 1976-82; missionary Internat. Mission Bd., So. Bapt. Conv., The Philippines, 1983-86; pastor Downtown Bapt. Ch., Orlando, Fla., 1986-88; pres. Clear Creek Bapt. Bible Coll., Pineville, Ky., 1988—. Author: Preparing to Preach, 1999, Korean edit. 2002; columnist Western Recorder newspaper, 1988—; editor: Ky. Bapt. Heritage, 2001—. Bd. dirs. Coalition for the Homeless, Cen. Fla. YMCA, Orlando, 1986-88; mem. Ky. Bapt. Archives Adv. Bd. Mem. Assn. Bible Colls. (accredited, del. 1988—), Assn. So. Bapt. Colls. and Schs. (del. 1988—), So. Assn. Coll. and Schs. (del. 1999 ), Kiwanis (pres. Pineville chpt. 1994-95, dist. 6 lt. gov. 1997-98), Ky. Bapt. Conv. (pres. 1980). Baptist. Home and Office: 300 Clear Creek Rd Pineville KY 40977-9752 Business E-Mail: bwhittaker@ccbbc.edu.

**WHITTAKER, JEANNE EVANS,** retired journalist; b. Detroit, Jan. 1, 1934; d. Alfred Heacock and Margaret (Evans) W.; m. Charles Martin Hines Jr., Sept. 29, 1962 (div. Feb. 1970); children: Charles M. Hines III, Margaret Helen Whittaker Zimmerman. Student, Northwestern U., 1952-53; BS in History, U. Mich., 1956. Clubmobile worker UN forces ARC, Republic of Korea, 1956—58; staff programmer ARC France, Chaumont, Evreux, 1958—61; dir. Bexar County chpt. youth ARC, San Antonio, 1961—62; staff writer/columnist Detroit Free Press, 1970—75; editor Mich. Social Register, 1975—77; Lifestyle editor Observer and Eccentric newspapers, Birmingham, Mich., 1977—87; staff writer, columnist Detroit News, 1987—91; cons. in field, 1992—. Mem. adv. com. Wayne State U. Press, 2000—. Contbr. articles to mags. Bd. dirs. Detroit chpt. ARC, 1989-92; Mem. Univ.-Liggett Sch. Aumni Bd., 2003—; mem. adv. bd. Greenfield Village Antiques Show, 2000-05. Recipient Penney-Mo. award U. Mo., 1984; 1st place lifestyles/Family award Mich. Press Assn., 1982, 84, Gen. Excellence award 1982, 86; Gen. Excellence award Suburban Newspaper Assn., 1979. Mem. Detroit Hist. Soc. (bd. dirs. 1986-91), Detroit Inst. Arts Women's Assn. Episcopalian. Avocations: writing, reading, travel. Home: 552 Cadieux Rd Grosse Pointe MI 48230-1508 Personal E-mail: jeannewhittaker@aol.com.

**WHITTAKER, JUDITH ANN CAMERON,** lawyer; b. N.Y.C., June 12, 1938; d. Thomas Macdonald and Mindel Cameron; m. Kent E. Whittaker, Jan. 30, 1960; children: Charles Evans II, Catherine Cameron. BA, Brown U., 1959; JD, U. Mo., 1963. Bar: Mo. 1963, U.S. Dist. Ct. (we. dist.) Mo. 1963, U.S. Ct. Appeals (8th cir.) 1965, U.S. Supreme Ct. 1980, D.C. 1987. Assoc. and ptnr. Sheffrey, Ryder & Skeer, Kansas City, Mo., 1963-72; asst. and assoc. gen. coun., exec. v.p. gen. coun. Hallmark Cards, Inc., Kansas City, 1972—2004; dir., v.p., gen. coun. Univision Holdings, Inc., Kansas City, 1988-92; sec., bd. dirs. Crown Media Holdings, Inc., 2000—04; of counsel Shook, Hardy & Bacon, Kansas City, Mo., 2004—. Bd. dirs. Am. Arbitration Assn., 1997-2003. Trustee Brown U. Providence, 1977-83, U. Mo. Law Found., Kansas City, 1977-90; dir. Kansas City (Mo.) Indsl. Devel. Authority, 1981-84, Legal Aid Kansas City, 1971-77, De La Salle Sch. Episcopalian. Avocations: reading, skiing, hiking, piano, golf. Office: Shook Hardy & Bacon 2555 Grand Blvd Kansas City MO 64198-2613

**WHITTAKER, WILLIAM L. (RED WHITTAKER),** engineering educator, research scientist; b. Holidaysburg, Pa., 1958; m. Kathleen M. Whittaker. BS, Princeton U., 1973; MS, Carnegie Mellon U., 1975, PhD, 1979. Chief sci. RedZone Robotics, Homestead, Pa.; chief sci., founder Robotics Engring. Consortium Carnegie Mellon U.; prin. rsch. sci. Robotics Inst. Carnegie Mellon U., 1986—96, founder, dir. field robotics ctr., 1986—, Fredkin Prof. Robotics. Mem. com. to provide interim oversight of U.S. Dept. Energy nuc. weapons complex NAS, 1988—89, mem. peer rev. com. on U.S. Dept. Energy environ. mgmt. technologies, 1994—95; mem. commn. on engring. and tech. systems, com. on advanced space techonologies Nat. Rsch. Coun. Contbr. articles to profl. jours. Named Man of Yr. in Tech., Pitts., 1994; named one of Top 100 U.S. Innovators, Sci. Digest mag., 1987; recipient Smithsonian award, Computerworld, 1992, Teare award for Tchg. Excellence, Carnegie Mellon U. Fellow: Am. Assoc. Artificial Intelligence; mem.: Am. Nuc. Soc. Robotics and Remote Systems Divisn., Ctr. Comml. Devel. of Space Studies Inst. Office: Carnegie Mellon U Robotics Inst 5000 Forbes Ave Pittsburgh PA 15213 E-mail: red@ri.cmu.edu.*

**WHITTELL, POLLY (MARY KAYE WHITTELL),** editor, journalist; b. Washington, Oct. 20; d. Alfred Whittell Jr. and Mary Halsey (Patchin) Hopper. BA in English, U. Calif., Berkeley; postgrad., Radcliffe Coll.; postgrad. in journalism, Columbia U. Rschr. Nat. Rev. Mag., N.Y.C., 1970-71; asst. to presdl. speech writer The White House, Washington, 1971-72; asst. editor TravelAge East Mag., Dun & Bradstreet Publs., N.Y.C.,

1973-75; copy editor Ski Mag. Skier's Guides, Times Mirror Mags. and Am. Express, N.Y.C., 1975-76; asst. editor to sr. editor Hearst Mags., Motor Boating & Sailing Mag., N.Y.C., 1977-2000; contbg. editor Powerboat Mag., 2000—01, Hearst Mags., 2002—. Contbg. author: (anthology) Against the Sea, 1998; contbr. articles to other nat. and internat. consumer mags. Mem. charity benefit com. Youth Counseling League, N.Y.C., 1975-85, Am. Cancer Soc., 1998-99, and others; v.p. Knickerbocker Rep. Club, N.Y.C., 1979-80; elected mem. N.Y. Rep. County Com., N.Y.C., 1980-84. Mem. Boating Writers Internat. (award for environ. article 1995), Soc. Profl. Journalists, Princeton Club (N.Y.), SandBar Beach Club (v.p. membership 1980-82). Episcopalian. Avocations: photography, travel, boating, skiing. Personal E-mail: pollywhitt@aol.com.

**WHITTEMORE, ALICE,** biostatistician; b. NYC, July 5, 1936; BS, Marymount Manhattan Coll., 1958; MA, Hunter Coll., 1964; PhD in Mathematics, CUNY, 1967. From asst. prof. to assoc. prof. math. Hunter Coll., N.Y.C., 1967-74; adj. assoc. prof. environ. med. N.Y.U., 1974-76, mem. faculty dept. statistics, 1976-87; prof. epidemiology dept. health rsch. and policy Stanford U., Palo Alto, Calif., 1987—. Recipient Sloan Found. rsch. grant, Soc. Ind. and Applied Math. Inst. Math and Soc., 1974-76, Rockefeller Found rsch. grant 1976-77. Mem. NAS Inst. Medicine, AAAS, Soc. Indsl. and Applied Math, Am. Math Soc., Math Assn. Am., Sigma Xi Office: Stanford U Sch Medicine Dept Health Rsch and Policy HBP Redwood Bldg Stanford CA 94305-5092

**WHITTEMORE, ANTHONY DUNSTER,** vascular surgeon; b. Boston, Nov. 5, 1944; s. Anthony Rogers Whittemore and Kathrine Gansevoort Binnian Nowe; m. Rhoda Belknap Stetson, June 18, 1966; children: Anthony Rogers, Joshua Stetson, Sarah Belknap. BS, Trinity Coll., 1966; MD, Columbia U., 1970. Resident in surgery Columbia Presbyn. Med. Ctr., 1970-76; research assoc. Columbia U., N.Y.C., 1972-73, NIH trainee, 1975-76; vascular fellow Peter Bent Brigham Hosp., Boston, 1976-77; chief vascular surgery Naval Regional Med. Ctr., Portsmouth, Va., 1977-79; instr. surgery Harvard Med. Sch/Peter Bent Brigham Hosp., Boston, 1979-80; asst. prof. surgery Harvard U., Boston, 1981-87, assoc. prof. surgery, 1987-93, prof. surgery Harvard Med. Sch., 1993—; dir. surg. tng. program Harvard Med. Sch./Brigham and Women's Hosp., 1979; mem. med. staff Brigham and Women's Hosp., 1979—, chief divsn. vascular surgery 1990-1999, apptd. dir. Vascular Ctr., 1991, chief medical officer, 1999—; cons. Bard CardioSurgery, Billerica, Mass., 1982—, Meadox Medicals, Oakland, N.J., 1983—, instrumentation Labs., North Andover, Mass., 1980—; investigator grants NIH, 1979, 83. Contbr. articles to profl. jours. Served to lt. comdr. USN, 1977-79. Recipient Commendation USN, 1979. Fellow ACS; mem. Assn. Acad. Surgery, Am. Surg. Assn., Am. Soc. for Artificial Internal Organs (program com. 1982—), Am. Surg. Soc., Soc. U. Surgeons, Boston Surg. Soc., Internat. Cardiovascular Soc., Soc. Vascular Surgery, New Eng. Surg. Soc., New Eng. Soc. Vascular Surgery, Soc. Internat. de Chirurgie, The Country Club; patents in field. Home: 148 Farm Rd Sherborn MA 01770-1622 Office: Brigham & Women's Hosp 75 Francis St Boston MA 02115-6106 Office Phone: 617-732-8515.

**WHITTEMORE, BRIAN,** media consultant, advertising executive; Anchor morning news, dir. news Sta. WGY-AM, Albany, NY, 1983—86; anchor morning news WHDH Radio, Boston, 1987—90; dir. news and program WBZ Radio, Boston, 1990—95; v.p., gen. mgr. Sta. KDKA-AM, Pitts., 1996—98, Sta. WCCO-AM, Mpls., 1999—2003; pres. Best/Whittemore Prodns., LLC, Prior Lake, Minn., 2003—.

**WHITTEMORE, EDWARD REED, II,** poet, retired educator; b. New Haven, Sept. 11, 1919; s. Edward Reed and Margaret Eleanor (Carr) W.; m. Helen Lundeen, Oct. 3, 1952; children: Catherine Carr, Edward Reed III, John Lundeen (dec.), Margaret Goodhue. AB, Yale U., New Haven, Conn., 1941; postgrad., Princeton U., 1945-46; Litt.D., Carleton Coll., Northfield, Minn., 1971. Mem. faculty Carleton Coll., 1947-67, prof. English, 1962-67, chmn. dept., 1962-64; program assoc. Nat. Inst. Pub. Affairs, 1966-68; cons. in poetry Libr. of Congress, 1964-65, 84-85; Bain-Swiggett lectr. Princeton, 1967; prof. U Md , 1968-84, prof. emeritus, 1984—; poet laureate State of Md., 1985-88. Lit. editor New Republic, 1969-74. Author: Heroes and Heroines, 1947, An American Takes a Walk, 1956, The Self-Made Man, 1959, The Boy From Iowa, 1962, The Fascination of the Abomination, 1963, Poems, New and Selected, 1967, From Zero to the Absolute, 1967, 50 Poems 50, 1970, The Mother's Breast and the Father's House, 1974, William Carlos Williams: Poet from Jersey, 1975, The Poet as Journalist, 1976, The Feel of Rock, 1982, Pure Lives, 1988, Whole Lives, 1989, The Past, the Future, the Present, 1990, Six Literary Lives, 1993; editor: Furioso, 1939-53, Browning, 1960, Carleton Miscellany, 1960-64, Delos mag., 1988-91. Capt. USAAF, 1941-45. Decorated Bronze star, 1945. Home: 4526 Albion Rd College Park MD 20740-3610

**WHITTEMORE, LAURENCE FREDERICK,** bank executive; b. Bangor, Maine, Mar. 7, 1929; s. John Cambridge and Elizabeth Payson (Prentiss) Whittemore; m. Sarah Lee Arnold, Aug. 9, 1958; children: Arianna, Gioia, Lia, Nike. BA, Yale U., 1951; MBA, Harvard U., 1953; student, Balliol Coll., Oxford U., Eng., 1950. Account mgr. Brown Bros. Harriman, N.Y.C., 1956-72, gen. mgr., 1972-74; ptnr. Brown Bros. Harriman & Co., N.Y.C., 1974—2003, ltd. ptnr., 2004—. Dir. Manhattan Life Ins. Co., N.Y.C., Albany Ins. Co., N.Y.C.; mem. investment adv. com. Union Investment GmbH, Frankfurt, Germany, 1973—2002; mem. Chgo. Stock Exch., 1975—2003. Trustee Sarah Lawrence Coll., 1988-2000, hon. trustee, 2001—; trustee Am. Inst. Contemporary German Studies, 1994—2002, Asia Soc., 1998—; mem. Nat. Com. on USA China Rels., N.Y.C., 1982—, Chgo. Coun. on Fgn. Rels., 1980—; del. Assn. Yale Alumni, New Haven, 1982-86; chmn. Yale 35th Reunion Gift Drive, 1983-86; gov. Opportunity Internat., 1996—; dir. New Eng. Air Mus., 1999—. Fellow Sterling fellow, Yale U., 2001—. Mem.: Chgo. Club, Yale Club, Links Club. Republican. Episcopalian. Office: Brown Bros Harriman & Co 140 Broadway New York NY 10005-1101

**WHITTEMORE, PAUL BAXTER,** psychologist; s. Harry Ballou and Margaret B. Whittemore; m. Jane Moore, Apr. 22, 1995. BA in Religion, Ea. Nazarene Coll., 1970; MDiv., Nazarene Theol. Sem., 1973; MA in Theology, Vanderbilt U., 1975, PhD in Theology, 1978; PhD in Clin. Psychology, U. Tenn., 1987. Cert. in clin. psychology Am. Bd. Profl. Psychology, lic. psychologist Calif. Asst. prof. philosophy and edn. Trevecca Nazarene Coll., Nashville, 1973—76; asst. prof. philosophy and theology Point Loma Coll., San Diego, 1976—80; asst. prof. philosophy Mid. Tenn. State U., Murfreesboro, 1980—83; clin. psychology intern Los Angeles County/U. So. Calif. Med. Ctr., L.A., 1986—87; postdoc. behavior health ctr. Calif. Med. Ctr., L.A., 1987—88; clin. asst. prof. family medicine U. So. Calif. Sch. Medicine, L.A., 1988—; pvt. practice psychologist Newport Beach, Calif., 1989—. Mem. behavioral sci. faculty Glendale Adventist Family Practice Residency Program, Glendale, Calif., 1989—90; inpatient group therapist Ingleside Hosp., Rosemead, Calif., 1990—92; founder, pres. Date Coach, 1992—2000. Contbr. articles to profl. jours. Recipient Andrew W. Mellon Postdoctoral Faculty Devel. award, Vanderbilt U., 1981. Mem.: AAUP (chpt. v.p. 1982—83), APA, Orange County Psychol. Assn. (bd. dirs. 1996—2001), Calif. Psychol. Assn. (media divsn. sec.-treas. 1997—98), Am. Philos. Assn., Am. Acad. Religion. Achievements include discovery of link between phenylthiocarbamide tasting and depression. Office: 1001 Dove St Ste 145 Newport Beach CA 92660-2123

**WHITTEN, CHARLES ALEXANDER, JR.,** physics professor; b. Harrisburg, Pa., Jan. 20, 1940; s. Charles Alexander and Helen (Shoop) W.; m. Joan Emann, Nov. 20, 1965; 1 son, Charles Alexander III. BS summa cum laude, Yale U., 1961; PhD in Physics, Princeton U., 1966. Research asso. A.W. Wright Nuclear Structure Lab., Yale U., 1966-68; asst. prof. physics UCLA, 1968-74, assoc. prof., 1974-80, prof., 1980—; vice chmn. physics dept., 1982-86. Vis. scientist Centre d'Etudes Nucléaires de Saclay-Moyenne Energie, 1980-81, 86-87. Contbr. articles to profl. jours. Mem. Am. Phys. Soc., Sigma Pi Sigma, Phi Beta Kappa. Home: 9844 Vicar St Los Angeles CA 90034-2719 Office Phone: 310-825-1691. E-mail: whitten@physics.ucla.edu.

**WHITTEN, JERRY LYNN,** chemistry professor; b. Bartow, Fla., Aug. 13, 1937; s. John Graves and Dorothy Iola (Jordan) W.; m. Mary Hill (div. Sept. 1977); 1 child, Jerrard John; m. Adela Chrzeszczyk, June 21, 1980; 1 child, Christina. BS in Chemistry, Ga. Inst. Tech., 1960, PhD, 1964. Cert. chemist. Rsch. assoc. to instr. Princeton (N.J.) U., 1963-65; asst. prof. chemistry Mich. State U., East Lansing, 1965-67, SUNY, Stony Brook, 1967-68, assoc. prof., 1968-73, prof., 1973-89, chmn. chemistry dept., 1985-89; prof. chemistry, dean Coll. Phys. and Math. Scis. N.C. State U., Raleigh, 1989-99. Vis. prof. Centre Europèen de Calcul Atomique et Molèculaire, Orsay, France, 1974-75, Univ. Bonn and Wuppertal, Fed. Republic Germany, 1979-80, Eidgenossische Technische Hochschule, Zurich, Switzerland, 1984, U. Wuppertel, 2005. Contbr. more than 180 articles to profl. jours. Bd. dirs. N.C. Sch. Sci. and Math Found., chair; bd. dirs. Burroughs Wellcome Fund. Recipient Alexander von Humboldt U.S. Sr. Scientist award, 1979; grantee Petroleum Rsch. Fund, 1966-67, 74-76, 77-81, NSF, 1967-72, U.S. Dept. Energy, 1977—; SDIO/ONR grantee, 1991-92; Alfred P. Sloan fellow, 1969-71. Mem. AAAS, Am. Phys. Soc., Am. Chem. Soc., N.Y. Acad. Scis., Sigma Xi (pres. N.C. chpt.), Phi Beta Kappa, Phi Kappa Phi. Democrat. Episcopalian. Avocations: boating, tennis, skiing. Office: NC State U Coll Dept Chemistry PO Box 8204 Raleigh NC 27695-0001 Office Phone: 919-515-7960. E-mail: j_whitten@ncsu.edu.

**WHITTEN, LESLIE HUNTER, JR.,** writer, poet, reporter; b. Jacksonville, Fla., Feb. 21, 1928; s. Leslie Hunter and Linnora (Harvey) W.; m. Phyllis Webber, Nov. 11, 1951; children: Leslie Hunter III, Andrew, Daniel, Deborah Wilson Engle. BA in Journalism/English magna cum laude, Lehigh U., 1950, LHD, 1989. Journalist Radio Free Europe, 1952-57, I.N.S., 1957-58, U.P.I., 1958, Washington Post, 1958-63; with Hearst Newspapers, 1963-66, asst. bur. chief Washington, 1966-92; sr. investigator Jack Anderson's Washington Merry-Go-Round, 1969 92; pres. Athanor Inc., 1977-93. Vis. assoc. prof. Lehigh U., 1967-69; adj. prof. So. Ill. U., 1984. Author: Progeny of the Adder, 1965, Moon of the Wolf, 1967, Pinion the Golden Eagle, 1968, The Abyss, 1970, F. Lee Bailey, 1971, The Alchemist, 1973, Conflict of Interest, 1976, Washington Cycle, 1979, Sometimes a Hero, 1979, A Killing Pace, 1983, A Day Without Sunshine, 1985, The Lost Disciple, 1989, The Fangs of Morning, 1994, Sad Madrigals, 1997, Moses, the Lost Book of the Bible, 1999, The Rebel, 2005; contbr. numerous poems to anthologies and other publs. Vol. Hospice, 1987-2003. Served with AUS, 1946-48. Recipient hon. mention pub. service Washington Newspaper Guild, 1963, Edgerton award ACLU, 1974 Home and Office: 114 Eastmoor Dr Silver Spring MD 20901-1507 Office Phone: 301-593-5943. Personal E-mail: lhwhitjr@aol.com.

**WHITTEN, MARY LOU,** nursing educator; b. Vandalia, Ill., Apr. 8, 1946; d. Otto M. and Lucille (Mattes) Elam; m. Dennis L. Whitten, Aug. 27, 1966; children: Michael, Christopher, Andrew. BSN, Baylor U., 1968; MS in Nursing, So. Ill. U., 1990. RN, Ill. Instr. health occupations Okaw Vocat. Sch., Vandalia, Ill.; head nurse med.-surg. Fayette County Hosp., Vandalia; DON Kaskaskia Coll., Centralia, Ill. CPR instr. Am. Heart Assn. Vol. ARC. Mem. Am. Assn. of Women in C.C. Ill., Ill. Coun. Dirs. of Nursing, Phi Kappa Phi. Home: RR 3 Box 848 Vandalia IL 62471-9204 Office: Kaskaskia Coll 27210 College Rd Centralia IL 62801-7800 Office Phone: 618-545-3331. Business E-Mail: mwhitten@kaskaskia.edu.

**WHITTENBERG, IRA ORVILLE,** lawyer; b. Ft. Worth; s. Ira Orville and Thyra Finch Whittenberg; m. Emma Jo Noland, Apr. 14, 1962; children: Ira Grant, Cheryl Lynn, Wendy Ann. BS in Indsl. Engring., So. Meth. U., 1957, LLB, 1961, LLM, 1977. Bar: Tex. 73. Contract mgr., corp. counsel Bell Helicopter Textron, Ft. Worth, 1961—89; dir. contracts, corp. counsel Murdock Engring., Irving, Tex., 1989—91; pvt. practice cons., mediator Colleyville, Tex., 1991—. Capt. USAF, 1955—57. Fellow: Nat. Contract Mgmt. Assn. (pres. 1962—); mem.: State Bar Tex. (award 2002), Toastmasters Internat. (chpt. pres. 1982—). Republican. Presbyterian. Avocations: sailing, bicycling. Home and Office: 3607 Cliffwood Dr Colleyville TX 76034 Office Phone: 817-498-8141. E-mail: docwh@comcast.net.

**WHITTENBURG, JUSTIN M.,** lawyer; b. Amarillo, Tex., Nov. 8, 1974; s. Mack Whittenburg and Catherine Leftwich Reavis; m. Blythe Dayne Martindale, Feb. 27, 1999; children: Mack, David Earl, Dane. BA in Econs., U. Tex., Austin, 1998; JD, U. Houston, 2004. Project controls Zachry Constrn. Corp., San Antonio, 2001—2001, ABB Lummus Global, Houston, 2001—02. Office: Baker & McKenzie LLP 711 Louisiana St Ste 3400 Houston TX 77002 Business E-Mail: justin.m.whittenburg@bakernet.com.

**WHITTERS, JAMES PAYTON, III,** lawyer, educator; b. Boston, Oct. 23, 1939; s. James P. Jr. and Norene (Jones) W.; m. Elizabeth Robertson, July 19, 1969; children: James P. IV, Catharine A. BA in History, Trinity Coll., Hartford, Conn., 1962; JD, Boston Coll., 1969; MA in Am. studies, U. Mass., Boston, 2002. Bar: Mass. 1969, US Dist. Ct. Mass. 1970, US Ct. Appeals (1st cir.) 1972. Assoc. Ely, Bartlett, Brown & Proctor, Boston, 1969-74, Gaston Snow & Ely Bartlett, Boston, 1974-79, ptnr., 1979-88, Gaston & Snow, Boston, 1988-91; of counsel Peabody & Brown, Boston, 1991-95; dir. Office Career Devel., Suffolk U. Law Sch., Boston, 1995—2004, adj. prof. Am. legal history, 1997—. Bd. dirs., sec. Robertson Factories, Inc., Taunton, Mass., 1979-04; v.p. The Alkalol Co., Boston, 1976-97, sr. v.p., 1997-05, pres., treas., gen. counsel, 2005—; vis. tchr. Groton Sch., Mass., 1993-94; mem. Mass. Conflict Intervention Mediation Team, 1995—. Bd. dirs. New Eng. com. NAACP Legal Def. Fund, 1982-2006, Beacon Hill Nursery Sch., 1976-78, Mass. Appleseed Ctr. Law and Justice, 1997—, The Esplanade Assn., 2005—; chmn. Mass. Outdoor Advt. Bd., Boston, 1975-81; vice chmn. Mass. Jud. Nominating Coun., Boston, 1983-87; trustee Trinity Coll., 1984-95; trustee, sec. Hurricane Island Outward Bound Sch., 1977-87; bd. dirs. Mass. affiliate Am. Heart Assn., 1979-98, chmn., 1989-91; bd. dirs. Greater Boston Legal Svcs., 1982-84, 93-99, Mass. Assn. Mediation Programs and Practitioners, 1993 98; founder Beacon Hill Seminars, 2000 2001, bd. dirs. 2001-02; facilitator City Wide Dialogues on Racial and Ethnic Diversity, 2003-. Lt. (j.g.) USN, 1962-65. Recipient Alumni Excellence award Trinity Coll., 1987. Mem.: ABA, Boston Bar Assn. (standing com. on work-life balance, children's outreach task force, pub. svc. and criminal justice task force), The Country Club (Brookline, Mass.). Democrat. Episcopalian. Avocations: mountain climbing, jogging, yoga, reading. Home: 44 Mount Vernon St Boston MA 02108-1302 Office Phone: 617-248-8822. Personal E-mail: jpwhit3@aol.com.

**WHITTIER, BARBARA J (BOBBIE),** retired biology educator, retired chemistry educator; b. New Rochelle, NY, July 13, 1943; d. Gordon F. and Elinor E. Whittier. BS, Cornell U., Ithaca, NY, 1965; MAT, Harvard U., Cambridge, Mass., 1966. Postgraduate Professional License Va. State Bd. of Edn., 1968, Collegiate Professional Va. State Bd. of Edn., 1966. Sci. educator Wakefield HS, Arlington, Va., 1966—98, sci. dept. chair, 1990—95; ret., 1998. Cons. Arlington Pub. Schools, 1998—2003; project asst. Biotechnology Inst., Arlington, Va., 2003—; softball coach Wakefield H.S., 1983—90. Mem., elder, clk. of session, meals on wheels Arlington Presbyn. Ch., 1980—2006; pnc liaison and mem., com. ministry Nat. Capital Presbytery, Washington, 2000—06; com. mem. Va. Jr. Acad. Sci., Richmond, 1982—2006, sponsor, 1982—2006; mem. Wakefield Alumni Assn., Arlington, 2003—06. Named to Wakefield HS Hall of Fame, 2005; recipient Presdl. award for Excellence in Sci. and Math. Tchg. (PAESMT), NSF, 1986, Outstanding Educator award, Joint Bd. on Sci. and Engring. Edn. and the Wash. Acad. of Sci., 1984, Nat. Sci. Week award, NSF, 1958. Mem.: Va. Assn. of Sci. Teachers (Va. Jr. Acad. Sci. rep. 2005—06), Nat. Assn. of Biology Teachers (life), Delta Delta Delta. Presbyn. Avocation: sports. Home: 2424B S Walter Reed Dr Arlington VA 22206-4086 Personal E-mail: bwhittier@aol.com.

**WHITTINGHAM, CHARLES ARTHUR,** library director, publishing executive; b. Chgo., Feb. 11, 1930; s. Charles Arthur and Virginia (Hartke) W.; m. Jean Bragger Whittingham, June 4, 1955; children: Mary Elizabeth, Charles Arthur III, Philip Alexander, Leigh Ann. BS in English Lit. cum laude, Loyola U. Chgo., 1951. With McCall Corp., Chgo., 1956-59, Time,

Inc., Chgo., 1959-62; pub.'s rep. Fortune mag., Time, Inc., N.Y.C., 1962-65, mgr. San Francisco, 1965-69; asst. to pub. Fortune, N.Y.C., 1969-70, asst. pub., 1970-78; pub. Life mag., N.Y.C., 1978-88; sr. v.p. N.Y. Pub. Libr., 1989-92; exec. prodr. Kunhardt Prodns., Inc., 1995—. Lt. j.g. USNR, 1951—55. Named to Athletic Hall of Fame Loyola U., Loyola Acad. Mem.: Century Assn., The Pilgrims, Brook Club. Home and Office: 800 Fifth Ave 8C New York NY 10021

**WHITTINGHAM, HARRY EDWARD, JR.,** retired banker; b. Albany, N.Y., Dec. 25, 1918; s. Harry E. and Mary (Baer) Whittingham; m. Gladys D. Willstaedt, Sept. 2, 1942; children: Jeffrey A., Neal E. Grad., Stonier Grad. Sch. Banking, 1961. With Schenectady Trust Co., 1947-84, pres., chief exec. officer, 1974-82, chmn., chief exec. officer, 1982-84. Author (with Purdy, Schneider, Aldom): Automation in Banking, 1962. Vestryman Episcopal Ch. With AUS, 1941—46. Home: 2025 Cockrell Pt NW Kennesaw GA 30152

**WHITTINGHAM, M(ICHAEL) STANLEY,** chemist; b. Nottingham, Eng., Dec. 22, 1941; came to U.S., 1968, naturalized, 1980; s. William Stanley and Dorothy Mary (Findlay) W.; m. Georgina Judith Andai, Mar. 23, 1969; children: Jenniffer Judith, Michael Stanley. BA in Chemistry, Oxford U., 1964, MA, DPhil, 1968. Rsch. assoc., head solid state electrochemistry group Materials Ctr., Stanford U., 1968-72; mem. staff Exxon Rsch. Co., Linden, N.J., 1972—; group head solid state chem. physics, 1975-78; dir. solid state scis., 1978-80; mgr. chem. engring. tech., 1980-84; dir. phys. scis. Schlumberger Co., Ridgefield, Conn., 1984-88; prof. chemistry and materials sci. and engring., dir. The Inst. for Materials Rsch., SUNY, 1988—; vice provost for rsch. SUNY, 1994-2000; vice-chair bd. dirs. Rsch. Found., 1995-2001. Cons., lectr. in field; JSPS fellow U. Tokyo. Author, editor papers in field; author 5 books. Recipient Gas Coun. scholarship, Oxford U., 1964-67. Mem. Electrochem. Soc. (Young Author award 1971, N.Y. chmn. 1980-81, Battery Rsch. award 2002, fellow 2004), Am. Chem. Soc. (chmn. solid state sect. 1987, chmn. Binghamton sect. 1991), Am. Phys. Soc., Materials Rsch. Soc. Achievements include patents in field; reversible (rechargeable) lithium batteries and methods for making intercalation batteries; method for making TiS2 mixed material cathodes, high briteness luminescent displays. Home: 396 Meeker Rd Vestal NY 13850-3230 Office: SUNY Dept Chemistry Binghamton NY 13902 Office Phone: 607-777-4623. E-mail: stanwhit@binghamton.edu.

**WHITTINGTON, ANNE ELIZABETH,** diabetes educator; b. Berea, Ohio, Apr. 4, 1957; d. Richard Murphy and Eleen Elizabeth (Cooney) Whittington. ADN, Sante Fe Coll., 1979; BSN, U. N.C., 1983; MSN, Med. Coll. Ga., 1990; MBA, Brenau U., 1997. Tchr. Nat. Cert. Bd. for Diabetes Educators; cert. water aerobics instr. Staff nurse U. Fla. Teaching Hosp., Gainesville, 1979-80, New Hanover Meml. Hosp., Wilmington, N.C., 1980-81, Cape Fear Meml. Hosp., Wilmington, 1983-84; home health nurse New Hanover Home Health Agy., Wilmington, 1984-85, Comprehensive Home Health Care, Augusta, Ga., 1985; coord. outreach edn. for Ga. Dept. of Human Resources Grant, Augusta, 1990—2000; dir. diabetes programs Naval Med. Ctr., San Diego, 2001—, dir. Paws for Healing program, 2005—. Docent Augusta Richmond County Mus., 1987-91; dir. Our Lady of Peace Choir, North Augusta, 1990—; co-founder Cen. Savannah River Area Arthritis Support Group, Augusta, 1991—; Cath. chaplaincy Augusta Correctional Instn., 1991—. Recipient Woman of Excellence award Cen. Savannah River Area, 1992; named Outstanding Diabetes Educator, GADE, 1992, Outstanding Alumnus, Med. Coll. Ga. Sch. Nursing, 1992, Outstanding Diabetes Educator, Am. Assn. Diabetes Edn., 1993; torchbearer Atlanta Olympics, 1996. Mem.: Arthritis Health Profl. Assn., Ga. Nurses Assn., U. N.C. Sch. Nursing Alumni Assn. (bd. dirs. 1989—93), Am. Diabetes Assn., Am. Assn. Diabetes Educator (sec. visual impaired preson speciality practice group 1994—97, chair visual impaired person speciality group 1997—2000, bd.dirs. 1999—2002, treas. 2002—), Greater Augusta Diabetes Educators (chmn. profl. edn. 1991—2000, pres. 1995—97), ANA, Sigma Theta Tau (Grad. Student of Yr. 1991). Democrat. Roman Catholic. Avocations: music, water aerobics. Mailing: Attn: Health Promotion Dept 34800 Bob Wilson Dr San Diego CA 92134-1301

**WHITTINGTON, FELICIA TRENISE,** social services administrator, educator; b. New Orleans, Feb. 2, 1971; d. Audrey Mea Whittington-Simmons. MA, Jackson State U., Miss., 1996. Exec. dir. Family Life Ctr. Tougaloo (Miss.) Coll., 1996—, asst. dir. Owens Health & Wellness Ctr., 2002—. Adj. prof. dept. criminal justice Jackson State U., 1997—. Mem. youth adv. bd. United Way, Jackson, 2000—02; dir. Family and Cmty. Violence Prevention Program. Named one of Outstanding Young Women of Am., 1997; grantee, Office of Minority Health Family and Cmty. Violence Prevention Program, 1995—, Target Stores, 2002, Dept. Edn., 2001, 2002. Mem.: Delta Sigma Theta. Avocations: community service projects, reading. Office: Tougaloo Coll Family Life Ctr 500 W County Line Rd Tougaloo MS 39174 E-mail: felicia.whittington@tougaloo.edu.

**WHITTINGTON, LORIN DALE,** music educator; b. Balt., Nov. 1, 1951; s. Cicero Edward Whittington and Dorothy Virginia Peters. MusB, Appalachian State U., 1979. Cert. tchr. music k-12 N.C. Tchr. Hall Fletcher Mid. Sch., Asheville, NC, 1979—81, Hill St. Mid. Sch., Asheville, 1979—81, Owen H.S., Swannanoa, NC, 1981—97, Owen Mid. Sch., Swannanoa, 1997—. Chorus master Mid-Atlantic Opera Co., Asheville, 1985—86. Composer: (sound recording) Rochelle, 1972. Mem.: Music Educators Nat. Conf. Achievements include performance by Owen Middle School Chorus at Carnegie Hall, 2005. Avocations: genealogy, art, computer graphics, guitar, travel. Home: 19 Clairmont Ave Asheville NC 28804 Office: Owen Mid Schl 730 Old US 70 Swannanoa NC 28778 Office Phone: 828-686-7739. Personal E-mail: vytiense@att.net.

**WHITTINGTON, RALPH EDWARD,** curator, librarian; b. Washington, Jan. 13, 1945; s. Ralph John and Mildred May Whittington; m. Jennifer Kay Rutland, June 7, 1969 (div.); 1 child, Amanda Anne. Grad., Surrattsville H.S., Clinton, Md., 1963. Deck attendant Libr. of Congress, Washington, 1963—76, searcher libr. materials locator, 1976—85, curator main reading rm., 1985—2000; cons. Mus. Sex, N.Y.C., 2001—. Avocation: vinyl record collector. Home: 9204 Greenfield Ln Clinton MD 20735

**WHITTINGTON, STEPHEN LUNN,** museum director; b. Washington, Jan. 31, 1956; s. Charles Lunn and Alice Marie (Doyle) W.; m. Christine Ann Carlson, Aug. 18, 1979; children: Daniel, Joseph. AB in Anthropology, U. Chgo., 1977; MA, Pa. State U., 1981, PhD, 1989. Dir. Proyecto Arqueologico Ostuman, Copan, Honduras, 1989, U. Maine Hudson Mus., 1991—2002, Teozacoalco Archaeol. Project, 2002—; asst. curator collections Wyo. Hist. and Geol. Soc., Wilkes-Barre, Pa., 1989-90; cooperating assoc. prof. dept. anthropology U. Maine, 1991—2002. Dir. Iximche Osteological Project, 1992—95; adj. assoc. prof. dept. anthropology Wake Forest U., dir. Mus. Anthropology, 2002—. Author: Archaeology and Ethnohistory of Iximche, 2003; editor: Bones of the Maya, 1997; contbr. articles to profl. jours. Active Maine State Mus. Comm., 1998—2002; mem. Southeastern Mus. Conf. Coun., 2005—; chair Hispanic Arts Initiative Steering Com., 2005. Grantee Wenner-Gren Found. for Anthrop. Rsch., 1992-93, NSF, 1989, Inst. Internat. Edn., 1988, Found. for the Advancement of Mesoamerican Studies, 1995, 99, 2002, NEH, 1997, 2005. Mem. Am. Assn. Mus., N.C. Mus. Coun., Soc. for Am. Archaeology, Southeastern Mus. Conf. Avocations: jogging, fencing, bicycling. Home: 1307 Brookwood Dr Winston Salem NC 27106 Office: Wake Forest Univ Mus Anthropology PO Box 7267 Winston Salem NC 27109 Office Phone: 336-758-5827. E-mail: whittisl@wfu.edu.

**WHITTINGTON-BROWN, VANESSA ELIZABETH,** secondary school educator; b. Boston, Apr. 15, 1960; d. Samuel Wall and Ernestine (Brazand Hundley) Whittington; m. Alphonso Brown, July 25, 1992. BS, Bridgewater State U., 1978; postgrad., Cambridge Coll., 1992—. Elem. tchr. Boston (Mass.) Pub. Schs., 1983—, Pauline A. Shaw, Dorchester, Mass., 1987-92; tchr. The Josiah Quincy Sch., Boston, 1992—. Adult edn. sec. Boston Pub. Schs., 1982, 83, mem. graphic learning com., 1983, impact II tchr. adaptor;

musician cable TV program Gospel Expressions Prodns.; tutor Metco (after sch. program); mem. Primary Summer Source Inst., 1991; local pres. Sunshine Band, 1986, state pres., 1989-92. Composer: Lord I'm Coming Home, 1986. Mem. Children's Mus. and the Mus. Sci., Women's Heritage Trail, 3 Regent St. Young Adult Choir, Women's Choir, Boston Writing Project, Professional Dev. Program; co-dir. Specially Trained Youth Leadership in Excellence (STYLE), 1997; church musician Church of God in Christ Church, 1976-92. With USAR, 1979-91. Mem. Assn. Supervision and Curriculum Devel., Greater Boston Reading Coun., Boston Tchrs. Union, Black Educators Alliance of Mass., Nat. Coun. Tchrs. English, Women's Heritage Trail, African Meeting House. Democrat. Avocations: music, bowling, racquetball, basketball, poetry. Office Phone: 617-635-8497. E-mail: vewb@myway.com.

**WHITTLESEY, JUDITH HOLLOWAY,** public relations executive; b. Bartlesville, Okla., Dec. 28, 1942; d. Harry Haynes and Suzanne (Arnote) Holloway; m. Dennis Jeffrey Whittlesey, Aug. 3, 1968; children: Kristin Arnote, Kevin Jeffrey. BA, U. Okla., 1964; postgrad., Tulsa U., 1965, U. Va., 1971-72. Staff aide Office of the V.P. of U.S., Washington, 1979-81, Com. for Future of Am., Washington, 1981-82; dep. dir. scheduling and advance Mondale-Ferraro Campaign, Washington, 1984; dir. media rels. Susan Davis Internat., Washington, 1986-87, v.p., 1987-88, exec. v.p., 1988—. Bd. dirs. Cultural Alliance of Greater Washington, 1983-93, Washington Project for the Arts, 1987-93, Levine Sch. Music, 1993-98, Food Rsch. and Action Ctr., 1993—; bd. dirs. Decatur House, Suited For Change, Leadership Washington, 2004. Avocation: contemporary art. Office: Susan Davis Internat 1350 I St NW Washington DC 20005 Office Phone: 202-408-0808. Business E-Mail: judy@susandavis.com.

**WHITTON, LYNDA JEAN,** librarian, foundation administrator; b. Shreveport, La., Sept. 18, 1942; d. Lynford and Rowena Laurence (Belgard) Feazel; m. John Evan Whitton Jr., June 22, 1963 (div. Mar. 1990); children: Suzette F., Patricia L., Brian E., Charles L.; m. Thomas Eugene Henley, Dec. 12, 1992 (dec. May 2002). BA in Sociology, Corpus Chrsiti State U., 1991, MS in Counseling, 1992; MLS, U. Tex., 1995. Crew leader U.S. Census Bur., Ft. Worth, 1980; ind. market researcher, coord. Arbitron, Ft. Worth, 1980-87; field interviewer U.S. Census Bur., Corpus Christi, Tex., 1983-87; youth counselor City of Corpus Christi, 1987; career counselor Corpus Christi Pub. Libr., 1987-94, bus. libr. II, 1994-97, mgr. N.W. Br. Libr., 1997—. Mem. ALA, Pub. Libr. Assn., Tex. Libr. Assn. (vol. coord. 1994), N.W. Bus. Assn. Baptist. Avocations: reading, gardening, painting, quilting. Office: Corpus Christi Pub Libr NW Br 3202 McKinzie Rd Corpus Christi TX 78410-2442 Business E-Mail: lyndafw@stx.rr.com.

**WHITTUM-HUDSON, JUDITH ANNE,** education educator, researcher; d. Edith Thayer Hunter and Ward Maxim Whittum; m. Alan Paul Hudson, Dec. 24, 1983. PhD, U. Conn., 1980. Asst. prof. Johns Hopkins U., Balt., 1982—89, assoc. prof., 1989—98; prof. Wayne State U., Detroit, 1998—. Grantee, NIH, 1984—. Fellow: Infectious Disease Soc. of Am.; mem.: Am. Soc. for Microbiology, Am. Assn. of Immunologists, Am. Coll. of Rheumatology. Achievements include patents for anti-chlamydial vaccine and oral delivery. Office: Wayne State Univ Sch Med 550 E Canfield Ave 363 Lande Bldg Detroit MI 48201 Office Phone: 313-577-5501. Office Fax: 313-577-5559. Business E-Mail: jhudson@med.wayne.edu.

**WHITTY, JEFF,** playwright, actor; b. 1972; s. John Whitty. BA, U. Oregon, 1993; MFA, NYU Tisch Sch. of the Arts. Actor: (TV series) As the World Turns; author: (plays) The Plank Project, Suicide Weather, Balls, The Hiding Place, (Broadway plays) Avenue Q, 2003 (Tony award best book of a musical, 2004, Drama Desk nom. for outstanding book of a musical, 2004); actor: (plays) Freedomland, The Beard of Avon. Office: John Golden Theatre 252 W 45th St New York NY 10010

**WHITWORTH, HALL BAKER,** forest products company executive; b. St. Paul, NC, Feb. 15, 1919; s. A. Frederick and Maude Ethel (Baker) W.; m. Mary Margaret Mease, May 18, 1946; children: Hall Baker, Laura Ellen, David Allen. Student, Miss. So. Coll., 1942, U. N.C., 1957. With Champion Internat., Canton, NC, 1936-62, mgr. materials, 1956-62, dir. materials packages div. Chgo., 1962-65, dir. purchase U.S. Plywood-Champion Papers, Inc. (now champion Internat. Corp.) Hamilton, Ohio, 1965-68, dep. dir. corporate materials services, 1966, v.p., dir. purchase, 1968-75, v.p. materials Stamford, Conn., 1975—, dir., 1975—, now ret.; v.p., dir. So. Agrl. Co., 1985—; pres., dir. H. Whitworth Enterprises, Inc., 1985—. Bd. dirs. Pathfork-Harlan Coal Co., Elmac Corp. Served with U.S. Army, 1942-46. Recipient Thomas award Carolina-Va. Purchasing Agts. Assn., 1963 Mem. Am. Paper Inst. (chmn. energy subcom.), Am. Mgmt. Assn. (v.p. purchasing, transp. and phys. distbn. div. council) Clubs: Canton Toastmasters (founder, 1st pres.). Lodges: Elks; Lions. Methodist. Home and Office: 1111 S Lakemont Ave Apt 442 Winter Park FL 32792-5473 Office Phone: 407-306-9412. Personal E-mail: hall_whitworth@msn.com.

**WHITWORTH, HORACE ALGERNON,** mechanical engineer; b. Kingston, Jamaica, W.I., Mar. 24, 1953; came to U.S., 1967; s. Egbert Leopold and Violet Cecilia (Trouth) W. BSME, U. Mass., 1975; MS, George Washington U., 1977, DSc, 1983. Asst. prof. Howard U., Washington, 1983-89, dir. grad. studies dept. mech. engring., 1988-96, assoc. prof. mech. engring., 1989-99, prof. mech. engring., 1999—, chmn. dept. mech. engring., 2004—. Contbr. articles to profl. jours. Bd. dirs. Jamaica Support Found., Washington, 1991-95. Recipient Sr. Fellows Found. award Pacific Telesis Found., 1988, Prof. Acad. award Honeywell Corp., 1992; rsch. grantee in field. Mem. ASME (bd. dirs. Washington chpt. 1994—, Instr. of Yr. student chpt. 1985-86, 87-89), Am. Soc. Metals, Soc. for Exptl. Mechanics. Democrat. Methodist. Achievements include development of mathematical models to evaluate fatigue damage development in fibrous composite materials. Office: Howard U 2300 6th St NW Washington DC 20059-2323 Office Phone: 202-806-6600. Business E-Mail: hwhitworth@howard.edu.

**WHITWORTH, KATHRYNNE ANN,** professional golfer; b. Monahans, Tex., Sept. 27, 1939; d. Morris Clark and Dama Ann (Robinson) W. Student, Odessa Jr. Coll., Tex., 1958. Joined tour Ladies Profl. Golf Assn., 1959—. Named to Hall of Fame Ladies Profl. Golf Assn., Tex. Sports Hall of Fame, Tex. Golf Hall of Fame, World Golf Hall of Fame; Capt. of Solheim Cup, 1990-92. Mem. Ladies Profl. Golf Assn. (sec. 1962-63, v.p. 1965, 73, 88, pres. 1967, 68, 71, 89, 1st mem. to win over $1,000,000). Office: care Ladies Profl Golf Assn 2570 Volusia Ave Daytona Beach FL 32114-8144

**WHITWORTH, WILLIAM A.,** magazine editor; b. Hot Springs, Ark., Feb. 13, 1937; s. William C. and Lois Virginia (McNabb) W.; m. Carolyn Hubbard, Dec. 27, 1969; children— Matthew, Katherine. BA, U. Okla., 1960. Reporter Ark. Gazette, Little Rock, 1960—63; reporter N.Y. Herald Tribune, 1963—65; staff writer The New Yorker, 1966—72, assoc. editor, 1973—80; editor-in-chief The Atlantic Monthly, Boston, 1981—99, editor emeritus, 1999—; editor-at-large The American Scholar, Washington, 2002—04. Office: 600 New Hampshire Ave NW Washington DC 20037 Personal E-mail: ww131@comcast.net.

**WHOLLEY, MICHAEL CHRISTOPHER,** retired military officer, lawyer; b. Lawrence, Mass., Oct. 7, 1944; m. Kathleen S. Sheehy, Sept. 3, 1966; children: Griffin, Clayton. BA in History and Lit., Harvard U., Cambridge, Mass., 1966; JD, U. Va. Law Sch., 1977; LLM in Environ. Law and Land Use, George Washington U., 1985; MA in Nat. Security and Strategic studies, Naval War Coll., 1989. Naval aviator, 1968; commd. USMC, 1966, advanced through grades to brig. gen., 1993; officer Chu Lai, Vietnam, 1969-70; with 54th Squadron, Coningsby, England, 1972-74; reviewing legal billets/assignments 2nd Marine Divsn., Camp Lejeune, NC, 1977-81; mil. judge, chief judge Navy & Marine Corps Judiciary, 1981, 92-93; staff judge advocate to cmndt., dir. judge advocate divsn., Hdqs. USMC, Washington, 1993-96; gen. coun. NASA, Washington, 2004—. Dir. Cherry Point Fed. Credit Union, Havelock, N.C., 1986-88; chmn. supervisory com. Navy Fed.

Credit Union, Vienna, Va., 1993—. Mem. FBA, Va. Bar Assn., Judge Advocates Assn., Marine Corps Assn., Marine Corps Aviation Assn. Avocation: sailing. Office: NASA 300 E St SW Washington DC 20546-0005 Office Phone: 202-358-2450. Office Fax: 202-358-2741.

**WHORISKEY, ROBERT DONALD,** lawyer; b. Cambridge, Mass., May 9, 1929; s. John Joseph and Katherine Euphemia (MacDonald) W.; m. Martha Beebe Poutas, Apr. 16, 1966; children: Alexandra, Jonathan, Eliza. AB, Harvard U., 1952; JD, Boston Coll., 1958; LLM, NYU, 1960. Bar: Mass. 1958, NY 1963, U.S. Tax Ct. 1961, U.S. Claims Ct. 1969, U.S. Dist. Ct. (so. dist.) NY 1969, U.S. Customs 1971, U.S. Ct. Appeals (2d cir.) 1972, U.S. Supreme Ct. 1974, U.S. Ct. Appeals (3d cir.) 1983, U.S. Ct. Appeals (DC cir.) 1991. Sr. trial atty. Office Chief Counsel, IRS, NYC, 1960-67; assoc. Curtis, Mallet-Prevost, Colt & Mosle, NYC, 1967-70, ptnr., 1970-2000, of counsel, 2001—, exec. coun. 1978-82, chmn. tax dept., 1982-87. Bd. dirs. InterNat. Tax Inst., v.p., lectr., 1980-84, chmn. bd., pres., lectr., 1985-87; lectr. Practicing Law Inst., World Trade Inst., Tax Execs. Inst., Am. Mgmt. Assn., Coun. for Internat. Tax Edn.; bd. dirs. Life Ins. Co. of Boston and NY, Inc. Author: Foreign Trusts, 1977, Annual Institute on International Taxation, 1966, 80, 81, (with Sidney Pine, Ralph Seligman) Tax and Business Benefits of the Bahamas, 1986; contbg. author: International Boycotts, CCH Federal Tax Service, 1988, CCH Smart Tax CD-ROM: Third Party Information, John Wiley and Sons, Inc.'s Transfer Pricing, 1993, Transfer Pricing Under IRC & 482: Overview and Planning, Part I, 1996, Accuracy Related Penalty Regulations for Transfer Pricing, Part II, 1997, Third Party Information, Part III, 1997, U.S. Taxation of International Operations, Warren, Gorham Lamont, 1998; mem. editl. adv. bd. Corp. Bus. Taxation Monthly, 2000—. Trustee, treas. Montessori Sch. Westchester, 1974-77; mem. bd. ethics Village of Larchmont, NY, 1988—. With U.S. Army, 1952-54. Mem. ABA (com. on alternative tax sys. tax sect. 1994-2004, com. on ct. procedure tax sec. 1997-2004), NY State Bar Assn. (com. on practice and procedure tax sect. 1990—), Harvard Club, Larchmont Yacht Club. Democrat. Roman Catholic. Office: Curtis Mallet-Prevost Colt & Mosle 101 Park Ave 35th Fl New York NY 10178-0061 Office Phone: 212-696-6031. Personal E-mail: rwhoriskey@aol.com. Business E-mail: rwhoriskey@cm-p.com.

**WHORTON, M. DONALD,** physician, epidemiologist; b. Las Vegas, N.Mex., Jan. 25, 1943; s. R. H. and Rachel (Siegal) Whorton; m. Diana L. Obrinsky, Apr. 9, 1972; children: Matthew Richard, Laura Elizabeth, Julie Hannah. Student, U.S. Naval Acad., 1961—62; B of Biology, N.Mex. Highlands U., 1964; MD, U. N.Mex., 1968; MPH, Johns Hopkins U., 1973. Intern Boston City Hosp., 1968—69; resident in pathology U. N.Mex., Albuquerque, 1969—71; instr., resident in medicine Balt. City Hosp., 1972—74; instr. Johns Hopkins U., Balt.; assoc. dir. divsn. emergency medicine Balt. City Hosps., 1974—75; clin. asst. prof. divsn. ambulatory and cmty. medicine U. Calif. Sch. Medicine, San Francisco, 1975—77; lectr. U. Calif. Sch. Pub. Health, San Francisco, 1975—79; med. dir. labor occup. health program Inst. Indsl. Rels., Ctr. for Labor Rsch. and Edn., 1975—79, assoc. clin. prof. occup. medicine, 1979—87; prin. Environ. Health Assocs., Inc., Oakland, 1978—88; v.p. ENSR Health Scis., 1988—94; pvt. practice Alameda, Calif., 1994—2001; with WorkCare, 2001—. Chmn. adv. com. for hazard evaluation svc. and info. system Indsl. Relations Dept., State of Calif., 1979—84; cons. in field; chmn. statewide adv. com. on occupl. and environ. health U. Calif. Ctrs., 1996—. Contbr. articles to profl. jours. Recipient Upjohn Achievement award, 1968; scholar, Robert Wood Johnson Found., 1972—74. Fellow: Am. Coll. Occupl. and Environ. Medicine, Am. Coll. Epidemiology; mem.: APHA, Inst. Medicine NAS, Calif. Med. Assn. (adv. panel on occupl. and environ. medicine), Soc. for Occupl. and Environ. Health, Alpha Omega Alpha. Office: WorkCare 1320 Harbor Bay Pkwy # 115 Alameda CA 94502-6556 Office Phone: 510-748-6900 ext. 201. Personal E-mail: whobrin@lmi.net. Business E-mail: dwhorton@workcare.com.

**WHYATT, ROBIN M.,** healthcare educator; d. Robert C. Murphy and Nathalie H. Osborn; m. Thomas E. Whyatt, May 12, 1974; children: Erin E. Cercena, Matthew D. BA, Earlham Coll., 1966; MPH, Columbia U., 1985, DrPH, 1995. Exec. dir. Scenic Hudson Inc., Poughkeepsie, NY, 1977—81; sr. project scientist Natural Resources Def. Coun., N.Y.C., 1984—90; sr. staff assoc. Columbia U., N.Y.C., 1990—97, assoc. rsch. scientist, 1997—2000; dep. dir. Columbia Ctr. for Children's Environ. Health, 1998—; asst. prof. dept. pub. health Columbia U., 2000—04, assoc. prof., 2004—. Condr. workshops in field; mem. sci. adv. bd. Cin. Children's Environ. Health Ctr., 2000—; co-chair chem. exposure workgroup Nat. Children's Longitudinal Cohort Study, 2002—; mem. sci. adv. bd. Trichlorethylene Health Risk Assessment, U.S.EPA, 2002. Contbr. numerous articles and abstracts to profl. jours. Founding mem. Citizens Against Aerial Spraying, 1981; mem. PCB citizen's adv. com. EPA, Region II, 1980—81; bd. dirs. Alice Desmond and Hamilton Fish Libr., Garrison, NY, 1991—93; coach Odyssey of the Mind, Garrison Union Free Sch., 1992—96. Grantee, NIEHS, 2004—, 2003—06, NIEHS/EPS, 1997—, EPA, 2000—03, N.Y.C. Coun. Spkrs. Fund for Biomed. Rsch., 2002—04. Mem.: APHA, Internat. Soc. for Exposure Analysis. Avocations: canoeing, hiking. Office: Dept Environmental Health Sci Columbia Univ Mailman Sch Pub Health 60 Haven Ave New York NY 10032

**WHYBARK, DAVID CLAY,** business educator, researcher; b. Tacoma, Sept. 18, 1935; s. Clay Alfred and Irene (Stanton) W.; m. Neva Jo Richardson, July 6, 1957; children: Michael David, Suzanne Marie (dec.). BS, U. Wash., 1957; MBA, Cornell U., 1960; PhD, Stanford U., 1967. Rsch. assoc. Stanford (Calif.) U., 1962-67; asst. prof. Ariz. State U., Tempe, 1965-66; assoc. prof. Purdue U., West Lafayette, Ind., 1967-76; prof. Ind. U, Bloomington, 1976-90; Macon G. Patton disting. prof. U. N.C., Chapel Hill, 1990—. Vis. prof. Shanghai Inst. Mech. Engring., 1986-87, Chinese U. of Hong Kong, 1996, Victoria U., New Zealand, 1996, Canterbury U., New Zealand, 1996; adj. prof. Inst. for Mgmt. Devel., Lausanne, Switzerland, 1981-82, 85-90; dir., founder Global Mfg. Rsch. Group, 1990—; cons. in field. Author: Master Production Scheduling: Theory and Practice, 1979, Manufacturing Planning Control Systems, 1984, International Operations Management, 1989, Integrated Production and Inventory Management, 1993, Why ERP?, 2000, Manufacturing Planning and Control Systems for Supply Chain Management, 2004; editor: Internat. Jour. Prodn. Econs., 1991-95, Global Manufacturing Practices, 1993. Recipient Lilly Alumni MBA Tchg. Excellence award, 1990, Disting. Rsch. award, Kenan-Flagler Sch., 1998. Fellow: Pan Pacific Bus. Assn. (mem. coun.), Internat. Soc. Inventory Rsch. (mem. coun., pres. 2000—02), Decision Scis. Inst. (past pres., Disting. Svc. award 1984); mem.: Ops. Mgmt. Assn. (pres. 1992—93), Am. Prodn. Inventory Control Soc. Avocations: travel, winemaking. Office: U NC Kenan-Flagler Sch Chapel Hill NC 27599-3490 Office Phone: 919-962-3206. Business E-Mail: clay_whybark@unc.edu.

**WHYBROW, PETER CHARLES,** psychiatrist, educator, author; b. Hertforshire, Eng., June 13, 1939; U.S. citizenship, 1975; s. Charles Ernest and Doris Beatrice (Abbott) W.; children: Katherine, Helen Student, U. Coll., London, 1956—59; MB BS, U. Coll., 1962; diploma psychol. medicine, Conjoint Bd., London, 1968; MA (hon.), Dartmouth Coll., 1974, U. Pa., 1994. House officer endocrinology U. Coll. Hosp., 1962, sr. house physician psychiatry, 1963—64; house surgeon St Helier Hosp., Surrey, England, 1963; house officer med. Prince of Wales Hosp., London, 1964; resident psychiatry U. N.C. Hosp., 1965—67, instr., rsch. fellow, 1967—68; mem. sci. staff neuropsychiat. rsch. unit Charshalton, Surrey, 1968—69; dir. residency tng. psychiatry Dartmouth Med. Sch., Hanover, NH, 1969—71; prof. psychiatry, 1970—84, chmn. dept., 1970—78, exec. dean, 1980—83; prof., chmn. dept. psychiatry U. Pa., Phila., 1984—86, Ruth Meltzer prof. psychiatry, 1992; chief psychiatrist Hosp. U. Pa., 1984—96; prof. psychiatry and biobehavioral scis., chmn. dept. psychiatry Sch. Medicine UCLA, 1996—, dir. Semel Inst. for Neurosci. and Human Behavior, 1996—; physician-in-chief Neuropsychiat. Hosp., 1996—99, Judson Braun disting. prof. psychiatry, 1999—. Dir. psychiatry Dartmouth Hitchock Affiliated Hosp., 1970-78; vis. scientist NIMH, 1978-79; cons. VA, 1970—, NIMH, 1972—; chmn. test com. Nat. Bd. Med. Examiners, 1977-84; rschr. psychoendocrinology Author: Mood Disorders: Toward a New Psychobiology, 1984, The Hibernation Response, 1988, A Mood Apart, 1997, American Mania: When More Is Not Enough,

2005; editor: Psychosomatic Medicine, 1977 (Ann. Book award NIH 2005); mem. editl. bd. Cmty. Psychiatry, Psychiat. Times, Directions in Psychiatry, Neuropsychopharmacology, Depression; contbr. articles to profl. jours Recipient Anclote Manor award psychiat. rsch. U. N.C., 1967, Sr. Investigator award Nat. Alliance for Rsch. into Schizophrenia and Depression, 1989; scholar Josiah Macy Jr. Found., 1978-79; fellow Ctr. Advanced Studies in Behavioral Sci., Stanford, 1993-94; recipient Lifetime Investigator award NDMDA, 1996; decorated Knight of Merit, Sovereign Order of St. John of Jerusalem, 1993; Disting. Prof. U. Calif., 2004 Fellow AAAS, Am. Psychiat. Assn., Royal Coll. Psychiatrists (founder), Am. Coll. Psychiatrists, Ctr. Advanced Study of Behavioral Scis. (hon.), Soc. Psychosomatic Rsch. London (hon.); mem. Am. Assn. Chmn. Depts. Psychiatry (pres. 1977-78), Royal Soc. Medicine, Am. Psychopath Assn., Am. Coll. Neuropsychopharmacology, Soc. Biol. Psychiatry, N.Y. Acad. Scis., Soc. Neurosci., Sigma Xi, Alpha Omega Alpha Office: UCLA Semel Inst Neuroscience & Human Behavior 760 Westwood Plz Los Angeles CA 90095-8353 Office Phone: 310-206-1233. Fax: 310-825-3942. Business E-Mail: pwhybrow@mednet.ucla.edu.

**WHYTE, BRUCE LINCOLN,** management executive, marketing professional; b. N.Y.C., Mar. 13, 1941; s. Lincoln Dodge and Louise (Connor) W. BS, Fordham U., NY, 1962; MS, NYU, 1963; PhD in Bus. Adminstrn., San Francisco Internat. U., 2005. Editor corp. planning Am. Airlines, NYC, 1963—65; sr. mktg. analyst Ea. Airlines, NYC, 1965—67; v.p. Deckcraft Corp., NYC, 1967—69; founder, pres. Original Print Collectors Group, NYC, 1972; chmn. bd. OPCG (Subs. Reader's Digest), NYC, 1980—84; pres. Bruce Whyte Enterprises, internat. fine arts bus., NYC, 1984—92, Bruce Whyte Bus. Devel. Co., 1998—, Bruce Whyte Cons., 1998—. Cons. mktg. The Prudential Co., N.Y.C., 1986, Am. Express, 1987; sr. mktg. cons. A.R.T. Corp., 1988; bus. cons. Mystic Seaport Mus., Mass., 1990-; Am. Art liaison Dr. of the World, Paris, 1992; chmn. Bus. Incubator Group Corp. Kingston, N.Y., 1993-; gen. mgr. Sherpa's Pet Trading Co., N.Y.C., 1996; exec. v.p. Sanctuary, Inc., 1996-99, chmn. nat. bd. advisors, 2000-. v.p. bd. dir., 2004-; cons. N.Y. State coun. on the Arts, 1996-97; registered expert witness Dept. Treasury, 1983-; mng. dir. Venture Capital Forum, 1995-96; tech. assistance program cons. N.Y. State Govt., 1996-; trustee Integrity Global Asset Mgmt., 1999-; gen. devel. dir. First Alert, Rockville Centre, N.Y., 1998-2002; pres. disaster recovery plans and response devel. Disaster Recovery Experts, Inc., Rockville Centre, 1999—; trustee Dow Jones Internet Index Fund/Dow Jones, Global Biotech. Index Fund, Dow Jones Global Wireless Commn. Fund Index, Wakefield, RI, 1999-2001; hon. chmn. Congl. Bus. Adv. Coun., 2002, spkr. Congress, 2003—; dep. dir. gen. Am.'s Internat. Biog. Ctr., 2000—. Editor: Art Newsletter OPCG Newsletter, 1972-84 (Best award in U.S.A. 1983-84). Sr. advisor U.S. Congl. Adv. Bd., Washington, 1981-83; chmn. Com. U.S. Senatorial Bus. Adv. Bd., Washington, 1981-83, 2002—; advisor NY Dept. State, 1993; trustee, v.p. Hist. Preservation Soc., NYC 1986-92, U.S. art liaison Found. Mitterand (The Universal Declaration of Human Rights) on behalf of Amnesty Internat., UN, UNESCO, High Commn. on Refugees, Nat. Mus., Heads of State, Paris, NYC, 1989; consumer art protection legis. advisor, atty. gen. NY State Senate and Assembly, 1981; pres. Ulster Arts Alliance, 1993-96; chmn. Kingston Carnegie Libr./Pub. Mus., 1993, Mus. Arts and Tech. Old City Hall, 1994-95; trustee Entrepreneurial Catalyst Forum, 1994-96; advisor Congl. Bus. Commn., 2002—, sustaining hon. chmn., 2003—; Conn. Congl. Com. voting del. to U.S. Congress, The White House and IRS, 2002—; mem. nat. adv. bd. Am. Security Coun., 1981-2005; dep. dir. gen. Ams. Internat. Biog. Ctr., 2002—, presenter of NYC homeland security awards to former NYC police commr. Bernard Kerrick on behalf of Sept. 11 disaster recovery efforts, 2002, and police commr. Raymond Kelly, 2003; dep. dir. gen. for Americas of the Internat. Biog. Ctr., Eng., 2002-; hon. co-chmn. Ann. Formal Pres.'s Dinner, 2003, Ann. Bus. Adv. Coun. Bd. Meeting honoring Pres. George W. Bush, 2003. Recipient Best of Art Catalogues award, Sroge Colorado Springs, 1983, Gold medal Congress Majority Whip Tom DeLay, 2002-03, Internat. Order of Merit, 2003, U.S. Senate Medal of Freedom; named to U.S. Congl. Bus. Honor Roll, 2002, Nat. Rep. Exec. Com. Congl. Spkrs. Cir., 2002; Artist fellow, 1988-; named U.S. Businessman of Yr. Congl. Bus. Adv. Coun., 2003, 2004. Mem. Fine Arts Publ. Assn. (bd. dirs. 1984—), Nat. Arts Club (gov., treas. 1972-74, 86—), U.S. C. of C. Office Phone: 203-367-0629. Personal E-mail: bruce.whyte@snet.net.

**WHYTE, GEORGE KENNETH, JR.,** lawyer; b. Waukegan, Ill., Oct. 10, 1936; s. George K. and Ella Margaret (Osgood) W.; m. Ann B. Challoner, June 20, 1964; children: Mary, Douglas. AB in Polit. Sci., Duke U., 1958; LLB, U. Wis., 1965. Bar: Wis. 1965. Law clk. to chief justice Wis. Supreme Ct., Madison, 1965-66; assoc. Quarles & Brady, Milw., 1966-73, ptnr., 1973—2004; ret., 2004. Lt. USN, 1958—62. Mem. ABA (employment law sect.), Wis. Bar Assn. (former chmn. labor and employment law sect.), Rotary (pres. 2002-03), The Town Club, Milw. Country Club. Congregationalist. Home: 1026 W Shaker Cir Mequon WI 53092-6034 E-mail: gkw@quarles.com.

**WHYTE, KELLY ANN,** music educator; b. Chgo., Ill., June 12, 1969; d. Edward John and Judy Ann Kistinger; m. David Bruce Whyte, Apr. 3, 1993; children: Ethan David, Jacob Matthew. MusB, Millikin U., 1991. Music choir tchr. Coal City Dist. 1, Ill., 1991—93, Minooka Sch. Dist. 201, Ill., 1993—2000, Richland Grade Sch., Crest Hill, Ill., 2000—. Worship leader Larkin Bapt. Ch., Joliet, 2000—, choir dir., 2002—; mem. Evang. Choir, Joliet, 2003—04. Mem.: Music Educator Nat. Conf. Avocations: cooking, camping. Home: 333 E 4th St Lockport IL 60441

**WHYTE, MICHAEL P.,** genetics educator, researcher, director; b. N.Y.C., Dec. 19, 1946; s. Michael Paul and Sophie (Dziuk) W.; m. Gloria Frances Golenda, Oct. 26, 1974; 1 child, Catherine Alexandra. BA in Chemistry, NYU, 1968; MD, SUNY, Bklyn., 1972. Diplomate Am. Bd. Internal Medicine, Nat. Bd. Med. Examiners. Intern, 1st yr. resident dept. medicine NYU Sch. Medicine Bellevue Hosp., N.Y.C., 1972-74; clin. assoc. devel. and metabolic neurology nr. Nat. Inst. Neurol. and Communicative Disorders and Stroke NIH, Bethesda, Md., 1974-76; fellow divsn. bone and mineral metabolism dept. medicine Washington U. Sch. Medicine, 1976-79, instr. dept. medicine, 1979-80, asst. sci. dir. Clin. Rsch. Ctr., 1979—; asst. physician Barnes Hosp., 1979—; staff physician St. Louis Children's Hosp., 1979—; NIH clin. assoc. physician Clin. Rsch. Ctr. Washington U. Sch. Medicine, 1980-82, asst. prof. medicine dept. medicine, 1980-86, assoc. prof. medicine dept. medicine, 1986-91, asst. prof. pediat. Edward Mallinckrodt dept. pediat., 1982-89, assoc. prof. pediat. Edward Mallinckrodt dept. pediat., 1989-92, prof. medicine dept. medicine, 1991—, prof. pediat. Edward Mallinckrodt dept. pediat., 1992—, prof. genetics James S. McDonell dept. genetics, 1997—; med. dir. Metabolic Rsch. Unit Shriners Hosp. for Children, St. Louis, 1982-2000, mem. staff—1983—; assoc. attending physician Jewish Hosp., 1983—. Mem. editl. bd. Calcified Tissue Internat., 1995-2000, Jour. Bone and Mineral Rsch., 1994—; med. adv. bd. Osteogenesis Imperfecta Found., 1986—, med. adv. panel Paget's Disease Found., 1986—; chmn. med. adv. com., bd. dirs. Osteogenesis Found., 1995—; med.-sci. dir. Ctr. for Metabolic Bone Disease and Molecular Rsch. Shriners Hosp. for Children, St. Louis, 2000—. Assoc. editor: Primer on Metabolic Bone Diseases and Disorders of Mineral Metabolism, 1990, 93, 96, 99, 2003, 06; assoc. editor Calcified Tissue Internat., 1989-2000; contbr. chpts. to books, articles to profl. jours. Lt. comdr. USPHS, 1974-76. Fellow Am. Coll. of Endocrinology; mem. Am. Soc. Cell Biology, Am. Soc. Clin. Investigation, Am. Coll. Physicians (assoc.), Am. Fedn. Clin. Rsch., Am. Soc. Advancement Sci., Am. Soc. Bone and Mineral Rsch. (ednl. com. 1987—, Fuller Albright award 1987, Young Investigator award 1983, Dr. Boy Frame award 1997), Am. Soc. Human Genetics, Endocrine Soc., Soc. Exptl. Biology and Medicine, Japanese Soc. Inherited Metabolic Disease (hon.), N.Y. Acad. Scis. Office: Barnes-Jewish Hosp 216 S Kingshighway Blvd Saint Louis MO 63110-1026 Office Phone: 314-872-8305. Business E-Mail: mwhyte@shrinenet.com.

**WHYTE, NANCY MARIE,** performing arts educator; b. Myrtlepoint, Oreg., Mar. 12, 1948; d. Lawrence Edward and Carol Elizabeth (Johnson) Guderian; m. Anthony John Whyte, Aug. 7, 1967 (div. Sept. 1968); 1 child,

Charles Lawrence; m. Douglas Brian Graff, June 27, 1971 (div. Oct. 1974); m. Lawrence Hanson, Mar. 12, 1976 (div. Aug. 1984); m. Joseph Paul Deacon, Aug. 10, 1985; 1 child, Nina Alexandra. Student, U. Wash., 1969-72, Am. Sch. Dance, 1972; BA, Evergreen State Coll., 1987. Owner, dir. Nancy Whyte Sch. Ballet, Bellingham, Wash., 1969—; artistic dir. Garden Street Dance Players, Bellingham, 1969-72, MT Baker Ballet, Bellingham, 1975—, Alpha and Omega Worship Dancers, 2003—; co-dir. Exptl. Performance Workshop, Bellingham, 1975-77; instr. creative dance St. Paul's Primary Sch., Bellingham, 1993-97; facilitator dance workshop Allied Arts/Whatcom Co., Bellingham, 1995—. Guest lectr. Western Wash. U., Bellingham, 1976—83, 1996—2003; guest faculty Dance Theatre N.W., Tacoma, 1995—; liturgical dance cons. Assumption Cath. Sch., 2001—04; artistic dir. Alpha and Omega Worship Dancers, 2003—. Author: Memoirs of a Child of Theatre Street, 1993; soloist Raduga Folk Ballet/N.Y. Character Ballet, N.Y.C., 1978-79; choreographer numerous ballets, 1972—. Mem. Nat. Dance Assn., Dancers Over 40, Sacred Dance Guild, Vancouver Ballet Soc. Democrat. Avocations: voice, writing. Office: MT Baker Ballet 1412 Cornwall Ave PO Box 2393 Bellingham WA 98227-2393 Office Phone: 360-734-9141. E-mail: isadorables@msn.com.

**WHYTE, RAYMOND A.,** artist; b. Canmore, Alta., Can., Aug. 3, 1923; s. Adolf Whyte and Mary McGuire; m. Erica Giller Whyte, June 12, 1953. Student, Art Students League, N.Y.C. Mural, Austral Oil Co., Houston, 1965. Represented in permanent collections Gerald B. Kara, N.Y.C., B. Gerald Cantor, one-man shows include Galerie de Tours, San Francisco, 1962—81, Crocker Art Mus., Sacramento, 1967, E. Kulik Gallery, N.Y.C., 1972, exhibited in group shows at Nat. Acad., 1949, portrait and painting commns. With Royal Can. Air Force, 1942—45. Avocations: skiing, photography, classical music, painting, painting Napoleonic tin soldiers on horses. Home: 1276 Meredith Dr Spring Hill FL 34608

**WHYTE, RONALD M.,** judge; b. 1942; BA in Math., Wesleyan U., 1964; JD, U. So. Calif., 1967. Bar: Calif. 1967, U.S. Dist. Ct. (no. dist.) Calif. 1967, U.S. Dist. Ct. (cen. dist.) Calif. 1968, U.S. Ct. Appeals (9th cir.) 1986. Assoc. Hoge, Fenton Jones & Appel, Inc., San Jose, Calif., 1971-77, mem., 1977-89; judge Superior Ct. State of Calif., 1989-92, U.S. Dist. Ct. (no. dist.) Calif., San Jose, 1992—. Judge pro-tempore Superior Ct. Calif., 1977-89; lectr. Calif. Continuing Edn. of Bar, Rutter Group, Santa Clara Bar Assn., State Bar Calif.; legal counsel Santa CLara County Bar Assn., 1986-89; mem. county select com. Criminal Conflicts Program, 1988. Bd. trustees Santa Clara County Bar Assn., 1978-79, 84-85. Lt. Judge Advocate Gen.'s Corps, USNR, 1968-71. Recipient Judge of Yr. award Santa Clara County Trial Lawyers Assn., 1992, Disting. Svc. award Berkeley Ctr. Law and Tech., 2001; nmaed Fed. Judge of Yr., Santa Clara (Calif.) County Trial Lawyers Assn., 2003. Mem. Calif. Judges Assn., Assn. Bus. Trial Lawyers (bd. govs. 1991-93), Santa Clara Inn of Ct. (exec. com. 1993—), San Francisco Bay area Intellectual Property Inn of Ct. (exec. com. 1994—). Office: US Courthouse 280 S 1st St Rm 2112 San Jose CA 95113-3002

**WIACEK, RAYMOND J.,** lawyer; b. Detroit, Dec. 5, 1950; BA, Yale U., 1973; JD, Harvard U., 1976. Bar: Mich. 1976, D.C. 1977. Lawyer Jones, Day, Reavis & Pogue, Washington; ptnr. fin. affairs and tax group coun. Jones Day, Washington. Adj. prof. taxation Georgetown Univ. Law Ctr. Mem. Phi Beta Kappa. Office: Jones Day 51 Louisiana Ave NW Washington DC 20001-2113 Office Phone: 202-879-3908. Office Fax: 202-626-1700. Business E-Mail: rjwiacek@jonesday.com.

**WIANT, SARAH KIRSTEN,** law librarian, educator, director; b. Waverly, Iowa, Nov. 20, 1946; d. James Allen and Eva (Jorgensen) W.; m. Robert E. Akins (dec.) BA, Western State Coll., 1968; MLS, U. North Tex., 1970; JD, Washington & Lee U., 1978. Asst. law libr. Res. Tech. U., 1970—72, Washington & Lee U., Lexington, Va., 1972—, dir., 1978—, asst. prof. law, 1978-83, assoc. prof. law, 1984-92, prof. law, 1993—. Participant Conf. on Fair Use, NII, 1995-98. Co-author: Copyright Handbook, 1984, Libraries and Copyright: A Guide to Copyright Law in the 1990s, 1994, UCITA Encyclopedia of Lib. and Information Science, 2d edit., 2003, 3d edit., 2005; co-author: (Va. sect.) Legal Research in the District of Columbia, Maryland and Virginia, 2005; co-author: (admiralty chpt.) Specialized Legal Research, 2005; co-author: Developments on Copyright Law, 2005; mem. adv. bd. Westlaw, 1988—93, 2003—; contbr. chapters to books. Mem.: ABA (com. on librs. 1987—93), U.S. Trademark Assn., Maritime Law Assn., Spl. Librs. Assn. (chair copyright com. 1990—96, John Cotton Dana award 1997), Am. Assn. Law Schs. (chmn. sec. on librs. 1990—92, accreditation com. 1991—94), Am. Assn. Law Libs. (mem. exec. bd. 1981—84, mem. copyright com. 1990—94, chmn. 2003—04, copyright office rep., Pres.' award 2001, Spl. Dist. Svc. award Southeastern chpt. 1997). Office: Washington & Lee U Law Libr Lewis Hall Lexington VA 24450 Office Phone: 540-458-8540. Business E-Mail: wiants@wlu.edu.

**WIATT, JAMES ANTHONY,** theatrical agency executive; b. LA, Oct. 18, 1946; s. Norman and Catherine (Sonners) W.; m. Randie Laine. BA, U. So. Calif., 1969. Campaign coord. Tunney for Senate, L.A., 1969-71; adminstrv. asst. Senator John V. Tunney, L.A., 1972-75; agt. FCA, L.A., 1976-78; lit. agt. Internat. Creative Mgmt., L.A., 1978-81, motion picture agt., 1981-83, head of motion picture dept., 1983-85, pres., COO, from 1985, co-chmn., co-CEO Beverly Hills, Calif.; to 1999; pres., co-CEO William Morris Agy., Beverly Hills, 1999—. Mem. bd. councilors USC Sch. Cinema-TV; mem. bd. govs. Music Ctr. L.A., Am. Film Inst.; mem. exec. bd. med. scis. UCLA; exec. coun. The Quills. Named one of 50 Most Powerful People in Hollywood, Premiere mag., 2004—06. Office: William Morris Agy 151 S El Camino Dr Beverly Hills CA 90212-2775 E-mail: jwiatt@wma.com.*

**WIBERG, DONALD MARTIN,** electrical engineering educator, consultant; b. Battle Creek, Mich., Sept. 20, 1936; s. Martin and Lina (Havstein) W.; children: Erik M., Kristin A., Kenneth C. BS, Calif. Inst. Tech., 1959, MS, 1960, PhD, 1965. Registered profl. engr., Calif. Sr. design engr. Convair, San Diego, 1964-65; asst. prof. elec. engring. UCLA, 1965-71, assoc. prof., 1971-77, prof., 1977-94, prof. anesthesiology, 1979-94, vice chmn. dept. elec. engring., 1985-86, prof. emeritus, 1994-2001; prof. emeritus dept. elec. engring. U. Calif., Santa Cruz, 2001—, rsch. prof. Ctr. for Adaptive Optics, 2002—. Cons. in field; vis. prof. German Rsch. Orgn. for Air and Space Flight, Munich, 1969-70, dept. elec. engring. and computer sci. U. Newcastle, Australia, 1989-90, Inst. for Systems Rsch., U. Md., College Park, 1994, Ajon U., Suwon, Korea, 2006. Author: State Space and Linear Systems, 1971; co-editor: Regulation of Breathing, 1983. Mem. adv. bd. Parthenia Sch., Los Angeles, 1971-74. Sr. NATO research fellow KFZ Karlsruhe, W.Ger., 1973; sr. Fulbright fellow, Copenhagen, 1976-77, Trondheim, Norway, 1983-84 Fellow IEEE (applications assoc. editor Trans. on Automatic Control 1983, assoc. editor-at-large 1987-89, 92-94, named Congl. fellow legis. asst. office Senator Tom Harkin, D-IA 1995), Am. Physiol. Soc. (assoc. editor Modelling Methodology Forum 1980-91), Sigma Xi. Home: 2395 Delaware Ave #153 Santa Cruz CA 95060-5716 Business E-Mail: wiberg@ee.ucla.edu.

**WIBERG, KENNETH BERLE,** chemist, educator; b. Bklyn., Sept. 22, 1927; s. Dan and Solveig Berle W.; m. Marguerite Koch, Mar. 18, 1951; children: Patricia, Robert, William. BS, Mass. Inst. Tech., 1948; PhD, Columbia, 1950. Mem. faculty U. Wash., 1950-62, prof. chemistry, 1958-62, Yale U., 1962—; Whitehead prof., 1968-90, chmn. chem. dept., 1968-71, Eugene Higgins prof., 1990—97, Eugene Higgins prof. emeritus, 1997—. Boomer lectr. U. Alta., Can. 1959; Mem. chemistry advisory panel Air Force Office Sci. Research, 1960-66, NSF, 1965-68, chmn., 1967-68 Author: Laboratory Technique in Organic Chemistry, 1960, Interpretation of NMR Spectra, 1962, Physical Organic Chemistry, 1964, Computer Programming for Chemists, 1966, also articles.; Editor: Oxidation in Organic Chemistry, 1966, Sigma M.O. Theory, 1970; mem. editorial bd.: Organic Syntheses, 1963-71, Jour. Organic Chemistry, 1968-72, J. Computer Chem., 1982—, Tetrahedron, 1981—, Chemical Revs., 1986—; bd. editors: Jour. Am. Chem. Soc, 1969-72. Recipient James Flack Norris award, 1973, Arthur C. Cope award 1988; Sloan Found. fellow, 1958-62; Guggenheim fellow, 1961-62;

Cope scholar, 1986. Mem. AAAS, Am. Acad. Scis., Nat. Acad. Scis., Am. Chem. Soc. (exec. com. organic div. 1961-63, Calif. sect. award 1963, Linus Pauling award 1992). Office: Yale U Chemistry Dept 225 Prospect St New Haven CT 06520-5107

**WIBERG, LARS-ERIK,** occupational compatibility consultant; b. Wakefield, Mass., June 1, 1928; s. Sverker Claesson and Ingrid (Heurlin) W.; m. Elizabeth Margaret (Allenbrook), Oct. 18, 1957; children: Kirsten, Margaret, Brenda. BS in Geology, MIT, 1950; MAT, Harvard U., 1952. From engr. to dir. corp. comm. EG and G Inc., Boston and Bedford, Mass., 1956—69; from asst. v.p. to v.p. compensation, orgnl. planning and ombudsman for officers First Nat. Bank of Boston, 1969—81; cons. Rockport, Mass., 1981—. Lectr. human resources mgmt. Boston U., 1988—92; lectr. job search and career planning U. Karlstad, Sweden, 1992. Author: It's Your Move, 1991; inventor in the field of Occupl. Compatibility; interviewed in Rockport Recollected. Mem. Gov. John A. Volpe's Mgmt. Engring. Task Force, 1965; mem. planning bd., Rockport, 1965-72, chmn., 1969-72; pres. ch. coun. Swedenborg Chapel, Cambridge, Mass., 1984-2004; dir. Mass. New Ch. Union, 1990-2004; mem. zoning bd. appeals, Rockport, 1986-2006, chmn., 2006—, mem. site rev. com., 1999-2001; v.p., founder The Uses Trust, Ltd., 2005. 1st lt., USAF, 1953-55. Mem. Affiliated New Eng. Cons. (founding mem. Lexington, Mass. 1985), Life Ext. Found., Heritage Found., Swedenborg Sci. Assn. Avocations: home repair, music, cooking, reading. Home and Office: 90 South St Rockport MA 01966-1916 Business E-Mail: bjara@gis.net.

**WIBISONO, MAKARIM,** diplomat; b. Mataram, Indonesia, May 8, 1948; married; 3 children. Degree in internatl rels., Gajahmada U., Jogjakarata, Indonesia, 1970; MS in Internat Studies, Johns Hopkins U., 1984; MA in Polit. Economy, Ohio State U., 1986, PhD, 1987. Editor Express News Mag., Jakarta, Indonesia, 1970-72; head U.S. desk Dept. Fgn. Affairs, Indonesia, 1972-76, head N.Am. sect., 1976-77; head info. and cultural divsn. Indonesian Embassy, Brasilia, Brazil, 1977-81; dep. dir. trade and exhbns. Fgn. Affairs Dept., Indonesia, 1977-81, dep. dir. info. affairs, 1987-88; head info. divsn. Indonesian Embassy, Washington, 1988-91; min. counsellor, head econ. divsn. Indonesia UN Mission, 1991-93; dir. multilateral econ. coop. Dept. Fgn. Affairs, Indonesia, 1993-94; dep. permanent rep. from Indonesia UN, 1994-97; permanent rep. to UN Govt. Indonesia, N.Y.C., 1997—2001; dir.-gen. for fgn. econ. rels. Dept. Fgn. Affairs, Republic of Indonesia, UN, 2001—02; dir. gen. for Asia Pacific and Africa Affairs Indonesia Mission, UN, 2002—. Office: Permanent Mission Rep Indonesia to UN 325 E 38th St New York NY 10016-2745

**WIBLE, JULIE LYNN,** human services administrator, military officer; m. Larry Edward Wible, July 25, 1992. AA in Liberal Arts, Las Positas CC, 1994; BS in Orgnl. Behavior, U. San Francisco, 1995; MS in Pub. Adminstrn., Calif. State U., Stanislaus. Chief line 349th Aerospace Medicine Squadron, Travis AFB, Calif., 2001—03, med. readiness offcr, 2003—05, health svcs. adminstr., 2005—. Assoc. govt. program analyst Dept. Edn., Sacramento, 1998—2005. Decorated Air Force Commendation medal USAFR; recipient Air Force Outstanding Unit award with Valor, Nat. Def. Svc. medal, Air Force Longevity Svc. award, Armed Forces Res. medal, Meritorious Civilian Svc. medal, USN, 1993, 1995, Global War on Terrorism Svc. medal, USAFR, 2005. Mem.: VFW, Med. Svc. Corps Officers Assn., Res. Med. Svc. Corps Officer Assn., Assn. Mil. Surgeons of the US, Res. Officers Assn. Avocations: travel, reading, fitness. Home: 1177 Ishi Goto St Stockton CA 95206 Office: 349 Aerospace Medicine Squadron 531 Waldron St Ste D Travis Afb CA 94535-2149 Office Phone: 707-424-3814. Office Fax: 707-424-3813. Business E-Mail: julie.wible@travis.af.mil.

**WICHA, MAX S.,** oncologist, educator; b. N.Y.C., Mar. 24, 1949; m. Sheila Crowley; children: Jason, Allyson. BS in Biology summa cum laude with honors, SUNY, Stony Brook, 1970; MD, Stanford U., 1974. Diplomate Am. Bd. Internal Medicine; lic. physician, Mich.; Ill. Intern in internal medicine U. Chgo. Hosps. and Clinics, 1974-75, jr., sr. resident in internal medicine, 1975-77; rsch. assoc. lab. pathophysiolog Nat. Cancer Inst./NIH, Bethesda, Md., 1977-79, fellow in clin. oncology, 1978-80, investigator lab. pathophysiology, 1979-80; asst. prof. internal medicine divsn. hematology and oncology U. Mich., Ann Arbor, 1980-83, assoc. prof., 1983-88, prof., 1988—, mem. tumor metastasis, extracellular matrrix, reproductive endocrinology programs, 1982—; dir. divsn. hematology and oncology, dir. Simpson Meml. Rsch. Inst., 1984-93, mem. program in cellular and molecular biology, 1984—, dir. Comprehensive Cancer Ctr., 1987—. Mem. cancer rsch. com. U. Mich., 1981—, sci. adv. bd. dental rsch. inst., 1983—, dean's adv., 1988—, reproductive endocrinology selection com., breast care ctr. exec. com., 1988—, exec. dir.'s adv. coun., 1992—, chair instl. rev. com. gene therapy program project., 1992—, dean's adv. com. Howard Hughes Med. Inst., 1992—, strategic planning policy and organizational com. health scis. info. tech. and networking, 1992—; vis. prof. Mich. State U., 1985, Harvard U., Boston, 1986, Wash. State U., 1986, Boston U., 1986, Wayne State U./Harper Grace Hosps., 1987, U. Ill., 1987, Med. Coll. Wis., 1987., U. Chgo., 1987, Eppley Inst. for Rsch. in Cancer and Allied Diseases, Omaha, 1988, U. Nebr., Omaha, 1988, U. Minn./Minn. VA Hosp., 1988, MD Anderson Cancer Ctr., Houston, Mt. Sinai Med. Ctr., N.Y.C., Am. Cancer Soc., Kalamazoo, 1989, Gainesville, Fla., 1990, Orlando, Fla., 1990, Pezcoller Symposium, Rovereto, Italy, 1990, Prince Henry's Hosp., Melbourne, Australia, 1990, Northwestern U. Med. Ctr., Chgo., 1990, Meml. Sloan-Kettering Cancer Ctr., N.Y.C., 1990, Tex. S.W. U., Dallas, 1990, Mich. State U., 1991; lectr. U. Mich., 1990; mem. NIH Site Visit team U. Calif. Cancer Rsch. Lab., Berkeley, 1985; ad hoc mem. cell biology and physiology study sect. NIH, 1985, 86, study sect., Bethesda, 1991; mem. NCI Site Visit team Norris Cotton Dartmouth Cancer Ctr, 1989, Howard U., Wash., 1989, Howard U. Parent Com., 1989, MD Anderson Cancer Ctr., Houston, 1992; sci. advisor U. Colo. Cancer Ctr., Denver, 1990, Samuel Waxman Cancer Rsch. Found., Mt. Sinai Med. Ctr., N.Y.C., 1988-93; mem. NCI Adv. Panel, Bethesda, 1991; mem. sci. adv. com. U. Tex. San Antonio Cancer Ctr., U. Miami Sylvester Cancer Ctr., Mich. State U., East Lansing, Norris-Cotton Cancer Ctr., Dartmouth-Hitchcock Med. Ctr., Hanover, N.H., Mich. Cancer Found., Detroit, V. T. Lombardi Cancer Rsch. Ctr., Georgetown U., Washington, 1992—, MD Anderson Cancer Ctr., Houston, 1992—; mem. extramural sci. adv. bd. UCI Clin. Cancer Ctr., U. Calif. Irvine, Orange, 1992—; mem. NCI SPORE in Prostate Cancer Study Sect., 1992; chair NCI Cancer Ctr. Support Rev. Com., 1993; NCI Site Visit chair Jefferson Cancer Ctr., Phila., 1992, Worcester (Mass.) Cancer Found., 1993, Duke U. Cancer Ctr., Durham, N.C., 1993, Lineberger Comprehensive Ctr., Chapel Hill, N.C., 1993; mem. NCI Comprehensive Cancer Ctrs. Review, 1993, chmn. parent com. Cancer Ctr. Support Rev. Com., 1992—; cons. Warner Lambert Co., 1980—. Assoc. editor: Molecular and Cellular Differentiation, 1993; co-editor: The Hematopoietic Microenvironment, 1993; mem. editorial bd. Blood, Molecular and Cellular Differentiation, Jour. Lab. and Clin. Medicine, Cancer Rsch., 1993—, Oncology, Cancer Prevention Internat.; reviewer Nature, Science, Proceedings of NAS, Jour. Clin. Investigation, Jour. Cell Biology, Exptl. Cell Rsch., Exptl. Hematology, Cancer., Clin. and Exptl. Metastasis, Jour. Nat. Cancer Inst., Tissue & Cell, Am. Inst. Biol. Scis., Am. Jour. Pathology, Jour Immunology, Jour. Med. Scis., NSF, Oncology Rsch., Lab. Investigation, Breast Cancer Rsch. and Treatment; contbr. over 110 articles and to profl. jours., chpts. to books; invited lectr. in field. With USPHS, 1977-80. Recipient NSF RSch. award SUNY, 1969, Eli Luke and David Jacob Rsch. award Stanford U. Sch. Medicine, 1974, Upjohn Achievement Excellence in Medicine award, Outstanding Med. Resident award U. Chgo. Hosps., 1977, Jerome Conn Excellence in Rsch. award, 1983; grantee NIH, 1991—, 93—, Am. Cancer Soc., 1992—, Suntory Rsch. Inst., 1992-93. Mem. AAASN, Am. Assn. for Cancer Rsch. (state legis. com. 1992—, finance com. 1992—), Am. Fedn. for Clin. Rsch. (selections com. midwest sect. 1986—, comm. com., 1986—, awards com., 1986—), Am. Soc. for Cell Biology, Am. Soc. Hematology (com. on publs. 1991-93), Assn. Am. Cancer Insts. (bd. dirs. 1993—), Am. Soc. for Clin. Investigation, Am. Soc. Clin. Oncology (award selection com. 1992—), Ctrl. Soc. for Clin. Rsch., Mich. Soc. Hematology and Oncology, Southwest Oncology Group, Assn. Community Cancer Ctrs. Achievements include patents for antibodies to human mammary cell growth inhibitor and methods of production and use,

human mammary cell growth inhibitor and methods of production and use; research in regulation of cell growth and differentiation, molecular mechanisms of tumor metastasis. Mailing: 6302 CCGC 0942 1500 E Medical Ctr Dr Ann Arbor MI 48109

**WICHERN, DEAN WILLIAM,** business educator; b. Medford, Wis., Apr. 29, 1942; s. Arthur William and Rebecca Ann (Ambler) W.; m. Dorothy Jean Rutkowski, Dec. 7, 1968; children: Michael, Andrew. BS in Math., U. Wis., 1964, MS in Stats., 1965, PhD in Stats., 1969. Instr. Sch. Bus. U. Wis., Madison, 1967-69, asst. prof., 1969-72, assoc. prof., 1972-76, prof., 1976-84, chmn. quantitative analysis dept., 1975-78; prof. Mays Bus. Sch. Tex. A&M U., 1984—, head info. and ops. mgmt. dept., 1984—88, Tex., 1997—98, 2004—, assoc. dean, 1988-95, John E. Pearson prof. bus. adminstrn., 1985—. Vis. prof. Math. Rsch. Ctr., 1978-79. Co-author: Intermediate Business Statistics, 1977, Applied Multivariate Statistical Analysis, 5th edit., 2002, Business Statistics: Decision Making With Data, 1997, Business Forecasting, 8th edit., 2005; mem. editl. bd. Jour. Bus. and Econ. Stats., 1983—91. Mem. Royal Statis. Soc., Am. Statis. Assn., Inst. Oper. Rsch. and Mgmt. Sci., Internat. Inst. of Forecasters, Beta Gamma Sigma, Phi Kappa Phi. Home: 9217 Riverstone Ct College Station TX 77845-8333 Office: Tex A&M U Mays Bus Sch 4217 TAMU College Station TX 77843-4217 Business E-Mail: d-wichern@tamu.edu.

**WICK, DOUGLAS,** producer; m. Lucy Fisher; 3 children. Grad. cum laude, Yale U. Owner Red Wagon Prodns., Culver City, Calif. Assoc. prodr. Starting Over 1979; prodr. Wolf, 1994, The Craft, 1996, Hush, 1998, Working Girl (six Acad. Award Nomiations, five Golden Globes including Best Picture), 1988, Stuart Little, 1999, Girl, Interrupted, 1999, Gladiator, 2000, The Hollow Man, 2000, Stuart Little 2, 2002, Peter Pan, 2003, Win A Date With Tad Hamilton, 2004, Bewitched, 2005, Memoirs Of A Geisha, 2005, Jarhead, 2005. Office: Red Wagon Prodns Hepburn West Bldg 10202 W Washington Blvd Culver City CA 90232 Fax: 310-244-1480.

**WICK, MICHAEL M.,** biotechnology executive; MD, PhD in Chemistry, Harvard U. Chief melanoma clinic and lab. molecular dermatol. oncology Dana Farber Cancer Inst., Boston, 1980—92; assoc. prof. Harvard Med. Sch., Boston, 1981—94; exec. dir. oncology/immunology and clin. rsch. Lederle Labs. (divsn. Am. Cyanamid), 1990—95; sr. v.p. rsch. CV Therapeutics, 1995—97, cons., 1997; bd. dirs. Telik, Inc., South San Francisco, Calif., 1997—, exec. v.p R&D, COO, 1997—98, pres., 1998—, CEO, 1999—, chmn. bd. dirs., 2000—. Office: Telik Inc 3165 Porter Dr Palo Alto CA 94304-1213

**WICK, MITCHELL A.,** physician; b. NYC, July 15, 1954; s. Edwin and Doris Wick. BA in Chemistry, U. South Fla., 1976; postgrad., U. Miami, Coral Gables, Fla., 1972—73; D.O., Kirksville Coll. Osteo. Medicine, Mo., 1980. Diplomate Am. Osteo. Bd. Family Physicians, Am. Acad. Pain Mgmt., Am. Assn. Integrative Medicine. Intern Southeastern Med. Ctr., N. Miami, Fla., 1980—81; resident Parkview Hosp., Toledo, 1981—83; staff physician Walk-in Family Medicine Ctr., Boynton Beach, Fla., 1983—86; physician Davie-Dania Med. Ctr., Fla., 1986—96; staff physician Meml. Pembroke Hosp., Pembroke Pines, Fla., 1991—. Author: Megaphysics, A New Look at the Universe, 2003. Mem.: Fla. Osteo. Med. Assn., Am. Osteo. Assn. Achievements include research and copywrite on physics theory regarding the fractal nature of spacetime manifolds and how matter and energy interact with thereof utilizing string theory. Avocations: physics, tensor calculus. Home: 914 S Chippewa Cir Boynton Beach FL 33436 Office Phone: 561-736-2000. Personal E-mail: wobsaxoshin@comcast.net.

**WICK, ROBERT THOMAS,** retired food service executive; b. St. Louis, Nov. 26, 1927; s. Robert Berninger and Katherine (Burke) W.; m. Virginia Rose Allen, Sept. 6, 1952; children: Susan, Patrick, Nancy, Robert J. BS, St. Louis U., 1955; cert. in food distbn., Mich. State U., 1956. Sales mgr. Nat. Tea Co., St. Louis, 1966-68, asst. div. mgr., 1968-69, div. mgr. Sioux City, Iowa, 1969-71, Milw., 1971-73, Chgo., 1973-74; v.p., gen. mgr. A&P Food Stores, Indpls., 1975-77; div. v.p. Colonial Food Stores- Grand Union, Norfolk, Va., 1977-79; pres., chief exec. officer Bonnie Be-Lo Markets, Inc., Norfolk, 1979-90, ret., 1990. Bd. dirs. Virginia Beach (Va.) Community Svcs. Bd., 1985-89; mem. adv. bd. Straight, Inc., Chesapeake, Va., 1987-91; dir. Community Alternatives, Inc., Virginia Beach, 1991-92. Tech. cpl. U.S. Army, 1946-48. Recipient Citizen of Yr. award St. Louis Argus Newspaper, 1968. Mem. Food Mktg. Inst. (bd. dirs. 1982-89), Va. Food Dealers Assn. (bd. dirs. 1981-87), Tidewater Retail Mchts. Assn. (pres., bd. dirs. 1981-91). Conservative. Roman Catholic. Avocations: travel, golf. Home: 801 Winthrope Dr Virginia Beach VA 23452-3940 Personal E-mail: rwick@cox.net.

**WICK, WILLIAM SHINN,** clergyman, chaplain, pastor; b. West Chester, Pa. s. William R. and Barbara (Shinn) W.; m. Debra R. Smith, Apr. 1, 1989; 1 child, Christopher R. BA, Trinity Internat. U., Deerfield, Ill., 1975; MDiv, Trinity Evang. Div. Sch., Deerfield, 1978. Ordained to ministry Evang. Free Ch. Am., 1978. Pastor Bradford (Vt.) Evang. Free Ch., 1978-85, Cornerstone Evangelical Free Ch., Vt., 1985-89, Grace Evang. Free Ch., Northfield, Vt., 1989-96; chaplain Norwich U., Northfield, 1989—; interim pastor First Bapt. Ch., Barre, Vt., 2001—03, Resurrection Bapt. Ch., Montpelier, Vt., 2003—04, Orange Christian and Missionary Alliance Ch., 2004—05, Websterville Baptist Ch., 2006—. Mem. bd. govs. Trinity Western U., Langley, B.C., Can., 1999—. Capt. CAP, 2005—. Mem.: Profl. Ski Instrs. Am. Mem. Evangelical Free Ch. Am. Avocations: alpine skiing, racquetball, tennis, scuba diving, sailing, astronomy. Home: 763 S Main St Northfield VT 05663-5601 Office: White Chapel Norwich U 158 Harmon Dr Northfield VT 05663-1000 Office Phone: 802-485-2128. Personal E-mail: theskiingrev@hotmail.com. Business E-Mail: chaplain@norwich.edu.

**WICKENS, DREW C.,** finance director; b. Yankton, SD, July 30, 1968; s. Donaldson V. and Carolyn F. Wickens; m. Nada A. Karam, Aug. 27, 1995; children: Kyla D., Kate D., Tiffany D. BA in Econ., Emory U., Atlanta, 1990; MBA, HEC Sch. Mgmt., Paris, 1996. Cert. Mgmt. Acct., Inst. Mgmt. Accts., NJ, 2003, Cert. Fin. Mgr., Inst. Mgmt. Accts., NJ, 2004, Cert. Internal Auditor, Inst. Internal Auditors, Fla., 2004, Certified Fraud Examiner, ACFE/Tex., 2004. Dir. fin. planning and budget Am. U. Beirut, New York, 2002—. Mem.: Soc. for Coll. and U. Planning, Assn. Cert. Fraud Examiners, Inst. Internal Auditors, Inst. Mgmt. Accts. Office: Am Univ of Beirut 3 Dag Hammarskjold Plz 8th Fl New York NY 10017-2303 Office Phone: 212-583-7600. Office Fax: 212-583-7650. Personal E-mail: wickens@aub.edu.

**WICKER, CHRISTOPHER EUGENE,** public health service officer; b. Lackey, Ky., July 8, 1955; s. Worley and Geneva Wicker; m. Winata Warawdekar, July 6, 1982; children: Ryan Christopher, Rohan Suneet. BS in Environ. Health, Ind. State U., Terre Haute, 1981, MS in Health & Safety Adminstrn., 1987. Cert. in mgmt. accountability & control, USDA, 2004; registered environm. health specialist Nat. Environ. Health Assn. 1994. Electronic intelligence analyst US Air Force, 1973—77; intern Oakland County Health Dept., Pontiac, Mich., 1979—79, Council Bluffs Health Dept., Iowa, 1980—80; preventive medicine officer US Navy, 1982—95; pub. health advisor Def. Commissary Agy., Fort Lee, Va., 1995—. Dep. dir. pub. health, safety and security Def. Commissary Agy., 1995—2005; agy. rep. Armed Forces Pest Mgmt. Bd., 1995—. Cub scout pack leader Boy Scouts Am., Chester, Va., 1995—2000, boy scout troop leader, 2000—02. Decorated Good Conduct medal US Air Force, Nat. Def. Svc. medal US Navy, Navy Overseas Svc. medal, Navy Achievement award, Navy Commendation medal, Armed Forces Expeditionary medal, Joint Meritorious Unit award; recipient Superior Civilian Svc. award, Dept. Def., 1997. Mem.: Nat. Environ. Health Assn. (licentiate). R-Consevative. Hindu. Avocation: travel. Home: 10707 Hamlin Way Chester VA 23831 Office: Defense Commissary Agy 1300 E Ave Fort Lee VA 23801-1800 Office Phone: 804-734-8448. Office Fax: 804-734-8960. Personal E-mail: cewicker@comcast.net. Business E-mail: christopher.wicker@deca.mil.

**WICKER, NANCY LYNN,** art history educator; b. Shelbyville, Ind. m. Matthew Leigh Murray, May 17, 1991. BA in Art History and Art Studio, Ea. Ill. U., 1975; MA in Art History, U. Minn., 1979, PhD in Ancient Studies, 1990. Adj. instr. Minn. State U., Mankato, 1986, asst. prof., 1990-95, assoc. prof., 1995-2000, prof. Mankato, 2000—02. dir. Scandinavian Studies Program, 2000—02; adminstr. asst. U. Minn., Mpls., 1986-90; prof., chair art dept. U. Miss., University, Miss., 2003—. Editor: Beyond Gender Theory, 1999, Gender and the Archaeology of Death, 2001; contbr. articles to profl. jours. Birka Internat. scholar, 1992; Am.-Scandinavian Found. fellow, 1982, NEH fellow, 2001-02; grantee Am. Coun. Learned Socs., 1990, Am. Numismatic Soc., 1994, Norwegian Ministry Fgn. Affairs, 1996, Norwegian Info. Svc., 1996, Am. Scandinavian Found., 1996, Berit Wallenberg Found., 1997, Am. Philos. Soc., 1997, Internat. Rsch. and Exchs. Bd., 1997, NEH, 2000-2001, Kress Found. grant, 2003. Mem. European Assn. Archaeologists, Internat. Sachsensymposion, Nat. Council Art Adminstrs., Soc. Am. Archaeology, Archaeol. Inst. Am., Medieval Acad. Am., Internat. Ctr. Medieval Art (bd. dirs. 2003-06), Coll. Art Assn., Nat. Coun. Art Adminstrs., Soc. Advancement Scandinavia Study (bd. dirs. 2001-05), Soc. Medieval Feminist Scholarship, Soc. Medieval Archaeology, Soc. Historians Scandinavia (bd. dir. 2005—). Office: Univ Mississippi Art Dept PO Box 1848 University MS 38677 Office Phone: 662-915-7193.

**WICKER, ROGER F.,** congressman, lawyer; b. Pontotoc, Miss., July 5, 1951; s. Fred and Wordna Wicker; m. Gayle Long; 3 children. BA in Polit. Sci. and Journalism, U. Miss., 1973; JD, Ole Miss Law Sch., 1975. Judge adv. USAF, 1976—80; mem. staff rules com. Staff of US Rep. Trent Lott, Miss., 1980-82; pvt. practice, 1982—; pub. defender Lee County, Miss., 1984—87; mem. Miss. State Senate, 1987—94, US Congress from 1st Miss. dist., 1995—, dep. majority whip; mem. House appropriations com., 1995—, House Task Force for a Drug Free America, Rep. Policy Com., 2001—, subcommittee on labor, health and human svcs. and edn., subcommittee on def., subcommittee on energy and water devel., subcommittee on fgn. ops., budget com., 2003—; former chmn. Tenn. Valley Authority Congl. Caucus. Mem. Cmty. Devel. Found., Lions Club, Tupelo First Baptist Church, Miss. With USAF, 1976—80, positions up to lt. col. USAFR, 1980—2004. Recipient Nat. Pub. Svc. award, Am. Heart Assn., 1998, Capitol Dome award, Am. Cancer Soc., 2003, Award, Mfg. Excellence, NAM, 2003. Republican. Office: US House Reps 2455 Rayburn House Bldg Washington DC 20515-2401*

**WICKER, THOMAS CAREY, JR.,** retired judge; b. New Orleans, Aug. 1, 1923; s. Thomas Carey and Mary (Taylor) Wicker; m. Jane Anne Trepanier, Dec. 29, 1995; children: Thomas Carey III, Catherine Anne. BBA, Tulane U., 1944, LLB, 1949, JD, 1969. Bar: La. 1949. Law clk. La. Supreme Ct., New Orleans, 1949—50; asst. U.S. Atty., New Orleans, 1950—53; ptnr. Simon, Wicker & Wiedemann, New Orleans, 1953—67, Wicker, Wiedemann & Fransen, 1967—72; dist. judge Jefferson Parish, La., 1972—85; judge La. Ct. Appeal 5th cir., 1985—98. Mem. faculty Nat. Jud. Coll., 1979—93, Tulane U. Sch. Law, 1978—83. Co-author (with others): Judicial Ethics, 1982, Modern Judicial Ethics, 1992; editor: Tulane Law Rev., 1949. Past bd. visitors Tulane U.; bd. dirs. La. Jud. Coll.; past pres. Sugar Bowl. Lt. (j.g.) USNR, 1944—46. Mem.: ABA (jud. divsn. coun.), La. Dist. Judges Assn. (past. pres.), Am. Judicature Soc., Jefferson Parish Bar Assn., La. Bar Assn. (chmn. jr. bar sect. 1958—59, gov. 1958, ho. of dels. 1960—72), Tulane U. Alumni Assn. (past pres.), Order of Coif, Metairie Country Club, Rotary (pres. 1971—72), Pi Kappa Alpha, Beta Gamma Sigma. Episcopalian. Avocations: golf, photography, military history.

**WICKERT, JONATHAN ADAM,** engineering educator; b. El Paso, Tex. BS, U. Calif.-Berkeley, 1985, MS, 1987, PhD, 1989. Rsch. fellow U. Cambridge, England, 1989—90; prof. mech. engring. Carnegie Mellon U., Pitts., 1990—. Mem. Wickert Consulting Svcs. LLC, Allison Park, Pa., 2003—. Author: (textbook) An Introduction to Mechanical Engineering, (articles) Applied Mechanics Revs., Internat. Jour. Nonlinear Mechanics, Jour. Acoustical Soc. Am., Shock and Vibration Digest, Jour. Vibration and Acoustics, Jour. Manufacturing Sci. and Engring., Jour. Tribology, Jour. Micromechanics and Microengring.; associate editor Jour. Info. Storage Systems. Recipient George Tallman Ladd Rsch. award, Carnegie Mellon U., 1993, Ralph Teetor Ednl. award, Soc. Automotive Engrs., 1996, Marsha and Philip Dowd Faculty Fellowship, Carnegie Mellon U., 1998, Benjamin Teare Ednl. award, 2000, Curtis McGraw Rsch. award, Am. Soc. for Engring. Edn., 2002, Tech. Achievement award, Info. Storage Industry Consortium, 2003, Curriculum Innovation award, ASME, 2005; fellow, NSF/NATO, 1989—90; grantee rsch. in dynamics, applied mechanics, and vibration, NSF, 1991—2006. Fellow: ASME; mem.: AAUP, Soc. Automotive Engrs., Am. Soc. Engring. Edn. Achievements include patents for Damper for Brake Noise Reduction - Brake Drums; Damper for Brake Noise Reduction; research in high-density computer data storage; machine dynamics; manufacture of sheet metal, fiberglass, polymer materials; design of automotive disk brakes. Avocations: long distance running, woodworking. Office: Carnegie Mellon Univ 5000 Forbes Ave Pittsburgh PA 15213

**WICKES, GEORGE,** English literature educator, writer; b. Antwerp, Belgium, Jan. 6, 1923; came to U.S., 1923; s. Francis Cogswell and Germaine (Attout) W.; m. Louise Westling, Nov. 8, 1975; children by previous marriage: Gregory, Geoffrey, Madeleine (dec.), Thomas, Jonathan. BA, U. Toronto, Ont., Can., 1944; MA, Columbia U., 1949; PhD, U. Calif., Berkeley, 1954. Asst. sec. Belgian Am. Ednl. Found., N.Y.C., 1947-49; exec. dir. U.S. Ednl. Found. in Belgium, 1952-54; instr. Duke U., Durham, N.C., 1954-57; from asst. prof. to prof. Harvey Mudd Coll. and Claremont Grad. Sch., Calif., 1957-70; prof. English and comparative lit. U. Oreg., Eugene, 1970—, dir. comparative lit., 1974-77, head English dept., 1976-83. Lectr. USIS, Europe, 1969, Africa, 1978. 79, vis. prof. U. Rouen, France, 1970, U. Tübingen, Germany, 1981, U. Heidelberg, Germany, 1996. Editor: Lawrence Durrell and Henry Miller Correspondence, 1963, Henry Miller, Letters to Emil, 1989, Henry Miller and James Laughlin: Selected Letters, 1995; Author: Henry Miller, 1966, Americans in Paris, 1969, The Amazon of Letters, 1976; translator: The Memoirs of Frederic Mistral, 1986. With U.S. Army, 1943—46. Fulbright lectr. France, 1962-63, 66, 78; sr. fellow Ctr. for Twentieth Century Studies, U. Wis.-Milw., Milwaukee, 1971, Creative Writing fellow Nat. Endowment Arts, 1973, Camargo fellow, 1991. Mem.: PEN. Office: U Oreg English Dept Eugene OR 97403

**WICKESBERG, ALBERT KLUMB,** retired management consultant; b. Neenah, Wis., Apr. 2, 1921; s. Albert Henry and Lydia (Klumb) W.; m. Dorothy Louise Ahrensfeld, Oct. 28, 1944; children— Robert, William, James. BA, Lawrence Coll., 1943; MBA, Stanford U., 1948; PhD, Ohio State U., 1955. Staff accountant S.C. Johnson & Son, Inc., Racine, Wis., 1948-50; asst. prof. Sacramento State Coll., 1950-51; prof. U. Minn., Mpls., 1953-86, prof. emeritus, 1987—, chmn. dept. bus. adminstrn., 1959-62, dir. grad. studies, 1963-66, chmn. dept. mgmt. and transp., 1971-77. Author: Management Organization, 1966. Served with AUS, 1943-46, 51-52. Soc. Advancement Mgmt. fellow, 1972 Mem. Acad. Mgmt., Soc. Advancement Mgmt. (pres. Twin Cities chpt. 1961-62). Congregationalist. Home: 4501 Roanoke Rd Minneapolis MN 55422-5268

**WICKFIELD, ERIC NELSON,** investment company executive; b. Bryn Mawr, Pa., Feb. 14, 1953; s. Paul Gilbert Jacobs and Patricia Ruth (Nelson) Davies; m. Kristine Margaret Erickson, June 21, 1974 (div. 1976); m. Sara Lou Datt, July 23, 1977 (div. 1990); 1 child, Eric N. Jr.; m. Leslie Walsh Willingham, June 8, 1990; 1 child, Douglas N. BS, Rochester Inst. Tech., 1974; MBA, Boston U., 1990. Project mgr. Flight Safety Internat., Wichita, Kans., 1976-82; v.p. Aufleger-Garrett, Stillwater, Okla., 1982-86; demonstration pilot citation div. Gen. Dynamics, Wichita, 1986-87; pres. Prompt Fin. Inc., Concord, Mass., 1987—, bd. dirs.; adj. faculty Boston U. Grad. Sch. Mgmt., 1997—. Co-author: Sustaining High Performance, 1990; author: Management Manual, 1987; author: Financial Users Network User's manual, 1997, Losing Situational awareness, 2001, Communicating the Loss of SA, 2004. Bd. dirs. Groton Ctr. for The Arts. Mem. Internat. Operator's Coun., Aircraft Owner's & Pilot's Assn., Aero Club New Eng. (bd. dirs.). Republican. Methodist. Avocation: skiing. Office: Prompt Fin Inc 30 Monument Sq Concord MA 01742-1858

**WICKHAM, DIANNE,** nursing administrator; b. Dillon, Mont., Feb. 26, 1952; d. William Byron Wickham and Margaret Dewalt (Lovell) Starkweather. ADN, No. Mont. Coll., 1974; BSN, Mont. State U., 1978, MSN, 1980. RN, Mont. Clin. dir. St. Patrick Hosp., Missoula, Mont., 1980-81; asst. prof. Lewis Clark State Coll., Lewiston, Idaho, 1981-83, Mont. State U., Bozeman, Mont., 1983-86; home health nurse West Mont. Home Health, Helena, 1986-87; dir. clin. svcs., 1987-90; critical care nurse St. James Hosp., Butte, Mont., 1986-87; exec. dir. Mont. State Bd. of Nursing, Helena, 1990—. Mem. long term care com. Gov. Task Force on Aging, Helene, Mont., 1993-95, mem. task force to develop. investigator tng. Nat. Com. of State Bds. Nursing, Chgo., 1993—, mem. adj. faculty Mont. State U., Bozeman, 1993—, cons. in field, 1994—. Judge Soroptomists scholarship award, 1993, JC Penneys Golden Rule award, Helena, 1995. Recipient State award for excellence Am. Acad. Nurses Practitioners, 1994.

**WICKHAM, JOHN ADAMS, JR.,** retired army officer; b. Dobbs Ferry, N.Y., June 25, 1928; s. John Adams and Jean Gordon (Koch) W.; m. Ann Lindsley Prior, June 18, 1955; children: Lindsley, John Adams, Matthew. BS, U.S. Mil. Acad., 1950; MA, Harvard U., 1955, M.P.A., 1956; grad., Nat. War Coll., 1967. Commd. 2d lt. U.S. Army, 1950, advanced through grades to gen., 1979; asst. prof. social scis. U.S. Mil. Acad., 1956-60; bn. comdr. 1st Cavalry Div., Republic of Vietnam, 1967; brigade comdr., chief of staff 3d Inf. Div., Fed. Republic of Germany, 1969-70; army mem. chmn.'s staff group Office of Chmn. Joint Chiefs of Staff, Washington, 1970-71; dep. chief of staff for econ. affairs Mil. Assistance Command, Republic of Vietnam, 1971-73; dep. chief, negotiator U.S. del. Four Party Joint Mil. Commn., Republic of Vietnam, 1973; sr. mil. asst. to Sec. Def. Washington, 1973-76; comdr. 101st Airborne Div. (Air Assault), Ft. Campbell, Ky., 1976-78; dir. Joint Staff Orgn. Washington, 1978-79; comdr. in chief UN Command, Republic of Korea-U.S. Combined Forces Command, Korea, 1979-82; vice chief of staff U.S. Army, Washington, 1982-83, chief of staff, 1983-87, ret., 1987; pres., chief exec. officer Armed Forces Communications and Electronics Assn., Fairfax, Va., 1987-92. Bd. dirs. Cooper Instr. for Aerobic Rsch., Xsirius, Inc., Honeywell Fed. Sys., Advanced Photonics, Nortel Inc. Author: Korea on the Brink, 2000. Pres. Sun City Town Coun., 1996—99, Sun City Found., 2001—03; elder St. Andrews Presbyn. Ch., 2001—. Decorated D.S.M. (8), Silver Star (2), Legion of Merit (4), Bronze Star with V device, Air medal (11), Purple Heart, Legion of Honor (France), Order of Mil. Merit (Rep. of Korea), Royal Order of Polar Star (Sweden); recipient Disting. Grad. award West Point, 2006. Mem. Assn. U.S. Army, 101st Airborne Assn., Retired Officers Assn. Home: 13590 N Fawnbrooke Dr Tucson AZ 85737 E-mail: j55wick@comcast.net.

**WICKIEWICZ, JESSICA-LAUREN CHARLOTTE,** academic administrator; b. Greensboro, N.C., Sept. 11, 1976; d. Janice E. Keegan. MA in Psychology, Adelphi U., 2002. Rsch. asst. Derner Inst., Garden City, 2002—03; program dir. Adelphi U., Garden City, NY, 2002—, sr. resident dir., 2003—, coord. Greek life, 2004—. Presenter White Ribbon Campaign, Garden City, 2004—05. Recipient Women's Recognition for Svc. award, Adelphi U., 2003, 2004, 2005. Master: Sigma Delta Tau (assoc.; advisor 2001—05); mem.: Psi Chi (life). Achievements include research in affect of an open adoption on the adoptee. Office: Adelphi Univ 1 South Ave Garden City NY 11530 Office Phone: 516-877-6740, Office Fax: 516-877-3653.

**WICKLEIN, JOHN FREDERICK,** journalist, educator; b. Reading, Pa., July 20, 1924; s. Raymond Roland and Parmilla Catherine (Miller) W.; m. Myra Jane Winchester, July 31, 1948 (dec. 2002); children: Elizabeth, Peter, Joanna. LittB, Rutgers U., 1947; MS in Journalism, Columbia, 1948. Reporter Newark (N.J.) Evening News, 1947-51; news mng. editor Elec. World (McGraw-Hill weekly), N.Y.C., 1951-54; reporter, editor N.Y. Times, 1954-62; news dir. Sta. WNET-TV, N.Y.C., 1962-64; exec. producer news Sta. WABC-TV, N.Y.C., 1964-67; exec. producer Washington Bur. chief Pub. Broadcast Lab. (Nat. Edni. TV), 1967-70; mng. news and pub. affairs broadcasts Sta. WCBS-TV, N.Y.C., 1970-71; gen. mgr. Sta. WRVR, N.Y.C., 1971-74; prof. journalism and broadcasting Boston U., 1974-80; dean Sch. Public Communication Boston U., 1974-78; vis. prof. communication Meth. U., São Paulo, Brazil, 1979; program officer for news and pub. affairs programs Corp. for Pub. Broadcasting, 1980-84; Willard M. Kiplinger chair in pub. affairs reporting, dir. Kiplinger mid-career program for journalists Ohio State U., 1984-89, mem. adv. bd. Kiplinger program, 2004—; Fulbright rsch. scholar Charles Sturt Univ., Bathurst, NSW, Australia, 1990. Lectr., cons. Rutgers U. Media Resources Ctr., Cracow, Poland, 1992, 94; Ayers vis. prof. journalism Jacksonville (Ala.) State U., 1992-93; prodr. news documentaries for pub. and comml. TV; ind. writing, reporting and editing coach for newspapers including Washington Post, Buffalo News, Memphis Comml. Appeal, 1994—; coord. Working Group for Pub. Broadcasting, 1987-89; spl. com. on regulation of media ACLU, 1988-92; adj. faculty Poynter Inst. for Media Studies, 1988; adj. prof. journalism for rsch. Ohio State U., 1991-93; media ethics com. Nat. Coun. Chs., 1975-92; fellow Inst. Dem. Comm. Boston U., 1975-78; newsroom trainers group Poynter Inst., 1995—; lectr., cons. in field. Author: (with Monroe Price) Cable Television: A Guide for Citizen Action, 1972, Electronic Nightmare: The New Communications and Freedom, 1981; editor: Investigative Reporting: The Lessons of Watergate, 1975; contgb. editor The Washington Monthly, 1969-72; contbr. to Am. Journalism Review, The Progressive, TV Quar., Atlantic Monthly, Columbia Journalism Rev., Archeology, Quill, Australian Journalism Rev., others. Recipient George Polk award, 1963, documentary award, Venice Film Festival, 1968, DuPont award, 1973, Brechner Freedom Info. prize, 1987. Mem.: ACLU, Soc. Profl. Journalists, Amnesty Internat. USA, Phi Beta Kappa. Democrat. Home and Office: 7 Riverwoods Dr C116 Exeter NH 03833   Office   Phone:   603-772-4032.   Personal   E-mail: jfwicklein@comcast.net.

**WICKLUND, DAVID WAYNE,** lawyer; b. St. Paul, Aug. 7, 1949; s. Wayne Glenwood and Elna Katherine (Buresh) W.; m. Susan Marie Bubenko, Nov. 17, 1973; children: David Jr., Kurt, Edward. BA cum laude, Williams Coll., 1971; JD cum laude, U. Toledo, 1974. Bar: Ohio 1974. Assoc. Shumaker, Loop & Kendrick, Toledo, 1974-80, ptnr., 1981—. Adj. instr. law, U. Toledo, 1988. Editor-in-chief U. Toledo Law Rev. 1973-74. Mem.: ABA, Toledo Bar Assn., Ohio State Bar Assn. (bd. govts. antitrust sect. 1994—2001), U. Toledo Coll. Law Alumni Assn. (pres. 1999—2000), Inverness Club. Office: Shumaker Loop & Kendrick N Courthouse Sq 1000 Jackson St Toledo OH 43624-1573 Office Phone: 419-321-1213. Business E-Mail: dwicklund@slk-law.com.

**WICKMAN, JOHN EDWARD,** librarian, historian; b. Villa Park, Ill., May 24, 1929; s. John Edward and Elsie (Voss) W.; m. Shirley Jean Swanson, Mar. 17, 1951; children— Lisa Annette, Eric John. AB, Elmhurst Coll., 1953; A.M., Ind. U., 1958, PhD, 1964; LL.D., Lincoln Coll., 1973. Instr. history Hanover (Ind.) Coll., 1959-62, Southeast Campus, Ind. U., Jeffersonville, 1962; asst. prof. history Northwest Mo. State Coll., Maryville, 1962-64; asst. to Gov. William H. Avery of Kans., Topeka, 1964-65; asst. prof. history Regional Campus, Purdue U., Fort Wayne, Ind., 1965-66; dir. Dwight D. Eisenhower Libr., Abilene, Kans., 1966-89; ret., 1989. Contbr. articles on Am. West, archival mgmt., adminstrv. history, oral history to profl. publs. Served with U.S. Army, 1953-55. Nat. Ctr. for Edn. in Politics faculty fellow, 1964-65; Am. Polit. Sci. Assn. Congl. fellow, 1975-76 Mem. Oral History Assn. (v.p. 1971-72, pres. 1972-73), Western History Assn. (coun. 1972-75), Kans. Hist. Soc. (2d v.p. 1974-75, pres. 1976-77, dir.). Home: 411 W 4th St PO Box 325 Enterprise KS 67441-0325

**WICKMAN, LESLIE,** research scientist, science administrator; b. Wash. d. Walter and Joan Wickman. BA, Willamette U., 1980; MS, Stanford U., 1983, PhD, 1994. Cert. tchr. Calif., 1998. Faculty mem., dir. Ctr. Rsch. in Sci. Azusa Pacific U., Calif., 1999—; rsch. scientist The RAND Corp., Santa Monica, Calif., 1999—; mem. faculty AuSable Inst., Grand Rapids, Mich., 2004—;

campus pastor Parkcrest Christian Ch., Long Beach, Calif., 2005—. Cons. Wickman Enterprises, Long Beach, Calif., 1997—; Celebration of Roses guest spkr. Azusa Pacific U., 2003; NSF guest guestr. Whitworth Coll., 2003. Primary author (tech. paper) Lunar Life Support System Study: Metabolic Energy and Water Considerations, Load-Carrying in Reduced Gravities-Operational Considerations, Locomotion while Load-Carrying in Reduced Gravities; author: (tech. paper) Zero-Gravity Induced Osteoporosis, The Effects of Automation on Work in Space, Hubble Space Telescope - Dawn of the Era of Serviceable Spacecraft, Space-Based Servicing, (science article) Mars: Mission Possible?, (doctoral dissertation) The Influence of Reduced Gravity on Human Load-Carrying and Preferred Load Placement; co-author: (book) Absorbing Air Force Fighter Pilots: Parameters, Problems, and Policy Options, (tech. report) Crew Volume Estimating, (rsch. report) Comparing Animal and Robot Capabilities for Military Missions; prodr.: (exhbn.) Space Technology Transfer to Earth Health and Medical Applications; singer: (Christian music CD) Prepare the Way. Volleyball player CBVA, FIVB, Athletes in Action, 1982—2006; football player Calif. Quake Women's Football Team, Long Beach, 2001—06; adv. com. Acad. Evang. Scientists and Ethicists, Madison, Wis., 2005—; rev. panel mem. Jet Propulsion Lab Mars Sci. Lander; vis. faculty mem. Internat. U., Strausbourg, France. Nominee Tech. Adv. Com. US Sec. of Def., Aerospace Industry, 1990; recipient award, AAUW, 1980, Mark O. Hatfield prize in polit. sci., Willamette U., 1980, Space Sta. Program commendations, Lockheed Missiles and Space Co., 1986, Commendations space sta. EVA simulations, McDonnell Douglas Corp., 1986, Lockheed Corp. Astronaut tng. and designation, Lockheed Missiles and Space Co., 1986—96, Commendations Hubble Space Telescope Program, NASA and Lockheed, 1990, Disting. Alumni award, Willamette U., 2000, Transformational Scholarship Champion award, Azusa Pacific U. Provost's Office, 2004; Stanford Honors Coop. Grad. Program scholarship, SRI Internat. and Lockheed, 1981—83, 1988—90, Rsch. grant, NASA and Stanford U., 1990—94, Tchg. Learning Tech. Roundtable grant, Azusa Pacific U., 2001, Rsch. grant, Christian Scholars Found., 2003—06, Azusa Pacific U. Faculty Rsch. Coun., 2004—05, inducted into, Seaside H.S. Hall of Fame, 2003. Mem.: AIAA, Azusa Pacific U. Faculty Rsch. Coun., Human Factors and Ergonomics Soc., Soc. Automotive Engrs. (Arch T. Colwell Merit award 1997), Aerospace Med. Assn. (Presentation award 1995), Cornerstone Soc., Stanford U. Alumni Assn., Sigma Rho Phi. Achievements include Willamette University Pentathlon All-Time Record Holder; member Women's Football World Bowl Championship Team member and Conference All-Star. Avocations: football, volleyball, surfing, skiing, music.

**WICKMAN, PETER M.,** sociologist, educator; b. Sault Ste Marie, Mich., Feb. 23, 1923; s. John Silas and Estelle (MacAdam) W.; m. Helen L. Colborne, Mar. 19, 1949 (div. 1964); 1 child, Stephen B.; m. Winona Moore Marsh, Sept. 1, 1984; 1 child, Matthew L. Marsh. BA in History, Greenville Coll., 1948; MA, Northwestern U., 1949; EdD, Mich. State U., 1960. Instr. soc. sci. John Wesley Coll., Owosso, Mich., 1950-54; asst., assoc. prof. Greenville (Ill.) Coll., 1954-60; asst. prof. U. Fla., Gainesville, 1960-63; assoc. prof. Nassau Comm. Coll., Garden City, N.Y., 1963-67; prof. in soc. and crim. SUNY, 1967-92, emeritus prof. sociology crim. and pub. policy; instr. Coll. Within Prison Walls, Colo., Ariz., 1992-94. Vis. prof. Troy (Ala.) State U., 1961, dir., cons. St. Law Regional, Canton N.Y., 1971-72, evaluation rschr. Assoc. Coll., Potsdam, N.Y., 1974-75, conf. organizer SUNY EEOP, 1969, Internat. White Collar Cr. 1980, rschr. UUP & SUNY Sabbatic, 1983-84; spkr. in field; adj. prof. sociology and criminology, SUNY Oswego and Canton, 1995-98; dir. rsch. Housing of Aging, N.Y., 1971, Regional Cmty. Corrections, Study, LEAA, 1971-72; evaluation field rschr. Kircshner Assocs., Albuquerque, 1973-80; rsch. of prisons reform in Nordic countries, 1974-75; participant in combind Congress of Japanese Soc. Control of Internat. Social Assn., Hiroshima, 1976. Editor: Readings in Soc. Prob's, 1973-76, Soc. Prob's Con' Per's, 1977, co-editor: Readings in Criminology, 1978, White Collar Crime, 1982, Contemporary Perspectives on Social Problems, 1977, others; co-author: Criminology Perspect's, 1980, Perspectives on Crime: Readings in Criminology, 1979; USIA Symposium lectures Am. Justice Sys., Estonia Nat. Pub. Svc. Acad., Nov. 1993; contbr. articles to profl. jours. Mem. bd. dirs. Potsdam Food Co-op, 1977-79, St. Francis Acad., Lake Placid, 1985-92, Reach-Out Crisis Line, Potsdam, N.Y., 1986-89; WWII vet. Mem. Am. Soc. of Criminology. Episcopalian. Avocations: tennis, reading, hiking, mountain climbing, travel. Home: 4 Somerset Dr Potsdam NY 13676-1635

**WICKNER, SUE HENGREN,** biochemist; BS, American U., 1967; MS, Georgetown U., 1970; PhD, Albert Einstein Coll. Med., 1973. Rsch. chemist lab molecular biology Nat. Cancer Inst., NIH, 1977—94, chief molecular biology, lab. molecular biology, 1994—. Recipient Merit award, NIH, 1995; Postdoctoral Rsch. fellow, 1974—76, Staff fellow, 1976—77. Mem.: Nat. Acad. Scis. Office: Nat Cancer Inst NIH Lab Molecular Biology Bldg 37 Rm 2D19 37 Convent Dr MSC 4255 Bethesda MD 20892-4255*

**WICKRAMASINGHE, HEMANTHA KUMAR,** electrical engineer, physicist; b. Colombo, Sri Lanka, May 31, 1949; naturalized U.S. citizen, 1996; s. Percival Herbert and Therese Elizabeth (Soysa) W.; m. Sophie Marie de La Porte, Nov. 17, 1973; children: Lucille Samantha, Anita Elizabeth. BSc in Electronic Engring., U. London, 1970, PhD in Electronic and Elec. Engring., 1974. Assoc. rsch. asst. dept. electronic and elec. engring. U. Coll. London, 1974-75, lectr. dept. electronic and elec. engring., 1978-83; rsch. assoc. E.L. Ginzton Lab. Stanford (Calif.) U., 1975-78; from mgr. phys. measurements T.J. Watson Rsch. Ctr. to fellow IBM, Yorktown Heights, NY, 1984—2000, fellow T.J. Watson Rsch. Ctr., 2000—, sr. mgr. nanoscale and quantum studies Almaden Rsch. Ctr. San Jose, Calif., 2002—03, sr. mgr. nanoscale sci. and tech., 2003—05, chief tech. officer sci. and tech., 2005—. Cons. Hirst Rsch. Ctr. GE Co., London, 1980-83, U.K. Atomic Energy Authority, Harwell, Eng., 1980-82; adj. prof. Poly. Inst. N.Y., Bklyn., 1985-87; mem. editl. bds. Nanotech., 1991-96, Advances in Nanoscale Physics, electonics and Engring., 1991—, Rev. of Sci. Instruments, 1996—. Editor: Scanned Probe Microscopy, 1992; co-editor: Determining Nanoscale Properties of Materials by Microscopy and Spectroscopy, 1994; contbr. over 150 articles to profl. jours.; holder numerous patents in field. Recipient V.K. Zworykin premium, Inst. Elec. Engrs., 1983, Disting. Corp. Inventor award, Nat. Inventors Hall of Fame, 1998, Morris E. Leeds award, IEEE, 1992, Joseph F. Keithley award, Am. Phys. Soc., 2000. Fellow: IBM, Royal Microscopical Soc., Inst. of Physics, IEEE, Am. Phys. Soc. (centennial spkr. 1999); mem.: Nat. Acad. Engring. Achievements include first introduction of vibrating mode atomic force microscopes, atomic force microscopes into manufacturing lines, first deployment of a magnetic force microscope capable of imaging nanometer scale magnetic properties, work in areas of optics, acoustics, photoacoustics, metrology and scanning probe microscopy. Home: 1261 Echo Valley Dr San Jose CA 95120 Office: IBM Almaden Rsch Ctr 650 Harry Rd San Jose CA 95120 Personal E-mail: wickla@sbcglobal.net

**WICKS, DAVID O., JR.,** communications executive; b. Boston, May 17, 1941; s. David O. and Elizabeth L. Wicks; m. Joan Gagnebin, Sept. 7, 1963; children: Perrin, Sara. BA, Trinity Coll., Hartford, Conn., 1963; MBA, U Va., 1968. With nat. divsn. Chem. Bank, 1963—66; specialist in venture capital and cable TV Warburg Paribas Becker, NYC, 1968—83, mng. dir., 1979—83; gen. ptnr. Becker Venture Assoc., Becker Comms. Assoc. II; sr. ptnr. Criterion Venture Ptnr., Houston, 1983—88. Mng. dir. Criterion Investments, Inc., 1983-88; pres. Criterion Investments, Inc., 1985-88; v.p. Cablevision Sys. Corp., Bethpage, NY, 1996-2002; pres. Devonshire Comms. Assocs., cons., 2002-; ptnr. The Alwyn Group, LLC, 2002—; exec. NASA Mid Continent Tech. Transfer Ctr., 1992-95; adj. professor Columbia U., N.Y.C., 2004—; expert witness on cable TV, US Congress and state regulatory bodies. Contbr. articles to profl. jour. Chmn. Cable Positive, Inc., 2003—05; elected pioneer CATV, 2000; bd. dirs. Vis. Nurse Assn. NY, Union Chapel Shelter Island, Friends of Cath. Univ. in Chile. Recipient Vanguard award Nat. Cable TV Assn., 1978. Mem.: Shelter Island Yacht Club, Univ. Club. Office Phone: 516-695-2951. Personal E-mail: dwicksjr@aol.com.

**WICKS, DWIGHT EARL,** elementary school educator; b. Clearwater, Idaho, Aug. 23, 1947; s. Marshall Robert and Edith Vivian Wicks; m. Leann Adele Gehrke, May 18, 1974. BS, Lewis Clark State Coll., Lewiston, Idaho, 1974. Tchr. Prairie Mid. Sch., Cottonwood, Idaho, 1989—. With U.S. Army, 1968—71, Vietnam. Home: 674 Powerline Rd Grangeville ID 83530 Office: Prairie Mid Sch PO Box 158 Cottonwood ID 83522

**WICKS, JOHN R.,** lawyer; b. Ottumwa, Iowa, Dec. 8, 1937; m. Nedra Morgan, Mar. 27, 1964; children: Catherine, John. BSC, U. Iowa, 1959, JD, 1964. Bar: Iowa 1964, Minn. 1966. Assoc. Dorsey & Whitney LLP, Mpls., 1966-71, ptnr. Rochester, Minn., 1972-2000, of counsel Mpls., 2001—. Fellow: Am. Coll. Trusts and Estates Counsel; mem.: Minn. State Bar Assn. (probate and trusts law coun. 1989—92). Office: Dorsey & Whitney LLP 50 S 6th St Minneapolis MN 55402-1498 Office Phone: 612-340-8898. E-mail: wicks.john@dorsey.com.

**WICKS, WILLIAM WITHINGTON,** retired public relations executive; b. Chgo., Dec. 20, 1923; s. William and Alice (Withington) W.; m. Frances M. Horner, Nov. 29, 1947; children: Barbara Anne, Christine Frances. BNS, U. Notre Dame, 1944, AB in Journalism magna cum laude, 1947. Staff corr. United Press Assn., Milw., 1947; pub. rels. mgr. Internat. Harvester Co., Louisville, 1948-58; mgr. field svcs. pub. rels. Std. Oil Co. (Ind.), Chgo., 1959—60; v.p. pub. rels. Griswold-Eshleman Co., Chgo., 1961-68; dir. pub. rels. G. D. Searle & Co., Chgo., 1968-74; from dir. pub. rels./investor rels. to v.p. Kimberly-Clark Corp., Neenah, Wis., 1974—89, v.p. Dallas, 1989-92, asst. to CEO, 1989—92, ret., 1982. Chmn. pub. relations sect. Pharm. Mfrs. Assn., Washington, 1974. Pres. Jr. Achievement Neenah-Menasha, 1978-81; bd. mem. Friends of the Irving Pub. Libr., 1997-99. Served to lt. (j.g.) USNR, 1942-46, PTO. Recipient Silver Anvil award Pub. Rels. Soc. Am., 1963, 79, J. Sinnott Meyer's Burse for Journalism award, U. Notre Dame, 1946-47. Mem. PRSA (founder, pres. Bluegrass chpt. 1957-58), Optimist (pres. South End Club in Louisville 1957), Publicity Club of Chgo. (pres. 1967-68), Las Colinas Sports Club (Irving), USN Meml. Found. (plank owner), Navy League U.S., Patrol Craft Sailors Assn. Republican. Roman Catholic. Home: 1312 Travis Cir S Irving TX 75038-6243

**WICKSTEAD, LAURA STUART,** librarian, archivist; d. John J. Wickstead Jr. and Alexandria Stuart Wickstead. BA, Kenyon Coll., 1979; MLS, Clarion U. PA, 1999. Exec. dir. Crawford County Hist. Soc., Meadville, Pa., 2001—03; libr., archivist Meadville Pub. Libr., Pa., 1999—2001; libr. VA Rm. Roanoke Pub. Librs., Va., 2004—. Scholar Modern Archives Inst., Colonial Dames of Am., 2001. Office: Roanoke Pub Libr 706 South Jefferson St Roanoke VA 24016 Home: 2350 Berkeley Ave Roanoke VA 24016 Office Phone: 540-853-2073.

**WICKSTROM, ERIC,** biophysical chemist, educator; b. Chgo., Dec. 21, 1946; s. Eric Lester and Lillian (Partnoy) W.; m. Lois June Sinsheimer, July 1, 1967; children: Erica Lorraine, Eileen Anitra. BS in Biology with honors, Calif. Inst. Tech., 1968; PhD in Chemistry, U. Calif., Berkeley, 1972. Research assoc. U. Colo., Boulder, 1973-74; asst. prof. U. Denver, 1974-81; sr. research scientist So. Biotech, Tampa, Fla., 1981-82; vis. assoc. prof. U. South Fla., Tampa, 1982-83, asst. prof., 1983-87, assoc. prof., 1987-91, prof., 1991-92, Thomas Jefferson U., Phila., 1992—. Mem. Inst. Biomolecular Sci., Tampa, 1984-92; guest rschr. Nat. Cancer Inst., Bethesda, Md., 1986, Max Planck Inst. Molecular Genetics, Berlin, 1986, Kimmel Cancer Ctr., 1992-. Editor: Prospects for Antisense Nucleic Acid Therapy for Cancer and AIDS, 1991, Clinical Trials of Genetic Therapy with Antisense DNA and DNA Vectors, 1998; mem. editl. bd. Biotech. Healthcare, Bioconj. Chem., Oligonucleotides. Grantee, NSF, 1976—81, Nat. Inst. Gen. Med. Sci., 1976—89, Luekemia Soc. Am., 1986—87, U.S. Army, 1986—88, Nat. Cancer Inst., 1987—, Am. Found. AIDS Rsch., 1989—90, Fla. High Tech. Indsl. Coun., 1988—91, Genta, Inc., 1989, Am. Cancer Soc., 1990—96, Dept. of Energy, 2000—. Mem.: Internat. Soc. Nuclsds, Nucltds and Nucleic Acids, Am. Assn. Cancer Rsch., Am. Soc. Biochem and Molecular Biology, Am. Chem. Soc. Democrat. Jewish. Office: Thomas Jefferson U Dept Biochemistry/Molecular Biol 233 S 10th St Rm 219 Philadelphia PA 19107-5541

**WICKSTROM, JON ALAN,** telecommunications executive, consultant; b. San Antonio, Apr. 17, 1949; s. Stanley Alan and Louise W.; m. Mary Carmen Sparkman, Jan. 25, 1969 (div. Jan. 1978); children: Dana Marie, Jon Alan Jr.; m. Jane Bielbey Slawson, June 19, 1988. BS, Tex. Tech. U., 1975; MS, U. Tex., 1998. Ptnr. Hensley & Assocs., Albuquerque, 1976—78; mgr. dealer svcs. Gulf States Toyota, Houston, 1978—80; mgr. comms. Hughes Tool Co., Houston, 1980—85; mgr. network svcs. Tenneco Oil Co., Houston, 1986—89; mgr. comms. Clarke Am., San Antonio, 1989—94; info/tech. planner USAA, San Antonio, 1994—96; sr. mgr. MMC Ernst & Young LLP, San Antonio, 1996—2000, Cap Gemini Ernst & Young, 2000—02; prin. Comm. Tech. Cons., Houston, 1980—96, 2002—. Author: (reference) 1976 Population Estimates for Bernallio County, New Mex., 1976. Rep. precinct chmn. Bexar County, Tex., 1992-94; cons. Houston Symphony Orch., 1988. Mem. Alamo Area Telecomms. Assn. (bd. dirs 1990-94, pres., 1992-93), S.W. Comms. Assn. (bd. dirs. 1981-85, pres. 1982-84), Tex. Telecomms. Conf. (bd. dirs. 1982-84, chmn. 1983), Am. Mensa. Avocations: sailing, golf, music, investing.

**WICKUS, JAMES D.,** food service executive; m. Judee Wickus; 3 children. BSBA, Spencerian Bus. Coll., 1964. Various positions Baraboo Food Products (now Sysco Food Svcs.), Wis., 1964—78; pres. ops. Sysco Corp., 1978—96, pres., CEO Detroit, 1996—2003, sr. v.p. food svcs. ops. Canton, Mich., 2003—. Office: Sysco Corp 41600 Van Born Rd Canton MI 48188-2797

**WICKWIRE, PATRICIA JOANNE NELLOR,** psychologist, educator; d. William McKinley and Clara Rose (Pautsch) Nellor; m. Robert James Wickwire, Sept. 7, 1957; 1 child, William James. BA cum laude, U. No. Iowa, 1951; MA, U. Iowa, 1959; PhD, U. Tex., Austin, 1971; postgrad., U. So. Calif., UCLA, Calif. State U., Long Beach. Lic. edni. psychologist, marriage and family therapist, Calif. Tchr. Ricketts Ind. Schs., Iowa, 1946-48; tchr., counselor Waverly-Shell Rock Ind. Schs., Iowa, 1951-55; reading cons., head dormitory counselor U. Iowa, Iowa City, 1955-57; tchr., sch. psychologist, adminstr. S. Bay Union H.S. Dist., Redondo Beach, Calif., 1962-82, dir. student svcs. and spl. edn. Cons. mgmt. and edn.; pres. Nellor Wickwire Group, 1981—; mem. exec. bd. Calif. Interagy. Mental Health Coun., 1968-72, Beach Cities Symphony Assn., 1970-82; chmn. Friends of Dominguez Hills, Calif., 1981-85. Contbr. articles in field to profl. jours. Pres. Calif. Women's Caucus, 1993-95, 2003—. Mem. APA, AAUW (exec. bd., chpt. pres. 1962-72), Nat. Career Devel. Assn. (media chair 1992-98), Am. Assn. Career Edn. (pres. 1991—), L.A. County Dirs. Pupil Svcs. (chmn. 1974-79), L.A. County Pers. and Guidance Assn. (pres. 1977-78), Assn. Calif. Sch. Adminstrs. (dir. 1977-81), L.A. County SW Bd. Dist. Adminstrs. for Spl. Edn. (chmn. 1976-81), Calif. Assn. Sch. Psychologists (bd. dirs. 1981-83), Am. Assn. Sch. Adminstrs., Calif. Assn. for Measurement and Evaluation in Guidance (dir. 1981, pres. 1984-85, 98-2000, 04-05), ACA (chmn. Coun. Newsletter Editors 1989-91, mem. on women 1989-92, mem. com. on rsch. and knowledge 1994—, chmn. 1995—, mem. and chmn. bylaws com. 1998-2001, rep. to joint com. on testing practices 2001—), Assn. Measurement and Eval. in Guidance (Western regional editor 1985-87, conv. chair 1986, editor 1987-90, exec. bd. dirs. 1987-91), Calif. Assn. Counseling and Devel. (exec. bd. 1984—, pres. 1988-89, jour. editor 1990—), Nat. Assn. for Ind.-Edn. Coop. (bd. dirs. 2002-05), Internat. Career Assn. Network (chair 1985—), Pi Lambda Theta, Alpha Phi Gamma, Psi Chi, Kappa Delta Pi, Sigma Alpha Iota. Office: The Nellor Wickwire Group 2900 Amby Pl Hermosa Beach CA 90254-2216 Office Phone: 310-376-7378.

**WIDDER, EDITH ANNE,** biologist; b. Boston, June 11, 1951; d. David Vernon and Vera Adela (Ames) Widder; m. David Charles Smith, Feb. 9, 1972. BS magna cum laude in Biology, Tufts U., 1973; MS in Biochemistry, U. Calif., Santa Barbara, 1977, PhD in Neurobiology, 1982. Cert. sci. rsch. pilot for atmospheric diving sys. submersibles 1984. Lab. asst.

phycology U. Mass. Field Sta. Environ. Scis., 1968—69; rsch. assoc. NIH Resource Lab. Electron Probe Microanalysis Harvard U. Med. Sch., Boston, 1973-75; assoc. rschr. ONR bioluminescence prog. U. Calif., Santa Barbara, 1977-83, postdoctoral rsch. biologist, 1983-85, asst. rsch. biologist, co-prin. investigator Marine Sci. Inst. and Neuroscience Rsch. Inst., 1985-89; asst. scientist, prin. investigator Harbor Br. Oceanog. Inst., Ft. Pierce, Fla., 1989-91, assoc. scientist, prin. investigator, 1991—93, acting divsn. dir., 1993—94, sr. scientist, prin. investigator, 1993—2005; prof. biol. scis. Fla. Inst. Tech., 1991—; pres., sr. scientist Ocean Rsch. & Conservation Assn., 2005—. Sci. cons. Dynamics Tech., Inc., LA. 1987—89; disting. scientist adj. Monterey Bay Aquarium Rsch. Inst., 1998—; adj. rsch. prof. earth and planetary scis. dept. Johns Hopkins U., 2000—; affiliate prof. dept. biol. scis. Fla. Atlantic U., 2000—; adj. sr. rsch. scientist Bigelow Lab. Ocean Scis., 2005—. Contbr. articles to profl. jours.; mem. editl. bd.: Marine Tech. Soc. Named Earle C. Anthony fellow, 1978; recipient Women of Discovery award, Sea, Wings WorldQuest, 2006; grantee, NSF, 1986—88, 1990—91, 1991—; MacArthur Fellow, John D. and Catherine T. MacArthur Found., 2006. Mem. AAAS, Am. Soc. Limnology and Oceanography, Am. Soc. Zoologists, Soc. Neuroscience, Soc. Photo-Optical and Instrumentation Engrs., Internat. Soc. Bioluminescence and Chemiluminescence (councilor), Am. Acad. Underwater Scis., Explorers Club. Achievements include patents in field; first to make video recordings of bioluminescence in the ocean, 1985. Office: Ocean Rsch & Conservation Assn 1420 Seaway Dr Fort Pierce FL 34949 E-mail: ewidder@oceanrecon.org.*

**WIDDER, KENNETH JON,** pathologist, educator; b. Chgo., Jan. 14, 1953; s. Alan A. and Edith Widder. BS, Carleton Coll., 1974; MD, Northwestern U., Evanston, Ill., 1979. Intern Duke U., Durham, N.C., 1979-80, resident in pathology, 1980-81; asst. clin. prof. pathology U. Calif., San Diego, 1981-84, assoc. clin. prof., 1984—, cons., chief exec. officer Molecular Biosystems, Inc., San Diego, 1981—. Cons. Eli Lilly & Co., Indpls., 1978-83; mem. adv. com. Congl. Sci. and Tech. Com., Washington, 1986-88. Editor: Methods in Enzymology: Drug and Enzyme Targeting, 1985; patentee in field. Recipient Wiley J. Forbus award N.C. Sco. Pathology, 1981. Mem. AAAS, Am. Soc. Clin. Pathologists, Young Pres. Orgn., Sigma Xi. Office: Santarus Inc 10590 W Ocean Air Dr Ste 200 San Diego CA 92130

**WIDDICOMBE, RICHARD PALMER,** librarian; b. Paterson, N.J., Apr. 12, 1941; s. Robert Lord and Elvira Barbara (Guttilla) W.; m. Martha Elizabeth Bruyn, Feb. 26, 1972 BA, Alfred U., 1963; MS L.S., Syracuse U., 1964. Asst. librarian Yonkers Pub. Library, NY, 1964-65; asst. librarian Cooper Union, N.Y.C., 1965-66, Stevens Inst., Hoboken, NJ, 1966-72, dir. library, 1973—. Trustee Alfred U., NY, The Sagamore Inst., 2006—; trustee, chmn. bd. Hoboken Hist. Mus., 2002—. Episcopalian. Home: 103 Big Moose Lake Eagle Bay NY 13331-9704 Office: SC Williams Libr Stevens Inst Hoboken NJ 07030 Office Phone: 201-216-5421. Business E-Mail: richard.widdicombe@gmail.com.

**WIDEMAN, IDA DEVLIN,** science educator; d. John Cole and Lillie Alma Devlin; m. Leroy Wideman, May 12, 1945; children: Michael Andre, Leroy Maurice. BS, SC State U., 1964—68; MAT, U. of SC, 1976—77. Sci. tchr. West Side H.S., Newark, 1971—73, Hopkins Jr. H.S., Hopkins, SC, 1976—83, St. Andrews Mid. Sch., Columbia, SC, 1983—. Co-dir. NSF grant Ctr. for Sci. Edn., U. S.C.; master tchr. sci. U. S.C., Columbia, Aiken; presenter in field. Mem. Nat. Assn. of U. Women, Columbia, SC, 1990. Named Tchr. of Yr., St. Andrews Middle Sch., state winner, Presdl. Awards for Excellence in Math. and Sci. Tchg. Mem.: Richland County Edn. Assn., SC Edn. Assn., NEA, SC Earth Sci. Teachers Assn. (past pres., v.p. 1988—90), SC Sci. Coun., NSTA, Delta Sigma Theta Sorority (life). United Methodist. Avocations: walking, reading. Home: 446 Koon Store Rd Columbia SC 29203 Office: St Andrews Middle Sch 1231 Bluefield Rd Columbia SC 29210 Office Phone: 803-731-8910. Home Fax: 803-333-0542; Office Fax: 803-731-8913. Personal E-mail: lwideman@sc.rr.com. E-mail: iwideman@richlandone.org.

**WIDEMAN, JOHN EDGAR,** English literature educator, novelist; b. Washington, June 14, 1941; married; 3 children. BA, U. Pa., 1963; BPhil, Oxford U., Eng., 1966; postgrad., U. Iowa Writers Workshop, 1967; DLitt (hon.), U. Pa., 1985, Rutgers U. Mem. faculty U. Wyo., Laramie, prof. English, 1974—85, U. Mass., Amherst, Mass., 1986—2001, disting. prof. English, 2001—; prof. dept African studies Brown U, Providence. USIS lectr. in Ea. Europe. Author: A Glance Away, 1967, Hurry Home, 1969, The Lynchers, 1973, Hiding Place, 1981, Damballah, 1981, Sent for You Yesterday, 1983 (PEN Faulkner award for fiction, 84), Brothers and Keepers, 1984, Reuben, 1987, Fever, 1989, Philadelphia Fire, 1990 (PEN Faulkner award for fiction, 91), The Homewood Books, 1992, The Stories of John Edgar Wideman, 1992, All Stories Are True, 1993, Fatheralong, 1994, The Cattle Killing, 1996, Two Cities, 1998, Hoop Roots, 2001, God's Gym, 2005; co-author (with Mumia Abu-Jamal): Live from Death Row, 1995; author: (short stories) Weight, 2000 (O. Henry award, 2000); contbr. numerous articles and revs. to profl. jours., mags. Recipient Lannan award, 1991; fellow Kent fellow, MacArthur fellow, 1993; grantee, Nat. Endowment for Humanities; scholar Ben Franklin scholar, Rhodes scholar. Mem.: MLA, Am. Acad. Arts Scis., Am. Studies Assn. (mem. coun. 1980—81), Am. Assn. Rhodes Scholars (dir.). Office: Brown U Dept African Studies Providence RI 02912 Home: 383 Grand St New York NY 10002

**WIDENER, CHARLENE,** theater director, educator; d. Richard Widener and Helen Chism; m. Patrick Reading, Oct. 30, 1993. MA, Hutchinson C.C., Kans.; BSc, Master's, Kans. State U., Manhattan. Dir. theatre Hutchinson C.C., Kans., 2002—. Dir.: (theatrical prodn.) Death of A Salesman, Macbeth, How I Learned to Drive, A Moon for the Misbegotten. Bd. mem. Hutchinson Theatre Guild, 2004—. Recipient Horizon award, Phi Theta Kappa, 2004, Paragon Advisor award, 2005. Mem.: NEA (membership chairperson 2000—06), Hutchinson C.C. Faculty Senate (prof. 2000—). Office: Hutchinson Community Coll 1300 N Plum Hutchinson KS 67501 Office Phone: 620-665-3544.

**WIDENER, HIRAM EMORY, JR.,** judge; b. Abingdon, Va., Apr. 30, 1923; s. Hiram Emory and Nita Douglas (Peck) Widener; children: Molly Berentd, Hiram Emory III. Student, Va. Poly. Inst., 1940—41; BS, U.S. Naval Acad., 1944; LLB, Washington and Lee U., 1953, LLD, 1977. Bar: Va. 1951. Pvt. practice, Bristol, Va., 1953—69; judge U.S. Dist. Ct. (we. dist.) Va., Abingdon, 1969—71, chief judge, 1971—72; judge U.S. Ct. of Appeals (4th cir.), Abingdon, 1972—. U.S. commr. Western Dist. Va., 1963—66; mem. Va. Election Laws Study Commn., 1968—69. Chmn. Rep. 9th Dist., Va., 1966—69; state exec. com. Va. Rep. State Ctrl. Com., 1966—69. Lt. (j.g.) USN, 1944—49, lt. USNR, 1951—52. Decorated Bronze Star with combat V. Mem.: Va. State Bar, Va. Bar Assn., Am. Law Inst., Phi Alpha Delta. Republican. Presbyterian. Office: US Courthouse 180 E Main St Rm 123 Abingdon VA 24210-2839 Office Phone: 276-628-3138.*

**WIDENER, MARY LEE,** non-profit financial executive; b. Schaal, Alaska, July 6, 1938; d. Mert and Johnnie (Newton) Thomas; children: Warren Jr., Michael, Stephen. Diploma, Heald Bus. Coll., 1956; Pub. Adminstrn. Program, U. San Francisco Sch. Profl. Studies, 1978; LLD (hon.), John F. Kennedy U., 1979. Adminstrv. asst. to exec. v.p. U. Calif., Berkeley, 1959-69, office mgr. gifts and endowments, 1959-69; urban program coord. Fed. Home Loan Bank Bd., Washington, 1972-73; housing cons. Ford Found., N.Y.C. 1973-74; exec. dir. Oakland Neighborhood Housing Svcs., Oakland, 1973-74; program cons. Urban Reinvestment Task Force, Washington, 1974-76; pres., CEO Neighborhood Housing Svcs. of Am., Inc., Oakland, 1974—. Chmn., Fed. Home Loan Bank, San Francisco, 1994-2003, Social Compact, 2004-06; bd. dirs. The PMI Group, S.H. Cowell Found., The First Am. Corp.; bd. trustees Nat. Housing Conf., 2000—. Author: (with others) Housing America, 1993. Trustee, San Francisco Found., 1988-98, chair, 1996-98; trustee Ptnrs. for Livable Cmtys.; adv. bd. PEW Charitable Trusts Partnership for Civic Change, Phila.; former mem. KQED, San Francisco, United Way Bay Area, Univ. YWCA, BRIDGE Housing Corp., John F. Kennedy U., program adv. coun. Inst. Nonprofit Orgn. Mgmt., U. San Francisco; former state chair Calif.

Dem. Ctrl. Com., San Francisco; former mem. U.S. Senate Housing Task Force, Washington, Commn. on Homelessness, Oakland; former chair affordable housing adv. coun. Fed. Home Loan Bank, San Francisco; former mem. Fannie Mae's Adv. Coun.; former participant Internat. Exch. Housing Profls. Recipient award Nat. Coalition of 100 Black Women, N.Y., 1989, San Francisco LWV Women who could be Pres. award, 1996; named Housing Person of Yr., Nat. Housing Conf., Washington, 2000. Democratic. Methodist. Avocations: tennis, travel, golf. Office: Neighborhood Housing Svc Am 1970 Broadway Fl 4 Oakland CA 94612-2212 Office Phone: 510-287-4201.

**WIDERA, GEORG ERNST OTTO,** mechanical engineering educator, consultant; b. Dortmund, Germany, Feb. 16, 1938; arrived in U.S., 1950; s. Otto and Gertrude (Yzermann) Widera; m. Kristel Kornas, June 21, 1974; children: Erika, Nicholas. BS, U. Wis., 1960, MS, 1962, PhD, 1965. Asst. prof. then prof. dept. materials engring. U. Ill., Chgo., 1965-82, prof. mech. engring., 1982-91, head dept., 1983-91, acting head indsl. sys. engring. dept., 1985-86, dir off-campus engring. programs, 1987-88; prof., chmn. mech. and indsl. engring. dept. Marquette U., Milw., 1991—2002, dir. Ctr. Joining and Mfg. Assembly, 2002—, dir. Discovery Learning Ctr., sr. assoc. dean Coll. Engring., 1999—, interim dean Coll. Engring., 1998—99, 2003. Gastdozent U. Stuttgart, Germany, 1968; vis. prof. U. Wis.-Milw., 1973—74, Marquette U., Milw., 1979—80; cons. Ladish Co., Cudahy, Wis., 1967—76, Howmedica, Inc., Chgo., 1972—75, Sargent & Lundy, 1970—48, Nat. Bur. Stds., 1980, bd. dirs.; cons. Engrs. and Scientists Milw., 1996—98; vis. scientist Argonne Nat. Lab., Ill., 1968. Editor: Procs. Innovations in Structural Engring., 1974, Pressure Vessel Design, 1982; assoc. editor: Pressure Vessel Tech., 1977—81, 2003—, Applied Mechanics Revs., 1987—94, Mfg. Rev., 1991—95, mem. editl. adv. bd.: Acta Mechanica Sinica, 1990—, mem. editl. bd.: Pressure Vessels and Piping Design Technology, 1982, tech. editor: Jour. Pressure Vessel Tech., 1982—93, 2005—; co-editor: SME Handbook of Metalforming, 1985, 1994, Design and Analysis of Plates and Shells, 1986. Fellow Std. Oil Co. Calif., 1961—63, NASA, 1966, von Humboldt, Fed. Republic Germany, 1968—69. Fellow: WRC (chmn. subcom. design procedures for shell intersections 1983—87, chmn. com. reinforced openings and external loads 1987—91, vice chmn. com. polymer pressure components 1991—99, chmn. com. shells and ligaments 1994—97, pressure vessel rsch. coun.), ASCE (sec.-treas. structural divsn. Ill. sect. 1972—73, chmn. divsn. 1976—77, chmn. peer rev. com., tech. coun. rsch. 1984, coun. structural plastics), ASME (chmn. machine design div. Chgo. sect. 1967—68, exec. com. Chgo. sect. 1970—73, editor newsletter Chgo. sect. 1971—73, chmn. jr. awards com. applied mechanics divsn. 1973—76, chmn. design and analysis com. pressure vessel and piping divsn. 1980—83, chmn. pressure vessel rsch. com. 1982—87, bd. editors 1983—93, mem. exec. com. and program chmn. pressure vessel and piping divsn. 1985—89, vice-chmn., sec. pressure vessel and piping divsn. 1989—90, mem. bd. pressure tech. codes and stds. 1989—94, chmn. 1990—91, mem. materials and structures group 1990—91, historian, senate pressure vessel and piping divsn. 1992—93, honors and awards chmn. Milw. sect. 1992—95, mem. coun. engring. 1992—96, v.p., materials and structures group 1993—96, mem. tech. execs. com. 1993—96, bd. editors 2005—, Pressure Vessel and Piping medalist 1995), Wis. Mfg. Curriculum Com. (vice-chmn. exec. com. 1998—2002), 2d China Nat. Stds. Com. Pressure Vessels (hon. cons. 1989—94), Internat. Coun. Pressure Vessel Tech. (chmn. Am. regional com. 1988—, internat. chmn. 1992—96, 2003—06), Am. Soc. Engring. Edn., Soc. Mfg. Engrs. (sr.), French Pressure Vessel Assn.; mem.: Wis. Assn. Rsch. Mgmt. (v.p. 2003—04, pres. 2004—05). Achievements include research in mechanics of composite materials, plate and shell structures, stress analysis, pressure vessels, mechanics of deformation processing. Office: Marquette U Coll Engring PO Box 1881 Milwaukee WI 53201-1881 Office Phone: 414-288-4427. Business E-Mail: geo.widera@marquette.edu.

**WIDGER, CHRIS,** professional baseball player; b. Wilmington, Del., May 21, 1971; m. Theresa Kidwell, Dec. 27, 1996. Student, George Mason U. Catcher Seattle Mariners, 1992—95, Montreal Expos, 1996—. Office: The New York Yankees Yankee Stadium 161st St and River Ave Bronx NY 10451 Address: 95 Fort Mott Rd Pennsville NJ 08070-2839

**WIDING, ERIC P.,** auction specialist; BA in Art History, Williams Coll. Head, american paintings dept. Christie's, NYC, sr. v.p. Contbr. articles to art jours. Mem.: Phi Beta Kappa. Office: Christie's NY 20 Rockefeller Plz New York NY 10020 Office Phone: 212-636-2140. Office Fax: 212-636-4924. Business E-Mail: ewiding@christies.com.

**WIDLUND, OLOF BERTIL,** computer science educator, mathematician; b. Stockholm, Feb. 11, 1938; s. Sten O. and Dagmar W.; m. Nadine H. Taub, June 13, 1972. MS in Engring., Royal Inst. Tech., Stockholm, 1960, PhD, 1964; habilitation, Uppsala U., Sweden, 1966. Asst. prof. NYU, N.Y.C., 1968-72, assoc. prof., 1972-75, prof. computer sci., 1975—, chmn. dept. computer sci., 1980-86. Contbr. articles to profl. jours. and a rsch. monograph. Achievements include research in numerical solutions of partial differential equations. Office: NYU Courant Inst 251 Mercer St New York NY 10012-1110 Business E-Mail: widlund@cims.nyu.edu.

**WIDMAN, GARY LEE,** lawyer; b. Fremont, Nebr., June 1, 1936; s. Benjamin H. and Alice C. (Negley) W.; m. Mary Margaret Donnelly, Mar. 5, 1972(div. 1988); children: Andrew Scott, Natalie Claire. BS, U. Nebr., 1957; JD, Hastings Coll. Law U. Calif., 1962; LLM, U. Mich., 1966. Bar: Calif. 1962, D.C. 1982. Assoc. Thelen, Marrin, Johnson & Bridges, San Francisco, 1962-65; assoc. prof. law U. Denver, 1966-69; prof., dir. resource and environ. law program Hastings Coll. Law U. Calif., San Francisco, 1969-80; gen. counsel Coun. Environ. Quality, Exec. Office Pres., Washington, 1974-76; lectr. U. Calif. at Davis, 1978, Boalt Hall, 1977-79; assoc. solicitor Dept. Interior, Washington, 1980-81; of counsel Fulbright & Jaworski, 1981-85; atty. staff attys. U.S. Ct. of Appeals (9th cir.), San Francisco, 1985-87; atty. Bronson, Bronson & McKinnon, San Francisco, 1988-95, chief counsel State Dept. Parks and Recreation, Sacramento, 1996-99; prof. law Santa Clara (Calif.) U. Law Sch., 1998-99; sr. mediator Concur Inc., Berkeley, Calif., 2001—04. Trustee Rocky Mountain Mineral Law Found., 1969-74, 77-80; apptd. by gov. P. Wilson to Bay-Delta Oversight Coun., 1993-95. Author and project dir.: Legal Study of Oil Shale on Public Lands, 1969. Bd. dir. Sustainable Bus. Inst., Achenbach Graphic Arts Coun., Fine Arts Mus. San Francisco, 2004—. Served with U.S. Army, 1957-59. Mem. ABA (coun. sect. natural resources 1975-77, spl. com. energy law 1977-82, coun. lawyers and scientists 1984-90), Fed. Bar Assn. (chmn. com. natural resources 1977), Calif. Bar Assn., Trout Unltd. Calif. (pres. 1986-90), Calif. Heritage Coun. (pres. 2004-06), Fort Point Presidio and Hist. Assn (v.p 2004-06, 2006-). Home: 28 Marinero Cir Apt 31 Tiburon CA 94920-1644 Office Phone: 415-435-0360. E-mail: gwidman@mindspring.com.

**WIDMAN, PHILLIP C.,** machinery manufacturing executive; Fin. and opers. positions Asea Brown Boveri Ltd., 1987—98, v.p., CFO, supply mgmt., 1997—98; exec. v.p., CFO Philip Svcs. Corp., 1998—2001, ind. cons., 2001—02; sr. v.p., CFO Terex Corp., Westport, Conn., 2002—. Office: Terex Corp 500 Post Rd E Ste 320 Westport CT 06880

**WIDMER, CHAD L.,** marine biologist, researcher; b. Tacoma, Wash., Feb. 25, 1970; s. Clyde D. and Carol L. Widmer. BS, Humboldt State U., 1996, MA, 2000. Cert. asst. SCUBA instr. Nat. Assn. Underwater Instrs., 1996, intermediate mapping GIS Cert. Tng. Course, Calif. State U., 2004, Learning ArcGIS 9 2004. Marine sci. instr. Seacamp, Big Pine Key, Fla., 1994—96, Catalina Island Marine Inst., Two Harbors, Calif., 1997—98; edn. specialist Monterey Bay Aquarium, Monterey, 1999—2001, sr. jellyfish aquarist, rschr., 2001—. Cons. Monterey Bay Jellyfish Supply, Pacific Grove, Calif., 2003—. Contbr. articles to profl. jours. Vol. mentor Student Oceanography Club, Monterey, Calif., 1999—2002. Sgt. Army and Calif. Army N.G., 1988—96, Fort Riley, Kans. and Eureka, Calif. Decorated Top Gun Tank Gunnery Platoon U.S. Army, mem. Honor Platoon; recipient Chpt. Top Teke, Tau Kappa Epsilon, 1993. Mem.: Hydrozoan Soc. (assoc.), Sigma Xi, Theta Epsilon Alumni Assn. (Top Alumnus 2001). Green Party. Achievements include first to culture and describe the entire lifecycle for the cross jellyfish,

Mitrocoma cellularia; on the team responsible for collecting and maintaining the worlds only living great white shark in captivity; on the team that were the first in the world to collect and display the orange spotted comb jellyfish, Leucothea pulchra. Avocations: Harley Davidson motorcycles, scuba diving, surfing, geocaching, hiking. Office: Monterey Bay Aquarium 886 Cannery Row Monterey CA 93940 Office Fax: 831-644-7597. Business E-Mail: cwidmer@mbayaq.org.

**WIDMER, ERIC,** headmaster; BA in History, Williams Coll.; PhD in History and Far Ea. Languages, Harvard U. Tchr. Brown, 1969—94; headmaster Deerfield Acad., Mass., 1994—. Mem. bd. dirs. Am. Secondary Schs. for Internat. Students and Teachers; bd. trustees Am. Community Sch., Beirut. Co-editor: (books) The Transcendent Mirror: A Bicentennial Anthology for Deerfield, Crossings Frontiers: Culture, Language & Bilingualism; co-author: Owned By the Land, Global Education and the Environment, 2001; author: Russian Ecclesiastical Mission in Peking During the 18th Century, Les relations fraternelles des adolescents. Mem.: New England Assn. of Schs. and Colleges (chmn. visiting com.). Office: Deerfield Acad 7 Boyden Lane Deerfield MA 01342

**WIDNALL, SHEILA EVANS,** aeronautical educator, former secretary of the airforce, former university official; b. Tacoma, July 13, 1938; d. Rolland John and Genievieve Alice (Krause) Evans; m. William Soule Widnall, June 11, 1960; children: William, Ann. BS in Aero. and Astronautics, MIT, 1960, MS in Aero. and Astronautics, 1961, DSc, 1964; PhD (hon.), New Eng. Coll., 1975, Lawrence U., 1987, Cedar Crest Coll., 1988, Smith Coll., 1990, Mt. Holyoke Coll., 1991, Ill. Inst. Tech., 1991, Columbia U., 1994, Simmons Coll., 1994, Suffolk U., 1994, Princeton U., 1994. Asst. prof. aeros. and astronautics MIT, Cambridge, 1964-70, assoc. prof., 1970-74, prof., 1974-93, head divsn. fluid mechanics, 1975-79; dir. Fluid Dynamics Rsch. Lab., MIT, Cambridge, 1979-90; chmn. faculty MIT, Cambridge, 1979-80, chair com. on acad. responsibility, 1991-92, assoc. provost, 1992-93; sec. USAF, 1993-97; Inst. prof. MIT, Cambridge, 1997—. Bd. dirs. Gen. Corp., Chemfab Inc., Bennington, Vt., Aerospace Corp., L.A., Draper Labs., Cambridge, Gencorp; past trustee Carnegie Corp., 1984-92, Charles Stark Draper Lab. Inc.; mem. Carnegie Commn. Sci., Tech. and Govt, mem. Columbia Accident Investigation Bd., 2003-. Co-author: Lean Enterprise Value: Insights from MIT's Lean Aerospace Initiative, 2002 (Engring. Sci. Book award Internat. Acad. Astronautics 2003); contbr. articles to profl. jours.; patentee in field; assoc. editor AIAA Jour. Aircraft, 1972-75, Physics of Fluids, 1981-88, Jour. Applied Mechanics, 1983-87; mem. editorial bd. Sci., 1984-86. Bd. visitors USAF Acad., Colorado Springs, Colo., 1978-84, bd. chair, 1980-82; trustee Boston Mus. Sci., 1989-93, Sloan Found., 1998-. Named to Nat. Women's Hall of Fame, 2003; recipient Washburn award, Boston Mus. Sci., 1987. Fellow AAAS (bd. dirs. 1982-89, pres. 1987-88, chmn. 1988-89), AIAA (bd. dirs. 1975-77, Lawrence Sperry award 1972, Durand Lectureship for Pub. Svc. award 1996, pres. 2000-01), Am. Phys. Soc. (exec. com. 1979-82); mem. ASME (Applied Mechs. award 1995, Pres. award 1999), NAE (coun. 1992-93, v.p. 1998—), NAS (panel on sci. responsibility), Am. Acad. Arts and Scis., Soc. Women Engrs. (Outstanding Achievement award 1975), Internat. Acad. Astronautics, Seattle Mountaineers. Office: MIT Bldg 33-411 77 Massachussetts Ave Cambridge MA 02139 Office Phone: 617-253-3595. E-mail: sheila@mit.edu.*

**WIDNER, RALPH RANDOLPH,** retired public administrator; b. Phila., Oct. 21, 1930; s. Ralph Litteer and Viola (Cunningham) W.; m. Joan Sundelius Ziegler, July 9, 1955; children: Jennifer Anne, Wendy Widner Ducharme. BA, Duke U., 1952; postgrad., NYU, 1957, Georgetown U., 1958; DHL (hon.), Union Coll., Ky., 1970, Capital U., Columbus, Ohio, 1971. Journalist Paterson (N.J.) Evening News, 1955-56, N.Y. Times, 1956-58; Congressional fellow Am. Polit. Sci. Assn., 1958; dir. pub. affairs Pa. Dept. Forests and Waters, 1959-60; asst. dir. Pa. Planning Bd., 1960-62; legis. asst. to U.S. Senator Clark, 1962-65; exec. dir. Appalachian Regional Commn., 1965-71; pres. Acad. for contemporary problems, 1971-82; adj. prof. pub. adminstrn. and city planning Ohio State U., 1971-82; pres. Nat. Tng. and Devel. Service for State and Local Govt., 1979-81; staff v.p. Urban Land Inst., 1982-83; exec. dir. Greater Phila. First Corp., 1983-88; chmn. emeritus Fairfax House Internat. Fellow Nat. Acad. Pub. Administrn. (sr.). Democratic. Home: 65 Elm Rd Princeton NJ 08540 Office: PO Box 7517 Alexandria VA 22307-0517 Home: 2210 Belle Haven Rd Alexandria VA 22307-1100 Office Phone: 609-924-9184. Personal E-mail: fxhouse@compuserve.com.

**WIDNER, ROBERTA ANN,** accountant, artist; b. El Paso, Tex., Sept. 27, 1940; d. Wilburn Alton and Frances (Martin) Leavelle; m. Jerry Wesley Widner, Jan. 21, 1959; children: Kim, Mark. Attended, Fechin Inst., 1986. Civil serv. Fed. Govt., 1958, cert. state merit system State of N.Mex, 1958. Stenographer Employment Security Commn. Legal Dept., Albuquerque, 1958, Cannon AFB Comdr.'s Office, Clovis, 1958; sec. to pres. Walker Wholesale Hardware, Jacksonville, 1959; stenographer Household Fin. Corp., San Diego, 1960—61; temp. clk. U.S. Post Office, Clovis, 1974; sec./acctg. Coop. Ext. Svc./Dir. - 4-H - NMSU Rodeo Dept., Las Cruces, 1977. - Sec. N.Mex Employment Security Commn., Albuquerque, 1958; state triticale sec. N.Mex Triticale Assn., Clovis; profl. improvement com. Coop. Ext. Svc., Las Cruces, 1983—84. Oils, pastels, watercolors. Planning com. fashion fund raisers Am. Cancer Soc., Las Cruces, 1991—92; planning com. pan. renaissance fair Dona Ana Arts Coun., Las Cruces, 1985—85; planning com. nat. maid of cotton fashion show Cotton Inc., Las Cruces. Recipient Pres.'s Star Performer award, NMSU, 2002. Mem.: Border Book Festival, Dona Ana Coun., Mesilla Valley Arts Guild (treas. 1985). Achievements include juried Exhibit - El Paso Museum of Art, 1987; juried - Internat. Penwomens' Mex./U.S. Exhibit; juried Art - Cinco Pintores - Linda Lundeen Gallery/Las Cruces; juried - Southern New Mexico Arts Profls., 1990; juried - Rio Grande Arts Invitational, 1998. Avocations: painting, Mexican/European travel, ballooning, sewing, water-skiing. Business E-Mail: rwidner@nmsu.edu.

**WIDOM, BENJAMIN,** chemistry professor; b. Newark, Oct. 13, 1927; s. Morris and Rebecca (Hertz) W.; m. Joanne McCurdy, Dec. 21, 1953; children: Jonathan, Michael, Elisabeth. AB, Columbia U., 1949; PhD, Cornell U., 1953; DSc (hon.), U. Chgo., 1991; Doctor honoris causa, U. Utrecht, 1999. Rsch. assoc. U. N.C., Chapel Hill, 1952-54; instr. chemistry Cornell U., Ithaca, NY, 1954-55, asst. prof., 1955-59, assoc. prof., 1959-63, prof., 1963-83, Goldwin Smith prof., 1983—; van der Waals prof. U. Amsterdam, Netherlands, 1972; vis. prof. Harvard U., Cambridge, Mass., 1975; IBM vis. prof. Oxford (Eng.) U., 1978. Lorentz prof. U. Leiden, The Netherlands, 1985; vis. prof. Kath. U. Leuven, Belgium, 1988, U. Aix Marseille, France, 1995; Kramers/Debye prof. U. Utrecht, 1999. Co-author: (with J.S. Rowlinson) Molecular Theory of Capillarity, 1982; author: Statistical Mechanics, 2002. With U.S. Army, 1946-47. Recipient Clark disting. tchg. award Cornell U., 1973, Dickson prize for sci. Carnegie-Mellon U., 1986, Hirschfelder Prize in Theoretical Chemistry U. Wis., 1991, Bakhuis Roozeboom medal Royal Netherlands Acad. Arts & Scis., 1994, Onsager medal U. Trondheim, Norway, 1994, Boltzmann medal Internat. Union of Pure and Applied Physics, Commn. on Statis. Physics, 1998. Fellow Am. Phys. Soc., Am. Acad. Arts and Scis., N.Y. Acad. Scis. (Boris Pregel award for chem. physics rsch. 1976); mem. NAS, Am. Philos. Soc., Am. Chem. Soc. (Langmuir award in chem. physics 1982, Hildebrand award in theoretical and exptl. chemistry of liquids 1992, Theoretical Chemistry award 1999). Home: 204 The Parkway Ithaca NY 14850-2247 Office: Cornell U Chemistry Dept Ithaca NY 14853 Office Phone: 607-255-3363. Business E-Mail: bw24@cornell.edu.

**WIDOM, HAROLD,** mathematician, educator; b. Newark, Sept. 23, 1932; s. Morris and Rebecca (Hertz) W.; m. Lois Sanow, Mar. 20, 1955 (div. Sept. 1976); children: Barbara, Jennifer, Steven; m. Linda Novick, May 26, 1985. MS, U. Chgo., 1952, PhD, 1955. From instr. to prof. Cornell U., Ithaca, N.Y., 1955-68; prof. U. Calif., Santa Cruz, 1968—. Author: (book) Lectures on Measure and Integration, 1969, Lectures on Integral Equations, 1969; contbr. over 70 articles to scholarly and profl. jours.; mem. editorial bd. Jour. Integral Equations Operator Theory, 1977—, Jour. Asymptotic Analysis, 1988—. NSF postdoctoral fellow, 1959, Alfred P. Sloan Found. fellow, 1961, J.S. Guggenheim Found. fellow, 1967, 72; NSF grantee, 1970—. Fellow: Am. Acad. Arts and Sciences; mem.: Am. Math. Soc. Office: Professor Emeritus Math Dept 353B Baskin Engineering Santa Cruz CA 95064 Office Phone: 831-459-2652. Office Fax: 831-459-3260. E-mail: widom@ucsc.edu.*

**WIDOM, JONATHAN,** biology professor; b. Ithaca, NY, Oct. 25, 1955; BA in Chemistry, Cornell U., 1973—77; PhD in Biochemistry, Stanford U. Sch. Medicine, 1977—82. Rsch. collaborator biology dept. Brookhaven Nat. Lab., 1982—83; Jane Coffin Childs Meml. Fund postdoctoral fellowship Med. Rsch. Coun. Lab. Molecular Biology, Cambridge, England, 1983—85; asst. prof. dept. chemistry U. Ill. Urbana-Champaign, 1985—91, asst. prof. biochemistry, 1985—91, asst. prof. Beckman Inst. Advanced Sci. and Tech., 1989—91, asst. prof. biophysics, 1989—91; assoc. prof. dept. biochemistry, molecular biology and cell biology Northwestern U., 1991—98, assoc. prof. dept. chemistry, 1991—98, prof., 1998—, Coord. prof. biochemistry, molecular biology and cell biology, 2001—. Dir. NIH Molecular Biophysics Tng. Prog., 1992—98; dir. Ctr. Structural Biology Northwestern U., 1994—2000, chmn. dept. biochemistry, molecular biology and cell biology, 1998—2004; vis. prof. Rockefeller U., 2003—04. Contbr. articles to profl. jours.; mem. editl. bd.: Current Opinion in Microbiol., 1998—2001, Gene, 1999—. Recipient Presdl. Young Investigator award, 1988—93. Office: Dept Biochemistry Molecular Biology and Cell Biology Northwestern U 2153 Sheridan Rd Evanston IL 60208-3500 E-mail: j-widom@northwestern.edu.*

**WIDRAN, JERROLD JOSEPH,** urologist; b. Chgo., Dec. 1, 1926; s. Louis Widran and Bess Lanoff; m. Lita June Soible, June 12, 1957; children: Susan, Deborah, Sanford. MD, U. Ill., Chgo., 1950. Diplomate Am. Bd. Urology. Surg. urologist, Ill. Pres. surg. staff Skokie Valley Hosp., 1983—85; pres. Grant Hosp., 1985—88; v.p. staff Our Lady of Resurrection, 2000—01. Contbr. articles to profl. jours. With USN, 1943—46. Fellow: ACS; mem.: Am. Urol. Assn., Chgo. Urol. Soc., Ill. Urol. Soc. Achievements include patents in field. Avocations: tennis, golf, bridge. Home: 939 Mesa Grande Dr Palm Desert CA 92211 Fax: 760-345-5167. Personal E-mail: widranjj@verizon.net.

**WIDYOLAR, SHEILA GAYLE,** dermatologist; b. Vancouver, B.C., Can., June 11, 1939; d. Walter Herbert and Olive Louise (O'Neal) Roberts; Kithi K. Widyolar, 1960 (div. 1979); 1 child, Keith. BS, Loma Linda U., 1962; MD, Howard U., 1972. Resident U. Calif., Irvine, 1973-76; dermatologist pvt. practice, Laguna Hills, Calif., 1976—. Clin. instr. U. Calif. Sch. Medicine, 1978—86. Chmn. bd. dirs. Opera Pacific, Costa Mesa, Calif., 1996-97. Fellow Am. Acad. Dermatology, Am. Soc. Dermatopathology; mem. AMA, Calif. Med. Assn., Dermatol. Soc. Orange County (pres. 1983), Alpha Omega Alpha. Avocations: music, travel. Office: Ste 403 23911 Calle de Mag Dalena Laguna Hills CA 92653 Office Phone: 949-452-3814.

**WIE, MICHELLE SUNG,** professional golfer; b. Honolulu, Oct. 11, 1989; d. Byung-Wook and Hyun-Kyong Sung Wie. Played in major LPGA Tournaments US Women's Open, 2003, Kraft Nabisco Championship, 2003, 2004; winner Jennie K. Wilson Invitational, 2001, Hawaii State Women's Stroke Play Championship, 2001, USGA Women's Amateur Pub. Links Championship, 2003; profl. golfer, 2005—. Named one of 100 Most Influential People, Time Mag., 2006. Mem.: Hawaii State Jr. Golf Assn. Achievements include youngest player to win Hawaii State Women's Stroke Play Championship, Jennie K. Wilson Internat., and US Amateur Pub. Links Championship; youngest player to make an LPGA cut, playing in the Kraft Nabisco Championship; youngest player to ever compete and win the Curtis Cup, 2004. Avocations: reading, drawing, computers. Office: c/o LPGA 100 Internat Golf Dr Daytona Beach FL 32124-1092*

**WIEBE, LEONARD IRVING,** pharmacist, educator; b. Swift Current, Sask., Can., Oct. 14, 1941; s. Cornelius C. and Margaret (Teichroeb) W.; m. Grace E. McIntyre, Sept. 5, 1964; children: Glenis, Kirsten, Megan BSP, U. Sask., 1963, MS, 1966; PhD, U. Sydney, Australia, 1970, DSc, 2002; D.Pharm.Sci (hon.), Meiji Pharm. U., Japan, 2002; D.Pharm.Sci, Health Sci. U. Hokkaido, 2003. Pharmacist Swift Current Union Hosp., 1963-64; sessional lectr. U. Sask., Can., 1965-66; asst. prof. U. Alta., Can., 1970-73, assoc. prof., 1973-78, prof., 1978—, dir. Slowpoke Reactor Facility, 1975—89, 2001—02, asst. dean rsch. Can., 1984-87, assoc. dean, 1990-99; prof. dept. exptl. oncology, 1999—; sessional lectr. U. Sydney, Australia, 1973; pres. Internat. Biouncleonics Cons. Lts., 1991—, BioCyDex Inc., 2003—. Rsch. assoc. Cross Cancer Inst., Edmonton, 1978—, Med. Rsch. Coun. Can.; vis. prof. Royal P.A. Hosp., Sydney 1983-84, Searle vis. profl., 1986; MRC vis. prof., Toronto, 1987; PMAC vis. prof., 1988; McCalla prof. U. Alta, 1993-94; radiopharmacy cons. Australian Atomic Energy Commn., Sydney, 1983-84; mem. MRC standing com. on sci. and tech., 1995-98; cons. IAEA, 2001, 03; hon. liason prof. Peoples U. Bangladesh. Editor: Liquid Scintillation: Science and Technology, 1976, Advances in Scintillation Counting, 1983; guest editor Jour. of Radioanalytical Chemistry, 1981; editor Internat. Jour. Applied Radiation Instrumentation Sect. A, 1988-90; regional editor Internat. Jour. Nuclear Biology and Medicine, 1992-95; mem. editl. bd. Jour. Pharmacy & Pharm. Sci., Jour. Applied Radiation Isotopes, 1995—. Recipient Janssen-Ortho Rsch. award, 1998, McNeil award, 1988; Commonwealth Univs. Exchange grantee, 1966; Alexander von Humboldt fellow, 1976-79, 82. Mem. Pharm. Bd. of New South Wales, Sask. Pharm. Assn., Soc. Nuclear Medicine, Assn. Faculties of Pharmacy of Can. (McNeil Rsch. award 1988), Can. Radiation Protection Assn., Can. Assn. Radiopharm. Scientists, Am. Pharm. Assn., Am. Assn. Pharm. Sci., Internat. Assn. Radiopharmacy (exec. sec. 1991-95), Can. Assn. Pharm. Scis. (founding), Univ. Club (Edmonton) (pres. 1985). Mem. Mennonite Ch.

**WIEBE-BROWN, BEVERLY,** music educator; b. York, Nebr., Aug. 29, 1949; d. Klaus H. Friesen and Bertha E. Mierau Friesen; m. William A. Brown, Aug. 7, 1999; children: Heath Wiebe, Erin Wiebe Woods, Stephen Brown, Kara Wiebe Nedich, Bryce Wiebe. BA in Sacred Music, Grace U., Omaha, 1971; BS in Music Edn., Okla. Panhandle State U., Goodwell, 1990; MFA in Music Edn., U. Nebr., Kearney, 1999. Organist Trinity Presbyn. Ch., Perryton, Tex., 1987—94; music dir. Frist Christian Ch., Perryton, 1988—94; choral aide, accompanist Perryton Ind. Sch. Dist., 1990—92, middle sch. choral dir., 1992—94; K-12 music educator Centura Pub. Sch., Cairo, Nebr., 1994—. Attendee Voice Care Network, Collegeville, Minn., 2001—05. Mem.: ACDA, NCDA, MENC, NMEA, Alpha Delta Kappa (corr. sec. 2004—06). Home: 208 S Suez PO Box 595 Cairo NE 68824-0595

**WIEBENSON, DORA LOUISE,** architectural historian, editor, writer; b. Cleve., July 29, 1926; d. Edward Ralph and Jeannette (Rodier) W. BA, Vassar Coll., 1946; MArch, Harvard U., 1951; MA, NYU, 1958, PhD, 1964. Architect, N.Y., 1951-66; lectr. Columbia U., 1966-68; assoc. prof. U. Md., 1968-72, prof., 1972-77; vis. prof. Cornell U., 1974; prof. U. Va., Charlottesville, 1977-92, prof. emeritus 1992—, chmn. div. archtl. history, 1977-79, assoc. fellow U. Va. Ctr. Advanced Studies, 1982-83; pres. Archtl. Publs., N.Y.C., 1982—; editor-in-chief Centropa, 2000—. Editor: Marsyas XI 1962-64, 1965, Essays in Honor of Walter Friedlaender, 1965; Architectural Theory and Practice from Alberti to Ledoux, 1982, rev., 1983, Spanish transl., 1988; Guide to Graduate Degree Programs in Architectural History, 1982, rev., 1984, 86, 88, 90; co-editor: The Architecture of Historic Hungary, 1998, Hungarian transl., 1998; author: Sources of Greek Revival Architecture, 1969, Tony Garnier: The Cité Industrielle, 1969, Japanese transl., 1983, The Picturesque Garden in France, 1978, Mark J. Millard Architectural Collection, Vol. I: French Books: Sixteenth through Nineteenth Centuries, 1993; contbr. articles to profl. jours. Student fellow Inst. Fine Arts, 1961-62, 62-63; grantee Am. Philos. Soc., 1964-65, 70, Samuel H. Kress Found., 1966, 72-73, 98, Gen. Rsch. Fund, U. Md., 1969, 74, 76, NEH, 1972-73, Am. Coun. Learned Socs., 1976, 81, 85, Ctr. Advanced Studies, U. Va., 1980, 81, 97, Graham Found. Advanced Studies Fine Arts, 1982, 93, Archtl. History Found., 1996; fellow Yale Ctr. Brit. Art, 1983; sr. rsch. fellow NEH, 1986-87. Mem. Soc. Archtl. Historians (bd. dirs. 1974-77, 80-83, chair edn. com. 1976-90), Coll. Art Assn., Am. Assn. Advancement Slavic Studies, Am. Soc. Eighteenth Century (mem. exec. bd. 1991-94). Business E-Mail: centropa@rcn.com.

**WIEBERG, KAREY ROSE,** music educator, director; b. Jefferson City, Md., July 12, 1979; d. Larry William and Peggy Anne Wieberg; 1 child, Kaylin Berendzen. BS in Music Edn., S.W. Mo. State U., Springfield, Mo., 2002. Dir. choir Webster Groves Sch. Dist., St. Louis, 2003—04, Francis Howell Sch. Dist., St. Charles, Mo., 2004—. Singer: St. Louis (Mo.) Chamber Choir, 2003—. Nominee Dist. Tchr. of Month, Francis Howell H.S., 2005. Mem.: Music Educators Nat. Conf., Am. Choral Dirs. Assn. Avocations: swimming, reading, movies. Office: Francis Howell High Sch 7001 Hwy 94 South Saint Charles MO 63304

**WIEBERS, DAVID OWEN,** physician; b. Mar. 26, 1951; MD, U. Nebr., 1975. Diplomate Am. Bd. Psychiatry and Neurology. Intern in medicine U. Minn., Mpls., 1975-76; resident in neurology Mayo Clinic, Rochester, Minn., 1976-80, chair divsn. cerebrovasc. diseases, 1994—2002, head sect. neurology, 1987-96, dir. Mayo Stroke Ctr., 1994—; prof. neurology Mayo Med. Sch., Rochester, Minn., 1991—. Vis. prof. more than 70 acad. med. ctrs. Author: 6 books, 4 med. textbooks; co-author: 1 med. textbook; contbr. more than 330 articles to profl. jours. Chair, bd. dirs. Humane Soc. U.S., Washington, 1999—, Human Soc. Internat. (bd. dirs. 1994—), Earth Voice Internat. (bd. dirs. 1995—). Recipient 19 internat. and 51 U.S. awards for sci. and med. achievement. Mem.: Humane Soc. US Leg. Fund (chair bd. dirs. 1999), World Soc. Protection of Animals (bd. dirs. 1997—, London). Office: Mayo Clinic Dept Neurology 200 1st St SW Rochester MN 55905-0002 Office Phone: 501-284-9735. Business E-Mail: wiebers.david@mayo.edu.

**WIECHA, JOSEPH AUGUSTINE,** language educator; b. Chorzów II, Poland, Sept. 20, 1926; came to U.S., 1955, naturalized, 1958; s. Karol and Gertruda (Rudzki) W.; m. Mary Ruth Moore, 1953; children: Joseph Damian, Charles Francis, John Moore. BA with honors, Nat. U. Ireland, 1950; PhD with distinction, NYU, 1963. Instr. fgn. langs. U.S. Third Air Force, London, 1951-55; instr. German and Spanish U. Md., London, 1951-55; tchr. Spanish and math. Bklyn. Friends Sch., 1955-56; instr. German NYU, N.Y.C., summer, 1958; lectr. German and humanities Harvard U., Boston, 1959-63; lectr. German lit. Colby Coll., summer 1963; prof. German SUNY, Oswego, 1963-69, chmn. dept. fgn. langs. and lit., 1963-69, chmn. dept. Germanic and Slavic langs. and lit., 1969-72, disting. teaching prof., 1973-92, disting. tchg. prof. emeritus, 1992—; chmn. SUNY Fgn. Studies Ctr., 1972-73. Lectr. and cons. methodology of tchg. fgn. langs., 1959—; condr. seminars tchg. methodology fgn. langs. Nat. U. Pedro Enriquez Ureña, Santo Domingo, 1973, U. Pisa, Italy, 1974, Moscow State Pedagogical Inst.; Fgn. Langs., USSR, 1976; vis. prof. U. Wroctaw, Poland, 1977. Developed Wiecha Progressive-Reflex method of teaching fgn. langs. Served as officer 2d Polish Corps Brit. VIII Army, 1944-47. Decorated Bronze medal Polish Army, Brit. Def. medal; French Star; Star of Italy; recipient diploma of apit. recognition U. Nat. Pedro Enriquez Ureña, 1973; Galileo medal U. Pisa, 1974; Ogden Butler fellow, 1958-59, Fels fellow, 1956-59, Kosciuszko Found. fellow, 1959. Mem. MLA, N.Y. State Assn. Fgn. Lang. Tchrs. (dir. 1975-78, Disting. Tchr. award 1975, Disting. Bd. Dirs. award 1978, Spl. Contbn. to Teaching Fgn. Langs. award 1979), Am. Assn. Tchrs. of German, Polish Inst. Arts and Scis. in Am., Nat. Spanish Honors Soc. (hon.), Am. Coun. on Edn. (nat. honor roll), Delta Phi Alpha (hon.), Dobro Slovo (hon.). Home: 710 Copa De Oro Marathon FL 33050-5406 also: 22 Bayside Rd Northport ME 04849-4435 E-mail: josephmaryWiecha@bellsouth.net.

**WIECHERT, ALLEN LEROY,** educational association administrator; b. Independence, Kans., Oct. 25, 1938; s. Norman Henry and Serena Johanna (Steinke) W.; m. Sandra Swanson, Aug. 19, 1961; children: Kristin Nan, Brendan Swanson, Megan Ann. BArch, Kans. State U., 1962. Lic. Lic. arch., Kans., cert. Nat. Coun. Archtl. Registration Bds. Arch. in tng. McVey, Peddie, Schmidt & Allen, Wichita, Kans., 1962-63; arch. Kivett & Myers, Kansas City, Mo., 1963-68; asst. to vice chancellor plant planning and devel. U. Kans., Lawrence, 1968-74, assoc. dir. facilities planning, 1974-78, univ. dir. facilities planning, 1978-92, univ. arch., 1993-95; campus planner Gould Evans Assocs., Lawrence, 1995-96; code enforcement officer City of Prairie Village, Kans., 1997-2001; ret.; project mgr. subs. corp. Kans. Bd. Regents, 2003—04; architect Kans. State Hist. Preservation Office, 2004—05; long range physical planning cons., 2005—. Mem. long range phys. planning com. Kans. Bd. Regents, 1971-95; designer, archtl. programmer ednl. facilities; bd. dirs. Kans. U. Fed. Credit Union, 1972-81, pres. bd., 1974. Editor, contbr.: Physical Development Planning Work Book, 1973. Chmn. horizons com. Lawrence Bicentennial Commn.; designer Kaw River Trail, 1976; mem. Action 80 Com., 1980-81, Lawrence-Douglas County Horizon 2020 Task Group, 1993-95; mem. standing com. Kans. Episcopal Diocese, 1976-80, pres. com., 1981, mem. diocesan coun., 1982-84, chmn. coll. work com., 1982-84, commn. on ch. arch. and allied arts, 1986-99, long range planning com., 1988; sr. warden Trinity Episc. Ch., Lawrence, 1977-80, 2001-02, mem. vestry, 1997-99; trustee Kans. Sch. Religion, 1973-80, 82-95, v.p., 1984-85, pres., 1986-92, trustee friends of the dept. of religious studies, 1995-2005; mem. adv. bd. Salvation Army, 1990-2005; bd. dirs. Trinity Group Care Home, 1973-79; advancement chmn. troop com. Boy Scouts Am., 1981-87, dist. com. Pelathe dist., 1984—, vice chmn., 1985-87; exec. bd. Heart of Am. Coun., 1985-87. 1st lt. Kans. Air N.G., 1961-67. Recipient Dist. Award of Merit, Boy Scouts Am., 1988, Silver Beaver award, 1991, Follow Me Boys award, 2002. Mem. AIA, Assn. Univ. Archs. (sec.-treas. 1986-87, v.p. 1987-88, pres. 1988-89), Nat. Hist. Trust, Kans. U. Endowment Assn. (sec. 1981-85, founder, exec. bd. Hist. Mt. Oread Fund divsn.), Nat. Cathedral Assn. (regional co-chairperson 1993-2005). Home: 813 Highland Dr Lawrence KS 66044-2431

**WIECHERT, BARBARA THERESA,** school nurse practitioner; d. Dominick Michael and Lillian Kolar Marino; m. Paul Joseph Wiechert, July 1, 1972; children: Paul Joseph Jr., Sarah Anne. BSN, Loyola U., 1972; MEd, Govs. State U., 2003. Cert. vision technician, Ill., 1987, audiometric technician, Ill., 1987, type 73, Ill., 1990. Staff nurse Palos Cmty. Hosp., Palos Heights, Ill., 1976—80; staff nurse Med. Ctr. Loyola U., Maywood, Ill., 1980—85; staff nurse outpatient Mulchay Outpatient Ctr., Maywood, 1985—87; sch. nurse Aero Spl. Edn. Coop., Burbank, Ill., 1987—94, Ridgeland dist. 122, Oaklawn, Ill., 1994—. Supr. sch. nurse interns Nat. Coll. Edn., Evanston, Ill., 1989, 1997—98; involved with nat. incentive Every Child Needs a Sch. Nurse Am. Fedn. Tchrs., DC, 2003—. Exhibitions include Loyola U. Art Show, 1972 (Hon. Mention award, 72). Asst. leader Girl Scouts Am., Chgo., 1992—96. Grantee, Ill., 1988—90. Mem.: PTA (various coms. 1994—), Am. Fedn. Tchrs., Ill. Assn. Sch. Nurses, Nat. Assn. Sch. Nurses. Avocations: travel, ceramics, reading, music, walking. Office: Ridgelan Pub Schs 6500 W 95th St Oak Lawn IL 60453

**WIECHMANN, ERIC WATT,** lawyer; b. Schenectady, NY, June 12, 1948; s. Richard Jerdone and Ann (Watt) W.; m. Merrill Metzger, May 22, 1971. BA, Hamilton Coll., 1970; JD, Cornell U., 1974. Bar: Conn. 1975, U.S. Dist. Ct. (so. and ea. dists.) N.Y. 1975, U.S. Dist. Ct. Conn. 1975, U.S. Dist. Ct. D.C. 1981, U.S. Ct. Appeals (2nd cir.) 1975, U.S. Ct. Appeals (9th cir.) 1980, U.S. Ct. Appeals D.C. 1982, U.S. Ct. Appeals (5th cir.) 1986, U.S. Ct. Appeals (10th cir.) 1989, U.S. Supreme Ct. 1978. Assoc. Cummings & Lockwood LLC, Stamford, Conn., 1974—82, ptnr., 1982—2003, mng. ptnr. Hartford office, bd. dirs., 1996—2003, bus. clients exec. com., 2003; ptnr. McCarter & English LLP, Hartford, Conn., 2003—, mng. ptnr., Hartford office, 2003—04. mem. exec. com., 2003—, mem. compensation com., 2003—. Spl. pretrial master U.S. Dist. Ct. Conn., 1984—; state atty. trial referee, 1986—, mem. evidence code oversight com., 2002—; civil task force, 1995—, civil jury instrn. com. Conn. Superior Ct., 1996-2000, docket control com., 2001—; comml. arbitrator Am. Arbitration Assn. Contbr. articles to profl. jours. Mem. Zoning Bd. Appeals, New Canaan, Conn., 1984-85; bd. dirs. Conn. Rivers coun. Boy Scouts Am., trustee; bd. dirs. Internat. Assn. Def. Counsel Found., pres., 2005—. Mem. ABA (vice-chmn. toxics and hazardous law com. TIPS sect.), Def. Rsch. Inst., Internat. Assn. Def. Counsel (faculty Def. Trial Acad. 1996, chmn. toxic and hazardous substance com. 1998-99, chmn. CLE bd. 2000-02), Internat. Soc. Barristers, Conn. Bar Assn. (exec. com. antitrust sect.) 1982—, ct. rules adv. com, chmn. 1991-93), Conn. Bar Found., Golf Club

Avon. Republican. Episcopalian. Home: 10 Langley Park Farmington CT 06032-1541 Office Phone: 860-275-6731. Personal E-mail: ewiech@yahoo.com. Business E-Mail: ewiechmann@mccarter.com.

**WIECZOREK, DENNIS E.,** lawyer; b. June 4, 1952; AB magna cum laude, Washington Univ., St. Louis, 1974; JD, Duke Univ., 1977. Bar: Ill. 1977, US Dist. Ct. (no. dist.) Ill. Ptnr., co-chair Franchise & Distribution practice group DLA Piper Rudnick Gray Cary, Chgo. Lectr.; contbr. articles to profl. jours.; co-author: Annual Franchise & Distribution Law Delelopments, 2002, Franchising: A Planning & Sales Compliance Guide; author (contributing): Fundamentals of Franchising. Mem.: ABA, Chgo. Bar Assn., Ill. Bar Assn. Office: DLA Piper Rudnick Gray Cary Ste 1900 203 N LaSalle St Chicago IL 60601-1293 Office Phone: 312-368-4087. Office Fax: 312-236-7516. Business E-Mail: dennis.wieczorek@dlapiper.com.

**WIECZOREK, JOHN RICHARD,** application developer, systems analyst; b. River Falls, Wis., Mar. 8, 1963; s. John Richard Vichorek and Sara Ellen Wieczorek; life ptnr. Eileen Anne Lacey. AB in Physics, Cornell U., 1984. Programmer, analyst Mus. of Vertebrate Zoology, U. Calif., Berkeley, 1997—. Mem. sci. subcom. data access and database interoperability Global Biodiversity Info. Facility, Copenhagen, 2004—; co-convenor of geospatial info. subgroup Taxonomic Databases Working Group, 2004—. Co-developer (distributed database protocol) Distributed Generic Information Retrieval. Recipient Ebbe Nielsen prize, Global Biodiversity Info. Facility, 2006. Avocations: volleyball, travel. Office: U Calif Mus Vertebrate Zoology 3101 VLSB Berkeley CA 94720 Office Phone: 510-642-5409. Office Fax: 510-643-8238. E-mail: tuco@berkeley.edu.

**WIED, GEORGE LUDWIG,** physician; b. Carlsbad, Czechoslovakia, Feb. 7, 1921; came to U.S., 1953, naturalized, 1960; s. Ernst George and Anna (Travnicek) W.; m. Kayoko Y. Yamauchi, 1980; 1 child, George. MD, Charles U., Prague, 1945, Hon. Med. Degree, 1995. Intern County Hosp., Carlsbad, Czechoslovakia, 1945; intern U. Chgo. Hosps., 1955; resident in ob-gyn U. Munich, Fed. Republic Germany, 1946-48; practice medicine specializing in ob-gyn West Berlin, 1948-53; asst. ob-gyn Free U., West Berlin, 1948-52; assoc. chmn. dept. ob-gyn Moabit Hosp., Free U., West Berlin, 1953; asst. prof., dir. cytology U. Chgo., 1954-59, assoc. prof., 1959-65, prof., 1965-91, mem. bd. adult edn., 1964-68, prof. pathology, 1967-91, Blum-Riese prof. ob-gyn, 1968-91, acting chmn. dept. ob-gyn, 1974-75. Editor-in-chief Jour. Reproductive Medicine, Acta Cytologica, Analytical and Quantitative Cytology, Clinical Cytology; editor: Introduction to Quantitative Cytochemistry, Automated Cell Identification and Cell Sorting, Compendium on Clinical Cytology, Compendium on the Computerized Cytology and Histology Laboratory, Compendium on Quality Assurance in Clinical Cytology; sr. editor Gen. and Diagnostic Pathology. Hon. dir. Chgo. Cancer Prevention Ctr., 1959-83; chmn. jury Maurice Goldblatt Cytology award, 1963-92. Recipient Cert. of Merit, U.S. Surgeon Gen., 1952, Maurice Goldblatt Cytology award, 1961, George N. Papanicolaou Cytology award, 1970, Masubuchi Gold Medal award 13th Internat. Cytology Congress, 1998, Kazumsa Masubuchi Lifetime Achievement award, 1998. Mem. Am. Soc. Cytology (pres. 1965-66), Mex. Soc. Cytology (hon.), Spanish Soc. Cytology (hon.), Brazilian Soc. Cytology (fgn. corr.), Indian Acad. Cytology (hon., Lifetime Achievement award 1998), Latin-Am. Soc. Cytology (hon.), Japanese Soc. Cytology (hon.), Internat. Acad. Cytology (pres. 1977-80), German Soc. Cytology (hon.), Ctrl. Soc. Clin. Rsch., Chgo. Path. Soc., Chgo. Gynecol. Soc. (hon.), Am. Soc. Cell Biology, German Soc. Ob-Gyn, Bavarian Soc. Ob-Gyn, German Soc. Endocrinology, Russian Assn. Cytologists (hon.), Swedish Soc. Medicine (hon.), Austrian Soc. Clin. Cytology (hon.), Sigma Xi. Home and Office: 1640 E 50th St Chicago IL 60615-3161 E-mail: wied@cytology.

**WIEDEMANN, CHARLES LOUIS,** dentist; b. Belvidere, NJ, May 6, 1936; s. Charles and Clothilde Paulina (Fischer) W.; m. Jacqueline Burdzy, June 11, 1960; children: Lorraine Carol, Julie Patricia. BA in Biol. Sci., Rutgers U., 1957; DDS with honors, Fairleigh Dickinson U., 1962; grad., U.S. Army Med. Field Svc. Sch., 1962; postgrad. student, Inst. for Grad. Dentists, 1968-69, St. Clare's Hosp. Continuing Edn., N.J., 1972—; U. Pa., 1974-75, Boston U. Sch. Grad. Dentistry, 1977. Pvt. practice dentistry, Hackettstown, N.J., 1966—. Founder dental sect. staff dept. surgery Hackettstown Regional Med. Ctr., chief dentistry, 1973-75, 77-78, chief of staff dental sect. dept. surgery, 1974, 80, 85; dental health dir. Clarence W. Sickles Med. Ctr., Hackettstown, 1970-90; co-dir. Stargazer, Bd. of Ed. Online Mag. telecomm. sys., 1985-86; pres. Rexxcom Sys. Electronic Pub. and Computer Software, Co., 1990—; lectr. in field. Author: The Now Philosophy for Dentistry, 1972, Fantastic Facts About Dental Health, 1975, (computer software) The Format Machine, 1987, Autofont, 1990, The Magic Font Machine (Magifont, Magivue, Magishow), 1990, News 1, 1991, Digipad, 1993, The Autofont Titler, 1994; co-author: Autodoc, 1990, rev. edit., 1993, Font Mania, 1991:: rev. edit., 1996, XL1000, 1993, XL2000, 1993, XL2001, 1994, rev. edit., 1995, E-Z Book, 1995, Autofont Titler, 1995; editl. adv. panel: Dental Econs. Jour., 1979—80; editor: DPA News, 1993—95; contbr. articles to profl. jours. and mags.; columnist: Hackettstown Gazette, 1983—85. Chmn. Bd. of Health, Washington Twp., Morris County, N.J., 1975-78; co-dir. telecomm. sys. Hunterdon Ctrl. Regional H.S., 1989-98; presentations to Morris, Warren, and Sussex Counties, N.J. elem. schs. ann., 1966-93. Capt. Dental Corps., U.S. Army, 1962-65. Recipient cert. Stuart L. Isler Found. for Preventive Dentistry, 1986. Fellow Acad. Gen. Dentistry, Am. Endodontic Soc. (Harold Katz Meml. award 1983); mem. ADA (panel on quar. survey of pvt. practitioners 1990-93), Digital Pub. Assn. (founder, bd. dirs.), Am. Analgesia Soc., Internat. Analgesia Soc., N.J. Dental Assn., Warren-Sussex Dental Soc., Tri-County Dental Soc. (tchr. dental practice adminstrn. 1970-71), Hackettstown Dental Study Group (co-founder 1974-2006), Found. for Motivation in Dentistry (founder, chmn., bd. dirs.), Hosp. Assn. Neighborhood Dentists. Republican. Achievements include design of computer fonts, modules, graphics simulations; giant talking toothbrush, talking molar; development of painless dental injections; improved nerve-block anesthesia technique; first to develop electronic publishing software; invention of Rexxcom character set. Office: 110 Mill St Hackettstown NJ 07840-2343 Office Phone: 908-852-0880.

**WIEDEN, DAN G.,** advertising executive; b. 1945; m. Bonnie Wieden. BS journalism, Univ Oreg., 1967. With Georgia-Pacific Corp., Portland, Oreg., 1967-72; free-lance writer, 1972-78; with McCann-Erickson, Portland, 1978-80, William Cain, Portland, 1980-82; pres., exec. creative dir. Wieden & Kennedy Internat., Portland, 1982—. Named to Hall of Achievement, Sch. Journalism and Comm., Univ. Oreg., 2000. Office: Wieden & Kennedy Internat LLC 224 NW 13th Ave Portland OR 97209-2953

**WIEDER, BRUCE TERRILL,** lawyer, electrical engineer; b. Cleve., Dec. 9, 1955; s. Ira J. and Judith M.W. BSEE, Cornell U., 1978; MBA, U. Tex., 1980, JD with honors, 1988. Bar: Tex. 1988, U.S. Dist. Ct. (we. dist.) Tex. 1989, U.S. Patent and Trademark Office 1989, U.S. Ct. Appeals (fed. cir.) 1990, D.C. 1991, U.S. Supreme Ct. 1992, U.S. Dist. Ct. (no. dist.) Tex. 1995, Va. 1997, U.S. Dist. Ct. (ea. dist.) Va. 1997. Engr. Motorola, Inc., Austin, Tex., 1979-85; assoc. Arnold, White & Durkee, Austin, 1988-90; law clk. U.S. Ct. Appeals (Fed. cir.), Washington, 1990-91; assoc. Burns, Doane, Swecker & Mathis, Alexandria, Va., 1991-97, ptnr., 1998—2005; mem. Dow Lohnes, Washington, Pa., 2006—. Adj. prof. Georgetown U. Law Ctr., 1998—. Mem. IEEE, ABA, Am. Intellectual Property Law Assn., Alpha Phi Omega, Beta Gamma Sigma. Office: Dow Lohnes 1200 New Hampshire Ave NW Washington DC 20036-6802 Office Phone: 703-836-6620. E-mail: bwieder@dowlohnes.com.

**WIEGAND, ELIZABETH,** musician, educator; b. Michigan City, Ind., Sept. 25, 1931; d. Leo Theodore and Ella Martha Grieger; m. Lee Paul Wiegand, June 17, 1950; children: David Lee, Elaine Martha Johnson, Susan Elizabeth, Christine Mary. Cert. music tchr., Valparaiso U. Cert. Nat. Cert. Music Tchrs., permanent cert. Music Tchrs. Nat. Assn. Organist Queen All Sts. Ch., Michigan City, 1954—92; organist, choir dir. St. Stanislaus Kostka Consolation Choir, Michigan City 1992—, spl. Eucharistic min., 1998—; chapel organist St. Anthony Meml. Hosp., Michigan City, 1998—; organist, pianist LaPorte Presbyn. Ch., Ind., 2001—. Competition judge Nat. Tchrs. Music Conf., Nat. Assn. Organ Tchrs. Musician: Tex. Women's U. Repository, 1999, Cath. of Antwerp, 1998, St. Williams Ch. Named Music Educator of the Yr., Am. Music Conf., 1995—2005. Fellow: Nat. Fedn. Music Clubs; mem.: ASCAP (Popularity award 1980—2006), Am. Coll. Musicians (1st Pl. gold medal Internat. Rec. Competition). Roman Catholic. Avocations: embroidery, art, photography. Home: 7421 W Johnson Rd Michigan City IN 46360 Office Phone: 219-878-9511.

**WIEGEL, ROBERT LOUIS,** consulting engineering executive; b. San Francisco, Oct. 17, 1922; s. Louis Henry and Antionette L. (Decker) W.; m. Anne Pearce, Dec. 10, 1948; children: John M., Carol E., Diana L. BS, U. Calif. at Berkeley, 1943, MS, 1949. Mem. faculty U. Calif. at Berkeley, 1946—, prof. civil engring., 1963-87, prof. emeritus, 1987—, asst. dean Coll. Engring., 1963-72, acting dean, 1972-73; dir. state tech. svcs. program for Calif. U. Calif., 1965-68, sec. acad. senate, 1988-89; vis. prof. Nat. U. Mex., summer 1965, Polish Acad. Sci., 1976, 88, U. Cairo, 1978; sr. Queen's fellow in marine sci. Australia, 1977; cons. to govt. and industry, 1965—. Chmn. U.S. com. for internat. com. oceanic resources, mem. marine bd. Nat. Acad. Engring., 1975-81; pres. Internat. Engring. Com. on Oceanic Resources, 1972-75, hon. mem., 1988; mem. coastal engring. research bd. Dept. Army, 1974-85; mem. IDOE adv. panel NSF, 1974-77, Gov. Calif. Adv. Commn. Ocean Resources, 1967, Calif. Adv. Commn. on Marine and Coastal Resources, 1967-73, Tsunami Tech. Adv. Council, Hawaii, 1964-66; U.S. del. U.S.-Japan coop. sci. programs, 1964, 65 Author publs. in field; editor Shore and Beach jour., 1988-96; patentee in field. V.p., bd. dirs. Am. Shore and Beach Preservation Assn., 1988-95, dir. emeritus, 1995—; mem. Nat. Rsch. Coun. com. on Beach Nourishment and Protection, 1992-95. 1st lt. U.S. Army, 1942-46. Recipient Outstanding Civilian Svc. medal Dept. Army, 1985, Berkeley citation U. Calif., 1987, Joe W. Johnson Outstanding Beach Preservation award Calif. Shore and Beach Preservation Assn., 1993, Coastal Zone Found. award, 1993, Morrough P. O'Brien award Am. Shore and Beach Preservation Assn., 1995, Oral History award Bancroft Libr., U. Calif., 1997; Robert L. Wiegel scholar, 2001—. Fellow AAAS; mem. NAE, ASCE (hon., chmn. exec. com. waterways, harbors, coastal engring. div. 1974-75, vice chmn. coastal engring. rsch. coun. 1964-78, chmn. 1978-92, chmn. task com. wave forces on structures 1960-67, chmn. com. on coastal engring. 1970-71, Rsch. prize 1962, Moffatt-Nichol Coastal Engring. award 1978, Internat. Coastal Engring. award 1985), Japan Soc. Civil Engrs. (hon.), Sigma Xi. Home: 1030 Keeler Ave Berkeley CA 94708-1404 Office Phone: 510-642-7340.

**WIEGLEY, ROGER DOUGLAS,** lawyer; b. Buffalo, Dec. 8, 1948; s. Richard John and Georgianna (Eggleston) W. BA, SUNY, Buffalo, 1970; JD magna cum laude, U. Wis., 1977. Bar: Wis. 1977, Hawaii 1978, N.Y. 1982, D.C. 1982, Calif. 1986. Spl. asst. U.S. atty. U.S. Justice Dept., Honolulu, 1978-81; spl. asst. to gen. counsel Dept. of the Navy, Washington, 1981-82; assoc. Sullivan & Cromwell, Washington, 1982-88; ptnr. Sidley & Austin, Washington, 1988-94, Winthrop, Stimson, Putnam & Roberts, Washington, 1994-98; dir. Credit Suisse First Boston, N.Y.C., 1999—2001, Winterthur Ins. Group, N.Y.C., 2001—. Arbitrator nat. panel Am. Arbitration Assn., 1988—98. Co-author: Trade and Export Finance, 2d edit., 2000; contbr. numerous articles to profl. jours. Served with USN, 1973-82. Mem. Assn. of Bar City of N.Y. (chmn. banking law com. 2000-03). Address: 50 Old South Salem Rd Ridgefield CT 06877 Personal E-mail: roger.wiegley@srsmail.com.

**WIEGMAN, EUGENE WILLIAM,** minister, academic administrator; b. Fort Wayne, Ind., Oct. 27, 1929; s. A. Henry and E. Catherine (McDonald) W.; m. Kathleen Wyatt, Apr. 26, 1952; children: Kathryn, Rose Marie, Mark, Jeanine, Gretchen, Matthew. BS, Concordia Coll., 1953; MS, U. Kans., Lawrence, 1956, EdD, 1962; grad., Pacific Luth. Theol. Sem., 1985. Tchr., coach Trinity Luth. Sch., Atchison, Kans., 1954-58; prin. tchr. St. John's Coll., Winfield, Kans., 1958-61; prof. Concordia Coll., Seward, Nebr., 1961-65; administrv. asst. to Rep. Clair Callan, Lincoln, Nebr., 1965-66; asst. to administr. fed. extension service Dept. Agr., Washington, 1966-67; dean community edn. Fed. City Coll., Washington, 1967-69; pres. Pacific Luth. U., Tacoma, 1969-75. Independent Colls. Wash., 1975-76; dir. Wash. Office Community Devel., 1977-78; commr. Dept. of Employment Security, 1978-81; exec. dir., pres., CEO emeritus Family Counseling Service of Tacoma and Pierce County, Wash., 1987-97; assoc. pastor Luther Meml. Ch., Tacoma, 1987-90; pastor Gethsemane Luth. Ch., Tacoma, 1990-98, Luther Meml. Ch., Tacoma, 1998—2002; dean clin. pastoral edn. Grad. Sch. of Korea, 1992—. Mem. Wash. State Employment and Tng. Council; mem. cabinet Gov. of Wash., 1977-81. Candidate for U.S. Congress from 6th dist. Wash., 1976; mem. Council on Washington's Future; exec. bd. dirs. Pacific Harbors Coun. Boy Scouts Am.; bd. dirs. Tacoma Area Urban Coalition; past chmn. Wash. Friends Higher Edn.; bd. dirs. Tacoma Urban League, Bellarmine Prep. Sch., Tacoma, Camp Brotherhood, Nativity House; trustee Tacoma Gen. Hosp., Pacific Sci. Center; mem. Commn. on Children, Youth and Families for Tacoma and Pierce County; mem. com. Faith Homes for Young Women; pres. Second City chamber of Tacoma. Recipient Disting. Teaching award City Winfield, Kans., 1960, Freedom Found. Teaching award, 1961, Disting. Eagle Scout award, 1982, Pres. award St. Martins Coll., 1980. Mem. Kiwanis, Phi Delta Kappa. Home: 405 N Stadium Way Tacoma WA 98403-3228 Personal E-mail: eugenewiegman@msn.com.

**WIEGNER, EDWARD ALEX,** manufacturing executive; b. Waukesha, Wis., Dec. 13, 1939; s. Roy Edward and Margaret (Kuehnlein) Wiegner; m. Cathryn J. Mullens, Oct. 16, 1970; children: Carlin, Ryan; 1 child from previous marriage, Christine. BBA, U. Wis., 1961, MS in Econs., 1965, PhD in Econs., 1969. Asst. prof. bus. adminstrn. Marquette U., Milw., 1965-71; assoc. prof U. Wis., Madison, 1972-73; sec. Wis. Dept. Revenue, Madison, 1971-74; sr. v.p. fin. bd. dirs. Wis. Power and Light Co., Madison, 1974-76, tr., v.p. comptroller, pub. und fin. affairs, dir., 1976 80, exec. v.p., bd. dirs., 1980-82; v.p., CFO, bd. dirs. Am. Natural Resources Co., 1982-85, exec. v.p.; chief adminstrv. officer, bd. dirs., 1985-86; sr. v.p. Coastal Corp., 1985-86; sr. v.p., chief fin. officer Household Internat., Inc., 1986-88; exec. v.p., CFO Progressive Corp., Mayfield Heights, Ohio, 1988-91, pres. fin. svcs. div., 1989-93; gen. ptnr. Aurora Ptnrs., 1994-96; vice chmn. 1st Am. Ins. Co., Kansas City, Mo., 1994-97; chmn., CEO First Am. Fin. Corp., 1997-98; chmn. Geologix, Inc., Placerville, Calif., 1998—, Ins. Distbn. Solutions, LLC, Jacksonville, Fla., 1999—. Contbr. articles to profl. jours. Mem.: Grand Harbor Country Club. Home and Office: 151 Shores Dr Indian River Shores FL 32963 Personal E-mail: edward@wiegner.com.

**WIEHE, FRED,** writer; b. Cin., Apr. 15, 1955; s. Fred Wiehe and Elizabeth Elfers; m. Suzanne Brenner, Nov. 25, 1989; children: Jesse Brenner-Wiehe, Ian Brenner-Wiehe. BA, U. Cin., 1974—78. Case mgr. Zonta Children's Ctr., San Jose, Calif., 1984—86; tchr. Children's Health Coun., Palo Alto, Calif. 1986—91; author San Jose, Calif. Author: (novels) Strange Days, 1993, 2d edit., 2005, (novels) Starkville, 1996, 2001, Night Songs, 1998, The Burning, 2003, Strange Days, 2005. Mem.: Horror Writers Assn. Personal E-mail: fwiehe@fredwiehe.com.

**WIEHOFF, JOHN P.,** trucking executive; With Arthur Anderson, 1984—92; contr., treas. C.H. Robinson Worldwide, 1992—98, sr. v.p., CFO, 1998—99, pres., 1999—, CEO, 2002—, chmn. elect, 2006—. Office: 8100 Mitchell Rd Eden Prairie MN 55344*

**WIELAND, GILBERT DARRYL,** medical researcher, anthropologist, gerontologist; b. Hagerstown, Md., Oct. 31, 1951; s. Gilbert Hugh and Joan Kanaga Wieland; m. Manhal A. Wieland, Apr. 26, 1980; 1 child, Christopher. BA cum laude in Anthropology, Am. U., 1972; PhD in Anthropology, U. Rochester, 1982; MPH in Health Svcs., UCLA, 1983. Sr. rsch. scientist VA Geriatric Rsch., Edn. and Clin. Ctr., Sepulveda, Calif., 1982—96; rsch. dir. Beverly Found., Pasadena, Calif., 1987—90; assoc. rsch. prof. divsn. geriat. UCLA, 1991—96; prof. U. S.C. Sch. Medicine, Columbia, 1996—; rsch. dir. geriat. Palmetto Health Richland, Columbia, 1998—. Dep. editor Journal of Gerontology: Medical Sciences, 2005—; assoc. editor Aging: Clinical and Experimental Research, 2005—, mem. editl. bd., reviewer 30 med. and sci. jours., —. Fellow: Gerontol. Soc. Am. (chair pub. policy com. 2000—02, chair rsch. taskforce), Am. Geriatrics Soc. (mem. rsch. com. 2000—05); mem.: Columbia Choral Soc. Office Phone: 803-434-4330. E-mail: darryl.wieland@palmettohealth.org.

**WIELAND, JOHN,** real estate executive; m. Sue Wieland; 2 children. BA magna cum laude, Amherst Coll., 1958; MBA with high distinction, Harvard Bus. Sch., 1964; LHD (hon.), Amherst Coll., 1993. Chmn. John Wieland Homes and Neighborhoods, Inc., Atlanta, 1970—. Bd. dirs. Fed. Res. Bank Atlanta. Internat. bd. dirs. Habitat for Humanity; bd. dirs. Piedmont Hosp. Found., Atlanta Neighborhood Devel. Partnership; former chmn. High Mus. Art; former vice chmn. Woodruff Arts Ctr.; chmn. Adv. Coun., Emory U. Ctr. Ethics. Mem. Nat. Assn. Home Builders (life bd. dirs.), Atlanta (Ga.) C. of C. (mem. exec. com), Phi Beta Kappa. Office: 1950 Sullivan Rd Atlanta GA 30337-5706 Business E-mail: john.wieland@jwhomes.com.

**WIELAND, WILLIAM DEAN,** healthcare consulting executive; b. Peoria, Ill., Feb. 15, 1948; s. George William and Virginia Lee (Delicath) W.; m. Joyce Lumia; 1 child, William Michael. BBA, Bradley U., 1971. Asst. adminstr. Galesburg (Ill.) Cottage Hosp., 1973-74; v.p. Anton & Damian, Iowa City, 1975-76; mgr. Clifton, Gunderson & Co., Peoria, 1977-80; v.p. OHMS Health Mgmt. Services, Columbus, 1980-84; dir., cons. VHA Cons. Svcs., Tampa, Fla., 1984-88; divsn. mgr. VHA, Inc., Tampa, Fla., 1988-95; sr. cons. mgr. Cost Sys. Group, Inc., Tampa, Fla., 1995-96; prin. Medifax Assocs., Tampa, Fla., 1997-98; project mgr. U. Cmty. Health, Tampa, Fla., 1998—. Small bus. cons. Clifton, Gunderson & Co., 1977-80; cons. OHMS Health Mgmt. Svcs., Columbus, 1980-84. Mem.: Healthcare Info. and Mgmt. Sys. Soc., Am. Bus. Club, Sigma Nu (Zeta Phi chpt.). E-mail: wwieland@tampabay.rr.com.

**WIEMAN, CARL E.,** physics professor; b. Corvallis, Oreg., Mar. 26, 1951; m. Sarah Gilbert. BS, MIT, 1973; PhD, Stanford U., 1977; DS (hon.), U. Chgo., 1997. Asst. rsch. physicist dept. physics U. Mich., Ann Arbor, 1977—79, asst. prof. physics, 1979—84; assoc. prof. physics U. Colo., Boulder, 1984—87, prof., 1987—97, disting. rsch. prof., 1997—; fellow Joint Inst. for Lab. Astrophysics, Boulder, 1985—. Loeb lectr. Harvard U., 1990—91; Rosenthal Meml. lectr. Yale U., 1988, Columbia U., 1988; Cherwell-Simon Meml. lectr. Oxford U., 1999; vis. scholar Phi Beta Kappa, 1999—2000. Recipient Ernest Orlando Lawrence Meml. award, U.S. Dept. Energy, 1993, Einstein medal for laser sci., Soc. Optical and Quantum Electronics, 1995, Fritz London prize for low temperature physics, 1996, Newcomb Cleveland prize, AAAS, 1996, King Faisal Internat. prize for Sci., 1997, Sci. award, Bonfils Stanton Found., 1998, Lorentz medal, Netherlands Royal Acad. Sci., 1998, Benjamin Franklin Medal in Physics, 2000, The Nobel Prize in Physics, 2001, Nat. Sci. Found. Dir. Award for Disting. Teaching Scholars, 2001, U.S. Outstanding Doctoral and Rsch. Univ. Prof., Coun. for Advancement and Support of Edn. & Carnegie Found. for Advancement of Tchg., 2004, Nat. Prof. of the Year, Carnegie Found. for the Advancement of Teaching & the Council for Advancement & Support of Edn., 2005. Fellow: Guggenheim, 1990-1991, Hertz Found., 1973-1977, am. Phys. Soc. (Davisson-Germer prize 1994, Schawlow prize in laser sci. 1998); mem.: NAS, 1995, Am. Physical Soc. (fellow, 1990), Am. Acad. Arts and Sci., 1998, Am. Assn. Physics Tchrs. (Richtmyer lectr. award 1996), Optical Soc. Am. (R.W. Wood prize 1999). Achievements include first to achieve Bose-Einstein condensation, 1995. Office: Dept Physics and JILA CB440 Univ Colo Boulder CO 80309-0440*

**WIEMER, ROBERT ERNEST,** film and television producer, writer, director; b. Highland Park, Mich., Jan. 30, 1938; s. Carl Ernest and Marion (Israelian) W.; m. Rhea Dale McGeath, June 14, 1958; children: Robert Marshall, Rhea Whitney. BA, Ohio Wesleyan U., 1959. Ind. producer, 1956-60; dir. documentary ops. WCBS-TV, N.Y.C., 1964-67; ind. producer of television, theatrical and bus. films N.Y.C., 1967-72; exec. producer motion pictures and TV, ITT, N.Y.C., 1973-84, pres. subs. Blue Marble Co., Inc., Telemontage, Inc., Alphaventure Music, Inc., Betaventure Music, Inc., 1973-84; founder, chmn., chief exec. officer Tigerfilm, Inc., 1984—; chmn., bd. dirs. Golden Tiger Pictures, Hollywood, Calif., 1988—; pres, CEO Tuxedo Pictures Corp., Hollywood, Calif., 1993—. Bd. dirs., v.p. prodn. Las Vegas Internat. Film Festival; v.p. prodn. Cinevegas. Writer, prodr., dir.: (feature films) My Seventeenth Summer, Witch's Sister, Do Me a Favor, Anna to the Infinite Power, Somewhere, Tomorrow, Night Train to Kathmandu; exec. prodr.: (children's TV series) Big Blue Marble (Emmy and Peabody awards); dir. (TV episodes) New York Undercover, seaQuest DSV, Star Trek: The Next Generation, Deep Space Nine, The Adventures of Superboy; composer (country-western ballad) Tell Me What To Do. Capt. USAF, 1960-64. Recipient CINE award, 1974, 76, 77, 79, 81, Emmy award, 1978. Mem. NATAS, ASCAP, Info. Film Producers Assn. (Outstanding Producer award), Nat. Assn. TV Programming Execs., Am. Women in Radio and TV, N.J. Broadcasters Assn., Dirs. Guild Am., v.p., bd. mem. CineVegas The Las Vegas Internat. Film Festival. Office: Golden Tiger Pictures 3896 Ruskin St Las Vegas NV 89147-1097

**WIENER, HESH (HAROLD FREDERIC WIENER),** publishing executive, consultant; b. Bklyn., July 20, 1946; s. Jesse Leonard and Regina (Rappaport) W. BS in Polit. Sci., MIT, 1969; LLB with honors, Open U., London, 2002. Mem. staff systems devel. Data Gen. Corp., Southboro, Mass., 1969-70; dir. computer edn. project U. Calif., Berkeley, 1970-72; editor Computer Decisions Mag., Rochelle Park, NJ, 1973-78; editor, pub. Tech. News Am., N.Y.C., 1976-88; pres. Tech. News of Am. Co., Inc., N.Y.C., 1982—; mng. dir. Tech. News Ltd., London, 1992—. Webmaster, tech-news.com, 1996—, primrosehill.com, 1998—, luminum.com, 2000—; pub. Computer and Comms. Buyer Newsletter, 1979-95, Mainstream Newsletter, 1980-82, Infoperspectives Newsletter, 1982—, Storage Tech. Monitor, 1984-87, Infoperspectives Internat. (U.K.), 1989—, (Mid. East), 1991—, The Four Hundred Newsletter (U.K.), 1990-97, The Four Hundred Newsletter (U.S.), 1990-97; editor Infoperspectives Internat. (Italy), 1991-98, The Four Hundred Newsletter (Italy), 1995—; pub. U.S. edit. Computergram Internat. Newsletter, 1985-90; contr. Processeurs mag., 1989-99; cons. Hewlett-Packard Co. (Paris), 1971-72, Xerox Corp., 1972-73; advisor NSF, 1975; columnist 451.com, 2000—. Author: Big Blue and You, The IBM Atlas, The Mainframe; corr. Computer Weekly, U.K., 1975-81, Computable, Amsterdam, 1976-87, Computing Can., 1977-78, Infoperspectives Paris, 1977-89, Data News, Brussels, 1979-86, Informatics, U.K., 1981-85, Datanytt, Copenhagen, 1982-89, Mgmt. Tech. mag., 1983-85; editor BusinessWeek Newsletter for Info. Execs., 1987-90, Datamation Mag., 1983-90, Infoperspectives Internat. (Milan), 1991—; contbg. editor Bus. and Soc. Rev., 1978-85; contbr. N.Y. Times Syndicate, Los Angeles Times Syndicate, N.Am. Newspaper Alliance Wireservice, Newsday, Manhattan, Inc., Rom Mag., Informatique (Paris), The Economist (London), Dun's Bus. Month, Software News, Intermedia, Digital News, Data Communications, Bus. Week Newsletter for Info. Execs., Bus. Strategy Internat., Nikkei Watcher on IBM (Tokyo), 1989-96; contbg. editor Midrange Svc. Pubs., 2002-05, IT Jungle Pubs., 2003—; contbg. editor Big Iron News, 2005—; webmaster tech-news.com, 1995—, luminum.com, 1999—; webmaster PrimroseHill.com, 1997—. Mem.: Overseas Press. Home: 246 6th Ave Brooklyn NY 11215-2103 Office: Tech News Am 123 7th Ave Brooklyn NY 11215-1383

**WIENER, JACQUES LOEB, JR.,** federal judge; b. Shreveport, La., Oct. 2, 1934; s. Jacques L. and Betty (Eichenbaum) Wiener; m. Sandra Mills Feingerts; children: Patricia Wiener Shifke, Jacques L. III, Betty Ellen Wiener Spomer, Donald B. BA, Tulane U., 1956, JD, 1961. Bar: La. 1961, U.S. Dist. Ct. (we. dist.) La. 1961. Ptnr. Wiener, Weiss & Madison, Shreveport, 1961—90; judge U.S. Ct. Appeals (5th cir.), New Orleans, 1990—. Mem. coun. La. State Law Inst., 1963—; master of the bench Am. Inn of Ct., 1990—98. Pres. United Way N.W. La., 1975. Shreveport Jewish Fedn., 1969—70. Fellow: La. Bar Found., Am. Bar Found., Am. Coll. Trust and Estates Counsel; mem.: ABA, Am. Law Inst., Shreveport Bar Assn. (pres. 1982), La. Bar Assn., Internat. Acad. Estate and Trust Law (academician). Avocations: fly fishing, upland game bird hunting, photography, travel. Office: Court of Appeals Building 600 Camp St Rm 244 New Orleans LA 70130-3425*

**WIENER, JOEL HOWARD,** historian, educator; b. NYC, Aug. 23, 1937; s. Philip Wiener and Elizabeth Weissman; m. Suzanne Wolff Wiener, Sept. 4, 1961; children: Paul, Deborah, Jane. BA, NYU, 1959; postgrad., U. Glasgow, Scotland, 1961—63; PhD, Cornell U., 1965. Asst. prof. history Skidmore Coll., Saratoga Springs, NY, 1964—67, CUNY, 1967—71, assoc. prof. history, 1972—78, prof. history, 1978—2000, emeritus prof. history, 2000—. Dir. study abroad program in Eng. CUNY, 1971—73; prof. history doctoral program, 1980—2000, chmn. dept. history, 1981—85; cons., advisor Cornell U. Press, U. NC Press, Victorian Studies, NEH, English Lit. in Transition, 1880-1920, Princeton U. Press, Greenwood Press, UK Social Sci. Rsch. Coun., Ill. U. Press, Victorian Periodicals Rev., Am. Journalism, Albion, Jour. Brit. Studies, Rutgers U. Press, PSC-CUNY, Dictionary Labour Biography, Harvester Press; mem. editl. bd. Media History; mem. adv. bd. Dictionary of Nineteenth-Century Journalism. Author: The War of the Unstamped, 1969, A Descriptive Finding List of Unstamped British Periodicals, 1830-1836, 1970, William Lovett, 1989, Radicalism and Freethought in Nineteenth-Century Britain, 1983; editor: Great Britain: Foreign Policy and the Span of Empire, 4 vols., 1972, Great Britain: The Lion at Home, 4 vols., 1974, Innovators and Preachers, 1985, Papers for the Millions, 1988; contbr. articles to profl. jours.; assoc. editor Dictionary of National Biography, 1999—2004. Grantee, Oxford Bibliog. Soc., 1971—72, Am. Philos. Soc., 1971—72. Fellow: Royal Hist. Soc.; mem.: Am. Journalism Historians Assn. (rsch. com. 1998—), Rsch. Soc. for Victorian Periodicals (v.p., pres. 1981—85). Avocations: travel, theater, cinema. Home: 267 Glen Ct Teaneck NJ 07666 Office Phone: 201-837-5452. Home Fax: 201-837-8658. Personal E-mail: jwiener267@aol.com.

**WIENER, JON,** history professor; b. St. Paul, Minn., May 16, 1944; s. Daniel N. and Gladys (Aronsohn) Spratt. BA, Princeton U., 1966; PhD, Harvard U., 1971. Acting asst. prof. UCLA, 1973-74; asst. prof. history U. Calif.-Irvine, 1974-83, prof., 1984—. Plaintiff Freedom of Info. Lawsuit against FBI for John Lennon Files, 1983—. Author: Social Origins of the New South, 1979; Come Together: John Lennon in His Time, 1984, Professors, Politics, and Pop, 1991, Gimme Some Truth: The John Lennon FBI File, 2000, Historians in Trouble, 2005; contbg. editor The Nation mag.; contbr. articles to profl. jours. including The New Republic and New York Times Book Rev. Mem. Am. Hist. Assn., Nat. Book Critics Circle, Orgn. Am. Historians, Liberty Hill Found. (bd. dirs.). E-mail: wiener@uci.edu.

**WIENER, JOSEPH,** pathologist, educator; b. Toronto, Sept. 21, 1927; arrived in U.S., 1949, naturalized, 1960; s. Louis and Minnie (Salem) W.; m. Judith Hesta Ross, June 20, 1954; children: Carolyn L., Adam L. MD, U. Toronto, 1953. Intern Detroit Receiving Hosp., 1953-54; resident to chief resident pathology Mallory Inst. Pathology, 1954-55, 57-60; from asst. to assoc. prof. pathology Columbia U., N.Y.C., 1960-68; prof. pathology N.Y. Med. Coll., N.Y.C., 1968-78, Wayne State U., Detroit, 1978—, chmn. dept., 1978-90. Cons. NIH, 1970— Served to capt. M.C. U.S. Army, 1955-57. Grantee Heart, Lung and Blood Inst., 1971-93; fellow Coun. for High Blood Pressure Rsch., 1982. Fellow Am. Heart Assn., Am. Stroke Assn., Coll. Am. Pathologists; mem. AAAS, Am. Soc. Investigative Pathology, Am. Soc. Cell Biology, Mich. Path. Soc., Internat. Acad. Pathology, Am. Heart Assn., U.S./Can. Acad. Pathology, Mich. Heart Assn. (dir.), Internat. Soc. Hypertension. Achievements include rsch. on cellular/molecular biology of experimental hypertension. Office: 540 E Canfield St Detroit MI 48201-1928 Office Phone: 313-577-1157. Business E-mail: jwiener@med.wayne.edu.

**WIENER, MALCOLM HEWITT,** historian, writer; b. Tsingtao, China, July 3, 1935; (parents Am. citizens); s. Myron and Ethel (Zimmerman) W.; m. Carolyn Talbot Seely, June 8, 1990; children: Kate, Elizabeth, Thomas, Jonathan. BA, Harvard U., 1957, JD, 1963; LittD (hon.), U. Sheffield, 1997; PhD (hon.), Eberhard-Karl U., Tübingen, Germany, 1998; Doctorate (hon.), U. Athens, Greece, 1998. Bar: N.Y. 1964. Atty., N.Y.C., 1963-71; pvt. practice investing, 1971-98; chmn. Millburn Corp., N.Y.C., 1977-98; chmn. bd. trustees Malcolm Hewitt Wiener Found., N.Y.C., 1984—. Columnist Newsday. Co-dir. Aegean Bronze Age Colloquium, NYU Inst. Fine Arts, 1975—; founder, exec. dir. Inst. Aegean Prehistory, 1982-89, pres., 1990—; trustee Am. Sch. Classical Studies in Athens, Metro. Mus. Art; mem. adv. bd. Malcolm Wiener Ctr. for Social Policy, Kennedy Sch. Govt. Harvard U.; mem. Coun. Fgn. Rels., chmn. Indep. Task Force Non-lethal Tech. Mil. Implications and Options, 1995. With USN, 1957-60. Fellow: AAAS, Soc. Antiquaries London, Archaeol. Inst. Am. (life); mem.: ABA, Chevalier de l'Ordre des Arts et des Lettres, Österreichische Akademie Wissenschaften (corr.), Royal Swedish Acad. Letters, History and Antiquities (corr.), Austrian Archaeol. Inst. (corr.). Office: Villa Candia 66 Vista Dr Greenwich CT 06830 Office Phone: 203-862-9334. Business E-mail: cpadgett@instap.org.

**WIENER, MARVIN S.,** rabbi, editor, executive; b. N.Y.C., Mar. 16, 1925; s. Max and Rebecca (Dodell) W.; m. Sylvia Bodek, Mar. 2, 1952; children: David Hillel, Judith Rachel. BS, CCNY, 1944, MS, 1945; BHL, Jewish Theol. Sem. Am., 1947, MHL, Rabbi, 1951, DD (hon.), 1977. Registrar, sec. faculty Rabbinical Sch., Jewish Theol. Sem. Am., 1951-57; cons. Frontiers of Faith TV Series, NBC, 1951-57; dir., instr. liturgy Cantors Inst.-Sem. Coll. Jewish Music, Jewish Theol. Sem. Am., 1954-58; faculty coord. Sem. Sch. and Women's Inst., 1958-64; dir. Nat. Acad. for Adult Jewish Studies, United Synagogue Am., N.Y.C., 1958-78; editor Burning Bush Press, 1958-78, United Synagogue Rev., 1978-86; dir. com. congrl. stds. United Synagogue Am., 1976-86, cons. cmty. rels. and social action, 1981-82, editor, exec. joint retirement bd., 1986—. Mem. Joint Commn. on Rabbinic Placement, 1951-57, Joint Prayer Book Commn., 1957-62; mem. exec. coun. Rabbinical Assembly, 1958-86, summer Rabbi, Forest Hills Jewish Ctr., 1961-64; editl. cons. N.Y. Bd. Rabbi, 1987-89; trustee joint retirement bd. Jewish Theol. Sem. Am. Rabbinical Assembly and United Synagogue Am., 1959-86, sec. 1968-76, 84-85, vice chmn., 1976-82, 85-86, chmn. 1982, treas., 1983-84; co-chmn. Jewish Bible Assn., 1960-64; chmn. bd. rev. Nat. Coun. Jewish Audio-Visual Materials, 1968-69; mem. exec. com. Nat. Coun. Adult Jewish Edn., 1966—; mem. exec. bd., editl. adv. bd., v.p. Jewish Book Couns., 1976-96; chmn. Internat. Conf. Adult Jewish Edn., Jerusalem, 1972. Editor: Nat. Acad. Adult Jewish Studies Bull., 1958-78, The High Holy Days, Book I (Herman Kieval), 1959, The Jewish Dietary Laws (Samuel H. Dresner and Seymour Siegel), 1959, Past and Present: Selected Essays (Israel Friedlaender), 1961, Heart of Wisdom, Book I (Bernard S. Raskas), 1962, Book II, 1979, Judaism: Profile of a Faith (Ben Zion Bokser), 1963, The Wisdom of Solomon Schechter (Bernard Mandelbaum), 1963, Jewish Tract Series, 1964-78 (15 titles), Foundations of A Faith (Simon Greenberg), 1967, Judaism and the Christian Predicament (Ben Zion Bokser), 1967, The Maturing of the Conservative Movement (Bernard Mandelbaum), 1968, The Sabbath (Samuel L. Dresner), 1970, Adult Jewish Edn., 1958-78, Talmudic Law and the Modern State (Moshe Silberg), 1973, Self-Incrimination in Jewish Law (Aaron Kirschenbaum), 1970, Sex and the Family in the Jewish Tradition (Robert Gordis), 1970; contbr. articles to numerous periodicals. Mem. Am. Acad. Jewish Rsch., Assn. Jewish Studies, N.Y. Bd. Rabbis, Rabbinical Assembly. Home: 67-66 108th St Apt D-46 Forest Hills NY 11375-2974 Office: Joint Retirement Bd Ste 1515 One Penn Plaza New York NY 10119

**WIENER, RONALD MARTIN,** lawyer; b. Phila., June 1, 1939; s. William V. and Sylvia Wiener; children: Carol Jan, Alan Mark. AB, U. Pa., 1961; JD magna cum laude, Harvard U., 1964. Bar: DC 1965, Pa. 1966. Law clerk U.S. Tax Ct., 1964-66; assoc. Wolf, Block, Schorr and Solis-Cohen, LLP, Phila., 1966-72, ptnr., 1972—. Mem. commr.'s adv. group IRS, 1992—93. Fellow: Am. Coll. Tax Counsel (regent 3rd cir. 1996—2003); mem.: ABA, Phila. Bar Assn. (chair tax sect. 1989—90), Pa. Bar Assn. Office: Wolf Block Schorr and Solis-Cohen LLP 1650 Arch St 22d fl Philadelphia PA 19103-2678 Office Phone: 215-977-2266. Business E-mail: rwiener@wolfblock.com.

**WIENER, THOMAS ELI,** lawyer; b. Dallas, Nov. 29, 1940; s. Samson and Fan (Gardner) W.; m. Felice Gloria Goodwin, Jan. 24, 1970; children: Gary Allen, Debra Roslyn, Allison Beth, Todd David. BA, U. Tex., 1962, JD with honors, 1968. Bar: Tex. 1968, D.C. 1969, Pa. 1972, U.S. Supreme Ct. 1972. Atty.-advisor office chief counsel IRS, Washington, 1968-72; assoc. Pepper Hamilton & Scheetz, Phila., 1972-74; Abrahams & Loewenstein, Phila., 1974-76, Goodis, Greenfield, Henry & Edelstein, Phila., 1976-77, Mesirov, Gelman, Jaffe, Cramer & Jamieson, Phila., 1977-78; prin. Franklin, Margulies & Huntington, 1978-91, Riley & DeFalice, P.C., Phila., 1991-92, Wiener & Caplan, P.C., Phila., 1992-95; pvt. practice Bala Cynwyd, Pa., 1995—. Bd dirs. Lufkin (Tex.) Industries, Inc. Author: (with others) Tax Problems of Fiduciaries, 1977. Trustee Golden Slipper Club; pres. Main Line Reform Temple, 1992-94, pres. brotherhood 1981-83; pres. Rotary Gundaker Found., 1986-87; 1st v.p. N. Am. Fedn. Temple Brotherhoods, 1999-01; v.p. Phila. Fedn. Reform Synagogues, 1993-98; chmn. Synagogue Fedn. Coun. of Phila., 1994-97; trustee Union Am. Hebrew Congregations, 1995—, exec. com., 2001-05, ARZA/World Union N.Am. Mem. D.C. Bar Assn., Pa. Bar Assn., Tex. Bar Assn., Phila. Bar Assn., Am. Law Inst., Order of Coif, Masons (32 degree K.C.C.H., past master), Rotary (pres. chpt. 1985-86). Home: 1233 Remington Rd Wynnewood PA 19096-2329 Office: One Belmont Ave Ste 605 Bala Cynwyd PA 19004-1609 Office Phone: 610-667-8999. E-mail: twiener@aol.com.

**WIENER, VALERIE,** state senator, writer, communications executive; BJ, U. Mo., 1971, MA, 1972, U. Ill., Springfield, 1974; postgrad., McGeorge Sch. Law, 1976—79. Prodr. Checkpoint Sta. KOMU-TV, Columbia, Mo., 1972-73; v.p., owner Broadcast Assocs., Inc., Las Vegas, 1972-86; pub. affairs dir. First Ill. Cable TV, Springfield, 1973-74; editor Ill. State Register, Springfield, 1973-74; prodr. and talent Nev. Realities Sta. KLVX-TV, Las Vegas, 1974-75; account exec. Sta. KBMI (now KFMS), Las Vegas, 1975-79; nat. traffic dir. six radio stas., Las Vegas, Albuquerque and El Paso, Tex., 1979-80; exec. v.p., gen. mgr. Stas. KXKS and KKJY, Albuquerque, 1980-81; exec. adminstr. Stas. KSET AM/FM, KVEG, KFMS and KKJY, 1981-83; press sec. U.S. Congressman Harry Reid, Washington, 1983-87; adminstrv. asst Friends for Harry Reid, Nev., 1986; press sec. U.S. Senator Harry Reid, Washington, 1987-88; owner Wiener Comm. Group, Las Vegas, 1988—; mem. Nev. Senate, Dist. 3 Clark County, 1996—, minority whip, 2001—; owner PowerMark Pub., 1998—. Author: Power Communications: Positioning Yourself for High Visibility (Fortune Book Club main selection 1994, Money Book Club selection 1995), Gang Free: Friendship Choices for Today's Youth, 1995, 2d edit., 1996, The Nesting Syndrome: Grown Children Living at Home, 1997, Winning the War Against Youth Gangs, 1999, Power Positioning: Advancing Yourself as The Expert, 2000 (Nat. award), Power-Master HandBook Series, 2000— (seven nat. awards); contbg. writer The Pacesetter, ASAE's Comm. News. Sponsor Futures for Children, Las Vegas, Albuquerque, El Paso, 1979—83; mem. El Paso Exec. Women's Coun., 1981—83; media chmn. Gov.'s Coun. Small Bus., 1989—93; mem. Clark Coun. Sch. Dist. and Bus. Cmty. PAYBAC Spkrs. and Partnership Programs, 1989—, chair legis. com. on juvenile justice, 1999—2000; chair Common. on Sch. Safety and Juvenile Violence, 1999—2000; various state and nat. legis. commn.s and coms.; vice chmn. Congl. Awards Coun., 1989—93, Gov.'s Commn. on Postsecondary Edn., 1992—96; mem. Nev. Technol. Crimes Task Force, 2001—03, Nev. Drug Commn., 1997—2000, Nev. Commn. on Aging, 1997—, Nev. Anti-Bullying Task Force, 2001—03, Gov.'s Task Force on Corrections, 2002, chair legis. com. on obesity, 2003—04; mem. VIP bd. Easter Seals, El Paso, 1982; med. dir. 1990 Gov.'s Conf. on Women; steering com. Youth Recovery Network, 2001—02; founding mem. Nev. team Action Healthy Kids; bd. dirs. BBB So. Nev., 1994—, Pub. Edn. Found., 1997—. Named Nev.'s Disting. Sr. Athlete, 2000, Outstanding Vol., United Way, El Paso, 1983, SBA Nev. Small Bus. Media Adv. of Yr., 1992, Disting. Sr. Athlete in Nev., 2000, So. Nev. Health Care Policy Hero, 2003, Nev. Legislator of Yr., Soc. Pub. Health Educators, 2004; named one of 27 Health Sch. Heroes in U.S., 2002; named to Hall Fame, Leadership Las Vegas, 2006; recipient 161 Comm. awards, 1989—, Outstanding Achievement award, Nat. Fedn. Press Women, 1991, Disting. Leader award, Nat. Assn. Cmty. Leadership, 1993, Gold medals in fitness and weightlifting, Nev. Sr. Olympics, 1998—2003, 2005, Gold medals in swimming, 2002—03, 2005, Walking Silver medal, 2005, Outstanding Women Adv. for Edn. award, Va. Commonwealth U., 2000, Internat. Comm. Svc. award, Internat. New Thought Alliance, 2001, Winner Nev. 100 Fitness Challenge, Nev. State Legis. Session, 2005. Mem. Nat. Assn. Women Bus. Owners (media chmn., nat. rep. So. Nev. 1990-91, Nev. Adv. of Yr. award 1992), Nev. Press Women, Nat. Spkrs. Assn., Small Pubs. Assn. N.Am., Dem. Press Secs. Assn., El Paso Assn. Radio Stas. U.S. Senate Staff Club, Las Vegas C. of C. (Circle of Excellence award 1993), Soc. Profl. Journalists. Democrat. Avocations: reading, writing, fitness and weightlifting training and competition, public speaking, community involvement. Office: 1500 Foremaster Ln Ste 2 Las Vegas NV 89101-1150

**WIENS, ANN,** artist, writer, editor, art critic; East Coast editor, then sr. editor, and editor New Art Examiner, 1991—98, art critic New City, 1998—2000; contbr. articles to Art and Antiques, Chicago Magazine, CS, dialogue, New City, Chicago Reader, Chicago Collection; exhibits paintings in numerous group and solo shows throughout the Midwest and East Coast, represented by Byron Roche Gallery, Chgo. Mem.: Chgo. Art Critics Assn. Address: 2010 W Eastwood Ave Chicago IL 60625 Office Phone: 312-344-8631. E-mail: a.wiens@comcast.net.

**WIENS, ARTHUR NICHOLAI,** psychology professor; b. McPherson, Kans., Sept. 7, 1926; s. Jacob T. and Helen E. (Kroeker) W.; m. Ruth Helen Avery, June 11, 1949; children: Barbara, Bradley, Donald. BA, U. Kans., 1948, MA, 1952; PhD, U. Portland, 1956. Diplomate: Am. Bd. Examiners Profl. Psychology. Clin. psychologist Topeka State Hosp., 1949-53; sr. psychologist outpatient dept. Oreg. State Hosp., Salem, 1954-58, chief psychologist, 1958-61, clin. psychology internship program, 1958-61; clin. instr. U. Oreg. Med. Sch., Portland, 1958-61, asst. prof., 1961-65, assoc. prof., 1965-66; prof. med. psychology, 1966—96; prof. emeritus med. psychology, 1997—. Field assessment officer Peace Corps, 1965; cons. psychologist Portland Ctr. for Hearing and Speech, 1964—67, Dammasch State Hosp., 1967—69, Raleigh Hills Hosp., 1968—84, Oreg. Vocat. Rehab. Divsn., 1973—2001, mem. state adv. com., 1976—93; cons. William Temple Rehab. House, Episcopal Laymen's Mission Soc., 1968—88; chmn. State Oreg. Bd. Social Protection, 1971—84, State of Oreg. Bd. Psychologist Examiners, 1963—66, 1974—77; v.p. bd. dirs. Raleigh Hills Rsch. Found., 1974—80. Contbr. articles to profl. jour. Fellow AAAS, APA (chmn. com. on vis. psychologist program 1972-76, chmn. accreditation com. 1978, mem. task force edn. and credentialing 1979-84); mem. Am. Assn. State Psychology Bd. (pres. 1978-79), Nat. Register Health Svc. Providers in Psychology (bd. dirs. 1985-92, chmn. 1989-92), Profl. Exam. Svc. (bd. dirs. 1982-88, 90-96, chmn. 1986-88), Sigma Xi. Home: 74 Condolea Way Lake Oswego OR 97035-1010 Office: Oreg Health Scis U Portland OR 97201 Business E-Mail: wiensa@ohsu.edu.

**WIER, PATRICIA ANN,** publishing executive, consultant; b. Coal Hill, Ark., Nov. 10, 1937; d. Horace L. and Bridget B. (McMahon) Norton; m. Richard A. Wier, Feb. 24, 1962; 1 child, Rebecca Ann. BA, U. Mo., Kansas City, 1964; MBA, U. Chgo., 1978. Computer programmer AT&T, 1960-62; lead programmer City of Kansas City, Mo., 1963-65; with Playboy Enterprises, Chgo., 1965-71, mgr. systems and programming, 1971; with Ency. Britannica, Inc., Chgo., 1971—; v.p. mgmt. svcs. Ency. Britannica USA, 1975-83, exec. v.p. adminstrn., 1983-84; v.p. planning and devel. Ency. Britannica, Inc., Chgo., 1985—; pres. Compton's Learning Co. divsn., 1985; pres. Ency. Britannica (USA), 1986-91, Ency. Britannica N.A., 1986—94; exec. v.p. Ency. Britannica, Inc., 1986-94; pres. Ency. Britannica N.Am., 1986—94; mgmt. cons. pvt. practice, Chgo., 1994—. Cons. pvt. practice, Chgo., 1994—; bd. dirs. Alcas Corp., Mannatech Inc. Life mem. coun. Grad. Sch. Bus., U. Chgo.; mem. bd. regents Lewis U. Mem. Direct Selling Assn. (bd. dirs. 1984-93, chmn. 1987-88, named to Hall of Fame 1991), Women's Coun. U. Mo. Kansas City (hon. life) Com. 200, The Chgo. Network. Roman Catholic. Office: Patricia A Wier Inc 175 E Delaware Pl Ste 8305 Chicago IL 60611-7748 Personal E-mail: wier@prodigy.net.

**WIER, RICHARD ROYAL, JR.,** lawyer; b. Wilmington, Del., May 19, 1941; s. Richard Royal and Anne (Kurtz) W.; m. Anne E. Edwards, Nov. 25, 1978; children— Melissa Royal, Emma Kurtz; children from previous marriage: Richard Royal, III, Mimi Poole. BA in English, Hamilton Coll., 1963; LLB, U. Pa., 1966; postgrad., Temple U., 1981-82. Bar: D.C. 1967, Del. 1967, Pa. 1980, U.S. Dist. Ct. Del., U.S. Ct. Appeals (3d cir.), U.S. Supreme Ct. Assoc. Connolly, Bove & Lodge, Wilmington, 1966-68; dep. atty. gen. State of Del., Wilmington, 1968-70; state prosecutor Del. Dept. Justice, Wilmington, 1970-74; atty. gen. State of Del., Wilmington, 1975-79; ptnr. Prickett, Jones, Elliott, Kristol & Schnee, Wilmington, 1979-92; pvt. practice Wilmington, 1993—. Lectr. criminal and labor law various instns. Active United Way campaign, 1976-77; supervisory bd. Gov.'s Commn. on Criminal Justice; bd. dirs. Del. Coun. Crime and Justice, 1982-89; adv. coun. Diabetes Control, 1990-92; dir. Project Assist, 1992-95, Commn. on Outreach, 1994—. Recipient Law Enforcement award Newark Police Dept., 1974; Law Enforcement Commendation medal Nat. Soc. SAR, 1976; Ideal Citizen award Am. Found. for Sci. Creative Intelligence, 1976; Commendation Del. Gen. Assembly Senate, 1976-77, 80; named one of Top Labor/Employment Attys. in Del., Del. Today, 1999—. Mem. ABA, Nat. Dist. Attys. Assn. (state dir.), Del. Bar Assn. (chmn. criminal law sect. 1987-91, co-chmn. on drug crisis 1993—, vice chmn. labor law sect. 1987-88, chmn. 1989-90), Pa. Bar Assn., D.C. Bar Assn., Nat. Assn. Attys. Gen. (hon. life, exec. com.), Soc. Attys. Gen. Execs. (emeritus), Am. Judicature Soc., Am. Del. Trial Lawyers Assn., Nat. Assn. Extradition Ofcls. (hon. life, regional v.p., exec. dir.), Italian Radio/TV Assn. (hon., Outstanding Achievement award), Internat. Platform Assn., Pi Delta Epsilon. Achievements include inventor in field. Office: Two Mill Rd Ste 200 Wilmington DE 19806 Business E-Mail: rwier@wierlaw.com.

**WIERMAN, JOHN CHARLES,** mathematician, educator; b. Prosser, Wash., June 30, 1949; s. John Nathaniel and Edith Elizabeth (Ashley) W.; m. Susan Shelley Graupmann, Aug. 13, 1971; 1 child, Adam Christopher. BS in Math., U. Wash., 1971, PhD in Math., 1976. Asst. prof. math. U. Minn., Mpls., 1976-81; asst. prof. Johns Hopkins U., Balt., 1981-82, assoc. prof., 1982-87, prof., 1987—, chmn. math. scis. dept., 1988-2000; dir. entrepreneurship and mgmt. program, 1996—, dir. Ctr. for Leadership Edn., 2004—. Sr. rsch. fellow Inst. Math. and Its Applications, Mpls., 1987—88; Navy ASEE fellow Naval Surface Warfare Ctr., 2001—02. Co-author: First-Passage Percolation on the Square Lattice, 1978; contbr. articles to profl. jours. Grad. fellow, NSF, 1971—74, NSF rsch. grantee, 1976—93, sabbatical fellow, Navy-ASEE, 2001—02. Fellow Inst. Math. Stats. (organizer spl. session on percolation theory 1982, organizer spl. session on probability and math. stats. 1986), Inst. of Combinatorics and its Applications; mem. Am. Soc. Quality, Inst. Math. Stats., Am. Math. Soc., Am. Statis. Assn., Math. Assn. Am., Sigma Xi, Phi Beta Kappa. Office: Johns Hopkins U Dept Applied Math and Stats 34th & Charles Sts Baltimore MD 21218 Office Phone: 410-516-7211. Business E-Mail: wierman@jhu.edu.

**WIERNIK, PETER HARRIS,** oncologist, educator; b. Crocket, Tex., June 16, 1939; s. Harris and Molly (Emmerman) W.; m. Roberta Joan Fuller, Sept. 6, 1961; children: Julie Anne, Lisa Britt, Peter Harrison. BA with distinction, U. Va., 1961, MD, 1965; Dr. honoris causa, U. Republic, Montevideo, Uruguay, 1982. Diplomate Am. Bd. Internal Medicine, Am. Bd. Med. Oncology (mem. writing com. 1981-87). Intern Cleve. Met. Gen. Hosp., 1965—66, resident, 1966—70; resident Osler Svc. Johns Hopkins Hosp., Balt., 1970—71; sr. asst. surgeon USPHS, 1966, advanced through grades to med. dir., 1976; sr. staff assoc. Balt. Cancer Rsch. Ctr., 1966—71, chief med. oncology sect., 1971—76, chief clin. oncology br., 1974—76, 1976—82; assoc. dir. cancer treatment divsn. Nat. Cancer Inst., 1976—82; assoc. dir. Albert Einstein Cancer Ctr., Bronx, 1982—98, prof. medicine, 1983—98, prof. radiation oncology, 1996—98, head med. oncology divsn. Asst. prof. medicine U. Md. Sch. Medicine, Balt., 1971-74, assoc. prof., 1974-76, prof., 1976-82; prof. medicine radiation oncology NY Med. Coll., 1998—; cons. hematology med. oncology Union Meml. Hosp., Greater Balt. Med. Ctr., Franklin Sq. Hosp.; bd. dirs. Balt. City unit Am. Cancer Soc., 1971-78; chmn. patient care com., 1972-75, profl. edn. grants com., NYC divsn., 1983-90, nat. clin. fellowship com., 1984-96; med. adv. com. Nat. Leukemia Assn., 1976-88, chmn. med. adv. com., 1989—; chmn. adult leukemia com. Cancer Leukemia Group B, 1976-83; prin. investigator Ea. Coop. Oncology Group, 1982-94, 96—; chmn. gynecol. oncology com., 1986-88, chmn. leukemia com., 1988-94; sci. cons. Vt. Regional Cancer Ctr., 1987—; dir. OLM Comprehensive Cancer Ctr., NY Med. Coll., 1998—. Editor: Controversies in Oncology, 1982, Supportive Care of the Cancer Patient, 1983, Neoplastic Diseases of the Blood, 1985, 4th edit., 2003, Adult Leukemias, 2001; editor: (assoc.) Medical Oncology and Tumor Pharmacotherapy, 1987—91; editor: (sr.), 1991—; editor (assoc.) Am. Jour. Therapeutics, 1994—; co-editor: Year Book of Hematology, 1986—98, Handbook of Hematologic and Oncologic Emergencies, 1988—98, Bone Marrow Transplantation (textbook), 1995, Am. Jour. Medical Scis., 1976—81; editor: Jour. of Cancer Rsch. and Clin/ Oncology, 1986—89, Jour. Clin. Pharmacology, 1985—; mem. editl. bd. Cancer Treatment Reports, 1972—76, Leukemia Rsch., 1977—86, 1991—2005, Leukemia, 1986—2003, Cancer Clin. Trials, 1977—, Jour. of Therapeutic Rsch., 1994—, Hospital Practice, 1979—, Jour. of Clin. Oncology, 1989—91, Leukemia and Lymphoma, 1989—, PDQ National Cancer Inst., 1987—94, Cancer Investigation, 1998—, Serbian Archives Medicine, 2005—; contbr. articles to profl. jours., chapters to books. Recipient Z Soc. award U. Va., 1961, Byrd S. Leavell Hematology award U. Va. Sch. Medicine, 1965, Gold medal 1st Polish Congress Oncology, 2002. Fellow AAAS, ACP, Am. Coll. Clin. Pharmacology (awards com. 1999—), Internat. Soc. Hematology, Royal Soc. Medicine (London), NY Acad. Medicine; mem. Am. Soc. Clin. Investigation (instl. rep. 1997—), Am. Soc. Clin. Oncology (chmn. edn. tng. com. 1976-79, 84, subcom. clin. investigation 1980-82, program com. 1990, pub. issues com., 1990-95, com. rsch. awards 1996-2000, com. health svcs. rsch. 2000-2003), Am. Assn. Cancer Rsch. (clin. cancer rsch. com. 2002—), Am. Soc. Hematology, Am. Fedn. Clin. Rsch., Am. Acad. Clin. Toxicology, Internat. Soc. Exptl. Hematology, NY Acad. Sci., Am. Soc. Hosp. Pharmacy, Am. Soc. Clin. Pharmacology Therapeutics, Am. Radium Soc. (program com. 1992-93, exec. com. 1988-95, publ. com. 1988-92, sec. 1990-91, pres.-elect, 1992-93, pres. 1993-94, Janeway medalist 1996), Polish Oncology Soc. (hon., finalist Gold medal), Harvey Soc. (assoc.), Uruguayan Hematology Soc. (hon.), Acad. Medicine Uruguay (corr.), European Assn. Cancer Rsch., European Soc. Hematology, Phi Beta Kappa (assoc.), Sigma Xi, Alpha Omega Alpha, Phi Sigma (award 1961). Office: Comprehensive Cancer Ctr Our Lady Mercy Med Ctr 600 E 233rd St Bronx NY 10466-2604 Office Phone: 718-304-7220. Personal E-mail: pwiernik@aol.com. Business E-Mail: wiernik@jimmy.harvard.edu, pwiernik@olmhs.org. *Always remember why you entered a profession in the first place. Leave the politics to those who have forgotten.*

**WIERSBE, WARREN WENDELL,** clergyman, writer, lecturer; b. East Chgo., May 16, 1929; s. Fred and Gladys Anna (Forsberg) W.; m. Betty Lorraine Warren, June 20, 1953; children: David, Carolyn, Robert, Judy. B.Th., No. Baptist Sem., 1953; D.D. (hon.), Temple Sem., Chattanooga, 1965, Trinity Ev-Div. Sch., 1986; LittD (hon.), Cedarville U., 1987. Ordained to ministry, Bapt. Ch., 1951. Pastor Central Bapt. Ch., East Chicago, 1951-57; editl. dir. Youth for Christ Internat., Wheaton, Ill., 1957-61; pastor Calvary Bapt. Ch., Covington, Ky., 1961-71; sr. min. Moody Ch., Chgo., 1971-78; bd. dirs. Slavic Gospel Assn., Wheaton, 1973-87; columnist Moody Monthly, Chgo., 1971-77; author, conf. minister, 1978-80; pres. ScripTex, Inc., Lincoln, Nebr., 1982—. Vis. instr. pastoral theology Trinity Div. Sch., Deerfield, Ill.; gen. dir. Back to the Bible Radio Ministries, Lincoln, Nebr., 1984-89; writer-in-residence Cornerstone Coll., Grand Rapids, Mich.; disting. prof. preaching Grand Rapids Bapt. Sem. Author: over 150 books including William Culberson, A Man of God, 1974, Live Like a King, 1976, Walking with the Giants, 1976, Be Right, 1977, (with David Wiersbe) Making Sense of the Ministry, 1983, Why Us? Why Bad Things Happen to God's People, 1984, Real Worship: It Can Transform Your Life, 1986, The Integrity Crisis, 1988, Be What You Are, 1988, The New Pilgrim's Progress, 1989, Living

With the Giants, 1993, Preaching and Teaching with Imagination, 1994, Be Myself, 1994, The Bible Exposition Commentary, 6 vols., 2004. Home and Office: 441 Lakewood Dr Lincoln NE 68510-2419

**WIERSMA, G. BRUCE,** dean, forester, educator; b. Paterson, N.J., Oct. 26, 1942; s. George and Marjorie (Zeedyk) W.; m. Ann Becker, Aug. 15, 1964; children: Heather, Robin, Jennifer, Joshua. BS, U. Maine, 1964; MF in Forestry, Yale U., 1965; PhD Coll. Environ. Sci. & Forestry, SUNY, 1968. Teaching asst., 1965-66; rsch. biologist Coll. Environ. Sci. and Forestry SUNY, 1968; combat devels. staff officer U.S. Army Inst. Land Combat, Alexandria, Va., 1968-70; head monitoring sect. EPA, Washington, 1970-72, chief ecol. monitoring branch, 1972-74, chief pollutant pathways br. Las Vegas, Nev., 1974-79, sr. ecologist, 1979-80; mgr. environ. earth scis. group, Idaho Nat. Engring. Lab. EG&G Idaho, Inc., 1980-87; instr. Idaho Falls Campus of Higher Edn. U. Idaho, 1981-90, affiliate grad. faculty Coll. Forestry Wildlife and Range Scis., 1988-90; mgr., dir. Ctr. Environ. Monitoring and Assessment Environ. Sci. and Tech. Group, 1989-90; dir. Ctr. Environ. Monitoring and Assessment Idaho Nat. Engring. Lab., EG&G Idaho, Inc., Idaho Falls, 1988-90; dean Coll. Forest Resources, assoc. dir. Maine Agrl. Experiment Sta., prof. Forest Resources U. Maine, Orono, 1991-93, dean Coll. Natural Scis., Forestry and Agr., dir. Maine Agrl. and Forest Exptl. Sta., 1993—. Dir. Ctr. Environ. Monitoring and Assessment, Idaho Falls, Idaho, 1980-90; mem. ad-hoc task force to plan global environ. monitoring sys., 1993-95; trustee Nature Conservancy, 1993-95; mem. UN ad hoc task force to plan global terrestrial observing sys., 1993-95; bd. dirs. Maine Forest Products Coun., 1993—; U.S. Nat. Com. on Data for Sci. and Tech., 1990-92; chmn. com. on databased NRC, 1990-94, mem. com. on marine monitoring, 1986-90; mem. forest resources adv. com. U.S. Sec. Agr., 1998—; mem. Gov. Maine's Com. on Sawmill Biomass Conversion, 1999. Contbr. chpts. to books, articles to profl. jours; editor, founder Jour. Environ. Monitoring and Assesment. Pilot, Maine wing CAP. Capt. U.S. Army, 1968-70. Recipient numerous rsch. grants from various sources. Mem. NRC (chair com. on databases, 1990-94, com. on marine monitoring, 1986-90, Nat. Assn. Profl. Forestry Schs. (exec. com. 1993-98), Assn. Expt. Sta. Dirs. (exec. com. N.E. region 1996-2000, chmn. 1998-99, com. on policy 1997—). Avocations: jogging, swimming, cross country skiing, backpacking. Home: 103 Wildwood Estates Dr Holden ME 04429-7344 Office: Univ of Maine/Coll Natural Scis Forestry and Agr 5782 Winslow Hall Orono ME 04469-5782 Office Phone: 207-581-3794. Business E-Mail: wiersma@maine.edu.

**WIERSMA, KEVIN,** lab administrator; Various positions, fin. and opers. mgmt. Medtox Scientific, Inc., St. Paul, 1992—98, v.p., 1998—, COO, lab. divsn., 2000—, CFO, 2002—. Office: Medtox Scientific Inc 402 W County Rd D Saint Paul MN 55112

**WIERZCHOLSKI, WUNSCHIK CHRISTOPH,** mechanical engineer, mathematician, information scientist; b. Znin, Poland, Mar. 18, 1939; s. Henryk and Kanarkowska Maria Wunschik; m. Anna Poznanska, Apr. 27, 1974; 1 child, Michalina. M of Engring., Tech. U., Poznań, Poland, 1967, ScD, PhD, 1970; MSc in Math., U. Poznań, 1967. Asst. prof. Tech. U., Lublin, Poland, 1983-85, Szczecin, Poland, 1985-90, prof., 1990—, Maritime U. Gdynia, 2000, Golansk U. Tech., 2003—. Head dept. applied math. U. Szczecin, 1986-88; head dept. tech. mechanics Agrl. Acad. Szczecin, 1990-94; lectr., Tech. U. Hannover, Germany, 1992, guest prof. mech. engr., Tech. U. Essen, Germany DFG, German Rsch. Found., 1997; coord. EU Grantee Transfer of Knowledge, 2004—. Contbr. over 350 articles to profl. scientific jours. in field of tech. mechanics tribology. Coord. EU Grant Transfer of Knowledge, 2004—. Polish grant, 1990, 94, 97, 99, 2001, 2003 German grantee DLR-Berlin-POL, 198-96; recipient Scientific State award in topic hydrodynamic lubrication, 1981. Mem. Polish Math. Soc., Polish Acad. Scis. (sect. of biomechanics 1999—), Polish Tribological Soc. (mem. mgmt. 1997—), Scientific Soc. of Szczecin, N.Y. Acad. Roman Catholic. Avocation: numerical and analytical applications in biomechanics. Home: Seledynowa PL 70781 Szczecin Poland Office: Seledynowa st 9/7 PL70-781 Szczecin Poland Address: Stettin Seledynowastr 9/7 PL70781 Szczecin Poland

**WIES, BARBARA,** publishing executive, editor; b. Dec. 5, 1939; BA, U. Conn., 1961; student, New Sch. for Social Rsch., 1961-62. Product devel. Fearn Soya, Melrose Park, Ill., 1973-75; product devel. Modern Products, Milw., 1973-75; editor, pub. Bestways Mag., Carson City, Nev., 1977-89; pub. The Healthy Gourmet Newsletter, 1989-91, Fine Wine Good Food Newsletter, 1991—; publicity dir. Nev. Artists Assn., 1994—; owner Gualala (Calif.) Galleries, 1989-90; assoc. pub., mgr. Gola Range Mag., 1998—. Owner, operator cooking sch. Greensboro N.C. 1969-73; instr. Very Spl. Arts Nev., 1997. Author: Natural Cooking, 1968, Wok and Tempura, 1969, Japanese Home Cooking, 1970, The Wok, 1971, Super Soy, 1973, The Health Gourmet, 1981, International Healthy Gourmet, 1982; editor: Desert News, 2004—; one-woman show paintings Dolphin Gallery, Gualala, Calif., 1990, River Gallery, Reno, 1994; 2 women show 1992, 94, 96, Dolphin Gallery, Calif., 1994, solo exhbn. Nev. Artists Assn. Gallery, 1993, 95, 96, 97; featured artist Nev. State Libr., 1996, Silver State Gallery, Reno, 1998, West Nev. C.C., 1996, art show judge, 1997; restaurant critic Reno Gazette Jour., 1995-2001; editor, designer Nev. Episcopal Diocesan newsletter Desert Spirit, 2004—; Bishop's Staff, Episcopal Diocese of Nevada, 2005-, 2006. Performer Nev. Arts sponsored Tumblewords, 2000—; staff assoc. Wilmington Children's Mus., NC; del. Nev. Episcopal Diocese Convention, 2002, Vestry St. Peter's Episcopal Ch., 2003—; sr. warden, 2005. Grantee Nev. Arts Coun., 2002; recipient First Place adult fiction Nev. State Lit. Co., 1995, First Place fiction State Lit. Comp., 1998, 2d Place fiction Writers Block; Nev. Arts Coun. fellow, 1999-2000. Mem. Nat. League Am. Pen Women (chair 1st and 2d ann. lit. competition Reno br., chairperson 1st Nat. Lit. award), Inst. Food Technologists, Pastel Soc. of the West Coast, Inst. Am. Culinary Profls.

**WIESCHAUS, ERIC F.,** molecular biologist, educator; b. South Bend, Ind., June 8, 1947; BS, U. Notre Dame, 1969; PhD in Biology, Yale U., 1974. Rsch. fellow Zool. Inst., U. Zurich, Switzerland, 1975-78; group leader European Molecular Biol. Lab., Germany, 1978-81; from asst. prof. to assoc. prof. Princeton U., 1981-87; prof. molecular biology Princeton U., 1987—. Fellow Lab. de Genetique Moleculaire, France, 1976; vis. rscher. Ctr. Pathobiology, U. Calif., Irvine, 1977; mem. sci. adv. coun. Damon Runyon-Walter Winchell Cancer Fund, 1987-92. Contbr. articles to numerous profl. jours. Recipient Nobel prize in physiology or medicine, 1995. Fellow Am. Acad. Arts and Scis.; mem. NAS. Office: Princeton U MOF 435 Dept Molecular Biology Washington Rd Princeton NJ 08544-0001*

**WIESE, DANIEL EDWARD,** marketing and communications researcher; b. Cedar Rapids, Iowa, June 16, 1936; s. Erwin Edward and Bernice Virginia (Cristy) W.; m. Mary Virginia Smith, Nov. 3, 1958 (div. 1982); children: Anne, John, Amy; m. JoBeth Kuehl, Aug. 6, 1982; children: Jamie, Jill, Eric. BS, Iowa State U., 1958. Agy. assoc. ConnGen Life Ins., Hartford, Conn., 1959—61; rsch. assoc. Meredith Pub. Co., Des Moines, 1961—65; rsch. dir. Popular Sci. Pub. Co., N.Y.C., 1966—67; assoc. rsch. dir. Reader Digest Assn., N.Y.C., 1966—67; rsch. dir. Successful Farming divsn. Meredith Corp., Des Moines, 1967—77; mgr. Agtrack divsn. Chilton Rsch. Svcs. Radnor, Pa., 1977—80; v.p., dir. rsch. svcs. Creswell, Munsell, Fulta & Zirbel, Inc., Cedar Rapids, Iowa, 1980—86; pres. Dan Wiese Mktg. Rsch., Cedar Rapids, Iowa, 1986—. Mem. editl. adv. bd. Agrimarketing mag., 1989. Bd. dirs. Plymouth Congl. Nursery Sch., Des Moines, 1975; mktg. com. Cedar Rapids Symphony, 1984; mem. adv. bd. Cedar Rapids Better Bus. Bur., Area Mktg. Task Force, Linn County I-Club Bd., 1991-92; bd. dirs., chmn. mktg. com. Witwer Sr. Ctr., 2001—. Capt. U.S. Army, 1959.mem. Celebration of Agr. com., 1999—. Mem. Nat. Agri-Mktg. Assn. (chmn. mktg. rsch. com. 1982-83, Cornbelt chpt. bd. 1995-2001), Advt. Fedn. Cedar Rapids (1st v.p. 1988-89, pres. 1989-90, bd. dirs. 1987-90, mem. adv. bd. 2002—, inducted Hall of Fame 2003), Cedar Rapids C. of C. (agr.-bus. com.), Ag-Maizing Cedar Rapids (exec. com. 1998-99), Rotary. Home and Office: 2108 Greenwood Dr SE Cedar Rapids IA 52403-2727 Office Phone: 319-364-2866. Business E-Mail: danwiese@mchsi.com.

**WIESE, GLENDA COPPERSMITH,** librarian, archivist; b. Oskaloosa, Iowa, May 6, 1948; d. Franklin Carlisle and Genevieve Burdock Coppersmith; m. Carlton Edwin Wiese, Mar. 24, 1968; children: Elizabeth Coppersmith, Audrey Carlisle. BA, Marycrest Coll., 1972; MA, U. Iowa, 1973, PhD, 2003. Head children's svcs. Bettendorf Pub. Libr., Iowa, 1973—81; spl. collections libr., archivist Palmer Coll. Chiropractic, Davenport, 1980—. Co-author: Principles and Practice of Chiropractic, Fundamentals of Chiropractic, Chiropractic Success; editor: Chiropractic: An Illustrated History; contbr. articles to profl. jours. Grant writer Jr. League of the Quad-Cities, Davenport, 1998. Recipient Murray Gottlieb Prize, Med. Libr. Assn., 1993, Outstanding Faculty of 1987, Palmer Coll. of Chiropractic, 1987, Outstand Faculty of the Yr., 1995, Thelma FordyceMack Faculty Recognition Award, 2002, 2004—05. Mem.: Mid-West Archives Conf., Soc. Am. Archivist, Med. Libr. Assn. (chair chiropractic librs. sect. 1991—93), Quad-Cities Heritage League, Assn. History Chiropractic (exec. dir. 1996—2000, bd. dirs. 2004—). Avocations: gardening, boating, reading, travel, camping. Office: Palmer Coll Chiropractic 1000 Brady St Davenport IA 52803 Office Phone: 563-884-5894. Office Fax: 563-884-5267. E-mail: wiese_g@palmer.edu.

**WIESE, WOLFGANG LOTHAR,** physicist, researcher; b. Tilsit, Germany, Apr. 21, 1931; came to U.S., 1957; naturalized, 1965; s. Werner Max and Charlotte (Donath) W.; m. Gesa Ladehoff, Oct. 12, 1957; children: Margrit, Cosima. BS, U. Kiel, Fed. Republic Germany, 1954, PhD, 1957, PhD (hon.), 1993. Rsch. assoc. U. Md., College Park, 1958-59; rsch. physicist Nat. Bur. Standards, Gaithersburg, Md., 1960-62, chief plasma spectrosc. sect., 1962-77, chief atomic and plasma radiation div., 1978-91, chief atomic physics div., 1991—2004; ret., 2004; NIST rsch. assoc., 2005—. Lectr. U. Calif., 1963, 64. Author: Atomic Transition Probabilities, Vol. I., 1966, Vol. II, 1969, Vol. III, 1988, Vol. IV, 1988, Atomic Transition Probabilities for C, N, and O, 1996, Spectral Data for Highly Ionized Atoms, 2000. Recipient Silver Medal award Dept. Commerce, 1962, Gold Medal award, 1971, Humboldt award, 1986, A.S. Fleming award U.S.C. of C., 1971, Disting. Career in Sci. award Wash. Acad. Sci., 1992, Disting. Postdoctoral award U. Md., 2003; Guggenheim fellow, 1966. Fellow Am. Phys. Soc., Optical Soc. Am., Wash. Acad. Sci.; mem. Internat. Astron. Union. Lutheran. Home: 8229 Stone Trail Dr Bethesda MD 20817-4555 Office Phone: 301-975-3201. Business E-Mail: wiese@nist.gov.

**WIESEL, ELIE,** writer, educator; b. Sighet, Romania, Sept. 30, 1928; arrived in Paris, 1945; came to US, 1956, naturalized, 1963; s. Shlomo and Sarah (Feig) W.; m. Marion Erster, 1969; 1 son, Shlomo Elisha; 1 stepchild, Jennifer. Student, The Sorbonne, Paris, 1948-51; LittD (hon.), Jewish Theol. Sem., NYC, 1967; LHD (hon.), Hebrew Union Coll., 1968, Manhattanville Coll., 1972, Yeshiva U., 1973; D of Hebrew Letters (hon.), Spertus Coll. Judaica, 1973; PhD (hon.), Bar-Ilan U., 1973; LHD (hon.), Boston U., 1974; LLD (hon.), Hofstra U., 1975; LittD (hon.), Marquette U., 1975, Simmons Coll., 1976; LHD (hon.), Coll. St. Scholastica, 1978; LLD (hon.), Talmudic U. Fla., 1979; LHD (hon.), Wesleyan U., 1979; LLD (hon.), U. Notre Dame, 1980; LHD (hon.), Brandeis U., 1980; LittD (hon.), Anna Maria Coll., 1980, Yale U., 1981; LHD (hon.), Kenyon Coll., 1982, Hobart/William Smith Coll., 1982, Emory U., 1983, Siena Heights Coll., 1983, Fla. Internat. U., 1983, Fairfield U., 1983, Dropsie Coll., 1983, Moravian Coll., 1984, Colgate U., 1984; LittD (hon.), Wake Forest U., 1985; LHD (hon.), SUNY, Binghamton, 1985, Lehigh U., 1985; LittD (hon.), Haverford Coll., 1985; HHD (hon.), U. Hartford, 1985; LHD (hon.), Coll. New Rochelle, 1986, Tufts U., 1986, Georgetown U., 1986; LittD (hon.), Capital U., 1986; LHD (hon.), Hamilton Coll., 1986, Rockford Coll., 1986; PhD (hon.), U. Haifa, 1986; LittD (hon.), LI U., 1986; LHD (hon.), Villanova U., 1987, Coll. St. Thomas, 1987, U. Denver, 1987, Walsh Coll., 1987, Loyola Coll., 1987; LittD (hon.), U. Paris, Sorbonne, 1987; HHD (hon.), Lycoming Coll., 1987; LittD (hon.), U. Conn., 1988; PhD (hon.), Ben Gurion U., 1988; LittD (hon.), U. Cen. Fla., 1988; LLD (hon.), La Salle U., 1988; LHD (hon.), Ohio U., 1988; HHD (hon.), U. Miami, 1988; LittD (hon.), Wheeling Jesuit Coll., 1989, Wittenberg U., 1989; HHD (hon.), Brigham Young U., 1989; DSc (hon.), U. Health Scis./Chgo. Med. Sch., 1989; LHD (hon.), Concordia Coll., 1990, NYU, 1990, Fordham U., 1990, Conn. Coll., 1990; ThD (hon.), U. Åbo Akadem, 1990; LHD (hon.), Upsala Coll., 1991, Duquesne U., 1991, Roosevelt U., 1991, Hunter Coll., 1992, Susquehanna U., 1992, Am. U., 1992; LittD (hon.), Fairleigh Dickenson U., 1993; LHD (hon.), Millersville U., 1993; degree (hon.), U. Dayton, 1993, U. Mich., 1993, U. Bordeaux, 1993; LHD (hon.), Gustavus Adolphus Coll., 1994, McGill U., 1994, Mt. Sinai Med. Sch., 1994, Spelman Coll., 1995; Doctorat (hon.), U. Catholique de Louvain, 1995; LLD (hon.), Bates Coll., 1995; LHD (hon.), Sacred Heart U., 1995; D (hon.), U. Buenos Aires, 1995; Docteur (hon.), U. de Picardie Jules Verne, Amiens, France, 1996; LHD (hon.), Briar Cliff Coll., 1996, Clark U., 1996, Phila. Coll. Textiles, 1996, U. Mass., Dartmouth, 1997, U. South Fla., 1997; LHD (hon.), Fla. Atlantic U., 1997, U. R.I. 1997, U. Mass., Lowell, 1997; LLD (hon.), U. Guelph, 1997; LHD (hon.), De Paul U., 1997, Seton Hall U., 1998; LittD (hon.), St. John's U., 1998; LHD (hon.), Eckerd Coll., 1998, Appalachian State U., 1998; LHD (hon.), Merrimack U., 1998; D. (hon.), Cedar Crest Coll., 1998; LHD (hon.), Gettysburg Coll., 1998, Loyola U., Chgo., 1999; HHD (hon.), Mich. State U., 1999; Doutor (hon.), U. do Estado do Rio de Janeiro, 1999; Docteur (hon.), U. Montreal, 1999; LHD (hon.), St. Norbert Coll., 1999; St. Joseph's U., 2000, U. Fla., 2000; PhD (hon.), Hebrew U., 2000, U. Bologna, 2000; EdD (hon.), Regis U., 2001; Docteur (hon.), U. Paris, Sorbonne, 2001; LHD (hon.), Hebrew Coll., 2001; EdD (hon.), Stockton Coll., 2003, Meredith Coll., 2003, Old Dominion U., 2003, Elon U., 2004, Case Western Reserve U., 2004; LHD (hon.), Chapman U., 2005, Israel Inst. Tech., 2005, MsDaniel Coll., 2005, Chapman U., 2005; HHD, McDaniel Coll., 2005. Disting. prof. Judaic studies CCNY, 1972-76; Andrew W. Mellon prof. in the humanities Boston U., 1976—, prof. religious studies and univ. prof., 1976—, prof. philosophy, 1988—. Disting. vis. prof. Henry Luce, 1982-83, Yale U.; lectr. Andrew W. Mellon Ann. Lecture Series Boston U., 92d St. YMHA, YWHA Ann. Lectr. Series, ann. radio broadcast series, 1966-86, advisory bd. Rena Costa Ctr. for Yiddish Studies at Bar-Ilan U., 1994, advisory coun. Carnegie Commn. on Preventing Deadly Conflict, 1994, chmn US Pres's Commn. on the Holocaust, 1979-80, US Holocaust Meml. Coun., 1980-86; hon. chmn. Holocaust Studies Ctr. of Bronx HS Sci., Nat. Jewish Resource Ctr., NYC; hon. coun. Vancouver Holocaust Ctr. Soc., 1992—, Ctr. Christian-Jewish Understanding, Sacred Heart U.; Am. Friends of Ghetto Fighter's House; co-chmn. Children of Chernobyl/Children at Heart, 1995—; steering com. The Balkan Inst., 1996—; mem. Nat. hon. com. Darius Milhaud Soc.; mem. coun. Ethic Accord Project on Ethic Rels., (hon.) Am. Friends of Neve Shalom/Wahat al-Salam, 1996—; leadership coun. Tanenbaum Ctr. Interreligious Understanding, 1996—; founder Elie Wiesel Found. for Humanity, 1987; founding pres. Paris-based Universal Acad. Cultures, 1993; pres. Am. Friends Kiryat Ungvar-Jerusalem, 1990—; hon. pres. Comité Français Pour "Yad Vashem," Am. Gathering of Jewish Holocaust Survivors, 1985, Am. Kurdish Info. Network, 1997, adv. bd., 1997; v.p. Internat. Rescue Com., 1985—; adv. bd. The Raoul Wallenberg Commn. of US, 1981—, Friends of LeChambon, 1982, Boston U. Inst. for Philosophy & Religion, 1986, Boston U. Students for a Free Tibet, Nat. Inst. Against Prejudice & Violence, Internat. Ctr. in NY, 1986—, Friends of Akim USA, 1991, Sholom Aleichem Meml. Found., Nat. Law Students Assn., 1995—, AmeriCares, 1995, React Take Action Awards, 1996—, No Greater Love, 1996—, Inst. Study of Violence, 1996—, Global Lawyers and Physicians: Working Together for Human Rights, 1997; internat. adv. bd. Elmhurst Coll. Holocaust Edn. Project, 1996—; Am. bd. adv. The Moscow Ctr.; advisory coun. US Com. Refugees, 1996—, Nat. Endowment for Democracy, 1996—; Helsinki adv. com. Human Rights Watch; bd. govs. Haifa U., (mem. emeritus) Tel Aviv U. 1976—, Massuah - Inst. Study of Holocaust, Israel; bd. dirs. Nat. Com. on Am. Fgn. Policy, Elaine Kaufman Cultural Ctr., Humanitas, Am. Assocs. Ben-Gurion U. of the Negev, Mut. of Am., France Libertés, bd. dir. HIAS; bd. trustees Annenberg Rsch. Inst., 1983-89, Am. Jour. World Svc., 1985—; Haifa U.; Tel-Aviv U., Yeshiva U., 1977—, Am. Jewish Heritage Ctr., Mus. Jewish Heritage, NY; patron Internat. Peace U., Berlin, 1995—; colleague Cathedral St. John the Divine, 1975—; mem. jury Nessuit Internat. Prize Lit., 1984; mem. Task Force Apprehending Indicted War Criminals, 1998—. Author: Night (Oprah's Book Club 2006) 1960, Dawn, 1961, The Accident, 1962, The Town Beyond the Wall, 1964, The Gates of the Forest, 1966, The Jews of Silence, 1966, Legends of Our Time, 1968, A Beggar in Jerusalem,

1970, One Generation After, 1970, Souls on Fire, 1972, The Oath, 1973, Ani Maamin, 1973, Zalmen, or the Madness of God, 1974, Messengers of God, 1976, A Jew Today, 1978, Four Hasidic Masters, 1978, The Trial of God, 1979, The Testament, 1980, Le Testament D'Un Poète Juif Assassiné (France's Prix Livre-Inter 1980), Bourse Goncourt, 1980, Prix des Bibliothécaires, 1981), 1985, Images from the Bible, 1980, Five Biblical Portraits, 1981, Somewhere A Master, 1982, Paroles d'Étranger, 1982, The Golem, 1983, The Fifth Son (Grand Prix de la Littérature, City of Paris), 1985, Signes d'Exode, 1985, Against Silence (3 vols., ed. Irving Abrahamson), 1985, Job ou Dieu dans la Tempête, 1986, A Song for Hope, 1987, The Nobel Address, 1987, Twilight, 1988; (essays) Silences et Mémoire d'hommes, 1989, L'Oublié, 1989, From the Kingdom of Memory, 1990, Célébration Talmudique, 1991, Sages and Dreamers, 1991, The Forgotten, 1992, (with John Cardinal O'Connor) A Journey of Faith, 1990, (with Albert Friedlander) The Six Days of Destruction, 1988, (dialogues with Philippe-Michaël Saint-Cheron) Evil and Exile, 1990, commentaries to A Passover Haggadah, 1993, All Rivers Run To The Sea (a memoir), 1995, (with Jorge Semprun) Setaire est Impossible, 1995, (with François Mitterand) Memoir in Two Voices, 1996, Et la Mer N'est Pas Remplie, Memoirs II, 1996, Célébration Prophétique, Portraits et Légendes, 1998, Les juges, 1999, King Solomon and His Magic Ring, 1999, And the Sea is Never Full (English transl. of Et la mer n'est pas remplie, Memoirs II 1999), The Judges, 2002, (dialogues with Michael de Saint Cheron) Le Mal et L'Exil/Dix ans après, 1999, (essays) D'où viens-tu? (pub. by Le Seuil), 2001, After the Darkness, 2002, Wise Men and Their Tales, 2003, The Time of the Uprooted, 2005, (essays) Et où vas-tu?, 2004; editorial and adv. bds. Midstream, Religion and Lit. (U. Notre Dame), Sh'ma: Jour. of Responsibility, Hadassah Mag., Acad. of the Air for Jewish Studies, Holocaust and Genocide Studies: An Internat. Jour., Passages, Religion and the Arts; subject of more than 55 books; journalist Israeli, French and Am. newspapers. Chmn. adv. bd. World Union Jewish Students, 1985—; comité d'Honneur Ligue International Contre le Racisme et l'Antisemitisme, 1985—; founder Nat. Jewish Ctr. Learning and Leadership, 1974; mem. soc. fellows Ctr. Judaic Studies, U. Denver, 1980, bd. overseer Bar-Ilan U., 1970—. Recipient Prix Rivarol, 1963, Prix de l'Universite de la langue Francaise, 1963, Ingram Merrill award, 1964, Jewish Heritage award, Haifa U., 1975, Remembrance award, 1965, Prix du Souvenir, 1965, Nat. Jewish Book Council award, 1965, 1973, Prix Médicis, 1968, Prix Bordin, French Acad., 1972, Eleanor Roosevelt Meml. award, NY United Jewish Appeal, 1972, Am. Liberties medallion, Am. Jewish Com., 1972, Martin Luther King Jr. medallion, CCNY, 1973, Ann. award for Disting. Service to Am. Jewry, Nat. Fedn. of Jewish Men's Clubs, 1973, Faculty Disting. Scholar award, Hofstra U., 1974, Rambam award, Am. Mizrachi Women, 1974, Meml. award, NY Soc. Clin. Psychologists, 1975, First Spertus Internat. award, 1976, Myrtle Wreath award, Hadassah, 1977, King Solomon award, 1977, Liberty award, HIAS, 1977, Jewish Heritage award, B'nai B'rith, 1966, Avodah award, Jewish Tchrs. Assn., Jewish Tchrs. Assn., 1972, Humanitarian award, B'rith Sholom, 1978, Joseph Prize for Human Rights, Anti-Defamation League, 1978, Zalman Shazar award, State of Israel, 1979, Presdl. Citation, NYU, 1979, Inaugural award for Lit., Israel Bonds Prime Minister's Com., 1979, Jabotinsky medal, S.Y. Agnon medal, State of Israel, 1980, Rabbanit Sarah Herzog award, Emunah Women of Am., 1981, Le Grand Prix Littéraire du Festival Internat. Deauville, 1983, Internat. Lit. prize for Peace, Royal Acad. Belgium, 1983, Lit. Lions award, NY Pub. Libr., 1983, Jordan Davidson Humanitarian award, Fla. Internat. U., 1983, Anatoly Scharansky Humanitarian award, 1983, Grand Officer, Legion of Honor, France, Congl. gold medal, 1985, Voice of Conscience award, Am. Jewish Congress, 1985, Remembrance award, Israel Bonds, 1985, Anne Frank award, 1985, 4 Freedoms award, FDR 4 Freedoms Found., 1985, Medal of Liberty award, Statue of Liberty Presentation, 1986, Nobel Peace Prize, 1986, First Herzl Lit. award, First David Ben-Gurion award, Nat. UJA, Gov.'s award, Shaarei Tzedek, Internat. Kaplun Found. award, Hebrew U. Jerusalem, Scopus award, 1974, Am.-Israeli Friendship award, Disting. Writers award, Lincolnwood Library, 1984, First Chancellor Joseph H. Lookstein award, Bar-Ilan U., 1984, Sam Levenson Meml. award, Jewish Cmty. Rels. Coun., 1984, Comenius award, Moravian Coll., 1985, Henrietta Szold award, Hadassah, 1985, Disting. Cmty. Svc. award, Mut. Am., 1985, Covenant Peace award, Synagogue Coun. Am., 1985, Jacob Pat award, World Congress Jewish Culture, 1985, Humanitarian award, Internat. League Human Rights, 1985, Disting. Fgn.-Born Am. award, Internat. Ctr. NY, Inc., 1986, Freedom Cup award, Women's League Israel, 1986, First Jacob Javits Humanitarian award, UJA Young Leadership, 1986, Boston City Coun. Commendation, 1986, medal of Jerusalem, 1986, Freedom award, Internat. Rescue Com., 1987, Achievement award, Artist and Writers for Peace in the Mid. East, 1987, La Grande Médaille de Vermeil de la Ville de Paris, 1987, La Médaille de la Chancellerie de l'Université de Paris, 1987, La Médaille de l'Université de Paris, 1987, First Eitinger prize, U. Oslo, 1987, Lifetime Achievment award, Present Tense mag., 1987, Spl. Christopher award, The Christophers, 1987, Achievement award, State Israel, 1987, Sem. medal, Jewish Theol. Sem. Am., 1987, Metcalf Cup and Prize for Excellence in Teaching, Boston U., 1987, Spl. award, Nat. Com. on Am. Fgn. Policy, 1987, Grã-Cruz da Ordem Nacional do Cruzeiro do Sul, Brazil's highest distinction, 1987, Profiles in Courage award, B'nai B'rith, 1987, Centennial medal, U. Scranton, 1987, Citation from Religious Edn. Assn., 1987, Golda Meir Sr. Humanitarian award, 1987, Presdl. medal, Hofstra U., 1988, Bicentennial medal, Georgetown U., 1988, Human Rights Law award, Internat. Human Rights Law Group, 1988, Janus Korczak Humanitarian award, INTERPHIL, 1989, Count Sforza award in Philanthropy, Am. Hungarian Found., 1989, Lily Edelman award for Excellence in Continuing Jewish Edn., B'nai B'rith Internat., 1989, George Washington award, NAHE, Kent State U., 1989, Bicentennial medal, NYU, 1989, Humanitarian award, Human Rights Campaign Fund, 1989, Internat. Brotherhood award, C.O.R.E., 1990, Frank Weil award for Disting. Contbn. to adv. of N.Am., Jewish Culture Jewish Cmty. Ctrs. Assn. N.Am., 1990—, 1st Raoul Wallenberg award, U. Mich., 1990, Award of Highest Honor, Soka U., 1991, Facing History and Ourselves Humanity award, 1991, La Medaille de la Ville de Toulouse, 1991, 1st Internat. Primo Levi award, 1992, Lit. Arts award, Mus. Found. for Jewish Culture, 1992, Ellis Island Medal of Honor, 1992, Guardian of the Children award, AKIM USA, 1992, Bishop Francis J. Mugavero award for religious and racial harmony Cath. Newman Ctr. Queens Coll., 1994, Golden Slipper Humanitarian award, 1994, Interfaith Coun. on the Holocaust Humanitarian award, 1994, Crystal award Davos World Economic Forum, 1995, First Niebuhr award, Elmhurst Coll., 1995, Mathilde Schecter award Women's League Conservative Judaism, 2000, Manhattan award Nat. Arts Club, 2000, Benediction medal The Delbarton Sch., 2001, Humanitarian award Israel Cancer Rsch. Fund, 2004, Inaugural award Louise T. Blouin Found., 2005, Grifo d'Oro award Mayor of Genoa, Italy, 2005, Light of Truth award Internat. Campaign Tibet, 2005; named Humanitarian of the Century Coun. Jewish Orgns., Presdl. medal Freedom, 1992; Beth Hatefutsoth hon. fellow, 1988; honors established in his name: Elie Wiesel award for Holocaust Rsch., U. Haifa, Elie Wiesel Chair in Holocaust Studies, Bar-Ilan U., Elie Wiesel Endowment Fund for Jewish Culture, U. Denver, 1987, Elie Wiesel Disting. Svc. award, U. Fla., 1988, Elie Wiesel awards for Jewish Arts and Culture B'nai B'rith Hillel Founds., 1988, Elie Wiesel Chair in Judaic Studies Coll., 1990, Disting. Libery award N.Y.C. Refugee Employment Project, 1995, Freedom award Nat. Civil Rights Mus., 1995, Humanitarian award Queensborough Comty. Coll./Holocaust Resource Ctr. Archives, 1995, Socio Honorario de la Sociedad Hebrai ca Argentina, 1995, Pres. award Quinnipac Coll., 1996, Golden Plate award Am. Acad. Achievement, 1996, Lotos medal of Merit, The Lotos Club, 1996, Guardian of Zion award Ingeborg Rennert Ctr. Jerusalem Studies, Bar-Ilan U., 1997, Eisenhower Leadership prize Eisenhower World Affairs Inst. Gettysburg Coll., 1997, Canterbury medalist Becket Fund for Religious Liberty, 1998, ABA ann. award, 1998, Rabbi Marc H. Tanenbaum award for Advancement Interreligious Understanding, 1998, Yitzhak Rabin Peacemaker award Merrimack Coll., 1998, Aesop prize Children's Am. Folklore Soc. for King Solomon and His Magic Ring (Children's Folklore sect. 1999), Raoul Wallenberg Internat. Humanitarian award The Am. Jewish Joint Distbn. Com., 1999, Comdr.'s Cross, Order of Merit, Republic of Hungary, 2004, King Hussein award, Hashemite Kingdom of Jordan, 2005, Hon. Citizen City of Santa Margherita, Italy, 2005; named Man of Year Tel Aviv Mus. Art, 2005; named one of 100 Most Influential People, Time Mag., 2006. Fellow Jewish Acad. Arts and Scis., Am. Acad. Arts and Letters (dept. lit.), Am. Acad. Arts

& Scis., Modern Lang. Assn. Am. (hon.), Timothy Dwight Coll. Yale U.; mem. Fgn. Press Assn. (hon. life), Amnesty Internat., PEN (New England coun. 1993—), Writers & Artists for Peace in Middle East, Writers Guild of Am. East, The Author's Guild, Royal Norwegian Soc. Scis. and Letters, Soc. des auteurs Paris, European Acad. of Arts, Sci. and Humanities, Albert Einstein Soc. (hon., Phila.), Phi Beta Kappa (Assocs. award 1994). Office: Boston U 147 Bay State Rd Boston MA 02215

**WIESEL, SAM W.,** medical educator, academic administrator; b. Birmingham, Ala., July 7, 1945; MD, U. Pa., 1971. Intern Hosp. U. Pa., 1971—72, fellow in orthopedics, 1972—73, resident in orthopedics, 1973—76; exec. v.p. health studies, exec. dean sch. medicine Georgetown U. Med. Ctr., Washington, 1996—2002, sr. v.p., dean clin. affairs, 2002—, chmn. dept. orthop. surgery sch. medicine. Office: Georgetown U Main Campus and Med Ctr 37th and O St NW Washington DC 20057

**WIESEL, TORSTEN NILS,** neurobiologist, educator; b. Upsala, Sweden, June 3, 1924; arrived in U.S., 1955; s. Fritz Samuel and Anna-Lisa Elisabet (Bentzer) Wiesel; 1 child, Sara Elisabet. MD, Karolinska Inst., Stockholm, 1954; D Medicine (hon.), Karolinska Inst, Stockholm, 1989; AM (hon.), Harvard U., 1967; D Medicine (hon.), Linköping U., 1982; ScD (hon.), NYU, 1987, U. Bergen, 1987. Instr. physiology Karolinska Inst., 1954—55; asst. dept. child psychiatry Karolinska Hosp., 1954—55; fellow in ophthalmology Johns Hopkins U., 1955—58, asst. prof. ophthalmic physiology, 1958—59; assoc. in neurophysiology and neuropharmacology Harvard U. Med. Sch., Boston, 1959—60, asst. prof. neurophysiology and neuropharmacology, 1960—64, asst. prof. neurophysiology, dept. psychiatry, 1964—67, prof. physiology, 1967—68, prof. neurobiology, 1968—74, Robert Winthrop prof. neurobiology, 1974, 83, chmn. dept. neurobiology, 1971—82; Vincent and Brooke Astor prof. neurobiology, head lab. Rockefeller U., NYC, 1982—98, pres., 1991—98, pres. emeritus, 1998—, dir. Shelby White and Leon Levy Ctr. for Mind, Brain & Behavior, 1998—; sec. gen. Human Frontier Sci. Program, 2000. Ferrier lectr. Royal Soc. London, 1972, NIH lectr., 75; Grass lectr. Soc. Neurosci., 1976; lectr. Coll. de France, 1977; Hitchcock prof. U. Calif.-Berkeley, 1980; Sharpey-Schafer lectr. Phys. Soc. London; George Cotzias lectr. Am. Acad. Neurology, 1983; chmn. bd. govs. NY Acad Scis., 2001—. Contbr. numerous articles to profl. jours. Recipient Jules Stein award, Trustees for Prevention of Blindness, 1971, Lewis S. Rosenstiel prize, Brandeis U., 1972, Friedenwald award, Assn. Rsch. in Vision and Ophthalmology, 1975, Karl Spencer Lashley prize, Am. Philos. Soc., 1977, Louisa Gross Horwitz prize, Columbia U., 1978, Dickson prize, U. Pitts., 1979, Nobel prize in physiology or medicine, 1981, W.H. Helmerich III award, 1989. Mem.: AAAS, Inst. Medicine (chmn. com. on human rights 1994—2004, David Rall medal 2005), Royal Swedish Acad. Scis. (fgn.), Royal Soc. (fgn.), Soc. Neurosci. (pres. 1978—79), Swedish Physiol. Soc., Nat. Acad. Arts and Scis., Am. Acad. Arts and Scis., Am. Philos. Soc., Am. Physiol. Soc., Physiol. Soc. (Eng.) (hon.). Office: Rockefeller U 1230 York Ave New York NY 10021-6399 E-mail: wiesel@mail.rockefeller.edu.*

**WIESEN, DONALD GUY,** retired diversified manufacturing company executive; b. N.Y.C., July 4, 1928; s. Benjamin and Grace (Heath) W.; m. Patricia Ann Elfers, Apr. 29, 1950; children: Mara, Caitlin, Elizabeth, Anne, Megan. BS, Columbia U., 1948, MS, 1954. C.P.A., N.Y. Sr. tax specialist Price Waterhouse & Co., N.Y.C., 1950-58; with Chesebrough-Pond's Inc., Greenwich, Conn., 1958-87, gen. mgr. ops. Europe, 1965-70, treas., 1970-72, group v.p., chief fin. officer, 1972-77, group v.p., internat., 1977-82, sr. group v.p., 1982-84, vice chmn., chief fin. officer, 1984-87, also dir., ret., 1987. Bd. dirs. Skandia Am. Corp., 1985-91. Trustee Greenwich Libr., 1974-80; bd. govs. St. Bernard Coll., Cullman, Ala., 1973-75; rep. Columbia U. Alumni, Geneva, 1968; bd. dirs. Inter-City Found. for Charity and Edn., Bridgeport, Conn., 1992-93. Capt. USMC, 1951-54. Mem. AICPA, Indian Harbor Yacht Club, Univ. Club (N.Y.). Roman Catholic.

**WIESENBERG, RUSSEL JOHN,** statistician; b. Kaukauna, Wis., Apr. 9, 1924; s. Emil Martin and Josephine (Appelbaker) W.; m. Jacqueline Leonardi, Nov. 23; children: James Wynne, Deborann Donna. BS, U. Wis., 1951; postgrad. Cornell U., 1960-61, U. Mich., 1969, George Washington U., 1976. Analyst, GE, West Lynn, Mass., 1951-56; specialist Internat. GE, Rio de Janeiro, 1956-59; statistician Gen. Motors Corp., Lockport, NY, 1959-65, sr. statistician, Harrison Radiator divsn., 1965-78, sr. reliability engr., 1978-82, sr. reliability statistician, 1982-87. Auditor Cmty. Chest Fund, 1952-55; umpire Little League Baseball, 1962-65; committeeman Buffalo Area coun. Boy Scouts Am., 1962—, Cub Scout committeeman, 1962-64, Webelos cubmaster, 1963-64; mem. Nat. Congress Parents and Tchrs., 1963—; heart fund Vol. Heart Assn., 1968; tournament dir. Am. Legion Baseball, 1975; vol. United Way campaign, 1983, nat. telethon March of Dimes, 1983-84. Served with AUS, 1943-46. Decorated Bronze Star. Mem. AAAS, Am. Statis. Assn., Nat. Register Sci. and Tech. Pers., U. Wis. Alumni Assn., Artus, Internat. Platform Assn., Phi Kappa Phi. Lutheran. com.). Contbr. articles to profl. jours. Home: 14 Norman Pl Buffalo NY 14226-4233

**WIESENFELD, BESS G.,** interior designer; b. Elizabeth, N.J., May 6, 1915; d. Morris and Rebecca (Sokolov) Gazevitz; m. Benjamin Wiesenfeld, Oct. 23, 1938 (dec.); children: Myra Judith Wiesenfeld Lewis, Elaine Phyllis Wiesenfeld Livingston, Ira Bertram (dec.), Sarah Ann Wiesenfeld Wasserman BFA, N.Y. Sch. Interior Design, 1982. Pres. Anasarca Corp., 1958—; real estate devel. Colonia, NJ, 1961—; pres. Carolier Lns., Inc., 1986—, BGW LLC, Bess & Co. Patron Met. Opera; sustaining mem. N.J. Symphony Orch. Mem.: AAUW, Am. Soc. Interior Designers (allied), Friends of Music at Princeton, Friends of Art Mus. Princeton, N.J., Mus. Modern Art, Met. Mus. Art. Jewish. Home: 374 New Dover Rd Colonia NJ 07067-2713 also: 2600 S Ocean Blvd Palm Beach FL 33480-5484

**WIESENFELD, KURT ARN,** physicist, researcher; b. Roslyn Heights, N.Y., Feb. 12, 1958; s. David and Elaine Kaye (Dattner) W.; m. Karla Mari Jennings, Aug. 17, 1985; children: Alexis Elaine and Sophia Stella (twins). BS in Physics, MIT, 1979; MA in Physics, U. Calif., Berkeley, 1982, PhD in Physics, 1985. Lectr., rschr. physics U. Calif., Santa Cruz, 1984-85; rschr. Brookhaven Nat. Lab., Upton, NY, 1985-87; asst. prof. Ga. Inst. Tech. Atlanta, 1987-92, assoc. prof., 1992-97, prof., 1997—. Contbr. numerous articles to sci. jours. Fellow Am. Phys. Soc. Office: Ga Inst Tech Sch Physics 837 State St Atlanta GA 30332-0001 Business E-Mail: Kurt.wiesenfeld@physics.gatech.edu.

**WIESER, SIEGFRIED,** planetarium executive director; b. Linz, Austria, Oct. 30, 1933; came to Can., 1955; s. Florian Wieser and Michaela Josepha (Kaufmann) Wieser-Burgstaller; m. Joan Xaven Quick, Sept. 8, 1962; children: Leonard Franz, Bernard Sidney. BS in Physics, U. Calgary, Alta., Can., 1966. Lead chorus singer, dancer Landes Theatre, Linz, 1949-53; project engr. EBG, Linz, 1952-54; with Griffith Farms Ltd., Eng., 1954-55; seismic computer operator Shell Can., Calgary, 1956-61; GTA systems analyst U. Calgary, 1961-66; planetarium dir. Centennial Planetarium, Calgary, 1966-84, exec. dir., 1984-91; exec. dir. emeritus Alberta Sci. Ctr., 1991—. Cons. Electro Controls, Salt Lake City, 1978-79. Contbr. articles to profl. publs. Recipient Violet Taylor award U. Calgary, 1964, Immigrant of Distinction Arts and Culture award, 2002; Queen Elizabeth scholar Province Alta., 1961; Paul Harris fellow Rotary Internat. Mem. Calgary Region Arts Found. (pres. 1999-2000), Alberta Coll. of Art Alumni Assn. (pres. 1991-92). Anglican. Avocations: swimming, hiking, astronomy, lecturing. E-mail: sigwies@shaw.ca.

**WIESLER, JAMES BALLARD,** retired banker; b. San Diego, July 25, 1927; s. Harry J. and Della B. (Ballard) W.; m. Mary Jane Hall, Oct. 3, 1953; children: Tom, Jim, Larry. BS, U. Colo., 1949; postgrad., Rutgers U., 1962, Advanced Mgmt. Program, Harvard U., 1973. With Bank of Am., NT & SA, 1949-87; v.p., mgr. main office San Jose, Calif., 1964-69; regional v.p. Cen. Coast adminstrn., 1969-74; sr. v.p., head No. European Area office Frankfurt, Fed. Republic of Germany, 1974-78; exec. v.p., head Asia div. Tokyo, 1978-81; exec. v.p., head N.Am. div. Los Angeles, 1981-82; vice chmn., head retail banking San Francisco, 1982-87; ret., 1987. Bd. dirs. Visa USA, Visa Internat., Sci. Applications Internat. Corp.; bd. dirs., chmn. Bank Adminstrn. Inst., 1986-87. Pres. Santa Clara County United Fund, 1969, 70, San Jose C. of C., 1968; fin. chmn. Santa Clara County Reps., 1967-74; bd. dirs. San Diego Armed Svcs., YMCA, Sidney Kimmell Cancer Ctr.; mem. bd. of trustees Borrego Cmty. Health Found.; trustee, chmn. bd. dirs. Sharp Meml. Hosp.; hon. consul-gen. for Japan, 1990-95. With USN, 1945-46. Mem. San Diego Hosp. Assn. (bd. dirs., treas.), San Diego Zool. Soc., Greater San Diego C. of C. (pres., CEO 1998-99), Bohemian Club, DeAnza Country Club, San Diego Yacht Club. Presbyterian. Home: 605 San Fernando St San Diego CA 92106-3312 Office: Bank Am Nat Trust & Savs 450 B St San Diego CA 92101-8001

**WIESNER, DAVID,** illustrator, children's writer; b. Bridgewater, N.J. m. Kim Khang; 2 children. BFA in Illustration, R.I. Sch. Design. Illustrator Houghton Mifflin, N.Y.C. Author (illustrator): (books) Free Fall, 1988 (Caldecott Honor book), Hurricane, 1990, Tuesday, 1991 (Caldecott medal, 1992), June 29, 1999, 1991 (Reading Rainbow book), Sector 7, 1999, Three Pigs, 2001 (Caldecott medal, 2002, Prix Sorcières); illustrator (books) Kite Flier, 1986, The Sorcerer's Apprentice, 1989, The Rainbow People, 1989, Tongues of Jade, 1991, Man From the Sky, 1992, Night of the Gargoyles, 1994, creator (CD-ROM) The Day the World Broke; one-man shows include Nat. Ctr. for Children's Illustrated Lit., Abilene, Tex., 1999. Office: Houghton Mifflin 222 Berkeley St Boston MA 02116

**WIESNER, JOHN JOSEPH,** retail chain store executive; b. Kansas City, Mo., Mar. 31, 1938; s. Vincent A. and Jane Ann (Hagerty) W.; m. Georgiana Schild, Oct. 15, 1960; children: Susan, John V., Gretchen. BS in Bus. Adminstrn., Rockhurst U., 1960. Vice pres., contr. Fisher Foods, Cleve., 1970-77; asst. corp. contr. Richardson Vicks, N.Y.C., 1960-70; sr. exec. v.p. Pamida, Inc., Omaha, 1977-85, vice chmn., chief exec. officer, 1985-87; CEO C.R. Anthony Co., Oklahoma City, 1987-97, chmn., CEO, 1992-97; dir. Stage Stores, 1997—. Bd. dirs. Elder Beerman, Dayton, Lamonts, Inc., Kirkland, Wash. Bd. dirs. Omaha Area Council on Alcohol and Drug Abuse, 1983—; bd. dirs. Fontenelle Forest, Omaha, chmn., 1983, 84, A Chance to Change Fedn.; mem. bd. regents Rockhurst U, Okla. City Golf & Country Club, Oklahoma City, Kansas City. Mo. Named Bus. Assoc. of Yr., Am. Bus. Women's Assn., 1983. Mem. Nat. Assn. Accts. Republican. Roman Catholic. Home: 1476 S San Joaquin Dr Palm Springs CA 92264-8685

**WIESNET, DONALD RICHARD,** retired hydrologist; b. Buffalo, Feb. 7, 1927; s. Charles Anthony Wiesnet and Rose Elizabeth Nee Hildenbrand; m. Evelyn Elaine Jordan, Dec. 27, 1952; children: Peter Christopher, Ellen Elaine, Andrew John, Elizabeth Ann. AS, Syracuse U., 1947; BA in Geology, SUNY, Buffalo, 1950, MA in Geology, 1951. Teaching Certificate NY State Bd. Regents, 1952. Geologist US Geol. Survey, Washington, 1952—61, hydrogeological map editor, 1961—64; rsch. hydrologist US Naval Oceanog. Office, Suitland, Md., 1967—71; sr. rsch. hydrologist NOAA / Nat. Environ. Satellite Svc., Camp Springs, Md., 1971—80; chief, land sciences br. NOAA / Nat. Environ. Satellite Data & Info. Svc., Camp Springs, Md., 1980—82; CEO Satellite Hydrology, Inc., Vienna, Va., 1982—90. Author: (book) Satellite Hydrology; contbr. (book) Manual of Remote Sensing, V. II, Manual of Photographic Interpretation, Facets of Hydrology. Del. White House Conf. on Aging, Washington, 1995; silver rep. (11th) Nat. Silver Haired Congress, Alexandria, Va., 1996—2004; advisor on sr. affairs Rep. Tom Davis III US Congress, 1993—2004. Capt. USNR - Ret., 1965—87. NY State Veterans' Scholarship, NY State, 1951, Govt. Employee Grad. Scholarship, US Geol. Survey, 1964, Monetary Grant - Antarctic Mapmaking, NSF, 1978. Fellow: Am. Soc. Photogrammetry & Remote Sensing, Geol. Soc. of Am.; mem.: Nat. Assn. Ret. Fed. Employees (chpt. pres. 1993—94). Roman Catholic. Achievements include pioneer in the application of remote-sensing techniques and satellite data to snow measurements, river basin parameters, flood mapping, ocean currents, and estuarine tidal flows. Avocation: ornithology. Home: 601 McKinley St NE Vienna VA 22180

**WIESSLER, DAVID ALBERT,** news correspondent; b. Cambridge, Mass., July 20, 1942; s. Albert Francis and Vivian Mary Wiessler; m. Mary Judith Burton, Dec. 28, 1968. AB, Princeton U., 1964; MA, U. Tex., 1968. Editor UPI, Dallas, N.Y.C., Washington, 1966-82; assoc. editor U.S. News & World Report, Washington, 1982-84; Washington Bur. chief UPI, Washington, 1984-90; sr. polit. editor, 1990-93; news editor Bloomberg News Svc., 1994-95; editor nat. news Reuters, Washington, 1995-98, sr. Wash. corr., 1998—. Recipient Best Feature Writer award, Dallas Press Club, 1970. Mem.: Washington Gridiron Club. Avocations: reading, travel, cooking.

**WIEST, DIANNE,** actress; b. Kansas City, Mo., Mar. 28, 1948; Student, U. Md. Appeared in numerous plays including Ashes (off-Broadway), 1976, Leave It to Beaver is Dead, The Art of Dining (Obie award, 1979, Theatre World award 1983), Bonjour La Bonjour, Three Sisters, Serenading Louie (Obie award, 1983), Othello, After the Fall, Heartbreak House, Our Town, and Hunting Cockroaches, 1987, In the Summer House, 1993, Blue Light, 1994, Memory House, 2005, Third, 2005; appeared in films including It's My Turn, 1980, I'm Dancing as Fast as I Can, 1982, Independence Day, 1982, Footloose, 1984, Falling in Love, 1984, The Purple Rose of Cairo, 1985, Hannah and Her Sisters, 1986 (Acad. award for Best Supporting Actress 1987), Radio Days, 1987, Lost Boys, 1987, September, 1987, Bright Lights, Big City, 1988, Parenthood, 1989 (Acad. award nominee), Cookie, 1989, Edward Scissorhands, 1990, Little Man Tate, 1991, Cops and Robbersons, 1994, The Scout, 1994, Bullets Over Broadway, 1994 (Golden Globe award Best Supporting Actress-Drama 1995, Acad. award for Best Supporting Actress 1995), Drunks, 1995, The Birdcage, 1996, The Associate, 1996, Practical Magic, 1998, The Horse Whisperer, 1998, Portofino, 1999, I Am Sam, 2001, Dr. Rey!, 2002, (voice) Robots, 2005; TV appearances include The Wall, 1982, The Face of Rage, 1983, Simple Life of Noah Dearborn, 1999, The 10th Kingdom, 2000.*

**WIG, ROBERT CURTIS,** retired music educator, conductor; b. Montevideo, Minn., Oct. 10, 1934; s. Emil Corneilius and Melda Dena Wig; m. Marilyn Ruth Berg, Oct. 16, 1960; children: Curtis, Karen, Kathleen. BS, St. Cloud State U., 1957, MS, 1963. Registered music educator Music Educators Nat. Conf., Washington, 1991. Music tchr. Dassel (Minn.) Pub. Sch., 1957—64, Milaca (Minn.) Pub. Sch., 1964—93, Pease (Minn.) Christian Sch., 1999—2000; ret. Mem., past condr. St. Cloud (Minn.) Mcpl. Band, 1957—; dir. Alleluia Singers, Milaca, 1993—. Recipient Commendation Mcpl. Band, City of St. Cloud, Minn. Mem.: NEA (life), Assn. Concert Bands, Ret. Assn. Music Minn. (life), Minn. Edn. Assn. (life), Windjammers Unlimited Inc., Lions Club (past pres.). Lutheran. Avocations: gardening, golf, bowling, music. Home: 525 2nd Ave SW Milaca MN 56353

**WIGAN, GARETH,** film company executive; b. London, Dec. 2, 1931; m. Patricia Wigan. Agent MCA, London, 1957—60, John Redway & Associates, 1960—61, Gregson & Wigan, 1961—68; co-founder London Internat., 1968—70; independent film prodr., 1975—77; v.p. creative affairs 20th Century Fox, Los Angeles, 1975—76, v.p. production, 1976—83; co-founder W.W. Productions, 1983—87; production consultant Columbia Pictures, 1987—93, exec. v.p., 1993—97; co-vice chair Sony Pictures Entertainment, 1997—98, Columbia Tristar Motion Picture Group, 1998—. Office: Columbia TriStar Motion Picture Group 10202 Washington Blvd Culver City CA 90232-3119

**WIGFIELD, RITA L.,** elementary school educator; b. Mpls., Dec. 14, 1945; d. Willard Ernest and Bernice Eleanor (Peterson) Ahlquist; m. Vernon Carter Wigfield, Oct. 9, 1982. BS, U. Minn., 1967; grad., St. Thomas Coll.; postgrad., Hamlin U. Cert. elem. educator, Minn. Tchr. Alice Smith Sch., Hopkins, Minn., 1967-80, Meadowbrook Sch., Hopkins 1980-86, Gatewood Sch., Hopkins, 1986—. Owner Swede Country Antiques, Minnetonka, Minn., 1983—; elem. team leader Prin.'s Adv. Bd.; chmn. bldg. tech. com. Hopkins Sch. Dist., past supr. bldg. sch. patrol; coop. tchrs. Gustavus Adolphus Coll.; cons. and presenter in field. Author: We Love Literature, 1991 (Grand Prize

Scholastic Inc., 1991). Mem. Wooddale Choir Evang. Christian Ch., decorating com., Mission commn., organizer fellowship dinners; mem. Loaves and Fishes, Minn. Landscape Arboretum. Recipient Hon. Mention Learning Mag., 1990, Nat. Coun Econ. edn./Internat. Paper Col. Found., 1992, 2d pl. Minn. Coun. Econ. Edn., 1992, Ashland Oil award, 1994; named Minn. Tchr. of Yr., 1992. Mem. ASCD, Nat. Assn. Miniature Enthusiasts, Am. Quilting Soc., Internat. Reading Assn., Minn. Edn. Assn., Hopins Edn. Assn. (bldg. rep., treas.), Delta Kappa Gamma (pres. Beta Beta chpt.), Kappa Delta Pi. Avocations: miniatures, quilting, flowers, cross-stitch, antiques. Office: Gatewood Elem Sch 14900 Gatewood Dr Minnetonka MN 55345-6731 Home: 7610 Smetana Ln Apt 201 Eden Prairie MN 55344-4751

**WIGGIN, KENDALL FRENCH,** state librarian; b. Manchester, N.H., Aug. 21, 1951; s. Ralph M. Jr. and Frances (Miltimore) W.; m. Elaine M. Elliott, June 2, 1973 (div. Jan. 1989); children: Sara, Douglas; m. Laura A. Larson, May 26, 1990 (div. May 26, 1990); children: Lindsey, Tess; m. Patricia Copes, Sept. 5, 2004. BA, U. N.H., 1974; MS in LS, Simmons Coll., 1975. Libr. Litchfield (N.H.) Pub. Libr., 1975; dir. Merrimack (N.H.) Pub. Libr., 1975-83; coord. tech. svcs. Manchester City Libr., 1983-90; state libr. N.H. State Libr., Concord, 1990-99, Conn. State Library, Hartford, 1999—. Mem. ALA, New Eng. Libr. Assn., N.H. Libr. Assn., Chief Officers State Libr. Agys., Chief Officers State Libr. Agys. in N.E., N.H. Writers and Publishers Project. Republican. Presbyterian. Avocations: stamp collecting/philately, gardening. Office: 231 Capitol Ave Hartford CT 06106 Office Phone: 860-757-6510. Business E-Mail: kwiggin@cslib.org.

**WIGGINS, BARBARA SUE,** pharmacist, educator; b. St. Louis, Va., Mar. 5, 1969; d. Earl Leonard and Carrie Sue Pigg; m. John Wesley Wiggins, Nov. 4, 1962; children: Luke James, Lauren Grace. BS in Pharmacy, St. Louis Coll. Pharmacy, 1992; PharmD, Va. Commonwealth U./Med. Coll. Va., 1998. Bd. cert. pharmacotherapy specialist with added qualifications in cardiology. Clin. specialist - cardiology U. Wash. Med. Ctr., Seattle, 1999—2002; clin. instr. U. Wash. Sch. Pharmacy, Seattle, 1999—2002; ACLS instr. Am. Heart Assn., Seattle, 1999—2002; pharmacy clin. specialist- cardiology U. Va. Health Sys., Charlottesville, 2002—; clin. instr. Sch. Nursing U. Va., Charlottesville, 2002—; ACLS instr. Am. Heart Assn., Richmond, Va., 2002—; clin. instr. Sch. Medicine U. Va., 2003. Contbg. editor and reviewer Springhouse (Pa.) Pub., 1998. Contbr. chapters to books, articles to profl. jours. Chair profl. affairs Wash. Soc. Health Sys. Pharmacists, Seattle, 2002—02. Lt. USN, 1993—99. Recipient Merck Award for Clin. Rsch., 1998. Mem.: Am. Soc. Health Sys. Pharmacists, Va. Soc. Health Sys. Pharmacists (assoc.), Am. Heart Assn. (assoc.), Rho Chi. Achievements include 1996 United States Olympic Marathon Trials Qualifier. Avocations: running, tennis, bicycling, hiking. Office: Univ Va PO Box 800674 Charlottesville VA 22908-0674 E-mail: bsw4v@virginia.edu.

**WIGGINS, CHARLES HENRY, JR.,** lawyer; b. Balt., July 15, 1939; s. Charles Henry and Kathryn Wilson (Walker) W.; m. Wendy Jane Horn, June 20, 1964 (div. 1996); children: Charles Hunter, Rebecca Rae, Melinda Marie; m. Karen Ann Kowal, Apr. 26, 1997 (div. 2002). BSEE, U. Ill., Urbana, 1962; JD with honors, U. Ill., 1965. Bar: Ill. 1965, U.S. Dist. (no. dist.) Ill. 1970, U.S. Tax Ct. 1974, U.S. Ct. Appeals (7th cir.) 1983. Assoc. Vedder, Price, Kaufman & Kammholz, Chgo., 1969-73, ptnr., 1974—. Mem. zoning bd. appeals Village of Indian Head Pk., Ill., 1984-91. Capt. U.S. Army, 1965-68. Mem. Chgo. Bar Assn., University Club (Chgo.), Edgewood Valley Country Club (LaGrange, Ill., bd. dirs. 1991-98), SAR. Avocations: golf, tennis, bridge. Office Phone: 312-609-7525. Business E-Mail: cwiggins@vedderprice.com.

**WIGGINS, D. SCOTT,** headmaster; m. Susan Wiggins. BA, Boston U.; JD, Ariz. State U. Coll. of Law. Former sci. & math teacher Fessenden Sch., West Newton, Mass., former dir. athletics; former dir. admissions Fountain Valley Sch., Colorado Springs, Colo.; various positions including dean of students, dir. of residential life, and mathematics chair Indian Mountain Sch., Lakeville, Conn.; former principal Metairie Park Country Day Sch., La.; headmaster Lawrence Acad., Groton, Mass., 2003—. Office: Lawrence Acad Powderhouse Rd PO Box 992 Groton MA 01450

**WIGGINS, DAVID STEWART,** state supreme court justice; b. Chgo., Oct. 19, 1951; s. Kalman G. and Joan (Feldman) W.; m. Marsha Wiggins, Dec. 23, 1973; children: Samantha, Sydney, Taylor. BA in Philosophy, U. Ill., Chgo., 1973; JD, Drake U., 1976. Bar: Iowa 1976, U.S. Dist. Ct. (no. and so. dists.) Iowa 1976, U.S. Ct. Appeals (8th cir.) 1976, U.S. Ct. Claims, 1979, D.C. Ct. Appeals, 1979, U.S. Supreme Ct. 1979. Assoc. to ptnr. Williams, Hart, Lavorato & Kirtley, 1976—79; ptnr. Wiggins & Anderson P.C. (now Anderson & Tully), West Des Moines, 1979—2003; justice Iowa Supreme Ct., 2003—. Mem. Iowa Judicial Com. on Cost of Litigation, 1988, Iowa Judicial Adv. Com. on Rules of Civil Procedure, 1991—97, Iowa Judicial Fax Tech. Com., 1992—95; chair Iowa Judicial Qualifications Commn., 2000—03; mem. Iowa Judicial Redistricting Commn., 2002; adv. Am. Bd. Trial Advs., 1993—. Fellow Iowa Acad. Trial Lawyers, Iowa Trial Lawyers Assn. (pres. 1986-87, Meritorious Achievement award 1999), Iowa State Bar Assn. (bd. governors), Am. Coll. Barristers (sr. counsel), C. Edwin Moore Am. Inn of Ct. (master emeritus). Office: Jud Br Bldg 1111 East Ct Ave Des Moines IA 50319*

**WIGGINS, DEWAYNE LEE,** financial executive; b. Stillwater, Okla., Jan. 6, 1949; s. Lloyd Lee Wiggins and Joyce Yvonne Blair; m. Susan Sochinski, Sept. 9, 1978. BS in Acctg., Okla. State U., 1972; MBA, Ind. U., 1984. Pilot Braniff Internat., Dallas, 1977-82; investment analyst Duff & Phelps, Inc., Chgo., 1984-86; portfolio mgr. Centerre Trust Co., St. Louis, 1986-88; pres. Lindbergh Capital Mgmt., Inc., St. Louis, 1988—; founder, pres. Lindbergh Signature Fund, St. Louis, 1999—. Capt. USAF, 1972-76. Mem. Ind. U. Alumni Assn., Beta Gamma Sigma. Roman Catholic. Avocations: reading, tennis, gardening. Office: Lindbergh Capital Mgmt Inc 5520 Telegraph Rd Ste 204 Saint Louis MO 63129-3570

**WIGGINS, JAMES L.,** lawyer; b. Savannah, Ga., Aug. 13, 1946; BS in Criminal Justice, Armstrong State Coll., 1972; JD, Mercer U., 1975. Pub. defender Oconee Jud. Cir. Ga., 1978—80, dist. atty., 1981—84; U.S. atty. for mid. dist. Ga. U.S. Dept. Justice, Macon, Ga., 1994-96; ptnr. Almand & Wiggins, Macon. Mem.: Macon Bar Assn., Ga. State Bar (gov. bd. govs. Oconee jud. cir. 1989—). Office: Almand & Wiggins 1922 Forsyth Street PO Box 1605 Macon GA 31202-1605

**WIGGINS, JOY L.,** education educator; b. New Braunfels, Tex., May 11; d. David Edward and Cynthia Cook Wiggins. BA, Tex. Tech U., 1996; MEd, Western Wash. U., 2000; PhD, Ohio State U., 2005. Cert. K-8 tchr. Tex. English tchr. Zhejiang U. of Tech., Hangzhou, China, 2000—01; adj. instr. Ohio Dominican U., Columbus, 2002—03; vis. prof. Otterbein Coll., Westerville, Ohio, 2003—04; grad. asst. Ohio State U., Columbus, 2001—04; 6th grade tchr. Dallas Ind. Sch. Dist., 2004—05; asst. prof. U. Tex., Arlington, 2005—. Presenter in field. Contbr. to ency. Rolfe E. Wood and Michael L. Wood Meml. scholar, Ohio State U., 2004. Mem.: Nat. Coun. Tchrs. English, Am. Ednl. Rsch. Assn. (reviewer 2005—06). Achievements include research in constructions of preservice teachers' biographies: mediations of a socio-political text. Office Phone: 817-272-0988.

**WIGGINS, KIM DOUGLAS,** artist, appraiser, dealer; b. Roswell, N.Mex., Apr. 8, 1959; s. Walton Wray Wiggins and Barbara Jo Chesser; m. Mary Allison Raney, Sept. 4, 1977 (div. May 1984); children: Rebekah, Mona; m. Maria C. Trujillo, June 17, 1995; children: Gianna Josiah, Elisha Douglas, Eden Renee. Student, Ea. N.Mex., U., Roswell, 1977, 83-84, San Antonio Coll., 1978-79, Ind. Bapt. Coll., Dallas, 1982-83, Santa Fe Inst. Fine Art, 1989. Dir. Clarke-Wiggins Fine Art, Palm Springs, Calif., 1986-89; owner, mgr. Wiggins Fine Art, Santa Fe, 1989-93, Wiggins Studio, Roswell, 1991—. Cons. Mus. N.Mex., Santa Fe 1992—, Cline Fine Art, Santa Fe, 1993—98; lectr. in field SE Cowboy Symposium, Atlanta, 2004. One man shows include Altermann Morris Galleries, Houston, Dallas, Santa Fe, 1992-2006, Studio

Gallery, Laguna Beach, San Diego, 1998, Roswell Mus. and Art Ctr., 2006; exhibited in group shows at Pa. Acad. Fine Art, Phila., 1992-96, M.H. DeYoung Mus., San Francisco, 1993-96, Autry Mus. Western Heritage, L.A., 1999-2006, Desert Caballeros Western Mus., Wickenburg, Ariz., 2000, Denver Art Mus., 2000, The Corcoran Gallery of Art, 2001, Joslyn Art Mus., 2002, Art Inst. Chgo., 2003, Booth We. Art Mus., Atlanta, 2005, C.M. Russell Mus., 2006; represented in permanent collections Mus. N.Mex., Sante Fe, Anschutz Collection, Denver, Staples Ctr., L.A., Autry Mus. Western Heritage, L.A., Booth Western Art Mus., Atlanta; editor: K. Douglas Wiggins: Sense of Spirit, 1993; pub., contbr.: Art of the American West, 1999, Painters and the American West, 2000, The Trail of Painted Ponies, 2001, Gathered by Grace, 2002, Grace for the Moment, 2005. Mem. NRA, HOG, CMA, Internat. Platform Assn., Soc. Am. Impressionists, Coun. for Art of West, Gladney Ctr., Assurance Home, Other Side of the West. Republican. Avocations: printmaking, poetry, motorcycling, scuba diving, fencing. Home: 6 El Arco Iris Dr Roswell NM 88201-7711 Studio: Altermann Galleries 225 Canyon Rd Santa Fe NM 87501-2755

**WIGGINS, MARY ANN WISE,** small business owner, educator; b. Coushatta, La., Dec. 25, 1940; d. George Wilkinson and Maitland (Allums) Wise; m. Gerald D. Paul (div. Nov. 1977); children: John Barron, James Gordon, Brenda Michelle; m. Billy J. Wiggins, Oct. 3, 1981; children: Marshall Wade, Brian David, William Joshua, George Justin; stepchildren: Joseph James, Winona Gail. BA, Northwestern State U., Natchitoches, La., 1964, postgrad., 1994, Weatherford Coll., 1967, North Tex. State U., 1968; grad., La Tech U., 2005. Lic. ins. agt., real estate agt., La., pvt. pilot. Tchr. U.S. Army Schs., Nuremberg, Germany, 1964—66, Mineral Wells Ind. Sch. Dist., 1967—70; bookkeeper Wise Dept. Store, Coushatta, La., 1966—67; amb. of good will Vietnam, 1971; owner, mgr. Mary Ann's Furniture & Hardware, Coushatta, 1977—97; tchr. Springville Mid. Sch., 1994—96, Red River Parish Alternative Sch., 1996—98, tchr. Ware Youth Ctr., 1998—. Com. mem. Instrn. and Profl. Devel. Com. La. Assn. Educators, 1998-2000, vice chmn. 1999-2002; v.p. La. Juvenile Detention Tchrs. Assn., 1999—; tchr. leader La. Tech., 2002-03. Columnist: Wise Old Owl Coushatta Citizen, 2004—. Chmn. Am. Cancer Soc., Conway, Ark., 1972, Red River Parish United Way, Coushatta, 1985; treas., bd. dirs. Hall Summit United Meth. Ch.; pres. Red River Parish Assn. Educators Polit. Action Com. Recipient German-Am. hospitality award Orgn. German-Am. Women, Nuremberg, 1965. Mem. NEA, La. Assn. Educators (chmn. legis. com. 2000-04), Red River Assn. Educators (v.p. 1994, pres. 1998-2001), U.S.C. of C., Coushatta-Red River C. of C. (charter), Pi Kappa Sigma, Sigma Kappa. Democrat. Methodist. Avocations: gardening, swimming, horseback riding, computers, week-enders with family, landscaping. Home: 2217 E Carrol St Coushatta LA 71019-8567

**WIGGINS, NANCY BOWEN,** real estate broker, market research consultant; b. Richmond, Va., Oct. 9, 1948; d. William Roy and Mary Virginia (Colson) Bowen; m. Samuel Spence Saunders, Aug. 16, 1969 (div. 1977); m. Edwin Lindsey Wiggins, Jr., Apr. 16, 1983 (div. 1999); children: Neal Bowen, Mark Edwin. AA, St. Mary's Coll., Raleigh, N.C., 1968; postgrad., Trinity U., 1968-69; BA, U.S. Internat. U., San Diego, 1970; MA, U. Tex., Arlington, 1975; postgrad., Tulane U., 1976-77. Cert. comml. investment mem. Bank teller Bank of Am., San Diego, 1971-72; lectr. U. Tex., Arlington, 1974-76; instr. Johnson C. Smith U., Charlotte, NC, 1977-78; human svcs. planner Centralina Coun. of Govt., Charlotte, 1978-80; mktg. rsch. analyst First Union Nat. Bank, Charlotte, 1980-81; mktg. rep. Burroughs Corp., Charlotte, 1981-83; ptnr., mktg. researcher George Selden & Assocs., Charlotte, 1983-84; pres., broker Bowen Wiggins Co., Charlotte, 1984-92; pres. WRB, Inc. (merger Bowen Wiggins Co. and W. Roy Bowen Co., Inc.), Charlotte, 1992-96; mgr., ptnr. Nancy Wiggins, LLC, Charlotte, 1996—; ptnr. Buster & Wiggins Internat., Myrtle Beach, SC. Instr. U. N.C., Charlotte, 1984-85, 87-90, Winthrop U., Rock Hill, S.C., 1985-86, 91-92; bd. dirs. Roy Bowen, Inc., Frogmore, S.C., v.p., sec., 1990. Contbr. articles to profl. jours. Vice chmn. United Cerebral Palsy Coun., Charlotte, 1984; chmn. bd. dirs. Carriage House Condominium Assn., Charlotte, 1980-82; mem. Charlotte Mayor's Budget Adv. Com., 1980-81, Charlotte-Mecklenburg Planning Commn., 1994-99, mem. planning com., 1994-95, zoning com., 1995-97, vice-chmn. zoning com., 1997, planning com. 1998, vice chmn. planning com. 1998—, exec. com., 1997—; pres. Mecklenburg Dem. Women's Club, 1990; mem. state exec. com. N.C. Dem. Party, 1991-95, 99-2000; mem. Mecklenburg County Solid Waste Adv. Bd., 1991-92 commn. recycling com., 1991-94, 95-96; mem. Comml. Investment Real Estate Inst., 1997-98, bd. dirs. N.C. chpg., 1999. Mem. AAUW, Charlotte Region Comml. Bd. Realtors, N.C. Assn. Appraisers (bd. dirs., pres. 1989-90), Internat. Coun. Shopping Ctrs., Internat. Real Estate Fedn. (Paris, U.S. del. Retail Conf. at World Congress 1998, U.S. vice chair trade missions, sec.-gen. exch. com. 1999-2000), Am. Planning Assn., Charlotte C. of C. (bd. advisors 1997), Multimillion Dollar Club, Tournament Players Club Piper Glen, Rose Soc., Good Friends, Nat. Assn. Realtors, FIABCI, Paris, Internat. Trade Mission Com. (sec. gen. internat. exch. com.), N.C. Citizens for Bus. and Industry, NAR Charlotte (region comml. bd.), CCIM (N.C. chpt. bd. dirs.), Pi Sigma Alpha. Democrat. Episcopalian. Avocations: gardening, art collecting. Home: 6611 Gaywind Dr Charlotte NC 28226-6902

**WIGGINS, NORMAN ADRIAN,** academic administrator, law educator; b. Burlington, N.C., Feb. 6, 1924; s. Walter James and Margaret Ann (Chason) W.; m. Mildred Alice Harmon. AA, Campbell Coll., 1948; BA, Wake Forest Coll., 1950, LLB, 1952; LLM, Columbia U., 1956, JSD, 1964; Exec. Program, U. N.C., 1968-69; LLD, Gardner-Webb Coll., 1972. Deacon Wake Forest Baptist Ch., Winston-Salem, N.C., 1963-66, Buies Creek (N.C.) Bapt. Ch., 1973—; deacon, tchr. Sunday sch., 1952—; lay preacher, 1953—; pres. N.C. Found. of Ch.-Related Coll., 1969-70, Campbell U., Buies Creek, 1967—, prof. law, 1976—. Mem. Chief Justice Commn. on Professionalism, 2004—. Author: Wills and Administration of Estates in North Carolina, 1964—, (with Gilbert T. Stephenson) Estates and Trusts, 1973; Editor: N.C. Will Manual, 1958—, Trust Functions and Services, 1978; Contbr. articles to legal jours. Chmn. Gov.'s Task Force Com. on Adjudication of the Com. on Law and Order, 1969-71; mem. Com. on Drafting Intestate Succession Act for N.C., 1957-59; mem. Com. for Revision of the Laws Relating to the Adminstrn. of Descs.' Estates, 1959-67, chmn., 1964-67; trustee Sunday Sch. Bd., So. Bapt. Conv., 1975—, chmn. bd. trustees, 1978—, nominations com., 1988—; pres. Bapt. State Conv. N.C., 1983-85; bd. dirs. N.C. Citizens for Bus. and Industry. Recipient Outstanding Civilian Svc. award Dept. Army, 1985, Comdr.'s award for Pub. Svc., 1995, Internat. Freedom of Mobility award, 1995, Patriotic Civilian Svc. award U.S. Dept. Army, 1998, award longest tenure as univ. pres. Coalition Christian Cols. and Univs., 1998, The Order of the Long Leaf Pine award, 1998, John J. Parker award, 1999, NC Baptist Heritage award, 2005, Baptist State Conv., 2005, The Charles D. Johnson Outstanding Educator award, 2005, James Iredell award, 2006; Campbell Law Sch. renamed in his honor the Norman Adrian Wiggins Sch. of Law, 1989; recognized for outstanding svc. to high edn. and legal edn. Newcomen Soc. U.S., 1993; named to List of 100 Influential Bapt. Leaders in 20th Century, 2000. Mem. ABA, Nat. Assn. Coll. and Univ. Attys. (pres. 1972-73, Disting. Svc. award 1991), Am. Assn. Presidents Ind. Colls. and Univs. (pres. 1981-83), N.C. Assn. Colls. and Univs (exec. com. 1980—, pres. 1984-85), N.C. Assn. Ind. Colls. and Univs. (pres. 1972-73, exec. com. 1980-81), N.C. Bar Assn., Harnett County Bar Assn., Nat. Fellowship Baptist Men (pres. 1987-90), Jay Waugh Evang. Assn. (dir./pres. 1970-72), Dunn Area C. of C., Wake Forest Alumni Assn., Rotary (hon. mem. Dunn club), Phi Alpha Delta, Phi Kappa Phi, Omicron Delta Kappa. Office: Campbell U PO Box 280 Buies Creek NC 27506-0127 Business E-Mail: byrde@webster.campbell.edu.

**WIGGINS, RITA CASSIDY,** poet; b. Chgo., Oct. 2, 1926; d. Thomas Francis Cassidy and Anastacia Charlotte Higgins; m. John Lawson Wiggins, Aug. 16, 1947 (dec. Sept. 27, 2002); children: Laura, John, Thomas, Martha, Caroline, Paul, James, Edward. Degree in English lit., Barat Coll., 1947. Sales rep. Marshall Field's, Chgo., 1948, Bloomingdale's, NJ, 1968—70; owner Which-Crafts, NJ, 1972—74; fin. dir. Fashion Inst. of Design and Merchandising, San Francisco, 1981—83. Author: (poetry) Shedding Light, 2000, Art Scan - Napa Valley, 2000, Love, Honor and Value, 2002. Bd. dirs. Calistoga

(Calif.) Caregivers, 2000—02; mem. Fair Housing, L.A., 1965—; mem. bd. Warren (Ill.) Pub. Libr., 1980—82. Recipient Hon. Mention award, Jassamyn West, Napa, Calif., 1991, 2d prize, Napa Arts Coun., 1995. Mem.: Nat. League Am. Pen Women. Democrat. Roman Catholic. Avocations: writing, travel, theater, music. Home: 1329 Madrona Ave Saint Helena CA 94574 Personal E-mail: naparita@aol.com.

**WIGGINS, STEPHEN EDWARD,** physician; b. Phila., May 7, 1951; s. Ralph Cannon and Bernice J. (Maslovitz) W.; m. Rebecca del Carmen, Oct. 3, 1992; children: Daniel Stephen, Elizabeth Rebekah. BA, Rutgers U., 1973; MD, Med. Coll. Va., 1977. Diplomate Am. Bd. Family Practice. Resident in family practice Riverside Hosp., Newport News, Va., 1977-80; staff emergency physician North Arundal Hosp., Glen Burnie, Md., 1980-81, So. Md. Hosp. Ctr., Clinton, 1982-84; med. dir. Convenient Health Care, Waldorf, Md., 1984—. Ptnr. Old Line Med. Partnership, Waldorf, 1990-97, Convenient Health Care Mgmt., Waldorf, 1989-97; instr. family practice Georgetown U. Sch. Medicine, Washington, 1995—2005; pres. 640 Old Line Ctr. L.P., 1997—; pres. Old Line Med. Svcs. P.C., 1997—. Vol. physician and citizen diplomat Gesundheit Inst., Russia, 1991; citizen diplomat U.S.-China Peoples Friendship Assn., China, 1988; vol. physician March of Dimes Walk-a-thon, Md., 1985-86. William Demarest scholar, Rutgers U., New Brunswick, N.J., 1969-73. Fellow Am. Acad. Family Physicians; mem. Med. and Chirurg. Faculty of the State of Md., Md. Acad. Family Physicians, Charles County Med. Soc. Avocation: scuba diving. Office: Convenient Health Care 12090 Old Line Ctr Waldorf MD 20602-2556

**WIGGLEWORTH, MARGARET,** property manager; b. Potomac, Md. Student, U. Md. Staff mem. judiciary com. and govtl. affairs com. Senator Charles McC. Mathias, Jr., Md., 1980—85; asst. dir. nat. affairs NPR, 1985—87; exec. dir. U.S. Coalition Svc. Industries, Inc., 1987—98; pres., CEO Colliers Internat. Property Consultants USA Inc., Boston, 1998—. Office: Colliers Internat Property Consultants USA Inc 20th Fl 50 Milk St Boston MA 02109

**WIGGS, EUGENE OVERBEY,** ophthalmologist, educator; b. Louisville, Apr. 27, 1928; s. Eugene Overbey and Marie Helen (Martin) W.; m. Kathleen; children: Susan, Christopher, Karen, Mark. AB, Johns Hopkins U., 1950; MD, Duke U., 1955. Intern Denver Gen. Hosp., 1955-56; resident in ophthalmology Wilmer Inst. Johns Hopkins Hosp., 1956-59; ophthalmic plastic fellow Byron Smith, MD, N.Y.C., 1969; pvt. practice specializing in oculoplastic surgery Denver, 1961—. Clin. prof. emeritus U. Colo. Med. Ctr.; lectr. ophthalmic plastic surgery various med. ctrs. Contbr. articles to med. jours. With USNR, 1959-61. Mem. Denver Med. Soc., Colo. Med. Soc., Am. Soc. Ophthalmic Plastic and Reconstructive Surgery, Am. Acad. Ophthalmology (svc. award 1982), Colo. Ophthalmology Soc. Republican. Roman Catholic.

**WIGHT, PATRICIA ANNE,** neuroscience educator; b. Providence, June 10, 1955; d. Howard Morrison Jr. and Nancy Lee (Phillips) W.; m. Mark David Crew, Jan. 15, 1988; children: Joseph David, Kyle Douglas, Michael Patrick. BS, U. Calif., Irvine, 1978; PhD, U. Calif., Riverside, 1988. Rsch. asst., tchg. asst. U. Calif., Riverside, 1981—88; postdoctoral fellow UCLA, 1988—92; asst. prof. U. Ark. Med. Scis., Little Rock, 1992—99, assoc. prof., 1999—2006, prof., 2006—. Contbr. articles to profl. jours. Mem. AAAS, Am. Soc. Neurochemistry, Am. Physiol. Soc., Soc. for Neurosci., Sigma Xi. Roman Catholic. Avocations: hiking, skiing, swimming. Office: U Ark Med Scis 4301 W Markham St # 750 Little Rock AR 72205-7101 Office Phone: 501-686-5366. E-mail: pwight@uams.edu.

**WIGHTMAN, ALEC,** lawyer; b. Cleve., Jan. 23, 1951; s. John and Betty Jane (Follis) W.; m. Kathleen A. Little, June 19, 1976; children: Nora, Emily. BA, Duke U., 1972; JD, Ohio State U. 1975. Bar: Ohio 1975, U.S. Tax Ct. 1982, U.S. Ct. Appeals (6th cir.) 1983. Assoc. Krupman, Fromson & Henson, Columbus, Ohio, 1975-77; ptnr. Krupman, Fromson, Bownas & Wightman, Columbus, 1978-82; assoc. Baker & Hostetler, Columbus, 1982-83, ptnr., 1984—, exec. ptnr., 2004—. Bd. trustees The Arthur G. James Cancer Hosp., Richard J. Solove Rsch. Inst.; bd. dirs. Cleve. Rock & Roll., Inc. Mem. ABA, Ohio Bar Assn., Columbus Bar Assn., Ohio Oil and Gas Assn. Avocation: tennis. Office: Baker & Hostetler 65 E State St Ste 2100 Columbus OH 43215-4260 Office Phone: 614-462-2636. Business E-Mail: awightman@bakerlaw.com.

**WIGHTMAN, ARTHUR STRONG,** physicist, researcher; b. Rochester, NY, Mar. 30, 1922; s. Eugene Pinckney and Edith Victoria (Stephenson) W.; m. Anna-Greta Larsson, Apr. 28, 1945 (dec. Feb. 11, 1976); 1 child. Robin Letitia (dec. Mar. 2, 2001); m. Ludmilla Popova, Jan. 14, 1977. BA, Yale U., 1942; PhD, Princeton U., 1949; DSc, Swiss Fed. Inst. Tech., Zurich, 1969, Göttingen U., 1987. Instr. physics Yale, 1943-44; from instr. to asso. prof. physics Princeton, 1949-60, prof. math. physics, 1960-92; prof. emeritus, 1992—; Thomas D. Jones prof. math. physics Princeton, 1971-92. Vis. prof. Sorbonne, 1957, École Polytechnique, 1977-78. Served to lt. (j.g.) USNR, 1944-46. NRC postdoctoral fellow Inst. Teoretisk Fysik, Copenhagen, Denmark, 1951-52; NSF sr. postdoctoral fellow, 1956-57; recipient Dannie Heineman prize math. physics, 1969, Poincaré prize Internat. Assn. Math. Physics, 1997. Fellow NAS, Am. Acad. Arts and Scis., Royal Acad. Arts. Am. Phys. Soc.; mem. AAAS, Am. Math. Soc. Office: Princeton U 350 Jadwin Hl Princeton NJ 08544-0001 Office Phone: 609-258-5835. Business E-Mail: wightman@princeton.edu.

**WIGHTMAN, SHARON LEILANI,** librarian; d. Frank Bacon and Hazel Elizabeth Drake; m. James Ernest Wightman, Oct. 9, 1965; children: Wendy Joy, Kim Diane, Dawn Lyn, Robin Gail. BS in Liberal Arts, Cazenovia Coll., 1995; MLS, Syracuse U., 1999. Cert. pub. libr. N.Y. State. Tailor, owner Wightman Tailoring, Cazenovia, NY, 1982—88, admissions rep. Cazenovia Coll., 1988—95; sales lead coord. Inchcape Testing, Cortland, NY, 1995—97; children's libr. Fayetteville (N.Y.) Free Libr., 1999—2001; libr. ITT Tech. Inst., Liverpool, 2001—. Notary pub. N.Y. Dept. of State, 2000—. Author: (online publ.) Digital Libraries Initiative, 1998. Bd. dirs. 4-H Found., Madison County, 2001—04. Named Employee of the Quar., ITT Tech. Inst. 2002, Employee of the Yr., 2002; recipient Achievement in Profl. Devel. Reference Adult Svc. Sect., N.Y. Libr. Assn., 2004. Mem.: ALA, AAUW, Am. Soc. Notaries, NY Libr. Assn., Librn. Unltd. (v.p. 2004—05, pres. 2005—). Republican. Avocations: travel, reading, gardening, surf fishing. Office: ITT Tech Inst 235 Greenfield Pkwy Liverpool NY 13088 Office Phone: 315-461-8000. Personal E-mail: swightman@hotmail.com.

**WIGINGTON, RONALD LEE,** retired chemical information services executive; b. Topeka, May 11, 1932; s. Oscar and Virginia C. (Ritchie) W.; m. Margaret E. Willey, Aug. 17, 1951; children: Linda (dec.), Carol, David, Brian. BS in Engring. Physics, U. Kans., 1953; MEE, U. Md., 1959; PhD in Elec. Engring., U. Kans., 1964; postgrad. in Advanced Mgmt., Harvard Bus. Sch., 1976-77. Tech. staff Bell Telephone Labs., Murray Hill, NJ, 1953-54; divsn. chief Dept. Def., Washington, 1956-68; dir. R & D Chem. Abstracts Svc., Am. Chem. Soc., Columbus, Ohio, 1968-84; dir. Washington ops. Am. Chem. Soc., 1984-86; CEO, dir. Chem. Abstracts Svc., Am. Chem. Soc., Columbus, 1986-91; dir. info. tech. Am. Chem. Soc., Columbus, 1991-94. Chmn. bd. Online Computer Libr. Ctr., Dublin, Ohio, 1985-87, trustee, 1978-92; lectr. Am. U., Washington, 1967-68; adj. assoc. prof. Ohio State U., 1969-78. Contbr. chpts. to books; contbr. articles to profl. jours. Pres., various positions PTA Prince George's County, Md., 1966-68; moderator, treas. Cmty. Assn. Upper Arlington (Ohio) Schs., 1970-74; mem. Upper Arlington Civic Orch., 1970-84, pres., 1973-76; bd. dirs. Material Property Data Network, 1987-94, Ohio Ctr. of Sci. and Industry, 1988-93; trustee Health Coalition of Ctrl. Ohio. Columbus, 1991-99, treas., 1994-99, vice-chmn., 1996-99. With U.S. Army, 1954—56. Named Honor Man of U. Kans, 1953; named to Topeka H.S. Hall of Fame, 2001; recipient Nat. Capital award, D.C. Coun. Engring. and Archtl. Socs., 1967, Meritorious Civilian Svc. award, Dept. Def., 1967; Summerfield scholar, U. Kans., 1949. Fellow: Internat. Coun. Sci. and Tech. Info. (exec. bd. and treas. 1992—94, fellow 1995—),

Nat. Fedn. Abstracting and Info. Svcs. (bd. dirs. 1979—84, pres. 1982—83, hon. fellow 1995—); mem.: IEEE (sr.), Am. Chem. Soc., Sigma Xi. Avocations: gardening, music, genealogy. Home: 2470 Wimbledon Rd Columbus OH 43220-4212 Personal E-mail: rwigingt@columbus.rr.com.

**WIGLESWORTH, MICHAEL BLAND,** advertising executive; b. Balt. Apr. 13, 1949; s. Reginal A. and Janice (Peppler) W.; m. Barbara Atkinson, Aug. 5, 1972 (div. Apr. 1980); m. Shari Kulik, Dec. 7, 1997. BS, Va. Commonwealth U., 1975. Account exec. Richmond (Va.) Newspapers, 1973—75; v.p. mktg. Bunch & Laughon Advt., Richmond, 1975—76; pres. Collier & Wiglesworth, Inc., Richmond, 1976—80; v.p. account svcs. Brand Edmonds Bolio, Richmond, 1980—82; v.p. sales promotion Eisner & Assocs., Balt., 1983—85; dir. promotion J. Walter Thompson, L.A., 1985—87; mgmt. supr. Einson Freeman, Paramus, NJ, 1987—89; sr. v.p.; mgmt. supr. SAI/Earle Palmer Brown Promotions, Phila., 1989—94; sr. v.p. acct. svc. Hadley, N.Y.C., 1994—96; ptnr. Allegis Mktg., 1996—2000; sr. v.p. acct. svcs. SAI Mktg., 1996—2000; v.p. promotional mktg. Marketsource, Cranbury, NJ, 2000—01; group dir., relationship mktg. Carlson Mktg. Group, Phila., 2001—03; sr. v.p. Mastermind Mktg., Phila., 2003—; ptnr. Dreamscapes Builders, LP, Houston, 2004—. Pres. M & W Ventures, Richmond, 1977-83; ptnr. Recreation Unltd., Inc., Richmond, 1979-80. Recipient best in Show award Am. Newspaper Assn., N.Y.C., 1979, Maxi award Direct Mail Assn., 1992, Reggie award Promotional Marketers Assn. Am., 1993, Pro award Coun. of Sales Promotion Agencies, 1994. Mem. Am. Advt. Fedn. (Retail Advt. award 1979), Am. Mktg. Assn. (Effie award 1980, Spire award 1992), Phi Kappa Sigma. Republican. Avocations: jogging, skiing, scuba diving, travel, music. Home: 520 Station Ave Glenside PA 19038-1419 Office: Mastermind Mktg 1450 W Peachtree St NW Atlanta GA 30309 Office Phone: 678-420-4007. E-mail: mike.wiglesworth@mastermindmarketing.com, mwiglesworth@comcast.net.

**WIGLEY, MARK ANTONY,** architecture educator; BArch, U. Auckland, New Zealand, 1979; PhD, 1987. Interim dean, prof. arch. Columbia U., 2003—04, dean Grad. Sch. of Architecture, Planning & Preservation, 2004—. Actor; author: The Architecture of Deconstruction: Derrida's Haunt, 1993, White Walls, Designer Dresses: The Fashioning of Modern Architecture, 1995, The Architectural Cult of Synchronization, 2000, Network Fever, 2001; editor (with Catherine de Zegher): The Activist Drawing: Retracing Situationist Architectures from Constant's New Babylon to Beyond, 2001. Recipient Internat. Com. Archtl. Critics Triennial award for archtl. criticism, 1990; grantee, Graham Found., 1997; Resident fellow, Chgo. Inst. for Arch. and Urbanism, 1989. Office: Columbia Sch Architecture, Planning & Preservation 402 Avery MC 0358 2960 Broadway New York NY 10027-6902

**WIGMORE, BARRIE ATHERTON,** investment banker; b. Moose Jaw, Sask, Canada, Apr. 11, 1941; m. Deedee Dawson, Aug. 24, 1964 BEd. U. Sask., Can., 1962, BA, 1963; MA, U. Oreg., 1964; BA, Oxford U., Eng., 1966, MA, 1971; LLD (hon.), U. Saskatchewan, 2002. Investment banker Goldman Sachs Group Inc., NYC, 1970—. Author: The Crash and Its Aftermath, A History of U.S. Securities Markets 1929-33, 1985, Securities Markets in the 1980s, 1997. Trustee Metropolitan Mus. Art. Hon. fellow Worcester Coll., Oxford. Mem.: Hudson Nat. Golf Club. Avocations: financial history, golf. Home: 1 W 72nd St New York NY 10023-3486 Office Phone: 212-902-5272.

**WIGMORE, STEVEN P.,** lawyer; s. Alfred A. and Patricia D. Wigmore; m. Christine A. Wigmore, June 1, 1994; children: C., W., E. JD, Cath. U. Am., Washington, 1998. EIT Md.; bar: Ga. 2000, US Patent & Trademark Office 1997. Mech. engr. EG&G Wash. Analytical Svcs. Ctr., Alexandria, Va., 1993—93; patent examiner US Patent & Trademark Office, Alexandria, 1993—96; patent agt. Birch, Stewart, Kolasch, and Birch LLP, Falls Church, Va., 1996—99; intellecual property lawyer King & Spalding LLP, Atlanta, 1999—. Sec Atlanta Electronic Commerce Forum, 2004—. Mem.: ABA, ASME (sec., newsletter editor Atlanta sect. 2004—, Atlanta Sect. Mem. of Yr. 2004—05), Atlanta Bar Orgn., Am. Intellectual Property Law Assn. Avocation: tennis. Office: King & Spalding LLP 1180 Peachtree St NE Atlanta GA 30309-3521 Office Phone: 404-572-2884. Office Fax: 404-572-5134. Business E-Mail: swigmore@kslaw.com.

**WIGSTON, DAVID LAWRENCE,** biologist, dean; b. London, Dec. 12, 1943; came to U.S., 1993; s. Frederic Roland Wigston and Joan Mavin; m. Patricia Anne Werner, May 25, 1991; 1 child, Alexa Joan Dobinson. BSc with 1st class honors, U. Exeter, Eng., 1965; PhD in Forest Ecology, U. Exeter, 1972. Lectr. in biology Exeter Coll., 1967-69; sr. lectr. biology Coventry (Eng.) U., 1970-74; reader environ. sci. Plymouth (Eng.) U., 1974-82; prof., chair dept. forestry Papua New Guinea U. Tech., Lae, 1982-86; prof. environ. sci. No. Territory U., Darwin, Australia, 1986-93, dean faculty of sci., 1986-92; rsch. prof. U. Fla., Gainesville, 1993-96; rsch. assoc. dean U. Mich. Flint, 1996—. Vis. fellow St. Cross Coll. Oxford (Eng.) U., 1980; cons. Swedish Biomass Energy Program, 1981-82; chief wildlife scientist No. Territory (Australia) Govt., 1992-93. Narrator (symphonic works) Peter & The Wolf, Jungle Book, Hassan, 1961—. Cons. Internat. Convention Biodiversity, Australia, 1992-93; pres., bd. dirs Gainesville Symphony Orch., 1994-96. Fellow Australian Inst. Biology (sec. No. Territory br. 1987-93); mem. Ecol. Soc. Am., Soc. Human Ecology, Soc. Econ. Botany. Avocations: music, theater, art, literature. Office: U Mich 303 Kearsley St Flint MI 48502

**WIGTON, CHESTER MAHLON,** physician; b. Pueblo, Colo., Jan. 12, 1928; s. Washington Irving and Bessie Marie (Ramsey) W.; m. Marjorie Chanak, Aug. 29, 1953 (dec. Jan. 1981); children: Robin, Renee, Kent, Lance, Bruce, Scott; m. Anita Kay Nelson, July 4, 1993; children: Sallie Michelle Short, Sadie Kay Short. BS cum laude, Colo. Coll., 1950; MD, U. Colo., Denver, 1954. Diplomate Am. Bd. Family Practice. Intern Swedish Hosp., Seattle, 1954-55; pvt. practice family medicine, Durango, Colo., 1957—; emeritus active Med. Mercy Hosp., Durango, 1990—; vp. staff, 1970-73. Med. dir. Hacienda Nursing Home, Bloomfield, N.Mex., 1992-95. Pres. CAMP Inc., Durango, 1970, CEOW Inc., Durango, 1964; treas. Tamarron Owners Assn. Bd., Durango, 1986-95; sec. Durango Sch. Bd., 1969-73; dir. San Juan Devel., Durango, 1971. Lt. (j.g.) USPHS, 1955-57; sec. Cmty. Hosp. Bd., Durango, 1986-92. Fellow Am. Acad. Family Practice; mem. Durango C. of C. (pres. 1965-66), Durango Rotary Club (pres. 1968), Electra Lake Sporting Club (pres. 1982-85), Delta Epsilon, Sigma Nu, Nu Sigma Nu. Republican. Presbyterian. Avocations: skiing, tennis, golf, fishing, hunting. Home: 151 Riverview Dr Durango CO 81301-4349 Personal E-mail: cwigton@frontier.net.

**WIJNBERG, SANDRA S.,** professional services company executive; b. Aug. 1, 1956; BA English, UCLA; MBA, U. So. Calif., L.A. With Morgan Stanley & Co. Inc.; joined PepsiCo as v.p., treas., 1994; sr. v.p., CFO KFC Corp. Divsn.; sr. v.p., treas. Tricon Global Restaurants Inc, 1997—2000; sr. v.p., CFO Marsh & McLennan Cos., N.Y.C., 2000—. Bd. dirs. Pvt. Sector Coun., 2001—, Tyco Internat. Ltd., 2003—. Office: Marsh & McLennan Co 1166 6th Ave New York NY 10036*

**WIKMAN, MICHAEL RAYMOND,** advertising executive; b. Mpls., Dec. 28, 1950; s. Charles Pierce and Jeanne Elizabeth W.; m. Carrie Brandt, Feb. 7, 1981; children: Caroline Celeste, Charles Michael. B in Elected Studies, U. Minn., 1973. Analyst, supr. media services Cambell-Mithun Advt., Mpls., 1973-77, account mgr., 1977-80; pres. MWA Direct, Mpls., 1980—. Mem. Direct Mktg. Assn. (Echo award 1987), Midwest Direct Mktg. Assn. (Art, Response and Copy award 1987). Avocations: art collecting, downhill skiing, tennis, sailing. Home: 5404 Richmond Ln Minneapolis MN 55436-2437

**WIKSTROM, LORETTA WERMERSKIRCHEN,** artist; b. Willow River, Minn., Mar. 2, 1938; d. Jacob Joseph and Anna Bertha (Doege) Wermerskirchen; m. Donovan Carl Wikstrom, Aug. 16, 1958; children: Bradley Donovan, Kendra Kay, Brock Karl. Student, St. Paul Sch. of Art, 1956-57, U. Minn., 1957-58, Honolulu Acad. of Art, 1963-66, Dayton Art Inst., 1985-87. Exhibited in group shows at Sinclair Coll., 1985, Arts Venture, 1985,

one-woman shows include Bevercreek Libr., 1986, City of Englewood, 1986. Vol. artist Boy Scouts Am., Charleston, SC, Minn., 1967—74; vol. artist, tchr. Girl Scouts U.S., O'Fallon, Ill., 1975—76; vol. art judge pub. elem., jr. and sr. HS, Charleston, Mascoutah, Ill., 1969—78, Ill. State Hist. Libr., Belleville, 1979, Belbrook (Ohio) HS, 1988, 1989. Recipient 2d pl., hon. mention, Nat. Nature and Wildfowl Show, 1987, hon. mention, Wyoming (Ohio) Pub. Arts Comm. show. 1987. Mem.: Dayton Soc. Painters and Sculptors, Beavercreek Creative Artists Assn. (sec. 1987—, v.p. 1988—90), St. Louis Artists Guild, Gateway East Artists Guild, Minn. Artists Assn., Charleston Artists Guild, Guild S.C. Artists. Home: 395 12 Oaks Trl Dayton OH 45434-5873 Personal E-mail: lwikstrom@aol.com.

**WILANSKY, HEYWOOD,** retail executive; Graduate, Canaan Coll. With May Dept. Stores Co., 1976—95, pres., CEO Filene's div., 1991—92, pres., CEO Foley's div., 1992—95; pres., CEO Bon-Ton Stores Inc., 1995—2000; prof. of mktg. Univ. Md., 2000—03; pres., CEO Filene's Basement Inc., 2003—04, Retail Ventures Inc., Columbus, Ohio, 2004—. Office: Retail Ventures Inc 3241 Westerville Rd Columbus OH 43224

**WILBANKS, JAN JOSEPH,** retired philosopher; b. Lynchburg, Ohio, Dec. 17, 1928; s. James Odell and Bernice Elizabeth (Daugherty) W.; m. Alice Ramona Pacheco, Nov. 14, 1953; children— Elise, Anita, Jennifer. BS, Cin. Coll. Pharmacy, 1951; PhD in Philosophy, Ohio State U., 1964. Instr. philosophy Purdue U., 1961-64; mem. faculty Marietta (Ohio) Coll., 1964-89, prof. philosophy, 1973-89. Author: Hume's Theory of Imagination, 1968, also articles. With AUS, 1951-53. Home: 122 High St Marietta OH 45750-2636 Personal E-mail: janwilbanks@msn.com.

**WILBER, ROGER ALAN,** history supervisor, writer; b. Ravena, N.Y., Sept. 14, 1946; s. John Henry Wilber, Jr. and Sarah Frances (Krom) Wilber; m. Cyndy Michele Borowski, July 21, 1969; children: Roger Alan Wilber, Jr., Ami Leah (Wilber) Mosher. Diploma, A.P. Bible Sch., 1975, Moody Bible Inst. Corr. Sch., 1975; tchg. cert., Albany Bible Inst., 1978—79. Cert. C.P.R. Instr. ARC, 1982. Supr. libr. clk. III N.Y.S. Edn. Dept., Albany, 1981—. Deacon Apostolic Pentecostal Ch., Glenmont, NY, 1976—77; head deacon U.C.C. Ch., Ravena, NY, 1991—92; co-sec, treas. Capital Dist. Friends of Jung, Albany, 1994—96; facilitator Parallel Orgn. N.Y.S. Libr., Albany, 2000—04; N.Y.S. libr. rep. Collections Stewardship Team Cultural Edn. Ctr., Albany, 2000—, floor marshal for Tenant Safety Orgn., 2001—05; guest lectr. Ravena-Coeymans Hist. Soc., 2004, 05. Author: (historical book) Teacher, Soldier, Doctor - The Life of John H. Wilber, M.D. (Copyrighted, 2003), William W. Wilber & the 113th Regiment - N.Y. Volunteers - 7th Heavy Artillery, NY in the Civil War (Copyright, 2004), Call To Duty - The Town of Coeymans in The Civil War (Copyright, 2004); editl. bd. and contbg. author: newsletter NYS Library Staff Information Bulletin, 1997—2000, NYS Library Information Bulletin, 2000—; contbg. author Schoharie County Hist. Review, 2003; contbr. articles to profl. jours. Book repair instr. Ravena Free Libr., NY, 1992—92; guest lectr. Ravena-Coeymans Hist. Soc., 2004, 2005; adult bible study tchr. Ravena, Glenmont, & Albany, NY, 1970—2004. CTA 2 USN, 1966—68. Decorated Nat. Def. Svc. Medal U.S. Navy; recipient NYS Merit awards, 1974, 1977, 1983, 1984, 20 Yrs. Svc. award, N.Y.S. Edn. Dept., 1990, 25 Yrs. Svc. award, 1995, 30 Yrs. Svc. award, 2000, 35 Yr. Svc. award, 2005, Commr. Richard P. Mills Supr. Cert., 2003. Mem.: editorial bd. NYS Library Info. Bulletin. Independent. Avocations: coin collecting/numismatics, paper clip collecting, writing, historical research, fishing. Home: 3 Jefferson Avenue Ravena NY 12143-1120 Office: New York State Rsch Libr Cultural Education Center Albany NY 12230

**WILBERDING, MERLE FRANCIS,** lawyer; b. Carroll, Iowa, Mar. 8, 1944; s. Anthony Francis Wilberding and Evelyn Louise Goecke; children: Abigail (Wilberding) Pavell, James Grandison. BA, St. Mary's U., Winona, Minn., 1966; JD, U. Notre Dame, South Bend, Ind., 1969; LLM in Taxation, George Washington U., Washington, D.C., 1972; MBA, U. Dayton, Ohio, 1975; MLIS, U. Wis., Milw., 2006. Bar: Iowa 1969, D.C. 1969, Ohio 1973. Lawyer Arent, Fox, Kintner & Plotkin, Washington, 1969—73, Coolidge, Wall, Woosley & Lombard, Dayton, Ohio, 1973—. Dir. First Nat. Bank, Germantown, Ohio, 1980—, Germantown Ind. Telephone Co., Germantown, Ohio, 2001—. Author: Bobsleds and Farmsteads, 150 Years of Cool Law, 2003, Dumplings and Doughnuts, 2004. Capt. U.S. Army, 1969—73. Home: 1013 Rubicon Rd Dayton OH 45409 Office: Coolidge Wall Womsley and Lombard 33 W First St Dayton OH 45402 Office Phone: 937-449-5772. Office Fax: 937-223-6705.

**WILBERG, MACK J.,** conductor, composer; b. Price, Utah, Feb. 20, 1955; s. LaMar Joseph and Helen McNeil Wilberg; m. Rebecca Susan Wilcox, Dec. 8, 1984; children: Kirstin, Jeffrey, James, Cara. MusB, Brigham Young U., 1979; MusM, U. So. Calif., L.A., 1981, D in Musical Arts, 1985. Prof. music Brigham Young U., Provo, Utah, 1984—99; assoc. music dir. Mormon Tabernacle Choir, Salt Lake City, 1999—. Mem.: Am. Choral Dirs. Assn. (life). Office: Mormon Tabernacle Choir 50 E North Temple St Salt Lake City UT 84150 Office Phone: 801-240-4150.

**WILBUR, COLBURN SLOAN,** foundation consultant and trustee, former executive; b. Palo Alto, Calif., Jan. 20, 1935; s. Blake Colburn and Mary (Sloan) W.; m. Maria Grace Verburg, Sept. 1, 1961; children: Marguerite Louise, Anne Noelle. BA in Polit. Sci., Stanford U., 1956, MBA, 1960. Asst. cashier United Calif. Bank, San Francisco, 1960-65; v.p. Standata, San Francisco, 1965-68; administr. mgr. Tab Products, San Francisco, 1968-69; exec. dir. Sierra Club Found., San Francisco, 1969-76, David and Lucile Packard Found., Los Altos, Calif., 1976—99, bd. dirs., 1999—; sr. fellow Council on Found., 1999—2000, interim pres., CEO, 2004. Bd. dirs. Colo. Coll., Colorado Springs. Bd. dirs. Philanthropic Ventures Found.; former bd. dirs., mem. adv bd. Global Fund Women, Palo Alto, Calif.; past bd. dirs. Big Bros. San Francisco, Calif. Confederation Arts, Peninsula Grantmakers, Women's Fund Santa Clara; former bd. dirs., pres. Big Bros. Peninsula, North Fork Assn., Peninsula Conservation Ctr.; past bd. dirs., chmn. No. Calif. Grantmakers; bd. dirs., mem. adv. bd. Sierra Club Found., Stanford Theater Found., Palo Alto, Calif. San Francisco/Inst. Nonprofit Orgn. Mgmt. With U.S. Army, 1957-58. Mem. Commonwealth Club (bd. advisors). Office: David & Lucile Packard Found 300 2nd St Los Altos CA 94022-3694 E-mail: c.wilbur@packfound.org.*

**WILBUR, COLLEEN PATRICIA,** elementary school educator, principal; b. Detroit, Mar. 20, 1949; d. John Martin and Rita Marie (Hurley) Cooney; m. Otis Gray Wilbur, Dec. 16, 1972; 1 child, John. BS, Kent State U., 1971; BA in Edn., Fla. Atlantic U., Boca Raton, Fla., 1983; student MS tng., edn. leadership program, Nova Southeastern Univ., Ft. Lauderdale, Fla., 2001—. Cert. Early Childhood, Elem. Edn., Fla. Tchr. Merrell Day Sch., Lauderdale Lakes, Fla., 1978-83, St. Coleman Sch., Pompano Beach, 1983-94, St. Mark's Sch., Ft. Lauderdale, 1994—99, lower sch. prin., prek3 - grade 4, 1999—2005, head lower sch., 2005—. Peer tchr. St. Coleman Sch., 1987-88, 92-93, coord. grades kindergarten through 4, 1992-94. Named Tchr. of Yr., St. Coleman Sch., 1987—88. Mem.: Fla. Kindergarten Coun. (pres. 2003—). Avocations: gardening, sailing, gourmet cooking. Home: 6731 NW 23rd Ter Fort Lauderdale FL 33309-1405 Office: St Marks Sch 1750 E Oakland Park Blvd Fort Lauderdale FL 33334-5299 Business E-Mail: cwilbur@saintmarks.com

**WILBUR, E. PACKER,** investment company executive; b. Bridgeport, Conn., Sept. 9, 1936; s. E. Packer and Elizabeth (Wells) Wilbur; m. Laura Mary Ferrier, Sept. 17, 1965; children: Alison Mary Thompson, Andrew Packer, Gillian Elizabeth Stratmann. BA, Yale U., New Haven, Conn., 1959; MBA, Harvard U., Cambridge, Mass., 1965. Cons. McKinsey & Co. Inc., N.Y.C., 1964-67; dir. corp. planning Am. Express Co., N.Y.C., 1967-69; v.p. Van Alstyne Noel & Co., N.Y.C., 1969-70; exec. v.p., dir. mem. exec. com. Newburger Loeb & Co. Inc., N.Y.C., 1970-73; pres. E. P. Wilbur & Co., Inc., Southport, Conn., 1973—. Southport Fin. Corp., 1986—. Chmn. bd. dirs. Criterion Mgmt., Inc., Trend Mgmt., Inc., Fairfield Advisors, Inc., EPW Securities, Inc.; gen. ptnr. Embankment Properties Ltd., London; others;

former allied mem. N.Y. Stock Exch., N.Y.C. Contbr. articles to fin. jours. Bd. dirs. Discovery Mus., Bridgeport, Wakeman Meml. Boys/Girls Club, Southport, Greater Bridgeport Jr. Hockey League, Pequot Libr., Southport, Northfield-Mt. Hermon Sch., Mass., Charter Revision Commn., Harbor Mgmt. Commn., Fairfield, Conn.; mem. dean's coun. John F. Kennedy Sch. Govt Harvard U., mem. bd. Inst. Social and Econ. Policy in Mid. East; mem. dean's internat. coun. Harris Sch. Pub. Policy Studies U. Chgo. With U.S. Army, 1959—60. Mem.: Royal Victorian Aero. Club, Royal No. Yacht Club (Scotland), Yale Club (NYC), Country Club Fairfield, Pequot Running Club (Southport, founder), Pequot Yacht Club (Southport). Office: 2507 Post Rd Southport CT 06890-1259 Home: PO Box 669 227 Main St Southport CT 06890

**WILBUR, MARCIA KAORU,** writer; d. Willard Leroy and Masayo Wilbur; children: Tina, Zack, Cordell, Alex Emmett Marian. AAS, Three Rivers, Norwich, CT, 1999—2000; BS, Ariz. State U., 1998—2002. Intern Free Software Found., Cambridge, Mass., 2002; ind. contractor/writer Aries Tech., Tempe, 2003—04; contract tech. writer NCS Pearson, Mesa, Ariz., 2004. Author: (book) Digital Millennium Copyright Act; author: (subject matter expert) (computer based curriculum) Linux Essentials; editor: (online directory) DMCA editor, (online journal) Computing Life; author: Binary Freedom/ System Toolbox. Com. mem. Digital Speech Project - FSF, Cambridge, Mass., 2002—03. Personal E-mail: aicra@well.com.

**WILBUR, RICHARD PURDY,** writer, educator; b. NYC, Mar. 1, 1921; s. Lawrence L. and Helen (Purdy) W.; m. Mary Charlotte Hayes Ward, June 20, 1942; children: Ellen Dickinson, Christopher Hayes, Nathan Lord, Aaron Hammond. AB, Amherst Coll., 1942, AM, 1952, DLitt (hon.), 1967; AM, Harvard U., 1947; LHD (hon.), Lawrence Coll., Washington U., Williams Coll., U. Rochester, SUNY, Potsdam, 1986, Skidmore Coll., 1987, U. Lowell, 1990; LHD (hon.), Mass. Coll. Liberal Arts, 2002; DLitt (hon.), Clark U., Am. Internat. Coll., Marquette U., Wesleyan U., Carnegie-Mellon U.; DLitt. (hon.), Lake Forest Coll., 1982, Smith Coll., 1996, Sewanee U., 1996; DD (hon.), St. Mary's Sem. and U., 2001. Jr. fellow Harvard U., Cambridge, Mass., 1947-50, Asst. prof. English, 1950-54; assoc. prof. Wellesley Coll., 1955-57; prof. Wesleyan U., 1957-77; writer in residence Smith Coll. 1977-86. Author: The Beautiful Changes, 1947, Ceremony, 1950, A Bestiary, 1955, 2d edit., 1993, Things of This World, 1956, Poems 1943-56, 1957, Advice to a Prophet, 1961, Poems of Richard Wilbur, 1963, Walking to Sleep, 1969, The Mind-Reader, 1976, Seven Poems, 1981, The Whale, 1982, New and Collected Poems, 1988 (Pulitzer prize for poetry, 1989), Bone Key and Other Poems, 1998, Mayflies: New Poems and Translations, 2000, Collected Poems 1943-2004, 2004, (children's books) Loudmouse, 1963, Opposites, 1973, More Opposites, 1991, A Game of Catch, 1994, Runaway Opposites, 1995, The Disappearing Alphabet, 1998, Opposites, More Opposites and Some Differences, 2000, The Pig in the Spigot, 2000, (criticism) Responses, 1976, expanded edit., 2000, (prose pieces) The Catbird's Song, 1997; co-author (with Lillian Hellman): (comic opera) Candide, 1957; co-author: (with William Schuman) (cantata) On Freedom's Ground, 1986; translator (Moliere): The Misanthrope, 1955, Tartuffe, 1963 (co-recipient Bollingen Translation prize, 1963), The School for Wives, 1971, The Learned Ladies, 1978, Four Comedies, 1982, Lovers' Quarrels, 2006; translator: (Racine) Andromache, 1982, Phaedra, 1986, The Suitors, 2001; translator: Moliere's The School for Husbands, 1992, Imaginary Cuckold, 1993, Molière's Amphitryon, 1995, Don Juan, 1998, Molière's The Bungler, 2000; editor: Complete Poems of Poe, 1959, Poems of Shakespeare, 1966, Selected Poems of Witter Bynner, 1978, Edgar Allan Poe: Poems and Poetics, 2003. Decorated chevalier Ordre des Palmes Academiques; recipient Harriet Monroe prize Poetry mag., 1948, Oscar Blumenthal prize, 1950, Prix de Rome, Am. Acad. Arts and Letters, 1954, Edna St. Vincent Millay Meml. award, 1957, Nat. Book award, 1957, Pulitzer prize, 1957, Sarah Josepha Hale award, 1968, Bollingen prize, 1971, Brandeis U. Creative Arts award, 1971, Prix Henri Desfeuilles, 1971, Shelley Meml. award, 1973, Harriet Monroe Poetry award, 1978, St. Botolph's Club Found. award, 1983, Drama Desk award, 1983, Aiken-Taylor award, 1988, Bunn award, 1988, Washington Coll. Lit. award, 1988, St. Louis Lit. award, 1989, Grand Master award Birmingham-So. Coll., 1989, Gold Medal for Poetry, Am. Acad. Inst. Arts and Letters, 1991, Edward MacDowell medal, 1992, Nat. Arts Club Medal of Honor for Lit., 1994, PEN/Manheim Medal for Translation, 1994, Milton Ctr. prize, 1995, Acad. Am. Achievement award, 1995, Robert Frost medal Poetry Soc. of Am., 1996, T.S. Eliot award, 1996, Wallace Stevens award, 2003, Ruth Lilly prize, 2006; Guggenheim fellow, 1952-53, 63, Ford fellow, 1960-61, Camargo Found. fellow, 1985; named U.S. Poet Laureate, Libr. Congress, 1987, Nat. Medal of the Arts, 1994; named to Theater Hall of Fame, 2003. Fellow: MLA (hon.); mem.: PEN (Transl. award 1983), ASCAP, AAAL (pres. 1974—76, chancellor 1976—78, 1980—81), Dramatists Guild, Acad. Am. Poets (chancellor emeritus), Am. Acad. Arts and Scis. Home: 87 Dodwells Rd Cummington MA 01026-9705

**WILBUR, RICHARD SLOAN,** medical association administrator, physician; s. Blake Colburn and Mary Caldwell (Sloan) Wilbur; m. Betty Lou Fannin, Jan. 20, 1951; children: Andrew, Peter, Thomas. BA, Stanford U., 1943, MD, 1946; JD, John Marshall, 1990. Cert. ABIM (Gastroenterology Am. Bd. Internal Medicine, 1954. Intern San Francisco County Hosp., 1946—47; resident Stanford Hosp., 1949—51, U. Pa. Hosp., 1951—52; postgrad. tng. U. Mich. Hosp., 1957, Karolinska Sjukhuset, Stockholm, 1960; staff Palo Alto (Calif.) Med. Clinic, 1952—69; dep. exec. v.p. AMA, Chgo., 1969—71, 1973—74; asst. sec. for health and environment dept. def., 1971—73; sr. v.p. Baxter Labs., Inc., Deerfield, Ill., 1974—76; exec. v.p. Council Med. Splty. Socs., 1976—91, sec. accreditation coun. for continuing med. edn., 1979—91; assoc. prof. medicine Georgetown U. Med. Sch., 1971—77, Stanford Med. Sch., 1952—69; pres. Nat. Resident Matching Plan, 1991—92. Chmn. bd., CEO Inst. for Clin. Info., 1994—99; sr. v.p. healthcare Buckeye Corp. Pte. Ltd., Singapore, 1997—2000; CEO Medic Alert, 1992—94; pres. Am. Bd. Med. Mgmt., 1992; mem. Am. Bd. Electrodiagnostic Medicine, 1993—98; chmn. med. adv. bd. Med. City, Bangalore, India, 1997—2000; bd. vis. Drew U. Postgrad. Med. Sch. Contbr. articles to profl. jours. Bd. govs. ARC; chmn. Mid-Am. Blood Svcs. Bd., Lifesource Blood Bank, 1996—98; Vice-chmn. Rep. Cen. Com. Santa Clara County, Calif., 1966—89; bd. dirs. Nat. Adv. Cancer Coun., Nat. Health Coun., 1993—95; chmn. bd. dirs. Medic Alert Found.; chmn. bd. Calif. Med. Assn., 1968—69, Calif. Blue Shield, 1966—68, Am. Medico-Legal Found., 1987—; pres. Royal Soc. Medicine Found., 1998—2004. With USNR, 1942—58. Recipient Disting. Svc. medal, Dept. Def., 1973, Scroll of merit, Nat. Med. Assn. 1971. Fellow: ACP, Am. Coll. Physician Execs. (bd. regents 1985—89, pres. 2006—, 1988—89), Am. Coll. Legal Medicine (pres. 2006—), Internat. Coll. Dentistry (hon.); mem.: Am. Soc. Internal Medicine, Am. Gastroent. Assn., Santa Clara County Med. Soc. (hon.), Lake County Med. Soc., Ill. Med. Assn., Inst. Medicine, Union League Phila., Cedars Club, Pacific Interurban Clin. Club, Alpha Omega Alpha, Phi Beta Kappa. Home: 985 Hawthorne Pl Lake Forest IL 60045-2217 Office: APT Management Inc 736 N Western Ave #222 Lake Forest IL 60045 E-mail: aptmgmnt@aol.com.

**WILBURN, JOHN,** editor; B in Govt., Coll. William and Mary; M in History, George Mason U. Fact checker Reader's Digest; joined Houston City Mag., 1979; founder San Antonio Light's Viva Mag., 1983; editor Dallas Morning News' Sunday mag. Dallas Life, 1985, Houston Press, 1989—93; assoc. prodr. David Frost's PBS TV Interview Program, 1993—97; exec. prodr. The Houston Sidewalk website, 1997—2000; news and ops. mgr. KHOU-TV website, 2000—02; asst. mng. editor Houston Chronicle, 2002—03, interim mng. editor, 2003—04, mng. editor, 2004—. Office: Houston Chronicle 801 Texas St Houston TX 77002

**WILBURN, MARY NELSON,** lawyer, writer, poet, translator; b. Balt., Feb. 18, 1932; d. David Alfred and Phoebe Blanche (Novotny) Nelson; m. Adolph Yarbrough Wilburn, Mar. 5, 1957; children: Adolph II, Jason David. AB cum laude, Howard U., 1952; MA, U. Wis., 1955, JD, 1975; cert. in translation, Georgetown U., 1997. Bar: Wis. 1975, U.S. Supreme Ct. 1981. Commr. Nat. Coun. of Negro Women Commn. on Edn., 1986—2000; English lang. officer U.S Dept. of State, Washington, 1999—. Vol. One Ch. One Family, 1995—

bd. dirs., 1997—; mem. bd. Office Employee Appeals, D.C., 1997—2001; vol. Black Revolutionary War Patriots' Found., 1998—; judge Leadership Am., 1991—; bd. dirs. Remington Ctr. Endowment Inc., U. Wis. Law Sch.; mem. bd. edn. Cath. Archdiocese of Washington, 1995—2000. Mem. Internat. Fedn. Women Lawyers (exec. coun. 1996—), Internat. Fedn. Women Lawyers (mem. coun. 1996—, UN rep. 2000-02, internat. sec. 2002—), Am. Translators Assn., Links, Inc., Leadership Greater Washington (bd. dirs. 1992-94, v.p. 1995-96), Zonta Internat., Friends of Remington Ctr. Endowment, Law Sch., U. of Wis. (bd. dirs.). Office Phone: 202-277-3557. E-mail: mnwilburn@juno.com.

**WILCHER, LARRY K.,** lawyer; b. Lebanon, Ky., July 19, 1950; s. Dwain LaRue and Juanita (Tungate) W.; m. Mary Jo Hayden, Aug. 21, 1971; children: Emily Jane, Joseph Keith. BS in Pharmacy, St. Louis Coll. Pharmacy, 1973; JD, No. Ky. U., 1984; program of instrn. for lawyers, Harvard U., 1987, 91, 94. Dir. real estate SuperX Drugs Corp., Cin., 1975-84; dir. real estate, real estate counsel Dollar Gen. Corp., Goodlettsville, Tenn., 1984-85, gen. counsel, 1985—2002; dir. U.S. Bank, 1995—; pres. Nations Title Co., Inc., 1999—2002; ptnr. Wyatt, Tarrant & Combs, 2002—. Dir. US Bank South Ctrl. Ky., 1995—, Ky. Auth. for Ednl. TV, 2005—. Contbr. to book: Kentucky Business Organizations, 1989; presenter in field. Sec., dir. Scottsville-Allen County Indsl. Devel. Authority, Inc., 1991—, Scottsville-Allen County Leasing Corp., 1992—; dir. Leadership Ky., 1994—2000, mem. exec. com., 1997—2000; dir. Bowling Green-We. Ky. U. Symphony Orch., 1998—2000; mem. internat. bus. adv. coun. Gordon Ford Coll.; chmn. Warren County Young Reps, Bowling Green, Ky., 1979, Scottsville-Allen County Planning Commn., 1997—. Named to Hon. Order Ky. Cols., 1968, One of Outstanding Young Men of Am., U.S. Jaycees, 1978; recipient Johnson & Johnson award St. Louis Coll. Pharmacy, 1973, Thurston B. Morton Leadership award Ky. Young Rep. Fedn., 1979. Mem. ABA, Nat. Assn. Corp. Dirs., Ky. Bar Assn. (recognition award 1987), Def. Rsch. Inst. Republican. Baptist. Office: Wyatt Tarrant & Combs LLP 918 State St Bowling Green KY 42101 Office Phone: 270-842-1050. Business E-Mail: lwilcher@wyattfirm.com.

**WILCHINS, HOWARD MARTIN,** lawyer; b. Paterson, N.J., Mar. 6, 1945; s. Philip Aaron and Esther (Blake) Wilchins; m. Margaret Mandon, Sept. 6, 1970 (dec. July 2001); children: Julie, Daniel; m. Sue Renay Rubinstein, Mar. 21, 2004. AB, Mich. State U., 1966; JD, U. Chgo., 1969. BAR: D.C. 1969, U.S. Supreme Ct. 1975. Trial atty. FPC, Washington, 1969-70; spl. asst. to N.Y. Public Service Commn., Albany, 1970-72; dep. sect. chief AEC, Washington, 1972-75; dep. gen. counsel-litigation U.S. Ry. Assn., Washington, 1975-81, gen. counsel, 1981-84; dep. chief enforcement div. FCC Common Carrier Bur., Washington, 1984-90; v.p. Arnold S. Tesh Advisors, Washington, 1990-92; sr. litigation atty. Office Nuclear Safety Enforcement, U.S. Dept. Energy, Washington, 1992—. Mem. faculty Trial Practice Inst., U.S. CSC, 1977-79 Bd. dirs. United Jewish Appeal Greater Washington, 1984-90, 92-96; bd. dirs. Charles E. Smith Jewish Day Sch., 1983—, v.p., 1986-88, pres., 1988-90; mem. Hillel of Greater Washington, 1990—, v.p., 1992-94, pres., 1994-96; bd. dirs., mem. Capital Camps, 1990-96; bd. dir. Jewish Edn. Svc. N.Am., 1996—, asst. treas., 2000-02, treas., 2003-05, v.p., 2005—; bd. dirs. Tikvat Israel Congregation, Rockville, Md., 2000-04, Gersher Jewish Day Sch., 2005-. Mem. ABA, D.C. Bar Assn., Fed. Comm. Bar Assn. (co-chmn. com. on arbitration and mediation 1991-94). Home: 10308 Snowpine Way Potomac MD 20854-3940 Office: US Dept Energy Office Nuclear Safety Enforc Washington DC 20585-0001 E-mail: howard.wilchins@hq.doe.gov.

**WILCOX, ALLEN JAMES,** epidemiologist; b. Columbus, Ohio, Sept. 30, 1946; s. Alfred Thomas and Virginia Wilcox; m. Claire Berteel Wilcox; children: Lauren, Joseph. BA, U. Mich., 1969, MD, 1973; MPH, U. N.C., Chapel Hill, 1976, PhD, 1979. Diplomate Am. Bd. Preventive Medicine. Sr. investigator Nat. Inst. Environ. Health Sci./NIH, Durham, NC, 1979—, chief epidemiology br., 1991—2001. Editor-in-chief: Epidemiology, 2001—. Cofounder Durham Ctrl. Park, Inc., Durham, NC, 1995—. Recipient Outstanding Svc. medal, U.S. Pub. Health Svc., 1990, Disting. Svc. medal, Pub. Health Svc., 2002, Herman Tyroler Dist. Alumni award, U. N.C., 2000, Dir.'s award, NIH, 2001. Fellow: Am. Coll. Epidemiology; mem.: Am. Epidemiol. Soc. (President 2002—03), Soc. Epidemiol. Rsch. (President 1997—98), Soc. Perinatal Epidemiol. Rsch. (President 1995—96). Office: Nat Inst Environ Health Sci 111 S Alexander Dr Durham NC 27709 Office Phone: 919-541-4660.

**WILCOX, BENSON REID,** cardiothoracic surgeon, educator; b. Charlotte, NC, May 26, 1932; s. James Simpson and Louisa (Reid) W.; m. Lucinda Holderness, July 25, 1959 (div. June 2003); children: Adelaide, Alexandra, Melissa, Reid; m. Harriet H. Davis, Aug. 15, 2005. BA, U. N.C., 1953, MD, 1957. Diplomate Am. Bd. Surgery, Am. Bd. Thoracic Surgery (chmn. 1991-93). Resident Barnes Hosp., St. Louis, 1958—59, N.C. Meml. Hosp., Chapel Hill, 1959—60, 1962—64; clin. assoc. Nat. Heart Inst., Bethesda, Md., 1960—62; instr. U. N.C., Chapel Hill, 1963—65, asst. prof., 1965—68, assoc. prof., 1968—71, chief cardiothoracic surgery divsn., 1969—98, chief emeritus, 1998—, prof. surgery, 1971—. Cons. NIH Grant Com., Bethesda, 1986—89; pres. Atlantic Coast Conf., Greensboro, NC, 1980—81; dir. Am. Bd. Thoracic Surgery, 1983—93, chmn., 1991—93; mem. coun. for grad. edn., 1993—96; bd. dirs. Nat. Residency Matching Program, 1998—, pres., 2001—02, vice chmn. res. rev. com. for thoracic surgery, 2001—03, sec., treas., 2003—. Author (with others): Atlas of the Heart, 1988, Surgical Anatomy of the Heart, 1992, 3d edit., 2004; contbr. articles to profl. jours. Recipient Samaritan's Purse award, 1999; Markle scholar John and Mary Markle Found., 1967; recipient Hadassah Myrtle Wreath award, 1979, Disting. Alumnus award Darlington Sch., Rome, Ga., 1997. Mem.: ACS (mem. adv. coun. cardiothoracic surgery 1992—, chmn. 1998—2002), Grad. Med. Edn. (coun. 1993—), Womack Soc. (pres. 1991—93), Thoracic Surgery Dirs. Assn. (pres. 1985—87), So. Surg. Assn., Soc. Univ. Surgeons, Soc. Thoracic Surgeons (treas. 1980—86, pres. 1994—95), Am. Surg. Assn., Am. Assn. Thoracic Surgery, CTS Net Corp. (bd. dirs. 1999—2005). Democrat. Presbyterian. Avocations: medical history, golf, hiking. Office: U NC Med Sch Womack Bldg CB 7065 3040 Burnett Chapel Hill NC 27599-0001 Office Phone: 919-966-3381. Personal E-mail: bensonreid@aol.com. Business E-Mail: benson@med.unc.edu.

**WILCOX, DAVID ERIC,** electrical engineering educator, consultant; b. Cortland, N.Y., Sept. 4, 1939; s. James A. and Lucille (Fiske) C.; m. Phyllipa Ann Wilcox, Jan. 23, 1977; children: Terri L., Cinda A., Jana L. 0postgrad., Syracuse U., 1965; BSEE, U. Buffalo, 1961; 0postgrad., Marist Coll., Rutgers U.; MS, U. Bridgeport, 1977. Registered profl. engr., N.Y. Rsch. engring. mgr. input/output devices Rome (NY) Air Devel. Ctr., 1966—70; dir. sales Mercom Inc., Winsooki, Vt., 1970-73, dir., 1972—73; pres. Wilcox Tng. Sys., Newburgh, NY, 1973—98; pres., CEO Global Skills Exch., Alexandria, Va., 2003—. Exec. dep. dir., Nat. Skill Stds. Bd., 1998-2003, bd. dirs.; prin. Exec. Effectiveness, Inc., NYC; instr. Dale Carnegie courses. Author: Information System Sciences, 1965; contbr. articles to profl. jours.; patentee in field. Pres. N.Y. State Jaycees, 1972-73, chmn., 1973-74; dir. U.S. Jaycees, 1970-71; bd. dirs., v.p. N.Y. State Spl. Olympics, 1972-73; bd. dirs., treas. Family Counseling Svc., Inc.; mem. Orange County Pvt. Industry Coun., N.Y. State Excelsior Examiner, 1995. Lt. USAF, 1961-65. Mem. IEEE, Soc. Info. Display, N.Y. State Soc. Profl. Engrs., Internat. Transactional Analysis Assn., Internat. Platform Assn., Am. Soc. Quality Control. Methodist. also: 30 W 60th St New York NY 10023-7902 Office: Global Skills Exch 1410 King St Alexandria VA 22314 Home: 413 N Fairfax St Alexandria VA 22314-2321 Office Phone: 703-684-5067. Business E-Mail: dwilcox@gskillsxchange.com.

**WILCOX, HARRY HAMMOND,** retired anatomist; b. Canton, Ohio, May 31, 1918; s. Harry Hammond and Hattie Estelle (Richner) W.; m. D. June Freed., June 21, 1941; children: Joyce L. Wilcox Graff, Margaret J. (Mrs. Grayson S. Smith); James Hammond. BS, U. Mich., 1939, MS, 1940, PhD, 1948. Asso. prof. biology Morningside Coll., Sioux City, Iowa, 1947-48; asso. in anatomy U. Pa., 1948-52; mem. faculty U. Tenn. Center for Health Scis.,

1952-83, Goodman prof. anatomy, 1966-83, emeritus prof. anatomy, 1983—. Assoc. editor: Anat. Record, 1968-83. Docent Memphis Zoo, 1983—, emeritus, 2005. With U.S. Army, 1945—46. Mem.: AAAS, Soc. for Integrative and Comparative Biology, Am. Assn. Anatomists, Sigma Xi. Home: 1031 Marcia Rd Memphis TN 38117-5513

**WILCOX, HARRY WILBUR, JR.,** retired manufacturing executive; b. Phila., Feb. 13, 1925; s. Harry Wilbur and Justine Elizabeth (Doolittle) W.; m. Colleen Ann Cerra, Apr. 6, 1946 (dec. 2004); children: Justine, Harry Wilbur III; m. Elizabeth W. Crowther, 2006. BS, Yale U., 1949. With Gen. Electric Co., N.Y.C., 1949-50; mfg. supt. Sylvania Electric Products, 1951-67; v.p., gen. mgr. Granger Assocs. (electronics), Palo Alto, Calif., 1967-70; pres. Am. ITT-Cannon Electric Co., Phoenix, 1970-72; pres. Hills McCanna Co., Carpentersville, Ill., 1972-75, VSI, and group v.p. IU Internat. Corp., 1975-78; exec. v.p. ITT-Grinnell, 1978-85; pres. ITT Indsl. and Constrn. Divsn., Lancaster, Pa., 1985-88. Dir. Meyer Industries, Nat. Temperature Control Centers, Paul N. Howard Co.; former chmn. VSI, VSI-UK. Patentee in electroluminescence. Mem. adv. com. Town of Sherborn, Mass. Served with U.S. Army, 1943-46. Decorated Bronze star. Mem. Yale Club of Treasure Coast, Grand Harbor Golf and Beach Club (Vero Beach). Home: 1135 Harbor Links Cir Vero Beach FL 32967 also: 47 Middle Beach Rd Madison CT 06443 E-mail: harcon13@comcast.net.

**WILCOX, HARVEY JOHN,** lawyer; b. Elyria, Ohio, Nov. 1, 1937; s. Hubbard Clyde and Sylvia (Wahter) W.; m. Leslie Louise Coleman, Apr. 11, 1970. BA cum laude, Amherst Coll., 1959; LLB, Yale U., 1962. Bar: Ohio 1962, Va. 1994. Mem. firm Wilcox & Wilcox, 1962-78; with office gen. counsel Dept. Navy, Washington, 1966-94, asst. to gen. counsel, 1972-76, counsel Naval Air Systems Command, 1972-76. Navy dep. gen. counsel, 1976-94, coms. atty., arbitrator, 1994—. Guest lectr. U.S. Army Logistics Mgmt. Center; mem. Navy Contract Adjustment Bd., 1968-72 Designed Arlington County (Va.) flag, 1983. Bd. dirs. Navy Fed. Credit Union, 1974-77, sec.-treas., 1974-75, 2d v.p., 1975-77; mem. Def. Adv. Panel on Streamlining Acquisition Laws, 1991-92. Lt. USNR, 1963-66. Recipient Meritorious Exec. rank 1980, Disting Exec. rank, 1981, 89, Navy Disting. Civilian Svc. award, 1989, Defense Disting. Civilian Svc. award, 1994. Mem. Ohio Bar Assn., Va. State Bar, Charlottesville-Albemarle Bar Assn., Nat. Trust Hist. Preservation, Nature Conservancy, Piedmont Environ. Coun. Home: PO Box 338 Turner Mountain Rd Ivy VA 22945-0338 E-mail: wilcoxny@earthlink.net.

**WILCOX, HELENA MARGUERITA (RITA),** music educator; b. Manhattan, Kans., Feb. 16, 1930; d. Virgil Otis Jones and Helena Mary Viers-Jones; children: Charles E., Marguerita E., Patricia A. MusB, State U. Iowa, 1952, MA, 1959. Cert. music tchr. Ariz., 1959, Calif., 1967, Jr. Coll. Calif., 1972. Pvt. kindergarten, Springerville, Ariz., 1959—60; art supr. Yuma (Ariz.) Elem. Sch. Dist., 1960—67; violin tchr. Ariz. Western Cmty. Coll., Yuma, 1965—67; string instrument tchr. Stockton (Calif.) Unified Sch. Dist., 1967—2002; Suzuki violin tchr. San Joaquin Delta Coll., Stockton, 1972—; musician Stockton (Calif.) Symphony, 1967—; tchr. summer arts Stockton (Calif.) Arts Commn.; organ. Symphony Orch., Yuma, 1962—67. Production grant, Stockton Unified Sch. Dist., 1980. Mem.: Nat. Music Educators, Calif. Tchrs. Assn., Suzuki Assn. of the Am., Music Tchrs. Assn. of Calif., Stockton Br. (pres. 2003—), Am. String Tchrs. Assn. (pres. 1975). Democrat. Unitarian. Home: 2348 W Alpine Ave Stockton CA 95204 Personal E-mail: ritaviola@sbcglobal.net.

**WILCOX, JAROSLAVA ZITKOVA,** physicist; d. Antonin Zitek and Barbora Zitkova; children: Elizabeth, Marc. MS, Charles U., 1966; PhD in Physics, UCLA, 1972. Rsch. assoc. Czech Acad. Scis., Prague, Czech Republic, 1966—68; prof. Tufts U., Medford, Mass., 1972—74; sr. tech. staff TRW, Redondo Beach, Calif., 1974—90; sr. tech. staff Caltech JPL, Pasadena, Calif., 1990—. Cons. BW9 Inc., Calif., 1998—2000; presenter in field. Contbr. over 100 publs. in field; exhibitions include include Czech Consulate, Lee Strasberg Theater, JPL. Recipient Tech. Achievement Roll Hon., TRW, 1983; fellow, Czech Acad. Scis., 1966—68, Tufts U., 1973; grantee, TRW, 1980—90, NASA, 1998, 2001, 2003, 2005. Mem.: West L.A. Artists (organizer 2000—). Achievements include invention of the AEXS instrument, vibrational microgyroscope, several diode laser concepts, SAW devices; patents in field. Avocations: travel, photography, drawing, painting. Home: 235 N Kenter Avenue Los Angeles CA 90049 Office: Jet Propulsion Laboratory - Caltech Pasadena CA 91109 Office Phone: 818-354-3556. Business E-Mail: jzw@jpl.nasa.gov.

**WILCOX, JOHN CAVEN,** lawyer, financial executive; b. NYC, Nov. 12, 1942; s. Daniel A. and Jessie Alexandra (Caven) W.; m. Vanessa Guerrini-Maraldi, Sept. 30, 1983; children Daniel D.G., William G.M., Julia G.M. BA magna cum laude, Harvard U., 1964; MA, U. Calif., Berkeley, 1965; JD, Harvard U., 1968; LLM, NYU, 1981. Bar: N.Y. 1973. Account exec. Georgeson & Co. Inc., NYC, 1973-79, mng. dir., 1979-90, chmn., 1990—99; vice chmn. Georgeson Shareholder Comm., Inc., 1999—2005; sr. v.p. head corp. governance TIAA-CREF, 2005—. Dir. GSC Proxitalia, 1999-05; bd. govs. Internat. Corp. Governance Network, 2002- 05; chair ICGN com. on cross-border voting practices. Trustee Woodrow Wilson Nat. Fellowship Found., 1996, vice chmn. 1996—; trustee Family Dynamics, Inc., NYC, 1979-96, Bennington Coll., 1998—. With US Army, 1968-70. Vietnam. Woodrow Wilson fellow. Mem. ABA, NYSE (mem. shareholders comm. com. 1989-95, com. on corp. laws), Am. Soc. Corp. Secs., Nat. Assn. Security Dealers (mem. issuer affairs com 1990—), Nat. Assn. Corp. Dirs. (mem. adv. bd. N.Y. chpt.), The Brook, Harvard Club (NYC), Phi Beta Kappa. Democrat. Home: 580 West End Ave New York NY 10024-1723 Office: TIAA-CREF 730 Third Ave New York NY 10017 Office Phone: 212-916-5404. Business E-Mail: jwilcox@tiaa-cref.org.

**WILCOX, JON P.,** state supreme court justice; b. Berlin, Wis., Sept. 5, 1936; m. Jane Ann; children: Jeffrey, Jennifer. AB in Polit. Sci., Ripon Coll., 1958; JD, U. Wis., 1965. Pvt. practice Steele, Smyth, Klos and Flynn, LaCrosse, Wis., 1965-66, Hacker and Wilcox, Wautoma, Wis., 1966-69, Wilcox, Rudolph, Kubasta & Rathjen, Wautoma, 1969-79; mem. Wis. State Legislature, 1969—75; judge Waushara County Cir. Ct., 1979-92; justice Wis. Supreme Ct., 1992—. Commr. Family Ct., Waushara County, 1977-79; del. Wis. Conservation Congress, 1975-80; vice chmn., chmn. Wis. Sentencing Commn., 1987-92; chief judge 6th Jud. Dist., 1985-92; mem. State-Fed. Jud. Coun., 1992-99, Jud. Coun. Wis., 1993-98; mem. Prison Overcrowding Task Force, 1988-90; mem. numerous coms. Wis. Judiciary; mem. faculty Wis. Jud. Coll., 1985-96; chmn. Wis. Chief Judges Com., 1990-92; co-chair comm. on judiciary as co-equal br. of govt. Wis. State Bar, 1995-97; lectr. in field. Contbr. (with others): Wisconsin News Reporters Legal Handbook: Wisconsin Courts and Court Procedures, 1987. Bd. visitors U. Wis. Law Sch., 1970—76. Lt. U.S. Army, 1959—61. Named Outstanding Jaycee Wautoma, 1974; recipient Disting. Alumni award Ripon Coll., 1993. Fellow Am. Bar Found.; mem. ABA (com. on continuing appellate edn.), Wis. Bar Assn. (bench bar com., chmn. appellate practice sect.), Wis. Law Found. (bd. dirs.), Tri-County Bar Assn., Dane County Bar Assn., Trout Unltd., Ducks Unltd., Rotary, Phi Alpha Delta. Office: Supreme Court State Capitol PO Box 1688 Madison WI 53701-1688*

**WILCOX, MARK DEAN,** lawyer; b. May 25, 1952; s. Fabian Joseph and Zeryle Lucille (Tase) W.; m. Catherine J. Wertjes, Mar. 12, 1983; children: Glenna Lynn, Joanna Tessie, Andrew Fabian Joseph. BBA, U. Notre Dame, 1973; JD, Northwestern U., 1976; CLU, Am. Coll., 1979, ChFC, 1992. Bar: Ill. 1976, U.S. Dist. Ct. (no. dist.) Ill. 1976, Trial Bar 1982, U.S. Ct. Appeals (7th cir.) 1987, U.S. Supreme Ct. 1989. Staff asst. Nat. Dist. Attys. Assn., Chgo., 1974-75; trial asst. Cook County States Atty., Chgo., 1975; intern U.S. Atty. No. Dist. Ill., Chgo., 1975-76; assoc. Lord, Bissell & Brook, LLP, Chgo., 1976-85. ptnr. 1986—2005; founding ptnr. Walker Wilcox Matousek, LLP, Chgo., 2005—. Mem. YMCA Met. Chgo., Trinity United Meth. Ch., No Bats Baseball Club, Irving Park YMCA; venue ofcl. Internat. Spl. Olympics. Fellow Am. Bar Found.; mem. ABA (tort and ins. practice sect.), Am. Soc. CLU and ChFC, Chgo. Bar Assn. (ins. law com.), Am. Health Lawyers Assn.,

Nat. Assn. Ins. and Fin. Advisors, Def. Rsch. Inst., Soc. Fin. Svc. Profls., Trial Lawyers Club Chgo., Notre Dame Nat. Monogram Club, Union League Club, Chgo. Lions Rugby Football Club, Beta Gamma Sigma. Office Phone: 312-244-6722.

**WILCOX, MARY MARKS,** retired Christian education consultant, educator; b. Madison, Wis., Apr. 23, 1921; d. Roy and Mary Celia (Leary) Marks; m. Ray Everett Wilcox, Nov. 28, 1942; children: Peter, Anne, Susan, Steven. BA, U. Wis., 1942; MRE, Iliff Sch. Theology, Denver, 1968. Cert. Christian educator. Cons. local chs., Lakewood, Littleton, Wheat Ridge, Colo., 1963–74; instr., leader numerous seminars throughout U.S. and Can., 1963—; interim parish cons. 1st Presbyn. Ch., Lakewood, 1988-90, profl. assoc. for faith devel., 1993-97; adj. prof. Iliff Sch. Theology, 1970—; ret., 2002. Author: Developmental Journey, 1979; co-author: Viewpoints, 1998; contbr. articles to various publs., chpts. to books. Trustee, mem. exec. bd. Nat. Ghost Ranch Found., Abiquiu, N. Mex., 1983-93. Recipient award Iliff Alumni Assn., 1989. Mem.: Assn. Presbyn. Christian Educators (past mem. exec. bd.). Democrat. Presbyterian. Home: 3590 Estes St Wheat Ridge CO 80033-5933 E-mail: marywilcox@aol.com.

**WILCOX, MAUD,** editor; b. N.Y.C., Feb. 14, 1923; d. Thor Fredrik and Gerda (Ysberg) Eckert; m. Edward T. Wilcox, Feb. 9, 1944 (dec. 1998); children: Thor(dec.), Bruce, Eric, Karen. AB summa cum laude, Smith Coll., 1944; A.M., Harvard U., 1945. Teaching fellow Harvard U., 1945-46, 48-51; instr. English Smith Coll., Northampton, Mass., 1947-48, Wellesley Coll., Mass., 1951-52; exec. editor Harvard U. Press, 1958-66, humanities editor, 1966-73, editor-in-chief, 1973—89; freelance editorial cons. Cambridge, 1989—; ret. Cons., panelist NEH, Washington, 1974-76, 82-84; cons. Radcliffe Pub. Course, 1991. Mem. MLA (com. scholarly edits. 1982-86), Assn. Am. Univ. Presses (chair com. admissions and standards 1976-77, v.p. 1978-79, chair program com. 1981-82), Phi Beta Kappa. Democrat. Episcopalian. Home and Office: 63 Francis Ave Cambridge MA 02138-1911 Personal E-mail: maudwilcox@post.harvard.edu.

**WILCOX, RAYMOND L,** oil industry executive; b. Mar. 19; BSME cum laude, U. Mich., 1968; postgrad., London Bus. Sch., 1994. Design and constrn. engr. Chevron, 1968—81, mem. fgn. ops. staff, 1981—86, ops. supt. Lafayette, La., 1986—90; mng. dir. Chevron Asiatic, Melbourne, Australia, 1990—96; v.p., gen. mgr. marine transp. Chevron Shipping Co., San Ramon, Calif., 1996—99; gen. mgr. asset mgmt. Chevron Nigeria Ltd., 1999—2000, chmn., mng. dir., 2000—01; mng. dir. Nigeria/Mid-Africa strategic bus. unit ChevronTexaco Corp., 2001—02; pres. ChevronTexaco Exploration and Prodn. Co., 2002—06; v.p. ChevronTexaco Corp., Houston; pres., CEO Chevron Phillips Chem. Co. LLC, 2006—. Bd. dirs. Dynergy Inc., 2003—. Bd. dirs. Spindletop Charities, Greater Houston Partnership; chmn. Century divsn. United Way of Tex. Gulf Coast, 2003. Mem.: Am. Petroleum Inst. (mem. upstream com.). Office: Chevron Phillips Chem Co 10001 Six Pines Dr The Woodlands TX 77380

**WILCOX, SHIRLEY JEAN LANGDON,** genealogist; b. Arcata, Calif., Dec. 10, 1942; d. Elmore Harold and Alberta May (Starkey) Langdon; m. Wayne Kent Wilcox, June 22, 1963; 1 child, Harold Bonner. BS, U. Md., 1964. Cert. Bd. for Certification of Genealogists. Tchr. Prince George's County (Md.) Sch. System, 1964-67, substitute tchr., 1968-73; profl. genealogist Lanham, Md., Arlington, Va., 1973—; genealogy tchr. Fairfax County Pub. Schs., 1995-99. Level II coord. Mid-Atlantic Genealogy and History Inst., George Mason U., Fairfax, Va., 1986; trustee bd. for Certification of Genealogists, 2000—. Editor: A Bibliography of Published Genealogical Source Records, Prince George's County, Maryland, 1975, Prince George's County Land Records, Vol. A, 1696-1702, 1976, 1850 Census Prince George's County, Maryland, 1978, 1828 Tax List Prince George's County, Maryland, 1985; author: The National Genealogical Society: A Look at Its First One Hundred Years, 2003. Elder Presbyn. Ch., 1970-73, 95-98. Fellow Nat. Geneal. Soc. (chmn. conf. program subcom. 1990, 2d v.p. 1990-94, councilor 1994-96, pres. 1996-2000); mem. DAR (libr. Belle Air chpt. 1985—, Outstanding Jr. Mem. award 1979), Assn. Profl. Genealogists (pres. 1991-93, pres. Nat. Capital area chpt. 1994-96, dir. region 3 2004—, Grahame Thomas Smallwood Jr. award of merit 1996), Va. Geneal. Soc. (gov. 2001—), Prince George's County Geneal. Soc. (pres. 1973, 75-76, book rev. editor 1976-96, Jane Roush McCafferty award of excellence 1985), Fairfax Geneal. Soc. (pres. 1986-89), Soc. Mayflower Descs. in D.C., Paperweight Collectors Assn. (pres. Md.-D.C.-Va. chpt. 1988-90), Clay Family Soc. (dir. 2002-06), numerous others Avocation: collecting paperweights. Home: 1500 23rd St S Arlington VA 22202-1523

**WILCOX, STEVEN ALAN,** lawyer; b. Providence, Mar. 1955; s. Donald W. and Edna Wilcox; m. Nancy Wilcox, Aug., 1980. BA summa cum laude, Boston Coll., 1977, JD cum laude, 1980. Bar: Mass. 1980. Assoc. Ropes & Gray, Boston, 1980-89, ptnr. corp. dept., 1989—, head life sci. practice group. Mem. ABA, Mass. Bar Assn., Boston Bar Assn. Office: Ropes & Gray 1 International Pl Boston MA 02110-2624 Office Phone: 617-951-7319. Office Fax: 617-951-7050. Business E-Mail: swilcox@ropesgray.com.

**WILCOX, T.J.,** filmmaker; b. Seattle, 1965; BFA, Sch. Visual Arts, N.Y., 1989; MFA, Art Ctr. Coll. Design, Pasadena, 1995. Filmmaker: (one-man shows include) Gavin Brown's Enterprise, 1996, 1997; Daniel Buccholz, 1997; Inst. Contemporary Arts, 1993; Walker Art Ctr. 1998; Henry Art Gallery, 1999; (group shows include) Art Ctr. Coll. Design, 1994, 1995; Pasadena Plaza, 1994; Guggenheim Gallery, Chapman U., 1995; Bradbury Bldg., 1995; Marc Foxx Gallery, 1996; LACE, 1996; L.A. Ctr. Photographic Studies, 1996; Kunsthalle, 1996; Kunstlerhaus Bethanien, 1996; David Zwirner Gallery, 1996; Venice Biennale, 1997; Mus. of Art, 1997; Armand Hammer Mus. Art, UCLA, 1997; Whitney Mus. Am. Art, 1997; Mus. Abteilberg 1998. Office: c/o Gavin Brown's Enterprise Corp 620 Greenwich St New York NY 10014-3304

**WILCOXSON, ROY DELL,** plant pathologist, researcher, educator; b. Columbia, Utah, Jan. 12, 1926; m. Iva Wall, 1949; children: Bonnie, Paul, Karren, John. BS, Utah State U., 1953; MS, U. Minn., 1955, PhD in Plant Pathlgy, 1957. Asst. prof., 1957-66; prof. plant pathology U. Minn., St. Paul, 1966-91, prof. emeritus, 1991—. Spl. staff mem. Rockefeller Found.; vis. prof. Indian Agrl. Inst., New Delhi; dir. Morocco project U. Minn. 1983-87; adj. prof. Inst. Agronomy and Vet. Medicine, Hassan II, Rabat, Morocco, 1985—. Fellow Am. Phytopath Soc., Indian NAS, Indian Phytopath Soc., AAAS. Achievements include research in diseases of forage crops and cereal crops; cereal rust diseases. Office: 1669 County Road 8230 West Plains MO 65775-5766 Address: Dept Plant Path U Minn Saint Paul MN 55101

**WILCZAK, PAUL FRANCIS,** psychologist; b. Buffalo, N.Y., July 31, 1941; s. Francis Joseph Wilczak and Louise Ren; m. Priscilla Anne Kontak, Dec. 27, 1969; children: Sean, Kimberly, Sara. BA in Music, Cath. U. Am., 1964; MA in Religion, Cath. U. Am., 1964; MA in Religion and Psychol. Studies, U. Chgo., 1970, PhD in Religion and Psychol. Studies, 1973. Lic. psychologist Mo., Pa. Asst. prof. Coll. New Rochelle, NY, 1965—68; assoc. prof. St. Meinrad (Ind.) Seminary, 1972—78; staff Cr. for Pastoral Ministry, Kansas City, Mo., 1978—81; intern, resident and clin. staff Midwest Xian Counseling Ctr., Kansas City, Mo., 1981—91; lic. psychologist The Samaritan Ctr., Lancaster, Pa., 1991—94, Pa. Counseling Svc. Inc., Lebanon, 1995—2001, Wellspan Behavioral Health, York, Pa., 2001—. Address: 441 Coach House Ln Lititz PA 17543-9396 Office Phone: 717-481-7840. E-mail: pfwilczak@dejazzd.com.

**WILCZEK, FRANK ANTHONY,** physics professor; b. Mineola, NY, May 15, 1951; s. Frank John and Mary Rose (Cona) W.; m. Elizabeth Jordan Devine, July 3, 1973; children: Amity, Mira. BS in Math., U. Chgo., 1970; MA in Math., Princeton U., 1972, PhD in Physics, 1974; Doctorate (hon.), Université de Montréal, 2001. Instr. Princeton U., NJ, 1974, asst. prof. NJ, 1974-76, 1977—78, assoc. prof. NJ, 1978—80, prof. NJ, 1980-81, U. Calif., Santa Barbara, 1980—88, Inst. for Theoretical Physics, Santa Barbara, Calif.,

1981-88; prof., Sch. of Natural Scis. Inst. for Advanced Study, Princeton, 1989—2000. Vis. fellow Inst. for Advanced Study, Princeton, 1976-77; Chancellor Robert Huttenback prof. of physics U. Calif., Santa Barbara, 1984-90; vis. prof. Harvard U., 1987-88; J. Robert Oppenheimer prof. Inst. for Advanced Study, 1997-2000; Herman Feshbach prof. MIT, 2000-; adj. prof. Centros Estudios Cientificos, 2002-; vis. Schrodinger-prof. City of Vienna, Austria, 2002; Leland J. Haworth Disting. Scientist, Brookhaven Nat. Lab., 1994-97; lecturer at several universities and soc.; serves on several advisory bds. Author: Longing for the Harmonies, 1988, Geometric Phases in Physics, 1989, Fractional Statistics and Anyon Superconductivity, 1990; editor-in-chief Annals of Physics, 2001-; editl. advisor, Daedalus, 2002-; contbr. articles to profl. jours. Trustee U. Chgo., 1998—2004. Recipient J.J. Sakurai prize Am. Phys. Soc., 1986, Dirac medal UNESCO, 1994, Michelson-Morley prize Case Western Res. U., 2002, Lorentz medal, 2002, Lilienfield prize Am. Physics Soc., 2003, Europhysics prize, 2003; named A.P. Sloan fellow, 1975-77, MacArthur fellow, 1982-87, Regent's Fellow, Smithsonian Astrophysical Observatory, 1986-88; co-recipient High Energy and Particle Physics prize, European Physical Soc., 2003, Nobel Prize in Physics, 2004, King Faisal prize (sci.), King Faisal Found., 2005. Fellow: AAAS, Am. Philos. Soc., Am. Philos. Soc.; fgn. mem. Royal Netherlands Acad. Arts and Sci. (Lorentz medal, 2002; mem. NAS, Am. Acad. Arts & Scis. Achievements include discovery of asymptotic freedom in the theory of the strong interaction. Avocations: chess, music, logic puzzles. Home: 4 Wyman Rd Cambridge MA 02138-2218 Office: MIT Ctr for Theoretical Physics 6-305 77 Massachusetts Ave Cambridge MA 02139 Office Phone: 617-253-0284. Business E-Mail: wilczek@mit.edu.

**WILCZYNSKI, CHRISTIE LOUISE,** secondary school educator, counselor; b. Wyandotte, Mich., Oct. 28, 1948; d. Chris E. and Dorothy M. (Benham) Maghielse; m. Joseph S. Wilczynski, Mar. 13, 1971; 1 child, Christy Marie. BS, Ea. Mich. U., 1972, MS, 1981, MA, 1991. Cert. secondary continuing edn., Mich.; lic. profl. counselor. Counselor, tchr. adult edn. and sociology Wyandotte Pub. Schs., 1975—82, 1984—89; tchr. sociology and family life, 1989; counselor, tchr. adult edn. and sociology Wyandotte Pub. Schs., 1997—99, tchr. secondary sch., 1999—. Grad. asst. Ea. Mich. U. Honors Program, 1989—91; employment counselor Downriver Cmty. Conf., 1992—95; commr. Wyandotte Planning and Rehab. Commn., 1993—94; presenter parenting workshops Wyandotte Cmty. Edn. Co-author: (script) Applewood: Living and Caring Together, 1983; contbr. articles to periodicals; freelance Christian music songwriter: Jesus I love You, 2003, There Is a Town Called Bethlehem, 2003, Holy Father Hear Me Now, 2003, Jesus the Price Did Pay, 2003, The Rock Higher than I, 2004, Forgive My Weakness, 2004, We Pledge Our Love, 2005, Annastyn's Song, 2005. Mem.: Mich. Counseling Assn., Ea. Mich. U. Home Econs. Alumni Assn. (editor), Phi Kappa Phi, Zeta Tau Alpha (past treas. chpt.), Chi Sigma Iota. Home: 19142 Wedgewood Rd Riverview MI 48193-7861

**WILCZYNSKI, JANUSZ S.,** manufacturing executive, retired physicist; b. Warsaw, May 12, 1929; came to US, 1962; m. Brahna Lauger. Diploma in Indsl. Mechanics, Mining Acad., Cracow, Poland, 1954; MSc in Physics, Jagellonian U., Cracow, Poland, 1957; PhD in Physics and Optics, Imperial Coll. U. London, 1961. Physicist Watson, Intl. U., London, 1961-62; rsch. staff mem. T.J. Watson Rsch. Ctr., IBM, Yorktown Heights, NY, 1962-63, mgr. tech. optics, 1963-83, 2d level mgr., 1983-84, sr. mgr., 1984-86, dir., 1986-93; gen. ptnr. Wilc Instruments LLP, 1995. Contbr. over 60 articles to profl. jours. Recipient 13 Invention awards, 1966-98, 7 Outstanding Innovation awards IBM, 1968-91; IBM fellow, 1981. Fellow Optical Soc. Am. (McClarthan medal 1988); mem. NAE. Avocation: astronomical optics. Home: PO Box 790 Sandia Park NM 87047-0790 Office Phone: 505-286-8285. Office Fax: 505-286-8272. Personal E-mail: wilczyn@swcp.com.

**WILD, EARL,** composer; b. Pitts., Nov. 26, 1915; Grad., Pitts. Carnegie Tech. (now Carnegie Mellon U.), 1937. Performer KDKA Radio, Pitts., 1927—33; pianist Pitts. Symphony Orch., 1929; staff pianist NBC Network, 1937—44; staff pianist, conductor, composer ABC Network, 1944—68; composer The Caesar Hour, 1952—56. Musician US Navy; tchr. Ctrl. Conservatory of Music, Beijing, Toho-Gakuen Sch. Music, Tokyo, SunWah Sch., Seoul, Manhattan Sch. Music, Ohio State U.; disting. vis. artist Carnegie Mellon U., Pitts.; founder, artist dir. & pianist Concert Soloist of Wolf Trap, Vienna, 1978—82. Named Instrumentalist of Yr., Musical Am., 2005; recipient Alumni Merit award, Carnegie Mellon U., 1996, Disting. Achievement award, 2000, Grammy award, 1997. Achievements include becoming first artist to perform a piano recital on US television, 1939; being youngest American piano soloist ever engaged by NBC Symphony; performing for 6 consecutive presidents (Herbert Hoover to Lyndon Johnson). Mailing: c/o Michael Rolland Davis Prodn 2233 Fernleaf Ln Columbus OH 43235*

**WILD, JAMES ROBERT,** biochemistry and genetics professor; b. Sedalia, Mo., Nov. 24, 1945; s. Robert Lee and Frances Elleta (Wheeler) W.; m. Ann Lynn Brenner, Aug. 1, 1973; 1 child, Kalli Ann. BA in Zoology, U. Calif., Davis, 1967; PhD in Cell Biology, U. Calif., Riverside, 1971, post doctoral fellow, 1972. From asst. to assoc. prof. genetics and biochemistry Tex. A&M U., Coll. Sta., Tex., 1975-84, prof., chair genetics faculty, 1984—, prof. biochemistry & genetics, 1984—2000, head biochemistry and biophysics dept., 1986-90, exec. assoc. dean Coll. Agr. and Life Scis., 1987—92, prof., head dept. biochemistry and biophysics Coll. Agr. and Life Scis., 1994—2000, chmn. faculty genetics. Fellow faculty Tex. Agrl. Experiment Sta., 1999. With USN, 1972-75. Recipient So. Regional award for excellence in coll. anduniv. tchg. in food and agrl. scis., Higher Edn. program USDA, 1992. Fellow AAAS. Methodist. Office: Tex A&M U 2128 Biochemistry Bldg Rm 332 College Station TX 77843-2128 Office Phone: 979-845-6539. Business E-Mail: j-wild@tamu.edu.

**WILD, JOHN JULIAN,** surgeon, researcher, medical educator; b. Sydenham, Kent, Eng., Aug. 11, 1914; came to U.S., 1946; s. Ovld Frederick and Ellen Louise (Cuttance) W.; m. Nancy Wallace, Nov. 14, 1949 (div. 1966); children: John O., Douglas J.; m. Valerie Claudia Grosenick, Aug. 9, 1968; 1 child, Ellen Louise. BA, U. Cambridge, Eng., 1936, MA, 1940, MD, 1942, PhD, 1971. Intern, resident U. Coll. Hosp., London, 1938-42; intern U. College Hosp., London, 1938-42; staff surgeon Miller Gen., St. Charles and North Middlesex Hosps., London, 1942-44; venereologist Royal Army Med. Corps, 1944-45; rsch. fellow, instr. depts. surgery and elec. engring., prin. investigator U. Minn., Mpls., 1946-51; dir. rsch. Medico-Technol. Rsch. Dept. St. Barnabas Hosp., Mpls., 1953-60; dir. Medico-Technol. Rsch. Unit Minn. Found., St. Paul, 1960-63; pvt. practice Mpls., 1966—; dir. Medico-Technol. Rsch. Inst. Mpls., St. Louis Park, Minn., 1965—. Lectr. in field of medical instruments, ultrasound. Contbr. articles to profl. jours. Recipient Japan prize in Medical Imaging, Sci. and Tech. Found. Japan, 1991, 1st Frank Annunzio award Christopher Columbus Fellowship Found., 1998, lifetime achievement award U. Minn. Med. Sch., 2000, Ian Donald Tech. Achievement award ISUOG, 2000. Fellow Am. Inst. Ultrasound in Medicine (Pioneer award 1978); mem. AMA, World Fedn. Ultrasound in Medicine and Biology, Minn. State Med. Assn., Hennepin County Med. Soc., N.Am. Alvis Owners Club; hon. mem. Brit. Inst. Radiology, Japan Soc. of Ultrasound in Medicine. Achievements include patents in field; origination of ultrasonic medical imaging instruments and diagnostic techniques; origination of the field of pulse-echo ultrasonic diagnostic medicine. Home and Office: Medico-Technol Rsch Inst 4262 Alabama Ave S Minneapolis MN 55416-3105

**WILD, NELSON HOPKINS,** lawyer; b. Milw., July 16, 1933; s. Henry Goetseels and Virginia Douglas (Weller) W.; m. Joan Ruth Miles, Apr. 12, 1969; children: Mark, Eric; m. Diana Morris, Sept. 7, 2002. AB, Princeton U., 1955; LL.B., U. Wis. 1961. Bar: Wis. 1962. Cert. 1967; cert. specialist in probate, estate planning and trust law State Bar of Calif. Research assoc. Wis. Legis. Council, Madison, 1955-56; assoc. Whyte, Hirschboeck, Minahan, Harding & Harland, Milw., 1961-67, Thelen, Marin, Johnson & Bridges, San Francisco, 1967-70; sole practice law San Francisco, 1970—. Mem. State Bar Calif. Client Trust Fund Commn., 1983, mem. exec. com. conf. dels., 1985-88. Contbr. articles to legal jours. Bd. dirs. Neighborhood Legal Assistance Found., San Francisco, 1974-85, chmn. bd., 1978-81. Served with

USAF, 1956-58. Mem. ABA, Calif. Bar Assn., San Francisco Bar Assn., Am. Bar Found., Lawyers of San Francisco Club (gov. 1975, treas. 1981, v.p. 1982, pres.-elect 1983, pres. 1984), Calif. Tennis Club (bd. dirs. 1995-97, pres. 1997). Office: 332 Pine St Ste 710 San Francisco CA 94104-3230 Personal E-mail: nwildlaw@aol.com.

**WILD, RICHARD P.,** lawyer; b. NYC, Aug. 13, 1947; s. Alfred P. and Harriet C. (Hoffman) W.; m. Deirdre L. Felbin, June 15, 1969; children: Nicholas B., Daniel M. AB, Columbia U., 1968; JD, Yale U., 1971. Bar: Pa. 1971, U.S. Dist. Ct. (ea. dist.) Pa. 1971, U.S. Tax Ct. 1973, U.S. Claims Ct. 1977. Assoc. Dechert LLP, Phila., 1971-78, ptnr., 1978—. Mem. Phila. Bar Assn. (tax sect.). Office: Dechert LLP Circa Ctr 2929 Arch St Philadelphia PA 19104-2808

**WILD, ROBERT ANTHONY,** academic administrator; b. Chgo., Mar. 30, 1940; s. John Hopkins and Mary Dorothy (Colnon) Wild. BA in Latin, Loyola U., Chgo., 1962, MA in Classical Lang., 1967; STL, Jesuit Sch. Theology, Chgo., 1970; PhD in Study of Religion, Harvard U., 1977. Ordained priest 1970. From asst. to assoc. prof. Marquette U., Milw., 1975—83; vis. prof. Pont. Istituto Biblico, Rome, 1983—84; dir. Jesuit philosophate program Loyola U., Chgo., 1984—85, assoc. prof. theology, 1985—92; provincial superior Chgo. Province S.J., 1985—91; pres. Weston Jesuit Sch. Theology, Cambridge, Mass., 1992—96, Marquette U., Milw., 1996—. Trustee Jesuit Sch. Theology, Berkeley, 1985—90, Weston Sch. Theology, Cambridge, Mass., 1985—96, Marquette U., 1990—, St. Louis U., 1994—2002, Milw. Rsch. Park, 2002—05, Greater Milw. Commn., 2002—, Wis. Assn. Ind. Colls. and Univs., 1996—, chmn., 2001—, St. Joseph's U., Pa., 2004—. Author: Water in the Cultic Worship of Isis and Sarapis, 1981; co-editor: Sentences of Sextus, 1981; contbr. articles to profl. jours. Mem.: Cath. Bibl. Soc., Soc. Bibl. Lit. Office: Marquette Univ O'Hara Hall PO Box 1881 Milwaukee WI 53201-1881 Office Phone: 414-288-7223. Business E-Mail: robert.wild@marquette.edu.

**WILD, ROBERT WARREN,** lawyer; b. Syracuse, N.Y., Mar. 25, 1942; s. Robert Sumner and Evelyn I. (Yorman) W.; m. Elizabeth Trowbridge, Sept. 5, 1965; children: Robert Mason, Alexander Lewis, Elizabeth Anne. BS, MIT, 1964; JD, Cornell U., 1970. Bar: N.Y. 1971, D.C. 1973. Engr. Smithsonian Astrophysical Obs., Cambridge, Mass., 1965-67; atty., advisor U.S. Dept. Justice, Washington, 1970-72; law clk. to Hon. Justice William H. Rehnquist U.S. Supreme Ct., Washington, 1972-73; ptnr. Nixon Peabody LLP, Rochester, NY, 1973—. Mem. Monroe County Bar Assn. (trustee 1990-91, 92-94, treas. 1992-94, counsel 1994—). Office: Nixon Peabody LLP Clinton Sq PO Box 31051 Rochester NY 14603-1051 Office Phone: 585-263-1302. Business E-Mail: rwild@nixonpeabody.com.

**WILDASIN, DAVID E(ARL),** economics professor; b. Willimantic, Conn., Dec. 2, 1950; m. Kathleen Ann Preslin, Aug. 10, 1973. BA in Econs., U. Va., 1972; PhD Econs., U. Iowa, 1976. Asst. prof. U. Ill., Chgo., 1976—79, Ind. U., Bloomington, 1979—82, assoc. prof., 1982—86, prof. econs., 1986—93, prof. West European studies, 1993; prof. econs. Vanderbilt U., Nashville, 1993—2000; endowed prof. pub. fin. Martin Sch. Pub. Policy and Adminstrn., prof. econs. U. Ky., Lexington, 2000—, dir. Inst. Federalism and Intergovtl. Rels., 2005—. Cons. World Bank, 1992—2002, long-term cons. policy rsch. dept. pub. econs. divsn., 1995—96; vis. assoc. prof. Queen's U., Kingston, Ont., Canada, 1982—83; vis. prof. U. Cath. Louvain, Louvain-la-Neuve, Belgium, 1986—87, Sch. of Higher Studies in Social Scis., Marseille, France, 1995; summer fellow U. Bonn, Germany, 1990; vis. scholar Interuniv. Ctr. for Econ. Studies, Gadjah Mada U., Indonesia, 1990, Ctr. for Econ. Studies U. Munich, 1991, U. B.C., Canada, 1992; econ. policy rsch. unit Copenhagen Bus. Inst., 1996; lectr. in field; cons. in field. Author: Urban Public Finance, 1986; co-author: Public Sector Economics, 1984; editor: Fiscal Aspects of Evolving Federations, 1997; assoc. editor: Regional Sci. and Urban Econs., 1987—2004, Jour. Regional Sci., 1989—, Jour. Urban Econs., 1991—, Internat. Tax and Pub. Fin., 1993—, Rev. Internat. Econs., 1994—, Nat. Tax Jour., 1998—, Jour. Pub. Econ. Theory, 1999—, Jour. Pub. Econs. 1999—2003, Papers in Regional Sci., 1999—2001, German Econ. Rev., 2000—, Finanzarchiv, 2000—, CESifo Econ. Studies, 2003—, Contbns. to Econ. Analysis, 2004—, Founds. and Trends in Microecons., 2005, referee: profl. jours.; contbr. over 85 articles to Am. Econ. Rev., Econ. Jour., others. Grantee, NSF, 1978—81; Ameritech fellow, Ind. U., 1988—89, Rsch. fellow, Ctr. for Ops. Rsch. and Econometrics, U. Cath. de Louvain, Belgium, 1986—87, U. Bonn, Germany, 1990, Rsch. fellow, Ctr. for Econ. Studies (CESifo), U. Munich, 1999—, Inst. for Study of Labor, U. Bonn, Germany, 2000—. Mem. Am. Econ. Assn., Econometric Soc, Nat. Tax Assn., Tax Inst. Am. Office: U Ky Martin Sch Pub Policy Lexington KY 40506-0027 Office Phone: 859-257-2456. Business E-Mail: dew@davidwildasin.us.

**WILDE, CARLTON D.,** lawyer, director; b. Houston, Apr. 11, 1935; s. Henry Dayton and Louise (Key) W.; m. Martha Cloyes, July 26, 1958; children: Carlton D. Jr., Jennifer. Student, Coll. of William and Mary, 1953-55; BA, U. Tex., 1957, JD, 1959. Assoc. Bracewell & Giuliani, Houston, 1959-62, ptnr., 1962-67, 85—, mng. ptnr., 1967-85. Fellow Am. Bar Found., Tex. Bar Found., Houston Bar Found.; mem. ABA, State Bar Tex., River Oaks Country Club, Coronado Club (Houston), Biltmore Forest Country Club (Asheville, N.C.). Republican. Home: 3105 Reba Dr Houston TX 77019-6209 Office: Bracewell & Giuliani 2300 S Tower Pennzoil Pl 711 Louisiana Ste 2300 Houston TX 77002-2781 Business E-Mail: carlton.wilde@bracewellgiuliani.com.

**WILDE, DANIEL UNDERWOOD,** computer engineering educator; b. Wilmington, Ohio, Dec. 27, 1937; s. Arthur John and Ruby Dale (Underwood) Wilde. BSEE, U. Ill., 1960; MS, M.I.T., 1962, PhD, 1966. Research instr. medicine Boston U. Med. Sch., 1964-66; asst. prof. elec. and computer. engring. U. Conn., 1966-69, assoc. prof. 1970-75, prof. 1976-87, assoc. dir. New Eng. Rsch. Application Ctr., Storrs, Conn., 1966-72, dir., 1973-85, NASA Indsl. Application Ctr., 1972-91; pres. NERAC Inc., Tolland, Conn., 1985-99. Cons. NERAC Inc., 1999-2004; trustee Engring. Index, Inc.; cons. Am. Soc. Metals, 1973-76; bd. dirs. Internat. Coun. Sci. Info. Author: Author: Introduction to Computing: Problem Solving, Algorithms and Data Structures, 1973; contbr. articles to profl. jours. With USAF. Recipient NASA Public Service award, 1975 National Tech. Fedn. Abstracting and Indexing Svcs. (hon.), Internat. Coun. Sci. Info. (hon.); mem. IEEE, Am. Soc. Info. Sci., Assn. Computing Machinery, Assn. Info. and Dissemination Centers (sec.-treas. 1976-79, pres. 1979-81).

**WILDE, EDWIN FREDERICK,** retired mathematics professor; b. Lombard, Ill., Jan. 14, 1931; s. Edwin Frederick and Carrie Belle (Hammond) W.; m. Connie Mae Rawlings, Aug. 23, 1952 (dec. July 2002); children— Brad Alan, Bruce Ramon, Elizabeth Lynn; m. Kathleen Wright, Sept. 25, 2004. BS, Ill. State U., Normal, 1952, MS, 1953; MA, U. Ill., 1955, PhD, 1959; postgrad., U. Wis., part time, 1955-58, Stanford U., Calif., 1964-65. With Beloit Coll., Wis., 1955-76, prof. math., dean faculty Wis., 1969-71, v.p. for planning Wis., 1971-75; dean Roger Williams Coll., Bristol, RI, 1976-80; provost, dean of faculty U. Tampa, Fla., 1980-86; vice chancellor U. S.C., Spartanburg, 1986-91, prof. math., 1991-99; ret., 1999. Cons. AID insts., India, 1964, Insts. Internat. Edn., East Pakistan, 1969 NSF Sr. Sci. Faculty fellow, 1964-65 Mem. Math. Assn. Am. (bd. govs. 1968-69, 72-75). Home: 275 James Rd Gaffney SC 29341-4013 E-mail: efw1931@yahoo.com.

**WILDE, HAROLD RICHARD,** college president; b. Wauwatosa, Wis., May 14, 1945; s. Harold Richard and Winifred (Wiley) W.; m. Benna Brecher, Feb. 4, 1970; children: Anna, Henry, Elizabeth Ty. BA, Amherst Coll., 1967; MA, PhD, Harvard U. Cambridge, Mass., 1973. Spl. asst. to gov. Office of Gov., State of Wis., Madison, 1972-75; cons. minister of Commr. of Ins., State of Wis., Madison, 1975-79; spl. asst. to pres. U. Wis. System, Madison, 1979-81; v.p. for external affairs Beloit (Wis.) Coll., 1981-91; pres. North Ctrl. Coll., Naperville, Ill., 1991—. Bd. dirs. Ctr. for Pub. Representation, Inc., Madison, 1981-87, Beloit Community Found., 1988-91, Budget Funding Corp., 1993-99, Naperville Devel. Partnership, 1996—. Mem.: Phi Beta

Kappa. Home: 329 S Brainard St Naperville IL 60540-5401 Office: North Ctrl Coll 30 N Brainard St Naperville IL 60540-4607 Office Phone: 630-637-5454. Business E-Mail: hrwilde@noctrl.edu.

**WILDE, WILSON,** insurance company executive; b. Hartford, Conn., Sept. 24, 1927; s. Philip Alden and Alice Augusta (Wilson) W.; m. Joanne Gerta Menzel, June 19, 1953; children— Stephen W., David W., Elisabeth L., Richard A. Student, Swarthmore Coll., 1945-46; BA, Williams Coll., 1949. Sales agt. Conn. Gen. Life Ins. Co., Hartford, 1949-53; with Hartford Steam Boiler Inspection & Ins. Co., 1953-70, exec. v.p., 1970-71, pres., CEO 1971—, from chmn., CEO to chmn. emeritus, 1993-98, chmn. emeritus, 1998—. Corporator Inst. Living, Hartford; hon. bd. dirs. Hartford Stage Co., 1973—, Jr. Achievement, Old State House Assn., 1976—; trustee Loomis-Chaffee Sch., 1974—, chmn. bd., 1988-98. With USNR, 1945-47, 51-53. Office: PO Box 5024 Hartford CT 06102-5024

**WILDEMANN, GREGORY NYLUND,** writer; b. Hartford, Conn., Sept. 19, 1956; s. Michael Nylund and Diana L. Wildemann. Student in Fgn. Svc., Georgetown U., 1974—79; AA, Tompkins-Cortland CC, 1984; BA, SUNY, Albany, 1985. Instr. Sch. Fgn. Svc., Georgetown U., Washington, 1974—79; press aide NY State Assembly, Albany, NY, 1985—89. Author (under pseudonym): The Rag and Bone Shop, 2001, Letters From an Age of Reason, 2001, The Sound of Trees, 2002, Scorched Earth, 2002, For Courage Tomorrow, 2005; author: numerous poems. Recipient Medal of Honor, Order of Loyola, 2003; Baker scholar. Mem.: Hudson Valley Writer's Guild. Democrat. Methodist. Home: 32 Robin St Albany NY 12206-2719 E-mail: aquametaphors@yahoo.com.

**WILDENTHAL, C(LAUD) KERN,** physician, educator; b. San Marcos, Tex., July 1, 1941; s. Bryan and Doris (Kellam) W.; m. Margaret Dehlinger, Oct. 15, 1964; children: Pamela, Catharine. BA, Sul Ross Coll., 1960; MD, U. Tex. Southwestern Med. Ctr., Dallas, 1966; PhD, U. Cambridge, Eng., 1970. Intern Bellevue Hosp., N.Y.C., 1964-65; resident in medicine, fellow cardiology Parkland Hosp., Dallas, 1965-67; rsch. fellow Nat. Heart Inst., Bethesda, Md., 1967-68; vis. rsch. fellow Strangeways Rsch. Lab., Cambridge, 1968-70; asst. prof. to prof. internal medicine and physiology U. Tex. Southwestern Med. Ctr., Dallas, 1970-76, prof., dean grad. sch., 1976-80, prof., dean Southwestern Med. Sch., 1980-86, prof., pres., 1986—. Hon. fellow Hughes Hall, U. Cambridge, 1994—. Author: Regulation of Cardiac Metabolism, 1976, Degradative Processes in Heart and Skeletal Muscle, 1980; contbr. articles to profl. jours. Bd. dirs. Lasker Found., Dallas Ctr. Performing Arts, Dallas Symphony, Dallas Opera, Dallas Mus. Art, Dallas Citizen's Coun., Greater Dallas C. of C., Cambridge in Am., Hoblitzelle Found., Reves Found. Recipient rsch. career devel. award NIH, 1972; spl. rsch. fellow USPHS, 1968-70; Guggenheim fellow, 1975-76. Mem. AMA, Inst. Medicine/NAS, Am. Soc. Clin. Investigation, Am. Coll. Cardiology, Royal Soc. Medicine Gt. Britain, Am. Physiol. Soc., Internat. Soc. Heart Rsch. (past pres. Am. sect.), Am. Fedn. Clin. Rsch., Assn. Am. Med Colls., Assn. Am. Physicians, Am. Heart Assn. (past chmn. sci. policy com.), Assn. Acad. Health Ctrs. (past chmn. sci. policy com.), Brit. N.Am. Com. Home: 4001 Hanover Ave Dallas TX 75225-7010 Office: U Tex Southwestern Med Ctr 5323 Harry Hines Blvd Dallas TX 75390-7208 Office Phone: 214-648-2508.

**WILDER, C. JOHN (JOHN WILDER),** energy executive; b. Mo. m. Susan Burford; three children. BS magna cum laude in Bus. Adminstrn., S.E. Mo. State U., 1980; MBA, U. Tex., Austin, 1994. With Royal Dutch/Shell Group of Cos., asst. treas.; dir. econs. and fin. Shell Exploration and Prodn. Co.; asst. treas. Shell Oil Co.; CEO Shell Capital, 1998; exec. v.p., CFO Entergy Corp., New Orleans, 1999—2004; pres., CEO TXU Corp., Dallas, 2004-05, chmn., pres., CEO, 2005—. Mem. adv. bd. McCombs Sch. Bus., U. Tex., Austin, Global Energy Mgmt. Inst., U. Houston, A.B. Freeman Sch. Bus., Tulane U. Named Best CFO in Am., Institutional Investor, 2003. Mem.: Edison Elec. Inst., World Econ. Forum. Methodist. Office: TXU Corp Energy Plz 1601 Bryan St Dallas TX 75201-3411

**WILDER, DAVID RANDOLPH,** retired materials engineer; b. Lorimor, Iowa, June 11, 1929; s. Rex Marshall and Ethel Marie (Busch) W.; m. Donna Jean Moore, June 17, 1951; children: Susan, Michael, Margaret, Bruce. BS, Iowa State U., 1951, MS, 1952, PhD, 1958. Registered profl. engr., Iowa (inactive). Engr. Ames Lab., 1951-81; faculty mem. dept. materials sci. and engring. Iowa State U., Ames, 1955—, prof. engring., chmn. dept., 1961-89, prof. engring., 1989-91, prof. emeritus, 1991—; cons. to various industries, fed. agys, 1955—. Contbr. numerous tech. paper to profl. lit.; patentee in field. Fellow Am. Ceramic Soc., Accreditation Bd. for Engring. and Tech.; mem. Nat. Inst. Ceramic Engrs., Am. Soc. for Engring. Edn., Keramos. Home: 1214 Ridgewood Ave Ames IA 50010-5208

**WILDER, DWIGHT SAFFORD,** academic administrator; b. Plainfield, N.J., Dec. 24, 1946; s. Glenn Safford and Marion Seaver (Fiske) W.; children: Thomas, Douglas; m. Margaret Ruth Holland, Sept. 9, 1995. BA, Johns Hopkins U., 1969; postgrad., Harvard U., 1969-70; MBA, So. N.H. U., 1981; postgrad., Rivier Coll., 2002—03. Mem. faculty Hebron (Maine) Acad., 1969-70; assoc. dir. continuing edn. N.H. Coll., Manchester, 1975-78, seminar adminstr., 1978-80, asst. to dean, 1980-84; program design specialist N.H. Job Tng. Council, Concord, 1984-89; apprentice program mgr. Portsmouth Naval Shipyard, 1989-92; coord. Seacoast Tech. Prep. Consortium, 1992-96; sch.-to-career coord. Timberlane Sch. Dist., Plaistow, NH, 1996—2004, asst. prin., 2004—. Mng. editor Jour. Ednl. Computing Research, 1983-84. Mem. Cold River Camp Cons., 1999— Mem. Am. Soc. Tng. and Devel., Appalachian Mountain Club (vol. educator and cons., 1975—, sec. North Country bd. 1980-87), N.H. Personnel and Guidance Assn., N.H. Sch. Prins. Assn., Chatham Trails Assn. (pres. 2002-05), Old Johannian Assn. (U.S. rep. 2001—), Toastmasters (pres. Navy Brunswick chpt. 1973-74, pres. Manchester chpt. 1982-83) Avocations: hiking, backpacking, painting. Home: 15 Pinecrest Dr Somersworth NH 03878 Office: Timberlane Sch Dist 36 Greenough Rd Plaistow NH 03865 Office Phone: 603-382-6541. Personal E-mail: dwilder@timberlanehs.com.

**WILDER, GENE,** actor, film director, writer; b. Milw., June 11, 1935; s. William J. and Jeanne (Baer) Silberman; m. Mary Joan Schutz, Oct. 27, 1967 (div. 1974); 1 child, Katharine Anastasia; m. Gilda Radner, 1984 (dec.); m. Karen Boyer, Sept. 8, 1991. BA, U. Iowa, 1955; postgrad., Bristol Old Vic Theatre Sch., 1955-56. Appeared in Broadway play: The Complaisant Lover, 1962 (Clarence Derwent award); appeared in London production of Laughter on the 23rd Floor, 1996; appeared in motion pictures: Bonnie and Clyde, 1966, The Producers, 1967 (Acad. award nom. best supporting actor), Start the Revolution Without Me, 1968, Quackser Fortune Has a Cousin in the Bronx, 1969, Willy Wonka and the Chocolate Factory, 1970, Everything You Always Wanted to Know About Sex, 1971, Rhinoceros, 1972, Blazing Saddles, 1973, The Little Prince, 1974, Silver Streak, 1976, The Frisco Kid, 1979, Stir Crazy, 1980; Hanky Panky, 1982, See No Evil, Hear No Evil, 1989, Funny About Love, 1990, Another You, 1991; (TV films) Murder in a Small Town, 1999, Alice in Wonderland, 1999, The Lady in Question, 1999; dir., writer, actor film: The Adventures of Sherlock Holmes' Smarter Brother, 1975, The World's Greatest Lover, 1977, Sunday Lovers, 1980, The Woman in Red, 1984, Haunted Honeymoon, 1986; actor, co-writer film: Young Frankenstein, 1974 (Acad. award nomination); TV appearances include: The Trouble With People, 1973, Marlo Thomas Spl., 1973, The Scarecrow, 1972, Thursday's Games, 1973, (series) Something Wilder, 1994-95; guest appearances TV series The Defenders, 1962, The DuPont Show of the Week, 1962-63, The Frank Skinner Show, 1997, Will & Grace, 2002-03 (Emmy award best guest actor 2003); author: Kiss Me Like a Stranger: My Search for Love and Art, 2005. Campaigned with Elaine May and Rene Taylor for Eugene McCarthy, Allard Lowenstein and Paul O'Dwyer, 1968. Served with U.S. Army, 1956-58. Actors Equity Assn., Am. Federation of Television & Radio Artists, DGA, WGA. Office: c/o David Shapira & Assoc Ste 235 15821 Ventura Blvd Encino CA 91436

**WILDER, JANET MARY,** performing company executive; d. Robert and Jean; m. Ward Wilder; children: Suzanne, Robert. BS, U. Colo., 1966. Cecchetti tchr. cert. Cecchetti Coun. Am., tchr. cert. Dance Nat. Dance Masters Assn., tchg. cert. Calif. Tchr. Santa Venetia Mid. Sch., San Rafael, Calif., 1967—68; fitness/dance instr. Am. Wives' Club, Ghedi, Brescia, Italy, 1969—71; instr. Julie Ward Sch. Dance, Rapid City, SD, 1972—77, Spokane Ballet, Wash., 1981—83, Capitol City Ballet, Sacramento, 1985—87, Marguerite Phares Sch. Dance, Sacramento, 1985—87; artistic dir. Dakota Repertory Dance Co., Rapid City, 1975—77, San Antonio Dance Theatre, 1983—85, Dance Theatre NW, Spokane, 1994—2004, Ballet Spokane, 2003—; instr., co-dir. Entenman Sch. Dance, Bellvue, Nebr., 1978—81; dancer Omaha Ballet, 1979—81; dir. Ballet Arts, San Antonio, 1983—85; co-dir. Ballet Arts Acad., Spokane, 1987—94; co-founder, dir. Theatre Ballet Spokane, 1987—94; choreographer/prodr./dir. Coeur d'Alene (Idaho) Summer Theatre, 1991—96; resident choreographer Spokane/Coeur d'Alene Opera, 1987—; owner, dir. Acad. Dance, Spokane Valley, Wash., 1994—. Founder/mem. Inland NW Dance Assn., Spokane, 1989—; ballet adv. bd. mem. Greater Spokane Music & Allied Arts Festival, 1988—2000, MusicFest NW, Spokane, 2000—; dance edn. del. to China People to People, Bejing, 1996. Author: (book) Terms Every Dancer Should Know; writer, prodr., dir.: (ballets) The Toy Shelf; choreographer (over 150 ballets, operas & musicals). Mem. Rapid City Svc. League, 1975—77; mem./officer PTA, Rapid City, 1975—77; com. mem. First Night Spokane, 2003; mem. entertainment com. Diamonds & Divas, Spokane, 2000—05. Recipient Outstanding Mem., Ghedi Air Force Wives' Club, 1971, Ellsworth Officer's Wives' Club, 1977, Outstanding Young Women of Am., Outstanding Young Women of Am. program, 1973, Wash. State Dance Sch. Dir., Dance Excellence Internat. Festival for Young Dancers, 1992—95, Bowl Games of Am./CocaCola Olympic City, 1996, Jim Chase Asset builder, Chase Youth Commn., 1997, Dir. in charge - Teen Group Creativity Award, 2000, Dir. in charge - Teen Group Cmty. Svc. Hon. Mention, 2001. Mem.: Nat. Dance Edn. Orgn., Nat. Dance Assn., MusicFest NW, Inland NW Dance Assn. (v.p. 2002—04). Avocations: writing, scuba diving, skiing, boating. Office Phone: 509-922-3023. Personal E-Mail: janetwilder123@aol.com.

**WILDER, JOHN SHELTON,** lieutenant governor; b. Fayette City, Tenn., June 3, 1921; s. John Chamblee and Martha (Shelton) W.; m. Marcelle Morton, Dec. 31, 1941; children: John Shelton Wilder, II, David Morton. Student, U. Tenn.; LLB, U. Memphis, 1957. Bar: Tenn. 1957. Engaged in farming, Longtown, Tenn., 1943—; supr. mgmt. Longtown Supply Co.; judge Fayette County Ct.; mem. Tenn. Senate, 1959—60, 1966—; mem. senate 81st, 85th, 86th through 102nd Gen. Assemblies; lt. gov., spkr. senate State of Tenn., Chester, Crockett, Fayette, Hardeman, Hardin, others, 1971—, pres. senate, 1971—. Past pres. Nat. Assn. Soil Conservation Dists., Tenn. Soil Conservation Assn., Tenn. Agrl. Council; exec. com. So. Legis. Conf., Conf. Lt. Govs.; dir. Bank Tenn., Cumberland Bank; chmn. Cumberland BanCorp, Inc. Served with U.S. Army, 1942-43. Mem. Tenn. Cotton Ginners Assn. (past pres.), Shriner, Scottish Rite, Mason, Delta Theta Phi. Clubs: Shriners. Democrat. Methodist. Office: Office Lt Governor 1 Legislative Plz Nashville TN 37243-0026 also: 4020 Highway 59 Mason TN 38049 Office Phone: 615-741-2368, 901-465-4647. Office Fax: 615-741-9349.*

**WILDER, L(AWRENCE) DOUGLAS,** mayor, former governor; b. Richmond, Va., Jan. 17, 1931; children: Lynn, Larry, Loren. BS, Va. Union U., 1951; JD, Howard U., 1959. Bar: Va. Mem. Va. Senate, 1969-85; lt. gov. State of Va., 1986-89, gov., 1989-93; Al Douglas Wilder Disting. prof. Va. Commonwealth U., 1988—; mayor Richmond, Va., 2005—. Del. Democratic Nat. Conv., 1980; agt. NAACP Legal Def. Fund. Bd. dirs. United Givers Fund; chmn. bd. Red Shield Boys' Club. Served with U.S. Army, 1952-53 Decorated Bronze Star; named one of 100 Most Influential Black Americans, Ebony mag., 2006; recipient Spingarn Medal, NAACP, Anna Eleanor Roosevelt Medallion of Honor, Thurgood Marshall Award of Excellence. Mem. ABA, Va. Bar Assn., Nat. Bar Assn., Am. Judicature Soc., C. of C., Urban League (bd. dirs. Richmond), Omega Psi Phi. Clubs: Masons; Shriners. Democrat. Office: Virginia Commonwealth Univ 919 W Franklin St PO Box 842028 Richmond VA 23284-2028 also: Mayor's Office Rm 201 900 E Broad St Richmond VA 23219 Office Phone: 804-828-4971, 804-646-7970. Office Fax: 804-646-7987.*

**WILDER, MICHAEL STEPHEN,** former insurance company executive; b. New Haven, Sept. 8, 1941; BA, Yale U., 1963; JD, Harvard U., 1966. Bar: Conn. 1966. Atty. Hartford (Conn.) Fire Ins. Co., 1967-69, asst. gen. counsel, 1969-71, assoc. gen. counsel, 1971-75, gen. coun., sec., 1975-87, sr. v.p., gen. counsel, sec., 1987-95; sr. v.p., gen. counsel The Hartford Fin. Svcs. Group, Inc., 1995—2001; ret., 2001. Mem. ABA, Conn. Bar Assn. Home: 85 Emily Way West Hartford CT 06107-3136

**WILDER, ROLAND PERCIVAL, JR.,** lawyer; b. Malden, Mass., June 21, 1940; s. Roland Percival and Clarissa (Hunting) W.; m. Susan McAra Randell, Sept. 3, 1965 (dec. Jan. 1996); children: Roland Percival III, William Randell; m. Carolyn Sue Whisenhunt, Nov. 26, 2004. BA, Washington and Jefferson Coll., 1963; JD, Vanderbilt U., 1966. Bar: D.C. 1967, U.S. Dist. Ct. D.C. 1967, U.S. Dist. Ct. Md. 1994, U.S. Dist. Ct. Colo. 1997, U.S. Dist. Ct. (ea. dist.) Mich. 1999, U.S. Ct. Appeals (D.C. cir.) 1967, U.S. Ct. Appeals (4th, 5th and 6th cirs.) 1976, U.S. Ct. Appeals (8th and 9th cirs.) 1977, U.S. Ct. Appeals (2d cir.) 1978, U.S. Ct. Appeals (11th cir.) 1981, U.S. Ct. Appeals (3d cir.) 1997, U.S. Ct. Appeals (7th cir.) 2002, U.S. Supreme Ct. 1972. Atty. Office of Solicitor U.S. Dept. Labor, Washington, 1967-69; asst. counsel civil rights office of solicitor U.S. Dept. Labor, Washington, 1969-70, counsel civil rights office of solicitor, 1970-71; supr. atty. office gen. counsel NLRB, Washington, 1972-74; assoc. gen. counsel Internat. Brotherhood Teamsters, Washington, 1974-85; sr. mem. Baptiste & Wilder P.C., Washington, 1985—. Lectr. in field. Mng. editor Vanderbilt U. Law Rev., 1965-66; contbr. articles to profl. jours. V.p Arlington (Va.) Cubs Youth Club, Inc., 1975-81; coach Fairfax (Va.) Hockey Club, 1979-83. Mem. ABA, D.C. Bar Assn., Assn. Trial Lawyers Am., Phi Delta Phi, Pi Sigma Alpha, Phi Alpha Theta, Roosevelt Soc., Joint Council Flight Attendant Unions (hon. flight attendant 1985). Democrat. Avocations: history, tennis, skiing. Office: Baptiste & Wilder PC 1150 Connecticut Ave NW Ste 500 Washington DC 20036-4194 Office Phone: 202-223-0723. Business E-Mail: rpwilderjr@bapwild.com.

**WILDER, RONALD PARKER,** economics professor; b. Freeport, Tex., Jan. 15, 1941; s. J. Barton and Lois (Parker) W.; m. Charlotte D. Pearson, Sept. 4, 1965; children: Erika, Rachel, David. BA, Rice U., 1963, MA, 1964; PhD, Vanderbilt U., 1969. Asst. prof. econs. U. S.C., Columbia, 1970-75, assoc. prof., 1975-80, prof., 0180—2006, prof. emeritus, 2006—, chmn. dept. econs., 1987—2002. Co-author: Stock Life Insurance Profitability, 1986; mem. editorial bd. So. Econ. J., 1978-80; contbr. articles to profl. jours. Capt. U.S. Army, 1968-70. Fellow Ford Found., Vanderbilt U., 1964-65. Mem. Am. Econ. Assn., So. Econ. Assn., Omicron Delta Epsilon. United Methodist. Avocations: hiking, canoeing. Office: U of SC Dept Of Econs Columbia SC 29208-0001

**WILDERMUTH, ANITA JEAN,** art educator; b. La Crosse, Wis., July 20, 1939; d. Arthur and Aleda Marie (Thompson) Thurin; m. Robert Berl Wildermuth, Aug. 15, 1970. BA, Luther Coll., 1961; MA in Tchg., Rockford Coll., 1977. Cert. tchr., Wis. Tchr. art Dodgeville Pub. Schs., Wis., 1961—62, Viroqua Pub. Schs., Wis., 1962—66, Beloit Sch. Dist., Wis., 1966—98; ret., 1998. Supr. art Sch. Dist. Beloit, 1968-98; owner Thurin Apts., Viroqua, Wis.; sec.-treas. Wildermuth Farms, Inc. EMT, Turtle Fire Dept., Beloit, 1980-2005; mem. U. Wis. Ext. Homemakers, So. Wis. Interest Macintosh Computer Soc. Mem. Wis. Art Educators Assn., Nat. Art Educators Assn. (amb. to China for art edn. 1988), Nat. Farmers Orgn., Art League Beloit, Nat. Assn. Photoshop Profls., Beloit Area Ret. Educators Assn. Avocations: art, computer graphics, painting, crafts, golf. Home: 10001 S Clinton Corners Rd Clinton WI 53525-8308 Office Phone: 608-676-4684. E-mail: wilderm@jvlnet.com.

**WILDERMUTH, BRUCE R.,** lawyer; b. Bklyn., Feb. 19, 1952; BA in History, George Washington U., 1974; JD, St. John's U., 1979. Bar: NY 1980, US Dist. Ct. Ea. Dist. NY, US Dist. Ct. So. Dist. NY, US Dist. Ct. No. Dist. NY. Ptnr. Wilson, Elser, Moskowitz, Edelman & Dicker LLP, NYC. Mem.: NY State Bar Assn. Office: Wilson Elser Moskowitz Edelman & Dicker LLP 150 E 42nd St 3rd Fl New York NY 10017-5639 Office Phone: 212-490-3000 ext. 2142. Office Fax: 212-490-3038. Business E-Mail: wildermuthb@wemed.com.

**WILDEROTTER, JAMES ARTHUR,** lawyer; b. Newark, July 25, 1944; s. Arthur Walter and Dorothy Theresa (King) W.; children: James, Kristin, Kathryn. BA, Georgetown U., 1966; JD, U. Ill., 1969. Bar: D.C. 1969, U.S. Supreme Ct. 1974. Assoc. Covington & Burling, Washington, 1969-71; spl. asst. to Under Sec. Commerce, Washington, 1971-73; exec. asst. to Sec. HUD, Washington, 1973-74; assoc. dept. atty. gen. U.S. Washington, 1974-75; assoc. counsel to Pres. U.S., 1975-76; gen. counsel U.S. Energy Research and Devel. Adminstrn., Washington, 1976-77; of counsel Morgan, Lewis & Bockius, Washington, 1977-78; ptnr. Jones, Day, Reavis & Pogue, Washington, 1978—91, 1995—2006; gen. counsel U.S. Trade and Devel. Agy., Washington, 1991-94; gen. counsel U.S. Trade and Devel. Agy., Washington, 1991-94; gen. counsel U. S. Trade and Devel. Agy., Washington, 1991-94; gen. counsel U. S. Trade and Devel. Agy., Washington, 2006—. Editor in chief: U. Ill. Law Rev., 1968-69. Gen. counsel rules com. Rep. Nat. Conv., 1980; sec. James S. Brady Presdl. Found., 1982-88; gen. counsel Nat. Sudden Infant Death Syndrome Found., 1986-90, sec. Sudden Infant Death Syndrome Alliance, 1990-93. With USN, 1962-68. Mem. ABA Republican. Roman Catholic. Home: 5903 Mount Eagle Dr Alexandria VA 22303 Office: US Trade and Devel Agy 1000 Wilson Blvd Ste 1600 Arlington VA 22209 Office Phone: 202-879-3832. Personal E-mail: jawilder@yahoo.com. Business E-Mail: jwilderotter@ustda.gov.

**WILDEROTTER, MAGGIE (MARY AGNES WILDEROTTER),** software executive, former cable television executive; b. Neptune, N.J., Feb. 9, 1955; d. Denis James and Constance Rosemary (Shields) Sullivan; m. Philip Jay Wilderotter; children: Christopher, Daniel. BA in Econs., Holy Cross Coll., 1977. Accts. receivable supr. CableData, Sacramento, 1979-80, mgr. acctg. svcs., 1980-82, mgr. reg. support, 1982, mktg. mgr., 1982-83, dir. mktg., 1983, dir. nat. accts., 1983-85, v.p., 1985—87, sr. v.p., sales & mktg., 1987—91; sr. v.p. McCaw Cellular Communications, 1991—95; exec. v.p., nat. ops. & CEO, Aviation Communications div. AT&T Wireless Svcs., 1995—97; pres., CEO Wink Communications, 1997—2002; sr. v.p., bus. strategy Microsoft Corp., 2002—04; pres., CEO Citizens Communications, 2004—05, chmn., CEO, 2005—. Bd. dirs. Phoenix Cable Ptnrs., San Rafael, Calif., 1988—, Satellite Video Ctr., Rancho Cordova, Calif., 1988—, CableData Europe Ltd., Leeds, Eng., 1989—, Citizens Communications, 2004-, Xerox Corp., 2006-. Outstanding Mentor award, Women in Cable and Telecommunications Found., 1999. Mem. Nat. Cable TV Assn. (bd. dirs. 1987—), Women in Cable (exec. mem.), Cable TV Adminstrn. & Mktg. Soc., Calif. Cable TV Assn., Nat. Acad. Cable Programming. Republican. Roman Catholic. Office: Citizens Communications 3 High Ridge Park Stamford CT 06905

**WILDHACK, WILLIAM AUGUST, JR.,** lawyer; b. Takoma Park, Md., Nov. 28, 1935; s. William August and Martha Elizabeth (Parks) W.; m. Martha Moore Allston, Aug. 1, 1959; children: William A. III, Elizabeth L. BS, Miami U., Oxford, Ohio, 1957; JD, George Washington U., 1963. Bar: Va. 1963, D.C. 1965, Md. 1983, U.S. Supreme Ct. 1967. Agt. IRS, Va., 1957-65; pvt. prac. Washington, 1965—69; v.p., corp. counsel B.F. Saul Co. and affiliates, Chevy Chase, Md., 1969-87, Chevy Chase Bank, F.S.B. and affiliates, 1987-90; atty. pvt. practice, Arlington, Va., 1990—. Sec. B.F. Saul Real Estate Investment Trust, Chevy Chase, 1972-87. Mem. ABA, Md. Bar Assn., D.C. Bar, Va. Bar, Arlington County Bar Assn. (chmn. trusts and estates sect. 2002—), Nat. Acad. Elder Law Attys., Soc. Corp. Secretaries and Governance Profls.

**WILDING, DIANE,** computer scientist, consultant; b. Chicago Heights, Ill., Nov. 7, 1942; d. Michael Edward and Katherine Surian; m. Manfred Georg Wilding, May 7, 1975 (div. 1980). BSBA in Acctg. magna cum laude, No. Ill. U., DeKalb, 1963; postgrad., U. Chgo., 1972—74; cert. in German lang., Goethe Inst., Rothenburg, Germany, 1984; cert. in internat. bus. German, Goethe Inst., Atlanta, 1994; cert. in Web page design, Kennesaw State U., Ga., 2000. Lic. cosmetologist. Sys. engr. IBM, Chgo., 1963-68, SAP cons. Atlanta, 1993—; data processing mgr. Am. Res. Corp., Chgo., 1969-72; system R & D project mgr. Continental Bank, Chgo., 1972-75; fin. industry mktg. rep. IBM Can., Ltd., Toronto, Ont., 1976-79; regional telecom. mktg. exec. Control Data Corp., Atlanta, 1980-84; gen. mgr. The Plant Plant, Atlanta, 1985-92. Pioneer installer on-line automatic teller machines Pos Equipment, 1977. Mem. Chgo. Coun. Fgn. Rels.; bd. dirs. Easter House Adoption Agy., Chgo., 1974—76. Mem.: Internat. Brass Soc., Mensa, Goethe Inst., Libertyville Racquet Club, Royal Ont. Yacht Club, Ponte Verde Club (Fla.). Avocations: travel, gourmet cooking, languages, antiques. Home: PO Box 723055 Atlanta GA 31139-0055 Office: IBM 1600 Riveredge Pkwy NW Atlanta GA 30328-4697 E-mail: diane.wilding@gmail.com.

**WILDING, LAWRENCE PAUL,** retired pedology educator, soil science consultant; b. Winner, SD, Oct. 1, 1934; s. William Kasper and Ruth Inez (Root) W.; m. Gladys Dora Milne, Nov. 25, 1956; children: Linda Kay, Doris Bertha, Charles William, David Lawrence. BSc, S.D. State U., 1956, MSc, 1959; PhD, U. Ill., 1962. Asst. in agronomy S.D. State U., Brookings, 1956-59; rsch. fellow U. Ill., Urbana, 1959-62; prof. agronomy Ohio State U., Columbus, 1962-76; prof. pedology Tex. A&M U., College Station, 1976—2003, prof. emeritus, 2003, ret., 2003—. Vis. prof. U. Guelph, Ont. Can., 1971-72; mem. NATO Advanced Rsch. Workshop on Expansive Soils, Cornell U., 1990-91; mem. U.S. Nat. Com. on Soil Sci.; mem. NRC-NAS, 1998-2000; mem. exec. com. Am. Geol. Inst. Coun., 1998-2001. Author and/or editor 4 books; assoc. editor Catena Verlag, 1989, Geoderma, 1988-92; contbr. over 150 articles to profl. jours., chpts. to books. Sgt. S.D. N.G., 1956-59. Recipient Mem. award Sigma XI, 1988, Superior Svc. Group award sci. rsch. USDA, 1993; Campbell Soup fellow, 1959-62, Faculty fellow Tex. A&M U.; grantee USDA, AID, 1986—. Fellow AAAS, Am. Soc. Agronomy (cert.), Soil Sci. Soc. Am. (Soil Sci. Rsch. award 1987, opportunities in soil sci. com., chmn. subcomm. B 1989-92, chmn. divsn. S-5, bd. dirs. rep., mem. steering com. 1990-91, pres. elect 1992-93, pres. 1993-94, past pres. 1994-95), Am. Inst. Chemists; mem. Soil Scientists Assn. Tex., Internat. Union Soil Scis. (hon. mem., prof. emeritus 2003-), Soil and Water Conservation Soc. Am., Tex. A&M Faculty Club, Gamma Sigma Delta. Democrat. Presbyterian. Avocations: golf, woodworking, travel, sports, antiques. Office: Texas A&M U Dept Soil And Crop Scis College Station TX 77843-0001 Business E-Mail: wilding@tamu.edu.

**WILDING, RICHARD,** library director; Bus. mgr. Mid-Continent Pub. Libr. (MCPL), Independence, Mo., asst. dir., 1998—2006, dir. Libraries, 2006—. Office: Mid-Continent Pub Libr 15616 E 24 Highway Independence MO 64050 Office Phone: 816-836-5200. Office Fax: 816-521-7253.*

**WILDMAN, GARY CECIL,** chemist, researcher; b. Middlefield, Ohio, Nov. 25, 1942; s. Gerald Robert and Frances Jane (Swager) W.; m. Linda Bufkin, Mar. 27, 1999; children: Debbie, Eric. AB in Chemistry, Thiel Coll., 1964; PhD in Chemistry, Duke U., 1970. Research asst. B.F. Goodrich Research, Brecksville, Ohio, summer 1964; instr. Duke U., 1966—67; research chemist Hercules Research Center, Wilmington, Del., 1968-71; assoc. prof. polymer sci. U. So. Miss., Hattiesburg, 1971-76, prof., 1976-83, chmn. dept., 1971-76, dean Coll. Sci. and Tech., 1976-83; v.p. research and devel. Schering Plough, Memphis, 1983—. Mem. Am. Chem. Soc., So. Soc. Coatings Tech., Soc. Plastics Engrs., Am. Crystallographic Assn., Phi Beta Kappa, Sigma Xi, Phi Lambda Upsilon, Sigma Pi Sigma, Omicron Delta Kappa. Clubs: Rotary. Republican. Methodist. Home: 2140 Johnson Rd Germantown TN 38139-3500 Office: PO Box 377 Memphis TN 38151-0002

**WILDMAN, MAX EDWARD,** lawyer, director; b. Terre Haute, Ind., Dec. 4, 1919; s. Roscoe Ellsworth and Lena (Shaw) W.; m. Joyce Lenore Smith, Sept. 25, 1948; children: Leslie, William. BS, Butler U., 1941; JD, U. Mich., 1947; MBA, U. Chgo., 1952. Bar: Ill., Ind. Ptnr. Kirkland & Ellis, Chgo., 1947-67;

mng. ptnr. Wildman, Harrold, Allen & Dixon, Chgo., 1967-89. Dir. Colt Industries, N.Y., Nat. Blvd. Bank, Ill. Contbr. articles to profl. jours. Trustee Butler U., Indpls., Lake Forest Hosp., Ill., Lake Bluff Library Bd., Ill.; chmn. Lake Bluff Zoning Bd. Served to lt. col. USAF, 1943-46; PTO Fellow Am. Coll. Trial Lawyers; mem. Soc. Trial Lawyers, Law Club, Legal Club, Trial Lawyers Club of Chgo. Clubs: Anglers (Chgo.), Pere Marquette Rod and Gun (Baldwin, Mich.), Shoreacres (Lake Bluff), Univ. of Chgo. Presbyterian. Office: Wildman Harrold Allen & Dixon 225 W Wacker Dr Chicago IL 60606-1224 Office Phone: 312-201-2627.

**WILDMAN, PETER ROBERTS,** mathematics professor; b. Glendale, Calif., Aug. 18, 1959; s. Neol Roberts and Maria Anna Wildman; m. Karen Louise Muehl, June 15, 1985; children: Daniel, Andrew, Matthew. BA, Occidental Coll., 1981; MS, N.Mex. State U., 1992. Instr. Murlborough Sch., L.A., 1982—90; asst. N.Mex. State U., Las Cruces, N.Mex., 1990—92; instr. math. Casper (Wyo.) Coll., 1992—. Co-dir. Wyo. Math and Sci. Coalition, Casper, 1995—2003. Bd. dirs., fundraiser Sci. Zone Mus., Casper, 2004—; cubmaster, den leader Boy Scouts Am., Casper, 1997—. Mem.: Nat. Coun. Tchrs. Math., Math. Asn. Am., Wyo. Math. Assn. Two Yr. Colls. (pres. 2000—02), Am. Math. Tchrs. Two Yr. Coll. (v.p. ctrl. region 2004—). Tchr. Excellence award 2001), Phi Theta Kappa (Tchg. award 2004). Democrat. Baptist. Home: 4920 E 18th Casper WY 82609 Office: Casper Coll 125 College Dr Casper WY 82601 Office Phone: 307-268-2506.

**WILDNAUER, RICHARD HARRY,** pharmaceutical executive; b. New Kensington, Pa., Feb. 14, 1940; s. Richard Michael and Rosemary Elizabeth (Moore) Wildnauer; m. Sharon Ann Novick, Jan. 22, 1966; 1 child, Tara Lynne. BS in Chemistry, St. Vincent Coll., 1962; PhD in BioChemistry, W.Va. U., 1966; MBA in Mgmt., Rider Coll., 1974. NIH trainee W.Va. U., 1963—66; sr. rsch. assoc. in skin biology, exploratory rsch. divsn. Johnson & Johnson Domestic Operating Co., New Brunswick, NJ, 1975—77, assoc. mgr. tech. planning, exploratory rsch. divsn., 1975—77; sr. project coord., new products, pharm. divsn. McNeil Labs., Ft. Washington, Pa., 1979—82; dir. new product devel. Janssen Pharmaceutical Inc., New Brunswick, 1979—82, v.p. R&D, 1982—88; v.p. tech. and bus. devel. Johnson & Johnson Corp., New Brunswick, 1988—92; pres. Baker Cummins Dermatologicals, Inc., Lakewood, NJ, 1992—95; pres., CEO NeoStrata Co., Inc., Princeton, NJ, 1995—. Contbr. articles to profl. jours. Trustee, bd. dirs. United Way Ctrl. N.J., 1988—95, pres., 1991—93. Mem.: Soc. Co. Chemists, N.Y. Acad. Scis., Soc. Investigative Dermatology, Am. Acad. Dermatology, Sigma Xi. Roman Catholic. Office: NeoStrata Co Inc 307 College Rd E Princeton NJ 08540-6618 Office Phone: 609-520-0715. Business E-Mail: rwildna@Neostrata.com.

**WILDONER, NANCY SCHAMU,** music educator, fine arts department chairman; b. Syracuse, NY, June 8, 1957; d. Frederick William and Marlyn Meyer Schamu; m. Robert Sterling Wildoner, Aug. 15, 1987; children: Melody June, Robert Sterling III. BA in Music Edn., Fredonia State U., 1979; MusM, Binghamton U., 1983; studied organ with M. Searle Wright and Paul Jordan. Tchng. Cert. NY. Music tchr. Norwich Sch. Dist., NY, 1979—81; grad. asst. Binghamton U., NY, 1981—83; substitute tchr. Broome County, Binghamton, NY, 1983—85; K-12 music tchr. Chenango Forks Sch., Binghamton, NY, 1984—; choir dir., organist First Congregational Ch., Binghamton, NY, 2002—. Church organist various chs., 1977—2005; exec. coun. mem. Broome County Music Educators Assn., Binghamton, NY, 2000—05; pvt. piano and organ tchr., Binghamton, NY, 2001—05. Womens aux. mem. Sanitaria Springs Fire Dept., NY, 1989—2005. Mem.: Broome County Music Educators Assn., NY Sch. Music Assn., Music Educators Nat. Conf., Am. Guild of Organists. Protestant. Avocations: theater, travel. Home: 778 Brotzman Rd Binghamton NY 13901 Office: Chenango Forks elem Sch 6 Patch Rd Binghamton NY 13901 Business E-Mail: wildonern@cforks.org.

**WILDRICK, KENYON JONES,** minister; b. Rahway, N.J., June 14, 1933; s. Stanley B. and Adele (Jones) W.; BA, Trinity Coll., Hartford, Conn., 1955, BD, Princeton U., 1958, ThM, 1962, DD, Trinity Coll., Conn., 1985; m. Nancy Ruth Mersfelder, Aug. 23, 1958; children: Catherine Ruth, Margaret Jeanne, Kenyon Douglas. Ordained to ministry Presbyterian Ch., 1958; asst. minister Community Congregational Ch., Short Hills, N.J., 1958-61, assoc. minister, 1961-67, sr. minister, 1967-93, min. emeritus, 1993—; sr. min. Pilgrim Congregational Ch., Warren, N.J., 1993—; campus ministry Middle Atlantic Conf., 1962-65. Bd. dirs. Milburn-Short Hills chpt. ARC, 1963-64; ch. and ministry com. N.J. Assn., 1965—; trustee Ctr. Theol. Inquiry, Princeton, N.J., 1985—; pres. bd. trustees Overlook Protestant Chaplaincy Program, 1973—; trustee investment com. Fellowship Conn. Congregational Chs., 1996—; trustee, vice-chmn. Presbyn. Homes N.J., 1981—. Mem. Millburn Clergy Assn. (chmn. 1987—), Rotary (dir. Milburn Club 1973), Delta Phi. Home: 214 Preston Dr Gillette NJ 07933-1439 Office: 105 Mountainview Rd Warren NJ 07059-5020

**WILDS, BONNIE,** writer, volunteer; b. Phila. m. Walter Warren Wilds; children: Stephanie Wilds Shea Blackhurst, Eugenia Wilds Ardrey, Vanessa Wilds Cunningham Wassenar, Pamela Wilds Cole. BA, Sarah Lawrence Coll.; MA, PhD, U. Pitts. Desk officer Dept. State, Washington, economist. Author: A Critical Edition of El Animal Profeta by Antonio Mira de Amescua, 1979. Women's com. Carnegie Mus. Art, Pitts.; social svc. bd. Shadyside Hosp., Pitts.; pres. women's aux. bd. Magee Women's Hosp., Pitts; v.p. Bethany Lenox Hill Day Care Ctr., N.Y.C.; bd. dirs., v.p. Mary Walton Children's Ctr., N.Y.C.; bd. dirs Musicians Emergency Fund., pres.; bd. dirs., pres., past pres. Hospitality Com. for UN Dels.; resource coordinator Inst. of Internat. Edn.; past v.p. Hospitality Com. for UN Dels. Recipient Pub. Svc. citation, City of Pitts. Fellow: Frick Collection, Pierpont Morgan Libr.; mem.: MLA, UN Assns., USA Fgn. Policy Assn., The New Eng. Soc., Preservation Soc. Newport County, St. George's Soc., Church Club, Union Club, The Pilgrims, Colony Club (N.Y.). Republican. Episcopalian. Avocations: community service, travel, reading. Home: 20 E 68th St New York NY 10021-5837

**WILDS, DANIEL O.,** health products executive; BA, Calif. State U., L.A.; MBA, Northwestern U., Evanston, Ill. With Baxter Internat., 1968—92, pres. chemotherapy svc. divsn., pres., COO diagnostic joint venture with Genentech, gen. mgr. Mexico City ops., gen. mgr. Container Devel. Bus. Ctr., dir. strategy devel., v.p. corp. alliances; pres., CEO Medisense, Inc., Adeza Biomed. Corp., 1992—96, Shiloov Biotechnologies (USA) Inc., 1997—98; pres., CEO, dir. Northwest Biotherapeutics, Inc., Boethell, Wash., 1998—. Office: Northwest Biotherapeutics Inc 22322 20th Ave SE #150 Bothell WA 98021-8446

**WILDSTEIN, EVAN,** venture capitalist; BBA, U. Mich., Ann Arbor. Fin. analyst acquisition and pvt. fin. group Dean Witter Reynolds, Inc.; joined Kohlberg & Co., 1994, prin., 1999. Bd. dirs. Allied Aerospace Industries, Inc., Holley Performance Products, Inc., Tinnerman Palnut Engineered Products LLC. Office: Kohlberg & Co 111 Radio Cir Mount Kisco NY 10549 Office Phone: 914-241-7430. Office Fax: 914-241-7476.

**WILE, JOAN,** composer, lyricist, singer; b. Rochester, N.Y., July 17, 1931; d. Louis and Janet Louise (Wile) Meltzer; children: Ron Wasserman, Diana Wasserman McCloskey. BA, U. Chgo., 1952. Freelance composer, lyricist, singer, mus. book writer. Rec. artist Vanguard Records, 1954; singer Storyville, 1954, The Crystal Palace, 1957; mem. vocal-revue act The Neighbors performances include The Village Vanguard, Le Ruban Bleu, The Bon Soir and The Living Room; singer, lyricist feature film The Happy Hooker, 1974; singer radio and TV jingles, movie sound tracks, supper clubs, hotels, TV music spls. and variety shows; lyricist, composer mus. Tobacco Road, 1974, Seven Ages of Woman, 1987 (named most promising new musical); writer, producer When They Turned on the Tap at the Watergate, The Truth Come Pourin' Out; lyricist songs for Romper Room, 1983; lyricist, composer, writer People is People, 1983; lyricist, composer script for children's albums for Golden and Peter Pan Records, others; lyricist, composer material in Julius Monk's Upstairs at the Downstairs, 1958; lyricist, composer, performer Nancy's Economic Plan, 1980; lyricist, composer Mothers and Daughters,

1984; lyricist, composer, author The Symposium, 1987; lyricist, composer From There to Here, 1987; writer Rhyme, Women and Song; lyricist, librettist, composer Museum of Natural Sex History, 1992; composer Women Walking, 1997, composer-lyricist What A Woman (Homage to Peggy Lee), 2003; founder, singer The NY Granny Chicks, 2005. Organizer Women in Def. Eleanor Roosevelt, N.Y.C., 1989—; founder, dir. Grandmothers Against the War, 2003; founder, organizer Revolt Against the Tax Refund, 2001; founder Granny Peace Brigade, 2005; treas. bd. dirs. Soc. Singers, 2002. Runner-up Am. Song Festival, 1976 Mem.: ASCAP (Popular award 1970—2005), AFTRA, SAG, Theatre Artists Workshop, Dramatists Guild, Soc. of Singers (bd. dirs.). Avocation: political and musical activities. Home and Office: 263 West End Ave Apt 4B New York NY 10023-2613 E-mail: jwile@prodigy.net.

**WILENS, MICHAEL ENGBER,** information technology executive, researcher, educator; b. Chgo., Aug. 23, 1953; s. Charles E. and Norma J. (Myers) W. S.B. in Elec. and Computer Engring., MIT, 1975, S.M. in Elec. and Computer Engring., 1976; M.S. in Computer Sci., U. Mich., Ann Arbor, 1979, Ph.D. in Computer Sci., 1984, M.B.A., 1980. Sr. systems analyst Digital Equipment Corp., 1972-73; computer scientist Naval Surface Weapons Ctr., White Oak, Md., 1973-74; teaching asst. elec. engring. MIT, 1975, project mgr. Sloan Sch. Ctr. for Info. Systems Research, 1975-76; teaching fellow computer sci. U. Mich., Ann Arbor, 1976-80, project mgr. Info. Systems Research Group, 1976-80, research asst. Grad. Sch. Bus., 1981, instr. software engring, elec. engring., 1981-82; staff cons. Infosystems Mgmt., Ann Arbor, 1981; pres., CEO Computerized Office Services, Inc., Ann Arbor, 1982; sr. mgmt. positions Groupe Lagardere, Lawyers Coop. Publishing and HCIA; pres., CEO legal & regulatory group, Thomson Corp.; exec. v.p., CTO West Group, 1996-2000; pres., CEO N. Am. Legal, Thomson Lcgal and Regulatory 2000; exec. v.p., CTO Thomson Corp. 2006-. Cons. mil. services. Instr. fin. planning and control Midwest Assn. of Housing Coops., Ann Arbor. Named for Teaching Excellence U. Mich., 1979. Mem. Assn. of Computing Machinery (reviewer Computing Revs. jour.), IEEE, Ann Arbor Computer Bus. Assn. (pres. 1983), AAAS, Sigma Xi. Office: Thomson Corp Metro Ctr One Station Pl Stamford CT 06902*

**WILENSKY, GAIL ROGGIN,** economist, researcher; b. Detroit, June 14, 1943; d. Albert Alan and Sophia (Blitz) Roggin; m. Robert Joel Wilensky, Aug. 4, 1963; children: Peter Benjamin, Sara Elizabeth. AB (hon.), U. Mich., 1964, MA in Econs., 1965, PhD in Econs., 1968; degree (hon.), Hahnemann U., 1993, Rush U. 1997, U. Scis., Phila., 2002. Economist President's Commn. on Income Maintenance Programs; exec. dir. Md. Coun. of Econ. Advs., 1969-71; sr. rschr. Urban Inst., Washington, 1971-73; assoc. rsch. scientist, pub. policy and pub. health U. Mich., Ann Arbor, 1973-75, vis. asst. prof. econs., 1973-75; sr. rschr. Nat. Ctr. for Health Svcs. Rsch., Hyattsville, Md., 1975-83; assoc. profl. lectr. George Washington U., 1976-78; v.p. div. health affairs Project HOPE, Millwood, Va., 1983-90; adminstr. Health Care Fin. Adminstrn., Washington, 1990-92; dep. asst. to the pres. for policy devel. White House, 1992-93; sr. fellow Project HOPE, Bethesda, Md.; 1993—, chair phys. payment rev. com., 1990-. Medicare Payment Adv. Commn., 1997—2001; co-chair Pres.'s Task Force to Improve Healthcare Delivery for Vets., 2001—03. Contbr. 100 articles in field to profl. jours. Dir. Am. Heart Assn., 1980-85, bd. dirs., 2002—; mem. health adv. com. Compt. Gen. U.S., 1987-90; bd. dirs. United Healthcare Corp., Cephalon, ManorCare, Gentiva Health Svcs., Inc., Quest Diagnostics; mem. vis. com. med. sch. U. Mich., 1993-97; trustee United Mine Workers Am. Retirement Fund, 1993—; commr. WHO Commn. on the Social Determinants of Health, 2005-. Flinn Found. disting. scholar, 1985; recipient Dean Conley award Am. Coll. Healthcare Execs., 1989. Mem. NAS (mem. inst. medicine 1989—); Am. Econ. Assn. (women's com. 1982-84), Fedn. Orgn. of Profl. Women (chmn. econ. task force 1981-83), Am. Statis. Assn., Nat. Tax Assn., Washington Women Economists, Assn. Health Svc. Rsch. (dir. 1984-87), Found. Health Svc. Rsch. (bd. dir. 1987-90), Acad. Health (chair bd. dir. 2000—, Cosmos Club (Washington). Home: 2807 Battery Pl NW Washington DC 20016-3439 Office Phone: 301-656-7401. Business E-Mail: gwilensky@projecthope.org.

**WILENSKY, HAROLD L.,** political science professor, sociologist, researcher; b. New Rochelle, NY, Mar. 3, 1923; s. Joseph and Mary Jane (Wainsten) W.; children: Stephen David, Michael Alan, Daniel Lewis. Student, Goddard Coll., 1940-42; AB, Antioch Coll., 1947; MA, U. Chgo., 1949, PhD, 1955. Asst. prof. sociology U. Chgo., 1951-53, asst. prof. indsl. relations, 1953-54; asst. prof. sociology U. Mich., Ann Arbor, 1954-57, assoc. prof., 1957-61, prof., 1961-62, U. Calif., Berkeley, 1963-82, prof. polit. sci., 1982—, research sociologist Inst. Indsl. Relations, 1963—, project dir. Inst. Internat. Studies, 1970-90; project dir. Ctr. for German and European Studies, Berkeley, 1994-96, Inst. Govtl. Studies, 1996—. Mem. rsch. career awards com. Nat. Inst. Mental Health, 1964—67; cons. in field. Author: Industrial Relations: A Guide to Reading and Research, 1954, Intellectuals in Labor Unions: Organizational Pressures on Professional Roles, 1956, Organizational Intelligence: Knowledge and Policy in Government and Industry, 1967, The Welfare State and Equality: Structural and Ideological Roots of Public Expenditures, 1975, The New Corporatism, Centralization, and the Welfare State, 1976, Rich Democracies: Political Economy, Public Policy, and Performance, 2002, (with C.N. Lebeaux) Industrial Society and Social Welfare, 1965, (with others) Comparative Social Policy, 1985, (with L. Turner) Democratic Corporatism and Policy Linkages, 1987; editor: (with C. Arensberg and others) Research in Industrial Human Relations, 1957, (with P.F. Lazarsfeld and W. H. Sewell) The Uses of Sociology, 1967; contbr. articles to profl. jours. Pilot USAAF, 1943—45. Recipient aux. award Social Sci. Rsch. Coun., 1962, Book award McKinsey Found., 1967; fellow Ctr. for Advanced Study in Behavioral Scis., 1956-57, 62-63, German Marshall Fund, 1978-79; Harry A. Millis rsch. awardee U. Chgo., 1950-51. Fellow AAAS; mem. AAUP, Internat. Sociol. Assn. Internat. Polit. Sci. Assn., Indsl. Relations Research Assn. (exec. com. 1965-68), Assn. for Study Social Problems (chmn. editorial com.), Am. Polit. Sci. Assn., Am. Sociol. Assn. (exec. council 1969-72, chmn. com. on info. tech. and privacy 1970-72), Council European Studies (steering com. 1980-83). Democrat. Jewish. Avocations: music, trumpet, skiing. Office: U Calif Dept Polit Sci 1950-210 Barrows Hall Berkeley CA 94720-1902 E-mail: hwilensk@socrates.berkeley.edu.

**WILENTZ, SEAN,** historian, educator, writer; b. NYC, Feb. 20, 1951; s. Elias and Jeanne Marie (Campbell) W.; m. Christine Stansell, Jan. 30, 1980; children: James Thomas Farrell, Hannah Cady Rose. BA, Columbia Coll., 1972, U. Oxford, Eng., 1974; MA, Yale U., 1975, MPhil, 1976, PhD, 1980. Asst. prof. Princeton (NJ) U., 1979-85, assoc. prof., 1985-87, Dayton-Stockon prof., history, 1987—, dir. program in Am. studies, 1995—. Author: Chants Democratic, 1984, anniversary edition, 2004, The Rise of American Democracy, 2005 (Bancroft prize for history, Columbia Univ., 2006), Andrew Jackson: The Seventh President, 1829-1837, 2005; editor: Rites of Power: Symbolism, Ritual and Politics Since the Middle Ages, 1985; co-author: The Kingdom of Matthias, 1994; co-editor: The Key of Liberty, 1993, The Rose & the Briar: Death, Love and Liberty in the American Ballad, 2004; editl. bd. Dissent, NYC, 1992—; contbg. editor The New Republic, Washington, 1995—. Recipient Alfred Beveridge award Am. History Assn., 1984, Frederick Jackson Turner award Orgn. Am. Historians, 1985; Guggenheim fellow John Simon Guggenheim Meml. Found., 1990-91. Fellow Soc. Am. Historians (exec. bd. 1986—). Democrat. Avocations: baseball, jazz. Office: Dept History Princeton U Princeton NJ 08544-0001*

**WILES, ANDREW J.,** mathematician, educator; b. England, Apr. 11, 1953; married. BS in Math., Oxford U., England; PhD in Math., Cambridge U., England; DSc (hon.), Yale Univ., 2005. Lectr. Inst. Advanced Studies, Princeton, NJ; asst., assoc. prof. math. Harvard U., Cambridge, Mass.; prof. math. Princeton U., 1982—88, 1990—. Recipient Wolf prize in math., Wolf Found., Israel, 1995, NAS award in Math., 1996, Royal medal, Royal Soc., 1996, Frank Nelson Cole prize in algebra, Am. Math. Soc., 1996, Frank Nelson Cole prize in number theory, 1997; fellow John D. and Catherine T.

MacArthur Found. fellow, 1997. Achievements include solving (with Richard Taylor) Pierre de Fermat's last theory of 1637. Office: Princeton U Dept Math, 602 Fine Hall Princeton NJ 08544-0001*

**WILES, BETTY JANE,** accountant; b. Scott County, Ark., Dec. 21, 1940; d. Edd and Nellie Margaret (Richey) Staggs; m. Ralph A. Wiles, July 18, 1959; children: Ralph A. Jr., Penny Margaret. BBA magna cum laude, Henderson State Coll., 1983. CPA Ark. Sec. Royalty Holding Co., Oklahoma City, 1959-65, Rector & Eubanks, Mena, Ark., 1966-69; paralegal Shaw & Shaw Attys., Mena, Ark., 1969-83; pvt. practice acctg. Mena, Ark., 1984—. Cons. adv. bd. Mena H.S., 1985-86; cons. adv. bd. St. John Libr., Rich Mountain C.C., 1987-90, mem. svc. adv. com., 1988-90; trustee Mena Hosp. Com., 1991—. Mem. AAUW (pres. Mena br. 1993-95), Ark. Soc. CPAs (emergency assistance com., govt. acct. and auditing com. 1993-95), Ouachita Chpt. CPAs (v.p. 1996-97, pres. 1997-98, 2004), Quachita Writer's Guild. Baptist. Avocation: poetry. Home: PO Box 522 Mena AR 71953-0522 Office: 601TB Hwy 71 N Mena AR 71953-3337

**WILES, CHARLES PRESTON,** minister; b. Frederick, Md., Aug. 5, 1918; s. Charles Wesley and Nellie (Burgess) W.; m. Mary McCallum; children: Mary Margaret, Charles Preston, Wade Burgess. AB, Washington Coll., 1939; postgrad., U. Va., 1940; MA, Duke U., 1945, PhD (Univ. fellow 1947-51, Kearns Honor fellow 1949-50), 1951; B.D., Va. Theol. Sem., 1947. Ordained to ministry Episc. Ch., 1947. Priest-in-charge St. Joseph's Ch., Durham, N.C., 1947-51; rector St. Mary's Episcopal Ch., Burlington, N.J., 1951-64; pres., trustee Burlington Coll., 1951-64, faculty cons., 1956-64; mem. faculty Phila. Div. Sch., 1959-62, lectr. ch. history, 1960-62; dean St. Matthew's Episcopal Cathedral, Dallas, 1964-87, dean emeritus, 1989; assoc. priest St. Luke's, Dallas, 1987 -. Faculty U.S. Army War Coll., Carlisle, Pa., 1964; dep. gen. Conv. from Diocese Dallas, 1967, 69, 70, 73, 76, 79; del. Provincial Synod from Diocese Dallas, 1966, 69, 72, 75, 78; mem. exec. council Diocese Dallas, 1967-77, 84-86, pres. mem. standing com., 1970-73, pres., 1971-73, mem. bd. missions, 1967-69, chmn. dept. coll. work, 1965-71, mem. bd. examing chaplains, 1965-71; mem. standing liturgical commn.; dean, warden Cathedral Center for Continuing Edn. and Pastoral Concern, 1971-87, Commn. Ministry, 1971-76; dean Dallas Deanery, 1965-69, 84-86, Bicentennial preacher, 1975; pres. convocation and clericus Diocese of N.J., 1961-64; examining chaplain, mem. bd. missions, mem. bd. Christina edn., dean Burlington-Trenton convocation; instr., dean Drew Conf. for Adults in N.J., 1952-56; retreat conductor St. Martin's House, Bernardsville, N.J., St. John Bapt. Convent, Mendhan, N.J.; dean Diocesan Sch. Religion, N.J., 1962-63, Anglican Sch. Theology, 1971-75; parish life lab. and weekend conductor Nat. Dept. Christian Edn., 1962; co-founder, dean Princeton (N.J.) Conf., 1956-64; mem. Goals for Dallas Com.; co-chmn. N.Am. Cathedral Deans' Conf., 1980-81 Author: Sacrament and Sacrifice, 2d edit., 1973, Lancelot Andrews, Caroline Divine, 1951, Lift Up Your Hearts, 1956, A Manual of Prayers, 1975, The Holy Eucharist: Word and Sacrament, 1993, The Gate of Heaven, 1993, A Centennial Narrative History of the Episcopal Diocese of Dallas, 1995, Troubadours of God, 1998, Windows for Faith, 2000. Trustee Gen. Theol. Sem., 1968-80; bd. dirs. Evergreen Home for Aging, St. Philip's Community Center, Overseas Mission Soc. Named Priest of Yr., 1969. Mem. Navy League, Ch. Hist. Soc. (dir. 1960-68), Kiwanian Club (Disting. Svc. award 1951, Disting. Citizen award Brunswick, Md. 1986), Dallas Athletic club, Chaparral, Vesper (Phila.) Club, Burlington County Country Club. Home: 7023 Northwood Rd Dallas TX 75225-2439 Personal E-mail: dr.cpwiles@dallastexas.com.

**WILES, DAVID ERNEST,** academic administrator; b. Washington, Jan. 19, 1954; s. Ernest Gallienne and Dorothy (Buglass) Wiles; m. Esther Parkes, June 12, 1976; children: Heather Wiles Molendyk, Mark David, Bonnie Louise, Jay William. BS, Miami Christian Coll., 1976; MS in Edn., U. Miami, 1979, PhD, 1995. Admissions counselor Miami Christian Coll. (now Trinity Internat. U.), 1976—80, fin. aid dir., 1979—85, dir. enrollment svcs., 1980—85; rsch. analyst U. Miami, Coral Gables, 1985—88, mgr. testing ctr., 1988—2000, asst. dir. planning & instl. rsch., 1996—2000, dir. testing ctr., 2000—04, exec. dir. testing ctr., 2004—. Pres. Measurement Svcs. SIG, Am. Ednl. Rsch. Assn., 1992—93, treas., 2000—02. Leadership Miami Greater Miami C. of C., 1992—93. Recipient Outstanding Grad. award, Miami Christian Coll., 1976. Mem.: Nat. Coun. Measurement in Edn., Nat. Coll. Testing Assn., Am. Ednl. Rsch. Assn., Delta Epsilon Chi. Office: U Miami PO Box 249086 Coral Gables FL 33124-4222 Office Phone: 305-284-2450. Business E-Mail: dwiles@miami.edu.

**WILES, DAVID MCKEEN,** chemist; b. Springhill, NS, Can., Dec. 28, 1932; s. Roy McKeen and Olwen Gertrude (Jones) W.; m. Valerie Joan Rowlands, June 8, 1957; children: Gordon Stuart, Sandra Lorraine. BSc with honors, McMaster U., 1954, MSc, 1955; PhD in Chemistry, McGill U., 1957. Rsch. officer chemistry divsn. NRC Can., Ottawa, 1959-66, head textile chemistry sect. chemistry divsn., 1966-75, dir. chemistry divsn., 1975-90; pres. Plastichem Cons., Victoria, B.C., Canada, 1990—. Chmn. Can. High Polymer Forum, 1967—69; v.p. N.Am. Chem. Congress, Mexico City, 1975. Contbr. articles to profl. jours.; mem. editl. adv. bd. numerous profl. jours.; patentee in field. Can. Ramsay Meml. fellow, 1957-59. Fellow Chem. Inst. Can. (chmn. bd. dirs. 1972-74, pres. 1975-76, Dunlop Lectr. award 1981), Royal Soc. Chem. London, Royal Soc. Can.; mem. Am. Chem. Soc. (Polymer Chem. divsn.). Home and Office: 3965 Juan Fuca Terr Victoria BC Canada V8N 5W9 Office Phone: 250-721-0732. Personal E-mail: dmwiles@telus.net.

**WILES, LESSLEY DECKER,** foundation administrator, preservationist; b. Pitts., Apr. 19, 1939; d. John Ellsworth and Irma Evelyn Decker; m. William Wharton Wiles, Aug. 20, 1961; 1 child, Kenneth William. BA, U. Ky., 1960. Statistician Wis. State Employment Svc., Madison, 1962—65, U.S. Dept. Labor, Wash., 1965—67; project mgr. HUD, Wash. 1967—72, new cmty. program officer, 1977—83, sr. program specialist, 1983 -91, dir. maintenance mgmt. divsn., 1991—92, sr. program officer, 1992—95; self-employed housing cons. York, Pa., 1996—. Mem., FHA commr.'s asset mgmt. strategy working team HUD, Wash., 1993—94. Mem. and com. chair Arlington/Tyson's Civitan Clubs, Fairfax County, Va., 1985—2005; ch. counsel sec. Walker Chapel United Meth. Ch., Arlington, 1988—97, flower com. chair, 1995—2002; mem. Arlington Cmty. Residences, Inc., 1982—88. Recipient Civitan of Yr., Arlington Civitan Club, 1991, 1992. Mem.: Pa.-Del. AHMA. Liberal. United Methodist. Avocations: crafts, gardening, volunteering. Home: 2635 Twin Lane York PA 17402-8248

**WILES, MICHAEL E.,** lawyer; b. July 23, 1953; AB, Georgetown U., 1975; JD, Yale U., 1978. Bar: NY 1979. Assoc. Debevoise & Plimpton LLP, NYC, 1978—87, litig. ptnr., 1987—. Mem.: ABA, Assn Bar of City NY. Office: Debevoise & Plimpton LLP 919 Third Ave New York NY 10022 Office Phone: 212-909-6653. Office Fax: 212-909-6836. E-mail: mewiles@debevoise.com.

**WILES, WILLIAM WHARTON,** retired federal government official; b. Knoxville, Tenn., June 9, 1931; s. James H. and Sally May (Wharton) W.; m. Lessley K. Decker, Aug., 1961; 1 child, Kenneth W. BA, Murray State U., 1953; MBA, U. Ky., 1959; PhD, U. Wis., 1973. Instr. U. Ky., 1959-61; with Fed. Res. Sys., Washington, 1964-98, sec. of bd., 1981-98. With U.S. Army, 1954-56. Home: 2635 Twin Ln York PA 17402 E-mail: Lessleyva@aol.com.

**WILETS, LAWRENCE,** physicist, educator; b. Oconomowoc, Wis., Jan. 4, 1927; s. Edward and Sophia (Finger) W.; m. Dulcy Elaine Margoles, Dec. 21, 1947; children: Ileen Sue, Edward E., James D.; m. Vivian C. Wolf, Feb. 8, 1976. BS, U. Wis. 1948; MA, Princeton U., 1950, PhD, 1952. Rsch. assoc. Project Matterhorn, Princeton, NJ, 1951-53, U. Calif. Radiation Lab., Livermore, 1953; NSF postdoctoral fellow Inst. Theoretical Physics, Copenhagen, 1953-55; staff mem. Los Alamos (N.Mex.) Sci. Lab., 1955-58; mem. Inst. Advanced Study, Princeton, 1957-58; mem. faculty U. Wash., Seattle, 1958—, prof. physics, 1962-95, prof. emeritus, 1995—. Cons. to pvt. and govt. labs.; vis. prof. Princeton U., 1969, Calif. Inst. Tech., 1971. Author: Theories of Nuclear Fission, 1964, Nontopological Solitons, 1989; contbr.

over 180 articles to profl. jours. Del. Dem. Nat. Conv., 1968. NSF sr. fellow Weizmann Inst. Sci., Rehovot, Israel, 1961-62; Nordita prof. and Guggenheim fellow Lund (Sweden) U., Weizmann Inst., 1976—; Sir Thomas Lyle rsch. fellow U. Melbourne, Australia, 1989; recipient Alexander von Humboldt sr. U.S. scientist award, 1983. Fellow Am. Phys. Soc., AAAS; mem. Fedn. Am. Scientists, AAUP (pres. chpt. 1969-70, 73-75, pres. state conf. 1975-76), Explorers Club, Phi Beta Kappa (chpt. pres. 1996-97), Sigma Xi. Achievements include research on theory of nuclear structure and reactions, nuclear fission, atomic structure, atomic collisions, many body problems, subnuclear structure and elementary particles. Office: U Wash Dept Physics PO Box 351560 Seattle WA 98195-1560 Personal E-mail: wilets@comcast.net. Business E-mail: wilets@u.washington.edu.

**WILEY, C. MARK,** lawyer; b. High Point, NC, Oct. 9, 1963; BS cum laude, Wake Forest U., 1985, JD cum laude, 1988; LLM in Taxation, NYU, 1989. CPA 1988; bar: NC 1988, admitted to practice: US Dist. Ct. (Mid. Dist. NC) 1988, US Tax Ct. 1989, US Fed. Ct. of Claims 1990. Clk. Carruthers & Roth, P.A., Greensboro, NC, 1987; mem. Womble Carlyle Sandridge & Rice PLLC, Winston-Salem, NH, leader, tax practice group, 1998—2002, mem. mgmt. com. Mem. Wake Forest Law Review, 1988. Mem. Forsyth County Estate Planning Council. Recipient Wake Forest Law Faculty Scholar, I. Beverly Lake award. Mem.: Northwest Piedmont Chpt. CPA, NC Assn. CPA, ABA, NC Bar Assn., Forsyth County Bar Assn. Office: Womble Carlyle Sandridge & Rice PLLC One W 4th St Winston Salem NC 27101 Mailing: Womble Carlyle Sandridge & Rice PLLC PO Box 84 Winston Salem NC 27102 Office Phone: 336-721-3605. Office Fax: 336-733-8406. Business E-mail: mwiley@wcsr.com.

**WILEY, CARL ROSS,** timber company executive; b. Astoria, Oreg., Apr. 17, 1930; s. Hamilton Ross and Ada Ellen (Smith) W.; m. Dolores Eileen Brice, Dec. 19, 1953; children: Susan, Steven, Kenneth. BS in Indsl. Engring., Oreg. State U., 1958; grad. exec. tng. program, MIT, 1974. Quality control engr. Oreg. Metall. Corp., 1958-59; indsl. engr. Osborne Electronics Corp., Portland, Oreg., 1959-62; v.p. timber and mfg. Boise Cascade Corp., Idaho, 1962-80; exec. v.p. Roseburg (Oreg.) Lumber Co., 1980-85; chief exec. officer Puget Sound Plywood, Tacoma, 1986-93; pres., CEO Lane Plywood, Eugene, Oreg., 1993-96; retired, 1996. Bd. dirs. Boise YMCA, 1975-78. With AUS, 1951-53. Mem. Am. Plywood Assn. (trustee), Western Wood Products Assn. (bd. dirs., chmn. econ. svcs. 1974-80). Lutheran. E-mail: wileycd@juno.com.

**WILEY, DAVID COLE,** television producer; b. Long Beach, Calif., Sept. 12, 1948; s. Norman Cole and Bettigene Rosamond W. Ind. prodr., 1987—. Prodr.: Abduction-the UFO Soap, 1987, Speak-Out, 1988-89, Coal Canyon BMX, 1989, PC 101-Computer Repair, 1989, Young Lives, 1990, A Slice of Life, 1990, 91, Hidden Talents, 1992, Rock Talk, 1992—, History of the Santa Ana Canyon, 1994-2001, Buena Park Journal, 1994-2001, Avenging Angel, 2001, O.D.O.C. Returns, 2005; (documentaries) In Search of the Butterfield Trail, 1990, George Key Ranch - Centennial Celebration, 1993, Visitors from Catalan, 1996, History of the Santa Ana River, 1997, The Steam Kalliope, 1998, Plan 10 from Outer Space, 1998, History of Orange County, 2002, The Rocky Road, 2003. Vice-pres. Santa Ana Canyon Hist. Coun., 1995-2001. Recipient Western Access Video Excellence award Nat. Fedn. Local Cable Programmers, 1992, CABY Comcast Cablevision, 1996, Communicator award of distinction, 2005, Videographer award of distinction, 2005-06. Mem. Alliance Cmty. Media. Address: PO Box 6481 Fullerton CA 92834-6481

**WILEY, EDWIN PACKARD,** retired lawyer; b. Chgo., Dec. 10, 1929; s. Edwin Garnet and Marjorie Chastina (Packard) W.; m. Barbara Jean Miller, May 21, 1949; children: Edwin Miller, Clayton Alexander, Stephen Packard. BA, U. Chgo., 1949, JD, 1952. Bar: Wis. 1952, Ill. 1952, U.S. Dist. Ct. (ea. dist.) Wis. 1953, U.S. Supreme Ct. 1978. Assoc. Foley & Lardner, Milw., 1952-60, ptnr., 1960-98; ret. Bd. dirs. Genetic Testing Inst., Inc., other corps. and founds. Co-author: Bank Holding Companies: A Practical Guide to Bank Acquisitions and Mergers, 1988, Wisconsin Uniform Commercial Code Handbook, 1971; author: Promotional Arrangements: Discrimination in Advertising and Promotional Allowances, 1976; editor in chief U. Chgo. Law Rev., 1952. Bd. dirs. Blood Ctr. Southeastern Wis., pres., 1978-82; pres. Blood Ctr. Rsch. Found., Inc., 1983-87; v.p. Friends of Schlitz Audubon Ctr., Inc., 1975-87; active United Performing Arts Fund of Milw.; pres. Wis. Conservatory ofMusic, 1968-73; pres. First Unitarian Soc. Milw., 1961-63; v.p. Mid-Am. Ballet Co., 1971-73, Milw. Ballet Co., 1973-74; pres. Florentine Opera Co., 1983-86; bd. dirs. Milw. Symphony Orch., pres., 1993-95; bd. dirs. Milw. Pub. Mus., Inc., sec., 1992-2005; bd. dirs. Wis. History Found., v.p., 1998-2005; bd. dirs. Preserve Our Parks, Inc., 1999—; mem. Wis. Gov.'s Commn. on Historic Sites, 2002-2003. Mem. ABA, State Bar of Wis., Milw. Bar Assn., Am. Law Inst., Order of Coif, Univ. Club, Phi Beta Kappa (pres. Greater Milw. assn. 1962-63). Home: 929 N Astor St Unit 2101 Milwaukee WI 53202-3488 Office Phone: 414-297-5780. Personal E-mail: ewiley@mac.com. Business E-mail: ewiley@foley.com.

**WILEY, GREGORY ROBERT,** publisher; b. Sept. 21, 1951; s. William Joseph and Terese (Kunz) W.; children: Kathleen, Mary Glennon. BA in Pers. Adminstrn., U. Kans., 1974. Dist. sales mgr. Reader's Digest, St. Loius, 1976-80, regional sales dir. Chgo., 1980-82; nat. sales mgr. retail divsn. Rand McNally & Co., Chgo., 1982-83, nat. sales mgr. premium incentive divsn., 1983-86, nat. sales mgr. bookstore and mass market sales, 1986-88; book pub. The Sporting News, St. Louis, 1988-90; v.p. mktg. Marketmakers Internat., St. Louis, 1990-93, Sofsource Inc., St. Louis, 1993—96; eastern regional v.p. Handleman Co., St. Louis, 1996—2002; dir. sales and marketing, books The Sporting News, St. Louis, 2002—. Mem. Nat. Premium Sales Execs., Promotional Mktg. Assn. Am. Roman Catholic. Avocations: private pilot, historic restoration, golf. Home: 4245 Maryland Ave Saint Louis MO 63108-2905

**WILEY, JAMES DEE,** retired history and biology educator, national park service ranger; b. Douglas, Ariz., May 14, 1950; s. James David Wiley and Harriett D. Rattliff. BS in Edn., No. Ariz. U.; MS in Edn., Corpus Christi State U.; PhD, Kensington U., London, 1998. Cert. instr. Ariz. Assn. Cmty. Colls., 2000. Tchr./coach Douglas Pub. Schs., Ariz., 1985—2001; instr. Cochise C.C., Douglas, 1991—2001; pk. ranger Nat. Pk. Svc.-Independence NHP, Phila., 2003—. Cons. Douglas Wild Life Zoo, 1990—2001. Lobbyist Douglas Edn. Assn., 1991—2001, Douglas Pub. Schools, 1991—2001, Ariz. Edn. Assn., Phoenix, 1991—99. Mem.: NSTA (assoc.), NEA (life; polit. action com. 1991—95, Reach for the Stars award 1994), SW Herpalogical Assn. (assoc.), Ariz. Herpalogical Assn. (assoc.), Nat. Biology Teachers Assn. (assoc.), Douglas Edn. Assn. (life; pres. 1994—98), Ariz. Edn. Assn. (life; polit. action com. 1991—99), Sons of Confederate Veterans (assoc.). Avocations: travel, reading, carving, photography. Home: 421 Locust St Philadelphia PA 19106-3716 Personal E-mail: dr_jim_wiley@excite.com.

**WILEY, JASON LARUE, JR.,** neurosurgeon; b. Canandaigua, N.Y., Dec. 2, 1917; s. Jason LaRue and Eva Althea (Moore) W.; m. Alma Williams, Jan. 4, 1944 (div. Feb. 1956); children: Robert W., Richard L.; m. Ann Valentine Gerrish, Apr. 14, 1956 (div. July 1979); children: Martha V., Pamela M., Catherine A. Student, Antioch Coll., 1934-37; MD, Harvard U. 1941. Diplomate Am. Bd. Surgery, Am. Bd. Neurol. Surgery. Intern Kings County Hosp., Bklyn., 1941-42; asst. resident surgery Ellis Hosp., Schenectady, NY, 1948-49; from asst. to assoc. resident surgery Rochester (N.Y.) Gen. Hosp., 1949-51; from asst. to assoc. to chief resident neurosurgery Yale U. and Hartford Hosp., New Haven and Hartford, Conn., 1951-54; practice medicine specializing in neurosurgery Kansas City, Mo., 1954—56, Rochester, NY, 1956—89. Chief neurosurgery Rochester Gen. Hosp., 1959-71, community neurosurgeon, 1989—; clin. assoc. prof. neurosurgery U. Rochester, 1961-88. Mem. Bd. for Profl. Med. Conduct, N.Y. State Dept. Health, Troy, N.Y., 1985-2004. Served to lt. comdr. USN, 1942-47, PTO. Mem. Med. Soc.

County Monroe, Med. Soc. State N.Y., N.Y. State Neurosurg. Soc., Congress Neurol. Surgeons, Am. Assn. Neurol. Surgeons. Republican. Episcopalian. Avocations: sailing, skiing, fishing, genealogy. Office: 1445 Portland Ave Rochester NY 14621-3036

**WILEY, JOHN D.,** academic administrator; BS in Physics, Ind. U., 1964; MS in Physics, U. Wis., Madison, 1965, PhD in Physics, 1968. Tech. staff Bell Telephone Labs., Murray Hill, NJ, 1968—74; Alexander von Humboldt rsch. and tng. fellow Max Planck Inst., Stuttgart, Germany, 1974—75; mem. elec. and computer engring. faculty U. Wis., Madison, 1975—, co-founder Ctr. for X-Ray Lithography and Engring. Rsch. Ctr. for Plasma-Aided Mfg., chair Materials Sci. program, 1982—86, assoc. dean for rsch., Coll. Engring., 1986—89, dean, Grad. Sch., and sr. rsch. officer, 1989—94, provost & vice chancellor for acad. affairs, 1994—2000, chancellor, 2001—. Office: U Wis 161 Bascom Hall 500 Lincoln Dr Madison WI 53706*

**WILEY, JOHN EDWIN,** cytogeneticist; b. Roanoke, Va., Mar. 2, 1951; s. James Edwin and Marie Rita (Cassell) W. BA, U. N.C., Greensboro, 1973, MA, 1976; PhD, N.C. State U., 1981. Diplomate Am. Bd. Med. Genetics-Clin. Cytogenetics, Biomed. rschr. St. Paul's Coll., Lawrenceville, Va., 1981-82; postdoctoral trainee U. Wis., Madison, 1982-84; mem. faculty East Carolina U. Sch. Medicine, Greenville, NC, 1984—. Contbr. articles to profl. jours. Biomed. rsch. support grantee United Way, Greenville, 1986-87, USPHS, Washington, 1987-90. Mem. AAAS, Am. Soc. Human Genetics, Am. Soc. Zoologists, Am. Soc. Ichthyologists and Herpetologists. Democrat. Achievements include observation that certain genes on frog chromosomes seem to move frequently around, that chromosome constitution in many breast cancer tumors seems normal, that in some patients with ring X chromosomes the ring may not be turned off, that the addition of tumor promoting agents helps white blood cells in many vertebrates to divide, and that DNA sequences on ends of frog chromosomes are the same as those on the ends of human chromosomes. Office: East Carolina U Brody Sch Medicine 600 Moye Blvd Greenville NC 27834-4300 Home: 206 Ravenwood Dr Greenville NC 27834-6737 Office Phone: 252-744-2525. E-mail: wileyj@ecu.edu.

**WILEY, MICHAEL E.,** oil industry executive; BS in Petroleum Engring., U. Tulsa; MBA, U. Dallas. Various engring. and operational positions ARCO Gas and Oil Co., various locations, 1972, sr. and exec. v.p., pres., 1993—2000, COO, 1998—2000; pres. Vastar, 1993—94, CEO, 1994—96, chmn. bd. dirs.; chmn., pres., CEO Baker Hughes Inc., Houston, 2000—. Office: Baker Hughes Inc 3900 Essex Ln Ste 1200 Houston TX 77027-5177

**WILEY, RICHARD ARTHUR,** lawyer; b. Bklyn., July 18, 1928; s. Arthur Ross and Anna Thorsen (Holder) W.; m. Carole Jean Smith, Aug. 13, 1955; children: Kendra Elizabeth, Stewart Alan, Garett Smith. AB, Bowdoin Coll., Brunswick, Maine, 1948, LLD, 1994; BCL, Oxford U., Eng., 1951; LLM, Harvard U., 1959. Bar: Mass. 1954, U.S. Ct. Mil. Appeals 1954, U.S. Dist. Ct. Mass. 1962, U. S. Supreme Ct. 1985. Atty. John Hancock Mut. Life Ins. Co., Boston, 1956-58; from atty. to mng. ptnr. Bingham, Dana & Gould, Boston, 1959-76; gen. counsel, asst. sec. Dept. Def., 1976-77; v.p., counsel First Nat. Bank Boston, 1977-78, exec. v.p., 1978-85, Bank of Boston Corp., 1985; ptnr. Csaplar & Bok, Boston, 1986-90, mem. exec. com., 1987-90, chmn., 1989-90, of counsel, 1990, Gaston & Snow, Boston, 1990-91; dir. Powers and Hall P.C., Boston, 1991-94, of counsel, 1994-95, Hill & Barlow, Boston, 1995—2002, Foley & Hoag LLP, Boston, 2002—. Bd. dirs., chmn. Automated Assemblies Corp., Mass. Higher Edn. Assistance Corp.; bd. dirs. Edn. Rsch. Inst., Nomadic Structures, Inc., Nypro, Inc., Carlo Gavazzi Mupac, Inc.; lectr. Boston U. Law Sch., 1961-64; past vice chmn. New Eng. Conf. on Doing Bus. Abroad; trustee New Eng. Legal Found., chmn., 1980-83; adj. prof. govt. and legal studies Bowdoin Coll., 1995-2002; adj. prof. law Boston Coll. Law Sch., 1998—Author: Cases and Materials on Law of International Trade and Investment, 1961; contbr. articles to profl. jours. Bd. overseers Bowdoin Coll., 1966-81, pres., 1977-80, trustee, 1981-93, trustee emeritus, 1993—; mem. Mass. Edn. Financing Authority, 1986-91, chmn., 1987-91; mem. Wellesley (Mass.) Town Meeting, 1971-75, mem. fin. adv. com., 1973-74; chmn. Mass. Bd. Regents of Higher Edn., 1991; bd. regents Task Force on Student Fin. Aid, 1987; mem. Mass. Higher Edn. Coord. Coun., 1991-95, vice chmn., 1991-93, chmn., 1993-95; chmn. lawyers divsn. United Way Mass. Bay, 1975; mem. devel. com., trustees of donations Episcopal Diocese Mass., 1971-75; trustee, exec. com. North Conway Inst., mem., 1980-92, chmn., 1988-92; bd. trustees Internat. Coun. Trust, Boston; trustee, mem. exec. com., chmn. Mass. Taxpayers Found., 1989-92; chmn. bd. trustees World Peace Found., Boston, 1983-95; corporator Schepens Eye Rsch. Inst., 1991-95; dep. chmn. planning Mass. rep. state com., 1971, vice chmn. fin. com., 1971-72. Officer USAF, 1953-56. Decorated Air Force Commendation medal; recipient Dep. Def. Disting. Pub. Svc. medal, 1977; Rhodes scholar, 1949. Mem.: ABA (vice chmn. fgn. and internat. bus. law com. 1967—69), Boston Bar Assn. (exec. com., antitrust com. 1965—68), Boston Com. on Fgn. Rels. (chmn. 1980—83), Coun. on Fgn. Rels., Phi Beta Kappa.

**WILEY, RICHARD EMERSON,** lawyer; b. Peoria, Ill. July 20, 1934; s. Joseph Henry and Jean W. (Farrell) W.; m. Elizabeth J. Edwards, Aug. 6, 1960; children: Douglas S., Pamela L. BS with distinction, Northwestern U., 1955, JD, 1958; LLM, Georgetown U., 1962; LLD (hon.), Cath. U. of Am., 1998. Bar: Ill. 1958, DC 1972. Pvt. practice, Chgo., 1962—70; gen. counsel FCC, Washington, 1970—72; mem., 1972—74, chmn., 1974—77, chmn. FCC's adv. com. on advanced TV svc., 1987—96; mng. ptnr. Wiley Rein & Fielding, Washington, 1983—; Nat. co-chmn. lawyers Bush-Quayle campaign, 1992, Bush-Cheney campaign, 2000. Prof. law John Marshall Law Sch., U. Chgo., 1963-70. Chmn. bd. Media Inst., 1999-, Inst. for Tele-Info., Columbia U., 1997—. Capt. AUS, 1959-62. Recipient Medal of Honor, Electronic Industries Am., 1996, Emmy award Nat. Acad. TV Arts & Sci. 1997, Disting. Svc. award Nat. Assn. Broadcasters, 2002, named one of 75 Best Lawyers, Washingtonian mag., 2002, Internat. Achievement award N.Am. Broadcasters Assn., 2004; named to Most Influential Lawyers in Am. six times, and recognized as an enduring influence in 2003, by Nat. Law. Jour., named Rep. Lawyer of Yr. by Rep. Nat. Lawyers Assn. 2004. Fellow: Am. Bar Found.; mem.: ABA (chmn. Forum com. on comm. 1985—87, ho of dels. 1969—71, 1977—84, chmn. young lawyers sect. 1977—84, chmn. bd. editors ABA Jour. 1984—89, chmn. com. on scope and correlation of work 1989, chmn. adminstrv. law & regulatory practice 1993—94, chmn. nat. law day 2003), Rep. Nat. Lawyers Assn. (bd. mem., co-chmn. judicial advocacy panel), Adminstrv. Conf. U.S. (coun., sr. fellow), Chgo. Bar Assn., Ill. Bar Assn., Fed. Comm. Bar Assn. (pres. 1987), Fed. Bar Assn. (pres. 1977), Phi Delta Kappa, Phi Delta Phi. Methodist. Office: Wiley Rein & Fielding 1776 K St NW Ste 1100 Washington DC 20006-2332 Office Phone: 202-719-7010. Business E-mail: rwiley@wrf.com.

**WILEY, SHIRLEY WINONA WALTERS,** adult education educator, artist; b. Denver, Colorado, May 20, 1920; d. John and Cressie (Gottschalk) Walters; m. Lee Grandison Wiley, Aug. 20, 1941; 1 child, Lee Walters. BFA, U. Tex., 1938—41; EdM, U. Houston, 1951; attended, C.C., Houston, Tex., 1984—97, Rice U. Continuing Edn., 1982—89, Carnegie Mellon U., Pitts., 1984, The Breadloaf Sch. of English, Santa Fe, N.Mex., 1993. Cert. Tex. Bilingual tchr. El Paso Elem. Pub. Sch., El Paso, Tex., 1942; English tchr. Reagan H.S., Houston, 1947—54; chmn. English dept. Bellaire Sr. H.S., Houston, 1954—69; master tchr. Rice U., Houston, 1965—92, U. dir. film study for teachers, 1969—75, lectr. in edn. dept., 1970—71; English tchr. curriculum design H.S. for Performing Arts, Houston, 1970—73; chmn. English dept. The Kinkaid Sch., Houston, 1987; citation Nat. Found. for Advancement in the Arts, Miami, Fla., 1991; English tchr. The Kinkaid Sch., Houston, 1974—95; tchr., specialized writing Women's Inst., Houston, 1997—. Guest lectr. Art History The Kinkaid Sch., Houston, 1997; AP cons., lectr. CEEB, So. West Region, 1993—95; leader,advanced composition workshop HISD Area1, Houston, 1977—78; lit. com. CEEB, Princeton, NJ, 1964—70; adv. bd. Rice U., Houston, 1963—64; lectr. Harris County Writing for Tchr., Houston, 1963—64. Author: (book) The English Book Sci. Rsch. Assoc., 1981, The Composition Book 1 and Book 2, 1970, (extra mural studies) The

Epic,U. Kans. Press, 1969, (book) Understanding the Novel, Am. Writers, 1962, Understanding the Novel, Brit. Writers, 1962, Team Tchg. HISD, 1960. Lectr. Women's Inst., Houston. Recipient First Film Student Made, KUHT T.V. Sta., 1953, sponsor, Creative Writing Club, Bellaire Sr. H.S., 1956—59, Nat. Honor Soc., Bellaire Sr. H.S., 1958—63, Dist. Judge, S.W. Area Nat. Coun. of English Writing, 1959—63, speaking, So. Tex. Regional Conf. of NEA, 1961, Tex. Joint Com. for Secondary Sch. and Coll., 1962, art dir., Conv. of Nat. Coun. of Teachers of English, 1966, Tchr. of the Yr., Jr. Chamber of Commerce, 1967, Harvard U., 1967, cons., Open U.: The Humanities, U. of Houston, 1975, maj. spkr., Nat. Coun. of Teachers of English, Secondary, 1976, lectr., Advanced Placement Workshops, Houston, 1977—78, Advanced Placement Workshops, Galveston, Tex., 1977, Advanced Placement Workshops, Albuquerque, 1977, Adv. Placement Workshops Austin,Tex., 1979, Advanced Placement Workshops, El Paso,Tex., 1980, Advanced Placement Workshops, Oklahoma City, 1981, Advanced Placement Workshops, W. Orange Cove, ISD, 1982, Advanced Placement Workshops, Orange Consol. Sch. Dist., 1983, Citation, So. Meth. U., 1985, Spl. Recognition CEEB Award, AP Commn., 1985, Columbianna Award for Outstanding Tchg. at Kinkaid, Kinkaid Sch., 1993, U. Citation, Tufts U., 1994. Mem.: Citywide Creative Writing Anthology, Cum Laude, Houston Soc.division of Phi Beta Kappa. Achievements include Awards to students studying with Shirley Wiley; Five Woodrow Wilson Fellows; Nat. Coun. of Teachers of English Writing Awards, 1961-1965; Atlantic Monthly Crative Writing Awards, 1966-1975. Avocations: painting, sculpting. Home: 2929 Post Oak Blvd Apt 1308 Houston TX 77056-6116

**WILEY, WILLIAM T.,** artist; b. Bedford, Ind., Oct. 21, 1937; BFA, San Francisco Art Inst., 1961, MFA, 1962. Assoc. prof. U. Calif., Davis, 1962-73; instr. San Francisco Art Inst., 1963, 66-67, U. Nev., Reno, 1967, Wash. State Coll., Pullman, 1967, U. Calif., Berkeley, 1967, Sch. Visual Art, N.Y.C., 1968, U. Colo., Boulder, 1968. (solo exhbns.) Staempfli Gallery, NYC, 1960, 1962, 1964, Hansen Fuller Gallery, San Francisco, 1968, 1969, 1971, 1972, 1974, 1978, What Is Not Music?, Frankfurter Kunstverein, Frankfurt, West Germany; Galerie Grita Insam, Vienna, Austria, 1987, What Is Not Drawing?, L.A. Louver, Venice, Calif., 1987, William T. Wiley-Recent Work, Max Protetch, 1991, One Man's Moon..., Marian Locks Gallery, Phila., Pa., 1992, Wm. T. Wiley, Walker Hill Museum, 1994, Nothing Lost From The Original, M.H. deYoung Museum, 1995, Concentrations 3: Wm. T. Wiley, The Contemporary Museum, 1996, Locks Gallery, Phila.- Pa., 1996, Wm. T. Wiley, 60 Works for 60 Years, Albrecht-Kemper Museum, 1997, Recent and Relevant, Riva Yares Gallery, Scottsdale, Ariz., Santa Fe, NMex., 2000, Unobjektive Art, Marsha Mateyka Gallery, Washington, DC, 2001, No Bull, Morgan Gallery, Kansas City, MO, 2001, Before & After, Rena Bransten Gallery, San Francisco, CA, 2002 and several others; (traveling exhbns.) American Painting of the 1970's, Albright-Knox Art Gallery, Buffalo, NY, traveled to Newport Harbor Art Museum, Newport Beach, Calif.; Cincinnati Art Mus., Cincinnati, Ohio; Art Mus. of Southern Tex., Corpus Christi; Krannert Art Mus., U. Ill. at Urbana-Champaign, 1978-79, 20th Century Drawings from the Whitney Museum of American Art, traveled to Nat. Gallery of Art, Washington, DC; The Cleveland Mus. Art; Calif. Palace of the Legion of Honor, San Francisco, Calif.; Ark. Arts Ctr., Little Rock; Whitney Mus. Am. Art, Fairfield County, Stamford, Conn., 1987, William T. Wiley: Struck! Sure? Sound/Unsound, The Corcoran Gallery of Art, Washington, DC, travelling to Contemporary Arts Ctr., Cincinnati, Ohio; Southeastern Ctr. for Contemporary Art, Laguna Beach, Calif. 1991; (group exhbns.) Am. Exhbn., Art Inst. Chgo., 1961, 1962, Whitney Biennial, Whitney Mus. Am. Art, NYC, 1968, When Attitudes Become Form, Kunsthalle, Berne, Switzerland, 1969, 100 Years of California Sculpture, Oakland Museum, Oakland, Calif., 1982, Language, Drama, Source, Vision, The New Mus., NYC, 1983, Phila. Collects: Art Since 1940, Phila. Mus. Art, 1986, Disarming Images: Art for Nuclear Disarmament, Bronx Mus. Arts, 1986, Boston Collects: Contemporary Painting & Sculpture, Mus. Fine Arts, Boston, MA, 1986, San Francisco Lives, San Francisco Mus. Modern Art, 1990, Calif. Classics: Art From the 1960's and 1970's, Bayly Art Mus., U. Vir., Charlottesville, Vir., 1991, Putting Things Together, The Art Mus. of Santa Cruz County, Calif., 1995, Signs & Symbols, Barbara Mathes Gallery, NYC, 1996, Drawings, Marsha Mateyka Gallery, Washington, DC, 1997, Art Making Book Making Art, San Francisco Art Inst., 1998, Piecing it Together: A Visual Journey, San Jose Mus. Art, Calif., 1999, Made in California, LA County Mus. Art, 2000, Celebrating Modern Art, The Anderson Collection, San Francisco Mus. Modern Art, 2000, Fallout, Meridian Gallery, San Francisco, Calif., 2000, Riva Yares 2000, The First 35 Years, Riva Yares Gallery, Scottsdale, Ariz., Santa Fe, NMex., 2000, Music in My Soul, Portsmouth Museums, Portsmouth, Vir., 2001 and several others; (pub. collections) Am. Acad. & Inst., NYC, Art Inst. Chgo., Balt. Mus. Contemporary Art, Carnegie Inst., Pittsburgh, PA, City of Columbus, Ohio, City of Hayward, CA, City of San Francisco, Dallas Mus. Art, Denver Art Mus., Hirshhorn Mus. and Sculpture Garden, Smithsonian Institution, Washington, DC, LA County Mus., Mus. Fine Arts, Boston, MA, Mus. Modern Art, NYC, Nat. Gallery of Victoria, Victoria, Australia, Nat. Mus. Am. Art, Washington, DC, Philadelphia Mus. Art, Corcoran Gallery of Art, Washington, DC, Weatherspoon Art Gallery, Whitney Mus. Am. Art, NYC, Worcester Art Museum, Worcester, Mass., Yale University Art Gallery, New Haven, CT and several others. Recipient Painting prize, Calif. Sch. Fine Arts, 1959, First prize, Calif. Sch. Fine Arts Festival, 1960, Fletcher award, Calif. Sch. Fine Arts, 1960, First prize in Painting, Oakland Annual, 1960, New Talent award, Art in America, 1961, Sculpture prize, LA County Mus. Art Painting prize, 1962, 65th Annual Exhbn., The Art Inst. Chgo., 1962, Nealie Sullivan award, San Francisco Art Inst. Purchase prize, Whitney Mus., NYC, 1968Creative Arts award, U. Calif. at Davis, 1968, Bartels prize, 72nd American Exhbn., The Art Inst. Chgo., 1976, Travelling Grant to Australia, Australian Arts Coun., 1980. Address: c/o Wanda Hansen 615 Main St Sausalito CA 94965-1317 also: c/o Rena Bransten Gallery 77 Geary St San Francisco CA 94108 Office Phone: 415-332-0325, 415-982-3292.

**WILEY-HART, DEBRA,** musician, educator; d. Nathaniel D. Duberstein and Miriam Scott Levine; m. Michael Andrew Hart, Apr. 17, 1994. BA, Hunter Coll., 1978; MA, NYU, 1988. Tchr., coach to singers and actors, NYC, 1982—; acting and voice tchr. Henry St. Settlement, NYC, 1988—92; acting tchr. Harlem Sch. for Arts, NYC, 1989, Marymount Manhattan, NYC, 2004—05, Lee Strasberg Theater and Film Inst., NYC, 1995—2005; voice specialist Montclair (NJ) State U., 2004—; head voice and acting divsn. ABC Film and Video, LLC, NYC, 2005—. Dir., coach Mannes Coll. Music, NYC, 1998; acting tchr. for musical theater Disney Theatrical Prodns., NYC, 2001; guest artist Dalcroze Inst., Juilliard Sch., NYC, 2002—03. Singer, actor: Songs and Sonnets of Edna St. Vincent Millay, 2001; singer: NY State Tchrs. Assn. Vocal Pedagogy Seminar, 2004. Tchr. New Triad for Collaborative Arts, Lincoln Ctr., NY, 2006. Mem.: Guild Mus. Artists, Actors Equity Assn. Office: ABC Film & Video LLC 303 5th Ave New York NY 10016 Office Phone: 212-686-3490. Personal E-mail: debra@abcfilmvideo.com.

**WILFERT, CATHERINE M.,** medical association administrator, pediatrician, epidemiologist, educator; b. LA, July 26, 1936; m. Samuel L. Katz; children: Rachel, Catherine stepchildren: John, David, William, Deborah, Susan, Penelope. BA with distinction, Stanford Coll., 1958; MD cum laude, Harvard U., 1962. Med. intern Boston City Hosp., 1962—63; resident in pediat. Children's Hosp., Boston, 1964—66, fellow in infectious diseases, 1966—68; asst. prof. pediat. and virology Duke U., 1969—73, assoc. prof. pediat., 1974—79; prof. pediat. and microbiology, chief pediatric infectious diseases, 1980—96, prof. emeritus; sci. dir. Elizabeth Glaser Pediat. AIDS Found., Santa Monica, Calif., 1997—. Chair Adv. Com. on Immunization Practices, 1980, Perinatal Working Group of Prevention Trials Network, NIH; mem. adv. com. Office of AIDS Rsch., 1999—2005. Mem.: NIH AIDS Coms., Inst. Medicine, Infectious Diseases Soc. Am. (pres. 2000). Office: Elizabeth Glaser Pediatric AIDS Found 1917 Wildcat Creek Rd Chapel Hill NC 27516-9786 Office Phone: 919-968-0008. Home Fax: 919-968-0447. Personal E-mail: wilfert@mindspring.com.

**WILFORD, JOHN NOBLE, JR.,** science news correspondent; b. Murray, Ky., Oct. 4, 1933; s. John Noble and Pauline (Hendricks) W.; m. Nancy Everett Watts, Dec. 25, 1966; 1 child, Nona. Student, Lambuth Coll., 1951-52; BS, U. Tenn., 1955; MA, Syracuse U., 1956; Internat. Reporting fellow, Columbia, 1961-62; DHL (hon.), R.I. Coll., 1987; DSc (hon.), Middlebury Coll., 1991. Reporter Comml. Appeal, Memphis, summers 1954-55; reporter Wall St. Jour., N.Y.C., 1956, 59-61; contbg. editor Time mag., N.Y.C., 1962-65; sci. reporter N.Y. Times, 1965-73, asst. nat. editor, 1973-75, dir. sci. news, 1975-79, sci. corr., 1979—. Vis. journalist Duke U., 1984; McGraw lectr. Princeton U., 1985; Disting. prof. journalism, U. Tenn., Knoxville, 1989-90; mem. Am. Mus.-Mongolian Gobi Expdn., 1991, Dir.'s Visitor, Inst. for Advanced Study, 1995. Author: We Reach The Moon, 1969, The Mapmakers, 1981, The Riddle of the Dinosaur, 1985, Mars Beckons, 1990, The Mysterious History of Columbus, 1991; co-author: The New York Times Guide to the Return of Halley's Comet, 1985, (with William Stockton) Spaceliner, 1981, Israel: The Historical Atlas, 1997; editor: Scientists at Work, 1979, Cosmic Dispatches, 2000. With CIC AUS, 1957-59. Recipient Book award Aviation/Space Writers, 1970, Writing award Aviation/Space Writers, 1983, G.M. Loeb Achievement award U. Conn, 1972, Press award Nat. Space Club, 1974, AAAS-Westinghouse Sci. Writing award, 1983, Ralph Coats Roe medal ASME, 1995, Pulitzer prize, 1984, N.Y. Times Pulitzer Prize Winning Team, 1987, N.Y.C. Mayor's award, 2001, Am. Geol. Inst. award, 2001, Sagan award Coun. Sci. Soc. Pres., 2001. Mem. Nat. Assn. Sci. Writers, Authors Guild, Soc. Profl. Journalists, Am. Geog. Soc. (councilor 1994—), sec. 2000—), Am. Acad. Arts and Scis., Century Assn., Sigma Chi, Phi Beta Kappa. Home: 232 W 10th St New York NY 10014-2976 Office: 229 W 43rd St New York NY 10036-3913 Office Phone: 212-556-7485. Business E-Mail: wilford@nytimes.com.

**WILHELM, DAVID C.,** investment company executive; m. Degee Dodds; children: Luke, Logan. BA, Ohio U., 1977; MPP, Harvard U., 1990; Doctorate (hon.), U. Charleston. Rsch. dir. pub. employee dept. AFL-CIO, 1981-83; campaign mgr. Senator Paul Simon, 1984, Senator Joseph Biden for Pres., Iowa, 1985-87, Richard M. Daley for Mayor, Chgo., 1989, 91, Gov. Bill Clinton for Pres., 1991-92; exec. dir. Citizens for Tax Justice, Washington, 1985-87; pres. The Strategy Group, Chgo., 1988-91; chmn. Nat. Dem. Com., 1993-94; sr. mng. dir. investment banking Kemper Securities, Inc. (now First Union), Chgo., 1995-97; founder, sr. v.p. Wilhelm & Conlon, Inc., Chgo., 1998—2004; founder, pres. Woodland Venture Mgmt., Chgo., 2002—; founder, ptnr. Adena Ventures, 2002—, Hopewell Ventures, 2004—; founder, pres. The Strategy Group. Lectr. U. Chgo.; bd. dirs. Christian Century Mag., League of Chgo. Treasures, Children's Meml. Hosp., Chgo., Ill. Venture Capital Assocs., Chicagoland Entrepreneurial Ctr., Ill. Ventures. Bd. dirs. Chgo. Project for Violence Prevention, Ctr. for Tax and Budget Accountability. Fellow Inst. of Politics, Harvard U., 1996, recipient hon. Dr. of Public Service, Ohio Univ. Office: Woodland Venture Mgmt 20 N Wacker Dr Ste 2200 Chicago IL 60606 E-mail: wilhelm@woodlandvc.com.

**WILHELM, EDWARD W.,** corporate financial executive; Grad., U. of Detroit. With PricewaterhouseCoopers, 1981—91; contr., v.p./contr. Kmart Corp., 1991—94; v.p. fin. Borders Group, Ann Arbor, Mich., 1994—97, v.p. planning, reporting and treasury, 1997—2000, sr. v.p., CFO, 2000—. Office: Borders Group 100 Phoenix Dr Ann Arbor MI 48108-2202*

**WILHELM, FRANK L.,** publisher, writer; Children: David Donne, Anita Sue, Laura Jean. BA in English, U. Ill., 1950, MS in Vocat. Counseling, 1951. Registered social worker, Ill. Tchr. English, Bd. Edn., Windsor and Clifton, Ill., 1951-53; personnel mgr. J.P. Smith Shoes, Chgo., 1953-55; outside sales Ency. Britannica, Chgo., 1955-57; vocat. counselor, supr. tng. Cook County, Ill. and State of Ill., Chgo., 1957-89; owner Books of Am., Evanston, Ill., 1998—. Author: (poetry) Poetry City, USA, 1997, (novels) Orphan's Odyssey, 2002. Folk dancer Folk Dance Coun. Chgo. With USN, 1944-46. Avocations: bridge, chess, gardening, cooking, ancient mid-east history. Home: 2940 W Sherwin Ave Chicago IL 60645-1210 Office: BOA Pub Co PO Box 6272 Evanston IL 60204-6272 Personal E-mail: xopo@aol.com

**WILHELM, GARY BRETZ,** physician; s. Norman E. and Madeleine Bretz Wilhelm; m. Katherine Jean Kuhlman; 1 child, John Hunter. MD, U. Tex. Health Sci. Ctr., San Antonio, 1974; PhD in Human Anatomy and Neuroscis., U. Tex. Med. Br., Galveston, 1986; BA in Biology, Capital U., Columbus, Ohio, 1974. Postdoctoral fellow dept. pathology U. Tex. Health Sci. Ctr., San Antonio, 1980—81, instr. in human anatomy, 1980—82; intern Brooke Army Med. Ctr., Fort Sam Houston, Tex., 1986—87; orthopedic resident William Beaumont Army Med. Ctr., Fort Bliss, Tex., 1991—96; commd. 2d lt. US Army, 1986, advanced through grades to maj.; physician extender staff US Army Acad. Health Scis., San Antonio, 1990—91; resident physician Acad. Health Scis., Fort Bliss, Tex., 1991—96; chief, phys. exams clinics and aerospace medicine Munson Army Health Ctr., Ft. Leavenworth, Kans., 1996—; flight surgeon Mo. Army Nat. Guard, Jefferson City, 1996—. Chief, phys. exams clinics and aerospace medicine Munson Army Health Ctr., Fort Leavenworth, Kans., 1996—; orthopedic tech. course dir. Acad. Scis., Fort Sam Houston, 1990—91. Contbr. articles to profl. publs. Co-dir. Nat. Student Rsch. Forum, Galveston, 1978—79. Col., flight surgeon Mo. Army NG. Decorated Meritourious Svc. medal US Army; named Flight Surgeon of Yr.; recipient Civilian Achievement award. Episcopalian. Avocations: flying, fox hunting, reading. Office: Munson Army Health Center 550 Pope Avenue Fort Leavenworth KS 66048 Office Phone: 913-758-0585.

**WILHELM, GRETCHEN,** retired secondary school educator, volunteer; b. Ames, Iowa, Sept. 30, 1938; d. Harley Almey Wilhelm and Orpha Elizabeth Lutton. BS in Math., Iowa State U., 1960; MS in Math., Oreg. State U., 1969. Permanent profl. endorsement for math. grades 7-12 and gen. sci. Iowa, life endorsement math. grades 7-12 and all scis. grades 7-12 Minn. Math. tchr. Shenandoah (Iowa) H.S., 1960—63, Robbinsdale (Minn.) Sr. H.S., 1963 68; jr. mathometician on faculty inst. Atomic Rsch. Iowa State U., Ames (Iowa) Lab. U.S. Atomic Energy Commn., 1969; math. tchr. Robbinsdale Cooper Sr. High, New Hope, Minn., 1969—94, math. dept. chmn., 1974—76; ret., 1994. Dist. math. curriculum devel. com. Robbinsdale Sch. Dist., New Hope, 1984—89. Election judge, New Hope, 1994, 1996, 1998, 2000; charter mem. Plymouth (Minn.) Creek Christian Ch., 1978, bd. mem., 1978—79, 1982—84, 1989—91, 1997—2001. Recipient NSF Math. Inst. stipend, Oreg. State U., Corvallis, 1962, 1963, 1964, 1965. Mem.: AAUW (life; Mpls. br. bd. dirs., adv. rep. 1997—98), NEA (life), Minn. Geneal. Soc., Iowa Geneal. Soc., Women Descs. Ancient and Hon. Arty. Co., US Daus. War of 1812 (state registrar 2000—), Thomas Stanton Soc., Thomas Minor Soc., New Eng. Women Descs. (state registrar 2005—), Dau. Am. Colonists, Colonial Dames the XVII Century (state sec. 1997—99), Colonial Dames Am., Nat. Soc. DAR (life; chpt. 2nd vice regent 1987—88, chpt. registrar 1988—94, State constn. week chmn. 1992—95, chpt. 1st vice regent 1994—96, state registrar 1995—97, state officers club v.p., chaplain 1995—97, chpt. chaplain 1996—98, state DAR good citizen chmn. 1997—99, chpt. regent 1998—2000, bd. mgmt., state regent 2001—03, charter mem. State Regents Club, Officers Club 2001—), hon. state regent 2003—, state membership chmn. 2003—05, chair Holt Cogswell Nursing scholar 2004—, speaker staff 2005—). Republican. Mem. Christian Ch. (Disciples Of Christ). Avocation: genealogy. Home: 3925 Winnetka Ave N Minneapolis MN 55427

**WILHELM, JOHN L.,** health facility administrator; b. Chgo., 1943; MPH, U. Ill., Chgo., 1979; MD, Loyola U. Stritch Sch. Medicine. Internist Mercy Hosp., Chgo., 1969—71; resident, physn. Northwestern-Wesley Hosp. Chgo., 1971—73; resident, gyn. endocrinology Michael Reese Hosp., 1974—75; chief, bur. pub. health Chgo. Health Dept., 1990; dep. commr. Chgo. Dept. Pub. Health, commr. 2000—05; exec. dir. Infant Welfare Soc. Chgo., 2005—. Office: Infant Welfare Soc Chgo 3600 W Fullerton Chicago IL 60647

**WILHELM, JOHN W.,** labor union administrator; m. Elizabeth B. Gilbertson, 1969; 2 children. B with high honors, Yale Coll., 1967. Org. & bus. agent Local 217 Conn./R.I. Hotel and Restaurant Employees Internat. Union,

1969—71, sec., treas., 1971—83, bus. mgr., 1978—86; internat. v.p. Hotel Employees and Restaurant Employees Internat. Union (HERE), 1982-1996, gen. sec.-treas., 1996-98, gen. pres., 1998—2004; pres. hospitality industry UNITE HERE, Washington, 2004—. Trustee Welfare/Pension Funds Hotel and Restaurant Employees Internat. Union, 1988—; trustee S. Nevada Culinary and Bartenders Pension Fund, 1995—; commr. Nat. Gambling Impact Study Commn., 1997—99. Mem.: Phi Beta Kappa. Office: UNITE HERE 1775 K St NW Ste 620 Washington DC 20006 Office Phone: 202-393-4373.*

**WILHELM, KATE (KATY GERTRUDE),** author; b. Toledo, June 8, 1928; d. Jesse Thomas and Ann (McDowell) Meredith; m. Joseph B. Wilhelm, May 24, 1947 (div. 1962); children: Douglas, Richard; m. Damon Knight, Feb. 23, 1963; 1 child, Jonathan. PhD in Humanities (hon.), Mich. State U., 1996. Writer, 1956—. Co-dir. Milford Sci. Fiction Writers Conf., 1963-76; lectr. Clarion Fantasy Workshop Mich. State U., 1968-94. Author: More Bitter Than Death, 1962; (with Theodore L. Thomas) The Clone, 1965, The Nevermore Affair, 1966, The Killer Thing, 1967, Let the Fire Fall, 1969, The Year of the Cloud, 1970, Abyss: Two Novellas, 1971, Margaret and I, 1971, City of Cain, 1971, The Clewiston Test, 1976, Where Late the Sweet Birds Sang, 1976, Fault Lines, 1976, Somerset Dreams and Other Fictions, 1978, Juniper Time, 1979; (with Damon Knight) Better Than One, 1980, A Sense of Shadow, 1981, Listen, Listen, 1981, Oh! Susannah, 1982, Welcome Chaos, 1983, Huysman's Pets, 1986; (with R. Wilhelm) The Hills Are Dancing, 1986, The Hamlet Trap, 1987, Crazy Time, 1988, Dark Door, 1988, Smart House, 1989, Children of the Wind: Five Novellas, 1989, Cambio Bay, 1990, Sweet, Sweet Poison, 1990, Death Qualified, 1991, And the Angels Sing, 1992, Seven Kinds of Death, 1992, Naming the Flowers, 1992, Justice for Some, 1993, The Best Defense, 1994, A Flush of Shadows, 1995, Malice Prepense, 1996, The Good Children, 1998, Defense for the Devil, 1999, No Defense, 2000, The Deepest Water, 2000, Desperate Measures, 2001, Skeletons, 2002, Clear and Convincing Proof, 2003, The Unhidden Truth, 2004, Storyteller, 2005, The Price of Silence, 2005; (multimedia space fantasy) Axoltl, U. Oreg. Art Mus., 1979, (radio play) The Hindenburg Effect, 1985; editor: Nebula Award Stories #9, 1974, Clarion SF, 1976; contbr. articles to popular mags., profl. jours. Mem. Nat. Writers Union, Mystery Writers Am., Authors Guild. Address: 1645 Horn Ln Eugene OR 97404-2957 E-mail: kate@katewilhelm.com.

**WILHELM, MORTON,** retired surgeon; b. Roanoke, Va., June 22, 1923; s. Walter LeRoy and Della Mae (Turner) W.; m. Jean Osborne, June 3, 1949; children: Melissa, Christina. BS, Va. Mil. Inst., 1944; MD, U. Va., 1947. Diplomate Am. Bd. Surgery. Intern, resident in surgery VA Mason Hosp., Seattle, 1947-51, 52-53; fellow, instr. surgery Med. Ctr. U. Va., Charlottesville, 53-54, 56-66, assoc. prof. surgery Med. Ctr., 1966-80, prof. surgery Med. Ctr., 1980-93, chief dept. surg. oncology Med. Ctr., 1990-93, Joseph Farrow prof. surg. oncology Med. Ctr., 1990-93. Pres. Va. div., mem. nat. bd. dirs. Am. Cancer Soc., Meritorious Svc. award, Horsley award, Nat. Teresa Lasser award. Lt. U.S. Army, 1951-53. Fellow ACS (vice chmn. commn. on cancer 1989-90, pres. Va. chpt., mem. bd. govs.); mem. So. Surg. Assn., So. Soc. Clin. Surgeons, Soc. Surg. Oncology. Avocations: tennis, golf, woodworking.

**WILHELM, ROBERT OSCAR,** lawyer, civil engineer; b. Balt., July 7, 1918; s. Clarence Oscar and Agnes Virginia (Grimm) W.; m. Grace Sanborn Luckie, Apr. 4, 1959. BSCE, Ga. Tech. Inst., 1947, MSIM, 1948; JD, Stanford U., 1951. Bar: Calif. 1952, U.S. Supreme Ct. Mem. Wilhelm, Thompson, Redwood City, Calif., 1952—92; gen. cousnel Bay Counties Gen. Contractors; pvt. practice civil engring., Redwood City, 1952—. Pres. Bay Counties Builders Escrow, Inc., 1972-88. Author: The Manual of Procedures for the Construction Industry, 1971, Manual of Procedures and Form Book for Construction Industry, 9th edit., 1995, Construction Law for Contractors, Architects and Engineers; columnist Law and You in Daily Pacific Builder, 1955-2001. With C.E., AUS, 1942-46. Named to Wisdom Hall of Fame, 1999. Mem. Bay Counties Civil Engrs. (pres. 1957), Peninsula Builders Exch. (pres. 1958-71, dir.), Calif. State Builders Exch. (treas. 1971), Del Mesa Carmel Cmty. Assn. (bd. dirs. 1997-99), Masons, Odd Fellows, Eagles, Elks. Home: 134 Del Mesa Carmel Carmel CA 93923-7950 Office: 600 Allerton St Ste 202 Redwood City CA 94083

**WILHELM, WILLIAM JEAN,** civil engineering educator; b. St. Louis, Oct. 5, 1935; s. Maurice Ferdinand and Winifred Eileen (McClintock) W.; m. Patricia Jane Zietz, Aug. 17, 1957; children: William, Robert, Andrew, Mary, David. BME, Auburn U., 1958, MS, 1963; PhD, N.C. State U., 1968. Lic. profl. engr., Kans. Structural engr. Palmer & Baker Engrs., Mobile, Ala., 1958-60; instr. engring. graphics Auburn U., 1960-64; asst. prof. civil engring. W.Va. U., Morgantown, 1967-72, assoc. prof., 1972-76, prof., 1976-79, chmn., 1974-79; dean engring., prof. Wichita State U., 1979-2000, dean, prof., emeritus, 2000—, dir. Ctr. for Productivity Enhancement 1984-86, exec. dir. Ctr. Tech. Application, 1988-93. Bd. dirs. Kans. Tech. Enterprise Corp., Orthopaedic Rsch. Inst. Via Christi Regional Med. Sys.; chair bd. dirs. Envision. Found. Contbr. articles to profl. jours. Officer 2d Lt. U.S. Army, 1959, 62. Recipient Recognition award Wichita State U. Alumni Assn., 1993, Engr. Svc. award Wichita Coun. Engring. Socs., 2000. Fellow NSPE, ASCE, Am. Soc. Engring. Edn. (George K. Wadlin award 1998, MidWest sect. Spl. Appreciation award 2001), Am. Concrete Inst. (Joe W. Kelley award 1986, Henry L. Kennedy award 1994); mem. Soc. Women Engrs. (sr., Rodney D. Chipp Meml. award 2000), Kans. Soc. Profl. Engrs. (pres. 1994-95, Outstanding Engr. of Yr. award 1989, Career Recognition award 2000), Order of the Engr., Sigma Xi, Phi Kappa Phi, Tau Beta Pi, Pi Tau Sigma, Chi Epsilon (chpt. mem. U. Wa. U. 1979), Golden Key (hon.). Roman Catholic. Home: 7014 E 25th St N Wichita KS 67226-1734 Personal E-mail: billwilhelm1@cox.net.

**WILHELMI, CYNTHIA JOY,** information technology manager, information scientist, consultant; Student, Iowa State U., Ames, 1964—66, BA in Art and Edn., 1966; MA in Comm., U. Nebr., Omaha, 1996. Master Artist-in-Residence Nebr. Arts Coun., Omaha, 1985—91; grad. tchg. asst., tchg. fellow U. Nebr., Omaha, 1993—95; Family Friends of Eastern Nebr. program coord. Vis. Nurse Assn., Omaha, 1996—97; instr. Midland Luth. Coll., Fremont, Nebr., 1997—99; info. tech. cons., project mgr., test engr., bus. analyst Bass & Assocs., Omaha, 1999—2000; info. tech. cons. Robert Half Internat. Cons., 2000, Maxim Group/TEKSystems, 2000—02, Client Resources Inc., 2003; data mgr. TEKsystems, 2003; govt. bid proposal coord. NuGenSof cons. co., 2003—04; bus. sys. analyst Wells Fargo; farmer, 2001—05; data mgr. Raytheon, 2003, proposal coord., 2003—04; bus. sys. analyst Praxis Tech. Group, 2005; sr. quality assurance, testing engr. Acacia Tech. Svcs. Inc., 2006; project mgr. and coord. Profl. Project Ptnrs., Inc., 2006—. Sr. project mgr., bus. analyst Alegent Health, Ameritrade, Omnium Worldwide, Lincoln Benefit Life, Raytheon, Wells Fargo, Praxis Tech. Group; IT data mgr., govt. info. tech. proposal coord.; sr. test engr. Ameritrade, Lincoln Benefit Life, Ameritas, Alegent Health, Nationwide Ins., 2006—; project mgr. Alegent Health, Ameritrade, Lincoln Benefit Life; engr. Omnium Worldwide, Raytheon, Northrop Grumman Mission Sys., Ameritrade; 3d-party vendor mgr. Alegent Health, Lincoln Benefit Life; CD installation tester Lincoln Benefit Life; tech. documentor Alegent Health, Omnium Worldwide, Ameritrade, PerClick-dot-com, Ameritas, Raytheon Sys., Inacom; data mgr. Northrop Grumman Mission Sys.; bus. sys. cons. Wells Fargo, Nationwide Agribusiness Ins., Nationwide Insurance Agile Tech.; project mgr., corp. enterprise field ops. software release coord. Wells Fargo Corp. Offices. Editor, pub., contbg. author Salaam mag., 1985-86. Mem. adv. coun. Foster Grandparents, Omaha, 1999-2005; bd. dirs., pub. rels./publicity chair U. Nebr. Friends of Art, Omaha, 1997-99; bd. dirs. Nebr. SIDS Found., 2002—03 Named Outstanding Grad. Tchg. Asst., U. Nebr., Omaha, 1995, Adm. in the Gt. Navy of Nebr., 1990. Mem. AAUW, Am. Meteor. Soc., Soc. for Tech. Comm. (bd. dirs., chair pub. rels. 1999), Nebr. Adms. Assn., Soc. for Collegiate Journalists (hon.), Phi Delta Gamma, Mensa (Nebr., Western Iowa exec. com. 2003-05, SIGHT coord. 2003-05, mem. nat. nominating com. 2004-05, 06—). Republican. Personal E-mail: cwi813@earthlink.net.

**WILHELMSEN, HAROLD JOHN,** accountant; b. Kansas City, Mo., July 13, 1928; s. Karl John and Cora Irene (Reynolds) W.; m. Audrey Loraine Woodard, Oct. 14, 1950. BBA, U. Wis., 1950. CPA, Wis. With S.C. Johnson & Son Inc., Racine, Wis., 1953-90. dir. fin. South Pacific, 1970-72, mgr. overseas fin. svcs., 1972-76, contr. U.S. ops., 1976-78, v.p., contr. internat. ops., 1978-90, ret., 1990. Pres. Racine Symphony Orch. Assn., 1957-60; trustee Carthage Coll., Kenosha, Wis., 1984-91, dir., sec. Pinnacle Peak Country Club Estates, 1992-95; dir., 1993-97, pres. Pinnacle Peak Country Club, 1996-97; treas. Christ the Lord Luth. Ch. Served with U.S. Army, 1950-52. Mem.: Ranch Village Health Club and Spa, Pinnacle Peak Country Club. Republican. Lutheran. Avocations: golf, squash, bridge, reading, music. Personal E-mail: hjw-az@cox.net.

**WILHIDE, STEPHEN D.,** medical association administrator; BA in Social Scis., Frostburg State U., Md., 1965; MSW, U. Md., 1972; MPH, U. Pitts. 1976. Exec. dir. So. Ohio Health Svcs. Network, 1976—2002, Nat. Rural Health Assn., Alexandria, Va., 2002—. Vol. VISTA, NC. With U.S. Army, Vietnam. Named one of Most Powerful People in Healthcare, Modern Healthcare mag., 2003. Office: National Rural Health Associ 1600 Prince St Ste 100 Alexandria VA 22314-2836 Office Phone: 703-519-7910. Business E-Mail: wilhide@nrharural.com.

**WILHJELM, CHRISTIAN,** conductor, artist; b. Long Branch, N.J., Nov. 6, 1949; s. Carl and Alice Wilhjelm; m. Jacqueline Sarracco; children: Carl, Hannah, Erik, Emma. BA in Music, New Eng. Conservatory, 1972; MA Edn., Coll. of NJ, 1978; EdD, Columbia U., 1998. Musician-French horn Richmond Symphony, Richmond, Va., 1972—76; band dir. North Brunswick Twp. HS, 1977—79, Ridgewood HS. NJ, 1979—82, Rye HS. NY, 1982—84, Pascack Hills HS, Montvale, NJ, 1984—; NYU Wind Ensemble, NYC, 2006—; music dir. Ridgewood Concert Band, Ridgewood, 1983—; artist Montclair State U., NJ, 1996—2003; condr., music dir. The Goldman Band, NYC, 2000—05. Bd. dirs. Classical NJ, Westfield, NJ, 1998, Bergen Youth Orch., Engelwood, NJ, 2001—. Contbr. book Spotlight on Bands. Recipient Sudler Award of Merit, John Philip Sousa Found., 1998; fellow Paul Harris Fellowship, Rotary Internat., 1992. Mem.: Music Educator's Nat. Conf., Coll. Band Dir. Nat. Assn., Am. Fedn. of Musicians. Personal E-mail: cwilhjelm@msn.com.

**WILK, JOSHUA,** psychologist; b. Flemington, NJ, Mar. 6, 1970; s. Stan and Rhona Wilk. PhD, U. Md., College Park, 1999. Lic. psychologist Md. Dir. workforce and grad. med. edn. studies Am. Psychiat. Assn., Arlington, Va., 2001—. Recipient New Investigator award, NIMH, 2005.

**WILK, PAMELA JUNE,** elementary school educator; b. Chgo., Ill., Aug. 11, 1944; d. Ralph Robert and June Fleurette Landers; m. Walter William Wilk, May 4, 1968; children: Thomas, Jennifer. BA, Mundelein Coll., 1966. Tchr. Whittier Sch., Northlake, Ill., 1966—68, Riley Sch., Northlake, Ill., 1968—69, St. Ferdinand Sch., Chgo., 1978—91, St. Theresa Sch., Palatine, Ill., 1991—; v.p., mem. Liturgical Com., Chgo., 1978—91; den mother Cub Scouts, Chgo., 1978; mem. Home and Sch. Assn., Chgo., 1976—85. Mem.: ASCD, Nat. Cath. Edn. Assn., Nat. Cath. Edn. Assn. Avocations: travel, reading, opera, theater. Home: 710 Cherry Ct Itasca IL 60143 Office: St Theresa Sch 445 N Benton St Palatine IL 60067 Office Phone: 847-359-1820.

**WILK, RONALD,** physician; b. N.Y.C., Nov. 27, 1944; BA, L.I. U., Bklyn., 1966; MD, U. Bologna, Italy, 1972. Diplomate Am. Acad. Neurology, 1980. Intern, resident Mt. Sinai Hosp., N.Y.C., chief resident, 1977. Fellow: Royal Soc. Medicine, Am. Acad. Neurology.

**WILK, STUART,** publishing executive; Reporter, asst. city editor Milwaukee Sentinel; night city editor The Dallas Morning News, 1980, metro editor, asst. mng. editor, dep. mng. editor, mng. editor, 1996—2004, v.p., assoc. editor, 2004—, Belo Corp. (parent co. of The Dallas Morning News), 2004—. Discussion leader Am. Press Inst.; profl. in residence Marshall U. W. Page Sch. Journalism, 2001; faculty Cross-Media Journalism Pilot Program, Robert C. Maynard Inst. of Journalism Edn. Bd. dir. Freedom of Information Found. Tex. Mem.: Associated Press Mng. Editors (pres., mem. exec. com., chair, Mktg., Ethics and Diversity Com., supervised nationwide survey on diversity in the newsroom 1996). Office: Dallas Morning News 508 Young St Dallas TX 75202 Office Phone: 214-977-8222. Business E-Mail: swilk@dallasnews.com.

**WILKE, LEROY,** retired church administrator; m. Jane Wilke. Grad., Golden Valley Lutheran Coll.; MA, Minn. State U.; LittD (hon.), Concordia U., 1999. Chaplain's asst. US Army; adminstr., dir. Christian Edn., Mpls. 1969; prof. edn. Concordia Coll., St. Paul, 1976; exec. dir. dist. and congl. svcs. Luth. Ch.-Mo. Synod, St. Louis, 1985—2005. Sec. Karpenko Inst. for Nurturing and Developing Leadership Excellence, 2005—. Lutheran. Office: KINDLE c/o Emmauel Luth Ch 3120 Irving St Denver CO 80211-3632 Office Phone: 303-433-3303. Office Fax: 303-433-2280. E-mail: leroy.wilke@lcms.org.*

**WILKE, SABINE,** language educator; b. Wiesbaden, Germany, July 21, 1957; d. Hans and Klara Wilke; m. Richard T. Gray, Dec. 6, 1984; 1 child, Cora L. Wilke-Gray. MA, U. Mainz, Germany, 1982, PhD, 1986. Asst. prof. German, Stanford U., Calif., 1986—89, U. Wash., Seattle, 1989—92, assoc. prof., 1992—97, prof., 1997—. Vis. prof. Harvard U., Cambridge, Mass., 2000—. Author books. Fellow Fulbright-DAAD fellow, 1983—84, NEH, 1990—91, Humboldt Found., 1996—97; Fulbright fellow, 2003—04, Guggenheim fellow, 2003—04. Office: U Wash Dept Germanics Box 353130 Seattle WA 98195 Office Phone: 206-543-4580. Business E-Mail: wilke@u.washington.edu.

**WILKENING, LAUREL LYNN,** academic administrator, aerospace scientist; b. Richland, Wash., Nov. 23, 1944; d. Marvin Hubert and Ruby Alma Wilkening; m. Godfrey Theodore Sill, May 18, 1974 BA, Reed Coll., Portland, Oreg., 1966; PhD, U. Calif., San Diego, 1970; DSc (hon.), U. Ariz., 1996. From asst. prof. to assoc. prof. U. Ariz., Tucson, 1973—80, dir. Lunar and Planetary Lab., head planetary scis., 1981—83, vice provost, prof. planetary scis., 1983—85, v.p. rsch., dean Grad. Coll., 1985—88; divsn. scientist NASA Hdqrs., Washington, 1980; prof. geol. scis., adj. prof. astronomy, provost U. Washington, Seattle, 1988—93; prof. earth system sci., chancellor U. Calif., Irvine, 1993—98. Dir. Rsch. Corp., 1991-2003, Seagate Tech., Inc., 1993-2000, Empire Ranch Found., 1998-2003, 2005—; vice chmn. Nat. Commn. on Space, Washington, 1984-86, Adv. Com. on the Future of U.S. Space Program, 1990-91; chair Space Policy Adv. Bd., Nat. Space Coun., 1991-92; co-chmn. primitive bodies mission study team NASA/European Space Agcy., 1984-85; chmn. com. rendezvous sci. working group NASA, 1983-85; mem. panel on internat. cooperation and competition in space Congl. Office Tech. Assessment, 1982-83; trustee NASULGC, 1994-97, UCAR, 1989-89, 97-98, Reed Coll., 1992-2002. Editor: Comets, 1982. Recipient trainee, NASA, 1967—70; grantee fellow, U. Calif Regents, 1966—67. Fellow Meteoritical Soc. (councilor 1976-80), Am. Assn. Advanced Sci.; mem. Am. Astron. Soc. (chmn. div. planetary scis. 1984-85), Am. Geophys. Union, AAAS, Planetary Soc. (dir. 1994-2000, v.p. 1997-2000), Phi Beta Kappa. Democrat. Avocations: gardening, camping, swimming.

**WILKERSON, ANDREA LETA,** musician, educator; d. James Leonard Baker and Betty Lee Ragsdale; m. Stephen Craig Wilkerson, May 14, 1979; 1 child, Chancellor Kenton. B of Music Edn., U. Tulsa, 1977; MusM, Pitts. State U., Kans., 1991. Profl. singer (as Andrea Baker) Skyline Records, Dana Records, Powerhouse Records, 1968—; jazz clinician nationwide, 1975—; music instr. Mt. San Antonio Coll., Walnut, Calif., 1989—94; tchr. Monrovia (Calif.) Unified Sch., 1990—96; prof. music Pasadena (Calif.) City Coll., 2001—05. Actor: (various mus. theater prodns.), 1972—; prodr. (CDs) Shaw Nuff, Blues Sort of Thing, 1999—2000; prodr., dir.: DVDs Art of Jazz Saxophone, 1991. Vol. Cystic Fibrosis orgns., ARC. Named Miss Grand

Lake, Miss Coveen Country, 1974, 3d runner-up and top talent winner, Miss Okla. Mem.: AFM. Presbyterian. Avocations: travel, gardening, training dogs, physical fitness. Office: PO Box 5063 Covina CA 91723

**WILKERSON, H. DEAN, JR.,** association and organization executive; Gen. counsel MADD, Dallas, 1990—93, exec. dir. Irving, Tex., 1993—2004, Amer. Coll. of Emergency Physicians, 2004—. Office: Amer Coll of Emergency Physicians 1125 Executive Cir PO Box 619911 Irving TX 75261-9911

**WILKERSON, ISABEL,** journalist, writer; With NY Times, NYC, bureau chief Chgo. Bur. Chgo., 1991—95, sr. writer NYC, 1995—2003. Author: The Great Migration, 1995. Recipient Pulitzer Prize for feature writing, 1994.*

**WILKERSON, JANET STAFFORD,** publishing executive, educator; d. Laroy W. Stafford and Jeanne F. Bergman; m. David Allen Wilkerson, July 21, 1942; children: Tracy LaVerne, Jordan Thomas, Robert Scott Stillman, Sean David, Kelly Lynn Wikerson, Lani Jeanne'. BS, Ind. State U., 1970; MAT, Ind. U., 1976. Lic. profl. tchr. Ind. Bd. Edn., 1975. C.s practitioner self-employed, Silver Spring, Md., 1986—2003; owner, pres. Braden River Pub., Sarasota, Fla., 2004. Pub. spkr. C.S. (COP), Silver Spring, Fla., 1978—2004; min. (armed forces & prison) C.S., 1995—2004; tchr. Auburn U., Montgomery, 1976—82, Evelyn Wood Reading Dynamics, Boomington, Ind., 1970—76, Indpls., 1970—76, Muncie, 1970—76, Terre Haute, 1970—76; spkr. in field. Author: Keep Thy Heart; With All Thine Heart; watercolor paintings, Pelicans and Flowers in Window; prodr.(compiler, collector): (children's story books) First Grade Stories. Rep. ofcl. Manatee County Exec. Com., Bradenton, Fla., 2002—04; vol. White Ho., Washington, 2001—02; rep. ofcl. Montgomery County Ctrl. Com., 1990—2002; stop era chair States Ind./ State Ala., Montgomery, 1974—77; cs min. to armed svcs. and prisons C.S., 1995—2002; bd. mem., chair, supt. First Ch. Christ, Scientist, Silver Spring, 1989—2002; officer PTA, Silver Spring, 1989—2001; cmty. vol. Schools, Nursing Homes, 1989—2002. Named Family of Yr., Md. State PTA, 2000. Mem.: Rep. Club (assoc.; media chair 2002—04). Conservative. Christian Science. Avocations: photography, violin, piano, singing, art, animals. Office: Braden River Publishing PO Box 20538 Braden River FL 34204 Personal E-mail: janet@70x7.org. E-mail: brp@70x7.org.

**WILKERSON, LUANN,** dean, medical educator; BA magna cum laude, Baylor U., 1969; MA in English, U. Tex., 1972; EdD, U. Mass., 1977. Tchg. asst. dept. English U. Tex., Austin, 1970-72; tchr. grade 8 lang. arts Quabbin Regional H.S., Barre, Mass., 1974-75; rsch. asst. Clinic to Improve Univ. Tchg. U. Mass., Amherst, 1974-76, staff assoc., 1976-77; dir. tchg. and media resource ctr., asst. prof. speech and theatre Murray (Ky.) State U., 1977-80; acting dir., coord. faculty devel. office ednl. devel. and resources Coll. Osteopathic Medicine Ohio U., Athens, 1980-81; assoc. dir. office curricular affairs, asst. prof. family medicine Med. Coll. Wis., Milw., 1981-83; ednl. specialist ednl. devel. unit Michael Reese Hosp. and Med. Ctr., Chgo., 1983-84; dir. faculty devel. office ednl. devel. Harvard Med. Sch., Boston, 1984-91, lectr. in med. edn., 1988-91; dir. Ctr. for Ednl. Devel. and Rsch. UCLA Sch. Medicine, 1992-99, asst. dean med. edn., 1992-94, assoc. prof. medicine, 1992-95, prof. medicine, 1996—, assoc. dean med. edn., 1995-97, sr. assoc. dean med. edn., 1998—. Mem. editl. bd. Advances in Health Scis. Edn., 1995—, Med. Edn., 1995—, Acad. Medicine, 2001—; reviewer: Acad. Medicine, 1989—, Tchg. and Learning in Medicine, 1990—, Jour. Gen. Internal Medicine, 1988—, Am. Ednl. Rsch. Assn., 1987—, Rsch. Med.Edn. Ann. Conf., 1988—; contbr. articles to profl. jours. and chpts. to books; lectr. in field. Recipient Clinician Tchr. award Calif. Regional Soc. Gen. Internal Medicine, 1995, Excellence in Edn. award UCLA Sch. Medicine, 1998. Mem. Am. Assn. Med. Colls. (mem. rsch. med. edn. com. 1990-93, western chair group on ednl. affairs 1995-97, co-dir. fellowship in med. edn. rsch. 1995-97, convenor spl. interest group on faculty devel. 1997-98, chair group on ednl. affairs 1997—), Am. Ednl. Rsch. Assn., Profl. and Orgnl. Devel. Network (mem. nat. core com. 1977-80, 84-86, exec. dir. 1984-85), Phi Beta Kappa. Office: UCLA Sch Mcdicine Ctr Ednl Devel & Rsch PO Box 951722 Los Angeles CA 90095-1722 E-mail: lwilkerson@mednet.ucla.edu.

**WILKERSON, MATHA ANN,** retired oil company executive; b. Mill Creek, Okla., Sept. 1, 1937; d. Frank and Lottie Evelyn (Cordell) Stie; m. Ronald Gene Wilkerson, Dec. 22, 1956; 1 child, Mitchell Linn. BS in Edn., East Ctrl. U., Ada, Okla., 1966. Elem. sch. tchr. Moore (Okla.) Pub. Schs., 1966—74; office mgr. S. S. Sanbar, M.D., Oklahoma City, 1974—78; ops. mgr., acct. John A. Taylor Oil Co., Oklahoma City, 1978—84; office mgr., controller Lance Ruffel Oil & Gas Corp., Oklahoma City, 1984—2005; ret. Mem. Coun. of Petroleum Accounts Soc. (com. mem. 1979—). Baptist. Avocations: crafts, reading, theater, cooking.

**WILKERSON, WILLIAM HOLTON,** banker; b. Greenville, N.C., Feb. 16, 1947; s. Edwin Cisco and Agnes Holton (Gaskins) W.; m. Ellen Logan Tomskey, Oct. 27, 1973; 1 child, William Holton Jr. AB in Econs., U. N.C., 1970. Asst. v.p. 1st Union Nat. Bank, Greensboro, NC, 1972-77; v.p. Peoples Bank & Trust Co., Rocky Mount, NC, 1977-79, exec. v.p., 1987-89, pres., 1989-90; sr. v.p. Hibernia Nat. Bank, New Orleans, 1979-86; group exec. officer, vice chmn. bd. dirs. Centura Banks, Inc., Rocky Mount, 1990-97, pres., 1998—2001, Wilkerson Co., Inc., Greenville, NC, 2001—. Bd. visitors U. N.C., Chapel Hill, 1999-2003; mem. Greenville Mus. of Art. Mem. Greenvillee-Pitt Assn. Realtors, Rocky Mount C. of C. (bd. dirs. 1989-96, vice chmn. 1992-94, chmn. 1995), Omicron Delta Epsilon, Chi Beta Phi, Phi Sigma Pi. Republican. Home: 407 Rutledge Rd Greenville NC 27858 Office: PO Box 2095 Greenville NC 27836-0095 E-mail: wwilkerson1@cox.net.

**WILKES, BRENT AMES,** management consultant; b. Melrose, Mass., Sept. 30, 1952; s. Gordon Borthwick and Frances (Ames) W.; 1 child, Erin; m. Linda Dadourian, Oct. 18, 1998. Bachelor, U. Mass., 1974; M of Pub. Affairs, U. Conn., 1977. Cert. assn. exec., 1998, assoc. risk mgmt., 1998, ins. cons., 2004. Administr. asst. Town of Tolland, Conn., 1975-76; mgmt. specialist Mass. Dept. Community Affairs, Boston, 1976-79; adminstrv. asst. to mayor City of Gloucester, Mass., 1979-80; assoc. dir., dir. of field svcs. Mass. Mcpl. Assn., Boston, 1980-89; v.p., treas. Mass. Interlocal Ins. Assn., Boston, 1984-89; pres. MMA Consulting Group, Inc., Boston, 1989-94, MMA Mgmt. Svcs. Inc., Boston, 1995-98, N.E. Pub. Risk, Inc., Boston, 1998. Northeast Assn. Mgmt., Inc., Boston, 1999—; v.p., treas. Pub. Employer Risk Mgmt. Assn., Albany, NY, 1989—97, pres., 1997—; bd. dirs. NLC Mut. Ins. Co., 1994—2000. Bd. dirs. Assn. Govt. Risk Pools, 2000—, pres., 2003—03; adj. prof. Suffolk U. Grad. Sch. Mgmt., Boston, 1980—82; lectr. numerous regional and nat. trade assns. Author and editor: Managing Small Towns, 1986; contbr. articles to profl. jours. Mem. fin. com. Town of Acton, Mass., 1977-79; mem. town meeting Town of Reading, Mass., 1987-89; pres. Unitarian Universalist Ch. of Reading, 1990-93. Mem. Am. Soc. Assn. Execs., Internat. City Mgmt. Assn. (cert. in mgmt.), Mass. Mcpl. Mgmt. Assn. Democrat. Unitarian Universalist. Avocations: golf, tennis, volleyball, reading, boating. Office: 9 Cornell Rd Latham NY 12110 Office Phone: 518-220-9815. E-mail: bwilkes@neami.com.

**WILKES, DELANO ANGUS,** architect; b. Panama City, Fla., Jan. 25, 1935; s. Burnice Angus and Flora Mae (Scott) W.; m. Dona Jean Murren, June 25, 1960. BArch, U. Fla., 1958. Cert. nat. Coun. Archtl.; registration bds. cert. personal trainer, older adult specialty cert. Am. Coun. on Exercise. Designer Perkins & Will Partnership, Chgo., 1960-63; designer, job capt. Harry Weese, Ltd., Chgo., 1963-66; project arch. Fitch Larocca Carrington, Chgo., 1967-69; arch. Mittelbusher & Tourtelot, Chgo., 1970-71; assoc. Bank Bldg. Corp., Chgo., 1972-75; sr. assoc. Charles Edward Stade & Assocs., Park Ridge, Ill., 1975-77; sr. arch. Consoer Morgan Arch., Chgo., 1977-83, mktg. coord., 1980-83; design cons. Chamlin & Assocs., Peru and Morris, Ill., 1969-82, dir. arch., 1983-86, v.p. arch., 1986-2000. Archtl. cons Sweet's divsn. McGraw Hill, Inc., Chgo., 1984-90; ptnr. Deri Wilkes Assocs., 1990-95; trainer Fitness Barn, 1995-96, Q Sports Club, 1998, Alpha Fitness, 1999-2001; ptnr. River Town Properties, Comml. Devel., Palatka, Fla., 2004. Author: Colonel

Ebenezer Folsom, 1778-1789, North Carolina Patriot and Tory Scourge, 1975, Shrangri-La's New Face, 2006; editor Folsom Bull., 1977-80; prodr. documentary film The Angry Minority, Menninger Found., 1978. Mem. coord. com. Dune Acres Plan Commn. (Ind.), 1983-91; bldg. commr. City of Dune Acres, 1984-89, Arch. Rev. Bd. Marsh Creek Country Club, St. Augustine, Fla., 1988—, chair natural landscape com., 2001—; chmn. Ind. party Dune Acres, 1987; elected trustee Dune Acres Town Bd., 1988-91, pres., 1988-89; mem. Dune Acres Civic Improvement Found., 1988-91 (leadership recognition for drive to restore Dune Acres Clubhouse); cons. Inst. of Crippled and Disabled, N.Y.C., 1978-83; guest lectr. field trip guide Coll. DuPage, Glen Ellyn, Ill., 1968-76; guest arch. med. adv. com. to Pres.'s Com. for Handicapped, 1977, 78; vice chmn. Westchester County Dem. Precinct, Porter County, Ind., 1986; chmn. selection com. Dem. Hdqrs., Porter County, 1986; treas. Com. to Elect Kovach to Coun., Porter County, 1986; vice chmn. Duneland Dems., 1988-92; pres. Ocean House Condominium Assn. St. Augustine, Fla., 1993-94. Mem.: Putnam County Hist. Soc., New Eng. Hist. Geneal. Soc., N.C. Geneal. Soc., Am. Soc. Interior Design (coord. Info. Fair 1979), Chgo. Assn. Commerce and Industry (display dir. 1979 mtg.), Art Inst. Chgo., Chgo. AIA (chmn. design awards display com. 1978-79, prodr. New Mem. Show 1979, chmn. pub. rels. com. 1980), AIA, Folsom Family Assn. Am. (pres. 1978-82, v.p. 1982-, nominating chmn. 1983, host ann. meeting, Chgo. 1981), Businessmen for Pub. Interest, Wilkes Family Rsch. Assn., Marsh Creek Country Club (chmn. Fla. landscape com.), German Shorthaired Pointer Club North Fla., Gargoyle, Soc. Colonial Wars, Cook County Hist. Soc., Chgo. Lyric Opera Guild. Democrat. Unitarian Universalist. Home: 332 Marsh Point Cir Saint Augustine FL 32080-5858 Office Phone: 904-471-6956. Personal E-mail: dawilkes@bellsouth.net.

**WILKES, DONNA NATALIE,** historian; b. Washington, Feb. 8, 1954; d. Roland A. and Grace D. (Vaughn) W. BS cum laude, Georgetown U., 1977; MA, Harvard U., 1982. Research fellow Sch. Medicine Georgetown U., Washington, 1974, counselor, tutor Office for Minority Students, 1976-77; editor, researcher Ctr. for Applied Psych., Washington, 1978-79; historian U.S. Naval Research Lab., Washington, 1979; freelance editor Washington, 1980-85; cons. historian History Assoc., Inc., Rockville, Md., 1985—92, U.S. Dept. Energy, Washington, 1987-89, Smithsonian Instn., Washington, 1988-89. Mem. Nat. Council on Pub. History, Washington, 1985—. Vol. Media Community Relations Com., 1986-92, Providence Hosp., 1985; bd. dirs. D.C. Ind. Living Service, Inc., 1982; mem. Mayor's Com. on Handicapped, Washington, 1982, Archdiocesan Com. on Handicapped, Washington, 1981, Planning Com. for UN Day Celebration, Washington, 1981. Grantee NSF, 1980-82, 86; recipient Cert. of Appreciation Fed. Emergency Mgmt. Agy., Washington, 1986, Outstanding Alumni award Georgetown U., 1986, Cert. of Merit Washington Acad. Sci., 1971, Nat. Contbn. award Internat. Yr. of the Disabled Person, 1981, Joy Evans award Mayor of Washington, 1998, Letter of Commendation Pres. William J. Clinton, 1999; named Washington Woman of Yr., 1987. Mem. History of Sci. Soc., Soc. for History in Fed. Govt., Mensa. Democrat. Roman Catholic. Avocations: piano, tai chi, recorder. Home: 3720 Upton St NW # A356 Washington DC 20016-2299

**WILKES, JEFFREY BLAINE,** real estate appraiser; s. William Francis and Betty June Wilkes; m. Cathy G. Wilkes, Apr. 30, 1988; children: Jeffrey Samson, William Scott. Studied, Columbia Coll., Sioux Falls, S.D. 1975—77. Cert. Appraiser Assessor S.D. Dept. Revenue, 1985, S.D. Asssessor S.D. Assn. Assessing Officers, 2001. Supr., residential bldg. permits Minnehaha County, Sioux Falls, SD, 1984—. Nat. chmn. USJC Outstanding Young Farmer Congress, Sioux Falls, SD, 1982—83; internat. dir. Sertoma Internat., Sioux Falls, SD, 1996—98; pres. Sioux Falls Jaycee, SD, 1984—85, S.D. Jaycee Camp for Handicapped, Sioux Falls, 1988—89, S.D. Jaycee Internat. Senator, Sioux Falls, 1990—91, Sioux Falls Noon Sertoma, SD, 1994—95; dist. gov. S.D. Sertoma, Sioux Falls, 1995—96; devel. v.p. S.D. Sch. of the Deaf Found., Sioux Falls, 1997—; chmn., Newton Hills Dist. Boy Scouts of Am., Sioux Falls, SD, 2001—, camp visitation team, Ctrl. Region, 2001—. Photographer's mate first class USN, 1970—74, South Pacific. Mem.: Sioux Falls Noon Sertoma (life; pres. 1994—95, Gold Honor Pres. 1995), Am. Legion (life), DAV (life), VFW (life). Home: 217 W 19th Sioux Falls SD 57105 Personal E-mail: wilkesjb@hotmail.com.

**WILKES, JOHN MICHAEL,** military officer, auditor; b. Pitts., Dec. 16, 1950; s. John Joseph Wukits and Anne Lebanik. *Father John J. Wukitis served as a sergeant in the Third Army with the 787th Field Artillery Battalion during World War II and participated in the Central Europe and Rhineland campaigns. He later worked as an auditor for the Defense Contract Audit Agency. Mother Anne Lebanik was employed by the Bell Telephone Company of Pennsylvania.* BA in Econs. and Polit. Sci., U. Pitts., 1972; student, La Roche Coll., 1984—88, BS in Acctg. magna cum laude, 1991, MS in Human Resources Mgmt., 1995; AS in Math. and Physics with honors, C.C. Allegheny County, 1998; BS in Natural Scis., U. Pitts., 2004. Spl. accounts mgr. Dell Fastener Corp., Pitts., 1974—78; commd. ens. USN, 1980, advanced through grades to lt. comdr., 1990; auditor Office of Insp. Gen. US Dept. Agr., Hyattsville, Md., 1988—90; sales Sun Book Co., Pitts., 2000—04; asst. engring. dept. Destroyer squadron 10, USS STUMP, 1980—81; lt. missile sys. Destroyer Squadron 22, USS Fahrion, 1983—84; surface combatant with Task Group 60.4 Beirut, 1983—84; asst. tng. officer, staff duty officer Commander Naval Surface Group Mediterranean, 1985—89; pers. officer Naval Embarked Adv. Team, 1996—97. Asst. So Others Might Eat, Wash., DC, 1989—90. Decorated Naval Expeditionary Medal, Nat. Def. Svc. Medal, Sea Svc. Deployment Ribbon. Republican. Cath. Achievements include invention of Decorative Door Guard system; Illuminated Decorative Door Guard System. Avocations: golf, jogging. Home: 208 Lucille St Glenshaw PA 15116

**WILKEY, ELMIRA SMITH,** illustrator, artist, writer, educator; b. Kankakee, Ill., Dec. 13, 1936; d. Edmond Anthony and Dorothy Agnes (Schilling) Smith; m. Lowell Gene Wilkey; children: Anthony, Eric, Martin, Barry, Tad, Jeremy. BA cum laude, Loretto Heights Coll. (now Regis U.), Denver, 1958. Mgr. Duncan Assocs., Champaign, Ill., 1960-61; English/drama speech tchr. Kankakee Sch. Dist., 1958-60; substitute tchr. Kankakee County, 1965-80; art instr. Kankakee C.C., 1988, 2000; behavior couns. Nutri-Sys., Bourbonnais, Ill., 1987-91; English tchr. Bishop McNamara H.S., Kankakee, 1994-2000; founder, co-owner, printer Studio Sans Serif Divsn., Bronte Press Ltd. Edits., Manteno, Kankakee, Bourbonnais, 1977—. Textbook art coms. DSP, Boston, 1965-74; art adj. Olivet Coll., Bourbonnais, 1993-94; writer, art presenter W.C. Workshops Olivet Coll., Kankakee Art League, 1980-90, design cons. for histories Sisters, Servants of the Holy Heart of Mary, 2002-04; lectr. in field. Illustrator: Come Spring, History of Rockville, Hoofbeats, 2001; with Children's Book Program, cable TV, Manteno, Ill., 1996-99, ten books including classic, historical prose, poetry, folklore, herbal subjects, and 2 children's books; columnist Pat's Meanders, 1992—; one woman shows include Galesburg Civic Art Ctr., 1984, Tall Grass Art Assn., ONU Brandenberg Gallery, 1994; exhibited in solo shows at Prairie State Coll., 1980, Western Mich. U.; group shows include Ill. Women in the Arts Invitation, Prairie State Coll., 1980, Copley Soc., Boston, 1986, Tall Grass Art Assn., 2001, 05, 06, Xavier U., 2004, 05, Vanderpoel, Chgo., 2004-05, Tall Grass Gallery, Park Forest, Ill., 2005, 06, Sanctuary Gallery, Ill., 2005, 06. Cmty. arts. coun. Kankakee; cmty. art adv. bd. Kankakee C.C.; donates artwork annually to Hospice, Catholic Charities, United Way. Recipient numerous awards in art; Straw Series Signature art technique, V.I.P. Mem. Nat. League Am. Penwomen (Ill. state pres, Chgo. br. v.p. 1979—, treas. 2002—04), Ill. State Poetry Soc. (charter), Transparent Watercolor Soc. Am., Nat. Mus. Women in Arts, Great Books (charter, pres. 1980-85), Miniature Book Soc., Christians in Visual Arts. Republican. Roman Catholic. Avocations: walking, herb/plant identification, singing, piano, camping. Home and Office: Studio Sans Serif Divsn The Bronte Press 4136 W 6940N Rd Bourbonnais IL 60914-4208 Office Fax: 815-936-9913. Personal E-mail: miraswilkey@yahoo.com.

**WILKEY, MALCOLM RICHARD,** retired ambassador, retired judge; b. Murfreesboro, Tenn., Dec. 6, 1918; s. Malcolm Newton and Elizabeth (Gilbert) W.; m. Emma Secul Depolo, Dec. 21, 1959. AB magna cum laude,

Harvard U., 1940, LLB, 1948; LLD (hon.), Rose-Hulman Inst. Tech., 1984. Bar: Tex. 1948, NY 1963, US Supreme Ct. 1952, DC 1970. US atty. So. Dist. Tex., 1954-58; asst. atty. gen. US, 1958-61; ptnr. Butler Binion Rice & Cook, 1961-63; gen. counsel, sec. Kennecott Copper Corp., 1963-70; judge US Ct. Appeals DC Cir., 1970-85; US amb. to Uruguay, 1985-90. Ofcl. in charge fed. forces at Little Rock Sch. Crisis, Dept. Justice, 1958; mem. US-Chile Arbitration Commn., 1991-97; lectr. internat. constl. and adminstrv. law London Poly., 1979, 80; lectr. Tulane U. Law Summer Sch., Grenoble, France, 1981, 83, San Diego Law Summer Sch., Oxford, Eng., 1983, Brigham Young Law Sch., 1984, 93; vis. fellow Wolfson Coll., Cambridge U., 1985; chmn. Pres.'s Commn. on Revision Fed. Ethics Laws, 1989; spl. counsel to Atty. Gen. for inquiry into the House Banking Facility, 1992. Author: Is It Time For A Second Constitutional Convention, 1995, As the Twig is Bent, 2003. Del. Rep. Nat. Conv., 1960. Served from 2d lt. to lt. col. AUS, 1941-45. Named Am. mem., Fulbright Commn., 2002—; hon. fellow, Wolfson Coll., Cambridge. Fellow Am. Bar Found.; mem. Am. Law Inst. (adv. com. restatement fgn. rels. law of US), Jud. Conf. US (com. on standards for admission to fed. cts. 1976-79), Phi Beta Kappa, Delta Sigma Rho, Phi Delta Phi (hon.). Republican. Address: Av El Bosque 379 Providencia Santiago Chile E-mail: mrw@wilkey.us.

**WILKIE, DONALD WALTER,** retired biologist, aquarium administrator; b. Vancouver, BC, Can., June 20, 1931; s. Otway James Henry and Jessie Margaret (McLeod) W.; m. Patricia Ann Archer, May 18, 1980; children: Linda, Douglas, Susanne. BA, U. B.C., 1960, M.Sc., 1966. Curator Vancouver Pub. Aquarium, 1961-63, Phila. Aquarama, 1963-65; exec. dir. aquariummus. Scripps Instn. Oceanography, La Jolla, Calif., 1965-93, exec. dir. emeritus, 1993—; founding dir. Birch Aquarium of Scripps, 1992. Cons. aquarium design, rschg. exhibit content; sci. writer and editor naturalistmarine edn. programs. coach, Scholastic Clay Targets Prog. Author books on aquaria and marine ednl. materials; contbr. numerous articles to profl. jours. Bd. mem. San Diego Shotgun Sports Assn.; pres. UCSD Retirement Assn. 1999-02. Mem. San Diego (Calif.) Zool. Soc. Home: 4548 Cather Ave San Diego CA 92122-2632 Office: U Calif San Diego Scripps Instn Oceanography Libr 9500 Gilman Dr La Jolla CA 92093-0219 E-mail: dwilkie@ucsd.edu, donwilkie1@mac.com. *As a biologist and teacher my major goal has been to increase public interest in learning about our environment and promoting proper use of the earth's resources.*

**WILKIN, RICHARD EDWIN,** clergyman, religious organization administrator; b. nr. Paulding, Ohio, Nov. 3, 1930; s. Gaylord D. and Beulah E. (Tarlton) W.; m. Barbara A. Zehender, Aug. 10, 1952; children— Richard Edward, James Lee, Deborah Ann. Student, Giffin Jr. Coll., 1948-49; BS, Findlay Coll., 1952, D.D., 1975; postgrad., Ind. U., 1959-60. Ordained to ministry Churches of God Gen. Conf., 1953; pastor Neptune Ch. of God, Celina, Ohio, 1952-59, Wharton (Ohio) Ch. of God, 1959-64, Anthony Wayne Ch. of God, Ft. Wayne, Ind., 1964-70; adminstr., chief exec. Chs. of God Gen. Conf., Findlay, Ohio, 1970-87; supr. mission work India, Bangladesh, Haiti, 1970-85; dir. field edn. and Inst. for Biblical Studies, faculty mem. Winebrenner Theol. Sem., Findlay, 1987-92, adj. facultt O.T., 1993-97; interim sr. pastor Coll. 1st Ch. of God, Findlay, 1992-93. Dir. summer youth camps, sec., mem. exec. com. Ohio Conf., 1952-59, state clk., pres., 1959-64; chmn. Commn. on Edn., mem. exec. com. Ind. Conf., 1964-70; adv. com. Am. Bible Soc.; steering com. U.S. Ch. Leaders, 1979; pres. Ft. Wayne Ministerial Assn.; bd. dirs. Associated Chs. of Ft. Wayne and Allen County, 1966-70; tchr. Center Twp. Jr. High Sch., Celina, Mendon (Ohio) Union High Sch., Van Del High Sch., Van Wert, Ohio, 1954-59; interim pastor Shawnee First Ch. of God, Lima, Ohio, 1987-88, ch. cons., 1987-93. Vice pres. bd. trustees Winebrenner Haven, mem. adv. com. in race rels. regarding sch. reorgn. and busing, Ft. Wayne, 1967-69; trustee Winebrenner Theol. Sem., 1980-87, sec. bd. trustees; trustee U. Findlay, 1985—, chmn. com. trustees; sec. bd. of pensions Gen. Conf., Ch. of God, 1986-99; bd. dirs. Found. Great Lakes, Conf. Chs. of God, 1998-2006, chmn. adminstr.'s adv. com., 1998-2003. Recipient Outstanding Tchr. award, 1958; Disting. Alumnus award Findlay Coll., 1973, Outstanding Leadership award Ohio Conf. Chs. of God, 1986, Disting. Assoc. award U. Findlay, 1992; named Hon. Alumnus Winebrenner Theol. Sem., 1978.

**WILKINS, AMY P.,** publishing executive; BA, Holy Cross Coll. Assoc. pub., advt. dir. Health Mag. 1994—95, pub., 1995—97; pres. Petersen Youth Group1, 1997—98; pub. Biography Mag., 1998—2000, Smithsonian, Smithsonian Air & Space Mag., 2000, Better Homes and Gardens Mag., Country Home, 2006—. Office: Country Home Mag Meredith Publ 375 Lexington Ave New York NY 10017-5514*

**WILKINS, BARRATT (GEORGE WILKINS),** librarian; b. Atlanta, Nov. 6, 1943; s. George Barratt and Mabel Blanche (Brooks) W. BA, Emory U., 1965; MA, Ga. State U., 1968, U. Wis., 1969. Reference libr. SC State Libr., Columbia, 1969-71; instl. libr. cons. Mo. State Libr., Jefferson City, 1971-73; asst. state libr. State Libr. Fla., Tallahassee, 1973-77, state libr., 1977—2003; div. div. Libr. and Info. Svcs. State Fla., Tallahassee, 1986—2003; acting asst. sec. state Fla. Dept. of State, 1987. Abstractor Hist. Abstracts, 1967—71; dir. survey project Nat. Ctr. Edn. Stats., 1976—77, chmn. state libr. agys. survey steering coun., 2003—; bd. dirs. S.E. Libr. Network, Inc., 1979—82, treas., 1980—81, vice chmn., 1981—82; mem. adv. coun. US Pub. Printer, 1983—86, S.E. Atlantic Regional Med. Libr. Svcs., 1986—89; mem. planning com. Fla. Automated Edn. Commn., 1989—94; del The White House Conf., Libr. Info. Svcs., 1991; mem. steering com. pub., state libr. surveys Nat. Ctr. Edn. Stats., 1992—; mem. adv. coun. Fla. State Bd. Ind. Colleges, Universities, 1995—98, Fla. State U. Sch. Info. Studies, 1999—2000; mem. pub. libr. surveys Nat. Ctr. Ednl. Stats., 1997—2003; mem. privacy, tech. task force State Fla., 2000—01; mem. Speakers Legis. Hist. Preservation Com., 2000—03; mem. libr. stats. revision com. Nat. Info. Stds. Orgn., 2001—03; del The White House Conf. Sch. Librs., 2002; bd. dirs. First Am. Found., Inc., Fla. Distance Learning Network, Inc.; mem. planning com. Fla. Gov.'s Conf. Libraries, Info. svcs.; cons. in field. Contbr. articles profl. jours. Mem. adv. com. statewide jail project Mo. Assn. Social Welfare, 1971-73; bd. dirs. ctrl. divsn., 1971-73; mem. State Univ. System Interinstl. Lib. Com., 1977-2003; bd. dirs. Fla. Ctr. for Libr. Automation, 1984-2003, Fla. Ctr. for the Book, 1984—, Fla. Coll. Ctr. for Libr. Automation, 1990-2003, Coun. for Fla. Librs., 1981—; pres. Rose Hollow Homeowners Assn., 2004—; patron Atlanta Hist. Soc., Hist. Oakland Found. Recipient Leadership Achievement award Assn. Specialized and Coop. Libr. Agys., 1991, Outstanding Pub. Svc. award Gov. of Fla., 1991, Keppel award and Lorenz award Nat. Ctr. Edn. Stats., 1995—, Profl. Achievement award Assn. Specialized and Coop. Libr. Agencies, 2003, Disting. Alumni award U. Wis. Sch. Libr. and Info. Studies, 2003; U. Wis. fellow, 1969. Mem. ALA (coun. 1981-85, legis. com. 1982-86, com. on orgn. 1988-90, planning com., 1993-95, standards, 1996-98, legis. honor roll 1996), Assn. State Libr. Agys. (pres. 1976-77), Assn. Hosp. Instl. Librs. (bd. dirs. 1973-74), Am. Correctional Assn. (chair instrn. libr. com 1975-80), Southeastern Libr. Assn. (pres. 1982-84), Assn. Specialized and Coop. Libr. Agys. (bd. dirs. 1981-85, 87-89, sscls. rev. 1997—2003, chair awards com., 2003-05, chair legis. com., 2005-), Fla. Libr. Assn. (hon. life mem.), Libr. Adminstrn. and Mgmt. Assn. (chair govt. affair com 1984-86), Chief Officers of State Libr. Agys. (bd. dirs. 1980-82, pres. 1990-92, chair legis. com. 1992-96, chair rsch. & stats. com. 1998-2003), Univ. Club, Gov.'s Club, Beta Phi Mu, Phi Alpha Theta. Episcopalian. E-mail: barratt.wilkins@mac.com.

**WILKINS, BURLEIGH TAYLOR,** philosophy educator; b. Bridgetown, Va., July 1, 1932; s. Burleigh and Helen Marie (Taylor) W.; children: Brita Taylor, Carla Cowgill, Burleigh William. BA summa cum laude, Duke U., 1952; MA, Harvard U., 1954, Princeton U., 1963, PhD, 1965. Instr. MIT, Cambridge, 1957-60, Princeton U., 1960-61, 63; asst. prof. Rice U., Houston, 1965-66, assoc. prof., 1966-67, U. Calif., Santa Barbara, 1967-68, prof., 1968—. Author: Carl Becker, 1961, The Problem of Burke's Political Philosophy, 1967, Hegel's Philosophy of History, 1974, Has History Any Meaning?, 1978, Terrorism and Collective Responsibility, 1992. Mem. Phi Beta Kappa. Office: U Calif Dept Philosophy Santa Barbara CA 93106

**WILKINS, CAROLINE HANKE,** advocate, political organization worker; b. Corpus Christi, Tex., May 12, 1937; d. Louis Allen and Jean Guckian Hanke; m. B. Hughel Wilkins, 1957; 1 child, Brian Hughel. Student, Tex. Coll. Arts and Industries, 1956—57, Tex. Tech. U., 1957—58; BA, U. Tex., 1961; MA magna cum laude, U. Ams., 1964. Instr. history Oreg. State U., 1967-68; administr. Consumer Svcs. divsn. State of Oreg., 1977-80, Wilkins Assoc., 1980—. Mem. PFMC Salmon Adv. subpanel, 1982-86. Author: (with B. H. Wilkins) Implications of the U.S.-Mexican Water Treaty for Interregional Water Transfer, 1968. Dem. precinct committeewoman, Benton County, Oreg., 1964-90; publicity chmn. Benton County Gen. Election, 1964; chmn. Get-Out-the-Vote Com., Benton County, 1966; vice chmn. Benton County Dem. Ctrl. Com., 1966-70; vice chmn. 1st Congl. Dist., Oreg., 1966-67, chmn., 1967-68; vice chmn. Dem. Party of Oreg., 1968-69, chmn., 1969-74; mem. exec. com. Western States Dem. Conf., 1970-72; vice chmn. Dem. Nat. Com., 1972-77, mem. arrangements com., 1972, 76, mem. Dem. Charter Commn., 1973-74; mem. Dem. Nat. Com., 1972-77, 85-89, mem. size and composition com., 1987-89, rules com., 1988; mem. ethics commn., Oreg. Govt., 1974-76; del., mem. rules com. Dem. Nat. Conv., 1988; 1st v.p. Nat. Fedn. Dem. Women, 1983-85, pres., 1985-87, parliamentarian, 1993-95, 99-2001, chair Pres.'s coun., 2001-2003, chair by-laws com., 2003-05, parlimentarian, 2005-, we. regional dir., 2005—, western region dir., 2005-; mem. Kerr Libr. bd. Oreg. State U., 1989-95, pres., 1994-95; mem. Corvallis-Benton County Libr. Found., 1991-2001, sec., 1993, v.p., 1994, pres., 1995, mission and goals com. chair 2000-01; bd. dirs. Oreg. chpt. U.S. Lighthouse Soc., pres., 1997-98; bd. dirs. Oreg. State U.-Corvallis Symphony, 1998-2001, v.p. 1999-2000, resources com.; pres. Oreg. Fedn. Dem. Women, 1997-2001, Oreg. State-Corvallis chpt., UNIFEM, 1998-2002; bd. dirs. Oreg. State U. Acad. Lifelong Learning, 2003—; mem. Women and Philanthropy, Oreg. State U. Giving Cir., 2003; mem. Oreg. Jud. Fitness and Disability Commn., 2004-, vice chair, 2005-. Named Outstanding Mem. Nat. Fedn. Dem. Women, 1992, Woman of Achievement, Oreg. State U. Women's Ctr., 1998. Mem.: Soc. Consumer Affairs Profls., Nat. Assn. Consumer Agy. Adminstrs., Oreg. State U. Folk Club (pres. faculty wives 1989—90, scholarship chair 2000—01, grants com. 2002—03), Zonta Internat. (vice area bd. dirs. dist. 8 1992—94, bd. dist. 8 1994—96, by laws and resolutions chair 1997—98, internat. rels. coord. dist. 8 2000—02, chair dist. 8 nominating com. 2003—06, parliamentarian 2006—). Office: 3311 NW Roosevelt Dr Corvallis OR 97330-1169

**WILKINS, CHARLES L.,** chemist, educator; b. L.A., Aug. 14, 1938; s. Richard and Lenore M. Wilkins; m. Ingrid Fritsch, 1997; children: Mark R., Connor W. Fritsch, Eric. BS, Chapman Coll., 1961; PhD, U. Oreg., 1966. Prof. chemistry U. Nebr., Lincoln, 1967-81; prof. U. Calif., Riverside, 1981-98; disting. prof. U. Ark., Fayetteville, 1998—. Recipient Frank H. Field and Joe L. Franklin award for Outstanding Achievement in mass spectrometry, Am. Chem. Soc., 1997, Eastern Analytical Symposium award in the fields of Analytical Chemistry, 2002, Alumni Disting. Achievement award, Ark. U., 2003, Alumni Achievement award, U. Oreg. Dept. Chemistry, 2004. Office: U Ark Dept Chem & Biochem Fayetteville AR 72701 Office Phone: 479-575-3160. E-mail: cwilkins@uark.edu.

**WILKINS, CHRISTOPHER PUTNAM,** conductor; b. Boston, May 28, 1957; s. Herbert Putnam and Angela (Middleton) W. BA, Harvard U., 1978; MusM, Yale U., 1981. Condr.-in-residence SUNY, Purchase, 1981-82; asst. condr. Oreg. Symphony, Portland, 1982-83, Cleve. Orch., 1983-86; assoc. condr. Utah Symphony, Salt Lake City, from 1986; condr. Colo. Springs Symphony Orch., 1989-96, artistic advisor, 1998—; music dir. San Antonio Symphony, 1992—. Condr. Exxon Arts Endowment, 1982-86. Office: San Antonio Symphony Po Box 658 San Antonio TX 78293-0658 Home: 11 Edmonds Rd Concord MA 01742-2649

**WILKINS, DAVID BRIAN,** law educator; b. Chgo., Jan. 22, 1956; BA in Govt., Harvard U., 1977, JD, 1980. Bar: DC 1982. Law clk. to Hon. Wilfred Feinberg US Ct. Appeals 2nd Cir., NY, 1980—81; law clk. to Justice Thurgood Marshall US Supreme Ct., 1981—82; assoc. Nussbaum, Owen & Webster, Washington, 1982—86; asst. prof. law Harvard Law Sch., Cambridge, Mass., 1986—92, prof., 1992—, Kirkland and Ellis prof. law, 1996—, dir. Program on the Legal Profession, 1991—. Office: Harvard Law Sch 1563 Massachusetts Ave Cambridge MA 02138 Office Phone: 617-495-0958. Office Fax: 617-496-4880. Business E-Mail: dwilkins@law.harvard.edu.

**WILKINS, DAVID GEORGE,** fine arts educator; b. Battle Creek, Mich., Sept. 12, 1939; s. George Henry and Marjorie Ewing (Pierce) Wilkins; m. Ann Thomas, June 25, 1961; children: Rebecca Louise, Katherine May. BA, Oberlin Coll., 1961; MA, U. Mich., 1963, PhD, 1969. Instr. U. N.H., Durham, 1963—64; prof. dept. history of art and arch. U. Pitts., 1967—, chair, 1989—92, 1998—2004, dir. univ. art gallery, 1976—92. Faculty mem summer sessions Sarah Lawrence Col-Univ Mich, Florence, Italy, 1975—81. Author (with Bernard Schultz and Katheryn M Linduff): Art Past/Art Present, 2004; author: (with Bonnie Bennett) Donatello, 1984, Maso di Banco, 1985; author: (with K J Arbitman) The Illustrated Bartsch, Vol 53, Pre-Rembrandt Etchers, 1985, The Art of the Duquesne Club, 2002; author: (with Mark M Brown and Lu Donnelly) The History of the Duquesne Club, 1989; author: (with F. Hartt) History of Italian Renaissance Art, 6th edit., 2006; editor (with Rebecca L Wilkins): The Search for a Patron in the Middle Ages and the Renaissance, 1996; editor: (with Sheryl Reiss) Beyond Isabella: Secular Women Patrons of Art in the Italian Renaissance, 2001; editor: The Collins Big Book of Art, 2005. Mem Humanities Coun, 1984—88; mus adv panel Pa Coun Arts, 1985—87; bd dirs Pittsburgh Cir Arts, 1979—98; Mendelssohn Choir Pittsburgh, 1979—84. Recipient Chancellor's Disting. Tchg. award, U. Pitts., 1987; fellow William E. Suida, Kress Found, Kunsthistorisches Inst, Florence, 1966—67. Mem.: Renaissance Soc. Am., Italian Art Soc., Coll. Art Assn. (Disting. Tchg. Art History award 2005). Democrat. Home: 1217 Shady Ave Pittsburgh PA 15232-2811 E-mail: dgw2@pitt.edu.

**WILKINS, DAVID HORTON,** ambassador, former state legislator; b. Greenville, SC, Oct. 12, 1946; m. Susan Clary; children: James, Robert. BA (hon.), Clemson U., 1968; JD, U. SC, 1971; degree (hon.), Med. U. SC, Citadel. Bar: S.C. Mem. S.C. Ho. of Reps., 1980—2005, chmn. judiciary com., 1986—92, speaker pro tempore, 1992-95, speaker, 1995—2005; US amb. to Can. US Dept. State, Ottawa, 2005—. Adj. prof. Greenville Tech. Coll., 1972—94; chmn. Greenville County Legis. Del., 1985—86; pres. Nat. Speakers Assn., 1998—2005; fellow Am. Acad. Matrimonial Lawyers. Served in U.S. Army, 1971 USAR, 1973—76. Recipient Friend of the Taxpayer award S.C. Assn. Taxpayers, others; named Outstanding Legislator of Yr. by S.C. C. of C., Dept. Probation of Parole, S.C. Sch. Bds. Assn., S.C. Troopers Assn., others, Nat. Republican Legislator of Yr. Nat. Rep. Legis. Assn. Republican. Baptist. Office: DOS Amb 5480 Ottawa Pl Washington DC 20521-5480*

**WILKINS, EARLE WAYNE, JR.,** retired surgery educator; b. Albany, N.Y., Aug. 17, 1919; s. Earle Wayne and Mildred Anna (Dana) W.; m. Suzanne Porter, Aug. 26, 1944; children: Clinton Porter, Wendy Dana Wilkins Hopkins, Wayne Lawrence. AB, Williams Coll., 1941; MD, Harvard U., 1944. Diplomate Am. Bd. Surgery, Am. Bd. Thoracic Surgery. Surg. resident Mass. Gen. Hosp., Boston, 1944-46, 48-51, mem. staff, 1952-59, vis. surgeon, 1968-78; mem. staff Harvard Med. Sch., Boston, 1953—, clin. prof. surgery, 1979-89, prof. emeritus, 1989—. Fulbright vis. prof. Allgemeines Krankenhaus, Vienna, Austria, 1964-65; vis. prof. Nat. Def. Med. Ctr., Taipei, Taiwan, 1989; surgeon Boston Bruins Hockey Club, 1969-85; physician tech. advisor Divsn. Emergency Med. Svcs., Washington, 1977-81, med. dir. Mass. Region IV, Boston, 1980-82; chmn. bd. Boston Med. Flight, 1985-87; Earle W. Wilkins, Jr. vis. prof. MGH, 1998. Editor: Current Therapy in Cardiothoracic Surgery, 1989, Esophageal Cancer, 1988, Emergency Medicine: Scientific Foundations and Current Practice, 1989; contbr. numerous articles to profl. jours. Trustee Williams Coll., Williamstown, Mass., 1971-89, pres. Soc. of Alumni, 1967-69. Lt. (j.g.) USNR, 1946-48. Recipient Sports Illustrated Silver Anniversary All-Am. award Time Inc., N.Y.C., 1965, Commonwealth award Commonwealth of Mass., 1986, Disting. Alumnus award Albany Acad., 1988, Rogerson Cup Williams Coll., 1991, Bicentennial medal

Williams Coll., 1993. Fellow ACS, Am. Surg. Assn.; mem. AMA, Mass. Med. Soc., Boston Surg. Soc., Am. Assn. Thoracic Surgery (councillor 1984-88), Soc. Thoracic Surgeons, New England Surg. Soc. (pres. 1980-81), Gen. Thoracic Surg. Club, Taconic Golf Club (pres. 1990-95). Republican. Achievements include Emergency Dept. No. Adams Regional Hosp., 2004, named in honor of. Avocations: golf, tennis, skiing, travel, stamps. Home: 240 South St Williamstown MA 01267-2822

**WILKINS, FLOYD, JR.,** lawyer, educator; b. Fowler, Calif., Sept. 8, 1925; s. Floyd and Kathryn (Springborg) W.; m. Holly Blee, June 18, 1949 (div. Jan. 1964); children: Douglas B., Janet H., Steven B., Kevin D.; m. Sybil Ann Perrault, Feb. 22, 1964. BS, U. Calif., Berkeley, 1946; LLB, Harvard U., 1952. Bar: N.Y. 1953, Calif. 1959. Assoc. Dwight, Royall, Harris, Koegel & Caskey, N.Y.C., 1952-58; v.p., trust officer San Diego Trust & Savs. Bank, 1958-63; assoc., then ptnr., prin. Seltzer Caplan Wilkins & McMahon, P.C. and predecessors, San Diego, 1963-91. Lectr. U. So. Calif. Tax Inst., L.A., 1975, Title Ins. and Trust Co., L.A. and Santa Ana, Calif., 1973, 78, 83, Trust Svcs. of Am. Tax Forum, San Diego, U. Calif. Continuing Edn. of Bar, San Diego, 1977-91. Bd. dirs., pres. San Diego County Citizens Scholarship Found. Served with USNR, 1944-46. Mem. ABA, State Bar Calif., San Diego County Bar Assn. Republican. Avocations: travel, photography, wine, gardening. Home: 2005 Soledad Ave La Jolla CA 92037-3904 Personal E-mail: fwilkins@san.rr.com.

**WILKINS, FRED CLAYTON,** physician, educator, engineer; b. Barnwell, SC, Aug. 18, 1958; s. Fred C. Wilkins and Mary Josephine Erskine; m. Sharon Rawls Wilkins, Dec. 1, 1990 (dec. June 26, 2004); 1 child, Marshall Clayton. BS in Applied Sciences and Engring., US Mil. Acad., West Point, 1980; MS in Systems Mgmt., U. So. Calif., 1988; MD, U. Miss. Med. Ctr., 1997; M in Biomedical Sci., U. Miss., Jackson, 2004. Cert. flight instr. FAA, 1991. Airborne inf. officer Inf. Ctr., Fort Benning, Ga., 1980—81; flight instr. Army Aviation Ctr., Fort Rucker, Ala., 1982—84; aviation platoon leader Fourth Squadron, Seventh US Cav., Uijongbu, Republic of Korea, 1984—85; aviation maintenance co. comdr. Fifth Squadron, Seventeenth Air Cav., Fort Hood, Tex., 1986—88; sr. test program engr. USAF, Eglin, Fla., 1989—90; state aviation standardization officer Miss. Army N.G., Jackson, 1990—91; family practice resident Naval Hosp. Pensacola, Fla., 1997—98; dir. clin. services, sr. med. officer Naval Air Sta. Whiting Field, Pensacola, 1999—2002; naval aviator, flight surgeon dual designator Chief Naval Air Tng., Pensacola, 2003—. Adj. prof. Pensacola Jr. Coll., Fla., 2003—. Editor: (aviation textbook) Naval Helicopter Aerodynamics. Maj. U.S. Army, 1980—93, Republic of Korea, with USN, 1997—. Recipient Proctor and Gamble Profl. Opportunity award, Am. Physiology Soc., 1993, Outstanding Student award, Miss. State Legislature and Bd. Higher Edn., 1997; fellow, Glaxo Rsch. Inst., 1993-1995; Hearin-Hess Scholarship, U. Miss., 1991-1992, Dean's Scholarship, 1992-1995, Health Profession Scholarship, USN, 1993-1997. Mem.: Am. Bd. Utilization Rev. and Quality Assurance (assoc.), US Naval Inst. (life), Army Aviation Assn. Am. (life; treas. 1982—83), Assn. Mil. Surgeons of the US (life). Christian. Avocations: flying, travel, sailing, scuba diving, tennis. Personal E-mail: clay.wilkins@navy.mil.

**WILKINS, J. ERNEST, JR.,** mathematician, educator; b. Chgo., Nov. 27, 1923; s. J. Ernest and Lucille B. (Robinson) W.; m. Gloria Louise Stewart, June 22, 1947 (dec.); children: Sharon Wilkins Hill, J. Ernest III; m. Maxine G. Malone, June 2, 1984 (dec.); m. Vera Anderson, Sept. 12, 2003. BS, U. Chgo., 1940, MS, 1941, PhD, 1942; BME, NYU, 1957, MME, 1960. Mathematician Am. Optical Co., Buffalo, 1946-50; mgr. R&D Internat Nuclear Corp., White Plains, N.Y., 1950-60; assoc. dir. lab. Gen. Atomic Co., San Diego, 1960-70; Disting. prof. applied math. physics Howard U., Washington, 1970-77; vis. scientist Argonne (Ill.) Nat. Lab., 1976-77, fellow, 1984-85; v.p., dep. gen. mgr. EG & G Idaho, Idaho Falls, 1977-84; Disting. prof. Clark Atlanta U., 1990—. Chmn. Army Sci. Bd. Dept. Army, 1978-81; mem. Adv. Com. on Reactor Safeguards, Washington, 1990-94, chmn., 1993-94. Contbr. articles to profl. jours. With AUS, 1946-47. Recipient Outstanding Civilian Svc. medal U.S. Army, 1980. Mem. NAE, Am. Nuclear Soc. (pres. 1974-75, cons. 1987-90), Am. Math. Soc., Am. Math. Assn. Am., Oak Ridge Assn. Univs. (coun. 1990-2003).

**WILKINS, JEFFREY M.,** computer company executive; Co-founder CompuServe, 1969; founder Discovery Sys., 1985-91; pres., CEO Metatec Corp., Dublin, Ohio, 1991—, chmn. bd. dirs. Office: Metatec Internat Inc 7001 Metatec Blvd Dublin OH 43017-3219

**WILKINS, JOHN P.,** university librarian; BA, Antioch Coll., 1979; MA in English, U. Va., 1980; MLS, U. Tenn., 1986. Rsch. libr. resident U. Mich., Ann Arbor, 1986—88, data svcs. libr., English selector, 1988—92, head Humanities Text Initiative, 1994—96, head Digital Libr. Production Svc., 1996—, interim assoc. dir. Digital Libr. Svcs., 2002, assoc. univ. libr. Libr. Info. Tech., 2003—, interim co-univ. libr., 2006—; sys. libr. info. svcs. U. Va., Charlottesville, 1992—94. Contbr. articles to profl. jours. Office: Libr Adminstrn U Mich 818 Hatcher S Ann Arbor MI 48109-1205 Office Phone: 734-764-9356. Office Fax: 734-763-5080. E-mail: jpwilkin@umich.edu.*

**WILKINS, JOHN WARREN,** physics professor; b. Des Moines, Mar. 11, 1936; s. Carl Daniel and Ruth Elizabeth (Warren) W. BS in Engring, Northwestern U., 1959; MS, U. Ill., 1960, PhD, 1963; DTech (hon.), Chalmers Tekniska Hogskola, Göteborg, 1990. NSF fellow U. Cambridge, Eng., 1963-64; asst. prof. physics Cornell U., 1964-68, assoc. prof., 1968-74, prof., 1974-88; eminent scholar, prof. physics Ohio State U., 1988—. Vis. prof. H.C. Ørsted Inst., Copenhagen, 1968, Nordita, Copenhagen, 1972-73, 75-76, 79-81; cons. Los Alamos Nat. Lab., 1984—, Lawrence Livermore Nat. Lab., 1997—; adv. com. U. Chgo. Sci. and Tech., 1990—. Assoc. editor Physica Scripta, 1977-85, Phys. Rev. Letters, 1982-85, Rev. Modern Physics, 1990-93, mem. editorial bd. Phys. Rev. B, 1991 94; coord. Comments on Condensed Matter Physics, 1985-90. Sloan fellow, 1966; Guggenheim fellow, 1985. Fellow AAAS, Am. Phys. Soc. (publs. oversight com. 1995-97, chmn. 1995-96, councillor divsn. condensed matter physics 1993-94, exec. com. divsn. biol. physics 1997-73, vice-chair through past chair divsn. condensed matter physics 2001—); mem. European Phys. Soc. Office: OSU Physics 191 W Woodruff Ave Columbus OH 43210 E-Mail: wilkins@mps.ohio-state.edu.

**WILKINS, MICHAEL JON,** state supreme court justice; b. Murray, Utah, May 13, 1948; s. Jack L. and Mary June (Phillips) W.; m. Diane W. Wilkins, Nov. 9, 1967; children: Jennifer, Stephanie, Bradley J. BS, U. Utah, 1975, JD, 1976; LLM, U. Va., 2001. Bar: Utah 1977, US Dist. Ct. Utah 1977, U.S. Ct. Appeals (10th cir.) 1987, U.S. Supreme Ct. 1986. Mng. ptnr. Wilkins, Oritt & Headman, Salt Lake City, 1989-94; judge Utah Ct. Appeals, 1994—2000; justice Utah Supreme Ct, 2000—03, assoc. chief justice, 2003—, mem. jud. coun., 2000—. Mem. Gov.'s Adv. Com. on Corp., Salt Lake City, 1989-94; mem. Utah Supreme Ct. Complex Steering Com., 1993-94; mem. Judiciary Standing Com. on Tech., 1995-2000, chmn., 1995-2000; mem. Legis. Compensation Commn., 1994-95. Trustee Utah Law Related Edn. Project, Inc., Salt Lake City, 1991-95, chmn., 1992-94. 1st lt. U.S. Army, 1968-72. Mem. Lds Ch. Office: Utah Supreme Ct 450 S State St PO Box 140210 Salt Lake City UT 84114-0210*

**WILKINS, RAYFORD, JR.,** telecommunications industry executive; b. Waco, Tex. m. Lorena Wilkins; 1 child. BBA, U. Tex., Austin, 1974. Comml. asst. Southwestern Bell Tel., Houston, 1974; with SBC Comm., 1983—2005, pres. Kans. & western Mo. area, pres. Pacific Bell Bus. Comm. Svcs., 1997, pres. SBC Comm. Svc., 1997—99, pres. CEO Southwestern Bell Tel., pres. SBC bus. comm. svcs., 1999—2000, pres., CEO Pacific Bell, 2000, grp. pres. SBC mktg. & sales, 2000, grp. pres., CEO SBC enterprise bus. svcs.; grp. pres. internat. ops. AT&T Inc. (merger of SBC Comm. with AT&T Corp.), San Antonio, 2005—. Mem. bd. Cingular Wireless; bd. mem. H&R Block, Telefonos de Mexico, Am. Movil. Bd. mem. AT&T Found., Tiger Woods Found., Tiger Woods Learning Ctr.; mem. adv. coun. U. Tex. McCombs Sch. Bus., Austin. Named CEO of Yr., Minority Supplier Coun., 1997; named one of Top 50 African Ams., Black Enterprise mag., 1999, Nation's 50 Most

Powerful Black Execs., Fortune mag., 2002, 50 Most Important African Ams. in Tech., eAccess Corp., 2002, 2005, 75 Most Powerful African Ams. in Corp. Am., Black Enterprise mag., 2005, 100 Most Important Blacks in Tech., US Black Engr. & Info. Tech. mag., 2006, Top 100 Blacks in Corp. Am., Black Profl. mag., 2006; recipient Eagle award, Nat. Eagles Leadership Inst., 1997. Mailing: AT&T Inc 175 E Houston St PO Box 2933 San Antonio TX 78299-2933*

**WILKINS, ROBERT HENRY,** neurosurgeon, educator, editor; b. Pitts., Aug. 18, 1934; s. George H. and Mary M. (Lemon) W.; m. Gloria A. Kohl, Dec. 28, 1957; children: Michael I., Jeffrey K., Elizabeth A. BS, U. Pitts., 1955, MD, 1959. Diplomate Am. Bd. Neurol. Surgery. Intern, resident gen. surgery Duke U. Med. Ctr., Durham, NC, 1959-61, resident in neurosurgery, 1963-68, asst. prof. neurosurgery, 1968-72, prof. neurosurgery, 1976—2004, chief divsn. neurosurgery, 1976-96, emeritus prof. neurosurgery, 2005—; clin. assoc. surgery br. Nat. Cancer Inst., Bethesda, Md., 1961-63; chmn. dept. neurosurgery Scott and White Clinic, Temple, Tex., 1972-75; assoc. prof. neurosurgery U. Pitts., 1975-76. Lectr. Cook County Grad. Sch. Medicine, Chgo., 1976-96; attending neurosurgeon Durham VA Hosp., 1968-72, 78-98; mem. Nat. Adv. Coun. Nat. Inst. Neurol. Disorders and Stroke, 1989-92. Co-editor: Neurosurgery, 2d edit., 3 vols., 1996, Neurosurgery Updates I and II, 1990, 91, Neurosurgical Operative Atlas, 1991-2000, Principles of Neurosurgery, 1994; editor Clin. Neurosurgery, 1972-75; assoc. editor Surg. Neurology, 1975-76; founding editor Neurosurgery, 1977-82, mem. editl. rev. bd., 1997-2001; mem. editl. bd. Jour. Neurosurgery, 1987-96, chmn., 1996-97, mem. adv. bd., 1997—; neurosurgery editor Key Neurology and Neurosurgery, 1993-96, Yr. Book of Neurology and Neurosurgery, 1994-97. Recipient Travel award Copenhagen, Nat. Inst. Neurol. Diseases and Blindness, 1965, Royal Australasian Coll. Surgeons, Found. lectr. Adelaide 1986. Fellow ACS (gov. 1996); mem. Congress Neurol. Surgeons (pres. 1979-80), Am. Assn. Neurol. Surgeons (treas. 1989-92), So. Neurosurg. Soc. (sec. 1988-91, pres. 1992-93), Soc. Neurol. Surgeons (v.p. 1995-96), Am. Bd. Neurol. Surgery (dir. 1991-97, chmn. 1996-97), Phi Beta Kappa, Alpha Omega Alpha. Democrat. Avocation: medical writing and editing. Office: Duke U Med Ctr PO Box 3807 Durham NC 27710-0001 E-mail: rhwilkins@aol.com.

**WILKINS, ROBERT L.,** lawyer; b. Muncie, Ind., 1963; BS cum laude, Rose-Hulman Inst. Tech., 1986; JD, Harvard Law Sch., 1989. Bar: DC, US Dist. Ct. Appeals DC Circuit, US Dist. Ct. DC, US Dist. Ct. Md., US Supreme Ct. Clk. US Dist. Judge, 1989; with DC Pub. Defender's Office, 1990—2000; ptnr., Corp. Def. White Collar, Comml. Litigation, Appellate Litigation practices Venable LLP, 2000—. Vis. instr. Harvard's Law Sch. Trial Advocacy Workshop, 1996, 99; mem. DC Truth-in-Sentencing Commn., 1997—98, DC Adv. Com. Sentencing, 1998—2000, DC Juvenile Justice Adv. Group, 1998—2000, DC Access to Justice Commn., 2005—; lectr. Georgetown Univ. Law Ctr., Washington Coll. Law, Am. Univ., George Washington Univ. Contbr. articles to profl. jours. Founder Nat. African Am. Mus. and Cultural Complex, 1999. Named a Top Washington Lawyer, Washingtonian Mag., 2004; named Practitioner Yr. award, U. Md. Black Law Student Assn., 1999, Pro Bono Atty. Yr., Am. Civil Liberties Union Md., 2001; named one of 40 Under 40 Most Successful Young Litigators in Am., Nat. Law Jour.; recipient Henry W. Edgerton Civil Liberties award, Am. Civil Liberties Union Fund Nat. Capital Area, 2001. Office: Venable LLP 575 7th St NW Washington DC 20004 Office Phone: 202-344-4058. Office Fax: 202-344-8300. Business E-Mail: rlwilkins@venable.com.*

**WILKINS, ROBERT PEARCE,** writer, lawyer; b. Jesup, Ga., Sept. 10, 1933; s. Ransom Little and Sarah (Pearce) W.; m. Rose Truesdale, Jan. 7, 1956; children: Robert Pearce, Chisolm Wallace (dec.), Sarah Ruth Weiss, Rose Anne Brooks. BA, U. S.C., 1953, JD, 1954; LL.M., Georgetown U., 1957. Bar: S.C. 1954; cert. mediator and arbitrator, S.C. Atty. Office Gen. Counsel, Sec. Army, Washington, 1956; trust officer First Nat. Bank S.C., Columbia, 1957-60; practice law Columbia, 1960-64; ptnr. McLain, Sherrill & Wilkins, Columbia, 1964-68, McKay, Sherrill, Walker, Townsend & Wilkins, Columbia, 1969-75; sole practice law Columbia and Lexington, S.C., 1975-88; of counsel Nelson, Mullins, Riley & Scarborough, Lexington, 1988—. Pres. Sandlapper Press, Inc., 1967-72, pub. Sandlapper Mag. S.C., 1968-72; editor Sandlapper Mag. S.C., 1968-69, 89—; editor, pub. S.C. History Illustrated, 1970; pres. R.P.W. Pub. Corp.; mem., chmn. S.C. Splty. Adv. Bd. Estate Planning and Probate, 1982-85; lectr. in law U. S.C., 1971-78. Author: Draftin Wills and Trust Agreements in South Carolina, 1971, Drafting Wills and Trust Agreements in Michigan, 1978, Wills and Trust System (Arkansas), 1978, Drafting Wills and Trust Agreements: A Systems Approach, 1998, 3d edit., 1999, software edit., 50 Things to Do with the Rest of Your Life, 2003; (with others) Word Processing for a Law Office, 1979, also articles; editor: The Lawyer's Microcomputer, 1982-85, The Lawyer's PC, 1983-97, What a Lawyer Needs to Know to Buy and Use a Computer, 1984, The Perfect Lawyer, 1990-97, The Lawyer's Word, 1991, Shepard's Elder Care/Law Newsletter, 1991-95, Hot docs Toolbox, 1996-97, Drafting Wills and Trust Agreements Newsletter, 1997. Del., Spl. Liaison Tax Com. Southeastern Region, 1967-70; exec. com. Richland County Rep. Com., 1960-64; sec.-treas. Richland County Rep. Club, 1960; bd. dirs. Ctrl. Tb-RD Assn.; trustee Sch. Dist. 1, Lexington County, S.C., 1971-78, sec., 1972-75, chmn., 1975-78; mem. S.C. Commn. on Higher Edn., 1978-80, S.C. Commn. on Lawyer Competence, 1980-82; bd. dirs. Crime Stoppers of the Midlands, 1983-85, RPW Learning Ctr., 1987-94, Mt. Hope Cemetary, 1991—, also v.p., 1992—; v.p. 11th cir. Alumni Coun. U. S.C., 1993-95, mem. awards com., 1995-97; mem. commn. Riverbanks Zoo, 1986—, sec., 1991-95, chmn., 1995-96, 97—, vice-chmn., 1996-97. With AUS, 1954-55. Recipient Compleat Lawyer award Law Sch. U. S.C., 1997, Diamond Circle award U. S.C. Coll. Journalism and Mass Comms., 1998. Fellow Am. Bar Found., Am. Coll. Trust and Estate Counsel (publs. com. 1984-87, bd. regents 1986-87, mem. tech. com. 1988-89, Am. Coll. Tax Counsel, Coll. Law Practice Mgmt (charter, trustee 1994-98), S.C. Bar (tax coordinating com. 1968-70, chmn. legal econs. com. 1973-75, ho. of dels. 1978-80, editor S.C. Lawyer 1989-91, chmn. alternative dispute resolution sect. 1993—), S.C. Bar Found. (life, bd. dirs. 1984-88, v.p. 1986-87, pres. 1987-88); mem. ABA (ho. of dels. 1986-87, chmn. valuation subcom., estate and gift tax com., taxation sect. 1967-73, vice chmn. svc. and assistance to law student div. com. gen. practice sect. 1971-72, vice chmn. corp. counsel com. gen. practice sect. 1972-74, editor econs. of law practice sect. legal econs. 1974-78, sec. 1977-78, vice chmn. 1978-79, chmn. 1980-81, mem. standing com. assn. comm. 1981-84, real property, probate and trust law, mem. publs. com. 1985-89, editor Probate and Property, 1986-89), Richland County Bar Assn. (chmn. probate sect. 1973-74, unauthorized practice of law com. 1976), Lexington County Bar (chmn. mediation com. 1994—), Columbia Jaycees (sec.-treas. 1958-59), Columbia Estate Planning Coun. (pres. 1964-65), Am. Y-Flyer Yacht Racing Assn. (area v.p. 1971, internat. dir. 1972-73), Omicron Delta Kappa, Sigma Chi Clubs: Columbia Sailing (dir. 1968-71), Columbia Tip Off (dir. 1968-73), Columbia (pres. 1971-72). Home: 124 Lake Murray Ct Lexington SC 29072-9104 also: PO Box 729 Lexington SC 29071-0729 E-mail: rpw@50thingstodo.com.*

**WILKINS, WILLIAM WALTER,** federal judge; b. Anderson, S.C., Mar. 29, 1942; s. W. Walter Wilkins and Evelyn Louise (Horton); m. Debra Ann Dill, Aug. 19, 1999; children: Lauren, Lyn, Walt. BA, Davidson Coll., 1964; JD, U. S.C., 1967. Bar: S.C. 1967, U.S. Dist. Ct. S.C. 1967, U.S. Ct. Appeals (4th cir.) 1969, U.S. Supreme Ct. 1970. Law clk. to Hon. Clement F. Haynsworth Jr. U.S. Ct. Appeals (4th cir.), 1969—70; legal asst. to U.S. Senator Strom Thurmond, 1970—71; ptnr. Wilkins & Wilkins, Greenville, SC, 1971—78; solicitor 13th Jud. Cir., 1974—81; judge U.S. Dist. Ct. Greenville, 1981—86; U.S. Ct. Appeals (4th cir.), 1986—, chief judge, 2003—. Lectr. Greenville Tech. Coll., 1973—97, Taft Seminar, Clemson Univ., SC, 1973—97; chmn. U.S. Sentencing Commn., 1985—94; chmn. com. on criminal law Jud. Conf. U.S., 2000—03; disting. prof. Charleston Sch. Law, 2004—. Editor-in-chief: S.C. Law Rev., 1967; contbr. articles to profl. jours. With USAR, 1967—69, with USAR, 1969—83, with S.C. Army Nat. Guard, 1983—94. Mem.: S.C. Bar Assn., Wig and Robe. Republican. Baptist. Office: US Ct Appeals 4th Cir 300 E Washington St Greenville SC 29601-0857*

**WILKINS-CORDERY, RENEE HELENE,** psychologist; b. Grand Rapids, Mich., Mar. 4, 1959; d. Monica Carole Thomaszewski; m. Herbert Carr Wilkins, Oct. 12, 2002; m. Russel Lee Cordery, May 24, 1975 (div. Sept. 5, 1999); children: Geoffrey Lee Cordery, Jason Michael Cordery. D in Psychology, Wright State U., 1999; cert. in psychopharmacology, N.Mex State U., 2005. Lic. psychologist N.Mex, 2004, clin. psychologist Ill., 2000. Psychologist sr. doctorate State of Wis., Winnebago, 2000—04; staff psychologist (forensic) Las Vegas (N.Mex.) Med. Ctr., 2004—05; dir. psychology Cibola County Correctional Ctr., Milan, N.Mex., 2005—. Recipient Redman award, Wright State U. Sch. Profl. Psychology, 1996; grantee, N.Mex Higher Edn. Dept, 2005—. Mem.: APA. Democrat. Avocation: travel. Office: Cibola County Correctional Center 2000 Cibola Loop Milan NM 87021 Office Phone: 505-285-6991 302. Personal E-mail: rhcordery@aol.com.

**WILKINSON, ALAN HERBERT,** nephrologist, educator; b. Johannesburg, July 11, 1948; came to U.S., 1985; s. Raymond C. and Nonie (Levick) W.; m. Angelika A. E. Adami, Dec. 22, 1973; one child: Rebecca Kate Adami. BS in Physiology, Biochemistry, Philosophy, U. Witwatersrand, South Africa, 1969, BS in Biochemistry with honors, 1970, MB, BCh, 1975; cert. health care mgmt., U. Calif., Irvine, 1998. Fellow Royal Coll. Physicians (U.K.), specialist in clin. hypertension. Vis. assoc. Dept. Internal Medicine U. Iowa, Iowa City, 1987-88; assoc. prof. of medicine UCLA Sch. Med., 1988-95, prof. med., 1995—; dir. clin. nephrology UCLA Dept. Med., 1988-93, dir. kidney and pancreas transplantation, 1993—. Contbr. articles to profl. jours. Mem. steering com. Nat. Kidney Found.; mem. U.S. Transplant Games, L.A., 1992; bd. dirs. So. Calif. Renal Disease Coun., 2002-04, med. adv., 2004—. Recipient Exceptional Svc. award Nat. Kidney Found., 1992; Nat. Kidney Found. fellow. Mem. Am. Soc. Transplantation, Internat. Nephrology Soc., Am. Soc. Nephrology. Avocations: ornithology, gardening. Office: UCLA Dept Med 200 Medical Plz Box 951693 Los Angeles CA 90095-1693

**WILKINSON, ALBERT MIMS, JR.,** lawyer; b. Nashville, June 29, 1925; s. Albert Mims and Mary Nelle (Derryberry) W.; m. Edythe Bush, Mar. 27, 1953 (div.); children: William Terry, Elizabeth Ann, David Bush; m. Dolores Jean Attard, Oct. 22, 1971 (div.); 1 child, Mary Dolores. Student, Emory U., 1942-43; JD, U. Ga., 1949. Bar: Ga. 1948. Pvt. practice law, Atlanta, 1950-85; gen. counsel GEC-Marconi Avionics Inc., Atlanta, 1985-98; hon. legal adviser to Brit. Consul Gen. at Atlanta. Author: The Winning of the Revolutionary War in the South, 1976, The Rights of Unsecured Creditors-The Law in Ga., 1979; editor: Chronicles of the Old Guard of the Gate City Guard of Atlanta, 1858-2001 (3 vols.), 2002. Mem. DeKalb County Bd. Elections, 1966-72; chmn. 44th Congl. Dist. Republican Exec. Com., 1968-70, Ga. State Rep. Exec. Com., 1968-74; 1st vice chmn. Ga. Rep. Party, 1972-74, asst. gen. counsel, 1974-75; vice chmn., trustee Atlanta Counseling Center, Inc., 1960-83. Served with USCGR, 1943-46. Decorated Order Brit. Empire. Fellow Comml. Law Found.; mem. BA, Ga. Bar Assn., Atlanta Bar Assn., Ga. Soc. (pres. 1962-63), SAR, Southeastern Mem.'s Assn. (pres. 1960-61), Comml. Law League (dir.), Ga. Soc. Colonial Wars, Old Guard of Gate City Guard (comdt. 1986), N.C. Soc. of Cincinnati, Sphinx Club, Gridiron Club, Commerce Club, Civitan, Masons, Blue Key, Omicron Delta Kappa. Baptist. Home and Office: 66 Demorest Ln # 333 Sky Valley GA 30537-2581 *By precept and example my parents pointed out the upward way in life, on a foundation of religious faith. "To do justly, to love mercy, to walk humbly with thy God." Later a beloved teacher taught the lines from Ulysses as he prepared to set sail, "To strive, to seek, to find and never yield." Their inspiration has continued throughout my life.*

**WILKINSON, ANTHONY J.,** social studies educator; b. Decatur, Ind., Nov. 15, 1969; s. Dennis R. and Joyce A. Wilkinson; m. Laura L. Wilkinson, Aug. 8, 1998; children: Abigail Rose, Katherine Louise. BS in Secondary Edn., Ind. U., Bloomington, 1992; MS in Ednl. Adminstrn., No. Ill. U., DeKalb, 2005. Social studies tchr. Mannheim Sch. Dist., Melrose Park, Ill., 1993—.

**WILKINSON, CHARLES P.,** ophthalmologist; b. Syracuse, 1940; MD, Johns Hopkins U. Sch. Medicine, 1966. Intern Johns Hopkins Hosp., 1966—67; resident Wilmer Inst., Balt., 1967—70; fellow U. Miami, 1970—71; chmn. dept., prof. ophthalmology Johns Hopkins U. Sch. Medicine. Co-author: Michels Retinal Detachment, 1996. Mem.: Am. Bd. Ophthalmology (vice chmn. 2003, chmn. 2004). Avocation: golf. Office: Greater Balt Med Ctr 6569 N Charles St #505 Towson MD 21204-5809 Office Phone: 443-849-2196.*

**WILKINSON, CLAUDE HENRY,** writer, artist, English literature educator; b. Memphis, Dec. 17, 1959; s. Henry Bridgforth and Lula (Moncrief) W. BSc, U. Miss., 1981; cert. d'excellence, Alliance Française, Memphis, 1991; MA, U. Memphis, 1992. Instr. English McNeese State U., Lake Charles, La., 1990-91, U. Memphis, 1991-92, Lane Coll., Jackson, Tenn., 1992-94, LeMoyne-Owen Coll., Memphis, 1998-99; owner Claude Wilkinson Fine Art Studio, Nesbit, Miss., 1984—. Editor River City Mag., Memphis, 1991; John and Renée Grisham So. writer in residence U. Miss., 2000-01. Author: Reading the Earth, 1998 (Naomi Long Madgett Poetry award, 1998), Joy in the Morning, 2004; author poetry; contbr. articles to profl. jours. Recipient New Poets award, Ursus Press, 1984, Grand prize, Miss. Poetry Soc., 1985, W.M. Whittington Jr. Purchase award, Cottonlandia Mus. Juried Exhbn., 1993, 1st prize in painting, Carnegie Ctr. for Arts and History, 1994, Pioneer Br. Poetry award, Ark. Writers' Conf., 1995, Kenneth Beaudoin Meml. award, Mid-South Poetry Festival, 1995, Paul Laurence Dunbar Poetry award, Detroit Black Writers Guild, 1998, Whiting Writer's award, Mrs. Giles Whiting Found., 2000; Provost Scholar, U. Miss., 2006, Walter E. Dakin fellow, Sewanee Writers' Conf., 1999. Avocations: music, mythology, nature study. Office Phone: 662-429-4935.

**WILKINSON, DANIEL MELVIN,** music educator; b. San Miguel de Tucuman, Argentina, Feb. 14, 1959; arrived in U.S., 1967; s. Melvin Leon and Carol Evangeline Wilkinson. BS in Music Edn., Trevecca Nazarene U., Nashville, 1983; MM in Performance, Western Ky. U., 1984. Instr. Madisonville (Ky.) C.C., 1990—98; assoc. prof. Hopkinsville (Ky.) C.C., 1998—. Contbr. poetry and photography to The Round Table; vocalist, accompanist: Town and Gown Chorale, 1998—2005, musician piano and organ recitals, performance in master class before Madame Marie-Louise Langlais. Mem.: Am. Guild Organists (sub-dean Evansville chpt. 2002—04), Hopkinsville Art Guild. Republican. Avocations: reading, composition, travel, movies, photography. Home: 622 Foxfield Rd Hopkinsville KY 42240 Office: Hopkinsville C C PO Box 2100 North Dr Hopkinsville KY 42240 Office Phone: 270-707-3864. Business E-mail: dwilkins@hopkinsville.net.

**WILKINSON, DAVID STANLEY,** pathologist, consultant, researcher, educator; b. Richmond, Va., Feb. 2, 1945; s. Herbert Carroll and Hattie Mae (Vaughan) Wilkinson; m. Judith Farish Pace, June 16, 1967; children: Jill Marie, Julie Lynne, Virginia Ann. BS in Chemistry, Va. Mil. Inst., Lexington, 1967; PhD in Exptl. Oncology and Pathology, U. Wis.-Madison, 1971; MD, U. Miami, 1978. Diplomate Am. Bd. Pathology. Fellow McArdle Lab. Cancer Rsch. U. Wis., 1967—71; asst. prof. biochemistry U. South Fla., Tampa, 1972—76; resident in pathology Walter Reed Army Med. Ctr., Washington, 1978—82; instr. pathology Uniformed Svc. U. Health Sci., Bethesda, 1979—82; chief clin. pathology Eisenhower Army Med. Ctr., Ft. Gordon, Ga., 1984—84; instr. pathology Med. Coll. Ga., Augusta, 1982—84; assoc. prof. pathology George Washington U. Med. Ctr., 1984—89, dir. clin. pathology div., 1984—92, prof. pathology, 1989—93; med. dir. George Washington U. Hosp., 1992—93; prof. pathology, chmn. dept. pathology Va. Commonwealth U., 1993—. Lectr. in field. Editor: (other) Clinical Laboratory Management Review, 1989—2004; contbr. articles to profl. jours. Commd. 2nd lt. U.S. Army, 1967, advanced through grades to maj. U.S. Army, 1982. Fellow: Coll. Am. Pathologists, Am. Soc. Clin. Pathology; mem.: AMA, Assn. Pathology Chairs (pres. 2004—06), Med. Soc. Va. (del.), Richmond Acad. Medicine (trustee), U.S. and Canadian Acad. Pathology, Am. Soc. Investigative Pathology, Am. Assn. Blood Banks, Clin. Lab. Mgmt. Assn., Am. Assn. Clin. Chemistry, Soc. Exptl. Biology and Medicine, Am.

Assn. Cancer Rsch., VMI Keydet (Lexington, Va.). Republican. Office: Va Commonwealth Univ Dept Pathology PO Box 980662 Richmond VA 23298-0662 Business E-mail: dswilkin@vcu.edu.

**WILKINSON, DORIS,** medical sociology educator; b. Lexington, Ky., June 13, 1936; d. Howard Thomas and Regina Wilkinson. BA, U. Ky., 1958; MA, Case Western Res. U., 1960, PhD, 1968; MPH, Johns Hopkins U., 1985; postgrad., Harvard U., summer 1991. Asst. prof. U. Ky., Lexington, 1968-70; assoc. prof., then prof. Macalester Coll., St. Paul, 1970-77; exec. assoc. Am. Sociol. Assn., Washington, 1977-80; prof. med. sociology Howard U., Washington, 1980-84; vis. prof. U. Va., 1984-85; prof. sociology U. Ky., Lexington, 1985—. Chmn. panel women in sci. program NSF, Washington, 1976; rev. panelist Nat. Inst. Drug Abuse, Washington, 1978—79; mem. bd. sci. counselors Nat. Cancer Inst., Bethesda, Md., 1980—84; vis. scholar Harvard U., Cambridge, Mass., 1989—90, vis. prof. (summers), 1992, 93, 94, 97; Rapoport vis. prof. social theory (summers) Smith Coll., 1995, 96; bd. dirs. Nat. Conf. for Cmty. Justice, 1992—96; dir. Heritage Project, 2000—. Author: Workbook for Introductory Sociology, 1968; editor: Black Revolt: Strategies of Protest, 1969; co-editor: The Black Male in America, 1977, Alternative Health Maintenance and Healing Systems, 1987, Race, Gender and the Life Cycle, 1991, Race, Class and Gender, 1996; social history photographic exhbn. "The African American Presence in Medicine" Harvard Med. Libr., 1991, Pearson Mus.- So. Ill. U. Med. Sch., 1992, N.J. Coll. Medicine and Dentistry, 1993, Louisville Mus. History and Sci., 1994, U. Cin. Med. Sch. Libr., 1994, Albert Einstein Coll. of Medicine, 1995, Midway Coll., 1996; contbr. articles to profl. jours. Bd. overseers Case Western Res. U., Cleve., 1982-87; apptd. Ky. Commn. on Women, 1993-96. Recipient Pub. Humanities award U. Ky., 1990, Midway Coll. Women's History Month award, 1991, Gt. Tchr. award Nat. Alumni Assn. U. Ky., 1992, Disting. Scholar award Assn. Black Sociologists, 1993, Cmty. Svc. award Frankfort-Lexington Links, Inc., 2005-, Cmty. Svc. award Girl Scout Wilderness Road Coun., Lexington, Ky., 2005; inducted into Hall of Disting. Alumni, U. Ky., 1989, Ida Lee Willis Mem. award, 2006; fellow Woodrow Wilson Found., 1959-61, Ford Found., 1989-90; grantee Social Sci. Rsch. Coun., 1975, Nat. Inst. Edn., 1978-80, Nat. Cancer Inst., 1986-88, Ky. Humanities Coun., 1988, 01, Am. Coun. Learned Soc., 1989-90, NEH, 1991; Disting. Prof. in Coll. Arts and Scis., U. Ky., 1992-93, Coll. of Social Work Hall of Fame, U. Ky., 1999; Disting. Lectureship named in hon. AASR Program, 2000. Mem.: Ea. Sociol. Soc. (v.p. 1983—84, pres. 1992—93, I. Peter Gellman award 1987), Soc. Study Social Problems (v.p. 1984—85, pres. 1987—88), DC Sociol. Soc. (pres. 1982—83), So. Sociol. Soc. (honors com. 1993—94), Am. Sociol. Assn. (exec. assoc. 1977—80, budget com. 1985—88, v.p. 1991—92, mem. coun. 1994—97, elected History of Sociology sect. 2003, Dubois-Johnson-Frazier award 1988), Phi Beta Kappa.

**WILKINSON, EDWARD ANDERSON, JR.,** retired military officer, manufacturing executive; b. Selma, Ala., Sept. 21, 1933; s. Edward Anderson and Alice Margaret (Moorer) W.; m. Barbara Anne Parker, June 4, 1955 (dec. June 1991); children: Daryl Edward, Daniel Bryan, Edward Anderson III, David Park; m. Sondra Marie Moore, Oct. 2, 1994. BS, U.S. Naval Acad., 1955; MS in Mech. Engring., 1964; grad., Nat. War Coll., 1972. Commd. ensign U.S. Navy, 1955, advanced through grades to rear adm., 1979; dir. Anti-Submarine Warfare Systems Program Office, Washington, 1978-79; dep. dir. Def. Mapping Agy., Washington, 1979-81; cmdr. Patrol Wings, U.S. Atlanta Fleet, Brunswick, Maine, 1981-83; dir. Def. Mapping Agy., Washington, 1983-85; ret., 1985; exec. v.p. Internat. Fed. Systems Intergraph Corp., Reston, Va. Decorated Legion of Merit, D.S.M. (Dept. Def.) Methodist. Home: 9680 Perdido Vista Dr Elberta AL 36530-6028 Office Phone: 703-264-5644. E-mail: andy.wilkinson@intergraph.com.

**WILKINSON, EUGENE PARKS,** nuclear engineer, director; b. Long Beach, Calif., Aug. 10, 1918; s. Dennis William and Daisy Amelia (Parks) W.; m. Janice Edith Thuli, Mar. 28, 1942; children: Dennis Eugene, Stephen James, Marian Lynn, Rodney David. AB in Chemistry, San Diego State U., 1938. Instr. chemistry San Diego State U., 1938-39; commd. ensign U.S. Navy, 1940, advanced through grades to vice adm., 1970; served various locations including 1st comdg. officer USS Nautilus (1st nuclear-powered submarine), 1953-57; 1st comdg. officer USS Long Beach, 1959-63, 1st nuclear-powered surface ship; ret., 1974; exec. v.p. Data Design Labs., Cucamonga, Calif., 1977-80; pres., chief exec. officer Inst. Nuclear Power Ops., Atlanta, 1980-84, pres. emeritus, 1984—. Chmn. bd. dirs. MDM Svcs. Corp., Laguna Niguel, Calif. Decorated Legion of Merit, Silver Star, D.S.M. with three oak leaf clusters, others, Second Order Sacred Treasure Japan; recipient George Westinghouse Gold medal ASME, 1983, Oliver Townsend medal Atomic Indsl. Forum, 1984, Gold medal Uranium Inst., 1989. Mem. Am. Soc. Naval Engrs., Am. Nuclear Soc. (Henry DeWolf Smyth Nuclear Statesman medal 1994, Walter Zinn award 1998), Navy League, Submarine League, Nat. Acad. Engring. Avocations: tennis, bridge. Home: 1449 Crest Rd Del Mar CA 92014-2530

**WILKINSON, FRANCES CATHERINE,** librarian, educator; b. Lake Charles, La., July 20, 1955; d. Derrell Fred and Catherine Frances (O'Toole) W.; div.; 1 child, Katrina Frances. BA in Comm. with distinction, U. N.Mex., 1982, MPA, 1987; MLS, U. Ariz., 1990. Mktg. rsch. auditor Mktg. Rsch. N.Mex., Albuquerque, 1973—78; freelance photographer, 1974—75; from libr. supr. gen. libr. to assoc. dean libr. svcs. U. N.Mex., Albuquerque, 1978—2001, interim dean libr. svcs., 2001—02, assoc. dean librs., 2002—06, interim dean, 2006—. Cons., trainer ergonomics univs. and govt. agys. across U.S., 1986—; bd. dirs. Friends of U. N.Mex. Librs., Albuquerque, 1997-04; mediator Mediation Alliance, 1991-94, U. N.Mex. Faculty Dispute Resolution, 1999—; mediation coach U. N.Mex., 1999-2000. Author, editor books; editor jour. columns; contbr. articles to profl. jours. Counselor, advocate Albuquerque Rape Crisis Ctr., 1981-84. Recipient James Fulton Zimmerman award for adminstry. excellence, Friends of U. N.Mex. Librs., Inc. Mem.: ALA (com. 1990—2000, 2003—), Leadership in Libr. Acquisitions award 2000), N.Mex. Assn. Rsch. Librs., N.Mex. Preservation Alliance (vice chair 1995—96), N.Mex. Libr. Assn., N.Am. Serials Interest Group (com. 1994—97, exec. bd. 1997—2001, com. 2001—03), Pi Alpha Alpha, Phi Kappa Phi (chpt. treas. 1991—92, chpt. pres. 1992—94). Home: PO Box 8102 Albuquerque NM 87198-8102 Office: U N Mex Univ Librs MSC 05 3020 1 University of New Mex Albuquerque NM 87131-0001 Office Phone: 505-277-4241. Business E-mail: fwilkins@unm.edu.

**WILKINSON, HARRY EDWARD,** management educator, consultant; b. Richmond Heights, Mo., June 30, 1930; s. Harry Edward and Virginia Flo (Shelton) W.; m. Sara Beth Kikendall, Aug. 30, 1958; children: Linda Beth, Cheryl Susan. BA in Physics, Princeton U., 1952; MBA, Washington U., St. Louis, 1957; D Bus. Adminstrn., Harvard U., 1960. Lic. psychologist, Mass. Staff engr. Southwestern Bell Tel. Co., St. Louis, 1954-57; traffic engr. New Eng. Tel. & Telegraph Co., Boston, 1957-60; sr. mgmt. cons. Harbridge House Inc., Boston, 1961-65; dean bus. adminstrn., dir. Mgmt. Inst., Northeastern U., Boston, 1965-67; pres., chmn. bd. Univ. Affiliates Inc., North Port, Fla., 1967-2000; vis. prof. mgmt. Rice U., Houston, 1990-94, 97-2000, dir. office of exec. devel., 1993-97. Cons. to various industries and govt., 1961—. Author: Influencing People in Organizations, 1993; contbr. articles to mgmt. jours. Lt. (j.g.) USNR, 1952-54, Korea. Mem. APA, Acad. Mgmt., N.Am. Case Rsch. Assn., Harvard Bus. Assn. E-mail: wilkinso@rice.edu.

**WILKINSON, J. HARVIE, III, (JAMES HARVIE WILKINSIN III),** federal judge; b. NYC, Sept. 29, 1944; s. James Harvie and Letitia (Nelson) W.; m. Lossie Grist Noell, June 30, 1973; children: James Nelson, Porter Noell. BA, Yale U., 1963-67; JD, U. Va., 1972; JD (hon.), U. Richmond, 1997, U. SC, 1998; LLD (hon.), Christopher Newport U., 2003. Bar: Va. 1972. Law clk. to Hon. Lewis F. Powell, Jr. US Supreme Ct., Washington, 1972-73; asst. prof. law U. Va., 1973-75, assoc. prof., 1975-78; editor Norfolk Virginian-Pilot, Va., 1978-81; prof. law U. Va., 1981-82, 83-84; dep. asst. atty. gen. Civil Rights div. Dept. Justice, 1982-83; judge US Ct. Appeals (4th cir.) 1984—, chief judge, 1996—2003. Author: Harry Byrd and the Changing Face of Virginia Politics, 1968, Serving Justice: A Supreme Court Clerk's View,

1974, From Brown to Bakke: The Supreme Court and School Integration, 1979, One Nation Indivisible: How Ethnic Separatism Threatens America, 1997. Bd. Visitors U. Va., 1970-73; Republican candidate for Congress from 3d Dist. Va., 1970; bd. dirs. Fed. Jud. Ctr., 1992-96, James Madison Meml. Found., 2003-. Served with U.S. Army, 1968-69. Recipient Thomas Jefferson Found. medal Law, U. Va., 2004. Mem. Va. State Bar, Va. Bar Assn., Am. Law Inst. Episcopalian. Office: US Ct Appeals 255 W Main St Ste 230 Charlottesville VA 22902-5058 Office Phone: 434-296-7063.*

**WILKINSON, JOHN HART,** lawyer; b. Newton, Mass., Dec. 31, 1940; s. Roger Melvin and Margaret (Carter) Wilkinson; children: Heather, Carter. BA, Williams Coll., 1962; LLB, Fordham U., 1965. Bar: NY 1965, US Dist. Ct. (so. and ea. dists.) NY 1968, US Ct. Appeals (2d cir.) 1981, US Ct. Appeals (11th cir.) 1982, US Ct. Appeals (3d cir.) 1984, US Ct. Appeals (5th cir.) 1987. Assoc. Donovan, Leisure, Newton & Irvine, NYC, 1965, 67-73, ptnr., 1973-98; editor, contbg. author firm's ADR Practice Book, 1990; law clk. presiding justice US Dist. Ct. (so. dist.) NY, 1967-68; of counsel Fulton, Rowe & Hart, NYC, 1998—. Spkr. field. Contbr. articles to profl. jours. Bd. dirs., pres. Childfind Am., Inc., 1993—94; vol. learning disabled children Chelsea Neighborhood, NYC, 1965—67; v.p. bd. dirs. Pelham (NY) Family Svc., 1982—85; bd. dirs. Catskill Ctr. Conservation Devel., 1993—. Recipient Am. Jurisprudence award, Fordham U. Mem.: ABA (alt. dispute resolution com. 1989—93), Assn. Bar City NY (profl. responsibility com. 1987—89, pub. assistance com. 1991—94), NY State Bar Assn. (alt. dispute resolution com. 1989—93). Avocations: woodworking, fly fishing, bicycling, camping. Office: Fulton Rowe & Hart One Rockefeller Plz New York NY 10020 Office Phone: 914-663-0700. Personal E-mail: johnhwilkinson@msn.com.

**WILKINSON, LAURA,** Olympic athlete; b. Houston, Nov. 17, 1977; d. Ed and Linda Wilkinson; m. Eriek Hulseman. Student, U. Tex.; BS in pub. rels., U. Tex. at Austin. Mem. World Cup Team, 1995, 1997, 2000, 2002, 2004, capt., 2004; mem. US Olympic Team, 2000, 2004, World Championship Team, 1998, 2003, Goodwill Games Team, 1998, 2001, Pan Am Games Team, 2003. Pub. spkr. Named USA Diving Athlete of Yr., 2000, 2004. Achievements include World Cup Bronze Medalist in Platform Synchro, 1995; placed 5th World Championships, 1998; Goodwill Games Platform Gold Medalist, 1998; Olympic Platform Gold Medalist, Sydney Olympics, 2000; World Cup Platform Gold Medalist, 2004. Avocations: drawing, writing, watching movies. Office: US Diving Inc 201 S Capitol Ave Ste 430 Indianapolis IN 46225 E-mail: diver@laurawilkinson.com

**WILKINSON, LESTER F., JR.,** lawyer; b. Mass., Nov. 12, 1956; BA, Bates Coll., 1978; JD, U. San Diego, 1981. Bar: Maine 1981, U.S. Dist. Ct. Maine 1981. Mng. shareholder Bernstein, Shur, Sawyer & Nelson, PA, Augusta, Maine. Instr. real estate law U. Maine, Augusta, 1988—89. Bd. dirs. Children's Ctr., 1990—93, pres., 1994; bd. dirs. Maine Gen. Health Assocs., 1997—2000. Mem.: Kennebec County Bar Assn., Maine State Bar Assn. (bd. govs., treas. 1994—2001, prest.-elect 2002, pres. 2003), Kennebec Valley C. of C. (dir. 1988—, pres. 2001). Office: Bernstein Shur Sawyer and Nelson 146 Capitol St Po Box 5057 Augusta ME 04330-5057

**WILKINSON, LOUISE CHERRY,** psychology professor, dean; b. Phila., May 15, 1948; BA magna cum laude, Oberlin Coll., 1970; EdM, EdD, Harvard U., 1974. Prof., chmn. dept. ednl. psychology U. Wis., Madison, 1976-85; prof., exec. officer Grad. Sch. PhD Program CUNY, N.Y.C., 1984-86; disting. prof., dean Grad. Sch. Edn. Rutgers U., 1986—2003; dean Sch. Edn. Syracuse (NY) U., 2003—05, disting. prof. edn., psychology and comm. scis., 2003—. Chair ednl. strategic planning Rutgers U.; mem. nat. rev. bd. Nat. Inst. Edn., 1977, 85, 87; cons. Nat. Ctr. for Bilingual Rsch., 1982, 84, US Dept. Edn., 1995—96; adv. bd. Nat. Reading Rsch. Ctr., 1992—98; vis. prof. U. London, 2006—; honored guest prof. Beijing Normal U., 2001—05. Co-author: Communicating for Learning, 1991; editor: Communicating in Classroom, 1982, Social Context of Instruction, 1984, Gender Influences in the Classroom, 2002; co-editor: Literacy and Language Learning, 2004; contbr. articles to profl. jours.; mem. editl. bds. various publs.: Fellow: APA, Am. Assn. for Applied and Preventive Psychology, Am. Psychol. Soc.; mem.: NJ Coun. Acad. Policy Advisors, Am. Ednl. Rsch. Assn. (v.p. 1990—92, program chair 1997). Home: 525 Plum St # 208 Syracuse NY 13204

**WILKINSON, MILES FROME,** healthcare educator, researcher; b. Edinburgh, Scotland, Feb. 14, 1957; arrived in U.S., 1959; s. John Frome Wilkinson and Rowena Pattee Kryder; m. Deepti Srinivas, June 6, 2002; 1 child, Vishaala Satya. BA in Biology, U. Calif., San Diego, 1980; PhD, U. Warwick, England, 1984. Postdoc. fellow Scripps Clinic, La Jolla, Calif., 1984—85, U. Calif., San Diego, 1985—87; asst. prof. Oreg. Health Scis. U., Portland, Oreg., 1987—93, assoc. prof., 1993—94; assoc. prof. M.D. Anderson Cancer Ctr. U. Tex., Houston, 1994—2001, prof. M.D. Anderson Cancer Ctr., 2001—. Contbr. over 100 articles to profl. jours. Grantee numerous grants. Office: University of Texas MDACC 1515 Holcombe Blvd Houston TX 77030 Business E-mail: mwilkins@mdanderson.org.

**WILKINSON, RALPH RUSSELL,** retired biochemistry educator, toxicologist; b. Portland, Oreg., Feb. 20, 1930; s. Tracy Chandler and Lavern (Russell) W.; m. Evelyn Marie Wickman, Aug. 5, 1956. BA, Reed Coll., 1953; PhD, U. Oreg., 1962; MBA, U. Mo., Kansas City, 1974. Rsch. chemist VA Hosp., Kansas City, Mo., 1973-74; sr. rsch. chemist Midwest Rsch. Inst., Kansas City, 1975-84; prof. Rockhurst Coll., Kansas City, 1985-86, Cleve. Chiropractic Coll., Kansas City, 1987-99, prof. emeritus, 1999—. Cons. in biochemistry, toxicology, environ. impact, tech. assessment, Kansas City, 1984—. Author: (book) Neurotoxins and Neurobiological Function, 1987; contbr. articles to profl. jours. Mem. Southtown Coun., Kansas City, Mo., 1989—, Spina Bifida Assn. Am., Kansas City, 1989—. Recipient NSF fellowship, 1959-60. Mem. Am. Chem. Soc., Sigma Xi. Avocations: travel, history, biography, music, antiques. Home: 7911 Charlotte St Kansas City MO 64131-2175

**WILKINSON, ROSEMARY REGINA CHALLONER,** poet, writer; b. New Orleans, Feb. 21, 1924; d. William Lindsay Challoner Jr. and Julia Regina (Sellen) Challoner/Schillo; m. Henry Bertram Wilkinson, Oct. 15, 1949; children: Denis James, Marian Regina, Paul Francis, Richard Challoner. Lifetime credential to teach poetry, San Francisco State U., 1978; LHD (hon.), Livre U., Pakistan, 1975; DLitt (hon.), World Acad. Arts & Culture, Rep. of China, 1981. Lectr./reader of poetry. Author: (poetry) A Girl's Will, 1973, California Poet, 1976, Earth's Compromise, 1977, It Happened to Me, 1978, I Am Earth Woman, 1979, The Poet and the Painter, 1981, Poetry and Arte, 1982, Gems Within, 1984, Nature's Guest, 1984, In the Pines, 1985, Longing for You, 1986, Purify the Earth, 1988, Sacred in Nature, 1988, Earth's Children, 1990, New Seed, 1991, Angels and Poetry, 1992, Cambrian Zephyr, 1993, Collected Poems, 1994; Poetry: Nature, 1996, Poetry: Spiritual, 1997, Poetry Calendar 2000, 1999, A Song in the Wind with Love, 2001, My Plea, 2001, Selected Verses, 2001, Blessing of Poetry, 2002, Living Spring Water, 2005, 2006, others; (play) An Historical Epic, 1974, Epic of the Ships Captain, 1986. Founder Poetry-Fine Arts Divsn. of San Mateo (Calif.) County Fair, 1977, Dr. Williams Poetry Workshop, Burlingame H.S., 1985; sec.-gen. World Acad. Arts and Culture-USA, San Francisco, 1985—95, pres., 1994—2003. Mem.: Authors League Am., The Authors Guild, Acad. Am. Poets, Poetry Soc. of Am., Nat. League Am. Pen Women Inc. (Washington 4th and 5th v.p. 1986—90, Berkeley, Calif. pres. 1988—90, Lake Tahoe br. 1988—), World Acad. of Arts and Culture/World Congress of Poets, World Congress of Poets (Taipei, Taiwan bd. dirs. 1973—2003, San Francisco pres. 1981, sec.-gen. 1985—95, pres. 1994—2003). Soroptimist Internat. (hon.). Democrat. Roman Catholic. Avocations: reading, research, brush painting, lecturing. Home: 3146 Buckeye Ct Placerville CA 95667-8334

**WILKINSON, SIGNE,** cartoonist; b. Wichita Falls, Tex. married. BA in English, 1972; student, Pa. Acad. Fine Arts. Reporter West Chester (Pa.) Daily Local News, Academy of Natural Scis., Phila.; freelance cartoonist Phila. and N.Y. publs.; cartoonist San Jose (Calif.) Mercury News, 1982-85, Phila. Daily

News, 1985—. Illustrator: Abortion Cartoons in Demand, 1992, You Bet Your Tomatoes, 2002, How to Grow the $735 Tomato, 1999; contbr. to Univ. Barge Club News, various mags. Bd. dirs. Fair Hill Burial Ground. Recipient Pulitzer Prize for edit'l. cartooning, 1992, Overseas Press Club award, 1997, 2001, Robert F. Kennedy award, 2002. Mem. Assn. Am. Edit'l. Cartoonists (pres. 1994-95). Avocations: gardening, rowing. Office: Phila Daily News PO Box 7788 400 N Broad St Philadelphia PA 19130-4015 Business E-mail: wilkins@phillynewes.com.

**WILKINSON, TOM,** actor; b. Leeds, West Yorkshire, Eng., Dec. 12, 1948; m. Diana Hardcastle, Jan. 5, 1988; children: Alice, Molly. Diploma in Eng. and Am. Lit., U. Kent; attended, Royal Acad. Dramatic Arts; LittD (hon.), U. Kent, 2001. Actor: (films) The Shadow Line, 1976, Bones, 1984, Sylvia, 1985, Wetherby, 1985, Sharma and Beyond, 1986, Paper Mask, 1990, In the Name of the Father, 1993, All Things Bright and Beautiful, 1994, Prince of Jutland, 1994, A Business Affair, 1994, Sense and Sensibility, 1995, The Ghost and the Darkness, 1996, The Full Monty, 1997, Wilde, 1997, Gillian Armstrong's Oscar and Lucinda, 1997, The Governess, 1998, Rush Hour, 1998, Shakespeare in Love, 1998, Ride with the Devil, 1999, The Patriot, 2000, Chain of Fools, 2000, In the Bedroom, 2001, Another Life, 2001, Black Knight, 2001, The Importance of Being Earnest, 2002, An Angel for May, 2002, Girl with a Pearl Earring, 2003, Eternal Sunshine of the Spotless Mind, 2004, A Good Woman, 2004, Ripley Under Ground, 2005, Batman Begins, 2005, The Exorcism of Emily Rose, 2005, Separate Lies, 2005, The Night of the White Pants, 2006, The Last Kiss, 2006; (TV films) Squaring the Circle, 1984, Strangers and Brothers, 1984, A Pocket Full of Rye, 1985, The Woman He Loved, 1988, The Attic: The Hiding of Anne Frank, 1988, First and Last, 1989, Prime Suspect, 1991, Underbelly, 1992, An Exchange of Fire, 1993, Measure for Measure, 1994, Crossing the Floor, 1996, Cold Enough for Snow, 1997, The Gathering Storm, 2002, Normal, 2003. Office: The Gersh Agy 232 N Canon Dr Ste 201 Beverly Hills CA 90210*

**WILKINSON, WARREN SCRIPPS,** manufacturing executive; b. Detroit, Feb. 2, 1920; s. Almadus DeGrasse and Harriet Gertrude (Whitcomb) W.; m. Joan Todd, June 14, 1941; m. Mireille De Bary, Dec. 17, 1966. Grad., Hotchkiss Sch., Lakeville, Conn., 1937; BS in Math, Harvard U., 1941; student, Calif. Inst. Tech., 1941-42. With U.S. Rubber Co., Detroit, 1942-43, Hanson Van Winkle-Munning Co., Matawan, NJ, 1946-64, pres., 1961-64; v.p., gen. mgr. Hanson-Van Winkle-Munning div. M & Chems. Inc., 1964-66; chmn. RPI Designs, Marlette, Mich., 1966—. Mem. Detroit Hist. Commn., 1994—2006; mem. overseer's com. on univ. resources Harvard U. With USN, 1943—46. John Harvard fellow, 1996. Home: 2 Woodland Pl Grosse Pointe MI 48230-1920

**WILKINSON, WILLIAM SHERWOOD,** lawyer; b. Williston, ND, Sept. 6, 1933; s. John Thomas and Evelyn (Landon) W.; m. Carol Ann Burns, Aug. 20, 1960; children— Leslie Ann, Richard Sherwood, Greta Diann. BS in Bus, U. Idaho, 1955; JD, U. Denver, 1960. Bar: Colo. 1960, Mich. 1966. Practiced in, Canon City, Colo., 1960-66; asst. dist. atty. 11th Jud. Dist., Colo., 1961-65; gen. counsel, sec. Mich. Farm Bur. Family Cos., Lansing, 1966-96. Lectr. Pre-Parole Release Center, Colo. State Penitentiary, 1961-65; instr. adult edn., Canon City, 1965; counsel Canon City Recreation Dist., 1964-65 Mem. lay adv. bd. St. Thomas More Hosp., Canon City, 1963-66; Del., county, dist. and congl. convs. Republican party, 1964. Served to capt. USAF, 1955-58. Recipient Cmty. Disting. Svc. award Canon City Jr. C of C., 1964; named to Outstanding Young Men of Am., 1965. Mem. ABA, Colo. Bar Assn., Mich. Bar Assn., Am. Judicature Soc., Am. Corp. Counsel Assn., Nat. Coun. Farmer Coops. (legal, tax and acctg. com.), Phi Delta Phi, Tau Kappa Epsilon. Methodist (lay leader, mem. ch. ofcl. bd.). Home: 1707 Foxcroft Rd East Lansing MI 48823-2131 E-mail: wwilca@aol.com.

**WILKISON, DAVID,** editor; BA, U. W. Va. Corr. AP, Morgantown, W.Va., Newark, 1996—97, news editor Des Moines, 1997—99, Phila., asst. bur. chief, bur. chief Ky., regional news dir. Phoenix, Mid-Atlantic bur. chief Washington, 2006—. Office: AP Washington Bur 6th Fl 2021 K St NW Washington DC 20006-1082 Office Phone: 202-776-9400. Office Fax: 202-776-9570.*

**WILKS, PAUL ALMY, JR.,** engineering executive; b. Springfield, Mass., June 16, 1923; s. Paul A. and Mary Ethyl (Libby) Wilks; m. Laura May Parsons, Oct. 4, 1947; children: Donald(dec.), Mark, Sandra. BS, Harvard Coll., 1945. Dir. mktg. Parkin Elmer Corp., Norwalk, Conn., 1944—57; v.p., co-founder Conn. Unstrument Corp., Wilton, 1957—63; founder, pres. Wilks Scientific Corp., Norwalk, 1963—77, Gen. Analysis Corp., 1977—98, Wilks Enterprise, Inc., 1998—. Author: Happiness is Being in the Winner's Circle, 1981; contbr. articles to profl. jours. Mem.: Coblentz Soc. (founding mem. 1954, William-Wrights award 1981). Achievements include first to commercial development of IR-absorption cells; commercial applications of attenuated total reflection; development of gas chromatographs. Avocations: sailing, breeding horses. Home: 179 Middlesex Rd Darien CT 06820 Office: Wilks Enterprise Corp 140 Water St Norwalk CT 06854 Office Phone: 203-855-9166.

**WILKS, THOMAS MILTON,** religious studies educator, minister; b. Mansfield, La., Feb. 14, 1945; s. Milton E. and Bernice (Thompson) W.; m. Jacquelin Holsomback, Jan. 28, 1972; children: T. David, Bryan E. BA, La. Coll., Pineville, 1967; ThM, New Orleans Bapt. Theol. Sem., 1971; DMin, So. Bapt. Theol. Sem., Louisville, 1977. Lic. field traumatologist, in-svc. guidance dir. Youth min. First Bapt. Ch., Bastrop, La., 1968; pastor Magnolia Bapt. Ch., Vancleave, Miss., 1969-71; youth associa., pastoral intern First Bapt. Ch., Pine Bluff, Ark., 1971-73, pastor Charleston, Mo., 1973-78; min. Bapt. Metro Campus, St. Louis, 1970-80; assoc. dean students for counseling, univ. chaplain Okla. Bapt. U., Shawnee, 1980-84, asst. prof. applied ministry, dir. in-svc. guidance, 1984-87, assoc. prof. applied ministry, dir. in-svc. guidance, 1987-93, prof. applied ministry, dir. in-svc. guidance, 1993-94, dir. off-campus programs and insvc. guidance, prof., 1994-96, prof. applied ministry, dir. in-svc. guidance, 1996-97, Jewell and Joe Huitt prof. religious edn., 1998—, dir. in-svc. guidance, 1998—. Adj. prof. psychology Oklahoma City U. Grad. Sch., 1983-84; adj. prof. pastoral leadership Southwestern Bapt. Theol. Sem., 1996, 98; cons. family ministry Bapt. Gen. Conv. Okla., Oklahoma City, 1999—; mem. bd. Summit Youth Camps, Edmond, Okla., 1994—; mem. long-range planning co. In-Svc. Guidance Conf. Assn., 1992-99, pres., 1991, bd. dirs., chmn. bd. dirs., 2002-2004; mem. Youth Matrix Team, Lifeway Christian Resources, Nashville, 1996—; state cons. in family ministry Bapt. Gen. Conv. Okla., 1998—; mem. Nat. Task Force on Bi-Vocat. Ministry, 1992; spkr. various civic clubs and orgns., graduations and faculty devel. workshops for schs. and colls. Author: Blind Faith, 1995; co-author: Devotionals For Guys Who Like Movies, 2002, Transforming Student Ministry, 2005; writer youth ministry, local ch. and missions internship, preaching, counseling, pastoral care and pastoral ministry study guides Pres. North Rock Creek Bd. Edn., Shawnee, 1998; treas. Shawnee H.S. Quarterback Club, 1994-95; chmn. bd. dirs. Therapeutic Horsemanship Program Harvest Farms, 2004-06. Recipient Lewis W. Newman award, In Svc. Guidance Assn., 2005. Mem. Nat. Network Youth Ministries, In-Svc. Guidance Assn. (chmn. exec. com. 1996-99, bd. dirs. 1999—, chmn. bd. dirs. 2002-04), Assn. Theol. Field Educators. Republican. Avocations: coach, youth baseball, basketball, soccer, track. Home: 18 Woodcrest Shawnee OK 74804-9048 Office: Okla Bapt U Box 61248 Shawnee OK 74804 E-mail: tom.wilks@okbu.edu.

**WILL, ANNE MARILYN,** retired elementary school educator; b. Maryville, Mo., Mar. 9, 1940; d. Paul Gordon and Louise Madeline (Burke) Seymour; (div.); children: Eric Scott, LeAnne Elizabeth. BS Elem. Edn., N.W. Mo. State U., 1962, MEd, Mo. U., 1983. Tchr. 5th and 6th grades, Des Moines, 1962—64; tchr. 4th grade Salem R-80, Mo., 1964—83, tchr. math. chpt. I, 1983—99; ret., 1999. Methodist. Avocation: reading. Home: HC 82 Box 98 Salem MO 65560-8608

**WILL, CLIFFORD MARTIN,** physicist, researcher; b. Hamilton, Ont., Can., Nov. 13, 1946; m. Leslie Saxe, June 26, 1970; children: Elizabeth, Rosalie. BS, McMaster U., Hamilton, 1968; PhD, Calif. Inst. Tech., 1971. Enrico Fermi fellow U. Chgo., 1972-74; asst. prof. physics Stanford U., Palo Alto, Calif., 1974-81; assoc. prof. physics Washington U., St. Louis, 1981—85, prof. physics, 1985—2005, James McDonnell prof. physics, 2005—, chmn. dept. physics, 1991—2002. Chmn. com. on time transfer in satellite systems Air Force Studies Bd., Washington, 1984-86; chmn. sci. adv. com. NASA Gravity Probe B, 1998—. Assoc. editor Physical Rev. Letters, 1989-92, Physical Rev. D, 1999-2001; author: Theory and Experiment in Gravitational Physics, 1981, new edit., 1993, Was Einstein Right?, 1986, rev. edit., 1993. Alfred P. Sloan Found. fellow, 1975-79, J.S. Guggenheim Found. fellow, 1996-97, J.W. Fulbright fellow, 1996-97; recipient Sci. Writing award Am. Inst. Physics, 1987, Disting. Alumni award, McMaster U., 1996. Fellow Am. Phys. Soc. (exec. com. astrophysics divsn. 1988-90, vice chair, chair elect, chair topical group on gravitation 1997-2001), Am. Acad. Arts and Scis.; mem. Am. Astron. Soc., Am. Assn. Physics Tchrs. (Richtmyer Meml. Lectr. 1987), Internat. Soc. Gen. Relativity and Gravitation (pres. 2004—). Office: Washington U Dept Physics Campus Box 1105 1 Brookings Dr Saint Louis MO 63130-4899

**WILL, FREDERIC,** university administrator, writer; b. New Haven, Dec. 4, 1928; s. Samuel F. and Constance B. Will; m. Julie Omotejohwo, July 27, 1995; children: Barbara, Alex, Chris, Carson, Kyle. BA, Ind. U., 1948; PhD, Yale U., 1954. Asst. prof. classics Dartmouth, Hanover, N.H., 1952-54, Pa. State U., University Park, 1955-60; prof. classics U. Tex., Austin, 1960-65; prof. comparative lit. U. Iowa, Iowa City, 1965-70, fellow Inst. Advanced Studies, 1985-92; prof. comparative lit. U. Mass., Amherst, 1971-84; pres. Mellen U., Mt. Vernon, Iowa, 1995—2000; prof. Am. studies U. Ivory Coast, 2000—02; vis. prof. classics Cornell Coll., Iowa, 2002; vis. prof. Hunan Normal U., China, 2003; prof. U. Robert de Boron, France, 2004—. Vis. prof. Deep Springs Coll., 2003—06. Author: Intelligible Beauty in Aesthetic Thought, 1956, Mosaic and Other Poems, 1959, A Wedge of Words, 1963, The Twelve Words of the Gypsy, (trans.) 1964, Metaphrasis, 1964, Flumen Historicum, 1965, Hereditas, 1965, Literature Inside Out, 1966, The King's Flute (trans.), 1966, From A Year in Greece, 1967, Planets, 1968, Archilochos, 1969, Herondas, 1972, Brandy in the Snow, 1972, The Fact of Literature, 1973, The Knife in the Stone, 1973, The Jargon of Authenticity, (trans.) 1973, Guatemala, 1973, Botulism, 1975, The Generic Demands of Greek Literature, 1976, Belphagor, 1977, Epics of America, 1977, One Thousand Year Old bodies: Selected Poems, 1980, Shamans in Turtlenecks, 1984, The Sliced Dog, 1984, The Fall and The Gods 3 vols., 1988-92, Entering the Open Hole, 1989, Big Rig Souls, 1992, Translation Theory and Practice, 1993, Literature as Sheltering the Human, 1993, Singing with Whitman's Thrush, 1993, Recoveries, 1993, Trips of the Psyche, 1993, Textures, Spaces, Wonders, 1993, Bananas, Corn and Cheese, 2002, Be the Sweat of Thy Brow, 2002, Miroirs d'Eternité, 2002, Flesh and the Colour of Love, 2002, English for Success, 2002, Social Reflections on Work, 2002, Field Research in North American Agricultural Communities, 2002, Three Essays on Mellen University: Early Life and Times, 2004, The Male's Midlife Rite of Passage: Three Imagined Lives, 2006, China a Modern History, 2006; founding editor Arion, 1962, Micromegas, 1965—; lit. papers archived in Humanities Rsch. Ctr., U. Tex., Austin. Fellow Fulbright Found., Greece, 1952, Germany, 1957, Tunisia, 1976, Cote d' Ivoire, 200-02, Chad, 2003; Bollingen Found. fellow, 1956, Am. Coun. Learned Socs. fellow, 1957, Nat. Endowment Arts fellow, 1960; Ford Found. tchg. intern, 1953; recipient Tex. Inst. Letters award, 1962, NY Quar. prize, 1962; grantee Coun. Lit. Mags., 1962-67, PEN Club/Writers' Union awards, 1962-67. Roman Catholic. Home: 617 7th St NW Mount Vernon IA 52314 Personal E-mail: samuelw981@aol.com

**WILL, GEORGE FREDERICK,** editor, journalist, commentator; b. Champaign, Ill., May 4, 1941; s. Frederick L. and Louise Will; m. Madeleine Marion, 1967 (div.); children: Jonathan, Geoffrey, Victoria; m. Mari Maseng, Oct. 12, 1991; 1 child, David. BA, Trinity Coll., 1962, Oxford U., Eng., 1964; MA, PhD in politics, Princeton U., 1967; LLD (hon.), U. San Diego, 1997; LittD (hon.), Dickinson Coll., Georgetown U., 1978; degree (hon.), U. Ill., 1988. Prof. polit. philosophy Mich. State U., 1967-68, U. Toronto, 1968-70; mem. staff of Sen. Gordon Allott US Senate, Washington, 1970-72; Washington editor The Nat. Rev., 1973-76; syndicated columnist The Washington Post Writers Group, 1974—; contbg. editor, columnist Newsweek mag., 1976—; founding panel mem. This Week program (formerly This Week with David Brinkley), ABC, 1981—; contbg. analyst ABC News. Author: Statecraft as Soulcraft, 1983, The New Season: A Spectator's Guide to the 1988 Election, 1987, Men at Work: The Craft of Baseball, 1989, Restoration: Congress, Term Limits and the Recovery of Deliberative Democracy, 1992, (collections of columns) The Pursuit of Happiness and Other Sobering Thoughts, 1978, The Pursuit of Virtue and Other Tory Notions, 1982, The Morning After: American Successes and Excesses 1981-86, 1986, Suddenly: The American Idea Abroad and at Home 1986-1990, 1990, The Leveling Wind: Politics, the Culture & Other News 1990-94, 1994, The Woven Figure: Conservatism and America's Fabric 1994-97, 1997, With a Happy Eye But...America and the World 1997-2002, 2002, (collection of essays) Bunts: Curt Flood, Camden Yards, Pete Rose, and Other Reflections on Baseball, 1998. Bd. governors Negro Leagues Baseball Mus. Named Young Leader Am., Time mag., 1974, Best Writer, Any Subject, Washington Journalism Rev., 1985; named one of 25 Most Influential Washington Journalists, Nat. Jour., 1997; recipient Pulitzer Prize for Commentary, 1977, Nat. Headliners Award, 1978, Silurian Award for Edit'l. Writing, 1980, 1991. Avocation: baseball. Address: ABC Pub Rels 77 W 66th St New York NY 10023-6201 Office: Washington Post Writers Group 1150 15th St NW Washington DC 20071

**WILL, JAMES FREDRICK,** academic administrator, former steel company executive; b. Pitts., Oct. 12, 1938; s. Fred F. and Mary Agnes (Ganter) W.; m. Mary Ellen Dowser, Dec. 19, 1964; children: Mary Beth, Kerry Ann. BSEE, Pa. State U., 1961; MBA, Duquesne U., 1972. Works mgr. Kaiser Steel Corp., Fontana, Calif., 1976-78, v.p. ops., 1978-80, v.p. planning, 1980-81, exec. v.p., 1981, pres., 1981-82; exec. v.p., pres. indsl. group Cyclops Corp., Pitts, 1982-86, pres., chief operating officer Pitts., 1986-88, pres., chief exec. officer, 1989-92; pres., chief oper. officer Armco Inc., Parsippany, NJ, 1992-93, pres., chief exec. officer Pitts., 1994-96, chmn., pres., CEO, 1996—2000; pres. Saint Vincent Coll., Latrobe, Pa., 2000—06, pres. emeritus, vice chancellor, 2006—. Vice-chmn. chmn. 1995, Specialty Steel Industry of N.Am. Office: Saint Vincent Coll 300 Fraser Purchase Rd Latrobe PA 15650-2690*

**WILL, KATHERINE HALEY,** academic administrator; m. Oscar Henry Will, III; 4 children. Student, Carleton Coll., 1970-73; BA in English, Tufts U., 1974; MA in English, U. Ill., Urbana, 1975, PhD in English, 1986. Instr. English Augustana Coll., Sioux Falls, S.D., 1977-86, asst. prof. English, 1986-90, faculty dir. new student seminar program, 1987-91, assoc. prof. English, 1990-96, dean grad. study, dir. gen. edn., 1991—96; provost, prof. English Kenyon Coll., Gambier, Ohio, 1996-99; pres. Whittier Coll., Calif., 1999—2004, Gettysburg Coll., Pa., 2004—. Participant Mgmt. Devel. Seminar for Higher Edn. Adminstrs., Harvard U., summer 1992; cons. and presenter in field. Contbr. articles to profl. jours. Bd. dirs. United Way Great L.A. NEH fellow Summer Seminar in Romanticism and Gender, UCLA, 1989. Mem.: Annapolis Group (exec com.), Coun. Ind. Colls. (bd. dirs.), Nat. Assn. Ind. Colls. and Univs. (bd. dirs.). Office: Gettysburg Coll Pennsylvania Hall, 3 Fl W 300 N Washington St Gettysburg PA 17325 Office Phone: 717-337-6011. Office Fax: 717-337-6008. E-mail: kwill@gettysburg.edu.*

**WILL, ROLAND TRACY, II,** writer, editor, journalist, publisher, actor; b. Schenectady, N.Y., May 18, 1954; s. Albert Roland and Constance Mary (Headley) W.; m. Gay Adair Strandemo, July 1, 1989; children: Roland Leigh Leonard, Glenn Tracy. BA, U. Wis., 1988. Polit. sci. and comm. arts editor, pub., journalist Wis. Health Policy Report, Wis. Ind. News Svc., Madison, 1994—99. Author: (Compass Am. Guide) Wisconsin, 1994, 3d edit., 2001, History of Dane the Capital County, 2000; (plays) Packer Glory, 1984, Fatal Time to Final End, 1986; actor (plays) Bombs Away Enola Gay, 1983, Hans Brinker and Silver Skates: Rock Musical on Roller Skates, 1984, Light My Fire—Jim Morrison, 1985, The Cherry Orchard, 1985, The Hangwoman, 1986, The Phantom of Shopppko, 1987, Joe a Life: The Story of Joe McCarthy, 1988, Chain Reaction, 1996; series editor, contbr. Wisconsin: Buildings of America, 2006; writer, asst. prodr. (TV spl.) Spanish Spoken Here, 2005 (named Best Documentary, Wis. Broadcasters Assn. 2005). Bus. mem. Dane County Hist. Soc., Madison, 1995; sec. bd. dirs. Broom St. Theater, Madison, 1984-2005; curator photography exhibit Wis. Hist. Mus.; TV host/prodr. Wisconsin Stories, Wis. Pub. TV, 1999-2002; mem. curriculum com. Wannakee Sch. Bd., 2005; vestry St. Dunstan's Episcopal Ch., Madison. Episcopalian. Avocations: history, architecture, travel. Personal E-mail: tracy.will@yahoo.com.

**WILL, TREVOR JONATHAN,** lawyer; b. Ashland, Wis., Aug. 11, 1953; s. William Taylor and Geraldine Sue (Trevor) W.; m. Margaret Ann Johnson, Aug. 28, 1976; children: Tyler William, Alexandra Marie, Jennifer Catherine. BA summa cum laude, Augustana Coll., 1975; JD cum laude, Harvard U., 1978. Bar: Wis. 1978, U.S. Dist. Ct. (ea. dist.) Wis. 1978, U.S. Dist. Ct. (we. dist.) Wis. 1980, U.S. Ct. Appeals (7th cir.) 1983, U.S. Supreme Ct. 1984, U.S. Dist. Ct. (ea. dist.) Mich. 1985. Assoc. Foley & Lardner LLP, Milw., 1978-87, ptnr., 1987—, chmn. product liability practice group. Adj. law prof. Marquette U. Law Sch., 1994-00. Mem. ABA, State Bar Wis., Milw. Bar Assn., Def. Rsch. Inst. Office: Foley & Lardner LLP 777 E Wisconsin Ave Ste 3800 Milwaukee WI 53202-5306 Office Phone: 414-297-5536. Office Fax: 414-297-4900. Business E-mail: twill@foley.com.

**WILLADSEN, MICHAEL CHRIS,** marketing professional, sales executive; b. Cheboygan, Mich., Sept. 18, 1946; s. Chris Jens and Helen Margaret (Barr) W.; m. Kay Ann Brooks, Dec. 10, 1964, (div. Dec. 10, 1989); children: Michael Jr., Erik; m. Linda Sue Degroff, Apr. 4, 1992; children: Stephanie, Gretchen, Ross. Student, Delta Coll., 1964—66; A in Bus. Mgmt., Northwood Inst., 1968, BA in Bus. Mgmt., 1969. Mktg. rep. Detroit dist. Petemco, Inc., 1970-73, mktg. rep. Indpls. Dist., 1973-74; dist. mgr. Petemco Inc.-Ind. Ohio Mich., Ind., Ohio, Mich., 1974-76, Consolidated Stas. Marathon Oil, Oshkosh, Wis., 1976-79; sales mgr. Champaign (Ill.) Dist. Marathon Oil, 1981-82, supr. Credit Card Ctr. Findlay, Ohio, 1982-84; wholesale mktg. profl. Marathon Brand Mktg./Ohio, Mich., Ky., 1982-84; jobber sales Marathon Oil/Ohio, Pa., W.Va., Ohio, Pa., W. Va., 1984-92, Marathon Oil/Ill., Wisc., Chgo., Chgo., 1992-2000, Marathon Ashland Petroleum, Atlanta, Ga., 2000—, N.C., S.C., Ala. Named to Nat. Assn. Intercollegiate Athletes Sml. Coll. All-State Football Team/Dist. 23, 1968; inducted into Mich. Touch Football Hall of Fame/Team Category, 2002. Mem. Cleve. Petroleum Club (v.p. 1988-91), Chgo. Oilmens. Republican. Presbyterian. Avocations: camping, softball, basketball, physical work out. Office: Marathon Petroleum Co PO Box 1007 Cumming GA 30028 Office Phone: 678-947-5808. Business E-Mail: mcwilladsen@marathonpetroleum.com.

**WILLAMS, MICHAEL,** editor; b. 1963; Grad., Harvard U. Copy editor Japan Times, Asahi News Svc., Tokyo; sr. editor Bus. Tokyo mag., NYC, 1991—92; from news editor to econ. & polit. corr. Wall St. Jour., Tokyo, 1992—96, asst. fgn. editor NYC, 1996—99, bur. chief Tokyo, 1999—2003, S. Europe bur. chief Paris, 2003—06; editor Wall St. Jour. Europe, 2006—. Co-recipient Bob Considine award, Overseas Press Club, 1997. Office: Wall Street Journal 200 Liberty St New York NY 10281 Office Phone: 212-416-2000.*

**WILLAN, LARRY CHARLES,** secondary school educator, art educator, photographer; b. Frankfurt, Germany, Oct. 30, 1961; arrived in U.S., 1962; s. Leonard Oliver and Carolyn Sue Willan; m. Leslie Joann Reeder, July 1, 1989. BS in Visual Arts Edn., Ball State U., 1989; MS in Guidance Counseling, Butler U., 2002. Football coach John Marshall H.S., Indpls., 1982—84; art tchr. Crispus Attucks Jr. High, Indpls., 1989—91, Eastwood Middle Sch., Indpls., 1991—2003, Westlane Middle Sch., Indpls., 1991—2002, North Ctrl. H.S., Indpls., 2002—. Profl. photographer, profl. painter/artist L. Willan Studio, Indpls. Avocations: hiking, rafting, ornithology, open-wheel racing.

**WILLANS, JEAN STONE,** bishop, religious organization administrator; b. Hillsboro, Ohio, Oct. 3, 1924; d. Homer and Ella (Keys) Hammond; m. Richard James Willans, Mar. 28, 1966; 1 dau., Suzanne Jeanne. Student, San Diego Jr. Coll.; DD (hon.), Am. Coll. Sems., 1996. Ordained archdeacon, 1996, ordained priest 1997, consecrated bishop 1998, Ch. of the East. Asst. to v.p. Family Loan Co., Miami, Fla., 1946-49; civilian supr. USAF, Washington, 1953-55; founder, dir. Blessed Trinity Soc.; editor Trinity mag., L.A., 1960-66; co-founder, exec. v.p., dir. Soc. of Stephen, Altadena, Calif. 1967—; exec. dir. Hong Kong, 1975-81. Lectr. in field. Author: The Acts of the Green Apples, 1974, rev. edit. 1995, Chinese edit., 2003; co-editor: Charisma in Hong Kong, 1970, Spiritual Songs, 1970, The People Who Walked in Darkness, 1977, The People Who Walked in Darkness II, 1992, 2d edit., 2000; works archived at Fuller Theol. Sem., 2004. Recipient Achievement award Nat. Assn. Pentecostal Women, 1964; monument erected in her honor Kowloon Walled City Park, Hong Kong Govt., 1996. Republican. Office: Soc of Stephen PO Box 6225 Altadena CA 91003-6225

**WILLARD, GREGORY DALE,** lawyer; b. Pittsfield, Ill., Feb. 8, 1954; s. Wesley Dale and Rosmary (Stark) W.; m. Ann Julia Grier, June 3, 1978; children: Michael, David, John. BA summa cum laude, Westminster Coll., Fulton, Mo., 1976; JD cum laude, U. Ill., 1979. Bar: Mo., U.S. Dist. Ct. (ea. dist.) Mo., U.S. Ct. Appeals (8th Cir.). Staff asst. to Pres. Exec. Office of the Pres. The White House, Washington, 1976-77; ptnr. Bryan Cave LLP, St. Louis, 1979—, group leader Bankruptcy, Restructuring and Creditors' Rights. Co-chmn. bankruptcy com. Met. Bar Assn., St. Louis, 1983-84. Bd. Dirs. St. Louis Children's Hosp., 1985-89, Found. for Spl. Edn., 1990—, Congress Neurol. Surgeons, 1998—. Mem. Congress of Neurol. Surgeons, Noonday Club. Office: Bryan Cave One Metropolitan Square 211 N Broadway Saint Louis MO 63102-2733 E-mail: gdwillard@bryancave.com.

**WILLARD, H(ARRISON) ROBERT,** electrical engineer; b. Seattle, May 31, 1933; s. Harrison Eugene and Florence Linea (Chelquist) Willard. BSEE, U. Wash., 1955, MSEE, 1957, PhD, 1971. Lic. profl. engr., Wash. Staff assoc. Boeing Sci. Rsch. Labs., Seattle, 1959-64; rsch. assoc. U. Wash., 1968-72; sr. engr., rsch. prof. applied physics lab., 1972-81; sr. engr. Boeing Aerospace Co., Seattle, 1981-84; dir. instrumentation and engring. MetriCor Inc. (formerly Tech. Dynamics, Inc.), Redmond, Wash., 1984-92; sr. engr. B.E. Meyers & Co., Inc., Redmond, 1992—. Contbr. articles to profl. jours. With U.S. Army, 1957—59. Mem.: IEEE, Am. Geophys. Union, Sigma Xi, Phi Beta Kappa, Tau Beta Pi. Achievements include patents in field. Office: 14540 NE 91st St Redmond WA 98052-4939

**WILLARD, JOHN GERARD,** communications executive, consultant, writer, educator; b. Pitts., Nov. 20, 1952; s. Cornelius Merle and May E. (Hinds) W.; m. Lorraine L. Franze, Sept. 2, 1978; children: Mary Elizabeth, Kristen Anne, Lisa Lorraine, Jessica Kathleen. BA in Journalism, Duquesne U., 1974. Producer, dir. air talent Sta. WDUQ-FM, Pitts., 1971-73; master control tech. dir. Sta. KDKA-TV, Pitts., 1973; cons. comms. Better Bus. Bur., Pitts., 1974; asst. account exec. Marc & Co. Advt., Pitts., 1975; adminstr. employee benefit adminstrn. Rockwell Internat. Corp., Pitts., 1975-80, adminstr. relocation and corp. personnel procedures, 1980-81, mgr. corp. policy, 1981-82; pres. John G. Willard Cons., 1982—. Contbr. articles to profl. jours. Office: 360 Middlegate Dr Bethel Park PA 15102-1438 Office Phone: 412-831-5650. E-mail: jgw7@telerama.com.

**WILLARD, LOUIS CHARLES,** librarian; b. Tallahassee, Fla., Sept. 28, 1937; s. Bert and Rose (De Milly) W.; m. Nancy Bush, June 22, 1963. BA, U. Fla., 1959; BD, Yale, 1965, MA, 1967, PhD, 1970. Tchr. Tripoli (Lebanon) Boys' Sch., 1959-62; ordained to ministry Presbyn. Ch., 1965; acting librarian Princeton Theol. Sem., 1968-69, librarian, 1969-86; librarian, mem. faculty Harvard Div. Sch., 1986-99; dir. accreditation and instnl. evaluation Assn. Theol. Schs., 1999—. Mem. A.L.A., Theol. Library Assn., Soc. Bibl.

Lit., Am. Acad. Religion, Phi Beta Kappa, Chi Phi. Office: Assn Theol Schs 10 Summit Park Dr Pittsburgh PA 15275-1103 Home: 970 Villeroy Greens Dr PO Box 5040 Sun City Center FL 33573 Office Phone: 412-788-6505. Business E-mail: willard@ats.edu.

**WILLARD, NANCY MARGARET**, writer, educator; b. Ann Arbor, Mich. d. Hobart Hurd and Margaret (Sheppard) W.; m. Eric Lindbloom, Aug. 15, 1964; 1 child, James Anatole. BA, U. Mich., 1958, PhD, 1963; MA, Stanford U., 1960. Lectr. English Vassar Coll., Poughkeepsie, NY, 1965—. Author: (poems) In His Country: Poems, 1966; Skin of Grace, 1967; A New Herball: Poems, 1968, Testimony of the Invisible Man: William Carlos Williams, Francis Ponge, Rainer Maria Rilke, Pablo Neruda, 1970, Nineteen Masks for the Naked Poet: Poems, 1971, The Carpenter of the Sun: Poems, 1974, A Visit to William Blake's Inn: Poems for Innocent and Experienced Travelers, 1981 (Newbery Medal 1982), Household Tales of Moon and Water, 1983, Water Walker, 1989, The Ballad of Biddy Early, 1989; (short stories) The Lively Anatomy of God, 1968, Childhood of the Magician, 1973; (juveniles) Sailing to Cythera and Other Anatole Stories, 1974, All on a May Morning, 1975, The Snow Rabbit, 1975, Shoes Without Leather, 1976, T0e Well-Mannered Balloon, 1976, Night Story, 1986, Simple Pictures are Best, 1977, Stranger's Bread, 1977, The Highest Hit, 1978, Papa's Panda, 1979, The Island of the Grass King, 1979, The Marzipan Moon 1981, Uncle Terrible, 1982, (adult) Angel in the Parlor: Five Stories and Eight Essays, 1983, The Nightgown of the Sullen Moon, 1983, Night Story, 1986, The Voyage of the Ludgate Hill, 1987, The Mountains of Quilt, 1987, Firebrat, 1988; (novel) Things Invisible To See, 1984, Sister Water, 1993; (play) East of the Sun, West of the Moon, 1989, The High Rise Glorious Skittle Skat Roarious Sky Pie Angel Food Cake, 1991, A Nancy Willard Reader, 1991, Pish Posh said Hieronymus Bosch, 1991, Beauty and the Beast, 1992; illustrator: The Letter of John to James, Another Letter of John to James, 1982, The Octopus Who Wanted to Juggle (Robert Pack), 1990, (novel) Sister Water, 1993, (essays) Telling Time, 1993, (juvenile) A Starlit Somersault Downhill, 1993, (juvenile) The Sorcerer's Apprentice, 1993; author, illustrator: An Alphabet of Angels, 1994; (juvenile) Gutenberg's Gift, 1995, The Good Night Blessing Book, 1996, Cracked Corn and Snow Ice Cream, 1997, The Tortilla Cat, 1998; (poems, with Jane Yolen) Among Angels, 1995, Swimming Lessons, 1996, The Magic Cornfield, 1997; editor: (anthology of poems) Step Lightly: Poems for the Journey, 1998, The Tale I Told Sasha, 1999, (juvenile) Shadow Story, 1999, (juvenile) The Moon and Riddles Diner and the Sunny Side Cafe, 2001, (juvenile) The Mouse, the Cat and Grandmother's Hat, 2003, (scholastic) Cinderella's Dress, 2003, (young adult) Paradise Lost, 2004, Sweep Dreams, Little Brown, 2005 Recipient Hopwood award, 1958, Devins Meml. award, 1967, John Newbery award, 1981, Empire State award, 1996; Woodrow Wilson fellow, 1960; NEA grantee, 1987. Mem. The Lewis Carroll Soc. Office: Vassar Coll Dept English Raymond Ave Poughkeepsie NY 12604-0001

**WILLARD, RALPH LAWRENCE**, surgeon, educator, physician, retired academic administrator; b. Manchester, Iowa, Apr. 6, 1922; s. Hosea B. and Ruth A. (Hazelrigg) W.; m. Norma L. Hattel, Nov. 12, 1943 (div. 1968); children: Laurie, Jane, Ann, H. Thomas; m. Margaret Dyer Dennis, Sept. 26, 1969. Student, Cornell Coll., 1940-42, Coe Coll., 1945; D.O., Kirksville Coll. Osteo. Medicine, 1949; EdD (hon.), U. North Tex., 1985; ScD (hon.), W.Va. Sch. Osteo. Medicine, 1993. Intern Kirksville Osteo. Hosp., 1949-50, resident in surgery, 1954-57; chmn. dept. surgery Davenport Osteo. Hosp., 1957-68; dean, prof. surgery Kirksville Coll. Osteo. Medicine, 1969-73; asso. dean acad. affairs, prof. surgery Mich. State U. Coll. Osteo. Medicine, 1974-75; dean Tex. Coll. Osteopathic Medicine, 1975-76, pres., 1981-85, prof. surgery, 1985-87; v.p. med. affairs North Tex. State U., Denton, 1976-81; assoc. dean W.Va. Sch. Osteo. Medicine, Lewisburg, 1988-91. Mem. Nat. Adv. Council Edn. for Health Professions, 1971-73, Iowa Gov.'s Council Hosps. and Health Related Facilities, 1965-68; chmn. council deans Am. Assn. Colls. Osteo. Medicine, 1970-73, pres., 1979-80 Served with USAAF, 1942-45; Served with USAF, 1952-53; col. USAFR, ret. Decorated D.F.C., Air medal with 4 oak leaf clusters, Meritorious Svc. medal, Legion of Merit; recipient Robert A. Kistner Educator award Am. Assn. Colls. Osteo. Medicine, 1989; named Disting. scholar Acad. Osteo. Medicine Nat. Acads. Practice, 2000. Fellow Am. Coll. Physician Execs., Am. Coll. Osteo. Surgeons; mem. Am. Osteo. Assn. (Disting. Svc. cert. 1992), Tex. Osteo. Assn., W.Va. Soc. Osteo. Medicine, Am. Acad. Osteopathy, Acad. Osteo. Dirs. Med. Edn., Quiet Birdmen, Davis-Monthan Officers Club, Masons, Shriners, Rotary (Paul Harris fellow), Internat. Comanche Soc., Order of Daedalians. Democrat. Episcopalian. Address: PO Box 79267 Fort Worth TX 76179-0267 Personal E-mail: willardrl@aol.com. *The wise man has faith, the fool is he who betrays that faith.*

**WILLARD, RICHARD KENNON**, lawyer, former pharmaceutical company executive; b. Houston, Sept. 1, 1948; s. Fair McDaniel Willard and Elsbeth Rowe (Kennon) Willard Armistead; m. Leslie Harral Hopkins, July 10, 1976; children: Stephen Hopkins, Lauren Suzanne. BA, Emory U., 1969; JD, Harvard U., 1975. Bar: D.C. 1988, Tex. 1978, Ga. 1975. Law clk. US Ct. Appeals, San Francisco, 1975-76, US Supreme Ct., Washington, 1976-77; atty. Baker & Botts, Houston, 1977-81; counsel for intelligence policy US Dept. Justice, Washington, 1981-82, dep. asst. atty. gen. civil divsn., 1982-83, asst. atty. gen., 1983-88; ptnr. Steptoe & Johnson, Washington, 1988-99; sr. v.p., gen. counsel The Gillette Co., Boston, 1999—2005; sr. v.p. gen. counsel Bristol-Myers Squibb Co., NYC, 2005—06. Adj. prof. Georgetown U. Law Ctr., 1991-96, Boston U. Law Sch., 2002-05. Note editor: Harvard U. Law Rev., 1974-75. Gen. counsel Republican Party of Tex., Austin, 1980-81. Served to 1st lt. U.S. Army, 1969-72. Mem. Met. Club. Episcopalian.

**WILLARD, ROBERT F.**, career military officer; b. LA; Grad., U.S. Naval Acad., 1973. Advanced through grades to admiral, 2005—; F-14 naval aviator; served with Fighter Squadrons Two (VF-2), Twenty Four (VF-24), and One Twenty Four (VF-124) NAS Miramar; ops. and exec. officer, instr. Navy Fighter Weapons Sch. (Top Gun); exec. and commdg. officer Screaming Eagles; commdr. USS Tripoli, 1994, USS Abraham Lincoln, 1995—98; commdr. Carrier Group 5 USS Kitty Hawk, 2000—01; dep. chief of staff, comdr. U.S. Pacific Fleet, 2001; comdr. Seventh Fleet, 2002—04; vice chief naval ops. USN, 2005—. Aerial coord. (films) Top Gun, 1986. Decorated Def. Disting. Svc. Medal, Disting. Svc. Medal, four Legions of Merit, others; named Pacific Fleet Tailhooker of Yr., 1982. Office: USN 2000 Navy Pentagon Washington DC 20350*

**WILLAUER, WHITING RUSSELL**, retired manufacturing executive, systems engineer; b. Boston, May 24, 1931; s. Whiting and Louise Knapp (Russell) Willauer-Jackson; m. Julie Mackie McConihe, Mar. 15, 2001 (div.); m. Julie Matheson Arnold, July 11, 1959 (div.); children: Whiting Russell, Jr., William Arnold. BS, Princeton U., 1955, MS, 1959; PhD, Georgetown U., 1964. Research assoc. joint research com. Dept. Def., 1951-52; ops. mgr. Civil Air Transport Airline Taiwan, 1952-53; scientist Analytic Services, Inc., 1958-61; asst. prof. astronomy Georgetown U., 1965-68; mgr. TRW Systems Group support to chief Naval ops., McLean, Va., 1968-73, TRW support to U.S. Navy Antisubmarine program, 1973-79, TRW Amphibious Ship Bldg. program, 1979-85; advanced systems mgr. TRW Systems Integration Group, 1985-90, cost estimating mgr., 1990-95, sr. cons., 1995-99; sr. v.p., chief strategist K12Nation.net, 1999-2000. Cons. Nat. Geog. Soc., 1961-65, U. Tex., 1962, NSF, 1963, Booz-Allen & Hamilton, 1966-67. Mng. editor: Jour. Astronautical Scis, 1969-71; Designer: Orrery Planetarium Nat. Geog. Soc. Asst. chief steward Alpine Venue XIII Olympic Winter Games, Lake Placid, 1980; mem. U.S. Olympic Com., bd. dirs., 1987-94, sec. nat. governing bodies, 1989-92, mem. membership svcs. com., 1988-92, mem. athletic devel. com., 1992-96; chef de mission Winter Pan Am. Games, Las Lenas, Argentina, 1990; asst. chief de mission XVI Winter Olympics, Albertville, France, 1992; U.S. Olympic Com. liaison to VI Paralympic Winter Games, Lillehammer, Norway, prime 1994. Research fellow Georgetown U., 1961-65. Fellow AAAS (coun.); mem. Am. Astronautical Soc. (v.p. fin.), Blue Ridge Ski Coun. (pres. 1976-78), U.S. Ski Assn. (pres. 1982-87, Julius Blegan award 1988, Mary and Bud Little award 1998), U.S. Ski and Snowboard Assn. (vice chmn. 1994-96, trustee emeritus 1997—), Internat. Ski Fedn.

(chmn. U.S. del. 1983, 85, chmn. recreational skiing com. 1987-98, eligibility com. 1988-98), Ea. Ski Assn. (treas. 1980-82), Pan Am Sports Orgn. (winter games adv. com. 1988—), Sigma Xi, Chevy Chase Club (Md.), Nantucket Yacht Club (Mass.) (commodore 1981-83, bd. govs. 1957-59, 68—), Nantucket IOD Fleet Assn. (fleet capt. 2002-04), Arthur Knapp Prize 2003 IOD World Championship, USCG Aux. Flotilla 11-7 (sec. 2003—, Mem. of Yr. 2004), Nantucket Alliance Substance Abuse Prevention (pres. 2004-05, Nantucket Island Bd. Selectman 2005—, chmn. 2006-). Personal E-mail: whitey@willauer.com.

**WILLBANKS, JILL ANN**, home economist, educator; b. Big Spring, Tex., Jan. 22, 1956; d. C.W. and Sue (Sutton) W. BS in Home Econs., Tex. Tech U. 1977. Cert. elem. and secondary tchr., Tex. Home econs. tchr. Spur (Tex.) High Sch., 1978-82, Big Spring (Tex.) High Sch., 1982—. Counselor Camp Boothe Oaks Girl Scouts USA, Sweetwater, Tex., 1976-80. Mem. Tex. Fedn. Tchrs., Phi Upsilon. Roman Catholic. Avocations: macrame, reading, sewing, gardening, quilting. Home: 602 W 18th St Big Spring TX 79720-4252 Office: Big Spring High Sch 708 E 11th Pl Big Spring TX 79720-4648

**WILLBANKS, ROGER PAUL**, publishing and book distributing company executive; b. Denver, Nov. 25, 1934; s. Edward James and Ada Gladys (Keller) W.; m. Beverly Rae Masters, June 16, 1957; children: Wendy Lee, Roger Craig BS, U. Denver, 1957, MBA, 1965. Economist, bus. writer, bus. forecaster Quest, Denver, 1959—66; dir. pub. rels. Denver Bd. Water Commrs., 1967—70; pres. Royal Publs. Inc., Denver, 1971—, Nutri-Books Corp., Denver, 1971—, Inter-Sports Book and Video, Denver, 1986—. Editor: Mountain States Bus., 1962—66, Denver Water News, 1967—70. Active Gov. of Colo.'s Revenue Forecasting Com., 1963-66. Capt. U.S. Army, 1957-60 Recipient Pub. Rels. award Am. Water Works Assn., 1970, Leadership award Nat. Inst. Nutritional Edn., 1989, Medal of Freedom, U.S. Senate, 1994 Mem. Am. Booksellers Assn., Nat. Nutritional Foods Assn., Pub. Rels. Soc. Am. (charter health sect.), Denver C. of C., SAR, Auburn Cord Duesenberg Club, Rolls Royce Owners Club, Classic Car Am. Club, Denver U. Chancellor's Soc., Ferrari Owners Club Republican. Lutheran. Address: Royal Publs Inc PO Box 5793 Denver CO 80217-5793

**WILLBORN, STEVEN L.**, dean, law educator; BA magna cum laude, Northland Coll., 1974; MS in Counseling, U.Wis.-Madison, 1976; JD cum laude, U. Wis. Law Sch., 1976. Asst. prof. law U. Nebr.-Lincoln Coll. Law, 1979, assoc. prof., 1982, prof., 1985, Richard C. & Catherine Stuart Schmoker Prof. Law, 1999—, dean, 2001—. Pvt. practice, 1976—79; vis. prof. University Mich. Law Sch., 1992. Co-author: Employment Law: Cases and Materials, The Statistics of Discrimination: Using Statistical Evidence in Discrimination Cases, 2002; contbr. articles to law jours. Grantee Lincoln Coll., Oxford U., 1993; vis. scholar Australian Nat. U., Canberra, 1988, U. Toronto, 1991; Fulbright Scholar, Inst. Advanced Legal Studies, U. London, 1985—86. Office: U Nebr-Lincoln Coll Law Ross McCollum Hall PO Box 830902 Lincoln NE 68583 E-mail: willborn@unl.edu.

**WILLE, JOHN JACOB, JR.**, medical products executive, biologist; b. N.Y.C., June 24, 1937; s. John J., Sr. and Beatrice Wille; m. Myra L. Mitchell, Feb. 11, 1995; children: Chris, Julia, Rachel, Konrad. BA, Cornell U., 1960; PhD (USPHS scholar 1961-64), Ind. U., 1965. From postdoctoral to sr. postdoctoral rschr. Argonne (Ill.) Nat. Lab., 1968; asst. prof. U. Cin., 1968—71; assoc. prof. La. State U., Baton, 1975—80; rschr., prof. Mayo Med. Sch., Rochester, Minn., 1980—84; sect. head cell biology So. Rsch. Inst., Birmingham, Ala., 1984—89; dir. skin rsch. Bristol Myer Squibbs, Skillman, NJ, 1989—97; pres. Hygiene Biomedical Corp., Charlotte, NC, 1997—2001, also bd. dirs.; pres. Bioderm Techs., Inc., Trenton, NJ, 1997—. Cons. Ortec Internat., Inc., N.Y.C., 1998—2001. Editor: Biochemical Modulation of Skin Reaction, 2000; contbr. articles to profl. jours. Grantee, NIH, 1986—89, USDA, 1999. Mem.: Soc. Cosmetic Chemists, Soc. Investigative Dermatology, Am. Assn. Cancer Rsch. Achievements include patents in field. Avocations: antiques, furniture restoration, piano, tennis. Office: Bioderm Technologies Inc 4 Lina Ln Mount Holly NJ 08060-5414 Office Phone: 609 261 1488.

**WILLE, LOIS JEAN**, retired editor; b. Chgo., Sept. 19, 1931; d. Walter and Adele S. (Taege) Kroeber; m. Wayne M. Wille, June 6, 1954. BS, Northwestern U., 1953, MS, 1954; Litt.D. (hon.), Columbia Coll., Chgo., 1980, Northwestern U., 1990, Rosary Coll., 1990. Reporter Chgo. Daily News, 1958-74, nat. corr., 1975-76, assoc. editor charge editorial page, 1977; assoc. editor charge editorial and opinion pages Chgo. Sun-Times, 1978-83; assoc. editor editorial page Chgo. Tribune, 1984-87, editor editorial page, 1987-91, ret., 1991. Author: Forever Open, Clear and Free: the Historic Struggle for Chicago's Lakefront, 1972, At Home in the Loop: How Clout and Community Built Chicago's Dearborn Park, 1997. Recipient Pulitzer prize for public svc., 1963, Pulitzer prize for editorial writing, 1989, William Allen White Found. award for excellence in editorial writing, 1978, numerous awards Chgo. Newspaper Guild, numerous awards Chgo. Headline Club, numerous awards Nat. Assn. Edn. Writers, numerous awards Ill. AP, numerous awards Ill. UPI. Home: 1530 S State St Apt 1011 Chicago IL 60605 Personal E-mail: lowille@aol.com.

**WILLE, ROSANNE LOUISE**, educational consultant; b. Hackensack, N.J., Aug. 4, 1941; d. Albert Wille and Rose Marie (Rock) Eberhardt; m. George B. Jacobs, Mar. 12, 1980; children: Leigh, Steven, Alexander, Jeffrey. M Pub. Adminstrn., Rutgers U., 1986; PhD, N.Y.U., 1980. Dept. chair Rutgers U., Newark, 1978-84, Lehman Coll., Bronx, NY, 1984-87, dean, 1987-92, provost, sr. v.p., 1992—2002; cons. for higher edn., 2002. Contbr. articles to profl. jours. Bd. dirs. Family Support Svcs., Bronx, N.Y., 1994-2002, bd. dirs. South Bronx Overall Economic Devel., Inc., Bronx, 1991-2002. Recipient Vision award Family Support Svcs., Bronx, 1996, Thousand Points of Light award Pres. George Bush, Washington, 1991. Mem. N.Y. Acad. Scis., N.Y. Acad. Medicine, Am. Assn. Higher Edn. Avocations: aviation, golf. Address: PO Box 4148 South Hackensack NJ 07606-4148 Personal E-mail: rlwille@earthlink.net.

**WILLE, WAYNE MARTIN**, retired editor; b. Des Plaines, Ill., Nov. 17, 1930; s. Clarence Louis and Lois Naomi (Martin) W.; m. Lois Jean Kroeber, June 6, 1954. BSJ, Northwestern U., 1952, MSJ, 1953. Reporter Chgo. Sun Times, 1956-57; dir. press info. WBBM-TV and CBS-TV, Chgo., 1957-58; feature editor Sci. and Mechanics mag., 1958-60, mng. editor, 1960-62; news editor Nat. Safety Council, Chgo., 1962-64, asst. dir. pub. info., 1964-67; mng. editor World Book Year Book, Chgo., 1967-69; exec. editor World Book Yr. Book, 1969-83; mng. editor World Book Yr. Book and Sci. Yr. and Health & Med. Ann., 1983-91. Served with AUS, 1953-55. Mem. Chgo. Headline Club (pres. 1967-68), Soc. Profl. Journalists, Art Inst. Chgo., Oriental Inst. Clubs: La Salle Street Rod and Gun.

**WILLEN, LIZ**, reporter; Staff writer, edn. reporter Newsday, NYC, 1989—2000; reporter, sr. writer Bloomberg News, NYC, 2000—. Co-recipient Spl. citation, Edn. Writers Assn., 1994, George Polk award for health reporting, 2006, IRE award, Investigative Reporters & Editors Jour., 2006; recipient Breaking News Story award, Edn. Writers Assn., 1994. Office: Bloomberg News 731 Lexington Ave New York NY 10022 Office Phone: 212-617-2300. Office Fax: 917-369-5000. E-mail: ewillen@bloomberg.net.*

**WILLENBECHER, JOHN**, artist; b. Macungie, Pa., May 5, 1936; s. John George and Geneva (Bacon) W. BA, Brown U., 1958; postgrad., N.Y.U., Inst. Fine Arts, 1958-61. Sculptor-mem. N.Y.C. Art Commn., 1980-92; mem. commn. for plaza and pavillion, Mpls. Inst. Arts, 1991. Exhibited in one-person shows including Hamilton Gallery Contemporary Art, N.Y.C., 1977, 80, 82, U. Mass. Art Gallery, Amherst, 1977, Wright State U. Art Gallery, Dayton, Ohio, 1977, Jaffe-Friede Gallery, Dartmouth Coll., Hanover, N.H., 1977, Fine Arts Ctr. U. R.I., Kingston, 1978, Neuberger Mus., SUNY at Purchase, 1979, Allentown (Pa.) Art Mus., 1979, Mpls. Inst. Arts, 1991, U. N.Mex. Art Gallery, Albuquerque, 1996, 5 Myles Gallery, Bklyn., 2003, CUNY Grad. Ctr., N.Y.C., 2003; exhibited in numerous group shows including

Albright-Knox Art Gallery, Buffalo, 1963, Whitney Mus. Am. Art, N.Y.C., 1964-68; represented in permanent collections including Solomon R. Guggenheim Mus., N.Y.C., Met. Mus., N.Y.C., Whitney Mus. Am. Art, Albright-Knox Art Gallery, Phila. Mus. Art, Centre d'Art et Culture Georges Pompidou, Paris, Hirshhorn Mus. and Sculpture Garden, Washington, Art Inst. Chgo. Nat. Endowment for Arts grantee, 1977, Esther and Adolph Gottlieb Found. grantee, 1994. Achievements include being subject of profl. articles and catalogues.

**WILLENBRINK, ROSE ANN**, retired lawyer; b. Louisville, Ky., Apr. 20, 1950; d. J.L. Jr. and Mary Margaret (Williams) W.; m. William I. Cornett Jr. Student, U. Chgo., 1968-70; BA in Anthropology with highest honors, U. Louisville, 1973, JD, 1975. Bar: Ky. 1976, U.S. Dist. Ct. (we. dist.) Ky. 1976, Ohio 1999. Atty. Mapother & Mapother, Louisville, 1976-79; v.p., counsel Nat. City Bank, Louisville, 1980-99, v.p., sr. atty. Cleve., 1999—2004, Louisville, 2004—05, ret., 2005. Mem. Ky. Bar Assn., Phi Kappa Phi. Home: 6803 Chadworth Pl Prospect KY 40059 Personal E-mail: willenbrink@yahoo.com.

**WILLENS, SCOTT**, pharmacologist, military officer; b. Englewood, N.J., Apr. 9, 1971; s. Leonard and Dana Elizabeth Willens; m. Melanie Lynn Wigsmoen, Apr. 3, 2004; children: Haley Danielle Fitch, Emily Ann Fitch, Matthew Isaac. BS, Rutgers U., 1992; DVM, U. Minn., St. Paul, 1996; PhD, NC State U., Raleigh, 2005. Asst. hosp. dir. and assoc. veterinarian North Bergen Animal Hosp., NJ, 1996—97; assoc. veterinarian Bergenfield Animal Clinic, Bergenfield, 1998; vet. intern Mystic Aquarium and Inst. Exploration, Conn., 1998—99; doctoral candidate N.C. State U., Raleigh, 1999—2005; commd. maj. U.S. Army, 2004; vet. pharmacologist and chief neurobehavioral toxicology br. U.S. Army Med. Rsch. Inst. Chemical Def., Aberdeen Proving Ground, Md., 2004—. Actor: (musical) Pippin; singer: (vocal competition) Military Idol (Ft. Myer installation winner and nat. finalist, 2005), D.A. Stars of Tomorrow Competition, (musical) 231st Annual Army Birthday Ball; contbr. chapters to books, articles to peer-reviewed profl. jours. V.p. Rising Hills Home Owners Assn., Rising Sun, Md., 2005—06; mem. Vet. Adv. Bd. Cecil County Health Dept., North East, Md., 2006. Decorated Army Achievement medal; recipient Robert F. Hammer Meml. award, U. Minn. Coll.Vet. Medicine, 1995, Best Student Presentation in Basic Rsch. award, Internat. Assn. Aquatic Animal Medicine, 1999; scholar, Am. Soc. Animal Sci., 1992; George H. Cook scholar, 1992. Mem.: Am. Vet. Med. Assn., Internat. Assn. Aquatic Animal Medicine, Am. Legion, Alpha Psi (historian 1994—95), Sigma Alpha Mu (alumni chmn. 1991—92). Jewish. Office: USAMRICD 3100 Ricketts Point Rd Aberdeen Proving Ground MD 21010-5400 Office Phone: 410-436-4132. Office Fax: 410-436-1960. E-mail: scott.willens@us.army.mil.

**WILLER, EDWARD HERMAN**, real estate broker; b. Concord, N.C., June 12, 1941; s. Emil Francis and Mary (McKinley) W.; m. Cornelia Campbell, Nov. 30, 1963; children: Laura Campbell, Edward Groves. AB, Davidson Coll., 1963. V.p., sales mgr. Bacon & Co., Realtors, Raleigh, N.C., 1971-84; pres. residential div. York Properties, Inc., Raleigh, 1984—2001. Treas. N.C. Real Estate Ednl. Found., Greensboro, 1984, pres., 1988; bd. dirs. Rex Hosp. Found., Raleigh, 1988-89, Relo, The Internat. Referral Network, Inc., Chgo., dir., 1988-92, treas., 1992. Author: Real Estate Exam Ready Book, 1984; contbr. articles to profl. jours. Bd. dirs. Ea. N.C. Multiple Sclerosis Soc., Raleigh, 1982-85; campaign chair United Way of Wake County, 1996, bd. dirs., 1994-2000, mem. exec. com., 1996-97, treas., 2001—. 1st lt. U.S. Army, 1963-66, Vietnam. Named Realtor of the Year, 1984. Mem. Nat. Assn. Realtors (cert.), N.C. Assn. Realtors (bd. dirs. 1978-82), N.C. Real Estate Ednl. Found. (pres.), Raleigh Bd. Realtors (pres. 1979), Greater Raleigh C. of C. (bd. dirs. 1991-94), Quite Birdmen Club. Democrat. Presbyterian. Avocations: teaching, flying, woodworking. Home: 1512 Saint Mary's St Raleigh NC 27608-2217 Office: York Simpson Underwood 311 Oberlin Rd Raleigh NC 27605-3125 Office Phone: 419-582-1695.

**WILLERSON, JAMES THORNTON**, internist, educator; MD, Baylor U., 1965. Prof. medicine U. Tex. Health Sci. Ctr., Houston, 1976—, dir. divsn. cardiology, 1977—; Edward Randall III prof., chair. U. Tex. Med. Sch., Houston, 1989—. Mem. NAS-Inst. Medicine. Office: U Tex Health Sci Ctr Sch Medicine Dept Internal Med 6431 Fannin St Rm 1-150 Houston TX 77030-1501

**WILLES, MARK HINCKLEY**, media specialist; b. Salt Lake City, July 16, 1941; s. Joseph Simmons and Ruth (Hinckley) W.; m. Laura Fayone, June 7, 1961; children: Wendy Anne, Susan Kay, Keith Mark, Stephen Joseph, Matthew Bryant. AB, Columbia Coll., 1963, PhD, 1967. Staff banking and currency oper. Ho. of Reps., Washington, 1966-67; asst. prof. fin. Wharton Sch. U. Pa., Phila., 1967-69; economist Fed. Res. Bank, Phila., 1967, sr. economist, 1969-70, dir. rsch., 1970-71, v.p., dir. rsch., 1971, 1st v.p., 1971-77; pres. Fed. Res. Bank of Mpls., 1977-80; exec. v.p., chief fin. officer Gen. Mills, Inc., Mpls., 1980-85, pres., COO, 1985-92, vice-chmn., 1992-95; chmn., pres., CEO Times Mirror Co., L.A., 1995-2000; pub. L.A. Times, 1997-99; disting. prof. mgmt. Brigham Young U., Provo, Utah, 2000, 2004—; pres. Hawaii Honolulu Mission, ch. of LDS, 2001—04. Office: Brigham Young Univ 3651 N 100 E Ste 300 Provo UT 84604 *My success is based on adherence to principles I learned in the home, which is the most basic and important organizational unit in the world. Three of those principles stand out in my mind: Be just, honest and moral—do things not only because they are required, but because they are right. Have mercy—care enough about others to be fair and kind. Be humble—you can get more done effectively with the help of others than you can on your own.*

**WILLET, E. CROSBY (EVERETT CROSBY WILLET)**, artist; b. Phila., Jan. 8, 1929; s. Henry Lee and Katharine Muriel (Crosby) W.; m. Augusta Winter, Nov. 27, 1954; children: William, Nancy Lee, Katharine Crosby, Henry Lee II. BA, Lafayette Coll., 1950; DFA (hon.), Orthodox Cath. Archdiocese, Phila., 1982. Apprentice Blenko Glass Co., Milton, W.Va., 1950; craftsman Willet Stained Glass Studio Inc., Phila., 1950-54, v.p., 1954-64, pres., 1964—. Works include: Portsmouth Priory, R.I., 1966, Folger Bay Washington Cathedral, 1973, Assocs. Dining Room, Smithsonian Instn., 1976, 2d Bapt. Ch., Houston, 1985-86, Gethsemane Cathedral, Fargo, N.D., 1992-95, Peachtree Road United Methodist Church, Atlanta, 2001, St. Martins Episcopal Ch., Houston, 2004. Recipient George Washington Kidd award Lafayette Coll., 1985, Elbert M. Conover award AIA/IFRAA, 2002. Fellow Stained Glass Assn. Am. (exec. bd. 1958-78, 81, pres. 1964-66); mem. InterFaith Forum, Religion, Art and Architecture (exec. bd. 1979-2001, Conover award, 2002), Am. Soc. Appraisers (sr. mem.), Appraisers Assn. Am., Nantucket Yacht Club, Moorings Club. Republican. Presbyn. Home and Office: Willet Stained Glass Studio 10 E Moreland Ave Philadelphia PA 19118-3539 Office Phone: 215-247-5721. E-mail: ecwillet@earthlink.net.

**WILLETT, DON R.**, state supreme court justice; BBA, Baylor U.; JD, MA in Polit. Sci., Duke U. Former law clerk to Judge Jerre S. Williams U.S. Ct. of Appeals for Fifth Circuit, Tex.; atty. Haynes and Boone, LLP, 1993—96; legal adv. to gov. Tex., 1996—2000; dep. atty. gen. for legal counsel Tex., 2000—04; justice Tex. Supreme Ct., 2005—. Served on Bush-Cheney 2000 Presidential Campaign and Transition Team; supreme ct. liaison Tex. Ctr. for Legal Ethics and Professionalism. Former mem. Tex. Commn. on Volunteerism & Community Svc.; bd. mem. Nat. Fatherhood Initiative, Big Brothers Big Sisters of Central Tex., SafePlace, the Tex. Lyceum Assn. Fellow: Tex. Bar Found.; mem.: Tex. Assn. for Ct. Administration (judicial adv. bd.), Am. Law Inst. Office: Tex Supreme Ct PO Box 12248 Austin TX 78711*

**WILLETT, JOHN A.**, lawyer; b. NYC, Aug. 4, 1946; BA, Bucknell U., 1968; MBA, JD, Stanford U., 1972; LLM, NYU, 1976. Bar: Calif. 1972, N.Y. 1973. Ptnr., N.Y.C. Office Mgt. Arnold & Porter, N.Y.C. Fellow, Am. Coll. Investment Counsel; mem. ABA, State Bar Calif., Assn. of Bar of City of N.Y. Office: Arnold & Porter 399 Park Ave Fl 35 New York NY 10022-4690 Office Phone: 212-715-1001. Office Fax: 212-715-1399. Business E-mail: john.willett@aporter.com.

**WILLETT, RICHARD**, writer, editor; b. L.A., Apr. 11, 1959; s. Bob and Vera (Kerr) W. Grad. high sch., North Vancouver, B.C., Can. Clk. Classic Bookshop, Vancouver, B.C., Can., 1977-78, clk./asst. mgr. N.Y.C., 1978-84; asst. to pres. Dramatists Play Svc., Inc., N.Y.C., 1984-88; freelance editor N.Y.C., 1988—. Prodr./treas. New Directions Theater, N.Y.C., 1994-2001; co-artistic dir. New Directions Theater, N.Y.C., 2001—; active Alliance of Resident Theatres/N.Y., Theatre Comm. Group. Author: (plays) Certain Doubts, 1987, The Godsend, 1991 (Off-Off-Broadway Rev. award 1997), Boys Will Be Boys, 1995, S.O.S., 1995, Hot Air, 1998, Triptych, 1999, Random Harvest, 1999, The Flid Show, 2000, Public Speaking, 2000, Weekend at the Willard, 2002, Tiny Bubbles, 2002, 9/10, 2003; contbr. short stories to Christopher Street, Oxalis, Hawaii Rev., Karamu. Edward F. Albee Found. fellow, 1990; Tennessee Williams scholar Sewanee (Tenn.) Writers' Conf., 1993. Mem.: Dramatists Guild, Writers Guild Am. (assoc.).

**WILLETT, ROBERT E.**, lawyer; b. Glendale, Calif., June 21, 1943; BA, San Fernando Valley State Coll., 1971; JD, U. Calif., Berkeley, 1974. Bar: Calif. 1974, U.S. Supreme Ct. 1987, U.S. Tax Ct. 1988. Lawyer O'Melveny & Myers, L.A. Mem. state bar com. for adminstrn. of justice, 1987-90. Assoc. editor Calif. Law Rev., 1972-73, notes and comments editor, 1973-74. Mem. ABA sections on litigation and antitrust, L.A. County Bar Assn. sections on antitrust and litigation (vice chair ct. improvements com. 1985-87), Order of Coif. Office: O'Melveny & Myers LLP 400 S Hope St Los Angeles CA 90071-2899 Office Phone: 213-430-6355. Office Fax: 213-430-6407. Business E-Mail: rwillett@omm.com.

**WILLETT, ROSLYN LEONORE**, public relations executive, food service consultant, writer, editor; d. Edward and Celia (Stickler) Sternberg; m. Edward Willett (div.); 1 child, Jonathan Stanley. BA, Hunter Coll., NYC; postgrad., Columbia U., CUNY, NYU, New Sch. Dietitian YWCA, NYC; tech. and patents libr., food technologist in charge tech. svcs. and devel. Stein Hall & Co., NYC; editor McGraw-Hill, Inc., NYC, Harcourt Brace Jovanovich, Inc., NYC; pub. rels. writer Farley Manning Assocs., NYC; cons. pub. rels. and food svc. Roslyn Willett Assocs., Inc., NYC, 1959—. Adj. prof. Hunter Coll., Poly U., Columbia U. Sch. Pub. Health; dir. West End Writers Workshop, 1998—2002; seminar presenter in field. Author: The Woman Executive in Woman in Sexist Society, 1971, also short stories and essays; assoc. editor Timber Creek Rev., Words of Wisdom, 2001—, Bulls Head Creek Rev., 2004—. V.p. North Shore Ams. for Dem. Action; orl. rapporteur Post-Assembly Tech. Sessions, WHO; juror Am. Film Festival, Arts and Scis., 1962—88; chmn. Women's Polit. Caucus, Inc. NY, NJ, Conn, 1971—73; v.p. Mid Hudson Arts and Sci. Ctr., Poughkeepsie, NY; apptd. to regional adv. coun. Fed. SBA, 1976—78; chmn. image of woman com. NOW; bd. dirs. Small Bus. Task Force, Assn. for Small Bus. and Professions, 1981—85, Rhinebeck Chamber Music Soc., 1985—86, Will Inst., New Paltz, 1980—2001, Women Studies Abstracts, 1971—81; pres. Hunns Lake Assn. 1999—2001. Mem. Pub. Rels. Soc. Am. (accredited), Food Svc. Cons. Soc. Internat. (bd. dirs. 1978-80), NY Acad. Scis., Inst. Food Technologists, Juilliard Assn., Assn. for Japanese Art in Am., Inc., Alliance Française, Paris Club, NY Print Club. Avocations: writing, dance, art collecting, hiking, swimming. Home: 97 W Hunns Lake Rd Stanfordville NY 12581-5606 Office: 441 West End Ave New York NY 10024-5328

**WILLETT, TERI KAY**, art educator; b. Jefferson City, Mo., May 15, 1953; d. Robert Jewell and Esther Marie Cunningham; m. Roger Gregory Willett, Aug. 7, 1976; children: Sarah Ellen Willett-Otto, Jesse Timothy, Anthony Carter. BA, St. Mary Coll., 1975; M in religious Edn., Loyola U., New Orleans, 1987; MA, Ctrl. Mo. State U., 1997. Cert. tchr. Mo. Educator Holy Family Sch., Independence, Mo., 1985—87, Nativity of Mary Sch., Independence, 1986—87, St. Mary's H.S., Independence, 1987—. Workshop presenter Mo. Art Edn. Assn., 1996—. Exhibitions include St. Mary Coll., Leavenworth, Kans., 1975, 1993, 1994, Visitors Ctr., Arrow Rock, Mo., 1995, Rozier Gallery, Jefferson City, Mo., 1996, 1999, Ea. Mo. State U., Warrensburg, 1997, St. Joseph, Mo., 1998, Mo. Art Edn. Assn., Lake of the Ozark, 1999, Winston Churchill Meml., Fulton, Mo., 2001, 2002, 2005, Lake of the Ozarks, Mo., 2001, 2005, Period Gallery, Omaha, 2001, Parklane Gallery, Kirkland, Wash., 2001, Joyfeli Gallery, Kansas City, Mo., 2001—02, Images Gallery, Kansas City, 2003, 2005, 2006, St. Louis, 2004, Old Blake Mus., Independence, Mo., 2004, Goppert Gallery, Leavenworth, Kans., 2005, Unity Temple, Kansas City, 2005, North Ctrl. Mo. Coll., Trenton, 2005, Cornerstone Gallery, Independence, 2006. Merit badge counselor Boy Scouts Am., Kansas City, Mo., 1993—2003. Named Secondary Tchr. of Yr., Nat. Cath. Educators Assn., 1994; recipient Tchrs. Honor award, Nelson/Atkins Mus. Art, 1996, Grand prize, 1999. Mem.: Kans. Watercolor Soc. (assoc.), Mo. Watercolor Soc. (assoc. Signature Status 2002), Mo. Art Edn. Assn. (assoc.; dist. #3 rep. 1993—2006). Home: 3602 N Osage Independence MO 64050 Office: St Mary's High School 622 N Main Independence MO 64050 Personal E-mail: terikay@comcast.net. E-mail: twillett@stmhs.org.

**WILLETT, THOMAS EDWARD**, lawyer; b. NYC, Nov. 8, 1947; s. Oscar Edward and Alice (Fleming) W.; m. Marilyn Kenney, Dec. 28, 1969; children: Thomas Justin, Christopher Joseph. BS, USAF Acad., Colo., 1969; JD with distinction, Cornell U., 1972. Bar: N.Y. 1973, U.S. Claims 1973, U.S. Supreme Ct. 1977. Judge advocate USAF, Syracuse, NY, 1973-75, Kincheloe AFB, Mich., 1975-77, USAF Hdqs., Washington, 1977-79; assoc. Harris Beach LLP, Rochester, NY, 1979-84, ptnr., 1985—. Pres. Monroe County Legal Assistance Corp., Rochester, 1983-89. Capt. USAF, 1969-79. Mem. ABA, N.Y. State Bar Assn., Monroe County Bar Assn., Order of Coif. Office: Harris Beach LLP 99 Garnsey Rd Pittsford NY 14534 Office Phone: 585-419-8646. E-mail: twillett@harrisbeach.com.

**WILLETT, WALTER CHURCHILL**, epidemiologist, educator; b. Hart, Mich., June 20, 1945; s. Elwin Lintin and Lawain (Churchill) W.; m. Gail Valerae Pettiford, June 11, 1973; children: Amani, Kamali. Studied food sci., Mich. State U., 1963-66; MD, U. Mich., 1970; MPH, Harvard U. 1973, DPH 1980. Diplomate Am. Bd. Internal Medicine. Lectr. in medicine U. Dar es Salaam, Tanzania, 1974-75, head community health dept., 1975-77; fellow clin. epidemiology Channing Lab. Med. Sch., Harvard U., Boston, 1977-80; asst. prof. epidemiology Sch. Pub. Health, Harvard U., Boston 1980-84, assoc. prof. epidemiology, 1984-88, Fredrick John Stare prof. epidemiology and nutrition, 1987—, chmn. dept. nutrition, 1991—; prof. epidemiology and nutrition Harvard Med. Sch., 1992—. Statis. cons. New Eng. Jour. Medicine, Boston, 1987—; spkr. in field. Author: Nutritional Epidemiology, 1989, Eat, Drink and Be Healthy: The Harvard Medical School Guide to Healthy Eating, 2001, Nutritional Epidemiology, 2nd Edit.; contbr. over 900 articles to sci. publs. Recipient Charles S. Mott prize, GM Cancer Rsch. Found., 2001, Brinker award, Komen Found., 2003, Linus Pauling Inst. Prize for Health Rsch., 2003, Rogers award, AAMC, 2003, Discovery Health Channel Med. Honors, 2004. Mem. Am. Epidemiol. Soc., Soc. for Epidemiol. Rsch., Am. Inst. Nutrition, Alpha Omega Alpha. Avocations: gardening, woodworking, skiing, bicycling, kayaking. Office: Harvard Sch Pub Health Dept Nutrition Bldg II Rm 311 651 Huntington Ave Boston MA 02115 Office Phone: 617-432-4680.*

**WILEY, CHARLES WAYNE**, lawyer; b. Dillon, Mont., Oct. 7, 1932; s. Asa Charles and Elizabeth Ellen Willey; m. Helene D., July 21, 1962 (div.); children: Stephen Charles, Heather Helene, Brent David, Scott D.; m. Alexis W. Grant, Jan. 26, 1986. BS with honors, Mont. State U., 1954; JD with high honors, U. Mont., 1959. Bar: Mont. 1959, Calif. 1960, U.S. Ct. Claims 1975, U.S. Tax Ct. 1975, U.S. Ct. Appeals (9th cir.) 1959, U.S. Ct. Appeals (Fed. cir.) 1983, U.S. Supreme Ct. 1972. Law clk. to presiding judge U.S. Ct. Appeals (9th cir.), 1959-60; ptnr. Price, Postel & Parma, Santa Barbara, Calif., 1960-77; pvt. practice Santa Barbara, 1977-97; shareholder Hollister & Brace, Santa Barbara, 1998-2001. Prof. law corp.; instr. Santa Barbara City Coll., 1961—63, U. Calif., Santa Barbara, 1963—64; lectr. Mont. Tax Inst., 1990, 92, Am. Agr. Law Assn., 1993, 96; adj. prof. law U. Mont., 2005. Chief editor Mont. Law Rev., 1958—59. Pres. Legal Aid Found. Santa Barbara, 1970; mem. Laguna Blanca Sch. Bd., pres. 1980-81; v.p. Phoenix of Santa Barbara. Served to capt. USAF, 1954-56. Mem.: State Bar of Mont. (chair sect. bus., estates, tax, trusts and real estate 2004—05), State Bar of Calif.,

Santa Barbara County Bar Assn. (pres. 1972—73), Rotary, Kiwanis, Phi Delta Phi, Phi Eta Sigma, Phi Kappa Phi. Republican. Episcopalian. Avocations: reading, writing, travel. Office: 806 Parkview Way Missoula MT 59803

**WILLHAM, RICHARD LEWIS**, zoology educator; b. Hutchinson, Kans., May 4, 1932; s. Oliver S. and Esther B. (Hurt) W.; m. Esther B. Burkhart, June 1, 1954; children: Karen Nell, Oliver Lee. BS, Okla. State U., 1954; MS, Iowa State U., 1955, PhD, 1960. Asst. prof. Iowa State U., Ames, 1959-63, assoc. prof., 1966-71, prof. dept. animal sci., 1971-78, Disting. prof., 1978—; assoc. prof. Okla. State U., Stillwater, 1963-66. Cons. in field; tchr. livestock history; guest curator exhbn. Art About Livestock, 1990. Author: A Heritage of Leadership - The First 100 Years of Animal Science at Iowa State University, 1996. Recipient Svc. award Beef Improvement Fedn., 1974, Edn. and Rsch. award Am. Polled Herefore Assn., 1979, Rsch. award Nat. Cattlemen's Assn., 1986, 91, Disting. Alumnus award Okla. State U., 1978, Regents Faculty Excellence award Iowa State U., 1993; named to Hall of Fame Am. Hereford Assn., 1982, Am. Angus Assn., 1988. Fellow Am. Soc. Animal Sci. (animal breeding and genetics award 1978, industry service award 1986). Home: 2316 Hamilton Dr Ames IA 50014-8201 Office: Iowa State U Dept Animal Sci Ames IA 50011-0001 E-mail: rwillham@iastate.edu.

**WILLI, STEVEN MATTHEW**, physician, educator, researcher; s. John Edward and Doris Mae (Smith) Willi; m. Maria Szpiech, July 27, 2002. BA cum laude, Johns Hopkins U., 1981, MD, 1985. Diplomate in pediatrics and pediatric endocrinology Am. Bd. Pediatrics. Resident in pediat. Children's Hosp. of Phila., 1985—88; fellow in pediatric endocrinology Children's Hosp. Phila., 1988—91; instr. pediat. U. Pa., Phila., 1991—92, assoc. prof. pediat., 2004—; asst. prof. pediat. Med. U. S.C., Charleston, 1992—98, assoc. prof., 1998—2004. Contbr. chpts. to books, articles to profl. jours. Med. dir. Camp Adam Fisher for Children with Diabetes, Summerton, S.C., 1995-2003; bd. dirs. Juvenile Diabetes Found., 1995-99; dir. Diabetes Ctr. for Children, Children's Hosp. of Phila., 2004—. Recipient Nat. Rsch. Svc. award NIH, 1990, Clin. Assoc. Physician award NIH, 1996; Healfman scholar, 1985. Fellow Am. Acad. Pediatrics; mem. Endocrine Soc., Lawson Wilkins Pediatric Endocrine Soc., Am. Diabetes Assn. (profl. sect., mem. youth svcs. com. 1993—), So. Med. Assn., Charleston County Med. Soc. Avocations: tennis, bicycling, photography, golf. Office: Childrens Hosp of Phila Divsn Endocrinology/Diabetes 34th St Civic Ctr Blvd Philadelphia PA 19104-0001

**WILLIAM, DAVID**, theater director, actor; b. London, Eng., June 24, 1926; arrived in Can., 1986; s. Eric Hugh and Olwen (Roose) W. BA, U. Coll., Oxford, Eng., 1950. Artistic dir. Glasgow Citizen's Theatre, The Nottingham Playhouse, The New Shakespeare Co., London, The National Theatre of Israel, Stratford Festival, Can., 1989-93. Vis. prof. theater dept. De Paul U., Chgo., 1985-88; founder, 1st artistic dir. Ludlow Festival. Profl. debut as Rosencrantz to Richard Burton's Hamlet, Old Vic Theatre, London, 1953; theatre directing credits include: Bacchae, The Importance of Being Earnest, The Tempest, Entertaining Mr. Sloane, Love Letters, Treasure Island, Hamlet, Love for Love, The Shoemaker's Holiday, Murder in the Cathedral, Troilus and Cressida, The Winter's Tale, She Stoops to Conquer, Antigone, Separate Tables, Romeo and Juliet, Othello, King Lear, Volpone, Albert Herring, The Merry Wives of Windsor, Twelfth Night; directing world premiers of operas include: Therese, Royal Opera House Covent Garden, The Lighthouse, Edinburgh festival, Red Emma; other operas directed include Iphigenie en Tauride, The Fairy Queen, Lisbon, La Traviata, Scottish Opera, Il Re Pastore, Camden Festival, Albert Herring, Aldeburgh Festival, Cosl Fan Tutte, Opera St. Louis, Tosca, Can. Opera Co., Mrs. Mozart, Hartford Symphony Orch., 1999; appeared in Uncle Vanya as Serebryakov, As You Like It as Jaques, Twelfth Night as Malvolio; appeared in numerous TV prodns. most notably as Richard the Second in the BBC series An Age of Kings; compiled, directed and acted in My Shakespeare, Stratford Festival and CBC Radio; played A.E.H. in The Invention of Love, Guthrie Theatre, Mpls., 2000, Studio Theater, Washington, 2001, Boyet in Love's Labours Lost, Nat. Arts Ctr, Ottawa, 2005; played in Under Milk Wood, St. Mary's, Ont., 2004. Home: 194 Langarth St E London ON Canada N6C 1Z5 Personal E-mail: may.king@rogers.com.

**WILL.I.AM, See ADAMS, WILLIAM JR.**

**WILLIAMES, LEE JOHN**, academic administrator, history professor; b. Phila., July 4, 1942; m. Frances, Feb. 24, 1968; 3 children. BA in Pre-Law and Liberal Arts, LaSalle U., 1964; MA in European History, Niagara U., 1966, ACS in Soviet Studies, 1966; PhD in History, SUNY, Binghamton, 1981. Prof., honors dir. Coll. Misericordia, Dallas, Pa., 1966-86; asst. provost, prof. U. Scranton, Pa., 1987-92; v.p. acad. affairs, prof. history U. St. Thomas, 1992—2000, acting pres. summer, 1997, now prof. history and emeritus v.p. acad. affairs, 2000—; vis. prof. Mary Immaculate Coll., U. Limerick, Ireland, 2000. Frequent spkr. Russian univs.; sec. gen. internat. coun. U. St. Thomas, 1995-97. Author: Anton Chekov: Iconoclast, 1989; (curriculum exercises) Odyssey of the Mind, 1988-96, written over 20 articles on history and on teaching, Commr. Northeastern Pa. coun. Boy Scouts Am., 1988-92, v.p., 1984-88; mem. water safety bd. ARC, N.E. Pa., 1988-91; chair steering com. St. Thomas/Shell Oil/Helms Collaboration, 1997—. Recipient Silver Beaver medal Boy Scouts Am., 1984, St. George medal Cath. Com. on Scouting, 1986, Jubalarian medal La Salle U., Phila., Centennial medal U. Scranton. Fellow Am. Coun. on Edn. (exec. com. coun. fellows 1989-92); mem. Mid. Atlantic Hist. Assn. of Cath. Colls. and Univs. (editor jour. 1985-92), Am. Assn. for Advancement of Slavic Studies. Roman Catholic. Avocations: swimming, canoeing, martial arts, stained glass, antique restoration. Office: U St Thomas 3800 Montrose Blvd Houston TX 77006-4626 Office Phone: 713-525-3810. E-mail: williames@stthom.edu.

**WILLIAMS, ALAN KEISER**, management consultant; b. Harrisburg, Pa., Dec. 19, 1928; s. Paul Rupp and Margaret Helen (Keiser) W.; m. Barbara Elaine Hanson, Aug. 7, 1952 (div. Aug. 1975); children: Margaret Vivian Williams Westfall, Bryn Barbara Williams Stuart, Andrew Hanson Williams; m. Peggie Lucille Hall, May 29, 1988. BA, U. No. Colo., 1952. Sr. rsch. mgr. Dow Chem. Co., Golden, 1952-74; v.p. Allied-Gen. Nuclear Svc., Barnwell, S.C., 1974-83; prin. engr., project mgr. Bechtel Nat. Inc., San Francisco, 1983-91; sr. program analyst Sci. Applications Internat. Co., Germantown, Md., 1991-95; pvt. cons., 1995—. Contbr. articles to Jour. Electro Chem. Soc. Tech. co-chmn. ENC-3 Brussels, 1982. With U.S. Army, 1946-47. Fellow Am. Nuclear Soc. (chmn. Savannah River sect 1980, bd. dirs. 1982-85); mem. AAAS, Am. Chem. Soc. Achievements include research in processing and handling actinide elements, principally uranium, plutonium and americium. Home and Office: 39531 S Moonwood Dr Tucson AZ 85739 Personal E-mail: akwplw@wbhsi.net.

**WILLIAMS, ALFRED B.**, retired management educator; b. Oakland City, Ind., Sept. 17, 1940; s. Ross Merl and Jesse Adell (Helsley) W. BS cum laude, Oakland City U., 1963; MS, Ind. U., 1964; PhD, Ga. State U., 1974. Tchr. Arlington H.S., Indpls., 1964-65, Oakland City (Ind.) U., 1965-69; editor Southwestern Pub. Co., 1969-72, cons., 1981-93; adj. prof. Ga. State U., Atlanta, 1972-74; prof. mgmt. and bus. commn. U. La., Lafayette, 1975—2002, chmn. dept., 1986-96, prof. emeritus, 2002—; ret., 2002; adj. prof. U. La., Lafayette, 2004—05. Cons. John Wiley Pub. Co., N.Y., 1988-89, Irwin Pub., 1989. Author study guides; editor Info. Systems Bus. Comm. Jour., 1983, 93. Reading mentor Help One Student to Succeed reading program N. Lewis Elem. Sch., New Iberia, La., 2003—. Mem. AAUP, Assn. Bus. Communicators (bd. dirs. 1986-90, Francis W. Weeks Merit award 1984), La. Assn. Higher Edn., Sierra Club, Phi Delta Kappa, Phi Kappa Phi, Delta Pi Epsilon, Beta Gamma Sigma. Methodist.

**WILLIAMS, ALLEN W., JR.**, lawyer; b. Milw., Sept. 8, 1944; AB cum laude, Harvard U., 1966; JD cum laude, Columbia U., 1970, MBA, 1970. Bar: Wis. 1970. Legal counsel to Gov. Patrick J. Lucey State of Wis., 1971-72; ptnr. Foley & Lardner LLP, Milw., chmn. regulatory practice dept. Chmn., bd. trustees Med. Coll. Wis., 1984-87; mem. legal com. Edison Electric Inst.,

1981—. Mem. bd. editors Columbia Law Review, 1969-70. Bd. dirs. Planned Parenthood Wis., 1974-76. Mem. State Bar Wis., Milwaukee County Zool. Soc. (bd. dirs. 1977—, pres. 1984-86), Med. Coll. Wis. (chmn. 1984-1987), Edison Electric Inst. (legal com. 1981). Office: Foley & Lardner LLP Firstar Ctr 777 E Wisc Ave Milwaukee WI 53202 Office Phone: 414-297-5808. Office Fax: 414-297-4900. Business E-Mail: awilliams@foley.com.

**WILLIAMS, AMY MCDANIEL**, lawyer; b. Birmingham, Ala., Sept. 7, 1962; BA cum laude, Duke Univ., 1985; JD magna cum laude, Cornell Univ., 1990. Bar: Va. 1990. Assoc. Hunton & Williams LLP, Richmond, Va., 1992—99, ptnr., bus. practice group, 1999—, chmn. ethics com., 2002—. Sr. note editor Cornell Law Rev., 1990. Mem.: ABA, Met. Richmond Women's Bar Assn., Nat. Assn. Women Lawyers. Office: Hunton & Williams LLP Riverfront Plz East Tower 951 E Byrd St Richmond VA 23219-4074 Office Phone: 804-788-7388. Office Fax: 804-788-8218. Business E-Mail: awilliams@hunton.com.

**WILLIAMS, ANDREW W.**, energy executive; Degree, N.C. State U., 1971; MBA, Loyola Coll., 1984. From v.p. energy and mkt. policy and devel. to sr. v.p., CFO Pepco Holdings, Washington, 1994—2000, sr. v.p., 2000—, CFO, 2000—. Office: Pepco Holdings 701 Ninth St NW Room 4230 Washington DC 20068

**WILLIAMS, ANITA MARIE**, publishing executive, writer; b. Detroit, Feb. 4, 1963; d. Lawrence Trevone Bartell and Bernadia Hankerson; m. Paul Thomas Williams, Jr., Aug. 25, 1984 (dec. Oct. 16, 1991); children: Ebony Renee, Paul Thomas David III. BA in Africana studies, Wayne State U., 1999, BA in Speech Comm., 1999, MA in African-Am./African History, 2003. CEO/founder Metro Detroit Intellectual Soc., Detroit, 1997—; CEO African-Princess0204 Pub. and Photos, Detroit, 1997—; founder, CEO Creating a Legacy for Our Sister and Daughters, Detroit, 1999—; columnist Gazette News, Detroit, 1999—2000, My Life Time Mag., Detroit, 2003. Author, rschr.: historical biography Katherine Dunham: An African-American Cultural Icon; photo exhbn., Eyes of the AfricanPrincess0204; author: (photographic essay) Eyes of the AfricanPrincess0204; prodr.: (multi-media cd) Eyes of the AfricanPrincess0204, Hankerson Family Reunion. Recipient Coleman A. Young scholarship, Africana Studies Dept., Wayne State U., 1998, Dudley Randall scholarship, 1997, Mich. Nat. Bank/Detroit Urban League scholarship, Detroit Urban League, 1999, Dudley Randall scholarship, Africana Studies Dept., Wayne State U., 1998, Coleman Young scholarship, 1999. Achievements include research in Uncovering pertinent data pertaining to the African Diaspora. Office Phone: 313-931-5446. Personal E-mail: awill27595@aol.com.

**WILLIAMS, ANN CLAIRE**, federal judge; b. Detroit, Aug. 16, 1949; m. David J. Stewart. BS, Wayne State U., 1970; MA, U. Mich., 1972; JD, U. Notre Dame, 1975; degree (hon.), Lake Forest Coll., 1987, U. Portland, 1993, U. Notre Dame, 1997. Law clk. to Hon. Robert A. Sprecher, 1975-76; asst. U.S. atty. U.S. Dist. Ct. (no. dist.) Ill., Chgo., 1976-85; faculty Nat. Inst. for Trial Advocacy, 1979—, also bd. dirs.; adj. prof., lectr. Northwestern U. Law Sch., 1979—, John Marshall Law Sch., 1979—; judge U.S. Dist. Ct. (no. dist.) Ill., 1985-99, U.S. Ct. Appeals (7th cir.), Chgo., 1999—. Chief Organized Crime Drug Enforcement Task Force for North Ctrl. Region, 1983-85; mem. ct. adminstrn. and case mgmt. com. Jud. Conf. U.S., 1990-97, chair, 1993-97. Sec. bd. trustees U. Notre Dame; founder Minority Legal Resources, Inc. Recipient Earl Burns Dickerson award, Chgo. Bar Assn., 1997, Tradition of Excellence award, Minority Legal Resources, Inc., 1997, Thurgood Marshall Jurist of Year, Legal Ministry of Second Baptist Church, 1997, Alumni of Year, Black Law Students Assn. U. Notre Dame, 1997, Morton A. Brody Disting. Jud. Svc. award, Colby Coll., 2002. Mem. FBA, Fed. Judges Assn., Ill. State Bar Assn., Ill. Jud. Coun., Cook County Bar Assn., Women's Bar Assn. Ill., Black Women's Lawyers Assn. Greater Chgo. Office: US Ct Appeals 7th Circuit 219 S Dearborn St Ste 2612 Chicago IL 60604-1803*

**WILLIAMS, ANTHONY**, lawyer; b. NYC, Jan. 12, 1946; s. Patrick and Palma (Leone) W. AB in Govt. cum laude, Harvard U., 1968; JD, NYU, 1973. Bar: N.Y. 1974, Calif. 1977, US Supreme Ct. 1980. Assoc. Coudert Bros., N.Y.C., 1973-75, San Francisco, 1976-79, ptnr. N.Y.C., 1981—, adminstrv. ptnr., 1982-85, chmn., 1993—2001, head Global Life Sci. practice. Bd. chmn. Fenn, Wright & Manson, England; bd. vice chmn. Senetek PLC; mem. internat. adv. bd. Intelligent Engineering Ltd., Trautman Wasserman & Co.; dir. Brook Capital Corp., DBT America Inc., German Am. C. of C., Plymouth Holdings Ltd., British Virgin Islands, River Ventures Inc., Hong Kong. Editor (in chief): NYU Jour. Internat. Law; contbr. articles to profl. jours. Vice chmn. HELP USA Inc.; bd. mem. City Univ. of NY, Friends of Heidelberg Ctr. for Am. Studies, Harvard MIT Div. of Life Sci. & Tech., Metro Internat. NY, Robert F. Kennedy Mem. Ctr. for Human Rights, Sheltering Arms Svc. Served U.S. Army, 1968-70. Mem. ABA, N.Y. Bar Assn., Assn. Bar of City of N.Y., Calif. Bar Assn. Avocations: reading, baseball, golf. Office: Coudert Bros 1114 Avenue Of The Americas Fl 4 New York NY 10036-7710 Office Phone: 212-626-4418. Office Fax: 212-626-4120. Business E-Mail: williamsa@coudert.com.

**WILLIAMS, ANTHONY A.**, mayor; b. 1951; s. Lewis and Virginia W.; m. Diana Lynn Simmons; 1 child, Asantewa Foster. BA in Polit. Sci. magna cum laude, Yale U., 1982; JD, M of Pub. Policy, Harvard U., 1987. Law clk. to Hon. David Nelson US Dist. Ct., Boston, 1987-88; asst. dir. Boston Redevel. Authority, 1988-89; exec. dir. Cmty. Devel. Agy. State, 1989-91; dep. comptr. State of Conn., Boston, 1991-93; exec. dir. Cmty. Devel. Agy., St. Louis, 1989-91; dept. contr. State of Conn., 1991-93; CFO Dept. Agr., Washington, 1995—; 981 mayor Washington DC, 1999— Adj. prof. pub. affairs Columbia U., NYC, 1992-93. Pres. pro tempore, chmn. cmty. devel. com. Conn. Bd. Alderman, 1980-83; dir. comm. Conn. Spkr. House and Assembly Dem., 1983; second v.p., Washington, DC-based National League of Cities (NLC), 2002-. Named one of 100 Most Influential Black Americans, Ebony mag., 2006; Kellogg Found. Nat. fellow, 1991. Democrat. Office: Office of the Mayor 1350 Pennsylvania Ave NW 6th Fl Washington DC 20004 Office Phone: 202-393-8669.*

**WILLIAMS, ANTHONY ERVIN**, music educator; b. Nashville, Aug. 25, 1960; s. Albert Osborne and Marion Ervin Williams. MusB, U. Cin., 1982; MusM, U. Mich., 1984. Music dir., organist Good Shepherd United Meth. Ch., Dearborn, Mich., 1983—86; instr. music, univ. organist Fisk U., Nashville, 1986—90; instr. music, univ. organist Dillard U., New Orleans, 1990—. Dir. Fisk Jubilee Singers Fisk U., Nashville, 1987—90. Musician organ recitals. Bd. dirs. New Orleans Mission, 1992—2004. Recipient Strader Organ scholarship, U. Cin., Coll. Conservatory of Music, 1978—82. Mem.: Mus. Arts Soc. New Orleans (bd. dirs. 2002—2006), Am. Guild of Organists (bd. dirs. New Orleans chpt. 1992—94). Avocations: cooking, travel, ballroom dancing. Office: Dillard Univ 2601 Gentilly Blvd New Orleans LA 70122 Home: 3603 Batavia St Nashville TN 37209-2530 Office Phone: 504-816-4854. Home Fax: 504-242-5122. Personal E-mail: awilli6034@aol.com. E-mail: awilliams@dillard.edu.

**WILLIAMS, ARTHUR L., JR.**, retired insurance company executive; married; 2 children. BA, Miss. State U.; MS, Auburn U. HS football coach; part time ins. salesman; founder A.L. Williams and Associates, 1977—89; retired, 1990. Lectr. in field. Author: The Leader's Role, The Winning Edge, Do It, Passion Selling, The Power of Believing In You, COACH The A.L. Williams Story. Named one of Forbes' Richest Americans, 2006.*

**WILLIAMS, ASHLEE JEAN**, English educator, psycho-social rehabilitation specialist; b. Boise, Idaho, Aug. 28, 1976; d. Clare Marie Kipp and Scott W. Williams. Grad. in Secondary Edn., U. of Idaho, 2001. Cert. secondary edn. tchr. Idaho, 2001. Reading and English tchr. for high risk juveniles Twin Falls Sch. Dist., Idaho, 2003—. Psycho-social rehab. specialist Alliance

Family Svcs., Twin Falls, Idaho, 2005—. Mem.: Idaho Edn. Assn. Office: Snake River Detention and CDC 2515 Wright Ave Twin Falls ID 83301 Office Phone: 208-736-5048. E-mail: williamsas@tfsd.k12.id.us.

**WILLIAMS, B. JOHN, JR.,** retired federal agency administrator, lawyer; b. Lancaster, Pa., Dec. 13, 1949; s. Bernard John and Sarah Elizabeth (Sykes) W.; m. Martha Caroline Roberts, Aug. 6, 1977; children: Robert, Sarah, Anne, Bernard. BA, George Washington U., 1971, JD, 1974. Bar: D.C., Pa., U.S. Tax Ct., U.S. Ct. Appeals (3rd, 9th and fed. cirs.), U.S. Supreme Ct. Law clk. to judge U.S. Tax Ct., Washington, 1974-76; assoc. Ballard, Spahr, Andrews & Ingersoll, Phila., 1976-81; spl. asst. to chief counsel IRS, Washington, 1981-83; dep. asst. atty. gen. Tax Div. Dept. Justice, Washington, 1983-84; ptnr. Morgan, Lewis & Bockius, Washington, 1984-85; judge U.S. Tax Ct., Washington, 1985-90; ptnr. Morgan, Lewis & Bockius, Washington, 1990-2000, Shearman & Sterling, Washington, 2000—02; chief counsel, IRS U.S. Dept. Treasury, Washington, 2002—03. Mem. adv. com. U.S. Ct. Appeals, Fed. Cir. Fellow Am. Coll. Tax Counsel; mem. ABA, Am. Law Inst., Phi Beta Kappa, Omicron Delta Kappa. Republican.

**WILLIAMS, BARBARA ANNE,** retired academic administrator; b. Camden, N.J., Oct. 14, 1938; d. Frank and Laura Dorothy (Szweda) W. BA cum laude, Georgian Ct. U., 1963; MLS, Rutgers U., 1965; MA, Manhattan Coll., 1973; postgrad., NYU, 1976—81, postgrad., 1993—. Cert. English tchr., N.J.; joined Sisters of Mercy, 1957. Sec. Camden Cath. H.S., 1956-57; registrar Georgian Ct. U., Lakewood, NJ, 1960-66, dir. libr. svcs., 1966-74, dean acad. affairs, 1974-80, pres., 1980-2000, sci. and math. libr., 2000—04, pres. emerita, 2000—, archivist, 2003—. Bd. dirs. N.J. Natural Gas Co., 1986-91 Mem. editl. bd. N.J. Woman mag. Bd. dirs., mem. ednl. adv. coun. Diocese of Trenton, N.J., 1983-90; mem. adv. bd. Ocean County Ctr. for Arts, Lakewood, N.J., 1983-91; mem. Ocean County Pvt. Industry Coun., 1983-92; bd. dirs. Monmouth/Ocean Devel. Coun., 1981-84; mem. State of N.J. Student Assistance Bd., 1995-99; mem. Ocean County School-to-Career Com., 1996-2000; mem. art adv. coun. Nat. Mus. Cath. Art and History, 2000—; mem. Mid-Atlantic Regional Archives Conf., 2003—; trustee Camden Cath. H.S., 2005—. Named Outstanding Woman N.J. Assn. Women Bus. Owners, 1983; recipient Humanitarian award Monmouth/Ocean Devel. Coun., 1985, Salute to Policymakers award Exec. Women N.J., 1986, Woman in Leadership award Monmouth Coun. Girl Scouts, 1987, Citizen of Yr. Alcoholism & Drug Abuse Coun. Ocean County, 1993, Brotherhood/Sisterhood award Monmouth/Ocean County chpts. NCCJ, 1994, Friend of Scouting award Boy Scouts Am. Jersey Shore Coun., 1999, Leadership award Mercy Higher Edn. Colloquium, 2000. Mem. Assn. Mercy Colls. (pres. 1981-83, sec. 1996-98), Mercy Higher Edn. Colloquium (mem. exec. com. 1980-87), Ocean County Bus. Assn. (trustee 1982-84), Nat. Assn. Inc. Colls. and Univs. (secretariat 1981-83, 87-91), NAIA (coun. of Ind. mem. 1997-2000), Soc. Am. Archivists. Home and office: Georgian Ct Univ 900 Lakewood Ave Lakewood NJ 08701-2600 Office Phone: 732-987-2441. E-mail: williamssb@georgian.edu.

**WILLIAMS, BARBARA IVORY,** educational researcher; b. Detroit, Apr. 28, 1936; d. Henry Oliver and Willa Mae (Frazier) I.; m. Alney Elliott Whitener, Jan. 1, 1987 (dec.). BS, Wayne State U., 1957, MEd, 1960; PhD, U. Washington, 1973. Tchr. Detroit Pub. Schs., 1957-68; program assoc. Mich.-Ohio Regional Lab., Detroit, 1968-70; lectr. predoctoral U. Wash., Seattle, 1970-73; sr. program assoc. Far West Lab. for Ednl. Research and Devel., San Francisco, 1973-76; sr. cons. E.H. White & Co. San Francisco, 1976-77; sr. program assoc. Northwest Regional Lab., Portland, Oreg., 1977-84; area coord. Ednl. Testing Service, Washington, 1984-85; edn. group dir. Research and Evaluation Assocs., Washington, 1985-87; ind. cons. Washington, 1987-89; assoc. dir. edn. studies Westat, Rockville, Md., 1989—. Mem. Am. Ednl. Research Assn., Am. Psychol. Assn., Nat. Assn. Black Sch. Educators, Phi Delta Kappa, Alpha Kappa Alpha (pres. Portland chpt. 1980-84). Democrat. Baptist. Avocation: needlecrafts. Home: 13601 Belle Chasse Blvd Unit 414 Laurel MD 20707-9433 Office Phone: 301-251-4249. E-mail: barbaraji@mac.com.

**WILLIAMS, BARBARA STAMBAUGH,** editor; b. Jenkins, Ky., Nov. 22, 1937; d. James Cosby and Jessie Kate (Bise) Stambaugh; m. Manning Williams, Sept. 11, 1963. BS in Journalism, U. Tenn., 1959. Polit. reporter News and Courier, Charleston, S.C., 1961-63, 67-76, asst. mng. editor, 1976-81; city hall reporter Camden (N.J.) Courier Post, 1963-67; editor The Evening Post, Charleston, S.C., 1981-90, The Evening Post and News Courier, Charleston, S.C., 1990-91, The Post and Courier, Charleston, S.C., 1991—. Pres. Nat. Coun. Editl. Writers, Rockville, Md., 1992. Bd. dirs. Charleston Sci. and Cultural Edn. Fund. Named Outstanding Newspaper Woman in S.C. S.C. Press Assn., 1962. Mem. Sigma Delta Chi (ByLiner award 1973). Achievements include first woman editor of a daily newspaper in South Carolina. Office: The Post & Courier 134 Columbus St Charleston SC 29403-4800 Office Phone: 843-937-5526. E-mail: barbara@postandcourier.com.

**WILLIAMS, BART H.,** lawyer; b. Orleans, France, Oct. 24, 1962; BA, Yale U., 1984, JD, 1987. Bar: Calif. 1988, US Dist. Ct., Central Dist. Calif. 1988. Assoc. Munger Tolles & Olson, 1987—91; asst. US atty., Criminal Divsn., Major Frauds Section Central Dist. Calif., 1991—94; ptnr. Munger, Tolles & Olson LLP, LA, 1994—. Lawyer del. Ninth Circuit Judicial Conf., 1997—99; mem. bd. trustees Charles R. Drew U. Medicine and Sci.; mem. LA County Bar Assn. Task Force on Criminal Justice System; dep. gen. counsel LA Police Commn. Independent Review Panel; co-chair ABA Lit. Section's Expert Witness Com.; adj. prof. law Loyola Law Sch.; adj. prof. Nat. Inst. Trial Advocacy. Bd. dirs. Alliance Children's Rights. Named Prosecutor Yr., Internat. Assn. Credit Card Investigators, 1993; named one of Top 20 Lawyers in State of Calif. Under 40 Yrs. Age, Calif. Law Bus. Mag., 2002, 45 Under Forty-Five, Am. Lawyer Mag., 2003, Am. Top Black Lawyers, Black Enterprise Mag., 2003, Calif. Superlawyers, Law & Politics Mag., 2004; recipient Potter Stewart prize, Yale Moot Ct. Appeals. Mem.: ABA (mem. sections on lit., criminal law, mem. task force on independent counsel act 1997—98), State Bar Calif. Office: Munger Tolles & Olson LLP 355 S Grand Ave 35th Fl Los Angeles CA 90071

**WILLIAMS, BENJAMIN, IV,** headmaster, history educator; m. Ginger Williams; children: Ben, Grace, Carson. BA in Am. Studies, Williams Coll.; MA in Am. Civilization, Brown U. With First Boston, NYC; history and English teacher, dir. of development St. Sebastian's Sch., Mass.; dean of middle and upper schools St. John's Sch., Houston, 1993—97; headmaster Cate Sch., Carpinteria, Calif., 1997—. Office: Cate Sch 1960 Cate Mesa Rd PO Box 5005 Carpinteria CA 93013

**WILLIAMS, BENJAMIN R.,** health facility administrator; CIO Horizon/CMS Healthcare Corp., Albuquerque; v.p., info. services & CIO St. Joseph Health Sys., Orange, Calif., 1998, now sr. v.p., strategic innovation & chief info. officer. Spkr. in field. Recipient Innovator of Yr. award., Coll. of Healthcare Info. Mgmt. Executives, 2004. Office: St Joseph Health Sys 500 S Main St Ste 1000 PO Box 14132 Orange CA 92863-1532*

**WILLIAMS, BERNARD,** Olympic athlete; b. Balt., Jan. 19, 1978; Student, Barton County C.C., Great Bend, Kans., U. Fla., 2000—. Co-winner Gold Medal 4X100 meter relay U.S.A. Track and Field Team, Sydney, 2000; gold medal 4x100m relay US Team World Outdoor Champions, 2001; silver medal winner 200m Olympics, 2004. Office: USA Track and Field Team One RCA Dome Ste 140 Indianapolis IN 46225

**WILLIAMS, BERNIE (BERNABE FIGUEROA WILLIAMS),** professional baseball player; b. San Juan, P.R., Sept. 13, 1968; Outfielder New York Yankees, 1991—. Named ALCS MVP, 1996; named to Am. League All-Star team, 1997—2001; recipient Am. League Gold Glove Award, 1997—2000. Achievements include being a member of World Series Champion New York Yankees, 1996, 1998-2000; led American League in batting average (.339), 1998. Office: New York Yankees Yankee Stadium E 161 St and River Ave Bronx NY 10451*

**WILLIAMS, BETHTINA QUBRÉ,** minister; d. Cleophus Noble Marshall and Marilyn Etta Marshall-Pierce; m. Stanley Davis Williams, Feb. 28, 1986; children: Stanley II, Jonathan, Joshua. BA. Friends Internat. Christian U., Merced, Calif., 1990, MA, 1996, DMin, 2001. Ordained min. Living Word Christian Ctr., Inc., 1996. Adminstrv. asst. Tex. Tech. U., Lubbock, Tex., 1983—84; health and safety coord., tchr. Kinder Care Pre-Sch., Lubbock, 1985—87; assoc. mgr. Paul Harris Store, Lubbock, 1987—89; libr. asst. Torreion (Spain) AFB, 1990—91; co-founder, co-pastor, exec. adminstr. Lighthouse of Faith Cmty. Ch., Ft. Walton Beach, Fla., 1997—; network pastor Life Cmty. Fellowship, 2001—05. Adv. bd. West Navarre Elem. Sch., 2004—05. Author: Women of Character and Destiny, 2005. Dir. outreach in humanitarian svc. Landstuhl (Germany) Base Chapel, 1993. Recipient Appreciation cert., Wayland Bapt. U., 1986, Commdr.'s Commendation medal, USAF, Ramstein, Germany, 1995, Appreciation cert., USAF, 2000, Commdr.'s medal, Hurlbut Field AFB, Fla., 2000, cert. of honor, King of Shai State, Ghana, 2004. Avocations: writing, exercise, singing, travel, public speaking. Office: Lighthouse of Faith Church Inc 755 Lovejoy Rd NW Fort Walton Beach FL 32548

**WILLIAMS, BETTY JEAN,** medical/surgical nurse; b. Spokane, Wash., Mar. 14, 1922; d. Charles Howard and Ellen Christine (Hedren) Williams. Registered nurse, Tacoma Gen. Hosp. Sch. Nursing, 1944. Cert. RN Wash. Staff nurse U.S. Army Nurse Corps., Menlo Pk., Calif., 1944—45, Tokyo, 1945—46, Manila, 1945, Harborview Hosp., Seattle, 1946—48; clin. nurse, scrub nurse Dr. Walter Scott Brown, Seattle, 1948—85. Lt. U.S. Army Nurse Corp., 1944—46, Calif., Japan. Recipient Dist. Svc. award, Am. Soc. Plastic and Reconstructive Surgery, 1995. Mem.: Am. Soc. Plastic Surgical Nurses (hon.; regional chair Pacific NW 1975—77). Democrat. Avocations: gardening, travel, symphony concerts.

**WILLIAMS, BRADLEY BENNETT,** historian; b. LA, Mar. 5, 1948; s. Robert E. and Helen L. Williams; m. Susan E. Poster, May 25, 1980. BA, U. So. Calif., 1972; MA, San Diego State U., 1977; PhD, U. Iowa, 1984. Cert. fundraising U. Calif., 1996. Dir. Heritage Mus., Coralville, Iowa, 1983—84; assoc. registrar LA County Mus. Art, 1984—85; registrar Skipball Mus., Hebrew Union Coll., LA, 1985—86; assoc. for alumni devel. Loyola Marymount U., LA, 1990—92; dir. Ninth Judicial Cir. Hist. Soc., Pasadena, 1992—. Editor: (scholarly jour.) Western Legal History, 1992—. Pres. Southwest Oral History Assn., 1997—98; mem. bd. dirs. Theodore Payne Found., LA, 1993; v.p. Pasadena Arts Council, 1987—90. Recipient Trustee's award, State Historical Soc. of Iowa, 1983, Svc. award, Southwest Oral History Assn., 1999; NEH Challenge Grant, Pasadena Hist. Soc., 1989. Mem.: Southwest Oral History Assn. (pres. 1997—98), Oral History Assn., Am. History Assn., Am. Assn. for State and Local History, Northwest Oral History Assn. (pres. 2005—). Home: 952 E Athens St Altadena CA 91001 Office: Ninth Judicial Cir Historical Soc 125 S Grand Ave Pasadena CA 91105 E-mail: historyconsultant@hotmail.com.

**WILLIAMS, BRIAN,** network news anchor; m. Jane Stoddard; 2 children. Student, George Washington U., Cath. U. Am.; Doctorate (hon.), Elmira Coll., Providence Coll. Corr. various stas., Phila., Washington, Pittsburgh, Kans.; anchor, corr. Sta. WCBS-TV, N.Y.C.; anchor, mng. editor NBC Nightly News Sat., N.Y.C., 1993—99; chief White House corr. NBC, Washington, 1994—96; anchor, mng. editor The News with Brian Williams MSNBC/CNBC, N.Y.C., 1996—2004; anchor, mng. editor NBC Nightly News, N.Y.C., 2004—. Former vol. firefighter, NJ. Named Father of Yr., Nat. Father's Day Com., 1996, Best Anchor, USA Today, Man of Yr., GQ Mag., 2001; recipient Emmy award, 1987, 1993, 2001. Office: NBC News 30 Rockefeller Plz Fl 3 New York NY 10112

**WILLIAMS, BROWN F,** media specialist, consultant; b. Evanston, Ill., Dec. 22, 1940; s. Jack Kermit Williams and Virginia Helen (Benjamin) Likar; m. Linda Francee Ludt, Sept. 1961 (div. 1968); 1 child, Eden Carol Williams McCarthy; m. Martha Amidon Powers, Sept. 1970 (div. 1974); m. Sandra Ann Matkowski, Jan. 1984 (dec. May 2000); 1 child, Bronwyn Emily. AB in Math. and Physics, U. Calif., Riverside, 1962, MA in Physics, 1964, PhD in Physics, 1966. Mgr. Electro-Optics Lab., Princeton, NJ, 1969-75; dir. RCA Labs., Princeton, 1976-82, v.p., 1982-87; pres. Williams Cons. Group, Princeton, 1988-90. CEO, chmn. Princeton Video Image, 1990—2004; v.p. R&D Evergreen Solar, 2004- Fellow IEEE; mem. AAAS, Am. Phys. Soc., Sigma Xi. Avocations: skiing, sailing, horseback riding. Office Phone: 609-648-2652. E-mail: bfwilliams1@comcast.net.

**WILLIAMS, BRYAN,** dean, medical educator; b. Longview, Tex., July 28; s. Lewis Bryan and Margaret Louise (Smart) W.; m. Frances Montgomery, Mar. 31, 1950; children: Harrison, Amy, Philip, Nickolas, Margaret, Lincoln. MD, Southwestern Med. Sch., 1947. Diplomate Am. Bd. Internal Medicine. Pvt. practice, Dallas, 1957-70; prof. internal medicine, assoc. dean student affairs Southwestern Med. Sch., 1970-90, prof. internal medicine emeritus, dean student affairs emeritus. Fellow ACP; mem. Inst. Medicine Nat. Acad. Scis. (charter)

**WILLIAMS, CARL CHANSON,** insurance company executive; b. Cin., Oct. 16, 1937; s. Charles J. and Alcie (Brazile) W.; m. Claire Bathé, May 26, 1985; 1 child, Michelle. A.S., U. Cin., 1965; BS, SUNY-Brockport, 1974; MBA, U. Rochester, 1975. Mgr. fin. systems Xerox Corp., Rochester, N.Y., 1972-77; dir. info. mgmt. Am. Can Co., Greenwich, Conn., 1977-79, mng. dir. info. mgmt., 1979-80, mng. dir. ops. control, 1980-82; sr. v.p., dir. mgmt. info. systems DDB Needham Worldwide, N.Y.C., 1982-91; pres. The Intertechnology Group, Inc., N.Y.C., 1990-91; v.p. infosystems and tech. Macmillan Pub. Co., N.Y.C., 1991-93; gen. mgr. info. tech. Amoco Corp., Chgo., 1993-94, v.p. info. tech., 1994-97; sr. v.p., chief info. officer Principal Fin. Group, Des Moines, Iowa, 1997—. Cons. Stamford (Conn.) Bd. Edn., 1981-82; lectr. U. Rochester, N.Y., 1975-77; adj. prof. Fordham U., 1991—. Exec. dir. Concerned Assn. Rochester, N.Y., 1971-75; bd. dirs. Stamford Cmty. Arts Coun., 1983-84; trustee Roosevelt U., 1995-97, U. Rochester, 1999—, Exec. Leadership Found., 2000—; mem. Exec. Leadership Coun. 1993—. Mem. Soc. Info. Mgmr. (exec. coun. 1980-83, pres. 1985, pres. coun. 1986—), Exec. Leadership Coun. (found. bd. trustees). Office: Principal Fin Group 711 High St Des Moines IA 50392-0002 Home: 2420 Vintage Hill Dr Durham NC 27712-9476 E-mail: william@principal.com.

**WILLIAMS, CARLISLE M., JR.,** municipal official, insurance company executive; b. Painter, Va., June 27, 1937; s. Carlisle M. and Evelyn Hickman Williams; m. Barbara Belle Schuyler, July 11, 1987; m. Barbara Evans Taylor, June 15, 1958 (div. Mar. 19, 1987); children: Carlisle M. III, Valerie Taylor. AA, Goldey-Beacom Coll. Wilmington, Del., 1958; BA, East Carolina U., Greenville, 1960; DHL (hon.), Mary Washington Coll. 2003. County adminstr. County of Accomack, Va., 1966—83, County of Stafford, Va. 1984—2003; corp. officer, v.p. Silver Co., Fredericksburg, Va., 2005—; corp. officer, sec. Vaco Reins. Co. Ltd., Brit. Virgin Islands, 2006—. Adminstrv. officer & sec./treas. George Washington Boyhood Home Found., Stafford, 1992—99; chmn. Fredericksburg Area Met. Planning Orgn., Va., 2001—03, VACO Group Self Ins. Assn., Roanoke, Va., 2001—05; pres. Va. Local Govt. Mgmt. Assn., Richmond, Va., 1981—82; sec./treas. Cedar Island Bridge and Beach Authority, Accomac, Va., 1975—83. Chmn. com. Stafford County Mus.; mem. adv. com. Stafford County Cable Commn.; sec.-treas. Accomack County Indsl. Devel. Authority, Cedar Island Bridge and Beach Authority; mem. new bldg. com. Fredericksburg Area Mus. and Culture Ctr., 2004—; chmn. Fredericksburg Area Met. Planning Orgn., 2001—03; local govt. chmn. Rappahannock United Way, 2000—01; mem. adv. bd. Salvation Army; chmn. supervisory bd. Va. Assn. Counties Group Self-Ins. Assn., 2001—05; mem. supervisory bd. Va. Assn. Counties Risk Pool, 2001—05; pres. Ea. Shore Jaycees, Onancock, Va., 1967—68, Onancock Rotary Club, 1981—82; bd. dirs. Mary Washington Hosp. Found., 2003—; U. Mary Washington Found., 2006—, Rappahannock United Way, Rappahannock Regional Criminal Justice Acad., Rappahannock Regional C. of C. Recipient Jefferson Cup, Va. Assn. Counties, 2000, James Monroe Medal, Mary Washington Coll., 2003. Mem. Am. Soc. Pub. Adminstrn., Urban Land Inst., Nat. Assn. County Adminstrs., Nat. Civic League, Nat. Trust for Hist. Preservation, Internat.

City/County Mgmt. Assn., Va. Emergency Mgmt. Assn., Va. Innovations Group, Stafford County Hist. Soc., No. Va. Mgrs. Assn., Va. Local Govt. Mgmt. Assn. Methodist. Avocation: sailing. Home: 12 Aiken Rd Fredericksburg VA 22405-3340 Office: County of Stafford 1300 Courthouse Rd PO Box 339 Stafford VA 22555-0339 E-mail: cmwjr@co.stafford.va.us.

**WILLIAMS, CAROL H.,** advertising executive; b. Chgo. d. Clarence Earl Williams and Betty Jane Norment-Williams; m. Tipkins Hood; children: Tipkins Hood Jr., Carol Hood. Student, Northwestern U. Creative dir., sr. v.p. Leo Burnett Agy., Chgo., 1969—80, Foote-Cone & Belding, San Francisco, 1980—82; prin. owner Carol H. Williams Advt., Inc., Oakland, Calif., 1986—. Active US Dream Acad. Recipient Outstanding Women in Mktg. and Comms. award, Ebony Mag., 2001, Women to Watch award, Ad Age, 2002, Bus. Achievement award, Nat. Coalition 100 Black Women, Inc., 2003, Ad Agency of Yr., Black Enterprise Mag., 2004. Mem.: NAACP, TEC Internat., Rainbow/PUSH Coalition. Office: Carol H Williams Advertising Inc 555 12th St Ste 1700 Oakland CA 94607-4058

**WILLIAMS, CAROLE LEE,** secondary school educator; b. Oak Park, Ill., Sept. 13, 1942; d. Leland Charles and Eleanor Irene (Breen) Carstens; m. Lawrence Robert Williams, July 3, 1965; children: Amy, Kate, Molly. BA in Art/English and Journalism, U. Evansville, 1965; MS in Art/English, Ind. U. 1985. Tchr. art/English Rudyard (Mich.) H.S., 1967-69, Shawe Meml. H.S., Madison, Ind., 1982—. Tchr. English Crane House, Ctr. for Asian Study, Fujian Province, Hunan Province, 1991, 92, 94, 95, Guangdong Province, 1998; Fulbrigh-Hayes Summer Sem. to Turkey and Cyprus, 2004. Editor: (books) Mom's Poetry, 1982; one-woman photo show: Hanover Coll. Art Gallery, Ind., 1993. Fellow Coun. for Basic Edn., NEH, Washington, 1991, 93, NEA, Washington, 1993; named Art Tchr. of the Yr., Ind. Alliance for Arts Edn., Indpls., 1991-92; named Outstanding Secondary Art Educator, Ind., 1995-96; Tchr. Creativity fellowship Eli Lily, 2005 Mem. Art Edn. Assn. of Ind. (dist. rep. 1993-95), Nat. Art Edn. Assn., Delta Kappa Gamma (treas., v.p.). Republican. Methodist. Avocation: travel. Office: Shawe Meml High Sch 201 State St Madison IN 47250 Home: 2339 Woods Edge Dr Madison IN 47250 Office Phone: 812-273-2150.

**WILLIAMS, CECILIA LEE PURSEL,** optometrist; b. Lewisburg, Pa., Nov. 15, 1948; d. Lee LaVerne and Geraldine May (Steininger) Pursel; m. Richard Lee Williams, May 17, 1975; 1 son, Kent Lee. Student, Lycoming Coll., 1966-68; BS, Pa. Coll. Optometry, 1970, OD, 1972. Lic. and/or cert. optometrist, D.C., Pa., N.Y., N.J., Va. Rsch. optometrist in soft lens materials Gumpelmayer Optik, Vienna, Austria, 1973; optometrist Sterling Optical Co. Contact Lens Ctr., Washington, 1974-79; pvt. practice optometry Springfield, Va., 1980—. Recipient Clin. Efficiency award Pa. Coll. Optometry, 1972; Women's Aux. of Pa. Optometrists scholar, 1968-70, 70-72; Pa. State grantee, 1968-70, 70-72. Mem. Optometric Ctr. of Nation's Capital (dir. 1977-80), Am. Optometric Assn., Va. Optometric Assn., No. Va. Optometric Soc., Nat. Honor Soc. for Optometry, Omega Delta. Home: 3600 Wilton Hall Ct Alexandria VA 22310-2176 Office: 7241 Commerce St Springfield VA 22150-3411 Office Phone: 703-866-9364.

**WILLIAMS, CHARLES EDWARD,** engineer; b. Warsaw, N.Y., July 9, 1939; s. Charles Dwight and Oletha (Davenport) W.; m. Grace Norma Robertson, June 30, 1965 (div. 1970); 1 child, Eric Charles; m. Virginia Vee Parker, May 3, 1980. BS in Ceramic Engring., Alfred U., 1961; MS in Phys. Metallurgy, Denver U., 1968. Ceramic engr. Rocky Flats plant Dow Chem., Golden, Colo., 1961-65; ceramic engr. Coors Porcelain Co., Golden, 1965-69; packaging engr. Fairchild Semiconductor, San Diego, 1969-71; sales engr., cons. Otto Jahnke and Assocs., San Diego, 1971-72; plant engr. Tecate (Mex.) Internat., Baja California, 1972-73; prodn. engr. ceramic divsn. Buckbee Mears, San Diego, 1973-75; mem. group tech. staff Tex. Instruments, Dallas, 1975—. Contbr. articles to profl. jours.; 13 patents in field; performer (audiocassette) Up The Trail, 1993. Exec. v.p. Acad. We. Artists, Ft. Worth, 1995-99. Mem. IEEE, Internat. Microelectronic and Packaging Soc. Republican. Presbyterian. Avocations: cowboy poetry, professional storytelling, pottery. Home: 6245 Chesley Ln Dallas TX 75214-2118 Office: Tex Instruments m/s 8719 12500 TI Blvd Dallas TX 75243-4136 E-mail: c-williams7@ti.com.

**WILLIAMS, CHARLES JUDSON,** lawyer, writer; b. San Mateo, Calif., Nov. 23, 1930; s. John Augustus and Edith (Babcock) W.; children: Patrick, Victoria, Apphia. AB, U. Calif., Berkeley, 1952, LLB, 1955. Bar: Calif. 1955, U.S. Supreme Ct., 1970. Assoc. Kirkbride, Wilson, Harzfeld and Wallace, San Mateo County, Calif., 1956-59; sole practice Solano County, Calif., 1959-64, Martinez, Calif., 1964—2002, Benicia, Calif., 1981-88; city atty. Pleasant Hill, 1962-80, Yountville, Calif., 1965-68, Benicia, 1968-76, 80-82, Lafayette, Calif., 1968—, Moraga, Calif., 1974-92, Danville, Calif., 1982-88, Pittsburg, Calif., 1984-93, Orinda, Calif., 1985-97; of counsel Best, Best and Krieger, 2002—04; atty. pvt. practice, Martinez, Calif., 2004—. Lectr. Calif. Continuing Edn. Bar 1964-65, U. Calif. Extension 1974-76, John F. Kennedy U. Sch. Law 1966-69; spl. counsel to various Calif. cities; legal advisor Alaska Legis. Council 1959-61; advisor Alaska sup. ct. 1960-61; advisor on revision Alaska statues 1960-62; atty. Pleasant Hill Redevel. Agy. 1978-82; sec., bd. dirs. Vintage Savs. & Loan Assn., Napa County, Calif., 1974-82; bd. dirs. 23d Agrl. Dist. Assn., Contra Costa County, 1968-70. Author: California Code Comments to West's Annotated California Codes, 3 vols., 1965, West' California Code Forms, Commercial, 2 vols., 1965, West's California Government Code Forms, 3 vols., 1971, Supplement to California Zoning Practice, 1970, 80, 82, 84, 85, 87, 89, 91, 94, 96, 98, 2000, 01; contbr. articles to legal jours. Mem. ABA, Calif. Bar Assn., Contra Costa County Bar Assn. Office: 1330 Arnold Dr Ste 149 Martinez CA 94553-6538 Office Phone: 925-228-3840. Personal E-mail: chaslaw@sbcglobal.net.

**WILLIAMS, C(HARLES) K(ENNETH),** poet, educator, literature educator; b. Newark, N.J., Nov. 4, 1936; s. Paul Bernard and Dossie (Kasdin) W.; m. Sarah Dean Jones, June, 1966 (div. 1975); 1 child, Jessica Anne; m. Catherine Justine Mauger, Apr. 15, 1975; 1 child, Jed Mauger. BA, U. Pa., 1958. Vis. prof. lit. Beaver Coll., Jenkintown, Pa., 1975, Drexel U., Phila., 1976, U. Calif., Irvine, 1978, Boston U., 1979-80, Bklyn. Coll., 1982-83; Mellon vis. prof. lit. Franklin and Marshall Coll., Lancaster, Pa., 1977; prof. writing Columbia U., N.Y.C., 1981-85; prof. lit. George Mason U., Fairfax, Va., 1982-95. Halloway lectr. U. Calif., Berkeley, 1986, Princeton U., 1995—. Author: A Day for Anne Frank, 1968, Lies, 1969, I Am the Bitter Name, 1972, With Ignorance, 1977, The Lark, The Thrush, The Starling, 1983, Tar, 1983, Flesh and Blood, 1987, Poems, 1963-1983, 1988, The Bacchae of Euripides, 1990, Helen, 1991, A Dream of Mind: Poems, 1992, Selected Poems, 1994, The Vigil, 1997, Poetry and Consciousness, 1998, Repair, 1999, Misgivings, A Memoir, 2000, The Singing: Poems, 2003; contbg. editor Am. Poetry Rev., 1972—; translator: Women of Trachis (Sophocles), 1978. Sponsor People's Fund, Phila., 1967—. Recipient Nat. Book Critics Circle award in poetry, 1987, Morton Dauwen Zabel prize, Am. Acad. of Arts and Letters, 1989, Lit. prize, 1999, Harriet Monroe prize, 1993, Berlin prize, Am. Acad. in Berlin, 1998, Pulitzer prize, 2000, Book award, L.A. Times, 2000, Weathertop prize, 2000, Pen Marth Albrand Memoir prize, 2001, Nat. Book award, 2003, Lifetime Achievement award, 5th Internat. Conf. on AIDS, India, 2005; fellow, Guggenheim Found., 1975, Nat. Endowment for Arts, 1985, 1993; grantee, Lila Wallace-Reader's Digest, 1993—95. Mem. PEN (Voelcker Career Achievement award 1998), Poetry Soc. Am., Am. Acad. Arts and Scis., Am. Acad. Arts and Letters. Avocations: piano, guitar, drawing. Home: 245 Moore St Princeton NJ 08540 Business E-Mail: cknms@princeton.edu.

**WILLIAMS, CHARLES LAVAL, JR.,** retired preventive medicine physician; b. New Orleans, Jan. 19, 1916; s. Charles Laval and Lewise (McLaurine) W.; m. Ellen Clendenin Ustick, Dec. 14, 1946; children: Ellen Clendenin, Katherine McLaurine. Student, U. Va., 1933-35; MD, Tulane U., 1940; M.P.H., U. Mich., 1945. Diplomate: Am. Bd. Preventive Medicine and Pub. Health. Intern U.S. Marine Hosp., New Orleans, 1941; with USPHS, 1941-67; assigned N.C. State Health Dept., 1941-44, USPHS States Relations div., 1944, U. Mich., 1944-45, Am. Acad. Pediatrics Nat. Study Child Health Services, 1945-47; chief planning unit, asst. chief div. commd. officers,

1947-51; with US/AID Div. Pub. Health, 1951-62; chief pub. health adviser AID Mission to Peru, 1959-62; asso. dir. internat. relations Office Internat. Health, 1962-64; chief Office Internat. Research, NIH, Bethesda, Md., 1965-66; dep. dir., then dir. Office Internat. Health, Office Surgeon General, USPHS, Washington, 1966-67; dep. dir. Pan Am. Health Orgn., 1967-79; ret.; exec. v.p. Am. Assn. World Health, 1980-84. U.S. del./alt. or advisor to eight world health assemblies between 1955 and 1967, and to ten sessions of the Directing Coun. of the Pan Am. Health Orgn. between 1953 and 1966. Fellow Am. Pub. Health Assn.; mem. U.S.-Mexico Border Pub. Health Assn., Phi Kappa Phi, Delta Omega. Home: 5600 Wisconsin Ave Apt 1009 Chevy Chase MD 20815-4411

**WILLIAMS, CHARLES WESLEY,** engineering executive, researcher; b. Palestine, Ark. s. Fredrick Charles and Fannie Rochet (Southall) W.; m. Nancy Sue Rhea, Sept. 5, 1959; children: Brent L., Brian E. BSEE, U. Tenn., 1959, MS, 1963. Registered profl. engr., Ohio. Devel. engr. Mead Rsch. Lab., Chillicothe, Ohio, 1959-60, Oak Ridge (Tenn.) Nat. Lab., 1960-63; tech. mgr. EG & G Ortec, Oak Ridge, 1963-76, tech. dir. phys. and life sci., 1976-81, dir. positron emission tomograph sys., 1981—85; pvt. practice Oak Ridge, 1985—. Contbr. articles to profl. jours. Fellow IEEE (life, v.p. NS 1979). Baptist. Personal E-mail: charles02@comcast.net.

**WILLIAMS, CHERYL A.,** secondary school educator; b. Neosho, Mo., July 7, 1957; d. Travestine Williams. BS in Math., Tex A&M U., 1978, postgrad., 1978-79, Rose State Coll., 1980-81, Sheppard Tech. Tng. Ctr., 1980-81; MS in Math., U. Tex., 1997. Computer scientist Tinker AFB, Oklahoma City, 1980-81, Defense Comm. Agy., Washington, 1986; tchr. Parent Child Inc., San Antonio, 1989; asst. sec. Antioch Bapt. Ch., San Antonio, 1989-92; substitute tchr. San Antonio Ind. Sch. Dist., 1990-93; instrnl. asst. Northside Ind. Sch. Dist., San Antonio, 1995-96, asst. tchr., 1994-95, North East Ind. Sch. Dist., San Antonio, 1996—2001; rep. West Telemarketing, 1998-99; math. tutor Alamo C.C. Dist., 1998—99; instr. math., 1998—, St. Philips Coll., 1998—2001; math. tutor Trave and G.G.'s Tutorial Svc., 1999—; instr. math. Guardian Angel Performing Arts Acad., 2002—. Asst. mgr. Fashion Pl., San Antonio, 1994—95; tax preparer H&R Block, 1994—95; distbr. Avon, 1999—2001; indep. beauty cons. Mary Kay Cosmetics, 1999—; scorer Harcourt Brace Corp., 2001, Randstad, 2001; rep. Express Svcs., 2001; cons. Prepaid Legal Svcs., Inc., 2003; ind. bus. owner Cyberwize, 2004. Counselor YMCA, San Antonio, 1989-91; active Girl Scouts U.S., 1964-86; mem. choir, asst. sec. area ch., 1972, tutor 1970—, tchr. Sunday Sch., 1973-86, asst. sec. Sunday Sch., 1973-86, 88—, asst. ch. sec., 1988-91; mem. Dorcas Circle, Lupus Found. Am., Biomed. Rsch. U. Tex., 1995—; mem. Epilepsy Found. Am., Tex. Head Injury Assn., Nat. Head Injury Assn., Smithsonian Instn.; vol. Cancer Therapy Rsch. Ctr., 2003—, Am. Cancer Soc., 2003—. Mem. NEA, Tex. Edn. Assn., Mu. Alpha Theta. Avocations: jigsaw puzzles, bowling. Office Phone: 210-601-4732.

**WILLIAMS, CHRISTOPHER,** investment company executive; BArch, Howard U.; MBA, Dartmouth Coll. Former sr. v.p. Lehman Brothers, NY; former pres. Williams Finl. Mkts.; CEO Williams Capital Group, LP, NYC; chmn. Williams Capital Mgmt., LLC, 2002—, CEO, 2002—; co-CEO EH Williams Capital Mgmt. Bd. dirs. Wal-Mart, Harrah's Entertainment. Bd. dirs. NYC Partnership, Nat. Dance Inst., Alvin Ailey Dance Found., WNYC Radio. Mem.: Century Assoc., Young President's Org., Nat. Assoc. Securities Professionals (bd. dirs.), Securities Industry Assn. (bd. dirs. N.Y. dist.), Econ. Club N.Y. (bd. dirs.). Office: Williams Capital Group LP 650 5th Ave 11th Flr New York NY 10019*

**WILLIAMS, CHRISTOPHER,** music educator; b. Madison, Wis., Jan. 3, 1977; s. DuWayne and GraceAnn Williams; m. Jennifer Kalscheuer, May 29, 2005. Choral and Gen. Music Edn., U. Wis., Platteville, 1995—2000. Vocal music dir. Cuba City Pub. Schools, Wis., 2003—, Sch. Dist. of Alma Ctr. Humbird/Merrilan, Alma Center, Wis.; vocal music tchr. internship Southwestern Cmty. Schools, Hazel Green, Wis., 2000; singer Heartland Singers, Whitewater, Wis., 2001—. Singer and soloist Platteville Chorale, Wis., 1998—; asst. dir. Heartland Festival Children's Summer Prodn., Platteville; choral condr. St. Raymond's Parish, Fall Creek, Wis., 2003, Peace Luth. Ch., Platteville, 2001; guest condr. Six Rivers Honors Choir, Platteville, 2004; condr. Arioso, Platteville, 2004—; asst. condr. and singer Pine Tones/SPEBSQSA Chpt., Black River Falls, Wis., 2001—03; choral condr. Dubuque Oratorio Soc., Iowa; liturgical vocal soloist First English Luth. Ch., Platteville, 1998—2000. Recipient Performance award, Am. Choral Directors Assn., 2002, Wis. Choral Directors Assn., 2005, Wis. State Music Assn. 2004, 2000. Mem.: Music Edn. Nat. Conf. (corr.), Am. Choral Dir. Assn. (corr.), Phi Mu Alpha Sinfonia (life; parlimentarian 1998—2000, Cream of the Crop 1998).

**WILLIAMS, CHRISTOPHER,** photographer; b. LA, 1965; Exhibitions include Carnegie Museum, Pittsburgh, Pa., Museum Boijmans Van Beuningen, Rotterdam, Lenbachhaus, Munich, Mus. Contemporary Art, LA, The UBS Corp. Art Coll., exhibited in group shows at Whitney Biennial, Whitney Mus. Art, NYC, 2006, David Zwirner Gallery, NYC. Office: c/o David Zwirner Gallery 525 W 19th St New York NY 10002*

**WILLIAMS, CLARA A.,** sculptor; b. Nashville, Sept. 16, 1972; Attended, Sch. Visual Arts; MFA, Yale U. Exhibited in group shows at P.S. 1 Some Young New Yorkers, 1997, PPOW Gallery, 1999, Richard Tells Gallery, 1999, Friedrich Petzel Gallery, 1999, Mus. Contemporary Art, San Diego, 2000, Zobeide & Man With Bags, Nicole Klagsbrun Gallery, 2000, The Price, Pub. Art Fund, 2003, Man with Luggage, Pierogi Gallery, 2000. Fellow Comm. Commn. on Arts, 2001, Guggenheim Meml. Found., 2004. E-mail: williams_greaterny@hotmail.com.

**WILLIAMS, CLAY RULE,** lawyer; b. Milw., Sept. 25, 1935; s. George Laverne and Marguerite Mae (Rule) W.; m. Jeanne Lee Huber, Jan. 18, 1986; children: Gwynne, Amy, Daniel, Sarah. BA, Lawrence U., 1957; LLB, U. Mich., 1960. Bar: Wis. 1960, U.S. Dist. Ct. (ea. and we. dists.) Wis. 1964, U.S. Ct. Appeals (7th cir.) 1965, U.S. Ct. Mil. Appeals 1963, U.S. Supreme Ct. 1963. Assoc. Gibbs, Roper & Fifield, Milw., 1963-67; sr. counsel Von Briesen & Roper, S.C., Milw., 1967-99, of counsel, 1999—. Mem. Gov.'s Task Force Creation Bus. Ct., 1994-99; instr. profl. seminars. Author: Berry, Davis, Deguire and Williams, Wisconsin Business Corporation Law, 1992; contbr. articles to profl. jours. Active Shorewood (Wis.) Sch. Bd., 1976-79. Capt. USAF, Judge Adv. Corps., 1960-63. Fellow Wis. Bar Found.; Fellow, ABA Found., mem. ABA (sect. antitrust law, corp. counseling com.), Wis. Bar Assn. (co-chmn. com. to revise corp. laws 1986-90, chmn. standing com. on bus. corp. law 1990-97, Pres.'s Award of Excellence 1990, 97), Milw. Bar Assn. (probate and real property sect., joint bench-bar com. Ct. Appeals, 1986-88, long-range planning com. 1987), Am. Law Inst., Milw. Club, Univ. Club. Republican. Episcopalian. Avocations: hunting, fishing, skiing, reading. Office: von Briesen & Roper SC 411 E Wisconsin Ave Milwaukee WI 53202 Office Phone: 414-273-7000. Business E-mail: cwilliam@vonbriesen.com.

**WILLIAMS, CLORETTA MAE,** retired elementary school educator; b. St. Johns County, Fla., Apr. 17, 1932; d. Daniel and Flossie Evelana Cohen, Paul and Susie Green; married, Dec. 10, 1952; children: Janice Edmond, Audrey Jackson, Renee, Curtis. BS, Fla. Meml./Indl. Coll., 1952; postgrad., numerous univs. Music and 3d grade tchr. Flagler County H.S., Bunnell, Fla., 1951—53; 1st grade tchr. Coleman Elem. Sch., Pompano, Fla., 1956—58; head start, 1st, 3d, 4th and 5th grade tchr. Charles Drew Elem. Sch., Pompano, Fla., 1958—86, ret., 1986. Sch. rep. Broward County North Area Advisory, Pompano, Fla., 1997; mem. adv. bd. Am.'s Choices Networking, Pompano, Fla., 2005. Recipient Tchr. of Yr. award, Charles Drew Sch.-Broward County Sch. Bd., 1964, Honored Pioneer of Broward County award, Broward County Hist. Com., 1999. Mem.: AARP, So. Poverty Law Ctr. (Plaque on Wall 2005), Heart Found. Democrat. Baptist. Home: 2738 NW Fourth Ct Pompano Beach FL 33069 Office: Mitchell/Moore Srs Program 910 NW Tenth St Pompano Beach FL 33060 also: E Pat Larkins Sr Program 520 Martin Luther King Jr Blvd Pompano Beach FL 33069

**WILLIAMS, CONSTANCE,** state senator; b. June 27, 1944; m. Sankey V. Williams; 2 children. BA, Barnard Coll., 1966; MBA, U. Pa., 1980. Rep. Pa. House of Reps., Harrisburg, 1996—2001; mem. Pa. State Senate, Harrisburg, 2001—. Democrat. Jewish. Office: 352 Main Capital Senate Box 203017 Harrisburg PA 17120-3017 Business E-mail: chwilliams@pasenate.com.

**WILLIAMS, CRAIG STEWART,** organist, music educator, director; b. Lynwood, Calif., Sept. 17, 1962; s. Barry Edward and Malvina Louise Williams; m. Lee Nielsen Williams, July 8, 1990; children: Abigail Leigh, Stewart Thomas. MusB, U. So. Calif., 1984; MusM, Juilliard Sch., 1986, Rider U., 1997. Organist Peace Luth. Ch., Tustin, Calif., 1981—84; organist, dir. music Covenant Ch. LI, Floral Park, NY, 1986—87, 1st Presbyn. Ch., Jamaica, NY, 1987—94; organist JFK Internat. Airport Protestant Chapel, Jamaica, NY, 1987—95; organist, dir. music Calvary Bapt. Ch., NYC, 1995—2000, Cadet Chapel, US Mil. Acad., West Point, NY, 2000—. Commr. NYC Presbytery, 1992—95; demonstrator, recitalist Baldwin Organ Co., Babylon, NY, 1993—97; adj. faculty Rider U., 1999—, Nyack Coll., 2003—; cons. pipe organ project Calvary Bapt. Ch., NYC, 2001—03. Worship and workshop music leader Kiwanis Club, Middletown, NY, 2001—02; participant Mohonk Mountain House, Shawangunk, NY, 2003; vis. lectr. U. Redlands, Calif., 2003. Mem.: Hymn Soc. Am., Am. Guild Organists (dean 1990—92), Pi Kappa Lambda. Avocations: gardening, poetry. Office: Cadet Chapel US Mil Acad Bldg 722 West Point NY 10996 Office Phone: 845-938-7352. Business E-mail: craig.williams@usma.edu.

**WILLIAMS, CRISSA MARY VAN VLECK,** museum administrator; b. Salem, Oreg., Nov. 18, 1967; d. Richard William and Barbara Elaine Van Vleck; m. John Brendan Williams, Jan. 2, 2005. Diploma, Cordon Bleu Cookery Sch., London, 1987; AA in Liberal Studies, C.C. Vt., Waterbury, 2000; BA in English Lit., San Francisco State U., 2003; MA in Mus. Studies, John F. Kennedy U., 2006. Asst. baker Sonoma Mission Inn and Spa, Boyes Hot Springs, Calif., 1989—90; pastry chef Bix, San Francisco, 1992—94, Bistro Roti, San Francisco, 1994—95, Fullers, Seattle Sheraton, 1997—98, Zoe, NYC, 1995—96, Jackson Ho. Inn, Woodstock, Vt., 1998—2000; pastry cook Auberge Du Soleil, Rutherford, Calif., 1997—98; asst. registrar rights and reproductions Calif. Hist. Soc., San Francisco, 2000—02, asst. curator edn. and programs, 2002—03, asst. to exec. dir., programs and spl. events mgr., 2003; asst. archivist Charles Schluz Mus., Santa Rosa, Calif., 2004; dir. edn. Marin History Mus., San Rafael, Calif., 2004—06. Mem.: Am. Assn. State and Local History, Orgn. Am. Historians, Am. Studies Assn., Western Museums Assn., Calif. Assn. Museums, Am. Assn. Museums. Office Phone: 415-454-8538 ext. 3.

**WILLIAMS, DANNA BETH,** reading specialist; b. Aurora, Ill., Apr. 13, 1956; d. Daniel Strango and Roberta Arlene Roberts; m. Norman Charles Williams, June 25, 1988; children: Scott, Samuel, Spencer. BSc, U. Nev., Reno, 1978; postgrad. in Curriculum and Instrn., Concordia U., Irvine, Calif., 2006—. Cert. TESOL Nev. Lic. of Edn., tchg.credential Calif. Reading specialist Job Corps, Stead, Nev., 1979; tchr. Churchill County Schools, Fallon, 1979—88; sub. tchr. Irvine Sch. Dist., Calif., 1988—90, Mission Viejo Sch. Dist., 1989—90; tchr. pvt. schools Orange County, 1990—96; tchr. Orange Unified Sch. Dist., 1996—2000, reading specialist, 2000—. Lang. arts mentor, tchr. Orange Unified Sch. Dist., 1999—2001, English lang. learner adv., 2005—; Consortium on Reading Excellence trainer fifth grade tchrs., 2003—04. Religious educator San Francisca Solano, 1988—91, 2002—04, Cath. Ch., 1983—88. Mem.: ASCD, Calif. Teachers Assn. Internat. Reading Assn. Roman Catholic. Home: 21022 Los Alisos Blvd Apt 614 Rancho Santa Margarita CA 92688 Office: Cambridge Elem Sch 425 N Cambridge Orange CA 92866 Office Phone: 714-997-6103. E-mail: dwilliam@orangeusd.k12.ca.us.

**WILLIAMS, DARCEL PATRICE,** writer, editor; b. Houston, Nov. 23, 1958; d. Leroy and Estelle Forch Williams; m. Jason LaRue Williams, Sr., May 26, 1979 (div. Sept. 0, 1985); 1 child, Jason LaRue H. Student, Tex. So. U., 1977—81; U. Houston, 1985—88. Lic. massage therapist City of Tulsa, 1993. Acctg. Taft Broadcasting, Houston, 1981—85; office mgr. DeColores Prodns., Houston, 1989—90; cmty. ctr. dir. Helping Hands - Riverview Pk., Tulsa, 1995; author Am. Book Pub. Group, Salt Lake City, 1999—, sr. editor, 1999—2003. Creative adviser/cons. Various Ind. Entrepreneurial Enterprises, Tulsa, 1989—2003. Author: (novel) Soaring On Clipped Wings (Book of Month, 2004), (screenplay) Fighting to Love; senior editor: novels Cryer's Valley, Have No Mercy, writer, dir.: Sadie's Soap Suds TV Show, 2004; web designer, writer (web site) www.DarcelWilliams.com;, author poetry; contbr. Named Humanitarian of Month, 2003; recipient Best New Writer of Yr. Disilgold Mag. award, Younity Reviewers Guild, 2004. Mem.: Younity Revs. Guild Worldwide, Disilgold Lit. Network Assn., Nat. Writers Union, Authors Den Forum (life). Achievements include design of safety product for use in vehicular transportation of children; product for walking in hazardous environmental conditions. Avocations: singing, music, sewing and design, swimming, reading. Office Phone: 918-499-8722. Personal E-mail: eagledfly@yahoo.com.

**WILLIAMS, DARLENE F.,** federal agency administrator; BA, Howard U.; MBA, Chgo. U.; PhD, Stanford U. Mgr. mktg., planning and rsch. Ryder Systems, Inc.; corp. policy mgr. TXU; gen. dep. asst. sec. policy devel. and rsch. HUD, Washington, 2003—05, gen. dep. asst. sec., 2005, asst. sec., 2005—. Office: HUD 451 Seventh St SW Main Code R Rm 8100 Washington DC 20410-6000 Office Phone: 202-708-1600. Office Fax: 202-619-8000.*

**WILLIAMS, DARRICK SHAD,** mathematician; b. Batesville, Ark., May 20, 1970; s. Thomas Edward and Lou Ann Williams; children: Kathrynn Marie, Thomas Konrad, Austin Ross. BA in Math., Lyon Coll., Batesville, Ark., 2005. Adj. prof. UACCB, Batesville, Ark., 2005—. Mem. Lyon Coll. Bagpipe Band, Batesville, Ark. With USAR, 1989—94. Decorated Kiwati Liberation Medal U.S. Navy Independent. Home: 1002 N Hill St Newark AR 72562 Office: UACCB PO Box 3350 Batesville AR 72503-3350 Office Phone: 870-793-1223. Personal E-mail: darrickshad@yahoo.com.

**WILLIAMS, DARRYL MARLOWE,** medical educator; b. Denver, Apr. 3, 1938; s. Archie Malvin and Dorothy Merle (Grapes) W.; m. Susan Arlene Moore, June 24, 1966; children: Carol Ruth, Peter Todd, Sarah Elizabeth. Student, U. Colo., 1956—58; BS, Colo. State U., 1963; MD, MS in Anatomy, Baylor U., 1964; MPH, U. Tex., 2001. Diplomate Am. Bd. Internal Medicine, Am. Bd. Hematology. Intern and resident Baylor Affiliated Hosps., Houston, 1964-66, 67-68; resident U. Utah, Salt Lake City, 1966-67, fellow in hematology, 1968-73, asst. prof., 1973-77; assoc. prof. La. State U., Shreveport, 1977-81, prof., 1981-90, chief hematology sect., 1977-85, asst. dean/rsch., 1981-85, dean Sch. Medicine, 1985-90; prof. medicine, dean Sch. Medicine Tex. Tech U. Health Scis. Ctr., Lubbock, 1990-95; prof. medicine, exec. dir. office border health, project dir. Hispanic Ctr. of Excellence Tex. Tech. Health Scis. Ctr., El Paso, 1997—; dir. curriculum planning office, 2002—, also bd. dirs., 1995—, dir. med. edn. Cmty. Partnership, 1995—2001, dir. health caucus opportunity program, 2005—. Mem. hemophilia adv. com. La. Legislature, Baton Rouge, 1977-83; vice chair La. Lung and Cancer Bd., New Orleans, 1984-90; pres. N.W. La. AIDS Task Force, Shreveport, 1987. Mem. editl. bd. Tex. Jour. Rural Health, 1990—2004. Mem. Am. Heart Assn., Lubbock chpt., Shreveport Biracial Commn., 1988, Lubbock Indigent Health Care Coalition Task Force, 1991-92, Health Professions Edn. Adv. Com., Lubbock Friends of Pub. Radio; vice chair health profls. edn. adv. com. Tex. Coord. Bd. Higher Edn., 1992-95; sec. Health Edn. and Tng. Consortium of Tex., 1990-99, vice chmn., 1999-2002, chmn., 2002-04; mem. steering com. Border Vision Fronteriza, 1995-2000; bd. dirs. El Paso Cancer Consortium; project dir. Hispanic Ctr. of Excellence, 2001—; adv. com., Tex. State Dept. Health Cmty. Health Workers, 2003—05; exec. dir. Health Edn. Tng. Ctr. Alliance of Tex., 2003—; project dir. Tex. Tech. Regional Ctr. Pub. Health, Medicine Edn., 2003-. Recipient award Nat. Ski Patrol Sys., Salt Lake City, 1975, Disting. Svc. award Multicultural Diversity, 2005, Disting. Svc. award Tex. Tech U. Sch. Medicine, 2005 Fellow ACP, Am. Coll. Nutrition; mem. Am. Soc. Hematology, Am. Inst. Nutrition, Am. Soc. Clin. Nutrition, Tex. Med. Assn. (physicians oncology com.), Am. Cancer Soc. (bd. dirs. El

Paso unit 1999-2004, pres. 2001-03), Alpha Omega Alpha. Office: Tex Tech Health Sci Ctr at El Paso 4800 Alberta Ave El Paso TX 79905-2709 Office Phone: 915-545-5742. Business E-Mail: darryl.williams@ttuhsc.edu.

**WILLIAMS, DAVE HARRELL,** investment company executive; b. Beaumont, Tex., Oct. 5, 1932; s. George Davis and Mary (Hardin) W.; m. Reba White, Mar. 15, 1975. BS in Chem. Engring. U. Tex., 1956; MBA (Baker scholar, Teagle fellow), Harvard U., 1961. Chartered fin. analyst. Chem. engr. Exxon Corp., Baton Rouge, 1959; security analyst deVegh & Co., N.Y.C., 1961—64; dir. research Waddell & Reed, Kansas City, Mo., 1964—67; exec. v.p. Mitchell Hutchins, Inc., N.Y.C., 1967—77; chmn. bd. Alliance Capital Mgmt. Corp., N.Y.C., 1977—2001, chmn. emeritus, 2001—04. Contbr. articles to profl. jours. Trustee U.S.S. Intrepid Mus. Found. Served with USNR, 1956-59. Named one of Top 200 Collectors, ARTnews Mag., 2004, 2006. Mem. Fin. Analysts Fedn. (past officer, dir.), N.Y. Soc. Security Analysts (past pres.), Bond Club N.Y., Econ. Club N.Y., Knickerbocker Club, Grolier Club. Presbyterian. Avocation: Collector of Am. Prints. Office: White Williams Holdings 41 W 57th St New York NY 10019 E-mail: dwilliams@white-williams.com.*

**WILLIAMS, DAVID ALEXANDER,** retired chief pilot; b. Helena, Mont., May 29, 1939; s. Daniel samuel and Dorothy (Alexander) W.; m. Jacquoline anders, Feb. 14, 1964 (div. Mar. 1988); children: Daniel Alexander, Darryl Jackson. BA, U. So. Calif., L.A., 1962. Lic. airline transport pilot, FAA. Commd. ensign USNR, 1963, advanced through grades to capt., 1985; tng. and test pilot McDonnel Douglas, Long Beach, Calif., 1980-87, chief pilot flight stds. and safety, 1987-97, Douglas Products divsn. Boeing, Long Beach, 1997-99; ret., 1999. Mem. internat. adv. com. Flight Safety Found., Washington, 1987-99; mem. windshear tng. aid task force FAA/industry, Washington, 1985-87; mem. CFIT tng. com. Flight Safety Found./FAA, 1992-96, joint safety analysis team FAA Industry, 1997-99. Author: Turbulence Education and Training Aid FAA/Industry, 1996-97. Mem.: Mil. Officers Assn. Am., Naval Res. Assn. Avocations: cycling, sailing, scuba diving. Home: 223 Mission Ln San Luis Obispo CA 93405 Personal E-mail: davew805@gmail.com.

**WILLIAMS, DAVID ALFRED,** elementary school educator; b. Jacksonville, Fla., May 24, 1961; s. Merle W. Long and John Alfred Williams, James Elbert Toby Long (Stepfather). A, Brewton Parker Coll., 1982; BFA in Music Edn., Tift Coll./Mercer U., 1984; M in Sch. Adminstrn. and Leadership, Cambridge Coll., 2006. Profl. tchr. Ga., 2006, cert. Ga. Real Estate Bd., 2004. Music specialist Appling County Elem. Sch., Baxley, Ga., 1987—; owner, event cons. Seasonings, LLC; owner, artist, instr. The Studio. Musician (pianist/vocalist): (albums) Reflections & Memories; musician: Remember When. Mem. First Bapt. Ch., Baxley, Ga., 2000—05. Mem.: Ga. Music Educators Assn. (assoc.), Nat. Music Educators Assn. (assoc.), Friends of Johnny Mercer (assoc.), Waycross Heritage Soc. (assoc.). Baptist. Avocations: swimming, travel, cake decorating, music, cooking. Home: 556 Pineview Ave Baxley GA 31513 Office: Appling County Elem Sch 680 Blackshear Hwy Baxley GA 31513 Office Phone: 912-367-8640. Home Fax: 912-367-5992; Office Fax: 912-367-8649. Personal E-mail: david@thekeyboardkid.com. E-mail: dwilliams@appling.k12.ga.us, dwilliams@accessatc.net.

**WILLIAMS, DAVID HOWARD,** lawyer; b. Las Vegas, Nev., Sept. 21, 1945; s. Howard Cummins and Alice Emma (Taufenbach) W.; m. Kathleen Graham, Sept. 2, 1967; children: David Howard Jr., Jonathan Graham. BA in History cum laude, Denison U., 1967; MA in Polit. Sci., Columbia U., 1969; JD cum laude, Ohio State U., 1973. Bar: Ohio 1973, Ga. 1980. Assoc. Vorys, Sater, Seymour & Pease, Columbus, Ohio, 1973-79; from assoc. to ptnr. Powell, Goldstein, Frazer & Murphy, Atlanta; ptnr. Hunton & Williams, Atlanta; now ptnr. Schiff Hardin LLP, Atlanta, co-leader Employee Benefits and Exec. Compensation Group. Adj. prof. U. Ga. Sch. Law, 1995-97; lectr. in field. Bd. dirs. Atlanta Ballet, 1991-92, Ga. Assn. for Primary Health Care; former trustee, co-pres. parents' assn. Trinity Sch., Atlanta; former trustee Northside Youth Orgn., Atlanta; former asst. gen. counsel Ga. Rep. Party; former mem. coun. legal advisors Rep. Nat. Com.; mem. Benefits Coun., ASPA, Atlanta, 1998-99, Midtown Leadership Program, Atlanta, 2001. Mem. ABA, State Bar Ga., Atlanta Bar Assn.; Am. Soc. Pension Actuaries, ASPA Benefits Coun. of Atlanta, ESOP Assn. Office: Schiff Hardin LLP One Atlantic Ctr, Ste 2300 1201 W Peachtree St Atlanta GA 30309-3574 Office Phone: 404-437-7010. Office Fax: 404-437-7100. E-mail: dwilliams@schiffhardin.com.*

**WILLIAMS, DAVID J.,** diversified financial services company executive; BA, Yale U., 1965; MBA, Harvard U., 1974. Chartered fin. analyst. Portfolio mgr. T. Rowe Price Assocs., Balt.; chief investment officer Horizon Trust Co., Morristown, NJ; from sr. portfolio mgr. to mng. dir. U.S. Trust Co. N.Y., 1987—92; lead mgr. Excelsior Value & Restructuring Fund, Boston, 1992—. Mem.: Assn. Investment Mgmt. and Rsch.

**WILLIAMS, DAVID RUSSELL,** retired music educator; b. Indpls., Oct. 21, 1932; s. H. Russell and Mary Dean (Whitmer) W.; m. Elsa Bühlmann, Jan. 30, 1960. AB, Columbia U., 1954, MA, 1956; PhD, U. Rochester, 1965. Dir. music Windham Coll., Putney, Vt., 1959-62; opera coach Eastman Sch. Music, Rochester, NY, 1962-65, assoc. prof. theory, adminstr. of MusM program, 1965-80; prof., chmn. dept. music U. Memphis (formerly Memphis State U.), 1980-87, profl. music, 1980-98, prof. emeritus, 1998—. Bd. dirs. Memphis Youth Symphony, Memphis Symphony, 1984-90; mem. exec. bd. Opera Memphis, 1980-87, Salute to Memphis Music, 1980-87. Author: Bibliography of the History of Music Theory, 1971, Conversations with Howard Hanson, 1988, Music Theory from Zarlino to Schenker: A Bibliography and Guide, 1990; producer: Highwater Records album 8201 featuring John Stover, classical guitar, 1983; composer Suite for Oboe, Clarinet and Piano, 1968, Five States of Mind, 1970. Bd. dirs., sec. Rochester Philharm. Orch., 1976-78, v.p., bd. dirs. Rochester Chamber Orch., 1974-78, pres., bd. dirs. Opera Theatre of Rochester, 1973-74; bd. dirs., chmn. Am. Ritual Theatre, 1979-80; bd. sponsors Met. Opera Mid. South Region, Memphis, 1983—. Served as cpl. U.S. Army, 1957-59. Recipient Eastman Sch. Music Pub. award, 1970. NARAS (treas. Memphis chpt. 1984-86), Coll. Music Soc. (sec. 1973-83), Music Tchrs. Nat. Assn. Sci. (state chmn 1971-74), Nat. Assn. Schs. of Music (chmn. region 8 1989-92), Tenn. Assn. Music Execs. in Colls. and Univs. (pres. 1986-87), Rochester Club, Univ. Club, Summit Club, Pi Kappa Lambda (pres. U. Memphis chpt. 1988-90), Phi Beta Kappa, Phi Mu Alpha, Sigma Alpha Iota. Avocations: language study, word puzzles. Home: 273 W Central Park St Apt 1 Memphis TN 38111-4570 E-mail: drwillms@memphis.edu. *Having had a family background that was superior in so many ways has helped me to sharpen my purpose in life, in that it has made me realize to what an extent affirmative action is necessary in order to provide a milieu in which truly equal opportunity can exist. Many doors of opportunity have been held open for me; those of disadvantaged access are often not aware that these doors exist. The more individuals I can lead to these portals, the more I will have achieved in my lifetime.*

**WILLIAMS, DEBORAH LEE,** foundation administrator; b. L.A., Feb. 11, 1954; d. Eleazer Deming and Jeanne Sanford Williams; m. Charles (Skip) Robert Roy, Apr. 6, 1985; 1 child, Andrew Roy. BA, Pomona Coll., 1975; JD, Harvard U., 1978. Bar: Alaska 1979. Atty. solicitors honors program Dept. Interior, Washington, 1978—79, atty. Nat. Pk. Svc. and Nat. Fish and Wildlife Svc. Anchorage, 1979—81, spl. asst. to sec. for Alaska, 1994—98; exec. dir. Alaska Consumer Advocacy Program, Anchorage, 1981—82; atty. Hellen, Partnow and Condon, Anchorage, 1983—86, 1989—93; exec. dir. Am. Lung Assn. Alaska, Anchorage, 1993—94; Alaska Conservation Found., Anchorage, 1999—. Pres. bd. dirs. Trustees for Alaska, Anchorage, 1982—85; bd. dirs. TransAlaska Pipeline Liability Fund, Washington, 1994—98; adj. prof. Alaska Pacific U., Anchorage, 1993—94, U. Alaska, Anchorage, 1987—88; commr. Anchorage Mcpl. Health Commn., 1981—85. Founder, editor Harvard Environ. Law Rev., 1976; contbr. law rev. articles to profl. jours. Trustee Exxon Valdez Oil Spill Trustee Coun., Anchorage, 1994—98. Recipient Nat. Performance Rev. award, V.P. of U.S., 1997, 1998. Mem.: Green Star (bd. dirs. 2002—), Planned Parenthood of Alaska (bd. dirs., chair nominating com.

1997—2003), Rotary Internat., Phi Beta Kappa. Achievements include making appearances on 60 Minutes, 60 Minutes Australia, BBC, and many Alaskan TV shows; being the subject of cover stories in Alaska Business Monthly, We Alaskans and other publications. Avocations: backpacking, travel, building. Office: Alaska Conservation Found 441 W 5th Ave Ste 402 Anchorage AK 99501 Business E-Mail: dwilliams@akcf.org.

**WILLIAMS, DOCIA SCHULTZ,** small business owner; b. St. Louis, Mo., Sept. 12, 1930; d. John Frederick and Statira Jim (Thornton) Schultz; m. Stanley Good Southworth Jr. (div. 1983); 1 child, Sarah Elizabeth Southworth; m. Roy Donald Williams, Dec. 1, 1984. BA, Tex. Womans U., 1951. Fashion coordinator Ike Clark of Dallas, Dallas, 1951—53, Harveys Dept. Store, Nashville, Tex., 1953—55; model, coordinator Freelance, San Antonio, 1968; owner, boutique shop San Antonio, 1973—79; tour mgr. numerous travel co., 1979—89; owner, operator Mission City Tours, San Antonio, 1989—. With S.A. Writers Guild, San Antonio; writer C.S. Journal, San Antonio Conservation Soc., San Antonio, 2003—. Author: Spirits of San Antonio, 1992, When Darkness Falls, 1994, Ghosts Along The Texas Coast, 1993, Phantoms of the Plains, 1995, Best Tales of Texas Ghosts, 1998, Exploring San Antonio with Children, 2000, History and Mystery of the Menger Hotel, 2000; speaker (various profl. conventions). Nat. pres. Tex. Woman's U. Assn. of Former Students, 1982—84. Named one of Ten Outstanding Women in San Antonio, Express News Pub. Co., 1973; recipient Spirit of San Antonio award, San Antonio Hotel and Lodgings Assn., 2003. Mem.: Nat. Assn. Women Bus. Owners (Entreprenurial Spirit award 2004), Tour Guides Assn. of S.A. (charter mem., Disting. Svcs. award 2004), S.A. Coun. Presidents, San Antonio Hist. Soc., Nat. Soc. Arts and Letters. Republican. Meth. Avocations: music, travel, creative writing, antiques. Home and Office: 1319 Vista Del Monte San Antonio TX 78216 Office Phone: 210-493-2454. Personal E-Mail: dociasw@aol.com.

**WILLIAMS, DONALD JOHN,** physicist, researcher; b. Fitchburg, Mass., Dec. 25, 1933; s. Tolvo John and Ina (Kokkinen) Williams; m. Priscilla Mary Gagnon, July 4, 1953; children: Steven John, Craig Mitchell, Elno Stenroos. BS, Yale U., 1955, MS, 1958, PhD, 1962. Sr. staff physicist Johns Hopkins U. Applied Physics Lab., 1961-65; head particle physics br. Goddard Space Flight Center, NASA, 1965-70; dir. Space Environ. Lab., NOAA, Boulder, Colo., 1970-82; prin. investigator Energetic Particles expt. NASA Galileo Mission, 1977—2003; prin. staff physicist Johns Hopkins U. Applied Physics Lab., 1982-89, dir. Milton S. Eisenhower Rsch. Ctr., 1990-96, chief scientist rsch. ctr., 1996-99, ret., 1999. Mem. nat. and internat. sci. planning coms.; chmn. com. solar-terrestrial rsch. NAS, 1989—93; sci. adv. bd. USAF, 1993—97. Assoc. editor Jour. Geophys. Rsch., 1967—69, Revs. Geophysics and Space Rsch., 1984—86; editor (with G. D. Mead): Physics of the Magnetosphere, 1969, Physics of Solar-Planetary Environments, 1976; mem. editl. bd. Space Sci. Revs., 1975—85; author (with L. R. Lyons): Quantitative Aspects of Magnetospheric Physics, 1983; contbr. articles to profl. jours. Lt. USAF, 1955—57. Recipient Sci. Rsch. award, NOAA, 1974, Disting. Authorship award, NOAA and Johns Hopkins Applied Physics Lab., 1976, 1985, 1997. Fellow: Am. Geophys. Union; mem.: Internat. Acad. Astronautics, Internat. Assn. Geomagnetism and Aeronomy (pres. 1991—95), Am. Phys. Soc., Sigma Xi. Home: 117 Tivoli Trace Ct Poinciana FL 34759 Personal E-Mail: donaldwfl@verizon.net.

**WILLIAMS, DONALD R.,** social sciences educator; b. Hamilton, Ohio, Feb. 11, 1956; BBA, U. Wis., Milw., 1977; PhD, Northwestern U., Evanston, Ill., 1984. Asst. prof. econs. Kent State U., Ohio, 1983—88, assoc. prof. econs., 1988—94, prof. econs., 1994—, assoc. dean grad. sch. of mgmt., 2003—06, assoc. dean Coll. Bus. Adminstrn., 2006—. Sr. rsch. assoc. CEPS/INSTEAD, Differdange, Luxembourg, 2002—; vis. prof. KU Leuven, Belgium, 2003—. Mem.: European Assn. Labour Economists, Soc. Labor Economists, Am. Econ. Assn. Office: Kent State Univ Coll Bus Administration Kent OH 44242 Office Phone: 330-672-2772. Business E-Mail: dwilliam@kent.edu.

**WILLIAMS, DONNA M.,** social studies educator; 1 child, Riley. AA, Blair C.C., Colo. Springs, Colo., 1984; BS, U. So. Colo., Pueblo, Colo., 1991 Tchr. social studies Bethune (Colo.) Elem. Sch., 1991—. Adv. Nat. Hon. Soc., Bethune, 2004—. Mem.: DAR. Office: Bethune R-5 145 W 3rd Ave Bethune CO 80805

**WILLIAMS, DOROTHY STANDRIDGE,** retired food products manager, civic worker; b. Powder Springs, Ga. d. Robert Anderson and Bertie Mae Standridge; m. Harold Thomas Barfield (div.); 1 child, H. Gregory; m. J. Arden Williams (div.). Student, DeKalb Coll., Atlanta, 1982—83, U. Que., 1997, U. Laval, Que., 1998, U. Paris-Sorbonne, 2000. Assoc. promotion mgr., promotion coord. Coca-Cola USA, Atlanta, 1978-83, promotions mgr., 1983-86; mgr. internat. promotion svcs. The Coca-Cola Co., Atlanta, 1986-90, mgr. global promotion svcs., 1990-94. Cons., judge Point-of-Purchase Advt. Inst., 1995. Attaché Atlanta Conv. and Visitors Bur., 1992—; vol. Welcome South Ctr., Atlanta, 1995—; bd. advisors Life Coll. for Knowledge and Tng., 1995—; chmn. cmty. rels. com. Life Coll., 1995-96, vice chmn. bd. adv. Knowledge and Tng. program, 1997-98, chmn. bd. advisors Knowledge and Tng. program, 1998-99. Mem. Ga. Trust for Hist. Preservation, Atlanta High Mus. Art, Atlanta Bot. Garden, Alliance Francaise, Smyrna Hist. Soc. Avocations: travel, french language, interior design, hiking, bridge.

**WILLIAMS, DOYLE Z.,** finance educator; b. Shreveport, La., Dec. 18, 1939; s. Nuell O. and Lurline (Isbell) Williams; m. Maynette Derr, Aug. 20, 1967; children: Zane Derr, Elizabeth Marie. BS, Northwestern State U., 1960; MS in Acctg., La. State U., 1962, PhD, 1965. CPA Tex. Mgr. spl. edn. projects AICPA, N.Y.C., 1967—69; assoc. prof. Tex. Tech. U., Lubbock, 1969—71, prof. acctg., 1972—73; prof. area acctg., coord., 1973—78; prof. acctg. U. So. Calif., L.A., 1978—93, dean Sch. Acctg., 1979—87, interim dean Sch. Bus., 1986—88; dean Walton Coll. Bus. U. Ark., Fayetteville, 1993—2005, dean emeritus, 2005—, prof., 2005—06; sr. scholar Kennesaw State U., 2006—. Vis. prof. U. Hawaii, Honolulu, 1971—72. Contbr. articles to profl. jours. Chmn. Acctg. Edn. Change Commn., 1989—93. Named Mem. of the Yr., N.Y. chpt. Nat. Assn. Accts., 1967, Outstanding Acctg. Educator, Beta Alpha Psi, 1982; recipient Disting. Faculty award, Calif. CPA Found., 1983, Nat. Leadership award, Acad. Bus. Administrs., 1995, Lifetime Achievement award, Ark. Soc. CPA. Mem.: AICPA (coun. 1983—91, v.p. 1987—88, bd. dirs. 1987—91, Outstanding Educator award 1990, Gold medal 2002), Assn. Advance Coll. Schs. Bus. Internat. (chair acctg. accreditation com. 1995—97, bus. accreditation com. 1995—97, chair acctg. accreditation com. 1999—2000, bd. dirs., vice chair 2003—04, chair 2004—05), S.W. Bus. Deans Assn. (pres. 1998—99), Adminstrs. Acctg. Programs (pres. 1977—78), Fedn. Schs. Accountancy (pres. 1982, Faculty Merit award 1993), Am. Acctg. Assn. (dir. edn. 1973—75, pres. 1984—85, Outstanding Educator award 1996).

**WILLIAMS, DREW DAVIS,** surgeon; b. San Augustine, Tex., Jan. 18, 1935; s. Floyd Everett and Villamae (Morehead) W.; m. Marilyn Raus, June 27, 1958; children: Leslie, Cynthia, Matthew, Jennifer, Amelia. BS, Tex. A&M Coll., 1957; MD, U. Tex., 1960; grad., naval flight surgeon, U.S. Naval Sch. Aviation Medicine, 1963. Diplomate Am. Bd. Surgery, Am. Bd. Quality Assurance and Utilization Rev. Physicians. Intern USPHS Hosp., Seattle, 1960-61; resident in gen. surgery U. Tex. Med. Br., Galveston, 1961-62, 64-68; resident in pulmonary sch. M.D. Anderson Hosp., Houston, 1968; pvt. practice Baytown, Tex., 1968—. Active staff San Jacinto (Tex.) Meth. Hosp., 1968-95, chief of surgery, 1972, 73, pres. med. staff, 1976; mem. courtesy staff Bay Coast Hosp., Baytown, 1968-95; cons. staff Baytown Med. Ctr. Hosp., 1972-95; 1st chmn. dept. surgery in devel. of family practice residency program affiliated with Tex. Med. Sch., Houston, 1977; mem. Tex. State Bd. Med. Examiners, 1983-89, sec.-treas., 1984-88, pres., 1988-89; unit med. dir., clin. instr. dept. preventive medicine and cmty. health U. Tex. Med. Br., Galveston, 1995-99. Contbr. chpt. to book and articles to profl. jours. Flight surgeon USN, 1962-64; lt. comdr. USNR, ret., 1967. Clin. fellow, Am. Cancer Soc., 1966—67. Mem.: SAR (past pres. local chpt.), AMA (Physicians Recognition award), ACS, Ret. Physicians Orgn. (med. reserve com.).

Houston Surg. Soc. (past pres.), Baytown Surg. Soc., East Harris County Med. Soc. (pres. 1982), Harris County Med. Soc. (exec. bd. 1994, chmn. coun. med. splty., co-chmn. disaster response com. of ret. physician orgn.), Singleton Surg. Soc. (past pres.), Tex. Surg. Soc., Tex. Med. Assn., Sovereign Colonial Soc.-Am. of Royal Descent, Colonial Order of the Crown, Descendents of Colonial Clergy, Sir William Osler Soc., Sons of Republic of Tex. (at large life), Magna Carta Barons, Am. Cancer Soc. (pres. Baytown chpt. 1970—71), Knights Templar, Shriners, Masons (32 degree). Democrat. Mem. Ch. of Christ. Avocations: hunting, fishing, genealogy, painting, gardening. Home and Office: 1217 Kilgore Rd Baytown TX 77520-3912 Office Phone: 281-422-7969. Business E-Mail: ddw@hal-pc.org.

**WILLIAMS, E. FAYE,** lawyer, political organization executive, health products executive; BS, Grambling State U.; MPA, U. So. Calif.; JD, Howard U.; PhD in Pub. Adminstrn., City Univ. of LA; D of Ministry, Wesley Theol. Seminary. Former counsel US Congress; legis. counsel DC City Coun.; chief of staff to DC Coun. Mem. Marion Barry; pres., CEO Natural Health Options, Inc., Washington. Former prof. internat. law So. U. Law Ctr., Baton Rouge; pub. affairs dir. WWGB, Washington; commentator La. Radio Network. Bd. mem. Shundahia Network. Named one of Most Influential Black Americans, Ebony mag., 2006; recipient Star Performer Award, Asian Benevolent Soc., Humanitarian Award, African Hebrew Israelites, Winnie Mandela Endurance with Dignity award, Support A Child Found., Inc., 2001, Cmty. Svc. award, Nation of Islam, Woman Entrepreneur of Yr. award, Indiana Black Expo. Mem.: Nat. Congress of Black Women (nat. chair 2006—, past gen. counsel). Office: Nat Congress Black Women Ste 200 1224 W St, SE Washington DC 20020 Office Phone: 301-562-8000.*

**WILLIAMS, EDDIE NATHAN,** retired think-tank executive; b. Memphis, Aug. 18, 1932; s. Ed and Georgia Lee (Barr) W.; m. Jearline F. Reddick, July 18, 1981; children: Traci Lynne, Edward Lawrence, Terence Reddick. BS, U. Ill., 1954; postgrad., Atlanta U., 1957, Howard U., 1960; LLD, U. D.C., 1986; DHL, Bowie State Coll., 1980, Chgo. State U., 1994, Dillard U., 2001; LLD, Benedict Coll., 2003, Clark-Atlanta U., 2005. Reporter Atlanta Daily World Newspaper, 1957-58; staff asst. U.S. Senate Com. on Fgn. Relations, Washington, 1959-60; fgn. service res. officer U.S. Dept. State, Washington, 1961-68; v.p. U. Chgo., 1968-72; pres., CEO, Joint Ctr. for Polit. and Econ. Studies, Washington, 1972—2004, pres. emeritus, 2005—; pres. CEO Eddie Williams & Assocs., 2004—. Vis. pub. policy fellow Howard U., 2005. Editorial columnist: Chgo. Sun Times, 1970-72; contbr. articles to profl. jours. Am. Polit. Sci. Assn. fellow, 1958, MacArthur Found. fellow, 1988, Nat. Acad. Pub. Adminstrn. fellow, 1993, Am. Acad. Arts and Scis. fellow, 1998; recipient Adam Clayton Powell Award Congl. Black Caucus, 1981, Washingtonian of Yr. award Washingtonian Mag., 1991, Alumni of Yr. award U. Ill. Alumni Club of Greater Washington, 1994, Outstanding Leadership award Korean Am. Alliance, 1994. Mem. Kappa Tau Alpha, Omega Psi Phi, Sigma Pi Phi. Office: Eddie Williams & Assocs 1250 Connecticut Ave NW Ste 200 Washington DC 20036 Office Phone: 202-558-3521. Business E-Mail: ewilliams@eddiewilliamsllc.com.

**WILLIAMS, EDWARD DAVID,** information technology management consultant; b. Scranton, Pa., June 20, 1932; s. David Thomas and Mabel (Sims) W. m. Natalie Innadze, Oct. 18, 1952; children: Denise, Claudia. BBA, Hofstra U., 1961; postgrad. in Bus. Adminstrn., Fairleigh Dickenson U., 1979. Cons. Cresap, McCormick and Paget, N.Y.C., 1964—65; sr. mgmt. cons. Union Carbide Corp., N.Y.C., 1965—67; asst. contr. data processing We. Union, N.Y.C., 1967—69; v.p. mgmt. info. sys. ABC, Hackensack, NJ, 1970—86; v.p., chief info. officer Blue Cross Blue Shield of N.J., Newark, 1986—88; v.p. Chantico Pub. Co., Carrellton, Tex., 1989—90; pres. SMC-BIS Inc., Basking Ridge, NJ, 1990—93; pres., CEO Strategic Outsourcing Svcs. Inc., Mountain Lakes, NJ, 1993—97; sr. v.p. Computer Horizons Corp., Mountain Lakes, 1997—99; exec. v.p. PRT Group Inc., Windsor, Conn., 1999; pres. Ed Williams Assoc. Ltd., Franklin Lakes, NJ, 1995—. Spkr. in field. With U.S. Army, 1948-52. Decorated Silver Star with oak leaf cluster, Bronze Star with V; recipient Purple Heart with 2 oak leaf clusters, Combat Info. Badge. Mem. Soc. Mgmt. Info. Systems, N.J. C. of C., Profit Oriented Systems Planning Bd. (bd. dirs.). Masons. Republican. Home and Office: Ed Williams Assoc Ltd 662 Cheyenne Dr Franklin Lakes NJ 07417 Office Phone: 201-847-9148. Personal E-Mail: Edward.D.Williams@att.net.

**WILLIAMS, EDWARD EARL, JR.,** entrepreneur, educator; b. Houston, Aug. 21, 1945; s. Edward Earl and Doris Jewel (Jones) W.; m. Susan M. Warren, June 28, 1983; children: Laura Michelle, David Brian. BS, U. Pa., 1966; PhD, U. Tex., 1968. Asst. prof. econs. Rutgers U., New Brunswick, NJ, 1968-70; assoc. prof. fin. McGill U., Montreal, Que., Canada, 1970-73; v.p. Svc. Corp. Internat., Houston, 1973-77; prof. adminstrv. sci. Rice U., Houston, 1978-82, Henry Gardiner Symonds prof., 1982—, prof. stats., 1995—. Chmn. bd. dirs. Edward E. Williams & Co., Houston, 1976-92; chmn. bd., pres. Tex. Capital Investment Co., 1979-95; chmn. bd. First Tex. Venture Capital Corp., 1983-92; mng. dir. First Tex. Venture Capital, LLC, 1992-2000, Svc. Corp. Internat., Simugram Sys., Inc.; adv. dir. Frost Nat. Bank Author: Prospects for the Savings and Loan Industry, 1968, An Integrated Analysis for Managerial Finance, 1970, Investment Analysis, 1974, Business Planning for the Entrepreneur, 1983, The Economics of Production and Productivity: A Modeling Approach, 1996, Entrepreneurship and Productivity, 1998, The N.Y. Times Pocket MBA Series: Business Planning, 1999, Models for Investors in Real World Markets, 2003, Preparing an Entrepreneurial Business Plan, 2004; contbr. articles to profl. jours. Benjamin Franklin scholar, Jesse Jones scholar U. Pa., 1966; fellow Tex. Savs. and Loan League, fellow NDEA U. Tex., 1968. Mem. Am. Statis. Assn., Coll. Innovation and Entrepreneurship, Fin. Mgmt. Assn., So. Pacific Hist. and Tech. Soc., Santa Fe Rlwy. Hist. and Modeling Soc., Soc. on Econs. and Mgmt. in China, Raveneaux Country Club, Jewish Comm. North, Beta Gamma Sigma, Alpha Kappa Psi. Republican. Home: 7602 Wilton Park Dr Spring TX 77379-4672 Office: Rice U Jesse H Jones Grad Sch Mgmt Houston TX 77251 Business E-Mail: jmkeynes@rice.edu.

**WILLIAMS, EDWARD F(OSTER), III,** environmental engineer; b. N.Y.C., Jan. 3, 1935; s. E. Foster Jr. and Ida Frances (Richards) W.; m. Sue Carol Osenbaugh, June 5, 1960; children: Cecile Elizabeth, Alexander Harmon. BS in Engring., Auburn U., 1956; MA in History, U. Memphis, 1974. Registered profl. engr., Tenn. Engr. Buckeye Cellulose Corp. (subs. of Procter & Gamble), Memphis, 1957, process safety engr., 1960, resident constrn. engr. Perry, Fla., 1960-61, staff engr. Memphis, 1961-70; chief engr., v.p. Enviro-trol, Inc., Memphis, 1970-73; from v.p. to pres. Ramcon Environ. Corp., Memphis, 1973-80; pres. E.F. Williams & Assocs., Inc., Memphis, 1980-98; v.p. engring. Environ. Testing & Cons. of the Americas, Inc., 1998—2001, pres., 2001—. Chmn. bd. EFW Comml. Ventures, Inc., 1990—, Spiridon Press, Inc., 1998-99; bd. dirs. Mobile Process Tech. Inc., Memphis; v.p. Environ. Testing and Cons., Inc., Memphis, 1985-94; environ. coord. Shelby County, Tenn., 1995-96. Author: Fustest with the Mostest, 1968, Early Memphis and Its River Rivals, 1969, Great American Civil War Trivia Book, 1998; editor Environ. Control News for So. Industry, 1971-2001 State rep. Tenn. Gen. Assembly, 1967-68; mem. Shelby County Bd. Commrs., Memphis, 1978-94, chmn., 1987-88, 90-92, Shelby County Records Commn., 1978-, chmn., 1993-, Chickasaw Basin Authority, 1980-94, 98—, vice chmn., 1982-94; historian Shelby County, 1994—; environ. coord. Shelby County Mayor's staff, 1995—96; trustee Belton Coll., 1982-, chmn., 1987-88, 90-92; del. Rep. Nat. Conv., 1988; state chmn. Nat. Conf. Rep. County Ofcls., 1993—96; vice chmn. Shelby County Stormwater Steering Com., 1998—2002; vice-chmn. Memphis-Shelby local Emergency Planning Com., 1986—2003; vice chmn. Shelby County Courthouse Hist. Preservation Commn., 2000—, Mid-South Commn. on Aging, 2003; bd. dirs. Better Bus. Bur. Memphis, 1995—; chmn. Shelby County Hist. Commn., 1997—98; pres. Christ United Presbyn. Ch. Corp., 1995—98; del. Rep. Nat. Conv., 1992, 1996, state exec. com., 1994—2002; bd. dirs. Southwest Tenn. C.C. Found., 2001—; v.p. Memphis Belle War Meml. Found., 2000—05; adv. com. Boy Scouts of Am., Chickasaw Coun., 1980—; vice chmn. Rep. Party of Shelby County, 2003—05. Lt. USAF, 1957—60, capt. res. USAF, 1961, wing comdr. staff, 1958, Chem., Biol., & Radiol. Warfare. Named Tenn. Water Conserva-

tionist of Yr., Tenn. Conservation League, 1973, Tenn. Legis. Conservationist of Yr., Nat. Wildlife Fedn., 1974, Memphis Outstanding Engr., Memphis Joint Engrs. Coun., 1980; recipient Shelby County Environ. Improvement award, 1983, Tenn. Lifetime Environ. Stewardship award Tenn. Dept. Environ. and Conservation, 1995. Mem. NSPE, ASME, Am. Acad. Environ. Engrs. (diplomate), Environ. Assesment Assn., TSPE, Water Environ. Fedn., Am. Indsl. Hygiene Assn. (chpt. pres.), Am. Soc. Safety Engrs. (Outstanding Achievement award 1995-96), Air and Waste Mgmt. Assn., Engrs. Club Memphis (bd. dirs. 1979-80, 98-2002, pres. 2000-01), Tenn. Water and Wastewater Assn., Rotary, C. of C. (environ. coun. chmn. 1988-2000, chmn. emeritus 2000—), Tenn. Hist. Soc. (v.p. 1972), Tenn. Hist. Commn. (vice-chmn. 1987-99), West Tenn. Hist. Soc. (pres. 1983-85), Am. Hist. Assn., Memphis Belle Meml. Assn. (bd. dirs. 2004-05) Memphis-Shelby County Tenn. Bicentennial Commn. (chmn. 1994-96), Davies Manor Assn. (pres. 1999-2000), Miss. Hist. Soc. Republican. Avocation: history. Home: 148 Perkins Ext Memphis TN 38117-3127 Office: ETC of the Americas Inc 751 E Brookhaven Cir Memphis TN 38117-4501 also: PO Box 241813 Memphis TN 38124-1813 also: Shelby Co Office 150 Washington Ave Rm 210 Memphis TN 38103 Office Phone: 901-685-2077. E-mail: efwilliams@etcamemphis.com. *It has been my observation that history does not repeat itself, but human nature does. Knowledge of this principle can be put to use in politics, business, and other endeavors if one knows history.*

**WILLIAMS, EDWARD FRANK,** poet, entertainment company executive; b. N.Y.C., Oct. 3, 1949; s. Frank and Maggie W.; m. B.L. Williams, 1980 (div. 1985). AAS, Kingsborough C.C., Bklyn., 1970. Instr. bd. edn. Cmty. Sch. Dist. # 13, Bklyn., 1971-99; FCC 3rd class permit FCC, 1980—; performance poet Poet and Writers Inc., N.Y.C., 1980—; CSAC State of N.Y., 1990—; CEO, pres. Libra Prodns./Entertainment Inc., Bklyn., 1998. Author: E.F. Williams, Urban Poet, 1985, (CD version), 1999. Avocations: lyricist, motivational speaker, educational consultant. Home: 1633 Sterling Pl Apt 4H Brooklyn NY 11233-4970

**WILLIAMS, EDWARD W.,** information technology executive; BS in Mgmt., Rutgers U.; degree in Bus., Stanford U. Various postions RCA and The Gen. Electric Co., 1959—87; from mem. staff to sr. v.p., CFO ITT Industries, White Plains, NY, 1987—2002, sr. v.p., 2002—, CFO, 2002—. Mem. exec. com. ITT Industries. Office: ITT Industries 4 West Red Oak Lane White Plains NY 10604-3617

**WILLIAMS, EDWIN NEEL,** newspaper editor; b. Rives, Mo., Jan. 14, 1942; s. Carl Edwin and Vina Marie (Edmonston) W.; m. Marylyn Lentine, 1973; 1 child, Jonathan Lentine. BA in History, U. Miss., 1965. Reporter Clarksdale (Miss) Press-Register, 1965; reporter, editor Delta Dem.-Times, Greenville, Miss., 1967-72; Nieman fellow Harvard U., Cambridge, Mass., 1972-73; writer, researcher Ford Found., N.Y.C., 1973; editorial writer Charlotte (N.C.) Observer, 1973-76, editor of editorial pages, 1976-80, 87—. Chmn. KinderMourn, Charlotte, 1988, N.C. Harvest, 1993-94; bd. dirs. N.C. Ctr. for Pub. Policy Rsch., Raleigh, 1992-95. With U.S. Army, 1965-67. Baptist. Home: 916 Mount Vernon Ave Charlotte NC 28203-4845 Office: Charlotte Observer PO Box 30308 Charlotte NC 28230-0308 Office Phone: 704-358-5012. E-mail: ewilliams@charlotteobserver.com.

**WILLIAMS, ELEANOR JOYCE,** retired government air traffic control specialist; b. College Station, Tex., Dec. 21, 1936; d. Robert Ira and Viola (Ford) Toliver; m. Tollie Williams, Dec. 30, 1955 (div. July 1978); children: Rodrick, Viola Williams Smith, Darryl, Eric, Dana Williams Robinson, Sheila Williams Watkins, Kenneth. Student, Prairie View A&M Coll., 1955-56, Anchorage Community Coll., 1964-65, U. Alaska-Anchorage, 1976. Clk./stenographer FAA, Anchorage, 1965-66, adminstrv. clk., 1966-67, pers. staffing asst., 1967-68, air traffic control specialist, 1968-79, air traffic control supr. San Juan, P.R., 1979-80, Anchorage, 1983-85, airspace specialist Atlanta, 1980-83, with Washington, 1985-87; area mgr. Kansas City Air Rt. Traffic Control Ctr., Olathe, Kans., 1987-89, asst. mgr. Quality Assurance, 1989-91, supr. traffic mgmt., 1991, supr. system effectiveness section, 1991-93, asst. air traffic mgr., 1993-94; air traffic mgr. Cleve. Air Route Traffic Control Ctr., Oberlin, Ohio, 1994-97; acting mgr. sys. mgmt. br. Des Plaines, Ill., 1995-96; mem. human resource reform team task force Washington, 1996—; acting regional exec. mgr. Great Lakes Region Des Plaines, Ill., 1996-97. Propr. Williams Apts., Anchorage. Sec. Fairview Neighborhood Coun., Anchorage, 1967-69; mem. Anchorage Bicentennial Commn., 1975-76; bd. dirs. Mt. Patmos Youth Dept., Decatur, Ga., 1981-82; mem. NAACP; del. to USSR Women in Mgmt., 1990; v.p. A&M Consol. Lincoln H.S. Alumni Assn., 2000—; mem. citizens amb. program People to People Internat.; mem. adv. bd. Lincoln Recreation Ctr. Recipient Mary K. Goddard award Anchorage Fed. Exec. Assn. and Fed. Women's Program, 1985, Sec.'s award Dept. Transp., 1985, Pres. VIP award, 1988, C. Alfred Anderson award, 1991, Disting. Svc. award Nat. Black Coalition of Fed. Aviation Employees, 1991, Paul K. Bohr award FAA, 1994, Nat. Performance Rev. Hammer award from V.P. Al Gore, 1996, Regional Adminstrs. award for meritorious svc. Gt. Lakes Regional Adminstrn., 1997, Top Flight award for outstanding svc. FAA, 1997; A salute to Her Name in the Congl. Record 104th Congress, 1995, Execs. in Profile award for exemplary career performance Region Ten Blacks in Govt., 1998, Pres.'s award for outstanding svc. Lincoln Former Students Assn.; named Disting. Alumnus Lincoln H.S., 2000; named Youth Advocate Cmty. Champion State of Tex., Tex. Commn. Alcohol and Drug Abuse, 2001; inducted into Black Aviation Hall fame, 2001, Woman of Yr. award North to the Future Bus. and Profl. Women's Club, Anchorage, 2006 Mem.: Women in Mgmt. (del. Soviet Union), Internat. Platform Assn., Fed. Mgrs. Assn., Air Traffic Contrs. Assn., Profl. Women Contrs. Orgn., Nat. Black Coalition of Fed. Aviation Employees (pres. cen. region chpt. 1987—92, Over Achievers award 1987, Disting. Svc. award 1988, Sojourner Truth award Great Lakes region 1997), Blacks in Govt., Nat. Assn. Negro Bus. and Profl. Women USA Inc. (North to the Future club, charter pres. 1975—76), Gamma Phi Delta. Democrat. Baptist. Avocations: singing, sewing. Home: 7931 Old Seward Hwy Apt 8 Anchorage AK 99518-3265 Personal E-Mail: ejw4atc@aol.com, ejtwmsent@msn.com.

**WILLIAMS, ELIZABETH,** human services administrator; d. Sylvester and Lucinda Williams; m. Willie Alfred Oden (div.); 1 child, Robert Earl Oden (dec.). Student, Hammel Bus. Coll., Akron, Ohio, 1960—61, Washtenaw CC, Ann Arbor, Mich., 1962—63, Econ. Inst. Christian Edn., Stanford, Conn., 1968, Norwalk CC, Conn., 1969—70, Roosevelt U., Chgo., 1972, City Coll. NY, Manhattan, 1972—74. LCSW Mich., 1974. Founder, owner Al's Restaurant, Akron, 1964—68; head sports dept. Lord and Taylors, Stanford, 1968—70; supr., planner, bd. dirs. Washtenaw County Neighborhood Svcs., Ypsilanti, Mich., 1970—76; founder, exec. dir. New Bethel Cmty. Ctr., Ypsilanti, 1976—80, People's Choice Multi Purpose Ctr., Inc., Ypsilanti, 1976—80, founder, pres. LA, 1981—87; program dir. Watts Labor Com. Action, LA, 1980—81; founder, pres. EOW Enterprises, LA, 1987—94, SLW Fin. and Investment Corp., 1993—, EW Capital Sys. Enterprises, 2002—. Founder Sr. Citizens Edn. and Tutoring Program, 1970—76; program dir. campus svc. E. Mich. U., Ypsilanti, 1979—80; coord. youth tng. Mich. Tech. Inst., Ann Arbor, 1980; program coord. U. Mich. Dept. Continuing Edn. for Women. Founder Washtenaw County Lit. Coun., Ann Arbor, Mich., 1976—80; mem. Solid Front for Unity in Am., 1982—93, Nat. Orgn. Black Lawyers, Calif., Nat. Coun. Aging, Calif., Ypsilanti Orgn. Social Workers, Nat. and State Orgn. Social Workers, Calif., Ypsilanti area Coll. Life-Long Learning, Wayne State U., Detroit; rep. Bd. Licenses and Regulations, Mich.; spl. program dir. Mt. Zion Ch. of God in Christ, Ypsilanti, 1973—81; bd. mem. YWCA, Stanford, Conn.; state chair Conf. Black Women, Stanford; mem. Stanford Housing Project, MLK Birthday Commn., LA, 1982—85; program planner, program dir.; recruiter, trustee Hong Kong Internat. Humanitarian Self Liquidating Loan Program, 1991—2005; mem., bd. dirs. Nat. Orgn. Social Workers; mem. exec. com. United Way, Calif.; mem. Mich. State Steering Com.; mem. bd. dirs. extended opportunity program Boy Scouts of Am., Ypsilanti. Named Exec. Adminstr. of Yr., Compton, Calif., 1983—84, Bus. Woman of Yr. CBS TV, 1984, Citizen of Week, KNX News, 1985, Bus. Woman of Yr. ACC News, 1986, Miss Christianity, ACC Churches and Cmty. News, 1987; recipient Pauline award, Ministers Alliance, LA,

1983—84, Entrepreneur award, Philanthropist Christian Club, LA, 1983—84, Agy. of Yr. award, Calif., 1983—84, Excellent Cmty. Svc. award, NAACP, 1984, Outstanding Svc. to LA Cmty. award, IRS, 1985, Humanitarian award, People's Choice bd. dirs., 1986, Keys to the City, Compton, 1987, Feeding the Hungry spl. award, 1987; Unique Partnership in Conservation award grant, So. Calif. Gas Co., 1986. Avocations: checkers, chess, cooking, dominoes, interior decorating.

**WILLIAMS, ELIZABETH ANN,** museum program director; b. Kansas City, Mo., Apr. 26, 1965; d. John Paul and Carol Ann Williams. BS in Interior Design, U. Mo., Columbia, 1987; MA in Art H istory, U. Mo., Kansas City, 2005. Interior designer R. Felkner and Associates, Inc., Leawood, Kans., 1987—98; interior designer, owner Eteriors, 2000—05; rsch. intern decorative arts dept. Nelson-Atkins Mus. Art, Kansas City, 2003—05; grad. tchg. asst. art history dept. U. Mo., 2004—05; rsch. assoc. decorative arts dept., 2006—. Dir. leadership tng. Jr. League, Kansas City, 2003—04, dir. tng., 2000. Mem.: Am. Soc. Eighteenth-Century Studies, Midwest Art History Soc., Am. Assn. Mus., Coll. Art Assn., Am. Soc. Interior Designers (assoc.), Phi Upsilon Omicron, Pi Beta Phi. Office Phone: 816-751-1347.

**WILLIAMS, ELLA MARILYN,** mathematics educator; b. Raleigh, NC, Aug. 15, 1950; d. Thomas Harold and Ella W. BA, Bennett Coll., 1972; MA, N.C. Cen. U., 1973. Cert. math. tchr., D.C. Tchr. D.C. Pub. Schs., Washington, 1973, Greensboro (N.C.) Pub. Schs., 1973-77; math. specialist U. D.C., Washington, 1977-80; tchr. DC Pub. Schs., Washington, 1980—. Participant in Honors Tchrs. Workshop, Mich. State U., East Lansing, 1987, St. John's Ins. Inst. for Educators, 2003, Nat. Security Agy. Summer Inst., 2005. Nominee for Presidential award, DC Pub. Schs. Math. Dept., Washington, 1987 Mem. Nat. Coun, Tchrs. of Math (rep standards implementation com., rep. 2000—, chmn. nominating com. 1989-2005, Rep., 1999—), D.C. Coun. Tchrs. of Math. (nominating com. 1989-2006). Home: 3715 Alabama Ave SE # B Washington DC 20020-2403 Office: DC Pub Schs Eastern High 1700 E Capitol St NE Washington DC 20003 Office Phone: 202-698-4500. Personal E-mail: emarilynw@aol.com.

**WILLIAMS, EREKA ROCHELLE,** education educator; b. Windsor, NC, Dec. 6, 1973; d. Franklin D. and Mamie Bell Williams. BS, Fayetteville State U., NC, 1995, MA, 1998; PhD, U. NC, Greensboro, 2003. Cert. elem. educator NC, spl. edn. educator NC. Prof. NC A&T State U., Greensboro, 2003—, elem. edn. undergrad. coord., 2004—. Mem. COPC rsch. adv. bd. NC A&T State U., 2005; mem. Nat. Multicultural Edn., Nat. Coun. Social Studies, Am. Ednl. Rsch. Assn., Kappa Delta Pi (counselor 2004, 5 yr. Membership award 2003). Achievements include research in African American parental perceptions of school efficacy; service learning in the elementary social studies. Avocations: travel, music. Home: PO Box 1696 Greensboro NC 27402 Office: NC A&T State U 1601 E Market St Greensboro NC 27411 Office Phone: 336-334-7841. E-mail: ewilliam@ncat.edu.

**WILLIAMS, ERIC JOSEPH,** transportation executive; b. Havana, Cuba, Nov. 15, 1945; came to U.S., 1961; s. Ereic and Frances (Waterhouse) W.; m. Maria Julia Williams, Mar. 30, 1984; children: Jason, Natasha. BS in Fgn. Svc., Georgetown U., 1968. With Emery Worldwide, Miami, Fla., 1970-88, regional mgr. S.Am., 1977-81, dist. mgr. L.Am.-Caribbean, 1984-86, dir. L.Am.-Caribbean sector, 1986-88; dir. L.Am.-Caribbean region LEP Internat., Miami, 1988-90; mng. dir. sales L.Am. divsn. Fed. Express, 1990-96; sr. mgr. L.Am. sales Fritz Co., 1996-98; v.p. internat. Pilot Air, 1999—2003; v.p. D.F. Young Logistics, 2003—; pres. G.O.A.L., 2004—. Adult edn. tchr., Miami, 1973-75; chmn. Air Cargo Ams., 1999. Exec. bd. Hist. Mus. South Fla.; active Miami Beacon Coun., 1995-97; founder, chmn. America's Relief. 1st lt. U.S. Army, 1968-70. Mem. Soc. Ams., Coral Gables C. of C., Georgetown U. Alumni Assn. (com.), Coconut Grove Sailing Club (com. 1975-76), DACOR. Episcopalian. Home: 501 Raven Ave Miami FL 33166-3950 Office Phone: 786-433-2004. Personal E-mail: ejoe04@aol.com. Business E-Mail: ericw@goalintl.com.

**WILLIAMS, ERVIN EUGENE,** religious organization administrator; b. Corning, N.Y., Feb. 25, 1923; s. Douglas Lewis and Mina P. (Barnes) Williams; m. Ruth Evelyn Snyder, June 12, 1945; children: Roger Eugene, Virginia Ruth. Student, Toccoa Falls (Ga.) Bible Coll., 1939, Cornell U., 1942; BA, Pa. State U., 1949; MA, Mich. State U., 1961, PhD in Communications, 1971. Ordained to ministry Ind. Bapt. Ch., 1950. Acad. dean Greensburg (Pa.) Bible Inst., 1949-51; min. Bapt. Ch., New Kensington, Pa., 1951-53; instr. Pa. State U., 1953-55; sr. min. East Lansing (Mich.) Trinity Ch., 1955-71; vis. prof. Trinity Evang. Div. Sch., Deerfield, Ill., 1968-71, prof. comm. and practical theology, 1971-77, dir. D Ministry program, 1975-76; gen. dir. Am. Missionary Fellowship, Villanova, Pa., 1977-92; exec. min. Ch. of the Apostles, Atlanta, 1993-95; ch. and instl. cons. Smyrna, Ga., 1995—; sr. pastor New Life Bible Ch., Man-O-War Cay, Abaco, The Bahamas, 1997—98; assoc. Mattocks & Assoc., Inc., Fairfax, Va., 2005—. Chaplain Mich. State U., East Lansing, 1955—71; cons. Haggai Inst. Advanced Leadership Tng., Atlanta, 1969—95; lectr. Calvary Bapt. Coll., Kansas City, Mo., 1962, Haggai Inst. Third World Leaders, Singapore, 1970—95; cons. to mission bds., 1967—76; assoc. dir. Camp of Woods, Speculator, NY, 1971—77; Staley lectr. Robert Wesleyan Coll., North Chill, NY, 1973, Judson Coll., Elgin, Ill., 1977—79. Author: 3 books; contbr. articles to religious periodicals. Trustee Gospel Vols., Speculator, 1963—93, Dorothy H. Theis Meml. Found., Sierra Vista, Ariz., 1987—95; mem. bd. regents Owosso (Mich.) Coll., 1971—73. Pilot USAAF, 1942—45, prisoner of war, ETO. Decorated DFC, Air medal with 2 oak leaf clusters, POW medal, ETO Campaign medal with 6 clusters, Victory medal; recipient Presdl. citation. Mem.: Mich. Acad. Arts and Scis., Christian Assn. Psychol. Studies, Aircraft Owners and Pilots Assn., Nat. Sunday Sch. Assn., Phi Beta Kappa, Alpha Kappa Delta, Phi Kappa Phi, Pi Gamma Mu, Office Phone: 703-727-2259. E-mail: misupsu@bellsouth.net. *It is much more difficult to conceal ignorance and prejudice than it is to acquire knowledge and fairness.*

**WILLIAMS, FRANK J.,** state supreme court chief justice, historian, writer; b. Providence, Aug. 24, 1940; s. Frank and Natalie L. (Corelli) W.; m. Virginia E. Miller, Aug. 24, 1966. BA, Boston U., 1962, JD, 1970; MS in Taxation, Bryant Coll., 1986, LHD (hon.), 2004, Lincoln Coll., 1987; LLD (hon.), So. New England Sch. Law, 2001; LHD (hon.), Johnson & Wales U., 2002; Lincoln diploma of honor, Lincoln Meml. U., 2002; LLD (hon.), Roger Williams U., 2004, Mass. Sch. Law, 2004, U. R.I., 2006. Bar: R.I. 1970, U.S. Dist. Ct. R.I. 1970, U.S. Supreme Ct. 1976. Assoc. Tillinghast, Collins & Graham, Providence, 1970-75, Leonard Decof Ltd., Providence, 1976-78; law clk. Graham, Reid, Ewing & Stapleton, Providence, 1969; law clk., adminstrv. asst. RI Atty. Gen., Providence, 1967-68; pres. Frank J. Williams Ltd., attys.-at-law, Providence, 1978-95; assoc. justice RI Superior Ct., 1995-2001; chief justice RI Supreme Ct., 2001—. Judge of probate Town of Hopkinton, RI, 1978-82, 84-90, solicitor, 1978-82, 84-87; judge of probate Town of West Greenwich, RI, 1984-86, 92-95, solicitor, 1984-92, asst. solicitor, 1992-95; dep. judge of probate, 1987-92; solicitor Town of Coventry, RI, 1972-74, 76-78, Town of Barrington, RI, 1993-95, Town of Bristol, RI, 1995, Town of South Kingstown, RI, 1995; past spl. counsel Towns of Westerly, Bristol, Hopkinton, South Kingstown, City of Providence; atty. Town of Smithfield Sewer Authority, 1974-90; legis. counsel RI Retail Fedn., 1975-93, Credit Info. Bur., RI Mortgage Bankers Assn., 1992-95; adj. prof. Roger Williams U. Sch. of Law, 1997—, US Naval War Coll., 2003—; lectr. bus. and legal practice RI Sch. Design, Providence, 1976-80; panel of arbitrators Am. Arbitration Assn., panel of mediators RI Superior Ct., 1993-95; mem. RI Bd. Bar Examiners, 1987-95, chair, 1995; chair RI Housing and Mortgage Fin. Corp., 1995, Lincoln Forum, 1996—; apptd. by pres. to Mil. Commns. Rev. Panel for mil. tribunals, Guantanamo Bay, Cuba, 2004—. Pres. Lincoln Group of Boston, 1976—88, Abraham Lincoln Assn., Springfield, Ill., 1986—95, Ulysses S. Grant Assn., 1990—; elected del. RI Constnl. Conv., 1986; elected town moderator Richmond, RI, 1992—95; dist. moderator Chariho Regional Sch. Dist., 1994; chmn. Lincoln adv. com. Brown U.; mem. Lincoln prize adv. com. Gettysburg Coll.; bd. dirs. John E. Fogarty Found. for

Persons with Mental Retardation, 1975—, South County Hosp., 1995—2004, R.I. Coun. for the Humanities, 2001—, Narraganset Coun. Boy Scouts Am., 1969—80, 1998—2001. Capt. U.S. Army, 1962—67, Germany and Vietnam. Decorated Bronze Star, Combat Infantryman's badge, Army Commendation medal, Air medal with 2 oak leaf clusters, Republic of Vietnam Gallantry Cross with silver star; named Hon. Brigadier Gen., R.I. Militia, 2003; named to RI Heritage Hall of Fame, 2004; recipient Disting. Eagle Scout award, 2005. Fellow: ATLA (jud.); mem.: RI Bar Assn. (chmn. new lawyers adv. com. 1976—87, ho. of dels. 1986—93, chmn. mcpl. law com. 1993), Conf. Chief Justices (bd. dirs. 2004—06), Am. Law Inst., Nat. Assn. for Ct. Mgmt., Am. Judges Assn., Am. Antiquarian Soc., Phi Alpha Delta, Alpha Phi Sigma, Phi Sigma Alpha. Roman Catholic. Office: 250 Benefit St Providence RI 02903 Office Phone: 401-222-3290.

**WILLIAMS, FRANKLIN CADMUS, JR.,** bibliographer; b. Palestine, Tex., July 30, 1941; s. Franklin Cadmus and Cathryn Lucille (Pessoney) W. BA, Baylor U., 1963; MA, Stephen F. Austin State U., 1965; PhD, U. Wis., 1975. Cert. in secondary edn. English and History. Teaching fellow Stephen F. Austin State U., Nacogdoches, Tex., 1964-65, U. Wis., Madison, 1965-68; instr. English Austin Peay State U., Clarksville, Tenn., 1970-71; adj. asst. prof. East Tex. State U., Commerce, 1975; asst. prof. English Jarvis Christian Coll., Hawkins, Tex., 1976-78, 79-81; ind. scholar Palestine, Tex., 1981—; owner, bibliographer Goldsmith Archive, Palestine, 1981—. Cons. Diocese of Galveston-Houston, 1977-84, Tex. State Hist. Assn., Austin, 1988; speaker, editor Jarvis Christian Coll., Hawkins, Tex., 1976-78, 79-81; nat. teaching fellow Office Edn., Washington, 1976-77; del. to Baylor U., U. Wis. System, Madison, 1981. Author: Lone Star Bishops: The Roman Catholic Hierarchy in Texas, 1997; contbr. articles to profl. jours. Mem. Modern Lang. Assn., Tex. State Hist. Assn., Tex. Cath. Hist. Soc., Baylor Alumni Assn. (life), Wis. Alumni Assn. (life), Sigma Tau Delta. Avocations: reading, record collecting, historical genealogy, tennis, swimming. Office: PO Box 96 Palestine TX 75802-0096

**WILLIAMS, FREDERICK BOYD,** priest; b. Chattanooga, Apr. 23, 1939; s. Walter Howard and Matlyn (Goodman) W. BA, Morehouse Coll., 1959; MS, Howard U., 1960; STB, Gen. Theo. Sem., 1963; DMin, Colgate-Rochester Divinity Sch, 1975; DCL, Commonwealth U., 1993. Rsch. mathematician NASA, Greenbelt, Md., 1959-60; curate St. Luke's Episc. Ch., Washington, 1963-65; rector St. Clement's Episc. Ch., Inkster, Mich., 1966-72, Church of the Intercession, N.Y.C., 1972—. Hon. canon Diocese of Botswana, Gaborone, Africa, 1979—. Contbr. articles to profl. jours. Com. mem. HIV curriculum N.Y.C. Bd. Edn., 1991—; chmn. Harlem Churches for Community Improvement, Inc., N.Y.C., 1991—, Nat. Conf. on AIDS, N.Y.C. 1992—; commr. Black Leadership Commn. on AIDS, N.Y.C., 1991—; mem. adv. bd. Anglican Rep. to UN, N.Y.C., 1992—; founder, treas. Conf. on Afro-Anglicanism, London, 1984—; trustee Rockefeller Found. Recipient scholarship Ford Found. 1955-59, Merrill fellow Harvard U. 1984. Mem. Kappa Alpha Psi, Pi Mu Epsilon, Delta Sigma Rho, Alpha Phi Gamma. Avocations: travel, photography, cooking. Office: 550 W 155th St New York NY 10032-7801

**WILLIAMS, GARY MURRAY,** pathologist, educator; b. Regina, Sask., Can., May 7, 1940; s. Murray Austin and Selma Ruby (Domstad) W.; m. Julia Christine Lundberg; children: Walter, Jeffrey, Ingrid. BA, Washington and Jefferson Coll., 1963; MD, U. Pitts. 1967. Diplomate Am. Bd. Pathology, Am. Bd. Toxicology. Assoc. prof. pathology Temple U., Phila., 1971-75; mem. Fels Rsch. Inst., Phila., 1971-75; rsch. prof. N.Y. Med. Coll., Valhalla, 1975-98, prof. pathology, environ. pathology and toxicology, dir., 1999—. Mem. working group Internat. Agy. Rsch. on Cancer, Lyon, France, 1976, 80, 82-83, 85-87, 89, 91, 96-99; mem. subcom. on upper reference levels of nutrients NRC, 1999-03, com. health effects dioxin, 2004-06; advisor joint expert com. on food additives WHO, 2001-06. Founding editor: Cell Biology and Toxicology, 1984—; mem. editl. bd. Archives of Toxicology, 1988—, European Jour. Cancer Prevention, 1991—, Drug and Chem. Toxicology, 1994—, Toxicologic Pathology, 2003—, assoc. editor, 2005—, Food and Chemical Toxicology, 2005—; contbr. more than 490 articles to profl. jours.; editor or co-editor 8 books. Lt. comdr. USPHS, 1969-71. Recipient Sheard-Sanford award Am. Soc. Clin. Pathologists U. Pitts., 1967, Dean's Disting. Rsch. award NY Med. Coll., 2006, 50th Anniversary 5 Yr. Svc. medal WHO, 2006; named Disting. Scientist Am. Chem. Soc., 2005. Fellow Internat. Acad. Toxicol. Pathology (accreditation com. 2000), Royal Coll. Pathologists; mem. Soc. Toxicology (Arthur J. Lehman award 1982, Lectr. award 1996, Advancement Animal Welfare award 2002), Soc. Toxicologic Pathology, Phi Beta Kappa, Alpha Omega Alpha. Home: 8 Elm Rd Scarsdale NY 10583-1410 Office: Dept Pathology NY Med Coll Valhalla NY 10595-1549 Office Phone: 914-594-4146. Business E-Mail: gary_williams@nymc.edu.

**WILLIAMS, GEORGE CHRISTOPHER,** biologist, ecology and evolution educator; b. Charlotte, N.C., May 12, 1926; s. George Felix and Margaret (Steuart) W.; m. Doris Lee Calhoun, Jan. 25, 1951; children: Jacques, Sibyl, Judith, Phoebe. AB, U. Calif., Berkeley, 1949; PhD, UCLA, 1955; ScD (hon.), Queen's U., Kingston, Ont., Can., 1995, SUNY, Stony Brook, 2000. Instr. and asst. prof. Mich. State U., East Lansing, 1955-60; assoc. prof. dept. ecology and evolution SUNY, Stony Brook, 1960-66, prof., 1966-90. Adj. prof. Queens U., Kingston, Ont., Can., 1980-95. Author: Adaptation and Natural Selection, 1966, Sex and Evolution, 1975, Natural Selection: Domains, Levels and Challenges, 1992, The Pony Fish's Glow, 1997; co-author: (with R.M. Nesse) Why We Get Sick: The New Science of Darwinian Medicine, 1995; co-editor: (with James Paradis) Evolution and Ethics, 1989; editor Quar. Rev. Biology, SUNY, 1965-98. With U.S. Army, 1944-46. Recipient Eminent Ecologist award Ecol. Soc. Am., 1989, Daniel Giraud Elliot medal Nat. Acad. Sci., 1992, Royal Swedish Acad. Crafoord prize, 1999; fellow Ctr. Adv. Study Behavioral Sci., Stanford, 1981-82, Guggenheim Found., 1988-89. Fellow AAAS, Soc. Study Evolution (v.p. 1973, pres. 1989), Nat. Acad. Sci., Am. Soc. Ichthyologists and Herpetologists, Am. Soc. Naturalists (editor 1974-79), Icelandic Natural History Soc. Office Phone: 631-632-8600.

**WILLIAMS, GEORGE EARNEST,** retired engineer, retired corporate financial executive; b. Bartow, Fla., Nov. 27, 1923; s. Earnest Roscoe and Ruby Barnett (Mathews) W.; m. Muriel Theodorsen, June 9, 1949. BS in Engring. with honors, USCG Acad.; 1944; postgrad., Harvard U., 1945-46; SM in Mgmt., MIT, 1949. Registered profl. engr. 2 states. Project engr., bus. cons. Ebasco, N.Y.C.; design engr., prodn. supr. Minute Maid Corp., Orlando, Fla.; asst. contr., div. contr., group contr., corp. dir. fin. planning and analysis United Technologies Corp., Hartford, 1957-76, v.p., 1977-82; sr. v.p. fin. Otis Elevator Co., N.Y.C., 1976-77; sr. v.p. Kensington Mgmt. Cons., 1982-84; ret., 1984. Mem. exec. com. Conn. Commn. Services and Expenditures, 1971, Under then Gov. Meskill. Contbr. articles to fin. jours., chpts. to books. Served with USCG, 1941-47, PTO and Atlantic. Mem. AIAA, Fin. Execs. Inst., Army and Navy Club (Washington), Naples Yacht Club, Port Royal Club. Achievements include originating pricing system purchase of Fla. oranges for concentrate mfg. which is still in use and has made a great change in citrus horticulture with an emphasis on sweeter juice vs. outside appearance. Avocation: yachting. Home: Unit A-301 114 Moorings Park Dr Naples FL 34105-2109

**WILLIAMS, GEORGE LEO,** historian, retired secondary school educator, landmark director; b. N.Y.C., June 29, 1931; s. Leo Dominick and Cathryn Margaret (Schellderfer) W.; m. Adelia Gilda Musa, Feb. 26, 1958; children: Adelia, Marina, Gilda. BA, CUNY, 1953, MA, 1955; PhD, NYU, 1966. Tchr. Port Washington (N.Y.) Pub. Schs., 1953, chairperson integrated studies, 1960-65, coord. Amherst project, 1968-69, chairperson English dept., 1970-90; adminstrv. asst. secondary and higher edn. dept. NYU, N.Y.C., 1965-66. Adj. prof. NYU, 1966-74, Adelphi U., Garden City, N.Y. 1967-69, Hofstra U., Hempstead, N.Y., 1967-74; chmn. profl. growth and devel. com. Port Washington Pub. Schs., 1973-90, chmn. bicentennial com. 1989-90, mem. policy bd. Port Washington Tchr. Ctr., 1987-90; mem. alumni bd. Queens Coll. History Dept., 1996-2000; dir. Sandminers Monument, Inc., 2004—. Co-author: (play) The Triumph of the Constitution, 1988, Secession: A

Township Divided, 2005; author: Fascist Thought and Totalitarianism in Italy's Secondary Schools: Theory and Practice, 1922-1943, 1993, Port Washington in the Twentieth Century: Places and People, 1995, Papal Genealogy: The Families and Descendants of the Popes, 1998, (play) Remembrances of the First Colonial Settlement, 1993, A Family HIstory, Book I, 1990, Book II, 2006; contbg. author: Erziehungsstaaten, 1998; editor Port Arrow Community Newsletter, 1973-84, Cow Neck Peninsula Hist. Soc. Newsletter, 1974-77, Cow Neck Peninsula Hist. Soc. Jour., 2001—; contbg. editor L.I. Forum, 1985-2004; author, prodr. (video) Port Washington into the 21st Century, 1996. Chair landmarks com. Cow Neck Peninsula Hist. Soc., Port Warhington, 1980—97, trustee Port Washington, 1974—77, trustee emeritus, 2005—; commr. landmarks com. Village of Port Washington North, 1983—; pres. Hist. Soc. North Hempstead, 2001—04, pres. emeritus, 2005—; mem., chairperson Hist. Landmark Preservation Commn., North Hempstead, NY, 1984—, chmn., 1991—; chairperson 1701 Roslyn Grist Mil Com., 1997—; mem. Port Washington Continuing Edn. Adv. Coun., 1988—97; co-chair Roslyn Clock Tower Com., 1994—96; mem. Preservation League of N.Y., Bigelow Soc., N.Y. Pub. Libr., W.A.R. Goodwin Soc.; grant writer Dodge House Restoration Com.; mem. orgnl. com. Landmark on Main St., 1984—90; mem. Cow Neck Peninsula Hist. Soc. Dodge House Restoration Com., 1992—; adv. bd. records Town of North Hempstead, 1994—; mem. 1998 ann. com. L.I.R.R. to Port Washington; trustee Sand Miners Meml., Inc., 2003—; trustee emeritus Hist. Soc. North Hempstead, 2005; mem. Bay Walk Nautical Arts Com., 2006—. Recipient environ. award Residents for a More Beautiful Port Washington, 1994, numerous Certs. of Appreciation, Civic award for Outstanding Cmty. Svc., Port Washington Rotary, 2001, Cert. of Appreciation, Port Washington Police Dist., 2001, Exec. Citation, Nassau County, 2001, citation N.Y. State Assembly, 2001, Legis. citation Nassau County, 2001, Queens Coll. Dept. History Cert. Appreciation, 2002, Town of North Hempstead's Proclamation, 2002. Mem.: Friends of the Arts, Friends of Planting Fields, Nat. Trust Hist. Preservation, N.Y. State Mus. Assocs., Fulbright Assn., Am. Hist. Assn. (cert. recognition 1988), Port Washington Tchrs. Assn. (v.p. 1963—64, bd. dirs. 1966—74, newsletter editor 1990—92, founder and 1st pres. ret. tchrs. chpt. 1991), Soc. for Preservation L.I. Antiquities, Assn. Pub. Historicans of N.Y. State, N.Y. State Hist. Assn., N.Y. Geneal./Biog. Soc., Residents for a More Beautiful PortWashington (Environ. Quality Recognition award 2003), Roslyn Landmark Soc., Pi Sigma Alpha, Phi Alpha Theta, Phi Beta Kappa. Home: 84 Radcliff Ave Port Washington NY 11050-1600 E-mail: geoleowms@aol.com.

**WILLIAMS, GEORGE WALTON,** language educator; b. Charleston, SC, Oct. 10, 1922; s. Ellison Adger and Elizabeth Simonton (Dillingham) W.; m. Harriet Porcher Simons, Nov. 28, 1953; children: George Walton Jr., Ellison Adger II, Harriet Porcher Stoney. BA, Yale U., 1947; MA, U. Va., Charlo Phi, 1957. Asst. cashier Carolina Savs. Bank, Charleston, 1949-54; asst. prof. English, Duke U., 1957-63, assoc. prof., 1963-67, prof., 1967, chmn. dept. English, 1982-86, prof. emeritus, 1993—. Dir. summer inst. Commn. on English, Coll. Entrance Exam. Bd., 1962; pres. Durham Savoyards, Ltd., 1966-68, 81-82; sr. fellow Coop. Program in Humanities, Duke-U. N.C., 1969; Historiographer, Diocese of S.C., 1960-78; vis. prof. U.S. Mil. Acad., 1982-83 Author: St. Michael's, Charleston, 1751-1951, 1951, rev. edit., 2001, Image and Symbol in the Sacred Poetry of Richard Crashaw, 1963, The Craft of Printing and the Publication of Shakespeare's Plays, 1985, 5 children's books; editor: Romeo and Juliet, 1964, Complete Poetry of Richard Crashaw, 1970, Jacob Eckhard's Choirmaster's Book, 1971, Shakespeare's Speech-Headings, 1997; contbg. editor Dramatic Works of Beaumont and Fletcher, 1966-96; assoc. gen. editor Arden Shakespeare, 1996—. With U.S. Army, 1943—45, ETO. Decorated Combat Inf. badge; recipient Outstanding Civilian Service medal Dept. Army, 1983; Guggenheim Found. fellow, 1977-78; Huntington Library fellow, 1981 Mem. MLA (com. on new variorum 1980-92, chmn. Shakespeare divsn. 1990), South Atlantic MLA (pres. 1980-81, J.H. Fisher award 2001), Southeastern Renaissance Conf. (editor 1960-70, 91-95, pres. 1973, hon. life 2002), Royal Soc. Arts London, S.C. Hist. Soc., Malone Carolina Yacht Club (Charleston), St. Cecilia Soc. (Charleston), Elizabethan Club Yale U., N.Am. Guild of Change Ringers, Phi Beta Kappa, Phi Kappa Phi. Home: 1 Tradd St Charleston SC 29401 Office: Duke U Dept English PO Box 90015 Durham NC 27708-0015 Office Phone: 919-684-5827.

**WILLIAMS, GERALD ARNETT,** academic administrator; b. Jacksonville, Fla., May 7, 1975; s. Gerald Arnett and Clara Mae Williams; m. Joi D. Jones, Jan. 21, 2006. BA in Legal Studies, Valdosta State U., 1997, MPA, 1999, MEd, 2003; EdD, Argosy U., 2006; D Religious Studies, Trinity Coll. and Theol. Sem., 2006. Acct. dir. student life, adj. faculty mem. Valdosta (Ga.) State U., 2003—05; acting dir. housing Thomas U., Thomaville, Ga., 2005, dir. student life Thomasville, Ga., 2005—. Exec. dir. Rhema Word Ministries, Valdosta, 2004—05. Bd. dirs. Big Bros. of Valdosta 2002—03, Teen Plus, Valdosta, 2003—04. Named Advisor of Yr., Valdosta State U., 2004. Mem.: Ga. Housing Officers, Nat. Assn.Colls. and Employers, Nat. Assn. Student Pers. Adminstrs., Order of Omega, Phi Beta Sigma (pres. 2001—03), Omicron Delta Kappa (hon.). Republican. Avocations: reading, golf, weightlifting. Office: Thomas U 1501 Millpond Rd Thomasville GA 31792 Office Phone: 229-226-1621.

**WILLIAMS, GERALD R.,** law educator; s. Ross Gerald and Luana Williams; m. Claudia Grace Clark, Dec. 17, 1965; children: Colette Williams Callister, Jennifer Williams Anderson, Nicole Williams Bruderer, Michael Gerald, Daniel Clark. B.A., Brigham Young U., Provo, Utah, 1966; JD, U. Utah, Salt Lake City, 1969. Bar: Utah 1969, U.S. Dist. Ct. Utah 1969. Legal advisor to the prosecutor Navajo Tribe, Window Rock, Ariz., 1969—70; fellow Internat. Legal Ctr., Kabul, Afghanistan, 1970—72; prof. of law Brigham Young U. Law Sch., Provo, Utah, 1973—. Vis. prof. Ariz. State U. Coll. Law, Tempe, 1972—73, U. Cairo Faculty of Law, 1978—80; expert panel Internat. Devel. Law Inst., Rome, 1983—; pres., bd. of dirs Utah Legal Svcs., Inc., Salt Lake City, 1990—07, vis prof. Harvard Law Sch., Cambridge, Mass., 1986; editl. bd. Alternatives to the High Cost of Litig., N.Y.C., 1991—; editl. advisor Dispute Resolution Jour., Washington, 1992—; bd, dirs. Am. Arbitration Assn., Washington, 1992—96. Author: (book) Legal Negotiation and Settlement, article. Pres. Bd. of Edn., Provo, Utah, 1995—98. Grantee, NSF, 1973-76. Mem.: ABA (mem. standing com. dispute resolution 1989—92), Assn. for Conflict Resolution. Office: Brigham Young Univ 538 JRCB Provo UT 84602 Office Phone: 801-422-2032. Business E-Mail: gerald.williams@byu.edu.

**WILLIAMS, H. THOMAS (TOM WILLIAMS),** academic administrator, physicist, educator; b. Hampton, Va. BS in Physics, U. Va., 1965, PhD in Physics, 1967. NSF post-doctoral rsch. fellow Nat. Bur. Stds., 1967—69; rschr. Inst. for Theoretical Physics, U. Erlangen-Nuernberg, Germany, 1970—71; staff scientist Kaman Scis. Corp., Colorado Springs, Colo., 1971—73; mem. faculty Washington and Lee U., Lexington, Va., 1974—, Edwin A. Morris prof. physics, 1994—, chair dept. physics, 1989—2000, assoc. dean, 1986—89, chief acad. officer, provost, 2003—. Cons. Nat. Bur. Stds., 1974—86, Los Alamos Sci. Lab., 1987—93. Office: Washington and Lee Univ Lexington VA 24450 Business E-Mail: williamsh@wlu.edu.

**WILLIAMS, HANK, JR., (RANDALL HANK WILLIAMS),** country music singer, songwriter; b. Shreveport, La., May 26, 1949; s. Hank and Audrey Williams; m. Gwen Yeargain (div.); 1 child, Hank III; m. Becky White (div.); children: Hilary, Holly; m. Mary Jane Thomas, July 1, 1990; children: Katharine Diane, Samuel. Performer throughout US; recorded song Ain't Misbehavin'; latest albums include: Montana Cafe, 1986, Hank Live, 1987, Born to Boogie, 1987, Wild Streak, 1988, Greatest Hits III, Lone Wolf, 1990, Pure Hank, 1991, (with Clink Black) Maverick, 1992, Out of Left Field, 1993, A Tribute to My Father, 1993, (with Waylon Jennings and Ray Charles) Greatest Hits, vol. 2, 1994, Hog Wild, 1995, High Notes: Original Classic Hits Vol. 8, 1995, American Legends: Best of The Early Years, 1995, 20 Hits Special Collection Vol. 1, 1995, A.K.A. Wham Bam Sam, 1996, The Hits, 1997, The Complete Hank Williams Jr., 1999, Stormy, 1999, I'm One of You, 2003; composer All My Rowdy Friends, 1993, TV film Willa, 1979 (also actor); singer in films The Dangerous Days of Kiowa Jones, 1966, Kelly's

Heroes, 1970, The Moonshine War, 1970, actor A Time to Sing, 1968, Roadie, 1980, (voice) Tom Sawyer, 2000, TV series (voice) The Simpsons; author Living Proof: An Autobiography, 1979. Recipient 18 Gold albums, 5 Platinum albums, 1 Double Platinum album, Entertainer of Yr. award, Country Music Assn., 1987, 1988, Music Video of Yr. award, 1987, Entertainer of Yr. award, Acad. Country Music., 1987—89, Video of Yr. award, 1987—89, Album of Yr., 1989, Grammy award, 1990, Johnny Cash Visionary award, Country Music TV, 2006. Office: c/o Ken Levitan and Ross Schilling Vector Mgmt PO Box 120479 Nashville TN 37212 also: Curb Records 48 Music Sq E Nashville TN 37203*

**WILLIAMS, HAROLD LEE,** religious studies educator, minister, coach, director; b. Norfolk, Va., June 26, 1960; s. Harries Benjamin and Madge Virginia Williams; m. Regina Ann Blackstock, July 19, 1986; children: Harold Lee II, Quintin Lemar. AA, Chowan Coll., Murfreesboro, NC; BS, W.Va. U. Inst. Tech., Montgomery; M in Religious Edn., Interdenominational Bible Inst., Lawrenceville, VA. Tchr., coach Brunswick County Pub. Schs., Lawrenceville, Sussex County (Va.) Pub. Schs., Greensville County Schs., Emporia, Va.; instr., athletic dir., coach St. Paul's Coll., Lawrenceville; asst. pastor First Bapt. Ch., Lawrenceville. 1st v.p. NAACP, Lawrenceville; treas. Brunswick Youth Devel. League, Lawrenceville; moderator Unified Shiloh Bapt. Assn., Southside, Va.; bd. dirs. Brunswick-Mayfield Recreation Ctr., chaplain. Mem.: NEA (assoc.), Va. HS Coaches Assn., Inc. (assoc.), Brunswick Edn. Assn. (assoc.), Va. Edn. Assn. (assoc.), Omega Psi Phi (hon.). Democrat. Baptist. Avocations: reading, mentoring youth, sports, chess. Home: PO Box 481 Lawrenceville VA 23868 Office: Brunswick HS 2171 Lawrenceville Plank Rd Lawrenceville VA 23868 Office Phone: 434-848-0320. Office Fax: 434-848-6303. E-mail: harold.williams@brun.k12.va.us.

**WILLIAMS, HAROLD MARVIN,** lawyer, retired foundation administrator, retired academic administrator, retired federal agency administrator; b. Phila., Jan. 5, 1928; s. Louis W. and Sophie (Fox) W.; m. Nancy Englander; children: Ralph A., Susan J., Derek M. AB, UCLA, 1946; JD, Harvard Law Sch., 1949; postgrad. in law, U. So. Calif., 1955-59; DHL (hon.), Johns Hopkins U., 1987, Occidental Coll., 1997, Calif. State U., 1998. Bar: Calif. 1950. Pvt. practice, LA, 1950, 1953—55; with Hunt Food and Industries Inc., 1955-68, v.p., 1958-60, exec. v.p., 1960-68; gen. mgr. Hunt-Wesson Foods, 1964-66, pres., 1966-68, Hunt Food and Industries Inc., 1968; chmn. bd., fin. com. Norton Simon, 1968—70; prof. mgmt. UCLA, 1970-77; chmn. SEC, Washington, 1977-81; pres., CEO J. Paul Getty Trust, 1981-98, pres. emeritus; of counsel Skadden Arps et al, 1998—. Pres., dir. Special Investments Securities, Inc., 1961—66. Pub. mem. Nat. Advt. Review Bd., 1971—75; trustee Nat. Humanities Ctr., 1987—93; mem. Coun. Fgn. Rels., Com. Econ. Devel., Pres.' Com. Arts, Humanities, 1993—2001, Commn. Econ. Devel. State Calif., 1973—77; energy coord. City of LA, 1973—74; regent U. Calif., 1983—94; commn. rev. master plan higher edn. State Calif., Calif., 1985—87; co chair Calif. Citizens Commn. Higher Edn.; dir. Ethics Resource Ctr.; mem. Commn. Acad. Presidency; co-chmn. Pub. Comm. LA County Govt.; dir. Pub. Policy Inst. Calif., 1995—2003, Calif. Endowment, 1995—2004, Alliance for Coll. Ready Schs., Alliance for Excellent Edn.; chair bd. visitors UCLA Sch. Arts and Arch. 1st lt. AUS, 1951—53, Korea. Decorated Bronze Star. Mem.: State Bar Calif. Office: J Paul Getty Trust 1200 Getty Center Dr Ste 1100 Los Angeles CA 90049-1668 also: Skadden Arps Slate Meagher Flom LLP 300 S Grand Ave Ste 3400 Los Angeles CA 90071 Office Phone: 310-440-6417, 213-687-5370. E-mail: hwilliams@getty.edu.

**WILLIAMS, HAROLD ROGER,** economist, educator; b. Arcade, N.Y., Aug. 22, 1935; s. Harry Alfred and Gertrude Anna (Scharf) W.; m. Lucia Dorothy Preuschoff, Apr. 23, 1955; children: Theresa Lynn, Mark Roger. BA, Harpur Coll., SUNY, Binghamton, 1961; MA, Pa. State U., 1963; PhD, U. Nebr., 1966; postgrad., Harvard U., 1969-70. Instr., Pa. State U., 1962-63; Instr. U. Nebr., 1965-66; mem. faculty Kent (Ohio) State U., 1966—, prof. econs. and internat. bus., 1972—, chmn. dept., 1974-81, dir. Internat. Bus. Program, Grad. Sch. Mgmt., 1980-86, chmn. faculty senate, 1988-89, now prof. emeritus; assoc. dean Grad. Sch. Mgmt., 1994-96; program dir. Kent State-Geneva Program, Geneva, 1996-97. Econ. cons. and adv. to numerous govt., bus. and internat. orgns. Author over 100 books and articles in field. Served with AUS, 1954-57. Grantee NSF. Mem. Am. Econ. Assn., Internat. Econs. Assn., Acad. Internat. Bus., Midwest Econ. Assn. (v.p. 1969-70), So. Econ. Assn., Phi Gamma Mu, Omicron Delta Epsilon, Beta Gamma Sigma, Phi Beta Delta. Home: 415 Suzanne Dr Kent OH 44240-1933 Office: Rm 478 Dept Econs Kent State U Kent OH 44242-0001 Office Phone: 330-672-1085. E-mail: Hwilliam@BSA3.Kent.edu.

**WILLIAMS, HENRY WARD, JR.,** lawyer, writer; b. Rochester, N.Y., Jan. 12, 1930; s. Henry Ward and Margaret Elizabeth (Simpson) W.; m. Barbara Dimmick; children: Edith Williams Linares, Margaret Williams Warren, Sarah Williams Farrand, Ann Williams Treacy, Elizabeth DeLancey, Victoria Maureen AB, Dartmouth Coll., 1952; LLB, U.Va., 1958. Bar: N.Y. 1959, U.S. Dist. Ct. (we. dist.) N.Y. 1959, U.S. Dist. Ct. (so. dist.) Mich. 1982, U.S. Ct. Appeals (2d cir.) 1963, U.S. Tax Ct. 1960, U.S. Supreme Ct. 1968, D.C. 1978. Ptnr. Harris, Beach & Wilcox, Rochester, 1958—78, Robinson, Williams, Angeloff & Frank, Rochester, 1979—80, Weidman, Williams, Jordon, Angeloff & Frank, Rochester, 1980—82, The Williams Law Office, Rochester, 1982—. Exec. editor Va. Law Rev., 1957-58 Chmn. Genesee Finger/Lakes Regional Planning Coun., 1973-89; majority leader Monroe County Legislature, 1967-73; councilman Town of Wheatland, N.Y., 2002—; mem. adv. coun. Dartmouth Coll., 1995-99; mem. # 8020 Nat. Ski Patrol Sys. Lt. (j.g.) USN, 1952-55 Mem. ABA, N.Y. State Bar Assn., Monroe County Bar Assn. (trustee 1982-85), Rochester Yacht Club, Royal Can. Yacht Club, Lake Yacht Racing Assn. (pres. 1985-87, hon. pres. 1988-90), Royal Ocean Racing Club, Royal Nfld. Yacht Club, Raven Soc., Order of Coif, Omicron Delta Kappa Office: The Williams Law Office PO Box 8 Scottsville NY 14546-0008 Office Phone: 585-889-3000.

**WILLIAMS, HOWARD RUSSELL,** law educator; b. Evansville, Ind., Sept. 26, 1915; s. Clyde Alfred and Grace (Preston) W.; m. Virginia Merle Thompson, Nov. 3, 1942 (dec. 2000); 1 son, Frederick S.T. AB, Washington U., St. Louis, 1937; LLB, Columbia U., 1940. Bar: N.Y. 1941. With firm Root, Clark, Buckner & Ballantine, N.Y.C., 1940-41; prof. law, asst. dean U. Tex. Law Sch., Austin, 1946-51; prof. law Columbia U. Law Sch., N.Y.C., 1951-63; Dwight prof. Columbia Law Sch., 1959-63; prof. law Stanford U., 1963-85, Stella W. and Ira S. Lillick prof., 1968-82, prof. emeritus, 1982, Robert E. Paradise prof. natural resources, 1983-85, prof. emeritus, 1985—. Oil and gas cons. President's Materials Policy Commn., 1951; mem. Calif. Law Revision Commn., 1971-79, vice chmn., 1976-77, chmn., 1978-79 Author or co-author: Cases on Property, 1954, Cases on Oil and Gas, 1956, 5th edit., 1987, Decedents' Estates and Trusts, 1968, Future Interests, 1970, Oil and Gas Law, 8 vols., 1959-64 (with ann. supplements/rev. 1964-95), abridged edit., 1973, Manual of Oil and Gas Terms, 1957, 11th edit., 2000. Bd. regents Berkeley Bapt. Divinity Sch., 1966-67; trustee Rocky Mountain Mineral Law Found., 1964-66, 68-85. Pvt., maj. U.S. Army, 1941—46. Recipient Clyde O. Martz Tchg. award Rocky Mountain Mineral Law Found., 1994. Mem.: Phi Beta Kappa. Democrat. Home: 360 Everett Ave Apt 4B Palo Alto CA 94301-1422 Office: Stanford U Sch Law Nathan Abbott Way Stanford CA 94305 Office Phone: 650-725-5875.

**WILLIAMS, HOWARD WALTER,** aerospace engineer, engineering executive; b. Evansville, Ind., Oct. 18, 1937; s. Walter Charles and Marie Louise (Bollinger) W.; m. Phyllis Ann Scofield, May 4, 1956 (div. Sept. 1970); m. Marilee Sharon Mulvane, Oct. 30, 1970; children: Deborah, Steven, Kevin, Glennn, Lori, Michele. *Howard and Marilee's descendants are in Montana: Deborah and Cliff Mantha; their sons are Rhian, Jordan, and David. Son, Rhian (and wife Jenny) have child, Anne. Son, Jordan (and wife Susan) live in Reno. Steven and Sandy Williams have Joshua and Mitchell. In Sacramento, Lori and Brett Clover have Brett II and Aaron. Michele Didway has Jason and Jessica with Scott Shearer, who has Kim, Kristy, David, and Kassie. Howard and Marilee moved from southern California to Sacramento, Phyllis to Montana, in the 1970s. Kevin lives in Sacramento. Glen and*

*Rebecca live in Portland. Sister Janet Ragsdale lives in Sacramento and brother Harold lives in Corona.* AA, Pasadena City Coll., 1956; BSME, Calif. State U., Los Angeles, 1967; BSBA, U. San Francisco, 1978; PhD in Comml. Sci. (hon.), London Inst. Rsch., 1992. Turbojet, rocket engr. Aerojet-Gen. Corp., Azusa, Calif., 1956-59, infrared sensor engr., 1959-60, rocket, torpedo engr., 1960-66, power, propulsion mgr. propulsion divsn. Sacramento, 1967-73, high speed ship systems mgr., 1974-78, combustion, power mgr., rocket engine and energy mktg. mgr., 1979-89, dir. strategic planning, 1989-94; strategic analyst, program mgr. Pratt & Whitney Space Propulsion, West Palm Beach, Fla., 1995—2003. Mgmt. cons., 2004—. Author: (with others) Heat Exchangers, 1980, Industrial Heat Exchangers, 1985, History of Liquid Rocket Engine Development in the U.S., 1992, Aerojet: The Creative Company, 1997; co-inventor Closed Cycle Power System, 1969. Recipient Energy Innovation award U.S. Dept. Energy, 1985. Mem. AIAA (sr., Best Paper 1966), Am. Soc. Metals (organizing dir. indsl. heat exch. conf. 1985). Avocation: bicycling. *Personal philosophy: I hope to be as good a parent and grandparent as mine have been.*

**WILLIAMS, HUGH ALEXANDER, JR.,** retired mechanical engineer, consultant; b. Spencer, NC, Aug. 18, 1926; s. Hugh Alexander and Mattie Blanche (Megginson) W.; m. Ruth Ann Gray, Feb. 21, 1950; children: David Gray, Martha Blanche Williams Heidengren. BS in Mech. Engring., N.C. State U., 1948, MS in Diesel Engring., 1950; postgrad., Benedictine U. Inst. Mgmt., 1977. Registered profl. engr., Ill. Jr. engr.-field svc. engr. Baldwin-Lima Hamilton (Ohio) Corp., 1950-52, project engr., 1953-55, Electro-Motive divsn. Gen. Motors Corp., La Grange, Ill., 1955-58, sr. project engr., 1958-63, supr. product devel. engine design sect., 1963-86, staff engr. advanced mech. tech., 1986-87. Editor So. Engr., 1947-48; contbr. articles to profl. jours. Trustee Downers Grove (Ill.) San. Dist., 1965-92, pres., 1974-91, v.p., 1991-92; pres. Ill. Assn. San. Dists., 1976-77, bd. dirs., 1977-89; mem. statewide policy adv. com. Ill. EPA, 1977-79; mem. DuPage County Intergovtl. Task Force Com., 1988-92; elder Presbyn. Ch. Served with USAAC, 1945. Recipient Trustee Svc. award Ill. Assn. San. Dists., 1986, Citizens award Downers Grove Evening cpt. Kiwanis, 1991; Norfolk So. R.R. fellow, 1950. Fellow ASME (chmn. honors and awards com. 1993-96, Diesel and Gas Engine Power Divsn. Spkr. awards 1968, 84, Divsn. citation 1977, 97, Internal Combustion Engine award 1987, exec. com. Internal Combustion Engine divsn. 1981-87, 88-92, chmn. 1985-86, sec. 1988-92); mem. Soc. Automotive Engrs. (life), ASME (chmn. Soichiro Honda medal com. 1987-92, chmn. Internal Combustion Engine Award com. 1993-98), Ill. Assn. Wastewater Agys. (Outstanding Mem. award 1990, hon. mem. 1992), Raleigh Host Lions Club (pres. 1996-97), SAR (pres. Raleigh cpt. 2000-01), St. Andrew's Soc. N.C., Jamestowne Soc. (1st N.C. co. lt. gov. 2006—), Masons (32 degree), Sigma Pi. Republican. Achievements include patentee in field. Home: 2108 Weybridge Dr Raleigh NC 27615-5562 Personal E-mail: Hector26@aol.com.

**WILLIAMS, IAN GEORGE,** writer; b. Liverpool, Eng., Sept. 21, 1949; s. Edward and Margaret (Cooper) W.; m. Anora Mahmudova, Nov. 30, 2002; children: Alexander James, Ian Anton Norbek. BA with honors, Liverpool U., 1973. Speechwriter for Neil Kinnock UK Labor Party, 1987; pres. UN Corr. Assn., 1995—96, v.p., 1997—98. Author: The Alms Trade, 1989, The UN For Beginners, 1995, Deserter: Bush's War on Military Families, Veterans and His Own Past, 2004, Rum: A Social and Sociable History of the Real Spirit of 1776, 2005; contbr. chapters to books, numerous articles to mags. and profl. publs. Mem. Royal Inst. Internat. Affairs, London Press Club, Overseas Press Club (N.Y.C.), Nat. Press Club (Washington). Avocations: theater, reading, bicycling, sailing. Office: The Nation Mag 33 Irving Pl New York NY 10003 Office Phone: 212-686-8884. E-mail: uswarreport@igc.org.

**WILLIAMS, IDA JONES,** consumer and home economics educator, writer; b. Coatesville, Pa., Dec. 1, 1911; d. William Oscar and Ida Ella (Ruth) Jones; m. Charles Nathaniel Williams, Mar. 17, 1940 (dec. July 1971). BS, Hampton Inst., 1935; MA, U. Conn., 1965. Cert. high sch. tchr., English, sci., home econs., Va., Pa. Tchr. sci. and home econs. Richmond County H.S., Ivondale, Va., 1935—36; tchr. English and home econs. Northampton County H.S., Chesapeake, Va., 1936 40, tchr. consumer and home econs Machipongo, Va., 1940—70, Northampton Jr. H.S., Machipongo, 1970—76. Author: Starting Anew After Seventy, 1980 (plaque 1980), News and Views of Northampton County High Principals and Alumni, 1981, Great Grandmother, Leah's Legacy-Remember You're Free, 2000; co-author: The History of Virginia State Federation of Colored Women's Clubs, Inc., 1996; editor: Fifty Year Book 1935-1985 - Hampton Institute Class, 1985, Favorite Recipes of Ruth Family & Friends, 1986. V.p. Ea. Lit. Coun., Melfa, Va., 1987-89; active Ea. Shore Coll. Found., Inc., Melfa, 1988-2000, Gov.'s Adv. Bd. on Aging, Richmond, Va., 1992-94; instr. Ladies Community Bible Class, 1976-80 (Plaque 1980); sec., treas., v.p. Hospice Support of Ea. Shore, 1980-94; mem. Northampton/Accomack Adv. Coun., 1992-94; marshall 28th anniv. commencement Ea. Shore C.C., 1996; bd. dirs. Ea. Shore C.C. Found., 1998-2000; com. mem. Va. State Legis., 1995-2002 Named Home Econs. Tchr. of Yr., Am. Home Econs. Assn. and Family Cir., 1975, Woman of Yr., Prog. Women of E.S., 1997, Ida J. Williams scholarship in her honor, Keller Ch. Christ, 1999; recipient Jefferson award, Am. Inst. Pub. Svc., Wavy-TV-Bell Atlantic and Mattress Discounters, 1991, Nat. Sojourner Truth Meritorious Svc. award, Negro Bus. and Profl. Women's Clubs, Gavel Ea. Shore Ret. Tchrs. Assn., 1994, Gov.'s award for vol. excellence, 1994, Contribution to Edn. award, Ea. Shore Coll. Found., 1997, plaque, Southeastern Assn. Colored Women's Clubs, Inc., 2001, Leadership award, 2001, Dedicated Svc. award, Nat. Assn. Colored Women's Club, 1998, Exemplary Svc. award, 2001, Svc. award, E.S. C.C. Found., Inc., 2000, plaque 1st Black Northampton County, Ea. Shore Va. C. of C., 2002, Black Achievement award, Ebenezer A.M.E. Ch., 2003, Achievement award, Chester County Hist. Soc. of Pa., 2003, Ednl. Achievement award, Northampton County H.S. Alumni Assn., 2003, Dedicated Svc. award, S.E. Assn. Colored Women's Clubs Inc., 2003—05; honored at ceremony for mother Ida Ella Ruth Jones at hist. road marker on Route 82, Pa., 2004. Mem. AARP (Citation award 1996, Mem. of Yr. 1997, v.p. Northampton chpt. 1998-2000), Progressive Women of Ea. Shore (pres. 1985-93, Gold Necklace 1993, Woman of Yr. 1997), C. of C., Univ. Women (v.p. Portsmouth br. 1985-87), Ea. Shore Ret. Tchrs. (pres. 1977-84), Dist. L Ret. Tchrs. (pres. 1989-91, chmn. legis. com. 1998, 99, 2001, chmn. edn. and scholarship com. 2001-05, Dedicated and Outstanding Svc. award 2003), Va. State Fedn. Colored Women's Club (pres. 1990-94, editor history com. 1994-96) Mem. Ch. of Christ. Avocations: crafts, travel, writing, lecturing. Home and Office: PO Box 236 14213 Lankford Hwy Eastville VA 23347-0236

**WILLIAMS, J. BRYAN,** lawyer; b. Detroit, July 23, 1947; s. Walter J. and Maureen June (Kay) Williams; m. Jane Elizabeth Eisele, Aug. 24, 1974; children: Kyle Joseph, Ryan Patrick. AB, U. Notre Dame, 1969; JD, U. Mich., 1972. Bar: Mich. 1972, U.S. Dist. Ct. (ea. dist.) Mich. 1972. Atty. Dickinson Wright, PLLC (and predecessor firm), Detroit, 1972—, CEO Bloomfield Hills, Mich., 1991-2000. Pres. U.S. Law Firm Group, Inc., 2002. Mem.: ABA, Detroit Legal News Co. (bd. dirs.), Econ. Club Detroit (bd. dirs. 1996—2001), Mich. Bar Assn., Detroit Regional C. of C. (bd. dirs. 1994—2003, vice chmn. 1998—2002), Nat. Club Assn. (bd. dirs. 1994—2006, treas. 1997—98, v.p. 1998—2002, chmn. 2002—03, sec. 1995—97), Oakland Hills Country Club, Notre Dame Club Detroit (pres. 1984), Roman Catholic. Home: 993 Suffield Ave Birmingham MI 48009-1242 Office: Dickinson Wright PLLC 38525 Woodward Ave Ste 2000 Bloomfield Hills MI 48304 Office Phone: 248-433-7289. Business E-Mail: jwilliams@dickinsonwright.com.

**WILLIAMS, J. LINDA,** librarian; b. Bethesda, Md., June 30, 1945; d. Joseph Gordon and Annie Louise (Whitfield) DiMisa. BS in Secondary Edn./English and History, Radford U., 1966; MLS, U. Md., 1977; cert. adminstrn., supr., Bowie (State Coll.), 1987. Cert. tchr., librarian. Tchr. English, history Prince William County Pub. Schs., Woodbridge, Va., 1967—73; tchr. English Charles County Pub. Schs., LaPlata, Md., 1973—76; library media specialist St. Mary County Pub. Schs., Leonardtown, Md., 1977—84; staff specialist Md. Dept. Edn., Balt., 1985—94; supr. media and

instrnl. materials Prince George's County Pub. Schs., Landover, Md., 1994—99; dir. libr. media svcs. Anne Arundel County Pub. Schs., Annapolis, Md., 1999—. Named Alumnus of Yr. Coll. Library and Info. Svcs., 1988 U. Md.; profl. devel. grantee 3M, 1981. Mem. ALA (pres.-elect 2004-05), AASL (pres. 2005-06), Md. Libr. Assn., Md. Edn. Media Assn. (pres. 1998-99), Beta Phi Mu. Home: 1726 Farmington Ct Crofton MD 21114-2307 Office: 1657 Crofton Centre Crofton MD 21114 E-mail: lwilliams@aacps.org, jw177@aol.com.

**WILLIAMS, J. VERNON,** retired lawyer; b. Honolulu, Apr. 26, 1921; s. Urban and W. Amelia (Olson) W.; m. Malvina H. Hitchcock, Oct. 4, 1947 (dec. May 1970); children— Carl H., Karin, Frances E., Scott S.; m. Mary McLellan, Sept. 6, 1980. Student, Phillips Andover Acad., 1937-39; BA cum laude, Amherst Coll., 1943; LL.B., Yale, 1948. Bar: Wash. 1948. Assoc. Riddell, Riddell & Hemphill, 1948-50, ptnr., 1951-55; sr. prin. emeritus Riddell Williams, P.S., Seattle, 1996—. Sec., dir. Airborne Freight Corp., 1968-79, gen. counsel, 1968-96. Chmn. March of Dimes, Seattle, 1954-55; Mem. Mayor's City Charter Rev. Com., 1968-69; chmn. Seattle Bd. Park Commrs., 1966-68; co-chmn. parks and open space com. Forward Thrust, 1966-69; dir. bd. and commrs. br. Nat. Recreation and Parks Assn., 1968-69; chmn. Gov.'s adv. com. Social and Health Services, 1972-75; Bd. dirs. Seattle Met. YMCA, 1965—, pres., 1976-79; trustee Lakeside Sch., 1971-79; mem. alumni council Phillps Andover Acad., 1970-73, Yale Law Sch., 1969-77; chancellor St. Mark's Cathedral, Seattle, 1964-2000. Served with USAAF, 1943-45. Mem. Univ. Club, Seattle Tennis Club, Birnam Wood Golf Club. Home: 2061 43rd Ave E #201 Seattle WA 98112 Office: 4500 1001 4th Ave Plz Seattle WA 98154-1065

**WILLIAMS, JACK MARVIN,** research chemist; b. Delta, Colo., Sept. 26, 1938; s. John Davis and Ruth Emma (Gallup) W. BS with honors, Lewis and Clark Coll., 1960; MS, Wash. State U., 1964, PhD, 1966. Postdoctoral fellow Argonne (Ill.), Nat. Lab., 1966-68, asst. chemist, 1968-70, assoc. chemist, 1970-72, chemist, 1972-77, sr. chemist, group leader, 1977—; vis. guest prof. U. Mo., Columbia, 1980, 81, 82, U. Copenhagen, 1980, 83, 85. Chair Gordon Rsch. Conf. (Inorganic Chemistry), 1980. Bd. editors: Inorganic Chemistry, 1979-96, assoc. editor, 1982-93. Crown-Zellerbach scholar, 1959-60; NDEA fellow, 1960-63; recipient Disting. Performance at Argonne Nat. Labs. award U. Chgo., 1987, Centennial Disting. Alumni award Wash. State U., 1990. Mem. AAAS, Am. Crystallographic Assn., Am. Chem. Soc. (treas. inorganic div. 1982-84), Am. Phys. Soc., Phi Beta Kappa. Office: Chemistry Div 9700 S Cass Ave Lemont IL 60439-4803

**WILLIAMS, JACK RAYMOND,** civil engineer; b. Barberton, Ohio, Mar. 14, 1923; s. Charles Baird and Mary Williams; m. Mary Berneice Jones, Mar. 5, 1947 (dec.); children: Jacqueline Rae, Drew Alan; m. Betty Ruth Scholfield, Nov. 9, 1990 (dec.). Student, Colo. Sch. Mines, 1942—43, Purdue U., 1944—45; BS, U. Colo., 1946. Gravity and seismograph engr. Carter Oil Co., Western U.S. and Venezuela, 1946-50; with Rock Island R.R., Chgo., 1950-80, structural designer, asst. to engr. bridges, asst. engr., 1980-82, engr. bridges system, 1963-80; sr. bridge engr. thomas K. Dyer Inc., 1980-82; v.p. Alfred Benesch & Co., 1982-96. Served with USMCR, 1943-45. Fellow ASCE (life); mem. Am. Concrete Inst., Am. Ry. Bridge and Bldg. Assn. (past pres.), Am. Ry. Engring. Assn. (hon. mem., past chmn. com. 8, Concrete and Foundations, past chmn. com. 10 concrete ties). Home: 293 Minocqua St Park Forest IL 60466-1942

**WILLIAMS, JAMES A.,** labor union administrator; b. 1951; m. Gerrie Williams; 4 children. Elected pres., bus. mgr. Glaziers, Archtl. Metal and Glass Workers' Local 252, Phila., 1975, former co-chmn. Pension, Annuity, Health & Welfare and Vacation Funds; region gen. v.p. Union of Painters and Allied Trade, 1994—95, sec. and treas., 1995—2002, pres., 2003—. Mem. exec. council AFL-CIO, 2004—. Contbr. articles to profl. jours. Served in U.S. Army, 1969—71, Vietnam. Decorated 2 Bronze Stars, Army Accommodation medal, Air medal; recipient Labor Man of the Yr. award, Israeli Bond Assoc., 1990, Vietnam Veterans Labor Leader of the Yr award, 1992. Office: Internat Union Painters & Allied Trade 1750 New York Ave NW Washington DC 20006*

**WILLIAMS, JAMES ARTHUR,** retired military officer, information technology executive; b. Paterson, N.J., Mar. 29, 1932; s. Charles M. and Elsie (Kretszchmar) W.; m. Barbara Widnall, June 26, 1959; children: Steven, Karen. BS, U.S. Mil. Acad.; MA in Latin Am. Studies, U. N.Mex. Commd. 2d lt. U.S. Army, 1954, advanced through grades to lt. gen.; asst. army attache U.S. Def. Attache Office, Caracas, Venezuela, 1966-72; exch. officer State-Def. Exch. Program Office of Sec. Def., Washington, 1972-74; comdr. 650th MI Group, Shape, 1974-76; dep. dir. estimates Def. Intelligence Agy., Washington, 1977-80; dep. chief staff for intelligence U.S. Army, Europe, 1980-81; dir. Def. Intelligence Agy., Washington, 1981-85; ret., 1985; v.p. PSC Corp., 1986; pres. Direct Info. Access Corp., Annandale, Va., 1987—; chmn. bd. dirs. Info. Ops. Inc., 2000—04; pres. Info Assure, 2004—. Sr. fellow Joint Forces Staff Coll., 1998; intelligence advisor Dept. Homeland Security, 2004. Bd. visitors Joint Mil. Intelligence Coll., 1996. Decorated Legion of Merit, Bronze Star with oak leaf cluster, Air medals, D.S.M., Nat. Intelligence D.S.M.; Legion of Honor (France); named Disting. Mem. Mil. Intelligence Hall of Fame. Mem. Assn. U.S. Army, Nat. Mil. Intelligence Assn. (chmn. bd. 1986—). Methodist. Office: Info Assure Inc 1298 Bay Dale Dr Ste 207 Arnold MD 21012-2815 Office Phone: 410-757-4188.

**WILLIAMS, JAMES BRYAN,** banker; b. Sewanee, Tenn., Mar. 21, 1933; s. Eugene G. and Ellen (Bryan) W.; m. Betty G. Williams, July 11, 1980; children: Ellen, Elizabeth, Bryan. AB, Emory U., 1955. Pres. Peachtree Bank & Trust Co., Chamblee, Ga.; chmn. bd. First Nat. Bank & Trust Co., Augusta, Ga.; pres. Sun Banks, Inc., Orlando, Fla., Trust Co. of Ga., Atlanta; chmn. exec. com. SunTrust Banks, Inc., Atlanta; retired, 1998. Bd. dirs. The Coca-Cola Co., Atlanta, 1979-, Genuine Parts Co., Atlanta, Rollins, Inc., Ga.-Pacific Corp., Atlanta, RPC, Inc., Atlanta, Genuine Parts Co., Atlanta. Trustee Emory U.; chmn. bd. trustees Robert W. Woodruff Health Scis. Ctr.; nat. trustee Boys & Girls Clubs Am.; trustee Robert W. Woodruff Found.; trustee emeritus Westminster Schs. Atlanta. Lt. USAF, 1955-57. Mem. Bankers Roundtable, Ga. C. of C. (dir. emeritus), Peachtree Golf Club, Augusta Country Club, Commerce Club, Capital City Club, Ocean Forest Golf Club, Piedmont Driving Club, Phi Beta Kappa, Omicron Delta Kappa. Office: SunTrust Banks Inc PO Box 4418 25 Park Pl NE Atlanta GA 30303-2900*

**WILLIAMS, JAMES BUCHANAN,** retired surgeon; b. El Paso, Tex., May 28, 1919; s. Jasper Buchanan and Clara Belle Williams; m. Willeen Agnes Brown, May 30, 1951; children: Brenda Joyce, James Buchanan II. BS, N.Mex. A&M, State College, 1947; MD, Creighton U. Sch. Medicine, Omaha, 1951; MS in Surgery, Creighton Med. Sch., Omaha, 1956. Cert. MD Nebr., 1956, Am. Bd. Surgery, 1957. Pres. Creighton U. Sch. Medicine, 1982—84, Cook County Physician, Chgo., 1982—84. *On April 12, 1945, Dr. Williams was one of 101 Tuskegee Air Force officers who protested segregated facilities at Freeman Field. His actions contributed to the desegregation of the Air Corps and its change of name to the Air Force in 1949. At St. Barnard, Dr. Williams was appointed chief of surgery in 1970 and was approved for a Type A Institutional Preceptorship. He and brother Jasper saved an infant shot in his mother's uterus; the first infant to survive a gun shot wound to the chest and abdomen in utero. Dr. Williams met with President Kennedy to request an amendment to prevent discrimination against patients, he co-founded Williams Clinic Ltd. with his brothers, he was Martin Luther King's Chicago physician, and he presented a movie at the American College of Surgery and Thoracic Endometriosis in 1972.* Bd. dirs. N.Mex. State U. Las Cruces, 1985—90, Creighton Med. Planning Adv. Bd., Omaha, 1981—86. First lt. U.S. Air Corps, 1942—46. Recipient Alumni Merit award, N.Mex. A&M, 1961, Outstanding Alumni award, N.Mex. State U., 1967, Alumni Merit award, Creighton U. Sch. Medicine, 1999. Master:

NAACP (life); fellow: Am. Coll. Surgeons; mem.: Alpha Omega Alpha Soc. Catholic. Achievements include establishing Clara B. Williams scholarship, N.Mex. A&M, 1985; street named in his honor (Williams Ave.), 1967. Avocations: fishing, hunting.

**WILLIAMS, JAMES CASE,** metallurgist; b. Salina, Kans., Dec. 7, 1938; s. Luther Owen and Clarice (Case) W.; m. Joanne Rufener, Sept. 17, 1960; children: Teresa A., Patrick J. BS in Metall. Engring. U. Wash., 1962, MS, 1964, PhD, 1968. Rsch. engr., lead engr. Boeing Co., Seattle, 1961-67; tech. staff N.Am. Rockwell Corp., Thousand Oaks, Calif., 1968-74; mgr. interdivisional tech. program N.Am. Aerospace group, 1974, program devel. mgr. structural materials, 1974-75; prof. metallurgy, co-dir. Ctr. for Joining of Materials, Carnegie-Mellon U., Pitts., 1975-81; pres. Mellon Inst., Pitts., 1981-83; dean Carnegie Inst. Tech., Carnegie-Mellon U., Pitts., 1983-88; gen. mgr. materials dept. GE Aircraft Engines, 1988-99; prof., Honda chair Ohio State U., Columbus, 1999—, dean engring., 2001—04. Bd. dirs. com. on engring. and tech. systems NRC, 1996-2001; chmn. Nat. Materials Adv. Bd., 1988-95, materials and structures com. NASA Aero. Adv. Com. 1992-97; mem. NASA Propulsion Rsch. and Tech. Com., 1997-99; mem. Materials Sci. and Engring. Study, 1986-88; bd. govs. Inst. for Mechs. and Materials, U. Calif., San Diego, 1989-95; trustee Min. Math. Sci. and Engring., Cin., 1988-99; mem. sci. adv. bd. USAF, 1996-2001; mem. materials rsch. com. Def. Advanced Rsch. Projects Agy., 1981-2000; adv. com. Divsn. Engring. and Phys. Sci., NRC, 2001-04. Co-author: Titanium, 2003; co-editor: Scientific and Technological Aspects of Titanium and Titanium Alloys, 1976; contbr. numerous articles to tech. jours. Trustee Oreg. Grad. Inst. Sci. and Tech., 1988-94; cons. Cubmaster Boy Scouts Am., 1976-77. Recipient Ladd award Carnegie Inst. Tech.; Adams award Am. Welding Soc.; Boeing doctoral fellow. Fellow: TMS-AIME, Am. Soc. Metals (Disting. lectr. on materials and soc. 1997, Campbell lectr. 1999, Gold medal 1992); mem.: AIME (Leadership award 1993, App to Pract award 2002), NAE, ASM, Internat. Ti Assn. (Achievement award 2003), Alpha Sigma Mu. Republican. Episcopalian. Home: 7711 Charlotte Hull Ct New Albany OH 43054-9680 Office Phone: 614-292-7251. Business E-mail: williams.1726@osu.edu.

**WILLIAMS, JAMES EUGENE,** management consultant; b. Macon, Ga., June 23, 1927; m. Linda K. Magnuson, June 23, 1984; children: Paul David, Lisa Jane Williams Robertson, Philip Alan, Gail Ellen Williams Feeney, Amanda Allen Thompson, Jason Douglas Allen, Joel Winston Allen BS in Aero. Engring., Iowa State Coll., 1950. Engr., Robins AFB, Ga., 1950-54, Hdqrs. USAF, Washington, 1954-61; dep. asst. sec. Office Asst. Sec. Air Force, Washington, 1961-85; dir. govt. bus. policy Northrop Corp., Washington, 1988-88; pvt. practice mgmt. cons. Tempe, Ariz., 1988—. Co-founder The Williams Inst. for Ethics and Mgmt., Tempe, 1993—. Recipient Presdl. Meritorious Exec. award, 1981, Presdl. Disting. Exec. award, 1982. Home: 955 E Knox Rd Unit 129 Chandler AZ 85225 Personal E-mail: LJWMS@aol.com.

**WILLIAMS, JAMES FRANCIS, JR.,** religious organization administrator; b. Coffeyville, Kans., June 20, 1938; s. James Francis and Sarah Kathryn (Tavenner) W.; m. Alice Carol Kinney, June 1, 1963; children: James F. III, Todd Alexander, Leslie. BA, So. Meth. U., 1960; ThM, Dallas Theol. Sem., 1964; HHD, U. Tex., 1988. Ordained min. N.W. Presbyn. Ch., 1967. Campus dir. Campus Crusade for Christ, Dallas, 1961-64, area dir. various North Tex. locations, 1964-68; dir. music campus Crusade for Christ, Arrowhead, Calif., 1967-71; regional dir. Campus Crusade for Christ, 1968-71, nat. dir. tng. U.S., 1971-72; founder, min. at large Probe Ministries, Internat., Dallas, 1973—, pres., 1973—98. Dir. music Campus Crusade for Christ, Arrowhead, Calif., 1967-71. Soloist, chorus Dallas Opera, 1982-84. Named one of Outstanding Young Men in Am. Dallas Jaycees, 1965. Mem. Evangelical Christian Ch. Office: Probe Ministries 1900 Firman Dr Ste 100 Richardson TX 75081-6796 Office Phone: 972-480-0240.

**WILLIAMS, JAMES FRANKLIN, II,** dean, librarian; b. Montgomery, Ala., Jan. 22, 1944; s. James Franklin and Anne (Wester) W.; m. Madeline McClellan, Jan. 1966 (div. May 1988); 1 child, Madeline Marie; m. Nancy Allen, Aug. 1989; 1 child, Audrey Grace. BA, Morehouse Coll., 1966; MLS, Atlanta U., 1967. Reference libr. Wayne State U. Sci. Libr., Detroit, 1968-69; document delivery libr. Wayne State U. Med. Libr., Detroit, 1969-70, head of reference, 1971-72, dir. med. libr. and regional med. libr. network, 1972-81, regional dir., 1975-82; assoc. dir. of librs. Wayne State U., 1981-88; dean librs. U. Colo., Boulder, 1988—. Bd. regents Nat. Libr. Medicine, Bethesda, Md., 1978-81; bd. dirs. Denver Art Mus., 1997—; pres. 1999—; bd. dirs. Ctr. Rsch. Librs., 1998—; pres. Big Twelve Plus Libr. Consortium, 2000; bd. dirs. Coun. on Librs. and Info. Resources. Mem. editl. bd. Portal: Libraries and the Academy; contbr. articles to profl. jours., chpts. to books; book editor and author. Bd. dirs. Educom, 1997-98, Boulder Cmty. Hosp., 2000—. Subject of feature interview in centennial issue Am. Librs. jour., 1976. Mem. ALA (Visionary Leader award 1988, Melvil Dewey medal 2002), Portal (editl. bd.), Assn. Rsch. Librs. (bd. dirs. 1994-96, 2000-03), Boulder C. of C. (bd. dirs.). Avocations: bicycling, travel, fishing. Office: U Colo Office Dean Librs PO Box 184 Boulder CO 80309-0184 Office Phone: 303-492-7511. Business E-Mail: james.williams@colorado.edu.*

**WILLIAMS, JAMES HENRY, JR.,** mechanical engineer, educator, consultant; b. Newport News, Va., Apr. 4, 1941; s. James H. Williams and Margaret L. (Holt) Mitchell; children: James Henry III, Mariella Louisa. Student, Newport News Apprentice Sch., 1965; BS, MIT, 1967, MS, 1968; PhD, Cambridge U., 1970. Sr. design engr. Newport News (Va.) Shipyard, 1960-70; asst. prof. mech. engring. MIT, 1970-74, assoc. prof., 1974-81, prof., 1981—2000, duPont prof., 1973, Edgarton prof., 1974-76, prof. writing and humanistic studies, 2000—. Cons. in field. Contbr. articles on stress analysis, materials and nondestructive testing to profl. jours. Named Prof. of Tchg. Excellence, Sch. Engring., 1991, C.F. Hopewell faculty fellow, 1993; recipient Charles F. Bailey Bronze medal, 1961, Silver medal 1962, Gold medal, 1963, Baker award, 1976. Mem. ASME, Am. Soc. Nondestructive Testing, Nat. Tech. Assn. Office: MIT Room 3-360 77 Massachusetts Ave Rm 3-360 Cambridge MA 02139-4307 Office Phone: 617-253-2221. Business E-Mail: jhwill@mit.edu.

**WILLIAMS, JAMES LEE,** finance company executive; b. Tampa, Fla., Nov. 5, 1941; s. Donald Clark and Nell (Medlin) W.; m. Linda Taylor, Dec. 28, 1968; children: Donald Clark II, Taylor Lee. AA, St. Petersburg Jr. Coll., Fla., 1965; BS, Fla. State U., 1967. Mgmt. Ryder Truck Lines, Jacksonville, Fla., 1967—69; dept. mgr. underwriting divsn. U.S. Leasing Corp., Dallas, 1969—73; area v.p. Mfrs. Hanover Leasing Corp., Houston and London, 1973—79; v.p. corp. fin. Underwood Neuhause & Co. Inc., Houston, 1979—81; chmn., CEO 1st City Leasing Corp., Houston, 1981—85; mng. dir. capital markets 1st City Bancorp., Houston, 1985—89; mng. dir. fin. svcs. M.P.S.I. Sys. Inc., Dallas, 1989—90; pres., CEO Strategic Decisions Holdings Corp., Dallas, 1990—92; sr. mng. dir. Williams and Assocs., 1992; pres. Global Svcs. Capital Corp., Houston, 1993—96; v.p. dist. CFO Ikon Hou Adminstrv. Svc. Ctr., Houston, 1997—98; CFO Insync Internet Svcs., Houston, 1998—99, Walkabout Software, 1999—2001; pres. BancLeasing, Inc., 2001—03; mng. dir. Global Svcs., Houston, 2003—04; exec. dir. SIRE-Therapeutic Equestrian Ctrs., 2004—. Served with USN, 1959-62. Mem. Equipment Leasing Assn. (fed. govt. rels. com. 1984-88, 95—), Tex. Assn. Equipment Lessors (bd. dirs. 1983-89), Greater Houston Partnership (Arabian horse and Announcer's com., Houston Livestock Show and Rodeo), Houston Ctr. Club (bd. dirs. 1985-89), Lakeside Racquet Club (athletic com. 1986-89), Forum Club Houston. Republican. Presbyterian. Avocations: golf, jogging, swimming. Office: SIRE 24161 Spring Dr Hockley TX 77447 Business E-Mail: jimm@sire-htec.org.

**WILLIAMS, JAMES M.,** foundation administrator; BS in engring., U. Mich.; MBA in fin., U. Chgo. Mgr. pension asset mgmt. dept. Ford Motor Co.; pres. Harbor Capital Advisors, Harbor family of mutual funds; v.p., chief investment officer J. Paul Getty Trust, LA, 2002—. Office: J Paul Getty Trust 1200 Getty Ctr Dr Los Angeles CA 90049-1679 Office Phone: 310-440-7300.*

**WILLIAMS, JANE MICHELE,** elementary school educator; d. James and Michele Higbee; m. Scott Williams, Apr. 14, 2001. BS in Advt./Pub. Rels., Tex. Christian U., Ft. Worth, 2000. Asst. media planner BBDO/Team Frito-Lay, Dallas, 2000—02; tchr. 5th grade Mesquite ISD, 2003—. Office Phone: 972-882-5180. Personal E-mail: janiewilliams45@yahoo.com.

**WILLIAMS, JANICE H.,** business executive; d. William Leroy and Mamie Louise Abernathy; m. Ruben J. Williams, Sr., 1966; children: Ruben J. Williams, Jr., Chauncey J., Anjalon D.K.Assoc. Degree, Davenport Bus. Sch., 1981; Degree, Grand Rapids Jr. Coll., 1981; Bachelor Degree, Davenport Bus. Sch., 1987; Divinity Cert., Oral Roberts U., 1998. Cert. personal ins. Inst. Cert., 1976, comml. ins. Inst. Cert., 1977. Exec. sec. Christman Constrn., Grand Rapids, Witmark Co., Grand Rapids; underwriter St. Paul Ins., Grand Rapids; asst. underwriter Aetna Ins., Grand Rapids; exec. sec. Spartan Stores, Grand Rapids; investigator Ford Motor Credit, Grand Rapids; pres., CEO Lakeside Orgn., Inc., Grand Rapids. Reporter St. Paul Ins., Grand Rapids, 1982—84; employment cons. Lakeside Orgn., Inc., 1994—2004; Power Point videographer Chrisman Constrn., Grand Rapids, 1999—2000. Amb., task force mem., vol. 4-H Mich. State U., 1990—2002; adult literacy trainer Kent County Lit. Coun., Mich., 1992—96; charter mem., fin. supporter Trail Blazer Girl Scouts, Grand Rapids, 1996—. Recipient Booker T. Washington Vol. Svc. to Children award, Kent County Child Abuse and Neglect, 1993, Vol. Svc. award, Nat. Assn. Negro Bus. Assn., 1994. Mem.: Cambridge England Adv. Coun. (hon.), Historic Mount Vernon Legacy (leader 2002—05), Girl Scouts of Am. (life). Avocations: poetry reading, golf, sewing, photography. Home: 2240 Delange Dr SE Grand Rapids MI 49506

**WILLIAMS, JASON CHANDLER,** professional basketball player; b. Belle, W.Va., Nov. 18, 1975, s. Terry Williams; m. Denika Williams; 2 children. Student, U. Fla. Guard Sacramento Kings NBA, 1998—2001, Memphis Grizzlies, 2001—05, Miami Heat, 2005—. Named Schick All-Rookie First Team, 1998—99. Mailing: The HEAT Group 601 Biscayne Blvd Miami FL 33132

**WILLIAMS, JEANNE,** writer; b. Elkhart, Kans., Apr. 10, 1930; d. Guy Edwin and Louella Isabel (Salmon) Kreie; m. Gene F. Williams, Jan. 18, 1949 (div. 1968); children: Michael, Kristian; m. John Creasey, 1970 (div. 1973); m. Robert Joseph Morse, Feb. 13, 1981. Student, U. Okla. Author: Mission to Mexico, 1958, The Horsetalker, 1961, River Guns, 1962, Beasts with Music, 1967, New Medicine, 1972, A Lady Brought with Rifles, 1976, A Woman Clothed in Sun, 1977, Bride of Thunder, 1978, Daughter of the Sword, 1979, The Valiant Women, 1980, Harvest of Fury, 1981, The Cave Dreamers, 1983, A Mating of Hawks, 1983, The Heaven Sword, 1985, So Many Kingdoms, 1986, Texas Pride, 1987, Lady of No Man's Land, 1988, No Roof but Heaven, 1990, Home Mountain, 1990, Island Harp, 1991, The Longest Road, 1993, Daughter of the Storm, 1994, The Unplowed Sky, 1994, Home Station, 1995, Wind Water, 1997, The Underground Valley, 2004, The Hidden Valley, 2004, The Trampled Fields, 2005; author: (as Jeane Crecy) Hands of Terror, 1972, The Lightning Tree, 1973, The Evil Among Us, 1975, My Face Beneath the Stone, 1975, The Winter Keeper, 1975, The Night Hunter, 1982; author: (as Jeanne Foster) Deborah Leigh, 1981, Eden Richards, 1982, Women of the Three Worlds, 1984; author: (as Kristin Michaels) To Begin with Love, 1975, Enchanted Twilight, 1976, A Special Kind of Love, 1976, Enchanted Journey, 1977, Make Believe Love, 1977, Song of the Heart, 1977, Voyage to Love, 1977, Magic Side of the Moon, 1979; author: (as Deirdre Rowan) Dragon's Mount, 1973, Silver Wood, 1973, Ravensgate, 1977, Shadow of the Volcano, 1975, Time of the Burning Mask, 1976; author: The Confederate Fiddle, 1962, rev. edit., 1995, Coyote Winter, 1966, Freedom Trail, 1973, Oh! Susanna, 1963, Oil Patch Partners, 1967, Promise of Tomorrow, 1959, Tame the Wild Stallion, 1957, To Buy A Dream, 1958, Trails of Tears, 1972, new edit., 1993, Winter Wheat, 1975. Bd. dirs. Internat. Soc. Animal Rights, Clark's Summit, 1982—86, Defenders Wildlife, Washington, 1988—90; vol. EMT, Portal, Ariz., 1986—98. Mem.: Authors Guild, Tex. Inst. Letters, Western Writers Am. (pres. 1974—75, Levi Strauss Golden Saddleman 1962, Spur award Best Novel of the West 1981, 1991, Best Western Juvenile 1962, 1974). Democrat. Unitarian Universalist. Avocations: hiking, travel, gardening. Home: Cave Creek Canyon Rd Portal AZ 85632 E-mail: jeannewilliams30@hotmail.com.

**WILLIAMS, JEFFERY LYNN,** secondary school educator, consultant; b. Zanesville, Ohio, Sept. 17, 1965; s. Barbara June and Glenn Eugene Harris (Stepfather); Jeffrey James Williams; life ptnr. William Don LaRiccia. BS in Edn., Ohio State U., 1990; Med, John Carroll U., Ohio, 2003. Cert. Tchr. Ohio Dept. of Edn., 2006. Tchr. Whitehall (Ohio) City Schools, 1990—93, Chagrin Falls (Ohio) Exempted Village Sch. Dist., 1993—2000; K-12 dist. literacy tchr. leader and reading recovery tchr. Solon (Ohio) City Schs., 2000—; adj. prof. Ashland (Ohio) U., 2001—. Ednl. cons. Solon (Ohio) City Schs., 1998—. Siri adv. com. Ohio Dept. Edn., Columbus, 2001—04. Sgt. U.S. Army, 1984—86. Recipient Tchr. of Yr., Chagrin Falls Schs., 1998, Tchr. of Month, Cuyahoga County Edn. Svc. Ctr., 1998. Mem.: Internat. Reading Assn., Reading Recovery Coun. of N.Am., Golden Key Nat. Honor Soc., Pi Lambda Theta Nat. Honor Soc., Phi Kappa Phi, Phi Delta Kappa. Liberal. Roman Catholic. Achievements include development of Literacy Learning. Avocations: travel, writing, genealogy, cross country skiing, cooking. Home: 18844 Rivers Edge Dr Chagrin Falls OH 44023 Office: Solon City Schs 6795 Solon Blvd Solon OH 44139 Office Phone: 440-349-7757 5721. Business E-Mail: jwilliams@solonboe.org.

**WILLIAMS, JEFFREY P.,** investment banker; b. July 13, 1951; BArch, U. Cin., 1975; MBA, Harvard U., 1979. Mng. dir. Morgan Stanley, N.Y.C., 1979-96; exec. v.p. McGraw-Hill, N.Y.C., 1996-98; ptnr. Greenhill & Co., LLC, N.Y.C., 1998—. E-mail: jwilliams@greenhill-co.com.

**WILLIAMS, JIMY,** professional athletics manager; b. Santa Maria, CA, Oct. 4, 1943; m. Peggy Sallee, Feb. 19, 1977; children: Monica, Brady, Shawn, Jenna. BS, Fresno State U. Mgr. Quad Cities affiliate Midwest League Angels, 1974; 3d base coach Blue Jays, 1986—89; mgr. Boston Red Sox, 1996—2001, Houston Astros, 2001—04. Named Mgr. of Yr., Pacific Coast League, 1976, 1979, AL Mgr. of Yr., 1999.

**WILLIAMS, JOBETH,** actress; b. Houston, Dec. 6, 1948; m. John Pasquin, 1982; children: Nick, Will. Grad., Brown U. Appeared in plays A Coupla White Chicks Sitting Around Talking, 1980, Gardenia, 1982, Idiot's Delight, 1986, Cat on a Hot Tin Roof, 1993; films include Kramer vs. Kramer, 1979, The Dogs of War, 1980, Stir Crazy, 1980, Poltergeist, 1982, Endangered Species, 1982, The Big Chill, 1983, American Dreamer, 1984, Teachers, 1984, Desert Bloom, 1986, Poltergeist II, 1986, Memories of Me, 1988, Welcome Home, 1989, Switch, 1991, Dutch, 1991, Stop! Or My Mom Will Shoot, 1992, Me, Myself and I, 1993, Wyatt Earp, 1994, Parallel Lives, 1994, Little City, 1997, Just Write, 1997, Jungle 2 Jungle, 1997, When Danger Follows You Home, 1997, Justice, 1998, Repossessed, 2002, The Rose Technique, 2002, Into the Fire, 2004, Fever Pitch, 2005; TV movies include Fun and Games, 1980, The Big Black Pill, 1981, Adam, 1983 (Emmy award nominee, Golden Globe award nominee), The Day After, 1983, Kids Don't Tell, 1985, Adam: His Song Continues, 1986, Murder Ordained, 1987, Baby M, 1988 (Emmy award nominee, Golden Globe award nominee), Nurse is Bill W., 1989, Child in the Night, 1990, Victim of Love, 1991, Jonathan: The Boy Nobody Wanted, 1992, Sex, Love and Cold Hard Cash, 1993, Chantilly Lace, 1993, Voices from Within, 1994, Lemon Grove, 1994, Parallel Lives, 1994, Voices from Within, 1994, Season of Hope, 1994, Ruby Jean and Joe, 1996, Breaking Through, 1996, It Came From the Sky, 1998, A Chance of Snow, 1998, Justice, 1999, Jackie's Back!, 1999, Trapped in a Purple Haze, 2000, The Ponder Heart, 2001, Homeward Bound, 2002, 14 Hours, 2005; TV series include The Guiding Light, 1977-81, Somerset, 1975-76, (voice) Fish Police, 1992, John Grisham's The Client, 1995-96, (voice) Stories from My Childhood, 1998, Payne, 1999; co-exec. prodr.: (TV movie) Bump in the Night, 1991; dir. (films): On Hope, 1994 (Acad. award nominee for Best Live Action Short Film 1995), Winona's Web, 2001.

**WILLIAMS, JODY,** political organization administrator; b. Rutland, Vt., Oct. 9, 1950; BA, U. Vt.; MA, Sch. Internat. Tng.; MA in Internat. Studies, Johns Hopkins U.; PhD (hon.), Briar Cliff Coll., Marlboro Coll., U. Vt., Williams Coll., Pa. State U., Royal Mil. Coll. Canada, Wesleyan U., Franklin Pierce Coll., Regis U., Shensu U., Rockhurst U., Gustaus Adolphus Coll., Lehman Coll., Smith Coll. Former coord. Nicaragua-Honduras Edn. Project, Washington; assoc. dir. Children's Project Med. Aid El Salvador, L.A./El Salvador, 1986—92; internat. Campaign to Ban Landmines Vietnam Vet. Found. Am., Washington, 1991—; amb. Internat. Campaign to Ban Landmines, Alexandria, Va., 1997—; founder Sponsor a Mine-Detection Dog program, 1998—. Patron Internat. Peace Found., Vienna, 1998—; adv. com., arms divsn. Human Rights Watch, 1998—; adv. com. Code of Conduct on the Arms Trade, Arias Found. for Peace and Human Progress, 1998—, Rep. Eddie Bernice Johnson's Women for World Peace Fund, 2003—; disting. vis. prof. social work and global justice Univ. Houston, Tex., 2004—. Contbr. articles to profl. jours, co-author: After the Guns Fall: The Enduring Legacy of Landmines, 1995. Founder Nobel Women's Initiative, 2006. Co-recipient Nobel Peace Prize, 1997; named one of 100 Most Powerful Women in World, Forbes Mag., 2004; recipient Distinguished Peace Leadership award, Nuclear Age Peace Found., 1998, Fiat Lux award, Clark U., Hollywood Humanitarian award, 2002. Address: ICBL 33 rue de Bruxelles 1470 Genappe Belgium E-mail: williams@icbl.org.

**WILLIAMS, JOHN A. (JACK WILLIAMS),** newspaper publishing executive; b. Springfield, Ill., May 1, 1950; m. Judy Williams; children: Suzanne, Michel. BBA, U. Ill., 1972. Part-time employee Ill. State Jour. & Register, Springfield, 1968-72; bus. mgr. San Francisco Progress, 1972-74; gen. mgr. Yakima (Wash.) Herald Republic, 1975-80, Modesto (Calif.) Bee, 1980-85; v.p. sales & mktg. Seattle Times Co., 1985-89, exec. v.p., 1989—95; v.p. bus. devel. Gannett, 1995—2003, sr. v.p. bus. & devel., newspaper div., 2003—06; pres. Gannett Digital, 2006—. Dir., 1st v.p. Direct Mktg. Puget Sound, Inc., Times Communications Co., Inc, Times Distribution, Inc., Times Info. Svcs., Inc.; v.p., dir. Yakima Herald-Republic, Inc., Rotary Offset Press, Inc., Times Community Newspapers, Inc., mgmt. com. Gannett. Chmn. bd. Leadership Tomorrow, bd. dirs., 1987—; mem. strategic planning com. United Way, 1991—; bd. dirs. Corp. Coun. Arts, 1989—. Mem. Newspaper Assn. Am. (dir.), Newspapers First (dir., exec. com.), Glendale Country Club, The Lakes Club, The Rainier Club, Washington Athletic Club, Bellevue Athletic Club. Office: Gannett Co Inc 7950 Jones Branch Dr Mc Lean VA 22107*

**WILLIAMS, JOHN ANDREW,** physiology educator, consultant, medical educator; b. Des Moines, Aug. 3, 1941; s. Harold Southall and Marjorie (Larsen) W.; m. Christa A. Smith, Dec. 26, 1965; children: Rachel Jo, Matthew Dallas. BA, Cen. Wash. State Coll., 1963; MD, PhD, U. Wash., Seattle, 1968. Staff fellow NIH, Bethesda, Md., 1969-71; research fellow U. Cambridge, Eng., 1971-72; from asst. to prof. physiology U. Calif., San Francisco, 1973-87; prof. physiology, chair dept. physiology, prof. internal medicine U. Mich., Ann Arbor, 1987—. Mem. gen. medicine study sect. NIH, Bethesda, 1985-88, NIDDK, DDK-C study sect., 1991-95. Contbr. numerous articles to profl. jours.; editor Am. Jour. Physiology: Gastrointestinal Physiology, 1985-91; assoc. editor Jour. Clin. Investigation, 1997-01; sect. editor Ann. Rev. Physiology, 2002-05. Trustee Friends Sch. in Detroit, 1992—2000. Grantee, NIH, 1973—. Fellow Am. Assn. Advancement Sci.; mem. Am. Physiol. Soc. (Hoffman LaRoche prize 1985, mem. coun. 1996-99, pres. 2003-04), Am. Soc. Cell Biology, Am. Soc. Clin. Investigation, Am. Gastroenterology Assn., Am. Pancreatic Assn. (pres. 1985-86), Assn. Am. Physicians. Democrat. Home: 1115 Woodlawn Ave Ann Arbor MI 48104-3956 Office: Dept Molecular & Intergrative Physiology Univ of Mich Med Sch Ann Arbor MI 48109 E-mail: jawillms@umich.edu.

**WILLIAMS, JOHN CHARLES, II,** data processing executive; b. Dayton, Ohio, Jan. 29, 1955; s. John Charles and Frances Jerline (McKean) W.; m. Diane Catherine Busch, Feb. 11, 1978 (div. Jan. 1996); 1 child, Tabitha Anne; m. Linda A. Blair, Nov. 24, 2001. BSBA, U. Phoenix, 2001, MBA, 2003. Programmer Kino Starr, Tucson, 1977-78, City of Boise (Idaho), 1978; data processing mgr. Nat. Assn. Ind. Businesses, Inc., Boise, 1978-79; chief exec. officer Williams Rsch. Assoc., Boise, 1979-80, MRW Data Systems, Inc., Tucson, 1981-82, Computer Security, Tucson, 1983-86, Modern Magic, Tucson, 1986-88; tech. support dir. Program Sources, Inc., Tucson, 1988-89; chief exec. officer Cactus Explosives Corp., 1989-90, Systems Cons. Assocs., Tucson, 1990-94; sr. systems analyst Desert Diamond Casino, 1994-97; systems analyst Muscular Dystrophy Assn., Tucson, 1997—. CEO/pres. Highland Mushroom Farms Inc., Tucson, 2004—. Area coord. Kolbe For Congress Campaign, Tucson, 1984; Ariz. Rep. State Committeeman, 1986—; mem. Ariz. Sonora Desert Mus., Tucson, 1983—. Mem.: Am. Heraldry Soc. (dir. edn.). Republican. Avocations: horsemanship, coin collecting/numismatics.

**WILLIAMS, JOHN EDWARD,** lawyer; b. Atlanta, May 21, 1946; s. Edward Carl and Mary E. (Griffin) W.; m. Kristin Forsberg, May 22, 1976; children: Alexandra, Courtney, Charles. BA, Yale U., 1968; JD, U. Va., 1974; LLM in Taxation, Georgetown U., 1977. Bar: Va. 1974, D.C. 1975, U.S. Dist. Ct. D.C. 1975, U.S. Tax Ct. 1975, U.S. Ct. Appeals (D.C. cir.) 1975, U.S. Supreme Ct. 1977. Law clk. to Judge Charles R. Richey U.S. Dist. Ct. (D.C. dist.), 1974-75; assoc. Patton, Boggs & Blow, Washington, 1975-78 Cadwalader, Wickersham & Taft, Washington, 1978-81; asst. to the commr. IRS, Washington, 1981-84; tax counsel Ropes & Gray, Washington, 1984-86; ptnr. David & Hagner, P.C., Washington, 1986-90, Winston & Strawn, Washington, 1990-2000; atty. Law Offices of John E. Williams, 2000—. Editl. bd. U. Va. Law Review, 1972-74; mem. Jud. Conf. of D.C. Cir., 1978, 82, 85, 87, 92. With USAR, 1968—74. Recipient IRS Commissioner's award, 1984. Mem. ABA (tax sect., chmn. tech. subcom., adminstrv. practice com. 1986-88), Met. Club, Yale Club N.Y.C., Heritage Hunt Club. Office: 3213 Duke St Ste 601 Alexandria VA 22314 Office Phone: 703-838-2939. Business E-Mail: johnedwardwilliams@earthlink.net.

**WILLIAMS, JOHN HORTER,** civil engineer, energy industry executive; b. Havana, Cuba, Aug. 17, 1918; s. Charles P. and Alice Magruder (Dyer) W.; m. Emily Alice Ijams, June 6, 1942 (dec.); children: John H., Burch I., S. Miller; m. Joanne Harwell Simpson., Feb. 1, 1975. BS, Yale U., 1940; PhD (hon.), 2006. Registered profl. engr., Okla., Minn. With The Williams Cos. Inc., Tulsa, 1940-42, 46-50, pres., dir., 1950-70, chmn., chief exec. officer, 1971-78, now hon. dir. Bd. dirs. Apco Argentina, Inc., Unit Corp.; hon. bd. dirs. Willbros Group, Inc. Served with USNR, 1942-46. Decorated Order of Condor of Andes (Bolivia); named Okla. Hall of Fame, 1977; recipient Outstanding Okla. Oil Man award Okla.-Kans. Oil and Gas Assn., 1982, Disting. Svc. award Nat. Petroleum Hall of Fame, 1985; inducted into Okla. Commerce and Industry Hall of Honor, 1986, Tulsa Hall of Fame, 1990. Mem. ASCE, Yale Engring. Assn. Office: The Williams Cos Inc Ste 4500 One Williams Ctr Tulsa OK 74172 Personal E-mail: k4blr@triad.rr.com.

**WILLIAMS, JOHN JAMES, JR.,** architect; b. Denver, July 13, 1949; s. John James and Virginia Lee (Thompson) W.; m. Mary Serene Morck, July 29, 1972. BArch, U. Colo., 1974. Registered architect, Colo., Calif., Idaho, Va., Utah, N.Mex., Wyo., Ohio, Nebr., Mo., Mo. Project architect Gensler Assoc. Architects, Denver, 1976, Heinzman Assoc. Architects, Boulder, Colo., 1977, EZTH Architects, Boulder, 1978-79; prin. Knudson/Williams PC, Boulder, 1980-82, Faber, Williams & Brown, Boulder, 1982-86, John Williams & Assocs., Denver, 1986-97; John Williams Architecture P.C., 1997—. Panel chmn. U. Colo. World Affairs Conf.; vis. faculty U. Colo. Sch. Architecture and Planning, Coll. Environ. Design, 1986-91; mem. dean's adv. bd. Coll. Arch. and Planning, 2000-04. Author (with others) State of Colorado architect licensing law, 1986. Commr. Downtown Boulder Mall Commn., 1985-88; bd. dirs. U. Colo. Fairway Club, 1986-88; mem. Gov's. Natural Hazard Mitigation Coun., State of Colo., 1990. Recipient Tchg. Honorarium, U. Colo. Coll. Architecture and Planning, 1977-80, 88, Excellence in Design and Planning award City of Boulder, 1981-82, Citation for Excellenc, WOOD Inc., 1982, 93, Disting. Profl. Svc. award Coll. Environ. Design U. Colo., 1988, James Sudler Svc. award AIA, Denver, 1998 Mem. AIA (sec. 1988, bd.

dirs. Colo. North chpt. 1985-86, chair Colo. govtl. affairs com. 1995-98, Design award 1993, 2001, pres. 1990, sec. Colo. chpt. 1988, ednl. fund Fisher I traveling scholar 1988, state design conf. chair 1991, North chpt. Design award 1993, treas. Denver chpt. 1998, v.p. 1999, pres. edn. Colo. chpt. 2001, Disting. Svc. award Colo. chpt. 2001, Architects and Planners of Boulder (v.p. 1982), Nat. Coun. Architect Registration Bd., Nat. Golf Found. (sponsor), Kappa Sigma (chpt. pres. 1970). Avocations: golf, political history, fitness and health. Home: 1031 Turnberry Cir Louisville CO 80027-9594 Office: John Williams Architecture PC 350 Interlocken Blvd Ste 240 Broomfield CO 80021 Business E-Mail: johnw@jwarchitecture.com.

**WILLIAMS, JOHN LEE,** lawyer; b. Nashville, Dec. 23, 1942; s. Leslie Elwood and Gladys Mae (Ridings) W.; m. Norma Jean Givens, May 27, 1967; 1 child, Jacob Andrew. BA, Tenn. Technol. U., 1964; JD, U. Tenn., 1967. Bar: Tenn 1967. Ptnr. Porch, Peeler & Williams, Waverly, Tenn., 1967-78, Porch, Peeler, Williams & Thomason, Waverly, 1978—; asst. dist. atty. 23d Jud. Cir. Ct. Tenn., 1972-74; judge Ct. Gen. Sessions of Humphreys County, Tenn., 1978-82. County atty. Humphreys County, 1968—72, 1982—86, 1994—; city atty. City of Waverly, 1968—, City of McEwen, Tenn., 1978—, City of Lobelville, Tenn., 1985—89; gen. counsel Meriwether Lewis Elec. Coop., Centerville, Tenn., 1980—. State legal counsel Tenn. Jaycees, 1970; treas., sec. Humphreys County Dem. Exec. Com., 1978-2001; chmn. Humphreys County Election Commn., 1968-72. Col. U.S. Army ret. Mem.: Humphreys County Bar Assn. (pres. 1978—), Tenn. Bar Assn. (ho. of dels.), Masons (master 1985, 1999, 2005). Home: 1739 Ogden Rd Mc Ewen TN 37101 Office Phone: 931-296-7741. Business E-Mail: john.williams@porchpeeler.com.

**WILLIAMS, JOHN N.,** dean, dental educator; BA with honors, Transylvania U., Lexington, KY, 1974; DMD Dental-Gen. Practice, U. Louisville, 1980, MBA, 1987. Asst. u. provost U. Louisville, 1988—91; dean U. Louisville Sch. Dentistry, 1999—2005; assoc. dean for ednl. programs U. of Louisville Sch. of Dentistry, 1991—98; prof. dept. periodontics, endontics and dental hygiene U. Louisville Sch. Dentistry; dean U. N.C. Sch. Dentistry, Chapel Hill, NC, 2005—. Mem. editl. bd. Jour. Contemporary Dental Practice. Mem.: Am. Acad. Devel. Medicine and Dentistry. Avocations: boating, classical & choral singing. Office: Sch Dentistry NC Univ CB #7450 1090 Old Dental Bldg Chapel Hill NC 27599-7450 Office Phone: 919-966-2731. Business E-Mail: john_williams@dentistry.unc.edu.*

**WILLIAMS, JOHN RODMAN,** theologian, educator, clergyman; b. Clyde, N.C., Aug. 21, 1918; s. John Rodman and Odessa Lee (Medford) W.; m. Johanna SerVaas, Aug. 6, 1949; children: John, Lucinda Lee, David Bert. AB, Davidson Coll., 1939; BD, Union Theol. Sem., 1943, ThM, 1944; PhD, Columbia U., 1954. Ordained to ministry Presbyn. Ch., 1943. Chaplain USNR, 1944—46; chaplain, assoc. prof. philosophy Beloit Coll., 1949—52; pastor First Presbyn. Ch., Rockford, Ill., 1952—59; prof. systematic theology and philosophy of religion Austin Presbyn. Theol. Sem., 1959—72; prof. Christian doctrine, pres. Melodyland Sch. Theology, Anaheim, Calif., 1972—82; prof. Christian theology Regent U., Virginia Beach, Va., 1982—. Author: Contemporary Existentialism and Christian Faith 1965, The Era of the Spirit, 1971, The Pentecostal Reality, 1972, Ten Teachings, 1974, The Gift of the Holy Spirit Today, 1980, Renewal Theology, Vol. 1, God, the World, and Redemption, Vol. 2, 1988, Salvation, the Holy Spirit and Christian Living, Vol. 3, 1990, The Church, the Kingdom, and Last Things, 1992, Renewal Theology, 3 vols. in one, 1996. Home: 608 Fleet Dr Virginia Beach VA 23454-7344 *There is only one ultimate "Who", Jesus of Nazareth, in whose light all the rest of us are but dimly burning candles.*

**WILLIAMS, JOHN TAYLOR,** lawyer; b. Cambridge, Mass., June 19, 1938; s. Paul Merchant Taylor and Audrey Arlene Dowling; m. Leonora Hall; children: Caleb, Jared, Nathaniel. AB, Harvard U., 1960; LLB, U. Pa., 1965. Bar: Mass. 1965, U.S. Dist. Ct. Mass., U.S. Ct. Appeals (1st cir.), U.S. Supreme Ct. Corp. loan officer State St. Bank & Trust Co., Boston, 1960-62; from assoc. to ptnr. Haussermann, Davison & Shattuck, Boston, 1965-83; ptnr. Palmer & Dodge, Boston, 1983—2021, Hill & Barlow, Boston, 2001—02; prin. Fish & Richardson PC, Boston, 2003—. Lectr. on 1st amendment, copyright, pub. and intellectual property law for Practicing Law Inst., Mass. CLE/New Eng. Law Inst., Nat. Assn. Archivists, Boston Patent Lawyers Assn., others; apptd. mem. U.S. Courthouse Arts Comm., U.S. State Dept. Del. to China, 1993; mem. lit. panel Nat. Endowment for the Arts, 1990, 91, 94, mem. presentation and creation panel, 1996. Author: (screenplay) Rolf in the Woods, 1987, (screenplay) Toussaint L'Overture, 1989, (with E. Gabriel Perle) Perle and Williams on Publishing Law, 2 vols. (revised annually); contbg. author: Legal Problems in Book Publishing, 1981, 84, 86; contbg. editor: Small Voices and Great Trumpets: Minorities and the Media, 1980. Bd. dirs. City of Cambridge Arts Coun., 1973-83, chmn., 1981-83; bd. dirs. Ploughshares Inc., 1988-89; trustee Arthur Fiedler Meml. Inc., 1983—87, Boston Philharm. Orch., 1983-85, Petra Found., 1988—2003; trustee, gen. counsel Inst. Contemporary Art, 1970-92; mem. corp. Mass. Gen. Hosp., 1985—; mem. Patent and Tech Conflicts Coms., 1985-91; clk. John F. Kennedy Meml. Commn. Inc., 1986—; trustee, co-chair Provincetown Fine Arts Work Ctr., 1992—. Named one of Boston's top lawyers, Boston Mag., 2002; recipient Learned Hand award, Am. Jewish Com., 2005. Mem. ABA (sect. patent, trademark, copyright law, comm. com. on authors 1978-81, comms. and entertainment law forum coms.), Boston Bar Assn. (former chmn. com. on delivery of legal svcs. to indigent), Lawyers' Com. for Civil Rights under Law (chmn. steering com. 1988-91), Mass. Bar Assn. (bus. law and computer law sects.), Nat. Lawyers' Com. for Civil Rights (bd. dirs. 1989—95), Tavern Club (Boston). Office: Fish & Richardson PC 225 Franklin St Boston MA 02110 Office Phone: 617-521-7820. Office Fax: 617-542-8906. Business E-Mail: jtwilliams@fr.com.

**WILLIAMS, J(OHN) TILMAN,** insurance company executive, real estate agent, municipal official; b. Detroit, Feb. 26, 1925; s. Aubrey and Martha (Lou) W.; m. Sally Jane Robinson, Aug. 22, 1947; children: Leslie Ann, Martha Lou. BS in Agr, Mich. State U., 1951. Pres. Satellite Ins. Brokerage, Garden Grove, Calif., 1959—. Pres. Satellite Real Estate, Satellite Mortgage & Loan Co. Mayor Garden Grove, 1976-78, re-elected, 1987, mem. coun., 1980-92, apptd. vice mayor, 1989—; mem. Ad Hoc Com. on Property Tax to Limit Govt. Spending with Spirit of 13 Initiative; elected to Orange County Dem. Cen. Com., 68th Assembly Dist., 1996; past pres. Garden Grove High Sch. Band Boosters; trustee Garden Grove Unified Sch. Dist., 2000—; Dem. candidate for Congress, 2004. With USAAF, World War II, PTO. Mem. Bd. Realtors, Ind. Ins. Agts. Assn., Orange County Esperanto Assn. (pres. 1985—), Am. Legion, VFW. Clubs: Toastmasters (Anaheim, Calif.), Fifty-Plus Sr. Citizens of Garden Grove (pres. 1986—). Lodges: Lions, Elks. Democrat. Home: 11241 Chapman Ave Garden Grove CA 92840-3301 Office: 12311 Harbor Blvd Garden Grove CA 92840-3809 Office Phone: 714-750-4333. *Service to one's fellowman and community is the greatest avocation and pleasure one can follow.*

**WILLIAMS, JOHN TOWNER,** composer, conductor; b. LI, NY, Feb. 8, 1932; s. John and Esther Williams; m. Barbara Ruike, 1956 (dec. 1974); children: Jennifer, Mark, Joseph; m. Samantha Winslow, 1980. Student, UCLA; student with Mario Castelnuovo-Tedesco, Los Angeles; student Juilliard Sch.; studied with Madame Rosina Lhevinne, NYC; degree (hon.), Berklee Coll. Music, Boston, Northeastern U., Tufts U., U. So. Calif., Boston U., New Eng. Conservatory Music, Providence Coll. Pianist Columbia & Twentieth Century-Fox, 1956—; condr. Boston Pops Orch., 1980—93, laureate condr., 1993—; artist-in-residence Tanglewood Music Ctr., Boston, 1993—94. Guest condr. with orchestras including Cleveland Orch., Denver Symphony, Indianapolis Symphony, London Symphony Orch., Los Angeles Philharmonic, Montreal Orch., Philadelphia Orch., and Toronto Orch. Works include: composer (film scores) I Passed for White, 1960, Because They're Young, 1960, The Secret Ways, 1961, Bachelor Flat, 1962, Diamond Head, 1962, Gidget Goes to Rome, 1963, The Killers, 1964, John Goldfarb, Please Come Home, 1964, None But the Brave, 1965, How to Steal a Million, 1966, The Rare Breed, 1966, Not With My Wife, You Don't, 1966, The Plainsman, 1966, Penelope, 1966, A Guide for the Married Man, 1967, Valley of the

Dolls, 1967 (Acad. award nominee), Fitzwilly, 1968, Sergeant Ryker, 1968, The Reivers, 1969 (Acad. award nominee), Daddy's Gone A-Hunting, 1969, Goodbye, Mr. Chips, 1969 (Acad. award nominee), The Story of A Woman, 1970, Fiddler on the Roof, 1971 (Acad. award for musical adaptation 1971), The Cowboys, 1972, The Poseidon Adventure, 1972 (Acad. award nominee), Images, 1972 (Acad. award nominee), Pete 'n' Tillie, 1972, The Paper Chase, 1973, The Long Goodbye, 1973, The Man Who Loved Cat Dancing, 1973, Cinderella Liberty, 1973 (Acad. award nominee), Tom Sawyer, 1973 (Acad. award nominee), Sugarland Express, 1974, Earthquake, 1974, The Towering Inferno, 1974 (Acad. award nominee), Conrack, 1974, Jaws, 1975 (Acad. award, Grammy award, Golden Globe award 1976), The Eiger Sanction, 1976, Family Plot, 1976, Midway, 1976, The Missouri Breaks, 1976, Raggedy Ann and Andy, 1977, Black Sunday, 1977, Star Wars, 1977 (Acad. award, 3 Grammy awards, Golden Globe award 1977), Close Encounters of the Third Kind, 1977 (2 Grammy awards, Acad. award nominee 1978), The Fury, 1978, Jaws II, 1978, Superman, 1978 (2 Grammy awards 1979), Meteor, 1979, Quintet, 1979, Dracula, 1979, "1941", 1979, The Empire Strikes Back, 1980 (2 Grammy awards, Acad. award nominee 1980), Raiders of the Lost Ark, 1981 (Grammy award, Acad. award nominee 1982), Heartbeeps, 1981, E.T., 1982 (Acad. award for best original score, 3 Grammy awards, Golden Globe award 1982), Monsignor, 1982, Yes, Giorgio, 1982 (Acad. award nominee), Superman III, 1983, Return of the Jedi, 1983 (Acad. award nominee), Indiana Jones and the Temple of Doom, 1984 (Acad. award nominee), The River, 1984 (Acad. award nominee), Space Camp, 1986, Emma's War, 1986, The Witches of Eastwick, 1987 (Acad. award nominee), Empire of the Sun, 1987 (Acad. award nominee), Jaws: The Revenge, 1987, Superman IV: The Quest for Peace, 1987, The Secret of My Success, 1987, The Accidental Tourist, 1988 (Acad. award nominee, Indiana Jones and the Last Crusade, 1989 (Acad. award nominee), Always, 1989, Born On The Fourth of July, 1989 (Acad. award nominee), Stanley and Iris, 1990, Presumed Innocent, 1990, Home Alone, 1990 (Acad. award nominee), Hook, 1991 (Acad. award nominee), JFK, 1991 (Acad. award nominee), Far and Away, 1992, Home Alone II, 1992, Jurassic Park, 1993, Schindler's List, 1993 (Acad. award 1993, Grammy award 1994), Sabrina, 1995 (Acad. award nominee for best original score 1996), Nixon, 1995 (Acad. award nominee 1996), Sleepers, 1996, Rosewood, 1997, The Lost World: Jurassic Park, 1997, Seven Years In Tibet, 1997 (Acad. award nominee), Amistad, 1997 (Acad. award nominee), Saving Private Ryan, 1998 (Acad. award nominee, Grammy award 1998), Stepmom, 1998, Star Wars Episode I: The Phantom Menace, 1999, Angela's Ashes, 1999 (Acad. award nominee, Grammy award 2000), The Patriot, 2000 (Acad. award nominee), Artificial Intelligence, 2001 (Acad. award nominee), Harry Potter and The Sorcerer's Stone, 2001 (Acad. award nominee), Minority Report, 2002, Star Wars Episode II: Attack Of The Clones, 2002, Harry Potter: The Chamber of Secrets, 2002, Catch Me If You Can, 2002 (Acad. award nominee), Harry Potter: The Prisoner of Azkaban, 2004, The Terminal, 2004, Star Wars Episode III: The Revenge of the Sith, 2005, War of the Worlds, 2005, Harry Potter and the Goblet of Fire, 2005, Memoirs of a Geisha, 2005 (Broadcast Film Assn. award, 2006, Best Original Score-Motion Picture, Hollywood Fgn. Press Assn., Golden Globe award) 2006), Munich, 2005, Superman Returns, 2006; composer music for songs including:(from Sabrina, lyrics by Alan and Marilyn Bergman) Moonlight, 1995 (Acad. award nominee 1996); composer:(TV programs) Heidi, 1969 (Emmy award), Jane Eyre, 1971 (Emmyaward), Masterpiece Theatre, 1971, Malcolm in the Middle, 2000, Smallville, 2001, (main theme) Jack & Bobby, 2004, others; composer numerous concert pieces and symphonies including Jubilee 350 Fanfare for the Boston Pops, 1980, theme to the 1984 Summer OlympicGames, Liberty Fanfare, 1987; recorded numerous albums with Boston Pops Orch. including Pops in Space, That's Entertainment (Pops on Broadway), Pops on the March, Pops Aroundthe World (Digital Overtures), Aisle Seat, Pops Out of This World, Boston Pops on Stage, America, the Dream Goes On; collaborator: (with Jessye Norman) With A Song in My Heart, Swing, Swing, Swing, Unforgettable; guest condr. major orchs. including London Symphony Orch., Cleve. Orch., Phila. Orch., Toronto Orch., Montreal Orch. Served with USAF, 1952-54. Recipient several gold and platinum records Rec. Industry Assn. Am., Kennedy Ctr. Honors, John F. Kennedy Ctr. Performing Arts, 2004. Composer of over seventy-five film scores. Office: Boston Symphony Orch 301 Mass Ave Boston MA 02115 also: The Gorfaine Schwartz Agency Inc 4111 W Alameda Ave Ste 509 Burbank CA 91505-4171*

**WILLIAMS, JOSEPH DALTON,** pharmaceutical executive; b. Washington, Pa., Aug. 15, 1926; s. Joseph Dalton and Jane (Day) W.; m. Mildred E. Bellaire, June 28, 1973; children: Terri, Daniel. BS in Pharmacy, U. Nebr., 1950; DSc (hon.), Union U., 1991, U. Nebr., 1989; LHD (hon.), Albany Coll. Pharmacy, Union U., 1980, Rutgers U., 1987, Long Island U., 1988; DSc (hon.), Phila. Coll. Pharmacy and Sci., 1988, Long Island U., 1988, Albany Coll. Pharmacy of Union U., 1991; D Human Svcs. (hon.), Caldwell Coll., 1989; LLD (hon.), Bethune-Cookman Coll., 1990, Coll. St. Elizabeth, 1990, Seton Hall U., 1990, U. Md., 1991, St. Augustine Coll., 1992. Pres. Parke-Davis Co., Detroit, 1973-76; pres. pharm. group Warner-Lambert Co., Morris Plains, NJ, 1976-77; pres. Internat. Group, 1977-79; pres., dir. Warner-Lambert Corp., 1979-80, pres., chief operating officer, 1980-84, chmn., CEO, 1985-91, chmn. exec. com., 1991-97; retired, 1997. Bd. dirs. AT&T, 1984-1997, J.C. Penney & Co., 1985-1998, Exxon Corp., 1985-1997, Rockefeller Fin. Svcs. Inc., Rockefeller and Co., 1992-1999, Eckerd Corp., 1997-2000. Trustee emeritus Columbia U. With USNR, 1943—46. Mem. Am. Pharm. Assn., Links Club, Pine Valley Golf Club, Baltusrol Golf Club, Mid Ocean Club. Office: Warner-Lambert Co 55 Madison Ave Morristown NJ 07960-7397 Office Phone: 973-285-3277.

**WILLIAMS, JOY,** writer; b. Chelmsford, Mass., Feb. 11, 1944; d. William Lloyd and Elisabeth (Thomas) W.; m. Rust Hills; 1 child, Caitlin. MA magna cum laude, Marietta Coll., 1963; MFA, U. Iowa, 1965. Rschr., data analyst USN, Siesta Key, Fla., 1967-69; now writer. Vis. instr. U. Houston, 1982, U. Fla., 1983, U. Calif., Irvine, 1984, U. Iowa, 1984, U. Ariz., 1987. Author: State of Grace, 1973, The Changeling, 1978, Taking Care, 1982, The Florida Keys: A History and Guide, 1986, Breaking and Entering, 1988, Escapes, 1991, The Quick and the Dead (Pulitzer Prize finalist), 2000, Honored Guest, 2004; contbr. short stories to numerous anthologies and mags. Guggenheim fellow, 1974; NEA grantee, 1973; recipient Nat. Mag. award for fiction, 1980, Harold and Mildred Strauss Livings award Am. Acad. Arts and Letters, 1993, Rea Short Story award Ill Nature essays, 2002. Mem. Phi Beta Kappa. Democrat. Office: 1425 E magee Rd Tucson AZ 85718 also: Amanda Urban ICM 40 W 57th St New York NY 10019-4001

**WILLIAMS, JOYCE HALL,** secondary school educator; b. Viola, Tenn., Feb. 6, 1926; d. Albert White and Byrde Groom Hall; m. Lewis Blanton Williams, Dec. 14, 1948; children: Susan Joyce Boada, Nancy Hall West, Lewis B.(dec.). BA, U. Tenn., Knoxville, 1947; postgrad., U. Miami, 1967; MA, U. North Ala., 1982. Cert. tchr. Fla., Ala. Tchr. Gulliver Preparatory Sch., Coral Gables, Fla., 1967—70, 1975—79, Am. Internat. Sch., New Delhi, 1970—73, Internat. Inst. Tropical Agr., Ibadan, Nigeria, 1974—79; faculty Faulkner U., Florence, Ala., 1981—88, N.W. C.C., Muscle Shoals, Ala., 1981—88; adj. tchr. U. North Ala., 1994. Owner Off-Ctr. Pub. Co., Ala., 1985. Author: A Volunteer in Romania, 1999, Sunshine and Shadows, 2001, In the Cradle of Mankind, Let's Play Ball and the Taj Mahal!, Roamin Around Romania, 2004, (children's coloring book) Can Cousin Kunja Cut a Kanga?. Vol. tchr. Headstart, Handy Ctr., Florence, 2001—03; tchr., vol. Adult Basic Edn., Handy Ctr., 2001—03; vol. ch. libr. Edgemont Meth. Ch., 1987—. Named Tchr. of the Yr., Gulliver Acad.; recipient Diploma of Recognition, Israelite Heritage Instn. for excellence in Bible Study, 1967, winner, Ernest Hemingway Internat. Writing Competition, Key West, Fla. Mem.: AAUW, Assn. Ala. Writers, United Meth. Women. Avocation: golf. Home: 3412 Kolbe Ln Florence AL 35631-1842

**WILLIAMS, JUAN,** news correspondent; BA philosophy, Haverford College, 1976. Editl. writer, op-ed columnist, White House corr. Washington Post, 1976—97; host, Talk of the Nation Nat. Public Radio (NPR), 2000—01, sr. nat. corr.; polit. contbr. FOX News Channel, 1997—, weekend anchor. Regular panelist, FOX News Sunday with Tony Snow FOX News Channel.

Author: Eyes on the Prize: America's Civil Rights Years, 1954-1965, 1988, Thurgood Marshall: American Revolutionary, 2000, My Soul Looks Back in Wonder: Voices of the Civil Rights Experience, 2004; contbr. articles to Fortune, Atlantic Monthly, Ebony, GQ, New Republic; guest appearances Nightline, ABC, Washington Week in Review, PBS, Oprah. Office: FOX News Channel 400 N Capitol St NW Ste 550 Washington DC 20001

**WILLIAMS, JUANITA ROSALIE,** artist; b. Zanesville, Ohio, Aug. 7, 1933; d. Joseph Russell and Gladys Lucille (Worden) Somers; m. Roy George Williams, Feb. 16, 1952 (div. 2002); children: Karin Sue Williams Brandi, Kenneth Roy. Grad. high sch., Zanesville. Juror Bexley (Ohio) Art Guild, Capital U., 1984. One-woman shows include Collector's Gallery Columbus Mus. Fine Art, Ohio, 1972, Pomerene Fine Arts Ctr., 1991, McDonough Gallery, Marietta Coll., 1991, Blue Sky Gallery, Columbus, 1992, exhibited in group shows at Zanesville Art Ctr., 1981, 1990, Franklin U., Columbus, Ohio, 1985, Marietta (Ohio) Coll., 1991, Pomerene Fine Arts Ctr., Coshocton, Ohio, 1991, No. Ariz. U., 1992, French Art Colony, Gallipolis, Ohio, 1992, Soc. Layerists in Multi-Media, San Miguel Allende, Mex., 1996, Marlborough, Eng., 1997, Sirius Gallery, Santa Fe, 2001, Represented in permanent collections Zanesville Art Ctr., Ohio, Soc. Bank Cleve., Edward Cherry Corp., Columbus, Nat. WaterColor Soc. Bd. dirs. Zanesville Art Ctr., 1986-90. 92-95. Recipient 1st award Rocky Mountain Nat., 1984, Elsie and David Wu-Ject Key award Am. Watercolor Soc., 1989, 4th award San Diego Watercolor Soc., 1993. Mem. Nat. Watercolor Soc., Soc. Layerists in Multi-Media, Ohio Watercolor Soc. (silver Buckeye award 1986), Southeastern Ohio Watercolor Soc. (co-founder, 1st pres. 1978-79). Avocations: gardening, interior decorating, reading, metaphyics, travel. Mailing: 9908 Wild Turkey NW Albuquerque NM 87114 Office Phone: 505-792-7782. E-mail: juan1aran@aol.com.

**WILLIAMS, JULIE FORD,** retired finance company executive, economist; b. Long Beach, Calif., Aug. 7, 1948; d. Julious Hunter and Bessie May (Wood) Ford; m. Walter Edward Williams, Oct. 20, 1984; 1 child, Andrew Ford. BA in Econs., Occidental Coll. 1970. Legal sec. Kadison, Pfaelzer, Woodard, Quinn & Rossi, L.A., 1970-71, 74-77; legal sec. Fried, Frank, Harris, Shriver & Jacobson, N.Y.C., 1971-72, Pallot, Poppell, Goodman & Shapo, Miami, Fla., 1973-74; adminstrv. asst. Capital Research-Mgmt., Los Angeles, 1978-82; corp. officer Cash Mgmt. Trust Am., 1982—, Bond Fund Am., 1982—, Tax-Exempt Bond Fund Am., 1982—, AMCAP Fund, 1984-98, 2000—, Am. Funds Income Series, 1985—, Am. Funds Tax-Exempt Series II, 1986—, Capital World Bond Fund, 1987—, Am. High-Income Trust, 1987—, Intermediate Bond Fund Am., 1987—, Tax-Exempt Money Fund Am., 1989—, U.S. Treasury Money Fund Am., 1991—, Fundamental Investors, 1992-2000, Ltd. Term Tax-Exempt Bond Fund Am., 1993—, Am. High-Income Mcpl. Bond Fund, 1994—; v.p. fund bus. mgmt. group Capital Rsch. Mgmt., 1986—; sec. Growth Fund of Am., 1998-2000, Am. Mutual Fund, 2000—05; ret., 2005. Pres. alumni bd. govs. Occidental Coll., 1997—98, bd. trustees, 1999—2003. Democrat. Episcopalian. Office: Capital Rsch & Mgmt Co 333 S Hope St 55th Floor Los Angeles CA 90071-1452

**WILLIAMS, JULIE LLOYD,** federal agency administrator, lawyer; b. Washington, May 24, 1950; d. Walter Herbert and Jean (Grabill) W.; m. Don Scroggin, May 9, 1981; 1 child, Patrick Conner. BA, Goddard Coll., 1971; JD, Antioch Sch. Law, 1975. Bar: Va. 1975, D.C. 1976. Assoc. Fried, Frank, Harris, Shriver, Washington, 1975-83; assoc. gen. counsel Fed. Home Loan Bank Bd., Washington, 1983-86, dep. gen. counsel, 1986-89; dep. chief counsel Office of Thrift Supervision, Washington, 1989-91, sr. dep. chief counsel, 1991-93; dep. chief counsel Comptr. of Currency, Washington, 1993-94, chief counsel, 1994-98, acting comptr., 1998, 2004—05, first sr. dep. comptr., chief counsel, 1999—; bd. dir. FDIC, 2004—. Co-author: (handbook) How to Incorporate: A Handbook for Entrepreneurs & Professionals, 1987; author: Savings Institutions: Mergers, Acquisitions & Conversions, 1988, National Banks and the Dual Banking System, 2003. Mem. ABA (banking law com.), Women in Housing and Fin. Home: 3064 Q St NW Washington DC 20007-3080 Office: Office of Comptroller Currency 250 E St SW Washington DC 20219

**WILLIAMS, KAREN HASTIE,** lawyer; b. Washington, Sept. 30, 1944; d. William Henry and Beryl (Lockhart) Hastie; m. Wesley S. Williams, Jr.; children: Amanda Pedersen, Wesley Hastie, Bailey Lockhart. Cert., U. Neuchatel, Switzerland, 1965; BA, Bates Coll.. 1966; MA, Tufts U., 1967; JD, Cath. U. Am., 1973. Bar: D.C. 1973. Staff asst. internat. gov. relations dept. Mobil Oil Corp., N.Y.C., 1967-69; staff asst. com. Dist. Columbia U.S. Senate, 1970, chief counsel com. on the budget, 1977-80; law clk. to judge Spottswood Robinson III U.S. Ct. Appeals (D.C. Cir.), Washington, 1973-74; law clk. to assoc. justice Thurgood Marshall U.S. Supreme Ct., Washington, 1974-75; assoc. Fried, Frank, Harris, Shriver & Kampelman, Washington, 1975-77, 1975-77; adminstrv. Office Mgmt. and Budget, Washington, 1980-81; of counsel Crowell & Moring, Washington, 1982, ptnr., 1982—2004; ret., 2005. Bd. dirs. Chubb Corp., Gannett Co., Inc., Sun Trust Bank, Inc., Washington Gas Light Co., Continental Airlines. Trustee, past chair Greater Washington Rsch. Ctr. Mem. ABA (pub. contract law sect., past chair), Nat. Bar Assn., Washington Bar Assn., Nat. Contract Mgmt. Assn., NAACP (legal def. fund, bd. dirs.). Office: Crowell & Moring 1001 Pennsylvania Ave NW Ste 1100 Washington DC 20004-2595

**WILLIAMS, KAREN JOHNSON,** federal judge; b. Orangeburg, SC, Aug. 4, 1951; d. James G. Johnson and Marcia Johnson (Reynolds) Dantzler; m. Charles H. Williams, Dec. 27, 1968; children: Marian, Ashley, Charlie, David. BA, Columbia Coll., 1972; postgrad., U. S.C., 1973, JD cum laude, 1980. Bar: S.C. 1980, U.S. Dist. Ct. S.C. 1980, U.S. Ct. Appeals (4th cir.) 1981. Tchr. Irmo (S.C.) Mid. Sch., 1972—74, O-W H.S., Orangeburg, 1974—76; assoc. Charles H. Williams PA, Orangeburg, 1980—92; judge U.S. Ct. Appeals (4th cir.), 1992—. Exec. bd. grievance commn. S.C. Supreme Ct., Columbia, 1983—92. Child devel. bd. First Bapt. Ch., Orangeburg; bd. dirs. Orangeburg County Mental Retardation Bd., 1986—94, Orangeburg-Calhoun Hosp. Found., Columbia Coll., 1988—92, Reg. Med. Ctr. Hosp. Found., 1988—92; adv. bd. Orangeburg-Calhoun Tech. Coll., SC, 1987—92. Mem.: ABA, Nat. Assn. of Women Judges, Bus. and profl. Women Assn., S.C. Trial Lawyers Assn., Orangeburg County Bar Assn. (co-chair Law Day 1981), S.C. Bar Assn., Fed. Judges Assn., Am. Judicature Soc., Rotary, Order of Coif, Order of Wig and Robe, Order of the Crop Rd Orangeburg SC 29115-8185 Office: Lewis F Powell Jr US Cthse Annex 1100 E Main St Ste 617 Richmond VA 23219-3517*

**WILLIAMS, KATIE DEPASCALE,** voice educator; b. Athens, Ga., May 24, 1974; d. Ernie and Linda (McMullen) DePascale; m. Richard Harris Williams, Nov. 4, 2000; 1 child, James Lafayette. MusB, Converse Coll., Spartanburg, S.C., 1996; M.Music Edn., U. Ga., Athens, 2002. Chorus tchr. Winder Barrow Mid. Sch., Winder, Ga., 1996—99, Hart County H.S., Hartwell, Ga., Oconee County H.S., Watkinsville, Ga., 2000—. Mem.: Am. Choral Dirs. Assoc., Nat. Assn. Music Educators, Ga. Music Educators Assn.

**WILLIAMS, KEITH ROY,** museum director; b. Sunnyside, Wash., Sept. 5, 1958; s. Charles N. Williams and Ruth Arlene (Plank) Hicks; m. Nancy Maxson, 1980 (div. 1984); m. Deanna Lynn Murphy, Oct. 26, 1987; children: Steven, Jeremy. AA in Gen. Studies, Columbia Basin C.C., Pasco, Wash., 1979; BA in Anthropology, Wash. State U., 1981, MA in History/Pub. History, 1984, PhD in History, 1991. Interpretive ranger Nez Perce Nat. Hist. Pk. Nat. Pk. Svc., 1984, historian Alaska regional office Anchorage, 1986; dir. Wenatchee Valley Mus. and Cultural Ctr., Wenatchee, Wash., 1987—. Cons. Office Archaeology and Hist. Preservation, 1985, Batelle N.W. DOSE Reconstruction Project, Hanford, 1987, 88; instr. Wenatchee Valley C.C., 1988, 93—; Wash. state adviser Smithsonian Instn. exhibit Barn Again. 2000-01; field assessor and surveyor Am. Assn. Museums Mus. Assessment program, 1996—; pres., co-owner Spirit Voices Prodns., Inc., 2003—; spkr. in field. Author: (video, booklet) The People and The Plow, 1987, (audio CD) Bullfrogs Amuck: On the Yakima River, 2003; contbr. articles to profl. jours. Active Wash. State Heritage Coun., Olympia, 1988-90, Wash. Centennial

Com., Wenatchee, 1989; mem. design com. Wenatchee Downtown Assn., 1993-96; bd. dirs. Wash. Friends Humanities, Seattle, 1990—, Wenatchee Centennial Com., 1992, Wash. Commn. for the Humanities, 2001—. Grantee Assn. Humanities Idaho, Wash. Commn. Humanities, various other founds; nominee Paul Harris Rotary fellow for cmty. leadership, 2004. Mem. Wash. Mus. Assn. (bd. dirs. 1988-90, 94-96), Kiwanis (bd. dirs. 1998-99, past pres.). Avocations: boating, gardening, hunting, camping, reading. Office: Wenatchee Valley Mus and Cultural Ctr 127 S Mission St Wenatchee WA 98801-3039 Office Phone: 509-664-3340. E-mail: k.williams@wenatcheevalleymuseum.com.

**WILLIAMS, KENNETH SCOTT,** entertainment company executive; b. Tulsa, Okla., Dec. 31, 1955; s. David Vorhees Williams and Mary Louise (Newell) Rose; m. Jann Catherine Wolfe, May 20, 1989; children: Catherine Eloise, Michael Holbrook. BA, Harvard Coll., 1978; MS, Columbia U., 1985. Bank officer Chase Manhattan Bank, N.Y.C., 1978-82; asst. treas. Columbia Pictures Entertainment, N.Y.C., 1982-84, v.p., treas., 1984-89, sr. v.p. fin. and adminstrn. Burbank, Calif., 1990-91; sr. v.p. corp. ops. Sony Pictures Entertainment, Culver City, Calif., 1991-95, exec. v.p., 1995-96; pres. Digital Studio divsn. Sony Pictures Entertainment, 1996-2000, Technicolor Digital Cinema, Burbank, Calif., 2002; pres., CEO Stan Lee Media, Inc., Encino, Calif., 2000—02; COO Ascent Media Group, Santa Monica, Calif., 2002—03, pres., CEO, 2003—. Past pres., bd. dirs. L.A. Conservancy; former chmn. Entertainment Tech. Ctr. U. So. Calif.; former trustee U. Calif., Riverside; bd. dirs. L.A. Music Ctr., L.A. Pub. Access TV Channel 36, L.A. Master Chorale; mem. Blue Hill Troupe, N.Y.C., 1979—. Mem. N.Y. Soc. Securities Analysts, Acad. Television Arts and Scis., Fin. Execs. Inst. (v.p.), Digital Coast Roundtable (bd. dirs.), Harvard Club So. Calif. (exec. v.p., bd. dirs.), Beta Gamma Sigma. Home: 457 Cuesta Way Los Angeles CA 90077-3434 Office: Ascent Media Group 5th Fl 520 Broadway Santa Monica CA 90401 E-mail: kwilliams@ascentmedia.com.

**WILLIAMS, KEVIN W.,** automotive executive; b. Lexington Park, Md., Sept. 27, 1961; B in Bus. Mgmt., Tenn. State U., 1983; M in Bus. Adminstrn., Ctrl. Mich. U., 1989. Reliability analyst GM, Flint, Mich., 1983—89; gen. supr. prodn. Lansing Craft Ctr., 1989—91; program readiness mgr. GM EV1 electric vechicle program, 1991—93; reliability engr. N. Am. Truck Group, 1993—95, asst. prodn. supr. Janesville, Wis., 1995—96, area mgr. gen. assembly, 1996; dir. supplier quality GM Europe, 1997—2000; exec. dir., supplier quality GM N. Am., 2000—03, v.p. quality, 2003—. Bd. dirs. Motor Enterprises Inc.

**WILLIAMS, LANCE,** journalist; Sports staff writer San Francisco Chronicle. Contbr. articles to numerous profl. jours.; numerous appearances on sports radio and television shows; author: (Sports Book) Game of Shadows, 2006. Recipient Dick Schaap Excellence in Sports Journalism award, 2004, George Polk award, 2004, Edgar A. Poe, White House Correspondents' Assn., 2004. Office: San Francisco Chronicle 901 Mission St San Francisco CA 94103-2988*

**WILLIAMS, LARRY R.,** music educator; b. Dodge City, Kans. s. Ross O. and Agnes M. (Adams) Williams; m. Rita G. Williams; children: Patricia Kristine DeLano, Lori Ann, Lindsey Rose. MusB in Edn., Southwestern Coll., 1960; MusM in Edn., U. Kans., 1966. Educator music Ottawa (Kans.) Pub. Schs., 1960—65, Topeka (Kans.) Pub. Sch., 1965—68; dir. orch. string Lawrence (Kans.) Pub. Sch., 1968—78, U. Kans., Lawrence, 1978—79, Winfield (Kans.) Pub. Sch., 1979—86, Sumner Acad. Arts & Scis., Kans. City, 1986—95; prof. music Baker U., Baldwin City, Kans., 1995—2005. Dir. orch. string Southwestern Coll., Winfield, 1979—86; adj. prof. N.W. Mo. State U., Maryville, Mo., 2005—; guest condr. in field. Pres. Kans. City (Mo.) Civic Orch., 1990—2006, bd. dirs., 1990—2006. With USAR, 1957—89. Mem.: Kans. Am. String Tchrs. Assn. (dist. pres.), Kans. Music Educators Assn. (pres. 1988—89, named to Music Educators Hall Fame), Jaycees (named Outstanding Young Educator Kans. 1972), Rotary (bd. dirs. 1983—2005), Presbyn. Home: 8224 Malsey Lenexa KS 66215

**WILLIAMS, LAWRENCE SOPER,** photographer; b. Balt., July 8, 1917; s. Lawrence S. and Ida (Exall) W.; m. Avilda Leyshon Williams, Nov. 21, 1940; children: Jay Stephen, Wendy Lauren. Student, Md. Inst. Wirephoto operator AP, Balt., 1937—38; news photographer Balt. Sun Papers, 1938—40, Harris and Ewing News Photos, Washington, 1940—41; war corr., photographer Bur. Info. U.S. War Dept., Washington, 1941—45; picture editor Holiday mag., Phila., 1945—48; freelance photographer Havertown, Pa., 1949—59; pres. Lawrence S. Williams, Inc., Upper Darby, Pa., 1959—83, chmn., 1983—93. Pres. Archtl. Photographers Assn., N.Y.C., 1968-70, Paoli (Pa.) Woods Homeowner's Assn., 1985-86; chmn. archtl. landscape com. Robynwood Village, Hershey's Mill; vol., TV audio instr. West Chester Sch. Dist. Recipient Gold medal Artist Guild of Phila., 1965, Silver medal Artist Guild of Pa., 1964, George W. Berry trophy Soc. Comml. Photographers Del. Valley, 1961, 66, 78, 79, 82, Best of Show trophy Am. Mus. Photography, Phila., 1966, 71, 77, 79, 82, Best Comml. Print trophy Guild of Profl. Photographers Del. Valley, 1971, 70, Award of Excellence Am. Advtg. Assn. Pa., 1978, Pres.'s Cup Profl. Photographers Assn. Pa., 1971, Silver medal for Sixty Years World in Colour, Internat. Photo competition, Hague, Netherlands, 1973, numerous archtl., comml., indsl., pictorial awards. Fellow Am. Soc. Photographers; mem. Soc. Comml. Photographers Del. Valley (life), Profl. Photographers Assn. Pa. (life), Profl. Photographers Am. Inc. (life, master photography degree 1966, craftsman photography degree 1968), Shriners. Republican. Lutheran. Achievements include assembly of the largest collection of architectural photographs in U.S. consisting of over 250,000 negatives which are now in the archives of the Athenaeum of Philadelphia, Pa. Avocation: travel. Home: 14410 Shannondell Dr Audubon PA 19403-5609 Office: PO Box 694 Kimberton PA 19442-0694 E-mail: larryvil@sdlifestyle.com.

**WILLIAMS, LEAFORD CLEMETSON,** writer, political scientist; b. St. Elizabeth, Jamaica, Oct. 3, 1924; came to U.S., 1948; s. Jeremiah and Alice Williams; m. Bertha M. Bussey, May 19, 1950; children: Valerie, Kharl, Brenda. Student, Georgetown U., 1957-60; BA in Internat. Rels., Am. U., Washington, 1961, MA in Internat. Rels., 1972. Fgn. svc. officer USIA, Washington, 1961-67; pub. affairs officer U.S. Civil Svc. Dept. Transp., Washington, 1968-79; asst. to dir. White House Coun. on Small Bus., Washington, 1979-80. Chief mission, Taegu, Korea; cultural attache, Bombay, India; pub. affairs officer Am. Embassy, Seoul, Korea. Author: Rebirth of a Nation, 1954, Journey Into Diplomacy, 1996, Boys Without Dads: When Dads Abandon Homes, 2000. City Coun. candidate Dem. Party, Washington, 1974; chmn. Disciples Men Christian Ch., Washington, 1990; chmn. UN Assn., Washington, 1980-90; bd. mem. Immigration and Refugees Svcs., Washington, N.Y.C., 1992—. With USAF, 1950-56. Decorated Bronze Star. Mem. Thursday Luncheon Group Dept. State (program officer 1980-84). Avocations: golf, public speaking, writing. Home and Office: 1037 Crittenden St NE Washington DC 20017-2718 E-mail: fort@erols.com.

**WILLIAMS, LENA,** sportswriter; b. Washington, Mar. 2, 1950; BA cum laude in English, Howard U., 1972; MS in Journalism, Columbia U., 1973. Assoc. editor Black Sports Mag.; clk. NY Times, 1974—76, reporter, 1976—88, sports writer, 1988—. Author: It's the Little Things: The Everyday Interactions That Get Under the Skin of Blacks and Whites, 2000. Named one of Outstanding Women in Mktg. and Comms., Ebony Mag., 2001; recipient Excellence award, Nat. Assn. Black Journalism, 1997, Black Achievers award, Young Men's Christian Assn. Mem.: Newspaper Guild (chair of Times-Guild unit). Office: NY Times Sports Desk 229 W 43d St New York NY 10036 Office Phone: 212-556-7371. Office Fax: 212-556-5848.*

**WILLIAMS, LEOLA WILKERSON,** social worker, writer; d. David and Albertha Jones Wilkerson; m. Lafayette H. Williams, Sr., Apr. 30, 1977; children: Byron, Lafayette Jr., Langston, Joseph. BS, Tuskegee U., Ala., 1971; MSW, Fla. State U., 1985. Social worker Dept. Health and Rehab. Svcs., Jacksonville, 1971—85; case worker Children's Home Soc., Jacksonville,

1985—93; owner Spl. Occasions Party Shop, Jacksonville, 1993—95; counselor Youth Crisis Ctr., Jacksonville, 1995—98; social worker Fresenius Med. Care-Dialysis Clinic, Jacksonville, 1998—2002, St. Catherine Laboure Manor, Jacksonville, 2002—. Author: How Joseph Met the President, 2001. Mem. Friends of the N.W. Br. Libr., Jacksonville, 2001—02, Open Arms Christian Assembly. Mem.: Tuskegee Alumni Club, Delta Sigma Theta. Democrat. Avocations: reading, walking, real estate investing, writing, serving the Lord. Home: 5012 Princely Ave Jacksonville FL 32208 Office Phone: 904-308-4707.

**WILLIAMS, LILLIAN SERECE,** historian, social studies educator; BA, U. Buffalo, 1966, MA, 1973, PhD, 1979. Tchr. Buffalo Bd. Edn., 1966—69; asst. prof. U. Buffalo, 1972—76, vis. asst. prof., 1985—87, assoc. prof., dept. chair, 2002—; asst. prof. Howard U., Washington, 1976—85; from asst. to assoc. prof. U. Albany, NY, 1987—2002. Historian NAACP, Balt., 1992—93, Girl Scouts U.S.A., N.Y.C., 1995—97, N.Y. State Mus., Albany, 1997—98; dir. Inst. for Rsch. on Women U. Albany, 1998—2002. Author: Strangers in the Land of Paradise, 1999; editor: (documentary) Records of the National Association of Colored Women, 1993, 1994; assoc. editor: Jour. African Am. History, Afro-Ams. in N.Y. Life and History. Mem. exec. bd. Assn. for Study African Am. Life and History. Named one of 8 Outstanding Citizens of Western NY, Buffalo News, 2006; recipient Nuala McGann Drescher award, United. Univ. Profls., Lifetime Achievement award, Niagara County Black Achievers, Niagara Falls, N.Y., 2000, Augspurger award in local history, Buffalo and Erie County Hist. Soc., 2006; State Farm Ins. fellow, Nat. African Am. Women Leadership Inst., 2001. Mem.: Afro-Am. Hist. Assn.the Niagara Frontier, Orgn. Am. Historians, Delta Sigma Theta. Avocations: reading, art, interior decorating. Office: SUNY Buffalo African Amer Studies Dept 732 Clemens Hall Buffalo NY 14260 Office Phone: 716-645-2082

**WILLIAMS, LINDA C.,** lawyer; b. Portsmouth, Va., Apr. 4, 1956; BA with high honors, Univ. Va., 1978, JD, 1982. Bar: Calif. 1984. Law clk. Judge Albert Tate, Jr., US Ct. Appeals (5th cir.), New Orleans; ptnr., head Corp. Securities & Fin. Inst. group Pillsbury Winthrop Shaw Pittman, San Francisco. Instr. Univ. San Francisco Sch. Law. Mem.: Order of the Coif. Office: Pillsbury Winthrop Shaw Pittman 50 Fremont St San Francisco CA 94105 Office Phone: 415-983-7334. Office Fax: 415-983-1200. Business E-Mail: linda.williams@pillsburylaw.com.

**WILLIAMS, LISA A.,** special education educator; d. Ida M. Williams. B. Music Edn., Howard U., Washington, 2000, M. Music Edn., 2003; MEd in Spl. Edn., U. San Diego, Calif., 2002; EdS in Spl. Edn., Fla. State U., Tallassee, 2005. Cert. tchr. Music K-12 Calif., Va., Fla., 2000, tchr. spl. edn. Fla., 2004. Tchr. spl. edn. San Diego City Schs., San Diego, 2000—02; tchr. music Fairfax County Schs., Fairfax, Va., 2002—03; tchr. spl. edn. Leon County Schs., Tallahassee, 2004—06, San Diego Unified Sch. Dist., 2006—. Acad. counselor Fla. State U., Tallahassee, 2003—04; site coord. Leon County Schs. Title I Program, Tallahassee, 2004; dir. children's choir Bethel AME Ch., San Diego, 2000—02. Named Riley Minority Educator of Yr., 2006; Spl. Edn. and Minority scholar, Howard U., Grad. asst., 2002—03, Doctoral fellow, Phi Delta Kappa Internat., 2003—04, Childhood Edn., Reading and Disability Svcs. fellow, Fla. State U., 2005—06. Mem.: Nat. Assn. Music Educators, Phi Delta Kappa Internat., Internat. Clarinet Assn., Nat. Assn. for Black Sch. Educators, NEA, Coun. for Exceptional Children, Tau Beta Sigma, Alpha Kappa Alpha (Ednl. Advancement Found. scholar 2005), Sigma Alpha Iota (life). Personal E-mail: pindrop26@aol.com.

**WILLIAMS, LOUIS CLAIR, JR.,** public relations executive; b. Huntington, Ind., Nov. 7, 1940; s. Louis Clair and Marian Eileen W.; children— Terri Lynn, L. Bradley, Lisa C.; m. Mary Clare Moster. B.A., Eastern Mich. U., 1963. Copywriter, Rochester (N.Y.) Gas and Electric Co., 1963-65, editor RG&E News, 1965-66; employee info. specialist Gen. Ry. Signal Co., Rochester, 1966-67, supr. employment and employee rels., 1967-69; supr. pub. rels. Heublein, Inc., Hartford, Conn., 1969-70; dir. corp. communications Jewel Cos., Inc., Chgo., 1970-71; account exec. Ruder & Finn of Mid-Am., Chgo., 1971-73, v.p., 1973-76, sr. v.p., 1976-78; cons. Towers, Perrin, Forster & Crosby, Los Angeles, 1978-79; exec. v.p., gen. mgr. Harshe-Rotman & Druck, Inc., Chgo., 1979, pres. midwest region, 1979-80; v.p. Hill & Knowlton, Inc., Chgo., 1980-81, sr. v.p., 1981-83; pres. Savlin Williams Assocs., Evanston, Ill., 1983-85, L.C. Williams & Assocs., Chgo., 1985—. Mem. Internat. Assn. Bus. Communicators (chmn. found., pres., chmn. Chgo. chpt. 1979-80), Inst. Pub. Rels. (chmn. 1989), Pub. Rels. Soc. Am., Publicity Club Chgo. Personal E-mail: LCWA@att.net.

**WILLIAMS, LOWELL CRAIG,** lawyer, employee relations executive; b. Tehachapi, Calif., Dec. 3, 1947; s. Lyndon Williams and Gertrude (White) Sievert; m. Marsha Mendelssohn; children: John S., Jeffrey A. Beschenigungeschichte, Georg August U., Germany, 1968; BA, U. Calif., Santa Barbara, 1969; JD, Columbia U., 1972. Bar: N.Y. 1973, U.S. Ct. Appeals (2nd cir.) 1974, U.S. Supreme Ct. 1974. Assoc. Sullivan & Cromwell, N.Y.C., 1972-75; v.p. Elf Aquitaine, Inc., N.Y.C., 1976-95; v.p. Compagnie des Machines Bull, N.Y.C., 1995—; exec. v.p. group human resources, 1998-99; exec. dir. Exult Inc., N.Y.C., 1999—2001; sr. advisor TPI Sourcing Inc., The Woodlands, Tex., 2002—03; v.p. global human resource svcs., gen. counsel EquaTerra, Inc., Houston, 2003—. Past pres. Scarsdale Synagogue. Mem. Internat. Bar Assn., German Law Assn. (dir.). Office: EquaTerra Inc 3262 Westheimer Blvd #120 Houston TX 77098-1002 Office Phone: 914-661-7904. Business E-Mail: lowell.williams@equaterra.com.

**WILLIAMS, LOWELL E.,** theater educator; b. Louisville, Sept. 22, 1944; s. Samuel R. and Virginia E. Williams; children: Romy Riddick, Justin L. BA, Kent State U., Ohio, 1965, MA, 1968; MFA, Temple U., Phila., 1979. Rehab. psychologist Temple Cmty. Mental Health, Phila., 1969—79; bus. rep. Actors Equity Assn., N.Y.C., 1986—89, SAG, N.Y.C., 1989—2003; lectr. dept. theatre arts U. Miami, Fla., 2003—. Bd. dirs. Edison Sr. H.S., Miami, 2006. Recipient Off Broadway award, OBIE, 1983; Soc. Devereaux fellow, Devereaux Found., 1968. Avocations: cooking, exercise. Home: 7483 SW 82d St # A 108 Miami FL 33143 Office: Dept Theatre Arts U Miami PO Box 248273 Coral Gables FL 33124-8273

**WILLIAMS, LUCINDA,** country musician; b. Lake Charles, La., 1953; d. Miller W.; m. Greg Sowders (div.). Albums include: Ramblin' On My Mind, 1979, Happy Woman Blues, 1980, Lucinda Williams, 1988, Passionate Kisses, 1989 (Grammy award Best Country Song 1994), Sweet Old World, 1992, Car Wheels on a Gravel Road, 1998 (Grammy award for best contemp. folk album, 1999), Essence, 2002 (Grammy award for best female rock vocal); contbr. songs to: Sweet Relief, 1993, Born to Choose, 1993.

**WILLIAMS, LUTHER STEWARD,** research scientist; b. Sawyerville, Ala., Aug. 19, 1940; s. Roosevelt and Mattie B. (Wallace) W.; m. Constance Marie Marion, Aug. 23, 1963; children: Mark Steward, Monique Marie. BA magna cum laude, Miles Coll., 1961; MS, Atlanta U., 1963; PhD, Purdue U., 1968, DSc (hon.), 1987, U. Louisville, 1992, Capitol Coll., 1996, Bowie State U., 1996, Tuskegee U., 1997, U. DC, 1999. NSF lab. asst. Spelman Coll., 1961-62, Atlanta U., 1962-63, instr. biology, faculty rsch. assoc., 1963-64, asst. prof. biology, 1969-70, prof. biology, 1984-87; grad. tchg. asst. Purdue U., West Lafayette, Ind., 1964-65, grad. rsch. asst., 1965-66, asst. prof. biology 1970-73, assoc. prof., 1973-79, prof., 1979-80, NIH Career Devel. awardee, 1971-75, asst. provost, 1976-80; dean Grad. Sch., prof. biology Washington U., St. Louis, 1980-83; v.p. acad. affairs, dean Grad. Sch. U. Colo., Boulder, 1983-84; Am. Cancer Soc. postdoctoral fellow SUNY-Stony Brook, 1968-69; assoc. prof. biology MIT, 1973-74; spl. asst. to dir. Nat. Inst. Gen. Med. Scis., NIH, Bethesda, Md., 1987-88; dep. dir. Nat. Inst. Gen. Med. Scis. NIH, Bethesda, 1988-89; sr. advisor to dir. NSF, Washington, 1989-90, asst. dir. for edn. and human resources, 1990-99; visiting scholar Payson Ctr. Internat. Devel./Tech., Arlington, Va., 1999-2000, edn. cons., 2000—; Educator, cons., 2000—; dir. edn., sr. advisor to dir. Mo. Bot. Garden, St. Louis, 2001-05; chmn. rev. com. MARC Program, Nat. Inst. Gen. Med. Scis., NIH, 1972-76; grant reviewer NIH, 1971-73, 76, NSF, 1973,

76-80, Med. Rsch. Coun. of N.Z., 1976; mem. life scis. screening com. recombinant DNA adv. com. HEW, 1979-81; mem. nat. adv. gen. med. sci. council NIH, 1980-85; mem. adv. com. Office Tech. Assessment, Washington, 1984-87; chmn. fellowship adv. com. NRC Ford Found., 1984-85; mem.-at-large Grad. Record Exam. Bd., 1981-85, chmn. minority grad. edn. com., 1983-85; mem. health, safety and environ. affairs. com. Nat. Labs., U. Calif., 1981-87; mem. adv. panel Office Tech. Assessment, US Congress, 1985-86; mem. fed. task force on women, minorities and the handicapped in sci. and tech., 1987-91; mem. adv. panel to dir. sci. and tech. ctrs. devel. NSF, 1987-88; mem. nat. adv. com. White House Initiative on Historically Black Colls. and Univs. on sci. and Tech., 1986-89; numerous other adv. bds. and coms. Contbr. sci. articles to profl. jours. Vice-chmn. bd. advisors Atlanta Neighborhood Justice Ctr., 1984-87; bd. dirs. Met. Atlanta United Way, 1986-87, Butler St. YMCA, Atlanta, 1985-87; trustee Atlanta Zool. Assn., 1985-87, Miles Coll., 1984-87, Atlanta U., 1984-87, 90-96; mem. nominating com. Dana Found.; mem. St. Louis CC Found. Bd., 2004-. NIH predoctoral fellow Purdue U., 1966-68; recipient William A. Hinton Rsch. Trng. award, Am. Soc. Microbiology, 1998, trustee award Acad. Scis. St. Louis, 2004; named to Black Coll. Hall of Fame, 2002. Fellow Am. Acad. Microbiology; mem. Am. Soc. Microbiology, Am. Chem. Soc., Am. Soc. Biol. Chemists (mem. ednl. affairs com. 1979-82, com. on equal opportunities for minorities 1972-84). Home and Office: 15286 Brightfield Manor Dr Chesterfield MO 63017 Office Phone: 314-577-5139. Personal E-mail: lswilliams1960@sbcglobal.net. Business E-Mail: luther.williams@mobot.org.

**WILLIAMS, MARGARET M. (MEG WILLIAMS),** insurance company executive; Joined Scottsdale Ins. Co., 2003, chief info. officer, v.p. info. tech. Named one of Premier 100 IT Leaders, Computerworld, 2005. Office: Scottsdale Ins Co 8877 N Gainey Ctr Dr Scottsdale AZ 85258 Office Phone: 480-365-4000. Office Fax: 480-483-6752.*

**WILLIAMS, MARIO,** professional football player; b. Richlands, NC, Jan. 31, 1985; Studied Pro Sports Mgmt., NC St. Univ., 2004—06. Defensive end Houston Texans, 2006—. Named Nat. Preseason Defensive Player Yr., Blue Ribbon Coll. Football, 2005; named to NC Shrine Bowl Team, 2002, first team All-ACC, 2006; recipient Bob Warren award for Integrity and Sportsmanship. Achievements include first overall selection in 2006 NFL Draft. Office: Houston Texans Two Reliant Park Houston TX 77054*

**WILLIAMS, MARION LESTER,** government official; b. Abilene, Tex., Dec. 1, 1933; s. Martin Lester and Eddie Faye (Wilson) W.; m. Johnnie Dell Ellinger, Dec. 14, 1957; children: Tammy Dawn Cole, Pamela DeAnn Ritterbush. BS, Tex. A&M U., 1956; MS, U. N.Mex., 1967; PhD, Okla. State U., 1971. Test engr. Sandia Nat. Labs., Albuquerque, 1959-61; weapons sys. engr. Naval Weapons Evaluation Facility, Albuquerque, 1961-66; ops. rsch. analyst Joint Chiefs of Staff/Joint Task Force II, Albuquerque, 1966-68; chief reliability div. Field Command DNA, Albuquerque, 1969-71; prin. scientist SHAPE Tech. Ctr., The Hague, Netherlands, 1971-74; chief tech. advisor HQ AF Test & Evaluation Ctr., Albuquerque, 1974-81; chief scientist HQ AF Operational Test & Evaluation Ctr., Albuquerque, 1981-89, tech. dir., 1989—. Vis. adv. com. Okla. State U., Stillwater, 1988—; adv. com. U. N.Mex., Albuquerque, 1985—. Editor T&E Tech. Jour., 1987—; contbr. articles to profl. jour. Sci. advisor N.Mex. Sci. & Tech. Oversight Com., Albuquerque, 1988; bd. advisors U. N.Mex. Cancer Ctr., 1987—; bd. dirs. Contact Albuquerque, 1986-87. 1st lt. USAF 1956-59. Recipient Presdl. Rank award, 1987, 92. Fellow Mil. Ops. Rsch. Soc. (pres. 1982-83, bd. dir. 1976-81, Wanner award 1991), Internat. Test & Evaluation Ctr. (bd. dirs. 1984-86, 88-90, v.p. 1990, pres. 1992-93), Ops. Rsch. Soc. Am., Tau Beta Pi, Phi Eta Sigma, Alpha Pi Mu, Sigma Tau, Kappa Mu Epsilon. Baptist. Avocations: skiing, computers. Home: 1416 Stagecoach Ln SE Albuquerque NM 87123-4429 Office: HQ AF Operational Test Ctr Kirtland AFB Albuquerque NM 87117-0001 E-mail: mlw505@yahoo.com.

**WILLIAMS, MARK DIDRIK,** music educator, composer; b. Harlingen, Tex., Mar. 31, 1959; s. Vincent D. and Verla A. Williams. BA, Luther Coll., Decorah, IA USA, 1980; MA, U. of Iowa, Iowa City, IA USA, 1980—82; Mus D musical arts, U. of Ill., Urbana-Champaign, IL USA, 1984—88. Music performance instr. Lake Tahoe C.C., South Lake Tahoe, Calif., 2000—; adj. instr. of music Western Nev. C.C., Carson City, Nev., 1993—99; adj. asst. prof. of music Millikin U., Decatur, Ill., 1987—90. Composer (lyricist): (musical) Beauty; author: (website) Singing Voice, (article) Music Educators Jour.; composer: (musical) Guilty Pleasures. Recipient Who's Who Among Am. Teachers, 2002. Mem.: Nat. Assn. of Teachers of Singing, Am. Soc. of Composers, Authors and Publishers, MENSA. Independent. Christian. Avocations: musicals, reading, movies, skiing, hiking, computers. Office: Lake Tahoe Comty Coll One College Dr South Lake Tahoe CA 96150 Personal E-mail: voxdoc@yahoo.com. E-mail: williams@ltcc.edu.

**WILLIAMS, MARK ELLIS,** artist, educator; b. Elyria, Ohio, July 19, 1956; s. Wilbur Forrest and Evelyn Wintefred Williams; m. Carol Louise Wakeman, Oct. 24, 1981; children: Keri Michelle, Kevin Mercer. BA, Malone Coll., Canton. Ohio, 1979; MA, Bowling Green State U., Ohio, 1991. Cert. art educator Ohio, 1979. Art instr. Pandora-Gilboa Schs., Pandora, Ohio, 1983—. Ceramic artist. Recipient Strong award, Bowling Green State U. Art Dept., 1991, Coach of Yr., Putnam County League, 1986, 1988, 1996, Blanchard Valley Conf., 1988, 2003, Dist. 8 Volleyball Coach of Yr., 1999, 2005. Mem.: NEA, N.W. Ohio Art Edn. Assn., Ohio State Volleyball Coaches Assn. (life; trustee 2000—), Sportsmanship, Ethics, and Integrity award 2001, Lifetime Achievement award 2005). Achievements include design of dual chamber downdraft kiln with bisqueing capabilities during glaze firing sequence. Home: 401 S Jefferson Pandora OH 45877 Office: Pandora-Gilboa Schs 410 Rocket Ridge Pandora OH 45877 Office Phone: 419-384-3275 E-mail: williamm@pg.noacsc.org.

**WILLIAMS, MARSHA E.,** broadcast executive; BA, Conn. Coll.; MA, Washington U. With The Psychological Corp., Cleve., San Antonio, Children's TV Workshop (now Sesame Workshop), 1991—95, MTV Networks Co., NYC, 1996—, v.p. rsch. and planning Nickelodeon Networks, sr. v.p. rsch. and planning Nickelodeon Networks, 2006—. Office: MTV Networks Co Nickelodeon Networks 1515 Broadway 42d Fl New York NY 10036*

**WILLIAMS, MARSHA RHEA,** computer scientist, educator, researcher, consultant; b. Memphis, Aug. 4, 1948; d. James Edward and Velma Lee W. Cert., Schiller Coll., West Berlin, Germany, 1968; BS in Physics, Beloit Coll., 1969; MS in Physics, U. Mich., 1971; MS in Sys. and Info. Sci., Vanderbilt U., 1976, PhD in Computer Sci., 1982. Cert. data processor. Engring. coop. student Lockheed Missiles & Space Co., Sunnyvale, Calif., 1967-68; asst. transmission engr. Ind. Bell Tel. Co., Indpls., 1971-72; sys. analyst, instr. physics Memphis State U., 1972-74; computer-assisted instrn. project programmer Fisk U., 1974-76; mem. tech. staff Hughes Rsch. Labs., Malibu, Calif., 1976-78; assoc. sys. engr. IBM, Nashville, 1978-80; rsch. and tchg. asst. Vanderbilt U., Nashville, 1980-82, spl. asst. to dean Grad. Sch., spring 1981, minority engr. advisor, 1975-76; cons. computer-assisted instrn. project Meharry Med. Coll., Nashville, summer 1982; assoc. prof. computer sci. Tenn. State U., Nashville, 1982-83, 84-90, full tenured prof., 1990—, univ. marshal, 1992-97. Assoc. prof. U. Miss., Oxford, 1983-84, faculty senator; assoc. program dir. Applications of Advanced Techs. Sci. and Engring. Edn., NSF, 1987-88, apptd. USRA Sci. and Engring. Edn. Coun., Advanced Design Program, 1992-94; cons. on minority scientists and engrs. Univ. Space Rsch. Assn., Washington, 1988; vis. scientist CSNET-Minority Instn. Networking Project Bolt, Beranek & Newman, Cambridge, Mass., 1989; mem. tech. staff Bell Comm. Rsch., Red Bank, N.J., 1990; prin. investigator NSF Computer Sci., Engring. & Math. Scholarships Project, 2002-03; presenter papers profl. meetings. Editor-in-chief newspaper Pilgrim Emanuel Bapt. Ch., 1975-76. Advisr Chi Rho Youth Fellowship, Temple Bapt. Ch., 1975-81, adv. com. Golden Outreach Sr. Citizens Fellowship, 1979-80, 86-87, 89-93, Women's Day spkr., 1979-81, Ebenezer Missionary Bapt. Ch., 1993; adviser Nat. Soc. Black Engring. Students, 1983-84; founder, coord. Tenn. State U. Assn. for

Excellence in Computer Sci., Math. and Physics (AE-COMP), 1986-87; coord. Tech. Opportunities Fair, 1986, 87; dir. Tenn. State U. Minorities in Sci., Engring. and Tech. Rsch. Project-MISET, 1989—; child sponsor World Vision, 1981—; mem.; newsletter staff Lake Providence Missionary Bapt. Ch. Recipient Disting. Instr. award, 1984, Disting. Svc. citation Beloit Coll. Alumni Assn., 1994; grantee Digital Equipment Corp., 1989-92; rsch. grantee Tenn. State U., 1993, 94, NSF, 2002-03. Mem. AAUP, NAACP (nat. judge ACT-SO sci. olympics 1992), Assn. Computing Machinery, Assn. Info. Tech. Profls. (edn. chmn., bd. dirs. 1986), Tenn. Acad. Sci., Phi Kappa Phi. Home: PO Box 281946 Nashville TN 37228 Office: Tenn State U Dept Computer Sci PO Box 9604 Nashville TN 37209

**WILLIAMS, MARTHA ETHELYN,** information science educator; b. Chgo., Sept. 21, 1934; d. Harold Milton and Alice Rosemond (Fox) Williams. BA, Barat Coll., 1955; MA, Loyola U., 1957. With IIT Rsch. Inst., Chgo., 1957-72, mgr. info. scis., 1962-72, mgr. computer search ctr., 1968-72; adj. assoc. prof. sci. info. Ill. Inst. Tech., Chgo., 1965-73, lectr. chemistry dept., 1968-70; rsch. prof. info. sci., coordinated sci. lab. Coll. Engring. U. Ill., Urbana, also dir. info. retrieval rsch. lab., 1972—, prof. info. sci. grad. sch. of libr. info. sci., 1974—, affiliate, computer sci. dept., 1979—. Chair large data base conf. Nat. Acad. Sci./NRC, 1974, mem. ad hoc panel on info. storage and retrieval, 1977, numerical data adv. bd., 1979-82, computer sci. and tech. bd., nat. rsch. network rev. com., 1987-88, chair utility subcom., 1987-88, subcom. promoting access to sci. and tech. data for pub. interest; task force on sci. info. activities NSF, 1977; U.S. rep. review com. for project on broad system of ordering, UNESCO, Hague, Netherlands, 1974; vice-chair Gordon Rshc. Conf. on Sci. Info. Problems in Rsch., 1978, chair, 1980; mem. panel on intellectual property rights in age of electronics and info. U.S. Congress, Office of Tech. Assessment; program chmn. Nat. Online Meeting, 1980-2001; founder, pres. Info. Market Indicators, Inc., 1982-; cons. in field; invited lectr. Commn. European Communities, Industrial R&D adv. com., Brussels, 1992. Editor-in-chief: Computer-Readable Databases Directory and Data Sourcebook, 1976—89, founding editor:, 1989—; editor: Ann. Rev. Info. Sci. and Tech., 1976—2001, Online Rev., 1979—92, Online and CD-ROM Rev., 1993—2000; mem. editl. adv. bd.: Database, 1978—88, mem. editl. bd.: Info. Processing and Mgmt., 1982—89, The Reference Libr., founding editor: Online Info. Rev., 2000—; contbr. articles to profl. jours. Trustee Engirng. Info., Inc., 1974-87, bd. dirs., 1976-91, chmn. bd. dirs., 1982-91, v.p., 1978-79, pres., 1980-81; regent Nat. Libr. Medicine, 1978-82, chmn. bd. regents, 1981; mem. task force on sci. info. activities NSF, 1977-78; mem. nat. adv. com. ACCESS ERIC, 1989-91. Recipient best paper of year award H. W. Wilson Co., 1975; Travel grantee NSF, Luxembourg, 1972, Honolulu, 1973, Tokyo, 1973, Mexico City, 1975, Scotland, 1976 Fellow: AAAS (mem. nominating com. 1983, 1985), Nat. Fedn. Abstracting and Info. Svcs. (hon.), Inst. Info. Scis. (hon.); mem.: NAS (mem. joint com. with NRC on chem. info. 1971—73), Internat. Fedn. for Documentation (U.S. nat. com.), Assn. Sci. Info. Dissemination Ctrs. (v.p. 1971—73, pres. 1975—77), Assn. Computing Machinery (pub. bd. 1972—76), Am. Soc. Info. Sci. (councilor 1971—72, mem. publs. com. 1974—, pres. 1987—88, councilor 1987—89, contbg. editor bull. column 1974—78, Award of Merit 1984, Pioneer Info. Sci. award 1987, Watson Davis award 1995), Am. Chem. Soc. Home: 2134 Sandra Ln Monticello IL 61856-8036 Office: U Ill 1308 W Main St Urbana IL 61801-2307 E-mail: m-will13@uiuc.edu.

**WILLIAMS, MARY ALICE BALDWIN,** retired home economist, volunteer; b. St. Louis, Mar. 24, 1928; d. Ulysses Grant and Irene (Jenkins) Gray; m. Earl Randolph Baldwin, June 24, 1952 (div. 1973); 1 child, Arlene Denise; m. Robert Williams Jr., Dec. 21, 1985. BS, Lincoln U., 1952; MA, Webster U., 1971; postgrad., Harris Stowe Tchrs. Coll., 1976-78, Cen. Mo. State U., 1979-80, U. Mo., 1981-82. Cert. home economist, Mo. Tchr. home econs. Cen. H.S., Hayti, Mo., 1952-53, Cleve. Pub. Schs., 1953-56; tchr. elem. sch. St. Louis Pub. Schs., 1958-67, tchr. home econs., 1968-83, curriculum supr. home econs., 1984-93, cons. home econs. and character edn., 1993; ret., 1993; vol. cons. Family & Consumer Sci. Fiber Art, 1993—. Presenter in field. Author curriculum materials in home econs. and character edn. Fund raising com. Annie Malone Children's Home, St. Louis, 1987-90; 75th anniversary com. YYWCA Phylliss Wheatley, St. Louis, 1988 Mem Nat Assn Univ. Women (del. 1992, Woman of Yr. 2001, N. Ctrl. sectional lay mem. 1999-2003), Am. Home Econs. Assn. (ethics com. 1990-92, population com. 1990-91), Mo. Home Econs. Assn. (tchr. rep. 1988-90), Am. Vocat. Assn., Mo. Vocat. Assn. (legis. com.), St. Louis Home Econs. Tchrs. Assn. (founder, adviser), Lincoln Univ. Alumni Assn. (chair founders day), Delta Sigma Theta. Avocations: sewing, clothing design, music, reading, travel, designer and quilter African Am. history and story quilts. Home: 4910 Maffitt Pl Saint Louis MO 63113-1727

**WILLIAMS, MARY ELLEN COSTER,** federal judge; b. Flushing. NY, 1953; married; 2 children. BA in Latin and Greek summa cum laude, Cath. U., 1974, MA in Latin, 1974; JD, Duke U., 1977. Assoc. Fulbright and Jaworski, Washington, 1977—83; asst. US atty. civil divsn. US Dept. Justice, Washington, 1983—87; ptnr. Jamis, Schuelke and Weschler Law Firm, Washington, 1987—89; adminstrv. judge GSA Bd. of Contract Appeals, Washington, 1989—2003; judge US Ct. of Fed. Claims, Washington, 2003—. Editl. bd. Duke Law Jour. Fellow: Am. Bar Found. (life); mem.: DC Bar (sec.), DC Young Lawyers Sect. (chair), Bar Assn. of DC (found. pres., trustee, bd. dirs.), ABA (sect. rep. com. of ethics and professionalism 1998—2000, commn. on evaluation of rules of profl. conduct 1998—2000, presdl. task force on govt. lawyers 2000—01, chair elect. pub. contract law 2002—, chair elect, vice chair, sec., sect. rep. ho. delegates 2004—). Office: US Ct of Fed Claims 717 Madison Pl NW Washington DC 20005

**WILLIAMS, MARY IRENE,** business education educator; b. Hugo, Okla., June 30, 1944; d. Primer and Hylar B. (Tarkington) Jackson; m. Lee A. Williams (div. June 1981); 1 child, Monica Ariane. BS in Bus. Edn., Langston U., 1967; MS in Bus., Emporia State U., Kans., 1973; EdS, U. Nev., Las Vegas, 1977; DBA in Internat. Bus., Alliant U., 1992. Instr. Spokane (Wash.) C.C., 1967-70; tchr. bus. Topeka Pub. Schs., 1970-73; prof. C.C. So. Nev., Las Vegas, 1973—, assoc. dean of bus., 1978—93, dean acad. support svcs., 1993—95, prof. bus./mgmt., 1997—, chmn. bus. adminstrn. dept., 2006—; prof. bus./mgmt., asst. to assoc. v.p., asst. coord. bus. Langston U., Tulsa, 1995—97. Adj. prof. So. Nazarene U., 1996-97; adj. prof. Tulsa Jr. Coll., 1997. Author: A Journey Upward, 2004. Named Educator of Yr. Nucleus Plaza Assn., 1985, New Visions, Inc., 1986. Mem. AAUW, Nat. Bus. Edn. Assn., Alpha Kappa Alpha Avocations: exercising, studying languages, reading. Office: CCSN 6375 W Charleston Blvd W2C Las Vegas NV 89146-1164 Personal E-mail: marywmslvnv@aol.com.

**WILLIAMS, MARY PEARL,** judge; b. Brownsville, Tex., Jan. 12, 1928; d. Marvin Redman and Theo Mae (Kethley) Hall; m. Jerre Stockton Williams, May 28, 1950; children: Jerre Stockton, Shelley Wiliams Austin, Stephanie Williams Laden. BA, U. Tex., 1948, JD, 1949. Bar: Tex. 1949. U.S Supreme Ct. 1955, U.S. Dist. Ct. (we. dist.) Tex. 1987. Asst. atty. gen. State of Tex., Austin, 1949-50; relief judge Mcpl. Ct., Austin, 1964; asst. instr. dept. govt. U. Tex., Austin, 1966-67; atty. Office of Emergency Preparedness, Exec. Office of Pres., Washington, 1968-70; labor arbitrator, mem. arbitration panel Am. Arbitration Assn., 1972-73; judge County Ct. Law 2, Travis County, Tex., 1973-80, 53d Jud. Dist. Ct., Austin, 1981-2000, sr. judge, 2000—. Cons. HEW, 1966—67. Mem. adv. com. Juvenile Bd. Travis County, 1964—67; trustee United Way, 1974—78. Named Outstanding Woman, Austin Am.-Statesman, 1974, Austin Citizen, 1978, Woman of the Yr., Austin Dist. Bus. and Profl. Women, 1977; named to Austin HS Hall of Fame, 1996. Fellow: ABA, Am. Bar Found.; mem.: Inst. Jud. Adminstrn., Am. Judicature Soc., Am. Law Inst., Travis County Bar Assn., Coll. State Bar Tex., State Bar Tex., Jr. League Austin, Kappa Alpha Theta, Delta Kappa Gamma (hon.). Democrat. Methodist. Home: Apt 137 4100 Jackson Ave Austin TX 78731-6034 Office: Travis County Courthouse PO Box 1748 Austin TX 78767-1748 E-mail: greatimpy@aol.com.

**WILLIAMS, MEG See WILLIAMS, MARGARET**

**WILLIAMS, MELVIN DONALD,** anthropologist, educator; b. Pitts., Feb. 3, 1933; s. Aaron and Gladys Virginia (Barnes) W.; m. Faye Wanda Strawder, June 20, 1958; children: Aaron Ellsworth, Steven Rodney, Craig Haywood. AB, U. Pitts., 1955, MA, 1969, PhD, 1973. Owner, operator Wholesale Periodical Distbn. Co., Pitts., 1955-66; instr. dept. sociology and anthropology Carlow Coll., 1969-71, asst. prof., 1971-75, chmn. dept. sociology and anthropology, 1973-75; assoc. prof. anthropology U. Pitts., 1976-79, adj. prof., 1979-82; prof. anthropology Purdue U., 1979-83, U. Md., College Park, 1983-88, U. Mich., Ann Arbor, 1988—. Olie B. O'Connor prof. Am. instns. Colgate U., 1976-77 Author: On the Street Where I Lived, Community in a Black Pentecostal Church, The Human Dilemma, The Black Middle Class, An Academic Village, Race for Theory; editor: Selected Readings in Afro-American Anthropology; contbr. articles to profl. publs. Co-chmn. project area com. Urban Redevel. Authority, Pitts., 1972—; co-dir. interdisciplinary family community project Western Psychiat. Inst. and Clinic, 1973-76; bd. dirs. Cath. Social Svc. of Allegheny County, Pa., 1973-76; coll. ombudsman, 1991-93, faculty senate, 1993-96. Career Svc. award U. Mich., 2004; fellow NSF, 1967, NDEA, 1969; grantee NSF, 1969-72, Cmty. Action Pitts., 1969-71, Social Sci. Rsch. Coun., 1974-75, Lilly Endowment, 1980-83, 85-86. Fellow Am. Anthrop. Assn.; mem. African Studies Assn., AAAS, AAUP, Am. Sociol. Assn., Assn. Study Afro-Am. Life and History, Soc. for Psychol. Anthropology, Am. Author's Assn. (planning commn. 2005). Home: 520 W Washington St Ann Arbor MI 48103-4232 Office: University of Michigan Dept Anthropology 101 West Hall 108 S University Ave Ann Arbor MI 48109-1107 Office Phone: 734-764-7274. Business E-Mail: mddoublu@umich.edu. *Personal philosophy: An abiding interest in people has stimulated me to discover more and more about humankind and has been an ever-present motivation to develop, grow and experience.*

**WILLIAMS, MICHAEL ANTHONY,** lawyer; b. Mandan, N.D., Sept. 14, 1932; s. Melvin Douglas and Lucille Ann (Gavin) Williams; m. Marjorie Ann Harrer, aug. 25, 1962 (div. 1989); children: Ann Margaret, Douglas Raymond, David Michael; m. Dorothy Ruth Hand, 1989. BA, Coll. of St. Thomas, 1954; LL.B., Harvard U., 1959. Bar: Colo. 1959, N.D. 1959, U.S. Dist. Ct. Colo. 1959, U.S. Ct. Appeals (10th cir.) 1959, U.S. Supreme Ct. 1967. Assoc. Sherman & Howard and predecessor Dawson, Nagel, Sherman & Howard, Denver, 1959—65, ptnr., 1965—91; pres. Williams, Youle & Koenigs, P.C., Denver, 1991—2002; prin. Michael A. Williams LLC, Denver, 2002—. Served as 1st lt. USAF, 1955—57. Mem.: ABA, Coll. Comml. Arbitrators, Colo. Bar Assn., Am. Law Inst., Colo. Bar Found., Am. Bd. Trial Advs., Am. Coll. Trial Lawyers. Office: 950 17th St Ste 1800 Denver CO 80202-2811 Office Phone: 303-785-7999. Business E-Mail: mwilliams@wyk.com.

**WILLIAMS, MICHAEL EDWARD, SR.,** dean; b. Mobile, Ala., July 30, 1960; s. Charles Edward and Ollie Jo (Hayes) Williams; m. Roberta Jean Norton, Nov. 28, 1987; children: Michael Edward Jr., Joshua Cody, Carey Alan. BS in Secondary Edn. Hist., Troy State U., 1982; MA in Hist., Auburn U., 1984; MDiv, Souwestern Bapt. Theological Sem., 1987, PhD in Ch. Hist., 1993. Grad. tchg. asst. Auburn (Ala.) U., 1982—84; pastor Trinity Hills Bapt. Ch., Benbrook, Tex., 1987—94; tchg. fellow ch. hist. Southwestern Bapt. Theological Sem., Fort Worth, Tex., 1991, adj. prof. ch. hist., 1994; adj. prof. hist. Dallas (Tex.) Bapt. U., 1991—94, asst. prof. hist., 1995—96, prof. hist., 1996—, dean coll. humanities and social scis., 1996—. Edtl. bd. Bap. Hist. Heritage Jour., 1997—, Jour. Tex. Bapt. Hist., Dallas, 1998—2002; academic book review editor Bapt. Hist. Heritage Jour., Nashville, 2003—. Author: Isaac Taylor Tichenor: The Creation of the Baptist New South, 2005, To God Be The Glory: The Centennial History of BBU, 1998 (TBHS Ch. Hist. award, 1998), Victory Thru Faith: A History of the Risen Heights Baptist Church, 1996 (TBHS Ch. Hist. award, 1996); contbr. articles various profl. jours. Named Prof. of Yr., Dallas Bapt. U., 1999—2000; recipient Hon. Alumnus award, Decatur Bapt. Coll., 1999. Mem.: So. Hist. Assn., Fellowship Bapt. Historians (sec.), Bapt. Hist. and Heritage Soc. Independent. Bapt. Avocations: sports, jogging, bicycling, swimming, movies. Home: 169 Deer Creek Dr Aledo TX 76008 Office: Dallas Bapt U 3000 Mt Crest Pkwy Dallas TX 75211

**WILLIAMS, MICHAEL G.,** publishing executive; b. NY, Aug. 1956; married. With Aetna Life and Casulaty Co., Emery Air Freight Corp.; chief info. officer Seagram Asia-Pacific; v.p., info. tech., chief tech. officer spirits and wine group Seagram Co., 1992—98; v.p., chief info. officer NY Times, 1998—, NY Times Co., 2000—04. Working coun. for chief info. officers Corp. Adv. Bd. Co. Office: New York Times Co 229 W 43rd St New York NY 10036-3959

**WILLIAMS, MICHAEL JAMES,** lawyer; b. Breckenridge, Minn., July 13, 1954; s. Robert L. and Carol J. (Edenborg) W.; m. Sherry L. Schnieder, Oct. 27, 1984; children: Taylor Michael, Tory Lyn. AA, N.D. State Coll. Sci. 1974; Bachelor's, U. N.D., Grand Forks, 1976, JD, 1979. Bar: N.D. 1979, U.S. Dist. Ct. N.D., 1982, U.S. Dist. Ct. Minn. 1982, U.S. Ct. Appeals (8th cir.) 1982, Minn. 1985. Atty. Kapsner & Kapsner, Bismarck, N.D., 1979-82; ptnr. Miller Norman Kenney & Williams, Moorhead, Minn., 1983-89; atty. Hagen Law Office, Fargo, N.D., 1989-92; ptnr. Maring Williams Law Office, Fargo, 1992—. Mem. N.D. Bar Assn. (pres. 2005), N.D. Trial Lawyers Assn. (prers. 2004). Minn. Trial Lawyers Assn., Minn. Bar Assn. Avocation: sports. Office: Maring Williams Law Office PC 1220 Main Ave Ste 105 PO Box 2103 Fargo ND 58107-2103

**WILLIAMS, MICHELLE,** actress; b. Kalispell, Mont., Sept. 9, 1980; d. Larry and Carla; 1 child, Matilda Rose. Actor: (films) Lassie, 1994, Species, 1995, Timemaster, 1995, A Thousand Acres, 1997, Halloween H20: 20 Years Later, 1998, Dick, 1999, But I'm a Cheerleader, 1999, Perfume, 2001, Prozac Nation, 2001, Me Without You, 2001, The United States of Leland, 2003, The Station Agent, 2003, A Hole in One, 2004, Imaginary Heroes, 2004, Land of Plenty, 2004, The Baxter, 2005, Brokeback Mountain, 2005 (Critics Choice award, best supporting actress, Broadcast Film Critics Assn., 2006), The Hawk is Dying, 2006; (TV series) Raising Caines, 1995, Dawson's Creek, 1998—2003; (TV films) My Son Is Innocent, 1996, Killing Mr. Griffin, 1997, If These Walls Could Talk 2, 2000. Named one of 21 Hottest Stars Under 21, Teen People mag., 1999. Avocations: reading, boxing. Office: Creative Artists Agy 9830 Wilshire Blvd Beverly Hills CA 90212*

**WILLIAMS, MICHELLE (TENETRIA MICHELLE WILLIAMS),** singer; b. Rockford, Ill., July 23, 1980; Mem. Destiny's Child, 2000—05. Singer: (albums) Heart to Yours, 2002, Do You Know, 2004; singer: (with Destiny's Child) (songs) Say My Name, 2000 (MTV Video Music award, 2000, Grammy Award for best group R&B performance, best R&B song, 2001), (albums) Survivor, 2001 (MTV Video Music award, 2001, Am. Music award, Favorite Pop Album, 2002, Grammy award for best group R&B vocal performance, 2002), 8 Days of Christmas, 2001, Destiny Fulfilled, 2004 (Am. Music award, Favorite R&B Album, 2005); actor: (Broadway plays) Aida, 2002. Recipient Best Female Group, BET, 2001, Favorite R&B Group, Am. Music Awards, 2001, 2002, 2005, Image award for Outstanding Duo or Group, NAACP, 2001, 2005, 2006, Brit award, Best Internat. Group, 2002, World's Best-Selling Group, World Music Awards, 2002, World's Best-Selling Pop Group, 2002, 2006, World's Best-Selling R&B Group, 2002, 2006, Best-Selling Female Group of All Time, 2006. Address: 1505 Hadley Houston TX 77002 Office Phone: 212-833-3000. Office Fax: 713-772-5175.*

**WILLIAMS, MILLER,** retired poet, educator; b. Hoxie, Ark., Apr. 8, 1930; s. Ernest Burdette and Ann Jeanette (Miller) W.; m. Lucille Day, Dec. 29, 1951 (div.); m. Rebecca Jordan Hall, Apr. 11, 1969; children: Lucinda Robert, Karyn. BS, Ark. State Coll., 1951; MS, U. Ark., 1952; postgrad., La. State U., 1951, U. Miss., 1957; HHD (hon.), Lander Coll., 1983; DHL, Hendrix Coll., 1995. Instr. in English La. State U., 1962-63, asst. prof., 1964-66; vis. prof. U. Chile, Santiago, 1963-64; assoc. prof. Loyola U., New Orleans, 1966-70; Fulbright prof. Nat. U. Mex., Mexico City, 1970; co-dir. grad. program in creative writing U. Ark., 1970-84, assoc. prof., 1971-73, prof. English and fgn. langs., dir. program in transl., 1973-87, univ. prof., 1987—2004, dir. poetry-in-the prisons programs div. continuing edn., 1974-

79, chmn. program in comparative lit., 1978-80; ret., 2004. Fellow Am. Acad. in Rome, 1976—, mem. adv. coun. Sch. Classical Studies, 1985-91; first U.S. del. Pan Am. Conf. Univ. Artists and Writers, Concepcion, Chile, 1964; invited del. Internat. Assembly Univ. Press Dirs., Guadalajara, Mex., 1991; mem. poetry staff Bread Loaf Writers Conf., 1967-72; founder, exec. dir. Ark. Poetry Cir., 1975; founding dir. U. Ark. Press, 1980-97; participant Assn. Am. Univ. Presses Soviet Mission, 1989. Author: (poems) A Circle of Stone, 1964, Recital, 1965, So Long At the Fair, 1968, The Only World There Is, 1971; (criticism) The Achievement of John Ciardi, 1968, The Poetry of John Crowe Ransom, 1971; (with John Ciardi) (criticism) How Does a Poem Mean?, 1974; (poems) Halfway From Hoxie: New & Selected Poems, 1973, Why God Permits Evil, 1977, Distractions, 1981, The Boys on Their Bony Mules, 1983; translator: (poems) Poems & Antipoems (Nicanor Parra), 1967, Emergency Poems (Nicanor Parra), 1972, Sonnets of Giuseppe Belli, 1981; editor: (poems) 19 Poetas de Hoy en Los Estados Unidos, 1966, (with John William Corrington) Southern Writing in the Sixties: Poetry, 1967, Southern Writing in the Sixties: Fiction, 1966, Chile: An Anthology of New Writing, 1968, Contemporary Poetry in America, 1972, (with James A. McPherson) Railroad: Trains and Train People in American Culture, 1976, A Roman Collection: An Anthology of Writing about Rome and Italy, 1980, Ozark, Ozark: A Hillside Reader, 1981, (criticism) Patterns of Poetry, 1986, (poetry) Imperfect Love, 1986, Living on the Surface: New and Selected Poems, 1989, Adjusting to the Light, 1992, Points of Departure, 1995, The Ways We Touch, 1997, Some Jazz A While: The Collected Poems, 1999, The Lives of Kevin Fletcher: Stories Mostly Short, 2002, Making a Poem: Some Throughts About Poetry adn the People Who Write It, 2006; poetry editor La. State U. Press, 1966-68; contbr. articles to profl. publs. Named Bread Loaf fellow in poetry, 1963; recipient Henry Bellaman Poetry award, 1957, award in poetry, Arts Fund, 1973, Prix de Rome, Am. Acad. Arts and Letters, 1976, Nat. Poets prize, 1990, Charity Randall citation, Internat. Poetry Forum, 1993, John William Corrington award for excellence in lit., Centenary Coll., Shreveport, La., 1994, Acad. Lit. award, AAAL, 1995, Presdl. Inaugural Poet, 1997. Mem. MLA, PEN, AAUP, South Ctrl. MLA, Am. Lit. Translators Assn. (v.p. 1978-79, pres. 1979-81), Authors' Guild, Soc. Benemerito dell'Assn. Centro Romanesco Trilussa (Rome). Home: 1111 Valley View Dr Fayetteville AR 72701-1603 Personal E-mail: mwms1000@aol.com, mwms1000@cox.net.

**WILLIAMS, MONICA BERNADETTE ELLEN,** jewelry designer; b. Port Jefferson, N.Y., July 5, 1980; d. Bernard Gerard Williams and Monica Ellen Donnelly. BA summa cum laude, SUNY, Stony Brook, 2003; postgrad. in Art History and Criticism, SUNY Stony Brook, 2004—. Jewelry designer, costume jewelry dealer Grandma's Top Drawer Jewelry Boutique, Port Jefferson, 1998—. Mem.: Vintage Fashion and Costume Jewelry, Welcome Inn Soup Kitchen, Sigma Beta, Golden Key, Phi Beta Kappa. Roman Catholic. Personal E-mail: liquidsilver9@att.net.

**WILLIAMS, MONTEL,** television talk show host; m. Rochele See (div.); children: Ashley, Maressa; m. Grace Morley, 1992 (div. 2000); children: Montel, Wyntergrace. Host The Montel Williams Show, 1990—. Actor(TV films): Perry Mason: The Case of the Telltale Talk Show Host, 1993, Educating Matt Waters, 1996, (TV series): A Different World, The New Adventures of Robin Hood, JAG; co-author: Bodychange, 2001; author: A Dozen Ways to Sunday, 2001, Mountain Get Out of My Way; co-author: Climbing Higher, 2004. Recipient Daytime Emmy Award for Outstanding Talk Show Host, 1996. Office: 433 W 53rd St New York NY 10019-5603*

**WILLIAMS, NANCY,** lawyer; b. Kansas City, Mo., Jan. 2, 1945; BS in Journalism, Northwestern U., 1967; JD magna cum laude, U. Wash., 1980. Bar: Wash. 1981, US Ct. Appeals (9th Cir.), US Dist. Ct. (We. Dist.) Wash., US Dist. Ct. (Ea. Dist.) Wash. Volunteer PeaceCorp, 1967—69; pub. info. officer US Dept. Labor, 1973—78; ptnr. Perkins Coie LLP, Seattle, mem. exec. com., chmn. Labor & Employment Practice Area Seattle Office. Co-editor: Washington Employment Law Letter, 1994—; rev. asst. Equal Employment Law Update, 1996, 1997, 1998; contbg. editor: (rev. asst.) Equal Employment Law Update, 2003—, Employment Discrimination Law, 1996. Mem.: ABA (Labor & Litig. Sect.). Office: Perkins Coie LLP 1201 Third Ave Ste 4800 Seattle WA 98101-3099 Office Phone: 206-359-8473. Office Fax: 206-359-9000. Business E-Mail: nwilliams@perkinscoie.com.

**WILLIAMS, NEIL, JR.,** lawyer; b. Charlotte, N.C., Mar. 22, 1936; s. Lyman Neil and Thelma (Peterson) W.; m. Sue Knight, Mar. 23, 1958; children: Fred R., Susan S. AB, Duke U., 1958, JD, 1961. Bar: Ga. 1962, U.S. Dist. Ct. (no. dist.) Ga. 1977, U.S. Ct. Appeals (11th cir.) 1977. Assoc. Alston & Bird (and predecessor firm), Atlanta, 1961—61, ptnr., 1966—99, mng. ptnr., 1984-96; gen. counsel, global ptnr. Amvescap PLC, Atlanta, 1999—2002; ret., 2002. Bd. dir. Printpack, Inc., Atlanta, Acuity Brands, Inc., Atlanta. Chmn. bd. trustees Duke U., 1983—88, trustee, 1980—93; chmn. bd. trustees Vasser Woolley Found., Atlanta, 1975—, Leadership Atlanta, 1976—80; trustee Brevard Music Ctr., 1977—86, 1991—2001, Presbyn. Ch. USA Found., Jeffersonville, Ind., 1983—90, Research Triangle Inst., 1983—88, The Duke Endowment, Charlotte, NC, 1997—, Halle Found., Atlanta, 2005—; bd. dir. Atlanta Symphony Orch., 1970—76, 1984—93, 1995—98, pres., 1988—90; bd. dir. Woodruff Arts Ctr., 1987—98, 1999—, chmn., 2001—; bd. counsellors The Carter Ctr., Atlanta, 1987—96, Ctrl. Atlanta Progress, 1984—96; bd. dir. Am. Symphony Orch. League, Washington, 1990—2000, chmn. 1995—99. Recipient Disting. Alumni award Duke U., 1991, Rhyne award, 1996, Learned Hand award Am. Jewish Com., 2006. Mem. ABA, Am. Bar Found., State Bar Ga., Am. Law Inst., Atlanta C. of C. (bd. dirs. 1992-97, vice chmn. 1994-97), Piedmont Driving Club, Commerce Club (Atlanta), University Club (N.Y.C.), Phi Beta Kappa, Omicron Delta Kappa. Home: 3 Nacoochee Pl NW Atlanta GA 30305-4164 Office: Alston & Bird LLP 1201 W Peachtree St Atlanta GA 30309-3424 Office Phone: 404-881-7883. Business E-Mail: neil.williams@alston.com.

**WILLIAMS, NEVILLE,** solar power corporation executive; b. Muncie, Ind., Mar. 28, 1943; s. Donald Charles and Rose Eileen (Boughton) W. Student, U. Colo., 1964-66, U. Neuchatel, Switzerland, 1967. Freelance corr., Vietnam, 1968-69; freelance journalist Montreal, Que., Can., 1970-71, London, 1971-73; writer, prodr. Sta. WNBC-TV News, NYC, 1973-74; freelance writer Telluride, Colo., 1975-79; media liaison Office of Solar Energy U.S. Dept. Energy, Washington, 1979-80; dir. of mktg. Telluride Ski Resort, Inc., 1981-83; owner, operator Hist. Sheridan Opera House, Telluride, 1983-85; nat. media dir. Greenpeace USA, Washington, 1987-89; chmn. exec. dir., founder Solar Electric Light Fund, Washington, 1990—97. Chmn., CEO, founder Solar Electric Light Co., 1997-2003; chmn. SELCO-India, 1995-2005; founder, chmn. Standard Solar, Inc. Author: The New Exiles, 1971, Chasing the Sun, 2005, (monograph) Great Telluride Strike, 1977; contbr. articles to NY Times mag., Penthouse, Outside, New Times, The Nation, The New Republic, Nature, Solar Today; others. Apptd. mem. Adv. Com. for Commerce and Devel., State of Colo., 1980-85; apptd. mem. Gov.'s Motion Picture & TV Commn., 1981-85. Recipient Corp. Excellence award, U.S. Dept. of State, 2001. Fellow Internat. Solar Energy Soc. Business E-Mail: neville@standardsolar.com.

**WILLIAMS, NIAMA LESLIE JOANN,** writer, educator; b. L.A., Mar. 25, 1962; d. Lewis Oscar and Lessie Beatrice W., Marian Claudette W. (Stepmother). B in Comparative Lit., Occidental Coll., 1985; MA in Profl. Writing, U. So. Calif., 1991; MA in African Am. studies, Temple U., 1994; postgrad., 2005. Tchg. asst. African-Am. studies Temple U., Phila., 1993—94; Frederick Douglass tchg. fellow West Chester U., Pa., 1998; adj. prof. English Temple U., 2004—. Adj. prof. English Camden County Coll., 1995—96, C.C. Phila., 1995—97, LaSalle U., Phila., 1997; hourly instr. West L.A. Coll., Culver City, Calif., 2000—03, L.A. Trade-Tech. Coll., 2000—02; part-time instr. Loyola Marymount U., L.A., 2000—01. Author: poems (Hon. Mention, Rhyming Poem Category, Writers Digest Competition, 2000, Hon. Mention Rhyming Poem Category, Writers Digest Competition, 2004), short stories; contbr. articles. Career day presenter, writing and libraries Bret Harte Prep. Mid. Sch., L.A., 1992, 2002; career day guest poet Westwood Elem. Sch., L.A.,

2002. Recipient honorable mention in non-rhyming category, Writers Digest competition, 2004. Mem.: E-drum, Creative Writers Opportunities List, Internat. Black Writers and Artists. Democrat.

**WILLIAMS, NIKKIA SEKEENA,** science educator; b. Norfolk, Va., Jan. 23, 1980; d. Walter Alfonso and Deborah Skyles; m. Ryan Levar Williams, June 19, 2004. A in Edn., BS in Biology, Norfolk State U., 2003. Tchr. sci. Suffolk Pub. Schs./ Turlington Woods Sch., Va., 2003—. Drug free liaison Suffolk Pub. Schs., Va., 2004—. Dir. prodr. (play/performance) Black History Month Program. Tutor First Bapt. Ch. South Hill, Chesapeake, Va., 2005. Named Rookie Tchr. of the Yr., Suffolk Pub. Schs./ Turlington Woods Schs., 2004. Baptist. Avocations: singing/music, travel. Office: Suffolk Pub Schs 629 Turlington Rd Suffolk VA 23434 Office Phone: 757-925-5525. Office Fax: 757-925-5583. Personal E-mail: ryanandnikkia@aol.com. E-mail: nikwilliams@spsk12.net.

**WILLIAMS, NOEL BROWN,** information technology executive; CIO Am. Svc. Group, Tenn.; with HCA-Hosp. Corp. of Am. Info. Svcs., 1979—93; v.p. info. svcs. HCA Information Svcs., 1993—95; cons., 1995—96; chief info. officer Am. Svc. Group/ Prison Health Svcs., Inc., 1996—97; sr. v.p., chief info. officer HCA Inc., Nashville, 1997—. Office: HCA Inc One Park Pl Nashville TN 37203

**WILLIAMS, O'BANION, III,** lawyer; b. Houston, 1956; BA, Tex. Tech. U., 1979; JD, St. Mary's U. Sch. Law, 1983. Bar: Tex. 1983. Ptnr., Energy Transactions, Real Estate Andrews Kurth LLP, Houston, treas., Lawyers for Am. Com. Sr. assoc. editor St. Mary's Law Jour. Mem.: Houston Bar Assn., State Bar Tex., ABA, Phi Delta Phi. Office: Andrews Kurth LLP 600 Travis Ste 4200 Houston TX 77002-3090 Office Phone: 713-220-4340. Office Fax: 713-238-7147. Business E-Mail: owilliams@andrews-kurth.com.

**WILLIAMS, OLIVER FRANKLIN,** priest, educator; b. West Orange, N.J., Dec. 4, 1939; s. Justin James Williams and Ruth Amelda Flammer. BS in Chem. Engring., U. Notre Dame, 1961, MTh, 1969; PhD, Vanderbilt U. 1974. Prof. U. Notre Dame, Ind., 1973—, dir. MDiv program Ind., 1974—77, assoc. provost Ind., 1987—94, dir. Ctr. for Ethics and Religious Values in Bus. Ind., 1994—. Chmn. bd. Leadership Devel. Program U.S. - South Africa, Washington, 1995—2004; mem. adv. coun. U.S. Cos. in South Africa (Sullivan Principles), 1997—1994; trustee St. Augustine's U., Johannesburg, 1996—; bd. dirs. UN Global Compact Learning Forum Academic Network, 2002—; vis. prof. U. Cape Town, Stellenbosch U., 2003—; bd. dirs. Found. for UN Global Compact, 2006—. Co-author: Economic Imperatives and Ethical Values, 2001; author: The Apartheid Crisis, 1986; editor, contbr.: Global Codes of Conduct: An Idea Whose Time Has Come, Business, Religion and Spirituality: A New Synthesis, 2003. Bd. dirs. Edn. Africa, Johannesburg, 1993, Catholic Charities, Diocese of Fort Wayne, South Bend, 1986—92, King's Coll., Pa., 2004—. Recipient Charles C. Slater Meml. award, Jour. Macromarketing, 1992. Mem.: Assn. for Practical and Profl. Ethics, Soc. for Bus. Ethics, Acad. Mgmt. (chair social issues divsn. 1990—91). Roman Catholic. Avocations: hiking, travel, writing. Home: 400 Siegfried Hall Notre Dame IN 46556 Office: U of Notre Dame 255 Mendoza Coll Bus Notre Dame IN 46556 Office Phone: 574-631-5761 x 6072. Business E-Mail: williams.80@nd.edu.

**WILLIAMS, PATRICIA ANNE,** philosopher, writer; b. Alexanderia, Va., May 26, 1944; d. Samuel Leonard and Kay Cloaninger Williams. BA, Coll.William and Mary, 1966; MA in English, U. Va., 1967, MA in Philosophy, 1985; PhD, U. Guelph, 1989. Lectr. La Trobe U., Melbourne, Victoria, Australia, 1968—71; asst. prof. Va. State U., Petersburg, 1990—95. Del. Citizen Amb. People to People Program, China, 1993. Author: (book) Doing without Adam and Eve: Sociobiology and Original Sin, 2001 (Outstanding Acad. Title award Choice Mag., 2002), Where Christianity Went Wrong, When, and What You Can Do About It, 2001, Hazardous Engagement: God Makes a Friend, 2006; editor: Evolution and Human Values, 1995, (Jour.) Universalist Friends, 2005-; contbr. articles to profl. jours. and encys. Mem. ACLU, 1973—; charter mem. U.S. Holocaust Meml. Mus., Washington, 1993—; mem. So. Poverty Law Ctr. Wall of Toleration, Montgomery. Fellow, Westar Inst., 2005—; NEH fellow, 1989. Fellow: Quaker Universalist; mem.: Inst. on Religion in an Age of Sci., Internat. Soc. for History, Philosophy, and Social Studies of Biology (program chmn. 1992—93), Philosophy of Sci. Assn., Am. Philos. Assn., Friends Assn. Higher Edn. Mem. Soc. Of Friends. Avocations: travel, hiking. Home: PO Box 69 Covesville VA 22931 Personal E-mail: theologyauthor@aol.com.

**WILLIAMS, PATRICIA J.,** law educator; b. Boston, 1951; BA, Wellesley Coll, 1972; JD, Harvard Univ, 1975. Bar: Calif, US Ct Appeals, 9th cir. Dep. city atty. LA City Atty. Office, 1976—78; atty. Western Ctr. on Law & Poverty, LA, 1978—80; asst. prof. Golden Gate Coll., 1980—84, assoc. prof., 1984—85, CUNY, 1984—88; prof. Univ. Wis., Madison, 1988—93, Columbia U., NYC, 1991—; James L. Dohr prof. law. Trustee Wellesley Coll. Columnist The Nation; author: The Alchemy of Race & Rights, 1991, The Rooster's Egg: On the Persistence of Prejudice, 1995, Seeing a Color-Blind Future: The Paradox of Race, 1997. Grantee MacArthur Fellowship, 2000. Office: Columbia Law Sch 435 W 116th St New York NY 10027-7297 E-mail: williams@law.columbia.edu.

**WILLIAMS, PAUL,** retired federal agency administrator; b. Jacksonville, Ill., Aug. 6, 1929; s. Russell and Bernice (Wheeler) W.; m. Ora B. Mosby; 1 child, Reva Williams. BA, Ill. Coll., 1956, LHD, 1980. Dir. fin. City of Chgo., 1956-63; assoc. dir. fin. United Planning Orgn., Washington, 1964-65; internat. admnistry. officer U.S. Dept. State, Washington, 1965-68; dir. office mgmt. U.S. HUD, Washington, 1968-93, gen. dep. dept. fair housing and equal opportunity, 1993-94, dep. ops. and mgmt., 1994-97, ret., 1997. Cons. S.E. Econ. Devel. Corp., nat. Exec. Svc. Corp., 1998; Buzan learning instr. for mind mapping, 2000-2002. Author: Questionnaire on Execution of Urban Renewal Programs, 1959. Pres. Bel Pre Civic Assn., Wheaton, Md., 1978, bd. dirs., 1971, 79; pres. Bel Pre PTA, Wheaton, 1973, Rossmoor Kiwanis Club, 2002, Rossmore Kiwanis Found., 2004-05; bd. dirs. Rockville C. of C., African Am. C. of C. Sgt. U.S. Army, 1948-52. Recipient letter of recognition for 36 yrs. fed. svc. U.S. Pres., letter of recognition for 36 yrs. govt. svc. Senators of Md., citation for 36 yrs. dedicated govt. svc. Gov. of Md., cert. of recognition Nat. Assn. Black and Minority C. of C., 1987. Baptist. Avocations: reading, jogging, golf, tai chi. Home: Unit 306 2900 N LeisureWorld Blvd Silver Spring MD 20906-2321 Office Phone: 301-598-2899. Personal E-mail: owilli7738@aol.com.

**WILLIAMS, PAUL DAVID,** mathematics professor; m. Rebecca Ann Williams; 1 child, Kristin Ann. EdD, U. Pitts., 1980. Prof. math and computer sci. dept. California U. Pa., 1986—, math lab dir., 1986—. Contbr. articles to profl. jours. Judge Pa. Jr. Acad. Sci., California, 1986—2006. Perkins Vocat. Edn. grantee, 1986—94. Mem.: State Sys. Higher Edn. Math. Assn. (vice chair, chair 1990—94), Nat. Coun. Tchrs. Math. Office: Math and Computer Science Dept California University of Pennsylvania California PA 15419 Office Phone: 724-938-5894.

**WILLIAMS, PAUL ROBERT,** lawyer, foreign policy analyst; b. Pasadena, Calif., June 3, 1965; s. Robert David and Janice Martha W.; m. Kathleen Elizabeth, June 3, 1965, July 24, 1964. AB in Polit. Sci., U. Calif. Davis, 1987; JD, Stanford U., 1990; PhD, U. Cambridge, 1997. Bar: Calif. 1990. Law clk. to Justice William H. Erickson Colo. Supreme Ct., Denver, 1990-91; atty., adviser U.S. State Dept. Office of Legal Adviser, Washington, 1991-93; Fulbright Rsch. scholar U. Cambridge, 1993-96; exec. dir. Pub. Internat. Law and Policy Group, 1994—; sr. assoc. Carnegie Endowment for Internat. Peace, 1996—. Author: Treatment of Detainees, 1990; contbr. articles to profl. jours. Nominee Nobel Peace Prize, 2005. Mem. ABA, Am. Soc. Internat. Law. Lutheran. Home: 6908 Fairfax Dr Unit 300 Arlington VA 22213-1021*

**WILLIAMS, PAUL STRATTON,** lawyer; b. San Francisco, Oct. 9, 1959; s. Henry Stratton and Frances (Spurlock) W.; m. Laura Dawn Coleman, Sept. 15, 1984; children: Scott Coleman, Ryan Stratton. AB, Harvard Coll., 1981; JD, Yale U., 1984. Bar: Calif. 1984, Ohio 1987. Assoc. Gibson, Dunn & Crutcher, LA, 1984-87, Vorys, Sater, Seymour & Pease, Columbus, Ohio, 1987-90; gen. counsel Info. Dimensions, Inc., Dublin, Ohio, 1994-95; v.p., asst. gen. counsel Cardinal Health, Inc., 1995—99, sr. v.p., dep. gen. counsel, 2000—01, exec. v.p., chief legal off. and sec., 2001—. Bd. dir. State Auto Fin. Corp. Mem. ABA, Ohio Bar Assn., Columbus Bar Assn., Harvard Club Central Ohio, Yale Club Central Ohio. Democrat. Avocations: running, tennis. Office: Cardinal Health Inc 7000 Cardinal Pl Dublin OH 43017-1092 Office Phone: 614-717-7768, 614-757-5000.

**WILLIAMS, PEARL See GOOD, EDITH**

**WILLIAMS, PEGGY RYAN,** academic administrator; b. Montreal, Que., Can., May 27, 1947; d. Fred Smith and Carol (Kennedy) Ryan; m. David A. Williams, May 30, 1970. BA psychology, U. Toronto, St. Michael's Coll., Can., 1968; MEd, U. Vt., 1976; EdD, Harvard U. 1983. Caseworker, children's svcs. Monroe County Dept. Social Svcs., Rochester, NY, 1968-72; med. social worker Med. Ctr. Hosp. of Vt., Burlington, 1972; coord. instrn, academic advisor CC of Vt., Lamoille County, 1973—75, project dir. Northwestern Vt., 1975—76, regional dir. Montpelier, 1976-82; part-time instr. C.C. Vt., 1978—85; asst. to the pres. Johnson (Vt.) State Coll., summer 1981; tchg. fellow Harvard U., 1981; dir. ednl. and pers. svcs., office of chancellor Vt. State Colleges, Waterbury, 1982-85; assoc. prof. Trinity Coll., Burlington, 1985—89, chair, dept. bus & economics, 1985-88, assoc. acad. dean, 1988-89; pres. Lyndon State Coll., Lyndonville, Vt., 1989-97, Ithaca (N Y) Coll, 1997—; dir. Coun. Ind. Colls. Adj. faculty Johnson State Coll., 1984—86. Active The Ithaca Downtown Partnership Cmty. Adv. Bd.; bd. mem. Sacred Heart Sch. Montreal, bd. chair, 1998—2001; bd. mem. Tompkins Trust Co., 1999—; com. mem. Cornell U. Johnson Mus. Art Cmty. Adv. Coun.; mem. adv. coun. Finger Lakes Land Trust, 2000—03. Recipient Jackie M. Gibbons Leadership award, Am. Coun. Edn./Nat. Identification Program, 1984, Margaret R. Williams Emerging Profl. award. Mem. Am. Assn. Higher Edn., 1973-, Am. Coun. on Edn., 1981- (bd. dirs., 2000-), Nat. Assn. Women in Edn., 1985-, Office: Ithaca Coll Job Hall Ithaca NY 14850

**WILLIAMS, PETRA SCHATZ,** antiquarian, director; b. Poughkeepsie, N.Y., Sept. 2, 1913; d. Grover Henry and Mayme Nickerson (Bullock) Schatz; m. J. Calvert Williams, Nov. 26, 1946; children: Miranda, Frederica, Valerie. AB, Skidmore Coll., 1936; JD, Fordham U., 1940. Founder Fountain House, Phoenix, 1953, Fountain House East, Jefferstontown, Ky., 1966. Author: Flow Blue China, An Aid to Identification, 1971, Flow Blue China II, 1973, Flow Blue China and Mulberry Ware, 1975, Staffordshire Romantic Transfer Patterns, 1979, Staffordshire III Romantic Transfer Patterns, 1986, L'Envoi, 1998. Past pres. Meml. Hosp. Aux., Phoenix, Heard Mus. Guild, Phoenix; bd. dirs. Ky. Humane Soc. Mem. Nat. Soc. Interior Designers: nat. dir. for Ariz. 1957-58, Ky. 1968, pres. Ky. 1967-68), DAR, Ky. Hist. Soc., Flow Blue Internat. Collectors Club (hon.). Clubs: Filson. Mem. Soc. Of Friends. Address: PO Box 99298 Jefferstontown KY 40269-0298

**WILLIAMS, PHARRELL,** music producer, arranger, vocalist; b. Virginia Beach, Va., Apr. 5, 1974; Music prodr., performer (with Chad Hugo) The Neptunes; prodr., performer, group mem. N.E.R.D. Prodr. for artists including Jay-Z, LL Cool J, Britney Spears, Kelis, No Doubt, Bow Wow, Toni Braxton, Snoop Dogg, Busta Rhymes, N'Sync, Mystikal, Ol' Dirty Bastard, Usher, Nelly, and many others, singer, prodr., with the Neptunes (albums) Neptunes Present...Clones, 2003; singer: (albums) (with N.E.R.D.) In Search of..., 2002, Fly or Die, 2004, (songs) Lapdance, 2001, Rock Star, 2002, Live in Paradiso, 2003, She Wants to Move, 2004, (with Jay-Z) Frontin', 2003; background vocals with Justin Timberlake (songs) Rock Your Body, 2002, background vocals with Jay-Z Change Clothes, 2003. Recipient Songwriter of Yr., BMI, 2001, 2002, Prodr. of Yr., Source Awards, 2002, 2003, R&B and Hip Hop Best Prodr. award, Billboard, 2003, Urban Prodr. of Yr., BMI, 2003, Prodr. of Yr. (Neo-Classical), Grammys, 2003. Achievements include selling first song with Chad Hugo, "Rump Shaker," to Wreckx N Effect while still in high school in 1992; signing with Chad Hugo Star Trak Entertainment label to Arista Records in 2002.

**WILLIAMS, PHILIP COPELAIN,** gynecologist, obstetrician; b. Vicksburg, Miss., Dec. 9, 1917; s. John Oliver and Eva (Copelain) W.; B.S. magna cum laude, Morehouse Coll., 1937; M.D., U. Ill., 1941; m. Constance Shielda Rhetta, May 29, 1943; children— Philip, Susan Carol, Paul Rhetta. Intern, Cook County Hosp., Chgo., 1942-43, resident in ob-gyn, 1946-48; resident in gynecology U. Ill., 1948-49; practice medicine specializing in ob-gyn, Chgo., 1949—; mem. staff St. Joseph Hosp., Ill. Masonic Hosp., Cook County Hosp., McGaw Hosp.; clin. prof. Med. Sch. Northwestern U., Chgo. Bd. dirs. Am. Cancer Soc. Chgo. unit and Ill. div. Served with U.S. Army, 1943-45. Recipient Civic award Loyola U., 1970; Edwin S. Hamilton Interstate Teaching award, 1984; diplomate Am. Bd. Ob-Gyn, Fellow ACS, Internat. Coll. Surgeons; mem. AMA, Chgo., Ill. med. socs., AMA, Chgo. Gynecol. Soc. (treas. 1975-78, pres. 1980-81), Am. Fertility Soc., Inst. Medicine, N.Y. Acad. Scis., AAAS. Presbyn. Clubs: Barclay, Carlton, Plaza. Contbr. articles to profl. jours. E-mail: pwill2oo@aol.com. Home: 1040 N Lake Shore Dr Chicago IL 60611 E-mail: pwill200@sbcglobal.net.

**WILLIAMS, PHYLLIS CUTFORTH,** retired realtor; b. Moreland, Idaho, June 6, 1917; d. William Claude and Kathleen Jessie (Jenkins) Cutforth; m. Joseph Marsden Williams, Jan. 21, 1938 (dec. 1986); children: Joseph Marlis, Bonnie Lou Williams Thompson, Nancy Kay Williams Stewart, Marjorie Williams Karren, Douglas Claude, Thomas Marsden, Wendy Kathleen Williams Clark, Shannon Irene Williams Ostler. Grad., Ricks Coll., 1935. Tchr. Grace (Idaho) Elem. Sch. 1935-38: realtor Williams Realty, Idaho Falls, Idaho, 1972-77; mem. Idaho Senate, Boise, 1977. Owner, mgr. river property. Compiler: Idaho Legisladies Cookbook, Cookin' Together, 1981. With MicroFilm Ctr., LDS Ch. Mission, Salt Lake City, 1989-90; former block chmn., vol. Cancer Drive; active Idaho State Legisladies Club, 1966-84, v.p., 1982-84; mem. Bonneville County (Idaho) Rep. Women. Avocations: genealogy, music, politics, cooking, attending grandchildren's special events.

**WILLIAMS, QUINN PATRICK,** lawyer; b. Evergreen Park, Ill., May 6, 1949; s. William Albert and Jeanne Marie (Quinlan) W.; children: Michael Ryan, Mark Reed, Kelly Elizabeth. BBA, U. Wis., 1972; JD, U. Ariz., 1974. Bar: Ariz. 1975, N.Y. 1984, U.S. Dist. Ct. Ariz. 1976. V.p., sec., gen. counsel Combined Comm. Corp., Phoenix, 1975-80; sr. v.p. legal and adminstrn. Swensen's Inc., Phoenix, 1980-86; ptnr. Winston & Strawn, Phoenix, 1985—89, Snell & Wilmer, Phoenix, 1989—2002; shareholder Greenberg Traurig, 2002—; pres. Enterprise network, 2001. Bd. dirs. Ariz. Tech. Coun., 2001—, Ariz. Venture Capital Conf., 1993-2000; co-chmn. Gov.'s Small Bus. Advocate Exec. Coun., 1993—; chair, bd. dirs. Greater Phoenix Econ. Coun., 1996-2000; vice-chair Gov. Regulatory Coun., 1995-97; sec. GSPED High Tech. Cluster, 1993—; mem. Gov.'s Coun. on Innovation and Tech., 2003—; exec. com. A2Tech Coun., 2002—. With USAF, 1967-73. Mem. ABA, State Bar Ariz., Maricopa County Bar Assn., N.Y. Bar Assn., Internat. Franchise Assn., Scottsdale C. of C. (bd. dirs.), Paradise Valley Country Club, Scottsdale Charros. Office: Greenberg Traurig 2375 E Camelback Rd Ste 700 Phoenix AZ 85016-9000 Office Phone: 602-445-8344. Business E-Mail: williamsq@gtlaw.com.

**WILLIAMS, RALPH CHESTER, JR.,** physician, educator; b. Washington, Feb. 17, 1928; s. Ralph Chester and Annie (Perry) W.; m. Mary Elizabeth Adams, June 23, 1951; children: Cathy, Frederick (dec.), John (dec.), Michael, Ann AB with distinction, Cornell U., 1950, MD, 1954; MD (hon.), U. Lund, Sweden, 1991. Diplomate Am. Bd. Internal Medicine. Intern Mass. Gen. Hosp., Boston, 1954-55, asst. resident in internal medicine, 1955-56; resident in internal medicine N.Y. Hosp., 1956-57; chief resident Mass. Gen. Hosp., Boston, 1959-60; guest investigator Rockefeller Inst., N.Y.C., 1961-63; physician in internal medicine and rheumatology, 1963—; assoc. prof. U.

Minn., Mpls., 1963-68, prof., 1968-69; prof., chmn. dept. medicine U. N.Mex., Albuquerque, 1969-88; Schott prof. rheumatology and medicine U. Fla., Gainesville, 1988-98; with rheumatology dept. U. N.Mex. Sch. Medicine, Albuquerque, 1998, emeritus prof. medicine, 1998—. Assoc. editor: Jour. Lab. and Clin. Medicine, 1966-69; mem. editl. bd.: Arthritis and Rheumatism, 1966—; contbr. articles to profl. jours. Capt. USAF, 1957—59. Recipient Regents' Meritorious Svc. award, U. N.Mex., 2003. Master Am. Coll. Rheumatology (Gold medal 2004); fellow ACP; mem. Am. Assn. Immunology, Assn. Am. Physicians, Am. Fedn. Clin. Rsch., Am. Soc. Clin. Investigation, Ctrl. Soc. Clin. Rsch., Western Soc. Clin. Investigation, Phi Beta Kappa, Alpha Omega Alpha. Achievements include research in immunologic processes and connective tissue diseases. Home: 624 E Alameda St Apt 13 Santa Fe NM 87501-2293 Personal E-mail: coolypatch22@aol.com.

**WILLIAMS, RALPH WATSON, JR.,** retired security firm executive; b. Atlanta, July 2, 1933; s. Ralph Watson and Minnie Covington (Hicks) W.; m. Nancy Jo Morgan, Mar. 19, 1955 (dec. Dec. 1989); children: Ralph Watson III, Nancy Jane, John Martin Hicks; m. Almonese Brown Clifton, Nov. 24, 1990. Grad., Sewanee Mil. Acad., 1951; BBA, U. Ga., 1955. Trainee banking Trust Co. Ga., Atlanta, 1955; mcpl. sales staff Courts & Co., Atlanta, 1955-57; v.p., salesman securities First Southeastern Corp., Atlanta, 1957-60; br. mgr. Francis I. duPont & Co., 1960-69; spl. partner duPont Glore Forgan Inc., N.Y.C., 1969-70, gen. partner, 1970, exec. v.p., 1971—, sr. v.p., 1972—; also dir.; sr. v.p., dir., mem. exec. com. duPont-Walston Inc., 1973-74; sr. v.p. E.F. Hutton & Co. Inc., 1974-81; exec. v.p., dir. E.F. Hutton & Co., Inc., 1981-88; exec. v.p. Shearson Lehman Hutton Inc., Atlanta, 1988-89; ret., 1989. Former bd. trustees, chmn. fin. com. St. Andrews Sewanee (Tenn.) Sch. Mem. Nat. Assn. Security Dealers (chmn. dist. com. 7), Benedicts Atlanta, Phi Delta Theta. Clubs: Commerce (Atlanta), Capital City (Atlanta), Piedmont Driving (Atlanta). Presbyterian. Home: 3504 Dumbarton Rd NW Atlanta GA 30327-2614 Home Fax: 404-237-1812. Personal E-mail: ralphnesie@comcast.net.

**WILLIAMS, REBA WHITE,** corporate financial executive, writer, researcher; m. Dave H. Williams. BA in Enlgish, Duke U., Durham, N.C.; MBA, Harvard U., Cambridge, Mass.; MA in Art History, Hunter Coll., N.Y.C.; MA in Philosophy, CUNY, PhD in Art History. Former rschr. McKinsey & Co., Inc.; securities analyst Mitchell Hutchins, Inc. Dir. spl. projects, mem. bd. dir. Alliance Capital Mgmt.; vice chmn. White Williams Holdings, Ltd., 2001—. Mem. editl. bd. Print Quar.; contbr. articles to Am. Artist, Bus. and Soc., Instl. Investor Chgo. Daily News, Fin. Analysts Jour., others; author catalog essays. Mem. Manhattan Cmty. Bd. 8, 1999-2000; mem. Art Commn. City NY, 1995-98, pres., 1997-98; mem. NY State Coun. on the Arts, 1996-99, vice chmn., 1999; hon. keeper of Am. prints The Fitzwilliam Mus., Cambridge, Eng. Decorated Polish Order of Merit, cavalier of grand cross Order of Poland 1st class; recipient Pacesetter award NY City Coun., 1999, Disting. Cultural Leadership award NY Rep. County Com., 1999, Augustus Graham medal Bklyn. Mus., 1998; named one of Top 200 Collectors, ARTnews Mag., 2004, 2006, others. Mem. Cosmopolitan Club. Avocation: Collector of Am. Prints. Office: 258 Atlantic St Stamford CT 06901 Office Phone: 212-752-1705. Business E-Mail: reba@rebawhitewilliams.com.

**WILLIAMS, REDFORD BROWN,** medical educator; b. Raleigh, NC, Dec. 14, 1940; s. Redford Brown Sr. and Annie Virginia (Betts) W.; m. Virginia Carter Parrott, August 9, 1940; children: Jennifer Betts, Lloyd Carter. AB, Harvard U., 1963; MD, Yale U., 1967. Diplomate Am. Bd. Internal Medicine. Intern, then resident Yale-New Haven Med. Ctr., 1967-70; sr. surgeon USPHS, Bethesda, Md., 1970-72; asst. prof. Duke U. Med. Ctr., Durham, NC, 1972, prof. psychiatry, 1977—, prof. psychology, 1990—, dir. behavioral medicine rsch. ctr., 1985—; CEO Williams LifeSkills, Inc., 1997—. Cons. NIH rev. coms., Bethesda, 1977—. Author: The Trusting Heart, 1989, Anger Kills, 1993, Lifeskills, 1998, In Control, 2006; contbr. articles to profl. jours. Dir. NC Heart Assn., Chapel Hill, 1980-83. Recipient Rsch. Scientist award NIMH, 1974—; NIH grantee, 1976—. Fellow Soc. Behavioral Medicine (pres. 1984-85, Upjohn Disting. Scientist award 1992), Acad. Behavioral Medicine Rsch. (pres. 1995—); mem. Am. Psychosomatic Soc. (bd. dirs. 1978-81, pres. 1992), Internat. Soc. Behavioral Medicine (pres.-elect 2004-06, pres. 2006-08). Unitarian Universalist. Avocation: tennis. Office: Duke U Med Ctr PO Box 3926 Durham NC 27710-0001 Office Phone: 919-684-3863. Business E-Mail: redfordw@duke.edu.

**WILLIAMS, RICHARD CHARLES,** computer programmer, consultant; b. Boston, Dec. 25, 1955; s. Richard Clayton and Nancy Karolyn (Kerr) W. BA, SUNY, New Paltz, 1991. Cert. in software engring. Programmer/cons. Shared Ednl. Computing, Poughkeepsie, NY, 1976-78; systems programmer, comms. mgr. Cornell U. Med. Sch., N.Y.C., 1978-79; staff programmer IBM Corp. Hdqrs., White Plains, NY, 1979-84; systems programmer IBM Data. Systems Div., Poughkeepsie, 1984-86; adv. programmer IBM Network Systems, White Plains, 1986-89; open systems cons. IBM Large Systems, Kingston, NY, 1989-95; sr. R/3 basis architect, cert. SAP cons. IBM-SAP Competency Ctr., Phila., 1996-97; sr. architect, 1997—. Cons. IBM Hudson Valley Fed. Credit Union, Poughkeepsie, 1986—, C-Net, Broomfield, Colo., 1988-89, Toastmasters Bd. Dirs., Santa Ana, Calif., 1987, Landmark Edn., N.Y.C., 1989—. Author: Lasting Legacy, 1987; co-author: Migrating to TSO from VSPC, 1986; inventor, patentee. Bd. dirs. Hudson Valley FCU, 1995-2001, 2d vice chair, 1996-97, 1st vice-chair, 1997—; bd. dirs. SUNY Alumni Bd. Named one of Outstanding Young Men of Am., 1985, VoL. of Yr., NA-CUSAC, 1995. Mem. IEEE, ACM, SUNY Alumni Assn. (bd. dirs. 1994-99), Poughkeepsie Toastmasters Internat. (chpt. pres. 1982, dist. gov. 1985, Toastmaster of Yr. 1984), Open Online Transactional Programming Users Group (planning bd. 1995-97). Democrat. Methodist. Avocations: skiing, community organizing, travel. SAP Neurottstrasse 16 D-69190 Walldorf Germany Home: 1105 Toedli Dr Boulder CO 80305-8524

**WILLIAMS, RICHARD DWAYNE,** physician, educator, urologist; b. Wichita, Kans., Oct. 7, 1944; s. Errol Wayne and Roseanna Jane (Page) W.; m. Beverly Sue Ferguson, Aug. 29, 1964; 1 child, Wendy Elizabeth. BS, Abilene Christian U., 1966; MD, Kans. U., 1970. Diplomate Am. Bd. Urology, Nat. Bd. Med. Examiners. Intern, then resident in gen. surgery U. Minn., Mpls., 1970-72, resident in urology, 1972-76, asst. prof., 1976-79, U. Calif., San Francisco, 1979-84, assoc. prof., 1984—; prof., chmn. dept. urology U. Iowa, Iowa City, 1984—. Chief urology VA Med. Ctr., San Francisco, 1979-84, VA Med. Ctr., Iowa City, 1984-88; mem. task force on bd. exams Am. Bd. Urology, 1981-85, guest examiner Oral exams, 1984-, trustee, 1994-2000; Rubin H. Flocks chair in urology U. Iowa, 1994; mem. nat. adv. coun. NIDDK, NIH. Author: (with others) Advances in Urologic Oncology, 1987, Genitourinary Cancer: Basic and Clinical Aspects, 1987, Adult and Pediatric Urology, 1987, General Urology, 1988, Textbook of Medicine, 1988, also others; editor: Advances in Urologic Oncology, 1987; guest editor Seminars in Urology, 1985, Problems in Urology: Prostate Cancer, 1989; bd. editors Jour. Urology, 1980-88; mem. editorial bd. Urology, Jour. Urology; also articles. Bd. dirs. Iowa chpt. Nat. Kidney Found., 1985; bd. advisors 1989-92; pres. Am. Found. Urologic Diseases, 2003-05. Maj. USAR, 1971-77. Bordeau scholar Kans. U. Med. Ctr., 1968-69; NIH, VA, Am. Cancer Soc. grantee. Fellow ACS (chmn. urology sect. No. Calif. chpt. 1980-82, chmn ann. meeting programs 1988, mem. residency rev. com. urology 1993-99, vice chair 1995, chair 1997); mem. AAAS, Iowa Med. Soc., Iowa Urologic Soc., Am. Urologic Assn. (dir. seminar on residency evaluation 1987, bd. editors alt. 1988-, rep. North Ctrl. sect., prodr. slide presentation 1988, recipient prizes 1982, 87, com. mem. 1987-, bd. dirs. 1994, pres.-elect 1997), Am. Assn. for Cancer Rsch. Am. Soc. Clin. Oncology, Am. Assn. GU Surgeons, Clin. Soc. Genitourinary Surgeons (sec.-treas. 1997-2000), Am. Soc. Internat. D'Urologie (pres. US sect. 2003-06), Soc. Univ. Urologists (chmn. com. on residency evaluation 1986-88, councillor 1987-, pres. 1993), Soc. Surg. Oncology, Soc. Urologic Oncology (chmn. membership com. 1987-90, sec. 1990-94, pres.-elect 1995, pres. 1996), Johnson County Med. Soc., Flock's Soc., Western Urologic Forum, Alpha Omega Alpha. Republican. Office: U Iowa Dept Urology 200 Hawkins Dr Iowa City IA 52242-1009 Office Phone: 319-356-0760. Business E-Mail: richard-williams@uiowa.edu.

**WILLIAMS, RICHARD LEROY,** federal judge; b. Morrisville, Va., Apr. 6, 1923; s. Wilcie Edward and Minnie Mae (Brinkley) W.; m. Eugenia Kellogg, Sept. 11, 1948; children: Nancy Williams Davies, R. Gregory, Walter L., Gwendolyn Mason. LLB, U. Va., 1951. Bar: Va. 1951. Ptnr. McGuire, Woods & Battle and predecessor firms, 1951-72; judge Cir. Ct. City of Richmond, 1972-76; ptnr. McGuire, Woods & Battle, 1976-80; dist. judge U.S. Dist. Ct., Richmond, Va., 1980—, sr. judge, 1992—. 2d lt. Air Corps., U.S. Army, 1940-45. Fellow Am. Coll. Trial Lawyers; mem. Va. State Bar, Va. Bar Assn., Richmond Bar Assn. Office: US Dist Ct/Lewis F Powell Ste 305 1000 E Main St Richmond VA 23219-3525 Office Phone: 804-916-2240.

**WILLIAMS, RICHARD LUCAS, III,** electronics executive, director, lawyer; b. Evanston, Ill., Oct. 30, 1940; s. Richard Lucas Jr. and Ellen Gene (Munster) W.; m. Karen Louise Carmody, Nov. 11, 1967 AB, Princeton U., 1962; LLB, U. Va., 1965. Bar: Ill. 1965, D.C. 1968, U.S. Supreme Ct. 1968. Assoc. Winston & Strawn, Chgo., 1968-74, ptnr., 1974-79; sr. v.p., gen. counsel Gould Inc., Rolling Meadows, Ill., 1979-81, sr. v.p., adminstrn., gen. counsel, 1981-90, also bd. dir., 1985-88; ptnr. Smith Williams and Lodge, Chgo., 1990-95, Vedder, Price, Kaufman & Kammholz, Chgo., 1995—. Bd. dirs. GNB Batteries, Inc., 1984-86, ULINE Inc., Waukegan, Ill. Bd. dirs. 1990—, Internat. Tennis Hall of Fame, Newport, R.I., 1993-97; v.p. Chgo. Dist. Tennis Assn., 1968-70; vice chmn. Am. Cancer Soc., Chgo., 1984; bd. dirs., pres. Lake Shore Found. for Animals, Chgo., 1990-94. With JAGC USNR, 1965-68. Mem. ABA, Ill. Bar Assn., Chgo. Bar Assn., Execs. Club Chgo. (co-chmn. Western Europe internat. com. 1990-97, 2003—), The Lawyers Club (Chgo., 1997—), Meadow Club (Rolling Meadows, gov. 1979-90, chmn. 1985-90), Club Internat. Home: 1200 N Lake Shore Dr Chicago IL 60610-2370 Office: Vedder Price 222 N La Salle St Ste 2600 Chicago IL 60601-1104

**WILLIAMS, RICHARD THOMAS,** lawyer; b. Evergreen Park, Ill., Jan. 14, 1945; s. Raymond Theodore and Elizabeth Dorothy (Williams) W. AB with honors, Stanford U., 1967, MBA, JD, Stanford U., 1972. Bar: Calif. 1972, U.S. Supreme Ct. 1977. Assoc.,then ptnr. Kadison Pfaelzer Woodard Quinn & Rossi, L.A., 1972-87; ptnr. Whitman & Ransom, 1987-93, Whitman, Breed, Abbott & Morgan, L.A., 1993-2000, Holland & Knight, LLP, L.A. 2000—. Contbg. editor Oil and Gas Analyst, 1978-84. Mem. ABA, L.A. County Bar Assn. Office: Holland & Knight LLP 633 W 5th St Los Angeles CA 90071-2005 Office Phone: 213-896-2410. Business E-mail: richard.williams@hklaw.com.

**WILLIAMS, RICHMOND DEAN,** library consultant and appraiser; b. Reading, Mass., Dec. 10, 1925; s. Theodore Ryder and Anabel Lee (Hutchison) W.; m. Eleanor Davidson Washbourne, Sept. 26, 1953; children—Richmond Lyttleton, Eleanor Davidson, Anne Ryder. AB cum laude, Williams Coll., 1950; MA, U. Pa., 1952, PhD, 1959. Instr., asst. dean Williams Coll., Williamstown, Mass., 1954-56; dir. Wyo. Hist. and Geol. Soc., Wilkes-Barre, Pa., 1956-60; asst. dir. Am. Assn. State and Local History, Madison, Wis., 1960-61; dir. libraries Eleutherian Mills-Hagley Found., Wilmington, Del., 1962-87. Instr. Acad. Lifelong Learning U. Del., 1996—; cons. archivist M.S. Hershey Found., Pa., 1981—; Md. Dept. Housing and Cmty. Devel., 1993-94; bd. dirs. Rhistoric Inc. Co-author: A Look at Ourselves, 1962; author: They Also Served, 1965; compiler: Directory of Historical Records in Delaware, 1995, (ann. series) Writing Haiku—, 1996-05. Sec., U. Del. Library Assocs., Wilmington, 1972-86; mem. adv. bd. Del. Hist. Records, Dover, 1976-02; mem. Del. Humanities Forum, Wilmington, 1984-91; trustee Conservation Ctr. Phila., 1984-86. Served to 1st lt. AUS, 1943-47. Pennfield fellow U. Pa., 1953 Mem. Econ. History Assn (sec.-treas. 1975-88), Mid-Atlantic Regional Archives Com., Am. Assn. State and Local History (pres. 1974-76), Am. Antiquarian Soc., Libr. Co. Phila., Phi Beta Kappa. Avocations: golf, book collecting. Home and Office: 202 Brecks Ln Wilmington DE 19807-3011 Office Phone: 302-654-0986. Business E-Mail: rdwms@udel.edu.

**WILLIAMS, RICKY (ERRICK LYNNE WILLIAMS),** professional football player; b. San Diego, May 21, 1977; s. Errick and Sandy Williams; children: Marley, Prince. Grad. U. Tex. Running back/receiver New Orleans Saints, 1999—2002; running back Miami Dolphins, 2002—04, 2005—06, Toronto Argonauts, 2006—. Actor: (films) Stuck On You, 2003. Founder Run Ricky Run Foundation. Recipient Heisman Trophy, 1998; named to Pro-Bowl, 2002 Achievements include led NFL in rushing yards, 2002. Office: Toronto Argonauts Ste 3300 One Blue Jays Way Toronto ON M53 1J3 Canada Office Fax: 416-341-2714.*

**WILLIAMS, RITA TUCKER,** lawyer; b. Atlanta, Jan. 26, 1950; d. Claude Edward and Lillian Bernice (Barber) Tucker; m. Raymond Williams, Jr., Jan. 1, 1973; children: Monet Danielle, Brandon Raynard, Blake Hassan. BA, Spelman Coll., 1972; MA, U. Mich., 1976; JD, Emory U., 1987. Bar: Ga. 1987. Tchr. pub. schs., Suisun, Calif., 1977-82; assoc. Alston & Bird, Atlanta, 1987-89, Bernard & Assocs., Decatur, Ga., 1989-90; prin. Williams & Assocs., Decatur, Ga., 1990—. Instr. seminar Nat. Inst. Trial Advocacy, Emory U., Atlanta, spring 1992-95, tutor 1st yr. law students, 1996. Named Outstanding Alumna, Emory U. Law Sch., 1996. Mem. ABA, State Bar Ga. Assn., Ga. Trial Lawyers Assn., Omicron Delta Kappa. Democrat. Office: 220 Church St Decatur GA 30030-3328 Office Phone: 404-370-3783. Personal E-mail: ritw@atlonline.com.

**WILLIAMS, ROBERT CHADWELL,** history professor; b. Boston, Oct. 14, 1938; s. Charles Reagan and Dorothy (Chadwell) W.; m. Ann Bennett Kingman, Aug. 27, 1960; children: Peter, Margaret, Katharine. BA, Wesleyan U., 1960; A.M., Harvard U., 1962, PhD, 1966. Asst. prof. history Williams Coll., Williamstown, Mass., 1965-70; prof. history Washington U., St. Louis, 1970-86; dean of faculty, prof. history Davidson Coll., N.C., 1986-98, Vail prof. history, 2000—03. Pres. Central Slavic Conf., 1971-72; v.p. History Assocs. Inc., Gaithersburg, Md., 1980—; sr. research assoc. St. Antony's Coll., Oxford, 1985. Author: Culture in Exile, 1972, Artists in Revolution, 1976, Russian Art and American Money, 1980 (Pulitzer nominee), The Other Bolsheviks, 1986, Klaus Fuchs, Atom Spy, 1987, Russia Imagined, 1997, Ruling Russian Eurasia, 2000, The Historian's Toolbox, 2003, Horace Greeley, 2006; co-author: Crisis Contained, 1982; mem. editorial bd.: Slavic Rev., 1979-82. Trustee Wesleyan U., 1996-99, Agnes Scott Coll., 2003-. Fellow Kennan Inst., 1976-77; fellow Am. Council Learned Socs., 1973-74, W. Wilson Found., 1960-61 Mem. Am. Assn. for Advancement of Slavic Studies, Phi Beta Kappa, Sigma Xi Presbyterian. E-mail: bob03harmony@yahoo.com.

**WILLIAMS, ROBERT E.,** lawyer; BA with highest honors, U. Calif., Santa Barbara, 1973; JD, Harvard U., 1976. Bar: Calif. 1976. Ptnr. Fin. and Bankruptcy Practice Group Sheppard, Mullin, Richter & Hampton LLP, LA. Mem.: Am. College of Real Estate Lawyers, Phi Beta Kappa. Office: Sheppard, Mullin, Richter & Hampton LLP 48th Fl 333 S Hope St Los Angeles CA 90071 Office Phone: 213-617-4169. Office Fax: 213-620-1398. Business E-mail: rwilliams@sheppardmullin.com.

**WILLIAMS, ROBERT HENRY,** oil industry executive; b. El Paso, Jan. 12, 1946; s. William Frederick and Mary (Page) W.; m. Joanne Marie Mudd, Oct. 22, 1967; children: Lara, Michael, Suzanne, Jennifer. BS in Physics, U. Tex., El Paso, 1968; PhD in Physics, U. Tex., Austin, 1973; MS in Physics, Va. Poly. Inst., 1971. Dir. Gulf Oil R&D, Houston, 1978-81; tech. mgr. Gulf Oil Internat., Houston, 1981-83; exploration mgr. Gulf Oil Co., Houston, 1983-85; mgr. geophys. rsch. Tenneco Oil Co., Houston, 1985-87, mgr., chief geophysicist, 1987-88; founder, mng. dir. Dover Energy, Houston, 1988—; exec. v.p. Tatham Offshore Inc, Houston, 1989-95, also bd. dirs.; chmn., CEO Dover Tech Inc., Houston, 1990—. Cons. Tenneco Inc., Houston, 1990—; DeepTech Internat., 1992-95; Ukraine Acad. Sci., 1993; bd. dirs., exec. v.p. DeepTech Inc., 1991-95; founder, pres. Westway tech. Assocs., 1986—; co-founder, chmn. CEO Castaway Graphite Rods, Inc., 1990—; owner, CEO Team Tex., Inc., 1993—; Bulldog Lures, Inc., 1994—; founder, CEO Houston Books Inc., 1994—; founder, CEO, chmn. Dover Energy Exploration, 1995—; pres. Westway Interests; chmn., CEO, bd. dirs. W.B. Oil & Gas Inc.,

1997-2001, Dover (Belize), 1996-2002; bd. dirs. Tatham Offshore, Swep, Inc.; CEO Norman Lures, 1997—; founder, bd. dirs., CEO Win Leisure Products, 1997—; dir./founder William Found., 1998—; CEO, chmn. bd. dirs. Airrus Fishing Products, 2003-06. Contbr. articles to profl. jours. Coun. mem. Boy Scouts Am., Houston, 1995—; leader Girl Scouts U.S., Houston, 1989—. Mem. Soc. Exploration Geophysics, Am. Assn. Petroleum Geologists, Am. Geophys. Union. Republican. Avocations: scuba diving, book collecting, fishing. Office: Dover Tech 14420 Westway Ln Houston TX 77077

**WILLIAMS, ROBERT JOSEPH,** retired museum director, educator; b. Bennington, Vt., June 21, 1944; s. Joseph and Ruthe Allison (Moody) Williams. BS in Edn., U. Vt., 1970; MA in Interdisciplinary Social Sci., San Francisco State U., 1981. Tchr. adult edn. Mt. Anthony Union H.S., Bennington, Vt., 1972-74; columnist Bennington Banner, 1972-77; tchr. San Francisco State U., 1976-79; founder, dir. NORRAD Drug Rehab. Ctr., San Francisco, 1986-88; mus. curator Shaftsbury (Vt.) Hist. Soc., 1989—2005; ret., 2005. Founder, dir. Bennington Tutorial Ctr., 1971-74. Author: Toward Humanness in Education, 1981, Chalice of Leaves: Selected Essays and Poems, 1988, Modern Salvation: Guidelines from Cosmology, 1994, Superstring Displacement as a Common Factor in Gravity, Electromagnetic Radiation and Molecular Adhesion, 2004; author: (with others) Intimacy, 1985. Recipient Edmunds Essay medal Vt. Historical Soc., Montpelier, 1961, award League Vt. Writers, 1972, Golden Poet award World of Poetry, Sacramento, Calif., 1990. Democrat. Avocation: cosmology. Home: 102 Putnam St Bennington VT 05201-2348 *I sought the truth, and sought to live by it.*

**WILLIAMS, ROBERT JOSEPH,** behavioral health services executive, psychologist; b. Durango, Colo., Feb. 14, 1948; s. Owen C. and Florence K. Williams; m. Kay Lynn Williams, Mar. 24, 1973; children: Robin, Matthew, Nicholas. BA, U. Colo., 1970; MA, U. No. Colo., 1976; PhD, U. Minn., 1979. Diplomate Am. Bd. Psychol. Specialties. Tchr. math. Jefferson County Schs., Lakewood, Colo., 1970-76; psychologist Pikes Peak Mental Health Ctr., Colorado Springs, Colo., 1979-82, clin. dir., 1982-83; dir. Inst. for Family and Personal Devel., Colorado Springs, 1983-86; mng. ptnr. Marriage and Family Treatment Ctr., Colorado Springs, 1986-90; COO Quinco Behavioral Health Systems, Columbus, Ind., 1990-92, pres., CEO, 1992—. Feedback cons. Ctr. for Creative Leadership, Colorado Springs and San Diego, 1986-96; facilitator Franklin Covey Ctr., Columbus, 1994-99; cons. Trustee Leadership Tng. Program, Indpls., 1991-98; adj. faculty U. Denver, U. Colo., Colorado Springs, 1981-90. Contbr. articles to profl. jours. Trustee Bartholomew Consol. Sch. Corp., Columbus, 1996-2001, pres., 1999-2000; past pres., moderator Leadership Bartholomew County; mem. Healthy Communities Coun. 1995—, co-chmn. 2004-05; bd. dirs. Columbus Ind. Philharmonic, 2001—, pres. 2003-04; bd. mem. Rotary, 2004-05, Columbus Area C. of C., 2005—. Sgt. USMCR, 1970—76. Boettcher Found. scholar, 1966-70; Regents scholar, 1966. Mem. Rotary Club, Masons. Democrat. Presbyn. Avocations: hiking, reading, motorcycling, weight training. Office: Quinco Behavioral Health Sys 720 North Marr Rd Columbus IN 47201 E-mail: rjwilliams@quincoinc.com.

**WILLIAMS, ROBERT LEON,** retired psychiatrist, neurologist, educator; b. Buffalo, July 22, 1922; s. Leon R. and L. Paulyne (Ingraham) W.; m. Shirley Glynn Miller, Feb. 5, 1949; Karen, Kevin BA, Alfred U., 1944; MD, Albany Med. Coll., Union U., 1946. Chief neurology and psychiatry Lackland AFB Hosp., USAF, San Antonio, 1952-55; cons. neurology and psychiatry to USAF Surgeon Gen., 1955-58; faculty Coll. Medicine, U. Fla., Gainesville, 1958-72, prof., chmn. dept. psychiatry, 1964-72; prof. psychiatry Baylor Coll. Medicine, Houston, 1972-92, chmn. dept., 1972-90, prof. neurology, 1976-92, acting chmn. dept., 1976-77, prof. emeritus psychiatry and neurology, 1992—; ret. Mem. faculty various univs., part time 1949-58 including Albany Med. Coll. at Union U., Columbia Coll. Physicians and Surgeons, Boston U., U. Tex., Georgetown U. Author: (with W.B. Webb) Sleep Therapy: A Bibliography and Commentary, 1966, (with others) EEG of Human Sleep: Clinical Applications, 1974; editor: (with Ismet Karacan and Carolyn J. Hursch) Psychopharmacology of Sleep, 1976, Sleep Disorders: Diagnosis and Treatment, 1978, 2d edit., 1988; (with others) Phenomenology and Treatment of Anxiety, 1979, of Alcoholism, 1980, of Psychophysiological Disorders, 1982, of Psychosexual Disorders, 1983, of Psychiatric Emergencies, 1984 Served from 1st lt. to lt. col. USAF, 1949-58; col. Res., ret. Recipient Cert. Profl. Achievement USAF Surgeon Gen., 1967 Mem. Am. Psychiat. Assn., Am. Electroencephalographic Soc., Am. Coll. Psychiatrists (pres. 1982-83), Am. Acad. Neurology, AMA, Group for Advancement of Psychiatry, Benjamin Rush Soc. (pres. 1986-88), Accreditation Coun. for grad. Med. Edn. (residency rev. com. for psychiatry 1985-93), Alpha Omega Alpha. Achievements include research and publs. on basic psychophysiology of human sleep.

**WILLIAMS, ROBERT P., II,** lawyer; b. Albuquerque, 1959; BA, Johns Hopkins Univ., 1981; JD, Univ. Ga., 1984. Bar: Ga. 1984. Assoc. Troutman Sanders LLP, Atlanta, 1984—92, ptnr., govt. law group, 1993—, and practice group leader, telecom. and electronic commerce. Staff mem. Ga. Jour. Internat. & Comparative Law, 1982—83; editor: Ga. Jour. Internat. & Comparative Law, 1983—84. Mem.: ABA, State Bar Ga. (secy, adminstrv. law sect. 1989—91, vice chmn., adminstrv. law sect. 1991—92, chmn., adminstrv. law sect. 1993—94), Phi Delta Phi. Office: Troutman Sanders LLP Ste 5200 600 Peachtree St NE Atlanta GA 30308-2216 Office Phone: 404-885-3438. Office Fax: 404-962-6721. Business E-mail: robert.williams@troutmansanders.com.

**WILLIAMS, ROBERT SANDERS (SANDY WILLIAMS),** dean, academic administrator, educator, researcher; b. Athens, Ga. m. Jennifer Williams; children: Molly, Nicholas, Owen. Degree, Princeton U., 1970; MD, Duke U., 1974; internship and residency internal medicine, Mass. Gen. Hosp., 1974—76; fellowship in cardiology, Duke U. Med. Ctr., 1977—80. Asst. prof. medicine, physiology, cell biology Duke U. Sch. medicine, 1980—84; assoc. prof. medicine and microbiology Duke U. Sch. Medicine, 1986—90, dean, vice chancellor acad. affairs, 2001—; chief cardiology, prof. internal medicine, biochemistry, and molecular biology, dir. Ryburn Ctr. for Molecular Cardiology U. Tex. Southwestern Med. Ctr., 1990—2001. Rschr. in field; vis. prof. dept. biochemistry Oxford U., 1984—85; vis. scientist Cold Spring Harbor Lab., NY, 1995—96; dir.'s adv. com. NIH; bd. external advisors Nat. Heart, Lung and Blood Inst. Contbr. more than 150 scholarly articles to biomed. jours.; Proceedings of the Nat. Acad. Scis. Recipient Disting. Alumnus Award, Duke U. Sch. Medicine, 2000. Fellow: AAAS; mem.: NAS, Inst. of Medicine, Assn. Univ. Cardiologists, Am. Heart Assn. Achievements include being the leader of the Dallas Heart Disease Prevention Project, an innovative program of research in the genetic epidemiology of cardiovascular disease. Office: Duke U Sch Medicine Box 2927 Durham NC 27710*

**WILLIAMS, ROBIN,** actor, comedian; b. Chgo., July 21, 1951; s. Mr. and Mrs. Robert W.; m. Valerie Velardi, June 4, 1978 (div. 1988); m. Marsha Garces, Apr. 30, 1989; 2 children. Attended, Claremont Men's Coll., Marin Coll., Juilliard Sch., N.Y.C. Started as stand-up comedian in San Francisco clubs, including Holy City Zoo, The Boardinghouse; appeared in TV series Laugh-In, The Richard Pryor Show, America 2-Night, Happy Days, Homicide: Life on the Streets, 1993 (Emmy nomination, Guest Actor - Drama Series, 1994); Mork and Mindy, 1978-82 (People's Choice award), (cable) Robin Williams: An Evening at the Met, 1986 (Grammy award), host of HBO's Shakespeare: The Animated Tales, 1993 (CableAce Award, Best Entertainment Host); film appearances include: Popeye, 1980, The World According to Garp, 1982, The Survivors, 1983, Moscow on the Hudson, 1984, The Best of Times, 1986, Club Paradise, 1986, Seize the Day, 1986, Good Morning Vietnam, 1987 (Golden Globe award 1988, Acad. Award nominee for best actor), The Adventures of Baron Munchausen, 1988, Dead Poets Society, 1989 (Best Actor nomination Golden Globe award, 1994, nominated best actor Acad. award), Cadillac Man, 1990, Awakenings, 1990, Dead Again, 1991, The Fisher King, 1991 (Golden Globe award, Acad. award nominee for best actor 1991), Dead Again, 1991, Hook, 1991, Aladdin (voice) (Spl. Achievement award Hollywood Fgn. Press, Nat. Bd. Rev. 1992), 1992, Toys, 1992, Mrs. Doubtfire, 1993 (Best Picture, Best Actor in a Musical or

Comedy, Golden Globe, 1994, Best Picture, Best Actor, People's Choice award, also prodr.), Nine Months, 1995, Jumanji, 1995, The BirdCage, 1996, Jack, 1996, The Secret Agent, 1996, Hamlet, 1996, Deconstructing Harry, 1997, (TV series, voice) Great Minds Think for Themselves, 1997, Father's Day, 1997, Flubber, 1997, Good Will Hunting, 1997, What Dreams May Come, 1998, Patch Adams, 1998, Bicentennial Man, 1999, Jakob the Liar (also exec. prodr.), 1999, Artificial Intelligence (voice), 2001, One Hour Photo, 2002, Death to Smoochy, 2002, Insomnia, 2002, The Final Cut, 2004, The House of D, 2004, Noel, 2004, Robots (voice), 2005, RV, 2006, The Night Listener, 2006; theatre: Waiting for Godot, 1988; recorded albums: Reality, What a Concept, 1979 (Grammy award), Throbbing Python of Love, A Night at the Met (Grammy award); host Comic Relief, 1986; appeared in TV variety programs, ABC Presents a Royal Gala, 1988 (Emmy award, 1988), Carol, Carl, Whoopi & Robin, 1987 (Emmy award), Robin Williams: Live at the Met, 1986, Robin Williams Live, 1986, Comic Relief, 1986, Young Comedians All Star Reunion, 1988, Robin Williams: Live on Broadway, 2002 (Emmy nomination, Grammy award, 2003) Recipient Golden Apple award Hollywood Women's Press Club, ACE award, Am. Comedy award, 1987, 88, Grammy award for best comedy rec., 1987, Man of Yr. award Hasty Pudding Theatricals, 1989, People's Choice award Favorite Comedy Motion Picture Actor, 1994, ShoWest Conv. award Male Star of Yr., 1994, Cecil B. DeMille award, Hollywood Fgn. Press, 2005.*

**WILLIAMS, ROGER,** state official; m. Patty Williams; children: Jaclyn, Sabrina. B, Tex Christian U. Pres. & CEO Jack Williams Automall, 1974—95; profl. basketball player Atlanta Braves farm team, 1971—74; owner & operator San Antonio Brewers profl basketball club, 1972—75; asst. head coach to head coach-basketball team Tex. Christian U.; sec of state State of Tex., 2004—. Chmn. bd. Roger Williams Automall, Weatherford, Victory Fin. Corp. Republican. Office: Office of Secretary of State PO Box 12887 Austin TX 78711 Office Phone: 512-463-5770. Office Fax: 512-475-2761. E-mail: secretary@sos.state.tx.us.*

**WILLIAMS, ROGER LAWRENCE,** historian, educator; b. Boulder, Colo., June 22, 1923; s. Raymond Ustick and Mabel (Woolf) W. BA, Colo. Coll. 1947; MA, U. Mich., 1948, PhD, 1951. Asst. prof. Minn. State Coll., Mankato, 1950-52, MIT, Cambridge, 1952-55; vis. prof. Mich. State U., East Lansing, 1955-56; assoc. prof. Antioch Coll., Yellow Springs, Ohio, 1956-65; prof. U. Calif., Santa Barbara, 1965-71, U. Wyo., Laramie, 1971-78, Disting. prof., 1978-88. Author: French Revolution of 1870-71, 1969, The Mortal Napoleon III, 1971, The Horror of Life, 1980, Aven Nelson of Wyoming, 1984, Gérard and Jaume: Two Neglected Figures in the History of the Jussiaean Classification, 1988, Napoleon III and the Stoffel Affair, 1993, The Letters of Dominique Chaix, Botanist-Curé, 1997, Botanophilia in 18th Century France: The Spirit of the Enlightenment, 2001; co-author: How Modernity Came to a Provençal Town, 1988, Handbook of Rocky Mountain Plants, 1992, A Guide to Rocky Mountain Plants, 2002, French Botany in the Enlightenment: the Ill-fated Voyages of La Pérouse and His Rescuers, 2003, A Region of Astonishing Beauty, the Botanical Exploration of the Rocky Mountains, 2003, An Intellectual Biography of Elie-Abel Carrière, 2004, Revolution and Madness: Blanqui and Trelat, 2005, From Malesherbes to Tocqueville, The Legacy of Liberalism, 2006; mem. editl. bd.: Antioch Rev., 1958—64. Vol. Rocky Mountain Nat. Park, Estes Park, Colo., 1986-87. Mem. French Hist. Studies (life), History Sci. Soc. (life), Hist. Soc. Nat. Coun. for History Edn., N.Y. Bot. Soc., Denver Bot. Soc. Home: 1701 S 17th St Laramie WY 82070-5406

**WILLIAMS, RONALD A.,** health insurance company executive; b. Chgo., Nov. 11, 1949; m. Cynthia Williams; 1 child. BA in Psychology, Roosevelt U., 1970; MS in Mgmt., MIT, 1984. Sr. v.p. mktg. and specialty products to exec. v.p. group and network svc. Blue Cross Calif., 1987—95, pres., 1995—99; sr. v.p. Vista Health Corp.; group mktg. exec. Control Data Corp.; pres., co-founder Integrative Sys.; pres. large group divsn. WellPoint Health Networks Inc., 1999—2001; exec. v.p., chief of health operations Aetna Inc., 2001—02, pres., 2002—, COO 2006—. Bd. dirs. Aetna Inc., 1992—, Lucent Technologies, 2003—; trustee Conference Bd.; mem. dean's advisory coun Mass. Inst. Tech, mem. corp. vis. com, mem. Alfred P. Sloan Mgmt. Soc. Avocations: jazz, movies. Office: Aetna Inc 151 Farmington Ave Hartford CT 06156*

**WILLIAMS, RONALD DAVID,** telecommunications industry executive; b. Marshall, Ark., Mar. 15, 1944; s. Noble Kentucky and Elizabeth (Karns) W.; m. Beth L. Williams, Nov. 1977; children: Stephanie Noble, Keith Michael. BA, Columbia U., 1966, BS, 1967, MBA, 1973. Process engr. DuPont, Deepwater, NJ, 1966; design engr. Combustion Engring. Co., Hartford, 1971; cons. Arthur Andersen & Co., N.Y.C., 1973-76; corp. planner Amax Inc., Greenwich, Conn., 1976-77, group planning adminstr., 1978-80; mgr. corp. planning and analysis, 1980-94, dir. fin. analysis, 1984-86; project mgr. Olin Corp., Stamford, Conn., 1977-78; mgr. ops. planning and analysis Savin Corp., Stamford, 1986-88; dir. fin. Bandgap Tech. Corp., Broomfield, Colo., 1988-90, v.p. fin. and adminstrn., 1990-93; v.p., gen. mgr. Bandgap Chem. Corp., 1992-94; contr. Heraeus PMR, Inc., Alden, NY, 1994-95, v.p. fin. and adminstrn., 1995-96; gen. mgr. Acoustiflo, Boulder, Colo., 1996-97; sr. fin. staff analyst Energy Corp., New Orleans, 1998-99; mgr. fin. planning Energy Tech. Co., 1999—. Mem. Fred's team Meml. Sloan Kettering Cancer Ctr. With USN, 1967-70, Vietnam. NASA trainee, 1971; S.W. Mudd scholar, 1971. Mem. AAAS, Am. Chem. Soc., Am. Mgmt. Assn., Utility Telecom. Coun., Ark. Hist. Assn., Westport Hist. Soc., Colo. Hist. Soc., Appalachian Mountain Club, Boulder Road Runners, Chalmette Track Club, New Orleans Track Club, Gulf Coast Running Club, Pine Belt Pacers, Mesa Monument Striders, West Bank Track Club. Home: 7361 S Meadow Ct Boulder CO 80301-3951 Office: 639 Loyola Ave New Orleans LA 70113-3125 Business E-Mail: rwill16@entergy.com.

**WILLIAMS, RONALD DEAN,** minister, religious organization administrator; b. Decatur, Ill., Oct. 23, 1940; s. Henry Lawrence and Ella Loudica Williams; m. Carole Jeanette Lane, June 16, 1962; children: Scott Allan, Mark Lawrence, Derek James. BTh, LIFE Bible Coll., LA, 1965; DD, Internat. Ch. Foursquare Gospel, LA, 1992. Ordained to ministry Internat. Ch. Foursquare Gospel, 1966. Pastor Foursquare Gospel Ch., Surrey, Canada, 1965-69, missionary Hong Kong, China, 1969-85; prof. Life Bible Coll., 1985-95; mng. editor Foursquare World Advance, 1993—2002; comm. officer Internat. Ch. Foursquare Gospel, 1988-2000. Bd. dirs. Foursquare Gospel Ch., denominational historian, 2004—; pres. exec. bd. Internat. Pentecostal Press Assn., Oklahoma City, 1990—98; comm. officer Pentecostal/Charismatic Ch. N.Am., Memphis, 1994—2005; coord. E. Coun. Foursquare Miss., 1979—82. Editor: The Vine and The Branches, 1992; mng. editor: Foursquare World Advance mag., 1985—2002. Coord. 19th Pentecostal World Conf., 2001. With USAF, 1958—61. Avocations: writing, golf, reading, music. Office: Internat Ch Foursquare Gospel 1910 W Sunset Blvd Ste 200 Los Angeles CA 90026-3295 Business E-mail: rworld@foursquare.org.

**WILLIAMS, RONALD DOHERTY,** lawyer; b. New Haven, Apr. 6, 1927; s. Richard Hugh and Ethel W. (Nelson) w.; m. Laura Costarelli, Aug. 25, 1951; children: Craig F., Ronald D., Ellen A., Jane E. BA, U. Va., 1951; LLB, 1954. Bar: Conn. 1954. Assoc. Pullman, Comley, Bradley & Reeves, Bridgeport, Conn., 1954-60; ptnr., 1960-88, Williams, Cooney & Sheehy, 1989—. Mem. Fed. Jud. Com., 1988-91, com. unauthorized practice law, 1988-94, com. to study rules civil practice & procedure, 1984-86; atty. state trial referee, 1984-90. Selectman Town of Easton (Conn.), 1975-85, justice of the peace, 1977—, town atty., 1985-2000; mem. Bridgeport Area Found., 1971-90, emeritus dir., 1991—; adv. com. U. Bridgeport Law Sch., 1982-92; mem. statewide grievance com., 1985-91, chmn., 1989-91; mem. exec. bd. Sch. Law Quinnipiac Coll., 1994—. Served with U.S. Army, 1945-46. Fellow Am. Coll. Trial Lawyers; mem. ABA, Conn. Bar Assn. (del. govs. 1975-78), Bridgeport Bar Assn. (pres. 1975), Conn. Def. Lawyers Assn. (pres. 1984-85). Republican. Roman Catholic. Home: 14 Newman Dr Easton CT 06612-1915 Office: 799 Silver Ln Trumbull CT 06611-0753 Office Phone: 203-380-1741. E-mail: wilcooshee@aol.com.

**WILLIAMS, RONALD OSCAR,** mathematician; b. Denver, May 10, 1940; s. Oscar H. and Evelyn J. (Johnson) Williams. BS in Applied Math., U. Colo., Boulder, 1964; postgrad., U. Colo., 1968—70; postgrad. in continuing edn. U. Denver, 1975; postgrad. Advanced Tech. Edn. Program, Hughes Aircraft Co., 1980—89; postgrad., George Washington U., DC, 1985. Computer programmer Apollo Sys. dept. Missile and Space div. Gen. Electric Co., Kennedy Space Ctr., Fla., 1965-67, Manned Spacecraft Ctr. (now called Johnson Space Ctr.), Houston, 1967-68; computer programmer Grad. Sch. Computing Ctr. and Lab. Atmospheric and Space Physics U. Colo., Boulder, 1968-73; computer programmer analyst Def. Sys. divsn. Sys. Devel. Corp. for NORAD, Colorado Springs, 1974-75; engr. def. sys. and command-and-info. sys. Martin Marietta Aerospace, Denver, 1976-80; sys. engr., def. info. sys. divsn. space and comm. group Hughes Aircraft Co., Aurora, Colo., 1980-89; rsch. analyst Math. Rsch. Ctr., Littleton, Colo., 1990—, dir., sr. rsch. mathematician, 1996—. Vol. fireman Clear Lake City (Tex.) Fire Dept., 1968; officer Boulder Emergency Squad, 1969-76, rescue squad officer, 1969-76, liaison officer to cadets, 1971, pers. officer, 1971-76, mem. exec. bd., 1971-76, EMT, 1973—; res. dispatcher A-1 Ambulance, Boulder, 1973; spl. police officer Boulder Police Dept., 1970-75; spl. dep. sheriff Boulder County Sheriff's Dept., 1970-71; mem. nat. adv. bd. Am. Security Coun., 1979-91, Coalition of Peace Through Strength, 1979-91. Non-commd. officer USMCR, 1958—66. Decorated Organized Res. medal; recipient award of merit Boulder Emergency Squad, 1971, 72, Dedicated Svc. award Boulder Emergency Squad, 1976, Cost Improvement Program award, Sys. Performance Improvement award, Top Cost Improvement Program award in Def. Sys. Div., Space and Comm. Group Hughes Aircraft Co., 1982. Mem. AAAS, AIAA (sr.), Math. Assn. Am., Am. Math. Soc. Soc. Indsl. and Applied Math., Math. Study Unit of Am. Topical Assn., Armed Forces Comm. and Electronics Assn., Assn. Old Crows, Nat. Def. Indsl. Assn., Former Intelligence Officers, Nat. Mil. Intelligence Assn., U.S. Naval Cryptologic Vet. Assn., Marine Corps Assn., Marine Corps Heritage Found., Air Force Assn., U.S. Naval Inst., Nat. Geog. Soc., Smithsonian Inst., Nat. Space Soc., Soc. Amateur Radio Astronomers, Radio History Soc., Met. Opera Guild, Colo. Pub. Radio (classical music), Colo. Hist. Soc., Hist. Denver, Hist. Boulder, Hawaiian Hist. Soc., Denver Bot. Gardens, Denver Mus. Nature and Sci., Denver Zool. Found., Alumni Assn. U. Colo. Boulder, South High Alumni and Friends Denver, Marine Corps Assn., Air Force Assn., Marine Corps Heritage Found. (charter), Am. Mensa Ltd., Denver Mile-Hi, Mensa, Acoustic Neuroma Assn., Nat. Brain Tumor Found., Wings Over Rockies Air & Space Mus., Denver Zool. Found., Crystal Cathedral Ministries Sparrows Club. Lutheran.

**WILLIAMS, ROY,** college basketball coach; b. Spruce Pine, N.C., Aug. 1, 1950; m. Wanda; children: Scott, Kimberly. BA, U. N.C., 1972, MAT, 1973. Asst. coach UNC Tarheels, 1978—88; head coach U. Kansas Jayhawks, 1988—2003, UNC Tarheels. asst. coach USA Senior National Team, 2003, U.S. Olympic Team, Athens, 2004. Named Nat. Rookie Coach of Yr., Basketball Times, 1989, Nat'l Coach of the Year 1990-92, 1997, 2006, Big 8 Coach of the Yr. seven times, Coach of the Yr., AP, 1992, 2006. Achievements include coaching NCAA Nat. Champion UNC Tarheels, 2005. Office: UNC Athletic Dept PO 2126 Chapel Hill NC 27514*

**WILLIAMS, ROY,** professional football player; b. Odessa, Tex., Dec. 20, 1981; Attended, Univ. Tex., 2004. Wide receiver Detroit Lions, 2004—. Vol. HAVEN domestic violence shelter, 2004—, Boys and Girls Club, Detroit, 2004—. Actor: (films) Friday Night Lights, 2002. Named to All-American Dream Team, NFL Draft Report, 2004. Office: Detroit Lions 222 Republic Dr Allen Park MI 48101*

**WILLIAMS, ROY L.,** public relations executive, advocate; m. Patricia Ryder Williams, 1961; 2 children. M of Urban Planning, Wayne State U.; postgrad., U. Manchester, Eng. Exec. asst. to Gov. William G. Milliken; pres. and CEO Detroit Urban League; mgr. cmty. rels. Chrysler Corp., 1984—; chmn. spl. contbn. fund NAACP, mem. nat. bd. dirs. Chmn. Mich. State Housing Devel. Authority; mem. steering com. Detroit Neighborhood Housing Svcs.; past pres. Nat. Coun. State Housing Bds.; exec. v.p. HP Devco; bd. dirs. Detroit City Planning Commn. Named Citizen of Week, WWJ Radio; recipient Human Rights award, Nat. Jewish Labor Com., 1995. Mem.: Highland Pk. C. of C. (v.p.) Office: NAACP 4805 Mt Hope Dr Baltimore MD 21215

**WILLIAMS, ROY L.,** fraternal organization administrator; m. Barbara Williams; 2 children. BA, U. Tex., Arlington, 1971. Dist. exec. Longhorn Coun. Boy Scouts of Am., Fort Worth, Tex., 1972, dist. exec. Abilene, Tex., fin. dir. Little Rock, 1978, scout exec. Jayhawk Area Coun. Topeka, 1981, dir. Boy Scout Div., Nat. Coun., scout exec. Narragansett Coun. Providence, 1990, regional dir. Western Region Tempe, Ariz., chief scout exec. Irving, Tex., 2000—. Vet. USAF. Recipient Vigil Honor, Order of Arrow, Disting. Svc. Award. Mem.: Tribe of Mic-O-Say. Office: Boy Scouts of Am National Coun PO Box 152079 Irving TX 75015-2749*

**WILLIAMS, SALLY J.,** psychologist, educator; b. Waukesha, Wis., Mar. 30, 1953; d. Warren Charles and E. Jane Williams; children: Pamela Ann Kososki, David Warren Kososki. BA in Clin. Psychology, Alveno Coll., 1994; postgrad., Marquette U., 1995—96; D in Psychology, Wis. Sch. Profl. Psychology, Milw., 2005. Behavioral technician/intake specialist/group therapist Aurora Psychiat. Hosp., Wauwatosa, Wis., 1994—2003; psychol. assoc. B Wis. Dept. of Corrections, Fond du Lac, Wis., 2004—. Instr. (part-time) Alverno Coll., Milw., 2004—. Mem. St. Mary's Episcopal Ch., Dousman, Wis., 1987—2006. Mem.: APA. Home: 1023 Oxford Rd Waukesha WI 53186 Office: Taycheedah Correctional Institution 751 County Road K Fond Du Lac WI 54935-2946 Office Phone: 929-920-7153. Personal E-mail: sjwilliams999@wi.rr.com. E-mail: sally.williams@doc.state.wi.us.

**WILLIAMS, SANDRA LYNN,** ethics educator; b. Evanston, Ill., May 11, 1955; d. Robert Chandler and Evelyn Clauson Williams. BS in Fine and Applied Arts, U. Ill., 1977, MBA in Fin. Mgmt., 1980, PhD in Human Resource Devel., 2001. Banking officer Continental Bank N.A., Chgo., 1980, 2nd v.p., 1981—84, v.p., 1984—89, sector credit officer, 1989—93, mng. dir., 1993—94; v.p. Bank of Am., Chgo., 1994—99, human capital cons., 1996—99; pvt. pub. spkr. and cons., 1999—. Tng. mgr. and instr. corp. and instnl. banking tng. dept. Continental Ill. Nat. Bank, N.A., Chgo., 1984—92; guest instr. dept. human resources U. Ill., Coll. Edn., Champaign, Ill., 1999—2001; grad. tchg. asst. dept. human resource edn. U. Ill., 1999—2001; presenter in field. Author: Human Capital Management and Development, 2001, (booklet/guide) Human Capital Planning Guidebook, 1998; contbr. articles to profl. jours. Mem. adv. bd. Ill. Fatherhood Initiative, Chgo., 1997—99; active Rep. Nat. Com., Washington, 1994—2005; judge of elections Maine Twp., Cook County, Ill.; legis. adv. Ill. Connection, Urbana, 1997—; elder, mem. mgmt. session Park Ridge (Ill.) Presbyn. Ch., 1996—99, moderator worship, music and arts com., 1998—99. Recipient Stewart Wesbury award for vol. achievement, Mid-Am. Chpt. ARC, 1992; William Chandler Bagley fellow, 1999, 2000. Mem.: Robert Morris Assocs. (mem. N.Am. pvt banking steering com. 1992—98), Acad. Human Resource Devel., U. Ill. Alumni Assn. (life; dir./MBA pres., Constituent Leadership award 1993, Disting. Svc. award 1996), Union League Club Chgo. (chmn. internat. dinners program 1990—92, pub. affairs com., urban affairs sub-com, cultural affairs com. 1992—99, mem. women's initiative network group 1993—), chmn. mem. activities com., co-chair pub. affairs com. 1996—97, dir. 1996—99, chair comm. com. 1997—99, pub. affairs sr. counselor, pers. and adminstrn. com. mem. 2001—04, mem. fin. com. 2002, mem. admissions com. 2002—, corp. sec. 2005—, Bd. Recognition award 1999). Avocations: hiking, swimming, singing, piano. Office: 1468 Parkside Dr Park Ridge IL 60068-1559

**WILLIAMS, SANKEY VAUGHAN,** health services researcher, internist; b. San Antonio, Apr. 15, 1944; s. James Sankey and Helen (Long) W.; m. Constance Hess, June 27, 1972; children: Elizabeth Helen, Jennifer Lee. AB, Princeton U., 1966; MD, Harvard U., 1970. Diplomate Am. Bd. Internal Medicine. Intern Hosp. of U. Pa., 1970-71, jr. resident, 1971-72, chief med.

resident, 1974-75; assoc. dir. clin. rsch. Ctr. for Study of Aging, U. Pa., 1982-86; assoc. dir. for med. affairs Leonard Davis Inst. for Health Econs., U. Pa., 1978-90; dir. clin. scholars program U. Pa., Phila., 1988-96; prof. health care systems Wharton Sch., U. Pa., Phila., 1989—; prof. medicine U. Pa., Phila., 1989—, chief div. gen. internal medicine, 1992—, Sol Katz prof. medicine, 1992—. Commr. Prospective Payment Assessment Commn., U.S. Congress, Washington, 1988-91; chairman health svcs. rsch. devel. grants study sect. Agy. for Health Care Policy and Rsch., 1991-94; counselor for med. affairs to the pres. U. Pa., 1990-92. Co-editor: The Physician's Practice, 1980; author 35 revs, chpt. or editorials; contbr. 62 articles to various sci. jour., assoc. editor, annals of Internal Medicine, 2003-. Lt. comdr. USPHS, 1972-74. Recipient Career Devel. award Henry S. Kaiser Family Found., 1981-86. Mem. ACP (master, chmn. clin. privileges com. 1989-93, Soc. for Med. Decision Making (pres. 1985-86), Soc. for Gen. Internal Medicine (coun. 1979-84, editor Jour. Gen. Internal Medicine 1994-99, pres. 2000-01). Office: Hosp Univ of Pa Divsn Gen Internal Medicine 1220 Blockley Hall 423 Guardian Dr Philadelphia PA 19104-6021

**WILLIAMS, SERENA,** professional tennis player, apparel designer; b. Saginaw, Mich., Sept. 26, 1981; Prof. tennis player WTA Tour, 1995—; designer Aneres clothing line. TV appearances include: My Wife and Kids, 2002; Law and Order: Special Victims Unit, 2004; The Division, 2004; (voice) The Simpsons, 2001. Named WTA Most Improved Player, 1999, Player of the Year, TENNIS Mag., 1999, Female Athlete in the World, AP, 2002, WTA Tour Player of the Year, 2002, #1 most marketable female athlete, Sports Business Daily, 2003; recipient Espy award for Best Female Athlete, ESPN, 2003, Espy award for Best Female Tennis Player, 2003, 2004. Achievements include winner of 26 career singles titles, 10 career doubles titles, and 2 mixed doubles titles, WTA tour; Grand Slam Championships: US Open, 1999, 2002, Wimbledon, 2002, 2003, Roland Garros, 2002, Australian Open, 2003, 2005; winner of doubles titles (with Venus Williams) at Australian Open 2001, 2003, Wimbledon, 2000, 2000, Roland Garros, 1999, US Open, 1999, Mixed Doubles (w/ Max Mirnyi), Wimbledon, 1998; winner of doubles gold medal (with Venus Williams), Sydney Olympic games, 2000; winning 4 Grand Slam tournaments in a row, 2002-2003; signing largest endorsement deal to date by a female athlete with Nike, 2003. Office: c/o USTA 70 W Red Oak Ln White Plains NY 10604-3602*

**WILLIAMS, SHANNON RENEE,** mental health services professional; d. Joyce Bromley Wright; m. Anthony Markell Williams, July 5, 1997; children: JaHarold, Justin, Jamilla. BS, Bowie State U., 1990, MA, 1993; PhD, Howard U., 2004. Lic. clin. profl. counselor Md. Mental health assoc. Regional Inst. for Children and Adolescents, Rockville, Md., 1990—94; correctional psychologist assoc. Dept. Pub. Safety and Correctional Svcs., Jessup, Md., 1994—2005; therapist Wash. Assessment and Therapy Svc., Lanham, Md., 2005—; psychotherapist Bowie Counseling Svcs., 2006—. Coord. Diamonds in the Rough womanhood tng. program Paramount Bapt. Ch., Washington, 2000—. Mem.: APA, Am. Counseling Assn. Avocations: reading, singing.

**WILLIAMS, SHERYL KATHERYN,** archivist, librarian; b. Big Rapids, Mich., Feb. 5, 1948; d. Walter and Constance Virginia Van Welden; m. Gerry C. Williams, Aug. 12, 1972; children: Jeffrey A., Andrew T., Peter A. BA, Kalamazoo Coll., 1970; MLS, U. Okla., 1977. Libr. U. Okla., Norman, 1977, manuscripts processor, 1978—79; asst. curator Kans. collection U. Kans., Lawrence, 1979, curator Kans. collection, 1979—, univ. archivist 1994—2004. V.p. Midwest Archives Conf., 2003—04; mem. Kans. State Hist. Records Adv. Bd., 1979—. Recipient Chancellor's award for disting. librarianship, U. Kans., 1994. Mem.: Orgtn. Am. Historians, Soc. Am. Archivists (mem. coun. 2005—). Avocations: gardening, needlecrafts, collage. Home: 1101 W 27th St Lawrence KS 66046 Office: U Kans Spencer Rsch Libr 1450 Poplar Ln Lawrence KS 66046

**WILLIAMS, SONDRA BETH,** social studies educator, department chairman; b. Valdosta, Ga., Sept. 13, 1957; d. Benjamin Norwood and Janice Lanier Williams. BA, BS, Ga. State U., Atlanta, 1997. Social studies tchr. Tower HS, Decatur, Ga., 1997—, dept. chair, 2005—. Mem.: ACLU, NEA, Nat. Coun. Social Studies, Amnesty Internat., Sierra Club. Green Party. Avocation: stained glass art. Home: 555 Oakdale Rd NE Atlanta GA 30307 E-mail: sbwilliams@mindspring.com.

**WILLIAMS, SONIA KAY,** retired secondary school educator; b. Duluth, Minn., Jan. 13, 1939; d. Allen Parke and Ruth Adelaide (Mitchell) Swayne; m. William Fedrick Williams, Mar. 26, 1960; children: Keith Douglass, Jennifer Gay. BMus, U. Tenn., Chattanooga, 1960; M in Secondary Tchg. of English, Statesboro U., 1975; edn. specialist, Valdosta State U., 1988. Tchr. North Chattanooga Jr. H.S., 1960-61; music tchr. Savannah (Ga.) Country Day Sch., 1968-72; English tchr. Appling County Jr. H.S., Baxley, Ga., 1972-74, Appling County Comprehensive H.S., Baxley, 1974—2001; ret., 2001. Accompanist Appling Applause, Baxley, 1978-92; drama tchr. Appling County H.S., 1990-92. Prodr. videotape Sonia's Signya's, 1991. Bd. dirs., Sunday sch. tchr. First United Meth. Ch., Baxley, 1980-94; pres. Friends of Libr., Baxley, 1990-92; charter mem. Appling Hist. Soc., Baxley, 1980—; bd. dirs., 1992-94; mem. Appling Heritage Com., Baxley, 1992-2006; vol. ARC, Am. Cancer Soc., Sue Care Hosp., Appling Co. Food Bank, 2003-06, CASA, 2002-06; apptd. spl. adv. for abused and neglected children. Named Star Tchr., Appling County C. of C., 1984, outstanding Retired Educator of Yr. Altamaha Tech. Coll., 2004; recipient Outstanding Educator award Ga. Retired Educators Assn., 2001, Cmty. Svc. award, 2003. Mem. Nat. Coun. Tchrs. English, Ga. Assn. Educators (instrnl. and profl. devel. com. 1992-97, Dist. Tchr. of Yr. 1997-98), Lions Internat., Delta Kappa Gamma (pres. Alpha Pi chpt. 1997-99). Avocations: reading, writing, swimming, drama. Home: 177 Torrance Rd Baxley GA 31513-6726

**WILLIAMS, STEPHEN,** anthropologist, educator; b. Mpls., Aug. 28, 1926; s. Clyde Garfield and Lois (Simmons) Williams; m. Eunice Ford, Jan. 6, 1962; children: Stephen John, Timothy. BA, Yale U., 1949, PhD, 1954; MA, U. Mich., 1950; MA (hon.), Harvard U., 1962. Asst. anthropology dept. Peabody Mus., Yale U., 1950-52; mem. faculty Harvard U., Cambridge, Mass., 1958—, prof. anthropology 1967-72, Peabody prof., 1972-93, prof. emeritus, 1993—, chmn. dept., 1967-69; rsch. fellow Peabody Mus., Harvard U., Cambridge, 1954-57, mem. staff, 1954—, dir. mus., 1967-77. Curator N.Am. Archaeology, 1962-93, hon. curator 1993—; dir. rsch. of Peabody Mus.'s Lower Miss. Survey, 1958-93. Author books and articles on N.Am. archaeology, "Fantastic" archaeology and the history of Am. archaeology. Home: 1017 Foothills Trail Santa Fe NM 87505-4537 Office: PO Box 22354 Santa Fe NM 87502-2354 Office Phone: 505-983-8836. Personal E-mail: williamsstephen@msn.com.

**WILLIAMS, STEPHEN EDWARD,** lawyer; b. Clarksburg, Va., Dec. 8, 1948; AB, Harvard U., 1970; JD, W.Va. U., 1974. Bar: W.Va. 1974. Lawyer Consolidated Gas, 1974-78, sr. lawyer, 1978-82, gen. lawyer, 1982-84, asst. gen. counsel, 1984-87; sec., gen. counsel Consolidated Natural Gas, 1987-92, assoc. gen. counsel, 1992, sr. v.p., gen. counsel, 1992—. Mem. Am. Corp. Counsel Assn., Pa. Bar Assn., Fed. Energy Bar Assn., W.Va. State Bar, Pitts. Symphony Soc. (bd. dirs., exec. com.). Office: Consolidated Natural Gas Co CNG Tower Fl 21 625 Liberty Ave Pittsburgh PA 15222-3110

**WILLIAMS, STEPHEN FAIN,** federal judge; b. NYC, Sept. 23, 1936; s. Charles Dickerman and Virginia (Fain) Williams; m. Faith Morrow, June 11, 1966; children: Susan, Geoffrey Fain, Sarah Margot Nu, Timothy Dwight Nicholas Morrow. BA, Yale U., 1958; JD, Harvard U., 1961. Bar: N.Y. 1962, Colo. 1977. Assoc. Debevoise, Plimpton, Lyons & Gates, N.Y.C., 1962—66; asst. atty. US Dist. Ct. (so. dist.), NY, 1966—69; asst. prof. law U. Colo., Boulder, 1969—77, prof., 1977—86; judge US Ct. Appeals (D.C. cir.), Washington, 1986—2001, sr. judge, 2001—. Vis. professor UCLA, 1975—76; vis. prof., fellow in law and econs. U. Chgo., 1979—80; vis. William L. Hutchison prof. energy law So. Meth. U., 1983—84; cons. Adminstry. Conf. U.S., 1974—76, FTC, 1983—85; mem. Boulder Area Growth Study

Commn., 1972—73. Contbr. articles to profl. jours. and mags. With U.S. Army, 1961—62. Mem.: ABA, Fed. Energy Bar Assn., Am. Law Inst. Office: US Courthouse 333 Constitution Ave NW Washington DC 20001 E-mail: SFWilliams@cadc.uscourts.gov.*

**WILLIAMS, STEVEN A., JR.,** former federal agency administrator; b. Bellows Falls, Vt. m. Beth Williams; 2 children. B in Environ. Resource Mgmt., Pa. State U., D in Forest Resources; MS, U. N.D. Grad. tchg. asst. U. N.D., 1979—81, Pa. State U., 1981—85; wildlife biologist Mass. Divsn. Fisheries and Wildlife, 1985—89, asst. dir. for wildlife, 1989—92; dep. exec. dir. Pa. Game Commn., 1992—95; sec. Kans. Dept. Wildlife and Parks, 1995—2002; dir. Fish and Wildlife Svc. U.S. Dept. Interior, Washington, 2002—05. Mem.: Wildlife Soc., Internat. Assn. Fish and Wildlife Agys.

**WILLIAMS, STEVEN D.,** plastic surgeon; b. Mpls., Minn. m. Yvonne Christian William, June 1, 1991. BA, U. Chgo., 1979; MD, Loyola U. Maywood, Ill., 1985. Former cert. State Med. Bd. OH, Mich. Bd. Medicine, former lic. State Med. Bd. OH, Mich. Bd. Medicine, cert. State Ill. Med. Bd., Fed. Drug Enforcement Adminstrn., lic. State Ill. Med. Bd., Fed. Drug Enforcement Adminstrn., bd. cert. Nat. Bd. Med. Examiners, Am. Bd. Plastic Surgery, splty. bd. cert. Am. Bd. Plastic Surgery, 1998. Resident, intern, gen. surgery U. Ill., 1985—89, chief resident, gen. surgery, 1989—90; fellow, staff attending-burn fellowship, dir. ICU Cook County Hosp., 1990—91; resident, plastic and reconstructive surgery Med. Coll. OH, Toledo, 1991—92, adminstrv. chief resident, plastic and reconstructive surgery, 1992—93; attending physician, plastic surgeon, pvt. practice Ctr. Reconstructive Surgery, 1993—95, Cmty. Health Ctr. Bourbonnais, 1995—. Chmn., chief surgery Riverside Med. Ctr. & St. Mary's Hosp., 2005—, chmn. operating room coms.; mem. Med. Ctr. Trauma Com., Kankakee, Ill., Riverside Med. Ctr. Dept. Profl. Edn., Kankakee, Riverside Med. Ctr. Opcr. Rm. Com., Kankakee, Riverside Med. Ctr. Physicians Adv. Bd., Kankakee, Provena St. Mary's Hosp. Oper. Rm. Com., Ill.; presenter, spkr. in field; med. dir. Riverside Ambulatory Surgery Ctr. Contbr. articles to profl. jours. Mem. Am. Breast Cancer Found., Am. Cancer Soc., Am. Diabetes Assn., Am. Found. for Blind, Am. Fedn. Police, Am. Heart Assn., Am. Inst. Cancer Rsch., Alzheimers Assn., Amnesty Internat., Arthritis Found., Cath. Charities, Covenant House, Cystic Fibrosis Found., Feed the Children, Hospice Edn. Inst., Internat. Humane Soc., Habitat for Humanity, Macular Degeneration Rsch. Found., Mercy Home Boys & Girls, Multiple Sclerosis Assn. Am., NAACP, Nat. Found. Cancer Rsch., Nat. Geog. Soc., Nat. Hort. Soc., Nat. Humane Soc., Nat. Osteoporosis Found., Nat. Parkinsons Found., Nat. Pub. & Chgo. Pub. Radio, Oblate Missions, Pub. TV, United Negro Coll. Found., USO, Sacred Heart League, World Conf. Religion & Peace; ptnr. Spl. Olympics; vol., vision and blood pressure screening test; mem. Big Bros./Big Sisters Met. Chgo., Chgo. Anti-Cruelty Soc., Harbor House Kankakee, Maryknoll Fathers and Bros., So. Poverty Law Ctr., St. Jude's Childrens Hosp. Assn., St. Labre Am. Indian Sch., LWV; chr. lector. Fellow: Am. Coll. Surgeons, ACS; mem.: AMA, Kankakee County Med. Soc., Phenylketonuria Action Group, Karl A. Meyer Surg. Soc. of Cook County Hosp., Kankakee County Med. Soc. (v.p. 2005—, pres. 2006—), Chgo. Med. Soc., Ill. State Med. Soc., Am. Burn Assn., Chgo. Soc. Plastic Surgeons, Midwest Assn. Plastic Surgeons (treas.), Am. Soc. Plastic Surgeons, VFW, Am. Vets. Assoc., Paralyzed Vets. Found., Consumers Union, U. Chgo. Varsity Athletic Letterman's Club, Phi Gamma Delta. Avocations: bicycling, hiking, guitar, photography, travel.

**WILLIAMS, STUART ALAN,** lawyer; b. Brownsville, Pa., Nov. 18, 1953; s. Max J. and Sylvia S. Williams; m. Francine W. Williams; children: Louis Samuel, Nicole Beth. B.A. with highest distinction, Pa. State U., 1975; J.D., Georgetown U., 1978. Bar: Pa. 1978, U.S. Dist. Ct. (we dist.) Pa. 1978. Ptnr. Eckert, Seamans, Cherin & Mellott, Pitts., 1978; DKW Law Group; chief legal officer Mylan Laboratories Inc. 2002-; adj. prof. labor law Duquesne U. Sch. Law, Pitts., 1980—. pres. Meadows Real Estate, Inc., 1986—, Washington Trotting Assn., 1986—. Bd. dirs. Washington County Council on Econ. Devel. Mem. Pa. Bar Assn. (sec.-treas. labor law sect. 1981, vice chairperson 1982), ABA (com. on devel. law under Nat. Labor Relations Act), Phi Delta Phi, Phi Beta Kappa, Phi Kappa Phi, Omicron Delta Kappa. Assoc. editor The Tax Lawyer; contbr. articles to legal jours. Office: Mylan Labs 1500 Corporate Dr Canonsburg PA 15317

**WILLIAMS, SUE,** artist; b. Chicago Heights, Ill., 1954; Student, Cooper Union, 1973; BFA, Calif. Inst. Arts, 1976. One-woman shows include Laughelton Gallery, N.Y.C., 1989, Amy Lipton Gallery, 1991, Stuart Regen Gallery, L.A., Gallery 210, St. Louis, 1992, 303 Gallery, 1992, 1994, 1996, 1998, San Francisco Art Inst., 1993, Vera Vitagioia, Naples, 1993, Galerie Rizzo, Paris, 1993, Galerie Walcheturm, Zurich, 1994, Modulo, Lisbon, Portugal, 1994, 1996, Galleria Il Capricorno, Venice, Italy, 1994, 1997, Jack Hanley Gallery, San Francisco, 1995, Galerie Metropol, Vienna, Austria, 1995, Regen Projects, L.A., 1996, Jean Bernier Gallery, Athens, Greece, 1996, 1998, Galerie Ghislaine Hussenot, Paris, 1996, Johnen & Schottle, Cologne, Germany, 1997, Ctr. d'Art Contemporain, Geneva, 1997, Sadie Coles, London, 1998, Neue Galerie un Landesmus. Joanneum, Graz, Austria, 1998, exhibited in group shows at Adam Baumgold Fine Art and Simon Capstick-Dale Fine Art, N.Y.C., 1996, Freidrich Petzel Gallery, 1996, Galerie Andreas Binder, 1996, Spiral Wacoal Art Ctr., Tokyo, 1996, Weatherspoon Art Gallery, Greensboro, N.C., 1997, Elizabeth Harris Gallery, 1997, Fine Arts and Lehmann Maupin, N.Y.C., 1997, Mus. d'Art Contemporani Barcelona, 1997, Whitney Mus. Am. Art, 1997, Emory U., 1998, The Aldrich Mus. Contemporary Art, Ridgefield, Conn., 1998, Pat Hearn and Mattehw Marks Gallery, N.Y.C., 1998, Landesgalerie Oberosterreich, Linz, Austria, 1998, Kunsthalle Krems, Austria, 1998, numerous others, Represented in permanent collections; performer The New Mus., N.Y.C., 1996. Contbr. articles to profl. jours., reviewer in field. Office: c/o 303 Gallery 525 West 22d St New York NY 10011

**WILLIAMS, SUE DARDEN,** library director; b. Miami, Fla., Aug. 12, 1943; d. Archie Yelverton and Bobbie (Jones) Eagles; m. Richard Williams, Sept. 30, 1989. BA, Barton Coll., Wilson, N.C., 1965; M.L.S., U. Tex., Austin, 1970. Cert. librarian, N.C., Va. Instr. Chowan Coll., Murfreesboro, NC, 1966-68; libr.'s asst. Albemarle Regional Libr., Winston, NC, 1968-69; br. libr. Multnomah County Pub. Libr., Portland, Oreg., 1971-72; asst. dir. Stanly County Pub. Libr., Albemarle, NC, 1973-76, dir., 1976-80; asst. dir. Norfolk (Va.) Pub. Libr., 1980-83, dir., 1983-94, Rockingham County Pub. Libr., Eden, NC, 1996—2004, Albemarle Regional Libr., Winton, NC, 2004—. Mem. ALA (coun. 1987-91, orientation com. 1990-92, chair 1991), Libr. Adminstrv. and Mgmt. Assn. (pub. rels. sec. 1985-87bd. dirs. 2004—), Southeastern Libr. Assn. (staff devel. com. 1986-88, Rothrock award com. 1984-86, sec. pub. libr. sect. 1982-84), Va. Libr. Assn. (SELA rep. 1993-96, coun. 1984, 88-91, 93-96, ad hoc conf. guidelines com. 1985-86, chmn. conf. program 1984, awards and recognition com. 1983, mem. SELA outstanding libr. program award com. 2002), Pub. Libr. Assn. (bd. dirs.-at-large Met. area 1986-89), Va. State Libr. (coun. com. 88-89), N.C. Libr. Assn. (scholarship com. 1999-2005, chair 2001-2005), LAMS. Home: 109 Chowan Rd Murfreesboro NC 27855 Office: Albermarle Regional Libr PO Box 68 303 W Tryon St Winton NC 27986 Office Phone: 252-358-7832. E-mail: swilliams_arl@yahoo.com.

**WILLIAMS, SUE M.,** federal agency administrator, writer; b. Sumter, S.C., Aug. 20, 1942; d. Perry Harrington and Ida (Sumter) Taylor; 2 children. Diploma, cert., Comms. Inst. Am., 1968; BA, U. Colo., 1974; R. Sc. F., Ernest Holmes Coll. Ch. of Religious Sci., 1979; M in Mgmt. Sci., Regis U., Denver, 1999. Ordained to ministry. Long distance operator Mountain Bell/Penn Bell, Phila. & Colorado Springs, 1969-74; reservations clk. Frontier Airlines, Colorado Springs, 1969-74; ops. trainee Cen. Bank of Denver, 1974-75; legal specialist USAFR, Lowry AFB, Colo., 1975-77; asst. mgr. Western Airlines, L.A., 1974-87; supr. reservation sales Delta Air Lines, L.A., 1987-88; sr. svc. office mgr. U. Colo., Denver, 1988-89; sales coord. Hewlett Packard Co., Englewood, Colo., 1989-90; supr. U.S. Sprint (United Telecom), Denver, 1990—2006; supr. distbn. ops. U.S. Postal Svc., sr. bus. svc. specialist, 2006—. Contbr. articles to profl. jours. Mem. Vets. Club, Colorado Springs, 1973-74; various offices L.A. Election Dept., 1983-85; appointed vet. com.

Calif. Reps., L.a., 1985; participant Hands Across Am., L.A., 1985, The Bolder Boulder, various walking races for local charity; charter mem. Women in Mil. Meml. Found., Washington, 1990. With USAF, 1961-63. Mem. Am. Legion, Coll. Devine Metaphysics Alumni Assn. (area v.p. 1982—).

**WILLIAMS, SUNITA L.,** astronaut; b. Euclid, Ohio, Sept. 19, 1965; d. Deepak N. and Ursaline B. Pandya; m. Michael J. Williams. BS in Physical Sci., U.S. Naval Acad., 1987; MS in Engring. Mgmt., Fla. Inst. Tech., 1995. Commn. ensign USN, 1987, advanced through grades to lt. comdr., various assignments, 1987—89, overseas combat, 1989—92; officer in charge Hurrican Andrew Relief Ops. USS Sylvania, 1992—93; various assignments USN, 1993—95; served on USS Saipan, Norfolk, Va., 1995—98; astronaut NASA, Houston, 1998—. Decorated Commendation medal USN, Achievement medal USN & USMC, Humanitarian Svc. medal USN. Mem.: Soc. Flight Test Engrs., Soc. Exptl. Test Pilots, Am. Helicopter Assn. Office: Astronaut Office CB NASA Johnson Space Center Houston TX 77058

**WILLIAMS, SUSAN MARIE,** music educator; b. Indpls., July 19, 1958; d. John Stanley and Kathleen Ann Slamkowski; m. Stuart Clifford Williams, June 27, 1981; children: Zachary, Benjamin. BS, Clarke Coll., 1980; MA in Liberal Studies, Valparaiso U., Ind., 1987. Musc tchr. Union Twp. Sch., Wheeler, Ind., 1981—85; music tchr. elem., high sch. LaCrosse (Ind.) Sch., 1985—87; music tchr. elem., middle and high sch. Morgan Twp. (Ind.) Sch., 1987—88; elem. music. Portage (Ind.) Twp. Schs., 1988—2001, dept. chair. Choir dir. Ctrl. Elem., Portage, 1988—; rep. area I curriculum/assessment guide Ind. Acad. Stds. for Music, 2000. Facilitator Compassionate Friends, 1995—. Grantee Ind. Portfolio grant, Ind. Dept. Edn., 1999—2001. Mem.: Music Educators Nat.Conf., Ind. Music Educators. Avocations: running, water-skiing, skiing, bicycling, travel. Office: Ctrl Elem Sch 2825 Russell Portage IN 46368 Office Phone: 219-763-8015. E-mail: swilliams@portage.k12.in.us.

**WILLIAMS, SUSAN SHIDAL,** language educator; b. Atlanta, Jan. 7, 1963; d. L. Neil and Sue (Sigmon) W. BA, Yale U., 1985, PhD, 1991. Asst. prof. English Ohio State U., Columbus, 1991-97, assoc. prof. English, 1997—2006, prof. English, 2006—. Author: Confounding Images: Photography and Portraiture in Antebellum American Fiction, 1997, Reclaiming Authorship: Literary Women in America 1850-1900, 2006; co-editor: Reciprocal Influences: Literary Production Distribution, and Consumption in America, 1999, American Periodicals; manuscript reviewer and contbr. articles to profl. jours. Mem. Columbus Symphony Orch. Chorus, 1992-98. Whiting fellow Yale Univ., New Haven, Conn., 1990-91, Steven Botein fellow Am. Antiquarian Soc., Worcester, Mass., 1997; Coca-Cola Crit. Difference for Women Rsch. grantee Ohio State U., 1996-97, Nat. Endowment for the Humanities, 2006. Mem. MLA, Am. Studies Assn., Soc. History of Authorship, Reading & Pub., Rsch. Soc. Am. Periodicals (mem. adv. bd. 1997-2005). Office: Ohio State Univ English Dpt 164 W 17th Ave Columbus OH 43210-1370 Office Phone: 614-688-3147. E-mail: williams.488@osu.edu.

**WILLIAMS, SUZANNE,** state senator; b. Oklahoma City, Feb. 3, 1945; m. Ed Williams; 2 children. BA in Edn., Baylor U.; MA in Spl. Edn., U. Colo. Educator; state sen. dist. 41 Colo. Senate, Denver, 1996—, mem. edn. and transp. and energy coms. Recipient Gov.'s award for curriculum innovation, 1985, Gov.'s Action Plan award, 2000, Insider award, Aurora Sentinel, 1994, Leadership award, Colo. Edn. Assn., 1999, Outstanding Leadership Legis. award, AIA, Colo., 2001, cert. appreciation, Denver Indian Family Resource Ctr., 2002. Mem.: AAUW, Colo. Soc. Sch. Psychologists, Assn. Sch. Nurses, Colo. Assn. Edn. Young Children, Women in Govt., Aurora Sister Cities Internat., Delta Kappa Gamma. Democrat. Avocations: reading, music, exercising. Office: State Capitol # 271 200 E Colfax Ave Denver CO 80203 Office Phone: 303-866-3432.

**WILLIAMS, TED VAUGHNELL,** physical education educator; b. Bronx, N.Y., Apr. 1, 1952; s. Joseph Alexander and Annie (Canady) W. BS, Springfield Coll., 1977. Cert. tchr., N.Y. Substitute tchr. Valhalla (N.Y.) High Sch., 1977; tchr. aide for handicapped children, tchr. spl. edn. Rye Lake Campus, Valhalla, 1978; supr. recreation activities Springfield (Mass.) Girl's Club Family Ctr., 1979; assoc. dir. boy's and men's phys. edn. dept. Trenton YMCA, 1979—; house supr. Cardinal McCloskey's Group Home, Tappan, N.Y., 1980-81; phys. edn. tchr. Our Lady of Refuge Sch., Bronx, N.Y., 1982-83; tchr. phys. edn. various Cath. elem. schs. Yonkers, N.Y., 1983—. With ops. dept. Hudson Valley Nat. Bank, 1990-92. Active Walk Am. for Healthier Babies, March of Dimes, 1990-93. Recipient Ed Steitz award Basketball Hall of Fame, 1975, Capitol award Nat. Leadership Coun., 1991; named to Wall of Tolerance, Civil Rights Meml. Ctr., Montgomery, Ala. Mem. ASCD, AAHPERD, Am. Assn. Leisure and Recreation, Hudson Valley Leisure Svcs. Assn. Democrat. Baptist. Home: 49 Bradford Ave White Plains NY 10603-2143 Office Phone: 914-965-2356. E-mail: tedww@aol.com.

**WILLIAMS, TERRIE MICHELLE,** public relations executive; b. Mt. Vernon, NY, May 12, 1954; MA, BA cum laude, Brandeis U., 1975; MS, Columbia U., 1977. Exec. dir. World Inst. of Black Community, NYC, 1982; dir. pub. rels. Essence Communications Inc., NYC, 1982-86, v.p., 1986-88; pres. The Terrie Williams Agy., NYC, 1988—. Med. soc. worker N.Y. Hosp., NYC, 1977-80; program adminstr. Black Filmmaker Found., N.Y.C., 1980-81; exec. dir. Black Owned Communications Alliance, N.Y.C., 1981-82. Author: The Personal Touch, 1995. Recipient Entrepeneur of the Yr. award Nat. Assn. Market Developers, 1990, Flo Kennedy Media award, 1990, Matrix award N.Y. Women in Communications, 1991. Mem. Women in Communications, NOW, Brandeis U. Alumni Assn. (bd. dirs.), NY TV Acad. Arts and Scis., Pub. Rels. Soc. Am. (D. Parke Gibson award 1981). E-mail: tmwm@terriewilliams.com.

**WILLIAMS, THELMA B.,** retired principal; d. Joseph and Floria Bush; m. McDonald Williams, Oct. 9, 1955; children: Donald J., Patricia A. Johnson. BS in Edn., Paine Coll., 1963; EdM, U. Ga., 1974, EdS, 1981. Tchr. Levi White Elem., Augusta, Ga., 1963—72; reading specialist Richmond County Schs., Augusta, 1972—76; asst. prin. Glenn Hills High Augusta, 1976—81; prin. W.S. Hornsby Elem., Augusta, 1981—99. Edn. vol. Richmond County Schs., 1999—2002; founder after-sch. tutorial program, 2005—. Commn. mem. Augusta Richmond County Hist. Commn., 1995—2003; mem. several ministries Macedonia Bapt. Ch., organizer after school tutorial program, 2004; mem. Augusta Classic, 1998—, Alzheimer's Assn., Augusta, 1983—2003. Recipient Meritorious Svc. award, Richmond County Prin. Assn., 1999, Pres.'s award, Paine Coll., 2001, Disting. award of edn., Nat. Assn. Equal Opportunity in Higher Edn., 2002, United Negro Coll. Fund award, Tom Joyner Found., 2003, Yough Svc. award, Ga. Rep. Quincy Murphy, 2004, Outstanding Educators award, W.S. Hornsby and East Augusta Cmty. Neighborhood Assn. and PCS Nitrogen, 1998. Mem.: Richmond County Ret. Tchrs. Assn., Art Factory for Creative Arts (sec. 1990—92), Loyal Kristian Women Civic Group (v.p. 2006—, vice chmn. 2006—), Paine Coll. Alumni Assn. (chmn. ballot com. 1997—99, pres. Augusta chpt. 2001—), Phi Delta Kappa (pres. Platinum Club 1983—, lectr. Founder's Day 1994, nat. chairballots 1997—99, chmn. ballots com. 1997—99, local pres. 2001—03, pres. Augusta chpt. 2001—), Zeta Phi Beta (Founder's Day Lectr. 1994). Avocations: travel, reading, baking, teaching. Personal E-mail: TBW51@comcast.net.

**WILLIAMS, THEODORE JOSEPH,** engineering educator; b. Black Lick, Pa., Sept. 2, 1923; s. Theodore Finley and Mary Ellen (Shields) W.; m. Isabel Annette McAnulty, July 18, 1946; children: Theodore Joseph, Mary Margaret, Charles Augustus, Elizabeth Ann. BSCh.E., Pa. State U., 1949, MSCh.E., 1950, PhD, 1955; MS in Elec. Engring., Ohio State U., 1956. Research fellow Pa. State U., University Park, 1947-51; asst. prof. Air Force Inst. Tech., 1953-56; technologist Monsanto Co., 1956-57, sr. engring. supr., 1957-65; prof. engring. Purdue U., Lafayette, Ind., 1965-94, prof. emeritus, 1995—, dir. control and info. systems lab., 1965-66; dir. Purdue Lab. Applied Indsl. Control, 1966-94, dir. emeritus, 1995—; cons., 1964—. Vis. prof. Washington

U., St. Louis, 1962-65; hon. prof. Inst. Automation, Academia Sinica, Shenyang, China, 1992. Author: Systems Engineering for the Process Industries, 1961, Automatic Control of Chemical and Petroleum Processes, 1961, Progress in Direct Digital Control, 1969, Interfaces with the Process Control Computer, 1971, Modeling and Control of Kraft Production Systems, 1975, Modelling, Estimation and Control of the Soaking Pit, 1983, The Use of Digital Computers in Process Control, 1983, Analysis and Design of Hierarchical Control Systems - With Special Reference to Steel Plant Operations, 1985, A Reference Model for Computer Integrated Manufacturing (CIM) - A Description from the Viewpoint of Industrial Automation, 1989, The Purdue Enterprise Reference Architecture, 1992; editor: Computer Applications in Shipping and Shipbuilding, 6 vols., 1973-79, Proceedings Advanced Control Confs., 19 vols., 1974-93, Architectures for Enterprise Integration, 1996. Served to 1st lt. USAAF, 1942-45; to capt. USAF, 1951-56. Decorated Air medal with 2 oak leaf clusters. Fellow AAAS, AIChE, Instrument Soc. Am. (hon. mem., pres. 1968-69, Albert F. Sperry gold medal 1990, Lifetime Achievement award 1995), Am. Inst. Chemists, Inst. Measurement and Control (London, Sr. Harold Hartley silver medal 1975), Indsl. Computing Soc.; mem. IEEE (sr.), Internat. Fedn. for Info. Processing (Silver Core award 1978), Soc. for Computer Simulation (hon.), Am. Chem. Soc., Am. Automatic Control Coun. (pres. 1965-67), Am. Fedn. Info. Processing Socs. (pres. 1976-78), Sigma Xi, Tau Beta Pi, Phi Kappa Phi, Phi Lambda Upsilon. Home: 208 Chippewa St West Lafayette IN 47906-2123 Office: Purdue U Potter Rsch Ctr Inst Interdisciplinary Engring Studies West Lafayette IN 47907-1293 Office Phone: 765-494-7434. Business E-mail: tjwil@ecn.purdue.edu.

**WILLIAMS, THOMAS ALAN,** elementary school educator, small business owner; b. Kingston, Pa., Dec. 15, 1961; s. Thomas Elwin and Lois Jean (Vanderhoff) W.; m. Jeanne Ann Sweinberg, July 10, 1993; children: Lindsay Nicole, Thomas Lee. BS in Edn., Bloomsburg (Pa.) U., 1983; MS in Counselor Edn., U. Scranton, Pa., 1987. Cert. secondary counselor, elem. counselor. Tchr. N.W. Sch. Dist., Shickshinny, Pa., 1983-84; tchr. grades 4-6 Lake-Lehman (Pa.) Sch. Dist., 1984-88, tchr. social studies grades 7-8, 1988-93, tchr. social studies grades 10-12, 1993-99, tchr. grades 4-6, 1999—, asst. athletic dir., 2001—04; pres. T&J Williams Enterprises Inc., 2001—; owner Curves, Lehman, 2001—, Plains, 2001—, Hanover, 2001—, Nanticoke, 2004—, Wilkes-Barre Twp., 2004—. Wrestling coach Lake-Lehman Sch. Dist., 1984-99. Wrestling official Pa. Interscholastic Athletic Assn., Wilkes-Barre, 1981—. Named Pa. N.E. Regional Coach of Yr., Regional Wrestling Com., 1991, 95, Coach of Yr., Times-Leader, 1990, 91, 92, 94, 95, 96, 97. Mem. Nat. Wrestling Coaches Assn., Pa. State Athletic Dirs. Assn., Pa. Wrestling Coaches Assn., Dist 2 Pa. Interscholastic Athletic Assn., Wrestling Coaches Assn. (Coach of Yr. 1992, 95, Sportsmanship award 1995), Masons, Shriners, Caldwell Consistory. Republican. Methodist. Avocations: fishing, collectibles, photography, travel, gardening. Home: 1087 Mountain View Dr Dallas PA 18612-9539 Office: Lake-Lehman H S Lehman PA 18627 Personal E-mail: TNJWilly@aol.com.

**WILLIAMS, THOMAS ARTHUR,** biomedical computing consultant, psychiatrist; b. Racine, Wis., May 11, 1936; s. Robert Klinkert and Marion Ane (Wisneski) Williams; m. Christine Frances Fannon, July 3, 1970; children: Jennifer, Thomas, Hailey, Renate, Luke. BA, Harvard Coll., 1958; MD, Columbia U., 1963; postgrad., NIH, 1967-68. Diplomate Nat. Bd. Med. Examiners, Am. Bd. Psychiatry and Neurology. Intern in surgery Columbia Presbyn. Med. Ctr., N.Y.C., 1963-64; resident in psychiatry Columbia Presbyterian Med. Ctr., N.Y. State Psychiat. Inst., N.Y.C., 1964-67; chief depression rsch. NIMH, Bethesda, Rockville, Md., 1967-71; asst. prof. U. Pitts., 1969-70; assoc. prof. U. Utah, Salt Lake City, 1971-77; prof., chmn. dept. psychiatry Eastern Va. Med. Sch., Norfolk, Va., 1977-78; clin. dir. Sheppard & Enoch Pratt Hosp., Towson, Md., 1978-80; U. South Fla., Tampa, 1980-83; practitioner psychiat. medicine, med. dir. St. Augustine (Fla.) Psychiat. Ctr., 1983-89, 89-90; prin. Williams & Assocs., Palm Harbor, Fla., 1990—. Treas., pres. Klinkert Realty Co., Inc., Racine, Wis., 1960—85. Chief editor: Psychobiology of Depression, 1972, Mental Health in the 21st Century, 1979; contbr. numerous articles to profl. jours. and chpts. to books. Mem. Gov.'s Adv. Com. on Mental Health, Salt Lake City, 1971-77, Gov.'s Adv. Com. on Penal Code, Richmond, Va., 1978, Dist. Mental Health Bd., Tampa, 1980-83; mem. U.S. Govt. Mission on Psychiatry to USSR, 1974; sponsor, coach Forest Hills Little League Baseball, Tampa, 1980-83. Sr. surgeon USPHS, 1958-67. Recipient Predoctoral fellowship NIMH, 1960-61, Alumni Rsch. award N.Y. State Psychiat. Inst., 1964, Rush Bronze Medal award Am. Psychiat. Assn., 1973, Rsch. grants VA, 1977-78. Mem. AMA, Fla. Med. Assn., Hillsborough County Med. Assn., Columbia U. Alumni Club (dir. 1995—), Harvard Club of the West Coast of Fla. Avocations: computers, classical music, opera, basketball. Home: 3844 Muirfield Ct Palm Harbor FL 34685 Personal E-mail: tawmd@verizon.net.

**WILLIAMS, THOMAS EUGENE,** pediatric hematologist, pediatric oncologist, pharmaceutical executive; b. Texarkana, Ark., May 13, 1936; s. Thomas Earle and Frankie Jo (Garner) W.; m. Peggy Jane O'Neill, May 31, 1958; children: Thomas Eugene, Elizabeth Anne, James David. BA, Yale U., 1958; MD, U. Tex. Southwestern Med. Sch., 1962. Diplomate Am. Bd. Pediat., Am. Bd. Pediat. Hematology and Oncology. Rotating intern Hermann Hosp., Houston, 1962-63; pediat. resident Children's Med. Ctr., Dallas, 1963-65; fellow pediat. hematology U. Va. Sch. Medicine, Charlottesville, 1967-68; rsch. assoc. Cancer Rsch. Lab., U. Va., Charlottesville, 1968-69; asst. prof. pediat. and pathology U. Tex. Health Sci. Ctr., San Antonio, 1969-72, assoc. prof. pediat., asst. prof. pathology, 1972-73, assoc. prof. pediat. and pathology, 1973-79, assoc. prof. pediat., 1985-94. Med. dir. Santa Rosa Children's Hosp. Cancer Rsch. and Treatment Ctr., 1974—79, South Tex. Comprehensive Hemophilia Ctr., 1977—79; dir. pediat. bone marrow transplantation program, 1986—93; sr. clin. rsch. scientist Burroughs Wellcome Co., 1979—85; dir. new drug devel. Orphan Med., Inc., 1994—96; dir. med. affairs Ilex Oncology Svcs., Inc., 1997—98, ILEX Oncology Products, Inc., 1998—2002; clin. assoc. prof. pediat. U. N.C. Sch. Medicine, 1979—85; clin. fellow bone marrow transplantation program Johns Hopkins U. Sch. Medicine, Balt., 1985; sr. dir. Divsn. Oncology ICON Clin. Rsch., Inc., 2002—. Contbr. articles to profl. jours. Exec. dir. Episcopal Med. Missions Found., 1997—. Lt. cmmdr. USNR, 1965—67. Recipient travel award Am. Soc. Pharmacology and Exptl. Therapeutics, 1968; Am. Cancer Soc. advanced clin. fellow, 1968-69, 70-72. Mem. Am. Soc. Clin. Oncology, Am. Soc. Hematology, Am. Assn. for Cancer Rsch. Episcopalian. Office: 1174 Highland Terrace Dr Canyon Lake TX 78133-5271 Office Phone: 215-616-3250. Personal E-mail: drtommd@satx.rr.com. Business E-mail: williamst@iconus.com.

**WILLIAMS, THOMAS FRANKLIN,** physician, educator; b. Belmont, N.C., Nov. 26, 1921; s. T. F. and Mary L. (Deaton) Williams; m. Catharine Carter Catlett, Dec. 15, 1951; children: Mary Wright, Thomas Nelson. BS, U. N.C., 1942; MA, Columbia U., 1943; MD, Harvard U., 1950; DSc (hon.), Med. Coll. Ohio, 1987, U. N.C., 1992; DMS, Thomas Jefferson U., 2003. Intern Johns Hopkins, Balt., 1950—51, asst. resident physician, 1951—53; resident physician Boston VA Hosp., 1953—54; research fellow U. N.C., Chapel Hill, 1954—56, instr. dept. medicine and preventive medicine, 1956—57, asst. prof., 1957—61, assoc. prof., 1961—68, 1968; attending physician Strong Meml. Hosp., Rochester, NY, 1968—; cons. physician Genesee Hosp., Rochester, NY, 1973—; prof. medicine, preventive medicine and cmty. health U. Rochester, 1968—92, prof. radiation biology and biophysics, 1968—91, on leave, 1983—91, prof. emeritus, 1992—; clin. prof. medicine U. Va., 1983—89; lectr. medicine Johns Hopkins U., 1983—89; clin. prof. depts. family medicine and medicine Georgetown U., 1983—89; dir. Nat. Inst. on Aging NIH, 1983—91; asst. surgeon gen. USPHS, 1983—91, ret., 1991; attending physician Monroe Cmty. Hosp., Rochester, 1991—, vice-chmn. cmty. coalition for long term care, 1991—; disting. physician VA Med. Ctr., Canandaigua, NY, 1995—98. Adv. bd. U. Rochester Sch. Medicine and Dentistry, 1968—83; med. dir. Monroe Cmty. Hosp., Rochester, 1968—83; mem. rev. coms. Nat. Ctr. for Health Svcs. Rsch.; adv. bd. St. Ann's Home; mem. gov. bd. NRC, 1981—83; sci. dir. Am. Fedn. Aging Rsch., 1992—; cons. in field. Contbr. articles to profl. publs. With

USNR, 1943—46. Recipient Civic award for health care, Rochester N.Y. C. of C., 1998; fellow, USPHS, 1966—67; scholar Markle scholar, 1957—61. Fellow: ACP, APHA; mem.: NAS (coun. 1980—83, governing bd. 1981—83, Gustav O. Lienhard award Inst. Medicine 1969), AAAS, Am. Clin. Climatol. Assn., N.C. Coun. for Human Rels. (chmn. 1963—66), Rochester Regional Diabetes Assn. (pres. 1977—79), Am. Gerontol. Soc., Am. Geriatrics Soc., Soc. Exptl. Biology and Medicine, Am. Fedn. Clin. Rsch., Am. Diabetes Assn. (bd. dirs. 1974—80), Monroe County Med. Soc., N.Y. State Med. Soc., Assn. Am. Physicians, Inst. Medicine. Episcopalian. Home: 287 Dartmouth St Rochester NY 14607-3202 Office: Monroe Community Hosp Office Med Dir Rochester NY 14620 Office Phone: 585-760-6357.

**WILLIAMS, THOMAS RHYS,** anthropologist, educator; b. Martins Ferry, Ohio, June 13, 1928; m. Margaret Martin, July 12, 1952; children: Rhys M., Ian T., Tom R. BA, Miami U., Oxford, Ohio, 1951; MA, U. Ariz., 1956; PhD, Syracuse U., 1956. Asst. prof., asso. prof. anthropology Calif. State U., Sacramento, 1956-65; vis. asso. prof. anthropology U. Calif. Berkeley, 1962; vis. prof. anthropology Stanford U., 1976; prof. anthropology Ohio State U., Columbus, 1965-78, chmn. dept. 1967-71, mem. grad. council, 1969-72, mem. univ. athletic council, 1968-74, chmn. univ. athletic council, 1973-74, exec. com. Coll. Social and Behavior Scis., 1967-71; dean Grad. Sch. George Mason U., Fairfax, Va., 1978-81, prof. anthropology, 1981—, dir. Ctr. for Rsch. and Advanced Studies, 1978-81, fed. liaison officer, 1978-81, chmn. faculty adv. bd. grad. degree program in conflict resolution, 1980-86. Author: The Dusun: A North Borneo Society, 1965, Field Methods in the Study of Culture, 1967, A Borneo Childhood: Enculturation in Dusun Society, 1969, Introduction to Socialization: Human Culture Transmitted, 1972, Socialization, 1983, Cultural Anthropology, 1990; editor, contbg. author: Psychological Anthropology, 1975, Socialization and Communication in Primary Groups, 1975; contbr. articles to profl. jours. Mem. United Democrats for Humphrey, 1968, Citizens for Humphrey, 1968. With USN, 1946—48. Rsch. grant NSF, 1958, 62, Am. Council Learned Socs.-Social Sci. Rsch. Council, 1959, 63; Ford Found. S.E. Asia, 1974, 76; recipient Disting. Faculty award Calif. State U., Sacramento, 1961, George Mason U., 1983; Disting. Tchg. award Ohio State U., 1968, 76 Fellow Am. Anthrop. Assn., Royal Anthrop. Inst. Gt. Britain; assoc. mem. Current Anthropology; mem. AAAS, Sigma Xi. Office: George Mason U Robinson Hall B-315 MS 3G5 4400 University Dr Fairfax VA 22030-4444

**WILLIAMS, THOMAS W.,** electrical engineer; b. Rochester, N.Y., Aug. 3, 1943; s. Thomas Alfred and Mary Anne (Boryszewski) W.; m. Suzane Louise Sawyer, Dec. 26, 1964 (div. 1982); children: Megan Ren+245, David Thomas; m. Candace Merrill, Mar. 16, 1985. BSEE, Clarkson U., 1965; MA in Maths., Binghamton U., 1968; PhD in Elec. Engring., Colo. State U., 1971. From staff to sys. designer IBM, Endicott, NY, 1968-73, mem. ISI design rules and control group Boulder, Colo., 1973-77, from sr. engr., mgr. to sr. tech. staff, mgr. VLSI Design, 1977-1998; Synopsys fellow Test Technology, Synopsys, Inc. Guest prof., Robert Bosch fellow, Universitaet Hannover, Germany, 1985, 1996-98; adj. prof. U. Calgary, Can. Contbr. articles to profl. jours. Grantee NSF. Fellow IEEE (W. Wallace McDowell award 1989); mem. IEEE (bd. govs. 1987-93, 95-, bd. dirs. 2001-02), Phi Kappa Phi, Eta Kappa Nu. Office Phone: 303-245-0493. E-mail: t.williams@computer.org.

**WILLIAMS, TODD EDWARD,** plastic surgeon; s. Larry and Connie Williams; m. Deborah K. Allen, Apr. 11, 1999; children: Kendall, Sydney. BS, Ea. Ill. U., 1988; MD, So. Ill. U., 1992. Gen. surgery resident So. Mich. U., East Lansing, 1992—98; plastic surgery residency So. Ill. U., 1998—2000; pvt. practice San Juan Plastic Surgery, Farmington, N.Mex., 2000—. Office: San Juan Plastic Surgery 2300 E 30th St Bld B Ste 103 Farmington NM 87401 Office Phone: 505-327-1754.

**WILLIAMS, TONDA,** entrepreneur, consultant; b. NYC, Nov. 21, 1949; d. William and Juanita (Rainey) W.; 1 child, Tywana. Student, Collegiate Inst., N.Y.C., 1975-78, C.W. Post Coll., 1981-83; BA in Bus. Mgmt., Am. Nat. U., Phoenix, 1983; grad., L.I. Bus. Inst., 1996. Notary pub. N.Y. Asst. controller Acad. Ednl. Devel., N.Y.C., 1971-81; mgr. office Chapman-Apex Constrn. Co., Bayshore, NY, 1982-84; specialist computer RGM Liquid Waste Removal, Deerpark, NY, 1985-87; contr. LaMar Lighting Co., Freeport, NY, 1987—; owner, pres. Omni-Star, Bklyn., 1981—; pres. Omni-Data Tech., Bayshore, NY, 1996—. Author: Tonda's Songs in Poetry, 1978, The Magic of Life, 1991; co-author: Computer Management of Liquid Waste Industry, 1986. Recipient Golden Poet award World of Poetry, 1992. Mem. Am. Mus. Natural History, Am. Soc. Notary Pubs. Avocations: bowling, chess, singing. Home: 74 Cedar Dr Bay Shore NY 11706-2419 Office Phone: 631-968-0016. Office Fax: 631-968-1016. E-mail: tonda@omnidatatech.com.

**WILLIAMS, TREAT (RICHARD TREAT WILLIAMS),** actor; b. Rowayton, Conn., Dec. 1, 1951; s. Richard Norman and Marian (Andrew) W.; m. Pam Van Sant, 1988. BA, Franklin and Marshall Coll., 1973. Appeared in Broadway plays Over There, Grease; (repertory plays) Servant of Two Masters, Ohio, Claptrap, Cambridge, Mass., 1985, Pirates of Penzance at N.Y. Shakespeare Festival, Glass Menagerie, Long Wharf, New Haven, 1986, Bobby Gould in Hell, 1989; (films) Deadly Hero, 1976, Eagle Has Landed, 1976, Hair, 1979, Why Would I Lie, 1980, Pursuit, 1981, Prince of the City, 1981, Once Upon a Time in America, 1984, Flashpoint, 1984, Smooth Talk, 1985, Men's Club, 1986, Sweet Lies 1988, Dead Heat, 1988, The Heart of Dixie, 1989, Russicum, 1989, Where the Rivers Flow North, 1993, Handgun, 1994, Things to do When You're Dead, 1995, The Phantom, 1996, Mullholland Falls, 1996, The Devil's Own, 1997, Deep Rising, 1997, The Deep End of the Ocean, 1999, Skeletons in the Closet, 2000, Critical Mass, 2000, Crash Point Zero, 2000, Venemous, 2001, The Circle, 2001, Gale Force, 2002, Hollywood Ending, 2002, Miss Congeniality 2: Armed and Fabulous, 2005; TV movies Jack Dempsey Story, 1982, Streetcar Named Desire, 1983, Some Men Need Help, 1983, Hoover, Sweet Lies, 1986, Things To Do in Denver When You're Dead, 1995, In the Shadow of Evil, 1995, The Late Shift, 1996, Escape Human Cargo, 1998, Substitute 2: School's Out, 1998, 36 Hours to Die, 1999, The Substitute 3: Winner Takes All, 1999, Journey to the Center of the Earth, 1999, Guilty Hearts, 2002; (TV series) Good Advice, 1993-94, Everwood, 2002-; TV appearances Faerie Tale Theatre, 1987, Tales from the Crypt, 1992, Road to Avonlea, 1993, UC Undercover, 2002, Going to California, 2002. Mem. AFTRA, SAG, Actors Equity Assn. Episcopalian.

**WILLIAMS, UNA JOYCE,** psychiatric social worker; b. Youngstown, Ohio, June 24, 1934; d. Samuel Wilfred and Frances Josephine (Woods) Ellis; children: Wendy Louise, Christopher Ellis, Sharon Elizabeth. *Una Williams is descendant of the Ellis family of great-grandparents Thomas and Mary Ellis from Staffordshire, England. Mary came to America with her children after the death and burial of Thomas in Staffordshire. Her grandson, Sam Ellis, was an engineer with Saturn Rockets and her grandson, Sam Ellis, was a professional baseball player. She is also descended from pioneering families Scott and Woods, who migrated via wagon train into North Georgia from Virginia and the Carolinas in late 1700s and early 1800's. These families were farmers of Scotch-Irish lineage, and both have members who served in the Revolutionary and Civil Wars as well as WWI, WWII and Vietnam.* BA, U. Ala., 1957; MSW, Adelphi U., 1963. Diplomate in profl. counseling Internat. Acad. Behavioral Medicine, Counseling and Psychotherapy. Dir. Huntington Program Sr. Citizens, 1963—67; psychiat. social worker-supr. N.Y. State Dept. Mental Hygiene, Suffolk Psychiat. Hosp., Central Islip, 1969—72; info.-referral counselor Mental Health Assn. Nassau County, Hempstead, NY, 1993—; therapist Madonna Heights Family Clinic, Dix Hills, NY, 1994—99; med. and psychiat. social worker Northport VA Med. Ctr., NY, 1994—2005, psychiat. social worker acute psychiat. treatment svcs., 2005—, med. social worker dialysis svcs., 2005—. Cons. on programs for aging Luth. Social Svcs. Met. N.Y., 1959, sr. citizens programs, Bd. Edn. Port Jefferson, N.Y., 1961-63. Chmn. Huntington Twp. Com. Human Rels., 1970; sec. bd. trustees Unitarian Universalist Fellowship Huntington, 1984. Mem. NASW (diplomate in social work), Am. Assn. Family Counselors and Mediators,Germany Philatelic Soc. (pres. chpt. 30, 1990, Mem. of Yr. 1987). Avocations: painting, stamp collecting/philately, music (voice & piano), genealogy. Home: 316 Lenox Rd Huntington Station NY 11746-2640 Office Phone: 631-261-4400 2349.

**WILLIAMS, VANESSA (VANESSA LYNN WILLIAMS),** recording artist, actress; b. Millwood, N.Y., Mar. 18, 1963; d. Milton and Helen; m. Ramon Hervey II, 1988 (div. 1997); children: Melanie, Jillian, Devin; m. Rick Fox, 1999 (div.); 1 child, Sasha Gabriella Fox. Recording artist, 1988—. Stage appearances include: (Broadway) Kiss of the Spider Woman, 1993-95 (Theatre World award, 1995), Into the Woods, 2002(nominee Drama Desk award for Outstanding Actress in a Musical, 2002, Tony award Best Actress in a Musical, 2002); film appearances include Pick-up Artist, 1987, Under the Gun, 1988, Another You, 1991, Harley Davidson and the Marlboro Man, 1991, Eraser, 1996, Hoodlum, 1997, Soul Food, 1997, Dance with Me, 1998, The Adventures of Elmo in Grouchland, 1999, Light It Up, 1999, Shaft, 2000, Johnson Family Vacation, 2004,(TV films) Full Exposure: The Sex Tapes Scandal, 1989, The Kid Who Loved Christmas, 1990, Perry Mason: The Case of the Silenced Singer, 1990, Stompin' at the Savoy, 1992, Jacksons: An American Dream, 1992, Nothing Lasts Forever, 1995, Bye Bye Birdie, 1995, The Odyssey, 1997, Futuresport, 1998, Courage to Love, 2000 (also exec. prodr.), Don Quixote, 2000, A Diva's Christmas Carol, 2000, WW3, 2001, Keep the Faith, Baby, 2002, (TV mini series) Nothing Lasts Forever, 1995, (TV series) Ugly Betty 2006-; guest appearances Partners in Crime, 1984, T.J. Hooker, 1986, The Love Boat, 1986, The Fresh Prince of Bel-Air, 1990, Between Brothers, 1997, Vanessa Williams and Friends: Christmas in N.Y. 1996, Star Trek: Deep Space Nine, 1996, L.A. Doctors, 1999, Ally McBeal, 2002, Boomtown, 2003, South Beach, 2006; albums: The Right Stuff, 1988, The Comfort Zone, 1991, The Sweetest Days, 1994, Star Bright, 1996, Next, 1997, Alfie, the Best of Vanessa, 1998; # 1 hit single Save the Best for Last; vocalist (soundtracks) Beverly Hills 90210, 1990, Harley Davidson and the Marlboro Man, 1991, Adventures of Priscilla, Queen of the Desert, 1994, The Mask, 1994, Pocahontas, 1995, Eraser, 1996, Dance with Me, 1998, The Adventures of Elmo in Grouchland, 1999, Isn't She Great, 2000; host Style World, 2000; spokesperson for Proactive Solution (Acne Medication); commercial appearances Radio Shack. Recipient 8 Grammy award nominations; named one of 50 Most Beautiful People, People Mag. Achievements include being the first Black to be named Miss America, 1983 (resigned title 1983). Office: Mercury Records care Dawn Bridges 825 8th Ave New York NY 10019-7416 also: Mercury Records 11150 Santa Monica Blvd Los Angeles CA 90025-3380 Address: William Morris Agy 151 El Camino Dr Beverly Hills CA 90212*

**WILLIAMS, VAUGHN CHARLES,** lawyer; b. LA, Mar. 2, 1945; s. David Welford and Ovida M. (White) W. AB, Harvard U., 1966; JD, Stanford U., 1967. Bar: Calif. 1969, D.C. 1971, N.Y. 1977, U.S. Ct. Appeals (2d cir.) 1977, U.S. Ct. Appeals (5th, 8th and 9th cirs.), U.S. Supreme Ct. 1981. Law clk. to Hon. Carl McGowan U.S. Ct. of Appeals (D.C. cir.), Washington, 1969-70; counsel U.S. Senate, Dist. Col. Comm., Washington, 1970-71; assoc. Wilmer Cutler & Pickering, Washington, 1971-74; gen. counsel U.S. Coun. on Wage-Price Stability, Washington, 1975-76; assoc. Skadden Arps Slate Meagher & Flom, N.Y.C., 1977-79, ptnr., 1979—. Dir. N.Y.C. Campaign Fin. Bd., 1994—; mem. Merit Selection Panel So. Dist. of N.Y. Dir. Lincoln Ctr. for Performing Arts, N.Y.C., Bklyn. Acad. Music, God's Love We Deliver, Inc., Lawyers For Children, Inc.; vice chmn. Fund for the City of N.Y. Named to Am.'s Top Black Lawyers, Black Enterprise mag., 2003. Mem. Assn. Bar of City of N.Y. (Bainbridge-Smith com., com. for future, former mem. long range planning com.), University Club. Office: Skadden Arps Slate Meagher & Flom 4 Times Sq Fl 24 New York NY 10036-6595 E-mail: vwilliam@skadden.com.

**WILLIAMS, VENUS,** professional tennis player; b. Lynwood, Calif., June 17, 1980; d. Richard and Oracene Williams. Profl. debut Bank of West Classic, Oakland, Calif., 1994; owner V Starr Interiors; designer Venus Williams Collection Wilson's Leather Co. Mem. U.S. Fed Cup Team, 1995, 99, 2003, U.S. Olympic Tennis Team, Sydney, 2000, Athens, 04. Recipient ESPY award for outstanding women's tennis player, 2001, Espy award for Best Female Tennis Player, 2001, 2006, Espy award for Best Female Athlete, 2002; named Most Impressive Network Newcomer award, 1997, TENNIS Mag. Most Improved Player, WTA Tour, 1998; winner mixed doubles (with Gimelstob) Australian Open, 1998, Roland Garros, 1998, doubles (with Serena Williams) French Open, 1999, U.S. Open, 1999, Australian Open, 2001, 03, Wimbledon, 2002, 2005, singles and doubles gold medal winner, Sydney Olympics, 2000, singles U.S. Open, 2000, 01, Wimbledon, 2000, 2001; winner 31 Career Singles Titles and 9 Career Doubles Titles, WTA Tour. Mem.: WTA Tour Players' Coun. Jehovah'S Witness. Avocations: interior decorating, fashion design. Office: US Tennis Assn 70 W Red Oak Ln White Plains NY 10604-3602*

**WILLIAMS, VERONICA MYRES,** psychotherapist, social worker; b. Shreveport, La., May 11, 1947; d. McEura and Margie Virgina (Reagan) Myres; divorced; children: Nicole Leann, Jennifer Lyn, Erica Maria. BA, La. Tech. U., Ruston, 1969; MSW, U. Mich., Ann Arbor, 1977; PhD, So. Calif. U., 2001. Diplomate Am. Bd. Clin. Social Workers, Am. Psychotherapy Assn.; cert. social worker, Mich. Probation counselor Citizens Probation Authority, Flint, Mich., 1970-72; unit dir., therapist Svcs. to Overcome Drug Abuse Among Teenagers, Flint, 1972-74; psychiat. therapist Psycho-Therapeutic Treatment Clin., P.C., Flint, 1974-77; psychiat. social worker Hurley Med. Ctr., Flint, 1977-79; field instr. Sch. Social Work U. Mich., Ann Arbor, 1978-79, 86—; psychiat. social worker Inst. Mental Health, Flint, 1979-81, Psychotherapeutic Treatment Clinic, 1981-83; clin. social worker Flint Bd. Edn., 1979-83; pupil appraisal spl. edn. Caddo Parish Sch. Bd., Shreveport, La., 1983—85; psychiat. therapist Mott Children's Health Ctr., 1986—92, Oakland Psychol. Clinic, P.C., 1991—92; owner and dir. V. Williams, PhD, MSW, ACSW, BCD, PC, Flint, Mich., 1992—. Developer dropout prevention program Flint Bd. Edn., 1986-98; Recipient Svc. Dist., 1998-2006. Bd. dirs. Boys & Girls Club. Mem. NASW, ACSW, NEA, Mich. Edn. Assn. Democrat. Office: Ste 110 225 E 5th St Flint MI 48502 Office Phone: 810-232-0018. E-mail: drvmw@yahoo.com.

**WILLIAMS, VIVIAN LEWIE,** retired counseling administrator; b. Columbia, SC, Jan. 23, 1923; d. Lemuel Arthur Sr. and Ophelia V. (McDaniel) Lewie; m. Charles Warren Williams, Apr. 4, 1947 (div. 1967); children: Pamela Ann Williams-Coote, Charles Warren Jr. (dec.). BA, Allen U., 1942; MA in Psychology, U. Mich., 1946, postgrad., 1946, 48; MS, U. So. Calif., 1971, postgrad., 1971-72. Cert. marriage and family therapist, Calif.; cert. Calif. C.C. counselor. Asst. prof. psychology Tenn. State Agrl. and Indsl. U., Nashville, 1946-47; asst. prof. edn. Winston-Salem (NC) State U., 1947—50; asst. prof. edn., dir. tchr. edn. Allen U., Columbia, SC, 1951-53; specialist reading, coord. lang. arts Charlotte (N.C.) Mecklenburg Schs., 1963-67, cons. comprehensive sch. improvement project, 1967-69; asst. prof. edn., psychology Johnson C. Smith U., Charlotte, 1967-69; counselor, team leader Centennial, U. So. Calif. Tchr. Corps, L.A., 1970—73; counselor Compton (Calif.) C.C., 1973—2003, adv. fgn. student, 1975-85; ret., 2003. Co-developer Hyde Park Estates and The Moors, Charlotte, N.C., 1960-63. Pres. bd. dirs. Charlotte Day Nursery, 1956-59; bd. dirs. Taylor St. USO, Columbia, S.C., 1951-53; sec. southwest region Nat. Alliance Family Life, 1973-74; sec. bd. dirs. NCCJ, Charlotte, 1959-62. Recipient Faculty Audit Program award Ford/Carnegie Found., Harvard U., Cambridge, Mass., 1968, Pub. Svc. Achievement award WSOC Broadcasting Co.; fellow U. Mich., 1946. Mem. NAACP (life, Golden Heritage mem. 1992), AAUW (life), NEA (life), Am. Fedn. Tchrs., Faculty Assn. Calif. C.C., Nat. Acad. Counselors and Family Therapists (life, clin. mem., pres. S.W. region 1989), C.C. Counselors Assn., The Links, Inc. (Harbor area chpt. historian 1985-87, chaplain 1990-94, 96-98), Jack and Jill Am. (charter mem., organizer Charlotte chpt., pres. 1954-56), Women on Target, Calif. Tchrs. Assn., Delta Sigma Theta, Alpha Gamma Sigma (Golden Apple award 1981). Democrat. Methodist. Avocations: sewing, crafts, photography. Home: 6621 Caro St Paramount CA 90723-4755

**WILLIAMS, VIVIAN (VINNIE) MARIE,** publishing executive, editor, writer; b. Charleston, S.C., July 16, 1920; d. Joseph Harry Ahlsweh and Vivian Estelle Francis; m. Roy Raymond Williams, Mar. 15, 1945 (dec. Dec. 1978); 1 child, Marie DeWitt. BS in Social Work/Sociology, Fla. State Coll. for Women, 1941; LLD, Fla. State U., 1961. Social worker State of Fla., Fla.,

1941—44; reporter Sarasota (Fla.) Herald-Tribune, 1944—45; instr. Fla. State Coll. Women, Tallahassee, 1945—46; reporter McDuffie Progress, Thomson, Ga., 1964—71; freelance writer Atlanta Jour. Constn., 1964—71, Augusta (Ga.) Chronicle, 1971—81; owner, pub., editor The Oconee Enterprise, Watkinsville, Ga., 1986—2003. Co-organizer Wrightsboro (Ga.) Quaker Cmty. Found., Ga., 1968—; organizer, individual/sole sponsor Oconee Firefighters/1st Responders; coord. Watkinsville (Ga.) Christmas Parade, 1997—2003, Watkinsville Annual Awards Dinner, 1998—2003. Author: (novels) The Fruit Tramp, 1957 (Best Ga. award, 1957), Walk Egypt, 1960 (Best Ga. award), I Resign You, Stallion, 1965, Greenbones, 1966 (Best Ga. award, 1966). Vol. firefighters Oconee County. Recipient hon. life mem., Bartram Trail Horse Club, 1977. Mem.: Oconee County C. of C. (vol., com. mem., Vol. of the Yr. 2001), Ga. Press Assn. Democrat. Presbyterian/Methodist. Avocation: gardening. Address: Box 501 Watkinsville GA 30677 Office: The Oconee Enterprise Box 535 Watkinsville GA 30677 Office Phone: 706-769-5175.

**WILLIAMS, W. VAIL,** psychologist; b. Denver, Apr. 13, 1940; s. Warren J. and Edna M. (Follen) W.; m. Sandra M. Eisenrich (div. 1972); 1 child, Jason; m. Linda Lou Fain, Dec. 27, 1975; children: Ken, Dan, Davis, Jeremiah. BS, Bradley U., 1963, MA, 1964; PhD, U. Okla., 1968. Lic. psychologist, S.D., Colo., Calif. Owner Social Systems Devel., 1970-78; sr. psychologist Ft. Logan Mental Health Ctr., Denver, 1968-74; sr. rsch. assoc. Mental Rsch. Inst., Palo Alto, Calif., 1974-78; assoc. prof. Med. Sch. U. S.D., Sioux Falls, 1978—; chmn. curriuclum and evaluation com. Sch. Medicine U. S.D., Sioux Falls, 1989-92, mem. exec. com. dept. psychiatry Sch. Medicine, 1999—. Bd. dirs. Univ. Physicians, U. S.D. Sch. Medicine, 1997—; cons. Sioux Valley Behavioral Health, Sioux Falls, 1989-94, 99—, Woodfield Home, LSS, 1998—; clin. dir. Psychiatry Assocs., 1989—. Contbr. to books and articles to profl. jours. Bd. dirs. S.D. Jr. Football Assn., Sioux Falls, 1988-92, Citizens Against Rape and Violence, Sioux Falls, 1988-89, Post 15 Baseball Program, 1995-98. Fellow Am. Orthopsychiat. Assn.; mem. APA, AAAS, S.D. Psychol. Assn. (pres. Div. 1 1993-94), Woodlake Athletic Club, El Raid Shrine. Avocation: computers. Office: Psychiatry Assoc 1000 E 21st St Ste 4000 Sioux Falls SD 57105-1015 Home: 3700 S Westport Ave Sioux Falls SD 57106-6344 E-mail: wwilliam@usd.edu.

**WILLIAMS, WALKER RICHARD, JR.,** social services administrator; b. Dayton, Ohio, July 11, 1928; s. Walker Richard Sr. and Addie Mary (Smith) W.; m. Eddora L. Saunders, Aug. 6, 1949 (dec. Sept. 1966); 1 child, Yvette R.; m. Emma Jean Griffin, Sept. 4, 1971; children: Timotny E., Walker R. III. Student, U. Dayton, 1946-48. Commd. 2d lt. U.S. Army, 1952; advanced through grades to capt. USAF, Wright Patterson AFB, Ohio, 1963, supply cataloger, supr., 1963, employee rels. specialist, pers. mgmt. specialist, 1966-71; EEO investigator and grievance examiner, chief EEO and affirmative action programs Army and Air N.G., Wright Patterson AFB, Ohio, 1971-88; retired USAR, 1988; program dir. Youth Svc. U.S.A.-Dayton, 1988-89; pvt. contractor Dayton, 1989—. Mem. Adjutant Gen. Ohio Minority Recruiting Adv. Com., 1988—; bd. dirs. Dayton Opportunities Industrialization Ctr., 1976—, Wright Patterson Domestic Action Programs, Inc., 1984—; pres. Jefferson Twp. Bd. Edn., 1980—; mem. Nat. Black Caucus of Black Sch. Bd. Mems., 1980—, Nat. Black Caucus Local Elected Officials, Gov.'s Com. to Preserve Statue of Liberty, 1987, Citywide Vocat. Ednl. Com., 1986—; adv. com. Dayton Bd. Edn., 1980—, Miami Valley Mil. Affairs Assn., Black Elected Democrats of Ohio. Recipient Air Force Civilian Svc. award, Dayton C. of C., Internat. Personnel Mgmt. Assn. Employee of the Yr., Blacks in Govt. Pres.'s award, Federally Employed Women's Supr. of the Yr. runner up, Hispanic Heritage Wk. Spl. award, NAACP Humanitarian award, Community Svc. award, Dayton Bd. Edn., James W. Cisco award, Vocat. Ednl. award Wilberforce U., Urban League Humanitarian award, Svc. to Youth award Girl Scouts U.S., Spl. award United Negro Coll. Fund, Beautillion Militaire Legacy award, Jack & Jill, 7 Air Force Logistics Command Significant Achievement awards, AG of Ohio award, Ohio State U. award, Black Studies Group award, Russell Lyle award Wright Patterson AFB Quarter Century Club, Student Intervention Program Radcliff Sch., Blacks in Glvt. Mediation award, others; a day named in his honor, Dayton, 1987, 88, Svc. award Jefferson Township Bd. Edn. Mem. Miami Valley Pers. Assn., Internat. Pers. Mgmt. Assn., Retired Officers Assn., Air Force Assn., NAACP, Urban League, Blacks in Govt., Dayton Intergovt. EEO Coun. (chmn.), historian 1967—), Miami Valley Mil. Affairs Assn., Wright Patterson Quarter Century Club (past pres.). Democrat. Avocations: reading, photography. Home: 5050 Fortman Dr Dayton OH 45418-2233

**WILLIAMS, WALTER E.,** economics professor; b. Phila. BA in Econ., Calif. State Univ.; MA in Econ, PhD in Econ, UCLA; LHD (hon.), Va. Union Univ., Grove City Coll.; LLD (hon.), Washington & Jefferson Coll.; Doctor Honoris Causa en Ciencias Sociales (hon.), Univ. Francisco Marroquin, Guatemala. Life-time std. teaching credential State Calif. Group supr., juvenile delinquents LA Co. Probation Dept., 1963—67; faculty LA City Coll., 1967—69, Calif. State Univ., 1967—71, Temple Univ., Phila. 1973—80, George Mason Univ., Fairfax, Va., 1980—, now John M. Olin Disting. Prof. Econ. Adj. scholar Cato Inst., HeritageFound.; assoc. scholar Ethics and Pub. Policy Ctr. Author: The State Against Blacks, 1982, America: A Minority Viewpoint, 1982, All It Takes Is Guts, 1987, South Africa's War Against Capitalism, 1989, revised edit., 1990; contbr. articles to profl. jours.; mem. editl. bd. Jour. Labor Rsch.; mem. editl. rev. bd. Current Mag.; numerous debates, lectures, TV and radio appearances including appearances on Milton Friedman's Free to Choose, WQLN's Star Spangled Spenders, WTBS Debate Series Counterpoint, William F. Buckley's Firing Line, ABC Nightline, CBS Nightwatch, Face The Nation, Crossfire, MacNeil/Lehrer News Hour, CNN's Larry King Show, C-Span, Inside Story; former commentator NPR Radio, All Things Considered; commentator PBS Nightly Business Report, 1991-93; nationally syndicated columnist Creators Syndicate, 1980—; past weekly columnist Phila. Tribune; frequent appearance on network and local TV and radio news. Mem. adv. bd. Abraham & Sarah Found., Alexis de Rocqueville Inst., Atlas Econ. Rsch. Found., Buckeye Ctr. Pub. Policy Solutions, Capitol Rsch. Ctr., Ctr. for Rebldg. America's Schs., Commonwealth of Va., Gov.'s Adv. Coun. on Self-Determination and Federalism, Consumer Alert, Contemporary Econs. and Bus. Assn., Destiny Mag., Drury Coll., Breech Sch. Bus. Adminstrn., The Dumont Inst., Family Security Found., Free Enterprise Edn. Ctr., Ind. Inst., Inst. Econ. Affairs, Jour. Inst. Socioecon. Studies, Landmark Legal Found. Ctr. Civil Rights, Libertarian Alliance, London, Lincoln Inst., Nat. Found. Teaching Entrepreneurship to Handicapped and Disadvantaged Youth, Inc., Nat. Tax Limitation Com., Nellie Thomas Inst. Learning, Rep. Nat. Com., Rev. Bd. Econ. Studies NSF, Taxpayer's Found., Young Americans for Freedom; bd. overseers Hoover Instn. on War, Peace and Revolution, Stanford U.; bd. dis. Citizens for a Sound Economy, Reason Found. UCLA grad. opportunity fellow, Ford Found. dissertation fellow, Hoover Inst. War, Revolution and Peace Nat. fellow, Heritage Found. disting. scholar, 1978-79, UCLA Inst. Govt. and Pub. Affairs fellow; recipient Honor award Freedoms Found. at Valley Forge, 1977, Ann. award Alpha Kappa Psi Found., 1978, Nat. Svc. award Inst. Socioecon. Studies, 1980, George Washington medal of honor Freedoms Found., 1983, Disting. Alumnus award Calif. State U., 1987, L.A. City Commendation award, 1987, Adam Smith award Assn. Pvt. Enterprise Edn., 1989, Wilson S. Johnson award Nat. Fedn. Ind. Businesses, 1991, Robert J. Courtney award LaSalle U., 1993, U.S. News Media award VFW, 1993, award Heartland Inst., 1994, Warren Brooks award Am. Legis. Exch. Coun., 1994. Mem. Mt. Pelerin Soc., Am. Econ. Assn. Address: Creators Syndicate Ste 700 5777 W Century Blvd Los Angeles CA 90045 Office: Econ Dept George Mason Univ MSN 3G4 4400 University Dr Fairfax VA 22030-4444 Office Phone: 703-993-1148. Office Fax: 703-993-1133. Business E-mail: wwilliam@gmu.edu.

**WILLIAMS, WALTER JOSEPH,** lawyer; b. Detroit, Oct. 5, 1918; s. Joseph Louis and Emma Geraldine (Hewitt) W.; m. Maureen June Kay, Jan. 15, 1944; 1 child, John Bryan. Student, Bowling Green State U., 1935-36; BSBA, Ohio State U., 1940; JD, LL.B., U. Detroit, 1942. Bar: Mich. 1942. Title atty. Abstract & Title Guaranty Co., 1946-47; corp. atty. Ford Motor Co., 1947-51, Studebaker-Packard Corp., 1951-56; asst. sec., house counsel Am.

Motors Corp., Am. Motors Sales Corp., Am. Motors Pan-Am. Corp., Evart Products Co., Ltd., 1956-65, corp. sec. house counsel, 1965-72; asst. corp. sec., dir. Am. Motors (Can.) Ltd.; dir. Evart Products Co., 1959-72; dir., corporate sec., house counsel Jeep Corp., Jeep Sales Corp., Jeep Internat. Corp., 1968-72; partner Gilman and Williams, Southfield, Mich., 1972-74 atty. Detroit Edison Co., 1974-75; asst. sec., sr. staff atty. Burroughs Corp. (and subsidiaries), 1975-84; pvt. practice, pres. Walter J. Williams P.C., Bloomfield Hills, Mich., 1984—. Charter commr. City of Dearborn Heights, Mich., 1960-63; dir. Detroit Met. Indsl. Devel. Corp., 1962-72, also asst. sec. Served to capt. U.S. Army, 1942-46. Mem. ABA, Detroit Bar Assn. (chmn. corp. gen. counsel com. 1965-68), Fed. Bar Assn., State Bar Mich., Ohio State U. Alumni Assn. (pres. Detroit 1961-63), U. Detroit Law Alumni, Delta Theta Phi. Clubs: Oakland Hills Country. Home and Office: 3644 Darcy Dr Bloomfield Hills MI 48301-2125

**WILLIAMS, WALTER WAYLON,** lawyer, agricultural products supplier; b. Gause, Tex., Nov. 12, 1933; s. Jesse Nathaniel and Lola Fay (Matthews) W.; m. Velmalene Von Gonten, Mar. 6, 1953; children— Diana Lee, Virginia Marie. BBA with honors, U. Tex., 1959, JD with honors, 1960. Bar: Tex. bar 1960. Since practiced in. Houston; mem. firm Fulbright, Crooker, Freeman, Bates & Jaworski, 1960-63, Bates & Brock, 1964-66, Brock, Williams & Boyd, 1966-79, Williams & Boyd, 1979-88; pres. Nat. Pecan Growers Coun., 1976-78, Tex. Pecan Growers Assn., 1976-78. Served with AUS, 1953-55. Named Outstanding Soldier of Second Army, 1955 Mem. ABA, Houston Bar Assn., State Bar Tex., Tex. Trial Lawyers Assn. (dir. 1972-76), Houston Trial Lawyers Assn. (dir. 1969), Nat. Trial Lawyers Am., Chancellors, Beta Gamma Sigma, Phi Delta Phi. Home: 545 Williams Rd Yoakum TX 77995-5320

**WILLIAMS, WAYNE M.,** music educator, b. Potsdam, N.Y., Mar. 12, 1953; s. Earl Raymond and Jean Marie Williams; m. Diane Elizabeth Williams, July 3, 1976; children: Elaine, Elizabeth, Elyse. B in Music Edn., SUNY, Potsdam, 1975, M in Music Edn., 1980; diploma in piano tuning, Am. Sch. Piano Tuning, 2001; postgrad., Ind. Wesleyan U. Cert. tchr. N.Y. Jr. high instrumental music Sydney (Can.) Bd. Sch. Commr., 1977—84; grades K-8 gen./instrumental music tchr. Cape Breton Dist. Sch. Bd., Sydney, 1984—91; grades 4-12 instrumental music tchr. Schroon Lake (N.Y.) Ctrl. Sch., 1991—. First chair french horn Adirondack C.C. Concert Band, Lake George Chamber Orch., Glens Falls, NY, 1995—; organist, choir dir. Chestertown (N.Y.) Cmty. United Meth. Ch., 2001—; performer various brass and woodwind quintets/ensembles; bell staff Sagamore Resort, Bolten Landing, NY. Mem.: Schroon Lake C. of C. (brass dir. 1991—), Soc. for the Preservation and Encouragement Barbershop Quartet Singing in Am., Inc., Essex County Sch. Music Assn., Ctrl. Adirondack Sch. Music Assn., N.Y. State Sch. Music Assn., Music Educators Nat. Conf., Town of Schroon Lions Club (bd. dirs. 1996—, pres. 1999—2000), Phi Mu Alpha Sinfonia Fraternity Am. Inc. Republican. Methodist. Avocations: hockey, gardening, guitar. Home: 11 Continental Dr Schroon Lake NY 12870 Office: Schroon Lake Ctrl Sch Main St Schroon Lake NY 12870 E-mail: finetuning@nycap.rr.com.

**WILLIAMS, WESLEY S., JR.,** real estate company executive; BA, Harvard U.; JD, HArvard U.; MA, Tufts U.; LLM, Columbia U. Bar: N.Y., Washington. Co-chair bd., co-CEO, mem. exec. com. Lockhart Cos., Inc., St. Thomas, V.I., 1987—; co-chair Lockhart Ins. Holding Co., Ltd., Lockhart Fin. Svcs. Corp.; dir. Lockhart Real Estate Corp.; ptnr. Covington & Burling, Washington, 1975—. San Francisco, 1975—, London, 1975—, Brussels, 1975—, Paris, 1975—. Bd. trustees, mem. exec. com. Penn Mut. Lofe Ins. Co.; bd. mgrs. Blackstar LLC; bd. dirs. Blackstar Commn., Inc., Carr/Am. Realty Corp., Fed. Res. Bank, Richmond, Va.; adj. prof. real estate fin. and fin. svcs. law Georgetown U. Law Ctr. Mem.: N.Y. State Bar Assn., D.C. Bar Assn., Am. Law Inst. Office: PO Box 7020 St Thomas VI 00801

**WILLIAMS, WESLEY SAMUEL, JR.,** lawyer; b. Phila., Nov. 13, 1942; s. Wesley Samuel and Bathrus Amanda (Bailey) W.; m. Karen Roberta Hastie, Aug. 17, 1968; children: Amanda Pedersen, Wesley Hastie, Bailey Lockhart. BA in French Lit. magna cum laude, Harvard U., 1963, JD, 1967; MA (Woodrow Wilson fellow), Fletcher Sch. Law and Diplomacy, 1964; LLM, Columbia U., 1969. Bar: D.C., U.S. Supreme Ct., N.Y. Spl. counsel D.C. City Council, 1967-69; assoc.-in-law Columbia U. Law Sch., 1968-69; legal counsel Com. on D.C. U.S. Senate, 1969-70; assoc. Covington & Burling, Washington, 1970-75, ptnr., 1975—. Trustee Penn Mut. Life Ins. Co., Phila., 1978—; bd. dirs. Broadcast Capital Cos., 1979-92, chmn., 1989-92, Carr Realty, Co., Inc., 1993—; mem. Pres.'s U.S. Circuit Judge Nominating Commn., 1977-80; gen. counsel D.C. Bar, 1979-81; adj. prof. Georgetown U. Law Sch., 1971-73; mem. exec. com. Washington Lawyers Com. Civil Rights Under Law, 1972—; mem. editorial bd. D.C. Real Estate Reporter; vice chmn., bd. dirs. Lockhart Cos., St. Thomas, U.S. Virgin Islands, 1987—, co-chief exec. officer, 1989—; vice chmn., bd. dirs. Blackstar Communications, Cos., 1987—. Author legal articles, texts. Pres. bd. trustee Nat. Child Rsch. Ctr., 1980-82; bd. overseers Harvard U., 1985-91, chmn. vis. com. Harvard U. Div. Sch., 1986-91; bd. dirs. World Affairs Coun. Washington, D.C., Inc., 1980—, Nat. Symphony Orch. Assn., 1977-92; bd. dirs. Family and Child Svcs. Washington, 1970—, pres., 1973-76; exec. com. community adv. com. Jr. League Washington, 1977-86; pres. standing com. Epsic. Diocese of Washington, 1983-88; sec. bd. trustees Protestant Episc. Cathedral Found., 1982-90; bd. regents Smithsonian Inst., 1993—. Fellow Am. Bar Found.; mem. ABA, Am. Law Inst., Nat. Bar Assn., Fed. Bar Assn., D.C. Bar Assn., Washington Bar Assn., Harvard Law Sch. Assn. (pres.), Order Hosp. St. John Jerusalem, Harvard Club, City Tavern Club, Met. Club, Chevy Chase Club, Univ. Club, Alpha Phi Alpha, Sigma Pi Phi.

**WILLIAMS, WILLIAM COREY,** theology educator, consultant; b. Wilkes-Barre, Pa., July 12, 1937; s. Edward Douglas and Elizabeth Irene (Schooley) W.; m. Alma Simmenroth Williams, June 27, 1959; 1 child, Linda. Diploma in Ministerial Studies, NE Bible Inst., 1962; BA in Bibl. Studies, Cen. Bible Coll., 1963, MA in Religion, 1964; MA in Hebrew and Near Ea. Studies, NYU, 1966, PhD in Hebrew Lang. and Lit., 1975; postgrad., Hebrew U., 1977-78, Inst. Holyland Studies, 1986. Ref. libr. Hebraic section Libr. Congress, Washington, 1967-69; prof. Old Testament So. Calif. Coll./Vanguard U., Costa Mesa, 1969—; adj. prof. Old Testament Melodyland Sch. Theology, Anaheim, Calif., 1975-77; vis. prof. Old Testament Fuller Theol. Sem., Pasadena, Calif., 1978-81, 84, Asian Theol. Ctr. Evangelism Missions, Singapore and Sabah, E. Malaysia, 1985, Continental Bible Coll., Saint Pieters-Leeuw, Belgium, 1985, 2000-01; Mattersey Bible Coll., England, 1985, Inst. Holy Land Studies, Jerusalem, 1986, Regent U., 1994. Transl. cons. reviser New Am. Std. Bible, 1969-94; transl. cons. New Internat. Version, 1975-76, New Century Version, 1991, The New Living Translation, 1992-95, New Internat. Version, Reader's Version, 1993-94; transl. cons. editor Internat. Children's Version, 1985-86. Author: (books, tapes) Hebrew I: A Study Guide, 1980, Hebrew II: A Study Guide, 1986, They Spoke From God, 2004; contbr. articles to International Standard Bible Encyclopedia, New International Dictionary of Old Testment Theology and Evangelical Dictionary of Biblical Theology; contbr. articles to profl. jours.; contbr. notes to Spirit Filled Life Study Bible; editor: They Spoke From God, 2004. Nat. Def. Fgn. Lang. fellow NYU, 1964-67; Alumni scholar N.E. Bible Inst., 1960-61; NEH fellow, summer 1992; recipient Disting. Educator's award Assemblies God, 1997. Mem. Soc. Bibl. Lit., Evang. Theol. Soc. (exec. office 1974-77), Inst. Bibl. Rsch., Lockman Found., Costa Mesa, 1992-94, mem. editl. bd. 1974-94). Home: 1817 Peninsula Pl Costa Mesa CA 92627-4591 Office: Vanguard U 55 Fair Dr Costa Mesa CA 92626-6520 Office Phone: 714-556-3232 239. Business E-mail: wwilliams@vanguard.edu.

**WILLIAMS, WILLIAM EARLE,** artist, educator, curator; b. Vicksburg, Miss., Apr. 19, 1950; s. Willie and Estella (Steele) W.; m. Mary Katherine Meermans, Aug. 19, 1978; children: Emily Katherine, Daniel Earle. BA, Hamilton Coll., Clinton, NY, 1973; MFA, Yale U., 1978. Prof. art, curator photography Haverford (Pa.) Coll. Author: Party Pictures, 1985; author, editor: Photographers of Sculpture, 1988; editor: Japanese Wood Block Prints, 1987, Gettysburg: Journey in Time, 1997; one-man shows include

Cleve. Mus. of Art, 1990, South East Mus., 2001, Bryn Mawr Coll., 2002, exhibited in group shows at Allentown Mus. Art, 1995, Bardini Mus., Florence, Italy, 1990, Phila. Mus. Art, 2000, Princeton U. Mus., 2006, Represented in permanent collections Phila. Mus. Art, Met. Mus. Art, others. Fellow in photography, Pa. Coun. on the Arts, 1986, 1997, 2002, Pew fellow, 1997, Guggenheim fellow, 2003. Mem.: Soc. Photog. Edn. (bd. dirs. 1996—2003, vice chair 2000, treas. 2001), Phila. Athenaeum, Franklin Inn Club. Avocations: running, bicycling, walking. Home: 753 College Ave Haverford PA 19041-1301 Office: Haverford Coll 370 Lancaster Ave Haverford PA 19041-1336 Office Phone: 610-896-1259.

**WILLIAMS, WILLIAM HARRISON,** retired librarian; b. Seattle, Apr. 18, 1924; s. William E. and Letah M. (Hollenback) W.; m. Mary Helen Sims, Apr. 19, 1945; children: Linda Lee, Dee Ann. BS, Brigham Young U., 1969, M.L.S., 1970. Dir. Provo Pub. Library, Utah, 1969-70; Wyo. State Librarian, 1970-78; dir. Wyo. state Archives and Hist. dept., 1971-78; exec. sec. Wyo. Hist. Soc., 1971-78; pa. research analyst Wyo. Taxpayers Assn., 1978-84. Served to lt. col. USAAF, 1943-64. Decorated USAF commendation with oak leaf cluster. Mem. Masonic Order, Order of the Ea. Star, Order of the Amaranth, Beta Phi Mu, Phi Alpha Theta. Home: 18616 N 99th Ave Apt 1028 Sun City AZ 85373 E-mail: weewilli@juno.com.

**WILLIAMS, WILLIAM JOHN, JR.,** lawyer; b. New Rochelle, NY, Feb. 6, 1937; s. William John and Jane (Gormley) W.; m. Barbara Reuter. BA, Holy Cross Coll., Worcester, Mass., 1958; LLB, NYU, 1961. Bar: N.Y. 1961. Assoc. Sullivan & Cromwell LLP, NYC, 1962—68, ptnr., 1969—2004, of counsel, 2005—. Mem. legal adv. bd. NASD, 1988—94; mem. legal adv. com. NYSE, 1997—2000, 2003—. Trustee NYU Law Sch. Found., 1977—, Holy Cross Coll., 1988-96; chmn. bd. Sofia Am. Sch. in Bulgaria; past gen. counsel, chmn. rules golf com., sec., v.p. and pres. US Golf Assn., 1974-88. Fellow Am. Bar Found.; mem. ABA, Am. Law Inst., N.Y. State Bar Assn., N.Y.C. Bar Assn. Democrat. Roman Catholic. Office: Sullivan & Cromwell LLP 125 Broad St Fl 32 New York NY 10004-2498

**WILLIAMS, WILLIAM JOSEPH,** hematologist, educator; b. Bridgeton, N.J., Dec. 8, 1926; s. Edward Carlaw and Mary Hood (English) W.; m. Margaret Myrick Lyman, Aug. 12, 1950 (dec. Aug., 1985); children: Susan Lyman, William Prescott, Sarah Robb; m. Karen A. Hughes, Feb. 18, 1989. Student, Bucknell U., 1943-45; MD, U. Pa., 1949. Diplomate: Am. Bd. Internal Medicine. (hematology com. 1976-80). From intern to assoc. prof. U. Pa., Phila., 1949—61, assoc. prof. to prof. medicine, chief hematology, 1961—69; sr. research microbiology Case W. Res. U., 1952; asst. prof. medicine Washington U., St. Louis, 1959—60; rsch. fellow Oxford U., England, 1960—61; mem. hematology tng. com. Nat. Inst. Arthritis and Metabolic Disease, 1964—68, mem. rsch. career program com., 1968—72; chmn. dept. medicine SUNY Health Sci. Ctr., Syracuse, 1969—92, prof. medicine, 1969—, Disting. Svc. prof., 2002—, interim dean Coll. Medicine, 1991—92, dean coll. medicine and v.p. biomed. scis., 2002—04, disting. svc. prof., 2002—, dean emeritus Coll. Medicine, 2004—. Vis. scientist Walter and Eliza Hall Inst., Melbourne, Australia, 1980; vis. prof. Monash U., Melbourne, 1980; mem. thrombosis adv. com. Nat. Heart and Lung Inst., 1969-73, chmn., 1971-73; adv. coun. Nat. Arthritis, Metabolism and Digestive Diseases, 1975-79; mem. residency rev. com. internal medicine Accreditation Coun. Grad. Med. Edn., 1983-89, mem. bd. appeals panel for internal medicine, 1989-2000; mem. N.Y. State Coun. Grad. Med. Edn., 1987-89. Editor-in-chief: Hematology, 1972, 4th edit., 1989, Williams Hematology Companion Handbook, 1996; co-editor: Williams Manual of Hematology, 2003; contbr. articles to med. lit. Trustee Everson Mus. Art, 1975-81, 83-89. With USNR, 1944-46, 52-54. Recipient Research Career Devel. award Nat. Heart Inst., 1963-68; Daland fellow Am. Philos. Soc., 1955-57; Markle scholar, 1957-62 Mem. ACP (gov. Upstate N.Y. 1976-81), Am. Soc. Biochemistry and Molecular Biologists, Am. Soc. Clin. Investigation, Assn. Am. Physicians. Am. Clin. and Climatol. Assn., Am. Soc. Hematology, Interurban Clin. Club (sec. 1964-70), Alpha Omega Alpha. Mem. Soc. Friends. Home: 5160 Peck Hill Rd Jamesville NY 13078-9724 Office: 750 E Adams St Syracuse NY 13210-2306 Office Phone: 315-464-9788. Business E-Mail: williamw@upstate.edu.

**WILLIAMS, WILLIAM MAGAVERN,** headmaster; b. Niles, Mich., Dec. 22, 1931; s. Errol Edwin and Mary Elizabeth (Magavern) W.; m. Linda Carol Grush, June 15, 1958; children: Diana, William Jr., Sarah. BA, Williams Coll., 1953, LHD (hon.), 1984; postgrad. in Philosophy, Columbia U., 1954-58, MA in Ednl. Psychology, 1966. Tchr. elem. English, history, phys. edn. McTernan Sch., Waterbury, Conn., 1953-54; head guidance, boarding, and humanities depts., instr. English, coach varsity wrestling Riverdale Country Sch., Bronx, NY, 1955-66; headmaster Doane Acad., Burlington, NJ, 1966-70, Poly. Prep. Country Day Sch., Bklyn., 1970-00, headmaster emeritus, 2000—. Trustee Bklyn Inst. Arts and Scis., 1972-79, Bklyn. Ctrl. YMCA, 1974-78, Profl. Children's Sch., 1976-79, Bklyn. Children's Mus., 1979-82, Plymouth Ch. Pilgrims, 1979-86, N.Y. State Assn. Ind. Schs., 1980-86, Northern Stage, 2003-; chmn. bd. dirs Stafford (Vt.) Sch., 2002-03, United Ch. of Stafford, 2003—. Mem. Headmasters' Assn., Country Day Sch. Headmasters' Assn. (v.p. 1998-99, pres. 1999-2000), Cum Laude Soc. (regent dist. III 1971-87, dep. pres. gen. 1981-87, pres. gen. 1987-96, regent-at-large 1996—), Guild Ind. Schs. N.Y. (pres. 1986-88). Avocations: sailing, skiing, chess, travel, civil war history. Home: 15 Beacon Hill Rd Strafford VT 05072 Personal E-mail: wmw232@aol.com.

**WILLIAMS, WILLIAM PROCTOR,** literature educator; b. Glade, Kans., Sept. 1, 1939; s. Joseph Earl and Mildred Bernice Williams; m. Antonia Forster, June 2, 1984; children: Elizabeth Anne Dewbray, William Proctor II. BA, Kans. State U., 1961, MA, 1964, PhD, 1968. Asst. prof. English No. Ill. U., DeKalb, 1967—70, assoc. prof. English, 1970—78, prof. English, 1978—99, assoc. dean rsch., grad. sch., 1982, dir. librs., 1982—83; vis. prof. English Mary Baldwin Coll., Staunton, 2004—04; sr. lectr. English U. of Akron, Ohio, 2000—. Editor Analytical and Enumerative Bibliography, DeKalb, 2000—2002. Author: An Introduction to Bibliographical and Textual Studies, 1985, A Bibliography of the Writings of Robert Graves, 1987; contbr. articles to profl. jours. Reader gen. ordination exam. Episcopal Ch., 1974—77. Fellow, Newberry Libr., 1974; sr. rsch. fellow, Fulbright Comm., 1983, Charlton Hinman fellow, Folger Shakespeare Libr., 2003—04, Rsch. grantee, Nat. Endowment for Humanities, 1978. Fellow: Bibliog. Soc. Am.; mem.: Malone Soc., Soc. Textual Scholarship, Midwest MLA (mem. exec. com. 1987—90), Shakespeare Assn. Am. Achievements include discovery of Castle Ashby manuscripts. Avocations: gardening, historic aircraft, cricket. Home: 2006 White Pond Dr Akron OH 44313 Office: U Akron Dept English Akron OH 44325 Business E-Mail: wpw@uakron.edu.

**WILLIAMS, WILLIE, JR.,** physicist, researcher; b. Independence, La., Mar. 24, 1947; s. Willie Sr. and Lee Anner (Booker) W.; 1 child, Willie Williams III. BS, So. U., 1970; MS, Iowa State U., 1972, PhD, 1974. Mem. faculty Lincoln U., Lincoln University, Pa., 1974—, assoc. prof. physics, 1979-84, prof. physics, 1984—, chmn. dept., 1976-95, chmn. sci. and math. div., 1978-80, 83-88, founder, dir. Lincoln Advance Sci. and Engring. Reinforcement (LASER) Program, 1980-96, dir. pre-engring., 1976-96, prin. investigator Early Alert-Young Scholars Program, 1992-96. Bd. dirs. women tech. program Lincoln U. Urban Ctr., Phila.; vis. prof. Ctr. for Teaching Innovation, Drexel U., 1975; liaison officer Nat. Assn. for Equal Opportunity in Higher Edn., Dept. Def. Program., 1987—; mem. steering com. NSF Comprehensive Ctr. for Minorities, Phila.; bd. dirs. Prime Inc., Phila. Contbr. articles to profl. jours. Chmn. Cheyney Lincoln Temple Cluster, 1974-78; pres. The Men Fedn., So. U., 1968-69. Recipient Lindback award for Outstanding Teaching, 1976, Outstanding Scientist award White House Initiative, 1988; named one of Outstanding Young Men of Am., 1987 by NASA, 1979, Mobil Oil Corp., 1977, Nat. Bur. Standards, 1979, Dept. Def., 1980-81, Navy fellow, 1982 Mem. AAAS, AAUP (pres. Lincoln U. chpt. 2001-03), Am. Assn. Physics, N.Y. Acad. Scis., Math. Assn. Am., Am. Phys. Soc., Nat. Soc. Black Physicists, Nat. Geog. Soc., Iowa State Alumna Assn., Sigma Xi, Sigma Pi Sigma. Baptist. Home: 448 W Baltimore Pike West Grove PA 19390-9201 Office: Lincoln U Dept Physics Lincoln University PA

19352 Office Phone: 610-932-8300 ext. 3474. E-mail: wwillie2@aol.com. *Throughout my life I have always striven to achieve the very best and have held on to the belief that wherever possible improve upon today, so that everyone might have a better tomorrow! I have been guided by the principle of being selective in my endeavors, having specific objectives, followed by detailed analysis, concise actions, and intense work with continous review.*

**WILLIAMS, WILLIE ALVIN,** retired literature educator; b. Windom, Tex., Oct. 16, 1919; s. Elie Williams and Louease Kimble-Williams; m. Trula Amanda Sloan, Sept. 23, 1943; 1 foster child, Jacqueline L. Maxwell. BA, Wiley Coll., 1948. Tchr. English Rhodes H.S., Daingerfield, Tex., 1948—49, Pemberton H.S., Marshall, Tex., 1950—77, Toyei Boarding Sch., Ganada, Ariz., 1977—83; ret., 1983. Water safety instr. ARC Gregg County, Longview, Tex., 1968—77. Author: Cousins, Unlimited, 2003, booklets. Mem. local chpt. NAACP, 1984—89; mem. Gregg County Hist. Com., 1990—; mem. disaster team ARC, Longview, 1986—89; tchr. Sunday Sch. Wesley/McCabe United Meth. Ch., Longview, 1967—; bd. dirs. Longview chpt. ARC, Longview, 1987—89; bd. dirs Habitat for Humanity, Longview, 1984—87. Master sgt. U.S. Army, 1940—45. Named Sunday Sch. Tchr. of Yr., Wesley/McCabe United Meth. Ch., 2001; recipient Martin Luther King Humanitarian award, Pan Hellenic Coun., Longview, 1987. Democrat. Avocations: swimming, fishing, woodworking. Home: 2102 Armond Dr Longview TX 75602 E-mail: kimsharwaw@aol.com.

**WILLIAMS, YOLANDA YVETTE,** music educator; d. Ernest Thomas Williams and Thelma Christina Williams (Lewis). BA, Hamline U., 1979; MusB, U. Minn., Mpls., 2004. Adj. faculty music dept. Mpls. (Minn.) Cmty. and Tech. Coll., 1991—; adj. faculty African-Am. Studies U. of Minn., Minneapolis, Minn., 1998—; dir. of worship and music Redeemer Luth. Ch., Mpls., 2003—. Singer: (opera) La Purpura de la Rose, Porgy and Bess, (musical) Chatouranga, A.My Name Is Alice, The Greenwood Encyclopedia of African American Folklore, 2006, (oratorio) Requiem Mass. Mem. steering com. J-Train, St. Paul, 2003. Avocations: reading, composing. Office: University of Minnesota 267 19th Ave S 808 Soc Sci Minneapolis MN 55455-0471 E-mail: willi233@tc.umn.edu.

**WILLIAMS-DE SILVA, LISA ANNETTE,** small business owner, adult nurse practitioner; d. Joice Renee and Charles Braden (Stepfather); m. Lionel De Silva, June 12, 2003. BS in Bus., Ariz. State U., 1988, BSN, 2000, MSN, Nurse Practitioner, 2003. Cert. Achievement Cynosure Laser, Cert. Proficiency, Aesthetic Laser Sys. Sciton Aesthetic. Pres. Medical-Legal Support Svcs., Inc., Scottsdale, Ariz., 1998—. Owner and nurse practitioner Ultra Smooth Skin, Inc., Scottsdale, 2003—. Faculty Wives Club scholar, Ariz. State U., 1998—2000, STAR Program scholar, 1998—2000. Mem.: Dermatology Nurses Assn., Internat. Acad. of Laser Medicine and Surgery (assoc.), Am. Assn. of Legal Nurse Consultants (assoc.), Am. Coll. of Phlebology (assoc.), Am. Acad. of Nurse Practitioners (assoc.), Am. Soc. of Laser Medicine and Surgery (assoc.). Avocations: hiking, travel, scuba diving. Office: Med-Legal Support Svcs Inc 14891 N Northside Scottsdale AZ 85260 Office Phone: 480-699-1244.

**WILLIAMSEN, DANNYE SUE,** publishing executive, writer; b. Memphis, Mar. 26, 1949; d. Roy Fauntly and Arliss Wyleen Goodroe; m. Jon Charles Beckum, Dec. 23, 1969 (div. Mar. 1972); m. John Dean Williamsen, Dec. 24, 1986. BA cum laude, U. Memphis, 1995. Adminstr. Security Investments, Inc., Memphis, 1972—75; nightclub owner, investor Memphis, 1976—78; internat. tech. analyst ContiCommodity, Inc., Memphis, 1977—80; owner, tech. analyst Commodity Cons., Inc., Memphis, 1981; project mgr. B&P Devel. Co., Austin, Tex., 1982—84; asst. to pres. Memphis C. of C., 1984—86; owner, dental technician Williamsen Dental Lab., Memphis and Prophetstown, Ill., 1986—; ptnr., editor Personal Edn. Network, Prophetstown, Ill., 2001—; owner Networx Pub., Prophetstown, 2002—05, Williamsen Pub., Smyrna, Ga., 2006—. Bd. dirs. Heartland Equine Assisted Therapeutic Ctr., Rock Falls, Ill., 2000—01; columnist Penmanship mag., 2005—; pub. Williamsen Pubs., 2000—. Author: Illusions, 1998, IT'S YOUR MOVE! Transform Your Dreams from Wishful Thinking to Reality, 2004; editor: Creative Living-an evolving approach to bus. life, 2001—, (e-newsletter) Metaphysical Minute, 2003—04; columnist: Penwomanship Mag, 2005; editor: (newsletter) MindSlap!; author: Metaphysical Minute-Philosophy on the Run, 2006. Mem. AAUW (pres. 1998-99), APA, NOW, NAFE, Am. Bus. Women's Assn., Assn. for Humanistic Psychology, Nat. Assn. Women Writers, Small Pubs. Assn. N.Am., Pubs. Mktg. Assn., Psi Chi, Chi Beta Phi. Avocations: reading, counseling. Office: Williamsen Publs PO Box 680924 Marietta GA 30068-0016 Office Phone: 770-438-0889. Business E-Mail: dannyew@williamsenpublications.com.

**WILLIAMS III, ROBERTON CAPELL,** economics professor; b. Keflavik, Iceland, Dec. 2, 1972; s. Roberton Capell Williams, Jr. and Jane Carlile Hilder. AB, Harvard Coll., 1990—94; PhD, Stanford U., 1994—99. Asst. prof. U. Tex., Austin, 1999—. Faculty rsch. fellow Nat. Bur. Econ. Rsch., Cambridge, Mass., 2000—; Andrew W. Mellon fellow in econ. studies Brookings Instn., Washington, 2002—03; vis. rsch. scholar Stanford Inst. Econ. Policy Rsch., 2003—04. Mem. editl. coun.: Jour. Environ. Econs. & Mgmt., Berkeley Electronic Jour. in Econ. Analysis & Policy; contbr. papers to profl. jours. and pubs. Grantee Grad. fellowship, NSF, 1994—97, STAR Grad. fellowship, EPA, 1997—99. Mem.: Assn. Environ. and Resource Economists, Nat. Tax Assn., Am. Econ. Assn., Austin Yacht Club. Avocations: sailboat racing, travel, landscape photography. Office: Dept Econs Univ Tex 1 University Sta #C3100 Austin TX 78712-0301 Office Phone: 512-475-8522. Business E-Mail: rwilliam@eco.utexas.edu.

**WILLIAMS MADDOX-BROWN, JANICE HELEN,** nurse; b. Boston; d. Arthur Hamilton Wade and Edith Josephine (Weekes) Williams; m. Larry Maddox, May 21, 1977 (dec.); m. Richard Brown, Mar. 11, 2000. BS in Nursing, Boston U., 1957; MA, Atlanta U. Sch. Edn., 1971; MPH, Emory U., 1976; PhD, Union Inst., Cin., 1998. Staff nurse Beth Israel Hosp., Boston, 1958, N.Y. Hosp.-Cornell U. Med. Ctr., N.Y.C., 1958-59; ward supr. Jewish Meml. Hosp., Boston, 1959-61; staff and pvt. duty nurse Mass. Gen.Hosp., Boston, 1961-63; pub. health nurse Boston Health Dept., 1963-64; intravenous nurse Hughes Spalding Hosp., Atlanta, 1964-66; pub. health nurse Fulton County (Ga.) Health Dept., 1966-69; sr. tchr. Atlanta Southside Comprehensive Health Ctr., 1970-73, acting dir. edn., 1973-74, assoc. dir. clin. nursing, 1974-76; assoc. dir. mental health planning project So. Region Edn. Bd., Atlanta, 1976-78; nursing cons. Dept. Health and Human Svcs., Atlanta, 1978-81; head nurse VA Med. Ctr., Atlanta, 1982-85; br. mgr. Am. Home Health Care of Ga., Inc., Jonesboro, 1985-86; ind. contractor Med. Emergency Clinic-Grady Meml. Hosp., 1986—91; project dir. Morehouse Sch. Medicine Initiative, W.K. Kellogg Found., 1991-95; assoc. prof. Ctrl. Mich. U., 2000—01. Evening coord., instr. for innovative practical nursing program for health para-profl. Atlanta Area Tech Sch., 1971-83; admissions com. M. Pub. Health program Emory U. Sch. Medicine, 1979-91. Women's Day com. Ctrl. United Meth. Ch., Atlanta, Ben Hill United Meth. Ch Recipient spl. recognition Am. Cancer Soc., 1975.

**WILLIAMSON, ALAN BACHER,** literature educator, poet, writer; b. Chgo., Jan. 24, 1944; s. George and Jehanne (Bacher) W.; m. Anne Winters, Oct. 12, 1968 (div. Feb. 1988); 1 child, Elizabeth Kilner. BA, Haverford Coll., 1964; MA, Harvard U., 1965, PhD, 1969. Asst. prof. U. Va., Charlottesville, 1969-75; Briggs-Copeland lectr. Harvard U., Cambridge, Mass., 1977-80; Fannie Hurst lectr. Brandeis U., Waltham, Mass., 1980-82; prof. English, U. Calif., Davis, 1982—. Poetry panelist Nat. Endowment for Arts, 1989. Author: (criticism) Pity the Monsters, 1974, Introspection and Contemporary Poetry, 1984 Eloquence and Mere Life, 1994, Almost a Girl, 2001, (poetry) Presence, 1983, The Muse of Distance, 1988, Love and the Soul, 1995, Res Publica, 1998, The Pattern More Complicated: New and Selected Poems, 2004, Westernness: A Meditation, 2006. Poetry fellow Nat. Endowment for Arts, 1973; Guggenheim fellow, 1991. Mem. MLA (exec. com. div. on poetry 1987-91). Democrat. Buddhist. Office: U Calif Dept English Davis CA 95616 Business E-Mail: abwilliamson@ucdavis.edu.

**WILLIAMSON, BARRY SCOTT,** conductor, performing arts educator; b. Washburn, Wis., Dec. 13, 1955; s. Mortimer Leo and Esther Edna Williamson; 1 child, Caitlin Rose. MusB, Concordia Coll., Moorhead, Minn., 1978; MusM in Choral Conducting, U. of Ariz., 1982; Dr. of Mus. Arts in Choral Conducting, U. Tex., 1993. Vocal instr./coach Williamson Vocal Studio, Austin, Tex., 1986—; founding artistic dir. and condr. Tex. Choral Consort, Austin, 1997—; choir dir. and organist Koenig Ln. Christian Ch., Austin, 1998—. Dir. of music ministries St. John Neumann Cath. Ch., Austin, 1989—91; choir dir. Hyde Pk. Christian Ch., Austin, 1987—89; vocal music dir. Cholla H.S., Tucson, 1982—86; choirmaster and organist St. Alban's Episc. Ch., Tucson, 1984—86; condr., univ./cmty. chorus U. of Ariz., Tucson, 1981—82; asst. dir. Tucson Ariz. Boys Chorus, 1981—82; paid singer St. Phillip's On the Hill Episc. Ch., Tucson, 1981—82; vocal music dir. Rice Lake Sr. H.S., Rice Lake, Wis., 1980—81; choir dir. Bethany Luth. Ch., Rice Lake, 1980—81; vocal music dir.- grades 7-12 Kasson-Mantorville Jr-Sr. H.S., Kasson, Minn., 1978—80; dir. of music ministries NW Hills United Meth. Ch., Austin, 1996—98; choir dir. St. John's Luth. Ch., Kasson, Minn., 1978—80; choir dir.,Concordia choir Concordia Coll., Moorhead, Minn.; dir. of choral activities U. of Tex. at El Paso, 1993—96; choirmaster and organist St. Francis On the Hill Episc. Ch., El Paso, Tex., 1993—95; dir. of choral activities Trinity U., San Antonio, 1992—93; artistic dir. and condr. Austin Civic Chorus, Austin, 1987—91; condr. chorus U. of Tex. at Austin, 1986—88; asst. chorus dir., asst. to the condr. Austin Lyric Opera, Austin, 1986—88; dir. of music ministries Good Shepherd Episc. Ch., Austin, 1991—92. Mem.: Chorus Am., Tex. Choral Dirs. Assn., Am. Choral Dirs. Assn. Office: Texas Choral Consort PO Box 300597 Austin TX 78703-0010 Office Phone: 512-372-3233. E-mail: barry@txconsort.org.

**WILLIAMSON, BRIAN DAVID,** information systems executive, consultant; b. Danbury, Conn., May 14, 1973; s. Robert Garth and Celeste Marie (D'Alessio) W. AA in Specialized Bus., Art Inst. Phila., 1993; BS in Gen. Studies, Teikyo Post U., 1994; postgrad. in Tech. Mgmt., Polytech. U., 1997. Asst. mgr. The New Milford (Conn.) Music Ctr., 1991-93; prodn. asst. Med. Broadcasting Co., Conshohocken, Pa., 1993; CIO Custom Designs, Inc., Danbury, Conn., 1991—; info. systems and telecomms. analyst Datahr Rehab. Inst., Brookfield, Conn., 1996-97; LAN adminstr. Praxair, Inc., Danbury, Conn., 1998—. Video technician Danbury Corp., Bethel, Conn., 1992-97. Author, writer (film script) The Senior, 1994. Republican. Roman Catholic. Avocations: tennis, computer graphics, movies, music, hiking. Office: Praxair Inc 39 Old Ridgebury Rd Ste 7 Danbury CT 06810-5109 Home: 12 Tandem Ln Sherman CT 06784-1918

**WILLIAMSON, BRUCE A.,** gas industry executive; b. Great Falls, Mont. B in Fin., U. Mont., 1981; MBA, U. Houston. With Royal Dutch/Shell Group, 1981—95; sr. v.p. fin. bus. develop. and risk mgmt. PanEnergy Corp., v.p. fin., 1995—97; pres., CEO Duke Energy Internat., 1997—2001, Duke Energy Global Markets, 2001—02, Dynegy Inc., Houston, 2002—, chmn., 2004—, CEO, 2002—. Chancellor's nat. adv coun. U. Houston, Dean's adv. bd., C.T. Bauer Coll. Bus.; bd. dir. Greater Houston Partnership. Office: 1000 Louisiana Ste 5800 Houston TX 77002 Office Phone: 713-507-6400, 877-439-6349. Office Fax: 713-767-6652, 713-507-3871.*

**WILLIAMSON, CARL AUGUSTUS,** engineering executive; b. Newport News, Va., Sept. 7, 1950; s. Marvis Harrison Sr. and Annie Lucille (Amos) W.; m. Bonnie Bernel Mitchell, Sept. 21, 1973; 1 child, Carl Michael; 1 stepson, Leon Mitchell. BS, Norfolk State Coll., 1972; MBA, Northeastern U., 1982; DEng, MIT, 1987. Cert. secondary edn. tchr. Electrical estimator Stone & Webster, Boston, 1973-74; instr. D.C. Pub. Schs., Washington, 1974-76; sales engr. Westinghouse, Framingham, Mass., 1976-78; cost engr. Gilbert Commonwealth, Jackson, Mich., 1978-80; instr. Boston Pub. Schs., Boston, 1980-82; cons. Gilbert Commonwealth, Washington, 1983—. Col. U.S. Army, 1968-72. Mem. NRA, MBA Assn., Washington Tchrs. Union. Baptist. Avocations: sports, arts, dance. Home and Office: Apt 207 2700 Martin Luther King Jr Ave # A Washington DC 20032-2601

**WILLIAMSON, CHARLES R.,** retired energy company executive; PhD in Geology, U. Tex., Austin, 1978. Rsch. assoc. Sci. and Tech. Divsn. Unocal Corp., Brea, Calif., 1977-83, chief exploration geologist U.K., 1983-86; exploration mgr. U. Unocal Netherlands, The Hague, 1986-89; v.p. exploration Uncoal Thailand, Bangkok, 1989-92; v.p. Energy Resources Divsn. Unocal, 1992-94, v.p. planning and info. svcs., 1994-95, v.p. corp. planning and econs., 1995-96, group v.p. internat. opers., 1996-97, group v.p. Asia Opers., 1997-99; exec. v.p. internat. energy ops. Unocal Corp., El Segundo, Calif., 1999—2001; CEO, chmn. Unocal (acquired by Chevron Corp.), 2001—05; exec. v.p., mem. exec. com. Chevron Corp., 2005. Mem. adv. bd. earth scis. dept. Stanford U.; bd. dir. Weyerhaeuser Co., 2004—, Talisman Energy Inc., 2004—, PACCAR Inc., 2006—. Mem. Am. Soc. Petroleum Geologists, Soc. Econ. Paleontologists and Mineralogists, Soc. Petroleum Engrs., Internat. Assn. Sedimentologists. Mailing: PACCAR Inc Bd Directors PO Box 1518 Bellevue WA 98009*

**WILLIAMSON, CHARLES READY, III,** lawyer; b. Boston, Jan. 2, 1944; s. Charles Ready and Anne Margaret (Livingstone) W.; m. Julie Anne Williamson, Nov. 6, 1971; 1 dau., Anne Lucinda. B.A., Colgate U., 1965; LL.B., Suffolk U., 1968. Bar: Mass. 1968, Oreg. 1970, U.S. Supreme Ct. 1977. Law clk. to Judge Joseph B. Silverio, Mass. land ct., Boston 1968-69; VISTA atty., dep. dir. Multnomah County Legal Aid Service, Portland, 1970-74; assoc. Kell, Alterman & Runstein, Portland, 1974-78, 88—; pvt. practice, Portland, 1978-88; pres. Oreg. Legal Service Corp., 1976-77; mem. Oreg. Bd. Psychology Examiners, 1973-74; chmn. Oreg. Grad. Sch. Profl. Psychology, Pacific U. Pres. Oreg. Consumer League, 1972-74; councilor Met. Service Dist. 1978-84; treas. Democratic Bus. Forum 1982-84. Mem. ABA, Oreg. Bar Assn. (pres., pres.-elect 2002-03, pres. 2003-04), Multnomah County Bar Assn. Club: Portland City. Contbr. in field. Office: Kell Alterman & Runstein 520 SW Yamhill Ste 600 Portland OR 97204-1329

**WILLIAMSON, DONALD ELLIS,** public health service officer, state agency administrator; b. Louisville, Miss., June 17, 1955; m. Anita Hudspeth; 1 child, Jonathan Stuart. Student, East Miss. Jr. Coll., 1972-73, Miss. State U., 1973-75; MD cum laude, U. Miss., 1979. Diplomate Am. Bd. Internal Medicine. Intern, resident in internal medicine U. Va. Hosp., Charlottesville, 1979-82; with East Miss. State Hosp., Meridian, 1979; state tb control oficer Miss. State Dept. Health, 1982-86; dir. divsn. disease control Ala. Dept. Pub. Health, 1986-88, dir. bur. preventive health svcs., 1988-92, state health officer, 1992—. Faculty mem. Injury Control Rsch. Ctr. U. Ala., Birmingham; clin. assoc. prof. dept. internal medicine U. South Ala.; presenter in field. Contbr. articles to profl. jours. Chmn. Ala. Pub. Health Care Authority, Ala. Radiation Adv. Bd. Health; mem. Ala. Commn. Aging, State Bldg. Commn., Statewide Health Coordinating Coun., Ala. Youth Svcs. Bd., Ala. Child Abuse & Neglect Prevention Bd., Ala. Resource Devel. Com., Ala. Anat. Bd., Planning and Adv. Coun. Devel. Disabilities, Ala. Bd. Med. Scholarship Awards, Pesticides Adv. Com., Gov.'s Interagy. Coordinating Coun., Ala. Juvenile Justice Coordinating Coun., Emergency Med. Svcs. Adv. Coun., 1986-92, Legis. Adv. Com. AIDS, 1988-90, Atty. Gen.'s Task Force Med.Waste, 1989, Water Resources Adv. Coun., and Ala. Children's Svcs. Facilitation Team, 1993—; mem. med. adv. com. ARC. Recipient Mosby Book award, 1979, Dr. Robert Ramsey award, 1993; Pub. Health Leadership Inst. scholar, 1996. Mem. APHA, Assn. State and Territorial Health Ofcls. (exec. com. 1995-2000, pres. 1997-98), Am. Acad. of Pediatrics (Child Health Advocate of the Yr. award 1999), Pub. Health Found. (Theodore R. Ervin award 1999) Med. Assn. State Ala., Ala. Pub. Health Assn. (bd. dirs. 1991—, chmn. disease control and epidemiology Sect. 1991-92, D.G. Gill award 1997), Pub. Health Found. (bd. dirs. 1995-99, treas. 1997—), Phi Theta Kappa, Phi Kappa Phi, Alpha Omega Alpha. Home: 8113 Lichfield Ct Montgomery AL 36117-5124 Office: Ala Dept Pub Health PO Box 303017 201 Monroe St Montgomery AL 36104-3735

**WILLIAMSON, DONALD RAY,** retired career Army officer; b. Amarillo, Tex., Oct. 13, 1943; s. Floy Edwin and Dorothy Lorene (Orr) W.; m. Beverly Ann Howard, Aug. 31, 1963; children: Rebecca Ann, Catherine Paige. BS in

Econs., W. Tex. State U., 1966; MA in Bus., Cen. Mich. U., 1977; degree, Dept. Def. Program Mgrs., 1982, U.S. Army Command and Gen. Staff Coll. 1980. Commd. 2d lt. U.S. Army, 1966, advanced through grades to lt. col., 1982, retired, 1986, comdg. officer combat support co. Ft. Hood, Tex., 1973-74, comdg. officer 2d aviation co. 1974-75, dep. insp. gen. Ft. Leavenworth, Kans., 1975-78, comdg. officer 213th aviation co. Rep. of Korea, 1978-79, asst. program mgr. advanced scout helicopter program, 1981-86; owner Witan Group, Chesterfield, Mo., 1986-88; pres., owner Sys. Test Evaluation Inc., Huntsville, Ala., 1988-99; gen. mgr. LESCO, Huntsville, Ala., 1999-2000. Contbr. articles to profl. jours. Decorated Bronze Star, 37 Air medals with "V" device, D.F.C. with oak leaf cluster, Legion of Merit. Mem. Army Aviation Assn. Am., Assn. U.S. Army, Lansing Jaycees (past pres.), Mensa. Avocations: flying, reading, tennis. Home: 2110 Greenslope Trl NE Huntsville AL 35811-2608

**WILLIAMSON, DOUGLAS FRANKLIN, JR.,** lawyer; b. Anniston, Ala., Mar. 23, 1930; s. Douglas Franklin and Elizabeth Louise (Connor) W.; m. Barbara Tuerk, Dec. 28, 1957; children: Mary Leyden, Douglas Franklin III, Bruce Reynolds. AB summa cum laude, Amherst Coll., 1952; LLB, Yale U., 1955. Bar: NY 1958, Fla. 1976. Assoc. Breed, Abbott & Morgan, N.Y.C., 1957-63, ptnr., 1963-72, Williamson & Hess and predecessor firm, N.Y.C., 1972-79; of counsel Winthrop, Stimson, Putnam & Roberts, N.Y.C., 1979-81, ptnr., 1982-95, sr. counsel, 1996-2000, Pillsbury Winthrop Shaw Pittman LLP and predessors, N.Y.C., 2001—. Bd. dirs. World Wildlife Fund, Washington, 1979-88, treas., 1986-88, mem. nat. coun., 2008-2006; bd. dirs. Conservation Found., Washington, 1985-88, treas., 1986-88; bd. dirs. Ea. N.Y. chpt. Nature Conservancy, Mt. Kisco, N.Y., 1976-87, 93-97, sec., 1976-87, hon. dir., 1987—, chmn., 1993-94; bd. dirs. Oblong Land Conservancy, Pawling, N.Y., 1990-98, chmn. 1996-98; bd. dirs. Quaker Hill Civic Assn., Pawling, 1974-2000, past pres.; chmn. Pawling Assessment Rev. Bd., 1976-2001. With U.S. Army, 1955-57. Fellow: N.Y. State Bar Found.; mem.: Am. Bar City N.Y. (life), English Speaking Union, Old Guard Soc. Palm Beach, Soc. Colonial Wars, Everglades Club, Quaker Hill Country Club (pres. 1980—81), Phi Beta Kappa, Phi Beta Kappa Soc. (sec. 1975—77, v.p. 1977—79). Office: Pillsbury Winthrop Shaw Pittman LLP 1540 Broadway New York NY 10036-4039 Office Phone: 212-858-1000.

**WILLIAMSON, EDWIN DARGAN,** lawyer, former federal official; b. Florence, SC, Sept. 23, 1939; s. Benjamin F. and Sara (Dargan) W.; m. Kathe Gates, July 12, 1969; children: Samuel Gates, Edwin Dargan Jr., Sara Elizabeth. BA cum laude, U. of the South, 1961, DCL (hon.), 1992; JD, NYU, 1964. Bar: NY 1965, DC 1988. Assoc. Sullivan & Cromwell LLP, NYC, 1964-70, ptnr., 1971-76, London, 1976-79, NYC, 1979-88, Washington, 1988-90, 93—; coord. internat. trade and investment practice area; legal adviser US Dept. State, Washington, 1990-93. Mem. Permanent Ct. Arbitration, 1991—2004; mem. U.S. adv. NTT DoCoMo, 2002—04. Regent U. of the South, Sewanee, Tenn., 1981-87, chmn., 1985-87, coun. fgn. rels., 1995—; bd. dirs. Nat. Dance Inst., NYC, 1984-88, Episcopal Ch. Found., NYC, 1986-90; vestryman St. James Episcopal Ch., NYC, 1984-88; bd. mem. SC Govs. Sch. for Sci. and Math. Found., 2003-04. Mem. US Coun. Internat. Bus., Bus. and Industry Adv. Com. to OECD (vice chmn. com. on multinat. enterprise and investments 1993—2004, mem. BIAC expert group on multilat agt. on investment 1996-99, vice-chmn. 1998-2004, mem. exec. com. USCIB 1999—, chmn. task force corp. govt. 2002-04), Met. Club. Republican. Office: Sullivan & Cromwell LLP 1701 Pennsylvania Ave NW Washington DC 20006-5805 Office Fax: 202-293-6330. Personal E-mail: edwinwilliamsonsr@msn.com. Business E-Mail: williamsone@sullcrom.com.

**WILLIAMSON, (EULAH) ELAINE,** elementary school educator; b. N.Y.C., July 27, 1945; d. Eddie Lee and Eulah Genola (Hardie) Riley; m. George Leslie Williamson, Feb. 17, 1973 (div. 1999); children: George Todd, Michelle Elaine, Heather Dawn BA, Hampton U., 1967; MA in Urban Edn., Jersey City State Coll., 1998; postgrad., St. Peter's Coll., Jersey City. Cert. elem. tchr. K-8, supr., N.J. Tchr. elem. Englewood (N.J.) Pub. Schs., 1967-78, Irvington (N.J.) Pub. Schs., 1988-97; tchr. math. Hackensack (N.J.) Pub. Schs., 1997—. Mem. NEA, Nat. Mid. Sch. Assn., Nat. Coun. Tchrs. Math., Nat. Black Child Devel. Inst., N.J. Edn. Assn., Hackensack Edn. Assn., Profl. and Bus. Women NAACP, Phi Delta Kappa Democrat. Bapt. Avocations: photography, football, horseback riding. Office: Hackensack Mid Sch 360 Union St Hackensack NJ 07601-4394 also: 5/6 Sch 320 State St Hackensack NJ 07601 Office Phone: 201-646-8170. E-mail: blackie727@aol.com.

**WILLIAMSON, FLETCHER PHILLIPS,** real estate broker; b. Cambridge, Md., Dec. 16, 1923; s. William Fletcher and Florence M. (Phillips) Williamson; m. Betty June Stoker, Apr. 6, 1943 (div. 1972); 1 child, Jeffrey Phillips; m. Helen M. Stumberg, Aug. 28, 1972 (dec. Jan. 2002). Student, U. Md., 1941—42. Test engr. engring. lab. Glen Martin Co., 1942-43; salesman Corkran Ice Cream Co., Cambridge, 1946-50; real estate broker, 1950—. Chmn. bd. Williamson Real Estate, Dorchester Indsl. Devel. Corp., 1963—72; dir. Dorchester indsl. Devel. Corp.; vice-chmn. bd., dir. Nat. Bank Cambridge, 1970—; dir. Cam-Storage, Inc., Delmarva Bank Data Processing Ctr.; co-receiver White & Nelson, Inc.; v.p Delmarva Bank Shares. Bd. dirs. Delmarva coun. Boy Scouts Am., Dorchester County Pub. Libr.; past pres. Cambridge Hosp., United Fund Dorchester County; bd. dirs., v.p. Game Conservation Internat., Del. Mus. Natural History. Sgt. AUS, 1943—46, ETO. Methodist. Home: 310 E Wildwood Dr San Antonio TX 78212-1756 E-Mail: fpworldtraveler@aol.com.

**WILLIAMSON, JACK (JOHN STEWART),** writer; b. Bisbee, Ariz., Apr. 29, 1908; s. Asa Lee and Lucy Betty (Hunt) W.; m. Blanche Slaten Harp, Aug. 15, 1947 (dec. Jan. 1985); stepchildren: Keign Harp (dec.), Adele Harp Lovorn. BA, MA, Eastern N.Mex. U., 1957, LHD (hon.), 1981; PhD, U. Colo., 1964. Prof. English Eastern N.Mex. U., Portales, 1960-77, prof. emeritus, 1977—. Author numerous sci. fiction books including The Legion of Space, 1947, Darker Than You Think, 1948, The Humanoids, 1949, The Green Girl, 1950, The Cometeers, 1950, One Against the Legion, 1950, Seetee Scock, 1950, Seetee Ship, 1950, Dragon's Island, 1951, The Legion of Time, 1952, (with Frederik Phhl) Star Bridge, 1955, Dome Around America, 1955, The Trial of Terra, 1962, Golden Blood, 1964, The Reign of Wizardry, 1965, Bright New Universe, 1967, Trapped in Space, 1968, The Pandora Effect, 1969, People Machines, 1971, The Moon Children, 1972, H.G. Wells: Critic of Progress, 1973, Teaching SF, 1975, The Early Williamson, 1975, The Power of Blackness, 1976, The Best of Jack Williamson, 1978, Brother to Demons, Brother To Gods, 1979, Teaching Science Fiction: Education for Tomorrow, 1980, The Alien Intelligence, 1980, The Humanoid Touch, 1980, Manseed, 1982, The Queen of a Legion, 1983, Wonder's Child: My Life in Science Fiction, 1984 (Hugo award 1985), Lifeburst, 1984, Firechild, 1986, Mazeway, 1990, Undersea Quest, 1954, Undersea Fleet, 1955, Undersea City, 1956, The Reefs of Sapce, 1964, Starchild, 1965, Rogue Star, 1969, The Farthest Star, 1975, Wall Around a Star, 1983, Land's End, 1988, Mazeway, 1990. (with Frederik Phol) The Singers Of Time, 1991, Beachhead, 1992, Demon Moon, 1994, The Black Sun, 1996, The Fortress of Utopia, 1998, The Silicon Dagger, 1999, The Stone from the Green Star, 1999, Terraforming Earth, 2001, The Stonehenge Gate, 2005; (with Miles J. Breuer) The Birth of an New Republic, 1981. Served as staff sgt. USAAF, 1942-45. Mem. Sci. Fiction Writers Am. (pres. 1978-80, Grand Master Nebula award 1976), Sci. Fiction Research Assn. (Pilgrim award 1968), World Sci. Fiction, Planetary Soc. Avocations: travel, astronomy, photography. Home: PO Box 761 Portales NM 88130-0761 Office: Ea NMex U Golden Libr Portales NM 88130 Business E-Mail: Jack.Williamson@enmu.edu.

**WILLIAMSON, JOEL RUDOLPH,** humanities educator, writer; b. Anderson County, S.C., Oct. 27, 1929; s. James Henry and Carrie Mae (Swaney) W.; m. Marie Ahearn, Nov. 17, 1953 (div. May 1983); children: Joelle, William, Alethea; m. Anna Woodson, Oct. 18, 1986. AB, U.S.C., 1948, MA, 1951; PhD, U. Calif., 1964. Instr. dept. history U. N.C., Chapel Hill, 1960-64, asst. prof., 1964-66, assoc. prof., 1966-69, prof., 1969-85, Lineberger prof. in humanities, 1985—. Resident fellow Rockefeller Ctr., Bellagio, Italy, 1988; Eudora Welty prof. in so. studies Millsaps Coll., 1984; disting. vis. prof.

Rhodes Coll., 1984; vis. prof. dept. history, assoc. Lowell House Harvard U., 1981-82. Author: After Slavery: The Negro in South Carolina During Reconstruction, 1861-1877, 1965, The Origins of Segregation, 1968, New People: Miscegenation and Mulattoes in the United States, 1980, The Crucible of Race, 1984 (Francis Parkman prize Soc. Am. Historians, Ralph Waldo Emerson award Phi Beta Kappa, Mayflower Cup, Frank L. and Harriet C. Owsley award 1985, Robert Francis Kennedy Book award, Pulitzer prize in History nomination 1985), A Rage for Order, 1986, William Faulkner and Southern History, 1993 (Pulitzer prize in History nomination 1994, Mayflower Cup), also articles. Lt. USN, 1951-55. Fellow Guggenheim Found., 1970-71, NEH, 1987-88, Ctr. for Advanced Study in Behavioral Scis., Stanford, Calif., 1977-78, summer 1979, 80, 81, So. fellow, 1961-62, Charles Warren Ctr., 1981-82. Mem. Soc. Am. Historians, Orgn. Am. Historians, Am. Hist. Assn., So. Hist. Assn., So. Assn. for Women Historians. Avocation: travel. Home: 211 Hillsborough St Chapel Hill NC 27514-3522 Personal E-mail: annaleoww@aol.com.

**WILLIAMSON, JOHN PRITCHARD,** retired utilities executive; b. Cleve., Feb. 22, 1922; s. John and Jane (Pritchard) W.; m. Helen Morgan, Aug. 3, 1945; children: John Morgan, James Russell, Wayne Arthur. BBA, Kent State U., 1945; postgrad., U. Toledo, 1953-56, U. Mich., 1956. CPA, Ohio, ret. Sr. acct. Arthur Andersen & Co., Detroit and Cleve., 1945-51; dir. methods and procs. Toledo Edison Co., 1951-59, asst. treas., 1959-60, sec., 1960-62, sec.-treas., 1962-65, v.p. finance, 1965-68, sr. v.p., 1968-72, pres., chief exec. officer, 1972-79, chmn., chief exec. officer, 1979-86; founding chmn. Centerior Energy Corp. (now First Energy Corp.), 1985—86. Chmn. emeritus Toledo Edison Co.; dir. emeritus, chmn. 1st Nat. Bank of Toledo, 1974-75; chmn. N.Am. Electric Reliability Coun., 1984-87; chmn. Nat. Electric Security Coun., 1987-88; guest lectr. U. Toledo, 1976-. Pres. Ohio Electric Utility Inst., 1972; chmn. East Cen. Area Power Coordination Pool, 1971-72, mem. exec. com. Edison Electric Inst., 1981-85; mem. Ohio Devel. Adv. Coun., 1973-79; trustee Assn. Edison Illuminating Cos., 1982-84; pres. Toledo C. of C., 1970; chmn. Ohio C. of C., 1979-81, life dir.; pres. Toledo Symphony Orch., 1985-86; hon. trustee Toledo Mus. Art, Toledo Hosp., Toledo Symphony; trustee U. Toledo Found., 1980-87; hon. trustee Kent State U. Found.; vice chmn. Greater Toledo Corp., 1984-86; trustee, treas. Rio Verde Cmty. Ch., 1989-92; founding elder Covenant Presbyn. Ch., Stephen minister, 1996; pres. Toledo Cmty. Chest, 1972; chmn. Greater Toledo Area United Way, 1971, Epworth Meth. Ch. Found.; dir. Rio Verde Cmty. Assn., 1998-2003 Named Toledo Area's Outstanding Citizen, 1976; recipient Kent State U. medallion, 1992; Williamson Alumni Ctr. named in his honor, 1991. Mem. Fin. Analysts Soc. Toledo (pres. 1968-69), Sys. and Procs. Assn. (internat. treas. 1960), Inst. Pub. Utilities (chmn. exec. com. 1969-70), Toledo Boys Club (Echo award 1974), Kent State U. Alumni Assn. (pres. 1971-72, Outstanding Alumnus 1974), Belmont Country Club, Rio Verde Country Club, Inverness Club (gov., treas. 1967-76, com. chair 1979 U.S. Open, 1986 PGA Championship, winner 1965 Amateur Invitational), Rio Verde Saddle Club (past pres.), Kiwanis (past pres. Toledo chpt., Disting. Svc. award 1977, 02, past internat. pres. award 2002), Blue Key, Delta Sigma Pi, Beta Alpha Psi (hon.), Beta Gamma Sigma (hon.), Delta Upsilon. Republican. Home: 10661 Cardiff Rd Perrysburg OH 43551-3404 also: 18524 E Poco Vista Rio Verde AZ 85263-7125

**WILLIAMSON, JOHN THOMAS, SR.,** minerals company executive; b. Atlanta, Oct. 1, 1925; s. Walter Berry and Clare (Mathews) W.; m. Ava Gene Shealy, June 11, 1949; children: John Thomas, Ava Clare, Robin E., Leila Ann. Diploma, N. Ga. Coll., 1942-43; BS in Indsl. Engring., Ga. Inst. Tech., 1949. Registered profl. engr. and land surveyor, Ga. Chief engr. Thiele Kaolin Co., Sandersville, Ga., 1949-57; assoc. W.C. Davis and Assocs., Atlanta and Tallahassee, 1957-60; chief engr. So. Clays Inc., Gordon, Ga., 1960-63; asst. gen. mgr. Freeport Kaolin Co., N.Y.C., 1972-77, v.p., gen. mgr., 1977-78, pres., 1978-85; cons., gen. mgr. Gordon ops. Engelhard Corp., N.J., 1985-86; pres. IMPEX Corp., Milledgeville, Macon, Brunswick, Ga., 1987—. Bd. dirs. Freeport Export Corp., Freeport Overseas Sales Co., 1978-83. Patentee on processing kaolins; contbr. articles to profl. jours. Mem. adv. bd. Ga. Coll., 1979-82, found. bd., 1983-98, emeritus, 1998—, vice chmn. found. bd., 1988-89, chmn., 1989-90; mem. nat. adv. bd. Ga. Tech. Inst., 1979-85, emeritus; adv. bd. sch. mgmt. U. Ga., 1979-80; mem. Ga. Mil. Coll. Found. Bd., 1993—, exec. com., 1st v.p., 1995. With USNR, 1943-46. Recipient Robert Earll McConnell award AIME, 1996, GMC Hon. Alumni award, 2000. Mem. TAPPI, China Clay Prodrs., Ga. State Mining Assn., Ga. Soc. Profl. Engrs., Ga. Bus. and Industry Assn. (bd. dirs. 1978-83), Bus. Coun. Ga. (bd. dirs. 1983-88), Ga. Soc. Mining Engrs., Ga. C. of C., Jaycees, Lions (pres. 1957), Baldwin County Progressive Farmers Club, Alpha Tau Omega. Baptist (deacon). Home: 1810 Tanglewood Rd Milledgeville GA 31061-2461 Office: PO Box 1028 Milledgeville GA 31059-1028 also: IMPEX Corp 157 Darien Hwy Brunswick GA 31525-2423 also: IMPEX Corp 2474 Kingsley Dr Macon GA 31204-1757

**WILLIAMSON, KEITH HARVEY,** lawyer; b. St. Louis, May 16, 1952; s. Irving Alexander and Elizabeth Rebecca (Giddings) W.; m. Addie L. Perkins, Oct. 29, 1988.; 1 child. BA, Brown U., 1974; MBA, JD, Harvard U., 1978; LLM in Taxation, NYU, 1986. Bar: DC 1978, NY 1982. Assoc. Covington & Burling, Washington, 1978-81, Reavis & McGrath, NYC, 1981-88; dir. taxes Pitney Bowes Credit Corp., Shelton, Conn., 1988-94, asst. gen. counsel, 1993—94, v.p., sec., gen. counsel, 1994—98; sr. assoc. gen. counsel, mergers and acquisitions Pitney Bowes Inc., 1998—99, pres., capital svcs. divsn., 1999—. Bd. dirs. Stamford (Conn.) Mus. and Nature Ctr., New Canaan Country Sch.; founder Minority Corp. Counsel Assn.; mem. Black Exec. Exch. Program, Urban League. Office: Pitney Bowes Cap Svcs 27 Waterview Dr Shelton CT 06484

**WILLIAMSON, KENNETH LEE,** chemistry professor; b. Tarentum, Pa., Apr. 13, 1934; s. James D. and Mary June (Becker) W.; m. Mary Louise Hoerner, Sept. 15, 1956; children: Christopher Lee, Tania Louise, Kevin Keith. BA cum laude (Nat. scholar), Harvard, 1956; PhD (Allied Chem. and Dye Co. fellow), U. Wis., 1960. Mem. faculty Mt. Holyoke Coll., 1961—prof. chemistry, 1969—, Mary E. Woolley prof. chemistry, 1984-99, Mary E. Woolley prof. chemistry emeritus, 1999—. Mem. Grad. faculty U. Mass., 1965—; vis. prof. Cornell U., 1966, Dartmouth Coll., 1986-87, Harvard U., 1989-90, U. Trondheim, Norway, 1991, U. Louis Pasteur, Strasbourg, France, 1991, U. Amsterdam, Basel U., Switzerland, 1992, U. Canterbury, New Zealand and U. Auckland, New Zealand, 1994; vis. prof. MIT, 1996, 97, Calif. Inst. Tech., 2000. Author papers and books in field; patentee in field. Mem. South Hadley Hist. Commn., 1983—, South Hadley Cultural Coun., 2000-03; chair, Sycamores Com., South Hadley Hist. Soc., 1992-. NIH postdoctoral fellow Stanford, 1960-61; NSF sci. faculty fellow U. Liverpool, Eng.; also fellow of univ., 1968-69; Guggenheim fellow, 1975-76; Oxford (Eng.) U. fellow of univ., 1976, 1983; research assoc., Calif. Inst. Tech., 1975, 82. Mem. Am. Chem. Soc., AAAS, Sigma Xi. Congregationalist. Avocations: sailing, cabinetry. Home: 43 Woodbridge St South Hadley MA 01075-1138 E-mail: williamson98@comcast.net.

**WILLIAMSON, KIM ANN,** biology educator; d. H.W. and S.A. Williamson. BS, Wright State U., Dayton, Ohio, 1979; MA, Miami U., Oxford, Ohio, 1999. Nat. Bd. Cert. Tchr. Sci. tchr. Twin Valley S. HS, W. Alexandria, Ohio, 1979—89, E. Clinton HS, Lees Creek, Ohio, 1989—. Mem. labor mgmt. com. E. Clinton Unified Sch. Dist., Lees Creek, Ohio, 2006. Recipient Tchr. of Yr. award, E. Clinton Unified Sch. Dist., 1997, 2004. Mem.: Ohio Edn. Assn. Avocation: reading.

**WILLIAMSON, LAIRD,** theater director, actor; b. Chgo., Dec. 13, 1937; s. Walter B. and Florence M. (Hemwell) W. BS in Speech, Northwestern U., 1960; MFA in Drama, U. Tex., 1965. Dir. Am. Conservatory Theatre, San Francisco, 1974-2002; stage dir. A Christmas Carol, 1976-81, The Matchmaker (tour of Soviet Union), 1976, A Month in the Country, 1978, The Visit, 1979, Pantaleize, 1980, Sunday in the Park, 1986, End of the World, 1988, Imaginary Invalid, 1990, Machinal, 1997, Long Day's Journey, 1999, Master Harold and the Boys, 2001, The Glass Menagerie, 2002, The Dazzle, 2003, A Moon for the Misbegotten, 2005; dir. Oreg. Shakespearean Festival, Ashland,

1972-2002, Western Opera Theatre, San Francisco, 1976-77, Theater Fest. Santa Maria, Calif., 1971-84, Denver Theater Ctr., 1981-2002, Bklyn. Acad. Music, 1981, Seattle Repertory Theatre, 1990, Old Globe Theatre, San Diego, 1977, 92, 94, 97; artistic dir. Theater Fest, Solvang, Calif., 1983-84, Intiman Theatre, 1986, 88, Berkeley Shakespeare Festival, 1990, Guthrie Theatre, 1991, 93, The Shakespeare Theatre, Washington, 1995, 96, 98; actor in Othello, 1973, Twelfth Night, 1974, Cyrano, 1974, Enrico IV, 1977, Judas, 1978, Hamlet, 1979, The Bacchae, 1981, Hamlet, 2000, Shrew, 2000. Mem. Soc. Stage Dirs. Actors Equity Assn., Screen Actors Guild. Mailing: c/o Geary Theatre 415 Geary St San Francisco CA 94102

**WILLIAMSON, MARILYN,** retired secondary school educator; b. St. Louis, Apr. 6, 1930; d. Herschel and Estella (Wollf) W. BA, Roosevelt U., Chgo., 1951; MEd, U. Ill., 1955; life reading spl. cert., Harris-Stowe State Coll., St. Louis, 1968; postgrad., Washington U., St. Louis. Cert. life elem. and secondary tchr., reading specialist, Mo. Elem. tchr. St. Louis Pub. Schs., tchr. verbal skills, head lang. arts dept., reading specialist. Historian met. St. Louis chpt. Coalition 100 Black Women; sec. St. Louis chpt. Top Ladies Distinction; active ch. orgns.; co-chair Lane Tabernacle Scholarship. Recipient Retirement award Top Ladies Distinction St. Louis chpt., 50 Yr. Membership plaque Lane Tabernacle C.M.E. Ch., Cmty. Svc. award Top Ladies Distinction, Inc., 2005; named Top Lady of Yr., top Ladies of Distinction Inc., 1994 Mem. NAACP, Internat. Reading Assn., Mo. Tchrs. Assn., Nat. Coalition of 100 Black Women, (Shero award, Cmty. Svc. award 2004), Nat. Coun. Negro Women, Phi Delta Kappa (past pres., chair founder's day, v.p. Alpha Nu chpt.), Iota Phi Lambda (Apple for Tchr. award 1984), Delta Sigma Theta. Home: 5236 Vernon Ave Saint Louis MO 63113-1522

**WILLIAMSON, MARILYN LAMMERT,** literature educator, academic administrator; b. Chgo., Sept. 6, 1927; d. Raymond Ferdinand and Edith Louise (Eisenbies) Lammert; m. Robert M. Williamson, Oct. 28, 1950 (div. Apr. 1973); 1 child, Timothy L.; m. James H. McKay, Aug. 15, 1974. BA, Vassar Coll., 1949; MA, U. Wis., 1950; PhD, Duke U., 1956. Lectr. Duke U., Durham, NC, 1955-56, 58-59, N.C. State U., Raleigh, 1957-58, 61-62; asst. prof. Oakland U., Rochester, Mich., 1965-68, assoc. prof., 1968-72; prof. English Wayne State U., Detroit, 1972-90, Disting. prof. English, 1990-97, Disting. prof. emerita, 1997—, chmn. dept. English, 1972-74, 81-83, assoc. dean Coll. Liberal Arts 1974-79, dir. women's studies, 1976-87, dep. provost Detroit, 1987-91, sr. v.p. for acad. affairs, provost, 1991-95, 98-200. Pres. Assn. Depts. English, 1976-77. Author: Infinite Variety, 1974, Patriarchy of Shakespeare's Comedies, 1986, British Women Writers 1650-1750, 1990, Tales of Two Dogs, 2005; editor: Renaissance Studies, 1972, Female Poets of Great Britain, 1981, Shakespeare Studies: Middle Comedies, 2003; contbr. articles to profl. jours. Pres. LWV, Rochester, 1963-65. Recipient Detroit Disting. Svc. award, 1986, Faculty Recognition award Bd. Govs., Wayne State U., 1991, 30 Yr. award Mich. Humanities Coun., 2004; Bunting Inst. fellow, 1969-70, AAUW fellow, 1982-83, J.N. Keal fellow, 1985-86. Mem.: MLA (exec. coun. 1977—80, mem. editl. bd. 1992—94), Fed. State Humanities Coun. (bd. dirs. 1994—2001, chair 1997—99), Mich. Coun. Humanities (bd. dirs. 1988—2001, chair 1997—99), Mich. Acad. (pres. 1978—79). Democrat. Home: 2275 Oakway Dr West Bloomfield MI 48324-1855

**WILLIAMSON, MARVEL,** dean, nursing administrator, sexologist, educator, writer; b. Holton, Kans., Nov. 4, 1953; d. Thomas Arthur and Lois M. (Ihrig) Ansley; m. Paul Williamson, May 12, 1973; children: Marcus W., Sean W. BS in Nursing, Wichita State U., 1976; MS in Nursing, U. Ky., 1978; PhD, U. Iowa, 1987. Cert. sex educator. Prof. U. Iowa, Iowa City, 1980-89; dir. patient svcs. Ransom Meml. Hosp., Ottawa, Kans., 1989-91; dir. schs. nursing at Rolla, Sikeston and Kansas City Park Coll., Parkville, Mo., 1991-97; prof. Albany (Ga.) State U., 1997-99; sexologist Silver Spring, Md., 1999—2001; dean Kramer Sch. Nursing, Oklahoma City U., 2001—. Contbr. articles to profl. jours. Mem. ANA, Am. Assn. Sex Educators, Counselors and Therapists, Sigma Theta Tau. Home and Office: 3141 NW 18th St Oklahoma City OK 73107 Office: Oklahoma City U 2501 N Blackwelder Oklahoma City OK 73106 Office Phone: 405-521-5900.

**WILLIAMSON, OLIVER EATON,** economics professor, law professor; b. Superior, Wis., Sept. 27, 1932; m. Dolores Jean (Celeni); children: Scott, Tamara, Karen, Oliver, Dean. BS, Mass. Inst. Tech., 1955; MBA, Stanford U., 1960; PhD, Carnegie Mellon U., 1963; PhD (hon.), Norwegian Sch. Econ. and Bus. Adminstrn., 1986; PhD in Econ. sci. (hon.), Hochschule St. Gallen, Switzerland, 1987, Groningen U., 1989, Turku Sch. Econ. and Bus. Admin, St. Petersburg, Russia, 1996, HEC, Paris, 1997, Copenhagen Bus. Sch., 2000, U. Chile, 2000, Valencia U., 2004, Nice U., 2005. Project. engr. U.S. Govt., 1955-58; asst. prof. econ. U. Calif., Berkeley, Calif., 1963-65; assoc. prof. Pa. State U., Phila., 1965-68, prof., 1968-83, Charles and William L. Day prof. econ. and social sci., 1977-83; Gordon B. Tweedy prof. econ. law and orgn. Yale U., 1983-88; Transam. prof. of bus., econ. and law U. Calif., Berkeley, Calif., 1988-94, Edgar F. Kaiser prof. bus. adminstrn., prof. econ. and law, 1994—. Spl. econ. asst. to asst. atty. gen. for antitrust Dept. Justice, 1966—67; dir. Ctr. for Study of Orgnl. Innovation, U. Pa., 1976—83; cons. in field. Author: The Economics of Discretionary Behavior, 1964; Corp. Control and Bus. Behavior, 1970; Markets and Hierarchies, 1975; The Econ. Instn. of Capitalism, 1985; Econ. Orgn., 1986, Antitrust Economics, 1987; The Mechanisms of Governance, 1996; assoc. editor, Bell. Jour. Econ., 1973-74; editor, 1975-82; co-editor Jour. Law, Econ. and Orgn., 1983—2003. Fellow Ctr. for Advanced Study in Behavioral Sci., 1977-78; Guggenheim fellow, 1977-78; Fulbright scholar, 1999; Am. Acad. Arts and Sci. fellow, 1983; recipient Alexander Henderson Award Carnegie-Mellon U., 1962, Alexander von Humboldt Rsch. prize, 1987, Irwin award Acad. Mgmt., 1988, John von Newmann lectr., 1999, H.C. Recktenwald prize in econs., 2004. Fellow Econometric Soc., Am. Acad. Polit. and Social Sci., Acad. Internat. Bus. (eminent scholar); mem. NAS, Internat. Soc. for New Instnl. Econ. (pres. 1999-2001), Am. Econ. Assn. (v.p. 2000-01), Am. Law and Econ. Assn. (pres. 1997-98), Western Econ. Assn. (pres. 1999-2000), Internat. Indsl. Econ. Assn., Office: Univ Calif Dept Econ Berkeley CA 94720-0001

**WILLIAMSON, PETER DAVID,** lawyer; b. Houston, Oct. 13, 1944; s. Sam and Sophie Ann (Kaplan) W.; m. Patricia Golemon; children: Heather, Amber, Asia, Ginger. BA, U. Ill., 1966; JD, U. Tex., 1969. Bar: NY 1969, U.S. Supreme Ct. 1974, U.S. Ct. Appeals (4th, 5th, 6th, 8th, 9th, 10th, 11th and D.C. cirs.); lic. commdl. pilot. Pvt. practice, Houston, 1971—. Founder IMMLAW, The Nat. Consortium of Immigration Law Firms. Mem. Am. Immigration Lawyers Assn. (pres. 1994-95). Home: 1522 Park St Houston TX 77019-5324 Office: 500 Jefferson Ste 2040 Houston TX 77002 Office Phone: 713-751-0222. Business E-Mail: pwilliamson@pdwlaw.com. *I do not believe in the existence of national boundaries. The philosophy of my practice of the law is to help my clients achieve the ability to pass freely through such artificial political barriers.*

**WILLIAMSON, PHILEMONA,** artist; b. NYC; BA, Bennington Coll., 1973; MA, NYU, 1979. Various positions Harlem Sch. Arts, 1978—83; vis. artist Norfolk (Va.) State U., 1982; artist Met. Mus. Art, 1983; artist. tchr. workshops Arts Connection, 1986—89; vis. artist Ctr. D'Art, Port-Au-Prince, Haiti, 1987; artist-in-residence Very Spl. Arts, 1987—88; supr. student tchrs. dept. post-baccalaureate edn. Sch. Visual Arts, 1988—89; adj. faculty R.I. Sch. Design, 1989—90; painting faculty Bard Coll. Milton Avery Grad. Sch. Arts, 1991; adj. faculty Parsons Sch. Design, 1991—92, vis. artist MFA program, 1994. Mem. adv. bd. Getty Ctr. Edn. in Arts, 1989—98; panelist in field; artist-in-residence Millay Colony for Arts, Austerlitz, NY, 1983. One-woman shows include The Queens (N.Y.) Mus. Art, 1988, Wenger Gallery, L.A., 1989, Fine Arts Gallery, Southampton (N.Y.) Coll. L.I. U., 1990, June Kelly Gallery, N.Y.C., 1990, 1992, 1995, 1998, African Am. Mus., Hempstead, N.Y., 1991, Powers Art Gallery, East Stroudsburg (Pa.), 1992, Pa. State U., University Park, 1993, Flushing Coun. on Culture and Arts, N.Y.C., 1993, John Michael Kohler Arts Ctr., Sheboygan, Wis., 1999, exhibited in group shows at The Mint Mus. Art, Charlotte, N.C., 1991, U. Wis. at Milw. Fine Arts Gallery, 1992, Lehman Coll. Art Gallery and Krasdale Foods Arts Gallery, Bronx, 1994, Anderson Gallery, Buffalo, 1994, Kingsborough C.C. Art Gallery of CUNY, Bklyn., 1996, Pratt Manhattan Gallery,

N.Y.C., 1996, Rubelle and Norman Schafler Gallery, Pratt Inst., Bklyn., 1996, Spelman Coll. Mus. Fine Art, Atlanta, 1996, numerous others, Represented in permanent collections pub. and corp. collections. Recipient Arts in Transit Poster Commn., Union Sq. Sta., N.Y., 1992, Joan Mitchell Found. award in painting, 1997; fellow Fellow in painting, NEA, 1987—88, fellow in painting, N.Y. Found. Arts, 1991; grantee exhbn. grantee, Artist Space, 1988; Pollock-Krasner Found. grantee, 1989—90, Ludwig Vogelstein grantee, 1993—94. Office: 11 LaSalle Rd Montclair NJ 07043

**WILLIAMSON, R. MARK,** lawyer; b. Pensacola, Fla., Oct. 7, 1960; MusB, La. State Univ., 1981; MusM, Univ. North Tex., 1983; JD with highest honors, Fla. State Univ., 1991. Bar: Wis. 1991, Ga. 1996. Assoc. Foley & Lardner Law Firm, Milw.; ptnr., co-leader, wealth planning group Alston & Bird LLP, Atlanta. Adj. prof. law Univ. Wis., Madison, Wis. Exec. editor Fla. Law Rev. Recipient Best Young Author award, Estates and Trusts Mag., 1997. Fellow: Am. Coll. Tax and Estate Counsel; mem.: Order of Coif. Office: Alston & Bird LLP One Atlantic Ctr 1201 W Peachtree St NW Atlanta GA 30309-3424 Office Phone: 404-881-7993. Office Fax: 404-881-7777. Business E-Mail: mwilliamson@alston.com.

**WILLIAMSON, RICHARD CARDINAL,** physicist; b. Minocqua, Wis., Sept. 10, 1939; s. Lyman Olaf and Edna (Cardinal) W.; m. Christine Bauer, Sept. 2, 1961; children— Kari, Meagan, Heidi, Ryan BS in Physics, MIT, 1961, PhD in Physics, 1966. Staff physicist NASA Electronics Research Ctr., Cambridge, Mass., 1965-70; staff mem. and assoc. group leader MIT Lincoln Lab., Lexington, Mass., 1970-80, group leader applied physics, electrooptic device rsch., 1980-95, sr. staff electro-optical devices and materials group, 1995—. Contbr. articles to jours., chpts. to books; patentee in field Fellow IEEE (Centennial award 1984, Sonics and Ultrasonics Achievement award 1985); mem. IEEE, Am. Phys. Soc., Optical Soc. Am., Sigma Xi. Methodist. Home: 21 Pendleton Rd Sudbury MA 01776-1612 Office: 244 Wood St Rm C317 Lexington MA 02420-9108 Office Phone: 781-981-7857. Business E-Mail: williamson@ll.mit.edu.

**WILLIAMSON, RICHARD HALL,** federal agency administrator; b. Canton, N.C., July 29, 1940; s. James Eustace and Gwendolyn (Nevada) H.; m. Julia Draper Brown, Nov. 7, 1965 (div. Jan. 1981); children: Shawn Nicol, Kevin Carson; m. Janie E. Shaheen, Nov. 18, 1998. BS in Physics, N.C. State U., 1962, MS in Nuclear Engring., 1970, postgrad., 1972. Instr. N.C. State U., Raleigh, 1968-72; chief, energy systems analysis AEC, Washington, 1972-75; asst. dir., energy analysis U.S. Energy R & D Adminstrn., Washington, 1975-77; dir., program analysis U.S. Dept. Energy, Washington, 1977-80, dir., policy devel., 1980-84, dep. asst. sec. for internat. affairs, 1984-94; dep. exec. dir. U.S. Energy Assn., Washington, 1995-99. Bd. dirs. Houston World Energy Congress Inc., 1994-99; chmn. Worth Assocs. Inc., Flint Hill, Va., 1998—. Author: A Group Strategy for Energy Research, Development and Demonstration, 1980; contbr. articles to jours. in field. Football ofcl. Atlantic Coast Conf., Greensboro, N.C., 1980-2002, Rose Bowl, Pasadena, Calif., 1995; treas. Sigma Alpha Mu Endowment Fund, 1994—, Sigma Alpha Mu Found., 1989—; treas. St. Simons Island Newcomers Club, 2001—03. 1st lt. U.S. Army, 1962-64; col. USAR, 1964-93. NSF fellow, 1964-65; AEC fellow, 1965-68; recipient Outstanding alumnus award IFC, N.C. State U., 1971, Presdl. Rank award U.S. Dept. Energy, 1990, Atlantic Coast Conf. Svc. to Football Officiating award, 2000, Mem. Atlantic Coast Conf. Ret. Football Ofcls. Assn. (ret. 2002), Sigma Alpha Mu (nat. pres. 1984-86), Tau Beta Pi, Phi Kappa Phi, Omicron Delta Kappa, Sigma Pi Sigma, Pi Mu Epsilon. Republican. Methodist. Avocations: stamp collecting/philately, tennis, golf, skiing. Home: 906 Champney Saint Simons Island GA 31522-5464 Office: Worth Assocs PO Box 456 820 Fodderstack Rd Flint Hill VA 22627 Office Phone: 540-675-1250.

**WILLIAMSON, RICHARD SALISBURY,** ambassador; b. Evanston, Ill., May 9, 1949; s. Donald G. and Marion (Salisbury) W.; m. Jane Thatcher, Aug. 25, 1973; children: Elizabeth Jane, Craig Salisbury, Richard Middleton. AB with honors, Princeton U., 1971; JD, U. Va., 1974. Bar: Ill. bar 1974, D.C. bar 1975. Legis. counsel, adminstrv. asst. to Congressman Philip M. Crane of Ill., 1974-76; assoc. firm Winston & Strawn, Washington, 1977-80, ptnr., 1980; asst. to Pres. for intergovtl. affairs, Washington, also assoc. dir. President's Task Force on Regulatory Relief, 1981-83; U.S. ambassador Vienna, 1983-85; sr. v.p., corp. and internat. relations Beatrice Cos., Inc., Chgo., 1985-86; ptnr. Mayer, Brown & Platt, Chgo., 1986—2001; asst. sec. of state internat. orgn. affairs U.S. Dept. State, Washington, 1988-89; alt. repr. to the U.N. for special polit. affairs U.S. Dept. State, Washington, 2002—. Rep. UN Orgns., Vienna, 1983-85; dep. ref. with rank of ambassador IAEA. Editor: Trade & Economic Growth, 1993, United States Foreign Policy and the United Nations System, 1996; co-editor: (with Paul Laxalt) A Changing America: Conservatives View the 80's From the United States Senate, 1980; author: Reagan's Federalism: His Efforts to Decentralize Government, 1990, The United Nations: A Place of Promise and of Mischief, 1991, Disorder in the New World, 1997, Seeking Firm Footing: America in the World in the New Centur7, 2001. Chmn. Ill. Rep. Party, 1999-2002. Republican. Office: US Mission UN 799 United Nations Plz New York NY 10017-3505

**WILLIAMSON, ROBERT F.,** pharmaceutical executive; BA, Pomona Coll.; MBA, Stanford U. Rsch. asst. Fed. Res. Bd. Govs.; v.p., dir. The Boston Cons. Group, 1991—99; pres., CEO, dir. DoubleTwist, Inc., Oakland, Calif., 1999—2002; pres., CEO Eos Biotechnology, 2002—03; CEO Arriva Pharms., Inc., Alameda, 2003—. Office: Arriva Pharmaceuticals, Inc 2020 Challenger Dr Alameda CA 94501 Office Phone: 510-337-1250.

**WILLIAMSON, SAMUEL RUTHVEN, JR.,** historian, educator; b. Bogalusa, La., Nov. 10, 1935; s. Samuel Ruthven and Frances Mitchell (Page) Williamson; m. Joan Chaffe Andress, Dec. 30, 1961; children: George Samuel, Treeby Andress, Thaddeus Miller. BA, Tulane U., 1958; AM, Harvard U., 1960, PhD, 1966, grad. in Advanced Mgmt., 1986; degree (hon.), Furman U., Va. Theol. Sem., Centre Coll., The U. of the South, 2006. Asst. prof. U.S. Mil. Acad., 1963—66; from instr. history to asst. dean Harvard U., 1966—69, asst. to dean of Harvard Coll., 1966—70; rsch. assoc. Inst. Politics, faculty assoc. Ctr. for Internat. Affairs, 1971—72; mem. faculty J.F. Kennedy Sch. Govt., 1971—72; from assoc. prof. history to provost U. N.C., Chapel Hill, 1972—84, provost univ., 1984—88; pres., vice chancellor U. of South, Sewanee, Tenn., 1988—2000, vice chancellor emeritus, prof. history, 2000—05, Robert M. Ayres Jr. disting. univ. prof., 2001—05. Cons. historian's office Office of Sec. Def., 1974—76; vis. fellow Churchill Coll., 1976—77; mem. vis. com. Harvard Coll., 1986—92; dir. Rsch. Triangle Inst., 1984—88; mem. bd. visitors Air U., 1994—2002. Author: The Politics of Grand Strategy: Britain and France Prepare for War 1904-1914, 1969, 1990; co-author: The Origins of U.S. Nuclear Strategy, 1945-53, 1993, July 1914: Soldiers, Statesmen, and the Coming of the Great War, 2003; editor: The Origins of a Tragedy, July 1914, 1981, War and Soc. Newsletter, 1973—88; co-editor: Essays on World War I: Origins and Prisoners of War, 1983, Austria-Hungary and the Origins of the First World War, 1991. Mem. cen. com. Morehead Found., 1978—93; vice chmn. bd. visitors Air U., 1996—98, chmn. bd. visitors, 1998—2000. Capt. U.S. Army, 1963—66. Fellow, NEH, 1976—77, Nat. Humanities Ctr., 1983; grantee, Ford Found., 1976; Fulbright scholar, U. Edinburgh, 1958—59, Woodrow Wilson Ctr. scholar, Washington, 2002, Woodrow Wilson fellow, 1958—63, Danforth fellow, 1958—63. Mem.: Nat. Assn. Colls. and Univs. (vice chmn., chmn. bd. dirs. 1993—95), Internat. Inst. Strategic Studies, Am. Hist. Assn. (George Louis Beer prize 1971). Democrat. Episcopalian. Home: PO Box 837 Sewanee TN 37375-0837 Office: U of South duPont Libr Sewanee TN 37383-1000 Business E-Mail: swilliam@sewanee.edu.

**WILLIAMSON, SUSAN,** mathematician, educator; b. Boston, Dec. 29, 1936; d. Richard Phillip and Mary Elizabeth Williamson. AB, Radcliffe Coll., Cambridge, Mass., 1958; MA, PhD, Brandeis U., Waltham, Mass., 1963. Instr. Cardinal Cushing Coll., Brookline, Mass., 1962—63; asst. prof. Boston Coll., Chestnut Hill, Mass., 1963—64, Regis Coll., Weston, Mass., 1965—67, asst. prof., 1967—71, acad. dean, 1973—75, prof., 1971—2002, prof. emerita, 2002—. Reviewer Math. Revs., Ann Arbor, Mich., 1968—. Contbr.

articles to profl. jours. Overseer DeCordova Mus., 2004—. Mem.: AAUP, Assn. Harvard Coll. Class Secs. and Treas., History Edn. Soc., Math. Assn. Am., Am. Math. Soc. Avocation: drawing. Home: 37 Hagen Rd Newton Center MA 02459

**WILLIAMSON, THOMAS ARNOLD,** publishing executive; b. Sagamore, Pa., Oct. 4, 1939; s. Thomas and Mabel (Kennedy) Williamson; m. Kathryn Steiner White, Mar. 1, 1980; 1 child, Thomas J. Grad., Phillips Exeter Acad., 1957; AB, Harvard U., 1961. From sales person to sr. v.p. Harcourt Brace & Co., N.Y.C., 1962—88, sr. v.p., 1988—95; pres. Psychol. Corp., San Antonio, 1982—88; v.p. Holt Rinehart & Winston Harcourt Brace, 1989—95, pres. sch. publs., 1989—93; pres. Learning Initiative, Austin, Tex., 1994—, T. Williamson Assocs., Inc., Austin, 1995—2005, Focused Learning, Ltd., Austin, 1998—2005; assoc. Keller Williams Realty, Austin, 2003—. Bd. dirs. The Austin Project. Co-chmn. vis. com. to psychology dept. U. Tex., Austin, 1986—89, 1995—98; vol., chair chpt. 249 SCORE, 2003—04. Mem.: Hills Country Club, Town and Gown Club, Harvard Club N.Y.C. Home: 5 Cheverly Ct Austin TX 78738-1511 Office: Keller Williams Realty 1927 Lohmans Crossing Ste 102 Austin TX 78734 Office Phone: 512-263-6709. Personal E-Mail: tawilliamson@austin.rr.com.

**WILLIAMSON, VIKKI LYN,** university official, financial executive; b. Huntington, W.Va., June 30, 1956; d. Ernest E. and Wanda C. (Cole) W. BA in Secondary Edn., English, Temple U., 1978; postgrad. in Acctg. and Fin., U. Cin., 1984-86; MA in Mgmt., Antioch U., 2002. CPA, Ohio; cert. tchr., Tenn., Ohio. Tchr. Springfield Christian Acad., Tenn., 1978-79; acctg. asst. Children's Hosp. Med. Ctr., Cin., 1979-84; asst. dir. fin. svcs. U. Cin. Med. Ctr., 1984-85, dir. fin. svcs., 1985-88, dir. fin. and adminstrn., 1988-91, dep. dir., CFO, 1991-2000; chief fin. adminstrv. officer Antioch U McGregor, Yellow Springs, Ohio, 2000—02; dir. budget and fin. planning Ctrl. State U., 2002—05, asst. v.p. adminstrn. and fin., 2005—. Bd. dirs. Contemporary Dance Theatre, 1987-90; mem. fin. oversight com. Beavercreek City Schs., 2004—. Bd. dirs. Habitat for Humanity-Hamilton, 1991-94, v.p., 1991, pres., 1992; v.p. PTA, 1997-98, pres., 1989-99, treas. 1999-2001; treas., bd. dirs. Tawawa Cmty. Devel. Found., 2002—05. Mem. AICPA, Healthcare Fin. Mgmt. Assn., Am. Assn. Blood Banks, Ohio Assn. Blood Banks (fin. com. 1986-90, treas. 1991-97), Am.'s Blood Ctrs. (fin. com. 1991-2000, alt. trustee 1991-2000), Assn. Women Adminstrs. (fin. com. 1987-90), Assn. Mid-Level Adminstrs. (bd. dirs. 1987-90), Ohio Assn. Coll. and Univ. Bus. Officers (exec. com. 2004—, sec. 2005, v.p. 2005, pres. 2006—), Alpha Epsilon Theta, Beta Gamma Sigma, Delta Mu Delta. Office: Central State Univ PO Box 1004 Wilberforce OH 45384 Office Phone: 937-376-6632. Business E-Mail: vwilliamson@centralstate.edu.

**WILLIAMSON, WALTER BLAND,** lawyer; b. Selma, Ala., Apr. 6, 1938; s. Walter Bland and Tina (Matheny) W.; children: Michael Davis, Amy Caroline; m. Dana Leigh Freiburger, Jan. 2, 1999. BS, Stetson U., 1959; JD, Emory U., 1963. Bar: Okla. 1969, Ga. 1963, U.S. Ct. Mil. Appeals 1963, U.S. Supreme Ct. 1969. Atty. Office Gen. Counsel Fed. Deposit Ins. Corp., Washington, 1967; atty. Office Std. Policy U.S. Dept. Commerce, 1968-69; shareholder Pray, Walker, Jackman, Williamson & Marlar and predecessors, Tulsa, 1969—, pres., 1993-98. Steering com. conf. on nuclear power generation Nat. Energy Law and Policy Inst., 1981; adv. com. on natural gas allowables Okla. Corp. Commn., 1983, 88. Mem. Okla. Energy Resources Bd., 1997-96; trustee Grace and Franklin Bernsen Found., Philbrook Mus. Art; bd. dirs. Indian Nations Coun., Boy Scouts Am.; governing bd. Jasmine Moran Childrens Mus. Capt. U.S. Army, 1963-67. Mem. ABA (vice-chmn. natural gas mktg. and transp. com., natural resource sect. 1986-88, co-chmn. energy com. adminstrv. law and regulatory practice sect. 1998-2000), Okla. Bar Assn. (chmn. mineral law sect. 1982), Tulsa County Bar Assn. (chmn. mineral law sect. 1979), Ind. Petroleum Assn. Am. (regional v.p. 1991-95), Okla. Ind. Petroleum Assn. (chmn. legal com. 1979-83, gen. counsel 1983—, Mem. of Yr. 1987), Energy Advocates (coord. 1987-88, 91), Phi Delta Phi. Home: 1228 E 19th St Tulsa OK 74120-7419 Office: 900 Oneok Plz Tulsa OK 74103 Office Phone: 918-581-5504. E-mail: wbw@praywalker.com.

**WILLIAMSON, WAYNE C.,** internist, geriatrician; b. Hammond, Ind., 1952; BA, Northwestern U., 1974; MD, U. Cin., 1978. Cert. Am. Bd. Internal Medicine, 1984, in Geriatric Medicine 1992. Intern Rush Presbyn., St. Luke's Med. Ctr., Chgo., 1978—79, resident, internal medicine, 1979—81, physician; asst. prof. Rush Med. Coll.; physician Northwestern Meml. Hosp., 1999—; mem. faculty Steinberg Sch. Medicine, 1999—. Office: Northwestern Meml Hosp Galter Pavillion 201 E Huron 11-105 Chicago IL 60660 Office Phone: 312-942-7493.

**WILLIAMSON, WILLIAM PAUL, JR.,** journalist; b. Des Moines, Mar. 30, 1929; s. William Paul and Florence Alice (Dawson) W.; m. Vania Torres Nogueira, Nov. 27, 1959; children: Mary Liz, Jon Thadeus, Margaret Ann Student, Mexico City Coll., 1952, U. Havana, 1955; BA, U. No. Iowa, 1953; MA, U. Iowa, 1954. Editor Brazilian Bus., Rio de Janeiro, 1958-60; mng. ptnr. Editora Mory Ltd., Rio de Janeiro, 1960-79; editor Brazil Herald, Rio de Janeiro, 1960-80; exec. dir. Inter Am. Press Assn., Miami, Fla., 1981-94, hon. life mem., mem. adv. coun., 1994—, dir., 1966-80, chmn. awards com., 1975-80. Solo navigator 1st passage Madeira Island, Portugal-Madeira Island, Brazil, 1994-95. Editor for Brazil, Fodor's South America, 1970-79; contbr. articles to various newspapers and mags. Pres. Am. Soc., Rio de Janeiro, 1968; bd. dirs. Instituto Brasil-Estados Unidos, Rio de Janeiro, 1977-80, Am. C. of C. for Brazil, Rio de Janeiro, 1964-68; rear commodore Seven Seas Cruising Assn., 2000—. Served with USMC, 1946-48. Decorated Order of Rio Branco (Brazil); recipient Citizen of Rio de Janeiro award State Legislature, 1975; Hon. Carioca award O Globo Newspaper, Rio de Janeiro, 1972; Ralph Greenberg award Am. Soc. Rio de Janeiro, 1977; Outstanding Svc. to Freedom of Expression and Newspapers awards Internat. Fedn. of Newspaper Pubs. and Internat. Assn. of Broadcasting, 1994; Benemeritous Citizen award Mcpl. Legislature, Itaquai, Brazil, 1995. Mem. Am. Soc. Assn. Execs., South Fla. Soc. Assn. Execs. (pres. 1987), Soc. Profl. Journalists, Overseas Press Club Am., Brazil Fgn. Corr. Assn. (founder, mem. honor), Rio Yacht Club, Ilha da Madeira Yacht Club, Kappa Tau Alpha. Home: 3051 NE 47th Ct Apt 204 Fort Lauderdale FL 33308-5304 Personal E-Mail: billvania@yahoo.com.

**WILLIAMS-THOMAS, ELIZABETH A.,** financial planner, consultant; b. San Francisco, Jan. 16, 1948; d. John and Myrtle Mary (Thierry) W.; children: Brian, Jonathan. Degree, U. Calif., 1979, MBA. Manpower coord., fed. programs U.S. Govt., San Francisco; patient svc. rep. Health Care Svc., Oakland, Calif.; ins. and real estate cons.; pres. Investments Unlimited, Oakland, EWJ & Assocs. Mktg. Firm; planning commr. City of Pitts.; CEO Ultimate Vacations Inc. Human rels. commr. Contra Costa County. Recipient Pub. Speaking award; European Investment fellow. Mem. AAUW, NAFE, NAACP, Nat. Real Estate Owners Assn., Nat. Notary Assn., Order Ea. Star, Heroines Jericho, Daus. Isis, Soropotimist Inc., Toastmistress Club, Beta Phi Sigma. Home: PO Box 523 Pittsburg CA 94565-0052

**WILLIE, CHARLES VERT,** social sciences educator; b. Dallas, Oct. 8, 1927; s. Louis James and Carrie (Sykes) W.; m. Mary Susannah Conklin, Mar. 31, 1962; children: Sarah Susannah, Martin Charles, James Theodore. BA, Morehouse Coll., 1948, DHL (hon.), 1983; MA, Atlanta U., 1949; PhD, Syracuse U., 1957, DHL (hon.), 1992; Yale U., 1972, R.I. Coll., 1983, Johnson C. Smith U., Charlotte N.C., 1991, Franklin Pierce Coll., Rindge, NH, 1996, Haverford Coll., 2000; DD (hon.), Gen. Sem., 1974, Episcopal Div. Sch., 2004; MA (hon.), Harvard U., 1974; DL (hon.), Framingham State Coll., Mass., 1992; D of Engring. Tech. (hon.), Wentworth Inst. Tech., 1996; D of Canon Law (hon.), Seabury-Western Theol. Sem., 2005. Instr. to asst. prof. sociology Syracuse U., NYC, 1952-63, assoc. prof., 1964-67, prof., 1968-74, chmn. dept. sociology, 1967-71, v.p., 1972-74; prof. edn. and urban studies Grad. Sch. Edn. Harvard U., Cambridge, Mass., 1974-98, Charles William Eliot prof. edn. Grad. Sch. Edn., 1998-99, prof. emeritus Grad. Sch. Edn., 1996—. Instr. dept. preventive medicine SUNY Upstate Med. Center, Syracuse, 1955-60; rsch. dir. Washington Action for Youth delinquency prevention project, Pres.' Com. on Juvenile Delinquency and Youth Crime,

Washington, 1962-64; vis. lectr. lab. dept. psychiatry Harvard U. Med. Sch., Boston, 1966-67; vis. lectr. Episcopal Div. Sch., Cambridge, Mass., 1966-67; commr. Pres.'s Commn. on Mental Health, 1977-78; mem. tech. adv. bd. Maurice Falk Med. Fund, 1968-99; bd. dirs. Social Sci. Rsch. Coun., 1969-75; master Boston Sch. Desegregation case, Fed. Dist. Ct., 1975; mem. nat. adv. com. Maxwell Sch. Syracuse U., 1992-00, Hogg Found. Mental Health, 1998-02, Morehouse Rsch. Inst., 1997-02; bd. overseers Boston Sci. Mus., 1997-01, overseer emeritus, 2002—; corporator Emerson Hosp., Concord, Mass., 1998—; chmn. bd. dirs. Judge Baker Children's Ctr., Boston, 2001-03; mem. nat. adv. com. The History-Makers, 2002—. Author: Church Action in the World, 1969, The Family Life of Black People, 1970, Black Students at White Colleges, 1972, Race Mixing in the Public Schools, 1973, (with B. Brown and B. Kramer) Racism and Mental Health, 1973, Black/Brown/White Relations, 1977, Oreo, 1975, (with R. Edmonds) Black Colleges in America, 1978, (with R. Reddick) A New Look at Black Families, 1976, 5th edit., 2003, The Sociology of Urban Education, 1978, The Caste and Class Controversy on Race and Poverty, 1979, 2d edit., 1989, The Ivory and Ebony Towers, 1981, (with S. Greenblatt) Community Politics and Educational Change, 1981, Race, Ethnicity and Socioeconomic Status, 1983, School Desegregation Plans That Work, 1984, Black and White Families, 1985, Five Black Scholars, 1986, (with Michael Grady) Metropolitan School Desegregation, 1986, Effective Education, 1987, (with Inabeth Miller) Social Goals and Educational Reforms, 1988, (with Michael Grady and Richard Hope) African-Americans and the Doctoral Experience, 1991, (with A. Garibaldi and W. Reed), The Education of African-Americans, 1991, Theories of Human Social Action, 1994, (with P. Rieker, B. Kramer and B. Brown) Mental Health, Racism and Sexism, 1995, (with Michael Alves) Controlled Choice, 1996, (with Ralph Edwards) Black Power/White Power in Public Education, 1998, (with Edwards and Alves) Student Diversity, Choice and School Improvement, 2002, (with R. Reddick and R. Brown) The Black College Mystique, 2006. Hon. trustee Episcopal Div. Sch., Cambridge; invited mem. United Negro Coll. Fund, pres. assembly, 1989-90; chair bd. dirs. Dana McLean Greeley Found. for Peace and Justice, 1989-92; mem. nat. exec. coun. Episcopal ch., 1967-74, v.p. gen. conv. House of Deps., 1970-74; host Inner City Beat nat. pub. affairs weekly TV program, monitor channel, 1991-92. Recipient faculty svc. award Nat. Univ. Ext. Assn., 1969, 50th Anniversary Disting. Alumnus award Syracuse U. Maxwell Sch., 1974, Spirit of Pub. Svc. award, 1994; Lee-Founders award Soc. for Study Social Problems, 1983, Family Scholar award, 1986; Disting. Career Contbn. award com. on role and status of minorities in edn., Am. Ednl. Rsch. Assn., 1990, Benjamin E. Mays Svc. award Morehouse Coll., 1994, Father John LaFarge, S.J. award Fairfield U., 1995, Disting. Career award Assn. Black Sociologists, 1996, Outstanding Book award for mental health, racism and sexism Myers Ctr. for Study of Human Rights, 1996, Arents Alumni award Syracuse U., 2000, Outstanding Tchr. award, Harvard U., 2005, Oustanding Contbns. to Discipline, Professions and Exptl. Econs. and Social Sci. award, 2006. Mem. Am. Ednl. Rsch. Assn., Am. Sociol. Assn. (coun. 1980-83, 95-98, v.p. 1996-97, DuBois-Johnson-Frazier award 1994, William Foote Whyte award 2004, Career Disting. Scholarship award 2005), Assn. Black Sociologists, Ea. Sociol. Soc. (past pres., Robin M. Williams Disting. Lectureship award, 1994), Phi Beta Kappa, Alpha Phi Alpha. Episcopalian. Home: 41 Hillcrest Rd Concord MA 01742-4615 Office: Harvard U Grad Sch Edn 405 Gutman Libr 6 Appian Way Cambridge MA 02138-3704 Office Phone: 617-495-4678. Personal E-Mail: cvmswillie@aol.com.

**WILLIFORD, DRURY FISHER, JR.,** historical researcher, writer, editor; b. Memphis, Nov. 27, 1929; s. Drury Fisher and Irene Frances (Dawson) Williford; m. Virginia Lucile Jackson, Dec. 1950 (div. Sept. 1971); children: Peggy Leigh, Virginia Fisher, Alan Lyle, Mark Edward; m. Shirley Ann Hagedom, Aug. 1981. BA, W.Va. U., 1986. Cert. police firearms instr. Fed. Law Enforcement Tng. Ctr. Audit clk. Nat. Bank of Commerce, Memphis, 1953-54; patrolman Memphis Police Dept., 1954-55; patrol insp. U.S. Border Patrol, El Paso, Tucson and Buffalo, 1955-57; from insp. to ops. officer U.S. Customs Svc., Toronto, Ont., 1957-63, Buffalo, 1963-72, Washington, 1972-81; ret., 1981. Freelance photographer. Contbr. articles to profl. jours. Boys hockey coach Amherst (NY) Hockey Assn., 1964—72, Wheaton (Md.) Hockey Club, 1972—73, Morgantown (W.Va.) Hockey Club, 1981—82; literacy vol. tutor, 1985—88. With USN, 1950—52. Named Marion County Tutor of the Yr., 1987; named to Hockey Hall of Fame, Amherst, 1984; recipient High Quality Performance award, Dept. of Treasury, 1975, 1976, 1979, Spl. Achievement award, 1981; Judith Hemdon fellow, W.Va. Legislature, 1984. Democrat. Avocations: animal protection, habitat conservation, ultralight aircraft builder and pilot. Home: PO Box 734 Reedsville WV 26547-0734

**WILLIFORD, VELMA JEAN,** minister; b. Anderson, S.C., May 15, 1947; d. Eugene and Zora Etrulia Hagood; m. Claude Riley Williford, Apr. 14, 1965; children: Claude Rodriques, Maximo Jermaine, William Lamont. DMin, Christian Life Sch. Theology, Columbus, Ga., 1994—2004. Pres. Tabernacle of Faith Min., Inc., Anderson, SC, 1991—2005. Mem.: Gold Reagents. Avocations: reading, cooking, camping. Office: Gospel Tabernacle Faith Ch 1613 S Main St Anderson SC 29624 Office Phone: 864-261-6107. Business E-Mail: gospeltfc@bellsouth.com.

**WILLIG, KARL VICTOR,** computer company executive; b. Idaho Falls, Idaho, June 4, 1944; s. Louis Victor and Ethel (McCarty) W.; m. Julianne Erickson, June 10, 1972; 1 son, Ray. BA magna cum laude, Coll. of Idaho, 1968; MBA (Dean Donald Kirk David fellow), Harvard U., 1970. Pres. Ariz. Beef, Inc., Phoenix, 1971-73; group v.p. Ariz.-Colo. Land & Cattle Co., Phoenix, 1973-76; v.p. Rufenacht, Bromagen & Hertz, Inc., Chgo., 1976-77; pres. Sambo's Restaurants, Inc., Santa Barbara, Calif., 1977-79; ptnr. Santa Barbara Capital, 1979-85; pres. EURUSA Equities Corp., 1985-86; pres., chief exec. officer InfoGenesis, 1986—2004; chmn. bd. Am. Commn., 2005—. Trustee Am. Bapt. Sem. of West, 1977-85; mem. Chgo. Merc. Exch., 1976-77, mem. audit com. and membership coms., 1976-77 Bd. dirs. Santa Barbara Rescue Mission, 2002—, Los Padres coun. Boy Scouts Am., 2004—. Named one of Outstanding Young Men of Am., 1972; recipient Assn. of U.S. Army award, 1964; named Entrepenour of Year, South Coast Bus. and Tech. awards, 2005 Baptist.

**WILLIG, KENNETH C. H.,** lawyer; b. NYC, Mar. 3, 1949; BA cum laude, Bklyn. Coll., 1970; MA, Univ. Pa., 1971, PhD, 1975, JD, 1980; Mombusho vis. scholar, Univ. Osaka, Japan, 1972—75. Bar: NY 1981. Ptnr., joint global leader Comml. practice group, chmn. Project Fin. practice group DLA Piper Rudnick Gray Cary, NYC. Editor: Univ. Pa. Law Rev.; mem. adv. bd. Jour. of Internat. Econ. Law. Mem.: ABA, NY State Bar Assn., Assn. Bar City of NY. Office: DLA Piper Rudnick Gray Cary 1251 Ave of the Americas New York NY 10020-1104 Office Phone: 212-835-6240. Office Fax: 212-835-6001. Business E-Mail: kenneth.willig@dlapiper.com.

**WILLIG, ROBERT DANIEL,** economics professor; b. Bklyn., Jan. 16, 1947; s. Jack David and Meg W.; m. Virginia Mason, July 8, 1973; children: Jared Mason, Scott Mason, Brent Mason, Alexandra Mason. BA, Harvard U., 1967; MS in Ops. Rsch., Stanford U., 1968, PhD in Econs. 1973. Lectr. Stanford U., Palo Alto, Calif., 1971-73; tech. staff Bell Labs., Holmdel, NJ, 1973-77, supr. dept. econs. rsch., 1977-78; prof. econs. and pub. affairs Princeton U., 1978—; task force on future of postal svc. Aspen Inst., 1978-80; dep. asst. atty. gen. U.S. Dept. Justice, Washington, 1989-91. Cons. in field; rsch. fellow U. Warwick, Eng., 1977; organizing com. Telecom Policy Rsch. Conf., 1977-78; rsch. adv. bd. Am. Enterprise Inst., 1980-88; mem. N.J. Gov.'s Task Force on Market-Based Pricing of Electricity, 1987; bd. dirs. Consultants in Industry Econs., Inc., 1992-2005, Competition Policy Assocs., Inc., 2002-2005, mem. Def. Sci. Bd. Task Force on Antitrust for the Def. Industry, 1993-94. Transp. Rsch. Bd. Task Force, 1995-96; advisor Inter-Am. Devel. Bank, 1997-00. Author: Welfare Analysis of Policies Affecting Prices and Products, 1973, Contestable Markets and the Theory of Industry Structure, 1982; editor: Handbook of Industrial Organization, 1986, Can Privatization Deliver: Infrastructure for Latin America, 1999, Second Generation Reforms in Infrastructure Services, 2002; contbr. articles to profl. jours.; mem. editl. bd. MIT Press Series on Govt. Regulation, 1978—, Am.

Econ. Rev., 1980-83, Jour. Indsl. Econs., 1985-89, Utility Policy, 1989-2001. Adv. bd. B'nai B'rith Hillel Found., Princeton U., 1978-89. Grantee, NSF, 1979—85. Fellow Econometric Soc. (program com. 1978-81); mem. Am. Econ. Assn. (nominating com. 1980-81). Office: Princeton Univ Economics Dept Princeton NJ 08540

**WILLINGHAM, CLARK SUTTLES,** lawyer; b. Houston, Nov. 29, 1944; s. Paul Suttles and Elsie Dell (Clark) W.; m. Jane Joyce Hitch, Aug. 16, 1969; children: Meredith Moores, James Barrett. BBA, Tex. Tech U., 1967; JD, So. Meth. U., 1971, LLM, 1984. Bar: Tex. 1971. Ptnr. Kasmir, Willingham & Krage, Dallas, 1972—86, Finley, Kumble et al, Dallas, 1986—87, Brice & Mankoff, Dallas, 1988—98, Moseley Law PC, Dallas, 1998—. Contbr. articles to profl. jours. Bd. dirs. Dallas Summer Musicals, 1971—, exec. com., 1979-93, 97-2003, pres. 1994. Mem. ABA (chmn. agrl. com. tax sect. 1984-86), State Bar Tex. (chmn. agrl. tax com. 1985-87), Dallas Bar Assn., Am. Law Inst., Tex. Rangers Law Enforcement Assn.(bd. dirs.), Nat. Cattlemen's Beef Assn. (bd. dirs., pres. 1998), U.S. Meat Export Fedn. (exec. com. 1991-93), Beef Industry Coun. (exec. com. 1990-91, promotion chmn. 1992-94), Tex. Cattle Feeders Assn. (bd. dirs., pres. 1988), Tex. Bd. Vet. Med. Examiners (pres. 1994), Tex. Beef Coun. (bd. dirs., pres. 1989), Dallas Country Club. Republican. Episcopalian. Home: 3824 Shenandoah St Dallas TX 75205-1702 Office: Moseley Martens LLP 3878 Oak Lawn Ave Fl 4 Dallas TX 75219-4460 Office Phone: 214-525-3940. E-mail: clarkw@airmail.net.

**WILLINGHAM, DEBORAH N.,** information technology executive; BS in Indsl. and Systems Engrng., Ga. Inst. Tech. Various sr. mgmt. pos. IBM Corp.; v.p., support, Enterprise Customer Unit Microsoft, Redmond, Wash., 1993—96, v.p., Enterprise Customer Unit, 1996—99, v.p., bus. and enterprise divsn. mktg., sr. v.p. human resources. Mem. Nat. Bd. Advisors Coll. Bus. and Pub. Administrn., U. Ariz.; mem. indsl. and systems engring. alumni adv. bd., pres.'s adv. bd. Ga. Inst. Tech.

**WILLINGHAM, EDWARD BACON, JR.,** ecumenical minister, administrator; b. St. Louis, July 27, 1934; s. Edward and Harriet (Sharon) W.; m. Angeline Walton Pettit, June 14, 1957; children: Katie, Carol. BS in Physics, U. Richmond, 1956; postgrad., U. Rochester, 1958—59; MDiv., Colgate Rochester Div. Sch., 1960. Ordained to ministry Am. Bapt. Ch., 1960. Min. Christian edn. Delaware Ave. Bapt. Ch., Buffalo, 1960-62; dir. radio and TV Met. Detroit Coun. Chs., 1962-75; exec. dir. Christian Communication Coun. Met. Detroit Chs., 1976-98. Broadcast cons. Mich. Coun. Chs., 1965-75; guest cons. religious broadcasting Germany, 1968; coord. com. Mich. Ecumenical Forum, 1986, 90-92, chmn., 1991-92. Bd. mgrs. Broadcasting and Film Commn., Nat. Coun. Chs., 1965-73; mem. Muslim-Christian-Jewish Leadership Forum, 1987—; bd. deacons 1st Bapt. Ch. Birmingham, chmn., 1994-95. Recipient Gabriel award Cath. Broadcasting Assn., 1972, 1st Ann. Ecumenical award Am. Bapt. Chs. Mich., 1992, Race Rels. award Booker T. Washington Bus. Assn. Detroit, 1983, Brotherhood award Bethal AME Ch., Detroit, 2000 Mem. Assn. Regional Religious Communicators (pres. 1969-71), World Assn. Christian Comm. (cen. com. 1973-78, chmn. N.Am. Broadcast sect. 1970-71, bus. mgr., 1972-98, Pioneer in Broadcasting Com. award 2004), Phi Gamma Delta, Sigma Pi Sigma. Office: 21440 Lathrup St Southfield MI 48075-4218

**WILLINGHAM, JEANNE MAGGART,** performing arts educator, performing company executive; b. Fresno, Calif., May 8, 1923; d. Harold F. and Gladys (Ellis) Maggart. Student, Tex. Woman's U., 1942; student profl. dancing schs. worldwide. Tchr. dance Beaux Arts Dance Studio, Pampa, Tex., 1948—; artistic dir. Pampa Civic Ballet, 1972—. Mem. Tex. Arts and Humanities Coun. Mem. Tex. Arts Alliance, Pampa C. of C. (fine arts com.), Pampa Fine Arts Assn. Office: Pampa Civic Ballet Beaux Arts Dance Studio 315 N Nelson St Pampa TX 79065-6013 Office Phone: 806-669-6361.

**WILLINGHAM, MARY MAXINE,** fashion retailer; b. Childress, Tex., Sept. 12, 1928; d. Charles Bryan and Mary (Bohannon) McCollum; m. Welborn Kiefer Willingham, Aug. 14, 1950; children: Sharon, Douglas, Sheila. BA, Tex. Tech U., 1949. Interviewer Univ. Placement Svc., Tex. Tech U., Lubbock, 1964-69; owner, mgr. buyer Maxine's Accent, Lubbock, 1969—. Speaker in field. Leader Campfire Girls, Lubbock, 1964-65; sec. Cmty. Theatre, Lubbock, 1962-64. Recipient Golden Sun award Dallas Market, 1985, Woman of Excellence award in Bus., YWCA, 2001; named Outstanding Mcht., Fashion Retailer Mag., 1971, also Outstanding Retailer. Mem. Ranch and Heritage Ctr.

**WILLINGHAM, WARREN WILLCOX,** psychologist; b. Rome, Ga., Mar. 1, 1930; s. Calder Baynard and Eleanor (Willcox) W.; m. Anna Michal, Mar. 17, 1954; children: Sherry, Judith, Daniel. Student, Ga. Inst. Tech., 1952; PhD, U. Tenn., 1955. Rsch. assoc. World Book Co., N.Y.C., 1959-60; dir. evaluation studies Ga. Inst. Tech., Atlanta, 1960-64; dir. rsch. Coll. Bd., N.Y.C., 1964-68, dir. access rsch. office Palo Alto, Calif., 1968-72; asst. v.p., disting. rsch. scientist Ednl. Testing Svc., Princeton, NJ, 1972—. Vis. prof. U. Minn., 1988; mem. adv. bd. on ednl. requirements on Sec. Navy, 1968; leader Psychometric Seminar, Nat. Inst. Testing and Evaluation, Jerusalem, 1999; cons. to numerous schs., colls. U.S. Office Edn. Author: Free Access Higher Education, 1970, Source Book for Higher Education, 1973, College Placement and Exemption, 1974, Assessing Experimental Learning, 1977, Selective Admissions in Higher Education, 1977, Personal Qualities and College Admissions, 1982, Success in College, 1985, Testing Handicapped People, 1988, Predicting College Grades, 1990; Gender and Fair Assessment, 1997; editor: Measurement in Education, 1969-72; mem. editl. bd. Jour. Ednl. Measurement, 1971-75, Alternate Higher Ed., 1976-80, Am. Ednl. Rsch. Jour., 1968-71; contbr. articles, tech. reports to profl. jours. Served to lt. USNR, 1955-59. Recipient Ann. award So. Soc. Philosophy and Psychology, 1958 Fellow Am. Psychol. Assn., AAAS; mem. Nat. Council on Measurement in Edn. (dir.), Am. Ednl. Research Assn., Am. Psychol. Soc., CAEL (hon. life mem.), Sigma Xi. Mailing: 131 Bertrand Dr Princeton NJ 08540

**WILLIS, BEN,** writer, artist; b. Racine, Wis., Dec. 4, 1930; s. Ben Sherlock Willis and Beryl Hester (Smith) Young; div. 1971. Attended, Phila. Coll. Art, 1953—54, Pa. Acad. Fine Arts, 1954—55, Academie Julian, Paris, 1955—57. Author: The Tao of Art, 1987, Internet reprint edit., 2001; collaborator: The Art of Oriental Embroidery, 1980; exhibited in group shows Salmagundi Club, N.Y.C., 1971-75, 1980, Am. Watercolor Soc., Nat. Acad. Design, N.Y.C., 1978, Cicchinelli Galleries, N.Y.C., 1980, Nat. Arts Club, N.Y.C., 1980, Manasquan Group Artists, 1981, Pastel Soc., N.Y.C., 1982, Allied Artists Am., N.Y.C., 1982, Am. Artists Profl. League, N.Y.C., 1984; represented in numerous pvt. collections. Seaman 1st class, USN, 1948-52, Korea. Recipient 1st prize N.Y.C. Ctr., 1960, Manasquan Outdoor Art Show, 1981, Best in Show award Manasquan Group Artists, 1981, others. Fellow Alumni Fellowship Pa. Acad. Fine Art, Author's Guild. Episcopalian. Avocations: languages, music, reading, Judo. Home: 10 C Bennington Ln Whiting NJ 08759-1621

**WILLIS, BEVERLY ANN,** architect; d. Ralph William and Margaret Amanda (Porter) W. BFA, U. Hawaii, 1954; PhD in Fine Arts (hon.), Mt. Holyoke Coll., 1983. Registered architect, Calif. Prin. Willis Atelier, Honolulu, 1954-58, Willis & Assocs., Inc., San Francisco, 1958-88. Pres. Beverly Willis Architecture Found., 2002—; pres., dir. Architecture Rsch. Inst., Inc., NYC, 1993—2005; co-chair Rebuild Downtown Our Town Coalition, 2002; prof. Internat. Women's U., Kassel, Germany, 2000. Author: Invisible Images: The Silent Language of Architecture, 1997; contbg. author: City and Gender-International Discourse on Gender, Urbanism and Architecture, 2003, Creating Sustainable Urban Environments: Future Forms and Design for Sustainable Cities, 2005; prin. works include Union St. Stores (merit award San Francisco AIA, award of distinction State of Calif.), Nob Hill Cts. (merit award AIA), 1970, Margaret Hayward Park (grand and merit awards Pacific Coast Bldg. Con., Honor award Design Internat.), 1983, San Francisco Ballet Bldg., 1984, Manhattan Village Acad. H.S., N.Y.C., 1995; contbr. articles to profl. jours., chpts. to books. Founding trustee Nat. Bldg. Mus., Washington,

1976—; bldg. rsch. adv. bd. Nat. Acad. Sci., 1971-79, chair Fed. Construction Coun., 1976-79; pres. Beverly Willis Architecture Found., NYC, 2002-. Recipient Phoebe Hearst Gold Medal award, 1969. Fellow AIA (v.p. Calif. coun. 1979, pres. 1980); mem. Achievement Rewards for Coll. Scientists, Internat. Women's Forum, Lambda Alpha (pres. San Francisco chpt. 1981-82), Villa Taverna and Nat. Arts Club. Avocations: poetry, sketching, tennis. Office Phone: 212-577-1200. Business E-Mail: bevwillis@architect.org.

**WILLIS, BRUCE DONALD,** judge; b. Mpls., Jan. 29, 1941; s. Donald Robert and Marie Evelyn (Edwards) W.; m. Elizabeth Ann Runsvold, July 17, 1971; children: Andrew John, Ellen Elizabeth. BA in English, Yale U., 1962; LLB, Harvard U., 1965. Bar: Minn. 1965, U.S. Dist. Ct. Minn. 1965, U.S. Ct. Fed. Claims 1989, U.S. Ct. Appeals (8th cir.) 1991, U.S. Supreme Ct. 1992. Assoc. Popham, Haik, Schnobrich & Kaufman, Ltd., Mpls., 1965-71, ptnr., 1971-95; judge Minn. Ct. Appeals, 1995—. Mem. jud. adv. bd. Law and Orgnl. Econs. Ctr., U. Kans., 1997—2001; adv. bd. Minn. Inst. Legal Edn. 1986—2003. Contbr. articles to profl. jours. Del. Rep. Nat. convs., 1976, 88; vice chmn. Ind.-Rep. Party Minn., 1979-81; mem. State Ethical Practices Bd., 1990-95, sec. 1990-91, vice chmn. 1991-92, chmn., 1992-93; mem. Minn. Commn. on Jud. Selection, 1991-94; mem. Minn. Bd. Jud. Stds., 1997—2005; mem. adv. com. on rules of civil appellate procedure Minn. Supreme Ct., 1997—. Named one of 1990's Lawyers of Yr., Minn. Jour. Law and Politics, 1991, one of Minn.'s Best Trial Lawyers, Minn. Lawyer, 1991. Mem.: ABA, Minn. Bar Assn. (professionalism com. 1998—). Mem. United Ch. of Christ. Home: 2940 Walnut Grove Ln N Plymouth MN 55447-1567 Office: Minn Jud Ctr 25 Rev Dr Martin Luther King Jr Blvd Saint Paul MN 55155-1500 E-mail: bruce.willis@courts.state.mn.us.

**WILLIS, CAROL,** museum director; b 1949; m Mark Willis. BA in Art History, Boston U. Founder, dir., curator Skyscraper Mus., N.Y.C., 1996—. Arch. historian, prof. urban studies Columbia U. Author: Form Follows Finance: Skyscrapers and Skylines in New York and Chicago, 1995 (AIA book award), The Lower Manhattan Plan: Visions for Downtown New York. Office: The Skyscraper Museum 39 Battery Pl New York NY 10280-1501

**WILLIS, CHRISTOPHER SCOTT,** school psychologist, writer; b. Cranston, R.I., Feb. 26, 1952; s. James Albert and Margaret Scott Willis; m. Gretchen Marie Williams, July 21, 1979; 1 child, Andrew Scott. BA in Psychology, Philosophy, U. RI, 1977; MS in Sch. Psychology, Albany State U., 1979; PhD in Psychology, U. RI, 1999. Sch. psychologist Newport County Spl. Edn., Portsmouth, RI, 1979—. Author: Shore Diving in Rhode Island, 1986, (screenplays) Love it or Leave it, 2006. Bd. govs. Masonic Learning Ctr., Cranston, RI, 2001—. Mem.: NASP (del. 2002—, exec. coun. 2003—, R.I. Sch. Psychologist of Yr. 1993, 1996, finalist Nat. Sch. Psychologist of Yr. 2001), R.I. Sch. Psychologist Assn. (pres. 2000—02). Office: Newport County Regional Spl Edn 1 Frank Coelho Dr Portsmouth RI 02871 Office Phone: 401-683-3570. E-mail: drchriswillis1@netscape.net.

**WILLIS, CLAYTON,** broadcaster, former government official, educator, arts consultant; b. Washington, Aug. 11, 1933; s. William H. and Elizabeth Carl (Keferstein) W. Student, The Sorbonne, Paris, 1953-54; BA, George Washington U., 1957; student, U. Oslo, 1953; grad., N.Y. Inst. Fin., 1966, Assn. Commodities Exch. Firms Inc., 1966. Spl. assignment Am. Embassy, London, 1957; writer NBC Network radio show Tex and Jinx, 1958; spl. corr. NBC News, La Paz, Bolivia, 1959; spl. Washington corr. Fin. News TV Network (now CNBC), N.Y.C., 1988; contbr., anchor, TV prodr., corr. Saudi Arabian TV, Newsweek mag., Phillips News Svc. The Hope (Ark.) Star; contbr., corr. Christian Sci. Monitor, L.A. Times-Mirror Syndicate, The Palm Beach (Fla.) Post, The Greenwich (Conn.) Time, Fin. News TV Network, New York, The Mainichi, Tokyo, The China Post, Taipei, Taiwan, Chattanooga Times, The Nashville Tennessean, the Daily Nation of Kenya, The Khartoum Echo, Sudan, The Washington Daily News, Washington Post, Cape Argus of Capetown, South Africa, Bangkok Post, Irish Times, Dublin; reporter, movie, art critic Albuquerque Tribune, 1959-61; asst. editor Newsweek Mag., N.Y.C., 1961-62; TV broadcaster-writer UPI Newsfilm, N.Y.C., 1962; White House corr., chief bur., anchor World Radio News, Houston; White House, Washington corr. WAVA Radio Sta., Washington, 1963-65; editorial writer, Hearst Newspapers, N.Y.C., 1965; press officer UN, N.Y.C., 1965-66; spl. assignment Am. Embassy, Reykjavik, Iceland, 1967; editorial writer, critic, corr. N.Y. Amsterdam News, N.Y.C., 1967-68; contbg. govt., law, and ethics programs Ford Found., N.Y.C., 1968-69; dir. pub. affairs U.S. EEOC, Washington, 1969-70; cons. OEO, Washington, 1970, Pres.'s Nat. Coun. on Indian Opportunity, Washington, 1970-71, Community Rels. Svc., U.S. Dept. Justice, Washington, 1970-73, Cabinet Com. on Opportunities for Spanish-Speaking People, 1971-72, Fed. Energy Administrn., Washington, 1973-74; dir. pub. affairs Office of Petroleum Allocation, U.S. Dept. Interior, 1973-74; dir. Congl. rels., dir. pub. affairs Pres.'s Nat. Commn. on Fire Prevention and Control, 1971-73; pub., editor, owner Four Corners Chieftain, Ignacio and Durango, Colo., 1972-73; lectr. Sch. of Bus., U. D.C., Washington, 1973-74; owner, White House corr., photojournalist Willis News Svc., Washington, 1974—; pub. affairs dir. Inaugural Vets. Com., 1976-77; White House corr., anchor Channel 33, Arlington, Va., 1991—. Adviser to Fernando E.C. de Baca, spl. asst. to the Pres., White House, 1974-76; lectr. nat., internat. affairs, Haiti, art, communications, energy; corr.-broadcaster Sta. KTEN-TV, Ada, Okla., 1985; mem. staff presdl. transition office U.S. Pres. Bush, 1988-89, 90; dir. and curator L. Clayton Willis Art Collection, Palm Beach, Fla.; anchor, corr. Channel 33 Arlington, Va., 1991—; pres., White House corr., congressional corr., photojournalist, The Evening News Broadcasting Co., Willis News Service; prodr., anchor documentary programs Saudi Arabian TV, 1992—; exec. prodr., anchor Glimpses of the World documentaries, 1993; White House corr., photojournalist Hope (Ark.) Star, 1994—; dir., curator L. Clayton Willis Art Collection, Palm Beach; chmn. emeritus Haitian Art Mus., Delray Beach, Fla.; exec. prod., host, commentator The Clayton Willis Talk Show, WPBR, Palm Beach, Fla, 2000-. Co-author: Capital Farce 1977 Lott-Willis Pictorial Digest of U.S. Presidential Elections and Inaugurations, 1997; host/exec. prodr., commentator The Clayton Willis Talk Show, WPBR, 1998-; pres.'s White House corr. Evening News Broadcasting Co., Washington, 2000; contbr. articles to Daily Mail, London, London Sunday Express, Umtali Post, Zimbabwe, Gwelo (Zimbabwe) Times, To the Point news mag., Johannesburg, The Citizen, Johannesburg, Hartford Courant, Sacramento Union, Chattanooga Times, UPI Radio Networks, Washington Post, The Hope (Ark.) Star, Phillips News Svc., also other mags. and newspapers. Broadcaster with Bush/Quayle Nat. Campaign Hdqrs., Washington, 1988; adviser Presdl. Transition Office of Pres. George Bush, 1988-89; loaned Haitian paintings for spl. exhbn. to Haitian Embassy, Washington, 1991, Milw. Art Mus., 1992, Hypoluxo Town Hall, Fla., 2005. Recipient Outstanding Svc. award Harlem Prep. Sch., Johannes Gutenberg medal (Mainz, Germany), 1984, Letters of Cert. Appreciation Pres. of U.S., 1989. Covered Vietnam, Congo, Mid. East, Rhodesian and South African wars; covered Clarence Thomas and Robert Gates U.S. Senate confirmation hearings, 1991; covered 2000 presdl. election and re-count, Palm Beach, Fla.; covered Haitian rebellion and fall of Pres. Aristide, Haiti, 2004; covered the 2004 Kerry-Bush Presidential Campaign. Office Phone: 561-688-1777. Personal E-mail: lclaytonwillis@aol.com.

**WILLIS, CONNIE (CONSTANCE E. WILLIS),** writer; b. Denver, Dec. 31, 1945; m. Courtney Willis; 1 child. Tchr. elem. and jr. H.S., Branford, Conn., 1967-69. Author: (short stories) Letter from the Clearys, 1982 (Nebula award, 1982, Hugo award, 1983), Even the Queen, 1992 (Nebula award, 1992, Hugo award, 1993), Death on the Nile, 1993 (Hugo award, 1994), The Soul Selects Her Own Society, 1996 (Hugo award, 1997), (novels) Water Witch, 1982, Fire Watch, 1985 (Nebula award, 1982, Hugo award, 1983), Lincoln's Dreams, 1987 (John W. Campbell Meml. award), Doomsday Book, 1992 (Nebula award, 1992, Hugo award, 1993), Impossible Things, 1993, Uncharted Territory, 1994, Uncharted Territory, 1994, Remake, 1995, Bellwether, 1996, To Say Nothing of the Dog, 1997 (Hugo award, 1999), Miracle, 1999, Promised Land, 1997, Miracle and other Christmas Stories, 1999, Passage, 2001 (Locus award, Hugo award nominee, 2002, Nebula award nominee, 2002), Inside Job, 2005, (novellas) The Last of the Winnebagos, 1989 (Nebula award, 1988, Hugo award, 1989), The Winds of Marble

Arch, 2000 (Hugo best novella nominee, 2000). Named Best Sci. Fiction/Fantasy Author of Nineties Locus Mag. Address: 1716 13th Ave Greeley CO 80631-5418 E-mail: conniewillis@juno.com.

**WILLIS, CRAIG DEAN,** academic administrator; b. Cambridge, Ohio, Mar. 21, 1935; s. John Russell and Glenna (Stevens) W.; m. Marilyn Elaine Foster, June 9, 1956; Mark Craig, Bruce Dean, Todd Laine, Garth John. BA, Ohio Wesleyan U., 1957; MA, Ohio State U., 1960, PhD, 1969. Registrar Ohio Wesleyan U., 1964-69; dir. admissions Wright State U., 1970-72, dean, 1971-77; v.p. acad. affairs Concord Coll., 1977-82; pres. Lock Haven U. Pa., 1982—2004, Eastern Mich. U., Ypsilanti, 2004—. Chmn. internat. affairs com. Am. Assn. State Colls. and Univs.; A.C.E. pres.'s commn. on internat. edn.; vice chmn. Clinton region Mellon Bank Ctr., 1987, chmn., 88, also bd. dirs.; bd. dirs. Lock Haven U.; cons. Ellis Assocs., Princeton, W.Va., 1980—82. Chmn. bd. Kirkmont Preschool, Beavercreek, Ohio, 1974-77, Beavercreek Library, 1976-77, Regional Edn. Service Agy., Beckley, W.Va., 1978-82; mem. N.E.-Midwest leadership Coun., 1989—. Recipient Disting. Alumnus award dept. edn. Ohio Wesleyan U. 1991; scholar Sohio Oil, 1953, Govt. of France, Paris, 1964, Shell Oil Co, 1967. Mem. Commn. State Coll. and Univ. Pres., Assn. State Colls. and Univs., Clinton County C. of C. (pres.), Rotary (v.p., pres. elect, Citizen of Yr. award Lock Haven 1989), Ohio Wesleyan U. Alumni Assn. (Disting. Sesquicentennial Alumnus of the Edn. 1992), Phi Kappa Phi, Kappa Kappa Psi, Phi Delta Kappa, Kappa Delta Pi. Presbyterian. Office: Eastern Mich U 202 Welch Hall Ypsilanti MI 48197 Business E-Mail: cwillis@lhup.edu.

**WILLIS, DONTRELLE,** professional baseball player; b. Oakland, Calif., Jan. 12, 1982; Pitcher Fla. Marlins, Miami, 2003—. Mem. Team USA, World Baseball Classic, 2006. Named Nat. League Rookie of the Yr., 2003, California High School Player of the Year, 2000; named to, Nat. League All-Star Team, 2003, 2005. Achievements include member of World Series Champion Florida Marlins, 2003. Office: c/o Florida Marlines Pro Player Stadium 2267 Dan Marino Blvd Miami FL 33056*

**WILLIS, EDWARD OLIVER,** management consultant, state agency administrator; b. St. Louis, Apr. 6, 1948; s. George Washington and Mary (Fantroy) W.; m. Jennifer Linnea Johnson, June 17, 1972 (div. Dec. 1991); children: Linnea, Eric; m. Linda Diane Clark, Aug. 8, 1992. AA, Am. River Coll., Sacramento, 1972; BS in BA, Calif. State U., Sacramento, 1974; MBA in Mgmt., Golden Gate U., San Francisco, 1978. Divsn. ops. supr., casualty claims investigator Allstate Ins. Co., Menlo Park, Sacramento, 1974-75; budget analyst Dept. Fin., State of Calif., Sacramento, 1975-77; assoc. govtl. program analyst Dept. Health, Medi-Cal Procurement Project, State of Calif., Sacramento, 1977-78; chief fiscal br. solid waste mgmt. bd. State of Calif., Sacramento, 1978-79; mgr. adminstrv. svcs. state lands commn., 1979-80; asst. to assoc. supt. pub. instrn. dept. edn., 1980-82, dep. dir. adminstrv. dept. fish and game, 1982-90, acting administr. office of oil spill prevention and response, 1990-92, dep. dir. adminstrv. dept. developmental svcs., 1992-93, dep. dir. adminstrv. svcs. program dept. toxic substances, 1993-94, asst. sec. policy devel. Calif. Environ. Protection Agy., 1994-95, chief dep. dir. Calif. Conservation Corps, 1995—98; owner, prin. cons. WW Assocs., 1994; chief adminstrv. officer Santa Clara Valley Water Dist., San Jose, Calif., 1998—2002; interim exec. dir. Calif. Coun. Developmental Disabilities, Sacramento, 2005. Part-time instr. Cosumnes River Coll., Sacramento, 1980-83. Author: Business Employment Equity Plan, 1994. Vol. United Way Campaign, United Negro Coll. Fund, Sacramento Children's Home, YMCA; 1st v.p. Nat. Black Child Devel. Inst., Sacramento, 1981-82; chmn. Black Adv. Com. to State Pers. Bd., 1984-85; mem. St. Francis of Assisi Sch. Bd., Sacramento, 1996—, pres., 1991-93; bd. trustees Black Advocates in State Svc., 1992; bd. dirs. Nat. Forum for Black Pub. Adminstrs., Washington, 1993-04, 2d v.p., 2003-04; Little League coach, 1996—. With USAF, 1966-70. Decorated Air medals (4). Mem. Nat. Forum for Black Pub. Adminstrs. (Sacramento chpt. bd. dirs. 1993—, 1st v.p. 1990-91, pres. 1991-93), Am. Soc. Pub. Adminstrn. (Pub. Adminstr. of the Yr.). Avocations: golf, softball. Home: 2208 E Leo Pl Chandler AZ 85249

**WILLIS, FRANK EDWARD,** retired air force officer; b. Clinton, Ill., June 19, 1939; s. William Edward and Bernardine (Saveley) W.; m. Clarice Marie Hull, June 7, 1961; children: Michael, Steven, William. BS in Engring., USAF Acad., Colorado Springs, Colo., 1961; MA in Bus. Mgmt., U. Nebr., 1973. Commd. 2d lt. USAF, 1961, advanced through grades to maj. gen., 1989; dep. comdr. 314th Tactical Airlift Group, Little Rock AFB, 1978-79, comdr., 1979-80; vice comdr. 374th Tactical Airlift Wing, Clark Air Base, The Philippines, 1980-81, comdr., 1981-83, 317th Tactical Airlift Wing, Pope AFB, N.C., 1983-84; vice comdr. Air Force Manpower and Pers. Ctr., Randolph AFB, Tex., 1984-85; comdt. Air Command and Staff Coll., Maxwell AFB, Ala., 1985-88; vice comdr. 22d Air Force, Travis AFB, Calif., 1988-89; dir. and dep. chief of staff for requirements Air Mobility and Mil. Airlift Command, Scott AFB, Ill., 1989-93; ret., 1993; co-owner retail hobby shop Tinker Town, Inc., St. Louis, 1994—. Decorated D.S.M. (2), Legion of Merit (2), Air medal (7), Meritorious Svc. medal (2). Presbyterian. Avocations: electronics, computer, model building. Home: 1901 Mistflower Glen Ct Chesterfield MO 63005-4713 Personal E-mail: frank@willis.net.

**WILLIS, FRANK ROY,** historian, educator; b. Prescot, Lancashire, Eng., July 25, 1930; s. Harry and Gladys Reid (Birchall) W.; children from previous marriage, Jane, Clare, Geoffrey. BA, Cambridge U., Eng., 1952, cert. in edn., 1955, diploma in devel. econs., 1974; PhD, Stanford U., Calif., 1959. Instr. Stanford U., 1959-60; from instr. to assoc. prof. history U. Wash., Seattle, 1960-64; assoc. prof. then prof. U. Calif., Davis, 1964—. Author: The French in Germany, 1962, France, Germany and the New Europe, 1945-1967, 1968, Europe in the Global Age, 1968, Italy Chooses Europe, 1971, Western Civilization: An Urban Perspective, 1973, World Civilizations, 1982, The French Paradox, 1982, Western Civilization: A Brief Introduction, 1987. Fellow, Rockefeller Found., Paris, 1962—63 Guggenheim Found. Rome 1966—67, Social Scis. Rsch. Coun., Cambridge, 1973—74. Avocation: travel. Office: U Calif Dept History Davis CA 95616

**WILLIS, GLADDEN WILLIAMS,** pathologist, scientific photographer, tree farmer; b. Minden, La., Mar. 26, 1939; s. John Stillmon and Virgie Williams Willis; m. Lydia Hall, May 14, 1966; children: Charles Austin, Loye Stillmon. BS, Centenary Coll., 1960; MD, Tulane U., 1964. Intern La. State U. Med. Ctr., Shreveport, 1964-65, resident, 1965-69; fellow Meml. Sloan-Kettering Med. Ctr., NYC, 1969-71; pathologist St. Luke's Hosp., Houston, 1971-72, St. Mary's Hosp., Roswell, N.Mex., 1972-73, Ochsner Clinic Found., New Orleans, 1973—2005, dir. anat. pathology, 1976—2003, vice chmn. lab. medicine, 1996—2003. Contbr. articles to profl. jours., more than 1480 sci. photographs to encys. and books. Past pres. Jefferson Performing Arts Soc., Metarie, La. Capt. USAF, 1966—72. Recipient George Washington Honor medal, Valley Forge Found., 1996. Fellow Arthur Purdy Stout Soc., Royal Microscopical Soc.; mem. Assn. Dirs. of Anatomic Pathology, Internat. Acad. Pathology, Am. Soc. Media Photographers, NY Acad. Scis. Republican. Methodist. Avocation: photography. Home and Office: PO Box 719 Doyline LA 71023 E-mail: gladdenwillis@direcway.com.

**WILLIS, ISAAC,** dermatologist, educator; b. Albany, Ga., July 13, 1940; s. R.L. and Susie M. (Miller) W.; m. Alliene Horne, June 12, 1965; children: Isaac Horne, Alliric Isaac. BS, Morehouse Coll., 1961, DSc (hon.), 1989; MD, Howard U., 1965. Diplomate Am. Bd. Dermatology. Intern Phila. Gen. Hosp., 1965-66; fellow Howard U., Washington, 1966-67; resident fellow U. Pa., Phila., 1967-69, assoc. in dermatology 1969-70; mem. staff Phila. Gen. Hosp., 1969-70; instr. dept. dermatology U. Pa., Phila., 1970-72; mem. staff Moffit Hosp. U. Calif., San Francisco, 1970-72; asst. prof. Johns Hopkins U., Johns Hopkins Hosp., Balt., 1972-73; mem. staff Johns Hopkins Hosp., Balt. City Hosp., Good Samaritan Hosp., Balt., 1972-72; asst. prof. Emory U., Atlanta, 1973-77; mem. staff Crawford W. Long Meml. Hosp., Atlanta, 1974—, West Paces Ferry Hosp., Atlanta, 1974-2000; assoc. prof. Emory U., Atlanta, 1977-82; prof. Morehouse Sch. Medicine, Atlanta, 1982—, chief dermatology, 1982-96—2003. Contbr. articles to profl. jours.; mem. staff Piedmont Hosp., Atlanta, 2000—. Dep. commdr. of 3297th USA Hosp. (1000B), 1990-; mem. gen. medicine group

IA study sect., NIH, 1985-; mem. grants review panel EPA, 1986—; adv. bd. Arthritis and Musculoskeletal and Skin Diseases, 1991-, U. Pa. Sch. Medicine, 1995-, adv. bd. U. of Calif. Sch. of Engring. LaJolla, 2000-, Emory U., 1994-; chmn. inst. review bd., mem. pharmacy and therapeutic com.; bd. dirs. Comml. Bank Gwinnett, Comml. Bank of Ga., Heritage Bank, Landmark Bank Fla., Learning Framework, West Paces Med. Ctr., Lupus Specialists, Inc., InterVu, Inc., Lupus Erythematosus Found., Jacquelyn McClure Lupus Erythematosus Clinic, Skin Cancer Found., World Network Solutions; bd. dirs., chmn. audit com. Comml. Bank of Ga., 2000-, Landmark Bank of Fla., 1999-; mem. med. staff Piedmont Hosp., 2000-; adv. bd. Enable, Inc.; mem. adv. coun. U. Calif. Jacobs Sch. Engring., San Diego, 2001-; vice coun. Internat. Biographical Ctr., 2002; cons. in field. Author: Textbook of Dermatology, 1971; contbr. articles to profl. jours. Trustee Friendship Bapt. Ch., Atlanta, 1980-82; mem. gov.'s commn. on effectiveness and economy in govt. State of Ga. Human Resources Task Force, 1991—, Ga. State Bd. of worker's Compensation Med. subcom., 1997—; mem. nat. alumni coun. U. Pa., 1995—; mem. coun. of advisors U. Calif. San Diego Jacobs Sch. Engring., 2001--. Col. USAR, 1983-95. Recipient Benny Trailblazer award, Morehouse Coll., 2004. Fellow Am. Acad. Dermatology, Am. Dermtol. Assn., Am. Soc. Laser Medicine and Surgery, Inc.; mem. AAAS, AMA, Nat. Cancer Inst., Soc. Investigative Dermatology, Nat. Med. Assn., Internat. Soc. Tropical Dermatology, Pan Am. Med. Assn., Am. Fedn. Clin. Rsch., Am. Soc. Photobiology, U. Pa. Nat. Alumni Adv. Coun., State of Ga. Dermatology Found., Frontiers Internat., Sportsman Internat., Phi Beta Kappa, Omicron Delta Kappa. Achievements include a patent for the development of a shaving composition and method for preventing Pseudofollientitis Barbae, 1999; subspecialties in the areas of dermatology and cancer research (medicine). Home: 1141 Regency Rd NW Atlanta GA 30327-2719 Office: NW Med Ctr Ste 342 3280 Howell Mill Rd NW Ste 342 Atlanta GA 30327-4109 Office Phone: 404-351-8306. Personal E-mail: iwmd2@bellsouth.net.

**WILLIS, JOHN PATRICK,** chemist; b. Albany, NY, Mar. 10, 1947; s. John James and Mary Catherine (Varden) W.; m. Tientje Jane Dirzuweit, July 22, 1972. BS, Iona Coll., 1969; MS, SUNY, Oswego, 1974; PhD, U. Conn., 1977. Assoc. prodn. chemist Winthrop Labs., Rensselaer, N.Y., 1970-72; rsch. chemist Uniroyal, Inc., Middlebury, Conn., 1977-79; postdoctoral rschr. U. Minn., Mpls., 1979-80; mgr. chem. rsch. Nova Biomed Corp., Newton, Mass., 1980-83; founder, chmn. Ilex Corp., Marlboro, Mass., 1983-87; med. cons. 1987-88; founder T.J. Assocs., Biomed. Cons., 1987-89; v.p., chief oper. officer Sharon Drive Corp., Westlake, Ohio, 1988-93; dir. rsch. Medisense, Inc., Waltham, Mass., 1997-93; v.p. R&D Marathon Med. Techs., Inc., Worcester, Mass., 1997-98; exec. v.p., chief tech. officer BioValve Techs., Inc., North Grafton, Mass., 1999-2000; pres., CEO Teknow Source Inc., Shirley, Mass., 2000—02; chmn., CEO North Country Naturals, Inc., Shirley, Mass., 2000—05; tech. dir. biotech. Mohawk Innovative Tech, Inc., Albany, NY, 2001—04; rsch. prof. dept. chemistry and chem. biology Rensselaer Polytechnic Inst., Troy, NY, 2004—05; founder, chmn. Ultradian Diagnostics LLC, 2004—. Mem. adv. bd. Clin. Lab. Practice, Mass. Dept. Pub. Health, 1986-87, 128 Entrepreneurs' Ctr., Waltham, Mass., 1986-88; mem. tech. adv. coun. Edison Biotech. Ctr., Cleve., 1988-90. U. Conn. Rsch. Found. fellow, 1976. Fellow Am. Inst. Chemists; mem. Am. Chem. Soc., Electrochem. Soc., Am. Assn. Clin. Chemistry, N.Y. Acad. Scis., Sigma Xi, Phi Kappa Phi, Phi Lambda Upsilon. Achievements include research in bioelectrochemistry, organic electrochemistry and biosensors; patents in field. Office: Ultradian Diagnostics LLC 5 Univ Pl Ste A324 Rensselaer NY 12144 Office Phone: 518-618-0046. Personal E-mail: jwillis@tiac.net.

**WILLIS, JOHN T.,** former secretary of state; b. Nov. 1, 1946; m. Kathy S. Mangan; children: Karen M., James T. BA in Econs. cum laude, Bucknell U., 1968; JD, Harvard Law Sch., 1971. Clk. Army Ct. of Mil. Rev., 1971-74; legal asstance officer Aberdeen Proving Grounds, 1974-75; pvt. practice atty. Westminster, Balt. City, Md., 1975-90; chief of staff County Exec. of Prince George's County, 1990-94; apptd. sec. of state State of Md., 1995—2003. Adj. prof. McDaniel Coll.(formerly Western Md. Coll.), 1999—; past chmn. Gov.'s Commn. on Md. Mil. Monuments; adv. bd. U. Balt.'s Schaefer Ctr. for Pub. Policy; adj. prof. govt. and pub. adminstrn. U. Balt. Author: Presidential Elections in Maryland, 1984; contbg. author: Western Maryland: A Profile, 1980, Justice and the Military, 1992; contbr. articles to profl. jours.; editor: The Advocate, 1973-74. Vice-chmn. Md. Dem. Party, 1987-89; mem. various coms. and del. to Dem. Nat. Convs., 1976-2000; former chair Dem. Secs. of State. Judge advocate gen. corps U.S. Army, 1968-75. Mem. Md. Bar Assn., Carroll County Bar Assn., Md. Hist. Soc., Carroll County Arts Coun. (past pres.). Democrat. U Balt 1420 N Charles St Baltimore MD 21201 E-mail: jwillis@ubalt.edu.

**WILLIS, JUDY ANN,** lawyer; b. Hartford, Conn., July 7, 1949; d. Durward Joseph and Angeline Raphael (Riccardo) Willis. BA, Ctrl. Conn. State U., 1971; postgrad., U. Conn. Law Sch., 1976—77; JD, Boston Coll., 1979. Bar: Mass. 1979, U.S. Dist. Ct. Mass. 1980, Calif. 1990. Sr. atty. H.P. Hood Inc., Charleston, Mass., 1979-83; v.p. law Parker Bros., Beverly, Mass., 1983-89; sr. v.p. bus. affairs Mattel, Inc., El Segundo, Calif., 1989—. Office: Mattel Inc M1-0848 333 Continental Blvd El Segundo CA 90245-5012 E-mail: judy.willis@Mattel.com.

**WILLIS, KEVIN,** airport administrator; Mgr. Atlanic City Internat. Airport, until 1996; compliance specialist FAA, Washington, 1996—. Office: FAA Airport Safety and Compliance Branch AAS-310 800 Independence Ave SW Washington DC 20591-0001 Business E-mail: kevin.willis@faa.gov.

**WILLIS, NANCY CAROL,** artist, illustrator, writer; b. Wilmington, Del., Apr. 20, 1952; d. Robert L. and Kathryn (Bowsher) W.; m. A. Laurence Field, Oct. 24, 1987 (dec. 2001). BS in Graphic and Advt. Design, U. Del., 1974; MBA, Wilmington Coll., 1986. Pub. rels. specialist New Castle County, Wilmington, 1975-80; graphic design supr. DuPont Co., Wilmington, 1980-88; owner Nancy Carol Willis Studios, Middletown, Del., 1988—; prof. Wilmington Coll., New Castle, Del., 2003—. Owner Birdsong Books, Middletown, Del., 1998—; ednl. cons. Artist Profl. Artists League Grand Nat. Juried Exhbns., 1989, 90; cover artist Manhattan Arts Mag., 1992 (award of excellence); illustrator: (books) Growing With Kindermusik, 1994, Kindermusik Adventures, 1996, The Rock, 1996, Birds of Delaware, 1999; author, illustrator: (book) The Robins In Your Backyard, 1996 (Parent Coun. Seal, Del. Diamonds Book award, Accelerated Reader Program); author, illustrator Kids Page Outdoor Del. mag. 1997-98, Delaware Bay Shorebird Guide, 1998, Delaware Watersheds, 2001, Raccoon Moon, 2002 (Accelerated Reader Program, Del. Diamonds Book award, Children's Book award Internat. Reading Assn., 2003, BookSense 76 Children's Booklist, named Your Big Backyard Read-to-Me book Nat. Wildlife Fedn., 2005), Red Knot: A Shorebird's Incredible Journey, 2006 (Del. Diamonds Book award Accelerated REader Program), (interpretive display) Gordon's Pond State Pk., 2002, Brandywine Creek State Pk., 2003. Vol. Tri-State Bird Rescue and Rsch., Newark, Del., 1988-92; gallery dir. Luther Towers II Art Gallery, Wilmington, 1989-90; vol. Del. Wildlife Rehabilitators Assn., 1994—; elder, New Covenant Ch., 1999—, dir. Arts Ministry program, 2000—. Grantee Earthwatch, 1994; recipient Good Egg Achievement award Tri-State Bird Rescue and Rsch., 1990, 1st pl. watercolor award Cape May County Art League, 1991; James Gervan art scholar, 1974. Mem. Del. Found. Visual Arts, Soc. Children's Book Writers and Illustrators, Pubs. Mktg. Assn. Avocations: birding, photography, dog agility competition, sketching. E-mail: ncwillis@nancycarolwillis.com.

**WILLIS, PAUL ALLEN,** librarian, dean; b. Floyd County, Ind., Oct. 1, 1941; s. Clarence Charles and Dorothy Jane (Harriott) Willis; m. Barbara Marcum, June 15, 1963; children: Mark, Sally. AB, U. Ky., 1963, JD, 1969; MLS, U. Md., 1966. Cataloger Libr. of Congress, Washington, 1963; head descriptive cataloging Sci. and Tech. Info. Facility NASA, College Park, Md., 1963-66; law libr., prof. law U. Ky., Lexington, 1966-73, dir. librs., 1973—2002, acting dean Coll. Libr., 1975-76, 78; dean of librs. U. SC, Columbia, 2002—. Exec. sec. Ky. Jud. Retirement and Removal Commn., 1977-81; adv. com. Ctr. for Jud. Conduct Orgns., Am. Judicature Soc., Chgo., 1979-81; chmn. Southea. Libr. Network, Atlanta, 1998-99; exec. com. Ky.

Hist. Soc., 1984-88; mem. Ky. Adv. Coun. on Librs., 1985-2002, adv. com. Online Computer Libr. Ctr., 1986-90; cons. S.E. Consortium for Internat. Devel., U. Sriwijaya, Palembang, Sumatera, Indonesia, 1987-88, Hanoi U. Tech., 1999, 2001, Vietnam Nat. U., Ho Chi Minh City, 1999 Sr. fellow, UCLA, 1982. Mem. Assn. Southeastern Rsch. Librs. (chair 1986-88, bd. dirs. 2002-), Assn. of Rsch. Librs. (bd. dirs. 2002-2003). Home: 111 Dene Ct Georgetown SC 29440-1095 Office: U SC Thomas Cooper Library 1322 Green St Columbia SC 29208-0001 Office Phone: 803-777-6212. Business E-mail: willis@sc.edu.

**WILLIS, RALPH HOUSTON,** mathematics professor; b. McMinnville, Tenn., Dec. 26, 1942; s. Carl Houston and Carrie Lee (Hill) W.; m. Gayle Catherine Celestin, June 29, 1973 (div. Apr. 1985); m. Velma Inez Church, Aug. 10, 1985; 1 stepchild, Bobbie Lynn White Buckner. BS in Math., Mid. Tenn. State U., 1964, MA in Math., 1966. Cert. secondary edn. tchr. Instr. depts. math. and computer sci. Western Carolina U., Cullowhee, NC, 1968-73, asst. prof., 1973-83, assoc. prof., 1983—. Co-founder State Math Contest com., 1977-78, western regional rep. exec. steering com., 1978—, recording sec., 1978—; co-founder NC Math. League, 1981-82, mem. problem writing com., 1981-84. Editor: (newsletters) Abelian Grapevine-Secondary Math, 1970-88, The Child of Mathematics-Elementary-Middle Grade Math., 1972-78; mem. editl. bd. The Centroid, 1995-2000; contbr. articles to profl. jours. Founder, dir., coord. H.S. Math. Contest, Western Carolina U., 1970—, solicitor-coord. Math. Contest Scholarship Program, 1971-82, founder, coord. math dept. student awards program, 1970—, initiator-coord. math. dept.'s Vis. Prof. Program, 1974-77; founder, faculty sponsor NC Coun. Tchrs. Math. Student Affiliate, Western Carolina U., Cullowhee, 1988—; coord. state road paving project Univ. Heights Cmty. Devel. Orgn., 1974-76, chmn., founder cmty. watch., 1978-79, coord. pub. water sys. upgrade project, 1980-84; founder, coord., bd. dirs., trustee Hunerwadle Cmty. Cemetery Assn., Beersheba, Tenn., 1983—; co-founder NC State Math. Contest and Contest Network, 1977-78. Recipient hon. mention NC Gov.'s award for Excellence, 1991, Exemplary Site award State Math. Contest Com., 1990, Paul A. Reid Disting. Svc. award for Faculty, 1991, Coll. Arts and Scis. Disting. Career Svc. award, 2003. Mem. Nat. Coun. Tchrs. Math., NC Coun. Tchrs. Math. (state bd. dirs. 1993-98, historian 1993-98, Innovator award 1994, editl. bd. Centroid 1995-2000, W.W. Rankin award 2001), Phi Kappa Phi, Kappa Mu Epsilon. Avocations: genealogy, gardening, military history, model building, die cast model collector. Office: Western Carolina U Math Dept Stillwell Bldg Cullowhee NC 28723

**WILLIS, RALPH WALKER,** retired firefighter; b. Redondo Beach, Calif., Nov. 21, 1921; s. Achatius Walker and Elizabeth Margaret (Dehm) Willis; m. Helen Elizabeth Willis, May 18, 1946 (dec. June 2006). Grad. h.s., San Diego. Firefighter Richmond (Calif.) Fire Dept., 1946-67; pres. Firefighters Union IAFF AFL CIO, 1964—67. Author: Sansei Banzai, 1986, War and Rememberance Revisited, 1988, The Eternal Regiment, 1995, My Life as a Jarhead, 1999 (The Ernie Pyle WWII Roundtable award). Sgt. USMC, 1941-45. Mem.: VFW (life), American's for Historical Accuracy, Iwo Jima Survivors Assn. American Independent Party. Avocations: travel, painting, writing. Home: 866 Camino De Oro San Jacinto CA 92583-6807 E-mail: jarheadhandr@aol.com.

**WILLIS, RUTH,** freelance/self-employed theater director, actress; b. Toledo, Nov. 7, 1932; d. Thomas LeRoy and Ruth Caroline (Ehmann) Ramsey; m. Charles Perrin Willis, Nov. 14, 1956; children: David, Laura. BE cum laude, U. Toledo, 1954. Grade sch. tchr. Toledo Pub. Schs., 1954—61; acting tchr. Cin. Children's Home, 1958—59, Contemporary Arts Mus., Houston, 1972, Jewish Cmty. Ctr., 1969—72; dir. Exptl. Wing Country Playhouse, 1968—72; mem. Actor's Studio Ariz. State U., Phoenix, 1980—81; dir. Plays for Living Family and Children's Svcs., Pitts., 1984—87; adult acting tchr. Point Park Coll. Conservatory, 1987—2001; artistic dir. Open Stage Theatre, 1991—. Dir.: (over 100 major prodns.); actor: (plays) The Women (named Best Actress, Assn. Cmty. Theatres, Cin.), The Sleeping Prince (named Best Actress, Country Playhouse, Houston), Sweet Bird of Youth (named Best Actress, Stagebrush Theatre, Scottsdale, Ariz.); dir.: Candida (named Best Dir.), Lucia Mad (Best Top Ten Evenings of Theatre, Pitts. Gazette, 1997). Gen. bd. mem. Mariemont Players, Cin., 1958—60, Phoenix Children's Theatre, 1978—81; exec. bd. mem., v.p. Phoenix Theatre, 1978—79, exec. bd. mem., v.p.; 1980—81; founder Open Stage Theatre, Pitts., 1991. Recipient Svc. award, Phoenix Little Theatre Bd. Dirs., 1981. Mem.: Charlevoix Garden Club, Nat. Soc. Arts and Letters, Pi Epsilon Delta. Avocations: piano, painting, yoga, gardening, decorating.

**WILLIS, SELENE LOWE,** electrical engineer, application developer, consultant, information technology manager; b. Birmingham, Ala., Mar. 4, 1958; d. Lewis Russell and Bernice (Wilson) Lowe; m. André Maurice Willis, June 12, 1987. BSEE, Tuskegee U., Ala., 1980; postgrad., UCLA, 1993—94, U. So. Calif., 1996, UCLA, 1999. Component engr. Hughes Aircraft Corp., El Segundo, Calif., 1980—82; reliability and lead engr. Aero Jet Electro Sys. Corp., Azusa, Calif., 1982—84; sr. component engr. Rockwell Internat. Corp., Anaheim, Calif., 1984, Gen. Data Comm. Corp., Danbury, Conn., 1984—85; design engr. Lockheed Missile and Space Co., Sunnyvale, Calif., 1985—86; mgr. property Penmar Mgmt. Co. L.A., 1987—88; aircraft mechanic McDonnell Douglas Corp., Long Beach, Calif., 1989—93; unix sys. adminstrn. Santa Cruz Ops., Calif., 1994; bus. ops. mgr., cons. New Start, Santa Monica, Calif., 1995; software developer Nat. Advancement Corp., Calif., 1996; entrepreneur Datatronics, Calif., 1996—; exec. v.p., owner L.A. Network Engr. Jet Propulsion Lab., 1996—2000; software engr., network engr., application engr., lead engr. Jet Propulsion Lab., Pasadena, Calif., 1996—2000, project mgr., 1999—2000, lead UNIX engr. L.A., 1998—2000; mgmt. sys. engr. Tech. Jet Propulsion Lab., Pasadena, 1998—2000, mgr. project element, 1999—; cons., sr. project mgr. Amgen, Thousand Oaks, Calif., 1999—2000, sr. sys. engr., 2000—; mgr. project So. Calif. Edison, 2002—03, mgr., settlements, 2003—, mgr. energy supply and mgmt., 2003—05, mgr. structured contracts, 2005—. Cons., software designer Kern and Wooley, atty., Westwood, Calif., 1995; software developer Nat. Advancement Corp., Santa Ana, Calif., 1995—. Vol. Mercy Hosp. and Children's Hosp., Birmingham, Ala. 1972-74; mrm. L.A. Gospel Messengers, 1982-84, West Angeles Ch. of God and Christ, L.A., 1990; cons., mgr. bus. ops. New Start, Santa Monica (Calif.) Bay Area Drug Abuse Coun., 1995; vol. Pres. Clinton's Going-To-Coll. Program through Univ. Calif. at Los Angeles, 1997—; chair Univ. Calif. at Los Angles Transfer Coll. Scholarship Program, 1998-99. Scholar Bell Lab., 1976-80, Univ. Calif. at Los Angles, 1994, Gem Award, UTA, 1999, Outstanding Group Award, JPL, 1999. Mem. IEEE, ASME, Aerospace and Aircraft Engr., So. Calif. Profl. Engring. Assn., Tuskegee U. Alumni Assn., UCLA Alumni Assn. (scholarship and adv. com.), Eta Kappa Nu, Christian Ch. Avocations: piano, computers, softball, real estate.

**WILLIS, SOLOMON LEE,** mathematics educator; s. Eddie and Brenda Willis. BS in Math., Gardner Webb U., 1999; MA in Math. Edn., Appalachian State U., 2004. Cert. tchr. NC HS math. tchr. Gaston Day Sch., Gastonia, NC, 2000—06; adj. coll. math. tchr. Cleve. CC, Shelby, NC, 2002—; math. instr. Western Piedmont C.C., 2006—. T-cubed regional instr. Tex. Instruments, Dallas, 2003—. Dir., organizer talent show Gaston Day Sch.; educator adv. bd. Discovery Pl., Charlotte, NC, 2003—04. MELT scholar, Appalachian State U., 2002—04, Te@ch Tech. grantee, Best Buy, 2004. Mem.: Math. Assn. Am. (assoc.), Nat. Coun. Tchrs. Math. (assoc. Trust Fund scholar 2002—03). Personal E-mail: solomon.willis@yahoo.com.

**WILLIS, WALTER BRUCE (BRUCE WILLIS),** actor, vocalist; b. Idar-Oberstein, Fed. Republic Germany, Mar. 19, 1955; came to U.S., 1957; s. David and Marlene Willis; m. Demi Moore, Nov. 21, 1987 (div. Oct. 18, 2000); children: Rumer Glenn, Scout Larue, Tallulah Belle. Student, Montclair State Coll.; studied with Stella Adler. Mem. First Amendment Comedy Theatre. Actor: (off-Broadway prodns.) Heaven and Earth, 1977, Fool for Love, 1984, The Bullpen, The Bayside Boys, The Ballad of Railroad William, (TV film) Trackdown, (feature films) Prince of the City, 1981, The Verdict, 1982, Blind Date, 1987, Sunset, 1988, Die Hard, 1988, In Country, 1989

(Golden Globe nomination 1990), Look Who's Talking (voice), 1989, Die Hard 2: Die Harder, 1990, Bonfire of the Vanities, 1990, Mortal Thoughts, 1991, Hudson Hawk, 1991, Billy Bathgate, 1991, The Last Boy Scout, 1991, Death Becomes Her, 1992, Striking Distance, 1993, Color of Night, 1994, North, 1994, Pulp Fiction, 1994, Nobody's Fool, 1994, Die Hard With a Vengeance, 1995, 12 Monkeys, 1995, Four Rooms, 1995, Last Man Standing, 1996, The Jackal, 1997, The Fifth Element, 1997, Mercury Rising, 1998, Armageddon, 1998, The Siege, 1998, Breakfast of Champions, 1999, The Sixth Sense, 1999, The Story of Us, 1999, The Whole Nine Yards (also prodr.), 2000, The Kid, 2000, Unbreakable, 2000, Bandits, 2001, Harts War, 2002, Grand Champion, 2002, True West, 2002, Tears of the Sun, 2003, Rugrats Go Wild! (voice), 2003, Charlie's Angels: Full Throttle, 2003, The Whole Ten Yards, 2004, Hostage, 2005, Sin City, 2005, Alpha Dog, 2006, 16 Blocks (also prodr.), 2006, Lucky Number Slevin, 2006, Over the Hedge (voice), 2006, Fast Food Nation, 2006; exec. prodr.: Crocodile Hunter: The Collision Course, 2002, (TV) True West, 2002, guest star (TV series) Miami Vice, The Twilight Zone; regular (TV series) Moonlighting, 1985-89 (People's Choice award 1986, Emmy award 1987, Golden Globe award 1987), musician (TV spl.) The Return of Bruno, 1986; rec. artist (album) The Return of Bruno, 1987, If It Don't Kill You, It Just Makes You Stronger, 1989; appeared in numerous commls. Named Internat. Broadcasting Man of Yr. Hollywood Radio and TV Soc.; recipient Star on Walk of Fame, 1998, People Choice award, 2000, Order of Arts & Letters, Govt. France, 2005 Office: Creative Artists Agency c/o Arnold Rifkin 9830 Wilshire Blvd Beverly Hills CA 90212*

**WILLIS, WILLIAM DARRELL, JR.,** neuroscientist, educator; b. Dallas, July 19, 1934; s. William Darrell and Dorcas (Chamberlain) W.; m. Jean Colette Schini, May 28, 1960 (dec. Jan. 1, 2006); 1 child, Thomas Darrell. BS, BA, Tex. A&M U., 1956; MD, U. Tex. Southwestern Med. Sch., 1960; PhD, Australian Nat. U., 1963. Postdoctoral research fellow Nat. Inst. Neurol. Diseases and Blindness, Australian Nat. U., 1960-62, Istituto di Fisiologia, U. Pisa, Italy, 1962-63; from asst. prof. to prof. anatomy, chmn. dept. U. Tex. Southwestern Med. Sch., Dallas, 1963-70; chief lab. comparative neurobiology Marine Biomed. Inst., prof. anatomy and physiology U. Tex. Med. Br., Galveston, 1970—, dir. Marine Biomed. Inst., 1978—2004, chmn. dept. anatomy and neurosci., 1986—2004, Ashbel Smith prof., 1986-95, Cecil and Ida Green prof., 1995—. Mem. neurology B study sect. NIH, 1968-72, chmn., 1970-72, mem. neurol. disorders Program rev. com., 1972-76, Nat. Adv. Neurol. and Communicative Disorders and Stroke Coun., 1987-90; tng. grant com. Nat. Inst. of Neurol. Disorders and Stroke, 1994-98. Mem. editl. bd. Neurosci., Exptl. Neurology, 1970-90, Archives Italienne Biologie, Neurosci. Letters, 1976-92; chief editor Jour. Neurophysiology, 1978-83, Pain, 1986-89; assoc. editor Jour. Neurosci., 1986-89, editor-in-chief, 1993-94; sect. editor Exptl. Brain Rsch., 1990-92, 1995-2004. Mem. AAAS, Am. Assn. Anatomists (exec. com. 1980-86), Am. Pain Soc. (pres. 1982-83), Internat. Assn. Study Pain (coun. 1984-90), Am. Physiol. Soc., Soc. Exptl. Biol. Medicine, Soc. Neurosci. (pres. 1984-85), Internat. Brain Rsch. Orgn., Cajal Club, Sigma Xi, Alpha Omega Alpha. Home: 2925 Beluche Dr Galveston TX 77551-1511 Office: U Tex Med Br 301 University Blvd Galveston TX 77555-1069 Office Phone: 409-772-2103. Business E-Mail: wdwillis@utmb.edu.

**WILLIS, WILLIAM ERVIN,** lawyer; b. Huntington, W.Va., Oct. 11, 1926; s. Asa Hannon and Mae (Davis) W.; m. Joyce Litteral, Sept. 1, 1949; children: Kathryn Cunningham, Anne Dresser, William. Student, Ind. U., 1944, NYU, 1945; AB, Marshall U. 1948; JD, Harvard, 1951; LHD (hon.), Marshall U., 1997. Bar: N.Y. 1952. Pvt. practice, N.Y.C., 1951—; ptnr. Sullivan & Cromwell, 1960-94, sr. counsel, 1994—. Lectr. Practising Law Inst., 1963—; trustee Fed. Bar Council, 1968-72; mem. 2d Circuit Commn. on Reduction Burdens and Costs Civil Litigation, 1977-82. Co-author Doing Business in America; contbr. Edn. Civil Practice Law Rev. Forms and Guidance for Lawyers, also articles to legal jours. Mem. panel arbitrators Pub. Resources; trustee Tenafly (N.J.) Nature Ctr., 1994—2001, pres., 1997—2001; bd. dirs. Soc Yeager Scholars, Marshall U., Huntington, 1995—2004, v.p., 2001—04, pres., 2004—. With AUS, 1944—46. Fellow Am. Coll. Trial Lawyers, Am. Bar Found.; mem. ABA (standing com. on fed. judiciary 1987-95, chair 1992-93, 94-95), N.Y. Bar Assn. (chmn. antitrust sect. 1976-77, exec. com. 1976-83), Assn. Bar City of N.Y. (chmn. profl. discipline com. 1983-86, chmn. ethics 2000 com. 1999—2003, judicial conduct 2000—), Fed. Bar Coun. (trustee 1969-72), Am. Judicature Soc., Am. Arbitration Assn. (panel arbitrators), N.Y. Law Inst., N.Y. County Lawyers, Inc. Sud. Adminstrn., India House. Home: 190 Tekening Dr Tenafly NJ 07670-1219 Also: Otterhole Rd West Milford NJ 07480 Office: Sullivan & Cromwell 125 Broad St 28th Fl New York NY 10004-2498 Business E-Mail: wewillis@nysbar.com.

**WILLISCROFT-BARCUS, BEVERLY RUTH,** retired lawyer; b. Conrad, Mont., Feb. 24, 1945; d. Paul A. and Gladys L. (Buck) W.; m. Kent J. Barcus, Oct. 1984. BA in Music, So. Calif. Coll., 1967; JD, John F. Kennedy U., 1977. Bar: Calif. 1977. Elem. tchr. Sunnyvale, Calif., 1968-72; legal sec., legal asst. various law firms, 1972-77; assoc. Neil D. Reid, Inc., San Francisco, 1977-79; sole practice Concord, Calif., 1979—2004. Exam. grader Calif. Bar, 1979-2001; real estate broker, 1980-88; tchr. real estate King Coll., Concord, 1979-80; judge pro-tem Mcpl. Ct., 1981-93; mem. Stage Right Drama Group, Concord, Calif., 1999—; lectr. in adoption law. Co-author: Adoption Law in California, Adoption Practice, Procedure and Pitfalls in California; lectr. in field. Bd. dirs. Contra Costa Musical Theatre, Inc., 1978-82, v.p. adminstrn., 1980-81, v.p. prodn., 1981-82; mem. community devel. adv. com. City of Concord, 1981-83, vice chmn., 1982-83, mem. status of women com., 1980-81, mem. redevel. adv. com., 1984-86, planning commnr. 1986-92, chmn., 1990; mem. exec. bd. Mt. Diablo coun. Boy Scouts Am., 1981-85; bd. dirs. Pregnancy Ctrs. Contra Costa County, 1991-2001, chmn., 1993-2000 Mem. Concord C. of C. (bd. dirs., chmn. govt. affairs com. 1983-84, v.p. 1985-87, pres. 1988-89, Bus. Person of Yr. 1986), Calif. State Bar (chmn. adoptions subcom. north, 1994), Contra Costa County Bar Assn., Christian Legal Soc., Todos Santos Bus. and Profl. Women (co-founder, pres. 1983-84, pub. rels. chmn. 1982-83, Woman of Achievement 1980, 81), Soroptimists (fin. sec. 1980-81). Office: PO Box 981 Pittsburg CA 94565-0098

**WILLISON, BRUCE GRAY,** dean; b. Riverside, Calif., Oct. 16, 1948; s. Walter G. and Dorothy (Phillips) W.; m. Gretchen A. Illig; children: Patrick, Bruce G., Kristen, Jeffery, Geoffrey, Lea. BA in econs., UCLA, 1970; MBA, U. So. Calif., 1973. With Bank of Am. LA, 1973-79; joined First Interstate Bancorp, LA, 1979, dir. mktg., 1981, sr. v.p., mem. mng. com., 1981—82; sr. v.p. trust divsn. First Interstate Bank of Calif., LA, 1982—83, exec. v.p. world banking group, 1983-85; pres., CEO First Interstate Bank Ltd., LA, 1985-86; chmn., CEO First Interstate Bank Oreg., Portland, 1986-91; chmn., pres., CEO First Interstate Bank of Calif., LA, 1991—96; vice chmn. First Interstate Bancorp, LA, 1995—96; pres., COO H.F. Ahmanson and Co., Irwandale, Calif., 1996—99; dean UCLA Anderson Sch. Mgmt., 1999—, John E. Anderson chair in mgmt. Bd. dirs. IndyMac Bancorp., Inc., Sun America, Inc., Health Net Inc., 2000—, Homestore, Inc., 2002—. Bd. dirs. United Way of LA, Operation Hope Inc. Served to lt. USN, 1970—72. Office: UCLA Anderson Sch Mgmt Dean's Office F-407 PO Box 951481 Los Angeles CA 90095-1481 Office Phone: 310-825-7982. E-mail: bruce.willison@anderson.ucla.edu.

**WILLITS, ARLENE,** secondary school educator; b. Newark, Jan. 14, 1950; d. Bernard Walter and Elsie M. (Olson) K. BA, Upsala U. 1972; MA, Georgian St. U., 1988. Nat. bd. cert. in adolescent sci. Tchr. Marlboro (N.J.) Bd. Edn., 1973—, choreographer, 1992-94, choreographer, dir. summer arts program, 1994. Co-author: Exploring Marlboro, 1980. Tchr. artist Met. Opera Co., N.Y.C. 1990-92. Fellow Taft Inst. 1983; recipient James F. Murray award N.J. Hist. Soc. 1982; grantee N.J. Hist. Commn., 1979-95. Mem. NEA, ASCD, N.J. ASCD, Battleground Hist. Soc. (program dir. 1978-79, trustee 1979-81), N.J. Edn. Assn., Monmouth County Edn. Assn., Marlboro Twp. Edn. Assn.

**WILLKE, THEODORE LAWRENCE,** research facility director; b. Indpls., Dec. 27, 1944; s. Myron Gustav and Freda (Payne) W.; m. Sue Ellen Koenig, Aug. 1, 1976; children: Theodore II, Chad, Bradford. BS in Astronautical Engring. & Engring. Sci., U.S. Air Force Acad., 1967; MS in Nuclear Engring., MIT, 1968; MBA, U. Dayton, 1971; PhD in Indsl. and Sys. Engring., Ohio State U., 1974. Registered profl. engr., Ohio, Wash. Sys. engr. Battelle, Columbus, Ohio, 1974-77; sect. mgr. Pacific N.W. Labs., Richland, Wash., 1977-82; dir. tech. assessment Gas Rsch. Inst., Chgo., 1982-84, divsn. dir. adminstrn., 1984-86, v.p., 1987-97; dir., CEO Carnegie Mellon Rsch. Inst., Pitts., 1997—2001; pres. TLW Solutions Inc., Pitts., 2002—. Mem. PRC Internat., Arlington, Va., 1994-97; chmn. Internat. Gas Union Com., Chgo., 1994-97; adj. prof. mech. engring. U. Wash., 1979; vis. disting. svc. prof. Carnegie Mellon U., 2001-02. Contbr. articles to profl. jours. including Pub. Utilities Fortnightly, Internat. Jour. Sys. Sci. Mem. tech. adv. com. pipeline safety U.S. Dept. Transp., 1996—; mem. Leadership Pitts. XVI, 1999-2000. Capt. USAF, 1967-71. Recipient award NSPE, 1975. Mem. ASME (mem. bd. on rsch. and tech. devel. 1988-90), AAAS. Achievements include patent in field. Office: TLW Solutions Inc One Oxford Ctr 37th Fl Pittsburgh PA 15219

**WILLKE, THOMAS ALOYS,** academic administrator, statistician, educator; b. Rome City, Ind., Apr. 22, 1932; s. Gerard Thomas and Marie Margaret (Wuennemann) W.; m. Geraldine Ann Page, Dec. 28, 1954; children: Richard, Susan, Donald, Jeanne, Mary, Kathleen. AB, Xavier U., 1954; MS, Ohio State U., 1956, PhD, 1960. Sr. engr. N.Am. Aviation, Columbus, Ohio, 1959-60; instr. math. Ohio State U., Columbus, 1960-61, asso. prof., 1966-70, assoc. prof. statistics, 1970-72, prof., 1972-73, dir. stats. lab., 1971-73, vice provost Arts and Scis., 1973-86, acting dean Univ. Coll., 1983-86, dean undergrad. studies Arts and Scis., 1986-87; prof. math. scis. Otterbein coll., Westerville, Ohio, 1987-97, chmn. dept. math. scis., 1988-96; rsch. mathematician U.S. Nat. Bur. Standards, Washington, 1961-66; asst. prof. math. U. Md., College Park, 1963-66; prof. statistics, undergrad. dean Ohio State U., 1987—; prof. math. scis. emeritus Otterbein Coll., 1997—. Contbr. articles on statis. non parametric methods and robustness to profl. jours. Mem. Am. Statis. Assn., Math. Assn. Am. Roman Catholic. Home: 4375 Mumford Dr Columbus OH 43220-4438

**WILLKIE, WENDELL LEWIS, II,** lawyer; b. Indpls., Oct. 29, 1951; s. Philip Herman Willkie and Rosalie (Heffelfinger) Hall; m. Carlotta Fendig; children: Alexandra Elizabeth, Diana Fendig, Caroline Heffelfinger. AB, Harvard U., 1973; BA cum laude, Oxford U., Eng., 1975, MA rhodes scholar, 1983; JD, U. Chgo., 1978. Bar: N.Y. 1979. Assoc. Simpson Thacher and Bartlett, N.Y.C., 1978-82; gen. counsel NEH, Washington, 1982-84; assoc. counsel to Pres. The White House, Washington, 1984-85; chief of staff, counselor to Sec. U.S. Dept. Edn., Washington, 1985, gen. counsel, 1985-88; counsel Office of the Pres.-elect, Washington, 1988-89; gen. counsel Dept. of Commerce, Washington, 1989-93; v.p. Westvaco Corp., N.Y.C., 1995-96, sr. v.p., gen. counsel, 1996—2002; sr. v.p., gen. counsel, sec. MeadWestvaco Corp. (formerly Westvaco Corp.), 2002—. Vis. fellow Am. Enterprise Inst., Washington, 1993-94. Co-author, editor: (with J.R. Lilley) Beyond MFN: Trade with China and American Interests, 1994. Harvard U. scholar, 1969-73, Rhodes scholar, 1973-75. Republican. Episcopalian. Office: Westvaco Corp 1 High Ridge Park Stamford CT 06905

**WILLNER, ALAN ELI,** electrical engineer, educator; b. Bklyn, Nov. 16, 1962; s. Gerald and Sondra (Bernstein) W.; m. Michelle Frida Green, June 25, 1991. BA, Yeshiva U., 1982; MS, Columbia U., 1984, PhD, 1988. Summer tech. staff David Sarnoff Rsch. Ctr., Princeton, NJ, 1983, 84; grad. rsch. asst. dept. elec. engring. Columbia U., NYC, 1984-88; postdoctoral mem. tech. staff AT&T Bell Labs., Holmdel, NJ, 1988-90; mem. tech. staff Bell Comm. Rsch., Red Bank, NJ, 1990-91; prof. U. So. Calif., LA, 1992—, assoc. dir. Ctr. Photonic Tech., 1994—. Head del. Harvard Model UN Yeshiva U., 1982; instr. Columbia U., 1987; rev. panel mem. NSF, Washington, 1992, Washington, 93, Washington, 94, invited optical comm. workshop, 94; chair panel on optical info. and comm., 94; co-chair Conf. on Lasers and Electro-Optics; steering com. and tech. com. mem. Conf. Optical Fiber Comm. Author 1 book; contbr. articles to profl. jours.; editor-in-chief Jour. Lighwave Tech., IEEE Jour. Selected Topics in Quantum Electronics; assoc. editor Jour. Selected Areas in Comm. Mem. faculty adv. bd. U. So. Calif. Hillel Orgn., 1992. Recipient Disting. Lectr. award, IEEE Lasers and Electro-Optics Soc., Armstrong Found. prize, Columbia U., 1984, Best Engring. Tchr. award, USC/TRW, young investigator award, NSF, 1992, Eddy Paper Award, 2001, USL Assoc. Award for Univ. Wide Excellence in Tchg.; fellow, Semiconductor Rsch. Corp., 1986, Sci. and Engring., David and Lucile Packard Found., 1993, presdl. faculty, NSF, 1994, sr. scholar, Fulbright Found., 1997; grantee NSF, Advanced Rsch. Projects Agy., Packard Found., Powell Found., Ballistic Missile Def. Orgn. Fellow: IEEE, Optical Soc. Am. (symposium organizer ann. mtg. 1992, panel organizer ann. mtg. 1993, symposium organizer ann. mtg. 1995, panel organizer ann. mtg. 1995, program com. for conf. on optical fiber commn. 1996, 1997, program co-chair ann. mtg. 2001, vice chair optical comm. group, tech. council chair-photonics divsn., co-chair sci. and engring. coun., bd. dirs.; program co-chair of OSA Annual Mtg., tech. coun. chair photonics divsn.); mem.: IEEE (sr.; editor-in-chief IEEE/OSA Jour. Lightwave Tech.), Soc. Photo-Instrumentation Engring. (program chair telecomm. engring. photonics west 1995, chmn. conf. on emerging techs. for all-optical networks photonics west 1995, program com. for Conf. on Optical Fiber Comm. 1996, conf. program com. components for WDM), IEEE Lasers and Electro-Optics Soc. (chmn. optical comm. subcom. ann. mtg. 1994, bd. govs. 1998—2001, v.p. tech. affairs, mem. optical comm. tech. com., bd. govs., mem. optical networks tech. com., various awards coms., chmn. optical commn. tech. com., awards com. mem. Quantum Electronics, IEEE Fellow, pres.-elect, Disting. Lectr. award), Sigma Xi. Achievements include patents for localized photochemical etching of multilayered semiconductor body, optical star coupler utilizing fiber amplifier tech., and one-to-many simultaneous optical WDM 2-dim plane interconnections. Home: 9326 Sawyer St Los Angeles CA 90035-4102 Office: U So Calif Dept Elec Engring Eeb 538 Los Angeles CA 90089-0001 Business E-Mail: willner@usc.edu.

**WILLNER, ANN RUTH,** political scientist, educator; b. N.Y.C., Sept. 2, 1924; d. Norbert and Bella (Richman) W. BA cum laude, Hunter Coll., 1945; MA, Yale U., 1946; PhD, U. Chgo. 1961. Lectr. U. Chgo., 1946-47, rsch. assoc. Ctr. for Econ. Devel. and Cultural Change, 1954-56, 61-62; advisor on orgn. and tng. Indonesian Ministry for Fgn. Affairs, Jakarta, 1952-53; expert for small scale indsl. planning Indonesian Nat. Planning Bur., Jakarta, 1953-54; fgn. affairs analyst Congl. Reference Svc., Libr. of Congress, 1960; asst. prof. polit. sci. Harpur Coll., Binghamton, NY, 1962-63; postdoctoral fellow polit. sci. and Southeast Asian studies Yale U., New Haven, 1963-64; rsch. assoc. Ctr. Internat. Studies, Princeton U., 1964-69; assoc. prof. polit. sci. U. Kans., Lawrence, 1969-70, prof., 1970-98. Vis. prof. polit. sci. CUNY, 1975; cons. govt. agys. and pvt. industry Polit. sci. editor: Ency. of the Social Scis., 1961; mem. editl. bd. Econ. Devel. and Cultural Change, 1954-57, Jour. Comparative Adminstrn., 1969-74, Comparative Politics, 1977—; author: The Neotraditional Accomodation to Political Independence, 1966, Charismatic Political Leadership: A Theory, 1968, The Spellbinders, 1984, 2004; also monographs, jour. articles, book chpts., newspaper columns. Grantee Rockefeller Found., 1965, Social Sci. Rsch. and Am. Coun. Learned Socs., 1966. Mem. Am. Polit. Sci. Assn. (gov. coun. 1979-81), Nat. Press Club. Home: 560 N St SW # N405 Washington DC 20024-4605 Office Phone: 202-484-2092. Personal E-mail: arwill@earthlink.net.

**WILLNER, BARRY A.,** lawyer; BA cum laude, Lafayette Coll., 1969; JD, Georgetown U., 1972. Bar: NY 1974, US Dist. Ct., So and Ea. Dists. NY, US Ct. Appeals, 2nd Cir. Ptnr. Kaye Scholer LLP, NYC, 1980—, mng. ptnr., mem. exec. com. Co-author: The Shadow Government, 1972. Mem. ABA, Assn. Bar of City NY. Office: Kaye Scholer LLP 425 Park Ave New York NY 10022 Office Phone: 212-836-8421. E-mail: bwillner@kayescholer.com.

**WILLNER, DOROTHY,** anthropologist, educator; b. NYC, Aug. 26, 1927; d. Norbert and Bella (Richman) W. Ph.B., U. Chgo., 1947, MA, 1953, PhD, 1961; postgrad., Ecole Pratique des Hautes Etudes, U. Paris, France,

1950—51. Anthropologist Jewish Agy., Israel, 1955-58; tech. asst., adminstrn. expert in community devel. UN, Mexico, 1958; asst. prof. dept. sociology and anthropology U. Iowa, Iowa City, 1959-60; research assoc. U. Chgo., 1961-62; asst. prof. dept. sociology and anthropology U. N.C., Chapel Hill, 1962-63; Hunter Coll., N.Y.C., 1964-65; assoc. prof. dept. anthropology U. Kans., Lawrence, 1967-70, prof., 1970-90; professorial lectr. Johns Hopkins U. Sch. Advanced Internat. Studies, 1992. Cons. Washington Action for Youth, United Planning Orgn., 1964; rsch. in field. Author: Community Leadership, 1960, Nation-Building and Community in Israel, 1969. Contbr. numerous articles to profl. publs. Fellow Am. Anthrop. Assn., Soc. Applied Anthropology, Royal Anthrop. Inst.; mem. Cen. States Anthrop. Soc. (past pres.), Assn. Polit. and Legal Anthropology (past pres.). Home: N 407 560 N St SW Washington DC 20024-4605

**WILLNER, JAY R.,** consulting company executive; b. Aurora, Ill., Sept. 22, 1924; s. Charles R. and Ida (Winer) W.; m. Suzanne Wehmann, July 17, 1958; 1 child, Adam. Student, UCLA, 1946—48; BS in Chem. Engring. and Econ., MIT, 1950; MBA, Rutgers U., 1959. Rschr. Andrew Brown Co., L.A., 1950-52; tech. salesman Glidden Co., L.A., 1952-54; market rschr. Roger Williams Inc., N.Y.C., 1954-59; sr. market analyst Calif. Chem. Co., San Francisco, 1959-63; mgr. planning chem. coatings divsn. Mobil Chem. Co., N.Y.C., 1963-68; pres. WEH Corp., San Francisco, 1968—. Lectr. U. Calif., Berkeley, 1962—; adj. faculty U. San Francisco, 1977—; U.S. corr. German mag. Farbe & Lack. Contbg. editor Jour. Protective Coatings and Linings; editor The WEH Report; author 2d Ann. Comprehensive Survey for Steel Structures Painting Coun. Supporter San Francisco Mus. of Modern Art; 2d lt. A.C., AUS, 1943-46. Mem. Am. Chem. Soc. (50-yr. mem.), Steel Structures Painting Coun., Mechs. Libr., Chemists Club (N.Y.C.), MIT Club No. Calif. Home: 700 Presidio Ave San Francisco CA 94115-2956 Office: WEH Corp PO Box 470038 San Francisco CA 94147-0038 Office Phone: 415-567-3336. Business E-Mail: jrw@wehcorp.com.

**WILLNER, JUDITH P.,** clinical geneticist, pediatrician, educator; b. Bay Shore, N.Y., July 27, 1945; d. Harman and Edith (Sclank) Pleasure; m. Joseph Harrison Willner, June 22, 1969; children: Daniel, Rachel, Jonathan. AB, Harvard U., 1967; MD, NYU, 1971. Cert. Am. Bd. Pediatrics, Am. Bd. Med. Genetics. Asst. prof. ob-gyn. and pediatrics N.Y. Hosp./Cornell U. Med. Ctr., N.Y.C., 1982-89; asst. prof. pediatrics, clin. geneticist Mt. Sinai Sch. Medicine, N.Y.C., 1977-80, asst. prof. pediatrics, 1989-93, assoc. prof. human genetics and pediatrics, 1993—. Pres. N.Y. State Genetics Task Force, N.Y. 1996—. Mem. sch. com. Harvard U., Radcliffe Coll., 1974—; co-chair 30th reunion Radcliffe Coll., Cambridge, Mass., 1996—. Mem. Human Genetics. Office: Dept Human Genetics Mt Sinai Hosp 1 Gustave L Levy Pl New York NY 10029-6500

**WILLNER, KENNETH M.,** lawyer; b. Topeka, Kans., Feb. 2, 1962; BA with distinction, U.Va., 1984, JD, 1987. Bar: Va. 1987, DC 1988, cert.: U.S. Supreme Ct., U.S. Ct. Appeals, third, fourth, eighth, tenth & D.C. cir., U.S. Dist. Ct., Ea. Dist. Va., U.S. Dist. Ct., S.D.C., U.S. Dist. Ct., We. Dist. Pa. Profl. pers. ptnr. Paul, Hastings, Janofsky & Walker LLP, Washington. Mem.: D.C. Bar Assn. (employment law sect.), Va. Bar Assn. (employment law sect.), ABA (employment law sect.). Business E-Mail: kenwillner@paulhastings.com.

**WILLOCK, MARCELLE MONICA,** retired medical educator; b. Georgetown, Guyana, Mar. 30, 1938; came to U.S. 1954; d. George and Renee W. BA, Coll. New Rochelle, 1958; MD, Howard U., 1962; MA, Columbia U., 1982; MBA, Boston U., 1989. Diplomate Am. Bd. Anesthesiology. Asst. clin. prof. med. ctr. NYU, 1968-72, assoc. clin. prof. med. ctr., 1972-74; asst. prof. clin. anesthesiology Columbia U., NYC, 1978-82; prof. Boston U., 1982, chmn. dept. anesthesiology, 1982—98, asst. provost cmty. affairs, 1998—2002; dean Coll. Medicine Charles R. Drew U., L.A., 2002—05; ret., 2005. Sec. The Med. Found., Boston, 1991-94. Contbr. articles to profl. jours. Pres. Louis and Marthe Deveaux Found., Panama, 1965—; trustee Coll. New Rochelle, NY, 1976-82, 2006—. Mem. Am. Soc. Anesthesiologists (del. 1986—, alt. dir. 1990-94, bd. dirs. 1994—, asst. sec. 1999-2001), Mass. Soc. Anesthesiologists (pres. 1988-89), Soc. Acad. Anesthesia Chairs (sec.-treas. 1989-91, pres.-elect 1993-94, pres. 1994—), Alpha Omega Alpha. Roman Catholic. Home: 85 East India Rd Apt 31E Boston MA 02110

**WILLOCKS, ROBERT MAX,** retired librarian; b. Maryville, Tenn., Oct. 1, 1924; s. Willis Lemuel and Hannah (Emert) W.; m. Neysa Nerene Ferguson, May 23, 1947; children— Margret Sharon, Samuel David, Mark Timothy, Robert Daniel, Kent Max. BA, Maryville Coll., 1949; B.D., Golden Gate Bapt. Theol. Sem., 1951, Th.M., 1962; MA in Library Sci, Peabody Coll., 1962. Ordained to ministry Bapt. Ch., 1950; pastor in Calif., 1950-56; missionary to Korea So. Bapt. Fgn. Mission Bd., Taejon, 1956- 65; assoc. dir. library Heidelberg Coll., Tiffin, Ohio, 1965-67; dir. library Columbia Coll., SC, 1967-70; asst. dir. libraries Syracuse U., NY, 1970-76; assoc. dir. libraries U. Fla., Gainesville, 1976-83, acting dir. libraries, 1983-84, dep. dir. libraries, 1984-89, ret., 1989; pastor Northwood Bapt. Ch., Gainesville, 1981-92; libr. Bapt. Theol. Sem., Lusaka, Zambia, 1994-97, Ghana Bapt. Sem., Kumasi, 1998—2006. Acting dir. Fla. Ctr. for Libr. Automation, 1984; cons. Choong Chung Nam Province Library Assn., Republic of Korea, 1962—65; dir. Korea Bapt. Press, 1959—61; prof. ch. history Korea Bapt. Sem., 1957—65, acting pres., 1958—59, librarian, 1959—65; vice chmn. Korea Bapt. Mission, 1962—64; del. Fla. Gov.'s Conf. on Libraries, 1978. Editor: Korean translations Thus it is Written, 1963, The Progress of Worldwide Missions, 1965. Chmn. trustees Wallace Meml. Bapt. Hosp., Pusan, Korea, 1963-65; pres. bd. dirs. Phoenix Homeowners Assn., 1980-88. With USNR, 1943-46. Mem. ALA (chmn. telefacsimile com. 1976-78, tech. com. 1980-84, chmn. standards com. 1985-88), Fla. Libr. Assn., Southeastern Library Assn., AAUP, Peabody Coll. Alumni Assn. (pres. S.C. 1968 69) Home: 1326 E Earll Dr Phoenix AZ 85014

**WILLOUGHBY, SARAH-MARGARET C.,** retired chemist, educator, chemical engineer, consultant; b. Bowling Green, KY, Oct. 15, 1917; d. Austin Burrell Claypool and Minerva Dallas Renfrow-Claypool; m. John Richard Evans, II, Aug. 30, 1938 (dec. Dec. 1942); 1 child, Richard Claypool Evans; m. Olief Glenn Willoughby, June 18, 1948 (dec.); children: Sarah, Stephen(dec.). BS, Western Ky. U., 1938; PhD, Purdue U., 1950. Registered profl. engr., Ind., Tex. Chemist Devoe-Reynolds, Inc., Louisville, 1941—42; jr. engr. chem. lab. div. Curtiss-Wright Corp., Louisville, 1942—44; tech. asst. Purdue U., West Lafayette, Ind., 1944—46, fellow, 1946—50; rsch. chemist, coatings divsn. Monsanto Chem. Co., Boston, 1950—52; assoc. prof. of chemistry U. Tex., Arlington, 1954—84, co-dir. Ctr. for Microcrystalline Polymer Rsch. Studies, 1978—82, prof. emeritus chemistry, 1984. Cons. Albert H. Halff Assocs., Dallas, 1980—86. Co-edit., author Engineer-in-Training Manual, 1970. Nominee Dallas-Ft. Worth Trailblazer award, 1996; named to Hall of Fame Alumni, Western Ky. U., 1994, Am. Men and Women of Sci., Personalities of the South, 1974, Cmty. Leaders and Noteworthy Americans, 1978, Notable Women of Tex., 1984—85, Daughters of Guilds of Colonial Artisans and Tradesmen, 2005; recipient Outstanding Chem. Engr. award, Purdue U., 1996, Cmty. Growth Contbn. award, Arlington Hist. Soc., Tex. Fellow: Am. Inst. Chemists; mem.: Am. Chem. Soc. (emeritus mem.), Peyton Soc. Va. (life), Gold Star Wives Am. (life), NY Acad. Sci. (life), Soc. Women Engrs. (sr.), Nat. Soc. Daughters of Founders and Patriots (v.p. N.E. Tex. chpt. 1997—, pres. N.E. Tex. chpt. 2006—08), Plantagenet Soc., Colonial Dames Am., Nat. Soc. DAR (chpt. regent 1967—69, nat. bicentennial com. mem. 1975—76, Nat. Women's Issues essay award 2006), Nat. Soc. Children of Am. Revolution (Tex. sr. state pres. 1968—70), Nat. Soc. Colonial Dames of XVII Century (chpt. regent 1980—82), Nat. Soc. Magna Carta Dames (Tex. state pres. 1986—88), Colonial Order of the Crown, Soc. Descendants of Knights of the Most Noble Order of the Garter, Sovereign Colonial Soc. Ams. of Royal Descent, Friends of St. George, Order Ky. Cols., Sigma Xi (pres. 1966—68, emeritus mem.), Alpha Chi Omega (Lambda Epsilon chapt.). Home: 1630 Pecan Park Dr Arlington TX 76012

**WILLOUGHBY, STEPHEN SCHUYLER,** mathematics professor; b. Madison, Wis., Sept. 27, 1932; s. Alfred and Elizabeth Frances (Cassell) W.; m. Helen Sali Shapiro, Aug. 29, 1954; children: Wendy Valentine (Mrs. Peter Gallen), Todd Alan. AB (scholar), Harvard U., 1953, AM in Teaching, 1955; EdD (Clifford Brewster Upton fellow), Columbia U., 1961. Tchr. Newton (Mass.) Pub. Schs., 1954-57, Greenwich (Conn.) Pub. Schs., 1957-59; instr. U. Wis., Madison, 1960-61, asst. prof. math. edn. and math., 1961-65; prof. math. edn. and math. NYU, 1965-87, dir. math. edn. dept., 1967-83, chmn. math., sci. and stats. edn. dept., 1970-80, 86-87, chmn. U. Faculty Coun., 1981-82; prof. math. U. Ariz., Tucson, 1987—2002; prof. emeritus math. and math. edn. NYU, 1987—; prof. emeritus math. U. Ariz., Tucson, 2002—. Mem. nat. bd. advisor Sq. One TV, 1983-94; U.S. Commn. on Math. Instrn., 1984-95, chmn., 1991-95; math. adv. com. Nat. Tchr. Exam. Successor (Praxis), 1989-94; edn. panel New Am. Schs. Devel. Corp., 1991-97; U.S. nat. rep. Internat. Commn. on Math. Instrn., 1991-95. Author: Contemporary Teaching of Secondary School Mathematics, 1967, Probability and Statistics, 1968, Teaching Mathematics: What Is Basic, 1981, Mathematics Education for a Changing World, 1990, Real Math, 1981, 85, 87, 91, Math: Explorations and Applications, 1998, College Mathematics Through Applications, 1999, The Other End of the Log: Memoirs of an Education Rebel, 2002, SRA Real Math, K-6, 2007; contbr. articles to profl. jours. and encys., chpts. to yearbooks and anthologies. Recipient Leadership in Math. Edn. Lifetime Achievement medal, 1995. Mem. Nat. Coun. Tchrs. Math. (dir. 1968-71, pres. 1982-84), Coun. Sci. Soc. Pres. (chmn. 1988). Home: 5435 E Gleneagles Dr Tucson AZ 85718-1805 Office: U Ariz Dept Math Tucson AZ 85721-0001 Personal E-mail: sswill@aol.com.

**WILLOUGHBY, WILLIAM FRANKLIN, II,** retired physician, researcher; b. Washington, Feb. 4, 1936; s. William Westel and Patricia (DeZychlinska) W.; m. Mary Scott Fishburne, 1963 (div. 1974); children: Westel Woodbury, William Franklin III, Laura Fishburne, Mary Scott; m. Judith Eleanor Barbaras, Oct. 25, 1975; 1 child, Robert Alexander Willoughby. AB, Johns Hopkins U., 1957, MD, 1965, PhD in Microbiology, 1965; grad. with distinction, USAF War Coll., 1985. Diplomate Am. Bd. Pathology. Intern then resident in pathology Johns Hopkins Hosp., 1965-67; asst. prof. depts. pathology and microbiology Case Western Res. U., Cleve.; dir. Virginia Mason Rsch. Ctr., Seattle, 1972-75; assoc. prof. dept. pathology Sch. Medicine, Johns Hopkins U., Balt., 1975-87; prof., chmn. dept. pathology Sch. Medicine, U. S.C., Columbia, 1987-92; dir. labs. Cook County Hosp., Chgo., 1992-98, interim med. dir., 1994-96; ret., 1998. Cons. NIH, Bethesda, Md., 1979-98, mem. pathology A study sect., 1982-86; cons. NRC, Washington, 1981-84; mem. res. component med. coun., Dept. Def., Pentagon, 1991-93; dep. surgeon gen. for res. affairs USAF, Bolling AFB, D.C., 1993-95; asst. surg. gen. USAF, Operation Desert Storm/Desert Shield, 1990-91. Mem. editorial bd. Am. Rev. Respiratory Disease, 1978-84; contbr. articles to profl. jours., reviewer numerous sci. manuscripts. Vestryman Trinity Episcopal Ch., Long Green, Md., 1984-87; bd. dirs. Ctrl. S.C. chpt. ARC, Columbia, 1989-92; bd. fellow Norwich U., 1992-95. Maj. USAFR, 1975-95, advanced through grades to maj. gen., 1992-95. Decorated D.S.M., Legion of Merit; recipient Edwin E. Osgood prize Va. Mason Rsch. Ctr., 1973; Arthritis Found. fellow Scripps Clinic and Rsch. Found., 1967-69; Poncine scholar Poncine Found., 1972-74; NIH rsch. grantee, 1976-91. Fellow Coll. Am. Pathologists; mem. AAAS, Am. Lung Assn. (nat. rsch. grant rev. com. 1978-82, chmn., 1981-82), Am. Soc. Investigative Pathology, Am. Assn. Immunologists, Am. Soc. Cell Biologists, Chgo. Coun. Fgn. Rels., Internat. Acad. Pathology, Assn. Pathology Chmns., Aerospace Med. Assn., Soc. USAF Flight Surgeons (bd. govs. 1993-96), Am. Thoracic Soc., Assn. Mil. Surgeons U.S., Soc. Med. Cons. to Armed Forces, Army Navy Club, Air Force Assn., Univ. Club, Met. Club, Silver Wings Club Avocations: music, genealogy, antique automobiles, Chinese art. Home: 1416A S Federal St Chicago IL 60605-3057 Personal E-mail: wwilloughb@aol.com.

**WILLOUGHBY-SMITH, DOLORES ANNE,** elementary school educator, consultant; b. Chickasha, Okla., Jan. 6, 1938; d. Loranzie Dawl and Anna Mae (Montgomery) Wilkes; m. Don Jeral Willoughby, Apr. 8, 1956 (dec. Apr. 1975); m. Clarence (John) Smith, Aug. 1, 1999; children: Danny Michael, Melissa Dawn Willoughby Onesalt. BS, U. Sci. and Arts Okla., 1969; MEd, Southwestern Okla. State U., 1976; postgrad. Okla. State U., 1985-90, Ctrl. State U., Edmond., 1975; postgrad., U. Okla., 1985-89, 92. Cert. K-8 sci., math., reading, and social studies tchr., Okla. Teller Okla. Nat. Bank, Chickasha, 1957-66; tchr. Verden (Okla.) Pub. Schs., 1969-82, Amber-Pocasset (Okla.) Schs., 1982-89; tchr. sci., computer coord. Chickasha Intermediate Sch., 1989-92; elem. tchr. Grand Avenue Sch., Chickasha, 1992—2001; sci. tchr. Chickasha Intermediate Sch., 2001—02. Evaluation com. North Ctrl. Accreditation, Oklahoma City, 1993; sci. curriculum alignment com. Chickasha Schs., 1992-93, site chmn. for sci. and computer programs, 1993-94; reviewer CHIME newsletter, 1986; assesment adminstr. Nat. Assessment Ednl. Progress, 2005; instr. Canadian Valley Vocat.-Tech. Contbr. articles to profl. jours. Vice chair adv. bd. Chickasha Pub. Libr., 1993—; pres. Grady County Ret. Tchrs., 2005—; program coord. Rx for Okla. Washita Valley Cmty. Action Coun. Recipient Okla. medal of Excellence for Elem. Teaching Okla. Found. for Excellence, 1995, Okla. Elem. Sci. Tchr. of Yr. award Okla. Sci. Tchrs. Assn., 1995, Grady County Ret. Tchr. award, 2003. Mem. NSTA (space adv. bd. 1990-94, gen. rev. panel 1994-96, NASA Educators' Workshop Math and Sci. Tchrs. award 1994), Nat. Assesment Ednl. Progress (assesment adminstr.), Okla. Writers, Norman Galaxy of Writers, Friday Writers Group, Grady County Ret. Educators (pres. 2005-2006). Democrat. Baptist. Avocations: bobbin lace-making, travel, reading, telecommunication, genealogy. Home: 116 S 13th St Chickasha OK 73018-3107 Office Phone: 405-224-5831 ext 107. Personal E-mail: dlrssmith@netscape.net.

**WILLS, CHARLES FRANCIS,** retired religious organization administrator; b. Avalon, NJ, July 26, 1914; s. Charles H. and Anna Margaret (Diemand) W.; m. Charlotte Emily Robson, Aug. 22, 1936; children: C. Frederic, Emily, Sally and Larry (twins). BS, Wheaton Coll., Ill., 1935; B.D., Eastern Bapt. Theol. Sem., 1938, Th.M., 1941; grad., Air War Coll., 1961. Commd. 1st lt. U.S. Army, 1941; advanced through grades to col. U.S. Air Force, 1963; chaplain AUS, 1941-49, U.S. Air Force, 1949-67; ret., 1967; exec. dir. chaplaincy services Am. Bapt. Chs., Valley Forge, Pa., 1969-75, exec. dir. profl. services, 1975-78; assoc. sec. Bapt. World Alliance, Washington, 1978-80, treas., 1980-81. Mem. Commn. on Doctrine and Interchurch Cooperation, 1980-90. Decorated Legion of Merit, Bronze Star, Purple Heart. Mem. Mil. Chaplains Assn., Mil. Order of Purple Heart.

**WILLS, DAVID WOOD,** minister, educator; b. Portland, Ind., Jan. 25, 1942; s. Theodore Oscar Mitchell and Elizabeth Lochore (Wood) W.; m. Carolyn Reynolds Montgomery, Aug. 22, 1964; children: John Brookings, Theodore Worcester, Thomas Churchill. BA, Yale U., 1962; BD, Princeton Theol. Sem., 1966; PhD, Harvard U., 1975. Ordained to ministry Presbyn. Ch., 1970. Asst. prof. Sch. of Religion, U. So. Calif., 1970-72; asst. prof. dept. of religion Amherst Coll., Mass., 1972-78, assoc. prof., 1978-83, prof., 1983-90, prof. religion and Black studies, 1990-94, Winthrop H. Smith '16 prof. Am. history and Am. studies, dept. religion and Black studies, 1994—, also dir. Luce Program in Comparative Religious Ethics 1978-88. Author: Christianity in the United States, 2005; editor (with Richard Newman) Black Apostles at Home and Abroad, 1982, (with Albert Raboteau) Afro-American Religion: A Documentary History Project, 1987—, Christianity in the United States, 2005. Kent fellow Danforth Found., 1966-70, 75, Ford Found. fellow, 1972, Inst. for Ecumenical and Cultural Rsch. fellow, 1972, Nat. Humanities Ctr. fellow, 1980-81, 94, NEH fellow for Coll. Tchrs., 1988-89, W. E. B. DuBois Inst. for Afro-Am. Rsch. fellow, 1989-91. Mem. Am. Acad. Religion (chair Afro-Am. religious history group 1975-78), Am. Hist. Assn., Am. Soc. Ch. History, Am. Studies Assn., Orgn. Am. Historians, Phi Beta Kappa. Home: 47 Stagecoach Rd Amherst MA 01002-3527 Office: Amherst Coll Dept Religion Amherst MA 01002 Office Phone: 413-542-2470. E-mail: dwwills@amherst.edu.

**WILLS, GARRY,** historian; b. Atlanta, May 22, 1934; s. John and Mayno (Collins) Wills; m. Natalie Cavallo, May 30, 1959; children: John, Garry, Lydia. BA, St. Louis U., 1957; MA, Xavier U., Cin., 1958, Yale U., 1959, PhD, 1961; LittD (hon.), Coll. Holy Cross, 1982, Columbia Coll., 1982, Beloit Coll., 1988, Xavier U., 1993, St. Xavier U., 1993, Union Coll., 1993, Macalester Coll., 1995, Bates Coll., 1995, St. Ambrose, 1997, George Washington U., 1999, Spring Hill Coll., 2000, Siena Heights U., 2001, Gettysburg Coll., 2002, Am. U., 2003, Muhlenberg Coll., 2004. Fellow Ctr. Hellenic Studies, 1961—62; assoc. prof. classics Johns Hopkins U., 1962—67, adj. prof., 1968-80; Henry R. Luce prof. Am. culture and public policy Northwestern U., 1980—88, adj. prof., 1988—2005, prof. history emeritus, 2005—. Author: (book) Chesterton, 1961, Politics and Catholic Freedom, 1964, Roman Culture, 1966, Jack Ruby, 1967, Second Civil War, 1968, Nixon Agonistes, 1970, Bare Ruined Choirs, 1972, Inventing America, 1978, At Button's, 1979, Confessions of a Conservative, 1979, Explaining America, 1980, The Kennedy Imprisonment, 1982, Lead Time, 1983, Cincinnatus, 1984, Reagan's America, 1987, Under God, 1990, Lincoln at Gettysburg, 1992 (Pulitzer Prize for gen. non-fiction, 1993), Certain Trumpets: The Call of Leaders, 1994, Witches and Jesuits: Shakespeare's Macbeth, 1994, John Wayne's America, 1997, St. Augustine, 1999, A Necessary Evil, 1999, Papal Sin, 2000, Venice, Lion City, 2001, St. Augustine's Childhood, 2001, James Madison, 2002, Why Am I a Catholic, 2002, St. Augustine's Memory, 2002, Mr. Jefferson's University, 2002, St. Augustine's Sin, 2003, Negro President, 2003, St. Augustine's Conversion, 2004, The Rosary, 2005, Henry Adams and the Making of America, 2005, St. Augustine's Confessions, 2006, What Jesus Meant, 2006, What Paul Meant, 2006. Recipient Merle Curti award, Orgn. Am. Historians, Nat. Book Critics Cir. award (2), Wilbur Cross medal, Yale U., Peabody award, NEH Presdl. medal, 1998, John Hope Franklin award, First Freedom award, Coun. for the First Freedom, Lincoln Laureate, State of Ill. Mem.: AAAL, Am. Philos. Soc., Am. Antiquarian Soc., Am. Acad. Arts and Scis., Mass. Hist. Soc. Roman Catholic. Office: Northwestern U Dept History Evanston IL 60208 Business E-Mail: g-wills@northwestern.edu.

**WILLS, J. ROBERT,** academic administrator, theater educator, writer; b. Akron, Ohio, May 5, 1940; s. J. Robert and Helen Elizabeth (Lapham) W.; m. Barbara T. Salisbury, Aug. 4, 1984 (dec. 1998); m. Jeanne Hokin, June 2002. BA, Coll. of Wooster, 1962; MA, U. Ill., 1963; PhD, Case-Western Res. U., 1971; cert. in arts adminstrn, Harvard U., 1976. Instr. to asst. prof., dir. theatre Wittenberg U., Springfield, Ohio, 1963-72; assoc. prof., dir. grad. studies, chmn. dept. theatre U. Ky., Lexington, 1972-77, prof. theatre, dean Coll. Fine Arts, 1977-81; prof. drama, dean Coll. Fine Arts U. Tex., Austin, 1981-89; Effie Marie Cain Regents chair in Fine Arts, 1986-89; provost, prof. theatre Pacific Luth. U., Tacoma, 1989-94; prof. theatre, dean coll. fine arts Ariz. State U., Tempe, 1994—2006. Cons. colls., univs., arts orgns., govt. agencies Author: The Director in a Changing Theatre, 1976, Directing in the Theatre: A Casebook, 1980, rev. edit., 1994; dir. 95 plays; contbr. articles to profl. jours. Bd. dirs. various art orgns., Ky., Tex., Wash., Ariz. Recipient grants public and pvt. agencies. Mem. Nat. Assn. State Univs. and Land-Grant Colls.(chmn. commn. on arts 1981-83), Coun. Fine Arts Deans (exec. com. 1984-89, sec./treas. 1986-89), Univ. and Coll. Theatre Assn. (pres. 1981-82), Assn. for Communication Adminstrn. (pres. 1986-87), Ky. Theatre Assn. (pres. 1976). Office: Ariz State U PO Box 872102 Tempe AZ 85287-2102 Business E-Mail: bob.wills@asu.edu.

**WILLS, JOHN ELLIOT, JR.,** retired historian, writer; b. Urbana, Ill., Aug. 8, 1936; s. John Elliot and George Anne (Hicks) W.; m. Carolin Connell, July 19, 1958; children: Catherine, Christopher John, Jeffrey David, Joanne, Lucinda. BA in Philosophy, U. Ill., 1956; MA in East Asian Studies, Harvard U., 1960, PhD in History and Far Ea. Langs., 1967. History instr. Stanford (Calif.) U., 1964-65, U. So. Calif., L.A., 1965-67, asst. prof., 1967-72, assoc. prof., 1972-84, prof., 1984—2004, prof. emeritus, 2004—, acting chair East Asian Langs. and Cultures, 1987-89; dir. East Asian Studies Ctr. USC-UCLA Joint East Asian Studies Ctr., L.A., 1990-94. Rsch. abroad in The Netherlands, Taiwan, China, Japan, Macao, Philippines, Indonesia, India, Italy, Spain, Portugal, Eng. Author: Pepper, Guns, and Parleys: The Dutch East India Company and China, 1974, Embassies and Illusions: Dutch and Portuguese Envoys to K'ang-hsi, 1666-1687, 1984, Mountain of Fame: Portraits in Chinese History, 1994, 1688: A Global History, 2001; co-editor: (with Jonathan D. Spence) From Ming to Ch'ing: Conquest, Region, and Continuity in Seventeeth-Century China, 1979; editor: Eclipsed Entrepots of the Western Pacific: Taiwan and Central Vietnam, 1500-1800, 2002; contbr. articles to profl. jours. Grantee Nat. Acad. Scis., 1985, Am. Coun. Learned Soc., 1979-80; Younger Humanist fellow NEH, 1972-73. Mem. Assn. for Asian Studies, Am. Hist. Assn., Phi Beta Kappa, Phi Kappa Phi (recognition award 1986, 95). Avocation: travel. Business E-Mail: jwills@usc.edu.

**WILLS, KATHERINE V. TSIOPOS,** language educator; b. St. Louis, Sept. 30, 1957; d. Vasilios and Kalliope Stratos Tsiopos; m. Howard William Wills. BA in English and Anthropology, Washington U., St. Louis, 1979; MA in English and Writing, Ind. U., Bloomington, 1991; PhD in Composition and Rhetoric, U. Louisville, 2004. Cert. in Allied Health Technique in Histological Method St. Joseph's Hosp., 1990. Pres. Port of Nashville, Inc. LLC, 1986—90; lectr. English Ind. U.-Purdue U. Columbus, 1991—; v.p. Workplace Training Assocs., Inc., 1993—. Presenter in field. Contbr. over 60 articles in creative jours. Recipient essay award Scholastic Mag., Inc., 1973, award for acad. excellence and community svc. Am. Hellenic Progressive and Edn. Assn., poetry award Wednesday Club of St. Louis, Mo., 1977, Roger Conant Hatch hon. mention for writing, Washington U., 1977. Mem.: MLA, AAUP, Writing Program Adminstrs., Writers' Ctr. Indpls., TechRhet-Listserv, Rhetorical Soc. Am., Conf. Coll. Composition and Communication, Nat. Conf. Tchrs. English, Multi-ethnic Lit. US, Cultural Studies Assn., Assn. Tchrs. Tech. Writing, Assn. Bus. Communication, Phi Kappa Delta. Greek Orthodox. Avocations: scuba diving, motorcycling, fishing. Home: 7772 Bellsville Rd Nashville IN 47448-8995 Office Phone: 812-348-7215. E-mail: kwills@iupui.edu.

**WILLS, MICHAEL STEPHEN,** nutritionist, quality assurance professional; b. Roslyn, NY, Mar. 10, 1953; s. Thomas Francis and Catherine Ann Wills; m. Svetlana Victorivna Shiryaeva, Jan. 26, 1994 (div. Aug. 2005); m. Barbara Ann Keegan, Jan. 15, 1979 (div. June 30, 2005); stepchildren: Charles Clancy, Kseniya Andreevna Shiryaeva 1 child, Sean Michael. BS with high honors, U. Ariz., 1975. Registered dietitian Am. Dietetics Assn., Ill., 1976. Newspaper carrier LI Newsday, Albertson, NY, 1966—69; dietetic technician Ariz. Med. Ctr., Tucson, 1972—73; dietetic practicum U.S. Army, San Francisco, 1973—73; dietetic technician Tucson Med. Ctr., 1973—75; dietetic internship U. Ariz., Tucson, 1975—76; dir. of food svc. Catskill (N.Y.) Meml. Hosp. and Nursing Home, 1976—77; food svc. dir. New Rochelle (N.Y.) Nursing Home, 1977—79; dir. of food svc. Grace Plz., Inc., Great Neck, NY, 1979—82; corp. dietitian Data Control Info., Inc., Hornell, NY, 1982—84; dir. devel., 1984—86; quality assurance and customer support rep. The CBORD Group, Inc., Ithaca, NY, 1986—87; mgr. support and quality assurance, 1987—88; mgr. quality assurance, 1988—98; dir. quality assurance, 1998—. Cons. ServiceMaster, Downers Grove, Ill., 1986—94, Abbot Labs., Chgo., 1987—88, Brown U., Providence, 1987—92, Hallmark Cards, Kansas City, Kans., 1987—94, 1988 Winter Olympics, Calgary, Alberta, Canada, 1987—88, Disneyland, Paris, 1993—93, The Walt Disney World Co., Orlando, Fla., 1993—, Cornell U., Ithaca, NY, 1995, Kaiser Permanente, L.A., 2001—03, NSW Dept. Health, Sydney, NSW, Australia, 2002—04, Disneyland, Anaheim, Calif., 2003, H.E.B. Markets, San Antonio, 2004—, Calif. Inst. of Tech., Pasadena, Calif., 2004—04; presenter in field. Contbr. articles to profl. jours. Alumni bd. dirs. U. Ariz. Coll. Agrl. & Life Scis., 2005—; mem. Unitarian Universalist Assn., Ithaca, 1992—2004. Recipient Photography award, Photographic Soc. Am., 2005; scholar Promising Student, Herricks H.S. PTA, 1971, U. Ariz., 1973—74; NY State Regents scholar, N.Y. State Dept. Edn., 1971, Syntex Dietetic Internship scholar, Syntex Corp., 1975. Mem.: Am. Dietetic Assn. (licentiate), Amercian Soc. for Quality (assoc., paper reviewer 2002—04), Photographic Soc. Am. (assoc.), Kappa Omicron Nu. Democrat. Roman Catholic. Achievements include development of functional reliability approach for software develop-ment; method for calculating probability of concurrence for multi-user software applications; design of CBORD_performance: a software application for measuring software performance benchmarks. Avocations: photography, astronomy, writing, backpacking. Home: PO 258 20 West Malloryville Rd Freeville NY 13068 Office: The CBORD Group Inc 61 Brown Rd Ithaca NY 14850 Office Phone: 607-257-2410. Personal E-mail: mwills@twcny.rr.com. Business E-Mail: msw@cbord.com.

**WILLS, ROBERT HAMILTON,** retired publishing executive; b. Colfax, Ill., June 21, 1926; s. Robert Orson and Ressie Mae (Hamilton) W.; m. Sherilyn Lou Niersthermer, Jan. 16, 1949; children: Robert L., Michael H., Kendall J. BS, MS, Northwestern U., 1950. Reporter Duluth (Minn.) Herald & News-Tribune, 1950-51; reporter Milw. Jour., 1951-59, asst. city editor, 1959-62; city editor Milw. Sentinel, 1962-75, editor, 1975-91; exec. v.p. Jour./Sentinel, Inc., Milw., 1991-92, pres., 1992-93; vice-chmn., 1993; also bd. dirs. Jour./Sentinel, Inc., Milw.; pub. Milw. Jour. Sr. v.p., bd. dirs. Jour. Communications; pres. Wis. Freedom of Info. Council, 1979-86, charter mem., 1979; Pulitzer Prize juror, 1982, 83, 90. Mem. media-law rels. com. State Bar Wis., 1969-99; vice chmn. privacy coun. Wis. Pub. Svc. Commn., 1996-97; mem. Wis. Privacy Coun., 1994-95. Recipient Leadership award Women's Ct. and Civic Conf. Greater Milw., 1987; inducted into Journalism Hall of Achievement Medill Sch. Northwestern U., 1997, Wis. Newspaper Assn. Found. Hall of Fame, 2001. Mem. Wis. Newspaper Assn. (pres. 1985-86, Disting. Svc. award 1992), Wis. AP (pres. 1975-76, Dion Henderson award Svc. 1993), Am. Soc. Newspaper Editors, Internat. Press Inst., Milw. Press Club (Media Hall Fame 1993), Soc. Profl. Journalists (prs. Milw. chpt. 1979-80, nat. pres. 1986-87), Sigma Delta Chi Found. (bd. dirs. 1993-96, Wis. Newsman of Yr. 1973, Freedom of Info. award Milw. chpt. 1988). Home: 2064 Tiger Links Dr Henderson NV 89012-6111 E-mail: wills2064@juno.com.

**WILLS, WILLIAM RIDLEY, II,** retired insurance company executive, historian; b. Nashville, June 19, 1934; s. Jesse Ely and Ellen (Buckner) W.; m. Irene Weaver Jackson, July 21, 1962; children: William Ridley III, Morgan Jackson, Thomas Weaver. BA, Vanderbilt U., 1956. Agt., staff mgr. Nat. Life & Accident Ins. Co., Nashville, 1958-62, supr., 1962-64, asst. sec., 1964-67, asst. v.p., 1967-70, 2d v.p., 1970-75, v.p., 1975-81, sr. v.p., 1981-83, Am. General Services Co., 1982-83; dir. Nat. Life & Accident Ins. Co., Nashville, 1976-83; pres. Tenn. Hist. Soc., 1985-87; bd. dirs. Nat. Trust for Hist. Preservation, 1988-91. Author: History of Belle Meade: Mansion, Plantation and Stud, 1991, Old Enough to Die, 1996, Touring Tennessee: A Post Card Panorama, 1989-1955, 1996, Tennessee Governors at Home, 1999, Belle Meade Country Club: The First One Hundred Years, 2001, Gentleman, Scholar, Athlete: The History of Montgomery Bell Academy, 2005. Nat. chmn. Living Endowment Drive Vanderbilt U., 1974; pres. Cumberland Mus. and Sci. Ctr., Nashville, 1977; gen. chmn. campaign United Way, Nashville and Mid. Tenn., 1978; pres. YMCA of Met. Nashville, 1984; trustee Ladies Hermitage Assn., 1981—90; mem. Tenn. Hist. Commn.; chmn. YMCA Found. Mid. Tenn., 1998—99; chmn. bd. Montgomery Bell Acad., 1988—97, gen. chmn. $43 million capital campaign, 1999—2000; mem. adv. bd. Pub. Libr. of Nashville and Davidson County, 2002—; pres. Monteagle Sunday Sch. Assembly, 2002—04; bd. dirs. Vanderbilt U. 1988—. Lt. USN, 1956—58. Recipient awards YMCA, 1977, 1983, United Way De Tocqueville award, 1989, Tenn. History Book award Tenn. Libr. Assn. and Tenn. Hist. Commn., 1991, Disting. Alumnus award Montgomery Bell Acad., 1996, H.G. Hill award YMCA of Mid. Tenn., 2003. Fellow Life Office Mgmt. Assn.; mem. Assn. Preservation Tenn. Antiquities (pres. Nashville chpt. 1987-89), Belle Meade Country Club, Coffee House Club, Round Table Literary Club. Presbyterian. Personal E-mail: ridleywills@aol.com.

**WILLSE, JAMES PATRICK,** newspaper editor; b. NYC, Mar. 17, 1944; s. Sherman Stokes and Katherine (Mackey) W.; m. Sharon Margaret Stack, Sept. 15, 1973; 1 child, Elizabeth Ruth. BA, Hamilton Coll., 1967; MS, Columbia U., 1968. Nat. editor AP, NYC, 1969-74, news editor San Francisco, 1975-78; city editor San Francisco Examiner, 1978-82, mng. editor, 1982-84, NY Daily News, 1984-89, editor, 1989—93, pub., 1992—93; dir. news media Advance Publications, Inc., 1993—94; editor Star Ledger, Newark, 1995—. Named Beveridge Editor of Yr. Nat. Press Found., 2000; fellow Stanford U., 1975. Mem. Am. Soc. Newspaper Editors, AP Mng. Editors. Office: Star Ledger 1 Star Ledger Plz Newark NJ 07102-1291 Office Phone: 973-392-4127. E-mail: jwillse@starledger.com.*

**WILLSIE, SANDRA KAY,** provost, dean, internist, educator; BS in Med. Tech., Pittsburg State U., Kans., 1975; DO, Kansas City U. Medicine and Bioscis., Mo., 1983. Diplomate in internal medicine, pulmonary diseases and critical care medicine Am. Bd. Internal Medicine, Am. Bd. Osteo. Internists, 2000. Rotating intern Univ. Hosp., Kansas City, Mo., 1983-84; resident in internal medicine U. Mo.-Kansas City Affiliated Hosps., 1984-87; fellow in pulmonary diseases and critical care medicine Truman Med. Ctr.-West, Kansas City, Mo., 1987-89; instr. medicine U. Mo.-Kansas City Sch. Medicine, 1984-89; med. dir. pulmonary clinic Truman Med. Ctr., 1991-2000; asst. prof. medicine U. Mo. Kansas City Sch. Medicine, 1989-94, assoc. prof. medicine, 1994-99; dep. asst. dean, 1994—97, asst. dean, 1997-2000, prof. medicine, 1999-2000, Kansas City U. Medicine and Bioscis., 2000—02, vice dean acad. affairs, adminstrn., med. affairs, 2002—, exec. v.p. acad. affairs, provost, dean, 2002—. Invited bd. question author Am. Bd. Internal Medicine, 1995—, relevance reviewer for pulmonary disease bd. exam, 1996—; internal medicine subspecialty program pre-reviewer Accreditation Coun. for Grad. Med. Edn., 1997—2000; credentials com. Truman Med. Ctr., Inc., 1990—96, med. intensive care unit com., 1992—2000, intermediate care unit com., 1992—2000, exec. com. Truman Health Sys., 1998—2000, profl. standards com., 1998—2000. Contbr. articles to profl. jours. Bd. dirs. Girls to Women, 1995—2000, v.p. bd. dirs., 1996—2000. Fellow: Am. Coll. Physicians (state activities com. 1991—95, chair, state activities com. 1994, scientific presentations judge 1995—96, coun. mem. 1998—2004), Am. Coll. Osteo. Internists (program com. 2000—, rsch. com. 2003—, Rschr. of Yr. 2004); mem.: Met. Med. Soc. (chair women in medicine com. 1995—2000, pres. com. 1995—2000, bd. dirs. 1997—2000, exec. com. 1999—2000, chair women in medicine com. 2000—), Am. Osteo. Assn., Kans. City Pulmonary Roundtable (pres.), Soc. Critical Care Medicine, Am. Lung Assn. Mo. (bd. mem.), Jackson County Osteo. Assn., Mo. Assn. Osteo. Physicians and Surgeons, Am. Thoracic Soc., Am. Coll. Chest Physicians (chair, basic sci. com. 1995—98, scientific program com. 1995—2003, membership com. 1997—2001, gov. for Mo. 1997—2001, chair, scientific presentations and awards com. 1998—2000, vice chair, scientific program com. 1999—2000, chair, scientific program com. 2000—01, regent 2004—, Young Investigator award 1992). Office: Kansas City Univ Medicine and Bioscis 1750 Independence Ave Kansas City MO 64106-1453 Office Phone: 816-283-2308. Business E-Mail: swillsie@kcumb.edu.

**WILLSON, C. GRANT,** chemical engineering and chemistry professor; b. Vallejo, Calif., Mar. 30, 1939; s. Carlton P. and Margaret Ann (Cosner) W.; m. Deborah Jeanne Merritt, Dec. 13, 1975; children: William, Andrew. BS in Chemistry, U. Calif., Berkeley, 1962, PhD in Organic Chemistry, 1973; MS in Organic Chemistry, San Diego State U., 1969. With propellent rsch. Aerojet Gen. Corp., Sacramento, 1962-64; tchr., coach Fairfax H.S., La., 1964-67; prof. Calif. State U., Long Beach, 1973-74, U. Calif., San Diego, 1974-78; mgr. polymer sci. and tech. IBM Almaden Rsch. Ctr., San Jose, Calif., 1978-93; prof. chemistry, chem. engring. U. Tex., Austin, 1993—. Contbr. articles to profl. jours.; patentee in field. Recipient Kosar award, Soc. Imaging Sci. and Tech., 1998, Aristotle award, Semicondr. Rsch. Corp., Photopolymer Sci. award, Japan, 2003. Mem. NAE, AAAS, Soc. Photog. and Instrumentation Engrs., Am. Phys. Soc., Am. Chem. Soc. (Arthur K. Doolittle award 1986, ACS Chemistry of Materials 1991, Carothers award 1992, Coop. Rsch. award in Polymer Sci. 1993, Applied Polymer Sci. Award, 2004, Heroes of Chemistry award, Arthur Dehon Little award 2005), NAS (award for chem. in svc. to soc. 1999, SPIE Fritz Zernike award, 2005), Coun. for Chem. Rsch. (Malcom Pruitt award 1997), St. Francis Yacht Club, Sigma Xi. Avocations: sailing, skiing. Office: U Tex Dept Chem and Chem Engring Austin TX 78712 Business E-Mail: willson@che.utexas.edu.

**WILLSON, CLYDE D.,** biologist, educator; b. Omaha, May 7, 1935; s. Paul Gallup and Elise Willson; m. Greta Jean Olsen, July 17, 1954; children: Ian, Bjorn, Scott, Gillian. BA in Biochemistry, U. Calif., Berkeley, 1956, PhD in Chemistry, 1960. Postdoctoral fellow Pasteur Inst. NIH, Paris, 1960—62; asst. prof. biology U. Calif., Berkeley, 1962—67, Miller fellow, 1967—69; prof. biology and chemistry Laney Coll., Oakland, Calif., 1969—. Chair biology dept. Laney Coll., 1975—77, 1995—2002, rep. Acad. Senate, 1990—2002. Contbr. articles to profl. jours. Natural scis. docent Oakland Mus., 1969—72. Mem.: AAUP (sec.-treas., U. Calif. at Berkeley 1963—64), No. Calif. Parasitologists, West Coast Bacterial Physiologists. Avocation: keyboard performance. Home: 136 International Blvd Oakland CA 94606 Office: Laney College 900 Fallon St Oakland CA 94607

**WILLSON, DAVID ALLEN,** retired reference librarian, writer; b. Seattle, June 30, 1942; s. Robert Richard and Alice Hansine (Aspen) W.; m. Penelope Poeschl, Dec. 13, 1972 (div. Mar. 1986); children: Mungo Park, Darcy Monroe; m. Michele Geraldine DeBruyne, Mar. 8, 1986; children: Joaquin Sandoval, Alice Maria. BA, U. Wash., 1964, MLS, 1970. Reference libr. Green River C.C., Auburn, Wash., 1970—2000. Author: REMF Diary, 1988, The REMF Returns, 1992, In the Army Now, 1995; co-editor: Vietnam War Literature, 1996, Viet Nam War Jour., 2000—. With U.S. Army, 1966—67. Recipient Disting. Faculty award Puget Power, 1996, Vietnam Vets. Am. Contbn. to Am. Culture award, 1997. Mem.: Popular Culture Assn., Vietnam Vets. Am. Democrat. Lutheran. Avocations: movies, listening to the blues, especially fred mcdowell. Home: 23630 201st Ave SE Maple Valley WA 98038-8633 E-mail: dawillson@earthlink.net.

**WILLSON, DAVID E.,** music educator; b. Jackson, Miss., Aug. 18, 1951; s. Duncan Willson; m. Joan Harrington Willson. B of Music Edn., U. Miss., 1973, M of Music Edn., 1975. Band dir. Independence H.S., Miss., 1975—76; jr. band dir. Greenwood Pub. Schs., Miss., 1976—77; dir. bands Caldwell H.S., Columbus, Miss., 1978—85, Clinton Pub. Schs., Clinton, Miss., 1985—91, U. Miss., Oxford, 1991—. Recipient Music Educator of Yr. award, NEFIMA, 1992, Miss. Band Dir. of Yr. award, 1995. Mem.: Miss. Band Masters, Nat. Band Assn., Phi Beta Mu (internat. v.p. 2001—05). Avocations: jogging, automobiles, travel. Office: Univ Miss 103B E Scruggs Music University MS 38677

**WILLSON, JAMES DOUGLAS,** aerospace transportation executive; b. Edinburgh, Scotland, May 24, 1915; came to U.S., 1921; s. George William and Margaret (Douglas) W.; m. Genevieve Best, Nov. 11, 1939; children: James Douglas, Stephen J., Wendy. BS with honors, Ohio State U., 1937, MBA, 1938. C.P.A., N.Y. Sr. auditor Arthur Andersen & Co. (C.P.A.'s), N.Y.C., 1938-42; controller Stinson div. Consol. Vultee Aircraft Corp., 1946-48, Plaskon div. Libbey-Owens-Ford Glass Co., 1948-53; treas. Affiliated Gas Equipment Co., Cleve., 1953; v.p. finance, treas. Norris-Thermador Corp., Los Angeles, 1957-59; controller, mgr. finance Tidewater Oil Co., Los Angeles, 1959-60, v.p. finance, 1960-66, Northrop Corp., Los Angeles, 1966-70, sr. v.p. finance, treas., 1970-80, also dir. Author: Controllership, 1952, 63, 81, 90, 95, Business Budgeting and Control, 1956, 57, Internal Auditing Manual, 1983, 89, Budgeting and Profit Planning, 1983, 89, 92, Financial Information Systems, 1986. Served to lt. comdr. USNR, 1942-46. Mem. Nat. Assn. Accts. (Lybrand Gold medal 1960), Am. Inst. C.P.A.s, Controllers Inst. Am. Home: 1715 Chevy Chase Dr Beverly Hills CA 90210-2709

**WILLSON, PRENTISS, JR.,** retired lawyer; b. Durham, NC, Sept. 20, 1943; s. Prentiss and Lucille (Giles) W. AB, Occidental Coll., 1965; JD, Harvard U., 1968. Bar: Calif. 1969, U.S. Dist. Ct. (no. dist.) Calif. 1971, U.S. Ct. Appeals (9th cir.) 1971, U.S. Tax Ct. 1971, U.S. Supreme Ct. 1975. Instr. law Miles Coll., Birmingham, Ala., 1968-70; ptnr. Morrison & Foerster, San Francisco, 1970-98, Ernst & Young, San Francisco, 1998—2001; ret., 2002. Prof. Golden Gate U., 1971-84; lectr. Stanford U. Sch. Law, 1985-88. Contbr. articles to profl. jours. Mem. ABA, Calif. Bar Assn. Democrat. Home: 66 Ardmore Rd Larkspur CA 94939-2124 E-mail: prentiss.willson@ey.com

**WILLSTEIN, GARY JAY,** orthopedic, surgeon; b. NYC, Sept. 21, 1959; s. Louis and Edna Helen Willstein; m. Lynne Edgington Swanson, Nov. 14, 1992; children: Hannah, Sarah, Benjamin. BS with honors, Iowa State U., Ames, 1981; MD, U. Iowa, Iowa City, 1985. Diplomate Am. Bd. Orthopedic Surgery. Orthopedic surgeon Orthopedic Surgeos Colo., Englewood, 1990—2000, Western Mont. Clinic, Missoula, 2000—; med. dir. Providence Surgery Ctr., Missoula, 2002—. Mem.: Missoula Med. Assn. Avocations: sailing, skiing, hiking. Office: Western Mont Clinic 500 W Broadway Missoula MT 59802

**WILLUMSON, GLENN GARDNER,** curator, art historian; b. Glendale, Calif., June 22, 1949; s. Donald Herbert and Aileen Ann (Gardner) W.; m. Margaret Julia Moore, June 20, 1970; children: Erik Ryan, Ashley Aileen. BA, St. Mary's Coll., 1971; MA, U. Calif., Davis, 1984; PhD in Art History, U. Calif., Santa Barbara, 1988. Asst. curator Nelson Art Gallery, Davis, Calif., 1982-83; curator Getty Rsch. Inst., L.A., 1988-92; sr. curator Palmer Mus. of Art Pa. State U., University Park, Pa., 1992-2001; assoc. prof. art history, dir. mus. studies U. Fla., 2001—. Fellow Nat. Writing Project, 1987; vis. prof. U. Calif., Irvine, 1990; affiliate prof. art history Pa. State U., University Park, 1994-2001. Author: W. Eugene Smith and the Photo-Essay, 1992 (grantee J. Paul Getty Trust 1991), Collecting With a Passion, 1993; mem. editl. bd. History of Photography mag., London, 1991-94, Cambridge Univ. Press., N.Y.C., 1993-97. Haynes fellow Huntington Libr., 1990-96, Univ. Tchr.'s fellow NEH, 1997-98. Mem. Am. Studies Assn. (Annette K. Baxter prize 1987), Coll. Art Assn., Soc. Photog. Edn. (mem. governing bd. Mid-Atlantic region 1993-97), Assn. Historians Am. Art. Mus. Assn. (bd. com. mus. profl. tng. 2004—) Office: Coll Fine Arts U Fla PO Box 115801 Gainesville FL 32611

**WILLUMSTAD, ROBERT B.,** insurance company executive, retired bank executive; b. Bklyn., Aug. 22, 1945; m. Carol Willumstad; 2 children. Grad. Adelphi U., LLD (hon.), 2005. Various ops., retail banking and computer systems positions Chemical Bank, 1967—87; chmn., CEO consumer finance svcs. Travelers Group; chmn., CEO Global Consumer Group, Citigroup Inc., 2000—03; pres. Citigroup, Inc., 2002—05, COO, 2003—05; pres., CEO Citibank N.A., 2003—05; bd. dir., chmn. elect Am. Internat. Group, NYC, 2006—. Vice chmn. MasterCard Internat.; bd. dirs. S.C. Johnson & Son Inc.; dir., chmn. elect Fin. Services Roundtable. Bd. dirs. Habitat for Humanity Internat., 2001—; bd. trustee Am. Scandinavian Found.; bd. trustees Adelphia U., 2005—. Recipient Frederick Douglass award, NYC Urban League, 2002. Mem.: Financial Services Roundtable (bd. dirs.). Office: Am Internat Group 70 Pine St New York NY 10270*

**WILMER, ANN,** public relations executive; b. Waynesboro, Pa., Oct. 18, 1952; d. Vaughn Edward and Frances Laura (Hudson) W. BS in Journalism cum laude, U. Fla., 1975, cert. of East Asian studies, 1975; EdM, Salisbury State Coll., 1979. Pub. rels. dir. Delmarva Adv. Coun., Salisbury, Md., 1975-77; advt. mgr. Ahtes & Hanna Ptnrs., Inc., Salisbury, 1979-80; substitute tchr. Wicomico County Sch. Bd., Salisbury, 1979-82; instr. Wor Wic Tech. C.C., 1982-85; pub. affairs officer Md. Dept. State Planning, Balt., 1985-87; publs. administr. Md. Dept. Housing and Cmty. Devel., 1988; pub. affairs officer Md. Dept. Natural Resources, 1988-97; pres. Capital Letters, Salisbury, Md., 1997—. Lectr. journalism, media studies Salisbury U., 1998—; freelance editor, pub. rels. cons. Active Md. State Dem. Com., 1982-86; nat. committeewoman Young Dems. of Am., Md., 1984-86; mem. Preservation Trust of Wicomico, Inc., 1990-96, pres., 1991-95; trustee Salisbury Area Property Owners Assn., 1991-92; founder Green Ribbon Campaign for Open Records, 2000. Named Outstanding Young Woman of the Yr., Salisbury Jaycees, 1982. Mem. Soc. Profl. Journalists (v.p. U. Fla. chpt. 1973-74, Pres. award 1975). Avocations: opera, needle arts, genealogy. Office: Capital Letters 408 N Division St Ste A Salisbury MD 21801-4274 Office Phone: 410-548-5588. Business E-Mail: alwilmer@salisbury.edu.

**WILMER, ROBIN LOUISE,** music educator; d. Elizabeth Jean and Forrest Aubrey Hettinger; m. Michael Jack Wilmer, May 3, 1985. BA in music, Calif. State U. at Sacramento, 1972—77. Life tchg. credential in music: K-jr. coll. Calif., credential (adminstrn.) in ednl. leadership and policy studies. Mid. sch. music tchr. Albert Einstein Mid. Sch., Sacramento, 1977—2004; music tchr. Rosemont H.S., Sacramento, 2004—. Lead tchr., creative and performing arts small learning cmty. Rosemont H.S., 2004—. Contbr. articles. Recipient Sacramento Area Tchr. of the Yr., Wal Mart, 2005, Thanks to Teachers - Regional Finalist, Apple Computers, 1990. Mem.: Calif. Music Educators Assn. (pres. 200—02). Avocations: reading, photography. Office: Rosemont H S 9594 Kiefer Blvd Sacramento CA 95827 Office Phone: 916-228-5844. Office Fax: 916-228-5743. E-mail: robinwi@sac-city.k12.ca.us.

**WILMERDING, JOHN,** art historian, educator, curator; b. Boston, Apr. 28, 1938; s. John Currie and Lila Vanderbilt (Webb) W. AB, Harvard U., 1960, AM, 1961, PhD, 1965. Asst. prof. art Dartmouth Coll., 1965-68, assoc. prof., 1968-73, Leon E. Williams prof., 1973-77, chmn. dept. art, 1968-72, chmn. humanities divsn., 1971-72; sr. curator Am. art Nat. Gallery of Art, 1977-83, dep. dir., 1983-88; Sarofim prof. Am. art Princeton U., 1988—, chmn. dept. art and archeology, 1992-99. Vis. lectr. history of art Yale U., 1972; vis. prof. fine arts Harvard U., 1976; vis. prof. art U. Md., 1979; vis. prof. art history U. Del., 1982; hon. curator painting Peabody Mus., Salem, Mass.; vis. curator Met. Mus., 1988—. Author: Fitz Hugh Lane, American Marine Painter, 1964, A History of American Marine Painting, 1968, Pittura Americana dell' Ottocento, 1969, Robert Salmon, Painter of Ship and Shore, 1971, Fitz Hugh Lane, 1971, Winslow Homer, 1972, The Genius of American Painting, 1973, American Art, 1976, American Light, The Luminist Movement, 1980, American Masterpieces from the National Gallery of Art, 1980, An American Perspective, 1981, Important Information Inside, 1982, Andrew Wyeth, The Helga Pictures, 1987, Paintings by Fitz Hugh Lane, 1988; American Views: Essays on American Art, 1991, The Artist's Mount Desert: American Painters on the Maine Coast, 1994, Compass and Clock: Defining Moments in American Culture, 1999, Signs of the Artist: Signatures and Self-Expression in American Paintings, 2003, American Art in the Princeton University Art Museum, Vol. 1, 2004. Trustee Nat. Gallery of ARt, Washington, Coll. of the Atlantic, Bar Harbor, Maine, Solomon R. Guggenheim Mus., NYC, N.E. Harbor Libr., Maine, Wyeth Endowment for Am. Art, Wilmington, Del., Nat. Portrait Gallery, Washington. Guggenheim fellow, 1973-74. Fellow Phila. Atheneum (hon.); Mem. Coll. Art Assn., Am. Studies Assn. Office: Princeton U Dept Art and Archaeology 105 McCormick Hall Princeton NJ 08544-1018 Office Phone: 609-258-3785. E-mail: wilmerdg@princeton.edu.

**WILMERS, ROBERT GEORGE,** bank executive; b. NYC, Apr. 20, 1934; s. Charles K. and Cecilia (Eitingon) W.; m. Elisabeth Roche de la Rigodiere; children: Robert G. Jr., Christopher C. BA, Harvard U., 1956; postgrad., Harvard Bus. Sch., 1958-59. Dep. fin. adminstr. City of N.Y., 1966-70; v.p. Morgan Guaranty Trust Co., N.Y.C. and Belgium, 1970-80; chmn. M&T Bank Corp., Buffalo, 1982—2005. Bd. dirs. Vivian Beaumont Theater Inc., Buffalo Fiscal Stability Authority, The Bus. Coun. N.Y. State, Fin. Svcs. Roundtable. Decorated officer de l'Ordre de la Couronne (Belgium); also: 1 W 64th St New York NY 10023-6734 Office: M&T Bank 1 M&T Plz Buffalo NY 14203 Office Phone: 716-842-5425. Business E-mail: rwilmers@mandtbank.com.

**WILMORE, DOUGLAS WAYNE,** surgeon, educator; b. Newton, Kans., July 22, 1938; s. Waldo Wayne and Hilda Gard (Adrian) W.; m. Judith Kay Shabert; 1 child, Carol Kristann. BA, Washburn U., 1960; MD, Kans. U., 1964; MS (hon.), Harvard U., 1979; PhD (hon.), Washburn U., 1995. Diplomate Am. Bd. Surgery. Intern Hosp. U. Pa., Phila., 1964-65, resident, fellow, 1965-71; chief clin. rsch. and staff surgeon U.S. Army Inst. Surg. Rsch., Ft. Sam Houston, 1971-79; staff surgeon Brigham and Women's Hosp., Boston, 1979—; Frank Sawyer prof. surgery Harvard Med. Sch., Boston, 1989—. Editor Scientific American Surgery, 1988, ACS Surgery, 2001—. Mem. Inst. Medicine, 1999. Lt. Col. U.S. Army, 1971-74. Achievements include development of safe modern techniques for providing parenteral nutrition to critically-ill patients; rehabilitation program for individuals with severe gastrointestinal disease; first to use growth factors and specialized nutrition to rehabilitate patients with the short bowel syndrome; use the amino acid L-glutamine in clinical nutrition.

**WILMOT, IRVIN GORSAGE,** former hospital administrator, educator, consultant; b. Nanking, China, June 30, 1922; s. Frank Alonzo and Ethel (Ranney) W.; m. Dorothy Agnes Mohlfeld, Feb. 6, 1943; children: Marcia Beth, David Michael. BS, Northwestern U., 1955; MBA, U. Chgo., 1957. With Internat. Register Co., Chgo., 1946-47; buyer U. Chgo., 1947-49 adminstrv. asst., then asst. supt. U. Chgo. Clinics, 1949-61; adminstr. NYU Med. Ctr.-Univ. Hosp., 1961-68, exec. v.p., 1968-81, Blue Cross-Blue Shield Greater N.Y., 1981-83, dir., 1977-81; exec. v.p., COO Montefiore Hosp. and Med. Ctr., N.Y.C., 1984-85; healthcare cons., 1985—. Instr. then asst. prof. U. Chgo., 1957-61; assoc. prof. NYU, 1961-68; prof., 1968—; assoc. dir. U. Chgo. Grad. Program Hosp. Adminstrn., 1959-61; mem. hosp. rev. and planning coun. State of N.Y., 1979-87. Bd. dirs N.Y. Blood Ctr., 1978-81. With USAN, 1940-46. Fellow Am. Coll. Hosp. Adminstrs. (life, chmn. ctrl. com. insts. 1959-65, regent N.Y. State and P.R. 1974—); mem. Assn. U. Programs Hosp. Adminstrs. (exec. sec. 1959-61), Am. Hosp. Assn. (mem. coun. rsch. and planning 1965-68, coun. on mgmt. 1979-80, coun. on fin. 1981-84, trustee 1979-81), Am. Med. Colls. (chmn. coun. tchg. hosps. 1970-71), Greater N.Y. Hosp. Assn. (bd. govs., pres. 1973-74), Hosp. Assn. N.Y. State (trustee, chmn. 1976-77). Home: 34 Helen Ave Rye NY 10580-2447

**WILMOTH, MARSHA HOPE,** elementary school educator; d. J.C. and T. Bearnease Bolden; m. Charles DeWayne Wilmoth, Mar. 18, 1972 (dec.); children: Michele H., Sharon L., Leslie D. AA, Coffeyville (Kans.) Cmty. Jr. Coll., 1972; BS in Edn., Pittsburg State U., 1974; cert. reading specialist, Emporia State U., 1986. Mid. sch. English tchr. Wann (Okla.) Sch., 1974—75; Title 1 reading and math. tchr. K-9th grade, Indian edn. tutoring coord. and tchr. Lincoln Meml. Grade Sch., Caney, 1978—; Title 1 reading tchr. Caney (Kans.) HS, 1981—82; elem. tchr. Caney, 1982—2006; substitute tchr. Duncanville (Tex.) Schs., 1976—77. Sponsor youth activities Assemblies of God and Bapt. chs. Named High Qualified Tchr., Kans. State Dept. Edn.; recipient recognition, Unified Sch. Dist. 436, Parent award. Mem.: NEA, Internat. Reading Assn., No. Cherokee Nation, Caney Valley Tchr. Assn., Kans. Edn. Assn., Ducks Unltd., Order Ea. Star, Alpha Upsilon Alpha, Kappa Delta Pi. Avocations: cooking, photography. Office: Caney Valley Unified Schs 201 E 1st Ave Caney KS 67333-1903 E-mail: mwilmoth@caney.com.

**WILMOTT, TIMOTHY J.,** recreational facility executive; m. Nancy Wilmott; 1 child, Meghan. BS magna cum laude in Indsl. Engring., MS magna cum laude in Indsl. Engring., Lehigh U.; MBA in Corp. Fin., U. Pa. From mem. staff to COO Harrah's Entertainment Inc., Las Vegas, 1987—2003, COO, 2003—. Office: Harrahs Entertainment Inc One Harrahs Ct Las Vegas NV 89119

**WILMOUTH, ROBERT K.,** commodities trader; b. Worcester, Mass., Nov. 9, 1928; s. Alfred F. and Aileen E. (Kearney) W.; m. Ellen M. Boyle, Sept. 10, 1955; children: Robert J., John J., James P., Thomas G., Anne Marie. BA, Holy Cross Coll., 1949; MA, U. Notre Dame, 1950, LLD, 1984. Exec. v.p., dir. 1st Nat. Bank Chgo., 1972-75; pres., chief adminstrv. officer Crocker Nat. Bank, San Francisco, 1975-77; pres., chief exec. officer Chgo. Bd. Trade, 1977-82; chmn. LaSalle Nat. Bank, 1982-99. Pres., chief exec. officer Nat. Futures Assn., 1982-2002, Spl. Policy Adv. Nat. Futures Assn., 2003-. Life trustee U. Notre Dame; mem. adv. coun. Kellogg Grad. Sch. Mgmt., Northwestern U. Mem. Chgo. Club, Barrington Hill Country Club. Office: Nat Futures Assn 200 W Madison St Ste 1600 Chicago IL 60606-3415

**WILNER, ALAN M.,** judge; b. Balt., Jan. 26, 1937; AB, Johns Hopkins U., 1958, MLA, 1966; JD, U. Md., 1962. Assoc. Sherbow, Shea & Doyle, Balt., 1962-65; asst. atty. gen. State of Md., 1965-68; assoc. Venable, Baetjer & Howard, Balt., 1968-71; asst., then chief legis. officer, govs. staff, 1971-77; assoc. judge Ct. of Spl. Appeals, 1977-90, chief judge, 1990-96; judge Md. Ct. of Appeals, 1996—. Adj. faculty U. Md. Sch. of Law, U. Balt. Sch. of Law; with Judicial Inst. Md., 1997—; chmn. bd. dirs., 1999—; mem. Md. Alternative Dispute Resolution Commn., 1998—. Mem. ABA, Md. Bar Found., Md. State Bar Assn., Balt. County Bar Assn. Office: Md Ct of Appeals County Courts Bldg 401 Bosley Ave Towson MD 21204*

**WILNER, MARION LEONARD,** art educator; b. N.Y.C., Sept. 27, 1929; d. Jack Frank and Madeline (Leff) Leonard; m. Myron Wilner, May 28, 1950; children: Andrew, Matthew, David. BS, NYU, 1950, MA, 1952. Prof. of art, coord. art transfer program Bristol Community Coll., Fall River, Mass., 1966-89, prof. emerita, 1993. Advisor dean's adv. coun. coll. visual and performing arts U. Mass., Dartmouth, 1993; lectr. Sacred Hearts Convent, 1992, R.I. Jewish Hist. Soc., 1992, Brandeis U. Nat. Women's Com., 1991, 90, Universidade Nova, Lisbon, 1988, Universidade Dos Acores, 1987; vis. scholar U. Mass., Dartmouth, 1992; mem. Higher Edn. Nominating Coun. 1990; judge Ea. Edison Poster and Essay Contest, 1989, R.I. Regional Scholastic Art Awards, 1987, Ann. Regional Art Exhbn. Fall River Festival, 1985; writer art Fall River Herald News, 1994-. Prin. works exhibited in numerous one-woman and group shows including DeBlois Gallery, Newport, R.I., 1992, 94, Bert Gallery, Providence, 1991, Dodge House Gallery, Providence, 1990, Fall River Hist. Soc., 1988, Newport Art Mus., 1987, Escola Superior de Belas Artes, Lisbon, 1986, Eastbourne Gallery, Newport, 1977, Facets Gallery, Fall River, 1993, New England Ctr. Gallery, U. N.H., 1992, Fed. Res. Bank Boston, 1992, Deblois Gallery, Newport, RI, 2003, Perkins Gallery, Mass., 2004, Retrospective at Bristol C.C., Fall River, Mass., 2005, Bristoli Art Mus., RI, 2006; prin. works represented in numerous collections including Duro Industries, Inc., Bristol C.C., Providence Art Club Mems. Show, Cianfarani award, 1998, R.I. Econ. Devel. Corp., 1999, Juried R.I. State Com., Nat. Mus. Women in Arts, 2000, Providence Art Club, Printmaking award, 2001, Deblois Gallery, Newport, R.I., 2001, Newport Art Mus., 2002, KRAUSE Gallery, 2003. Trustee Swain Sch. Design, New Bedford, Mass., 1977-91, Fall River Pub. Libr., 1978-91; active Fall River Cultural Commn., 1988—, Fall River Arts Lottery Coun., 1989—; mem. adv. bd. SMU Ctr. for Jewish Culture, 1983; visual arts dir. Festival '82; graphic designer for various community orgns. Gulbenkian grantee Lisbon, Portugal, 1986, 88; recipient Outstanding Cmty. Svc. award Fall River Area C. of C. and Industry, 1996, Ruth Findley award Providence Art Club, 2002. Mem.: Deblois Gallery, 19 on Paper. Home: 786 Madison St Fall River MA 02720-5718 E-mail: mandmwilner@yahoo.com.

**WILNER, THOMAS BERNARD,** lawyer; b. Toronto, July 7, 1944; came to U.S., 1944; s. Morton H. and Zelda (Dunkelman) W.; m. Jane Ten Broeck; children: Amanda, Adam, David. BA, Yale U., 1966; LLB, U. Pa., 1969. Clk. to Chief Judge William Hastie U.S. Ct. Appeals, Phila., 1969-70; assoc. Debevoise Plimpton, N.Y.C., 1970-72; counsel Amtrak, Washington, 1972-73; ptnr. Arnold & Porter, Washington, 1973-89, Shearman & Sterling, Washington and Tokyo, 1989—. Office: 801 Pennsylvania Ave NW Washington DC 20004-2604 Office Phone: 202-508-8050. Business E-mail: twilner@shearman.com.

**WILOCH, THOMAS,** poet, editor; b. Detroit, Feb. 3, 1953; s. Joseph and Jane W.; m. Denise Gottis, Oct. 10, 1981. BA, Wayne State U., Detroit, 1978. Rsch. asst. Wayne State U., Detroit, 1976; editl. asst. The Gale Group, Farmington Hills, Mich., 1977-78, asst. editor, 1978-81, sr. asst. editor, 1981-85, sr. writer, 1985-89, assoc. editor, 1989—2004; freelance writer, 2004—. Prose poem collections include: Stigmata Junction, 1985, 2d edit., 2005, Paper Mask, 1988, The Mannikin Cypher, 1989, Tales of Lord Shantih, 1989, Mr. Templeton's Toyshop, 1995; prose poems collections include Screaming in Code, 2006, cut-up haiku: Night Rain, 1991, Decoded Factories of the Heart, 1991, Narcotic Signature, 1992, Lyrical Brandy, 1993, Neon Trance, 1997; editor (with Leonard Kniffel): Directory of Michigan Literary Publishers, 1982, Contemporary Authors, New Revisions Series (asst. editor) Vols. 1-5, 1982—85, (sr. asst. editor) Vols. 6-15, 1982—85, (sr. writer) Vols. 16-27, 1986—89, (assoc. editor) Vols. 28-117, 1989—2003; editor Grimoire mag., 1982—85; author: Crime: A Serious American Problem, 2004, National Security, 2004, Prisons & Jails, 2005; contbr. to over 200 periodicals, including Pub.'s Weekly, Bloomsbury Rev., Fiction Rev., Small Press Rev., Factsheet 5, Kayak, Asylum, Wormwood Rev., others. Mem.: Nat. Assn. for Self Employed, Assn. Literary Scholars and Critics. Address: 42015 Ford Rd Ste 226 Canton MI 48187 Personal E-mail: twiloch@wowway.com.

**WILPON, FRED,** professional sports team executive; b. Bklyn., Nov. 22, 1936; s. Nathan and Frances (Altman) W.; m. Judith Anne Kessler, Sept. 27, 1958; children: Jeffrey Scott, Robin Lynn, Bruce Nathan. BA, U. Mich., 1958. Vice pres. Hanover Equities Corp., N.Y.C., 1959-69, Peter Sharp & Co., N.Y.C., 1969-71; chmn. bd. Sterling Equities, Inc., Manhasset, NY, 1971—; pres. N.Y. Mets Profl. Baseball Team, 1980—, now also chief exec. officer, 1980—; owner Brooklyn Cyclones, 2000—. Mem. Vol. Urban Cons. Group, Mayor N.Y.C. Housing Task Force; trustee Jewish Inst. Geriatric Care, New Hyde Park, N.Y., 1976—, Green Vale Sch., Glen Head, N.Y., 1977—. Served with USAF, 1959. Mem. Young Pres. Orgn. Clubs: KP. Achievements include unveiling of new NY Mets Stadium plans, 2006.

**WILS, MADELYN,** film company executive; b. Queens, NY, 1955; Owner, prodr. Bread and Butter TV; pres., CEO Tribeca Film Inst., NYC, 2004—. Trustee Alliance Downtown NY, Inc., Conservancy Hist. Battery Pk., Gateway Sch. NY; dir. Hudson River Park Trust; bd. mem. Lower Manhattan Devel. Corp., NYC, 2001—. Office: Tribeca Film Inst 375 Greenwich St New York NY 10013

**WILSON, ALICE MCATEER,** secondary school educator; b. S.I., N.Y., July 28, 1947; d. Charles Francis Jr. and Clorinda)Mardus) McAteer; m. Van Ray Wilson, 1979; 1 child, Clorinda Ann. BA in Math., Wells Coll., 1969; MS in Secondary Math. Edn. with honor, CUNY, 1971. Permanent tchr. cert., N.Y. State; cert. tchr., N.Y.C. Tchr. math. Tottenville H.S., S.I., 1970—2005, Gov. Livingston H.S., NJ, 2005—. Mem. alumnae coun. Wells Coll., Aurora, N.Y., 1992—. Mem. Phi Beta Kappa. Avocations: piano, sewing, swimming, sailing. Home: 599 Oakland Ave Staten Island NY 10310

**WILSON, ARMIN,** retired chemist; b. Sapulpa, Okla., Dec. 13, 1916; s. Joseph Bartholomew and Amelia (Heller) W.; m. Evelyn Hodes, June 8, 1943; children: Jonathan, Robert. BA, Rice U., 1939, MA, 1941; AM, PhD, Harvard U., 1945. Sr. chemist Merck Labs., Rahway, N.J., 1945-53; dept. head Bristol Myers, Hillside, N.J., 1953-68; prof. Rutgers U., New Brunswick, N.J., 1968-78. Contbr. articles to profl. jours. Fellow N.Y. Acad. Scis., mem. Phi Beta Kappa, Sigma Xi. Avocation: poetry. Home: 112 Crosslands Dr Kennett Square PA 19348-2014

**WILSON, BLENDA JACQUELINE,** foundation administrator; b. Woodbridge, N.J., Jan. 28, 1941; d. Horace and Margaret (Brogsdale) Wilson; m. Louis Fair Jr. AB, Cedar Crest Coll., 1962; AM, Seton Hall U., 1965; PhD, Boston Coll., 1979; DHL (hon.), Cedar Crest Coll., 1987, Loretto Heights Coll., 1988, Colo. Tech. Coll., 1988, U. Detroit, 1989; LLD (hon.), Rutgers U., 1989, Ea. Mich. U., 1990, Cambridge Coll., 1991, Schoolcraft Coll., 1992, DHL (hon.), Marysville U., 1994, Mt. St. Mary's Coll., 1996, Antioch U., 1999, Cambridge Coll., 2001, Salve Regina U., 2002, Merrimack Coll., 2001; D Pub. Svc. (hon.), U. Mass., 2002, Mass. Coll. Liberal Arts, 2003. Tchr. Woodbridge Twp. Pub. Schs., 1962-66; exec. dir. Middlesex County Econ. Opportunity Corp., New Brunswick, N.J., 1966-69; exec. asst. to pres. Rutgers U., New Brunswick, N.J., 1969-72; sr. assoc. dean Grad. Sch. Edn. Harvard U., Cambridge, Mass., 1972-82; v.p. effective sector mgmt. Ind. Sector, Washington, 1982-84; exec. dir. Colo. Commn. Higher Edn., Denver, 1984-88; chancellor and prof. pub. adminstrn. & edn. U. Mich., Dearborn, 1988-92; pres. Calif. State U., Northridge, 1992-99, Nellie Mae Found.,

Quincy, Mass., 1999—. Am. del. U.S./U.K. Dialogue About Quality Judgments in Higher Edn.; adv. bd. Mich. Consol. Gas Co., Stanford Inst. Higher Edn. Rsch., U. So. Colo. Dist. 60 Nat. Alliance, Nat. Ctr. for Rsch. to Improve Postsecondary Tchg. and Learning, 1988-90; bd. dirs. Alpha Capital Mgmt.; mem. higher edn. colloquium Am. Coun. Edn., vis. com. Divsn. Continuing Edn. in Faculty of Arts and Scis., Harvard Coll., Pew Forum on K-12 Edn. Reform in U.S., The Coll. Bd., Federated Dorchester Neighborhood House, Fed. Res. Bank of Boston; bd. dirs. Ptnrs. Healthcare Sys., Medco Health Solutions, Inc. Dir. U. Detroit Jesuit High Sch., Northridge Hosp. Med. Ctr., 1993-99, Arab Cmty. Ctr. for Econ. and Social Svcs., Union Bank, J. Paul Getty Trust, James Irvine Found., 1996-99, Internat. Found. Edn. and Self-Help, Achievement Coun., L.A.; dir., vice chair Met. Affairs Corp.; exec. bd. Detroit area coun. Boy Scouts Am.; bd. dirs. Commonwealth Fund, Henry Ford Hosp.-Fairlane Ctr., Henry Ford Health System, Met. Ctr. for High Tech., United Way Southeastern Mich.; mem. Nat. Coalition 100 Black Women, Detroit, Race Rels. Coun. Met. Detroit, Women & Founds., Greater Detroit Interfaith Round Table NCCJ, Adv. Bd. Valley Cultural Ctr., Woodland Hills; trustee assoc. Boston Coll.; trustee emeritus Cambridge Coll.; trustee emeritus, bd. dirs. Found. Ctr.; trustee Henry Ford Mus. & Greenfield Village, Sammy Davis Jr. Nat. Liver Inst. Mem. AAUW, Assn. Governing Bds. (adv. coun. of pres.'s), Edn. Commn. of the States (student minority task force), Am. Assn. Higher Edn. (chair-elect), Am. Assn. State Colls. & Univs. (com. on policies & purposes, acad. leadership fellows selection com.), Assn. Black Profls. and Adminstrs., Assn. Black Women in Higher Edn., Women Execs. State Govt., Internat. Women's Forum, Mich. Women's Forum, Women's Econ. Club Detroit, Econ. Club, Rotary. Office: Nellie Mae Edn Found 1250 Hancock St 205N Quincy MA 02169-4331 Business E-Mail: bwilson@nmefdn.org.

**WILSON, BONNIE JEAN,** lawyer, educator, investor; b. Alameda County, Calif. d. August and Violet Adeline (Lockard) Ritzenthaler; m. Allan Nicholas Wilson (dec.); children: Albert Clyde, Bruce Allan. BA, U. Calif., Berkeley, cert. in elem. tchg.; JD, Thomas Jefferson SOL, 1981. Bar: Calif.; cert. tchr., Calif. Elem. sch. tchr. Contra Costa and San Diego Counties; intern San Diego County Dist. Atty. Office, 1981; pvt. practice La Jolla, Calif., 1982—. Mem. La Jolla Presbyn. Ch., San Diego Symphony Assn., Friends of the La Jolla Libr.; adv. dir. San Diego Opera Assn.; edn. activist, 1972-76. Mem. Calif. State Bar Assn., San Diego County Bar Assn., La Jolla Newcomer's Club (bd. dirs. 1968-69), U. Calif. Berkeley Alumni Club (bd. dirs. San Diego chpt. 1961-62), Am. Assn. Ind. Investors (bd. dirs. 1991-97), Pi Lambda Theta, La Jolla Beach and Tennis Club. Presbyterian. Home: 2235 Bahia Dr La Jolla CA 92037-7007

**WILSON, BRENDA MARIE,** secondary school educator; b. New Orleans, Feb. 4, 1951; d. Chester Simmons, Jr. and Lillie Mae Simmons; m. Eli Wilson, Jr., June 19, 1971; children: Eli III, LaVar Antoine. AS, So. U., 1972; BSc, Rochester Inst. Tech., NY, 1984; MSc, LI U., 1990. Adj. tchr. L.I. (N.Y.) U., 1987—89, asst. dean, 1989—93; tchr. Bd. Edn., Bklyn., 1997—98; with accts. payable Chempiah Ministries, Queens, NY, 1998—2000; tchr. Orange County Pub. Schs., Orlando, Fla., 2001—. Mem. sch. adv. com. Orange County Pub. Schs., 2002—. V.p. Eli Wilson Ministries, Orlando, 2002—03. Named Tchr. of Yr., Orange County Pub. Schs., 2004. Mem.: Phi Gamma Nu, Alpha Kappa Alpha. Baptist. Office: Cerokee School 550 S Eola Dr Orlando FL 32801-3999 Home: 6503 Hawdsmoor Dr Orlando FL 32818

**WILSON, BRENT LAWRENCE,** lawyer, mediator; b. New Orleans, Jan. 9, 1952; s. Commodore Waddell and Mildred Louise (Quave) W.; m. Trojanell Theresa Bordenave, June 22, 1974. BA, Morehouse Coll., 1973; postgrad., U Ga., 1973-74; JD, SUNY, Buffalo, 1976. Bar: La. 1976, Ga. 1979, U.S. Dist. Ct. (no. dist.) Ga. 1979, U.S. Ct. Appeals (5th and 11th cirs.) 1979, U.S. Ct. Appeals (3d cir.) 1982, U.S. Ct. Appeals (6th cir.) 1986. Field atty. NLRB, Atlanta, 1976-80; assoc. Elarbee, Thompson & Trapnell, Atlanta, 1980-87; ptnr. Elarbee, Thompson, Sapp & Wilson, Atlanta, 1987—. Lectr. Atlanta U., 1984; adj. prof. law Emory U., Atlanta, 1984-85; mem. Study Commn. on Employment Laws, 1997-98. Contbr. articles to profl. jours. Mem. Fulton County Bd. Ethics 1991, Homelessness Task Force United Way of Metropolitan Atlanta, 2005; exec. bd. dirs. Boys and Girls Clubs of Metro Atlanta, 1999—, exec. com., 2005; bd. dirs. St. Judes Recovery Ctr., Inc., 1989—, bd. chair, 2005; mem. Christ our Hope Cath. Ch. Named one of Top 100 Ga. Super Lawyers, 2004, 2005; named to Am.'s Top Black Lawyers, Black Enterprise Mag., 2003; recipient, Ga. Legal Elite, 2003, Best Lawyers for Bus., Chambers USA, 2005. Mem.: Indsl. Rels. Rsch. Assn., ABA (mem. labor and employment law mgmt. com.), NAACP (life), Atlanta Soc. African Am. Human Resources, Soc. Human Resource Mgmt. (legis. com. co-chmn. 1987—88, 1990—91), Nat. Employment Law Coun., Nat. Assn. Securities Dealers (arbitrator), State Bar Ga. (co-chair Ga. Diversity Prog. 1998—99), Nat. Bar Assn. (mem. comml., labor and arbitration sect.), Gate City Bar Assn., Atlanta Bar Assn. (sec., treas. labor and employment law sect. 1985, vice chmn. labor and employment law sect. 1986, chmn. labor and employment law sect. 1987), 100 Blackmen of Atlanta, Lawyers Club of Atlanta, Atlanta Morehouse, Lawyers Club Atlanta, 191 Club, Atlanta Bus. League, Am. Inns. Ct., Phi Alpha Delta, Omega Psi Phi. Avocations: spectator sports, racquetball, reading, travel. Office: Elarbee Thompson Sapp & Wilson 229 Peachtree St NE Ste 800 Atlanta GA 30303-1614 Office Phone: 404-659-6700. Business E-Mail: bwilson@elarbeethompson.com.

**WILSON, BRIAN ANDREW,** computing performance consultant, educator, writer, editor; b. Denver, July 10, 1967; s. Leonard Tom Jr. and Mary Ann (Slutz) W.; m. Amy Michelle Duncan, Apr. 28, 2001. BA in Music, Cleve. Inst. Music, 1990; BA, Case Western Reserve U., 1990; M in Info. Tech., Am. Intercontinental U., 2002. Cert. Mercury Cert. Product Cons., Mercury cert. instr. Software support, SQA engr. Borland Internat., Inc., Scotts Valley, Calif., 1990-92, software cons., 1992—94; pres., founder OnRamp Internet Svcs., Inc., Atlanta, 1995—96; founder Internet Gadsden, 1995—96, Internet Tuscaloosa, 1995—96; founder, ptnr. TechSouth Consulting, Suwanee, Ga., 1996—. Vis. faculty Ga. Inst. Tech., Atlanta, 2005—. Author: Quattro Pro for Windows: Everything you Need, 1992; tech. editor: Using Quattro Pro 3, 1991, Using Quattro 4, 1992, Using Quattro Pro for Windows, 1992, Paradox for Windows: Programming, 1993, dBase IV 2.5: Quick Reference, 1993. Mem. Ga. Inst. Tech. Coll. Computing Ind. Ptnrs. Assn., Assn. Computing Machinery, Software Contractor's Guild, Berkeley Hills Country Club. Avocations: golf, sailing, tennis, sky-diving. Office: 471 Henderson Lake Dr Canton GA 30115

**WILSON, BRIAN CHARLES,** music educator; b. Birmingham, Ala., Aug. 3, 1973; s. Tenison D. and Janice Roberson Wilson; m. Christy Jane Pruitt, June 24, 2000. BS in Music Edn., U. Ala., 1997; MEd in Music Edn., Auburn U., 2004. Cert. tchr. Ala. Dept. of Edn. Dir. of bands Tarrant (Ala.) Mid. Sch., 1998—2001; asst. dir. of bands Pinson Valley H.S. and Rudd Mid. Sch., Pinson, Ala., 2001—04; dir. of bands North Jefferson Mid. Sch., Kimberly, Ala., 2004—. Interim dir. Leeds (Ala.) Cmty. Band, 1997; interim orch. dir. Shades Mountain Bapt. Ch. Celebration Orch., Vestavia Hills, Ala., 2001. Musician, worship leader Shades Mountain Bapt. Ch., Vestavia Hills, 1999—. Mem.: Music Educators Nat. Conf., Ala. Music Educators Assn., Ala. Bandmasters Assn. Southern Baptist. Avocations: golf, travel, gardening, home improvement. Office Phone: 205-379-4000. E-mail: brianwilson@jefcoed.com.

**WILSON, BRUCE BRIGHTON,** lawyer, retired transportation executive; b. Boston, Feb. 6, 1936; s. Robert Lee and Jane (Schlotterer) Wilson; m. Elizabeth Ann MacFarland, Dec. 31, 1958; children: Mabeth, Mary, Bruce, Robert, Caroline Daly. AB, Princeton U., 1958; LLB, U. Pa., 1961. Bar: Pa. 1962. Assoc. Montgomery, McCracken, Walker & Rhoads, Phila., 1962-69; atty. US Dept. Justice, Washington, 1969-79, dep. asst. atty. gen. antitrust div., 1971-76; spl. counsel Consol. Rail Corp., Phila., 1979-81, gen. counsel litigation and antitrust, 1981-82, v.p., gen. counsel, 1982-84, v.p. law, 1984-87, sr. v.p. law, 1987-97, sr. v.p. merger, 1997. Dir. Carload Express, Inc., Phila. Indsl. Devel. Corp., Wayne Sr. Ctr., The Phila. Singers; mem. mgmt. com. Concord Resources Group, 1989-91. Chmn. Radnor Twp. Cable Commn. Com., 1993—2000, mem., 2002—; Radnor Twp. Ethics

Commn., 2000—01. Fellow Salzburg Seminar in Am. Studies (Austria), 1965; fellow Felz Inst. State and Local Govt., 1967. Mem. ABA, Phila. Bar Assn., Corinthian Yacht Club, Merion Cricket Club, Beach Club Cape May. Republican. Episcopalian. Home: 224 Chamounix Rd Wayne PA 19087-3606 Personal E-mail: brucewilson224@comcast.net.

**WILSON, BRUCE KEITH,** men's health nurse; b. Alton, Ill., Aug. 18, 1946; s. Lewis Philip and Ruth Caroline Wilson; children: Sarah Ann, Andrew James. BSN, U. Tex., San Antonio, 1975, MSN, 1977; PhD, North Tex. State U., Denton, 1987. Coord. Pan Am. U., Edinburg, Tex., 1982-83; house supr. HCA Rio Grande Regional Hosp., McAllen, Tex., 1986-87; program dir. Tex. Southmost Coll., Brownsville, 1983-86; prof. U. Tex.-Pan Am., Edinburg, 1986—. Author: Logical Nursing Math., 1987; contbr. chpts. to books, numerous articles to profl. jours. With U.S. Army, 1966-68. Mem. Am. Assembly for Men in Nursing (bd. dirs. 1997-2001), Tex. League for Nursing (bd. dirs. 1993-97). Avocations: photography, computer. Home: 1702 Ivy Ln Edinburg TX 78539-5367 Office: U Tex-Pan Am Dept Nursing Edinburg TX 78539 Personal E-mail: wilson@hiline.net.

**WILSON, C. DANIEL, JR.,** library director; b. Middletown, Conn., Nov. 8, 1941; s. Clyde D. and Dorothy M. (Neal) W.; m. M. April Jackson, Apr. 1986; children: Christine, Cindy, Clyde, Ben. BA, Elmhurst Coll., 1967; MA, Dominican U., 1968; MPA, U. New Orleans, 1995. Trainee Chgo. Pub. Libr., 1967-68; instr. U. Ill., 1968-70; asst. dir. Perrot Meml. Libr., Greenwich, Conn., 1970-76; dir. Wilton Pub. Libr., Wilton, Conn., 1976-79; assoc. dir. Birmingham Pub. Libr., Birmingham, Ala., 1979-83; dir. Davenport (Iowa) Pub. Libr., 1983-85, New Orleans Pub. Libr., 1985-97, St. Louis County Libr., 1997—. With USMC, 1962-65. Mem. ALA, Internat. Assn. Met. Librs. (pres. 1998-2002), Mo. Libr. Assn., Am. Soc. Pub. Adminstrs., Rotary, Pi Gamma Mu. Episcopalian. Home: 511 W 4th St Hermann MO 65041 E-mail: dwilson@slcl.lib.mo.us.

**WILSON, CARL,** information technology executive; V.p. info. mgmt. Pillsbury Co. Inc.; sr. v.p., mgmt. info. svc., food and internat. retailing secorts Grand Met. Plc.; v.p. & CIO, info. resources Ga. Pacific Corp.; exec. v.p., dir. & chief info. officer Marriott Internat. Inc., Washington, 1997—. Bd. dir. Global Exchange Services, enamics, Inc., Software Architects, Inc.; bd. dir. (independent mem.) Rivermine, 2005—; mem. AT&T Client Adv. Coun., Microsoft Global Exec. Roundtable. Office: EVP & CIO Marriott Internat One Marriott Dr Washington DC 20058 also: EVP & CIO Marriott Internat 10400 Fernwood Rd Bethesda MD 20817*

**WILSON, CARL WELDON, JR.,** construction company executive, civil engineer; b. Norfolk, Va., Sept. 4, 1933; s. Carl Weldon and Janie Marie (Ludford) W.; m. Jean Roberts, Feb. 13, 1960; children: Lisa Ann, Carl Weldon III. BCE, Tex. A&M U., 1954. Registered profl. engr., Tex. Engr. Magnolia Petroleum Co., Morgan City, La., 1954-55, Brown & Root, Houston, 1957-60; project mgr. Claude Everett Constrn. Co., Houston, 1960-62; pres. Falcon Constrn. Co., Houston, 1962-63; pres., owner Wilson Engring. and Constrn. Co., Houston, 1963-68; v.p. Divcon, Inc., Houston, 1968-71, Wilson Industries, Inc., Houston, 1971-81; pres., prin. owner BS&B Engring. Co., Inc., Houston, 1981-86; chmn., majority shareholder Task Internat., Inc., Houston, 1986—. Served to 1st lt. U.S. Army, 1954-57. Republican. Episcopalian. Avocations: tennis, running, painting. Home: 750 Bison Dr Houston TX 77079-4401 Office: Task Internat Inc PO Box 940121 Houston TX 77094-7121 Office Phone: 281-217-4388. Personal E-mail: taskintcww@aol.com. Business E-Mail: cwilson@silverfox.com.

**WILSON, CAROL SUE MAPLES,** business administration educator; b. Scammon, Kans., Mar. 25, 1939; d. Floyd Grant and Mary Marie (Whitescarver) Maples; m. Charles Curtis Wilson, June 11, 1967; 1 child, Derek Kyle. BS in Edn., Pittsburg (Kans.) State U., 1960, MS in Edn., 1963; postgrad., U. No. Colo., 1965-66. Instr. Fredonia (Kans.) HS, 1960-63, Independence (Kans.) CC, 1963-64, Ft. Hays State U., Hays, Kans., 1964-65; asst. prof. Pittsburg State U., 1965-69; part-time instr. Crowder Coll., Neosho, Mo., 1970-71, Adult Edn. Program, St. Charles, Mo., 1971-72, Lindenwood Coll., St. Charles, 1972-73, Tulsa CC, 1974-84, Okla. State U., Tulsa, 1992—99; asst. prof. Oral Roberts U., Tulsa, 1975—, pres. Sch. Bus., 1992—95. Spkr. in field. Co-dir. vacation Bible sch. First United Meth. Ch., Neosho, 1970; sec. Kans. Bus. Edn. Assn., 1965—67; bd. dirs., sec. Kans. Credit Union, Pittsburg, 1967—69; v.p. Welcome Wagon Club, Neosho, 1970—71; pres. Newcomers Club, St. Charles, 1972—73. Named Outstanding Faculty Mem., Oral Roberts U. Sch. Bus., 2002; recipient Bus. Svc. award, 2003. Mem.: Assn. Bus. Comm., Okla. Bus. Edn. Assn. (Outstanding Collegiate Tchr. of the Yr. 1999), Mountain Plains Bus. Edn. Assn. (conv. program chair 2004, Outstanding Collegiate Tchr. of the Yr. 2002), Nat. Assn. Bus. Edn., Pi Omega Pi (nat. sec., historian 1966—70), Delta Pi Epsilon. Avocations: bowling, walking, reading, collecting. Office: Oral Roberts U Sch Bus 7777 S Lewis Ave Tulsa OK 74171-0001 Office Phone: 918-495-6563. Business E-Mail: cwilson@oru.edu.

**WILSON, CAROLYN ROSS,** retired school system administrator; b. Lake Charles, La., June 25, 1941; d. Charles Wesley and Lucille Gertrude (Payne) Ross; m. James David Wilson, Apr. 10, 1971; 1 child, Charlise. BS in Music Edn. cum laude, Xavier U., 1962; MMus in Music Edn., Cath. U., Washington, 1968; postgrad., U. D.C., 1985-86, George Washington U., 1987-88, Harvard U., 1989. Tchr. Xavier U. Jr. Sch. Music, New Orleans, 1960-61, Orleans Parish Schs., New Orleans, 1962-63, D.C. Pub. Schs., Washington, 1964-87, curriculum writer, summer 1984, 85, adminstrv. intern Ea. High Sch., 1987-88, asst. prin. Cardozo High Sch., 1988-89, asst. prin. Duke Ellington Sch. of Arts, 1989-93; prin. Duke Ellington Sch. Arts, Washington, 1993-97—; proposal reader U.S. Dept. Edn., 1998, 98, 99. Curriculum writer music dept. D.C. Pub. Schs., Washington, 1984-85, dir. All City High Sch. Chorus, 1973. Composer: A Dedication to Federal City Alumnae Chapter of Delta, Sigma Theta Sorority, Inc., 1973. Lector Immaculate Conception Ch., Washington, 1986—; named D.C. Tchr. of the Yr., 1987. Recipient Cert. of Merit-Outstanding Tchr. and Prin. award D.C. Govt., 1994; U.S. Dept. Edn. Effective Schs. grantee, Washington, 1992. Mem. ASCD, Instn. for Devel. Ednl. Activities (6th yr. fellow, session chair 1988, seminar leader 1991, 92, 93, 94), Delta Sigma Theta (Federal City Alumnae chpt.). Roman Catholic. Avocations: reading, travel, bowling, musical arranging, playing the piano.

**WILSON, CARRIE LEE STROUD,** principal; b. Bellevue, La., Dec. 14, 1948; d. Jeffrie Edward Stroud and Mary Elizabeth Jones-Stroud; m. Victor George Wilson, Apr. 19, 1972; children: Geoffrey Victor, Kimberly Georgina Elizabeth, James Anderson Stuart. B.A., U. Redlands, 1971; MA in Edn., U. Calif.-Berkeley, 2003. Preliminary Adminstrv. Intern Servicing Credential Calif. Tchg. Credentialing Com., 2002, Preliminary Adminstrv. Servicing Credential Calif. Tchr. Credentialing, 2004, Emergency Tchg. Credential Calif. Tchg. Credentialing, 2001. Counselor Upward Bound/U. Redlands, Vallejo, Calif., 1967; asst. to teen prof dir. Redlands City Recreation Dept., Redlands, Calif., 1968; recreation leader Redlands Recreation Dept., Calif., 1969—70, art instr., 1971; docent U. Calif., Berkeley, 1971—72; tchr./ drawing and composition-photography Vallejo City Unified Sch. Dist., 1998—99, asst. prin., 2002—03, vice prin., 2004—; tchr. Berkeley Unified Sch. Dist., Berkeley, Calif., 1973—74; real estate agt. Calif. Sch. Real Estate, Oakland, 1979—80; substitute tchr. Vallejo City Unified Sch. Dist., 1980—84, tchr. 1884—2000; art instr./exploratory art for young people Calif. Coll. Arts and Crafts, Oakland, 1985—86; tchr./summer sch. Vallejo City Unified Sch. Dist., 1999—2000, tchr./secondary/jr. high-middle sch., 1983—98, tchr/art-photography, 1998—99; academic dir. Jesse Bethel HS, Vallejo, 1999—2001, asst. prin. 2002—03, vice prin., 2003—; Chairperson/facilitator Springstowne Jr. HS, Vallejo, 1985—98, dept. head, 1991—98; state conf. presenter Calif. League of Mid. Schs., San Francisco, 1991—92; mentor-master-coach tchr. Springstowne Jr. HS, Vallejo, 1992—98; tchr. leader Jesse Bethel HS, Vallejo, 1998—2001, chairperson digital grant application to the state, 1999—2001, state standardized test coord., 2000—, chairperson com. for accreditation, 2001—02, state sch. intervention program for student achievement, 2001—03. Author: (poetry) What Time Is Fishin Time (pub. Famous Poets Soc., 1995), (essay) The

Importance of Nature (pub. Nat. Essay Press, 1967); exhibitions include oil & acrylic painting thesis Journey of Self Expression, ceramics, Vase (Nat. Mus. of Arts- Wash., D.C., 1968), portraits on canvas/oil paintings (Patton State Hospital-Rehabilitation Ctr. For Young Women, 1969), Personal Expressions of African American Suburb Experience (Participant in Exhibit, 1968); contbr. (Cert./Black History Month, 1969); Compilation of Perspectives of an African American Woman (Cert. of Participation/Watts Summer Festival of Arts, L.A., 1965). Mem. ednl. reform programs for student achievement Vallejo City Unified Sch. Dist., 1995—2005; min. Jehovah's Witnesses, Vallejo, 1973—2005; mem. Vallejo Artist Guild, 1990—96; contbr. Continental Omega Boys and Girls Club, Vallejo, 2001—05; advisor Willie B. Atkins Tanner Project, Vallejo, 1998—2005. Nominee Tchr. of Yr., Calif. League Mid. Sch.; recipient, Elks B.P.O.E.; grantee Ednl. Opportunity Grant, Fed. Govt., 1967—71; Behring Scholar, U. Calif. Berkeley, Prin. Leadership Inst., 2001—03. Mem.: Vallejo Schs. Mgrs. Assn., ASCD, Assn. Calif. Sch. Adminstrs. Jehovah'S Witness. Achievements include recipient Phillip Harris Memorial Scholarship; missionary Ministry for Jehovah's Witnesses. Avocations: writing, art. Home: 119 Toni Ct Vallejo CA 94591-4272 Office: Jesse Bethel HS 1800 Ascot Pkwy Vallejo CA 94591-4272 Office Phone: 707-556-5700.

**WILSON, CASSANDRA,** singer; b. Jackson, Miss., 1955; Albums include Point of View, 1986, Blue Skies, 1988, Days Aweigh, 1987, Jumpworld, 1990, She Who Weeps, 1991, Cassandra Wilson Live, 1992, Blue Light 'Till Dawn, 1993, Dance to the Drums Again, 1993, After the Beginning Again, 1994, New Moon Daughter, 1996, Travelling Miles, 1999, Belly of the Sun, 2002, Glamoured, 2003. Office: Blue Note Records 150 5th Ave New York NY 10011-4311

**WILSON, CECILIA ANN,** special education educator; b. Corning, NY, Feb. 8, 1959; d. Leroy Eugene and Helen Esther (Rodman) W. BA, Manhattanville Coll., Purchase, N.Y., 1981; M Spl. Edn., Mansfield (Pa.) U., 1986. Cert. tchr., tchr. asst., N.Y. Asst. tchr. mid. sch. Corning (N.Y.)-Painted Post Sch. Dist.; jr.-sr. high sch. tchr. spl. edn. Steuben-Allegany Bd. Coop. Ednl. Svcs., Bath, N.Y.; mid. sch. tchr. spl. edn. Penn Yan (N.Y.) Sch. Dist.; jr.-sr. high sch. resource room tchr., chmn. com. spl. edn. Avoca (N.Y.) Cen. Sch.; resource room tchr. Elmira (N.Y.) City Sch. Dist., varsity coach swimming, diving, cheerleading, softball, jr. varsity softball and volleyball. Mem. com. special edn. Resource Room, Cohocton (N.Y.) Ctrl. Sch. Dist.; coord. student affairs Empire State Speech & Hearing Clinic, Inc. Sec. N.Y. State area 15 Spl. Olympics; chairperson Relay for Life, 2004, youth chairperson. Mem. NEA. Home: 223 Pritchard Ave Corning NY 14830-1735

**WILSON, CHARLES BANKS,** artist; b. Springdale, Ark., Aug. 6, 1918; s. Charles Bertram and Bertha Juanita (Banks) W.; children: Geoffrey Banks, Carrie Vee. Student, Art Inst. Chgo., 1936—41. Mag. and book illustrator, 1943-60; head art dept. N.E. Okla. A. & M. Coll., Miami, Okla., 1947-61; painter, printmaker. Executed murals, Okla. State Capitol, 1975; represented in permanent collections Met. Mus., N.Y.C., Libr. of Congress, Washington, U.S. Capitol Bldg., D.C. Corcoran Gallery, Smithsonian Inst., Will Rogers Meml. Mus., Philbrook Art Ctr., Tulsa, Nat. Cowbow Hall of Fame, Oklahoma City, Okla. State Capitol; illustrator numerous books; appeared on (TV spl.) AETN-TV, Okla., 2006, AENBETN-TV, Ark., 2006. Bd. dirs. Thomas Gilcrease Mus. History and Art, Tulsa, 1957-61; chmn. Pub. Libr. Bd., Miami, Okla., 1954-59. Named to Okla. Hall of Fame, Okla. Historians Hall of Fame, 2001, named an Okla. Treasure, State of Okla. Arts Commn., 2001; named Charles Banks Wilson Bldg. in his honor Northeast Okla. A&M Coll.; recipient Western Heritage award Cowboy Hall of Fame, Disting. Svc. citation U. Okla., Lifetime Achievement award Ark. Art Coun., 2006; subject of books The Lithographs of Charles Banks Wilson, 1989, Search for the North American Purebloods, 2000, An Oklahoma Portrait, 1989. Mem. Internat. Inst. Arts and Letters (Geneva). Home and Office: 1611 E Mission Blvd Fayetteville AR 72703-3043 Office Phone: 479-442-9891. Personal E-mail: nag-pra-106@earthlink.net. Business E-Mail: cvwilson@mail.uark.edu.

**WILSON, CHARLES H. (CHARLES HARRISON WILSON),** retired air force officer, financial planner, human resource development professional; b. Chgo., Sept. 6, 1941; s. Charles W. and Lorraine F. (Parker) W.; m. Mona Dickerson, July 2, 1988; children: Audrey M., Angela M., Andrew M., Aaron M. BS, So. Ill. U., 1964; BA, U. Md., 1976; MBA, Webster U., 1979. Commd. 2d lt. USAF, 1964, advanced through grades to lt. col., 1986, dep. logistics agy. Washington personnel dir. Wright-Patterson AFB, Ohio, 1980-83, ret., 1984; exec. dir. exec. leadership program Dept. Def. (Pentagon), Washington, 1976-88. Mil. liaison Republic of China, 1977-80; adj. prof. Park Univ., St. Louis, 1977-80; mcpl. cons. City of Dayton, Ohio, 1980; pres. Advanced Ethonomics. Sch. bd. Alexandria Pub. Sch., Alexandria, Va., 2003—; bd. dir. Credit Union No. Va. Fellow D.C. Life Under Writers Tng. Coun.; mem. Classification and Compensation Soc., Am. Soc. Tng. and Devel., Internat. Pers. Mgmt. Assn. (human rights commn.), Omega Psi Phi, Toastmasters; elected to Alexandria City Sch. Bd. Democrat. Methodist. Achievements include invention of microwave oven carousel. Avocation: flying. Home: 6101 Edsall Rd Apt 703 Alexandria VA 22304-6004 Office Phone: 202-429-9393. E-mail: chaswill@juno.com.

**WILSON, CHARLES REGINALD,** federal judge; b. Pensacola, Fla., 1954; BS, U. Notre Dame, 1976, JD, 1979. Bar: Fla. 1979. Law clk. to Hon. Joseph W. Hatchett U.S. Ct. Appeal for 11th Cir., 1979—80; asst. county atty. Hillsborough county, Fla., 1980—81; county judge 13th Jud. Cir. of Fla., 1986—90; pvt. practice Fla., 1981—86; U.S. magistrate judge U.S. Dist. Ct. (mid. dist.) Fla., 1990—94, U.S. atty., 1994—99; U.S. cir. judge U.S. Ct. Appeals 11th Cir., Tampa, Fla., 1999—. Mem.: Ferguson-White Inn of Am. Inn of Ct., Fed. Bar Assrs., Am. Law Inst. Office: 11th Cir Ct Appeals 801 N Florida Ave Ste 14B Tampa FL 33602-3849*

**WILSON, CHARLES STEPHEN,** cardiologist, educator; b. Geneva, Nebr., June 14, 1938; s. Robert Butler and Naoma Luella (Norgren) Wilson; m. Linda Stern Walt, Aug. 21, 1960; children: Michael Scott, Amy Lynn, Cynthia Lee. BA cum laude, U. Nebr., 1960; MD, Northwestern U., 1964. Diplomate Am. Bd. Internal Medicine subsplty. bd. cardiovascular disease, Nat. Bd. Med. Examiners. Intern Fitzsimons Gen. Hosp., Denver, 1964-65; fellow in internal medicine and cardiology Mayo Grad. Sch. Medicine, Rochester, Minn., 1968-72; practice medicine specializing in cardiology Lincoln, Nebr., 1972—; attending staff Bryan Meml. Hosp., 1972—, chmn. cardiology, 1976-79; clin. prof. medicine and cardiology U. Nebr. Med. Ctr., Omaha; med. dir. Bryan LGH Med. Ctr. Ultrafast CT Scanner, Lincoln, 2001—, Sch. Allied Health, Bryan LGH Coll. of Health Scis., 2002—. Mem. Mayor's Coun. on Emergency Med. Svcs., Lincoln, 1974-78; founder, chmn. Nebr. State Hypertension Screening Program; med. dir. Lincoln Mobile Heart Team, 1977-80, Lincoln Cardiac Rehab. Program, 1978-79; co-founder, pres. Nebr. Heart Inst., 1987; co-founder Lincoln Cardiac Transplant Program, 1987. Contbr. articles to profl. jours.; editorl. cons. Chest, 1975-76; assoc. editor Nebr. Med. Jour., 1981-88. Trustee U. Nebr. Found., 1983—, chmn. Nebr. Coordinating Commn. for Postsecondary Edn., 1984-88; mem. bd. regents U. Nebr., 1991—, chmn. 1994, 2001. Served as maj., M.C., USAR, 1963-68. Gen. Motors Nat. scholar, 1956-60, Nat. Found. med. scholar, 1960-64, Mead Johnson scholar ACP, 1968-71. Fellow ACP, Am. Coll. Cardiology (bd. govs. 1990-93, pres. Nebr. affiliate 1992-93), Am. Coll. Chest Physicans, Am. Heart Assn. (dir. Nebr. affilate 1973-80, pres. 1976-77); mem. Mayo Cardiovascular Soc., Nebr. Cardiovascular Soc. (pres. 1989-90), Nebr. Coun. on Pub. Higher Edn. (steering com. 1991—), Lincoln Heart Assn. (dir. 1972-75, pres. 1974-75), AMA, Nebr. Med. Assn. Lancaster County Med. Soc., Am. Soc. Internal Medicine, Lincoln Found., U. Nebr. Chancellor's Club, Lincoln U. Club (dir. 1981-84), U. Nebr. Pres. Club, Phi Beta Kappa, Sigma Xi, Alpha Omega Alpha, Phi Delta Theta (pres. Nebr. Alpha chpt. 1959-60). Home: 7430 N Hampton Rd Lincoln NE 68506-1624 Office: Bryan LGH Ultrafast CT Scanner 1500 S 48th St Lincoln NE 68506

**WILSON, CHERYL RENEÉ,** municipal official; b. Fairfield, Ala., Feb. 06; d. Donald Edward and Amanda Anetta Wilson; children: Joe Tolbert, Ashley Tolbert. BS in Biology, Stillman Coll., 1985; MA in Profl. Devel., Dallas Bapt. U., 2006. Cert. code enforcement officer Tex. Lab. technician Dallas County Health Dept., 1990; environmental health specialist City of Dallas, 1990—94, City of Arlington, 1994—2000, field ops. mgr., 2000—. Mem.: Nat. Environ. Health Assn., Code Enforcement Assn. Tex., Tex. Environ. Health Assn. (mem. governing coun. 2001—04, pres. 2002—03, chmn. code enforcement com. 2005). Avocations: travel, bowling, exercise, reading. Office: City of Arlington 201 E Abram # 720 Arlington TX 76013

**WILSON, CHERYL YVONNE,** elementary school educator, secondary school educator; b. Dayton, Ohio, Sept. 25, 1958; d. Samuel Wesley Wilson Sr. and Hazel Oneida Wilson; m. Henry Heard Cofield Jr., July 27, 1985. Student, Ohio State U., 1976—81; AA, Miami U., 1987. Legal sec. Raymond W. O'Neal, Sr. Atty. at Law, Middletown, Ohio, 1982—83; reorder buyer Dason's Hardware Ctr., 1984—85; Writer's Digest Novel Writing Workshop Middletown City Sch. Dist., 1986—87; deputy clk. Butler County Clk. Cts., Hamilton, 1990—91; mail room clk. Butler County Printing Co., 1992—95; mail courier, security officer Johnson Controls Svcs., Inc., 1998—2000; mail room clk. Dayton Daily News Cox Ohio Publ., 2003—04. Pres., CEO Ohio Writer's Pub. Co., Middletown, 1987—1991—; dept. sec. House Reparations 40, 2005—. Columnist: Dept. Health Regulation Forty Indsl. Inst., 2004—; author: numerous poems, —. Mem. 2006-1966 U.S. Bicentennial Commn., 2003—, curator, exec. dir. 2003. Nominee 87th Spingarn medal award, NAACP, 1998, 2001, Coretta Scott King book award, 2002, Oprah Winfrey Angel Network Use Your Life award, 2003. Mem.: NAACP (life Bronze Plaque award 2002), Nat. African Am. Genealogy Rsch. Pub. Assn., Internat. African Am. Genealogy Rsch. Pub. Assn. (curator 2003—, exec. dir. 2003—), Middletown Hist. Soc. (life). Republican. Mem. Lds Ch. Avocations: writing, reading, photography. Office Phone: 513-424-7749. Personal E-mail: ohioafriamerhistmo@sbcglobal.net.

**WILSON, CHRISTOPHER J.,** lawyer; b. Pensacola, Fla., May 25, 1965; BA cum laude, Thomas More Coll., 1988; JD cum laude, U. Notre Dame, 1991. Bar: Ohio 1991. Ptnr. Frost Brown Todd LLP; assoc. gen. counsel, asst. corp. sec. Cincinnati Bell, Inc. (formerly Broadwing, Inc.), Cincinnati, Ohio, 1999—2003, v.p., gen. counsel, 2003—. Mem. adv. coun. Nat. Assn. Minority and Women Owned Law Firms; mem. steering com. Gr. Cincinnati Minority Counsel Program. Mem.: Ohio State Bar Assn., Cincinnati Bar Assn. Office: Cincinnati Bell Inc 201 E Fourth St Cincinnati OH 45202 Office Phone: 513-397-6351. Office Fax: 513-721-7358. E-mail: christopher.wilson@cinbell.com.

**WILSON, CLARK R.,** geophysicist, educator; BA with high honors in Physics, U. Calif. San Diego Revelle Coll., 1970; MS in Earth Sci., U. Calif. San Diego Scripps Instn. Oceanography, 1973, PhD in Earth Sci., 1975. Asst. prof. to assoc. prof. U. Tex., Austin, 1976—89, prof., 1989—, Wallace Pratt prof. geophysics 1992—. Chmn. dept. geol. scis. U. Tex., Austin, 1990—94, 2004—; geodynamics and geopotential fields prog. specialist NASA, Washington, 1996—99; head Geophys. Fluids Ctr. Hydrology, 1999—2004; mem. directing bd. Internat. Earth Rotation Svc., 2000—. Contbr. articles to sci. jours.; assoc. editor geodesy: Jour. Geophys. Rsch., 1993—99. Office: Geol Scis Dept U Tex 1 Univ Sta C1100 Austin TX 78712-0254 E-mail: crwilson@mail.utexas.edu.*

**WILSON, CLAUDE RAYMOND, JR.,** lawyer; b. Dallas, Feb. 22, 1933; s. Claude Raymond and Lottie (Watts) W.; m. Emilynn Wilson; children: Deidra Wilson Graves, Melissa Woodard Utley, Michele Woodard Dunn. BBA, So. Meth. U., 1954, JD, 1956. Bar: Tex. 1956; CPA, Calif., Tex. Assoc. firm Cervin & Melton, Dallas, 1956-58; atty. Tex. & Pacific R.R. Co., Dallas, 1958-60; atty. office regional counsel IRS, San Francisco, 1960-63, sr. trial atty. office chief counsel Washington, 1963-65; ptnr. Wilson & White, Dallas, 1965-98, Vial, Hamilton, Koch & Knox LLP, Dallas, 1998—. Chmn., Dallas dist. dir. IRS Adv. Commn., 1990-91. Chmn. Dallas Hist. Soc., 2000-01; mem. fin com Dallas Arboretum and Bot. Gardens, 2003—, City of University Park, 2004—; bd. govrs., mem. fin. com., mem. ethics com. Dallas Symphony Orch., 2004—. Mem.: AICPA (coun. 1989—93, tax exec. com. 1998—2001), ABA, Tex. Soc. CPAs (pres. 1989—90, pres. Dallas chpt. 1983—84), Dallas Bar Assn. (pres. sect. taxation 1969—70), State Bar Tex., Greater Dallas C. of C. (chmn. appropriations and tax com. 1990—91), Dallas Petroleum Club, Masons, Delta Theta Phi., Delta Sigma Phi. Episcopalian. Office: Vial Hamilton Koch & Knox 1700 Pacific Ave Ste 2800 Dallas TX 75201-7388 Office Phone: 214-712-4418. E-mail: cwilson@vialaw.com.

**WILSON, CLEO FRANCINE,** foundation administrator; b. Chgo., May 7, 1943; d. Cleo Antonio Chancey and Frances (Page) Watson; divorced; children: SuLyn Silbar. BA in English with distinction, U. Ill., 1976. Supr. Playboy Enterprises, Inc., Chgo., 1980-82; grants mgr. Playboy Found., Chgo., 1982-84, exec. dir., 1984—, v.p. pub. affairs, 2001—. Pres. Intuit: The Ctr. for Intuitive and Outsider Art, 1996—, 2000—. Pres. AIDS Found. Chgo., 1990-93; v.p. Donors Forum Chgo., 1986-88; sec. Chgo. Women in Philanthropy, 1986-87; advisor Chgo. Dept. Cultural Affairs, 1988-90. Recipient Kizzy Image award Black Woman Hall of Fame, 1984;, Friend for Life award Howard Brown Health Ctr, 1991, Handy L. Lindsey award for inclusiveness in philanthropy, 2004; honored by AIDS Found, Chgo, 1999; named one of Chgo's. Up and Coming by Dollars & Sense mag., 1985, Phenomenal Woman award An Expo for Today's Black Woman, 1997. Home: 6571 N Glenwood Ave Chicago IL 60626-5121 Office: Playboy Enterprises Inc 680 N Lake Shore Dr Fl 15 Chicago IL 60611-4455

**WILSON, COLIN HENRY,** writer; b. Leicester, Eng., June 26, 1931; s. Arthur and Anetta Wilson; m. Joy Stewart; children: Sally, Damon, Rowan; 1 child from previous marriage, Roderick. Writer-in-residence Hollins (Va.) Coll., 1966—67; vis. prof. U. Wash., Seattle, 1967, Rutgers U., New Brunswick, NJ, 1974. Author: The Outsider, 1956, The Glass Cage, 1967, (novels) The Occult, 1971, The Black Room, 1971, The Space Vampires, 1975, Mysteries, 1978, others, (books) Access to Inner World, 1982, A Criminal History of Mankind, 1983, The Essential Colin Wilson, 1984, The Personality Surgeon, 1986, Spider World, 1987, The Misfits, 1988, Beyond the Occult, 1988, Written in Blood, 1989, Atlantis & The Neanderthals, 2006; author: (with Donald Seaman) Modern Encyclopedia of Murder, 1983, The Serial Killers, 1989; author: (with Damon Wilson) Encyclopedia of Unsolved Mysteries, 1987, Crimes of Passion, 2006; author: others, (plays) Mozart's Journey to Prague, 1991, Spider World: The Magician, 1992, The Strange Life of P. D. Ouspensky, 1993, From Atlantis to The Sphinx, 1996, Atlas of Holy Places and Sacred Sites, 1996, Alien Dawn, 1998, The Books in My Life, 1998, The Devil's Party, 2000, Spider World: The Magician, 2002, Spider World: Shadowland, 2003; author: (with Damon Wilson) Unsolved Mysteries Past and Present, 1993; author: (with Rand Fle'math) Atlantis Blueprint, 2000; author: (autobiography) Dreaming to Some Purpose, 2004. Mem. PTO. Mem.: Savage. E-mail: cdin@chwilson.demon.co.uk.

**WILSON, D. EDWARD, JR.,** lawyer; b. New Orleans, Dec. 23, 1951; s. Donald Edward and Nellie (Courtney) W.; m. Lynn Whittlesey, Sept. 10, 1981; children: Robert Donald, Thomas Courtney, John Whittlesey. BA, U. Va., 1973; JD, Georgetown U., 1976. Bar: D.C. Law clk. to Judge R.L. Kunzig U.S. Ct. Appeals (fed. cir.), Washington, 1976-77; assoc. Morgan, Lewis & Bockius, Washington, 1977-81; assoc. counsel to the pres. The White House, Washington, 1981-84, gen. counsel Office of Adminstrn., 1984-85; prin. dep. asst. sec. for mgmt. Dept. of the Treasury, Washington, 1985-86, acting gen. counsel, 1986-88; pvt. practice, 1988—; ptnr., Banking & Fin. Svc., Internat. Bus. practices Venable LLP, Washington, 2003—. Author monographs. Chmn Goodwin House, Inc., 1996-2001, Goodwin House Found., 2005-06; mem. vestry St. Peter's Episcopal Ch., Arlington, Va., 1988-91. Recipient Disting. Svc. award Sec. Dept. Treasury, 1988, Gen. Counsel's award, 1988, Chief Counsel's award IRS, 1988. Mem. ABA, D.C. Bar, La. State Bar Assn., So. Yacht Club (New Orleans), Met. Club

(Washington). Republican. Episcopalian. Office: Venable LLP 575 7th St NW Washington DC 20004 Office Phone: 202-344-4000. Office Fax: 202-344-8300. Business E-Mail: dewilson@venable.com.

**WILSON, DANIEL H.,** robotics engineer, writer; b. Tulsa, 1978; MS in Robotics, Data Mining, Carnegie Mellon Univ., PhD in Robotics, 2005. Rsch. intern Intel Rsch. Seattle, Microsoft Rsch., Palo Alto Rsch. Ctr. Author: How To Survive a Robot Uprising, 2005 (Wired Mag. Rave award, 2006). Achievements include being co-holder of 4 patents. Mailing: Bloomsbury USA Author Mail Ste 300 175 Fifth Ave New York NY 10010 Home: Portland OR*

**WILSON, DANIEL RICHARD,** anthropologist, physician; b. Fort Dodge, Iowa, Feb. 22, 1956; m. Sandra Lea Davis; 1 child, Victoria Elizabeth. BA Anthropology, Yale U., 1979; MD, U. Iowa, 1983; PhD Anthropology, Cambridge U., 1995; diploma mental health mgmt., Case Western Res. U., 1996. Cert. FABPN, 1989. Resident in psychiatry Harvard Med. Sch., 1987; neuropsychiatrist McLean Hosp. - Harvard Med. Sch., Belmont, Mass., 1987—92; assoc. prof. psychiatry U. Cin., 1993—98; med. dir. ODMH - Lewis Ctr., 1993—2000, ODMH - Statewide ISS, 1998—2000; prof. psychiatry U. Cin., 1998—2000; prof., chmn. psychiatry, prof. anthropology Creighton U., Omaha, 2000—. Named Nat. Tng. Program of Yr., Nat. Alliance for Mentally Ill, 1995; recipient Huston award, U. Iowa Coll. Medicine, 1983, Nat. Exemplar Training Program award, Am. Psychiat. Assn., 1994; vis. fellow, Clare Hall, Cambridge U., 1992—93, Slyster scholar, AMA, 1982—83, Burroughs-Wellcome fellow, Am. Psychiat. Assn., 1985—87, Overseas fellow, Royal Anthropol. Inst., 1997—, Rotary fellow, Cambridge U., England, 1992—93. Fellow: Am. Bd. Forensic Medicine (life); mem.: World Psychiat. Assn. (chair Psychotherapy 2004—), Internat. Soc. Police Surgeons (life), Alpha Omega Alpha (life). Office: Creighton U Sch Med 3528 Dodge St Omaha NE 68131 Office Phone: 402-345-8828.

**WILSON, DARREN DUANE,** social studies educator, basketball coach; b. Hemett, Calif., Feb. 23, 1971; s. Wayne and Mary Margarett Wilson; m. Diane Lynn Wismann, June 29, 1996; children: Jake Andrew, Emily Marie. MEd, Stephen F. Austin State U., Nacogdoches, Tex., 1995, BS in Kinesiology, 1993. Cert. tchr. social studies Tex. Edn. Agy., tchr. phys. edn. Tex. Edn. Agy. Tchr. Silverlake Elem. Grapevine Colleyville Ind. Sch. Dist., Grapevine, Tex., 1995—97, tchr., coach Grapevine H.S., 1997—. Geography team leader Grapevine H.S. Grapevine Colleyville Ind. Sch. Dist., Grapevine, 1997—, head girls basketball coach Grapevine H.S., 1999—2005. Named N.E. Tarrant County Girls Basketball Coach of the Yr., Ft. Worth Star Telegram, 2001. Mem.: United Educators Assn., Tex. Girls Coaches Assn., Tex. Assn. of Basketball Coaches. Republican. Roman Catholic. Avocations: military history, gardening, cooking, pinball collector, reading. Office: Grapevine H S 3223 Mustang Dr Grapevine TX 76051 Office Phone: 817-251-5210. Office Fax: 817-481-5957. E-mail: darren.wilson@gcisd.net.

**WILSON, DAVE,** editor; Mng. editor Broward bur. Miami Herald, mng. news editor, 2006—. Office: Miami Herald 1 Herald Plz Miami FL 33132-1693 Office Phone: 954-538-7130. Office Fax: 305-376-5287. E-mail: dwilson@miamiherald.com.*

**WILSON, DAVID JAMES,** chemistry researcher, educator; b. Ames, Iowa, June 25, 1930; s. James Calmar and Alice Winona (Olmsted) W.; m. Martha Carolyn Mayers, Sept. 6, 1952; children: John Wesley, Charles Steven, William David, Andrew Lyman, Joyce Ballin. BS in Chemistry, Stanford U., 1952; postgrad., 1952-53, 55-57; PhD, Calif. Inst. Tech., 1958. Mem. faculty U. Rochester, NY, 1957-69, assoc. prof. NY, 1963-67, prof. phys. chemistry NY, 1967-69; prof. Vanderbilt U., Nashville, 1969-95, prof. chemistry and environ. engring., 1977-95, prof. emeritus, 1995—; Alexander Heard disting. service prof., 1983-84; sr. rsch. assoc. Eckenfelder/Brown and Caldwell, Nashville, 1988-95; sr. rsch. fellow, 1995—. Vis. sr. lectr. chemistry U. Ife, Nigeria, 1964-65; vis. prof. U. Málaga, Spain, 1993-94; mem. Rochester Com. for Sci. Info., 1960-69, v.p., 1966-69; chmn. Nashville Com. for Sci. Info., 1971-74. Author: (book) Foam Flotation: Theory and Applications, Hazardous Waste Site Soil Remediation, Modeling of In Situ Techniques for Treatment of Contaminated Soils. Pres. Tenn. Environ. Coun., 1985-87. Sp-3 U.S. Army, 1953—55, Army Chem. Ctr., Md. Recipient award Monroe County Conservation Coun., 1967, Tenn. Conservation League, 1971; Alfred P. Sloan Found. fellow, 1964-66. Mem. AAAS, Am. Chem. Soc., Tenn. Acad. Sci., Sigma Xi, Phi Beta Kappa. Avocations: ornithology, music, travel, hiking. Home: 11544 Quirk Rd Belleville MI 48111 Office Phone: 734-699-7623. Personal E-mail: djw1ls0n@sbcglobal.net.

**WILSON, DEAN,** professional golfer; b. Kaneohe, Hawaii, Dec. 17, 1969; Student, Brigham Young U. Profl. golfer, 1992—; mem. PGA Tour, 2003—. Named Rookie of Yr., Japan PGA, 2000. Achievements include winning Japan Golf Tour events including the Aiful Cup, 2000, Japan PGA Championship, 2001, Ube Kosan Open, 2001, Japan PGA Matchplay Championship, 2001, Tsuruya Open, 2002, Gateway To The Open Mizuno Open, 2002; winner, the International on the PGA Tour, 2006. Office: PGA Tour 112 PGA Tour Blvd Ponte Vedra Beach FL 32082*

**WILSON, DEBORA J.,** broadcast executive; m. Larry Wilson; 1 stepchild, Kevin; 1 child, Christine. BS in Fin. and Bus. Adminstrn., George Mason U. With Bell Atlantic Network Svcs.; joined The Weather Channel, 1994, sr. v.p. new bus. devel., exec. v.p., gen. mgr. online svcs.; pres., CEO The Weather Channel Interactive, 1999—2003; COO The Weather Channel Network and The Weather Channel Interactive, 2003—04; pres. The Weather Channel Cos., 2004—. Recipient Tami Award, 2000. Mem.: Interactive Adv. Bureau, Cable & Telecom. Assoc., National Cable Television Assoc., bd. of dir. Lightbridge, Inc. Office: 300 Interstate North Pkwy SE Atlanta GA 30339-2403

**WILSON, DEBORRAH,** physical education educator; b. Tachikowa, Japan, Aug. 18, 1950; BS in Phys. Edn. and Health, U. Del., 1972; MEd, Wilmington Coll., 2000. Elem. phys. edn. tchr. Downes Elem. Sch.; instr. of programs. teen dir. YWCA, 1972—78; phys. edn. specialist Christina Sch. Dist., 1978—. Recipient Outstanding Alumni award U. Del., 1993, Disting. Svc. award Maclary PTA, 1993, Del. Congress Parents and Tchrs. Inc.; named Ea. Region Elem. Sch. Phys. Edn. Tchr. of Yr., Nat. Assn. Sport and Phys. Edn., 1993, Elem. Phys. Edn. Tchr. of Yr., Del. Assn. of Yr., Elem. Sch., 2000. Home: 731 Art Ln Newark DE 19713-1208 Office Phone: 302-454-2133. E-mail: dekeencat@aol.com.

**WILSON, DENA SUZETTE,** elementary school educator; b. Lubbock, Tex., Aug. 22, 1964; d. James Leroy and Rena Glyndell Louthan; m. Robert Hugh Wilson Jr., Dec. 16, 1989. BA in Family and Consumer Sci., U. Houston, 1986; M in Elem. Edn., Berry Coll., M. Berry, Ga., 2000. Cert. vocat. home econs. tchr. Tex., 1987, kindergarten tchr. Tex., 1988, self-contained elem. tchr. Tex., 2002, tchr. (pre-kindergarten through eighth grades) Ga., Tex., tchr. (grades sixth through twelfth) Ga., Tex. Tchr. pre-kindergarten Spring Ind. Sch. Dist., Tex., 1986—90; store mgr. Suzette's Cards & Gifts, 1990—97; tchr. grades 1 and 2 Bartow County Schs., Cartersville, Ga., 1997—2002; tchr. grade 3 Llano Ind. Sch. Dist., Tex., 2002—, Renaissance reading leadership team mem., 2006—. Site based leadership team Llano Ind. Sch. Dist., Tex., 2004—, team leader, 2004—. Sec. Child Welfare Bd., Llano, 2004—, Llano Corp. Children in Crisis, 2005—; dir. Awana 1st Bapt., 2003—, dir. vacation bible sch., 2006. Mem.: Internat. Reading Assn., Delta Kappa Gamma. Avocations: reading, antiques, cooking. Home: 407 W Sandstone Llano TX 78643 Office: Llano Elem Sch 1600 Oatman St Llano TX 78643 Mailing: PO Box 56 Llano TX 78643

**WILSON, DENISE See EARLY, TERI**

**WILSON, DON MATTHEW, III,** corporate banking executive; b. Ravenna, Ohio, Jan. 24, 1948; s. Don Matthew and Helen Jane (Strimple) W.; m. Lynn Suzanne Byron, Oct. 13, 1984. AB cum laude, Harvard U., 1970; MBA,

Dartmouth Coll., Hanover, N.H., 1973. Mng. dir. Chem. Bank, N.Y.C., 1973—. Republican. Congregationalist Clubs: Harvard (N.Y.C.); Rockaway Hunting (L.I.) Office: Chem Bank 277 Park Ave New York NY 10172-0003

**WILSON, DONALD EDWARD,** internist, educator, dean; b. Worcester, Mass., Aug. 28, 1936; s. Rivers Rivo and Licine (Bradshaw) Wilson; m. Patricia C. Littell, Aug. 27, 1977; children: Jeffrey D.E., Sean D., Monique, Sheila L. AB, Harvard U., 1958; MD, Tufts U., 1962. Diplomate Am. Bd. Internal Medicine. Intern St. Elizabeth Hosp., Boston, 1962—63; resident in medicine, research fellow in gastroenterology VA Hosp. and Lemuel Shattuck Hosp., Boston, 1963—66; assoc. chief gastroenterology Bklyn. Hosp., 1968—71; instr. medicine SUNY Downstate Med. Center, Bklyn., 1968—71; asst. prof. medicine U. Ill., Chgo., 1971—73, asso. prof., 1973—75, prof., 1975—80, acting head dept. medicine, 1976—77; dir. divsn. gastroenterology U. Ill. Hosp., Chgo., 1971—78, chief of gastroenterology, 1973—80; physician-in-chief, 1976—77; prof., chmn. dept. medicine SUNY Downstate Med. Center, Bklyn., 1980—91; physician-in-chief State U. and Kings County Hosp., 1980—91; dean U. Md. Sch. Medicine, Balt., 1991—, v.p. of med. affairs, 1999—. Vis. prof. medicine U. London, Kings Coll. Med. Sch., 1977—78; mem. gastrointestinal drugs adv. bd. FDA, 1985—87, chmn., 1986—87; mem. Part II test com. Nat. Bd. Med. Examiners, 1985—88; mem. nat. digestive adv. bd. NIH, 1985—87, chmn., 1986—87, mem. gen. clin. rsch. ctrs. com., 1987—; mem. nat. adv. com. Agy. for Health Care Policy and Rsch., Dept. HHS, 1991—94, chmn., 1992—94; mem. residency rev. com. for internal medicine Acque, 1993—; mem. nat. com. fgn. med. edn. and accreditation U.S. Dept. Edn., 1994—; mem. nat. adv. rsch. resources com. NIH, 1997—2000; bd. dirs. Provident Bank Corp., 2002—. Contbr. articles to med. jours.; mem. editl. bd. Tufts Med. Alumni Bulletin, 1993—2002. Bd. vis. Harvard Sch. Pub. Health, 1992—94; bd. overseers Tufts U. Med. Sch., 2002—; bd. dirs. Balt. Symphony Orch., 1997—2004, Kernan Hosp., Balt., 1991—98, bd. dirs. Endowment Fund, 1996—; bd. dirs. Alliance to End Childhood Poisoning, 1992—95, The Baer Sch., Balt., 1992—, Mercy Med. Ctr., Balt., 1991—, U. Md. Med. Sys., 1991—. Capt. M.C. USAF, 1966—68. Recipient Rsch. award, HEW, 1971, 1974, John A. Hartford Found., Inc., 1972—79, Distilled Spirits Coun. U.S., 1972—74, VA, 1974. Master: ACP; mem.: AAAS, NAS, Inst. of Medicine, Assn. Profs. Medicine (sec.-treas. 1990—91), Am. Clin. and Climatol. Assn., Nat. Med. Assn., Assn. for Acad. Minority Physicians (sec./treas. 1986—), Assn. Am. Physicians, Chgo. Soc. Gastrointestinal Endoscopy (pres. 1979—80), N.Y. Soc. Gastroenterology, N.Y. Acad. Medicine, N.Y. Acad. Scis., Soc. Exptl. Biology and Medicine, Midwest Gut Club, Digestive Disease Found., Chgo. Soc. Gastroenterology (pres. 1978—79), Ctrl. Rsch. Club, Ctrl. Soc. Clin. Rsch., Accreditation Coun. Grad. Med. Edn. (rev. com. internal medicine), Am. Assn. Study Liver Disease, Am. Fedn. Clin. Rsch., Am. Gastroent. Assn., Md. Med Comprehensive Ins. Trust (mem. 1998—, chmn. 1998—2000, 2002—04), The Ctr. Club (Balt.), Med. Club Bklyn., 14 West Hamilton St. Club (Balt.), Harvard Club (Chgo., N.Y.C.), Sigma Pi Phi (grand boule). Office: U Md Sch Medicine 655 W Baltimore St Rm 14029 BRB Baltimore MD 21201-1509 Office Phone: 410-706-7410. Office Fax: 410-706-0235.*

**WILSON, DONALD GREY,** management consultant; b. Bridgeport, Conn., Sept. 20, 1917; s. William Gray and Jeannetta McAvoy (Kerr) W.; m. Elizabeth Jean Lanning, Apr. 24, 1943 (div. Mar. 1971, dec. Mar. 2002); children: Kirk Lanning, Craig Gardner, William Grey. BSEE, Rensselaer Poly. Inst., 1938; SM, Harvard U., 1939, MES, 1947, PhD, 1948. Mgr. automatic fire alarm divsn. Sealand Corp., Bridgeport, Conn., 1939-40; instr. elec. engring. Rensselaer Poly. Inst., 1940-42; staff mem. Radiation Lab. MIT, 1942-45; prof. elec. engring. U. Kan., Lawrence, 1947-55, chmn. dept., 1948-55; dir. Phila. Brass & Bronze, 1962-64, Mallory-Xerox Corp., 1964-65. Cons. U.S. Naval Ordance Test Sta., China Lake, Calif., 1953-54; assoc. dir. rsch. dept. Stromberg-Carlson Co., San Diego, 1955-59, gen. mgr., 1959, asst. v.p., 1959-60; v.p. rsch. P.R. Mallory & Co., Indpls., 1960, v.p. rsch. and engring., 1961-71, v.p. rsch., engring. and environ. affairs, 1971-75; alt. dir. Mallory Metal. Products, Inc., 1967; pres. Contemporary Custom Cabinets, San Diego, 1975-76; v.p. Continental Resources and Minerals Corp., Dayton, Ohio, 1978-79; sr. v.p. Tanzi Mergers/Acquisitions, San Diego, 1983-86; mgmt. cons., 1976—; sr. lectr. U. Rochester, 1956-57; lectr. dept. elec. engring. San Diego State U., 1981-92, asst. dean coll. engring., 1987, prof. emeritus, 1992—; mng. dir., exec. bd. Nat. Bur. Cert. Cons., 1988-94, sr. adv. counsel, 1994-2001. Contbr. articles to profl. jours. Bd. dirs. Speech and Hearing Clinic, Indpls., 1960-66, Washington Twp. Sch. Dist., 1964-68, pres., 1966-67. Recipient Outstanding Acad. Advisor award San Diego State U., 1992. Fellow AAAS; mem. IEEE (sr. life, exec. com. San Diego sect. 1986-2003, 2004—, chmn. S.W. area region 6 1999-2000, sec. region 6 2001-02, ethics and mem. conduct com. 2002-03, R&D policy com. 2000—, Third Millennium medal, Internat. IEEE Outstanding Br. Counselor award 1992), Affiliation Profl. Cons. Orgns. (chmn. bd. govs. 1991-93 San Diego Engring. Coun. Outstanding Svc. award 2000), Intertel, Sigma Xi, Sigma Phi Epsilon, Tau Beta Pi, Eta Kappa Nu. Home: 1950 Silverleaf Cir 310 Carlsbad CA 92009 Personal E-mail: don.wilson@ieee.org

**WILSON, DONALD HURST, III,** mediator, biopharmaceutical industry executive; b. Balt., Mar. 1, 1946; s. Donald H. and Winifred W.; m. Catharine A. MacKinnon, June 21, 1968 (div. 1972); m. Beverly Lee Wright, Oct. 3, 1975 (div. 1998); m. Constance Fisher Neely, Sept. 23, 2000; children: Beverly Callaway, Sarah Elizabeth. AB, Yale U., 1968; MBA, JD, Harvard U., 1976. Bar: Mass. 1977, N.C. 2003; cert. Superior Ct. mediator N.C. Dispute Resolution Commn. Cons. Boston Cons. Group, 1976-78; dir. mktg. I/C divsn. Black & Decker, Hampstead, Md., 1978-83; pres. MWI Tng. Svcs., Inc., Hunt Valley, 1983—96; v.p. Innoversity Edn. Ctrs., Global Knowledge Network, Inc., Md., 1996—97; pres. and COO Endacea, Inc. (formerly Link Tech., Inc.), Raleigh, 1997—98, pres. and CEO, 1998—2000, v.p. and COO, 2001—02, v.p., gen. counsel, 2003, pres., CEO and gen. counsel, 2004—. Bd. dirs. Endacea, Inc. (formerly Link Tech., Inc.) Raleigh. Mem. vestry St. John's Episcopal Ch., 1993-96, lay eucharistic min., 1995-98; dir. The Bishop Claggett Ctr., 1995-97. Mem.: Info. Tech. Tng. Assn. (founder and dir. 1992—95), Assn. Microcomputer Distbrs. (founder and dir. 1988—90), Archaeol. Soc. Md. (trustee 1994—98). Republican. Avocations: archaeology, golf. Home: 1112 Baslow Brook Ct Raleigh NC 27614-8866

**WILSON, DONALD WALLIN,** academic administrator, communications educator; b. Poona, India, Jan. 9, 1938; s. Nathaniel Carter and Hannah Myrtle Wilson; children: Carrie, Jennifer, Gregory, Andrew. BA, So. Missionary Coll., 1959; MA, Andrews U., 1961; PhD, Mich. State U., 1966. Dean applied arts and tech. Ont. (Can.) Colls., North Bay, 1968-73; acad. dean Olivet Coll., 1973-76; pres. Castleton State Coll., 1976-79, Southampton Coll., 1979-83, prof. communications and history, 1973-83; pres., prof. Pittsburg State U. (Kans.), 1983-95; pres. Kilang Nusantara Pacific, 1995—; exec. v.p. Shepherd of the Hills Entertainment Group, Branson, Mo., 1997—. Author: The Untapped Source of Power in the Church, 1961, Long Range Planning, 1979, The Long Road From Turmoil to Self Sufficiency, 1989, The Next Twenty-Five Years: Indonesias Journey Into The Future, 1992, The Indispensable Man: Sudomo, 1992. Mem. Kans. Adv. Coun. of C.C.'s; bd. dirs. Internat. Thailand; pres. Internat. Univ. Found. Named Adminstr. of Achievement Andrews U., 1981; recipient Outstanding Alumni award Mich. State U., 1984. Mem. Speech Communication Assn., Assn. Asian Studies, Internat. Univ. Found. Republican. Methodist. Office: Kilang Nusantara Pacific Office of Pres Frontenac KS 66763 Address: 503 Ohio St Pittsburg KS 66762-6429 E-mail: wdonaldwilson@aol.com

**WILSON, DONNA ELIZABETH,** music educator; b. Springfield, Ohio, Oct. 30, 1917; d. Howard Earl Sise and Gertrude Wright (Gordon) Sise McCallister; m. William Richard Wilson, June 7, 1944 (dec. 1964); children: Judith Wilson Hubbard, Gordon Richard (dec.), Rodger Mark (dec.) Cert. in tchr. tng., Wittenberg Coll., 1937; BS in Edn., West Tex. State U., 1957, MEd, 1967. Elem. tchr. Springfield (Ohio) Pub. Schs., 1937-41; elem. tchr. music Norman (Okla.) Pub. Schs., 1956-58, Canyon (Tex.) Ind. Schs., 1958-82; tchr. Payap U., Chiang Mai, Thailand, 1982-86; ret., 1986. Choir dir. Presbyn. Ch., Canyon, 1949-77, ordained elder, 1980-82, mem. mission interpretation task

group, Lubbock, Tex., 1989-91, mission itineration coord., 1989-91 Recipient Tex. Panhandle Disting. Women's Svc. award Women's Forum, 1987. Mem. AAUW (leadership growth team), Tex. Music Educators Assn. (chmn. state elem. div. 1977-79).

**WILSON, DORIS H.,** volunteer; b. Akron, Ohio, Jan. 26, 1921; d. Charles Peter and Emma Clara (Howald) Huff; m. Angus Francis Wilson, June 14, 1952; children: Ann Wilson Lambertus, Lea Wilson MacInnis. BS, U. Akron, 1945; postgrad., Framingham State Coll., 1965, Salem State Coll., 1968. Adminstrv. asst. divsn. comml. engr. Ohio Bell Tel. Co., Akron, 1941-52; adminstr. Framingham Ctr. Kindergarten and Nursery Sch., 1965-68. Author: (book) A History of Great Neck, Ipswich, 1984, 1996. Vol. nurse's aide ARC, Akron, 1940; active Gov.'s Coun. Civilian Def., Boston, 1960—66; cofounder, charter mem. Hospice at Home, Wayland, Weston, Natick, Sudbury, Mass., 1978; chmn. W. Suburban Area Boston Symphony Orch., 1978—81; docent Gt. Ho. at Castle Hill, Ipswich, Mass., 1984—2005, Whipple Ho., Ipswich, 1985—2002; treas. Nuc. Freeze Coun., Ipswich, 1986—87; charter mem., bd. dirs. Aplastic Anemia Found. Am. New Eng. region, Brookline, Mass., 1987—92; vol. office asst. Habitat for Humanity, St. Petersburg, Fla., 1988; mem. Ipswich Women's Club, 1981—2006. Recipient Election Poll Officer citation, Gov. of Mass., 1980, 1st pl. Ann. Short Story Contest, Gen. Fedn. Women's Club, 2002. Mem.: AAUW (Mass. state parliamentarian 1966—76, charter, pres. Framingham-Wellesley br., North Shore br., grantee 1974), Ipswich Citizens Advocating Renewable Energy, Friends Glen Magna (Danvers, Mass. dir. 1991—93), Ipswich Hist. Soc., Boston Symphony Assn. Vols., Peace Action, Ipswich Bay Yacht Club (dir. 1981—82), Wayland Women's Club (hon.; pres.). Democrat. Roman Catholic. Home: 8 Bowdoin Rd Ipswich MA 01938-2807

**WILSON, DOUGLAS FREDERICK,** professional sports team executive, retired professional hockey player; b. Ottawa, Ont., Can., July 5, 1957; s. Douglas and Verna Wilson; m. Katherine Ann Kivisto, July 11, 1981; children: Lacey Anne. Defenseman Chgo. Blackhawks, 1977—91, San Jose Sharks, 1991—93, dir. pro devel., 1997—2003, gen. mgr., 2003—; coord. player rels. and bus. devel. NHL Players Assn., 1993—97. Account exec. Coca-Cola, Chgo. Recipient James Norris Meml. Trophy for best NHL defenseman, 1981-82. Avocations: golf, travel. Office: San Jose Sharks 525 W Santa Clara St San Jose CA 95113*

**WILSON, DOUGLAS LEONARD,** minister, educator; b. Lumberton, NC, June 8, 1964; s. James Martin and Ruby Wilson; m. Julia Kaye Roberts, May 19, 1983; children: Martin, Samuel. BS in Math. magna cum laude, N.C. State U., 1986; MRE, Foundations Bible Coll., Dunn, N.C., 1990; DRE, Founds. Bible Coll., 1993. Ordained to ministry 1992. Tchr. Raleigh Christian Acad., NC, 1986-90; bookkeeper First Free Will Bapt. Ch., Raleigh, 1987-90; acct. Oscar N. Harris and Assocs., P.A., Dunn, 1990-93; dean Christian Edn. Founds. Bible Coll., Dunn, 1993—. Tchr. Founds. Christian Acad., Dunn, 1993—, prin., 1999—. Vol. Prisoners Hope Ministry, Lillington, NC, 1996—. Recipient Faculty Forum award, Founds. Bible Coll., 1995. Office: PO Box 1166 Dunn NC 28335-1166

**WILSON, E. B.,** manufacturing executive, consultant, writer; b. Albany, NY, May 13, 1931; s. Harold Edgar and Marie Elizabeth (Brush) W.; m. Mary Beth Weilbacher, Aug. 2, 1956. BA, St. Lawrence U., 1953, PhD (hon.), 2002; MBA, Harvard U., 1955. Mkt. dir. Richardson-Vicks, Inc., NYC, Paris, Manila, 1957-64; CEO Japan Kimberly-Clark Corp., Neenah, Wis., 1964-68, France, 1968-71; pres. CEO French ops. Kimberly-Clark, Corp., Neenah, Wis., 1968—73; v.p. internat. div., gen. mgr. Pillsbury Co., Mpls., 1971-76; exec. v.p. Shaklee Corp., San Francisco, 1976-79; pres., CEO Hisway Cosmetics, Inc., NYC, 1979-84, Hathaway Group of Warnaco, NYC, 1984—89; chmn. Global Brands, Inc., NYC, 1989—; found., pres. EBI, Inc., Chatham, Mass., 1995—. Chmn., chief exec. officer Sero Co., Branford, Conn., Mortin Jonap, Ltd., Hauppauge, NY; bd. dirs. William Schneider, Inc., Miami, HMI, Inc., Norwood, Mass. Author: The Committee on Trustees, 2001; contbr. to columns Trusteeship jour. Trustee Chatham Hist. Soc., 2006-, St. Lawrence U. Canton, NY, 1986-2001, chmn. bd. trustees, 1995-2001, Boston Conservatory, 2000-, San Francisco Ballet, 1978, New Horizons Project, Cambridge, Mass., 2001-; devel. dir. Cen. Park Conservancy, NYC, 1983-89. With USAR, 1955-57. Mem. Eastward Ho Club (v.p., gov. 1985-91), Harvard Club NY, Harvard Club Boston, Eagle Scout. Republican. Avocations: cooking, running, golf, reading, international travel. Home and Office: 1114 Orleans Rd North Chatham MA 02650 E-mail: ebi@cape.com.

**WILSON, E. DAVID,** toy company executive; Sr. v.p., sales Hasbro, Inc., Parker Brothers, 1990-95; pres. Milton Bradley, 1990—95, Hasbro Games Group, 1995—97, Hasbro Americas, 1997—99; sr. v.p. & sector head, games Hasbro, Inc., 1999—2001, pres., games, 2001—. Office: Hasbro Inc 1027 Newport Ave Pawtucket RI 02862

**WILSON, EDWARD CONVERSE, JR.,** oil and natural gas production company executive; b. Cambridge, Mass., Jan. 1, 1928; s. Edward Converse and Jean (McLean) W.; m. Patricia Ann Cairns, Sept. 10, 1953; children: Amy Cairns, Sarah Converse. AB, Harvard U., 1949. Brokerage trainee Estabrook & Co., Boston, 1951; Midwest Stock Exch. clk. Paul H. Davis & Co., Chgo., 1951-52; mem. Chgo. Bd. Trade, 1952-78, dir. 1966-67, chmn. 1970-71; ptnr. Nolan & Wilson Co. (specialists on Midwest Stock Exchange), 1965-72; sr. ptnr. Wilson Prodn. Co., Ft. Smith, Ark., 1972-74. Mem. devel. com. Chgo. chpt. Nat. Multiple Sclerosis Soc., 1970; mem. vis. com. on univ. resources Harvard, 1971-74, 76-81; bd. dirs. Franklin Blvd. Community Hosp., 1970-74. Served with USAAF, 1946-47. Mem. Racquet Club (Chgo.). Home: 11114 Wickwood Dr Houston TX 77024-7523

**WILSON, EDWARD NATHAN,** mathematician, educator; b. Warsaw, NY, Dec. 2, 1941; s. Hugh Monroe and Margaret Jane (Nunlaing) W.; m. Mary Katherine Schooling, Aug. 19, 1976; children: Nathan Edward, Emily Katherine. BA, Cornell U., 1963; MS, Stanford U., 1965; PhD, Washington U., St. Louis, 1971. Instr. Ft. Valley (Ga.) State Coll., 1965-67, Washington U., St. Louis, 1968-69, U. Calif., Irvine, 1970-71, Brandeis U., Waltham, Mass., 1971-73; asst. prof. Washington U., St. Louis, 1973-77, assoc. prof., 1977-87, dean grad. sch., 1983-93, dean univ. coll., 1986-88, prof., 1987—, chair dept. math., 1995-99. Mem. Grad. Record Exams. Bd., Princeton, N.J., 1986-90; sec.-treas. Assn. Grad. Schs. Contbr. articles to profl. jours. Mem. Brentwood Sch. Bd., Mo., 1984. Woodrow Wilson fellow, 1963; NSF fellow, 1963-65; NDEA fellow, 1967-70. Mem. Am. Math. Soc., Math. Assn. of Am. Democrat. Office: Washington U Campus Box 1146 1 Brookings Dr Saint Louis MO 63130-4899 Office Phone: 314-935-6729. Business E-Mail: enwilson@math.wustl.edu.

**WILSON, EDWARD OSBORNE,** biologist, educator, writer; b. Birmingham, Ala., June 10, 1929; s. Edward Osborne and Inez (Freeman) W.; m. Irene Kelley, Oct. 30, 1955; 1 child, Catherine Irene. BS, U. Ala., 1949, MS, 1950, LHD (hon.), 1980; PhD, Harvard U., 1955; DPhil, Uppsala U., Sweden; DSc (hon.), Duke U., 1978, Grinnell Coll., 1978, U. West Fla., 1979, Lawrence U., 1979, Fitchburg State Coll., 1989, Macalester Coll., 1990, U. Mass., 1990, Oxford U., 1993, Ripon Coll., 1994, U. Conn., 1995, Ohio U., 1996, Bates Coll., 1996, Coll. Wooster, 1997, U. Guelph, 1997, U. Portland, 1997, Kenyon Coll., 2002, U. of the South, 2002, Harvard U., 2004, Clark U., 2005, LHD (hon.), Hofstra U., 1986, Muhlenburg Coll., 1998, Yale U., 1998, Pa. State U., Bradford Coll., 1987, Duke U., 2003; DHC, U. Madrid Complutense, 1995, U. Montreal, 2004; LLD, Simon Fraser U.; DrRerNat, U. Würzburg, 2000. Jr. fellow Soc. Fellows, Harvard U., 1953—56, faculty, 1956—, Baird prof. sci., 1976—94, Pellegrino U. prof., 1994—97, rsch. prof., 1997—2002, curator entomology, 1971—97, hon. curator entomology, 1997—. Selection com. Guggenheim Found., 1982—89; bd. dirs. World Wildlife Fund, 1983—94, Organ. Tropical Studies, 1984—91, N.Y. Bot. Garden, 1994—95, Am. Mus. Natural History, 1992—2002, Am. Acad. Liberal Edn., 1993—2004, Nature Conservancy, 1994—2002, Conservation Internat., 1997—. Author: The Insect Societies, 1971, Sociobiology: The New Synthesis, 1975, On Human Nature, 1978

(Pulitzer prize for non-fiction, 1979), Promethean Fire, 1983, Biophilia, 1984, Success and Dominance in Ecosystems, 1990, The Diversity of Life, 1992 (Nat. Wildlife Assn. award, Deutsche Umweltstiftung Book award, Sir Peter Kent Conservation prize), Naturalist, 1994 (L.A. Times Book prize sci., 1995), In Search of Nature, 1996, Consilience: The Unity of Knowledge, 1998 (Forkosch award Internat. Acad. Humanism, 2000), Biological Diversity: The Oldest Human Heritage, 1999, The Future of Life, 2002 (Natural World Book prize, U.K., 2002), Pheidole in the New World: A Dominant, Hyperdiverse Ant Genus, 2003 (Julia Ward Howe prize, 2003), From So Simple A Beginning, 2005, Nature Revealed, 2006; author: (with R.H. MacArthur) The Theory of Island Biogeography, 1967; author: (with C.J. Lumsden) Genes, Mind and Culture, 1981; author: (with Bert Holldobler) The Ants, 1990 (Pulitzer prize for non-fiction, 1991), Journey to the Ants, 1994 (Phi Beta Kappa prize sci., 1995); others. Recipient Cleve.-AAAS Rsch. prize, 1967, Mercer award, Ecol. Soc. Am., 1971, Nat. Medal Sci., 1976, Disting. Svc. award, Am. Inst. Biol. Scis., 1976, Archie Carr medal, U. Fla., 1978, Leidy medal, Acad. Natural Sci., Phila., 1979, Tyler Ecology prize, 1984, Silver medal, Nat. Zool. Park, 1987, German Ecol. Inst. prize, 1987, Weaver award scholarly letters, Ingersoll Found., 1989, Crafoord prize, Royal Swedish Acad. Scis., 1990, Prix d'Inst. de la Vie, Paris, 1990, Revelle medal, 1990, Gold medal, Worldwide Fund for Nature, 1990, Achievement award, Nat. Wildlife Fedn., 1992, Shaw medal, Mo. Bot. Garden, 1993, Internat. prize biology, Govt. of Japan, 1993, Eminent Ecologist award, 1994, Ecol. Soc. Am. Audubon medal, Audubon Soc., 1995, Pub. Understanding Sci. award, AAAS, 1995, John Hay award, Orion Soc., 1995, Schubert prize, Germany, 1996, Washburn medal, Mus. Sci., 1996, Hutchinson medal, Garden Club Am., 1997, Stone award, New Eng. Aquarium, 1999, Nonino prize, Letters and Sci., Italy, 2000, King Faisal Internat. prize for ecology, 2000, Kistler prize, Found. for the Future, 2000, Phillips Meml. medal, World Conservation Union, 2000, Lewis Thomas prize, Rockefeller U., 2001, Nierenberg prize, Scripps Oceanographic Inst., 2001, Thoreau medal, Thoreau Soc., 2001, Lifetime Achievement award, Time, 2001, Global Environment Citizens award, Harvard U., 2001, Busk medal, Royal Geog. Soc., 2002, Presdl. medal, Republic of Italy, 2002, Silver Cross of Christopher Columbus, Dominican Republic, 2003, Lowell Thomas award, Explorers Club, 2004, Frances Hutchinson medal, Chgo. Bot. Garden, 2004, Gov.'s award, Island Alliance, Mass., 2004, Rachel Carson award, Internat. Soc. Ecotoxicology and Chemistry, 2004, Rungius medal, Am. Mus. Wildlife Art, 2005, Prince William of Orange medal, Leiden U., 2006, others; Guggenheim Found. fellow, 1978. Fellow: Deutsche Akad. Naturforsch, Am. Philos. Soc. (Franklin medal 1998), Am. Acad. Arts and Scis.; mem.: NAS, Royal Soc. Sci. Uppsala (Sweden), Russian Acad. Sci., Royal Entomol. Soc., Finnish Acad. Sci. and Letters, Royal Soc. London, Netherlands Entomol. Soc. (hon. life), Royal Soc. Edinburgh (life), Assn. Tropical Biology (hon. life), Acad. Humanism (hon. life), Am Humanist Assn. (Disting. Svc. award 1982, hon. life, Humanist of Yr.), Zool. Soc. London (hon. life), Entomol. Soc. Am. (Founders Meml. award 1972, L.O. Howard award 1985, hon. life), Brit. Ecol. Soc. (hon. life), Am. Genetics Assn. (hon. life), Explorers Club (life, hon. life). Home: Apt A-208 1010 Waltham St Lexington MA 02421 Office: Harvard U Mus Comparative Zoology Cambridge MA 02138 Office Phone: 617-495-2315. Business E-Mail: ewilson@oeb.harvard.edu.

**WILSON, EDWIN,** theater director; b. Nashville, Tenn., Nov. 10, 1927; s. E. Edwin and Catherine (Jones) Wilson; m. Catherine Stuart, July 8, 1967. BA cum laude, Vanderbilt U., 1950; grad. in English, U. Edinburgh, Scotland, 1951; MFA, Yale U., 1957, DFA, 1958. Prof. Yale U. Drama Sch., New Haven, 1957—58, Hofstra U., 1958—60, Vanderbilt U., Nashville, 1959; prof. Grad. Ctr. Hunter Coll. CUNY, N.Y.C., 1966—91; theater critic Wall St. Jour., N.Y.C., 1972—94, sr. cultural writer, 1994—96; moderator TV interviews CUNY-TV, PBS, N.Y.C., 1993—93; chair dept. theater and film CUNY Hunter Coll., 1980—83; v.p. faculty Hunter Coll., N.Y.C., 1973—75; exec. dir. Martin E. Segal Theater Ctr. Hunter Coll., 1987—2003. Mem. N.Y. Drama Critics Cir., 1972—94, pres., 1982—84; mem. Pulitzer Prize Drama Jury, 1977—78, 1979—80, 2000—03; mem. nominating com. Tony awards, N.Y.C., 1975—77, N.Y.C., 1988—99; rep USIA to Romania and German Dem. Republic, 1984. Author: The Theater Experience, 1976, 9th edit.; 2004; co-author (with Alvin Goldfarb): Art, 2005, Lving Theater 4th edit., 2004; editor (and introduction author): Shaw on Shakespeare, 1961; dir.: (plays, for profit companies as well as student performers.); prodr.(numerous off-Broadway plays and one Broadway Play): Agatha Sue I Love You; playwright: plays Waterfall, The Bettinger Prize, Musical Great Expectations. Pres. Theater Devel. Fund, 1982—84; mem. playwright's com. Rockefeller Found., 1983—86; bd. dir. Theater Devel. Fund, 1981—2003, 1981—, John Golden Fund, 1980—. Grantee grant to report on contemporary Japanese theatre, Milwaukee Rep and Japanese-Am. Friendship Commn., 1978—79. Mem.: Am. Theater Critics Assn., Century Assn., Coffee House Club, Phi Beta Kappa. Home: 55 Central Park W New York NY 10023-5003

**WILSON, ELDON RAY,** minister; b. Tieton, Wash., Apr. 16, 1931; s. Frank Madison and Beatrice Jane (Snider) W.; m. LouCelle Charlotte Seward, Aug. 3, 1957; children: Randall Wayne, Gary Ray. BTh, Internat. Bible Coll., San Antonio, 1967; PhD, Sussex Coll., Hayward's Heath, Eng., 1972. Ordained to ministry Emmanuel Ch., 1956. Founder, pastor Emmanuel Tabernacle, Port Arthur, Tex., 1958-63; evangelist U.S., Can., 1963-65; founder, pastor Gospel Tabernacle, Ilion, NY, 1965-70; pastor Full Gospel Ch., Halifax, N.S., Canada, 1970-72; missionary Europe, Africa, 1972-77; founder, pastor New Covenant Ch., Columbus, Ohio, 1977-84; missionary New Covenant Ministries, Columbus, 1984-97; acad. dean City Bible Coll., Utica, NY, 1998-2001. Bd. dirs. Good News Mission, Bogota, Colombia, 1985—; trustee Mission Teams Internat., Elkton, Md., 1989—. Author: The New Creation, 1975. Bd. dirs. Kuyahoora Valley Libr., Newport, N.Y., 1985—; overseer Shekinah Ministries, Amsterdam, The Netherlands, Bread of Life Ministries, Bastogne, Belgium. With USN, 1951-55. Republican. Home: 7417 West St Newport NY 13416 Office: PO Box 317 Newport NY 13416 Personal E-mail: loucelle.wilson@juno.com.

**WILSON, ELIZABETH SAWIN,** psychiatrist; b. Cambridge, Mass., Oct. 16, 1939; d. Horace John and Katherine Biddle (Rhoads) Sawin; m. Robert Woodrow Wilson, Sept. 4, 1958; children: Philip, Suzanne, Randal. BA with honors, USC, 1962; MD with honors, Ross U., Roseau, Dominica, 1987. Diplomate Am. Bd. Neurology and Psychiatry, added certification in geriatric psychiatry and addictions psychiatry. Resident in psychiatry U. Medicine and Dentistry N.J., Piscataway, 1991; pvt. practice Hazlet, N.J., 1991—. Avocations: travel, gardening. Home: 9 Valley Point Dr Holmdel NJ 07733-1320 Office: 1 Bethany Rd Ste 38 Hazlet NJ 07730-1661 Office Phone: 732-888-7911.

**WILSON, ERIC F.G.,** information technology executive; BSc with honors, Guelph U. Sr. v.p., chief info. officer Philip Svcs. Corp., Houston, 1997—2000; sr. v.p. operations, chief tech. officer Fusionstorm, San Francisco, 2000—03; sr. v.p., chief info. officer Raley's, West Sacramento, Calif., 2003—. Office: Raleys 500 W Capitol Ave West Sacramento CA 95605

**WILSON, EUGENE ROLLAND,** retired foundation executive; b. Findlay, Ohio, Jan. 14, 1938; s. Clair and Ethel Bernice (Cryer) W.; m. Mary Ann Dalton; children: Jeff, Andy. BA, Bowling Green State U., 1960; MS, Syracuse U., 1961. Dir. devel., asst. to pres. Bowling Green (Ohio) State U., 1966-70; mgr. radio-TV advt. Columbia Gas of Ohio, Inc., Columbus, 1964-66; assoc. dir. devel. Calif. Inst. Tech., Pasadena, 1971-77, v.p. for inst. rels., 1979-80; assoc. dir. ARCO Found., L.A., 1977-79, exec. dir., 1980-83, pres., 1984-94; pres. youth devel. Ewing Marion Kauffman Found., Kansas City, Mo., 1995-2000, sr. v.p., 2000—03; int., 2003; sr. fellow Ctr. for Philanthropy and Pub. Policy, U. So. Calif.; sr. fellow Midwest Ctr. for Nonprofit Leadership, U. Mo., Kansas City. Chmn. contbns. coun. Conf. Bd.; sr. advisor Coun. of Founds. Founding trustee Arcadia (Calif.) Edn. Found.; elder trustee Presbyn. Ch. Named Outstanding Young Man Bowling Green Jaycees, 1967; recipient hon. service award Hugo Reid Sch. PTA, 1977, Corp. Social Responsibility award Mex.-Am. Legal Def. and Edn. Fund, 1989, Nat. Leadership award in edn. Inst. for Ednl. Leadership, 1992. Mem. Bowling

---

Green State U. Alumni Assn. (pres. 1965), Gnome and Athenaeum Clubs of Caltech, Omicron Delta Kappa. Home: 14117 W 56th Ct Shawnee KS 66216-4696 *Our values and judgments are shaped by our roots. The special relationships developed in small-town rural America, and the many opportunities to enjoy a variety of leadership experiences, prove invaluable later in life to cope with the broader, more vexing problems of pluralistic society. Later sophistication— tempered by the humility of those early roots— then becomes more meaningful.*

**WILSON, FLOYD C.,** oil industry executive; children: Christopher, Andrew. Founder, chmn., pres., CEO Hugoton Energy Corp., 1987—98; chmn., CEO 3TEC Energy Corp., 1999—2003; founder, pres., CEO Petrohawk Energy Corp., Houston, 2003—, chmn., 2004—; ptnr. Wilson Group Companies. Office: Petrohawk Energy Corp 1100 Louisiana Ste 4400 Houston TX 77002*

**WILSON, FRANCES C.,** career military officer; BS, Mich. State U.; MEd, Pepperdine U.; MA in Psychology, U. No. Colo.; MS in Bus. Mgmt., Salve Regina Coll.; PhD in Edn., U. So. Calif. Commd. 2d lt. USMC, 1972, advanced through grades to maj. gen.; air traffic control officer Marine Corps Air Sta., Yuma, Ariz., Kaneohe, Hawaii, 1975; tchr. instrnl. mgmt. Marine Corps Devel. & Edn. Ctr., Quantico, Va.; staff sec. 3d Marine Divsn., Okinawa, Japan, 1980-81; asst. prof., co. officer brigade of midshipmen U.S. Naval Acad., Annapolis, Md.; mgmt. analyst HQ USMC, Washington; spl. asst. for gen. and flag officer matters Joint Staff, Pentagon, exec. asst. to vice dir., 1987; comdr. 4th Recruit Tng. Battalion, Parris Island, S.C., 1988-90, Camp H.M. Smith, Svc. Battalion Marine Corps Pacific; sec. Joint Staff, until 1997; commanding gen. Marine Corps Base, Quantico, 1997-99, Third Force Svc. Support Group, Okinawa, Japan, 1999—2001; dir. pers. mgmt. divsn. M&RA Hdqrs. USMC, 2001—03; comdt. Indsl. Coll. Armed Forces, Nat. Def. U., Ft. McNair, DC, 2003—. Decorated Def. Superior Svc. medal, Def. Meritorious Svc. medal, Meritorious Svc. medal, Navy Commendation medal, Navy Achievement medal.

**WILSON, FRANCES HELEN,** retired occupational therapist; b. Pitts., Oct. 17, 1929; d. J. Vernon and Margaret Hassler (Prugh) Wilson. BA, Conn. Coll., 1951; advanced standing cert., Columbia Sch. Occupl. Therapy, 1953. Therapist Washington (Pa.) County Soc. Crippled Children and Adults, 1953-54; staff therapist Oakland VA Hosp., U. Pitts., 1955-66; supr. Occupl. Therapy Clinic, Aspinwall VA Hosp., Pitts., 1966-74, 81-85, Occupl. Therapy Clinic, Oakland VA Hosp., Pitts., 1974—85, ret., 1985. Active Jr. League Pitts., Inc.; vol. Pitts. (Pa.) Children's Mus. Mem. Western Pa. (treas. 1967-69), Am. Occupl. Therapy Assns., Presbyn. Univ. Hosp. Pitts. Vol. Assns., Pitts. (Pa.) Symphony Assn., Acad. Lifelong Learning, Conn. Coll. Club (treas. 1971-94), Twentieth Century Club (Pitts.). Republican. Presbyterian. Home: Washington Plz 1116 1420 Centre Ave Pittsburgh PA 15219

**WILSON, FRANKLIN D.,** sociology educator; b. Birmingham, Ala., Sept. 3, 1942; s. Ernest and Ollie Lee (Carter) W.; m. Marion F. Brown; children: Rachel, Chareese BA, Miles Coll., 1964; postgrad., Atlanta U., 1964-65; MA, Wash. State U., 1971, PhD, 1973. Instr. Grambling (La.), 1965-66; Williams H. Sewell-Bascom prof. sociology U. Wis.-Madison, 1973—, chmn. dept. Afro-Am. studies, 1984-87, chmn. dept. sociology, 1988-91, dir. Ctr. for Demography and Ecology, 1994-99. Author: Residential Consumption, Economic Opportunities and Race, 1979; deputy editor Demography, 1995-98; co-editor Am. Sociol. Rev. Bd. of Census adv. com. Profl. Assns., 1993-99. Served with U.S. Army, 1966-69; Vietnam Decorated Purple Heart, Silver Star, Vietnam medal of Valor; Census fellow Am. Statis. Assn., NSF, 1991-92, Population Coun. fellow, 1971-72. Mem. Population Assn. Am., Sociol. Rsch. Assn., Assn. Black Sociologists, Am. Sociol. Assn. (sec. 2003—). Unitarian Universalist. Avocations: swimming, reading. Office: U Wis Ctr for Demography and Ecology Social Sci Bldg Madison WI 53713 Business E-Mail: wilson@ssc.wisc.edu

**WILSON, FRED M., II,** ophthalmologist, educator; b. Indpls., Dec. 10, 1940; s. Fred Madison and Elizabeth (Fredrick) W.; m. Karen Joy Lyman, Sept. 10, 1959 (div. June 1962); 1 child, Teresa Wilson Kulick; m. Claytonia Leigh Pemberton, Aug. 28, 1964; children: Yvonne Wilson Hacker, Jennifer Wilson DeLong, Benjamin James. AB in Med. Scis., Ind. U., 1962, MD, 1965. Diplomate Am. Bd. Ophthalmology. Intern Sacred Heart Hosp., Spokane, Wash., 1965-66; resident in ophthalmology Ind. U., Indpls., 1968-71, fellow in ophthalmology, 1971-72, F.I. Proctor Found., San Francisco, 1972-73; from asst. prof. to assoc. prof. ophthalmology Ind. U., Indpls., 1972-76, prof. ophthalmology, 1981—2005, prof. emeritus 2005—. Med. dir. Ind. Lions Eye Bank, Inc., Indpls., 1973-99; cons. surgeon Ind. U., Indpls., 1973-2005. Contbr. articles to profl. jours., chapters to books. Lt. comdr. USNR, 1966-68, PTO. Mem. Am. Acad. Ophthalmology (assoc. sec. 1988-93, Sr. Teaching award 1989), Assn. Proctor Fellows, Soc. Heed Fellows, Am. Ophthalmol. Soc., Am. Bd. Ophthalmology (bd. dirs. 1993-2000), Ill. Soc. Ophthalmology (hon.), Mont. Acad. Ophthalmology (hon.), Pacific-Coast Ophthalmol. Soc. (hon.). Republican. Avocations: photography, guitar, history, language, natural history. Home: 12262 Crestwood Dr Carmel IN 46033-4323 Office: Ind U Sch Medicine Dept Ophthalmolgy 702 Rotary Cir Indianapolis IN 46202-5133

**WILSON, FREDERIC SANDFORD,** pharmaceutical company executive; b. Schenectady, NY, Mar. 28, 1947; s. Robert Omer and Isabel May (Sandford) W.; children: Amy Kathleen, Adrienne Ann; m. Judith Ann Goettsche, Feb. 7, 1973; children: Marla Ann, Brian Bennett, Jessica Lea, Jennifer Lynn. BS, Syracuse U., 1968. Acct. exec. Mastropaul Design Inc., Syracuse, N.Y., 1969-70; copy editor Norwich Eaton Pharms., Norwich, N.Y., 1970-72, sales rep. Gary, Ind., 1972-73, asst. product mgr. Norwich, 1974-75, mktg. svcs. mgr., 1975-76, product mgr., 1977-81, bus. devel. mgr., 1981-83, sr. product mgr., 1983-85, mgr. med. foods, 1986-89, assoc. mktg. mgr. P&G Pharms., Norwich, 1989-92; dir. profl. rels. P & G Pharms., Cin., 1993-96; mgr. mktg. svcs. P&G, Cin., 1997-98; category mgr. CME P&G Pharms., Cin., 1998—. Cons. Sandoz Nutrition Corp., Mpls., 1992., bd. dir. Nat. Bd. of Osteopathic Med. Examiners. Inventor Jejunostomy Kit, 1981, Vivonex T.E.N. med. food, 1983, Tolerex med. food, 1987. Bd. dirs. Syracuse U. Minority Access Program, 1989-91; mem. nat. task force on continuing med. edn. Providence Industry Collaboration, chmn. pharm. alliance, 1996-98 Mem.: AMA (affiliate). Office: Procter & Gamble Box 2075 8700 Mason-Montgomery Rd Mason OH 45040-9462 Office Phone: 513-622-5456. Business E-Mail: wilson.fs@pg.com.

**WILSON, FREDERICK ALLEN,** gastroenterologist, educator, health facility administrator, medical educator; b. Winchester, Mass., Aug. 22, 1937; s. Warren Archibald and Alice Jane (Springall) W.; m. Lynne Stewart Cantley, Feb. 24, 1962; children: Douglas, Victoria. AB, Colgate U., Hamilton, N.Y., 1959; MD, Albany Med. Coll., N.Y., 1963. Intern Hartford Hosp., Conn., 1963-64, resident in medicine, 1964-66; fellow in gastroenterology Albany Med. Coll., 1966-67; USPHS postdoctoral fellow in gastroenterology U. Tex. Southwestern Med. Sch., Dallas, 1969-72; asst. prof. medicine Vanderbilt U. Sch. Medicine, Nashville, 1972-76, assoc. prof., 1976-82, mem. adv. com. clin. rsch. ctr., 1978-81; prof. medicine, chief div. gastroenterology Milton S. Hershey Med. Ctr., Pa. State U., Hershey, 1982-90; prof. medicine, dir. divsn. gastroenterology Med. U. S.C., Charleston, 1990-94, dir. fellowship tng. program in gastroenterology and hepatology, 1990—2003, now prof. medicine divsn. gastroenterology and hepatology, dept. medicine. Mem. ACP Med. Knowledge Self-Assessment Program VI, 1980-81; mem. gastroenterology and clin. nutrition rev. group Nat. Inst. Arthritis, Diabetes, Digestive and Kidney Disease, NIH, Bethesda, Md., 1985-89; pre-reviewer Am. Coun. Grad. Med. Edn., 1994-95. Contbr. numerous articles, abstracts, chpts. to profl. publs.; reviewer for sci. jours. Served to maj. M.C., U.S. Army, 1967-69. Recipient Clin. Investigator award VA Med. Ctr., Nashville, 1972-75; recipient Investigator award Howard Hughes Med. Inst., Vanderbilt U., 1975-78; NIH Fogarty Internat. Ctr. sr. internat. fellow Max Planck Inst. for Biophysics, Frankfurt, Germany, 1979-80. Mem. Am. Fedn. Clin. Rsch., Ctrl. Soc. Clin. Rsch., Am. Gastroenterology Assn., Am. Assn. Study Liver Diseases, Am. Soc. Clin. Investigation, N.Y. Acad. Scis., SC Med. Assn., Ea.

---

Gut Club, Pa. Soc. Gastroenterology. Office: Med U SC Div Gastroenterology 96 Jonathan Lucas St #210 Charleston SC 29425-0001 Office Phone: 843-792-2301. Business E-Mail: wilsonfa@musc.edu.

**WILSON, GARY DEAN,** lawyer; b. Wichita, Kans., June 7, 1943; s. Glenn E. and Roe Zella (Mills) W.; m. Diane Kay Williams, Dec. 29, 1965; children: Mark R., Matthew C., Christopher B. GA, Stanford U., 1965, LLB. 1968. Bar: D.C. 1970, U.S. Dist. Ct. D.C. 1970, U.S. Ct. Appeals (D.C. cir.) 1972, U.S. Ct. Appeals (7th cir.) 1979, U.S. Ct. Appeals (2d cir) 1983. Law clk. U.S. Ct. Appeals, 2d cir., N.Y.C., 1968-69, U.S. Supreme Ct., Washington, 1969-70; assoc. Wilmer, Cutler & Pickering, Washington, 1970-75, ptnr., 1976—. Acting prof. law Stanford (Calif.) Law Sch., 1981-82. Bd. visitors Stanford Law Sch., 1990-92, 2000—. Democrat. Home: 4636 30th St NW Washington DC 20008-2127 E-mail: gwilson@wilmer.com, dwilson1@erols.com.

**WILSON, GARY LEE,** airline company executive; b. Alliance, Ohio, Jan. 16, 1940; s. Elvin John and Fern Helen (Donaldson) W.; children: Derek, Christopher. BA, Duke U., 1962; MBA, U. Pa., 1963. V.p. fin., dir. Trans-Philippines Investment Co., Manila, 1964-70; exec. v.p., dir. Checchi & Co., Washington, 1971-73; exec. v.p. Marriott Corp., Washington, 1973-85; exec. v.p., chief exec. officer The Walt Disney Co., Burbank, Calif., 1985—89; co-chmn. bd. Northwest Airlines, Inc., St. Paul, 1991—97, chmn. bd., 1997—. Bd. of govs. Internat. Air Transport Assn.; bd. dirs. Walt Disney Co., Burbank, Calif., 1985—, Yahoo! Inc., 2001—, CB Richard Ellis, Inc. Mem. NCAA Leadership Advisory Board; bd. trustees Duke U., Keck Sch. of Medicine, U. So. Calif. Office: Northwest Airlines 5101 Northwest Dr Saint Paul MN 55111-3027*

**WILSON, GARY THOMAS,** engineering executive; b. Pitts., Sept. 26, 1961; s. Charles Zachary and Doris Jean (Alexander) Wilson; m. Georgiann E. Wilson, Dec. 31, 1994. AB, Dartmouth Coll., 1983, BEEE, 1984; MSEE, Calif. State U., Long Beach, 1992; postgrad., UCLA, 1992-99. Elec. engr. AiResearch, Man., Garrett, Torrance, Calif., 1983; sr. mem. tech. staff TRW Space & Electronics Group, Redondo Beach, Calif., 1984-93; v.p. of R&D CZAND Assocs., L.A., 1993—; rsch. asst. UCLA Flight System Rsch. Ctr., Westwood, Calif., 1994-96; sr. scientist payload sys. Hughes Space & Comms., 1996-2000; sr. project mgr. Boeing Satellite Systems, 2000—01; dir. advanced systems Mission Rsch. Corp., 2001—04; v.p. space and sensors sector ATK Mission Rsch., 2004—06; pres. Zuma Engring. & Rsch., 2006—. Cons. CZAND Assocs., L.A., 1985-93; instr. electronics UCLA Smarts Program. Tutor math. and sci. Recipient Meritorious Svc. award United Negro Coll. Fund, 1989; TRW master's fellow, doctoral incentive fellow Calif. State U., 1993. Mem. IEEE, Nat. Soc. Black Engrs., Dartmouth Soc. Engrs. Avocations: tennis, golf, chess, basketball, bicycling. E-mail: gwmsee@aol.com.

**WILSON, GEORGE MACKLIN,** history educator, cultural studies center administrator; b. Columbus, Ohio, Apr. 27, 1937; m. Joyce DeCoster Klain, June 11, 1960; children: George David, Elizabeth Adeline. AB in Politics and Russian Studies, Princeton U., 1958; AM in East Asian Regional Studies, Harvard U., 1960, PhD in History and Far Ea. Langs., 1965. From instr. to asst. prof. history U. Ill., Urbana-Champaign, 1964-67; assoc. prof. history Ind. U., Bloomington, 1967-76, assoc. prof. East Asian langs. and cultures, 1975-76, prof., 1976—, dir. East Asian studies program, 1970-71, 72-73, assoc. dean rsch. and advanced studies, assoc. dean internat. programs, 1972-75, dean internat. programs office of pres., 1975-78, dir. grad. studies dept. history, 1980-83, acting chair dept. history, 1983-84, summer 1981, summer 1982, dir. East Asian studies ctr., 1987—; dir. Title VI nat. resource ctr. East Asian studies, 1991-2000. Vis. lectr. Japanese history U. Mich., Ann Arbor, 1963-64, summer 1964; vist. asst. prof. history summer sch. arts and scis. Harvard U., 1966, assoc. prof. history summer sch., 1975, rsch. assoc. East Asian rsch. ctr., 1966, 75, 78-79; rsch. assoc. faculty letters Kyoto U., 1971-72, vis. prof. faculty edn., 1985; mem. chair various coms. Ind. U., mem. bd. advisors East Asian summer lang. inst., 1985—, chair Japan forum, 1990—; cons. internat. divsn. Ford Found., 1974-77, cons. history Midwest univs. consortium internat. activities, 1979-80; mem. rev. panel divsn. pub. programs NEH, 1978-80; mem. adv. screening com. Japan Coun. Internat. Exch. Scholars, 1978-81, chair, 1980-81; mem. adv. panel Annenberg Sch. Comm. and Corp. Pub. Broadcasting, 1982-84; cons. East Asian history Am. Hist. Rev., 1985-91; mem. Gov. Robert Orr's Higher Edn. Del. to Ind.'s Sister State, Zhejiang Province, China, 1988; chair I.U. Japan Forum, 1988-94; bd. dirs. Ind. Consortium Internat. Programs, 1972-78; Ind. U. mem. bd. dirs. Interuniversity Ctr. Japanese Lang. Studies in Yokohama, 1988—; presenter in field. Author: Radical Nationalist in Japan: Kita Ikki, 1883-1937, 1969, Japanese edit., 1971, Patriots and Redeemers in Japan: Motives in the Meiji Restoration, 1992; editor, contbg. author: Crisis Politics in Prewar Japan: Institutional and Ideological Problems of the 1930s, 1970; Editl. advisor for Japanese and Korean history Encyclopaedia Britannica, 1969-99; book manuscript reader U. Hawaii Press, Ind. U. Press, Princeton U. Press; article manuscript evaluator Am. Hist. Rev., Comparative Studies Soc. and History, Jour. Asian Studies; contbr. articles and book revs. to profl. jours. Grantee U. Ill., 1965, Harvard U., 1966, 75, Ind. U., 1967, 68, 72, Am. Philos. Soc., 1968, Am. Coun. Learned Socs., 1971; Grad. Sch. Arts and Scis. fellow Harvard U., 1959-60, Fgn. Area Tng. fellow Ford Found., 1960-63, Fulbright-Hays Sr. fellow, 1971-72, Profl. fellow Japan Found., 1985. Mem. Am. Hist. Assn. (convener 1984 and 1988 ann. meetings, chair conf. Asian history 1989—), Midwest Conf. Asian Affairs (mem. nominating com. 1990-91), Midwest Univs. Consortium Internat. Activities, Inc. (liaison officer for Ind. U. 1973-78, bd. dirs. 1974-78, sec. corp. 1974-78), Assn. Asian Studies (mem. program com., Japan rep. 1985 ann. meeting), Japan-Am. Soc. Ind., Inc. (founding, mem. steering com. 1987-88, bd. dirs. 1988—), Hudson Inst. (pub.). Office: Indiana University East Asian Studies Ctr Memorial Hall W Rm 207 Bloomington IN 47405

**WILSON, GERALD EVERETTE,** funeral services company executive; b. Houston, Nov. 2, 1953; s. Clifford Dennis and Naomi Betty (Falls) W.; m. Marsherria Ervin, Aug. 14, 1974; 1 child, Gerrad Everette. BA in Econs., MA in Econs., Stanford U., 1976; MS in Acctg., U. Houston, 1978. CPA, Tex.; cert. fin. planner. Mem. staff Arthur Young & Co., Houston, 1976-80 mgr., 1980-84, prin., 1984-86; founder, assoc., chmn. Wilson Fin. Group, Inc., Houston, 1986—. Bd. dirs. Cedar Crest Funeral Home Inc., Dallas, Thompson Funeral Home Inc., Sacramento, So. Funeral Home Inc., Memphis, Whitehaven Chapel Inc., Memphis, Mainland Funeral Home, LaMarque, Tex., Morris-Bates Funeral Home, Ft. Worth, Paradise Funeral Home, Houston, Carl Barnes Funeral Home, Inc., Houston. Bd. dirs. Stanford U. Athletic Bd., Palo Alto, Calif., 1985—, Leadership Houston, 1985-87, Houston Proud, 1988; chmn. sec. Steering Com. Harris County Parks, Tex., 1986—; mem. adv. bd. Houston Ind. Sch. Dist., 1986—. Named Outstanding Young Houstonian Houston Jaycees, 1985, Outstanding Young Texan Tex. Jaycees, 1985, Outstanding Black Houstonian Riverside Hosp., 1986. Mem. Am. Inst. CPA's, Tex. Soc. CPA's, Inst. Fin. Planning, Houston C. of C., Katy C. of C. Democrat. Baptist. Avocations: golf, jogging. Office: Wilson Fin Group Inc 15415 Katy Fwy Ste 500 Houston TX 77094-1816*

**WILSON, GLENN,** economist, educator; b. East St. Louis, Ill., Feb. 4, 1929; s. Herschel and Regina (Hayes) W.; m. Helen Janice O'Dell, Jan. 28, 1951; children— David, Thomas, Ann. BA, U. Okla., 1951; MA, 1952. Adminstr. Welfare and Retirement Fund United Mine Workers, Pitts., Knoxville, Tenn., 1952-58; dir. med. care research Nationwide Ins. Co., Columbus, 1958-62; exec. dir. Community Health Found., Cleve., 1962-68; exec. v.p. Kaiser Community Health Found., Cleve., 1968-69; assoc. dean U. N.C. Med. Sch., Chapel Hill, 1970-88, prof. dept. social medicine, 1977—, chmn. dept., 1977-89. Cons. Sault Ste. Marie and Dist. Group Health Assn.; health adv. Mayor Stokes, Cleve., 1967-69 Contbr. articles to profl. jours. Home: 214 Glandon Dr Chapel Hill NC 27514-3816 Office: U NC Med Sc Dept Social Medicine Chapel Hill NC 27514 E-mail: glenn_wilson@unc.edu.

**WILSON, GRETCHEN,** vocalist; b. Granite City, Ill., June 26, 1973; 1 child, Grace. Signed by Epic Records, 2003—. Singer: (singles) Redneck Woman, 2004 (Breakthrough Video of Yr., Country Music Television Music award, 2005), When I Think About Cheatin, 2004 (Female Video of Yr., Country Music Television Music award 2005), (five singles) 5-Mo-Fo-Ya, 2005, (albums) Here for the Party, 2004, All Jacked Up, 2005; TV appearances include: In The Moment, 2004. Named Female Vocalist of Yr., Country Music Assn., 2005; recipient Horizon award, 2004, Favorite New Artist, Am. Music Awards, 2004, Favorite Female Country Artist, 2005, Female Country Artist of Yr., Billboard Music Awards, 2004, New Country Artist of Yr., 2004, Top New Artist, Acad. Country Music Awards, 2005, Top Female Vocalist, 2005. Achievements include first new artist to debut at #1 on Billboard's Country LP chart. Office: Sony Music 34 Music Sq E Nashville TN 37203-4323*

**WILSON, G(ROVER) GRAY,** lawyer; b. Louisville, Ky., Apr. 1, 1951; BA, Davidson Coll., 1973; JD, Duke Univ., 1976. Bar: NC 1976. Fellow: Am. Coll. Trial Lawyers; mem.: Am. Bd. Trial Advocates, NC Assn. of Def. Attorneys, Forsyth County Bar Assn., NC Bar Assn. (pres. 2004), Phi Beta Kappa. Office: Wilson & Iseman LLP Ste 400 110 Oakwood Dr Winston Salem NC 27103

**WILSON, HAROLD BATTING,** treasurer; b. NYC, June 24, 1910; s. William Johnson and May LaForest Wilson; m. Edna Anita Helmling, Jan. 9, 1937 (dec. Apr. 1996). Cert. in acct. and bus. law, Fordham U., 1930—32. Registered pub. acct., N.Y., 1974; cert. data processor Data Processing Mgmt. Assn., 1963, computer technology Inst. Advanced Technology, 1967. Office boy Arthur Andersen & Co., NYC, 1929—32, acct./auditor, 1933—38; acct. Office of Comptr., NYC, 1938—40; prin. systems analyst Divsn. of Employment, NY State, Albany, 1941—70; investment adv. Registered with S.E.C., Naples, Fla., 1975—90; treas. Theatre '90 Inc., Syracuse, NY, 1990—. Corp. dir. Theatre '90 Inc., Syracuse, 1990—. Author: (book) How to Beat Wall St., 1991. Sgt. USAF, 1943—45, US. Recipient NY State cert. of merit, Gov. Nelson A. Rockefeller, 1971. Mem.: SAR Nat. Soc. Avocations: writing, sports. Home: 7235 Canton St Rd Baldwinsville NY 13027

**WILSON, HAROLD STACY,** history professor, writer; b. Neva, Tenn., June 22, 1935; s. Joseph Hooker Wilson and Bertie Hazel Reece; m. Henrietta Sheppard Fair, June 21, 1968; children: Katherine McCall, Kyle Stacy. BA, King Coll., 1957; MA, Johns Hopkins U., 1959; PhD, Emory U., 1966. Asst. prof. Wesleyan Coll., Macon, Ga., 1962—66, Old Dominion U., Norfolk, Va., 1966—68, assoc. prof., 1968—2003, prof. history, 2003—, chair, history dept., 1991—98, mem. faculty senate, 1999—, vice-chair faculty senate, 2001—03. Fulbright prof. Fu Ren U., Taipei, Taiwan, 1971—72, Tamkang U., Taipei, 1971—72, Nat. U. Singapore, 1978—80; exch. prof. Kitakyushu U., Japan, 1991. Author: (history book) McClure's Magazine and the Muckrakers, 1970, Confederate Industry: Manufacturers and Quartermasters in the Civil War, 2002; editor: Textile History Rev., 1963—66; assoc. editor: Wesleyan Quar. Rev., 1964—66, editl. asst.: The Great American and The Blue and the Gray; contbr. 26 scholarly articles and 20 book revs. in field. Supporter Union Mission, Norfolk, Va., 1966—, Salvation Army, Norfolk, 1966—, Young Life, Norfolk, 1966—, Stas. WHRO-TV, WHRV-TV, Norfolk, 1966—, Norfolk Pub. Libr., 1966—; founder, Patrick scholarship King Coll., Bristol, Tenn., 1996—; short-term missioner South Am. Missionary Soc., Honduras, 2002—; founding mem. Christ the Redeemer Anglican Ch., Norfolk, 2005—. Nominee Peter Seaborg award, 2002; grantee Tech. And Tchg. grant, U. 21st Century, 1992; Rsch. grant, Nat. Found. Arts and Humanities, 1968, Faculty Field Rsch. grant, US Mil. Acad., 1987. Mem.: So. Hist. Assn. (chair arrangements com. 1987—88), Friends of Old Dominion U. Perry Libr. (life). Independent-Republican. Baptist. Avocations: hiking, swimming, travel. Home: 626 W Princess Anne Rd Norfolk VA 23517-1806 Office: Old Dominion Univ Hampton Blvd Norfolk VA 23529 Office Phone: 757-683-3949. Personal E-mail: hwilson@odu.org. Business E-Mail: hwilson@odu.edu.

**WILSON, HEATHER ANN,** congresswoman; b. Keene, NH, Dec. 30, 1960; d. George Douglas Wilson and Martha Lou Wilson-Kernozicky; m. Jay Hone; 3 children. BS in Internat. Politics, USAF Acad., Colo., 1982; MPhil in Internat. Rels., U. Oxford, Eng., 1984, PhD in Internat. Rels., 1985. US mission NATO, Brussels, 1987—89; dir. def. policy and arms control NSC, Washington, 1989—91; pres. Keystone Internat., Inc., Albuquerque, 1991—95; cabinet sec. N.Mex. Dept. Children, Youth and Families, Santa Fe, 1992—98; mem. US Congress from 1st N.Mex. dist., 1998—, mem. energy and commerce com., mem. permanent select com. on intelligence, chair tech. and tactical intelligence subcommittee. Adj. prof. U. N.Mex.; mem. Def. Adv. Com. on Women in the Svcs. Contbr. articles to profl. jours. Capt. USAF, 1982—89. Named Rhodes scholar, 1982; recipient Hero of the Taxpayer award, Ams. for Tax Reform, 1999, 2002, Spirit of Free Enterprise award, US C. of C., 2000, Guardian of Small Bus. award, Nat. Fedn. Ind. Bus., 2000, Golden Bulldog award, Watchdog of Treasury, 2000, Disting. Cmty. Health Superhero award, Nat. Assn. Cmty. Health Ctrs., Inc., 2005, Javits-Wagner-O'Day Champion award, 2005. Mem.: Kiwanis. Republican. Methodist. Avocations: hiking, skiing. Office: US Ho Reps 318 Cannon Ho Office Bldg Washington DC 20515-3101 Office Phone: 202-225-6316.*

**WILSON, HUGH MAL,** lawyer; b. Rutherfordton, NC, May 3, 1930; s. H. Mal and Ruth C. (Scruggs) W.; m. Martha Whitehead, Aug. 18, 1956; children: Karen, Lynne, Robert. AA, Mars Hill Coll., 1949; BBA, Wake Forest U., 1951, JD, 1956. Bar: N.C. 1956. Pvt. practice, Lenoir, N.C., 1957-62; ptnr. Wilson, Palmer & Lackey, Lenoir, 1962—2001, Wilson, Lackey & Rohr, Lenoir, 2001—. Bd. dirs. 1st Union Nat. Bank, Lenoir. Trustee Caldwell C.C., Lenoir, 1972-74, 87—; chmn. State Bd. Elections, Raleigh, 1974-76. Cpl. USAF, 1951-53. Mem. Assn. Trial Lawyers Am., N.C. Trial Lawyers Assn., N.C. State Bar, N.C. Bar Assn., Caldwell County Bar Assn. (pres.), Republican, Baptist. Office: Wilson lackey & Rohr PO Box 638 Lenoir NC 28645-0638

**WILSON, HUGH STEVEN,** lawyer; b. Paducah, Ky., Nov. 27, 1947; s. Hugh Gipson and Rebekah (Dunn) W.; m. Clare Maloney, Apr. 28, 1973; children: Zachary Hunter, Samuel Gipson. BS, Ind. U., 1968; JD, U. Chgo., 1971; LLM, Harvard U., 1972. Bar: Calif. 1972, U.S. Dist. Ct. (ctrl. dist.) Calif. 1972, U.S. Dist. Ct. (so. dist.) Calif. 1973, U.S. Ct. Appeals (9th cir.) 1975, U.S. Dist. Ct. (no. dist.) Calif. 1977, U.S. Supreme Ct. 1978, U.S. Dist. Ct. (ea. dist.) 1980. Assoc. Latham & Watkins, L.A., 1972-78, ptnr. San Diego, 1978—2004; mng. ptnr. Tennenbaum Capital Ptnrs., LLC, Santa Monica, Calif., 2005—. Recipient Jerome N. Frank prize U. Chgo. Law Sch., 1971. Mem. Calif. Club, Coronado Yacht Club, Order of Coif. Republican. Avocations: literature, zoology. Office: Tennenbaum Capital Ptnrs 2951 28th St Ste 1000 Santa Monica CA 90405 E-mail: steve.wilson@tennenbaumcapital.com.

**WILSON, I. DODD,** dean; b. St. Peter, Minn., July 10, 1936; m. Ginger Wilson; 2 children. AB summa cum laude, Dartmouth Coll., 1958; MD, Harvard U., 1961. Diplomate Am. Bd. Internal Medicine. Intern dept. medicine U. Minn. Hosps., Mpls., 1961—62; med fellow Dept. of Medicine, 1962-63, 65-66; instr. dept. of medicine U. Minn. Med. Sch., Mpls., 1967—68, asst. prof., 1968—71, assoc. prof., 1971—76, dir. sect. of gastroenterology, 1972—83, vice chmn. dept. of medicine, 1983—86, prof. medicine, 1976—86; dean, prof. medicine U. Ark. Coll. of Medicine, Little Rock, 1986—; exec. vice chancellor U. Ark. Med. Scis., 1994—2000, chancellor, 2000—. Mem. Univ. Hosp. Consortium Rsch. Task Force, 1994; adv. bd. UALR Donaghey Project, 1994—; mem. State Crime Lab. Bd., 1992—, chmn. 1991-92; bd. dirs. First Comml. Nat. Bank, Ark. Children's Hosp. Rsch. Inst., Inc.; mem. Ark. Rice Depot Bd., 1988-94; mem. State Med. Examiner's Commn., 1986-90; med. bd. Univ. Hosp., 1986—; mem. chancellor's cabinet U. Ark. for Med. Scis., 1986-2000; chmn. U. Minn. Clin. Assocs., ad hoc com. for fin matters 1986; vice chmn. U. Minn. Clin. Assocs., 1986, clin. assoc. exec. com., 1985; mem. univ. com. Univ. Press, 1985-86; clin. assoc. planning and mktg. com. U. Minn., 1985; mem. Hosp. Quality Assurance Steering com., 1984-96, chmn. hosp. utilization mgmt. com., 1985;

mem. Univ. Bookstore com., 1985; mem. Univ. Senate, 1985-86; chmn. dept. medicine search com. for Dir. of Gen. Internal Medicine, 1985; chmn. med. sch. search com. head of dept. dermatology U. Minn., 1984, chmn. dept. medicine search com. for dir. pulmonary sect. 1984, mem. hosp. bd. govs. com. on planning and devel., 1983-86, med.-surg. hosp. facilities com., 1982-83, mem. steering com. of self-study task force U. of Minn. Med. Sch., 1982-83, many more coms. Contbr. numerous articles to profl. jours. Lt. USNR, 1963—65. Fellow ACP; mem. AMA, Am. Fedn. for Clin. Rsch., Am. Gastorenterol. Assn., Ctrl. Soc. for Clin. Rsch., Am. Assn. for the Study of Liver Disease, Ark. Med. Soc. (editl. bd. 1988-93, ex-officio mem., coun. 1987—), Pulaski County Med. Soc., Assn. of Am. Med. Colls. (coun. of deans, chair 1995-96, mgmt. edn. program planning com. 1993—, adv. panel on strategic positioning for health care reform 1992-95, exec. coun. 1992-97, adminstrv. bd. 1992-97, DEANS-VA coordinating com. 1990-94, ad hoc com. on nursing svcs. and the tchg. hosp. 1989, adv. com. on medicare regulations for payment of physicians in tchg. hosps. 1989), So. Med. Phi Beta Kappa, Alpha Omega Alpha. Office: Univ Ark for Med Scis Mail Slot #541 4301 W Markham St Little Rock AR 72205-7101

**WILSON, IAN EDWIN,** cultural organization administrator, archivist; b. Montreal, Que., Can., Apr. 2, 1943; s. Andrew and Marion (Mundy) W.; m. Ruth Dyck, Mar. 24, 1979. BA, Queen's U., Kingston, Ont., 1968, MA History, 1974; DLitt York U. (hon.), 2001. Archivist Queen's U., Kingston, Ont., Canada, 1966-76; provincial archivist Sask. (Can.) Archives, 1976-86; archivist of Ont. Ont. Govt., Toronto, 1986-99; dir. gen. info. resource mgmt. divsn. Ministry Culture, Tourism and Recreation, Toronto, 1990-93; nat. archivist Canada, 1999—2004; v.p. Internat. Coun. on Archives, 2000—04; librarian and archivist of Can., 2004—. Sec. Kingston Hist. Soc., 1967-72, v.p.; 1972-76; chair cons. group Social Sci. and Humanities Rsch. Coun. Can., Ottawa, 1979-80; adj. prof. Faculty Info. Studies U. Toronto, 1993-2002; spkr. in field. Author: (with J. Douglas Stewart) Heritage Kingston, 1973; editor: Kingston City Hall, 1975; producer: (with J. William Brennan) Regina Before Yesterday, 1978; contbr. articles to profl. jours. Chmn. congregation Mennonite Ch., Regina, 1981-84; mem. Sask. award merit selection com., 1985-86; chair Sask. Heritage adv. bd., 1978-83; Ont. dir. Forum for Young Canadians, 1995-99. Recipient Queen Elizabeth II silver and gold jubilee medal, 1977, 2002, W.G. Leland cert. commendation Soc. Am. Archivists, 1981, W. Kaye Lamb prize Assn. Can. Archivists, 1983; Woodrow Wilson hon. fellow, 1967; apptd. mem. Order of Can., 2002; apptd. comdr. l'ordre des arts et des lettres, France, 2003. Fellow Soc. Am. Archivists; mem. Ont. Hist. Soc. (exec. coun. 1970-73; v.p. 1973-75, pres. 1975-76), Can. Hist. Assn. (past chmn., vice chmn., pres. archives sect. 1972-74), Champlain Soc. (bd. dirs., v.p. 1989-95, pres. 1995-2003). Home: 10 Bayport Priv Ottawa ON Canada K1V 0Z3 Office: Libr and Archives Canada 550 Boul de La Cite Gatineau PQ Canada K1A 0N4 Office Phone: 613-934-5800. E-mail: ian.wilson@lac-bac.gc.ca.

**WILSON, IAN HOLROYDE,** management consultant, futurist; b. Harrow, Eng., June 16, 1923; came to U.S., 1954; s. William Brash and Dorothy (Holroyde) W.; m. Page Tuttle Hedden, Mar. 17, 1951 (div. Dec. 1983); children: Rebecca, Dorothy, Ellen, Holly, Alexandra; m. Adrianne Marcus, July 12, 1992. MA, Oxford U., 1948. Orgn. cons. Imperial Chem. Industries, London, 1948-54; various staff exec. positions in strategic planning, mgmt. devel. Gen. Electric Co., Fairfield, Conn., 1954—80; sr. cons. to maj. U.S. and internat. cos. SRI Internat., Menlo Park, Calif., 1980-93; prin. Wolf Enterprises, San Rafael, Calif., 1993—. Exec. in residence Va. Commonwealth U., Richmond, 1976; fellow Va. Ctr. for Creative Arts, 1994, 98, 2000. Author: Planning for Major Change, 1976, The Power of Strategic Vision, 1991, Rewriting the Corporate Social Charter, 1992, Managing Strategically in the 1990s, 1993, Executive Leadership, 1995, The New Rules of Corporate Conduct, 2000, The Subtle Art of Strategy, 2003; co-author: The Scenario Planning Handbook, 2006; contbg. editor: Learning from the Future, 1998; mem. editl. bd. Planning Rev., 1973—81; Am. editor: Long Range Planning Jour., 1981—89; sr. editor, mem. editl. bd. Strategy and Leadership, 1993—2004. Mem. adv. bd. Technol. Forecasting and Social Change, 1989—99; chmn. Citizen's Long Range Ednl. Goals Com., Westport, Conn., 1967—70; mem. strategic process com. United Way of Am., Alexandria, Va., 1985—94. Capt. Brit. Army, 1943—45, ETO. Mem. AAAS, Assn. for Strategic Planning, World Future Soc. Unitarian Universalist. Avocations: travel, writing, photography. Home and Office: 79 Twin Oaks Ave San Rafael CA 94901-1915 Office Phone: 415-454-6062. Personal E-mail: jason415xx@aol.com.

**WILSON, ISABEL GOMEZ,** elementary school educator, consultant; b. Bogota, Colombia, Dec. 19, 1939; arrived in U.S., 1951; BS, Fla. Internat. U., 1983; MEd, U. Miami, 1984; PhD, So. Ill. U., 1993. ESL instr. BiNat. Ctr., Bogota, 1970-71; chpt. 1 tchr. Dade County Pub. Sch., Miami, Fla., 1983-84, Oceanside Unified Sch. Dist., Oceanside, Calif., 1990—. Mem. Coalition for Peace, Carlsbad, 1990—. Recipient Bilingual Edn. Promotion award Yeshiva U., 1982. Mem. Nat. Assn. for Bilingual Edn., Coun. for Exceptional Children. Office: St Thomas U 16400 NW 32nd Ave Miami Gardens FL 33054

**WILSON, JACK,** aeronautical engineer; b. Sheffield, Yorkshire, Eng., Jan. 5, 1933; arrived in U.S., 1956; s. George and Nellie (Place) W.; m. Marjorie Reynolds, June 3, 1961 (div. Jan 1991); children: Tanya Ruth, Cara; m. Carol Blixen, Jan. 3, 1997. BS in Engring., Imperial Coll., London, 1954; MS in Aero. Engring., Cornell U., 1958, PhD in Aero. Engring., 1962. Sr. scientific officer Royal Aircraft Establishment, Farnborough, England, 1962-63; prin. rsch. sci. Avco-Everett Rsch. Lab., Everett, Mass., 1963-72; vis. prof. Inst. Mecanique des Fluides, Marseille, France, 1972-73; sr. scientist U. Rochester, NY, 1973-80; sr. rsch. assoc. Sohio/BP Am., Cleve., 1980-90; sr. engring. specialist Sverdrup Tech. Inc., Cleve., 1990-93, NYMA, Brook Park, 1994-98, DYNACS Engring. Co., Inc., Brook Park, 1998-2001, QSS Group Inc., Fairview Park, Ohio, 2001—06, ASRC Aerospace Corp., Fairview Park, Ohio, 2006—. Author: (chpt.) "Gas Lasers" of Applied Optics in Engineering VI, 1980, "Laser Sources" of Techniques in Chemistry XVII, 1982; contbr. articles to profl. jours. Co-recipient Manly award, Soc. Automotive Engrs., 1995; recipient Soaring Gold Badge award, Fedn. Aero. Internat., Paris, 1998. Fellow AIAA (assoc.; tech. com. 1991-92). Achievements include first to demonstrate gas-dynamic laser, measurement of air ionization rate at high speeds, wave rotor performance, and unsteady ejector thrust augmentation; patents in application of high speed flow to gas laser media, devel. of antimony dopant sources. Office: ASRC Aerospace Corp 21000 Brookpark Rd Cleveland OH 44135-3127 Office Phone: 216-977-1204. Business E-Mail: jack.wilson@grc.nasa.gov.

**WILSON, JACK FREDRICK,** retired federal government official; b. Salt Lake City, Apr. 2, 1920; s. John Lorimer and Mayme J. (James) W.; m. Gwendolyn Gwynn, Nov. 20, 1947; children: Wendy, Elaine, Barbara Ann, Laurel, John F. Jr., James C. BS, Brigham Young U., 1942; postgrad., Mont. State U., 1962, Pa. State U. 1965. Range conservationist Bur. Land Mgmt., Rawlins, Wyo., 1949-57, dist. mgr. Burley, Idaho, 1957-67, dist. and land office mgr. Riverside, Calif., 1967-72; dir. Boise Interagy. Fire Ctr., Idaho, 1972-81; dir. Office Aircraft Services U.S. Dept. Interior, Boise, 1981-87; dir. Boise Interagy. Fire Ctr., 1987-92; ret., 1992. Contbr. articles to profl. jours. Dir. county disaster com. ARC, 1982-88. Maj. USAF. 1942-47 Recipient Meritorious award U.S. Dept. Interior, 1976, Disting. Service award, 1981, EEO Performance award, 1985; Outstanding Contbn. to Fire Mgmt. award U.S. Dept. Agr. Forest Service, 1976, Pub. Lands Found. Life Time Svc. Award 2002. Mem. Am. Foresters (chmn. fire com. 1980-82), Am. Soc. Range Mgmt. (sec. pres. 1967), So. Calif. Assn. Foresters and Fire Wardens, Lions (sec. 1954-57). Mem. Ch. of Jesus Christ of Latter-day Saints. Avocations: long range weather forecasting, genealogy, reading, golf. Home: 1820 Sunrise Rim Rd Boise ID 83705-5138 Personal E-mail: jfwilson4@cableone.net.

**WILSON, JAMES CHARLES, JR.,** lawyer; b. Birmingham, Ala., Sept. 13, 1947; s. James C. and Angelina (Serio) W.; m. Ann Bullock, Mar. 1, 1975; children: Brent Trammell, Lucy Bullock. BA, Tulane U., 1969, JD, 1972;

MBA, Samford U., 1995. Ptnr. Bradley, Arant, Rose & White, Birmingham, 1972-90, Lange, Simpson, Robinson & Somerville, Birmingham, 1990-93, Sirote & Permutt, P.C., Birmingham, 1993-96; v.p. and gen. counsel Shop-A-Snak Food Mart, Inc., Birmingham, 1996; pres. Lucent Holdings, Inc., Golden, Miss., 1997-98; ptnr. Baker, Johnston & Wilson LLP, Birmingham, Ala., 1999—2002; shareholder Baker Donelson, Bearman, Caldwell & Berkowitz, PC, Birmingham, 2003—. Adj. prof. internat. bus. transactions and internat. law U. Ala., Tuscaloosa, 1983-85, 89-96; internat. bus. transactions Cumberland Sch. Law, 1990-95, adj. prof. corp. fin., 2001—, adj. prof. securities regulation, 2003—. Author: Alabama Business Corporation Law, 1980; co-author: Corporate Law for the Healthcare Provider: Organization, Operation, Merger and Bankruptcy, 1993, Alabama Business Corporation Law Guide, 1995. Adv. bd. Jr. League of Birmingham, 1984; bd. dirs. Ala. chpt. Am. Liver Found., 1993-97, sec., 1994-95; trustee The Altamont Sch., 1995-2001, v.p., 1996-98, pres., 1998-2000. With U.S. Army, 1972-76. Mem.: ABA (sect. internat. law, tax and corp., banking and bus. law), Birmingham Bar Assn. (chmn. pub. rels. com. 1990, chmn. spl. projects com. 2002, chmn. membership benefits com. 2003), Ala. Law Inst., Ala. Bar Assn., Am. Law Inst., Birmingham Golf Assn. (pres., v.p., treas. 1982—84), Rotary (pres. Birmingham-Sunrise club 1986—87, bd. dirs. 2006—). Office: 1600 South Trust Tower 420 North 20th St Birmingham AL 35203 Office Phone: 205-244-3829. Business E-Mail: jwilson@bakerdonelson.com.

**WILSON, JAMES HARGROVE, JR.,** lawyer; b. Oliver, Ga., Nov. 26, 1920; s. James Hargrove and Louise (Sealy) W.; m. Frances Audra Schaffer, Dec. 24, 1942 (dec. Nov. 1990); children: Susan Frances, James Hargrove. AB with honors, Emory U., 1940; LL.B. summa cum laude, Harvard U., 1947. Bar: Ga. 1947, D.C. 1951. Assoc. firm Sutherland, Tuttle & Brennan (now Sutherland, Asbill & Brennan LLP), Atlanta and Washington, 1947-53, ptnr., 1953—. Lectr. Emory U., 1959, chmn. bd. visitors, 1967-68; trustee The Northwestern Mut. Life Ins. Co., Milw., 1972-91; mem. advisory group Commr. of Internal Revenue, 1963-64 Pres.: Harvard Law Review, 1946-47. Chmn. bd. trustees Met. Atlanta Crime Commn., 1970-71; mem. Harvard U. Overseers Com. to Visit Law Sch., 1959-65; trustee Emory U., 1983-90, trustee emeritus, 1990—. Served to lt. comdr. USNR, 1942—46. Fellow Am. Bar Found.; Am. Coll. Tax Counsel; mem. ABA, State Bar Ga., D.C. Bar, Atlanta Bar Assn., Am. Law Inst. (coun. 1974—), Lawyers Club Atlanta (pres. 1960-61), Am. Judicature Soc., Harvard Law Sch. Assn. (coun. 1981-85), Emory U. Alumni Assn. (pres. 1966-67), Capital City Club, Piedmont Driving Club, Peachtree Club, Phi Beta Kappa, Omicron Delta Kappa, Kappa Alpha. Methodist. Home: 3171 Marne Dr NW Atlanta GA 30305-1931 Office: Sutherland Asbill & Brennan LLP 999 Peachtree St NE Ste 2300 Atlanta GA 30309-3996

**WILSON, JAMES LAWRENCE,** retired chemical company executive; b. Rosedale, Miss., Mar. 2, 1936; s. James Lawrence and Mary Margaret (Klingman) W.; m. Barbara Louise Burroughs, Aug. 30, 1958; children: Lawrence Burroughs, Alexander Elliott. B.Mech. Engring., Vanderbilt U., 1958; MBA, Harvard, 1963. Vice pres. Nyala Properties, Inc., Phila., 1963-65; staff assoc. Rohm & Haas Co., Phila., 1965-67, exec. asst. to pres., 1971-72, treas., 1972-74, regional dir. Europe, 1974-77, group v.p., 1977-86, vice-chmn., 1986-88, chmn., CEO, 1988-99; ret., 1999. Treas. Warren-Teed Pharms., Inc., Columbus, Ohio, 1967-68, v.p., 1969; pres. Consol. Biomed. Labs., Inc., Dublin, Ohio, 1970-71; bd. dirs. Vanguard Group Investment Cos., Cummins Inc., MeadWestvaco Corp., AmeriSourceBergen Corp. Trustee Vanderbilt U., 1987—, Culver Ednl. Found., 1988—; chmn. Phila. High Sch. Acads., 1989-99. Mem. Chem. Mfrs. Assn. (bd. dirs. 1988-99, chmn. 1996). Office: 175 Strafford Ave Ste 1 Wayne PA 19087-3331

**WILSON, JAMES LEE,** retired geology educator, consultant; b. Waxahachie, Tex., Dec. 1, 1920; s. James Burney and Hallie Christine (Hawkins) W.; m. Della I. Moore, May 8, 1944; children: James Lee Jr., Burney Grant, Dale Ross (dec.). Student, Rice U., 1938-40; BA, U. Tex., 1942, MA, 1944; PhD, Yale U., 1949. Geologist Carter Oil Co., Tulsa, 1943-44; asst. and assoc. prof. U. Tex., Austin, 1949-52; rsch. geologist Shell Devel. Co., Houston, 1952-66; prof. Rice U., Houston, 1966-79, U. Mich., Ann Arbor, 1979-86; geol. cons. New Braunfels, Tex., 1986—. Cons. Erico Corp., London, 1985-88, Masera Corp., Tulsa, 1988—, Coyote Geol. Svcs., Boulder, Col., 1990—; adj. prof. Rice U., 1986—. Author: Carbonate Facies in Geologic History, 1975; contbr. articles to tech. jours. With C.E., U.S. Army, 1944-46, Italy. Grantee NSF. Fellow: Geol. Soc. Am. (Sloss award); mem.: Con. Soc. Petroleum Geologists, South Tex. Geol. Soc., West Tex. Geol. Soc., Am. Assn. Petroleum Geologists (hon. Disting. Educator award), Paleontological Soc., Econ. Econ. Paleontology and Minerology (pres. 1972—73), field trip guide books 1989, Sidney Powers Meml. award 2002, Twenhofel award, Hedberg award), Internat. Sedimentological Soc. Avocations: piano, languages. Home and Office: 1316 Patio Dr New Braunfels TX 78130-8505 Office Phone: 830-625-6612. Personal E-Mail: jlwilson@nbtx.com.

**WILSON, JAMES MILLER, IV,** cardiovascular surgeon, educator; b. Atlanta, Mar. 11, 1946; s. James Miller Wilson III and Sara Sharp; m. Lisa VanLandingham; children: James Miller V, Robert Paul, Michael Simpson, Sara Ann. Student, Emory U.; MD, Duke U., 1971. Diplomate Am. Bd. Surgery, Am. Bd. Thoracic Surgery. Intern N.Y. Hosp., 1971-72; resident N.Y. Hosp.-Cornell Med. Ctr., 1972-73, U. Calif., San Francisco, 1975-80; attending staff Christ Hosp., Cin., 1980—, Bethesda Hosp., Cin., 1980—, Jewish Hosp., Cin., 1980—, Univ. Hosp., Cin., 1982—, Deaconess Hosp, Cin., 1982—, VA Med Ctr., Cin., 1983—, Children's Hosp., Cin., 1984—, Good Samaritan Hosp., Cin., 1994—; assoc. prof. clin. surgery U. Cin. Coll. Med., 1985—; chmn. dept. cardiovasc. surgery Deaconess Hosp., 1985—2001; dir. cardiac surgery Mercy Hosp., 2001—. Open heart surgery adv. com., Ohio, 1995—; tech. adv. panel on cardiac surgery Nat. Quality Forum; mem. Thoracic Surgery Found.; lectr. in field. Contbr. articles to profl. jours. Lt. Comdr. submarine svc. USN, 1973-75. Fellow ACS, Am. Coll. Cardiology, Am. Heart Assn. (cardiovasc. coun.), Am. Coll. Chest Physicians; mem. AMA, U.S. Naval Submarine League, UDT/SEAL Assn., U.S. Submarine Vets., Inc., Am. Thoracic Surgery, Thoracic Surgery Found., Assn. Acad. Surgery, Soc. Thoracic Surgeons, Ohio State Med. Assn., Cin. Acad. Medicine, Howard C. Nafziger Soc. Avocations: music, diving, hiking, skiing, horses. Office: Heart Hosp #33S 3050 Mack Rd Fairfield OH 45014 Office Phone: 513-603-8600. E-mail: jmwilson@alumni.duke.edu.

**WILSON, JAMES RAY,** international business educator; b. Mar. 7, 1930; s. Ray Crawford and Ruth Lee (Walthers) W.; m. Carolyn Dempsey, Feb. 1, 1952; children: Robin E., Victoria, Mark, Jamie. BA, U.S. Navy Coll. Tng. Program scholar), Miami U., Oxford, Ohio, 1951; postgrad., Miami U., 1967—68; MA, Ohio State U., 1969, PhD, U. Minn., 1984. Grad. asst. Ohio State U., 1955—56; grain mcht. Cargill Inc., Balt., 1956-58; pres. Granexport Corp., Manilla, Philippines, 1959—66; mng. dir. Tradax Graanhandel B.V., Amsterdam, 1966—67; instr. dept. geography Miami U., 1967—68; pres. Cargill Agricola S.A., Sao Paulo, Brazil, 1968—78; dir. indsl. div. Tradax Geneve S.A., Geneva, 1978—80; corp. v.p. Cargill Inc., Mpls., 1980—83; pres. Cargill S.E. Asia, Ltd, Singapore, 1984—88; internat. bus. prof. Miami U. of Ohio, Oxford, Ohio, 1988—92, prof. mgmt., 1994—98; chmn. Cargill Tech. Svcs., Ltd., Thame, England, 1992—94; proprietor Antiquarian Bookstore, Ohio, 1998—. Served with USN, 1952-55. Fellow Royal Geog. Soc. Congregationalist. Home: 6533 Buckley Rd Oxford OH 45056-9727 Office: Books in Shandon 4795 Cincinnati-Brookville PO Box 8 Shandon OH 45063 Office Phone: 513-738-2962.

**WILSON, JAMES REID, JR.,** publishing executive; b. Phila., Aug. 5, 1934; s. James Reid Wilson and Florence Dunn; m. Eve-Ann Jones; children: Suzanne Winters, Diantha Curtis. BS in Econs., U. Pa., 1956. Assoc. dir. western hemisphere promotion The NY Times, NYC, 1966-69, mgr. indsl. advt., 1969-74; mgr. corp. advt. US News & World Report, NYC, 1974-79, advt. mgr., 1979-85, mktg. mgr., 1985-86; sr. v.p. Newspaper Advt. Bur., NYC, 1986-93; dir. Izvestia/Hearst, WeMbl, NYC and Moscow, 1993-94; pres. Media Ptnr., NYC, 1995-97; ad sales dir. Forbes SIP, NYC, 1997-2000, v.p., 2000—03; mng. dir. Hollywood Stars, 2004—05. Pres. Pa. Assn. Retarded Citizens, 1969-71; sr. v.p. Assn. Retarded Citizens US, Arlington,

Tex., 1975-77, pres. 1977-79; bd. mem. Walker Ctr., One-to-One. Mem. St. Nicholas Soc., Union League, Scarsdale Golf Club, Penn Club, NY Sons of the Revolution. Republican. Presbyterian. E-mail: 329wilson@comcast.net.

**WILSON, JAMES ROSS,** communications educator, broadcast executive; b. Petaluma, Calif., Nov. 25, 1939; s. Stanley Thomas and Billie (Ross) W.; m. Elizabeth Ann Buckleman; Dec. 29, 1964 (div. 1982); children: Greg, Tom. BA, Fresno State Coll., 1961; MA, Calif State U., Fresno, 1976. Radio and TV instr. Dept. Def. Info. Sch., Ft. Slocum, N.Y., 1962-65; news dir. Sta. KVON, Napa, Calif., 1965; Sta. KTIM, San Rafael, Calif., 1966; news reporter Sta. KMJ, Fresno, 1966-67, news dir., 1967-71; program dir. Sta. KMJ/KNAX-FM, Fresno, 1971-78, v.p., gen. mgr., 1978-82; news assignment editor Sta. KFSN-TV, Fresno, 1982-83; prof. mass comm., gen. mgr., faculty advisor KFSR-FM Calif. State U., Fresno, 1983—; jazz disk jockey Sta. KVPR, Valley Pub. Radio, Fresno, 1984-90; weekend news anchor KMPH-FM News Radio, 1994-96. Co-author: Mass Media/Mass Culture, 4th edit., 1997, 5th edit., 2000. Recipient Best Newscast award Calif. AP-TV-Radio Assn., 1971, Best News Documentary award Calif. AP-TV-Radio Assn., 1973-74, Broadcast Excellence award Billboard mag., 1976; Calif. State U. grantee, 1987. Mem. Broadcast Edn. Assn., Cen. Calif. Broadcasters Assn. (treas., bd. dirs. 1980-83), Assn. for Edn. in Journalism and Mass Communication, Soc. Profl. Journalists, Alpha Epsilon Rho, Phi Kappa Phi. Home: 4747 E Holland Ave Fresno CA 93726-2914 Office: Calif State U Dept Mass Comm Journalism Fresno CA 93740-0001 E-mail: james_wilson@csufresno.edu.

**WILSON, JANE,** artist; b. Seymour, Iowa, Apr. 29, 1924; d. Wayne and Cleone (Marquis) Wilson; m. John Gruen, Mar. 28, 1948; 1 child, Julia Gruen. BA, U. Iowa, 1945, MA, 1947. Mem. fine arts faculty Parsons Sch. Design, 1973-83, 89-90. Vis. artist U. Iowa, 1974; adj. assoc. prof. painting and drawing Columbia U., 1975—85, assoc. prof., 1985—86, prof., 1986—88, acting chair, 1986—88; Andrew Mellon vis. prof. painting Cooper Union, 1977—78. One-woman shows include Hansa Gallery, N.Y.C., 1953, 1955, 1957, Stuttman Gallery, 1958, 1959, Tibor de Nagy Gallery, 1960—66, Graham Gallery, 1968, 1969, 1971, 1973, 1975, Fischbach Gallery, 1978, 1981, 1984, 1988, 1990, 1991, 1993, 1995, 1997, Munson-Williams-Proctor Inst., Utica, N.Y., 1980, Cornell U., Ithaca, N.Y., 1982, Compass Rose Gallery, Chgo., 1988, Am. U., Washington, 1989, U. Richmond, Va., 1990, Earl McGratgh Gallery, LA, 1990—91, 1993, Dartmouth Coll., Hanover, N.H., 1991, Amot Mus., Elmira, N.Y., 1993—94, Parrish Mus., Southampton, N.Y., 1996, Glenn Horowitz Gallery, East Hampton, N.Y., 1996, D. C. Moore Gallery, N.Y.C., 1999, 2001, 2003, 2004, Heckscher Mus., Huntington, N.Y., 2001, McKinney Ave. Contemporary, Dallas, 2003, Represented in permanent collections Met. Mus., Mus. Modern Art, Whitney Mus., Wadsworth Athenaeum, Heron Art Mus., NYU Rockefeller Inst., Vassar Coll., Pa. Acad. Fine Arts, Hirsch Horn Mus., Washington, Nelson-Atkins Mus., Kansas City, Mo., San Francisco Mus. Modern Art, Heckscher Mus., L.I. Mus., Stony Brook, others. Recipient Eloise Spaeth award, Guild Hall, East Hampton, N.Y., 1968, Lifetime Achievement award, 2001, Purchase prize, Childe Hassam Fund, 1971, 1973, 1981, Ranger Fund Purchase prize, 1977; Ingram-Merrill grantee, 1963, Louis Comfort Tiffany grantee, 1967. Mem.: Nat. Acad. Design (academician 1974—, pres. 1992—94), Am. Acad. Arts and Letters (award in Art 1985), Phi Beta Kappa. E-mail: jwi1010@aol.com.

**WILSON, JASON,** chef; m. Nicole Wilson, 2001. Degree in Culinary Arts, Calif. Culinary Acad., 1995. Cook Aqua, San Francisco, Flying Saucer, San Francisco, Stars, Singapore, 1996, exec. chef Seattle, 1998; founder The Morning Grind coffee cart, South Lake Union, Wash.; caterer Duck Pond Winery, 2001—04; co-owner, exec. chef Crush, Seattle, 2005—. Recipient Best New Chef award, Food and Wine Mag., 2006. Office: Crush Restaurant 2319 E Madison St Seattle WA 98112 Office Phone: 206-302-7874.

**WILSON, JEAN DONALD,** endocrinologist, educator; b. Wellington, Tex., Aug. 26, 1932; s. J. D. and Maggie E. (Hill) Wilson. BA in Chemistry, U. Tex., 1951, MD, 1955. Diplomate Am. Bd. Internal Medicine. Intern, then resident in internal medicine Parkland Meml. Hosp., Dallas, 1955—58; clin. assoc. Nat. Heart Inst., Bethesda, Md., 1958—60; instr. internal medicine U. Tex. Southwestern Med. Sch., Dallas, 1960—61, prof., 1968—. Editor: Jour. Clin. Investigation, 1972—77. Sr. asst. surgeon USPHS, 1958—60. Recipient Fuller prize, Am. Urol. Assn., 1983, Lita Annenberg Hazen award, 1986, Dale medal, Soc. for Endocrinology, 1991, Pincus medal, Worchester Found., 1992. Fellow: Royal Coll. Physicians; mem.: NAS, Endocrine Soc. (Oppenheimer award 1972, Koch award 1993), Am. Soc. Biochemistry and Molecular Biology, Soc. Exptl. Biology and Medicine, Am. Philos. Soc., Assn. Am. Physicians (Kober medal 1999), Am. Soc. Clin. Investigation, Inst. Medicine, Am. Acad. Arts and Scis. (Amory prize 1977). Office: U Tex Southwestern Med Ctr Dept Internal Medicine 5323 Harry Hines Blvd Dallas TX 75390-8857 Fax: 214-648-8917. Office Phone: 214-648-3685. E-mail: jwils1@mednet.swmed.edu.

**WILSON, JEAN LOUISE,** retired state legislator; b. Phila., June 13, 1928; d. Horace and Catherine (Lennox) Terry; m. Benjamin H. Wilson (dec.); children: Sheryl J. Gordon, Denise T. Munn. BS in Edn., Pa. State U., 1949. Tchr. Columbia Inst., Phila., 1949-50, Wilkes Coll., Wilkes Barre, Pa., 1950-51; office mgr., exec. sec. Camden Fibre Mills, Warminster, Pa., 1969-82; mem. Pa. Ho. of Reps., 1988-92. Legis. chmn. Doylestown V.I.A.; active Benj. H. Wilson Sr. Ctr. for Learning in Retirement, Del. Valley Coll.; former mem. bd. Bucks County Opportunity Coun.; former treas. Bucks County chpt. Fox Chase Cancer Ctr. Avocations: duplicate bridge, golf. Home: 12 Far View Rd Chalfont PA 18914-2511

**WILSON, JERRY CLARK,** language educator; b. Boise, Idaho, Jan. 1, 1940; s. Gerald Vern and Betty Lou Wilson; m. Brenda Jean Urvin, June 3, 1960; children: Angela Sue Wilson Newburg, Stephen Jerry. BA in Religion, N.W. Nazarene Coll., Nampa, Idaho, 1963; cert. of Spanish, Inst. Mexicano Am., Mexico City, 1967; MA in Missiology, Fuller Theol. Sem., Pasadena, 1987; MA in Spanish, U. Calif., Santa Barbara, 1998. Dir. sem. Ch. of the Nazarene, Chiclayo, Peru, 1967—72, dir. bilingual sem. Boca Cuseo Alto Morano Jungle, Peru, 1975—78, sem. Panama City, Panama, 1976—78, dir. study/work program Santo Domingo, Dominican Republic, 1979—83; Spanish prof. Point Loma Nazarene U., San Diego, 1987—. Avocations: reading, repairing old cars, sports.

**WILSON, JOE (ADDISON GRAVES WILSON),** congressman, former senator, lawyer; b. Charleston, SC, July 31, 1947; s. Hugh deVeaux And Wray Smart (Graves) Wilson; m. Roxanne Dusenbury McCrory, Dec. 30, 1977; children: Michael Alan, Addison Graves, Julian Dusenbury, Hunter Taylor. BA, Washington and Lee U., Lexington, Va., 1969; JD, U. SC, Columbia, 1972. Bar: SC 1972. Staff mem. Staff of US Senator Strom Thurmond, Washington, 1967, Staff of US Rep. Floyd Spence, Columbia, SC, 1970-72; ptnr. Kirkland, Wilson, Moore, Taylor & Thomas, West Columbia, 1972—2001; mem. US Congress from 2nd SC dist., 2002—, mem. armed svcs. com., mem. edn. and the workforce com., mem. internat. rels. com., asst. majority whip. Dep. gen. counsel US Energy Sec. Jim Edwards, Washington, 1981-82; bd. dirs. Bank Am., Lexington, SC; mem. SC State Senate, Columbia, 1984-2001; presdl. appointee Intergovernmental Adv. Coun. Edn., 1990-91; mem. Internat. Observation Del. for 1990 Bulgarian parliamentary election Vice chmn. SC Rep. Party, 1972-74; campaign mgr. Staff of US Rep. Floyd Spence, Columbia, 1974, 78, 80, 82, 98; dist. campaign mgr. Staff of Gov. Carroll Campbell, 1986 Served in USAR, 1972—75, positions to col. SC Army N.G., 1975—2003. Mem. Rotary, Masons, Shriners. Republican. Presbyterian. Office: US Ho Reps 212 Cannon Ho Office Bldg Washington DC 20515 Office Phone: 202-225-2452.*

**WILSON, JOHN ATKINS, II,** application developer; b. Exeter, N.H., Jan. 19, 1961; s. John Atkins and Janice Lee (Deppe) W.; m. Rhonda Louise Eaton, Mar. 16, 1985; children: Daryl Atkins, Sarah Ellen, Hillary Elizabeth. BS magna cum laude in Computer Sci., U. N.H., 1983; MS in Software Engring., Wang Inst., 1988. Computer scientist U. N.H. Rsch. Computing

Ctr., Durham, 1980-83; mem. tech. staff MITRE Corp., Bedford, Mass., 1983-89, group leader, 1989-93, assoc. dept. head, 1993-95, dir. software prototyping, 1995-97, mgr. internet techs., 1997-2000, dir. info. tech., 2002—; sr. mgr. Kara Comm., 2000—01. Adj. faculty computer info. systems N.H. Coll., Nashua, 1989—96; adj. faculty computer sci. Boston U., 1996—, Daniel Webster Coll., 1996—. Avocation: electronic music. Office: MITRE Corp 202 Burlington Rd Bedford MA 01730-1420 E-mail: jawilson@mitre.org.

**WILSON, JOHN D.,** lawyer; b. Rockford, Ill., 1952; BA magna cum laude, 1974; JD, U. Pa., 1979. Bar: Ill. 1979, NY 1983. Former staff mem. US House of Rep. Conf. (John B. Anderson, Ill.), 1974—75; ptnr. Shearman & Sterling LLP, London, Paris, NYC, San Francisco, 1988—; mng. ptnr., Menlo Park, Calif. Arthur Littleton Instr. Office: Shearman & Sterling LLP 525 Market St San Francisco CA 94105 also: Shearman And Sterling Attn Todd 710 Bair Island Rd Apt 408 Redwood City CA 94063-5553 Office Phone: 415-616-1215, 650-838-3621. Office Fax: 415-616-1199, 650-838-3699. Business E-Mail: jwilson@shearman.com.

**WILSON, JOHN PASLEY,** law educator; b. Newark, Apr. 7, 1933; s. Richard Henry and Susan Agnes (Pasley) Wilson; m. Elizabeth Ann Reed, Sept. 10, 1955 (div.); children: David Cables, John Pasley, Cicely Reed. AB, Princeton U., 1955; LLB, Harvard U., 1962. Bar: N.J. 1962, U.S. Dist. Ct. N.J. 1962, Mass. 1963, U.S. Dist. Ct. Mass. 1963. Budget examiner Exec. Office of Pres., Bur. of Budget, Washington, 1955-56; assoc. Riker, Danzig, Scherer & Brown, Newark, 1962-63; asst. dean Harvard U. Law Sch., Cambridge, Mass., 1963-67; assoc. dean Boston U. Law Sch., 1968-82; dean Golden Gate U. Sch. Law, San Francisco, 1982-88, prof., 1988—2003, prof. emeritus, dean emeritus, 2003—. Vis. prof. dept. health policy and mgmt. Harvard U., 1988; cons. Nat. Commn. Protection Human Subjects Biomedical and Behavioral Rsch.; mem. Mass. Gov.'s Commn. Civil and Legal Rights Developmentally disabled; former chmn. adv. com. Ctr. Cmty. Legal Edn., San Francisco. Author: (book) The Rights of Adolescents in the Mental Health System; contbr. chapters to books, articles to profl. jours. Bd. dirs. Greater Boston Legal Svcs., Chewonki Found.; mem. Health Facilities Appeals Bd., Mass.; assoc. mem. Dem. Town Com., Concord; chmn. Bd. Assessors, Concord; bd. overseers Boston Hosp. Women, past chmn. med. affairs com.; past mem. instl. rev. bd. Calif. Pacific Hosp., San Francisco. Served to lt. (j.g.) USNR, 1956—59. NIMH grantee, 1973. Mem.: Nat. Assn. Securities Dealers (arbitrator). Office: Golden Gate U Sch Law 536 Mission St San Francisco CA 94105-2967 Office Phone: 415-442-6651. Personal E-mail: jwlsn7@comcast.net. Business E-mail: jwilson@ggu.edu.

**WILSON, JOHN THOMAS,** microbiologist; b. El Paso, Tex., Apr. 30, 1947; s. John Thomas and Marjorie Wilson; m. Barbara Hallum Wilson, Oct. 17, 1981; children: Toby Elizabeth, Carl Smith, Charles Smith, Ivan Smith. BS, Baylor U., Waco, Tex., 1969; MA, U. Calif., Berkeley, 1971; PhD, Cornell U., Ithaca, N.Y., 1978. Rsch. microbiologist U.S. EPA, Ada, Okla., 1979—. Contbr. articles to profl. jours. Dist. chmn. Harry Miller dist. Boy Scouts Am., Ada, Okla., 2004—06. Mem.: Rotary. Achievements include patents for biodegradation of halogenated aliphatic hydrocarbons. Home: 2013 Foster Dr Ada OK 74820 Office: RS Kerr Environmental Rsch Center 919 Kerr Research Dr Ada OK 74820 Office Phone: 580-436-8534. Office Fax: 580-436-8703. E-mail: wilson.johnt@epa.gov.

**WILSON, JONATHAN C.,** lawyer; b. Bristol, Tenn., Dec. 6, 1958; BA pers. mgmt., U. Wyo., 1980, JD with honors, 1983. Bar: Tex. 1983, admitted to practice: US Dist. Ct. (So. Dist.) Tex., US Dist. Ct. (Ea. Dist.) Tex., US Dist. Ct. (We. Dist.) Tex., US Dist. Ct. (No. Dist.) Tex., US Ct. Appeals (5th Cir.), US Ct. Appeals (6th Cir.), US Supreme Ct., cert.: State Bar Tex., Bd. Legal Specialization (specialist), Tex. Supreme Ct. Ptnr. Haynes and Boone LLP, Dallas, chmn., Labor and Employment Law Practice Group. Spkr. in field. Staff editor Wyo. Land & Water Law Rev., 1981—82. Named one of Best in Am. in labor and employment law, Corp. Counsel Mag., 2004. Mem.: Dallas Bar Assn., Tex. State Bar, ABA, Order of Coif. Office: Haynes and Boone LLP 901 Main St Ste 3100 Dallas TX 75202-3789 Office Phone: 214-651-5646. Office Fax: 214-200-0381. Business E-Mail: jonathan.wilson@haynesboone.com.

**WILSON, JOSEPH CHARLES, IV,** former ambassador; b. Bridgeport, Conn., Nov. 6, 1949; s. Joseph Charles III and Phyllis (Finnell) W.; m. Susan Dale Otchis, Apr. 27, 1973 (div. 1986); m. Valerie Elise Plame, Apr. 3, 1998; children: Sabrina Cecile, Joseph Charles, Trevor Rolph, Samantha Finnell Diana. BA in History, U. Calif., Santa Barbara, 1972. Fgn. svc. officer Dept. of State, Washington, 1976-98; congl. fellow Am. Polit. Sci. Assn., Washington, 1985-86; dep. chief of mission Am. Embassy, Bujumbura, Burundi, 1982-85, Brazzaville, Congo, 1986-88, Baghdad, Iraq, 1988-91; amb. Gabon, Sao Tome and Principe, 1992-95; polit. adv. to Commander in Chief U.S. Armed Forces Europe, 1995-97; spl. asst. to pres., sr. dir. for African affairs Nat. Security Coun., Washington, 1997-98; pres. JC Wilson Internat. Ventures, Washington, 1998—. Adj. scholar Mid. East Inst., 2002—04. Author: The Politics of Truth: Inside the Lies That Led to a War and Betrayed My Wife's CIA Identity--A Diplomat's Memoirs, 2004 (N.Y. Times Bestseller). Decorated comdr. Order of Equatorial Star (Gabon); recipient Disting. Alumni award U. Calif. Santa Barbara, 1991, 1995, Disting. Def. Dept. Civilian award, 1997; recipient Ron Ridenhour prize, 2003, Am. Patriot award Ams. for Informed Democracy, 2003. Mem. Am. Fgn. Svc. Assn. (William R. Rivkin award 1987), U. Calif. Santa Barbara Alumni Assn., San Onofre Surfing Club. Avocations: golf, bicycling, exercise, skiing.

**WILSON, JOSEPH MORRIS, III,** lawyer; b. Milw., July 26, 1945; s. Joseph Morris Jr. and Phyllis Elizabeth (Cresson) W.; children: Elizabeth J., Eric M.; m. Dixie Lee Brock, Mar. 23, 1984. BA, Calif. State U., Chico, 1967; MA, U. Washington, 1968; JD summa cum laude, Ohio State U., 1974. Bar: Alaska 1976, U.S. Dist. Ct. Alaska 1976, U.S. Ct. Appeals (9th cir.) 1986. Recruiter and vol. U.S. Peace Corps, Republic of Benin, 1969-73; legal intern U.S. Ho. of Reps., Washington, 1975; ptnr. Guess & Rudd P.C., Anchorage, 1976-88, chmn. comml. dept., 1981-82, ptnr. compensation com., 1982-84; mgr. Alaska taxes, sr. tax atty. BP Exploration Inc., Alaska, 1990-99. Bus. law instr. U. Alaska, Anchorage, 1977-78. Mem. Alaska Bar Assn., World Affairs Coun. Democrat. Avocations: music, sports, travel. Home and Office: 2556 Palmera Cir Las Vegas NV 89121-4016 Office Phone: 702-369-7105. E-mail: jsphwlsn@aol.com.

**WILSON, KAREN LEE,** museum staff member, researcher; b. Somerville, NJ, Apr. 2, 1949; d. Jon Milton and Laura Virginia (Van Dyke) W.; m. Paul Ernest Walker, 1980; 1 child, Jeremy Nathaniel. AB, Harvard U., 1971; MA, NYU, 1973, PhD, 1985. Rsch. assoc., dir. excavation at Mendes, Egypt Inst. Fine Arts, NYU, 1979-81; coord. exhbn. The Jewish Mus., N.Y.C., 1981-82, adminstrv. cataloguer, 1982-83, coord. curatorial affairs, 1984-86; curator Oriental Inst. Mus. U. Chgo., 1988-96, mus. dir., 1996—2003, rsch. assoc., 1988—; coord. Kish Project Field Mus. Natural History, Chgo., 2004—. Rsch. asso. Oriental Inst. U. Chgo. Author, editor: Mendes, 1982; contbr. articles to profl. jours. Mem.: Calif. Art Assn., Am. Oriental Soc. Office Phone: 312-665-7184. Business E-Mail: k-wilson@uchicago.edu.

**WILSON, KATHY KAY,** former foundation administrator, consultant; b. Monticello, Ind., Jan. 25, 1961; d. Kenneth L. and Janet I. Kruger; m. Douglas M. Wilson, July 20, 1991. AS, Ball State U., 1981; BS, Ind. Wesleyan U., 1989. Legal sec. Nesbitt Law Firm, Rensselaer, Ind., 1981-84; asst. to dir. Office of Patents and Copyrights Purdue Rsch. Found., West Lafayette, Ind., 1984-86; legal sec. Barnes & Thornburg, Indpls., 1986-87; rsch. and info. specialist Ind. U. Found., Indpls., 1987-91, rsch. mgmt. and info. svcs. Bloomington, 1991-98, dir. Office of Devel. Svcs., 1998-2001; prin. Wilson Cons., 2003—. Cons. Prospect Rsch., 1991—; mem. faculty Fund Raising Sch., 1988-90. Mem. adv. coun. Bloomington Hosp., 1992-2001. Mem. Am. Prospect Rsch. Assn. (v.p. bd. dirs. 1991, pres. 1992, Ind. chpt. pres. 1988-90), Phi Gamma Nu, Delta Delta Delta. Business E-Mail: wilsondk@home.ffni.com.

**WILSON, KEITH B.,** rehabilitation educator; b. Spartanburg, S.C., Feb. 19, 1962; s. George and Helen Annette Wilson; m. Beverly Jean Gaither, June 13, 1992; 1 child, Aliya Imani. BA, Wilberforce U.; MEd, Kent State U., 1985; PhD, Ohio State U., 1997. Cert. rehab. counselor. Case mgr. Ohio Bur. Vocat. Rehab., Canton, 1985; counseling coord. Savannah (Ga.) State U., 1986—89; dir. counseling svc. Brewton-Parker Coll., Mt. Vernon, Ga., 1989—94; grad. program asst. Ohio State U., Columbus, 1994—95, tchg. asst., 1995—97; asst. prof. Pa. State U., State College, 1997—. Cons. Brewton-Parker Coll., Mt. Vernon, 1993; mem. adv. bd. Pa. Office Vocat. Rehab., Harrisburg, 1998—; cons. Indiana U. Pa., 2000. Author: (newsletter) Mosaic, 2001; co-editor: Rehab. Counseling Bull., 2002. Judge Pa. State Grad. Exhbn., State College, 2001; chairperson Multicultural Ad. Com., Harrisburg, 2002—; bd. dirs. Inst. Sci. Advancement, Harrisburg, 2001. Recipient Bobbie Atkins Rsch. award, Nat. Assn. Multicultural, 2001. Mem.: Pa. Counseling Assn. (Named Outstanding Rschr. 2000), Pa. Rehab. Assn., Phi Beta Kappa. Home: 109 Berwick Dr Boalsburg PA 16827 Office: Pa State U Counselor Edn 308 Cedar Bldg State College PA 16802-3110 Office Phone: 814-863-2413. Business E-Mail: kbw4@psu.edu.

**WILSON, KEITH DUDLEY,** media and music educator, consultant, dean; b. Windermere, July 13, 1936; s. Charles Alexander and Fanny (Shaw) Wilson; 1 child, Nicholas. BA with honors, Kings Coll., Cambridge, 1957, MA, 1960; LittD (hon.), U. Salford, Manchester, Eng., 2000. Lectr. Brit. Coun./Zagreb Univ., Croatia, 1957-58; assoc. prof., dir. TV Brit. Coun. Tehran U., Iran, 1958-64; reader Brit. Coun. Osmania U., Hyderabad, India, 1964-66; head of liberal edn. Salford (Eng.) Coll. Tech., 1967-72, head of humanities, 1972-85; head of performing arts and media U. Coll. Salford, 1985-90; dir. Ctr. Media Performance and Comm. U. Salford, 1990-96, founding chief exec. Internat. Media Ctr., 1993-99, dean faculty of media, music and performance, 1996-99. Tutor, counsellor Open U., 1972—90; dir. TVUK, Adelphi Prodns., Salford, 1988—99, Channel M, 1997—2000; chair PRS John Lennon awards, 1990—93; co-chair NYNEX Cable TV, Manchester, 1993—95; vis. acad. Brit. Coun., Republic of Korea, 1992; founder over 30 higher edn. courses in music, media, drama, rec., entertainment orgns., media and sci., new media; European edn. advisor, cons. media, music and rec. industries, 2000—; resident broadcasts and recs. Edinburgh Internat. Festival, 1986—97. Musician: (concert tours) Brazil, Belgium, The Netherlands, Iceland, Norway, Denmark, Greece, Ecuador, Russia, Hungary; contbr. articles to profl. jours. and nat. papers. Mem. City of Salford LS Lowry Centenary, 1988, The Lowry, Nat. Landmark Millennium Project for Arts, Digital World Ctr.; founder Salford U. Brass Band, Wind Band, Big Band, Soundworks, Jazz Ensembles, Groove Machine, Aspects Theatre; mem. City Pride Initiative, Manchester, 1993—97, Fellowship Gt. Britain Sasakawa Found., Japan, 1991; mem. centenary com. U. Salford, 1994—96. Fellow: Royal Soc. Arts (chmn. N.W.); mem.: Prodrs. Assn. Cinema and TV, Brit. Acad. Film and TV, Brit. Film Inst., Royal TV Soc. Avocations: wine, walking. Home and Office: 60 Central Rd Didsbury Manchester M204ZA England

**WILSON, KENNETH GEDDES,** physics research administrator; b. Waltham, Mass., June 8, 1936; s. E. Bright and Emily Fisher (Buckingham) Wilson; m. Alison Brown, 1982. AB, Harvard U., 1956, DSc (hon.), 1981; PhD, Calif. Tech. Inst., 1961; PhD (hon.), U. Chgo., 1976. From asst. prof. to prof. physics Cornell U., Ithaca, NY, 1963—88, James A. Weeks prof. in phys. sci., 1974—87; Hazel C. Youngberg Trustees Disting prof. The Ohio State U., Columbus, 1988—. Co-author: Redesigning Education, 1974. Recipient Nobel prize in physics, 1982, Dannie Heinemann prize, 1973, Boltzmann medal, 1975, Wolf prize in physics, Wolf Found., Israel, 1980, A.C. Eringen medal, 1984, Franklin medal, 1982, Aneesur Rahman prize, 1993. Mem.: NAS, Am. Acad. Arts and Scis., Am. Phys. Soc., Am. Philos. Soc.

**WILSON, KENNETH JAY,** writer; b. Oklahoma City, Aug. 25, 1944; s. Kenneth J. and Betty Wallace (Bleakmore) W. BA magna cum laude, Yale U., 1966, M.Phil., 1969; postgrad. Queen's Coll., Oxford U., Eng., 1969-70; PhD, Yale U., 1973. From instr. to assoc. prof. English U. Rochester, NY; assoc. Clare Hall, Cambridge U., England; vis. assoc. prof. English Coll. William and Mary, Williamsburg, Va.; dir. of rights and permissions Princeton U. Press. Cons. USIA, 1985 Editor: Letters of Sir Thomas Elyot, 1976, English Works of Thomas More, 1978; author: Incomplete Fictions, 1985, Pope John Paul II, 1992; contbr. essays, book revs. and short fiction to mags. and profl. jours. Woodrow Wilson fellow, 1966, 83; sr. fellow Folger Shakespeare Library, Washington, 1976; Am. Philos. Soc. grantee, 1976; Am. Council Learned Soc. fellow, 1977 Mem. Mory's Club, Elizabethan Club (New Haven), Yale Club (NYC), Palm-Aire Country Club, Phi Beta Kappa. Democrat. Roman Catholic. Home: 5570 Country Club Way Sarasota FL 34243-3759 E-mail: nuboy@comcast.net.

**WILSON, L. MICHELLE,** lawyer; b. Boise, Idaho, Jan. 20, 1963; d. Tom Martin and George Ann Wilson. BA, U. Wash., Seattle, 1985; JD, U. Chgo., 1988. Ptnr. Perkins Coie, Seattle, 1988—; assoc. gen. counsel Amazon.com Inc., Seattle, 1999—99, v.p., gen. counsel, sec., 1999—. Recipient Dow Jones award Wall St. Jour., 1985. Mem. ABA, Washington State Bar Assn., Order of Coif, Phi Beta Kappa, Beta Gamma Sigma. Office: Amazon.com Inc 1200 12th Ave S Ste 1200 Seattle WA 98144-2734 Office Phone: 206-266-1000. Office Fax: 206-266-1821.

**WILSON, LANFORD,** playwright; b. Lebanon, Mo., Apr. 13, 1937; s. Ralph E(ugene) and Violetta (Tate) W. Student, San Diego State Coll., 1955-56; PhD in Humanities (hon.), U. Mo., 1985, Grinnell Coll., 1994; PhD in Lit. (hon.), L.I. U., 1995. Playwright, 1962—; resident playwright, dir., co-founder Cir. Repertory Co., NYC, 1969-93. Instr. playwriting U. Houston, 2003—. Author: (plays) So Long at the Fair, 1963, Home Free!, 1964, No Trespassing, 1964, The Sandcastle, 1964, The Madness of Lady Bright, 1964, Ludlow Fair, 1965, Balm in Gilead, 1965, This is the Rill Speaking, 1965, Days Ahead, 1965, Sex is Between Two People, 1965, The Gingham Dog, 1966, The Rimers of Eldritch, 1966, Wandering, 1966, Lemon Sky, 1969, Serenading Louie, 1970, The Great Nebula in Orion, 1970, The Hot L Baltimore, 1972, The Family Continues, 1972, The Mound Builders, 1975, Fifth of July, 1978, Brontasaurus, 1978, Talley's Folly, 1979, A Tale Told, 1981, Angels Fall, 1983, A Betrothal, 1984, Talley & Son, 1985, Burn This, 1987, A Poster of the Cosmos, 1987, The Moonshot Tape, 1990, Redwood Curtain, 1991, Trinity, 1993, I'm Not the Ocean, 1995, Sympathetic Magic, 1996, A Sense of Place (or Virgil is Still the Frogboy), 1997, Your Everyday Ghost Story, 1997, Book of Days, 1998, Rain Dance, 2003; translator Three Sisters, 1984, Ghosts, 2002; author: (books) Balm in Gilead and Other Plays, 1966, The Rimers of Eldritch and Other Plays, 1968, The Gingham Dog, 1969, Lemon Sky, 1970, The Hot L Baltimore, 1973, The Mound Builders, 1976, Fifth of July, 1979, Talley's Folly, 1980, Angels Fall, 1983, Serenading Louie, 1985, Talley & Son, 1986, Burn This, 1988, Redwood Curtain, 1992, 21 Short Plays, 1994, By the Sea, 1996, Collected Plays, Vol. I, 1997, Vol. II, 1999, Vol. III, 1999, Vol. IV, 2006, A Sense of Place, 1999, Sympathetic Magic, 1999, Book of Days, 2001, Rain Dance, 2005. ABC Yale fellow, 1969; Rockefeller grantee, 1967, 73, Guggenheim grantee, 1970, NEA grantee, 1990; recipient Vernon Rice award, 1966-67, Inst. Arts and Letters award, 1970, Obie award, 1972, 75, 84, 97, Outer Critics Circle award, 1973, Drama Critics Circle award, 1973, 80, Pulitzer prize, 1980, Brandeis award, 1981, John Steinbeck award, 1990, Edward Albee Last Frontier award, 1994, Am. Acad. of Achievement award, 1995, Am. Assn. Theatre Critics Best Play award, 1998, Guild Hall Lifetime Achievement award, 2000, William Inge Lifetime Achievement award, 2001; inducted into Theater Hall of Fame, 1996, Mo. Writers Hall of Fame, 1998; recipient Lucille Lortel's Edith Oliver award for Sustained Excellence, 2001. Mem. Am. Acad. Arts and Letters, Dramatists Guild Am. Council.

**WILSON, LAURA ANN,** newspaper editor; b. Otis AFB, Mass., Oct. 3, 1967; d. Robert Carl Laidacker, Emmett Adkins, Jr. and Wanda June (Laidacker); m. Charles John Wilson, Dec. 12, 1992; children: Brendan, Emily. Cert., Lucas Travel Sch., 1988; AA, Pierce Coll., 1993; BS, U. So. Fla., 1997. Intern The Tampa Tribune, Fla., 1996, bus. clerk Fla. 1996; mgn.

editor The Pinellas News, St. Petersburg, Fla., 96-98; cmty. editor The Star Democrat, Easton, Md., 1998-2000, spl. sects. editor, 2000—03; editl. specialist Shore Health System, 2003. Spkr. Career Day, Clearview Elem. Sch., St. Petersburg, Fla., 1997, Easton Middle Sch., Md., 1998: guest spkr. Md. Nonprofits, Balt., 1999; student mentor, Talbot Mentors, Easton, 1999—. Mem. The Writers Guild (v.p. USF chpt. 1994), Soc. Profl. Journalists (pres. USF chpt. 1996). Avocations: bowling, walking, reading, travel, movies. Office: Shore Health Sys 219 S Wash St Easton MD 21601 E-mail: lwilson@chespub.com.

WILSON, LELAND EARL, retired petroleum engineer; b. Ft. Recovery, Ohio, Oct. 28, 1925; s. John Huffman and Matilda Caroline (Sunderhaus) W.; m. Marian Ruthetta Trygstad, Nov. 27, 1948; children: Kathleen Ann, Linda Kay, Mary Lee, John Russell. BS in Petroleum Engring., Tulsa U., 1950. Registered profl. engr., Alaska, Tex. Drilling engr. Atlantic Refining Co., Tex., Ark., and La., 1950-56, drilling supr. La., Tex., 1956-65; drilling supt. Atlantic Richfield, Anchorage, 1965-67, prodn. and drilling supt., 1967-72; ops. mgr. ARCO Oil Prodn. Co., London, 1972-75; resident mgr. ARCO Greenland, Copenhagen, 1975-78; pres. ARCO Indonesia, Inc., Jakarta, 1978-82; v.p. ARCO China, Hong Kong, 1982-85; petroleum cons. Lindale, Tex., 1985—. Author family history Dear John, 1989; contbr. articles to profl. jours.; inventor in field. Aviation cadet AAF, 1943-45. Recipient Pioneer award, East Tex. Soc. Petroleum Engrs., 2004. Mem. NSPE, Tex. Soc. Profl. Engrs., Soc. Petroleum Engrs., Petroleum Club (pres. Anchorage 1971-72), Indonesian Petroleum Assn. (pres. 1981-82). Republican. Roman Catholic. Avocations: genealogy, golf, travel.

WILSON, LEONARD GILCHRIST, medical educator; b. Orillia, Ont., Can., June 11, 1928; s. George Edward and Mary Agnes (MacPhee) W.; m. Adelia Katherine Hans, June 7, 1969; 1 child, George Edward Hans. BA, U. Toronto, Can., 1949; M. U. London, 1955; PhD, U. Wis., Madison, 1958. Lectr. Mount Allison U., Sackville, N.B., Canada, 1950-53; vis. instr. U. Calif., Berkeley, 1958-59; asst. prof. Cornell U., Ithaca, NY, 1959-60, Yale U., New Haven, 1960-65, assoc. prof., 1965-67; prof., head dept. history of medicine U. Minn., Mpls., 1967-98, prof. emeritus, 1998—. Author: Charles Lyell: The Years to 1841: The Revolution in Geology, 1972, Medical Revolution in Minnesota, 1989, Lyell in America: The Trans Atlantic Years, 1841-1853, 1998; editor: Benjamin Silliman and His Circle, 1979, Sir Charles Lyell's Scientific Journals on the Species Question, 1971; editor Jour. History Medicine and Allied Scis., 1973-82; co-editor: Readings in History of Physiology, 1966; mem. bd. mgrs. Jour. Hist. Medicine, 1962—. Fellow AAAS; mem. Am. Assn. History of Medicine, Am. Hist. Assn., History of Sci. Soc., Minn. Acad. Medicine (pres. 1984-85, sec.-treas. 1989-98), Brit. Soc. for the History of Sci., Soc. for the History of natural History. Home: 797 Goodrich Ave Saint Paul MN 55105-3344 Business E-Mail: wilso004@umn.edu.

WILSON, LEVON EDWARD, lawyer, educator; b. Charlotte, N.C., Apr. 2, 1954; s. James A. and Thomasina Wilson. BSBA, Western Carolina U., 1976; JD, N.C. Ctrl. U., 1979; Ed D, 2001. Bar: N.C. 1981, U.S. Dist. Ct. (mid. dist.) N.C. 1981, U.S. Tax Ct. 1981, U.S. Ct. Appeals (4th cir.) 1982, U.S. Supreme Ct. 1984; lic. real estate broker, N.C.; cert. mediator N.C. Alternative Dispute Resolution Commn., arbitrator BBB. Pvt. practice, Greensboro, NC, 1981-85; assist. county atty. Guilford County, Greensboro, 1985-88; asst. prof. N.C. Agrl. & Tech. State U., Greensboro, 1988-91, Western Carolina U., Cullowhee, NC, 1991-96, prof., 1996—, prof., head dept. bus. adminstrn., law and mktg., 1996—2002; pres. Integrated Mgmt. Resources, Inc., 2000—; prof. Sch. Acctg., Ga. So. U., Statesboro, 2005—. Pres. Trade Brokers Cons.; legal counsel, bd. dirs. Rhodes Assocs., Inc., Greensboro, 1982—; legal counsel Guilford County Sheriff's Dept., Greensboro, 1985-88; bd. dirs. Webster Enterprises, Inc. Contbr. articles to profl. jours. Bd. dirs. Post Advocacy Detention Program; active mem. Prison Litigation Study Task Force, Adminstrn. Justice Study Com. Recipient Svc. award Blacks in Mgmt., 1980, Excellence in Tchg. award Jay I. Kneedler Found. of Western Carolina U., 1994-95, 2003-2004; Student in Free Enterprise fellow, Bd of Govs. award for Excellence in Tchg. U. NC Sys, 2004-05. Mem. ABA, N.C. Bar Assn., Acad. Legal Studies in Bus., Southeastern Acad. Legal Studies in Bus. (former editor-in-chief Jour. of Legal Studies in Bus., mng. editor), N.C. Assn. Police Attys., N.C. Real Estate Educators Assn., So. Acad. Legal Studies in Bus., Phi Delta Phi, Beta Gamma Sigma. Democrat. Methodist. Office: Ga So U Sch Accountancy PO Box 8141 Statesboro GA 30460-8141 Home: PO Box 1414 Statesboro GA 30459-1414 Personal E-mail: levonwilson@msn.com. Business E-Mail: lwilson@georgiasouthern.edu.

WILSON, LEWIS LANSING, insurance executive; b. Cobleskill, N.Y., Jan. 26, 1932; s. Clarence A. and Ordella (Walker) W.; m. Barbara Jane Kathan, June 7, 1952; children: Susan W. Coleman, Joan, Peter L. (dec.) Grad. high sch., Cobleskill. Cert. profl. ins. agt., ins. cons. Mgr. claims Sterling Ins. Co., Cobleskill, 1950—57; ins. agt. State Farm Ins. Co., Cobleskill, 1957—59; pres. Lewis L. Wilson Inc., Cobleskill, 1959—91, Fire Mark Ins. Agy., Inc., Cobleskill, 1991—. Pres. Redington Amb. Resort, North Redington, Fla., Point Pleasant Resort, St. Thomas, V.I., bd. dirs.; owner Wilson Travel Agy., 1978—, Wilson Tel. Exch., Cobleskill, 1978-86, Wilson Security, Inc., Cobleskill, 1981-86; rep. N.Y. Mapp Program, 1985-88 Town chmn. Cobleskill Rep. Party, 1978-83; chmn. Schoharie County Rep. Com., N.Y., 1983—, Cobleskill SUNY Found. Fund Drive; commr. Schoharie County Bd. Elections, 1983—; pres. Cobleskill Ctrl. Sch. Bd., Cmty. Hosp. Schoharie County, Cobleskill; dir. Schoharie Colonial Heritage; past chmn. Nat. PIA PAC (chmn. nat. gov. affairs, 1st v.p.); pres. Cobleskill Cemetery Assn., 1999—; chmn. Two Million One Hundred Thousand Rescue Fund Recipient Gold medal, Ronald Reagan, 2004. Mem. Profl. Ins. Agts. (pres. 1989, bd. dirs., v.p. 1987, 1st v.p. 1988, pres. 1989-90, nat. v.p., Ins. Agt. of Yr. 1986), N.Y. Ind. Ins. Agts. (regional v.p.), N.Y. Life Underwriters, Rotary (pres. Cobleskill chpt., gov. dist. 719 1982, Paul Harris fellow 1985-86), Elks (exalted ruler, hon. founder nat. found. 1980), Nat. Assn. Profl. Ins. Agts. (v.p. 2000—, Person of Yr. 1997) Republican. Methodist. Home: 168 Grandview Dr Cobleskill NY 12043 Office: PO Box 39 Cobleskill NY 12043-0039 Office Phone: 518-234-2534.

WILSON, LINDA, librarian; b. Rochester, Minn., Nov. 17, 1945; d. Eunice Gloria Irene Wilson. BA, U. Minn., Morris, 1967; MA, U. Minn., 1968. Libr. rsch. svcs. U. Calif., Riverside, 1968-69, head dept. phys. scis. catalog, 1969-71; city libr. Belle Glade (Fla) Mcpl. Libr., 1972-74; instr. part-time Palm Beach Jr. Coll., Belle Glade, 1973; head adult-young adult ext. Kern County Libr. Sys., Bakersfield, Calif., 1974-80; dir. dist. libr. Lake Agassiz Regional Libr. System, Crookston, Minn., 1980-85; supervising libr. San Diego County Libr., 1985-87; county libr. Merced (Calif.) County Libr., 1987-93; learning network mgr. Merced Coll., 1994-95; city libr. Monterey Park (Calif.) Bruggemeyer Libr., 1995—. Mem. Leadership Merced, 1987-88, East Site Based Coordinating Coun., Merced, 1990-92, Merced Gen. Plan Citizens Adv. Com., 1992-95, Sister City Com., Merced, 1992-95. Recipient Libr. award Eagles Aux., 1984, Woman of Achievement award Commn. on the Status of Women, 1990, Libr. award Calif. Libr. Trustees and Commrs., 1990, Woman of Yr. award Merced Bus. and Profl. Women, 1990, People Who Make a Difference award Monterey Pk. United Dems., 2003, Woman of Yr. award 29th Congl. Dist., 2004. Mem. ALA (sec. pub. libr. sys. sect. 1988-89), Met. Coop. Library Sys. (pres. 1999-2000), Calif. Libr. Assn. (sec. govt. rels. com. 1991-92, continuing edn. com. 1993-96, pub. rels. 1997-2000, nominations com. 2000-01), Minn. Libr. Assn. (pres. pub. libr. divsn. 1985), Merced County Mgmt. Coun. (pres. 1989), Merced Bus. and Profl. Women (Woman of Yr. 1984, pres. 1988-89), East L.A.-Montebello Bus. and Profl. Women (v.p. 1998-2002, pres. 2002-05), Rotary (pres. Monterey Park chpt. 1999-2000). Democrat. Lutheran. Avocations: travel, walking, reading, swimming, stamp collecting/philately. Home: 1000 E Newmark Ave Apt 22 Monterey Park CA 91755-3129 Office Phone: 626-307-1418. Business E-Mail: lwilson@montereypark.ca.gov. E-mail: lindalwilson@juno.com.

WILSON, LINDA SMITH, retired academic administrator; b. Washington, Nov. 10, 1936; d. Fred M. and Virginia D. Smith; m. Malcolm C. Whatley, June 29, 1957 (div. 1969); 1 child, Helen K. Whatley; m. Paul A. Wilson, Jan.

22, 1970; 1 stepchild, Beth A. BA, Tulane U., 1957, HLD (hon.), 1993; PhD, U. Wis., 1962; DLitt (hon.), U. Md., 1993. Rsch. assoc. U. Md., College Park, 1962—64, rsch. asst. prof., 1964—67; vis. asst. prof. U. Mo., St. Louis, 1967—68; asst. to vice chancellor for rsch., asst. vice chancellor for rsch., assoc. vice chancellor for rsch. Washington U., St. Louis, 1968—75; assoc. vice chancellor for rsch. U. Ill., Urbana, 1975—85; assoc. dean U. Ill. Grad. Coll., Urbana, 1978—85; v.p. for rsch. U. Mich., Ann Arbor, 1985—89; pres. Radcliffe Coll., Cambridge, Mass., 1989—99, pres. emeritus, 1999; sr. lectr. Harvard Grad. Sch. Edn., 1989—2003; bd. dirs. Myriad Genetics, Tulane U., Tulane Murphy Found., Friends of DaPonte String Quartet; ret., 2003. Rsch. resources adv. coun. NIH, Bethesda, Md., 1987—, mem. Nat. Commn. on Rsch., Washington, 1978—80; dir.'s adv. coun. NSF, Washington, 1980—89; com. on govt.-univ. relationships NAS, 1981—83, govt.-univ.-industry rsch. roundtable, 1984—89, coord. coun. for edn., 1991—93; energy rsch. adv. bd. Dept. of Energy, 1987—90; chmn. adv. com. office sci. and engring. pers. NRC, 1990—96; adv. com. edn. and human resources NSF, Washington, 1990—95; sci., tech. and states task force Carnegie Commn. on Sci., Tech. and Govt., 1991—92; overser Mus. Sci., Boston, 1992—2001; trustee Mass. Gen. Hosp., 1992—99, hon. trustee, 1999—2002; trustee Com. on Econ. Devel., 1995—; bd. dirs. Inacom, Inc., 1997—2003, Citizens Fin. Group, Inc., 1997—2000, Value Line, Inc., 1998—2000; bd. vis. Coll. Letters and Sci. U. Wis., 1999—2005; dean's adv. coun. Newcomb Coll., 1999—. Contbr. articles to profl. jours. and book chpts. Adv. bd. Nat. Coalition for Sci. and Tech., Washington, 1983—87; bd. govs. YMCA, Champaign, Ill., 1980—83. Named One of 100 Emerging Leaders, Am. Coun. Edn. and Change Mag., 1978; recipient Centennial award, Newcomb Coll., 1986, Disting. Alumni award, U. Wis., 1997, Radcliffe medal, 1999. Fellow: AAAS (bd. dirs. 1984—88); mem.: Am. Coun. Edn. (commn. on women in higher edn. 1991—93, chair 1993), Inst. Medicine (commn. mem. 1986—89, com. on setting NIH priorities, com. on govt.-industry collaboration in biomed. edn. and rsch.), Assn. for Biomed. Rsch. (bd. dirs. 1983—86), Nat. Coun. Univ. Rsch. Adminstrs., Soc. Rsch. Adminstrs. (Disting. Contbr. to Rsch. Adminstrn. award 1984), Am. Assn. Univ. Women (com. on chemistry and pub. affairs 1978—80), Phi Kappa Phi, Phi Delta Kappa, Alpha Lambda Delta, Sigma Xi, Phi Beta Kappa. Home: 47 Keene Neck Rd Bremen ME 04551

WILSON, LIZABETH ANNE, dean, library director; b. Waterloo, Iowa, May 21, 1954; d. Martin Lucien and Joanne Hausser Wilson; m. Dean August Pollack, Sept. 1, 1983. BA, Northwestern U., 1972—77; MLS, U. of Ill., 1977—78. Asst. architecture and art libr. U. Ill., 1979—80, asst. undergrad. libr., 1980—86, asst. dir. libr. undergrad. and instrnl. svcs., 1986—92; assoc. dir. libr. for rsch. and instrnl. svcs. U. Wash., Seattle, 1992—2000, dean univ. librs., 2001—. Chair of bd. of trustees OCLC, Inc., Dublin, 2003—; exec. dir. Leopoldo Cicognara Program+, Urbana-Champaign, Ill., 1987—2004; co-founder UWired collaboration at the University of Washington. Author (co-author): (journal article) The Bottom Line; contbr. chapters to books, articles. Recipient Margaret E. Monroe Libr. Adult Services award, RUSA/Am. Libr. Assn., 1995, Miriam Dudley Instrn. Libr. award, Assn. of Coll. and Rsch. Libraries, 1995, EDUCAUSE Award for Systemic Progress in Tchg. and Learning, EDUCAUSE, 2000. Mem.: Greater Western Libr. Alliance (pres. 2004), Digital Libr. Fedn. (mem. exec. com. 2004—), OCLC Membs. Coun. (pres. 1999—2000), Assn. Rsch. Librs. (bd. dirs. 2003—), Instrn. Sect. of ACRL (chair 1990—91), Assn. Coll. and Rsch. Librs. (pres. 2000—01, Excellence in Academic Libr. award 2004). Achievements include development of Office: U Wash Box 352900 Seattle WA 98195-2900 Office Phone: 206-543-1763. Business E-Mail: betsyw@u.washington.edu.

WILSON, LLOYD LEE, registrar, educator; b. Elkton, Md., Sept. 14, 1947; s. Clifton Laws and Betty Raye (Bare) W.; m. Susan Sieg Wilson, 1992; children: Asa, Ryan, Morgan, Daniel. BS in Mgmt., MIT, 1969, MS in Mgmt., 1977. Bus. mgr. med. clinics Mass. Gen. Hosp., Boston, 1970-73; ptnr. Willow Co., mgmt. cons., Cambridge, Mass., 1974-77; dir. community relations Wilson Neuropsychiat. Hosp., Charlottesville, Va., 1977-78; exec. dir. Jefferson Area United Transp. Inc., Charlottesville, Va., 1978-80, Va. Mountain Housing Inc., Blacksburg, 1980-82; gen. sec. Friends Gen. Conf. Religious Soc. Friends, Phila., 1982-85; dir. rsch. and devel. Va. Mountain Housing, Inc., Christiansburg, 1985-88, dir. multifamily housing, 1989-91, regional dir., 1991-92; pres. Friendly Mgmt. Svcs. Corp., Norfolk, Va., 1992-95, Not-for-Profit Mgmt., Inc., Norfolk, Va., 1995—2004; registrar Chowan U., Murfreesboro, NC, 2002—, asst. prof. religion, 2006—. Dir. instnl. rsch. Chowan Coll., Murfreesboro, N.C., 2000—; asst. prof. of acctg., 2001—; pres., dir. Va. Housing Coalition, Inc., 1981-82; treas., bd. dirs. Cedar Grove Consulting, LLC, 2004—, Fiddle Hill Farm, Inc., Barboursville, Va., 1982-89; bd. mgrs. Bible Assn. Friends in Am., Phila., 1983-85; mem. com. rec. ministers Balt. Yearly Meeting Friends, Sandy Spring, Md., 1984-86; asst. sec.-treas. Friends Meeting House Fund, Inc., Phila., 1984-85; asst. presiding clk. Comm. Commn. of Friends United Meeting, Richmond, Ind., 1987-88; recorded min. of gospel, Soc. of Friends, 1989— (presiding clk. Va. Beach monthly meeting 1990-92); dir. coordinating cabinet Va. Coun. Chs., 1988; presiding clk. N.C. Yearly Meeting of Friends, 1991-92. Author: Essays on the Quaker Vision of Gospel Order, 1993, Wrestling with one Faith Tradition, 2005; contbr. articles to profl. jours. Treas., bd. dirs. Norfolk (Va.) Quaker House, Inc., 1995-2000; bd. dirs. New Dominion Housing, Inc., Norfolk, 1992-94; vice chmn. Montgomery County Cmty. Svc. Commn., Christianburg, Va., 1980-82; mem. ednl. coun. MIT, 1977-89; bd. dirs. Am. Friends Svc. Com., Inc., Phila., 1980-83; bd. dirs. Interfaith Housing Corp. Cambridge, Inc., 1975-77, treas., 1976-77, also numerous others. Home: PO Box 647 Woodland NC 27897-0647 Office Phone: 252-398-6246. Business E-Mail: llwilson@alum.mit.edu.

WILSON, LOIS FAIR, retired school system administrator; b. Redlands, Calif., Mar. 17, 1924; d. James Albert and Emma (Lederer) Fair; m. Herbert Blair Wilson (dec. Nov. 1989). BA, U. Redlands, 1945; MEd, U. So. Calif., LA, 1954 EdD, U. Ariz., 1972 Fla u h lu Tung Sch (Calif) City Sch in San Bernardino County, 1945-51; curriculum cons. Office of San Bernardino (Calif.) County Schs., 1951-61; asst. prof., coord. elem. edn. U. Redlands, Calif., 1961-64; supr. student tchrs. Calif., 1988—; program asst. to coord. for kindergartens Tucson Unified Sch. Dist., 1965-72; curriculum coord. to elem. prin., 1972-84; supr. student tchrs. Calif. State U., San Bernardino, 1985-88, ret., 1988; travel escort Hillsen's Tours and Travels, Redlands, 1984-92, Laura's Travel Svc., Redlands, 1992—95; escort San Diego Opera Summer Music Festival, 1993, 94; supr. student tchrs. interim program Summer Demonstrations Sch. Tchr. hard of hearing Easter Seal Pre-Sch., 1964-65; summer faculty World Campus Afloat, Chapman Coll., 1974-75, No. Ariz. U., 1978, 80; mem. steering com. Ariz. Young Readers' Conf., U. Ariz., 1975-84; mem. kindergarten curriculum guide com. State of Ariz.; tchr. Stanford U., 1956-58, team staff curriculum workshop, 1959. Contbr. articles to profl. jours. Mem. pre-sch. com. Tucson, 1967-68; bd. dirs. Town and Gown U. Redlands, 1985-92, pres., 1991-92, membership, sec., historian (Hon. Svc. award 1993); chair San Bernardino County Agrl. Stabilization and Conservation Svc. Com., 1986-1990; mem. Assocs. of the Redlands Bowl, Assistance League of Redlands, 1988—, heritage aux. 4th grade program, 3d grade drug awareness program, Kimberly Jrs. Reunion Com., 1991; bd. dirs. Redlands Hist. Mus., 2d v.p Recipient Cert. of Appreciation Dept. Edn. State of Ariz., 1984. Mem. AAUW, PEO (chpt. treas. 1994-95), ASCD (pres. 1960, pres. Ariz. chpt. 1980), Calif. Women for Agr., Ret. Edn. Mgrs. of Calif. (region 12), Calif. Ret. Tchrs. Assn. (v.p. Redlands-Yucaipa div. 1990-92), U. Redlands Pan Hellenic Alumnae (bd. dirs. 1984-90, class rep. 1996-98, alumni bd. 1994-1998), Redlands Assn. and Symphony Guild (bd. dirs., 2d v.p. 1988-90, 2003-05, chmn. youth music com. 1988-91, mem. adv. com. 1994-99), Inland Orange Conservancy, Redlands Conservancy, Friends A.K. Smiley Libr., Lincoln Shrine Assn., Redlands Sister City Assn., Redlands Hist. Glass Mus., Redlands Contemporary Club, April Morning Club (membership com. 1988-89, publicity 1989-90, yearbook 1991-92, pres. 1994-95), Alpha Delta Kappa Fidelis Iota (sec.), Redlands American Assn. Hist. Soc., U. Redlands Ret. Faculty Assn., Easter Seal Soc. (tchr. pre-sch. fostering learning deaf), Kimberly-Shirk Assn. Republican. Presbyterian. Avocations: travel, reading, classical music, research and writing, volunteerism. Home: 1131 Kimberly Pl Redlands CA 92373-6786

WILSON, LOIS M., minister; b. Winnipeg, Man., Can., Apr. 8, 1927; d. Edwin Gardiner Dunn and Ada Minnie (Davis) Freeman; m. Roy F. Wilson, June 9, 1950; children: Ruth, Jean, Neil, Bruce BA, United Coll., Winnipeg, 1947, BDiv, 1969; Diploma in TV prodn., Ryerson Tech. Inst., 1974; DDiv (hon.), Victoria U., Toronto, 1978, United Theol. Coll., Montreal, 1978, Wycliff Coll., 1983, Queens U., Kingston, 1984, U. Winnipeg, 1986, Mt. Allison U., 1988; LLD (hon.), LLD (hon.), Dalhousie U., 1989, Ripon Coll., Wis., 1992; LLD (hon.), U. Toronto, 2005, U. Manitoba, 2006; DCL, Acadia U., 1984; DHuml (hon.), Mt. St. Vincent, Halifax, 1984. Ordained to ministry United Church of Can., 1965. Minister, Thunder Bay, 1965-69, Hamilton, 1969-78, Kingston, 1978-80; moderator United Church of Can., Kingston, 1980-82, McGeachy sr. scholar, 1989-91; pres. Can. Council of Chs., Toronto, Ont., 1976-79; co-dir. Ecumenical Forum Can., Toronto, Ont., 1983-89; pres. World Council of Chs., Geneva, 1983-91; chancellor Lakehead U., Thurder Bay, Ont., 1990-2000; chmn. contemporary theology Lafayette-Orinda (Calif.) Presbyn. Ch., 1995; ind. senator Senate of Can., 1998—2002; apptd. ecumenist in residence Toronto Sch. Theology, 2006—. Mem. adv. coun. internt. devel. studies U. Toronto, 1987-93, Fair Oto Can., Across Boundries Multifaith Inst., Mining Watch Can.; spokesperson Project Ploughshares, 1st and 2d UN Conf. on Disarmament, N.Y.C., 1978-82; officer Human Rights Commn., Ont., 1973; mem. bd. regents Victoria U., 1990—; chief Can. Fact finding Mission to Sri Lanka, 1992; team mem. Ctrl. Am. Monitoring Group to El Salvador and Guatemala, 1993; spl. envoy of Can. to The Sudan, 1999-02; lectr. in field. Author: Like a Mighty River, 1980, Turning the World Upside Down, 1989, Miriam, Mary and Me, 1992, Telling Her Story, 1992, Stories Seldom Told, 1997, Nuclear Waste, 2000; mem. adv. bd.: Can. Woman Studies Jour., York U., 1993—2004; contbr. articles to profl. publs.; author: Transforming the Faith of our Fathers. Apptd. Can. Senator, 1998; pres. Social Planning Coun., Thunder Bay, 1967—68, Can. Com. for Scientists and Scholars, Toronto, 1982; mem. Refugee Status Adv. Com., 1985—89; chmn. Urban Rural Mission, Can., 1990—96; mem. environ. assessment panel Can. Nuclear Fuel Waste Mgmt. and Disposal Concept, 1989—96; bd. dirs. Elizabeth Fry Soc., Hamilton, 1976—79, Amnesty Internat., 1978—90, Can. Inst. for Internat. Peace and Security, 1984—87, Energy Probe, 1981—86, Internat. Ctr. Human Rights and Dem. Devel., 1997—98, Can. Univ. Svc. Overseas, 1983—85; trustee Nelson Mandela Fund, 1990—92. Decorated Order of Can., Order of Ont., Companion of Order of Can.; sr. fellow Massey Coll. U. Toronto, 2005—; recipient Queens Jubilee medal, Commemorative medal for 125th Anniversary of Confederation of Can., 1992, World Federalist Peace award, 1985, Pearson Peace medal UN Assn. of Can., 1985; named hon. pres. Student Christian Movement of Can., Toronto, 1976. Mem. DPR Korea Assoc., Canada (chmn. 2002-), Women, Peace and Security (co-chair 2001-), CAW (pub. rev. bd. 1986—), Can. Assn. Adult Edn. (bd. dirs. 1986-90), Friends Can. Broadcasting (bd. dirs. 1986-94, v.p.), Civil Liberties Assn. (v.p. 1986—), UNIFEM (nat. v.p. 1993-95, mem. CCIC team to monitor El Salvador election 1994), World Federalists (pres. Can. chpt. 1996-2000, v.p. World Federalist Movement intern, 1998-, acting pres., 2004-), Parliament of World's Religions (del. 1993), Christian-Jewish Dialogue Jerusalem (keynote speaker 1994). Mem. United Ch. Of Can. E-mail: royandlois.wilson@sympatico.ca.

WILSON, LUKE, actor; b. Dallas, Sept. 21, 1971; Actor: (films) Bottle Rocket, 1996, Telling Lies in America, 1997, Best Men, 1997, Scream 2, 1997, Bongwater, 1998, Dog Park, 1998, Home Fries, 1998, Rushmore, 1998, Kill the Man, 1999, Blue Streak, 1999, My Dog Skip, 2000, Committed, 2000, Preston Tylk, 2000, Charlie's Angels, 2000, Legally Blonde, 2001, Soul Survivors, 2001, The Royal Tenenbaums, 2001, The Third Wheel, 2002, Masked & Anonymous, 2003, Old School, 2003, Alex and Emma, 2003, Legally Blonde 2: Red, White & Blonde, 2003, Charlie's Angels: Full Throttle, 2003, Around the World in 80 Days, 2004, Anchorman: The Legend of Ron Burgundy, 2004, Mini's First Time, 2006, Hoot, 2006, My Super Ex-Girlfriend, 2006, Idiocracy, 2006; (TV series) The X Files, 1993, That '70s Show, 1998; actor, dir.: (films) The Family Stone, 2005; The Wendell Baker Story, 2005. Office: c/o Creative Artists Agy 9830 Wilshire Blvd Beverly Hills CA 90212*

WILSON, LYNTON RONALD, retired telecommunications industry executive; b. Port Colborne, Ont., Can., Apr. 3, 1940; s. Ronald Alfred and Blanche Evelyn (Matthews) W.; m. Brenda Jean (Black), Dec. 23, 1968; children: Edward Ronald, Margot Jean, Jennifer Lyn. BA, McMaster U., 1962, LLD, 1995; MA, Cornell U., 1967; D (hon.), U. Montreal, 1995; D in Civil Law, Bishop's U., Lennoxville, Que., Can., 1997; LLD, U. Cape Breton, 1998, Mount Allison U., 2000, Brock U., 2003. Dep. minister Ministry Industry and Tourism, Ont., Canada, 1978-81; pres. CEO Redpath Industries, Ltd., Toronto, Canada, 1981-88; mng. dir. N.Am. Tate and Lyle, PLC, 1986-89; chmn. bd. Redpath Industries, Ltd., Toronto, Canada, 1988-89; vice chmn. Bank of N.S. Toronto, Canada, 1989-90; pres., COO BCE, Inc., Montreal, Canada, 1990-92, pres., CEO, 1992-93, chmn., pres., CEO, 1993-96, chmn., CEO, 1996-98, chmn. bd. dir., 1998-2000. Chmn. bd. dir. CAE, Inc.; chmn. emeritus Nortel Networks Corp.; chmn. Daimler Chrysler Can. Adv. Coun.; mem. supervisory bd. Daimler Chrysler AG; chmn. bd. dirs. Allergen NCE. Founding co-chmn. HISTORICA Found., Canada. Decorated officer Order of Can. Mem. The Mount Royal Club of Montreal, York Club, Toronto Golf Club, Rideau Club, Mount Bruno Country Club. Home: 2038 Lakeshore Rd E L6J 1M3 Oakville ON Canada Office: 483 Bay Ste 7th Fl N Tower M5G 2C9 Toronto ON Canada Office Phone: 416-364-4612.

WILSON, M. ROY, academic administrator, medical educator; b. Yokohama, Japan, Nov. 28, 1953; BS, Allegheny Coll., 1976; MD, Harvard Med. Sch., 1980; MS in Epidemiology, UCLA, 1990. Diplomate Nat. Bd. Medicine, Am. Bd. Ophthalmology. Intern Harlem Hosp. Ctr., NYC, 1980-81; resident in ophthalmology Mass. Eye & Ear Infirmary/Harvard Med. Sch., Boston, 1981-84, glaucoma, 1984-85; clin. fellow in ophthalmology Harvard Med. Sch., 1980-85, clin. assist. ophthalmology, 1985-86; clin. instr. dept. surgery. Divsn. Ophthalmology Howard U. Sch. Medicine. Washington, 1985-86; asst. prof. ophthalmology UCLA, 1986-91; asst. prof., chief Divsn. Ophthalmology Charles R. Drew U. of Medicine and Sci., L.A., 1986-90, assoc. prof., chief Divsn. Ophthalmology, 1991-94, acad. dean, 1993, dean, 1995-98, prof., 1994-98, UCLA, 1994-98; dean sch. medicine Creihton U., Omaha, 1998—, interim v.p., 1999-2000, vice pres. health scis., 2001—; pres. Tex. Tech. U. Health Sci. Ctr., Lubbock, 2003—06; chancellor U. Colo at Denver Health Scis. Ctr., 2006—. Asst. in ophthalmology Mass. Eye and Ear Infirmary, 1985-86; cons. ophthalmologist, Victoria Hosp., Castries, St. Lucia, 1985-86; hosp. appointment, UCLA; chief physician Martin Luther King, Jr. Hosp., L.A., 1986—; project dir. Internat. Eye Found., Ministry of Health, 1985-86; biology lab instr., Allegheny coll., 1975; instr. in biochemistry Harvard U. Summer Sch., 1977-78; instr. Harvard Med. Sch., 1980-85, others; cons. and presenter in field; participant coms. in field. Mem. AMA, APHA, Assn. Rsch. in Vision and Ophthalmology, Chandler-Grant Glaucoma Soc., Nat. Med. Assn., Am. Acad. Ophthalmology, Inst. Medicine (elected 2003), Soc. Eye Surgeons Internat. Eye Found., Mass. Eye and Ear Infirmary Alumni Assn., So. Calif. Glaucoma Soc., West Coast Glaucoma Study Club, Assn. Univ. Profs. in Ophthalmology, L.A. Eye Soc., Glaucoma Soc. Am. Assn. Glaucoma Soc., Soc. Epidemiol. Rsch. Office: U Colo at Denver Health Scis Ctr 35 SYS Boulder CO 80309-0035*

WILSON, MAGGIE ISABELLE LOVELL, secondary school educator, literature educator; b. Branchville, Ala., Jan. 26; d. Winston Porter and Ruth Kate (Buckner) Lovell. AB, Samford U., Birmingham, Ala., 1971; MA, EdS, U. Ala., 1978; MFA, Loyola U., 1979; PhD, Sussex (Eng.), U., 1981. Cert. elem./secondary tchr. Tchr. English Birmingham Pub. Schs., 1972-92; tchr. English secondary edn. Terrell County Schs., Dawson, Ga., 1992-93. Author, illustrator: Carousel of Creative Communication, 1976, Leeds, Her Story, 1979; author: Creative Expressions, 1980, Into Our Third Century, 1984, From Brush Arbor Days to the Twentieth Century, 1992. Historian Leeds (Ala.) First United Meth. Ch., 1990-99; docent Birmingham Mus. Art, 1970-80; pres. Sylacauga dist. United Meth. Women, 1981-84. Recipient numerous awards Ala. Watercolor Soc., Birmingham, 1970—, Pres. award Kappa Pi, Samford U., Birmingham, 1971, Art of Distinction Salon Des Nations, Paris, 1984. Mem. AAUW, Internat. Biog. Assn., Ala. Coun. Tchrs.

English (bd. mem. 1976—), Leeds Art Coun., Leeds Hist. Soc., Birmingham Art Assn., Internat. Soc. Artists, Leeds Bus. and Profl. Women (pres. 1971-76, 86, 88—, Woman of Yr. 1996-97), Leeds United Meth. Women (pres. 1972-76, 84—, pres. Sylacauga dist. 1981-84), La. Watercolor Soc. (awards 1986-99), So. Watercolor Soc., Kappa Delta Epsilon, Phi Gamma Mu. Home: 1110 Montevallo Rd SW Leeds AL 35094-1926

WILSON, MALCOLM CAMPBELL, investment trust management executive; b. Phila., Dec. 9, 1942; s. James Murray and Janet (Haines) Wilson; m. Barbara Ann Bahmermann, June 10, 1989; children from previous marriage: Jennifer Marie, David Campbell, Andrew Russel. BS in Bus. Adminstrn., Drexel U., 1966, MBA in Fin., 1968. Chartered fin. analyst. Rsch. analyst Provident Nat. Bank, Phila., 1971—77, co-mgr. rsch. dept., 1977—78, dir. equity rsch., 1978—84, dir. econ. and investment rsch., 1984—88, chief investment officer PNC Fin. div., 1986—88, sr. v.p., mgr. personal svcs. group, 1989—92; exec. v.p., mgr. investment mgmt. and trust Phila. market PNC Bank, N.A., 1993—95; sr. v.p., mgr. Personal Svcs. Group, Mercantile-Safe Deposit and Trust Co., Balt., 1996—98, exec. v.p., mgr. investment mgmt. and trust, 1998—2003; mng. dir., ptnr. Davidson Capital Mgmt., Devon, Pa., 2003—. With USN, 1968—73. Fellow: Fin. Analysts Fedn.; mem.: N.Y. Soc. Security Analysts, Mayflower Soc., Pa. Soc. SAR. Republican. Episcopalian. Avocations: hunting, fishing, golf. Home: 103 Cawley Ct Chester Springs PA 19425 Office: Davidson Capital Mgmt 20 N Waterloo Rd Devon PA 19333 Office Phone: 610-254-2045. Business E-Mail: swilson@davidsoncapmgt.com.

WILSON, MARC FRASER, art museum director; b. Akron, Ohio, Sept. 12, 1941; s. Fraser Eugene and Pauline Christine (Hoff) W.; m. Elizabeth Marie Fulder, Aug. 2, 1975. BA, Yale U., 1963, MA, 1967. Departmental asst. Cleve. Mus. Art, 1964; translator, project cons. Nat. Palace Mus., Taipei, Taiwan, 1968-71; assoc. curator of Chinese art Nelson Gallery-Atkins Mus., Kansas City, Mo., 1971-73, curator of Oriental art, 1973—, interim dir., 1982; curator Oriental art Nelson-Atkins Mus. Art, Kansas City, 1982-99, dir./CEO, 1999—. Mem., rapporteur Indo-US Subcom. on Edn. and Culture, Washington, 1976-79; mem. adv. com. Asia Soc. Galleries, N.Y.C., 1984—; China Inst. in Am., 1985—. Mem. adv. com. Muni-Art Commn. on Urban Sculpture, Kansas City, 1984-87; com. mem. Kansas City-Xi'an, China, Sister City program, 1986—; mem. humanities coun. Johnson County Cmty. Coll., 1976-79; commr. Japan-U.S. Friendship Commn., Washington, 1986-88; panelist Japan-U.S. Cultural and Edn. Cooperation, Washington, 1986-88; mem. mayor's task force on race relations, 1996—; mem. indemnity adv. panel, 1995—; v.p. Brush Creek Ptnrs. 1996—. Recipient The William Yates Medallion Civic Svc. award William Jewell Coll., 1995, Disting. Svc. award Baker U., 1997. Mem. Assoc. Art Mus. Dirs. (treas., trustee 1988-90, chmn. works of art com. 1986-90), Mo. China Coun., Fed. Coun. Arts and Humanities (chmn. arts and artifacts indemnity adv. panel 1986-89, 1995-98). Office: Nelson-Atkins Mus Art 4525 Oak St Kansas City MO 64111-1818 E-mail: mwilson@nelson-atkins.org.

WILSON, MARGARET BUSH, lawyer; b. St. Louis, Jan. 30, 1919; married; 1 child, Robert Edmund. BA cum laude, Talladega Coll., 1940; LL.B., Lincoln U., 1943. Ptnr. Wilson & Wilson, St. Louis, 1947-65; now with firm Wilson & Assocs. Asst. dir. St. Louis Lawyers for Housing, 1969-72; asst. atty. gen. Mo., 1961-62; atty. Rural Electrification Adminstrn., Dept. Agr., St. Louis, 1943-45; instr. civil procedure St. Louis U. Sch. Law, 1971; chmn. St. Louis Land Reutilization Authority, 1975-76; mem. Mo. Coun. Criminal Justice, 1972—; chmn. Intergroup Corp., 1985-87; bd. dirs. Mut. of N.Y. Mem. gen. adv. com. ACDA, 1978-81; trustee emeritus Washington U., St. Louis; chmn. bd. trustees Talladega Coll., Ala., 1988-92; nat. bd. dirs. ARC, 1975-81, United Way, 1978-84, Police Found., 1976-93; treas. NAACP Nat. Housing Corp., 1971-84, chmn. nat. bd., 1975-84; dep. dir./acting dir. St. Louis Model City Agy., 1968-69; adminstr. Mo. Commn. Svc. and Continuing Edn., 1967-68. Recipient Bishop's award Episcopal Diocese Mo., 1962; Juliette Derricotte fellow, 1939-40, Disting. Lawyer award Bar Assn. Metro St. Louis, 1997; Margaret Bush Wilson Endowed Professorship in Arts and Scis. established at Washington U., St. Louis, 2004. Mem. ABA (women. youth edn. for citizenship 1991-94, chmn. Nat. Law Day 1998-2000), Nat. Bar Assn., Mo. Bar Assn., Mound City Bar Assn., St. Louis Bar Assn., Alpha Kappa Alpha. Office: Wilson & Assocs 4054 Lindell Blvd Saint Louis MO 63108-3202 Office Phone: 314-534-4400. Office Fax: 314-534-4403.

WILSON, MARGARET MARY GEORGIANA, geriatrician, researcher, physician; d. Victoria Arit and Andrew Iyere Wilson. MBBS, U. Ibadan, Nigeria, 1977, MB, 1983. Diplomate Am. Bd. of Internal Medicine, 2000. Sr. registrar U. of Ibadan, Oyo, Nigeria, 1988—90; dir. clin. svcs. St. Louis U., 2004—; clin. rsch. fellow Hammersmith Hosp., London, 1990—91, St. Louis U., 1994—97; assoc. prof. St Louis U., 2000—; med. dir. Tower Village NH, 2000—, Integrated Health Svcs., Big Bend Woods, Mo., 2003—04, Nat. Healthcare, Town and Country, Mo., 2004—. Mem. Nat. Coun. Nutrition, 2001—; mem. editl. bd. Jour. Gerontology: Med. Scis., St. Louis, 2000—; guest editor Clinics in Geriatric Medicine, Phila. Mem. MCC, St Louis, Mo., 2002—04. Recipient Chevening Medicine award, Brit. Fgn. and Commonwealth Office, 1990, Vincent Uzodike; Internal Medicine, Nat. Postgraduate Coll. of Physicians, Nigeria, 1991, Sunderland DGH Excellence in Clin. Presentation, Sunderland DGH, Eng., 1993, Sir William Osler Tchg. award, St. Louis U., 2003, Kathy Humphrey award, 2004, Fellow, Nat. Nigerian Med. Postgrad. Coll. Fellow: Nat. Postgrad. Coll. Physicians Nigeria, Acad. Minority Physicians (assoc.); mem.: Royal Coll. Physicians U.K., Am. Geriatric Soc., Brit. Clean. Study Fellows, Am. Med. Dirs. Assn. Christianity. Achievements include development of Geriatric Appetite Evaluation Instrument. Avocation: non-fiction works. Office: Geriatric Div St Louis U 1402 S Grand Blvd Rm M238 Saint Louis MO 63104 Office Phone: 314-977-8462. Business E-Mail: wilsonmg@slu.edu.

WILSON, MARGARET SCARBROUGH, retail executive; b. Aug. 7, 1930; Student, Smith Coll., 1948-50; BA, U. Tex., 1952. Mem. staff Bayway Refinery Exxon Corp., NJ, 1960-61; mem. staff psychiat. ward VA Hosp., Houston, 1962; from mem. staff to chmn. Scarbroughs, Austin, Tex., 1952—74, chmn. bd., CEO, 1974—. Mem., bd. dirs. audit and contbns. coms. R.J. Reynolds Industries, 1978-85; hon. bd. dirs. Internat. Longevity Ctr., N.Y.C.; bd. dirs. Scarbrough Devel. Corp., Nat. Retail Fedn., 1991-2002, Am. Productivity & Quality Ctr., 1991-2002; chmn. San Antonio br. Fed. Res. Bank Dallas, 1975-76; trustee Nat. Policy Assn., 1997-98; pres., treas. Scarbrough Ventures LLC, 2001-, MSW-NSG Mgmt. LLC, 2000-, MSW-NSG Enterprises Ltd., 2000-, MSW-NSG Real Estate Ventures Ltd., 2001-. Trustee Com. Econ. Devel., 1973—, Cooper Inst. for Aerobics Rsch., Dallas, 1980-93, St. Stephen's Sch., Austin, 1979-83; mem. Nat. Com. U.S.-China Rels., 1976—, dir. 1980-94; mem. U.S. Coun. Internat. Bus., 1977—, mem. exec. com., 1978—, trustee, 1978—; bd. vistors Babcock Grad. Sch. Mgmt.-Wake Forest U., Winston-Salem, N.C., 1983-86; mem. bus. coun. S.W. Tex. State U., 1983-86; mem. deptl. vis. com. dept. home econs. U. Tex.-Austin, 1983-84, pres.'s assocs., 1992—; mem. univ. coun. Rockefeller U., N.Y., 1982-86; mem. chancellor's coun. U. Tex. Sys., 1994—; mem. Tex. Rsch. League, 1977—, dir. audit com. 1986—; Friends of L.B.J. Libr., 1980—; assoc. mem. George Bush Presdl. Libr., 1995—; bd. dirs. World Bus. Coun., 1980-89; mem. adv. coun. Coll. Bus. Adminstrn., U. Tex.-Austin, 1964-68, Dean's Assocs. Coll. Fine Arts, 1985-87, Friends of Free Enterprise com. Coll. Engring., 1985-87; mem. India-U.S. Bus. Coun., 1976-82, dir., 1978-82; mem. Pres.'s Commn. on Pers. Interchange, 1972-73, UN Day Com., 1971-74; mem. Mayor's Bus. Roundtable, Austin, 1985-87; mem. Houston Com. Fgn. Rels., 1994—, Dallas Com. Fgn. Rels., 1997—, SRI Internat. Assocs. Program, 1998-99; mem. Conf. Bd. Mem. Alliance Francaise, Asia Soc. (adv. bd. Houston chpt.) 1991-94, mem. N.Y. chpt.), Houston World Affairs Coun., Austin World Affairs Coun., English Speaking Union, Tex. Assn. Taxpayers, Retail Industry Trade Action Coalition (trustee 1984), Nat. Planning Assn. (trustee 1985-97), Am. Enterprise Inst. Am. Mgmt. Assn. (dir. 1969-72), Internat. C. of C., British Am. Bus. Inc., U.S. C. of C. (bd. dirs. 1980-82), Tex. Asian C. of C. (mem. adv. coun. 1997—), Tex. State Soc. Wash., World Econ. Devel. Congress (mem. adv. bd. 1993),

Internat. Indsl. Conf. (mem. adv. coun. 1996-97), Coun. Fgn. Rels., World Econ. Forum, Bus. Coun. Internat. Understanding, Ctr. Strategic and Internat. Studies (Washington Round Table 1998—), Am. Enterprise Inst., Pacific Coun. on Internat. Policy, World Pres.'s Orgn. (internat. chpt., met. chpt., Dallas chpt., Houston chpt., Cen. Tex. chpt.), Pres.'s Cir. Nat. Acad. Scis., Inst. of Medicine and Inst. Engrs., Houston Forum, Brookings Instn., Bretton Woods Com., Brit.-N.A. Com., Tarry House, The University Club N.Y., Met. Club (Washington), Headliners Club, Tex. Breakfast Club of Washington, Kappa Kappa Gamma, numerous other local and nat. orgns. Office: 517 W 39th St Austin TX 78751-4904 E-mail: Margaret.Wilson@Scarbroughs.com.

WILSON, MARGARET SULLIVAN, retired executive dean, consultant; b. Norwich, Conn., Mar. 21, 1924; d. John Joseph and Margaret Ellen (Connelly) Sullivan; BS, Eastern Conn. State U., 1944; MA, U. Conn., 1949; m. William Robert Wilson, July 20, 1950 (dec.); children: Margaret Ellen, William Robert. Reading cons. Greenwich (Conn.) Pub. Schs., 1948-50; asst. prof. early childhood, chmn. dept. early childhood Eastern Conn. State U., Willimantic, 1967-77, exec. asst. to pres., 1977-78, v.p. adminstrv. affairs, 1978-80, exec. dean, 1980-89, emeritus dean, 1989—; commr. Nat. Commn. Prevention Infant Mortality, 1986-93, chair Norwich Econ. Devel. Commn., 1988-91, Southeastern Connecticut regional Planning Commn., 1999-2001(mem. 1993—); dir. Rose City Community Land Trust Housing, Com. on City Plan, 1992—; del. White House Conf. on Children, 1970, 80, White House Conf. on Travel and Tourism, 1995; corporator Chelsea Groton Savs. Bank, Norwich, Conn. Mem. Conn. Mental Health Bd., 1979-83; mem. adv. bd. Norwich Hosp.; chmn. rev. com. Conn. Health Coordinating Council; mem. Eastern Regional Mental Health Bd., 1976-83, chmn., 1979-81; mem. Norwich Bd. Edn., 1954-69, 80-83, adv. coun. head start and day care programs, 1986-91; mem. Conn. Dem. Cen. Com., 1966-82, Dem. Town Com., 1964-82, 86-90; chmn. Blue Ribbon Commn. To Establish Goals for U. Conn. Health Ct., 1975-76; sr. warden Ch. of Resurrection, Norwich, 1988-91, Dio Com on Ministry Higher Edn. Named Citizen of Yr., C. of C., 1970; recipient Disting. Alumni award Eastern Conn. State U., 1972, Mental Health Bell award Conn. Mental Health Assn., 1972, Valiant Women award Council Ch. Women, 1976, Woman of Yr. award Bus. and Profl. Women, 1978, Jefferson award Inst. Pub. Service, 1982, pres. Norwich Mus. Trust, Inc., 1992—; mem., vice chair Southeastern Conn. Regional Planning Commn., 1993—; dir. Family Svc. Southeastern Conn., 1995—, Southeastern Conn. Enterprise Region, Norwich Comm. and Tech. Learning Ctr.; past-pres. Eastern Conn. Cmty. Found.; del. White House Conf. on Aging, 1995. Mem. Norwich Area C. of C. (dir. 1979-81), Greater Willimantic C. of C. (edn. com. 1980-88), United Ch. Women Conn. (bd. dirs.). Democrat. Office: 83 Windham St Willimantic CT 06226-2211 Home: 5 Mills Ln Collinsville CT 06022

WILSON, MARIE C., foundation administrator; b. Ga. 5 children. D in Cmty. Svc. (hon.), Drake U. Dir. women's programs Drake U.; mem. DesMoines City Coun.; pres. Ms. Found. for Women, N.Y.C., 1984—. Co-creator Take Our Daus. To Work Day, 1993—; U.S. govt. del. UN Fourth World Conf. on Women, Beijing, 1995; co-founder, pres. The White House Project, 1998—. Co-author: Mother Daughter Revolution, 1993; author: Closing the Leadership Gap: Why Women Can and Must Help Run the World, 2004. Recipient Robert W. Scrivner award for creative grantmaking, Leadership for Equity and Diversity award, Women & Philanthropy. Office: Ms Found for Women 120 Wall St 33rd Fl New York NY 10005

WILSON, MARK, corporate financial executive; BS in Agrl. Econs.; MBA in Fin. and Acctg., Cornell U. V.p. Thomas Learning MacAndrews & Forbes; CFO Towers Perrin, Stamford, Conn., 2001—. Office: Towers Perrin 1 Stanford Plz Stamford CT 06901

WILSON, MARTIN D., pharmaceutical executive; Pres., COO D & K Healthcare Resources, Inc., St. Louis. Office: D&K Healthcare Resources Inc PO Box 16989 Saint Louis MO 63105-1389

WILSON, MARY ALICE, musician, educator; b. Nov. 2, 1939; MusB, Northwestern U., Evanston, Ill., 1961. Orch. band dir., pvt. tchr. Luth. Schs., Deerfield Pub. Schs., 1961-64; pvt. tchr. violin and piano Cleve., 1964-77; dir. Suzuki Program, violin tchr. W.Va. U., 1977—, chmn. music divsn., 2005; founder, leader Seneca String Quartet, Morgantown, W.Va., 1986—. Accompanist. Ch. vol. tchg. and music, Cleve., Chgo., Morgantown, 1960—. Recipient Outstanding Tchr. award, W.Va. U. Music Dept., 2005. Mem.: Am. String Tchrs. Assn. (co-developer, chmn. 5th yr. state solo competition, state sect. 2003—05), W.Va. Music Tchrs. Assn. (dist. chmn. of strings 1977—), state officer pub. 1989—, State Outstanding Tchr. Yr. 1996), Music Tchrs. Nat. Assn. (state office of composition contest 1989—). Home: 237 Poplar Dr Morgantown WV 26505-2519 E-mail: cbwilson@mail.wvu.edu, bigmacwil@hotmail.com.

WILSON, MARY ELIZABETH, epidemiologist, physician, educator; b. Indpls., Nov. 19, 1942; d. Ralph Richard and Cateryn Rebecca (Kurtz) Lausch; m. Harvey Vernon Fineberg, May 16, 1975. AB, Ind. U., 1963; MD, U. Wis., 1971. Diplomate Am. Bd. Internal Medicine, Am. Bd. Infectious Diseases. Tchr. of French and English Marquette Sch., Madison, Wis., 1963-66; intern in medicine Beth Israel Hosp., Boston, 1971-72, resident in medicine, 1972-73, fellow in infectious diseases, 1973-75; physician Albert Schweitzer Hosp., Deschapelles, Haiti, 1974-75, Harvard Health Svcs., Cambridge, Mass., 1974-75; asst. physician Cambridge Hosp., 1975-78; hosp. epidemiologist Mt. Auburn Hosp., Cambridge, 1975-79, chief of infectious diseases, 1978—2002, dir. Travel Resource Ctr., 1996—2002, mem. consulting staff, 2003—05. Mem. adv. com. immunization practices CDC, Atlanta, 1988—92; mem. acad. adv. com. Nat. Inst. Pub. Health, Mexico, 1989—91; cons. Ford Found., 1988; site dir. GeoSentinel Network, 1999—2002, spl. cons., 2002—; instr. medicine Harvard Med. Sch., Boston, 1975—93, asst. clin. prof., 1994—99, assoc. prof. medicine, 1999—2004, assoc. clin. prof., 2004—; assoc. Ctr. Health and Global Environment, 1996—2000; asst. prof. depts. epidemiology and population and internat. health Harvard Sch. Pub. Health, 1994—99, assoc. prof. population and internat. health, 1999—; lectr. Sultan Qaboos U., Oman, 1991; chair Woods Hole Workshop, Emerging Infectious Diseases, 1993. Author: A World Guide to Infections: Diseases, Distribution, Diagnosis, 1991; editor (with Richard Levins and Andrew Spielman): Disease in Evolution: Global Changes and Emergence of Infectious Diseases, 1994; mem. editl. bd. Current Issues Pub. Health, 1999—2003, Emerging Infectious Diseases, Global Change and Human Health, 1999—2003; sect. editor travel medicine and tropical diseases: Infectious Diseases Clin. Practices; mem. editl. bd. Infectious Diseases Clin. Practices, 2006—; assoc. editor: Jour. Watch Infectious Diseases, 1997—; mem. editl. adv. bd. Clin. Infectious Diseases, 1999—2004, spl. sect. editor Emerging Infections, Clinical Infectious Diseases, 2006—. Mem. Cambridge Task Force AIDS, 1987—90; bd. dirs. Horizon Comm., West Cornwall, Conn., 1990—97. Recipient Lewis E. and Edith Phillips award, U. Wis. Med. Sch., 1969, Cora M. and Edward Van Liere award, 1971, Mosby Scholarship Book award, 1971, Leo Blacklow Tchg. award, 1999; fellow, Ctr. Advanced Study Behavioral Scis., Stanford, Calif., 2002; scholar-in-residence, Bellagio (Italy) Study Ctr., Rockefeller Found., 1996. Fellow: ACP, Royal Soc. Tropical Medicine and Hygiene, Infectious Diseases Soc. Am.; mem.: Soc. for Epidemiol. Rsch., Internat. Union Against Tuberculosis and Lung Disease, Soc. for Vector Ecology, Wilderness Med. Soc., Internat. Soc. Travel Medicine, Peabody Soc., Mass. Infectious Diseases Soc., Am. Soc. Tropical Medicine and Hygiene, N.Y. Acad. Scis., Am. Soc. Microbiology, Aesculapian Club, Alpha Omega Alpha, Phi Sigma Iota, Sigma Sigma. Avocations: flute, hiking, reading, travel. Business E-Mail: mary_wilson@harvard.edu.

WILSON, MELVIN EDMOND, retired civil engineer; b. Bremerton, Wash., Aug. 3, 1935; s. Edmond Curt and Madeline Rose (Deal) W.; m. Deanna May Stevens, Nov. 22, 1957 (div. Mar. 1971); children: Kathleen, Debra Wilson Frank. BSCE, U. Wash., 1957, MSCE, 1958. Registered profl. engr., Wash. Asst. civil engr. City of Seattle, 1958-60, assoc. civil engr., 1960-64, sr. civil engr., 1964-66, supervising civil engr., 1966-75, sr. civil engr., 1975-77, mgr.

X, 1977-88; owner Wilson Cons. Svcs., Seattle, 1988-89; transp. sys. dir. City of Renton, Wash., 1989-96, ret., 1996. Owner Mel Wilson Photographer, Seattle, 1975-84. Contbr. reports to profl. jours. Rep. Renton transp. work group King County (Wash.) Growth Mgmt. Policy Com.; rep. Renton tech. adv. com. South County Area Transp. Bd., King County, 1992-96, developer svc. policy (adopted by Puget Sound Govtl. Com.) to encourage travel by transit. successfuly led effort to make Renton first suburban city to receive direct transit svc. under Met. King County Plan, 1994; vol. personal trainer, 1988—; vol. trainer for medical patients, 1988—. Mem. ASCE, Am. Pub. Works Assn., Inst. Transp. Engrs., Tau Beta Pi, Sigma Xi. Avocations: weightlifting, art.

WILSON, MICHAEL E., lawyer; b. Rantoul, Ill., Oct. 28, 1951; BA cum laude, Washington U., 1973, JD, 1977. Bar: Mo. 1977. Principal Greensfelder, Hemker & Gale, P.C., St. Louis. Instr. legal writing Washington U. Sch. Law, 1979-82; mem. nat. panel constrn. industry arbitrators and co-chmn. St. Louis Constrn. Adv. Com. 1987-97. Mem. ABA, The Mo. Bar (contbr. jour.), Bar Assn. Metro. St. Louis (contbr. jour.), Order Coif. Office: Greensfelder Hemker & Gale PC 2000 Equitable Bldg 10 S Broadway Saint Louis MO 63102-1712

WILSON, MICHAEL HOLCOMBE, investment banker, former Canadian government official; b. Toronto, Ont., Can., Nov. 4, 1937; s. Harry Holcombe and Constance L. (Davies) W.; m. Margaret Catherine Smellie, Oct. 17, 1964; children: Cameron (dec.), Geoffrey, Lara. Student, Upper Can. Coll.; B in Comm., U. Toronto, 1959. With Harris & Partners Ltd., Toronto, 1961-63, 65-73, v.p.; 1972; exec. v.p. following merger with Dominion Securities Ltd., 1973-79; mem. Can. Ho. of Commons, Ottawa, 1979-93; min. of state for internat. trade Govt. Can., Ottawa, 1979-80, min. of fin., 1984-91, min. of industry, sci. & tech., min. internat. trade, 1991-93; bus. advisor Michael Wilson Internat., Toronto, 1993—2000; vice chmn. RBC Dominion Securities Inc., 1995-2000; chmn. UBS Global Asset Mgmt. Co. (formerly Brinson Can. Co.), Canada, 2000—04, UBS Can., 2004—. Mem. bd. Ctr. for Addiction and Mental Health Found., 2000; chmn. Mental Health Implementation Task Force; bd. mem. Cmty. Found. for Greater Toronto; bd. dirs. BP PLC, Manulife Fin.; chmn. Neurosci. Can. Partnership, Can. Coun. Pub.-Pvt. Partnerships, Can. Coalition for Good Governance; chancellor Trinity Coll. Mem. Toronto Club, Toronto Golf, Badminton and Racquet Club, Osler Bluff Ski Club, Mad River Golf Club, Kappa Alpha. Progressive Conservative. Anglican. Office: UBS Can 161 Bay St Ste 4100 PO Box 617 Toronto ON Canada M5J 2S1

WILSON, MICHAEL JOSEPH, newspaper executive; b. Houston, June 11, 1953; s. Joseph Henry and Mary Beth (Kelley) W.; m. Lynne Freeman, June 24, 1978; children: Stephanie Elizabeth, Amanda Leigh. BJ, U. Tex., 1975. Advt. sales rep. Dow Jones, Houston, 1977-80; sales rep. Wall Street Jour. subs. Dow Jones, N.Y.C., 1980-83; advt. exec. Wall Street Jour. subs. Dow Jones & Co., N.Y.C., 1983-86, internat. advt. dir., 1986-87, mktg. dir. for spl. reports Hong Kong, 1987-89; dir. advt., pub. Asian Wall Street Jour., Hong Kong, 1987-89, former pub., 1989; advt. sales Dallas Morning News; v.p., advt. Austin American-Statesman, Tex., 2005—. Mem. Internat. Advt. Assn., Nat. Investor Rels. Inst., Am. C. of C. in Hong Kong, Hong Kong Pubs. Soc. (treas. 1990-91, dep. chmn. 1991, chmn. 1991). Office: Austin American-Statesman 305 S Congress Ave Austin TX 78704*

WILSON, MICHAEL MOUREAU, lawyer, physician; b. Cheverly, Md., Dec. 30, 1952; s. Kenneth Moureau and Helen (Rice) Smith. BS, MIT, 1974; JD, Georgetown U., 1977, MD, 1986. Bar: D.C. 1977, N.Y. 1980, U.S. Dist. Ct. D.C. 1980, U.S. Dist. Ct. Md. 1992, U.S. Ct. Appeals (D.C. cir.) 1980, U.S. Supreme Ct. 1981. Law clk. Hon. John B. Hannum U.S. Dist. Ct., Phila. 1977—78; assoc. Cravath Swaine & Moore, N.Y.C., 1978—79; asst. to gen. counsel NSF, Washington, 1979—82; resident in psychiatry St. Elizabeth Hosp., 1986—89; pvt. practice med. malpractice litigation, 1989—. Notes editor Am. Criminal Law Rev., 1976-77. Mem. ABA, Assn. Trial Lawyers Am., D.C. Trial Lawyers Assn., Phi Beta Kappa. Office: 1120 19th St NW Ste LL-11 Washington DC 20036 Office Phone: 202-223-4488. E-mail: wilson@wilsonlaw.com

WILSON, MIKE, journalist; Police bur. corr. New York Times. Office: The New York Times Police Bur One Police Plz Rm 202C New York NY 10038 Office Phone: 212-349-0193. Office Fax: 212-556-1337. Business E-Mail: wilsonm@nytimes.com.*

WILSON, MIRIAM GEISENDORFER, retired physician, educator; b. Yakima, Wash., Dec. 3, 1922; d. Emil and Frances Geisendorfer; m. Howard G. Wilson, June 21, 1947; children—Claire, Paula, Geoffrey, Nicola, Marla. BS, U. Wash., Seattle, 1944, MS, 1945; MD, U. Calif., San Francisco, 1950. Mem. faculty U. So. Calif. Sch. Medicine, L.A., 1965—, prof. pediatrics, 1969—2004, emeritus prof. pediatrics, 2004—. Office: U So Calif Med Ctr 1129 N State St Rm 1g24 Los Angeles CA 90033-1044

WILSON, MYRON ROBERT, JR., retired psychiatrist; b. Helena, Mont., Sept. 21, 1932; s. Myron Robert, Sr. and Constance Ernestine (Bultman) Wilson. BA, Stanford U., 1954, MD, 1957. Diplomate Am. Bd. Psychiatry and Neurology. Dir. adolescent psychiatry Mayo Clinic, Rochester, Minn., 1965-71; pres., psychiatrist in chief Wilson Ctr., Faribault, Minn., 1971-86, chmn., 1986-90; ret., 1990. Assoc. clin. prof. UCLA, 1985—99. Contbr. articles to profl. jours. Chmn., CEO C. B. Wilson Found., LA, 1972—; bd. dirs. Pasadena (Calif.) Symphony Orch. Assn., 1987; vestryman, treas. St. Thomas' Parish, LA, 1993—96. Lt. comdr. USN, 1958—60. Fellow, Mayo Grad. Sch. Medicine, Rochester, 1960—65. Fellow: Internat. Soc. Adolescent Psychiatry (founder, treas. 1985—88, sec. 1985—88, treas. 1988—92), Am. Soc. Adolescent Psychiatry, Am. Psychiat. Assn.; mem.: Sigma Xi (Mayo Found. chpt.). Episcopalian. Personal E-mail: mrobertwilson@aol.com.

WILSON, NICHOLAS ADAM, finance educator; b. Pitts., Apr. 8, 1982; s. Donald Eugene and Beverly Ann Wilson. BS in Econs., St. Vincent Coll., 2004, BS in Math., 2004; postgrad., Carnegie Mellon U., 2004—. Counselor and coord. Pathways to Success, Latrobe, Pa., 2001—03; intern, media coord., website content developer Partners in Progress, Ligonier, Pa., 2002—; tchg. asst. profl. speaking and fin. analysis Carnegie Mellon U., Pitts., 2005—. Treas., bd. mem. Partners in Progress, Ligonier, 2005—06. Recipient President's award, St. Vincent Coll., 2004; grantee Internship Opportunity Fund, H. J. Heinz III Sch. of Pub. Policy and Mgmt, Carnegie Mellon U., 2005; scholar, KC, 2000—04, Pa. Governor's Sch. for Excellence in Internat. Studies, 2000—04; acad. scholar, St. Vincent Coll., 2000—04, Leadership scholar, 2000—04, George Washington fellow, St. Vincent Coll. Economic's Dept., 2002. Mem.: KC. Roman Catholic. Avocations: metal detecting, soccer, researching history of southwestern Pennsylvania, aviation, stamp collecting/philately. Business E-Mail: nwilson@andrew.cmu.edu

WILSON, NORMAN GLENN, church administrator, writer; b. Rensselaer, N.Y., Nov. 3, 1936; s. Lawrence Wilbur and Wilhelmena Augusta (Knapp) W.; m. Nancy Ann Deyo, Nov. 17, 1956; children: Beth, Lawrence, Jonathan. BRE in Religious Edn., United Wesleyan Coll., 1958, DD (hon.), 1986; MA in Biblical Studies, Winona Lake Sch. Theology, 1968. Pastor The Wesleyan Ch., 1958-76, Gloversville, NY, 1963-66, North Lakeport, Mich., 1966-70, Owosso, Mich., 1970-76, dir. comm. Indpls., 1992—. Program prodr., speaker The Wesleyan Hour, Indpls., 1975—; mem. gen. adminstrn. coun. The Wesleyan Ch., Indpls., 1992—; disting. lectr. Staley Found., 1986. Author: How to Have a Happy Home, 1976, Christianity in Shoe Leather, 1978, The Constitution of the Kingdom, 1989, People Just Like Us, 1994, Follow the Leader, A Daily Spiritual Journey, 1996; editor; contbr.: Journey Into Holiness, 2000; The Call to Contentment, 2002; editor The Wesleyan Advocate, 1992-2004, Wesleyan Life, 2004-. Mem. Nat. Religious Broadcasters (bd. dirs. 1984-2005, Merit award 1984). Mem. Wesleyan Ch. Avocations: painting, antique cars. Home: 304 Scarborough Way Noblesville IN 46060-3881 Business E-Mail: wilsonn@wesleyan.org.

**WILSON, OWEN,** actor; b. Dallas, Nov. 18, 1968; s. Robert and Laura Wilson. BA in English, U. Tex., Austin, 1991. Actor: (TV films) Heat Vision and Jack, 1999; (TV series) King of the Hill, 1997; assoc. prodr. (films) As Good as It Gets, 1997, The Royal Tenenbaums, 2001; writer, actor: films Bottle Rocket, 1996; prodr., actor (films) You, Me and Dupree, 2006; actor: (films) The Cable Guy, 1996, Anaconda, 1997, Armageddon, 1998, Permanent Midnight, 1998; exec. prodr., actor: (films) Rushmore, 1998, The Minus Man, 1999, Breakfast of Champions, 1999, The Haunting, 1999, Shanghai Noon, 2000, Meet the Parents, 2000, Zoolander, 2001, Behind Enemy Lines, 2001, I Spy, 2002, Shanghai Knights, 2003, The Big Bounce, 2004, Starsky & Hutch, 2004, The Life Aquatic with Steve Zissou, 2004, Meet the Fockers, 2004, The Wendell Baker Story, 2005, Wedding Crashers, 2005, (voice) Cars, 2006. Recipient Favorite On-Screen Match-Up (with Vince Vaughn), People's Choice Award, 2006, Best On-Screen Team (with Vince Vaughn), MTV Movie awards, 2006. Office: United Talent Agy 9560 Wilshire Blvd Ste 500 Beverly Hills CA 90212*

**WILSON, OWEN MEREDITH, JR.,** lawyer, mediator, arbitrator; b. Oakland, Calif., Dec. 22, 1939; s. O. Meredith and Marian Wilson; m. Sandra A. Wilson (div.); children: Ann, Melissa, Jennifer; m. Teddi Anne Wilson; children: Amanda, Lisa. Student, U. Utah, 1957-59; AB, Harvard U., 1961; LLB, U. Minn., 1965. Bar: Oreg. 1965, Wash. 1985. Ptnr. Lane Powell Spears Lubersky, Portland, Oreg., 1969—2005; prin. Wilson Dispute Resolution, 2005—. Mem. mediation panel U.S. Dist. Ct., 1986—. Mem. bd. visitors Law Sch. U. Minn., 1990-96. Mem. ABA, Oreg. State Bar Assn., Wash. State Bar, Multnomah Bar Assn. Office: 1211 SW 5th Ave Ste 2950 Portland OR 97204-3158 Office Phone: 503-972-5090. Business E-Mail: met@wilsonadr.com.

**WILSON, PATRICIA POTTER,** librarian; b. Jennings, La., May 3, 1946; d. Ralph Harold and Wilda Ruth (Smith) Potter; m. Wendell Merlin Wilson, Aug. 24, 1968. BS, La. State U., 1967; MS, U. Houston-Clear Lake, 1979; EdD, U. Houston, 1985. Cert. tchr., learning resources specialist (libr.), Tex. Tchr. England AFB (La.) Elem. Sch., 1967-68, Edward White Elem. Sch./Clear Creek Ind. Schs., Seabrook, Tex., 1972-77; libr. C.D. Landolt Elem. Sch., Friendswood, Tex., 1979-81; instr./lectr. children's lit. U. Houston, 1983-86; with U. Houston/Clear Lake, 1984-87, asst. prof. libr. sci. and reading, 1988-94, assoc. prof. learning resources and reading edn., 1994—2001, assoc. prof. emerita, 2001—. Cons. Hermann Hosp., Baywood Hosp., 1986-87, Bedford Meadows Hosp., 1989-90, Wetcher Clinic, 1989; co-owner, v.p. Potter Farms, Inc., 1994—; mem. devel. bd. NASA and CCISD, Longhorn, 2005-. Author: Happenings: Developing Successful Programs for School Libraries, 1987, The Professional Collection for Elementary Educators, 1996, Premiere Events: Library Programs That Inspire Elementary Patrons, 2001, Leadership for Today's School Library, 2001, Igniting the Spark: Library Programs that Inspire High School Patrons, 2001, Center Stage: Library Programs That Inspire Middle School Patrons, 2002; editor: A Review Sampler, 1985—86, 1989—90; contbg. editor: Tex. Libr. Jour., 1988—94; contbr. articles to profl. jours. Trustee Freeman Meml. Libr., Houston, 1982—87, v.p., 1985—86, pres., 1986—87; trustee Evelyn Meador Libr., 1993—94, adv. bd., 1994—; mem. bd. dirs. Houston Symphony League-Bay Area, 2004—05, chair ann. fund campaign, 2005; founder Friends of Neumann Libr., 1998—2001; chmn. hospitality com. Lunar Rendevous Festival, 1998—; gen. chmn. Lunar Rendezvous Festival, 2002, mem. adv. bd., 2002—; mem. Assistance League of the Bay Area, 1997—; vol. Houston: A Visit from St. Nicholas Com., 2004—, co-chmn. kick-off event, 2005; mem. adv. bd. Bay Area Soc. Prevention Cruelty Animals, 1994—98, Bay Area Turning Point, 1998—; bd. dirs. Sta. KUHT-TV, 1984—87, Friends of Neumann Libr., 1998—99, Bay Area Houston Ballet and Theatre, 2001—04, vice chair bd. dirs., 2003—04, chmn. kickoff event, 2003; dir. Learning Resources Book Rev. Ctr., 1989—90; bd. dirs. Armand Bayou Nature Ctr., Houston, 1989—94; mem. Bay Area Houston Econ. Partnership, 2002—, mem. banquet com., 2002—. Named Outstanding Vol. of Yr., Houston's Nat. Philanthropy Day, 1999; named one of 10 Men and Women of Heart, Bay Area Turning Point, 2001; recipient Rsch. award, Tex. State Reading Assn., 1993, Pres. award, Tex. Coun. Tchrs. English, Disting. Tchg. award, Enron Corp., 1996, Disting. Alumni award, U. Houston-Clear Lake, 1998, Disting. Alumna award, U. Houston, Coll. Edn., 2002, Disting. Alumni award, Univ. Houston Ctrl., 2005; grantee, Tex. Libr. Assn., 1993. Mem. ALA, NASA, CCISD (Longhorn devel. bd. 2005—), Am. Assn. Sch. Librs., Internat. Reading Assn., Nat. Coun. Tchrs. English (Books for You rev. com. 1985-88, 97-98, Your Reading rev. com. 1993-96), Tex. Coun. Tchrs. English, Antarctican Soc., Bay Area Houston Econ. Partnership (banquet com. 2002-), Clear Lake Panhellenic Assn., Lakewood Yacht Club, Travelers' Century Club, Bay Oaks Country Club, Phi Delta Kappa, Phi Kappa Phi (sec. 1997-98, pres. 1998-99). Methodist.

**WILSON, PAUL HOLLIDAY, JR.,** lawyer; b. Schenectady, NY, Sept. 4, 1942; s. Paul H. and Sarah Elizabeth (MacLean) W.; m. Elaine Hawley Griffin, May 30, 1964; children: Hollace, Paul, Kristen, Katherine. AB, Brown U., 1964; LLB, MBA, Columbia U., 1967. Bar: N.Y. 1967, U.S. Dist. Ct. (so. dist.) 1968. Law clk. U.S. Dist. Ct. (so. dist.) N.Y., N.Y.C., 1967-68; assoc. Debevoise & Plimpton LLP, N.Y.C., 1968-75, ptnr., 1976—, fin. ptnr., 1980-88, 91-93, 2001—, dep. presiding ptnr., 1993-98. Vice-chmn., trustee St. Michael's Montessori Sch., N.Y.C., 1977-79, chmn. bd. trustees, 1979-81. Mem. ABA, Assn. Bar City N.Y. (mem. commn. on securities regulations 1985-88). Clubs: Vineyard Haven Yacht (Mass.) (vice-commodore 1985, commodore 1986-87). Avocations: sailing, reading, music. Office: Debevoise & Plimpton LLP 919 Third Ave 46th Fl New York NY 10022-6225 Office Phone: 212-909-6000. Business E-Mail: phwilson@debevoise.com.

**WILSON, PAUL LOWELL,** mortgage company executive, lawyer; b. May 12, 1951; s. James Joseph and Edna Vivian (Halterman) W.; children: Meredith Elaine, Taylor Halterman; m. Abigail Mayer. AB, W.Va. U., 1973; JD, Coll. of William of Mary, 1976. Bar: W.Va., 1976, U.S. Dist. Ct. (so. dist.) W.Va. 1976, U.S. Dist. Ct. (ea. dist.) Va. 1991 Assn. Private & Peyton, Charleston, W.Va., 1976-78; title atty. Lawyers Title Ins. Corp., Williamsburg, Va., 1978-80; assoc. S.J. Baker, Williamsburg, 1981-83; counsel edn. com. W.Va. Legislature, Charleston, 1977-78; gen. counsel A J & L Corp., Williamsburg, 1983-85, v.p., gen. counsel, 1985-91; prin. First Capital Comml. Funding, Inc., 1997—. Bd. dirs. 503 Cert. Devel. Co., Richmond, Sta. WHRO-TV. Mem. York County Sch. Bd., 1986-94, chmn., 1992-94; pres. Nat. Housing Corp., 1986-93, The Preservation Group, Inc., 1991-97. Mem. W.Va. State Bar, Sigma Phi Epsilon. Presbyterian. Office: 3312 Windsor Dr Charlotte NC 28209 Office Phone: 704-552-8659. E-mail: pwilson@firstcapitalcref.com.

**WILSON, PEGGY JO,** secondary school educator; b. Marysville, Kans., Oct. 8, 1950; d. Allen L. and June A. (Ritter) Holeman; m. John Frederick Wilson, May 27, 1972; children: Bradley, Craig. BA in Math. cum laude, Kans. State U., 1972, MEd, 1975. Cert. tchr., Kans. Tchr., math. Unified Sch. Dist. #501, Topeka, 1972—79, Seaman Unified Sch. Dist. #345, Topeka, 1979—80; tech. asst. Menninger Found., Topeka, 1980—82; tchr., math. Auburn-Washburn Unified Sch. Dist. #437, Topeka, 1984—. Active Friends of Topeka Libr., Friends of Topeka Zoo, Friends of KTWU. Mem. NEA, Auburn Washburn NEA, Nat. Coun. Tchrs. of Math., Phi Kappa Phi, Phi Delta Kappa. Methodist. Avocations: reading, piano, walking. Office: Washburn Rural High Sch 5900 SW 61st St Topeka KS 66619-2008 Office Phone: 785-339-4100.

**WILSON, PEGGY MAYFIELD,** retired chemist; d. Isaac Newton and Ella Lockwood Mayfield; m. Irving Ray Dunlap Jr. (dec.); m. William W. Wilson III, July 25, 1975 (dec.). BS in Chemistry, U. Tex., Austin, 1948, PhD in Chemistry, 1952. Spl. instr. U. Tex., Austin, 1952—53; from rsch. technologist to sr. rsch. technologist Mobil Rsch. Devel. Corp., Dallas, 1953—84, group mgr. dept. rsch., 1984—89; pres. Greater Duncanville Indsl. Corp., Tex., 1991—2000, Stone Gap Indsl. Corp., Duncanville, 1991—2000; ret. 2000. Regent East Tex. State U., Commerce, 1981—87. Founder, econ. devel. City of Cedar Hill, Tex., 1991—96; adv. bd. Cedar Valley C.C.; coun. mem. City of Cedar Hill, 1996—98; active State Rep. Exec. Com., Tex., 1971—80; bd. dirs., treas. Internat. Mus. Cultures. Named Outstanding Rep. Woman, Tex. Fedn. Rep. Women, 1973; recipient Jean Harris award, Rotary, 1998, Golden Cedar Lifetime award, Cedar Hill C. of C., 2001. Mem.: Am. Chem. Soc., Cedar Hill Assn. for Cultural Arts, Cedar Summit Book Club. Republican. Methodist. Achievements include patents in field. Avocation: gardening.

**WILSON, PETER SCOTT,** lawyer; b. Edinburgh, Scotland, July 15, 1955; B in Commerce, McGill U., 1976; JD, Harvard U., 1979. Bar: N.Y. 1980. Assoc. Cravath Swaine and Moore, N.Y.C., 1979-87, ptnr., corp., 1987—. Mem. ABA, N.Y. State Bar Assn., Assn. Bar City of N.Y., Internat. Bar Assn. Democrat. Presbyterian. Office: Cravath Swaine & Moore Worldwide Plaza 825 8th Ave New York NY 10019-7475 Office Phone: 212-474-1767. Office Fax: 212-474-3700. Business E-Mail: pwilson@cravath.com.

**WILSON, PHILL,** foundation administrator; Grad., Ill. Wesleyan U. AIDS coord. City LA, 1990—93; co-chair LA County HIV Health Comn., 1990—95; dir. Policy and Planning, AIDS Project LA, 1993—96; appointee HRSA AIDS Advisory Com., 1995—98; founder, exec. dir. Black AIDS Inst., LA; founder, dir. African Am. AIDS Policy and Tng. Inst., U. Southern Calif. Coord. Internat. Cmty. Treatment and Sci. Workshop (12th, 13th, 14th and 15th Internat. AIDS Confs. in Geneva, Switzerland, Durban, South Africa, Barcelona, Spain, and Bangkok, Thailand); mem. US Delegation 1994 World AIDS Summit, Paris; co-founder Nat. Black Lesbian & Gay Leadership Forum, Nat. Task Force on AIDS Prevention; involved in the founding of the following orgns. Chris Brownlie Hospice, AIDS Healthcare Found., Nat. Minority AIDS Coun., LA County Gay Men of Color Consortium, CAEAR Coalition; worked extensively on HIV/AIDS policy, rsch., prevention and treatment issues in Russia, Latvia, Ukraine, UK, Holland, Germany, France, Mexico, South Africa, Zimbobwe, Zambia, Tanzania, India and Botswana. Published articles in La Times, NY Times, LA Weekly, Essence, Ebony, VIBE, Jet, Poz, HIV+, and Arise. Named one of Leadership for Changing the World, Ford Found., 2001, 2005 Black History Makers in the Making, Balck Entertainment TV (B.E.T.); recipient Award of Courage, amFAR Found. Honoring with Pride, 2001, Delta Spirit award, Delta Sigma Theta (LA chpt.), Discovery Health Channel Medical Honor, 2004. Office: Black AIDS Inst 1833 W 8th St Ste 200 Los Angeles CA 90057 Office Phone: 213-353-3610. Office Fax: 213-989-0181. Business E-Mail: phillw@blackaids.org. E-mail: phillw@aaainstitute.org.

**WILSON, R. DALE,** marketing educator; b. Ironton, Ohio, July 16, 1949; s. Robert J. and Treva L. (Shively) Wilson; m. Emily J. Ray, June 19, 1971; 1 child, Travis Ray. BBA cum laude, Ohio U., 1971; MBA, U. Toledo, 1972; PhD, U. Iowa, 1977. Asst. prof. mktg. Pa. State U., University Park, 1976-80; v.p., dir. mktg. scis. Batten, Barton, Durstine & Osborn, Inc., NYC, 1980-83; vis. prof. Cornell U., Ithaca, NY, 1983-84; assoc. prof. Mich. State U., East Lansing, 1984-87, prof., 1987—. Cons. in field. Contbr. articles to profl. jours. Youth baseball and basketball coach, East Lansing, 1989—98. Grantee, Pa. State U., Mich. State U., IBM Corp. Mem.: Am. Soc. Competitiveness, Inst. Ops. Rsch. and Mgmt. Scis. (assoc. editor interfaces, cert. recognition 1983), Am. Mktg. Assn., Am. Acad. Advt., Beta Gamma Sigma. Office: Mich State U Eli Broad Grad Sch Mgmt Dept Mktg/Supply Chain Mgmt N322 N Business Complex East Lansing MI 48824-1122 Office Phone: 517-432-5535 x239. Business E-Mail: wilsonrr@msu.edu.

**WILSON, RALPH COOKERLY, JR.,** professional football team executive; b. Columbus, Ohio, Oct. 17, 1918; s. Ralph Cookerly and Edith (Cole) W.; children: Christy Cole, Linda Brown, Edith Denise. AB, U. Va., 1940; postgrad., U. Mich., 1940-41. Pres. Ralph C. Wilson Jr. Enterprises (privately owned family bus.); engaged in profl. football, roadbuilding Detroit, 1946—; pres., owner Buffalo Bills Profl. Football Club, 1959—. With USNR, 1941-46. Decorated Commendation medal. Mem. Ocean Club of Fla., Country Club of Detroit, Grosse Pointe (Mich.) Club, Buffalo Country Club, Shriners. Presbyterian.

**WILSON, RALPH SLOAN,** retinal surgeon; b. El Dorado, Ark., Nov. 12, 1937; s. George Evander and Lauree Eta (Doss) W.; AB, Davidson Coll., 1959; BS, U. Ark., 1963, MD (Research fellow) 1963; m. Sarah Mignon Ross, Dec. 27, 1958; m. Ann Jameson, 1987; children: Ralph Sloan, William Gregory, Steven Robert, John Matsek (stepson). Intern, U. Ark. Hosps., Little Rock, 1963-64; postgrad. ophthalmology Harvard Med. Sch., Boston, 1964-65; resident ophthalmology U. Ark. Hosps., 1965, U. Tex. Med. Br., Galveston, 1965-67; Heed fellow retinal pathology and surgery Mass. Eye and Ear Infirmary, Harvard Med. Sch., Boston, 1969; asst. prof. and dir. retina services dept. ophthalmology U. Ark. Med. Center, Little Rock, 1970-75, assoc. prof., 1975-81, prof., 1981—95, prof. emeritus, 1995-, acting chmn. ophthalmology dept., 1974-75; practice medicine specializing in retinal surgery Retinal Group, LTD., Little Rock, 1975-99; mem. Ark. State Bd. Dispensing Opticians; dir. Retina Service, US VA Hosp., Little Rock; chief staff, exec. com. Doctors Hosp.; dir. Ritchie Grocer Co., S.W. Trading Corp. Chmn. admissions com. U. Ark. Coll. Medicine; trustee Lyon Coll. (formerly Ark. Coll.), 1982-; pres., bd. dirs Retinal Research Fund; bd. dirs. Ark. Eye & Kidney Bank, Ark. Soc. for Prevention of Blindness, 1971-73. Served to lt. comdr. USNR, 1967-69. Diplomate Am. Bd. Ophthalmology (examiner 1973-83); Hoffmann La Roche grantee, 1966-67; recipient AMA Physicians Recognition awards, 1969-99. Mem. Am. Acad. Ophthalmology (speakers bur., hon. award, sr. hon. award Pub. Info. Com.), Am. Acad. Retinal Surgeons (formerly Vitreous Soc., charter mem.), Assn. Rsch. and Vision in Ophthalmology, AMA, Ark., Pulaski County med. socs., Am., Ark. Assns. Ophthalmology, Am. Ophthal. Soc. (athletic chmn.), AAUP, Research to Prevent Blindness, So. Med. Assn., Pan Am. Soc. Ophthalmology, Société Française d'Ophthalmologie, Sociedad Boliviana de Oftalmología, New Orleans Acad. Ophthalmology, Soc. Eye Surgeons, Internat. Eye Found., U. Tex. Med. Br. Ophthalmology Alumni Assn. (pres. 1970-72), Univ. Med. Group, Am. Heed Fellows, Little Rock Acad. Surgery, Retina Soc., Ark. Acad. Ophthalmology (pres. 1975-76), Ark. Found. for Med. Care, Assn. VA Ophthalmologists, Ark. Ophthalmology sect. of Ark. Med. Soc. (pres. 1977-78), Assn. Mil. Surgeons, Alpha Omega Alpha, Alpha Tau Omega, Sigma Xi. Contbr. articles to profl. jours., Research in ocular melanomas, ocular fireworks injuries, mechanism of human accomodation and multiple ocular surgical techniques; holder patents in field. Home: 140 Washington Rd Rye NH 03870 E-mail: cottagers@aol.com.

**WILSON, RHYS THADDEUS,** lawyer; b. Albany, Ga., May 9, 1955; s. Joseph Farr Jr. and Betty Ann (Wilkins) W.; m. Carolyn Reid Saffold, June 2, 1984. AB, Duke U., 1976; JD, U. Ga., 1979; LLM, Emory U., 1985. Bar: Ga. 1979. Pvt. practice law, Atlanta, 1979-89; sr. v.p., gen. counsel Monarch Capital Group, Inc., Atlanta, 1989-92, Jackson & Coker, Inc., Atlanta, 1992-93; pres. Jackson & Coker Locum Tenens, Inc., Atlanta, 1993-95; ptnr. Robins, Kaplan, Miller & Ciresi, Atlanta, 1995, Nelson Mullins Riley & Scarborough LLP, 2006—. Spkr. continuing legal edn. seminars. Contbr. articles to profl. jours. Bd. dirs. Atlanta Opera Co. Mem. ABA, Ga. Bar Assn. (chmn. internat. law sect. 1987-88, exec. com. corp. and banking law sect. 1987-89, editl. bd. Ga. State Bar Jour. 1986-89), Atlanta Bar Assn. (editor newsletter 1984-86, Outstanding Svc. award 1986), Assn. for Corp. Growth, Atlanta Tech. Angels (dir.), Visage Internat., Capital City Club. Episcopalian. Office Phone: 404-817-6000.

**WILSON, RICHARD A.,** oil and gas industry support services executive; b. 1938; BS in Petroleum Engring., U. Wyo. Pres. Energy Svc. Co. Inc., Dallas, 1988-89; sr. v.p.- ops., 1989—. Formerly with ESSO Exploration; past v.p. Global Marine Drilling Co.; various positions, then exec. v.p. Schlumberger Tech. Corp. Office: ENSCO 500 N Akard St Ste 4300 Dallas TX 75201-3331

**WILSON, RICHARD CHRISTIAN,** engineering firm executive; b. Bethlehem, Pa., July 17, 1921; s. Christian and Laura Barrows (Campbell) W.; m. Jean M. Avis, July 16, 1949; children:—Richard A., Christy. BS, Carnegie-Mellon U., 1943; MS, Lehigh U., 1947; PhD, U. Mich., 1961. Mfg. engr. Westinghouse Electric Corp., East Pittsburgh, 1943; instr. mech. engring. Carnegie-Mellon U., Pitts., 1943-44; vacuum test engr. Kellex Corp., N.Y.C., 1944; area supr. Carbide & Carbon Chem. Co., Oak Ridge, 1945-46; apparatus engr. Westinghouse Electric Corp., Jackson, Mich., 1947-55; instr. indsl. and operation engring. U. Mich., 1955-61, asst. prof. 1961-63, assoc. prof., 1963-66, prof., 1966-85, chmn. dept., 1973-77, assoc. dean Coll. Engring., 1968-72; pres. Techware, Inc., 1985-86, ret., 1986. Dir. Cascade Data Corp., 1969-72 Contbr. articles to profl. jours. Bd. dirs. Ecumenical Assn. Internat. Understanding, 1970-87, pres., 1975-76, 86-87; dir. Washtenaw Trombones and Jazzbones, 1995—. Mem. IEEE, Inst. Mgmt. Sci., Am. Inst. Indsl. Engrs., Ops. Research Soc. Am., Sigma Xi, Beta Theta Pi, Phi Kappa Phi. Clubs: Rotary. Home: 805 Mount Pleasant Ave Ann Arbor MI 48103-4776 Office: U Mich Dept Indsl Engring Ann Arbor MI 48109

**WILSON, RICHARD E.,** music educator; b. Natrona Heights, Pa. BS, Clarion U., Pa., 1979; M in Music Edn., Indiana U. Pa., 1993. Music tchr. Kiski Sch. Dist., Vandergrift, Pa., 1979—80; tchr. instrumental music Diocese of Greensburg, 1980—87; tchr. Hempfield Area Sch. Dist., Greensburg, Pa., 1987—. Mem.: Pa. Music Educators Assn., Hempfield Area Edn. Assn., Westmoreland County Music Educators Assn., Music Educators Nat. Conf., Phi Beta Mu.

**WILSON, RICHARD EDWARD,** composer, music educator, pianist; b. Cleve., May 15, 1941; s. James F. and Edith Ann (Zingler) Wilson; m. Adene Stevenson Green, May 15, 1971; children: Katherine Blanca, James Graham. AB magna cum laude, Harvard U., 1963; MA, Rutgers U., 1966. Asst. prof. music Vassar Coll., Poughkeepsie, NY, 1966-70, assoc. prof. music, 1970-76, prof. music, 1976—, chmn. dept. music, 1979-82, 85-88, 95-98, Mary Conover Mellon Chair, 1988—. Composer-in-residence Am. Symphony Orch., 1992—. Composer: Music for Violin and Violoncello, 1969; composer. (four string quartets); composer: Eclogue for Piano Solo, 1974 (Burge prize, 1979), Figuration, 1980, Two Symphonies, 1984, 1987, Agitations, 1994, Pamietam, 1995, Five Love Songs, 1995, Transfigured Goat, 1996, A Child's London, 1997, Triple concerto for horn, bass clarinet, marimba and orch., 1998 (Koussevitzky commn.), Intimations for Piano and Orch., 2000, Revelry for Full Orchestra, 2002, Peregrinations for Viola and Orchestra, 2002, others; composer: (opera) Aethelred the Unready, 1994. Recipient Walter Hinrichsen award, Am. Acad. Inst. Arts and Letters, 1986, Cleve. Arts prize, 1988, Exec.'s award Dutchess County, 1989, Stoeger prize, Chamber Music Soc. Lincoln Ctr., 1994, Acad. award in music, Am. Acad. Arts and Letters, 2004;, Guggenheim fellow, 1992. Mem.: ASCAP, Am. Music Ctr., Century Assn., Harvard Club, Phi Beta Kappa. Home: 27 Vassar Lake Dr Poughkeepsie NY 12603-3120 Office: Vassar Coll Dept Music PO Box 18 Poughkeepsie NY 12604-0001

**WILSON, RICHARD F.,** academic administrator; b. Point Pleasant, W.Va. m. Pat Wilson; children: Adam, Rachel. B in Math. Alderson-Broaddus Coll., 1968; MA in Higher Edn., U. Mich., 1970, PhD in Higher Edn., 1978. Math. tchr. Spencerville (Ohio) H.S., 1968—69; dir. admissions Alderson Broaddus Coll., Philippi, W.Va., 1970—74; project asst. to Dr. William Haberl, spl. asst. to the exec. officers U. Mich., Ann Arbor, 1974—75, grad. student rsch. asst. Office Acad. Planning and Analysis, 1975—76, rsch. assoc. Office Acad. Planning Analysis, 1976—78; asst. dir. Office Planning and Evaluation U. Ill. Urbana-Champaign, 1978—80, adj. asst. prof. higher edn., 1981—84, asst. vice chancellor for acad. affairs, 1981—86, assoc. chancellor, 1986—94, interim dir. corp. and found. rels., 1991, adj. prof. higher edn., 1994—2004, assoc. chancellor for devel., 1994—2004; dep. dir. U. Ill. Found., 1994—96, v.p., 1996—2004; pres. Ill. Wesleyan U., 2004—. Mem. Applie Higher Edn. Adv. Group, 1992—. Office: Ill Wesleyan Univ Pres Office Holmes Hall 204 PO Box 2900 Bloomington IL 61702

**WILSON, RICHARD LEE,** political science professor; b. Worthington, Minn., Dec. 20, 1944; s. G. Roy and Dorothy Eileen (Johnson) W.; m. Carolyn Ann Dirks, Aug. 24, 1968 (div.); 1 child, Kevin Richard. BA, U. Chgo., 1966, postgrad., 1966-67; PhD, Johns Hopkins U., 1971; postgrad., Columbia U., 1988, Stanford U., 1992. Congl. aide 4th Congl. Dist. Md., 1971; asst. prof. polit. sci. U. Tenn., Chattanooga, 1971-76, assoc. prof., 1976-87, prof., 1988—. Registrar-at-large Hamilton County Election Commn., 1977-84; lectr. Robert A. Taft Inst. Govt., U. Tenn., Nashville, 1978, 79, 81; supr. state legis. and mer. internship program U. Chattanooga, 1972-86; vis. prof. Govt. Fgn. Affairs Coll., Beijing, 1986-87; Fulbright prof. govt. Beijing U., 1988-89, Samford U., Birmingham, Ala., 1991-93. Author: Tennessee Politics, 1976, American Government, 1993, 2d edit., 1995, American Political Leaders, 2002 (Choice award 2003); editor: Encyclopedia of American Government, 2001; co-editor: Ready Reference: Censorship, 1997 (named Outstanding Ref. Source 1998 ALA), Encyclopedia of the Supreme Court, 2000 (named OUtstanding Ref. Scouce 2002 ALA); contbr. chpts. to books. Chmn. Hamilton County Health Planning Adv. Council, 1975-79; bd. dirs. Ga.-Tenn. Regional Health Commn., 1978-82; active Tenn. State Health Coordinating Council, 1977-81; exec. com. State Health Coordinating Council, 1979-81. Named Outstanding Educator of Yr., Signal Mountain (Tenn.) Jaycees, 1973, Outstanding Prof. of Yr., SGA, 1985-86, Oustanding Reference Source ALA, 2002; recipient Polit. Edn. award NAACP, 1980, Excellent Prof. award Fgn. Affairs Coll., Beijing, 1987, UTC Exceptional Merit award, 1990, 94; NEH grantee, 1988, 92. Mem. So. Polit. Sci. Assn., Midwest Polit. Sci. Assn., Am. Polit. Sci. Assn. (nat. rsch. grant 1995), Nat. Soc. Internships and Exptl. Edn., SAR, China People's Friendship Assn., Aircraft Owners and Pilots Assn. Methodist. Office: Univ of Tenn Dept Political Sci Fletcher Hall 414 Chattanooga TN 37403 Office Phone: 423-425-4226. E-mail: richard-wilson@utc.edu.

**WILSON, RICHARD RANDOLPH,** lawyer; b. Pasadena, Calif., Apr. 14, 1950; s. Robert James and Phyllis Jean (Blackman) W.; m. Catherine Goodhugh Stevens, Oct. 11, 1980; children: Thomas Randolph, Charles Stevens. BA cum laude, Yale U., 1971; JD, U. Wash., 1976. Bar: Wash. 1976, U.S. Dist. Ct. (we. dist.) Wash. 1976, U.S. Ct. Appeals (9th cir.) 1977. Assn. Hillis, Phillips, Cairncross, Clark & Martin, Seattle, 1976-81, ptnr., 1981-84, Hillis, Cairncross, Clark & Martin, Seattle, 1984-87, Hillis Clark Martin & Peterson, Seattle, 1987—, mem. mgmt. com., 1991—. Pres. Plymouth Housing Group, Seattle, 1998—2000, trustee, 1994—2001, bd. dirs., 2001—05, Quality Child Care Svcs., Inc., Seattle; lectr. various bar assns., 1980—. Contbr. articles to profl. jours. Chmn. class agts. Yale U. Alumni Fund, New Haven, 1985—87, class agt., 1971—2001, mem. class coun., 1991—96, mem. Western Wash. exec. com., 1994—96, Yale capital campaign, 1992—97, vice chmn. leadership gifts com. Yale 25th reunion, 1995—96, 30th reunion, 2000—01; mem., vice chmn. Medina (Wash.) Planning Commn., 1990—92; trustee, performer Gilbert & Sullivan Soc., 1984—91; chmn. capital campaign Plymouth Congl. Ch., 1995, moderator, pres. ch. coun. Seattle, 1998—2000, ch. corp., 2004—05. Mem. ABA, Wash. State Bar Assn. (dir. environ. and land use law sect. 1985-88), Seattle-King County Bar Assn., Kingsley Trust Assn. (trustee 2003—), pres. 1996-98), Yale Assn. We. Wash. Congregationalist. Avocations: acting, singing, rare book collecting. Home: 2305 86th Ave NE Bellevue WA 98004-2416 Office: Hillis Clark Martin & Peterson 1221 2nd Ave Ste 500 Seattle WA 98101-2925 Office Phone: 206-623-1745. Business E-Mail: rrw@hcmp.com. Notable cases include: Barrie vs. Kitsap County, 1980; Sore vs. Snohomish County, 1983; Conv. Ctr. Coalition vs. City of Seattle, 1986; Orion Corp. vs. State, 1987, Cougar Mountain Assocs. vs. King County, 1988; King County vs. Central Puget Sound Growth Management Hearings Board, 1998, 1999; Quadrant Corp. vs. Central Puget Sound Growth Mgt. Hearings Bd., 2005.

**WILSON, RITA,** actress; b. LA, Oct. 26, 1958; m. Tom Hanks; 2 children. Actor: (films) The Day It Came to Earth, 1979, Cheech & Chong's Next Movie, 1980, Volunteers, 1985, The Bonfire of the Vanities, 1990, Sleepless in Seattle, 1993, Mixed Nuts, 1994, Now and Then, 1995, That Thing You Do!, 1996, Jingle All the Way, 1996, No Dogs Allowed, 1996, Psycho, 1998, Runaway Bride, 1999, The Story of Us, 1999, Perfume, 2001, Auto Focus, 2002; (TV films) Barbarians at the Gate, 1993, If These Walls Could Talk, 1996, From the Earth to the Moon, 1998, Invisible Child, 1999; prodr.: (films) My Big Fat Greek Wedding, 2002, Connie and Carla, 2004; (TV series) My Big Fat Greek Life, 2003.

**WILSON, ROBERT ALLEN,** religion educator; b. Geff, Ill., Oct. 7, 1936; s. Perry Arthur and Eva Mae (Dye) W.; m. Patsy Ann Jarrett, June 1, 1957; children: Elizabeth Ann, Angela Dawn, Christine Joy. AB, Lincoln Christian Coll., 1958, Hanover Coll., 1961; MRE, So. Bapt. Sem., 1965, EdD, 1972. Ordained to ministry Ch. of Christ, 1958. Min. Fowler Christian Ch., Ind., 1955—59, Zoah Christian Ch., Scottsburg, Ind., 1959—64; min. edn. and youth Shively Christian Ch., Louisville, 1964—69; prof. Christian edn. and family life Lincoln Christian Seminary, Ill., 1969—2004. Pres. Christian Marriage and Family Enrichment Services, Lincoln, 1980—. Contbr. articles to profl. jours. Mem. Nat. Assn. Profs. Christian Edn. (editor newsletter 1975-79, pres. 1979-80), Religious Edn. Assn. Lodges: Rotary (bd. dirs. Lincoln chpt. 1988—, pres. 1993-94). Home: 330 Campus View Dr Lincoln IL 62656-2106 Office: Christian Marriage & Family Enrichment Svcs 330 Campus View Dr Lincoln IL 62656 Office Phone: 217-732-1629. Personal E-mail: wilsondrbob99@aol.com.

**WILSON, ROBERT E.,** lawyer; b. Wichita Falls, Tex., Oct. 3, 1943; BBA, So. Meth. U., 1966, JD, 1969. Bar: Tex. 1969. Ptnr., Real Estate, Fin., Corp. Haynes and Boone LLP, Dallas, mng. ptnr. of firm, bd. dir. Contbr. articles to profl. jour.; editor-in-chief Law Jour., 1969. Named a Super Lawyer, D Magazine, Tex. Monthly. Mem.: The Real Estate Coun. (cmty. leadership com.), Am. Coll. Mortgage Attys., US-Japan Bus. Coun., Am. Coll. Real Estate Lawyers (bd. govs.), State Bar Tex. (real property, probate and trust law sect. 1984—), ABA (chmn. mortgages and other debt financing com., real property, probate and trust law sect.), Tex. Bar Assn., Dallas Bar Assn. (chmn. real property law sect. 1982). Office: Haynes & Boone LLP 901 Main St Ste 3100 Dallas TX 75202-3789 Office Phone: 214-651-5601. Office Fax: 214-200-0550. Business E-Mail: robert.wilson@haynesboone.com.

**WILSON, ROBERT FOSTER,** lawyer; b. Windsor, Colo., Apr. 6, 1926; s. Foster W. and Anne Lucille (Svedman) W.; m. Mary Elizabeth Clark, Mar. 4, 1951 (div. Feb. 1972); children: Robert F., Katharine A.; m. Sally Anne Nemec, June 8, 1982. BA in Econs., U. Iowa, 1950, JD, 1951. Bar: Iowa 1951, U.S. Dist. Ct. (no. and so. dists.) Iowa 1956, U.S. Ct. Appeals (8th cir.) 1967. Atty. FTC, Chgo., 1951-55; pvt. practice, Cedar Rapids, Iowa, 1955—. Pres. Lawyer Forms, Inc.; dir. Lawyers Forms, Inc.; mem. Iowa Reapportionment Com., 1968; del. to U.S. and Japan Bilateral Session on Legal and Econ. Rels. Conf., Tokyo, 1988, Moscow Conf. on Law and Bilateral Rels., Moscow, 1990; U.S. del. to Moscow Conf. on Legal and Econ. Rels., 1990. Mem. Iowa Ho. of Reps., 1959-60; pres. Linn County Day Care, Cedar Rapids, 1968-74. Sgt. U.S. Army, 1944-46. Mem. ATLA, Am. Arbitration Assn. (panel arbitrators), Iowa Bar Assn., Iowa Trial Lawyers Assn., Linn County Bar Assn., Am. Legion (judge adv. 1970-75, 87-93), Cedar View Country Club, Elks, Eagles, Delta Theta Phi. Democrat. Home: 2179 Blake Blvd SE Cedar Rapids IA 52403-1128 Office: 810 Dows Bldg Cedar Rapids IA 52403-7010 Office Phone: 319-364-1538. Personal E-mail: rwilsonlaw@aol.com.

**WILSON, ROBERT FRANK,** retired real estate broker, artist; b. Oxford, Pa., Aug. 26, 1949; s. Robert Thomas and Claudine Wilson; m. Barbara Wise. BA, U. Del., 1973; real estate cert., NYU, 2001. Prin. Blue Hen Graphics, NYC, 1980—98; dir. property mgmt. Tier II Mgmt./Andrews Bldg. Corp., NYC, 1998—. Prin.-Cliff View Real Estate Corp., NYC, 2006; dir. ops. Andrews Art Gallery, 2004—; editor, publisher Andrews Report. Bd. pres. Housing Coop., N.Y.C., 1988—, N.Y.C. Bus. Improvement Dist., 2003; dir. Andrews Art Gallery, N.Y.C. Recipient Achievement award, Cooperator Mag., 2001. Mem.: Salmagundi Club, NYC, Caledonian Club, NYC. Democrat. Avocations: collecting poster stamps, Kitsch, watercolor painting, travel. Home: 3 Great Jones St New York NY 10012

**WILSON, ROBERT GODFREY,** radiologist; b. Montgomery, Ala., Mar. 18, 1937; s. Robert Woodridge and Lucille (Godfrey) W.; m. Dorothy June Waters, Aug. 31, 1957; children: Amy Lucille, Robert Darwin, Robert Woodridge II, Lucy Elizabeth. BA, Huntingdon Coll., 1957; MD, Med. Coll. Ala., 1961. Diplomate Nat. Bd. Med. Examiners, Am. Bd. Radiology, Am. Bd. Nuclear Medicine. Intern Letterman Gen. Hosp., San Francisco, 1961-62; resident in radiology U. Okla. Med. Center, Oklahoma City, 1965-68, clin. instr. in radiology, 1968—; practice medicine specializing in diagnostic and therapeutic radiology, nuclear medicine Shawnee, Okla., 1968—; mem. med. staff Shawnee Med. Center, Mission Hill Meml. Hosp., Shawnee, 1968—. Served to capt. M.C., USAF, 1960-65. Mem. AMA, Okla., Pottawatomie County med. socs., Okla., Greater Oklahoma City radiol. socs., Am. Coll. Radiology, Soc. Nuclear Medicine, Radiol. Soc. N.Am. Methodist. Home: 26 Sequoyah Blvd Shawnee OK 74801-5570 Office: 5606 Aquarius Shawnee OK 74804-9387

**WILSON, ROBERT GORDON,** investment banker; b. Mt. Vernon, NY, Dec. 16, 1933; s. Gerald and Ella Baxter (Close) W.; m. Valerie Ann Wilson, Apr. 25, 1966 (div. 1986); children: Jennifer Lynn, Kimberly Ann; m. Anne Marie Henriquez, Sept. 27, 1986; 1 child, Anthony H. Crotti. BA, Haverford Coll., 1955; MBA, Columbia U., 1957. Gen. ptnr. Goldman Sachs & Co., N.Y.C., 1967-80, ltd. ptnr., 1981-89; pres. Goldman Sachs Internat., London, 1977-80; chmn., pres. Ecologic Waste Svcs., Inc., Miami, Fla., 1990-94; vice chmn. Carter Kaplan & Co., Richmond, Va., 1993-94; dir., founder LendingTree, Inc., Charlotte, NC, 1997—99. Former chmn. bd. trustees YMCA Greater N.Y., N.Y.C., 1985. Republican. Avocations: golf, wines, travel. Home and Office: Ziani Internat Capital Inc 151 Crandon Blvd Apt 1127 Key Biscayne FL 33149-1596 E-mail: rgw.55@hotmail.com.

**WILSON, ROBERT JAMES MONTGOMERY,** investment company executive; b. Millbrook, N.Y., Feb. 8, 1920; s. Albert James Montgomery and Charlotte (Kaye) W.; m. Yvette Laneres, May 10, 1952; children— Robert James Montgomery, Olivia Laneres Wilson Welbourn, Geoffrey Laneres. Grad., Choate Sch., 1938; AB, Yale U., 1942. Securities analyst buying dept. Union Securities Corp., N.Y.C., 1946-49; securities analyst Union Service Corp., N.Y.C., 1949-59, v.p., 1959-62; pres., dir. Surveyor Fund, Inc. (formerly Gen. Public Service Corp.), N.Y.C., 1962-71; with Rockefeller Family and Assos., 1972-75; pres. Adams Express Co., N.Y.C., 1975-86, also bd. dirs., 1975—; pres. Petroleum & Resources Corp. (formerly Petroleum Corp. Am.), N.Y.C., 1975-86, also bd. dirs., 1975—. Mem. adv. investment com. Md. State Retirement Systems, 1979-82; bd. dirs. Assn. Publicly Traded Investment Cos., 1968-71, chmn., 1969-71. Mem. 1940 Fahnestock Expdn. of Am. Mus. Natural History to South Seas. Served to capt. AUS, World War II. Mem. Md. Club.

**WILSON, ROBERT M.,** diversified financial services company executive; b. St. Louis, Aug. 10, 1952; s. William H. and Mary E. (Sacksteder) W.; m. Joli S. Schneeberger, Oct. 7, 1978; 1 child, William Wilcox. BS, Miami U., Oxford, Ohio, 1974; JD, Cleve. State U., 1977. Bar: Ohio; CPA, Ohio. Ptnr. Touche Ross & Co., Dayton, Ohio, 1972-88, Roberds, Inc., Dayton, 1988-2000, pres., 1998—2000; exec. v.p. Wealthport, Inc., 2000—01; COO CCA Global Ptnrs. Inc., 2001—. Chmn. Dayton Ballet Assn., 1979-91; trustee Carillon Park, 1988-94, City-Wide Devel. Corp., 1991-2000, Cath. Social Svcs., 1995-2000; assoc. bd. Dayton Art Inst., 1995. Mem. ABA (com. chmn. 1990-92), Ohio Soc. CPAs (pres. 1985-86). Republican. Roman Catholic.

**WILSON, ROBERT WARNE,** philanthropist; b. Detroit, Nov. 3, 1926; s. Clarence Warne Wilson and Margaret Ballantyne; m. Marillyn Buelow, Apr. 1957 (div. 1977). BA in Econs. magna cum laude, Amherst (Mass.) Coll., 1946; MA in Econs., U. Mich., 1947; postgrad., Mich. Law Sch., 1948-49. Trainee First Boston Corp., NYC, 1949-50, 52-53; securities analyst Bank of Detroit, 1953-58; securities analyst to v.p. Gen. Am. Inv., NYC, 1958-62; securities analyst A.G. Becker & Co., NYC, 1962-68; investor, 1968—86; philanthropist, 1987—. Bd. dirs. Bklyn. Mus., 1974-88, Bklyn. Botanic Garden, 1974-88, NYC Opera, 1977-98, chmn. 1981-93; adv. bd. Met. Opera, 1979-81; trustee Environtl. Def., 1986—, Lyric Opera of Chgo. Nat. Bd., 1995-01, Manhattan Inst., 1986-02, Whitney Mus. of Am. Art, 1978— v.p., World Monuments Fund, 1990— vice chmn., Deafness Rsch.

Found., 1998-01. U.S. Army, 1951—52. Mem.: Phi Beta Kappa. Republican. Avocations: opera, museums, theater, movies, sightseeing. Office: 520 83rd St Brooklyn NY 11209-4520 Office Phone: 718-748-6113.

**WILSON, ROBERT WOODROW,** radio astronomer; b. Houston, Tex., Jan. 10, 1936; s. Ralph Woodrow and Fannie May (Willis) W.; m. Elizabeth Rhoads Sawin, Sept. 4, 1958; children: Philip Garrett, Suzanne Katherine, Randal Woodrow. BA with honors in Physics, Rice U., 1957; PhD, Calif. Inst. Tech., 1962. Research fellow Calif. Inst. Tech., Pasadena, 1962-63; mem. tech. staff AT&T Bell Labs., Holmdel, NJ, 1963-76, head wireless tech. rsch. dept., 1976-94; sr. sci. Harvard-Smithsonian Ctr. for Astrophysics, Cambridge, Mass., 1994—. Adj. prof. SUNY, 1978—. Discoverer 3 deg. k microwave background radiation, 1965, CO and other molecules in interstellar space using their millimeter wavelength radiation;. Named Fairchild Disting. scholar, Caltech., 1987; recipient Henry Draper medal, Royal Astron. Soc., London, 1977, Nobel prize in physics, 1978, Herschel Medal, 1977; fellow NSF fellow, 1958—61, Cole fellow, 1957—58. Mem.: AAAS, NAS (Herschel medal 1977), Internat. Sci. Radio Union, Am. Phys. Soc., Internat. Astron. Union, Am. Astron. Soc., Sigma Xi, Phi Beta Kappa. E-mail: rwilson@cfa.com.*

**WILSON, ROBERTA BUSH,** retired psychotherapist, accountant; b. Watertown, NY, Dec. 23, 1937; d. Robert King and Barbara P. (Wiggins) Banks; m. Marvin D. Bush, Feb. 28, 1959 (div. 1977); m. Asa A. Wilson, July 29, 2004. BA, Glenville State Coll., 1977; MS, W.Va. U., Morgantown, 1985. Lic. profl. therapist W.Va. Acct. GE Plastics, Parkersburg, W.Va., 1959—77; lit. vol. Parkersburg, 1977—89; outpatient site head Abraxas, Parkersburg, 1989—95; psychotherapist Westbrook Health Svc., Parkersburg, 1996—97; ret., 1997. Pres., bd. dirs. Lit. Vol. Program of Wood County, Parkersburg. Mem.: Profl. Women's Assn. (pres., bd. dirs., Hall of Fame 1995). Episcoplian. Home: 111 Canterbury Dr Parkersburg WV 26104-8057

**WILSON, ROBERTA LOUISE,** writer, editor, journalist, activist; b. Hollywood, Calif., June 2, 1954; d. Robert Louis and Noreen Irvine Wilson; life ptnr. Jeff Lynn Moore; stepchildren: Tyron, Dashal, Adrianne 1 child, Dova Lindsay Moore. BA in Psychology, Chapman U., 1976. Editor Career Publs., Orange, Calif., 1976—81; freelance journalist Agoura Valley News, Westlake Mag., Agoura Hills, Calif., 1977—79; tech. writer Ashton-Tate, Torrance, Calif., 1983—87; tech. writer/project lead Microsoft Corp., Redmond, Wash., 1988—2000; freelance tech. writer Aldus Corp., Seattle, 1989—91. Officer Washtech/CWA Local 37083, Seattle, 2002—. Performance art for antinuclear UNARM, Business as Usual; contbr. articles to mags., websites. Media/People Power coord. Gt. Peace Mar. for Global Nuc. Disarmament, L.A., 1986—86; state coordinating com. Green Party of Wash. State, Seattle, 2001—02; co-organizer/writer bill of rights resolution Bill of Rights Def. Com., Bainbridge Island, Wash., 2003. Mem.: Green Party of Kitsap County (v.p. 2000—05), Winslow Cohousing Group (bd. trustees 1991—93). Mem. Religious Soc. Of Friends. Achievements include walked across the country with the Great Peace March for Global Nuclear Disarmament; co-founding member of first owner-developed cohousing community in the United States.

**WILSON, ROBIN SCOTT,** retired academic administrator, writer; b. Columbus, Ohio, Sept. 19, 1928; s. John Harold and Helen Louise (Walker) W.; m. Patricia Ann Kirk, Jan. 20, 1951; children: Kelpie, Leslie, Kari, Andrew. BA, Ohio State U., 1950; MA, U. Ill., 1951, PhD, 1959. Fgn. intelligence officer CIA, Washington, 1959-67; prof. English Clarion State Coll., Pa., 1967-70; assoc. dir. Com. Instnl. Cooperation, Evanston, Ill., 1970-77; assoc. provost instrn. Ohio State U., Columbus, 1977-80; univ. pres. Calif. State U., Chico, 1980-93, pres. emeritus, 1993—. Author: Those Who Can, 1973, Death By Degrees, 1995, Paragons, 1996; short stories, criticism, articles on edn. Lt. USN, 1953-57. Mem. AAAS, Phi Kappa Phi E-mail: robinwilson@comcast.net.

**WILSON, ROBLEY CONANT, JR.,** language educator, editor, writer; b. Brunswick, Maine, June 15, 1930; s. Robley Conant and Dorothy May (Stimpson) W.; m. Charlotte A. Lehon, Aug. 20, 1955 (div. 1991); children: Stephen, Philip; m. Susan Hubbard, June 17, 1995. BA, Bowdoin Coll., 1957, D.Litt (hon.), 1987; M.F.A., U. Iowa, 1968. Reporter Raymondville Chronicle, Tex., 1950-1951; asst. publicity dir. N.Y. State Fair Syracuse, 1956; instr. Valparaiso U., Ind., 1958-63; asst. prof. English U. No. Iowa, Cedar Falls, 1963-69, assoc. prof., 1969-75, prof., 1975-2000, prof. emeritus, 2000—, editor N.Am. Rev. Cedar Falls, 1969-2000. Author: The Pleasures of Manhood, 1977, Living Alone, 1978, Dancing for Men, 1983 (Drue Heinz Lit. prize, 1982), Kingdoms of the Ordinary (Agnes Lynch Starrett award, 1986), Terrible Kisses, 1989, A Pleasure Tree, 1990 (Soc. Midland Authors Poetry award, 1990), The Victim's Daughter, 1991, A Walk Through the Human Heart, 1996, Everything Paid For, 1999, The Book of Lost Fathers, 2001, Splendid Omens, 2004, The World Still Melting, 2005; co-editor: 100% Pure Florida Fiction, 2000. Bd. dirs. Associated Writing Programs, Norfolk, Va., 1983-86; pres. Iowa Woman Endeavors, Inc., 1986-90. With USAF, 1951-55. Guggenheim fellow, 1983-84, Nicholl Screenwriting fellow, 1996. Mem.: PEN, Authors' Guild. Home: PO Box 4009 Winter Park FL 32793-4009

**WILSON, RONALD LAWRENCE,** professional hockey coach; b. Windsor, Ont., Can., May 28, 1955; BA in Econs., Providence Coll. Profl. hockey player Toronto Maple Leafs, 1975-85, Minn. North Stars, 1986-88; asst. coach Milw., Vancouver Canucks, 1989-90, Vancouver Canucks, 1990-93; interim coach Milw. Admirals, 1990; head coach Anaheim (Calif.) Mighty Ducks, 1993-97, Team USA, 1996, Washington Capitals, Landover, Md., 1997—2002, San Jose Sharks, 2002—. Coach Team U.S.A., World Cup of Hockey, 1996, 2004, U.S. Olympic Hockey Team, Nagano, Japan, 1998. Named to NCAA All-Am. East 1st team, 1974-76; Team USA World Cup Champaions, 1996. Office: San Jose Sharks 525 W Santa Clara St San Jose CA 95113

**WILSON, ROSS,** ambassador; b. Mnpls., 1955; m. Margo Squire; 2 children. BA, U. Minn., 1977; MA, Columbia U., 1979; Grad., Nat. War Coll., 1995. Intern Office of Soviet Union Affairs US Dept. State, Washington, 1978-80, econ. officer Office of Soviet Union Affairs, 1980-82, 87-90, polit. officer Office of Egyptian Affairs, 1982-84, econ.-comml. officer Prague, 1985-87, spl. asst. to under sec. for econ. & agrl. affairs. Washington, 1990-92, dep. exec. sec., 1992-94, U.S. Consul Gen. Melbourne, Australia, 1995-97, prin. dep. to amb.-at-Large, spl. advisor to sec. for new Independent States of the former Soviet Union Washington, 1997—2000, US amb. to Azerbaijan Baku, 2000—03; US sr. negotiator for the Free Trade Area of the Americas Office US Trade Rep., Washington, 2003—05; exec. asst. & chief of staff for dep. sec. US Dept. State, Washington, 2005, US amb. to Turkey Ankara, 2005—. Recipient Pres. Meritorious Svc. award, 2005, Azerbaijan Order of Honor. Office: Am Embassy 7000 Ankara Pl Washington DC 20521*

**WILSON, ROWAN D.,** lawyer; b. Pomona, Calif., Sept. 3, 1960; AB cum laude, Harvard Univ., 1981; JD cum laude, Harvard Univ., 1984. Bar: Calif. 1985, NY 1987. Law clk., Hon. James E. Browning US Ct. of Appeals, 9th Cir.; assoc. Cravath Swaine & Moore LLP, NYC, 1986—92, ptnr., litig., 1992—. Mem.: Assn. Bar City NY, Fed. Bar Coun., Neighborhood Defender Svc. of Harlem, Lawyers' Com. for Civil Rights. Office: Cravath Swaine & Moore LLP Worldwide Plz 825 Eighth Ave New York NY 10019-7475 Office Phone: 212-474-1348. Office Fax: 212-474-3700. Business E-Mail: rwilson@cravath.com.

**WILSON, RUSSELL EDWARD,** music educator; b. Atlanta, Ga., Jan. 25, 1963; s. Thomas Edward and Vivian Heaton Wilson. M of Music Edn., VanderCook Coll. Music, 1994; MusB, Ga. State U., 1985. Cert. elem. secondary tchr. Ga. Band dir. Hapeville HS, 1987, North Clayton Mid. Sch., College Park, 1987—92, Riverdale Mid. Sch., 1992—98, Mundy's Mill Mid. Sch., Jonesboro, Ga., 1998—2006, Lee Mid. Sch., 2006—, Coweta County, 2006—. Lead tchr. Clayton County Pub. Schools, Jonesboro, Ga., 2001—06; pvt. studio instrn. Oboe Studio, McDonough, Ga., 1981—. Musician (prin.

oboist): Tara Winds Concert Band, 1988—. Asst. orch. dir. First Bapt. Ch., Jonesboro, 2004—; comm. dir. Tara Winds Concert Band, Atlanta, 2005—06. Recipient Legion of Honor, John Philip Sousa Found., 2005. Mem.: Ga. Music Educators Assn. (dist. treas. 1990—92), Music Educators Nat. Conf., Internat. Double Reed Soc., Nat. Band Assn. Home: 366 Whitney Ln Mcdonough GA 30253 Personal E-mail: oboeman@aol.com.

**WILSON, RUTH YVETTE,** artist, educator; b. St. John, Canada, July 5, 1933; d. James Ritson Wilson; m. James Blair Wilson, June 15, 1964; 1 child, James Blair. Staff promotion artist Zellers Ltd., Montreal, 1953—56; advertising artist All Fla. Mag., Ocala, Fla., 1956—57; asst. promo. dir. Charm Mag., N.Y.C., 1957—59; advertising mgr. Velcro Sales, N.Y.C., 1959—60; fashion co-coord. artist Haggertys, Beverly Hills, Calif., 1960—61; fashion co-coord. stylist Christenson Studios, N.Y.C., 1961—62; instr. Can. Bedminster Workshops, 1962—, Muncy Greeting Card Corp., 2003—. Instr. watercolor Somerset Art Assn., Peapeck, NJ, 2003—; workshop instr. Corp. & Art Assn., Can., U.S.A.; pvt. classes Wilsons Watercolor Classes, Pluckernin, NJ, 1970—; gallery owner North Mountain Gallery, Muncy Valley, Pa., 1998—; Keystone Horseshoe Mountain Pk., 1995—. Prin. works include United States Equestrian, 1979—84, Tele. & Telegraph, 1981, greeting card co., 1996—98. Recipient Liquitex Art award, Bald Eagles art League, 2001, Best Non Equine award, Hunterdon County Edn. Found., 2002, Honorable Mention, Cultural Heritage Gallery, 2003, numerous others. Mem.: Am. Artist Profl. League, Sullivan Coun. of the Arts, Eagles Mere Friends of the Arts, Rartian Valley Arts Assn., Somerset Art Assn. (Award of Excellence 2003), Garden State Water Color Soc. (Silver Brush award 2000), N.J. Water Color Soc., Pa. Water Color Soc. (assoc.). Avocations: reading, painting, gardening, cooking, sewing. Office Phone: 908-526-9048.

**WILSON, SAMUEL MAYHEW,** surgeon; b. Phila., June 26, 1950; m. Dorothy Hay Barrus, June 9, 1990; children: Elisabeth, Mary. BA, Swarthmore Coll., 1972; MS, Drexel U., 1975; MD, Temple U., 1979. Diplomate Am. Bd. Surgery. Resident in surgery Temple U. Hosp., Phila., 1979-84; fellow in vascular surgery Presbyn.-U. Pa. Med. Ctr., 1984-86; attending surgeon Evang. Cmty. Hosp., Lewisburg, 1986-88, Albert Einstein Med. Ctr., Phila., 1988-95. Attending surgeon Elkins Park (Pa.) Hosp., 1988-95, Frankford Hosp., Phila., 1988-95, JFK Meml. Hosp., Phila., 1988-95; staff surgeon Bayhealth Med. Ctr.-Kent Gen. Hosp., Dover, 1996—, chair dept. surgery, 2006-; asst. clin. instr. surgery U. Pa. Med. Sch., Phila., 1984-85, assoc. clin. instr., 1985-86; clin. instr. surgery Temple U. Sch. Medicine, Phila., 1988-95. Contbr. articles to profl. jours. Active Christ Episcopal Ch., Dover, 1996—, vestry, 2005—. Corp. USMCR, 1972-78. Fellow ACS, Southeastern Surg. Congress; mem. AMA (Physician Recognition award), Med. Soc. Del., Kent County Med. Soc., Delaware Valley Vascular Soc., Ea. Vascular Soc. Avocations: sailing, skiing, hiking, photography, reading. Office: 540 S Governors Ave Ste 100A Dover DE 19904-3523

**WILSON, SAMUEL V.,** academic administrator; BA, Hampden-Sydney Coll., LLD, 1979; LHD, Longwood Coll., 1999. Pres. Hampden-Sydney Coll., Va., 1992—2000, pres. emeritus, 2000—, James C. Wheat Vis. Prof. in Leadership, 2000—. Office: Hampden-Sydney Coll Hampden Sydney VA 23943-0128 E-mail: swilson@hsc.edu.*

**WILSON, SCOTT THOMAS,** psychologist, researcher; b. Bayonne, NJ, July 29, 1969; s. John Thomas and Patricia Jean Wilson; m. Denise Figlar, May 16, 1999; children: Liam Patrick, Ella Kinsey. BA in Psychology, Rutgers U., 1992; PhD in Clin. Psychology, Columbia U., 2003. Lic. clin. psychologist NY. Predoctoral fellow Columbia U., NYC, 1999—2000, postdoctoral rsch. fellow in psychiatry, 2005—; rsch. scientist NY State Psychiat. Inst., NYC, 2002—05; pvt. practice NYC, 2005—. Cons. Amador and Assocs., LLC, NYC, 2004—. Contbr. Suicide in Schizophrenia. Fellow Nat. Rsch. Svc. award, NIMH, 1999. Mem.: APA. Achievements include research in patients with severe mental illnesses, including schizophrenia and borderline personality disorder. Office Phone: 212-543-6236. Business E-Mail: stw16@columbia.edu.

**WILSON, SHARON ROSE,** literature educator, researcher; b. Denver, May 13, 1941; d. John William Wilson and Rose Schlagel; m. Roger Lloyd Brown, May 5, 1973 (div. 1998); 1 child, Stephen Roger Wilson-Brown. BA, Colo. State Coll., 1963; MA, Purdue U., 1967; PhD in Eng., U. Wis., 1976. Cert. secondary edn., Colo. Teaching asst. Purdue U., West Lafayette, Ind., 1963-65, U. Wis., Madison, 1965-70; instr. U. Northern Colo., Greeley, 1970-73, asst. prof., 1974-78, assoc. prof., 1978-84, prof. eng., women's studies, 1985—. Vis. humanist Boulder County Women's Resources Ctr., 1980; speaker and lectr. in field. Author: Margaret Atwood's Fairy-Tale Sexual Politics, 1993, The Self-Conscious Narrator and His Twentieth-Century Faces, 1976; co-editor: Approaches to Teaching Atwood's The Handmaid's Tale and Other Works, 1996; editor: Margaret Atwood's Textual Assasinations; contbr. articles to profl. jours. Founding mem. local Nat. Orgn. for Women, 1982; women's issues chairperson League of Women Voters, Longmont, 1978-85; founding co-pres. Margaret Atwood Soc., 1983-88; v.p. Doris Lessing Soc., 2002-2005, pres. 2005—. Recipient numerous rsch. grants. Mem. MLA (organizer of spl. sessions 1980, 85, 88), Colo. Seminars (adv. bd. 1980—, coord. of program), Colo. Women's Studies Assn. (conf. coord. 1977), Margaret Laurence Soc., Samuel Beckett Soc. (charter), Internat. Assn. Fantastic in the Arts, Assn. for Canadian Studies in the U.S., Popular Culture Assn., Pacific Ctrl. Canadian Studies Network, Western Canadian Studies Assn., Rocky Mountain MLA. Avocations: swimming, reading, attending theatre and film performances, art. Office: U Northern Colo Sch English Lang & Lit Greeley CO 80639-0001 Office Phone: 970-351-2985. Business E-Mail: sharon.wilson@unco.edu.

**WILSON, SHIRLEY WILLINK,** music educator, musician; b. Corry, Pa., Jan. 16, 1946; d. Raymond Leon and Doris Marie Willink; m. Dean Kenneth Wilson, July 6, 1968. MusB, Houghton Coll., NY, 1967; MS, Ctrl. Conn. State U., New Britain, 1993. Cert. tchr. NY, 1977, Conn., 1978, Pa., 2002. Tchr. Pioneer Ctrl. Sch., Yorkshire, NY, 1967—73; piano tchr. private, Hartford, Conn., 1974; long-term sub. tchr. Newington Pub. Schs., Conn., 1974; tchr. Bloomfield Pub. Schs., Conn., 1974—2001; ch. organist Calvary Ch., West Hartford, Conn., 1978—2001; music assoc., organist First Presbyn. Ch. of Covenant, Erie, Pa., 2005—. Contbr. articles to profl. jours. Recipient Tchr. of Yr., Bloomfield Pub. Schs., 1996, Recognition award, Elem. & Mid. Sch. Principals' Assn. Conn., 1998; grantee Profl. grant for workshop for music tchrs., Conn. Music Educators Assn., 1996. Mem.: Presbyn. Assn. of Musicians, Christian Educators Assn. Internat. (pres. Greater Hartford Chpt. 1986—2001, 2005—2004, sec. of bd. dirs. 1998—2001), Am. Choral Directors Assn., Music Educators Conf. Presbyterian. Avocation: counted cross stitch. Office: First Presbyn Ch Covenant 250 W Seventh St Erie PA 16501 Office Phone: 814-456-4243. Business E-Mail: shirley.wilson@firstcovenanterie.org.

**WILSON, STANLEY CHARLES,** artist, educator, curator, art gallery director, consultant; b. LA, Feb. 2, 1947; s. Ernest Charles and Eleanor (Reid) W.; m. Jacquelyn Bellard, June 3, 1989; 1 child, Jendayi Asabi. BFA, Otis Art Inst., 1969, MFA, 1971. Asst. prof. Southwestern Coll., Chula Vista, Calif., 1972-73; prof. art Calif. Poly U., Pomona, 1973—; univ. gallery dir. Calif. Poly. U., Pomona, 1988—96; instr. Otis Parsons Watts Towers, L.A., 1981-88; prof. emeritus Calif. State Poly. U., Pomona, 2003—. Bd. artists Brockman Gallery Prodns., LA, 1980-85; bd. dirs. Watt Towers Art Ctr., LA; vis. artist dept. art U. Nev., Las Vegas, 1990; vis. prof. sculpture Otis Art Inst., LA, 1991-92; bd. advisors The Armory Gallery, Pasadena, Calif.; apptd. Nat. Edn. Com., Princeton, NJ, 1996; chair Pasadena (Calif.) Arts Commn., 1997; co-chair sculpture panel Coll. Art Assn., LA, 1999; Disting. artist lecture Calif. State U., Northridge, 2001; grad. reviewer Memphis Coll. of Art and Design, Memphis, 2001; co-curator exhbn. Armony Ctr. for Arts, Pasadena, 2002; slide lectr., disting. artist series Calif. State U., Northridge, 2002; vis. artist, grad. reviewer Memphis Coll. Art and Design, 2001; art adv. com. Pasadena Ctr., 2006. One-man shows include Sol Del Rio Gallery, San Antonio, 1980, Brockman Gallery, 1982, Daniel Maher Gallery, 1983, Southwest Coll., 1984; 2 person exhbn. Calif. State U., Bakersfield, 2002;

exhibited in group shows at Oranges/Sardines Gallery, 1984, Sparc Gallery, 1985, Mus. African Am. Art, 1985, L.A. Art Gallery, 1986, Muni Art Gallery Calif. State U. Dominguez Hills, Altars, Icons & Sacred Places, San Antonio Art Inst., 1992, Gallery 1078, Chico, Calif., Calif. State U., 2002, Calif. Poly. U., 2003, African AIDS Armory Ctr. for the Arts, Calif., 2004, Calif. African Am. Mus., 2005, Calif. AfroAm. Mus., L.A., 2005; represented in permanent collections Calif. Mus. Afro-Am. History and Culture, Prairie View Coll., 1977, Tex. A&M U., 1977, Atlanta Life Ins. Co., 1984, Golden State Life Ins., 1985, Broadway Fed. Savs. & Loan Corp., L.A., 1986, LACTC Metro Rail Commn.; artist in residence Studio Mus. Harlem, N.Y., Spokane (Wash.) Coll., (vis.) Graduate Review Memphis Coll of Art and Design, 2001, Pasadena Art Alliance, 2005; contbr. articles to profl. jours. Chmn. Pasadena Arts Commn. NEA fellow, 1986; Visual Arts fellow Pasadena Art Commn., 1991; advanced placement, Studio Art Devel. Com.; Brody visual art fellow, L.A., 1998; recipient Gold Crown award in visual arts Pasadane Arts Coun., 1998. Progressive. Avocations: music, gardening, architecture, sports. Office: Calif Poly U Dept Art 3801 W Temple Ave Pomona CA 91768-2557 Office Phone: 909-869-3519. Business E-mail: scwilson@csupomona.edu.

**WILSON, STEPHANIE D.,** astronaut; b. Boston, 1966; m. Julius B.J. McCurdy. BS in Engring., Harvard U., Divsn. Engring. and Applied Sciences, 1988; MS in Aerospace Engring., U. Tex., 1992. Loads and dynamic engr. astronautics group Martin Marietta, Denver, 1988—90; mem. attitude and articulation control subsystem for Galileo spacecraft Jet Propulsion Lab., Pasadena, Calif., 1992—96; astronaut NASA, Johnson Space Ctr., Houston, 1996—. Lead CAPCOM (capsule communicator) Columbia Mission, 2003; mission specialist, load master, operating robotic arm STS-121, Return-to-Flight test mission and assembly flight to Internat. Space Station, 2006. Mem.: AIAA. Achievements include research in control and modeling of large, flexible space structures; second African-American women in space. Avocations: skiing, music, astronomy, stamp collecting/philately, travel. Office: Astronaut Office/CB NASA Johnson Space Ctr Houston TX 77058*

**WILSON, STEPHEN RAY,** fertilizer manufacturing company executive; b. DuBois, Pa., Oct. 20, 1948; s. Richard C. and Marilyn J. (Stewart) W.; m. Susan K. Condon, Sept. 5, 1970; children: Jeffrey M., Elizabeth A. BA in Sociology, Northwestern U., 1970, MBA in Fin. and Acctg., 1974. CPA, Ill. Various positions Inland Steel Industries, Chgo., 1974-91, asst. treas., 1985-88; contr., treas. James T. Ryerson & Son, Chgo., 1988-89; v.p. info. mgmt. and fin. Joseph T. Ryerson & Son, Chgo., 1989-90; gen. mgr. corp. planning Inland Steel Industries, Inc., Chgo., 1990-91; sr. v.p., CFO, CF Industries, Inc., Long Grove, Ill., 1991—2003, pres., CEO, 2003—, chmn., 2005—. Bd. dirs. Northwestern Club Chgo., 1982-84; bd. trustees Chgo. Found. for Edn., 1993—. With U.S. Army, 1970-72. Mem. AICPA, Fin. Execs. Inst., Econ. Club Chgo. Avocations: running, golf, travel. Office: CF Industries Inc 1 Salem Lake Dr Long Grove IL 60047-8401*

**WILSON, STEVE,** museum director; BFA, U. So. Calif.; MFA in acting, Nat. Theatre Conservatory, Denver. Tchr., performing arts chmn. St. Mary's Acad., Colo.; faculty mem. Wolf Theatre Acad. and Stage Eleven; artist-in-residence Cherry Creek and Denver Pub. Sch. Dists., Denver Sch. Arts; exec. artistic dir., acting dir. Mizel Ctr. for Arts and Culture; dir. Wolf Theatre Acad. Office: Mizel Ctr Arts and Culture 350 S Dahlia St Denver CO 80246 Office Phone: 303-316-6363.

**WILSON, SUE,** newspaper editor; Bur. chief AP, Raleigh, N.C., 1999—. Address: 4020 Westchase Blvd Ste 300 Raleigh NC 27607-3960

**WILSON, SYLVIA ALYCE,** musician, educator; b. Mpls., June 19, 1950; d. Robert Leighton and Doris Mae (Seim) Butts; m. Dennis Charles Wilson, Sept. 12, 1970; children: Ryan Bradley, Virginia Anne Herzog. BS in Music Edn. with high distinction, U. Minn., 1972; MA in Music Edn., U. Minn., Mpls., 1987. Orch. tchr. Anoka-Hennepin Sch. Dist. No. 11, Coon Rapids, Minn., 1972—77, music tchr., 1986—89, 1992—; substitute music tchr. St. Louis Park (Minn.) Sch. Dist. No. 283, 1978—85; orch. tchr. Wayzata (Minn.) Sch. Dist. #284, 1985—86; orch./choir tchr. Roseville (Minn.) Area Pub. Schs. #623, 1989—90. Musician Lake String Quartet, Mpls., 1982—85; piano tuner, pvt. music tchr., 1982—86; preschool music tchr. West Bank Sch. Music, Mpls., 1983—85; judge Minn. State HS League, St. Paul, 2003—; presenter in field; MMEA State mentor Minn. Music Edn. Assn., 2006—. Contbr. articles to profl. jours. Violinist, violist Cantati Evangelica, Mpls., 1995—2001, Mpls. Civic Orch., 1970—; VBS tchr. First Bapt. Ch. Mpls., 1990—94, choir dir., bell choir dir., 1992—2000. Named Outstanding Sr., Am. Legion, 1968; recipient Meritorious Orch. Program award, Minn. String Tchrs. Assn., 1987, 2002; grantee, Anoka-Hennepin Ednl. Found., 1999—2001; scholar, U. Minn., 1968. Mem.: NEA, Minn. Educators of the Gifted and Talented, Anoka-Hennepin Edn. Minn. (bldg. rep. 2000—05), Am. String Tchrs. Assn., Music Educators Nat. Conf., Pi Kappa Lambda, Sigma Alpha Iota (pres., v.p., treas., corr. sec. 1970—, co-chair benefit music scholarships, Music scholar 1970, Sword of Honor 1971, Svc. to Chpt. award 2005, Rose of Honor 2006). Home: 2700 Joppa Ave S Saint Louis Park MN 55416 Office: Northdale Mid Sch 11301 Dogwood St Coon Rapids MN 55448 Personal E-mail: swilsonusf@yahoo.com.

**WILSON, TAYLOR,** lawyer; b. Dallas, Aug. 9, 1963; BA cum laude, Amherst Coll., 1985; JD, So. Meth. U., 1990. Bar: Tex. 1990. Ptnr., corp./securities, venture capital, mergers & acquisitions Haynes and Boone LLP, Dallas, Practice Group Leader, Bus. Trans. Sect., hiring ptnr., co-chmn., Investment Fund Practice Group. Assoc. sr. editor The Internat. Lawyer, 1989—90. Mem.: Dallas Bar Assn., State Bar Tex. (Bus. Law Sect., info./edn. com. 1996—), ABA (Bus. Law Sect., venture capital & pvt. equity com. 2001—). Office: Haynes and Boone LLP 901 Main St Ste 3100 Dallas TX 75202 Office Phone: 214 651 5615. Office Fax: 211 200 0617. Business E-Mail: taylor.wilson@haynesboone.com.

**WILSON, TERILYN BARRETT,** elementary school educator; b. Logan, W. Va., Aug. 17, 1950; d. Freeman J. and Marie P. Barrett; m. Kenneth Ray Wilson, Nov. 25, 1977; children: Melanie Brooke, Stephanie Marie. BA, Marshall U., 1972, M, 1973. Spl. edn. tchr. Putnam County Sch., Winfield, W.Va., 1972—73, Kanawha County Sch., Charleston, W.Va., 1973—74, Meade County Sch., Brandenburg, Ky., 1974—77, Logan County Sch., Logan, 1978, 1980—85, 2d grade tchr., 1985—90, spl. edn. tchr., 1998—2002, 5th grade tchr., 2003—. Chair, spl. edn. dept. Chapmanville Mid. Sch., Chapmanville, W.Va., 1990—2002, sec., faculty senate, 1994—98. Deacon, ch. bd. First Christian Ch., Logan, W.Va., 2003—05. Mem.: Internat. Reading Assn., Delta Kappa Gamma (v.p. 1992—96). Democrat. Avocations: reading, quilting, travel. Office: Chapmanville Mid Sch 300 Vance St Chapmanville WV 25508 Office Phone: 304-855-8378. Personal E-mail: tbkwilson@verizon.net.

**WILSON, THEODORE HENRY,** retired electronics executive, aerospace engineer; b. Eufaula, Okla., Apr. 23, 1940; s. Theodore V. and Maggie E. (Buie) W.; m. Barbara Ann Tassara, May 16, 1958 (div. 1982); children: Debbie Marie, Nita Leigh, Wilson Axten, Pamela Ann, Brenda Louise, Theodore Henry II, Thomas John, Margaret Mariana; m. Colleen Fagan, Jan. 1, 1983 (div. 1987); m. Karen L. Lerohl, Sept. 26, 1987 (div. 1997); m. Sandra Rivadeneira, Mar. 27, 1997. BSME, U. Calif., Berkeley, 1962; MSME, U. So. Calif., 1964, MBA, 1970, MSBA, 1971. Sr. rsch. engr. N.Am. Aviation Co. div. Rockwell Internat., Downey, Calif., 1962-65; propulsion analyst, supr. div. applied tech. TRW, Redondo Beach, Calif., 1965-67, mem. devel. staff systems group, 1967-71, sr. fin. analyst worldwide automotive dept. Cleve., 1971-72, contr. systems and energy group Redondo Beach, 1972-79, dir. fin. control equipment group Cleve., 1979-82, v.p. fin. control indsl. and energy group, 1982-85, mem. space and def. group Redondo Beach, 1985-93, ret., 1993. Lectr., mem. com. acctg. curriculum UCLA Extension, 1974-79. Mem. Fin. Execs. Inst. (com. govt. bus.), Machinery and Allied Products Inst. (govt. contracts coun.), Nat. Contract Mgmt. Assn. (bd. advisors), Aerospace

Industries Assn. (procurement and fin. coun.), UCLA Chancellors Assocs., Tau Beta Pi, Beta Gamma Sigma, Pi Tau Sigma. Republican. Avocations: golf, bridge. Home: 3617 Via La Selva Palos Verdes Peninsula CA 90274-1115

**WILSON, THOMAS DALE,** not-for-profit fundraiser; b. Lincoln, Nebr., June 2, 1952; s. Richard Barr and Charlotte Adele (Brown) Wilson; m. Susette Adele Eddinger, Mar. 9, 1973; children: Christine, Richard, Charles, Kathryn. B in Music Edn., U. Nebr., Lincoln, 1974; MusM, Northwestern U., Evanston, Ill., 1976. Dir. corp. found. rels. Field Mus. Natural History, Chgo., 1984—85; dir. devel. Phoenix Symphony, 1985—86; sr. campaign dir. Devel. Mgmt. Assn., L.A., 1986—89; v.p. devel. Oreg. Grad. Inst. Sci. & Tech., Portland, 1989—93; pres. Wilson and Assocs., Portland, Oreg., 1993—. Co-pres. Assn. Fundraising Profls. Oreg., Portland, 2002—03. Author: Great Grantsmanship, 1997, The Win Win Ask, 1999, Endowment Fundraising, 2000. Music dir. English Handbell Choir, 1989—94; trustee Valley Cmty. Presbyn. Ch. Found., 1989—94. Mem.: Nat. Soc. Fund Raising Execs. (Oreg. pres. 1990). Avocations: biking, reading, jazz saxophone. Office: Wilson & Assocs 4495 NW Malhuer Ave Portland OR 97229

**WILSON, THOMAS DOUGLAS, JR.,** lawyer; b. Winston-Salem, NC, Aug. 26, 1946; s. Thomas Douglas Wilson and Beatrice Burcham Chapman; m. Betsey Page Bent, Aug. 22, 1984; 1 child, Elizabeth. BA in Econs., U. N.C., Chapel Hill, 1968, JD, 1973. Bar: N.C. 1973, Ga. 1974; cert. arbitrator, mediator Ga.; arbitrator N.C. Trial atty. FTC, Atlanta, 1973-78; pvt. practice Atlanta, 1978-81; atty. Ga. Legal Svcs. Corp., Gainesville, 1981-84; mng. ptnr. Wilson, Cobb, Lichstenstein & Lao, Atlanta, 1984-93; pres. Ga. Emission Testing Co., Inc., Atlanta, 1993-95; assoc. McGuire, Wood & Bissette PA, Asheville, NC, 1995-98, mng. ptnr., 1999—2002. Vol. atty. Pisgah Legal Svcs., Asheville, 1996—, v.p., bd. dirs. Author: (manual) Social Security Disability Claims, 1984; co-author: (manual) North Carolina Construction Law: Rights and Remedies, 1998. Chmn. bd. dirs. RiverLink, Asheville, 1997-99; vice chmn. bd. dirs. Regional Waterh Authority Task Force, Asheville, 1996-99; mem. Asheville Econ. Devel. Task Force, 1999-2000; mem. Asheville Econ. Devel. Commn., 1997-99; youth basketball coach YMCA, Asheville Recreation League, 1997-2001; pres., bd. dirs. Asheville HS Booster Club. Mem. ABA, ATLA, Ga. Bar Assn., N.C. Bar Assn. (bd. dirs., constrn. law coun 2000—), N.C. Acad. Trial Lawyers, Asheville N.C. C. of C. (com. Asheville-Bumcombe Water Agreement). Home: 172 Marlborough Rd Asheville NC 28804 Office: 48 Patton Ave Asheville NC 28801-3321 Fax: 828-252-2437. E-mail: tdwilson@mwbavl.com.

**WILSON, THOMAS JOSEPH,** insurance company executive; m. Jill Garling; 3 children. BSBA, U. Mich., 1979; M of Mgmt., Northwestern U., 1980. Various fin. positions Amoco Corp., Chgo., 1980-86; mng. dir. mergers and acquisitions Dean Witter Reynolds, Chgo., 1986-93; v.p. strategy and analysis Sears, Roebuck and Co., Chgo., 1993-95; sr. v.p., CFO The Allstate Corp., Northbrook, Ill., 1995-98; chmn., pres. Allstate Fin., 1999—2002; pres. Allstate Protection, 2003—05; pres., COO The Allstate Corp., Northbrook, Ill., 2005—. Bd. dirs. Rush-Presbyn.-St. Luke's Med. Ctr. and Francis W. Parker Sch. Office: Allstate Ins Co 2775 Sanders Rd Northbrook IL 60062-6110

**WILSON, THOMAS LEON,** physicist, researcher; b. Alpine, Tex., May 21, 1942; s. Homer Marvin and Ogarita Maude (Bailey) W.; m. Joyce Ann Krevosky, May 7, 1978; children: Kenneth Edward Byron, Bailey Elizabeth Victoria. BA, Rice U., 1964, BS, 1965, MA, 1974, PhD, 1976. With NASA, Houston, 1965—, astronaut instr., 1965-74; high-energy theoretical physicist, 1969—. Author 3 books; contbr. articles to profl. jours. Recipient Hugo Gernsback award, IEEE, 1964; fellow, NASA, 1966—76. Mem.: AAAS, Am. Nuc. Soc., Am. Assn. Physicists in Medicine, NY Acad. Scis., Am. Phys. Soc. Achievements include research on grand unified field theory, relativistic quantum field theory, quantum chromodynamics, quantum probability theory, supergravity, quantum cosmology, astrophysics, deep inelastic scattering, neutrino astronomy, neutrino tomography; discoverer classical uncertainty principle; subspeciality: relativity and gravitation; patentee in field; contributor to design of NASA's proposed lunar base; originator olive branch as symbol of man's 1st landing on moon (on Susan B. Anthony and Eisenhower dollars); and manual Saturn takeover for Apollo moon program. Home: 206 Woodcombe Dr Houston TX 77062-2538 Office: NASA Johnson Space Ctr Houston TX 77058 Office Phone: 281-483-2147. Business E-Mail: twilson@ems.jsc.nasa.gov. E-mail: ThomasWilson@KickapooNovel.com

**WILSON, THOMAS MATTHEW, III,** lawyer; b. Ware, Mass., Feb. 22, 1936; s. Thomas Matthew Jr. and Ann Veronica (Shea) W.; m. Deborah Ord Lockhart, Feb. 10, 1962; children: Deborah Veronica, Leslie Lockhart, Thomas Matthew IV. BA, Brown U., 1958; JD, U. Md., 1971. Bar: Md. 1972, U.S. Ct. Appeals (4th cir.) 1976, U.S. Supreme Ct. 1977. Sales mgr. Mid-Ea. Box Mfg. Co., Balt., 1966-74; asst. atty. gen., chief antitrust divsn. State of Md., Balt., 1974-79; ptnr. Tydings & Rosenberg, LLP, Balt., 1979—. Author: Defending an Antitrust Action Brought by a State, 1987, The Spectre of Double Recovery in Antitrust Federalism, 1989; co-author: Reciprocity and the Private Plaintiff, 1972; mem. editl. adv. bd.: Bur. of Nat. Affairs Antitrust and Trade Regulation Report, 1979—. Mem. ABA (sect. on antitrust law 1974—, chmn. state antitrust enforcement com. 1986-89, antitrust sect. coun. 1990-93, council on legal edn. 1993-94), Md. Bar Assn. (antitrust subcom. 1975-78), Internat. Bar Assn. (sect. on bus. law, antitrust law and monopolies com. 1983—), Churchwarden's Chess Club, Annapolis Yacht Club. Republican. Achievements include patents for nail cartons. Home: Baobab Farm Hampstead MD 21074 Office: Tydings & Rosenberg LLP 100 E Pratt St Baltimore MD 21202-1009 Office Phone: 410-752-9708. Business E-Mail: twilson@tydingslaw.com.

**WILSON, THOMAS STRONG, JR., (IAM WILSON),** judge; b. Portland, Oreg., Aug. 13, 1944; s. Thomas Strong and Ruth (Isherwood) W. BA, Dickinson Coll., 1967; JD, U. Miami, 1971. Bar: Fla. 1971, D.C. 1972, U.S. Dist. Ct. (so. dist.) Fla., U.S. Ct. Appeals (5th cir.). Rsch. aide to Justice James Adkins Fla. Supreme Ct., Tallahassee, 1971-72; assoc. Preddy, Haddad, Kutner & Hardy, 1973, John R. Farrell, PA., 1973; asst. pub. defender Pub. Defender's Office, Dade County, Fla., 1973; sole practice Dade County, 1978-84; asst. state's atty. State's Atty.'s Office, Dade County, 1984-87, gen. master Family Divsn., 1987-90; judge Circuit Ct., Dade County, 1990. Served to ensign USNR, 1968-69. Named Judge of Yr., Am. Bd. Trial Advocates, Miami chpt., 1999, Dade County Trial Lawyers, 2003; recipient Steven Levine award. Mem. Iron Arrow, Skull and Key. Roman Catholic. Office: 73 W Flagler St Ste 624 Miami FL 33130 Office Phone: 305-349-5741, 305-349-7161.

**WILSON, TYLER J.,** medical association administrator; BA, Georgetown U., 1981; JD, Cath. U., 1986. Atty. legis. and regulatory affairs domestic policy divsn. U.S.C. of C.; v.p. govt. affairs Automotive Aftermarket Industry Assn.; exec. dir., sec. Am. Orthotic and Prosthetic Assn., 2000—06; pres., CEO Am. Assn. for Homecare, 2006—. Office: Am Assn for Homecare 625 Slaters Ln Ste 200 Alexandria VA 22314-1171 Office Phone: 703-836-6263. Office Fax: 703-836-6730.*

**WILSON, VALERIE PETIT,** health science association director; b. New Orleans, Jan. 24, 1950; d. Alvin Joseph and Lorraine Catherine (Kelly) Petit; children: Daniel Lawrence, Craig Anthony. BS, Xavier U. La., 1970; PhD, Johns Hopkins U., 1976. Dir. policy USPHS, Washington, 1990—92, dept. dir., 1992, asst. dir. nat. AIDS policy office, 1992—93; dir. health scis. policy Inst. Medicine Nat. Acad. Scis., Washington, 1993—98; dep. dir. Tulane/Xavier Ctr. Bio-Environ. Rsch., New Orleans, 1998—2003; exec. dir. leadership alliance, clin. prof. cmty. health Brown U., Providence, 2004—. Cons. NIH, Fairfax County Schs. Contbr. articles to profl. jours. Mem. AAAS, Am. Soc. Biochemists and Molecular Biologists. Avocations: quilting, gardening. Office: Brown U Leadership Alliance Cranston RI 02920-2699 Office Phone: 401-863-1474. Business E-Mail: valerie_wilson@brown.edu.

**WILSON, VAN CEDRIC,** academic administrator; b. Newark, July 21, 1960; s. Calvin Van and Helen Holder Wilson; m. Alma H. Hairston; children: Christin Victoria, Haleigh Lynette. BA, Western Carolina U., 1984, MPA, 1990; EdD, Appalachian State U., 2003. Asst. dir. acad. svcs. Western Carolina U., Cullowhee, NC, 1984—89, dir. retention svcs., 1989—91; dir. admissions Winston-Salem (N.C.) State U., 1991—99, exec. dir. enrollment mgmt., 1999—2002; v.p. student services Forsyth Tech. CC, Winston-Salem, 2002—. Mem. Crosby Scholars Cmty. Partnership Program, Winston-Salem, 2002, Leadership Winston-Salem, 2004—; YMCA, Winston-Salem, 2006—; co-chair Nat. Heritage Acad., Winston-Salem, 2000—03. Home: 1612 Cedarlimb Ct Winston Salem NC 27127 Office: Forsyth Tech CC 2100 Silas Creek Pky Winston Salem NC 27103 Office Phone: 336-734-7239. Business E-mail: wilsonvc42@aol.com. Business E-Mail: vwilson@forsythtech.edu.

**WILSON, VICKI LYNN,** executive secretary, administrative assistant; b. El Paso, Tex., Jan. 16, 1962; d. Theodore Elliott and Pamela Ann Wilson. AA, 2003—. Adminstrv. asst. Rsch. Analysis & Maintenance, Inc. (RAM), El Paso, Tex., 1990—2001; sec. Clint Ind. Sch. Dist., El Paso, Tex., 2001—02; exec. sec. San Marcos Consol. Ind. Sch. Dist., San Marcos, Tex., 2003—. Office: San Marcos CISD 500 West Hutchison San Marcos TX 78666 Home: 901 Hazelton St San Marcos TX 78666-3131 E-mail: vwilson62@hotmail.com.

**WILSON, W. DAVID,** corporate financial executive; b. 1954; At, DePauw U., 1975, Thunderbird Grad. Sch. of Intl. Mgmt., 1977. V.p. and CFO PolyOne Corp., Cleve., 2000—. Office: 33587 Walker RD Avon Lake OH 44012-1145

**WILSON, WALTER CLINTON,** retired gas industry executive; b. Brownwood, Tex., Sept. 21, 1942; s. Henry Eliga and Lottie Mae (Palmore) Wilson; m. Debra M. Thompson, Aug. 26, 1965; children: Walter Scott, Aimée Renee. BS cum laude, Howard Payne U., 1965. CPA Tex. Fin. mgmt. Exxon Co. USA, Kingsville, Corpus Christi, Houston, Tex., 1965-81; asst. contr. Superior Oil Co., Houston, 1982-85, fin. cons., 1985-87; contr. EOG Resources, Inc. (formerly Enron Oil and Gas Co.), Houston, 1987-88, sr. v.p., CFO, 1988-2000; ret., 2000. Mem. adv. bd. H. S. Grace & Co., Houston, 2001—. Trustee Fin. Exec. Rsch. Found., 1998—2001; chmn. pers. com. 1st Bapt. Ch., Houston, 1985—87, chmn. deacons, 1994—96; trustee Howard Payne U., Brownwood, 1999—, chmn., 2002—04; bd. dirs. Lyric Performing Arts Co., Brownwood, 2004—, chmn., 2004—. Lt. USNR, 1966—69, Vietnam. Mem.: Tex. Soc. CPAs (Houston chpt.), Fin. Execs. Internat. (Houston chpt.), Kingwood Country Club, Club Corp. Am.-Houston Soc. Republican. Personal E-mail: wwilson2@earthlink.net.

**WILSON, WARREN SAMUEL,** clergyman; b. New Orleans, May 15, 1927; s. Charlie Price and Warnie (Hart) W.; m. Lillie Pearl Harvey, Apr. 10, 1947; 1 child, Barbara LaJoyce. BA, So. U., Baton Rouge, 1950; DDiv, Moody Coll., Chgo., 1952; DDiv (hon.), Trinity Hall Coll. and Sem., Springfield, Ill., 1975. Ordained to ministry Ch. of God in Christ, 1952, crowned bishop, apptd. state bishop, Calif., 1970, chmn. internat. fin. and budget com. Min. St. Bernard St. Church of God in Christ, New Orleans, 1952—60, Fresno (Calif.) Temple Ch. of God in Christ, 1963—; jurisdictional biship Central Valley Ch. of God in Christ, 1970—; internat. fin. chmn. bd. of biships Ch. of God in Christ, 1974—. Served with USN, 1942-46, PTO. Mem. NAACP (life). Avocations: fishing, boating.

**WILSON, WENDY MARIE,** elementary school educator, consultant; b. Chgo., June 21, 1967; d. Richard John and Carol Lee (Orangias) Ziert; m. Chris Allan Wilson, June 17, 1989; children: Bailey Elizabeth, Grace Amelia Townley. BS in Edn., Loyola U., Chgo., 1991; MAT, Webster U., St. Louis, 1995. Cert. tchr. pre-K - 9 Ill., tchr. pre-K - 6 NY, tchr. gifted edn. ext. grades 5-9. Dir. Champlain Mill Presch., Winooski, Vt., 1990—91; tchr. Montessori K -2 and gifted grade 4 Savannah Chatham City Pub. Schs., Ga., 1991—94; coord. gifted students K - 8 Grant Mid. and Illini Elem. Schs., Fairview Heights, Ill., 1994—95; tchr. 3d grade Lexington Sch., Ky., 1999—2000; tchr. 4th grade Chesapeake Acad., Arnold, Md., 2000—01; tchr. gifted edn. and kindergarten Arlington Pub. Schs., Va., 2001—03; tchr. 1st grade Phelps and Clifton Springs Cen. Sch. Dist., NY, 2003—04; tchr. gifted edn. K-12 and social studies 8-12 Bloomfield Cen. Sch. Dist., NY, 2004—06; tchr. gifted and talented program grades 3-5 Canandaigua Elem/ Sch., NY, 2006—. Intern mus. edn. St. Louis Sci. Ctr., 1995; edn. cons. PBS Tchr. Source, Alexandria, Va., 2001—, mem. adv. bd., 2006—; Arlington County rep. No. Va. Coun. for Gifted/Talented Edn., Arlington 2001—02. Mem. stained glass restoration com. Dundee Presbyn. Ch., NY, 2005—06. Recipient Canandaigua Nat. Bank Tchr. Recognition award, 2006. Fellow: Wayne-Finger Lakes Leadership Inst. (scholarship 2005—); mem.: ASCD, PEO. Democrat. Avocations: cooking, historic preservation, travel, opera, reading.

**WILSON, WILLIAM CAMPBELL MCFARLAND,** gastroenterologist; b. Pitts., Pa., June 8, 1953; s. George Lincoln and Nancy Adair (Lytle) W.; m. Marlis Howland, June 25, 1977; children: Sarah, Stephen, Corrie. BS in Biology, Va. Tech, 1975; MD, Hahnemann U., 1979. Intern, residency R.I. Hosp., Providence, 1978-82; staff internist USAF Med. Ctr., Wright-Patterson AFB, Ohio, 1982-86; fellowship Hahnemann U., Phila., 1986-88; with Digestive Care, Dayton, Ohio, 1988—. Chmn. planning com. Dayton Gastroenterology Symposium, 1990—; com. patient edn. Miami Valley Hosp., Dayton, 1990—94, quality assurance com., 1992—, vice chmn. dept. medicine, 1994—96, chmn. dept. medicine, 1996—98, chief of staff-elect, 2002—04, bd. dirs., 2004—, chief of staff, 2004—06. Bd. dirs. Fairhaven Ch., Dayton, 1990—94, 2001—; physician 1993—2003; bd. dirs. In His Name Ministries, 2000—02. Physician USAF, 1979—86. Fellow ACP; mem. AMA, Am. Gastroenterological Assn., Am. Coll. Gastroenterology, Am. Soc. Gastrointestinal Endoscopy, Montgomery County Med. Assn., Alpha Omega Alpha. Avocations: tennis, woodworking, bicycling, photography, computers. Office: 75 Sylvania Dr Dayton OH 45440-3237 Office Phone: 937-320-5050. E-mail: wcmw@aol.com.

**WILSON, WILLIAM HARWELL,** psychiatrist, educator; b. Memphis, Feb. 6, 1951; s. Joseph Harwell Wilson and Helen Wilson (Cobb) Carruthers; m. Paula Rea, Oct. 18, 1986; children: Rea Xan, Sanford Shepherd. BA, Brown U., 1973; MD, U. Pa., 1981. Diplomate Am. Bd. Psychiatry and Neurology, Nat. Bd. Med. Examiners. Resident in psychiatry U. Wis., Madison, 1981-85; asst. prof. psychiatry U. Pitts. Sch. Medicine, 1985-86, Med. Coll. Pa., Phila., 1986-89, Oreg. Health Scis. U., Portland, 1989—93, asst. dir. pub. psychiatry tng. program, 1989—94, assoc. prof. psychiatry, 1993—2003, prof. psychiatry, 2003—. Dir. prof. edn. unit Dammasch State Hosp., Wilsonville, Oreg., 1989-94; attending psychiatrist Oreg. Health Scis. U. Hosp., 1994—; dir. Inpatient Psychiatric Svc., 2002-. Contbr. numerous articles on treatment of schizophrenia to sci. jours. Grantee NIMH, 1989-93; Recipient of Mental Health award of Excellence, State Oreg. Disting. fellow Am. Psychiat. Assn.; mem. Soc. for Biol. Psychiatry, Psychiatry, World Fedn. Mental Health, Nat. Alliance for Mentally Ill (Exemplary Psychiatrist award 1992, 98), Am. Soc. Clin. Psychopharmacology. Office: Oreg Health Scis U Mail Code UHN-80 3181 SW Sam Jackson Park Rd Portland OR 97239-3011 Office Phone: 503-494-7353. Business E-Mail: wilsonw@ohsu.edu.

**WILSON, WILLIAM J.,** language educator; b. Oxford, Ind., Sept. 18, 1932; s. William Woodward Wilson and Esta Ella (Burton) Dilley; m. Edith Lucille McElhaney, June 1, 1955 (dec. Mar. 1969); children: Susan Wilson Siener, Maura A., Kyle A. BS summa cum laude, Ill. State U., 1959; MA, Peabody-Vanderbilt U., Nashville, 1968; EdD, Nova U., Ft. Lauderdale, Fla., 1983. Tchr. Manteno (Ill.) High Sch., 1959-60; teaching asst. U. Ill., Urbana, 1960-61; tchr. Wheaton (Ill.) Central High Sch., 1961-67; editor Laidlaw Pubs., Chgo., 1968-69; asst. prof. Ball State U., Muncie, Ind., 1969-70; assoc. prof. English Palm Beach C.C., Lake Worth, Fla., 1970—. Test reader Ednl. Testing Svc., Princeton, N.J., 1965-96; pres. Am. Lang. Rsch. Found., Lake Worth, 1976—. Editor: New Approaches to Language and Composition, 1969; author children's mus. Winter Comes to Florida, 1974, children's mus.

play A Cruise on the S.S. Eternal, 1975, Arnold's Answering Apparatus, 1976. Bd. dirs. Village Green Condominiums, Palm Springs, 1985-86. With USN, 1951-55. No. Ill. U. fellow in linguistics, DeKalb, 1965—66, humanities fellow, Peabody-Vanderbilt U., Nashville, 1967. Mem. VFW, NEA, Am. Legion, Nat. Assn. Tchrs. English., Kappa Delta Pi, Sigma Tau Delta. Democrat. Episcopalian. Avocations: kairos prison ministry, sports, square dancing, travel, collecting timepieces. Home: 2100 Springdale Blvd Apt 216Y Palm Springs FL 33461-6366 Office: Palm Beach C C 4200 Congress Ave Lake Worth FL 33461-6366 Office Phone: 561-967-7222. Personal E-mail: barktree@bellsouth.net. Business E-mail: wilsonw@pbcc.edu.

**WILSON, WILLIAM JAMES,** healthcare executive; b. Racine, Wis., Oct. 9, 1948; s. William Henry and Eileen (Tate) W.; m. Deborah Ann Leon, Nov. 14, 1987; children: Jacob Leon, James Tate. Degree in adminstrn. of justice summa cum laude, Am. U., 1972. Asst. dir. promotions Jerry Lewis Telthon, Richmond, Va., 1975; dir. mktg. Mile High Publs., NYC, 1975-76; dir. bur. Travel Comm., Honolulu, 1976-78; founder Hawaii 800, 1979—; v.p. mktg. Video Vacations, NYC, 1982-84; founder Infovision, LA, 1984-87, Conv. TV; chmn. bd. Visitor Cable Network, Honolulu, 1978—; pres. Comcor, Hono-lulu, 1976—; pres. bus. devel. 3HO Superhealth Hollistic Treatment Ctr., Tucson, 1990-93; pres. Educational Discovery, 1993-94; CEO Advanced Learning Inst., 1994—; mng. dir. Vet. Inst. Integrated Medicine, 1996—98; founder, CEO Inst. Labs., 2001—. Founder Japan Am. News Network. Avocations: skiing, rugby. Home: 1109 Quince Ave Boulder CO 80304-0785 Office: PO Box 88377 Honolulu HI 96830-8377 Office Phone: 720-841-5897. Personal E-mail: jwiearnnow@aol.com.

**WILSON, WILLIAM JAMES,** marketing professional; b. Mpls., May 8, 1936; s. Elmo C. Wilson and Harriett (Ellis) Russo; m. Julie Steers, Sept. 24, 1960 (div. 1983); children: Amanda Jane, Heather May; m. Gabi Coatsworth, May 7, 1983. AB, Yale U., 1958; MA, Cambridge U., Eng., 1964; postgrad., U. Vienna, summer 1964. Internat. advt. devel. mgr. Reader's Digest, London, 1964-67; exec. v.p. dir. Internat. Rsch. Assn., N.Y.C., 1968-71; chair, CEO Roper Starch Worldwide, Harrison, NY, 1971—2001; exec. chmn. NOP World Roper ASW Inc., Harrison, 2001—. Bd. dirs. Roper Ctr. Storrs Ct.; U.S. rep. ESOMAR, The Netherlands 1982-88; chmn. Coun. of Am. Survey Rsch. Orgn., 1994, Coun. for Mktg. and Opinion Rsch., 1996—; past dir. Market Rsch. Coun; mem. bd. advisors MSMR program U. Tex., Arlington, A.C. Nielsen Ctr. for Market Rsch. U. Wis., Madison; mem. bd. dirs. Intersections Inc. Contbr. articles to profl. jours. Mem. Am. Mktg. Assn., Internat. Advt. Assn., Am. Assn. Pub. Opinion Rsch., World Assn. Pub. Opinion Rsch., European Soc. Opinion & Mktg. Rsch. Avocations: gardening, golf, reading, walking. Office: Roper ASW Inc 500 Mamaroneck Ave #103 Harrison NY 10528-1608

**WILSON, WILLIAM JULIUS,** sociology educator; b. Derry Twp., Pa., Dec. 20, 1935; s. Esco and Pauline (Bracy) W.; m. Mildred Marie Hood, Aug. 31, 1957; children: Colleen, Lisa; m. Beverly Ann Huebner, Aug. 30, 1970; children: Carter, Paula. BA, Wilberforce U., 1958; MA, Bowling Green State U., 1961; PhD, Wash. State U., 1966; LHD (hon.), U. Mass., 1982, L.I. U., 1982, Columbia Coll., Santa Clara U., Loyola Coll., 1988, De Paul U., 1989; LLD (hon.), Marquette U., Mt. Holyoke Coll., 1989; LHD (hon.), New Sch. for Social Rsch., 1991, Bard Coll., 1992, John Jay Sch. Criminal Justice 1992, U. Pa., 1993, So. Ill. U., 1993, Northwestern U., 1993, Bowling Green State U., 1994, SUNY, Binghamton, 1994, Princeton U., 1995, Columbia U., Rutgers U., Haverford Coll., 1996, Johns Hopkins U., Morehouse Coll., Niagara U., 1997, Dartmouth Coll., 1997, U. Amsterdam, 1998, Clarion U., 1999, Colgate U., 1999, Clark U., 1999, Bates Coll., 1999; D (hon.), Northeastern U., 1999, Macalester Coll. Ohio State U., 2001; DHL (hon.), Occidental Coll., 2001, Rensselaer Poly. Inst., 2001, Lawrence U., 2001, U Miami, 2002, others. Asst. prof. U. Mass., Amherst, 1965-69, assoc. prof., 1969-71; vis. assoc. prof. U. Chgo., 1971-72, assoc. prof. dept. sociology, 1972-75, prof., 1975—, chmn. dept. sociology, 1978—, Lucy Flower prof. urban sociology, 1980-84, Lucy Flower disting. service prof., 1984—; Lucy Flower Univ. prof., 1990-96; Malcolm Wiener Prof. of social policy Harvard U., 1996-98, Lewis P. and Linda L. Geyser Univ. Prof., 1998—. Mem. bd. univ. publs. U. Chgo. Press, 1975-79; bd. dirs. Ctr. for Nat. Policy, 1987 92, Ctr. Budget and Policy Priorities, 1987—, Ctr. for Advanced Study of Behavioral Scis., 1988-2002, Twentieth Century Fund (now called Century Found., 1992—, Jerome Levy Inst., 1992-2002, Manpower Demonstration Rsch. Corp., 1993—; bd. dirs. Pub./Pvt. Ventures, Phila., 1994-2002, 02- Author: Power, Racism and Privilege, 1973, Through Different Eyes, 1973, The Declining Significance of Race, 1978, The Truly Disadvantaged, 1987, The Ghetto Underclass, 1993, Sociology and the Public Agenda, 1993, When Work Disappears, 1996 (award Sidney Hillman Found. 1997), The Bridge Over the Racial Divide, 1999. Bd. dirs. Social Sci. Rsch. Coun., 1979-84, Chgo. Urban League, 1983-97, Spencer Found., 1987-97, George M. Pullman Found., 1986-93, Russell Sage Found., 1989-98, Nat. Humanities Ctr., 1990-95, PolicyLink, 2000-; mem. Com. on Sci., Engring. and Pub. Policy, NAS, 1995-2001; nat. bd. dirs. A. Philip Randolph Inst., 1981-, Inst. Rsch. on Poverty, 1983-87; trustee Spelman Coll., 1989-98, Bard Coll., 2001-;bd. govs. Levy Econs. Inst., 2001-; mem. Pres. Commn. on White House Fellowships, 1994-2001; mem. Pres. Com. Nat. Medal Sci., 1994-98; trustee Wilberforce U.; bd. advisors Frederick D. Patterson Rsch. Inst., 1995-, United Negro Coll. Fund, 1996—; mem. scholars' coun. Libr. of Congress, 2002-; nat. academic advisors Congl. Black Caucus Found., 2003-. With U.S. Army, 1958-60. Recipient Disting. Tchr. of Year award U. Mass., Amherst 1970, Regents Disting. Alumnus award Wash. State U., 1988, Burton Gordon Feldman award Brandeis U., 1991, Frank E. Seidman Disting. award in polit. econ., 1994, Martin Luther King Jr. Nat. award, 1998, Nat. Medal of Sci. 1998, A. Philip Randolph/Bayard Rustin Humanitarian award, 2003; Mac-Arthur Prize fellow, 1987. Fellow AAAS, Am. Acad. Polit. and Social Sci., Am. Acad. Arts and Scis. (Talcott Parsons Social Scis. prize, 2003); mem. NAS, Nat. Acad. Edn., Am. Philos. Soc., Inst. of Medicine, Brit. Acad., Am. Sociol. Assn. (pres. 1989-90, com. for pub. understanding of sociology award 1998, Sydney M. Spivack award 1977, DuBois, Johnson, Frazier award 1990, Lester F. Ward Disting. Contbns. to Applied Sociology award 1998), Soc. for Study Social Problems (C. Wright Mills award 1988), Sociol. Rsch. Assn. (pres. 1987-88), Consortium of Social Sci. Assn. (pres. 1993-94), Internat. Sociol. Assn., Chgo. Urban League (Beautiful People award 1979). Democrat. Home: 75 Cambridge Pkwy Unit E406 Cambridge MA 02142-1229 Office: John F Kennedy Sch Govt Harvard Univ 79 John F Kennedy St Cambridge MA 02138-5801

**WILSON, WILLIAM PRESTON,** psychiatrist, educator; b. Fayetteville, N.C., Nov. 6, 1922; s. Preston Puckett and Rosa Mae (VanHook) W.; m. Dorothy Elizabeth Taylor, Aug. 21, 1950; children: William Preston, Ben-jamin V., Karen E., Tammy E., Robert E. BS, Duke U., 1943, MD, 1947. Diplomate Am. Bd. Psychiatry and Neurology (examiner). Intern Gorgas Hosp., Ancon, Panama; from resident psychiatry to prof. emeritus Duke U. Med. Ctr., Durham, NC, emeritus prof. psychiatry, 1985—; assoc. prof. psychiatry, dir. psychiat. rsch. U. Tex. Med. Br., Galveston, 1958-60; dir. Inst. Christian Growth, Burlington, NC, 1985—; dist. prof. of counseling Carolina Evang. Divinity Sch., High Point, NC, 1996—. Chief neurophysiol. labs. VA Hosp., Durham, N.C., 1961-76; sec. Am. Bd. Qualification in Electroencepha-lography, 1971-77; mem. N.C. Gov.'s Task force on Diagnosis and Treatment; mem. med. adv. com. N.C. Found. Mental Health Rsch.; bd. dirs. nat. divsn. Contact Teleministry USA, also mem. internat. commnn. healing; cons. numerous area hosps.; Finch lectr. Fuller Theol. Sem., Pasadena, Calif., 1974; vis. prof. psychiatry Marshall U. Sch. Medicine, Huntington, W.Va., 1985-89. Co-author: The Grace to Grow; editor: Applications of Electroencephalogra-phy in Psychiatry; co-editor: EEG and Evoked Potentials in Psychiatry and Behavioral Neurology; contbr. articles to med. jours. Mem. ofcl. bd. Asbury United Meth. Ch., Durham; mem. program and curriculum com. United Meth. Ch., 1973-81; trustee Meth. Retirement Home, Durham; pres. United Meth. Renewal Svcs., Inc., 1978-82. Served with AUS, 1943-46. Recipient Ephraim McDowell award Christian Med. Found., 1982, Pioneer in Christian Psychia-try award Congress on Christian Counseling, 1998; named Educator of Yr., Christian Med. and Dental Soc., 1996; EEG Montreal Neurol. Inst. fellow, 1954-55, postdoctoral fellow NIMH. Mem. Am. Psychiat. Assn., So. Psy-

chiat. Assn. (pres. 1977-78), AMA, So. Med. Assn. (chmn. sect. neurology and psychiatry 1970), Med. Soc. N.C., Durham-Orange County Med. Soc. (chmn. student recruitment com. 1965), Soc. Biol. Psychiatry, Am. EEG Soc. (councillor), So. EEG Soc. (pres. 1964), Assn. Rsch. Nervous and Mental Diseases, Am. Epilepsy Soc., AAAS, Am. Acad. Neurology, Sigma Xi, Alpha Omega Alpha, U.S. Power Squadron Club (comdr. Durham 1971). Republi-can. Home: 1209 Virginia Ave Durham NC 27705-3263 Office: PO Box 2347 Burlington NC 27216-2347 Office Phone: 336-229-6049. Personal E-mail: williamwilson@verizon.net.

**WILSON, WILLIAM R., JR.,** federal judge; b. 1939; Student, U. Ark., 1957-58; BA, Hendrix Coll., 1962; LLB, Vanderbilt U., 1965. Atty. Autrey & Goodson, Texarkana, Ark., 1965-66, Wright, Lindsey & Jennings, Little Rock, 1969-72, Wilson & Hodge, Little Rock, 1972-74; prin. William R. Wilson Jr., P.A., Little Rock, 1974-80, Wilson & Engstrom, Little Rock, 1980-83, Wilson, Engstrom & Vowell, Little Rock, 1984, Wilson, Engstrom, Corum & Dudley, Little Rock, 1984-93; judge U.S. Dist. Ct. (ea. dist.) Ark., Little Rock, 1993—. Chair Ark. Supreme Ct. Com. on Model Criminal Jury Instrns., 1978—; active Ark. Supreme Ct. Com. on Civil Practice, 1982—. Lt. USN, 1966-69. Named Disting. Alumnus, Hendrix Coll., 1993, Outstanding Lawyer, Pulaski County Bar Assn., 1993. Mem. ABA, ATLA, Am. Bd. Trial Advocates (Nat. Civil Justice award 1992), Am. Coll. Trial Lawyers, Internat. Acad. Trial Lawyers, Internat. Soc. Barristers, Ark. Bar Assn. (Outstanding Lawyer 1991), S.W. Ark. Bar Assn., Ark. Trial Lawyers Assn. (pres. 1982, Outstanding Trial Lawyer 1988-89), Pulaski County Bar Assn. (Outstanding Lawyer 1993). Office: US Dist Ct Ea Dist 600 W Capitol Ave Ste 423 Little Rock AR 72201-3320

**WILSON, WILLIAM ROBERTS, JR., (BOB WILSON),** lawyer, apparel executive; b. Rosedale, Miss., July 6, 1941; s. William Roberts Wilson Sr. and Mary Elizabeth (Boatner) W.; m. Elizabeth Ann Smith; children: William Roberts Wilson III, Elizabeth Ann, Augusta Elliott. Student, Vanderbilt U., Tenn., 1964; JD, U. Miss., 1969. Pvt. practice, Jackson, Miss.; chmn. bd., owner Dunn's Mid.-South Sporting Goods Co. Chmn. founder The Charitable Food Bank, Miss. Sportsman Against Hunger; active mem. Rep. Nat. Com. Team 100, Newcomen Soc. of U.S., am. Intertrade Group, Presdl. Round Table, Rep. Senatorial Inner Circle. Mem. NRA (life mem.), Ala. State Bar Assn., Miss. Bar Assn., Miss. Trial Lawyers Assn. (life mem.), Assn. Trial Lawyers of Am. (sustaining mem.), Roscoe Pound Found. (fellow), Miss. State Bar Assn. (former commr.), Nat. Col. Advocacy, United Conservation Alliance (founding bd. mem.), Congressional Sportsmen Found. (bd. dirs.), Quail Unlimited (life mem., life sponsor), Miss. Wildlife Fedn. (life mem.), Ducks Unlimited (sponsoring mem.), Waterfowl, U.S.A., Delta Wildlife Found. (sponsoring founder), British Field Sport Soc. (life mem.), Catfish Point Hunting Club (gen. ptnr.), Athelstan Club, Country Club of Jackson Miss., Delta Kappa Epsilon (bd. dirs. R.O.A.R.), Delta Theta Phi. Office: PO Box 321444 Flowood MS 39232-1444

**WILSON, WILLIAM STANLEY,** oceanographer; b. Alexander City, Ala., June 5, 1938; s. Norman W. and Helen C. (Hackemack) W.; m. Anne M. Stout; children: Lauren, Jonathan (dec.). BS, William & Mary Coll., 1959, MA, 1965; PhD, Johns Hopkins U., 1972. Marine biol. collector Va. Inst. Marine Sci., Gloucester Point, 1959-62, computer systems analyst, 1964-65, Chesapeake Bay Inst., Balt., 1965-66; phys. oceanography program mgr. Office of Naval Rsch., Washington, 1972-78; chief oceanic processes program NASA, Washington, 1979-89, program scientist earth observing sys., 1989-92; asst. adminstr. for ocean svcs. and coastal zone mgmt. NOAA, Washing-ton, 1992-97, dep. chief scientist, 1997—2002; sr. scientist Nat. Environ. Satellite Data and Info. Svc., 2002—. U.S. rep. intergovtl. oceanographic commn. UNESCO, 1993—2003. Recipient Antarctica Svc. medal NSF, 1961, Superior Civilian Svc. award USN, 1979, Exceptional Sci. Achievement medal NASA, 1981, Disting. Achievement award MTS and Compass Publs., 1989, award Remote Sensing Soc., 1992, medal French Space Agy., 1994, Portuguese Naval Cross, 1997, Australian Antarctic Divsn. medal, 1998, Group Achievement award NASA, 2000. Mem. Am. Meteorol. Soc., Am. Geophys. Union (Ocean Scis. award 1984), Oceanography Soc. (com. chmn. 1989-92), Sigma Xi, Omicron Delta Kappa. Avocations: bicycling, scuba diving. Home: 219 Tunbridge Rd Baltimore MD 21212-3423 Office: NOAA/NESDIS 1325 E-W Hwy Silver Spring MD 20910 Business E-Mail: stan.wilson@noaa.gov.

**WILSON-MCKEE, MARIE,** museum director; Dir. Wyo. State Mus., Cheyenne. Office: Wyo State Mus Barrett Bldg 2301 Central Ave Cheyenne WY 82001-3173

**WILSON VANVOORHIS, CARMEN R.,** psychology professor; PhD, Iowa State U., 1995. Assoc. prof. U. Wis., La Crosse, 1996—. Office: U Wis La Crosse 1725 State St La Crosse WI 54601 Office Phone: 608-785-6879.

**WILSON-WEBB, NANCY LOU,** educational association administrator; b. Maypearl, Tex., Jan. 20, 1932; d. Madison Grady Wise and Mary Nancy Pearson-Bedford (Haney) Wilson; m. John Crawford Webb, July 29, 1972. BS magna cum laude, Abilene Christian U., Tex., 1953; EdM (hon.), Tex. Christian U., 1985. Cert. tchr., mid-mgmt., sch. adminstr., Tex. Tchr. elem. grades Ft. Worth Ind. Sch. Dist., 1953-67, adult edn. tchr., 1967-73; dir. adult edn. consortium for 38 sch. dists. Tex. Edn. Agy., 1973-2000. Pres. Nat. Commn. on Adult Basic Edn., "Most Outstanding adult ed. Admin. in US" by AAAC 1994-95; pres. Tex. Adult Edn. Adminstrn., 1994; apptd. mem. Tex. State Literacy Coun., 1987-94, Tex. State Sch. Bd. Commn., 1994-99; exec. bd. Tex. Coun. Co-op Dir., 1989-2001, Bd. Nat. Assn. of AAACE, 1988; pres., 1994—; apptd. to Gov. Ann Richard's Task Force for Edn.; ranch owner, mgr., 1998-2003. Cons. to textbooks, 1994-98; editor textbooks, 1999. Pres. Jr. Womans Club, Ft. Worth, 1969, Fine Arts Guild, Tex. Christian U., Ft. Worth, 1970-72, Ft. Worth Womens Civic Club Coun., 1970, pres. Aquarius Women's Club; active Exec. Libr. bd., Ft. Worth, 1990-2003, Jewel Charity Ball, 1988-2003; bd. dirs. Literacy Plus in North Tex., 1988-99, pres., 2001—; bd. dirs. Greater Ft. Worth Literacy Coun., 1976-88, 2002—, pres., 2001-03; commr. Ed-16 Task Forces Tex. Edn. Agy., 1993-94; literacy bd. dir. Friends of Libr., 1967-2002, Opera Guild Bd. Ft. Worth, 1965-85, Ft. Worth Ballet Guild, Johnson County (Tex.) Corr. Bd., 1990-2000; bd. dirs. Salvation Army, Ft. Worth, 1996-2003, Ft. Worth Libr.; active Tarrant County Bd. on Aging, 1997-98, Commn. Status of Women, Ft. Worth, 1973-99, Southside Ch. of Christ. Recipient Bevy award Jr. Womans Club, 1968, Proclamation Commr. Ct. Outstanding 43 Yr. Literacy Svc. to Tarrant County Com. Ctr., 1994, Tarrant County Woman of Yr. award, Fort Worth Star Telegram, 1995, Outstanding Leadership award Ft. Worth ISD Sch. Bd., 1985, 95, Mayor's Proclamation of Nancy Webb Week, 1996; named one of Most Outstanding Educators in U.S. Nat. Assn. Adult Edn., 1983, Most Outstanding Woman Edn., City of Ft. Worth, 1991, others; nominated to Tex. Hall of Fame for Women, 1991; named to Ft. Worth Hall of Fame, 1992; scholar Germany, 1983. Mem. NEA, DAR (Mary Isham Keith chpt. 1985-2002, Nat. Literacy award 1992, Leadership Literacy award 1985-87, 89, 94, Nat. Educators award 2003), AAUW, Am. Assn. Adult and Continuing Edn. (v.p. 1987-89, chair 1993 internat. conv. 1992, Nat. Adminstr. of Yr. in Adult Edn. 1998, Most Outstanding Adminstr. Adult Edn. in US 1999), Tex. Adult and Cont. Edn. (pres. 1985-86, Most Outstanding Adult Adminstr. in Tex. 1984), Tex. Coun. Adult Edn. Dirs. (pres. nat. com. on edn., Nat. Dept. Labor award 1992), Coun. World Affairs (bd. dir. 1980-2002), Am. Bus. Women's Assn., Ft. Worth C. of C., Lecture Found., Internat. Reading Assn. (Literacy Challenge award 1991), Ft. Worth Adminstrv. Assn., Southwest Cattle Raisers Assn., Ligon Assn., Zonta, Tanglewood Garden Club, Ft. Worth Garden Club (exec. bd. dirs. 2000-03), Woman's Club, Ft. Worth Petroleum Club, Carousel Dance Club, Met. Dinner Dance Club, Ridglea Country Club, Girls Svc. League, Aquarius (pres. 2001-02), Crescent Club (Dallas), Alpha Delta Kappa (Nat. Literacy award 1992), Greater Ft. Worth Literacy Coun. (pres. 2000-03), Phi Delta Kappa, Mary Isham Keith DAR (Nat. award 1993, Nat. Found. award 2003). Democrat. Mem. Lds Ch. Home: 3716 Fox Hollow St Fort Worth TX 76109-2616

**WILT, JEFFREY LYNN,** pulmonary and critical care physician, educator; b. Fairmont, W.Va., Nov. 15, 1963; s. Paul Lynn and Linda (Amos) W. BA, U. Mich., 1986, MD, 1988. Diplomate Am. Bd. Internal Medicine, Am. Bd. Pulmonary Diseases, Am. Bd. Critical Care Medicine, Am. Bd. Med. Examiners, Am. Bd. Nutrition Support; cert. ACLS instr. Fellow sect. pulmonary and critical care medicine W.Va. U., Morgantown, 1992-95; resident in internal medicine Blodgett-St. Mary's Hosp., Grand Rapids, Mich., 1988-91, chief med. resident in internal medicine, 1990-91; asst. dir. internal medicine residency St. Mary's Hosp., Grand Rapids, 1991-92; pvt. practice, Grand Rapids, 1995—. Asst. dir. med. ICU, Blodgett Meml. Med. Ctr., co-dir. transitional residency, 1997-98, COO internal medicine residency, 1998, program dir., 1998-99; assoc. program dir. internal medicine residency Mich. State U., Grand Rapids, 1999—, asst. prof. medicine, 1999-2003, assoc. prof., 2003—. Fellow ACP (Nat. Clin. Vignette winner 1991), Am. Coll. Chest Physicians (Young Investigators award 1993); mem. AMA, Am. Thoracic Soc., Soc. Crit. Care Medicine. Republican. Avocations: bicycling, Tae Kwon Do, magic, reading, chess. Home: 4995 Sequoia Dr SE Grand Rapids MI 49512-9622 Office: 1900 Wealthy St SE Ste 150 Grand Rapids MI 49506-2969

**WILTON, ELISABETH STARR,** management consultant; b. Cin., Apr. 1, 1936; d. Frank Starr Wilton Jr. and Bess Virginia (Clausen) Wilton; divorced; 1 child, Bart Wilton Jenkins. BA, Lawrence U., 1958; MEd, U. Md., 1970, PhD, 1978. Cert. clin. hypnotherapist Nat. Bd. Cert. Clin. Hypnotherapists, 2005. With U.S. Govt., Washington, 1959—98, ret., 1998; pres. Wilton Assoc., Inc., McLean, Va., 1999—. Author: Taking Charge: Conversations on Building Life Skills, 2006, (poem) Gifts of the Soul, 1999. Fulbright scholar, Germany, 1958—59. Mem.: Personality Assessment Sys. Found. (sec. 2004—). Home: 7008 Alicent Ct Mc Lean VA 22101 Office: Wilton Assoc Inc 7008 Alicent Ct Mc Lean VA 22101

**WILTROUT, ROBERT H.,** federal agency administrator; b. Kutztown, Pa., Sept. 13, 1950; BA, Kutztown U., 1972; MS in microbiology, Pa. State U., U. Park, 1975; PhD in immunology, Wayne State U., Detroit, 1979; studied, Queens U., Kingston, Ontario, Can., 1981. Postdoctoral studies Lab. Immu-nodiagnosis NIH; staff fellow Biol. Response Modifiers Program Nat. Cancer Inst. - Frederick Cancer Rsch. and Devel. Ctr.; head exptl. therapeutics sect. of Lab. Expt. Immunology Nat. Cancer Inst, 1986—, dir. Ctr. for Cancer Rsch., 2005—; assoc. dir. Nat. Cancer Inst. at Frederick, 2002—. Fellow USPHS, 1979. Mem.: Soc. Biol. Therapy, Soc. Leukocyte Biology, Am. Assn. Cancer Rsch., Am. Assn. Immunology. Office: Nat Cancer Inst at Frederick Bldg 560 Rm 31-18 1050 Boyles St Frederick MD 21702-1201 E-mail: wiltrour@mail.nih.gov.

**WILTSE, JAMES CLARK,** civil engineer; b. Dearborn, Mich., Apr. 14, 1927; s. Cecil C. and Mary G. (Brashear) W.; m. Marlyn R. Glatus, Feb. 14, 1953; children: Richard, Mary, Michael. BSCE, U. Mich., 1953. Registered profl. engr., Mass. Civil engr. U.S. Army C.E., Detroit, 1954-57; project engr. USAF Civil Engring., London, 1968-72; civil engr. USN Facilities Engring. Command, Norfolk, Va., 1973-75; chief engr. USN Resident Office, Keflavik, Iceland, 1976-81; staff civil engr. USAF Electronic Systems Div., Kaiserslau-tern, Germany, 1982-91; spl. asst. ROICC Norfolk, Lantnavfac Eng Com, Norfolk, Va., 1992-93; quality assurance engr. HQ Lantnavfac, 1993-94; ret., 1994. Sgt. U.S. Army, 1946-47, Japan. Fellow ASCE (life); mem. Soc. Am. Mil. Engrs. Home: 8555 Lawson Ave Norfolk VA 23503-5220 Personal E-mail: JCWILTSE@aol.com.

**WILTSE, JAMES CORNELIUS,** retired electrical engineer; b. Tanners-ville, N.Y., Mar. 16, 1926; s. James Cornelius and Leah Ida Wiltse; m. Helen Citron Wiltse, June 20, 1986; m. Margaret Lucille John, Jan. 27, 1950 (div. May 15, 1986); children: Linda Margaret, Paul James. BSEE, Rensselaer Poly. Inst., Troy, N.Y., 1946, MSEE, 1951; PhD, Johns Hopkins U., Balt., Md., 1959. Mgr. microwaves and antennas, 1959—63; dir. adv. tech. Electronic Comm., Inc., 1963—64; prin. rsch. scientist, lab chief Martin Marietta Corp., Orlando, Fla., 1964—68, mgr. Dept. Electromagnetics, 1968—72, dir. rsch. and tech., 1973—77, dir. Electronics Engring. Divsn., 1976; prin. rsch. engr. Ga. Inst. Tech., Atlanta, 1978—. Expert Dept. Electronics, New Delhi, 1993; assoc. dir. Ga. Tech Rsch. Inst., Atlanta, 1979—91. Contbr. articles to profl. jours.; editor, co-author: Millimeter Systems, 1981, Millimeter and Microwave Engineering for Communications and Radar, 1994. Lt. comdr. USNR, 1943—71. Named Author of Yr., Martin Marietta Corp, 1967, Engr. of Yr., Martin Marietta Corp., 1970, Govt. Engr. of Yr., Engrs. Greater Atlanta, 1984. Fellow: IEEE (Microwave Career award 2000), Soc. Photo-Optical Instrumentation Engrs. Independent. Achievements include research in fresnel zone plate antennas; millimeter wave engineering; electromagnetic engineering; development of terahertz technology. Home: 11138 Big Canoe; 9111 Shetland Trace Jasper GA 30143 Personal E-mail: james.wiltse@tds.net.

**WILTSE, RICHARD ARTHUR,** music educator; b. Grand Rapids, Mich., Sept. 10, 1972; s. David Arthur and MArjorie Powell (Ranck) Wiltse. Bach. Alma Coll., 1994; MusM, Western Mich. U., 2003. Dir. bands Bad Axe Pub. Schs., Mich., 1994—98, Berrien Springs Pub. Schs., 1998—. Musician: Southshore Concert Band, 1998—, Lake Effect Jazz Big Band, 2001—04. Original mem. Lake Effect Jazz Big Band, St. Joseph, 2001—04; counselor, dean West Mich. United Meth. Ch., Grand Rapids, Mich., 1990—2004. Mem.: Mich. Edn. Assn., Music Educators Nat. Conf., Mich. Sch. Band & Orch Assn. (dist. 6 music edn. rep. 1995—), Phi Kappa Phi. Avocation: jazz. Home: 412 S Kimmel St Berrien Springs MI 49103 Office: Berrien Springs Pub Schs 1 Sylvester Ave Berrien Springs MI 49103 Personal E-mail: banddir@prodigy.net.

**WILTSEY, SUSAN A.,** secondary school educator, priest; b. Richmond, Va., July 16, 1945; d. John M. and Marjorie G. Allman; 1 child from previous marriage, Katherine. AB, Randolph-Macon Woman's Coll., 1967; MA, U. Calif., Santa Barbara, 1977. Tchr. Dos Pueblos H.S., Goleta, Calif., 1971—91, Millcreek H.S., St. George, Utah, 1991—; priest in charge St. Luke's Episcopal Ch., Cedar City, Utah, 2005, Grace Episcopal Ch., St. George, Utah, 2006—. Democrat. Episcopalian. Home: 450 W Shinava Dr Ivins UT 84738 Office: Millcreek H S 2410 Riverside Dr Saint George UT 84790 Office Phone: 435-628-2462 ext 118. E-mail: swiltsey@kayenta.net.

**WILTZ, JAMES W.,** medical products executive; Sales & mgmt. positions Patterson Cos., St. Paul, 1969—80, v.p. midwest div., 1980—86, v.p. sales & dist., 1986—96, pres. dental supply unit, 1996—2003, pres., COO, 2003—05, pres., CEO, 2005—. Office: Patterson Cos 1031 Mendota Heights Rd Saint Paul MN 55120*

**WIMMER, KATHRYN,** retired elementary school educator; b. St. Louis, May 8, 1929; d. Arthur Jordan and Louise Clara Sykes; m. Harry William Wimmer, Aug. 4, 1951; children: Robert William, Richard Jordan. BS in Edn., U. Mo., 1951; postgrad., U. South Fla., 1971—72. Cert. tchr. Mo., Fla. Tchr. Affton (Mo.) Sch., 1951—52, Heege Sch., Affton, 1965—67, Gulf Gate Sch., Sarasota, Fla., 1972; piano tchr. Crestwood, Mo., 1963—65. Artist, musician, tchr. music and art; tutor IQ, employment and aptitude testing. Oil paintings, watercolor paintings. V.p. Southgate Cmty., Sarasota, 1989—90; pres. bd. dirs. Assoc. Women's Club, Sarasota, 1990—91, bd. dirs. 1986—93; vol. Gulf Gate Libr., Sarasota, 1993—2006. Recipient tennis trophy, Bath and Racquet Tennis Club, Sarasota, 1979, swimming trophy, Southgate Cmty. Assn., 1987, 1988, Wall of Honor cert., Roosevelt H.S., St. Louis, 2003. Mem.: Roosevelt H.S. Alumni Assn., U. Mo. Alumni Assn., Mysterium High IQ Soc., Delta Gamma (scholarship chmn., treas., rush chmn., social chmn.). Democrat. Presbyterian. Achievements include thirteen of the tutored students who were tested successfully were sent to Pine View School for the gifted. Avocations: embroidery, literature, travel, history, genealogy, embroidery. Personal E-mail: HarryKay@peoplepc.com.

**WIMPFFEN, OTTO RUDOLPH,** mathematics professor; b. Budapest, Hungary, June 21, 1938; arrived in U.S., 1952; s. John and Susan Wimpffen; m. Verlea Miller (div.); children: Steven, Suzanna Blanchard; m. Laurel Hetherington, Nov. 27, 1993. BS Mech. and Aerospace Engring., Ill. Inst. Tech., 1966; MBA, Loyola U., Chgo., 1972; postgrad., Chgo. State U., 1980—84. Mgr. engring. & prodn. Rep. Packaging, Chgo., 1963—68; engring. staff C. E. Niehoff & Co., Chgo., 1968—75; prof. math. Wilbur Wright Coll., Chgo., 1975—2006; ret., 2006. Bd. dirs. Am.-Spanish Inst., Chgo., 1976—80. 1st lt. N.G. U.S. Army, 1962—63. Recipient Excellence in Tchg. award, Wilbur Wright Coll., 2004—05; Inherited European Title Count Otto Rudolph Wimpffen. Mem.: Math. Assn. Am., Chgo. Yacht Club (race com. 1993—), Little Current Yacht Club. Avocations: sailing, skiing, auto racing, travel.

**WIMPRESS, GORDON DUNCAN, JR.,** management consultant, foundation administrator; b. Riverside, Calif., Apr. 10, 1922; s. Gordon Duncan and Maude A. (Waldo) Wimpress; m. Jean Margaret Skerry, Nov. 30, 1946; children: Wendy Jo, Victoria Jean, Gordon Duncan III. BA, U. Oreg., 1946, MA, 1951; PhD, U. Denver, 1958; LLD (hon.), Monmouth Coll., Ill., 1970; LHD (hon.), Tusculum Coll., Greenville, Tenn., 1971. Lic. comml. pilot. Dir. pub. rels., instr. journalism Whittier Coll., Calif., 1946-51; asst. to pres. Colo. Sch. Mines, Golden, 1951-59; pres. Monticello Coll., Alton, Ill., 1959-64, Monmouth Coll., Ill., 1964-70, Trinity U., San Antonio, 1970-77; vice chmn. S.W. Found. Biomed. Rsch., San Antonio, 1977-82, pres., 1982-92, also bd. govs.; pres. Duncan Wimpress & Assocs., Inc., San Antonio, 1992—. Chmn. scholarship commn. Valero Energy Corp.; bd. dirs. SW Rsch. Inst. Author: American Journalism Comes of Age, 1950. Mem. adv. bd. Alamo Area chpt. Am. Diabetes Assn.; ruling elder United Presbyn. Ch., U.S.A.; bd. dirs. ARC, Am. Heart Assn.; trustee San Antonio Med. Found. 1st lt. U.S. Army, 1942—45, ETO. Decorated Bronze Star. Mem.: Pilots Internat. Assn., Nat. Pilots Assn., Am. Assn. Higher Edn., Am. Acad. Polit. and Social Sci., Newcomen Soc. N.Am., Assn. Former Intelligence Officers, Greater San Antonio C. of C., Mensa, North San Antonio C. of C., Confederate Air Force, Aircraft Owners and Pilots Assn., San Antonio Golf Assn., Ptz. Club, San Antonio Country Club, Argyle Club, Rotary (dist. gov. San Antonio club 1983—84), Quiet Birdmen, Sigma Upsilon, Sigma Delta Chi, Pi Gamma Mu. Presbyterian. Avocations: golf, skiing, flying. Office Phone: 210-492-8173. Personal E-mail: duncan.w@sbcglobal.net.

**WIN, MOE Z.,** information scientist, educator; BSEE magna cum laude, Tex. A&M U., Coll. Sta., Tex., 1987; MSEE, U. So. Calif., L.A., 1989, MS in Applied Math., 1998, PhD in Elec. Engring., 1998. Rschr. Calif. Inst. Tech., Pasadena, Calif., 1987—91, with guidance and control sect., 1991—95, mem. tech. staff Jet Propulsion Lab., 1996; sr. tech. staff AT&T, Middleton, NJ, 1998—2000, prin. tech. staff, 2000—02; asst. prof. MIT, Cambridge, Mass., 2002—04, assoc. prof. Lab. Info. and Decision Sys., 2004—. Lectr. in field; cons. in field. Contbr. over 115 articles to profl. jours. Named Young Aerospace Engr. of Yr., AIAA, 2004; recipient numerous awards including, Disting. Alumni award, Mt. View Coll., 2002, Young Investigator award, Office Naval Rsch., 2003, Presdl. Early Career award, White Ho., 2004, Outstanding Internat. Collaboration award, Indsl. Tech. Rsch. Inst., Taiwan, 2004, Ednl. Innovation award, MIT, 2004; fellow, Inst. Advanced Study, 2004, Fulbright Found., 2004; Herman F. Heep scholar, Tex. A&M U., 1985. Fellow: IEEE (sec. radio comms. com. Comms. Soc. 2002—04, chmn. radio comms. com. Comms. Soc. 2006—, chmn. various confs., area editor Modulation and Signal Design, editor Wideband Wireless and Diversity, editorEqualization and Diversity 1998—2003, guest editor spl. issue 2002, Sergei A. Schelkunoff Transactions Paper prize 2003, Eric E. Sumner award 2006, Best Paper award 2006). Achievements include patents in field. Office: Mass Inst Technology Lab Info and Decision Sys 32 D668 77 Massachusetts Ave Cambridge MA 02139 Home: 30 Cambridge Pk Dr Ste 4135 Cambridge MA 02140

**WINANS, CECE,** gospel vocalist; b. Detroit, Oct. 8, 1964; m. Alvin Love; children: Ashley, Alvin II. Albums with Bebe Winans include Lord Lift Us Up, 1985, Bebe and Cece Winans, 1987, Heaven, 1988, Different Lifestyles, 1991, Noel, 1993, Relationships, 1994, Bebe & Cece Winans Greatest Hits, 1996; solo albums include For Always (1987 Grammy award for Best Female Gospel Performance), Don't Cry (1989 Grammy award for Best Female Gospel Performance), Alone In His Presence, 1995 (Grammy award 1995), Everlasting Love, 1998, His Gift, 1998, Alabaster Box, 1999, CeCe Winans 2001, Throne Room, 2001, Purified, 2005 (2 Grammy awards); appeared in films including White Men Can't Jump, 1992, Waiting to Exhale, 1995, The Prince of Egypt, 1998; appeared on TV shows including The Grammy Awards, Soul Train, Sesame Street, Martin, Living Single, Touched By an Angel, Christmas in Washington, Nat. Meml. Day Concert; host (TV program) Cece's Place, (radio program) On A Positive Note; author: Feel the Spirit, 1998. Recipient 10 Grammy awards, numerous Stellar and NAACP Image awards. Office: Capital Entertainment 1201 N St NW Apt A Washington DC 20005-5104*

**WINANT, CLINTON D.,** oceanographer, educator; b. Washington, May 18, 1944; s. Clinton and Janine Winant; m. Elizabeth M. Ogle, Mar. 21, 1997; children: Celeste, Chloe. PhD, U. So. Calif., L.A., 1972. Prof. oceanography Scripps Instn. Oceanography U. Calif., San Diego, 1972—.

**WINAWER, SIDNEY J.,** physician, educator; b. N.Y.C. s. Nathan and Sally Winawer; children: Cortez # 3 Chicago IL 60602 Office: Sears Holdings Corp 3333 Beverly Rd AC 153A Hoffman Estates IL 60179 Office Phone: 847-286-1259. Daniel, Jonathan, Joanna. BA, NYU, 1952; MD, SUNY, 1956; DSc (hon.), SUNY Downstate Med. Ctr., 2005. Asst. in medicine Harvard Med. Sch., Boston, 1962—66; asst. physician Harvard Med. Svc. Boston City Hosp., 1964—66; with Meml. Sloan-Kettering Cancer Ctr., N.Y.C., 1968—, chief gastroent. and nutrition svc., 1978—98, mem. with tenure of title, 1988—, Paul Sherlock chair, 1991—; prof. medicine Cornell U. Coll. Medicine, N.Y.C., 1980—, dir. integrative oncology program 1997—98. Head Cu Prevention Cancer WHO, Geneva, 1985—2000; liaison rep Nat Cancer Adv Bd, Washington, 1984—89; mem adv comt cancer prevention Am Cancer Soc, 1988—90; mem sci adv bd ICRF; consult varios rev comts Nat Cancer Inst, Washington. Editor: (book) Prevention Colorectal Cancer, 1980, Basic and Clinical Perspectives of Colorectal Polyps and Cancer, 1988, Lar Bowel Cancers: Policy, Prevention, Research and Treatment, 1991, Management of Gastrointestinal Disease, 1992, Gastrointestinal Cancer, 1992, Cancer of the Colon, Rectum and Anus, 1994, Cancer Free, 1995, Healing Lessons, 1998; contbr. chapters to books, articles to profl jours. Capt USAF, 1959—61. Recipient Clin. Achievement award, Sloan Kettering Meml. Cancer Ctr., 1997, Alumni award, 1998, SUNY Downstate Med. Ctr., 2000, SUNY, 2003, Constantine Medal, Italian Govt., 2002, Internat. Laurel award, Cancer Rsch. and Prevention Found., 2004; grantee Nat. Cancer Inst., 1974, 1977, 1980, 1985, 1988, 1990, 1993, 1999, 2003. Master: Am. Coll. Gastroenterology (pres. 1979—80, Baker Presdl. lectr. 1992, Disting. Sci. Achievement award 1982, Clin. Achievement award 1997); fellow: ACP; mem.: Internat. Digestive Cancer Alliance (co-chair), N.Y. Soc Gastrointestinal Endoscopy (founder, pres. 1978—79, ann. lectr. 1985), Am. Assn. Cancer Rsch., Am. Soc. Clin. Oncology (Am. Cancer Soc. award 2001), Am. Gastroenterol. Assn. (nat. chmn. cancer sect. 1989—91, U.S. multisoc. colorectal cancer task force, Joseph B. Kirsner award 1999), Am. Soc. Gastrointestinal Endoscopy (bd. dirs. 1974—78, disting. lectr. 1985, co-chair guidelines com. 1997—, Schindler award 1994). Jewish. Avocations: opera, cross country skiing, dance, swimming, bicycling. Office: Meml Sloan-Kettering Cancer Ctr 1275 York Ave New York NY 10065-6094 Office Phone: 212-639-7678. Business E-Mail: winawers@mskcc.org.

**WINBLAD, ANN,** investment company executive; BA in Math. and Bus. Adminstrn., U. St. Thomas, St. Paul, Minn., MA in Internat. Econs. and Edn.; LLD (hon.), U. St. Thomas. Systems programmer Fed. Reserve Bank; co-founder Open Systems, Inc., 1976-83; strategic planning cons., IBM, Microsoft, Price Waterhouse, and many start-ups; co-founding ptnr. Hummer Winblad Venture Ptnrs., San Francisco, 1989—. Bd. dirs. Dean & Deluca, Intacct, Market Wire, The Knot, Voltage Security, Arbor Software, Berkeley Systems, Net Perceptions; advisor The Software Forum, San Jose Ctr. for Software Develop., Stanford/MIT Venture Forum. Co-author: Object-Oriented Software, 1990; contbr. articles to profl. publs. Trustee U. St. Thomas, St. Paul, Mich. Office: Hummer Winblad Venture Partners 1 Lombard St Ste 300 San Francisco CA 94111-1130*

**WINCHELL, MICHAEL GEORGE,** lawyer; b. Ardmore, Okla., Oct. 30, 1949; s. George Stockwell and Willis Marion (Woolery) W.; m. Donna Jean Winchell; children: Merridith Elaine, Candace Michelle. BBA, Cen. State U., 1974; JD, U. Okla., 1976. Bar: Okla. 1977. Assoc. Sokolsky & Becker, Oklahoma City, 1977; asst. regional counsel GSA, Ft. Worth, 1977-87; adminstrv. judge EEOC Commn., Dallas, 1987-88; counsel S.E. bases USMC, 1988-89; chief counsel John F. Kennedy Space Ctr., 1993-97, Johnson Space Ctr., 1997—2004; ret. Lectr. law U. Okla., 2004—. Pres. GSA employee's assn., 1982-84; chief KSC Inter-Tribal Coun., 1993-97. Named Meritorious Exec. of the Federal Sr. Exec. Svc., Pres. Clinton, 2000; recipient Meritorious Civilan Svc. medal, USN, 1993, Exceptional Svc. medal, NASA, 2001. Mem. Fed. Bus. Assn. (pres. 1984-85), FBA (pres. Ft. Worth chpt. 1981-82, bd. dirs. younger lawyers' div. 1981-85, 2d v.p. 5th cir. 1982-83, v.p. 1983-84, sec. cir. officers 1983-84, dep. chmn. cir. officers 1984-85, chmn. rules com. 1985-86), Southeastern Cherokee Confederacy (chief Eagle Clan 1992-93). Office: 700 North 60th Noble OK 73068

**WINCHESTER, JAMES R.,** state supreme court justice; b. Clinton, Okla. m. Susan Winchester; 1 child, Davis. BA, U. Okla.; JD, Okla. City U. Pvt. practice, Weatherford, Okla., Hinton, Okla.; assoc. dist. judge Caddo County, Okla., 1983; dist. judge 6th Judicial Dist. Okla., 1983—97; U.S. adminstrv. law judge, 1997—2000; justice Okla. Supreme Ct., 2000—. Mem. exec. bd. Okla. Jud. Conference, pres., 1992-96. Recipient Outstanding State Trial Ct. Judge, Okla. Trial Lawyers Assn., 1986. Office: Oklahoma Supreme Ct Admin Office 1915 N Stiles Ste 305 Oklahoma City OK 73104-2861*

**WINCHESTER, JESSE GREGORY,** commercial real estate company executive; b. Charlotte, N.C., Mar. 2, 1957; s. Dewey Reece and Ruby Lee (Aldridge) W.; m. Jan Partain, May 14, 1983; children: Dustin, Mary-Elsye, Caleb, Sarah-Anne, Asa, Rebecca-Joy BSBA, U. N.C., 1979; founds. diploma, Am. Inst. Banking, 1979; advanced mgmt. program, Fuqua Sch. Bus. Duke U. Asst. v.p. 1st Nat. Bank Atlanta, 1979—83; exec. v.p. Lomas Mgmt. Inc., Dallas, 1983—96; mng. dir., owner TriMont Real Estate Advisors, Atlanta, 1996—; pres., owner Wineight, LLC. Campaign vol. United Way, Atlanta, 1982—83; participant Opportunity Dallas, 1985, Habitat for Humanity, Dallas and Atlanta, People Helping People, Dallas; Awana leader; cub scout leader Boy Scouts Am., scoutmaster; coach Hopewell Youth Assn., 2003—04, Upward Basketball; mem. Coppell (Tex.) Rep. Club, 1986; deacon Little River Ch., 2002—04. Named Hon. Citizen Charlotte, N.C Mem.: Mortgage Bankers Assn., Nat. Assn. Real Estate Investment Mgrs., Comml. Mortgage Securities Assn., Internat. Coun. Shopping Ctrs., Forsyth Christian Home Educators (adv. bd. dirs. 1999—2006), Appalachia Trail Soc., Nature Conservancy, Ga. Tech. Club, U. N.C. Alumni Assn., Haig Pt. Club, Am. Hiking Club, Alpha Phi Omega, Beta Gamma Sigma. Avocations: running, skiing, camping, white-water rafting, golf. Home: Meadowbrook Farm 16035 Westbrook Rd Alpharetta GA 30004-2887 Office: TriMont Real Estate Advisors 3424 Peachtree Rd NE Atlanta GA 30326

**WINCHESTER, RICHARD LEE, JR.,** lawyer; b. Memphis, May 21, 1924; s. Cassius Lee and Harriet Haywood (Bond) Winchester; m. Bette Anne Thompson, July 15, 1944; children: Robin Ann, Richard Lee Jr., John Thompson. LLB, U. Tenn., 1949, JD, 1965. Bar: Tenn. 1949. Sr. ptnr. Winchester Law Firm, Memphis, 1972—; atty. Shelby County, 1961—64; city atty. City of Arlington, Tenn., 1966—. Gen. counsel, bd. chmn. Cmty. Bancshares, Inc.; sec. Beachfront Condos, Inc., N. Fla. Chmn. Germantown Planning Commn., 1958—61; pres., bd. dirs. Mid-South Fair Assn.; bd. dirs. ARC; mem. Gov.'s Comm. on Human Relations, 1962—68; vice chmn., treas. Memphis and Shelby County Dem. Exec. Com., 1958—72; state exec. com., pres. Tenn. Young Dems., 1960—61; del. state and nat. Dem. convs., 1964—68; nat. elector from Tenn., 1960—72; pres. Episc. Planning Commn.; trustee U. Tenn., 1975—84, Episc. Girls Home, Bowld Hosp. Capt. inf. U.S. Army, 1942—46, PTO. Fellow: Tenn. Bar Found. (past pres. jr. sect.); mem.: Omicron Delta Kappa, Phi Kappa Phi, Nat. Assn. Legal Aid and Pub. Defenders, Am. Judicature Soc., Shelby County Bar Assn. (past pres. jr. sect.), Memphis Bar Assn. (past pres.), Tenn. Bar Assn., ABA (past del.), U. Tenn. Alumni Assn. (past bd. govs., 9th dist. rep.), Am. Legion (past post comdr., past state vice comdr.), Kiwanis, Tennessee, 40 and 8, Jesters, VFW (past post vice comdr.), Masons, Shriners, Phi Eta Sigma, Sigma Alpha Epsilon. Episcopalian. Office: Winchester Law Firm 6060 Poplar Ave Ste 38119 Memphis TN 38119 Office Phone: 901-685-9222. Business E-Mail: bmabie@winchesterlawfirm.com.

**WINCKLER, ALICIA JEAN,** human resources director; b. Yankton, SD, Aug. 16, 1972; d. Myron Mark and Barbara Jean Winckler; 1 child, Lucas Hansen. BS in Psychology and Alcohol and Drug Abuse Studies, U. SD, 1994; MA in Indsl. Orgnl. Psychology, U. Colo., Denver, 1997. Project mgr. HR Avantis, Denver, 1996—98; compensation analyst Watson Wyatt Worldwide, Denver, 1997; assessment systems cons. Sears, Roebuck & Co., Chgo., 1998—2000, mgr. testing and selection, 2000—01, mgr. orgnl. effectiveness, 2001—03, mgr. human resources, 2003—05; western region human resources dir. Sears Holdings Corp., Chgo., 2005—. Adj. faculty mem. Chgo. Sch. Profl. Psychology, 2004. Mem.: APA (assoc.), Kappa Alpha Theta, Omicron Delta Kappa. Democrat. Roman Catholic. Avocations: music, travel. Home: 1546 W Cortez # 3 Chicago IL 60602 Office: Sears Holdings Corp 3333 Beverly Rd AC 153A Hoffman Estates IL 60179 Office Phone: 847-286-1259. Personal E-mail: aliciawinckler@msn.com.

**WINCOR, MICHAEL Z.,** psychopharmacology educator, clinician, researcher; b. Chgo., Feb. 9, 1946; s. Emanuel and Rose (Kershner) W.; m. Emily E.M. Smyther; children: Meghan Heather, Katherine Rose. BS in Zoology, U. Chgo., 1966; PharmD, U. So. Calif., 1978. Rsch. project specialist U. Chgo. Sleep Lab., 1968-75; psychiat. pharmacist Brotman Med. Ctr., Culver City, Calif., 1979-83; asst. prof. U. So. Calif., L.A., 1983-97, assoc. prof., 1997—, interim chair dept. pharmacy, 2001—02, assoc. dean external programs, 2003—. Cons. Fed. Bur. Prisons Drug Abuse Program, Terminal Island, Calif., 1978—81, Nat. Inst. Drug Abuse, Bethesda, Md., 1981, The Upjohn Co., Kalamazoo, 1982—87, 1991—92, Area XXIV Profl. Stds. Rev. Orgn., L.A., 1983, Brotman Med. Ctr., Culver City, Calif., 1983—88, SmithKline Beecham Pharms., Phila., 1990—93, Tokyo Coll. of Pharmacy, 1991, G.D. Searle & Co., Chgo., 1992—97, 1999—2001, Pfizer, NY, 1998—2004, Wyeth-Ayerst, Phila., 1999—2001, Novartis, East Hanover, NJ, 2002—04, AstraZeneca, Wilmington, Del., 2003—04, Nat. Assn. Bd. Pharmacy Continuing Profl. Devel. Com., 2003—04, Sanofi-Aventis, 2004—, Takeda Pharms. N.Am., Inc., 2005—. Contbr. more than 75 articles to profl. jours., chpts. to books, papers presented at nat. and internat. meetings and reviewer. Mem. adv. coun. Franklin Avenue Sch., 1986-89; bd. dirs. K.I. Children's Ctr., 1988-89; trustee Sequoyah Sch., 1992-93; mem. tech. com. Ivanhoe Sch., 1993-96; U. So. Calif. Amb., 2000—. Recipient Cert. Appreciation, Mayor of L.A., 1981, Bristol Labs Award, 1978, DuPont Pharma Innovative Pharmacy Practice award, 1995, Pharmacy Coun. Mental Health award, 1996, Outstanding Chpt. Advisor award Am. Pharm. Assn.-Acad. of Students of Pharmacy, 2003; Faculty scholar U. So. Calif. Sch. Pharmacy, 1978. Mem. Am. Coll. Clin. Pharmacy (chmn. constn. and bylaws com. 1983-84, mem. credentials com. 1991-93, 95-97, ednl. affairs com. 1994, constn. and bylaws com. 1999-2000), Am. Assn. Colls. Pharmacy (focus group on liberalization profl. curriculum 1990-92, mem. pharmacy practice planning commn. 1996-97, chmn. pharmacy practice awards com. 1998-2000, mem. bylaws and policy devel. com. 2001-03, mem. computer tech. in edn. task force 2001-02, chmn. cur. of faculties strategic planning and resolutions com. 2001-03, mem. continuing pharmacy edn. ACPE liaison com., 2004-06), Am. Soc. Health-Sys. Pharmacists (chmn. edn. and tng. adv. working group 1985-88, chmn. com. on academia 1996-97), Am. Pharm. Assn. (del. ann. meeting ho. of dels. 1989, 1998), Sleep Rsch. Soc., Nat. Sleep Found., Am. Acad. Sleep Medicine, Calif. Pharmacists Assn. (trustee 1997-2001, chmn. editl. rev. com. 1998-2003), Hollywood-Wilshire Pharmacists Assn. (pres. 2006—), U. So. Calif. Sch. Pharmacy Alumni Assn. (bd. dirs. 1979—, pres. 1998—), Coll. Psychiat. Neurol. Pharmacists (chmn. recertification com. 2003-06, chmn. program com. 2006—), Rho Chi, Phi Lambda Sigma. Avocation: photography. Office: 1985 Zonal Ave Los Angeles CA 90089-9121

**WINDEBANK, ANTHONY J.,** dean; b. Bournemouth, Eng., Aug. 14, 1948; BA in biochemistry, Oxford U., 1970, MA in biochemistry, 1973, BMBCh in medicine, 1974. Cert. Am. Bd. Psychiatry and Neurology, Royal Coll. Physicians. Intern Radcliffe Infirmary, Oxford University, England, 1975, resident in internal medicine, 1975—76; resident in neurology Mayo Grad. Sch. Medicine, Mayo Clinic, Rochester, Minn., 1977—81, fellow in neurology, 1981—82; dean Mayo Clinic Coll. Medicine, Rochester, Minn., 1998—2005, also prof. of neurology and cellular neurobiology, dir., molecular neurosci. program. Named Mayo Grad. Sch. Tchr. of Yr., 1997; recipient Henry Woltman Award for Excellence in Clin.Neurology, Mayo Clinic, 1980, Tchr.-Investigator Devel. Award, NIH, 1982. Fellow: Am. Acad. Neurology, Royal Coll. Physicians.*

**WINDELS, JAMES H.R.,** lawyer; b. Oct. 25, 1963; BA magna cum laude, Princeton U., 1986; JD cum laude, Harvard U. Law Sch., 1989. Bar: N.Y. 1990, registered: U.S. Dist. Ct. So. & Ea. Dist. N.Y. 1990. Law clk. to Hon. Peter K. Leisure, U. Dist. Ct., So. Dist. N.Y., 1989—90; assoc. Davis, Polk & Wardwell, N.Y.C., 1990—97, ptnr., 1997—; chmn. firm pro bono com. Office: Davis, Polk & Wardwell 450 Lexington Ave New York NY 10017 Office Phone: 212-450-4978. Office Fax: 212-450-3978. Business E-Mail: james.windels@dpw.com.

**WINDELS, PAUL, JR.,** lawycr; b. Bklyn., Nov. 13, 1921; s. Paul and Louise E. (Gross) W.; m. Patricia Ripley, Sept. 10, 1955 (dec. 1995); children: Paul III, Mary H., James H.R., Patrick D. AB, Princeton U., N.J., 1943; LLB, Harvard U., Cambridge, Mass., 1948. Bar: N.Y. 1949. Spl. asst. counsel N.Y. State Crime Commn., 1951; asst. U.S. atty. Ea. Dist. N.Y., 1953-56; N.Y. regional adminstr. SEC, 1956-61, also spl. asst. U.S. atty. for prosecution securities frauds, 1956-58; lectr. law Am. Inst. Banking, 1950-57; mem. Windels, Marx, Lane & Mittendorf and predecessor firms, 1961—98, of counsel, 1998—. Author: Our Securities Markets-Some SEC Problems and Techniques, 1962. Trustee Bklyn. Law Sch.; trustee Lexington Sch. for the Deaf, Gerta Charitable Trust; past pres. Fed. Bar Coun. Capt. F.A., AUS, 1943-46, ETO; maj. USAR, ret. Recipient Flemming award for fed. svc.; decorated chevalier Order French Acad. Palms; officer Nat. Order Merit France. Fellow Am. Bar Found.; mem. ABA, N.Y. State Bar Assn., Assn. of Bar of City of N.Y. Republican. Presbyterian. Office: Windels Marx Lane & Mittendorf 156 W 56th St Fl 23 New York NY 10019-3867 Office Phone: 212-237-1210.

**WINDER, CLARENCE LELAND,** psychologist, educator; b. Osborne County, Kans., June 16, 1921; s. Clarence McKinley and Edna (Ikenberry) W.; m. Elizabeth Jane Jacobs, Aug. 14, 1943; children: David William, Christina Louise. Student, Santa Barbara State Coll., 1941; AB with honors, U. Calif. at Los Angeles, 1943; MA, Stanford U., 1946, PhD, 1949. From instr. to assoc. prof. Stanford U., 1949-61; dir. Psychol. Clinic, 1953-61; prof., dir. Psychol. Clinic, Mich. State U., 1961-62, prof. psychology, 1961-91, prof. emeritus, 1991—, chmn. dept., 1963-67; dean Coll. Social Sci. Mich. State U., 1967-74, assoc. provost, 1974-77, provost, 1977-86, provost emeritus, 1991—; prof., dir. Psychol. Svcs. Ctr., U. So. Calif., 1962-63. 1st lt. USAAF, 1943-45. Decorated Air medal with 7 clusters, D.F.C. Fellow APA, AAAS; mem. Sigma Xi. Achievements include research in psychol. aspects schizophrenia, parent-child rels., personality devel., and higher edn. adminstrn. Home: 1776 Hitching Post Rd East Lansing MI 48823-2144

**WINDER, ROBERT OWEN,** mathematician, computer engineer, geophysicist; b. Boston, Oct. 9, 1934; s. Claude V. and Harriet O. W.; m. Kathleen C. Winder; children by previous marriage: Katherine, Amy. AB, U. Chgo., 1954; BS, U. Mich., 1956; MS, Princeton U., 1958, PhD, 1962; MS, Ariz. State U., 2000. With RCA, 1957-78, group head Princeton and Somerville, NJ, 1969-75, dir. microprocessors, 1975-77; dir. systems, 1977-78; mgr. workstation devel. Exxon Enterprises, Inc., Princeton, 1978-85; v.p. Syntex Computer Systems Inc., Bordentown, NJ, 1985-88; mgr. product engring., Princeton Operation, Intel Corp., 1988-92; mgr. engring. ops. video products div., Intel, Chandler, Ariz., 1993-95. Vis. scholar dept. geol. scis., Ariz. State U., Tempe, 2001—. Contbr. articles to profl. jours.; patentee in field. NSF fellow, 1956-57; Recipient David Sarnoff award RCA, 1975. Fellow IEEE.

**WINDHAGER, ERICH ERNST,** physiologist, educator; b. Vienna, Nov. 4, 1928; came to U.S., 1954; s. Maximilian and Bertha (Feitzinger) W.; m. Helga A. Rapant, June 18, 1956; children: Evelyn Ann, Karen Alice. MD, U. Vienna, 1954. Rsch. fellow in biophysics Harvard Med. Sch., Boston, 1956—58; instr. in physiology Cornell U. Med. Coll., N.Y.C., 1958—61; vis. scientist U. Copenhagen, 1961—63; asst. to prof. physiology Cornell U. Med. Coll., N.Y.C., 1963—, Maxwell M. Upson prof. physiology and biophysics, 1978—2002, chmn. dept. physiology, 1973—2002, acting chmn. dept. cell biology, 1998—2002. Recipient Homer W. Smith award N.Y. Heart Assn., 1978, Berliner-Abbott award Am. Physiol. Soc., 1999. Office: Weill Med Coll Cornell U Dept Physiology 1300 York Ave New York NY 10021-4805 Office Phone: 212-746-6386. E-mail: ewindhag@med.cornell.edu.

**WINDHAM, DONALD ERIC,** bioinformatics analyst; b. Florence, SC, June 27, 1974; s. Donald Eugene Windham and Deborah Ann Robinson. BS in Zoology, NC State U., Raleigh, 1998, BS in Microbiology and Biology, 2002. Publs. staff NC State U. Computing Svcs., Raleigh, 1996—99; delivery lead IBM, Research Triangle Park, NC, 1999—2000, IT architecture specialist, 2000—02; bioinformatics specialist, sys. adminstr. NC State U. Fungal Genomics Lab, Raleigh, 2003—05; bioinformatics analyst NC State U. Ctr. Biology Nematode Parasitism, 2005—. Recipient One Team award, IBM, 2001. Mem.: Bioinformatics Orgn., Inc., Am. Soc. Microbiology. Office: NC State U Campus Box 7253 Raleigh NC 27603

**WINDHAM, JOHN FRANKLIN,** lawyer, educator; b. Fayette, Ala., Jan. 21, 1948; s. Grover B. Windham Jr. and Nancy Katherine (McAdams) Haynie; 1 child, John Franklin Jr.; m. Denise Roche McNair, Apr. 6, 1999; 1 stepchild, Brittany Danielle McNair. BA, U. West Fla., 1970; JD, U. N.C., 1975. Bar: Fla. 1975, U.S. Dist. Ct. (no. dist.) Fla. 1976, U.S. Ct. Appeals (11th cir.) 1983, U.S. Supreme Ct. 1984. Acctg. supr. Monsanto Co., Research Triangle Park, N.C., 1970-72; law clk. to U.S. Atty Pensacola, Fla., 1974; assoc. Beggs & Lane, Pensacola, 1975-79, ptnr., 1979—. Adj. assoc. prof. bus. law Troy State U., Pensacola, 1983-90. Mem. bd. dirs. Am. Cancer Soc., 1980-2005, exec. com. Fla. divsn., 1982-93, 95-2000, chmn. legacies and planned giving, 1984-88, chmn. income devel., 1980-91, chmn. ad hoc adv. com., 1991—, mem. risk adv. subcom., 1991-97, chmn. 1996-97, legal advisor, 1992—, vol. and staff devel. com., 1994-95, planning com., 1994-98, spokesperson tobacco media, 1995-96, mem. cause mktg. work group, 1995-96, mem. scholarship com., 1995-96, chmn. dist. VII steering com., 1995-96, v.p., 1996-97, mem. Winn Dixie adv. com., 1996-99, chmn. field ops., 1996-97, mem. task force volunteerism, 1996-99, dirsn. cell ctr. work group, 1996-98, mktg. and comms. com., 1997-2000, chmn. chartering com., 1997-98, chmn. elect bd. 1997-98, chmn. bd. 1998-99, personnel subcom., 1998-99, patient svc. ctr. work group, audit com., 1999-2000, nominating com., 1999-2005, evaluation adv. com., 2001-03, 05—; mem. Nat. Assembly, 2002—, mem. budget and fin. com., nom. ad hoc com., bd. governance task force, 1990—, chmn. bylaws com., 2002—; chmn. bd. Escambia Christian Sch., Pensacola, 1976-86; deacon Ch. of Christ, 1985-95, 1999-2002; adminstrv. team First City Ch., 2002-2004; elder First City Ch., 2004—; mem. adv. bd. Interim Healthcare, 1993-96, Panhandle Rehab. Injury Mgmt. and Evaluation, 1993-96; mem. found. bd. East Hill Christian Sch., 1995-97; bd. govs. Pensacola chpt. Order Granaderos & Dames de Galvez, 1990-98, pres. 1995-98; mem. U. West Fla. Found., 1983-85. Mem. Fla. Bar (workers compensation rules com., 1995-2001, drafting subcom., 2000-01), Fla. Def. Lawyers Assn., Fla. Workers Compensation Inst.,

Southeastern Admiralty Law Inst. (bd. dirs. 1986-89), Northwest Fla. Blood Ctr. Found. (treas. 2002-), U. West Fla. Nat. Alumni Assn. (bd. dirs.), Kiwanis (pres. Pensacola 1978-79, 88-89). Republican. Avocation: church activities. Office: Beggs & Lane PO Box 12950 Pensacola FL 32591-2950

**WINDHAM, REVISH,** poet; b. Panola, Ala., May 31, 1940; s. Ike, Sr. and Lillie (Queen) Windham; m. Janice L. Bowman, Sept. 22, 1985; 1 child, Veronice Wiggins-Windham. BA, Morris Brown Coll., 1962; MPA, NYU, 1989. Cert. mediator N.Y. Case worker N.Y.C. Dept. Social Svcs., 1968—70; youth counselor, group and family counselor, job developer N.Y. State Divsn. Youth, N.Y.C., 1970—90; investigator, unit supr. N.Y. State Divsn. Human Rights, N.Y.C., 1990—99; writer, poet NY, 1999—. Author: Shades of Black, 1970, Shade of Anger, 1972, I Wouldn't Take Nothing for My Journey, 2001, Blues Ain't Nothing but a Tonic, 2005; co-founder Black Forum; poetry editor: Black Forum, editor-in-chief:. Bd. dirs. S.E. Bronx (N.Y.) Neighborhood Ctr., Inc., 2000—, Philipsburg Manor (N.Y.) African Am. Adv. Bd., 2001—. With USN, 1964—68. Mem.: Morris Brown Coll. Alumni Assn., 369th Vets. Assn. (life), Shriners, Pentecost Consistory, Masons, Am. Legion (life), Corinthian, Phi Beta Sigma (life). Democrat. Baptist. Avocations: fishing, travel, reading, gardening. Home: 24 Hickory Rd Briarcliff Manor NY 10510

**WINDHAUSER, JOHN WILLIAM,** retired journalism educator, consultant; b. Rochester, NY, Jan. 30, 1943; s. Milton Edward and Mary Ellen (McDonald) W.; m. Marlene Marie Most. BS, Tri-State U., 1966; MA, Ball State U., 1967; PhD, Ohio U., 1975. Editor, reporter, advt. and pub. rels. positions, 1964—77; asst. prof. journalism Colo. State U., Ft. Collins, 1971—77, Bradley U., Peoria, Ill., 1977—78; assoc. prof., dir. rsch. ctr. U. Miss., Oxford, 1979—82; prof. La. State U., Baton Rouge, 1982—2005, U. Memphis, 2005—; cons. Jomar Assocs. Cons. in field; rsch. judge Soc. Profl. Journalists; editl. bd. Journalism Quarterly, Coll. Media Rev., Newspaper Rsch. Jour. Author: The Editorial Process, 1978, 2d edit., 1985; co-editor, co-author: The Media in the 1984 and 1988 Presidential Campaigns, 1991; contbr. numerous articles to profl. jours.; editor Profl. Jour., Coll. Press Rev., 1972-81. Recipient Life Membership award Nat. Coun. Coll. Publs. Advisers, 1981, Presdl. award, 1973-81. Mem. Assn. Edn. in Journalism

**WINDHORN, RICHARD J.,** dentist; b. Covington, Ky., Jan. 2, 1957; s. Raymond C. Windhorn and Doretta C. Moore; m. Debra J. Walburg, June 3, 1978; children: Michael D., Sarah E. BA, Wabash Coll., Crawfordsville, Ind., 1979; DMD, U. Ky., 1983. Lic. Am. Bd. Prosthodontics. Resident in prosthodontics US Army, Ft. Gordon, Ga., 1994—96, chief prosthodontics Heidelberg, Germany, 1996—99; mentor 2-yr. gen. dentistry residency USA Dental Activity, Ft. Hood, Tex., 1999—2002, chief prosthodontics Wurzburg, Bavaria, Germany, 2002—, officer in charge hosp. dental clinic, 2004—05; dep. dir. prosthodontic residence program U.S. Army Dental Activity, Ft. Gordon, Ga., 2005—. Col. U.S. Army. Fellow: Am. Coll. Prosthodontists. Avocations: softball, golf, woodworking, travel. Home: 1412 Andover Ct Evans GA 30809 Office: USA DENTAC Tingay Dental Clinic Fort Gordon GA 30905 Personal E-mail: richard.windhorn@us.army.mil.

**WINDHORST, JOHN WILLIAM, JR.,** lawyer; b. Mpls., July 6, 1940; s. John William and Ardus Ruth (Bottge) W.; divorced; 1 child, Diana Elizabeth. AB, Harvard U., 1962; LLB, U. Minn., 1965. Bar: Minn. 1965, U.S. Tax Ct., U.S. Ct. Appeals (8th cir.) 1965, U.S. Dist. Ct. Minn. 1967, U.S. Supreme Ct. 1975. Law clk. to Hon. H.A. Blackmun U.S. Cir. Ct., Rochester, Minn., 1965-66; assoc. Dorsey & Whitney, Mpls., 1966-70 with office of Revisor of Statutes State of Minn., 1967, 69; ptnr. Dorsey & Whitney, 1971-96, of counsel, 1997—. Bd. dirs. St. Paul Chamber Orch., 1980-86, Harry A. Blackmun Scholarship Found., 1996—, Minn. Taxpayers Assn., 1999—. Mem. ABA (com. on state and local taxes), Minn. Bar Assn., Hennepin County Bar Assn., Harvard Club of Minn. (pres. 1977-78). Home: 1235 Yale Pl Apt 1102 Minneapolis MN 55403-1946 Office: 50 S 6th St Ste 1500 Minneapolis MN 55402 Office Phone: 612-340-2645. Business E-Mail: windhorst.john@dorsey.com.

**WINDMAN, ARNOLD LEWIS,** retired mechanical engineer; b. N.Y.C., Oct. 17, 1926; s. Raphael and Anna (Wexler) W.; m. Patricia Foley, Dec. 13, 1967; children— Richard, Marjorie, Kevin, Colleen, Sean, JoAnn, Brian, William. B.M.E., Cornell U., 1947. Bar: registered profl. engr., N.Y., 13 other states. Project engr. F.E. Sutton, N.Y.C., 1947-50; with Syska & Hennessy, Inc., N.Y.C., 1950-90, pres., 1976-86, vice chmn., 1986-90, also bd. dirs. Pres. Am. Cons. Engrs. Coun., 1985-86; chmn. N.Y. State Bd. Engring. and Land Surveying, 1982-84; bd. dirs., v.p. Sea Pines Plantation, 1997-2000. Bd. dirs. Phelps Meml. Hosp., Tarrytown, N.Y., 1974-82; chmn. planning commn. Hilton Head Island, 2000. Mem. Am. Soc. Heating, Refrigerating and Air Conditioning Engrs., chpt. pres. (1965), N.Y. Assn. Cons. Engrs. (pres. 1981-82, dir. 1977), ASME, Tau Beta Pi, Pi Tau Sigma. Democrat. Jewish. Home: 1919 S Beach Club Vl Hilton Head Island SC 29928-4068 *Professional integrity, enthusiasm, and a continuing effort to train younger people for advancement are three key ingredients of a successful career.*

**WINDOM, HERBERT LYNN,** oceanographer, environmental scientist; b. Macon, Ga., Apr. 23, 1941; m. Patricia Woodruff, 1963; children: Kevin, Elizabeth. BS, Fla. State U., 1963; MS, U. Calif., San Diego, 1965, PhD in Earth Sci., 1968. Prof. oceanography Skidaway Inst. Oceanography, Savannah, Ga., 1968—94, acting dir., 1994-2001, prof. emeritus, 2001—. Mem. Am. Soc. Limnol. and Oceanography, Am. Geophys. Union, Oceanography Soc. Office: Skidaway Inst of Oceanography 10 Ocean Science Cir Savannah GA 31411-1011 E-mail: herb@skio.peachnet.edu.

**WINDOM, STEPHEN RALPH,** former lieutenant governor, lawyer; b. Florence, South Carolina, Nov. 6, 1949; s. Ralph and Connie (Hinds) W.; m. Mary (Becker); children: Robert Stephen, Thomas Patrick. BS, U. Ala., 1971, JD, 1974. Bar: Ala., 1974; U.S. Supreme Ct., 1980. Assoc. McDermott, Slepian, Kittrell, and Fleming, Mobile, Ala., 1974-77; ptnr. McDermott, Slepian, Windom, and Reed, Mobile, Ala., 1974-86, Sirote and Permutt, P.C., Ala., 1984—; mem. Ala. State Senate, 1989-99; lt. gov. State of Ala., 1999—2003. Lectr. in field, 1985—. Pres. Greater Gulf State Fair, Mobile, 1981; Cystic Fibrosis Found., Mobile, 1981. Capt. USAFR, 1971-82. Mem. Ala. State Bar Assn.; Mobile Bar Assn.; Am. Bankruptcy Inst.; Comml. Law League; Jaycees; Shriners; Masons; Phi Delta Phi. Republican. Avocations: hunting, water sports.

**WINDOM, WILLIAM,** actor; b. N.Y.C., Sept. 28, 1923; s. Paul and Isobel Wells (Peckham) W.; m. Patricia Veronica Tunder, Dec. 31, 1975; children: Rachel, Heather Juliet, Hope, Rebel Russell. Student, Williams Coll., 1942, The Citadel, 1943, Antioch Coll., 1943, U. Ky., 1943, Biarritz Am. U., 1945, Fordham U., 1946. Actor: (Army) Richard III, 1945—46, (Broadway appearances) Mlle. Colombe, 1954, Fallen Angels, 1956, USA, 1958, Androdes and the Lion, Alice in Wonderland, Time Remembered, Viva Madison Avenue, The World of Suzie Wong, Double in Hearts, Come Blow Your Horn; (films) To Kill a Mockingbird, 1962, For Love or Money, 1963, Cattle King, 1963, One Man's Way, 1964, The Americanization of Emily, 1964, Hour of the Gun, 1967, The Detective, 1968, The Angry Breed, 1969, The Gypsy Moths, 1969, Brewster McCloud, 1970, Echoes of a Summer, 1974, Sommersby, 1993, Attack of the 50 ft. Woman, 1993, Children of the Corn: The Gatherine, 1996; (TV series, leading role) The Farmer's Daughter, 1962—65, My World and Welcome to It, 1969—70 (Emmy award, 1970), (one-man theatrical presentation) Thurber I, 1972, Thurber II, 1975, Ernie Pyle I, 1976, Ernie Pyle II, 1979; (TV series) Murder She Wrote, Parenthood, 1990, (appearances in numerous TV movies including) A Great American Tragedy, The Day the Earth Moved, Guilty or Innocent: The Sam Sheppard Murder Case, Seventh Avenue, Blind Ambition, Portrait of a Rebel: Margaret Sanger, Desperate Lives, The Rules of Marriage, Miracle on 34th St., 1994, Fugitive X: Innocent

Target, 1996, The Thundering 8th, 1998, Early Bird Special, 1998, True Crime, 1999; actor, actor: others; mem.: Am. Repertory Theatre, 1946—47. Served with 508th parachute inf. AUS, 1943-46. Mem. Catboat Assn., Actors Equity Assn.

**WINDSOR, ADRIAN SHARON,** real estate broker, literature and language professor; b. Adrian, Mich., Oct. 19, 1938; d. LeRoy E. and Delores L. Wood; life ptnr. Ronald V. Knapp; children: Charles L. Proudfit, Kerren L. Bergman. BA, MA, U. Mich., Ann Arbor, PhD, 1967. Cert. internat. property specialist. Assoc. prof. English Colo. Women's Coll., Denver, 1968—77; dir. Sewall & Farrand acad. programs, assoc. prof. English U. Colo., Boulder, 1978—82; stock broker Dain Bosworth, 1982—85; real estate broker Adrian Windsor Broker, Irvine, Calif., 1988—; pres. Sovereign Holdings Internat. Corp. Dir. pub. rels. KGNU Pub. Radio, 1982—83; adj. prof. English Coastline CC 1991—2006. Author: (book) Seven Tools to Transform Genius Into Practical Power. Bd. mem. Colo. Music Festival, 1978—84, v.p. devel., 1978—84; bd. dirs. LA Fund Raising Reconstruction of Biblioteque Alexendrina. Recipient Outstanding Adj. Faculty award, 1996. Mem.: Fedn. Internation Real Estate Brokers, Calif. Assn. Realtors, Nat. Assn. Realtors, Inside Edge Found. Edn. (bd. dirs. 2002—03, program dir. 2003—). Democrat. Avocations: spiritual counseling, motivation, educational leadership, philanthropic project development. Office: 14252 Culver Dr #205A Irvine CA 92604 Office Phone: 949-369-3837. Office Fax: 949-369-9958. Personal E-mail: arealwin@aol.com.

**WINDSOR, HARRIET SMITH,** state official; children: James A. Smith Jr., Julia A. Smith-O'Hanlon. BA, Juniata Coll.; PhD, MA, U. Del. Cert. lay spkr. Peninsula Conf. Former English tchr. Seaford Sr. HS; dean instrn., dept. English Chmn. Del. Tech. and Cmty. Coll. Owens Campus; mem., dir. State Personnel Gov. Thomas R. Carper's Cabinet, 1993—2001; sec. of state State of Del., 2001—. Writer, spkr. numerous local, state and nat. bds. Serves Dist. Com. Ordained Ministry; mem., choir dir., organist, ch. sch. tchr., supt., administrv. bd. chmn., chmn. Pastor Parish Rels. Com. Millsboro Grace United Meth. Ch., lay leader, 2002—. Named Del. Mother of Yr., 1999, Woman of Yr., Sussex Ctrl. Jr. HS students; named to Del.'s Hall of Fame, 1997; recipient Millsboro's Woman of Year, 1989, Order of the First State, Governor Thomas R. Carper, Del., 2000. Democrat. Methodist. Office: Sec of State Townsend Bldg 401 Federal St Ste 3 Dover DE 19901 Office Phone: 302-739-4111. Office Fax: 302-739-3811. E-mail: hnsmith@state.de.us.

**WINDSOR, PATRICIA (KATONAH SUMMERTREE, PERRIN WINTERS, ANNA SEELING),** author, educator, lecturer; b. NYC, Sept. 21, 1938; d. Bernhard Edward and Antoinette (Gaus) Seelinger; m. Laurence Charles Windsor, Jr., Apr. 3, 1959 (div. 1978); children: Patience Wells, Laurence Edward; m. Stephen E. Altman, Sept. 21, 1986 (div. 1989). Student, Bennington Coll., 1956—58, Westchester C.C., AA, NYU. V.p. Windsor-Morehead Assoc., NYC, 1960—63; info. mgr. Family Planning Assn., London, 1974—76; faculty mem. Inst. Children's Lit., Redding Ridge, Conn., 1976—94, 1999—; editor-in-chief AT&T, Washington, 1978—80; instr. U. Md. Writers Inst., Open Univ., Washington, 1980—82; creative developer, faculty mem. Long Ridge Writer's Group, Danbury, Conn., 1988—2000, instr., 2006—; dir. Summertree Studios, Savannah, Ga., 1992—. Dir. Wordspring Lit. Cons., 1989—, Wordworks Writing Cons., 1999—, Born Author Lit. Cons., 2003-; dir. Devel. Writing Workshops, Katonah, NY, 1976-78; judge Internat. Assn. Bus. Communicators, Washington, 1979, 89; lectr. LI U., Jersey City State Coll., Skidmore Coll., others, 1987—; instr. Coastal Ga. Ctr. for Continuing Edn., 1996—, Armstrong Atlantic U. Continuing Edn., 1997-2000, Anne Arundel (Md.) C.C., 2000—, workshop coord., 2000—; dir., founder Born Author.com, 2002—; dir. Windsomethings Art & Crafts, 2004—; owner, designer Tiger Woman Crafts for Meditation, 2005-. Author: The Summer Before, 1973 (ALA Best Book award 1973, transl. 1980 Austrian State prize 1980, also Brit., Norwegian, German edits.), Something's Waiting for You, Baker D, 1974 (starred selection Libr. Jour., Brit., Japanese edits.) Home Is Where Your Feet Are Standing, 1975, Diving for Roses, 1976 (NY Times Outstanding Book for Young Adults award, starred selection Libr. Jour.), Mad Martin, 1976, Killing Time, 1980, Demon Tree, 1983 (pen name Colin Daniel), The Sandman's Eyes, 1985 (Edgar Allan Poe Best Juvenile Mystery award Mystery Writers Am.), How a Weirdo and a Ghost Can Change Your Life, 1986, The Hero, 1988 (highest rating Voice of Youth Advocate), Just Like the Movies, 1990, The Christmas Killer, 1991 (Edgar nominee, Brit., Danish, French edits.), Two Weirdos and a Ghost, 1991, A Weird and Moogly Christmas, 1991, The Blooding, 1996 (YALSA pick for reluctant readers), The House of Death, 1996, Nightwood (nominated Best Book 2006), 2006; columnist The Blood Rev., 1990-92, Savannah Parent, 1990-92; columnist Coastal Senior, 1997-99; also short stories in anthologies and mags.; actress: The Haunting of Hill House, City Lights Theatre Co., 1991; contr. articles Once Upon a Time Mag., 2003, 04, 05. Mem. City Lights Theatre Co., Savannah, Ga., 1991. Mem. Horror Writers Am., Internat. Women's Writing Guild, Children's Book Guild, Authors Guild, Poetry Soc. Ga., Savannah Storytellers. Avocations: skiing, painting, modern dance. Office: Born Author Dot Com PO Box 799 Severna Park MD 21146 E-mail: info@bornauthor.com.

**WINDSOR, WILLIAM EARL,** consulting engineer, sales representative; b. Evansville, Ind., Jan. 24, 1927; s. Charles H. and Lora E. (Archey) W.; divorced; children: Kim, William, Robert. Student, Purdue U., 1946-50. Field engr. Philco Corp., Phila., 1950-53, Europe, Africa, Arabia; studio ops. engr. Sta. WFBM, Indpls., 1953-55; field engr. RCA Svc. Co., Cherry Hill, NJ, 1955-56; audio facilities engr. ABC, N.Y.C., 1956-62; rsch. engr. Fine Recording, Inc., N.Y.C., 1962-66; chief engr. A & R Recording, Inc., N.Y.C., 1966-68; chief engr., corp. sec. DB Audio Corp., N.Y.C., 1968-70; pres. Studio Cons., Inc., N.Y.C., 1970-72; sr. v.p., v.p., gen. mgr. Quad Eight Electronics-Quad Eight/Westrex, San Fernando, Calif., 1972-85; sr. mktg. exec. Mitsubishi Pro Audio Group, San Fernando, Calif., 1985-89. Pres., CEO Quad Eight Electronics, Inc., Valencia, Calif., 1989-90; ind. cons., Valencia, 1991—. Inventor monitor mixer for multitrack audio consoles, 1967, update function for audio console automation, 1973; designer of new architecture for film scoring and film re-recording sound mixing consoles, 1974 (Acad. award 1974). Served with USNR, 1945-50. Fellow: Audio Engring. Soc. (chmn. NY sect. 1970). Avocations: photography, foreign travel, art collecting. Home and Office: 23112 Yvette Ln Valencia CA 91355-3060 Office Phone: 661-255-3265. Business E-Mail: wew@ispwest.com.

**WINE, L. MARK,** lawyer; b. Norfolk, Va., Apr. 16, 1945; s. Melvin Leon and Mildred Sylvia (Weiss) W.; m. Blanche Weintraub, June 8, 1969; children: Kim, Lara, Dana. BA with high honors, U. Va., 1967; JD, U. Chgo., 1970. Bar: D.C. 1970, U.S. Supreme Ct. 1977. Assoc. Kirkland & Ellis LLP, Washington, 1970-72, ptnr., 1978—; trial atty. land and natural resources divsn. Dept. of Justice, Washington, 1972-78. Mem. ABA. Office: Kirkland & Ellis LLP 655 15th St NW Ste 1200 Washington DC 20005-5793 Office Phone: 202-879-5024. Business E-Mail: mwine@kirkland.com.

**WINE, MARK PHILIP,** lawyer; b. Iowa City, Jan. 6, 1949; s. Donald Arthur and Mary Lepha Schneider; m. Carol Jean Sullivan; children: Nicholas Cox, Meredith Kathryn, Callie Ann, Cassidy Mae. AB, Princeton U., 1971; JD, U. Iowa, 1974. Bar: Iowa 1974, Minn. 1976, Calif. 1997, U.S. Dist. Ct. Minn. 1976, U.S. Ct. Appeals (8th cir.) 1976, U.S. Supreme Ct. 1984, U.S. Ct. Appeals (4th cir.) 1985, U.S. Ct. Appeals (7th and Fed. cirs.) 1992, U.S. Ct. Appeals (9th cir.) 1997, U.S. Dist. Ct. (so., no. and ctrl. dists.) Calif. 1997. Law clk. to judge U.S. Ct. Appeals (8th cir.), St. Louis, 1974-76; ptnr. Oppenheimer Wolff & Donnelly, 1976—2002, McDermott, Will & Emery, LA, 2002—. Mem. ABA, Internat. Assn. Def. Counsel, Calif. Bar Assn., L.A. Bar Assn., L.A. Intellectual Property Law Assn., Princeton Club So. Calif. Democrat. Avocations: cooking, reading, golf. Home: 6220 E Fox Glen Dr Anaheim CA 92807 Office: McDermott Will & Emery 2049 Century Park E Fl 34 Los Angeles CA 90067-3208 Office Phone: 310-551-9322. Personal E-mail: mpwineca@sbcglobal.net. Business E-Mail: mwine@mwe.com.

**WINE-BANKS, JILL SUSAN,** lawyer; b. Chgo., May 5, 1943; d. Bert S. and Sylvia Dawn (Simon) Wine; m. Ian David Volner, Aug. 21, 1965; m. Michael A. Banks, Jan. 12, 1980. BS, U. Ill., Champaign, Urbana, 1964; JD, Columbia U., 1968; LLD (hon.), Hood Coll., 1975. Bar: N.Y. 1969, U.S. Ct. Appeals (2d, 4th, 5th, 6th, 7th and 9th cirs.), U.S. Supreme Ct. 1974, D.C. 1976, Ill. 1980. Asst. press. and pub. rels. dir. Assembly of Captive European Nations, N.Y.C., 1965-66; trial atty. criminal divsn. organized crime & racketeering U.S. Dept. Justice, 1969-73; asst. spl. prosecutor Watergate Spl. Prosecutor's Office, 1973-75; lectr. law sem. in trial practice Columbia U. Sch. Law, N.Y.C., 1975-77; assoc. Fried, Frank, Harris, Shriver & Kampelman, Washington, 1975-77; gen. counsel Dept. Army, Pentagon, Washington, 1977-79; ptnr. Jenner & Block, Chgo., 1980-84; solicitor gen. State of Ill. Office of Atty. Gen., 1984-86, dep. atty. gen., 1986-87; exec. v.p., chief oper., officer ABA, Chgo., 1987-90; atty. pvt. practice, 1990-92; v.p., dir. transaction and govt. rels. Motorola Internat. Network Ventures, 1992-97; dir. strategic alliances Motorola Cellular Infrastructure Group, 1997—99; v.p. alliance mgmt. Maytag Corp., 1999-2001; CEO Winning Workplaces, Evanston, Ill., 2001—03; chief officer Chgo. Pub. Schs. Edn. to Careers, 2003—. Mem. EEC disting. vis. program European Parliament, 1987; chmn. bd. dirs. St. Petersburg Telecom., Russia, 1994-97, Omni Capital Ptnrs., Inc., 1994-97. Trustee Roosevelt U., 2004—; mem. adv. bd. Project Lead the Way, UIC Econ. Edn. Recipient Spl. Achievement award U.S. Dept. Justice, 1972, Meritorious award, 1973, Cert. Outstanding Svc., 1975; decorated Disting. Civilian Svc. Dept. Army, 1979; named Disting. Vis. to European Econ. Cmty. Mem.: The Chgo. Network, Internat. Women's Forum, Exec. Club (bd. dirs. 1999—2001), Econ. Club. Office: Chgo Pub Schs Edn to Careers 125 S Clark St 12th Fl Chicago IL 60603 Office Phone: 773-553-2460. Business E-Mail: jwine-banks@cps.k12.il.us.

**WINEBRENNER, WILLIAM PATRICK,** writer; b. West Columbia, W.Va., Sept. 26, 1933; s. Richard Arthur Winebrenner and Lucy Ethel Riley; children: Rita Jean Hreha, William Patrick II, Tonya Michelle Noel. Grad. h.s., Mason, W.Va. Journeyman Internat. Brotherhood Elec. Workers, Toledo, 1968-95; ret. Mem. adv. bd. Muskingum Area Tech. Coll., Zanesville, Ohio 1998; owner Valley Enterprises Pub., Stockport, Ohio, 1993-98. Author: (books) The Woodwalkers, 1993, Smoke in the Valley, 1995, Narrowbackin', 1997, From Out of the Forest, 1998, A Place of Evil, 1996. Mem. Elec. Workers Retirement. Democrat. Avocations: hunting, fishing, writing and promoting books. Home: 2300 State Route 376 Stockport OH 43787-9570

**WINEGAR, ALBERT LEE,** computer company executive; b. Beloit, Wis., Apr. 23, 1931; s. Albert Richard and Theo Rayneta (Hubbell) W.; m. Phyllis M. Everill, June 21, 1953; children: Bradford, Steven, Kristine, Kathleen. BBA, U. Wis., 1954. With IBM Corp., 1956-79, div. dir. mgmt. services, 1977-79; v.p. corp. planning, then group v.p. field ops. Olivetti Corp., Tarrytown, NY, 1979-80, pres., 1980-81; v.p. field ops. NBI Inc., Boulder, Colo., 1981-84; pres., chief exec. officer Sensory, Inc., Santa Clara, Calif., 1984-85, VICOM Systems, Inc., Fremont, Calif., 1985-91, ret., 1991. Bd. dirs. JRL Sys., Inc., Advanced Sys. Integration Group, Acad. Software Inc., Adams Globalization, Inc.; pres. Barton Creek Water Supply Corp. V.p. bd. trustees Valley Hosp., Ridgewood, N.J., 1978-81; pres. NJ Bus. Arts Found., 1977-78, Estates of Barton Creek Homeowners Assn., 1992-94; elder Westlake Hills Presbyn. Ch., stewardship chmn., 2002, fin. chmn., 2003 Capt. AUS, 1954-56. Sloan Exec. fellow, Stanford U., 1970. Mem. Computer and Bus. Equipment Mfrs. Assn. (dir. 1980-81), Barton Creek Country Club, Beta Theta Pi. Republican. Home: 8401 Hickory Creek Dr Austin TX 78735-1530 E-mail: alwinegar@aol.com.

**WINEKE, WILLIAM ROBERT,** reporter, minister; b. Madison, Wis., Apr. 4, 1942; s. Edward Ervin and Jennie Mae (Janssen) W.; m. Susan L. Detering, Dec. 9, 1964 (div. June 1975); children: Gregory, Andrew; m. Jacqueline Cone, Mar. 18, 1990. BS, U. Wis., 1965; BDiv, chgo. Theol. Sem., 1969. Reporter Wis. State Jour., Madison, 1963-65; writer United Ch. of Christ, N.Y.C., 1966-68; pub. rels. dir. Chgo. (Ill.) Theol. Sem., Chgo., 1968-69; reporter Wis. State Jour., Madison, 1969—; chaplain Wis. Rescue Mission, Madison, 1977—. Mem. bd. rev. Wis. Health Policy Network, Madison, 1994-2003. Fellow Religions Pub. Rels. Soc., 1974; recipient Disting. Svc. award State Med. Soc. Wis., 1992, Disting. Svc. award LWV, Madison, 1994. Democrat. Home: 1024 Ridgewood Dr Stoughton WI 53589-4125 Office: Wis State Jour 1901 Fish Hatchery Rd Madison WI 53713-1248

**WINER, WARD OTIS,** mechanical engineer, educator; b. Grand Rapids, Mich., June 27, 1936; s. Mervin Augustus and Ina Katherine (Wood) W.; m. Mary Jo Wielinga, June 15, 1957; children: Mathew Owen, James Edward, Paul Andrew, Mary Margaret. Asso., Grand Rapids Jr. Coll., 1956; BS, U. Mich., 1958, MS, 1959, PhD; PhD (Cavendish Lab. fellow), Cambridge U., Eng., 1964. Asst. prof. dept. mech. engring. U. Mich., Ann Arbor, 1963-66, assoc. prof., 1966-69; assoc. prof. mech. engring. Ga. Inst. Tech., 1969-71, prof., 1971-84, Regents' prof., 1984—, mem. exec. bd., 1983-88, chmn., 1984-86, dir. and chmn. Sch. Mech. Engring., 1988—, Eugene C. Gwaltney Jr. chair George W. Woodruff Sch. Mech. Engring., 2001—. Chmn. Gordon Research Conf. on Friction, Lubrication and Wear, 1980; mem. NRC, 1980-88; chmn. Com. on Recommendations for U.S. Army Basic Sci. Research, 1985-87; mem. div. mech., structural, materials engring. adv. bd. NSF Engring. Directorate, 1984-89. Co-editor: Wear Control Handbook, 1980; tech. editor: Jour. Lubrication Tech., 1980-84, Jour. of Tribology, 1984-87; contbr. articles to profl. jours. Democratic precinct chmn., 1967-68; Mem. exec. bd. Horace H. Rackham Sch. Grad. Studies, U. Mich., 1968. Recipient Disting. Faculty Svc. award Coll. Engring. U. Mich., 1967, Alumni Merit award, 1998, Cert. Recognition, NASA, 1977, Clarence E. Earle Meml. award Nat. Grease Lubricating Inst., 1979, Disting. Prof. award Ga. Inst. Tech., 1987; named Hon. Alumni, Ga. Tech., 2003. Fellow AAAS, ASME (hon.; bd. comms. 1987-91, v.p. rsch. 1989-93, Melville medal 1975, Centennial medallion 1980, Mayor D. Hersey award 1986, Charles Russ Richards Meml. award 1988), Soc. Tribologists and Lubrication Engrs. (bd. dirs. 1983-86, Internat. award 1997), Brit. Tribology Trust (gold medal 1987), Am. Soc. Engring. Educators (Benjamin Garver Lamme award 1995, Donald Marlowe award 1996); mem. NAE, Metro Atlanta Engring. Soc. (Engr. of Yr. 1989), Am. Acad. Mechanics, Soc. Rheology, Soc. Engring. Sci. (dir. 1980-84), AAUP (pres. Ga. Tech. chpt. 1972-74, v.p. state conf. 1973-75), Sigma Xi (chpt. pres. 1982-83, Sustained Rsch. in Engring. award 1975), Tau Beta Pi, Pi Tau Sigma, Phi Kappa Phi. Home: 1025 Mountain Creek Trl NW Atlanta GA 30328-3535 Office Phone: 404-894-3200. E-mail: ward.winer@me.gatech.edu.

**WINERIP, MICHAEL,** reporter; married; 4 children. B, Harvard Coll. Suburban reporter NY Times, columnist, investigative reporter, nat. politwriter, edn. writer, dep. metro editor, staff writer Sunday Mag., nat. edn. columnist. Author: 9 Highland Road: Sane Living for the Mentally Ill, 1995, (children's novel) Adam Canfield of the Slash, 2005. Office: NY Times 229 West 43rd St New York NY 10036 Office Phone: 212-556-4122. Office Fax: 212-556-3758. E-mail: winerip@nytimes.com.*

**WINESKI, LAWRENCE E.,** medical educator, biomedical researcher; b. Fort Dix, N.J., June 29, 1949; s. Max E. and Irene R. Wineski; m. Lynn C. Comerford, Aug. 16, 1980; children: Matthew C., Benjamin C. BA, Calif. State U., Fullerton, 1972; MA, San Francisco State U., 1976; PhD, U. of Ill., Chgo., 1980. Wetenschappelijk medewerker State U. of Groningen (Netherlands), 1980—81; postdoctoral scholar U. Mich., Ann Arbor, 1981—82; rsch. assoc. U. Ill., Chgo., 1982—83; asst. prof., assoc. prof. Morehouse Sch. of Medicine, Atlanta, 1983—. Mem. anatomy adv. bd. Lippincott Williams & Wilkins Publishers, Balt., 2005—. Author: (scientific papers) Jour. Zoology, Jour. Morphology, Jour. Experimental Zoology, Jour. Comparative Neurology, Acta Anatomica, Archives of Oral Biology, Cells Tissues Organs, (book chapter) Bones in the Basement: Postmortem Racism in 19th Century Medical Training, educational materials, CD-ROM; reviewer (various sci. jours.), 1991—2006. Grantee Rsch. Grants, NIH, NASA, 1989—2002. Mem.: Am. Assn. Advancement Sci., Ednl. Affairs Com., Soc. Integrative and Comparative Biology, Soc. Neurosci., Am. Assn. Clinical Anatomists, Am. Assn. Anatomists, AAAS Soc. for Neuroscience; Soc. for Integrative and

Comparative Biology (ednl. affairs com. 2004—). Avocations: soccer, travel. Office: Morehouse Sch of Medicine 720 Westview Dr SW Atlanta GA 30310-1495 Office Phone: 404-752-1563.

**WINET, HOWARD,** research scientist, medical educator; b. Chgo., Sept. 13, 1937; s. Maurice Winet and Lillian Silver; m. Carol Katherine Kasper; children: Evan Darwin, Wendy Lynn. BS in Zoology, U. Ill., 1959; MA in Zoology, UCLA, 1962, PhD in Zoology, 1969. Cert. tchr. secondary edn., Calif. Tchr. secondary sch. sci. L.A. City Schs., 1962—66; postdoctoral fellow engring. sci. Calif. Inst. Tech., Pasadena, 1970—74, rsch. engr., 1974—77; assoc. prof. physiology So. Ill. U., Carbondale, 1977—80; assoc. prof. rsch. orthopaedics U. So. Calif., L.A., 1980—88, assoc. rsch. biomed. engring., 1996—98; lectr. biomed. engring. UCLA, 1998—, adj. prof. orthop., 1998—. Cons. Commonwealth Sci. & Indsl. Rsch. Orgn., Canberra, Australia, 1979; vis. assoc. prof. math. U. Wis., Madison, 1982; Fogarty internat. fellow orthopaedics Gothenburg U., Sweden, 1984; sr. assoc. U.S. Army M.C., Walter Reed Hosp., Washington, 1990—92. Contbr. (book chpts.) Engineering Science, Fluid Dynamics, 1990, Encyclopedic Handbook of Biomaterials and Bioengineering, 1995, Clinically Applied Microcirculation Research, 1995, Bone Mechanics Handbook, 2001; mem. sci. editl. bd.: European Cells and Materials Jour. Grantee Rsch. grant, NIH, 1978—81, 1986—89, 1994—97. Mem.: Am. Rsch. Circulation Osseous (v.p.), Soc. Biomaterials (vice chair spl. interest groups 2002). Avocation: fly fishing. Office: Orthopaedic Hosp UCLA 2400 Flower St Los Angeles CA 90007 Office Phone: 213-742-1007. Business E-Mail: hwinet@ucla.edu.

**WINFIELD, JOHN BUCKNER,** rheumatologist, educator; b. Kentfield, Calif., Mar. 19, 1942; s. R. Buckner and Margaret G. (Katterfelt) Winfield; m. Patricia Nichols (div. 1968); 1 child, Ann Gibson; m. Teresa Lee McGrath, 1969 (div. 2000); children: John Buckner III, Virginia Lee; m. Leigh Fleming Callahan, 2001. BA, Williams Coll., 1964; MD, Cornell U., 1968. Diplomate Am. Bd. Internal Medicine. Intern in medicine N.Y. Hosp., N.Y.C., 1968-69; staff assoc. LI/Nat. Inst. Allergy and Infectious Diseases NIH, Bethesda, Md., 1969-71; resident in medicine, fellow in rheumatology U. Va. Sch. Medicine, Charlottesville, 1971-73; fellow in immunology Rockefeller U., N.Y.C., 1973-75; asst. prof. medicine U. Va. Sch. Medicine, Charlottesville, 1975-76, assoc. prof. medicine, 1976-78, U. N.C., Chapel Hill, 1978-81, prof. medicine, 1981—2006, chief div. rheumatology and immunology, 1978-99; dir. Thurston Arthritis Rsch. Ctr., U. N.C. Sch. Medicine, Chapel Hill, 1982—2001; dir Daughtridge Arthritis Ctr., Lenoir, NC, 2002—; Smith prof. medicine U. NC Sch. Med., Chapel Hill, 1987—2006, emeritus, 2006—, adj. prof. exercise sports physiology, 2003—; owner Winfield Medical, L.L.C., 2004—. Adv. coun. Nat. Inst. Arthritis and Musculoskeletal and Skin Diseases, NIH, 1988-92; chmn. edn. com. Am. Rheumatism Assn., Atlanta, 1980-84; immunol. scis. study sect. NIH, 1979-83, Arthritis Musculoskeletal and Skin study sect., 1992-96; vice-chair fellowship com. Arthritis Found., 1982; med. coun. Lupus Found. Am., 1987-96. Author more than 130 med. and sci. articles in peer reviewed rheumatology and immunology jours.; mem. editl. bd. Arthritis and Rheumatism, Bull. Rheumatic Diseases, Rheumatology Internat., Clin. Exptl. Rheumatology, Am. Jour. Medicine, Clin. Immunology, Current Rev. Rheumatology. Sr. asst. surgeon with USPHS, NIH, Bethesda, Md., 1968-71. Recipient Borden prize Cornell U. Med. Coll., 1964, numerous rsch. grants NIH and Arthritis Found., 1975—, Sr. Investigator award Arthritis Found., 1976-79, Kenan award U. N.C., 1985, NIH merit award, 1992. Fellow ACP; mem. Am. Assn. Immunologists, Am. Coll. Rheumatology, Am. Fedn. Clin. Rsch., Am. Soc. Clin. Investigation, Assn. Am. Physicians, Am. Clin. Climatol. Assn., Nat. Soc. Clin. Rheumatologists (treas. 1997-02), Henry Kunkel Soc. (councilor 2000-02), Chapel Hill Country Club. Republican. Episcopalian. Avocations: golf, on and off-road motorcycling, scuba diving instructor, skiing. Home: 102 Greenwood Ln Chapel Hill NC 27514-5957 Office Phone: 828-757-6414. Business E-Mail: john_winfield@med.unc.edu.

**WINFIELD, RICHARD NEILL,** lawyer; b. Chgo., Jan. 20, 1933; s. Richard Paul and Mary B. (Monaghan) Winfield; m. Deobrah Mary Trainer, June 13, 1959; children: Richard Neill Jr., Pamela, Nicole. AB, Villanova U., 1955; LLB, Georgetown U., 1961. Bar: Va. 1961, N.Y. 1962, U.S. Dist. Ct. (so. dist.) N.Y. 1963. Assoc. Donovan, Leisure, Newton & Irvine, N.Y.C., 1961-65; asst. counsel to Gov. Nelson A. Rockefeller Gov.'s Office, Albany, NY, 1965-67; assoc. Royall, Koegel, Rogers & Wells, N.Y.C., 1967-69; ptnr. Clifford Chance US LLP (formerly known as Rogers & Wells), N.Y.C., 1969—2002. Chmn. bd. consultors Sch. Law Villanova U., Pa., 1980—2004; faculty comm. law confs. Practising Law Inst., N.Y.C., 1977—2001, chmn. libel litig. confs., 1979—2000; prof. Columbia Law Sch., Fordham Law Sch., 2002—. Editor: Libel Litigation, PLI, 1979, 1981, 1984, 1986, 1988, 1990, 1992, 1994, 1996, 1998, 2000; contbr. articles to profl. jours. Chmn. bd. trustees Convent Sacred Heart Sch., N.Y.C., 1987—90; co-chmn. bd. dirs. Fund for Peace, 2000—; mem. bd. visitors Sch. Langs. and Linguistics, Georgetown U., Washington, 1987—93. Lt. USN, 1955—59. Recipient Alumni medallion, Coll. Liberal Arts & Scis. Villanova U., 1984, Loyalty award, Villanova U., 1986, First Amendment award, Deadline Club, 2002. Mem.: ABA (chmn. media law reform working group 1996—, Ctrl. Europe and Eurasian Law Initiative), Internat. Sr. Lawyers Project (co-founder, bd. dirs., treas.), Assn. Bar City of N.Y., N.Y. State Bar Assn., Century Assn. Republican. Roman Catholic. Avocations: travel, history. Home: 40 5th Ave New York NY 10011-8843 Office: Clifford Chance US LLP 31 West 52nd St New York NY 10019 Office Phone: 212-878-8233.

**WINFREY, CAREY WELLS,** journalist, editor; b. NYC, Aug. 1, 1941; s. William Colin and Mary (Robinson) W.; m. Jane Elizabeth Keeney, Feb. 13, 1982; children: Graham William, Wells Millar. AB, Columbia U., 1963, MS in Journalism, 1967. Assoc. editor Time Inc., N.Y.C., 1968-71; exec. producer Ednl. Broadcast Corp., N.Y.C. 1971-77; reporter, fgn. corr. for Africa N.Y. Times, N.Y.C., 1977-80; mag. editor CBS Mags., N.Y.C., 1981-90, editor Cuisine mag., 1983-84, v.p., editorial dir., 1985-87; founding editor-in-chief Memories mag. Diamandis Comm., Inc. (formerly mag. division CBS), N.Y.C., 1987-90; editor-in-chief Am. Health mag. Reader's Digest Publs., N.Y.C., 1990-96; dir. Delacorte Ctr. for Mag. Journalism, Columbia U., N.Y.C., 1996-98; asst. mng. editor People Mag., 1996—2001; editor-in-chief Smithsonian Mag., 2001—. Author: Starts and Finishes, 1975; exec. producer: (TV) Behind the Lines, 1971-75 (Emmy award 1973-74, NYU Don Hollenback award 1974), Assignment America, 1975, WNET Reports, 1976-77; columnist: "Eye on Books" for Book of the Month Club News, 1980, Parenting mag., 1986-89; prodr. CBS Cable; contbr. articles to Mags. Lt. USMC, 1963-66. Pulitzer Travelling fellow, 1967; recipient Meyer Berger award for Disting. Reporting Columbia U., 1978. Home: 3808 Reno Rd NW Washington DC 20008 Office: Smithsonian Mag MRC 951, PO Box 37012 Washington DC 20013-7012 Business E-Mail: cwinfrey@si.edu.*

**WINFREY, JOHN CRAWFORD,** economist, educator; b. Somerville, Tenn., July 2, 1933; s. Arthur Peter and Frances (Crawford) W.; m. Barbara Ann Strickland, July 20, 1957; 1 child, Mae Millicent. AB, Davidson Coll., 1957; PhD, Duke U., 1965. Asst. dir. data processing Hanes Hosiery, Winston Salem, NC, 1959-62; rsch. asst. in econs. Duke U., Durham, NC, 1963-64; asst. prof. econs. Washington and Lee U., Lexington, Va., 1965-68, assoc. prof., 1969-73, prof., 1974—. Vis. prof. Vanderbilt U., Nashville, 1966, Tufts U., Boston, 1975, UCLA, 1978, U. Ill., 1982, U. Va., 1986, Duke U., 1989, 95, U. Calif., Berkeley, 1993, U. Utrecht, Netherlands, 1995. Co-author: The Motion Commotion, 1972; author: Public Finance, Public Choice and the Public Sector, 1973, Social Issues, The Ethics and Economics of Taxes and Public Programs, 1997. Bd. dirs. Lexington Tennis Clinic, 1968-72, Rockbridge Area Conservation Coun., 1982-84, Rockbridge Area Social Svc., 2002—, Lexington Family Mentoring Program; mem. Rockbridge Area Behavioral Health Adv. Bd., 2001—; pres. Rockbridge Arts Guild, 1986-88, 2001-02. Recipient Cmty. Svc. award Lexington Jaycees, 1971; NEH fellow, 1975, 78, 82, 86, 89, 93; vis. fellow U. Coll. Oxford U., Eng., 1979, 95. Fellow Soc. for Values in Higher Edu.; mem. Am. Econ. Assn., So. Econ. Assn., History of Econs. Soc., Eastern Econ. Assn., High Wheelers Club

(Lexington), Sunrise Rotary Club. Democrat. Presbyterian. Home: 160 Kendal Dr #1035 Lexington VA 24450 Office: Washington and Lee U Dept Econs Lexington VA 24450 Business E-Mail: winfreyj@wlu.edu.

**WINFREY, MARCELLENE SEDETTA,** music educator, church musician; b. Chgo., Dec. 4, 1949; d. Arthur Semon and Nellye Mae Winfrey; m. Darryl Jones, Nov. 27, 1988 (div. Sept. 0, 1994); 1 child, Troy Lamar. B in Music Edn., Roosevelt U., 1980; MS in Elem. Edn., Xavier U., 1994. Cert. Orff-Schulwerk tchr. U. Cin., Coll. Conservatory Music, OH, 2004. Distbn. clk. USPS, Chgo., 1969—74; instr. Chgo. City Wide Coll., 1980—82; educator Chgo. Pub. Schs., 1982—87; adminstr. So. Bapt. Day Care, Cin., 1988—88; min. music Union Bapt. Ch., 1988—93; music specialist Cin. Pub. Schs., 1988—; ch. organist Quinn Chapel AME, 1994—97; ch. musician Allen Temple AME, 1997—. Mem. Local Sch. Dist. Mgmt. Com., Cin., 2004—. Mem., mentor Excel Club, Cin., 2004—05. Mem.: ASCD (assoc.), Ohio Music Educators Assn. (assoc.), Phi Delta Kappa (life). Avocations: travel, genealogy, gardening, walking, dance. Office: Western Hills HS 2144 Ferguson Rd Cincinnati OH 45238-3799 Office Fax: 513-363-8751. E-mail: winfrem@cpsboe.k12.oh.us.

**WINFREY, OPRAH,** television talk show host, actress, television producer; b. Kosciusko, Miss., Jan. 29, 1954; d. Vernon Winfrey and Vernita Lee. BA in Speech Comm. and Performing Arts, Tenn. State U. News reporter Sta. WVOL Radio, Nashville, 1971-72; reporter, news anchorperson Sta. WTVF-TV, Nashville, 1973-76; news anchorperson Sta. WJZ-TV, Balt., 1976—78, host morning talk show People Are Talking, 1978—83; host talk show A.M. Chgo. Sta. WLS-TV, 1984; host The Oprah Winfrey Show, Chgo., 1985—, Oprah After the Show, Chgo., 2002—; nationally syndicated, 1986—; host series of celebrity interview spls. Oprah: Behind the Scenes, owner, prodr., chmn., CEO Harpo Prodns., 1986—. Ptnr., co-founder Oxygen Media, an Internet and cable TV co., 1998—; founder, editl. dir. O, The Oprah Magazine in conjunction with Hearst Mags., 2000; launched (mag.)first internat. edit., O, The Oprah Magazine in South Africa, 2002-, Oprah, After the Show, 2002-, O at Home, 2004-, Oprah & Friends, XM Satelite Radio Holdings, Inc., 2006-; online leader, Oprah.com, launched Live Your Best Life, 2003-; started Oprah Book Club. Appeared in films The Color Purple, 1985 (nominated Acad. award and Golden Globe award), Native Son, 1986, There Are No Children Here, 1993, Beloved, 1998 (prodr.), About Us: The Dignity of Children, 1997 (TV), Before Women Had Wings, 1997 (TV; also prodr. ABC series Oprah Winfrey presents); prodr. Dr. Phil (TV series), 2002—; Listen Up: The Lives of Quincy Jones (TV spl.), 1990; prodr., actress ABC-TV mini-series The Women of Brewster Place, 1989, also series Brewster Place, 1990; co-prodr. The Color Purple (Broadway), 2005; exec. prodr. (ABC Movie of the Week) Overexposed, 1992; host, supervising prodr. celebrity interview series Oprah: Behind the Scenes, 1992, ABC Aftersch. Spls., 1991-93; host, exec. prodr. Michael Jackson Talks...to Oprah-90 Prime-Time Minutes with the King of Pop, 1993; exec. prodr. (TV) Nine, 1992, Oprah Winfrey Presents: Their Eyes Were Watching God, 2005; host Oprah Winfrey's Legends Ball, 2006; exec. prodr. TV miniseries: Oprah Winfrey Presents: The Wedding, 1998, David and Lisa, 1998, Tuesdays with Morrie, 1999, Amy and Isabelle, 2001, Their Eyes Were Watching God, 2005; voice (video) Our Friend, Martin, 1999; guest appearances The Fresh Prince of Bel-Air, 1992, Ellen, 1997, Home Improvement, 1999, The Hughleys, 1999, Mad TV, 2002 and several others. Established Oprah Winfrey Found., 1987—; Oprah's Angel Network, 1997—, ChristmasKindness South Africa, 2002—, Oprah Winfrey Scholars Program. Recipient Woman of Achievement award NOW, 1986, Emmy award for Best Daytime Talk Show Host, 1987, 91, 92, 94, 95, 97, Hon. Nat. Book Award for influential contbn. to reading and books, 1999, Nat. Book Found's 50th Anniversary gold medal, 1999, America's Hope award, 1990, Industry Achievement award Broadcast Promotion Mktg. Execs./Broadcast Design Assn., 1991, Image awards NAACP, 1989, 91, 92, 94, Entertainer of Yr. award NAACP, 1989. CEBA awards, 1989, 90, 91, George Foster Peabody's 1995 Individual Achievement award, 1996, Gold Medal award IRTS, 1996, Lifetime Achievement award NATAS, 1998, People's Choice award, 1997, 98, Horatio Alger award, 1993, Bob Hope Humanitarian award, 54th Ann. Primetime Emmy Awards, 2002, Marian Anderson Award, Phila., 2003, AAP Honors award, Assn. Am. Publishers, 2003, Disting. Svc. award, Nat. Assn. Broadcasters, 2004, Global Humanitarian Action award, UN Assn. U.S.A., 2004, Nat. Freedom award, Nat. Civil Rights Mus., 2005; ranked #1 Most Powerful In Industry, Entertainment Weekly, 1998, 200 Greatest Pop Culture Icons, VH1, 2003; named Broadcaster of Yr. Internat. Radio and TV Soc., 1988, TV Performer of Yr., TV Guide, 1997, Most Important Person in Books and Media, Newsweek, 1997; named one of 50 Most Beautiful in the World, People, 1997, America's 25 Most Influential People of the 20th Century, Time, 1998, 100 Most Powerful Women in Entertainment, Hollywood Reporter, 2004, 100 Most Influential People, Time Mag., 2004, 2005, Most Powerful Women, Forbes mag., 2005-2006, 50 Women to Watch, Wall St. Journal, 2005, 100 Most Influential People, Time Mag., 2006, 100 Most Influential Black Americans, Ebony mag., 2006; named to List American Billionaires, Fortune, 2003, 400 Richest Americans, 1999-, World's Richest People, 2003-; inducted to Television Hall of Fame, 1994, Broadcasting and Cable Hall of Fame, 2002, NAACP Hall of Fame, 2005; elected to Nat. Women's Hall of Fame, Seneca Falls, NY. Initiated a campaign to establish a national database of convicted child abusers, and testified before U.S. Senate Judiciary Committee on behalf of National Child Protection Act in 1991, as a result, President Clinton signed the "Oprah Bill" into Law on December 20, 1993, establishing the national database used by law enforcement agencies around the world; third woman in American entertainment industry to own her own studio; first African-American woman to reach billionaire status; after receiving Lifetime Acheivement Award in 1998, permanently withdrew name from Daytime Emmy Award consideration; Oprah and Oprah Winfrey Show received a total of 39 Daytime Emmy awards: seven for Outstanding Host; nine for Outstanding Talk Show; twenty one in the Creative Arts categories, and one for supervising producer of the ABC School Special, Shades of Single Protein; celebrated the 20th year anniversary of the Oprah Winfrey Show in November, 2005. Office: Oprah Winfrey Show Harpo Studios 1058 W Washington Blvd Chicago IL 60607 Address: Harpo Prodn PO Box 909715 Chicago IL 60607 Office Phone: 312-633-0808.*

**WING, ADRIEN KATHERINE,** law educator; b. Aug. 7, 1956; d. John Ellison and Katherine (Pruitt) Wing; children: Che-Cabral, Nolan Felipe. AB magna cum laude, Princeton U., 1978; MA, UCLA, 1979; JD, Stanford, 1982. Bar: N.Y. 1983, U.S. Dist. Ct. (so. and ea. dists.) N.Y. 1983, U.S. Ct. Appeals (5th and 9th cirs.). Assoc. Curtis, Mallet-Prevost, Colt & Mosle, N.Y.C., 1982-86, Rabinowitz, Boudin, Standard, Krinsky & Lieberman, 1986-87; assoc. prof. law U. Iowa, Iowa City, 1987-93, prof., 1993—, disting. prof. law, 2001—, assoc. dean faculty R&D, 2006—. Mem. alumni council Princeton U., 1983-85, 96-2000, mem. exec. com., 2002—, trustee Class of '78 Alumni Found., 1984-87, 93—; v.p. Princeton Class of 1978 Alumni, 1993-98, trustee Princeton U. 1995; mem. bd. visitors Stanford Law Sch., 1993-96; vis. prof. U. Mich., 2002. Mem. bd. editors Am. J. Comp. Law, 1993—. Mem. Iowa Commn. on African Ams. in Prisons, 1999—. Recipient Disting. Alum award, Newark Acad., 2004, Gertrude Rush award, 2006. Mem.: ABA (exec. com. young lawyers sect. 1985—87, law sch. site inspector 2002—), U.S. Assn. Constl. Law (bd. dir.), Am. Assn. of Law Schs. (minority sect. bd. 1996—, chair 2002), Am. Friends Svc. Com. (bd. dirs. Mid. East 1998—2004), Am. Soc. Internat. Law (exec. coun. 1986—89, exec. com. 1988—99, nominating com. 1991, 1993, group chair S. Africa 1993—95, membership com. 1994—95, exec. coun. 1996—99), Internat. Assn. Dem. Lawyers (UN rep. 1984—87), Nat. Conf. Black Lawyers (chmn. internat. affairs sect. 1982—95, UN rep.), Internat. Third World Legal Studies Assn. (bd. dirs. 1996—, nominating trustee Princeton com. 1997—2000), Coun. on Fgn. Rels., Iowa Peace Inst. (bd. dirs. 1993—95), Iowa City Fgn. Rels. Coun. (bd. dirs. 1989—94), Transafrica Scholars Forum Coun. (bd. dirs. 1993—95), Black Alumni of Princeton U. (bd. dirs. 1982—87). Democrat. Avocations: photography, writing, poetry. Office: U Iowa Sch Law Boyd Law Bldg Iowa City IA 52242 Office Phone: 319-335-9129. E-mail: adrien-wing@uiowa.edu.

**WING, JAMES DAVID,** lawyer; b. Milw., May 4, 1943; s. William H. and Elaine E. (Koehler) W.; children: Benjamin, Tracy, Nathaniel, John. BA, Beloit (Wis.) Coll., 1965; MA, U. Chgo., 1966, JD, 1969. Bar: Wis. 1969, Fla. 1975, U.S. Ct. Appeals (7th cir.) 1973, U.S. Dist. Ct. (mid. dist.) Fla. 1975, U.S. Ct. Appeals (5th cir.) 1978, U.S. Dist. Ct. (so. dist.) Fla. 1981, U.S. Ct. Appeals (11th cir.) 1981, U.S. Supreme Ct. 1979. Assoc. Whyte, Hirschboeck, Minahan, Harding & Harland, Milw., 1969-75, Carlton, Fields, Ward, Emmanuel, Smith & Cutler, Tampa, Fla., 1975-85, Myers, Kevin, Levinson, Frank & Richards/Shea & Gould, Miami, Fla., 1985-88, Fine, Jacobson, Schwartz, Nash, Block & England, Miami, 1988-94, Holland & Knight, Miami, 1994—. Fellow Ctr. for Internat. Legal Studies, Salzburg, Austria. Mem. Phi Beta Kappa, Phi Eta Sigma, Omicron Delta Kappa. Avocations: germanistics, tennis. Office: Holland & Knight LLP 701 Brickell Ave Ste 3000 Miami FL 33131 Fax: 305 789 7799. Office Phone: 305-374-8500, 305-789-7768. E-mail: james.wing@hklaw.com.

**WING, JOHN RUSSELL,** lawyer; b. Mt. Vernon, NY, Jan. 20, 1937; s. John R. and Elinore (Smith) W.; m. Mary Zeller, Aug. 24, 1963 (div. June 1975); children: Ethan Lincoln, Catherine Dorothy; m. Audrey Strauss, Aug. 12, 1979; children: Carlin Elinore, Matthew Lawrence. BA, Yale U., 1960; JD, U. Chgo., 1963. Bar: N.Y. 1964. Assoc. Sherman & Sterling, N.Y., 1963-66; U.S. atty. So. Dist. N.Y., N.Y.C., 1966-78; chief fraud unit U.S. Dist. Atty. So. Dist. N.Y., 1971-78; ptnr. Weil, Gotshal & Manges, N.Y.C., 1978—. Contbr. articles to profl. jours. Fellow Am. Coll. Trial Lawyers; mem. ABA (white collar crime com. criminal justice sect. 1978—, environ. task force com. 1983-85), Assn. Bar of City of N.Y. (criminal advocacy com. 1985-88), Fed. Bar Coun. (2d cir. cts. com. 1982-84), N.Y. Coun. Def. Lawyers (bd. dirs. 1986-90). Republican. Episcopalian. Avocation: sailing. Home: 52 Livingston St Brooklyn NY 11201-4813 Office: Weil Gotshal & Manges 767 5th Ave Fl Concl New York NY 10153-0119 Office Phone: 212-310-8364. Business E-Mail: john.wing@weil.com.

**WING, KENNARD THOMPSON,** educational organization official; b. Mobile, Ala., May 27, 1956; s. Kennard Loren and Phyllis Ellen (Thompson) W.; m. Cara Maureen McMenamin, Dec. 27, 1986; children: Thomas, Sara, James. BS, Brown U., 1978; MS, U. Pa., 1989. Cert. mgmt. acct. Statis. mgr. Gimbels, Phila., 1978-80; programmer, analyst Chase Econometrics, Bala Cynwyd, Pa., 1980-82; product mgr. Wharton Econometrics, Phila., 1982-84, acct. mgr., 1985-87; v.p. Thompson-Mayer, Phila., 1984-85; project dir. Interact, Bala Cynwyd, 1987-93; lectr. U. Pa., Phila., 1990-95; owner Kennard T. Wing & Co., Havertown, Pa., 1993-98, 2003—; project dir. OMG Ctr. for Collaborative Learning, Phila., 1998—2003. Adv. bd. Weston Inst., West Chester, Pa., 1988—89; adj. prof. Immaculata Coll., 2000. Contbr. articles to profl. jours. Co-founder Township Green, Haverford, Pa., 1990; vol. West Chester Small Bus. Devel. Ctr., Exton, Pa., 1991; pres. Haverford Twp. Adult Sch., 1994-95. Recipient Silver award, Soc. of Nat. Assn. Publs., 2003. Mem. Inst. Mgmt. Accts. Office: Kennard T Wing & Co 224 Kathmere Rd Havertown PA 19083

**WINGARD, CHRISTINE,** music educator; b. Chambersburg, Pa., Apr. 20, 1958; d. Jay Nelson and Jean Angie Wengert; m. Charles Edward Wingard, Aug. 13, 1983; children: Sarah, Andrew. MusB, Bridgewater Coll., 1980; MusM, James Madison U., 1990. Music tchr. Page County Pub. Sch., Luray, Va., 1980—85, sub. music tchr., 1988; pvt. piano instr. Harrisonburg, Va., 1980—91, 1996—2006. Tchr. Yamaha Music, Harrisonburg, 1991—96. Republican. Presbyn. Avocations: cooking, skiing, bicycling, cross stitch. Home: 1845 Park Rd Harrisonburg VA 22802

**WINGARD, JOHN REID,** medical educator; b. Charleston, S.C., Jan. 30, 1947; m. Frances Diane Phillips, 1974; children: Ellen, Emily, Sally, Benjamin. BA in English, Yale U., 1969; MD, The Johns Hopkins U., 1973. Diplomate Am. Bd. Internal Medicine, subspecialty of Med. Oncology. Intern City of Memphis Hosp./U. Tenn. Ctr. for Health Scis., 1973-74, resident, 1974-76; chief resident V.A. Hosp., Memphis, 1976-77; instr. in medicine U. Tenn. Ctr. for Health Scis., Memphis, 1976-77; fellow in oncology and internal medicine The Johns Hopkins U. Sch. Medicine, Balt., 1977-79, various to asst. prof. oncology, 1977-87, assoc. prof. oncology, 1987-91, assoc. prof. medicine, 1990-91; prof. medicine Emory U. Sch. Medicine, Atlanta, 1991-96, prof. Winship Cancer Ctr., 1992-96; dir. bone marrow transplant program, prof. medicine U. Fla., Gainesville, 1996—; dep. dir. U. Fla. Shands Cancer Ctr., 2004—. Dir. bone marrow transplant program Emory U. Sch. Medicine, 1991-96; dir. Bone Marrow Transplant Outpatient Clinic, Johns Hopkins Oncology Ctr., 1984-91; cons. Office of Disability Programs, Social Security Adminstrn., Balt., 1981-91; study group Nat. Inst. Allergy and Infectious Diseases, 1988—; adv. com. Internat. Bone Marrow Transplant Registry, 1989-91, 95—; sec.-treas., 1998—; chair, steering com. Blood and Marrow Transplant Clin. Trials Network, 2001—; bd. dirs. Found. Cellular Therapies. Contbr. articles to profl. jours.; contbr. chpts. to books; assoc. editor: Biology of Blood and Marrow Transplantation. Mem. Am. Soc. Microbiology, Am. Soc. Clin. Oncology, Am. Soc. Hematology, Internat. Soc. Exptl. Hematology, Am. Soc. Blood and Marrow Transplantation (pres. 2002-2003). Office: U Fla Coll Medicine PO Box 100277 Gainesville FL 32610-0277 Business E-Mail: wingajr@medicine.ufl.edu.

**WINGATE, BETTYE FAYE,** librarian, educator; b. Hillsboro, Tex., Oct. 31, 1950; d. Warren Randolph and Faye (Gilmore) W. BA summa cum laude, Baylor U., 1971; MA, 1975; MLS, Tex. Woman's U., 1985. Cert. prov. sec., learning resources endorsement. English tchr. Mexia HS, Tex.; reading tchr. Connally Ind. Sch. Dist., Waco, Tex.; reading tchr., libr. Grapevine-Colleyville Ind. Sch. Dist., Grapevine, Tex.; libr., ret., May 02 Crockett Mid. Sch., Irving, Tex. Mem. librs. coms., Campus Action Planning Com., 1989-93, Irving Ind. Sch. Dist. Site Based Decision-Making Com., 1992-94, mem. staff devel. coun., 1994-96, chair media fair com., 1996-2001; rev. Linworth Pub.; spkr., presenter in field. Founding sponsor Challenger Ctr., Air Force Meml. Found. Recipient Tex. Media awards, 1988, 89, 91. Mem. ALA, NEA, Am. Assn. Sch. Libr. (vol. libr. Kids Connect), Tex. State Tchr. Assn. (assn. rep.), Tex. Libr. Assn. (chmn. state media awards com. 1989-91), Tex. Assn. Edn. Tech., Computer Edn. and Tech., Assn. Ednl. Comm. and Tech., Planetary Soc., Nat. Space Soc., Nat. Parks & Conservation Assn., Baylor Alumni Assn., librs. (life), Wilderness Soc., Sierra Club, Beta Phi Mu, Delta Kappa Gamma (scholar 1985). E-mail: bettye.winate@yahoo.com.

**WINGATE, C. KEITH,** law educator; b. Darlington, SC, May 12, 1953; s. Clarence L. and Lilly W.; m. Gloria Farley; stepchildren: Brenda, Marvin, Terry and Oliver Champion. BA in Polit. Sci., U. Ill., 1974, JD cum laude, 1978. Bar: Calif., 1978. Assoc. litigation dept. Morrison & Foerster, San Francisco, 1978-80; from asst. to assoc. prof. law U. Calif.-Hastings, San Francisco, 1980-86, prof., 1986—. Dir. Coun. Legal Edn. Opportunity Region I Inst., 1989; vis. prof. law Stanford Law Sch., fall 1990, 94, spring 1998; chair Minority Law Tchrs.' Conf. Com., 1990; mem. acad. assistance work group, 1991; trustee Law Sch. Admission Coun., 1997-2001. Author: (with David I. Levine and William R. Slomanson) Cases and Materials on California Civil Procedure, 1991, (with William R. Slomanson) California Civil Procedure in a Nutshell, 1992, (with Donald L. Doernberg) Federal Courts, Federalism and Separation of Powers, 1994, 2nd edit., 2000. Bd. dirs. Cmty. Housing Devel. Corp., North Richmond, 1990-99. Recipient 10 Outstanding Persons award U. Ill. Black Alumni Assn., 1980; Harno fellow U. Ill., Coll. of Law, 1976. Mem. Assn. Am. Law Schs. (chair sect. minority groups 1990, exec. com. mem. sect. civil proceedure 1991), Charles Houston Bar Assn., Phi Sigma Alpha. Office: U Calif Hastings Coll Law 200 Mcallister St San Francisco CA 94102-4707

**WINGATE, CONSTANCE BLANDY,** retired librarian; b. Woodbury, N.J., Mar. 7, 1935; d. John Chase and Josephine Spond (Black) Blandy; m. Len B. Cooke Jr., 1978 (div. 1987); m. John B. Wingate, Mar. 12, 1999. BA, U. Pa., 1956; MA, U. Denver, 1957. Adult cons. Onondaga Library System, Syracuse, 1965-66; asst. dir. Mt. Vernon (N.Y.) Public Library, 1966-75; dep. dir. Queens Borough Public Library, Jamaica, NY, 1975-79, dir., 1980-94, ret., 1994. Founder pres. Literacy Vols. Mt. Vernon, 1972-74. Trustee METRO, 1980-91, v.p., 1985-88, pres., 1988-91; mem. N.Y. State Libr. Svcs.

and Constrn. Act Adv. Coun., 1982-88, chmn., 1986-87; bd. dirs. Queens Coun. on the Arts, 1988-94, v.p., 1989-93; bd. dirs. Queens Mus. of Art, 1988-98, v.p., 1994-96, pres. 1996-98; bd. dirs. Queens Libr. Found., 1996-2003. Mem.: ALA, Circumnavigators Club (internat. sec. 2002—06, internat. bd. govs. 2006—). Republican. Episcopalian. Home: 166-25 Powells Cove Blvd Beechhurst NY 11357

**WINGATE, ROBERT LEE, JR.,** internist; b. Columbia, S.C., May 28, 1936; s. Robert Lee and Helen (Owen) W.; m. Ritanne Cooper, Apr. 19, 1962 (div. 1965); 1 child, Elizabeth Anne Butterfield-Wingate; m. Jeannette DeLatte, Mar. 27, 1968 (div. 1980); children: Laura Owen Wingate, Charlotte Cramer; m. Ann Phyfer, Apr. 1, 1999; 1 child, Jeff Stamm. BS, U. S.C., 1957; MD, Med. Coll. S.C., 1961. Intern Cin. Gen. Hosp., 1961-62, jr. resident internal medicine 1964-65; asst. resident in internal medicine Med. Coll. of Va., Richmond, 1965-66; resident in internal medicine Charity Hosp. of La., New Orleans, 1966-67, resident in neurology, 1967-68; pvt. practice Columbia, 1968-78; PruCare physician Memphis, 1983-85; med. dir. M. Lowennstein and Celanese Corps., Rock Hill, SC, 1978-80; med. dir. nursing home care unit Dorn VA Hosp., Columbia, 1980-82; med. cons. disability determination div. Vocat. Rehab. S.C., 1982-83; cons. Student Health Ctr. U. S.C., Columbia, 1985-86; cons. Urgent Care Ctrs. S.C., 1986-87; pvt. practice Pelion, SC, 1987-92; staff internist, chief of staff, cons. internal medicine Western Mental Health Inst., Western Institute, Tenn., 1992-2000; with Memphis Mental Health Inst., 2000—03. Med. dir. Forest Hills Nursing Ctr., Columbia, 1968-78; med. cons. S.C. Commn. for Blind, Columbia, 1970-78, Mid-Carolina Coun. on Alcoholism, Columbia, 1970-74; instr. internal medicine U. S.C. Sch. Medicine, 1980-82; cons. internal medicine and urgent care Pelion Cmty. Care Ctr., 1989-92; instr. Sch. Nursing, Med. Coll. S.C., Winthrop divsn., 1978-80; lectr. in field; mem. adv. bd. Vector Med. Techs. and Nutrition Superstores; cardiology cons. Western Mental Health Inst., 2000-2003; pvt. practice gen. internal medicine, 2003. Contbr. articles to newspapers; reviewer Annal of Internal Medicine. Ofcl. physician Peanut Party S.C., 1990-92. Lt. comdr. M.C., USNR, 1958-66. Grantee Burroughs-Wellcome Co., 1958, Med. Coll. S.C., 1960, Congress of U.S. 1987. Fellow ACP; mem. AMA (life mem.), Physician's Recognition award 1969, 74, 79, 85, 86, 94-96, 96-99, 99-2002), Am. Soc. Internal Medicine, Am. Occupational Med. Assn., So. Med. Assn., West Tenn. Consolidated Med. Assembly, Soc. of 1824, State of Tenn. Med. Assn.Consol. Med. Assembly of West Tenn. Avocations: chess, hunting, fishing, gardening, billiards.

**WINGBLADE, LOREN CHARLES,** education educator; b. Chgo., Dec. 23, 1941; s. Loren Milton and Wanda S. Wingblade; m. Susan Leah Bozarth, Apr. 4, 1970. BS in Zoology, U. Wis., Madison, 1966; MA in Psychology, No. Ill. U., DeKalb, 1970; PhD in Psychology, Ind. U., Bloomington, 1977, MA in Sociology, 1988. Cert. bioethics Med. Coll. Wis.-Milw. Asst. prof. Westminster Coll., Fulton, Mo., 1977—83; vis. prof. Ind. U., 1983—89; prof. Jackson C.C., Mich., 1989—. Tchr. Ind. U.; Purdue U.; adj. instr. Siena Heights U. Mem. bioethics com. W.A. Foote Hosp., Jackson, 2001—. Mem.: North Ctrl. Sociol. Assn., Midwest Sociol. Assn., Carnegie Coun. on Ethics and Internat. Affairs, NEA, Am. Assn. for the Advancement of Sci., Am. Soc. Bioethics and Humanities, Am. Sociol. Asn., APA. Democrat. Lutheran. Achievements include development of IBM-PC exericzes for introductory psychology lab, assessment tool for introductory sociology course. Office: Jackson CC 2111 Emmons Rd Jackson MI 49201 Business E-Mail: loren_c_wingblade@jccmi.edu.

**WINGER, DEBRA,** actress; b. Cleve., May 16, 1955; d. Robert and Ruth W.; m. Timothy Hutton, March 16, 1986 (div.); 1 child, Emanuel Noah; m. Arliss Howard, Nov. 28, 1996; 1 child, Gideon Babe. Student, Calif. State U., Northridge. Made 1st profl. appearance in Wonder Woman TV series, 1976-77; appeared TV film Spl. Olympics, 1977; appeared in films Thank God It's Friday, 1978, French Postcards, 1979, Urban Cowboy, 1980, Cannery Row, 1982, An Officer and a Gentleman, 1982, Terms of Endearment, 1983, Mike's Murder, 1984, Legal Eagles, 1986, Black Widow, 1987, Made in Heaven, 1987, Betrayed, 1988, Everybody Wins, 1990, The Sheltering Sky, 1990, Leap of Faith, 1992, Wilder Napalm, 1992, Shadowlands, 1993 (Academy award nominee, Best Actress, 1993), A Dangerous Woman, 1993, Forget Paris, 1995, In the Wild: Pandas, 1995, Big Bad Love, 2001, Radio, 2003, Eulogy, 2004, (TV films) The Wizard of Oz in Concert: Dreams Come True, 1995; voice: Rumi: Poet of the Heart, 1998. Active Israel Def. Forces, 1972—73. Recipient Female Star of Yr. award, NATO, 1984. Office: care Creative Artists Agency 9830 Wilshire Blvd Beverly Hills CA 90212-1804

**WINGER, ROGER ELSON,** retired church administrator; b. Fisherville, Ont., Can., Dec. 25, 1933; s. Elson Clare and Bertha Caroline (Schweyer) W.; m. Della Bertha Lebien, June 7, 1958; children: Jeffrey, Karen Mohr, David, Thomas, Susan. AA, Concordia Jr. Coll., Ft. Wayne, Ind., 1953; BA, Concordia Sem., St. Louis, 1955, theol. diploma, 1958; DD (hon.), Concordia Luth. Sem., Edmonton, Alta., Can., 1991. Ordained to ministry, Luth. Ch., 1958. Pastor Holy Trinity Luth. Ch., London, 1958-64, Good Shepherd Luth. Ch., Coventry, Eng., 1964-69, Luth. Mission, Liverpool, Eng., 1969-72, Faith Luth. Ch., Dunnville, Ont., 1972-78, St. Matthew Luth. Ch., Smithville, Ont., 1972-78, St. Paul's Luth. Ch., Kitchener, Ont., 1978-91; pres. ea. dist. Luth. Ch.-Can., Kitchener, 1991-2000; ret., 2000. V.p. Ont. dist. Luth. Ch.-Can., 1982-88; sec. Luth. Ch.-Can., Winnipeg, Man., 1988-91; mem. bd. regents Concordia Luth. Sem., Edmonton, Alta., 1984-88, Concordia Luth. Sem., St. Catharines Ont., 1991-2000; bd. govs. Lutherwood; bd. dirs. Luth. Bible Translators Can. Lutheran. Avocations: photography, golf, woodworking. Home: 76 Deerwood Crescent Kitchener ON Canada N2N 1R3 E-mail: rogerdella@rogers.com.

**WINGERT, MICHAEL J.,** computer company executive; BSEE, Univ. Minn. With Maxtor Corp., Milpitas, Calif., 1994—96, v.p. engring., 1996—99, v.p. desktop engring., 1999—2001, sr. v.p. engring., 2001—04; pres., COO, CEO Cornice Inc., Longmont, Colo., 2004; pres., COO Maxtor Corp., Milpitas, Calif., 2004—06; exec. v.p. Maxtor integration Seagate Tech., Scotts Valley, Calif., 2006. Office: Seagate Technology 920 Disc Dr Scotts Valley CA 95066*

**WINGET, LARRY J., SR.,** automotive industry executive; Chmn., CEO, pres. Venture Global Engring. Indus., Fraser, Mich. Office: Venture PO Box 278 Fraser MI 48026-0278*

**WINICK, BERNYCE ALPERT,** artist, photographer; b. NYC; Student, Bklyn. Mus. Art Sch., 1938—41; BA in Fine Arts and Music, NYU; pvt. studies with, Mario Cooper, N.Y.C., 1969—86; student, Traphagen Sch. Fashion, 1958—61, Art Students League N.Y., 1961—64, Nat. Acad. Design Sch. Fine Arts, 1968—72. Artist, Woodmere, L.I., N.Y., 1969—. Designer, fashion artist, fashion con. in field. One-woman shows include Hewlett-Woodmere Pub. Libr., LI, 1969, Galerie Internat., NY, 1977, Thomas Moran (First prize Nat. Acad. Sch., 1972, Salmagundi Club 1981, 87, 90, Nat. Arts Club, 1985, Nat. Acad. Sch., 1972, First Prize Meml. award 2002), Gallery Internat. 57, NY, 1989, Discovery Art Gallery, Sea Cliff, LI, 1989, 96, 98, Glen Cove, NY, 1993-94, Chelsea Ctr., East Norwich, NY, 1993, 96, 98, 2000, 02, Z Gallery, SoHo, NY, 1994, County Exec. Bldg., 1997, Fine Arts Mus. LI, 1997, Town Hall, Hempstead, NY, 2000, Nat. Arts Club., NY 2002, NY Inst. Tech., 2004, Wisser Meml. Libr., 2003, N.Y. Inst. Tech., 2004; exhibited in group shows at Discovery Art Gallery, Glen Cove, NY, 1988, 91-93, 1996, 2000, 02, Nat. Acad. Sch. Fine Arts, NY, 1972, Long Beach Mus. LI, 1979, 81-85, 89 (2d prize 1989), Chen Chung Gallery of St. John's U., NY, 1980, Salmagundi Club, NY, 1980-81, 2002 (Thomas Moran Meml. award, 1st prize), Am. Watercolor Soc., NY, 1982, 85, 88, 92, Fine Arts Mus. LI, 1983, 88-89, 91-92, 96 (2d prize), 97, Nat. Arts Club, NY, 1985-86, 88-89, 2002, Nassau County Mus., LI, 1985-86, 88, Nat. Assn. Women Artists, NY, 1986, 88, 91-93, C.W. Post Coll., LI, LI Arts Coun. Freeport, 1995-96, 1999 (First prize in black and white photography), 2006 (Fabian Adler Meml. award), Chelsea Cultural Ctr., NY, 1995, 2001, (Suburban Art League award), Rockville Ctr. Guild for the Arts, NY, 1995, 97 (Best in Show for

photography), Chelsea Ctr. (Peacock Showcase award, First prize 2000), (Merit award 2001), East Norwich, NY, Discovery Art Gallery, Sea Cliff, NY, 1998, Canton Art Inst. Ohio, Galerie Internat., Gallery Internat. 57, Z Gallery, Salle Augustin-Chenier, Quebec, Can., Town Hall, Town of Hempstead, NY, 2000, NY Inst. Tech.; Wisser Meml. Libr., 2001, Nat. Arts Club (First photography prize 2002), Heckscher Mus., Huntington, NY, 2003, Mills Pond House, St. James, NY, 2002, 05 (1st prize watercolor), Nat. Arts Club, NY, 2001 (1st prize), NY Inst. Tech. Wissen Meml. Libr., Old Westbury, 2004, others; work included in U.S. Dept. State Art in Embassies program, pvt. and corp. collections; photographs in publs. including South Shore Record, 1995, Encyclopedia of Watercolour Landscape Techniques, 1996, Popular Photography, 1996-97, 99-2000, 04, Photography on America Online, 1997, 99-2000, New York: Sterling Pub. Co., Inc., 1998, Watercolor Planning and Painting, 1998, Abstracts in Watercolor, 1996, NY Times, 1999, 2001, NY Inst. Tech., 2003, Wisser Meml. Libr., Old Westbury, NY, 2004, Mills Pond House, St. James, NY, 2005 (1st prize watercolor); photography in (books) Capturing the Seen and Unseen in Photographs, 2001, Thirty Nine Musical Photographs, 2003, Town and Country Mag.; photographs exhibited in Mill Pond House, Salmagundi Club, NYU, Nat. Assn. Women Artists, Artists Unlimited, Tampa, Fla. Recipient award, Salmagundi Club, 2004, 2005, other awards, Fabian Adler Meml. award, L.I. Arts Coun., 2006. Fellow Royal Soc. Encouragement Arts Manufactures and Commerce (London); mem. Am. Watercolor Soc., Nat. Assn. Women Artists, Tri County Artists, Long Beach Art League, Nat. Arts Club, Salmagundi Club, Harvard Club and Arts Group. Avocations: fashion design, piano, poetry. Home and Office: 923 Beth Ln Woodmere NY 11598-1507

**WINICK, MYRON,** nutrition professor, physician; b. NYC, May 4, 1929; s. Charles B. and Ruth E. (Gesser) W.; m. Elaine L. Lasky, Sept. 19, 1964; children: Jonathan, Stephen. AB, Columbia U., 1951; MS, U. Ill., 1952; MD, SUNY, 1956. Intern U. Pa., Phila., 1956-57; asst. resident pediatrics Cornell U. Med. Coll., N.Y.C., 1957-59, chief resident, 1959-60; attending pediatrician Stanford U. Hosp., 1963-64; asst. prof. pediatrics Cornell U. Med. Coll., N.Y.C., 1964-68, assoc. prof. pediatrics and nutrition, 1968-70, prof., 1970-71; dir. Inst. Human Nutrition Columbia U. Inst. Human Nutrition, 1972-87, prof. pediatrics, 1972-89, R.R. Williams prof. nutrition, 1973-89, R.R. Williams prof. emeritus, 1990—; pres. U. Health Scis./Chgo. Med. Sch., North Chgo., Ill., 1990-93; dir. Ctr. for Nutrition, Genetics and Human Devel., 1975-87. Vis. prof. pediatrics U. Chile, Santiago, 1967; asst. attending pediatrician NY Hosp., NYC, 1964-68, assoc. attending pediatrician, 1968-70, attending pediatrician, 1970-71; attending pediatrician Presbyn. Hosp., NYC, 1972-89; cons. Pan Am. Health Orgn., 1966—; med. dir. Weight Watchers Internat., 1997—; sr. scientist Am. Health Found., 1999—. Author: Malnutrition and Brain Development, 1976; textbook Nutrition in Health and Disease, 1980; Growing Up Healthy, A Parent's Guide to Good Nutrition, 1982; For Mothers and Daughters: A Guide to Good Nutrition for Women, 1983; Your Personalized Health Profile: Choosing the Diet That's Right for You, 1985; Nutrition, Pregnancy and Early Infancy, 1989; The Fiber Prescription, 1992; editor: textbook Current Concepts in Nutrition, 1972—, Nutrition: Pre- and Postnatal Development, Vol. I, Human Nutrition: A Comprehensive Treatise, 1979, Columbia Ency. of Nutrition, 1988, (with Joan Lunden) Growing Up Healthy, 2004; contbg. editor Nutrition Revs., 1969-76; mem. editorial bd. Jour. Nutrition, 1972-76, 82-86, The Year in Metabolism (now Contemporary Metabolism), 1975—; assoc. editor Growth, 1984—; nutrition editor Cancer Prevention, 1994—. Trustee Found. for Internat. Child Health; mem. nutrition interdisciplinary cluster Pres.' Biomed. Research Panel, 1975; mem. panel on infants and children Pres.' Commn. on Mental Health, 1977; cons. Office of Tech. Assessment, U.S. Congress, 1976-78; mem. Food and Nutrition Bd. NRC, 1982-88. With USNR, 1960-62. Bank of Am.-Gianini Found. fellow Stanford, 1962; NIH Spl. fellow, 1963; recipient NIH Career Devel. award, 1968-71; E. Mead Johnson award pediatric research, 1970; Osborne and Mendel award Am. Inst. Nutrition, 1976; Agnes Higgins award March of Dimes Found., 1983 Fellow Royal Soc. Health, Am. Soc. Nutritional Scis., Am. Acad. Pediatrics; mem. AAAS, Am. Soc. Cell Biology, Soc. Developmental Biology, Harvey Soc., Soc. Pediatric Rsch., Royal Soc. Medicine, Brit. Nutrition Soc., Am. Soc. Clin. Nutrition, NY Acad. Scis., NY Acad. Medicine, (cons.), Soc. for Exptl. Biology and Medicine, Soc. for Neurosci., Internat. Soc. for Devel. Neurosci., Cosmos Club. Home: 165 West End Ave Apt 10K New York NY 10023

**WINICOV, ILGA BUTELIS,** biochemist, educator; b. Riga, Latvia, May 16, 1935; d. Arturs and Zenta (Gutmanis) Butelis; m. Herbert B. Winicov, Aug. 30, 1958 (div. 1979); children: Eric, Mark; m. Rodney E. Harrington, Jan. 26, 1979. AB, U. Pa., Phila., 1956, PhD, 1971; MS, U. Wis., Madison, 1958. Postdoctoral fellow Inst. Cancer Rsch., Phila., 1972-74, rsch. assoc., 1974-76; rsch. asst. prof. biochemistry Fels Rsch. Inst., Temple U., Phila., 1976-78; asst. prof. U. Nev. Sch. Medicine, Reno, 1979-85, assoc. prof., 1985-95, assoc. prof. microbiology, 1987-95, prof. biochemistry and microbiology, 1995-99; rsch. prof. plant biology Ariz. State U., Tempe, 1999—2002, ret., 2002—. Cons. biochemistry nucleic acids and molecular biology and plant biotechnology. Contbr. articles to profl. jours. Fellow: AAAS; mem.: Am. Soc. Plant Biologists, Internat. Soc. Plant Molecular Biology, Am. Assn. Cancer Rsch., Am. Soc. Microbiology, Am. Soc. Biol. Chemists. Achievements include patents in field. Business E-Mail: winicov@asu.edu.

**WINIK, JOANNE,** broadcast executive; BA, Dominican Coll. Continuity dir. KONO/KITY; auction mgr. KLRN-TV, San Antonio, 1972, pres., gen. mgr., 1987—. Board of directors PBS, 1999—. Recipient District 55 Comm. & Leadership Award, 2002—03. Office: KLRN-TV PO Box 9 San Antonio TX 78291-0009

**WINJUM, STEPHEN J.,** medical association administrator; b. Long Beach, Calif., 1963; BSBA cum laude in Acctg., Creighton U., 1985; JD cum laude, U. Notre Dame, 1988. Atty. Latham & Watkins, Katten Muchin Zavis Rosenman; prin., owner Chgo., 1990—94; founder NovaMed Eyecare Inc., Chgo., 1995—, pres., 1995—, CEO, 1995—, chmn. bd. Office: Novamed Eyecare Inc 3034 West Peterson Ave Chicago IL 60659

**WINKEL, RAYMOND NORMAN,** aerospace scientist, consultant, retired military officer; b. Flint, Mich., Dec. 8, 1928; s. Norman Martin and Evelyn Matilda (Hylen) W.; m. Ellen Stefula, Dec. 29, 1955 (dec. Feb. 2006); children: Raymond Norman, Ann, Maryellen. BS, U.S. Naval Postgrad. Sch., Monterey, Calif., 1964; MS, Villanova U., Pa., 1967; grad. advanced mgmt. program, Harvard U., 1973. Enlisted in USN, 1948, commd. ensign, designated naval aviator, 1951, advanced through grades to rear adm., 1979; service in Far East; comdg. officer Naval Electronics Systems Test and Evaluation Facility St. Inigoes, Md., 1969-71; dir. avionics US Navy, 1973-76; project mgr. Navy/Marine Corps heavy lift helicopter, 1976-78; gen. mgr. Navy/industry team to develop new ship/aircraft weapon system for anti-submarine warfare LAMPS Mark III, 1978-81; ret. USN, 1981; v.p. Washington ops. Telephonics Corp., Huntington, NY, 1981-82; v.p. programs and contracts Astronautics Corp. Am., Milw., 1982-94; aerospace industry cons. Heathsville, Va., 1994-95. Decorated Legion of Merit, Air medal, Navy Achievement medal. Mem. Exptl. Aircraft Assn., U.S. Naval Inst., Assn. Naval Aviation, Mil. Officers Assn. Am., Kiwanis, Indian Creek Yacht and Country Club, U.S. Power Squadron. Republican. Roman Catholic. Home: 1860 Island Point Rd Heathsville VA 22473-3729 E-mail: rwinkel@crosslink.net

**WINKELMANN, KURT JOSEPH,** science educator; BS, Va. Tech. U., 1995; PhD, Auburn U., 2000. Instr. Auburn (Ala.) U., 2000; postdoctoral rschr. Northwestern U., Evanston, Ill., 2000-01; asst. prof. Fla. Inst. Tech., Melbourne, 2001—. Office: Fla Inst Tech 150 W University Blvd Melbourne FL 32901 Office Phone: 321-674-7376.

**WINKELRIED, JON A.,** investment banker; b. Milburn, NJ, 1959; m. Abby Ellen Lipsey, Feb. 23, 1986. AB, U. of Chicago, 1981, MBA, 1982. Joined Goldman, Sachs & Co., Chgo., 1982, ptnr., 1990, head leveraged fin., 1995, mem. mgmt. com., 1999—, global co-head fixed income, currency and

commodities London, 2000; co-head investment banking divsn. The Goldman Sachs Group, Inc., 2005—06, pres., co-COO NYC, 2006—. Office: The Goldman Sachs Group Inc 85 Broad St New York NY 10004*

**WINKELSTEIN, WARREN, JR.,** physician, educator; b. Syracuse, NY, July 1, 1922; s. Warren and Evelyn (Neiman) W.; children: Rebecca Winkelstein Yamin, Joshua, Shoshana; m. Veva Kerrigan, Feb. 14, 1976. BA, U. N.C., 1942; MD cum laude, Syracuse U., 1947; MPH, Columbia U., 1950. Diplomate Am. Bd. Preventive Medicine. Intern Charity Hosp., New Orleans, 1947-48; with ICA (Vietnam), 1951-53; from dir. div. communicable disease control to 1st dep. comdr. local, environ. health svcs. Erie County Health Dept., 1953-62; from assoc. prof. to prof. SUNY, Buffalo, 1962-68; prof. epidemiology, dean pub. health U. Calif., Berkeley, 1972-96, prof. emeritus, 1996. Dir. Internat. Environ. Epidemiology Inst., 1997. Author: Basic Readings in Epidemiology, 1972; contbr. articles profl. jours. With AUS, 1944-46. Mem. APHA, AAAS, Internat. Am. Epidemiol. Socs., Am. Heart Assn. Address: Dept Epidemiol Univ Calif Sch Pub Health Berkeley CA 94720-7360

**WINKENWERDER, WILLIAM, JR.,** federal agency administrator; b. Ashville, NC, Apr. 27, 1954; BS, Davidson Coll., 1976; MD, U. N.C., 1981; MBA, U. Pa., 1986; postgrad., Stanford U., 1991. Resident internal medicine N.C. Meml. Hosp. U. N.C., 1981-84; instr. dept. medicine Sch. Medicine U. Pa., 1984-87; spl. asst. to adminstr. Health Care Financing Adminstrn. U.S. Dept. Health and Human Svcs., 1987-88; dir. quality assurance and utilization mgmt. Southeast Permanente Med. Group, Kaiser Permanente, Atlanta, 1988-90, assoc. med. dir., 1990-92; v.p. CMO so. ops. Prudential Health Care, Atlanta, 1992-95; v.p. primary care svcs. Emory Health Care, Atlanta, 1996-98; assoc. v.p. health affairs Robert Woodruff Health Scis. Ctr. Emory U., 1996-98; exec. v.p. health care svcs., vice chmn. Blue Cross Blue Shield Mass., Boston, 1998—; asst. sec. health affairs U.S. Dept. Def., Washington, 2001—. Mem. exec. com. Emory Healthcare, Emory Clinic, 1996-98; chmn. CMO com. Prudential Healthcare, 1992-95; bd. dirs. Care Sci. Corp., Wharton Sch. Bus. Health Care Alumni, Fed. Employees Program-Blue Cross Blue Shield Assn., The Reed and Barton Co.; founder HCFA Effectiveness Initiative, U.S. Dept. Health and Human Svcs., participant Task Forces on Health and Human Svcs. AIDS and Minority Health, 1987-88, U.S. Pub. Health Risk Assessment and Quality Assurance, Sec.'s Minority Health, Sec.'s Catastrophic Illness; rep. Prudential on Med. Dirs. Com. on Group Health Assn. Am.; spkr. in field. Contbr. articles to profl. jours. Kaiser Family Found. fellow, 1984-86, 87-88, Kellogg Pub. Health Policy fellow U. Pa., 1986, Wharton Washington fellow U. Pa., 1986. Mem.: AMA, Am. Soc. Internal Medicine, Health Care Forum's Physician Leader Network, Am. Assn. Health Plans (bd. dirs.), Am. Coll. Physician Execs., Am. Coll. Physicians, Davidson Coll. Alumni Assn. Office: US Dept Def Health Affairs 1200 Defense Pentagon Washington DC 20301-1200*

**WINKLEBACK, ARTHUR,** food products executive; BA in Bus. and Econs., UCLA; MBA, U. Pa. Exec. v.p., CFO C. Dean Metropoulos & Co., 1998—99; acting COO Perform.com, 1999—2001; CEO Freeride.com at Indigo Capital, 1999—2001; exec. v.p., CFO H.J. Heinz Co., Pitts., 2002—. Office: HJ Heinz Co 600 Grant St Pittsburgh PA 15219

**WINKLEBLECH, EILEEN,** computer technology educator, career planning administrator; b. Newark, N.J., Dec. 17, 1966; d. William John Glagola and Rose Sharon Reed; m. Vincent Anthony Winkleblech, July 12, 1992; children: Zachary Charles, Erik William, Cameron Allan. B in Edn., Caldwell Coll., NJ, 1988. Cert. Tchr. of Elem. Edn. N.J. State Dept. of Edn., 1988. Self-contained multidisciplinary instr. grade 8 Wash. Sch., Harrison, NJ, 1988—89, life skills, health, career edn., computer tech. edn. instr., 1999—2002; adult a.c.e. tech. grant program instr., 2000—01; basic skills math. instr. grades 6-8, 2003—05; after-school improvement program instr. grade 8, 2005; strategies in math. instr. grades 6—8, 2005; computer tech., career edn. instr. grades 6-8 Wash. Sch., Harrison, NJ, 2006—. Student/staff support team mem. Wash. Sch., Harrison, NJ, 1999—; a.c.e. tech. grant summer camp coord. Harrison (N.J.) Bd. of Edn., 2001; tech. com. chairperson Wash. Sch., Harrison, NJ, 2004—; after sch. improvement program coord. Wash. Sch./ Lincoln Sch., Harrison, NJ, 2004—05; math. team leader Wash. Sch., Harrison, NJ, 2006—. Office: Washington Sch 223 Hamilton St Harrison NJ 07029 Office Phone: 973-482-2285. Business E-Mail: ewinkleblech@harrison.k12.nj.us.

**WINKLEBLECH, JERRY A.,** band director; b. Monongahela, Pa., Jan. 17, 1973; s. William M. Winkleblech and Christine M. Collura; m. Shannon L. Jones, June 28, 1997; children: Arianne, Kendra. BS in Music Edn., Clarion U., Pa., 1995; postgrad., Duquesne U., 2001, postgrad., 2002. Substitute music tchr. Charleroi (Pa.) Sch. Dist., 1995—96; band idr. Punxsutawney (Pa.) Sch. Dist., 1996—98, East Allegheny Sch. Dist., North Versailles, Pa., 1998—. Choir dir. Peace Evang. Luth. Ch., Greenack, Pa., 1997—. Mem.: Music Educators Nat. Conf., Pa. State Edn. Assn., Pa. Music Educators Assn. Home: 420 Worthington St Mc Keesport PA 15132 Office: East Allegheny Sch Dist 1150 Jacks Run Rd North Versailles PA 15137 Office Phone: 412-824-9700.

**WINKLER, AGNIESZKA M.,** marketing executive; b. Rome, Feb. 22, 1946; came to U.S., 1953; naturalized, 1959; d. Wojciech A. and Halina Z. (Owsiany) W.; children from previous marriage: children: Renata G. Ritcheson, Dana C Sworakowski; m. Arthur K. Lund. BA, Coll. Holy Name, 1967; MA, San Jose State U., 1971; MBA, U. Santa Clara, 1981. Tchg. asst. San Jose State U., 1968-70; cons. to Ea. European bus. Palo Alto, Calif., 1970-72; pres./founder Commart Communications, Palo Alto, 1973-84; pres./founder, chmn. bd. Winkler Advt., Santa Clara, Calif., 1984—; chmn. bd. SuperCuts, Inc.; chmn., founder TeamToolz, 2000—04, The Winkler Group, 2004—. Bd. dirs. Reno Air, Lifeguard, Lifeguard Life Ins., IP Locks, C200, Inter-tel, Western Folklife Ctr.; exec. com. C200. Author: Warp Speed Branding, 1999. Trustee Santa Clara U., 1991—; trustee O'Connor Found., 1987-93, mem. exec. com., 1988—, mem. Capital Campaign steering com., 1989; mem. nat. adv. bd. Comprehensive Health Enhancement Support System, 1991—; mem. mgmt. west com. A.A.A.A. Agy., 1991—, vice chair no. Calif. coun., 1996—; project dir. Poland Free Enterprise Plan, 1989-92; mem. adv. bd. Normandy France Bus. Devel., 1989-92; mem. bd. regents Holy Names Coll., 1987—; bd. dirs. San Jose Mus. Art, 1987; mem. San Jose Symphony, Gold Baton, 1986; mem. nat. adv. com. Chess, 1991—; dir. Bay Area Coun., 1994—. Recipient CLIO award in Advt., Addy award, others; named to 100 Best Women in Advt., Ad Age, 1988, Best Woman in Advt., AdWeek and McCall's Mag., 1993, one of 100 Best and Brightest Women in Mktg. & Advt., Nat. Assn. Women Bus. Owners, 1996. Mem. Family Svc. Assn. (trustee 1980-82), Am. Assn. Advt. Agys. (agy. mgmt. west com. 1991), Bus. Profl. Advt. Assn., Polish Am. Congress, San Jose Advt. Club, San Francisco Ad Club, Beta Gamma Sigma (hon.), Pi Gamma Mu, Pi Delta Phi (Lester-Tinneman award 1966, Bill Raskob Found. grantee 1965). Office: The Winkler Group 633 Post # 515 San Francisco CA 94109

**WINKLER, CHARLES HOWARD,** investment company executive; b. NYC, Aug. 4, 1954; s. Joseph Conrad and Geraldine Miriam (Borok) W.; m. Joni S. Taylor, Aug. 28, 1993. BBA with highest distinction, Emory U., 1976; JD, Northwestern U., 1979. Bar: Ill. 1979, U.S. Dist. Ct (no. dist.) Ill. 1979. Assoc. Levenfeld & Kanter, Chgo., 1979-80, Kanter & Eisenberg, Chgo., 1980-84, ptnr., 1985-86, Neal Gerber & Eisenberg, Chgo., 1986-96; mng. dir., COO Citadel Investment Group, LLC, Chgo., 1996—2001; sr. mng. dir. Citadel Trading Group, Chgo., 1996—2000, Aragon Investments Ltd., Chgo., 1996—2000. Bd. dirs. Kensington Global Strategies Fund, Ltd., Antaeus Internat. Investments, Ltd., Jackson Investment Fund Ltd., Citadel Investment Group (Europe) Ltd., chief oper. officer, and sr. mng. dir. Amaranth Group Inc., 2001—; hedge fund mgr. Author: (with others) Basic Tax Shelters, 1982, Limited Liability Companies: The Entity of Choice, 1995; mng. editor Northwestern Jour. Internat. Law and Bus., 1979. Mem. ABA (mem. sect. on taxation), Beta Gamma Sigma. Office: Amaranth Group Inc One American Ln Greenwich CT 06831 Office Phone: 203-422-3320. Business E-Mail: cwinkler@amaranthllc.com.

**WINKLER, DOUGLAS J.**, secondary school educator; b. Kansas City, Mo., July 27, 1962; s. Jack and Martha Joe Ann Winkler; m. Stacy Lee Hobelman, May 13, 2000; 1 child, Emma Grace. B in Secondary Edn., U. Kans., Lawrence, 1985; M in US History, U. Mo., Kansas City, 2001. Tchr. North Kans. City Schs., 1986–2005, Liberty (Mo.) Pub. Schs., 2005–. V.p. North Kansas City Schs. Ednl. Found., 2004–05. Recipient Traditions of Excellence award, North Kansas City HS, 2003, Honor Cadre Traditions of Excellence in Tchg. award, North Kansas City Sch. Dist., 2003, Excellence in Edn. award, Northland C. of C., 2003. Mem.: Mo. State Tchrs. Assn. Republican. Baptist. Home: 5705 N Harden Kansas City MO 64151 Office: Liberty HS 200 Blue Jay Dr Liberty MO 64068-3810 Office Phone: 816-736-6000 ext. 2615. E-mail: dwinkler@liberty.k12.mo.us.

**WINKLER, GAIL CASKEY**, historian, writer; b. Chgo., Aug. 5, 1942; d. Robert E. and Ethel (Barquist) Caskey; m. Robert H. Winkler, Jan. 22, 1964 (div. 1976); m. Roger W. Moss, July 19, 1981. BA, Beloit (Wis.) Coll., 1964; MA, U. Wis., 1971, MS, 1977, PhD, 1988. Instr. U. Wis., Madison, 1976-81; sr. ptnr. LCA Assocs., Phila., 1982—; adj. faculty U. Pa., Phila., 1986—; asst. prof. U. Del., 1991-93. Author: Victorian Interior Decoration, 1986, Victorian Exterior Decoration, 1987, Floor Coverings for Historic Buildings, 1988, The Well-Appointed Bath, 1989, An Analysis of Drapery, 1993; (museum installations include), William Conner House, Conner Prairie, Fishers, Ind., Lanier Mansion, Madison, Ind., Tudor Hall in Pamplin Park, Petersburg, Va., Fairlawn Mansion, Superior, Wis., Adams House Mus., Deadwood, S.D., Villa Louis, Prairie du Chien, Wis., Hixon House, LaCrosse, Wis., Campbell House Mus., St. Louis, Dr. Richard Eells House, Quincy, Ill., (projects include) studies of the historic finishes and furnishings of the U.S. Senate and House, Chambers, Va. State Capitol, Richmond, City Hall, Phila., Capitol of the Commonwealth Pa., Rutherford B. Hayes house, Fremont, Ohio, Buchanan house, U.S. Naval Acad., Anderson Cottage (summer White House Abraham Lincoln), Washington, D.C., Wright Bros.' Printing Shop, Dayton, Ohio, Capitol of State of Va. Fellow Am. Soc. Interior Designers (bd. dirs. Pa. East chap. 1983-88, 2001—, Athena award 1989, Medallist award 1995), Found. Interior Design Edn. and Rsch. (rsch. com. 1986-96). Office: 604 S Washington Sq Philadelphia PA 19106-4118 Office Phone: 215-925-8367.

**WINKLER, HENRY FRANKLIN**, actor, film producer, director; b. NYC, Oct. 30, 1945; s. Harry Irving and Ilse Anna Maria (Hadra) W.; m. Stacey Weitzman, May 5, 1978; children: Zoe Emily, Max Daniel, (stepchildren) Jed Weitzman. BA, Emerson Coll., 1967, PhD, 1978; MA, Yale Sch. Drama, 1970. With Yale Repertory Theatre, 1970-71. Founder New Haven Free Theatre, 1968, Off The Wall N.Y., improvisation co., 1972; tchr. drama UCLA Adult Extension; founding mem. Children's Action Network. Off-Broadway shows, 1972-73, Cin. Playhouse, 1973; Broadway shows, The Dinner Party; films include The Lords of Flatbush, 1972, Crazy Joe, 1974, Heroes, 1977, The One and Only, 1977, Night Shift, 1983, Wes Craven's Scream, 1996, Ground Control, 1998, The Water Boy, 1998, Ugly Naked People, 1999, Elevator Seeking, 1999, Dill Scallion, 1999, P.U.N.K.S., 1999, Down to You, 2000, I Shaved My Legs for This, 2001, Holes, 2003, Fronterz, 2004, Unbeatable Harold, 2005, Berkeley, 2005, The Kid and I, 2005, The King of Central Park, 2006, Click, 2006; starred in TV series Happy Days, 1973-84, Fonz and the Happy Days Gang (voice), 1980, The Mork & Mindy/Laverne & Shirley with the Fonz Show (voice), 1982, Monty, 1994 (also exec. prodr.), Mr. Sunshine, (voice) Clifford's Puppy Days, 2003 (Performer for an animated program, Daytime Emmy award, Acad. TV Arts & Scis., 2005), Out of Practice, 2005-; appeared in TV films Katherine, 1975, America Salutes Richard Rodgers: The Sound of His Music, 1976, An American Christmas Carol, 1979 (ABC), Absolute Strangers, 1991 (CBS), The Only Way Out, 1994 (ABC), Truman Capote's One Christmas, 1994 (NBC), A Child is Missing, 1995 (CBS) (also exec. prodr.), Dad's Week Off, 1996 (Showtime), National Lampoon's Dad's Week Off, 1997, Detention: The Siege at Johnson High, 1997, Beverly Hills S.U.V., 2006; exec. producer (TV) Who Are the Debolts? Where Did They Get Nineteen Kids?, 1977, Starflight:The Plane That Couldn't Land, 1983, Ryan's Four, 1983, When Your Lover Leaves, 1983, Scandal Sheet, 1984, MacGyver, 1985-94 (several episodes), Mr. Sunshine, 1986, A Family Again, 1988, Starting Now, 1989, Sightings, 1992, Dead Man's Gun, 1997, 1999, So Weird, 1999, Sightings: Heartland Ghosts, 2002, WinTuition, 2002, Hollywood Squares, 2002-04, Young MacGyver, 2003, Unexplained Mysteries, 2003, Dallas Reunion: Return to Southfork, 2004, Happy Days: 30th Anniversary Reunion, 2005, Knots Landing Reunion: Together Again, 2005; prodr. (films) The Sure Thing, 1985; prodr., host home video Strong Kids, Safe Kids, 1985, PBS animated spl. Happy Ever After, 1985, Two Daddies to Love Me, 1988; prodr. (films) Young Sherlock Holmes, 1985; prodr. (TV films) Losing a Sister, 1988; pres. Fair Dinkum Prodns., Hollywood, Calif., 1979—, Winkler-Daniels Prodns., Hollywood, 1987-91; prodr. (TV) Run, Don't Walk for own co. JZM Prodns., 1981; dir. (TV) Joanie Loves Chachi, 1982; dir. (TV films) All the Kids Do It, 1984, A Smokey Mountain Christmas, 1986, Memories of Me, 1988, Cop and a Half, 1993, Dave's World, 1993, Too Something, 1995, Clueless, 1996, Sabrina, the Teenage Witch, 1996; TV guest appearances include Mary Tyler Moore, 1973, The Bob Newhart Show, 1974, Laverne & Shirley, 1976, 1979, Saturday Night Live, 1977, Mork & Mindy, 1978, Joanie Loves Chachi, 1982, Macgyver, 1990, (voice) Street Sharks, 1995, (voice) South Park, 1998, The Practice, 1999, 2000, (voice) The Simpsons, 1999, The Drew Carey Show, 2001, Law & Order: Special Victims Unit, 2002, Hollywood Squares, 2003, Arrested Development, 2003-05 (several episodes), Third Watch, 2004, Crossing Jordon, 2005; co-author (with Lin Oliver) (children's book series): Hank Zipzer:The World's Greatest Underachiever. Recipient Golden Globe award 1976, 77, 78, Golden Plate award Am. Acad. Achievement 1980, Daytime Emmy nomination best dir. All The Kids Do It, produced by JZM Prodns., 1985, Sorrisi e Canzoni Telegatto award (Italian TV award) 1980, Humanitarian award Women in Film, 1988, UN Peace prize, Chevalier de l'Ordre des Arts et des Lettres; named hon. youth chmn. Epilepsy Found., chmn. Toys for Tots, 1977, Best Actor in Comedy Series, Photoplay mag. 1976-77, King of Baccus, Mardi Gras, New Orleans 1977, Emmy nominee 1973, 74, 77, nat. spokesperson United Friends of the Children, 1982—. Mem. AFTRA, Screen Actors Guild, Actors Equity. Address: Evan Tripoli Internat Creative Mgmt 8942 Wilshire Blvd Beverly Hills CA 90211*

**WINKLER, HENRY RALPH**, retired academic administrator, historian; b. Waterbury, Conn., Oct. 27, 1916; s. Jacob and Ethel (Rieger) W.; m. Clare Sapadin, Aug. 18, 1940; children: Allan Michael, Karen Jean; m. Beatrice Ross, Jan. 28, 1973. AB, U. Cin., 1938, MA, 1940; PhD, U. Chgo., 1947; degree (hon.), Lehigh U., 1974, Rutgers U., 1977, No. Ky. U., 1978, St. Thomas Inst., 1979, Hebrew Union Coll., 1980, Xavier U., 1981, U. Akron, 1984, U. Cin., 1987, Thomas More Coll., 1989. Instr. U. Cin., 1939-40; asst. prof. Roosevelt Coll., 1946-47; mem. faculty Rutgers U., 1947-77, prof. history, 1958-77, chmn. dept., 1960-64; dean Faculty Liberal Arts, 1967, vice provost, 1968-70, acting provost, 1970, v.p. for acad. affairs, 1970-72, sr. v.p. for acad. affairs, 1972-76, exec. v.p., 1976-77, U. Cin., 1977, pres., 1977-84, pres. emeritus, 1984—, Univ. prof. history, 1977-86, prof. emeritus, 1986—. Mng. editor Am. Hist. Rev., 1964-68; vis. prof. Bryn Mawr Coll., 1959-60, Harvard, summer 1964, Columbia, summer 1967; faculty John Hay Fellows Inst. Humanities, 1960-65; bd. overseers Hebrew Union Coll., 1984—. Author: The League of Nations Movement in Great Britain, 1914-19, 1952, Great Britain in the Twentieth Century, 1960, 2d edit., 1966; editor: (with K.M. Setton) Great Problems in European Civilization, 1954, 2d edit., 1966, Twentieth-Century Britain, 1977, Paths Not Taken: British Labour and International Policy in the Nineteen Twenties, 1994, British Labour Seeks a Foreign Policy, 2000; mem. editorial bd. Historian, 1958-64, Liberal Edn., 1986—; mem. adv. bd. Partisan Rev., 1972-79; contbr. articles to jours., revs. Nat. chmn. European history advanced placement com. Coll. Entrance Exam. Bd., 1960-64; mem. Nat. Commn. on Humanities in Schs., 1967-68, Am. specialist Eastern Asia, 1968; exec. com. Conf. on Brit. Studies, 1968-75; chmn. bd. Nat. Humanities Faculty, 1970-73; chmn. adv. com. on history Coll. Entrance Exam. Bd., 1977-80; mem. council on acad. affairs, mem. bd. trustees, chmn., 1982-84; pres. Highland Park (N.J.) Bd. Edn., 1962-63; mem. exec. com. Nat. Assn. State Univs. and Land-Grant Colls., 1978-81, mem. Cin. Lit. Club, 1978—, pres., 1993—; bd. dirs. Am. Council on Edn., 1979-81; trustee Seasengood Good Govt. Found., 1979—, pres., 1991-93;

trustee Thomas More Coll., 1986-93; mem. Ohio Indsl. Tech. and Enterprise Bd., 1983-89; bd. dirs. Nat. Civic League, 1986—, Planning Accreditation Bd., 1988—; mem. adv coun. U. Va.'s Coll at Wise, Ohio Humanities Coun., 1994— With USNR, 1943-46. Recipient Lifetime Achievement award N.Am. Conf. on Brit. Studies, 1995, Bishop William Hughes award for disting. svc. to Cath. higher edn. Thomas More Coll., 1997, Leadership Medallion, Xavier U., 2003. Mem. Am. Hist. Assn., Phi Beta Kappa, Tau Kappa Alpha, Phi Alpha Theta. Clubs: Comml., Bankers, Cin., Lit. Office: U Cin 571 Langsam Library Cincinnati OH 45221-0001 Office Phone: 513-556-0125. Business E-Mail: Henry.Winkler@uc.edu.

**WINKLER, JEFFREY D.**, chemist; b. 1956; AB, Harvard Coll., 1977; MA, MPhil, PhD, Columbia U., 1981-83. Prof. chemistry U. Pa. Recipient NIH-NCI Rsch. Career Devel. award, 1988-93, Am. Cyanamid Young Faculty award, 1988-93, Arthur C. Cope scholar award Am. Chem. Soc., 2000; Alfred P. Sloan rsch. fellow, 1987-89. Achievements include research on total synthesis of naturally occurring compounds with important biological activity; development of new reactions and strategies in organic synthesis; design and synthesis of small molecules that mimic the functions of biological catalysts; preparation of macromolecular structures with well-defined structures and functions such as conducting or non-linear optical properties. Office: U Pa Dept Chemistry 231 S 34th St Philadelphia PA 19104-6323 Office Phone: 215-898-0052. E-mail: winkler@sas.upenn.edu.

**WINKLER, JOHN FREDERICK**, lawyer, educator; b. Gallipolis, Ohio, May 26, 1946; s. Carl Frederick and Anna (Reed) W.; m. Wendy Stephenson, May 2, 1970; children: Jonathan Reed, Asa Benjamin, Mary Susannah. BA, Yale U., New Haven, 1968; MA, McGill U., Montreal, 1972; AM, Harvard U., Cambridge, Mass., 1973; JD, Ohio State U., 1982. Bar: Ohio 1983, U.S. Supreme Ct. 1992. Assoc. Baker & Hostetler, Columbus, Ohio, 1983-90, ptnr., 1991-97, Christensen, Shoemaker & Winkler, Columbus, 1997—2002; counsel Ohio Supreme Ct. Rules Com., 1998—, Shoemaker, Winkler, Howarth & Taylor LLC, Columbus, 2003, Kisor & Winkler LLC, Columbus, Ohio, 2004—. Adj. prof. law Capital U., Columbus, 1987-98; teaching fellow Harvard U., Cambridge, Mass., 1974-77; lectr. in field. Author: (with M.L. Benedict) The History of Ohio Law, 2004; contbr. articles to profl. jours. Mem. ABA, Am. Inns. of Ct., Ohio Bar Assn., Columbus Bar Assn. (mem. editl. bd. 1995—1996). Home: 253 N Remington Rd Bexley OH 43209-1444 Office: Kisor & Winkler LLC 555 City Park Ave Columbus OH 43215-5799 Office Phone: 614-668-8221. E-mail: jwinkler@aya.yale.edu.

**WINKLER, JONATHAN REED**, historian, educator; b. Boston; PhD, Yale U., 2004. Asst. prof. history Wright State U., Dayton, Ohio, 2005—; adj. asst. prof. history U.S. Naval Acad., Annapolis, Md. Mem. Soc. for Historians of Am. Fgn. Rels. mem.: Phi Beta Kappa. Office: Wright State University 3640 Colonel Glenn Hwy Dayton OH 45435

**WINKLER, JOSEPH CONRAD**, former recreational products manufacturing executive; b. Newark, May 20, 1916; s. Charles and Mollie (Abrams) W.; m. Geraldine M. Borok, Sept. 20, 1953; children: Charles H., David J. BS, NYU, 1941. Gen. mgr. Indsl. Washing Machine Corp., New Brunswick, NJ, 1941-48; controller Mojud Corp., N.Y.C., 1948-52; controller, asst. treas. Barbizon Corp., N.Y.C., 1952-57; controller Ideal Toy Corp., N.Y.C., 1957-58, McGregor-Doniger, Inc., N.Y.C., 1958-59; dir. fin. and adminstrn. Ideal Toy Corp., N.Y.C., 1960-62, v.p. fin., 1962-68, sr. v.p. fin., 1968-78, exec. v.p., COO, dir., 1978-81, pres., dir., 1981-83; exec. in residence, bus. adv. coun. Sch. Bus. Adminstrn., Montclair (N.J.) State U., 1983-90. Dir. Ideal of Australia Ltd., Melbourne, 1963-82, Ideal of Canada Ltd., Toronto, 1963-82, Ideal of Japan Ltd., Tokyo and Kiowa, 1963-80, Ideal Toy Co. Ltd., High Wycombe and Wokingham, Eng., 1966-82, Arxon Spiel & Freizeit GmBH, Rotgau, Germany, 1968-82, Perfekta Ltd. and Hollis Industries Ltd., Hong Kong, 1970-74, Ideal Loisirs S.A., Paris, 1972-82. Mem. editl. bd. Issues in Internat. Bus., 1985-92. Committeeman, troop treas. Boy Scouts Am., Tenafly, N.J., 1965-71; bd. dirs. N.Y. League Hard of Hearing, 1982-88; active Nat. Roster Sci. and Splized. Pers., War Manpower Commn., 1941-46. Served with Office Statis. Control USAAF, 1945. Mem. Fin. Execs. Inst. Office Phone: 561-588-0952. E-mail: chada@worldnet.att.net.

**WINKLER, LEE B.**, business consultant; b. Buffalo; s. Jack W. and Caroline (Marienthal) W.; 1 child, James; m. Maria Mal Verde. BS cum laude, NYU, 1945, MS cum laude, 1947. Pres. LBW, Inc. (formerly Winkler Assocs. Ltd.), N.Y.C., Beverly Hills, Calif., 1948—, Winkler Assocs. Ltd., Beverly Hills, Calif., and N.Y.C., 1958—; exec. dir. Global Bus. Mgmt. Inc., Beverly Hills, 1967—. V.p. Bayly Martin & Fay Inc., N.Y.C., 1965-68, John C. Paige & Co., N.Y.C., 1968-71; cons. Albert G. Ruben Co., Beverly Hills, 1971— Served with AUS, 1943-45. Decorated chevalier comdr. Order Holy Cross Jerusalem, also spl. exec. asst., charge d'affaires, 1970; chevalier comdr. Sovereign Order Cyprus, 1970 Mem. Nat. Acad. TV Arts and Scis., Nat. Acad. Recording Arts and Scis., Beverly Hills C. of C., Phi Beta Kappa, Beta Gamma Sigma, Mu Gamma Tau, Psi Chi Omega. Office: 15250 Ventura Blvd Sherman Oaks CA 91403-3201 *In the final analysis, the bottom line, if you will—the only thing that truly matters in life are those friends and family that hold you dear to them. Success, and its attendant monies, rise and fall like the tides, and even vanish at times, but earned love is as constant as the earth's rotation is independent of the tides.*

**WINKLER, MATTHEW ADAM**, editor-in-chief, reporter, editor; b. June 1, 1955; m. Lisa Winkler; 3 children. AB in History, Kenyon Coll., 1977, LLD. Reporter Mount Vernon News, Ohio, 1976—77; pub. rels. specialist Gehrung Assocs., Keene, NH, 1977—78; reporter, asst. editor Bond Buyer, 1978—80; with Dow Jones Capital Markets Reports, 1980; reporter Wall Street Jour., 1980—90; European Fin. corr. Wall Street Jour. Europe, Jour. London, 1982—87; with Bloomberg L.P.; editor-in-chief Bloomberg News, N.Y.C., 1990—. Chmn. bd. trustees Kenyon Rev. Co-author: Bloomberg by Bloomberg, 1997. Trustee N.J. Symphony Orch., Overseas Club, 1998, Knight-Bagehot Fellowship Columbia U. Office: Bloomberg News 499 Park Ave New York NY 10022-1240

**WINKLER, MICHAEL**, computer company executive; BS in Electrical Engring., Lehigh U.; MBA, Harvard Bus. Sch. Various mgmt. positions Xerox Corp.; v.p., gen. mgr. comp. systems Toshiba Am. Info. Systems, Inc., 1992—95; sr. v.p., group gen. mgr Compaq Computer Corp. (later acquired by Hewlett-Packard Co.), Houston, 1996—2000, exec. v.p. global bus. units, 2000—01; exec. v.p. global ops. Hewlett-Packard Co., 2001—02, exec. v.p., chief mktg. officer, 2002—. Office: Hewlett-Packard Co 3000 Hanover St Palo Alto CA 94304-1185 Office Phone: 650-857-1501.

**WINKLER, PAUL FRANK, JR.**, astrophysicist, educator; b. Nashville, Nov. 10, 1942; s. Paul Frank and Estelle (Pye) W.; m. Geraldine Huck, Aug. 20, 1966 (div. 1979); children: Katharine Winkler Cocoran, Johanna Winkler Durrett; m. Janet Pippitt Beers, June 25, 1983; stepchildren: Sarah Creighton Beers, Nathan Pippitt Beers. BS, Calif. Inst. Tech., 1964; A.M., Harvard U., 1965, PhD, 1970. From instr. to prof. physics Middlebury Coll., Vt., 1969—84, William R. Kenan Jr. prof. physics, 1984-87, chmn. nat. scis. div., 1988-93, asst. to pres. for sci. planning, 1993-96, Gamaliel Painter Bicentennial prof. physics, 1997—. Vis. scientist MIT, Cambridge, 1973-74, 78-80; sr. vis. fellow Inst. Astronomy, U. Cambridge, 1985-86; vis. resident astronomer Cerro Tololo InterAm. Observatory, La Serena, Chile, 1990-91, 96-97; vis. fellow Joint Inst. for Laboratory Astrophysics, U. Colo., Boulder, 1991. Contbr. articles to profl. jours. NSF fellow, 1965-69, Alfred P. Sloan Found. fellow, 1976-80 Mem. Vt. Acad. Sci. and Engring., Am. Phys. Soc., Am. Astron. Soc., Internat. Astron. Union, Coun. on Undergrad. Rsch., Sigma Xi. Office: Middlebury Coll Dept Physics Middlebury VT 05753 Business E-Mail: winkler@middlebury.edu.

**WINKLER, SHELDON**, dentist, educator; b. N.Y.C., Jan. 25, 1932; s. Ben and Lillian (Barsh) W.; m. Sandra M. Cohen, Aug. 13, 1961; children: Mitchell, Lori. BA, Washington Sq. Coll., 1953; DDS, NYU, 1956. Asst. prof. denture prosthesis NYU Coll. Dentistry, N.Y.C., 1958-61, 66-68, rsch. asst.

prof., 1962-63; dir. materials rsch. Consol. Metal Products Industries Inc., Albany, NY, 1963-65, cons. materials rsch., 1966-68; asst. prof. removable prosthodontics sch. dentistry SUNY, Buffalo, 1968-70, assoc. prof., 1970-79; prof., chmn. dept. prosthodontics Temple U. Sch. Dentistry, Phila., 1979-86, 94-96, asst. dean for advanced studies, continuing edn./rsch., 1987-89, acting asst. dean, 1993-95, prof. restorative dentistry, 1996—2006; prof. dentistry Ariz. Sch. Dentistry and Oral Health, Mesa, 2006—. Asst. dir. dental dept. NYU Med. Ctr. Goldwater Meml. Hosp., NYC, 1966—68, vis. dentist dental dept., 1966—68; attending in prosthodontics E.J. Meyer Meml. Hosp., Buffalo, 1975—79; postgrad instr. First Dist. Dental Soc. NY, NYC, 1963—; cons. Coe Labs., Chgo., 1967—87, Hawthorn Ctr., Buffalo, Rosa Coplon Home & Infirmary, Buffalo, 1970—79, Erie C.C., Buffalo, 1979—, Lever Bros. Co., NYC, 1981—, VA Hosp., Phila., 1989—, Ivoclar N. Am., Amherst, NY, 2000—; lectr. dept. dental hygiene NYC C.C., 1967—68; hon. prof. Pierre Fauchard Sch. Dentistry, Asuncion, Paraguay, 1999—. Author: (with A. Davidoff and M.H.M. Lee) Dentistry for the Special Patient: The Aged, Chronically Ill and Handicapped, 1972, Essentials of Complete Denture Prosthodontics, 1979, 2d edit., 1988; editor: Resins in Dentistry, 1975, Complete Dentures, 1977, Removable Prosthodontics, 1984, (with B.R. Lang, F.R. Lauciello and G.P. McGivney) Contemporary Complete Denture Occlusion, 2001; editor Jour. Implant Dentistry, 1990-97; sr. editor Jour. Oral Implantology, 2000—; contbr. articles to profl. lit.; co-designer McGowan-Winkler complete denture trays. Served as capt. AUS, 1956-58, 61-62. Recipient Outstanding Layman award Vocat. Tech. Alumni and Student Assn., SUNY, Buffalo, 1974, Internat. Edn. award Internat. Congress Oral Implantologists, 1992, journalism award Internat. Coll. Dentists, 1993, Academic Devotion award Chulalongkorn U., Bangkok, 1995. Fellow Am. Coll. Dentists, Greater N.Y. Acad. Prosthodontics; mem. ADA, Internat. Assn. Dental Rsch., Am. Assn. Dental Schs., Am. Acad. Implant Prosthodontics (Outstanding Personality Implant Prosthodontics award, 2002), Sci. Rsch. Soc. Am., Acad. Plastics Rsch., Am. Prosthodontic Soc., Am. Soc. Geriatric Dentistry, Internat. Congress of Oral Implantologists, Sigma Xi, Sigma Epsilon Delta, Omicron Kappa Upsilon. Home: 8672 E Eagle Claw Dr Scottsdale AZ 85262-1058 Office: Ariz Sch Dentistry and Oral Health 5850 E Still Cir Mesa AZ 85206 Office Phone: 480-588-8062. E-mail: swinkdent@cox.net.

**WINLAND, THOMAS W.**, lawyer; b. Lancaster, Ohio, Mar. 18, 1949; BS, Ohio State U., 1971; JD, Duke U., 1974. Bar: Ohio 1974, D.C. 1982, U.S. Patent and Trademark Office, U.S. Ct. Customs and Patent Appeals 1980, U.S. Claims Ct. 1982, U.S. Ct. Appeals (fed. cir.) 1982. Ptnr. Finnegan, Henderson, Farabow, Garrett & Dunner, Washington. Named one of best lawyers in intellectual property law, Best Lawyers in Am., 2005—06. Mem. ABA (patent, trademark and copyright law sects., pub. contract law), Am. Intellectual Property Law Assn., D.C. Bar, Bar Assn. of D.C., Ohio State Bar Assn. Office: Finnegan Henderson Farabow Garrett & Dunner LLP 901 New York Ave NW Washington DC 20001-3315 Office Phone: 202-408-4000. Office Fax: 202-408-4400. Business E-Mail: tom.winland@finnegan.com.

**WINMILL, B. LYNN**, federal judge; m. Judy Jones; 4 children. BA, Idaho State U., 1974; JD, Harvard U., 1977. Atty. Holland and Hart, Denver, 1977-79, Hawley, Troxell, Ennis and Hawley, Pocatello, Idaho, 1984-87; judge Idaho Sixth Jud. Dist. Ct., Pocatello, 1987-95, US Dist. Ct. Idaho, Boise, 1995—, chief judge, 1999—. Adj. prof. law Idaho State Univ. 1991—95. Mem.: Colo. Bar Assn., 6th Dist. Bar Assn., Idaho State Bar Assn. Office: US Dist Ct Idaho US Courthouse 550 W Fort St 6th Fl Boise ID 83724-0001 Fax: 208-334-9209. Office Phone: 208-334-9145.

**WINN, ALBERT CURRY**, clergyman; b. Ocala, Fla., Aug. 16, 1921; s. James Anderson and Elizabeth (Curry) W.; m. Grace Neely Walker, Aug. 29, 1944; children: Grace Walker (Mrs. Stewart E. Ellis), James Anderson, Albert Bruce Curry, Randolph Axson. AB, Davidson Coll., 1942, LLD, 1968; BD, Union Theol. Sem., Va., 1945, ThD, 1956; ThM, Princeton Theol. Sem., 1949; LLD, Stillman Coll., 1975. Ordained min. Presbyn. Ch., 1945. Asst. prof. Davidson Coll., 1946-47; pastor Potomac Rural Parish, Va., 1948-53; prof. Bible Stillman Coll., 1953-60; prof. theology Louisville Presbyn. Theol. Sem., 1960-73, pres., 1966-73; pastor 2d Presbyn. Ch., Richmond, Va., 1974-81, N. Decatur Presbyn. Ch., Decatur, Ga., 1981-86. Moderator Presbyn. Synod Ala., 1958, Presbyn. Synod Ky., 1969, Gen. Assembly, Presbyn. Ch. in U.S., 1979; vis. prof. Union Theol. Sem. in Va., 1987, Columbia Theol. Sem., 1987, Louisville Presbyn. Theol. Sem., 1988; interim pastor Cen. Presbyn. Ch., Atlanta, 1989-90, St. Andrews Presbyn. Ch., Tucker, Ga., 1993-94; parish assoc. Trinity Prebyn. Ch., Winston-Salem, NC, 1999—. Author: Layman's Bible Commentary on Acts, 1960, The Worry and Wonder of Being Human, 1966, Where Do I Go From Here, 1972, Proclamation Two: Epiphany, 1980, A Sense of Mission, 1981, Christ the Peacemaker, 1982, Plain Talk about the Apostles' Creed, 1985, The Christian Primer, 1990, Ain't Gonna Study War No More, 1993. Chmn. trustees Stillman Coll., 1965-70. Served as chaplain USNR, 1945-46. Mem. Phi Beta Kappa, Beta Theta Pi, Omicron Delta Kappa. Office: 212 Oakwood Ct Winston Salem NC 27103-1952 E-mail: al.winn@juno.com.

**WINN, CAROLYN PAUTKE**, librarian, consultant; b. Detroit, June 5, 1927; d. Benno Edgar and Caroline Amelia (Milatz) Pautke; divorced; children: Eric, Gregory, Mathew. BS in Zoology, U. Mich., 1949, MA in Zoology, 1950; MLS, U. R.I., 1970. Cataloguer Mus. Zoology U. Mich., Ann Arbor, 1950-54; rsch. asst. U. Md., College Park, 1963-65, U. R.I., Kingston, 1965-67, cataloger, 1968-69, asst. ref. libr., 1969-70, instr. sci. ref. libr., 1970-73, asst. prof., sci. ref. libr., 1973-75; rsch. libr. Woods Hole (Mass.) Oceanographic Instn., 1975-95. Cons. Marine Biol. Lab./Woods Hole Oceanog. Instn. Libr., 1994—. Contbr. articles to profl. jours. Observer, vol. White House Conf. Librs. and Info. Svcs., Washington, 1979; adv. com. N.E. Academic Sci. Info. Ctr., New Eng. Bd. Higher Edn., 1978. Grantee U. R.I., 1974-75, Woods Hole Oceanographic Instn., 1976-77, 80-81, 86-87, Bur. Land Mgmt., 1982-84. Mem. ALA, Am. Geophys. Union (sub.mgr. electronic pub. 1983-87), Internat. Assn. Marine Sci. Librs. and Info. Ctrs. (editor jour. 1989-90, pres. 1982-83), New Eng. On-Line Users Group (database com. 1979-86), New Eng. Libr. Assn., R.I. Libr. Assn., R.I. Health Scis. Librs. Consortium, Nat. Micrographics Assn., Soc. Scholarly Pub., New Eng. Microcomputer Users Group, Boston Libr. Consortium (collection mgmt. com. 1992-94), Cape Librs. Automated Materials Sharing, Inc. (pres. 1989-90, mem. coms.) E-mail: cpwinn90@hotmail.com.

**WINN, H. RICHARD**, surgeon; b. Chester, Pa., 1942; BA, Princeton U., 1964; MD, U. Pa., 1968. Diplomate Am Bd. Neurol. Surgeons. Intern U. Hosp., Cleve., 1968-69, resident surgery, 1969-70; resident neurolog. surgery U. Hosp. Va., Charlottesville, 1970-74; neurol. surgeon U. Wash. Hosp., Seattle, 1983—2002; prof., chmn. neurol. surgery U. Wash., Seattle, 1983—2002; prof. neurosurgery and neurosci. Mt. Sinai Med. Sch., N.Y.C., 2003—. Bd. dirs. Am. Bd. Neurol. Surgery, 1995-2001, vice chmn., 2000-01. Founding editor Neurosurgical Clinics of North America; mem. editl. bd. Jour. Neurosurgery, 1995-2001, chair, 2001-2002; mem. editl. bd. Am. Physiology, 1995-2000, Am. Jour. Surgery. Recipient Disting. Alumnus, Haverford Sch., 2000. Fellow AAAS, Soc. Neurol. Surgeons (pres.); mem. AMA, Am. Assn. Neurol. Surgeons, Soc. Neurol. Surgeons (Grass prize 1999, Disting. Svc. award 2005), Congress Neurol. Surgeons. Office: Dept Neurosurgery Mount Sinai Sch Medicine One Gustave L Levy PO Box 1136 New York NY 10029 Office Phone: 212-241-9128. Business E-Mail: richard.winn@mountsinai.org.

**WINN, JAMES JULIUS, JR.**, lawyer; b. Colon, Panama, Nov. 7, 1941; came to U.S., 1941; s. James Julius and Molly (Brown) W.; m. Elizabeth Kokernot Lacy, Aug. 15, 1970; children: Mary Ann W. Burns, E. Lacy W. Sakellaris, James Julius VI. AB, Princeton U., 1964; JD cum laude, Washington and Lee U., 1970. Bar: Md. 1970, U.S. Dist. Ct. Md. 1971, U.S. Dist. Ct. D.C. 1982. Assoc. Piper & Marbury, Balt., 1970-78; ptnr. Piper Rudnick LLP, Balt., 1978—2004; mem. Winn Group LLC, 2001—; gen. counsel Kokernot 06 Ranch, Inc., 2006—. Bd. dirs. Columbia Bancorp. Assoc. editor, contbr. author Washington & Lee U. Law Rev., 1968-70. Counselor St. John's Ch., Western Run Parish, Glyndon, Md., 1974—; mem.

com. on canons and other bus. Episc. Diocese Md., 1986—; dir. Ctr. for Ethics and Corp. Policy, 1988-95, chmn., 1991-95; dir. Ctr. Stage, 1986-2004; dir. Oldfields Sch., 1991-96; v.p., dir. Ruxton Country Sch., 1988-91; dir. The Jemicy Sch., 1999—, chmn., 2005—, Mem. Md. State Bar Assn. (com. on corp. law of est. of bus. law). Office: DLA Piper Rudnick Gray Cary US LLP 6225 Smith Ave Baltimore MD 21209-3600

**WINN, JANICE GAIL,** food products administrator; b. Springfield, Mass., Nov. 2, 1954; d. Rose Eleanor (Draskawich) W. BA, Western New Eng. Coll., 1976. Gen. mdse. mgr. Mott's Shop-Rite, East Hartford, Conn., 1979-84; sr. merchandiser Imperial Distbrs., Auburn, Mass., 1984-85; dir. of gen. mdse. Waldbaums Food Mart, Holyoke, Mass., 1985-91; dir. health, beauty care and gen. mdse. Big Y Foods, Inc., Springfield, 1991—. Republican. Avocations: travel, spending time with partner and family. Office: Big Y Foods Inc 2145 Roosevelt Ave Springfield MA 01104-1650 Office Phone: 413-504-4410. E-mail: winni@charter.net.

**WINN, JOHN ARTHUR, JR.,** mathematics educator; b. Norfolk, Va., Apr. 8, 1945; s. John Arthur Sr. and Doris Marie (Beudert) W.; m. Elizabeth Ann Westcott, Dec. 17, 1988. BA with honors, SUNY, Oneonta, 1966; MS, C.W. Post Coll., 1969; PhD, Adelphi U., 1980. Cert. math. tchr., N.Y. Computer programmer Grumman Corp., Bethpage, N.Y., 1969-72; Electronic Assocs., Inc., Hampton Roads, Va., 1973-74; prof. math. SUNY, Farmingdale, 1974—. Coord. Discrete Math. Conf., Farmingdale, 1986; dir. Farmingdale Faculty Conf., 1987—. Author: Asymptotic Bounds for Classical Ramsey Numbers, 1988; contbr. articles to profl. jours. Mem. Math. Assn. Am. (del. 1987—, coord. regional conf. 1989), Am. Math. Soc. Avocation: playing trombone in charlie timm orchestra. Office: SUNY Melville Rd Farmingdale NY 11735-2221

**WINN, JOHN L.,** school system administrator; b. Brunswick, Ga., Oct. 23, 1948; BA, Fla. State U., 1970; MA in Philosophy, U. Fla., 1973. Dir. prevention ctr. Fla. Dept. of Edn., Tallahassee, 1987—89; edn. policy dir. to commr. of edn., 1989—91; dir. Office of Policy Rsch. and Accountability, 1991—96, coord. policy rsch., 1996—99, edn. policy coord. to gov., 1999—2001, asst. sec. of edn., 2001—02, dep. commr. for Accountability, Rsch., and Measurement, 2002—03, chief of staff to commr. of edn., 2003—04, commr. of edn., 2004—. Office: Fla Dept of Edn / Off of Commr Turlington Bldg, Ste 1514 325 W Gaines St Tallahassee FL 32399 Office Phone: 850-245-0505.

**WINN, JOSEPH LAMPHER,** retired electronics executive; b. Cambridge, Mass., Aug. 12, 1951; s. Joseph L. and Alicia M. (Muir) W.; m. Gail A. Cadogan, June 19, 1976; children: Kelly, Caroline, Joseph. BS in Fin., Boston Coll., 1973; MBA, Babson Coll., 1974. Fin. mgr. program Sanders Assocs. Inc., Nashua, N.H., 1974-78; fin. mgr. Digital Equipment Corp., Maynard, Mass., 1978-83; sr. v.p., controller Am. Cablesystems Corp., Beverly, Mass., 1983-88; exec. v.p., chief fin. officer Atlantic Radio Corp., Manchester, Mass., 1988—93; CFO & dir. Am. Radiosystems Corp., 1993—98; CFO Am. Tower Corp., Boston, 1998—2002, vice chmn., 2002—04. Bd. dirs. OnePIN, Westborough, Mass. Bd. trustees The Carroll Sch., 2002—03. Roman Catholic. Office: American Tower Corp 116 Huntington Ave Boston MA 02116-5749 E-mail: joe.winn@americantower.com.

**WINN, MORRIS X.,** former federal agency administrator; Grad., Prairie View A&M U. Divsn. dir. support svcs. Tex. Atty. Gen.'s Office, 1984—92, dir. employee rels., 1992—94; deputy commr. human resources Tex. Dept. Ins., 1994—99; divsn. mgr. human resources Tex. Comptroller Pub. Accts., 1999—2002; asst. adminstr. adminstrn. and resources mgmt. EPA, Washington, 2002—04.

**WINN, PAUL T.,** electronics executive; b. 1944; With IBM, Stamford, Conn.; pres., CEO, dir. Genicom Corp., Chantilly, Va., 1990—2000; pres. and CEO Powerquest, 2000—03; CEO Princeton Softech, Inc., Princeton, NJ, 2003—. Office: Princeton Softech Inc 111 Campus Dr Princeton NJ 08540-6400 Office Phone: 609-627-5500. Office Fax: 609-627-7799.

**WINN, STEVEN JAY,** critic; b. Phila., Apr. 25, 1951; s. Willis Jay and Lois (Gengelbach) W.; m. Katharine Weber, Sept. 15, 1979 (div. Dec. 1985); m. Sally Ann Noble, July 22, 1989; 1 child, Phoebe Ann. BA, U. Pa., 1973; MA, U. Wash., 1975. Staff writer, editor Seattle Weekly, 1975-79; theater critic San Francisco Chronicle, 1980—2002, arts and culture critic, 2002—. Co-author: Ted Bundy: The Killer Next Door, 1980, Great Performances: A Celebration, 1997; contbr. articles to various publs. Wallace Stegner fellow Stanford U., 1979-80; recipient first prize Excellence in Writing award Am. Assn. of Sunday and Feature Editors, 2002, 2003. Office: San Francisco Chronicle 901 Mission St San Francisco CA 94103-2905 Office Phone: 415-777-8869. E-mail: swinn@sfchronicle.com.

**WINNECKE, JOYCELYN,** editor; m. Bill Adee. Degree, U. So. Ind. Writer obituaries Evansville (Ind.) Courier and Press, 1977; reporter Wash. bur. Scripps Howard; city editor Indpls. Star; dep. metro editor, then metro news editor Chgo. Sun-Times, 1994—99; mng. editor Chgo. Sun Times, 1999—2002, Chgo. Tribune, 2002—. Office: Chgo Tribune 435 N Michigan Ave Chicago IL 60611

**WINNER, GEORGE HENRY,** lawyer; b. Elmira, N.Y., July 31, 1949; s. George H. and Beverly S. (Sweet) W.; m. Lynn Hardman, Dec. 4, 1976; children: Catherine H., Elizabeth H., Meredith F. BA, St. Lawrence U., 1971. Bar: N.Y. 1977, U.S. Dist. Ct. (no. and we. dists.) N.Y. 1977. Adminstrv. asst. N.Y. State Senate, Albany, N.Y., 1972-76, counsel, 1977-78, minority leader pro-tem, 1990—; N.Y. state assemblyman 127th Dist., Albany, NY, 1979—2004; ptnr., assoc. Winner, Suthern & Delaney, Elmira, NY, 1977-84; ptnr. Winner & Denton, Elmira, NY, 1984-94, Denton, Keyser, LaBreque & Moore, Elmira, 1995—2002, Keuster Maloney & Winner LLP, 2002—; sen. 53d Dist., Albany, 2005—. Dir. Peak Resorts, Inc., Virgil, N.Y., 1994—. Chemung County GOP exec. com., Elmira, 1980—. Mem. N.Y. State Bar Assn., Chemung County Bar Assn. Republican. Avocations: skiing, golf, scuba diving. Home: 15 Abbey Rd Elmira NY 14905 Office: Keyser Maloney & Winner 150 Lake St Elmira NY 14901-3401 Office Phone: 607-734-0990.

**WINNER, KARIN E.,** editor; b. White Plains, NY, Dec. 27, 1945; BA in Journalism, U. So. Calif. Editor San Diego Union-Tribune, 1995—. Office: San Diego Union-Tribune Pub Co 350 Camino De La Reina San Diego CA 92112-0191 Office 619-293-1201. E-mail: Karin.winner@uniontrib.com.

**WINNER, MICHAEL ROBERT,** film director, film producer, writer; b. London, Oct. 30, 1935; s. George Joseph and Helen (Zloty) W. Degree in law and econs. with honors, Cambridge U., Eng., 1956. Writer Fleet St. (newspapers), London, 1956-58. Columnist London Sunday Times, 1990, London News of the World, 1995. Engaged in film prodn., 1956; dir. films Play it Cool, 1962, West 11, 1963, The Mechanic, 1972, Death Wish II, 1981; dir., writer The Cool Mikado, 1962, You Must be Joking, 1965, The Wicked Lady, 1982; producer, dir. The System, 1963, I'll Never Forget What's 'isname, 1967, The Games, 1969, Lawman, 1970, The Nightcomers, 1971, Chato's Land, 1971, Scorpio, 1972, The Stone Killer, 1973, Death Wish, 1974, Won Ton Ton The Dog Who Saved Hollywood, 1975, Firepower, 1978, Scream for Help, 1983, Death Wish III, 1985; producer, writer, dir. films The Jokers, 1966, Hannibal Brooks, 1968, The Sentinel, 1976, The Big Sleep, 1977, Appointment With Death, 1987, A Chorus of Disapproval, 1988, Bullsey!, 1989, Dirty Weekend, 1992, Parting Shots, 1997; producer plays Nights at the Comedy, Comedy Theatre, London, 1960, The Silence of St. Just, Gardner Centre, Brighton, 1971, The Tempest, Wyndhams Theatre, London, 1974, A Day in Hollywood, A Night in the Ukraine, Mayfair Theatre, London, 1978, (TV series London Weekend TV) Michael Winner's TV Crimes, 1990, 91, 92, 93, 94; author: Winner's Dinners, 1999, rev. edit., 2000, Winner Guide to Whining and Dining, 2002, (autobiography) Winner Takes All, 2004, paperback edit., 2005; actor: (BBC film) For the Greater Good,

1990, Decadence, 1993, The Flump, 2000; actor and/or dir. commls. including Esure Ins., Kenco, Doritos, Books for Schs. Founder, chmn. Police Meml. Trust, 1984. Mem. Dirs. Guild Gt. Britain (coun.) Office: Scimitar Films Ltd 219 Kensington High St London W8 6BD England Office Phone: 0207 603 7272. E-mail: winner@ftech.co.uk.

**WINNICK, GARY,** communications executive; b. Roslyn, N.Y. married Karen; 3 children. Grad., C.W. Post Coll. With Drexel Burnham Lambert, Los Angeles, Calif.; founder Pacific Capital Group, 1985; chmn., founder Global Crossings Ltd., Beverly Hills, Calif., 1997—2002. Nat. adv. bd. Chase Manhattan Bank. Trustee Mus. Modern Art, N.Y.C.

**WINNIE, GLENNA BARBARA,** pediatric pulmonologist; b. Lansing, Mich., Oct. 14; d. Robert John and Irene (Fetchik) W.; m. Jeffrey Alan Cooper, Mar. 17, 1990; children: Robert Jefferson Cooper, David Jamison Cooper. BS, Mich. State U., 1973; MD, Vanderbilt U., 1977. Diplomate Am. Bd. Pediatrics, Am. Bd. Pediatric Pumonology. Resident in pediatrics Case Western Res. U./Babies and Childrens Hosp., Cleve., 1977-79, fellow in pediatric pulmonology, 1979-82; asst. prof. pediatrics Albany (N.Y.) Med. Coll., 1982-90, assoc. prof. pediatrcis, 1990-95, head pediatric pulmonology sect., 1982-95; adminstrv. dir. pulmonary divsn., co-dir. cystic fibrosis U. Pitts., 1995—. Dir. Albany Pediat. Pulmonary and Cystic Fibrosis Ctr., 1982—95; adminstrv. dir. pulmonary divsn. Children's Hosp. of Pitts., 1995—99; co-dir. Cystic Fibrosis Ctr., 1995—, dir. pulmonary divsn., 1999—, dir. pediatric sleep lab., 2001—, Children's Hosp. of Pitts., 2001—. Contbr. articles to profl. jours. Bd. dirs. Albany Ronald McDonald Ho., 1986-88, Cystic Fibrosis Found.-Western Pa. chpt., 1996—. Rsch. grantee Nat. Cystic Fibrosis Found., 1984-86, 88-90, 90-01, NIH, 1987-93. Mem.: Soc. Pediat. Rsch., Am. Acad. Sleep Medicine, Capital Dist. Pediatric Soc. (treas. 1985—90, pres. 1990—91), Am. Coll. Physician Execs., Am. Thoracic Soc. (rsch. fellowship review com. 1989—92), Am. Acad. Pediatrics (exec. com. chest sect. 1996—2001). Episcopalian. Achievements include description of role of Epstein Barr virus in pulmonary exacerbations in cystic fibrosis. Office: Childrens Nat Med Ctr 111 Michigan Ave NW Washington DC 20010-2970

**WINOGRAD, AUDREY LESSER,** retired advertising executive; b. NYC, Oct. 6, 1933; d. Jack J. and Theresa Lorraine (Elkind) Lesser; m. Melvin H. Winograd, Apr. 29, 1956; 1 child, Hope Elise. BA, U. Conn., 1953. Asst. advt. mgr. T. Baumritter Co., Inc., N.Y.C., 1953-54; asst. dir. pub. rels. and creative merchandising Kirby, Block & Co., Inc., N.Y.C., 1954-56; divsn. mdse. mgr., dir. advt. and sales promotion Winograd's Dept. Store, Inc., Point Pleasant, NJ, 1956-73, v.p., 1960-73, exec. v.p., 1973-86; pres., CEO AMW Assocs., Atlanta, 1976—2002, ret.. Editor bus. newsletters. Bd. dirs. Temple Beth Am, Lakewood, N.J., 1970-72, Temple Emanuel, Atlanta, 1999-2001; active Alley Cat Allies, Fund for Animals. Mem. NAFE, LWV, Jersey Pub. Rels. and Advt. Assn. (pres. 1982-83, bd. dirs.), Retail Advt. and Mktg. Assn. Internat. Monmouth Ocean Devel. Coun., Monmouth County Bus. Assn. (bd. dirs. 1985-97, pres. 1988-90, Woman of Yr. 1992-93, Person of Yr. 1995), N.J. Assn. Women Bus. Owners, Am. Soc. Advt. and Promotion, Ocean C. of C. (bd. dirs. 1994-97, award 1993, 94), Retail Advt. Conf. (Career Achievements and Contbns. to Soc. award 1993), Soc. Prevention Cruelty to Animals, Animal Protection Inst. Am., Human Soc., Internat. Fund Animal Welfare, World Wildlife Fund, Friends of Animals, Defenders of Wildlife, Nat. Humane Edn. Soc., In Defense of Animals, Atlanta Humane Soc., Sierra Club, Peta, Natural Resources Def. Coun., Delta Rescue, Last Chance for Animals, Best Friends, Humane Soc. of U.S., United Animal Nat., Wilderness Soc., Lifesavers Wild Horse Rescue, Environ. Defense, Audobon, Greenpeace. Avocations: collecting animal collectibles, gourmet cooking, environmental protection, exercise. Office: AMW Assocs 5304 Vernon Lake Dr Atlanta GA 30338-3527 Personal E-mail: audwin@comcast.net.

**WINOGRAD, NICHOLAS,** chemist; b. New London, Conn., Dec. 27, 1945; s. Arthur Selig Winograd and Winifred (Schaefer) Winograd Mayes; m. Barbara J. Garrison. BS, Rensselaer Poly. Inst., 1967; PhD, Case We. Res. U., 1970. Asst. prof. chemistry Purdue U., West Lafayette, Ind., 1970-75, assoc. prof. chemistry, 1975-79; prof. chemistry Pa. State U., University Park, 1979-85, Evan Pugh prof. chemistry, 1985—. Cons. Lawrence Livermore Lab., 1997-2003; mem. chemistry adv. bd. NSF, Washington, 1987-90, analytical chemistry adv. bd., 1986-89. Contbr. articles to profl. jours. A.P. Sloan Found. fellow, 1974; Guggenheim Found. fellow, 1977; recipient Founder's prize Tex. Instruments Found., 1984, Faculty Scholar's Pa. State U., 1985, Bennedetti Pichler award Am. Microchem. Soc., 1991, Outstanding Alumnus award Case We. Res. U., 1991. Fellow AAAS (award); mem. Am. Chem. Soc. Home: 138 Chemistry Ln Spring Mills PA 16875-9703 Office: Pa State U Dept of Chemistry 209 Chemistry Bldg University Park PA 16802-6300 Office Phone: 814-863-0001. Business E-Mail: nxw@psu.edu.

**WINOGRAD, SHMUEL,** mathematician; b. Tel Aviv, Jan. 4, 1936; came to U.S., 1956, naturalized, 1965; s. Pinchas Mordechai and Rachel Winograd; m. Elaine Ruth Tates, Jan 5, 1958; children: Daniel H., Sharon A. BSEE, MSEE, MIT; PhD in Math., NYU, 1968. Mem. research staff IBM, Yorktown Heights, NY, 1961-70, dir. math. sci. dept., 1970-74, 81-94; IBM fellow, 1972—. Permanent vis. prof. Technion, Israel. Author: (with J.D. Cowan) Reliable Computations in the Presence of Noise; research on complexity of computations and algorithms for signal processing. Fellow IEEE (W. Wallace McDowell award 1974), Assn. Computing Machinery, N.Y. Acad. Scis.; mem. NAS, Am. Math. Soc., Math. Assn. Am., Am. Philos. Soc., Soc. Indsl. and Applied Math. Am. Acad. Arts & Scis. Home: 235 Glendale Rd Scarsdale NY 10598-1533 Office: IBM Research PO Box 218 Yorktown Heights NY 10598-0218 Business E-Mail: swino@us.ibm.com.

**WINOKUR, MARISSA JARET,** actress; b. NYC, Feb. 2, 1973; Studied at, Am. Musical and Dramatic Acad. Actor: (plays, Broadway) Grease, 1995, Hairspray, 2002 (Tony award for best actress, 2003), 2005; (plays) Guys and Dolls, Peter Pan, Little Shop of Horrors, Romeo and Juliet, Nunsense II, Grandma Sylvia's Funeral, Hair, Happy Days; (films) Demo Real, 1998, Why Love Doesn't Work, 1999, Never Been Kissed, 1999, American Beauty, 1999, Sleep Easy, Hutch Rimes, 2000, Scary Movie, 2000, Amy's Orgasm, 2001, On Edge, 2001, Now You Know, 2002; (TV films) Beautiful Girl, 2003; co-exec. prodr. (TV films) Beautiful Girl, 2003; actor(guest appearances): (TV series) The Steve Harvey Show, 1998, Felicity, 1999, Dharma & Greg, 1999, 2000, Moesha, 2000, Curb Your Enthusiasm, 2000, Just Shoot Me, 2000, The Ellen Show, 2001, Boston Public, 2001. Office Phone: 310-288-5888. Office Fax: 310-288-5868.

**WINROTH, ANDERS,** historian, educator; m. Christina Winroth; children: Hjalmar, Elsa. BA, Stockholm U., 1990; PhD, Columbia U., 1996. Rsch. fellow U. Newcastle upon Tyne, 1996—98; asst. prof. dept. history Yale U. 1998—2003, assoc. prof., 2003—04, prof., 2004—. Author: The Making of Gratian's Decretum, 2000; co-editor: Charters, Cartularies and Archives: The preservation and transmission of Documents in the Medieval West, 2002. Morse fellow, Yale U., 2001—02, MacArthur Found. fellow, 2003. Office: Yale Univ Dept of History PO Box 208324 New Haven CT 06520 Office Phone: 203-432-7657.

**WINSHIP, FREDERICK MOERY,** journalist; b. Franklin, Ohio, Sept. 24, 1924; s. Wilbur William and Edna B. (Moery) W.; m. Joanne Tree Thompson, Aug. 29, 1967. AB, DePauw U., 1945; MS, Columbia, 1946. Corr. UPI, 1946—; assigned UN, 1947-49; editorial staff N.Y.C., 1950-60, cultural affairs editor, 1960-72, sr. editor, 1972-75, asst. mng. editor, 1975-80; sr. editor arts/theater N.Y.C., 1980-98; Broadway critic, 1985-98; arts critic at large, 2000—. Contbr. articles mags. Pres. Letters Abroad, Inc., 1962-83; chmn. Easter Seal Soc., N.Y.C., 1964-73, Oratorio Soc. N.Y., 1965-75, N.Y. Conf. Patriotic Socs., 1967-72; bd. dirs. Odell House-Rochambeau Hdgrs., 1965-75, N.Y. State Easter Seal Soc., 1969-72, Mus. of City of N.Y., 1974—, Am. Philharm. Orch., 1981-82, Friends of the Am. Theater Wing, 1990—. Recipient Am. Legion Journalism award, 1955; Whitelaw Reid Journalism fellow India, 1958; Creative Club Journalism award, 1962 Mem. S.A.R. (sec.

N.Y. chpt. 1963-68), St. Nicholas, Founders and Patriots, Mayflower Descs., Soc. Colonial Wars (bd. dirs.), S.R., Soc. Cincinnati, Sigma Delta Chi. Republican. Episcopalian. Home: 419 E 57th St New York NY 10022-3060

**WINSLET, KATE,** actress; b. Reading, Berkshire, Eng., Oct. 5, 1975; d. Roger and Sally Bridges Winslet; m. James Threapleton, Nov. 22, 1998 (div. Dec. 13, 2001); 1 child, Mia; m. Sam Mendes, May 24, 2003; 1 child, Joe Alfie. Appeared in plays including Peter Pan, What the Butler Saw (Manchester Evening News award for Best Supporting Actress), A Game of Soldiers, (musical) Adrian Mole; appeared in films including Heavenly Creatures, 1994 (Best Fgn. Actress award New Zealand Film and TV Awards, Best Brit. Actress London Film Critics Cir. Awards, Best Brit. Empire Mag. Awards), Sense and Sensibility, 1995 (SAG award, Brit. Acad. Film and TV award for Best Supporting Actress, Golden Globe nominee, Acad. Award nominee for Best Supporting Actress), A Kid in King Arthur's Court, 1995, Jude, 1996, Hamlet, 1996, Titanic, 1997 (BAFTA award, Best Brit. Actress Empire Mag., Golden Globe nominee, Best European Actress European Film Acad., Acad. Award nominee for Best Actress), Hideous Kinky, 1998, Holy Smoke, 1999, Faeries (voice), 1999, Quills, 2000 (Best Actress Evening Std. Brit. Film award, nominee Best Supporting Actress SAG award 2000), Enigma, 2001 (Best Brit. Actress Empire Awards), Christmas Carol: The Movie (voice), 2001, Iris: A Memoir of Iris Murdoch, 2001(Acad. Award nominee for Best Supporting Actress, Golden Globe nominee, BAFTA nominee), War Game, 2001 The Life of David Gale, 2003, Plunge: The Movie, 2003, Eternal Sunshine of the Spotless Mind, 2004 (Best Brit. Actress London Film Critics Cir. Awards, Best Brit. Actress Empire Mag. Awards, Acad. Award nominee, Golden Globe nominee, SAG nominee, BAFTA nominee), Finding Neverland, 2004 (BAFTA nominee), Romance & Cigarettes, 2005, All The King's Men, 2006, Little Children, 2006, Deep Sea 3D (narrator), 2006; appeared in TV movies including Pride (voice), 2004. Recipient Grammy award for best spoken word album for children, 2000, Best Actress, London Evening Std. Brit. Film Awards.*

**WINSLETT, STONER,** artistic director; b. Jacksonville, Fla., Aug. 17, 1958; m. Donald Paulding Irwin; children: Louise Gray Irwin, Elizabeth Irwin, Alexander Pankoff, Caroline Irwin. Student, Am. Ballet Theatre Sch., N.C. Sch. of the Arts; BFA summa cum laude, Smith Coll., 1980. Artistic dir. Richmond Ballet, 1980—. Pres. John Butler Found. Mem.: Phi Beta Kappa. Office: Richmond Ballet 407 E Canal St Richmond VA 23219-3811*

**WINSLOW, DAVID ALLEN,** chaplain, retired military officer; b. Dexter, Iowa, July 12, 1944; s. Franklin E. and Inez Maude (McPherson) W.; children: Frances, David. BA, So. Nazarene U., 1968; MDiv, Drew U., 1971, STM, 1974; cert. of achievement, Emergency Mgmt. Inst., FEMA, 1997. Ordained to ministry United Meth. Ch. Detroit Annual Conf., 1969; cert. FEMA instr. Clergyman, 1969—; assoc. min. All Sts. Episcopal. Ch., Millington, NJ, 1969-70; asst. min. Marble Collegiate Ch., NYC, 1970-71; min. No. NJ Conf. United Meth. Ch., 1971-75; joined chaplain corps USN, 1974, advanced through grades to lt. comdr., 1980, ret., 1995; chaplain Oak Knoll Naval Med. Ctr., Oakland, Calif., 1993-95; command chaplain USNS Mercy T-AH19, Oakland, 1993—95; disaster cons. Ch. World Svc., Cupertino, Calif., 1997—2001. Chaplain med. assistance team CA-6/nat. disaster med. sys. Contra/Costa County, Calif., 1997—2005; founding mem. Dept. Homeland Security, 2003; salesperson Dept. real estate State of Calif., 2000—. Author: The Utmost for the Highest, 1993, Epilogy: God Still Speaks, 1994, Be Thou My Vision, 1994, Evening Prayers At Sea, 1995, Wiseman Still Adore Him, 1995, God's Power At Work, 1996; (with Walsh) A Year of Promise: Meditations, 1995, editor: The Road to Bethlehem: Advent, 1993, Preparation for Resurrecton: Lent, 1994, God's Promise: Advent, 1994, The Way of the Cross: Lent, 1995; contbr. articles to profl. jours. Bd. dirs. disaster svcs. and family svcs. ARC, Santa Ana, Calif., 1988-91, Child Abuse Prevention Ctr., Orange, Calif., 1990-91; bd. dirs. Santa Clara County Coun. Chs., 1993-94, del., 1995-98; bd. dir. Salvation Army Adult Rehab. Ctr. Adv. Coun., San Jose, Calif., 1993-2003; bd. dirs. emergency svcs. Santa Clara Valley chpt. ARC, San Jose, 1995-98; bd. dirs. disaster svcs. Interfaith Svc., Inc., San Jose Internat. Airport. Recipient Navy Achievement medal, Navy Commendation medal with Gold Star in lieu of 2nd award, Navy Expeditionary medal, Humanitarian Svc. medal, Battle "E" award, Nat. Def. Svc. medal, sea svc. deployment ribbon with silver star. Fellow Am. Acad. Experts in Traumatic Stress (cert. expert), USN League (hon.), Disabled Am. Vets. (life), Sunrise Exch. Club (chaplain 1989-91), Dick Richards Breakfast Club (chaplain 1988-91), Kiwanis, Masons (life mem. Franklin lodge 0195, N.Y.), Shriners, Scottish Rite Avocations: golf, skiing, sailing. Office Phone: 408-858-5983.

**WINSLOW, DELANA LYNN,** business educator; b. Chgo., Aug. 8, 1949; d. George and Dorothy (Barnes) W.; children: Hans Koppenhoefer, Alicia Koppenhoefer. AAS, Orange County CC, 1969; BS in Orgnl. Mgmt., Nyack Coll., 1991; MS in Instructional Tech., NY Inst. Tech., 2001; postgrad., U. Albany, 2004. Acct. IBM, Hopewell Junction, N.Y., 1969-74; asst. office mgr., asst. to pres. Mid-Valley Petroleum, Newburgh, N.Y., 1979-85; dir. fin. Kahn, Inc., Newburgh, 1985-89; owner, mgr. Bus. Office Support Sys., Inc., Newburgh, 1989-97; tchr. Orange-Ulster BOCES, Goshen, NY, 1990-98, JS Burke Cath. Sch., 1988—99, Westchester Bus. Inst., White Plains, NY, 1999—2002; math. tchg. fellow Fordham Leadership Acad. for Bus. and Tech., NYC, 2003; virtual enterprises coord. NYC DOE Fordham Leadership Acad. for Bus. and Tech., Bronx, 2004—05; adj. coord. Bronx Cmty. Coll., 2005. Adj. instr. Bronx CC, 2005. Choir dir. Bethlehem Presbyn., Cornwall, N.Y., 1972-75; virtual enterprises coord. Foldham Leadership Acad. for Bus., adn Tech., 2004-05. Mem.: AAUW, Internat. Platform Assn. Republican. Methodist. Home: 32 Higgins Trl Monroe NY 10950-6624 E-mail: dlwinslowny@netscape.net.

**WINSLOW, HELEN LITTELL,** lawyer; b. Wilmington, Del., May 11, 1952; d. Julian Dallas and Jean (Littell) W.; m. Jonathan David Jaffe, Nov. 8, 1980; children: Kenan Winslow Jaffe, Nathaniel Harrington Jaffe, Saul Handler Jaffe. AB, Bryn Mawr Coll., 1974; JD, U. N.C., 1977. Bar: Del. 1977, U.S. Dist. Ct. Del. 1977, U.S. Ct. Appeals (3d cir.) 1980, U.S. Supreme Ct.1980. Law clk. to presiding judge U.S. Dist. Ct. Del., Wilmington, 1977-79; assoc. Richards, Layton & Finger, Wilmington, 1979—2001; asst. gen. counsel H.D. Lee Co., Inc., 2001—. Mem. ABA, Fed. Bar Assn. (v.p. Del. chpt. 1985-86, pres. Del. chpt. 1987—89), Del. Bar Assn. (pres.-elect 2004, pres. 2005-2006), Am. Judicature Soc., Bryn Mawr Del Club (Wilmington). Democrat. Jewish. Avocation: singing. Office: HD Lee Co 201 Baynard Building 3411 Silverside Rd Concord Pike Wilmington DE 19810

**WINSLOW, NORMAN ELDON,** small business owner; b. Oakland, Calif., Apr. 4, 1938; s. Merton Conrad and Roberta Eilene (Drennen) W.; m. Betty June Cagy, Jan. 14, 1962 (div. Aug. 1971); 1 child, Todd Kenelm; m. Ilene Ruth Jackson, Feb. 3, 1979. BS, Fresno (Calif.) State U., 1959. Asst. mgr. Proctors Jewelers, Fresno, 1959-62; from agt. to dist. mgr. Allstate Ins. Co., Fresno, 1962-69; ins. agt. Fidelity Union Life Ins., Dallas, 1969-71; dist. and zone mgr. 7-Eleven, Inc., Dallas, 1971-78; owner Ser-Vis-Etc. LLC, Fresno, Calif., 1978—. Arbitration/Calif. Superior Crs. Pub./editor FranchiserviceNews; author: Hands in Your Pockets, 1992; contbr. numerous articles to profl. jours. With USAFNG, 1961-67. Mem. Nat. Coalition of Assn. of 7-11 Franchises (affiliate, mem. adv. bd. 1984-90). Republican. Methodist. Avocations: gardening, photography, travel, model railroading. Home: 1293 N Fancher Ave Fresno CA 93727 Office: Ser-Vis-Etc LLC PO Box 8444 Fresno CA 93747-8444 Personal E-mail: elru2379@aol.com.

**WINSLOW, ROBERT A.,** real estate company executive; With IDC Real Estate (now JonesLangLaSalle), Tex., 1971; mktg. exec. IBM Corp.; co-founder, chmn., CEO US Equities Realty, Chgo., 1978—. Former co-chmn. Chgo. Devel. Coun.; mem. Mayor's Fellows Program, Fin. Rsch. and Adv. Com.; bd. mem. Metra, MB Fin. Inc. Founding chmn. Southgate Chgo.; former bd. mem. Mus. Contemporary Art; mem. bd. overseers Rush Med. Coll.; trustee Rush-Presbyn.-St. Luke's Med. Ctr., North Cntrl. Coll., Ill. Masonic Med. Ctr., Columbia Coll., Chgo.; active Boy Scouts Am./Chgo.

Area Coun., Bright New City, 1989—97; dir. Arts Club Chgo., The Marwen Found.; bd. mem. The Graham Found., Chgo. Pub. Libr. Found. Mem.: Chicagoland C. of C. (v.p. bd. dirs. 1982—91, bd. mem. 1990—, pres. adv. bd. 1991). Office: US Equities Realty Ste 400 20 N Michigan Ave Chicago IL 60602*

**WINSLOW, WALTER WILLIAM,** psychiatrist, educator; b. Lacombe, Alta., Can., Nov. 23, 1925; came to U.S., 1959, naturalized, 1964; s. Floyd Raymond and Lily Evangeline (Palmer) W.; m. Barbara Ann Spiker; children: Colleen Denise, Dwight Walter, Barbara Jean, Wendi Jae. BS, La Sierra Coll., 1949; MD, Loma Linda U., 1952. Diplomate: Am. Bd. Psychiatry and Neurology. Intern Vancouver Gen. Hosp., 1952; psychiat. resident Provincial Mental Hosp., Essondale, B.C., 1957-59, Harding Hosp., Worthington, Ohio, 1959-60; instr. dept. psychiatry and indsl. medicine U. Cin., 1960-66, dept. preventive medicine, 1964-66; asst. prof. psychiatry U. N.Mex., Albuquerque, 1966-68, assoc. prof. psychiatry, 1969-74, prof., chmn. dept. psychiatry, 1974-91, dir. mental health programs, 1976-91; med. dir. Charter Hosp. of Albuquerque, 1991-95, Charter-Heights BHS, Albuquerque, 1995—99; ret. Assoc. prof. psychiatry Georgetown U., Washington, 1968-69; dir. bernalillo County Mental Health/Mental Retardation Ctr., 1970-78, 81-91. Author: The History of Psychiatry in New Mexico, 1889-1989, 2005; contbr. articles to profl. jours. Recipient N.Mex. Gov.'s Commendation for 10 yrs. service in mental health, 1979 Fellow Am. Psychiat. Assn. (life, area VII rep. 1981-85, Assembly Speaker's award 1984), Am. Coll. of Psychiatrists (life), Am. Assn. Community Psychiatrists (hon.); mem. AMA, Am. Assn. Psychiatry and the Law, N.Mex. Psychiat. Assn. (pres. 1974-75) Republican.

**WINSON, ELLEN-MARIE (MACONE),** school system administrator, reading specialist; b. Woburn, Mass., Sept. 6, 1941; d. Fred Charles and Edna McKay Macone; m. Robert Arthur Winson, Aug. 7, 1971 (dec. Dec. 2005); children: Maura Jane Mann, Suzanne Marie DiPalma, Peter Robert. BS, U. of Mass., 1958—62; MEd, Northeastern U., 1963—66. Teacher Elementary K-8 Mass. Dept. of Edn., 1962, Reading Specialist K-12 Mass. Dept of Edn., 1965, Supervisor of Reading K-12 Mass. Dept. of Edn., 1968. Elem. tchr. Woburn Pub. Schools, Woburn, Mass., 1962—66, reading specialist k-12, 1966—76, Title 1 tchr., 1987—2000, Title 1 dir., 2000—. Remedial reading coord. Woburn Pub. Schools, Mass., 1968—77. V.p. Friends of the Libr., Woburn, Mass., 2001; bd. dirs. Title 1 Dissemination Project, Melrose, Mass., 1990—2005. Recipient State Leadership award, Nat. Assn. of Fed. Edn. Program Administrators, 2005. Mem.: Coun. of Administrators of Compensatory Edn. (rec. sec. 2003—05), Internat. Reading Assn. Avocations: travel, reading. Home: 23 Clinton St Woburn MA 01801 Office: Woburn Public Schools 55 Locust St Woburn MA 01801 Office Phone: 781-937-8233 x 230. Office Fax: 781-937-0715. Personal E-mail: ewinson@aol.com. E-mail: emwinson@woburnpublicschools.com.

**WINSTEAD, DWIGHT,** medical products executive; BS in Med. Tech., Delta State U. Health care salesman Worthington Diagnostics, Johnson & Johnson; dir. materials mgmt., adminstrv. dir. clin. labs. Alton Ochsner Found. Hosp., New Orleans; exec. v.p. VHA, Inc.; pres. Owen Healthcare, 1997—2001; grp. pres. Clin. Svcs. and Consulting Cardinal Health, 2001, group pres. Automation and Info. Svcs., COO Clin. Technologies and Svcs., grp. pres. Clin. Technologies and Svcs., 2006—. Bd. dirs. Sonus Pharms., 1995—. Office: Cardinal Health 7000 Cardinal Pl Dublin OH 43017*

**WINSTEAD, NASH NICKS,** academic administrator, plant pathologist; b. Durham County, N.C., June 12, 1925; s. Nash L. and Lizzy (Featherston) W.; m. Geraldine Larkin Kelly, Sept. 17, 1949; 1 dau., Karen Jewell. BS, N.C. State U., 1948, MS, 1951; PhD, U. Wis., 1953. Asst. prof. plant pathology, Raleigh, 1953-58; assoc. prof. N.C. State U., Raleigh, 1958-61, prof., 1961-90, prof. emeritus, 1991—, dir. inst. biol. scis., 1965-67, asst. dir. agrl. exptl. sta., 1965-67, asst. provost, 1967-73, assoc. provost, 1973-74, provost and vice chancellor, 1974-90, acting chancellor, 1981-82. Phillip Found. intern acad. adminstrn. Ind. U., 1965-66; bd. trustees N.C. Sch. Sci. and Math., 1985-90. Author: Home grown and Homemade, 1997, Mama's Book, 1998, The Provost's Office N.C. State U., An Informal History, 1955-93, 1999, The Civil War Campaigns Involving Corporal James Fletcher Winstead, 1999, Featherston Memories, 2002, Start Where You Are and Use What You've Got, 2005; contbr. articles profl. jours. Mem. N.C. Council on Higher Edn. for Adults, 1967-75; inst. rep. So. Assn. for Colls. and Schs., 1967-74; mem. Cooperating Raleigh Colls., 1968-90, pres., 1971-73, 83-85; chmn. interaction between protoplasm and toxicants com. So. Regional Edn. Bd., 1964-65; Bd. dirs. N.C. State U. YMCA, 1963-65; trustee Meth. Home for Children, 1980-88, pres., 1983-84, N.C. Wesleyan Coll., 1987-97. Served with USAAF, 1943-46. Recipient Sigma Xi research award, 1960 Fellow AAAS; Mem. Am. Phytopath. Soc. (chmn. disease, pathogen physiology com.), Am. Inst. Biol. Scis., N.C. Assn. Colls. and Univs. (exec. com. 1974-80, pres. 1978-79), Nat. Assn. State Univs. and Land Grant Colls. (edn. telecommunications com. 1980-85, equal opportunity com. 1985-88), Acad. Deans for So. States, N.C. Assn. of Acad. Officers (exec. com. 1986-89, v.p., pres. 1987-88), Sigma Xi, Phi Kappa Phi, Omicron Delta Kappa. Clubs: Torch Internat. (sec.). Home: 1109 Glendale Dr Raleigh NC 27612-4709

**WINSTED, DONALD EUGENE, III,** psychologist; b. Indpls., Apr. 4, 1962; s. Donald Eugene Winsted Jr. and Margorie Frances (Knapp) Winsted; m. Kimberly Salane Daniels-Winsted, Oct. 24; children: Dara, Ariel, Elliott. PhD, Ball State U., 1996. Lic. psychologist Tex. State Bd. Examiners of Psychologist. Prof. psychology Letourneau U., Longview, Tex., 1996—2005; lic. psychologist Shore and Assoc., Longview, 1996—. Psychologist Family and Protective Svcs., Longview, 1996—; Pathways Hosp., Longview, 2005—. With U.S. Army, 1986—92. Named Outstanding Sr., Ball State U., Dept. Psychological Sci., 1990; recipient Dist. Honor Graduate Class 3/89, U.S. Army Acad. Health Svcs.; Honors fellowship, Ft. Sam Houston, 1990. Mem.: Am. Psychological Assn. Meth. Avocations: guitar, basketball. Office: Shore and Assoc 107 Cmty Bk Blvd Ste 13 Longview TX 75605 Office Phone: 903-238-3030. Office Fax: 903-238-9051. Business E-Mail: dwinsted@charter.net.

**WINSTEN, SAUL NATHAN,** lawyer; b. Providence, Feb. 23, 1953; s. Harold H. and Anita E. Winsten; m. Patricia J. Miller, Aug. 7, 1977; children: David A., J. Benjamin, Jennifer M. BA, Beloit Coll., 1976; JD, Drake U., 1980. Shareholder DeWitt Ross & Stevens, Brookfield, Wis.; chmn. corp. counsel com. Wis. Mfrs. Commn., 2004—. Contbr. articles to profl. jours. Mem. Wis. Gov.'s Adv. Coun. on Internat. Trade, 1996-2003, co-chmn., 1999-2002; mem. Wis. Gov.'s Internat. Edn. Task Force, 1997-98; chmn. Wis. Mfrs. and Commerce Govt. Counsel Com., 2004—; mem. adv. com. Great Lakes Area IRS Adv. Com. Tax Exempt Orgn./Govt. Entities Coun., 2005—. Mem. ABA (chmn. com. young lawyers divsn. 1989-90, governing coun., antitrust, bus. and internat. law sects.), Wis. Bar Assn. (chair tax exempt orgn. com. of bus law sect. 2005—), Internat. Bar Assn., Japan-Am. Soc. Wis. (pres. 1993-94, co-founder 1990, sec. 1990-92), Nat. Assn. Japan-Am. Socs. (bd. dirs. 1991-97, exec. com. 1993-97), Order of Barristers, Hessen-Wisconsin, Inc. (bd. dirs.), Internat. Bar Assn. Office: DeWitt Ross & Stevens 13935 Bishops Dr Brookfield WI 53005-6605 Office Phone: 262-754-2852. Business E-Mail: snw@dewittross.com.

**WINSTON, ARNOLD,** psychiatrist, educator; b. N.Y.C., May 1, 1935; s. Irving and Eva (Barban) W.; m. Beverly M. Winston, Oct. 23, 1938; children: Roy, Eric, Michael. AB, U. Chgo., 1956; MD, SUNY Med. Ctr., Bklyn., 1960. Med. intern Downstate Med. Ctr-Kings County Hosp., Bklyn., 1960-61, psychiatry resident, 1961-62, 63-65, chief psychiatry treatment unit, 1966-72; chief of svc. South Beach Psychiat. Ctr., S.I., N.Y., 1972-74, dep. dir., 1974-75, dir., 1975-78; chmn. dept. psychiatry Beth Israel Med. Ctr., N.Y.C., 1978—. Asst. prof. psychiatry SUNY, Bklyn., 1971-75, clin. assoc. prof. psychiatry, 1975-78; prof. psychiatry Mt. Sinai Coll. Medicine, N.Y.C., 1978-94; prof. psychiatry Albert Einstein Coll. Medicine, Bronx, N.Y., 1994—, vice chmn. dept., 1996; Ostmarka lectr. U. Trondheim, 1989; vis. prof. U. Vt., 1983. Author: Short-Term Psychotherapy, 2002; contbr. numerous chpts. to books, articles to profl. jours. Psychotherapy rsch. grantee NIMH, 1993-95. Fellow Am. Psychiat. Assn. (disting. life), N.Y. Acad.

Medicine, Am. Coll. Psychiatrists; mem. Am. Bd. Psychiatry and Neurology (diplomate), Am. Assn. Psychiat. Adminstrs. (pres. N.Y. chpt. 1980-81). Avocations: tennis, skiing, gardening, golf. Office: Beth Israel Med Ctr 1st Ave & 16th St New York NY 10003 Office Phone: 212-420-2555. Business E-Mail: awinston@bethisraelny.org.

**WINSTON, FLAURA K.,** engineering researcher; Ph. D., Univ. of Penn. School of Medicine. Asst. physician Children's Hosp. of Phila., 1994—; founder, dir. TraumaLink. Recipient Melville medal ASME, 1995. Fellow: Bloomberg School of Public Health, John's Hopkins Univ. Office: The Children's Hosp of Phila 3535 TraumaLink 10th Fl 34th St and Civic Ctr Blvd Philadelphia PA 19104

**WINSTON, GEORGE,** solo pianist, guitarist, harmonica player; b. Hart, Mich., 1949; Ind. musician, 1967—; founder Dancing Cat Productions, Santa Cruz, Calif., 1983—. Ten solo piano albums including Ballads and Blues, 1972, Autumn, 1980, Winter Into Spring, 1982, December, 1982, Summer, 1991, Forest, 1994, Linus & Lucy: The Music of Vince Guaraldi, 1996, Plains, 1999, Night Divides the Day--The Music of the Doors, 2002, Montana, A Love Story, 2004; audiobook soundtracks: (with Meryl Streep) The Velveteen Rabbit, 1984, This is America Charlie Brown--Birth of the Constitution, 1988, (with Liv Ullmann) Sadako and the Thousand Paper Cranes Benefit CD, 1995, Remembrance-9/11 Memorial Benefit CD, 2001; prodr., co-prodr. 36 albums of the masters of traditional Hawaiian slack key (finger style) guitar. Office: c/o Dancing Cat Prodns PO Box 639 Santa Cruz CA 95061-0639 Office Phone: 831-429-5085. E-mail: ml@dancingcat.com.

**WINSTON, JUDITH ANN,** lawyer; b. Atlantic City, Nov. 23, 1943; d. Edward Carlton and Margaret Ann (Goodman) Marianno; m. Michael Russell Winston, Aug. 10, 1963; children: Lisa Marie, Cynthia Eileen. BA magna cum laude, Howard U., Washington, 1966; JD, Georgetown U., 1977. Bar: DC 1977, US Supreme Ct. Dir. EEO project Coun. Great City Schs., Washington, 1971-74; legal asst. Lawyers Com. for Civil Rights Under Law, Washington, 1975-77; spl. asst. to dir. Office for Civil Rights, HEW, Washington, 1977-79; exec. asst., legal counsel to chair U.S. EEO Commn., Washington, 1979-80; asst. gen. counsel U.S. Dept. Edn., 1980-86; dep. dir. Lawyers Com. for Civil Rights Under Law, 1986-88; dep. dir. pub. policy Women's Legal Def. Fund, Washington, 1988-90, chief employment discrimination com., 1979-88, ednl. cons., 1974-77; asst. prof. law Washington Coll. Law of Am. U., 1990-93, assoc. prof. law, 1993-95; gen. counsel U.S. Dept. Edn., Washington, 1993-2001; exec. dir. Pres.'s Initiative on Race, 1997-98; undersec. U.S. Dept. Edn., 2000-01; rsch. prof law Washington Coll. Law Am. U., Washington, 2001—; ptnr. Winston Withers & Assocs., LLC, Washington, 2002—. Author: (book) Desegregating Schools in the Great Cities: Philadelphia, 1970, Chronicle of a Decade 1961-70, 1970, Desegregating Urban Schools: Educational Equality/Quality, 1970; contbr. articles to profl jours. Pres. bd. dirs. Higher Achievement Program; bd. dirs. Ptnrs. for Dem. Change, Nat. Pub. Radio, So. Edn. Found., Nat. Law Ctr. on Poverty and Homelessness, Hist. Soc. DC Cir. Ct. Appeals, 2004—. Named Woman Lawyer of the Yr, Women's Bar Assn, 1997; recipient Margaret Brent, Am Bar Asn Comn Women in the Profession, 1998, Thurgood Marshall award, DC Bar, 1999. Fellow: ABA Found.; mem.: ACLU, Lawyers Com. Civil Rights Under Law, Nat. Bar Assn., Washington Bar Assn., Washington Coun. Lawyers, DC Bar Asn, Fed. Bar Assn., Links Inc., Phi Beta Kappa, Delta Theta Phi, Alpha Kappa Alpha. Democrat. Episcopalian. Home: 1371 Kalmia Rd NW Washington DC 20012-1444 Office: Winston Withers & Assocs 1730 M St NW # 413 Washington DC 20036 Office Phone: 202-887-8202. Business E-Mail: jwinston@winwithassocs.com.

**WINSTON, MARY A.,** publishing executive; BS in Acctg. and Info. Sys., U. Wis.; MBA, Northwestern U. Sr. auditor Arthur Andersen & Co., 1983—87; various positions Ameritech, 1987—91; dir. bus. devel. and strategy Biotech Divsn. Baxter Internat., 1991—95; sr. mgmt. positions Warner-Lambert, 1995—2002; v.p. Visteon Corp., 2002—04, treas., 2002—03, controller, 2003—04; exec. v.p. Scholastic Corp., N.Y., 2004—, CFO, 2004—. Office: Scholastic Corp 557 Broadway New York NY 10012

**WINSTON, MICHAEL RUSSELL,** foundation executive, historian; b. NYC, May 26, 1941; s. Charles Russell and Jocelyn Anita Prem Das Winston; m. Judith Ann Marianno, Aug. 10, 1963; children: Lisa Marie, Cynthia Eileen. BA magna cum laude, Howard U., 1962; MA, U. Calif.-Berkeley, 1964, PhD, 1974. Instr. dept. history Howard U., Washington, 1964-66, asst. dean Coll. Liberal Arts, 1968-69, asst. prof. dept. history, 1970-73, v.p. acad. affairs, 1983-90, prof. emeritus, 1990—; assoc. dir. Inst. Svc. to Edn., Washington, 1966; fellow Haus. Hof-und Staatsarchiv, Vienna, 1969; dir. Moorland Spingarn Rsch. Ctr., 1973-83; v.p., bd. dirs. Alfred Harcourt Found., Silver Spring, Md., 1992-93, pres., comptroller, 1993—. Cons. Smithsonian Instn., 1979—, nat. hist. Edn., 1978-85, NSF, 1985—. Author: (with R.W. Logan) The Negro in the United States, 1970, The Howard Univ.Dept. of History, 1913-73, 1973; editor: (with R.W. Logan) Dictionary of Am. Negro Biography, 1982, (with G.R. McNeil) Hist. Judgements Reconsidered, 1988; mem. editl. bd. Washington History, 1993-97. Mem. exec. bd. Nat. Capital Area coun. Boy Scouts Am., 1988—90; trustee spl. contbn. fund NAACP, 1980—82; trustee D.C. Pub. Defender Svc., 1985—88; bd. trustees Woodrow Wilson Nat. Fellowship Found., 1997—2006; bd. mgrs. Hist. Soc. Washington; bd. dirs. Harcourt Brace Jovanovich, 1980—91, D.C. Pub. Libr. Found., 1994—2002, pres., 1995—99, Nat. Coun. for History Standards; mem. bd. overseers' com. to visit dept. history Harvard U., 1996—; mem. nat. adv. com. and coun. of scholars Libr. of Congress; nat. adv. bd. Protect Historic Am.; mem. Commn. on Coll. and Univ. Nonprofl. Studies ABA; mem. Nat. Ctr. for History in the Schs. UCLA/NEH. Moten fellow U. Edinburgh, 1962, Wilson fellow U. Calif., 1962, Ford fellow, 1969-70, Woodrow Wilson Internat. Ctr. Scholars fellow, 1979-80; sr. scholar, 2001—. Mem.: Nat. Coun. for History Standards, Coun. on Foreign Relations, Atlantic Coun. of U.S., Hist. Soc. Washington, Am. Antiquarian Soc. Orgn Am Historians Am Hist. Assn., Grolier Club, Century Assn., Cosmos Club (Washington), Phi Beta Kappa (Ralph Waldo Emerson prize com. 2000). Democrat. Episcopalian. Home: 1371 Kalmia Rd NW Washington DC 20012-1444 Office: Alfred Harcourt Found 8401 Colesville Rd Silver Spring MD 20910-3352 Office Phone: 301-589-1551. E-mail: mwinston@erols.com. michaelrwinston@aol.com.

**WINSTON, ROLAND,** physicist, researcher; b. Moscow, USSR, Feb. 12, 1936; s. Joseph and Claudia (Goretskaya) W.; m. Patricia Louise LeGette, June 10, 1957; children: Joseph, John, Gregory. AB, Shimer Coll., 1953; BS, U. Chgo., 1956, MS, 1957, PhD, 1963. Asst. prof. physics U Pa., 1963-64; mem. faculty U. Chgo., 1964—, prof. physics, 1975—, chmn. physics dept., 1989-95. Recipient Kraus medal Franklin Inst., 1996, First Solar Personality of the Yr. award, Bangalore, India, 1999. Fellow: Am. Solar Engery Soc., Am. Optical Soc., Am. Phys. Soc., AAAS; mem.: Internat. Solar Energy Soc. ((Abbot award 1987, Farrington Daniels award 2001)), Franklin Inst. (hon.). Achievements include patent for ideal light collector for solar concentrators. Office: U Calif Merced Sch Natural Sci & Engring PO Box 2039 Merced CA 95344 Home: 3384 Locksley Ct Merced CA 95340-0751 E-mail: r-winston@uchicago.edu.

**WINSTON-MACAULEY, MARNIE,** columnist, writer; b. NYC, Sept. 1, 1948; d. Louis and Shirley Winston; m. Marnie Winston-Macauley, Apr. 21, 1979; 1 child, Simon Winston Macauley. MS, Columbia U., NYC, 1971. LCSW Nys Dept Edn., 1972. Sr. program specialist NYC Dept Corrections, NYC, 1971—75; dir. Pre-Trial Svcs. Inst Westchester, White Plains, NY, 1975—82; sr. program specialist NYC Dept Corrections, NYC, 1971—75. Adv. coun., NY State Senate, NY, 1979—81; v.p. State Assn. of Pre-Trial Svc. Agys., NY, 1979—81; bd. mem. Nat. Assn. Pre-Trial Svc. Agys., NY, 1977—80, Psychiat. Ctr. Advisor Com., Rockland County, NY, 1974—76. bd. mem. Las Vegas Ctr. for Edn., Media & the Arts, Nev., 2005—. Writer, columnist (syndicated advice columnist) Tribune, NY (nominated Emmy and Writers Guild award, Judith L. Ginsberg Meml. Award, Columbia U. Nat. Parenting Seal of Approval., 1971). Advisor Psychiat. Ctr. Adv. Com., NYC, 1977; bd. mem. Headstart, South Nyack, NY, 1974—76; mem. criminal

justice com. Adv. Coun., NY State Senate, NY, 1979—81; dir. of talent resources Las Vegas Ctr. for Edn., Media and the Arts, Las Vegas, 2005. Recipient Fed. Exemplary Project award, Fed. Govt.; Judith L. Ginsberg Meml. scholar, Columbia U. Independent. Jewish. Achievements include design of designed first classification system for prison, created development units in prisons, wrote 23 books, was syndicated advice columnist for Tribune Media, developed pre-trial services, Westchester, NY. Avocation: writing science fiction. Office Phone: 702-258-9904. Personal E-mail: asksadie@aol.com.

**WINT, DENNIS MICHAEL,** museum director; b. Macon, Ga., Mar. 17, 1943; s. Paul Kenneth and Mary (McClure) W. BS, U. Mich., 1965; tchr.'s cert., Lake Erie Coll., 1970; PhD, Case Western Res. U., 1977. Dir. environ. edn. Wiloughby Eastlake City Schs., 1968-70; dir. Ctr. Devel. Environment Curriculum, 1970-75; cons. Ohio Dept. Edn., 1975-77; dir. mus. and edn. Acad. Natural Scis., Phila., 1977-79, v.p., dir. natural history mus., 1979-82; dir. Cranbrook Inst. Sci., Bloomfield Hills, Mich., 1982-86; pres. St. Louis Sci. Ctr., 1986-95; pres., CEO The Franklin Inst., Phila., 1995—. Adj. asst. prof. Temple U.; past chmn. edn. and human resources adv. com. NSF, 1991-92; past pres. St. Louis Area Mus. Collaborative, 1991-92, mem. exec. com. Bd. govs. Greater Phila. 1st Partnership for Reform, 1995—98, mem. leadership com., 1995—98. Mem. Am. Assn. Mus. (bd. dirs. 2003-), Assn. Sci.-Tech. Ctrs. (mem. nominating com., v.p. 1993-95, pres. 1995-97, chmn. internat. com. 2000-05, strategic planning com. 2002-05), Greater Phila. Cultural Alliance (bd. dirs. 1996-05, chmn. strategic planning com. 2000-05), Benjamin Franklin Fed. Tchg. Commn. (co-chair). Home: 222 N 20th St Philadelphia PA 19103

**WINTER, CHESTER CALDWELL,** surgeon, educator, historian, writer; b. Cazenovia, NY, June 2, 1922; s. Chester Caldwell and Cora Evelyn (Martin) W.; m. Mary Antonia Merullo, Oct. 22, 1983; children by previous marriage: Paul, Ann, Jane. BA, U. Iowa, 1943, MD, 1946. Diplomate: Am. Bd. Urology. Intern Meth. Hosp., Indpls., 1946-47; med. resident St. Luke's Hosp., Cedar Rapids, Iowa, 1947; physician Calif., 1950-51; resident gen. surgery VA Hosp., Los Angeles, 1952-53; resident urology VA Hosp.-UCLA Med. Ctr., 1953-57; clin. asst. surgery UCLA, 1954-57, instr. surgery and urology, 1957-58, asst. prof. surgery and urology, 1958-59, asst. prof. Step II, 1959-60; prof. surgery and urology Ohio State U., 1960-88, prof. emeritus surgery and urology, 1988—, Louis Levy prof. urology, 1980-88. Dir. urology Ohio State U. Hosp., Columbus, 1960-78; cons. urology VA, Air Force hosps., Dayton, 1960-80. Radioisotope Renography, 1963, Correctable Renal Hypertension, 1964, Nursing Care of Patients with Urologic Diseases, 4th edit, 1977, Practical Urology, 1969, Vesicoureteral Reflux, 1969, A Concise History of the U.S. and the State of Ohio, 2002, A Bicentennial History of the State of Ohio, 2003, Ohio Cities: Historical Descriptions, 2004, Concise Biographies of Notable Ohioans, 2005; editl. cons. Exerpta Medica: Nuclear Medicine, Jour. AMA; mem. editl. bd. Andrology, Jour. Urology; contbr. articles to profl. jours. Served to capt. M.C. U.S. Army, 1943-46, 48-49. Fellow Am. Acad. Pediatricians, Am. Coll. Surgeons; mem. Am. Assn. Genitourinary Surgeons, Am. Urol. Assn., Soc. Univ. Surgeons, Soc. Pediatric Urology, Soc. Univ. Urologists, Internat. Soc. Urology, Urol. Investigators Forum, Ohio State Med. Assn., Columbus Surg. Soc., Central Ohio Urology Soc., Columbus Acad. Medicine, Ohio State U. Med. Soc. Home: 6425 Evening St Worthington OH 43085-3054 E-mail: cwinter3@ameritech.net.

**WINTER, DAMON,** photographer, photojournalist; Staff photographer LA Times, Dallas (Tex.) Morning News. Recipient Nat. Journalism award for photojournalism, Scripps Howard Found., 2006. Office: LA Times 202 W 1st St Los Angeles CA 90012 E-mail: dwinfo@damonwinter.com.*

**WINTER, DARIUS GERJON,** internist; b. Bucarest, Romania, Mar. 30, 1929; came to US, 1973; s. Alex Elek and Dora Winter; m. Jeanette Winter, Mar. 21, 1959; 1 child, Jacqueline. Bachelor's degree, Aurel Vlaicu, Bucarest, 1947; MD, Inst. Medicine and Pharmacy, Bucarest, 1953, PhD in Pharmacology, 1966. Bd. cert. diplomate in internal medicine. Pvt. practice, rschr., Romania, 1953-72; intern, resident in internal medicine Booth Meml. Med. Ctr., 1973-76; pvt. practice Rego Park, N.Y., 1976-98; group practice Mt. Sinai Med. Assoc., Rego Park, 1998—2002; pvt. practice Rego Park, 2002—; group practice Columbus Inst. Medicine, 2003—. Attending physician Parkway Hosp., Forest Hills., 1976—, N.Y. Hosp. Queens, 1976—, Mt. Sinai Hosp., N.Y.C., 1999, N. Shore U. Hosp. at Forest Hills, N.Y., 1999—. Contbr. numerous papers to profl. jours. Fellow ACP; mem. AMA, Am. Soc. Internal Medicine, N.Y. State Med. Soc. Avocations: travel, swimming. Office: 97-85 Queens Blvd Rego Park NY 11374 Office Phone: 718-261-9100. Personal E-mail: jdwinter2004@aol.com.

**WINTER, DAVID FERDINAND,** electrical engineering educator, consultant; b. St. Louis, Nov. 9, 1920; s. Ferdinand Conrad and Annie (Schaffer) W.; m. Bettie Jeanne Turner; children: Suzanne, Sharie Winter Chappeau. BSEE, Washington U., St.Louis, 1942; MSEE, MIT, 1948. Registered profl. engr., Mo. Staff mem. radiation lab. MIT, Cambridge, 1942-45, rsch. assoc. electronics lab., 1945-48; prof. elec. engring. Washington U., St. Louis, 1948-55, affiliate prof. elec. engring., 1955-67; v.p. engring. and rsch. Moloney Elec. Co., St. Louis, 1955-74; v.p. rsch. and engring. Blackburn div. IT&T, St. Louis, 1974-82; dir. advanced tech. devel., 1982-86; pvt. practice cons. St. Louis, 1986—. Ct. recognized tech. expert on sources, mitigation, and effects of stray voltage on dairy cattle cons. Wis. Pub. Svc. Commn.; cons. Naval Ordanance Lab. of Ind., Indpls., 1950-53, other industries, St. Louis, 1979—. Contbr. articles to profl. jours.; holder 28 patents. Elder, pastor Maplewood Bible Chapel, St. Louis. Recipient Alumni Achievement award, Wash. U., Sch. Engring. & Applied Sci., St. Louis Mo., 2003. Washington U., 2003. Fellow IEEE (life), Inst. Radio Engrs.; mem. NSPE, Am. Soc. Agrl. Engrs., Mo. Soc. Profl. Engrs., Sigma Xi, Tau Beta Pi, Eta Kappa Nu. Avocations: cabinet maker, photography, music instruments. Home and Office: 735 Harvard Ave University City MO 63130-3135 Office Phone: 314-727-4532. E-mail: dfwinter@hotmail.com.

**WINTER, DAVID LOUIS,** retired systems engineer, human factors scientist; b. Pitts., July 30, 1930; s. Louis A. and Gladys M. (Quinn) W.; m. Nancy L. Tear, July 1, 1952; children: Leeson, Blaise, Gregory, Lauren. BA, U. Pitts., 1952; MA, Columbia U., 1960; cert. computer sci., Northeastern U., 1971. Assoc. rsch. scientist Am. Insts. Rsch., Washington, 1961-66, sr. rsch. scientist Bedford, Mass., 1966-71, prin. rsch. scientist, 1976-94, retired, 1995; sr. systems analyst RCA Corp.-Sarnoff Labs., Princeton, NJ, 1971-73; mgr. systems engring. Codon Corp., Bedford, 1973-76. Computer systems cons. Mass. Dept. Mental Health, 1971-73. Pres. Mayo Peninsula Civic Assn., Edgewater, Md., 1964-65; v.p. Bedford Human Rels. Coun., 1992-94. Capt. USAF, 1952-64. Mem. Am. Acad. Polit. Sci., Human Factors Soc., Soc. Ednl. Tech. Democrat. Roman Catholic. Achievements include design and human factors test for 8 USAF electronic, intelligence and backscatter radar systems; design of 4 computer-assisted training systems for USAF E3 AWACS radar, computer displays, communications and navigation subsystems; cons. engr. for design and test of E6 Joint Stars battlefield surveillance system. Office: MicroVentures Ltd 27 Gould Rd Bedford MA 01730-1250

**WINTER, DONALD C.,** civilian military employee, former science administrator; BS in Physics with high distinction, U. Rochester, 1969; MS, U. Mich., 1970, PhD, 1972; grad., U. SC Mgmt. Policy Inst., 1979; grad. exec. program, UCLA, 1987; grad. program for sr. execs. in nat. and internat. security, Harvard U., 1991. Dir. rsch. & devel. in laser physics & applications TRW Sys., 1972—80, sr. sys. engring. & program mgr., 1982—90, v.p., gen. mgr. Def. Sys., Divsn. Space & Electronics, 1990—97, v.p., dep. gen. mgr. for group devel. space & electronics, 1998—99, pres., CEO, 2000—02; corp. v.p., pres. mission sys. Northrop Grumman Corp., L.A., 2002—05; program mgr. for space acquisition, tracking and pointing programs Def. Advanced Rsch. Projects Agy. US Dept. Def., 1980—82, sec. USN, 2006—. Bd. dirs. Wolf Trap Found., Electronic Industries Alliance, USO Met. Washington. Mem.: Nat. Acad. Engring. Office: US Dept Def Sec of Navy The Pentagon Rm 4E686 Washington DC 20350*

**WINTER, DOUGLAS E.,** lawyer, writer; b. St. Louis, Oct. 30, 1950; s. William E. and Dorothy E. (Schuster) W.; m. Lynne G. Turner, July 9, 1977; step-children: Carl, John, Stephen. BS, U. Ill., 1971, MS, 1972; JD, Harvard U., 1975; postgrad., Judge Advocate Gen.'s Sch., 1977. Bar: Mo. 1975, Ill. 1976, DC 1976. Clk. to Hon. William H. Webster U.S. Ct. Appeals (8th cir.), St. Louis, 1975-76; assoc. Covington & Burling, Washington, 1976-84; ptnr. Bryan Cave LLP, Washington, 1985—. Vis. prof. U. Iowa, Iowa City, 1980-81. Author: Stephen King, 1982, Shadowings: The Reader's Guide to Horror Fiction, 1983, Stephen King: The Art of Darkness, 1984, Faces of Fear, 1985, Black Wine, 1986, Splatter: A Cautionary Tale, 1987, Prime Evil, 1988, Darkness Absolute, 1991, Black Sun, 1994, Millennium, 1997, Revelations, 1997, Run, 2000, Clive Barker: The Dark Fantastic, 2001, Introduction to Legal Writing, 2004, American Zombie, 2006, A Little Brass Book of Full Metal Fiction, 2006; contbr. articles to popular mags. and nat. newspapers. Capt. US Army, 1973-77. Recipient world fantasy award World Fantasy Conv., 1986, award Internat. Horror Guild, 1995, 96, 98. Mem. Nat. Book Critics Circle, Horror Writers Assn. (chmn. grievance com. 1989—, trustee 1997—). Office: Bryan Cave LLP 700 13th St NW Fl 6 Washington DC 20005-3960 Office Phone: 202-508-6000. Business E-Mail: dewinter@bryancave.com.

**WINTER, FREDERICK ELLIOT,** fine arts educator; b. Barbados, WI, June 19, 1922; s. Edward Elliot and Constance Mabel (Gill) W.; m. Joan Elizabeth Hay, June 9, 1951; children: Elizabeth, Penelope, Mary, Michael. BA, McGill U., 1945; PhD, U. Toronto, 1957. Instr. U. Toronto, 1947-49, 50-51, lectr. 1951-57, asst. prof., 1957-61, asso. prof., 1961-68, prof., 1968-90, prof. emeritus, 1990—, chmn. dept. fine art, 1971-77, grad. coord. history of art, 1978-81, spl. lectr. history of art, 1990-98; chmn. U. Toronto Assn. Teaching Staff, 1968-69. Mem. mng. com. Am. Sch. Classical Studies, Athens, Greece, 1968-90, chair pers. com., 1975-77; mem. programme com. Can. Archaeol. Inst. at Athens, 1990-94; bd. dirs. Can. Acad. Inst., Athens. Author: (with G.S. Vickers, P.H. Brieger) Art and Man, Vol. I, 1963, Greek Fortifications, 1971, Studies in Hellenistic Architecture, 2006; contbr. articles Jour. Classical Assn. Can., Am. Jour. of Archaeology, Echos du Monde Classique/Classical Views. Recipient Gold medal in classics McGill U., 1945; Flavelle fellow U. Toronto, 1947-48; White fellow Am. Sch., Athens, 1949-50; spl. research fellow, 1977-78, 87-88; sr. assoc. fellow, 1982, 83-84, 86, 91; Am. Philos. Soc. grantee, 1957; grantee Soc. Sci. Humanities Rsch. Coun. Can., 1962, 68, 71, 75, 77-78, 82, 83-84, 86, 87-88, 91; grantee U. Toronto Humanities and Social Scis. Rsch. Com., 1993. Mem. Classical Assn. Can., Archeol. Inst. Am. (editorial adv. bd. Am. Jour. Archaeology 1981-85) Home: 164 Highgate Ave Willowdale ON Canada M2N 5G8

**WINTER, HARVEY JOHN,** retired government official; b. New Albion, NY, Apr. 6, 1915; s. George J. and Irene (Harvey) W.; m. Virginia M. Shaw, Sept. 2, 1939; 1 child, Jeffrey S. BA magna cum laude, U. Buffalo, 1938, MA, 1939; teaching fellow, George Washington U., 1939-40. Historian U.S. Nat. Park Service, 1940-42; archivist U.S. Nat. Archives, 1942-43; with U.S. Office Alien Property Custodian, 1943-51, chief reports and stats. sect., 1948-51; with State Dept., 1951—, chief internat. bus. practices div., 1959-61, asst. chief, 1961-70, chief bus. practices div., 1970-71, dir. office bus. protection, 1971-73, dir. office bus. practices, 1973-90; dir. office intellectual property and competition, 1991-92; U.S. del. European Productivity Agy. cartel meetings, Paris, 1958-60; mem. U.S. del. diplomatic confs. Internat. Design Agreement, The Hague, 1960, 17th session GATT, Geneva, 1960; U.S. alt. rep. 5th session Intergovtl. Copyright Com., London, 1960, 6th session, Madrid, 1961, 7th session, New Delhi, 1963; U.S. alt. rep. Interunion Coordinating Com., Geneva, 1963-69; U.S. observer African Seminar on Indsl. Property, Brazzaville, Congo, 1963; U.S. alt. observer Latin Am. Indsl. Property Seminar, Bogota, Colombia, 1964, Asian Indsl. Property Seminar, Colombo, Ceylon, 1966, Com. of Experts on Inventors' Certificates, Geneva, 1965, Com. of Experts on Adminstrv. Agreement, Geneva, 1965, Intellectual Property Diplomatic Conf., Stockholm, 1967, Diplomatic Conf. on Agreement for Classification of Indsl. Designs, Locarno, Switzerland, 1968, Diplomatic Conf. on Patent Cooperation Treaty, Washington, 1970, Diplomatic Conf. on Agreement for Internat. Patent Classification, Strasbourg, France, 1971, Diplomatic Conf. on Universal Copyright Conv., Paris, 1971; U.S. alt. rep. Diplomatic Conf. on Phonogram Conv., Geneva, 1971, Diplomatic Conf. on Indsl. Property, Vienna, 1973; U.S. rep. Com. Experts on Type Face Agreement, Geneva, 1972, Com. Experts on Communications Satellites Problems, Nairobi, Kenya, 1973; U.S. del. Diplomatic Conf. on Communications Satellites Conv., Brussels, 1974, Diplomatic Conf. on Treaty for Deposit Microorganisms, Budapest, Hungary, 1977, Diplomatic Conf. on Plant Protection Conv., Geneva, 1978, World Intellectual Property Orgn. Governing Bodies, Geneva, 1979-82, alt. del., 1983-91; alt. U.S. del. Diplomatic Conf. on Revision of Paris Conv., Geneva, 1980, 82, 83, 84 Nairobi, 1981; ret., 1992. U.S. del. UNESCO Experts on Rental of Videograms, Paris, 1984, Com. Govtl. Experts on Audiovisual Works and Phonograms, Paris, 1986, Com. Govtl. Experts on Internat. Register of Audiovisual Works, Geneva, 1988, Diplomatic Conf. on Treaty for Internat. Registration of Audiovisual Works, Geneva, 1989, Com. Experts on Disputes Steelement Treaty on Intellectual Property, 1990; chmn. Internat. Patent Classification Assembly, 1992. Recipient Superior Honor award Dept. State, 1971, 75, 89, 92, 50-Yr. Svc. award, 1990, Jefferson medal, N.J. Patent Law Assn., 1982; honoree Copyright Soc. U.S.A., 1989. Mem. Phi Beta Kappa. Episcopalian (vestry). Home: 1401 S Joyce St Apt 502 Arlington VA 22202-2137

**WINTER, HORST HENNING,** chemical engineer, educator; b. Stuttgart, Sept. 9, 1941; s. Simon Wilhelm and Hanna (Schwenn) W.; m. Karin Eckert, Aug. 29, 1969; children: Dirk Christopher, Lisa Susanne, Caroline Elke, Peter Benjamin. D of Engring., U. Stuttgart, 1973. Privatdozent U. Stuttgart, 1976-79; prof. U. Mass., Amherst, 1979—. Editor Rheologica Acta, 1989—; mem. edit. bd. Jour. Rheology, 1989—, Jour. Non-Newtonian Fluid Mechanics, 1989—; contbr. articles to sci. and profl. jours., 1977—. Recipient Bingham medal, 1996, NSF Creativity award, 1997, Alexander von Humboldt prize, 1999. Mem. Am. Soc. Rheology (exec. com. 1990-91), Am. Inst. Chem. Engrs., N.Y. Acad. Sci. Achievements include development of novel rheological techniques; discovery of self-similar relaxation of polymers at the gel point; universal time spectrum of linear flexible polymers of uniform length; invention of CSX process for making ultra-clean porous polymers; co-architect of the cyberinfrastructure platform for rheology. Office: U Mass Dept Chem Engring Amherst MA 01003 E-mail: winter@ecs.umass.edu.

**WINTER, JASON,** music educator; b. St. Louis, Mo., Feb. 13, 1975; s. Wayne and Anna Maria Winter; m. Pamela Fischer, May 26, 2003. MusB, DePauw U., 1997; MA in Tchg., Webster U., St. Louis, 2003. Cert. tchr. Mo. Vocal music tchr. Rockwood Sch. Dist., St. Louis, 1997—98, Wild Horse Elem. Sch., Chesterfield, Mo., 1998—2001; dir. Rockwood Children's Chorus, St. Louis, 2000—05; choir dir. Crestview Mid. Sch., Ellisville, Mo., 2001—. Music dir.: mus. Narnia, Joseph and the Amazing Technicolor Dreamcoat, Brigadoon, Cinderella, Oliver. Recipient Jeannie Simmons Mutz award, DePauw U., 1996, Outstanding Achievement award, Marquette Theater Co., 1999. Mem.: NEA, Mo. Music Educators Assn., Music Educators Nat. Conf., Mo. Choral Dirs. Assn., Am. Choral Dirs. Assn. Office Phone: 636-207-2520. Business E-Mail: winterjason@rockwood.k12.mo.us.

**WINTER, JOHN DAWSON, III,** blues guitarist, singer; b. Beaumont, Tex., Feb. 23, 1944; s. John Dawson II and Edwina (Holland) W. Grad. high sch. Organizer, performer numerous rock and blues bands, rec. artist, CBS Records, Inc., 1969—; TV and concert appearances through, U.S. and Europe, 1969—; albums include Johnny Winter, 1969, Second Winter, 1969, Johnny Winter-And, 1970, Live, 1971 (Gold Record award 1974), Still Alive and Well, 1973, Saints and Sinners, 1974, John Dawson Winter III, 1974, Captured Live, 1976, Nothin' But the Blues, 1977, White Hot and Blue, 1978, The Johnny Winter Story, 1980, Raisin' Cain, Serious Business, 1985 (Grammy nominee), 3rd Degree, 1986, The Winter of '88, 1988, Winter Scene, 1990, Let Me In, 1991, Hey Where's Your Brother, 1992, Scorchin' Blues, 1992, A Rock n' Roll Collection, 1994, Johnny Winter Live in New York City 1997, 1997; producer recs. by Muddy Waters; albums include Still

Hard (Artist of Yr., Rolling Stone mag. 1969), Hard Again, 1977 (Grammy award), I'm Ready, 1978 (Grammy award), Muddy Mississippi Waters Live, 1979 (Grammy award), King Bee, 1980. Mem. Broadcast Music Inc., Musicians Union.

**WINTER, JUDY ELAINE,** freelance/self-employed journalist, speaker; d. Lester App and Marie Pitcowicz; m. Richard Kent Winter, Aug. 7, 1976; children: Jenna Marie, Eric Richard(dec.). BA in Comm., Mich. State U., 1980. From advt. mgr. to corp. devel. assoc. WKAR-TV, East Lansing, Mich., 1985—88, corp. devel. assoc., 1988—92; freelance columnist DeWitt, Mich., 1996—. Co-author: A Special Kind of Love: For Those Who Love Children with Special Needs, 2004, Enabled in Words: The Real Lives, Real Victories of People with Disabilities, 2005; author: Breakthrough Parenting for Children with Special Needs: Raising the Bar of Expectations, 2006; contbr. articles to profl. jours. and periodicals. Co-chmn. Eric RicStar Winter Music Therapy Summer Camp, Mich. State U., 2003—. Named to Wall of Tolerance, Montgomery, Ala., 2003; recipient Cmty. Achievement award, Mich. Week, 2000, Disting. Achievement award, The Assn. Ednl. Pubs., 2000, 2002, Exceptional Parent award, Mich. Federated Chpts. Coun. Exceptional Children, 2002, Chief Everything Officer award, AOL and Dove, 2006. Avocations: travel, gardening, walking, photography, community outreach. E-mail: jappwinter@aol.com.

**WINTER, LEIGH ELLEN,** artist, educator; b. St. Louis, Mar. 31, 1969; d. Richard Lawrence and Vicki Hunt Winter, Kathryn Ann Winter (Stepmother); m. Gabriel Paul Katz, Sept. 29, 2001. BFA in Metalsmithing, U. Kans., Lawrence, 1992; MFA in Sculpture, Pratt Inst., N.Y.C., 1997. Asst. to art critic Robert C. Morgan, N.Y.C., 1996—98; artist's asst. Artist - Angiola Churchill, N.Y.C., 1997; curatorial asst./registrar Ian Woodner Family Collection, N.Y.C., 1998—99; asst. to the chair, art & design edn. Pratt Inst., Bklyn., instr., 2000—04, Sch. Visual Arts, N.Y.C., internship council., 2004—06, asst. dir. office career devel., 2006—. Artist's lecture Villa Duchesne, St. Louis, 1996; mem. grad. admissions com., art and design edn. Pratt Inst., Bklyn., 2000—04, mem. internship coun., 2001—04, mem. faculty search com., art and design edn., 2001—02, mem. peer rev. com., art and design edn., 2001—02, mem. sen. academic initiatives com., 2002—04. Exhibitions include Convergence, Pratt Inst., Bklyn., U. Kans., Lawrence, Kans., Wash. U., St. Louis, Mo., Olivette Cmty. Ctr. (Second Pl., 1984, Hon. Mention, 1984), St. Louis Artists Guild, Williamsburg Art and Hist. Soc., Bklyn., Caitlyn Gallery, St. Louis, Mo., The Bronx Mus. for the Arts, Bronx, N.Y., Monk Gallery, Williamsburg, Bklyn., N.Y., Mercer SS Gallery, NYC, 2004, prin. works include Point Lookout, East Windham, N.Y. Recipient Drawing and Painting, Villa Duchesne, Sculpture, Visual Arts; Artist's Residency, Vt. Studio Ctr., 2003, Artists in the Marketplace Program, Bronx Mus. of the Arts, 1997. Mem.: Nat. Assn. Colleges and Employers, Coll. Art Assn., Soc. Ethical Culture. Personal E-mail: leighwinter@optonline.net.

**WINTER, MARSHA TERRY,** French language educator; b. N.Y.C., Apr. 1, 1947; Student, Am. Acad. Dramatic Arts, 1962-63; AAS in Secretarial Sci., Queens Coll./CUNY, 1968, BA in French Lit., 1974, MA in French Lit., 1978; MPhil. in French Lit., Grad. Ctr./CUNY, 1981, PhD in French Lit., 1985. Cert. French tchr., N.Y. Asst. tchr. English lang. Coll. d'enseignement Secondaire, Amiens, France, 1974—75; tchr. French and English Cordozo High Sch., Bayside, N.Y., 1978; vis. asst. prof. French Fla. Atlantic U., Boca Raton, 1993. Adj. asst. prof. of French St. John's U., 1985; instr. conversational French program in pvt. enterprise, N.Y.C., 1986-93; instr. Gregg Steno Ballard Sch./YWCA; instr. sec. sci. Citibanc. Contbr. articles to The Writer, The N.Y. Times, profl. jours. and lit. mags. Participant Dark Shadows Festival, Newark; actress Colonial Ch. Players, Bayside, N.Y., 1985-86. Tchg. scholar French Govt., Amiens, 1974-75; fellow CUNY, 1980-81; grantee French Govt., Montpellier, 1981-82. Mem. MLA, Am. Assn. Tchrs. French, PhD Assn. Grad. Ctr. CUNY, CUNY Queens Coll. Alumni Assn. Avocations: writing literary and dark fantasy/horror novels, acting in community theatre.

**WINTER, MILDRED M.,** educational administrator; BA summa cum laude, Harris Tchrs. Coll.; MEd, U. Mo.; postgrad., Harvard U., U. Cin. Exec. dir. Parents As Tchrs. Nat. Cu. Inc., St. Louis. Tchr., cons., Mo., 1962 68; developer, dir. Ferguson-Florissant Parent-Child Early Edn. Program, Mo., 1969-72; first dir. early childhood edn. Mo. Dept. Elem. and Secondary Edn., 1972-84; sr. lectr. dept. elem. and early childhood edn. U. Mo., St. Louis; cons. in field. Contbr. articles to profl. jours. Named Outstanding Leader in Field of Edn., Mo. House of Reps., 1982, Outstanding Educator and Adv. for Young Children, Mo. Gov. Christopher S. Bond, 1984, Pioneer in Edn., State Bd. Edn., Mo. Dept. Edn., 1991, St. Louis Woman of Achievement in Edn., 1992; cited for Pioneering Leadership in Edn. Resolution, Mo. Senate, 1995; recipient Outstanding Svc. award Assn. Edn. of Young Children, 1984, Vol. Accreditation Leadership award, 1993, Spl. award Nat. Soc. Behavioral Pediat., 1992, Charles A. Dana Pioneering Achievements Health and Edn. Inst. Medicine award NAS, 1995. Office: Parents as Teachers Patnc 2228 Ball Dr Saint Louis MO 63146-8602

**WINTER, MIRIAM THERESE (GLORIA FRANCES WINTER),** nun, religious studies educator; b. Passaic, N.J., June 14, 1938; d. Mathias William and Irene Theresa (Marton) W. BMus, Cath. U. Am., 1964; M in Religious Edn., McMaster Divinity Coll., Hamilton, Ont., Can., 1976; PhD in Liturgical Studies, Princeton Theol. Sem., 1983; LHD (hon.), Albertus Magnus Coll., 1991, St. Joseph Coll., 1993, Mount St. Vincent U., 2004. Joined Med. Mission Sisters, Roman Cath. Ch., 1955. Dir. liturgy and liturgical music Med. Mission Sisters, Phila., 1960-76, pub. rels. dir., coord., 1963-72; assoc. prof. liturgy, worship and spirituality Hartford (Conn.) Sem., 1980-85, prof., 1985—, prof. liturgy, worship, spirituality, and feminist studies, 1994—; founder, dir. Women's Leadership Inst., 1996—. Mem. faculty St. Therese's Inst., Phila., 1964-68, acad. dir., 1968-72, Immaculate Conception Sem. Summer Program, Mo., 1969, Cath. U. Summer Grad. Program, Washington, 1970, Hope Ecumenical Inst., Jerusalem, summer 1974, 75, 76, McMaster Divinity Coll. Grad. Program, 1976, Continuing Edn. Program, 1976, N.Y. Archdiocesan Sch. Liturgical Music, summer 1980, 82, Vancouver Sch. Theology, summer 1982, USN Chaplains through Auburn Theol. Sem., 1990; mem. adj. faculty Union Inst., Cin., 1992-94; with emergency relief work Internat. Rescue Com., Cambodia, 1979-80, Malteser-Hilfsdienst Auslandsdienst, Germany, 1984, Med. Mission Sisters, Ethiopia, 1985; lectr., instr., performer, worship leader, song leader for various groups by invitation, nat. and internat., 1967—. Author: Preparing the Way of the Lord, 1978, God-With-Us: Resources for Prayer and Praise, 1979, An Anthology of Scripture Songs, 1982, Why Sing? Toward a Theology of Catholic Church Music, 1984, WomanPrayer, Woman Song: Resources for Ritual, 1987, WomanWord: A Feminist Lectionary and Psalter, 1990, WomanWisdom: A Feminist Lectionary and Psalter, Women of the Hebrew Scriptures, Part I, 1992 (1st pl. award for books on liturgy Cath. Press Assn., 1992), Woman-Witness: A Feminist Lectionary and Psalter, Women of the Hebrew Scriptures, Part II, 1992 (1st pl. award for books on liturgy Cath. Press Assn., 1993), The Gospel According to Mary: A New Testament for Women, 1993; co-author: Defecting in Place: Women Claiming Responsibility for Their Own Spiritual Lives, 1994 (2d pl. award for books on gender studies Cath. Press Assn., 1995), The Chronicles of Noah and Her Sisters: Genesis and Exodus According to Women, 1995 (2d pl. award for books on gender studies Cath. Press Assn., 1996), Songlines: Hymns, Songs, Rounds and Refrains, 1996, The Singer and the Song: An Autobiography of the Spirit, 1999, Out of the Depths, The Story of Ludmila Javorova, Ordained Roman Catholic Priest, 2001 (1st pl. award for books on popular presentation of the Cath. faith Cath. Press Assn., 2002), Eucharist with a small "e", 2005 (3d pl. award for books on liturgy, 2006); author: numerous songs including albums Keepsake, Hymns Re-Imagined, SpiritSong, WomanSong, WomanSong, Remember Me, Sandstone, Songs of Promise, RSVP: Let Us Pray, Gold, Incense and Myrrh, In Love, Seasons (Christian Oscar award Nat. Evang. Film Found., 1971), Knock, Knock, Praise the Lord in Many Voices (live rec. of Mass of a Pilgrim People premiered at Carnegie Hall), 1967, I Know the Secret, Joy is Like the Rain (Gold album in USA and Australia); contbr. articles to profl. jours. Bd. dirs. Capitol Region Conf. Chs., 1984-91, v.p., 1986-88. pres. bd. dirs., 1988-90, past pres., 1990-91, Archdiocesan Office Urban Affairs, 1986-95;

mem. Christian Conf. ann. event WINFEST, 1986, 87; mem. small christian communities design team Archdiocese of Hartford, 1987-91; mem. major events design team RENEW, 1986; subcommn. chair Archdiocesan Office of Synod, 1991; mem. New Eng. team Ministry of Money, 1984-90, 93; mem. The New Century Hymnal editl. com. United Ch. of Christ, 1993-95; active Pediats. AIDS Unit Yale-New Haven Hosp., Covenant to Care, Voices of Joy Gospel Choir women imprisioned at Niantic. Grantee Lilly Endowment, 1989-90, 91-93; recipient Ho. of Reps. citation Commonwealth of Pa., 1968, Women in Leadership Edn. award YWCA Conn., 1989, Convenant to Care award for ministry to children, 1993; named to McMaster U. Alumni Gallery, 1982, Celebration of 120 Women in Leadership, 1987, Bayley-Ellard H.S. Hall of Fame, 1993, Conn. Women's Hall of Fame, 2002. Mem. ASCAP (Popular Awards list 1968—), AAUW (Excellence in Equity award Conn. chpt. 1995), Nat. Assn. Pastoral Musicians, N.Am. Acad. of Liturgy, Societas Liturgica. Avocations: photography, calligraphy. Office: Hartford Sem 77 Sherman St Hartford CT 06105-2260 Office Phone: 860-509-9558.

**WINTER, PETER MICHAEL,** anesthesiologist, educator; b. Sverdlovsk, Russia, Aug. 5, 1934; arrived in U.S., 1938, naturalized, 1944; s. George and Anne Winter; m. Michelle Yakopec, Dec. 28, 1991; children: Karin Anne, Christopher George, Lia Lynn, Tori Anne. BA, Cornell U., 1958; MD, U. Rochester, 1962. Diplomate Am. Bd. Anesthesiology. Intern U. Utah, Salt Lake City, 1962-63; resident in anesthesiology, pharmacology and respiratory physiology Mass. Gen. Hosp., Boston, 1963-65; USPHS fellow Harvard U. Med. Sch., Mass., 1964-66; Buswell fellow dept. physiology, asst. prof. SUNY, Buffalo, 1966-69; assoc. prof. dept. anesthesiology Sch. Medicine, U. Wash., Seattle, 1969-74, prof., 1974-79; prof., chmn. dept. anesthesiology and critical care medicine U. Pitts. Sch. Medicine, 1979-96, Peter and Eva Safar prof. anesthesiology/critical care med., 1987—96, prof. emeritus, dir. faculty devel., 1996—. Anesthesiologist in chief Univ. Health Ctr. Hosps., Pitts., 1979—96. Editl. cons.: Anesthesiology CCMJ; contbr. chapters to books, papers and abstracts to pubs. With U.S. Army, 1953—56. Recipient Career Devel. award, NIH, 1971. Mem.: AMA, Assn. univ. Anesthetists, Internat. Anesthesia Rsch. Soc., Undersea Med. Soc., Soc. Critical Care Medicine, N.Y. Acad. Scis., Royal Soc. Medicine, Am. Soc. Anesthesiologists, Am. Coll. Chest Physicians, Morton Soc., Am. Alpine Club. Office: 3471 5th Ave Ste 910 Pittsburgh PA 15213-3221 Office Phone: 412-692-4500.

**WINTER, RALPH KARL, JR.,** federal judge; b. Waterbury, Conn., July 30, 1935; married. BA, Yale U., 1957, JD, 1960; JD (hon.), Bklyn. Law Sch., N.Y. Law Sch. Bar: Conn. 1973. Rsch. assoc., lectr. Yale U., 1962—64, from asst. prof. assoc. prof. law, 1967—78, William K. Townsend prof. law, 1978—82, adj. prof. law, 1982—; spl. cons. subcom. on separation of powers U.S. Senate Com. on Judiciary, 1968—72; sr. fellow Brookings Inst., 1968—70; adj. scholar Am. Enterprise Inst., 1972—82; judge U.S. Ct. Appeals (2d cir.), New Haven, 1982—97, chief judge, 1997—2000, sr. judge, 2000—. Vis. prof. law U. Chgo., 1966; adv. com. civil rules Jud. Conf. U.S., 1987—92, chmn. adv. com. rules evidence, 1993—96, exec. com., 1998—2000, chmn. exec. com., 1999—2000. Contbr. articles to profl. jours. Recipient Conn. Law Rev. award, Learned Hand award, Fed. Bar Coun. Office: US Ct Appeals 2nd Cir US Courthouse 141 Church St New Haven CT 06510-2030*

**WINTER, RICHARD LAWRENCE,** diversified financial services company executive; b. St. Louis, Dec. 17, 1945; s. Melvin Lawrence and Kathleen Jane (O'Leary) W.; children from previous marriage: Leigh Ellen, Jessica Marie, George Bradford; m. Kathryn Ann Geppert, Dec. 4, 1993. BS in Math., St. Louis U., 1967, MS in Math. (fellow), 1969; MBA, U. Mo., St. Louis, 1976. Rsch. analyst Mo. Pacific R.R., St. Louis, 1971-73; dir. fin. rels. Linclay Corp., St. Louis, 1973-74; asst. v.p. 1st Nat. Bank in St. Louis (now Centerre Bank, NA) subs. Boatmen's 1st Bank, 1974-79; v.p. fin. UDE Corp., St. Louis, 1979-81; pres. Health Care Investments, Ltd., St. Louis, 1981—, Larus Corp., St. Louis, 1981—, Garden View Care Ctr., Inc., O'Fallon, Mo., 1987—, Garden View Care Ctr. of Chesterfield, Inc., 1990—, Garden View Care Ctr. of St. Louis, Inc., Valley Park, Mo., 1998—. Exec. bd. Duchesne Bank, St. Peters, Mo., 1989-97; lectr. math. U. Mo., St. Louis, 1972-74, St. Louis U., 1982-90. Exec. adv. bd. St. Louis U. Coll. Arts and Scis., 2000—; chmn. Mo. State Coun. Arts, 2005—06; bd. dirs. Dance St. Louis, 1998—2004, 2006—, Mid-Am. Arts Alliance, 2005—06; cmty. adv. bd. Coll. Fine Arts and Comm. U. St. Louis, 2003—; fundraising staff St. Louis Symphony, Jr. Achievement, United Way St. Louis, Arts and Edn. Fund, St. Louis, 1974—79. With U.S. Army, 1969—71. Mem. Nat. Health Lawyers Assn., Mo. Athletic Club (St. Louis), Pi Mu Epsilon. Roman Catholic. Home: 725 S Skinker Blvd Unit 9N Saint Louis MO 63105 Office: Ste 170 12444 Powerscourt Dr Saint Louis MO 63131-3659 Office Phone: 314-965-1991. Business E-Mail: richard-l-winter@gvcc.com.

**WINTER, ROBERT FRANK,** biologist, educator; b. Fresno, Calif., Apr. 29, 1925; s. William T. and Zona (Roberts) Winter; m. Mary J. Guraro; children: Sandra, Philip, Rodney, Alan, Randy. BS, Fresno State U., Calif., 1950; MS, U. San Francisco. Jr. high tchr. Fresno City Unified Sch. Dist., 1951—59, sci. supvr., 1960—70; biology tchr. Fresno City Coll., 1951—. Dir. lab. for learning Fresno County Schs., 1966—70; biology instr. Colo. State U., Ft. Collins, 1980, Calif. State U., Fresno. Contbr. articles to profl. jours. Summer camp dir. Boy Scouts Am., Fresno, 1950—60; pres. Fresno Nat. Soc., 1958—60; chmn., organizer Fresno Jr. Mus. Discovery Ctr. Sgt. AC U.S. Army, 1943—46. Avocations: falconry, fly fishing. Home: 2080 N DeWolf Ave Fresno CA 93727

**WINTER, ROBIN OKNER,** health facility administrator; b. Newark, Mar. 10, 1953; BA, Haverford Coll., Haverford, Pa., 1974; MD, Albert Einstein Coll. Medicine, 1978; M in Med. Mgmt., Carnegie Mellon U., 1999. Diplomate Am. Bd. Family Medicine (cert. in geriatric medicine). Dir. family medicine residency program JFK Med. Ctr., Edison, NJ, 1989—. Assoc. Am. Family Medicine Residency Dirs. (pres. 2003—04). Office: JFK Med Ctr 65 James St Edison NJ 08818 Office Phone: 732-321-7493. Office Fax: 732-906-4986.

**WINTER, ROGER PAUL,** former federal agency administrator; b. Hartford, Conn., July 13, 1942; s. Raymond Gustav and Marion Nellie (Stafford) W.; m. Delorise Allen, Aug. 22, 1966; children: Jonathan, Raymond Todd, Nicole. BA in Psychology, Wheaton Coll., 1964; LLD (hon.), Holy Family Coll., 1993. Asst. sec. Md. Dept. Human Resources, Balt., 1970-79, Md. Dept. Budget and Fiscal Planning, Annapolis, 1979-80; dir. Office of Refugee Resettlement, HHS, Washington, 1980-81, U.S. Com. for Refugees, Washington, 1981-2001; exec. dir. Immigration and Refugee Svcs. Am., Washington, 1994-2001; dir. Office U.S. Fgn. Disaster Assistance, Washington, 2001—02; asst. adminstr. Bur. Democracy Conflict & Humanitarian Response USAID, Washington, 2002—05; spl. rep. to Sudan US Dept. of State, 2005—. Cons. on refugee affairs Women's Refugee Project, Washington, 1981-84; adv. bd. Refugee Policy Group, 1981-86; mem. bd. Refugee Voices, 1988-96; mem. exec. com. Coun. Washington Reps. on UN, 1989-91. Recipient Disting. Service Cambodian Assn. Am., 1982, Disting. Service award Indochina Resource Action Ctr., 1988. Mem. Nat. Ry. Hist. Soc.-Balt., Sudan Relief and Rehab. Assn. (bd. dirs., sec. 1991-93). Lodges: Eagles.

**WINTER, RUTH GROSMAN (MRS. ARTHUR WINTER),** journalist; b. Newark, May 29, 1930; d. Robert Delmas and Rose (Rich) Grosman; m. Arthur Winter, June 16, 1955; children: Robin, Craig, Grant. BA, Upsala Coll., 1951; MS, Pace U., 1989. With Houston Press, 1955-56; gen. assignment Newark Star Ledger, 1951-55, sci. editor, 1956-69; columnist L.A. Times Syndicate, 1973-78, Register and Tribune, syndicate, 1981-85, isyndicate.com, 1999-2001. Columnist myskinMD.com, 2000-01; contbr. to consumer mags.; instr. St. Peters Coll., Jersey City.; vis. lectr. mag. writing Rutgers U. Author: Poisons in Your Food, rev. edits., 1971, 91, 99, 2004, How to Reduce Your Medical Bills, 1970, A Consumer's Dictionary of Food Additives, 1972, 3d rev. edit., 1994, 99, 2004, Vitamin E, The Miracle Worker, 1972, So You Have Sinus Trouble, 1973, Ageless Aging, 1973, So You Have a Pain in the Neck, 1974, rev. edit., 2000, A Consumer's Dictionary of Cosmetic Ingredients, 1974, 4th rev. edit., 1994, 6th rev. edit., 2005, Don't

Panic, 1975, The Fragile Bond: Marriage in the 70's, 1976, Triumph Over Tension, 1976 (N.J. Press Women's Book award), Scent Talks Among Animals, 1977, Cancer Causing Agents: A Preventive Guide, 1979, The Great Self-Improvement Sourcebook, 1980, The Scientific Case Against Smoking, 1980, People's Guide to Allergies and Allergens, 1984, A Consumer's Guide to Medicines in Food, 1995, So What Can I Eat?, 2006; co-author: The Lean Line One Month Lighter Program, 1985, Thin Kids Program, 1985, Build Your Brain Power, 1986, Eat Right: Be Bright, 1988, A Consumer's Dictionary of Medicines: Prescription, Over-the-Counter and Herbal, 1994, 97, Super Soy,: The Miracle Bean, 1996, rev. edit., 2000, Pain in the Neck, 1997, rev. edit., 2000, Anti Aging Hormones, 1997, Brain Workout, 1997, 2003, Vitamin E: Your Protection Against Exercise Fatigue, Weakened Immunity, Heart Disease, Cancer, Aging, Diabetic Damage, Environmental Toxins, 1998, Smart Food, 1999, The Female Athlete's Body Book: Preventing and Treating Sports Injuries in Women and Girls, 2003, What Can I Eat? 2006. Recipient award of merit ADA, 1966, Cecil award Arthritis Found., 1967, Am. Soc. Anesthesiologists award, 1969, Arthritis Found. award, 1978; named Alumnus of Year Upsala Coll., 1971, Woman of Year N.J. Daily Newspaper Women, 1971, Woman of Achievement Millburn Short Hills Profl. and Bus. Women's Assn., 1991, Golden Triangle award Am. Dermatol. Assn., 1998. Mem. Soc. Mag. Writers, Authors League, Nat. Assn. Sci. Writers, Am. Med. Writers Assn. (Eric Martin Meml. award), N.J. Daily Newspaper Women (awards news series 1958, 70, named Woman of Achievement 1971, 83), Am. Soc. Journalists and Authors (pres. 1977-78, spl. service award 1983, Lifetime Achievement award 2004), N.J. Press Women (pres. 1982-84) Home and Office: 44 Holly Dr Short Hills NJ 07078-1318 E-mail: ruth@www.brainbody.com.

**WINTER, TERENCE,** writer; BA, NYU; JD, St John's U. Sch. Law. Practiced law (2 years), NYC. Co-prodr., writer (TV series) Sister, Sister, 1994, Flipper, 1995, DiResta, 1998, The PJs, 1999, exec. prodr., writer Brooklyn Rules, 2006, The Sopranos, 2000— (co-recipient, Writers Guild award and Edgar Award for the episode, Pine Barrens, 2001, Emmy award for Best Writing in a Drama Series for the episode, Long Term Parking, 2004, Emmy award for Outstanding Writing for a Drama Series the episode, Members Only, 2006), guest appearances (TV series), 2000, 2004; writer: TV series Diagnosis Murder, 1993; writer (TV series) The Cosby Mysteries, 1994, Charlie Grace, 1995, Xena: Warrior Princess (3 episodes: 1995, 1996, 1998), (TV episode) The Great Defender, 1995, Get Rich or Die Tryin', 2005, (video game) 50 Cent: Bulletproof. Mem.: Conn. Bar, NY Bar.*

**WINTER, THOMAS SWANSON,** publishing executive; b. Teaneck, N.J., Dec. 28, 1937; s. Frank J. and Beulah (Swanson) W.; m. Dawne Cina, Mar. 28, 1978; children: Victoria Ruth, Abigail Swanson. AB, Harvard U., 1959, MBA, 1961. Asst. editor Human Events newspaper Human Events, Inc., Washington, 1961-64, editor, 1964—, co-owner, pres., 1966-99, pres., editor-in-chief, 1999—; pres. Fund for Objective News Reporting. Treas. Conservative Victory Fund, Washington, 1975—; 1st vice-chmn. Am. Conservative Union, 1972—. Mem.: Nat. Press, Capitol Hill, Lutheran. Home: 16 4th St SE Washington DC 20003-3804 Office: Human Events 1 Massachusetts Ave NW Washington DC 20001-1401 Office Phone: 202-216-0600. Business E-Mail: twinter@eaglepub.com.

**WINTER, WILLIAM EARL,** retired beverage company executive; b. Granite City, Ill., Sept. 21, 1920; s. William M. and Ada M. (Compton) W.; m. Dorothy E. Schacher, Feb. 20, 1944 (dec. 1976); children: William C., Douglas E.; m. Mildred E. Stiebel, Mar. 18, 1977. AB, U. Ill., 1942. With Seven-Up Co., St. Louis, 1946-81, v.p., dir. mktg., 1969-71, exec. v.p., 1971-74, pres., chief operating officer, 1974-76, pres., chief exec. officer, 1976-79, chmn. bd., 1979-81, also former dir., cons.; chmn. emeritus, 1996—; cons. Cadbury Beverages/Seven-Up, chmn. emeritus, 1996. Bd. dirs. YMCA Greater St. Louis, U. Ill. Found.; mem. exec. bd. St. Louis Area coun. Boy Scouts Am. Capt. U.S. Army, 1942-46. Named to Promotion Mktg. Hall of Fame, 1979, Beverage World Hall of Fame, 1986 Mem. Am. Mktg. Assn., Sales and Mktg. Execs. St. Louis, Promotion Mktg. Assn. Am. (chmn. bd. 1971-72), Phi Beta Kappa, Phi Eta Sigma, Omicron Delta Gamma. Home: 14112 Baywood Villages Dr Chesterfield MO 63017-3421

**WINTER, WILLIAM ERNEST,** physician, educator; b. San Francisco, June 10, 1952; BS, U. Santa Clara, 1974; MD, Loyola U., 1977. Diplomate Am. Bd. Pediatrics, Am. Bd. Pediatric Endocrinology, Am. Bd. Clin. Chemistry; diplomate in chem. pathology Am. Bd. Pathology. Intern, resident in pediatrics U. Ky.-Albert B. Chandler Med. ctr., Lexington, Ky., 1977-80, chief resident in pediatrics, 1980-81; clin. fellow in pediatric endocrinology and diabetes U. Fla. Coll. Medicine, Gainesville, 1981-82, rsch. fellow in pediatric, endocrinology and diabetes, 1982—84, assoc. prof., 1990-96, prof., 1996—; clin. chemist Shands Hosp., Gainesville, 1992—. Office: U Fla Pathology Dept PO Box 100275 Gainesville FL 32610-0275

**WINTER, WILLIAM FORREST,** retired governor, lawyer; b. Grenada, Miss., Feb. 21, 1923; s. William Aylmer and Inez (Parker) W.; m. Elise Varner, Oct. 10, 1950; children: Anne, Elise, Eleanor. BA, U. Miss., 1943, LLB, 1949; LLD, William Carey Coll., 1980, Millsaps Coll., 1983, Troy State U., 1988, Davidson Coll., 1996, Miss. U. for Women, 2000, U. N.C., 2004, Tougaloo Coll., 2004. Bar: Miss. 1949. Practice in Grenada, 1949-58; practice in Jackson, Miss., 1968—; ptnr. Watkins, Pyle, Ludlam, Winter and Stennis, 1968-80; sr. ptnr. Watkins Ludlam Winter & Stennis, 1985—. Mem. Miss. Ho. of Reps., 1948-56; state tax collector, 1956-64; state treas., 1964-68; lt. gov. Miss., 1972-76; gov., 1980-84. Eudora Welty prof. So. studies Millsaps Coll., 1989; Jamie Whitten prof. law U. Miss., 1989; prof. pub. policy Miss. Valley State U., 2001—05; chmn. So. Growth Policies Bd., 1981, So. Regional Edn. Bd., 1982, MDC, Inc.; mem. Pres.'s Adv. Bd. on Race, 1997—99; chmn. Adv. Commn. on Intergovtl. Rels., 1993—97. Pres. bd. trustees Miss. Dept. Archives and History; chmn. Kettering Found., 1990-93, Appalachian Regional Commn., 1983, Commn. on Future of South, 1986, Nat. Civic League, 1987-88, Nat. Commn. on State and Local Pub. Svc., Stennis Ctr. for Pub. Svc., Found. for the Mid South, with AUS, 1943-46, 51. Harvard U. Inst. Politics fellow, 1985. Mem. Am., Miss., Hinds County bar assns., U. Miss. Alumni Assn. (pres. 1979), Phi Delta Phi, Omicron Delta Kappa, Phi Delta Theta. Clubs: Univ. (Jackson). Democrat. Presbyterian. Office: 633 N State St Jackson MS 39202-3306 Office Phone: 601-949-4800.

**WINTER, WINTON ALLEN, JR.,** lawyer, state senator; b. Ft. Knox, Ky., Apr. 19, 1953; s. Winton A. and Nancy (Morsbach) W.; m. Mary Boyd, July 28, 1978; children: Katie, Molly, Elizabeth. BA, U. Kans., 1975, JD, 1978. Bar: Kans. 1978. Ptnr. law firm Stevens & Brand, LLP, Lawrence, Kans., 1978—; v.p., gen. counsel Peoples, Inc., 2000-02; pres., CEO Peoples Bank, 2002—; pres. Corp. for Change; mem. Kans. Senate, 1982-92. Bd. dirs. Lawrence United Fund, Boys Club of Lawrence. Mem. ABA, Kans. Bar Assn., Douglas County Bar Assn. Kans. U. Law Soc., Rotary. Republican. Roman Catholic. Note and comment editor Kans. Law Rev., 1977-78. Office: PO Box 1795 4831 W 6th St Lawrence KS 66049 Office Phone: 785-842-4004. Personal: wwinter@epeoples.com. Business E-Mail: wwinter@bankingunusual1.com

**WINTER CHASER, VIVIAN JANICE,** elementary school educator; d. Lloyd Winter Chaser and Thelma Olive Winter Chaser Hawk Track. BS in Edn., U. S.D., Springfield, 1974; MA in Ednl. Adminstrn., U. S.D., 1978. Elem. tchr. SW Elem. Sch., Phoenix, 2000—; dir. pub. rels. Cook Coll. and Theol. Sch., Tempe, Ariz. Episcopal Ch. women Diocese of Ariz., Phoenix, 2004—05. Am. Indian fellow, 1977—78. Mem.: Ariz. Edn. Assn. Democrat. Episcopalian. Avocations: sewing, beading, watching old western movies. Home: 708 S Lindon Ln Tempe AZ 85281 Office: Cook College and Theological School 708 S Lindon Ln Tempe AZ 85281 Office Phone: 480-968-9354 x 134. Business E-Mail: vivian@cookcollege.org.

**WINTERER, PHILIP STEELE,** lawyer; b. San Francisco, July 8, 1931; s. Steele Leland and Esther (Hardy) W.; m. Patricia Dowling, June 15, 1955; children: Edward J., Amey W. Marrella. BA with hons., Amherst Coll., 1953;

LLB, Harvard U., 1956. Bar: N.Y. 1957, Republic of Korea 1958. Assoc., ptnr., head tax dept., dep. presiding ptnr. Debevoise & Plimpton, NYC, 1956—93, ret. ptnr., 1994, of counsel, 1994—96. Treas. Harvard Law Rev.; contbr. articles to profl. publs. Past pres. Am. Italy Soc.; life trustee Amherst Coll.; chmn. emeritus Sch. of Am. Ballet; chmn. exec. com. Phipps Houses; trustee emeritus N.Y. State Bd. Nature Conservancy; past chmn. Austen Riggs Ctr.; past vice chmn. Adelphi U.; mem. bd. govs. Emily Dickinson Mus.; Folger Shakespeare Libr.; mem. adv. coun., past v.p. Adirondack Trail Improvement Soc. Recipient Amherst Coll. medal for Eminent Svc., 1980, Pres. medal Adelphi U., 2004. Mem.: Am. Coll. Tax Counsel, Tax Forum, Citizens Housing and Planning Coun. N.Y., Am. Law Inst., Coun. Fgn. Rels., Century Assn., Ausable Club (trustee, pres.), Fellows Phi Beta Kappa Soc. (bd. dirs.). Home: 57 Gulf Brook Way Keene NY 12942 also: 1165 5th Ave New York NY 10029-6931 Office: Debevoise & Plimpton 919 3rd Ave New York NY 10022 Personal E-mail: winterhill95@aol.com.

**WINTERER, VICTORIA THOMPSON,** small business owner; b. Chgo., May 4, 1943; d. Henry Lawrence and Charlotte (Mather) Thompson; m. William George Winterer, Sept. 2, 1967; children: William G. Jr., Andrew H., Britton T., Mark L. Cert., Emma Willard Sch., Troy, N.Y., 1961; BA, Vassar Coll., 1965. Picture rschr. Time, Inc., N.Y.C., 1965-72; pres. bd. trustees Conn. River Mus., Essex, 1983-86; dir. Rockfall Found., Middletown, Conn., 1986-92; chairwoman Campaign for Emma Willard, Troy, 1992-97; v.p., trustee Emma Willard Sch., 1986-2000; owner, exec. Griswold Inn, Inc., Essex, 1972-96. Tutor in field. Bd. dirs. Conn. River Valley and Shoreline Visitors' Coun., Middletown, 1994-96; sec. Essex Twp. Bd. Trade, Essex, 1990-96; mem. Essex Rep. Town Com., 1976-84; trustee (life) Conn. River Mus.; mem. zoning subcom. Boca Grande Cmty. Planning Coun., 2004—; hon. trustee Emma Willard Sch., 2000—, trustee Uncle Larry's Fund, 2001—. Named Disting. Citizen of Yr., Middlesex County C. of C., 1996; recipient Disting. Alumnae award for Svc. to Emma Willard Sch., 1996, Tangeman medal, 1997. Home: Snail's Pace PO Box 1009 Boca Grande FL 33921-0640

**WINTERER-SCHULZ, BARBARA JEAN,** graphics designer, writer; b. Manchester, N.H., Apr. 1, 1938; d. John Edward and Elizabeth Virginia Grace; m. Allen George Winterer, Mar. 30, 1959 (div. 1977); children: Audrey Lyn Winterer-Chavez, Amy Jo Winterer DeNoble. AA, Mesa (Ariz.) CC, 1980; BS summa cum laude, U. Md., Heidelberg, Germany, 1996; postgrad. Sheriff's Tng. Acad., Montezuma County, Colo.; grad., U. Colo. 2004. Art designer Morningstar Art Design Studio, Dolores, Colo., 1988—. Interpreter Colo. State Pk.; U.S. rail ranger Durango-Silverton R.R.; master gardener Colo. State U.; bd. dirs. S.W. Cmty. Resources; health care provider Archuleta County Sch. Dist., Pagosa Springs, Colo.; farm medic; guest lectr. Northern Ariz. Univ.; Mesa Verda Nat. Pk., UNESCO World Heritage Ctr. Contbr. articles to newspapers and jours. Asst. dir. Ariz. Myasthenia Gravis Found., 1977—80; ofcl. U.S. reporter World Eskimo Indian Olympics, Fairbanks, Alaska, 1994; mem. disaster response team ARC, Pagosa Springs, mem. Durango chpt.; bd. dirs., chmn. pub. rels. com. Habitat for Humanity, Pagosa Springs; interpreter Chimney Rock Hist. Archeol. Site; interpretive docent, vol. Bur. Land Mgmt., Anasazi Heritage Ctr. Mus., 2004—; mem. Friends of Libr., Dolores, Colo. Recipient Humanitarian award, Phila. Inst. Human Potential, 1972, Chancellor of Germany award for Acad. Achievement, 1986, citation of Meritorious Achievement award in the Arts and Humanitarianism, Internat. Biog. Ctr., 1997; scholar, Chancellor of Germany. Mem.: AAUW, Colo. Archeology Soc., Hihitsanom Archeol. Soc., Pub. Lands Interpretive Assn., Libr. of Congress (assoc.), Internat. Rotary, Nat. Fedn. Garden Clubs, Cortez Garden Club (pres.), Colo. Fedn. Garden Clubs, Phi Theta Kappa, Alpha Sigma Lambda. Avocations: gardening, gourmet cooking. Office: Morningstar Art Design Studio PO Box 388 Dolores CO 81323-0388

**WINTERMAN, CRAIG L.,** lawyer; b. Denver, Oct. 29, 1950; BS, U. Oreg., 1973; JD, Southwestern U., 1976. Bar: Calif. 1977, U.S. Dist. Ct. (cen. dist.) Calif. 1977, U.S. Dist. Ct. (so. and no. dists.) Calif. 1980, U.S. Ct. Appeals (9th cir.) 1980, U.S. Supreme Ct. 1980. Ptnr. Herzfeld & Rubin, L.A., 1986—. Mem. State Bar Calif., Assn. So. Calif. Def. Counsel, Assn. Advancement Auto. Medicine, U. Oreg. Alumni Assn. (pres. so. Calif. chpt. 1999-2001). Office: Herzfeld & Rubin 1925 Century Park E Ste 600 Los Angeles CA 90067-2783 E-mail: cwinterman@hrla.net.

**WINTER-NEIGHBORS, GWEN CAROLE,** special education educator, art educator, consultant; b. Greenville, S.C., July 14, 1938; d. James Edward (dec. 2002) and Evelyn (Lee) Walters (dec. 1998); m. David M. Winter Jr., Aug., 1963 (dec. Feb. 1980); children: Robin Carole Winter, Charles G. McCuen, Dustin Winter TeBrugge; m. Thomas Frederick Neighbors, Mar. 24, 1989. BA in Edn. and Art, Furman U., 1960, MA in Psychology, 1967; cert. in guidance/pers., Clemson U., 1981; EdD in Youth and Mid. Childhood Edn., Nova Southeastern U., 1988; postgrad., U. S.C., Spartanburg, 1981-89; cert. clear specialist instrn. with honors, Calif. State U., Northridge, 1991; art edn. cert., Calif. State U., L.A., 1991; JD, Glendale U., 1999. Cert. tchr. art, elem. edn., psychology, secondary guidance, S.C. Tchr. 7th grade Greenville Jr. H.S., 1960—63; art tchr. Wade Hampton H.S., Greenville, 1963—67; prin. adult edn. Woodmont H.S., Piedmont, SC, 1983—85, Mauldin H.S., Greenville and Mauldin, SC, 1981; tchr. ednl. psychology edn. dept. Allen U., Columbia, SC, 1969; activity therapist edn. dept. S.C. Dept. of Corrections, Columbia, 1973—76; art specialist gifted edn. Westcliffe Elem. Sch., Greenville, 1976—89; tchr. self-contained spl. day class Elysian Heights Elem. Sch., Echo Park and L.A., Calif., 1989—91; art tchr. med. drawing Sch. Dist. Greenville County Blue Ridge Mid. Sch., Greer, 1991—95; tchr./asst. head edn. dept. N. Greenville Coll., 2001—02. Participant nat. conf. U.S. Dept. Edn./So. Bell, Columbia, 1989; com. mem. nat. exec. com. Nova Southeastern U., 1988—89; asst. chmn., tchr. edn. dept. North Greenville Coll., 2001, adm., staff, 01, U. S.C., Spartanburg; adj., student tchr., supr. U. SC, 2002; adv. bd. S.C. Gov. Sch. for Arts and Humanities, parent/adm. adv. bd. Spl. Edn.; adj. prof. U. SC Univ. Ctr., Greenville, 2002—03; ind. rep. Primerica Fin. Svs., 2003—05. Mozart Book, 1988; author: Let's Sing a Song About America, 1988 (1st pl. Nat. Music award, 1990), numerous poems; featured poet: Internat. Libr. Poetry, 2004. Life mem. Rep. Presdl. Task Force, 1970—; mem. voter registration com. Lexington County Rep. Party, 1970—80; grand jury participant 13th Jud. Ct. Sys., Greenville, 1986—88, guardian ad litem, 1988—2004; mem. arts educators adv. task force S.C. Gov. Sch. Arts and Humanities, 2002—04; mem. spl. edn. parent adv. bd. representing Sue Cleveland Elem. Sch. Greenville Co. Sch. Dist., Spl. Edn. Topics and Trends, 2001—06; poll mgr. Greenville Co.; bd. dirs., vice chmn. Stronghold Min, Webb-Atkins Inst. of Change, 2005—; vice chmn. bd. dirs. Webb-Atkins Inst. Change. Tchr. Incentive grantee Sch. Dist. Greenville County, 1986-88, Project Earth grantee Bell South, 1988-89, 94-95, Edn. Improvement Act/Nat. Dissimination Network grantee S.C. State Dept. Edn., 1987-88, Targett 2,000 Arts in Curricular grantee S.C. Dept. Edn., 1994-95, Alliance grantee Bus. Cmty. Greenville, 1992-95, Greater Art Rsch. grantee, 1993-94, S.C. Govs. Sch. Study grantee, 1994, Edn. Improvement Act Competitive Tchr. grantee S.C. Dept. Edn., 1994-95, Alliance Grand grant, 1995-96; recipient Am. Jurisprudence Bancroft-Whitney award Glendale U. Sch. Law, 1997, 98, Excellence Recognition in Real Property award Glendale Law Faculty, 1997, Excellence in Art of Appellate Advocacy, Glendale U. Sch. Law, 1998, Am. Jurisprudence Bancroft-Whitney award Constl. Law I, 1998. Mem.: ABA, Palmetto State Tchr. Assn., S.C. Art Edn. Assn., S.C. Arts Alliance, Nat. Mus. Women in Arts, Nat. Art Edn. Assn., Furman U. Singer Alumni, Phi Delta Kappa. Baptist Avocations: computers, art, writing, music. Office Phone: 214-499-4619. Personal E-mail: gwen.neighbors@gmail.com.

**WINTEROWD, NORMAN WADELL,** government agency administrator; b. Salmon, Idaho, Sept. 2, 1945; s. Wadell Finley and Grace Emily Winterowd; m. Susan Ellen Moore, Mar. 16, 1968; children: Michelle Reneé Endicott, Alisa Marie Sullivan, Aaron Troy. BA in Bus. Adminstrn., Bellevue U., Nebr., 1985. Ops. mgr. FEMA/MERS, Maynard, Mass., 1989—90, program officer, 1991—96, DHS/FEMA/MERS, Lakewood, Colo., 1996—. Pres. Colo. Mormon Chorale, Denver, 2002—. E-7 USAF, 1963—83. Avocations: golf, running, fishing. Office Phone: 303-235-4878.

**WINTEROWD, WALTER ROSS,** language educator; b. Salt Lake City, Jan. 24, 1930; s. Harold Ross and Henrietta Ethel (Fike) W.; m. Norma Graham, Aug. 2, 1952; children: Geoffrey Ross, Anthony Gordon. BS, Utah State U., 1952; PhD, U. Utah, 1962. Asst. prof. U. Mont., Missoula, 1962-66; assoc. prof. U. So. Calif., Los Angeles, 1966-71, prof. English, 1971-79, McElderry prof. English, 1979-97, prof. emeritus, 1997—. Author: Rhetoric: A Synthesis, 1967, Contemporary Rhetoric, 1975, The Contemporary Writer, 1975, Composition/Rhetoric: A Synthesis, 1986, The Culture and Politics of Literacy, 1989, The Rhetoric of the "Other" Literature, 1990, (with Geoffrey Winterowd) The Critical Reader, Thinker, and Writer, 1992, The English Department: A Personal and Institutional History, 1998, Searching for Faith, 2005, (with Judith Rodby) the Uses of Grammar, 2005. Served with U.S. Army, 1953-55. Mem. Nat. Council Tchrs. English, AAUP Democrat. Home: 17551 San Roque Ln Huntington Beach CA 92647-6641 Personal E-mail: wrossw@msn.com.

**WINTERS, ANNE,** poet, educator; b. St. Paul, Oct. 13, 1939; d. Warrington Woodruff and Helen Winters; 1 child, Elizabeth. BA, NYU, 1961; MA, Columbia U., 1963; Phd, U. Calif., Berkeley, 1993. Lectr. MIT, Cambridge, Mass., 1981—82, U. Calif., Davis, Calif., 1983—85; instr. St. Marys, Calif., 1985—87; asst. prof. Northwestern U., Evanston, Ill., 1991—94; mem. lit. faculty Bennington (Vt.) Coll., 1994—97; prof. English U. Ill., Chgo., 1997—. Lectr. Harvard U., Cambridge, 1995, 96; vis. assoc. prof. U. Chgo., 1997—98. Translator: Salamander: sel Poems of Robert Marteau, 1979 (Poetry prize, 1979); author: The Key to the City, 1986 (nominated Nat. Book Critics Circle prize, 1986), The Displaced of Capital, 2004 (W.C. Williams prize). Recipient Poetry award, Wellesley Coll., 1997, Lit. award, Am. Acad. Arts & Letters, 2003; grantee, NEA, 1985. Mem.: Writers Programs Am., Modern Lang. Assn. Democrat. Office: English Dept Univ Ill 601 S Morgan St Dept Mc162 Chicago IL 60607-7100

**WINTERS, BARBARA JO,** musician; b. Salt Lake City; d. Louis McClain and Gwendolyn (Bradley) W. AB cum laude, UCLA, 1960, postgrad., 1961, Yale, 1960. Mem. oboe sect. L.A. Philharm., 1961-94, prin. oboist, 1972-94; ret. Clinician oboe, English horn, Oboe d'amore. Recs. movie, TV sound tracks. Avocation: painting. Home: 3529 Coldwater Canyon Ave Studio City CA 91604-4060 Office: 151 S Grand Ave Los Angeles CA 90012-3013

**WINTERS, DARCY LAFOUNTAIN,** medical association administrator; b. Middletown, N.J., Aug. 27, 1955; d. Donald Mark LaFountain and Suzanne (Gilman) LaFountain Westergard; m. Leland Monte McNabb, July 4, 1981 (div. Feb. 1989); 1 child, Leland Monte Jr.; m. Stephen H. Winters, May 30, 1997. BBA in Internat. Fin. cum laude, U. Miami, 1977. Real estate agent, Grad. Realtor's Inst. Market rsch. asst. Burger King Corp., Miami, Fla., 1975-77, regional mktg. supr. Huntington Beach, Calif., 1977-78; mgr., restaurant planning Holiday Inns, Inc., Memphis, 1978-79, mgr., nat. promotions, 1979-83; dir. lodging and travel planning Holiday Corp., Memphis, 1983-86; affiliate broker The Hobson Co., Realtors, Memphis, 1986-88, Crye Leike, Memphis, 1988-92; sr. v.p. comm. and planning Medishares Mgmt. Group, Inc., Memphis, 1991-2000. Founder, Lunch for Two, LLC, 2001—. Active Friends Pink Palace Mus., Memphis, 1987-91, Family Link/Runaway, Memphis, 1980-88; chmn. Foster Care Rev. Bd., Memphis, 1988-98; bd. dirs. Bethany Home, Memphis, 1989—, pres., 1995, treas., 1998; bd. dirs. Am. Cancer Soc., 1994—, v.p. 2000, Univ. Club of Memphis, 2000—; mktg. com. Health Industry Coun., 1994-95. Named Profl. Vol. of Yr., Friends of Pink Palace Mus., Memphis, 1989, 93, U.S. Masters Swimming All-Am., 1993, 94; grad. Leadership Memphis, 1995; named Cmty. Hero for Olympic Torch Relay, 1996, named One of Fifty Women Who Make a Difference in 1998, Women's News, Mertie Buckman Empowerment award, 1999. Mem. Le Bonheur Club, Memphis Runners Track Club, Univ. Club (bd. dirs. 2000—). Republican. Episcopalian. Avocations: competitive long distance running, tennis, swimming. Home: 3030 Murano Bay Dr Boynton Beach FL 33435-2852

**WINTERS, DEAN,** actor; b. NYC, July 20, 1964; Grad. with honors, Colo. Coll. Actor: (TV films) The Playroom, 1996, Firehouse, 1997, Strip Search, 2004; (films) Conspiracy Theory, 1997, Lifebreath, 1997, Undercover Angel, 1999, Snipes, 2001, Bullet in the Brain, 2001, Hellraiser:Hellseeker, 2002, Love Rome, 2002, Brooklyn Bound, 2004; (TV series) Homicide: Life on the Street, 1993, NYPD Blue, 1993, New York Undercover, 1994, Millennium, 1996, Oz, 1997—2003, Sex and the City, 1999, Third Watch, 1999, Deadline, 2000, The Twilight Zone, 2002, Rescue Me, 2004— (TV miniseries) Law & Order: Special Victims Unit, 1999—2000, (guest appearance) I Love the '70s, 2003. Avocations: boxing, tai chi. Office: Fox Networks Group PO Box 900 Beverly Hills CA 90213-0900

**WINTERS, HAROLD FRANKLIN,** physicist; b. Renton, Wash., May 19, 1932; s. Walter Wade and Ruth Elizabeth (Meyer) W.; m. Marjorie Ann Neiswender, June 9, 1956; children: Kathie Moe, David Winters, John Winters, Janice Assadi, Judy Ahlquist. Attended, Biola Coll., 1950-51; BS, Whitworth Coll., 1958; PhD, Washington State U., 1963. Rsch. staff mem. IBM Almaden Rsch. Ctr., San Jose Calif., 1963-93, emeritus, 1993—. Vis. prof. Odense U., Denmark, 1979-80; past N.Am. rep. Subcom. on Plasma Chemistry, Internat. Union Pure and Applied Chemistry; past trustee Am. Vacuum Soc.; past lectr. numerous major nat. and internat. confs. throughout the world. Past mem. editl. bd. Plasma Materials Interactions, Jour. Nuc. Instruments and Methods; contbr. numerous articles to sci. jours. Corp. U.S. Army, 1952-54. Recipient (with John Coburn) Thinkers award Tegal Corp., 1983, Disting. Alumni Achievement award Wash. State U., 1992. Fellow Am. Vacuum Soc. (John A. Thornton Meml. award and lectr. 1993, plasma sci. divsn. named grad. student award in honor of John Coburn and Harold Winters 1994); mem. AAAS, Am. Sci. Affiliation. Achievements include patents for plasma processing, ion sources and ion pumps; scientific contributions in the fields of plasma science, surface science, thin films, ion bombardment of solids, dissociation of gases by electron impact. Home: 632 Lanfair Dr San Jose CA 95136-1947 Personal E-mail: htxc88a@yahoo.com. *My conversion to evangelical Christianity in high school led to a change in my attitude, lifestyle, behavior, and study habits. I changed from a poor student with a bad attitude to an excellent student with a great love for science. These changes led to a successful and enjoyable scientific career. I find no contradiction or conflict between science and my Christian faith; on the contrary science has increased my respect for God.*

**WINTERS, JACKIE F.,** small business owner, foundation administrator; b. Topeka, Apr. 19, 1937; m. Marc Winters; 4 children. Student, Oreg. State U. Cert. Policy Alternatives Flemming Fellow. Clk. Oreg. Med. Sch., 1959—69; asst. Oreg. Gov. Tom McCall, 1969—79, Oreg. Gov. Vic Atiyeh, 1979—87; owner Jackie's Ribs, 1985—; mem. Oreg. Ho. of Reps., 1998—2002, Oreg. Senate, 2003—. Campaign chair United Way Marion/Polk Counties; active Govs. Task Force on Mental Health, Cmty. Partnership Task Force Oreg. State Fair. Republican. Office: 900 Court St NE S-212 Salem OR 97301 Office Phone: 503-986-1710.

**WINTERS, JONATHAN,** actor; b. Dayton, Ohio, Nov. 11, 1925; s. Jonathan H. and Alice Kilgore (Rodgers) W.; m. Eileen Ann Schauder, Sept. 11, 1948; children: Jonathan IV, Lucinda Kelley. Student, Kenyon Coll., 1946; B.F.A., Dayton Art Inst., 1950. With radio sta. WING, Dayton, 1949; disc jockey sta. WBNS-TV, Columbus, Ohio, 1950-53. Appeared on: Garry Moore Show, 1954-63, Steve Allen Show, 1954-61, Omnibus, 1954, NBC Comedy Hour, 1956, Jonathan Winters Show, 1956-57, Jack Paar Show, 1963-64, Andy Williams Show, 1966-67, Dean Martin Show, 1966-67, Jonathan Winters Show, CBS-TV, 1968-69, Wacky World of Jonathan Winters, 1972-73; numerous appearances NBC Monitor show, 1963—; Hollywood Squares, 1975—; TV series include Mork & Mindy, 1982-83, Davis Rules, (Emmy award for best supporting actor) 1991-92, 5 spls. Showtime Cable TV; night club appearances, 1953-60; motion picture appearances: It's a Mad, Mad, Mad World, 1963, The Loved One, 1964, The Russians Are Coming, The Russians Are Coming, 1966, Penelope, 1967, The Midnight Oil, 1967, 8 On the Lam, 1967, Oh Dad, Poor Dad, 1968, Viva Max, 1969, The Fish That Saved Pittsburgh, 1979, The Longshot, 1986, Say Yes, 1986, Moon Over

Parador, 1988, The Flintstones, 1994, The Shadow, 1994, The Adventures of Rocky and Bullwinkle, 2000, Edward Fudwupper Fibbed Big, 2000, Swing, 2003; rec. artist, Columbia Records.; author: Mouse Breath, Conformity and Other Social Ills, 1965, Winter's Tales, 1987, Hang-Ups, 1990; voice: Arabian Knights, 1995, Santa vs. the Snoman, 1997, also numerous cartoon characters. Served with USMCR, 1943-46, PTO. Named to Comedy Hall of Fame U.S., 1993, Comedy Hall of Fame Can., 1994; recipient Grammy for Comedy Album of Yr., 1996, Mark Twain Prize for Am. Humor, Kennedy Center, 2000.*

**WINTERS, KEVIN L.,** dentist; DDS, U. Mo., Kansas City, 1989. Gen. practice resident U. Louisville-Humana Hosp., 1989—90; pvt. practice dentist Picture Perfect Smiles, Claremore, Okla., 1990—. Instr. Las Vegas Inst. for Advanced Dental Studies, 1997—; host mid-day news segment Dentist on Call Channel 2 KJRH; author Esthetic Procedures Update Dental Equipment and Materials mag. Recipient Outstanding Young Dentist of Okla. Award, 1995. Mem.: Okla. Dental Assn., Am. Acad. Cosmetic Dentistry, Acad. Gen. Dentistry, ADA, Crown Coun. (life). Office: Picture Perfect Smiles 1502 W Blue Starr Dr Claremore OK 74017 Office Phone: 918-341-4403. Office Fax: 918-341-4001. Business E-Mail: smilmkr95@aol.com.

**WINTERS, RICHARD ALLEN,** mineral economist; b. Butte, Mont., Feb. 19, 1963; s. Allen S. and Doris Ellen (Taylor) W. BS in Fin. and Econs., U. Mont., 1986; MS in Mineral Econs., Colo. Sch. Mines, 1990, postgrad., 1991-93. Office engr. Morrison Knudsen Engrs., Richland, Wash., 1986-88, project acct., 1987-88; ops. analyst Echo Bay Mines, Denver, 1989; instr. Colo. Sch. Mines, Golden, Colo., 1991-92; cons. Coors Brewing Co., Golden, 1991-92; sr. rsch. engr. Phelps Dodge Mining Co., Morenci, Ariz., 1992-94; gold analyst Robertson, Stephens and Co., San Francisco, 1994-95; v.p. corp. devel. Golden Star Resources Ltd., Denver, 1995-99; v.p. RMB Resources, 2000—. Pres. Mineral Econ. Grad. Student Assn., 1989-90. Mem. Soc. Mining, Metallurgy and Exploration, Assn. Environ. Resource Economists, Mineral, Econs. and Mgmt. Soc. Avocations: outdoors, jewelry craft. Office: 303 E 17th Ave Ste 700 Denver CO 80203-1260

**WINTERS, ROBERT CUSHING,** insurance company executive; b. Hartford, Conn., Dec. 8, 1931; s. George Warren and Hazel Keith (Cushing) W.; m. Patricia Ann Martini, Feb. 10, 1962; children: Sally, Beth. BA, Yale U., 1953; MBA, Boston U., 1963; LHD, Montclair State Coll., 1991, St. Peter's Coll., 1993. With Prudential Ins. Co. Am., 1953—; v.p. actuary, 1969-75, sr. v.p. Cen. Atlantic home office, 1975-78, exec. v.p., Newark, 1978-84, vice chmn., 1984-86, chmn., CEO, 1987-94, chmn. emeritus Newark, 1995—. Trustee, Episcopal Divinity Sch., Boston Symphony Orch. With U.S. Army, 1954-56. Fellow Soc. Actuaries; mem. Am. Acad. Actuaries (past pres.), Am. Coun. Life Ins. (chmn. bd. dirs. 1990-91), Sigma Xi. Office: Prudential Ins Co Am 751 Broad St 10th Fl Newark NJ 07102-3714 E-mail: robert.c.winters@prudential.com.

**WINTERS, SAM,** lawyer; b. Tex. BA, U. Tex., 1944, JD, 1948. Bar: Tex. 1948. Shareholder Clark, Thomas & Winters, Austin, Tex.; bd. govs. U.S. Postal Svc., Washington, 1991—2000, vice chair, 1996-97, chmn. bd. govs., 1994-95, 98. Chmn. Tex. Rsch. League, 1990, 91; past mem. Nat. Hwy. Safety Adv. Com.; mem. devel. bd. U. Tex., Austin With USN, World War II. Mem. ABA (past chair sect. pub. utilities, comm. and transp.), Am. Law Inst. (life), State Bar Tex. Office: Clark, Thomas & Winters PO Box 1148 Austin TX 78767

**WINTERS, STANLEY B.,** history professor, consultant, writer; b. N.Y.C., June 5, 1924; m. Helen Plavner, Sept. 12, 1948 (div. Dec. 1969); children: Jenifer O'Neill, Neal Winters; m. Zdenka Müllerová, Jan. 9, 1970. AB, NYU, 1948; AM, Columbia U., 1950; PhD, Rutgers U., 1966. Cert. secondary social studies educator, N.J. Artist, draftsman Art Glass Co., N.Y.C., 1942-43; instr. history NYU, 1949-50; dir. co-propr. Clinton Hill Day Sch., Newark, 1950-56; tchr. social studies Livingston (N.J.) H.S., 1956-57; disting. prof. history Newark Coll. Engring./N.J. Inst. Tech., 1957-91; disting. prof. emeritus history N.J. Inst. Tech., Newark, 1991 -. Adj. prof. history Rutgers U., Newark, 1980-91, rsch. assoc. Urban Studies Ctr., New Brunswick, 1961-62; cons., columnist Office of Info., Newark, 1972-80. Author: Karel Kramář's Early Political Career, 1966, From Riot to Recovery: Newark After Ten Years, 1979, T.G. Masaryk, 1850-1937: Thinker and Politician, 1990; co-author, editor: Intellectual and Social Developments in the Habsburg Empire, 1975, Great Britain, the USA and the Bohemian Lands 1848-1938 1991; editor: Dynasty, Politics and Culture, 1991, East Ctrl. Europe jour., 1975-91; mem. editl. bd. Bohemia-Zeitschrift, Munich, 1985-2003; columnist (pseudonymous weekly) NJ Afro-Am. newspaper, 1958-64; contbr. over 200 articles to profl. jours. and publs. Pres., co-founder Clinton Hill Neighborhood Coun., Newark, 1955-61; chmn. edn. com. br. NAACP, Newark, 1960-64; candidate city coun., Newark, 1962; candidate Essex County Freeholder, 1965; trustee Preservation and Landmarks Com., Newark, 1980-93; pres. Czechoslovak History Conf., Chapel Hill, N.C., 1988-90. Staff sgt. U.S. Army, 1943-46, ETO. Recipient Szendzimiri award, Polish Inst. Arts and Scis., N.Y.C., 1971, N.J. Inst. Tech. Pub. Svc. award, 1982, Josef Hlávka Meml. medal, Czechoslovak Acad. Scis., Prague, 1991, Disting. Svc. award, Czechoslovak History Conf., 1995, František Palacky Hon. medal, Acad. Scis. Czech Republic, 2003; grantee, NEH, 1967, N.J. Com. Humanities, 1976—77, 1985. Mem. Am. Hist. Assn. (life, nominated first Czech historian as hon. fgn. mem.), Organization Am. Historians, Am. Assn. Advancement Slavic Studies, Collegium Carolinum, Josef Pekař Hist. Soc. (hon.), Hist. Assn. of Czech Republic (hon.), Phi Beta Kappa. Avocations: chess, travel, walking, correspondence, pre-contemporary music. Home: 463 MacArthur Dr Port Charlotte FL 33954-3432

**WINTERS, WILLIAM THOMAS,** bank executive; b. N.Y.C., Sept. 27, 1961; s. William Thomas and Ann Wilson (Vickey) W.; m. Adriane Besonc, Sept. 19, 1984. BA, Colgate U., 1983; MBA, Wharton Bus. Sch., 1988. V.p., head global commodity swop group J P Morgan, N.Y.C., 1988-91. Office: J P Morgan 60 Wall St New York NY 10005-2888

**WINTERSHEIMER, DONALD CARL,** state supreme court justice; b. Covington, Ky., Apr. 21, 1931; s. Carl E. and Marie A. (Kohl) W.; m. Alice T. Rabe, June 24, 1961; children: Carl David D., Lisa Ann, Craig P., Amy T., Blaise Q. BA, Thomas More Coll., 1953; MA, Xavier U., 1956; JD, U. Cin., 1959; LHD (hon.), No. Ky. U., 1999. Pvt. practice, Covington, 1960-76; city solicitor City of Covington, 1962-76; judge Ky. Ct. Appeals, Frankfort, 1976-83; justice Ky. Supreme Ct., Frankfort, 1983—. Chmn. Ky. Supreme Ct. Criminal Rules Com., 1988-94. Continuing Jud. Edn. Com., 1983—. Rules Com., 1994—; del. Foster Parent Rev. Bd., 1985-2002; mem. adv. bd. Sta. WNKU-FM, 1984-94, Am. Soc. Writers on Legal Subjects. Published articles in Law Jour. of Nat. Legal Ctr. for Medically Disabled, Issues in Law & Medicine, Albany Law Review, Quinnipiac Law Review, Temple Law Review, No. Ky. U. Chase Law Rev., NYU Annual Survey of Am. Law. Trustee Sta. WNKU-FM. Recipient Cmty. Svc. award Thomas More Coll., 1968; recipient Disting. Alumnus award Thomas More Coll., 1982, Disting. Alumni award Coll. Law/U.Cin., 1998; named Disting. Jurist Chase Coll. Law, 1983, Outstanding Jurist Phi Alpha Delta Law Frat., 1990. Mem. ABA, Am. Judicature Soc., Ky. Bar Assn., Ohio Bar Assn., Cin. Bar Assn., Inst. Jud. Adminstrn., Am. Inns of Ct. (founder Chase chpt.). Democrat. Roman Catholic. Office: Ky Supreme Ct Capitol Building Room 235 700 Capitol Ave Frankfort KY 40601-3410 also: Ky Supreme Ct PO Box 387 Covington KY 41012 Office Phone: 859-292-6300.

**WINTERSTEIN, JAMES FREDRICK,** academic administrator; b. Copperas Cove, Tex., Apr. 8, 1943; s. Arno Fredrick Herman and Ada Amanda Johanna (Wagnr) W.; m. Diane Marie Bochmann, July 13, 1963; children: Russell, Lisa, Steven, Amy. Student, U. N.M., 1962; Dr of Chiropractic cum laude, Nat. Coll. Chiropractic, 1968; cert., Harvard Inst. for Ednl. Mgmt., 1988. Diplomate Am. Chiropractic Bd. Radiology; lic. chiropractic, Ill., Fla., S.D., Md. Night supr. x-ray dept. DuPage Meml. Hosp., Elmhurst, Ill., 1964-66; x-ray technologist Lombard (Ill.) Chiropractic Clinic, 1966-68, asst.

dir., 1968-71; chmn. dept. diagnostic imaging Nat. Coll. Chiropractic, Lombard, Ill., 1971-73, chief of staff, 1985-86; pres. Nat. U. Health Scis., Lombard, Ill., 1986—; pvt. practice West Chicago, Ill., 1968-73, Fla., 1973-85. Faculty Nat. U. Health Scis. Post-Profl., Grad. and Continuing Edn. 1967—; chmn. x-ray test com. Nat. Bd. Chiropractic Examiners, 1971-73; govs. adv. panel on coal worker's pneumoconiosis and chiropractic State of Pa., 1979; v.p. Am. Chiropractic Coll. Radiology, 1981-83; mem. adv. coun. on radiation protection Dept. Health and Rehabilitative Svcs. State of Fla., 1984-85; cons. to bd. examiners State of S.C., 1983-84, State of Fla., 1980-85; cons. to peer review bd. State of Fla., 1980-84; trustee Chiropractic Centennial Found., 1989-90; mem. adv. com. Aids Alternative Health Ptnrs., 1996-2000, Consortial Ctr. for Chiropractic Rsch., 1998—; bd. dirs. Fedn. Ill. Ind. Colls. and Univs., 1995—; bd. dirs. Alternative Medicine, Inc., 1999—; spkr. in field. Pub. Outreach (Nat. Univ. Health Scis. monthly); author numerous monographs on chiropractic edn. and practice; co-inventor composite shielding and mounting means for x-ray machines; contbr. articles to profl. jours. Chmn., bd. dirs. Trinity Luth. Ch., West Chgo., 1970-72, Luth. High Sch., Pinellas County, Fla., 1979-82, St. John Luth. Ch., Lombard, 1988; chmn. bd. edn. First Luth. Sch., 1975-79; chmn. First Luth. Congregation, Clearwater, Fla., 1979-82; chmn. bldg. planning com. Grace Luth. Ch. and Sch., St. Petersburg, Fla., 1984-85; bldg. planning com. ch. expansion, new elem. sch., First Luth. Sch., 1975-79; stewardship adv. coun. Fla./Ga. dist. Luth. Ch. Mo. Synod, 1983-85; trustee West Suburban Regional Acad. Consortium, 1993-99. With U.S. Army, 1961-64. Recipient Cert. Meritorious Svc. Am. Chiropractic Registry of Radiologic Technologists, Cert. Recognition for Inspiration, Guidance, and Support Delta Tau Alpha, 1989, Cert. Appreciation Chiropractic Assn. South Africa, 1988, 1st pl. Fund Raiser Ride for Kids award Pediat. Brain Tumor Found. U.S., 1997, Cert. Appreciation Ill. Chiropractic Soc., 1997, Hope and Support award Alternative Health Ptnrs., 1998, Chiropractor of Yr., Ill. Chiropractic Soc., 2000, Person of the Yr., Alternative Medicine, Inc., 2001, NUHS Bd. Trustees Disting. Svc. award, 2002, President's citation award Maryland Chiropractic Assn., 2003. Mem. APHA, Am. Chiropractic Assn., Am. Chiropractic Coll. Radiology (pres. 1983-85, exec. com. 1985-86), Am. Chiropractic Coun. on Diagnostic Imaging, Am. Chiropractic Coun. on Diagnosis and Internal Disorders, Am. Chiropractic Coun. on Nutrition, Nat. Univ. Alumni Assn., Am. Acad. Chiropractic Physicians (sec.), Assn. Chiropractic Colls. (sec.-treas. 1986-91), Coun. Chiropractic Edn. (sec.-treas. 1988-90, v.p. 1990-92, pres. 1992-94, immediate past pres. 1994-96), Fla. Chiropractic Assn. (chmn. radiol. health com. 1977-85, Disting. Svc. award 1999). Republican. Lutheran. Avocations: reading, automobile rehabilitation, harley-davidson motorcycles, fishing.

**WINTER-SWITZ, CHERYL DONNA,** travel company executive; b. Jacksonville, Fla., Dec. 6, 1947; d. Jacqueline Marie (Carroll) Winter; m. Frank C. Snedaker, June 24, 1974 (div. May 1976); m. Robert William Switz, July 1, 1981. AA, City Coll. of San Francisco, 1986; BS, Golden Gate U., 1990, MBA, 1992. Bookkeeper, agt. McQuade Tours, Ft. Lauderdale, Fla., 1967-69; mgr. Boca Raton (Fla.) Travel, 1969-76; owner, mgr. Ocean Travel, Boca Raton, 1976-79; ind. contractor Far Horizons Travel, Boca Raton, 1979-80; mgr. Tara/BPF Travel, San Francisco, 1981-84; mgr. travel. dept. Ernst & Whinney/Lifeco Travel, San Francisco, 1984-86; travel cons. Golden Gate U., San Francisco, 1986-99, Siemer & Hand Travel, San Francisco, 1989-99, Ravenel Travel, Charleston, SC, 1999-2000, Carlson Carolina Travel, Mt. Pleasant, SC, 2000—02, Sato/Navigant Travel, 2003—04; mgr. travel dept. WareOnEarth Comm., Inc., Charleston, 2004—. Instr. Golden Gate U., 1986-99, U. San Francisco. Mem. Amateur Trapshooting Assn., Hotel and Restaurant Mgmt. Club. Republican. Episcopalian. Avocations: trap shooting, gardening, cooking, travel, reading. Home: 1189 W Park View Pl Mount Pleasant SC 29466-7910 Office: WareOnEarth Comm Inc 2457 Aviation Ave Ste 200 N Charleston SC 29406

**WINTERTON, JOSEPH HENRY,** computer software executive; b. Oneida, N.Y., July 22, 1948; s. Stewart Grant and Margaret (Durant) W.; m. Susan Marie Briggs, May 29, 1971; children: Tamara Leigh, Danielle Marie, Derek James. AAS, Canton Coll., NY, 1968; BA, SUNY, Potsdam, 1970. Adv. programmer IBM Corp., Poughkeepsie, N.Y., 1970-81; mgr. R & D Candle Corp., L.A., 1981-83, dir. R&D White Plains, NY, 1983-96, sr. dir. R&D, 1996—2003; v.p., sr. mgr. Bank One, Columbus, Ohio, 2003—04; mgr. IBM Corp., Somers, NY, 2004—. Coach Yorktown (N.Y.) Athletic Club, 1988—2001; treas. Hudson Valley Christian Acad., Mahopac, NY, 1986—87, Yorktown Theatre Workshop, Yorktown Heights, NY, 1989—92; trustee Calvary Bapt. Ch., Ossining, NY, 1986, midnight run vol., 1993—; bd. dirs. Yorktown Theatre Co. With U.S. Army, 1970—76, N.G. Republican. Mem. Christian Ch. Avocations: photography, teaching Sunday sch., coaching youth sports, golf. Home: 1521 Hanover St Yorktown Heights NY 10598-4709 E-mail: jowinterton@aol.com.

**WINTERTON, SHAUN LESLIE,** entomologist, educator; B Applied Sci., U. South Queensland, Toowoomba, Australia, 1992; PhD, U. Queensland, Brisbane, Australia, 2000. Rsch. fellow N.C. State U., Raleigh, 2000—04; sr. insect biosystematist Calif. Dept. Food and Agr., Sacramento, 2004—. Rsch. assoc. U. Calif., Davis, 2004—. Recipient Phil Carne Prize winner, Australian Entomol. Soc., 2000. Mem.: Soc. Systematic Biologists. Office: Calif Dept Food & Agriculture 3294 Meadowview Rd Sacramento CA 95832 Office Phone: 916-262-1100. Business E-Mail: swinterton@cdfa.ca.gov.

**WINTHROP, JOHN,** wines and spirits company executive; b. Salt Lake City, Apr. 20, 1947; children: Grant Gordon, Clayton Hanford. AB cum laude, Yale U., 1969; JD magna cum laude, U. Tex., 1972. Bar: Calif. 1972. Law clk. 9th cir. U.S. Ct. Appeals, L.A., 1972-73; conseil juridique Coudert Freres, Paris, 1973-75; v.p. gen. counsel MacDonald Group, Ltd., L.A., 1976-82; pres., CEO MacDonald Mgmt. Corp. and MacDonald Group Ltd., L.A., 1982-86; pres., chief exec. officer MacDonald Corp. (gen. contractors), L.A., 1982-86; chmn., CEO Comstock Mgmt. Co., L.A., 1986—; pres., CEO Winthrop Investment Properties, Los Angeles, 1986—; CEO Veritas Imports, L.A., 1995—. Bd. dirs. Plus Prods., Tiger's Milk Prods., Irvine, Calif., 1977-80. Contbr. articles to profl. jours. Bd. dirs., sec. L.A. Sheriff's Dept. Found.; bd. dirs. L.A. Opera. Mem. Nat. Eagle Scout Assn. (life), French-Am. C. of C. (bd. dirs. 1982-87), Urban Land Inst., Yale Club N.Y., Calif. Club, The Beach Club, Elizabethan Club, Order of the Coif, Beta Theta Pi. Office: Veritas Imports Penthouse 9460 Wilshire Blvd Beverly Hills CA 90212-2720 E-mail: jwinthrop@veritaswine.com.

**WINTHROP, LAWRENCE FREDRICK,** judge; b. Apr. 18, 1952; s. Murray and Vauneta (Cardwell) W. BA with honors, Whittier Coll., 1974; JD magna cum laude, Calif. Western Sch., 1977. Bar: Ariz. 1977, Calif. 1977, U.S. Dist. Ct. Ariz. 1977, U.S. Dist. Ct. (so. dist.) Calif. 1981, U.S. Ct. Appeals (9th cir.) 1981, U.S. Dist. Ct. (cen. dist.) Calif. 1983, U.S. Supreme Ct. 1983. Assoc. Snell and Wilmer, Phoenix, 1977—83, ptnr., 1984—93, Doyle, Winthrop, P.C., Phoenix, 1993—2002; judge divsn. one Ariz. Ct. Appeals, Phoenix, 2002—. Judge pro tem Maricopa County Superior Ct., 1987-97; lectr. Ariz. personal injury law and federal and state and local tax law Tax Exec. Inst., Nat. Bus. Inst., Profl. Edn. Systems, Inc., Ariz. Trial Lawyers Assn., Maricopa County Bar Assn.; bd. dirs. Valley of the Sun Sch., 1989-97, chmn., 1994-96; mem. Vol. Lawyers Program, Phoenix, 1980-2002. Editor-in-chief: Calif. Western Law Rev., 1976-77. Fellow Ariz. Bar Found. (bd. dir. 2005-), Maricopa Bar Found.; mem. Calif. Bar Assn., Ariz. Bar Assn. (mem. com. on exam. 1995-2002), Ariz. Tax Rsch. Assn. (bd. dirs. 1989-93), Maricopa County Bar Assn., Ariz. Assn. Def. Counsel (bd. dirs., pres. 1988-89, chmn. med. malpractice com. 1993-95), Am. Bd. Trial Advs., Aspen Valley Club, Lorna Lockwood Inn Ct. (co-pres. 2005—), Forest Highlands Club Republican. Methodist. Avocations: music, golf, tennis. Home: 83 W Cypress St Phoenix AZ 85003 Office: 1501 W Washington St Phoenix AZ 85007 Office Phone: 602-542-1430. Business E-Mail: lwinthro@courts.sp.state.az.us.

**WINTLE, ROSEMARIE,** biomedical electronics engineer; b. Brigham City, Utah, Sept. 13, 1951; d. DeVere and Kathleen (Layton) W. Student, Weber State U., 1972-76, Brigham Young U., 1978-79, U. Utah, 1980-87, ITT

Electronic Tech. Inst., 1986-88, Utah State U., 1991-92. Engr. Morton Internat., Brigham City, Utah; computer technician Salt Lake City; engr. Nuclear Med., Mesa, Ariz., 1976-77, U. Utah Hosp. Lab., Salt Lake City, 1980-87; electronic engr. Varian Assocs., Salt Lake City, 1987-88; electronic bio-med. experiment and rsch. engr. Clin. Rsch. Assocs., Provo, Utah, 1988-89. Contbr. articles to profl. jours. Engr., builder Honeyville (Utah) town playground equipment; designer, mgr. Honeyville town water system. Recipient grant Brigham City. Mem. IEEE (pres.), NSPE, Inst. for Sci. Info., Am. Statis. Assn., Sci. Am. Libr., Computer Club, Amnesty Internat., Libr. of Science, Newbridge Book Club. Mem. Lds Ch. Avocations: chess, sports, computers. Personal E-mail: rosemarie.wintle@hotmail.com.

**WINTNER, MARK S.,** lawyer; b. Bronx, NY, 1947; BA cum laude, Queens Coll., 1968; JD, U. Chgo., 1972, LLM in Taxation, 1977. Bar: N.Y. 1973. Ptnr., employee benefits law, exec. compensation Stroock & Stroock & Lavan LLP, N.Y.C. Mem. ABA, N.Y. State Bar Assn., Order Coif. Office: Stroock & Stroock & Lavan LLP 180 Maiden Ln New York NY 10038-4982 Office Phone: 212-806-6020. Office Fax: 212-806-6006. Business E-Mail: mwintner@stroock.com.

**WINTON, CALHOUN,** literature educator; b. Ft. Benning, Ga., Jan. 21, 1927; s. George Peterson and Dorothy (Calhoun) W.; m. Elizabeth Jefferys Myers, June 30, 1948; children: Jefferys Hobart, William Calhoun. Student, Ga. Inst. Tech., 1944-46; BA, U. of the South, 1948; MA, Vanderbilt U., 1950, Princeton U., 1954, PhD, 1955. Instr. Dartmouth Coll., Hanover, NH, 1954-57; asst. prof. U. Va., Charlottesville, 1957-60; asst. prof. then assoc. prof., asst. dean Grad. Sch. U. Del., 1960-67; prof. head English U. S.C., Columbia, 1967-75, chmn. dept., 1970-73; prof. U. Md., College Park, 1975-97, dir. Rsch. Ctr. for Humanities, 1988-90, prof. emeritus, 1997—. Del. Joint Nat. Com. on Langs., Washington, 1986-90, 95-99. Author: (biography) Captain Steele, 1964, Sir Richard Steele, 1970; editor: Plays of Aaron Hill, 1981, John Gay and the London Theatre, 1993; author (with others) Colonial Book in the Atlantic World, 2000; contbr. entries Oxford Dictionary of National Biography, 2004. Pres. faculty guild U. Md., 1986-89; bd. dirs. Md. Fedn. Tchrs., Balt., 1986-89. Capt. USN, 1944-47, 50-52. Am. Philos. Soc. grantee, 1960; Guggenheim Found. fellow, 1965-66, Folger Shakespeare Libr. fellow, Washington, 1970, John Carter Brown Libr. fellow, Providence, 1995, 2003 Fulbright Commn. lectureship, Ankara, Turkey, 1979-80. Mem. MLA (exec. com. South Atlantic chpt. 1977-80), Am. Soc. 18th-Century Studies (founder 1970—), East Cen. Soc. 18th Century Studies (pres. 1987), Assn. Princeton Grad. Alumni (exec. bd. 1986-90), Cosmos Club Washington, Princeton Club (N.Y. and Washington), Am. Antiquarian Soc., Literary Soc. Washington. Democrat. Episcopalian. Avocations: swimming, book collecting. Office: The Univ of the South PO Box 3128 Sewanee TN 37375-3128 Business E-Mail: cwinton@mail.umd.edu.

**WINTON, LINDA,** international trainer and consultant; b. Phila. BA in Secondary Edn. and Spanish, La Salle Coll., Phila., 1971—75; MA in Spanish Lang. and Lit., NYU, Madrid, 1978—79; MS in Adult Edn. and Human Resource Tng. and Devel., U. So. Maine, Gorham, 1990—91. Cert. Tchr. Spanish Pa. Dept. Edn., 1975, NJ Dept. Edn., 1975, Tchr. French NJ Dept. Edn., 1977, Exhbn. Mgr. Internat. Assn. Exhbn. Mgmt., 2003. Spanish and French tchr. Willingboro HS, NJ, 1975—77; ESL instr. Camden Learning Ctr., NJ, 1975—77, Shell Oil Co., Madrid, 1977—79, Inst. Internat. Madrid, 1977—79, Aldeasa, Madrid, 1977—79; export sales Wheatland Tube Co., EMSI, Pa., 1979—81; Spanish and French tchr. Haddonfield HS, 1981—82; Spanish instr. U. Ky., 1982—84; dir. Gorham Adult and Cmty. Edn., Maine, 1989—93; prin. Tng. Assocs. Maine, 1990—91; sales rep., account exec. Diversified Expn., Maine, 1994—97; pres., CEO New Markets Internat. LLC, Falmouth, Maine, 1997—. Programmer Tampa Bay Coun. Internat. Visitors, Fla., 1986—87; sr. programmer Maine Coun. Internat. Visitors, 2000—. Recipient Ofines award for study linguistics, 1978; fellow, Nat. Endowment Humanities, 1984. Mem.: Meeting Profls. Internat. (internat. devel. com. 2000—01, global issues adv. group 2001—02, New Eng. chpt. fin. com. 2001—02, New Eng. chpt. internat. membership com. 2002—03, New Eng. chpt. membership com. 2002—04, New Eng. chpt. liaison to multicultural initiative 2003—05, New Eng. chpt. bd. dirs. 2004—05), Internat. Assn. Exhbn. Mgmt. (dept. commerce liaison com. 2001—03, CEM commn. 2003—). Office: New Markets Internat LLC 12 Arbor Rd Falmouth ME 04105 Office Phone: 207-781-2019. Business E-Mail: umi@maine.rr.com.

**WINTOUR, ANNA,** editor-in-chief; b. London, Nov. 3, 1949; arrived in U.S., 1976; d. Charles and Elinor Wintour; m. David Shaffer, Sept. 1984 (div. 2001); children: Charles, Kate; m. J. Shelby Bryan. Student, Queens Coll., 1963—67. Deputy fashion editor Harper's and Queen Mag., London, 1970—76; fashion editor Harper's Bazaar, NY, 1976—77; fashion and beauty editor Viva Mag., NY, 1977—78; contbg. editor fashion and style Savvy Mag., NY, 1980—81; sr. editor NY Mag., 1981—83; creative dir. US Vogue, NY, 1983—86; editor-in-chief British Vogue, London, 1986—87, House and Garden, NY, 1987—88, Vogue, NY, 1988—. Office: Vogue 4 Times Sq New York NY 10036*

**WINTROB, JAY S.,** insurance company executive; Grad. summa cum laude, U. Calif., Berkeley, 1979; JD, U. Calif., 1982. With O'Melveny & Myers, LA; asst. to chmn. AIG Sun Am., 1987, corp. v.p., 1987—89, sr. v.p., 1989—91, exec. v.p., 1991—95, vice chmn., 1995—98, CEO. 1998—2000, pres., 2000—, CEO. 2001—; exec. v.p.m Am. Internat. Group, 2002—; Bd. dirs. AIG Sun Am., AIG bd. trustees J. Paul Getty Trust, 2004—. Recipient Ecumenical Coun. Leadership award, Archdiocese LA, 2001, Luis Lainer Founder's award, Bet Tzedel Legal Services, 2002. Mem.: Order of Coif. Office: Am Internat Group 70 Pine St New York NY 10270*

**WINTRODE, RALPH CHARLES,** lawyer; b. Hollywood, Calif., Dec. 21, 1942; s. Ralph Osborne and Maureen (Kavanagh) W.; m. Leslie Ann O'Rourke, July 2, 1966 (div. Feb. 1994); children: R. Christopher, Patrick L., Ryan B.; m. Denise A. Beetham, Aug. 24, 1999. BS in Acctg., U. So. Calif., 1966, JD, 1967. Bar: Calif. 1967, N.Y. 1984, Japan 1989. From assoc. to ptnr. to of counsel Gibson, Dunn & Crutcher, Tokyo, L.A., Newport Beach and Irvine, Calif., 1967—. Sec. Music Ctr. Los Angeles County, 1986-88; bd. dirs. Coro Found., L.A. County, 1986-87. Mem. Newport Harbor Club, Am. Club Tokyo. Avocations: sailboat racing, auto racing, flying. Office: Gibson Dunn & Crutcher 4 Park Plz Ste 1400 Irvine CA 92614-8557 also: 333 S Grand Ave Ste 4400 Los Angeles CA 90071-1548 E-mail: wintrode@cox.net.

**WINTROL, JOHN PATRICK,** lawyer; b. Wichita, Kans., Feb. 13, 1941; s. Clarence Joseph and Margaret (Gill) W.; m. Janet Lee Mitchell; children: John Howard, Joanna Lee. BA cum laude, Rockhurst Coll., 1963; JD, Georgetown U., 1969. Bar: DC 1969, U.S. Ct. Appeals (4th, 5th, 11th and DC cirs.) 1981, U.S. Dist. Ct. MD 1984. Law clk. to Hon. Howard Corcoran U.S. Dist. Ct., Washington, 1969-71; assoc. Howrey & Simon, Washington, 1971-77; mng. ptnr. Perito, Duerk & Pinco, Washington, 1978-85; ptnr. Finley Kumble, Washington, 1985-87, Laxalt, Washington, Perito & Dubuc, Washington, 1988-91, McDermott, Will & Emery, Washington, 1991—2002; atty. John P. Wintrol L.L.C., Washington, 2003—. Mem. jud. conf. U.S. Ct. Appeals (D.C. cir.). Vol. Peace Corps, Turkey, 1963-65; pres. bd. trustees Holton Arms Sch. Mem.: ABA. Roman Catholic. Office: 2000 M St NW Ste 700 Washington DC 20036 Office Phone: 202-261-1056. Business E-Mail: jwintrol@jpwlaw.net.

**WINTROUB, BRUCE URICH,** dermatologist, educator, researcher; b. Milw., Nov. 8, 1943; s. Ernest Bernard and Janet (Zien) W.; m. Marya Kraus, Jan. 20, 1973; children: Anne Ben, Molly. Ba., Amherst Coll., 1965; MD, Washington U., St. Louis, 1969. Diplomate Am. Bd. Internal Medicine, Am. Bd. Dermatology. Intern in medicine Peter Bent Brigham Hosp., Boston, 1969-70, jr. asst. resident in medicine, 1970-71, jr. assoc. in medicine, 1976-80, asst. then attending physician, 1976-81; resident in dermatology Harvard Med. Sch., Boston, 1974-76, instr., 1976-78, asst. prof., 1978-82; assoc. prof. dermatology Sch. Medicine, U. Calif., San Francisco, 1982-85; attending physician med. ctr., 1982—, prof., mem. exec. com. dept. dermatology, 1985-95, 2000—, mem. dean's adv. com., governing bd. continuing med. edn., other coms., 1986-95; chmn. exec. com. dept. dermatology U. Calif.-San Francisco, 1985-95, 2000—, exec. vice dean Sch. Medicine, 1995-97, assoc. dean sch. medicine, 1990—95, 2000—04, vice-dean sch. med., 2004—; chief med. officer U. Calif.-San Francisco Stanford Health Care, San Francisco, 1997-99; assoc. dean Sch. Medicine Stanford (Calif.) U., 1997—99; dir. Dermatology Assocs., San Francisco, 1982-85; prof. & chair dept. dermatology U. Calif.-San Francisco, 1996—99, 1999. Cons. in dermatology Mass. Gen. Hosp., Boston, 1976-82, Beth Israel Hosp. and Children's Hosp. Med. Ctr., Boston, 1978-82, Parker Hill Med. Ctr., Boston, 1980-82; attending physician Robert B. Brigham Hosp. div. Brigham and Women's Hosp., Boston, 1980-81, assoc., 1982-85; chief dermatology svc. Brockton (Mass.) VA Med. Ctr., 1980-82; asst. chief dermatology VA Med. Ctr., San Francisco, 1982-85, mem. space com., 1984-85, dean's adv. com., 1985—, chmn. budget com., 1987—; clin. investigator Nat. Inst. Allergy, Metabolism and Digestive Disease, NIH, 1978; assoc. dean Sch. Medicine Stanford U., 1997—. Author: (with others) Biochemistry of the Acute Allergic Reactions, Fifth International Symposium, 1988; contbr. numerous articles, abstracts to profl. jours. Grantee Clin. fellow and grantee, NIH, 1967—69. Fellow Am. Acad. Dermatology (com. evaluations 1985—, coun. govt. liaison 1987—, congress on tech. plannning commn. 1988—, assoc. editor Dialogues in Dermatology jour. 1982-85, Stellwagon prize 1976); mem. Soc. Investigative Dermatology (chmn. pub. rels. com. 1987-88), Assn. Profs. Dermatology (chmn. program com. 1987—, bd. dirs.), Pacific Dermatol. Assn. (chmn. program com. 1987—), San Francisco Dermatol. Soc., Am. Fedn. Clin. Rsch. (chmn. dermatology program 1988-89), Am. Assn. Immunology, Dystrophic Epidermolysis Bullosa Rsch. Am. (bd. dirs. 1981), Internat. Soc. Dermatology, Internat. Soc. Cutaneous Pharmacology (founding mem.), Am. Soc. Clin. Investigation, Skin Pharmacology Soc., Calif. Med. Soc., San Francisco Med. Soc., Clin. Immunology Soc., Dermatology Found. (bd. dirs., exec. com.), AAAS, Am. Assn. Physicians, Calif. Acad. Medicine, Am. Dermatol. Assn., Sigma Xi, Alpha Omega Alpha. Avocation: golf. Office: Dept Dermatology U Calif San Francisco 1701 Divisadero St Rm 342 San Francisco CA 94143-0316 Office Phone: 415-353-7597. Business E-Mail: wintroub@medsch.ucsf.edu.

**WINWOOD, STEPHEN LAWRENCE,** musician, composer; b. Birmingham, Eng., May 12, 1948; s. Lawrence Samuel and Lillian Mary (Saunders) W.; m. Eugenia Crafton, Jan. 17, 1987; children: Mary Clare, Elizabeth Dawn, Stephen Calhoun, Lillian Eugenia. Rec. artist Spencer Davis Group, 1964-67, Blind Faith, 1970, Traffic, 1967-74; solo artist N.Y.C. and in England, 1974—. Dir. F.S. Ltd. Albums include: Arc of a Diver, 1980, Talking Back to the Night, 1982, Back in the High Life, 1986, Roll With It, 1988 (Grammy 1989), Chronicles, Refugees of the Heart, 1991, Traffic: Far From Home, 1994, Junction 7, 1997, About Time, 2003. Recipient 14 Gold Record awards, 4 Platinum Record awards, 2 Grammy awards, Lifetime Achievement award Ivor Novello's, 2002; inductee (with band Traffic) Rock 'N Roll Hall of Fame, 2004. Address: 41 Rodney Rd Cheltenham Gloucestershire GL50 1HX England

**WINZENREID, JAMES ERNEST,** lawyer, entrepreneur; b. Wheeling, W.Va., June 9, 1951; s. Ernest Christian and Dorothy Emma (Wolf) Winzenreid; m. Rebecca Lee Rice, Aug. 11, 1979; children: Diana Lee, Lauren Rice. AB, W. Liberty State Coll., W.Va., 1973; MBA, W.Va. U., 1979; JD, Duquesne U., Pitts., 1987; LLM, Wayne State U., Detroit, 1989. Bar: Pa. 1987, U.S. Dist. Ct. (we. dist.) Pa. 1987. Staff asst. Wheeling Pitts. Steel Corp., Wheeling, 1974—78, supr. indsl. rels., 1978; mgr. profl. planning and devel. Copperweld Corp., Pitts., 1978—79, mgr. human resources Glassport, Pa., 1979—81, plant mgr., 1981—83, group mgr. human resources Pitts., 1984—85, market program mgr., 1986—87; with lab. and employment dept. Eckert, Seamans, Cherin & Mellott, Pitts., 1986—87; corp. staff rep. Tecumseh (Mich.) Products Co., 1987—89; v.p. human resources devel. Lafarge (Va.) Corp., 1989—94; v.p. human resources western region Lafarge Constrn. Materials, Calgary, Alta., Canada, 1994—96, Lafarge Can. Inc., Calgary, Alta., Canada, 1996—99; mgr. union rels. GE, Bloomington, Ind., 2000—02; dir. labor rels. and compliance Metaldyne Corp., Plymouth, Mich., 2002—04; dir. employee rels. Lear Corp, Southfield, 2004—. Mng. editor: Juris mag., 1986. Bd. dirs. Wheeling Symphony Soc., 1977—86, Wheeling Jaycees, 1976—78; mem. adv. bd. Jr. Achievement Southwestern Pa., 1981—83. Named Outstanding Young Men, Am. U.S. Jaycees, 1979. Mem.: ABA, Indsl. Rels. Rsch. Assn., Human Resource Planning Soc., Am. Soc. Human Resources Mgmt., Allegheny Bar Assn., Pa. Bar Assn., Phi Alpha Delta. Republican. Lutheran. Avocations: golf, reading. Home: 924 Mill Pond Ct Northville MI 48167 Office: Lear Corp 21557 Telegraph Rd Southfield MI 48034 Personal E-mail: jimwinzenreid@aol.com.

**WIORKOWSKI, JOHN JAMES,** mathematics professor; b. Chgo., Sept. 30, 1943; BS, U. Chgo., 1965, MS, 1966, PhD, 1972. Rsch. assoc. U. Chgo., 1972; asst. prof. Pa. State U., University Park, 1973-74; assoc. prof. U. Tex. at Dallas, Richardson, 1975, assoc. prof. and program head Math. Scis. Program, 1979-81, prof., 1981—, asst. to v.p. acad. affairs, 1980-85, asst. v.p. acad. affairs, 1985-94, assoc. provost, 1994-2001, vice-provost, 2001—, head math. scis. program, 1996-98. Cons. to Fed. Energy Adminstrn., 1975, Tex. Instruments, 1977, Frito-Lay Inc., 1977-78, Republic Nat. Bank, 1979; mem. panel studying 55 mile per hour speed limit Nat. Acad. Sci. Contbr. articles to profl. jours. Served to capt. U.S. Army, 1968-71. Decorated Army Commendation medal, NSF grantee, 1975—; Am. Coun. Edn. fellow, 1981-82. Mem. Am. Statis. Assn. (chpt. pres. 1974, v.p. 1977, chpt. pres. 1978), AAAS, Inst. Math. Stats., Biometric Soc., Sigma Xi. Unitarian Universalist. Home: 9922 Lincolnshire Ct Rockwall TX 75087-4509 Office: U Tex at Dallas PO Box 830688 Richardson TX 75083-0688 Office Phone: 972-883-2274. E-mail: wiorkow@utdallas.edu, wiorkow@msn.com.

**WIOT, JEROME FRANCIS,** radiologist; b. Cin., Aug. 24, 1927; s. Daniel and Elvera (Weisgerber) W.; m. Andrea Koskritz, July 29, 1977; children: J. Geoffrey, Jason. MD, U. Cin., 1953. Diplomate: Am. Bd. Radiology (trustee, pres.). Intern Cin. Gen. Hosp., 1953-54, resident, 1954-55, 58-59; gen. practice medicine Wyoming, Ohio, 1955-57; mem. faculty U. Cin., 1959-67, 68—, prof., chmn. radiology, 1973-93, acting sr. v.p., provost for med. affairs, 1985-86, prof. emeritus, 1998—; practice medicine specializing in radiology Tampa, Fla., 1967-68. Contbr. articles to med. jours. Bd. dirs. Ruth Lyons Fund, U. Cin. Found., 1997—2003, U. Cin. Hosp., 2005—. Served with USN, 1945-46. Fellow Am. Coll. Radiology (pres. 1983-84, chmn. common. on diagnostic radiology); mem. Radiol. Soc. N.Am., Am. Roentgen Ray Soc. (pres. 1986-87), Am. Bd. Radiology (pres. 1982-84), Ohio Med. Assn., Cin. Acad. Medicine, Radiol. Soc. Greater Cin., Ohio Radiol. Soc. Office: U Cin Med Ctr Dept Radiology 234 Goodman St Cincinnati OH 45267-1000 Office Phone: 513-475-8755. E-mail: jfwiot@hotmail.com.

**WIPFLER, WILLIAM JOHN,** health facility administrator; s. William Louis and Pauline P. Wipfler; m. Valerie S. Libby, Aug. 10; children: Ashley, Michaela, Vanessa, Isaac. BA, Antioch Coll., Yellow Springs, Ohio, 1980; JD, MBA, Boston Coll., Newton, 1987. Atty. Pierce Atwood, Portland, Maine, 1987—88; asst. atty. gen. Maine Atty. Gen., Augusta, 1989—92; gen. counsel Maine Healthcare Fin. Corp., Augusta, 1992—94, exec. dir., 1994—96; CEO Eyecare Med. Group, Portland, 1996—2006, Orthop. Assocs., 2006—. Founder, bd. mem. Maine ASU Coalition, Portland, 2003—. Bd. mem. State of Maine Social Worker Bd., Augusta, 2000—04; bd. chair Inst. for Civic Leadership, Portland, 2002—; bd. Boys to Men, Portland, 2002—05. Office: Orthopaedic Assn 33 Sewall St Portland ME 04102

**WIPKE, W. TODD,** chemistry professor; b. Dec. 16, 1940; BS, U. Mo., Columbia, 1962; PhD, U. Calif., Berkeley, 1965. Rsch. chemist Esso Rsch. and Engring. Co., Baton Rouge, 1962; postdoctoral rsch. fellow Harvard U., 1967-69; asst. prof. Princeton U., 1969-75; assoc. prof. chemistry U. Calif., Santa Cruz, 1975-81, prof. chemistry, 1981—. Founder, sr. v.p. Molecular Design Ltd., San Leandro, Calif., 1978-91; founder, chmn. bd. GluMetrics Inc., 2002-04, dir. 2005—; cons. Ciba-Geigy, Basle, Switzerland, 1978-82, BASF, Ludwigshafen, Fed. Republic Germany, 1974-78, Squibb, Princeton, N.J., 1976-81; adv. EPA, 1984—; mem. sci. adv. bd. Pharmix, Scitegic, Tosk.

Editor: Computer Representation and Manipulation of Chemical Information, 1973, Computer-Assisted Organic Synthesis, 1977; editor-in-chief: (jour.) Tetrahedron Computer Methodology, 1987-92; editor: Tetrahedron and Tetrahedron Letters, 1987-92; contbr. articles to profl. jours. Capt. U.S. Army, 1966—67. Recipient Eastman Kodak Rsch. award, 1964, Texaco Outstanding Rsch. award, 1962, Alexander von Humboldt Sr. Scientist award, 1987; Merck Career Devel. grantee, 1970; NIH fellow, 1964-65. Mem. Am. Chem. Soc. (assoc., Computers in Chemistry award 1987, St. Charles Found. Alumni award 1996), Assn. Computing Machinery, Chem. Soc., Am. Assn. Artificial Intelligence (charter), Chem. Structure Assn. (charter), Internat. Soc. Study Xenobiotics. Office: U Calif Dept Chemistry Santa Cruz CA 95064

**WIRASINHA, HEMAMALI ANUSHKA,** computer scientist, researcher; b. Colombo, Sri Lanka, Mar. 1, 1972; d. Armyne Edwin and Hemamali Cornelia Wirasinha. Diploma in econ., London U., 1991; BS in Econ. with honors, U. London, 1994; postgrad., Harvard U., 1996; PhD in Computers and Info. Sci. (hon.), Cosmopolitan U., Miami, Fla., 2004. Jr. mgmt. exec. Ceylon Shipping Lines Ltd., Colombo, Sri Lanka, 1994—95; assisting lectr. in micro computers and info. tech. Harvard U., Cambridge, Mass., 1996—98. Dir. Ceylon Shipping Lines Ltd., Colombo, Sri Lanka, 1998—; author Prentice Hall India, Delhi, India, 2002—, Publish Am., Frederick, Md.; advanced level GCE AS/A2 examiner and moderator in computing U. London Edexcel; Sigma Xi ambassador Packard Internat. Sci. Networking Initiative, Sri Lanka, India, Maldives. Author: (book) Spread the Word Around: MS Word, 2001, Cyber Ethics, 2001, Study Buddy, 2001, Digital Art, 2001, Computer Tutor, 2001, Java Essence, 2002, PC Private Eye, 2002, Doctor PC, 2002, I Want to Teach the World to Click!: Computing for the Visually Impaired, 2002, Office Essentials: MS Office XP, 2002, Visually Learn PC (India Times Bestseller 2003), 2002, On Your Marks Net Set Go! Surviving in an E-World (India Times Bestseller 2003), 2002, Flash in a Flash: Web Development, 2002, Computing for the Asian Woman and the Curious Man, 2003, Microchip Militant, 2004. Establishing chpt. Young Politicians of Am., Cambridge, Mass.; contributory America's first responders alliance, Cambridge, Mass., 2004. Recipient Excellence award, Internat. Modeling and Talent Assn., 1997. Mem.: IEEE, AAAS, Brit. Computer Soc., Women in Tech. Internat., Assn. for Women in Computing, Am. Assn. for Artificial Intelligence, Harvard Faculty Club, Sigma Xi, Outstanding Student Honor Soc. Achievements include research in computer security; viability and usability of microchip implantations and advanced tech. to aid the visually impaired. Avocations: writing, travel, fashion, sports, swimming. Home: Apt 401 950 Massachusetts Ave Cambridge MA 02139 Address: 6 Charles Way Colombo 3 Sri Lanka Fax: 011 941 12575065. Office Phone: 617-864-0041. Home Fax: 617-864-1094. Personal E-mail: anushkawirasinha@post.harvard.edu. E-mail: anushka1@sigmaxi.org.

**WIRE, WILLIAM SHIDAKER, II,** retired apparel and footwear manufacturing company executive; b. Cin., Jan. 5, 1932; s. William Shidaker and Gladys (Buckmaster) W.; m. Alice Dumas Jones, Aug. 31, 1957 (dec.); children: Alice Wire Freeman (dec.), Deborah Wire Suber; m. Cheryl C Yates, Sept. 25, 2004. Student, U. of South, 1950; AB, U. Ala., 1954, JD, 1956; LLM, NYU, 1957. Bar: Ala. 1956. Atty. Hamilton, Denniston, Butler & Riddick, Mobile, 1959-60; with Talladega Ins. Agy., Ala., 1961-62, Genesco Inc., Nashville, 1962-94, former chmn. and CEO. Bd. dirs. Genesco Inc., Dollar Gen. Corp., Am. Endoscopy Svcs., Inc., Nashville Bank & Trust Co. Mem.: Burnt Pine Golf Club (Destin, Fla.), Golf Club Tenn., Univ. Club (NY), Belle Meade Country Club (Nashville), Kappa Alpha. Presbyterian. Home: 706 Overton Park Nashville TN 37215-2452

**WIRKEN, CHARLES WILLIAM,** lawyer; b. Moline, Ill., Aug. 29, 1951; s. Walter William and Elizabeth Claire Wirken; children: Nicole, Michelle. BS, U. Ariz., 1972, JD, 1975. Bar: Ariz. 1975, U.S. Dist. Ct. Ariz. 1976, U.S. Ct. Appeals (9th cir.) 1980, U.S. Ct. Appeals (Fed. cir.) 1985, U.S. Ct. Appeals (10th cir.) 2004, U.S. Supreme Ct. 1980. Assoc. Killian, Legg & Nicholas, Mesa, Ariz., 1975-79; ptnr. Killian, Nicholas, Fischer, Wirken, Cook & Pew, Mesa, 1980-97, Gust Rosenfeld P.L.C., 1997—. Pres. Vol. Lawyers Project, Phoenix, 1981-83; judge pro tem Ariz. Ct. Appeals, 1985-99, Maricopa County Superior Ct., 1986—; mem. civil study com. Maricopa County Superior Ct., 1984—; bd. dirs. Cmty. Legal Svcs., Phoenix, 1979-82. Exec. v.p. East Valley Partnership, Mesa, 1984; pres. Tri-City Cath. Social Svc., Mesa, 1983, 84; bd. dirs. East Valley Cultural Alliance, Mesa, 1984. Mem. State Bar Ariz. (bd. govs. 1995-06, pres. 2004-05), Maricopa County Bar Assn. (bd. dirs. 1983-91, pres. 1989-90), East Valley Bar Assn. (pres. 1979-80), Mesa C. of C. (dir. 1980-83, v.p. 1982-83), Rotary (bd. dirs. 1980-89, pres. 1987-88). Democrat. Roman Catholic. Home: 1708 E Knoll St Mesa AZ 85203-2171 Office: Gust Rosenfeld PLC 201 E Washington Ste 800 Phoenix AZ 85004-2327 Office Phone: 602-257-7959. E-mail: cwirken@gustlaw.com.

**WIRKEN, JAMES CHARLES,** lawyer; b. Lansing, Mich., July 3, 1944; s. Frank and Mary (Brosnahan) W.; m. Mary Morse, June 12, 1971; children: Christopher, Erika, Kurt, Gretchen, Jeffrey, Matthew. BA in English, Rockhurst Coll., 1967; JD, St. Louis U., 1970. Bar: Mo. 1970, U.S. Dist. Ct. (we. dist.) Mo. 1970. State prosecutor Jackson County, Kansas City, Mo., 1970-72; assoc. Morris, Larson, King, Stamper & Bold, Kansas City, 1972-75; dir. Spradley, Wirken, Reismeyer & King, Kansas City, 1976-88, Wirken & King, Kansas City, 1988-93; CEO The Wirken Law Group, Kansas City, 1993—. Adj. prof. law U. Mo., Kansas City, 1984-89, 2001—. Author: (books) Managing a Practice and Avoiding Malpractice, 1983, Wirken Tips: Law Office Marketing, Management and Economics, The Daily Record, 2003—; co-author: Missouri Civil Procedure Form Book, 1984—; mem. editl. bd.: jours. Missouri Law Weekly, 1989—, Lender Liability News, 1990—, Emerging Trends and Theories of Lender Liability, 1991, host: radio show Wirken on the Law, Sta. KMBZ, 1998—. Mem. ABA (exec. coun.), Nat. Conf. Bar Pres. (coun. 1992-96), Nat. Caucus of Met. Bar Leaders (exec. coun., pres. 1988-94), Am. Trial Lawyers Assn., L.P. Gas Group (founder, chair 1986-90, founder, chair lender liability group 1987-96), Mo. Bar Assn. (bd. govs. 1977-78, 2004—, chmn. econs. and methods practice com. 1982-84, quality and methods of practice com. 1989-91, vice chmn. young lawyers sect. 1976-78), Mo. Assn. Trial Attys. (bd. govs. 1983-85), Kansas City Met. Bar Assn. (pres. young lawyers sect. 1975, chair legal assistance com. 1977-78, chair tort law com. 1982, pres. 1990). Home: 47 W 53rd Kansas City MO 64112 Office: The Wirken Law Group PC 4740 Grand Blvd Ste 200 Kansas City MO 64112 Office Phone: 816-471-0330. Business E-Mail: jwirken@wirkenlaw.com.

**WIRSCHING, CHARLES PHILIPP, JR.,** retired brokerage house executive, securities trader; b. Chgo., Oct. 26, 1935; s. Charles Philipp and Marianne Ethel (York) W.; m. Beverly Ann Bryan, May 28, 1966. BA, U. N.C., 1957. Sales rep. Adams-Millis Corp., Chgo., 1963-67; ptnr. Schwartz-Wirsching, Chgo., 1968-70; sec., dir. Edwin H. Mann, Inc., 1971-74; stockbroker Paine Webber, Inc., Chgo., 1975-85, account v.p., 1986-95; ret., 1995. Cons. Paine Webber, Inc. Chgo., 1996-99. Adv. coun. John Nuveen & Co., Inc., 1993-95; trustee Wirsching Charitable Trust, 1987—. Mem.: Organ Hist. Soc., Salem (Ohio) Hist. Soc. Republican. Episcopalian. Avocation: foreign travel. Home and Office: 434 Clinton Pl River Forest IL 60305-2249

**WIRSZUP, IZAAK,** mathematician, educator; b. Wilno, Poland, Jan. 5, 1915; came to U.S., 1949, naturalized, 1955; s. Samuel and Pera (Golomb) W.; m. Pola Ofman, July 19, 1940 (dec. 1943); 1 son, Vladimir (dec. 1943); m. Pera Poswianska, Apr. 23, 1949; 1 dau., Marina (Mrs. Arnold M. Tatar). *Izaak Wirszup and his wife Pera (Poswianska Deull) are both survivors of the Nazi Holocaust. Izaak's entire family, including: his first wife Pola (Ofman), their 2 year old son Vladimir, both of Izaak's parents Samuel and Pera (Golomb) Wirszup, Izaak's brother Naum and sister Golda, and their families, were all killed by the Nazis. From September 1941, Izaak Wirszup was imprisoned first in the Ghetto Wilno, then in several Nazi concentration camps in Estonia and Germany. He was liberated by the American Army on April 30, 1945 from camp Allach-Dachau (near Munich, Germany).* Magister of Philosophy in Math, U. Wilno, 1939; PhD in Math, U. Chgo., 1955. Lectr. math. Tech. Inst. Wilno, 1939-41; dir. Bur. d'Études et de Statistiques

Spéciales, Société Centrale d'Achat-Société Anonyme des Monoprix, Paris, 1946-49; mem. faculty U. Chgo., 1949—, prof. math., 1965-85, prof. math. emeritus, 1985—, prin. investigator U. Chgo. Sch. Math. Project (sponsored by Amoco Found., also dir. resource devel. component), 1983—, dir. Internat. Math. Edn. Resource Ctr., 1988—. Dir. NSF Survey Applied Soviet Rsch. in Math. Edn., 1985-91; cons. Ford Found., Colombia, Peru, 1974-85, Sch. Math Study Group, 1960, 61, 66-68; participant, writer tchr. tng. material African Math. Program, Entebbe, Uganda, summer 1964, Mombasa, Kenya, summers 1965-66; assoc. dir. Survey Recent Ea. European Math. Lit., 1956-68, dir., 1968-84; dir. NSF program application computers to mgmt., 1976-83; cons. NSF-AID Sci. Edn. Program, India, 1969; mem. U.S. Commn. on Math. Instn., 1969-73; co-prin. investigator U. Chgo.-Polk Bros. Found. Program for the Devel. of Math. Tchrs. in Chgo. Pub. Schs., 1999—. *A December 1979 comparative studies report by Izaak Wirszup to the National Science Foundation, which revealed a crisis in mathematics and science education in the U.S., came to the attention of President Jimmy Carter. The President ordered a review of U.S. science and engineering education policies. Wirszup was subsequently invited to testify six times before the U.S. Senate. With an 8.4 million dollar grant from the Amoco Foundation, Wirszup founded the University of Chicago School Mathematics Project in 1983. More than three million students and teachers are now using UCSMP texts.* Contbr. articles to profl. jours.; Editor Math. books, transls., adaptions from Russian.; Adviser math.: Ency. Brit., 1971—. Recipient Llewellyn John and Harriet Manchester Quantrell award U. Chgo., 1958, Univ. Alumni Svc. medal, U. Chgo., 1994; resident master Woodward Ct., U. Chgo., 1971-85; endowed Wirszup Lecture Series, U. Chgo., 1986. Mem. NY Acad. Scis., Am. Math. Soc., Math. Assn. Am., AAAS, Nat. Council Tchrs. Math. (chmn. com. internat. math. edn. 1967-69, Lifetime Achievement medal for Leadership, Tchg., and Svc. in Math. Edn. 1996). Home: 5750 S Kenwood Ave Chicago IL 60637-1744 Office: U Chgo Dept Math 5734 S University Ave Chicago IL 60637-1514 Office Phone: 773-667-1967.

**WIRT, FREDERICK MARSHALL,** retired political scientist, educator; b. Radford, Va., July 27, 1924; s. Harry Johnson, Sr. and Goldie (Turpin) W.; m. Elizabeth Cook, Sept. 6, 1947; children: Leslie Lee, Sandra Sue, Wendy Ann. BA, DePauw U., 1948; MA, Ohio State U., 1949, PhD, 1956. Instr. to prof. polit. sci. Denison U., Granville, Ohio, 1952-66; vis. prof., lectr. U. Calif., Berkeley, 1966-68, 69-72; dir. policy scis. grad. program U. Md. Balt. County, 1972-75; prof. polit. sci. U. Ill., Urbana, 1975-2000; ret., 2000. Dir. Inst. for Desegregation Problems, U. Calif.-Berkeley, 1970-72; cons. Motion Picture Assn. Am., Rand Corp., Nat. Inst. Edn., SUNY Sch. Edn. Albany; vis. prof. U. Rochester, Nova U., U. Melbourne; acad. visitor London Sch. Econs. Author: Politics of Southern Equality, 1970 (honorable mention for best book 1972), Power in the City, 1974; (with others) School Desegregation in the North, 1967, The Polity of the School, 1975, Political Science and School Politics, 1977, Education, Recession, and the World Village, 1986, (with others) Culture and Education Policy in the American States, 1992, Aint' What We Was: Civil Rights in the New South, 1997 (Best Book on So. Politics award So. Polit. Sci. Assn., 1998), The Political Dynamics of American Education, 1997, 3d edit., 2005. Mem. Granville City Charter Commn., 1964. Grantee Am. Philos. Soc., Denison Rsch. Assn., U. Ill. Rsch. Bd., NEH, Ford Found., Ctr. Advanced Studies; fellow U. Ill., Dept. Edn., Spencer Found.; recipient Lifetime Achievement awards Am. Ednl. Rsch. Assn., 1995, Am. Polit. Sci. Assn., 1994. Mem. Am. Polit. Sci. Assn. (nat. council), Midwestern Polit. Sci. Assn., Am. Ednl. Rsch. Assn., Policy Studies Orgn. Office: U Ill Dept of Polit Sci Urbana IL 61801 Home: 2340 W Seltice Way Apt 129 Coeur D' Alene ID 83814 E-mail: f-wirt@uiuc.edu.

**WIRT, MICHAEL JAMES,** library director; b. Sault Sainte Marie, Mich., Mar. 21, 1947; s. Arthur James and Blanche Marian (Carruth) W.; m. Barbara Ann Hallesy, Aug. 12, 1972; 1 child, Brendan. BA, Mich. State U., 1969; MLS, U. Mich., 1971; postgrad., U. Wash., 1990. Cert. libr., Wash. Acting libr. U. Mich. Ctr. for Rsch. on Econ. Devel., Ann Arbor, 1971-72; instnl. svcs. libr. Spokane County (Wash.) Libr. Dist., 1972-76, asst. dir., 1976-79, acting dir., 1979, dir., 1980—. Mem. adv. com. Partnership for Rural Improvement, Spokane, 1982-85, Wash. State Libr. Planning and Devel. Com., 1984-85, Ea. Wash. U. Young Writers Project Adv. Bd., 1988-89; mem. issues selection com. Citizens League of Greater Spokane, 1991-93, City of Spokane Indian Trail Specific Plan Task force, 1992-95; mem. comm. com. United Way Spokane County, 1994, campaign chair local govt. divsn., 1996. Mem. Wash. Libr. Assn. (2d v.p. 1984-86, dir. 1989-91, pub. rels. com. 1993-2001, chair legis. planning com. 2003—, conf. coord. 2003-05, Merit award 1984, Pres. award 1998), Wash. Libr. Network (rep. Computer Svc. Coun. 1983-86, v.p., treas. State Users Group 1986-87), Am. Libr. Assn. (Pub. Libr. Affiliates Network 1990-93, PLA Bus. Coun. 1990-94, chmn. 1991-94), Spokane Valley C. of C. (local govt. affairs com. 1987-2000, co-chair 1996-98, pub. policy com. 2000-2005, mem. local governance com. 2003-2005, govenence com. 2005—), Spokane Regional C. of C. (local govt. com. 1990-94, human svcs. com. 1990-92, chmn. 1991-92, govt. reorgn. task force 1995), Spokane Civic Theatre (bd. dirs. 1996-2001, v.p. 1997-98, 2000, sec. 1998-2000), Inland N.W. Legis. Coalition, Momentum (local govt. strategy com. 1992-94), New Century (govt. collaboration com. 1997-98), Inland N.W. Coun. Librs. (bd. dirs. 1979—, chmn. 1997-98). Office: Spokane County Libr Dist 4322 N Argonne Rd Spokane WA 99212-1853 Office Phone: 509-924-4122. Business E-Mail: mwirt@scld.org.

**WIRTA, RAYMOND E.,** real estate company executive; b. 1944; Grad., Calif. State U.; M in Internat. Mgmt., Golden Gate U. With Golden West Fin. Corp., Bank of Am., The Irvine Co.; CEO Koll Real Estate Svcs., 1994-97, CB Richard Ellis, LA, 1999—. Office: CB Richard Ellis Group 865 S Figueroa St Los Angeles CA 90017

**WIRTH, FREMONT PHILIP, JR.,** neurosurgeon, educator, b. Nashville, July 23, 1940; s. Fremont P. and Willa (Dean) W.; children: Fremont Philip III, Andrew Simpson, Carolyn Howe. BA with honors in History, Williams Coll., 1962; MD, Vanderbilt U., 1966. Diplomate Am. Bd. Neurol. Surgery (guest examiner 1989, bd. dirs. 1992-98, vice chmn. 1997-98), Nat. Bd. Med. Examiners; cert. advanced trauma life support ACS. Surg. intern Johns Hopkins Hosp., Balt., 1966-67, resident and fellow in surgery, 1967-68; asst. resident in neurosurgery Barnes Hosp., Washington U., St. Louis, 1970-72, fellow in neurosurgery, 1972-74; pvt. practice, Savannah, Ga., 1974—. Asst. clin. prof. neurosurgery Med. Coll. Ga., Augusta, 1991—, vis. prof., 1978, 79, 86, 87; mem. staff, neurosurg. ICU, St. Joseph's Hosp., 1974—, dir. neurosurg. ICU, 1978—; mem. staff Meml. Med. Ctr., 1974-75, dir. rehab., 1983; mem. staff Candler Gen. Hosp., 1974—; med. dir. Head and Spinal Cord Injury Prevention Project for Ga., 1984-96; presenter in field, 1970—; vis. prof. U. Md., Balt., 1981, Tufts New Eng. Med. Ctr., Boston, 1982. Series editor (with R.A. Ratcheson) Concepts in Neurosurgery, 1986-93; editor: (with Ratcheson) Neurosurgical Critical Care, Concepts in Neurological Surgery, Vol. 1, 1987, Ruptured Cerebral Aneurysms, Concepts in Neurological Surgery, Vol. 6, 1994; contbr. articles and book revs. to med. jours., chpts. to books. Elder Skidaway Island Presbyn. Ch., 1981-83; mem. pack 57 com. Cub Scouts Am., Savannah, 1979-84; mem. troop 57 com. Boy Scouts Am., Savannah, 1980-85, mem. fin. com. Coastal Empire coun., 1987-90, mem. adv. bd., 1990-96; chmn. physicians' solicitation United Way Coastal Empire, 1987; bd. dirs. First Found., 1990-95. With USPHS, 1968-70. Fellow ACS (bd. govs. 1984-90, sr. mem. trauma com. 1991-93); mem. AMA (physician's recognition award 1973-76, 77-79, 80-82, 83-85, 88-91, 91-94, 95-98, 98—), Congress Neurol. Surgeons (profl. conduct com. 1989-93, v.p. 1985-86, Disting. Svc. award 1989), Am. Acad. Neurol. Surgeons, Neurosurg. Soc. Am., Am. Assn. Neurological Surgeons (nominating) com. 1994-96, bd. dirs. 1998-2001, v.p. 2002-03, pres. 2005-06), Brain Surgery Soc., Ga. Med. Soc. (pres. 1995, bd. trustees 1996-2001, chmn. 2000-01), Med. Assn. Ga. (editl. bd. 1987-93), Ga. Neurosurg. Soc. (exec. com. 1981-88, pres. 1988-89), So. Neurosurg. Soc. (exec. com. 1982-91, pres. 1988-89, Semmes lectr. 1997), N.Am. Skull Base Soc., Am. Heart Assn. (fellow stroke coun.). Avocations: golf, fly fishing, hunting. Office: Neurol Inst Savannah 4 E Jackson Blvd Savannah GA 31405-5810

**WIRTH, KELLEY K.,** state representative; b. Panorama City, Calif., Aug. 2, 1965; children: Kennedy, Meghan. BS, Oreg. State U., 1989; MS, U. So. Calif., 1992. State rep. dist. 16 Oreg. House Rep., Salem, 2001—; sys. analyst, planning commr. City of Corvallis, Oreg., 1996—; sys. analyst Asst. to 3d Infantry Divsn. Chief of Staff, 1993—99; adj. computer tech. faculty City Colls. Chgo.-Europe, 1992; bd. mem. Land Devel. Hearings Bd. City of Corvallis, 1998—, mem. Neighborhood Tech. Rev. Group, 1997—. Mem.: Corvallis LWV. Democrat. Episcopalian. Office: 900 Court St NE H-479 Salem OR 97301 Office Phone: 503-986-1416. Personal E-mail: wirthk@comcast.net.

**WIRTH, MICHAEL K. (MIKE WIRTH),** oil company executive; b. Oct. 1960; m. Julie Wirth; 4 children. BS, U. Colo. With Chevron Corp., 1982—; design engr., 1982, sr. retail mgr. mktg. Western Ops., 1998—99, gen. mgr. retail mktg., 1999—2000; pres. mktg. Caltex Corp., Singapore, 2000—01; pres. mktg. Asia/Middle East/Africa ChevronTexaco Corp, 2001—04, pres. Global Supply and Trading, 2004—06, exec. v.p. Global Downstream, 2006—. Office: Chevron Hdqs 6001 Bollinger Canyon Rd San Ramon CA 94583*

**WIRTH, PETER,** lawyer; b. Halgehausen, Germany, July 17, 1950; U.S., 1956; BA, U. Wis., 1972; JD, Harvard U., 1975. Bar: Mass. 1975. Assoc. Palmer & Dodge, Boston, 1975-81, ptnr., 1982-96, of counsel, 1996—; exec. v.p., chief legal officer Genzyme Corp., 1996—. Lectr. grad. tax program Boston U., 1982-85. Mem. ABA, Mass. Bar Assn., Phi Beta Kappa. Office: Genzyme Corporation 500 Kendall St Cambridge MA 02142 Office Phone: 617-768-6882, 617-252-7600.

**WIRTH, SANDRA LEE,** real estate company owner; b. Buffalo, June 8, 1945; d. Dominic A. and Santina (Lopez) Liberatore; 1 child, H. William III. Prin. Metro Sandra Lee Wirth Robshaw Gallery of Homes, Tonawanda, N.Y.; regional mgr. Paul Robshaw Galler of Homes, Tonawanda, N.Y., mgr. line Cheektowaga, N.Y.; broker assoc. B.W. Morris and Son Realtors, Buffalo; owner Metro Sandra Lee Wirth, Real Estate, Tonawanda, N.Y. Assembly, Dist. 148, Albany, 1994—. Chmn., past pres. West Seneca Druga Abuse Prevention Coun.; sponsor Call Home Free Program, Nat. Crime Prevention Coun.'s Nat. Night Out. Named Realtor of the Yr., Elma Bus. Person of the Yr. Mem. Nat. Assn. Realtors (cert.), N.Y. Assn. Realtors (state dir.), Greater Buffalo Bd. Realtors (1st v.p. 1988, treas. 1989, pres. elect 1990), Greater Buffalo Assn. Realtors (pres.), Buffalo and West Seneca C. of C. Office: NYS Assembly 148th District 5763 Seneca St Elma NY 14059-9615

**WIRTH, TAMARA L.,** music educator; b. Stuebenville, Ohio, July 18, 1968; d. William Harry and Elva Elizabeth Jones; m. Douglas Harry Wirth; children: Matthew Robert, Bradley Douglas. BS in Music Edn., Ind. U., Pa., 1990; MA in Edn., Marygrove Coll., 2005. Organist, choir dir. Paris (Pa.) Presbyn. Ch., 1985—92; organist Trinity United Meth. Ch., Spencerville, 1993—97; substitute tchr. various sch., Allen and Auglaize counties, Ohio, 1993—98; music tchr. St. Joseph Cath., Wapakoneta, Ohio, 1998—. Sec. St. Joseph PTO, Wapakoneta, 1999—2003, Spencerville PTO, 1998—2003. Democrat. Avocations: crafts, sewing, aerobics. Home: 8656 Deep Cut Rd Spencerville OH 45887 Office: St Joseph Cath Sch 1101 Lincoln Hwy Wapakoneta OH 45895

**WIRTH, TIMOTHY ENDICOTT,** foundation administrator, retired senator; b. Santa Fe, Sept. 22, 1939; s. Cecil and Virginia Maude (Davis) W.; m. Wren Winslow, Nov. 26, 1965; children: Christopher, Kelsey. BA, Harvard U., 1961, MEd, 1964; PhD, Stanford U., 1973; degree (hon.), U. Colo., Denver U., Colo. Coll., Washington Coll., Clark U. White House fellow, spl. asst. to sec. HEW, Washington, 1967; asst. to chmn. Nat. Urban Coalition, Washington, 1968; dep. asst. sec. for edn. HEW, Washington, 1969; v.p. Great Western United Corp., Denver, 1970; mgr. Rocky Mountain office Arthur D. Little, Inc. (cons. firm), Denver, 1971-73; mem. 94th-99th Congresses from 2d Colo. Dist., 1975-87, mem. energy and commerce com., sci. and tech. com., budget com., chmn. subcom. telecommunications, fin. and consumer protection; U.S. senator from Colo., 1987-93; counselor U.N. Dept. State, Washington, 1993-94, Under Sec. of State for global affairs, 1994-97. Mem. bd. overseers Harvard U.; chair vis. com. Harvard Grad. Sch. Edn. Recipient Disting. Service award HEW, 1969; Ford Found. fellow, 1964-66 Fellow: Am. Acad. Arts & Sci. Mem. White House Fellows Assn. (pres. 1968-69), Denver Council Fgn. Relations (exec. com. 1974-75), Alliance to Save Energy (chmn. 1987-93).

**WIRTHLIN, RICHARD BITNER,** researcher; b. Salt Lake City, Mar. 15, 1931; s. Joseph L. and Madeline (Bitner) W.; m. Jeralie Chandler, Nov. 23, 1956; children: Richard L., Mary Ann, J. Mark, Carolyn, Michael, Jill, Susan, John BS, U. Utah, 1956, MA, 1957; PhD, U. Calif.-Berkeley, 1964. Lectr. U. Calif. Med. Ctr., San Francisco, 1960-61; chmn. dept. econs. Brigham Young U., Provo, Utah, 1964-69; ptnr. Merrill-Wirthlin Assocs., Provo, 1964-69; pres., chmn. bd. dirs. Decision/Making/Info., McLean, Va., 1969-84; chmn. bd. dirs., CEO The Wirthlin Group, Salt Lake City, 1987—. Co-author (with Wynton C. Hall): (book) The Greatest Communicator: What Ronald Reagan Taught Me about Politics, Leadership, and Life. Dir. planning and strategy Reagan/Bush Campaign, 1980, campaign dir. research, planning and policy, 1980-81; dir. planning and evaluation Pres.-Elect Transition Com., 1980-81; cons. to Prime Minister Margaret Thatcher and Brit. Conservative Party, 1989—; bd. dirs. Harris Interactive. Recipient Disting. Alumni award U. Utah, 1986, Disting. Alumni Service award Brigham Young U., 1987; named Advt. Man of Yr., Advt. Age, 1981, Pollster of Yr. Polit. Cons., 1981. Mem. Acad. Polit. Sci., Am. Econ. Assn., Am. Mktg. Assn., Am. Assn. Pub. Opinion/Research, Council Survey Research Orgns., Sigma Chi, Omicron Delta Epsilon Republican. Office: Ste 550 406 W South Jordan Pkwy South Jordan UT 84095-3940

**WIRTSCHAFTER, DAVID,** talent agency executive; Agent William Morris Motion Picture Divsns., Beverly Hills, Calif.; pres. William Morris Agency, Beverly Hills, Calif., 2005—. Office: William Morris Agy Inc 151 S El Camino Dr Beverly Hills CA 90212-2775

**WIRTSCHAFTER, IRENE NEROVE,** tax specialist, consultant, military officer; b. Elgin, Ill., Aug. 05; d. David A. and Ethel G. Nerove; m. Burton Wirtschafter, June 2, 1945 (dec. 1966). BCS, Columbus U., 1942. Cert. tax profl., enrolled agt., IRS. Commd. ensign Supply Corps, USN, 1944, advanced through grades to capt., 1975; comdg. officer Res. Supply Unit, 1974—75; ret., 1976; agt. Office Internat. Ops. IRS, 1967—75; internat. banking specialist; real estate profl., appraiser, 1976—80; pvt. practice tax cons. Cocoa Beach, Fla. Sr. intern program U.S. Senate, 1981; mem. Sec. Navy's Adv. Com. Ret. Pers., 1984—86, VA Adv. Com. Women Vets., 1987—90. Past troop leader Girl Scouts U.S.A.; lt. col. and mission pilot CAP, 21 air races; comml. instrument pilot land and sea; Navy liaison officer Commd.'s Retiree Coun., Patrick AFB, 1985—89; mem. Nat. Com. Internat. Forest of Friendship, Atchison, Kans., 1976—; elected silver rep. Nat. Silver Haired Congress, 1977—2001; elected rep. Silver Haired Legis., 1984, Silver Haired Senate, 1988—; trustee Internat. Women's Air and Space Mus., 1993—, bd. dirs., 1999—; state rep. Nat. Soc. to Preserve Social Security and Medicare, 1999; bd. dirs., treas. Honor Am., 2001—05; sec. Navy League, 2000; cons. Jr. Achievement, 1989—94; founder sr. action com. Brevard County, 1981; chmn. College Park Airport Johnny Horizon Day, 1975; elected dir. Fla. Space Coast Philharm., 1985—, treas. 1986—92; bd. dirs., adv. mgr. Cocoa Beach Citizen's League, 1990—92; co-chmn. Internat. Women's Yr. Take Off Dinner, Washington, 1976; 1st v.p. Friends of Cocoa Beach Libr., 1988—90, pres., 1990—92, bd. dirs., 1993—; apptd. to Cocoa Beach Libr. Br., 1996—; mem. Cocoa Beach Bus. Improvement Coun.; elected senator Silver Haired Legislature, Fla., 1985—; vol., founding mem. Brevard Zoo; chmn. Cocoa Beach Code Enforcement Bd., 1989—96; co-chmn. sr. adv. com. Cape Canaveral Hosp., 1994—; trustee Assn. Naval Aviation, 1988—. Named Hon. Citizen, Winnipeg, Man., Can., 1966, Atchison, 1989, New Orleans, 1988, Hon. Dep. State Fire Marshal, Fla., 1987, Ky. Col., La. Col.; recipient cert. of appreciation, Cocoa Beach Women's Club, 2000, Svc.

Above Self award, Rotary, 1998. Mem.: RMGS, TROA, AAUW, Navy League (sec. 2001), WAVES Nat. (bd. dirs. chpt. 75 1989—, founder), Cocoa Beach Area C. of C., Assn. Enrolled Agts., Banana River Squadron (founder, comptr. 1984—), Assn. Naval Aviation (nat. trustee 1988—), Naval Order U.S. (treas. nat. capitol commandry), Naval Res. Assn. (nat. treas. 1975—77, nat. adv. com. 1985—, Nat. award of Merit 1992), Internat. Platform Assn. (life), Ninety Nines (past chpt. sect. and nat. officer, 99 achievement awards), Jazz Soc. Brevard, Patrick Women's Golf Assn. (treas. 1996—97), Silver Wings (nat. sec. 1986, bd. dirs. 1990—, nat. v.p. 2000—, Woman of Yr. award 1985), Tailhook Assn. (life), Rotary. Avocations: aviation, golf, music. Home: 1825 Minutemen Cswy Apt 301 Cocoa Beach FL 32931-2033 Personal E-mail: irenwirt@juno.com.

**WIRTZ, ELI J.,** lawyer, retail executive; b. West Bend, Iowa, Apr. 28, 1943; BBA, U. Iowa, 1966, JD, 1969. Assoc. to ptnr. Ahlers, Cooney, Dorweiler, Haynie Smith & Allbee, 1972—89; v.p., gen. counsel Casey's Gen. Stores, Ankeny, Iowa, 1989—. Mem.: Iowa State Bar Assn. Office: Caseys Gen Stores One Convenience Blvd PO Box 3001 Ankeny IA 50021 E-mail: legal@caseys.com.

**WIRTZ, WILLIAM WADSWORTH,** real estate company executive, professional sports team executive; b. Chgo., Oct. 5, 1929; s. Arthur Michael and Virginia (Wadsworth) Wirtz; m. Joan Roney, Dec. 15, 1950 (dec. May 1983); children: William R., Gail W., Karen K., Peter R., Alison M.; m. Alice Pirie Hargrave, Dec. 1, 1987. AB, Brown U., 1950. Pres. Chgo. Blackhawk Hockey Team, Inc., 1966—, Chgo. Stadium Corp., 1966—, Consol. Enterprises, Inc., Chgo., 1966—, Forman Realty Corp., Chgo., 1965—, 333 Bldg. Corp., Chgo., 1966—, Wirtz Corp., Chgo., 1964—. Chmn. bd. govs. Nat. Hockey League. Named to NHL Hall of Fame, 1976; recipient Lester Patrick trophy, 1978. Mem.: Sunset Ridge Country Club (Northbrook, Ill.), Fin and Feather Club (Elgin, Ill.), Mid-America Club (Chgo.), Racquet Club (Chgo.), Saddle and Cycle Club (Chgo.). Office: Wirtz 680 N Lake Shore Dr Fl 19 Chicago IL 60611-3495 also: United Ctr 1901 W Madison St Chicago IL 60612-2459 also: Nat Hockey Leage 1155 Metcalfe St Ste 960 Montreal PQ Canada H3B 2W2

**WIRUM, ANDREA A.,** lawyer; b. Okla. City, Feb. 24, 1956; BA, Mich. State Univ., 1977; JD, Univ. Calif., Hastings, 1980. CPA 1977; bar: Calif. 1980. Ptnr. Corp. & Securities practice, mem. mng. bd. Pillsbury Winthrop Shaw Pittman, San Francisco. Office: Pillsbury Winthrop Shaw Pittman 50 Fremont St San Francisco CA 94105 Office Phone: 415-983-1735. Office Fax: 415-983-1200. Business E-Mail: andrea.wirum@pillsburylaw.com.

**WISBAUM, WAYNE DAVID,** lawyer; b. Niagara Falls, N.Y., May 29, 1935; s. Franklin C. and Elizabeth (Boff) W.; m. Janet Katz, July 3, 1960; children: Karen, Wendy, Deborah. BA, Cornell U., 1956; LL.B., Harvard U., 1959. Bar: N.Y. 1960. Assoc. Kavinoky & Cook, Buffalo, 1960-66, sr. ptnr., 1966—. Pres., chmn. bd. dirs. Kleinhans Music Hall Mgmt. Inc., 1990-2000, life emeritus, 2003-. Pres. Buffalo Coun. on World Affairs, 1968-70; mem. Young Leadership Cabinet Nat. United Jewish Appeal, 1967-73; mem. com. on leadership devel. Nat. Coun. Jewish Fedn. and Welfare Funds, 1967—; mem. Mayor's Com. on Youth Opportunity; bd. dirs. Anti-Defamation League; mem. Coun. Internat. Studies, SUNY, Buffalo; chmn. Buffalo chpt. Am. Jewish Com.; pres., chmn. bd. dirs. Buffalo Found. Jewish Philanthropies, 2001—; bd. govs. United Jewish Fedn., Buffalo; chmn. bd. dirs. Buffalo Philharm. Orch. Soc.; bd. dirs., mem. exec. com. Burchfield Art Ctr.; bd. dirs., pres. Jewish Family Svc. of Erie County; vice chmn., bd. dirs. Artpark, Irish Classical Theatre; trustee Buffalo and Erie County Park Libr., Daeman Coll., 2004—; dir. emeritus Zool. Soc. Buffalo and Erie County, 2005—. Served to capt. U.S. Army, 1964. Recipient United Jewish Fedn. Buffalo Leadership award, 1967, Cmty. Rels. award Am. Jewish Com., 1985, Abram Pugash award Jewish Family Service, 1985, Cmty. Leadership award Israel Bonds, 2001, honoree Citation banquet Nat. Conf. for Cmty. and Justice, 2004, Citizen of Yr. award Buffalo News, 2003; named Harvard Alumnus of Yr., 1990. Mem. ABA, N.Y. State Bar Assn. (chmn. com. lawyers title guaranty funds, Root/Stimson award 2003), Erie County Bar Assn., Am. Law Inst., Harvard Law Sch. Assn. Western N.Y. (sec.), Zool. Soc. Buffalo (dir., mem. exec. com.), Harvard Club (pres. Buffalo chpt., mem. N.Y.C. chpt.), Buffalo Club, Cornell Club (N.Y.C. chpt.), Zeta Beta Tau. Home: 180 Greenaway Rd Buffalo NY 14226-4166 Office: Kavinoky & Cook 120 Delaware Ave Rm 600 Buffalo NY 14202-2793 Office Phone: 716-845-6000.

**WISDOM, PEGGY JEAN,** neurologist; b. OKeene, Okla., Nov. 4, 1947; d. Clarence W. and Grace V. Wisdom. BS in Biology/Chemistry, Northwestern State Coll., Evanston, Ill., 1968; MD, U. Okla., Norman, 1972. Diplomate Am. Bd. Psychiatry and Neurology. Resident in neurology U. Fla., 1972-76; asst. prof. neurology U. Okla., Oklahoma City, 1976-90, assoc. prof. neurology, 1990—2002, prof. neurology 2002—, vice chair dept. neurology 1981—; med. dir. neurologic rehab. O'Donoghue Rehab. Inst., Oklahoma City, 1981-89, chief of staff, 1986-90; chief neurology VA Med. Ctr., Oklahoma City, 1994-97, chief neurology/rehab., 1997—. Cons. Commn. on Accreditation of Rehab. Facilities, Tuscon, 1990—, Okla. Dept. Rehab. Svcs., Oklahoma City, 1993-96. Sci. adv. bd. Omniplex Mus., Oklahoma City, 1994—. Mem. Am. Acad. Neurology, Am. Acad. Neurology (chmn. women issues in neurology sect. 1999-2001), Assn. of VA Neurologists, Am. Epilepsy Soc. Republican. Presbyterian. Office: U Okla Health Scis Ctr # 215 711 Stanton L Young Blvd Oklahoma City OK 73104-5021 Office Phone: 405-270-5140. Business E-Mail: peggy-wisdom@ouhsc.edu.

**WISE, AARON NOAH,** lawyer; b. Hartford, Conn., Feb. 14, 1940; s. Joseph J. and Ethel (Sklar) W.; m. Genevieve Ehrlich, Dec. 17. 1966; children: Haywood Martin, Paul Russell, Renee Alicia AB, Boston U., 1962; JD, Boston Coll., 1965; LLM in Comparative/Internat. Law, NYU, 1971; certificat de Doctorat, d' Université en Droit U. Paris, 1970. Bar: N.Y. 1965, U.S. Dist. Ct. (so. dist.) N.Y. 1965. Internat. atty. Schering-Plough, Kenilworth, NJ, 1969-74; ptnr. Conboy Hewitt O'Brien & Boardman, NYC, 1974-80, Wise Lerman & Katz P.C. (formerly Rosenbaum Wise Lerman & Katz), NYC, 1981-95, Klepner & Cayea, NYC, 1995-98, Brand, Cayea & Brand, LLP, NYC, 1998-2000, Siller Wilk LLP, NYC, 2000—02, Gallet Dreyer & Berkey, LLP, NYC, 2002—. Author: International Sports Law and Business (Kluwer Law Internat., 1997, 3 vols.), Foreign Businessman's Guide to U.S. Law-Practice-Taxation, 2004; contbr. articles to pubs. in U.S. and Europe. Mem.: ABA, NY State Bar Assn. Avocations: multi-lingual including French, Spanish, Portuguese, Italian, Russian, Japanese and German. Home: 38 Cummings Cir West Orange NJ 07052-2264 Office: Gallet Dreyer & Berkey LLP 845 Third Ave New York NY 10022-6601 Office Phone: 212-935-3131. Business E-Mail: anw@gdblaw.com.

**WISE, ALLEN F.,** health care administrator; b. Wichita, Kans., Aug. 20, 1942; BS, Wichita State U. Exec. v.p. of operations Health Care Systems Inc., 1985—90; pres., CEO Keystone Health Plan, 1991-94; COO Independence Blue Cross, Phila., 1991—94; exec. v.p. Metra Health Co., 1994—95; pres., CEO Wise Health System, 1994; exec. v.p. United HealthCare Corp., 1995—96; pres., CEO Coventry Health Care, Inc., Bethesda, Md., 1996—2004, non-exec. chmn., 2004—. Bd. dir., chmn. HealthMarkets Inc.; bd. dir. Magellan Health Services Inc., NCP Group Inc. Office: 6705 Rockledge Dr Ste 900 Bethesda MD 20817-1814*

**WISE, BOB (ROBERT ELLSWORTH WISE JR.),** former governor, former congressman; b. Washington, Jan. 6, 1948; m. Sandy Casber; children: Robert, Alexandra. BA, Duke U., 1970; JD, Tulane U., 1975. Bar: W.Va. 1985. Sole practice, Charleston, W.Va., 1975—80; atty., legis. coun. for judiciary Gen. W.Va. Ho. of Dels., 1977—78; mem. W.Va. Senate, 1980—82, 97th-106th Congresses from 2nd W.Va. dist., Washington, 1983—2001; whip at large, 1986—2001; mem. govt. reform and oversight com., transp. and infrastructure com.; gov. State of W.Va., 2001—05. Pres. Alliance for Excellent Edn., Washington, 2005. Dir. West Virginians for Fair and Equitable

Assessment of Taxes, Inc. Mem.: ABA, W.Va. State Bar Assn. Democrat. Avocations: physical fitness, bluegrass music. Mailing: Alliance for Excellent Education Ste 901 1201 Connecticut Ave NW Washington DC 20036 Business E-Mail: gov@wvgov.org.*

**WISE, BRET W.,** chemical company executive; m. June Wise; 3 children. BS, Ind. U. CPA. Ptnr. KPMG; v.p., CFO WCI Steel, Inc., Warren, Ohio; sr. v.p., CFO Ferro Corp., Cleve., 1999—2002; CFO, sr. v.p. DENTSPLY Internat. Inc., York, Pa., 2002—05, exec. v.p., 2005—06, pres., COO, bd. dir., 2006—. Bd. dir. Dental Trade Alliance. Mem. AICPA, Fin. Execs. Inst. Office: DENTSPLY Internat Inc Susquehanna Commerce Ctr 221 W Philadelphia St York PA 17405*

**WISE, CARL STAMPS,** accounting educator; b. Brunswick, Ga., Sept. 2, 1955; s. George Lewis Jr. and Alice (Andrews) W. AA, SUNY, Albany, 1983; BS in Occupl. Edn., U. Wash., 1987; MPA, Ga. So. U., 1997, postgrad. in Edn., 1998—. Lic. mobile comm. technician. Enlisted USN, 1975, electronics technician, 1975-85; adj. prof. electronics tech. Fla. Jr. Coll., Jacksonville, 1983-84; comm. electronics technician Hasty's Comm. East, Brunswick, Ga., 1985-94; primary care give maternal grandmother Brunswick, Ga., 1994-95; electronics technician/purchase mgr./accounts receivable Thompson Comm., Savannah, Ga., 1996-97; adj. prof. acctg. Savannah Tech. Inst., Hinesville, Ga., 1997—; adj. prof. gen. studies Ctrl. Tex. Coll., Ft. Stewart and Hunter Army Airbase, Ga., 1998—. Computer upgrade/maintenance Ctrl. Tex. Coll. and Savannah Tech. Inst., Hinesville, 1998—. Recipient Sea Svc. Deployment ribbon, 1978, 79, 80. Mem. ASPA (East Ga. chpt. sec. 1998—), Personal Comm. Industry Assn. Republican. Episcopalian. Avocations: landscape painting, swimming, fishing, cooking. Office: Savannah Tech Inst 501 W General Screven Way Hinesville GA 31313-3059 Home: 88 Margaret Dr Midway GA 31320-7222 E-mail: jandrews@infoave.net.

**WISE, CHARLES DAVIDSON,** science educator; b. Huntington, W. Va., June 13, 1926; s. Fred Eugene Wise and Maggie M. Harshbarger; m. Juanita Irene Meadows, Mar. 22, 1947; 1 child, Sandra. AB, MS, W. Va. U., 1950; PhD, U. N.Mex., 1962. Cert. tchr. N.Mex., W. Va., Tex. Tchr. St. Albans (W. Va.) High Sch., 1951-53; lab. assst. Marshall U., 1950-51; grad. fellow U. N.Mex., Albuquerque, 1953-55, grad. asst., 1960-61; rsch. scientist U. Tex., Port Aransas, Tex., 1958-60; prof. Ball State U., Muncie, Ind., 1961-91; rep. Ind. State Legislature, Indpls., 1967-69; senator Ind. State Senate, Indpls., 1969-73. Contbr. articles to profl. jours., 1958—. Bd. dirs. Mental Health Svc. East Cen. Ind., 1974-77; pres. Muncie Bicentennial Festival Com., 1975-77. With U.S. Army, 1944-46. Recipient fellowship U. Ind., 1957, U. Tex., 1957-58, Marshall U. Alumni Community Achievement award, 1993; named Alumnus of Yr., East Bank High Sch., W.Va., 1977. Fellow Ind. Acad. Sci.; mem. Nat. Assn. State Legislators (life mem.), Nat. Audubon Soc., Ind. Audubon Soc. (past pres., conservation award 1977), E. Cen. Ind. Audubon Soc. (pres. 1988-90, conservation award 1984), Sigma Xi Rsch. Soc. (pres. Ball State U. chpt., bd. dir. Hoosier Environ. coun. 1990-93). Republican. Presbyterian. Avocations: birdwatching, travel, languages, genealogy, history. Home: 1032 Brickyard Ave Milton WV 25541 Office: Ball State Univ Muncie IN 47306-0001 Office Phone: 765-285-8820.

**WISE, CHARLES WILLIAM, III,** financial advisor; b. York, Pa., Oct. 7, 1951; s. Charles W. and Charlotte Louise; m. Holly Sue Smith, Dec. 7, 1974; 1 child, Heather Britta. BSBA, Ind. U. Pa., 1973. CPA Pa.; registered investment advisor rep. NASD. Staff, sr., in charge acct. Miller & Co. CPAs, York., Pa., 1973-77; supr. fin./operational audit Pa. Blue Shield, Camp Hill, Pa., 1977-79, various mgmt. positions audit, info. sys. audit, account svcs. and support, special investigations, 1979-85, dir. corp. audit, 1986-94; dir. audit/reimbursement Xact Medicare Svcs., Camp Hill, 1995—97; dir. audit and performance analysis HGSA, Camp Hill, 1998—99, dir. spl. projects, 1999—2000; chief security officer Highmark, Inc., Camp Hill, 2001—03; fin. advisor Citigroup/SmithBarney, 2004—. Life mem. Laurel Fire Co.; officer, bd. dirs. Strand Capitol Performing Arts Ctr.; mem. Art Forever Adv. Bd. Mem.: AICPA, York 100, Friends of Drum Corps Internat. Office: 204 N George St 3d Fl York PA 17401 Office Phone: 717-854-5553.

**WISE, GEORGE EDWARD,** lawyer; b. Chgo., Feb. 26, 1924; s. George E. and Helen L. (Gray) W.; m. Patricia E. Finn, Aug. 3, 1945; children: Erich, Peter, Abbe, Raoul, John. JD, U. Chgo. Bar: Calif. 1949, U.S. Dist. Ct. (no. dist.) Calif. 1948, U.S. Ct. Appeals (9th cir.) 1948, U.S. Dist. Ct. (cen. dist.) 1950, U.S. Supreme Ct. 1955. Law clk. Calif. Supreme Ct., 1948-49; sr. ptnr. Wise, Wiezorek, Timmons & Wise, Long Beach, 1949—; of counsel Wise Pearce Yocis & Smith, Long Beach. Mem. ABA. With USNR, 1943-45. Fellow Am. Coll. Trial Lawyers; mem. ABA, Los Angeles County Bar Assn., Long Beach Bar Assn. (pres. 1970, Atty. of Yr. 1990), Calif. State Bar. Home: 5401 E El Cedral St Long Beach CA 90815-4112 Office: Wise Pearce Yocis & Smith 249 E Ocean Blvd Ste 440 Long Beach CA 90802-4806 Personal E-mail: georgewise@yahoo.com.

**WISE, JACK RONALD,** music educator; b. Watseka, Ill., June 17, 1951; s. John Carroll and Rachel Mary Wise; m. Barbara Jean Given; children: Colin Jeffery, Erin Elizabeth, Sean Robert. BS in Music Edn., U. Ill., 1974; MusM, No. Ill. U., 1992. Cert. tchr. Ill., 1974. Tchr. music Decatur (Ill.) Pub. Schs., 1974—75, Orland Pk. (Ill.) Elem. Sch. Dist., 1975—76; from dir. band. elem. sch. to tchr. music Carpentersville (Ill.) Unified Sch. Dist., 1976—2001, tchr. music, 2001—. Cons. Crystal Lake (Ill.) Elem. Sch. Dist., 1992. Organizer, leader Appalachian Day, Project Trips, Hampshire, Ill., 1996—2004. Mem.: NEA, Ill. Music Educator's Assn., Ill. Edn. Assn., Local Edn. Assn. Dundee (bldg. rep. 2002—06), Music Educator's Nat. Conf., Pi Kappa Phi. Methodist. Avocations: reading, musical performance, sports, mechanical work on instruments, woodworking. Office: Algonquin Middle School C U S D 300 520 Longwood Place Algonquin IL 60102

**WISE, JOAN S.,** lawyer; b. Trenton, NJ, Aug. 11, 1941; BS in Edn., George Wash. U., 1976; MA in Remedial Reading, U. Calif., 1979; JD, Georgetown U. Bar: Md. 1984, DC 1987, US Supreme Ct. 1988. Asst. atty. gen. State of Md.; atty. to assoc. gen. counsel Am. Assn. Retired People (AARP), 1987—99, gen. counsel, 1999—. Mem.: Md. State Bar Assn., Inc., DC Bar Assn. Office: AARP 601 E St NW Washington DC 20049*

**WISE, JOHN AUGUSTUS,** lawyer, director; b. Detroit, Mar. 30, 1938; s. John Augustus and Mary Blanche (Parent) W.; m. Helga M. Bessin, Nov. 27, 1965; children: Monique Elizabeth, John Eric. Student, U. Vienna, 1957—58; AB honors cum laude, Coll. Holy Cross, 1959; JD, U. Mich., 1962; postgrad., U. Munich Law Faculty, 1962—63. Bar: Mich. 1963, D.C. 1966. Assoc. Dykema, Gossett, Detroit, 1962-64; asst. to pres. Internat. Econ. Policy Assn., Washington, 1964-66; assoc. Parsons, Tennent, Hammond, Hardig & Ziegelman, Detroit, 1967-70; pres. Wise & Marsac P.C., Detroit, 1970-2001; sr. ptnr. Williams, Mullen, Clark & Dobbins, PLLC, Detroit, 2001—04; of counsel, ptnr. Howard & Howard, P.C., Detroit, 2004—. Dir. Peltzer & Ehlers Am. Corp., 1975-80, Colombian Am. Friends Inc., 1974-89. Bd. dirs. Hyde Park Coop., 1974-77; trustee Friends Sch., Detroit, 1977-81, Brighton Health Svcs. Corp., 1991-94; Providence Hosp., 2001—; chmn. bd. dirs. Brighton Hosp., 1995—; mem. Detroit Com. on Fgn. Rels. Ford Found. grantee U. Munich, 1962-63. Mem. ABA, Mich. Bar Assn., Detroit Bar Assn., Internat. Bar Assn., Detroit Athletic Club, Detroit Econ. Club. Roman Catholic. Home: 1221 Yorkshire Rd Grosse Pointe Park MI 48230-1105 Office: Pinehurst Ctr Ste 101 39400 Woodward Ave Bloomfield Hills MI 48304-5151 Office Phone: 248-723-0435. E-mail: jwise@howardandhoward.com.

**WISE, JOHN MACGREGOR,** speech educator; b. Napa, Calif., May 13, 1966; BA in Comm. and English, Trinity U., San Antonio, 1988; MA in Speech Comm., U. Ill., Urbana, 1990, PhD in Speech Comm., 1995. Asst. prof. Clemson U., SC, 1995—99, Ariz. State U., Phoenix, 1999—2003, assoc. prof., chair, 2003—. Author: Exploring Technology and Social Space, 1997, Culture and Technology!, 2005, Mediamaking, 2d edit., 2005. Mem.: Nat. Comm. assn., Internat. Comm. Assn. Office: Ariz State U 4701 West Thunderbird Rd Glendale AZ 85306

**WISE, KIMBERLY ANNE (SCHILLACI),** music educator, musician; b. Painesville, Ohio, Apr. 15, 1975; d. Cynthia E and Kinton Connelly (Stepfather), Joseph S and Brenda Schillaci (Stepmother); m. Jeff Wise, June 16, 2000. MusB in Edn., Baldwin-Wallace Coll., 1998; MusM in Edn., VanderCook Coll. Music, 2004. Cert. tchr. N.C., 2002. Asst. dir. bands Parkwood Mid. and High Schs., Monroe, NC, 1998—2002; dir. bands and music East Lincoln Mid. Sch., Iron Station, 2002—; asst. dir. marching band East Lincoln H.S., Denver, 2002—. Brass performer Theatre Charlotte, 1999—99; asst. prin. horn Winthrop U. Olde English Wind Ensemble, Rock Hill, 2001—; prin. horn U. N.C. Charlotte Cmty. Band, 2003—. Musician: (performance) Winthrop Olde English Wind Ensemble (Selected to perform at the Am. Bandmasters Assn. Ann. Conv., 2005). V.p., sec. treas. VanderCook Coll. Music, 2004. Recipient John Philip Sousa Outstanding Band Mem. award, Riverside H.S. Band, 1993; scholar, U.S. Achievement Acad., 1997. Mem.: South Ctrl. Dist. Bandmasters Assn., Nat. Band Assn., Music Educator's Nat. Conf., Omicron Delta Kappa, Mu Phi Epsilon. Avocations: french horn, travel. Home: 12251 Fullerton Ct Charlotte NC 28214 Office: East Lincoln Mid Sch 4137 Highway 73 Iron Station NC 28080 Office Phone: 704-732-0761. Office Fax: 704-732-4456. Personal E-mail: kimberly@oldmedia.com. E-mail: kwise3@lincoln.k12.nc.us.

**WISE, LORRAINE E.,** educational consultant; d. Alonza Jerome and Elsie Virginia Beulah; 1 child, Hillary Lauren Beulah. BA, Fed. City Coll., 1974; MSW, Howard U., 1977. From program asst. to sr. policy specialist US Dept. Edn., 1974—94, sr. policy specialist student achievement and sch. accountability programs, 1994—. Nat. parental involvement expert US Dept. Edn., Office Elem. and Secondary Edn., Student Achievement ans Sch. Accountability, Washington, 1994—. Contbg. author Reaching All Families: Creating Family Friendly Schools, Family Involvement in Children's Education:Successful Local Approaches, discussant (various profl. symposiums), expert (various parental involvement programs); contbr. chapters to books. Recipient Plaque for Continued Support, Nat. Coalition Title I Chpt. 1 Parents Bd. Dirs., 2001, VIP award, Nat. Coalition Title I Parents, 2003, Plaque, NJ Assn. Parent Coord., Commitment and Dedication to Parents, 2003, Nat. Coalition of ESEA Title I Parents, 2005. Mem.: Am. Ednl. Rsch. Assn. Office: US Dept Edn 400 Md Ave SW Washington DC 20202 Office Phone: 202-260-1406. Business E-Mail: lorraine.wise@ed.gov.

**WISE, PATRICIA,** opera singer, educator; b. Wichita, Kans. d. Melvin R. and Genevieve F. (Dotson) W.; 1 child, Jennifer. B. Music Edn., U. Kans., Lawrence, 1966. Prof. voice Ind. U. Sch. Music, Bloomington, 1995—; tchr. master classes San Francisco, Vienna Conservatory, Salzburg (Austria) Mozarteum; voice tchr. Domingo Young Artist program Washington Opera. Debut as Susanna in Marriage of Figaro, Kansas City, 1966; prin. roles include Lucia, Gilda, Micaela, Juliette, Zerbinetta, Pamina, Musetta, Lulu, Violetta, Nedda, others; appeared with leading Am. opera cos. including, Chgo., Santa Fe, N.Y.C., San Francisco, Houston, San Diego, Miami, Balt., Phila., Pitts.; European appearances, 1971-76. London Royal Opera, Glyndebourne Festival, Vienna Volksoper, Geneva Opera; guest artist with Vienna, Hamburg, Munich, Cologne, Frankfurt, and Berlin State Operas; guest appearances in Madrid, Barcelona, Rome, La Scala Milan, Nice, Paris Chatelet, Zurich, Dresden, Salzburg Festival, Theatro Colon, Buenos Aires; appeared with orchs. including, Chgo. Symphony Orch., Los Angeles Symphony Orch., N.Y. Handel Soc., Israel Philharm. Orch., Vienna Philharm. Orch., N.Y. Philharm., Cleve. Orch., Berlin Symphonic Orch., BBC Orch., Nat. Orch. France; Angel Recordings; internat. TV, film appearances. Recipient Morton Baum award N.Y.C. Ctr., 1971, Dealey Meml. award Dallas Symphony, 1966, Naftzger young Artist award Wichita Symphony, 1966, Midland Young Artist award Midland (Tex.) Symphony Orch., 1966; M.B. Rockefeller Fund grantee, 1967-70; Sullivan Found. grantee, 1967-68; named Kammersänger Vienna Staatsoper, 1989. E-mail: patwise@indiana.edu.

**WISE, RICHARD EVANS,** corporate executive; b. Lancaster, Pa., Sept. 24, 1947; s. William Edmund and Dorothy Christelle (Evans) W.; m. Kathrine Suzanne Keller, Jan. 2, 1971; 1 child, Thomas Edmund. BS, West Chester (Pa.) U., 1970; MEd, Pa. State U., 1976, PhD, 1980. Project adminstrn. mgr. Hartford Ins. Group, 1977-80; v.p., tng. mgr. Conn. Nat. Bank, 1980-83; corp. tng. and devel. dir. Travelers Corp., Hartford, 1983-89, dir. corp. strategy and rsch., 1989-93; pres. ValueNet Internat., Inc., Hartford, 1993—. Adj. prof. Hartford Grad. Ctr.; pres. Am. Inst. Banking; bd. dirs. Admiral Farragut Corp., Human Tech. Partnership, Greenfield, Mass. Mem. editl. bd. Internat. Jour. Instrnl. Media; contbr. articles to profl. jours.; designer Travelers Mgmt. Devel. Continuum, 1984-86. Mem. Hartford mgmt. devel. adv. bd. Greater Hartford Arts Coun.; vice chmn. Windsor Govt. Study Commn., 1992-93; bd. dirs., v.p. Better Bus. Bur., Inc. Hartford; chmn. Grand Destiny capital campaign Pa. State U. Coll. Edn., 1997—; bd. dirs. Summer Wind Performing Arts Ctr., 2002—. Named Outstanding Alumnus Pa. State U., 1987; Chapter of Excellence Am. Inst. of Banking, 1983. Mem. Assn. for Ednl. Communications and Tech. (cert. of Merit, 1986, 88, Outstanding Practice award, 1983, div. coun. pres. 1990—), Am. Soc. for Tng. and Devel., Phi Delta Kappa. Independent. Methodist. Lodge: Masons. Avocations: sailing, skiing, music, golf, photography. Home: 8 Cobblestone Way Windsor CT 06095-2224 Office: ValueNet Internat Inc 100 Pearl St Hartford CT 06103 Office Phone: 860-559-5600.

**WISE, RICHARD REYNOLDS,** management consultant; b. Boston, July 15, 1964; s. Glenn Hershey and Ann Reynolds Wise; m. Carmela Vilar Vilar, Aug. 24, 1991; children: Isabel Vilar, Christopher Reynolds, Catherine Gatchalian. BA, U Pa., Phila., 1986; MBA, Wharton Sch., Phila., 1992. Mng. dir., strategy practice leader Mercer Mgmt. Cons., Boston, 2001—04; sr. ptnr., dir. brand strategy practice Lippincott Mercer, 2004—. Author: How to Grow When Markets Don't. Membership chair Wayland STC, Mass., 2005—06. Avocations: boating, squash, beer tasting. Office Phone: 617-424-3200. Personal E-mail: candrwise@comcast.net

**WISE, SANDRA CASBER,** lawyer; b. Macalester Coll., 1969; JD, U. Minn., 1972. Bar: Minn. 1972, D.C., 1986, W.Va., 1987. Legis asst. to Rep. Martha Keys, Washington, 1977-78; asst. to asst. to the pres. for women's issues Sara Weddington, The White Ho., Washington, 1979; staff sub-com. on pub. assistance Ho. Com. on Ways and Means, Washington, 1980, staff sub-com. on health, 1981-85; atty. White, Fine and Verville, 1986; staff dir. sub-com. on social security Ho. Com. on Ways and Means, Washington, 1987-94, minority counsel subcom. on social security, 1995-2000; first lady State of W.Va., 2001—.

**WISE, STEVEN FLETCHER,** art educator, artist; b. Oakland, Calif., Aug. 7, 1969; m. Kara Smith, Aug. 7, 1992. BA, Swarthmore Coll., 1991; MFA, U. Iowa, 1998. Art instr. U. Ark., Fayetteville, 2000—05; art tchr. Rogers (Ark.) Pub. Schs., 2005—. Drawing installation, Rejection Letters, internet website.

**WISE, WILLIAM JERRARD,** lawyer; b. Chgo., May 27, 1934; s. Gerald Paul and Harriet Muriel (Rosenblum) Wise; m. Peggy Spero, Sept. 3, 1959; children: Deborah, Stephen, Betsy, Lynne. BBA, U. Mich., 1955, MBA, 1958, JD with distinction, 1958. Bar: Ill. 1959. Spl. atty. Office Regional Counsel, IRS, Milw., 1959-63; with McDermott, Will & Emery, Chgo., 1963-70, Coles & Wise, Ltd., Chgo., 1971—80, Wise & Stracks, Ltd., Chgo., 1980—2000; Querrey & Harrow, Chgo., 2000—. Lectr., contbr. Ill. Inst. Continuing Legal Edn.; arbitrator Cir. Ct. Cook County Ill., 1990—. Bd. dirs. Blind Svc. Assn., Chgo., 1964—74; active Village of Winnetka, Ill., 1974—75; dir., treas. Suzuki Orff Sch. Young Musicians, Chgo., 1981—91. With U.S. Army, 1958—59. Mem.: Chgo. Bar Assn. Home: 1401 Tower Rd Winnetka IL 60093-1628 Office: Querrey & Harrow 175 W Jackson Blvd Ste 1600 Chicago IL 60604-2827 Office Phone: 312-540-7104. Personal E-mail: dididoe@yahoo.com. *I believe that one succeeds best in our society if one gives as little thought as possible to one's personal well being.*

**WISEHART, MARY RUTH,** retired religious organization administrator; b. Myrtle, Mo., Nov. 2, 1932; d. William Henry and Ora (Harbison) W. BA, Free Will Bapt. Bible Coll., 1955, George Peabody Coll. Tchrs., 1959, MA, 1960,

PhD, 1976. Tchr. Free Will Bapt. Bible Coll., Nashville, 1956-60, chmn. English dept., 1961-85; exec. sec.-treas. Free Will Bapt. Women Nat. Active for Christ, 1985-98. Author: Sparks Into Flame, 1985, Beyond the Gate, 1998; contbr. poetry to jours. Mem. Scribbler's Club. Free Will Baptist. Avocations: photography, music, drama. Personal E-mail: wisemrw@aol.com.

**WISEHEART, MALCOLM BOYD, JR.,** lawyer; b. Miami, Fla., Sept. 18, 1942; s. Malcolm B. and Dorothy E. (Allen) Wiseheart; m. Michele I. Romanens, Dec. 11, 1976. BA, Yale U., 1965; MA in English Jurisprudence, Cambridge U., 1973; JD with honors, U. Fla., 1970. Bar: Fla. 1970, Eng. 1970, Wales 1970, Jamaica 1970, Trinidad and Tobago 1971, DC 1980. Assoc. Helliwell, Melrose & DeWolf, Miami, 1970-72; pvt. practice Miami 1973—86, 1987—; sr. ptnr. Wiseheart & Joyce, P.A., Miami, 1986—87. Sec., gen. counsel Wiseheart Found., pres., 1985—2006; spl. master Dade County Property Appraisal Adjustment Bd., 1977—90; pres. Fla. Law Inst., 1980—2006; bd. dirs. Sta. WLRN Pub. Radio, 1982; dir. Yale Alumni Schs. Com. S. Fla., 2001—06; bd. dirs. Coun. Internat. Visitors. Bd. trustees Ransom Everglades Sch., 1995—97; bd. trustees, mem. exec. com. Players State Theater, 1982—84. Named Most Outstanding, U. Fla. Law Rev. Alumnus, 1981. Mem.: Gray's Inn of Ct., London (barrister), Order of Coif, Dade County Bar Assn. (dir. 1971—74, treas. 1974—75, sec. 1975—77, dir. 1986—89), Fla. Bar (chmn. grievance com. 1978—81), United Oxford and Cambridge Univs. Club (London), Yale Club (Miami pres. 1976—77). Office: Wiseheart Bldg 2840 SW 3rd Ave Miami FL 33129-2317 Office Phone: 305-285-1222. E-mail: mbwjr@bellsouth.net.

**WISEMAN, ALAN M(ITCHELL),** lawyer; b. Long Branch, NJ, July 6, 1944; s. Lincoln B. and Gertrude (Gorcey) W.; m. Paula Wiseman, July 8, 1965; children: Steven, David, Julie. BA, Johns Hopkins U., 1965; JD, Georgetown U., 1968. Bar: Md. 1968, Ill. 1970, DC 1973. Law clk. Hon. William J. McWilliams, Md. Ct. Appeals, 1968-69; assoc. Schiff, Hardin & Waite, Chgo., 1970-74; ptnr. Howrey Simon Arnold White, LLP, Washington, 1976—, co-chair antitrust practice group, chmn. pro bono and charitable activities com. Editor Georgetown Law Jour., 1967-68. Mem. US C. of C. (coun. antitrust policy 1983-2001). Office: 1299 Pennsylvania Ave NW Washington DC 20004-2400 Office Phone: 202-383-6638, 202-783-0800. Business E-Mail: wisemana@howrey.com.

**WISEMAN, CARTER STERLING,** writer, educator; b. NYC, Oct. 8, 1945; s. Mark Huntington Wiseman and Eleanor (Carter) Wood; m. Eileen Condon, Oct. 19, 1985; children: Emma, Owen, Damian. BA, Yale U., 1968; MA, Columbia U., 1972. Newsman AP, N.Y.C., 1972-74; assoc. editor Newsweek Mag., N.Y.C., 1974-77; sr. editor Horizon Mag., N.Y.C., 1977-79; mng. editor Portfolio Mag., N.Y.C., 1979-80; archtl. critic N.Y. Mag., N.Y.C., 1980-96; editor Yale Alumni Mag., New Haven, 1986—2002; lectr. Yale Sch. Architecture, New Haven, 2002—. Bd. dirs. MacDowell Colony, Peterborough, NH, pres., 1999—; tchr. The Reading Co., Westport, Conn. Author: Twentieth Century American Architecture, 2000, I.M. Pei, 2001; contbg. editor: ARTnews, 1996—. Chair Loeb Fellowship Harvard U., 1986—95. With U.S. Army, 1968—71. Recipient Spl. Citation award, Am. Inst. Arch., 1984, Inst. Honor award, Am. Inst. Archs., 1987, Interpretative Writing award, Soc. Silurians, 1985, Roger Starr award, Citizens Housing and Planning Coun., 1987, 1990; Loeb fellow, Harvard U., 1985. Mem.: Century Assn., Yale Club N.Y. Office: 16 W Branch Rd Weston CT 06883-2917 Personal E-mail: writertime@aol.com.

**WISEMAN, CRAIG,** song writer, publisher; b. Hattiesburg, Miss. With Almo Irving Music Publishing, 1990—2000, BMG Music Publishing, 2000—04; owner Big Loud Shirt Industries, 2004—. Mem. adv. bd. ASCAP. Writer: over 11 number one country singles including Young (Kenny Chesney), She's Got It All (Kenny Chesney), Everywhere (Tim McGraw), The Cowboy in Me (Tim McGraw), Just Another Day in Paradise (Phil Vasser), Tell Her (Lonestar), The Good Stuff (Kenny Chesney) (Country Song of Yr. Billboard Mag., 2002), writer (with Craig Wiseman) over 11 number one country singles including Live Like You Were Dying (Tim McGraw) (Song of Yr. Country Music Assn., 2004). Named Writer of Yr., Music Row Mag., 1997, Nashville Songwriters Assn., 1997. Mem.: Nashville Songwriter's Assn. Internat. (mem. exec. bd.), Country Music Assn. Office: Big Loud Shirt Industries LLC 1105 17th Ave S Nashville TN 37212

**WISEMAN, DOUGLAS CARL,** education educator, department chairman, dean; b. Nashua, NH, Feb. 28, 1935; s. Howard W. and Ruth D. (Aiken) W.; m. Donna Wiseman; children: Mark, Cynthia, Lori, Alan, Kathleen, Steve. BEd, Plymouth (N.H.) State Coll., 1961; MS, Ind. U., 1962, PED, 1970. Cert. tchr. health, math., phys. edn., sci. Tchr., track coach Nashua (N.H.) Pub. Schs., 1960-61, instr. baseball coach, 1962-63; tchr. asst. Ind. U., Bloomington, 1961-62; tchr. high sch., wrestling coach Portage (Mich.) High Sch., 1963-64; instr., asst. prof. soccer, wrestling and tennis coach Plymouth (N.H.) State Coll., 1964-69; asst. prof. Northeastern U., Boston, 1969-71; dir. athletics, chmn. phys. edn. dept. Plymouth State Coll., 1971-80, assoc. dean, dir. undergrad. studies, 1993-96, prof., accreditation coord., 1996-98, ret., 1998, prof. emeritus, 1998—; prof., chair dept. edn. Univ. Sys. of N.H., 1980—. Aquatics cons. Am./Nat. Red Cross, Laconia, N.H., 1971-98, State Dept. Edn., Concord, 1980-98. Author, contbg. editor: Adapted Physical Education, 1982, Practical Research, 1989, Quantitative Research, 1992, Physical Education for Exceptional Students, 1994, Introduction to Educational Research, 1995, Educational Research, 1996, Research Strategies for Education, 1999; contbr. more than 50 articles to profl. jours. Cert. police officer Ashland, N.H., 1992-98; chair sch. bd. Plymouth Regional Sch. Dist., 1989-91; divsn. staff officer-pub. edn., flotilla career counseling officer USCG Aux., 2001-2002. AAHPERD Ea. Dist. scholar, 1990-91. Republican. Avocations: reading, hiking, boating, Tae Kwon Do. Personal E-mail: seaquest05@msn.com.

**WISEMAN, ERIC C.,** apparel executive; BS, MBA, Wake Forest Univ. Exec. v.p. JanSport VF Corp., Greensboro, NC, 1995—98, pres. Bestform Intimates, 1998—2000, v.p. & chmn. global intimate apparel, 2000—03, v.p. & chmn. sportswear coalition, 2003—04, v.p. & chmn. outdoor & sportswear coalitions, 2004—05, exec. v.p. global brands, 2005—06, pres., COO, 2006—. Office: VF Corp 105 Corporate Ctr Blvd Greensboro NC 27408 Mailing: VF Corp PO Box 21488 Greensboro NC 27420-1488*

**WISEMAN, FLOYD LANDIS,** chemist; b. Oakland, Calif., Mar. 21, 1956; s. James Edward and Nora Gail Wiseman; m. Jacquelce Sue Snider, Jan. 13, 1978; children: James Matthew, John Mark, Fallon Rene. BS in Chemistry, U. Tenn., Martin, 1978; PhD in Chemistry, La. State U., Baton Rouge, 1982. Postdoctoral assoc. La. State U., 1982—84; commd. 2d lt. USAF, 1984, advanced through grades to maj., 1996; prof. USAF Acad., Colorado Springs, Colo., 1988—92, US Mil. Acad., West Point, NY, 1999—2004; ret. USAF, 2004; sr. scientist ENSCO, Inc., Melbourne, Fla., 2004—. Contbr. articles to profl. jours. Missions coord. River of Life Ch., Merritt Island, Fla. Decorated Commendation medal USAF, Meritorious Svc. medal. Republican. Mem. Assemblies Of God. Avocations: music, writing. Home: 1740 Curlaw Ct Viera FL 32955 Office: ENSCO, Inc 4849 N Wickham Rd Melbourne FL 32940

**WISEMAN, LAURENCE DONALD,** foundation executive; b. Washington, Feb. 24, 1947; s. Leon Robert and Marion (Wiseman) W.; m. Robin Lynn Jeweler, May 29, 1978; children: Justin J., David B. AB with highest distinction, Dartmouth Coll., 1969; M in Pub. Affairs, Princeton U., 1971. Exec. producer Sta. WQED-TV (pub. broadcasting), Pitts., 1971-75; prin. Moses, Epstein and Wiseman, Washington, 1975-78; v.p. Yankelovich, Skelly and White, N.Y.C., 1978-81, Am. Forest Council, Washington, 1981-84, pres., 1984—. Pres. Am. Forest Coun., 1984-92, Am. Forest Found., 1993—; external adv. bd. mem., Global Inst. Sustainable Forestry, Yale U., 2005-. Author: Coalition Building, 1977. Bd. dirs. Cystic Fibrosis Found., N.Y.C., 1979-80, Urban Philanthan., Washington, 1980-83, Sasha Bruce House, Washington, 1980-82; adv. com. Soc. for Profl. Journalists, Washington, 1984; trustee Nat. Ctr. for Housing and the Environment, 2001—; hon. trustee Nat. Arbor Day Found., Nebraska

City, Nebr., 1984—; chair Nat. Coun. on Pvt. Forests, 1997-98, Inst. for Journalism and Natural Resources, 1998—. Mem. Am. Forestry Assn., Soc. Am. Foresters, Pub. Rels. Soc. Am. Home: 10621 Democracy Ln Potomac MD 20854-4016 Office: Am Forest Found 1111 19th St NW Washington DC 20036-3603 Business E-Mail: lwiseman@forestfoundation.org. E-mail: lwiseman@affoundation.org.

**WISEMAN, MICHAEL MARTIN,** lawyer; b. NYC, Oct. 25, 1953; s. Robert Lawrence and Katherine Loise (Martin) W.; m. Helen Ann Garten, May 18, 1984. BA, Harvard U., 1975, JD, 1978. Bar: NY 1979, Mass. 1978, US Dist. Ct. (so. and ea. dists.) NY 1979, US Supreme Ct. 1988. Assoc. Sullivan & Cromwell, NYC, 1978-85, ptnr., 1985—, and mng. ptnr. fin. institutions practice area. Mem. NY State Bar Banking Law Com.; former mem. Russian-Am. Bankers Forum. Contbr. articles to profl. jours. Fellow Am. Bar Found.; mem. ABA (vice chair banking, currency and treasury com. of adminstrv. law sect. 1991-94), Assn. Bar City NY (chair com. on banking law 1985-91, chair 1988-91), Am. Law Inst. Office: Sullivan & Cromwell 125 Broad St Fl 28 New York NY 10004-2489 Office Phone: 212-558-3846. Office Fax: 212-558-3588. Business E-Mail: wisemanm@sullcrom.com.

**WISEMAN, THOMAS ANDERTON, JR.,** federal judge; b. Tullahoma, Tenn., Nov. 3, 1930; s. Thomas Anderton and Vera Seleta (Poe) W.; m. Emily Barbara Matlack, Mar. 30, 1957; children: Thomas Anderton III, Mary Alice, Sarah Emily. BA, Vanderbilt U., 1952, LL.B., 1954; LLM, U. Va., 1990. Bar: Tenn. Pvt. practice, Tullahoma, 1956-63; ptnr. Haynes, Wiseman & Hull, Tullahoma and Winchester, Tenn., 1963-71; treas. Tenn., 1971-74; ptnr. Chambers & Wiseman, 1974-78; judge U.S. Dist. Ct. (mid. dist.) Tenn. Nashville, 1978—, chief judge, 1984-91, sr. judge, 1995—; 6th cir. rep. Jud. Conf. of the U.S., 1990—2001, chair dist. judges conf., 1998-99. Mem. Tenn. Ho. of Reps., 1964-68; adj. prof. law Vanderbilt U. Sch. Law; cons. to judiciary of Brcko, Bosnia, 2002; mem. pattern jury instrn. com. 6th cir., 1988—. Asso. editor: Vanderbilt Law Rev, 1953-54. Democratic candidate for gov., Tenn., 1974; Chmn. Tenn. Heart Fund, 1973, Middle Tenn. Heart Fund, 1972. Served with U.S. Army, 1954-56. Fellow Tenn. Bar Found.; mem. Fed. Judges Assn. (bd. dirs. 1982-87, v.p. 1982-91, 87-91), Masons (33 deg.), Shriners, Amateur Chefs Soc. Presbyterian. Office: US Dist Ct 777 US Courthouse 801 Broadway Nashville TN 37203-3816

**WISEMAN, THOMAS G.,** lawyer; b. Bklyn., Sept. 8, 1947; BS, L.I. Univ., 1969; MS, Pa. State Univ., 1971; JD, Univ. Balt., 1982. Bar: Va. 1984, DC 1998, US Patent & Trademark Office. Primary patent examiner U.S. Patent & Trademark Office, 1972—83, supervising patent examiner, 1983—90, examiner in chief, 1990—91; acting patent branch chief Office Tech. Transfer, NIH, 1991—93; ptnr., Patent Prosecution, Intellectual Property Litigation practices Venable LLP, Washington. Lectr. L.I. Univ., 1972. Mem.: ABA, Am. Intellectual Property Assn., Va. State Bar Assn., DC Bar Assn., Am. Chemical Soc., Am. Assn. for Advancement of Sci. Office: Venable LLP 575 7th St NW Washington DC 20004 Office Phone: 202-344-4614. Office Fax: 202-344-8300. Business E-Mail: tgwiseman@venable.com.

**WISE MASTERS HUGHES, JANICE ANN,** school social worker; b. Leavenworth, Kans., Dec. 7, 1935; d. Paul Joel and Mae Valentine (Myer) Wise; m. DeArle Lee Masters, May 28, 1954; children: Gregory, Kathe Masters Owens. BS, Eastern Mich. U., 1965; MA, Mich. State U., 1970; postgrad., Nova U., 1989. Elem. tchr. pub. schs., Dryden, Lapeer and Haslett, Mich., 1960-69; sch. social worker Eaton County Intermediate Sch. Dist., Charlotte, Mich., 1969-71, Genesee Intermediate Sch. Dist., Flint, Mich., 1971—. Designer children and youth separation and/or divorce program; designer social thinking tools for children. Author: TA for You, 1978. Mem. NEA, Mich. Edn. Assn., Nat. Assn. Social Workers, Internat. Transactional Analysis Assn., Mich. Assn. for Emotionally Disturbed Children. Lodges: Zonta. Republican. Roman Catholic. Avocations: exhibitor and breeder of bearded collies and polish lowland sheepdogs, travel, cooking, reading.

**WISH, JAY BARRY,** nephrologist, specialist; b. Hartford, Mar. 30, 1950; s. Martin and Evelyn Lillian (Lassman) W.; m. Linda Kristina Hansen, June 29, 1971; (div. 1980); children: Allen Jeremy, Robin Lindsey; m. Diane Elizabeth Perkins, June 5, 1983 (div. 2006); children: Jeffrey Bryan, David Phillip. BA, Wesleyan U., 1970; MD, Tufts U., 1974. Diplomate Am. Bd. Internal Medicine, Am. Bd. Nephrology. Resident in medicine New England Med. Ctr., Boston, 1974-79; instr. in medicine Tufts U., Boston, 1978-79; lectr. in health sci. Northeastern U., Boston, 1978-79; asst. prof. of medicine Case Western Res. U., Cleve., 1979-85, assoc. prof. of medicine, 1985-96, prof. medicine, 1996—; dir. hemodialysis U. Hosps. of Cleve., 1980—, dir. continuing edn., 1987-95. Chmn. Med. Adv. Bd. Kidney Found. of Ohio, Cleve., 1985-88. Author: Renal Disease and Hypertension, 1982, Disorders of Potassium, 1984, Metabolic Diseases, 1986, Rheumatic Diseases of the Kidney, 1993, Acid-Base and Electrolyte Disorders in the Critically Ill Patient, 1993, Assuring Quality of Care in Dialysis Patients, 1994, Algorithms and Care Paths for Quality Improvement, 2000, Adequacy of Hemodialysis, 2002, Quality, Safety and Accountability in Dialysis, 2004; contbr. articles to med. jours. Chmn. med. rev. bd. End-Stage Renal Disease Network #22, Pitts., 1982-87, End-Stage Renal Disease Network #9, Indpls., 1992-2000, pres., 2001—; mem. exec. com. Forum of End-Stage Renal Disease Networks, 1992-2006, v.p. 1996-98, pres. 1998-2001; bd. dirs. Renal Phys. Assn., 1993-99, sec. 1996-97, treas. 1997-98; mem. Nat. Kidney Found. Fellow Am. Coll. of Physicians; mem. Cleve. Restoration Soc., Am. Soc. of Nephrology, Internat. Soc. of Nephrology, Alpha Omega Alpha. Democrat. Jewish. Avocation: performing arts. Office: U Hosps Cleve 11100 Euclid Ave Cleveland OH 44106-1736 Office Phone: 216-844-3163. Personal E-mail: jaywish@earthlink.net.

**WISH, LESLIEBETH BERGER,** psychotherapist, writer, management consultant; d. Irving L. and Miriam Solomon Berger; m. Peter A. Wish, Nov. 16, 1984; 1 stepchild, Carly Sidra. AB in History & English, Carnegie Mellon U., 1970; MA in English, Ohio U., 1971; MA in Social Svc. Mgmt., Byrn Mawr Coll., 1976; EdD in Human Devel., U. Mass., 1996. Lic. clin. social worker Md., 1980, Mass., 1982, Fla., 2003, diplomate clin. social work Bd. Examiners, 1988; cert. aquatics fitness instr., 2005. Post doctoral tng. in marriage & family therapy sys. Georgetown U. Med. Sch., 1979—82; dir. social work & families The Linwood Sch., Ellicott City, Md., 1980—81; dir. human resource devel. & clin. svcs. The New England Inst. Family Rels., Framingham, Mass., 1982—94; faculty coord., admissions acad. advisor Grad. Ctr. Bus. & Counseling Webster U., Sarasota, 2001—04; v.p. Gulfcoast Healthstyle, Sarasota, Fla., 1994—. Cons. in field. Author, contbg. editor: Trafalgar Publications, 2001—; author: (book) Incest, Women & Work, 1998; contbr. articles, fiction, and poems to numerous nat. magazines. Chair Sarasota Women's Advisory Commn., 1994—2001; pres. coun. Easter Seals, 2002—; co-coord. counseling network, spl. ops. Warrior Found., 2006—; co-coord. counselor network Spl. Ops. Warrior Found. Recipient Md.'s Best Small Press award, Md. Arts Commn., 1981. Mem.: Women's Leadership & Acad. Honor Society (mortar bd. 1970), Phi Kappa Phi. Achievements include pioneering the expansion of sex education and awareness of sexual issues at work and home for The New England Institute of Family Relations, the first sexual dysfunction clinic in New England; first to research, link and present in a book the connection between childhood sexual abuse and its impact on work and career in women; lecture in area of work and career; copyright on career-family history cinventory; introduced seminars and counseling at places of work. Avocations: travel, opera, writing, painting.

**WISHARD, DELLA MAE,** former newspaper editor; b. Bison, S.D., Oct. 21, 1934; d. Ervin E. and Alma J. (Albertson) Preszler; m. Glenn L. Wishard, Oct. 18, 1953; children: Glenda Lee, Pamela A., Glen Ervin. Grad. high sch., Bison. Mem. S.D. Ho. of Reps., Pierre, 1984-96; pub. editor Bison (S.D.) Courier, 1996-2000; owner Wishards Rentals, Rapid City, SD, 2004—. Columnist County Farm Bur. 1970-96. Committeewoman state Rep. Cen. Com., Perkins County, SD, 1980-84, 98-01; rep. precinct committeewoman Pennington County, 2006-. Mem. Am. Legis. Exch. Coun. (state coord. 1985-91, state chmn. 1991-96), Fed. Rep. Women (chmn. Perkins County chpt. 1978-84), S.D. Farm Bur. (state officer 1982), Perkins County Rep. (chmn. 2000-03). Lutheran. Avocations: writing, gardening. Home and Office: 3900 S Valley Dr Rapid City SD 57703 Office Phone: 605-348-2726. Personal E-mail: wishdg@rushmore.com.

**WISHARD, GORDON DAVIS,** lawyer; b. Indpls., Jan. 7, 1945; s. William Niles Jr. and Caroline (Davis) W.; m. Anne Emison; children: Claire Wishard Hoppenworth, Gordon Davis Jr. BA, Williams Coll., 1966; JD, Ind. U., 1969. Bar: Ind. 1969, U.S. Dist. Ct. (so. dist.) Ind. 1969, U.S. Ct. Appeals (7th cir.) 1976, U.S. Supreme Ct. 1980, U.S. Tax Ct. 1983. Ptnr. Ice Miller, Indpls. Mem. Am. Coll. Trust and Estate Coun. (Ind. chmn. 1990-95). Avocations: hunting, fishing. Office: Ice Miller 1 American Sq Indianapolis IN 46282-0020 Office Phone: 317-236-2331.

**WISHART, RONALD SINCLAIR,** retired chemical company executive; b. Bklyn., Mar. 1, 1925; s. Ronald Sinclair and Elizabeth Lathrop (Phillips) W.; m. Betty B. Burnup, Sept. 14, 1951 (dec. Dec. 1973); children: Michael Sinclair, James Ronald; m. Eleanor Dorothy Parrish Dooley, Jan. 11, 1975; stepchildren: Donna Dooley Willix, Arthur D. Dooley. BChemE, Rensselaer Poly. Inst., 1948. Engr., chemist Linde air divsn. Union Carbide Corp., Tonawanda, NY, 1948-51; sales rep. Chgo., Cleve., 1951-56; region mgr. Chgo., 1956-57; product mgr., mktg. mgr. Silicones divsn N.Y.C., 1957-64; gen. mgr., pres., 1964-66; pres. devel. and coating materials divsns., 1966-71; corp. dir. energy and transp. policy, 1972-82; v.p. fed. govt. rels., 1983-85; v.p. pub. affairs Danbury, Conn., 1985-90; chief of staff to chmn. of corp. Union Carbide, N.Y.C., 1984-85. Mem. adv. coun. Gas Rsch. Inst., Energy Modeling Ctr., Stanford U., 1979-83, Environ. and Energy Policy Ctr., John F. Kennedy Sch. Pub. Policy, Harvard U., 1980-87; energy com. Aspen Inst., 1976-88; chmn., exec. dir. Electricity Consumers Resource Coun., Washington, 1976-79. Author: The Marketing Factor, 1966; contbr. chpts. to books and articles to profl. jours.; patentee silicone formulas. Vol. Am. Field Svc., Burma, 1944-45; pres., trustee, elder White Plains (N.Y.) Presbyn. Ch., 1987-90; elder Palm City Presbyn. Ch., 1996-2002; treas., bd. dirs. St. Christopher's Jenni Clarkson Home, 1968-91; mem. exec. bd. Westchester Putnam coun. Boy Scouts Am., White Plains, 1985-91; v.p. Carbide Retiree Corps.; v.p. Hospice Martin and St. Lucie, Inc., 1994-99, pres. 2000-02; pres. Lancewood Assn., 1997. Mem. NAM (mem. energy com.), Am. Mgmt. Assn. (v.p. 1966-69), Chem. Mfrs. Assn. (chmn. energy com. 1974-78), Nat. Petroleum Refiners Assn. (v.p. 1972-76, chmn. issues com. 1985-89), Internat. Fedn. Ind. Energy Users (chmn. 1978), Am. Chem. Soc., Soc. Chem. Industry, U.S. C. of C. (mem. energy com.), Met. Club Washington, Harbor Ridge Yacht and Country Club. Republican. Presbyterian. Avocations: golf, reading, bridge. Home: 1329 Lancewood Ter Palm City FL 34990

**WISHNER, MAYNARD IRA,** retired finance company executive, lawyer; b. Chgo., Sept. 17, 1923; s. Hyman L. and Frances (Fisher) W.; m. Elaine Loewenberg, July 4, 1954; children: Ellen Kenemore, Jane Wishner, Miriam Segel. BA, U. Chgo., 1944, JD, 1947; LHD (hon.), Spertus Inst., 1998, Hebrew Union Coll., 2001, Spertus Coll. Judaica, 2001. Bar: Ill. 1947. Exec. dir. Chgo. Commn. on Human Relations, 1947-52; chief ordinance enforcement div. Law Dept., City of Chgo., 1952-55; mem. law firm Cole, Wishner, Epstein & Manilow, Chgo., 1955-63; with Walter E. Heller & Co., Chgo., 1963-86, pres., 1974-86; of counsel Rosenthal and Schanfield, Chgo., 1986-95, ret., 1995—. Dir. Walter E. Heller Internat. Corp., Am. Nat. Bank & Trust Co., and br. cos., Chgo. Pres. Jewish Fedn. Met. Chgo., 1987-89; chair Nat. Jewish Community Rels., 1992-94, pres. Coun. Jewish Fedn., 1993-96; chmn. bd. govs. Am. Jewish Com., 1977-80, nat. pres. 1980-83, hon. pres., recipient Human Rights medallion, 1975; bd. dirs. Nat. Found. for Jewish Culture; chmn. Ill. Humanities Coun.; commr. Nat. Hillel Found.; mem. vis. com. U. Chgo. Sch. Social Svc. Adminstrn. and Divsn. of the Humanities; chair Ill. Humanities Coun., 1991-93; bd. govs. Jewish Agy. for Israel. Recipient Rosenwald award Jewish Fedn. Met. Chgo., Officers Merit medal Republic of Poland, United Hellenic Leadership Coun. Frisis award, Civic Achievement award U. Chgo. Home: 1410 Sheridan Rd Wilmette IL 60091-1895 E-mail: maynwish@aol.com.

**WISHNICK, MARCIA MARGOLIS,** pediatrician, educator, geneticist; b. N.Y.C., Oct. 10, 1938; d. Hyman and Tillie (Stoller) Margolis; m. Stanley Wishnick, June 12, 1960; 1 child, Elizabeth Anne. BA, Barnard Coll., 1960; PhD, NYU, 1970, MD, 1974. Diplomate Am. Bd. Pediatrics, Nat. Bd. Med. Examiners. Rsch. technician Lederle Labs./Am. Cyanamid, Pearl River, NY, 1960-66; postdoctoral fellow N.Y. Pub. Health Lab., N.Y.C., 1970-71; resident in pediatrics NYU-Bellevue Med. Ctr., N.Y.C., 1974-77, asst. prof. pediatrics, 1977-82; clin. assoc. prof. pediatrics Bellevue Med. Ctr. NYU Med. Ctr., N.Y.C., 1982-87; clin. prof. pediatrics NYU-Bellevue Med. Ctr., N.Y.C., 1987—2003; pvt. practice, N.Y.C., 1977—2003. Contbr. articles to profl. jours. Fellow Am. Acad. Pediatrics; mem. AMA, N.Y. Pediatric Soc., N.Y. Med. Soc. Office Phone: 808-937-0312. Business E-mail: docwishnick@earthlink.net.

**WISKOCIL, ANGIOLINA,** telecommunications industry executive; b. Ecuador; B, Univ. Calif. Acctg. clerk Pacific Bell, 1973, v.p., network engring. West; now sr. v.p.-network svcs. AT&T Inc. (formerly SBC Comm., Inc.), San Antonio. Served on Calif. United Task Force to bridge digital divide; rep. to Leadership Am. Named one of 80 Elite Hispanic Women, Hispanic Bus. Mag., 2005, 50 Most Important Hispanics in Tech., Bus., Hispanic Engineer and Info. Tech. mag., 2005. Office: AT&T Inc 175 E Houston San Antonio TX 78205 Office Phone: 210-821-4105. Office Fax: 210-351-2071.*

**WISLER, DAVID CHARLES,** aerospace engineer; b. Pottstown, Pa., Apr. 21, 1941; s. Lloyd William and Ruth Georgiana (Enos) W.; m. Judith Ann Caleen, Aug. 22, 1964 (dec. Mar. 1979); children: Scott David, Cheryl Lynn; m. Beth Ellen Howard, Jan. 5, 1980; 1 child, Daniel James. BS in Aero Engring., Pa. State U., 1963; MS in Aero. Engring., Cornell U., 1965; PhD in Aero. Engring., U. Colo., 1970. Rsch. engr. GE R & D Ctr., Schenectady, 1965-67; mgr. aero tech. labs. GE Aircraft Engines, Evendale, Ohio, 1985—. Mgr. univ. programs and aero tech. labs.; adj. prof. Ohio State U., U. Cin., Tsinghua U., Beijing. Contbr. articles to profl. jours.; patentee in sloped trenches in compressors. Recipient Gas Turbine award ASME, 1990, 92. Fellow ASME (chmn. turbomachinery com. 1993-, bd. dirs. Internat. Gas Turbine Inst. 1997-, v.p. 2003—). Melville medal for best tech. paper 1989, 98, 2003, editor Jour. Turbomachinery, 2003—); mem. AIAA (assoc.), NAE. Avocation: photography. Home: 40 Trappist Walk Fairfield OH 45014-4465 Office: GE Aircraft Engines 1 Neumann Way # A-411 Cincinnati OH 45215-1915 Office Phone: 513-243-2905. E-mail: dave.wisler@ae.ge.com.*

**WISNER, FRANK GEORGE,** insurance company executive, former ambassador; b. NYC, July 2, 1938; s. Frank Gardiner W. and Mary Knowles (Fritchey) W.; m. Genevieve de Virel, July, 1969 (dec.) 1 dau., Sabrina; m. Christine de Ganay, June, 1976; 1 son, David; stepchildren: Caroline Sarkozy, Olivier Sarkozy. BA, Princeton U., 1961. With Fgn. Svc. Dept. U.S. Dept. State, Algiers, Morocco, 1962-64; from dep. ambassador's staff aide to sr. advisor Vietnamese province Tuyen Duc Agy. Internat. Devel., Vietnam, 1964-68; officer-in-charge Tunisian affairs U.S. Dept. State, Washington, 1968-71; chief econ.-comml. sect. Am. Embassy, Tunis, Tunisia, 1971-73, chief polit. sect. Dacca, Bangladesh, 1973-74; dir. plans and mgmt. Bur. Pub. Affairs, Washington, 1974-75; spl. asst. to dir., then dep. dir. Pres.' Interagy. Task Force Refugee Resettlement, Washington, 1975; spl. asst. to undersec. polit. affairs, 1975-76; dir. office So. African affairs U.S. Dept. State, Washington, 1976-77, dep. exec. sec., 1977-79; U.S. amb. to Zambia Lusaka, 1977-82; dep. asst. sec. African affairs U.S. Dept. State, Washington, 1982-86; U.S. amb. to Egypt Cairo, 1986-91; U.S. amb. to Philippines Manila, 1991-92; under sec. of state for internat. security affairs Washington, 1992-93; under sec. of def. for policy Dept. Def., Washington, 1993-94; U.S. amb. to India U.S. Dept. State, 1994-97; vice chmn. external affairs Am. Internat. Group Inc., N.Y.C., 1997—. Bd. dirs. EOG Resources; trustee Am. U. of Beirut, Am. U. Cairo; mem. bd. bus. Coun. Internat. Understanding; bd. U.S.-India Bus. Coun.; bd. refugees Internat., United Svcs. Orgn. Decorated Legion of Honor (Romania); recipient meritorious honor award Dept. State,

1973, superior honor award, 1992, disting. svc. award, 1997; recipient Mil. Medal of Honor Govt. Vietnam, 1968, Social Welfare medal of honor, 1968. Mem. Coun. on Fgn. Relations, Metropolitan Club (Washington), Ivy Club (Princeton, N.J.), Knickerbocker Club (N.Y.), Brook Club (N.Y.). Episcopalian. Office: Am Internat Group Inc 18th Fl 70 Pine St New York NY 10270-0002

**WISNER, PAMELA L.,** social worker; b. Stevensville, Newfoundland, Can., Dec. 4, 1958; d. John R. Wisner, Leslie S. Wisner. BA in Psychology and Sociology, U. Mobile, 1980; M in Counseling, La. Bapt. U., 1998. LCSW Ala. Bd. Social Work Examiners, 1995, cert. Cognitive Behavioral Therapist 1999, Forensic Counselor 1999, Addictions specialist, Domestic Violence Counselor endorsement 1999. Dir. cmty. svc. RAPHA, Mobile, Ala., 1995—96; coord., counselor Charter of Mobile, 1996—2000; therapist, family cons. Gulf Coast Therapeutic Program, Inc., Mobile, 2000—. Mem.: Nat. Bd. Cognitive Behavioral Therapists, Am. Psychotherapy Assn. (diplomate 1999). Avocation: Avocations: travel, reading, cats, crafts, cooking. Office: Therapeutic Programs 601 Bel Air Blvd Ste 200 Mobile AL 36606-3524 Home: 6213 Burnt Wood Dr S Mobile AL 36695

**WISNICKI, JEFFREY LEONARD,** plastic surgeon; b. NYC, May 15, 1957; s. Joseph and Lorraine (Justman) Wisnicki; m. Rebecca Lynn O'Shields, Feb. 2, 1997; children: Justin Robert, Brandon Lawrence. BS summa cum laude, Rensselaer Poly. Inst., 1976; MD cum laude with honors, Union U., 1980. Diplomate Am. Bd. Plastic Surgery. Intern in surgery Stanford (Calif.) U. Med. Ctr., 1980-81, resident in gen., plastic and reconstructive surgery, 1981-84, chief resident in plastic and reconstructive surgery, 1985-86; fellow in plastic and reconstructive surgery Dartmouth-Hitchcock Med. Ctr., Hanover, NH, 1984; active staff Good Samaritan Hosp., West Palm Beach, Fla., 1986—, Wellington Regional Hosp., West Palm Beach, 1986—; chief divsn. plastic surgery John F. Kennedy Meml. Hosp., West Palm Beach, 1990-93; chmn. dept. surgery Palms West Hosp., West Palm Beach, 1991-93, chief med. staff, 1994-97, chmn. bd. trustees, 1997—2002, trustee, 2002—03; chief divsn. plastic surgery Good Samaritan and St. Mary's Hosp., West Palm Beach, 1997—2001, Good Samaritan Hosp., 2004—. Clin. instr. surgery U. Calif., San Francisco, 1985; bd. dirs. Interplast, 1985-86, clin. faculty, 1986—90; presenter in field. Contbr. chpts. to books and articles to profl. jours. Named Best Plastic Surgeon, Palm Beach Mag., 1998. Fellow ACS; mem. Am. Soc. Plastic & Reconstructive Surgeons, Alpha Omega Alpha. Office: 2047 Palm Beach Lakes Blvd West Palm Beach FL 33409-6501 Office Phone: 561-798-1400.

**WISNIEWSKI, P. MICHELLE,** retired obstetrician, gynecologist; b. Oneida, NY, June 26, 1941; d. Henry Francis Wisniewski and Kathryn Starr Holloway; m. Anna Cebula Costello, Sept. 20, 1998; m. Louise Marie Benyovszky, Sept. 22, 1984 (div.); children: Ladislaus Michael, Alexander Paul. BS, Georgetown U., 1967; MD, Universidad Autonoma de Guadalajara, Mexico, 1975. Bd. Cert. Am. Bd. of Ob/Gyn, 1983, lic. Physician and Surgeon NJ, Pa., 1977, Residency in Ob/Gyn Hahnemann U., 1980. Chairperson, dept of ob/gyn Health Care Plan of NJ., Cherry Hill, NJ, 1980—82; attending physician ob/gyn NE Hosp., Phila., 1882—1987, Nazareth Hosp., Phila., 1984—90, Pa. Hosp., Phila., 1987—91; chairperson, dept. of ob/gyn Mercy Hosp., Wilkes-Barre, Pa., 1991—92. Author: (medical research) Journal of Reproductive Medicine (Fellowship, Internat. Soc. for the Study of Vulvovaginal Disease, 1987), (photographic exibit) The Natural and Scenic Beauty of the Florida Keys, 2003. Chairperson Fla. Keys Coun. for People with Disabilities, Key West, Fla., 2000—06; sr. dir. Disability and Disaster: Surviving the Fla. Keys; lobbyist Key West City Coun., Monroe County Commn., Key West, Fla., 2001—06; active plaintiff Assn. for Disabled Am., Miami, Fla., 2001—06, pres., 2006—. 1st lt. US Army, 1967—70, Rep. Vietnam. Decorated Air Medal for Valor USARV, Mil. Medal of Honor & Gallantry Cross Rep. Vietnam; recipient Hon. Conch Cert., Monroe Fla. County Mayor, 2002. Fellow: Am. Coll. Ob-Gyn. (life). Achievements include first to led the struggle to make the Florida Keys accessible for people with disabilities; aided passage of transgender civil rights legislation. Office: FKCFPWD Chairperson 1100 Simonton St Ste 2 257 Key West FL 33040 Personal E-mail: kwimages@bellsouth.net.

**WISNIEWSKI, STEPHEN ADAM,** professional football player; b. Rutland, Vt., Apr. 7, 1967; Student, Pa. State U. Offensive guard L.A. Raiders/Oakland Raiders, 1989—. Named All-Pro Team Guard by Sporting News, 1990-93, Coll. All-Am. Team, 1987, 88. Played in Pro Bowl, 1990-91, 93. Home: 36 El Alamo Ct Danville CA 94526-1455

**WISNIEWSKI, THOMAS JOSEPH,** music educator; b. Chgo., Sept. 17, 1926; s. George Wisniewski and Rose (Jelewski) W.; children: Dieter, Lisa Ann, Ericka (dec.). B.Mus., Am. Conservatory of Music, Chgo., 1948; M.Mus., No. Ill. U., 1964. Instr. string instrument Sch. Dist. 89, Maywood, Ill., 1950-55; orch. dir. Sch. Dist. 44, Lombard, Ill., 1955-67; dir. orchs. Glenbard East High Sch., Lombard, 1959-67; acting head extension in music, divsn u. extension U. Ill., Urbana, 1965—69, prof. music, 1967, emeritus prof., acting chair, 1994, chair music edn. div., 1988-92. Clinician and guest condr. internationally; music cons. Webster Internat. Illustrated Dictionary, 1993; ednl. cons. Wm. Lewis and Son, Chgo., 1965-70, Hal Leonard Pubs., Milw., 1975-84., Glaesel divsn. Selmer Corp., Elkhart, Ind., 1975-90. Prodr. films Playing the String Bass, 1967, Playing the Cello, 1968; developer (with Rodney Mueller) computer software program Visualized Vibrato, 1995, version 2.0, 1998; author: Learning Unlimited String Program, Vol. 1, 1975, (with John Higgins) Vol. 2, 1976; editor Orch. Pubs., 1990; music editor Webster International Illustrated Dictionary, 1994. Mem. Am. String Tchrs. Assn. Assn. (Disting. Svc. award Ill. unit 1991, Disting. Svc. award Tenn. unit 1993), Ill. Music Educators Assn. (Pres.'s award 1996), Music Educators Nat. Conf., Ill. String Tchrs. Assn. (editor 1967, 87, pres. 1970), Nat. Jazz Educators Assn. (nat. orch. chmn. 1976), Pi Kappa Lambda, Phi Mu Alpha. E-mail: thomaswisniewski@mac.com.

**WISS, GARY ALAN,** language educator; b. Astoria, Oreg., Nov. 30, 1935; s. Paul B. and Joanne L. Wiss; m. Cherilyn Elaine Leno, Sept. 21, 1986; children: Elisabeth Witt, Lawrence, Laura Wolosek, Geoffrey, Valorie, Nathaniel. BA in English, Walla Walla Coll., College Place, Wash., 1966; MA in English, U. Oreg., Eugene, 1969, ArtsD in English, 1976. Rsch. asst. U. Oreg. Med. Sch., Portland, Oreg., 1960—65; prof. English Walla Walla Coll., College Place, 1966—, writing coord., vice chair English dept., 1968—79, chair English dept., 1979—86. Tech. team leader U. Oreg. Med. Sch., Portland, 1962—65; editor in chief accreditation Walla Walla Coll., College Place, 1990—2000. Sgt. USAR, 1958—62. Recipient President's award for Excellence in Tchg., Walla Walla Coll., 1996. Republican. Seventh-Day Adventists. Avocations: backpacking, beach-combing, genealogy, films, carpentry. Office: Walla Walla Coll 204 S College Ave College Place WA 99324 Office Phone: 509-527-2782. Business E-mail: wissga@wwc.edu.

**WISS, MARCIA A.,** lawyer; b. Columbus, Ohio, May 15, 1947; d. John William and Margaret Ann (Cook) W.; m. Donald G. MacDonald (dec.); children: Christopher C. Wiss MacDonald, Joan Merle MacDonald. BS in Fgn. Svc., Georgetown U., 1969, JD, 1972. Bar: D.C. 1972. Econ. analyst World Bank, Washington, 1969; atty. U.S. Dept. Justice, 1972-73; atty. office gen. counsel Overseas Pvt. Investment Corp., 1973-78; gen counsel-designate Inst. for Sci. and Tech. Cooperation, 1979; ptnr. Kaplan Russin & Vecchi, 1987-92, Whitman & Ransom, 1992-93, Whitman, Breed, Abbott & Morgan, Washington, 1993-96; counsel Wilmer, Cutler & Pickering, 1996-2000; ptnr. Hogan & Hartson, 2000—. Gen. counsel Washington chpt., Soc. Internat. Devel., 1980-2001; gen. counsel, Assn. for Women in Devel., 1982—; bd. advisers, Procedural Aspects of Internat. Law Inst., 1985—; gen. counsel internat. policy coun. agr., adj. prof. of law Georgetown U. Law Ctr., 1984—; Johns Hopkins Sch. of Advanced Internat. Studies, 2001—. Editor Georgetown Law Ctr. Jour. Law and Policy in Internat. Bus., 1971-72. Chair Holy Trinity Parish Coun., Washington, 1976. Mem. Am. Fedn. Govt. Employees (chmn. 1975-76), D.C. Bar (steering com. divsn. 12, 1985-88, co-chmn. fin.

and banking com. 1985), Am. Soc. Internat. Law (v.p. 1991-94, exec. coun. 1987-90), Washington Fgn. Law Soc. (pres. 1983-84). Roman Catholic. Office: Hogan & Hartson 555 13th St NW Washington DC 20004 Office Phone: 202-637-5429.

**WISSEL-LITTMANN, JEFFREY G.,** health facility executive; b. May 1968; Pres., trustee TIRR Rehab. Ctr., Houston, 2003—. Office: TIRR Rehabilitation Ctr 4200 Montrose Ste 200 Houston TX 77006 Office Phone: 713-521-0020.

**WISSLER, ROBERT WILLIAM,** pathologist; b. Richmond, Ind., Mar. 1, 1917; s. William Oscar and Muriel (Thomas) W.; m. Elizabeth Anne Polk, Jan. 9, 1940; children: Barbara Anne Wissler-Mayers, Mary Linda Wissler Graham, David William, John Polk. AB, Earlham Coll., Richmond, 1939, DSc (hon.), 1959; MS, U. Chgo., 1943, PhD, 1946, MD with honors, 1948; MD (hon.), Heidelberg (Germany) U., 1973, U. Siena, Italy, 1982; DSc (hon.), UMDNJ, Newark, 1982, Ohio State U., 1990. From instr. to assoc. prof. U. Chgo., 1943-57, prof. McLean Inst., 1953-80, prof. dept. pathology, 1957-82, prof. in the Coll., 1965-80, chmn. dept. pathology, 1957-72, Donald N. Pritzker prof. pathology, 1972-87, Disting. Svc. prof. pathology, 1977-87, emeritus prof., 1987—. Vis. scientist Theodor Kocher Inst., U. Berne, Switzerland, 1963, Baker Inst. for Med. Rsch., Melbourne, Australia, 1985; vis. prof. pathology Nihon U. Sch. Medicine, Tokyo, 1974; mem. faculty Given Inst. Pathology, Aspen, Colo., 1964, 71-73, 78-81; dir. U.Chgo. Spl. Ctr. Rsch. Atherosclerosis, 1972-82., program dir. Pathobiol. Determinates Atherosclerosis Youth, 1985-96. Editor, co-editor monographs; contbr. chpts. to books, more than 300 articles to profl. jours. Scout leader Boy Scouts Am., Chgo., 1951-56, 61-67; trustee First Unitarian Ch., Chgo., 1960-64, chmn. bd., 1962-64; trustee Earlham Coll., 1968-71, 75-85, chmn. edn. com., 1977-85; mem. Hyde Park-Kenwood Cmty. Conf., Chgo., 1960—. Recipient award of merit Am. Heart Assn., Dallas, 1971, Disting. Achievement award Modern Medicine, 1977, Joseph B. Goldberger award AMA, 1979, Coeur d'Or award Chgo. Heart Assn., 1982, Gold Headed Cane award, Am. Assn. Pathologists, 1983, U. Chgo. Gold Key award, 1984, Career Achievement award Internat. Atherosclerosis So., 1994, Rising Sun award Emperor of Japan, 1995. Mem. Am. Soc. Exptl. Pathology (pres. 1961-62), Am. Heart Assn. (chmn. coun. on arteriosclerosis 1965-66), Assn. Pathology Chairmen (pres. 1967-68), Coll. Am. Pathologists (chmn. edn. com. 1985-95), Univ. Assocs. for Rsch. and Edn. in Pathology (bd. dirs., pres. 1969-71), Am. Assn. Pathologists and Bacteriologists, 1952-90 (pres. 1968), others. Avocations: gardening, photography, playing clarinet. Home: 5550 S South Shore Dr Apt 515 Chicago IL 60637-5053 Office: U Chgo Med Ctr MC 3083 5841 S Maryland Ave Chicago IL 60637-1463

**WISWALL, DOROTHY ROLLER,** language educator; b. Alpirsbach, Germany, Aug. 6, 1947; d. Albert and Else Roller; m. Thomas S. Wiswall, June 5, 1976; children: James, Karen. AB, Cornell Univ., 1971; AM, Univ. Mich., 1972, PhD, 1979. Instr. Sch. for Internat. Tng., Brattleboro, Vt., 1971; tchg. fellow Univ. Mich., Ann Arbor, 1971—75; adj. prof. Niagara Univ., 1981—91, Canisius Coll., Buffalo, 1991—2003, Buffalo State Coll., Buffalo, 2001—. Workshop presenter BOCES, Buffalo, 1998—99; vice pres. Am. Assn. of Teachers of German, Buffalo, 1998—2002; docent Buffalo Mus. Sci., 2004—; tutor Lit. Vols. Buffalo, 2004—. Author: A Comparison of Selected Poetic and Scientific Works of Albrecht von Haller, 1981. Treas. Grand Island Cmty. Chorus, 2006—; mem. coun. St. Timothy Luth. Ch. Grand Island, NY, 1999—2005, deacon, 2004—; pres. bd. dirs. STLCC Child Care Ctr., Grand Island, NY, 1995—99. Recipient 2d prize, Faculty divsn. Martin Luther King Poetry Contest at Canisius Coll., 2003; Travel grantee, U., Bern, Switzerland, 1977. Mem.: Am. Assn. Tchrs. German (v.p. 1998—2002), Zonta Internat. Club Buffalo (bd. 2004—06, sec. 2006—), Phi Sigma Iota. Lutheran. Avocations: swimming, playing violin, sewing, history of science, writing poetry. E-mail: wiswall@localnet.com.

**WISWALL, FRANK LAWRENCE, JR.,** lawyer, educator; b. Albany, NY, Sept. 21, 1939; s. Frank Lawrence and Clara Elizabeth (Chapman) W.; m. Elizabeth Curtiss Nelson, Aug. 9, 1975; children by previous marriage: Anne W. Kowalski, Frank Lawrence III. BA, Colby Coll., 1962, JD, Cornell U., 1965; PhD in Law, Cambridge U., 1967. Bar: Maine 1965, N.Y. 1968, U.S. Supreme Ct. 1968, D.C. 1975; lic. master near coastal steam and motor vessels, 1960—. Assoc. Burlingham, Underwood, N.Y., 1967-73; maritime legal adviser Rep. of Liberia, 1968-88; prof. (ad honorem) internat. maritime law Internat. Maritime Law, 1999; divsn. vice-capt. U.S. Coast Guard Aux., 2006—; writer, cons. in field internat. maritime law, 1988—. Legal com. Internat. Maritime Orgn., London, 1972-74, vice-chmn. 1974-79, chmn., 1980-84; tutorial supr. internat. law Clare Coll., Cambridge, Eng., 1966-67; vis. lectr. Cornell Law Sch., 1969-76, 82; lectr. U. Va. Law Sch. and Ctr. for Oceans Law and Policy, 1978-82; prof. law Cornell U., 1984; Johnsen prof. maritime law Tulane U., 1985; vis. prof. law World Maritime U., Malmo, Sweden, 1986-2003; prof..fellow Internat. Maritime Law Inst., Malta, 1991—, governing bd., 1992—; del. Internat. Conf. Marine Pollution, London, 1973; del. chmn. drafting com. Internat. Conf. Carriage of Passengers and Luggage by Sea, Athens, 1974; del. Internat. Conf. on Safety of Life at Sea, London, 1974, UN Conf. on Law of Sea, Caracas, Venezuela, 1974, NY, 1980; del.. chmn. com. final clauses Internat. Conf. on Limitation of Liability for Maritime Claims, London, 1976; del. UN Conf. Carriage of Goods by Sea, Hamburg, 1978, XIII Diplomatic Conf. on Maritime Law, Brussels, 1979; chmn. com. of the whole Internat. Conf. Carriage of Hazardous Substances by Sea, 1984; del. internat. conf. on Maritime Terrorism, Rome, 1988; counsel various marine casualty bds. of investigation, 1970-90, harbormaster, Port of Castine, 1960-62; chmn. joint internat. working group acts of piracy and maritime violence, 1998-2001, joint internat. working group criminal offenses on high seas Interpol, UN, ICC-IMB, ICS, CMI, ITF, 2004—. Author: The Development of Admiralty Jurisdiction and Practice Since 1800, 1970; editor-in-chief Benedict on Admiralty, Vols. 6, 6A-6F (Internat. Maritime Law), 1992—, Com. Maritime Internat. Handbook of Maritime Convs., 1997, 2001, 04; mem. editl. bd. Jour. Maritime Law and Commerce, 1993—, Benedict's Maritime Law Bull., 2002—, World Maritime U. Jour. Maritime Affairs; contbr. articles to profl. jours. Ofcl. prin. Diocese of Mid-Atlantic States, 1988—, Diocese of UK, 1997—, Anglican Cath. Ch.; chancellor Missionary Diocese of N.E., 1993—, Diocese Australia, 1998—; spkr. assembly laity Anglican Cath. Ch., 1995—; chmn. Am. Maritime Law Found., 2002—. Recipient Yorke prize U. Cambridge, 1968-69. Fellow Royal Hist. Soc.; mem. Nat. Lawyers Assn., Comité Maritime Internat. (titulary mem., exec. councillor 1989-96, v.p. 1997-2005, v.p. honoris causa 2005-), Maritime Law Assn. U.S. (chmn. com. on intergovtl. orgns. 1983-87, chmn. com. on CMI 1987-95), Ecclesiastical Law Soc., Selden Soc., Am. Soc. Legal History, Maine Bar Assn., US Navy League (pres. Penobscot coun. 1997), Oxford and Cambridge Club (London), Century Assn., Alpha Delta Phi, Phi Delta Phi. Office: PO Box 201 Castine ME 04421-0201

**WISZNIA, WALTER,** architectural firm executive; CEO, mgr., designer Wisznia and assocs., New Orleans. Office: Wisznia Associates 67 Tee Rd Lumberton MS 39455-5333

**WIT, DAVID EDMUND,** software company executive; b. N.Y.C., Feb. 25, 1962; s. Harold Maurice W. and Joan Leta (Rosenthal) Sovern; m. Kathleen Mary Bentley, Sept. 9, 1989. BA summa cum laude, Hamilton Coll., 1985. Rsch. assoc. E.M. Warburg Pincus and Co., N.Y.C., 1985-86; CEO Logicat Inc., N.Y.C., 1986—2002; co-CEO Micron Sys. Inc., Washington Crossing, Pa., 2003—; CEO Oakdale Capital, LLC, Larchmont, NY, 2003—. Mem. Phi Beta Kappa. Avocation: exercise. Home: 3 Stratford Rd Larchmont NY 10538-1341 Office Phone: 914-834-1343.

**WIT, HAROLD MAURICE,** retired investment banker, lawyer; b. Boston, Sept. 6, 1928; s. Maurice and Martha (Bassist) W.; children from previous marriage: David Edmund, Hannah Edna; 1 stepchild, Simon; m. Susan King, Sept. 16, 1999. AB magna cum laude, Harvard, 1949; JD (editor law jour.), Yale, 1954. Bar: N.Y. 1954. Assoc. Cravath, Swaine & Moore, N.Y.C., 1954-58; asst. sec. One William St. Fund, Inc., N.Y.C., 1958-59, v.p., sec.,

1959-60; assoc. Allen & Co., 1960-70; assoc Allen & Co., Inc., 1965—, v.p., 1965-70, exec. v.p., 1970-98, mng. dir., mem. exec. com.; ret. Mgr. Allen Investments II LLC. Former trustee South Folk-Shelter Island chpt. Nature Conservancy, 1993-2000; co-founder Group for South Fork; pres. South Fork Watchdogs; mem. Panel on Future of Govt. in N.Y., 1979-80; mem. vis. com. Harvard U. Div. Sch., 1990-97. With Mass. N.G.: 1947-50; lt. (j.g.) USNR, 1951-53, Korea. Mem. VFW, Am. Legion, Korean War Vets. Assn., University Club (N.Y.C.), Harvard Club (N.Y.C.), Phi Beta Kappa, Phi Delta Phi. Home: 150 E 69th St New York NY 10021-5704 also: 57 Cross Hwy East Hampton NY 11937-0348 Office: Allen & Co Inc 711 5th Ave New York NY 10022-3111 Office Phone: 212-832-8000.

**WITCHER, ROBERT CAMPBELL, SR.,** bishop; b. New Orleans, Oct. 5, 1926; s. Charles Swanson and Lily Sebastian (Campbell) W.; m. Elisabeth Alice Cole, June 4, 1957; 2 children. BA, Tulane U., 1949; MDiv, Seabury-Western Theol. Sem., 1952, DD, 1974; MA, La. State U., 1960, PhD, 1968; DCL (hon.), Nashotah House, 1989. Ordained priest Episcopal Ch., 1953; consecrated bishop, 1975. Priest-in-charge St. Andrew Ch., Clinton, La., Zachary, La., 1953-56, St. Augustine Ch., Baton Rouge, 1953-54, rector 1954-61; canon pastor Christ Ch. Cathedral, New Orleans, 1961-62; rector St. James Ch., Baton Rouge, 1962-75; coadjutor bishop L.I., 1975-77; bishop, 1977-91; prof. ch. history Mercer Sch. Theology, 1975-91; interim bishop of Armed Forces, 1989-90; bishop in residence Baton Rouge, New Orleans, 1991-92. Pres. Mercer Scholarship Fund; trustee Ch. Pension Fund, 1991-92; pres. bd. trustees estate belonging to Diocese of L.I., 1975-91; pres. Anglican Soc. N.Am., 1980-83; chmn. pastoral com. House of Bishops, 1980-90, Com. to Revise Title III, 1980-90; chmn. Com. on Developing Guidelines for Theol. Edn.; cons. Episc. Health Fund L.I.; historiographer Diocese of La. Author: The Episcopal Church in Louisiana, 1801-1861. Trustee U. of South, 1963 69, Seabury Western Theol. Sem., 1963-82, Gen. Theol. Sem., 1979 88, Ch. Pension Fund, 1985-91, Bch. Reins. Corp., Killough Charitable Trust, Gen. Health Med. Ctr., Gen. Health Fund.; pres. Episc. Health Svcs.; bd. dirs. Nat. Coun. Alcoholism, L.I. Coun. Alcoholism, Alcohol and Drug Abuse Coun., Baton Rouge, St. Mary's Hosp. for Children, Baton Rouge Green, La. Urban Forestry Coun., United Way, Gen. Health Sys., GHS Found.; bd. dirs., trustee St. James Place; active NCCJ (Baton Rouge chpt.). Capt. USNR, ret. Recipient Nat. Gold medal, SAR, Sesquicentennial medal, Tulane U., Gold Good Citizenship medal, NSSAR. Mem. N.Y. State Coun. Chs., L.I. Coun. Chs. (com. social justice), Am. Legion, Mil. Order of World Wars, Naval Res. Assn., Res. Officers Assn., Mil. and Hospitaller Order of St. Lazarus, Soc. Colonial Wars, Phi Kappa Phi, Phi Alpha Theta, Eta Sigma Phi. Episcopalian. Address: 1934 Steele Blvd Baton Rouge LA 70808-1673 Personal E-mail: cusnr@aol.com.

**WITCOFF, SHELDON WILLIAM,** lawyer; b. Washington, July 10, 1925; s. Joseph and Zina (Ceppos) W.; m. Margot Gail Hoffner, Sept. 6, 1953; children: Lauren Jill, David Lawrence, Lisa Ann, Julie Beth. BS in Elec. Engring, U. Md., 1949; JD, George Washington U., 1953. Bar: D.C. 1953, N.Y. 1955, Ill. 1956. Patent examiner Patent Office, Dept. Commerce, 1949-53; patent lawyer Bell Telephone Labs., Murray Hill, NJ, 1953-55; ptnr. Bair, Freeman & Molinare, Chgo., 1955-69, Allegretti, Newitt, Witcoff & McAndrews, Chgo., 1970-88, Allegretti & Witcoff, LTD, Chgo., 1988-95, Banner & Witcoff Ltd., Chgo., 1995—. V.p., dir. Art Splty. Co., Chgo., 1967-84; v.p. Caspian Fur Trading Co., N.Y.C.; co-founder Child Abuse Unit for Studies, Edn. and Svcs., Chgo. Fire and police commr., Skokie, Ill., 1960-63. Served with USNR, 1943-46. Mem. Am. Bar Assn., Intellectual Property Assn. of Chgo., Order of Coif, Tau Epsilon Phi, Phi Delta Phi., B'nai B'rith. Office: 10 S Wacker Dr Chicago IL 60606-7407 Office Phone: 312-463-5000. Personal E-mail: witcoff@hotmail.com. Business E-Mail: switcoff@bannerwitcoff.com.

**WITCOVER, JULES JOSEPH,** columnist, writer; b. Union City, NJ, July 16, 1927; s. Samuel and Sarah (Carpenter) W.; m. Marian Laverty, June 14, 1952 (div. Oct. 1990); children: Paul, Amy, Julie, Peter; m. Marion Elizabeth Rodgers, June 21, 1997. AB, Columbia Coll., 1949; MS, Columbia Grad Sch. Journalism, 1951. Reporter Hackensack (NJ) Star-Telegram, 1949-50, Providence Jour., 1951-52, Newark Star-Ledger, 1953, Washington Bur. Newhouse Newspapers, 1954-69, LA Times, Washington, 1970-72, Washington Post, 1973-76; columnist Washington Star, 1977—81, Balt. Sun, Washington, 1981—2005, Tribune Media Svcs., 1977—. Author: 85 Days: The Last Campaign of Robert Kennedy, 1969, The Resurrection of Richard Nixon, 1970, White Knight: The Rise of Spiro Agnew, 1972, (with Richard M. Cohen) A Heartbeat Away: The Investigation and Resignation of Vice President Spiro T. Agnew, 1974, Marathon: The Pursuit of the Presidency, 1972-76, 1977, (novel) The Main Chance, 1978, (with Jack W. Germond) Blue Smoke and Mirrors: How Reagan Won and Why Carter Lost the Election of 1980, 1981, (with Germond) Wake Us When It's Over: Presidential Politics of 1984, 1985, (with Germond) Whose Broad Stripes and Bright Stars?: The Trivial Pursuit of the Presidency 1988, 1989, Sabotage at Black Tom: Imperial Germany's Secret War in America, 1914-1917, 1989, Crapshoot: Rolling the Dice on the Vice Presidency, 1992, (with Germond) Mad as Hell: Revolt at the Ballot Box 1992, 1993, The Year the Dream Died: Revisiting 1968 in America, 1997, No Way to Pick a President: How Money and Hired Guns Have Debased American Elections, 1999, Party of the People: A History of the Democrats, 2003, The Making of an Ink Stained Wretch: Half a Century Pounding the Political Beat, 2005. With USN, 1945-46. Recipient Washington Corr. award Sigma Delta Chi, 1963, Alumni award Columbia Grad. Sch. Journalism, 1972; Reid Found. fellow, Europe, 1958. Roman Catholic.

**WITEK, JAMES EUGENE,** retired public relations executive; b. LaPorte, Ind., Sept. 14, 1932; s. Stanley and Victoria (Peret) W.; m. Mary Carolyn Hood, June 18, 1955; children: James Jay, Janet Marie, Jeffrey Patrick, Jean Theresa. AB, Ind. U., 1954; MA, U. Mo., 1970. Joined U.S. Army, 1954, commd 2d lt 1954, advanced through grades to lt. col., 1968; editor, pub. Infantry Mag., Fort Benning, Ga., 1968-70; advisor to Vietnamese Mil. Region IV Ranger Comdr., 1970-71; plans officer CINCPAC, Hawaii, 1971-75; exec. editor Soldiers, Washington, 1975-77, editor in chief, 1977-79; dir. public affairs Nat. Com. for Employer Support Guard and Res., Arlington, Va., 1979-82, ret., 1982; dep. dir. pub. relations Am. Legion, Washington, 1982-86; mgr. pub. rels. Dowty Aerospace, Sterling, Va., 1986-99; ret. Decorated Legion of Merit, Bronze Star, Air Medal, Purple Heart, Vietnamese Cross of Gallantry with Silver Star. Mem. Am. Legion, Ret. Officers Assn., Disabled Am. Vets., Phi Beta Kappa, Tau Kappa Alpha, Pi Kappa Phi. Roman Catholic. Home: 3240 Achates Alt Fairfax VA 22030-2128

**WITEK, JOHN W.,** history professor; b. Chgo., Sept. 13, 1933; s. John Andrew and Antoinette T. Witek. BA, Loyola U., 1957, MA, 1964; Ph. L., West Baden Coll., 1959; S.T.L., Bellarmine Sch. Theology, 1966; PhD, Georgetown U., 1973. Asst. prof. East Asian history Xavier U., Cin., 1973—75, Georgetown U., Wash., 1975—81, assoc. prof. East Asian history, 1981—2003, prof. East Asian history, 2003—. Mem.: Am. Hist. Assn., U. San Francisco, 1999—. Author: Controversial Ideas in China and in Europe, 1982; editor: Ferdinand Verbiest, 1623-1688, 1994, Dicionario Portugues-Chines, 2001, Monumenta Sinica, vol. 1, 2002. Mem. bd. dirs. Asian divsn. Libr. Congress Friends Soc., 2004—. Mem.: Am. Hist. Assn., Am. Cath. Hist. Assn. (2nd v.p. 1999—2001), Assn. Asian Studies (pres., Mid-Atlantic region 1989—90), Phi Beta Kappa. Roman Catholic. Home: Jesuit residence Georgetown U Washington DC 20057 Office: Dept History Georgetown U Washington DC 20057 Office Phone: 202-687-6061. Fax: 202-687-7245.

**WITHAM, CRAIG RAY,** biology and chemistry educator; b. Jacksonville, Ill., Aug. 21, 1959; s. Fred Lee and Martha Marie Witham; m. Carol Marie Hayden, Feb. 26, 1983; children: Kyle Read, Kegan Ray. BS in Biology and Chemistry, MacMurray Coll. Jacksonville, 1981; MS of Sci. Edn., So. Ill. U., Edwardsville, 1995. Cert. tchr. State of Ill. Analytical chemist Exolon ESK Corp., Hennepin, Ill., 1981—85; tchr. advanced placement biology and chemistry Carlinville (Ill.) H.S., 1987—. Named Carlinville Tchr. of Yr.,

2001; recipient Carlinville Creativity grant, Carlinville Schools Found., 1999—2005. Mem.: Nat. Sci. Tchr. Assn. (assoc.), Nat. Assn. of Biology Tchrs. (assoc.). Presbyterian. Home: 12453 Lake Catatoga Rd Plainview IL 62685 Office: Carlinville H S 829 W Main Carlinville IL 62626 Office Phone: 217-854-3104.

**WITHEE, DIANA KEERAN,** art historian, art dealer, educator; d. Royal Victor and Johanna Polterock Keeran; m. Gregory Wallace Withee, June 8, 1968 (div. 2006); children: Christopher Edward, Jefftrey Wallace, Brett Andrew. BA in Art History cum laude, Pomona Coll., Claremont, CA, 1969; MA in Art History, Tulane U., 1976; ABD in Art History, U. Md., College Park, 1994. Rsch. & prodn. asst., art documentaries Nat. Mus. of Am. Art, Washington, 1980—83; art history instr. Montgomery Coll., Rockville, Md., 1984—85; art history instr. & cons. Montgomery County Pub. Schs., Rockville, Md., 1986—87; curatorial asst., manuscripts and rare books Walters Art Gallery, Baltimore, Md., 1988—90; mus. educator Nat. Gallery of Art, Washington, 1990—93; guide supr., mus. educator Hillwood Mus., Washington, 1993—98; art dealer Sumner and Dene Gallery, San Diego, 1999—2002, Whitt-Krauss Objects of Fine Art, San Diego, 1999; art instr. Ctrl. Tex. Coll., San Diego, 2001—; art dealer Susan St. Fine Art Gallery, Solana Beach, Calif., 2002—; co-owner Keeran Properties, Helendale, Calif., 2004—. Cons. Time-Life Books, Alexandria, Va., 1992; bd. dirs. San Diego State U. Arts Coun.; panelist, art critic San Diego Inst. The Living Artist, 2002—05. Prodn. asst. (videotape) Anni Albers, William H. Johnson, Reuben Nakian, Jacob Kainen:Five Decades as an Artist, asst. prodr. Americans in Brittany and Normandy, curator (art exhibition) More than a Miniature: Works of Art in Medieval Manuscripts, (exhibition) The Power of the Press: Revolution & Communications 1450-1600; author: (mag. articles) The Walters Art Gallery Bulletin, (contributing author) Culture et Revolution: The French Revolution and Its Aftermath, (instructor's manual) The Inquiring Eye: The European Renaissance, (book) Teacher Programs in Art Museums: A Directory; contributing author (magazine) The Post, presenter (symposium paper) Intimate Portrayals of Napoleon's Family, (scholarly conference paper) Anatomical Observations of Women's Life Stages in the Frescoes of Thera, (scholarly conference presentation) An Altar in the Miniature Fresco at Thera and Its Implications, lecturer (scholarly lecture) Timeless Cycles: Youth, Beauty and Ag in the Bronze Age Frescoes of Thera, scholarly presenter (scholarly conference presentation) The Boxing Boys and Fishermen Frescoes at Thera: An Analysis of their Physical Ages and Its Implications, Physical Growth and Aging Characteristics Depicted in the Theran Frescoes at Thera, conference presenter (conference presentations) Developing Good Relationships Between Guides and Security, lecturer (museum lecture series) C.W.Post and the Breakfast Cereal Revolution, The Gilded Age: The Newport Mansions; editor: (newsletter) COVA Newsletter. Recipient Letter of Commendation, Nat. Gallery of Art, 1991, Cash Bonus award, 1992; scholar Grad. assistantship, U. Md., 1986-1988; Mus. fellowship, U. of Md., 1988-89, Travel fellowship, Wash. Chpt., Am. Inst. of Archaeology, 1991. Mem.: Phi Kappa Phi. Achievements include development of new methodology of deciphering Aegean Bronze Age art; ran numerous national programs in museum education for National Gallery of Art; re-organization of entire Hillwood guide program; volunteered to teach Navy & Marine personnel aboard the aircraft carrier John C. Stennis on its deployment to participate in war in Afghanistan two months after 9/11. Home: 850 State St #128 San Diego CA 92101 Personal E-mail: dkkeeran@cox.net.

**WITHERELL, DENNIS PATRICK,** lawyer; b. Dec. 15, 1951; s. Thomas William and Kathryn Marie (Savage) Witherell; m. Suzanne Witherell; children: Natalie, Jay stepchildren: Jodi Brouilette, Shelby Watson, Shane Allen. AB with highest honors, U. Mich., 1973; JD summa cum laude, Ohio State U., 1977. Bar: Ohio, U.S. Dist. Ct. (no. dist.) Ohio, U.S. Ct. Appeals (6th cir.). Law clk. U.S. Ct. Appeals (6th cir.), Cin., 1977—78; assoc. Shumaker, Loop & Kendrick LLP, Toledo, 1978—83, ptnr., 1983—. Mem. exec. bd. March of Dimes Birth Defects Found., N.W. Ohio chpt., Toledo, 1978—91, chmn., 1982—84; bd. trustees Kidney Found. of Northwest Ohio, 1988—94, pres., 1992—93; bd. trustee Life Connection of Ohio, 1991—2004, Vis. Nurse-Extra Care, 1994—99. Mem.: Nat. Multiple Sclerosis Soc. (bd. trustees Northwest Ohio chpt. 1999—, chmn. 2004—), Soc. of Ohio Hosp. Attys., Toledo Bar Assn, Ohio State Bar Assn. (chmn. health care law com. 1988—92), Am. Health Lawyers Assn., ABA. Roman Catholic. Home: 3218 Stonegate Dr Maumee OH 43537-9476 Office Phone: 419-321-1221. E-mail: dwitherell@buckeye-express.com.

**WITHERELL, MARY,** editor; Degree, Barnard Coll., 1983. Former acting mng. editor Cosmo Girl; mng. editor Ladies' Home Jour., N.Y.C., 2002—. Office: Ladies' Home Jour 125 Park Ave 20th Fl New York NY 10017-5516

**WITHERELL, MICHAEL S.,** physicist, educator; b. Toledo, Sept. 22, 1949; s. Thomas W. and Marie (Savage) W.; m. Elizabeth Hall. BS in Physics, U. Mich., 1968; MS, U. Wis., 1970; PhD in Physics, U. Wis., Madison, 1973. Instr. Princeton (N.J.) U., 1973-75, asst. prof., 1975-81, U. Calif., Santa Barbara, 1981-83, assoc. prof., 1983-86, prof., 1986-99, prof. physics, 2005—, vice chancellor for rsch., 2005—; dir. Fermi Nat. Accelerator Lab. (Fermilab), Batavia, Ill., 1999—2005. Guggenheim fellow John S. Guggenheim Found., 1989-90; recipient Gold award W.K.H. Soc. Energy, 2004 Fellow AAAS, Am. Physical Soc. (W.K.H. Panofsky prize 1990); mem. NAS Achievements include research in application of technologies to study particle physics: silicon vertex detectors and high-speed data acquisition sys. Office: U Calif Santa Barbara 3227 Cheadle Hall Santa Barbara CA 93106 Office Phone: 805-893-8270. Business E-Mail: witherell@research.ucsb.edu.

**WITHERS, ALDINA,** educational consultant; d. Jimmie Reddick and Shirley A. Frost; m. Michael Withers, Dec. 13, 2003; 1 child, Breanne N. Washington. BA, So. Calif. Coll., Costa Mesa, 1997; MBA, Keller Grad. Sch. Mgmt., Calif., 2000. Cons., grant writer Thirst 4 Knowledge, Lakewood, Calif., 2000—04. Bd. dir. Helping In Svc., Long Beach, Calif., 2004. Baptist. Avocations: travel, singing, arts and crafts, bicycling. Office: Thirst 4 Knowledge 4450 California Pl PMB350 Long Beach CA 90807 Office Phone: 562-544-2436. Office Fax: 562-685-0155. E-mail: t4knowledge@verizon.net.

**WITHERS, CARL RAYMOND,** lawyer; b. Reading, Pa., Jan. 26, 1924; s. Stuart Snable Withers and Edith Garman; m. Jenny Constance Cory, Sept. 2, 1950; children: Wren, Jill, Bradford. AB, Wittenberg U., 1950; JD, U. Mich., 1953. Bar: Ohio 1954. Pvt. practice, Cleve., 1954—. Former pres. mus. Shaker Hist. Soc., Shaker Heights, Ohio, 1970—; former trustee, treas. N.E. Inter Mus. Coun., Cleve., 1980—; exec. com. Cuyahoga County Rep. Party, Cleve., 1984-94; former deacon and trustee Fairmount Presbyn. Ch.; former trustee Cleve. Soldiers' and Sailors' Monument. Mem. Ohio State Bar Assn. (former coun. of dels. 1955), Cleve. Bar Assn., Am. Legion (Army-Navy Shaker post 54, former commdr., adjutant), Gt. Lakes Curling Assn. (treas., pres. 1985-96), Cleve. Grays, Estate Planning Coun. of Cleve., Cleve. Rotary Club (former trustee), Cleve. City Club, Beta Theta Pi (former pres.), Delta Theta Phi. Republican. Presbyterian. Avocations: curling, genealogy. Office: Ste 727 629 Euclid Ave Cleveland OH 44114-3003 Home: 103 Laurel Lake Dr Hudson OH 44236-2153 Office Phone: 216-781-4680.

**WITHERS, HUBERT RODNEY,** radiotherapist, radiobiologist, educator; b. Queensland, Australia, Sept. 21, 1932; arrived in U.S., 1966; s. Hubert and Gertrude Ethel (Tremayne) W.; m. Janet Macfie, Oct. 9, 1959; 1 child, Genevieve. MB BS, U. Queensland, Brisbane, Australia, 1956; PhD, U. London, 1965, DSc, 1982. Bd. cert. Ednl. Coun. for Fgn. Med. Grads. Intern Royal Brisbane and Associated Hosps., 1957; resident in radiotherapy and pathology Queensland Radium Inst. and Royal Brisbane Hosp., 1958-63; U. Queensland Gaggin fellow Gray Lab., Mt. Vernon Hosp., Northwood, Middlesex, England, 1963—65, Royal Brisbane Hosp., 1963-66; registrar Prince of Wales Hosp., Randwick, Sydney, Australia, 1966; vis. rsch. scientist lab. physiology Nat. Cancer Inst., Bethesda, Md., 1966-68; assoc. prof. radiotherapy sect. exptl. radiotherapy U. Tex. Sys. Cancer Ctr.M.D. Anderson Hosp. & Tumor Inst., Houston, 1968-71, prof. radiotherapy, chief sect. exptl. radiotherapy, 1971-80; prof. dir. exptl. radiation oncology dept. radiation oncology UCLA, 1980-89, 1991—94, prof. vice chair, dir. exptl.

radiation oncology dept. radiation oncology, 1991—94, Am. Cancer Soc. Clin. Rsch. prof. dept. radiation oncology, 1992—, interim dir. Jonsson Comprehensive Cancer Ctr., 1994—95, chmn. radiation oncology, 1994—2005. Assoc. grad. faculty U. Tex., Grad. Sch. Biomed. Scis. Houston, 1969-73, mem. grad. faculty, 1973-80; prof. dept. radiotherapy Med. Sch., U. Tex. Health Sci. Ctr., Houston, U. Tex. Med. Sch., Houston, 1975-80; prof., dir. Inst. Oncology, The Prince of Wales Hosp., U. NSW, Sydney, Australia, 1989-91; mem. com. mortality mil. pers. present-at-atmosphere tests of nuc. weapons Inst. Medicine, 1993-94; mem. radiation effects rsch. bd. NRC, 1993-99; mem. com. neutron dose reporting Internat. Commn. Radiation Units and Measurements, 1982-93, mem. report com. clin. dosimetry for neutrons, 1993-98; mem. task force non-stochastic effects radiation Internat. Com. Radiation Protection, 1980-84, mem. com. 1, 1982-90, mem. radiobiology com. Radiation Therapy Oncology Group, 1979-89, mem. dose-time com., 1980-89, mem. gastroenterology com., 1982-89; fellow Royal Australian Coll. Radiologists Edn. Bd., 1991-97; trustee Am. Bd. Radiology, 1995-04; mem. cancer rsch. coord. com. U. Calif., 1991-97, mem. standing curriculum com. Radiation biomed. physics grad. program, 1993—; cons. exptl. radiotherapy U. Tex. Sys. Cancer Ctr., 1980—. Mem. Am. editl. bd.: Internat. Jour. Radiat. Oncol. Biol. Phys., 1982-89, 91—, internat. editl. bd., 1989-91; cons. editor: The European Jour. Cancer, 1990-95; editl. bd. dirs.: Endocurietherapy/Hyperthermia Oncology, 1991—2001, Radiation Oncology Investigations, 1992-2002; assoc. editor: Cancer Rsch., 1993-94, editl. bd. 1995-97. Mem. Kettering selection com. Gen. Motors Cancer Rsch. Found., 1988-89, chmn., 2002-03, awards assembly, 1990-94, 2002-04, adv. coun., 1994—. Decorated officer Order of Australia, 1998; recipient Medicine prize Polish Acad. Sci., 1989, Second HS Kaplan Disting. Scientist award Internat. Assn. for Radiation Rsch., 1991, Gray medal Internat. Commn. Radiation Units, 1995, U.S. Dept. Energy Fermi award 1997, Radiation Rsch. Soc. Failla award, 1988, Gold medal Royal Australian and N.Z. Coll. Radiologists, 1997, Charles F. Kettering prize GM Cancer Rsch. Found., 1998; named Gilbert H. Fletcher lectr. U. Tex. Sys. Cancer Ctr., 1989, Clifford Ash lectr. Ont. Cancer Inst., Princess Margaret Hosp., 1987, Erskine lectr. Radiol. Soc. N.Am., 1988, Ruvelson lectr. U. Minn., 1988, Milford Schultz lectr. Mass. Gen. Hosp., 1989, Del Regato Found. lectr. Hahnemann U., 1990, Bruce Cain Meml. lectr. New Zealand Soc. Oncology, 1990, Emmanuel van der Schueren medal, 2004, Gold medal Gilbert H. Fletcher Soc., 2005, Radiol. Soc. N.Am., 2005, others. Fellow Am. Coll. Radiology, ACS Oncology Group (ethics com. oncology 2002—), Royal Australasian Coll. Radiologists (bd. cert., Gold medal 1997), Am. Bd. Radiology (bd. cert. therapeutic radiology, Am. Coll. Radiology adv. com. patterns of care study 1988-93, radiation oncology adv. group 1993-98, others, Gold medal 2004), Am. Radium Soc. (credential com. 1986-89, 93-94, treas. 1993-94, pres. 1996-97, others, Janeway medal 1994), Am. Soc. Therapeutic Radiology and Oncology (Gold Medal awards com. 1982, 93, 00, publs. com. 1993-97, vice-chair publs. com., 1996-97, keynote address 1990, Gold medal 1991), Nat. Cancer Inst. (ad-hoc rev. coms. 1970—, radiation sudy sect. 1971-75, cons. U.S.-Japan Coop. Study high LET Radiotherapy 1975-77, cancer rsch. emphasis grant rev. com. 1976, clin. cancer ctr. rev. com. 1976-79, toxicology working group 1977-78, reviewer outstanding investigator grants 1984-93, bd. sci. counselors, 1986-88)). Nat. Cancer Inst. Can. (adv. com. rsch. 1992-95), Pacific N.W. Radiol. Soc. (hon.), Tex. Radiol. Soc. (hon.), So. Calif. Radiation Oncology Soc. (sec., treas. 1992-94, pres. 1997-98), European Soc. Therapeutic Radiology and Oncology (hon.; Regaud lectr. 2000), Polish Oncology Soc. (hon., Gold medal 2002), Austrian Radiation Oncology Soc. (hon.), Phila. Roentgen Ray Soc. (hon.), Radiation Rsch. Soc. (pres. 1982-83, honors and awards com. 1984-88, ad hoc com. funds utilization 1987-89, adv. com. Radiation Rsch. Jour. 1988-96). Office: David Geffen Sch Medicine UCLA 10833 Le Conte Ave Los Angeles CA 90095-1714 Business E-Mail: hwithers@mednet.ucla.edu.

**WITHERS, RAMSEY MUIR,** retired federal agency administrator; s. William Muir and Alice Smith Hope Withers; m. Jean Alison Saunders, May 8, 1954; children:— James Scott, Leslie Susan, Deidre Ann BSc, Royal Mil. Coll. Can., Kingston, Ont., 1952, DEng (hon.), 1994; BSc in Elec. Engring., Queen's U., Kingston, 1954; D Mil. Sci. honoris causa, Royal Roads Mil. Coll., Victoria, B.C., 1992. Registered profl. engr., Ont. Commd. officer Can. Army, 1948, advanced through grades to gen., 1980; sta. in Can., Republic of Korea, Fed. Republic of Germany and U.K., 1952-76; comdr. Can. Forces Europe, Fed. Republic of Germany, 1976-77; vice chief. def. staff Can. Forces, 1977-80, chief def. staff, 1980-83, ret., 1983; dep. minister transport Dept. of Transp., Ottawa, Ont., 1983-88; pres., chief oper. officer Govt. Cons. Internat., Ottawa, 1988-93; dir. Can. Inst. Strategic Studies, 1990-96, ATS Aerospace Inc., 1993-97; chmn. Industry Govt. Rels. Group Inc. (IGRG Inc.), Ottawa, 1993-98—. V.p., sec. nat. coun. Boy Scouts Can., 1977-84, internat. commr., 1985-90, hon. v.p., 1990-2000; chmn. Can. War Mus. Com., 1988-95; trustee Can. Mus. Civilization, 1990-95; elected mem. Queen's U. Coun., Kingston, 1997-03. Decorated comdr. Order of Mil. Merit, comdr. Order of St. John, Can. Forces Decoration with two bars; Georgian Coll. fellow, 1987; recipient Outstanding Achievement Pub. Svc. award, 1986, Silver Wolf award Boy Scouts Can., 1990, Alumni Achievement award Queen's U., Kingston, 1995, Queen Elizabeth II Golden Jubilee medal, 2003. Mem.: Assn. Profl. Engrs. Ont., Royal Mil. Colls. Club Can. (hon. pres. 1997—). Avocation: boating. Home: 150 Waverly St Apt 2C Ottawa ON Canada K2P OV4 E-mail: withers1809@rogers.com.

**WITHERS, W. RUSSELL, JR.,** broadcast executive; b. Cape Girardeau, Mo., Dec. 10, 1936; s. Waldo Russell Sr. and Dorothy Ruth (Harrelson) W.; 1 child, Dana Ruth. BA, S.E. Mo. State U., 1958. Disc jockey Sta. KGMO Radio, Cape Girardeau, 1955-58; account exec. Sta. WGGH Radio, Marion, Ill., 1961-62; v.p. LIN Broadcasting Corp., Nashville, 1962-69; exec. v.p., dir. Laser Link Corp., Woodbury, NY, 1970-72; owner Withers Broadcasting of Hawaii, 1975-79, Withers Broadcasting of Minn., 1974-79, Withers Broadcasting Cos., Iowa, 1981—, Mood Music Ill., Mt. Vernon, 1973—, Mood Music Inc, Cape Girardeau, 1977—, Royal Hawaiian Radio Co., Inc., 1976—; Owner various radio and TV stas. including Sta. KREX-TV, Grand Junction, Colo., KREY-TV, Montrose, Colo., KREG-TV, Glenwood Springs, Colo., Page Ins. and Real Estate, Mt. Vernon, Ill.; chmn. bd., CEO Withers Beverage Corp., Mobile, Ala., 1973—79; chmn. adv. bd. Mut. Network; bd. dirs. Theatrevision, Inc., Turneffe Island Lodge, Ltd., Belize, Sta. WDTV, Clarksburg, W.Va., WMIX-AM-TV, Mt. Vernon, KGMO-KAPE, Cape Girardeau, KOKX AM-FM, Keokuk, Iowa, KTRC, Santa Fe, KRHW and KBXB, Sikeston, Mo., WKIB Anna, Cape Girardeau, WMOK, WREZ and WZZL, Paducah, Ky., WSDR-WSSQ, WZZL, Sterling Rock Falls, Ill., WILY, WRXX (FM), Centralia, Ill., WEBQ and WEBQ-FM, Harrisburg, Ill.; pres. Ill. Pub. Airports Assn.; co-chmn. TARPAC. Bd. dir., chmn. bd. Mt. Vernon Tourism and Conv. Bur.; chmn. Mt. Vernon Airport Authority; bd. regents Lincoln Acad.; past pres. IPAA; past chmn. Conv. & Visitors, Airport Authority; bd. dir. No. Colo. C.C., Libr. Am. Broadcasters, Radio Bd., AP. With U.S. Army, 1957-58. Mem. Mt. Vernon C. of C. (bd. dir.), Nat. Assn. Broadcasters (bd. dir., exec. com.), Ill. Broadcasters Assn., Stadium Club, Mo. Athletic Club, Elks, Moose, AmVets, Masons, Shriners, Sigma Chi. Christian Scientist. Home: 16074 Hawthorne Rd Mount Vernon IL 62864-2852 Office: PO Box 1508 Mount Vernon IL 62864-0030 Office Phone: 618-242-3500. E-mail: wrwithers@mvn.net.

**WITHERS, W. WAYNE,** lawyer; b. Enid, Okla., Nov. 4, 1940; s. Walter O. and Ruby (Mackey) W.; m. Patricia Ann Peppers, Dec. 12, 1974; children: Jennifer Lynn, Whitney Lee. BA, U. Okla., 1962; JD, Northwestern U., 1965. Bar: Okla. 1965, Mo. 1970, U.S. Ct. Appeals (8th cir.), 1972, U.S. Supreme Ct. 1972, U.S. Ct. Appeals (fed. cir.) 1984, U.S. Ct. Appeals (D.C. cir.) 1985, U.S. Ct. Claims, 1984. Staff atty. FTC, Washington, 1965-68; co. atty. Monsanto Co., St. Louis, 1968-78, asst. gen. counsel, 1978—82; v.p., gen. counsel Monsanto Agrl. Co., St. Louis, 1978—89; exec. v.p., sec., gen. counsel Emerson Electric Co., St. Louis, 1989—. V.p. Internat. Food Biotech. Coun., Washington, 1989-90; bd. dirs. Internat. Life Scis. Inst., Washington, 1988-89. Contbr. articles to profl. jours. Chmn. bd. Mo. Hist. Soc., 2002—04; trustee MHS, 1995—; bd. dirs. World Agrl. Forum, 1999—. Mem. ABA (sect. bus. law, com. gen. counsel, antitrust, litigation), Am. Law Inst., Bar Assn. Met. St. Louis, Am. Corp. Counsel Assn., Am. Soc. Corp. Secs., Supreme Ct.

Historic Soc., Warren E. Burger Soc., Nat. Ctr. for State Cts., Washington Legal Found., Indsl. Biotech. Assn. (chmn. law com. 1985-88), Environ. Law Inst. (assoc.), Nat. Agrl. Chem. Assn. (chmn. law com. 1983-85), The Conf. Bd. Coun. for Gen. Counsel (vice chmn. 1992-98), MAPI Law Coun. Office: Emerson Electric Co 8000 W Florissant Ave Saint Louis MO 63136-8506

**WITHERSPOON, CAROLYN BRACK,** lawyer; b. Little Rock, Mar. 29, 1950; d. Gordon Paisley and Mildred Louise (Lemon) Brack; m. Joseph Roger Armbrust, July 25, 1970 (div. 1976); 1 child, Catherine Paisley Armbrust; m. John Leslie Witherspoon, June 15, 1979. Student, U. Ark., 1968—70, So. Meth. U., 1970; BA, U. Ark., 1974, JD with honors, 1978. Bar: Ark. 1978, U.S. Dist. Ct. (ea. and we. dists.) Ark. 1978, U.S. Ct. Appeals (8th cir.) 1979, U.S. Supreme Ct. 1981. Asst. atty. City of Little Rock, 1978, chief dep. atty., acting city atty., 1984-85; assoc. House, Wallace & Jewell, Little Rock, 1985-87, ptnr., 1987-90; dir. McGlinchey Stafford Lang, Little Rock, 1990-97, Cross, Gunter, Witherspoon & Galchus, Little Rock, 1997—. Mem. com. Fed. Ct. Practice, 1988—91; mem. civil practice com. Ark. Supreme Ct., 1989—97, mem. continuing legal edn. bd., 1998—2001; chair adv. com. Civil Justice Reform Act, 1993—95; chair State Bd. Bar Examiners, 2001—05. Contbr. articles to profl. jours. Commr. Ark. Real Estate Commn., 1978—81; past chmn. Little Rock Housing Authority Bd. Commn.; past pres., bd. dirs. Advs. for Battered Women; past pres. Women's Found. Ark., Ark. Women's History Inst. Recipient Labor Law award, Am. Jurisprudence, 1977. Fellow: Coll. Labor and Employment Lawyers, Am. Bar Found. (Ark. Fellows chair); mem.: ABA (ho. dels. 1997—, trial and ins. practice sect., equal employment opportunity com.), Am. Employment Law Coun., William R. Overton Inn of Ct. (pres. 1992—93), Nat. Inst. Mcpl. Law Officers (state chmn. 1985—87, v.p. 1987—89), Pulaski County Bar Assn. (pres. 1989—90), Ark. Assn. Women Lawyers (pres. 1982—83), Ark. Bar Assn. (pres. 1995—96, Golden Gavel award 1989, Ark. Inst. Cont. Legal Edn. award 1991, Golden Gavel award 1993, Charles L. Carpenter award 2005), Transp. Lawyers Assn. (mem. exec. coun. 1997—99), Nat. Conf. Bar Pres. (mem. exec. coun. 1996—99), Am. Jur Soc., Am. Law Inst. Avocations: hunting, fishing, reading, travel. Office: Cross Gunter Witherspoon and Galchus 500 President Clinton Ave Ste 200 Little Rock AR 72201-1747 Office Phone: 501-371-9999. Business E-Mail: cspoon@cgwg.com

**WITHERSPOON, LYNN RALPH,** physician; b. Mt. Pleasant, Mich., Nov. 11, 1942; s. Ralph Leo and Kathleen Mae (Williams) W.; m. Glory Ann Smith, Jan. 27, 1980; children: Eric W., Kevin B., Heather A. BA, Fla. State U., 1964; MD, U. Wis. 1968. Diplomate Am. Bd. Nuclear Medicine, Am. Bd. Internal Medicine. With Ochsner Clinic/Alton Ochsner Med. Found., New Orleans, 1974—, dir. radioimmunology lab., 1975-95, chmn., dir. med. informatics, 1994-96; chief info. officer Ochsner Clinic, 1997—2001; chief info. officer, v.p. Ochsner Clinic Found., 2001—; intern, then resident in internal medicine Ochsner, New Orleans, 1968-70; fellow in nuclear medicine Duke U., Durham, N.C., 1972-74, chief resident in nuclear medicine, 1973-74. Contbr. numerous articles to profl. jours. Elder Jefferson (La.) Presbyn. Ch., 1982—; mem. adv. bd. Sta. WWNO, New Orleans, 1985—. Lt. comdr. USNR, 1970-72. Fellow ACP; mem. Soc. Nuclear Medicine, Southwestern Soc. Nuclear Medicine (v.p. 1980-81, sec. 1983-86, pres. 1988-89), Soc. Nuclear Medicine (trustee 1988-89). Presbyterian. Avocations: violin, swimming. Office: Ochsner Clinic 1514 Jefferson Hwy New Orleans LA 70121-2483 Office Phone: 504-842-7878. E-mail: lwitherspoon@ochsner.org.

**WITHERSPOON, MARIA BERNARDA PENA,** principal; b. San Cristobal, Dominican Republic, Dec. 20, 1955; came to U.S., 1969. d. Benjamin de Jesus and Belen Pena; m. James Howard Witherspoon, Aug. 6, 1977 (div. Feb. 1991). AA in Social Svcs., Pima CC, Ariz., 1980; BS in Child Devel. and Family, U. Ariz., 1981, MEd in Bilingual Edn., 1986, ednl. adminstrn. cert., 1989. Cert. basic elem. tchr. with bilingual endorsement Ariz., prin. Ariz., bilingual elem. edn. NY, sch. adminstr., supr. NY. Family counselor El Rio Neighborhood Ctr., Tucson, 1979; pre-sch. tchr. Project Head Start, Tucson, 1980; data collector U. Ariz., Tucson, 1982; bilingual educator Tucson Unified Sch. Dist., 1984-88; bilingual curriculum specialist Stafford Engring. and Tech. Magnct Sch., Tucson, 1988—; asst. prin. Leonardo da Vinci Intermediate Sch., 1999—2002; prin. Roberto Clemente Pub. Sch., 2002—. Mem. Spanish Lang. Arts Adoption com. Tucson Unified Sch. Dist. Mem. Task Force on Native Am. Studies, Tucson, 1986. Mem. AAUW, NEA, Tucson Edn. Assn. (alt. state del., assembly rep.), Nat. Assn. Bilingual Edn., Assn. for Supervision and Curriculum Devel., Am. Home Econs. Assn., Nat. Assn. Female Execs, N.Y.C. Elem. Sch. Prin.'s Assn., Assn. Family and Consumer Svc. Republican. Roman Catholic. Home: 5550 113th St South Richmond Hill NY 11419-1111 Office: Roberto Clemente Primary Sch PS19K 325 S 3d St Brooklyn NY 11211 Office Phone: 718-387-8554. E-mail: mwither@nycboe.net.

**WITHERSPOON, REESE (LAURA JEAN REESE WITHERSPOON),** actress; b. New Orleans, Mar. 22, 1976; d. John and Betty Witherspoon; m. Ryan Phillippe, June 5, 1999; children: Ava Elizabeth, Deacon. Co-owner prodn. co. Type A Films. Film appearances include The Man in the Moon, 1991, A Far Off Place, 1993, Jack the Bear, 1993, Freeway, 1996, Fear, 1996, Twilight, 1998, Overnight Delivery, 1998, Pleasantville, 1998, Cruel Intentions, 1999, Election, 1999, Best Laid Plans, 1999, American Psycho, 2000, Little Nicky, 2000, Legally Blonde, 2001, The Importance of Being Earnest, 2002, Sweet Home Alabama, 2002, Legally Blonde 2: Red, White & Blonde, 2003 (also exec. prodr.), Vanity Fair, 2004, Just Like Heaven, 2005, Walk the Line, 2005 (Best Actress, NY Film Critics Circle, 2005, Boston Soc. Film Critic award, 2005, Broadcast Film Assn., 2006, Nat. Soc. Film Critics award, 2006, Best Performance by an Actress in a Motion Picture-Musical or Comedy, Hollywood Fgn. Press Assn. (Golden Globe award), 2006, Outstanding Performance by a Female Actor in a Leading Role, Screen Actors Guild award, 2006, Actress in a Leading Role, British Acad. Film and TV Arts, 2006, Performance by an Actress in a Leading Role, Acad. Motion Picture Arts & Sciences, 2006, Choice Movie Actress: Drama/Action Adventure, Teen Choice awards, 2006), others; appeared in TV series Return to Lonsome Dove, 1993, Friends, 2000; voice (TV) King of the Hill, 2000, The Simpsons, 2002, (TV films) Wildflower, 1991, Desperate Choices: To Save My Child, 1992. Named 25 Most Intriguing People, People, 2001, 50 Most Beautiful People, 2002, Favorite Female Film Star, 2004; named one of 100 Most Influential People, Time Mag., 2006, 50 Most Powerful People in Hollywood, Premiere mag., 2006; recipient Catalan Internat. Film Festival Award Best Actress, 1997, Movieline Young Hollywood Award for Breakthrough Performance (Female), 1999, Online Film Critics Soc. Award for Best Actress, 1999, National Soc. of Film Critics Award for Best Actress, 1999, Favorite Leading Lady, People's Choice Award, 2006. Office: c/o 360 Mgmt 9111 Wilshire Blvd Beverly Hills CA 90210 Address: Endeavor 9601 Wilshire Blvd Beverly Hills CA 90210 also: Baker Winokur Ryder c/o Nancy Ryder 9100 Wilshire Blvd 6th Fl W Tower Beverly Hills CA 90212*

**WITHERSPOON, WALTER PENNINGTON, JR.,** orthodontist, volunteer; b. Sept. 3, 1938; s. Walter P. and Florence Evelyn (Jones) W.; m. Joyce Ann Smith, Sept. 6, 1970; 1 child, Annie Melissa. BS, U. S.C., 1960; DDS, U. N.C., 1964, MSO, 1969. Pvt. practice, Columbia 1969—. Med. staff Bapt. Med. Ctr., Columbia, 1970—, Lexington County Hosp., West Columbia, 1974—. Host Nite Line Broadcasting Co. Adv. bd. 1st Palmetto Bank and Trust, West Columbia, 1982; mem. adv. bd. 1st Citizens Bank; candidate S.C. Ho. of Reps., 1994; del. S.C. Rep. Com., 1989—; mem. platform com. S.C. Rep. Party Conv., poll com., 1992; del. Rep. Nat. Conv., Houston, 1992, rules com., task force on edn.; Rep. nat. committeeman, 1996—, rules com., rep. nat. com.; pres. Rep. Electoral Coll., 1996, 2000; bd. dirs. Southeastern Coll. Assemblies of God, Lakeland, Fla., 1984, Brookland Plantation Home for Boys, Orangeburg, S.C.; pres. Friends of Irmo Libr.; chmn. Lexington County Rep. Party; commr. Richland/Lexington Counties Commn. for Tech. Edn., S.C. Commn. on Alcohol and Drug Abuse; bd. dirs. Centerplace for Homeless; mem. Presdl. Visit-Ticket Com.; amb. Irmo C of C.; vol. lockup telethon Muscular Dystrophy Assn. Lt. USN, 1964-66. Recipient Century Mem. award Boy Scouts Am., 1984. Mem. ADA, Greater Columbia Dental Assn. (pres. 1975-76), U. NC Dental Alumni Assn. (bd. dirs.), SC Dental Assn. (ho. of dels. 1971-73, 91-96, legis. com. 1993), SC Orthodontic Assn. (ctrl. dist. dir., state rep.), Am. Assn. Orthodontists, (polit. action com.), Sertoma (pres. 1975-76), Am. Legion (mem. baseball com.), So. Assn. Orthodontists (SC rep. Am. Assn. Orthodontists polit. action com.), Cen. Dist. Dental Soc. Home: 250 Lancer Dr Columbia SC 29212-1216 Office: 205 Med Cir W West Columbia SC 29169-3653 Office Phone: 803-796-5300.

**WITHERSPOON, WILLIAM,** investment economist; b. St. Louis, Nov. 21, 1909; s. William Conner and Mary Louise (Houston) W.; m. Margaret Telford Johanson, June 25, 1938; children: James Tomlin, Jane Telford, Elizabeth Witherspoon McElroy. Student, Washington U. Evening Sch., 1928-47. Chartered fin. analyst; registered investment advisor. Rsch. dept. A. G. Edwards & Sons, 1928-31; pres. Witherspoon Investment Co., 1931-34; head rsch. dept. Newhard Cook & Co. Ltd., 1934-43, 45-53, economist, investment analyst, 1965—68; chief price analysis St. Louis Ordnance Dist., 1943-45; owner Witherspoon Investment Counsel, 1953-64; v.p. rsch. Stifel, Nicolaus & Co., 1968-81; registered investment advisor St. Louis, 1981—. Lectr. on investments Washington U., 1948-67. Contbr. articles to profl. jours. Mem. Clayton Bd. Edn., 1955-68, treas., 1956-68, pres., 1966-67; mem. Clayton Park and Recreation Commn., 1959-60; trustee Ednl. TV, KETC, 1963-64; mem. investment com. Gen. Assembly Mission Bd. Presbyn. Ch. (USA) Atlanta, 1976-79, mem. permanent com. ordination exams, 1979-85; cons. to investment com. Ctr. Theol. Inquiry, Princeton, N.J., 1995-97. Served as civilian Ordnance Dept., AUS, 1943-45. Mem. St. Louis soc. Fin. Analysts (pres. 1949-50), Mo. Athletic Club (St. Louis). Home: 6401 Ellenwood Ave Saint Louis MO 63105-2228 Personal E-mail: wwspoon@swbell.net. Many of the current social and ethical problems of today might be partially resolved if theology would be influenced by the 4th dimension of spacetime plus the 5th dimension of the mind, the 6th dimension of the spirit and the 7th dimension of God the Father.

**WITHEY, GARY DAVID,** biomedical researcher; b. Niskayuna, NY, Apr. 7, 1980; s. Gary David and Donna Perreault Withey. BS in Biomed. Engring., Johns Hopkins U., 2002. Intern GE, Niskayuna, NY, 2000—02; rsch. asst. Brown U., Providence, 2002—. Mem.: Sigma Xi. Home: 189 Williams St Apt # 6 Providence RI 02906 Office: Brown U 184 Hope St Box D Providence RI 02912 Office Phone: 401-863-3010. Personal E-mail: gary_withey@yahoo.com.

**WITHROW, GREGORY B.,** director, accountant; s. Roy Preston and Mary Leola Withrow; m. Jeanette Marie Cleveland, Mar. 18, 1989; 1 child, Julie Marie. MusB in Piano Performance magna cum laude, No. Ky. U., 1980, BS in Acctg., 1987; MBA, U. Ky., 1983; cert. in computer programming, Longview CC, Lee's Summit, Mo., 1997; cert. in mgmt., SUNY, Plattsburgh, 2004, cert. in strategic leadership, 2005. Internal auditor Fifth Third Bank, Cin., 1987—90; acct. Nazarene Theol. Sem., Kansas City, Mo., 1990—95; contr. Cleve. Chiropractic Coll., Kansas City, Mo., 1995—97; fiscal mgr. United Services Cmty. Action Agcy., Kansas City, Mo., 1997—98; dir. corp. services Ctr. for Mgmt. Assistance, Kansas City, Mo., 1998—2002; dir. student accounts SUNY Plattsburgh, 2003—. Dir. acad. rels. and ednl. projects Inst. Mgmt. Accts.-Kansas City Chpt., 1993—94, dir. program roster, 1994—95, treas., 1995—96; mem. steering com. NonprofitBooks (sponsored by B2P Commerce Corp.), Chgo., 2001—02; membership com. Cmty. Assn. Nonprofit Bus. Execs., Kansas City, 2002—02. Pianist Ch. of the Nazarene, Plattsburgh, NY, 2003—. Presdl. scholar, No. Ky. U., 1976—80. Avocations: piano, hiking. Office: SUNY Plattsburgh 101 Broad St Plattsburgh NY 12901 Office Fax: 518-564-3116.

**WITHROW, JAMES A,** music educator; b. Harrisburg, Pa., Nov. 24, 1964; s. James L. and Joyce M. (Yeckley) Withrow. BS in Edn., Clarion U. of Pa., Pa., 1987. Instructional II Pa., 1993. Music educator South Ea. Sch. Dist., Fawn Grove, Pa., 1988—; vol. Leo Enterprises/Red Lion Fire Co., Red Lion, Pa., 2005—. Yearbook adv. Delta-Peach Bottom Elem. Sch., Delta, Pa., 2001—. Vol. Leo Enterprises/Red Lion Fire Dept., Red Lion, Pa., 2005. Mem.: Pa. Music Educators Assn. (assoc.), Nat. Assn. tor Music Edn. (assoc.) Office: Delta-Peach Bottom Elem Sch 1081 Atom Rd Delta PA 17314 Office Phone: 717-456-5313.

**WITHROW, LUCILLE MONNOT,** nursing home administrator; b. Alliance, Ohio, July 28, 1923; d. Charles Edward Monnot and Freda Aldine (Guy) Monnot Cameron; m. Alvin Robert Withrow, June 6, 1945 (dec. 1984); children: Cindi Withrow Johnson, Nancy Withrow Townley, Sharon Withrow Hodgkins (dec.), Wendel Alvin. AA in Health Adminstrn., Eastfield Coll., Mesquite, Tex., 1976. Lic. nursing home adminstr., Tex.; cert. nursing home ombudsman. Held various clerical positions, Dallas, 1950-72; office mgr., asst. adminstr. Christian Care Ctr. Nursing Home, Mesquite, Tex., 1972-76; head adminstr. Christian Care Ctr. Nursing Home and Retirement Complex, Mesquite, 1976-91; nursing home ombudsman Tex. Dept. Aging and Tex. Dept. Health, Dallas, 1991-93; legal asst. Law Offices of Wendel A. Withrow, Carrollton, Tex., 1993—. Com. on geriatric curriculum devel. Eastfield Coll., Mesquite, 1979, 87; ombudsman adv. com. Sr. Citizens Greater Dallas; cons. in field. Vol. Dallas Arboretum and Bot. Soc.; mem. Ombudsman adv. com. Sr. Citizens of Greater Dallas; charter mem. Stage Show Prodns. Recipient Volunteerism award, Tex. Atty. Gen., 1987, Tex. Gov., 1992. Mem. Tex. Assn. Homes for Aging, Am. Assn. Homes for Aging, Health Svcs. Speakers Bur., White Rock Kiwanis. Mem. Ch. Of Christ. Avocations: reading, travel, theater. Home: 11344 Lippitt Ave Dallas TX 75218-1922 Office: Law Office of W A Withrow 1120 Metrocrest Dr Ste 200 Carrollton TX 75006-5872

**WITHROW, MARY ELLEN,** federal agency administrator; b. Marion, Ohio, Oct. 2, 1930; d. Clyde Welsh and Mildred (Stump) Hinamon; m. Norman David Withrow, Sept. 4, 1948; children: Linda Rizzo, Leslie Legge, Norma, Rebecca Gooding. Mem. Elgin Local Bd. Edn., Marion, Ohio, 1969-73, pres., 1972; safety programs dir. ARC, Marion, 1968-72; dep. registrar State of Ohio, Marion, 1972-75; dep. county auditor Marion County, Ohio, 1975-77, county treas. Ohio, 1977-83; treas. State of Ohio, Columbus, 1983-94; treas. of the U.S. Dept. Treasury, Washington, 1994—2001. Chmn. Ohio Bd. Deposits, 1983—. Mem. exec. com. Ohio Dem. Com., mem. exec. com. women's caucus; mem. Dem. Nat. Com.; mem. Met. Women's Ctr.; pres. Marion County Dem. Club, 1976; participant Harvard U. Strategic Leadership Conf., 1990; mem. Dem. Leadership Coun.; mem. Internat. Currency News Bd., 2002—; Robert Wood Johnson Fellowhip Bd, 1997—. Recipient Donald L. Scantlebury Meml. award, 1991, Women of Achievement award YWCA of Met. Columbus, 1993, Outstanding Govt. Svc. award Am. Numis. Assn., 1995; inducted Ohio Women's Hall of Fame, 1986; named Outstanding Elected Dem. Woman Holding Pub. Office, Nat. Fedn. Dem. Women, 1987, Advocate of Yr., SBA, 1988, Most Valuable State Pub. Ofcl., City and State newspaper, 1990; Women Execs. in State Govt. fellow Harvard U., 1987. Mem. LWV (dem. leadership coun.), State Assn. County Treas. (legis. com. 1979-83, treas. 1982), Nat. Assn. State Treas. (pres. 1992, Jesse Unruh award 1993, chair long range planning com., mem. exec. com.), Nat. Assn. State Auditors Comptrs. and Treas. (pres. 1990, strategic planning com., intergov. rels. com., chair state and mcpl. bonds com.), Treasury Hist. Assn., I Safe Bd, Coun. State Govts. (exec. com., internat. affairs com., orgnl. planning and coord. com., strategic planning task force), Women Execs. in State Govt. (chair fund devel. com.), Altrusa Bus. and Profl. Women's Club (hon.), Delta Kappa Gamma (hon.), Delta Sigma Pi (hon.). Clubs: Bus. and Profl. Women's.

**WITHROW, WILLIAM N., JR.,** lawyer; b. Toccoa, Ga., June 26, 1954; BA magna cum laude, U. Ga., 1975, JD magna cum laude, 1978. Bar: Ga. 1978. Law clk. to Hon. James C. Hill U.S. Ct. Appeals, 5th Cir., 1978-79; pnr., complex litig. Troutman Sanders LLP, Atlanta, 1986—, and sect. chief, litig. dept. Mem. ABA, State Bar Ga., Atlanta Bar Assn. Office: Troutman Sanders 5200 Bank of Am Plz 600 Peachtree St NE Ste 5200 Atlanta GA 30308-2216 Office Phone: 404-885-3244. Office Fax: 404-962-6726. E-mail: william.withrow@troutmansanders.com.

**WITHUHN, WILLIAM LAWRENCE,** curator, financial consultant; b. Portland, Oreg., Aug. 12, 1941; s. Vernon Lawrence and Ruth Eleanor (Ferguson) W.; m. Gail Joy Hartman, Nov. 22, 1964; children: James, Thomas, Harold. BA, U. Calif.-Berkeley, 1963; MBA with distinction, Cornell U., 1977, MA, 1980. Commd. regular 2d lt. USAF, 1963, advanced through grades to capt., 1967; indsl. engr., asst. dir. manpower and orgn. USAF at Western Transport Air Force, 1964-65; global, polar, tactical, and instr. navigator worldwide USAF, 1965-72, spl. ops. navigator Vietnam, 1968—70, select lead navigator Mil. Airlift Command, 1970-72; ret., 1972; intern, then staff asst. U.S. Ho. of Reps., 1973-74; v.p. Va. & Md. R.R. Co., Cape Charles, Va., 1977-81, Md. & Del. R.R., Federalsburg, Md., 1977-81; sr. v.p. Ont. Midland R.R., Ont. Cent. R.R., Sodus, N.Y., 1979-83; v.p. Rail Mgmt. Svcs., Inc., Syracuse, N.Y., 1979-83, RSA Leasing Co., Syracuse, 1980-83; exec. v.p. Am. Coal Enterprises, Inc., Akron, Ohio, 1980-82; v.p., gen. mgr. Allegheny So. Ry., Martinsburg, Pa., 1982-83; acting dir. R.R. Mus. of Pa., 1982-83; curator transp. Nat. Mus. Am. History Smithsonian Inst., Washington, 1983—, dep. chmn. dept. sci. and tech., 1984-91, splst. transp. to mus. dir., 1990-94. Bd. dirs., chmn. The Waring Group Inc., Transp. Cons., Salisbury, Md., 1983-89; cons. Nat. Pk. Svc., Pa. Hist. & Mus. Commn. UNESCO (India), Expo 2000 (Germany), Fed. Railroad Admnstrn., Nat. Transp. Safety Bd.; apptd. Garrett Morgan Transp. Futures Program steering com. U.S. Dept. Transp.; apptd. founding mem., history com., Transp. Rsch. Bd. Nat. Rsch. Coun.; apptd. mem., task force on transp. Nat. Parks and Pub. Lands, Transp. Rsch. Bd. Nat. Rsch. Coun. Author: Spirit of Steam, 1995; editor, co-author: Rails Across America, 1993; contbr. articles to profl. jours. Decorated D.F.C. with oak leaf cluster, Bronze Star, Air Medal with 12 clusters, Air Force Commendation Medal with cluster, Pres. Unit Citation, Antarctic Svc. Medal; De Karman fellow, 1979-80, Smithsonian fellow, 1980-81; recipient Gold Apple award Nat. Ednl. Film Festival, 1995. Mem. Nat. Parks Conservation Assn. (nat. coun.), Nat. Parks Mid-Atlantic Coun., Am. Inst. Indsl. Engrs., Lexington Group in Transp. History, Air Commando Assn., Disting. Flying Cross Soc., Internat. Assn. Ry. Oper. Officers, Brotherhood of Locomotive Engrs., Cornell Club Washington, Nat. Press Club, Theta Chi. Office: Nat Mus Am History Smithsonian Inst Rm 5210 Washington DC 20560-0628

**WITKE, DAVID RODNEY,** retired newspaper editor, consultant; b. Council Bluffs, Iowa, Mar. 24, 1937; s. Arnold and Rosamond Louise (Storer) W.; m. Priscilla Bill Smith, Oct. 8, 1960; 1 son, Carl. BS in Journalism, Northwestern U., 1959. Reporter, editor The Courier, Champaign-Urbana, Ill., 1962-66; copy editor The Register, Des Moines, 1966-70, city editor, 1970-73, asst. mng. editor adminstrn., 1973-74, asst. mng. editor electronics, 1974-75, mng. editor 1975-83, dir. ops., 1983-85, dep. editor, ombudsman, 1985-87, exec. sports editor, 1987-98, sr. editor, 1998—2002, ret., 2002; freelance cons., 2002—. Rep. Iowa Freedom of Info. Coun., Des Moines, 1973—, pres., 1986-88; vis. lectr. Drake U., 1986—, Iowa State U., 1990—; adj. faculty Simpson Coll., 2003—; juror Pulitzer Prize, 1989-91; tng. cons. The Register, Des Moines, 2003—. Bd. dirs. Des Moines Pastoral Counseling Ctr., 2005—. Served to lt. (j.g.) USN, 1959-62, PTO. Mem. Assoc. Press Mng. Editors Assn., Mid-Am. Newspaper Assn., AP Sports Editors Assn., Iowa Newspaper Found., The Prairie Club, Sigma Delta Chi. Unitarian Universalist. Achievements include early lectures on electronic applications to large newspaper production. Home and Office: 2521 48th Pl Des Moines IA 50310-2506 Office Phone: 515-274-0578.

**WITKIN, ERIC DOUGLAS,** lawyer; b. Trenton, NJ, May 14, 1948; s. Nathan and Norma Shirley (Stein) W.; m. Regina Ann Bilotta, June 8, 1980; children: Daniel Robert, Sarah Ann. AB magna cum laude, Columbia U., 1969; JD, Harvard U., 1972. Bar: N.Y. 1973, D.C. 1989, U.S. Dist. Ct. (so. and ea. dists.) N.Y. 1974, U.S. Dist. Ct. (we. dist.) N.Y. 2001, U.S. Ct. Appeals (2d and D.C. cirs.) 1974, U.S. Supreme Ct. 1977, U.S. Dist. Ct. D.C. 1989. Assoc. Poletti, Freidin, Prashker & Gartner, N.Y.C., 1972-80, ptnr., 1980-85; sr. atty. labor Kaye, Scholer, Fierman, Hays & Handler, N.Y.C., 1985-88; of counsel Akin, Gump, Strauss, Hauer & Feld, Washington, 1988-90; counsel Benetar, Bernstein, Schair & Stein, N.Y.C., 1990-99; ptnr. Roberts & Finger, LLP, N.Y.C., 1999-2001, Greble & Finger, LLP, N.Y.C. 2001; counsel Brown, Raysman, Millstein, Felder, & Steiner LLP, N.Y.C., 2001—. Treas., founder Property Owners Against Unfair Taxation, NYC, 1983-90; trustee Congregation Emanu-El of Westchester, 1996—, pres., 2002-04. Lawrence Chamberlain scholar Columbia U., NYC, 1968; recipient Alumni medal Alumni Fedn. Columbia U., 1982 Mem. ABA (labor and employment law sect.), N.Y. State Bar Assn. (labor and employment law sect., com. on equal employment opportunity law), Assn. of Bar of City of NY (spl. com. on sex and law 1975-82, com. on labor and employment law 1982-85, 92-94), Westchester County Bar Assn., Columbia Coll. Alumni Assn. (pres. 1988-90, bd. dirs. 1974—, Robert Lincoln Carey prize, Alumni prize 1969, Lions award 1990), Alumni Fedn. Columbia U. (alumni trustee nominating com. 1990-97, pres. 1997-99), Am. Soc. Pers. Adminstrn. (contbr. monthly newsletter 1986-88), Soc. Human Resource Mgmt., Soc. Columbia Grads. (bd. dirs. 1994-97), Human Resources Assn. NY, Phi Beta Kappa. Clubs: Harvard (NYC), Am. Yacht (Rye, NY) Avocations: piano, sailing. Home: 103 Wendover Rd Rye NY 10580-1939 Office: Brown Raysman Millstein Felder & Steiner 900 3rd Ave Fl 23 New York NY 10022 Office Phone: 212-895-2313. E-mail: ewitkin@brownrayman.com, ericwitkin@aol.com.

**WITKIN, EVELYN MAISEL,** retired geneticist; b. NYC, Mar. 9, 1921; d. Joseph and Mary (Levin) Maisel; m. Herman A. Witkin, July 9, 1943 (dec. July 1979); children: Joseph, Andrew. AB, NYU, 1941; MA, Columbia U., 1943, PhD, 1947. DSc honoris causa, N.Y. Med. Coll., 1978, Rutgers U., 1995. Mem. staff genetics dept. Carnegie Inst., Washington, 1950-55; mem. faculty State U. N.Y. Downstate Med. Center, Bklyn., 1955-71, prof. medicine, 1968-71; prof. biol. scis. Douglass Coll., Rutgers U., 1971-79, Barbara McClintock prof. genetics, 1979-83, Waksman Inst. Microbiology, 1983-91; Barbara McClintock prof. emerita Waksman Inst. Microbiology, Rutgers U., 1991—. Author articles; mem. editorial bds. profl. jours. Postdoctoral fellow Am. Cancer Soc., 1947-49; fellow Carnegie Instn., 1957; Selman A. Waksman lectr., 1960; Phi Beta Kappa vis. scholar, 1980-81; grantee NIH, 1956-89; recipient Prix Charles Leopold Mayer French Acad. Scis., 1977, Lindback award, 1979, Nat. Medal of Science award, 2002. Fellow AAAS, Am. Acad. Microbiology; mem. NAS, Am. Acad. Arts and Scis., Environ. Mutagen Soc., Am. Genetics Soc. (Thomas Hunt Morgan medal, 2000), Am. Soc. Microbiology. Home: 1 Firestone Ct Princeton NJ 08540-5220 E-mail: ewitkin@aol.com.

**WITKIN, JOEL-PETER,** photographer, poet; b. Bklyn., Sept. 13, 1939; s. Max and Mary (Pellegrino) W.; 1 child, Kersen Ahanu; m. Barbara Anne Gilbert, 2005. B.F.A., Cooper Union, 1974; M.F.A., U. N.Mex., 1986; student (fellow), Columbia U., 1973-74. Artist in residence Zerybthia Rome, Italy, summer 1996; represented by Hasted/Hunt Gallery, NYC, Galerie Baudoin Lebon, Paris; artist in residence Berlin, fall 1998, Paris, winter 1998. Lectr. Am. Acad. Rome, 1996, Camera Work, Berlin, El Escorial, Spain, 1996, Yale U., 2001, Soc. Photographic Edn., 1996. Exhibited in Projects Studio One, N.Y.C., 1980, Galerie Texbraun, Paris, 1982, Baudoin Lebon, Paris, 1982, 86, 90, 94, 97, 2000, 02, 04, Kansas Ctiy Art Inst., 1983, Stedelijk Mus., Amsterdam, 1983, Fraenkel Gallery, 1983-84, 87, 91, 93, 95, 97, Pace WildenStein MacGill Gallery, N.Y.C., 1983, 84, 87, 89, 91, 93, 95, 97, San Francisco Mus. Modern Art, 1985, Bklyn. Mus., 1986, Galerie Baudoin Lebon, Paris, 1987, 89, 91, 95, 97, 2000, 02, 04, Centro de Arte Reina Sofia Mus., Madrid, 1988, Palais de Tokyo, Paris, 1989, Fahey/Klein Gallery, L.A., 1987, 89, 91, 97, 98, 2005, Mus. Modern Art. Haifa, Israel, 1991, Photo Picture Space Gallery, Osaka, Japan, 1993, 95, 2001, Guggenheim Mus., N.Y.C., 1995, Interkamera, Prague, 1995, Il Castello di Rivoli Mus., Turin, 1995, Encontros de Fotografia, Colombia, Portugal, 1996, 98, Rencontres de la Photographie, Arles, France, 1996, Taipei Photo Gallery, Taiwan, 1994, 96, 98, Mus. of Fine Arts, Santa Fe, 1998, Wildenstein Gallery, Tokyo, 1998, Pace Wildenstein, L.A., 1998, Sternburg Mus., Prauge, 1999, Mesiac Fotografie, Slovakia, 1999, Hotel De Sully, Paris, 2000, Catherine Edelman Gallery, Chgo., 2000, 05, Athens Sch. Fine Art, 2000, Ctr. Contemporary Art, Honolulu, 2000, Etherton Gallery, Tucson, 2001, 05, Linda Durham Gallery, Santa Fe, 2005, Stadt Mus., Jena, 2002, Picture Photo Space, Osaka, 2002,

Infinito Gallery, Turin, 2002, Galeria Juana de Aizpuru, Madrid, 2003, Photoes Pana, Madrid, 2003, Le Garage Galerie, Toulouse, 2003, ARCO, Madrid, 2004, Gary Tatintsian Gallery, Moscow, 2005, Moscow House Photography, 2005, Witkin Vintage, Hasted/Hunt, NYC, 2006, Café Françoise, Brussels, Paris-Photo, 2006; group shows: Mus. Modern Art, N.Y.C., 1959, San Francisco Mus. Moder Art, 1981, Whitney Biennial, 1985, Palais de Tokyo, Paris, 1986, La Photographie Contemporaine en France, 1996, Foto Masson, Goteborg, Sweden, 1997, Hanlin Museum, So. Korea, 1997, Bogardenkapel, Bruges, 1998, Hayward Gallery, London, 1997, Strasborg Mus. d'Art Moderne et Contemporaine, 1998, The Ansel Adams Ctr., San Francisco, 1999, Camera Work, San Francisco, 1999, The Louvre, Paris, 2000, Musée Bourdelle, Paris, 2000, John Gibson Gallery, N.Y.C., 2000, The High Mus. Art, Ga., 2000, The Fotografie Forum, Frankfort, 2001, The Nat. Gallery of Can., 2002, Hotel de Sully, Paris, 2002, The Israel Mus., Jerusalem, 2002, The Whitney Mus., N.Y.C., 2002, H. Lunn Collection, Lille, 2003, Photology, Milan, 2003, Akira Ikeda Gallery, Berlin, 2003, Nat. Gallery of Can., Ottawa, 2004, Yancey Richardson Gallery, N.Y.C., 2004, Guggenheim, Bilbao, 2005, Bruce Silverstein, N.Y.C., 2005, Ctr. D'Art Del'Yonne, 2005, Wessel and O'Connor Fine Art, NYC, 2005, Mus. Contemporary Photography, Chgo., 2005, Cité Internat.: "The Book" M.E.P., Paris, 2006, Houston Ctr. for Photography, Silver Retrospective, 2006, others; represented in permanent collections, Mus. Modern Art N.Y.C., San Francisco Mus. Modern Art, 1980, Nat. Gallery Art, Washington, Victoria and Albert Mus., London, George Eastman House, N.Y., The Getty Collection, Moder Museet, Stockholm, Sweden, Whitney Mus., N.Y.C., The Guggenheim Mus., N.Y.C., Met. Mus., N.Y.C., Tokyo Met. Mus. Photography, Nat. Gallery Can., The Metropolitan Mus. Art, N.Y.C., Phila. Mus. Art; subject of monographs: Joel-Peter Witkin, 1985, 88-89, 91, 93, 95-96, 98, 99, 2000, 01, 02, 03; editor: Masterpieces of Medical Photography, 1987, Harms Way, 1994; visual editor: Songs of Experience, 2002, Songs of Innocence, 2003, Songs of Experience and Songs of Innocence, 2004, Bourgcoisie-in-de-Nile, 2006, The History of Hats in Art, 2006; artist residence, Paris, 1994, 98, 2000, Rome, 1996, Berlin, 1998, Buenos Aires, 2003, Moscow, 2005. Served with U.S. Army, 1961-64. Decorated Commander des Arts et de Lettres (France); recipient The Augustus Saint Gaudens medal The Cooper Union, 1996, Disting. Alumni award The Cooper Union, 1986, Internat. Ctr. Photography award, 1988, award for N.Y. Times "The Plague Yr.," Soc. Publ. Designers, 2000; Ford Found. grantee, 1977, 78, Nat. Endowment in Photography grantee, 1980, 81, 86, 92. Address: 1707 Five Points Rd SW Albuquerque NM 87105-3017 Office Phone: 505-843-6682. Personal E-mail: jwitkin1@comcast.net. *My need is to understand existence. That need becomes art when it reaches into the extreme limit of the possible but with grace and truth.*

**WITKINS, JAMES P.**, information technology executive; BS in Polit. Sci., U. Ill.; MSBA, Boston U. Grad. Sch. Mgmt. With Mfrs. Hanover Trust and Chemical Bank, 1977—2000; dir., svc. delivery & ops., corp. banking Barclays Bank PLC; mng. dir., tech. and ops. Fleet Boston Fin., 2000—05; sr. v.p., technology, chief info. officer Freddie Mac, 2005—. Rep., Fleet Boston Fed. Reserve Bd. of Governor's Interagency Review 9/11.

**WITKOP, BERNHARD**, chemist; b. Freiburg, Baden, Germany, May 9, 1917; came to U.S., 1947, naturalized, 1953; s. Philipp W. and Hedwig M. (Hirschhorn) W.; m. Marlene Prinz, Aug. 8, 1945; children: Cornelia Johanna, Phyllis, Thomas. Diploma, U. Munich, 1938, PhD, 1940, Golden Dr. Diploma, 1990; ScD, Privat-Dozent, 1947. Matthew T. Mellon research fellow Harvard U., 1947-48, mem. faculty, 1948-50; spl. USPHS fellow Nat. Heart Inst., NIH, 1950-52; vis. scientist Nat. Inst. Arthritis and Metabolic Diseases, 1953, chemist, 1954-55, chief sect. metabolites, 1956-87, chief lab. chemistry, 1957-87, scholar, 1987-92, hon. scholar emeritus, 1993; vis. prof. U. Kyoto, Japan, 1961, U. Freiburg, Fed. Repubic Germany, 1962; adj. prof. U. Md. Med. Sch., Balt.; Nobel symposium lectr. Stockholm-Karlskoga, 1981. Mem. bd. Internat. Sci. Exchange, 1974; exec. com. NRC, 1975; mem. Com. Internat. Exchange, 1977, Paul Ehrlich Award Com., Frankfurt, 1980-97; bd. dirs. Leo Baeck Inst., NY Editor: Fedn. European Biochem. Soc. Letters, 1979-90. Recipient Superior Svc. award USPHS, 1967; Paul Karrer Gold medal U. Zurich, 1971; Kun-ni-to (medal of sci. and culture 2d class) Emperor of Japan, 1975; Alexander von Humboldt award for sr. U.S. scientists, 1978 Mem. NAS, Am. Chem. Soc. (Hillebrand award 1958, Golden Membership 1997), Am. Acad. Arts and Sci., Am. Philos. Soc., Acad. Leopoldina (fgn.), Pharm. Soc. Japan (hon.), Chem. Soc. Japan (hon.), Japanese Biochem. Soc. (hon.), Acad. Scientarium et Artium Europaea, Rheinisch-Westfälische Akademie der Wissenschaften. Office: NIH-Dept Health Edn & Welfare 2A 04 Bldg 8 Bethesda MD 20892-0001 *A career between two worlds and two wars, spanning 50 years of research aims changing from structural to dynamic aspects, may be considered epigonal in the sense that my teacher H. Wieland (Nobel Prize 1928) always considered biochemistry as a neglected area of organic chemistry. In a small way I tried to follow his example and interests, such as oxidation mechanisms, natural products and highly active toxins.*

**WITKOWSKI, DEANNA DANIELLE**, musician; b. Exeter, N.H., Mar. 20, 1972; d. Michael and Dale Witkowski. MusB in Piano Performance, Wheaton Coll., Ill., 1993. Musician (composer): (albums) Wide Open Window, Having to Ask, Length of Days. Recipient winner, Gt. Am. Jazz Piano Competition, 2002. Mem.: Chamber Music Am., Rec. Acad. Arts and Scis., Internat. Assn. Jazz Edn. Personal E-mail: hello@deannawitkowski.com, deannawit@earthlink.net.

**WITMER, G. ROBERT**, retired state supreme court justice; b. Webster, N.Y., Dec. 26, 1904; s. George H. and Lillian (Woodhull) W.; m. Marian P. Costello, June 27, 1936; children: George Robert, John R., Thomas W., Sylvia Witmer Bissell. AB, U. Rochester, N.Y., 1926; LL.B., Harvard U., 1929. Bar: N.Y. 1929. Pvt. practice, Rochester, 1929-45; ptnr. Easton & Witmer, 1931-45; surrogate Monroe County, 1946-53; justice N.Y. State Supreme Ct., 1954-81, assoc. justice appellate div. 1st dept., 1963-67, appellate div. 4th dept., 1968 81; jud. adminstrv. officer, appellate div N.Y. State Supreme Ct. (4th dept.), 1981-94; adminstrv. judge N.Y. State Supreme Ct. (7th Jud. Dist.), 1962-68; ret., 1994. Town atty., Webster, 1934-35; served on N.Y. State Ct. Appeals, 1974. Co-author: N.Y. Pattern Jury Instructions-Civil, Vol. 1, 1965, rev. edit., 1974, Vol. 11, 1968; co-chmn. pub. com. Practitioner's Handbook for Appeals Appellate Divs. N.Y., 1979, Practitioner's Handbook for Appeals to the Court of Appeals of New York, 1981. Supr. Town of Webster and County of Monroe, 1936-45; chmn. Webster Republican Com., 1933-45, mem. exec. com. of Monroe County Republican Com., 1933-45. Mem. Am., N.Y. State, Monroe County Bar Assns., Am. Law Inst., Webster Grange, Univ. Club (Rochester), Masons, Theta Chi. Home: Apt 612 1570 East Ave Rochester NY 14610-1640

**WITMER, GEORGE ROBERT, JR.**, lawyer; b. Rochester, NY, Mar. 23, 1937; s. George Robert and Marian Pauline (Costello) W.; m. Nancy Rosetta Wenner, Dec. 28, 1968; children: Wendy Lynn, Heidi Dawn, George Robert, III, Frank David. AB, U. Rochester, 1959; LL.B., Harvard U., 1962. Bar: N.Y. 1962, U.S. Dist. Ct. (we. dist.) N.Y. 1963, U.S. Supreme Ct. 1967, U.S. Dist. Ct. (no. dist.) N.Y. 1977, U.S. Ct. Appeals (2d cir.) 1998. Assoc. Nixon, Hargrave, Devans & Doyle, Rochester, 1962-70, ptnr., 1970-99, Nixon Peabody, Rochester, 1999—2005, sr. counsel, 2005—. Instr. in bus. law U. Rochester, 1965-66; mem. com. to advise and coms. Jud. Conf. State N.Y. on Civil Practice Law and Rules, 1970-77; mem. N.Y. State Jud. Inst. on Professionalism in the Law, 1999—; mem. Adv. Group to N.Y. State and Fed. Jud. Coun., 1999—. Mem. N.Y. State Rep. Com., 1976—93; trustee Eastman Dental Ctr. Rochester, 1977—97, pres. bd. trustees, 1989—90; trustee U. Rochester, 1979—, chmn., 2003—. Fellow: ABA, N.Y. Bar Found. (dir. 1991—96); mem.: N.Y. State Bar Assn. (ho. dels. 1978—, environ. law sect. 1981—96, pres. 1994—95, Disting. Svc. award environ. law sect.), Monroe County (N.Y.) Bar Assn., Am. Law Inst. (life), ABA, Rotary (dir. Rochester club 1977—79, pres. 2001—02), Masons (master local lodge 1971), Phi Beta Kappa. Republican. Lutheran. Home: 892 Lake Rd Webster NY 14580-9008 Office: Nixon Peabody LLP PO Box 31051 Clinton Sq Rochester NY 14604-1729 Business E-Mail: grwitmer@nixonpeabody.com.

**WITMER, JOHN RICHARD**, librarian; b. Dallas, Dec. 26, 1949; s. John Albert and Doris May (Ferry) W.; m. Joyce Ann Pelzl, Nov. 25, 1972; 1 child, Katherine Anne. Student, Wheaton (Ill.) Coll., 1967-70; BS, West Tex. State U., 1971; MSLS, East Tex. State U., 1974; postgrad., Dallas Theol. Sem., 1978-81. Cert. secondary tchr., driving instr., learning resources specialist, Tex. Learning resources specialist Sherman (Tex.) Ind. Sch. Dist., 1974-76, Ector County Ind. Sch. Dist., Odessa, Tex., 1978-80; acting head libr. Calvary Bible Coll., Kansas City, Mo., 1976-77; head libr. Am. Christian Coll., Tulsa, 1977-78; tech. svcs. libr. Odessa Coll., 1980-82; tchr. county youth ctr. Ector County Ind. Sch. Dist., Odessa, Tex., 1985; reader svcs. libr. Wayland Bapt. U., Plainview, Tex., 1986-87; vis. tchr. Lubbock (Tex.) Ind. Sch. Dist., 1987-88; learning resources specialist Dallas Ind. Sch. Dist., 1988-90, 94-99; head libr. San Elizario Ind. Sch. Dist., El Paso, Tex., 1991-94; audio visual libr. Klein Ind. Sch. Dist., Houston, 1999—2003; literary cafe libr. Alief Ind. Sch. Dist., Houston, 2003—. Deacon Scofield Meml. Ch., Dallas, 1971-74, Odessa Bible Ch., 1981-86; mem. cast. crew Permian Playhouse, Odessa, 1979-82. Capt. U.S. Army, 1972-85. Mem. Tex. Libr. Assn. (life), Classroom Tchrs. Dallas (bldg. rep. 1989-90), Odessa Profl. Educators (sec., v.p., pres. state dist. rep. 1978-81), Odessa Univ. Kiwanis (v.p., pres. 1984-85). Republican. Avocations: collecting books and trivia, church work, contests, travel. Home: 15114 Runbell Pl Houston TX 77095-3228 E-mail: johnwitmer@juno.com.

**WITMEYER, JOHN JACOB, III**, lawyer; b. New Orleans, Dec. 18, 1946; s. John J. and Thais Audrey (Dolese) W. BS, Tulane U., 1968; JD with distinction, Duke U., 1971. Bar: NY. Assoc. Mudge Rose Guthrie & Alexander, NYC, 1971-76; ptnr. Ford Marrin Esposito & Witmeyer (now Ford, Marrin, Esposito, Witmeyer & Gleser LLP), NYC, 1976—. Bd. trustees Gregorian U. Found., 1999—; adv. coun. Paul Tulane Coll., Tulane U., 1998—; bd. dirs. Tulane Assocs., Tulane U., 2001—. Col. U.S. Army. Mem.: Order of the Holy Sepulchre (knight commander). Office: Ford Marrin Esposito Witmeyer & Gleser LLP Wall St Plz New York NY 10005-1875 Office Phone: 212-269-4900. E-mail: jjwitmeyer@fmew.com.

**WITOLD, KACZANOWSKI**, painter, sculptor; b. Warsaw, May 15, 1932; arrived in US, 1968; s. Feliks and Zofia Kaczanowski; divorced; children: Paul Kaczanowski, Paulina Kaczanowski, Wit Kaczanowski. Grad., Fine Art Acad., Warsaw, 1956. Exhibitions include Otis Art Inst., LA, 1973, Represented in permanent collections Conoco Oil Co., Houston, United Calif. Bank, Beverly Hills. Achievements include Co-designer Auschwitz Cultural Ctr. Home: 329 Detroit St Denver CO 80206 Studio: Zwirki 1 Wigury 53A Warsaw Poland

**WITT, ALICIA**, actress; b. Worcester, Mass., Aug. 21, 1975; d. Robert and Diane W. Home edn. Actress Internat. Creative Mgmt., Beverly Hills, Calif. TV appearances: Cybill, 1995-98, The Disappearance of Vonnie, 1994, Blackout, 1993, Twin Peaks, 1991, Hotel Room, Ally McBeal, 2000, Ring of the Nibelungs, 2004; film appearances: Dune, 1984, Liebestraum, 1991, Bodies, Rest and Motion, 1993, Fun, 1994 (Spl. Jury Recognition award Sundance Film Festival 1994), Four Rooms, 1995, Mr. Holland's Opus, 1995, Citizen Ruth, 1996, The Reef, 1997, Bongwater, 1998, Urban Legend, 1998, (voice) Gen 13, 1998, Cecil B. DeMented, 2000, Playing with Mona Lisa, 2000 (Best Actress award U.S. Comedy Arts Festival 2000), Vanilla Sky, 2001, Ten Tiny Love Stories, 2001, American Girl, 2002, Two Weeks Notice, 2002, The Upside of Anger, 2005; prodr. On the Wise, 2005; actor, prodr. Girls' Lunch, 2004; TV guest appearances Twin Peaks, 1990, Hotel Room, 1993, The Sopranos, 2000, Ally McBeal, 2000, The Twilight Zone, 2003, (mus. theater) The Gift, 2000. Recipient Spl. Jury Recognition for acting, Sundance Film Festival, 1994, Ind. Spirit Award nomination, 1995. Avocations: listening to big-band recordings, chess, backgammon, bowling.

**WITT, CATHERINE LEWIS**, neonatal nurse practitioner, writer; b. Burlington, Iowa, Nov. 21, 1957; d. Rodney Darrell and Neola Ann (Wharton) Lewis; m. John Robert Witt, Mar. 31, 1984; children: Jeffrey Lewis, Jennifer Diane. BSN, U. No. Colo., 1980; MSN, U. Colo., 1987. Cert. neonatal nurse practitioner. Staff nurse St. Joseph's Hosp., Denver, 1980-85; neonatal nurse practitioner Denver Children's Hosp., 1986-88; coord. neonatal nurse practitioner and neonatal transport Presbyn.-St. Luke's Med. Ctr., Denver, 1988—2002; neotal nurse practitioner NNP Svcs. of Colo., 2003—. Mem clin faculty neonatal nurse practitioner program Regis U. Column editor: Advances in Neonatal Care; contbr. chapters to books, articles to profl. jours. Troop leader Girl Scouts US; children's Bible tchr., altar guild Episcopal Ch. Mem. Nat. Assn. Neonatal Nurses (co-chair program com. 1992-94, bd. dir., dir.-at-large 1997-99, sec. 1999-2000, pres. 2003-04, past pres. 2005—), Nat. Cert. Corp. (test. com. 1994-96, nominations com. 2004-05). Democrat. Episcopalian. Avocations: altar guild, reading, sewing, dance. Home: 17586 E Dickenson Pl Aurora CO 80013-4180 Office: Presbyn-St Luke's Med Ctr 1719 E 19th Ave Denver CO 80218-1235 Office Phone: 303-839-7735. Personal E-mail: 70044.2401@compuserve.com, catherine.witt@healthonecares.com.

**WITT, DAVID L.**, curator, writer; b. Kansas City, Mo., Nov. 3, 1951; s. Lloyd Vernon and Dean Witt. BS in Polit. Sci., Kans. State U., 1974; M Liberal Studies, U. Okla., 2000. Naturalist Naish Nature Ctr., Edwardsville, Kans., summers 1967-70; asst. curator Seton Mus., Cimarron, N.Mex., summers 1972-74; curatorial asst. Riley County Hist. Mus., Manhattan, Kans., 1973-74; mus. asst. Millicent Rogers Mus., Taos, N.Mex., 1976-77; curator The Gaspard House Mus., Taos, N.Mex., 1978-79, The Harwood Found., Taos, N.Mex., 1979—2005, Acad. for Love of Learning, Santa Fe, 2005—. Author: The Taos Artists, 1984, Taos Moderns: Art of the New, 1992 (Southwest Book award Border Regional Libr. Assn. 1993), Modernists in Taos from Martin to Dasburg, 2002 (S.W. Book award Border Regional Libr. Assn. 2003), Ralph Emerson Twitchell award N.Mex. Hist. Soc. 2003); co-author: Spirit Ascendant: The Art and Life of Patrocíño Barela, 1996 (S.W. Book award Border Regional Libr. Assn. 2003), contbr. Taos Artists and Their Patrons, 1898-1950; contbr. articles to profl. jour. Organizer first N.Mex. Art History Conf., 1986; founder S.W. Art Hist. Coun., 1990. Mem. PEN, Am. Assn. Mus., N.Mex. Assn. Mus. (pres. 1986-88). Home: PO Box 317 Taos NM 87571-0317 Personal E-mail: davidlwitt@cybermesa.com

**WITT, EDWARD JOSEPH, JR.**, tax specialist, accountant; b. Miami, Fla., Oct. 4, 1951; s. Edward J. Sr. and Marie Eva Witt. BS in Physics, U. Fla., 1974; BBA in Acctg., Fla. Internat. U., 1979. Master tax adv. H&R Block, Inc., Tulsa, Okla., 1979—; acct. Stuart Cooper CPA, Hollywood, Fla., 1982—83; payroll clk. Pers. Pool, Ft. Lauderdale, Fla., 1983—84. Avocations: music, movies, reading, computers, astronomy. Home: 11519 W 91st St S Sapulpa OK 74066 Office: H&R Block Inc 1865 S Sheridan Tulsa OK 74112 E-mail: ttiwde777@yahoo.com.

**WITT, HUGH ERNEST**, manufacturing executive, consultant; b. Winchester, Ky., Nov. 18, 1921; s. Hugh E. and Louella (Milliken) W.; m. Janie Bryan (dec. Oct. 1990); m. Evelyn Chapman, Apr. 22, 1993. Student, Transylvania U., 1941-43; BS, U. Ky., 1945; MS, MIT, 1957. Asst. to dep. asst. sec. Dept. of Air Force, Washington, 1954-61, dep. asst. sec., 1961-70, Dept. of Navy, Washington, 1970-73; prin. dep. asst. Sec. of Def., Washington, 1973-74; fed. procurement policy adminstr. Office Mgmt. and Budget, Washington, 1974-77; dir., govt. liaison United Techs. Corp., Washington, 1977-81, v.p., govt. liaison, 1981-87, cons. to United Techs. Corp., 1987—. Pres. Old Town Civic Assn., Alexandria, Va., 1961-63; bd. dirs. Alexandria Hist. Found.; mem. Alexandria Bd. Archtl. Rev., 1964-77; trustee Alexandria Hosp. Found., 1992-94. Alfred P. Sloan fellow MIT, Cambridge, Mass., 1956-57. Fellow Nat. Contract Mgmt. Assn.; mem. Aerospace Industries Assn., Nat. Security Indsl. Assn., MIT Alumni Assn., Soc. Sloan Fellows, Kappa Alpha.

**WITT, JAMES LEE**, management consultant, former federal agency administrator; b. Dardanelle, Ark., 1944; m. Lea; children: Jimmy, Michael. Founder Witt Constrn. Co.; county judge Yell County, Ark.; state dir. Office Emergency Svcs., Ark.; dir. Fed. Emergency Mgmt. Agy. (FEMA), Washington, 1993—2001; chmn., CEO James Lee Witt Assoc., LLC, Washington,

2002—; CEO Internat. Code Coun., 2003—; nat. co-chmn. ProtectingAmerica.org, Washington, 2006—. Chmn. bd. Child Devel., Inc., charter; Gov.'s rep. state disasters, Presdl. disasters; bd. govs. ARC. Recognized for reinvention efforts Nat. Assn. Counties. Office: James Lee Witt Associates LLC 701 13th St NW Ste 800 Washington DC 20005-3967*

**WITT, JIM**, editor; Asst. mng. editor, news Star-Telegram Arlington, 1986—92, editor, 1992—95; publ. Star Telegram Northeast Tarrant County Ed., 1995—95; editor Ft. Worth Star-Telegram Knight-Ridder, Inc., Ft. Worth, 1996—. Office: Knight-Ridder Inc 400 W 7th St Fort Worth TX 76102-4701

**WITT, KIM LOU**, elementary school educator; b. Garden City, Kans., Aug. 23, 1951; d. J. Lee and Virginia Lou Carter; m. Jim George Witt, Aug. 18, 1973; children: Christopher George, Ryne Carter. BS in Family and Child Devel., Kans. State U., 1973, BS in Elem. Edn., 1976. Tchr. Gertrude Walker Elem., Garden City, 1976—78, Lincoln Elem., Dodge City, Kans., 1978—89, Sunnyside Elem., Dodge City, 1989—93, Town Ctr. Elem., Coppell, Tex., 1994—. Family mentor Christian Cmty. Action, Lewisville, Tex., 2001—04; leader Girl Scouts Am., 2003—; coord. Whitey's Pl. 1st United Meth. Ch., Coppell, 1996—2000; mission vol. Hackberry Creek Presbyn. Ch., Irving, Tex., 2004. Recipient Ruthe Jackson award, Keep Tex. Beautiful, 2005. Democrat. Presbyterian. Home: 131 Newport Dr Coppell TX 75019 Office: Town Ctr Elem 185 Heartz Rd Coppell TX 75019

**WITT, LEON GERARD**, school system administrator; b. Monett, Mo., May 1, 1954; s. Francis Leo and Mildred Josephine Witt; m. Theresa Ann Doyle, Aug. 7, 1952; children: Benjamin, Doyle, Caleb, Sharon, Margaret. BSE, MSSC, 1976; MSEA, SMSU, 1982. Tchr. St. Mary's Sch., Joplin, Mo., 1976—80; prin. St. Joseph's Sch., Springfield, Mo., 1980—2003; supt. Diocese Springfield, Cape Girardeau, Springfield, 2003—. Head staff devel. Springfield Catholic Schs., Springfield, Mo., 1992—96. Fundraising leader St. Joseph Ch., Springfield, Mo., 1998. Recipient Tolerance award, Tchg. Tolerance, 2001. Mem.: ASCD, NCEA, CACE. Roman Catholic. Avocation: golf. Office Phone: 417-866-0841. Office Fax: 417-866-1140. Business E-Mail: lwitt@dioscg.org

**WITT, ROBERT E.**, academic administrator; b. Sept. 16, 1940; m. Anne Witt; children: Peter, Karen. BA in Econs., Bates Coll., 1962; MBA, Dartmouth Coll., 1964; PhD in Bus. Adminstrn., Pa. State U., 1968. Rsch. asst. Amos Tuck Sch., Dartmouth Coll., Hanover, N.H., 1964-65; instr. mktg. Pa. State U., 1967-68; asst. prof. Coll. and Grad. Sch. Bus., U. Tex., Austin, 1968-71, assoc. prof., 1971-75, chmn. dept. mktg., 1973-83, prof., 1975-83, Zale Corp. centennial prof. bus., 1983-85, Betty and Glenn Mortimer centennial prof. bus., 1985-95, centennial chairperson bus. edn. leadership, 1986-95, acting dean, then dean, 1985—95; interim pres. U. Tex., Arlington, 1995-96, pres., 1996—2003, U. Ala., 2003—. Mem. budget coun. dept. mktg. adminstrn. U. Tex., Austin, 1969-85, mem. faculty exec. devel. program 1969—, mem. dean's coun., 1986—; mem. athletes adv. com. NCAA, 1986—; mem. acad. adv. bd. World Mgmt. Coun., 1988; mem. future directions coun. U. Tex. Ex-Students Assn., 1978-88, mem. exec. coun., 1981-83, 87-89; mem. adv. bd. dirs. Post Oak Bank, 1993—, Frost Nat. Bank, 1993—; mem. Acctg. Edn. Change Commn., 1992—; bd. dirs. Life Ptnrs. Group. Assoc. editor Social Sci. Quar., 1970-72; mem. editl. rev. bd. Jour. Mktg., 1971-73, 82-85; contbr. articles to profl. jours. Bd. dirs. Austin Symphony, 1991—, Univ. Coop. Soc., 1978-82. Recipient Top Hand award U. Tex. Ex-Students Assn., 1988. Mem. Am. Mktg. Assn. (fellow doctoral consortium 1967, program chmn. doctoral consortium 1972, reviewer, presenter), Assn. for Consumer Rsch. (treas. 1976, mem. exec. com. 1975-76, reviewer, conf. session chmn.), Am. Assembly Collegiate Schs. of Bus. (bd. dirs. 1991—, mem. visitation com. 1991, mem. govtl. rels. com. 1986-89, chmn. govtl. rels. com. 1987-89), So. Mktg. Assn. (conf. track chmn., presenter), Beta Gamma Sigma (v.p. U. Tex. chpt. 1973-74, pres. chpt. 1974-75), Phi Kappa Phi. Office: Office of Pres PO Box 870100 203 Rose Administration Tuscaloosa AL 35487-0100 Office Phone: 205-348-5100. Office Fax: 205-348-8377. E-mail: witt@pres.ua.edu.*

**WITT, TOM**, economics researcher, educator; b. Borger, Tex., Apr. 22, 1944; s. Eugene Thomason and Helen C. (Hathaway) W.; m. Grethe A. Myles, Mar. 4, 1976. BA, Okla. State U., 1966; MA, Washington U., St. Louis, 1968, PhD, 1974. Asst. prof. dept. econs. W.Va. U., Morgantown, 1970-75, assoc. prof. dept. econs., 1975-80, acting asst. dean Grad. Sch., 1977-78, exec. dir. Bur. Bus. Rsch., 1985—, dir. Ctr. Econs. Rsch., 1985—, acting assoc. dean Coll. Bus. and Econs., 1985-86, assoc. dean rsch. and outreach Coll. Bus. and Econs., 1994—. Cons. Nat. Regulatory Rsch. Inst., Columbia, Ohio, 1980-81, Am. Electric Power, 1995—, Allegheny Power, 1997—; exec. legis. br. Govt. W.Va., 1985—; cons., expert witness W.Va. Human Rights Commn., Charleston, 1984; expert witness W.Va. Atty. Gen., 1987-88, Ashland Oil, 1992-93. Author: Power from the Appalachians, 1989, also monographs; co-editor: West Virginia in the Nineties: Policies for Econ. Progress; econs. columnist The State Jour., Charleston; contbr. articles to profl. jours. Pres. Cheat Canyon Park Homeowners, Morgantown, 1979-87, Monongalia Arts Ctr., 1980-81; bd. dirs., treas. Friends of W.Va. Pub. Radio, Charleston, 1985-93, chmn., 1989-91; sec.-treas. Cheat Neck Pub. Svc. Dist., 1989-95; mem. Monongalia County Econ. Devel. Authority, 1994—. Mem. Am. Econ. Assn., Regional Sci. Assn., Assn. for Univ. Bus. and Econ. Rsch. (pres. 2000-2001). Home: 3202 Deerfield Ct Morgantown WV 26508-8612 Office: Bureau of Bus & Econ Rsch WV U PO Box 6025 Morgantown WV 26506-6025 Business E-Mail: twitt@wvu.edu.

**WITT, WALTER FRANCIS, JR.**, lawyer; b. Richmond, Va., Feb. 18, 1933; s. Walter Francis and Evelyn Virginia (Riggleman) W.; m. Rosemary Winter, Sept. 5, 1964; children: Leslie Anne Millman, Walter Francis III. BS, U. Richmond 1954 JD, 1966. Bar: Va. 1966, D.C, 1971. Annoc. Hunton and Williams, Richmond, 1966-74, ptnr., 1974—. Contbr. articles to profl. jours. 1st lt. U.S. Army, 1955-57. Mem. ABA (chmn. real property com. sect. gen. practice 1995-2000, Va. Bar Assn., Richmond Bar Assn., D.C. Bar Assn., Phi Beta Kappa, Phi Delta Phi. Home: 8901 Tresco Rd Richmond VA 23229-7725 Office Phone: 804-788-8391.

**WITTBRODT, EDWIN STANLEY**, financial planner, consultant, retired military officer; b. Flint, Mich., Aug. 13, 1918; s. Stanley Frank and Marie (Ross) W.; m. Joan Helen Miller, Apr. 22, 1950; children: Stephanie Rita, Candace Lee, Edwin Stanley. Student, Gen. Motors Inst. Tech., 1936-38, Grad. Sch. Dept. Agr. 1950-51, Indsl. Coll. Armed Forces, 1961-62, George Washington U., 1962, U. So. Calif., 1963-64. Joined U.S. Army, 1941, commd. 2d lt., 1942; advanced through grades to brig. gen. USAF, 1968; various assignments, 1941-49; budget officer Hdqrs. USAF, 1949-53, 56-61; dir. budget and acctg. Hdqrs. N.E. Air Command, Nfld., 1953-56; comptroller space systems div. Los Angeles, 1962-64; comptroller aero., systems div. Wright-Patterson AFB, 1964-66; asst. comptroller USAF, 1966-67; dir. acctg. and fin. Hdqrs. USAF, 1967-68; asst. comptroller air force for acctg. and fin., comdr. Air Force Acctg. and Fin. Ctr., Denver, 1968-71; v.p. systems Cen. Bank Denver, 1971-81, v.p. info. resources mgmt., 1981-84. Dir. Computer Congenerics Corp. Colo., Hasa Corp. Co-chmn. Combined Fed. Campaign, Denver, 1968-87; Hon. dir. USO, Denver, 1968-71; mem. council, 1971-87. Decorated D.S.M., Legion of Merit, Soldier's medal, Commendation medal with oak leaf cluster; recipient Gen. Jimmy Doolittle Disting. Fellow award, Flint No. Alumni Assn. Disting. Fellow award, 1990, Treas. Dept. Pioneer in Elec. Commerce award, 2005. Mem. Am. Soc. Mil. Comptrollers (past pres. Washington chpt., nat. v.p. 1968-70, pres. Denver chpt. 1971-72), Assn. Govt. Accountants, Assn. Mil. Banks (dir. 1974-84), Am. Inst. Banking, Denver C. of C. (chmn. mil. affairs com. 1979-82), Aurora C. of C. (def. coun. 1987—), Air Force Acctg. and Fin. Ctr., Denver, 1968-71; v.p. Silver and Gold chpt. 1972-73, state treas. 1976-83, pres. Mile High chpt. 1987-88) Clubs: Columbine Country. Home: 5225 S Prince St 509 Littleton CO 80123 *I have adopted two attitudes that I believe assisted me in all of my undertakings: (1)— that of being what I call a "responsible non-conformist" and (2)— "no problems— just opportunities".*

**WITTBRODT, ELIZABETH STRATTON,** education educator; b. Grand Rapids, Mich., Dec. 12, 1958; d. Eugene Robert and Irene Mackie Stratton; m. Gary Foster Wittbrodt, Apr. 27, 1985. BS in Occupl. Therpay, Western Mich. U., Kalamazoo, 1982; M Health Sci., Govs.State U., Chgo., 1990; EdD, Loyola U., Chgo., 1997. Cert. Nat. Bd. of Occupl. Therapy Bethesda, 1982. Staff occupl. therapist Jewish Hosp. of Cin., Cincinnati, Ohio, 1982—85; staff occupl. therapist neuro-trauma Loyola U. Med. Ctr., Maywood, Ill., 1985—86; clin. coord. Hinsdale Hosp., Hinsdale, Ill., 1986—87; assoc. prof. occupl. therapy Chgo. State U., Chgo., 1987—; registry staff Hinsdale Hosp., Hinsdale, Ill., 1990—. Roster ccreditation evaluators Accreditation Coun. for Occupl. Therapy Edn., Bethesda, Md., 2003—. Contbr. articles pub. to profl. jpur. Bd. mem. Riverside Twp. Mental Health Bd., Riverside Township, Ill. 2003; adv. bd. mem. Health Care Adv. Bd., Congressional Dist., 1999—2000; v.p. Youth Scholarship Com., North Riverside, Ill., 2000—. Recipient Faculty Excellence, Chgo. State U., 1993, 1994, 1996, 1997, 2001, Occupl. Therapist of the Yr., Ill. Occupl. Therapy Assn., 1995. Mem.: Ill. Occupl. Therapy Assn. (dir. membership 1997—, Ill. Occupl. Therapist of the Yr. 1995), Am. Occupl. Therapy Assn., Phi Delta Kappa. Office: Chgo State Univ 9501 King Dr Chicago IL 60628 Home Fax: 708-442-6585; Office Fax: 773-995-2839. Personal E-mail: elizawitt1@aol.com. Business E-mail: ewittbro@csu.edu.

**WITTCOFF, HAROLD AARON,** chemist; b. Marion, Ind., July 3, 1918; s. Morris and Bessie (Pruss) W.; m. Dorothy Brochin, 1946; 2 sons AB magna cum laude, DePauw U., Greencastle, Ind., 1940; PhD, Northwestern U., Evanston, Ill., 1943; grad., Advanced Mgmt. Program, Harvard U., Cambridge, Mass., 1964. From mem. staff to v.p., dir. chem. R&D Gen. Mills, Inc., Mpls., 1943—69; v.p., dir. corp. rsch. Gen. Mills Chemicals, Inc., 1969—79; dir. R & D Koor Chems., Beer Sheva, Israel, 1979-82; dir. process evaluation and rsch. planning Chem Systems, Tarrytown, N.Y., 1982-85; sci. adviser NEXANT/Chem Systems, White Plains, NY, 1985—; adj. prof. chemistry U. Minn., 1973-82. Vis. prof. Chulalongkorn U., Thailand, 1995-2005; adj. prof. chemistry Weizmann Inst., Israel, 1979-2005. Author: The Phosphatides, 1951, Industrial Organic Chemistry: A Perspective 2 vols. 1980; Pharmaceutical Chemicals in Perspective, 1989, Industrial Organic Chemicals, 1996, 2nd edit., 2004, Organic Chemistry Principles and Industrial Practice, 2003; patentee in field. Recipient Minn. award Am. Chem. Soc., 1976 Mem. Phi Beta Kappa, Sigma Xi, Phi Eta Sigma. Home: Box 307 Apt 4G-I Scarborough Manor Scarborough NY 10510 Office Phone: 914-609-0330. Personal E-mail: hawittcoff@yahoo.com. Business E-mail: hwittcoff@nexant.com.

**WITTE, ARNOLD STEWART,** neurologist; b. NYC, Dec. 14, 1952; s. Henry Dennis Witte and Shirley Block; m. Debra J. DeLuca, Apr. 29, 1984; children: Samantha, Russell, Daniel, Larissa. BS, SUNY, Stony Brook, 1973; MD, Tufts U., 1977. Diplomate Am. Bd. Internal Medicine, Am. Bd. Neurology & Psychiatry, Am. Bd. Electrodiagnostic Medicine, lic. NJ, Pa. Intern U. Hosps. Cleve., Cleve., 1977—78, resident 1978—79; resident in neurology Hosp. of U. Pa., Phila., 1980—81, fellow, 1982—83; asst. prof. neurology Thomas Jefferson U. Hosp., 1983—86; mem. staff Capital Health Sys. at Mercer, 1986—, chief dept. neurology 1989—96, 1999, vice chief dept. neurology, 2000—. Cons. Trenton Psychiat. Hosp., 1987—; Forensic Psychiat. Hosp., 1987—; courtesy staff St. Francis Med. Ctr., 1993—; active staff Robert Wood U. Hosp., Hamilton. Contbr. articles to profl. jours. Mem.: AMA, Mercer County Med. Soc., Am. Acad. Neurology, Alpha Omega Alpha. Office: 2 Princess Rd Lawrenceville NJ 08648 Office Phone: 609-895-9000.

**WITTE, DALE ANDREW,** choral director, educator; b. Marshfield, Wis., Nov. 20, 1967; s. David Albert and Dorothy Lee Witte; m. Renee Sue Heckendorf, June 22, 1991; children: Jonathan David, Hannah Beth. BS, Dr. Martin Luther Coll., New Ulm, Minn., 1989; M in Ch. Music, Concordia U., River Forest, Ill., 1997. Tchr., choir dir. St. Paul Luth. Ch., Tomah, Wis., 1989—93; choral dir., music tchr. Winnebago Luth. Acad., Fond du Lac, Wis., 1993—2006. Music Tech. Lab grantee, Internat. Paper, 2006. Mem.: Music Educators Nat. Conf. (assoc.), Am. Choral Dirs. Assn. (assoc.). Home: 51 E Arndt St Fond Du Lac WI 54935 Office: Winnebago Luth Acad 475 E Merrill Ave Fond Du Lac WI 54935 Office Phone: 920-921-4930.

**WITTE, JUSTIN,** painter; Student, Lacoste Sch. Fine Art, France, 1997, NY Studio Program, 1998; BA, Milw. Inst. Art and Design, 1999. Solo exhibitions, Ontploffing, Vox Populi, Phila., 2002, Lurk, 2004, work has also been exhibited at, NY Studio Program, 1998, Contemporary Mus., Balt., 2000, Vox Populi, 2001, 2002, Nexus Found. for Today's Art, Phila., 2003, Abington Art Ctr., Jenkintown, Pa., 2003, Space 1026, Phila., 2003, Basekamp, Phila., 2004, Cheltenham Ctr. for the Arts, Beaver Coll. Art Gallery, Artists Space, NYC. Pew Fellowship in the Arts, 2004, Independence Found. Fellowship in the Arts, 2004.

**WITTE, OWEN NEIL,** microbiologist, molecular biologist, educator; b. Bklyn., May 17, 1949; BS, Cornell U., 1971; MD, Stanford U., 1976. Predoctoral fellow Stanford U. Med. Sch., Palo Alto, Calif., 1971-76, MIT Ctr. Cancer Rsch., Cambridge, Mass., 1976-80; asst. prof. UCLA Dept. Microbiology, Molecular Genetics, 1980-82, assoc. prof., 1982-86, prof., 1986—, pres.'s chair in devel. immunology, 1989—; investigator UCLA Howard Hughes Med. Inst., 1986—; prof., microbiology & immunology UCLA Sch. Medicine, 1996—. Am. Cancer Soc. faculty scholar, 1982-87; recipient Faculty award UCLA, 1990, award in basic cancer rsch. Milken Family Med. Found., 1990, Richard and Hinda Rosenthal Found. award Am. Assn. Cancer Rsch., 1991, William Dameshek prize ASH, 1993; Outstanding Investigator grantee Nat. Cancer Inst., 50th Anniversary Commemorative award, Leukenia Soc. of Amer., 1999. Fellow Am. Acad. Arts and Scis., 1996, Am. Acad. Microbiology, 1997; mem. NAS, 1997, Inst. Medicine. E-mail: owenw@microbio.ucla.edu.

**WITTELS, BARNABY CAESAR,** lawyer, writer; b. Phila., Mar. 28, 1948; s. David G. and Beatrice Tanya (Graitcer) Wittels; m. Heidi Jo Linsk, Sept. 8, 1974 (div. Aug. 1997); children: Kate Sophie, William David; m. Mary M. Labaree, Sept. 20, 1998. BA cum laude, Temple U., 1970; MA in Pol. Sci., Boston U., 1972, JD, 1975. Bar: Pa. 1975, U.S. Dist. Ct. (ea. dist.) Pa. 1985, U.S. Dist. Ct. Appeals (2d, 3d and 4th cirs.) 1986. Asst. defender Defender Assn. Phila., 1975-80; law clk. to hon. Stanley Kubacki Ct. Common Pleas Phila. County, 1980-84; ptnr. Wittels, Newman & Bomstein, Phila., 1980-82; assoc. LaCheen & Alva, Phila., 1982-86; ptnr. LaCheen & Assoc., Phila., 1986—2003, LaCheen, Dixon, Wittels & Greenburg, Phila., 2003—. Advisor Temple U. Parliamentary Debate Team, 2004—. Contbr. columns in newspapers. Chair N.W. Victim Svcs., Phila., 1981—84, mem. counsel, 1984—90, bd. dirs., 1983—90, chair, 1997—2003, founding mem., mem. bd. dirs. counsel, 2003—; baseball coach Chestnut Hill Fathers Club, 1985—98, commr., 1991—93, 1992—98; vol. Lawyers Concerned for Lawyers, 2003—; committeeman 21st divsn. Dems., Phila., 1985—90; active various polit. and jud. campaigns, 1980—; mem. exec. com. N.W. Interfaith Movement, 1985—86. Mem.: ABA, NACDL, Phila. Bar Found. (Apothaker award 1983), Pa. Bar Assn., Phila. Bar Assn. (mem. fee dispute com. 1996—, mem. com. to elect good judges 1987—88, mem. lawyers assistance com. 2003—), Pa. Assn. Criminal Def. Lawyers. Jewish. Avocations: writing, baseball, football, reading, woodworking. Office: LaCheen Dixon Wittels & Greenberg 1429 Walnut St 13th Fl Philadelphia PA 19102 Fax: 215-735-4649. Office Phone: 215-735-5900. Personal E-mail: barnabyw@aol.com.

**WITTEMYER, JOHN,** lawyer; b. Boulder, Colo., Dec. 19, 1939; s. Leonard and Beatrice Augusta (Dickhut) W.; m. Nancy Jean Vincent, June 6, 1964; children—Jon Vincent, Christopher Glen, Luke Leonard. B.S.C.E., U. Colo., 1962, B.S. in Bus., 1962, LL.B., 1965. Bar: Colorado 1965. Law clk. U.S. Supreme Ct. Alaska, 1965; dist. atty. 1st Jud. Dist. Alaska, Juneau, 1966-67; sole practice, Boulder, 1967-73; ptnr. Moses, Wittemyer, Harrison & Woodruff, P.C., Boulder, 1973—; gen. counsel Platte River Power Authority, 1975—2002; chmn. & chief exec. officer Crowley land and Devel. Co., subs. Aetna Casualty and Surety Co., Ordway, Colo., 1970-75. Mem. ABA,

---

Colo. Bar Assn., Boulder Bar Assn., Colo. Cattlemen's Assn. Republican. Methodist. Club: Country. Home: Sunshine Canyon PO Box 4575 Boulder CO 80306-4575 Office: PO Box PO Box 1440 Boulder CO 80306-1440

**WITTEN, CHRISTOPHER JAS See WITTEN, JASON**

**WITTEN, DAVID MELVIN,** retired radiology educator; b. Trenton, Mo., Aug. 16, 1926; s. Buford Isom and Mary Louise (Melvin) W.; m. Netta Lee Watkins, Dec. 23, 1950; children—David Melvin, II, Michael Lee. Student, Trenton Jr. Coll., 1943-44, 46-47; AB, Washington U., St. Louis, 1950, MD, 1954; MS in Radiology, U. Minn., 1960. Diplomate: Am. Bd. Radiology. Intern Virginia Mason Hosp., Seattle, 1954-55; practice medicine specializing in family medicine Trenton, Mo., 1955-57; fellow in radiology Mayo Clinic/Mayo Found., Rochester, Minn., 1957-60; cons. in diagnostic roentgenology Mayo Clinic, 1960-70; instr. Mayo Grad. Sch. Medicine, Rochester, 1960-66, asst. prof. radiology, 1966-70; pvt. practice medicine specializing in radiology Aberdeen, Wash., 1970-71; clin. assoc. prof. U. Wash., 1970-71; prof. diagnostic radiology, chmn. dept. diagnostic radiology U. Ala., Birmingham, 1971-82; diagnostic radiologist in chief Univ. Hosp., Birmingham, 1971-82; prof., chmn. dept. radiology U. Mo., Columbia, 1982-87, prof. emeritus, 1987—, interim chmn. dept. radiology, 1998-99. Pres. U. Ala. Health Services Found., 1973-75 Author: Atlas of Tumor Radiology-The Breast, 1969, Clinical Urography, 1970, 77; contbr. articles on radiology of breast cancer, urologic and gastrointestinal disease to profl. jours.; mem. editorial bd. Am. Jour. Roentgenology, 1976-87, Applied Radiology, 1978-87, Urologic Radiology, 1979-87, Radiographics, 1983-87. Served with USNR, 1944-46. Fellow Am. Coll. Radiology; mem. AAAS, AMA, Radiol. Soc. N.Am., Am. Roentgen Ray Soc., Soc. Uroradiology (pres. 1981-82, Gold medal 2003), Soc. Uroradiology (gold medal 2003), Assn. Univ. Radiologists, Mo. Radiol. Soc. (pres. 1988-89), Mo. State Med. Assn., Can. Assn. Radiologists (hon.), Audubon Soc. (editor The Bluebird chpt. 1990-98). Home: 601 W Covered Bridge Rd Columbia MO 65203-9562 Office: Univ Mo Health Scis Ctr 1 Hospital Dr Columbia MO 65201-5276 Office Phone: 573-282-1026. Personal E-mail: dmw8@tranquility.net.

**WITTEN, EDWARD,** mathematical physicist; b. Balt., Aug. 26, 1951; s. Louis Witten; m. Chiara Nappi; 3 children. BA in history, Brandeis U., 1971; MA, Princeton U., 1974, PhD, 1976; PhD (hon.), Brandeis U., 1988, Hebrew U. of Jerusalem, 1993, Columbia U., 1996, U. Southern Calif., 2004. Postdoctoral fellow Harvard U., 1976—77, jr. fellow, 1977—80; prof. physics Princeton U., NJ, 1980—87; prof. Sch. Natural Scis, Inst. for Advanced Study, Princeton, NJ, 1987—; Charles Simonyi prof. Princeton U., NJ, 1997—. Vis. prof. Calif. Inst. Tech., 1999—2001. Contbr. articles to mags. and profl. jours.; co-author (with M.B. Green and J.H. Schwarz): Superstring Theory, Vol. 1 and 2, Cambridge Univ. Press. Bd. dirs. Americans for Peace Now, 1992—. MacArthur Fellow, 1982; recipient Einstein medal Einstein Soc. Berne, Switzerland, 1985, Phys. and Math. Sci. award N.Y. Acad. Sci., 1985, Dirac medal Internat. Ctr. Theoretical Physics, 1985, Alan Waterman award NSF 1986, Fields Medal, Internat. Union of Mathematicians, 1990, Madison medal, Princeton Univ., 1992, NJ Pride award, 1996, Award of the Golden Plate, Am. Acad. of Achievement, 1997, Klein medal, Stockholm U., 1998, Dannie Heineman prize, Am. Inst. of Physics, 1998, Nemmers prize in Math., Northwestern U., 2000, Clay Rsch. award, Clay Math. Inst., 2001, Shalom award, Americans for Peace Now, 2002, Nat. Medal of Science, 2002. Fellow: Am. Philosophical Soc., Am. Phys. Soc., Am. Acad. Arts & Scis., NAS; mem.: Acad. of Sciences of Paris (assoc.). Office: Inst for Advanced Study Sch Natural Scis Einstein Dr Princeton NJ 08540-4920

**WITTEN, JASON (CHRISTOPHER JAS WITTEN),** professional football player; b. Elizabethton, Tenn., May 6, 1982; Student, Univ. Tenn., 2002. TE Dallas Cowboys, 2003—. Named to Pro-Bowl, NFL, 2004; recipient All-American Hon., NCAA, 2002. Office: Dallas Cowboys One Cowboys Pkwy Irving TX 75063-4999*

**WITTEN, LOUIS,** physics professor; b. Balt., Apr. 13, 1921; s. Abraham and Bessie (Perman) W.; m. Lorraine Wollach, Mar. 27, 1949 (dec. 1987); children: Edward, Celia, Matthew, Jesse; m. Francis L. White, Jan. 2, 1992. BE, Johns Hopkins U., 1941, PhD, 1951; BS, NYU, 1944. Research assoc. Princeton U., NJ, 1951-53; research assoc. U. Md., College Park, 1953-54; staff scientist Lincoln Lab., MIT, 1954-55; assoc. dir. Martin Marietta Research Lab., Balt., 1955-68; prof. physics U. Cin., 1968-91, prof. emeritus, 1991—. Trustee Gravity Research Found. Editor: Gravitation: An Introduction to Current Research, 1962, Relativity: Procs. of Relative Conf. in Midwest of 1969, Symposium on Asymptotic Structure of Space-Time, 1976; patentee in field; contbr. numerous articles to sci. jours. Served to 1st lt. USAF, 1942-46 Fulbright lectr. Weitzmann Inst. Scis., Rehovot, Israel, 1963-64 Fellow Am. Phys. Soc.; mem. Am. Math. Soc., Internat. Astron. Union, AAAS. Office: Univ Cincinnati Dept Physics Cincinnati OH 45221-0011 Business E-mail: witten@physics.uc.edu.

**WITTEN, ROGER MICHAEL,** lawyer; b. Atlantic City, Nov. 13, 1946; s. H. Davis and Miriam P. (Popkin) Witten; m. Jill S. Judd, June 5, 1971; children: Wendy D., Katherine J. BA magna cum laude, Dartmouth Coll., 1968; JD cum laude, Harvard Univ., 1972. Bar: Mass. 1973, NY, US Supreme Ct. 1976. Law clk. Judge Harrison L. Winter, US Ct. Appeals (4th cir.), 1972—73; asst. spl. prosecutor Watergate Spl. Prosecution Force, Washington, 1973—74; ptnr. Wilmer Cutler Pickering, Washington, 1975—2004; ptnr., co-chmn. Internat. Litigation group, mem. mgmt. com. Wilmer Cutler Pickering Hale & Dorr, NYC, 2004—. Counsel Common Cause, 1982—; chmn. 20th Century Fund Working Group on Campaign Fin. Reform, 1998. Contbr. articles to profl. jours. Mem.: ABA (chmn. Election Law com. 1988—90), DC Bar Assn., Phi Beta Kappa. Office: Wilmer Cutler Pickering Hale & Dorr 399 Park Ave New York NY 10022 Office Phone: 212-230-8850. Office Fax: 212-230-8888. Business E-mail: roger.witten@wilmerhale.com.

**WITTENBERG, ALEXANDER,** museum publicist; b. Flushing, NY, Nov. 15, 1968; s. William and Carole Wittenberg; m. Batya L. Levin, May 30, 1999. BA, Yeshiva U., NYC, 1989. Comm. coord. The Jewish Mus., NYC, 1990—. Active Congregation Etz Chaim, Flushing, 1997. Democrat. Jewish. Office Phone: 212-423-3272.

**WITTENBERG, HENRY TAYLOR, JR.,** physician, surgeon; b. Kansas City, July 5, 1933; s. Henry Taylor and Ruby Lena (Pratt) Wittenberg; m. Helen Marie Marlar, Sept. 7, 1963; children: Heather Melanee, Henry Taylor III. BS in Pharmacy, U. Kans., Lawrence, 1956; DO, Kansas City U. Medicine and Bioscis., 1960. Lic. Mo., 1960, Okla., 1962, cert. Am. med. dir. 1998. Intern Lakeside Hosp., Kansas City, 1960—61; preceptor Claremore Health Ctr., Okla., 1962—64; physician pvt. practice, Independence, Mo., 1961—62, Blue Star Clinic, Claremore, 1962—, Claremore Regional Hosp., 1962—; interim home health med. dir., 2004—. Chief staff Claremore Regional Hosp., 1962—; founder, bd. mem. First Bank of Okla., 1977, v.p. bd., 1977—87; founding mem. Okla. chpt. Am. Med. Dirs., 1991, v.p. bd., 1991—95; med. dir. Wood Manor Nursing Home, 1987—, Claremore Nursing Home, 1989—, Trinity Hospice, 2000—, Colonial Care Nursing Home, 2002—; mem. gov.'s com. Emergency Med. Svc., 1995—2000; mem. adv. bd. Unicare Welfare HMO, 2002—04. Editor-in-chief: U. Kans. Jayhawker U. Kans. Yearbook, 1956. Founding mem., pres. Claremore Jaycees; chmn. Rogers County March of Dimes, 1965—67; Jaycee founder group, original cast mem. Claremore Gridiron, 1966—; lay reader St. Paul's Episcopal Ch., jr. warden, 1998, sr. warden, 1999. Named Physician of Yr., Claremore, Okla., 1996, Rep. of Yr., Nat. Rep. Congressional Com. and Bus. Adv. Coun., 2001; named one of Am.'s Top Family Doctors, Consumer Rsch. Coun. Am., 2004; recipient Omicron Kappa Kappa Scholastic award, Kans. U., Otto Schnellbacjer award Outstanding Contbr. Campus Life, Nat. Leadership award, Nat. Rep. Congressional Com. Mem.: Rogers County Med. Soc. (v.p. 1986, program dir. 1986—97), Okla. Osteo. Assn. (life), Shrine (Potentate's Honor award 2003), Scottish Rite, Masons 1958, Rho

---

Sigma Chi, Sigma Sigma Phi, Psi Sigma Alpha. Episcopalian. Achievements include delivery over 3000 babies. Office: Blue Star Clinic 206 E Blue Star Dr Claremore OK 74017 Office Phone: 918-341-4040.

**WITTENBERG, JON ALBERT,** accountant; b. Valparaiso, Ind., Mar. 22, 1939; s. Fred E. and Elizabeth (DeWaal) W.; m. Joann S. Zachwieja, May 13, 1967; children: Brad, Glen, Pam. BS, Ind. U., 1961. CPA, Ill. Auditor Ernst & Young, Chgo., 1961-66; fin. analyst Amoco Chems., Chgo., 1966-69; contr. Nat. Van Lines, Broadview, Ill., 1969-76, Consol. Millinery, Chgo., 1976—. Mem. AICPA, Ill. Soc. CPAs, Inst. Mgmt. Accts. Home: 1297 W New Britton Dr Hoffman Estates IL 60195-1764 Office: Consol Millinery Co 18 S Michigan Ave Ste 605 Chicago IL 60603-3283 Office Phone: 847-358-8851.

**WITTENBORG, KARIN,** university librarian; m. Michael B. Sullivan. BA, Brown U., 1969; MLS, SUNY-Buffalo, 1976. Positions with SUNY-Buffalo, 1976—79; info. mgmt. intern MIT, 1981—82; chief gen. reference dept. and curator social sci. collections Stanford U., 1979—85; assoc. univ. libr. collections UCLA, 1985—93; univ. libr. U. Va., 1993—. Adv. coun. Academic Computing and Libr. Stanford U.; mem. com. info. resources Brown U.; exec. com. Digital Libr. Fedn. Avocations: cooking, running, gardening. Office: U Va Libr PO Box 400113 Charlottesville VA 22904 Office Phone: 434-924-7849. Fax: 434-924-1431. E-mail: kw7g@virginia.edu.*

**WITTENBRAKER, RICK L.,** lawyer; b. New Castle, Ind., Mar. 25, 1948; BBA cum laude, Tex. Christian U., Ft. Worth, 1970; JD, U. Tex., Austin, 1973. Bar: Tex. 1973. Ptnr. Bracewell & Patterson LLP, Houston, 1983—2003; sr. v.p., gen. counsel, sec. Waste Mgmt. Inc., Houston, 2003—. Exec. com. bd. dirs. Spring Branch Edn. Found., Houston; bd. trustees Tex. Christian U.; bd. dirs. Assn. for Cmty. Broadcasting (Houston Pub. Broadcasting). Mem.: Beta Gamma Sigma. Office: Waste Mgmt Inc 1001 Fannin St Ste 4000 Houston TX 77002 Office Phone: 713-512-6361. Business E-mail: rwittenbraker@wm.com.

**WITTENBRINK, BONIFACE LEO,** priest; b. Evansville, Ill., June 30, 1914; s. Max C. and Catherine Rose (Pautler) W. PhL, Gregorian U., Rome, 1939; STL, Ottawa (Can.) U., 1943; MA, Cath. U. Am., 1947. Ordained priest Oblates of Mary Immaculate, Roman Cath. Ch., 1941. Instr. Latin, logic, history and religion St. Henry's Coll., Belleville, Ill., 1943-48; instr., registrar, prin. high sch. dept. Coll. of Our Lady of the Ozarks, Carthage, Mo., 1948-52; founding dir. King's House of Retreats, Buffalo, Minn., 1952-53; mission procurator Roman Cath. Ch., St. Paul, 1955-56, 59-62; prin. Alemany High Sch. for Boys, Oblate Western Province, San Fernando, Calif., 1956-59; permanent sec. Conf. Maj. Superiors of Men, Washington, 1963-69; exec. dir., sec. Found. for Community Creativity, Washington, 1970-71; founder, dir., then dir. devel. Radio Info. Svc. for Blind and Handicapped, Belleville, 1972-84; pres., then local dir. Friends of Eye Rsch., Boston, 1983-87; exec. v.p. Citizens for Eye Rsch., Belleville, 1987—. Pres. Oblate Ednl. Assn., St. Paul, 1961-62; sci. adv. bd. Nat. Acad. Child Devel., 1984-86; mem. com. Eye Experience St. Louis, 1984; adv. bd. Welfare of the Blind, Inc., 1984—; adv. coun. svcs. for print-handicapped Nat. Pub. Radio, 1976-77; active Internat. Christian Leadership, 1968-72; bd. dirs. LOGOS Translators, ptnr. CBMI. Bd. dirs. Technoserve, 1968-72, Internat. Book Svc., 1969-72; vol. Ill. Literacy Project, 1989-90; founding charter mem., bd. dirs. Washington Workshops Found.; mem. Vision Awards Dinner Com., 1998—. Recipient RPI Internat. Vision award, 27th Annual Vision Awards, Agrama Harmony Gold and Light award, 2000, Beverly Hills, Calif. Mem. Madison County Assn. Blind, Mo. Coun. Blind, Am. Coun. of Blind (ednl. radio com. 1974-76), Am. Found. for Blind (radio talking book com. 1973-76), Inst. for Study of Econ. Systems (bd. dirs. 1971-72), Ednl. Communications Assn., Coun. for Dept. of Peace, Wycliffe Bible Translators Assn., Vols. for Internat. Tech. Assistance, Ill. Radio Info. Svc., Soc. Internat. Devel., UN Assn., Rotary Internat. (Paul Harris fellow), Belleville Econ. Progress, Eagles, KC, Press Club St. Louis, Am. Assn. Ret. Persons. Avocations: reading, travel. Home: 200 N 60th St Belleville IL 62223-3951

**WITTENBURG, MICHAEL SHANE,** concert pianist, music educator; b. Saarbrücken, Germany, Nov. 26, 1973; s. John Steven and Margaret Wittenburg; 1 child, Karl Frederick. MusB in Performance-Piano, Eastman Sch. Music, 1996, MusM in Performance and Lit.-Piano, 1998; MusM in Performance-Orchestral Conducting, U. Tenn., Chattanooga, 2001. Instr. music Lee U., Cleveland, Tenn., 2001—04; asst. prof. music, 2004—; organist Christ United Meth. Ch., Chattanooga, 1999—; sect. violin Chattanooga Symphony and Opera, 1999—. Named Oustanding Grad. Student in Music: Performance, U. Tenn., Chattanooga, 2000; recipient Performer's cert. in Piano, Eastman Sch. Music, 1996; fellow Opera Coaching, 1996—98. Mem.: Am. Fedn. Musicians (mem. local 80), Pi Kappa Lambda (Faculty Inductee 2005). Conservative. Avocations: tennis, travel. Home: 621 Memorial Dr #1501 Chattanooga TN 37415 Office: Lee Univ Cleveland TN Personal E-mail: deliusfan@aol.com. E-mail: mwittenburg@leeuniversity.edu.

**WITTES, ROBERT E.,** physician, science foundation director; b. NYC, Mar. 20, 1943; married; 3 children. AB magna cum laude, Harvard U., 1964, MD cum laude, 1968. Intern in medicine Beth Israel Hosp., Boston, 1968-69, resident, 1969-70; rsch. assoc. lab. biochemistry Nat. Cancer Inst., NIH, Bethesda, Md., 1970-72; fellow in med. oncology Meml. Hosp., 1972-73, clin. asst. physician med. oncology svc., 1973-74, 74-75; physician to outpatients N.Y. Hosp., N.Y.C., 1974-76; asst. then assoc. attending physician solid tumor svc. Meml. Hosp., 1975-83, asst. chief, 1979-83; assoc. dir. cancer therapy evaluation program Nat. Cancer Inst., NIH, Bethesda, 1983-88, chief medicine br. clin. oncology program, 1990-95, dir. divsn. cancer treatment, diagnosis and ctrs., 1995—2002, dep. dir. extramural sci., 1997—2002; Physician in Chief Memorial Sloan-Kettering Cancer Center, 2002—. Asst. in medicine, Harvard U. Sch. Medicine, 1969-70; instr. medicine Georgetown U. Sch. Medicine, Washington, 1970-72; fellow in medicine, Cornell U. Med. Coll., 1972-74, instr. 1974-75, asst. prof., 1975-79, assoc. prof., 1980-83; vis. assoc. prof. Sloan-Kettering Inst. 1975-83; vis. physician Walter Reed Army Med. Ctr., Washington, 1987-88. Mem. editorial bd. Jour. clin. Oncology, 1983-86, Internat. Jour. Radiation Oncology, Biology and physis, 1987—, Am. Jour. clin. Oncology, 1985—, Cancer Investigation, 1983—, Current Opinion in Oncology, 1988—; editor-in-chief Cancer Treatment Reports, 1983-87, Primry Care and Cancer, 1982—, NCI Monographs, 1986-88, Jour. Nat. Cancer Inst., 1988, Oncology, 1987—. With USPHS. Fellow ACP; mem. AAAS, Am. Assn. Cancer Rsch., Am. Fedn. for Clin. Rsch., Am. Soc. Clin. Oncology, Internat. Assn. for Study of Lung Cancer, Soc. Head and Neck Surgeons (cons.). Office: Meml Sloan-Kettering Cancer Ctr 1275 York Ave New York NY 10021-0001

**WITTICH, JOHN JACOB,** retired academic administrator, finance company executive; b. Huntley, Ill., Nov. 13, 1921; s. John and Eva (Karl) W.; m. Leah Elliott, Apr. 2, 1944; children: Karen Ann Zvonar, Jane Ellen Tock, John Elliott. BA, DePauw U., 1943; LLD (hon.), 1971; MA, U. N.Mex., 1949; PhD, Stanford U., 1952; LHD (hon.), Ill. Coll., 1979; DPS (hon.), MacMurray Coll., 1980. Tchr. Albuquerque H.S., 1948-49; tchg. asst. Stanford, 1949-51; asst. prof. psychology Coll. of Pacific, Stockton, Calif., 1951-52; dean of admissions and fin. aid, assoc. prof. DePauw U., Greencastle, Ind., 1952-61; exec. dir. Coll. Center of Finger Lakes, Corning, NY, 1961-63, Coll. Student Personnel Inst., Claremont, Calif., 1963-68; adj. prof., dir. grad. studies in student pers. Claremont Grad. Sch., 1963-68; pres. MacMurray Coll., Jacksonville, Ill., 1968-80; dir. Fla. Assn. Colls. and Univs., 1980-84; dir. higher edn. program Stetson U., 1981-88; v.p. Capital Formation Counselors, Inc., Belleair Bluffs, Fla., 1983—2005. Contbr. articles to profl. jours. Exec. com. Divsn. Higher Edn., Ctrl. Ill. Conf. of United Meth. Ch., 1968-80; exec. com. Fedn. Independent Ill. Colls. and Assoc. Colls. Ill.; non-pub. adv. com. Ill. Bd. Higher Edn., 1972-78; mem. Nat. Merit Scholarship Selection Com., 1956, 61; cons. Calif. Gov.'s Conf. on Edn., 1965, on Youth, 1966; trustee Fla. Endowment for Humanities, 1982-85; recip. counsellor Stetson U., 1987—; bd. dirs. DeLand House Next Door, 1990-94; citizens adv. com. West Volusia Hosp. Authority, 1992-2002, vice-chmn., 2001-02; rsch. project evaluator for human subjects regional office U.S. FDA, 2003-05.

With USMC, 1943-46, PTO. Recipient DePauw Achievement award, 1969, Alumni citation DePauw U., 1994; Rockefeller fellow Aspen Inst. for Humanistic Studies, 1979. Mem. APA, Am. Coll. Pers. Assn. (commn. chmn.), Nat. Assn. Coll. Admissions Counselors (exec. bd. 1955-58), Cen. States Coll. Assn. (exec. com. 1969-77, sec.-treas. 1970-77), 4th Marine Divsn. Assn. WW II, Sigma Chi. Home: 918 Torchwood Dr Deland FL 32724-9407 Office Phone: 386-736-9006. Personal E-mail: jwittich@cfl.rr.com.

**WITTIG, DON,** judge; b. San Antonio, Sept. 18, 1941; s. Don A. and Miriam (Moon) W.; children: Jeffrey A., Marie C., Sarah Elizabeth. Student, U.S. Naval Acad., Annapolis, Md., 1960-61; BA in Govt., St. Mary's U., 1963, JD, 1965. Bar: Tex. 1965, U.S. Dist. Ct. (so. dist.) Tex. 1970, U.S. Ct. Claims 1965, U.S. Tax Ct. 1965, U.S. Ct. Customs and Patent Appeals 1965, U.S. Ct. Mil. Appeals 1965, U.S. Ct. Appeals (5th cir.) 1965. Ptnr. Lorance, Thompson & Wittig, Houston, 1972-80, Ellis, Wittig & Smith, Houston, 1984-85; pvt. practice Houston, 1985-88; judge 125th Dist. Ct., Houston, 1988—99; judge, sr. justice 14th Ct. Appeals, 1999—2001. Author: New Local Rules, 1988, A Practical Guide to Ct's. Charge, 1989, Streamlining Trial and Pretrial Practice, 1991. Mem. Internat. Com, Houston Livestock and Rodeo. Fellow Houston Bar Found.; mem. ABA (task force on fast track ligitation, cert. arbitrator & mediator), Nat. Arbitration Assn., State Bar Tex., Tex. Bar Found., Cameron County Bar Assn. Avocations: sailing, reading, golf. Office Phone: 956-233-9094. Business E-Mail: donwittig@ies.net.

**WITTIG, RAYMOND SHAFFER,** lawyer, intellectual property technology manager; b. Allentown, Pa., Dec. 13, 1944; s. Raymond Battie and Alice (Shaffer) Wittig; m. Beth Glover, June 21, 1975; children: Meaghan G., Allison G. BA, Pa. State U., 1966, MEd, 1968; JD, Dickinson Sch. Law, 1974. Bar: U.S. Ct. Appeals (DC cir.) 1978. Rsch. psychologist Intext Corp., Scranton, Pa., 1968; minority counsel Small Bus. Com., U.S. Ho. of Reps., Washington, 1975-84; pvt. practice Washington, 1984-92; tech. mgmt. group leader Geo-Ctrs., Inc., Newton Centre, Mass., 1992—2005; prin. Sci. Apps. Internat. Corp. Tech. Mgmt. Advisors, 2005—. Capt. U.S. Army, 1969—71. Mem.: ABA, AAAS, Assn. Univ. Tech. Mgrs., Am. Intellectual Property Law Assn., Fed. Lab. Consortium, Nat. Order Barristers, Licensing Execs. Soc. Office Phone: 202-841-0655. Personal E-Mail: wittigsall@aol.com.

**WITTLINGER, CHERYL A.,** elementary school educator; b. Lakewood, Ohio, Mar. 30, 1950; d. Richard Lawrence and Beverly Jane (Leighton) Riedel; children: Brian E., Jasen E, Ashley T. Student, Kent State U., 1968-70; AA, Lorain County Community Coll., Lorain, Ohio, 1977; BA in Visual Arts, Cleve. State U., 1982; postgrad., Coll. Mt. St. Joseph, Cin., 1987. Tchr. art Lorain (Ohio) City Schs., 1983—. Presenter in field; chmn. Lorain County Very Spl. Arts Festival, 1988; judge Lorain County Consortium for Gifted Edn. Fair, 1989. Endowment grant Lorain City Schs., 1987-88, 91, 98, 2000, 04 Mem. AAUW, Ohio Art Edn. Assn. (conf. presenter 1986-88, 90, Outstanding Art Tchr. for Northeastern Ohio region award 1991, 2001), N.E. Ohio Art Edn. Assn. (newsletter editor), Lorain Edn. Assn., Ohio Alliance for Arts Edn. Presbyterian. Avocations: breeding cocker spaniels, painting, travel, tole painting on clothes. Home: 527 Ashley Cir Avon Lake OH 44012-2131 Office: Longfellow Middle Sch 305 Louisiana Ave Lorain OH 44052

**WITTLINGER, TIMOTHY DAVID,** lawyer; b. Dayton, Ohio, Oct. 12, 1940; s. Charles Frederick and Dorothy Elizabeth (Golden) W.; m. Diane Cleo Dabney, May 20, 1967; children: Kristine Elizabeth, David Matthew. BS in Math., Purdue U., 1962; JD with distinction, U. Mich., 1965. Bar: Mich. 1966, U.S. Dist. Ct. (ea. dist.) Mich. 1966, U.S. Ct. Appeals (6th cir.) 1968, U.S. Supreme Ct. 1971. Assoc. Clark Hill (formerly Hill Lewis), Detroit, 1965-72, ptnr., 1973—, head litigation dept., 1976-91, gen. counsel, 1997—, chief legal officer, 1997—. Profl. assistance com. U.S. Dist. Ct. (ea. dist.) Mich., 1981-82; mem. Mich. Supreme Ct. Com. to Evaluate Mediation Ct. Rule, 1997-98; author; lectr. Ctr. for Internat. Legal Studies, 1999—; mem. coll. fellows Ctr. Internat. Legal Studies, Salzburg, Austria. Mem. ho. of deps. Episc. Ch., NYC, 1979-2003; vice chmn. Robert Whitaker Sch. Theology, 1983-87; sec. bd. trustees Episc. Ch., Diocese of Mich., Detroit, 1983—, sec. conv. Episc. Diocese of Mich., 1990—, ch. atty., 1997—, sec. Episc. nat. econ. justice implementation com., 1988-95, Episc. nat. exec. coun., 1991-97, nat. audit com., 2000-03; mem. Nat. Standing Commn. on Ministry Devel., 2000-06; ministry com. Nat. Episc. Jubilee, Salt Lake Episc. Coalition for Social Witness and Justice, Fifth Province Episc. Ecclesiastical Ct. Appeal, 1997-2000; trustee Episcopal Ch. Province V, 2006-; bd. dirs. Episc. Student Found., U. Mich., 1990-93, 2000-2002; chair Grubb Inst. Behavioral Studies Ltd., Washington, 1986—, London, 1986—; bd. dirs. Birmingham Village Playhouse, 2000—. Mem. ABA, Engring. Soc. Detroit, Assn. Profl. Responsibility Lawyers. Home: 736 N Glenhurst Dr Birmingham MI 48009-1143 Office: Clark Hill 500 Woodward Ave Ste 3500 Detroit MI 48226-3435

**WITTMAN, BRITTANY LYN,** design educator; b. Williamsport, Pa., Apr. 23, 1974; d. Kenneth Lynn Wittman and Linda Diane Cardene. BS in Textile Design cum laude, Phila. Coll. Textiles and Sci., 1997; MFA in Sculpture, U. Arts, 2004. Designer, project mgr. Knoll Textiles/Suzanne Tick, Inc., NYC, 1997—98; assoc. M. Finkel & Dau. Antiques, Phila., 2000; tech. assoc. Phila. U., 2000—04, co-dir. nonwovens design & engring. lab., 2004—05, profl., 2004—05. Adj. profl. Phila. U., 2002—04, vis. asst. prof., 2004—05; studio asst. Peters Valley Craft Ctr., Layton, NJ, 1996, Haystack Sect. Crafts, Deer Isle, Maine, 1999; adj. prof. Art Inst. Pitts. Online, 2006—. Exhibitions include Convergence, 2000, Da Vinci Art Alliance, Phila., 2001, Convergence, 2002, Phila. U. Faculty Show, 2002, Daegu Internat. Textile Design Exch., Korea, 2002, Convergence, 2003, East Falls, Phila., 2005, Premiere Vision, Paris, 2005, Gallery in the Garden, 2005. Asst. curator Lycoming County Hist. Soc., Williamsport, 1995. History Textiles & Costumes fellow, 1994—97. Address: La Maison de Brittany 817 Rural Ave Williamsport PA 17701-3035

**WITTMAN, VANESSA AMES,** communications executive; b. New London, Conn., Apr. 16, 1967; m. Drew M. Wittman; children: Parker, Mason. BS, U. N.C., 1989; MBA, U. Va., 1993. Assoc. Anderson Consulting, 1989—91; investment banker Morgan Stanley, 1993—96; ptnr. Sterling Payot, 1996—97; CFO Metricom, Inc., 1997—99; sr. dir. corp. devel. Microsoft Corp., 1999—2000; v.p., corp. devel. 360networks, 2000—02, CFO broadband network svcs., 2002—03; exec. v.p., CFO Adelphia Comm. Corp., 2003—. Bd. dirs. InfoSpace, Inc., Bellevue, Wash. Avocations: tennis, skiing. Office: Adelphia Comm Corp 5619 DTC Pkwy Greenwood Village CO 80111 Office Phone: 303-268-6300. Office Fax: 303-268-6495.

**WITTMANN, MARSHALL,** political organization worker; b. Waco, Tex., 1953; m. Karen Wittmann; 2 children. Student, NYU; BA in Elem. Edn., Univ. Mich., 1975. Campaign worker Ralph Yarborough, Lyndon B. Johnson, Eugene McCarthy; with United Farm Workers, 1975—76; lobbyist Nat. Treasury Employees Union, Washington, 1980—84, 1984—86; press sec. Linda Chavez for Senate campaign, Md., 1986, Connie Morella for Congress campaign, Md., 1986; dep. asst. sec. Dept. Health, Human Svcs., Washington, 1989—92; spokesman Christian Coalition, 1992—95; with Heritage Found., 1995—2000, Hudson Inst., 2000—02; press sec. John McCain, Washington, 2002—04; sr. fellow Dem. Leadership Coun., Washington, 2004—. Founder Jews for George, 1988. Jewish. Widely known as a political pundit and quotemeister. Office: Democratic Leadership Coun Ste 400 600 Pennsylvania Ave SE Washington DC 20003 Office Phone: 202-546-0007.*

**WITTMER, JAMES FREDERICK,** preventive medicine physician, educator; b. Carlinville, Ill., Dec. 30, 1932; s. Franklin Benjamin and Eva Caroline (Zihlman) W.; m. Juanita Lou Wilkey, June 29, 1962; children: Ellen, Carol, Nancy. MD, Washington U., St. Louis, 1957; MPH, Harvard U., 1961. Diplomate Am. Bd. Preventive Medicine. Intern U. Va. Hosp., Charlottesville, 1857-58; commd. capt. USAF, 1958, advanced through grades to col., 1971; ret., 1979; dean allied health U. Tex. Health Sci. Ctr., San Antonio, 1979-80; asst. prof. Conoco Oil Co., Ponca City, Okla.,

1980-81; assoc. med. dir. Mobil Oil Corp., N.Y.C., 1981-83; dir. health, environ. and safety ITT, N.Y.C., 1983-95, corp. v.p., 1990-95. Clin. prof. medicine Cornell U. Med. Coll., NYC, 1984—; lectr. environ. medicine NYU, NYC, 1984—; adj. prof. U. Tex. Sch. Pub. Health, Houston, 1987—, prof. occupl. health, 1996—97; nat. coord. com. on clin. preventive svcs. USPHS, 1994—97; cons. effective hearings and appeals U.S. Social Security Adminstrn., 1997—2003; cons. Met. Health Dist., San Antonio, 2002—. Mem. Pres.'s Com. on Employment People with Disabilities, Washington, 1986-2000, chmn. med. and ins. com., 1986-90. Fellow ACP, Am. Coll. Occupational and Environ. Medicine (bd. dirs. 1990-97, sec. 1992-94), Am. Coll. Preventive Medicine, Aerospace Med. Assn., N.Y. Acad. Medicine; mem. AMA, Tex. Occupational Med. Assn. Home and Office: 159 Sabine Rd Boerne TX 78006-6217 Office Phone: 830-537-4782. Business E-Mail: wittmer@gvtc.com.

**WITTMIER, DENISE DONELLE,** elementary school educator; b. Jamestown, N.D., Dec. 27, 1956; d. Boyd H. and Judith Williams; m. Dale M. Wittmier, June 17, 1978; children: Austin, Barret, Christa. B, Valley City (N.D.) State U., 1979. Tchr. elem. edn. Streeter (N.D.) Pub. Sch., 1979—97, Gackle (N.D.) Streeter Pub. Sch., 1997—, volleyball coach, 1996—. Mem. Am. Legin Aux. (sec. 1990—), N.D. Reading Assn., Streeter Homemaker's Club. Democrat. Lutheran. Home: 235 Helen St S Streeter ND 58483-7012 Office: Gackle Sch Dist 14 PO Box 375 Gackle ND 58442-0375

**WITTREICH, WARREN JAMES,** psychologist, consultant; b. Weehawken, N.J., Aug. 18, 1929; s. Andrew Otto and Muriel Viola (Wilson) Wittreich; m. Mary Shirley Wells, Sept. 10, 1951 (div. Sept. 1959); children: Michael(dec.); Peter; m. Lois Vivian Llewellyn, Sept. 8, 1959 (div. July 1996); children: Benjamin, Debra, Andrea; m. Eileen Burke, Aug. 20, 1996 (div. Sept. 1998); m. Diane L. Altif-Meyer, Jan. 8, 2000. AB in Psychology summa cum laude, Princeton U., 1951, MA in Psychology, 1953, PhD in Psychology, 1954; PhD in Clin. Psychology, Cath. U., Washington, 1958. Lic. psychologist, Pa. Guest scientist Naval Med. Rsch. Inst., Bethesda, Md., 1953-54; postdoctoral trainee VA, East Orange, NJ, 1954-55; clin. psychologist Lancaster and Phila. Pa., 1955—; exec. v.p. Nat. Analysts, Inc., Phila., 1959-64; pres. Daniel Yankelovich of Pa., Phila., 1964-67; pres., CEO Crossroads Career Planning Corp., Phila., 1967-85; adj. prof., rsch. cons. U. Pa., Phila., 1968-73; CEO Focus Group Assocs. Ltd., Bethlehem, Pa., 1995—. Advisor to Sec. of Transp., U.S. Dept. Transp., Washington, 1968-72; expert witness FTC, Washington, 1957, U.S. Congress, Washington, 1959, N.Y. State Supreme Ct., N.Y.C., 1963. Exhibited in 4 one-man shows; 2 commd. paintings; contbr. articles to profl. jours. Worker Robert F. Kennedy Campaign Com., Washington, 1967; mem. Citizens Adv. Com. on Transp. Quality, U.S. Dept. Transp., Washington, 1968-74. Recipient fellowship NSF, 1952-53. Fellow: Pa. Psychol. Assn.; mem.: APA, Sigma Xi, Phi Beta Kappa. Episcopalian. Avocation: painting. Home: 1581 Ralston Rd Bethlehem PA 18018

**WITTROCK, MERLIN CARL,** educational psychologist; b. Twin Falls, Idaho, Jan. 3, 1931; s. Herman C. and Mary Ellen W.; m. Nancy McNulty, Apr. 3, 1953; children: Steven, Catherine, Rebecca. BS in Edn. and Biology, U. Mo., 1953, MEd in Ednl. Psychology, 1956; PhD in Ednl. Psychology, U. Ill., 1960. Prof. grad. sch. edn. UCLA, 1960—, disting. tchr., founder Ctr. Study Evaluation, chmn. faculty, chmn. divsn. ednl. psychology, supr. UNEX Intern Tchr. Preparation Program, 1996—2006. Dir. math. and humanities program, co-founder Urban Tchr. Edn. Program; fellow Ctr. for Advanced Study in Behavioral Scis., 1967—68; vis. prof. U. Wis., U. Ill., Ind. U., Monash U., Australia; co-prin. investigator Calif. Reading Tchr's Insts.; chmn. com. on evaluation and assessment L.A. Unified Sch. Dist.; nat. adv. panel for math. scis. NRC of NAS; chmn. nat. bd. Nat. Ctr. for Rsch. in Math. Scis. Edn., U. Wis., Madison; chmn. charges com. UCLA; adv. bd. Kauffman Found.; dir. evaluation Calif. Reading Tchrs. Profl. Devel. Program; steering com. tchr. cert. program L.A. Unified Sch. Dist. Author, editor: The Evaluation of Instruction, 1970, Changing Education, 1973, Learning and Instruction, 1977, The Human Brain, 1977, Danish transl., 1980, Spanish transl., 1982, The Brain and Psychology, 1980, Instructional Psychology: Education and Cognitive Processes of the Brain, Neuropsychological and Cognitive Processes of Reading, 1981, Handbook of Research on Teaching, 3d edit., 1986, The Future of Educational Psychology, 1989, Research in Learning and Teaching, 1990, Testing and Cognition, 1991, Generative Science Teaching, 1994, Problem-Solving Transfer, 1996, Taxonomy for Learning, Teaching and Assessing, 2001. Mentor Edn. Leadership Program; bd. dirs. Wested R & D Ctr., 1989—2001. Capt. USAF, 1953—55. Recipient Disting. Tchr. of Univ., UCLA, 2005; grantee, Ford Found. Fellow: APA (pres. divsn. ednl. psychology 1984—85, assn. coun. 1988—91, award for Outstanding Svc. to Ednl. Psychology 1991, 1993, Disting. Svc. award for svc. to sci. adv. coun., Thorndike award for outstanding psychol. rsch. 1987), AAAS, Am. Psychol. Soc. (charter fellow); mem.: Am. Ednl. Rsch. Assn. (chmn. ann. conv., chmn. publs. 1980—83, assn. coun. 1986—89, bd. dirs. 1987—89, chmn. com. on ednl. TV, Outstanding Contbns. award 1986, Outstanding Svc. award 1989), Phi Delta Kappa. Office: UCLA 3021 Moore Hl Los Angeles CA 90095-1521 Office Phone: 310-825-8329. Business E-Mail: wittrock@ucla.edu.

**WITTRUP, KARL DANE,** chemical engineer, educator; BS in Chemical Engring., U. New Mexico, 1984; MS in Chemical Engring. & Biology, Calif. Inst. of Tech., 1986, PhD in Chemical Engring., 1988. Postdoctoral rsch. assoc. Amgen, Inc., Thousand Oaks, Calif., 1988—89; asst. prof. chemical engring. U. Illinois, Urbana, Ill., 1989—95, assoc. prof. chemical engring., biophysics, & bioengring., 1995—99, J. W. Westwater prof. chemical engring., biophysics, & bioengring., 1999; J.R. Mares prof. chemical engring. & bioengring. MIT, 1999—. Recipient Allan P. Colburn award, 1998, Presidential Young Investigator award, Nat. Sci. Found., 1990, A. McLaren White award, 1984. Office: MIT Chem Engring Dept Room 66-552 77 Massachusetts Ave Cambridge MA 02139

**WITTRY, DAVID BERYLE,** physicist, researcher; b. Mason City, Iowa, Feb. 7, 1929; s. Herman Joseph and Edna Pearl (Filbey) W.; m. Mildred Elizabeth DuBois, July 1, 1955; children: James David, Robert Andrew, Kristopher Lee, Diane Marie, Linda Beryle. BS, U. Wis., 1951; MS, Calif. Inst. Tech., 1953, PhD, 1957. Research fellow Calif. Inst. Tech., Pasadena, 1957-59; asst. prof. U. So. Calif., Los Angeles, 1959-61, assoc. prof. dept. elec. engring., 1961-69, prof. dept. materials sci. and elec. engring., 1969-98, disting. prof. emeritus, 1998—. Cons. Hughes Semiconductors, 1958-59, Applied Research Labs., Inc., 1958-83, Exptl. Sta., E.I. du Pont de Nemours & Co., 1962-71, Gen. Telephone and Electronics Research Labs., 1966-72, Autonetics div. N. Am. Aviation, 1961-63, Electronics Research div. Rockwell Internat., 1976-81, Atlantic Richfield Co. Corp. Tech. Lab., 1981-87, Jet Propulsion Lab., 1985-88, Hitachi Instruments, 1989-90; vis. scientist Japan Soc. Promotion of Sci., U. Osaka Prefecture, 1974. Editor 3 proceedings of cons. Contbr. articles to profl. jours. Patentee in field. Recipient first award essays on gravity, Gravity Research Found., 1949, Disting. Scientist award phys. scis. Microscopy Soc. Am., 1995, Disting. Svc. citation U. Wis. Coll. Engring., 1996; Guggenheim fellow, 1967-68; Knapp scholar U. Wis., 1949-51. Mem. IEEE, Electron Microscopy Soc. Am. (dir. phys. scis. 1979-81, pres. 1983), Microbeam Analysis Soc. (sec. organizing com. 1966, exec. council 1970-72, pres. 1988, Presdl. award 1980, Birks award 1987, 89, hon. mem.), Am. Phys. Soc., Sigma Xi. Methodist. Office: U So Calif Dept Materials Sci Los Angeles CA 90089-0001

**WITTRY, DIANE MARIE,** conductor, musician; d. David Beryl and Mildred Elizabeth Wittry; m. Richard Edward Peckham. MusB, U. So. Calif., 1983, MusM, 1985; studies with Leonid Korchmar, St. Petersburg Conservatory Music. Asst. condr. Pasadena Symphony, 1988—95; music dir., condr. Greater Miami (Fla.) Youth Symphony, 1989—91, Symphony S.E. Tex., Beaumont, 1991—2000, Allentown (Pa.) Symphony, 1996—, Norwalk (Conn.) Symphony, 2001—. Guest condr. LA Philharm., San Diego Symphony, N.J. Symphony, Houston Symphony, Fla. Philharm., others. Author: Beyond the Baton, 2005. Named Top prize winner, Conducting Competition, Italy, 2001; recipient Gold Crown award, City of Pasadena, 1991, Outstand-

ing Merit award, Chamber Music Am., 1992, Helen M. Thompson award, Am. Symphony Orch. League, 1996, Arts Ovation award, City of Allentown, 1999, Women of Excellence award, City of Beaumont, 1999, Women of Distinction award, Lehigh Valley, Pa., 2000, Florino Doro award, City of Vince, Italy, 2003. Mem.: Am. Symphony Orch. League, Condr.'s Guild (bd. dirs.), Phi Kappa Lambda. Methodist.

**WITTSTEIN, EDWIN FRANK,** theater director, set designer; b. Mt. Vernon, N.Y., Apr. 7, 1929; s. Nathan Harry and Miriam (Goldman) W. Student, Parsons Sch. Design, 1946-50; BS, NYU, 1950; postgrad., Cooper Union, 1950-52. Stage designer Dramatic Workshop prodn. The Inspector General, 1947; set designer Gertrude Stein's Yes Is for a Very Young Man; set and costume designer Ounga Opera, Phila., 1950, (opera) The Celebrated Jumping Frog of Calaveras County, Venice, Italy, 1953, The Transposed Heads, 1958, The Fantasticks, 1960-2002; designer Broadway prodn. Kean, 1961; set and costume designer The Gondoliers, N.Y.C. Opera, 1963, The Knack (directed by Mike Nichols), 1964, The Marriage of Figaro, N.Y.C. Opera, 1965, The Amen Corner, 1965, Happy Birthday Wanda June, Enter Laughing, 1965, The Room, A Slight Ache, 1965, The Yearling, 1965, Serjeant Musgrave's Dance, 1966 (Obie award 1966), You Know I Can't Hear You When the Water's Running, 1967, set designer Merchant of Venice, Shakespeare Festival Conn., 1967, As You Like It, Richard II, Shakespeare Festival Conn., 1968, The Man in the Glass Booth, 1968, The Basement, The Tea Party, Celebration, 1969, (for Cin. Playhouse) The Miser, Volpone, The Good Woman of Setzuan, Angel Street, He Who Gets Slapped, 1968-70, The Country Wife, Shakespeare Theatre, Conn., 1973, Ulysses in Nightown, 1974 (Tony award nomination 1974, Maharam award 1974), The Torchbearers, 1978, The Aspern Papers, 1978, Love's Labors Lost, 1983, Berkshire Theatre Festival, 1988, Tusitala, 1988, Tete a Tete, 1989, The Hasty Heart, 1990, Trains, 1991, (sets, costumes 30th anniversary tour) The Fantasticks, 1990, Sarah, Plain and Tall, 1991 (Emmy nomination 1991), Colette Collage, 1991, March of the Falsettos, 1991, Falsettoland, 1991, (prodn. designer Hallmark Hall of Fame TV) An American Story, 1992, (prodn. designer Hallmark Hall of Fame TV) Skylark, 1993, (prodn. designer Hallmark Hall of Fame TV) A Place for Annie, 1993, (set designer off-Broadway) I Do! I Do!, 1996, The Fantasticks, 2006; designer TV shows Armstrong Circle Theatre, The Tonight Show with Steve Allen, NBC operas Cosi Fan Tutte, La Traviata, La Boheme, Boris Godounov, Cavalleria Rusticana, Blithe Spirit, The Diary of Anne Frank, Camino Real, The Royal Family, The Prince of Homburg; prodn. designer TV series The Adams Chronicles (Emmy nomination 1975); designer TV films A Memory of Two Mondays, 1971, For Ladies Only, 1982, Legs, 1982, Samson and Delilah, 1983, Heartsounds, 1984; designer TV spl. Echoes in the Darkness, 1987; designer films Bananas, 1971, Play It Again Sam, 1971, The Seven-Ups, 1972; art dir. films Smile, 1975, Fame, 1979; prodn. designer film Endless Love, 1981; set and costume designer (ballet) Coppelia, 1992; one-man show (painting) Hammond Museum, N. Salem, N.Y., 1999; drawer, writer Positano Sketch Book, 2000. Home: 339 E 87th St New York NY 10128-4801

**WITTSTRUCK, THORNE MICHAEL,** physiologist; s. James Robert and Toni Lynn Wittstruck; m. Nyomi Kyra Wittstruck, July 22, 2001. BS in Exercise Sci., Winona State U., Minn., 1996. Registered exercise physiologist Am. Coll. Sports Medicine. Coord. cardiopulmonary rehab. St. Clare Hosp., Baraboo, Wis.; exercise physiologist Marshfield (Wis.) Clinic, Winona (Minn.) Cmty. Meml. Hosp. Tng. officer, team leader dive team Columbia County Sheriff's Office, Portage, Wis., 1998—; instr. hunter safety Wis. Dept. Natural Resources, Montello, Wis., 1996—2000. Mem.: Am. Assn. Cardopulmonary Rehab., Wis. Soc. Cardopulmonary Rehab. (coord. hons. gold games S.W. region). Avocations: scuba diving, skiing. Office: St Clare Hosp 707 14th St Baraboo WI 53913

**WITTY, CHRISTINE (CHRIS WITTY),** speed skater; b. West Allis, Wis., June 23, 1975; Student, Carroll Coll. Speed skater, 1985—. Mem. U.S. nat. team, 1988—. Recipient 1000 meter Silver medal Olympic Games, Nagano, Japan, 1998, 1500 meter Bronze medal, 1998; finished 2nd U.S. Olympic Team Trials, 2000. Achievements include U.S. flag bearer, Torino Olympic Winter Games, 2006. Avocations: cycling, movies, mountain biking. Home: PO Box 9694 Salt Lake City UT 84109-9694

**WITWER, SAMUEL WEILER, JR.,** lawyer; b. Chgo., Aug. 5, 1941; s. Samuel Weiler and Ethyl Loraine (Wilkins) W.; m. Susan P. Stewart, Sept. 18, 1971; children: Samuel Stewart, Michael Douglas. AB with honors, Dickinson Coll., 1963; JD, U. Mich., 1966. Bar: Ill. 1967, U.S. Dist. Ct. (no. dist.) Ill. 1967, U.S. Ct. Appeals (7th cir.) 1972, U.S. Supreme Ct. 1973, U.S. Ct. Appeals (6th cir.) 1985, U.S. Dist. Ct. (ea. dist.) Mich. 1987. Assoc. Witwer, Moran, Burlage & Atkinson, Chgo., 1967-74; ptnr. Witwer, Poltrock & Giampietro, 1974-2003, mem. Witwer and Waldron, LLC, 2003-; mem. Fed. Trial Bar Admissions Com. No. Dist. Ill., 1982-97. Governing mem. Chgo. Zool. Soc., 1986-90; trustee United Meth. Homes and Services, Chgo., 1974—, Dickinson Coll., Carlisle, Pa., 1976-97; mem. Cook County Home Rule Commn., Chgo., 1974-75; chmn. Agy. Appeals Com. Chgo., 1975-78; atty. Glenview Park Dist., 1982—; spl. asst. atty. gen. Auditor Gen. Ill., 1984-92. Mem. ABA, Meth. Bar Assn. (pres. 1972-73), Chgo. Bar Assn., Ill. Bar Assn., Law Club of Chgo., Sigma Chi, Phi Delta Phi. Republican. Methodist. Club: Union League. Home: 1330 Overlook Dr Glenview IL 60025-5166 Office: Witwer & Waldron LLC 1603 Orrington Ave Ste 2080 Evanston IL 60201 Office Phone: 847-332-2020. E-mail: witwer@wpglawyers.com.

**WITZEL, STEVEN M.,** lawyer; b. Chgo., Feb. 11, 1958; s. Howard B. and Sedelle K. Witzel; married. Adm. Dartmouth Coll., 1978; JD, Fordham U., 1983 Law clk. to Judge John M. Cannella U.S. Dist. Ct. (so. dist.) N.Y., N.Y.C., 1983—85; assoc. Cravath, Swaine & Moore, N.Y.C., 1985—89; asst. U.S. atty. So. Dist. N.Y., 1989—95; ptnr., assoc. gen. counsel PricewaterhouseCoopers LLP, N.Y.C., 1995—2005; ptnr. Fried Frank Harris Shriver & Jacobson LLP, N.Y.C., 2005—. Home: 164 Bank St PH A New York NY 10014 Office: Fried Frank Harris Shriver & Jacobson LLP One NY Plz New York NY 10004 Office Phone: 212-859-8592. Business E-Mail: steven.witzel@friedfrank.com.

**WITZIG, WARREN FRANK,** nuclear engineer, educator; b. Detroit, Mar. 26, 1921; s. Arthur Judson and Mary (Bender) W.; m. Bernadette Sullivan, Mar. 31, 1942; children: Eric, Leah, Marc, Lisa Witzig Davidson. BEE, Rensselaer Poly. Inst., 1942; MS, U. Pitts., 1944, PhD, 1952. Registered profl. engr., Pa., Wash. Rsch. engr. Westinghouse Research, Pitts., 1942-48; mgr. reactor physics, engr. Bettis Atomic, Pitts., 1948-60; co-founder, sr. v.p., dir. NUS Corp., Washington, 1960-67; head dept. nuclear engring. Pa. State U., 1967-87, emeritus, 1987—. Cons. nuclear engr. utilities industry; chmn. Pa. Gov.'s Com. on Atomic Energy Devel., 1970-80; mem. Saxton safety com., 1970-72; mem. waste com. Atomic Indsl. Forum, 1971-73; adv. com. Dept. Energy, 1980-82; mem. ops. rev. com. Tex. Utility; nuclear safety and compliance com., bd. dirs. GPU, 1983-92; mem. nuclear oversight com. PSE&G, 1983-91; mem. accrediting bd. Inst. Nuclear Power Ops., 1992-96; safety rev. bd. TVA, 1986-91; chmn. Westinghouse Nuclear Safety and Environ. Commn., 1988-93; chmn. safety audit bd. Centichem., 1989; safeguards com. Pa. State U., 1993—, interim dir. nuclear reactor, 1996-97. Designer S5W submarine reactor, 1956-60. Mem. bd. mgmt. YMCA, 1955-64. Fellow AAAS, Am. Nuc. Soc. (exec. com. edn. divsn., past chmn. nat. com. on public info., chmn. nuc. engring. dept. head com. 1980); mem. Am. Phys. Soc., IEEE (past chmn. nuc. engring. and plasma divsn.), Sigma Xi, Eta Kappa Nu, Pi Kappa Alpha, Sigma Pi Sigma (Power Engring. Educator spl. citation) Presbyterian (elder). Achievements include design of S5W submarine reactor; criticality engineer on Nautilus maiden voyage; developed continuing and long distance education in nuclear engineering. Home: 1900 Cliffside Dr Apt 309 State College PA 16801 Office: Pa State U Breazeale Nuclear Reactor University Park PA 16802-1408 E-mail: wfw1@psu.edu.

**WIVEL, NELSON AUBURN,** physician, medical researcher, educator; b. Denver, Sept. 4, 1935; s. Claude Burns and Aubrey (Angus) W.; m. Carol Henderson, June 16, 1963 (dec. 1999); children: Mark Auburn, Ashley Elizabeth. BS, Ea. N.Mex. U., 1957; MD, Stanford U., 1961. Diplomate Am. Bd. Pathology. Intern Cornell U., N.Y.C., 1961-62, asst. resident in medicine, 1962-63; asst. resident in pathology Stanford U., Calif., 1963-65; rsch. trainee in pathology Washington U., St. Louis, 1965-66; head ultrastructural studies sect. Nat. Cancer Inst., Bethesda, Md., 1966-70, head ultrastructural biology sect., 1970-86; med. officer for AIDS rsch. Gen. Clin. Rsch. Ctrs., NIH, Bethesda, 1986-89, dir. Office of Recombinant DNA Activities, 1989-96; dep. dir. Inst. Human Gene Therapy Sch. Medicine U. Pa., Phila., 1996—. Adj. prof. molecular and cellular engring., program chair ethics and pub. policy rsch. program U. Pa. Med. Ctr., Phila., 1996—; exec. dir. recombinant DNA adv. com. NIH. Assoc. editor Jour. Nat. Cancer Inst., 1968-70, Human Gene Therapy, 1993—, Jour. Biolaw and Bus., 1996—; Transplant Video Jour., 2002—, Pre Clinica 2003—; contbr. more than 100 articles to profl. jours. including Sci., Nature, Jour. of Virology, Virology. Recipient Commendation medal USPHS, 1990. Mem. Am. Soc. Cell Biology, Am. Soc. Virology, Am. Soc. Gene Therapy. Achievements include research on murine retroviruses that can function as moveable genetic elements (transposons). Office: U Pa Sch Med Inst Human Gene Therapy Translational Rsch Labs Ste 2000 125 S 31st St Philadelphia PA 19104-3403 Office Phone: 215-746-8939. Business E-Mail: naw@mail.med.upenn.edu.

**WIXOM, WILLIAM DAVID,** art historian, museum administrator, educator; b. Phila., July 17, 1929; s. Clinton Wood and Beatrice Rachel (Hunt) W.; m. Nancy Coe, Aug. 8, 1959; 3 children. BA, Haverford Coll., Pa., 1951; MA, Inst. Fine Arts NYU, 1963. Asst. curator to curator medieval and renaissance decorative arts Cleve. Mus. Art, 1958-78, chief curator early western art, 1979; chmn. dept. medieval art and The Cloisters Met. Mus. Art, N.Y.C., 1979-98, curator emeritus. Lectr. Barnes Found., Merion, Pa., 1951—52, curatorial cons. for medieval art, mem. curatorial adv. com., 2002—; adj. assoc. prof. history of art Case Western Res. U., Cleve., 1967—78, adj. prof., 1978, NYU, 1981—82; mem. adv. coun. Snite Mus. Art Notre Dame U., 1974—95. Author: Treasures from Medieval France, 1967, Renaissance Bronzes from Ohio Collections, 1975, Picturing the Apocalypse: illustrated Leaves from a Medieval Spanish Manuscript, 2002, A Glimpse at the Fountains of the Middle Ages, 2003, Medieval Sculptures at the Metropolitan, 800 to 1400, 2005; contbg. author The Royal Abbey of Saint Denis in the Time of Abbot suger, 1981, The Treasury of San Marco, 1985, Gothic and Renaissance Art in Nuremberg, 1986, Festschrift Gerhard Bott, 1987, Hommage a Hubert Landais, 1987, The Cloisters, Studies in Honor of the Fiftieth Anniversary, 1992, Festschrift Gerhard Schmidt, 1994, Enamels of Limoges 1100-1350, 1996, Studies in Honor of Kurt Weitzmann, 1995, The Dictionary of Art, 1996, The Glory of Byzantium, Art and Culture of the Middle Byzantine Era, AD-843-1261, 1997, Sculptures hors contexte, Louvre conférences et colloques, 1997, Mirror of the Medieval World, 1999, Romanesque Sculpture in American Collections, 1999, Tilman Riemenschneider, Master Sculptor of the Late Middle Ages, 1999; contbr. articles to profl. jours. Bd. dirs. Internat. Ctr. Medieval Art, N.Y.C., 1971-82, pres., 1971-74. Belgium-Am. Edn. Found. fellow, 1962; Nat. Endowment Arts grantee, 1973; fellow Pierpont Morgan Libr., 1979-2001; J. Paul Getty Mus. Guest Scholar, 1996. Fellow Soc. of Antiquaries of London; mem. Coll. Art Assn. (dir. 1979-83), Medieval Acad. Am., Internat. Ctr. Medieval Art. Mem. Soc. Of Friends. Office: Dept Medieval Art Met Mus Art New York NY 10028

**WIXON, HENRY N.,** lawyer; b. 1954; BS, Univ. Md., 1976, MS, 1980; JD, George Washington Univ., 1986. Bar: Md. 1986, DC 1989, US Patent & Trademark Office, US Supreme Ct. 1990. Ptnr., vice chmn. Intellectual Property dept. Wilmer Cutler Pickering Hale & Dorr, Washington. Mem.: Fed. Bar Assn. (past chmn. Comm. & IP Law sect., Patent, Trademark & Copyright com.), Am. Intellectual Property Law Assn. (charter mem. Biotechnology Practice com.), ABA, Md. Bar Assn. (mem. Com. on Representing Emerging Companies), DC Bar Assn., Biotechnology Ind. Assn. (mem. Intellectual Property Com.), Internat. Fedn. Advancement of Genetic Engring. & Biotechnology, No. Va. Biotechnology Council, Va. Biotechnology Assn. Office: Wilmer Cutler Pickering Hale & Dorr Willard Office Bldg 1455 Pennsylvania Ave NW Washington DC 20004 Office Fax: 202-942-8459, 202-942-8484. Business E-Mail: henry.wixon@wilmerhale.com.

**WIXTROM, DONALD JOSEPH,** translator; b. Republic, Mich., Oct. 14, 1928; s. Joseph Albert and Edith (Johnson) W.; m. Marilyn Jean Sjoquist, Oct. 14, 1961; children: Joe Alan, Lorna Jean, Aaron Matthew. Free lance translator, Republic, 1966—. Mem. Am. Translators Assn. Baptist. Home and Office: 6035 Dogwood Rd Republic MI 49879-9214

**WIZARD, BRIAN,** publisher, author; b. Newburyport, Mass., June 24, 1949; s. Russell and Ruth (Hidden) Willard. BA, Sonoma (Calif.) State U., 1976; D of Metaphysics, Universal Life Ch., 1997. Ordained to ministry Universal Life Ch., 1997. Pvt. practice as jeweler, sculptor and craftsman, Calif., 1974-79; Wallowa, Oreg., 1991—; prin. The Starquill Pub., Port Douglas, Queensland, Australia, 1981-86; owner Starquill Internat., Wallowa, Oreg. Author: (trilogy) The Will He Make it Saga (contender 1998 Pulitzer prize), Permission to Kill, 1985, Permission to Live, 1992 (Nobel Prize for lit. nominee 2000), Back in the World, 1995; (novels) Shindara, 1990, Heaven on Earth, 1998, Coming of Age, 1990, Pollution IV, 1993, Nigerian 419 Scam "Game Over!", 2000, Brazilian, Portuguese transl., 2005; (short stories) Tropical Pair, 1986, Metempsychosis, 1988 (In Search of) The Silver Lining, 1994, The Moon Whistling By on a Cloud, 1994, (The Princess of the) Wildflowers, 1995, Mushroom Magic, 1996, Vietnam 1999! Make Friends Not War, (novella) Beware of the Reload, 2003, Beware of Classified Ad Fraud, 2004, Psychology of Financial Terrorism, 2004, Beware of the 419 Employment Scam, 2005, Beware of the 419 Chat Scam, 2005, Space Egg, 2005; contbr. to Smithsonian Inst.'s The Vietnam War Generation, (audio version) Game Over!, 2002, combat helmet 2005—; contbr. to SpaceArc; prodr. (video documentary) Thunderhawks, 1987 (winner best documentary NY Ind. Film Festival 2005), Swift Action Newsteam, Tope Creek Lookout, 1995, Make Friends Not War: Return to Vietnam, 1999 (Aorence Vietnam Short Story winner); songwriter, prodr. (cassette) Brian Wizard Sings for His Supper, 1989 (cert. of achievement Billboard 1993); songwriter, singer, prodr. (I Don't Want) Permission to Kill, 1989, Busker's Theme Song, Living in North Queensland, Circus Act, Hitch Hiking Man, Self-Portrait, The Love We Share Will Never End, 1994, Never Met a Girl Like You, Folk-Rock Opera: A Cover Story: After That Ugly Saloon Incident; contbr. to America's Finest Songwriter and Lyricists CD, 1997, (novels, video and music) Brian Wizard's 20th Century Anthology, 1998 (nominee Nobel Prize in Lit. 2000), (video) Vietnam '99, (audio book) Nigerian 419 Scam Game Over, 2003, (opera) The Rocky Raccoon Folk Rock, 2004, Roadkill Stew, 2004; contbr. to TV documentaries History of the Machine Gun, 2000, Vietnam, The Personal Experience, 2001; contbr. (video documentary) Vietnam: Then and Again, 2005. Renovator hist. landmark The Tope Creek Lookout (Skyship); mem. Nat. Hist. Lookout Register; sponsor Adopt A Hwy., 1995; min. Universal Life Ch.; ambassador at large Africa Anti Fraud Alliance. With U.S. Army, 1967-70. Decorated Air medals (26), Aviator Flight Wings; recipient Cert. of Appreciation, Pres. Richard M. Nixon, Gold Book award, Mil. Writers Assn., Silver Book award, Am. Authors Assn., Best Documentary, NY Internat. Ind. Film Festival, Las Vegas, 2005. Mem. 145th Combat Aviation Bn. Assn., Vietnam Combat Vets. Assn., Vietnam Vets. Am., Vietnam Vets. Australia Assn., NRA (cert. handgun instr., 2002). Office: PO Box 42 Wallowa OR 97885-0042

**WIZDA, CHRISTINE ANNE,** history professor; b. Flemington, NJ, Sept. 21, 1977; d. Thomas Steven and Elaine Ann Wizda. BA, Rider U., 1999; MA, U. Houston, 2003, M in Applied Med. Anthropology, 2004, PhD, 2004—; Tutor Rider U., Lawrenceville, NJ, 1996—99; tchg. asst. U. Houston, 1999—2006. Named to The Chancellor's List, 2006; Murry Miller scholar, U. Houston, 2002, conf. grantee, 2003, scholar for field work in Belize, Office Internat. Studies, 2003. Mem.: Soc. Mil. History, Orgn. Am. Historians, Am. Hist. Assn., Phi Beta Delta, Phi Alpha Theta, Pi Gamma Mu. E-mail: cwizda@uh.edu.

**WIZWER, PHILLIP,** pharmacist, consultant; b. Holyoke, Mass., Apr. 2, 1943; s. Charles and Lillian Wizwer; m. Arlene Fiegleman, Aug. 16, 1969; children: Howard, Seth, Craig. BS, Mass. Coll. Pharmacy, 1966; MS, North Eastern U., 1968. Pharmacist Brigham Hosp., Boston, 1968—72; rsch. pharmacist Boston VA Hosp., 1972—75; pharmacist Mass. Coll. Pharmacy, Boston, 1975—. Coord. drug tng. for CNAs, Providence, 1999—2003; cons. in field. Trustee Temple Beth El, Lowell, Mass., 1998—2002; bd. dirs. Merimack Hebrew Acad., 1990—2000. Fellow: Am. Soc. Cons. Pharmacists (pres. (Mass. chpt.) 2005—); mem.: Am. Pharmacists Assn., Mass. Health Care Sys. Pharmacist, Mass. Pharmacists Assn. (bd. dirs. 1998—2006, pres. 2003—04, sec. 2005—06), Am. Soc. Aging, Am. Assn. Colls. Pharmacy. Office: Mass Coll Pharmacy 179 Longcrown Ave Boston MA 02115 Office Phone: 617-732-2972. Business E-Mail: pwizwer@mcphs.edu.

**WLADAWSKY-BERGER, IRVING,** communications executive; b. Cuba; MS in Physics, PhD in Physics, U. Chgo. Various managerial and professional positions, Thomas J. Watson Rsch. Ctr. IBM, Armonk, NY, 1970—84, v.p. computer sciences Thomas J. Watson Rsch. Ctr., 1984—85, various exec. positions large-systems develop. org., 1985—91, gen. mgr. POWER Parallel Systems Armonk, NY, 1991—95, gen. mgr. internet divsn. Somers, NY, 1995—99, v.p. tech. and strategy, 2000—. Mem. commn. on physical sciences, mathematics, and resources Nat. Rsch. Coun., 1984—87, founding mem. computer sciences and telecommunications bd.; mem. U. Chgo. bd. governors Argonne Nat. Laboratories; mem. technol. advisory coun. BP Internat.; co-chair President's Information Technol. Advisory Com., 1999—. Named one of 50 Most Important Hispanics in Tech., Bus., Hispanic Engineer and Info. Tech. mag., 2005; recipient Hispanic Engineer of the Year, 2001; fellow, Am. Academy of Arts and Sciences. Office: IBM Rte 100 Somers NY 10589*

**WLASCHIN, KEN,** cultural organization administrator, writer; b. Bradish, Nebr., July 12, 1934; s. Bernard A. and Lucy M. (Stevens) W.; m. Maureen N. Kennedy Martin, Mar. 22, 1961; 1 child, Scott Martin. BA, Dartmouth Coll., 1956; MA, U. Coll., Dublin, Ireland, 1957; postgrad., U. Poitiers, France, 1960. Program dir. Nat. Film Theater, London, 1969-83, London Film Festival, 1970-83; artistic dir. LA Film Expn., 1984-86; dir. exhbn. Am. Film Inst., LA, 1986-97, dir. creative affairs and preservation, 1998—. Theater critic Rome Daily Am. & Daily Sketch, Rome and London, 1962-67; art critic Art Voices Mag., Rome, 1962-68; film critic Films and Filming Mag., London, 1973-82; story editor London Weekend TV, 1968. Author: (TV play) Ticket to Trieste, 1961, (novel), The Italian Job, 1964, Rome A City, 1964, Guide to Cinema, 1970, Encyclopedia of Movie Stars, 1979, Faber Book of Movie Verse, 1994, Opera on Screen, 1997, Gian Carlo Menotti on Screen, 1999, Encyclopedia of Opera on screen, 2004, Encyclopedia of American Opera, 2005. With US Army, 1958-61, ETO. Mem. Brit. Film Inst., Brit. Film Acad. Avocation: opera. Home: 1050 E Ramon Rd #35 Palm Springs CA 92264 Office: Am Film Inst 2021 N Western Ave Los Angeles CA 90027-1625 Office Phone: 323-856-7708. Business E-Mail: kwlaschin@afi.com.

**WLEUGEL, JOHN PETER,** manufacturing executive; b. Hoyanger, Sogn, Norway, July 1, 1929; s. Johan and Helga (Faye) W.; m. Leonor Abaroa, Dec. 1959; children— Jan Andrew, Cecilia Maria. BA, U. Copenhagen, 1953; MBA, U. Toronto, 1957. With Belgium Machine Tool Assn., 1953-54, Massey-Ferguson Ltd., Toronto, 1954-71, treas., 1968-71; sr. v.p. Bata Ltd., Toronto; dir., officer several subsidiaries (Bata Shoe Orgn.), Don Mills, Ont., Canada, 1972-89; prof., exec. in-residence, internat. adv. bd. Schulich Sch. Bus., York U., North York, Canada, 1990—. Mem. Financial Execs. Inst., Univ. Club (Toronto). Home: 5 Campbell Crescent Toronto ON Canada M2P 1P1 Office: Schulich Sch Bus York U 4700 Keele St Toronto ON Canada M3J 1P3

**WLODARSKI, DAVID,** theater educator, director; s. Elvia Jordan and Franczisek Wlodarski; m. Michelle Olsen, Dec. 29, 2002. BS, Northeastern U., Boston, 1988; MFA, U. Idaho, 1997. Lectr. in stage technical mgmt. Hong Kong Acad. for the Performing Arts, 1998—2002; vis. asst. prof., theatre designer U. of Tex., El Paso; vis. asst. prof.; theatre tech. dir. Okla. State U., Stillwater, 2003—04; instr., theatre tech. dir. Western Ky. U., Bowling Green, 2004—05; asst. prof., theatre tech. dir. La. State U., Alexandria, 2005—06. Designer, tech. dir. (performance) Romeo & Juliet, designer (performance, exhibiton, publ.) Triumph of Love (Included in 2005 World Stage Design Catalog, 2005); contbr. exhibition; lighting designer (perfromance) Females Seeking (KC/ACTF Meritorious Achievement award for Lighting Design, 1997), set designer School for Scandal (KC/ACTF Meritorious Achievement award for Set Design, 1997), tech. dir. (performance) Top Girls (KC/ACTF Nat. Meritorious Prodn. award, 1996). Race participant The Matilda Bazaar & Sedan Chair Race Charities Fund, Hong Kong, 1999—2001. Mem.: U.S. Inst. Theatre Tech. Avocations: travel, hiking, dragon boat racing, woodworking.

**WLODAWER, ALEXANDER,** medical researcher; b. Poland; PhD, UCLA, 1974; Doctor Honoris Causa, Tech. U., Lodz, Poland, 2004. Postdoctoral training Stanford U.; joined Nat. Bur. Standards, 1976, ABL Basic Rsch. Program, Nat. Cancer Inst., Frederick, Md., 1987; chief Macromolecular Crystallography Lab. Nat. Cancer Rsch., Frederick, Md., 1999—, also head Protein Structure Sect. Vis. fellow Sidney Sussex Coll., U. Cambridge, 1998—99; adj. prof. biochemistry and molecular biology George Washington U., assoc. mem. Inst. Biomedical Sciences; mem. editl. bd. Jour. Biol. Chemistry, Protein Sci., Acta Biochimica Polonica. Mem.: Polish Acad. Sciences (fgn. mem.), Protein Soc., Am. Crystallographic Assn. Office: Macromolecular Crystallography Lab NCI Frederick Bldg 536 Rm 5 PO Box B Frederick MD 21702-1201 Office Phone: 301-846-5036. Office Fax: 301-846-6322. E-mail: wlodawer@ncifcrf.gov.

**WOBUS, REINHARD ARTHUR,** geologist, educator; b. Norfolk, Va., Jan. 11, 1941; s. Reinhard Schaffter and Oral (Phares) W.; m. Sheridan Whitcher, Mar. 18, 1967; children: Erik Reinhard, Cameron Wright. BA, Washington U., St. Louis, 1962; MA, Harvard U., 1963; PhD, Stanford U., 1966. Asst. prof. geology Williams Coll., Williamstown, Mass., 1966-72, assoc. prof., 1972-78, prof., 1978-85, Edna McConnell Clark prof. geology, 1985—, dept. chmn., 1988-96. Geologist U.S. Geol. Survey, Denver, 1967-86; vis. prof. Colo. Coll., Colorado Springs, 1976, 82-83, Colo. State U., Ft. Collins, summers 1977-84; bd. dirs. Colo. Outdoor Edn. Ctr., Florissant, Williamstown Rural Lands Found.; co-founder Keck Twelve-Coll. Geol. Consortium, mem. governing bd., 1986—, exec. com., 2005—. Contbr. maps and articles on Precambrian geology of So. Rocky Mountains to profl. jours. Danforth fellow, 1962, Woodrow Wilson fellow, 1962, NSF fellow, 1962-66. Fellow Geol. Soc. Am.; mem. Am. Geophys. Union, Nat. Assn. Geosci. Tchrs., Coun. on Undergrad. Rsch., Colo. Sci. Soc., Mineral Soc. Am., Phi Beta Kappa, Sigma Xi. Current work includes petrology and geochronology of Precambrian igneous and metamorphic rocks and mid-Tertiary volcanic rocks, so. Rocky Mountains, Silurian volcanic rocks, coastal Maine. Home: 20 Grandview Dr Williamstown MA 01267-2528 Office: Williams Coll Dept Geoscis Williamstown MA 01267 Office Phone: 413-597-2470. Business E-Mail: rwobus@williams.edu.

**WODICZKO, KRZYSZTOF,** artist, architect, educator; b. Warsaw, 1943; arrived in Can., 1977, arrived in US, 1991; MFA, Acad. Fine Arts, Warsaw, Poland, 1968. Designer Polish Optical Works; asst. prof. intermedia and photography Nova Scotia Coll. Art and Design, 1980—81; asst. prof. photography U. Hartford, 1988—89, Calif. Inst. Tech., 1991; prof. sculpture Ecole Nationale Superieure des Beaux Arts, France, 1991—95; joined faculty MIT, Cambridge, 1991, prof. visual art, 1997—, dir. Ctr. Advanced Visual Studies (CAVS), 1994—96, 2003—, dir. Interrogative Design Group, 1994—. Adj. prof. Warsaw Poly. Inst., 1970—75; vis. prof. design and mixed media Nova Scotia Coll. Art and Design, 1977—79; adj. prof. indsl. design Ont. Coll. Art, 1979; vis. prof. photography and studio art Calif. Inst. Arts, 1988; guest prof. sculpture Cooper Union Sch. Art, 1987, 89. One-man shows include Foksal Gallery, Warsaw, 1973, 1974, 1975, 1976, 1977, Hal Broom Gallery, NYC, 1977, 1978, 1980, 1984, 49th Paralle, 1986, Clocktower, 1988, Hirschhorn Mus., Washington, 1988, Galerie Gabrielle Maubrie, Paris, 1989, 1992, 1996, Exit Art, NYC, 1989—90, Josh Baer Gallery, 1991, Galerie Lelong, 1996, Hiroshima City Contemporary Art Mus., 1999, Zacheta Nat. Gallery Contemporary Art, Warsaw, Poland, (in preparation), 2006, others, exhibited in group shows at Edinburgh Festival, 1988, Wiener Festwochen, 1988, Whitney Mus., 1989, Ctr. Georges Pompidou, Paris, 1989, 1996—97, The Israel Mus., Jerusalem, 1990, Mus. Modern Art, San Francisco, 1991, Mus. d'Art Contemporain, Montreal, 1992, Mus. Fine Arts, Boston, 1993—94, Kunstmus., Bonn, Germany, 1994, Setagaya Mus. Art, Tokyo, 1995, Sonje Mus. Contemporary Art, Seoul, 1996, Louisiana Mus., Denmark, 1996, Nat. Mus. Modern Art, Kyoto, Japan, 1996, Uchwtz (The Handle), Museum Sztuki, Lodz, Poland, 1999, Venice Architectural Biennale, 2000, Whitney Biennale, Whitney Mus. Art, NYC, 2000, The Generali Found., Vienna, 2002, Internat. Ctr. Photography, NYC, 2003, Mass. Mus. Contemporary Art, 2004, Basque Mus. Contemporary Art, Spain, 2004, others, projections, The Bunker Hill Monument, Boston, 1998, The A-bomb Dome, Hiroshima, 1999, El Centro Cultural, Tijuana, Mex., 2001, The Central Library, St. Louis, 2004, Barcelona, 2005, others, instrumentations, Dis-Armor, 1999—, Aegis, 2000—, others; Commd. (with Julian Bonder) to design a Meml. to the Abolition of Slavery, City of Nantes, France, 2004—; author: Critical Vehicles: Writings, Projects, Interviews, 1999. Recipient Hiroshima Art Prize, 1998, Kepes Art Prize, Coun. for Arts, MIT, 2004, Artist Award for Disting. Body of Work, Coll. Art Assn., 2004. Office: MIT Ctr Advanced Visual Studies 265 Massachusetts Ave N51-315H Cambridge MA 02139*

**WODNICKI, ADAM JULIUSZ,** pianist, educator; s. Bronislaw Wodnicki and Malwina Wodnicka; m. Marta Janina Hoffman-Wodnicka, Nov. 15, 1973; children: Maya Andrea Wodnicka, Natalia Eva Wodnicka. MusM, Acad. of Music, Cracow, Poland, 1974. Faculty mem. Acad. of Music, Cracow, Poland, 1973—77; asst. prof. U. of Tex. at Austin, 1979—80; prof. of piano U. of North Tex. Coll. of Music, 1980—. Artistic co-dir. Internat. Piano Masterclasses, Varna, Bulgaria, 2000—; mem. bd. of artistic advisors Internat. Piano Festival and Course, Aveiro, Portugal, 2001—04. Performance editor (music score) I.J.Paderewski: Complete Works; performer: (albums) CDCM Computer Music Series, vol.1, Computer Music Compositions, K. Szymanowski: 12 Studies op.33, R. Muczynski: Piano Trios, I.J.Paderewski: Piano works, vol.1, I.J.Paderewski: Piano works, vol.2, D.Dzubay, R.Muczynski, D, Shostakovich:Sonatas for Cello and Piano, CDCM Computer Music Series, vol.27, J.Schwantner:and the Mountains Rising Nowhere, CDCM Computer Music Series, vol.14, Computer Music Currents 8. Recipient 3 prizes, VIII Festival of Polish Pianists, 1974, nat. competition prize, Chopin Soc., Warsaw, Poland, 1969—71, Worldwide Steinway Artists Roster, Steinway&Sons, NY, 1997—; Touring Artists Roster, Tex. Commn. on the Arts, 1996—. Mem.: Music Teachers Nat. Assn., Am. Liszt Soc. Office: Univ of North Tex Coll of Mus PO Box 311367 Denton TX 76203-1367 Office Phone: 940-565-3715. Personal E-mail: mnawod@juno.com.

**WOEHLER, JOEL LEE,** real estate asset manager; BA in Fin., U. No. Iowa, Cedar Falls, 1997; MBA, Drake U., Des Moines, Iowa, 2001. Cert. comml. investment mem. CCIM Inst., 1999. Asset mgr. AmerUs Capital Mgmt., Des Moines 1997—2001, Prinicpal Global Investors, Des Moines, 2001—04; sr. asset mgr. Prin. Global Investors, Des Moines, 2004—. Mem.: Beta Gamma Sigma. Avocations: running, weightlifting. Office: Principal Global Investors 801 Grand Ave Des Moines IA 50392 Office Phone: 515-248-0518.

**WOEHR, ANDREAS,** physics professor; b. Stuttgart, Baden-Wuerttemberg, Germany, Apr. 17, 1960; s. Peter Wolfgang Alexander and Anneliese Margarete Woehr. M in Physics, U. Stuttgart, 1986; Dr. rerum Naturalium, Johannes Gutenberg U., Mainz, Germany, 1992; cert. in med. physics, U. Kaiserlautern, Germany, 1999. Wissenschaftlicher angestellter Johannes Gutenberg U., Mainz; postdoctoral fellow Katholieke U., Leuven, Belgium, 1995—97; rsch. asst. Oxford U., England, 1998—2000; rsch. assoc. U. Md., College Park, 2001—03; rsch. asst. prof. U. Notre Dame, Ind., 2003—. Office: University of Notre Dame 225 Nieuwland Science Hall Notre Dame IN 46556 Office Phone: 574-631-9921. Office Fax: 574-631-9921. Business E-Mail: awoehr@nd.edu.

**WOELFEL, JAMES WARREN,** philosophy and humanities educator; b. Galveston, Tex., Aug. 16, 1937; s. Warren Charles and Mary Frances (Washinka) W.; m. Sarah Chappell Trulove, Nov. 24, 1982; children by previous marriages: Skye Caitlin, Allegra Eve, Sarah Judith; stepchildren: Ann Marie and Paul Trulove. BA, U. Okla., 1959; MDiv, Episcopal Div. Sch., Cambridge, Mass., 1962; MA, Yale U., 1964; PhD, U. St. Andrews, Scotland, 1967. Asst. prof. philosophy and religion U. Kans., Lawrence, 1966-70, asst. prof. philosophy, 1970-71, assoc. prof. philosophy and religion, 1971-75, prof. philosophy and religious studies, 1975-88, prof. philosophy, 1988—, acting chmn. dept. religious studies, 1983-84, dir. Humanities and Western civilization program, 1985—. Manuscript reader for various presses, jours. Author: Bonhoeffer's Theology, 1970, Borderland Christianity, 1973, Camus: A Theological Perspective (republished as Albert Camus on the Sacred and the Secular, 1987), 1975, Augustinian Humanism, 1979, The Agnostic Spirit as a Common Motif in Liberal Theology and Liberal Scepticism, 1990, Portraits in Victorian Religious Thought, 1997; co-editor (with Sarah Chappell Trulove): Patterns in Western Civilization, 1991, 3rd edit., 2002; contbr. essays, revs. to profl. jours.; contbr. articles to profl. jours.; author: The Existentialist on Legacy and Other Essays on Philosophy and Religion, 2006. Danforth grad. fellow Episcopal Div. Sch., Cambridge, Mass., 1959-62, U. St. Andrews, 1962-63, 65-66, Yale U., New Haven, 1963-65; Fulbright scholar U. St. Andrews, 1962-63, Pub. Scholar award Kans. Humanities Coun., 1997; grantee NEH, Exxon Found., Mellon Found., Menninger Found., Inst. for Ecumenical and Cultural Rsch. Mem. Am. Philos. Assn., Assn. for Core Texts and Courses, Phi Beta Kappa. Democrat. Avocations: piano, walking. Home: 808 Alabama St Lawrence KS 66044-3942 Office: U Kans Humanities & Western Civilization Program Bailey Hall 1440 Jayhawk Blvd Rm 308 Lawrence KS 66045-7574 Office Phone: 785-864-3011. E-mail: woelfel@ku.edu.

**WOERNER, ROBERT EUGENE,** editor, writer; b. Cadillac, Mich., Sept. 23, 1947; s. William Reginald and Ellen Hazel (Van Zoeren) W. BA in English with high honor, Grand Valley State U., 1969. Logistics coord. Colo. Outward Bound, 1979-80; writer, editor Bur. of Land Mgmt., U.S. Dept. Interior, Grand Junction, Colo., 1977-78, Elko, Nev., 1980-82, Craig, Colo., 1982-84, Denver, 1984—2006. Free-lance writer, Buena Vista, Colo., 1976-77; mem. computer tech. adv. bd. Warren Tech, Golden, Colo., 1994-97. Newsletter editor Outward Bound, Denver, 1989-95; author book rev.; contbr. articles to profl. jours. including Jour. of Forestry, Govt. Exec. Vol. Craig Hosp., Englewood, Colo., 1994. Capt. USAF, 1970-76. Honors scholar Grand Valley State U., 1966-69; recipient 4 STAR awards Bur. of Land Mgmt., 1999-2002, cert. Excellence in Accountability Reporting Assn. Govt. Accts. U.S. Dept of Interior, 2001. Mem.: So. Utah Wilderness Alliance, Sister Cities Internat., Japan Am. Soc. Colo. Avocations: hiking, astronomy, travel, reading, music. Office: Bur Land Mgmt PO Box 25047 Denver CO 80225-0047

**WOERTH, DUANE E.,** labor union administrator; b. Scribner, Nebr. BS, U. Nebr.; MA, U. Okla. First v.p. Air Line Pilots Assn., Herndon, Va., 1990—98, pres., 1998—. Former dir. Internat. Fedn. Air Line Pilots Assn., chmn. indsl. com.; former mem. bd. dirs. N.W. Airlines, 1993—98. Lt. col. USAF. Office: ALPA PO Box 1169 Herndon VA 20172

**WOERTZ, PATRICIA ANN,** agricultural company executive, retired oil company executive; b. Pitts., Mar. 17, 1953; married; 3 children. BS in Acctg., Pa. State U., 1974; grad. Internat. Exec. Devel. Program, Columbia U., 1994. Acct. Ernst & Young, Pitts., 1974—77 with Gulf Oil Corp., Pitts., 1977-81, Houston, 1981-85; with debt. reduction process, merger of Gulf and Chevron, 1985-87; fin. mgr. Chevron Info. Tech. Co., 1989-91, strategic planning mgr., 1991-93; pres. Chevron Can. Ltd., Vancouver, B.C., 1993-96, Chevron Internat. Oil Co., 1996-98; v.p. logistics and trading Chevron Products Co., Chevron Corp., 1996-98, v.p., 1998—2001; pres. Chevron Products Co., 1998—2001; exec. v.p. Global Downstream ChevronTexaco

Corp, San Francisco, 2001—06; pres., CEO Archer Daniels Midland Co., Decatur, Ill., 2006—. Bd. dirs. Archer Daniels Midland Co., 2006—. Bd. trustees U. San Diego; bd. visitors Pa. State U. Named a Disting. Alumna, Pa. State U., 2005; named one of Most Powerful Women in Bus., Fortune mag., 2005, 100 Most Powerful Women, Forbes Mag., 2006; recipient Alumni Fellow award, 2002. Mem.: Calif. C. of C. (bd. mem. 1999—), Am. Petroleum Inst. (bd. dirs.). Office: Archer Daniels Midland Co 4666 Faries Pkwy Decatur IL 62526*

**WOESE, CARL R.,** biophysicist, microbiology educator; b. Syracuse, N.Y., July 15, 1928; AB in Math. and Physics, Amherst Coll., 1950, DSc (hon.), 1985; PhD in Biophysics, Yale U., 1953; postgrad., U. Rochester, 1953-55; DSc (hon.), Syracuse U., 1994. Rsch. assoc. biophysics Yale U., New Haven, 1955-60; Biophysicist GE Rsch. Lab., 1960-63; prof. microbiology U. Ill., Urbana, 1964—. Stanley O. Ikenberry Endowed chair U. Ill., 1996. Contbr. articles to profl. jours. Recipient Bergey award Bergey's Manual Trust, 1983, John D. and Catherine T. MacArthur award, 1984, Leeuwenhoek medal 1990, 1992, 23d Brown-Hazen Lctrs. award, 1992, Roger W. Stanier Meml. Lctr. award U. Calif., Berkeley, 1993, Nat. Medal Sci., 2000, Crafoord prize, 2003; Univ. Sr. scholar U. Ill., 1986. Fellow Explorer's Club, Indian NAS, Am. Acad. Arts and Scis., Am. Acad. Microbiology; mem. Deutsche Gesellschaft fur Hygiene und Mikrobiologie (corr.), Deutsche Akademie Der Naturforscher Leopoldina, Bayerische Akademie der Wissenschaften (corr.), Max-Planck Soc., NAS (Selman A. Waksman award 1997), Ctr. Advanced Study U. Ill. Office: U Ill Chem & Life Scis Lab 131 Burrill Hall 601 S Goodwin Ave Urbana IL 61801-3709

**WOESTENDIEK, JOHN, JR., (WILLIAM JOHN WOESTENDIEK),** newspaper reporter; b. Winston-Salem, N.C., Sept. 5, 1953; s. William John Sr. and Josephine (Pugh) W.; 1 child, Joseph Yoon Tae. BJ, U. N.C., 1975. Reporter Ariz. Daily Star, Tucson, 1975-78; reporter, asst. city editor, city editor Lexington (Ky.) Herald-Leader, 1978-81; reporter Phila. Inquirer, 1981-90, nat. corr. West Coast bur. Newport Beach, Calif., 1990-93, reporter, 1994-96, columnist, 1996-2000; enterprise editor Charlotte (N.C.) Observer, 2000-01; reporter Baltimore Sun, 2001—. Recipient Paul Tobenkin Meml. award Columbia U., 1984, Nat. Headliners award Press Club Atlantic City, 1987, Pulitzer Prize for Investigative Reporting Columbia U., 1987, Ernie Pyle award, 1994, Best Feature Story award Ky. Press. Assn., 1978, Best Investigative Story award Ky. Press Assn., 1979, Nat. Arc of Excellence Nat. Assn. Retarded Citizens, 1984, Best News Reporting First Place award AP Mng. Editors Pa., 1985, Sigma Delta Chi award for Feature Writing, 1994, Best Feature Story award Chesapeake Associated Press, 2004; John S. Knight fellow Stanford U., 1988-89; named to N.C. Journalism Hall of Fame, 2003.

**WOETZEL, KURT D.,** banking executive; With Adolph Coors Co., 1978—84; joined The Bank of NY Co., Inc., 1985, now exec. v.p., chief info. officer. Named Leader in Fin., CNBC Tech. Leadership Awards, 2005; named one of Premier 100 IT Leaders, Computerworld, 2005. Office: The Bank of NY Co Inc One Wall St NY 10286 Office Phone: 212-495-1784. Office Fax: 212-809-9528. E-mail: kwoetzel@bankofny.com.*

**WOFFORD, CHLOE ANTHONY See MORRISON, TONI**

**WOFFORD, HARRIS,** senator, lawyer; b. N.Y.C., Apr. 9, 1926; s. Harris Llewellyn and Estelle (Gardner) W.; m. Emmy Lou Clare Lindgren, Aug. 14, 1948 (dec. Jan. 1996); children: Susanne, Daniel, David. BA, U. Chgo., 1948; study fellow, India, 1949, Israel, 1950; LLB, Yale U., 1954, Howard U., 1954. Bar: D.C. 1954, U.S. Supreme Ct. 1958, Pa. 1978. Asst. to Chester Bowles, 1953-54; law assoc. Covington & Burling, Washington, 1954-58; legal asst. to Rev. Theodore Hesburgh, Commn. on Civil Rights, 1958-59; assoc. prof. Notre Dame Law Sch., 1959-60, on leave, 1961-66; asst. to Senator Kennedy, 1960; spl. asst. to Pres. Kennedy, 1961-62; spl. rep. for Africa, dir. Ethiopian program U.S. Peace Corps, 1962-64; assoc. dir. Peace Corps, Washington, 1964-66; pres. Coll. at Old Westbury, SUNY, 1966-70, Bryn Mawr (Pa.) Coll., 1970-78; counsel firm Schnader, Harrison, Segal and Lewis, Phila., 1979-86; chmn. Pa. Dem. State Com., 1986; sec. labor and industry Commonwealth of Pa., 1987-91; U.S. senator from Pa., 1991-95; CEO Corp. Nat. Svc., Washington, 1995—2001; co-chair America's Promise: The Alliance for Youth, Alexandria, Va., 2001—04. Vis. lectr. Howard Law Sch. 1956; prof. of practice U. Md., 2003—. Author: It's Up to Us, 1946, (with Clare Wofford) India Afire, 1951, Of Kennedys and Kings, 1980; editor: Embers of the World, 1970; co-editor: Report of the U.S. Commission on Civil Rights, 1959. Mem. Coun. Fgn. Rels., 1968—; co-chmn. Com. for Study of Nat. Svc., 1977-80; mem. U.S. Adv. Com. on Nat. Growth Policy Processes, 1975-76; trustee The Am. Coll., Bryn Mawr, 1975-83; mem. coun. U.S.-South Africa Leader Exch. Program, 1971-87; bd. dirs. Internat. League for Human Rights, 1979-87, pres., 1980-81; bd. dirs. After-Sch. All-Stars, Campus Compact, Points of Light Found., Youth Svc. Am.; trustee Martin Luther King Ctr. for Nonviolent Social Change, 1983-87; governing coun. Wilderness Soc., 1983-87. With USAF, 1944-45. Mem.: ABA. Democrat. Roman Catholic. Home: 955 26th St NW Apt 501 Washington DC 20037-2040 E-mail: hlwofford@aol.com.

**WOFFORD, MILTON RUSSELL, JR.,** lawyer; b. Ft. Bragg, NC, Jan. 23, 1961; s. Milton Russell and Lucy Lynn Wofford; m. Dori Yvette Smith, Sept. 1991; children: Milton Russell III, Edward Smith, Richard Van. BA, Princeton U., 1983; MPhil, U. Glasgow, Scotland, 1988; JD, U. Chgo., 1991. Bar: Calif. 1991, Ga. 1996. Ms Cutchen, Doyle, San Francisco, 1991—95, Alston & Bird, Atlanta, 1995—2005; ptnr. Kilpatrick Stockton, Atlanta, 2005—. Contbr. articles to profl. jours. Sr. warden All Saints Episc. Ch., Atlanta, 2004—05, chmn. fin. com., 2005—; mem. ethics bd. Fulton County, Atlanta, 2001—03. Lt. U.S. Army, 1983—87. Mem.: ABA (vice chmn. com. antitrust sect. 2003—), Ga. Bar Assn. bd. antitrust sect. 2005—), Atlanta Young Lawyers (scholar). Episc. Office: Kilpatrick Stockton 1100 Peachtree St Atlanta GA 30309

**WOGAMAN, GEORGE ELSWORTH,** insurance company executive, financial consultant; b. Mikado, Mich., May 29, 1937; s. Edgar R. and Leah Katherine (McGuire) W.; m. Sandra Lee Jensen, Apr. 10, 1965; children: Jennifer, Christopher. Grad. various ins. courses. CLU, registered rep.; cert. ChFc. With Blair Transit Co., Dun & Bradstreet, Chrysler Engring. Co., 1955-61; exec. chief Westward Ho!, 1961-68; owner, mgr. George Wogaman Ins. Agy., Grand Forks, N.D., 1969—. Mem. pres. coun. Farmers Ins. Group, 1988—98, 1999—2003; alderman East Grand Forks (Minn.) City Coun., 1979—2000, v.p., 1982—2006. Corp. mem. Altru Health Sys., Grand Forks, 1982—; mem. Nat. Rep. Congl. Com., Rep. Presdl. Task Force; mem. Red River Valley Estate Planning Coun.; mem. Wesley United Meth. Ch., Grand Forks. Recipient Pub. Svc. award East Grand Forks City Coun., 1979. Mem. Am. Soc. CLU's, North Valley Life Underwriters Assn. (Life Underwriter of Yr. 1988), Farmers Ins. Group Pres.'s Coun., Famers Financial Solutions, 2001–. Home: 1818 19 h St NW East Grand Forks MN 56721-1013 Office: 2612 Gateway Dr Grand Forks ND 58203-1406 Office Phone: 701-772-7108. Business E-mail: gwogaman@farmersagent.com.

**WOHL, FRANK HAROLD,** lawyer; b. Richmond, Va., June 5, 1942; AB, Dartmouth Coll., 1963; JD, U. Chgo. Law, 1966. Bar: NY 1967. Asst. U.S. atty. So. Dist. NY, NYC, 1971—79; ptnr. Rosenman & Colin, NYC, 1979—84, Lankler Siffert & Wohl, LLP, NYC, 1984—. Chair NYC Civilian Complaint Rev. Bd., 1999—2002. Fed. RICO arbitrator. Fulton Fish Market, NYC, 1988—92; dir. Broodwood Child Care, Bklyn., 1992—99. Lt. comdr. JAGC USNR, 1967—71. Fellow: Am. Coll. Trial Lawyers (Access to Justice award 2004—); mem.: Fed. Bar Coun. (trustee 2004—), NY Coun. Def. Lawyers (bd. mem. 1998—2002), Fed. Bar Found. (dir. 1994—2002), Bar Assn. City of NY. Office: Lankler Siffert & Wohl LLP 500 Fifth Ave New York NY 10110-3398 Office Phone: 212-921-8399.

**WOHLBERG, BRENDT,** electrical engineer, researcher; b. Pietermaritzburg, South Africa, Jan. 22, 1969; s. Rolf and Lorna Wohlberg; m. Alison Sawyer; children: Olivia, Alexander. MSc in Applied Sci., U. Cape Town,

South Africa, 1993, PhD, 1996. Postdoctoral rschr. elec. engring. dept. U. Cape Town, 1997—98; postdoctoral rschr. Ctr. Nonlinear Studies Los Alamos Nat. Lab., 1999—2002, tech. staff mem. T-7 Math. Modeling and Analysis, 2002—. Contbr. articles to profl. jours. Office: Los Alamos Nat Lab T7 MS B284 Los Alamos NM 87545 Office Phone: 505-667-6886.

**WOHLEBER, LYNNE FARR,** archivist, librarian; b. Pitts., Mar. 16, 1939; d. Donald Elmer and Helen Rose (Lula) F.; m. David Louis Wohleber, Oct. 14, 1972 (div. Sept. 1989); 1 child, Jeffrey David. AB, Allegheny U., 1961; MLS, U. Pitts., 1991. Sec. comm. Aluminum Co. Am., Pitts., 1968—73; shop mgr. The Thread Shed, Pitts., 1986—90; libr. Coun. Am. Embroiderer's Libr., Carnegie, Pa., 1985—93; archivist Episcopal Diocese Pitts., 1989—. Cons. Calvary Episcopal Ch. Archives, Pitts., 1992—93, Bapt. Home Libr., Mt. Lebanon, Pa., 1994, First United Meth. Ch. Archives, Pitts., 1995, Episcopal Diocese of Albany, 2000; archival cons. Christ Ch., New Brighton, 2001, Old St. Luke's, Scott Twp., 2002, Grace Ch., Pitts., 2005; bldg. archives workshop instr., 1995, 2000—; presenter in field. Libr. com., bd. deacons, rec. sec. Bower Hill Cmty. Ch., 1999-99, nominating com. 1998-99, elder, 2003-06; contemporary svc. task force, 2002-04; coord. presch. program Am. Lung Assn., Pitts., 1977-87; capt., ward chair Am. Cancer Soc., Pitts., 1978-84; newsletter editor Mendelssohn Choir of Pitts., 1973-87; den leader Boy Scouts Am., Mt. Lebanon, Pa., 1983-84. Mem. Soc. Am. Archivists (planning com. 1999 Pitts. conf.), Mid-Atlantic Regional Archives Conf. (co-chair spl. events 1992, publs. com. 1996-2001, panelist 1999 spring conf., conf. local arrangements publicity com. 2003—04), Nat. Episcopal Historians and Archivists (Pitts. coord. for 1997 Episcopal Tri-History Conf., bd. dirs. 1996-2004, treas. 1999-2004, membership sect. 2005—), Hist. Soc. Episcopal Ch., Curators, Archivists and Record Profls. We. Pa. (co-chair Archives Week 1999 com.), Women's Episcopal History Project, Episcopal Archivists Network, Beta Phi Mu. Republican. Presbyterian and Episcopalian. Home: 110 Skylark Cir Pittsburgh PA 15234-1018 Office: Episcopal Diocese of Pitts 900 Oliver Bldg 535 Smithfield St Pittsburgh PA 15222-2403 Office Phone: 412-325-0087 ext. 138. Business E-mail: wohleber@pgh.anglican.org.

**WOHLEBER, ROBERT MICHAEL,** oil industry executive; b. Pitts., Feb. 15, 1951; s. Richard James Jr. and Mary (Gremer) W.; m. Jean Linda Joseph, Nov. 9, 1974; children: Taylor, Robin, Joseph, Charles. BBA, U. Notre Dame, 1973; MBA, U. Pitts., 1978. Investment officer Mellon Bank, Pitts., 1974-78; treasury rep. Copperweld Corp., Pitts., 1978-80, mgr. treasury svcs., 1980-82, asst. treas., 1982-86; dir. corp. fin. Freeport-McMoRan, Inc., New Orleans, 1986-87, asst. treas., 1987-89, treas., 1989-92, v.p., treas., 1992—94, v.p., exec. project mgr., 1994—96, sr. v.p., CFO, 1996, exec. v.p., CFO, dir., McMoRan Exploration Co., pres., CEO, Freeport-McMoRan Sulphur, 1997—99; sr. v.p., CFO Kerr-McGee Corp., 1999—. Guest lectr. Stetson U., Deland, Fla., 1983. Mem. Nat. Investment Sponsor Fedn. (membership chmn. 1985-86), Nat. Cash Mgmt. Assn., Pitts. Pension Fund Assn. (pres. 1984-85), Pitts. Cash Mgmt. Assn. (founder, pres. 1980-81). Republican. Reformed Presbyterian. Avocations: golf, skiing. Office: Kerr-McGee 123 Robert S Kerr Ave Oklahoma City OK 73125

**WOHLER, RUTH,** humanities educator; b. Manhattan, Kans., Aug. 9, 1947; d. L. Joseph and Wanda Marie Wedel; children: Dwayne, Bryan. BS, North West Mo. State U., 1969; EdM, Kans. State U, 1988. Elem. tchr. Unified Sch. Dist. 320, Wamego, Kans., 1969—73, Unified Sch. Dist. 329, Alma, Kans., 1977—79, Unified Sch. Dist. 320, Wamego, 1979—84; grad. tchr. asst. Kans. State U, Manhattan, 1987; instr. basic skills Barton County C.C., Ft. Riley, Kans., 1985—87; instr. English and tchr. edn. Mid Plains C.C., North Platte, Nebr., 1987—, chair humanities divsn. Instrnl. svc. Mid Plains Cmty. Coll., 1991—, chair Humanities div., 2002—; presenter Coll. Reading and Learning Assn., 1998. Recipient NISOD Excellence Award, Internat. Conf. on Tchg. and Leadership Excellence, 1997. Mem.: NEA (assoc.; former pres.), Coll. Reading & Learning Assn. (assoc.), Heartland Reading & Learning Assn. (assoc.; pres.), Delta Kappa Gamma, Phi Delta Kappa. Avocations: reading, walking, writing, gardening, music. Office: North Platte Community Coll 601 West State Farm Rd North Platte NE 69101 Home: 2588 Plains Rd Brutus MI 49716-9545 Office Phone: 308-535-3747.

**WOHLGENANT, RICHARD GLEN,** lawyer, director; b. Porterville, Calif., Dec. 2, 1930; s. Carl Ferdinand and Sara Alice (Moore) W.; m. Teresa Joan Bristow, Dec. 27, 1959; children: Mark Thomas, Tracy Patrice, Timothy James. BA, U. Mont., Missoula, 1952; LL.B., Harvard U., Cambridge, Mass., 1957. Bar: Colo. 1957, U.S. Dist. Ct. Colo. 1957. Assoc. Holme Roberts & Owen LLP, Denver, 1957-62; ptnr./mem. Holme Roberts & Owen, Denver, 1962-99, of counsel, 2000—. Bd. dirs. Adopt-A-Sch., Denver, 1976-80, St. Joseph Found., Denver, 1990-93, Denver Com. Coun. Fgn. Rels., 1988-98, Japanese-Am. Soc. Colo., 1993-98, Rocky Mountain chpt. U.S. Mex. C. of C., 1993-00; bi-nat. bd. U.S./Mex. C. of C., 2000—01; mem. Chamber of the Americas, 2001—03; adv. bd. Human Med. Genetics Prgm., U. Colo. H.S.C., 2000—03; trustee Helen K.and Arthur E. Johnson Found., 2003—. Mem. ABA, Colo. Bar Assn., Denver Bar Assn., Am. Coll. Real Estate Lawyers, Univ. Club, Law Club, City Club, Cactus Club, Denver Press Club. Republican. Roman Catholic. Home: 300 Ivy St Denver CO 80220-5855 Office: Holme Roberts & Owen LLP 1700 Lincoln St Denver CO 80203-4500

**WOHLMAN, MATTHEW JERRY,** legislative staff member; b. Redwood Falls, Minn., Sept. 29, 1979; s. Jerry and Domitilla Wohlman. MA, U. Minn., Duluth, 2006. Congl. intern Office of US Senator Mark Dayton, 2001—03; legis. asst. Office of Senator Yvonne Prettner Solon, 2003—. Food & environ. sci. curriculum com. U. Minn., pres. of student senate, 2000—01; campaign mgr. Marc Kimball for State Rep., Lake Elmo, Minn., 2003—04; academic chair, parliamentarian, treas., alumni assn. sec. Farm Ho. Frat., Saint Paul. Finalist Minn. state pork amb. award, Minn. Pork Prods. Dfl. Office: Minn State Senate 303 State Capitol Saint Paul MN 55155 Business E-Mail: matthew.wohlman@senate.mn.

**WOHLTMANN, HULDA JUSTINE,** pediatrician, endocrinologist; b. Charleston, S.C., Apr. 10, 1923; d. John Diedrich and Emma Lucia (Mohrmann) W. BA, Coll. Charleston, 1944; MD, Med. U. S.C., 1949. Diplomate Am. Bd. Pediatrics. Intern Louisville Gen. Hosp., 1949-50; resident in pediatrics St. Louis Children's Hosp., 1950-53, 1953-65, instr., 1953-58, asst. prof., 1958-65, postdoctoral fellow biochemistry, 1961-63; assoc. prof. pediatrics, head pediatric endocrinology Med. U. S.C., Charleston, 1965-70, prof., 1970-90, prof. emeritus, 1990—. Bd. dirs. Franke Home, Charleston, 1975-97, treas., 1989-91; mem. adv. bd. for ethics ctr. Newberry (S.C.) Coll., 1989—; trustee Luth. Theol. So. Sem., 1991-97. Contbr. articles to sci. jours. Mem. Am. Pediatric Soc., Ambulatory Pediatric Assn., Endocrine Soc., Am. Diabetes Assn., Am. Acad. Pediatrics, Midwest Soc. Pediatric Rsch., So. Soc. Pediatric Rsch., S.C. Diabetes Assn. (bd. dirs. 1970-86, pres. 1970-73, 84-85, v.p. 1982-83, Profl. Svc. award 1977), Lawson Wilkins Endocrine Soc., Sugar Club; fell. Am. Acad. Pediatrics. Lutheran. Home: 3 46th Ave Isle Of Palms SC 29451-2607

**WOHRLE, MARTA,** publishing executive; b. Manchester, Eng. Ptnr., co-founder Informed Sources, 1993—2002; dir. Mercer Mgmt. Cons., 2002—06; v.p., dir. digital media Hachette Filipacchi Media US, NYC, 2006—. Office: Hachette Filipacchi Media US 1633 Broadway New York NY 10019 Office Phone: 212-767-6000.*

**WOJCICKI, ANDREW ADALBERT,** chemist, educator; b. Warsaw, May 5, 1935; s. Franciszek Wojcicki and Janina (Kozlowa) Hoskins; m. Marba L. Hart, Dec. 21, 1968; children: Katherine, Christina. BS, Brown U., 1956; PhD, Northwestern U., 1960; postdoctoral fellow, U. Nottingham, Eng., 1960-61. Asst. prof. chemistry Ohio State U., Columbus, 1961-66, assoc. prof., 1966-69, prof., 1969-2000, prof. emeritus, 2001—, acting chmn., 1981-82, assoc. chmn., 1982-83, 84-86. Vis. prof. Academia Sinica, Taipei, Taiwan, 2002-03, Case Western Res. U., 1967, U. Bologna, Italy, 1988, Nat. Sci. Council Chemistry Rsch. Promotion Ctr., Taiwan, 1994, U. Sydney, Australia, 1998; vis. researcher U. Coll. London, 1969; sr. U.S. scientist Alexander von Humboldt Found., Mulheim/Ruhr, Germany, 1975-76; vis.

scholar U. Calif.-Berkeley, 1984; assoc. dean Coll. of Math. and Phys. Scis., Ohio State U., 1996-98. Contbr. articles to profl. jours. Guggenheim fellow U. Cambridge (Eng.), 1976; recipient Disting. Teaching award Ohio State U., 1968, Humboldt Sr. award Humboldt Found., 1975-76, Casimir Funk Natural Sci. award, Polish Inst. of Arts and Scis. in Am., 2001. Mem.: Am. Chem. Soc. (Columbus sect. award 1992), Phi Lambda Upsilon, Sigma Xi. Home: 825 Greenridge Rd Columbus OH 43235-3411 Office: Ohio State U 100 W 18th Ave Columbus OH 43210-1185 Office Phone: 614-292-4750.

**WOJCICKI, STANLEY GEORGE,** physicist, researcher; b. Warsaw, Mar. 30, 1937; came to U.S., 1950; s. Franciszek and Janina (Kozlow) W.; m. Esther Denise Hochman, Nov. 17, 1961; children: Susan Diane, Janet Maia, Anne Elizabeth. AB, Harvard U., 1957; PhD, U. Calif., Berkeley, 1962. Physicist Lawrence Radiation Lab., Berkeley, 1961-66; asst. prof. physics Stanford U., 1966-68, assoc. prof., 1968-74, prof., 1974—, chmn. dept., 1982-85, dep. dir. Superconducting Supercollider Central Design Group, 1984-89, chmn. physics dept., 2004—; chmn. Stanford Linear Accelerator Center Exptl. Program Adv. Com., 1979-81. Chmn. High Energy Physics Adv. Panel, 1990-96; spokesperson FermiLab Main Injector Neutrino Oscillation Search expt. Assoc. editor Phys. Rev. Letters for Exptl. High Energy Physics, 1978-80. Recipient Alexander von Humboldt Sr. Am. Scientist award, 1981; NSF fellow, 1964-65; Sloan Found. fellow, 1968-72; Guggenheim fellow, 1973-74 Fellow Am. Phys. Soc. Office: Stanford U Dept Physics Stanford CA 94305-4060 Office Phone: 650-926-2806. Business E-Mail: sgweg@slac.stanford.edu.

**WOJCIECH, MATUSIK,** computer scientist; BS EECS, U. Calif., Berkeley, 1997; MS EECS, MIT, 2001, PhD EECS, 2003. Vis. scientist Mitsubishi Elec. Rsch. Lab., 2003—; vis scientist computer graphics group MIT Lab. Computer Sci., 2003—. Contbr. articles to profl. jour. Named one of Top 100 Young Innovators, MIT Tech. Review, 2004. Office: Computer Graphics Group 77 Massachusetts Ave 32 D474 Cambridge MA 02139 Business E-Mail: wojciech@mit.edu.

**WOJCIK, BARBARA ELZBIETA,** statistician, researcher; d. Stanislaw and Stanislawa Marciniak; m. Zbigniew M. Wojcik, 1974; children: Martin R., Paulina M. BSEE, MSEE, Tech. U. Warsaw, 1973; PhD, Polish Acad. Scis., 1979. Supervisory statistician Ctr. for Healthcare Edn. and Studies, Fort Sam Houston, Tex., 1993—2001; dep. dir. Ctr. for AMEDD Strategic Studies, Fort Sam Houston, 2001—. Named one of the Top 25 Cancer Rschrs. in the U.S., Am. Cancer Soc., 1998. Mem.: APHA. Achievements include research in healthcare, epidemiology, statistics, rough sets. Office: Ctr for AMEDD Strategic Studies 1608 Stanley Rd Bldg 2268 Fort Sam Houston TX 78234 Office Phone: 210-221-9633. E-mail: barbara.wojcik@amedd.army.mil.

**WOJCIK, CASS,** decorative supply company executive, retired municipal official; b. Rochester, N.Y., Dec. 3, 1920; s. Emit M. and Casimira C. (Krawiecz) Wojcik; m. Lillian Laocada Lendzion, Sept. 25, 1948; 1 child, Robert Cass. Student, Lawrence Inst. Tech., 1941—43, 'Yale U., 1943—44, U.S. Sch. for European Pers., Czech Republic, 1945. Owner Nat. Florists Supply Co., Detroit, 1948—88, Nat. Decorative, Detroit, 1950—89; co-owner Creaton Ctr., Detroit, 1955—60, Wojcik Family Collection Collectqables Mktg., 1995—. Cons.-contr. hort-bot. design auto show displqays, TV prodrs., designers and decorators. Nen. Regional Planning and Evaluation Coun., 1969—75; city-wide mem. Detroit Bd. Edn., 1970—75; commr. Detroit Pub. Schs. Employees Retirement Commn., 1975; mem. Area Occupl. Ednl. Commn., Ednl. Task Force; chmn., grand marshal Ann. Gen. Pulaski Day Parade, Detroit, 1970—71; mem. Friends of Belle iSLE; mem. pastoral coun. Archdiocese of Detroit, '1983—86, 1988—92; v.p. rsch. Bama Coll., Ft. Lauderdale, Fla., 1989—94; vice chmn. '13th Congl. Dist. Rep. Party Mich., 1987—91; elected Electoral Coll., 1988. Withy U.S. Army, 1944—46. Decorated Bronze Star; recipient citation, Polish-Am. Congress, 1971, 3d prize Art in Park, City of Oakiland Park, Fla. Mem.: Mich. Heritage Coun., Internat. Platform Assn., Nat. Coun. Tchr. Retirement, Mcpl. Fin. Officers Assn. U.S., Nat. Coun. Great Cities Schs., Big Cities Sch. Bd. Com., Nat. Sch. Bd. Assn., Mich. Sch. Bd. Assn., S.E. Mich. Coun. Govts., Nat. Geog. Soc., Polish Century Club. Home: 1729 SW 14th Ct Fort Lauderdale FL 33312-4109 Office Phone: 561-750-9033.

**WOJCIK, JOHN CASIMIR,** music educator, director; b. South Haven, Mich., Aug. 19, 1952; s. Casimir Joseph and Mary Josephine Wojcik; m. Kimberly Kristine Allison, Mar. 25, 2000; 1 child, Jacob Casimir. MusB in Edn., Mich. State U., East Lansing, 1978; MusM in Trumpet Performance, U. Okla., Norman, 1981; MusD in Instrumental Conducting, U. Kans., Lawrence, 1989. Asst. dir. bands Enid (Okla.) HS, 1980—84; dir. bands Phillips U., Enid, 1984—87; Graceland U., Lamoni, Iowa, 1989—2001, Tex. A&M U., Corpus Christi, Tex., 2001—05, Delta State U., Cleve., Miss., 2005—. Contbr. articles to profl. jours. Mem.: Miss.Bandmasters Assn., Nat. Band Assn., Music Educators Nat. Conf., Coll. Band Dirs. Nat. Assn., Tau Beta Sigma, Kappa Kappa Psi, Pi Kappa Lambda, Phi Kappa Phi, Phi Mu Alpha Sinfonia (rec. sec. 1976—77, pres. 1977—78). Democrat. Roman Catholic. Avocations: golf, jogging, history. Office: Delta State U PO Box 3256 Cleveland MS 38733 Home: 1261 Avery St Cleveland MS 38732 Office Phone: 662-846-4629. Office Fax: 662-846-4605. Business E-Mail: jwojcik@deltastate.edu. E-mail: jkwojcik@bellsouth.net.

**WOJCIK, LAURA A.,** engineer, consultant; BS, Mich. State U., 1993; MSE, U. Mich., PhD, 1997. Registered profl. engr., Mich. Whitaker grad. fellow U. Mich., Ann Arbor, 1993—97; asst. prof. Va. Tech, Blacksburg, 1997—2000; sr. engr. Exponent, Farmington Hills, Mich., 2003—; dir. Packer Engring., Ann Arbor, Mich., 2003—. Office: Packer Engineering Ste B 1050 Highland Dr Ann Arbor MI 48130 Office Phone: 734-786-5000. Business E-Mail: law@packereng.com.

**WOJCIK, MARTIN HENRY,** not-for-profit executive; b. Chgo., May 10, 1948; s. Henry Martin and Mary Lorraine (Naughton) W. BS, Ill. Inst. Tech., 1970; M. in Humanities, Bonn U., W. Ger., 1975. Price adminstr. R.R. Donnelley & Sons., Chgo., 1970-72; dir. devel. Citizens for a Better Environment, Milw., 1976-79; pres. Chgo., 1979-85; dir. found. rels. Northwestern U., Evanston, Ill., 1987-89; dir. corp. and found. rels. Mayo Found., Rochester, Minn., 1989—2002; sr. v.p., COO, Scripps Health Found., La Jolla, Calif., 2002—04; dir. devel. The Biodesign Inst., Ariz. State U., Tempe, 2005—. Bd. dir. Citizens for Better Environment, Chgo., chmn. bd. dir., 1990—91, 1999—2001; mem. policy adv. com. III. EPA, Springfield, Ill., 1980—82. Bd. dir. Rochester Civic Theatre, 1991-97, pres. bd. dir. 1994-95; bd. dir. Wasie Found., 2003—; mem. advisory bd. Minn. State Arts Bd., 1995, 97, 99, 2001; adv. coun. KSDS Pub. Radio, San Diego, 2003-. Mem. Ill. Inst. Tech. Alumni Assn. Roman Catholic. Home: 8507 N 84th Pl Scottsdale AZ 85258-2401 Office Phone: 480-727-7435, Business E-Mail: martin.wojcik@asu.edu.

**WOJTASIK, JOSEPH T.,** retired military officer, small business owner; b. Middletown, Conn., Nov. 30, 1946; s. Theodore A. and Mary J. Wojtasik; m. Ruth Ann Kurtz, July 10, 1976; children: Christy, Joe Jr., Lance. BA in History, St. Leo (Fla.) Coll., 1968; grad. Officer Candidate Sch., 1970. Notary pub. Enlisted as pvt. Conn. Army N.G., 1968, promoted to sgt., 1969, commd. 2d lt., 1970, promoted to 1st lt., 1972; hdqs. commandant HQ 43d Infantry Brigade, 1977—80; tng. officer Fed. Mil. Technician Program; full-time adminstrv. officer HQ 242d Combat Engr. Battalion, 1980, exec. officer, 1981—84, battalion comdt., 1984—86; comdr. 242d Engr. Battalion, 1986—88; exec. officer 43d Infantry Brigade, 1988—90; ops. officer, post mobilization comdr., dep. dir. maintenance HQ State Area Command, 1990—96; promoted to col., 1996; dir. logistics, dep. chief of staff logistics Conn. Army N.G., 1999; ret., 2004; promoted to brig. gen. (ret.); owner Col. Joe's Personalized "Stuff"in. Decorated Legion of Merit, Meritorious Svc. medal, Army Commendation medal with 2 bronze oak leaf clusters, Air Force Commendation medal, Army Achievement medal, Army Res. Components Achievement medal with oak leaf clusters, Nat. Def. Svc. medal with 1 bronze svc. star device, Humanitarian Svc. medal with numeral 2, Armed

Forces Res. medal with gold hourglass device, Army Svc. Ribbon, Overseas Tng. Ribbon, Eisenhower award, Conn. medal of merit, Conn. Long Svc. medal with 35 yr. device, Conn. Emergency Svc. Ribbon with 6 oak leaf clusters; grantee Selective Res. Forces medal. Republican. Roman Catholic. Avocations: sports, swimming, walking, basketball, football. Home: 23 Doris St Wallingford CT 06492 E-mail: joseph.wojtasik@snet.net.

**WOJTASZEK, KEVIN JOSEPH,** director, video editor; b. Fraser, Mich., Aug. 26, 1979; s. Michael Stanislaus and Charlene Frances Wojtaszek. Asst. chief editor Sterling Video Prodns., Sterling Heights, Mich., 1995—99; IMC equipment supr. Fairleigh Dickinson U., Madison, NJ, 1999—. Home: 110 Ridgedale Ave Cedar Knolls NJ 07927 Office: Fairleigh Dickinson Univ 285 Madison Ave Madison NJ 07940 Office Phone: 973-443-8527. Office Fax: 973-443-8584. Personal E-mail: edicius@gmail.com. Business E-Mail: edicius@fdu.edu.

**WOLAK, FRANK ANTHONY,** economics professor; s. Francis Anthony and Jane Ellen Wolak; m. Michele Yvette Pridmore-Brown, June 10, 1989; children: Janelle Paulette, Clifton William, Paulette Frances. BA, Rice U., Houston; PhD, SM, Harvard U., Cambridge, Mass., 1981—85. Prof. economics Stanford U., Calif., 1986—. Home: 951 Shauna Ln Palo Alto CA 94306-3139 Office: Stanford U Dept Econs Stanford CA 94305-6072 Home Fax: 650-725-5702; Office Fax: 650-725-5702. Business E-Mail: wolak@zia.stanford.edu.

**WOLANDE, CHARLES SANFORD,** former computer company executive; b. Chgo., July 25, 1954; s. Sam C. and Marie Helene (Riccio) W.; children: Eric, Jill, Patrick, Ryan, Haley. B. St. Mary's Coll., Winona, Minn., 1976. Lab. tech. Jefferson Electric, Bellwood, Ill., 1976-73; pres. Comark, Inc., Glendale Heights, Ill., 1978—2002, also CFO Bloomingdale, Ill., 1978—2002. Named High Tech. Entrepreneur of the yr., Peat, Marwick, Mitchell, Chgo., 1987; named to CRN Industry Hall of Fame, 2003. Mem. C. of C. Glendale Heights. Republican. Roman Catholic. Avocations: golf, skiing. Office: 444 Scott Dr Bloomingdale IL 60108-3111

**WOLANIN, BARBARA ANN BOESE,** curator, art historian; b. Dayton, Ohio, Dec. 12, 1943; d. William Carl and Elisabeth Cassell Boese; m. Thomas R. Wolanin, 1966 (div. 1980); children: Peter, Andrew; m. Phillip F. Brown, 2001. AB, Oberlin Coll., 1966, AM, 1969; MAT, Harvard U., 1967; PhD, U. Wis., 1981. Art tchr. Newton (Mass.) Pub. Schs., 1969-71; asst. prof. art history Trinity Coll., Washington, 1978-83, James Madison U., Harrisonburg, Va., 1983-85; curator U.S. Capitol, Arch. of the Capitol, Washington, 1985—. Author: (exhbn. catalog) Arthur B. Carles, 1983, 2000, Constantino Brumidi, 1998; contbr. articles to profl. jours. Recipient Faculty Devel. award, James Madison U., 1985; Woodrow Wilson fellow, 1967, Kress fellow, U. Wis., 1974, Smithsonian fellow, 1976. Mem.: Am. Inst. Conservation, Coll. Art Assn., ArtTable (bd. dirs. DC chpt. 2003—05), Women's Caucus Art (pres. DC chpt. 1998—2001, nat. bd. dirs. 2002—), Phi Beta Kappa (pres. Trinity Coll. 1982—83). Home: 7807 Hamilton Spring Rd Bethesda MD 20817 Office: US Capitol Office Architect Washington DC 20515-0001

**WOLANIN, THOMAS RICHARD,** federal agency administrator, educator; b. Detroit, Dec. 1, 1942; s. Chester Richard and Helen Theresa (Luszki) W.; m. Donna M. Christian; children: Peter, Andrew. BA magna cum laude, Oberlin Coll., 1965; MA, Harvard U., 1970, PhD, 1972. Staff dir. subcom. on labor-mgmt. rels. House Edn. and Labor Com., 1975-77, dep. staff dir. subcom. on select edn., 1977-78; exec. asst. to pres. NYU, 1981-82; analyst Senate Budget Com., 1982-83; staff dir. subcom. on investigations House P.O. and Civil Svc. Com., 1983-85, 87-91; staff dir. subcom. on postsecondary edn. House Edn. and Labor Com., 1978-81, 85-87; 91-93; dep. asst. sec. legis. and congl. affairs U.S. Dept. Edn., Washington, 1993-96; sr. assoc. The Inst. for Higher Edn. Policy, Washington, 1996—. Instr. govt. Oberlin Coll., 1967-69; asst. prof. polit. sci. U. Wis., Madison, 1971-78; rsch. prof. edn. policy and polit. sci. George Washington U., Washington, 1997-00. Author: Presidential Advisory Commissions: Truman to Nixon, 1975; co-author: Congress and the Colleges: Higher Education in National Politics, 1976; contbr. articles to profl. jours. Bd. dirs. Am. Youth Policy Forum, Woodrow Wilson fellow, 1965-66, fellow Harvard U., 1965-67, 69-71, Congl. fellow, 1971-72, Spencer fellow Nat. Acad. Edn., 1975-81, Fulbright Found., 2005; grantee Ford Found., 1972-73, 73-74, USIA, 1990; scholar The Brookings Instn., 1970 Mem. Polish Am. Arts Assn. Washington, Congl. Fellowship Alumni Assn., Phi Beta Kappa. Democrat. Avocations: military history, polish history, literature. Office: Inst Higher Edn Policy 1320 19th St NW Ste 400 Washington DC 20036-1635 Office Phone: 202-861-8223 214. E-mail: tom@ihep.com.

**WOLAR, GLYNN G.,** history professor, lawyer; AB, Occidental Coll., 1974; MA in History, Calif. State U., L.A., 1976; JD, Western State U., 1979; PhD in History, U. Idaho, 1998. Bar: Mont.; cert. c.c. tchr. Ariz., Calif. Instr. history and polit. sci. Pasadena City Coll., Calif., 1982—87; instr. history L.A. Pierce Coll., Woodland Hills, Calif., 1986—87, No. Mont. Coll., Havre, Mont., 1988—89; atty. pvt. practice, 1987—91; instr. history and bus. law U. Idaho, Moscow, 1991—95, 1997—2004; instr. history Lewis-Clark State Coll., Lewiston, 1992—93; instr. history, philosophy, bus. law North Platte C.C., Nebr., 1999—; instr. history, ethics Chadron State Coll., 2001—05. Bd. dirs. Frontier Heritage Alliance, Sheridan, Wyo. Mem.: The Hist. Soc., Western History Assn., State Bar Mont. Avocations: mountain climbing, hiking, photography, baseball umpiring, reading. E-mail: wolarg@mpcc.edu.

**WOLBRINK, SHELLEY AMISTE,** history professor; b. Holland, Mich., July 21, 1969; d. Paul Henry and Vivian Lynn (Hutchison) Wolbrink; m. Jeffrey Allan VanDenBerg, Sept. 6, 1992; children: Avery Grace VanDenBerg, Evelyn Rose VanDenBerg. BA, Miami U., Oxford, Ohio, 1991; MA, PhD, U. Cin., 1998. Asst. prof. Drury U., Springfield, Mo., 1998—2004, assoc. prof. history, 2004—, divsn. chair social scis., 2005—, dir. Medieval studies, 2002—. Editor: Dictionary of World Biography: The Middle Ages, 2005; contbr. articles to profl. jours. Recipient Faculty award for excellence, Drury U., 1998; fellow Charles Phelps Taft Dissertation fellow, U. Cin., 1996—97; scholar Dr. A.F. Zimmerman scholar, Phi Alpha Theta, 1991. Mem.: Am. Cath. Hist. Assn., Medieval Acad. Am., Am. Hist. Assn., Phi Alpha Theta. Democrat. Avocations: reading, outdoors, travel. Office: Drury University 900 N Benton Ave Springfield MO 65802

**WOLCOTT, HUGH DIXON,** obstetrics and gynecology educator; b. NYC, Jan. 12, 1946; s. Charles Edmund and Joan Degrau (Loveland) W.; m. Jane Jarrell Smith; children: Allison, James. BS, U.S. Naval Acad., 1967; MSE, Princeton U., 1969; MD, Northwestern U., 1979. Diplomate Am. Bd. Ob-Gyn, Am. Bd. Med. Examiners. Commd. ensign USN, 1967, advanced through grades to capt., 1990; aviator, Fighter Squadron 14 Naval Air Station, Oceana, Va., 1971-74; test pilot Naval Air Test Ctr., Patuxent River, Md., 1974-76; staff physician Naval Hosp., Portsmouth, Va., 1984, Jacksonville, Fla., 1984-86, dir. colposcopy and laser clins. Portsmouth, Va., 1986-89, dir. ob-gyn. residency program, 1989-91, acting chmn. dept. ob-gyn., 1990-91; ret., 1991; asst. prof. Med. Coll. Hampton Roads, Norfolk, Va., 1991—. Chmn. dept. ob-gyn. Sentara Hosps, Norfolk, 1996—2001; ob-gyn. splty. advisor Sentara Health Mgmt. Corp., 2000—; chmn. bd. mgr.s Mid-Atlantic Women's Care, LLC, 2005—. Contbr. articles profl. jours. Mem. steering com. Sentara ObRight Patient Safety Initiative, 2005—. Awarded 1st prize scientific paper by resident physician Am. Coll. Obstetricans and Gynecologists; recipient Guggenheim fellowship Princeton U., 1967-68; Trident scholar U.S. Naval Acad., 1966-67. Fellow Am. Coll. Ob.-Gyns. (chmn. Navy sect. armed forces dist. 1989-91), Assn. Profs. Ob.-Gyns. (assoc.); mem. Am. Assn. Gynecol. Laparoscopists. Episcopalian. Home: 835 Botetourt Gdns Norfolk VA 23507-1814 Office: Woman Care Ctrs 811 Med Tower 400 Gresham Dr Norfolk VA 23507-1901 Office Phone: 757-623-3845. Personal E-mail: hdwolcott@aol.com.

**WOLCOTT, JOHN WINTHROP, III,** retired manufacturing executive; b. Balt., Dec. 3, 1924; s. John Winthrop, Jr. and Dorothy C. (Fraser) W.; m. Elizabeth Thelin Hooper, Apr. 24, 1948 (div. 1985); children: John Winthrop IV (dec.), Elizabeth T., Katherine C.; m. Karen E. Jones, Oct. 1, 1985; 1 child, Oliver Lund. B.Indsl. Engring., Gen. Motors Inst., 1951. Registered profl. engr., Ohio. With Gen. Motors Corp., 1946-53, Weatherhead Co., Cleve., 1957-60; v.p. H.K. Porter Co., Inc., Pitts., 1960-64; pres., dir., CEO Ametek, Inc., N.Y.C., 1964-66; v.p. Am. Machine & Foundry Co., 1966-77, group exec. process equipment group, 1967-70; exec. v.p. ops., dir. AMF, Inc., 1970-77; pres., chief exec. officer, dir. Transway Internat. Corp., N.Y.C., 1978-86, chmn. bd., 1982-86. Served with USCGR, 1943-46. Mem. Soc. Colonial Wars, Md. Club (Balt.) Episcopalian. Home: 210 Carrsbrook Dr Charlottesville VA 22901-1004 Personal E-mail: wol.cott@adelphia.net.

**WOLCOTT, KYLE B,** secondary school educator; b. Rochester, NY, Mar. 23, 1977; s. Bruce and Linda Wolcott; m. Sheryl Allen, May 5, 2003; 1 child, Brody R. BA in Secondary Edn., Pa. State U., 1999; M Gen. Edn., Nazareth Coll., 2003. Cert. secondary social studies tchr. NY. Tchr. Norman Howard Sch., Henrietta, NY, 2000—. Tchr. higher achievement program McQuaid SJ, Rochester, NY, 2000—03. Mem.: Nat. Coun. Social Studies (assoc.), Pa. State Alumni Assn. (life). Republican. Presbyterian. Avocations: sports, fishing, travel, woodworking. Home: 18 Foxpointe Cir Fairport NY 14450 Office: Norman Howard Sch 275 Pinnacle Rd Henrietta NY 14526 Office Phone: 585-334-8010 372. Personal E-mail: kbwolcott@normanhoward.org.

**WOLCOTT, VERNON,** music educator, musician; b. Hudson, NY, June 4, 1933; s. George and Edna Caroline Wolcott; m. Nancy Ester Bookout, July 6, 1956; children: Deborah, David. MusB, Curtis Inst., Phila., 1954; M in Sacred Music cum laude, Union Sem., NYC, 1956; D in Musical Arts, U. Mich., Ann Arbor, 1967. Faculty Hastings Coll., Nebr., 1956—57, Peabody Conservatory, Balt., 1957—62; prof. performance studies Coll. Musical Arts, Bowling Green State U., Ohio, 1962—. Organist St. Elizabeth's Ch., Phila., 1952—54, Franklin St. Presbyn. Ch., Balt., 1957—62, 1st Presbyn. Ch., Bowling Green, Ohio, 1963—, St. Peter's Luth. Ch., NYC, 1954—56; lectr., workshop presenter in field. Editor, performer: Disciple Variations (Wallace DePue), Christian Fellowship Art Music Composer's Nat. Conv., 1997; editor: A Christmas Carol to Peoria (Wallace DePue), 2000; composer: Eternite, O Perfect Love; performer: (recitals) Bowling Green New Music Festival, Prisms (Donald Wilson), 1968, C (Burton Beerman), 1973, Hymn Preludes (Paul Kennedy), 1994, 1996, How Lovely (Marilyn Shrude), 1997; featured recitalist.; Art of Fugue (J.S. Bach), 1984; performer: (organ dedicatory recitals) Meth. Ch., Ashland Ave. Bapt. Ch., St. Patrick's Ch., Sts. Peter and Paul Ch. Mem.: Am. Guild Organists, Music Tchrs. Nat. Assn. Avocation: art. Office: Bowling Green State Univ Coll Musical Arts Bowling Green OH 43403 Personal E-mail: vwolcot@bgnet.bgsu.edu.

**WOLD, JOHN SCHILLER,** geologist, former congressman; b. East Orange, NJ, Aug. 31, 1916; s. Peter Irving and Mary (Helff) W.; m. Jane Adele Pearson, Sept. 28, 1946; children: Peter Irving, Priscilla Adele, John Pearson. AB, St. Andrews U., Scotland and Union Coll., Schenectady, 1938; MS, Cornell U., 1939; LLD (hon.), U. Wyo., 1991. Dir. Fedn. Rocky Mountain States, 1966-68; v.p. Rocky Mountain Oil and Gas Assn., 1967, 68; mem. Wyo. Ho. of Reps., 1957-59; Wyo. Republican candidate for U.S. Senate, 1964, 70; mem. 91st Congress at large from Wyo.; chmn., CEO Wold Trona Co., Inc.; pres., chmn. Wold Talc Co.; ret. Wold Nuclear Co., Wold Mineral Exploration Co., Casper, Wyo.; founding pres. Wyo. Heritage Soc.; founder Central Wyo. Ski Corp. Chmn. Wyo. Natural Gas Pipeline Authority, 1987-91; chmn. bd. Nuclear Exploration and Devel. Corp., Mineral Engring. Co., chmn., CEO Gastech Contbr. articles to profl. jours. Chmn. Wyo. Rep. Com., 1960-64, Western State Rep. Chmns. Assn., 1963-64; mem. exec. com. Rep. Nat. Com., 1962-64; chmn. Wyo. Rep. State Fin. Com.; Active Little League Baseball, Boy Scouts Am., United Fund, YMCA, Boys Clubs Am.; former pres. bd. trustees Casper Coll.; trustee Union Coll. Served to lt. USNR, World War II. Named Wyo. Man of Yr. AP-UPI, 1968; Wyo. Mineral Man of Yr., 1979, Wyo. Heritage award, 1992, Wyo. Oil/Gas and Mineral Man of 20th Century, Am. Heritage Ctr. of U. Wyo., 1999; named Benefactor of Yr., Nat. Coun. for Resource Devel., 1993. Mem. Wyo. Geol. Assn. (hon. life, pres. 1956), Am. Assn. Petroleum Geologists, Ind. Petroleum Assn. Am., AAAS, Wyo. Mining Assn., Sigma Xi, Alpha Delta Phi. Episcopalian (past vestryman, warden). Home: 1231 W 30th St Casper WY 82601-5372 Office: Mineral Resource Ctr 139 W 2nd St Casper WY 82601-2473 Office Phone: 307-265-7252. Business E-Mail: trona@woldoil.com.

**WOLD, KENNETH JON,** music educator; b. Bemidji, Minn., June 3, 1940; s. Jon Martin and Lillian Kate Wold; m. Bonnie Louise Brammann, Sept. 2, 1961; children: Robin Lynette, Jon Kenneth, Brian David. Diploma in Bible and Christian edn., Oak Hlls Bible Inst., 1961; BS in Music Edn., St. Cloud State Coll., Minn., 1965; postgrad., Bemidji State U., 1968—72; MA in Music Ministry, Western Sem., Portland, Oreg., 1988. Music tchr. Mora (Minn.) Pub. Schs., 1965—68; instr. music Oak Hills Bible Inst., Bemidji, 1968—74; min. music 1st Presbyn. Ch., Duluth, 1974—75; instr. Oak Hills Christian Coll., Bemidji, 1975—. Chmn. Bemidji Area Ch. Musicians, 1995—; adult choir dir. Evang. Free Ch., Bemidji, 1988—. Recipient Friend of Arts award, Bemidji Arts Coun., 1999. Mem.: Am. Choral Dirs. Assn. Avocations: gardening, hiking, bicycling. Home: 613 15th St NW Bemidji MN 56601 Office: Oak Hills Christian Coll 1600 Oak Hills Rd SW Bemidji MN 56601 E-mail: kenwold@oakhills.edu.

**WOLDEGABRIEL, GIDAY,** research geologist; b. Mai Misham/Adwa, Tigray, Ethiopia, Sept. 3, 1955; arrived in U.S.; 1982; s. Giday WoldeGabriel and Mislal Mesfin; m. Almaz Berhane Tesfamichael, Jan. 15, 1994. BS in Geology with honors, Addis Ababa (Ethiopia) U., 1978, MS in Geology, 1980; PhD in Geology, Case Western Res. U., 1987. Lectr. geology Addis Ababa U., 1980-82; dir.'s postdoctoral fellow Los Alamos (N.Mex.) Nat. Lab., 1987-90, cons., 1990-92, mem. tech. staff, 1992—. Mem.: Am. Geophys. Union. Avocations: running, camping, skiing, body building, swimming. Home: PO Box 4694 Los Alamos NM 87544-3638 Office: Los Alamos Nat Lab EES-6 1 Ms D462 Los Alamos NM 87545-0001 Business E-Mail: wgiday@lanl.gov.

**WOLDEN, SUZANNE LEESA,** pediatric radiation oncologist; b. West Covina, Calif., June 30, 1969; MD, U. Calif. San Francisco Sch. Medicine, 1994. Cert. Radiation Oncology. Intern Cornell Med. Ctr., NY, 1994—95; resident Stanford U. Med. Ctr., Calif., 1995—98; asst. attending Meml. Sloan-Kettering Cancer Ctr., NY, 1998—. Contbr. articles to profl. jours. Office: Meml Sloan-Kettering Cancer Ctr 1275 York Ave New York NY 10021 Office Phone: 212-639-5148.*

**WOLDMAN, SHERMAN,** pediatrician; b. Buffalo, Apr. 1, 1932; s. Joseph Harry and Sadie (Weinstein). W. m. Fern Marlene Weinstein, Dec. 28, 1952; children: Deborah Janine Case, Scott Alan, Sabina Heide Muller. BS in Pharmacy magna cum laude, U. Buffalo, N.Y., 1953, MD with high honors, 1957. Diplomate Am. Bd. Pediat. Intern Millard Fillmore Hosp., Buffalo, 1957-58; resident in pediat. Womens & Children's Hosp., Buffalo, 1958—60, active staff, 1961—2004, emeritus, 2005; pvt. practice Buffalo, 1961-66, Cheektowaga, NY, 1962—2004; med. insp. Lover Twp. Elem. Schs., Cape May, NJ, 2005—; mem. active staff Millard Fillmore Hosp., Buffalo, 1961—2004, chmn. dept. pediat., 1985-91, emeritus, 2005; med. inspector Lower Twp. Elem. Sch., Cape May, NJ, 2005—; pediatrician pvt. practice, 2005, Clermont, 2006—. Adj. clin. asst. pediat. SUNY Sch. Medicine, Buffalo, 1962, clin. assoc. 1970, clin. asst. prof., 1973, clin. assoc. prof., 2001, preceptor Sch. Nursing, 1976-82; attending pediatrician Booth Meml. Hosp., Buffalo, 1969-72; sch. physician Williamsville (N.Y.) Cntl. Schs, 1962-94, chmn. of physicians, 1970-94; courtesy staff St. Joseph Intercmty. Hosp., Cheektowaga, 1963-80, Kenmore (N.Y.) Mercy Hosp., 1963-70, 1974-82, Sisters of Charity Hosp., Buffalo, 1991-2003, Erie County Med. Ctr., Buffalo, 1979-83, Buffalo Gen. Hosp., 1987-95; provisional staff Mercy Hosp., Buffalo, 1982-83, courtesy staff, 2000-03. Vol. Leukemia and Lymphoma Soc., 1975—, bd. trustees Western N.Y. and Finger Lakes chpt. 1975-2005, pres. 1977-79, v.p. 1979-81, mem. profl. edn. com. 1975-2005, mem. nat. bd.

trustees 1978-87, vice chmn. patient aid com., 1980-87; mem. task force on sch. health Erie County (N.Y.) Health Dept; trustee Temple Beth David Ner-Israel, Buffalo, 1964-65. Recipient (with Mrs. Fern Woldman) recognition cert. Cheektowaga C. of C., 1982; Myron L. Woldman Vol. of Yr. award Western N.Y. chpt. Leukemia Soc. Am., 1987, nat. chmn.'s citation 1999; Disting. Physician award Millard Fillmore Health Sys., 1995. Mem.: Maimonides Med. Soc. (pres. Buffalo chpt. 1982—83), Med. Soc. County of Erie, N.Y. (chmn. pub. health com. 1978—79), Buffalo Pediat. Soc. (pres. 1969—70), Med. Soc. State of N.Y., Am. Acad. Pediat. (PREP fellow 1979—85, 1992—94, 1994—96, 1997—99, 2000—02), Gibson Anat. Soc. (hon.), Phi Lambda Kappa (alumni pres. 1965, v.p. alumni 1980—81), Rho Chi, Alpha Omega Alpha. Avocations: gardening, computers. E-mail: swoldman@comcast.net.

**WOLD-OLSEN, PER,** pharmaceutical executive; b. Nov. 6, 1947; MBA in Econs. Adminstrn., Norwegian Sch. Mgmt., 1972; MBA in Mgmt. and Mktg., U. Wis., 1973. Mgmt. trainee Sarpsborg Paper Co., 1968—69; product mgr. trainee MSD Norway Merck & Co., Inc., 1973, European area intern, Rahway, 1974, spl. project mgr. MSD Norway, 1974, fin. and adminstrn. mgr. MSD Norway, 1975, mng. dir. MSD Norway, 1976, regional dir. Scandinavia, 1986, v.p. MSD Europe and regional dir. Scandinavia, 1990, sr. v.p. mktg. human health divsn., 1991—94; pres. Merck Human Health Merck & Co. Inc., Whitehouse Station, NJ, 1994—97, pres. Human Health Europe, Middle East & Africa, 1997—2005, pres. intercontinental health, 2005—. Office: Merck & Co Inc One Merck Dr PO Box 100 Whitehouse Station NJ 08889-0100

**WOLDRIDGE, SCOTT,** outsourced human resources company executive; Dir. info. tech. ops. Hewitt Associates LLC. Named one of Premier 100 IT Leaders, Computerworld, 2005.*

**WOLDT, HAROLD FREDERICK, JR.,** newspaper publishing executive; b. Atlanta, July 4, 1947; s. Harold Frederick and Dorothy Rose (Lansdowne) W.; m. Lisa Diane Neves; children: Lauren Rae, Katherine Neves, Caroline Neves. BS in Journalism, So. Ill. U., 1969. Classified advt. rep. Chgo. Tribune, 1969-70, classified automobile staff mgr., 1970-72; nat. advt. sales rep. Chgo. Tribune newspapers, N.Y.C., 1972-74, city circulation mgr., 1974-77; nat. circulation mgr. Chgo. Tribune, 1977-80, circulation mgr., 1980-84; v.p., circulation News & Sun Sentinel Co., Ft. Lauderdale, Fla., 1985; circulation dir. Newsday, Inc., Melville, NY, 1986-88, v.p., circulation LI, NY, 1988-94; sr. v.p. circulation Newsday, pres. Distbn. Systems. Am. subs. of Newsday, Inc., 1994-98; v.p. sales circulation mktg. The N.Y. Times, N.Y.C., 1998—2000; dir. circulation Omaha World-Herald; v.p. circulation San Jose (Calif.) Mercury News, 2001—04; sales dir. Publs. Circulation Fulfillment, Inc., 2006—. Speaker, participant Am. Press Inst.; bd. dirs. Abilities Health and Rehab. Svcs. (Nat. Ctr. for Disability Svcs.), Albertson, LI, N.Y., 1992-94. Bd. dirs. Robert R. McCormick Boys Club, Chgo., 1980-81; chmn. United Way campaign, Chgo. Tribune, 1980, Omaha World-Herald United Way Campaign, 1999-2000, bd. dir. San Jose Children's Discovery Mus. Calif., Ronald McDonald House Charities of the Bay Area, San Francisco, 2002—. Mem. Am. Pubs. Newspaper Assn. (circulation and readership com. 1988-93), Internat. Circulation Mgrs. Assn. (pres. 1991-92), Alpha Delta Sigma, Tau Kappa Epsilon. Office Phone: 408-529-1950. E-mail: hfwoldt@aol.com.

**WOLETZ, ROBERT G.,** editor; b. 1953; Cable tv advt. editor Paul Kagan & Assocs.; founder RGW Media, 1984; pub. rels. mgr. ABC Video Enterprises, 1985—86; with NY Times, 1986—, Vows columnist, Sunday Styles sect., Society News editor. Office: NY Times 229 W 43rd St New York NY 10036 Office Phone: 212-556-4588. Office Fax: 212-556-5999, 212-556-7689.*

**WOLF, AIZIK LOFT,** neurosurgeon; b. Bogota, Colombia, Jan. 17, 1956; came to U.S., 1963; s. Jose Wolf and Judy Grimberg Loft. AB, U. Chgo., 1977; MD, Yale U., 1981. Diplomate Am. Bd. Neurol Surgery Asst. prof. neurosurgery, chief epilepsy surgery U. Md. Hosp., Balt., 1987-93, asst. prof. neurology, chief Gamma knife skull base surgery, 1990-93; dir. Miami Neurosci. Ctr. Doctors Hosp., Coral Gables, Fla., 1993—. Office: Doctors Hosp 5000 University Dr Coral Gables FL 33146-2094 Office Phone: 786-308-3700. E-mail: drwolf@miamineurosciencecenter.com.

**WOLF, ALFRED A.,** physicist, educator; b. Phila., July 21, 1925; s. Jacob Wolf, Anna Wolf; m. Enid G. Wolf, Nov. 24, 1957 (div. Dec. 1981); children: Marcus M., Laurence J. BSEE, Drexel U., 1948; MSEE, U. Pa., 1954, PhD, 1958; ScD, U. Juarez, 1977, MD, 1978. Engr.-in-charge Naval Air Devel., Johnsville, Pa., 1949—56; chief scientist Gen. Dynamics, Rochester, NY, 1957—60; dir. rsch. Litton Industries, Silver Spring, Md., 1960—63; disting. prof. elec. engring. Drexel U., Phila., 1963—65; tech. dir. RCA, Burlington, Mass., 1965—67; assoc. tech. dir. Naval Ship R&D Ctr., Annapolis, Md., 1967—78; prime Rsch. Found., Annapolis, 1978—. Asst. prof. elec. engring. U. Pa., Phila., 1949—59; Pa. scholar, 1952—54; sr. sci. advisor USN, 1971—76; adj. assoc. prof. U. Rochester, 1960—62; adj. prof. U. Md., Annapolis, 1967—69, George Washington U., Washington, 1969—99. Author (prize winning): Biophysics of Wound Healing, 1989; contbr. 105 articles to profl. jours. (14 awards). Cpl. U.S. Army, 1943—46. Nominee Nobel Prize in Physics, 1972; named Notable Am. of Bicentennial Era, Am. Biog. Inst., 1976; recipient Citation of Honor, Drexel U., 1961, Honor citations (8), USN, 1972—83; grantee, NSF, 1956—59; Pa. scholar, 1952—54. Mem.: IEEE (life), Engring. in Medicine and Biology Soc. (chmn. Balt. sect. 1990—95), Sigma Xi. Democrat. Jewish. Achievements include discovery of first high temperature superconductor; 24 patents for electronics devices and systems. Avocation: writing. Home and Office: Prime Rsch Found 562 Ferry Point Rd Annapolis MD 21403-1308

**WOLF, ALICE KOERNER,** state legislator, former mayor; b. Vienna, Dec. 24, 1933; d. Frederick Koerner and Renee (Engel) K.; m. Robert A. Wolf, 1955; children: Eric Jeffrey, Adam Nathaniel. BS, Simmons Coll., 1955; MPA, Harvard U., 1978; EdD (hon.), Wheelock Coll., 2001. Residence staff MIT, Lincoln Lab, 1955-62, Computer Corp Am., 1967-71, pers. dir., 1971-76; mem. Cambridge Sch. Com., 1974-81, vicechairwoman, 1976-77, 80-81; chairwoman Ward 7 Dem. Com., 1976-85; committeewoman Mass. State Dem. Com.; 1983-90; mem. dist. 25 Middlesex Mass. Ho. of Reps., Boston. Del. Dem. Nat. Conv., 1980, 84, 88, 92, State Conv. Mem. NOW, Mass. Women's Polit. Caucus Cambridge Mental Health Assn., Am. for Dem. Action, Nat. Orgn. Women Am. Civil Liberties Union, Nat. Office: Mass Ho of Reps State House Rm 134 Boston MA 02133 Home: 48 Huron Ave Cambridge MA 02138-6706 Office Phone: 617-722-2400. Personal E-mail: alice@alicewolf.org. Business E-Mail: rep.alicewolf@hou.state.ma.us.

**WOLF, BARRY,** geneticist, pediatric educator; b. Chgo., June 19, 1947; s. Bert D. and Toby E. (Urkoff) W.; children: Michael Loren, Bryan Phillip. BS, U. Ill., 1969, MD, U. Ill. Coll. Medicine, 1974; PhD, U. Ill., 1974. Diplomate Am. Bd. Pediatrics, Med. and Biochem. Genetics. Intern, resident in pediatrics Childrens Meml. Hosp., Northwestern U., Chgo., 1974-76; fellow Yale U. Sch. Medicine, New Haven, 1976-78; prof. human genetics Med. Coll. Va., Richmond, 1978-2001, vice chair for rsch. dept. pediatrics, 1996-2000; dir. rsch. Conn. Children's Med. Ctr., 2001—05; assoc. chmn., dir. rsch. Dept. Pediats. Sch. Medicine U. Conn., 2001—01; chmn. Dept. Med. Genetics Henry Ford Hosp., Detroit, 2005—. Author over 175 jour. articles and book chpts. dealing with inherited disorders of metabolism and biochem. genetics, specifically disorders of biotin metabolism. Recipient E. Mead Johnson award for pediatric rsch. Am. Acad. Pediatrics, 1988, Borden award in nutrition Am. Inst. Nutrition, 1987, Outstanding Scientist of Va. award Va. Sci. Mus., 1986, Ounce of Prevention award Action for Prevention of Va., 1985. Mem. Am. Soc. Clin. Investigation, Am. Pediat. Soc., Soc. Pediatric Rsch., Soc. Inherited Metabolic Diseases, Soc. Study Inborn Errors of Metabolism, Am. Soc. Human Genetics. Avocation: japanese cloisonne. Office: Henry Ford Hosp Dept Med Genetics 2799 W Grand Blvd CFP-4 Detroit MI 48202 Office Phone: 313-916-3116. Business E-Mail: bwolf1@hfhs.org.

**WOLF, BARRY M.**, lawyer; b. NYC, Nov. 14, 1959; BS summa cum laude, SUNY, Albany, 1981; JD cum laude, U. Mich., 1984; LLM, NYU, 1989. Bar: N.Y. 1985. Ptnr. Weil, Gotshal & Manges LLP, NYC, co-head global corp. dept., 2000—. Mem.: ABA, Private Investment Fund Forum, N.Y. State Bar Assn. (tax sect.). Office: Weil, Gotshal & Manges LLP 767 Fifth Ave New York NY 10153 Office Phone: 212-310-8209. E-mail: barry.wolf@weil.com.

**WOLF, CARRIE IRENE**, religious organization administrator, musician; b. St. Louis, Oct. 30, 1974; d. Carolyn C and Vincent M Wolf. BS in music edn., SW Mo. State U., 1993—97. Music dir. St. Cletus, St. Charles, Mo., 2002—; youth min. St. Catherine Laboure, St. Louis, 1999—2002. Composer: (liturgical music) Various Psalms. Mem.: Nat. Pastoral Musicians (assoc.). Catholic. Avocations: musical theater, dance, camping.

**WOLF, CHARLES, JR.**, economist, educator; b. NYC, Aug. 1, 1924; s. Charles and Rosalie W.; m. Theresa van de Wint, Mar. 1, 1947; children: Charles Theodore, Timothy van de Wint. BS, Harvard U., Cambridge, Mass., 1943, M.P.A., 1948, PhD in Econs., 1949. Economist, fgn. service officer U.S. Dept. State, 1945-47, 49-53; mem. faculty Cornell U., 1953-54, U. Calif., Berkeley, 1954-55; sr. economist The Rand Corp., Santa Monica, Calif., 1955-67, head econs. dept., 1967-81; dean The Rand Grad. Sch., 1970-97, prof. pub. policy, 1997—, sr. econ. advisor, 1981—, corp. fellow in internat. econs., 1996—; sr. fellow Hoover Inst., 1988—. Bd. dirs. Capital Income Builder Fund, Capital World Growth Fund; lectr. econs. UCLA, 1960-72; mem. adv. bd. ctr. internat. bus. and edn. rsch., UCLA Anderson Grad. Sch. Bus., 1996—. Author: The Costs and Benefits of the Soviet Empire, 1986, Markets or Governments: Choosing Between Imperfect Alternatives, 1989, 2d edit., 1993, Linking Economic Policy and Foreign Policy, 1991, Long-Term Economic and Military Trends: The United States and Asia, 1994-2015, 1995, The Economic Pivot in a Political Context, 1997; co-author: Economic Openness: Many Facets, Many Metrics, 1999, Asian Economic Trends and Their Security Implications, 2000, European Military Prospects, Economic Constraints and the Rapid Reaction Force, 2001, Straddling Economics and Politics: Cross-Cutting Issues, in Asia, the United States and the Global Economy, 2002, Fault Lines in China's Economic Terrain, 2003, North Korean Paradoxes, 2005, The Russian Economy: Progress and Retreat on the Transitional Road, 2006; contbr. articles to profl. jours. Mem. Assn. for Public Policy Analysis and Mgmt. (pres. 1980-81), Am. Econs. Assn., Econometric Soc., Coun. on Fgn. Rels., Pacific Coun. Internat. Policy, Internat. Inst. Strategic Studies London. Clubs: Cosmos (Washington); Riviera Tennis (Los Angeles); Harvard (N.Y.). Office: The Rand Corp 1776 Main St Santa Monica CA 90407-2138 Office Phone: 310-451-6926.

**WOLF, CHARLES A.**, retail camera and photographic supplies executive; m. Missi Harnell; children: Alex, Tracey, Madeline. BBA, U. Okla., 1963. Founder Wolf Camera, Atlanta, 1974, now pres., CEO. Bd. dirs. First Union Bank. Bd. advisors Ga. State U. Bus. Sch.; bd. visitors Emory U.; bd. councilors the Carter Ctr., Atlanta; bd. dirs. Buckhead Coalition, Atlanta Symphony Orch., Atlanta C. of C., Paralympic Games, Ga. Ctr. for Children, Genesis Shelter, Jr. Achievement, United Way; chmn. adv. bd. united Way Drug Abuse Action Ctr.; chmn. Good-Touch/Bad-Touch, Atlanta. Named Retailer of Yr., Photographic Trade News mag., Entrepreneur of Yr. Bus. Atlanta mag., marketof of Yr. Atlanta chpt. Am. Mktg. Assn.; named to Ga. State U. Bus. Hall of Fame. Mem. Golf Club of Ga.

**WOLF, CHARLES BENNO**, lawyer; b. Chgo., Apr. 16, 1950; s. Ludwig and Hilde (Mandelbaum) W.; m. Sarah Lloyd, Sept. 1, 1973; children: Walter Ludwig, Peter Barton. AB, Brown U., 1972; JD, U. Chgo., 1975. Bar: Ill. 1975, U.S. Dist. Ct. (no. dist.) Ill. 1975, U.S. Ct. Appeals (4th, 5th, 6th, 7th, 8th, 9th, 10th, and 11th cirs.) 1985, U.S. Supreme Ct. 1985. Ptnr. Vedder, Price, Kaufman & Kammholz, Chgo., 1975—, exec. com., 1999—. Co-author: ERISA Claims and Litigation, 10th edit., 1995; contbr. articles to profl. jours. Fellow Am. Coll. Employee Benefits Counsel; mem. ABA (co-chair labor sect. subcom. on collective bargaining and employee benefits, past co-chair subcom. on multi-employer plans), Internat. Found. Employee Benefit Plans. Office: Vedder Price Kaufman & Kammholz 222 N La Salle St Ste 2600 Chicago IL 60601-1100 Office Phone: 312-609-7888. Business E-Mail: cwolf@vedderprice.com.

**WOLF, CHRISTOPHER ROBIN**, investment executive; b. Richmond, Va., Apr. 29, 1954; s. Rene Arthur and Charlotte Elizabeth W.; m. Lise Holt Honoré; children: Eleonor Charlotte, Elyssa Harriet. BA summa cum laude, univ. honors, Ohio Wesleyan U., 1978; MBA, Yale U., 1983. Pres. Computer Data Designs Co., San Francisco, 1978-81; v.p. investment banking Kidder, Peabody & Co., Inc., N.Y.C., 1983-88; sr. v.p., ptnr. mergers and acquisitions Oppenheimer & Co., Inc., N.Y.C., 1989-91; mng. ptnr. The Georgica Group, N.Y.C., 1991—96; group head investment banking Fahnestock & Co., Inc., N.Y.C., 1996—; exec. v.p., CFO Hyseq, Inc., Sunnyvale, Calif., 1996-99; pres., CEO Protogene Labs., Inc., Palo Alto, Calif., 1999—2001; CEO, chief investment officer KingsGate Capital Mgmt., LLC, San Francisco, 2001—. Adj. prof. Columbia U. Grad. Sch. Bus. Trustee Arneson Inst., Delaware, Ohio; ptnr. Blue Hill Ptnrs., N.Y.C., 604 Ptnrs., San Francisco, Rock Creek Ptnrs., Boulder, Colo. Mem. Knickerbocker Club, River Club, Yale Club, Phi Beta Kappa. Episcopalian. Avocations: travel, tennis, antiques, sailing, mountain climbing.

**WOLF, CONSTANCE JEANIE**, elementary school educator; b. Baldwin Park, Calif., May 26, 1948; d. Emil Richard and Connie (Rust) Schweikart, m. George Paul III Linehan (div.); m. H. William Wolf (div.). AA, Rio Hondo Jr. Coll., Whittier, Calif.; BA, MA, San Diego State U. Tchr. 5th-6th grade Grant Elem. Sch., San Diego, 1971—75; tchr. 6th grade Chesterton Elem. Sch., San Diego, 1975—80; tchr. 5th-8th grade San Diego Sch. Creative and Performing Arts, San Diego, 1980—. Named Tchr. of Yr., San Diego Unified Schs., 1992, Outstanding Tchr., San Diego State Coll., 2001—03. Avocation: sailing.

**WOLF, DALE B.**, health facility administrator, corporate financial executive; BA, Univ. Colorado; MBA, Univ. Denver. V.p. specialty ops. The Travelers, 1988—94; sr. v.p. bus. devel. MetraHealth Cos., Inc., 1995; exec. v.p. SpectraScan Health Svcs., Inc., 1995—96; sr. v.p. Coventry Health Care, Bethesda, Md., 1996—98, CFO, 1996—2004, treas., 1996—2004, exec. v.p., 1998—2004, CEO, 2004—. Bd. dir. HealthExtras Inc. Mem.: Soc. of Actuaries. Office: Coventry Health Care 6705 Rockledge Dr Bethesda MD 20817*

**WOLF, DALE EDWARD**, state official; b. Kearney, Nebr., Sept. 6, 1924; m. Clarice Wolf; 4 children. BSc, U. Nebr., 1945; PhD in Agronomy and Weed Control, Rutgers U., 1949. With Dept. Agr., 1946; assoc. prof. agronomy Rutgers U., 1949; with E.I. duPont de Nemours & Co., Inc., from 1950, dir. agrichem. mktg., then gen. mgr. biochem. dept., 1972-79; v.p. biochems., also chmn. bd. subs. Endo Labs., Inc., Wilmington, Del., from 1979; group v.p. Agrl. Products, Wilmington, Del. from 1983; dir. Del. Devel. Office, Dover, 1987-89; lt. gov. of Del. Dover, 1989-93; gov. State of Del., Dover, 1993. Vice chmn. WSFS Bank, 1998-2005, Emerald Bioagr. Corp., 2002—; trustee Christiana Care Health Svcs., 2002—. Co-author: Principles of Weed Control, 1951. Bd. dirs. Del. Health council. ARC, 1975; gen. campaign chmn. United Way Del., 1978, also bd. dirs.; gen. campaign chmn. Girls Club Del., 1987; chmn. Del. Found. for Literacy, 1993-98; mem. adv. bd. U. Del. Hotel, Restaurant Mgmt. Sch., 1994—; chmn. Stand Up For What is Right and Just, 2003—. 1st lt. AUS, 1943-46. Decorated Bronze Star, Purple Heart; recipient Josiah Marvel award, Del. State C. of C., 2005. Mem. Nat. Agrl. Chem. Assn. (chmn. 1981-83), Farm. Mfrs. Assn. (dir.), Masons, Farmhouse Fraternity, Sigma Xi, Alpha Zeta. Republican.

**WOLF, DICK (RICHARD A. WOLF)**, television producer; b. NYC, Dec. 20, 1946; m. Susan Scranton, 1970 (div. 1981); m. Christine Marburg, 1983; 3 children. Student, U. Pa. Exec. producer, pres. Wolf Films, Inc. Copywriter, producer over a dozen campaigns and 100 TV commls., 1969-76; producer, writer (screenplay) Skateboard, 1978, School Ties, 1992; writer, script cons. (TV series) Hill Street Blues, 1985 (Emmy award, Writer's Guild nominations for episode What are Friends For); writer, producer (film) No Man's Land, 1987; writer, producer and actor (film) Masquerade, 1988; writer, exec. producer 4 installments (series TV movies) Gideon Oliver, 1989; writer, creator, exec. producer (series TV movies) Christine Cromwell, 1989-90, (TV series) Nasty Boys, 1990, H.E.L.P., Law & Order, 1990, (Producers Guild Am. shared award Episodic TV 1996, Emmy award Outstanding Drama Series, 1996/97), Mann & Machine, 1992, The Human Factor, 1992, Crime and Punishment, 1993, South Beach, 1993, New York Undercover, 1994, Swift Justice, 1996, Arrest and Trial, 2000, Dragnet, 2003-04; creator, exec. producer (TV series) Feds, 1997, Players; exec. producer (TV series) Law & Order: Special Victims Unit, 1999—, D.C., 2000, Deadline, 2000-01, Law & Order Crime & Punishment, 2002—; exec. prodr., writer Law & Order Criminal Intent, 2001—; prodr. (TV documentary) Twin Towers, 2003. Office: Wolf Films Inc c/o Universal TV 100 Universal City Plz Universal City CA 91608-1002

**WOLF, EDWARD LINCOLN**, physicist, educator; b. Cocoa, Fla., Nov. 22, 1936; s. Norman Lincoln and Harriet (Burgess) W.; m. Carol Joyce Euwema, June 15, 1958; children: Douglas Wakefield, David Lincoln. BA, Swarthmore Coll., 1958; PhD, Cornell U., 1964. Postdoctoral fellow U. Ill. Dept. Physics, Urbana, 1964-66; research assoc. Eastman Kodak Co., Rochester, NY, 1967-75; prof. physics Iowa State U. Ames, 1975-85; head dept. physics, prof. Polytechnic U., Bklyn., 1986—95, prof. physics, 1986—. Sr. vis. fellow Cavendish Lab. U. Cambridge, U.K., 1973-74; vis. prof. U. Pa., Phila., 1982; program dir. condensed matter physics NSF, 1996-98. Author: Principles of Electron Tunneling Spectroscopy, 1985; editor: Materials and Mechanisms of Superconductivity, 1985, Nanophysics and Nanotechnology, 2004. Fellow Am. Phys. Soc.; mem. AAAS, Materials Rsch. Soc., Phi Beta Kappa, Sigma Xi. Presbyterian. Avocations: jogging, bicycling, music. Office: Polytechnic U Dept Physics Six Metrotech Ctr Brooklyn NY 11201-3850 Office Phone: 718-260-3629. E-mail: ewolf@poly.edu.

**WOLF, ELIZABETH ANN**, writer; d. Walter LeRoy and Ruth Estelle Wolf; children: Theresa Marie, Sharon Michelle, Robert Anthony. Comml. artist, freelance Gen. Store Inc., NJ, 1970—79; freelance Britt's Dept. Store, NJ, 1970—79; mktg. promotions, freelance Sear's Dept. Store, Am. appliance, Bamberger's Dept. Store, Kiiack Pools, Krupps, Litton Co., and Silverstone, NJ. Author: (poetry) Flights of Mind, 1996, (children's stories and audio books) Bedtime and Other Time Stories, 2001, Secret Places, 2002, Journey Down Story Book Lane, 2002, Alley Cat and Birdie Blue, 2002, Frogs in a Bogg, 2003, Mertyl's Magic Garden, 2004; author: (creator) Stories by Lamplight, 2004; music pub. Storytime Music BMI, reporting artist StoryBookZone.com. Mem.: Nat. Poet's Soc., Am. Fedn. Astrologers. Achievements include audio books with sound effects and music designed to be entertaining, especially for visually impaired children and adults; received awards for art and poetry. Avocations: art, woodcarving, meditation, walking, swimming. Office Phone: 877-633-1123.

**WOLF, FRANK RUDOLPH**, congressman, lawyer; b. Phila., Jan. 30, 1939; m. Carolyn Stover; children: Frank, Virginia, Anne, Brenda, Rebecca. Student, U. Miss., Oxford, 1957—58; BA, Pa. State U., 1961; LLB, Georgetown U. Sch. Law, 1965. Bar: Va., Washington, DC. Lawyer pvt. practice; legis. asst. Staff of US Rep. Edward G. Biester, Jr. of Pa., 1968-71; asst. Staff of US Sec. Interior Rogers C.B. Morton, 1971-74; dep. asst. sec. Congl. and Legis. Affairs US Dept. Interior, 1974-75; mem. US Congress from 10th Va. dist., 1981—. Mem. appropriations com., US Congress, mem. sci., the depts. of state, justice, and commerce, and related agencies subcommittee, 2001-. Served in U.S. Army, 1962—63, served in USAR, 1963—67. Republican. Presbyterian. Office: US Ho Reps 241 Cannon Ho Office Bldg Washington DC 20515-4610 Office Phone: 202-225-5136.*

**WOLF, FREDERICK GEORGE**, management educator; b. Paterson, NJ, Aug. 30, 1952; s. Frederick George and Doris (Miller) W. BS, U. S.C., 1974; postgrad., Clemson U., 1976-77; MS in Environ. Health, East Tenn. State U., 1978; MS in Sys. Mgmt., U. Denver, 1990; DBA in Mgmt., Nova Southeastern U., 2000. Phys. scientist U.S. Army Environ. Hygiene Agy., Edgewood, Md., 1974-75, S.C. Dept. Health and Environ. Control, Columbia, 1977-78; environ. scientist EPA, Atlanta, 1978-79, Boston, 1979—81, Seattle, 1981—86; mgr. hazardous waste sect. Parametrix Inc., Bellevue, Wash., 1986-88; regional mgr. environ. remediation Arkema, Inc., Tacoma, 1988—2006; clin. prof. mgmt. Pacific Luth. U. Sch. Bus., Tacoma, 2006—. Bd. dirs. Acad. of Hazardous Materials Mgmt.; Lt. USNR, 1974-87. Recipient Spl. Svc. award EPA, 1982, Bronze medal, 1983. Mem. Soaring Soc. Am. (Bronze badge number 338), Sigma Xi, Epsilon Nu Eta, Sigma Beta Delta. Office: Arkema Inc 2901 Taylor Way Tacoma WA 98421-4330

**WOLF, G. VAN VELSOR, JR.**, lawyer; b. Balt., Feb. 19, 1944; s. G. Van Velsor (dec.) and Alice Roberts (Kimberly) W. (dec.); m. Ann Holmes Kavanagh, May 19, 1984; children: George Van Velsor III, Timothy Kavanagh (dec.), Christopher Kavanagh, Elisabeth Huxley. BA, Yale U., 1966; JD, Vanderbilt U., 1973. Bar: N.Y. 1974, U.S. Dist. Ct. (so. dist.) N.Y. 1974, U.S. Ct. Appeals (2d cir.) 1974, Ariz. 1982, U.S. Dist. Ct. Ariz. 1982, U.S. Ct. Appeals (9th cir.) 1982. Agrl. advisor U.S. Peace Corps, 1966-70; assoc. Milbank, Tweed, Hadley & McCloy, N.Y.C., 1973-75; vis. lectr. law Airlangga U., Surabaya, Indonesia, 1975-76; editor-in-chief Environ. Law Reporter, Washington, 1976-81; assoc. Lewis & Roca, Phoenix, 1981-84, ptnr., 1984-91, Snell & Wilmer, Phoenix, 1991—. Vis. lectr. law U. Ariz., 1990, Vanderbilt U., 1991, U. Md., 1994, Ariz. State U., 1995; cons. Nat. Trust Hist. Preservation, Washington, 1981. Editor: Toxic Substances Control, 1980; editor in chief Environ. Law Reporter 1976-81; contbr. articles to profl. jours. Bd. dirs. Ariz. divsn. Am. Cancer Soc., 1985—96, sec. Ariz. divsn., 1990—92, vice-chmn. Ariz. divsn., 1992—94, chmn. Ariz. divsn., 1994—96, bd. dirs. S.W. divsn., 1996—2003, chmn., 1996—98, nat. bd. dirs., 1999—, bd. dirs. Gt. West divsn., 2003—, bd. dirs., Cancer Action Network, 2002—, pres. Cancer Action Network, 2003—04, nat. treas., 2004—; bd. dirs. Herberger Theatre Ctr., 1998—, sec., 2001—03, vice chmn., 2003—04; bd. dirs. Phoenix Little Theatre, 1983—90, chmn., 1986—88. Recipient St. George medal Am. Cancer Soc., 1998 Mem. ABA (vice-chmn. SONREEL commn. state and regional environ. coop. 1995-98, co-chmn. 1998-2000, vice-chmn. environ. audits task force 1998-99, vice-chmn. SONREEL ann. meeting planning com. 1998-99), Assn. of Bar of City of N.Y., Ariz. State Bar Assn. (coun. environ. & nat. res. law sect. 1988-93, chmn. 1991-92, CLE com. 1992-98, chmn. 1997-98), Maricopa County Bar Assn., Ariz. Acad., Union Club N.Y.C., Univ. Club Phoenix, Phoenix Country Club. Office: Snell & Wilmer 1 Arizona Ctr Phoenix AZ 85004-2202 Office Phone: 602-382-6201. Business E-Mail: vwolf@swlaw.com.

**WOLF, GERALYN**, bishop; b. Apr. 30, 1947; BS, West Chester U., Pa., 1968; MA in Edn., Trenton State Coll., NJ, 1971; MDiv, Episcopal Div. Sch., Cambridge, Mass., 1977. Tchr. George Sch., Newtown, Pa., 1970—74; ordained deacon, 1977, priest, 1978; served several Phila. area congregations, 1977—81; vicar St. Mary's Episcopal Ch. Phila., 1981—87; dean Christ Ch. Cathedral, Louisville, 1987—95; consecrated bishop, 1996; bishop Episcopal Diocese of RI, 1996—. Retreat leader and spkr. for the homeless. Author: Down and Out in Providence, various hymn texts. Episcopalian. Achievements include serving as the first female Dean of a Cathedral; mem. US Field Hockey Touring Team, Argentina, 1973. Office: Episcopal Diocese of RI Diocesan House & Resource Ctr 275 N Main St Providence RI 02903-1298 Office Phone: 401-274-4500. Office Fax: 401-331-9430. Business E-Mail: beeplepeople@cox.net.

**WOLF, HAROLD HERBERT**, pharmacy educator; b. Quincy, Mass., Dec. 19, 1934; s. John I. and Bertha F. (Sussman) W.; m. Joan Z. Silverman, Aug. 11, 1957; children: Gary Jerome, David Neal. BS, Mass. Coll. Pharmacy,

1956; PhD, U. Utah, 1961; LLD (hon.), U. Md., 1994. Asst. prof. pharmacology Coll. Pharmacy Ohio State U., 1961-64, assoc. prof., 1964-69, prof., 1969-76, Kimberly prof., 1975-76, chmn. divsn. pharmacology, 1973-76; dean Coll. of Pharmacy, U. Utah, Salt Lake City, 1976-89, prof. pharmacology, 1976—2005, dir. Anticonvulsant Drug Devel. Program, 1989—2002, prof. emeritus, 2005—. Vis. prof. U. Sains Malaysia, 1987-88, var. Nat. Joint Commn. on Prescription Drug Use, 1976-80; mem. NIH rev. com. Biomed. Rsch. Devel. Grant Program, 1978-79; external examiner U. Malaya, 1978, 92, 96, U. Sains Malaysia, 1980. Contbr. articles in field of ctrl. nervous sys. pharmacology and field of pharm. edn. Recipient Alumni Achievement award Mass. Coll. Pharmacy, 1978, Disting. Faculty award U. Utah, 1989, Rosenblatt prize, 1989, Disting. Alumnus award Coll. Pharmacy, U. Utah, 1991, Weaver prize, 2000. Fellow AAAS, Acad. Pharm. Scis.; mem. Am. Soc. Pharmacology and Exptl. Therapeutics, Am. Pharm. Assn. (task force on edn. 1982-84), Am. Assn. Colls. of Pharmacy (pres. 1977, Disting. Pharmacy Educator award 1988, scholar in residence 1989, chmn. commn. on implementing change in pharmacy edn. 1989-92, 95-96), Am. Soc. Hosp. Pharmacists (commn. on goals 1982-84), Am. Coun. on Pharm. Edn. (bd. dirs. 1985-88), Soc. Neurosci. Jewish. Home: 4467 Adonis Dr Salt Lake City UT 84124-3922 Office: Univ Utah Coll Pharmacy Salt Lake City UT 84112

**WOLF, JEFFREY STEPHEN**, physician; b. Hartford, Conn., July 30, 1946; s. Abraham and Norma Wolf; m. Nina Loving Lockridge; children: Sarah Loving, Lawren Hiley. BS, McGill U., 1968; MD, Med. Coll. Va., 1972, MS, 1973. Diplomate Am. Bd. Colon and Rectal Surgery. Intern in surgery Mt. Sinai Hosp., N.Y.C., 1972-73, resident, 1973-75, N.Y. Med. Coll.-Met. Hosp., N.Y.C., 1975-77; chief resident in surgery Met. Hosp., N.Y.C., 1977-78; fellow colon-rectal surgery Grtr. Balt. Med. Ctr., 1978-79; colon-rectal surgeon Portsmouth, Va., 1979—. Fellow ACS, Am. Soc. Colon and Rectal Surgery; mem. AMA, Portsmouth Acad. Medicine, Med. Soc. Va., Am. Soc. Colon and Rectal Surgeons, So. Med. Assn., Chesapeake Colon-Rectal Soc., S.E. Va. Soc. Colon-Rectal Surgeons. Office: 3235 Academy Ave Ste 200 Portsmouth VA 23703-3200 Office Phone: 757-484-9653.

**WOLF, JEROME THOMAS**, lawyer; b. Austin, Minn., June 13, 1937; s. William B. and Charlotte Elaine (Rosenstock) W.; m. Ellen L., Jan. 9, 1965; children: Margo Ann, Gregory Thomas. BA, Yale U., 1959; JD, Harvard U., 1962. Bar: Minn. 1962, Mo. 1966, Kans. 1984. Ptnr. Sonnerschein, Nath & Rosenthal, Kansas City, Mo., 1994—, founding mng. ptnr. Kans. City office, 1994-2000, chmn. firm mktg. com., 1999—. Co-chair Justice for All campaign Legal Aid of Western Mo., 2000—; mem. coun. of fellows Nelson Atkins Mus., Kansas City, Mo., 2001—; chmn. Jewish Cmty. Rels. Bur. Kansas City, 1973—79, 2001—; mem. CPR commn. on future of arbitration Best Lawyers in Am. Capt. JAGC U.S. Army, 1962—66. Mem.: ABA, Mo. Bar, Kansas City Bar Found. (pres. 1979—80, founding), Kansas City Bar Assn. (pres. 1979), Phi Beta Kappa. Democrat. Home: 2411 W 70th Ter Shawnee Mission KS 66208-2741 Office: 4520 Main St Ste 1000 Kansas City MO 64111 Office Phone: 816-460-2420. Business E-Mail: jwolf@sonnerschein.com.

**WOLF, JOAN MANGON**, nursing educator; b. Dover, Ohio, June 25, 1936; d. William James and Ruth (Metcalf) M.; m. Robert Charles Wolf, 1959 Diploma Nursing, St. Luke's Sch. Nursing, 1957; B. Kent State U., 1978; MS, U. Dayton, 1979. RN, Ohio, Fla.; cert. secondary tchr. sch. nurse, sch. guidance counselor, Ohio, Fla. Charge nurse St. Luke's Hosp., Cleve., 1957—58; staff nurse Union Hosp., Dover, Ohio, 1959—64; sch. nurse Buckeye Career Ctr., New Philadelphia, Ohio, 1980—82, instr. occupl. health, 1982—98; sch. nurse Indian Valley Sch. Dist., 2000—. Coord. adult edn. Nurse Aid tng. program Buckeye Career Ctr., New Philadelphia, 1991—98; inl. nurse provider, 1998—2005. Co-author Diversified Health Occupation Lab Mgmt Guide, 1992 Lay del. East Ohio conf. of Gnadenhutten United Meth. Ch., Lakeside, Ohio, 1991-2004, Order of St. Luke; vol. Am. Cancer Soc. New Philadelphia, 1960—, Am. Heart Assn. New Philadelphia, 1960—, Cmty. Bloodmobile Program, Canton, Ohio, 1980—, Tuscarawas County Hospice, 1998—; nurse, instr. ARC first aid and CPR Muskingum Lakes chpt., 1980—. Recipient Rockefeller Found. grant Ohio State U., 1959; Jennings scholar, 1996-97 Mem. Buckeye Edn. Assn., (chmn., founder scholarship com. 1986), Ohio Edn. Assn., NEA, AAUW (v.p. 2005-07), Am. Vocat. Assn., Ohio Vocat. Assn. Disting. Svc. award 1992, Pacesetter award 1995), Tuscarawas County Friends Libr., Avon Park Friends Libr., Alpha Tau Delta, Delta Kappa Gamma Office: Indian Valley Sch Dist 100 N Walnut St Gnadenhutten OH 44629

**WOLF, JOHN MICHAEL**, adult education seminar consultant; b. Upper Darby, Pa., Aug. 21, 1946; s. Herbert Michael and Elizabeth (Collins) W.; m. Gloria Ann Pettinati, Feb. 1, 1969 (div. 1978); m. Diane Elaine Batterson, Sept. 10, 1983 (div. 1994); children: John Michael Jr., Jessica Diane. BS, Drexel U., 1969; MBA, Temple U., 1972; PhD, Walden U., 1990. Salesman Lit Bros., Upper Darby, 1961-63, Cousins Shoes, Upper Darby, 1963-69; purchasing agt. Philco-Ford Co., Phila., 1969-70; sales rep. Conn. Gen. Life Ins. Co., Phila., 1970-75, Provident Life & Accident Ins. Co., Cherry Hill, N.J., 1975-78; pres. Associated Cons., Haddonfield, N.J. 1978-96; sr. ptnr. Lifelong Learning Ptnrs., Bradenton, Fla., 1996—. Cons. in field. Chmn. U.S. Jaycees, Haddonfield, 1979; co-chmn. March of Dimes, Haddonfield, 1983. Mem. Am. Mgmt. Assn., Soc. for Accelerative Learning & Tchg., Internat. Alliance Learning Creative Edn. Found., Statue of Liberty Found., Tau Kappa Epsilon. Avocations: soccer, music, travel, skiing. Office: Lifelong Learning Ptnrs 4115 Pinar Dr Bradenton FL 34210 Office Phone: 941-758-1800. Personal E-mail: wolfman73@aol.com.

**WOLF, JOHN S.**, ambassador, federal agency administrator; b. Sept. 12, 1948; BA, Dartmouth Coll., 1970; postgrad., Princeton U., 1978-79. Fgn. svc. officer, 1970—; prin. dep. asst. sec. for int. orgn. affairs U.S. Dept. State, 1989—92; amb. to Malaysia Kuala Lumpur, 1992—95; coord. APEC, 1996, amb., 1997; spl. advisor to Pres. and Sec. of State, Caspian Basin Energy Diplomacy, 1999—2000; asst. sec. for non-proliferation U.S. Dept. State, 2001—, chief U.S. Coordination Monitoring Mission (Middle East), 2003—. Recipient Pres.'s Meritorious Svc. award, 1992, APCAC award, Asia Pacific Coun. Am. C. of C., 1996. Office: US Dept State Non-Proliferation Bureau 2201 C St NW Washington DC 20520

**WOLF, JOSEPH ALBERT**, mathematician, educator; b. Chgo., Oct. 18, 1936; s. Albert M. and Goldie (Wykoff) W. BS, U. Chgo., 1956, MS, 1957, PhD, 1959. Mem. Inst. for Advanced Study, Princeton, 1960-62, 65-66; asst. prof. U. Calif., Berkeley, 1962-64, assoc. prof., 1964-66, prof., 1966—94, Miller research prof., 1972-73, 83-84, prof. grad. sch., 1994—; prof. honorario Universidad Nacional de Cordoba, Argentina, 1989. Vis. prof. Rutgers U., 1969-70, Hebrew U., Jerusalem, 1974-76, Tel Aviv U., 1974-76, Harvard U., 1979-80, 86 Author: Spaces of Constant Curvature, 1967, 5th edit., 1984, Unitary Representations on Partially Holomorphic Cohomology Spaces, 1974, Unitary Representations of Maximal Parabolic Subgroups of the Classical Groups, 1976, Classification and Fourier Inversion for Parabolic Subgroups with Square Integrable Nilradical, 1979; (with G. Fels, A.T. Huckleberry) Cycle Spaces of Flag Domains: A Complex Geometric Approach, 2005; co-editor, author: Harmonic Analysis and Representations of Semisimple Lie Groups, 1980, The Penrose Transform and Analytic Cohomology in Representation Theory, 1993, Geometry and Representation Theory of Real and P-adic Grps., 1997, Global Differential Geometry: The Mathematical Legacy of Alfred Gray, 2000; editor Letters in Math. Physics, Jour. of Group Theory in Physics; contbr. articles to profl. jours. Alfred P. Sloan rsch. fellow, 1965-67, NSF fellow, 1959-62; recipient Médaille de l'Université de Liège, 1995. Mem. Am., Swiss Math. Socs. Office: U Calif Dept Math Berkeley CA 94720-3840 Business E-Mail: jawolf@math.berkeley.edu.

**WOLF, KARL EVERETT**, aerospace transportation executive, communications executive; b. Hartford, Aug. 19, 1921; s. Carl Fred and Anna (Voss) W.; m. Lola Sue Stoner, Aug. 1, 1948; children: Paula R., Gloria J., Glenn K. BS, U.S. Mil. Acad., 1943; JD, U. Pa., 1953; SJD, George Washington U., 1963. Bar: D.C. 1953, Conn. 1953, U.S. Supreme Ct. 1960,

Calif. 1971, Mich. 1975. Commd. 2d lt. U.S. Army, 1943, advanced through grades to lt. col., 1959, ret.; 1963; assoc. counsel Philco. Corp., Phila., 1963-73; v.p., gen. counsel Ford Aerospace Corp., Detroit, 1973-88; ret., 1988. Mem. adv. bd. Bur. Nat. Affairs, Fed. Contract Reports, Washington, 1963-73 Author: State Taxation of Government Contractors, 1964. Decorated Silver Star, Bronze Star, Purple Heart, Croix de Guerre (Belgium). Mem. ABA, Calif. Bar Assn. Home: Apt 309 25412 Sea Bluffs Dr Dana Point CA 92629-2198 E-mail: karlwolf@cox.net.

**WOLF, KATIE LOUISE,** state legislator; b. Wolcott, Ind., July 9, 1925; d. John H. and Helen Munsterman; m. Charles W. Wolf, 1945; children: Mark, Marcia. Grad., Ind. Bus. Coll., 1944. Registration officer County of White, Ind., 1960, mgr. lic. bur. Ind., 1960-68; clk. 39th Jud. Cir. Ct., 1968-78; mem. Ind. Ho. of Reps., 1985-86, Ind. State Senate, 1987—. Mem. Dem. Nat. Com., 1968-90; del. Dem. nat. convs., 1972, 76, 80, 84. Named Woman of Yr., Bus. and Profl. Women's Club, 1984, Outstanding Freshman Legislator, 1985, Legislator of Yr., Ind. Conservation Offices Assn., Ind. Trial Lawyers Assn.; recipient award, Ind. Broadcasters Assn., 1985, Athen award, Monticello Greater C. of C., 1987, award, Nat. Fedn. Ind. Bus., 1998, Lifetime Achievement award, Monticello Greater C. of C., 2000, Sagamore of the Wabash award, Gov. O'Bannon, 2000, Dir.'s award, Purdue U., 2000, 4-Way Test award, Monticello Rotary, 2001, Child Case Devel. and Step Ahead award, White County. Lutheran.

**WOLF, LINDA S.,** retired advertising executive; Grad., Ohio Wesleyan U. Asst. account exec. Leo Burnett Group, Chgo., 1978; exec. v.p. new bus., dir. worldwide, group pres. N.Am. Leo Burnett Co., Inc., Chgo., 1978-2000; CEO Leo Burnett USA, Chgo., 2000—01; chmn., CEO Leo Burnett Worldwide, Chgo., 2001—05; ret., 2005. Bd. dir. Field Mus. Natural History, Children's Meml. Hosp., The Off The Street Club, Chgo. Coun. Fgn. Rels, Econ. Club Chgo.; adv. bd. Univ. Ill., Com. 200. Recipient Advt. Woman Yr., Women's Advt. Club Chgo., 2000.

**WOLF, MARTIN EUGENE,** lawyer, educator; b. Balt., Sept. 9, 1958; s. Eugene Bernard and Mary Anna (O'Neil) W.; m. Nancy Ann Reinsfelder, May 9, 1980; children: Matthew Adam, Allison Maria, Emily Elizabeth. BA, Johns Hopkins U., 1980; JD, U. Md., 1991. Bar: Md. 1991, U.S. Dist. Ct. Md. 1992, U.S. Ct. Appeals (4th cir.) 1992, U.S. Ct. Appeals (2nd cir.) 1993, U.S. Ct. Appeals (3rd cir.) 1998, U.S. Ct. Appeals (11th cir.) 2000, U.S. Ct. Appeals (Fed. cir.) 2003, U.S. Ct. Fed. Claims 2001. Mgmt. trainee Giant Foods, Inc., Landover, Md., 1980-82, dept. mgr., 1982-83, ops. analyst, 1983-86, fin. coord., 1986-89; law clk. Piper & Marbury, LLP, Balt., 1989—91, assoc., 1991—96; prin. Law Office of Martin E. Wolf, Abingdon, Md., 1996—99; ptnr. Quinn, Gordon & Wolf Chartered, Towson, Md., 2000—. Pres. bd. dirs. Chesapeake Search & Rescue Dog Assn., Inc., 2000—02. Mem. ABA, Md. State Bar Assn., Harford County Bar Assn., Harford County Bar Found. (Vol. Svc. award 1992, 94), Am. Trial Lawyers Assn. Democrat. Roman Catholic. Avocations: lacrosse, hockey. Home: 11 Mitchell Dr Abingdon MD 21009-1628 Office Phone: 410-825-2300. Business E-Mail: mwolf@quinnlaw.com.

**WOLF, MAURICE,** retired lawyer; b. London, Eng., Oct. 15, 1931; came to U.S., 1947; s. D.I. and Esther (de Miranda) W.; m. Yolanda Pazmino, May 4, 1963; children: J. David, Monica Maria. Cert., Universidad Nacional Autonoma de Mexico, Mexico City, 1959; BA with honors, UCLA, 1959; LLB, Columbia U., 1962. Bar: N.Y. 1962, D.C. 1964, U.S. Supreme Ct. 1980. Atty., advisor Office Satellite Communications, FCC, Washington, 1962-66, counsel, 1966-72; sr. counsel Inter-Am. Devel. Bank, Washington, 1972-77; sr. ptnr. Wolf, Arnold & Cardoso PC, Washington, 1977—2005; ret., 2005. Vis. prof. internat. law Am. U. Sch. Law, 1996-97, co-dir. summer internat. law program, Santiago, Chile, 1997; vis. lectr. U. Ga., 1998. Co-author: Doing Business With The International Development Agencies in Washington, 1983; mem. editl. adv. bd. Internat. Legal Materials, 1997—; contbr. articles to profl. jours. Parents fund coun. Williams Coll., 1984—90; parents adv. coun. Kenyon Coll., 1986—90, chmn. acad. affairs, 1988—; pres. Riverside Civic Assn., Fairfax, Conn., 1969—70, 1976—77, 2005—, v.p., 1977—80; co-chmn. Mt. Vernon Coun., Fairfax, 1969—70, v.p. Riverside, 2005—; bd. dirs. Inter-Am. Bar Found., 1995—2000. Harlan Fiske Stone scholar, Columbia U., 1962. Mem.: FBA, Inter-Am. Bar Found. (bd. dirs.), Internat. Bar Assn. (adv. editl. com.), Columbia Soc. Internat. Law (pres. 1961—62), Inter-Am. Bar Assn., Am. Soc. Internat. Law, DC Bar Assn. (chmn. internat. investment fin. subcom. 1978, vice-chair internat. law steering com. 1999—2000), NY Bar Assn., Am. Arbitration Assn. (internat. and comml. panels, large complex case panel, nat. arbitration forum panel), Williams Club. Avocations: photography, cooking. Office **Phone:** 202-857-0585. Business **E-Mail:** mwolf@interlawyers.com.

**WOLF, NAOMI,** writer; b. San Francisco, Nov. 12, 1962; d. Leonard and Deborah W.; m. David Shipley, Sept. 1993. BA, Yale U., 1984. Author: The Beauty Myth: How Images of Beauty Are Used Against Women, 1990, Fire With Fire: The New Female Power and How It Will Change the 21st Century, 1993, The Treehouse: Eccentric Wisdom from My Father on How to Live, Love and See, 2005; contbr. to periodicals including New Republic, N.Y. Times, Wall Street Journal. Rhodes scholar, 1986. Office: c/o John Brockman Inc 5 E 59th St New York NY 10022

**WOLF, PETER,** singer, composer; b. Bronx, NY, Mar. 7, 1946; m. Faye Dunaway, Aug. 7, 1974 (div. 1979). Disc jockey WBCN-FM; formed J. Geils Band, 1967. Singer (with J. Geils Band): (songs) Centerfold, 1981, (albums) The J. Geils Band, 1970, The Morning After, 1971, Bloodshot, 1973, Sanctuary, 1978, Freeze Frame, 1981, Showtime!, 1982, others; singer: (solo albums) Lights Out, 1984, Come as You Are, 1987, Up to No Good, 1990, Long Line, 1996, Fool's Parade, 1998, Sleepless, 2002; singer: (films) Fried Green Tomatoes, 1991, Miracle, 2004; composer, singer: (films) Lucky Numbers, 2000; composer: (films) Mr. Wrong, 1996, The Wedding Singer, 1998, Edtv, 1999, Love Stinks, 1999. Office: Artemis Records 130 5th Ave 7th Fl New York NY 10011

**WOLF, PETER MICHAEL,** investment manager, consultant, writer; b. New Orleans, Dec. 6, 1935; s. Morris and Ruth (New) W.; m. Alessandra Cantey, July 3, 1967; children: Phelan Godchaux, Alexis Ambler. BA, Yale U., 1957; MA, Tulane U., 1963; PhD, NYU, 1968. Ptnr. Wolf and Co., New Orleans, 1958-62; assoc. Wilbur Smith & Assocs., NYC, 1968-70; faculty mem. NYU, 1966-67, Pratt Inst., NYC, 1968-70; adj. prof. Cooper Union, NYC, 1971-87; chmn. bd. fellows, mem. faculty Inst. Arch. and Urban Studies, NYC, 1972-82; prin. Peter Wolf Assocs., NYC, 1970—. Participant, advisor Investment Policy com. Fiduciary Counsel Inc., 2000-04; organizer of exhbns. Mus. Modern Art, NYC, 1969; writer exhbns. Whitney Mus. Art, NYC, 1970; contrb. exhbns. Mus. Modern Art, NYC, 1973, Albany Inst Art, 1975; vis. scholar/artist Am. Acad. in Rome, 2001 Author: Hot Towns: The Future of the Fastest Growing Communities in America, 1999; Land in America: Its Value, Use and Control, 1981; On Streets, 1979; The Future of the City: New Directions in Urban Planning, 1974; The Evolving City, Urban Design Proposals by Ulrich Franzen and Paul Rudolph, 1974, Another Chance for Cities, 1970, Eugene Hénard and the Beginning of Urbanism in France 1900-1914, 1969. Trustee Guild Hall, East Hampton, NY, 1981-86, 99—, Van Allen Inst., 1995—; Godchaux Res. Plantation Fund, pres. 1994—; chmn. bd. trustees Van Allen Inst., NY, 1999-2000; adv. bd. Nat. Acad. Design, 1999—; dir. Franklin Realty Co., 2005—; trustee Village Preservation Soc. 2005— NEA Found. fellow, 1979; Graham Found. fellow, 1967-68, 94-95; Fulbright fellow, 1965-66; Ford Found. grantee, 1971-74; recipient Charles P. Shattuck award Nat. Rsch. Edn. Trust Fund, 1983. Mem.: Inst. Fn. Investors, Contemporary Arts Coun. Mus. Modern Art. Avocation: tennis. Home: 325 West End Ave New York NY 10023-8135 Office: 19 W 44th St Ste 812 New York NY 10036 Office Phone: 212-302-4240.

**WOLF, ROBERT EDWARD,** physician, educator; b. Houston, Jan. 20, 1942; s. John Eaton and Ruby Lucile (Bukowski) W.; m. Ann Elizabeth Killebrew, Dec. 23, 1967; 1 child, Robert Edward, Jr. BA, Baylor U., 1964;

MA, U. Tex. Med. Br., 1968, MD, 1969, PhD, 1973. Diplomate Am. Bd. Internal Medicine. Intern in internal medicine U. Tex. Med. Br., Galveston, 1969-70, resident in internal medicine, 1970-71; fellowship in rheumatology U. Tex. Health Scis. Ctr., Dallas, 1973-75; rsch. assoc. VAMC, Dallas, 1975-77; asst. prof. of medicine U. Tex. Health Scis. Ctr., Dallas, 1975-77; staff physician, chief rheumatology VA Med. Ctr., Shreveport, La., 1977—; chief rheumatology La. State U. Health Scis. Ctr., 1997—2003, assoc. prof. medicine, 1977-89, prof. medicine, 1989—2003, dir. Arthritis Ctr., 1990—2003, prof. emeritus, 2004—. Mem. faculty promotions com. La. State U. Health Scis. Ctr., 1994—98, rsch. adv. coun., 1992—2003, adminstrv. coun., 1994—2003, utilization rev. com., 1983—95. Contbg. author: Selected Topics in Clinical Chemistry, 1972, Serum Protein Abnormalities, 1975; contbr. articles to profl. jours. Undergrad. edn. com. Arthritis Found., Atlanta, 1979-82, pres., 1983-85, exec. com.; active Lupus Found., Shreveport. Lt. comdr. USPHS, 1971-73. Recipient Grand (Student) award Nat. Rsch. Forum, Galveston, 1968, 3rd (Resident) award, 1970, Multipurpose Arthritis Ctr. award NIH, Bethesda, Md., 1977, Ctr. of Excellence-Arthritis award State of La., Baton Rouge, 1990-2003. Fellow: Am. Coll. Rheumatology. Office: VA Med Ctr 510 E Stoner Ave Shreveport LA 71101

**WOLF, ROBERT JOHN,** music educator; b. East Chicago, Ind. s. Robert Wilson and Filumena (Balestra) Wolf. B Music Edn., Butler U., 1973; MM in Organ, U. Mich., 1979, DMA in Organ, 1987. Asst. tchr. U. Mich., Ann Arbor, Mich., 1974—76; dir. music St. Michael Ch., Monroe, Mich., 1973—80, Sacred Heart Ch., Dearborn, Mich., 1980—95, St. Patrick Ch., Brighton, Mich., 1995—; conductor Oratorio Soc. of city of Dearborn, Dearborn, Mich., 1988—90, Dearborn Ecumenical Chorus, Dearborn, Mich., 1990—95, The Grosse Pointe Cmty. Chorus, Grosse Pointe Shores, Mich., 1990—95. Workshop presenter Dioceses of Lansing, Lansing, Mich., 1995—; midwest rep. Nat. Pastoral Musicians, Silver Springs, Md., 2005—. Author: Index of Organ Works Based on Hymns From Worship III, 1991. Nat. chmn. of scholarships Nat. Pastoral Musicians, Silver Springs, Md., 2003—, dir. Lansing chpt., 1995—; treas. Detroit Chpt. Choristers Guild, Dallas, 2001—. Hoosier State scholarship, State of Ind., 1969, grant, The French Found., 1993—95, Sinfonia scholarship, Sinfonia, 1972. Mem.: Am. Guild English Handbell Ringers, Hymn Soc., Am. Guild Organists. Avocation: weightlifting. Home: 2226 Vinewood Blvd Ann Arbor MI 48104 Office: St Patrick Ch 711 Rickett Rd Brighton MI 48116 Office Phone: 810-229-9863 206. Office Fax: 810-220-0730. E-mail: musicdir@stpatchurch.org.

**WOLF, STEPHEN M.,** consumer products company executive, former airline executive; b. Oakland, Calif., Aug. 7, 1941; BA, San Francisco State U., 1965. Various positions Am. Airlines, Los Angeles, 1965-79, v.p. western div., 1979-81; sr. v.p. mktg. Pan Am. World Airlines, N.Y.C., 1981-82; pres., chief operating officer Continental Airlines, Houston, 1982-83; pres. Republic Airlines, Mpls., 1984-85, pres., chief exec. officer, 1985-86; chmn., pres., chief exec. officer Tiger Internat., Los Angeles, 1986-87, UAL Corp. and United Airlines, Chgo., 1987-92, chmn., CEO, 1992-94, former pres., dir.; adviser Air France, 1994-96; chmn., CEO USAIR Inc, Arlington, Va., 1996-98, chmn., 1998—2001, non exec. chmn., 2002—03; mng. ptnr. Alpilles LLC, 2003—; chmn. R.R. Donnelley & Sons Co., 2004—. Bd. dirs. Air Transport Assn., Bus. Roundtable, Washington, Altria Group Inc., conf. bd. N.Y. Internat. Air Transport Assn., Geneva, World Travel and Tourism Coun., London. Bd. dirs. Alzheimer's Disease and Related Disorders Assn., Chgo., Art Inst., Chgo., Chgo. Symphony Orch., Muscular Dystrophy Assn., Rush-Presbyn.-St. Luke's Med. Ctr., Chgo., J.L. Kellogg Sch. Bus. Adv. Coun., Northwestern U. Trustee Northwestern U., mem. bus. adv. com. Transportation Ctr.*

**WOLF, TIMOTHY VAN DE WINT,** food products executive; b. Apr. 27, 1953; s. Charles and Theresa Wolf; m. Mary Therese Merritt. BA in Econs. cum laude, Harvard U., 1974; MBA, U. Chgo., 1976. Fin. analyst to sr. fin. analyst Tennant Co., Mpls., 1976-79; mgr. mktg. planning and analysis Electrolux div. Consolidated Food Corp., Stamford, Conn., 1979-80; mgr. bus. planning Pepsi USA, Purchase, NY, 1980-81, mgr. bus. devel. and competitive analysis, 1981-82, dir. bus. planning fountain beverage div., 1982-84; sr. dir. bus. planning Taco Bell Corp., Irvine, Calif., 1984-86, v.p., controller, 1986—. Bd. dirs. Irvine Med. Ctr. Harvard Coll. scholar, Cambridge, Mass. Mem.: Harvard of So. Calif., U. Calif. Chancellor's (Irvine). Avocations: tennis, skiing, golf, German history, international relations. Office: Molson Coors Brewing Co 1225 17th St Ste 3200 Denver CO 80202

**WOLF, WERNER PAUL,** physicist, researcher; b. Vienna, Apr. 22, 1930; arrived in U.S., 1963, naturalized, 1977; s. Paul and Wilhelmina Wolf; m. Elizabeth Eliot, Sept. 23, 1954; children: Peter Paul, Mary-Anne Githa. BA, Oxford U., Eng., 1951, DPhil, MA, Oxford U., Eng., 1954; MA (hon.), Yale U., 1965. Rsch. fellow Harvard U., 1956-57; Fulbright travelling fellow, 1956-57; Imperial Chem. Industries rsch. fellow Oxford U., 1957-59, univ. demonstrator, lectr., 1959-62; lectr. New Coll., 1957-62; faculty Yale U., 1963—2001, prof. physics and applied sci., 1965-76, dir. grad. studies dept. engring. and applied sci., 1973-76, Becton prof., 1976-84, chmn. dept. engring. and applied sci., 1976-81, chmn. council engring., 1981-84, Raymond J. Wean prof. engring. and applied sci., prof. physics, 1984—2001, prof. emeritus, 2002—, dir. undergrad. studies dept. applied physics, 1987-94, dir. grad. studies coun. engring., 1989, chmn. dept. applied physics, 1990-97, chair commn. on econ. status of faculty, 1990-92, dir. editl. affairs for engring., 1994-99. Cons. Dupont Expt. Sta., Wilmington, Del., 1957, Hughes Aircraft, Culver City, Calif., 1957, GE Rsch. Lab., Schenectady, N.Y., 1960, Mullard Rsch. Labs., Salfords, England, 1961, IBM, Yorktown Heights, N.Y., 1962-66, Brookhaven Nat. Lab., 1966-80, GE R & D Ctr., Schenectady, 1966-93, U. Bridgeport, 1995-96, Nat. U. Singapore, 1994-96; vis. prof. Technische Hochschule, Munich, Germany, 1969; Sci. Research Council sr. vis. fellow Oxford U., 1980, 84; vis. fellow Corpus Christi Coll., 1984, 87; mem. program com. Conf. Magnetism and Magnetic Materials, 1963, 65, 86, chmn., 1968, mem. adv. com., 1964-65, 70-76, 85-88, chmn., 1972, steering com., 1970-71, conf. gen. chmn., 1971; mem. organizing, program coms. Internat. Congress on Magnetism, 1967, internat. program com., 1973-79, planning com., 1979-85; vis. physicist Brookhaven Nat. Lab., 1966, 68, vis. sr. physicist, 1970, research collaborator, 1972, 74, 75, 77, 80; mem. vis. com. dept. phys./sci. U. Del., 1980, 84, 86; mem. NATO Advanced Study Inst. Program Com., 1983, 85, internat. adv. bd. Yamada Conf. XXV on Magnetic Phase Transitions, 1990; mem. bd. visitors Fairfield U. Sch. Engring., 1996-2005. Editor: CASE Reports, 1988-90; contbr. articles to profl. jours. Named vis. guest fellow, Royal Soc. London, 1987; recipient sr. U.S. scientist award, Alexander von Humboldt Found, 1983, Sheffield Disting. Tchg. award, Yale U. Faculty Engring., 2000. Fellow IEEE (life), Am. Phys. Soc. (edn. com. 1977-80, program dir. Indsl. Grad. Intern Program 1978-79, chmn. fellowship com., Div. Condensed Matter Physics 1981-83); mem. Conn. Acad. Sci. and Engring., Yale Sci. and Engring. Assn. (Meritorious Svc. award 1985). Home: 37 Apple Tree Ln Woodbridge CT 06525-1258 Office: Yale U Dept Applied Physics PO Box 208284 New Haven CT 06520-8284 Business E-Mail: werner.wolf@yale.edu.

**WOLF, WILLIAM B., JR.,** lawyer; b. Washington, Sept. 11, 1927; s. William B. and Ruth (Pack) W.; m. Edna Russell Jacobs, Aug. 8, 1952 (div. Oct. 1976); children: Susan Marcia, William B. III, Victoria Katharine; m. Audrey Ann Riven, Nov. 29, 1980. AB, Princeton, 1948; postgrad., Oxford U., 1950; LLB, Yale U., 1951. Bar: D.C. 1951, U.S. Supreme Ct. 1954. Md. 1963. Ptnr. Wolf & Wolf, Washington, 1951-64, 82—; sole practice Washington, 1964-72, 75-81; ptnr. Wolf & Rosenblatt, Washington, 1972-75, Wolf, Amram & Hahn, P.C., Washington, 1981-82. Vice chmn. Security Nat. Bank, Washington, 1984-85. Author: Lawyers Are a Dime a Dozen, 1999. Pres. Nat. Capital USO, 1966—67, Jewish Hist. Soc. Greater WAshington, pres. 2000; Brotherhood Washington Hebrew Congregation, 1967-68. With USN, 1945, sgt. U.S. Army, 1946—48. Mem.: ABA, Bar Assn. D.C., University (Washington), Nassau (Princeton, N.J.), Edgartown (Mass.) Yacht, Woodmont Country. Republican. Jewish. Home: Watergate East 2700 Virginia Ave NW Washington DC 20037 Office: Wolf & Wolf 2510 Virginia Ave NW Washington DC 20037 Office Phone: 202-298-6000. E-mail: visible@abanet.org.

**WOLF, WILLIAM MARTIN,** computer company executive, consultant; b. Watertown, NY, Aug. 29, 1928; s. John and Rose (Emrich) Wolf; m. Eileen Marie Jolly, Aug. 19, 1952 (div. 1972); children: Rose(dec.), Sylvia, William. BS, St. Lawrence U., 1950; MS, U. N.H., 1951; postgrad., U. Pa., 1951—52, MIT, 1952—55. Programmer digital computer lab. MIT, Cambridge, 1952—54, dir., exec. dir. Tech. Capital Network, 1992—94; pres. Wolf R & D Corp., Boston, 1954—69, Wolf Computer Corp., Boston, 1966—76, Planning Sys. Internat., Boston, 1976—81, Micro Computer Software Inc., Cambridge, 1981—88, Tech. Acquisition Corp., Boston, 1989—91, Planning Internat., Inc., Boston, 1989—94, Wolfsort Corp., Boston, 1989—; chmn. Wolf & McManus, Brookline, Mass., 1995—; founder Year 2000 Software Corp., Brookline, Mass., 1996—2000; co-founder, pres., CEO Eureka.Com, Inc., Rockport, Mass., 1999—2000, FocuSystems, Inc., Rockport, Mass., 2000—; founder, pres., CEO Mass. Med. Agy., 2002—. Co-founder, pres. Assn. Ind. Software Cos., Washington, 1965—67, Design Sci. Inst., Phila., 1969—73, Nat. Coun. Profl. Svc. Firms, Washington, 1970—75; seminar leader MIT Sloan Sch., Cambridge, 2070; co-founder, bd. dirs. Harbor Nat. Bank, Boston. Author: (autobiography) No "e", 2005. Trustee Addison Gilbert Hosp., Gloucester, Mass., 1963; co-founder X-10 Orgn., Boston, 1962; v.p. Young Pres. Orgn., Boston, 1970; overseer Mus. Sci., Boston, 1989—97. Named Outstanding Young Man in Boston, Jaycees, 1962; recipient Spkr.'s award, Data Processing Mgmt. Assn., 1966. Mem.: World Bus. Coun., MIT Club (Alumni award 1991), Forty-Niners. Achievements include invention of management system; orbit calculator; patents for sorting method; method for solving Year 2000 problem. Office Phone: 978-273-0344. Personal E-mail: wmwolf@aol.com.

**WOLFBERG, MELVIN DONALD,** optometrist, educational association administrator, consultant; b. Altoona, Pa., June 24, 1926; s. Max Alex and Claire (Schiffman) Wolfberg; m. Audrey Iris Koch, Apr. 26, 1952; children: Debra Lynn, Michael Alex, Daniel Ben; m. Linda Diane Machesic, Dec. 4, 1979. OD, Pa. Coll. Optometry, Phila., 1951; D of Ocular Sci. (hon.), New England Coll. Optometry, 1989, Ill. Coll. Optometry, 1990; LHD (hon.), Pa. Coll. Optometry, 1998. Lic. optometrist, Pa. Pvt. practice and ptnr. optometric practice, Selinsgrove, Pa., 1951-79; pres. Pa. Coll. Optometry, Phila., 1979-89, chmn. bd., 1976-79; v.p. profl. rels. Bausch and Lomb, Rochester, NY, 1991-95; pres. In Vision Inst., Boston, 1991-95; ptnr./dir. Sylvan Learning Ctr., Vero Beach, Fla., 1996—. Cons. to sec. HEW, Washington, 1970-77; dir. Better Vision Inst., N.Y.C., 1960-80. Mem. Selinsgrove City Coun., 1961-62; pres. Selinsgrove Community Chest, 1957; chmn. Selinsgrove Sanit. Rep. Nat. Com., 1972, 76; chmn. Nat. Inter-Profl. Health Coun., Washington, 1972-77; dir. Univ. City Sci. Ctr., Phila., 1980-87; adv. com. Coun. Higher Edn., Commonwealth Pa., 1980-89. Served with U.S. Army, 1944-46, ETO. Decorated Purple Heart, Bronze Star, Silver Star; named Man of Yr. Central Pa. Optometric Soc., 1964, Alumnus of Yr. Pa. Coll. Optometry, 1970; recipient Carel C. Koch Meml. medal, 1989. Fellow Am. Acad. Optometry (pres. 1985-86, Eminent Svc. award, 2005); mem. Pa. Assn. Colls. and Univs. (exec. com. 1988-93), sec.-treas. 1985-88, vice chmn. 1988-89), Pa. Optometric Assn. (pres. 1959-61, Optometrist of Yr., Ewalt Meritorious Svc. award 2003), Am. Optometric Assn. (pres. 1969-70, Disting. Svc. award 1994, named to Nat. Optometry Hall Fame 2004), Pa. Coll. Optometry Alumni Assn. (pres. 1957), Beta Sigma Kappa. Office Phone: 772-299-0502. Business E-Mail: ilovesylvan@bellsouth.net.

**WOLFE, BARBARA L.,** economics professor, researcher; b. Phila., Feb. 15, 1943; d. Manfred and Edith (Heimann) Kingshoff; m. Stanley R. Wolfe, Mar. 20, 1965 (div. Mar. 1978); m. Robert H. Haveman, July 29, 1983; children: Jennifer Ann Wolfe, Ari Michael Wolfe. BA, Cornell U., Ithaca, N.Y., 1965; MA, U. Pa., 1971; PhD, U Pa., 1973. Asst. prof. Bryn Mawr (Pa.) Coll., 1973-76; rsch. assoc. Inst. Rsch. on Poverty, Madison, Wis., 1976-77, dir., 1994—2000; from asst. prof. to assoc. prof. U. Wis., Madison, 1977-88, prof., 1988—, dir., LaFollette Sch. Pub. Affairs, 2006—. Adj. prof. Australian Nat. U., 2002-; resident scholar NIAS, Wassenaar, Netherlands, 1984-85, 96-97; vis. scholar Russell Sage Found., N.Y., 1991-92. Co-author: Succeeding Generations, 1994; editor: (book) Role of Budgetary Policy in Demographic Transitions, 1994, contbr. articles to profl. jours. Mem. Commn. on Children with Disabilities, Washington 1994-95, Tech. Adv. Panel Social Security, Washington, 1994-95; vice chair bd. on children, youth and families IOM and NAS, 2005—. Recipient Best Article of Yr. award Rev. Income and Wealth, 1992, Fulbright award Coun. Internat. Exch. of Scholars, 1984. Mem.: Inst. of Medicine, Assn. Pub. Policy Mgmt. (policy coun. 2001—04), Internat. Inst. Pub. Fin. (bd. mgmt. 1994—2000, v.p. 2000—03), Am. Econ. Assn. (bd. com. 1989—92, exec. bd. 1996—99). Office: U Wis Inst Rsch on Poverty 1180 Observatory Dr Madison WI 53706-1320 Office Phone: 608-262-0662. E-mail: wolfe@LaFollette.wisc.edu, bwolfe@wisc.edu.

**WOLFE, CAMERON WITHGOT, JR.,** lawyer; b. Oakland, Calif., July 7, 1939; s. Cameron W. and Jean (Brown) W.; m. Frances Evelyn Bishopric, Sept. 2, 1964; children: Brent Everett, Julie Frances, Karen Jean. AB, U. Calif., Berkeley, 1961, JD, 1964. Bar: Calif. 1965, U.S. Dist. Ct. (no. dist.) Calif. 1965, U.S. Ct. Appeals (9th cir.) 1965, U.S. Tax Ct. 1966, U.S. Ct. Claims 1977, U.S. Ct. Appeals (3d cir.) 1980, U.S. Supreme Ct. 1986. Assoc., then ptnr. Orrick, Herrington & Sutcliffe, San Francisco, 1964—. Bd. dirs. Crowley Maritime Corp.; mem. steering com. Western Pension Conf. Pres. League To Save Lake Tahoe, 1979, 80; chmn. League To Save Lake Tahoe Charitable Truste, 1966-91, Piedmont Ednl. Fund Campaign, 1982-83; pres. Piedmont Ednl. Found., 1969-90; bd. dirs. Yosemite Fund, 1993—. With U.S. Army, 1957; with USAR, 1957-65. Mem. ABA (taxation com.), Calif. State Bar, San Francisco Bar Assn., San Francisco Tax Club (pres. 1997-98), Pacific Union Club, Claremont Country Club (Oakland, Calif.), Order of Coif, Phi Beta Kapa. Home: 59 Lakeview Ave Piedmont CA 94611-3514 Office: Orrick Herrington Sutcliffe 405 Howard St Fl 11 San Francisco CA 94105-2680

**WOLFE, CARL GUNDERSEN,** adult education educator; b. Hudson, N.Y., Mar. 16, 1956; s. James and Ellen Gundersen Wolfe. BS, U. Findlay, Ohio, 1978; MA, Marshall U., Huntington, W.Va., 1990; Cert., Internat. Summer Sch., Oslo, Norway, 1988. Instr. U. Rio Grande, Ohio, 1990—91; clk. Beckley Deli, W.Va., 2000—05; instr. Mountain State U., Beckley, W.Va., 2005—. Editor: (religious ency.) Travelers on the Long Road - A History of West Virginia Methodism. Mem.: Sons of Norway. Quaker. Home: 366 Mankin Ave Beckley WV 25801 Office: Mountain State Univ South Kanawha St Beckley WV 25801 E-mail: cwolfe@mountainstate.edu.

**WOLFE, CHARLES MORGAN,** electrical engineering educator; b. Morgantown, W.Va., Dec. 21, 1935; s. Slidell Brown and Mae Louise (Maness) W.; children— David Morgan, Diana Michele BS.E.E., W.Va. U., Morgantown, 1961, MS.E.E., 1962; PhD, U. Ill., 1965. Research assoc. U. Ill., Urbana, 1965; mem. staff MIT Lincoln Lab., Lexington, Mass., 1965-75; prof. elec. engring Washington U., St. Louis, 1975-97, Samuel C. Sachs prof., 1982-90, dir. semicondr. research lab., sr. prof., 1979-90. Cons. MIT Lincoln Lab., 1975-76, Fairchild Semicondr., Palo Alto, Calif., 1975-76, Air Force Avionics Lab., Dayton, Ohio, 1976-79. U. Ill., 1983-85 Author: Physical Properties of Semiconductors, 1989; editor: Gallium Arsenide and Related Compounds, 1979; contbr. articles to profl. jours., chpts. to books Served as sgt. USMC, 1955-58 Fellow IEEE (field awards com. 1984-87, Jack A. Morton award 1990); mem. NAE, AAAS, Electrochem. Soc. (Electronics divsn. award 1978).

**WOLFE, DAVID LOUIS,** lawyer; b. Kankakee, Ill., July 24, 1951; s. August Christian and Irma Marie (Nordmeyer) W.; m. Gail Lauret Fritz, Aug. 25, 1972; children: Laura Beth, Brian David, Kaitlin Ann. BS, U. Ill., 1973; JD, U. Mich., 1976. Bar: Ill. 1976, U.S. Dist. Ct. (no. dist.) Ill. 1976. Assoc., Gardner, Carton & Douglas, Chgo., 1976-82, ptnr., 1983—; chmn. mgmt. Com., HR law dept; lectr. ABA, Estate Planning Aid Assn. for Lutherans SMART Program, Chgo., 1980-84, Ill. Inst. Continuing Legal Edn., Employee Benefits Sec. Coun., Chgo. Bar Assn., Lake Shore Nat. Bank, Ill. State Bar Assn., Daughters Charity. Nat. Health Sys., Lutheran Health Sys., AM. Assn. Homes & Svcs. for Aging, Mich. Assn. Cert. Pub. Accts., Diversified Investment Advisors, Decalogue Soc., Conf Cons. Actuaries, Ind. Pension Conf., Inst Internat. Rsch., Lake Shore Bank Chgo. Contbr. articles to legal publs. Recipient Recognition award Ill. Inst. Continuing Legal Edn., 1981-84, Named to Best Laywers Am., 1993-2004. Mem. ABA (sects. on taxation, corp. banking and bus. law 1981—, lectr.), NFL Players Assn. (cert. contract advisor 1983—), NCAA (cert. contract advisor), Chgo. Assn. Commerce and Industry (employee benefit subcom. 1983—), Ill. State Bar Assn. (employee benefits sect. council, 1986-95, recognition award 1983), Phi Kappa Phi, Beta Alpha Psi, Beta Gamma Sigma, Sigma Iota Lambda, Phi Eta Sigma. E-mail: dwolfe@gcd.com. Office: Gardner Carton & Douglas LLP 191 N Wacker Dr Chicago IL 60606-1698 Office Phone: 312-569-1313. E-mail: dwolfe@gld.com.

**WOLFE, ELLEN DARLENE,** school librarian, elementary school educator; b. Mattoon, Ill., Dec. 16, 1952; d. Floyd Dale and Irma Jane (Hensley) Robinson; m. Walter Ray Wolfe, Mar. 12, 1994; children: Gregory David, William Scott, Joseph Dean, Brian Matthew, Joshua Paul. BS, Ind. State U., 1987. Cert. elem. educator, Ill. Reading tchr. Marshall (Ill.) Community Dist. 2, 1987-91; law librr. Robinson (Ill.) Correctional Ctr., 1991-94; libr. Palestine (Ill.) Cmty. Unit Sch. Dist. # 3, 1994—. Libr. City of Marshall, 1986—; dir. summer camp Clark County Handicapped Assn., Marshall, 1988—; law libr. Robinson Correctional Ctr., 1991. Coord. Jr. youth group St. Mary's Cath. Ch. Mem. Correctional Edn. Assn., Home Ext. Club, Kappa Delta Pi, Phi Delta Kappa, Roman Catholic. Home: 18993 E River Rd Palestine IL 62451-2430 Office: Robinson Correctional Ctr PO Box 1000 Robinson IL 62454-0919

**WOLFE, ETHYLE RENEE (MRS. COLEMAN HAMILTON BENEDICT),** academic administrator; b. Burlington, Vt., Mar. 14, 1919; d. Max M. and Rose (Saiger) Wolfe; m. Coleman Hamilton Benedict, Dec. 4, 1954. BA, U. Vt., 1940, MA, 1942; postgrad., Bryn Mawr Coll., 1942—43; PhD, NYU, 1950; LHD (hon.), CUNY, 1989; LittD (hon.), Iona Coll., 1989. Tchg. fellow U. Vt., 1940—42; rsch. fellow Latin Bryn Mawr (Pa.) Coll., 1942—43; instr. classics Bklyn. Coll., 1947—49, instr. classical langs., 1949—54, asst. prof., 1954—59, assoc. prof., 1960—68, prof., 1968—, acting chmn. dept. classics and comparative lit., 1962—63, chmn. dept., 1967—72; dean Bklyn. Coll. Sch. Humanities, 1971—78; exec. officer Bklyn. Coll. Humanities Inst., 1980—89; provost and v.p. for acad. affairs Bklyn. Coll., 1982—88, provost emeritus, 1989. Exec. com., chmn. com. on undergrad. affairs, com. on univ.-wide programs CUNY; study group AAAS, 1987—89, pub., 1987—89; dir. Nat. Core Visitors Programs, 1985—89, Fund for Improvement of Postsecondary Edn.-funded Ctr. for Core Studies, 1987—88; co-chair senate report Chancellor's Coll. Prep. Initiative, 1991; exec. com The Liberal Art of Sci.: Agenda for Action. Mem. editl. bd.: Classical World, 1965—71; co-editor: The Am. Classical Rev., 1971—76; contbr. articles to profl. jours. Named Ethyle R. Wolfe Inst. for the Humanities Bklyn. Coll. in her honor, 1989; named to Hall of Honor, U. Vt., 1991, Disting. U. Faculty Sen. Emeritus, CUNY, 1992; recipient Kirby Flower Smith award, 1939, Goethe prize, U. Vt., 1940, Alumni Achievement award, 1985, Nat. Presdl. medal, NEH, Charles Frankel prize, 1990; grantee, 1971, 1982—84, Mellon Found., 1982—85, 1986—89, Exxon, 1986—89. Josiah Macy, 1986—90. Mem.: Am. Soc. Papyrologists, Classical Assn. Atlantic States (exec. com.), Vergilian Soc. Am., Archeol. Inst. Am., Am. Philol. Assn., N.Y. Classical Club (past pres., exec. com.), Phi Beta Kappa (pres. 1988—90, past pres. Rho of N.Y. chpt., Spl. Citation of Honor on Sesquicentennial U. Vt. 1998). Home: 360 W 22nd St New York NY 10011-2600 Office: care Ethyle R Wolfe Inst Humanities Bklyn Coll Bedford Ave # H Brooklyn NY 11222

**WOLFE, GARY DONALD,** retired commissioner, librarian; b. Altoona, Pa., Mar. 19, 1941; s. Donald George and Norma Rosmond (Cooper) W.; m. Mary Susan Olex, Aug. 5, 1967; children: Mark Douglas, Michelle Marie. BS in Elem. Edn., St. Francis Coll., Loretto, Pa., 1970; MLS, U. Pitts., Pa., 1972. Libr. clk. Altoona Pub. Libr., 1959-61; acting children's libr. Coyle Free Libr., Chambersburg, Pa., 1961-63; asst. prof. librarianship St. Francis Coll., 1963-75; administr. Centre County Libr., Bellefonte, Pa., 1975-89; dir. libr. devel. State Libr. Pa., Harrisburg, Pa., 1989-95; dep. sec. edn., commr. for librs. State of Pa., Harrisburg, Pa., 1995—. Editor: Automated Circulation: A Study, 1981. Sgt. USAR, 1963-69. Recipient Disting. Alumni award St. Francis Coll., 1997, Cert. of Commendation, Am. Assn. Sch. Librs., 2003. Mem. ALA, Pa. Libr. Assn. (treas. 1983-85, cert. of merit 1986, Disting. Svc. award 1997), Pa. Citizens for Better Librs. Republican. Avocation: reading. Home: 2407 Wicklow Dr Harrisburg PA 17112-9620 Personal E-mail: garydwolfe@comcast.net.

**WOLFE, GEORGE C.,** theater director, producer, playwright; b. Frankfurt, Ky., Sept. 23, 1954; s. Costello and Anna Wolfe. BA, Pomona Coll., 1976; MFA, NYU, 1983. With Inner City Cultural Center, Los Angeles, Calif., 1975—78; teacher City Coll. of N.Y. & Richard Allen Ctr. for Cultural Art; resident dir. Public Theatre, N.Y.C., 1990—93; prodr. N.Y. Shakespeare Festival, N.Y.C., 1993—; head prodr. Public Theatre, N.Y.C., 1992—2004. Works include: writer, lyricist (plays) Paradise!, 1985; writer, dir. The Colored Museum, 1986 (Elizabeth Hull-Kate Warriner award, Dramatists Guild, 1986), Jelly's Last Jam, 1992 (Drama Desk award, 1992, Joe A. Callaway award, Stage Dirs. and Choreographers Found., 1993); writer Queenie Pie, 1987, The Wild Party, 2000; scene contbr. Urban Blight, 1988; curator Festival of New Voices, 1990, 92; adaptor, dir. Spunk, 1990 (Obie award best dir., 1990); dir., prodr. (Broadway shows) Angels in America: Millennium Approaches, 1992, (Tony award best dir., 1993), Angels in America: Perestroika, 1993 (Tony award nominee best dir., 1994), Twilight: Los Angeles, 1994, The Tempest, 1995, On the Town, 1998, Elaine Stritch At Liberty, 2002, Topdog/Underdog, 2002, Caroline, or Change, 2004 (Tony nom. best dir. of a musical, 2004); dir. (NY theater) Mother Courage and Her Children, 2006; prodr., lyrics, Bring in Da Noise, Bring in Da Funk, 1996 (Tony award for best dir., 1996); prodr. Golden Child, 1998, Take Me Out, 2003; dir. (TV movie), Lackawanna Blues, 2005 (Outstanding Directorial Achievement in Movies for TV, Director's Guild Am., 2005); actor: A Delicate Balance, 1996 (Tony award best leading actor, 1996). Grantee Rockefeller Found., Nat. Endowment for Arts, Nat. Inst. Musical Theatre; recipient Hull-Warriner award, 2 Audleco awards, The George Oppenheimer/Newsday award, CBS-FDG New Play award, NYU Disting. Alumni award, HBO/USA Playwrights award, Person of Yr. award Nat. Theatre Conf., Spl. Achievement award Audleco, Spirit of the City award, LAMBDA award, Career Achievement award, New Dramatists, 2000; named A Living Landmark, N.Y. Landmarks Conservancy. Mem. Dramatists Guild (mem. exec. bd.), Dir. Guild of Amer., Writers Guild of Amer., bd. dirs. Young Playwrights Festival, N.Y.C. Office: Joseph Papp Pub Theater 425 Lafayette St New York NY 10003-7087°

**WOLFE, GEORGE CROPPER,** retired private school educator, artist, writer; b. New Orleans, Sept. 6, 1933; s. Howard Edward and Amaryllis (Brannen) Wolfe; m. Catherine Vasterling, June 2, 1955; children: David, Michael, Philip. BFA, La. State U., 1956; MEd, U. New Orleans, 1972, MS in Urban Planning, 1975; postgrad., Tex. Tech U., Junction, 1986-93, Northwestern State U., La. Cert. tchr. art, social studies La. Elem. tchr. Live Oak Manor Sch., Waggaman, La., 1962-65; tchr. art Isidore Newman Sch., New Orleans, 1965-96; adj. prof. art Northwestern State U., Natchitoches, La., 1997-99; co-owner design studio Wolf Patrol Prodns. Author: (book) 3D-Wizardry: Design in Papier Mache Plaster and Foam, 1995, (video) Sculpture in Motion, 2000 (Silver Telly award, 2001), 3-D Wizardry (Telly award, 1996), Papier Maché Plaster and Foam; contbr. articles to profl. jours.; one-man shows include Hanchley Gallery, Northwestern U., 1999, exhibited in group shows at New Alexandria (La.) Mus. Art, commn. sculpture, Echo Totem, Alexandria Mus. Art, 1998, Alex the Red, 1998, Hands Supporting Hands, Wesley Found., 1999, Rhino, Northwestern State U., 2004, commn. life size puppets, Two by Two, Northwestern State U. Summer Theatre, 1998. With USCG, 1956—58. Mem. : La. Art Edn. Assn. (pres. 1978—79, coord. conf. 2005), Nat. Art Edn. Assn. (La. Art Educator of the Yr. 1990, Nat. Art Educator of the Yr. 2000—01, Victor Lowenfeld award 2002), Phi Delta Kappa (v.p., Rsch. award 1996), Kappa Delta Pi. Home: 342 Jefferson St Natchitoches LA 71457-4382

**WOLFE, GIL I.,** neurologist; b. N.Y.C., Apr. 26, 1963; s. Asher Wolfe and Haia Goldenberg; m. Amy Bolk, Dec. 10, 1989. MD, U. Tex., Dallas, 1989. Diplomate in neurology and clin. neurophysiology Am. Bd. Psychiatry and Neurology. Assoc. prof. U. Tex. Southwestern Med. Sch., Dallas, 2000—. Contbr. chapters to books, articles to profl. jours. Disting. chair in neuromuscular disease rsch. Dr. Bob and Jean Smith Found. Office: U Tex Southwestern Med Sch 5323 Harry Hines Blvd Dallas TX 75390-8897 Office Phone: 214-648-9574.

**WOLFE, GREGORY BAKER,** international relations educator; b. LA, Jan. 27, 1922; s. Harry Norton and Laura May (Baker) W.; m. Mary Ann Nelson, June 15, 1946; children: Gregory Nelson, Laura Ann, Melissa Helene. AB, Reed Coll., 1943; MA, Fletcher Sch. Law and Diplomacy, 1947, PhD, 1961; Dr. honoris causa, U. Autonoma de Guadalajara, Mex., 1984; D.H.L., S.E. Coll. Osteo. Medicine, Miami, Fla., 1985; DHL, U. Tecnologica Equinoccial, Quito, Ecuador, 2000, U. Tecnologica de Santiago, Dominican Republic, 2001. With internat. div. Arthur D. Little, Inc., Cambridge, Mass., 1951-57; dir. Greater Boston Econ. Study Com., 1957-61; dir. Latin Am. program Com. Econ. Devel., 1961-64; pres. Portland State U., 1968-74; dean Sch. Internat. Svc. Am. U., Washington, 1975-79; pres. Fla. Internat. U., Miami, 1979-86, prof. internat. rels., 1979—83, emeritus pres. and prof., 1983—; vis. scholar Cambridge U., Eng., 1986-87; chmn. Edbl. Facility Authority, Dade County, Fla., 1998—. Fed. negotiator Joint Transp. Com. Washington 1962-66 Contbr. articles to profl. jours. Chmn. bd. trustees Internat. Fine Arts Coll., 1993—2004, U. de Palermo Found., Buenos Aires, 1998—; bd. dirs. Chopin Found. U.S., Inc., 1988-96, Concert Assn. Fla., Inc., 1988—; founding chmn. Brickell Ave. Lit. Soc., 1 988-96. Recipient Fla. Internat. Ctr. award, 1980, Leonard Abess award, 1984, Orden del Merito Civil, King of Spain, 1986, Fulbright lectr., Ecuador, 1989. Personal E-mail: andes79@hotmail.com. Business E-Mail: wolfeg@fiu.edu.

**WOLFE, HARRIET MUNRETT,** lawyer; b. Mt. Vernon, NY, Aug. 18, 1953; d. Lester John Francis Jr. and Olga Harriet (Miller) Munrett; m. Charles Briant Wolfe, Sept. 10, 1983 (div. Dec. 2004). BA, U. Conn., 1975; postgrad., Oxford U., Eng., 1976; JD, Pepperdine U., 1978. Bar: Conn. 1979. Assoc. legal counsel, asst. sec. Citytrust, Bridgeport, Conn., 1979-90; v.p., sr. counsel, asst. sec. legal dept. Shawmut Bank Conn., N.A., Hartford, 1990-96, pvt. practice, 1996-97; exec. v.p., gen. counsel, sec. Webster Fin. Corp., Waterbury, Conn., 1997—. Govt. rels. com. Electronic Funds Transfer Assn., Washington, 1983—. Mem. ABA, Conn. Bar Assn. (legis. com. banking law sect.), Conn. Bankers Assn. (trust legis.com.), Guilford Flotilla Coast Guard Aux., U.S. Sailing Assn., Phi Alpha Delta Internat. (Frank E. Gray award 1978, Shepherd chpt. Outstanding Student award 1977-78). Home: 621 Northwood Dr Guilford CT 06437-1124 Office: Webster Fin Corp Webster Plaza Waterbury CT 06702 Office Phone: 203-578-2423. Business E-Mail: hwolfe@websterbank.com.

**WOLFE, JAMES RONALD,** retired lawyer; b. Pitts., Dec. 10, 1932; s. James Thaddeus and Helen Matilda (Corey) W.; m. Anne Lisbeth Dahle Eriksen, May 28, 1960 (dec. 1996); children: Ronald, Christopher, Geoffrey; m. Patricia D. Yoder, Oct. 30, 1999. BA summa cum laude, Duquesne U., 1954, DHL (hon.), 1997; LLB cum laude, NYU, 1959. Bar: N.Y. 1959. Assoc. Simpson Thacher & Bartlett, N.Y.C., 1959-69, ptnr., 1969-95, counsel, 1996-99, ret., 1999—. Co-editor: West's McKinney's Forms, Uniform Commercial Code, 1965. Served to 1st lt. U.S. Army, 1955-57. Mem. Assn. Bar City N.Y. Roman Catholic. Home: 500 SE 5th Ave Apt 601 Boca Raton FL 33432-5510 Office: Simpson Thacher & Bartlett 425 Lexington Ave New York NY 10017-3954

**WOLFE, JOAN L.,** non-profit organizations consultant; b. Detroit, May 2, 1929; d. William R. and Mary Lucinda (Deane) Luedders; m. Willard Wolfe, June 26, 1953; children: John Roberts, Peter Harper (dec.). BA in Econ., U. Mich., 1951; Dr. Pub. Svc. (hon.), Western Mich. U., 1973. Founder, chmn. West Mich. Environ. Action Coun., exec. dir., 1971-73; 1st woman mem. Mich. Natural Resources Commn., 1973-82, chair, 1977. Bd. dirs. Mich. League Conservation Voters, 1998—2004. Author: Making Things Happen: The Guide for Members of Volunteer Organizations, 1981, Making Things Happen: How to Be an Effective Volunteer, 1991. Named Conservationist of Yr. Mich. United Conservation Clubs, 1971, one of 500 Environ. Achievers, Friends of UN Environ. Programme, one of Mich. 50 Hist. Women to Know, Mich. History Mag., 2002; named to Mich. Women's Hall of Fame, 1996; recipient Women of Achievement and Courage award Mich. Women's Found., 1998, Environ. Quality award Mich. Soc. Internal Medicine, 1970, Conservation award Am. Motors Corp., 1973, others. Mem. Nat. Audubon Soc. (nat. bd. dirs. 1982-87).

**WOLFE, JOHN HALL,** medical researcher, educator, consultant; b. Davenport, Iowa, Oct. 16, 1947; s. Donald E. and Peggy V. (Hall) Wolfe; m. Ruth M. Lamdan, July 19, 1986. AB, Ripon Coll., Wis., 1965—69; VMD, U. Pa., Phila., 1978—82, PhD, 1978—86. Fellow Sloan-Kettering Inst. Cancer Rsch., NYC, 1985—87; prof. U. Pa., Phila., 1987—; adj. prof. Wistar Inst., Phila., 1993—; dir. W. F. Goodman Ctr. for Comparative Med. Genetics U. Pa. Sch. Vet. Medicine, Phila., 1998—; stokes investigator Children's Hosp. Phila., 1998—. Cons. NIH, 1990—; Welcome Trust, London; sci. adv. bd. Nat. MPS Soc., 2000—, Internat. Soc. Mannosidosis & Related Diseases, 2002—. Contbr. articles to profl. jours. Capt. U.S. Army, 1969—72, Germany. Decorated Commendation medal US Army; recipient Auxillary to SCAVMA prize, U. Pa. Sch. Vet. Medicine, 1982, SmithKline Beecham Rsch. award, 1991, Spl. Emphhasis Rsch. Career award, NIH, 1992—97; fellow, Med. Scientist Tng. Program of NIH, U. Pa., 1978—84; grantee Exxon Fellow, Sloan-Kettering Inst. Cancer Rsch., 1985—87; Rsch. grants, NIH, 1990—. Mem.: Am. Soc. Human Genetics, Soc. Neuroscience, Am. Soc. Gene Therapy, Am. Soc. Microbiology, Sierra Club (life). Achievements include patents for human neural stem cells. Avocation: sailing. Office: Univ Pa Childrens Hosp Phila 502G ARC 3516 Civic Ctr Blvd Philadelphia PA 19104

**WOLFE, JOHN LESLIE,** lawyer; b. Cuyahoga Falls, Ohio, Dec. 6, 1926; s. Leslie George and Phyllis (Bond) W.; m. Barbara Lou Carle, Dec. 27, 1950 (div.); children: David, Karla. Ab, U. Akron, 1950; JD, U. Mich., 1953. Bar: Ohio 1953, U.S. Dist. Ct. (no. dist.) Ohio 1955, U.S. Ct. Appeals (6th cir.) 1966, U.S. Supreme Ct. 1970. Sole practice, Akron, 1953—56; asst. pros. atty. Summit County, Akron, 1956—57; assoc. Hershey & Browne, Akron, 1957—61, ptnr., 1961—85, Wolfe, Williams & Abdenour, Akron, 1986—90; sole practice Akron, 1991—. Asst. atty. gen. State of Ohio, 1971-74; adj. prof. trial practice U. Akron, 1975-80; counsel Tri County Regional Planning Commn. of Portage, Summit and Medina Counties, 1960-74. Trustee Akron Law Libr., 1961—; past pres. Progress Through Preservation. Served with U.S. Army, 1945-47. Recipient Ohio Legal Ctr. Inst. award of merit, 1966. Mem.: ATLA, ABA, Nat. Employment Lawyers Assn., Ohio Acad. Trial Lawyers, Akron Bar Assn., Ohio State Bar Assn. Office: National City Center 1 Cascade Plz Ste 740 Akron OH 44308-1154 Office Phone: 330-535-2441. Personal E-mail: wolfe81@attglobal.net.

**WOLFE, LESLIE R.,** think-tank executive; Exec. dir. Ctr. for Women Policy Studies, Washington, D.C., pres. Office: Ctr Women Policy Studies 1211 Connecticut Ave NW Ste 312 Washington DC 20036-2709

**WOLFE, LINDA,** writer; b. N.Y.C., Nov. 15, 1932; d. Harry M. Friedman and Mina Romanoff Kaufman; m. Max Pollack; 1 child, Jessica Wolfe Bernstein; stepchildren: Deborah Pollack, Jude Pollack. MA, NYU, 1958. Editl. asst. Oxford U. Press, N.Y.C., 1955—60, Partisan Rev., N.Y.C., NY, 1958—60; writer, rschr. Time, Inc., N.Y.C., 1960—71; contbg. editor N.Y. Mag., N.Y.C., 1971—96; consulting editor Woman Mag. (Conde Nast), N.Y.C., 1990—90. Author: (book) The Literary Gourmet, 1962, The Cooking of the Caribbean Islands, 1970, Playing Around: Women and Adultery, 1975, The Cosmo Report: Women and Sex in the Nineteen-Eighties, 1981, Private Practices (a novel), 1981, The Professor and the Prostitute and Other True Tales of Murder and Madness, 1986, Wasted: The Preppie Murder, 1989

(Notable Book of Yr., N.Y. Times, 1989), Double Life: The Shattering Affair Between New York's Chief Judge Sol Wachtler & Socialite Joy Silverman, 1994, Love Me To Death: A Journalist's Memoir of the Hunt for her Friend's Killer, 1998, The Murder of Dr. Chapman: The Legendary Trials of Lucretia Chapman and Her Lover, 2004. Recipient Edgar Allan Poe award nominee, Mystery Writers of Am., 1989. Mem.: PEN (exec. bd. dirs. 1994—95), Nat. Book Critics Circle (v.p. 1997—2002, exec. bd. 2005—). Avocations: 18th century English dance, travel.

**WOLFE, LYNN ROBERT,** art educator; b. Red Cloud, Nebr., Sept. 11, 1917; s. Clyde Melvin and Eleanor Gilham Wolfe; m. Arlene Adele Chambers, Oct. 22, 1944 (dec.); children: Leslie, Lynne, Lisa. BFA, U. Nebr., 1941; MFA, U. Colo., 1948. Supr. Nebr. State Mus., Lincoln, 1941; instr. art U. Nebr., Lincoln, 1945—46; prof. fine art U. Colo., Boulder, 1946—84, prof. emeritus, 1984—. Vis. artist U. Alaska, 1965, U. Hawaii, Honolulu, 1983; curator U. Colo. Fine Arts Mus., Boulder, 1980—83. Stained glass, Presbyn. Hosp., Denver, 1964, sculpture, Danforth Chapel, Ft. Collins, Colo., 1955. Founder, exec. Plan Boulder, 1958; bd. dirs. Historic Boulder, 1974, Colo. Chautauqua Assn., Boulder, 1986—89. Capt. USAF, 1942—45. Democrat. Avocations: travel, hiking, rock gardening. Home: 701 Euclid Ave Boulder CO 80302 Office Phone: 303-442-8471.

**WOLFE, MARGARET RIPLEY,** historian, educator, consultant; b. Kingsport, Tenn., Feb. 3, 1947; d. Clarence Estill and Gertrude Blessing Ripley); m. David Earley Wolfe, Dec. 17, 1966; 1 child, Stephanie Ripley. BS magna cum laude, East Tenn. State U., 1967, MA, 1969; PhD, U. Ky., 1974. Instr. history East Tenn. State U., 1969-73, asst. prof., 1973-77, assoc. prof., 1977-80, prof., 1980—, sr. rsch. prof. history, 1999—2004, prof. history emerita, sr. faculty affiliate, 2004—. Disting. vis. prof. in history Washington and Lee U., 2006. Author: Lucius Polk Brown and Progressive Food and Drug Control, Tennessee and New York City, 1908-1920, 1978, An Industrial History of Hawkins County, Tennessee, 1983, Kingsport, Tennessee: A Planned American City, 1987, Daughters of Canaan: A Saga of Southern Women, 1995; gen. editor: Women in Southern Culture Series, 1995-2004; contbg. author to books, also introductions to books; contbr. articles to profl. jours. Mem. Tenn. Com. for Humanities, 1985-85, exec. coun. mem., 1984-85; mem. Women's Symphony Com., Kingsport, 1990-95; exec. com. Tenn. Commemorative Woman's Suffrage Commn., 1994-95; mem. state rev. bd. Tenn. Hist. Commn., 1995—2005. Haggin fellow U. Ky., 1972-73; recipient Disting. Faculty award East Tenn. State U., 1977, East Tenn. State U. Found. rsch. award, 1979, Alumni cert. merit, 1984. Mem. AAUP, ACLU (exec. com. Tenn. 1991-92), NOW, Tenn. State Employees Assn., Am. Studies Assn. (John Hope Franklin Prize com. 1992), Am. Hist. Assn., Orgn. Am. Historians, So. Assn. Women Historians (pres. 1983-84, exec. com. 1984-86), So. Hist. Assn. (com. on status of women 1987, program com. 1988, interim chair program com. 1988, mem. 1993, 94, 95, nominating com. 1994, chair nominating com. 1995, chmn. mem. com. 1998—), Smithsonian Assocs, Tenn. Hist Commn. (state rev. bd. 1995-2005), Tenn. Hist. Soc. (editl. bd. 1995—2004), Coordinating Com. for Women in History, East Tenn. Hist. Soc. (mem. editl. bd. Jour. East Tenn. History 1995-2004), St. George Tucker Soc., Phi Kappa Phi. Office: ETSU at Kingsport Kingsport TN 37660 also: East Tenn State U Dept History Johnson City TN 37614 Personal E-mail: mrwolfe47@earthlink.net. Business E-Mail: wolfem@etsu.edu.

**WOLFE, MAURICE RAYMOND,** retired museum director, educator; b. Paris (Neuilly), France, Oct. 13, 1924; s. Guy Ellsworth and Genevieve (Plion) W.; m. Warwick Ellen Griffin, Nov. 4, 1955; 1 child, Shavaun. BA, U. Calif. in Sociology, Berkeley, 1948; MA in Sociology, U. Calif., Berkeley, 1952; postgrad. study, U. Paris Sorbonne, 1951; Cert. of Completion Sch. of Edn., U. Calif., Berkeley, 1954, postgrad., 1955. Rsch. asst. dept. of edn. U. Calif., Berkeley, 1949; tchr. of English and history Castlemont H.S., Oakland, Calif., 1954; lectr. in anthropology, philosophy, sociology and edn. U. Md. Overseas, 1956-59; lectr., instr. in philosophy and sociology U. Md., Munich, 1960-62; faculty mem. Merritt Coll., Oakland, Calif., 1962-88, chmn. dept. behavioral scis., 1967-87; dir. and founder Merritt Coll. Anthropology Mus., Oakland, 1973-88; rsch. assoc. U. Calif. Lowie Mus. of Anthropology, 1985-89. Lectr. Pers. Mgmt. for Execs., U.S. Govt. Sponsored, Berkeley, Calif. 1966-67, San Francisco State U., 1967-68, Calif. State U., Hayward, Dept. Sociology, 1970-71; adj. instr. Monterey Peninsula Coll., 1990, 91, Hartnell Coll., Salinas, Calif., Chapman U., 1992-95, Golden Gate U., 1995-98; adj. prof. Golden Gate U., 1997—. Editor: (jour.) Sociologus, 1952. Recipient French Govt fellowship, Sorbonne, Paris, 1956; named to list of Great Teachers of Calif., Calif. Assn. Comty. Colls., Santa Barbara, 1984. Home: 33751 E Carmel Valley Rd Carmel Valley CA 93924-9303 Personal E-mail: warwickwolfe@aol.com.

**WOLFE, MICHAEL BRAMSON,** film producer, writer; b. Cin., Apr. 3, 1945; s. David Bramson and Violet Fosdick Wolfe; m. Cathian Summa Wolfe, Apr. 1, 1989. BA cum laude and phi beta kappa, Wesleyan U., 1968. Instr. Phillips Andover Acad., Mass., 1968—69; traveling poet's scholar Amy Lowell Found., Boston, 1970—73; businessman Self Employed, Calif., 1974—98; pub. Tombouctou Books, Bolinas, Calif., 1976—88; pres. Unity Prodns. Found., Santa Cruz, Calif., 1999—. Columnist Beliefnet.com, NYC, 1999—. Editor: (book: essay collection) Taking Back Islam: American Muslims Reclaim Their Faith (Wilbur award: Best Book Yr. on a Religious Theme, Religion Communicators Coun., 2003); author: (travel books) In Morocco, (volume of poetry) How Love Gets Around; editor: (anthology) One Thousand Roads to Mecca: Ten Centuries of Writing about the Muslim Pilgrimage; author: (book: travel narrative) The Hadj: An American's Pilgrimage to Mecca; prodr.(executive editor): (2-hour historical documentary film, pbs) Muhammad: Legacy of a Prophet (Cine Spl. Jury award: Best Profl. Documentary in Category of People and Places, 2004); prodr., writer, host-narrator (half-hour travel documentary film) ABC Nightline Special: The Hajj: An American's Pilgrimage to Mecca (Nominated for Emmy, George Polk, Overseas Press Club awards; Muslim Pub. Affairs Coun. Media 1997 award., 1997); contbr. television documentary; author: (fiction) Invisible Weapons, (volume of poetry) No, You Wore Red, World Your Own. Recipient Young Poet award, Atlantic Monthly, 1968, Poetry Prize, Glascock New England, 1968, Lowell Thomas award: Best Cultural Tourism award, Soc. Am. Travel Writers Found., 1998. Office: Unity Prodns Found PO Box 551 San Juan Bautista CA 95045 Office Phone: 831-818-9975. Personal E-mail: mbw@upf.tv.

**WOLFE, RICHARD PEEL,** lawyer; b. Brookhaven, Miss., May 31, 1937; s. Hubert Heuck and Nell (Peel) W.; m. Ann Perkins Terrell, Aug. 20, 1960; children: Susan W. Huppman, Emily W. Leigh. AB magna cum laude, Princeton U., 1959; JD, Harvard U., 1962; M in Civil Law, Tulane U., 1965. Bar: La. 1963, U.S. Dist. Ct. (ea. dist.) La. 1963, U.S. Ct. Appeals (5th cir.) 1963. Assoc. Monroe & Lemann, Attys., New Orleans, 1963—68, ptnr., 1968—96, sect. head, corp. sect., 1974—96, mgmt. com., 1989—93; ptnr. Jones, Walker, Waechter, Poitevent, Carrère & Denègre Attys., New Orleans, 1997—2005, of counsel, 2006—. Mem. IRS-Tax Lawyers S.W. Regional Liaison Com., 1976-77; presenter in field. Mem. Bd. Liquidation, City Debt for City of New Orleans, 2004—; bd. deacons St. Charles Ave. Presbyn. Ch., 1967—70, 1972—75, chmn., 1970; bd. dirs. New Orleans Opera Assn., 2005—; mem. planning com. Tulane Corp. Law Inst., Tulane Law Sch., 1988—2000; bd. dirs. Met. Crime Commn. of New Orleans, 1997—2001, Bur. Govtl. Rsch., 1984—90; trustee La. Nature and Sci. Ctr., 1980—84; chmn. Gallier Ho. Mus. Coun., Tulane U., 1986—88, trustee, 1978—86; mem. com. to nominate alumni trustees Princeton U., 1979—81, chmn., 1981; mem. Audubon Pk. Commn., New Orleans 1971—77; trustee Metairie Pk. Country Day Sch., 1973—77; mem. agy. rels. com. United Way of Greater New Orleans, 1973—75; bd. dirs. La. Mus. Found., 2006—. Mem.: ABA (corp. stockholder relationships com. 1967—77, sect. of taxation 1977—97), La. State Bar Assn. (liaison com. with dist. dir. IRS 1974—80, chmn. sect. on taxation 1975—76, task force on legal practice designation and specialization 1981—83, cert. tax law specialist 1986—96), Soc. of War of 1812, Cap and Gown Club (Princeton U.), Harvard Club (N.Y.C.), New Orleans Country Club, Boston Club, La. Club, New Orleans Lawn Tennis

Club, Phi Beta Kappa. Republican. Presbyterian. Home: 7916 Plum St New Orleans LA 70118 Office: Jones Walker 201 St Charles Ave Ste 5100 New Orleans LA 70170 Office Phone: 504-582-8182.

**WOLFE, SCOTT W.**, orthopedic hand surgeon; b. Rye, NY, Aug. 28, 1958; MD, Cornell U., 1984. Intern Roosevelt Hospital, NYC, 1984—86; orthopedics resident Hospital for Special Surgery, NYC, 1986—89; fellowship in hand surgery Columbia U. Coll. of Physicians & Surgeons, NYC, 1989—90; prof. Yale U. Sch. of Medicine, New Haven, dir. hand & upper extremity div.; prof. orthopedic surgery Cornell-Weill Med. Ctr., NYC; chief hand service Hospital for Special Surgery, NYC, clin. dir. orthopedic surgery & attending orthopedic surgeon, dir. hand surgical fellowship; assoc. dir. clinical rsch. Alberto Vilar Ctr. for Hand and Upper Extremity Surgery; chief hand and upper extremity surgery. Named one of NY Mag. Best Doctors in NY, 2001—05. Office: Hospital for Special Surgery 535 E 70th St New York NY 10021 Office Phone: 212-606-1529. Business E-Mail: wolfes@hss.edu.

**WOLFE, SHEILA A.**, journalist; b. Chgo. d. Leonard M. and Rena (Karn) W. BA, Drake U. Reporter Chgo. Tribune, 1956-73, asst. city editor, 1973-75; day city editor Chgo. Tribune, 1975-79; city editor Chgo. Tribune, 1979-81, met. coordinator, 1981-83, adminstrv. asst. to mng. editor, 1983-2000. Pres. City News Bur. Chgo. 1986-88, 94-96. Recipient Beck award for outstanding profl. performance Chgo. Tribune, 1979; recipient Disting. Service award Drake U., 1982 Mem. Phi Beta Kappa. Home: 71 E Division St Chicago IL 60610-8307 E-mail: chicagoshe@aol.com.

**WOLFE, SIDNEY MANUEL**, physician; b. June 12, 1937; s. Fred and Sophia Esther (Marks) W.; m. Suzanne M. Goldberg; children: Hannah, Leah, Rachel, Sarah. BS, Western Res. U., 1960, MD, 1965. Intern. Cleve. Met. Gen. Hosp., 1965-66, resident internal medicine, 1969-70; staff assoc. NIH, 1966-72; dir. Pub. Citizens Health Research Group, Washington, 1972—. Contbr. articles to med. jours. Served with USPHS, 1966-69. McArthur fellowship, 1990—. Office: Pub Citizen Health Rsch Group 1600 20th St NW Washington DC 20009

**WOLFE, STANLEY**, composer, educator; b. N.Y.C., Feb. 7, 1924; s. Bert S. and Dorothy (Sanders) W.; m. Marguerite Wiberg, Aug. 10, 1960; children: Jeffrey, Madeleine. Student, Stetson U., DeLand, Fla., 1946-47, Henry St. Music Sch., 1947-48; BS in Composition, Juilliard Sch. Music, N.Y.C., 1952, MS in Composition, 1955. Faculty Juilliard Sch., N.Y.C., 1955—2005, dir. extension div., 1956-89; adj. prof. music Lincoln Ctr. campus Fordham U., 1969-73; lectr. N.Y. Philharmonic Pre-Concert Series, 1985—. Prin. compositions include King's Heart; dance score, 1956, Canticle for Strings, 1957, Lincoln Square Overture, 1958, Symphony Number 3, 1959, String Quartet, 1961, Symphony Number 4, 1965, Symphony Number 5 (Lincoln Center Commn.), 1970, Symphony Number 6, 1981; Violin Concerto, 1987. Served with AUS, 1943-46. Recipient award Am. Acad. and Inst. Arts and Letters, 1990; Guggenheim fellow in composition, 1957; Nat. Endowment for Arts grantee, 1969, 70, 77 Mem. ASCAP, Am. Music Center, Am. Symphony Orch. League (Alice Ditson award 1961), U.S. Chess Fedn. Home: 32 Ferndale Dr Hastings On Hudson NY 10706

**WOLFE, THAD ALLISON**, air force officer; b. Coulee Dam, Wash., Oct. 26, 1942; s. Clyde Allison and Leona (Ruffner) W.; m. Jill Ann Strathern, June 4, 1964; children: Thori, Christian, Molly. BS in Mil. Sci., USAF Acad., 1964; MSEE, U. Wyo., 1969; grad., Squadron Officer Sch., 1972, Air Command and Staff Coll., 1978, Nat. War Coll., 1985; grad. sr. exec. program in nat. and internat. security, Harvard U., 1992. Commd. 2nd lt. USAF, 1964, advanced through grades to lt. gen., 1993; ops. flight comdr. 6950th Security Wing, RAF Sta. Chicksands, Eng., 1965-66; signals intelligence ops. officer 6994th Security Squadron, Pleiku, South Vietnam, 1966-67; devel. engr. Def. Intelligence Agy., Va., 1969-70; instr. pilot, flight comdr., asst. sect. comdr. Vance AFB, Okla., 1970-74; aircrew tng. Castle AFB, Calif., 1974-75; crew comdr., ops. officer 325th Bombardment Squadron, Fairchild AFB, Wash., 1975-77; readiness analyst, chief of pers. and adminstrn., exec. officer 325th directorate ops. and readiness Hdqs. USAF, Washington, 1978-81; comdr. 9th Bombardment Squadron, Carswell AFB, Tex., 1981; dep. comdr. for standardization and evaluation 1st Combat Evaluation Group, Barksdale AFB, La., 1982; command ctr. sr. contr. Hdqs. Strategic Air Command, Offutt AFB, Nebr., 1982-84; vice comdr., then comdr. 509th Bombardment Wing, Pease AFB, N.H. 1985-88; spl. asst. to comdr. for officer profl. devel. Hdqs. Strategic Air Command, Offutt AFB, Nebr., 1988, dep dir. nat. strategic target list, joint strategic target planning staff, 1988-90; comdr. Strategic Warfare Ctr., Ellsworth AFB, S.D., 1990-92; asst. dep. dir. for ops. Nat. Security Agy., Ft. George G. Meade, Md., 1992-93; vice comdr. Air Combat Command, Langley AFB, Va., 1993-95. Chmn., CEO Internat. Youth Inst., 1996—; chmn. profl. mil. edn. bd. dirs. Air Combat Command, Langley AFB, Va., 1993-95, chief environ. leadership coun., 1993-95; bd. dirs. Air U. Maxwell AFB, Ala., 1995, Inst. Environ. and Natural Resources, Rsch. and Policy, U. Wyo., Laramie, 1995—, Western Rsch. Inst., Laramie, 1995—. Chmn. membership Boy Scouts Am., Rapid City, S.D., 1991. Decorated D.D.S.M., D.S.S.M., Legion of Merit, Bronze Star, Meritorious Svc. medal with three oak leaf clusters, Air medal, Air Force Commendation medal, Vietnam Svc. medal with svc. star, Republic of Vietnam Campaign medal. Mem. USAF Acad. Assn. of Grads., U. Wyo. Alumni Assn., Air Force Assn., Daedalians. Avocations: reading, sports, antiques, gardening. Office: Internat Youth Inst Inc 128 S Royal St Alexandria VA 22314-3337

**WOLFE, TOM (THOMAS KENNERLY WOLFE JR.)**, writer, journalist; b. Richmond, Va., Mar. 2, 1931; s. Thomas Kennerly and Helen (Hughes) W.; m. Sheila Berger; children: Alexandra, Thomas AB, Washington and Lee U., 1951, DLitt (hon.), 1974; PhD in am. Studies, Yale U., 1957; DFA (hon.), Mpls. Coll. Art. 1971, Sch. of Visual Arts, 1987; LHD (hon.), Va. Commonwealth U., 1983, Southampton Coll., NY, 1984, Randolph-Macon Coll., 1988, Manhattanville Coll., 1988, Longwood Coll., 1989; DLitt (hon.), St. Andrews Presbyn. Coll., 1990, Johns Hopkins U., 1990, U. Richmond, 1993. Reporter Springfield (Mass.) Union, 1956-59; reporter, Latin Am. corr. Washington Post, 1959-62; city reporter N.Y. Herald Tribune, 1962-66; mag. writer N.Y. World Jour. Tribune, 1966-67; contbg. editor New York mag., 1968-76, Esquire Mag., N.Y.C., from 1977. Writer N.Y. Sunday Mag., 1962-66; contbg. artist Harper's Mag., N.Y.C., 1978-81. One-man show of drawings include Maynard Walker Gallery, N.Y.C., 1965, Tunnel Gallery, N.Y.C.; 1974; author: The Kandy-Kolored Tangerine-Flake Streamline Baby, 1965, The Electric Kool-Aid Acid Test, 1968, The Pump House Gang, 1968, Radical Chic and Mau-mauing the Flak Catchers, 1970, The Painted Word, 1975, Mauve Gloves and Madmen, Clutter and Vine, 1976, The Right Stuff, 1979 (Am. Book award 1980), In Our Time, 1980, From Bauhaus to Our House, 1981, The Purple Decades: A Reader, 1982, The Bonfire of the Vanities, 1987, A Man in Full, 1998, Ambush at Fort Bragg (audio), 1997, Hooking Up, 2000, I Am Charlotte Simmons, 2004; editor, contbr. The New Journalism, 1973; contbr. articles to Esquire Mag., others. Recipient Front Page awards for humor and fgn. news reporting Washington Newspaper Guild, 1961, Soc. Mag. Writers award for excellence, 1970, Frank Luther Mott Rsch. award, 1973, Harold D. Vursell Meml. award Am. Acad. and Inst. Arts and Letters, 1980, Columbia Journalism award, 1980, Nat. Sculpture Soc. citation for art history, 1980, John Dos Passos award, 1984, Gari Melchers medal, 1986, Benjamin Pierce Cheney medal Ea. Wash. U., 1986, Washington Irving medal St. Nicholas Soc., 1986, Theodore Roosevelt medal Theodore Roosevelt Assn., 1990, Wilbur Cross medal Yale Grad. Sch. Alumni Assn., 1990, St. Louis Literary award, 1990, Quinnipiac Coll. Pres. award, 1993; named Va. Laureate for Lit., 1977; Chicago Tribune Literary Prize for lifetime achievement, 2003. Office: Farrar Straus & Giroux Inc 19 Union Sq W 11th Fl New York NY 10003-3304

**WOLFE, VERDA NELL**, pension consultant, financial planner; b. Sulphur Springs, Tex., Jan. 31, 1927; d. Marvin Alvin and Winnie Davis (Bass) Hamier; m. James Braddy Wolfe, May 3, 1947; children: James Gordon, William Gregory, Charles Gary. Student, Baylor U., 1948-52, Tex. Tech U., 1974-76. CLU, CFP; cert. pension cons. Estate analyst Estate Fin. Planning Svc., Lubbock, Tex., 1973-76, Planning Cons., Lubbock, 1977-81; pres.

DDRW Fin. Svcs., Lubbock, 1982-85, Pension Concepts and Administration, Lubbock, 1986—. Mem. Soc. Fin. Svcs. Profls. (chpt. pres. 1988-89), Inst. Cert. Fin. Planners. Am. Soc. Pension Actuaries and Cons. Avocations: music, painting, gardening. Home: 2125 57th St Lubbock TX 79412-2625 Office: Pension Concepts & Adminstn 2811A 74th St Lubbock TX 79423-1437 Office Phone: 806-745-9781. Personal E-mail: v_wolfe@sbcglobal.net. Business E-Mail: vwolfe@door.net.

**WOLFE, WILLIAM JEROME**, librarian, language educator; b. Chgo., Feb. 24, 1927; s. Fred Wiley and Helen Dorothea (Lovaas) W.; m. ViviAnn Lundin O'Connell, June 25, 1960 (div. 1962); 1 child, Lund. AB, U. Chgo., 1948; BA, Roosevelt U., Chgo., 1953; MEd, Chgo. State U., 1963; AA with high honors, Pima C.C., 1992; BA in Art magna cum laude, U. Ariz., 1994. Tchr. English John Marshall High Sch., Chgo., 1956-60; libr. Safford Jr. High Sch., Tucson, Ariz., 1961-71, Santa Rita High Sch., Tucson, 1971-75, Tucson High Sch., 1975-87. Tutor Eastside Ctr., Literacy Vols. Tucson, 1988-2001, supr., 1993-2001. Co-founder Tucson Classic Guitar Soc., 1969-72; docent U. Ariz. Mus. Art, Tucson, 1989-2002; mem. adv. bd. U. Ariz. Sch. Music, 1995—; singer U. Ariz. Collegium Musicum, 1981-96, 2002-2004; mem. U. Ariz. Scholarship Devel. Adv. Coun., 2000—, liaison Coll. Fine Arts. With U.S. Army, 1945-46, ETO. Recipient U. Ariz. Alumni Assn. Slonaker award, 2001, Spirit Philantropy award, Assn. Fundraising Profls., 2004, Edward J. Sparling Alumni award, Roosevelt U., 2006. Mem.: Nat. Assn. of Scholars, Assn. Lit. Scholars and Critics, Tucson Guitar Soc. (treas. 2001—), Friends of the Sch. of Music U.Ariz., U. Ariz. Pres. Club, Phi Kappa Phi. Mem. Ch. of Christ Scientist. Avocations: poetry writing, drawing, singing, piano, classical guitar. Home: 8460 E Rosewood St Tucson AZ 85710-1702 Personal E-mail: wjwolfe@earthlink.net. *Through every turn of events, a pleasing composition of life develops from love of family, wise counsel of teachers, inspiration of friends, and trust in God.*

**WOLFEN, WERNER F.**, lawyer; b. Berlin, May 15, 1930; came to U.S., 1939; s. Martin and Ruth Eva (Hamburger) W.; m. Mary Glasier, July 1, 1956; children: Richard, James, Lawrence (dec.). BS, U. Calif., Berkeley, 1950, JD, 1953. Bar: Calif. 1953. Assoc. Irell & Manella, L.A., 1953-57, ptnr., 1957-98, sr. ptnr. emeritus, 1999—; pres. Capri Investment Co. LLC, 1999—. Bd. dirs. Broadcom Corp., Calhoun Vision, Inc., Pre-Cash Corp.; bd. visitors UCLA Sch. Arts and Arch., 1995—. Bd. dirs. UCLA Found., 1992-2003; bd. dirs. L.A. Goal, 1994-, pres., 1994-99. Mem. ABA. Democrat. Jewish. Office: Capri Investment Co LLC 1800 Avenue of the Stars Los Angeles CA 90067-4212 Office Phone: 310-203-7521. Business E-Mail: wwolfen@irell.com.

**WOLFENDEN, RICHARD VANCE**, biochemistry educator; b. Oxford, Eng., May 17, 1935; s. John Hulton and Josephine (Vance) W.; m. Anita Gaunitz, June 25, 1965; children: Peter, John. BA, MA, Exeter Coll., Oxford U., Eng., 1958; PhD, Rockefeller Inst., 1964. Asst. prof. chemistry Princeton U., NJ, 1964-70; assoc. prof. biochemistry U. N.C., Chapel Hill 1970-73, prof. biochemistry, 1973-83, alumni disting. prof., 1983—. Vis. fellow Exeter Coll., Oxford, 1969; vis. prof. U. Montpellier, France, 1976; mem. molecular biology panel NSF, Washington, 1973-76; mem. bio-organic and natural products study sect. NIH, Washington, 1981-86. Mem. editl. bd. Bioorganic Chemistry, 1983—, Biomed. Chem. Letters, 1993—. Fellow AAAS, Am. Acad. Arts and Scis.; mem. NAS, Am. Chem. Soc. (chair biol. divsn. 2000-02), Am. Soc. Biol. Chemists. Democrat. Home: 104 Jolyn Place Chapel Hill NC 27517 Office: U North Carolina Dept Biochemistry Chapel Hill NC 27514

**WOLFENSOHN, JAMES DAVID**, former diplomat, former President of the World Bank; b. Sydney, Australia, Dec. 1, 1933; naturalized U.S. citizen, 1980. s. Hyman and Dora (Weinbaum) W.; m. Elaine Ruth Botwinick, Nov. 26, 1961; children: Sara, Naomi, Adam. BA, U. Sydney, 1954, LLB, 1957; MBA, Harvard U., 1959. Bar: Supreme Ct. of Australia 1957. Lawyer Allen Allen & Hemsley, Australia; ptnr. Ord Minnett (brokers), Australia, 1963-65; mng. dir. Darling & Co. (investment bankers), Australia, 1965-67, J. Henry Schroder Wagg, London, 1968-70; pres. J. Henry Schroder Banking Corp., NYC, 1970-76, exec. dep. chmn., dir. Schroders Ltd., London; prin. exec. officer Schroder Group, London, 1974-77; exec. ptnr. Salomon Bros., NYC, 1977-81; chmn. Salomon Bros. Internat., London, 1977-81; pres., CEO James D. Wolfensohn, Inc., 1981-95; pres. The World Bank Group, Washington, 1995—2005; spl. Mid. East envoy for Gaza Strip withdrawal US Dept. State, Washington, 2005—06; sr. advisor Citigroup Corp., 2006—. Vis. lectr. fin. U. New South Wales, 1963-66; bd. dir. Rockefeller Univ.; mem. Coun. on Fgn. Rels., Century Assn. Contbr. articles to profl. jours. Mem. Australian Olympic Team, 1956; chmn. bd. dirs. John F. Kennedy Ctr. for the Performing Arts, Washington, 1990-95, chmn. emeritus, 1995—; bd. dirs. Met. Opera Assn., 1977-93, Joint Ctr. for Polit. Studies, 1978-88, mem. emeritus, 1988—; trustee Rockefeller Found., 1979-85, Population Coun., 1977-84; trustee Inst. for Advanced Study, Princeton, N.J., 1978—, chmn., 1986—; trustee Brookings Inst., 1983-90, hon., 1990—; trustee Rockefeller U., 1985-94, Howard Hughes Med. Inst., 1987-96; steering com. Bilderberg mtgs., treas. Am. Friends of Bilderberg, Inc., 1985—; pres. Internat. Fedn. Multiple Sclerosis Socs., 1977-83, Carnegie Hall, 1972—, bd. dirs., chmn., 1980-91, chmn. emeritus, 1991; mem. Nat. Multiple Sclerosis Soc., 1977-82. With Royal Australian Air Force, 1952-57. Recipient Business Com. for the Arts Leadership award, 1994, David Rockefeller prixe from Mus. of Modern Art NYC; decorated by govts. of Australia, Germany, France, Norway and Russia; honored by HM Queen Elizabeth of Eng. with KBE and HM, King of Morocco, 1995. Mem. Australian Olympic Fencing Team, 1956; Fellow Am. Acad. Arts and Scis.; mem. Coun. on Fgn. Rels., Century Assn., Harvard Club (NYC), Australian Club (Sydney).

**WOLFENSON, AZI U.**, electrical, mechanical and industrial engineer, consultant; b. Rumania, Aug. 1, 1933; arrived in Peru, 1937; s. Samuel G. and Polea S. (Ulanowski) Wolfenson; m. Rebeca Sterental, Jan. 10, 1983; 1 child, Michael Ben; children from previous marriage: Ida, Jeannette, Ruth, Moises, Alex. Mech., Elec. Engr. U. Nacional de Ingenieria, Peru, 1955; Indsl. Engr., U. Nacional de Ingenieria, 1967; MSc in Indsl. Engring., U. Mich., 1966; PhD in Engring. Mgmt., Pacific Western U., 1983; PhD in Engring. Energy, Century U., 1985; D in Philosophy of Engring. (hon.), World U. Roundtable, Ariz., 1987. Power engr. Peruvian Trading Co., 1956-57; gen. mgr. AMSA ingenieros S.A.. 1957-60; prof. U. Nacional de Ingenieria, Peru, 1956-72, dean mech. and elec. engring., 1964-66, dean indsl. engring., 1967-72; dir. SWSA Automotive Parts, Peru, 1954-77; project mgr. Nat. Fin. Corp., Cofide, 1971-73; Peruvian dir. Corporacion Andina de Fomento, CAF, 1971-73; rep. in Peru CAF, 1973-74; pres. DESPRO cons. firm, 1973-76; exec. pres. Electroperu, 1976-80. Cons. engr., 1964—; dir. Tech. Transference Studies, 1971—72. Author: (book) Work Communications, 1966, Programmed Learning, 1966, Production Planning and Control, 1968, Transfer of Technology, 1971, National Electrical Development, 1977, Energy and Development, 1979, El Gran Desafio, 1981, Hacia una politica economica alternativa, 1982, The Power of Communications: The Media, 1987; contbr. articles to newspapers and prof. mags. Mem. Nat. Coun. Fgn. Investment and Tech. Transfer, 1972—73, Superior Coun. Electricity, 1964—66; metal mech. expert for andean group, 1970—71; promoter, co-founder, gen. mgr. La Republica Newspaper, Peru, 1981; pres. PROA Project promotion AG, Switzerland, 1982—; chmn. Inst. for the Devel. of the Ams., Inc., Fla., 1993—; co-founder El Popular, 1983, El Nacional, 1985, Todo Sport, 1993, El Chino, 1994, La Reforma, 1997, El Men, 1999, La Razon, 2001; pres. bd. dirs. newspapers; v.p. bd. dirs. Island Way Cmty. Assn., 1995—97; mem. exec. bd. dirs. Miami State Israel Bonds, 1997; mem. consultative coun. Instituto Peruano de Deportes, 1999; mem. consultive coun. Min. Econ. and Fin., 1973—74; councilman at the Concejo Provincial De Lima, 1969—75; pres. Peruvian Jewish Cmty., 1966—70, Peruvian Hebrew Sch., 1976—78. Named Exec., Gente Mag., 1979; recipient Disting. Svc. awards, Order Merit, Peru, 1980, Disting. award, City Coun. Huancayo, 1980, Trujillo, 1978, Huaral, 1979, piura, 1980, Disting. Contbn. award, City of Lima, 1970, 1971, Disting. Contbn. to Elec. Devel. in Peru, 1979, El Sol Radiante, City Hall of Magdalena, Peru, 1995, Recognition award, Israel Govt., 1967, Disting. Comision Integracion Electrica Regional medal, CIER, 1984, Medal of

Honor, Electrical Engring. Colegio de Ingenieros del Peru, 2003. Fellow: Brit. Inst. Mgmt., Inst. Prodn. Engrs.; mem.: J.C.C. Fla., FCL, AIIE (sr.), ASME, MTM Assn., AAAS, World Assn. Newspapers (exec. mem. 2003), Asociacion Periodistas Peru, Circulo Periodistas Peru, Swiss sect. PEN Club Internat., Swiss Soc. Writers, United Writers Assn., Assn. Energy Engrs., Am. Nuc. Soc. (vice chmn. 1988, 1990, chmn. Swiss sect. 1991—93, Significant Contbn. to Advancement of Nuc. Sci. award 1995), Inst. Adminstrv. Mgmt., Asociacion Peruana Avance Ciencia, Assn. Mgmt. Sci. (dir. 1968), Am. Inst. Mgmt. Sci., Am. Soc. Engring. Edn., Asociacion Electrotecnica del Peru, Inst. Peruano Ingenieros Mecanicos (pres. 1965—66, v.p. 1967, dir. 1969, 1970, 1976), Colegio Ingenieros Peru (medal of honor award 2003), Alumni Assn. Mich., Pacific Western and Century U., Hebraica Club, Club de 2000. Home: 3781 NE 208th Ter Miami FL 33180-3835 Office: 3601 NE 207th St Ste 1205 Aventura FL 33180 Personal E-mail: aziwolfenson@aol.com.

**WOLFER, DALE**, retired music educator; b. Denver, June 2, 1928; s. George Earl and Hazel Grace Wolfer; m. Annette Baldwin, June 26, 1931; children: Chrisann, Suzanne, Michael Shane, Eric Jon. B in music edn., Colo. A&M, 1951; M in music edn., Denver U., 1958. Music dir. Olathe HS, Colo., 1953—54; choral dir. Grand Junction HS, Colo., 1954—58, Littleton HS, Colo., 1958—72, Lanier HS, U. Tex, Austin, Tex., 1972—88; music dir. Hillcrest Sch., Jos, Nigeria, 1988—90; prof. Lutheran Ch. HS, Bratislava, Slovakia, 1990—91; ret., 1991. Ch. worker Lutheran Hour Ministries, Istebna, Poland, 1998, Tikhovitsy, Russia, 99, Wittenberg, Germany, 2000. Summer music studies Western State Coll., Gunnison, Colo., 1948—50, U. Salzburg, Salzburg, Austria, 1968, Paul Waring Workshop, Paul Christiansen Workshop, 1968; mem. nat. com. Nat. Intercollegiate Band, Denver, 1951; ch. choir dir. various denominations, 1983—90, ch. handbell dir., 1994—2003. 1st lt. U.S. Army, 1951—53, Korea. Decorated Purple Heart US Army, Korea, Air medal. Mem.: Am. Choral Dir. (life). Lutheran. Avocations: travel, fishing, hiking, handbells, stained glass art. Home: 8018 S Pennsylvania Ct Littleton CO 80122-2854

**WOLFERSTEIG, ELOISE SMITH**, retired music educator; b. Bklyn., Oct. 7, 1930; d. George Francis and Louise C. (Becker) Smith; m. Robert Frederick Wolfersteig; 1 child, Patricia Lynn Albritton. MusB, West Minster Choir Coll., Princeton, N.J., 1953; MusM, Jamestown Coll., ND, 1958; MEd, Ga. Coll., 1973. Choir dir. St. Francis Assisi Cath. Ch.; tchr. Jacob Tome Inst., Md., 1953—54, Bainbridge (Md.) Elem. Sch., 1954—55; dir. Officers' Wives Nursery Sch., Bermuda, 1955—56; music tchr. Baldwin City Schs., Milledgesville, Ga., 1965—75; gifted edn. tchr. Bibb City Sch., Macon, Ga., 1975—90; music tchr. Cherokee City Sch., Andrews, NC, 1990—91; gifted edn. tchr. Clay City Schs., Hayesville, NC, 1991—95; tech. cons. Andrews, NC, 1995—99; dir. sch. age choirs Blairsville, Ga., 1998—. Finalist Excellence in Singing, Met. Opera, 1958; recipient District Star Tchr., Macon, Ga., 1985, Tchr. of Yr., Spl. Edn., Macon, Ga., 1988. Mem.: DAR (pres., regent), Delta Kappa Gamma, Phi Delta Kappa, Sigma Alpha Iota. Avocations: poetry, art, writing, drawing. Home: 5316 Pine Crest Rd Young Harris GA 30582 Personal E-mail: rfwolfer@alltel.net.

**WOLFERSTEIG, JEAN LOIS**, medical association administrator, educator; b. Kingston, NY, July 13, 1950; d. Evelyn Anna Schupp and John Raymond Wolfersteig; life ptnr. William Edward Miller. AS in Liberal Arts, Ulster County CC, 1970; BA in Secondary Edn., State U. Coll., 1972; MS in Pub. Svc. Adminstrn., Russell Sage Coll., Albany, New York, 1983. Unit mgr. Wassaic Devel. Ctr., Wingdale, NY, 1972—75, staff devel. specialist, 1976—79; dir. of staff devel. and tng. Westchester Devel. Disabilities Svcs. Office, Tarrytown, NY, 1979—84, Hudson River Psychiat. Ctr., Poughkeepsie, NY, 1984—92, quality mgmt. dir., 1992—98, dir. for facility admin. svcs., 1998—2002, CEO, 2002—. Bd. mem. Cmty. Adv. Bd. for Marist Coll., Poughkeepsie, 1985—90; adj. faculty Westchester CC, Valhalla, 1981—84; bd. mem. Adv. Bd. for Orange County CC Forensic Mental Health Program, Middletown, NY, 1985—85. Co-author: (international presentations) Balanced Scorecard and Performance Improvement. Chairperson of selection com. Herman B. Snow Scholarship Fund, Poughkeepsie, 1991—2001. Recipient Salute to Women in Industry, Dutchess County YWCA, 1992. Mem.: Nat. Assn. of State Mental Health Dirs., Phi Kappa Phi. Avocations: writing, sailing, travel, gardening. Office: Hudson River Psychiatric Center 10 Ross Cir Poughkeepsie NY 12601 Office Phone: 845-483-3400. Business E-Mail: hrqajlw@omh.state.ny.us.

**WOLFERT, FREDERICK E. (RICK WOLFERT)**, healthcare financial services company executive; BSBA, La. State U., 1976; grad. degree in banking, U. Del. With U.S. Leasing Corp., San Francisco, 1979—88; chmn., pres., CEO KeyCorp Leasing divsn., pres., CEO KeyBank USA divsn. KeyCorp, 1988—97; pres., CEO, bd. dirs. Heller Fin., 1997—2001; pres., CEO GE Capital Healthcare Fin. Svcs., Chgo., 2001—. Bd. dirs. Jr. Achievement, Chgo., Brookfield Zoo, Chgo., St. Joseph's Carondelete Child Ctr., Chgo., La. State U. Ourso Coll. Bus. Adminstrn. Mem.: Equipment Leasing Assn. (former chmn., chmn. membership com). Office: GE Healthcare Fin Svcs 500 W Monroe St Chicago IL 60661-3679

**WOLFF, ALAN WILLIAM**, lawyer; b. Malden, Mass., June 12, 1942; s. Louis K. and Etta (Bernstein) W.; m. Helene N. Novick, Mar. 3, 1965; children: Anna, Jeremy, Ewan. AB, Harvard U., 1963; LLB, Columbia U., 1966. Bar: Mass. 1967, N.Y. 1966, U.S. Supreme Ct. 1971, D.C. 1972, U.S. Ct. Appeals (fed. cir.) 1982, Ct. Internat. Trade 1993. Atty. Office Gen. Counsel, U.S. Treasury Dept., Washington 1968—73; dep. gen. counsel Spl. Trade Rep. (now U.S. Trade Rep.), Washington, 1973-74, gen. counsel, 1974-76, dep. spl. trade rep. (with rank of ambassador), 1977-79; ptnr. Verner, Liipfert et al, Washington, 1979-85, Dewey, Ballantine, Bushby, Palmer & Wood (now Dewey Ballantine), Washington, 1985—; mng. ptnr. & chmn. internat. trade practice group Dewey Ballantine LLP, Washington, 1992—. Mem. adv. com. for trade negotiations Office of the Pres., Washington, 1980—82; mem. policy adv. com. U.S. Trade Rep.'s Svcs., Washington, 1980—86; mem. adv. bd. Inst. Internat. Econs., Washington, 1981—, Ctr. Nat. Policy, Washington, 1988—, Econ. Strategy Inst., Washington, 1989—; mem. adv. com. on internat. econ. policy U.S. Dept. State, Washington, 1996—; mem. Nat. Academies Bd. Sci. tech. & Econ. Policy, Washington, 1997—2004; trustee U.S. Council for Internat. Bus., Washington, 1997; chmn. adv. bd. Internat. Comml. Diplomacy Project, Washington, 1999—. Co-author: The Microelectronics Race, 1987, Steel and the State, 1988, Conflict Among Nations: Trade Policy for the 1990s, 1992; contbr. articles to profl. jours. Mem. Coun. Fgn. Rels., 1979—; bd. advisors Am. Edn. and Health Found., 2002—; trustee Monterey Inst. Internat. Studies, 1992—2001. Mem. ABA, Am. Soc. Internat. Law, Council on Fgn. Rels. Democrat. Unitarian Universalist. Office: Dewey Ballantine LLP 1775 Pennsylvania Ave NW Washington DC 20006-4605 also: 1301 Avenue Of The Americas New York NY 10019-6022 Office Phone: 202-429-2352. Office Fax: 202-862-1093. Business E-Mail: awolff@dbllp.com.

**WOLFF, ALEJANDRO DANIEL**, ambassador; married; 2 children. Grad. magna cum laude, UCLA, 1978. Fgn. svc. officer US Dept. State, 1979—, mem. policy planning staff Washington, 1981—82, with Office of Soviet Union Affairs, 1988—89, with Office Under Sec. Polit. Affairs, 1989—91, dep. exec. sec., 1996—98, exec. assist. to Madeleine Albright and Colin Powell, 1998—2001, dep. U.S. rep. to UN NYC, 2005—; dep. chief of mission Am. Embassy, Paris, 2001—05. Office: US Dept State 140 E 45th St 7th Fl New York NY 10017

**WOLFF, BRIAN RICHARD**, metal products executive; b. LA, Dec. 11, 1955; s. Arthur Richard and Dorothy Virginia (Johnson) Wolff; children from previous marriage: Ashley Rachael, Taryn Nicole. BSBA, Calif. State U., Chico, 1980; postgrad., U. Phoenix, 1990—. Registered counseling practitioner Calif., cert. emergency response team Huntington Beach Fire Dept., 2003; ordained min. Prog. Universal Life Ch., 1996; registered guidance practitioner Calif. Supr. Federated Metals Corp./ASARCO, Long Beach, Calif., 1980-82, dist. sales mgr., 1983-84; sales mgr. Copper Alloys Corp., Beverly Hills, Calif., 1982-83; dir. mktg. Federated-Fry Metals/Cookson, Long Beach, Industry and Paramount, Calif., 1984-87; regional sales mgr.

Colonial Metals Co., L.A., 1987-91; nat. sales mgr. Calif. Metal X/Metal Briquetting Co., L.A., 1991-93; sales engr. Ervin Industries, Inc., Ann Arbor, Mich., 1993-95. Tech. sales mgr. GSP Metals & Chems. Co., 1987—91; cons. sales Calif. Metal Exch., L.A., 1987—91; Atlas Pacific, Inc., Bloomington, 1993—2005, mgr. sales, 2005—. Contbr. poetry to various publs. Mem. citizens adv. com. bus. Calif. Legislature, 1983; bd. trustees Newport Beach (Calif.) Alano Club, 2002—, pres., 2003—; bd. dirs. H.O.W. Hall, Huntington Beach, Calif., 2006—. Mem.: NRA, Soc. Die Cast Engrs., Am. Electroplaters Soc., Steel Structures Painting Coun., Calif. Cast Metals Assn., Am. Foundrymen Soc., Non Ferrous Founders Soc. Republican. Presbyterian. Avocations: scuba diving, tennis, fishing, trap shooting, hunting. Office Phone: 909-421-1200.

**WOLFF, CANDIDA (CANDI WOLFF)**, federal official; b. Sharon, Conn., June 9, 1964; m. Mark Roger Wolff; 2 children. BA in math & polit. sci., Mount Holyoke Coll., 1986; JD, George Washington U., 1989. Pub. policy lobbyist Akin, Gump, Strauss, Hauer & Feld, LLP, 1989—93; tax counsel Office of Senator Malcolm Wallop, 1993—95; legis. counsel Senate Steering Com. U.S. Senate, 1995—96, dep. staff dir. Senate Rep. Policy Com., 1997—2000; dep. asst. to v.p. for legis. affairs Office of Pres. of Senate (v.p. of U.S.), 2001—02, asst. to v.p. for legis. affairs., 2002—04; asst. to pres., dir. legis. affairs The White House, 2005—; ptnr. Washington Coun. Ernst & Young, 2004. Office: The White House 2nd Fl, West Wing 1600 Pennsylvania Ave NW Washington DC 20500 Office Phone: 202-456-2230. Office Fax: 202-456-0200.

**WOLFF, CATHERINE ELIZABETH**, opera company executive; b. Evanston, Ill., June 11, 1957; AB with honors, Vassar Coll., 1979; MA in Performing Arts Mgmt., Am. U., 1982. Administrv. asst. Opera Am., 1982-85; artistic administr. Pitts. Opera, 1985-94; exec. dir. Del. Symphony Orch., Wilmington, 1994-95; gen. dir. Syracuse (N.Y.) Opera Co., 1996—. Music panelist N.Y. State Coun. Arts, 2000—02, co-chair music panel, 2003. Mem. steering com. Arts and Culture Leadership Alliance Ctrl. NY, 2004—, founding pres., 2005—. McGuire fellow Vassar Coll., 1979. Mem. Opera Am., Am. Symphony Orch. League, Phi Beta Kappa. Office: Syracuse Opera Co PO Box 1223 Syracuse NY 13201-1223 E-mail: cwolff@syracuseopera.com.

**WOLFF, DEBORAH H(OROWITZ)**, lawyer; b. Phila., Apr. 6, 1940; d. Samuel and Anne (Manstein) Horowitz; m. Morris H. Wolff, May 15, 1966 (div.); children: Michelle Lynn, Lesley Anne; m. Walter Allan Levy, June 7, 1987. BS, U. Pa., 1962, MS, 1966; postgrad., Sophia U., Tokyo, 1968; JD, Villanova U., 1979, LLM, 1988. Tchr. Overbrook H.S., Phila., 1962-68; homebound tchr. Lower Merior Twp., Mongomery County, 1968-71; asst. dean U. Pa., Phila., 1975-76; law clk. Stassen, Kostos and Mason, Phila., 1977-78; assoc. Spencer, Sherr, Moses and Zuckerman, Norristown, Pa., 1980-81; ptnr. Wolff Assocs., Phila., 1981—. Lectr. law and estate planning, Phila., 1980—. Founder Take a Brother Program; bd. dirs. Germantown Jewish Ctr.; h.s. sponsor World Affairs Club, Phila., 1962-68; mem. exec. com., sec. bd. Crime Prevention Assn., Phila., treas., bd. dirs., 1965—; v.p. bd. dirs. U. Pa. Alumnae Bd., Phila., 1965—, pres. bd. dirs., 1965—; active Hahnaman Brain Tumor Rsch. Bd.; v.p., bd. dirs. organized classes, bd. crime prevention; chmn. urban conf. Boys Club Am., 1987, treas., 1999; active Hahnaman Brain Tumor Rsch. Bd.; v.p., bd. dirs. Crime Prevention; treas. Assn. of Alumnae ds.; mem. Alumni Class Leadership Counsel bd. U. Pa., 2001—, sec., 2006-. Recipient 3d Ann. Cmty. Svc. award Phila. Mayor's Com. for Women, 1984; named Pa. Heroine of Month, Ladies Home Jour., 1984. Mem.: Lions (pres. Germantown Club 1997—). Home and Office: 4242 W Mermaid Ln Philadelphia PA 19118-4204 Personal E-mail: debbyw@comcast.net.

**WOLFF, DERISH MICHAEL**, economist, department chairman; b. Boston, May 14, 1935; s. Nathan and Ruth Mae (Derish) W.; m. Maureen Robinson; children: Jeffrey Scott, Hayley Beth Kissel. BA, U. Pa., 1957; MBA, Harvard U., 1959. Fin. analyst Sigmund Werner, Inc., Belleville, NJ, 1959-61; devel. economist Louis Berger, Inc., East Orange, NJ, 1961-65, chief economist, 1965-67, v.p., 1968-75, exec. v.p., 1976-82, pres., CEO, 1982—2002, chmn., 2002—. Dir. Louis Berger Internat., CHELBI, Ammann & Whitney, Va. Maintenance Svcs., Klohn-Crippen, EA Engring., Sci. and Tech. Berger, Devine, Yaeger; guest lectr. UN, Fgn. Svc. Inst., Newark Inst. Tech., U. Nev., Ga. Inst. Tech., The New Sch., Harvard U., Rutgers U., U. Denver; vis. lectr. MIT, 2001—; mem. industry adv. panel Dept. of State, 2001-05; mem. Bretton Woods Com., 1987—. Mem. editl. bd. Modern Engring. Tech. 1978-80, Nat. Devel.-Modern Govt., 1972-79, Constrn. Bus. Review, 1991—. Mem. adv. com. N.J. Inst. Tech.; class chmn. U. Pa. Ann. Giving, 1975-82; mem. adv. bd. Huntsman Program Internat. Studies and Bus., U. Pa., 1997—; U.S. presdl. trade del. to Japan, 1986; indsl. sector adv. com. Dept. of Commerce, 1988-92; adv. com. US Trade and Devel. Program, 1989-92; bd. overseers N.J. Inst. Tech., 2006. Recipient Pres.'s medal for lifetime achievement, N.J. Inst. Tech., 2003. Mem. Am. Cons. Engrs. Coun. (chair internat. engring. com. 1983-85, vice chair 1986-93), Internat. Engring. and Constrn. Industries Coun. (del. 1986, 87, chmn. 1988-90), Bldg. Futures Coun. (co-chmn. 1994-). Ctr. for Strategic and Internat. Studies (steering group/GATT negotiations 1989), Phi Beta Kappa. Clubs: Harvard, Penn. Jewish. Office: Berger Group Holdings Inc 100 Halsted St East Orange NJ 07018-2699 Office Phone: 973-678-1960. Personal E-mail: dwolff@louisberger.com.

**WOLFF, DIANE PATRICIA**, writer, film and television producer; b. N.Y.C., Oct. 12, 1945; d. Irving Mark and Catherine Halkett (Grossman); m. Wallace Gorell (div.). BS, Columbia U., 1968; postgrad., U. Calif., Berkeley, 1977-78, Stanford U., 1978-79; student, Interuniv. Ctr. Tokyo. Prodr. Sta. KRON-TV, San Francisco, 1983-87; prodr. ind. films, 1990-92; prodr. CD-ROM projects, 1994-96; contbg. editor New Asia Pacific Review, Westport, Conn., 1996-98; ind. prodr. The BioNRG Show Genghis Prodns., 2006—. Journalist Nat. Interest, N.Y. Times, San Francisco Chronicle, San Jose Mercury News, Orlando Sentinel Author: Chinese Writing: An Introduction, 1975, Gone with the Gator, 2001; project editor: A Sun-Herald Serial Novel, Sack of Baghdad and Other Stories of Muslims and Mongols, Pitless Measurement of History: China and Tibet. Nat. def. fgn. lang. fellow Columbia U., 1967; recipient Most Notable Book award Am. Libr. Assn., 1975. Mem. Author's Guild, Am. Soc. Journalists & Authors, Assn. For Asian Studies, Asia Soc. Avocations: sailing, swimming, fitness, cooking, gardening. Home: 1184 Green Oak Trail Port Charlotte FL 33948 Office Phone: 941-456-4805. E-mail: dianepwolff@comcast.net.

**WOLFF, EDWARD**, physician; b. NYC, Apr. 15, 1941; s. Julius and Molly W.; m. Marilyn Alice Pels; children: Shanna, Loryn, Kimberly. BS, Muhlenberg Coll., 1962; MD, Georgetown U., 1966. Intern U. Ala. Hosp., Brimingham, 1966-67; resident N.Y. Med. Coll., N.Y.C., 1967-71; physician pvt. practice, Great Neck, NY, 1976—. Attending physician North Shore U. Hosp., Manhasset, NY, St. Francis Hosp. Heart Ctr., Roslyn, NY. Fellow Am. Coll. Physicians; mem. AMA, N.Y. State Med. Soc., Nassau County Med. Soc. Office: Ste 404 107 Northern Blvd Great Neck NY 11021 Office Phone: 516-498-1818.

**WOLFF, EDWARD ALVIN**, electronics engineer; b. Chgo., Oct. 31, 1929; s. Samuel S. and Lillian P. Wolff; m. Anna Lee Tishk, June 19, 1951; children: David Steven, Eliot Marvin, Susan Toby. BSEE, U. Ill., 1951, MS, 1953, PhD, U. Md., 1961. Electronic scientist Naval Research Lab., Washington, 1951-54; project engr. Md. Electronic Mfg. Corp., Litton Industries, College Park, Md., 1956-59, Electromagnetic Research Corp., College Park, Md., 1959-61; engring. mgr. Aero Geo Astro-Keltec Industries/Aiken Industries, Alexandria, Va., 1961-67; v.p. Geotronics, Inc., Falls Church, Va., 1967-71; supervisory electronics engr. NASA Goddard Space Flight Ctr., Greenbelt, Md., 1971—; system mgr. Network TDRS System, 1981-89, MRJ, Inc., Oakton, Va., 1989-98; cons. in field, 1998—. Instr. Tex. A&M U., 1967. Author: Spacecraft Technology, 1962, Antenna Analysis, 1966, 2d edit., 1988, Geoscience Instrumentation, 1974, Urban Alternatives, 1975, Microwave Engineering and Systems Applications, 1988. Mem. Md. Gov.'s Sci. Resources Adv. Bd., 1963—67; pres. U.S. Environment and Resources Coun.,

1972—75; treas. World Environment and Resources Coun., 1975—81. With U.S. Army, 1954—56. Fellow: IEEE (bd. dirs. 1971—72), Washington Acad. Scis.; mem.: NSPE, AIAA, Phi Eta Sigma, Sigma Tau, Eta Kappa Nu. Home: 16870 Island Cove Dr Apt 130 Jupiter FL 33477-2356 Personal E-mail: ewolff@bigfoot.com. *Everything I have done has been with the help of others. In return, as I have acquired management responsibilities, a primary objective has been to help others achieve their goals.*

**WOLFF, EDWARD NATHAN**, economist, educator; b. Long Branch, NJ, Apr. 10, 1946; s. Arthur Seymour and Ethel (Kalmenoff) Wolff; m. Jane Zandra Forman, Nov. 27, 1977; children: Spencer, Ashley. BA, Harvard U., 1968; PhD, Yale U., 1974. Rsch. assoc. Nat. Bur. Econ. Rsch., N.Y.C., 1974-77, 2001—; asst. prof. NYU, N.Y.C., 1974-79, assoc. prof., 1979-84, prof., 1984—; mng. editor Rev. Income and Wealth, 1987—2004; sr. scholar Levy Econs. Inst., 1999—. Cons. Aspen Inst., 1993, World Bank, 1994—97, Jerome Levy Econs. Inst., 1995—96, Century Found., 1999—2002, UN, 2000—02, 2005—06, Math. Policy Rsch., 2002—03, Econ. Policy Inst., 2000—06; others; vis. scholar Russell Sage Found., 2003—04. Author: Growth, Accumulation and Unproductive Activity, 1987, Top Heavy: A Study of Increasing Unequality of Wealth in America, 1995, Economics of Poverty, Inequality, and Discrimination, 1997, Retirement Insecurity, 2002, Does Education Really Help? Skill, Work and Inequality, 2006; editor: International Comparisons of Household Wealth Distribution, 1987, Research in Economic Inequality, Vol. 4, 1993, The Economics of Productivity, 1997, Quality of Life in Advanced Industrialized Nations, 2004; co-author: Productivity and American Leadership: The Long View, 1989, Competitiveness, Convergence, and International Specialization, 1993, Downsizing in America, 2003, Retirement Income: The Crucial Role of Social Security, 2005; co-editor: International Perspectives on Profitability and Accumulation, 1992, Poverty and Prosperity in the USA in the Late Twentieth Century, 1993, Convergence of Productivity, 1994, Assets for the Poor, 2001; contbr. articles to profl. jours. Grantee, NSF, 1984—90, Exxon Found., 1984—88, Fishman-Davidson Ctr. U. Pa., 1987—89, Sloan Found., 1990—98, 2006—, Mellon Found., 1991—95, Russell Sage Found., 1997—2003, Ford Found., 1997—2005, Kauffman Found., 2004—. Mem.: Eastern Econs. Assn. (pres. 2002—03), Internat. Input-Output Assn. (coun. 1995—2003), Internat. Assn. Rsch. Income and Wealth (coun. 1987—2004), Am. Econ. Assn. Avocations: tennis, skiing. Office: NYU Dept Econs 269 Mercer St Rm 700 New York NY 10003-6633 Office Phone: 212-998-8917. Business E-Mail: ew1@nyu.edu.

**WOLFF, EDWIN RAY**, retired construction engineer, consultant; b. Continental, Ohio, Mar. 24, 1933; s. Ray Simeon and Datha Ruth (Donaldson) W.; m. Elizabeth I. Sutterlin, Feb. 16, 1963; children: Sandra Jean, Donald Scott. BSME, U. Toledo, 1969. Registered profl. engr., Ohio. Mem. design staff City of Ft. Lauderdale, Fla., 1965-67; mem. design/spl. orders staff Devilbliss Co., Toledo, 1967-69; engineer, mem. R & D staff Toledo Scale, 1969-70; design/constrn. engr. Lucas County Engr., Toledo, 1970-98, ret., 1998. Cons. G.A.F., Inc., Oregon, Ohio, 1980—. Vol. Spl. Olympics, Lucas County, 1989—; trustee, bd. elders Fairgreen Ch., Toledo, 1975—; trustee Beneficial Union Pittsburg, 1986—; former bd. dirs. Lucas County ARC; bd. dirs. Cmty. Residential Svcs., Inc. With Combat Engrs. Corps, 1956-58. Mem. Phi Kappa Chi, Pi Kappa Alpha. Democrat. Presbyterian. Home: 4312 Grantley Rd Toledo OH 43613-3738

**WOLFF, ELEANOR BLUNK**, actress; b. Bklyn., July 10, 1931; d. Sol and Bessie (Schultz) Blunk; m. William Howard Wolff, June 19, 1955; children: Ellen Jill, Rebecca Louise. BA in Edn., Speech and Theatre, Bklyn. Coll., 1972, MS in Spl. Edn., 1975; postgrad., Adelphi U., Garden City, N.Y., 1980-81. Cert. tchr., N.Y. Fashion model Garment Ctr., N.Y.C., 1949—50; sec. to v.p. out-of-town/export sales Liebmann Breweries Inc., Bklyn., 1950—58; tchr. N.Y.C. Bd. Edn., Bklyn., 1971-76; sec. to dir. environ. programs, pub. affairs officers, speakers bur. project leader Power Authority State of N.Y., N.Y.C., 1976-85; tchr. Hewlett-Woodmere (N.Y.) Sch. Dist., 1986-89; instr. adult edn. County of Nassau, NY, 1986-97. Actress/model, N.Y.C., 1992—; mem. Love Creek Prodns. V.p. program devel. for youth ctr. Wavecrest Gardens Cmty. assn., Far Rockaway, N.Y., 1959-63; teen leader Far Rockaway Jewish Ctr. Youth Coun., 1965-68; pres. Parents Assn. P.S. 215Q, Far Rockaway, 1966-67; tutor N.Y.C. Bd. Sch. Vol. Program, Far Rockaway, 1969-71, New Ground Inc., Mineola, NY, 2004—; chair civic affairs Dem. Club, Far Rockaway, 1961-63; committeewoman Dem. Ctrl. Com., Queens County, N.Y., 1963-64, Nassau County Dem. Party, 1998—; v.p. membership, mem. constn. com. Nassau County Dem. Women's Caucus, 1988, 89; awards com. Bklyn. Coll., 1993-97, chair theatre arts affiliate, 1990-94, 2001-; mem. comm. adv. com. Hewlett-Woodmere Sch. Dist. 14, 1996-97; press/media steward vol. Goodwill Games, 1998; vol. program presenter Child Abuse Prevention Svcs., Roslyn, N.Y., 2003-05; vol. income tax assistance IRS, 2004-. Named Mother of Yr. Congregation Shaaray Tefila, Far Rockaway, 1968; recipient Merit award Wavecrest Gardens Cmty. Assn., 1960, Theater Arts Trophy for disting. svc. Bklyn. Coll. Alumni, 1992. Mem.: SAG (awards nominating com. 2000—01, 2006—), AFTRA, Actors Equity Assn., Alumni Assn. Bklyn. Coll. (life), Cmty. Garden Club of North Woodmere Park (corr. sec. 2001—03). Avocations: painting, piano, gardening. Personal E-mail: eleanorwolff@cs.com.

**WOLFF, ELROY HARRIS**, lawyer; b. NYC, May 20, 1935; s. Samuel and Rose Marian (Katz) W.; children: Ethan, Anna Louise. AB, Columbia U., 1957, LL.B., 1963. Bar: N.Y. 1963, D.C. 1969. Assoc. Kaye, Scholer, Fierman, Hays & Handler, N.Y.C., 1963-65; atty.-adviser to commr. FTC, Washington, 1965-67; sr. trial atty. Dept. Transp., 1967-69; assoc. Leibman, Williams, Bennett, Baird & Minow, Washington, 1969-70, ptnr., 1970-72, Sidley & Austin, Washington, 1972-99; sr. counsel Sidley Austin Brown & Wood, Washington, 2000—04 Mem. adv. com. on practice and procedure FTC, 1969-71; chmn. adv. com. on procedural reform CAB, 1975 Served to 1st lt. USAF, 1957-60. Mem. ABA (chmn. spring meeting program 1992-94, coun. 1995-98), Union Internationale des advocats (chmn. competition law com. 1994-98), Army and Navy Club. Office: 1501 K St NW Washington DC 20005 Office Phone: 202-736-8666. Business E-Mail: ewolff@sidley.com.

**WOLFF, FRANK PIERCE, JR.**, lawyer; b. St. Louis, Feb. 27, 1946; s. Frank P. and Beatrice (Stein) W.; m. Susan Scallet, May 11, 1984; children: Elizabeth McLane, Victoria Hancox. BA, Middlebury Coll., 1968; JD, U. Va., 1971. Bar: Mo. 1971, U.S. Ct. Appeals (5th cir.) 1974, U.S. Ct. Appeals (8th cir.) 1975, U.S. Supreme Ct. 1975. Ptnr. Lewis, Rice & Fingersh, St. Louis, 1971—90; ptnr., sect. leader, bus. and transactional counseling sect., mem. oper. group Bryan Cave LLP, St. Louis, 1997—. Bd. dirs. Misco Shawnee, Inc. Bd. dirs. Leadership St. Louis, 1985-88, Washington U. Child Guidance Clinic, St. Louis, 1976-79, Jewish Family and Children's Svc., St. Louis 1981-83, John Burroughs Sch., 1995-2000, BJC Health Sys., Inc., 1998-2001, The Butterfly House, 2001—; gen. counsel Mo. Bot. Garden, St. Louis, 1981—, Mo. Hist. Soc., St. Louis 1997—; trustee St. Louis Children's Hosp. 1995-2001, chairperson mission vision and values com., 1996-2001, mem. exec. com., 1997-99; co-chmn. Parks Task Force, 2004 Inc. Capt. USAR, 1968-76. Mem. ABA, Mo. Bar Assn., Bar Assn. Met. St. Louis (chmn. corp. sect. 1984-85), Noonday Club, Westwood County Club (chmn. fin. com. 1989-91, treas. 1989-91, v.p. 1991-93, pres. 1994-95, exec. com. 1989-95). Home: 17 Clerbrook Ln Saint Louis MO 63124-1202 Office: Bryan Cave LLP One Metropolitan Square 211 N Broadway Ste 3600 Saint Louis MO 63102-2733 Office Phone: 314-259-2330. Business E-Mail: fpwolff@bryancave.com.

**WOLFF, GRACE SUSAN**, pediatric cardiologist; b. Rome, NY; BS, Le Moyne Coll., 1961; MD, Med. Coll. Wis., 1965. Diplomate Am. Bd. Pediatrics, Pediatric Cardiology. Intern St. Vincents Hosp., N.Y.C., 1965-66; pediat. resident Babies Hosp.-Columbia Hospita, 1967-69; fellow in pediat. cardiology Childrens Hosp., Boston, 1969-71; chief divsn. pediat. cardiology U. Miami-Jackson Meml. Hosp., 1995—2005; prof. U. Miami, 1984; pediatrician, pediatric cardiologist U. Miami-Jackson Meml. Hosp., 1977—;

Mem. Am. Acad. Pediats., Am. Bd. Pediats., NASPE, Am. Acad. Pediat., Am. Coll. Cardiology, Am. Heart Assn. Office: U Miami-Jackson Meml Hosp PO Box 016960-R76 Miami FL 33101 Office Phone: 305-585-6683. Business E-Mail: gwolff@med.miami.edu.

**WOLFF, GREGORY STEVEN**, insurance company executive; b. Manchester, Conn., Dec. 10, 1951; s. Thomas J. and M. Elizabeth (Grandburg) W.; m. Elizabeth Mae Heppenstall, June 3, 1971; children: Keith J., James T., Kyle M. BA in Edn., U. Conn., 1974. Cert. fin. planner. Insurance salesman Northwestern Mut. Life, Glastonbury, Conn., 1974-76, Wolff-Zackin & Assocs., Inc., Vernon, Conn., 1976—2001; chmn. bd. dirs., mng. mem. Wolff-Zackin Fin. LLC, Vernon, 2001—. Lectr. in field; bd. dirs. Savs. Bank of Manchester Found., bd. dirs., Ea. Conn. Health Network, bd.overseers Internat. Inst. Sport. Contbr. articles to profl. jours.; co-author: Financial Need Analysis I, cassette prog. Co-founder Manchester Soccer Camp, 1981; bd. overseers Internat. Inst. of Sport. Mem. Nat. Assn. Life Underwriters, Conn. Assn. Life Underwriters, Hartford Assn. Life Underwriters (past pres.), Million Dollar Round Table, Ct. of Table. Methodist. Avocations: tennis, golf, coaching youth sports. Home: 126 Tamarac Dr Glastonbury CT 06033-1941 Office: Wolff-Zackin Fin LLC PO Box H Vernon Rockville CT 06066-1620

**WOLFF, HERBERT ERIC**, banker, former army officer; b. Cologne, Germany, May 24, 1925; s. Hugo and Juanna Anna (Van Dam) W.; m. Alice (Billy) Rafael, Nov. 13, 1946 (dec. July, 1987); children: Karen (dec. Jan., 1992), Herbert E., Allen R. BA, Rutgers U., 1953; BS, U. Md., 1957; MA, George Washington U., 1962; grad., U.S. Army War Coll., 1962, Harvard U., 1979. Commd. 2nd lt. U.S. Army, 1945, advanced through grades to maj. gen.; served in Fed. Republic of Germany, Greece, Iran, Republic of Korea, Australia, New Guinea, The Philippines, Japan and Socialist Republic of Vietnam; dep. dir. ops. NSA Chief CSS, Ft. Meade, Md., 1973-75; dep. corps. comdr. V. Corps U.S. Army, Frankfurt, Germany, 1975-77, comdr. gen. U.S. Army Western Command Hawaii, 1977-81; with First Hawaiian Bank, Honolulu, 1981-2000, sr. v.p., corp. sec., to 2000; hon. consul gen. (Dató) U.S. Pacific region Govt. of Malaysia, Honolulu, 1985—. Author: The Man on Horseback, 1962, The Tenth Principle of War Public Support, 1964, The Military Instructor, 1968. Exec. bd. Aloha coun. Boy Scouts Am.; bd. dirs. USO, Girl Scouts of US, Hawaii, March of Dimes, Found. Armed Forces Ctr. Security Studies; v.p. Hawaiii Com. Fgn. Rels.; past pres. Pacific Asian Affairs Coun.; pres. Hawaii Army Mus. Soc. Decorated Bronze Star with V and 3 oak leaf clusters, Air medal (24) U.S. Army, Purple Heart, Gallantry Cross with 2 palms, Gallantry Cross with palm and silver star Nat. Order 5th class South Vietnam, Order Nat. Security Merit Choen-Su S. Korea, D.S.M. with oak leaf clusters (2), Silver Star with oak leaf cluster U.S. Army, Legion of Merit with 3 oak leaf clusters, D.F.C., Combat Infantry Badge with two stars, master parachutist, Army aviator; named Citizen of Yr. Fed. Exec. Bd., 1987. Mem. 1st Inf. Divsn. Assn., 1st Cav. Divsn. Assn., Plaza Club (pres., bd. dirs.), Waialae Country Club, Rotary, Phi Kappa Phi. Office: First Hawaiian Ctr 999 Bishop St Honolulu HI 96813-0001 Personal E-mail: generalherbwolff@aol.com. *History is a gift we borrow and hope to pass on. Forget the past and be doomed to repeat it. Remember the past and accept the challenge to convince others.*

**WOLFF, JESSE DAVID**, lawyer; b. Mpls., Aug. 26, 1913; s. Maurice I. and Annalee (Weiskopf) W.; m. Elizabeth Hess, Nov. 22, 1939; children: Nancy Nicholas, Paula, Daniel Jesse. BA summa cum laude, Dartmouth Coll., 1935; JD, Harvard U., 1938. Bar: N.Y. 1938. Practiced in N.Y.C., 1938—; assoc., then ptnr., to counsel Weil, Gotshal & Manges, 1938-88, 88—, sr. mng. ptnr., 1966-86. Past dir., dep. chmn. Sotheby Parke Bernet Group (Eng.); past mem. adv. bd. Sotheby's Inc. Past hon. trustee Greater N.Y. ARC; past mem. exec. com. Salvation Army, N.Y.C. Served with AUS, 1942-45. Mem. ABA, Judge Adv. Gen. Assn. Office: Weil Gotshal & Manges 767 5th Ave 31st Fl New York NY 10153-0119 E-mail: jesse.wolff@weil.com.

**WOLFF, JOSH**, professional soccer player; b. Stone Mountain, Ga., Feb. 25, 1977; m. Angela Wolff, Nov. 11, 2000; 2 children. Attended, Univ. S.C. Forward Chgo. Fire, 1998—2003, Kansas City Wizards, 2003—. 47 caps, 10 goals U.S. Nat. Soccer Team, 1999—; mem. U.S. World Cup team, 2002, 06. Named to Major League Soccer All-Star team, 2002, 2004. Mailing: US Soccer Fedn 1801 S Prairie Ave Chicago IL 60616*

**WOLFF, KAREN LIAS**, music educator; BA in Music Edn., Morningside Coll., Iowa; MusM, U. Mich., PhD in Music. Faculty mem., Coll./Conservatory of Music U. Cin., 1978—87, acting dean, academic affairs, assoc. dean, academic affairs; dir. Sch. of Music U. Minn., 1987—91; dean, prof. music Oberlin Coll. Conservatory of Music, 1991—99; dean, Sch. of Music U. Minn., 2000, U. Mich., 2000—05, Paul C. Boylan Collegiate Prof. Music. Bd. mem. Minn. Orch., Minn. Opera, Minn. Composers Forum, Greater Twin Cities Youth Orch., Ohio Chamber Orch., U. Musical Soc., Mich. Shakespeare Festival, Interlochen Arts Acad., Ann Arbor Summer Festival; v.p. Nat. Assn. of Schools of Music; mem. Nat. Coun. on Arts Nat. Endowment for Arts, 2003—. Mailing: Nat Endowment for Arts 1100 Pennsylvania Ave NW Washington DC 20506*

**WOLFF, L. THOMAS**, physician, educator; b. Suffern, N.Y., 1942; MD, Albany Med. Coll., 1968. Dir. rural med. edn. program Upstate Med. U., Syracuse, NY; assoc. dir. N.Y. State Area Health Edn. Ctr.; disting. teaching prof. family medicine SUNY Upstate Med. U., NY. Co-investigator IDE-ATEL. Mem.: ABFP (pres. 1998—2003). Office: SUNY Upstate Med U Div Family Medicine 200 Madison Irving Med Ctr Syracuse NY 13210

**WOLFF, LARRY**, history professor; s. Robert and Renee Wolff; m. Perri Klass; children: Benjamin Orlando Klass, Josephine Charlotte Paulina, Anatol Elvis Klass. AB, Harvard Coll., Cambridge, Mass., 1979; PhD in History, Stanford U., Calif., 1984. Prof. of history Boston Coll., 1986—2006, NYU, 2006—. Author: (history book) Venice and the Slavs: The Discovery of Dalmatia in the Age of Enlightenment (Barbara Jelavich prize, 2002), Inventing Eastern Europe: The Map of Civilization on the Mind of the Enlightenment, Postcards from the End of the World: Child Abuse in Freud's Vienna, The Vatican and Poland in the Age of the Partitions, (novel) The Boys and their Baby. Fellow Guggenheim fellowship, Guggenheim Found., 2002, Am. Coun. of Learned Societies fellowship, Am. Coun. of Learned Societies, 1996, Fulbright fellowship, U.S. Fulbright Commn., 1981. Mem.: Soc. for Austrian and Habsburg History (assoc.; exec. com. mem. 2002—06), Am. Soc. for Eighteenth-Century Studies (assoc.; exec. bd. mem. 2005), Am. Assn. for the Advancement of Slavic Studies (assoc.), Am. Hist. Assn. (assoc.; officer, rsch. divsn. 2002—05), Am. Acad. of Arts and Sciences (life). Achievements include research in concerning the "invention" of Eastern Europe, how Europe came to be conceived as being divided into an East and a West, that is, Eastern Europe and Western Europe. Avocations: opera, baseball, music, movies. Office: NYU History Dept 53 Washington Square South New York NY 10012

**WOLFF, MANFRED ERNST**, medicinal chemist, pharmaceutical executive; b. Berlin, Feb. 14, 1930; came to U.S., 1933; s. Adolph Abraham and Kate (Fraenkel) W.; m. Helen S. Scandalis, Aug. 1, 1953 (div. 1971); children: Stephen Andrew, David James, Edward Allen; m. Susan E. Hurbert, Jan. 19, 1973 (div. 1975); m. A. Gloria Johnson, Dec. 25, 1982. BS, U. Calif. at Berkeley, 1951, MS, 1953, PhD, 1955. Registered U.S. patent agt. Rsch. fellow U. Va., 1955-57; sr. medicinal chemist Smith, Kline & French Labs., Phila., 1957-60; mem. faculty U. Calif., San Francisco, 1960-82, prof. medicinal chemistry, 1965-82, chmn. dept. pharm. chemistry, 1970-82; dir. discovery rsch. Allergan Labs, Irvine, Calif., 1982-84; v.p. discovery rsch. Allergan Pharms., Irvine, 1984-89; v.p. R & D Immunopharmaceutics Inc., San Diego, 1989-91, sr. v.p. R & D, 1991-95; pres. Intellepharm, Inc., Laguna Beach, Calif., 1997—. Adj. prof. medicinal chemistry U. So. Calif., 1982—; elected mem. U.S. Pharm. Conv. Com. of Revision, 1990—; lectr. Sch. Med. Chemistry Drew U., NJ, 1998-. Editor: Burger's Medicinal Chemistry and Drug Discovery, Vol. 1-5, 5th edit., 1995-97; asst. editor Jour. Medicinal Chemistry, 1968-71; mem. editl. bd. Medicinal Chemistry Rsch.,

1991-95, PharmSci., 1999-2004; contbr. articles to profl. jours.; patentee in field. Fellow AAAS, Am. Assn. Pharm. Scientists; mem. Am. Chem. Soc. Achievements include discovery of Alphagan and Lumigan medicines for glaucoma, Tazorac medicine for psoriasis, and Thelin medicine for pulmonary arterial hypertension. Office Phone: 949-494-5458. E-mail: drwolff@aol.com.

**WOLFF, MICHAEL A.,** state supreme court judge; Grad., Dartmouth Coll., 1967; JD, U. Minn., 1970. Lawyer Legal Svcs.; mem. faculty St. Louis U. Sch. Law, 1975-98; judge Mo. Supreme Ct., 1998—, chief justice, 2005—. Chief counsel to gov., 1993-94, spl. counsel, 1994-98. Co-author: Federal Jury Practice and Instructions, 4th edit; author monthly column Law Matters: Reflections of Chief Justice Michael A. Wolff, 2005. Chief counsel to Gov. St. Louis, 1993-94, spl. counsel, 1994-98. Office: Supreme Ct Mo PO Box 150 Jefferson City MO 65102-0150*

**WOLFF, OTTO J.,** federal agency administrator; b. 1942; BS in Fin., Pa. State U. Profl. staff mem. com. on house adminstrn. U.S. Ho. Reps.; dep. asst. sec. for adminstrn. US Dept. Commerce, 1981—93, asst. sec. for adminstrn., CFO Washington, 2001—. Office: US Dept Commerce 1401 Constitution Ave NW Washington DC 20230*

**WOLFF, PAUL MARTIN,** lawyer, sculptor; b. Kansas City, Mo., July 22, 1941; s. Joseph L. and Eleanor B. Wolff; m. Rhea S. Schwartz, Oct. 9, 1976. BA, U. Wis., 1963; LLB, Harvard U., 1966. Bar: D.C. 1968, U.S. Ct. Appeals (D.C. and 2d cir.) 1968, U.S. Supreme Ct. 1975, U.S. Ct. Appeals (10th and fed. cirs.) 1981, U.S. Ct. Appeals (8th cir.) 1982, U.S. Tax Ct. 1982, U.S. Ct. Claims 1984. Law clk. to Judge James R. Durfee U.S. Ct. Claims, Washington, 1966-67; assoc. Williams & Connolly, Washington, 1967-75, ptnr., 1976—. Adj. prof. Catholic U. Law Sch., 1970-73. Co-author: Forensic Sciences; contbr. articles to legal jours.; artist in one-man show, Trinity U., Washington, 2005, Zenith Gallery, Washington, 2005. Bd. dirs. Washington Coun. for Civil Rights Under Law, 1980-90, Renwick Alliance, Washington, 1987-93, Am. Jewish Com., Washington, 1988-92, Washington Legal Clinic for Homeless, 1988-99, Opportunities for Older Ams. Found., 1988-92, Emeritus Found., 1992-99; bd. dirs. Washington Performing Arts Soc., 1990-2002, hon. dir., 2002—; vice chmn. D.C. Pub. Charter Schs. Resource Ctr., 1999-2003; dir. D.C. Sports Commn., 1994-2000; dir. Com. Pub. Edn. 1994-99; trustee Fed. City Coun., bd. trustees, 1996—; trustee Am. U., 1996-2005; overseer Corcoran Mus. of Art, 1997-2005; mem. adv. bd. Woodrow Wilson Ctr. for Internat. Studies, 1999—; co-chmn. Triad Automotive Group LLC; mem. acquisitions com. Jewish Mus., 2003—. Recipient Learned Hand award, am. Jewish Com., 2004. Mem. Georgetown Club, Econ. Club Washington (dir.), Phi Beta Kappa. Independent. Avocations: photography, gardening, fly fishing, sculpting. Home: 4770 Reservoir Rd NW Washington DC 20007-1905 also: Oak Ridge Warrenton VA 20186 Office: Williams & Connolly 725 12th St NW Washington DC 20005-5901: 1250 Villager Sun Valley ID 83553 Fax: 202-434-5580. E-mail: pwolff@wc.com, dcpmw@aol.com.

**WOLFF, PETER ADALBERT,** physicist, researcher; b. Oakland, Calif., Nov. 15, 1923; s. Adalbert and Ruth Margaret W.; m. Catherine C. Carroll, Sept. 11, 1948; children: Catherine Mia, Peter Whitney. AB in Physics, U. Calif., Berkeley, 1945, PhD in Physics, 1951. Rsch. scientist Lawrence Radiation Lab., 1951-52; staff scientist Bell Telephone Lab., Murray Hill, NJ, 1952-63, dept. head, dir. electronic rsch. lab., 1964-70; prof. physics U. Calif., San Diego, 1963-64; prof. physics, head solid state and atomic physics div., assoc. dir. Material Sci. Ctr. MIT, Cambridge, 1970-76, dir. rsch. lab. of electronics, 1976-81, prof. physics Cambridge, 1976-89, prof. emeritus, 1994—, 1994—; dir. Francis Bitter Nat. Magnet Lab., 1981-87. Dir. Draper Lab. Contbr. articles to profl. jours. Served with C.E. U.S. Army, 1945-46. Fellow Nippon Electric Co. Rsch. Inst., Princeton, 1989-94. Mem. Am. Phys. Soc. Home: 321 Greew Way Wayland MA 01778

**WOLFF, RICHARD JOSEPH,** public relations executive, consultant, historian; b. Hackensack, N.J., Oct. 13, 1952; s. Richard Hamilton and Irene Marie (Ciruzzi) W. AB, Georgetown U., 1974; MA, Columbia U., 1976, PhD, 1979. Asst. dean, prof. St. John's U., Queens, NY, 1980-85; ptnr. pub. rels. Kekst & Co., Inc., N.Y.C., 1985-97; mng. dir. Eastern region and L.Am. Golin/Harris Internat., N.Y.C., 1997—2002, worldwide mng. divsn. G/H Fin., 1997—2002; CEO, The Global Cons. Group, N.Y.C., 2002—. Mem. Columbia U. Seminar on Modern Italy, N.Y.C., 1983—; founding mem. St. John's U. Seminar on Vatican Studies, Queens, 1994—; mem. Legatus, 2000—. Author: Between Pope and Duce, 1990, Dorothy Day, 1994; contbr. articles to profl. jours.; editor Catholics, the State and the European Radical Right, 1987. Chmn., commr. North Hudson Sewerage Authority, Hudson County, N.J., 1988—; mem. adv. com. Congressman Robert Menendez, Jersey City, N.J., 1994—. Recipient Howard Marraro prize Am. Cath. Hist. Assn., 1982, Internat. fellow Columbia U., 1977. Mem. Phi Beta Kappa. Roman Catholic. Avocations: golf, reading, travel, politics. Office: The Global Consulting Group 22 Cortlandt St 14th Fl New York NY 10007

**WOLFF, ROBERT PAUL,** philosophy educator; b. N.Y.C., Dec. 27, 1933; s. Walter Harold and Charlotte (Ornstein) W.; m. Cynthia Griffin, June 9, 1962 (div. 1986); children: Patrick Gideon, Tobias Barrington; m. Susan Gould, Aug. 25, 1987. AB, Harvard U., 1953, MA in Philosophy, 1954, PhD, 1957. Instr. Harvard U., 1958-61; asst. prof. philosophy U. Chgo., 1961-63; vis. lectr. Wellesley Coll., 1963-64; assoc. prof. philosophy Columbia, 1964-69, prof., 1969-71; prof. philosophy U. Mass., Amherst, 1971-92, prof. Afro-Am. studies, 1992—; grad. program dir. doctoral program in Afro-Am.; devel. cons. U. QwaQwa, South Africa, 1998—. Author: Kant's Theory of Mental Activity, 1963, A Critique of Pure Tolerance, 1965, Political Man and Social Man, 1966, Kant: A Collection of Critical Essays, 1967, Poverty of Liberalism, 1968, The Ideal of the University, 1969, In Defense of Anarchism, 1970, 2d edit., 1998, Ten Great Works of Philosophy, 1970, The Rule of Law, 1971, Styles of Political Action in America, 1971, Philosophy: A Modern Encounter, 1971, The Autonomy of Reason, 1973, 1984 Revisited, 1973, About Philosophy, 1975, 9th edit., 2005, Understanding Rawls, 1977, Understanding Marx, 1985, Moneybags Must Be So Lucky, 1988, Autobiography of an Ex-White Man, 2005. Exec. dir. Harvard-Radcliffe Alumni/ae Against Apartheid, 1988-90; pres., exec. dir. Univ. Scholarships for South African Students, 1990—; co-dir. Inst. Advanced Study in Humanities U. Mass., 1992-98, dir. Doctoral Program in Afro-Am. Studies, 1996—, dir. Undergrad. Mentoring and Achievement Program, 2006—. Home: 107 Buffam Rd Amherst MA 01002-9723 also: 17 rue Maître Albert 75005 Paris France Office Phone: 413-545-2751. Personal E-mail: rwolff12@comcast.net. Business E-Mail: rwolff@afroam.umass.edu.

**WOLFF, RONALD KEITH,** toxicologist, researcher; b. Brantford, Ont., Can., July 25, 1946; s. Roy Clifford and Agnes Audrey (Stratton) W.; m. Mary Carole Cromien Wolff, Aug. 26, 1972; children: Mark, Sarah, Andrew, Brian. BS, U. Toronto, 1964-68; MS, 1968-69, PhD, 1969-72. Diplomate Am. Bd. Toxicology, 1983. Rsch. assoc. McMaster U., Hamilton, Can., 1973-76; scientist Lovelace Inhalation Toxicology Rsch. Inst., Albuquerque, N.Mex., 1976-88; sr. rsch. scientist Eli Lilly and Co., Greenfield, Ind., 1988—2004; rsch. fellow Nektar Therapeutics, San Carlos, Calif., 2004—. Author: (book chpt.) Comprehensive Treatise on Pulmonary Toxicology, 1992, Comprehensive Toxicology, 1997; contbr. articles to profl. jours. Recipient Frank Blood award Soc. Toxicology, 1989, Thomas T. Mercer joint prize Am. Assn. for Aerosol Rsch. and Internat. Soc. Aerosols in Medicine, 2002. Mem. Am. Assn. for Aerosol Rsch., Internat. Soc. Aerosols in Medicine, Soc. Toxicology, Am. Indsl. Hygiene Assn. Avocations: camping, hiking, hockey. Office: Nektar Therapeutics 150 Industrial Rd San Carlos CA 94070 Office Phone: 650-620-6581. Business E-Mail: rwolff@ca.nektar.com.

**WOLFF, SANFORD IRVING,** lawyer; b. Chgo., Apr. 13, 1915; s. Herbert Barron and Libby (Levey) W.; m. Ann Barry, Mar. 21, 1970; children: Paul, David, Laura. BA, Knox Coll., 1936; grad., John Marshall Law Sch., U. Chgo., 1940. Bar: Ill. 1940, N.Y. 1973. Pvt. practice, Chgo. and N.Y.C. 1945—; chief exec. AFTRA, AFL-CIO, N.Y.C., 1968-85; of counsel Becker,

London & Kossow, N.Y.C., 1985—; chief exec. and counsel Am. Guild of Musical Artist, AFL-CIO, 1988-93. Trustee Harris Sch., Chgo. Served with AUS, 1940-45. Decorated Combat Inf. badge, Purple Heart, Bronze Star with cluster, Silver Star. Mem. ABA, Chgo. Bar Assn., NY Bar Assn. Home: 19 Prides Xing New Canaan CT 06840-5502 Office Phone: 203-966-0300.

**WOLFF, SHELDON,** radiobiology educator; b. Peabody, Mass., Sept. 22, 1928; s. Henry Herman and Goldie (Lipchitz) W.; m. Frances Faye Farbstein, Oct. 23, 1954; children: Victor Charles, Roger Kenneth, Jessica Raye. BS magna cum laude, Tufts U., 1950; MA, Harvard U., 1951, PhD in Biology, 1953. Teaching fellow Harvard U., 1952-53; sr. rsch. staff biology div. Oak Ridge Nat. Lab., 1953-66; prof. cytogenetics, anatomy and radiology U. Calif., San Francisco, 1966-94; prof. emeritus, 1994—; dir. Lab. Radiobiology and Environ. Health U. Calif., San Francisco, 1983-95; vice chmn., chief rsch. Radiation Effects Rsch. Found., Hiroshima, Nagasaki, Japan, 1996—2000. Vis. prof. radiation biology U. Tenn., 1962, lectr., 1953-65; cons. several fed. sci. agys.; mem. health and environ. rsch. adv. com. U.S. Dept. Energy, 1986—, chmn., 1987-95; co-chmn. Joint NIH/Dept. Energy Subcom. on Human Genome, 1989-94. Editor: Chromosoma, 1983-97; assoc. editor: Cancer Research, 1983-97; Editorial bd.: Radiation Research, 1968-72, Photochemistry and Photobiology, 1962-72, Radiation Botany, 1964-86, Mutation Research, 1964-97, Caryologia, 1967-96, Radiation Effects, 1969-81, Genetics, 1972-85; Contbr. articles to sci. jours. Mem. Marin County (Calif.) Civil Grand Jury, 2003—05; Marin County Grand Jury Assn., 2003—; Calif. Grand Jury Assn., 2004—. Recipient E.O. Lawrence meml. award U.S. AEC, 1973, 1st ann. Belle award, 1998. Mem. Genetics Soc. Am., Radiation Rsch. Soc. (counselor for biology 1968-72, Failla lectr. 1992, medal 1992), Am. Soc. Cell Biology, Environmental Mutagen Soc. (coun. 1972-75, pres. 1980-81, award 1982), Internat. Assn. Environ. Mutagen Socs. (treas. 1978-85), Sigma Xi. Democrat. Home: 41 Eugene St Mill Valley CA 94941-1717 Office: U Calif Dept Radiology San Francisco CA 94143-0628 Business E-Mail: shellyw@radmail.ucsf.edu.

**WOLFF, SIDNEY CARNE,** astronomer, science administrator; b. Sioux City, Iowa, June 6, 1941; d. George Albert and Ethel (Smith) Carne; m. Richard J. Wolff, Aug. 29, 1962 BA, Carleton Coll., 1962, DSc (hon.), 1985; PhD, U. Calif., Berkeley, 1966. Postgrad. research fellow Lick Obs, Santa Cruz, Calif., 1969; asst. astronomer U. Hawaii, Honolulu, 1967-71, assoc. astronomer, 1971-76; astronomer, assoc. dir. Inst. Astronomy, Honolulu, 1976-83, acting dir., 1983-84; dir. Kitt Peak Nat. Obs., Tucson, 1984-87, Nat. Optical Astronomy Observatories, 1987-2001; dir. Gemini Project Gemini 8-Meter Telescopes Project, 1992-94; astronomer, project scientist Large Synoptic Survey Telescope, 2001—04. Pres. SOAR Inc., 1999-2003; project scientist Large Synoptic Survey Telescope, 2002-04. treas. 2005; bd. mem. LSST Corp. Author: The A-Type Stars--Problems and Perspectives, 1983, (with others) Exploration of the Universe, 1987, Realm of the Universe, 1988, Frontiers of Astronomy, 1990, Voyages Through the Universe, 1996, 2nd edit., 2003, Voyages to the Planets, 1999, 2nd edit., 2003, Voyages to the Stars and Galaxies, 1999, 2nd edit., 2003; founding editor: Astronomy Edn. Rev., 2002; contbr. articles to profl. jours. Trustee Carleton Coll., 1989—, chair acad. affairs com., 1995-2005. Rsch. fellow Lick Obs. Santa Cruz, Calif., 1967; recipient Nat. Meritorious Svc. award NSF, 1994. Fellow Royal Astronical Soc.; mem. Astron. Soc. Pacific (pres. 1984-86, bd. dirs. 1979-85), Am. Astron. Soc. (coun. 1983-86, pres.-elect 1991, pres. 1992-94, Edn. prize 2006). Office: Nat Optical Astronomy Obs PO Box 26732 950 N Cherry Ave Tucson AZ 85719-4933 Business E-Mail: swolff@noao.edu.

**WOLFF, STUART,** online real estate executive; BSEE, Brown U.; MSEE, Princeton U., D in Elec. Engring. Former founder and CEO CareNet Am., others.; former v.p. And Interactive; former v.p. bus. svcs. TCI Interactive (subs. Telecomms. Inc.); chmn., pres. Real Select, Inc. (subs. Homestore-.com., Inc.), Thousand Oaks, Calif. Recipient MONBUSHO fellowship, Japanese Min. of Edn., Tokyo Inst. Technology, 1986. Office: Homestore.com Inc 225 W Hillcrest Dr Ste 100 Thousand Oaks CA 91360-7884

**WOLFF, TOBIAS (JONATHAN ANSELL WOLFF),** writer; b. Birmingham, Ala., June 19, 1945; s. Arthur Saunders and Rosemary (Loftus) Wolff; m. Catherine Dolores Spohn, 1975; children: Michael, Patrick, Mary Elizabeth. BA, Oxford Univ., 1972, MA, 1975, Stanford Univ., 1978; LHD (hon.), Santa Clara Univ., 1996. Mem. faculty Stanford (Calif.) U., Goddard Coll., Plainfield, Vt., Ariz. State U., Tempe, Syracuse (N.Y.) U., Stanford (Calif.) U., 1997—, dir. creative writing program, 2000—02; reporter Washington Post. Author: In the Garden of the North American Martyrs, 1981 (St. Lawrence award for fiction 1982), The Barracks Thief, 1984 (PEN/Faulkner award for fiction 1985), Back in the World, 1985, This Boy's Life: A Memoir, 1989 (L.A. Times Book prize 1989), In Pharaoh's Army: Memories of the Lost War, 1994 (Esquire-Volvo-Winterstone's award, Eng., 1994), The Night in Question, 1996, Old School, 2003 (PEN/Faulkner Award for Fiction finalist, 2004, Nat. Book Critics Circle finalist, LA Times Book award finalist, 2004, Prix de Medicis finalist, France, 2005); editor: Matters of Life and Death: New American Stories, 1983, The Stories of Anton Chekhov, 1987, Best American Short Stories, 1994, The Vintage Book of Contemporary American Stories, 1994, A Doctor's Visit: The Short Stories of Anton Chekov. Recipient Wallace Stegner fellowship in creative writing, 1975-76, Mary Roberts Rinehart award, 1979, Rea award, 1989, Whiting Writer's award, 1989, Lila-Wallace-Reader's Digest award, 1993, Lyndhurst Found. award, 1994, award merit Am. Acad. Arts and Letters, 2001, Fairfax prize for lit. George Mason U., 2003; Nat. Endowment for the Arts fellowship in creative writing, 1978, 85, Ariz. Coun. on Arts and Humanities fellowship in creative writing, 1980, Guggenheim fellowship, 1982. Office: Stanford U Dept English Stanford CA 94305-2087 Office Phone: 650-723-0504.

**WOLFF, VIRGINIA EUWER,** writer; b. Portland, Oreg., Aug. 25, 1937; d. Eugene Courtney and Florence Evelyn (Craven) Euwer; m. Art Wolff, July 19, 1959 (div. July 1976); children: Anthony Richard, Juliet Dianne. AB, Smith Coll., 1959; postgrad., Goddard Coll., Warren Wilson Coll., L.I. U., Portland State U., Lewis & Clark Coll. Cert. tchr., Oreg. Tchr. The Miquon Sch., Phila., 1968-72, The Fiedel Sch., Glen Cove, NY, 1972-75, Hood River Valley (Oreg.) H.S., 1976-86, Mt. Hood Acad., Govt. Camp, Oreg., 1986-98. 2d violinist Quartet con brio, Portland, 1989-94, Parnassius Quintet, Portland, 1996—. Author: Probably Still Nick Swansen, 1988, The Mozart Season, 1991, Make Lemonade, 1993, Bat 6, 1998, True Believer (Nat. Book award, Michael L. Printz honor, Pacific N.W. Booksellers Assn. award, Jane Addams Book honor, 2002), 2001, represented US, honor book, Internat. Board on Books for Young People, 2004. Violinist Mid-Columbia Sinfonietta, Hood River, 1976—92, Oreg. Sinfonietta, Portland, 1988—, Parnassius Chamber Ensemble, 2000-. Recipient Young Adult Book award Internat. Reading Assn., 1989, PEN U.S.A. Ctr. West, 1989, Best Young Adult Book of Yr. award Mich. Libr. Assn., 1993, Child Study Children's Book award Bank Street Coll., 1994, Oreg. Book award Oreg. Lit. Arts, 1994, 2001, Jane Addams Children's Book award Jane Addams Peace Assn. and the Women's Internat. League for Peace and Freedom, 1999, Nat. Book award, 2001, Printz Honor Book award, 2002, Jane Addams Honor Plaque, 2002, Evelyn Sibley Lampman award for svc. to the children of Oreg., Oreg. Libr. Assn., 2005; named to Carnegie medal Shortlist, ALA, 2002. Mem. Soc. Children's Book Writers/Illustrators (Golden Kite 1994, 2002), Chamber Music Soc. Oreg. Avocations: chamber music, swimming, hiking, playing violin, gardening. Office: Curtis Brown Ltd care Elizabeth Harding 10 Astor Pl Fl 3 New York NY 10003-6982

**WOLFF, WILLIAM F., III,** investment banker; b. NYC, Apr. 12, 1945; s. William F., Jr. and Nancy (Wimpfheimer) Wolff; m. Phyllis Fox, June 1, 1969; children: Kenneth, Laura, Jonathan, Gillian. BA, U. Mich., 1967; JD, Columbia U., 1970, MBA, 1971. Bar: N.Y. 1970. V-p. Salomon Bros., Inc. N.Y.C., 1971-78; prin. Morgan Stanley & Co. N.Y.C., 1978-83; mng. dir. Lehman Bros., N.Y.C., 1983-2000, UBS Warburg, N.Y.C., 2000—02, Endurance Capital, N.Y.C., 2002—03; mng. ptnr. Lykos Capital Mgmt., 2003—.

Trustee St. David's Sch., N.Y.C., 1985—2004; dir. City Harvest, 1999—2005. Mem.: Ocean Beach Club (Elberon, N.J.) (trustee 1985—89), Univ. Club (N.Y.). Office: 909 3d Ave New York NY 10022 Personal E-mail: rwolff3@yahoo.com.

**WOLFF, WILLIAM I.,** surgeon, educator; b. N.Y.C., Oct. 24, 1916; s. Julius Louis and Matilda (Brick) W.; m. Lillian Myrick, June 30, 1952 (div. 1967); children: Richard, Deborah, David, Alan, Lisa, Mitchell, George, Rebecca, Barbara; m. Rita T. Smith, Feb. 15, 1972. BS, NYU, 1936; MD, U. Md., 1940. Diplomate Am. Bd. Surgery, Am. Bd. Thoracic Surgery. Intern Cornell U. divsn. Bellevue Hosp., 1940-42, resident specializing in chest surgery Columbia U. divsn., 1942-43; resident, chief Bronx Vets. Hosp., 1946-48; chief thoracic surgery Deshon Vets. Hosp., 1949; practice medicine specializing in surgery N.Y.C., 1950—; emeritus dir. surgery Beth Israel Med. Ctr., N.Y.C., 1962-76; prof. surgery Mt. Sinai Sch. Medicine, N.Y.C., 1965—. 1st disting. lectr. soc. Am. Gastrointestinal Surgeons, 1987; vis. prof. or invited guest lectr. over 40 med. schs. univ. ctrs., over 150 tchg. hosps., numerous nat. and internat. cancer confs. in U.S., Eng., South Africa, Kenya, Israel, Mex., Can., USSR, France and P.R. Contbr. over 120 articles to med. jours., chpts. to books. Served to maj. M.C. AUS, 1943-46, ETO. Mem. ACS, Am. Coll. Gastroenterology (bd. govs.), Am. Assn. for Thoracic Surgery, Soc. Thoracic Surgeons (founding), Soc. for Surgery Alimentary Tract, Am. Coll. Chest Physicians, Am. Gastroenterologic Assn., Internat. Soc. Surgery, Internat. Cardiovasc. Surg. Soc., N.Y. Surg. Soc. (pres. 1980-81), N.Y. Acad. Medicine (chmn. sect. on surgery), Assn. Alumni Bellevue Hosp. (pres. 1982), Aspetuck Valley Country Club. Achievements include early contributor to subject of cardiac resuscitation by cardiac message; originator of scientific procedure of colonoscopy and removal of colonic polyps. Home: 200 E 24th St Apt 1503 New York NY 10010-3919 Office Phone: 212-755-4144.

**WOLFGANG, JARED DALE,** music educator; b. Salem, Ohio, May 25, 1980; s. Wayne Allen and Linda Kay Wolfgang. MusB in Edn., Ohio State U., 2003. Dir. of bands and choirs Newton Local Sch. Dist., Pleasant Hill, Ohio, 2003—. Mem.: NEA (local assn. pres. 2004—), Ohio Edn. Assn., Internat. Horn Soc., Ohio Music Edn. Assn. Methodist. Avocations: travel, reading. Office Phone: 937-676-3081.

**WOLFHARD, HANS GEORG,** retired research scientist; b. Basel, Switzerland, Apr. 2, 1912; arrived in U.S., 1956, naturalized, 1961; s. Albert Georg and Helen (Buerck) W.; m. Adelheid Rohde, Jan. 18, 1940 (dec. 1997); children: George, John (dec. 2002), Bernie; m. Clara Ralston, Jan. 4, 1997. Student, U. Berlin, 1934-35; Dr.Rer.Nat., U. Goettingen, 1938. Scientist Aero. Rsch. Sta., Brunswick, Germany, 1939—46; rsch. scientist Imperial Coll., London, Royal Aircraft Establishment, England, 1946—56; sr. prin. scientific officer Bur. Mines, Pitts., 1956—59; head dept. physics reaction motors divsn. Thiokol Chem. Corp., Denville, NJ, 1959—63; sr. rsch. staff Inst. Def. Analyses, Alexandria, Va., 1963—96; ret. Cons. Sverdrup Tech., AEDC-Arnold AFB, Tenn., 1996—2004. Co-author: Flames, 4th edit., 1979, Chinese transl., 1990. Fellow Ballistic Missle Def., Def. Dept.; recipient 1st Gen. Goodpastor award for Excellence in Rsch., 1983. Fellow Am. Optical Soc., Mil. Sensor Symposium (First Jamieson award); mem. AIAA, Combustion Inst. Episcopalian. Home: 711 Bright Ave Fayetteville TN 37334-2255

**WOLFINGER, NICHOLAS H.,** educator; b. Palo Alto, Calif., May 2, 1966; s. Raymond E. and Barbara Kaye Wolfinger; m. Jessica Lynn Koff, May 23, 1998. AB, U. Calif., Berkeley, 1990; MA, UCLA, LA, 1992, PhD, 1998. Assoc. prof. U. Utah, Salt Lake City, 2005—. Author: (research monograph) Understanding the Divorce Cycle. Liberal. Office: University of Utah 225 South 1400 East AEB 228 Salt Lake City UT 84102 Office Phone: 801-581-7491. Office Fax: 801-581-5156. Personal E-mail: nick.wolfinger@fcs.utah.edu.

**WOLFINGER, RAYMOND EDWIN,** retired political science professor; b. San Francisco, June 29, 1931; s. Raymond Edwin and Hilda (Holm) W.; m. Barbara Kaye, Aug. 7, 1960; 1 son, Nicholas Holm. AB, U. Calif.-Berkeley, 1951; MA, U. Ill., 1955; PhD, Yale U., 1961. Asst. prof. polit. sci. Stanford U., Calif., 1961—66, assoc. prof. Calif., 1966-70, prof. 1970-71, U. Calif., Berkeley 1971—; Heller prof. polit. sci., 1995—2006; ret., 2006. Dir. U. Calif. Data Archive and Tech. Assistance, 1980-92; chmn. bd. overseers Nat. Election Studies, Ann Arbor, Mich., 1982-86 Author: The Politics of Progress, 1974, (with others) Dynamics of American Politics, 1976, 80, (with Steven J. Rosenstone) Who Votes, 1980, (with others) The Myth of the Independent Voter, 1992; mem. editorial bd. Brit. Jour. Polit. Sci., 1980-84, Am. Polit. Sci. Rev., 1985-88. Bd. dirs. S.W. Voter Rsch. Inst., San Antonio, 1988-96, Consortium of Social Sci. Assns., 1987-93, pres. 1988-90. 1st lt. U.S. Army, 1951-53. Fellow Ctr. for Advanced Study in Behavioral Scis., 1960-61; Guggenheim fellow, 1965; Ford Found. faculty research fellow, 1970-71 Fellow Am. Acad. Arts and Scis. (chair Class III membership com. 1998-99); mem. Am. Polit. Sci. Assn. (sec. 1981-82), AAUP (council 1981-84), Western Polit. Sci. Assn. (v.p. 1988-89, pres. 1989-90). Democrat. Office: U Calif Dept Polit Sci Berkeley CA 94720-1950

**WOLFMAN, ALAN,** medical educator, researcher; b. Bronx, N.Y., Mar. 12, 1956; married. Postdoctoral fellow dept. biophysics U. Rochester Med. Ctr., 1988—90; assoc. staff dept. cell biology Cleve. Clinic Found., 1990—. Adj. prof. dept. biology Cleve. State U., 1994—. Contbr. articles to profl. jours.; periodic reviewer: Molecular Cell Biology, Jour. Biol. Chemistry, Biochemistry, BBA, ad hoc reviewer for program project: Nat. Inst. Diabetes and Digestive Kidney Diseases, 1995, invited reviewer: DRTC Pilot Project Ind. U., 1995—; presenter in field. Recipient Postdoctoral fellowship award, NIH, 1985—88, Established Investigatorship award, Am. Heart Assn. 1996—; grantee Cell Biology Tng., 1979, NIH First, 1988—93. Office: Cleve Clinic Found Rsch Inst Dept Cell Biology NC10 9500 Euclid Ave Cleveland OH 44195-0001

**WOLFMAN, BERNARD,** lawyer, educator; b. Phila., July 8, 1924; s. Nathan and Elizabeth (Coff) W.; m. Zelda Bernstein, Dec. 25, 1948 (dec. Oct. 1973); children: Jonathan L., Brian S., Dina A.; m. Toni A. Grotta, June 12, 1977. AB, U. Pa., 1946, JD, 1948; LLD (hon.), Jewish Theol. Sem., 1971, Capital U., 1990. Bar: Pa. 1949. Mass. 1976. Mem. law firm Wolf, Block, Schorr & Solis-Cohen, Phila., 1948-63; prof. law U. Pa. Law Sch., 1963-76, dean, 1970-75, Kenneth W. Gemmill prof. tax law and tax policy, 1973-76, chmn. Faculty Senate, 1969-70; Fessenden prof. law Harvard U., 1976—. Vis. prof. Stanford U. Law Sch., 1982, NYU Law Sch., 1987-88; Irvine lectr. Cornell U. Law Sch., 1980; Halle lectr. Case Western Res. U. Law Sch., 1983; Cleve. State U. Sch. Law; Sugarman lectr., 1989; Altheimer lectr. U. Ark. Sch. Law, Little Rock, 1994; Polisher lectr. Dickinson Coll. Law, 1998; mem. editl. bds. law divsn. Aspen Law & Bus. (formerly Little Brown & Co.), Jour. Corp. Taxation; gen. counsel AAUP, 1966-68, mem. coun., 1979-82; prof.-in-residence tax divsn. Dept. Justice, 2003; cons. to ind. counsel Lawrence E. Walsh (Iran-Contra prosecution), 1987-89; adv. group to commr. internal revenue, 1966-67; cons. tax policy U.S. Treasury Dept., 1963-68, 77-80; chmn. Task Force Univ. Governance, U. Pa., 1968-70; steering com. IRS project Administrv. Conf. US, 1974-80; vice chmn. bd. advs. NYU-IRS Continuing Profl. Edn. Project, 1981-85; mem. legal activities policy bd. Tax Analysts, 1974—; exec. com. Fed. Tax Inst. New Eng., 1976—; pres. Fed. Tax Inst. New Eng., 2004—. Author: (with Diane M. Ring)Federal Income Taxation of Corporate Enterprise, 1971, 4th edit., 2005; (with J. Holden and D. Schenk) Ethical Problems in Federal Tax Practice, 1981, 3dedit., 1995, (with J. Holden and K. Harris) Standards of Tax Practice, 1991, 6th edit. 2004; sr. author: Dissent Without Opinion: The Behavior of Justice William O. Douglas in Federal Tax Cases, 1975; contbr. articles to profl. jours. Adv. com. Commn. Philanthropy and Pub. Needs, 1973-75; mem. Phila. regional council Pa. Gov.'s Justice Commn., 1973-75; trustee Found. Center, NYC, 1970-76, Fedn. Jewish Agys. Greater Phila., 1968-74; bd. dirs. Phila. Lawyers Com. Civil Rights Under Law, 1970-74, Phila. Defender Assn., 1955-69; mem. Nat. Lawyers Adv. Council of Earl Warren Legal Tng. Program. Served with AUS, 1943-45. Fellow Am. Bar Found., Am. Coll. Tax Counsel (past regent 1st cir.); mem. ABA (past chmn. com. on taxation, coun. sect. individual rights and responsibilities 1978-82, coun. sect. taxation 1982-85),

Am. Law Inst., ACLU (nat. dir. 1973-75), Order of Coif (exec. com. 1982-91, v.p. 1986-89, pres. 1989-91), Phi Beta Kappa. Home: 229 Brattle St Cambridge MA 02138-4623 Office: Harvard Law Sch 1545 Mass Ave Cambridge MA 02138 Office Phone: 617-495-4623. Personal E-mail: wolfman@law.harvard.edu.

**WOLFMAN, EARL FRANK, JR.,** surgeon, educator; b. Buffalo, Sept. 14, 1926; s. Earl Frank and Alfreda (Peterson) W.; m. Lois Jeannette Walker, Dec. 28, 1946; children— Nancy Jeannette, David Earl, Carol Anne. BS cum laude, Harvard U., 1946; MD cum laude, U. Mich., 1950. Diplomate Am. Bd. Surgery. Intern U. Mich., Ann Arbor, 1950-51, asst. resident in surgery, 1951-52, resident in surgery, 1954-55, from jr. clin. instr. surgery to assoc. prof., 1955-66, asst. to dean, 1960-61, asst. dean, 1961-64; practice medicine specializing in surgery, 1957—, Sacramento, 1966—; prof. surgery Sch. Medicine, U. Calif., Davis, 1966—, founding chmn. dept. surgery, 1966-78, founding assoc. dean, 1966-76, mem. staff, chief surg. svcs. Med. Ctr., 1966-78, founding chmn. div. surg. scis., 1966-78. Contbr. articles to profl. jours. Served to lt. M.C. USNR, 1952-54. Fellow ACS; mem. AMA (del. 1987-99), Ctrl. Surg. Soc., Western Surg. Soc., Sacramento Surg. Soc., Pacific Coast Surg. Soc., Frederick A. Coller Surg. Soc., Soc. Surgery Alimentary Tract, Am. Assn. Endocrine Surgeons, Sierra Sacramento Valley Med. Soc., Calif. Med. Assn. (trustee 1991-2000), Am. Soc. Gen. Surgeons. Methodist. Office: U Calif Davis Sch Medicine Dept Surgery 2221 Stockton Blvd Fl 3 Sacramento CA 95817-2214 Business E-mail: efwolfman@ucdavis.edu.

**WOLFMAN, IRA JOEL,** editor, writer; b. Oct. 7, 1950; s. Aaron and Beatrice Ruth (Perlo) W.; m. Julia Diamant, June 24, 1979 (dec. 1982); m. Ronda Small, Dec. 20, 1991. BA cum laude, SUNY, Albany, 1971. News editor Washington Park Spirit, Albany, NY, 1971-73; sr. editor Smash mag., N.Y.C., 1975-76; Circus mag., N.Y.C., 1976-79; assoc. editor 3-2-1 Contact mag., N.Y.C., 1979-80; editor Sesame St Parents' Newsletter, N.Y.C., 1980-83; editor-in-chief Enter mag., N.Y.C., 1983-85, Sesame St. mag., Parents Guide, 1990-94; v.p., editor-in-chief Adult Consumer mags. Children's Television Workshop, N.Y.C., 1994-97, v.p., editorial dir. mags. and sch. products, 1997-2000, group v.p., publ. mags. Sesame Workshop, 2000-01; prin. POE Comms., 2001—; v.p. editl. Weekly Reader Pub., 2004—. Newsletter editor Found. for Grandparenting, Mt. Kisco, N.Y., 1984-87; editor Am. Writer, 1988-89; freelance writer and editor, contbr. to Travel & Leisure, Reader's Digest, Archtl. Record, Metropolis, N.Y. Daily News, Ms., Spy, 1985—. Author: Do People Grow on Family Trees? Genealogy for Kids and Other Beginners, 1991, My World and Globe, 1991, Climbing Your Family Tree: Online and Offline Genealogy, 2002, Jewish New York: Notable Neighborhoods and Memorable Moments, 2003. N.Y. State Legis. Corrs. scholar, 1970. Jewish. E-mail: iwolfman@weeklyreader.com.

**WOLFORD, KATHRYN FRANCES,** religious organization administrator; b. Reading, Pa., Dec. 12, 1957; d. Howard Francis Wolford and Katherine Eva (Auker) Carbaugh. BA in History, Gettysburg Coll., 1979; MA in Religious Studies, U. Chgo. Divinity Sch., 1980; MA in Pub. Policy, U. Chgo., 1981; PhD (hon.), Gettysburg Coll., 1995; PhD (hon.), Muhlenberg Coll., 2003. Country program rep. Ch. World Svc., Dominican Republic, 1983-85; regional rep. Nat. Coun. Chs., U.S.A., N.Y.C., 1985-90; program dir. for L.Am., Luth. World Relief, Balt., 1991-93, pres., 1993—. Named Md. Top 100 Women, Md. Daily Record, 2002, 2004. Democrat. Lutheran. Avocation: sailing.

**WOLFORD, RICHARD G.,** food products executive; With Dole Foods, 1967—87, pres. packaged foods, 1982—87; CEO HK Acquisition Corp., 1988—96, Del Monte Foods Co., San Francisco, 1997—, pres., 1998—, chmn., 2000—. Office: Del Monte Foods Co One Market The Landmark San Francisco CA 94105

**WOLFOWITZ, PAUL DUNDES,** President of the World Bank, former federal agency administrator; b. NYC, Dec. 22, 1943; s. Jacob and Lillian (Dundes) W.; m. Clare Selgin, Nov. 25, 1968; children: Sara Elizabeth, David Samuel, Rachel Dahlia. BA in Math. and Chemistry, Cornell U., 1965; MA, U. Chgo., 1967, PhD in Polit. Sci., 1972. Lectr., asst. prof. Yale U., 1970-73; with U.S. Arms Control and Disarmament Agy., 1973-77, spl. asst. to dir., 1974-75, dep. asst. dir., 1976, spl. asst. for Strategic Arms Limitation Talks (SALT), 1976-77; dep. asst. sec. of def., regional programs, program analysis and evaluation US Dept. Def., Washington, 1977-80; vis. assoc. prof. Paul H. Nitze Sch. of Advanced Intl. Studies, Johns Hopkins U., 1980-81, dean, prof. of intl. relations, 1994—2001; dir. policy planning staff US Dept. State, Washington, 1981-82, asst. sec. of state for East Asian and Pacific affairs, 1982-86, U.S. amb. to Indonesia Jakarta, 1986-89; undersec. def. for policy US Dept. Def., Washington, 1989—93, dep. sec., 2001—05; pres. The World Bank Group, Washington, 2005—. Recipient Presdl. Citizens medal. Office: The World Bank Group 1818 H St Washington DC 20433*

**WOLFRAM, CHARLES WILLIAM,** law educator; b. Cleve., Feb. 28, 1937; s. Carl P. and Dona M. (Minitch) W.; m. Nancy Russell Bass, Dec. 18, 1965; children: Catherine Dana, Peter Russell. AB, Notre Dame U., 1959; LLB, U. Tex., 1962. Bar: D.C. 1962, Minn. 1974. Assoc. Covington & Burling, Washington, 1962-64; mem. FAA Contract Appeals Panel, Washington, 1964-65; asst. prof. law U. Minn., 1965-67, assoc. prof., 1967-70, prof., 1970-81; prof. law Cornell U., Ithaca, N.Y., 1982-84, Charles Frank Reavis Sr. prof. law, 1984-99, Charles Frank Reavis Sr. prof. emeritus, 1999—. Assoc. dean acad. affairs Cornell U., Ithaca, 1986-90, interim dean, 1998-99; vis. prof. U. So. Calif. Law Center, 1976-77. Author: (with J. Morris Clark) Professional Responsibilty: Issues for Minnesota Attorneys, 1976, Modern Legal Ethics, 1986; contbr. chpts. to books, articles to profl. jours. Mem. Am. Law Inst. (chief reporter Restatement of Law Governing Lawyers, 1986-2000), Order of Coif. Democrat. Office: 2887 College Ave #148 Berkeley CA 94705 E-mail: charles.wolfram@pontofice.law.cornell.edu.

**WOLFRAM, DAVID ANTHONY,** information technology manager; b. Melbourne, Australia, Sept. 20, 1962; s. Hans Gerhard (dec.) and Bettine Rosalind (Kauffmann) W. BSc with honors, U. Melbourne, 1984, MSc, 1986; PhD, U. Cambridge (Eng.), 1990, U. Oxford (Eng.), 1991; MBA, Australian Grad. Sch. Mgmt., 2006. Cert. european engr., chartered IT profl., PMP; chartered engr. Rsch. asst. U. Oxford, 1990; jr. rsch. fellow Christ Ch., Oxford, 1990-94, BT fellow, 1994; lectr. in computer sci. Australian Nat. U., Canberra, 1995-2000, vis. fellow Rsch. Sch. Info. Sci. and Engring., 2000; with Microsoft Corp., USA, Redmond, Wash., 2000—02; project mgr. Expert Info. Svc. (now Infosys Tech. Australia), Melbourne, 2003—. Mem. program com CATS Computing: The Australasian Theory Symposium, 1999, 2000, 03, 04, program chair, 00, mem. steering com., 2002—. Author: The Clausal Theory of Types, 1993; contbr. articles to profl. jours.; guest editor: Electronic Notes in Theoretical Computer Science, Vol. 31, 2000; guest editor spl. issue Theoretical Computer Science, 2003. Fellow: Royal Soc. Australia, Cambridge Philos. Soc. (life); mem.: Project Mgmt. Inst. (bd. dirs. Melbourne chpt. 2006—), Assn. Computing Machinery, IEEE Computer Soc., N.Y. Acad. Sci., London Math. Soc., Brit. Computer Soc., Internat. Soc. for Philos. Enquiry (diplomate), Melbourne Cricket Club, Am. Australian Assn., Ordre du Tastevin (chevalier). Avocations: photography, tennis, chess.

**WOLFRAM, STEPHEN,** physicist, computer company executive; b. London, Aug. 29, 1959; came to U.S., 1978; Degree, Eton Coll., 1976, Oxford U., 1978; PhD in Theoretical Physics, Calif. Inst. Tech., 1979. With Calif. Inst. Tech., Pasadena, 1979-82, Inst. for Advanced Study, Princeton, NJ, 1983-86; prof. physics, math, computer sci. U. Ill., Champaign, 1986-90; founder, dir. Ctr. for Complex Sys. Rsch., 1996—98; pres., CEO Wolfram Rsch. Inc., Champaign, 1987—. Author: Theory and Applications of Cellular Automata, 1986, Mathematica: A System for Doing Mathematics by Computer, 1988, 2d edit., 1991, Mathematica Reference Guide, 1992, Mathematica: The Student Book, 1994, The Mathematica Book, 3rd edit., 1996, 5th edit., 2003, Cellular Automata and Complexity, 1994, A New Kind of Science, 2002; editor jour. Complex Systems, 1986— Fellow MacArthur Found., 1981; recipient World

Leadrers of Tomorrow award, World Economic Forum, 1999; named Scientist of Yr., R&D Mag., 2002. Office: Wolfram Rsch Inc 100 Trade Centre Dr Champaign IL 61820-7237 Business E-mail: s.wolfram@wolfram.com.

**WOLFRAM, THOMAS,** physicist, educator; b. St. Louis, July 27, 1936; s. Ferdinand I. and Audrey H. (Calvert) W.; m. Eleanor Elaine Burger, May 22, 1965; children: Michael, Gregory, Melanie, Susan, Steven. BA, U. Calif. Riverside, 1959, PhD in Physics, 1963; MA in Physics, UCLA, 1960. Engr. Atomics Internat., Canoga Park, Calif., 1960-63; mem. tech. staff N.Am. Aviation Corp. Sci. Ctr., Thousand Oaks, Calif., 1963-68; group leader in solid state physics Rockwell Internat. Sci. Ctr., Thousand Oaks, 1968-72, dir. div. physics and chemistry, 1972-74; prof. physics, chmn. dept. physics and astronomy U. Mo., Columbia, 1974-83; dir. phys. tech. divsn. AMOCO Corp., 1983-87; v.p., gen. mgr. AMOCO Laser Co., 1987-95; bus. cons., 1995—. Cons. in field. Author: The Venture, The Dragon Tamers; editor: Inelastic Electron Tunneling Spectroscopy, 1978; contbr. articles to profl. jours. Recipient Disting. Prof. award Argonne Univs. Assn., 1977 Fellow Am. Phys. Soc. Home and Office: 228 Trafalgar Ln San Clemente CA 92672 E-mail: ewolfram@cox.net. *Crisis is the catalyst for constructive change.*

**WOLFSON, AARON HOWARD,** radiation oncologist, educator; b. Nashville, May 13, 1955; s. Sorrell Louis and Jacqueline Adele (Falis) W.; m. Adrienne Sue Mates, Dec. 16, 1977; children: Alexis Ellyn, Andrew Lane. BA, U. Fla., 1978, MD, 1982. Diplomate Am. Bd. Radiology. Intern internal medicine Jackson Meml. Hosp., Miami, 1983—85; pvt. practice Palm Beach Gardens, Fla., 1985—86; resident in radiation oncology Med. Coll. Va., Richmond, 1986—89; from instr. to assoc. prof. radiation oncology U. Miami, Miller Sch. Medicine, 1989—2003, 2003—, vice chair dept. radiation oncology, 2005—. Co-dir. Gynecology Site dis. group Sylvester Cancer Ctr., 2001—. Contbr. articles to profl. jours. Bd. dirs. Children's Home Soc., Ft. Lauderdale, Fla., 1993—, Temple Beth Israel, Sunrise, Fla., 1994—; mem. spkrs. bur. U. Miami, 1993—; vol. spkr. Broward County Schs., 1990—; exec. v.p. Temple Beth Israel, 1996-98, pres., 1998-99. Sylvester Cancer Ctr. grantee, 1992. Mem. Gynecologic Oncology Group, Radiation Therapy Oncology Group, Am. Soc. Therapeutic Radiology and Oncology. Jewish. Achievements include research on malignant tumors of the female genital tract; patent for radiation implant for gynecologic cancer. Office: Univ Miami 1475 NW 12th Ave # D-31 Miami FL 33136-1002 Office Phone: 305-243-4210. Business E-mail: awolfson@med.miami.edu.

**WOLFSON, BARBARA LIBENSPERGER,** guidance counselor; b. Mar. 9, 1949; BS in Elem. Edn., Trenton State Coll., 1971, M in Student Pers. Svcs. Guidance, 1983. Elem. sch. tchr. Trenton (N.J.) Bd. Edn., 1971-83, guidance counselor, 1983—. Chmn. Raritan Township (N.J.) Zoning Bd. 1988-92; mem. Raritan Township Recreation Bd., 1992-93, Cable TV Bd., 1993-94, County com., 1986-2000. Mem. Daus. Am. Revolution, Order of Ea. Star (Ashler chpt.), Trenton Edn Assn. (chief del.), Cedar Mar. Yacht Club. Avocations: skiing, sailing. Home: 15 Blackwell Rd Flemington NJ 08822-1955

**WOLFSON, IRWIN M.,** insurance company executive; b. Bronx, May 29, 1937; s. Herman M. and Kate (Greenstein) W.; m. Pauline S. Frechtel, Dec. 25, 1962; children: Fran M., Lisa G. BS in Econs., NYU, 1960; grad., Life Underwriting Tng. Coun., 1975. Owner/CEO Wolfson Agency, Yonkers, NY, 1973—. Instr., owner Successful Adult Fin. Seminars, Yonkers, 1990—; mem. underwriter's tng. coun. Grad. Life Mem. operating bd. Child Abuse Prevention Ctr., White Plains, N.Y. Sgt. U.S. Army, 1960-66. Recipient Achievement award Congressman Elliot Engel, 1992, proclamation from T. Zaleski (Mayor) City of Yonkers, 1992, letter of Recognition from M. Cuomo (Governor) N.Y. 1992; Irwin M. Wolfson Day proclaimed by A. O'Rourk (County Exec.) N.Y. 1992. Mem. Yonkers Exch. Club (pres. 1990-91, NY dist. dir. 1991-95, 99--, NY dist. pres. 1996-97), Million Dollar Round Table. Home: 11 Jackson Ave Unit 4 Scarsdale NY 10583-3134 Office: Wolfson Agy 475 Tuckahoe Rd Yonkers NY 10710-5712 Office Phone: 914-779-1982.

**WOLFSON, JEREMY,** investment advisor; BS in Fin., Calif. State U., Northridge. Lic. internat. fin. analyst, cert. CFA. V.p., mgr. strategic projects Bank of Am., Glendale, Calif., 1992—94, v.p., mgr. sales project group, 1994—96, v.p., prin. fixed income sales L.A., 1996—2002, First Tenn. Bank-FTN Fin., Pasadena, 2002—05; sr. investment/compliance officer, portfolio mgr. City of L.A., 2005—. Mem.: Gov. Fin. Officers Assn., Calif. Assn. County Treas. and Tax Collectors, Calif. Soc. Mcpl. Fin. Officers, Calif. Mcpl. Treas. Assn., Internat. Rsch. Assn., L.A. Soc. Fin. Analysts, Assn. of Investment, Mgmt. and Rsch., Toastmasters, Sigma Alpha Epsilon. Home: 28007 Serra Ln Valencia CA 91355

**WOLFSON, JORDAN,** artist; b. NYC, 1980; BFA, Rhode Island Sch. Design, Providence, RI, 2003; studied, Konfstack Coll. Arts & Krafts, Stockholm, Sweden, 2003. One-man shows include Radar, Galleri Brandstrom & Stene, STOCKHOLM, 2002, Nostalgia is Fear, Irma Vep Lap, Champagne, France, 2004, Jordan Wolfson, Kunsthalle Zurich, 2004, Neverland, Jordan Wolfson, Yvon Lambert, Paris, 2005, Jiem-no-Pedti, t293 Naples, 2005, Wako Works of Art, Tokyo, 2006, exhibited in group shows at Fort Thuder, Providence, RI, 2000, Nada Art Fair, Miami, 2003, Palm D'Or Social Club, Berlin Art Fair, 2004, Festival of Dreams, Lombard-Freid Gallery, NYC, 2004, None of the Above, Swiss Inst., NYC, 2004, There is No Such Thing As The Real World, Galleri MGM, Oslo, 2005, BUIA Gallery, 2005, Post note, Midway Contemporary Art Mus., Minn., 2005, U-Move, Utopia and Image on the Move, Gallery Contemporary Art, Monfalcone, Italy, 2005, Sold Out, Spazio, More Fools In Town, Turin, 2005, Hudson Valley Ctr. Contemporary Art, 2006, Uncertain States of Am., 2006, Whitney Biennial, Whitney Mus. Art, 2006. Office: c/o Whitney Mus 945 Madison Ave New York NY 10021*

**WOLFSON, MARK ALAN,** investor, educator, dean; b. Chgo., Ill., Sept. 25, 1952; s. Jack and Maribelle (Simen) W.; m. Sheila Rae Aronesti, Aug. 3, 1975; children: Laura Rachel, Charles Michael. BS in Acctg. and Fin., U. Ill., 1973, M in Acctg. Sci., 1974; PhD in Acctg., U. Tex., 1977. Asst. prof. acctg. Stanford (Calif.) U., 1977-81, assoc. prof., 1981-85, prof., 1985-87, Joseph McDonald prof., 1987-92, assoc. dean, 1990-93, Dean Witter prof. acctg. and fin., 1992-96, cons. prof., 2001—; mng. ptnr. Oak Hill Capital Mgmt., 1998—; established Oak Hill Strategic Ptnrs., 1996—, Oak Hill Investment Mgmt., 2000—; prin. Oak Hill Platinum Ptnrs., 1999—, Oak Hill REIT Ptnrs., 2004—, Oak Hill Spl. Opportunities Fund, 2004—. Ford Found. vis. assoc. prof. U. Chgo., 1981-82; Thomas Henry Carroll vis. prof. Harvard U., Boston, 1988-89; cons. Fin. Acctg. Stds. Bd., Norwalk, Conn., 1985, 89-92; rsch. assoc. Nat. Bur. Econ. Rsch., Cambridge, Mass., 1988—; steering com. Stanford Inst. Econ. Policy Rsch., 1990-2000, exec. com. 2001-; task force Fed. Home Loan Bank Bd., 1989; v.p. Keystone Inc., 1995—; bd. dirs. eGain Comm., Fin. Engines, Inc., 230 Park Investors, Accretive Healthcare; mem. investment com. William and Flora Hewlett Found., 2004—. Contbr. numerous articles to profl. jours. Recipient Pomerance prize Chgo. Bd. Options Exch., 1981, Disting. Tchg. award Stanford U., 1990, Notable Contbn. to Lit. award AICPA-Am. Acctg. Assn., 1990, 92, Wildman award, 1991; named Disting. Accountancy Alumnus, U. Ill., 1989. Jewish. Office: Oak Hill Capital 2775 Sand Hill Rd Ste 220 Menlo Park CA 94025-7019

**WOLFSON, MICHAEL GEORGE,** retired lawyer; b. Chgo., Sept. 1, 1938; s. A. Lincoln M. Weingarten and Brina (Nelson) W.; m. Rita Sue Parsont, Sept. 11, 1966; children: Bethany Lynne, Sara Wynne, Deborah Kay. Student, MIT, 1956-58; BA, U. Chgo., 1961, JD, 1964, postdoctoral, 1964-65. Bar: Ill. 1964, N.Y. 1969. Assoc. Cravath, Swaine & Moore, N.Y.C., 1965-71, Brown, Wood, Fuller, Caldwell & Ivey, N.Y.C., 1971-73; ptnr. Sidley Austin LLP, NYC, 1974—2002, sr. counsel, 2003—06, ret., 2006. Mediator, specializing in comml. and internat. disputes. Woodrow Wilson fellow, 1961; Ford Found. fellow in internat. trade and devel., 1965. Fellow Am. Bar Found. (life); mem. ABA. Avocations: reading, photography, fly fishing, bicycling. Office Phone: 212-839-5321. Business E-mail: mwolfson@sidley.com.

**WOLGAMOTT, GARY DEAN,** medical educator; b. Weatherford, Okla., July 23, 1940; s. Kenneth Blaine and Winona Irene Wolgamott; m. Sandra Jean Wolgamott, Apr. 26, 1962; children: Thad Dean, Dotti D'Lane Wolgamott-Forehand. BS Biology and Chemistry, Northwestern Okla. State U., 1963; PhD Microbiology, Okla. State U., 1968. Postdoctoral fellow U. Iowa Coll. Medicine, Iowa City, 1971, NASA, Houston, 1974—75; chmn. allied health scis. Southwestern Okla. State U., Weatherford, 1975—, prof., 1968—, Bernhardt prof., 1996—, assoc. dean Sch. Health Scis., 1994—. Mem. med. tech. rev. com. Nat. Accrediting Agy. Clin. Lab. Scis., 1980—90. Named to Outstanding Profs. Acad., 1999—2000; recipient Outstanding Edn. Grad. award, Northwestern Okla. State U., 2006. Fellow: Okla. Acad. Sci. (chmn.collegiate acad. 1968—80, pres. 1980); mem.: Am. Soc. Microbiology (ednl. coord. 1971—79), Kiwanis (bd. dirs., pres. 1990—91), Lambda Tau (nat. sec.-treas., editor/author newsletter 1976—), Beta Beta Beta (nat. pres. 2001—). Methodist. Avocations: bicycling, running, backpacking, guitar, skiing. Office: Southwestern Oklahoma State U 100 Campus Dr Weatherford OK 73096-3001 Office Phone: 580-774-3079. Business E-Mail: gary.wolgamott@swosu.edu.

**WOLIN, NEAL STEVEN,** lawyer; b. Chgo., Dec. 9, 1961; s. Harry S and Doris (Wacker) Wolin. BA in history summa cum laude, Yale U., 1983; MS in devel. economics, U. Oxford, Eng., 1985; JD, Yale U., 1988. Bar: Ill 1989, DC 1989, US Supreme Ct 1995. Law clk. US Judge Eugene H. Nickerson, Bklyn., 1988-89; adj. asst. prof. of law Bklyn. Law Sch., 1989; assoc. Wilmer, Cutler & Pickering, Washington, 1989-90; spl. asst. to dir. ctrl. intelligence, 1990-93; dep. legal adviser Nat. Security Coun. The White House, 1993-94, exec. asst. to the nat. security adviser, 1994-95; dep. gen. counsel US Dept. Treasury, 1995-99, gen. counsel, 1999-2001; exec. v.p., gen. counsel The Hartford Fin. Services Group, Inc., Hartford, 2001—, also chief compliance officer, chief privacy officer. Vis. fellow Brookings Inst., Washington, 2001; adj. lectr. in pub. policy JFK Sch. Govt., Harvard U., 2001; bd. dirs. Greater Hartford Legal Assistance Found. Bd. overseers RAND Corp. Inst. Civil Justice; mem. bd. regents U. Hartford; mem. exec. com. Yale Law Sch. Assn.; mem. Presdl. Adv. Commn. on Holocaust Assets in US, 1999—2000. Named one of 100 People to Watch, Washingtonian mag., 1999; recipient Alexander Hamilton Award, Sec. Treasury, 2001; Charles and Julia Henry Fellow, Henry Trust, Oxford U., 1983—84, Coker Tchg. Fellow, Yale Law Sch., 1987—88. Mem.: Coun. Fgn. Rels., Phi Beta Kappa. Office: The Hartford Fin Svcs Group Inc Hartford Plz Hartford CT 06115 Office Phone: 860-547-3100. Business E-Mail: nwolin@thehartford.com.

**WOLIN, ROBERT EVERETT,** lawyer; BA, Lafayette Coll., 1969; JD, NYU, 1973. Bar: N.Y. 1974. Bar: Tex. 1983, US Dist. Ct. (so. N.Y., ea. Pa., No. Tex. dist.). Law clk. Judge James A. Coolahan, US Dist. Ct. N.J., 1973—75; adminstrv. ptnr. & mem. mgmt. com. Kirkpatrick & Lockhart Nicholson Graham LLP, Dallas. Mem.: ABA, N.Y. State Bar Assn., Tex. Bar Assn., Dallas Bar Assn., Phi Beta Kappa. Office: Kirkpatrick & Lockhart Nicholson Graham LLP Suite 1800 2828 N Harwood St Dallas TX 75201-6966 Office Phone: 214-939-4909. Office Fax: 214-939-4949. Business E-Mail: rwolin@klng.com.

**WOLINSKY, EMANUEL,** internist, educator; b. N.Y.C., Sept. 23, 1917; s. Jacob and Bertha (Siegel) W.; m. Marjorie Claster, Nov. 15, 1946; children: Douglas, Peter. Ba, Cornell U., 1938, MD, 1941. Diplomate Am. Bd. Med. Microbiology. Intern, resident medicine N.Y. Hosp., 1943-45; bacteriologist Trudeau Lab., Saranac Lake, NY, 1947-56; mem. faculty Case Western Res. U. Sch. Medicine, 1956-98, prof. medicine, 1968-88, prof. pathology, 1981-88, prof. emeritus 1988-98, ret., 1998. Dir. microbiology Cleve. Met. Gen. Hosp., 1959-91, acting dir. dept. pathology, 1980-86, chief div. infectious diseases, 1961-83. Co-editor Textbook of Pulmonary Diseases, 5th edit., 1993; Asso. editor: Am. Rev. Respiratory Diseases, 1973-79; Contbr. articles to profl. jours., textbooks. Mem. Tb panel U.S.-Japan Co-op. Med. Sci. Program, 1969-75. Recipient Crystal Cross award Ohio Thoracic Soc., 1995, Louis Weinstein award Clin. Infectious Diseases, 1995, Maurice Saltzman award Mt. Sinai Healthcare Found., 1999; named to Med. Hall of Fame, Cleve. Mag., 1998. Mem. Am. Soc. Microbiology (Gardner Middlebrook award 1998), Am. Thoracic Soc. (Trudeau medal 1986), Infectious Diseases Soc. Am. (Soc. Citation award 2004), Phi Beta Kappa, Alpha Omega Alpha. Home: 24761 S Woodland Rd Cleveland OH 44122-3327

**WOLINTZ, ARTHUR HARRY,** neurologist, ophthalmologist; b. Bklyn., May 30, 1937; s. Louis and Celia (Ragofsky) W.; m. Carol Sue Bergstein, Nov. 28, 1963; children: Robyn Joy, Ellen Sharon. Student, NYU, 1955-58; MD summa cum laude, SUNY, Bklyn., 1962; postgrad., Columbia U., 1967-68. Diplomate Am. Bd. Psychiatry and Neurology, Am. Bd. Ophthalmology; licensee Nat. Bd. Med. Examiners. U. State of N.Y. Intern Maimonides Hosp., Bklyn., 1962-63, jr. resident in medicine, 1963-64; resident Nat. Inst. Neurol. Diseases and Blindness, Bethesda, Md., 1964-66; chief resident Mt. Sinai Hosp., N.Y.C., 1966-67; clin. asst. prof. neurology Downstate Med. Ctr. SUNY, Bklyn., 1968-69, resident in ophthalmology 1969-71, from asst. prof. to prof., 1971—, prof. clin. ophthalmology and clin. neurology, 1977—, interim chief ophthalmology, 1983, acting regional chmn. dept. ophthalmology, 1984, prof. ophthalmology, 1987—, chmn. dept. ophthalmology, 1987-96; Disting. tchg. prof., chair emeritus dept. ophthalmology SUNY-Health Sci. Ctr. Bklyn., 1995, 96—; assoc. neurologist Presbyn. Hosp., N.Y.C., 1967-68; instr. neuropathology Coll. Physicians and Surgeons Columbia U., N.Y.C., 1967-68; instr. neurology Mt. Sinai Sch. Medicine, N.Y.C., 1967-68; assoc. dir. neurology Maimonides Med. Ctr., Bklyn., 1968-69; asst. neurologist Coney Island Hosp., Bklyn., 1968-69. Vis. neurologist Kings County Hosp. Ctr., Bklyn, 1968-69; chief divsn. ophthalmology and neuro-ophthalmology Kingsbrook Jewish Med. Ctr., Bklyn., 1971, sec. med. and dental staff 1976-77, v.p. 1978-79, pres. 1980-81, dir. ophthalmology 1981; attending physician State Univ. Hosp., Bklyn., 1971, Kings County Hosp. Ctr., Bklyn., 1971; conn. Luth. Med. Ctr. Beth Israel Med. Ctr., Brookdale Hosp. Med. Ctr., Bklyn., J.L. Coll. Hosp., Bklyn., Maimonides Med. Ctr., Cath. Med. Ctr. Bklyn. and Queens, Bklyn. VA Hosp. Author: Essentials of Clinical Neuro-Ophthalmology, 1976; contbr. chpts. to sci. textbooks and handbooks, articles to profl. jours. Pres. Flatbush Jewish Ctr., Bklyn. With USPHS 1964-66. Recipient J. Eugene Chalfin Meml. Lectr. award Alumni Assn. State Univ.-Kings County, 1981, Tchr. of Yr. award dept. ophthalmology Interfaith Med. Ctr., 1988, Greats in Ophthalmology in Bklyn. award, SUNY Downstate Med. Ctr. Dept. Ophthalmology, 2004. Fellow ACP, ACS, Am. Acad. Ophthalmology and Otolaryngology, Am. Acad. Neurology; mem. AMA, AAAS, Med. Soc. County Kings, Med. Soc. State N.Y., Bklyn. Ophthal. Soc., N.Y. Acad. Medicine, Am. Acad. Neurology, Alumni Assn. SUNY (pres.-elect 1989, pres. 1990-91), Richard C. Troutman M.D. Master Tchr. award in ophthalmology 1987, Disting. Alumni Achievement award 1997, Frank L. Babbott M.D. Meml. award 2002, Clarence and Mary Dennis Dedicated Svc. award 2004, Kingbrook Pres.'s award 2004), Oddfellows, Alpha Omega Alpha. Avocations: Torah reader, cantor. Home and Office: 100 Ocean Pky Apt 4H Brooklyn NY 11218-1755 Office Phone: 718-854-7360. Personal E-Mail: ahwolintz@aol.com.

**WOLITZER, STEVEN BARRY,** investment banker; b. Bklyn., Mar. 14, 1953; s. Philip and Regina (Wurm) W.; m. Joyce Sue Lindower, Dec. 7, 1985; children: David Joel, Scott Richard, Rachel. BS, NYU, 1973; MBA, Harvard U., 1977. CPA, N.Y. Mng. dir. Lehman Bros. Inc., N.Y.C., 1977—, head global mergers and acquisitions, 1996—. Home: 1185 Park Ave Apt 6A New York NY 10128-1309 Office: Lehman Bros Inc 745 Seventh Ave New York NY 10019 Business E-Mail: swolitze@lehman.com.

**WOLK, BRUCE ALAN,** law educator; b. Bklyn., Mar. 2, 1946; s. Morton and Gertrude W.; m. Lois Gloria Krepliak, June 22, 1968; children: Adam, Daniel. BS, Antioch Coll., 1968; MS, Stanford U., 1972; JD, Harvard U., 1975. Bar: D.C. 1975. Assoc. Hogan & Hartson, Washington, 1975-78; prof. U. Calif. Sch. Law, Davis, 1978—, acting dean, 1990-91, dean, 1995-98. Danforth Found. fellow, 1970-74, NSF fellow, 1970-72, Fulbright sr. research fellow, 1985-86. Mem. ABA, Am. Law Inst. Office: Univ Cal Davis Sch Law King Hall 400 Mrak Hall Dr Davis CA 95616-5201

**WOLKOFF, ALLAN WAYNE,** gastroenterologist, medical educator; b. Bklyn., Mar. 7, 1948; s. Martin and Evelyn Wolkoff; m. Claire Louise Freeman, Aug. 31, 1969; children: Steven Andrew, Hilary Joan. AB, Dartmouth Coll., 1968; B of Med. Sci., Dartmouth Med. Sch., 1970; MD, Albert Einstein Coll. of Medicine, 1972. Diplomate Am. Bd. of Internal Medicine, 1975, Subspecialty of Gastroenterology Am. Bd. of Internal Medicine, 1985. Prof. of medicine, anatomy and structural biology Albert Einstein Coll. of Medicine, Bronx, NY, 1976—, dir. Belfer Inst. for Advanced Biomedical Studies. Bd. dirs. Am. Liver Found., N.Y.C. Editor: (med. software series) Therapeutic Procedures in Medicine; assoc. editor (jour.) Hepatology, Am. Jour. of Physiology: Gastrointestinal and Liver Physiology, Seminars in Liver Disease. Surgeon USPHS, 1973—76. Recipient Outstanding Contbn. award, Am. Liver Found., 1986. Mem.: AAAS, Am. Soc. for Cell Biology, Am. Gastroent. Assn., Am. Assn. for the Study of Liver Diseases (councilor-at-large 1998—2001), Am. Physiol. Soc. (councilor 1998—2001), Assn. of Am. Physicians, Am. Soc. for Clin. Investigation, Internat. Assn. for Study of Liver, Interurban Clin. Club (pres. 2000—01), Phi Beta Kappa. Office: Albert Einstein Coll of Medicine 1300 Morris Park Ave Bronx NY 10461 Office Phone: 718-430-3798. Office Fax: 718-430-8975. Business E-Mail: wolkoff@aecom.yu.edu.

**WOLKOFF, EUGENE ARNOLD,** lawyer; b. NYC, June 9, 1932; s. Oscar and Jean (Zablow) W.; m. Judith Gail Edwards, Oct. 15, 1967; children—Mandy, Elana, Alexa, Justine. AB, Bklyn. Coll., 1953; LLB, St. John's U., 1961. Bar: N.Y. 1962, N.Mex. 1994. Practiced in N.Y.C and Santa Fe; mem. Callahan & Wolkoff, N.Y.C., 1965—; gen. counsel BGK Group of Cos. Bd. dirs. Babylon Enterprises, Inc., Hist. Newspaper Archives, Inc., Beacon Concessions, Inc.; mem. nat. panel arbitrators Am. Arbitration Assn. Served to lt. col. USAFR, 1953-75. Mem. N.Y State Bar Assn., N.Mex. Bar Assn., Pi Beta Gamma. Office: 2124 Broadway New York NY 10023-1722 also: 330 Garfield St Santa Fe NM 87501-2640 Office Phone: 505-992-5100, 212-332-9069. E-mail: gene@bgkgroup.com.

**WOLKOFF, NEAL L.,** stock exchange executive; married; 3 children. BA, Columbia U., 1977; JD, Boston U., 1980. Atty. NY Mercantile Exch., Inc., NYC, 1981—93, exec. v.p., 1993—2002, acting pres., 2000—01, exec. v.p., COO, 2002—03; cons. Am. Stock Exchange LLC, acting CEO, 2005, CEO, 2005—, chmn., 2005—. Office: Am Stock Exch LLC 86 Trinity Place New York NY 10006 Business E-Mail: neal.wolkoff@amex.com.

**WOLKOV, HARVEY BRIAN,** oncologist, researcher; b. Cleve., Feb. 8, 1953; s. Sidney and Norma Wolkov; m. Lauren Cronin, Jan. 9, 1993; 1 child, Nicole. BSc, Purdue U., 1975, MSc, 1977; MD, Medical Coll. Ohio, 1979. Diplomate Am. Bd. Radiology. Intern U. Calif., San Francisco, 1979-80; resident Stanford (Calif.) Med. Ctr., 1980-83; rsch. asst. Stanford U., 1982; from asst. clin. prof. to assoc. clin. prof. U. Calif., Davis, 1983-97, assoc. clin. prof., 1997—; med. dir. Mercy Hosps., Sacramento, 1987-90, Sutter Cancer Ctr. Dept. Radiation Oncology, Sacramento, 1990—. Mem. adv. bd. Nat. Graves Disease Found., Jacksonville, Fla., 1993—; dir. Sutter Gamma Knife Ctr., 1997—; co-prin. investigator radiation oncology Children's Oncology Group, 2001—. Author (with others): (book) Intraoperative Radiation, 1989, Frontiers in Radiation, 1991, Textbook Radiation Oncology, 2004; contbr. articles to profl. jours. Bd. dirs. Sutter Hosps. Found., Sacramento. Fellow: Am. Soc. Therapeutic Radiology and Oncology (bd. dirs. 2000—03, vice chair outcome rsch., corp. rels., workforce, comm., coronary artery radiation therapy coms., fin. com., Travel award 1987); mem.: Calif. Radiol. Soc. (exec. com. 2001—), Sutter Inst. Med. Rsch. (chair rsch. com. 1996—, hosp. chair oncology com. 2003—, neuroscience inst. leadership com. 2003—), Calif. Radiation Oncology Soc. (pres.-elect 1999, pres. 2000—01), Radiation Therapy Oncology Group (com. chair 1986—90, publ. com. 1990—, mem. com. 1990—, lung and brain com. 1990—), No. Calif. Radiation Oncology Soc. (pres. 1999—2001), Coun. Affiliated Radiation Oncology Soc. (pres. 1999—2000), Assn. Residents Radiation Oncology (exec. com. 1997-2000 1997—2000, advisor emeritus 2000—), Am. Cancer Soc. (reviewer 1990—, fellow 1978, 1983), Am. Coll. Radiology (chmn. stds. accreditation com. 1997—2003, councilor at large 1999, alt. councilor 2000—03, councillor 2003—, mem. expert panels, credentials com., fellow 1997) Avocations: painting, sculpture, travel. Office: Sutter Cancer Ctr 2800 L St Ste 10 Sacramento CA 95816-5616 Personal E-mail: hbwolkov@comcast.net. Business E-Mail: wolkovh@radiological.com.

**WOLL, HARRY J.,** electrical engineer; b. Farmington, Minn., Aug. 25, 1920; s. Henry L. and Clara M. (Fredrickson) W.; m. Mary V. Cowan, Feb. 15, 1947; children: Daniel, Alice. BSE.E., N.D. State U., 1940; postgrad., Ill. Inst. Tech., 1940-41; PhD, U. Pa., 1953. With RCA Corp., 1941-85, chief engr. aerospace systems div. Burlington, Mass., 1963-69, div. v.p. govt. engring. Moorestown, NJ, 1969-75; div. v.p., gen. mgr. RCA Automated Systems, Burlington, 1975-81; staff v.p., chief engr. RCA Electronic Products and Labs., Princeton, NJ, 1981-85. Patentee in field. Chmn. bd. trustees Moore Sch. Elec. Engring., U. Pa. 1976-90; trustee U. Pa., 1989-91. Recipient 50th Anniversary gold medal Moore Sch. Elec. Engring., U. Pa., 1973 Fellow AAAS, IEEE (past chmn. Phila. sect., past chmn. fellow com.), Aerospace Industries Tech. Council (past chmn.). Mem. KC, Sigma Phi Delta, Phi Kappa Phi. Roman Catholic. Home: PO Box 679 Concord MA 01742-0679 E-mail: hjwoll@cs.com.

**WOLLAN, CURTIS NOEL,** theater producer, theater director; b. Mpls., Nov. 10, 1951; s. Curtis Berdins and Lorraine Alice (Walser) Wollan; m. Jane Ellen Deter, May 17, 1980; children: Alexis Lorraine, Chet Curtis. BA in Speech and Theatre, Luther Coll., Decorah, Iowa, 1973; MFA in Directing, U. Iowa, 1976. Ptnr., artistic dir. Stage Two Prodns., Mpls., 1977-85; artistic dir. Chimera Theatre Co. St. Paul, 1985-87; ptnr., artistic dir. T.C.C. Prodns., Mpls., 1990-92; pres., prodr., dir. Troupe Am., Inc., Mpls., 1987—. Guest dir. Circa 21 Prodns., Rock Island, Ill., 1983—, Big League Theatricals, N.Y.C., 1988—93, Ryman Auditorium, Nashville, 1999, Lucas Theatre for the Arts, Savannah, 2001, Theatre Under the Stars, Houston, 2001, Dollywood Holiday Show, 2003, 2003—, Foothills Repertory Theatre, Worcester, Mass., 2004—05; past sec., bd. dirs. Midwest Citizens for Arts, Mpls., 1985—87; dir., asst. prodr. Sheehan Prodns. Medora Mus., Mpls., 1987—91; prodr., dir. Medora Musical, 1992—. Creator, dir. mus. concept revue: (plays) The Lovely Liebowitz Sisters, 1986—; dir.(nat. tour): Pump Boys and Dinettes, 1987—88, 1995, 2000, Big River, 1988—89, Oil City Symphony, 1989—90, Gifts of the Magi, 1990, Driving Miss Daisy, 1991—92, Steel Magnolias, 1992—93, Steven King's Ghost Stories, 1993, 1994, On Golden Pond, 1994, A Christmas Carol, 1996—2005, The Odd Couple, 1997, Moon Over Buffalo, 1998—99, Hank Williams, Lost Highway, 2000—01, The Sunshine Boys, 2001—05, Same Time, Next Year, 2002; co-author, dir. nat. tour: Mr. Pickwick's Christmas, 1987—92; prodr., dir. nat. tour 1940's Radio Hour, 1988, 1990; prodr.(nat. tour): A Child's Christmas in Wales, 1988—89, Forbidden Broadway, 1994—91, 1994, Babes in Toyland, 1992—96, 2004, Tap Dance Kid, 1995, Mahalia, 1996, Miracle on 34th St., The Musical, 1997—98, Schoolhouse Rock Live!, 1997—2000, Here's Love, 1999; prodr., dir.: Pump Boys and Dinettes, 1999—; Hank and My Honky Tonk Heroes, 1999—2003; Forever Plaid, 1999—; Church Basement Ladies, 2005—; How to Talk Minnesotan, The Musical, 2005—; actor: (films) Bix, 1990, The Childhood Friend, 1993. Recipient Best Prodn. award, Twin Cities Critics Cir., 1981, Best Direction award, 1981, Patriotism award, Am. Legion, 1995. Mem.: Southeastern Theatre Conf. Lutheran. Avocations: movies, restaurants, travel, history, horseback riding. Office: Troupe Am Inc 528 Hennepin Ave Ste 206 Minneapolis MN 55403-1810 Personal E-mail: cw@troupeamerica.com.

**WOLLE, CHARLES ROBERT,** judge; b. Sioux City, Iowa, Oct. 16, 1935; s. William Carl and Vivian (Down) W.; m. Kerstin Birgitta Wennerstrom, June 26, 1961; children: Karl Johan Knut, Erik Vernon, Thomas Dag, Aaron Charles. AB, Harvard U. 1959; JD, Iowa Law Sch., 1961. Bar: Iowa 1961. Assoc. Shull, Marshall & Marks, Sioux City, 1961-67, ptnr., 1968-80; judge Dist. Ct. Iowa, Sioux City, 1981-83; justice Iowa Supreme Ct., Sioux City and Des Moines, 1983-87; judge U.S. Dist. Ct. (so. dist.) Iowa, Des Moines, 1987-92, chief judge, 1992-99, sr. U.S. dist. judge, 2001—. Faculty Nat. Jud.

Coll., Reno, 1983-2004 Editor Iowa Law Rev., 1960-61. V.p. bd. dirs. Sioux City Symphony, 1972-77; bd. dirs. Morningside Coll., Sioux City, 1977-81. Fellow Am. Coll. Trial Lawyers; mem. Sioux City C. of C. (bd. dirs. 1977-78). Avocations: sports, art, music, literature, skiing. Office: Sr US Dist Judge US Dist Ct SD IA 110 E Ct St Des Moines IA 50309 Office Phone: 775-782-0293. Business E-Mail: charles_wolle@sdia.uscourts.gov.

**WOLLE, WILLIAM DOWN,** foreign service officer; b. Sioux City, Iowa, Mar. 11, 1928; s. William Carl and Vivian Lucille (Down) W.; m. Zanie L. Donahue, Feb. 7, 1992; children from previous marriage: Laila Jean, William Nicholas. BA, Morningside Coll., 1949; M.Internat. Affairs, Columbia U., 1951. Joined U.S. Fgn. Svc., 1951, consular officer Baghdad, Iraq, 1951-52, econ. officer, 1952—53, consular officer Manchester, England, 1954—56, trainee Arab lang. and area Beirut, 1957-58, fgn. service officer gen. Aden, Yemen, 1958—59, econ. officer Jidda, Saudi Arabia, 1959-62, internat. rels. officer, 1962-64; officer in charge Arab-Israeli affairs, 1965-67; detailed Nat. War Coll., 1967-68; counselor polit. affairs Kuwait City, Kuwait, 1968-70; econ. officer, dir. AID, Amman, Jordan, 1970-73; econ. officer Nairobi, 1973-74; ambassador to Oman, Muscat, 1974-78. Dir. Middle Eastern/South Asian Research Office, Dept. State, 1978-79; ambassador to United Arab Emirates, 1979-81; adviser internat. affairs Indsl. Coll. Armed Forces, 1982-84; chief sr. officer assignments, Washington, 1984-86. Served with AUS, 1946-47. Recipient Superior Service award Dept. State, 1974, Outstanding Civilian Service award Dept. Def., 1984. Home: 9659 Manassas Dr # 336 Manassas Park VA 20111

**WOLLER, JAMES ALAN,** lawyer; b. Adrian, Mich., Dec. 27, 1946; s. Robert Arthur and Florence Emma (Jacob) W.; m. Jill Ann Samis, Aug. 18, 1968 (div. Aug. 1978); 1 child, Emily Erin; m. Elizabeth Julia Frey, May 22, 1982 (div. Apr. 1999); m. Carol Pierini, Oct. 29, 1999. BA, U. Mich., 1969; JD, Columbia U., 1974. Bar: N.J. 1974, U.S. Dist. Ct. N.J. 1974, U.S. Tax Ct. 1976, U.S. Supreme Ct. 1995. Assoc. McCarter & English, Newark, 1974-79; v.p. Pfaltz & Woller, PA, Summit, NJ, 1979-86, pres., 1987—. Editor Columbia U. Human Rights Law Rev., 1973-74. Mem.: ABA, Summit Bar Assn. (pres. 1987—88), Union County Bar Assn., NJ Bar Assn., Columbia Law Sch. Assn. NJ (trustee 1992—97, pres 1997—2001, pres. 2001—03), Raritan Yacht Club (Perth Amboy, NJ) (fin. sec. 1988—89, treas. 1989—92, vice commodore 1993—94, commodore 1994—95), Downtown Club (trustee 1997—99, treas. 1999, v.p. 2000, pres. 2001). Republican. Methodist. Avocation: sailing. Home: 187 High St Perth Amboy NJ 08861 Office: Pfaltz & Woller PA 382 Springfield Ave Ste 217 Summit NJ 07901-2780 Office Phone: 908-273-1974. Personal E-mail: jimwoller@aol.com.

**WOLLER, KEVIN MARC PETER,** psychology professor, researcher; s. Tilman Wilhelm Meinrad and Helen Emma Rosa Woller; m. Kimberly Rachele Moore, Mar. 27, 1999; children: Taylor Danielle Hawkins, Logan Loyd Tilman, McKenzie Gabrielle Sara. BA, U. Wash., 1989; PhD, Kent State U., 1999. Acting asst. prof. La. Tech. U., Ruston, 1996—97; asst. prof. La. State U., Alexandria, 1997—2000; assoc. prof. Rogers State U., Claremore, Okla., 2000—. Mem. human subjects rev. bd. Rogers State U., Claremore, Okla., 2003—. Contbr. articles to profl. jours. Named Advisor of Yr., La. State U., Alexandria, 1998—99. Mem.: APA, Psi Chi (faculty advisor 2003—06). Office: Rogers State Univ 1701 W Will Rogers Blvd Claremore OK 74017 Office Phone: 918-343-7568. E-mail: kwoller@rsu.edu.

**WOLLERSHEIM, JANET PUCCINELLI,** psychology professor; b. Anaconda, Mont., July 24, 1936; d. Nello J. and Inez Marie (Ungaretti) Puccinelli; m. David E. Wollersheim, Aug. 1, 1959 (div. June 1972); children: Danette Marie, Tod Neil; m. Daniel J. Smith, July 17, 1976. AB, Gonzaga U., 1958; MA. St. Louis U., 1960; PhD, U. Ill., 1968. Lic. psychologist Mont. Asst. prof. psychology, asst. dir. testing/counseling ctr. U. Mo., 1968-71; prof. psychology U. Mont., Missoula, 1971—, dir. clin. psychology, 1980-87; chair Mont. Bd. Psychologists, 1977-78; cons. Mont. State Prison, 1971-85, Trapper Creek Job Corps, 1973—2003; pvt. practice Missoula, 1971—. Author numerous rsch. articles. Bd. dir. Crisis Ctr., Missoula, 1972-73; mem. profl. adv. bd. Head Start, Missoula, 1972-79. Recipient Disting. scholar award, U. Mont., 1991. Fellow Am. Psychol. Assn. (bd. dirs. div. clin. psychology 1990-92); mem. Rocky Mountain Psychol. Assn. (pres. 1983-84), Nat. Coun. Univ. Dirs. Clin. Psychology (bd. dirs. 1982-88). Home and Office: 105 Greenwood Ln Missoula MT 59803-2401 Office Phone: 406-543-6946. E-mail: jpwoller2000@yahoo.com.

**WOLLERT, GERALD DALE,** retired food products executive, securities trader; b. LaPorte, Ind., Jan. 21, 1935; s. Delmar Everette and Esther Mae W.; m. Carol Jean Burchby, Jan. 26, 1957; children— Karen Lynn, Edwin Del. BS, Purdue U., 1957. With Gen. Foods Corp., 1959-89, dir. consumer affairs White Plains, N.Y., 1973-74, mng. dir. Cottee Foods div. Sydney, Australia, 1974-76, gen. mgr. Mexico div. Mexico City, 1978-79, pres. Asia/Pacific ops. Honolulu; corp. v.p. worldwide coffee and internat. div. Kraft Gen. Foods Corp., Honolulu, 1979—89; ret., 1989; pres. GDW Investment Systems LLC, 2004—. Dir. Gen. Foods cos., Japan, Peoples Republic China, Korea, India, Taiwan, Singapore, Philippines. Webelos leader Boy Scouts Am., Mexico City, 1978-79; co. gen. chmn. United Fund campaign, Battle Creek, Mich., 1964-65, White Plains, N.Y., 1972-73. Served with U.S. Army, 1958. Mem. Asian-U.S. Bus. Coun., Oahu Country Club (Hawaii), Venice Golf and Country Club (Fla.), Legacy Hills (Ind.) Club.

**WOLLMAN, ERIC,** lawyer; b. Bklyn., May 26, 1951; s. Harry and Lillian (Levine) W. AA, Kingsborough Community Coll., 1970; BA, Bklyn. Coll., 1973; JD, Bklyn. Law Sch., 1993. Bar: N.J. 1994, N.Y. 1996. Exec. asst. to treas. Dept. Fin., N.Y.C., 1973-76; supervising investment analyst Office of Comptroller, N.Y.C., 1976-85, project mgr., 1985-90, adminstrv. mgr.proxy unit, 1990-92, dir. corp. governance, 1993-94, adminstrv. mgr., 1994-96, assoc. gen. counsel, 1996—2001, dep. dir. contracting, 2001—. Exec. prodr., host Second to None TV program, 1995-2001. Vice pres. Com. to Preserve Brighton Beach, Bklyn., 1989; aux. capt. N.Y.C. Police Dept., 1973—; mem. Pub. Works Forum, 1991-96, commr. of deeds. Recipient award of valor N.Y.C. Police Dept., award of merit United Fund of Greater N.Y., 30 Yr. Svc. award N.Y. Police Dept. Aux. Police. Mem. ABA, NRA, N.Y. County Lawyers Assn., Am. Assn. Jewish Lawyers and Jurists, Bklyn. Coll. Alumni Assn., Bklyn. Law Sch. Alumni Assn., Aux. Police Benevolent Assn., Phi Delta Phi. Democrat. Jewish. Home: 2209 E 28th St Brooklyn NY 11229-5057 Office: NYC Office of Comptroller 1 Centre St Rm 650 New York NY 10007-1602 Office Phone: 212-669-4766. Personal E-Mail: stnonradio@yahoo.com

**WOLLMAN, ROGER LELAND,** federal judge; b. Frankfort, S.D., May 29, 1934; s. Edwin and Katherine Wollman; m. Diane Marie Schroeder, June 21, 1959; children: Stephen James, John Mark, Thomas Roger. BA, Tabor Coll., Hillsboro, Kans., 1957; JD magna cum laude, U. S.D., 1962; LLM, Harvard U., 1964. Bar: S.D. 1964. Law clerk Hon. George T. Mickleson US Dist. Ct (So. Dist, SC), 1962—63; sole practice Aberdeen, 1964—71; states atty. Brown County, Aberdeen, 1966—71; justice S.D. Supreme Ct., 1971—85, chief justice, 1978—82; judge US Ct. Appeals (8th cir.), 1985—, chief judge, 1999—2002. Mem. Jud. Conference of US, 1999—2002. With U.S. Army, 1957—59. Mem.: Am. Jud. Soc. Office: US Ct Appeals US Courthouse & Fed Bldg 400 S Phillips Ave Rm 315 Sioux Falls SD 57104-6851*

**WOLLMER, RICHARD DIETRICH,** statistics and operations research educator; b. LA, July 27, 1938; s. Herman Dietrich and Alice Myrtle (Roberts) W. BA in Math., Pomona Coll., 1960; MA in Applied Math., Columbia U., 1962; MS in Engring. Sci., U. Calif., Berkeley, 1963, PhD Engring. Sci., 1965. Scientist Rand Corp., Santa Monica, Calif., 1965-70; prof. info. systems Calif. State U., Long Beach, 1970—, dept. chair, 2000—03, vis. prof. Northridge, 1981—82. Cons. McDonnell Douglas, Long Beach, Calif., 1978-80, 82, 85-91, Logicon, San Pedro, Calif., 1979-81, Behavioral Tech. Labs., U. So. Calif., 1973-75; vis. assoc. prof. Stanford U., 1976; rsch. scientist Electric Power Rsch. Inst., Palo Alto, Calif., 1977; rsch. engr. Jet Propulsion Lab., Pasadena, Calif., 1971. Contbr. articles to profl.

jours. Deacon Bel Air Presbyn. Ch., L.A., 1982-84, treas. 1983; mem. St. Andrews Presbyn. Ch., Newport Beach, Calif., 1999—. Mem.: Internat. Fedn. Ops. Rsch. Mgmt. Sci. (So. Calif.), Internat. Fedn. Ops. Rsch. Mgmt. Sci. (treas. 1999, sec. 2003, v.p. mem. 2006), Ops. Rsch. Soc. Am., So. Calif. Inst. Mgmt. Sci.-Ops. Rsch. Soc. (treas. 1979, vice chmn. 1980, chmn. 1981, vice chmn. 1988, chmn. 1989). Republican. Avocations: classical music, sports, reading, antique cars. Home: 6132 Fernwood Dr Huntington Beach CA 92648-5574 Office: Calif State U 1250 N Bellflower Blvd Long Beach CA 90840-8306 Business E-Mail: rwollmer@csulb.edu.

**WOLMAN, ERIC,** health care consultant; b. N.Y.C., Sept. 25, 1931; s. Leo and Cecil (Clark) W.; m. Sandra Rosman, July 27, 1963; children: Karin, Alastair. AB in Math., Harvard U., 1953; PhD in Applied Math., Harvard U., 1957. Mem. tech. staff AT&T Bell Labs., Murray Hill, Holmdel, NJ, 1957—66, dept. head traffic rsch. and network engring. Holmdel, NJ, 1966—77, dept. head ops. rsch. and computing syss. West Long Branch, NJ, 1977—82, dept. head human performance engring. Piscataway, Summit, NJ, 1983—87; v.p. cmty. programs and rsch. Mich. Cancer Found., Detroit, 1988—91; asst. leader cancer prevention and control program Prentis Comprehensive Cancer Ctr. Met. Detroit, 1990—94; mem. faculty grad. program in cancer biology Wayne State U. Sch. of Medicine, Detroit, 1992—96; vis. rsch. prof. dept. sys. engring and ops. rsch. George Mason U., Fairfax, Va., 1996—. Mem. evaluation panel for fire programs Nat. Bur. of Standards, Gaithersburg, Md., 1966-74, evaluation panel for nat. engring. lab., 1974-80, working group on info. tech. NSF, Arlington, Va., 1980-81. Contbr. articles to profl. jours. Trustee Rumson (N.J.) Country Day Sch., 1973-81, Sea Edn. Assn., Woods Hole, Mass., 1981—. Fellow AAAS; mem. Inst. Ops. Rsch. and The Mgmt. Scis. (coun. 1979-82), Seabright Beach Club, Harvard Club (N.Y.C.). Avocation: cruising. Home: 7806 Hidden Meadow Ter Potomac MD 20854-1792 Personal E-mail: eric.wolman@erols.com.

**WOLMAN, JONATHAN PALEY,** journalist; b. Madison, Wis., Aug. 1, 1950; s. Joseph Martin and Anne (Paley) W.; m. Deborah Eve Lamm, Sept. 24, 1978; children: Jacob, Emma, Sophia. BA, U. Wis., 1972. Reporter AP, Detroit, 1973-74, Madison, 1973, news editor Mich. news Mich., 1975, Urban Affairs Team Washington, 1976-77, news editor Wash. (D.C.) news, 1978-80, news editor, 1980-84, asst. bur. chief Washington (D.C.) Divsn., 1984-88, bur. chief Washington, 1989-98, mng. editor New York, 1998-2000, exec. editor, 2000—02, sr. v.p., 2002—04; editl. page editor Denver Post, 2004—. Mem. Am. Soc. Newspaper Editors, 1994—. Office: Denver Post 101 W Colfax Denver CO 80202 Office Phone: 303-954-1780. Business E-Mail: jwolman@denverpost.com.

**WOLMAN, M. GORDON,** geography educator; b. Balt., Aug. 16, 1924; s. Abel and Anna (Gordon) W.; m. Elaine Mielke, June 20, 1951; children: Elsa Anne, Abel Gordon, Abby Lucille, Fredericka Jeannette. Student, Haverford Coll.; AB in Geology, Johns Hopkins U., 1949; MA in Geology, Harvard U., 1951, PhD in Geology, 1953. Geologist U.S. Geol. Survey, 1951-58, part-time, 1958—; assoc. prof. geography Johns Hopkins U., Balt., 1958-62, B. Howell Griswold, Jr. prof. geography and internat. affairs, 1962—. Prof. Johns Hopkins U., 1962—, chmn. dept. geography and environ. engring., 1958—90, interim provost, 1987—90, prof. environ. health sci., 1998—; adv. com. geography U.S. Office Naval Rsch., Oak Ridge Nat. Lab.; exec. com. divsn. earth sci. NRC; internat. environ. programs com., environ. studies bd., com. water, com. mineral resources and environ., chmn. nat. comm. water quality policy NAS; chmn. NRC Com. Adv. U.S. Geol. Survey; chmn. NAS Commn. Geoscis., Environment and Resources, NRC Bd. Sustainability, 1995—2000; chmn. study land use and populationNRC Tri-Acad., China, India; environ. adv. com. Savannah River Tech. ctr.; chmn. U.S. Com. for IIASA, 1999—2003; chmn. adv. com. mgmt. and protection of water resources State. of Md., 2004—. Author: Fluvial Processes in Geomorphology, 1964; editl. bd.: Science mag. Pres. bd. trustees Park Sch., Balt.; pres. bd. dirs. Sinai Hosp., Balt., Resources for Future, 1980-87; adv. com. Inst. Nuc. Power Ops., 1982-85; active Balt. City Charter Revision Commn., Cmty. Action Com., Balt. With USNR, 1943-46. Recipient Meritorious Contbn. award Assn. Am. Geographers, 1972, Disting. Career award Geomorphology, 1993, D.L. Linton award Brit. Geomorphological Rsch. Group, 1994, Rachel Carson award Chesapeake Appreciation Inc., Ian Campbell medal Am. Geol. Inst., 1997, Nev. Med. Desert Rsch. Inst., Abel Wolman award Chesapeake sect. AWWA, 2003, Lifetime Achievement award Nat. Coun. for Sci. and the Environment, 2004, Outstanding Contbn. to Water Environment award Water Environment Fedn., 2004, Eisenhower medal Johns Hopkins U., 2005, Benjamin Franklin medal in Earth and Environ. Sci., Franklin Inst., 2006. Fellow Am. Acad. Arts and Scis., AAAS; mem. ASCE, NAS, NAE, Am. Geophys. Union (chmn. subcom. sedimentation, pres. hydrol. sect., Robert Horton medal 2000), Geol. Soc. Am. (v.p. 1983, pres. 1984, Penrose medal 1999), Am. Philos. Soc., Am. Geog. Soc. (councillor 1965-70, Cullum Geog. medal 1989), Washington Geol. Soc., Agrl. Hist. Soc., Md. Acad. Scis. (exec. com. 1970-75), Am. Geophysical Union, Phi Beta Kappa, Sigma Xi. Home: 2104 W Rogers Ave Baltimore MD 21209-4553 Office: Johns Hopkins U Dept Geography/Environ Engr Baltimore MD 21218 Office Phone: 410-516-7090. Business E-Mail: wolman@jhu.edu.

**WOLMAN, MARTIN,** lawyer; b. Albany, NY, Feb. 2, 1937; s. Benjamin S. and Sonya (Kogan) W.; children: Koren M. Wolman-Tardy, Barton T., William B., Brandon S. AB, Brown U., 1958; LLB, U. Calif., Berkeley, 1964. Bar: Calif., 1964, Conn., 1965. Atty. Conn. Bank & Trust Co., Hartford, 1964-67; assoc. Day, Berry & Howard, Hartford, 1967-72, ptnr., 1972—. Mem. Conn. Law Revision Commn., 1985-2002. Trustee Russell-Sage Coll., Troy, NY, 1990-96, Wadsworth Atheneum, 1994-2002, Lyme Acad. Coll. Fine Arts, 2003—; trustee Kingswood-Oxford Sch., West Hartford, Conn., 1980-93, chmn., 1986-89; bd. dirs Hartford Hosp., 1991—, chmn., 2003—; bd. dirs. Inst. Living, 1994, Hartford Health Care Corp., 1996—; bd. govs. Hill-Stead Mus., Farmington, Conn., 1990-94. Lt. (j.g.) USN, 1958-61. Fellow Am. Coll. Trust and Estate Counsel (chmn. Conn. chpt. 1981-86); mem. Conn. Bar Assn. (chmn. exec. com. probate sect. 1978-82). Office: Day Berry & Howard City Place I 25th Fl Hartford CT 06103-3499 Office Phone: 860-275-0221. Business E-Mail: mwolman@dbh.com.

**WOLMAN, WILLIAM,** economist, journalist, broadcaster; b. Montreal, Que., Can. s. Nathan and Toba (Wexler) W.; m. Ann Livia Colamosca, Jan. 7, 1982; children: John, Flora. BA, McGill U., 1948; PhD, Stanford U., 1957. Asst. prof. econs. Wash. State U., Pullman, 1954-60; v.p. Citicorp, N.Y.C., 1969-71, Argus Rsch. Corp., N.Y.C., 1971-74; chief economist CNBC, Ft. Lee, N.J., 1989—; econs. editor Bus. Week, N.Y.C., 1960-69, sr. editor, 1974-83, editor, 1984-89, exec. editor, 1983-84, chief economist, 1989—. Author: The Judas Economy: The Triumph of Capital and the Betrayal of Work, 1997, The Great 401K Hoax, 2002. Avocations: skiing, photography. Office: Bus Week 1221 Ave of Americas New York NY 10020-1001

**WOLNEK, STEPHEN S.,** religious organization administrator; Pres. United Synagogue of Conservative Judaism, NYC, 1997—2002, hon. pres., 2002—. V.p. Jewish Nat. Fund. Jewish. Office: United Synagogue of Conservative Judaism 155 5th Ave New York NY 10010-6802

**WOLPER, DAVID LLOYD,** motion picture and television executive; b. NYC, Jan. 11, 1928; s. Irving S. and Anna (Fass) W.; m. Margaret Dawn Richard, May 11, 1958 (div.); children: Mark, Michael, Leslie; m. Gloria Diane Hill, July 11, 1974. Student, Drake U., 1946, U. So. Calif., 1948. V.p., treas. Flamingo Films, TV sales co., 1948-50, v.p. West Coast Ops., 1954-58; chmn., pres. Wolper Prodns., L.A., 1958—. Cons., exec. producer Warner Bros., Inc., 1976—. TV prodns. include Race for Space, Making of the President 1960, 64, Biography series, Story of... series, The Yanks are Coming, Berlin: Kaiser to Khrushchev, December 7: Day of Infamy, The American Woman in the 20th Century, Hollywood and The Stars, March of Time Specials, The Rise and Fall of the Third Reich, The Legend of Marilyn Monroe, Four Days in November, Krebiozen and Cancer, National Geographic, Undersea World of Jacques Cousteau, China: Roots of Madness, The Journey of Robert F. Kennedy, Say Goodbye, George Plimpton, Appointment With Destiny, American Heritage, Smithsonian, They've Killed President

Lincoln, Sandburg's Lincoln, Primal Man, The First Woman President, Chico and the Man, Get Christie Love, Welcome Back, Kotter!, Collison Course, Roots, Victory at Entebbe, Roots: The Next Generations, Moviola, The Thorn Birds, North and South Books I, II, III, Napoleon and Josephine, Alex Haley's Queen, Men Of The Dragon, Unwed Father, The Morning After; feature films include The Hellstrom Chronicle, Devil's Brigade, The Bridge at Remagen, If It's Tuesday, This Must Be Belgium, Willy Wonka and The Chocolate Factory, Visions of Eight, This is Elvis, Murder in the First, Surviving Picasso, L.A. Confidential; live spl. events include Opening and Closing Ceremonies 1984 Olympic Games, Liberty Weekend July 3-6, 1986. Trustee L.A. County Mus. Art, Am. Film Inst., L.A. Thoracic and Cardiovascular Found., Boys and Girls Clubs Am., U.S. Golf Assn. Found.; bd. dirs. Amateur Athletic Assn. L.A., L.A. Heart Inst., Acad. TV Arts and Scis. Found., So. Calif. Com. for Olympic Games, U. Soc. Calif. Cinema/TV Dept.; bd. govs. Cedars Sinai Med. Ctr.; com. mem. U.S. Olympic Team Benefit; mem. adv. com. Nat. Ctr. Jewish Film. Recipient award for documentaries San Francisco Internat. Film Festival, 1960, 7 Golden Globe awards, 5 George Foster Peabody awards, Disting. Service award U.S. Jr. C. of C.; 40 Emmy awards, 145 Emmy nominations Acad. TV Arts and Scis.; Monte Carlo Internat. Film Festival award, 1964, Cannes Film Festival Grand Prix for TV Programs, 1964; Oscar award, 11 Oscar nominations, Jean Hersholt Humanitarian award Acad. Motion Picture and TV Scis., medal of Chevalier The French Nat. Legion of Honor, 1990; named to TV Hall of Fame, 1988. Mem. Nat. Acad. TV Arts and Scis., Acad. Motion Picture Arts and Scis., Producers Guild Am., Caucus for Producers, Writers and Dirs. Office: The David L Wolper Co Inc 617 N Rodeo Dr Beverly Hills CA 90210

**WOLPERT, ANN J.,** library director; BA, Boston U.; MLS, Simmons Coll., Boston. Libr. Boston Redevelopment Authority, 1967—76; with Arthur D. Little Inc., 1976—92, from tech. info. specialist, to mgr. Rsch. Libr., to dir. Cambridge Info. Ctr.; dir. Rsch. and Info. Svc. Harvard Bus. Sch., 1992—93, exec. dir. Libr. and Info. Svc.; 1993—95; dir. Mass. Inst. Tech. Librs., 1996—. Mem. Strategic Planning Com. Mass. Bd. Libr. Commr., 1992—; cons. U. N.Mex., Cornell U. Adelphi U., NYC, INCAE campuses, Costa Rica, Nicaragua, League European Rsch. Librs., Amsterdam, Nat. Libr. China, Malaysia U. Sci. and Tech.; spkr. in field; chmn. mgmt. bd. Mass. Inst. Tech. Press; bd. dirs. Tech. Rev., Inc. Mem. edtl. bd. Libr. and Info. Sci. Rsch., The Jour. Libr. Adminstrn., mem. adv. com. Sci. and Engring. Indicators; contbr. libr. papers to various publs.; reviewer Tech. Rev. Advisor Publ. Com. Mass. Med. Soc.; bd. dirs. Boston Libr. Consortium; hon. bd. trustees Simmons Coll.; mem. bd. dirs. Boston Libr. Consortium; NIH's Pub. Access Working Group, Steering Coms. Coalition Networked Info., Digital Libr. Fedn.; mem. Nat. Network Women Leaders Higher Edn. Am. Coun. Edn., Dean's Com., Pres.'s Acad. Coun., OpenCourseWare Faculty. Named to Nat. Network for Women Leaders in Higher Edn., Am. Coun. Edn. Mem.; Info. Tech. Strategic Planning and Resources Coordinating Coun., Coun. Ednl. Tech., Com. Intellectual Property and copyright com.). Rsch. Libr. (past pres. 2004—05, v.p. to pres., mem. intellectual property and copyright com.). Office: Building 14S-216 MIT 77 Massachusetts Ave Cambridge MA 02139-4307 Office Phone: 617-253-5297. Office Fax: 617-253-8894. E-mail: awolpert@mit.edu.

**WOLPERT-DEFILIPPES, MARY K.,** science administrator; BS in Pharmacy cum laude, Creighton U., 1963; MS in Pharmacology, U. Mich., 1966, PhD in Pharmacology, 1969; postdoctoral student, Yale U., 1969—. Rsch. assoc. in pharmacology Yale U., New Haven, 1970-71; staff fellow lab. chem. pharmacology NIH, Bethesda, Md., 1971-75, pharmacologist drug evaluation br., 1976-81, supervisory pharmacologist drug evaluation br., 1981-82, dep. chief drug evaluation br., 1982-85, pharmacologist Office of Assoc. Dir., 1985-88, program dir. Grants and Contracts Ops. Br., 1988-97, chief Grants and Contracts Ops. Br., 1997—. Contbr. articles to profl. jours.; patentee in field. Mem. Gamma Pi Epsilon, Rho Chi. Office: Nat Cancer Inst Divsn Cancer Treatment and Diagnosis Exec Pla N Rm 8150 Bethesda MD 20892 Office Phone: 301-496-8783. Business E-Mail: wolpertm@exchange.nih.gov.

**WOLPERT RICHARD, CHAVA,** artist; b. Frankfurt, Germany, Feb. 26, 1933; arrived in Palestine, 1934, arrived in U.S., 1958; d. Ludwig Y. and Else (Ahrens) Wolpert; m. Henry A. Richard, 1959 (dec. 1971). Student, Bezalel Acad. Arts and Design, Jerusalem, 1954—56. Artist-in-residence The Jewish Mus., N.Y.C., 1958—88. Painter, designer/creator of contemporary style ceremonial Judaica such as candelabra, Passover sets, Torah ornaments, decorative Judaica in enamel, silver, other metals, glass, porcelain, wood, acrylics, fabrics and oil painting; represented in 11 mus. collections in U.S., Australia, Europe, Israel. Pvt. Israeli Army, 1951—53. Recipient 2 Merit awards Interfaith Forum on Religion, Art and Arch., 1980, 83, Jurors' Choice award Liturgical Art Guild, 1991, Best in Judaica award Liturgical Art Guild, 1997. Mem. Judaic Art Guild, Liturgical Art Guild. Avocations: reflexology, healing with herbs. Office Phone: 718-896-4451.

**WOLRAICH, MARK LEE,** pediatrician, educator; BA, SUNY, Binghamton, 1966; MD, SUNY, Syracuse, 1970. Diplomate Am. Bd. Pediat. Pediatric intern SUNY, Syracuse, 1970-71; pediatric resident U. Okla. Health Scis. Ctr., Oklahoma City, 1973-74; pediatric fellowship U. Oreg. Health Scis. Ctr., 1974-76; asst. prof. U. Iowa, 1976-81, assoc. prof., 1981-86, prof., 1986-90, Vanderbilt U., 1990-2001, dir. divsn. child dcvel., dir. child dcvel. ctr., 1990-99, dir. ctr. for chronic illnesses and disabilities in children, 1990-2000; investigator J.F. Kennedy Ctr. for Rsch. on Edn. and Human Devel., 1990-2001; prof. pediat., dir. Child Study Ctr. Okla. U. Health Scis. Ctr., 2001—. Med. supr. U. Iowa Divsn. of Devel. Disabilities, 1980-90; vis. prof. Great Ormond St. Hosp. for Sick Children, London, 1983, U. Cape Town, Rondebosch Cape, South Africa, 1986, Columbus Children's Hosp., Ohio State U., Dept. Pediat., 1988; mem. Iowa State Foster Care Rev. Bd. Co-editor Advances in Developmental and Behavioral Pediatrics, 1981-92; cons. editor Am. Jour. on Mental Deficiency; edtl. adv. bd. A Guide to Parent Counseling; editor The Classification of Child and Adolescent Mental Disorders in Primary Care-Diagnostic and Statistical Manual for Mental Disorders in Primary Care Child and Adolescent Version, 1996; cons. reviewer Developmental Medicine and Child Neurology, Pediatrics, Medicine and Behavior, Jour. Pediatrics, Jour. of Social and Personal Relationships, Applied Rsch. in Mental Retardation, Jour. of Clin. Psychology, Jour. Developmental and Behavioral Pediatrics, Clin. Pediatrics, others; contbr. numerous articles to profl. publs. Recipient Disting. and Dedicated Svc. award Spina Bifida Assn. Iowa, 1979, Lou Holloway award Health Scis. Edn.; grantee NIMH, 1987-90, 98-2001, Nat. Inst. on Disability and Rehab. Rsch., 1987-89, NIH, 1988-91, Iowa Dept. Human Svcs., 1986-89, U. Iowa, 1979-87, United Cerebral Palsy Rsch. and Endl. Found., Inc., 1978-87, Iowa March of Dimes, 1980, Sugar Assn., Inc., 1983, Internat. Life Scis. Inst., 1988-91, W.T. Grant Found., 1989; MCH Lend grant, 1999—, CDC grant, 2002; named to Children and Adults with Attention-Deficit/Hyperactivity Disorder Hall of Fame, 2003. Fellow Am. Acad. Pediat. (com. 1992-2000, chair com. on psychosocial aspects of child and family health 1997-2000, chair child & adolescent health action group 2000-04, chair-elect mgmt. com., 2004-), Am. Acad. Cerebral Palsy and Devel. Medicine; mem. Soc. for Devel. and Behavioral Pediat. (pres. 1994-95, program dir. 1990-93), Soc. for Pediatric Rsch. (sr.), Am. Acad. Physician and Patient (charter), Am. Pediatric Soc. Office: Okla U Health Scis Ctr 1100 NE 13th St Oklahoma City OK 73117

**WOLSKI, VICTOR J.,** federal judge, lawyer; m. Lisa BA History, BS Econ., Univ. Pa., 1984; JD, Univ. Va., 1991. Bar: Calif., D.C., Oreg., Wash., U.S. Ct. Fed. Claims, U.S. Ct. Appeals, 9th & Fed. cir., U.S. Supreme Ct. Asst. to sec. USDA, 1988; asst. to gen. counsel US Dept. Energy; law clerk US Dist. Ct. (no. dist.) Calif., 1991—92; atty. Pacific Legal Found., 1992—97; tax counsel to Senator Connie Mack US Senate, Washington, 1997—2000; gen. counsel & chief tax atty. Joint Econ. Com. US Congress, 1999—2000; atty. Cooper & Kirk, Washington, 2000—03; judge US Ct. Fed. Claims, Washington, 2003—. Office: US Ct Fed Claims 717 Madison Pl NW Washington DC 20005

**WOLSKY, JACK,** retired art educator; b. Rochester, N.Y., Aug. 5, 1930; s. Benjamin and Mary Wolsky; m. Gladys Mindlin Wolsky, Dec. 20, 1953; children: Bonnie, Sharon, Marsha. AS, Rochester Inst. Tech.; 1951; BS, SUNY, Buffalo, 1955, MS, 1957. Prof. art SUNY, Brockport, NY, 1959—85, prof. emeritus, 1985—; ret., 1985. Mem. adv. bd. Jewish Cultural Arts Commn., Rochester, NY, Modern Arts Adv. Evaluation Com., Rochester and Monroe County, NY, Rochester Inst. Tech. Alumni Assn. Exec. Coun.; juror Western Gateway project N.Y. State Dept. Transp.; juror Monroe County-Greater Rochester Internat. Airport Competition, 2001—. Represented in permanent collections Meml. Art Gallery, Rochester, Munson-Williams-Proctor Inst., Utica, N.Y., State Univ. Coll. at Brockport, New Britain (Conn.) Mus. Am. Art, Rochester Inst. Tech. Adviser, vol. Rochester chpt. ARC, 1993—; bd. dirs. Temple B'rith Kodesh, Rochester, Friends of Sch. of Arts, Rochester. Recipient Kosciuszko Found. award, 1963, Juror's award, Rochester Finger Lakes Show, 1962, Harry Hoffman Meml. award, Albright Art Gallery, 1964, Rochester C. of C. Civic award in culture and arts, 1999, Chancellor's award for excellence in tchg., SUNY, 1979, SUNY Faculty Rsch. fellowship, 1968, 1970, 1973, Visual Arts award, Arts and Cultural Coun. Greater Rochester, 2002, Lillian Fairchild award, U. Rochester, Faculty Exch. scholarship, SUNY. Avocations: tennis, gardening. Home: 295 Washington St Spencerport NY 14559 Personal E-mail: gwolsky823@aol.com.

**WOLSON, CRAIG ALAN,** lawyer; b. Toledo, Feb. 20, 1949; s. Max A. and Elaine B. (Cohn) Wolson; m. Ellen Carol Schulgasser, Oct. 26, 1986; children: Lindsey, Michael, Geoffrey. BA, U. Mich., 1971, JD, 1974. Bar: NY 1975, US Dist. Ct. (so. and ea. dists.) NY 1975, US Ct. Appeals (2d cir.) 1975, US Supreme Ct. 1978. Assoc. Shearman & Sterling, NYC, 1974—81; v.p., sec., gen. counsel J.D. Mattus Co., Inc., Greenwich, Conn., 1985—88; also bd. dirs. J.D. Mattus Co., Inc. and affiliated cos., Greenwich, Conn.; v.p., asst. gen. counsel Chem. Bank, NYC, 1988—95; of counsel Williams & Harris, NYC, 1995-96; ptnr. Williams & Harris LLP, NYC, 1996-97; counsel Brown & Wood L.L.P., NYC, 1997-98, Mayer, Brown & Platt, NYC, 1999-2001; spl. counsel Schulte Roth & Zabel LLP, NYC, 2001—03; ptnr. Duane Morris, LLP, NYC, 2003—06; spl. counsel Cadwalader, Wickersham & Taft LLP, Charlotte, NC, 2006—. Dep. clk. Lucas County Courthouse, Toledo, 1968-69, 71-72. Articles and administrv. editor U. Mich. Law Rev., 1973-74. Mem.: ABA, Assn. of Bar of City of N.Y. (securities regulation com. 1994—97, corp. law com. 1997—2000, project fin. com. 2000—03, corp. law com. 2003—05, chmn. structured fin. com. 2000—), N.Y. State Bar Assn., Pi Sigma Alpha, Phi Eta Sigma, Phi Beta Kappa (NY Super Lawyer 2006). Avocations: reading, piano, theater. Home: 29 Punch Bowl Dr Westport CT 06880-2130 Office: Cadwalader Wickersham & Taft LLP 227 W Trade St Charlotte NC 28202 Office Phone: 704-348-5367. Business E-Mail: craig.wolson@cwt.com.

**WOLTER, JOHN AMADEUS,** librarian, federal official; b. St. Paul, July 25, 1925; s. Amadeus Frank and Marjorie (Wears) W.; m. Joan Patricia Venard, July 6, 1956; children: Mark, Thomas, Matthew, David. Student, Coll. of St. Thomas, 1950; BA, U. Minn., 1956, MA, 1965, PhD, 1975; postgrad., Georgetown U., 1957. Officer, seaman Isthmian Lines Inc., N.Y.C., 1943-50, 57-60; marine transp. officer Mil. Sea Transp. Ser., Washington, 1956-57; instr., map libr. U. Minn., 1961-64, asst. to dir. univ. librs., 1964-65, research fellow, 1965-66; asst. prof. Wis. State U., River Falls, 1966-68; asst. chief geography and map. div. Libr. of Congress, Washington, 1968-78, chief, 1978-91, acting dir. pub. svc. and collections MGMT I, 1989-90; cons. in geography, 1991-93. Mem. U.S. Bd. Geog. Names, 1969-83, vice chmn., 1980-81, chmn., 1981-83. Editor: Progress of Discovery: Johann Georg Kohl, 1993, Images of the World: The Atlas Through History, 1996, The Napoleonic War in the Dutch East Indies. The Minto Collection: Essay and Bibliography, 1999; rev. editor cartography divsn. Surveying and Mapping, 1971-72; mem. edtl. bd. Cartographica, 1971-80, Am. Cartographer, 1974-79, Terrae Incognitae, 1973-75, ACSM Bull., 1974-80, Surveying and Mapping, 1972-80; edtl. advisor The Portolan, 1986—; contbg. editor Imago Mundi, 1979-91; contbr. articles to profl. jours. Served with U.S. Army, 1950-56. Libr. of Congress Disting. Svc. award, 1992, Smithsonian Inst. Cert. of award, 1986. Mem. Internat. Geog. Union (U.S. nat. com. 1972-80, 84-88), Internat. Cartographic Assn. (U.S. mem. commn. on history of cartography 1972-76, corr. 1976-92, Assn. Am. Geographers (editorial bd. Annals 1988-92), Spl. Librs. Assn. (sec.-treas. geog. and map div. 1965), Soc. History Discoveries (sec.-treas. 1972-75, coun. 1976-78, v.p. 1983-85, pres. 1985-87), Am. Congress Surveying and Mapping (chmn. publs. com. 1978-80, Presdl. citation 1985), N.Am. Soc. Oceanic History, Soc. for History of Discoveries, Washington Map Soc., Soc. Nautical Rsch., U.S. Naval Hist. Found., Philip Lee Phillips Soc. (bd. dirs. ex officio), DAV, Am. Legion, Am. Mcht. Marine Vets., Theta Delta Chi. Home: 712 Canvasback Court Salisbury MD 21804 E-mail: jawjo@comcast.net.

**WOLTERING, MARGARET MAE,** retired educational association administrator; b. Trenton, Ohio, July 24, 1913; d. David Lindy and Nellie Stevenson; m. Elmer Charles Woltering, Apr. 9, 1938 (dec. Oct. 1994); 1 child, Eugene Anthony. Student, Mercy St. Nursing, Hamilton, Ohio, 1931-34; BS, Miami U., 1962, MEd, 1968, postgrad., 1975. RN Ohio, cert. tchr., curriculum supr., Ohio Pub. Health. Pub. health nurse Ohio State Dept. Health, Butler County, 1936-49; supr. Swedish Hosp., Seattle, 1944-45; various h.s. teaching positions Cin., 1968-78; ednl. cons. Ohio, 1981-94. Cons., Ohio, 1981—96; ednl. cons. specializing in curriculum devel., 1980—91; book reviewer Friends of Libr., 1991—93; lectr. Sr. Citizens Ctr., 1992—98; instr. Bible Study, 2000—05. Author: The National Library of Poetry Anthology, 2000—03, spelling book, numerous poems; contbg. author: Theater of the Mind, 2003. Chmn. Hosp. Svc. for Children, Hamilton, 1981—85; chmn. vol. tutorial program Hamilton H.S., 1989—93, 1994—2000; taught adults Bible Study, 1995—2005. Recipient Order of St. Louis IX medallion, 2003, Champion-Tenet award, 2003. Mem.: AAUW, Toastmasters, Democrat, Roman Catholic, Avocations: reading, theater, art collecting, China porcelain painting.

**WOLTERS, CURT CORNELIS FREDERIK,** foreign service officer; b. Nymegen, The Netherlands, Mar. 13, 1938; came to U.S., 1957; s. Frederik and Cornelia Johanna (Jansen) W.; m. Sara J. Daughters, June 10, 1962 (div. 1980); children: Gwyneth, Chad; m. Charlotte Cooper, Sept. 22, 1980 (div. 1988); children: Lottena, Cicely; m. Sylvana K. Perry, Apr. 1989; 1 child, Roger. Student, Wash. State U., 1958-61, U. Bonn, Fed. Republic Germany, 1962-63; BA, U. Oreg., 1964, MA, 1966; MBA, U. Washington, 1976; PhD, Pacific Western U., 1989. Asst. sec. Rep. Botswana Govt., Gaborone, 1966-68; program advisor The Ford Found., N.Y.C., 1968-74; sr. rsch. analyst Seattle C. of C., 1974-76; sr. assoc. Inst. Pub. Adminstrn. N.Y., N.Y.C., 1976-78; freelance economist Africa, 1978-79; econ. program officer, diplomat (AID) Dept. State, Washington, 1979—. Cons. Inst. for Puget Sound Needs, Seattle, 1975-76, Pacific Cons., Washington, 1976; chair Am. Cmty. Assoc., U.S. Embassy, Lusaka, Zambia, 1998—. Contbr. numerous articles to profl. jours.; author project evaluations. Mem. civic action com. Congress of Racial Equality, Eugene, Oreg., 1965-66; vol. campaign Dixie Lee Ray Gubernatorial Campaign, Seattle, 1976; treas., chmn. fin. com. Internat. Sch. Islamabad, 1989-92. Carnegie Found. fellow, 1964-65, Africa-Asia pub. svc. fellow Maxwell Sch., 1966-68, fellow German Govt., U. Bonn, 1962-63; recipient Air Def. Command Outstanding Achievement award USAF, 1960, Cmty. Svc. award U.S. Embassy, Islamabad, 1992-93, 93-94, Meml. Order of Tin Hats, Kabaw Valley Shellhole chpt. Lusaka, Zambia, 1997—. Mem. Am. Econ. Assn., Air Force Assn., Wilson Ctr. (assoc. of Smithsonian Instn.), Am. Fgn. Svc. Assn., Holland Am. Club (treas. Greater Seattle area 1975-76), Am. Legion. Officer: Dept Of State 210 Lusaka Pl Washington DC 20521-2310 E-mail: cuwolters@usaid.gov, curtwolters@yahoo.com.

**WOLTERS, RAYMOND,** historian, educator; b. Kansas City, Mo., July 25, 1938; s. Raymond M. and Margaret G. (Reilly) W.; m. Mary McCullough, June 23, 1962; children: Jeffrey, Kevin, Thomas. BA, Stanford U., 1960; MA, U. Calif.-Berkeley, 1962, PhD, 1967. Instr. dept. history U. Del., Newark, 1965-67, asst. prof., 1967-70, assoc. prof., 1970-75, prof., 1975-96, Thomas Muncy Keith prof., 1996—. Mem. edtl. adv. bd. Acad. Am. Ency.; author:

The New Negro on Campus, 1975, The Burden of Brown, 1984, Right Turn, 1996, Du Bois and His Rivals, 2002. Fellow NEH, 1971-72, Am. Coun. Learned Socs., 1978-79, Earhart Found., 1989-90; recipient Silver Gavel award ABA. Mem. Am. Hist. Assn., Orgn. Am. Historians, So. Hist. Assn. Home: 20 Bridlebrook Ln Newark DE 19711-2061 Office: U Del History Dept Newark DE 19716 Office Phone: 302-831-2378. Business E-Mail: wolters@udel.edu.

**WOLTERSTORFF, NICHOLAS PAUL,** philosophical theology educator; b. Bigelow, Minn., Jan. 21, 1932; s. Matthew and Agnes (Feenstra) W.; m. Claire Kingma, May 29, 1935; children: Amy, Eric, Robert, Klaas, Christopher. BA, Calvin Coll., 1953; MA, Harvard U., 1954, PhD in Philosophy, 1957; LittD (hon.), Northwestern Coll., 1989. Instr. Yale U., New Haven, 1957-59; prof. Calvin Coll., Grand Rapids, Mich., 1959-89; Noah Porter prof. philosophical theology Yale U., New Haven, 1989—2002, prof. emeritus, 2002—. Vis. prof. U. Tex., Austin, 1969, U. Mich., Ann Arbor, 1971, Princeton (N.J.) U., 1985, Notre Dame (Ind.) U., 1987; part-time prof. Free U., Amsterdam, The Netherlands, 1984-89; Wilde lectr. Oxford U., 1993. Author: On Universals, 1970, Reason Within Bounds of Religion, 1976, Works and Worlds of Art, 1980, Art in Action, 1980, Until Justice and Peace Embrace, 1983, Divine Discourse, 1995, John Locke and Ethics of Belief, 1996, Religion in the Public Square, 1997, Thomas Reid and the Story of Epistemology, 2001; co-edit. (with Alvin Plantinga) Faith and Rationality, 1984. Recipient Harbison award Danforth Found., 1980; NEH fellow, 1980. Mem. Am. Philos. Assn. (pres. 1991-92), Soc. Christian Philosophers (past pres.). Democrat. Avocations: gardening, woodworking. Office: Yale U Divinity Sch 409 Prospect St New Haven CT 06511-2167 Office Phone: 203-432-5343. Office Fax: 203-432-5356. E-mail: nicholas.wolterstorff@yale.edu.*

**WOLTZ, HOWARD OSLER, JR.,** retired metal products executive; b. Mt. Airy, N.C., Apr. 2, 1925; s. Howard Osler and Louise (Elliott) W.; m. Joan Elizabeth Moore, Dec. 29, 1949; children: Louise, Joan Woltz Robins, Howard O. III, Edwin Moore. LLB, U. Va., 1948. Bar: N.C., 1948. Ptnr. law firm, Mt. Airy, 1948-54; pres., founder Dixie Concrete Products, Inc., Mt. Airy, 1953-69; founder Dixie Exposaic, Inc., Mt. Airy, 1963; pres., chmn. bd. Insteel Industries (formerly Exposaic Industries, Inc.), Mt. Airy, 1969-89, chmn., CEO, 1989-91, non-exec. chmn., 2005—, ret. 2005. Mem. N.C. Ho. of Reps., 1951-53; chmn. Mt. Airy-Surry County Airport Authority, 1987-93; former pres. Greater Mt. Airy United Fund. Mem. Nat. Concrete Masonry Assn. (pres. 1965), N.C. Concrete Masonry Assn. (pres. 1959), Wire Reinforcement Inst. (chmn. 1982), Am. Wire Producers Assn. (bd. dirs. 1987-91), N.C. State Bar Assn., Mt. Airy C. of C. (Citizen of Yr. 1991). Rotary (past pres. Mt. Airy). Republican. Home: 243 Old Green Hill Rd Mount Airy NC 27030-9240 E-mail: howardwoltz@earthlink.net.

**WOLVERTON, EDWARD LEE ALLEN,** writer; b. Richmond, Calif., Oct. 8, 1952; s. Donald Lewis and Sally Lee Wolverton; m. Ura Marie Ivey, Apr. 15, 1985; children: Kristen, Edward Jr., Debbie, Cassie. Freelance journeyman machinist, San Francisco, 1988—2004; ret., 2004; artist, writer, 2000—. Author: (book of poetry) Red Rose, 2004, My Wild Irish Rose, 2006; contbr. anthologies (8 Editor's Choice awards Libr. Poetry); Exhibited in group shows at Phantom Art Gallery, Milpitas, Calif., 2005, online gallery, The Pedestal Mag.; contbr. poetry to websites; author: My Wild Irish Rose in Night Whispers, 2006. Sgt. U.S. Army, 1971—75. Nominee Poet of Yr., Internat. Soc. Poets, 2002, 2003, 2004. Avocations: writing, coin collecting/numismatics, stamp collecting/philately, painting. Home: 259 El Bosque Drive San Jose CA 95134

**WOLVERTON, THOMAS FRANK,** automotive company supervisor; b. Saginaw, Mich., Dec. 26, 1954; s. Francis Edward and Donna Muriel Wolverton; m. Holly Louise Muller, Dec. 20, 1978 (div. May 1980); 1 child, Brian Thomas; m. Trudy Renee Surprenant, Oct. 26, 1985; 1 adopted child, Renee Lynn. Cert. Trident submarine test dir.; Gen. Dynamics. With USN, 1974-83, missile technician Groton, Conn., 1974-80, lead instr., 1980-83; submarine test technician Gen. Dynamics, Groton, 1984, engring. asst., 1985, program coord., 1986, test dir., 1987-94; skilled trades supr. Aerotek Engring./GM, Flint, Mich., 1995—. V.p. Electric Boat Mgmt. Assn., Groton, 1992-94; vol. Big Bros. Am., Norwich, Conn., 1981-83. Mem. Am. Legion. Avocations: stamps, fishing, softball. Home: 9520 East Rd Burt MI 48417

**WOLYNES, PETER GUY,** chemistry researcher, educator; b. Chgo., Apr. 21, 1953; s. Peter and Evelyn Eleanor (Etter) W.; m. Jane Lee Fox, Nov. 26, 1976 (div. 1980); m. Kathleen Cull Bucher, Dec. 22, 1984; children: Margrethe Cull, Eve Cordelia, Julia Jean. AB with highest distinction, Ind. U., 1971; AM, Harvard U., 1972, PhD in Chem. Physics, 1976; DSc (hon.), Ind. U., 1988. Rsch. assoc. MIT, Cambridge, 1975-76; asst. prof. Harvard U., Cambridge, 1976-80; vis. scientist Max Planck Inst. für Biophysikalische Chemie, Gottingen, Fed. Republic Germany, 1977; assoc. prof. chemistry U. Ill., Urbana, 1980-83, prof. chemistry, 1983-2000, prof. physics, 1985-2000, prof. physics and biophysics, 1989-2000, mem. Ctr. for Advanced Study, 1989-2000; William H. and Janet LyCan prof. chemistry Ctr. for Advanced Study U. Ill., Urbana, 1993-96, Robert Eiszner prof., 1996-2000; prof. chemistry and biochemistry U. Calif., San Diego, 2000—; Francis H.C. Crick prof., 2001—, prof. physcis, 2003—. Vis. prof. Inst. for Molecular Sci., Okazaki, Japan, 1982, 87; vis. scientist Inst. for Theoretical Physics, Santa Barbara, Calif., 1987, Ecole normale Supérieure, Paris, 1992; Merski lectr. U. Nebr., 1986; Denkewalter lectr. Loyola U., 1986; Hinshelwood lectr. Oxford U., 1997; Harkins lectr. U. Chgo., 1997; FMC lectr. Princeton U., 1998; Matsen lectr. U. Tex., 2002; Rice lectr. U. NC, 2005. Contbr. numerous articles to profl. jours. Sloan fellow, 1981-83, J.S. Guggenheim fellow, 1986-87; Beckman assoc. Ctr. for Advanced Study, Urbana, 1984-85; Fogarty scholar NIH, 1994-98. Fellow AAAS, Am. Phys. Soc. (Biol. Physics prize 2004) Am. Acad. Arts and Scis., The Biophys. Soc.; mem. NAS, Am. Chem. Soc. (Pure Chemistry award 1986, Peter Debye award 2000, Edgar Fahs Smith award Phila. sect. 2005) NY Acad. Scis., Phi Beta Kappa, Sigma Xi, Phi Lambda Upsilon (Fresenius award 1988), Sigma Pi Sigma, Alpha Chi Sigma. Home: 12737 Sandy Crest Ct San Diego CA 92130-2795 Office: U Calif San Diego Dept Chem and Biochemistry 9500 Gilman Dr MC 0371 La Jolla CA 92093-0371 Office Phone: 858-822-4825. Business E-Mail: pwolynes@ucsd.edu.

**WOLYNIES, EVELYN See GRADO-WOLYNIES, EVELYN**

**WOLZ, ROBERT JOSEPH,** museum director; b. Salem, Ohio, June 24, 1946; s. Robert Cornelius and Mary Rosanna Wolz; m. Bonnie Robin Brothers, Jan. 7, 1973 (div. Aug. 16, 1986); children: Jason Alexander, Grant Robert. BA, Youngstown State U., Ohio, 1979. Owner Wolz's Plain & Fancy, East Palestine, Ohio, 1964—85; ops. mgr. Old Town Trolley Tours, Key West, Fla., 1986—87, gen. mgr., 1987—94; dir. Key West Ship Wreck Historeum Mus., 1994—99; exec. dir. Harry Truman Little White House, Key West, 1999—. Co-author (non fiction) The Legacy of the Truman Little White House: Presidents in Paradise, co-editor The National Security Legacy of Harry S. Truman. Sec. Key West Attractions Assn., 1990—95. Mem.: Fla. Assn. Museums, Am. Assn. for State & Local History, Am. Assn. Museums, Sons of Union Veterans of the Civil War (life; dept. comdr. 1968—72, sr. vice comdr. and chief 1974—76, jour. editor, Gettysburg 1981—84, nat. historian 1999—2006). R-Consevative. Roman Catholic. Office: Harry Truman Little White House Museum 111 Front St Key West FL 33040 Office Phone: 305-294-9911. Home Fax: 305-294-9988; Office Fax: 305-294-9988. Personal E-mail: bob.wolz@craftsmandesigns.com. Business E-Mail: bwolz@trumanlittlewhitehouse.com.

**WOLZIEN, CHARLES FREDERICK,** dean, music educator, musician; b. Washington, Jan. 20, 1951; s. Eldred Carl and Virginia Lorenz Wolzien; m. Sharon Lynn Kimmey, Nov. 14, 1959. MusB, San Francisco Conservatory Music, 1973; MusM, U. Colo., 1982, D in Musical Arts, 1989. Instr. music Met. State Coll., Denver, 1975—79; assoc. prof. music U. Colo., Boulder, 1990—, assoc. dean Coll. Music, 2003—. Guest lectr. Sydney (Australia)

Conservatorium Music, 1995. Author: Adrian Le Roy: French Renaissance Guitar Songs, Six Folksongs for Flute and Guitar, Music for Flute and Guitar, (column on early guitar literature) Guitar Found. Am. Jour.-Soundboard; musician: (CD recording) Dances, Grounds and Songs, Columbia Artists Community Concerts, Carnegie Recital Hall Debut; contbr. articles to profl. jours. Mem.: Pi Kappa Lambda (life). Avocation: motorcycling. Home: 2900 21st St Boulder CO 80304 Office: Univ Colo Boulder College of Music 301 UCB Boulder CO 80309-0301 Business E-Mail: wolzien@colorado.edu.

**WOMACK, EDGAR ALLEN, JR.,** energy executive, consultant, nuclear technology consultant; b. Humboldt, Tenn., Oct. 29, 1942; s. Edgar Allen Sr. and Lucy Opal (George) W.; m. Linda Jane Cochran, Dec. 28, 1963; children: Connie Britton, Cynthia Womack. BS, MIT, 1963, MS, 1965, PhD, 1969. With U.S. Atomic Energy Commn., Washington, 1968-73, Babcock and Wilcox Co., 1975-85, v.p. sales and mktg., 1983-85; v.p. R&D, chief tech. officer McDermott Internat., 1985—98; pres. COO BWX Techs., 1998—2002; prin. Cyncon LLC, 2003—. Mem. bd. Naval Submarine League. Patentee in field. Served to lt. USNR, 1968-70. Hon. Woodrow Wilson Found. fellow. Fellow ASME (ind. adv. bd. 1988—, chmn. 1997), AAAS, Indsl. Research Inst. (bd. 1989-96, pres. 1994-95), Sigma Xi. Presbyterian. Avocations: photography, diving, golf. Home: 401 Saint Andrews Cir Lynchburg VA 24503-3750 Personal E-Mail: cyncon@adelphia.net.

**WOMACK, JAMES ERROL,** college president; b. Eugene, Oreg., June 27, 1940; s. John Leon and Dorothy Laverne (Yarbrough) W.; m. Sharron Kay McCullough, June 8, 1963; children: Timothy, Stephen, Joseph, Marilee. BS, N.W. Christian Coll. 1963; M Teaching, Cen. Okla. State U., 1968; postgrad., Pacific Luth. U., 1958-60. U. Oreg., 1960-63. Phillips U., 1966-68, DHum (hon.), 1987. Cert. tchr., Okla., Calif.; cert. fund raising exec.; ordained to ministry Christian Ch. (Disciples of Christ), 1963. Youth min. Lowell (Oreg.) Christian Ch., 1962-63, First Christian Ch., The Dalles, Oreg., 1963-65; youth and edn. min. Putnam City Christian Ch., Oklahoma City, 1965-68; tchr. English and social studies, coach basketball Patterson (Calif.) High Sch., 1968-71; min. youth and edn. Maze Blvd. Christian Ch., Modesto, Calif., 1968-71; dir. devel. Nat. Benevolent Assn. (Colo. Christian Home), Denver, 1976-86; coord. campus activities, coach basketball N.W. Christian Coll., Eugene, 1971-73, dir. planned giving, 1973-76, pres., 1986—. Cons. Luth. Social Svcs. Colo., Denver, 1984-85, Dayton, Ohio, 1986-89, Florence Crittenton Home Svcs., Little Rock, 1985-98; presenter in field. Mem. devel. coun. Woodhaven Learning Ctr.; mem. fin. com. and nurture commn. Cen. Rocky Mountain Region Christian Ch.; chmn. N.W. Oklahoma City Youth Week Activities; trustee N.W. Christian Coll.; active Denver Planned Giving Roundtable; regional bd. dirs. N.W. Regional Ch., Christian Ch. in Kans. Recipient Book Award for Acad. Excellence Christian Bd. of Pub. Mem. Nat. Soc. Fund Raising Execs., Nat. Benevolent Assn. (trustee best of caring fund), Oreg. Ind. Coll. Assn. (mem. exec. com.), Colo. Assn. Fund Raisers (past sec., bd. dirs.), Emerald Empire Fellowship of Christian Athletes (charter mem., sec., bd. dirs.), Ministerial Alliance (chmn. migrant ministries), Rotary (mem. program com. Eugene chpt. 1990), Optimists (bd. dirs. Highland Park chpt.), Civitan, Denver City Club. Avocations: fishing, reading, sports. Home: 1363 Windsor St Springfield OR 97477-8107 Office: NW Christian Coll 828 E 11th Ave Eugene OR 97401-3745 E-mail: pres@nwcc.edu.

**WOMACK, JOHN W.,** pharmacist; b. St. Louis, Dec. 6, 1930; s. John Anderson and Della Long Womack; children: Peter Frank, Elin Vera, Brian William, John Anderson, Kimberly Ann. BS in pharmacy, U. Toledo, 1957. Registered Pharmacist Ohio. Chief pharmacist Cunningham Drug Co., Cleve., 1958—73, U. Pharmacy, Cleve., 1973—76, Revco Drug, Cleve., 1976—85, Neon, Cleve., 1985—. Mem. football camp Camp Stonem, Calif. 1953; mem. football team, 1954, AAU Basketball, Cleve., 1959; bd of trustees Free Clinic Greater Cleve., 1968—99; worker Carl Stokes Election, Cleve., 1968. Cpl. U.S. Army, 1952-54, Korea. Mem.: Nat. Pharm. Assn., Ohio State Pharm. Assn., Omega Psi Phi. Episcopal. Avocations: basketball, football. Home: 17707 Fed Rd Cleveland OH 44128

**WOMACK, LEE ANN,** country musician; b. Jacksonville, TX, Aug. 19, 1966; married; 2 children. Singer: (albums) Lee Ann Womack, 1997, Some Things I Know, 1998, I Hope You Dance, 2000, The Season for Romance, 2002, Something Worth Leaving Behind, 2002, Greatest Hits, 2004, There's More Where That Came From, 2005 (Album of Yr., Country Music Assn., 2005), (singles) The Fool, 1997, Does My Ring Burn Your Finger, 2000 (USA Today song of yr., 2001), I Hope You Dance, 2000, I May Hate Myself in the Morning, 2005 (Single of Yr., Country Music Assn., 2005); with Willie Nelson (duet) Mendocino County Line, 2002 (Country Music Assn. Vocal Event of Yr.). Studio: MCA Records Inc 60 Music Sq E Nashville TN 37203 Office: Richard De La Font Agency Inc Ste 505 4845 S Sheridan Rd Tulsa OK 74145 Office Phone: 615-244-8944, 918-565-6200.*

**WOMACK, THOMAS HOUSTON,** manufacturing executive; b. Gallatin, Tenn., June 22, 1940; s. Thomas Houston and Jessie (Eckel) Womack; m. Linda Walker, July 20, 1963 (div. Dec. 1989); children: Britton Ryan, Kelley Elizabeth; m. Pamela Ann Reed, Apr. 20, 1991. BSME, Tenn. Tech. U., Cookeville, 1963. Project engr. U.S. Gypsum Co., Jacksonville, Fla., 1963-65; project mgr. Maxwell House Divsn. Gen. Foods Corp., Jacksonville, 1965-68, mfg. mgr. Hoboken, NJ, 1968-71, divsn. ops. planning mgr., 1971-73; industry sales mgr. J.R. Schneider Co., Tiburon, Calif., 1973-79; pres. and CEO Womack Internat., Inc., Mare Island, 1979—; chmn. and CEO Ceramic Microlight Techs., Inc., 1995—; pres. and CEO Micronic Filtration Tech., LLC, 2005—. Mem.: Am. Soc. Chem. Engrs., Soc. Mfg. Engrs., Am. Filtration Soc., Soc. Tribologists and Lubrication Engrs. Achievements include patents for. Avocations: skiing, vintage exotic sports cars. Office: Womack Internat Inc PO Box 2175 Vallejo CA 94592-0175 Office Phone: 707-562-1000. Office Fax: 707-562-1010. Business E-Mail: womack@womack.com.

**WOMBLE, KEN,** theater educator, film director, writer, actor; s. Maxine Womble; m. Sandy Womble. BFA in Theatre, Fla. State U., Tallahassee, 1976; MFA in Theatre, So. Meth. U., Dallas, 1978. Dir. of performing arts St. Margaret's Episcopal Sch., San Juan Capistrano, Calif., 1997—2005; theatre instr. Saddleback Coll., Mission Viejo, 2000—05; asst. prof. theatre U. No. Colo., Greeley, 2005—. Author: (play) A Midsummer Night's Dream, An Adaptation, 2003; dir.: (documentary film) Wally Huntoon, A Life By Design, 2005; author: (play) Romeo and Juliet, An Adaptation, 2006; actor: (theater, film and television) Over 100 appearances. Mem.: AFTRA, SAG, Actors' Equity Assn. Office: Univ No Colo 501 20th St Campus Box 28 Greeley CO 80639 Office Phone: 970-351-1193.

**WOMBLE, WILLIAM FLETCHER,** lawyer; b. Winston-Salem, NC, Oct. 29, 1916; s. Bunyan Snipes and Edith (Willingham) Womble; m. Jane Payne Gilbert, Oct. 11, 1941; children: William Fletcher, Jr., Jane Womble Haver, Russell G., Ann Womble Strader. AB, Duke U., 1937, JD, 1939; LHT (hon.), High Point U., 2000. Bar: NC 1939. Assoc. Womble Carlyle Sandridge & Rice P.L.L.C. and predecessors, Winston-Salem, 1939-47, mem., 1947—. Campaign chmn. Forsyth County Cmty. Chest, 1949; mem. NC Gen. Statutes Commn., 1953—55, NC Bd. Higher Edn., 1955—57, 1960—63, NC Adv. Budget Commn., 1957—58; trustee, past chmn. High Point Coll. (now High Point U.), 1950—; trustee Winston-Salem State U., 1953—55; pres. Children's Home, 1959—75; bd. dirs. Triad United Meth. Home (now Arbor Acres United Meth. Retirement Cmty.), 1976—87, 1989—97, treas., 1975—79, pres., 1979—85; hon. chair United Way, Forsyth County, 1998; mem. People-to-People Citizen Amb. Program, 1981, 1986, NC Ho. of Reps., 1953—58, chmn. com. higher edn., vice chmn. fin. com., 1957; chmn. administrv. bd. Centenary United Meth. Ch., 1961—63, chmn. bd. trustees, 1983—85; trustee Sr. Svcs., Inc., 1998—2005, chair ann. fund., 2004—05. Served to maj. USAF, 1941—46. Named Trustee of the Yr., Gen. Bd. Global Mins. of United Meth. Ch., Health and Wlfare Minst. Dept., 1989. Fellow: Am. Coll. Trial Found. (life; state chmn. 1984—89, Fifty Yr. award 1995); mem.: ABA (ho. dels. 1978—87, bd. govs. 1982—85, exec. coun. Nat. Com. Bar Pres. 1985—88, ethics com. 1985—91, resource devel. coun. 1986—92, chmn. jud. code subcom. 1988—91, chair affiliate outreach com. 1994—97,

coun. mem. sr. lawyers divsn. 1995—97), Forsyth County Bar Assn. (pres. 1962), Am. Judicature Soc., NC State Bar (trustee Interest on Lawyers Trust Accounts 1983—91, vice chmn. 1989—91, Chief Justice's Professionalism award 2001), NC Bar Assn. (pres. 1966—67, chmn. endowment founders campaign 1986—87, chair sr. lawyers divsn. 1994—95, Judge John J. Parker award 1984), Soc. Cin., Winston-Salem C. of C. (pres. 1960—61), Old Town Club, Rotary (local pres. 1964). Democrat. Home: 1244 Arbor Rd 441 Winston Salem NC 27104-1139 Office: Womble Carlyle Sandridge & Rice One W 4th St Winston Salem NC 27101 Office Phone: 336-721-3603. Office Fax: 336-733-8369. Business E-Mail: wwomble@wcsr.com.

**WOMER, CHARLES BERRY,** retired hospital executive, management consultant; b. Cleve., Mar. 30, 1926; s. Porter Blake and Margaret (Berry) W.; m. Elizabeth Benson, Oct. 7, 1950; children: Richard B., Carol E., John C. MS in Hosp. Adminstrn., Columbia U., 1953; BS in Mech. Engring., Case Inst. Tech., 1949. Asst. dir. Univ. Hosps., Cleve., 1957-61, assoc. dir., 1961-65, pres., 1976-82; mgmt. cons., 1982-90; ret., 1990. Adminstr. Yale-New Haven Hosp., 1965-67, dir., 1968-76, pres., 1976; lectr. Yale U., 1965-78, 87-91; adj. asst. prof. Case Western Res. U., 1976-83; mem. Conn. Commn. on Hosps. and Health Care, 1973-76; bd. dirs. New Haven Savings Bank, 1969-76. Bd. govs. U. New Haven, 1972-76. Served with AUS, 1944-46. Fellow Am. Coll. Healthcare Execs. (life); mem. Am. Hosp. Assn. (chmn. coun. on mgmt. and planning 1977-79), Conn. Hosp. Assn. (trustee 1970-74, pres. 1972-73, Disting. Svc. award 1976), Assn. Am. Med. Colls. (exec. coun. 1974-77, 78-80, treas. 1975-76, chmn. 1979-80, adminstrv. bd. coun. tchg. hosps. 1972-77, chmn. 1975-76, Disting. Svc. Mem. 1982—). Home: 88 Notch Hill Rd Apt 382 North Branford CT 06471-1861

**WONDER, STEVIE (STEVELAND HARDAWAY JUDKINS, STEVLAND MORRIS),** musician; b. Saginaw, Mich., May 13, 1950; m. Syreeta Wright, 1971 (div. 1972); m. Kai Milla Wonder, 2001; children: Kailand, Mandla Kadjaly Carl Stevland Morris; children: Aisha, Keita, Mumtaz. Student pub. schs. in Detroit until age 12; then transferred to, Mich. Sch. for Blind. Recording artist Motown Records, Detroit, 1963—70; founder, pres. music pub. co. Black Bull Music, Inc., 1970—, Wondirection Records, Inc., 1982—. (singles) Fingertips, 1963, Uptight/Purple Raindrops, 1965, Someday At Christmas/The Miracles of Christmas, I'm Wondering/Everytime I See You I Go Wild, 1966, I Was Made To Love Her/Hold Me, 1967, Shoo-Be-Doo-Be-Doo-Da-Day/Why Don't You Lead Me To Love, You Met Your Match/My Girl, 1968, For Once In My Life, I Don't Know Why, My Cherie Amour, Yester-Me, Yester-You, Yesterday, Never Had a Dream Come True, Signed, Sealed, Delivered I'm Yours, Heaven Help Us All, I Wish (Grammy award, 1977), Don't You Worry 'Bout a Thing, You Haven't Done Nothin', Boogie on Reggae Woman (Grammy award, 1975), Isn't She Lovely, Sir Duke, Another Star, As, You Are the Sunshine of My Life (Grammy award, 1974), Superstition (Grammy award, 1974), Higher Ground, Living For the City (Grammy award, 1975), I Just Called to Say I Love You; singer: (albums) Tribute to Uncle Ray, 1962, With a Song In My Heart, 1963, The Jazz Soul of Little Stevie, 1963, The Twelve-Year-Genius, 1963, Stevie At The Beach, 1964, Down to Earth, 1966, Uptight, 1966, Someday at Christmas, 1967, I Was Made To Love Her, Someday At Christmas, 1967, Eivets Rednow (Featuring Alfie), 1968, For Once in My Life, 1968, Stevie Wonder's Greatest Hits, 1968, My Cherie Amour, Talk of The Town, 1969, Live at the Talk of the Town, 1970, Signed, Sealed and Delivered, 1970, Live In Person, 1970, Steve Wonder's Greatest Hits Vol. 2, 1971, Where I'm Coming From, 1971, Talking Book, 1972, Music of My Mind, Stevie Wonder Live, Where I'm Coming From, Talking Book, 1972, Portrait, 1976, Innervisions, 1973 (Grammy award, 1974), Fulfillingness' First Finale, 1974 (Grammy award, 1975), Songs In the Key of Life, 1976 (Grammy award, 1977), Looking Back, 1977, Stevie Wonder's Journey Through the Secret Life of Plants, 1979, Hotter than July, 1980, Stevie Wonder's Original Musiquarium, 1982, Woman in Red, 1984, In Square Circle, 1985 (best soul/R&B album of yr., Down Beat mag. Readers' poll, 1986), I Just Called to Say I love You, 1984 (Acad. award, Golden Globe award for single, 1984), Characters, 1987, Jungle Fever, 1991, Inner Peace, Motown Legends, 1995, Natural Wonders, 1995, Conversation Peace, 1996, Song Review, 1996, At the Close of a Century, 1999, The Definitive Collection, 2002, A Time to Love, 2005 (Grammy for Best Male Pop Vocal Performance, 2006), (Soundtrack) Bamboozled; actor: (films) Bikini Beach, Muscle Beach Party, 1964; frequent appearances (TV series) Mike Douglas Show, guest host Saturday Night Live. Named Musician of Year, Down Beat mag. Rock/Blues Poll, 1973—75, 1977—78, Best Selling Male Soul Artist of Year, Nat. Assn. Rec. Merchandisers, 1974; named to Songwriters Hall of Fame, 1982, Rock and Roll Hall of Fame, 1989; recipient Nelson Mandela Courage award, 1991, numerous Grammy awards, numerous awards for best singer/songwriter, Rock Music award, 1977, Am. Music award, 1978, Am. Video award for best rhythm and blues video for Ebony and Ivory, 1982, Century award, Billboard Music Awards, 2004, Grammy Award (with Beyonce) for Best R&B Performance by Duo, 2006, Lifetime Achievement award, Nat. Civil Rights Mus., 2006. Office: 4616 W Magnolia Blvd Burbank CA 91505-2731*

**WONDERS, PAMELA KIM,** music educator; b. East Liverpool, Ohio, Aug. 3, 1955; d. Richard Daniel and Lila Lee Wonders. BS in music edn., Trevecca Nazarene U., 1978; MEd, Tenn. State U., 1991. Band dir. Hillsboro H.S., Nashville, 1978—79, DuPont Elem., Nashville, 1979—80; choral dir. Maplewood H.S., Nashville, 1980—86, Hunters Lane H.S., Nashville, 1986—. Regional mgmt. team Sweet Adelweiss Internat., Tulsa, Okla., 2000—03, dir. musical activities, 1986—89; dir. Metro Nashville Chorus, 1988—. Mem.: Mid. Tenn. Vocal Assn., Music Educators Nat. Conf., Nat. Edn. Assn. Home: 590 Thomas Jefferson Circle Madison TN 37115 Office: Hunters Lane HS 1150 Hunters Lane Nashville TN 37207 Personal E-mail: wondersk@aol.com.

**WONDERS, WILLIAM CLARE,** geography educator; b. Toronto, Apr. 22, 1924; s. George Clarence and Ann Mary (Bell) W.; m. Lillian Paradise Johnson, June 2, 1951; children: Karen Elizabeth, Jennifer Anne, Glen William. BA with honors, Victoria Coll., U. Toronto, 1946; MA, Syracuse U., 1948; PhD, U. Toronto, 1951; Fil. Dr. h.c., Uppsala U., 1981. Teaching asst. dept. geography Syracuse U., 1946-48; lectr. dept. geography U. Toronto, 1948-53; asst. prof. geography dept. polit. economy U. Alta., 1953-55, assoc. prof. geography, 1955-57, prof., head dept. geography, 1957-67, prof. dept. geography, 1967-87, Univ. prof., 1983—, prof. emeritus, 1987—. Vis. prof. geography U.B.C., 1954, U. Okla., 1965-66, St. Mary's U., 1977, U. Victoria, 1989, J.F. Kennedy Inst., U. Berlin, 1990; guest prof. Inst. Geography, Uppsala (Sweden) U., 1962-63; rsch. fellow in Geography U. Aberdeen, Scotland, 1970-71, 78; vis. fellow in Can. Studies, U. Edinburgh, Scotland, 1987. Author: Looking at Maps, 1960, The Sawdust Fusiliers, 1991, Norden and Canada-A Geographer's Perspective, 1992, Alaska Highway Explorer, 1994; author: (with T. Drinkwater et al.) Junior Atlas of Alberta, 1979; contbr. editor: Canada's Changing North, 1971, rev. edit., 2003, The North, 1972, The Arctic Circle, 1976, Knowing the North, 1988, Geographica's Pocket World Reference, 2000, Frontiersmen & Settlers, 2002, Geordies, Yankees and Canucks, 2006; contbr. articles to jours. and encys., chapters to books. Active Nat. Assn. on Geog. Rsch., chmn. Boreal Inst. No. Studies (Can. Circumpolar Inst.), 1960-62; mem. Can. Permanent Com. on Geog. Names, 1981-94, Alta. Hist. Sites Bd., 1978-83, vice-chmn. 1982-83; policy bd. Can. Plains Rsch. Centre, U. Regina (Sask.), 1975-86; adv. bd. Royal Tyrrell Mus. Paleontology, 1984-89; bd. dirs. Muttart Found. 1986-93, 95-98, v.p., 1991-93. Decorated Order of Can., Can. Forces Decoration; recipient Queen's Jubilee medal; NSF sr. fgn. scientist fellow, 1965-66; Can. Coun. sr. rsch. fellow, 1969-70, 77-78; Nuffield Found. fellow, 1970-71. Fellow Arctic Inst. N.Am., Royal Soc. Can., Royal Can. Geog. Soc. (Massey medalist 1998); mem. Can. Assn. Geographers (past pres.), Can. Assn. Scottish Studies (councillor 1974-77), Scottish Soc. No. Studies (councillor 1981-86), Sigma Xi, Gamma Theta Upsilon. E-mail: wwonders@shaw.ca.

**WONG, AH-SAN,** planetary scientist, composer, writer; d. Chuen Wong and Mei Leung. MS in Physics, Calif. Inst. Tech., 1995, PhD in Physics, 2002; M in composition, Calif. State U., LA. Sr. rsch. fellow U. Mich., Ann Arbor, 2002—06. Mem.: Am. Astron. Soc. (mem. divsn. planetary sci.), Am. Geophys. Union.

**WONG, ANDREA,** broadcast executive; b. 1966; BS in Elec. Engring., MIT, 1988; MBA, Stanford Univ., 1993. Rschr. ABC News PrimeTime Live, 1993—94; exec. asst. pres. ABC TV Network, 1994—95, ABC, Inc., 1995, v.p., exec. asst. pres.; v.p. alt. series, spls. ABC Entertainment, 1998, exec. v.p. alt. programming, spls., late night, 2004—. Office: ABC 77 W 66th St New York NY 10023-6298*

**WONG, B.D.,** actor; b. San Francisco, Oct. 24, 1962; s. William D. and Roberta Christine (Leong) W.; 1 child, Jackson Foo. Grad. high sch., San Francisco. Bd. dirs. Alliance of Resident Theatres, N.Y.C.; lectr. Royce Carlton Inc. Speakers, N.Y.C., 1991—. Appeared (Broadway play) M. Butterfly, 1988-90 (Tony award, N.Y. Drama Desk award, N.Y. Outer Critics Circle award, Theatre World award, Clarence Derwent award, 1988), Pippin, 2005; (films) Family Business, 1990, The Freshman, 1990, Mystery Date, 1991, The Lounge People, 1991, Father of the Bride, 1991, The Lounge People, 1992, Jurassic Park, 1993, Men of War, 1994, The Ref, 1994, Father of the Bride II, 1995, Executive Decision, 1996, Stinkers, 1997, Seven Years in Tibet, 1997, Mulan, 1998, Slappy and the Stinkers, 1998, The Salton Sea, 2002, Stay, 2005; (TV movies) And the Band Played On, 1993, Judith Krantz's Dazzle, 1995, Dazzle, 1995, The Substitute 2: School's Out, 1998, (voice) Reflections on Ice: Michelle Kwan Skates to the Music of Disney's Mulan, 1998, Miss USA, 2004; (TV series) The X Files, 1996, Oz, 1997, Chicago Hope, 1999, Law & Order: Special Victims Unit, 2002—; TV guest appearances include (voice) Kim Possible, 2002. Recipient Arts in Leadership award, Coro Found., San Francisco, 1991, Jimmie award for Arts Advocacy, Assn. Asian- Pacific Am. Artists, L.A., 1991. Mem. SAG, AFTRA, Asian-Pacific Alliance for Creative Equality (co-founder 1990), Asian Am. Legal Def. and Edn. Fund (Justice in Action award, 1991), Actors' Equity Assn.*

**WONG, BELLA TOY FUNND,** lawyer; b. Boston, Feb. 5, 1961; d. Perry Wai Yee and Joan Hung (Lem) W.; m. Steven M. Brand, Sept. 18, 1993. BA, Harvard U., 1982, EdM, 1991; postgrad., Stanford U., 1982-84; JD, U. Calif., Davis, 1987. Bar: Calif. 1987, Mass., 1990; cert. gen. sci. and biology tchr., Mass. Assoc. LeBoeuf, Lamb, Leiby, MacRae, San Francisco, 1987-90; sci. instr. Lincoln Sudbury (Mass.) Regional H.S., 1991-98, head sci. dept., 1996-98; asst. supt. Wellesley (Mass.) Pub. Schs., 1998—. Mem. ABA, ASCD, Am. Assn. Sch. Personnel Officers, Calif. Bar Assn., Mass. Bar Assn., New Eng. Assn. Secondary Tchrs., Mass. Assn. Sch. Supts., Mass. Assn. Sch. Personnel Officers. Office: Wellesley Pub Schs 40 Kingsbury St Wellesley MA 02481-4831

**WONG, BRIAN JET-FEI,** surgeon; b. LA, Sept. 23, 1963; s. Richard Toy and Hazel F. (Lue) W. BS, U. So. Calif. 1985; postgrad., Oxford U., 1985-86; MD, Johns Hopkins U., 1990; PhD, U. Amsterdam, 2001. Resident U. Calif., Irvine, 1990-96, clin. instr., 1997-98, asst. prof., 1998—2001, assoc. prof., 2001—. Rsch. assoc. Beckman Laser Inst., Irvine, 1994—. Mem. ACS, Biomed. Optical Soc., SPIE, Am. Acad. Facial Plastic Surgery. Avocation: surfing. Office: U Calif Dept Otolaryngology 101 City Dr S # B25r81 Orange CA 92868-3201 Office Phone: 714-456-5753.

**WONG, CHING-PING,** chemist, materials engineer; b. Canton, China, Mar. 29, 1947; came to U.S., 1966; s. Kwok-Keung and Yun-Kwan W. BS in Chemistry, Purdue U., 1969; PhD in Organic/Inorganic Chemistry, Pa. State U., 1975. Postdoctoral scholar Stanford (Calif.) U., 1975-77; mem. rsch. staff AT&T Bell Labs., Princeton, NJ, 1977-82, sr. mem. tech. staff, 1982-87, disting. mem. tech. staff, 1987-92; AT&T Bell Labs. fellow, 1992-96; Regents, Charles Smithgall Inst. endowed chair, disting. prof. Sch. of Materials Sci. and Engring., Ga. Inst. Tech., Atlanta, 1996—; assembly, reliability and thermal mgmt. rsch. dir. NSF Packaging Rsch. Ctr. Program chmn. 39th Electronic Components Conf., 1989; gen. chmn. 41st Electronic Components and Tech. Conf., 1991; bd. govs. IEEE-Components, Hybrids and Mfg. Tech. Soc., 1987-89, tech. v.p., 1990-91, pres., 1992-93. Author, editor: Polymers for Electronic and Photonic Applications, 1993; contbr. articles to profl. jours. Recipient Outstanding Papers and Contbns. award IEEE-Components, Hybrids and Mfg. Tech. Soc., 1990, 91, 94, 96, 1998, 2001, Ga. Tech. Outstanding Faculty award, London, 1999, award of excellence Univ. Press, 2000, Ga. Tech. Disting. Profl award, 2004. Fellow: Nat. Acad. Engring., IEEE (Outstanding Sustained Tech. Contbns. award 1995, Millenium medal 2000, EAB Exceptional Continuation Edn. award 2001, CPMT Outstanding Exceptional Tech.Contbn. award 2002, CPMT Field award 2005). Achievements include over 50 U.S. and numerous internat. patents for integrated device passivation and encepsulation area; pioneer in application of gel polymers for device reliability without hermeticity, nano technology, a new application on electronic device packaging. Office: Ga Inst Tech Sch Materials Sci & Engring 771 Ferst Dr Atlanta GA 30332-0001 Office Phone: 404-894-8391. Business E-Mail: cp.wong@mse.gatech.edu.

**WONG, COLETTE L.,** apparel designer, educator; d. Burnell D. and Frances Hoffman; m. Timothy D. Wong, Sept. 19, 1982; children: Nicole, Derek. AAS, Fashion Inst. Tech., NYC, 1975; BS, Empire State Coll., NYC, 2000. Asst. designer women's & children's sleepwear SLT, Inc. & Christian Dior, USA, NYC, 1975—81; head designer, merchandiser jr. & women's lingerie Top Form Mills, Inc (formerlyBerkleigh Jr., Michael Berkowitz Co), 1981—86; creative designer lingerie & home products Silberman Mktg., 1988—90; freelance creative designer sleep & daywear Lady Ester Lingerie, 1986—87; freelance creative designer & illustrator L.V. Myles Co, 1987—89; freelance creative designer pvt. label Nap Industries, 1989—98; freelance creative designer & illustrator Carol Hochman Designs (divsn., Slumbertogs), 1992—93; assoc. prof., fashion design dept. Fashion Inst. Tech., 1984—, asst. chair, student related, fashion design dept. 2002—. Mentor intimate apparel students Femmy Gala/The Underfashion Club, Inc, NYC, 2004—; judge All Japan/AFT Internat. Fashion Sketch Contest, 2002—02; expert witness Coudert Bros. LLP, 2001—03; expert spkr., instr. Symposum on Universal Design Conf., 2000—01; project coord. scholarship & internship program SAIG Com., Underfashion Club, INC, 2003—; project dir. student competitions & fashion shows Nat. Osteoporosis Found./FIT/NOF, Beauty In All Forms. Author: Patient Osteoporosis Education Program/Procter & Gamble, (booklet) Style Wise: A Fashion Guide for Women with Osteoporosis. Recipient Chancellor's award Excellence Faculty Svc., Fashion Inst. Tech., 2004. Mem.: Underfashion Club. Achievements include development of creative course, Fashion In Corsetry. Avocations: travel, cooking, drawing, needlecrafts. Office Phone: 212-217-7667.

**WONG, DAVID T.,** biochemist, researcher; b. Hong Kong, Nov. 6, 1935; arrived in US, 1957; s. Chi-Keung and Pui-King Wong; m. Christina Lee, Dec. 28, 1963; children: Conrad, Melvin, Vincent. Student, Nat. Taiwan U., 1955—56; BS, Seattle Pacific U., 1961; MS, Oreg. State U., 1964; PhD, U. Oreg., 1966. Sr. biochemist Lilly Rsch. Labs., Indpls., 1968-72, rsch. biochemist, 1973-77, sr. rsch. scientist, 1978-89, rsch. advisor, 1990-97, Lilly rsch. fellow, 1997-99, cons., 2000—. Adj. prof. biochemistry and molecular biology Ind. U. Sch. Medicine, 1996—96, adj. prof. neurobiology, 1991—. Mem. editl. bd.: Chinese Jour. Physiology, 1996—2000; contbr. articles to sci. jours. Named Alumnus of Growing Vision, Seattle Pacific U., 1991, Alumnus of the Yr., 1998, Disting. Alumni Scientist award, Oreg. Health and Sci. U., 2004, alumni fellow, Oreg. State U., 2003; recipient Scientist of the Yr. Pres. award, Chinese Neurosci. Soc., 1991, Discoverers award, Pharm. Mfr. Assn., 1993, Lifetime Rsch. award, Mental Health Assn. Ind., 1996, World Difference award, Ind. Health Industry Forum, 1996, Pharm. Discoverer's award Prozac, Nat. Alliance Rsch. Schizophrenia and Depression, 1996, Outstanding Achievement in Neurosci. Rsch. award, Lilly Neuroscience Eli Lilly and Co., 2000, Cornerstone award, Am. Drugstore Mus. Indpls., 2000, Excellence award, Asian Am. Alliance, Inc., 2002, Pioneer Recognition award, Com. 100, 2002, Excellence award, U.S. Pan Asian Am. C. of C., 2002, Hon. Ga.

Citizen, mem. Goodwill Amb. Corp., State of Ga., 2003. Mem.: Ind. Chinese-Am. Profs. Assn. (pres. 2000), Soc. Chinese Bioscientists Am. (Disting. Scientist award for drug discovery 2004), Soc. Neurosci. (pres. Indpls. chpt. 1987, 1988), Am. Soc. Pharmacology and Exptl. Therapeutics, Am. Coll. Neuropsychopharamcology, Indpls. Assn. Chinese Ams. (pres. 1987). Achievements include patents in field; research in biochemistry and pharmacology of neurotransmission; discovery of and development of anti-depressant drug, Prozac (Fluoxetine); and Cymbalta (Duloxetine, a serotonine and norepinephrine uptake inhibitor); and other drugs including Strattera (Atomoxetive, a selective norepinephrine uptake inhibitor) for attention deficit hyperactivity disorder; dapoxetine (a serotonin uptake inhibitor); studies of potentially useful substances which enhance transmission of norepinephrine, dopamine, serotonin, acetylcholine, and GABA-neurons; studies of natural products led to the discovery of caboxylic ionophores: Narasin and A204, which increase transport of cations across biomembranes. Home: 5812 E Fall Creek Parkway N D Indianapolis IN 46226-1051 Home Fax: 317-254-8688. Personal E-mail: dtwongindy@iquest.net.

**WONG, DEBORAH M.,** science educator; b. Detroit, June 28, 1956; d. John T. and Elizabeth M. Pesta; m. Michael K. Wong, June 25, 2005; children: Cheryl L. Baranowski, Julie A. Baranowski. AA, Macomb CC, Mich., 1976; BA, Wayne State U., Detroit, 1992; Masters, Saginaw Valley State U., Mich., 2001. Cert. ASCP Mich. Med. lab. technician Mt. Clemens (Mich.) Gen. Hosp., 1977—89; tchr. New Haven (Mich.) Cmty. Schs., 1993—.

**WONG, ELAINE DANG,** foundation executive; b. Canton, China, June 3, 1936 (parents Am. citizens); d. Robert G. and Fung Heong (Woo) Dang; A.A. (Rotary scholar), Coalinga Coll., 1956; B.S. (AAUW scholar, Grad. Resident scholar), U. Calif., Berkeley, 1958, teaching credential, 1959; m. Philip Wong, Nov. 8, 1959; children— Elizabeth, Russell, Roger, Edith, Valerie. Tchr. acctg. San Mateo (Calif.) High Sch., 1959-60, acct., 1960-75; substitute tchr. Richmond County Schs., Augusta, Ga., 1975-77; comptroller Central Savannah River Area, United Way, Augusta, 1977-82; asst. controller Hammermill Hardwoods div. Hammermill Paper Co., Augusta, 1982-84; controller SFN Communications of Augusta, Inc. (WJBF-TV), 1984-85; acct. Med. Coll. Ga. Found., Inc., 1986-88, Nat. Sci Ctr. Found., Inc., 1988-89; cons. small bus.; pvt. tutor acctg. Mem. adv. bd. Richmond County Bd. Edn., 1985-87; bd. dirs. Cen. Savannah River chpt. Girl Scouts US, 1986-92. Panel judge Jr. Achievement Treas. award, 1980, 81; treas. Chinese Lang. Sch., 1973-75, Merry Neighborhood Sch., 1974-75. Recipient Achievement award Bank of Am., 1954. Mem. Nat. Assn. Accts. (dir. 1978-85, treas. 1982-84), Chinese Assn. Educators. Presbyterian.

**WONG, FAYE LING,** public health service officer; BS in Dietetics, U. Wash., 1972; MPH, U. Calif.-Berkeley, 1973. Registered dietitian, lic. Ga. Relief dietary supr. Va. Mason Hosp., Seattle, 1968—72; chief Bur. of Nutrition Coconino County Dept. Pub. Health, Flagstaff, Ariz., 1974—76; nutrition cons. Office of Cmty. Health Svcs., Oreg. State Health Divsn., Portland, 1976—81; dir. Sentinel Site project Detroit Health Dept., 1981—83; pub. health nutritionist field svcs. br. Ctr. for Health Promotion and Edn. CDC, Atlanta, 1983—89, program analyst Ctr. for Chronic Disease Prevention and Health Promotion, 1988—89, chief field svcs. br. divsn. nutrition, 1989—92, chief program ops., program svcs. br., 1992—94, asst. chief divsn. cancer prevention and control, 1994—95, asst. chief policy and devel., 1995—96, assoc. dir. diabetes edn., dir. nat. diabetes edn. program, 1996—2000, dir. Youth Media Campaign, 2001—. Contbr. numerous articles, abstracts to profl. jours.; to resource manuals. Recipient Award for Disting. Svc., Dept. Health and Human Svcs., 2000, Questar Internat. award, 2000, Thoth award., Pub. Rels. Assn. Am., 2000, Aesculapius Awards for Excellence, Nat. Diabetes Edn. Program, 1999, 1998, Award for Excellence in recognition of outstanding leadership and dedicated svc., Assn. of State and Territorial Pub. Health Nutrition Dirs., 1991. Mem.: Am. Diabetes Assn. (mem. health profls. sect. 1996—), Am. Assn. Diabetes Educators (mem. pub. health specialty practice group 1996—), Am. Dietetic Assn. (mem. diabetes care and edn. practice group 1996—, mem. nominating com. 1999—), APHA (mem. food and nutrition sect. 1975—, mem. exec. bd. pub. policy rev. and devel. com. 1995—97, chair editl. bd. Am. Jour. Pub. Health 1997—2000, pres. 2001—02, co-chair task force on aging 2001—03, chair, exec. dir. search com. 2001—, Apple award 1991). Office: 4770 Buford Hwy NE lc 94 Atlanta GA 30341 Business E-mail: fwong@cdc.gov.

**WONG, JAMES BOK,** economist, chemical engineer, technologist, consultant; b. Canton, China, Dec. 9, 1922; came to U.S., 1938, naturalized, 1962; s. Gen Ham and Chen (Yee) W.; m. Wai Ping Lim, Aug. 3, 1946, (dec.); children: John, Jane Doris, Julia Ann; m. Betty K.C. Yeow, May 25, 2002. BS summa cum laude in Agr., U. Md., 1949, BS summa cum laude in Chem. Engring., 1950; MS, U. Ill., 1951, PhD, 1954. Rsch. asst. U. Ill. Champaign-Urbana, 1950-53; chem. engr. Std. Oil of Ind., Whiting, 1953-55; process design engr., rsch. engr. Shell Devel. Co., Emeryville, Calif., 1955-61; sr. planning engr., prin. planning engr. Chem. Plastics Group, Dart Industries, Inc. (formerly Rexall Drug & Chem. Co.), L.A., 1961-66, supr. planning and econs., 1966-67, mgr. long range planning and econs., 1967, chief economist, 1967-72, dir. econs. and ops. analysis, 1972-78; dir. internat. techs., 1978-81; pres. James B. Wong Assocs., L.A., 1981—. Chmn. bd. dirs. United Pacific Bank, 1988—; tech. cons. various cos. Author: Jade Eagle, 2000; contbr. articles to profl. jours. Bd. dirs., pres. Chinese Am. Citizens Alliance Found.; mem. Asian Am. Edn. Commn., 1971-81. Served with USAAF, 1943-46. Recipient L.A. Outstanding Vol. Svc. award, 1977. Mem. AIChE, Am. Chem. Soc., Am. Inst. Chem. Engrs., VFW (vice comdr. 1959), Commodores (named to exec. order 1982), Sigma Xi, Tau Beta Pi, Phi Kappa Phi, Pi Mu Epsilon, Phi Lambda Upsilon, Phi Eta Sigma. Home: 2460 Venus Dr Los Angeles CA 90046-1646 *Personal philisophy: A man's reputation is his most prized possession.*

**WONG, JAMES ROBERT,** oncologist, educator; BA in Biochemistry summa cum laude, Harvard Coll., 1981, MD cum laude, 1986. Bd. cert radiation oncology. Rsch. fellow, assoc. Dana-Farber Cancer Inst., Harvard Med. Sch., 1986-87; intern internal medicine New Eng. Deaconess Hosp., Harvard Med. Sch., 1987-88; resident Harvard Joint Ctr. for Radiation Therapy, Harvard Med. Sch., 1988-92; asst. prof. radiology Cornell U. Med. Coll., 1992-97; chmn. dept. radiation oncology AHS/Morristown (N.J.) Meml. Hosp., 1997—. Tchg. asst. introductory biology Harvard Coll., 1980; organizer, lectr. tumor biology course for health professions program Harvard U., 1982-83; assoc. clin. prof. radiation oncology Columbia U., Coll. Physicians and Surgeons, 1998—; co-dir. dept. radiation oncology N.Y. Downtown Hosp., 1992-94, dir. Nasopharyngeal Cancer Ctr., 1993-95, dir. dept. radiation oncology, 1996-97; asst. attending dept. radiation oncology N.Y. Hosp./Cornell U. Med. Ctr., 1992-97, radiation oncology fellowship program dir. dept. radiation oncology, 1996-97, dir. brain tumor and stereotactic radiosurgery dept. radiation oncology, 1996-97, dir. radiation oncology rsch., 1996-97; presenter, lectr. in field. Contbr. articles to profl. jours. Recipient Essay Nat. Grand Prize awad Boehringer-Ingelheim Pharmacology, 1985, Physician's Rsch. Tng. Fellowship award Am. Cancer Soc., 1987, Young Oncologist Essay award Am. Radium Soc., 1992; Harvard Club scholar, 1978-81, Edward Wetmore scholar, 1979-81; Betty Lea Stone fellow Am. Cancer Soc., 1983. Mem. Am. Soc. for Therapeutic Radiology and Oncology (Traveling award 1990), Chinese Am. Med. Soc. (bd. dirs. 1995-98), Am. Coll. Radiology, Radiol. Soc. N.J., Oncology Soc. N.J., Phi Beta Kappa. Office: Morristown Meml Hosp 100 Madison Ave Morristown NJ 07960-6095

**WONG, JOE BING,** retired architect; b. Clifton, Ariz., Aug. 17, 1921; s. Hing Chong and Mock See Wong; m. Lillian Phyllis Jew, Dec. 19, 1942; children: Jeffrey(dec.), Judy Margaret. Student, U. Calif., Berkeley, 1938—41, Calif. Sch. Fine Arts, 1946—48. Registered arch., Calif., 1952, Ariz., 1954, Nev., 1963, Colo. 1968, Tex., 1990, Nat. Coun. Archtl. Registration, 1964. Ship conversion engr. Gen. Engring-Drydock, San Francisco, 1941—42; designer, chief draftsman Higgins & Root Archs., San Jose, Calif., 1946—53, Nichols-White Archs., Palo Alto, Calif., 1945—46; arch., owner Wong Assocs., Scottsdale, Ariz., 1954—98; ret., 1998. Pres.

Associated Scottsdale Archs., 1968—85. Active Scottsdale Libr. Bd. 1962—68; mem., chmn. Scottsdale Design Rev. Bd., 1968—71, Scottsdale Bldg. Adv. Bd., 1971—83, Scottsdale Adv. Bd. Appeals, 1983—90. With U.S. Army, 1943—46. Fellow: Internat. Inst. Arts and Letters (life); mem.: AIA (emeritus), Nat. Soc. Lit. and the Arts, Scottsdale Charros (life). Avocations: fishing, painting. Home: 7782 Via Sonrisa Scottsdale AZ 85258

**WONG, KUOK-SHOONG DANIEL,** research scientist; BSE in Elec. Engring., Princeton U., 1992; MS in Elec. Engring., Stanford U., 1994, PhD in Elec. Engring., 1998. Rsch. scientist Telcordia Techs., Red Bank, NJ, 1998—. Invited external phd examiner comput. sci. dept. Nat. U. of Singapore. Author: Wireless Internet Telecommunications; co-author: Wireless IP and Building the Mobile Internet; contbr. articles to profl. jours. including IEEE Transactions on Vehicular Tech., IEEE Jour. on Selected Areas in Comms., Internat. Jour. on Parallel and Distributed Sys. and Networks, IEEE Comms. Letters, IEEE Personal Comms. Mag., IEEE Comms. Mag. Pianist, leader small group bible studies Monmouth Chinese Christian Ch., NJ, 1999—2003. Fellowship, Stanford U. Sch. of Engring., 1992—93. Mem.: IEEE (sr.; vice-chair, NJ coast sect., comm. chpt. 2000—03, conf. tech. program com., session organizer, chair, tutorial tchr. 2001—, bd. dirs. Comsoc Sister Soc. 2004—), Sigma Xi, Phi Beta Kappa, Tau Beta Pi. Achievements include patents for Multicarrier personal access comms. sys. Address: B-09-3A Ken Condo Jalan SS 2/72 Petaling Jaya Selangor 47400 Malaysia

**WONG, LILIANE,** architect, educator; BA, Vassar Coll., 1981—81; MA, Harvard U., 1985. Registered arch. Assoc. Perry Dean Rogers & Ptnrs., Boston, 1985—94; prin. Mahon Wong Assocs., Cambridge, Mass., 1994—; assoc. prof. RISD, Providence, 1998—. Furniture line, Kore libr. furnishings line, 1995. Named Bulfinch Arch Competition winner, Hist. Neighborhood Found., 1987. Mem.: AIA, Boston Soc. Archs. (Women in Architecture award 1994, Women in Design aard 2002).

**WONG, MARGARET WAI,** lawyer; b. Hong Kong, July 27, 1950; d. Mien Lin and Kuan Kuo (Kwan) Hwang; m. Kam M. Chan, Jan. 3, 1983. AA, Ottumwa Heights Coll. (Iowa), 1971; BSc in Chemistry-Biology, Western Ill. U., 1973; JD, SUNY-Buffalo, 1976. Bar: Ohio 1977, N.Y. 1977, D.C. 1980, U.S. Dist. Ct. 1980, U.S. Ct. Appeals (6th cir.) 1983. Instr. bus. law SUNY-Fredonia, 1977; mgmt. trainee Cen. Nat. Bank, Cleve., 1977-78; chief legal and fin. officer Buffalo City Govt., 1979-80; assoc. Berger & Kirchenbaum, Cleve., 1980-81; prin. Margaret W. Wong & Assocs., Cleve., 1981—; co-founder, co-owner Pearl of the Orient Restaurant, Cleve., 1978—; co-founder, cons. Richmond Apothe-Care, Inc. Pharmcy, Cleve., 1982-95, Cleve. Apothe-Care, Inc. Pharmacy, 1986—. Contbr. articles to legal jours. Trustee, Women Space, Cleve., 1982—, Fedn. Community Planning, Cleve., 1983-84, Women City Club, Cleve., 1983—, Orgn. Chinese Ams., Cleve., 1983—, Cleve. Coun. Human Relations, 1983—; sec., trustee Chinese Assn. Greater Cleve., 1980—; bd. dirs. Greater Cleve. Growth Assn., Inter-Mus. Conservation Assn., Notre Dame Coll., Greater Cleve. Roundtable, NCCJ. Named one of Top Ten Outstanding Young Women, Glamour mag., 1983; YWCA Career Woman of Yr., 1984. Mem. ABA (vice chmn. immigration, naturalization and aliens sect. 1993-94), Fed. Bar Assn. (pres.-elect 1993, pres. 1994), N.Y. State Bar Assn., D.C. Bar Assn., Cuyahoga County Bar Assn., Cleve. Bar Assn., Ohio Bar Assn., Cleve. Trial Lawyers Assn., Am. Assn. Immigration Lawyers. Club: Zonta (trustee 1983-84) (Cleve.). Office: Margaret W Wong & Assoc 3150 Chester Ave Cleveland OH 44114 Office Phone: 216-566-9908. Business E-Mail: wong@imwong.com.

**WONG, MARTHA JEE,** state representative; b. Houston, Jan. 20, 1939; d. J.T. Jee and B.S. Joe. BS, U. Tex., 1960, M, 1977; EdD, U. Houston, 1983. Tchr. Houston Ind. Sch. Dist., 1973-76, prin., 1978-82, mgr. III, 1982-87; assoc. prof. Baylor U., Waco, Tex., 1987-88; dir. resource and community devel. Southwest Coll. HCCS, 1991-93; mem. Houston City Coun., 1994—2002, Ho. of Reps., Tex., 2003—. Cons. Tex. Ednl. Agency, Austin, 1983-86, SW Tech. Asst., Nacadoches, Tex., 1985-86; mem. state affairs com., Tex. Ho. of Reps., vice chair urban affairs com., rules & resolutions com. Contbr. articles to profl. jours. Bd. dirs Leadership Houston, 1985-88, Meyerland Improvement Assn., Houston, 1987-88; chair of bd. Vocat. Giudanmce Ctr.; founder Asian-Am. Coalition; vol. Ctr. Bd. Friends of Libr. Bd.; bd. mem. Orgn. of chinese Ams., Houston Chinese Lions, Am. Leadership Forum, Asia Soc., Houston Eye Bank, Greater Houston Women' Foun., Houston Mcpl. Employees Pension Bd. Named Outstanding Woman of the Yr. in Edn., YWCA, 1991. Mem. Tex. Council Women Sch. Execs. (chmn. career opportunities), Inst. for Chinese Culture and Language (bd. dirs.), Tex. Assn. Sch. Adminstrs., U. Houston Coll. Ednl. Alumni Assn. (bd. dirs.), Delta Kappa Gamma (v.p. 1985-87, scholar), Phi Delta Kappa, Phi Kappa Phi Honor Soc. Baptist. Office: Tex Ho of Reps PO Box 2910 Austin TX 78768

**WONG, NATHAN DONALD,** medicine and epidemiology researcher, educator; b. Downey, Calif., Apr. 18, 1961; s. Donald Wah and Mew Lun (Hee) W.; m. Mia K. Park, July 21, 1996; 1 child, David. BA, Pomona Coll., Claremont, Calif., 1983; MPH, Yale U., New Haven, Conn., 1985, PhD, 1987. Lectr. medicine Yale U., New Haven, 1987; asst. prof. U. Calif., Irvine, 1988—94, assoc. prof., 1994—2002, dir. preventive cardiology, dept. medicine, 1991—, prof., 2003—; prof. dept. epidemiology UCLA, 2003—. Prin. investigator Antihypertensive Lipid-Lowering to Prevent Heart Attack Trial and other lipid and cardiovasc. prevention trials, 1994—; co-prin. investigator Women's Health Initiative, 1995—; investigator NIH Mesa, Cardia studies; interviewed for various pub. and programs, including ABC Eyewitness News, L.A. Times, Orange County Register, CBS News, USA Today, N.Y. Times, others; profl. cons. Cedars-Sinai Med. Ctr., 2002—; editor-in-chief textbook Preventive Cardiology, Mcgraw-Hill, 2000, 2d edit, 2005 Mem. editl. bd.: Preventive Cardiology, Jour. Cardiovascular Drugs, Jour. Cardiovascular Risk, contbr. chapters to books, over 100 articles to profl. jours. Mem. Calif. Senate Hearing Panel on Youth Phys. Edn. and Fitness, 1991; chair Calif. Cardiovasc. Disease Prevention Coalition, 1998-99; spkr. numerous internat., nat. and local confs., hosps., and med. spkrs. burs. Rsch. grantee, Bristol Myers-Squibb, Pfizer. Fellow Am. Coll. Cardiology (membership and credentialing com. 2003—, prevention of cardiovasc. disease com. 2003-04, taskforce 4, 34th Bethesda Conf. 2003), Am. Heart Assn. Coun. on Epidemiology and Prevention. Achievements include research in computed tomography, metabolic syndrome, diabetes, lipids, hypertension, preventive cardiology, coronary and aortic calcium. Avocations: running, hiking, skiing, photography. Office: UCI Heart Disease Prevention Program C240 Medsci I Irvine CA 92697-0001 Office Phone: 949-824-5561. Fax: 949-824-5567. Business E-Mail: ndwong@uci.edu.

**WONG, OTTO,** epidemiologist; b. Canton, China, Nov. 14, 1947; came to U.S., 1967, naturalized, 1976; m. Betty Yeung, Feb. 14, 1970; children: Elaine, Jonathan. BS, U. Ariz., 1970; MS, Carnegie Mellon U., 1972, U. Pitts., 1973, ScD, 1975. Cert. epidemsiologist Am. Coll. Epidemiology, 1982. USPHS fellow U. Pitts., 1972-75; asst. prof. epidemiology Georgetown U. Med. Sch., 1975-78; mgr. epidemiology Equitable Environ. Health Inc., Rockville, Md., 1977-78; dir. epidemiology Tabershaw Occuopational Med. Assocs., Rockville, 1978-80; dir. occupational rsch. Biometric Rsch. Inst., Washington, 1980-81; exec. v.p., chief epidemiologist ENSR Health Scis., Alameda, Calif., 1981—; chief epidemiologist, pres. Applied Health Scis., San Mateo, Calif., 1991—. Adj. prof. epidemiology and biostats. Tulane U. Med. Ctr., New Orleans; vis. prof. epidemiology and occupl. health Nat. Def. Med. Ctr., Taipei, Taiwan, Shanghai Med. U.; adj. prof. dept. cmty. and family medicine Chinese U. Hong Kong; adj. prof. U. No. Tex. Med. Ctr.; hon. prof. cmty. medicine U. Hong Kong; cons. WHO, Nat. Cancer Inst., Nat. Inst. Occupl. Safety and Health, Occupl. Safety and Health Adminstrn., Nat. Heart, Lung and Blood Inst., Internat. Agy. for Rsch. on Cancer, U.S. EPA, Ford Motors Co., Gen. Electric, Mobil, Chevron, Union Carbide, Fairfax (Va.) Hosp., Agy. for Toxic Substances and Disease Registry, U. Ariz. scholar, 1967-68 Mem. editl. bd. The Annals of Epidemiology, Occupl. and Environ. Medicine.; contbr. articles to profl. jours. Fellow Am. Coll. Epidemiology,

Human Biology Council; mem. Am. Pub. Health Assn., Biometric Soc., Soc. Epidemiologic Rsch., Phi Beta Kappa, Pi Mu Epsilon. Republican. Office: Applied Health Scis PO Box 2078 181 2nd Ave Ste 628 San Mateo CA 94401-3812

**WONG, RAYMOND SHIU-LOONG,** radiologist; b. Hong Kong, Jan. 25, 1942; came to U.S., 1958; s. Jason Y. and Nancy L. (Tamm) W.; m. Jo-Lien Hsieh; 1 child, Florence W. BS in Chemistry, UCLA, 1962; MD, U. Chgo., 1966. Diplomate Am. Bd. Radiology with subspecialty in nuclear radiology, Am. Bd. Pediats. Diagnostic radiologist Hollywood Presbyn. Med. Ctr., L.A., 1981-94, Huntington Meml. Hosp., Pasadena, Calif., 1994—. Contbr. articles to profl. jours. Mem. Am. Coll. Radiology, Soc. Nuclear Medicine, Calif. Radiol. Soc., L.A. Radiol. Soc., Radiol. Soc. No. Calif. Office: Huntington Meml Hosp 100 W California Blvd Pasadena CA 91105-3097

**WONG, RICHARD,** music educator; b. Berkeley, Calif. s. Sun and Jik Wong. BA in Music, U. Calif., Berkeley, 1992; MA in Music, Calif. State U., Hayward, 1997. Cert. tchr. Calif. Music educator Am H.S., Fremont, Calif., 1995—. Elem. band dir., Fremont, Calif., 1996—. Musician: (concerts) Community Band. Named Staff Mem. of Month, Am. H.S., 2003; recipient Most Promising New Tchr. award, Fremont Unified Sch. Dist., 1995, Founder's Day award, Fremont Unified Sch. Dist. PTA, 2000; grantee, Fremont Edn. Found., 1999. Mem.: NEA, Internat. Soc. Music Edn., Calif. Music Educators Assn., Calif. Teachers Assn., Calif. Band Dirs. Assn., No. Calif. Band Assn., Internat. Assn. Jazz Educators, Nat. Assn. Music Edn., Am. Choral Dirs. Assn. (life). Avocation: reading. Office Phone: 510-796-1776.

**WONG, RONALD W.,** communications executive; BA in Polit. Sci., UCLA. Founding ptnr. Lang, Murakawa & Wong, 1994—97, dir., external comm., community relations svc. US Dept. of Justice, Washington, 1997; dep. polit. dir., gubernatorial campaign for Gray Davis, 1998; chief deputy appointments sec. to gov. Gray Davis Calif. Govt., 1998—2002; founder Imprenta Comm. Group, 2003; now pres., CEO Ronin Internat. Advisors. Mem. Pacific Council on Internat. Policy. Recipient Image award, Organization of Chinese Americans; grantee Sloan Found. Fellowship, U. Wash., Grad. Sch. of Public Affairs, Marshall Memorial Fellowship, Calif. Exec. Fellowship. Office: Imprenta Communications 400 Alhambra Rd San Gabriel CA 91775-2706

**WONG, STANTON D.,** lawyer; b. San Francisco, Nov. 4, 1957; AB, Univ. Calif., Berkeley, 1979, MBA, JD, Univ. Calif., Berkeley, 1983. Bar: Calif. 1983. Ptnr., ch-chmn. Securities practice Pillsbury Winthrop Shaw Pittman, San Francisco. Contbr. articles to profl. jours. Office: Pillsbury Winthrop Shaw Pittman 50 Fremont St San Francisco CA 94105 also: 2475 Hanover St Palo Alto CA 94304-1114 Office Phone: 415-983-1790. Office Fax: 415-983-1200. Business E-Mail: stanton.wong@pillsburylaw.com.

**WONG, STOVA,** law firm executive; Dir. networks and telecom. Paul, Hastings, Janofsky & Walker LLP; now chief info. officer. Named one of Premier 100 IT Leaders, Computerworld, 2005. Office: Paul Hastings Janofsky & Walker LLP 25th Fl 515 S Flower St Los Angeles CA 90071 Office Phone: 213-683-6000. Office Fax: 213-627-0705.*

**WONG, SUN YET,** engineer, consultant; b. Honolulu, Dec. 6, 1932; s. Chip Tong and Shiu Inn (Chang) W.; m. Janet Siu Hung Lau; children: Cathleen, Bryan, Jonathan. BS in Civil Engring. with honors, U. Hawaii, 1954; MS in Civil Engring., Yale U., 1955. Engr. N.Am. Aviation, Downey, Calif., 1955-58; mem. tech. staff Ramo Woolridge Space Tech. Labs., Redondo Beach, Calif., 1958-64; exec. v.p., treas., tech. dir. Mechanics Rsch. Inc., El Segundo, Calif., 1964-77; treas. System Devel. Corp., Santa Monica, Calif. 1977-79; chmn. bd., pres., treas. Applied Rsch. Inc., El Segundo, 1979-81; ind. cons. Rolling Hills Estates, Calif., 1981—. Cons. J.H. Wiggins Co., Redondo Beach, 1982—84, Intercon, Cerriots, Calif., 1982—84, Acurex, Mountain View, Calif., 1983, Applied Tech., Mountain View, Calif, 1983—85, Aston., Mountain View, 1983—85, Electromech. Sys. Inc., Anaheim, Calif., 1984, Measurement Analysis Corp., Torrance, Calif., 1984—96, MRJ, Fairfax, Va., 1984, Tompkins and Assocs., Torrance, 1984—2003, TRW, Redondo Beach, 1984, E Sys., Garland, 1986—93, Statis. Scis., Inc., Beverly Hills, Calif., 1986, Kodak Datatape, Pasadena, Calif., 1989, Odectics, Anaheim, 1990, Ampex, Redwood City, Calif., 1991, Swales & Assocs., Beltsville, Md., 1992—93, Hughes Space and Comms. Co., El Segundo, 1992, El Segundo, 94, El Segundo, 1996—2000, Lion Engring., Rancho Palos Verdes, Calif., 1994—2002, NASA Goddard, Greenbelt, Md., 1997, Boeing Space Sys., El Segundo, 2000—, Raytheon, El Segundo, 2000—02, Boeing Space and Intelligence, Seal Beach, 2003—, TriSept, Washington, 2003—. Recipient Intelligence Cmty. Seal medallion, U.S. Govt., 2001, Nat. Reconnaisance Office Dir.'s award, 2001, Tech. Excellence award, Boeing Co., 2002. Avocation: metal machining. Home and Office: 7 Club View Ln Rolling Hills Estates CA 90274 Office Phone: 310-534-4713. Personal E-mail: sywong@gte.net.

**WONG, SUZANNE CRAWBUCK,** librarian; b. Englewood, N.J., July 13, 1957; d. George Austin and Marion Elizabeth (Fournier) Crawbuck; m. Thomas Kay Wong, June 7, 1986; children: Jeremy Richard, Christina Elizabeth. BA in Humanities, St. Peter's Coll., Englewood Cliffs, N.J., 1980. Resources control clk. Ernst & Young (merged with Ernst & Whitney), N.Y.C., 1982-85, libr. asst., 1985—. Mem. Amateur Press Assns. (contbr. assn. jour. 1979-86) Democrat. Avocation: writing.

**WONG, THOMAS TANG YUM,** engineering educator; b. Hong Kong, July 27, 1952; arrived in U.S., 1976; s. Kwai Sun and Yee Yuen (Fung) W.; m. Mini-i Lee, June 9, 1984; children: Lillian Denise. BSc in Engring., U. Hong Kong 1975; MS Northwestern U., Evanston, Ill., 1978, PhD, 1981. Product engr. Motorola Semiconductor, Inc., Hong Kong, 1975-76; teaching asst. Northwestern U., 1976-78, rsch. asst., 1978-80, postdoctoral fellow, 1980-81; asst. prof. Ill. Inst. Tech., Chgo., 1981-86, assoc. prof., 1986-96, prof., 1996—, dir. grad. program dept. elec. engring., 1987-95, chmn. dept. elec. and computer engring., 2001—05; dir. rsch. and devel. Telecomm. Equipment Corp., Chgo., 1994—2001; chief sci. authority Quintech Electronics & Comms., Inc., Indiana, Pa., 1997-99. Cons. to pvt. industry, 1981—; chmn. Chicagoland Microwave Symposium, 1988. Author: Fundamentals of Distributed Amplification, 1993; contbr. articles to profl. jours.; book reviewer tech. publs.; Trustee Sch. Dist. 73.5, Ill., 1995—2001. GE fellow, 1983; rsch. grantee NASA, 1989-91, U.S. Dept. Energy, 1992—; pvt. industry, 1993—. Mem. IEEE (chmn. joint Chgo. chpt. Antenna Propagation and Microwave Theory Techniques Soc. 1987-88, mem. steering com. joint symposium Antennas Propagation Soc./Internat. Union of Radio Sci./Nuclear Electromagnetic Pulse 1992), AAUP, Am. Soc. Engring. Edn., Am. Phys. Soc., Tau Beta Pi, Eta Kappa Nu. Achievements include research and patents in the areas of microwave electronics and communications. Office: Ill Inst Tech Dept Elec/Computer Engring Chicago IL 60616 Business E-Mail: twong@ece.iit.edu.

**WONG, TIMOTHY C.,** language and literature educator; b. Hong Kong Jan. 24, 1941; came to U.S., 1951; s. Patrick J. and Rose (Poon) W.; m. Elizabeth Ann Steffens, Dec. 18, 1970; children: Sharon Elizabeth, Rachel Margaret, Laura Katherine. BA, St. Mary's Coll., Moraga, Calif., 1963; MA, U. Hawaii, 1968; PhD, Stanford U., 1975. Vol. U.S. Peace Corps, Thailand, 1963-65; asst. prof. Ariz. State U., Tempe, 1974-79, assoc. prof., 1979-85; resident dir. Coun. on Internat. Ednl. Exchange Peking Univ., China, 1984-85; assoc. prof. Ohio State U., Columbus, 1985-95; prof. Ariz. State U., Tempe, 1995—, dir. Ctr. for Asian Studies, 1995—2002, grad. dir. Asian langs. and civilizations program, 2002—. Author: Wu Ching-tzu, 1978, Stories for Saturday: Twentieth-Century Chinese Popular Fiction, 2003. Mem. Chinese Lang. Tchrs. Assn., Assn. Asian Studies, Am. Oriental Soc. (dir.-at-large 1996-2000, v.p. western br. 2000-01, pres. 2001-03). Democrat. Roman Catholic. Office: Ariz State U Dept Langs and Lits Tempe AZ 85287-0202 E-mail: timothy.wong@asu.edu.

**WONG, WAI HING,** marine biologist, researcher; b. Zibo, China; arrived in U.S., 2000; s. Naizhong Wang and Cuiying Chen; m. Ting Sun, Dec. 16, 1998. BS, Ocean U. Qingdao, China, 1993; MS, Ocean U. Qingdao, 1996; PhD, City U. Hong Kong, 2001. Rsch. asst. City U. Hong Kong, 1996—97; postdoctoral rsch. assoc. SUNY, Stony Brook, 2000—02, La. U. Marine Consortium, Chauvin, 2003—05, La. State U. Aquaculture Rsch. Sta., Baton Rouge, 2005—. Mem.: Marine Biol. Assn. Hong Kong, Nat. Shellfisheries Assn., Estuarine Rsch. Fedn. Achievements include discovery of evolutionary traits in digestive investments and feeding morphology of green mussels in different environments; demonstration of top-down control of bivalves on phytoplankton community with fatty acid analysis; elucidation of the selective feeding behavior of green mussels Perna viridis; discovery of the benthozooplankton loop (BZ loop) in the zebra mussel Dreissena polymorpha. Avocations: basketball, soccer, running. Office: La State U Aquaculture Rsch Sta 2410 Ben Hur Rd Baton Rouge LA 70820 Office Phone: 225-765-2848. Office Fax: 225-765-2877. Business E-Mail: wong@lsu.edu.

**WONG, WALLACE,** real estate investor; b. Honolulu, July 13, 1941; s. Jack Yung Hung and Theresa (Goo) W.; m. Amy Ju, June 17, 1963; children: Chris, Bradley, Jeffery. Student, UCLA, 1960-63. Chmn., pres. South Bay Coll., Hawthorne, Calif., 1985-86; chmn. Santa Barbara (Calif.) Bus. Coll., 1975—; gen. ptnr. W B Co., Redondo Beach, Calif., 1982—; CEO Pacific Am. Group, Rancho Santa Margarita, 1991-96; chmn., CEO Alpine, Inc., Rancho Santa Margarita, Calif., 1993-96; pres. Bayside Properties, Laguna Beach, Calif., 1993—, San Juan Capistrano, Calif., 1993—. Bd. dirs. Metrobank, L.A. FFF Enterprises; chmn. bd. 1st Ind. Fin. Group., San Juan Capistrano, 1994—. Acting sec. of state State of Calif., Sacramento, 1982; founding mem. Opera Pacific, Orange County, Calif., 1985; mem. Hist. and Cultural Found., Orange County, 1986; v.p. Orange County Chinese Cultural Club, Orange County, 1985. Named for Spirit of Enterprise Resolution, Hist. & Cultural Found., Orange Country, 1987; recipient resolution City of Hawthorne, 1973. Mem. Westren Accred Schs. & Colls. (v.p. 1978-79), Magic Castle (life), Singapore Club. Avocations: travel, skiing. Address: 884 Molokua Dr Kailua HI 96734 Business E-Mail: wwong1025@hawaii.rr.com.

**WONG, WING-YEN,** hematologist, educator; b. Malaysia; BA, Occidental Coll., L.A., 1979; MD, U. So. Calif., 1983. Intern U. So. Calif. Med. Sch., LA, 1979—83, resident, 1983—86, 1987, fellowship, 1987—91; dir., hemostasis and thrombosis Childrens Hosp. L.A., 2001—; assoc. prof. pediat. U. So. Calif., 2001—. Editl. bd. Haemophilia Forum, 2001—; jour. reviewer Jour. Pediatric Hematology-Oncology, Haemophilia, Lancet; adv. task force on pediatric hemostasis Nat. Hemophilia Found., 2002; med. dir. Hemophilia Found. So. Calif., 2002; mem. various rev. and study coms.; adv. com. blood safety and availability Sec. HHS, Washington, 2003—; expert in field. Contbr. articles to profl. jours., chapters to books. Physician Hemophilia Camp, 1997—. Mem.: Internat. Soc. Thrombosis and Haemostasis, World Fedn. Hemophilia, Am. Assn. Blood Banks, Hemophilia Rsch. Soc., Am. Soc. Hematology, Am. Acad. Pediat., Soc. Pediatric Rsch., Women Faculty Health Sci. Assn., We. Soc. Pediatric Rsch., L.A. Pediatric Soc., U. So. Calif. Salerni Collegium Alumni Assn. (bd. dirs. 1997—). Home: 631 Laurel Lane Monrovia CA 91016 Office: Childrens Hosp LA 4650 Sunset Blvd MS 54 Los Angeles CA 90027 Office Phone: 323-669-4141. Business E-Mail: wwong@chla.usc.edu.

**WONG, YANYI LIU,** physicist, researcher; arrived in US, 1998, naturalized, 2004; s. Mingpai Wong and Lilun Liu. BSEE, U. Md., Coll. Pk., 2001, MSEE, student, U. Md., Coll. Pk., 2004—. Tchg. asst. microelectronics U. Md., 2001—03; assoc. staff, applied physics lab. Johns Hopkins U., Laurel, Md., 2003—. Contbr. articles to profl. jours. Mem.: IEEE (finalist Best Paper award 2005). Buddhist. Office: Univ Maryland 2160 AV Williams Bldg College Park MD 20742 Office Phone: 240-899-0509. Business E-Mail: yanyi.wong@ieee.org.

**WONG, YAU-SUN,** music educator, conductor, composer; b. Hong Kong, Feb. 22, 1953; arrived in U.S. citizen, 1985; s. Man-Sun Wong and Shing King Mo; m. Ruth Ann Joslin, Nov. 24, 1979; children: Art, Allan. BA, Hong Kong Bapt. Coll., 1978; MusM, U. Tex., 1982; MusD, Fla. State U., 1993. Dir. ch. music divsn. Hong Kong Bapt. Theol. Sem., 1993—2000, assoc. prof., 1987—93, Union U., Jackson, Tenn., 2000; chair music dept. Bluefield Coll., Va., 2000—01; band dir. Ctrl. Bapt. Coll., Conway, Ark., 2001—02; condr. concert orch. Vanguard U., Costa Mesa, Calif., 2002—04; dir. chorale, band and orch. N.Mex. Jr. Coll., Hobbs, 2004—. Founder, dir. Costa Mesa Symphony, 2002—. Composer: Symphony No. 1, 1993. Composer grantee, Atlanta George Found., 1993. Mem.: Composers and Authors Soc. Hong Kong Ltd. Office: NMex Jr Coll 5317 Lovington Hwy Hobbs NM 88240 Office Phone: 505-392-4510. Business E-Mail: yswong@sluggy.net.

**WONG, Y(ING) WOOD,** real estate investment company executive, real estate development company executive, venture capital investment company executive; b. Hong Kong, Apr. 28, 1950; came to U.S., 1969; s. Loyee K.H. and Margaret M.C.L. Wong; m. Leslie K.P. Chan, Dec. 18, 1977; children: Joshua H., Jonathan H. AA in Biology, Menlo Coll., Atherton, Calif., 1971, BS in Bus. Adminstrn., 1974; BA in Zoology, U. Calif., Berkeley, 1972; MBA, Northwestern U., Evanston, Ill., 1976. Auditor Touche Ross & Co., CPAs, San Francisco, 1976-78; founder, mng. dir. Wong Properties, Palo Alto, Calif., 1976—; founder, venture capital ptnr. Wongfratris Investment Co., Palo Alto, 1986—; founder, ptnr. Corona Main Devel., L.L.C., Palo Alto, 2003—. Instr. Golden Gate U., 1977. Trustee Crystal Springs Uplands Sch., Hillsborough, Calif., 1993-98; advisor The Pei Ying Mid. Sch., Guangzhou, China, The Pui Ying Christian Svcs. Inc., Vancouver, Can.; bd. dirs. Peninsula Symphony, Los Altos, Calif., 2002-03. Named Hon. Citizen of Taishan City, China; established Wood Wong Fgn. Students Exch. Grant, Menlo Coll., 1997—; established Margaret Wong Meml. Music award endowment, Taishan (China) Pei Ying Mid. Sch., 2004—. Mem. Internat. Platform Assn., Commonwealth Club Calif., Beta Alpha Psi. Office: 51 Jordan Pl Palo Alto CA 94303-2903 E-mail: wood.wong@wongfratris.com.

**WONG-DIAZ, FRANCISCO RAIMUNDO,** lawyer, educator; b. Havana, Cuba, Oct. 29, 1944; came to U.S., 1961; s. Juan and Teresa (Diaz de Villegas) Wong; 1 child, Richard Alan. BA with honors, No. Mich. U., 1965; MA with highest honors, U. Detroit, 1967; PhD, MA, U. Mich., 1974; JD, U. Calif., Berkeley, 1976. Bar: Calif. 1980, U.S. Dist. Ct. (no. dist.) Calif. 1990, Fla. 1987. Prof. City Coll. San Francisco, 1975—, dept. chmn., 1978-85; rsch. atty. Marin Superior Ct., 1980-81; ct. arbitrator Marin Mcpl. Ct., 1985; atty. pvt. practice, Kentfield, Calif., 1980—. Adj. asst. prof. San Francisco State U., 1977; assoc. dean Miami-Dade Coll., 1986; dir. Cutcliffe Cons., Inc., Hawthorne, LaFamila Ctr., Inc., San Rafael, Calif., 1980-85, Small Bus. Inst., Kentfield, 1982-86; cons. ICC Internat., San Francisco, 1980-82; polit. commentator Univision KDTV, 1980—; bd. dirs. Pedro Pan Group, Inc.; prostate cancer devel. rsch. com. U. Calif. San Francisco Cancer Ctr. Author: American Politics in a Changing World, 1999, 2d edit., 2004; bd. editors Indsl. Rels. Law Jour., 1975-76; mem. editl. bd. Calif. Lawyer, 1991-93. Lector St. Sebastian's Ch., 1984—, parish coun., 1995; bd. dir. Am. Cancer Soc., 1999—; mem. devel. rsch. program, fellowship com. U. Calif.-San Francisco, 2002—; mem. adv. bd. Redes en Accion, 2002—; mem. Com. on the Present Danger; mem. World Assn. Internat. Studies. Vis. scholar U. Calif., Berkeley Sch. Bus., 1983-84, U.S. Dept. State scholar, Washington, 1976; Horace C. Rackham fellow U. Mich., 1970, summer fellow U. Calif. Berkeley, 1995, Nat. Security Law Ctr. U. Va., 1996; recipient Patient Courage award, ACS, 2004; named Best New Vol. of Yr., Am. Cancer Soc., 2000, One of One Hundred Most Influential Hispanics in the Nation, Hispanic Bus. Mag., Oct. 2000. Mem. ABA, Am. Polit. Sci. assn., Latino Ednl. Assn. (co-founder, treas. 1985), Cuban Am. Nat. Coun., World Affairs Coun. (sem. leader San Francisco 1980) World Assn. Internat. Studies, U. Calif. San Francisco PAC Advocates, Commonwealth Club. Roman Catholic. Office Phone: 415-239-3000. Business E-Mail: fwong@ccsf.edu.

**WONHAM, WALTER MURRAY,** electrical engineer, educator; b. Montreal, Que., Can., Nov. 1, 1934; m. Vera Anne Hale; children: Marjorie Jane, Cynthia Margaret. B of Engring., McGill U., Montreal, 1956; PhD, U.

Cambridge, Eng., 1961. Asst. prof. elec. engring. Purdue U., Lafayette, Ind., 1961-62; rsch. scientist Rsch. Inst. for Advanced Studies, Balt., 1962-64; assoc. prof. Brown U., Providence, 1964-69; rsch. assoc. NASA, Cambridge, Mass., 1967-69, cons., 1969; prof. elec. engring. U. Toronto, Ont., Canada, 1970—, J. Roy Cockburn prof., 1991-96, Cockburn chair, 1991, univ. prof., 1996—2000, univ. prof. emeritus, 2000—. Author: Linear Multivariable Control: A Geometric Approach, 1974, 3d edit., 1985 (Russian transl. 1980, Chinese transl. 1984); assoc. editor Soc. for Indsl. and Applied Math., Jour. on Control and Optimization, 1965-79, Sys. Control Letter, 1981-85. Recipient Brouwer medal Netherlands Math Soc., 1990; Athlone fellow, Gt. Britain, 1956-58; spl. scholar Nat. Rsch. Coun. Can., 1958-60; sr. postdoctoral resident rsch. assoc. NAS USA, 1967-69. Fellow IEEE (life, Control Sys. Sci. and Engring. award 1987), Royal Soc. Can.; mem. U.S. NAE (fgn. assoc.). Office: U Toronto Dept Elec Engring 35 St George St Toronto ON Canada M5S 3G4 Personal E-Mail: wonham@control.utoronto.ca.

**WONNACOTT, PAUL,** retired economics professor; b. London, Ont., Can., Mar. 16, 1933; s. Gordon Elliott and Muriel Johnston Wonnacott; m. Donna Elizabeth Cochrane, July 2, 1960; children: David, Ann, Alan, Bruce. BA, U. Western Ont., 1955; MA, Princeton U., 1957, PhD, 1959. Instr., asst. prof. econs. Columbia U., N.Y.C., 1958-62; assoc. prof. then prof. econs. U. Md., College Park, 1962-91, prof. emeritus, 1992; ret., 2000. Mem. Pres.'s Coun. Econ. Advisers, 1991-93; Alan Holmes prof. econs. Middlebury Coll., 1994-2000; rsch. staff Royal Commn. Banking and Fin., Toronto, 1962; sr. staff economist Coun. Econ. Advisers, Washington, 1968-70; assoc. dir. divsn. internat. fin. Fed. Res. Bd., Washington, 1974-75; vis. scholar Office Internat. Monetary Rsch., U.S. Treasury, 1980; econ. adviser to Under Sec. of State, 1990-91. Author: The Canadian Dollar, 1960, 2d rev. edit., 1965, (with R.J. Wonnacott) Free Trade between the United States and Canada: The Potential Economic Effects, 1967, (with H.G. Johnson and H. Shibata) Harmonization of National Economic Policies under Free Trade, 1968, Macroeconomics, 1974, 3d rev. edit., 1984, (with R.J. Wonnacott) Economics, 1979, 4th rev. edit. 1990, Spanish edit., 1981, 3d rev. edit., 1987, (with Y. and C. Crusius) Portuguese edit., 1982, 2d rev. edit., 1985, (with A. Blomquist) Can. edit., 1983, 4th rev. edit., 1994, Lithuanian edit., 1998, The United States and Canada: The Quest for Free Trade, 1987; contbr. articles to profl. jours. Fellow Brooking Inst., 1957-58, Ford Found., 1963-64; vis. fellow Inst. Internat. Econs., 1986, 93-94. Home: 10100 Bevern Ln Potomac MD 20854 E-mail: paulwon@wam.umd.edu.

**WONNACOTT, RONALD JOHNSTON,** economics professor; b. London, Ont., Can., Sept. 11, 1930; s. Gordon and and Muriel (Johnston) W.; m. Eloise Howlett, Sept. 11, 1954; children: Douglas, Robert, Cathy Anne. BA, U. We. Ont., 1955; AM, Harvard U., 1957, PhD, 1959. Mem. faculty U. We. Ont., London, 1958—96, prof. econs., 1964—96, chmn. dept., 1969—72, prof. emeritus, 1996—. Vis. assoc. prof. U. Minn., Mpls., 1961-62; cons. Resources for the Future, Econ. Council Can., Can.-Am. Com., Nat. Planning Assn., C.D. Howe Inst. Author: Canadian-American Dependence: An Interindustry Analysis of Production and Prices, 1961, Canada's Trade Options, 1975, Selected New Developments in International Trade Theory, 1984, The Economics of Overlapping Free Trade Areas and the Mexican Challenge, 1991, (with G.L. Reuber) The Cost of Capital in Canada, 1961, (with Paul Wonnacott) Free Trade Between the U.S. and Canada, 1967, Economics, 1979, 4th edit., 1990, (with Thomas H. Wonnacott) Introductory Statistics, 1969, 5th edit., 1990, Econometrics, 1970, 2d edit., 1979, Regression, 1981 Fellow Royal Soc. Can.; mem. Am. Econ. Assn., Can. Econ. Assn. (pres. 1981), London Hunt Club, Sunningdale Golf Club (Eng.), Hon. Co. Edinburgh Golfers, Craigleith Ski Club. Home: 171 Wychwood Pk London ON Canada N6G 1S1 Office Phone: 519-661-3500. Personal E-mail: wonnacot@uwo.ca.

**WONNER, PAUL JOHN,** painter; b. Tucson, Apr. 24, 1920; Student, Calif. Coll. Arts and Crafts; MA, MLS, U. Calif., Berkeley, 1953. Instr. painting UCLA, 1963-64, Otis Art Inst., 1966-68, Coll. Creative Studies, Santa Barbara, Calif., 1968-71, U. Calif., Davis, 1975-76, U. Calif., Long Beach, 1981. Represented in permanent collections Guggenheim Mus., N.Y.C., San Francisco Mus. Art, Nat. Collection Fine Arts, Smithsonian Inst., Oakland Mus., Joseph H. Hirshhorn Found., Boston Mus. Fine Arts, Charles A. Wustum Mus. Fine Art, Mpls. Inst. Art; one-man shows include San Francisco Art Assn. Gallery, Los Angeles, 1956, Whitney Mus. Am. Art, N.Y.C., 1959, Art Inst. of Chgo., 1961, 64, U. Ill., 1961, 63-65, Mus. Modern Art, N.Y.C., 1962, Waddington Galleries, London, 1965, Poindexter Gallery, N.Y.C., 1971, Charles Campbell Gallery, San Francisco, 1974, Calif. State U., Long Beach, 1975, 81, James Corcoran Gallery, Los Angeles, 1979, Los Angeles Munic Art Mus., 1982, John Berggruen, San Francisco, 1985-86, DC Moore Gallery, NYC, 1998, 99. Office: 403 Main St # 709 San Francisco CA 94105-2067 Address: John Berggruen Gallery 228 Grant St San Francisco CA 94108

**WOO, ALEX,** jewelry designer; BA, Cornell Univ. Owner and designer Alex Woo Jewelry, NYC, 1999—. Named NY's Rising Star, Crain's Bus. 40 Under 40, 2005, Rising Star, JCK Show, Design Ctr., 2006; named to Elite Women, Hispanic Bus. Mag., 2005; recipient Design Award, Women's Jewelry Assn., 1998. Office: Alex Woo Inc 70 Bowery Ste 208 New York NY 10013 Office Phone: 212-226-1352. Office Fax: 212-226-5533.*

**WOO, BENSON,** financial executive; BSEE, MIT; MBA, Harvard U. Various positions GM, 1979-94; v.p., treas. Case Corp., 1994-98; corp. v.p., CFO, York Internat. Corp., 1998—99; sr. v.p. Metris Cos., Inc., Minnetonka, Minn., 1999—2003; CFO TriMas Corp., Bloomfield Hills, Minn., 2003—.

**WOO, CAROLYN YAUYAN,** dean; b. Hong Kong, Apr. 19, 1954; arrived in US, 1972; m. David Bartkus; children: Ryan, Justin. BS in economics, Purdue U., 1975, MS in indsl. adminstrn., 1976, PhD in strategic mgmt., 1979. Asst. prof. mgmt. Purdue U., 1981—85, assoc. to full prof., 1985—93, assoc. exec. v.p. acad. affairs, 1995—97; dir. profl. master's programs Purdue U. Krannert Sch. Mgmt., 1993—95; Martin J. Gillen dean Mendoza Sch. Bus., Notre Dame U., 1997—, Ray and Milann Siegfried chair entrepreneurial studies, 1997—. Bd. dirs. Aon Corp., 1999—, Nisource Industries Inc., 1998—, Circuit City Stores Inc., 2001—. Bd. dirs. Catholic Relief Services, 2004—; bd. regents U. Portland, 2004—. Recipient TIEM Found. Disting. Scholar award, Internat. Coun. Small Bus., 1987, Excellence award for edn., Asian Am. Alliance, 2002, John S. Day alumni academic svc. award, Krannert Sch. Mgmt., Purdue U., 2003. Mem.: Com. of 100, Assn. to Advance Collegiate Schools Bus. Internat. (bd. dirs. 1999—, vice chair 2002—03, chair 2000-04). Office: Notre Dame Univ 204 Mendoza Coll Bus Notre Dame IN 46556-5646 Office Phone: 574-631-7992. Business E-Mail: Carolyn.Y.Woo.5@nd.edu.*

**WOO, DEREK,** electrical engineer, computer engineer; b. Sarnia, Ont., Can., Oct. 19, 1969; s. Charles and Shirley Woo; m. Yvonne Fennema, Mar. 9, 1996; children: Gabriel, Julian. BScEE, U. Western Ont., London, 1991. Design engr. Ont. Power Generation (Ont. Hydro), Toronto, 1989—93; cons. Siemens AG, Toronto, 1993—94, Accenture (formerly Andersen Consulting), Toronto, NYC, Chgo., 1994—96; pres. Eidetic Sys. Inc., NYC, 1996—; v.p., firmwide tech. Goldman, Sachs & Co., NYC, 2004—; Grantee, Govt. of China, 1987; scholar, Imperial Oil (Esso), 1987—91. Mem.: IEEE, IEEE Stds. Assn.

**WOO, JOHN See WU, YUSEN**

**WOO, KENNETH ROGER,** urologist; b. LA, July 27, 1969; s. Roger and Julie Woo; m. Christine H. Sohn, May 16, 1998. BS in Molecular Biology magna cum laude, UCLA, 1992; MD with distinction, Mt. Sinai Sch. Medicine, 1996. Resident urology NYU Med. Ctr., 1996—2002. Contbr. articles to profl. jours. Grantee Yamanouchi USA Rsch., 1999. Mem.: AMA, Endurol. Soc., Am. Assn. Clin. Urologists, Am. Urol. Assn., Golden Key, Phi Beta Kappa. Avocations: tennis, hiking. Office Phone: 410-879-4879. Personal E-mail: kennethwoo@comcast.net.

**WOO, S. B. (SHIEN-BIAU WOO),** retired state official, physicist, educator; b. Shanghai, Aug. 13, 1937; came to U.S., 1955; s. C.K. and Kuo-Ying (Chang) W.; m. Katy K.N. Wu, July 20, 1963; children: Chih-I, Chih-Lan. BS in Physics and Math. summa cum laude, Georgetown Coll., Ky., 1956; MS in Physics, Washington U., St. Louis, 1962, PhD in Physics, 1964. Prof. physics U. Del., Newark, 1966—2002; lt. gov. State of Del., Dover, 1985-89. Pres. Del. State Senate; chmn. Bd. Pardons; cons. E.I. DuPont Co., Wilmington, Del., 1968, Del. State Coll., Dover, 1980—81; steering com. 80-20 initiative, 1998—2001; pres. 80-20 PAC, 2001—, 80-20 Ednl. Found., 2005. Contbr. articles to profl. jours. Chmn. bd., chief exec. officer Chinese Am. Community Ctr., Hockessin, Del., 1982-83; sec. Asian-Am. caucus Democratic Nat. Conv., 1983-84; pres., co-chmn. Gov.'s Internat. Trade Council, 1985-89; chmn. Gov.'s task force on High Tech., 1985-89. Recipient Highest Achievement award Asian Am. High Tech. Conv., 1985; Army Rsch. grantee, 1972-87, NSF grantee, 1978-81; Inst. fellow Kennedy Sch., Harvard U. Mem. Am. Phys. Soc., AAAS, AAUP (exec. com. nat. council 1974-77), Orgn. Chinese Ams. (bd. dirs. 1977-79, nat. pres. 1990-91), Sigma Xi. Independent. Home: 5 Farm House Rd Newark DE 19711-7458 Office Phone: 866-367-8020. Business E-Mail: sbw@udel.edu.

**WOO, SAVIO LAU-YUEN,** bioengineering educator; b. Shanghai, June 3, 1942; naturalized; s. Kwok Chong and Fung Sing Woo; m. Patricia Tak-kit Cheong, Sept. 6, 1969; children: Kirstin Wei-Chi, Jonathan I-Huei. BSME, Chico State U., 1965; MS, U. Wash., 1966, PhD, 1971; DSc (hon.), Calif. State U., 1998. Rsch. assoc. U. Wash., Seattle, 1965—70; asst. research prof. U. Calif.-San Diego, La Jolla, 1970—74, assoc. rsch. prof., 1974—75, assoc. prof., 1975—80, prof. surgery and bioengring., 1980—90; vice chmn. for rsch., dir. Musculoskeletal Rsch. Ctr., U. Pitts., 1990—; prof. ortho surgery U. Pitts., 1990—93, prof. mech. engring., 1990—, Albert B. Ferguson Jr. prof. orthopaedic surgery, 1993—2004, prof. civil and environ. engring., 1994—2000, prof. rehab. sci. and tech., 1994—, W.K. Whiteford prof. bioengring., 1998—, Carnegie centenary prof., 2002—. Prin. investigator VA Med. Ctr., San Diego, 1972—90, Pitts., 1990—; cons. bioengr. Children's Hosp., San Diego, 1973—80; cons. med. implant cos., 1978—85; vis. prof. biomechanics Kobe (Japan) U., 1981—82; dir., CEO M&D Coutts Inst. for Joint Reconstrn. and Rsch., 1984—90; sci. adv. com. Whitaker Found., 1986—95, Steadman-Hawkins Sports Medicine Found., 1990—, Aircast Found., 1998—2004, OsteoArthritis Scis. Inc., 1992—95; adv. bd. Coll. Engring., Computer Sci. and Tech. Calif. State U., Chico, 1994—; adv. com. coord. grad. program in biomed. engring. U. Edmunton, U. Calgary, 1997—; bioengring. adv. com. Nat. Health Rsch. Inst., Taiwan, 1996—; biomed. engr. dept. adv. bd. Wayne State U., 1996—; bioengring. dept. adv. bd. Med. Coll. Ohio, 2004—. Assoc. editor Jour. Biomech. Engring., 1979—87, Jour. Biomechanics, 1978—, Jour. Orthopedic Rsch., 1983—92, Materials Sci. Reports, 1990—97, Proc. Inst. Mech. Engrs. (Part H), 1990—94, mem. internat. adv. bd. Knee Surgery, Sports Tramuatology, Arthroscopy, 1993—, mem. editl. bd. Jour. Ortho. Sci., 1995—, Jour. Ortho. Surgery, 1998—, Jour. Musculoskeletal Rsch., 1998—, Am. Jour. Sports Medicine, 1995, Am. Acad. Ortho. Surgery, 1995—, Healthcare Eng., 1999—, Tech. and Health Care, 2000—, Jour. Mechanics in Medicine and Biology, 2001—, Frontiers in Bioscience Jour., 2001—, Internat. Jour. on Bioengineering, 2001—, Acta Clinica, 2002—, Jour. Biomed. Engring., 2006—. Recipient Elizabeth Winston Lanier Kappa Delta award, 1983, 1986, awards for excellence in basic sci. rsch., Orthopaedic Rsch. Soc. and Am. Acad. Orthopaedic Surgeons, 1983, 1986, 1990, 1994, 2002, O'Donoghue award, Am. Orthopaedic Soc. Sports Medicine, 1990, 1997, Wartenweiler Meml. Lectureship, 1987, Citation award, Am. Coll. Sports Medicine, 1988, Rsch. Career Devel. award, NIH, 1977—82, Muybridge medal, Internat. Soc. Internat. Biomechanics, 1995, GOTS-Beiersdorf AG Res. award, 1996, Olympic Gold Medalist and prize, 1998, Cabaud Meml. award, AOSSM, 1999, Albert Trillat Young Inventors award, ISAKOS, 1999, Chancellor's Disting. Res. award, U. Pitts., 1999. Fellow: ASME (mem. exec. com. 1984—89, chmn. bioengineering divsn. 1986—87, sec., chmn. biomechanics com., chmn. honors com. bioengring. divsn., H.R. Lissner award 1991, Robert Henry Thurston award 2005), Japan Soc. Promotion Sci., Biomed. Engring. Soc. (bd. dirs. 1984—86, 2004—, Disting. Lectr. 2005), Am. Inst. Med. and Biol. Engring. (chmn. coll. fellows 1992—94, bd. dirs. 1992—94, founding); mem.; NAS, NAE, U.S. Nat. Commn. Biomechanics (chmn. 1994—97, exec. com. 1998—), European Orthopedic Rsch. Soc., Chinese Speaking Ortho Soc. (chmn. edn. com. 1997—, bd. dirs. 1997—), Internat. Soc. Fractures Repair (bd. dirs. 1986—94, v.p. 1987—90, pres. 1990—92), Am. Soc. Biomechanics (bd. dirs. 1977—87, pres. 1985—86, Giovanni Borelli award 1993), We. Orthopaedic Assn. (hon.), Can. Orthopedic Rsch Soc. (hon.), Orthopaedic Rsch. Soc. (chmn. program com. 1983—84, bd. dirs. 1983—87, pres. 1985—86), Am. Acad. Orthopedic Surgeons, World Coun. for Biomechanics (chmn. 1998—), Internat. Olympic Com. Olympic Acad. of Scis., Acad. Sinica, Inst. Medicine (chmn. sect. I 1996—98).

**WOOD, ANDRÉE ROBITAILLE,** archaeologist, researcher; b. Chgo., Feb. 10, 1929; d. Andrew George and Alice Marie (Fortier) Robitaille; m. Richard Lawrence Wood, Jan. 14, 1956; children: Mary Wood Molo, Matthew William Wood, Melissa Irene Wood, Elizabeth Wood Wesel, John Andrew Wood. BA, No. Ill. Univ., DeKalb, 1977, MA, 1982. Freelance archaeologist, 1981—84; rsch. asst. Prehistoric Project Oriental Inst., Univ. Chgo., Ill., 1984—98. Rsch., discovery, removal, analysis and identification of ancient blood residues on lithic material excavated at ten millenium old site, Çayönü in Ergani, Turkey. Contbr. articles to profl. jours. Avocations: poetry, boating, tennis. Home: 356 Old Sutton Rd Barrington IL 60010-9113 also: 8735 Midnight Pass Rd Apt 604B Sarasota FL 34242-2892

**WOOD, BENTON,** retired minister, priest; b. Arlington, Mass., Aug. 14, 1927; s. Edward E. Wood, Jr. and Dorothy Benton Wood; m. Joan Spodnyak Wood, Sept. 4, 1954; 1 child, John Benton. BS, Northwestern U., Evanston, IL, 1951; MS, State U. NY, Albany, NY, 1952; Religious Edn. Degree, Geneva Theol. Coll., Byfield, MA, 1974, Dr. (hon.) Humane Letters, 1979. Ordained Anglican Priest Diocese Albany, NY, 1957. Counsellor Camp Pasquaney, E. Hebron, NH, 1944—64; chaplain Northwood Sch., Lake Placid, NY, 1954—57, history dept. head, 1954—57; chaplain Trinity-Pawling Sch., Pawling, NY, 1958—62; dir. of studies, summer sch. St. Andrew's Sch., Boca Raton, Fla., 1962—65; headmaster York Sch., Monterey, Calif., 1965—67; academic dean Trinity Prepatory Sch., Winter Park, Fla., 1967—74; rector Ch. Annunciation, Anna Maria Island, Fla., 1975—88. Dir. St. Alban's Stamp Mission, Parrish, Fla., 1974—2001; editor Northwestern U. Alumni newsletter, Sarasota, Fla., 1990—2001; chaplain Baker St. Irregulars, 1980—. Author: (reference) Philatelic & Numismatic Holmes. Chaplain Anna Maria Fire Dept., Anna Maria Island, Fla., 1978—88. Pvt. U.S. Army, 1945—46. Recipient Two Shilling award, Baker St. Irregulars, 1997. Fellow: Am. Geog. Soc. Avocations: philatelist, sherlockian. Home: 9840 Sucia Circle Parrish FL 34219 Personal E-Mail: bwscannu51@aol.com.

**WOOD, BERENICE HOWLAND,** retired secondary school educator; b. Newport, R.I., Oct. 21, 1910; d. Horatio Gates and Margaret Lorraine (Doyle) W. AB, Vassar Coll., 1934; MA, Columbia U., 1936; postgrad., U. R.I., 1961-65. Clk. 1st Dist. Ct. R.I., Newport, 1942-50; home service dir. ARC, Newport, 1950-61; tchr. Cranston, R.I., 1961-62, Elmhurst Sch., Portsmouth, R.I., 1962-64, Newport, 1964-82. Sec. to mayor City of Newport, 1941. Pres. Coun. Social Agys., Newport, 1955—57; active Hist. Soc. Newport, Art Mus. Newport, Redwood Libr., Newport, Preservation Soc., Newport, Hill Assn., Newport. Mem. Point Assn. Newport, Nat. Trust Hist. Preservation. Roman Catholic. Avocations: maintaining and preserving antiquities, foreign travel. Home: 82 Mill St Newport RI 02840-3146

**WOOD, BETTY JEAN,** conceptual artist, art educator; b. Pitts., Ind., Mar. 2, 1942; d. Ralph Alphas and Mary Cordis Blanton; m. John E. Ayers, Aug. 25, 1963 (div. May 1987); children: Mark Ayers, Kristin Ayers Torres; m. Frederick Harrison Wood, Jr., Nov. 28, 1987 (dec. Jan. 2002); children: Andrew, Christopher. BA with honors, Pa. State U., 1984; MFA, U. Okla., 1992. Artist-in-residence Okla. Arts Coun., 1993—2003, Costa Rica; asst. instr. Okla. Arts Inst., Okla. State U., Stillwater, 1998; guest lectr. Southwestern State U., Weatherford, Okla., 2001; instr. Oklahoma City Mus. of Art.,

2002—; guest lectr. Goddard Art Ctr., Ardmore, Okla., 2003. Spl. project asst. ConservArt Assoc., Culver City, Calif., 1991—93; asst. preparator Fred Jones, Jr. Mus. of Art, U. Okla., 1992—2005, installation asst., 1992; co-coord. SummerWind Arts Festival, Norman, 1994—96; coord. Summer-Wind Arts Festival, Children's Events, 1995—; art cons. Dept. Edn., San Juan, 1986; bd. dirs. Children's Art Network, Norman, 1996—2001; coord./curator spl. exhbn. Ctrl. Pa. Festival of the Arts, State College, 1973—87; adj. prof. U. Okla., Norman, Okla., 1997—98, 2004—06; artist resident, Costa Rica. Author: (book reviews) Museologist, 1986—87, Community Based Art Education, 1995; one-woman shows include Bricktown Fin. Inst., Okla., numerous others, exhibited in group shows at 50th Anniversary Nat. Art Exhibit, Wind River Valley Artist's Guild, Wyo., Leslie Powell Gallery, Okla., IAO Gallery, Okla., Gallery on the Sq., Ky., Period Gallery, Nebr., Suite 2 Portfolio, Okla., Kirkpatrick Galleries of Omniplex, Okla., Goddard Art Ctr., Ardmore, Okla., East Ctrl. U., Ada, Okla., Purdue U., West Lafayette, Ind., Lamar U., Beaumont, Tex., Mus. Great Plains, Lawton, Okla., Soho Art Dist., NYC, Murray State Coll., Tishomingo, Okla., Mainsite Art Gallery, Norman, Okla., Internat. Print Exhbn., Barcelona, Spain, Taiwan, Ponca City Gallery, Okla., others, over 330 exhbns., Represented in permanent collections Sch. of Visual Arts, Pa. State U., Sch. of Art, U. Okla., Okla. Fred Jones, Jr. Mus. of Art, Okla. City Art Mus., Okla. Sch. of Arts and Scis., Okla. Visual Arts Coalition, Oklahoma City, pvt. collections U.S. and abroad. Recipient numerous awards for art. Mem.: Fred Jones Jr. Mus. Art, Oklahoma City Mus. Art, Mus. Women in Art, Nat. Mus. for Women in Art, Five to Nine Artists, Jacobson House Found., U. Okla. Art Alumni Assn. (pres. 1993), Pa. State U. Alumni Assn., Beta Sigma Phi Sorority (pres. 1983—84). Democrat. Avocations: children's/adult's workshops, reading, antiques, art. Home: 3316 Riviera Dr Norman OK 73072-7613 Office Phone: 405-850-2051. Business E-Mail: fredwood@ou.edu.

**WOOD, BRENDA JEAN,** pastor, evangelist; b. Patrick AFB, Fla., Sept. 24, 1961; d. Terry Robert Hubbard and Cherry Ann Marione, James William Redwine (Stepfather); m. Ross Landan Wood, Apr. 11, 1981; children: Jared Ross, Dwight Adam Myers, Christopher Wayne Pitts, Leslie Anne. AA, Weatherford Coll., Weatherford, Texas, 1981; BA Psychology, Calif. State U., San Bernardino, Calif., 1995; MS Marriage & Family Therapy, Fuller Theol. Sem., Pasadena, Calif., 1999, MA in Theology, 2002. Ordained min. Bethel Christian Ctr., 2004, lic. min. Assemblies of God, Calif., 1999. Youth pastor Full Gospel Assembly of God, Norco, Calif., 1995—97; intern counselor Turning Point Counseling, Diamond Bar, Calif., 1997—99; christian edn. dir. New Life Christian Fellowship, Riverside, Calif., 1998—98, youth pastor, 1998—98, sr. pastor, 1998—2004; pastor, founder Word of Life Ministries Internat., 2005—; evangelist Word of Life Ministries in Nigeria and India. Spkr. Religious and Civic Functions, 1995—; evangelist New Life Christian Fellowship, Mexico, 2002—, Nigeria, 2003, pastoral counselor, Calif., 1995—; parenting educator Safe Haven Program, Riverside, Calif., 2002—03. Chaplain Calif. Dept. of Forestry, Riverside, Calif., 2001—04; mem. Cops and Clergy, Riverside, Calif., 2002, bd. mem., 2002; mem. Jurupa C. of C., Riverside, Calif., 2003, Pastors Prayer Fellowship, Riverside, Calif., 2001. Scholar Music, Weatherford Coll., 1979. Assemblies Of God. Avocations: spending time with my family, gardening, travel. Home: 1804 Noah Dr Corona CA 92880 E-mail: pastorbrenda@theword.us.

**WOOD, CATHERINE T.,** special education educator; b. Mineola, N.Y., Jan. 17, 1950; d. Owen Joseph Sheehan and Dorothy Margaret Carnaghan; m. David Patrick Wood, Aug. 7, 1976; 1 child, Khalie Tamara. BS in Psychology, Spanish and Edn., Molloy Coll., Rockville Ctr., N.Y., 1971; MS in Spl. Edn., Hofstra U., 1975, postgrad. in Speech and Lang., 1975—; postgrad., Nov Southeastern U., 2005—. Cert. tchr. N.Y., in sign lang. Spl. edn. tchr. Malverne Sch. Dist., NY, 1971—80; spl. edn. math specialist Horizion Sch. for Perceptual Devel., Bayside, NY, 1980—84; spl. edn. tchr. Valley Stream Dist. 30, NY, 1984—. Pres. sch. bd. Our Lady of Peace Sch., Lynbrook, NY, 1995—97; mem. regional sch. bd. Region#24, Lynbrook, NY, 1995—97; religous edn. tchr. Our Lady of Peace, Lynbrook, NY, 1994—98. Vol. Full Cir., N.Y.C., 1969—73; tchr. vol. Vocat. Edn. Extension Bd., Hempstead, 1994—98. Recipient Master Tchrs. Award, Molloy Coll., N.Y., 1995. Mem.: ASCD, NY Student Speech Lang. Hearing Assn., Valley Stream Tchrs. Assn., Nassau Reading Coun., Nat. Coun. Tchrs. English, Nassau County Math Tchr. Assn., Kappa Delta Pi. Roman Catholic. Avocations: sewing, knitting, kayaking, music, pottery. Office: Forest Rd Sch 16 Forest Rd Valley Stream NY 11581

**WOOD, CHRISTOPHER L.J.,** real estate executive; b. London, Jan. 20, 1947; came to U.S., 1983; s. Sidney John and Lillian Ballantine (Pollock) W.; m. Pamela Wood, Dec. 14, 1978; 1 child, Alexander Wood. BSc, London U., 1969. Ptnr., dir. Debenham, Tewson & Chinnocks, London, 1972—96; COO America's Best, 1996—98; mng. dir. Peracon Inc.; prin. DTZ Debenham Thorpe Internat., 1996—. Mem. St. George's Soc. N.Y., Thames Rowing Club, Union League Club (Phila.). Office: DTZ PO Box 412 Pawling NY 12564

**WOOD, CONNIE GARRISON,** music educator; d. Maisie Smith and Ira Valdora, Jr. Garrison; m. James Ray Wood, Aug. 31, 1969; children: Allison Anne, Robert Garrison. B in Music Edn., Baylor U., 1970; M in Music Edn., Ind. U., 1982. Piano instr. The Conservatory at UMHB, Belton, Tex., 2000—; adj. piano instr. U. of Mary Hardin-Baylor, Belton, Tex., 2001—. Classroom music instr. NE Ind. Sch. Dist., San Antonio, 1971—76; piano instr. Pvt. Studio, Temple, Tex., 1980—2002; pianist First Bapt. Ch., Del Rio, Tex., 1982—83; profl. accompanist Temple I. S. D., Tex., 1993—, U. of Mary Hardin-Baylor, Belton, Tex., 1995—; pianist Immanuel Bapt. Ch., Temple, Tex., 1996—2002; profl. accompanist Temple Coll., Tex., 1996—2000. Actor: (civic theater production) Sound of Music, 2001; profl. accompanist (undergraduate recitals) Vocal and Instrumental Soloists and solo piano performances, 1998—, soloist (piano performance). Mem. and officer Parent-Teachers Orgn. in Temple I.S.D., Tex., 1983—2001. Mem.: Music Tchrs. Nat. Assn., Tex. Music Tchrs. Assn., Ctrl. Tex. Music Tchrs. Assn. (student affiliate membership chmn. 2000—04, competition chmn. 2000—04), Ctrl. Tex. Med. Alliance (hearing and vision screening com. 1984—93), Jr. League of Temple, Wildflower Guild (performance edn. instr. 1994—97), Mu Phi Epsilon. Avocation: reading. Office: U of Mary Hardin-Baylor & Conservatory Box 8012 Belton TX 76513

**WOOD, CORINNE GIESEKE,** former lieutenant governor; b. Barrington, Ill., May 28, 1954; m. Paul R. Wood; children: Ashley, Brandon, Courtney. BS, U. Ill., 1976; JD, Loyola U., 1979. Bar: Ill. 1979. Pvt. practice; counsel Ill. Savs. and Residential Fin. Bd.; atty. Hopkins & Sutter, Chgo.; gen. counsel Ill. Commr. of Banks and trusts; state rep. 59th dist. 90th Ill. Gen. Assembly, Springfield; rep. State of Ill., 1997—99, former Lt. Gov. Springfield, 1999—2003. Appointed spec. asst., Ill. Atty. Gen. Former co-capt. Shields Twp. Rep. Precinct; Lake Forest chmn. John E. Porter for Congress, 1994, 96; adv. mem. Coun. of Women Advisors to U.S. Congress; past 1st v.p., bd. dirs. Women's Rep. Club, past pres.; bd. mem. 10th Congl. Dist. of Lake Forest/Lake Bluff chpt.; past pres. (fin. chmn.), mem. bd. govs. Lake County Rep. Fedn.; bd. dirs. Allendale Shelter Club, Allendale Assn.; adv. bd. A Safe Place; transition bd. dirs. Anne M. Kiley Ctr. for the Developmentally Disabled; mem. LWV of Lake Forest/Lake Bluff; mem. Lake Forest Open Lands Assn.; former Lake Forest chmn., sustaining mem. Jr. League of Chgo.; former new mems. chair, membership com., Sunday sch. tchr. First Presbyn. Ch. of Lake Forest; den leader Pack 43, Boy Scouts Am.; plan commr. City of Lake Forest, 1993-97, sr. housing commr., 1993-97, ad hoc com. on sr. housing bd. mem. Recipient City of Lake Forest Spl. Recognition of Pub. Svc. award. Mem. ABA, Ill. Bar Assn., Lake County Bar Assn., Chgo. Bar Assn., House Financial Insts. Comm., Comm. on Aging, Edn. Appropriations Comm., Labor and Commerce Comm., appointed mem., Legislative Rsch. Bureau, bd. mem. Republican.

**WOOD, D. ANN,** language and music educator; b. Albuquerque, Aug. 20, 1949; adopted d. Arol Edmund and Margaret Dudley Beck, d. Ray Ruff and Jeanne Ann Short; m. Patrick David Kennedy, July 26, 1969 (div. Jan. 15, 1991); children: Ryan Patrick Kennedy, Deirdre Ann Kennedy; m. Brian

Claude Wood, Feb. 23, 1991; 1 child, Victoria Ann. BA in Speech and Theater, U. Mich., 1970; M Ch. Music, Concordia U. Wis., 2001. Ordained elder Presbyn. Ch. Instr. Wood Music Studio, Escanaba, Mich., 1977—; adj. faculty English and comm. Bay de Noc CC, Escanaba, 1981—2006; dir. music First Presbyn. Ch., Escanaba, 1989—. Musical dir. Bay de Noc Choral Soc., Escanaba, 1992—. Composer: (handbell composition) Amazing, Wondrous!. Bd. dirs. Bay Area Campus Ministry, Escanaba, 1997—2006. Named Outstanding Part-time Faculty Mem., Bay de Noc CC, 2005. Mem.: Choristers Guild, Suzuki Assn. Americas, Am. String Tchrs. Assn., Am. Choral Dirs. Assn., Am. Guild English Handbell Ringers (cert.). Presbyterian. Avocations: travel, community theater, music performance. Home: 2543 Lake Shore Dr Escanaba MI 49829 Office: Bay de Noc CC 2001 N Lincoln Rd Escanaba MI 49829 Office Phone: 906-786-5802 1248. Personal E-mail: dawood@charter.net.

**WOOD, DENNIS,** communications executive; Mgr. Berkeley Walcoverings Inc.; chmn. bd. dirs., pres., CEO C-MAC Industries, Montreal, Que., Canada. Bd. dirs. Gen. Trust Can., Maax Inc., Groupe Bocenor, Blue Mountain Coverings, Nat. Bank of Can. Bd. dirs Orchestre Metropolitaine of Montreal.

**WOOD, DIANE PAMELA,** federal judge; b. Plainfield, N.J., July 4, 1950; d. Kenneth Reed and Lucille (Padmore) Wood; m. Dennis James Hutchinson, Sept. 2, 1978 (div. May 1998); children: Kathryn Hutchinson, David Hutchinson, Jane Hutchinson. BA, U. Tex., 1971, JD, 1975; JD (hon.), Georgetown U., 2003, Ill. Inst. Tech., 2004. Bar: Tex. 1975, D.C. 1978, Ill. 1993. Law clk. U.S. Ct. Appeals (5th cir.), 1975—76, U.S. Supreme Ct., 1976—77; atty.-advisor U.S. Dept. State, Washington, 1977—78; assoc. Covington & Burling, Washington, 1978—80; asst. prof. law Georgetown U. Law Ctr., Washington, 1980—81, U. Chgo., 1981—88, prof. law, 1988—95, assoc. dean, 1989—92, Harold J. and Marion F. Green prof. internat. legal studies, 1990—95, sr. lectr. law, 1995—; spl. cons. antitrust divsn. internat. guide U.S. Dept. Justice, 1986—87, dep. asst. atty. gen. antitrust divsn., 1993—95; judge U.S. Ct. Appeals (7th cir.), 1995—. Contbr. articles to profl. jours.; bd. editors: Am. Jour. Internat. Law. Bd. dirs. Hyde Park-Kenwood Cmty. Health Ctr., 1983—85. Fellow: Am. Acad. Arts and Scis.; mem.: Am. Law Inst. (elected coun. mem. 2003), Am. Soc. Internat. Law, Phi Alpha Delta. Democrat. Office: US Courthouse 219 S Dearborn St Chicago IL 60604-1803*

**WOOD, DIRK GREGORY,** surgeon, physician, forensic consultant; b. Springfield, Ohio, Sept. 19, 1953; s. Carlos Paul and Evelyn Cecelia (Bird) W. BA magna cum laude, Urbana (Ohio) U., 1973; postgrad., Ohio State U., 1973-75; MD, UAG Facultad de Medicina, Guadalajara, Mexico, 1980; mini pupilage, Inns of Court School of Law, London, 1990; JD, Capital Law Sch., Columbus, Ohio, 1991. Diplomate Am. Bd. Ob-Gyn, Am. Bd. Forensic Medicine. Intern Bronx (N.Y.) Lebanon Hosp., 1981-82; resident William Beaumont Hosp., Royal Oak, Mich., 1982-86; physician, surgeon Her Care, Inc., Springfield, 1986—2001. CEO Just What the Doctor Ordered, Springfield, 1992-2001; dir. of obstetrics Mercy Med. Ctr., Springfield, Ohio, 1999-2000; chief collaborative physician Nurse Midwives Ctr., 1999-2000. Coroner Clark County, Ohio, 1991-97; mem. Clark County Rep. Ctrl. Com., Clark County Dist. 14, 1992-96. Named Ky. col., Ala. col. Fellow Internat. Coll. Surgeons, Am. Coll. Legal Medicine, Am. Coll. Forensic Examiners, Interam. Coll. Physicians and Surgeons; mem. SAR, Am. Soc. Law and Medicine, Phi Delta Epsilon (past chpt. pres.), Phi Alpha Delta. Republican. Avocations: scuba diving, bibliophilia, travel. Home: 2900 Cleveland Ave Saint Joseph MI 49085 Personal E-mail: drdirk@gcctv.com.

**WOOD, DONALD CRAIG,** retired marketing professional; b. Wilmington, Del., June 24, 1937; s. Thomas Henry and Madelyn (Brehm) W.; m. Elizabeth Haring, Apr. 28, 1962; children: Craig Standish, Allison Jean. BA, U. Del., 1959; MBA, Northwestern U., 1967. Sales mgr. NVF Corp., Broadview, Ill., 1960-62, Synthane Corp., Morton Grove, Ill., 1962-68; account exec., mgr. sales Donnelley Mktg. subs. Dun and Bradstreet Corp., Oakbrook, Ill., 1968-76, from dir. to v.p. market devel. to v.p. mktg. Stamford, Conn., 1977-1980; from v.p., gen. mgr. to pres. Donnelley Mktg. Info. Svcs. subs. Dun and Bradstreet Corp., Stamford, 1980-86; sr. v.p. Donnelley Mktg. Inc. subs. Dun and Bradstreet Corp., Stamford, 1987-90; v.p., gen. mgr. info. svcs. Triad Systems Corp., Livermore, Calif., 1990-96; ret., 1996. Served to 1st lt. U.S. Army, 1959-60. Home: 6312 Providence CC Dr Charlotte NC 28277

**WOOD, DONALD EURIAH,** retired lawyer; b. Guymon, Okla., May 27, 1935; s. Theodore and Lula Elizabeth (Rider) W.; m. Lynda Sharon Harris, Sept. 30, 1960; children: Donald Craig, Tana Dawn, Kristen Lynn. BA, Panhandle A&M Coll., 1958; LLB, Okla. U., 1964, JD, 1970. Bar: Okla. 1964. Asst. county atty., Texas County, 1964; county atty., 1965-67; dist. atty. Okla. 1st Jud. Dist., Guymon, 1967—2002; ret., 2002. Mem. adv. com. Criminal and Traffic Enforcement Systems, 1972; mem. Gov.'s Commn. Cmty. Affairs and Planning, 1972-75; mem. faculty Panhandle State Coll., 1974-92; mem. Okla. Dist. Atty. Tng. Coun., 1976-2001; mem. Okla. Bur. Narcotics and Dangerous Drugs Commn., 1992-98. Served with inf. AUS, 1958-60. Named Okla. Prosecutor of Yr., Assn. Okla. Narcotic Enforcers, 1994-95. Mem. Okla. Bar Assn. (legal ethics com. 1971-72), Texas County Bar Assn. (pres. 1966, 1970-71), Nat. Dist. Attys. Assn., Okla. Dist. Attys. Assn. (pres. 1972, exec. com. 1971-2001), Elks Club, Rotarian Club, Phi Alpha Delta. Presbyterian. Home: 605 Hillcrest Dr Guymon OK 73942-3345 Personal E-mail: done@ptsi.net.

**WOOD, DONALD F.,** lawyer; b. Bonne Terre, Mo., July 25, 1944; BSBA, Washington U., 1966; JD, Harvard U., 1969. Bar: Tex. 1970. Adminstrv. ptnr. Vinson & Elkins, L.L.P., Austin. Fellow Houston Bar Found. (chmn. 1991); mem. Beta Gamma Sigma, Omicron Delta Kappa. Office: Vinson & Elkins LLP 2801 Via Fortuna Ste 100 Austin TX 78746 Business E-Mail: dwood@velaw.com

**WOOD, DOUGLAS LYNN,** medical educator; b. Columbia, Mo., June 24, 1951; s. Cecil Vernon and Wilda Fay (Palmer) W.; m. Julia Ann Sandbothe, May 28, 1977; children: Ethan, Amanda, Paul, Benjamin. BA cum laude with distinction in Biology, Carleton Coll., 1973; MD magna cum laude, U. Mo., 1977. Diplomate Am. Bd. Internal Medicine, Am. Bd. Cardiovasc. Diseases. Asst. prof. medicine Mayo Grad. Sch. Medicine, Rochester, Minn., 1983—91, assoc. prof. medicine, 1991—2003, prof. medicine, 2003—. Cons. cardiovasc. diseases Mayo Clinic, Rochester, 1983—, vice-chair dept. medicine, 1993—; pres., CEO, chmn. bd. dirs. Immanuel-St. Joseph's Mayo Health Sys., Mankato, Minn.; chair Sec's Adv. Com. on Regulatory Reform, Dept. HHS, 2001-02, mem. practicing physicians adv. com., 2000-04. Contbr. articles to profl. jours. Mem. coun. on performance measurement Joint Commn. on Accreditation of Healthcare Orgns., Oakbrook Terrace, Ill., 1995—; mem. CPT editl. panel AMA, Chgo., 1994-97; chair fin. coun. St. Pius X Ch., Rochester, 1993-97; mem. Minn. Citizens Forum on Health Care Costs, 2003-04. Fellow ACP, Am. Coll. Cardiology; mem. Am. Coll. Physician Execs., Alpha Omega Alpha, Sigma Xi. Office: Mayo Clinic 200 1st St SW Rochester MN 55905-0002 Office Phone: 507-284-3725. Business E-Mail: wood.douglas@mayo.edu.

**WOOD, ELIJAH,** actor; b. Cedar Rapids, Iowa, Jan. 28, 1981; Appeared in films Back to the Future Part II, 1989, Internal Affairs, 1990, Avalon, 1990, Paradise, 1991, Radio Flyer, 1992, Forever Young, 1992, The Adventures of Huck Finn, 1993, The Good Son, 1993, North, 1994, The War, 1994, Flipper, 1996, The Ice Storm, 1997, Deep Impact, 1998, Black and White, 1999, The Bumblebee Flies Anyway, 2000, Chain of Fools, 2000, The Lord of the Rings: The Fellowship of the Ring, 2001, The Lord of the Rings: The Two Towers, 2002, The Lord of the Rings: The Return of the King, 2003, Spy Kids 3-D: Game Over, 2003, Eternal Sunshine of a Spotless Mind, 2004, Hooligans, 2005, Sin City, 2005, Everything is Illuminated, 2005; TV movies include Child in the Night, 1990, Day-O, 1992, Oliver Twist, 1997; also appeared in music video Paula Abdul's Forever Your Girl. Office: William Morris Agency c/o Nichole David 151 S El Camino Dr Beverly Hills CA 90212-2775

**WOOD, ELIZABETH ANN,** special education educator; b. Pittsfield, Mass., Aug. 2, 1979; d. Dennis Roy Luczynski and Tami Lee Daley; m. Jason Richard Wood, Aug. 31, 2000. BA in Sociology, BA in Early Childhood Edn., Mass. Coll. Liberal Arts, 2001, MEd in Spl. Needs, 2003. Cert. early childhood and moderate disability tcur. Mass. Mgr. Subway, North Adams, Mass., 1996—2002; lead pre-kindergarten tchr. North Berkshire YMCA, North Adams, 2001—03; spl. needs tchr. Hillcrest Edn. Ctrs., Pittsfield, Mass., 2003—. Mem.: Nat. Honor Soc. Roman Catholic. Avocations: sewing, exercise, scrapbooks. Home: 2 Daniels Ct Adams MA 01220 Office: Hillcrest Ednl Ctrs 1450 W Housatanic St Pittsfield MA 01201 Business E-Mail: lwood@hillcrestec.org.

**WOOD, EMILY CHURCHILL,** special education educator, social studies educator, consultant; b. Summit, N.J., Apr. 11, 1925; d. Arthur Burdett and Ruth Vail (Pierson) Churchill; m. Philip Warren Wood, June 22, 1946; children: Martha, Arthur, Warren, Benjamin. BA, Smith Coll., 1946; MA in Teaching, Manhattanville Coll., 1971; postgrad., U. Tulsa 1974-79, Langston U., 1990-92. Cert. tchr. social studies, learning disabilities, elem. edn., econs., Am. history, world history. Tchr. Miss Fines Sch., Princeton, NJ, 1946-47, Hallen Ctr. for Edn., Portchester, NY, 1973-74, Town and Country Sch., Tulsa, Okla., 1974-79, Tulsa Pub. Schs., 1979-97, Heritage Acad., Tulsa, 1998—; adj. instr. Tulsa C.C., Tulsa, 1998—. Ednl. cons. Tulsa, 1997—; exchange coord., Tulsa Pub. Sch., 2005—, culture box coord. Tulsa Global Alliance, 2004—; leader colloquia Bill of Rights Arts and Humanities Coun., Tulsa, 1989; mem. literacy task force Tulsa 2000 Edn. Com., 1990-92; chmn. internat. student exch. Eisenhower Internat. Sch., Tulsa, 1992—. Author: (with others) Visual Arts in China, 1988, Applauding Our Constitution, 1989, The Bill of Rights: Who Guarantees What, 1993; contbr. articles to profl. jours. Leader, founder Am. Field Svc., Tulsa, 1982—84; pres., v.p. Booker T. Washington H.S. PTA, Tulsa, 1985; campaign mgr. auditors race Dem. Party, Tulsa, 1988, 1992, 1994, 2006; bd. dirs. Smith Coll. Alumnae, Northampton, Mass., 1956—59, Sister Cities Internat., Tulsa, 1992—2001, nominations chair, 1999—2001; bd. dirs. Tulsa Global Alliance; trustee Okla. Found. for Excellence, 2000—. Named Tulsa Tchr. of Yr. Tulsa Classroom Tchrs. Assn. 1988, Nat. Elem. Tchr. of Yr., Nat. Bar Aux., 1992, Outstanding Elem. Social Studies Tchr., Nat. Cound. or Social Studies, 1999; recipient Elem. Medal of Excellence, Okla. Found. for Excellence, 1990, Valley Forge Tchrs. medal Freedoms Found., 1992, Paragon award Tulsa Commn. on Status of Women, 1996, Pinnacle award Mayor's Commn. on Status of Women, 1998, Liberty Bell award Tulsa Bar Assn., 1998, Global Vision award Tulsa Global Alliance, 2002. Mem. UN Assn. Ea. Okla. (pres. 1998-2000), Nat. Coun. Social Studies (religion program com. 1984—, bd. dirs. 1997—), DAR, Okla. Edn. Assn., Okla. Coun. Social Studies (pres. 1995, tchr. of yr. 1984), Okla. Bar Assn. (law related com. 1988—, tchr. of yr. 1990), Okla. Coun. Econ. Edn. (state and nat. awards 1981, 89, 92), Kent Place Alumnae Assn. (disting. alumna award 1992). Avocations: reading, swimming, travel, walking. Home: 3622 S Yorktown Pl Tulsa OK 74105-3452 E-mail: emily_wood46@hotmail.com.

**WOOD, EVAN RACHEL,** actress; b. Raleigh, NC, Sept. 7, 1987; d. Ira David Wood and Sara Lynn Moore. Actor: (films) Digging to China, 1998, Practical Magic, 1998, Detour, 1999, Little Secrets, 2001, S1m0ne, 2002, Thirteen, 2003, The Missing, 2003, Down in the Valley, 2005, Pretty Persuasion, 2005, The Upside of Anger, 2005; (TV films) In the Best of Families: Marriage, Pride & Madness, 1994, Search for Grace, 1994, A Father for Charlie, 1995, Death in Small Doses, 1995, Get to the Heart: The Barbara Mandrell Story, 1997, Down Will Come Baby, 1999; (TV series) Profiler, 1998—99, Once and Again, 1999—2002, (guest appearances) American Gothic, 1995—98, Touched by an Angel, 2000, The West Wing, 2002, CSI: Crime Scene Investigation, 2003.

**WOOD, FRANCES DIANE,** medical secretary, artist; b. Caddo, Okla., Mar. 7, 1950; d. Clovis Lynn and Hilda Dee (Guthrie) Wood; m. Samuel Dante Wolfe, Aug. 20, 1990 (div. Mar. 1992). BA, Southea. Okla. State U., 1972; postgrad., Grayson County Coll., 1987, Rose State Coll., 2002, U. Ctrl. Okla., 2004. Ins. clk. Sherman Cmty. Hosp., Tex., 1973—74; med. sec. Essin Clinic, Sherman, 1980—83; med. transcriptionist Texoma Med. Ctr., Denison, Tex., 1983—88, Wilson N. Jones Meml. Hosp., Sherman, 1989—95; CEO Designs by Diane, Caddo, 1995—. Conv. del. Blue Cross-Blue Shield Tex., Dallas, 1980—83; v.p. Jett Transcription, Denison, 1988. Exhibitions include paintings in cmty. art shows, Represented in permanent collections Shamrock Bank, Caddo, Indian Terr. Mus., Caddo. Charter mem. Caddo Edn. Found., Okla., 1993-95; sponsor Save the Children, Philippines, 1995. Mem. ASPCA, Friends Internat. Fellowship of Christians and Jews, Physicians Com. for Responsible Medicine, Nat. Trust Hist. Preservation, Okla. Sheriffs Assn. (hon.), Arts Coun. Co-op (life), Nat. Arbor Day Found., Sierra Club, Sacred Heart Auto League, People for Ethical Treatment Animals, Urban League Greater Oklahoma City Democrat. Avocations: pet care and pet psychology, interior decorating, astronomy, holistic and naturopathic medicine, gardening.

**WOOD, FRANK,** actor; b. Lincoln, Mass. Grad. acting program, NYU; grad. theater program, Wesleyan U. Broadway debut in Side Man (Tony award, 1999); actor: (plays) Three Sisters, Tomorrowland, King of Rats, Dark Ride, Hollywood Arms, 2002, The Rainmaker, 2006, Spring Awakening, 2006; many roles in Gil Kofman plays at Soho Rep, Adobe Theater and Dallas Theater Ctr., has worked with Fifty Second Street Project; actor: (TV appearances) Ed, 2001, The Sopranos, 2001, Third Watch, 2001, Law and Order, 2002; (films) Down to You, 2000, Small Time Crooks, 2000, Pollock, 2000, Thirteen Days, 2000, The Royal Tenenbaums, 2001, In America, 2002, People I Know, 2002, The Undeserved, 2004, King of the Corner, 2004, Keane, 2004, The Favor, 2006. Recipient 1995 Drama-Logue award for best ensemble in Kofman's Entrevista 187, Padua Hills Playwrights Festival. Mem.: East Coast Artists.*

**WOOD, FRANK MAXWELL,** prosecutor, lawyer; b. Forest Park, Ga. m. Suzanne Brunson; children: Frank, Sydney, James. BA, LaGrange Coll., 1981; JD, U. Ga., 1985. Law clk. Floyd County Superior Ct., 1985—87; staff atty. Pros. Attys.' Coun. Ga., 1992—94; asst. dist. atty. Ocmulgee Dist. Atty.'s Office, 1994—97; pvt. practice Macon, Ga.; US atty. (mid. dist.) Ga. US Dept. Justice, 2001—. Maj. Martha Bowman Meml. United Meth. Ch. With USAF, col. Ga. Air Nat. Guard. Office: US Attys Office Gateway Plz 300 Mulberry St 4th Fl Macon GA 31201 Office Phone: 478-752-3511.*

**WOOD, GARY STEWART,** dermatologist, researcher; BA, Northwestern U., Evanston, Ill., 1975; MD, U. Ill., Chgo., 1979. Cert. Anatomic pathology, dermatopathology Am. Bd. Pathology, 1983, Dermatology, dermatopathology Am. Bd. Dermatology, 1985. Asst. prof. dermatology and pathology Stanford U., Calif., 1986—89; assoc. prof. dermatology, pathology and oncology Case Western Res. U., Cleve., 1989—95, prof., 1995—2001; Johnson prof. dermatology U. Wis., Madison, 2001—. Chief dermatology Palo Alto VA Med. Ctr., Palo Alto, Calif., 1986—89, Cleve. VA Med. Ctr., 1989—2001; vice chmn. dermatology Case Western Res. U., Cleve., 1999—2001; chief dermatology Middleton VA Med. Ctr., Madison, Wis., 2002—; chmn., dept. dermatology U. Wis., Madison, 2002—. Author more than 280 publications. Grantee med. rsch., Va. Dermatology Found., 1986-present, NIH. Fellow: Am. Acad. Dermatology; mem.: Am. Assn. Va. Dermatologists (pres. 1993—95), Wis. Dermatol. Soc., Assn. Academic Dermatologic Surgeons, Assn. Profs. Dermatology, Am. Dermatol. Assn., Am. Soc. Dermatological Surgery, Am. Soc. Dermatopathology, Soc. Investigative Dermatology. Achievements include research in skin cancer and inflammation. Office: U Wis Dermatology One S Pk 7th Fl Madison WI 53715

**WOOD, GORDON STEWART,** historian, educator, writer; b. Concord, Mass., Nov. 27, 1933; s. Herbert G. and Marion (Friberg) W.; m. Louise Goss, Apr. 30, 1956; children: Christopher, Elizabeth, Amy. AB, Tufts U., 1955; AM, Harvard, 1959; PhD, Harvard U., 1964. Fellow Inst. Early Am. History and Culture, Williamsburg, Va., 1964-66; asst. prof. Harvard U., Cambridge, Mass., 1966-67; assoc. prof. U. Mich., Ann Arbor, 1967-69; prof. history Brown U., Providence, 1969—; Pitt. prof. Cambridge U., 1982-83. Bancroft lectr. U.S. Naval Acad., 1986; Anson G. Phelps lectr. NYU, 1986; Charles

Edmundson lectr. Baylor U., 1987; Samuel Paley lectr. Hebrew U., Jerusalem, 1987; presdl. lecture series on presidency, 1991; trustee, visiting prof. history & law Northwestern U., 2003; bd. trustees Tufts U. Author: The Creation of the American Republic, 1776-1787, 1969, The Rising Glory of America, 1760-1820, 1971; co-author: The Great Republic, 1977, The Radicalism of the American Revolution, 1992 (Pulitzer Prize for history 1993); co-editor: Imagined Histories: American Historians Interpret the Past, 1998, The American Revolution: A History, 2002, The Americanization of Benjamin Franklin, 2004, Revolutionary Characters: What Made the Founders Different, 2006. Mem. coun. Inst. Early Am. History and Culture, 1980-83; bd. trustees Colonial Williamsburg. With USAF, 1955-58. Recipient Bancroft prize Columbia U., 1970, Disting. Visitor award Australian-Am. Ednl. Found., 1976, Douglass Adair prize, 1984, Emerson prize Phi Beta Kappa, 1992, Kidger award New Eng. Tchrs. Assn., 2001, Boston Authors Club prize, 2005; Sunderland fellow U. Mich. Law Sch., 1990, All Souls Coll. fellow, 1991, Fletcher Jones Found. Disting. fellow The Huntington, 1997-98; Woodrow Wilson Ctr. guest-scholar, 1993-94; named to Rhode Island Heritage Hall of Fame, 2000; Dr. of Letters, La Trobe Univ., Australia. Mem. Am. Hist. Assn. (John Dunning prize), Orgn. Am. Historians, Soc. Am. Historians, Nat. Hist. Soc. (chmn. bd. advisors), Soc. Historians of the Early Am. Republic (pres.), Am. Acad. Arts and Scis., Am. Philos. Soc. Office: Brown Univ Dept of History Box N Providence RI 02912-9040*

**WOOD, HARLINGTON, JR.**, federal judge; b. Springfield, Ill., Apr. 17, 1920; s. Harlington and Marie (Green) W. AB, U. Ill., 1942, JD, 1948. Bar: Ill. 1948. Practiced in. Springfield, 1948-69; mem. firm Wood & Wood, 1948—58, 1961—69; U.S. atty. So. Dist. Ill., 1958-61; assoc. dep. atty. gen. for U.S. attys. Justice Dept., Washington, 1969-70, assoc. dep. atty. gen., 1970-72, asst. atty. gen. civil div. 1972-73; U.S. dist. judge So. Dist. Ill., Springfield, 1973-76; circuit judge U.S. Ct. Appeals (7th cir.), Springfield, 1976—92, sr. judge, 1992—. Adj. prof. Sch. Law, U. Ill., Champaign, 1993; disting. vis. prof. St. Louis U. Law Sch., 1996-2000. Chmn. Adminstrv. Office Oversight Com., 1988-90; mem. Long Range Planning Com., 1991-96. U.S. Army, 1942—46. Recipient Profl. Lifetime Achievement award, Inns of Ct., 2002. As rep. of US govt., his refusal to authorize use of force at Wounded Knee in 1973 is credited with helping bring a nonviolent end to the conflict. Office: US Ct Appeals PO Box 233 Petersburg IL 62675-0233

**WOOD, HEIDI**, commissioner; BA with honors, Brown U., 1987. Analyst SG Cowen; fin. cons. Shearson Lehman Hutton, Wedbush Morgan; from v.p., sr. analyst to exec. dir. Morgan Stanley, 1999—; commr. aerospace investment Aerospace Commn., Arlington, Va. Mem.: N.Y. Aerospace Analyst Soc. (treas.). Office: Aerospace Commn Crystal Gateway One Ste 940 1235 Jefferson Davis Hwy Arlington VA 22202-3283

**WOOD, H(OWARD) JOHN, III**, astrophysicist, astronomer; b. Balt., July 19, 1938; s. Howard John Jr. and Cara (Loss) W.; m. Austine Barton Read, June 10, 1961 (div. Jan. 1975); children: Cara Loss, Erika Barton; m. Maria Ilona Kovacs, May 22, 1977; 1 child, Andreas M. BA in Astronomy, Swarthmore Coll., 1960; MA, Ind. U., 1962, PhD, 1965. Lectr., asst. prof. then assoc. prof. U. Va., Charlottesville, 1964-70; staff astronomer European So. Obs., Santiago, Chile, 1970-75; Fulbright Resch. fellow U. Vienna Obs., 1976-78; rsch. assoc. Ind. U., Bloomington, 1978-81; asst. to the dir. Cerro Tololo Inter-Am. Obs., La Serena, Chile, 1982-83; physicist, astronomer NASA/Goddard Space Flight Ctr., Greenbelt, Md., 1984—, mgr. instrument synthesis and analysis lab., 2000—. Optics lead engr. Mars Observer Laser Altimeter, 1989-90, Hubble Space Telescope, 1990—; advisor optics and outreach James Webb Space Telescope, 1996—; advisor, participant Hubble Space Telescope Allen Comm., NASA, Danbury, Conn., 1990; co-chmn. Hubble Space Telescope Ind. Optical Rev. Panel, Columbia, Md., 1990-91; mem. panel The Townes/SAGE Panel-Jet Propulsion Lab., Pasadena, 1991-92 Co-author: (Book) Physics of Ap Stars, 1976; contbr. articles to profl. jours. Grantee NSF (10), 1965-82, Am. Astron. Soc., 1978. Mem. Internat. Astron. Union (Commn. 29 1962—), Optical Soc. Am. (chair optical tech. divsn. 1999-2001, co-chair ann. meeting 2002), Sigma Xi. Achievements include discovery of Balmer-Line variability of Ap stars; discovery of magnetic fields in southern Ap stars; alignment testing and delivery of the DIRBE photometric cryogenic telescope on the COBE spacecraft; alignment and optical prescription for Hubble Space Telescope while in orbit. Office: NASA/Goddard Space Flight Ctr Code # 551 Greenbelt MD 20771-0001 Office Phone: 301-286-8278. Business E-Mail: howard.j.wood@nasa.gov.

**WOOD, J. WARREN, III (JOSHUA WARREN WOOD III)**, lawyer; b. Portsmouth, Va., Aug. 31, 1941; s. Joshua Warren and Mary Evelyn (Carter) Wood; m. Marcia Neal Ramsey, Feb. 29, 1964; children: Lauren Elaine Yeh, Joshua Warren IV. AB, Princeton U., 1963; JD, U. Va., 1971. Bar: Va. 1971, NJ 1976, US Supreme Ct. 1977, NY 1982. Comml. banking asst. Bankers Trust Co., NYC, 1967-68; assoc. McGuire, Woods & Battle, Richmond, Va., 1971-75; v.p., gen. counsel, sec. Robert Wood Johnson Found., Princeton, NJ 1975—2003; pres., gen. counsel Global Ctr. Dispute Resolution Rsch., NYC, 2004—05; of counsel Greenbaum, Rowe, Smith & Davis LLP, Woodbridge, NJ, 2005—. Mem. AAA/ABA/AMA Commn. Alternative Dispute Resolution Health Care; master Marie L. Garbaldi Am. Inn Ct. Alternative Dispute Resolution. Mem. editl. bd. Va. Law Rev., 1969—71. Capt. arty. U.S. Army, 1963—67. Decorated Army Commendation medal. Mem.: ABA, Internat. Bar Assn. (mem. arbitration com.), Am. Arbitration Assn. (bd. dirs., mem. panel arbitrators, task force mass torts and alternative dispute resolution), NJ Bar Assn., Va. Bar Assn., NY Bar Assn., Princeton Bar Assn., Princeton Club, Order of Coif. Office: Metro Corp Campus One 99 Wood Ave S PO Box 5600 Woodbridge NJ 07095 Office Phone: 732-549-5600. Office Fax: 732-549-1881. E-mail: wwood@greenbaumlaw.com.

**WOOD, JACKIE DALE**, physiologist, educator, researcher; b. Picher, Okla., Feb. 16, 1937; s. Aubrey T. Wood and Wilma J. (Coleman) Wood Patterson. BS, Kans. State U., 1964, MS, 1966; PhD, U. Ill., 1969. Asst. prof. physiology Williams Coll., Williamstown, Mass., 1969-71; asst. prof. U. Kans. Med. Ctr., Kansas City, 1971-74, assoc. prof., 1974-78, prof., 1978-79; prof., chmn. dept. physiology Sch. Medicine, U. Nev., Reno, 1979-85; chmn. dept. physiology coll. medicine Ohio State U., Columbus, 1985-97, prof. physiology and internal medicine, 1997—. Cons. NIH, Bethesda, Md., 1982-88. Recipient Rsch. Career Devel. award NIH, 1974; named Hon. Citizen City of Atzugi Japan, 1987; Alexander von Humboldt fellow, W.Ger., 1976, grantee NIH, 1971—. Mem. AAAS, Am. Physiol. Soc. (assoc. editor 1984-96, rsch. award 1986), Soc. Neurosci., Am. Gastroent. Assn. Office: Ohio State U Dept Physiology and Cell Biology 304 Hamilton Hall 1645 Neil Ave Columbus OH 43210-1218 Office Phone: 614-292-5449. Business E-Mail: wood.13@osu.edu.

**WOOD, JAMES ANDERSON**, cardiac surgeon; b. Newton, Mo., Nov. 5, 1926; s. Frank and Lula Wood; m. Joann Wood, 1950; children: Diane, James, Jeff, Carol. BA, Reed Coll., 1953; MD, U. Oreg., 1957. Diplomate Am. Bd. Thoracic Surgery, Am. Bd. Surgery. Prof. cardiac surgery, 1974—94. Cofounder St. Vincent Hosp. Cardiac Surg. Program, Portland, VA Hosp. Cardiac Surg. Program, founder Bend OR Cardiac Surg. Program, Portland, Corvallis OR Cardiac Surg. Contbr. articles to profl. jours. With Marine Corps. Recipient Young Rschr. award Am. Heart Assn., Meritorious award AMA, 1965. Mem. AMA, Portland Surg. Soc., U.S. Polo Assn., Robert Wise Surg. Soc., El Dorado Polo Club, William Conklin Surg. Soc., Albert Starr Club, Am. Soc. of Thoracic Surgeons, Portland Acad. of Medicine, Dant Found., Wesley Eager Cardiac Surg. Found. (pres.), Pan Pacific Assn., Pacific Coast Surg., North Pacific Surg., Internat. Cardiovascular. Home: PO Box 5 North Plains OR 97133-0005

**WOOD, JAMES ARTHUR**, cartoonist; b. Miami, Fla., June 6, 1927; s. James Arthur and Baldwin Jennings Wood; m. Sallie Van Dyck, Nov. 10, 1951; children: James Arthur, Baldwin J., Elizabeth. BA cum laude, Washington & Lee U., 1950; M, Mich. State U., 1971. Contbg. cartoonist Washington Star, 1948—50; polit. cartoonist Richmond News Leader, Va., 1950—57, Pitts. Press, 1957—68; dir. info. U.S. Telephone Assn., Washington, 1968—80; editor, polit. cartoonist Farm Bur. News, 1975—91; founder,

dir. Nat. Gallery Caricature and Cartoon Art, 1994—97. Author: Great Cartoonists and Their Art. Elder Presbyn. Ch., 1967—. With USN, 1944—45. Recipient 12 awards and medals, Freedom Found., Valley Forge, Pa., 1950—68. Mem.: Assn. Am. Ednl. Cartoonists (pres. 1972), Nat. Cartoonists Soc., Sigma Delta Chi. Home: The Colonnades #389 2600 Barracks Rd Charlottesville VA 22901

**WOOD, JAMES EDWARD, JR.**, religion educator, author; b. Portsmouth, Va., July 29, 1922; s. James E. and Elsie Elizabeth (Bryant) W.; m. Alma Leacy McKenzie, Aug. 12, 1943 (dec. Oct. 2000); 1 son, James Edward III BA, Carson-Newman Coll., 1943; BD, So. Bapt. Theol. Sem., 1947, ThM, 1948; MA, Columbia U., 1949; postgrad., U. Tenn., 1943-44; cert. in Chinese, Yale U., 1949-50; Japanese diploma, Naganuma Sch. Japanese Studies, Tokyo, 1950-51; PhD., So. Bapt. Theol. Sem., 1957; LLD, Seinan Gakuin U., Japan, 1983; LLD (hon.), Capital U., 1996; DHC (hon.), Bucharest U., Romania, 1998. Ordained to ministry So. Bapt. Ch., 1942. Pastor Bapt. chs., Tenn. and Va., 1942-48; Bapt. missionary to Japan, 1950-55; prof. religion and lit. Seinan Gakuin U., Japan, 1951-55; assoc. prof. history of religions Baylor U., Waco, Tex., 1955-58; prof. hist. religions, dir. J. M. Dawson Inst. Ch. State Studies, 1958—73, 1980—99, 1st dir. honors program, 1959-64, founder chmn. interdeptl. grad. degree program in ch.-state studies, 1962-73, 80-95, founder Baylor Univ. Ch. State Rsch. Ctr., 1968, founder, chmn. faculty-student Far Eastern exch. program, 1970-72, Simon and Ethel Bunn Disting. prof. ch.-state studies, 1980-99, Simon and Ethel Bunn Disting. prof. emeritus, 1999—. Exec. dir. Bapt. Joint Com. on Pub. Affairs, Washington, 1972-80; mem. ctrl. panel Bapt. World Alliance Commn. on Religious Liberty and Human Rights, 1965-75, 80-2000, Commn. on Freedom, Justice and Peace, 1975-80; chmn. Bapt. Com. on USA Bicentennial, 1973-76; mem. So. Bapt. Inter-Agy. Coun., 1972-80, vice chmn., 1975-76, sec. 1976-76; fellow Internat. Acad. for Freedom of Religion and Belief, 1985-, pres. 1990-2000, hon. pres, 2000-; vis. prof. So. Bapt. Theol. Sem., 1974, N.Am. Bapt. Theol. Sem., Sioux Falls, S.D., 1974, 79, Okla. Bapt. U., Shawnee, 1977, vis. scholar, Christ Coll. Oxford U., 1983; vis. prof. Bulgarian Baptist Theol. Sem., Sofia, 1998, Faculty of Canon Law, Cath. U. Leuven, Belgium, 1999, others; vis. lectr. Tex. A&M U, 1962, 65, 68, Ashland (Ohio) Theol. Sem. 1971; Vernon Richardson lectr. U. Bapt. Ch., Balt., 1975, Ea. Bapt. Theol. Sem., Phila., 1975, Duquesne U., 1976, Wake Forest U., 1978. U. Richmond, 1979; lectr. First World Congress on Religious Liberty, Amsterdam, 1977, Rice U., 1977, 84, Notre Dame Law Sch., 1980, U. Kans., 1982, 2d World Congress on Religious Liberty, Rome, 1984, U. Faculty of Law, Warsaw, Poland, 1984, Loyola U., 1985, U. So. Calif., 1983, U. Oviedo, Spain, 1989, Chinese Inst. Religion, Beijing, 1986, Brigham Young U., 1986, 95, 97, 2005, Naval Coll. Chaplains, Providence, 1988-95, Union Theol. Sem. Va., 1989, U. Kans. Law Sch., 1990, U. Tirana, Albania, 1992, U. Malta, 1994, Austin Coll., 1989, 95, U. Pitts. Law Sch., 1997, U. Kiev, 1998; chair Internat. Consultation on Relig. Rights and Ethnic Identity, Budapest, 1992; co-chair Internat. Conf. Religious Freedom, Moscow, 1993; mem. internat. adv. bd. World Report on Freedom Conscience Human Rights Ctr., U. Sussex, Eng.; co-chair consultation on Freedom of Conscience and Belief, Moscow, 1993; chair Internat. Consultation Religious Liberty and Social Peace, Malta, 1994; Carver-Barnes lectr. Southeastern Bapt. Theol. Sem., 1981; Asian Found. lectr. Seinan Gakuin U., Japan, 1983; ecumenical consultation on edn. Nat. Coun. Chs., 1974; spkr. in field. Co-author: Church and State in Scripture, History and Constitutional Law, 1958; author: A History of American Literature: An Anthology, 1952, The Problem of Nationalism, 1969, Nationhood and the Kingdom, 1977, Secular Humanism and the Public Schools, 1986, Reflections on Church and State, 1995; (edited by Derek H. Davis) The Separation of Church and State Defended: Selected Writings of James E. Wood, Jr., 1995, Church-State Relations in the Modern World, 1999, Church and State In Historical Perspective, vol. 1, 2005, Church and State In The Modern World, vol. 2, 2005, and numerous others; editor: Markham Press Fund, Baylor U. Press, 1970-72; editor, contr.: Jewish-Christian Relations in Today's World, 1971, Baptists and the American Experience, 1976, Religion and Politics, 1983, Religion, the State, and Education, 1984. Religion and the State: Essays in Honor of Leo Pfeffer, 1985, Ecumenical Perspectives on Church and State, Protestant, Catholic and Jewish, 1988, Readings on Church and State, 1989, The First Freedom: Religion and the Bill of Rights, 1990, contr. co-editor: The Role of Religion in the Making of Public Policy, 1991, The Role of Government in Monitoring and Regulating Religion in Public Life, 1993, Problems and Conflicts Between Law and Morality in a Free Society, 1994, founding editor Jour. Ch. and State, 1959-73, 80-93, mem. editl. coun., 1973-80, mem. editl. bd., 1993-99; mem. editl. bd. Religion and Public Edn., Religious Freedom Reporter; area editor, contbr. Ency. So. Bapts., 1982, Church and State in Am. History, 1987; contbr. Changing Trends in Education, 1992, Law, Religion and Human Rights in Global Perspective, 1995, Dialogue of Democracy: An American Politics Reader, 1996, United Nations' Contributions to the Prevention and Settlement of Conflicts, 2003, The New Inquisitors, 2004, many others; contbr. over 300 articles to profl. jours. Sponsor Ams. for Pub. Schs., 1963-68; bd. dirs. Waco (Tex.) Planned Parenthood, 1966-72, pres., 1971-72; sponsor Christians Concerned for Israel, 1968—. Tex. Conf. Chs. Consultation on Religion and Public Edn., 1971, Nat. Christian Leadership Conf. for Israel, 1978—; pres. Waco area ACLU, bd. dirs. Tex. unit, 1968-72; pres. Nat. Coun. Religion and Pub. Edn., 1979-83, exec. com., 1975-90, bd. dirs., 1972-90; chmn. exec. com. Coun. Washington Reps. on UN, 1977-80, mem. council exec. com., 1973-80; exec. com. Nat. Coalition on Pub. Edn. and Religious Liberty, 1973-95; mem. religious liberty com. Nat. Coun. Chs. U.S.A., 1972—, mem. com. internat. concerns on human rights, 1973-80; Am. rep. Chs. Montreux Colloquium on Helsinki Final Act, 1977; v.p. Waco Conf. Christians and Jews, 1983-86, Internat. Acad. for Freedom of Religion and Belief, 1985-90, pres., 1990-2000, hon. pres., 2000—; mem. internat. adv. bd. World Report on Freedom of Conscience, Human Rights Ctr., U. Sussex, Eng.; trustee Internat. Devel. Conf., 1974-80; nat. coun. Am.-Israel Friendship League, 1977—; founder, chmn. Waco Human Rights Week, 1981-86; mem. ch. rels. com., U.S. Holocaust Meml. Coun., 1990-97; adv. on religious freedom abroad U.S. State Dept., 1998-2004. Recipient Disting. Alumnus award Carson-Newman Coll., 1974, Religious Liberty award Alliance for Preservation of Religious Liberty, 1980, Henrietta Szold award Tex. region Hadassah, 1981, Human Rights award Waco Conf. Christians and Jews, 1986, Cir. of Achievement award Baylor U. Mortar Bd., 1991, Religious Freedom Lifetime award Ams. United Ctrl. Tex., 1993, W.R. White Meritorious Svc. award, 1996, Human Rights Leadership award Freedom mag., 1998, Herbert H. Reynolds Exemplary award, 2004; hon. Tex. col., 1969; Alma M. and James E. Wood., Jr. endowed scholarship Baylor U., 2004—, Disting. Svc. in Promoting Religious Freedom award, Brigham Young U. Internat. Ctr. For Religious Studies, 2005. Mem. Am. Soc. Ch. History, Am. Acad. Religion, Am. Soc. Internat. Law, Am. Soc. Soc. Study of Religion, N. Am. Soc. Ecumenists, NCCJ (ad. com. on ch. state and taxation 1979-85), ACLU, Supreme Court Hist. Soc., Soc. for Scholarly Publishing, Va. Hist. Soc., Phi Eta Sigma, Pi Kappa Delta, Alpha Psi Omega. Democrat. Home: 203 Barrington Ln Yorktown VA 23693-5622 E-mail: james_wood@baylor.edu.

**WOOD, JAMES MICHAEL**, lawyer; b. Oakland, Calif., Mar. 22, 1948; s. Donald James and Helen Winifred (Reimann) Wood; m. Cynthia Ahart Wood; children from previous marriage: Nathan, Sarah, Ruth 1 stepchild, Alexandra. BA, St. Mary's Coll., 1970; JD, U. San Francisco, 1973. Bar: Calif. 1973, U.S. Dist. Ct. (no., ctrl. and so. dists.) Calif. 1973. Rsch. atty. Alameda County Superior Ct., Oakland, 1973-76; ptnr. Reed Smith LLP, Oakland, 1976—. Presenter profl. confs. Contbr. articles to profl. jours. Mem.: ABA (litig. sect., health litig. com., litig. products liability com.), Food Drug Law Inst. (bd. dirs., adv. com. 1999—), Nat. Health Lawyers Assn., Am. Acad. Hosp. Attys., Def. Rsch. Inst., Alameda County Bar Assn., No. Calif. Assn. Def. Counsel, State Bar Calif. Office: Reed Smith LLP 1999 Harrison St Ste 2200 Oakland CA 94612-3572 Office Phone: 510-466-6758. Business E-Mail: jmwood@reedsmith.com.

**WOOD, JAMES NOWELL**, museum director and executive; b. Boston, Mar. 20, 1941; s. Charles H. and Helen N. (Nowell) W.; m. Emese Forizs, Dec. 30, 1966; children: Lenke Hancock, Rebecca Nowell. Diploma, Universita per Stranieri, Perugia, Italy, 1962; BA, Williams Coll., Williamstown,

Mass., 1963; MA (Ford Mus. Tng. fellow), NYU, 1966. Asst. to dir. Met. Mus., N.Y.C., 1967-68, asst. curator dept. 20th century art, 1968-70; curator Albright-Knox Art Gallery, Buffalo, 1970-73, assoc. dir., 1973-75; dir. St. Louis Art Mus., 1975-80, Art Inst. Chgo., 1980—2004. Vis. com. visual arts U. Chgo., 1980-94; head com. Nat. Endowment Arts Mem. Intermuseum Conservation Assn. (past pres.), Assn. Art Mus. Dirs. Office: Art Inst Chgo 111 S Michigan Ave Chicago IL 60603-6492

**WOOD, JANIS LOUISE**, retired assistant principal; b. Wichita Falls, Tex., June 26, 1947; d. J. D. Richmond and Sarah Helena Stevens; m. Tommy Joe Kennedy (div.); 1 child, Pamela Kathleen Leidy; m. Jack Kelsey Wood, Aug. 7, 1970; 1 child, John David. AA, Eastfield Coll., Dallas, 1973; BA cum laude, U. Tex., Dallas, 1976; MEd, E. Tex. U., Commerce, 1997. Cert. tchr. Tex. Tchr. Plano Ind. Sch., Tex., 1978—82; owner, designer Wood Studios, Plano, 1984—90; tchr. Garland Ind. Sch. Dist., Tex., 1992—97, asst. prin., 1997—98, HS asst. prin., 1998—2001; ret., 2001. Instr. writing Collin County CC, Plano, 1992—94, Richland CC, Richardson, Tex., 1992—94; cons. human resources Millennium Cirs., Dallas, 2004—06. Bd. dirs. Garland Sports Hall of Fame, 2004—06. Recipient Super Tchr. award, Naaman Forest HS, 1992, Life Saving award, Garland Police, 2000. Mem.: Phi Theta Kappa. Republican. Avocations: gardening, reading.

**WOOD, JEREMY SCOTT**, architect, urban designer; b. Glen Ridge, N.J., Oct. 23, 1941; s. William Gamble and Alice-Marguerite (Scott) W.; m. Robin Benensohn-Rosefsky, June 14, 1970; children: Alexis, Jonas, Augusta. AB, Yale U., 1964, M in Architecture, 1970. Registered architect, Ma. Sr. assoc. TAC/The Architects Collaborative, Inc., Cambridge, Mass., 1970-94; sr. project mgr. Domenech Hicks & Krockmalnic, Inc., Boston, 1995-97; sr. project architect Elkus/Manfredi Architects, Ltd., Boston, 1997—. Instr. Boston Archtl. Ctr., 1970-76; head tutor dept. art history, history of modern architecture Yale U., 1969-70, Emerson Coll. Performance and Prodn. Ctr./Cutler Majestic Theatre Renovation, Boston, 2001-03. Author: (sect. and chpt. in books) Adaptive Reuse: Issues and Case Studies in Building Preservation, 1988, Office Buildings, 1989, Exposed Structure in Building Design, 1993; prin. works include Emerson Coll. Prodn. and Performance Ctr., Boston, 2001—03, Allen House Restoration & Condominiums, South End, Boston, 1998, MBTA/AMTRAK North-South Rail Link Stations (Boston), MBTA Subway Station Modernization State St. and Govt. Ctr. Stations (Boston), Complejo Medico de las Americas, Guatemala City, Guatemala, Health Care Internat. Hosp. and Hotel, Clydebank, Glasgow, Scotland, Copley, Place, Boston, The Westin Hotel at Copley Place, Boston, Liberty Ctr. and Vista Internat. Hotel, Pitts., Wellington Bus. Ctr. Offices, Medford, Mass., Two Portland (Maine) Sq. Office Bldg., One Mifflin Pl., Cambridge, Groton (Mass.) Sch. Dormitories, Coll. Engring. and Applied Sci., Shuwaikh Campus, Kuwait U., Kuwait City, Kuwait, Hosp. U. Pa., Phila.; asst. editor Perspecta 11; corr. Architecture and Urbanism, 1976; contbr. articles to profl. jours. Recipient Award of Excellence, Assn. Sch. Bus. Ofcls., Coun. Ednl. Facilities Planners, AIA, 1976, Concrete Industry Bd. Spl. Recognition award The Westin Hotel, Boston, 1983, Prestressed Concrete Inst. award, 1983, Honor award Associated Gen. Contractors of Mass., 1985, Grand award Urban Land Inst., 1988, hon. mention New Eng. Healthcare Design Awards, 1994, 1997 Move Massachusetts 2000 design award for engring. and arch. of North South Rail Link Project, Boston Preservation Alliance award for renovation of Cutler Majestic Theatre, 2003, Nat. Trust Hist. Preservation Honor award, 2004. Mem. AIA, Boston Soc. Architects (Honor awards), Mass. State Assn. Architects, Am. Planning Assn., Soc. Archtl. Hists. (life, Nat. chpt.), The Archtl. League N.Y. Home: 10 Pigeon Hill Rd Weston MA 02493-1620

**WOOD, JERILYN RUTH**, literature and language professor, secondary school educator, interior designer; b. El Paso, Tex., July 20, 1944; d. Floyd Fuston and Ruthie Bill Engler Stevens; m. Gordon D. Wood (dec.); 1 child, Megan Kathleen Douglas; m. Clifford Edward Kistner, Nov. 1, 1995. BA, No. Ariz. U., 1992, MA, 1995. Cert. tchr. secondary sch., adult edn., c.c. Owner, designer Woodshed Interiors, Yuma, Ariz., 1971—; instr. English dept. Ariz. Western Coll., Yuma, 1995—; chair English dept. Aztec HS, Yuma, 2002—. Coll. liaison Aztec HS, 2002—. Mem. Cultural Coun. of Yuma, 1987—93; mem. public art com. City of Yuma, 1997—2004, mem. arts and culture commn., 1998—2005, mem. planning and zoning com., 2005; mem. Vocat Adv. Bd., Yuma, Hospice Cmty. Bd.; chair Yuma Regional Arts Alliance. Avocations: reading, gardening, music, camping.

**WOOD, JERRY**, investment company executive; Former sr. mng. dir., fixed income sales Morgan Stanley, co-head, fixed income div. Credit Suisse First Boston, NY, 2003—. Office: Credit Suisse First Boston Eleven Madison Ave New York NY 10010 Office Phone: 212-325-2000.

**WOOD, JOHN ARMSTEAD**, planetary scientist, geological sciences educator, artist; b. Roanoke, Va., July 28, 1932; s. John Armstead and Lillian Cary (Hall) W.; m. Elisabeth Mathilde Heuser, June 12, 1958 (div.); children: Crispin S., Georgia K.; m. Julie Marie Nason, Sept. 9, 1989. BS in Geology, Va. Polytech. Inst., 1954; PhD in Geology, Mass. Inst. Tech., 1958; postdoctoral study, U. Cambridge, Eng., 1959-60. Staff scientist Smithsonian Astrophys. Obs., Cambridge, Mass., 1959, 1961—62, 1965—2004, ret., 2004; research asso. Enrico Fermi Inst. U. Chgo., 1962-65; prof. Harvard U., Geol. Scis. Dept., 1976-95; assoc. dir. Harvard-Smithsonian Center for Astrophysics, 1981—86. Vice chmn. Lunar Sample Analysis Planning Team, 1971—72; mem. NRC, Space Studies Bd., 1998—2001; chair Com. on Lunar and Planetary Exploration, 1999—2001. Author: Meteorites and the Origin of Planets, 1968, The Solar System, 1979, 2d edit., 2000. Recipient NASA medal for exceptional sci. achievement, 1973, J.L. Smith medal NAS, 1976, G.K. Gilbert award Geol. Soc. Am., 1992. Fellow AAAS, Am. Geophys. Union (F.L. Whipple award 2004), Meteoritical Soc. (pres. 1971-72, Leonard medal 1980); mem. NAS, Am. Acad. Arts and Scis., Cambridge Art Assn., Cosmos Club. Achievements include having asteroid no. 4736 named in his honor Johnwood. Home: 71 Langdon St Cambridge MA 02138-2501 E-mail: JAWood@alum.mit.edu.

**WOOD, JOHN MARTIN**, lawyer; b. Detroit, Mar. 29, 1944; s. John Francis and Margaret Kathleen (Lynch) Wood; m. Judith Anne Messer; children: Timothy Peter, Meagan Anne. BA, Boston Coll., 1966; JD, Cath. U. Am., 1969. Bar: D.C. 1970, Va. 2001, U.S. Dist. Ct. D.C. 1970, U.S. Dist. Ct. Va. 2001, U.S. Ct. Appeals (D.C. cir.) 1973, U.S. Ct. Appeals (3d cir.) 1973, U.S. Ct. Appeals (4th cir.) 1973, U.S. Supreme Ct. 1973. Trial atty. tax divsn. Dept. Justice, Washington, 1969-73; assoc. Reed Smith LLP, Washington, 1973-80, ptnr., 1980—, mng. ptnr., 1989-95, dir. legal pers., 1995-98. Dir. adv. bd. Salvation Army, Va. and Met. Washington, Leadership Washington, 1993—. Mem.: Fed. Bar Assn., Fairfax Bar Assn., The Currituck Club N.C., River Bend Golf and Country Club, Barristers Club Washington, Delta Sigma Pi, Phi Alpha Delta. Home: 9490 Oak Falls Ct Great Falls VA 22066-4143 Office: Reed Smith LLP 3110 Fairview Park Dr Ste 1400 Falls Church VA 22042 Office Phone: 703-641-4248. Business E-Mail: jwood@reedsmith.com.

**WOOD, JONATHAN STUART**, economist, educator; b. New Orleans, Nov. 14, 1944; s. John Joseph and Linelle Marie (Waguespack) W.; m. Ann M., Apr. 7, 1973; children: Elizabeth, Christopher, Julie, Jonathan. Grad., NASA Summer Inst. in Space and Engring., 1965; BS in Mech. Engring., Tulane U., 1966; MS in Aerospace Engring., Princeton U., 1970; MBA in Econs., NYU, 1975, MPhil in Econs. and Fin., 1978, PhD in Econs. and Fin., 1980. Rschr. on bio-engring study of neck whiplashes Tulane Med. Sch. and Tulane Sch. Engring. (for US Dept Health, Edn. and Welfare), 1963; materials tester and lab. analyst Svc. Foundry, New Orleans, 1964; ops. rsch. & econ. analyst Grumman Aerospace Corp., Bethpage, NY, 1969-74; sr. investment analyst, cons. to common stock dept. Prudential Ins. Co., Newark, 1974-76; instr. fin. & acctg. Sch. Bus. U. Conn., Storrs, 1976-78; Liberty Fund Rsch. fellow Stanford U. Inst. Humane Studies Rsch. Seminar in Econs., Palo Alto, Calif., 1977; asst. prof. fin. & econ. in fin. Tulane U., New Orleans, 1978-84; assoc. prof. econs. & fin. Coll. Bus. Adminstrn. Loyola U., New Orleans, 1984—. Prof. econs. and fin. Pace U. Grad. Sch. Bus. Adminstrn., N.Y.C., 1975-76; vis. prof. fin. Grad. Sch. Bus. Adminstrn NYU, 1980; vis. prof. fin. Grad. Sch.

Bus. Tulane U., 1985, 91, lectr., 1990; presenter in field.; cons. economist; expert in bus. valuation; adj. prof. in econ. and fin. Pace U. Grad. Sch. Bus. Adminstrn., N.Y., 1975-76; appeared on WWL-TV discussing current econ. and fin. events focusing on La. econ. matters; rschr., lectr. in field; conducted interviews and seminars in field. Author: Chemical Kinetic Influences, 1968, Chemical Kinetic Influences in Liquid Propellant Rocket Combustion Instability, 1969, 70, Effectiveness Evaluation of Orbital Observatories (with Joseph R. Fragola), 1975, Heterogeneous Expectations and Security Price Distributions, 1978, Entrepreneurship and the Co-Ordination of Expectations in the Stock Market, 1980, 82, Some Refinements in the Austrian Trade-Cycle Theory, 1984, Capital Formation Problems in the United States and the Question of a Capital Shortage, 1984, Methodologies for Valuation of Closely-Held Companies (with Dr. Michael A. Dalton and Robert I. Glover), 1989, Valuation of Closely-Held Companies & Professional Practices by Experts (with Dr. Michael A. Dalton and Dr. Robert I. Glover), 1989, Real Value of Damage Caps for Medical Malpractice in Louisiana (with Michael A. Dalton), 1989; contbr. chpts., reviews to books. Chmn. fin. com., mem. exec. bd. Short-Fern St. Neighborhood Assn., 1984-85; lectro, Eucharistic min., mem. com. Univ. Parish St. Thomas More Tulane U.; dir. Operation New Start, Inc.; softball coach Carrollton Boosters; elected to u. senate, 1986—; U. Senate Parking Com., 1986-87; faculty acad. affairs budget com., 1986-89, 89-92; Blue Ribbon Task Force for libr.'s acad. future, 1986-87; u. senate designatee to Fin. Com. of bd. trustees, 1991-92, 92-93; advisor to Endowment Com. of Bd. Trustees, 1991-93. Recipient MBA Top Gun award as Outstanding Tchr., Loyola U., 1993. Mem. Am. Econ. Assn., Am. Fin. Assn., We. Econ. Assn., We. Fin. Assn., So. Econ. Assn., So. Fin. Assn., Ea. Fin. Assn., Southwestern Social Scis. Assn., Opers. Rsch. Soc. Am./Inst. Mgmt. Sci., Pontchatrain Astronomy Soc., Student Recruitment Team, Grad. Edn. Task Force, Entrepreneurial Task Force, Curriculum Com., Advising Com. (chmn. 1986-87), MBA Curriculum Task Force. Avocations: astronomy, music. Home: 500 Arlington Dr Metairie LA 70001-5516 Business E-Mail: jswood@loyno.edu. E-mail: jsjewood@aol.com.

**WOOD, JOSEPH GEORGE**, neuroscientist, educator; b. Victoria, Tex., Dec. 8, 1928; s. Harold Robert and Frances Josephine (Marcak) W.; m. Jane L. Andrews; 1 dau., Marian. BS, U. Houston, 1954, MS, 1958; PhD, U. Tex., Galveston, 1962. Teaching asst. biology, U. Houston, 1956-58; instr. anatomy U. Tex. Dental Br., Houston, 1961, Yale U., 1962-63; asst. prof. U. Ark. Med. Sch., Little Rock, 1963-66; assoc. prof. U. Tex., San Antonio, 1966-70, asst. dean acad. devel., 1967-69, prof. and chmn. dept. neurobiology and anatomy Houston, 1970—84, prof. neurobiology and anatomy, 1984—88; prof., chmn. dept. anat. sci. U. Okla. Coll. Medicine, 1988-93; dir. Okla. Ctr. Neurosci., 1990-95. Guest prof. dept. pathobiology, cell biology and neuroanatomy U. Minn., 1993—96; sr. lectr. molecular and cell biology U. Tex., Dallas, 1997—, asst. dean pre-health professions, 1998—2002, assoc. dean pre-health edn., 2002—, clin. prof. human devel., 2002—; vis. prof. Philips U., Marburg, Germany, 1984. Served with AUS, 1954-56. Recipient Basic Sci. Tchg. award U. Ark. Med. Ctr., 1963, U. Tex. Houston, 1972, 75, 86, Disting. Alumnus award U. Tex. Med. Br., 1976 Mem.: Tex. Assn. Advisors for the Health Professions (chair), Tex. Soc. Electron Microscopy (pres. 1970—71, exec. coun. 1971—79), Am. Anatomy Chmn., Histochem. Soc., Assn. Am. Med. Colls., Soc. Neurosci. (exec. com. Houston chpt. 1971—77, pres. 1973—77, rsch. award 1962), Am. Assn. Anatomists (exec. com. 1974—78), Cajal Club, Alpha Omega Alpha, Sigma Xi, Golden Key, Phi Kappa Phi. Office: U Tex at Dallas MS FN II PO Box 830688 Richardson TX 75083-0688 Office Phone: 972-883-2571. Business E-Mail: woodj@utdallas.edu.

**WOOD, JULIENNE LOUISE**, librarian, historian; d. John Henry Wood and Lilas Naomi Lothen; m. Samuel Claude Shepherd, Jr., Sept. 2, 1978. BA magna cum laude, Gustavus Adolphus Coll., 1970; MA U.S. History, U. Wis., Madison, 1972; MLS, U. Wis., Milw., 1978; PhD U.S. History, U. Wis., Madison, 1994. Libr. copyright acquisitions Libr. Congress, Washington, 1979—80, sr. libr. copyright acquisitions, 1980—83, supr. libr. copyright office, 1983—85; dir. Barksdale Air Force Base Libr., Bossier City, La., 1985—87; lectr. history Centenary Coll., Shreveport, La., 1995—98; libr. govt. info. La. State U., Shreveport, 1999—2000, head rsch. svc. Noel Meml. Libr., 2000—. Subject advisor Hist. of the Americas, Gen. Works Libr. Sci., Bowkers Best Books for Academic Librs., 2002—04. Author: (hist. articles) Dictionary of American History, 2003, (biog. articles) American National Biography, 1999; book reviewer (reference book reviews) American Reference Books, Annual, 2001—, subject adv. Vol. 4 and Vol. 10, The Best Books, Inc., 2003. Co-chmn. program com. La. Hist. Assn., Forty-second ann. meeting, Lafayette, La., 2000; bd. dirs. La. Hist. Assn., 2004—; mem. bd. dir. Ark.-La.-Tex. Genealogical Assn., Shreveport, 1990; mem., treas., show chair. Red River Quilters, Shreveport, 1992—; grants reviewer Alliance Edn., Shreveport, 2001—. Higher Edn. Act Title II-B fellow, U. Wis.-Milw. Sch. Libr. Sci. Mem.: ALA (nat. com. 2000—), La. Libr. Assn. (state com. 2001—03), So. Hist. Assn., Orgn. Amer. Historians, Phi Kappa Phi, Beta Phi Mu, Phi Alpha Theta. Office: Noel Memorial Libr LSU Shreveport One Univ Pl Shreveport LA 71115-2399

**WOOD, KENNETH ANDERSON**, small business owner, display designer; b. Cleve., May 11, 1913; s. George Robert and Leonore (Anderson) Wood; m. Ruth Eleanor Diehm, Sept. 14, 1937 (dec. May 1999). Student, Fenn Coll., Cleve., 1932-34, Cleve. Inst. Art, 1935-45. Artist Patterson Displays, Cleve., 1934-35; art dir. Bailey Meter Co., Wickliffe, Ohio, 1936-71; owner Kenwood Designers and Assocs., Chesterland, Ohio, 1971—; designer of stained glass windows, 1979—. Pres. Artist and Craftsman Assocs., Cleve. 1940—44, Geauga Artists Assn., Geauga County, Ohio, 1950—53. Exhibitions include nat., regional and local, 1939—97, Represented in permanent collections Butler Mus. Am., Youngstown, Ohio, Inlander Collection of Gt. Lakes Regional Paintings, Cleve. Mus. Art, numerous pvt. collections; patents for product design. Mem.: Indsl. Designers Soc. Am. (life). Republican. Seventh Day Adventist Avocation: travel. Office: Kenwood Design and Assocs 11950 Sperry Rd Chesterland OH 44026-2225 Office Phone: 440-729-7778. E-mail: kennethwood@kennethwood.com.

**WOOD, KENNETH ARTHUR**, retired editor, writer; b. Hastings, Sussex, Eng., Feb. 25, 1926; came to U.S., 1965; s. Arthur Charles and Ellen Mary (Cox) W.; m. Hilda Muriel Harloe, Sept. 13, 1952. Editor Stamp Collector newspaper Van Dahl Publs., Albany, Oreg., 1968-80, editor emeritus, 1980—. Author (ency.) This Is Philately, 1982, (atlas) Where in the World, 1983, Basic Philately, 1984, Post Dates, 1985, Modern World, 1987; author several hundred articles and columns published in the U.K. and U.S.A., 1960—. Served with Brit. Army WW II. Recipient Disting. Philatelist award Northwest Fedn. Stamp Clubs, 1974, Phoenix award Ariz. State Philatelic Hall of Fame, 1979, Disting. Philatelist award Am. Topical Assn., 1979. Fellow Royal Philatelic Soc. (London); mem. Am. Philatelic Soc. (hon. life, Luff award 1987, Hall of Fame Writers Unit, 1984). Avocations: stamp collecting/philately, aviation history, modern history, gardening. Office: 2430 Tudor Way SE Albany OR 97322-5661

**WOOD, KENNETH EDWARD**, music educator, tenor; b. Houston, 1960; s. Waldon Edward and Elizabeth Ann Wood; m. Lucinda Carol Wilson, 1983; 1 child, Joshua Edward. All-level choral tchg. cert., Tex. Edn. Agy., 1983; MusB, North Tex. State U., 1983; MusM, U. North Tex., 1989; Dr. Musical Arts, U. Tex., Austin, 2000. Cert. classical singer Mag. and Comps., 2006. Pvt. music instr., Paige, Tex., 1990—2001; asst. prof. music Ctrl. Mo. State U., Warrensburg, Mo., 2001—05, assoc. prof. music, 2005—. Co. mem. Merola Opera Program, San Francisco, 1990; adjudicator Ctrl. Meth. Coll. Music Festival, Mo., 2003—04. Dir.: (exhbn.) Nat. Opera Assn. 49th Ann. Conv.; singer: (performance) National Opera Association 50th Annual Convention, Fort Worth Ballet, Western Opera Theatre, Sacramento Symphony, Texas Opera Theater, Lyric Opera of Dallas, Fort Worth Opera, Sedalia Symphony, Austin Choral Artists, Austin Chamber Music Festival, Austin Lyric Opera, Festival At Round Top, Austin Symphony, Opera Theatre of St. Louis. Adjudicator Mo. Pub. Schs., 2001—05, Kans. Pub. Schs., Kans., 2002—04; choir dir. Good Shepherd Luth. Ch., Bastrop, Tex., 1991—2001,

coun. pres., 1999—2001, coun. elder, 1993—99. Finalist, Internat. Opera Competition, 1984; recipient Sch. of Music Svc. award, North Tex. State U., 1979—83, Eugene Branscome Choral award, 1982—83, 5th pl., Tuesday Musical Club, 1984, U.S. Nat. Collegiate Award Winner, 1988, 3rd pl., Tuesday Musical Club, 1988, winner vocal divsn., Hemphill-Wells Sorantin Competition, 1990, Internat. Finalist, Ctr. for Contemporary Opera Singers Competition, 2003; scholar, Hamman Found., 1979—83; Mabel Farish Simmons scholar in opera, U. North Tex., 1987, Meet the Composer grantee, Mid-Am. Arts Alliance, 2003, Dr. and Mrs. Ernest C. Butler Endowed Presdl. scholar, U. Tex., Austin, 1994—95, Barbara Smith Conrad Endowed Presdl. scholar, 1995—96, Ann and Gordon Getty Found. scholar, 1996—97. Mem.: Am. Guild Musical Artists, Opera Am., Nat. Opera Assn., Nat. Assn. Tchrs. Singing (adjudicator 2002—04, site coord. state auditions 2004, paper presenter nat. conv. 2004, 1st pl. regional auditions 1987, 2d pl. regional auditions 1980—82), Pi Kappa Lambda, Phi Mu Alpha. Avocations: musical composition, travel, aquariums. Office: Ctrl Mo State Univ Dept Music Warrensburg MO 64093 E-mail: kwood@cmsu1.cmsu.edu.

**WOOD, KERRY**, professional baseball player; b. Irving, Texas, June 17, 1977; Pitcher Chicago Cubs, 1998—. Named Nat. League Rookie of the Yr., 1998; named to Nat. League All-Star Team, 2003. Achievements include led Nat. League in strikeouts (266), 2003; over 3,000 career strikeouts. Office: c/o Chicago Cubs 1060 W Addison Chicago IL 60613*

**WOOD, KIMBA M.**, federal judge; b. Port Townsend, Wash., Jan. 2, 1944. BA cum laude, Conn. Coll., 1965; MSc, London Sch. Econs., 1966; JD, Harvard U., 1969. Bar: U.S. Dist. Ct. D.C. 1969, U.S. Ct. Appeals D.C. 1969, N.Y. 1972, U.S. Dist. Ct. (ea. and so. dists.) N.Y. 1974, U.S. Ct. Appeals (2d cir.) 1975, U.S. Supreme Ct. 1980, U.S. Dist. Ct. (we. dist.) N.Y. 1981. Assoc. Steptoe & Johnson, Washington, 1969-70; with Office Spl. Counsel, OEO Legal Svcs., Washington, 1970-71; assoc., then ptnr. LeBoeuf, Lamb, Leiby & MacRae, N.Y.C., 1971-88; judge, U.S. Dist. Ct. (So. Dist.), NY, 1988—. Mem. ABA (chmn. civil practice, procedure com. 1982-85, mem. coun. 1985-88, pal. rep. 1989-91), N.Y. State Bar Assn. (chmn. antitrust sect. 1983-84), Fed. Bar Coun. (trustee from 1978, v.p., 1984-85), Am. Law Inst. Office: US Dist Ct US Courthouse 500 Pearl St Rm 1610 New York NY 10007-1316

**WOOD, L. LIN, JR.**, lawyer; b. Raleigh, N.C., Oct. 19, 1952; s. Lucian Lincoln and Josephine (Currin) W.; m. Deborah Anne Jamison, July 25, 1987; children:, Elizabeth Ashley, Matthew Carlton. BA cum laude Mercer U., 1974, JD cum laude, 1977. Bar: Ga. 1977, U.S. Dist. Ct. (no. and mid. dist.) Ga. 1977, U.S. Dist. Ct. Colo., U.S. Ct. Appeals (5th cir.) 1977, U.S. Ct. Appeals (11th cir.) 1981, U.S. Supreme Ct. Assoc. f Jones, Cork, Miller & Benton, Macon, Ga., 1977-80, Freeman & Hawkins, Atlanta, 1980-83; ptnr. Wood & Grant, Atlanta, 1983—. Mem. staff Mercer Law Rev., 1975-77. Recipient Am. Jurisprudence award 1976, 77, U.S. Law Week award, 1977. Mem. ABA (vice-chair Media Law & Defamation Torts com.), Assn. Trial Lawyers Am., State Bar Ga., Atlanta Bar Assn., Lawyers Club Atlanta, Ga. Trial Lawyers Assn. Republican. Methodist. Club: Atlanta City. Office: The Equitable Bldg Ste 2140 100 Peachtree St Atlanta GA 30303-1913 Office Phone: 404-522-1713. E-mail: llwood@linwoodlaw.com.

**WOOD, LARRY (MARY LAIRD)**, journalist, writer, public relations executive, educator, environmental consultant; b. Sandpoint, Idaho; d. Edward Hayes and Alice (McNeel) Small; children: Mary, Marcia, Barry. BA summa cum laude, U. Wash., 1939, MA summa cum laude, 1940; postgrad., Stanford U., 1940—43, U. Calif., Berkeley, 1946—47, U. Wis., 1971—72, U. Minn., 1971—72, U. Ga., 1972—73, U. Calif., Santa Cruz, 1974—76, Stanford Hopkins Marine Sta., 1977—80. Cert. secondary and jr. coll. tchr., Wash., Calif. Feature writer and columnist Oakland Tribune and San Francisco Chronicle, Calif., 1939—; archtl. and environ. feature and travel writer and columnist San Jose (Calif.) Mercury News (Knight Ridder), 1972-90; tchg. fellow Stanford U., 1940-43; dir. pub. rels. 2-counties, 65-park 100,000 acre East Bay Regional Park Dist., No. Calif., 1948-68; pres. Larry Wood Pub. Rels., 1946—; pub. rels. dir. Calif. Children's Home Soc., 1947-58. Prof. pub. rels., mag. writing, journalism, investigative reporting San Diego State U., 1974-75; disting. vis. prof. journalism San Jose State U., 1976; assoc. prof. journalism Calif. State U., Hayward, 1978; prof. sci. and environ. journalism U. Calif. Berkeley Ext. grad. divsn., 1979—; press del. nat. convs. Am. Geophys. Union Internat. Conf., 1986—, AAAS, 1989—, Nat. Park Svc. VIP Press Tour, Yellowstone after the fire, 1989—, Nat. Assn. Sci. Writers, 1989—, George Washington U./Am. Assn. Neurol. Surgeons Sci. Writers Conf., 1990, Am. Inst. Biol. Scis. Conf., 1990, Nat. Conf. Sci. Writers, Am. Heart Assn., 1995, Internat. Cardiologists Symposium for Med./Sci. Writers, 1995, Annenberg Program Electronic Media Symposium, Washington, 1995; EPA del. to USSR and Ea. Europe; expert witness on edn., pub. rels., journalism and copyright; cons. sci. writers interne project Stanford U., 1989—; spl. media guest Sigma Xi, 1990—; mem. numerous spl. press corps; selected White House Spl. Media, 1993—; selected mem. Duke U. 14th Ann. Sci. Reporters Conf., 1995; internat. press guest Can. Consulate Gen. Dateline Can., 1995—, French Govt. Tourist Office, 1996—, Ministerio delle Risorse Agricole Alimentari e Forestali and Assocs. Conf., 1995; appeared in TV documentary Larry Wood Covers Visit of Queen Elizabeth II. Contbr. over 5,500 articles to newspapers, nat. mags., nat. and internat. newspapers including L.A. Times-Mirror Syndicate, Knight-Ridder Syndicate, Washington Post, Phila. Inquirer, Chgo. Tribune, Miami Herald, Oakland Tribune, Seattle Times, San Francisco Chronicle, 36 Million Circulation Parade, San Jose Mercury News (Nat. Headliner award), Christian Sci. Monitor, L.A. Times/Christian Sci. Monitor Worldwide News Syndicate, Washington Post, Phila. Inquirer, Hawaiian Airlines In Paradise and other in-flight mags., MonitoRadio, Donnelly Pubs., Sports Illus., Life, Mechanix Illus., Popular Mechanics, Parents (contbg. editor), House Beautiful, Am. Home (assoc. mag. editor), Traveltoday, Better Homes and Gardens, Sunset, Archtl. Digest, National Geographic World Travel & Leisure, Chevron USA/Odyssey (Calif. Pub.'s award 1984), Xerox Edn. Publs., Europe's Linguapress, PSA Mag., Off Duty, Oceans, Sea Frontiers, AAA Westways, AAA Via, Travelin', others; home and garden columnist, editor, 5-part series Pacific Coast Ports, 5-part series Railroads of the West, series Immigration, Youth Gangs, Endangered Species, Calif. Lighthouse Chain, Lighthouses of the World, Pacific Coast Wetlands, Elkhorn Slough Nat. Estuarine Res., Ebey's Landing Nat. Hist. Island Res., Calif. Water Wars, BLM's Adopt a Horse Program, Mt. St. Helen's Eruption, Oreg's Covered Bridges, Loma Prieta Earthquake, Oakland Firestorm, Missing Children, Calif. Prison Reform, Columbia-Alaska's Receding Glacier, Calif. Underwater Parks, and many others; author: Wonderful U.S.A.: A State-by-State Guide to Its Natural Resources, 1989; co-author: McGraw-Hill English for Social Living, 1944, Fawcett Boating Books, 1956-66, Fodor's San Francisco, Fodor's California, 1982-89, Bell and Howell/Charles Merrill Focus on Life Science, Focus on Physical Science, Focus on Earth Science, 1983, 2d edit, 1987, State of California's Golden State Travel Guide, 1998; contbr. Earth Science 1987; 8 works selected for use by Europe's Woltors-Nordoff-Longman English Language Texts, U.K., Netherlands, 1988; author: (with others) anthology West Winds, 1989; reviewer Charles Merrill texts, 1983-84; book reviewer Profl. Communicator, 1987—; selected writings in permanent collections Oakland Pub. Libr., U. Wash. Main Libr.; environ. works included in Dept. Edn. State of Md. textbook; contbr. author Journalism Quar.; author script PBS/AAA America series, 1992; contbg. editor: Parents, Fashion Showcase, Spokane Mag. Nat. chmn. travel writing contest Assn. for Edn. in Journalism and Mass Comm. Soc. Am. Travel Writers, 1979-83; judge writing contest for Nat. Assn. Real Estate Editors, 1982—; cons. S.C. Dept. Parks, Recreation and Tourism, 1999—; invited Nat. Park Svc. Nat. Conf. Sci. Writers, 1985, Postmaster Gen.'s 1992 Stamps, 1991, Internat. Geodesy. Union Conf., 1982—, The Conf. Bd., 1995—, Corp. Comm. Conf., Calif. Inst. Tech. Media and Sci. Seminar, 1995—, Med. Writers Delegation to Russia and Estonia, 1997, N.Y. Times Opinion Rsch. Co. Corp. Image Conf., 1999, EPA and Dept. Energy Tech. Conf., 1992, Am. Soc. Photogrammetry and Remote Sensing Internat. Conv. Mapping Global Change, 1992, U.S. Conf. on Oceans, 1998, N.Y. Mus. Modern Art Matisse Retrospective Press Rev. and all media previews, 1992—; celebration 150th anniversary Oreg.

Trail, 1993, Nat. Coun. Advancement Sci. Writing, 1977-2003, Sigma Xi Nat. Conf., 1988-2003, Nat. Sci. Writers Confs., 1977-2003, PRSA Travel and Tourism Conf., 1993—, Internat. Conf. Environment, 1994, 95, Quality Life Europe, Prague, 1994, Calif. Sesquicentennial, 1996, 14th Ann. Sci. Writers Conf., 1996, Picasso Retrospective, 1996, others; mem. Gov.'s Conf. Tourism N.C., 1993-2002, Calif., 1976—, Fla., 1987—, N.C. Govs. conf. on tourism and film, 2000-, U.C. Irvine Calif. Computer Sci. Symposium, 2000, Sea Grant's conf. on sci. in the news, 2000, N.Y. conf. bd. conf. on environ. journalism, 2000, on economics, 2001; press guest 14 U.S. states and 12 fgn. countries' Depts. Tourism, 1986—; chmn. New Com. for Sci./Journalism Curricula U. Wash., 2006-. Named to Broadway Hall of Fame, U. Wash., 1984; recipient Broadway Disting. Alumnus award, 1995; citations for environ. writing Nat. Park Svc., U.S. Forest Svc., Bur. Land Mgmt., Oakland Mus. Assn., Oakland C. of C., Chevron USA, USN plaque and citation, Best Mag. articles citation Calif. Pubs. Assn., 1984, U.S. Treasury award, 1946; co-recipient award for best Sunday newspaper mag. Nat. Headliners, citation for archtl. features Oakland Mus., 1983; honoree for achievements in journalism Nat. Mortar Bd., 1988, 89; named one of 14 V.I.P. press 1989; one of Calif.'s top 40 Contemporary Authors, 1989; nat. honoree Social Issues Resources Series, 1987; recipient, Gov.'s Calif. Women of Achievement award, 1988-90. Mem.: AAAS, Calif. Acad. Scis., Am. Bd. Forensic Examiners, Pub. Rels. Soc. Am. (charter mem. travel, tourism, environment and edn. divsns.), Nat. Sch. Pub. Rels. Assn., Environ. Cons. N.Am., Am. Assn. Edn. in Journalism and Comm. (exec. bd. nat. mag. divsns. 1978, panel chmn. 1979—80, author Journalism Quart. jour.), Women in Comm. (nat. bd. officer 1975—77, book reviewer Prof. Communicator), Soc. Profl. Journalists (nat. bd. for hist. sites 1980—), Nat. Press Photographers Assn. (Bay area internet project 1989—, hon. life, honoree 1995), Investigative Reporters and Editors (charter), Nat. Assn. Sci. Writers, Bay Area Advt. and Mktg. Assn., Internat. Assn. Bus. Communicators, Am. Assn. Med. Writers, Soc. Am. Travel Writers, Am. Film Inst., Soc. Environ. Journalists (charter), Calif. Acad. Environ. News Writers, Am. Mgmt. Assn., Nat. Soc. Environ. Journalists (charter), Calif. Environ. Leadership Roundtable, Am. Heritage Found. (citation 1986—88), Fine Arts Mus., San Francisco, Calif. State Parks Found., Purple and Gold Soc., Mortar Board Alumnae Assn. (life honoree 1988—89), Stanford Alumni (life), U. Calif. (life; Berkeley Alumni (life; v.p., scholarship chmn. 1975—81), U. Wash. Com. (life; charter mem. ocean scis. alumni, dept. adv. sci. journalism, disting. alumni 1987), Nat. Parks and Conservation Assn., Calif. Environ. Leadership Roundtable (trustee), Nat. Wildlife Fedn., Oceanic Soc., Nature Conservancy, Smithsonian Audubon Soc., Internat. Oceanog. Found., Calif. Writers Club (state bd., Berkeley bd. 1989—, honoree ann. conv. Asilomar, Calif. 1990), Nat. Press Club, San Francisco Press Club, Seattle Advt. and Sales Club (former officer), Seattle Er. Advt. Club (charter), Phi Beta Kappa (statewide chmn. scholarship awards 1975—81, v.p. bd. dirs. Calif. Alumni Assn.), Pi Lambda Theta (charter 1995—, planning com.), Theta Sigma Phi. Home and Office: Piedmont Pines 6161 Castle Dr Oakland CA 94611-2737 Office Phone: 510-531-0977. *A creed I follow is Ralph Waldo Emerson's statement: "Nothing great was ever achieved without enthusiasm.".*

**WOOD, LEONARD JAMES**, lawyer; b. Camden, N.J., Dec. 21, 1949; s. Leonard and Virginia (Ferraro) W.; m. Catherine Mary Dugan, June 29, 1979; children: Leonard James III, Tara Kathleen. BA, Manhattan Coll., 1972; JD, Rutgers U., 1976. Bar: N.J. 1976, U.S. Ct. Appeals (3d cir.) 1977, U.S. Supreme Ct. 1980. Law clk. to presiding judge Chancery div. Superior Ct. of N.J., Camden, 1976-77; ptnr. Console, Marmero, Li Volsi, Wood, Curcio, Berlin, NJ, 1977-89, Ferreri and Wood, Voorhees, NJ, 1989-95, Morelli & Rinaldi, 1995-97; sole practice, 1997-99; ptnr. Wade & Wood LLC, 2000—02; mng. ptnr. Wade, Long, Wood & Kennedy, LLC, 2003—. Mem. Camden County Bar Assn. Office: 1250 Chews Landing Rd Laurel Springs NJ 08021-2816 Office Phone: 856-346-2800. Business E-Mail: lwood@mycomcast.net.

**WOOD, LESLIE ANN**, retail administrator; b. Chgo., Apr. 9, 1957; d. Howard Arnold and Anita Eleanor (Andler) W. AA, Harper Coll., 1977; BS in Comm. Scis., Ill. State U., 1979. MBA, Olivet Nazarene U., 1998. Advt. asst. Harry Alter Co., Chgo., 1979-80; clk. typist Career Guild, Evanston, Ill., 1980-81; reporter Aparacor, Evanston, 1981-82; sales mgmt. trainee Prudential Ins. Co. Am., Millburn, NJ, 1983-84; fin. cons. Summit Fin. Resources, Livingston, NJ, 1984; mgr. Chgo. area Renault Inc. divsn. AMC/Jeep/Renault, Elk Grove Village, Ill., 1985-87; customer rels. specialist Chrysler Motors, Lisle, Ill., 1987-88; dist. svc. and parts mgr. Chrysler, Lisle; dist. parts mgr. Subaru of Am., Addison, Ill., 1989-91, dist. fixed ops. mgr., 1992-95; univ. rep. Olivet Nazarene U., Schaumburg, Ill., 1996-97; mktg. cons. WZSR STAR 105.5, Crystal Lake, Ill., 1997-99; parts cons. Am. Isuzu Motors, Cerritos, Calif., 1999—2001, Hyundai Motor Am., Aurora, Ill., 2002—05; area mgr. Newgen Results, St, Louis, 2005—. Avocations: aerobics, circuit weight training, sewing, stained glass crafts. Home and Office: PO Box 517 O Fallon MO 63366-0517

**WOOD, LINCOLN JACKSON**, aerospace engineer; b. Lyons, NY, Sept. 30, 1947; s. William Hulbert and Sarah Brock (Strumsky) Wood. BS with distinction, Cornell U., 1968; MS in Aeronautics and Astronautics, Stanford U., 1969, PhD, 1972. Staff engr. Hughes Aircraft Co., El Segundo, Calif., 1974-77; tech. staff Jet Propulsion Lab. Calif. Inst. Tech., Pasadena, 1977-81, tech. group supr. Jet Propulsion Lab., 1981-89, tech. mgr., 1989-91, dep. tech. sect. mgr., 1991-99, dep. leader of Office of Excellence for Deep Space Comm./Nav. Sys., 2000—03, tracking and nav. sys. sys. mgr., deep space mission sys. engring. and ops. programs, 2003—04, program mgr., 2004—. Bechtel instr. engring. Calif. Inst. Tech., Pasadena, 1972—74, lectr. in sys. engring., 1975—76, vis. asst. prof., 1976—78, vis. assoc. prof., 1978—84; cons. in field. Contbr. articles to profl. jours. Bd. dirs. Boys Republic, Chino Hills, Calif., 1991, 1997—. Fellow: AIAA (assoc.; assoc. editor Jour. Guidance, Control and Dynamics 1983—89, tech. com. astrodynamics 1985—86, chmn. 1986—88); mem.: AAAS, IEEE (sr.), Am. Astron. Soc. (sr.; assoc. editor Jour. Astron. Scis. 1980—83, space flight mechanics com. 1980—97, gen. chmn. AAS/AIAA Space Flight Mechanics Meeting 1993, chmn. space flight mechanics com. 1993—95). Los Solteros (pres. 1991, 1997—2005), Sigma Xi. Office: Jet Propulsion Lab 4800 Oak Grove Drive Mail Stop 301-125L Pasadena CA 91109 Business E-Mail: lincoln.j.wood@jpl.nasa.gov.

**WOOD, LINDA MAY**, librarian; b. Ft. Dodge, Iowa, Nov. 6, 1942; d. John Albert and Beth Ida (Riggs) Wiley; m. C. James Wood, Sept. 15, 1964 (div. Oct. 1984). BA, Portland State U., 1964; M in Librarianship, U. Wash., 1965. Reference libr. Multnomah County Libr., Portland, Oreg., 1965-67, br. libr., 1967-72, adminstrv. asst. to libr., 1972-73, asst. libr., asst. dir., 1973-77; asst. city libr. L.A. Pub. Libr., 1977-80; libr. dir. Riverside (Calif.) City and County Pub. Libr., 1980-91; county libr. Alameda County Libr., Fremont, Calif., 1991—. Adminstrv. coun. mem. Bay Area Libr. and Info. Svcs., Oakland, Calif., 1991—. Chair combined charities campaign County of Alameda, Oakland, Calif., 1992; bd. dirs. Inland AIDS project, Riverside, 1990-91; vol. United Way of Inland Valleys, Riverside, 1986-87, Bicentennial Competition on the Constitution, 36th Congl. Dist., Colton, Calif., 1988-90. Mem. ALA (CLA chpt. councilor 1992-95), Calif. Libr. Assn. (pres. 1985, exec. com., ALA chpt. councilor 1992-95), Calif. County Librs. Assn. (pres. 1984), League of Calif. Cities (cmty. svcs. policy com. 1985-90), OCLC Users Coun. (Pacific Network del. 1986-89). Democrat. Avocations: dance, opera, reading. Office: Alameda County Libr 2450 Stevenson Blvd Fremont CA 94538-2326 Office Phone: 510-745-1536. E-mail: lwood@aclibrary.org.

**WOOD, LISA GODBEY**, prosecutor; b. Lexington, Ky., Jan. 28, 1963; married; 2 children. BA summa cum laude, U. Ga., 1985, JD summa cum laude, 1990. Bar: Ga. 1990. Law clk. to Hon. Anthony A. Alaimo US Dist. Ct. (so. dist.) Ga., 1990; assoc. Gilbert, Harrell, Summerford & Martin, Brunswick, Ga., 1991—2004, ptnr., 1995—2004; US atty. (so. dist.) Ga. US Dept. Justice, Savannah, Ga., 2004—. Adv. com. US Dist. Ct.; disciplinary review panel State Bar Ga.; mem. Ga. Bd. Pub. Safety. Mem.: ABA, Def. Rsch. Inst. Office: US Attys Office So Dist PO Box 8970 Savannah GA 31412*

**WOOD, MARCUS ANDREW,** lawyer; b. Mobile, Ala., Jan. 18, 1947; s. George Franklin and Helen Eugenia (Fletcher) W.; m. Sandra Lee Pellonari, July 25, 1971; children: Edward Alan, Melinda Janel. BA cum laude, Vanderbilt U., 1969; JD, Yale U., 1974. Bar: Oreg. 1974, U.S. Dist. Ct. Oreg. 1974, U.S. Ct. Appeals (9th cir.) 1982. Assoc., then ptnr. Rives, Bonihadi & Smith, Portland, Oreg., 1974-78; ptnr. Stoel Rives LLP and predecessor firms, Portland, 1974—. Pres., bd. dirs. Indochinese Refugee Ctr., Portland, 1980, Pacific Ballet Theatre, Portland, 1986-87; bd. dirs. Outside In, Portland, 1989—. Lt. USNR, 1969-71. Mem.: ABA, Phi Beta Kappa. Home: 9300 NW Finzer Ct Portland OR 97229-8035 Office: Stoel Rives 900 SW 5th Ave Ste 2300 Portland OR 97204-1229 Business E-mail: mwood@stoel.com.

**WOOD, MARGARET,** performing company executive; Entertainment and spl. events dir. Stratton Mountain Resort, Stratton, Va.; gen. mgr. Broward Ctr. for the Performing Arts, Ft. Lauderdale, Fla.; interim gen. dir. Anchorage Opera; gen. dir. Dance Conneticut, 2000—. Co-founder Performing Artservices Inc., NY; founder Dance Umbrella, 1975.

**WOOD, MARIAN STARR,** publishing executive; b. NYC, Mar. 30, 1938; d. Edward James and Betty (Starr) Markow; m. Anthony Stuart Wood, Mar. 21, 1963. BA, Barnard Coll., 1959; postgrad., Columbia U., 1959—64. Tchg. asst., lectr. Columbia U., N.Y.C., 1960-64; editor Praeger Pubs., N.Y.C., 1965-71; sr. editor Henry Holt & Co., N.Y.C., 1972-81, exec. editor, 1981-96, assoc. pub. Marian Wood Books, 1996-99; v.p. Marian Wood Books at G.P. Putnam's Sons, N.Y.C., 1999—. Recipient Roger Klein Found. award for career achievement, 2001. E-mail: Mwood@us.penguingroup.com.

**WOOD, MARK D.,** lawyer; b. Chgo., Jan. 8, 1966; BS with high honors, U. Ill., 1987; JD cum laude, U. Mich., 1990. CPA Ill., 1987; bar: Ill. 1990, US Dist. Ct., No. Dist. Ill. Ptnr., co-chair Securities Law Practice Group Katten Muchin Rosenman, LLP, Chgo. Mem.: ABA, Am. Bar Assn. Office: Katten Muchin Rosenman LLP 525 W Monroe St Chicago IL 60661 Office Phone: 312-902-5493. Office Fax: 312-577-8858. E-mail: mark.wood@kattenlaw.com.

**WOOD, MARY ELIZABETH,** retired secondary school educator, church musician; b. Berwyn, Ill., Apr. 15, 1929; d. Ralph Jerome Compton and Dora Mary Langlois; m. Harvey Eugene Wood, Aug. 21, 1954 (dec.); children: Joseph, Ann, Kim, Lynn, Christopher, Curtis, Carol, John, Nicole. BA in English and Edn., Marycrest U., Davenport, Iowa, 1951; MA in English and Edn., Mich. State U., East Lansing, 1958; AA in Music summa cum laude, Lansing C.C., Mich., 1980. Cert. permanent tchr. Mich. Tchr. H.S. Oxford (Iowa) Schs., 1951—52; tchr. jr. and sr. H.S. Gobles (Mich.) Schs., 1952—55; tchr. Cement City H.S., 1957—58, Portland H.S., 1958—60, Dimondale H.S., 1960—62; tchr. H.S. completion adults Holt Pub. Schs., 1965—95. Cantor Immaculate Heart Mary Ch., Lansing, Mich., 1970—84; dir. music Holy Cross Ch., Lansing, 1983—88, St. Peter Cath. Ch., Eaton Rapids, Mich., 1989—91, St. Jude Cath. Ch., DeWitt, Mich., 1992—2002; painter religious iconography. Singer: (albums) Jesus Lives by Fr. Lucien Deiss; composer: (children's operettas) The Country Cousin, 1984, The Touch, 1994, (liturgical music) Dedication Mass of St. Peter, 1992. Choir dir. Ch. Resurrection, Lansing, Mich. Mem.: Nat. Assn. Pastoral Musicians (co-chmn. Lansing chpt. 1995—). Roman Catholic. Avocations: sewing, reading, singing, music, writing. Home: 5102 Killarney Dr Holt MI 48842

**WOOD, MAURICE,** medical educator; b. Pelton, Eng., June 28, 1922; came to U.S., 1971; s. Joseph and Eugenie (Lumley) W.; m. Erica Joan Noble, May 1, 1948; children: Roger Lumley, Ashley Michael, Frances Jane. MB BS, U. Durham, Eng., 1945. Diplomate Am. Bd. Family Practice. Sr. ptnr. med. practice South Shields County, Durham, 1950-71; gen. practice teaching group U. Newcastle, Newcastle-on-Tyne, Eng., 1969-71; gen. clin. asst. dept. psychology-medicine South Shields Gen. Hosp., 1966-71; assoc. prof., dir. rsch. in family practice Med. Coll. Va.-Va. Commonwealth U., Richmond, 1971-73, prof., dir. rsch. in family practice, 1973-87, prof. emeritus, 1987—. Cons. advisor WHO, Geneva, 1979-90, chmn. working party to develop a classification for primary care, 1979-90; founding mem. exec. dir. N.Am. Primary Care Rsch. Group, Richmond, 1983-92, past pres., pres. emeritus, 1993—; chmn. com. on cmty. oriented primary care Insts. of Medicine, 1982-84. Assoc. editor Jour. Family Practice, 1976-83. Recipient award for meritorious svc. Va. Acad. Family Physicians, 1976; Maurice Wood award for career achievement in primary care rsch. founded in his honor, 1995. Fellow Royal Coll. Gen. Practitioners, Am. Acad. Family Physicians; mem. Inst. Medicine-Nat. Acad. Sci., Soc. Tchrs. Family Medicine (Curtis Hames Career Research award 1984), Inst. of Medicine, NAS, Ambulatory Sentinel Practice Network, Internat. Primary Care Network (treas., bd. dirs.), N.Am. Primary Care Rsch. Group (treas., bd. dirs., exec. dir. 1982-92). Lodges: Rotary. Episcopalian. Personal E-mail: wood150@verizon.net.

**WOOD, MICHAEL B.,** medical products executive; Grad., McGill U. Fellowship microvascular surgery, hand surgery U. Louisville; residency Mayo Grad. Sch. of Medicine; prof. of orthopedics Mayo Med. Sch., orthopedic surgeon, vice-chair bd. of gov. Mayo Regional Health Sys., Rochester, Minn.; CEO, pres. Mayo Found., 1999—2003, Pres. Emeritus, 2003—. Bd. dir. Steris Corp. Cubist Pharm. Inc. Pres. of bd. Malcolm Baldrige Nat. Quality Award Found., 2000. Mem.: bd. dir., Visionshare Inc. Am. Soc. Surgery of the Hand, Soc. of Med. Administrn., Minn. Med. Assn. Am. Med. Assn., Am. Soc. Reconstructive Microsurgery (pres. 1990—91). Office: Mayo Clinic 200 First St SW Rochester MN 55905 Office Phone: 904-953-2496. Business E-Mail: wood.michael@mayo.edu.

**WOOD, MICHAEL M.,** ambassador; married; 2 children. Co-founder, CEO Hanley Wood, LLC, 1976—2005; mem. bd. advisors Weronis Suhler Stevenson, 2005; founder Redwood Investments, LLC, 2005; U.S. amb. to Sweden, 2006—. Former mem. Harvard Joint Ctr. for Housing Studies, long range planning com. Nat. Assn. Home Builders. Recipient Top Exec. of Yr. award, Media Bus. mag., 2005. Office: US Embassy 5750 Stockholm Pl Washington DC 20521*

**WOOD, MICHAEL W,** lawyer; b. Austin, Tex. B, Rice Univ., Houston, 1967; JD, Univ. Tex., 1970. Bar: Tex. 1971, US Supreme Ct., US Ct. of Appeals (5th cir.), US Tax Ct. Co-founder Wood Campbell Moody & Gibbs, 1971; ptnr. Nathan Wood Sommers & Lippman; sr. v.p. and CEO Azurix Water Resources; co-ptnr. in charge of Houston office Akin Gump Strauss Hauer & Feld LLP, Houston, 2002—. Bd. trustees Houston Grand Opera; former bd. dir. Houston Ballet Found. and Wortham Theater Ctr. Mem.: ABA, Houston Bar Assn. Office: Akin Gump Strauss Hauer & Feld LLP 44th Fl 1111 Louisiana St Houston TX 77002-5200 Office Phone: 713-220-8111. Office Fax: 713-236-0822. Business E-Mail: mwood@akingump.com.

**WOOD, MYRA LINDEN FRANK,** consultant; b. Richmond, Va., Oct. 26, 1950; d. J. C. and Myra Teresa (Lanzaroe) Frank; m. Timothy Franklin Long (div. Jan. 1981); m. Robert Andrew Hudson (div. 1994); m. Frederick W. Wood, Sept. 25, 1999. BA, Erskine Coll., Due West, S.C., 1972; student, Inst. Fin. Edn., 1982-88. Chief activities therapist S.C. Dept. Corrections, Columbia, 1973-75, acting prin., 1975-77, coll. coord., 1977-78; owner, operator Carolina Coast Seafood, Aiken and Beaufort, S.C., 1978-80; from teller to savs. counselor Security Fed. Savs. & Loan, Aiken, 1981-83; customer svc. rep. Bankers 1st Savs. & Loans, Augusta, Ga., 1983-84, mgr. br. adminstrn., 1984-85; coord. automated teller machines, banking officer 1st Fed. Savs. Bank, Brunswick, Ga., 1985-88; ptnr., cons. electronic banking/software devel. RAH Systems, Brunswick, 1988-93; ptnr. specific application computer programming, software tng. Details & More, Greenville, S.C., 1989-90, ptnr. event planning, various mfg. positions and mktg./sales, 1989-91; cons. Mauldin, S.C., 1992-93. Lectr. S.C. Edn. Tchrs. Assn., Columbia, 1974, S.C. Assn. Social Workers, Columbia, 1975, Bus. and Profl. Women's Club, Columbia, 1978; small bus. owner, distbr. Nuskin Internat. line, 1987—90; ind. mktg. rep. Network 2000/U.S. Spring, 1988—92; computer specialist Top Food Svcs. Carolina, Inc., Duncan, SC, 1989—90; admintrv./sales mgr. Cusom Catering, Duncan, 1990; cons. Con-

tract Office/Computer Svcs., Greenville, 1992—2004; Shaklee ind. distbr., 1998—; dir., v.p., CFO FMW Holdings, Inc., 2000—; assoc. World Leadership Group/Global Equity Lending, 2004—; br. mgr. World Leadership Group/Global Equity Lending, 2005—. Book rev. writer A Class Act, Greenville, 1996—; appeared with Aiken Cmty. Theatre, 1981. Bd. dirs. Quest Soc., Greenville, 1992-95; mem. hospice com. Am. Cancer Soc., Augusta, 1981; lectr. St. John's United Meth. Ch., 1981-82, A Class Act, 1998; registrar, treas. Sugar Creek Soccer Club, Greenville, 1996-97. Mem. A Creative Gathering Writers Group, Writer's Roundtable. Democrat. Avocations: writing, reading, travel, study/research exploring the internet. Home and Office: PO Box 333 Mauldin SC 29662-0333 E-mail: cobfrank@charter.net.

**WOOD, NANCY ELIZABETH,** psychologist, educator; d. Donald Sterret and Orne Louise (Erwin) W. BS, Ohio U., 1943, MA, 1947; PhD, Northwestern U., 1952. Prof. Case We. Res. U., Cleve., 1952—60; specialist, expert HEW, Washington, 1960—62; chief rschr. USPHS, Washington, 1962—64; prof. U. So. Calif., L.A., 1965—. Learning disabilities cons., 1960-70; assoc. dir. Cleve. Hearing and Speech Ctr., 1952-60; dir. licensing program Brit. Nat. Trust, London; Author: Language Disorders, 1964, Language Development, 1970, Verbal Learning, 1975 (monograph) Auditory Disorders, 1978, Levity, 1980, Stoneskipping, 1989, Bird Cage, 1994, Out of Control, 1999. Pres. faculty senate U. So. Calif., 1987—88. Recipient Outstanding Faculty award, Trojan Fourth Estate, 1982, Pres.' Svc. award, U. So. Calif., 1992. Fellow APA (cert.), AAAS, Am. Speech and Hearing Assn. (legis. coun. 1965-68); mem. Internat. Assn. Scientists. Republican. Methodist. Office: U So Calif University Park Los Angeles CA 90089-0001 Personal E-mail: woodn@adelphia.net.

**WOOD, PAMELA SHARON,** music educator, soprano; b. San Francisco, Mar. 29, 1944; d. Clinton Barford and Pearl (Henderson) Wood; m. Eric Scott Fraley, Dec. 28, 1968 (div. 1981); children: Ayanna Fraley Moore, Amara Fraley; m. Stephen B. Ambush, July 25, 1982 (div. 1996). MusB Edn. summa cum laude, Howard U., 1967; Music Divsn. Honors, Yale U. Summer Sch. of Music and Art, 1968; Tchg. and Musicianship Cert., Kodaly Musical Tng. Inst., Inc., 1976; MusM in Vocal Performance, U. Mass., 1980; Advanced Assocs. Cert., Kodaly Ctr. Am., 2000. Music instr. and choral dir. Baccus and Hamilton Jr. High Schs., Wash., DC, 1967—69; music instr. and choral dir., elem. jr. high sch. music specialist pub. schs., Stoneham, Mass., 1969—70; mem. faculty, chmn. dept. music theory and edn. Elma Lewis Sch. of Fine Arts, Nat. Ctr. of Afro-American Artists, Inc., Boston, 1970—76; music tchr. Boston Pub. Schs. and Kodaly Ctr. of Am., 1981—82; voice tchr. Tufts U., Medford, Mass., 1982—87; music instr. Wheelock Coll., Boston, 1983—87, Roxbury CC, Boston, 1986—87; lectr. music MIT Sch. Humanities, Arts and Social Scis., Cambridge, Mass., 1987—96, sr. lectr. music, 1996—; voice tchr. Pine Manor Coll., Chestnut Hill, Mass., 2002—05. Voice tchr. Pine Manor Coll., Chestnut Hill, Mass., 2002—05, condr., 2004—05, Women's Inn at Pine St., Boston, 1995—2001, Sisters St. Joseph Cmty. Chorus, Brighton, Mass., 1996—2004; faculty Kodály Music Inst., Boston, 1999—; presenter in field. Singer (soprano soloist): Steve Reich & Musicians, 1974—88, NY and Israel Philharm., London, Boston, Chgo., San Francisco Symphonies, 1974—96; choral conductor: The Women's Inn at Pine St., 1995—2001, St. Joseph Cmty. Chorus, 1996—2004, Pine Manor Coll., 2004—05. Bd. overseers New Eng. Conservatory of Music, Boston, 1996—2004; assoc. bd. mem. Kodaly Ctr. Am., Wellesley, Mass., 1996—; bd. dirs. Boston Orch. & Chorale, 1991—94, Boston Children's Chorus, 2006—. Recipient Sponsors and Patrons award, Met. Opera Co., 1972, award, Nat. Assn. Tchrs. of Singing, 1981, Black Achiever, Greater Boston YMCA, 1994; honoree, Oberlin Black Musicians' Guild, Oberlin Conservatory of Music, 2003. Mem.: Orgn. Am. Kodaly Educators (nat. conf. team 2004—05), Nat. Assn. Study and Performance of African-Am. Music, Ctr. Black Music Rsch., Boston Area Kodaly Educators, Pi Kappa Lambda. Office: Mass Inst of Tech 77 Massachusetts Ave Cambridge MA 02139 Office Phone: 617-253-8778.

**WOOD, PATRICK HENRY, III,** former federal official; b. Port Arthur, Tex., July 4, 1962; m. Kathleen Ryder; 4 children. BS in Civil Engring., Tex. A&M U.; JD, Harvard Law Sch. Atty. Baker & Botts LLP, Washington; engr. Arco Indonesia; legal counsel to chmn. Tex. Railroad Commn.; advisor to Fed. Energy Regulatory Commr. Jerry Langdon Fed. Energy Regulatory Commn., US Dept. Energy, Washington, staff mem., 1993—94, chmn., 2001—05. Pub. Utility Commn. Tex., 1995—2001. Bd. dirs. SunPower Corp., 2005—; chmn. advisory bd. Airtricity N. Am., Chgo., 2006—. Office: Airtricity Inc 401 N Michigan Ave Ste 3020 Chicago IL 60611*

**WOOD, PAUL F.,** national health agency executive; b. Lockport, N.Y., Dec. 7, 1935; s. Dwight Edward and Frances (Fletcher) W.; m. Kathleen Frances Stretton, May 27, 1958; children: Paul S., Richard F. BA, Western Res. Univ., 1964; MA, Kent State U., 1970; PhD, Case Western Res. U., 1975. Assoc. exec. dir. United Way of Stark County, Canton, Ohio, 1967-70; owner Paul Wood Co., N. Canton, Ohio, 1970-86; dir. devel. The Salvation Army, N.Y.C., 1986-90; pres. Nat. Coun. on Alcoholism and Drug Dependence, N.Y.C., 1990-99; special asst. The Salvation Army, Cleve., 1999—2002; ret., 2002. Bd. dirs. Fairfield (Conn.) Chorale, 1991-94, Stepping Stones Found., 1996-99, Bedford Hills, N.Y.; fin. com. Westport United Meth. Ch., 1993-96. Mem.: Berlin Yacht Club (sec. 2006—). Avocations: sailing, computer programming. Office: The Salvation Army 2507 E 22nd St Cleveland OH 44115-3202 Personal E-mail: wood-paul@sbcglobal.net.

**WOOD, PHOEBE A.,** food products executive; Grad., Smith Coll.; MBA, UCLA. With Atlantic Richfield Co.; v.p. CFO Propel, Inc. divsn. Motorola, Inc.; exec. v.p., CFO Brown-Forman Corp., Louisville, 2002—. Office: Brown-Forman Corp 850 Dixie Hwy Louisville KY 40210

**WOOD, QUENTIN EUGENE,** oil industry executive; b. Mechanicsburg, Pa., Mar. 5, 1923; s. Lloyd Paul and Greta (Myers) W.; m. Louise Lowe, Apr. 14, 1958. BS, Pa. State U., 1948. Petroleum engr. Quaker State Oil Refining Corp., Parkersburg, W.Va., 1948-52, chief engr. Bradford, Pa., 1952-55, mgr. prodn., 1955-68, v.p. prodn. Oil City, Pa., 1968-70, exec. v.p., 1973-75, pres., chief ops. officer, 1973-75, pres., chief exec. officer, 1975-82, chmn., chief executive officer, 1982-88, chmn. bd., 1988-90, dir., 1990-93. Bd. dirs. Pa. Mfrs. Ins. Co.; chmn. industry tech. adv. com. U.S. Bur. Mines, 1960-70, Penn Grade Tech. Adv. Com., 1955-69, Pa. Oil and Gas Conservation Commn., 1961-71. Trustee Pa. State U., 1976-94, pres., 1979-87. 1st lt. USAAF, 1943-46. Mem. Am. Inst. Metall. Engrs., Pa. Grade Crude Oil Assn. (dir.), Pa. Oil Producers Assn. (past pres., dir. Bradford dist.), Am. Petroleum Inst. (dir.), Nat. Petroleum Refiners Assn. (dir.). Home: 1402 Spinnakers Reach Dr Ponte Vedra Beach FL 32082

**WOOD, R. L. (BOB WOOD),** chemicals executive; BA in History, U. Mich. With human resources, sales and mktg. depts. Dow Chem. Co., 1977—89; v.p. mktg. household products DowBrands, 1989—90, v.p. sales, 1990—93; group v.p., gen. mgr. household products DowBrands N.Am., 1993—94; v.p. polyolefins and elastomers Dow Plastics, Dow N.Am., 1994—95, bus. v.p. engring. plastics, 1995—97, bus. v.p. polyurethanes, 1997—2000; bus. group pres., mem. corp. operating bd. Thermosets and Dow Automotive, 2000—04; pres., CFO Crompton Corp., Middlebury, Conn., 2004—. Bd. dirs. Jarden Corp. Immediate past chmn. Big Bros./Big Sisters Am. Office: Crompton Corp 199 Benson Rd Middlebury CT 06762

**WOOD, R. STEWART, JR.,** retired bishop; b. Detroit, June 25, 1934; s. Raymond and Marjorie Wood; m. Kristin Lie Miller, June 25, 1955; children: Lisa, Raymond, Michael. AB, Dartmouth Coll., 1956; MDiv, Va. Theol. Sem., 1959; MA in Counseling and Sociology, Ball State U., 1973; postgrad., Va. Seminary. Ordained to diaconate and priesthood Epis. Ch., 1959. Assoc. rector St. Paul's, Columbus, Ind., 1959—60; vicar Episc. Ch., Seymour and Bean Blossom, Ind., 1960—63; assoc. rector Grace Ch., Muncie, Ind., 1963—66, rector, 1966—70; exec. dir. Episc. Cmty. Svcs., Indpls., 1970—76; rector All Saint's Episc. Ch., Indpls., 1973—76, Christ Ch., Glendale, Ohio, 1976—84, St. John's Ch., Memphis, 1984—88; elected Bishop Coadjutor

Diocese Mich., Detroit, 1988—89, diocesan bishop, 1990—2000; ret., 2000. Dir. summer camps, conf. ctr.; dep. Gen. Conv. 1970, 73, 76, 82; exec. coun. 1972-76, Coalition for Ordination of Women, bd. dirs. Episcopalian. Avocations: camping, golf, tennis, photography. Office: Box 968 255 Robert Frost Ln Quechee VT 05059-0968 Office Phone: 802-295-8912. E-mail: stemwood@aol.com.

**WOOD, RICHARD COURTNEY,** library director, educator; b. Spartanburg, S.C., Aug. 8, 1943; s. Herman Alva and Mildred Eloise (Porter) W.; m. Amy Louise Black, Aug. 16, 1974. BA, U. Tex., 1966; MLS, U. S. C., 1977. Head cataloging Wofford Coll. Libr., Spartanburg, 1969-78; hosp. libr. John Peter Smith Hosp., Ft. Worth, 1978-80; reference libr. Tex. Coll. Osteo. Medicine, Ft. Worth, 1980-82, assoc. dir. libr., 1982-91; exec. dir. librs., assoc. prof. Sch. Medicine, chair HCOM dept. Tex. Tech U. Health Scis. Ctr., Lubbock, 1991—. Cons. Tarrant County Med. Libr. Assn., Fort Worth, 1978-82, 84, Med. Plaza Hosp., Fort Worth, 1979-82, Grand Prairie (Tex.) Community Hosp., 1980-81, Cook-Fort Worth Children's Hosp., 1988-91. Patron Kimball Art Mus. Fort Worth, 1987—; spokesman Neighborhood Assn., Fort Worth, 1989; vis. exec. United Way, Fort Worth, 1990. Recipient Dean's award Sch. Nursing, Tex. Tech U. Health Sci. Ctr., 1998. Mem. Dallas-Tarrant County Consortium (chmn. 1980-81), Metroplex Consortium Health Scis. (chmn. 1980-81), South Cen. Regional Group, Med. Libr. Assn. (chmn. osteo. librs. sect. 1986-87), South Cen. Acad. Med. Librs. (bd. dirs. 1991—, past chair), Nat. Network Librs. Medicine (bd. dirs. South Cen. region 1991-93), Deutsche Gesellschaft für Heereskunde, LIS Users Group (chair exec. bd.), Sigma Tau Delta. Republican. Presbyterian. Avocations: languages, travel, history, gardening, music. Home: 1805 Bangor Ave Lubbock TX 79416-5518 Office: Preston Smith Libr Health Scis 3601 4th St Lubbock TX 79430-0001 Office Phone: 806-743-2203. E-mail: richard.wood@ttuhsc.edu.

**WOOD, RICHARD ROBINSON,** real estate company executive; b. Salem, Mass., Nov. 8, 1922; s. Reginald and Irene Margaret (Robinson) Wood; m. Pamela Vander Wiele, Mar. 8, 1951 (div. Apr. 1969); children: Christopher Robinson, Bryant Cornelius, Marcella Wood Mackenzie; m. Jane Philbin, Sept. 19, 1970. AB, Harvard Coll., 1944; postgrad., Mass. Inst. Tech., 1947-48. V.p. Hunneman & Co., Boston, 1959-72; trustee, sec. Mass. Real Estate Investment Trust, Boston, 1967-69; trustee Suffolk Franklin Savings Bank, 1967-74; pres., chmn. Continental Real Estate Equity, Boston, 1972-74; exec. v.p. ITEL Real Estate Corp., San Francisco, 1974-75; v.p. Baird & Warner, Chgo., 1976-80; pres., chmn. Renwood Properties, Inc., Cambridge, Mass., 1981—. Founder Real Estate Securities 2d Syndication Inst., 1972, pres., 1976—78; pres., chmn. ILCO Properties, Chgo., 1981—87; v.p., dir. Common Goal Capitol Group, Balt., 1986—; gen. ptnr. Common Goal Mortgage Fund, Balt., 1986—; mem. Coun. Rural Housing and Devel., 1988—; v.p., bd. dirs. St. Katherines Care Ctrs., 1990—; chmn. Inst. Responsible Housing Preservation, 1994—99, 19 Chauncy St. Trust, 1995—. Mem. Mayor's Citizen Adv. Bd., Boston, 1965—67, Coun. Rural Housing and Devel., 1988—; committeeman, treas. Mass. Rep. State Com., Boston, 1964—72; pres. Boston Rep. City Com., 1965—67. With M.C. U.S. Army, 1943—44. Mem.: Nat. Leased Housing Assn., White Mountain Ski Runners, Badminton and Tennis Club, Harvard Club N.Y., Longwood Cricket Club, Harvard Club Boston. Avocations: tennis, skiing. Home: 19 Chauncy St Cambridge MA 02138-2549 Office: Renwood Properties Inc Ste 44 875 Massachusetts Ave Cambridge MA 02139-3067 Office Phone: 617-876-4455. Personal E-mail: renwoodprops@aol.com.

**WOOD, ROBERT CHARLES,** lawyer, real estate developer; b. Chgo., Apr. 8, 1956; s. Roy Edward and Mildred Lucille (Jones) W.; m. Jennifer Jo Briggs, Oct. 1984; children: Jacqueline Jones, Reagan Keith. BA in History, So. Meth. U., 1979, BBA in Real Estate, 1979, JD, 1982. Bar: Tex. 1983. Appraiser McClellan-Massey, Dallas, 1977—79; rschr., acquisitions officer Amstar Fin. Corp., Dallas, 1979—80; prin. Robert Wood Cons., Dallas, 1981—98; ptnr. Welch & Wood Attys. and Y2K Cons., Dallas, 1998—2000; pvt. practice Dallas, 1995—; real estate investor and developer, 1998—. Cons. Plan Mktg. Cos., 1983-84; pvt. practice law, Dallas, 1983-84; gen. counsel Diversified Benefits, Inc., Dallas, 1984-86; nat. accts. mgr. Lomas & Nettleton Real Estate Group, Dallas, 1987-88; sr. pension cons., prin. Eppler, Guerin &Turner, 1988-93; chmn. adv. coun. on devel. Medisend, 1991; nat. consulting coord. fin. advisors coun., v.p. Callan Assocs., San Francisco, 1994-95; atty. at law, 1995—; exec. v.p., gen. counsel, Rushmore Investment Advisors, Plano, Tex., 2002-. Author: Electionomics: How the Money Managers View the Election, 1992, After the Congress Vote: How the Managers See Things Now, 1993, Y2K--The Year 2000 Issue: How Y2K Affects the Markets, 1998; mem. So. Meth. U. Law Rev., 1981-82; contbr. articles to profl. publs. Bd. dirs. Dallas unit Am. Cancer Soc., 1982-87, mem. spl. events com., 1986-87, mem. crusade com., 1987-88, mem. medisend adv. com., 1988-94, comm. corp. devel. bd., 1989-95. Mem. Tex. Bar Assn., Phila. Bar Assn., Phi Gamma Delta. Avocations: skiing, tennis, bicycling. Office Phone: 214-369-3209. E-mail: rccwood@aol.com.

**WOOD, ROBERT EMERSON,** pediatrics educator; b. Jacksonville, Fla., Nov. 15, 1942; s. Waldo E. and Verda V. Wood. BS in Chemistry magna cum laude, Stetson U., 1963; PhD in Physiology, Vanderbilt U., 1968, MD, 1970. Bd. cert. pediatrics; bd. cert. pediatric pulmonology. Intern in pediatrics Duke U. Med. Ctr., Durham, 1970-71, resident in pediatrics, 1971-72; fellow pediatric pulmonology Case Western Res. U., Cleve., 1974-76, asst. prof. pediatrics, 1976-82, assoc. prof. pediatrics, 1982-83; assoc. prof. pediatrics, chief divsn. pediatric pulmonary medicine Dept. Pediatrics, U. N.C., Chapel Hill, 1983-88, prof. pediatrics, chief divsn. pediatric pulmonary medicine, 1988-94, dir. pediat. ICU, 1984-86, dir. Ctr. Pediat. Bronchology, 1994-99; prof. pediats. and otolaryngology Cin. Children's Hosp. Med. Ctr., U. Cin., 1999—; chief, divsn. pulmonary medicine Children's Hosp. Med. Ctr., U. Cin., 2001—05. Mem. editorial bd.: Pediatric Pulmonology, 1992—, Jour. Bronchology, 1993—; contbr. chpts. to books and articles to profl. jours. Lt. comdr. USPHS, 1972-74. Named Grad. fellow Danforth Found., 1963-68, Med. Scientist fellow Life Ins. Med. Rsch. Found., 1965-70, Clin. Rsch. fellow Cystic Fibrosis Found., 1974-76. Mem. Am. Bronchesophagological Assn., Am. Assn. for Bronchology, Soc. for Pediatric Rsch., Am. Thoracic Soc., N.C. Pediatric Soc. Office: Cin Children's Hosp Med Ctr Pediat Pulmonary Medicine 3333 Burnet Ave Cincinnati OH 45229-3039 Fax: 513-636-7734. Office Phone: 513-636-2776. Business E-Mail: rewood@cchmc.org.

**WOOD, ROBERT L.,** chemicals executive; BA in History, U. Mich. Field seller Dow Chem. Co., Cleveland, Ohio, 1978—80, mktg. recruiting and placement dept. Midland, Mich., 1980—82, product sales mgr., 1982—84, mktg. mgr., 1984—87, dir. mktg., 1987—89, v.p. mktg. Indpls., 1989—90, v.p. sales, household products, 1990—93, group v.p. and gen. mgr. household products, 1993—94, v.p. polyolefins and elastomers, 1994—95, bus. v.p. engring. plastics, 1995—97, bus. v.p. polyurethanes, 1997—2000, bus. group pres. thermosets and Dow automotive, 2000—04; joined Crompton Corp., Middlebury, Conn., 2004; chmn., pres., CEO Chemtura Corp. (formed in merger of Crompton and Great Lakes), Middlebury, Conn., 2005—. Mem. Big Brothers Big Sisters of Am. Mem.: Jarden Corp. (bd. dirs.). Office: Chemtura Corp 199 Benson Rd Waterbury CT 06749

**WOOD, ROBERT WARREN,** lawyer; b. Des Moines, Iowa, July 5, 1955; s. Merle Warren and Cecily Ann (Sherk) W.; m. Beatrice Wood, Aug. 4, 1979; 1 child, Bryce Mercedes. Student. U. Sheffield, Eng., 1975-76; AB, Humboldt State U., 1976; JD, U. Chgo., 1979. Bar: Ariz. 1979, Calif. 1980, Wyo. 2000, NY 1989, D.C. 1993, Mont. 1998, US Tax Ct. 1980, Wyo.; Roll of Solicitors of Eng. and Wales, 1998. Assoc. Jennings, Strouss, Phoenix, 1979-80, McCutchen, Doyle, San Francisco, 1980-82, Broad, Khourie, 1982-85, Steefel, Levitt & Weiss, 1985-87, ptnr., 1987-91, Bancroft & McAlister, 1991-93; prin. Robert W. Wood, P.C., 1993—2005; ptnr. Wood & Porter, 2006—. Instr. in law U. Calif., San Francisco, 1981—82. Author: Taxation of Corporate Liquidations: A Complete Planning Guide, 1987, 2nd edit., 1994, The Executive's Complete Guide to Business Taxes, 1989, Corporate Taxation: Complete Planning and Practice Guide, 1989, S Corporations,

1990, The Ultimate Tax Planning Guide for Growing Companies, 1991, Taxation of Damage Awards and Settlement Payments, 1991, 3d edit., 2005, Office Tax Guide, 1991; co-author: (with others) California Closely Held Corporations: Tax Planning and Practice Guide, 1987, Legal Guide to Independent Contractor Status, 3d edit., 2000; editor: California Small Busines Guide, 4 vols., 1998, Home Office Money & Tax Guide, 1992, Tax Aspects of Settlements and Judgements, 1993, 2d edit., 1998, 3d edit., 2005; editor-in-chief The M & A Tax Report; editor: Limited Liability Companies: Formation, Operation and Conversion, 1994, 2d edit., 2001, Limited Liability Partnerships: Formation, Operation and Taxation, 1996; mem. editl. bd. Real Estate Tax Digest, The Practical Accountant, Jour. Real Estate Taxation. Fellow Am. Coll. Tax Counsel; mem. Calif. Bd. Legal Specialization (cert. specialist taxation), Can. Bar Assn., Bohemian Club, Law Coun. Australia. Republican. Office: Wood & Porter 333 Sacramento St San Francisco CA 94111 Office Phone: 415-834-1800. Business E-Mail: wood@woodporter.com.

**WOOD, RONALD,** musician; b. London, June 1, 1947; Owner Woody's on the Beach (nightclub), Miami, 1987—. Guitarist and bassist with Jeff Beck Group, 1966—69, Faces, 1969—75, Rolling Stones, 1975—, New Barbarians, 1979, solo (albums) Gimme Some Neck, 1979, I've Got My Own Album To Do, Now Look, albums (with Rolling Stones) Black and Blue, 1976, Love You Live, 1977, Some Girls, 1979, Emotional Rescue, 1979, Sucking in the Seventies, 1981, Tattoo You, Still Life, 1982, Undercover, 1983, Between the Sheets, 1985, Dirty Work, Rewind, 1986, Steel Wheel, 1988, Flashpoint, 1991, Voodoo Lounge, 1994 (Grammy award Best Rock Album), Bridges to Babylon, No Security, 1997, A Bigger Bang, 2005, (with Faces) Long Player, A Nod's As Good As A Wink..., To a Blind Horse, Ooh-La-La, (with Small Faces) First Step, Ogden's Nut Gone Flake, There Are But Four Small Faces, 1991, All or Nothing, 1992, films Let's Spend the Night Together, 1982, Digital Dreams, 1983 Named Greatest Touring Band of All Time, World Music Awards, 2006; named to Rock and Roll Hall of Fame, 1989. Office: Virgin Records 1540 Broadway New York NY 10036-4039

**WOOD, SHELTON EUGENE,** education educator, minister, consultant; b. Douglas, Ga., May 20, 1938; s. Shelton and Mae Lillie (Pheil) Wood; m. Edna Louise Wood, Aug. 25, 1961; children: Shelton John, Deirdre Louise. AA, St. John's U., 1958; BA, U. Nebr., 1959; MEd, Coll. William and Mary, 1971; PhD, Sussex U., 1973; EdD, Southeastern U., 1975; MBA, Univ. Mich. U., 1977; MA, U. Okla., 1980; D in Ministry, Wesleyan Bible Coll., 1999; Cert. in Internt. Rels., Fgn. Svc. Inst., 1971; Cert. in Mgmt., Indsl. Coll. Armed Forces, 1970. Area mgr. Marshall Fields Corp., Fla., 1957-58; transp. supr. Greyhound Corp., Jacksonville, Fla., 1959-62; officer US Army, 1963, advanced through grades to inf. col., 1966; with Redstone Readiness Group, 1977-80; chief studies and analysis divsn. Korean Inst. for Def. Analysis, 1981-83; faculty St. John River C.C., 1984-90; nat. and internat. bus. and mgmt. cons., 1995—; sr. pastor Fellowship Wesleyan Ch., Spring Hill, Fla., 1998—2005; asst. dist. supt. Fla., 2005—. Faculty Wesleyan Bible U., 1997—; pres. Georgetown Wesleyan U. of the Americas. Author: Strategic for Implementing A Family Life Ministry Ctr., 1997; contbr. articles to profl. jours. Active Boy Scouts Am., 1977—90; lay leader United Meth. Ch., Falls Ch., Va., 1977—79, St. James United Meth. Ch., 1986—90; mem. dist. bd. ministerial develop. Fla. Dist. of Wesleyan Ch., 1999, chair evangelism and ch. growth com., 1999—; bd. dirs. Baby Love. Decorated Bronze Star with 2 oak leaf clusters, Air medal with 3 oak leaf clusters, Purple Heart with 2 oak leaf clusters; Sussex Coll. fellow, 1969-70. Mem. NEA, Am. Soc. Trainers and Developers (pres. S.E. chpt. 1974-75), Am. Def. Preparedness Assn., Putnam County C. of C. (pres. 1990-91), Toastmasters Internat. (Disting. Toastmaster 1989), Kiwanis (pres. 1989-90), Phi Kappa Delta, Phi Delta Kappa. Address: 8485 Chatsworth St Spring Hill FL 34608 Personal E-Mail: ewood11@tampabay.rr.com.

**WOOD, STEPHEN WRAY,** minister, educator, legislator, singer, songwriter; b. Winston Salem, NC, Oct. 6, 1948; s. D.W. and Annie Lee (Harris) W.; m. Starr Smith, June 18, 1978; children: Allyson, Joshua. BTh., John Wesley Coll., 1970; BA, Asbury Coll., 1973; MA, U. N.C., 1979; DMin, Luther Rice Sem., Fla., 1980; MDiv, Houston Grad. Sch. Theology, 1990. Ordained to ministry Soc. of Friends, 1980. Asst. dean, asst. prof. John Wesley Coll., High Point, NC, 1975-81; min. Soc. of Friends, 1980—. Adj. prof. Luther Rice Sem.; assoc. prof. Houston Grad. Sch. Theology; pres. Triad Christian Counseling, Greensboro, 1979. Contbr. articles to hist., ednl. and religious jours., Dictionary of N.C. Biography, Oxford Internat. Roundtable, 1997—; composer, singer religious music. Trustee John Wesley Coll., High Point, 1981—; bd. dirs. Friends Ctr-Guilford Coll., Greensboro, 1982-89; vice chmn. Guilford County Rep. Party, N.C., 1981-85; mem. N.C. State Ho. Reps., 1985-86, 89-90, 91-92, 93-94, 95-96, 97—; spkr. pro tem, 1997—; chaplain High Point Jaycees. With U.S. Army, 1970-71; capt. N.C. State Militia. Mem. BMI (affiliate songwriter 1978—). Avocations: golf, book collecting, reading, cowboy boot collecting. Office: PO Box 5172 High Point NC 27262-5172 Office Phone: 336-883-9663. Personal E-mail: repstevewood@juno.com. I often reflect upon the maternal advice proffered me as a child, "Steve, if at first you don't succeed, try, try again." We may be down but not out. There is no such thing as the good old days because the future is just as bright as the promises of God. We conquer by continuing. Life is not a problem to be solved, it is a gift to be enjoyed.

**WOOD, TERRY LEE,** mathematics professor; BA, Mich. State U., 1964, MA, 1968, PhD, 1976. Cert. tchr. Mich. Elem. tchr. Lansing (Mich.) Pub. Schs., 1964-65, 66-68; tchr., researcher The Lab. Schs., Chgo., 1970-80; vis. asst. prof. Purdue U., West Lafayette, Ind., 1985-88, asst. prof. math. edn., 1988-93, assoc. prof., 1993-98, prof., 1998—. Co-editor: Transforming Children's Mathematics Education, 1990, Recreating Elementary Mathematics Education: Insights and Issues, 1993, Mathematics Teacher Education International Perspectives, 1999, Beyond Classical Pedagogy: Teaching Elementary School Mathematics, 2001; assoc. editor Jour. Math. Tchr. Edn.; mem. editl. bd. Ednl. Studies in Math., Jour. Tchr. Edn. Child Devel.; cons. editor Child Devel. Robert L. Snodgrass scholar. Mem. AAAS, APA, Am. Ednl. Rsch. Assn., Nat. Coun. Tchrs. Math., Psychology Math. Edn. Internat., Psychology Math. Edn. N.Am., Soc. Rsch. in Child Devel., Cognitive Devel. Soc. Office: Purdue U Curriculum & Instrn Beering Hall 100 N University St West Lafayette IN 47907-1622 Business E-Mail: twood@purdue.edu.

**WOOD, THOMAS E.,** lawyer; b. LA, Apr. 20, 1939; s. Louis Earl and Youda (Hays) Wood; m. Sally Ann Wood, June 22, 1963; children: Julia W. DeVuono, Melissa W. Brewster. BA, Amherst Coll., 1961; LLB, U. Pa., 1966. Bar: Pa. 1966. Assoc. Drinker Biddle & Reath LLP, Phila., 1966-72, ptnr., 1972—, ptnr.-in-charge Berwyn office, 2001—. Chmn. Easttown Zoning Hearing Bd., Easttown Twp., Pa., 1976—. Mem. Phila. Club. Office: Drinker Biddle & Reath LLP 1000 Westlakes Dr Ste 300 Berwyn PA 19312-2409 Office Phone: 610-993-2211. Office Fax: 610-993-8585. E-mail: thomas.wood@dbr.com.

**WOOD, THOMAS WESLEY,** humanities educator, editor; b. Hugo, Okla., Mar. 16, 1920; s. Thomas Wesley Wood Sr. and Alma Elora (Rogers) Daniel; m. L. Deloris Gray, May 31, 1968; m. Doreen Anderson, June, 1950 (div. 1966); children: John William, Thomas Wakefield. BA in History and Journalism, Tulsa U., 1951, MA in History, 1952; MS in Journalism, Northwestern U., 1953; PhD in European History, U. Okla., 1966. Reporter City News Bur. Chgo., 1952-54; prof. Tulsa (Okla.) U., 1954-73, So. Ill. U., Carbondale, 1973-78; vis. prof. Am. U., Cairo, Egypt, 1976-78, U. Ark., Little Rock, 1978-80; prof. Temple U., Phila., 1980-90, emeritus prof., 1990—. Reporter, corr. Tulsa World, 1954-84; editor, pub., founder Lost Generation Jour., Salem, Mo., 1973—. Author: Tulsa U. Editing Hankbook, 1956, 60, Tulsa U. Reporting Handbook, 1958, 60, 69, Outline History of American Journalism, 1961, Influence of the Paris Herald on the Lost Generation Writers, 1966; sub.-editor Egyptian Gazette, 1977-78. Recipient editing and writing award Mo. Press Women, 1985, writing award Pa. Press Club, 1983, writing award Ark. Press Women, 1979, 80, photography award Soc. Profl. Journalists, 1972. Mem. Overseas Press Club Am., Assn. Edn. Journalism and Mass Comm., Soc. Scholar Editors, Coun. Editors Learned

Journals, Pi Alpha Mu (nat. pres. 1956-60). Republican. Baptist. Avocations: fly fishing, travel, interviewing expatriate 20's americans. Home: RR 5 Box 134 Salem MO 65560-9008 Office: Lost Generation Jour RR 3 Box 387 Salem MO 65560-9315

**WOOD, THOMAS WILLARD,** health industry executive, retired military officer; b. Logan, Utah, Jan. 21, 1939; s. Elmer Douglas and Leola (Pitkin) W.; m. Blanche Loila Dowdle, Sept. 11, 1959 (div.); children: Dianna Wood Perry, Jeffery Thomas (dec.); m. Charlene Taulbee, Oct. 5, 1974; children: Douglas Winston Remington, Angela Christine Douglas, Thomas Willard II, Michael Joseph, Matthew David. BA, Utah State U., 1962; MS, Cen. Mich. U., 1975; postgrad., Indsl. Coll. Armed Forces, 1975, Armed Forces Staff Coll., 1976. Commd. 2d lt. USAF, 1962, advanced through grades to col., 1983; chief protocol Hdqrs. Air Force Logistics Command, Wright-Patterson AFB, Ohio, 1972-75; chief spl. project div. Hdqrs. 21st Air Force, McGuire AFB, N.J., 1977-78; chief inquiries br. Office Legis. Liaison, The Pentagon, Washington, 1978-82; dep. dir. Directorate Competition Advocacy Ogden Air Logistics Ctr., Hill AFB, Utah, 1982-85; air attache U.S. Def. Attache Office, Am. Embassy, Wellington, New Zealand, 1985-88; chief protocol, dep. dir. pub. and govtl. affairs Hdqrs. U.S. Comdr.-in-Chief Pacific, Camp Smith, Hawaii, 1988-89; ret., 1989; adminstrv. asst. to v.p. mktg. Hawaii Med. Svc. Assn., Honolulu, 1989-91; sr. account exec. client rels. Baxter Internat. Inc., San Antonio, 1991-92; sr. account exec. prescription svc. divsn. Caremark, Inc., San Antonio, 1992-95; with corp. accts. prescription svc. divsn. Caremark Inc., San Antonio, 1996-97; sr. account exec. field ops. Caremark Pharm. Svcs., Medpartners Inc., San Antonio, 1997-99; sr. acct. mgr. field ops. CaremarkRx Inc., San Antonio, 1999-2000. Sr. nat. acct. mgr. SBC Comms., Inc., Caremark, Inc., San Antonio, 2000-02, assoc. nat. acct. exec., 2003-04, strategic acct. exec., 2005—; dean New Zealand Mil. Attache Corps, 1986-88. High priest LDS Ch., also ch. organist, pianist, tchr.; music chmn., high coun. San Antonio North Stake, 2000—; mem. groundbreaking and dedication com. San Antonio Tex. Temple, 2002-05. Decorated DFC, Air medal with nine oak leaf clusters; Gallantry Cross with palm (Vietnam); named hon. Royal New Zealand Air Force Navigator, 1988. Mem. Disting. Flying Cross Soc. (pres. Alamo chpt.). Republican. Avocations: jogging, swimming. Home: 1351 Grey Oak Dr San Antonio TX 78213-1602 Office: CaremarkRx Inc 7034 Alamo Downs Pkwy San Antonio TX 78238-4509 Personal E-mail: alamowood@aol.com.

**WOOD, VIVIAN POATES,** mezzo soprano, educator; b. Washington, Aug. 19, 1923; d. Harold Poates and Mildred Georgette (Patterson) W. Studies with Walter Anderson, Antioch Coll., 1953-55; studies with Denise Restout, Saint-Leu-A-Forêt, France and Lakeville, Conn., 1960—62, studies with Denise Restout, 1964—70; studies with Paul A. Pisk, 1966—71; studies with Paul Ulanowsky, NYC, 1958—68; Elemer Nagy, 1965-68, Vyautas Marijosius, 1967-68; MusB, Hartt Coll. Music, 1968; postgrad. (fellow), Yale U., 1968; MusM (fellow), Washington U., St. Louis, 1971; PhD (fellow), 1973. Debut in recital series Internat. Jeunesse Musicals Arts Festival, 1953; solo fellowship Boston Symphony Orch., Berkshire Music Ctr., Tanglewood, 1964, St. Louis Symphony Orch., 1969, Washington Orch., 1949, Bach Cantata Series Berkshire Chamber Orch., 1964, Yale Symphony Orch., 1968. Appearances in U.S. and European recitals, oratorios, operas, radio and TV, 1953-68; soloist Landowska Ctr., Lakeville, 1969, Internat. Harpsichord Festival, Westminster Choir Coll., Princeton, N.J., 1973; prof. voice, head voice area Sch. of Music, U. So. Miss., Hattiesburg, 1971-2000, ret. 2000, prof. emerita, 2000—; asst. dean Coll. Fine Arts, 1974-76, acting dean, 1976-77; guest prof. Hochschüle für Musik, Munich, 1978-79; prof. Italian Internat. Studies Program, Rome, 1986; mem. Council Alliance for Arts Edn., Kennedy Ctr. Performing Arts, 1974—; mem. Miss. Gov.'s Adv. Panel for Gifted and Talented Children, 1974—; 1st Miss. Gov.'s Conf. on the Arts, 1974—. Author: Polenc's Songs: An Analysis of Style, 1971. Recipient Young Am. Artists Concert award N.Y.C., 1955; Wanda Landowska fellow 1961-68. Mem. Miss. Music Tchrs. Assn., Nat. Assn. Tchrs. of Singing, Music Tchrs. Nat. Assn., Am. Musicology Soc., Golden Key, Mu Phi Epsilon, Delta Kappa Gamma, Tau Beta Kappa (hon.), Pi Kappa Lambda. Democrat. Episcopalian.

**WOOD, WENDY DEBORAH,** filmmaker; b. N.Y.C., Oct. 4, 1940; d. John Meyer and Marion Emily (Peters) W.; m. William Dismore Chapple, Dec. 7, 1963; 1 child, Samuel Eliot. BA cum laude, Vassar Coll., 1962; MA, Stanford U., 1964. Tchg. asst. Stanford U., 1962-64; photographer, film editor Bristol (Eng.) U., 1964-66, asst. dir. Internat. Conf. Film Schs., 1966; tech. asst. biology dept. U. Conn., Storrs, 1970-72; sr. media specialist Aetna Life & Casualty Co., Hartford, Conn., 1972-89; media writer, prodr., dir. U. Conn. Ctr. for Media and Tech., Storrs, 1989—2006. Pres. Chapple Films, Inc., 1972—. Films include: Yankee Craftsman, 1972, Alcoholism, Industry's Costly Hangover, 1974, Draggerman's Haul, 1975, Flight Without Wings, 1977, Auto Insurance Affordability, 1981 (2 awards), Where Rivers Run to the Sea, 1981 (award), Our Town is Burning Down, 1982 (6 awards), Wellness at the Worksite, 1984 (4 awards), Aenhance, 1989 (3 awards), Tiffany: Magician in Glass. Mem. jury N.Y. Internat. Video and Film Festival; bd. dirs. Windham Regional Arts Coun., 1987, 88, 89; mem. peer rev. com. Conn. Commn. Higher Edn., 1992-96. Recipient CINE Golden Eagle award Coun. on Internat. Non-Theatrical Events, 1972, 76, 84, 1st Place award Indls. Photography, 1974, cert. Outstanding Creativity U.S. TV Commls. Festival, 1974, EFLA award Am. Film Festival, 1974, 76, Dir's. Choice award Sinking Creek Film Festival, 1975, award Columbus Film Festival, 1975, award Excellence Life Ins. Advts. Assn., 1975, Silver Screen award U.S. Indsl. Film Festival, 1976, 81, 1st place award Com. Film Festival, 1977, 1st prize Nat. Outdoor Travel Film Festival, 1978, 1st pl. Houston Film Festival, 1982, CINE Golden Eagle, 1982, 84, award Am. Film Festival, 1982, N.Y. Film Festival, 1982, 83, Silver CINDY award Assn. Visual Communicators, 1985, Conn. Film/Video Festival 1st pl. award, 1997, Gold award Conn. Film Festival, 1997, others. Mem. Info. Film Prodrs. Am. (nat. dir., pres. chpt. 1981-82, Cindy award 1971, 72, 81, 82, 85, 87), Internat. Quorum Motion Picture Prodrs., Audio Visual Communications Conn. chpt. 1985, treas. 1988). Democrat. Mem. Soc. of Friends. Home: 604 Phoenixville Rd Chaplin CT 06235-2211 E-mail: woodwendy@earthlink.net.

**WOOD, WILLARD MARK,** lawyer; b. Traverse City, Mich., Nov. 30, 1942; s. William Mark and Ebba Forsman Wood; m. Sharon McDermott, June 19, 1965; children: Sean, Pat, Kelly, Ryan, Casey. BA, Santa Clara U., 1964; JD, U. So. Calif., 1967. Bar: Calif., D.C., U.S. Supreme Ct. Judge advocate USMC, Vietnam, 1969-70; ptnr. O'Melveny & Myers, L.A., 1971—. Assoc. editor U. So. Calif. Law Review, 1966—67. Capt. USMC, 1967-71, Vietnam. Mem.: DC Bar, LA County Bar Assn., Order of the Coif, ABA, State Bar Calif. (chmn., local disciplinary com.), Phi Delta Phi. Roman Catholic. Office: O'Melveny & Myers 400 S Hope St Ste 1321 Los Angeles CA 90071-2899 Office Phone: 213-430-6220. E-mail: mwood@omm.com.

**WOOD, WILLIAM BARRY, III,** biologist, educator; b. Balt., Feb. 19, 1938; s. William Barry, Jr. and Mary Lee (Hutchins) W.; m. Marie-Elisabeth Renate Hartisch, June 30, 1961; children: Oliver Hartisch, Christopher Barry. AB, Harvard U., 1959; PhD, Stanford U., 1963. Asst. prof. biology Calif. Inst. Tech., Pasadena, 1965-68, assoc. prof., 1968-69, prof. biology, 1970-77; prof. molecular, cellular and developmental biology U. Colo., Boulder, 1977—, chmn. dept., 1978-83, disting. prof., 2004—. Mem. panel for developmental biology NSF, 1970-72; physiol. chemistry study sect. NIH, 1974-78; mem. com. on sci. and public policy Nat. Acad. Scis., 1979-80; mem. NIH Cellular and Molecular Basis of Disease Rev. Com., 1984-88' mem. bd. sci. edn. Nat. Acad. Scis., 2005- Author: (with J. H. Wilson, R.M. Benbow, L.E. Hood) Biochemistry: A Problems Approach, 2d edit., 1981, (with L.E. Hood and J.H. Wilson) Molecular Biology of Eucaryotic Cells, 1975, (with L.E. Hood and I.L. Weissman) Immunology, 1978, (with L.E. Hood, and J.H. Wilson) Immunology, 2d edit., 1984, (with L.E. Hood and I.L. Weissman) Concepts in Immunology, 1978; editl. rev. bd. Science, 1984-92; mem. editl. bd. Cell, 1984-87, Developmental Biology, 1995-1999; editor-in-chief, CBE Life Scis. Edn., 2005-; contbr. articles to profl. jours. Recipient U.S. Steel Molecular Biology award, 1969, Alexander von Humboldt Rsch prize, 2004; NIH Rsch. grantee, 1965—; Merit awardee, 1986-96; Guggenheim fellow,

1975-76. Fellow AAAS; mem. Nat. Acad. Scis., Am. Acad. Arts and Scis., Am. Soc. for Cell Biology, Genetics Soc. Am. Soc. for Developmental Biology. Office: Univ Colo Dept MCD Biology 347 UCB Boulder CO 80309

**WOOD, WILLIAM JEROME,** lawyer; b. Indpls., Feb. 14, 1928; s. Joseph Gilmore and Anne Cecilia (Morris) Wood; m. Joann Janet Jones, Jan. 23, 1954; children: Steven, Matthew, Kathleen, Michael, Joseph, James, Julie, David. Student, Butler U., 1945-46; AB with honors, Ind. U., 1950, JD with distinction, 1952. Bar: Ind. 1952. Mem. firm Wood, Tuohy, Gleason, Mercer & Herrin (and predecessor), Indpls., 1952—. Bd. dirs. Grain Dealers Mut. Ins. Co., Am. Income Life Ins. Co.; gen. counsel Ind. Cath. Conf.; city atty., Indpls., 1959—60; instr. Ind. U. Sch. Law, 1960—62. Author: (book) Indiana Pastor's Legal Handbook, 3d edit., 2001, Realtors' Indiana Legal Handbook, 2d edit., 1991. Mem. Ind. Legal Edn. Corp. Survey Commn., 1963—, chmn., 1977—86; mem. Ind. Corp. Law Study Commn., 1985—87, Ind. Non Profit Corp. Law Study Commn., 1989—91. With AUS, 1946—48. Recipient Brotherhood award, Ind. region NCCJ, 1973. Mem.: St. Thomas Moore Legal Soc. (pres. 1970), Indpls. Bar Found., Indpls. Bar Assn. (pres. 1972—73, coun. bd. mgrs. 1992—93), Ind. Bar Assn. (sec. 1977—78, award 1968), Audubon Soc., Indpls. Lit. Club (pres. 1973—74), Am. Legion. Democrat. Roman Catholic. Home: 3619 E 75th Pl Indianapolis IN 46240-3674 Office: Bank One Ctr Tower 111 Monument Cir Ste 3400 PO Box 44942 Indianapolis IN 46244-0942 E-mail: bwood@indylegal.com

**WOOD, WILLIAM MCBRAYER,** lawyer; b. Greenville, S.C., Jan. 27, 1942; s. Oliver Gillan and Grace (McBrayer) W.; m. Nancy Cooper, 1973 (dec. 1993); children: Walter, Lewis; m. Jeanette Dobson Haney, June 25, 1994. BS in Acctg., U. S.C., Columbia, 1964, JD cum laude, 1972; LLM in Estate Planning (scholar), U. Miami, 1980. Bar: S.C. 1972, Fla. 1979, D.C. 1973, U.S. Tax Ct 1977, U.S. Ct. Claims 1972, U.S. Supreme Ct. 1977; cert. mediator, SC, 2006. Intern ct. of claims sect., tax divsn. U.S. Dept. Justice, 1971; law clk. to chief judge U.S. Ct. Claims, Washington, 1972-74; ptnr. firm Edwards Wood, Duggan & Reese, Greer and Greenville, 1974-78; asst. prof. law Cumberland Law Sch., Samford U., Birmingham, Ala., 1978-79; faculty Nat. Inst. Trial Advocacy: N.E. Regional Inst., 1979, 83-90, 95-97, Fla. Regional Inst., 1989; teaching team 5th intensive trial techniques course Hofstra U., 1983; assoc. then capital ptnr. firm Shutts & Bowen, Miami, 1980-85; sole practice Miami, 1985—; also Rock Hill, S.C., 1994—; of counsel Griffin, Smith, Caldwell, Helder & Helms, Monroe, NC, 2001—. Lectr. Nat. Bus. Inst. Seminars, 2003—04. Contbg. editor: The Lawyers PC; Fla. editor: Drafting Wills and Trust Agreements; substantive com. editor ABA: The Tax Lawyer, 1983-2004 Pres. Piedmont Heritage Found., Inc. 1975-78; del. State Rep. Conv., 1985, 87, 90, Fla. State Rep. Conv., 1986, 88, 90, SC State Conv., 1978; exec. committeeman Miami-Dade County Republicans, 1985-94, Mecklenberg County, NC Rep. Party, 2005—; co-legal counsel, 1990-92; apptd. Miami-Dade County Indsl. Devel. Authority, 1990-94; mem. vestry Episc. Ch., 1993-94; committeeman, former cubmaster, Boy Scouts Am., Mint Hill, NC; With USAF, 1965-69, Vietnam. Decorated Air Force Commendation medal; recipient Am. Jurisprudence award in real property and tax I, 1971; winner Grand prize So. Living Mag. travel photo contest, 1969. Mem. ABA (taxation sect., teaching law com., 1994—), Greer C. of C. (pres. 1977, Outstanding leadership award 1976), Greater Greenville C. of C. (dir. 1977), Order Wig and Robe, Estate Planning Council South Fla., Omicron Delta Kappa. Club: Bankers (bd. govs. 1989-94). Lodge: Masons, Scottish Rite, Rotary. Office: 5345 Wilgrove Mint Hill Rd Charlotte NC 28227-3467 Office Phone: 305-374-4941. E-mail: wmwood@bellsouth.net.

**WOOD, WILLIAM PRESTON,** writer, lawyer; b. Bronxville, NY, Apr. 23, 1951; s. Preston and Eleanor Catherine (Auby) W. BA, Middlebury Coll., 1973; JD, U. of the Pacific, 1976. Bar: Calif. 1976, U.S. Dist. Ct. (ea. dist.) Calif. 1976. Dep. dist. atty. Sacramento County District Atty., Sacramento, 1977—82; dir. publs. Calif. Dist. Attys. Assn., Sacramento, 1984—85; chief counsel Office Sec. State, Sacramento, 1999—2003; commr. Calif. Dept. Corps., 2003—05, Calif. Undersecretary of State, 2005—; freelance writer, Sacramento, 1985—; commr. Author: (novels) Rampage, 1985, Gangland, 1988, Fugitive City, 1990, Court of Honor, 1991, Stay of Execution, 1994, The Bone Garden, 1994, Quicksand, 1998, Pressure Point, 2005, (motion picture) Rampage, 1992, Broken Trust, 1995; co-author (TV series) Kaz, 1978; contbr. articles to profl. jours. Pres. Citizens for a Better Sacramento, 1986. Mem. Writers Guild Am.-West. Republican. Episcopalian. Office Phone: 916-324-9011.

**WOOD, WILLIS BOWNE, JR.,** retired utilities executive; b. Kansas City, Mo., Sept. 15, 1934; s. Willis Bowne Sr. and Mina (Henderson) W.; m. Dixie Gravel, Aug. 31, 1955; children: Bradley, William, Josh. BS in Petroleum Engring., U. Tulsa, 1957; grad. advanced mgmt. program, Harvard U., 1983; JD (hon.), Pepperdine U., 1996. With So. Calif. Gas Co., L.A., 1960-74, from v.p. to sr. v.p., 1975-80, exec. v.p., 1983-84; pres., CEO Pacific Lighting Gas Supply Co., L.A., 1981-83; from sr. v.p. to chmn., pres., CEO, Pacific Enterprises, L.A., 1984-93, chmn., CEO, 1993-98; ret. 1998. Bd. dirs. Washington Mut., Seattle; with Automobile Club So. Calif., 2005; trustee U. So. Calif. Past trustee, past vice-chmn. Harvey Mudd Coll., Claremont, Calif., 1984-2005; trustee emeritus, past chmn. Calif. Med. Ctr. Found., L.A., 1983-2002; past trustee, past pres. S.W. Mus., L.A.; trustee John and Dora Haynes Found., 1998—; past bd. dirs. L.A. World Affairs Coun.; past dir., past chmn. bus. coun. for Sustainable Energy Future, 1994—; past dir. Pacific Coun. for Internat. Affairs. Recipient Disting. Alumni U. Tulsa, 1995; inductee U. Tulsa Engring. Hall of Fame, 2001. Mem. Soc. Petroleum Engrs., Calif. State C. of C. (past chmn.), Am. Automobile Assn. (dir. 1999-, chmn. 2002-05), NAM (past bd. dirs.), Hacienda Golf Club, Calif. Club, Shady Canyon Golf Club. Republican.

**WOODALL, DAVID MONROE,** engineer, researcher, dean; b. Perryville, Ark., Aug. 2, 1945; m. Linda Carol Page, June 6, 1966; 1 child, Zachary Page. BA, Hendrix Coll., 1967; MS, Columbia U., 1968; PhD, Cornell U., 1976. Registered profl. engr., Idaho. Nuc. engr. Westinghouse Corp., Pitts., 1968-70; asst. prof. U. Rochester, N.Y., 1974-77, U. N.Mex., Albuquerque, 1977-79, assoc. prof., 1979-83, chair dept., 1980-83, prof., 1984-86; group physics mgr. Idaho Nat. Engring. Lab. Idaho Falls, 1986-92; assoc. dean, dir. rsch. U. Idaho, Moscow, 1992-99, acting dean, 1999, assoc. dir. nanodel. sci., engring., math. U. Alaska, Fairbanks, 1999—2003; dir. Ctr. for Nanosensor Tech., 2001—03. Provost & v.p. for academic affairs, Oregon Inst. of Tech., 2003—, EAC commr. Accreditation Bd. Engring. Tech., 1990-95, bd. dir., 1997-2003; cons. in field. Contbr. articles to profl. jours. Grantee NSF, DOE, AFOSR, Office Naval Rsch., DMEA, others. Mem. Am. Nuc. Soc. (chpt. chair 1982-83), Am. Soc. Engring. Edn. (divsn. chair 1993, 95, chair engring. rsch. coun., v.p.). Office: Oregon Institute of Technology 3201 Campus Drive Klamath Falls OR 97601 E-mail: david.woodall@oit.edu.

**WOODALL, JERRY M.,** research scientist, educator; b. Tacoma Park, Md., Sept. 5, 1938; m. Susan Woodall; children: Chandler B., Marshall O., Debra M., Sunny L., Serena J. BS, MIT, 1960; PhD in Elec. Engring., Cornell U., 1982. Various positions, Thomas J Watson Rsch. Ctr. IBM; prof. microelectronics Charles William Harrison Dist. Purdue U., West Lafayette, Ind. 1993—99; C. Baldwin Sawyer prof. of elec. engring. and prof. of applied physics Yale U., New Haven, 1999—; also co-founder and Chief Sci. Officer LightSpin Tech. Inc., Bethesda, Md. Dir. NSF Materials Rsch. Sci. and Engring. Ctr. Tech. Enabling Heterostructural Materials. Recipient Heinrich Welker Gold medal Inst. Physics, 1988. Fellow IEEE (Jack A. Morton award 1984), Am. Vacuum Soc. (pres.-elect 1996-97, Medard Welch award 1990), Electrochem. Soc. (Solid State Sci. and Tech. award 1985), Am. Phys. Soc.; mem. Nat. Acad. Engring. Recipient Chief Sci Officer LightSpin Tech Inc PO Box 30198 Bethesda MD 20824-0198 also: Becton Ctr Rm 507 Yale Univ PO Box 208284 New Haven CT 06520-8284 E-mail: jerry.woodall@yale.edu.

**WOODALL, SAMUEL ROY, JR.,** lawyer; b. July 8, 1936; s. Samuel Roy Woodall; m. Jane Marvin Brock, Aug. 5, 1958; children: Samuel Roy III, Lawrence S., Claiborne A., George G. BA, U. Ky., 1958, LLB, 1961; postgrad., Yale U., 1959. Bar: Ky. 1962. Atty. Ky. Dept. Ins., 1962-64, gen. counsel, 1965-66; commr. ins. Commonwealth Ky., 1966-68; assoc. firm

Wyatt, Grafton and Sloss, Louisville, 1968-69, ptnr., 1969-72; pres. Western Pioneer Life Ins. Co. (and predecessors), Louisville, 1972-76; asst. to pres. Am. Life & Accident Ins. Co., Louisville, 1976-80; pres. Nat. Assn. Life Cos., Washington, 1980-93; v.p. and chief counsel state rels. Am. Coun. Life Ins., Washington, 1993-98; with Morris, Manning & Martin (Atlanta-based firm), Washington, 1998—2001; ins. cons. Congl. Rsch. Svc., Libr. of Congres, Washington, 2001—; sr. ins. policy analyst U.S. Treasury Dept., 2002—. Guest instr. ins. law U. Louisville, 1968—69. Note editor: U. Ky. Law Rev. 1961—62. Pres. Citizen's Met. Planning coun., Louisville, 1970—71; chmn. City of Louisville Riverfront Commn., 1970—75, Ky. Heritage Commn., 1964—77; bd. dirs. Bingham Child Guidance Clinic, Louisville, 1969—76, Youth Performing Arts Coun., 1979—80. Named one of Ky.'s 3 Outstanding Young Men, Ky. Jr. C. of C., 1968; recipient Sullivan medallion, U. Ky., 1958; fellow Woodrow Wilson, Yale U., 1959. Mem.: ABA, Fedn. Ins. Counsel, D.C. Bar Assn., Ky. Bar Assn., Phi Beta Kappa, Phi Alpha Delta (pres. chpt. 1961—62). Home: 2851 29th St NW Washington DC 20008-4111 Office: US Dept Treasury 15th and Pennsylvania Ave NW Washington DC 20220

**WOODALL, SUSAN KAY,** language educator, librarian; b. Terre Haute, Ind., Mar. 13, 1951; d. James H. and Frances E. (Erxleben) Anderson; m. John P. Ramsey, Aug. 8, 1978 (div. May 1987); children: Jamie Sue, Jessica Leora; m. John Omar Rodriguez, Nov. 21, 1990 (div. Oct. 1996); m. Michael Taylor Woodall, May 21, 2000. Student, Cambridge (Eng.) U., spring 1972; BA in Latin, English and Psychology cum laude, Valparaiso U., 1973; MA with distinction in English, Ind. State U., 1976, MA in Libr. Sci., 1985; gifted/talented edn. endorsement, Purdue U., 1990. Lic. lifetime tchr.; cert. tchr. secondary English, Latin and psychology, Ind.; cert. in elem. and secondary gifted and talented edn., Ind.; lic. lifetime elem. and secondary libr. Tchr. English and Latin Clinton (Ind.) H.S., 1973-77, Austin (Ind.) H.S., 1977-78; tchr. Latin, English and psychology South Putnam H.S., Greencastle, Ind., 1978-85, tchr., libr., 1986—, head dept., 1995—. Past drama coach, yearbook instr. South Putnam H.S.; acad. team coord., 1995-99; adj. instr. libr. sci. Ind. State U., Terre Haute, summers 1986, 87; Fulbright exch. tchr. Southwood Secondary Sch., Cambridge, Ont., Can., 1994-95; adj. tchr. gifted and talented edn., libr. cons. Sacred Heart Sch., Terre Haute, 1994-95; cons. Dist. III Ind. Classical Conf., 1975-77; state semifinalist English team coach; Ind. state workforce intern, 2004; state internship-Workone, 2004; participant Internat. Fulbright Assn. Conf., Athens, Greece; adj. prof. NY Tech. CC, 2005—; adj. instr. psychology and English Ivy Tech. CC, 2005—. Contbr. articles to profl. publs. Mem. VFW aux.; past participant Habitat for Humanity; mem. state com. for emeritus dir. INCOLSA, 2005—. Named Creative Latin Tchr. of Yr., Ind. Classical Conf., 1976, 77; recipient Exch. cert. Fulbright Assn., Washington, 1995. Mem. NEA, Ind. Collective Svcs. Auth. (South Putnam Sch. Corp. rep. 1989—, mem. exec. com. 1989-95), Stone Hills Area Libr. Svcs. Authority (bd. dirs. Bloomington, bd. dir. 1989-95, treas., bd. dirs. 1993, 94, cons., mem. com. for cons./dir. rev. 1992, Dedicated Svc. award 1995), Acad. Coaches Assn. (Ind. br.), Ont. Libr. Assn., Ind. Coop. Libr. Svcs. Auth. Episcopalian. Achievements include participant, Fulbright Internat. Conv., Athens, Greece, 2004. Avocations: writing, travel. Office: Ind South Putnam Libr Svcs 1780 E Us Highway 40 Greencastle IN 46135-8722 E-mail: psuedoll@aol.com.

**WOODALL, THOMAS A.,** state supreme court justice; b. Meridian, Miss., July 14, 1950; m. Debbie Bogan, 1972; children: Scott, Matthew, Claire. BA in History, Millsaps Coll., 1972; JD, U. Va., 1975. Former legal editor Michie Co.; with Rives and Peterson, Birmingham, Ala., 1975—91; ptnr. Woodall and Maddox, Birmingham, 1991—96; circuit judge Jefferson County, 1996—2001; assoc. justice Ala. Supreme Ct., 2001—. Mem. Ala. Pattern Jury Instrn.-Civil Com., 1985—2001, vice chmn., 1992—2001. Mem.: Birmingham Bar Assn. (chair com. on grievance, civil ct. procedures and membership). Republican. Methodist. Office: Ala State Supreme Ct 300 Dexter Ave Montgomery AL 36104-3741*

**WOODARD, ALFRE,** actress; b. Tulsa, Nov. 8, 1953; m. Roderick Spencer, 1983; 2 children. Student, Boston U. Appeared in (films) Remember My Name, 1976, Health, Cross Creek, 1983 (Acad. award nomination), Extremities, 1986, Scrooged, 1988, Mandela, 1988, Miss Firecracker, 1989, Grand Canyon, 1991, The Gun in Betty Lou's Handbag, 1992, Passion Fish, 1992, Heart and Souls, 1993, Rich in Love, 1993, Bopha!, 1993, Blue Chips, 1994, Crooklyn, 1994, How to Make an American Quilt, 1995, Statistically Speaking, 1995, Primal Fear, 1996, A Step Toward Tomorrow, 1996, Star Trek: First Contact, 1996, Follow Me Home, 1996, Down in the Delta, 1998, Brown Sugar, 1998, Mumford, 1999, What's Cooking, 2000, Love and Basketball, 2000, K-PAX, 2001, Baby of the Family, 2002, (voice) The Wild Thornberrys Movie, 2002, The Singing Detective, 2003, The Core, 2003, Radio, 2003, The Forgotten, 2004, Beauty Shop, 2005, Something New, 2006, (TV series) Tucker's Witch, 1982-83, Sara, 1985, St. Elsewhere, 1985-87, Hill Street Blues (Emmy award for guest appearance in drama series 1984), L.A. Law (Emmy award for guest appearance in drama series 1987), Desperate Housewives (Screen Actors Guild Award for outstanding performance by an ensemble in a comedy series, 2006), 2005-; (TV spls.) For Colored Girls Who Have Considered Suicide/When the Rainbow is Enuf, Trial of the Moke, Words by Heart, (TV films) A Mother's Courage: The Mary Thomas Story, Child Saver, Ambush Murder, Freedom Road, 1979, Sophisticated Gents, 1981, The Killing Floor, Unnatural Causes, 1986, Mandela, 1987, The Child Saver, Sweet Revenge, 1990, Blue Bayou, 1990, Race to Freedom: The Underground Railroad, 1994, Wizard of Oz in Concert, 1995, The Piano Lesson, 1995, Journey to Mars, 1996, Gulliver's Travels, 1996, Member of the Wedding, 1997, Miss Evers' Boys, 1997, Cadillac Desert (miniseries), 1997, Funny Valentines, 1999 (also exec. prodr.), Holiday Heart, 2000, A Wrinkle in Time (miniseries), 2003, The Water is Wide, 2005, others, (plays) For Colored Girls Who Have Considered Suicide, When the Rainbow is Enuf, (off-Broadway plays) A Map of the World, 1985, A Winter's Tale 1989, So Nice They Named Twice, Horatio, What's Cookin', 2000, Love and Basketball, 2000, Dinosaur, 2000. Recipient Emmy awards for guest appearance in drama series, Josephine Premice award for sustained excellence Classical Theatre of Harlem, 2006. Office: Touchstone TV 100 Universal Plz Bldg 2128 Ste G Universal City CA 91608*

**WOODARD, CAROL JANE,** educational consultant; b. Buffalo, Jan. 19, 1929; d. Harold August and Violet Maybelle (Landsittel) Young; m. Ralph Arthur Woodard, Aug. 19, 1950; children: Camaron Jane, Carsen Jane, Cooper Ralph. BA, Hartwick Coll., 1950; MA, Syracuse U., 1952; PhD, SUNY, Buffalo, 1972; LHD (hon.), Hartwick Coll., 1991; postgrad., Bank St. Coll., Harvard U. Cert. tchr., NY State. Tchr., Orchard Park, NY, 1950-51, Danville, Ind., 1951-52, Akron, NY, 1952-54; dir. Garden Nursery Sch. Williamsville, NY, 1955-65; tchr. Amherst Coop. Nursery Sch., NY, 1967-69; asst. prof. early childhood edn. SUNY, Buffalo, 1969-72; lab. demonstration tchr. and student teaching supr., 1969-76, assoc. prof., 1972-79, prof., 1979-88, prof. emeritus, 1988—; dir. Consultants in Early Childhood, 1988—. Cons. Lutheran Ch. Am., Villa Maria Coll., Hartwick Coll., Buffalo Mus. Sci., Headstart Tng. Programs, Erie Cmty. Coll., NY State Dept. Edn., numerous workshops.; cons. sch. systems, indsl. firms, pub., civic orgns. in child devel.; vis. prof. The Netherlands and East China Univ., Shanghai, People's Republic of China; sci. trainer The Wright Group, 1995. Author 7 books for young children, 2 textbooks in field; co-author: Physical Science in Early Childhood, 1987; co-author nat. curriculum for ch. sch. for 3-yr.-olds; author: (booklet) You Can Help Your Baby Learn; author/coord. TAKE CARE child protection project, 1987; contbr. chpt. to books, articles to profl. jour. Trustee Hartwick Coll., Oneonta, NY, 1978-87, trustee emeritus, 2004-; cons. EPIC Birth to Three Program, 1992; design cons. indoor playground Noah's Ark Jewish Ctr., Buffalo, 1992; Sites Project coord., 1994-2005; student tchg. supr. SUNY, Fredonia, 1994-2004. Mem. Nat. Assn. Edn. Young Children, Early Childhood Edn. Council Western NY, Nat. Assn. Childhood Edn. Internat., Phi Delta Kappa, Pi Lambda Theta. Home: 85 Ruskin Road East Aurora NY 14052-3028

**WOODARD, CATHERINE,** arts patron; m. Nelson Blitz Jr.; children: Perri Blitz, Allison Blitz. BA in History magna cum laude, Wake Forest Univ., 1981; MS in Journalism, Columbia Univ., 1982. Reporter Fort Worth Star-Telegram, Tex., 1982—84, NY Newsday, 1984—94; dep. editor Newsday Direct, 1994—95; news editor, iGuide News Corp., NYC, 1995—96. Named one of Top 200 Collectors, ARTnews Mag., 2004; recipient James Wright Brown Pub. Svc. award, Deadline Club, NY Newspaper Pub. award, Soc. of Silurians award. Mem.: Mus. Modern Art Print Associates, Artists Space (bd. dir., coord. new media), Phi Beta Kappa. Avocation: Collecting Viennese furniture, prints and works on paper, especially Much, Picasso, Kirchner and Johns.

**WOODARD, DIANE E.,** music educator; d. Harry Moore and Mary Purdy Woodard; m. Bruce N. Wardrep, Sept. 12, 1998. B in Music Edn., Ga. Coll. 1970; MusM, Ga. State U., 1975, cert. in edn. specialist, 1985, PhD, 1994. Cert. tchg. Ga. Choral dir. Babb Jr. HS, Forest Park, Ga., 1977-79, Jonesboro HS, Ga., 1979—2001, chair music dept., 1981—91; asst. choral dir. Woodward Acad., College Park, Ga., 2001—02; choral dir. Galloway Sch., Atlanta, 2002—. Music tchr. Fountain Jr. H.S., Forest Park, 1971—72. Organist, choir dir. St. Timothy's Luth. Ch., Forest Park, 1983—87; mem. Atlanta Symphony Orch. Chorus, 1983—. Mem.: MENC (so. divsn. bd. dirs. 1995—97, nat. assembly state pres. 1995—97), Am. Choral Dirs. Assn. (treas. Ga. chpt. 1977—80), Ga. Music Educators Assn. (organizing chair all-state chorus event 1978, 1979, chair choral divsn. 1979—81, organizing chair all-state chorus event 1982, 1983, 1985, region chair all-state chorus auditions 1994, pres. 1995—97, so. divsn. bd. nat. conf. 1995—98, nat. assembly state pres. 1997, exec. com. 1997—98, bd. dirs. 1997—98, region chair all-state chorus auditions 1998, 1999, 2000, 2002—05, dir. chair all-state chorus auditions 1990, coun. 1975—87, Music Educator of Yr. 2004). Office: Galloway Sch 215 W Wieuca Rd NW Atlanta GA 30342

**WOODARD, FREDRICK JAMES, JR.,** music educator, musician; b. Kansas City, Mo., Mar. 2, 1961; s. Fredrick James Woodard,Sr and Sandra Josephine Woodard, Barbara Ann Woodard (Stepmother); m. Rochelle Mareace Breeden, May 4, 1996; children: Kahmal London, Fredrick Woodard,III, Deniece. MusB, Berklee Coll. of Music, Boston, 1983; MEd, U. of Mass., Boston, 2000. Cert. Tchr. Mass., 1990, Ednl Administr. Mass., 2000. Gen. music tchr. St Joseph and St. Patrick Schs., Roxbury, Mass., 1992—94; guitar tchr. and instrumental ensemble dir. Belmont Hill Sch., Belmont, Mass., 1992—94; guitar,electric bass and strings tchr. Roland Hayes Divsn. of Music, Roxbury, Mass., 1994—; pres./owner Ujam Records, Roxbury, Mass., 1996—; bandleader The Fred Woodard Trio, Roxbury, Mass., 1988—; freelance musician Various bands in the Boston area, Boston, 1983—. Musician (guitarist,producer,composer,arranger): (jazz compact disc) Arrival, 1999, (compact disc) 1715, 2001 (GBOS Image Award Jazz Artist of the Yr., 2002). Mem. Dudley St. Neighborhood Initiative, Roxbury, Mass., 2001—02. Mem.: Mass. Music Educators Assn., Internat. Assn. for Jazz Edn. Avocations: history, photography, travel. Office: Ujam Records PO Box 190586 Boston MA 02119 Office Phone: 617-438-1719. E-mail: fwtrio@hotmail.com.

**WOODARD, GEOFFREY ESTY,** molecular physiologist; s. Paul Esty and Marion Kathryn Woodard. BA, Harvard U., 1988; PhD, U. of Cambridge, Eng., 2001, Rsch. fellow NIH, Bethesda, Md., 2001—. Mem.: Cambridge Philis. Soc., Am. Physiol. Soc., Order of the Founders and Patriots, Soc. of the War of 1812, SAR. Home: PO Box 5782 Bethesda MD 20824 Office: NIH 10 Center Dr Bethesda MD 20892

**WOODARD, JOSEPH LAMAR,** law librarian, educator; b. Auburndale, Fla., Dec. 28, 1937; s. Wilbur Allen and Florence Virginia (Ladd) Woodard; m. Eleanor Eugenia Cummings, Aug. 7, 1964; children: Robert Edward, James Frederick. BA, U. Fla., 1959, JD, 1962; MLS, Columbia U., 1964. Bar: Fla. 1962, U.S. Dist. Ct. (mid. dist.) Fla. 1970. Asst. reference libr. Columbia U., N.Y.C., 1962—64; asst. libr. Cahill, Gordon, Reindel and Ohl, N.Y.C., 1964—65; law libr. Tulane U., 1965—69; prof. Schuh, Schuh and Woodard, St. Petersburg, Fla., 1969—71; law libr. Stetson U., 1971—2001, prof. law, 1979—2001, law libr., prof. emeritus, 2001—. Pres. Tampa Bay Libr. Consortium, 1981, 1988—89. Stated clk. Presbytery Tampa Bay, 2005—06. With USAR, 1957—63. Mem.: ABA, Pinellas Pub. Libr. Coop. (sec.-treas. 1993—94, pres. 1994—95), Am. Assn. Law Librs. (sec.-treas. SE chpt. 1975—78), Fla. Bar Assn. Republican. Personal E-mail: lamar@woodardfamily.org.

**WOODARD, PETER CLARK,** music educator, musician; b. Bethesda, Md., May 17, 1950; s. Charles Clark and Catherine Marie Woodard; m. Lisa Anne Baker, Sept. 7, 1989 (div.); children: Clark, Kirk. MusB, U. Hartford, 1973; MusM, U. Conn., 1989. Music adv. Hartford (Conn.) Ballet Co., 1973—80; dance accompanist Mary Anthony Dance Theatre, NYC, 1980—84; faculty U. Hartford Hartt Sch., 1984—. Vocal accompanist undergrad. Cleve. Inst., 1968—69; vocal accompanist Hartt Sch., Hartford, 1969—73; chmn. jazz studies U. Hartford Hartt Sch., 1995—. Composer, performer (CD) Pictures from Fortaleza, 2001. Jazz performer, faculty Eleazar De Carvalho Festival, Fortaleza, Brazil, 2000—03; judge jazz piano competition Music Club Hartford, 1998; panelist Sinatra; Conf. Hofstra U., 1999; organizer, host Iraqi Forum, Hartford, 2002, Dorothy Day Forum, Hartford, 2003; organist St. Mary's Ch., Norwalk, Conn., 1964—68. Mem.: Conn. Composers Orgn., Pi Kappa Lambda. Democrat. Avocations: reading, literature. Office Phone: 860-768-4123. Business E-Mail: pwoodard@hartford.edu.

**WOODBRIDGE, JOHN DUNNING,** history professor; b. Salisbury, N.C., May 24, 1941; s. Charles Jahleel and Ruth (Dunning) W.; m. Susan Jane Frerichs, June 28, 1970; children: Elisabeth Anne, Joshua, David. BA in History, Wheaton Coll., 1963; MA in History, Mich. State U., 1965; PhD de Troisième Cycle, U. Toulouse, France, 1969; MDiv, Trinity Evang. Div. Sch., Deerfield, Ill., 1971. Vis. prof. history U. Toulouse, 1968-69; asst. prof. history Trinity Coll., Deerfield, 1970-74; prof. ch. history Trinity Evang. Div. Sch., Deerfield, 1970—; vis. prof. history Northwestern U., Evanston, Ill., 1988-95. Vis. prof. religion Hautes Etudes, Sorbonne, U. Paris, 1996, 99. Author: Biblical Authority, 1982, Revolt in Pre-revolutionary France, 1995; editor: Great Leaders of the Christian Church, 1988; co-editor: Historische Kritik und biblischer kanon, 1988; sr. editor Christianity Today, 1997-99. NEH fellow, 1973-74, Herzog August Bibliothek fellow, 1982, ACLS fellow, Paris, 1976-77; NEH summer grant, Chgo., 1995. Mem. Am. Soc. Eighteenth Century Studies, Soc. French History. Mem. Evangelical Free Ch. Avocation: composing music.

**WOODBRIDGE, JOHN MARSHALL,** architect, urban planner; b. NYC, Jan. 26, 1929; s. Frederick James and Catherine (Baldwin) W.; m. Sally Byrne, Aug. 14, 1954 (div. 1975); children: Lawrence F., Pamela B., Diana B. (dec. 2002); m. Carolyn Kizer, Apr. 8, 1975 BA magna cum laude, Amherst Coll., 1951; MFA in Architecture, Princeton U., 1956. Designer John Funk, Arch., San Francisco, 1957-58; designer, assoc. ptnr. Skidmore, Owings & Merrill, San Francisco, 1959-73; staff dir. Pres.'s Adv. Coun. and Pres.'s Temporary Commn. on Pennsylvania Ave., Washington, 1963-65; exec. dir. Pennsylvania Ave. Devel. Corp., Washington, 1973-77. Lectr. architecture U. Calif., Berkeley; vis. prof. U. Oreg., Washington U., St. Louis. Co-author: Buildings of the Bay Area, 1960, A Guide to Architecture in San Francisco and Northern California, 1973, Architecture San Francisco, 1982, San Francisco Architecture, 1992, rev., 2005 Recipient Fed. Design Achievement award Nat. Endowment for Arts, 1988; Fulbright scholar to France, 1951-52. Fellow AIA (emeritus); mem. Nat. Trust Hist. Preservation, Soc. Archtl. Historians, Phi Beta Kappa. Democrat. Episcopalian. Home: 19772 8th St E Sonoma CA 95476-3849

**WOODBRIDGE, NORMA JEAN,** nurse, writer; b. Flushing, N.Y., Apr. 21, 1931; d. Charles Jahleel Woodbridge and Ruth Eyman Dunning. BS in Nursing Edn., Temple U., 1958; RN, U. Pa., 1952; LittD, World Congress Poets, Cairo, 1990. RN Fla. Sr. RN, forensic State of Fla. Dept. Corrections,

1992-95; staff nurse Pines Village, North Ft. Myers, Fla., 1995—97; staff RN Lee Convalescent Ctr., Ft. Myers, Fla., 1997-98; unit mgr. Tandem Health Care, Norht Ft. Myers, 1998-99; nurse Cape Coral (Fla.) Gen. Staff Rehab., 1999—2005, Shady Rest Care Pavillion, 2005—. Author-in-residence Highland Park (N.J.) Sch. Sys., 1988-90. Author: African Realities and Dreams, 1987, Resting Places, 1988, Meditations of a Modern Pilgrim, 1990, Shining Splendor, 2005; contbr. Christmas Blessings, 2002; composer (jazz album) Watercolor Dreams, 1982; playwright Switch: Switch, 1998; poetry reading on NPR, 2001. Recipient Poet of the Millenium award, Internat. Poets Acad., 2000; fellow, Yaddo Writing Colony, 1988. Mem.: ASCAP, N.J. Poetry Soc. (v.p. 1987—88), Soc. Am. Poets, Peace River (Fla.) Writers Group. Avocations: travel, fishing, gourmet cooking, hiking, theater. Home: 2606 Zoysia Ln Fort Myers FL 33917-2476

**WOODBURN, NORMA DENMAN,** biology educator; b. N.Y., Nov. 19, 1921; d. George Griffin Denman and Rose Lillian Langtry; m. Robert P. Woodburn, July 21, 1946 (dec.); children: Lillian E., Pamela J., Preston M. Student in Biology, U. Mich., 1940—41; BA, Hunter Coll., N.Y., 1943; degree in Biology, Bridgewater State Coll., Mass., 1980; student, U. Mass., Dartmouth, Mass., 1981—82. Cert. tchr. N.J., Mass. Jr. chemist Celanese Corp., Newark, 1943; tchr. botany Salem Coll., Winston-Salem, NC, 1943—44; tchr. sci. Gardner Sch., N.Y., 1944—45, Leonard Sch., N.Y., 1945—47, Fay Sch., Boston, 1948—50, Middleboro (Mass.) H.S., 1950—87. Author: Unwilling Captive, 1996. Vol. Burkland Elem. Sch., Middleboro, 2000—06, U.S. Agrl. Dept., Taunton, Mass., 1988—90. Recipient Recognition cert., Middleboro (Mass.) Conservation Commn., 1986, Ret. award, NEA, 1987, Accomplishment award, Plymouth County Edn. Assn., 1987, Recognition cert., Middleboro (Mass.) Pub. Libr., 2003. Mem.: Nat. Biology Tchr. Assn. (life), Nat. Edn. Women's Clubs. Avocations: conservation, marine biology. Home: 4 Nook Rd Plymouth MA 02360

**WOODBURN, RALPH ROBERT, JR.,** lawyer; b. Haverhill, Mass., Nov. 3, 1946; s. Ralph Robert and Josephine Marie (McClure) W.; m. Janet M. Smith, Sept. 15, 1985. BA, Mich. State U., 1967; JD, Harvard U., 1972; LLM, Boston U., 1981. Bar: Mass. 1972, U.S. Tax Ct. 1987. Assoc. Bowers, Fortier & Lakin, Boston, 1972-76; from assoc. to ptnr. Haussermann, Davison & Shattuck, Boston, 1976-83; ptnr. Palmer & Dodge, Boston, 1983—2005, Edwards Angell Palmer & Dodge, Boston, 2005—. Tchr. Harvard Ctr. for Lifelong Learning, Cambridge, Mass., 1986-89; chmn. Wellesley Cable Access Bd., 1993-95. Contbr. articles to Boston Bar Jour. and Estate Planning. Treas. Exeter Assn. of New Eng., Boston, 1985-89, v.p., 1989-91, pres., 1991-93. Fellow Am. Coll. Trust and Estate Counsel; mem. ABA, Boston Bar Assn. (chmn. probate legislation 1983-93), Brae Burn Country Club (Newton, Mass.), Harvard Club of Boston, Boston Probate and Estate Planning Forum (program chair 1996-97, moderator 1997-98), Harvard Travellers Club. Home: 25 Cypress Rd Wellesley MA 02481-2918 Office: Edwards Angell Palmer & Dodge LLP 111 Huntington Ave Boston MA 02199-7613 Office Phone: 617-239-0123. Business E-Mail: rwoodburn@eapdlaw.com.

**WOODBURN, WILLIAM A.,** utilities executive; With Union Carbide, McKinsey & Co.; mgr. bus. devel. Gen. Electric Co., 1984—94; v.p., gen. mgr. GE Superabrasives, 1994—2000; exec. v.p., mem. office of the CEO GE Capital, 2000—01; pres., CEO GE Specialty Materials, 2001—.

**WOODBURY, DIXON JOHN,** physiologist, educator, research scientist; b. Seattle, Dec. 31, 1956; s. John Walter and Betty (Gunderson) Woodbury; m. Susan Diana Harvey, Mar. 20, 1980; children: James Dixon, Thomas Walter, Emily Susan, Kara Leigh. BS in Physics and Chemistry magna cum laude, U. Utah, 1980; PhD in Physiology and Biophysics, U. Calif., Irvine, 1986. Postdoctoral fellow in biochemistry Brandeis U., Waltham, Mass., 1986-89; rsch. assoc. Howard Hughes Med. Inst., Waltham, 1989-90; asst. prof. Wayne State U., Detroit, 1990-97, assoc. prof., 1997-2001, Brigham Young U., Provo, Utah, 2001—03, 2003—. Unitt mentor. Boy Scouts Am., 1984—86, 1996—98; bishopric Ch. Jesus Christ LDS, 1997—99. Fellow, U. Calif., 1980, 1981, 1985, Muscular Dystrophy Assn., 1986—88. Mem.: IEEE, Biophysical Soc., Soc. Neuroscience. Office: Brigham Young U 574 Widtsoe Bldg Provo UT 84602-5255 Office Phone: 801-422-7562.

**WOODBURY, MARDA LIGGETT,** librarian, writer; b. NYC, Sept. 20, 1925; d. Walter W. and Edith F. (Fleischer) Liggett; m. Philip J. Evans, Sept. 1948 (div. 1950); 1 child, Mark W. Evans; m. Mark Lee Woodbury, 1956 (div. 1969); children: Brian, Heather. Student, Bklyn. Coll., 1942-44; BA in Chemistry and Polit. Sci., Bard Coll., 1946; BS in L.S., Columbia U., 1948; postgrad., U. Calif., Berkeley, 1955-56, 60-61, MJ, 1995. Cert. tchr. Libr. various spl., med. and pub. librs., San Francisco, 1946-60, Coll. Pk. High Sch., Mt. Diablo, Calif., 1962-67; elem. sch. libr. Oakland and Berkeley, Calif., 1967-69; libr. dir. Far West Lab. Ednl. Rsch. & Devel., San Francisco, 1969-73; libr., editor Gifted Resource Ctr., San Mateo, Calif., 1973-75; libr. cons. Rsch. Ventures, Berkeley, Calif., 1975—2003; libr. dir. Life Chiropractic Coll., San Lorenzo, Calif., 1980-95. Author: A Guide to Sources of Educational Information, 1976, 2d edit., 1982, Selecting Instructional Materials, 1978, Selecting Materials for Instruction, Vol. I: Issues and Policies, 1979, Vol. II: Media and the Curriculum, 1980, Vol. III: Subject Areas and Implementation, 1980, Childhood Information Resources, 1985 (Outstanding Ref. Work, Assn. Ref. Librs. 1985), Youth Information Resources, 1987, Stopping the Presses: The Murder of Walter W. Liggett, 1998; mem. editorial bd. Ref. Libr., 1980-95. Home: 145 Monte Cresta Ave Apt 402 Oakland CA 94611-4809 Office Phone: 510-653-5876. Personal E-mail: mardawood@peoplepc.com.

**WOODBURY, MAX ATKIN,** mathematics professor; b. St. George, Utah, Apr. 30, 1917; s. Angus Munn and Grace (Atkin) W.; m. Lida Gottsch, May 30, 1947; children: Carolyn, Max TenEyck, Christopher, Gregory. BS, U. Utah, 1939; MS, U. Mich., 1941, PhD, 1948; M.P.H., U. N.C., Chapel Hill, 1977. Mem. faculty U. Mich., 1947-49; mem. Inst. for Adv. Study, Princeton, N.J., 1949-50; mem. faculty Princeton U., 1950-52, U. Pa., 1952-54; prin. investigator logistics research project Office Naval Research, George Washington U., 1954-56; faculty NYU, 1965-65; prof. computer sci. Duke U., prof. biomath. Med. Ctr., 1966-88, sr. fellow Ctr. for Study of Aging and Human Devel., 1975—, sr. fellow, sr. scientist Ctr. Demographic Studies, 1985—, prof. emeritus, 1987—. Pres. Biomed. Information-processing Orgn., 1961-62, Inst. for Biomed. Computer Research, 1961-71; cons. WHO, UNIVAC, CBS on computer election forecasts, 1952-62, sci. orgns., univs., govt. agys., corps. Contbr. articles to profl. jours. Served with USAAF, 1941-46, MTO. USPHS, NIH grantee, also other govt. agys., 1949-97; recipient MERIT award Nat. Inst. on Aging, NIH, June 1, 1988-May 31, 1998. Fellow AAAS, Am. Statis. Assn., Inst. Math. Statistics; mem. numerous sci., profl. socs., Phi Beta Kappa, Sigma Xi, Phi Kappa Phi (inventor of GoM methodology). Home: 1901 Hoke Ave Birmingham AL 35217-3523

**WOODBURY, RICHARD BENJAMIN,** anthropologist, educator; b. West Lafayette, Ind., May 16, 1917; s. Charles Goodrich and Marion (Benjamin) W.; m. Nathalie Ferris Sampson, Sept. 18, 1948. Student, Oberlin Coll., 1934-36; BS in Anthropology cum laude, Harvard U., 1939, MA, 1942, PhD, 1949; postgrad., Columbia U., 1939-40. Archeol. research, Ariz., 1938, 39, Fla., 1940, Guatemala, 1947-49, El Morro Nat. Monument, N.Mex., 1953-56, Tehuacan, Mex., 1964; archaeologist United Fruit Co. Zaculeu Project, Guatemala, 1947-50; assoc. prof. anthropology U. Ky., 1950-52, Columbia U., 1952-58; rsch. assoc. prof. anthropology interdisciplinary arid lands program U. Ariz., 1959-63; curator archeology and anthropology U.S. Nat. Mus., Smithsonian Instn., Washington, 1963-69; acting head office anthropology, 1965-66, chmn. office anthropology, 1966-67; prof., chmn. dept. anthropology U. Mass., Amherst, 1969-73, prof., 1973-81, prof. emeritus, 1981—, acting assoc. provost, dean grad. sch., 1973-74. Mem. divsn. anthropology and psychology NRC, 1954-57; bd. dirs. Archaeol. Conservancy, 1979-84, Valley Health Plan, Amherst, 1981-84, Mus. of No. Ariz., 1983-90; liason rep. for Smithsonian Instn., Com. for Recovery of Archeol. Remains, 1965-69; assoc. seminar on ecol. systems and cultural evolution Columbia U., 1964-73; mem. exec. com. bd. dirs. Human Relations Area Files, Inc., New Haven, Conn., 1968-70; cons. Conn. Hist. Commn., 1970-72.

Author (with A.S. Trik) The Ruins of Zaculeu, Guatemala, 2 vols., 1953, Prehistoric Stone Implements of Northeastern Arizona, 1954, Alfred V. Kidder, 1973, Sixty Years of Southwestern Archaeology, 1993, (chpt.) (with James A. Neely) The Prehistory of the Tehuacan Valley, Vol. 4, 1972; editor: (with I.A. Sanders) Societies Around the World (2 vols.), 1953, (with others) The Excavation of Hawikuh, 1966, Am. Antiquity, 1954-58, Abstracts of New World Archaeology; editor-in-chief: Am. Anthropologist, 1975-78; mem. editorial bd.: Am. Jour. Archeology, 1957-72. Mem. so. com., Shutesbury, Mass., 1979—82; chmn. fin. com. Friends of Amherst Stray Animals (Dakin Animal Shelter), 1983—85, trustee, 1991—; mem. Shutesbury Hist. Commn., 1998—, sec., 1999—2004. With USAF, 1942—45. Fellow. Mus. No. Ariz., 1985. Fellow AAAS (coun. rep. Am. Anthrop. Assn. 1961-63, com. on desert and arid zones rsch. Southwest and Rocky Mountains divsn. 1958-64, vice-chair 1962-64, com. arid lands 1969-74, sec. 1970-72), Am. Anthrop. Assn. (exec. bd. 1963-66, A.V. Kidder award 1989), Archeol. Inst. Am. (exec. com. 1965-67); mem. Soc. Am. Archeology (treas. 1953-54, pres. 1958-59, chmn. fin. com. 1987-89, Fiftieth Anniversary award 1985, Disting. Svc. award 1988), Ariz. Archeol. and Hist. Soc., Nature Conservancy, Archeol. Conservancy (life). Office: U Mass Dept Anthropology Machmer Hall Amherst MA 01003

**WOODBURY, ROBERT CHARLES,** lawyer; b. Sheridan, N.Y., July 7, 1929; s. Wendell F. and Lillian S. (Towne) W.; m. Martha Bayard Page, Jan. 25, 1958. BEE, Rensselaer Poly. Inst., 1950; JD, Cornell U., 1953. Bar: N.Y. 1954, U.S. Dist. Ct. (so. dist.) N.Y. 1965, U.S. Dist. Ct. (we. dist.) N.Y. 1979, U.S. Ct. Appeals (4th cir.) 1964, U.S. Ct. Claims 1961, U.S. Ct. Mil. Appeals 1956, U.S. Patent Office 1961; lic. profl. engr., N.Y. Project engr. Army reactors program U.S. Atomic Energy Commn., 1957-60; assoc. Reid & Priest, N.Y.C., 1962-70; pvt. practice Dunkirk, NY, 1971—; ptnr. Aular & Woodbury, Dunkirk, NY, 1973-81, Morten & Woodbury, Dunkirk, NY, 1982-88. Gen. counsel N.Y. State Temp. Commn. Environ. Impact Major Pub. Utility Facilities, 1970-71; del. N.Y. 8th Jud. Dist. Rep. Jud. Nominating Conv., 1985—; chmn. bd. dirs. Woodbury Farms, Ltd., 1965-98, Woodbury Vineyards, 1968-91. Assoc. trustee Buffalo Gen. Hosp. Found., 1994-96; trustees coun. Buffalo Gen. Healthcare Sys., 1996-98, steering com. 1996-98; mem. trustees coun. Kaleida Health Sys., Buffalo, 1998-2001, Kaleida Health Cmty. Coun., 2001—; founding pres. Chautauqua County Arts Coun., 1971; town atty. Town of Sheridan, 1972-75; dist. counsel city sch. dist. City of Dunkirk, 1973-82; co-founder No. Chautauqua Indsl. Roundtable, 1979; co-chmn. Chmn.'s Club, Chautauqua County Rep. Com. 1988-98; chmn., pres., dir., counsel Historic Harbor Renaissance, Inc., 1999—. Lt. USN, 1954-57. Fellow N.Y. Bar Found.; mem. N.Y. State Bar Assn. (chmn. com. atomic energy law 1967-69, chmn. com. pub. utility law 1969-71, mem. action unit 5 regulatory reform N.Y. 1988-83), Bar Assn. No. Chautauqua (pres. 1979), Cornell Law Assn., Rensselaer Alumni Assn., Dunkirk C. of C. (pres. 1979), Mid-Day Club Buffalo, Chautauqua Yacht Club. Republican. Presbyterian. Avocations: skiing, wine, sailing. Office: PO Box 800 87 E 4th St Dunkirk NY 14048-2225 Home: 80 Seel Acres Dunkirk NY 14048-3547 E-mail: bobhere@netsync.net.

**WOODCOCK, DAVID GEOFFREY,** architect, educator; b. Manchester, Eng., May 28, 1937; s. Herbert Edwin and Constance Mary (Bristol) Woodcock; m. Kathleen Mary Bishop, Oct. 1, 1960 (dec. 1964); 1 child, Jonathan Alfred; m. Valerie Frances Gubbins, July 4, 1964; children: Frances Mary, Penelope Jane. BA in Architecture with 1st class honors, U. Manchester, 1960, D in Town Planning, 1966. Registered arch., Tex. Lectr. U. Manchester, 1961; asst. prof. Tex. A&M U., College Station, 1962-66; sr. lectr. Kent. Inst. Art & Design, Canterbury, England, 1966—70; assoc. prof. Tex. A&M U., College Station, 1970—76, prof., 1976—; dir. Ctr. Heritage Conservation. Pvt. practice, Canterbury, 1966—70, College Station, 1980—. Bd. dirs. Opera and Performing Arts Assn., Tex. A&M U., 1980—83, 1988—91, pres., 1993—94; peer reviewer U.S. Gen. Svc. Adminstrn., 2004—; active Episc. Diocese Tex. Archtl. Commn., 1987—95; mem. adv. bd. Hammons Sch. Architecture Drury Coll., Mo., 1990—93, Savannah (Ga.) Coll. Arts and Design/Architecture, 1987—93. Recipient Rsch. Excellence award, Tex. Hist. Commn., 1991, Romieniec award for Archtl. Edn., Tex. Soc. Archs., 1995, Truett Latimer Profl. award, Preservation Tex., Inc., 1998. Fellow: AIA (hist. resource com. adv. group 2005—), Assn. Collegiate Schs. Architecture (regional dir. 1981—84, Disting. prof. 1991), Assn. Preservation Tech. Internat. (bd. dirs. 1990—, v.p. 1998—99, pres. 1999—2001, Harley J. McKee award 2003), Soc. Antiquaries London; mem.: Nat. Coun. Preservation Edn. Avocations: drawing, cross disciplinary education. Office: Tex A&M U Dept Architecture College Station TX 77843-3137 Office Phone: 979-845-7850. Business E-Mail: d-woodcock@tamu.edu.

**WOODCOCK, JANET,** federal official; b. Washington, Pa., Aug. 29, 1948; d. John and Frances (Crocker) W.; m. Roger Henry Miller, Nov. 16, 1981; children: Kathleen Miller, Susanne Miller. BS cum laude, Bucknell U., 1970; MD, Northwestern U., Chgo., 1977. Diplomate Am. Bd. Internal Medicine. Intern Hershey Med. Ctr./Pa. State U., 1977-78, resident in internal medicine, 1978-80, chief resident in medicine, 1980-81; fellow in rheumatology U. Calif./VA Med. Ctr., San Francisco, 1982-84; instr. medicine divsn. rheumatology and immunology VA Med. Ctr., San Francisco, 1984-85; med. officer divsn. biol. investigational new drugs Ctr. for Biologics Evaluation and Rsch./FDA, Rockville, Md., 1986-87, group leader divsn. biol. investigational new drugs, 1987-88, dep. dir. divsn. biol. investigational new drugs, 1988, dir. divsn. biol. investigational new drugs, 1988-90; dir. office of therapeutics rsch. and rev. Ctr. for Biologics Evaluation and Rsch., FDA, Rockville, Md., 1992-94, acting dep. dir., 1990-92; dir. Ctr. for Drug Evaluation and Rsch., FDA, Rockville, Md., 1994—2003; dep. commr. ops. FDA, Rockville, Md., 2003—. Instr. medicine, asst. prof. divsn. gen. internal medicine Hershey Med. Ctr./Pa. State U., 1981; analytical chemist rsch. divsn. A.B. Dick Co., Niles, Ill., 1971-73. Nat. Merit scholar Bucknell U., 1966, Pa. State scholar, 1966; Rsch. fellow Am. Rheumatism Assn.; VA Investigator grantee, 1985. Mem. Alpha Omega Alpha, Alpha Lambda Delta. Office: Ctr Drug Evaluation & Rsch US Food & Drug Admin 5600 Fishers Lane Rockville MD 20857

**WOODEN, JOHN ROBERT,** former college basketball coach; b. Martinsville, Ind., Oct. 14, 1910; s. Joshua Hugh and Roxie (Rothrock) W.; m. Nellie C. Riley, Aug. 8, 1932; children: Nancy Anne, James Hugh. BS, Purdue U., 1932; MS, Ind. State U., 1947. Athletic dir., basketball and baseball coach Ind. State Tchrs. Coll., 1946-48; head basketball coach UCLA, 1948-75. Lectr. to colls., coaches, business. Author: Practical Modern Basketball, 1966, They Call Me Coach, 1972; co-author: Wooden--a Lifetime of Reflections and Observations On and Off the Court, 1997, Inch and Miles--Pyramid to Success for Kids, 2004, One on One, 2004; contbr. articles to profl. jours. Served to lt. USNR, 1943-46. Named All-Am. basketball player Purdue U., 1930-32, Coll. Basketball Player Yr., 1932, to All-Time All-Am. Team Helms Athletic Found., 1943, Nat. Basketball Hall of Fame, Springfield (Mass.) Coll., as player, 1960, as coach, 1970, Ind. State Basketball Hall of Fame, 1962, Calif. Father of Yr., 1964, 75, Coach of Yr. U.S. Basketball Writers Assn., 1964, 67, 69, 70, 72, 73, Sportsman of Yr. Sports Illustrated, 1973, GTE Acad. All-Am., 1994; recipient Whitney Young award Urban League, 1973, 1st ann. Velvet Covered Brick award Layman's Leadership Inst., 1974, 1st ann. Dr. James Naismith Peachbasket award, 1974, Medal of Excellence Bellarmine Coll., 1985, Sportslike Pathfinder award to Hoosier with extraordinary svc. on behalf of Am. youth, 1993, 40 for the Age award Sports Illustrated, 1994, the 1st Frank G. Wells Disney award for role model to youth, 1995, Disting. Am. award Pres. Reagan, 1995, Svc. to Mankind award Lexington Theol. Sem., 1995, NCAA Theodore Roosevelt Sportsman award, 1995, Vince Lombardi award for excellence, 2000, Ind. Legend award, 2000, Presdl. Medal of Freedom, 2003, Pres. Ford award NCAA, 2006; named Basketball Coach of Century, 2000. *I have tried to live the philosophy of my personal definition of success which I formulated in the middle thirties shortly after I entered the teaching profession. Not being satisfied that success was merely the accumulation of material possessions or the attainment of a position of power or prestige, I chose to define success as "peace of mind which can be attained only through the self-satisfaction that comes from knowing you did your best to become the best that you are capable of becoming.".*

---

**WOODEN, ONTARIO SHERROD,** academic administrator; s. Dewayne Clyde and Jeanette McCray. BS, Albany State U., Ga., 2000; cert., Ind. U., 2003, MS, 2002, PhD, 2004. Cert. tchr. Ga. Prof. Standards Commn., 2000. Rsch. assoc. Ind. Project Academic Success, Bloomington, Ind., 2001—04; dir. honors program and academic success initiatives Albany (Ga.) State U., 2004—. Mem.: Nat. Assn. Student Affairs Profls. (mem. editl. bd. 2004), Assn. Study Higher Edn., Phi Delta Kappa, Am. Coll. Pers. Assn., Nat. Collegiate Honors Coun. Democrat. Seventh-Day Adventist. Avocations: reading, travel, writing, shopping. Office: Albany State University 504 College Drive Albany GA 31705 Home: 3419 Bellingham Ln Albany GA 31721 Office Phone: 229-430-1871. Office Fax: 229-420-1111. Personal E-mail: ontario.wooden@asurams.edu. E-mail: ontariowooden@yahoo.com.

**WOODFORD, ARTHUR MACKINNON,** retired library director, historian; b. Detroit, Nov. 23, 1940; s. Frank Bury and Mary-Kirk (MacKinnon) W.; m. Mary R. Woodford; children: Mark, Cristopher, Amy, Joyce, Kathleen, Lindsey. Student, U. Wis., 1958-60; BA in History, Wayne State U., 1963; AM in LS, U. Mich., 1964. Libr. Detroit Pub. Libr., 1964-74; asst. dir. Grosse Pointe (Mich.) Pub. Libr., 1974-77; dir. St. Clair Shores (Mich.) Pub. Libr., 1977—2005; ret., 2005—. Author: All Our Yesterdays, 1969, Detroit and Its Banks, 1974, Detroit: American Urban Renaissance, 1979, Charting The Inland Seas, 1991, Tonnancour, 1994, vol. 2, 1996, This Is Detroit: 1701-2001, 2001. With USNR, 1958-64. Mem. Mich. Libr. Assn. (v.p. 1988-89), Gt. Lakes Maritime Inst., Prismatic Club Detroit (pres. 1982), Algonquin Club of Detroit and Windsor (treas. 1983-93). Avocations: tennis, bridge, reading, model building. Home: 3284 S Channel Dr Harsens Island MI 48028 E-mail: woodfora@libcoop.net.

**WOODFORD, MICHAEL,** economics professor; AB, Univ. Chgo., 1977; JD, Yale Univ., 1980; PhD in Econ., MIT, 1983. Asst. prof., econ. Columbia Univ., 1984—86; John Bates Clark prof. polit. economy, 2004—; asst. prof. bus. econ. Univ. Chgo., 1986—89, assoc. prof., econ., 1989—92, prof., econ., 1992—95, Princeton Univ., 1995—98, Harold H. Helm prof. econ. and banking, 1998—2004. Co-editor (with J.B. Taylor): Handbook of Macroeconomics, 1999; co-editor: (with P. Aghion, R. Fryman, J. Stiglitz) Knowledge, Information and Expectations in Modern Macroeconomics, 2002; author: Interest and Prices: Foundations of a Theory of Monetary Policy, 2003 (Assn. Am. Publishers award for best profl./scholar book in econ., 2003); co-author (with J. Gali, S. Gerlach, J. Rotemberg, H. Uhlig): Monitoring the European Central Bank 5: The Monetary Policy Strategy of the ECB Reconsidered, 2004. Recipient NSF Graduate Fellowship, 1980—83, MacArthur Found. Prize Fellowship, 1981—86, NSF Rsch. Grants in Econ., 1987—, Guggenheim Mem. Found. Fellowship, 1998—99. Fellow: Am. Acad. Arts & Sci.

**WOODFORD, PETER C.,** lawyer; BA, Dartmouth Coll., 1971; JD with honors, George Washington U., 1978. Bar: Ill. 1978, US Ct. Appeals (3rd, 5th, 7th cir.), US Dist. Ct. (no. dist.) Ill., US Dist. Ct. (ea. dist.) Mich., US Tax Ct. Ptnr. Seyfarth Shaw LLP, Chgo., gen. counsel. Mem.: ABA. Office: Seyfarth Shaw LLP 55 East Monroe St Ste 4200 Chicago IL 60603 Office Phone: 312-269-8908. Office Fax: 312-269-8869. Business E-Mail: pwoodford@seyfarth.com.

**WOODHOUSE, GAY VANDERPOEL,** former state attorney general, lawyer; b. Torrington, Wyo., Jan. 8, 1950; d. Wayne Gaylord and Sally (Rouse) Vanderpoel; m. Randy Woodhouse, Nov. 26, 1983; children: Dustin, Houston. BA with honors, U. Wyo., 1972, JD, 1977. Bar: Wyo. 1978, U.S. Dist. Ct. Wyo., U.S. Supreme Ct. Dir. student Legal Svcs., Laramie, Wyo., 1976—77; assoc. Donald Jones Law Offices, Torrington, 1977—78; asst. atty. gen. State of Wyo., Cheyenne, 1978—84, sr. asst. atty. gen., 1984—89, spl. U.S. atty., 1987—89, asst. U.S. atty., 1990—95, chief dept. atty. gen., 1995—98, atty. gen., 1998—2000. Chmn. Wyo. Tel. Consumer Panel, Casper, 1982—86; advisor Cheyenne Halfway House, 1984—93; chmn. Wyo. Silent Witness Initiative Zero Domestic Violence by 2010, 1997, Wyo. Domestic Violence Elimination Coun., 1999—2001; mem. State Bar Commn. First Dist., 2002—05; spl. projects cons. N.Am. Securities Adminstrs. Assn., 1987—89; Chmn. bd. Pathfinder, 1987; S.E. Wyo. Mental Health. Mem.: Federalist Soc. for Law and Pub.Policy Studies (v.p., Wyo. chpt. 2003—04), Prevent Child Abuse Wyo. (pres. 2004—05), Laramie County Bar Assn., Cheyenne (Wyo.) C. of C., Cheyenne Rotary (bd. dirs.), Toastmasters, Rotary. Republican. Avocations: inline speed skating, stained glass. Address: 211 W 19th St Fl 3 Cheyenne WY 82001 Office: 123 Capitol Bldg Cheyenne WY 82002-0001 Office Phone: 307-432-9399. Personal E-mail: gaywoodhouselaw@aol.com. Business E-Mail: gay@woodhouselawoffice.com.

**WOODHOUSE, HELEN JACKSON,** music educator; b. Kanab, Utah, Aug. 19, 1940; d. Cleon Earl Jackson and Mildred Carpenter; m. Glenn Warren Woodhouse, Mar. 19, 1962 (dec.); children: Gregory James, Dorcas Sharon. AA, Coll. So. Utah, 1960; BS, Brigham Young U., 1989. Pvt. music tchr., Watsonville, Calif., 1993—. Mem.: ACLU, Nat. Guild Piano Tchrs., Commonwealth Club. Dfl. Mem. Lds Ch. Avocations: fossil hunting and collecting, volunteering.

**WOODHOUSE, JOHN FREDERICK,** food distribution company executive; b. Wilmington, Del., Nov. 30, 1930; s. John Crawford and Anna (Houth) W.; m. Marilyn Ruth Morrow, June 18, 1955; children: John Crawford II, Marjorie Ann Woodhouse Purdy. BA, Wesleyan U., 1953, DHL, 1997; MBA, Harvard U., 1955. Bus. devel. officer Can. Imperial Bank of Commerce, Toronto, Ont., Canada, 1955—59; various fin. positions Ford Motor Co., Dearborn, Mich., 1959—64, Cooper Industries, Inc., Mount Vernon, Ohio, 1964—67, treas. Houston, 1967—69, Crescent-Niagara Corp., Buffalo, 1968—69; exec. v.p., CFO Sysco Corp., Houston, 1969—71, pres., COO, 1972—83, pres., CEO, 1983—85, chmn., CEO, 1985—96, mem. exec. and fin. coms., 1996—98, chmn. bd. dirs., chmn. exec. com., 1998—2000, sr. chmn., 2000—. Bd. dirs., mem. exec. com. Shell Oil Co., 1991-2002; bd. dirs. Harvard Bus. Sch. Assocs., 1995-2001. Chmn. Mich. 16th dist. rep. Club, 1962-64; treas. Cooper Industries Found., 1967-69; trustee Wesleyan U., 1976-92, vice-chmn., 1986-92, chmn. comprehensive capital campaign, 1998-05; ruling elder Presbyn. Ch.; trustee, chmn. audit com., mem. exec. com. Mt. Holyoke Coll., South Hadley, Mass., 1996—; bd. dirs. Winrock Internat. Inst. Agrl. Devel., 1993-2000, mem. fin. com., mem. exec. com., chmn. investment com.; bd. advisors The Retail Food Industry Ctr., U. Minn., 1998-2002; trustee The Am. Inst. Food Distbn., Elmwood Pk., N.J., 2001—, The Food Inst., 2001—, Presbyn. Mo-Ranch Assembly, Hunt, Tex., 2002—, Meml. Park Conservancy, Houston, 2004—. Diplomate recognition Nat. Restaurant Assn., 2001, Hall of Fame award Nat. Frozen Foods Assn., 2002, Raymond Baldwin award disting. svc. Wesleyan U., 2005. Mem. Nat. Am. Wholesale Grocers Assn. (bd. dirs. 1990-2002, vice chmn. 1992, chmn. 1994-96), Internat. Foodservice Distbrs. Assn. (Herbert Hoover award 2000), Fin. Execs. Inst., Harvard Bus. Sch. Club, Sigma Chi (Significant Sig 1992). Avocations: backpacking, canoeing, tennis. Office: CLW Group 11111 Katy Freeway Ste 870 Houston TX 77079 Office Phone: 832-358-1700. Business E-Mail: woodhouse.john@corp.sysco.com, johnfwoodhouse1@yahoo.com.

**WOODHOUSE, MICHAEL A.,** restaurant holdings company executive; BS in Natural Scis., MS in Natural Scis., Queen's Coll., Cambridge, Eng. Exec. v.p., CFO S&A Restaurant Corp.; pres., internat. divsn. Pearle Health Svcs., Inc.; exec. v.p., CFO T.G.I. Friday's Inc., 1987; CFO Tia's Inc., Dallas; v.p., fin. Dallas Internat. Inc., 1993—94; sr. v.p., CFO, 1994—95; sr. v.p., fin., CFO CBRL Group, 1995—99, exec. v.p., COO, 1999—2000, pres., COO, 2000—01, pres., CEO, 2001—, chmn., 2004—. Bd. dirs. CBRL Group, 1999—. Office: CBRL Group 305 Hartmann Dr Lebanon TN 37088*

**WOODHOUSE, THOMAS EDWIN,** lawyer, trust company administrator; b. Cedar Rapids, Iowa, Apr. 30, 1940; s. Keith Wallace and Elinor Julia (Cherny) W.; m. Kiyoko Fujiie, May 29, 1965; children: Miya, Keith, Leighton. AB cum laude, Amherst Coll., 1962; JD, Harvard U., 1965. Bar: N.Y. 1966, U.S. Supreme Ct. 1969, Calif. 1975. Assoc. Chadbourne, Parke, Whiteside & Wolff, N.Y.C., 1965-68; atty./adviser AID, Washington, 1968-

---

69; counsel Pvt. Investment Co. for Asia S.A., Tokyo, 1969-72; ptnr. Woodhouse Lee & Davis, Singapore, 1972-74; assoc. Graham & James, San Francisco, 1974-75; asst. gen. counsel Natomas Co., San Francisco, 1975-81; mem. Lasky, Haas, Cohler & Munter, San Francisco, 1982-90; trust adminstr. Ronald Family Trust A, 1989—, Gordon P. Getty Family Trust, 1994—; sole practice Berkeley, 1990—2001. Of counsel Wilson, Sonsini, Goodrich & Rosati, Palo Alto, Calif., 1992-95; instr. law faculty U. Singapore, 1972-74; CEO, Vallejo Investments, 1997—. chmn. Police Rev. Com. of Berkeley (Calif.), 1980-84; mem. Berkeley Police Res., 1986—; bd. dirs. Friends Assn. of Svcs. for Elderly, 1979-84; clk. fin. com. Am. Friends Svc. Com. of No. Calif., 1979-83; pres. Zyzzyva Inc., lit. quar., 1985-87. Trustee Freedom from Hunger, 1989-99, Coun. of Friends Bancroft Libr., 1997-2002, chmn. 2002-2003, Coun. of Friends Amherst Coll. Libr., 1990-97, 2005-, Mark Twain Luncheon Club, 2002—, Dominican Sch. of Philosophy and Theology, 1998-2003; chmn. Friends of Amherst Coll. Libr., 1990-97, 2005—. With U.S. Army, 1958. Fellow Am. Bar Found. (life); mem. Calif. Bar Assn., Assn. Internat. de Bibliophile, Harvard Club, Univ. Club, Book Club Calif., Roxburghe Club, Travellers Club, Grolier Club, Faculty Club U. Calif.-Berkeley, Mira Vista Golf and Country Club. Republican. Roman Catholic. Home and Office: 1800 San Antonio Ave Berkeley CA 94707-1618 Personal E-mail: robert606@earthlink.net.

**WOODHURST, ROBERT STANFORD, JR.,** architect; b. Abbeville, S.C., July 12, 1921; s. Robert Stanford and Eva (Ferguson) W.; m. Dorothy Ann Carwile, Aug. 4, 1945; 1 son: Robert Stanford III. BS in Architecture, Clemson U., 1942. Registered arch., S.C., Ga., NCARB. Designer Harold Woodward, Arch., Spartanburg, SC, 1946-47; assoc. arch. F. Arthur Hazard, Arch., Augusta, Ga., 1947-54; prnr. Woodhurst & O'Brien, Architects, Augusta, Ga., 1954-83, Woodhurst Partnership, Augusta, Ga., 1983—. V.p. Southeastern Architects and Engrs., Inc., Augusta, 1964-83; lectr. history architecture N. Augusta Community Coll.; mem. nat. exam. com. Nat. Council Arch tl. Regis. Bds.; pres. Ga. State Bd. Archs. Chmn. Augusta-richmond County Planning Commn., 1966-68; trustee Hist. Augusta, Inc., active Mayor's Adv. Com., 1965-68; mem. Augusta Bldg. Code Bd. Appeals, 1955-58. Served to capt. U.S. Army, 1942-45. Decorated Air medal with 7 oak leaf clusters; Croix de Guerre avec palms (France); prisoner of war, Germany. Fellow AIA (Bronze medal 1942); mem. S.C. Assn. AIA (pres. 1977, Bronze medal 1977, Rothchild Silver Medal 1987), Soc. Archtl. Historians, Nat. Coun. Archtl. Registration Bds., Augusta Country Club, Pinnacle Club. Democrat. Baptist. Achievements include designed and built: Deacon 1st Bapt. Ch., Augusta, Univ. Hosp. Med Ctr., Augusta, Peabody Apts. and Irvin Towers, Augusta, W. Lake Country Club, Augusta, Med. Libr., Med. Coll. Ga., Libr. Voorhees Coll., Denmark, S.C., Ambulatory Care Ctr. Univ. Hosp. Augusta, Married Students Apts., Med. Coll. Ga., Covenant Presbyn. Ch., Augusta, Student Ctr. Voorhees Coll., Pres.' Home Voorhees Coll., others. Home: 810 Dogwood Ln Augusta GA 30909-2704 Office: Woodhurst Partnership 607 15th St Augusta GA 30901-2601 Office Phone: 706-724-4343. E-mail: twparch@aol.com.

**WOODLAND, IRWIN FRANCIS,** lawyer; b. NYC, Sept. 2, 1922; s. John James and Mary (Hynes) W.; m. Sally Duffy, Sept. 23, 1954; children: Connie, J. Patrick, Stephen, Joseph, William, David, Duffy. BA, Columbia U., 1948; JD, Ohio State U., 1959. Bar: Calif. 1960, Wash., 1991, U.S. Dist. Ct. (cen. dist.) Calif. 1960, U.S. Dist. Ct. (no. dist.) Calif. 1962, U.S. Dist. Ct. (so. dist.) Calif. From assoc. to ptnr. Gibson, Dunn & Crutcher, L.A., 1959-88. Bd. dirs. Sunlaw Energy Corp., Vernon, Calif. With USAF, 1942—45, ETO. Mem.: ABA, Wash. State Bar Assn., L.A. Bar Assn., Calif. Bar Assn., Jonathan Club, Phi Delta Phi. Roman Catholic. Address: Gibson Dunn & Crutcher 333 S Grand Ave Ste 4400 Los Angeles CA 90071-1548

**WOODLAND, N. JOSEPH,** retired optical engineer, retired mechanical engineer; b. Atlantic City, N.J., Sept. 6, 1921; BSME, Drexel U., 1947, DEng (hon.), 1998; MME, Syracuse U., 1956. Tech. asst. to unit chief, liquid thermal diffusion project for separating uranium isotopes Manhattan Project, Oak Ridge, Tenn., 1943—46; mech. designer Burlington Industries, 1947; lectr. in mech. engring. Drexel U., 1948—49, cons., 1987; cons. in aircraft hydraulics design, 1950; various positions at staff and sr. levels IBM Corp., 1951—87; cons., 1987—88. Named one of Drexel U.'s 100 Most Outstanding Alumni, 1992; recipient Nat. Medal Tech. for invention of bar code, 1992. Mem.: Anthony J. Drexel Soc. Achievements include patents in field.

**WOODLEY, DAVID TIMOTHY,** dermatology educator; b. Aug. 11, 1948; s. Raoul Ramos-Mimosa and Marian (Schlueter) W.; m. Christina Paschall Prentice, May 4, 1974; children: David Thatcher, Thomas Colgate, Peter paschall. AB, Washington U., St. Louis, 1968; MD, U. Mo., 1973. Diplomate Am. Bd. Internal Medicine, Am. Bd. Dermatology, Nat. Bd. Internal Medicine. Intern Beth Israel Med. Ctr., Mt. Sinai Sch. Medicine, N.Y. Hosp., Cornell U. Sch. Medicine, N.Y.C., 1973-74; resident in internal medicine U. Nebr., Omaha, 1974-76; resident in dermatology U. N.C., Chapel Hill, 1976-78, asst. prof. dermatology, 1983-85, assoc. prof. dermatology, 1985-88; prof. medicine, co-chief divsn. dermatology Cornell U. Med. Ctr., N.Y.C., 1988-89; prof., vice chair dept. dermatology Stanford (Calif.) U., 1989-93; prof., chair dept. dermatology Northwestern U., Chgo., 1993-99; co-chief dermatology U. So. Calif. Sch. Medicine, L.A., 1999—. Research fellow U. Paris, 1978-80; expert NIH, Bethesda, Md., 1983-89; prof., assoc. chmn. dermatology Stanford U Sch. Medicine, 1989-93; chmn. dermatology Sch. Medicine Northwestern U., 1993-99; prof., chmn. dermatology U So. Calif., 1999—; mem. study sect. NIH. Contbr. chpts. to books and articles in field to profl. jours. Mem. Potomac Albicore Fleet, Washington, 1982-83, Friends of the Art Sch., Chapel Hill, 1983—, Jungian Soc. Triangle Area, Chapel Hill, 1983—. Fellow Am. Acad. Dermatology; mem. ACS (assoc.), Dermatology Found., Am. Soc. for Clin. Investigation, Soc. Investigative Dermatology, Assn. Physician Poets, Am. Soc. for Clin. Investigation. Office: U So Calif Keck Sch Medicine Dept Dermatology UC Norris Cancer Ctr Topping tower 3905 1441 EAstlake Ave Los Angeles CA 90033 Office Phone: 323-865-0983. Business E-Mail: dwoodley@usc.edu.

**WOODLEY, FREDERICK WILLIAM,** molecular biologist, geneticist, educator; b. Yuba City, Calif., May 24, 1962; s. Frederick Vernon and Nadiene Elizabeth Woodley. BS in Biology and Physics, St. Francis U., Loretto, Pa., 1984; MS in Microbiology and Biology, Ind. U. Pa., 1989; PhD in Molecular and Cellular Biology, Ohio U., Athens, Ohio, 1997. Adj. prof. microbiology Columbus (Ohio) State C.C., 2000—; sr. clincal rsch. assoc. Columbus (Ohio) Children's Hosp., 2003—. Rsch. assoc. Ctr. Advanced Rsch. Neurogastrointestinal Disorders Columbus (Ohio) Children's Hosp., 2004—, rsch. assoc. Ctr. Healthy Weight and Nutrition, 2006—; tech. rsch. dir. Ctrl. Ohio Lion's Eyebank, Columbus, 1999—2000; adj. prof. of molecular genetics Cap. U., Columbus, 2006—. Scholar, Ind. U. of Pa., 1985—88, Ohio U., 1988—97. Fellow: Pediatric Academic Assn. (assoc.); mem.: KC (chief squire 1979—80), Gold's Gym, Phi Kappa Theta (life; sec. 1981—83), Alpha Phi Omega (life). Democrat. Roman Catholic. Achievements include research in pediatric gastroenterology and molecular biology. Home: 246 Blenheim Rd Columbus OH 43214 Office: Columbus Children's Hospital 100 Children's Drive Columbus OH 43205 Office Phone: 614-722-6413. Office Fax: 614-722-3062. Personal E-mail: frederickwoodley@yahoo.com. Business E-Mail: woodleyf@pediatrics.ohio-state.edu.

**WOODLEY, JOHN PAUL, JR.,** civilian military employee, lawyer; b. Shreveport, La., Sept. 28, 1953; s. John Paul and Hazel Eugenia (Iles) W.; m. Priscilla Anne Ingersoll, June 6, 1981; children: Elizabeth Ingersoll, Cornelia Ingersoll. BA, Washington & Lee U., 1974, JD, 1977. Bar: Va. 1977, U.S. Ct. Appeals (4th cir.) 1978, U.S. Dist. Ct. (ea. dist.) Va. 1979, U.S. Ct. Mil. Appeals 1979, U.S. Supreme Ct. 1982, U.S. Ct. Appeals (5th cir.) 1984, U.S. Ct. Appeals (11th and fed. cirs.) 1985. Law clk. to judge U.S. Dist. Ct., Richmond, Va., 1977-79; pvt. practice Richmond, 1985-86; ptnr. Woodley Simon & Woodley, Richmond, 1986—90; asst. commonwealth atty. Henrico county State of Va., 1990—94; dep. atty. gen. (govt. ops) Richmond, 1994—98, sec. nat. resources, 1998—2001; asst. dep. under sec. def. (environment) US Dept. Def., Washington, 2001—03; prin. dep. asst. sec. (civil works) US Army, 2004—05, asst. sec. (civil works), 2003—04, 2005—.

Treas. Richmond Rep. Com., 1988. Capt. JAGC, U.S. Army, 1979-85, maj. Res., 1986. Decorated Legion of Merit, Meritorious Svc. medal with 2 oak leaf clusters, Army Commendation medal with 1 oak leaf cluster, Army Achievement medal; recipient Sec. Def. medal for Outstanding Pub. Svc. Mem. ABA, Rep. Nat. Lawyers Assn. (bd. govs. 1988), Va. State Bar, Richmond Bar Assn., Assn. Trial Lawyers Am., Phi Beta Kappa, Assn. Va. Hearing Officers, Va. Trial Lawyers Assn., Va. Rep. Lawyers Assn. (chmn. 1987—), Richmond First Club. Roman Catholic. Avocation: skiing. Office: US Army 108 Army Pentagon Washington DC 20310

**WOODMAN, EDWARD,** dentist; 1 child, Ryan. Grad., Va. Commonwealth Sch. Dentistry, 1969. Founder, dentist Woodman Dentistry, Glen Cove, NY, 1972—. Office: Woodman Dentistry 11 Highland Rd Glen Cove NY 11542 Office Phone: 516-676-0250.

**WOODMAN, G. ROGER,** management consultant; b. Point Pleasant, N.J., Feb. 25, 1953; s. George Emil and Emma (Stringham) W.; m. Jean Wilson; 1 child, Kevin Richard. AS, Ocean County Coll., 1981; student, Trenton State Coll., 1987. Sr. operator, night supr. Ocean County Nat. Bank, Point Pleasant, 1973—85; constrn. ofcl. N.J. Dept. Cmty. Affairs, Trenton, 1985—87; pres., sr. cons. Cynosure Cons., Inc., Lakewood, NJ, 1987—. Environ. cons. Environ Health Inspections, Lakewood, 1988, N.J. Dept. Cmty. Affairs, Trenton, 1989-95, BNK, Restorations, Clifton, N.J., 1989—. Author: (with others) Uniform Construction Code, 1985. County committeeman Ocean County Reps., Lakewood, 1989-98; life mem. Bay Head Vol. Fire Co., 1971—; mem. Lakewood Rep. Club, 1989-98; mem. Fishermen's Meml. Fund, 1998—, chmn., 2001. Mem. Fire Protection Assn., N.J. Fireman's Assn., Am. Mgmt. Assn., Masons (Durand lodge master 1980, treas. 2000, sec. 2001—, jr. grand steward 2002-03, DRI 2003-). Avocations: gardening, hiking, travel, model trains, camping. Office: Cynosure Consultants 14 Marlow Dr Jackson NJ 08527-4678 Office Phone: 732-261-0288.

**WOODMAN, GREY MUSGRAVE,** psychiatrist; b. Birmingham, England, Jan. 26, 1922; came to U.S., 1959, naturalized 1963; s. Edward Musgrave and Ida (Cullen) W.; m. Irene Woodman; children: Sheila, Shonagh. BA, Oxford U., Eng., 1943, MA, BM, BChir, 1945; grad., Clinton Citizens Police Acad., 2001. Ship's surgeon Brit. Merchant Marines, 1946-48; intern Whipps Cross Hosp., London, 1949-50, med. registrar, 1951-53, Gen. Hosp., Newcastle-on-Tyne, England, 1953-54; gen. practice London, 1954-56; physician USAF Hosp., 1956-59; resident in psychiatry U. Okla. Med. Ctr., 1959-62; staff psychiatrist Western Mo. Mental Health Ctr., Kansas City, 1962-76; med. dir. Mental Health Ctr. Clinton County, Clinton, Iowa, 1976-87; pvt. practice Clinton, 1976—; founder, dir. Lincolnshire Clinic, The London Psychiat. Clinic, 1997—. Mem. staff Jane Lamb Health Ctr., Mercy Hosp., Comphealth; psychiat. cons. Mufon. Mem. Prevent Child Abuse Coun. Recipient Internat. Order of Merit, 1999. Fellow Royal Soc. Medicine (London, life); mem. AMA (life), Am. Psychiat. Assn. (life), Am. Acad. Med. Hypoanalysts (clin.), Brit. Med. Assn., World Fedn. Mental Health, Iowa Med. Soc. (past chmn. hospice com.), Internat. Assn. Social Psychiatry, Clinton Co. Prevent Child Abuse Coun., Am. Red Cross (mental health specialist 1996—), Oxford Club (life), Moose. Republican. Episcopalian. Home: 515 N 13th St Clinton IA 52732-4816 Office: London Psychiat Clinic 212 Wilson Bldg 5th Ave Clinton IA 52732 Office Phone: 563-243-7721.

**WOODMAN, HAROLD DAVID,** historian, educator; b. Chgo., Apr. 21, 1928; s. Joseph Benjamin and Helen Ruth (Sollo) W.; m. Leonora Becker; children— Allan James, David Edward. BA, Roosevelt U., 1957; MA, U. Chgo., 1959, PhD, 1964. Lectr. Roosevelt U., 1962-63; asst. prof. history U. Mo., Columbia, 1963-66, assoc. prof., 1966-69, prof., 1969-71, Purdue U., West Lafayette, Ind., 1971-97, Louis Martin Sears distng. prof., 1990-97, prof. emeritus, 1997—; chmn. Com. on Am. Studies, 1981-94. Author: Conflict and Consensus in American History, 1966, 9th rev. edit., 1996, Slavery and the Southern Economy, 1966, King Cotton and His Retainers, 1968, Legacy of the American Civil War, 1973, New South-New Law, 1995; mem. editl. bd. Jour. So. History, 1972-75, Wis. Hist. Soc., 1972-76, Bus. History Rev., 1971-77, Agrl. History, 1976-82, Am. Hist. Rev., 1981-84, Jour. Am. History, 1985-88. Served with U.S. Army, 1950-52. Recipient Otto Wirth award Roosevelt U., 1990; Woodrow Wilson Internat. Center for Scholars fellow, 1977; Faculty grant Social Sci. Rsch. Coun., 1969-70; Nat. Humanities Ctr. fellow, 1983-84 Mem. Am. Hist. Assn., Orgn. Am. Historians, Econ. History Assn., Agrl. History Soc. (pres. 1983-84, Everett E. Edwards award 1963), Soc. Am. Historians, Bus. History Conf. (pres. 1981-82), Ind. Assn. Historians (pres. 1983-84), So. Hist. Assn. (exec. coun. 1982-85, Ramsdell award 1965, pres. 1995-96). Home: 1100 N Grant St West Lafayette IN 47906-2460 Office: Purdue U Dept History West Lafayette IN 47907 Business E-Mail: hwoodman@cla.purdue.edu.

**WOODMAN, RYAN,** dentist; s. Edward Woodman. DMD, U. Pa. Sch. Dental Medicine, 1995. Resident Med. Col. Pa., 1995—96; dentist Woodman Dentistry, Glen Cove, NY, 1996—. Office: Woodman Dentistry 11 Highland Rd Glen Cove NY 11542 Office Phone: 516-676-0250. Business E-Mail: drryan@woodmandentistry.com.

**WOODMAN, STEWART,** chef; b. 1974; m. Heidi Woodman. Apprentice The Fairmont Banff Springs hotel, Alberta, Canada; sous chef Essex House, NYC, Le Bernardin, NYC; chef Mercer Kitchen, NYC, Jean Georges, NYC, Zoe, NYC, Restaurant Levain, Mpls.; co-owner, exec. chef Five Restaurant & Street Lounge, Mpls. Recipient Best New Chef award, Food and Wine Mag., 2006. Office: Five Restaurant & Street Lounge 2917 Bryant Ave S Minneapolis MN 55408 Office Phone: 612-827-5555.*

**WOOD PARRISH, VICTORIA ANN,** minister; b. Norwood, Mass., June 21, 1950; d. Ernest O. and Martha Lou (Foreman) Wood; children: Heather, Kathleen, W. James. B in Music Edn., DePauw U., 1972; MDiv, Princeton Theol. Sem., 1976, DMin, 1992. Ordained deacon United Meth. Ch., 1973, elder, 1979. Asst. pastor Arlington Ave. Presbyn. Ch., East Orange, N.J., 1973-74; chaplain Memphis City Hosp., 1974-75; asst. pastor Pearson Meml. United Meth. Ch., Trenton, N.J., 1975-76; assoc. pastor First United Meth. Ch., Franklin, Pa., 1977-79, Erie, Pa., 1979-85; pastor 10th St. United Meth. Ch., Erie, 1985-94, Park United Meth. Ch., North East, Pa., 1994—2000, First United Meth. Ch., Gilford, NH, 2000—. Clergy team mem. Erie Hospice, 1983-90. Mem. Coll. of Chaplains (profl. affiliate), Am. Assn. Pastoral Counselors Avocations: reading, music, genealogy, history. Home: PO Box 7408 Gilford NH 03247-7408 Office: First United Methodist Ch PO Box 7408 Gilford NH 03247-7408 Office Phone: 603-524-3289.

**WOODRESS, JAMES LESLIE, JR.,** language educator; b. Webster Groves, Mo., July 7, 1916; s. James Leslie and Jessie (Smith) W.; m. Roberta Wilson, Sept. 28, 1940. AB, Amherst Coll., 1938; A.M., NYU, 1943; PhD, Duke U., 1950; LittD, U. Nebr., 1995. News editor Sta. KWK, St. Louis, 1939-40; rewriteman, editor UPI, N.Y.C., 1940-43; instr. English, Grinnell (Iowa) Coll., 1949-50; asst. prof. English, Butler U., Indpls., 1950-53, asso. prof., 1953-58; prof., 1959-63, chmn. dept., 1959-63, dean letters and scis., 1963-65; prof. English, U. Calif.-Davis, 1966-87, chmn. dept., 1970-74; vis. prof. Sorbonne, Paris, 1974-75, 83. Author: Howells and Italy, 1952, Booth Tarkington: Gentleman from Indiana, 1955, A Yankee's Odyssey: The Life of Joel Barlow, 1958, Dissertations in American Literature, 1957, 3rd edit., 1968, Willa Cather: Her Life and Art, 1970, 3rd edit., 1981, American Fiction 1900-50, 1974, Willa Cather: A Literary Life, 1987; editor: Eight American Authors, 1971, American Literary Scholarship: An Annual, 1965-69, 75-77, 79, 81, 87, Critical Essays on Walt Whitman, 1983, Cather's The Troll Garden, 1983, (with Richard Morris) Voices from America's Past, anthology, 1961-62, 75. Served to lt. AUS, 1943-46. Ford Fund for Advancement Edn. fellow, 1952-53; Guggenheim fellow, 1957-58; Fulbright lectr. France, 1962-63; Fulbright lectr. Italy, 1965-66; recipient Hubbell medal, 1985 Mem. MLA (sec. Am. Lit. group 1962-63), AAUP, Phi Beta Kappa. Address: 892 Harrison Ave Claremont CA 91711-4128

**WOODRICK, ROBERT,** food products executive; Chmn. D W Food Ctrs., Grand Rapids, Mich. Emeritus trustee, Aquinas Coll.; trustee, Grand Rapids Community Coll. Office: D&W Food Ctrs 3001 Orchard Vista Dr SE Grand Rapids MI 49546-7078

**WOODRIFF, LEE,** company executive; s. Ray and Margaret; BS, Mont. State U., 1964; MS U. Wis.; PhD, Columbia Pacific U., 2002. Instr. Mont. State U., Bozeman, 1965—66, U. Wis., Milw., 1964—65; asst. prof. Middle East Tech. U., 1965—67, Humboldt State U., Arcata, Calif., 1967—70; prof. Menlo Coll., Menlo Park, Calif., 1970—96; CEO, pres. Naefels Ltd., Henderson, Nev., 1997—2006. Cons., founder Menlo Rsch. Assocs., Arcata, 1980—96; CEO Centro Ltd., Henderson, 1996—2005; pilot, flight instr. Recipient various tchg. awards. Mem.: AAUP, Am. Math. Assn., Math. Assn. Am. Avocations: sailing, skiing. Office: Naefels Ltd 1702 Millstream Henderson NV 89074 Office Phone: 702-347-9077.

**WOODRING, DEWAYNE STANLEY,** religious organization administrator; b. Gary, Ind., Nov. 10, 1931; s. J. Stanley and Vera Luella (Brown) Woodring; m. Donna Jean Wishart, June 15, 1957; children: Judith Lynn Bigelow, Beth Ellen Carey. BS in Speech with distinction, Northwestern U., Evanson, Ill., 1954; postgrad. studies in radio and TV broadcasting, Northwestern U., 1954—57; MDiv, Garrett Theol. Sem., 1957; LHD, Mt. Union Coll., 1967; DD, Salem Coll., 1970. Ordained to ministry Meth. Ch., 1955. Assoc. dir. youth Gary YMCA, 1950—55; min. edn. Griffith Meth. Ch., Ind., 1955—57; min. administrn. and program 1st Meth. Ch., Eugene, Oreg., 1957—59; dir. pub. rels. Dakotas area Meth. Ch., 1959—60, dir. pub. rels. Ohio area, 1960—64; administrv. exec. to bishop Ohio East area United Meth. Ch., Canton, 1964—77, asst. gen. sec. Gen. Coun. Fin. and Administr. Evanston, Ill., 1977—79, assoc. gen. sec., 1979—84; exec. dir., CEO Religious Conf. Mgmt. Assn., Indpls., 1982—. Staff dept. radio svcs. 2d Assembly World Coun. Chs., Evanston, 1954; vice-chmn. commn. entertainment and program North Ctrl. Jurisdictional Conf., 1968—72; chmn., 1972—76; mem. commn. gen. conf. United Meth. Ch., 1972—93, mgr., exec. dir., 1976—93, mem. divsn. interpretation, 1969—72; chmn. commn. Ohio Coun. Chs., 1961—65; exec. com. Nat. Assn. United Meth. Found., 1968—72, World Meth. Coun., 1986—2001; v.p. Ohio East Area United Meth. Found., 1967—75; chmn. bd. mgrs. United Meth. Bldg., Evanston, 1977—84; mem. adv. bd. Nassau/Paradise Island, 1997—99, Red Lion Hotels and Inns, P.R. Conv. Ctr., GMG Solutions; lectr., cons. in field. Creator (radio series) The Word and Music, prodr., dir. (TV series) Parables in Miniature, 1957—59. Adviser East Ohio Conf. Comm. Commn., 1968—76; bd. dirs. First Internat. Summit Edn., 1989; trustee, 1st v.p. Copeland Oaks Retirement Ctr., Sebring, Ohio, 1969—76; pres. Guild Assocs., 1971—. Named to, Ky. Cols., 1989, Hall of Leaders, Conv. Liaison Coun., 1994; recipient Cert. Meeting Profl. award, 1985, Cert. Expt. Mgr. award, 1988. Mem.: Marriot Customer Leadership Forum (mem. customer adv. bd.), Found. Internat. Meetings (bd. dirs.), Internat. Assn. Exhbn. Mgmt., Cert. Meeting Profls. (bd. dirs. 1983—92), Ind. Conv. Visitors Assn. (bd. dirs. 1996—2000), Def. Orientation Conf. Assn. (chaplain), Conv. Industry Coun. (bd. dirs., past chmn.), Meeting Profl. Internat., Ind. Soc. Assn. Execs. (Meeting Planner of the Yr. award 1990), Am. Soc. Assn. Execs. Home: 7224 Chablis Ct Indianapolis IN 46278-1540 Office: 1 RCA Dome Ste 120 Indianapolis IN 46225-1023 Office Phone: 317-632-1888.

**WOODROW, KENNETH B.,** retired retail company executive; BS, Yale U.; MBA, Harvard U. With Dayton Hudson Corp., 1970; pres. Target stores divsn. Target Corp., 1994-99, vice chmn. Mpls., 1999—2000. Bd. dirs. Shock Doctor, Inc, Duane Reade, Inc.; bd. dirs Delta Air Lines, Inc., 2004—; bd. dirs. Visteon Corp., 2004—.

**WOODRUFF, BOB,** newscaster; b. Bloomfield Hills, Mich., 1961; s. Robert N. and Fran Woodruff; m. Lee Woodruff, 1988; children: Mack, Cathryn, Nora, Claire. BA, Colgate U., 1983; JD, U. Mich., 1987. Atty.; law tchr. Beijing; translator during Tiananmen Sq. uprising CBS News, Beijing, 1989; corr., Justice Dept. ABC News, Washington, fgn. corr. Belgrade, Kosovo, Europe, Middle East, London bur. corr., corr. NYC, 2002; interim anchor ABC World News Tonight, NYC, 2005, co-anchor, 2006. Recipient Alfred I. Dupont award for 9/11 reporting, George Foster Peabody award for 9/11 reporting, David Bloom award for excellence in enterprise reporting, Radio & TV Corr. Assn., 2006. Fluent in Mandarin Chinese. Office: ABC News Press Rels Fl 2 47 W 66th St New York NY 10023-6201*

**WOODRUFF, C(HARLES) ROY,** retired professional association executive, consultant; b. Anniston, Ala., Sept. 27, 1938; m. Kay Carolyn Jernigan, June 26, 1962; children: Charles R. Jr., Earl David. BA, U. Ala., 1960; BD, So. Bapt. Theol. Sem., 1963, PhD in Psychology of Religion and Pastoral Care, 1966. Diplomate Am. Assn. Pastoral Counselors; lic. profl. counselor, Va. Asst. pastor Ft. Mitchell Bapt. Ch., South Ft. Mitchell, Ky., 1960-63; Protestant chaplain Silvercrest Hosp., New Albany, Ind., 1963-66; dir. dept. pastoral care and edn. Bryce State Hosp., Tuscaloosa, Ala., 1966-71; assoc. prof., chaplain supr. dept. patient counseling Med. Coll. Va., Richmond, 1971-76; assoc. prof., chmn. dept. psychology of religion and pastoral care Midwestern Bapt. Theol. Sem., Kansas City, Mo., 1976-78; exec. dir. Peninsula Pastoral Counseling Ctr., Newport News, Va., 1978-88, Am. Assn. Pastoral Counselors, Washington, 1988—2003; interim pastor Vienna (Va.) Bapt. Ch., 2004—06. Lecturing fellow Interpreter's House, Lake Junaluska, N.C., 1968-78; pastoral counselor, clin. supr. Psychol. Clinic, U. Ala., Tuscaloosa, 1969-71; adj. staff mem. The Counseling Inst., Kansas City, 1976-78, adj. prof., John Leland Ctr. for Theol. Studies, Fairfax, Va., vis. prof., Korea Profl. Inst. of Psychotherapy and Spirituality, Seoul, Korea. Author: Alcoholism and Christian Experience, 1968; (with others) Alcohol, In and Out of the Church, 1968, Work Adjustment: The Goal of Rehabilitation, 1973, Pastoral Theology and Ministry, Key Resources, 1983, The Dictionary of Pastoral Care and Counseling, 1990; also articles. Apptd. by Gov. of Va. to Bd. Profl. Counselors, Commonwealth of Va., 1987-95 (chmn. 1993-95); mem. Nat. Mental Health Leadership Forum, 1990-93; pres. Coalition on Ministry in Specialized Settings, 1996-2000; interim pastor Vienna Bapt. Ch., Va., 2004—. Recipient Disting. Contbns. award Am. Assn. Pastoral Counselors, 2003; United Meth. Ch. Gen. Bd. Christian Social Concerns grantee, 1965; So. Bapt. Theol. Sem. teaching fellow, 1965-66. Fellow Coll. Chaplains of Am. Protestant Hosp. Assn.; mem. Assn. for Clin. Pastoral Edn. (cert. supr.), Assn. Couples for Marriage Enrichment (cert.). Home: 10827 Burr Oak Way Burke VA 22015-2416

**WOODRUFF, ELLEN LOUISE,** chaplain; b. Bertha, Minn., Jan. 30, 1942; d. Harold Ernest and Ruth Eleanor (Olson) Klebs; m. John S. Woodruff, July 31, 1969; children: Ruth Ellen, Jonathan C. BA, U. Minn., 1969; Assoc. in Ministry, Luther Sem., St. Paul, 2000. Recreation therapist St. Mary's Hosp., Mpls., 1969, Belgrade Nursing Home, Minn., 1971—73; dir. youth camp Elks Assn., Brainerd, Minn., 1976—95; student chaplain Regions Hosp., St. Paul, 1997—98, Good Samaritan Homes, Mpls. & St. Paul, 1998—99; conservator St. Paul, 2000—03; chaplain St. Gertrude's Health and Rehab. Ctr., 2003—05, Hurricane Katrina Relief, 2005—. Mem. program com. Mid-States Camping Assn., Chgo., 1992—94; leader/spkr. Ch. Retreats, 1985—. Author (editor): Klebs Family History, 2001, Awesome Angels, 2000. Vol. chaplain Hurricane Katrina, 2005; active Shepherd of the Valley Luth. Ch. Recipient J.B. Fritzjerald award, Mpls. Park & Recreation, 1969; grantee, U. Minn., 1966—68. Mem.: Assn. Profl. Chaplains, Am. Camping Assn. (sec. newsletter 1983—95, bd. dirs 1980—83, 1990—93, Sue Tinker award 1993). Home: 9391 Knighton Woodbury MN 55125-3721

**WOODRUFF, FAY,** paleoceanographer, geological researcher; b. Boston, Jan. 23, 1944; d. Lorande Mitchell and Anne (Fay) W.; m. Alexander Whitehill Clowes, May 20, 1972 (div. Oct. 1984); m. Robert G. Douglas, Jan. 27, 1980; children: Ellen, Katerina. RN, Mass. Gen. Hosp. Sch. Nursing, Boston, 1966; BA, Boston U., 1971; MS, U. So. Calif., 1979. Rsch. assoc. U. So. Calif., L.A., 1978-81; rsch. faculty, 1981-96, conservator St. Paul, 2000—03; Hurricane Katrina Relief, 2005—. Mem. program com. Mid-States Camping Assn., Chgo., 1992—94. Internat. Symposium on Benthic Foraminifera, Sendai, Japan, 1990. Contbg. author: Geological Society of America Memoir, 1985; contbr. articles to profl. jours. Life mem. The Nature Conservancy, Washington, 1992; bd. dirs. Friends of

Friendship Park, Inc., 1995-2001; co-founder, v.p. Resources Families Adopted Ea. European Children, Inc., L.A., 1996-2000. NSF grantee, 1986-94. Mem. Am. Geophys. Union, Geol. Soc. Am., Internat. Union Geol. Scis. (internat. commn. on stratigraphy, subcommn. on Neogene stratigraphy 1991-99), Soc. Woman Geographers (sec. So. Calif. chpt. 1990-96), Soc. Econ. Paleontologists and Mineralogists (sec., editor N.Am. Micropaleontology sect. 1988-90), Sigma Xi. Office: U So Calif Earth Scis Los Angeles CA 90089-0001

**WOODRUFF, JAY NOEL,** editor, writer; b. Cooperstown, NY, Oct. 31, 1960; s. Robert Arnold Woodruff, Jr. and Marcia Shick Woodruff; m. Sarah Jean Carew, Oct. 1, 1988; children: Joseph Francis, Samuel Robert, Anne Elizabeth. BA in English, Harvard U., 1983; MFA, U. Iowa, 1987. Rsch., tchg. fellow Harvard U., Cambridge, Mass., 1987—91; mng. editor Double-Take Mag., Durham, NC, 1993—96; sr. editor Esquire Mag., New York, 1998—2000; asst. mng. editor Entertainment Weekly, New York, 2000—06, mng. editor EW.com, 2006—. Editor: (book) A Piece of Work, partic. essays; author: (short stories) various publications. Mem.: Am. Soc. Mag. Editors. Catholic. Office: Entertainment Weekly 1675 Broadway New York NY 10019 Personal E-mail: jnwoodruff@aol.com. Business E-Mail: jay_woodruff@ew.com.

**WOODRUFF, JUDY CARLINE,** broadcast journalist; b. Tulsa, Nov. 20, 1946; d. William Henry and Anna Lee (Payne) W.; m. Albert R. Hunt, Jr., Apr. 5, 1980; children: Jeffrey Woodruff, Benjamin Woodruff, Lauren Ann Lee. Student, Meredith Coll., 1964-66; BA, Duke U., 1968. News announcer, reporter Sta. WAGA-TV, Atlanta, 1970-75; news corr. NBC News, Atlanta, 1975-76, White House corr. Washington, 1977-83; anchor Frontline, PBS documentary series, 1984—90; corr. MacNeil-Lehrer News Hour, PBS, Washington, 1983-93; anchor, sr. corr. CNN, Washington, 1993—2005, prime anchor, sr. coord.; moderator Vice Presidential Debate, 1988, America Votes, 2003, 2004. Bd. advisors Henry Grady Sch. Journalism, U. Ga., 1979-82, Benton Fellowship in Broadcast Journalism, U. Chgo., 1984-90, Knight Fellowship in Journalism, Stanford U., 1985-99; bd. visitors Wake Forest U., 1982-89; trustee Duke U., 1985-97, emerita; founding bd. dirs. Internat. Women's Media Found.; vis. fellow, Joan Shorenstein Ctr.on the Press, Politics and Pub. Policy, Harvard U., 2005-; vis. prof. media and politics Duke U., 2006. Author: This is Judy Woodruff at the White House, 1982; corr: PBS Special Generation Next, 2006. Active Commn. on Women's Health, The Commonwealth Fund.; trustee Freedom Forum, Urban Inst.; trustee Nat. Mus. Am. History, 2006—. Recipient award Leadership Atlanta, Class of 1974, Atlanta chpt. Women in Comms., 1975, Edward Weintal award for excellence in fgn. policy reporting, 1987, Joan Shorenstein Barone award for series on def. issues, 1987, Helen Bernstein award for excellence in journalism N.Y. Pub. Libr., 1989, Pres.'s 21st Century award Nat. Women's Hall of Fame, 1994, CableAce award for best newscaster, 1995, CableAce Best Anchor Team award, 1996, Allen H. Neuharth award for excellence in journalism, 1995, News and Documentary Emmy award, 1997, Internat. Matrix award, Assn. for Women in Comm., 2003, Leonard Zeidenberg First Amendment award, Radio-Television News Directors Assn. and Found., 2003; named to Ga. Assn. of Broadcasters Hall of Fame, 2003; grantee Pru Charitable Trust, 2006—. Mem. NATAS (Atlanta chpt. Emmy award 1975), White House Corrs. Assn.

**WOODRUFF, KATHRYN ELAINE,** literature and language professor; b. Ft. Stockton, Tex., Oct. 12, 1940; d. James Arthur and Catherine H. (Stevens) Borron; m. Thomas Charles Woodruff, May 18, 1969; children: Robert Borron, David Borron. BA, Our Lady of the Lake U., San Antonio, 1963; MFA, U. Alaska, 1969; PhD, U. Denver, 1987. Cert. tchr., Tex., Colo. English and journalism U. Alaska, Fairbanks, 1963-64, Grand Junction (Colo.) Dist. 12, 1964-66; English tchr. Monroe High Sch., Fairbanks, Alaska, 1966-67; teaching asst. U. Alaska, Fairbanks, 1967-69, instr., 1969-70, U. Colo., Boulder, 1979, Denver, 1988-89, Regis Coll., Denver, 1987-89; asst. prof. Econ. Inst., Boulder, 1989—92; prof. English Colo. Christian U., Lakewood, 1993—. Tchr. Upward Bound, Fairbanks, 1968; instr. ethnic and women writers course U. Colo., Denver, 1988-93; mem. Assoc. Writing Programs; soprano Boulder Chorale, Cantabile Singers, St. John's Cathedral Choir, Augustana Chamber Choir; mem. Women's Studies Delegation to South Africa, 1998; active in missionary work in Ecuador, 1998, European Singing Tour with Augustana Arts, 1998, 2000; poetry readings various cities. Author: (poetry) Before the Burning, 1994; author numerous poems. Friend Chautauqua Music Festival, Boulder, 1985-2000; dir. 12th Annual Arts Festival, Fairbanks, 1969; mem. Augustana Chamber Chorus, St. John's Cathedral Choir; bd. dirs. Denver Bach Soc. Recipient Poet's Choice award Internat. Soc. Poetry, 1997; named one of Outstanding Young Women Am., 1966; NEH grantee, 1996. Mem. AAUW, MLA, Am. Assn. Univ. Professors, Assoc. Writing Programs, Soc. Internat. Devel. UN Assn., Nat. Women's Hall of Fame, Acad. Am. Poets, Denver Bach Soc. (bd. dirs. 2003-05), Internat. Women's Writing Guild. Democrat. Mem. Christian Ch. Avocations: singing, tennis, skiing, volleyball, travel. Office: Colo Christian U 8787 W Alameda Ave Lakewood CO 80226-1053 Business E-Mail: ewoodruff@ccu.edu.

**WOODRUFF, KAY HERRIN,** pathologist, educator; b. Charlotte, NC, Sept. 22, 1942; d. Herman Keith and Helen Thelma (Tucker) Herrin; m. John T. Lyman, May 3, 1980; children: Robert, Geoffry, Carolyn. BA in Chemistry, Duke U., 1964; MD, Emory U., 1968. Diplomate Am. Bd. Pathology (trustee 1993—, sec. 1998-2000, v.p. 2000-2001, pres. 2001—). Medicine and pediat. intern U. N.C., Chapel Hill, 1968-69, resident in anatomic pathology, 1969-70; chief resident in anatomic pathology, instr. U. Okla. Oklahoma City, 1970-71, fellow in electron microscopy-pulmonary pathology, instr., 1971-72; chief resident in clin. pathology U. Calif., San Francisco, 1972-74, asst. clin. prof. anatomic pathology, 1974-91, assoc. clin. prof., 1991—; chief electron microscopy VA Hosp., San Francisco, 1974-75; pvt. practice, San Pablo, Calif., 1981—. Pres. med. staff Brookside Hosp., San Pablo, 1994, med. dir. Regional Cancer Ctr., 1995-98; assoc. pathologist Children's Hosp., San Francisco, 1979-81, St. Joseph's Hosp., San Francisco, 1977-79; cons. pathologist Lawrence Berkeley (Calif.) Lab., 1974-93; med. dir. Bay Area Tumor Inst. Tissue Network, San Pablo, 1989—; asst. clin. prof. pathology health and med. scis. program U. Calif., Berkeley and U. Calif., San Francisco Joint Med. Program, 1985-91, assoc. clin. prof., 1991—, others. Contbr. articles and abstracts to med. jours. Mem. exec. bd. Richmond (Calif.) Quits Smoking, 1986-90, Bay Area Tumor Inst., Oakland, Calif., 1987—; mem. exec. bd. Contra Costa unit Am. Cancer Soc., Walnut Creek, Calif., 1985-87, mem. profl. edn. com., 1985-90, mem. pub. edn. com., 1985-86, mem. task force on breast health Calif. div., 1992-93; mem. transfusion adv. com. Irwin Meml. Blood Bank, San Francisco, 1977-83; chmn. transfusion adv. com. Alameda Contra County Blood Bank, 1989-92; commr. Calif. Bd. Med. Quality Assurance, 1978-80; pres. Brookside Found., San Pablo, Calif. 1998-2000. Recipient young investigator award Am. Lung Assn., 1975-77; Outstanding Svc. awards Am. Cancer Soc., 1986, 87, Disting. Svc. award, 1988; Disting. Clin. Tchg. award U. Calif., San Francisco and Berkeley Joint Med. Program, 1987, Outstanding Tchg. award, 1988, Excellence in Basic Sci. Instrn. award, 1990, Excellence in Tchr. Clin. Scis. award, 1993; cert. of recognition Cmty. Svc. Richmond, 1989. Mem. AMA, Coll. Am. Pathologists (editl. bd. CAP Today 1986-90, bd. govs. 1990-96, chmn. coun. on practice mgmt. 1994, William Kuhn award for outstanding comm. 1996, Presdl. Medal of Honor 1995, 96), Am. Med. Women's Assn. (exec. bd. 1984-87, regional bd. govs. 1984-87), No. Calif. Women's Med. Assn. (pres. 1982-84), Calif. Soc. Pathologists (bd. dirs. 1988-90), No. Calif. Oncology Group, South Bay Pathology Soc. (pres. 1987), Am. Assn. Blood Banks, Calif. Med. Assn., Alameda-Contra County Med. Soc., Am. Soc. Clin. Pathology, Calif. Pathology Soc. Avocations: classical music, music. Office: Doctors Med Ctr 2000 Vale Rd San Pablo CA 94806-3808

**WOODRUFF, LINDA GYJUAN,** mathematics educator; b. Nashville, Jan. 31, 1961; d. Jimmie Lee Woodruff and Emma Jean Harvey-Woodruff; 1 child, Emmanuel Dion. BS in Math., Tenn. State U., Nashville, 1985, MS in Math., 1997. Mech. engr. Buick divsn. GM Corp., Flint, Mich., 1980—81; claims examiner State of Tenn., Nashville, 1985—89; math. instr. Metro - Nashville

Pub. Schs., 1997—99, Tenn. State U., 1993—. Pvt. math tutor, Nashville, 1979—; math tutor Math Enrichment and Tutoring, 1999—2005; math cons. North Edgefield Organized Neighbors Assn., 2004—, Let's Make a Difference Woodbine Cmty. Edn. Program, 2004—; gen. edn. test coord. math dept. Tenn. State U., tutor cons. Mem. edn. team Tying Nashville Together, 2004—; angel tree coord. St. Vincent de Paul Ch., 1995—2000. Recipient certy. appreciation, Minority Enterprise Corp., 2003. Democrat. Roman Catholic. Avocations: reading, travel, movies, crossword puzzles. Office: Tenn State U 3500 John A Merritt Blvd Nashville TN 37209-1561 Office Phone: 615-963-5849.

**WOODRUFF, MARK REED,** magazine editor; b. Roanoke, Va., Jan. 3, 1957; s. James Moses and Elizabeth (Reed) W. BFA, Va. Commonwealth U., 1981; postgrad., San Francisco State U., 1983-84. Freelance writer, N.Y.C., 1984-88; features editor Taxi Mag., N.Y.C., 1988-90; mng. editor Spin Mag., N.Y.C., 1990-95; sr. editor Rolling Stone, N.Y.C., 1995-97, asst. mng. editor, 1997-98; editor-in-chief Tennis Mag., N.Y.C., 1998—. Mem. Am. Soc. Mag. Editors. Democrat. Avocation: tennis. Office: Tennis Mag 79 Madison Ave 8th Fl New York NY 10016 E-mail: mwoodruff@tennismagazine.com.

**WOODRUFF, THOMAS ELLIS,** electronics consulting executive; b. Stockton, Calif., Feb. 8, 1921; s. Ennis Casselberry and Gracella (Scotford) W.; m. Doris Elaine Walters, Jan. 14, 1947 (div. Aug. 1962); children: Mary Ann Woodruff Mahaffy, Patricia Lee; m. Ruth Elizabeth Craik, Feb. 25, 1964; 1 child, Robert Peter; stepchildren: Gordon Lee Vickers, Barbara Ann Vickers, Mary Jean Vickers. AA, Stockton Jr. Coll., 1941; BSEE, U. Calif., Berkeley, 1943. Registered profl. engr., Calif. Engr. GE, Syracuse, N.Y., 1944-47; staff engr. Hughes Aircraft Co., Culver City, Calif., 1947-56; mgr. electronics design Sanders Assocs., Nashua, N.H., 1956-58, chief engr. preliminary design, 1958-60, mgr. spl. programs div., 1960-62, corp. dir. systems, 1962-65, v.p., gen. mgr. corp. systems group, 1965-73, v.p. antisubmarine weapons and communications, 1966-72, dir., 1968-70, sr. dir., 1970-76, v.p. gen. mgr. ocean systems group, 1972-76, v.p. sci. and tech., 1976-88, corp. cons., 1989—; v.p. Sanders Nuclear Corp., Nashua, 1966-71. Mem. adv. com. Def. Intelligence Agy., Washington, 1978-83; joint adv. com. MIT Lincoln Lab., Bedford, Mass., 1988-89; cons. Superconductor Tech., Inc., Santa Barbara, Calif., 1988—, Oryx, Inc., Paramus, N.J., 1989—, Sanders/Lockheed, 1988-91, ret. 1992. Patentee, co-patentee 14 inventions in electronics for computers, control systems, video displays, submarine detection devices, others. Mem. IEEE (sr.). Republican. Avocations: skiing, photography, motorcycling, swimming. Home and Office: 8 Berkeley St Nashua NH 03064-2309 Office Phone: 603-882-5631. Personal E-mail: twuff@ieee.org.

**WOODRUFF, TRUMAN O(WEN),** physicist, emeritus educator; b. Salt Lake City, May 26, 1925; s. Wilford Owen and Evelyn (Ballif) W.; m. Ambrosina Lydia Jauregui, Sept. 14, 1948 (dec. June 1991); m. Patricia O'Keefe Vincent, Sept. 23, 1995. AB, Harvard U., 1947; BA, Oxford U., Eng., 1950; PhD, Calif. Inst. Tech., 1955. Nat. scholar Harvard, 1942-44, 46-47, Sheldon traveling fellow, 1947-48; Rhodes scholar Oxford U., 1948-50; Dow Chem. Co. fellow, Howard Hughes fellow Calif. Inst. Tech., 1950-54; research asso. physics U. Ill., 1954-55; physicist Gen. Elec. Research Lab., 1955-62; prof. physics Mich. State U., 1962-85, prof. emeritus, 1985—, chmn. dept., 1972-75; sr. scientist research labs. Hughes Aircraft Co., Malibu, Calif., 1986-87; cons. in physics Los Angeles, 1987-91. Vis. prof. Scuola Normale Superiore, Pisa, Italy, 1982—. Contbr. articles to sci. jours. Served with USNR, 1944-46. Fulbright fellow U. Pisa, 1968-69 Fellow Am. Phys. Soc.; mem. Assn. Harvard Chemists, Phi Beta Kappa, Sigma Xi.

**WOODRUFF, VALERIE,** state agency administrator; m. Frank Woodruff; 1 child, Scott 1 stepchild, Sheri. BEd in Secondary Edn., Alderson Broaddus Coll., W. Va.; MA in guidance and counseling, U. Del.; postgrad. studies in vocat. edn. and curriculum devel., Temple U., 1999—. From tchr. to prin. New Castle County, Del., Cecil County Md.; assoc. sec. for curriculum and instructional improvement Del. Dept. Edn., Dover, Del., 1992—99, acting sec., 1999—2000, sec. 2000—. Office: Del Dept Edn Townsend Bldg #279 401 Federal St Ste 2 Dover DE 19903-1402 Office Phone: 302-739-4601.

**WOODRUFF, VIRGINIA,** broadcast journalist, writer; b. Morrisville, Pa. d. Edwin Nichols and Louise (Meredith) W.; m. Raymond F. Beagle Jr. (div.); m. Albert Plaut II (div.); 1 child, Elise Meredith. Student, Rutgers U. News corr. Sta. WNEW-TV Metromedia, N.Y.C., 1967; nat., internat. critic-at-large Mut. Broadcasting System, 1968-75; lectr. Leigh Bur., 1969-71; byline columnist N.Y. Daily Mirror, N.Y.C., 1970-71; first Arts critic Teleprompter and Group W Cable TV, 1977-84; host/producer The First Nighter N.Y. Times primetime cable highlight program, 1977-84; pres., chief exec. officer Starpower, Inc., 1984-91; affiliate news corr. ABC Radio Network, N.Y.C., 1984-86; pres. Promarket People Inc., 1991-93; S.W. contbg. corr. Am. in the Morning, First Light, Mut. Broadcasting System, 1992; S.W. freelance corr. Voice of Am., USIA, 1992—. Perennial critic Off-Off Broadway Short Play Festival, N.Y.C., 1984—; was 1st Woman on 10 O'Clock News, WNEW-TV, 1967. Contbg. feature writer Vis a Vis mag., 1988-91. Mem. celebrity panel Arthritis Telethon, N.Y.C., 1976. Selected episodes of First Nighter program in archives N.Y. Pub. Libr., Billy Rose Theatre Collection, Rodgers and Hammerstein Collection, Performing Arts Rsch.Ctr. Mem. Drama Desk. Clubs: National Arts, Dutch Treat. Presbyterian. Personal E-mail: vwoodruff50@yahoo.com.

**WOODRUM, CLIFTON A., III,** lawyer, retired state legislator; b. Washington, July 23, 1938; s. Clifton A. Jr. and Margaret (Lanier) W.; m. Emily Abbitt, Aug. 10, 1963; children: Robert, Meredith W. Snowden, Anne. AB, U. N.C., 1961; LLD, U. Va., 1964. Bar: Va. 1964, U.S. Dist. Ct. (we. dist.) Va. 1964, U.S. Ct. Appeals (4th cir.) 1968, U.S. Supreme Ct. 1970. Assoc. Dodson, Pence & Coulter, Roanoke, Va., 1964-68; ptnr. Dodson, Pence, Viar, Woodrum & Mackey, 1968-95; counsel Dodson, Pence & Viar, 1995-98; mem. Va. Ho. of Dels., 1980—2004; ret., 2004—. Bd. dirs. Hometown Bank. Chmn. 6th Dist. Dem. Com., Va., 1972-76; mem. State Water Commn. 1981-2000, State Crime Commn., 1982-2000, chmn., 1995-98; chmn. Med. Malpractice Study Va., 1984-85, Freedom of Info. Study, 1998-2000; mem. Electric Utility Restructing Com., 1997-2003, Freedom of Info. Adv. Coun., 2000-2002, chmn.; bd. dirs. Va. Coalition Open Govt., 2004—, We. Va. Land Trust, 2004—, Libr. of Va., 2004—. Recipient Freedom of Info. award, Va. Coalition on Govt., 1999, 2003, Outstanding Legislator award, Va. Assn. Chiefs of Police, 1999, Child Advocate award, Am. Acad. Pediats. (Va. chpt.), 1997, Profiles in Courage award, Coalition of Labor Union Women, 2002, Outstanding Svc. award, Va. Firefighters Assn., 2003, McCain Fellow Advocacy award, ACOG, 2006. Mem.: ABA, Roanoke Bar Assn., Va. Bar Assn. Episcopalian. Home: 2641 Cornwallis Ave SE Roanoke VA 24014-3339 Office: Clifton A Woodrum PO Box 990 Roanoke VA 24005-0990 Office Phone: 540-982-5547.

**WOODRUM, PATRICIA ANN,** librarian; b. Hutchinson, Kans., Oct. 11, 1941; d. Donald Jewell and Ruby Pauline (Shuman) Hoffman; m. Clayton Eugene Woodrum, Mar. 31, 1962; 1 child, Clayton Eugene, II. BA, Kans. State Coll., Pittsburg, 1963; MLS, U. Okla., 1966. Br. libr. Tulsa City-County Libr. System, 1964-65, head ref. dept., 1965-66, head reference dept., 1966-67, chief extension, chief pub. svc., 1967-73, asst. dir., 1973-76, exec. dir., 1976-96; owner Paradigm Mgmt. Cons. Svcs., 1997—. Active Leadership Tulsa Alumni; interim exec. dir. Bot. Garden/Edn. and Rsch. Ctr.; bd. dirs. Tulsa Garden Ctr. Recipient Disting. Libr. award Okla. Libr. Assn., 1982, Leadership Tulsa Paragon award, 1987, Women in Comm. Newsmaker award, 1989, Outstanding Alumnus award U. Okla. Sch. Libr. Info. Studies, 1989, Headliner award Tulsa Press Club, 1996. Disting. Alumnus Coll. Arts and Scis., U. Okla., 2000; inducted into Tulsa City-County Libr. Hall of Fame, 1989, Okla. Womens Hall of Fame, 1993. Mem. ALA, Pub. Libr. Assn. (pres. 1993-94), Okla. Libr. Assn. (pres. 1978-79, Disting. Libr. award 1982,

Meritorious Svc. award 1996), Tulsa Press Club. Democrat. Episcopalian. Avocations: swimming, gardening. Office Phone: 918-728-2700. Business E-Mail: pwoodrum@tulsaconnect.com.

**WOODRUM, ROBERT LEE,** executive search consultant; b. Merkel, Tex., Mar. 3, 1945; s. Bill and Norma (Shea) W.; m. Linda Mary Larkin, July 20, 1968; children: Jennifer, Michael. BA, Calif. State U., Northridge, 1967; postgrad., U. Okla., 1974. Press sec. U.S. Senate, Washington, 1977-78; dir. pub. affairs U.S. Office Personnel Mgmt., Washington, 1979-80; pres. Corp. Communications, Washington, 1980-82; v.p. Norton Simon Inc., N.Y.C., 1982-83; spl. asst. to the commr. NFL, N.Y.C., 1983-84; exec. dir. Ritz Paris Hemingway Award, 1984-87; pres. Ritz Paris Internat., 1984-86; sr. v.p. AmBase Corp., 1986-91; mng. dir. Korn/Ferry Internat., N.Y.C., 1991—; dir. DataBuilt, Inc., 2000—. Advisor USIA, Washington, 1980-93, ARC, 1983, White House Vets. Com., 1979-80. Trustee N.Y.C. Meals on Wheels, Inc. Lt. comdr. USN, 1968-77. Mem.: Ocean Reef Club, S.C. Yacht Club. Office: 117 Harbour PSGE Hilton Head Island SC 29926-1265 Business E-Mail: woodrumr@kornferry.com.

**WOODS, ALLAN P.,** information technology executive; B in History and Philosophy, St. John's Univ., NYC. Officer Bankers Trust of NY, 1970—72; pres. several subs. Fidata/Bradford Computer and Sys; exec. v.p. and head info. svc. dept Mellon Fin. Corp., 1986—99, vice chmn. & chief info. officer, 1999—. Adv. bd. mem. Banking Industry Tech. Secretariat; bd. dir. Holy Family Inst., Duquesne Uni. (exec. com.); mem. visitors' bd. Univ. Pitts. Sch. of Library and Info. Sci.; tech. com. mem. Univ. Pitts. Med. Ctr. Capt. USMC, Vietnam. Mem.: Fin. Svc. Roundtable. Office: Vice Chair & CIO Mellon Fin Corp One Mellon Ctr Pittsburgh PA 15258-0001

**WOODS, BETTY,** insurance company executive; b. 1938, BA in Psychology, Seattle U., 1974. With Organizational Cons. of the Northwest, Seattle, 1974-76; pres., CEO Premera Blue Cross, 1976—2000; dir. Beckman Coulter Inc., Fullerton, Calif., 1994—, chmn., 2005—. Founding mem. Nat. Inst. Health Care Mgmt.; trustee Western Wash. Univ. Mem.: Seattle NW chpt., Nat. Assn. Corp. Directors. Office: Beckman Coulter Inc 4300 N Harbor Blvd PO Box 3100 Fullerton CA 92834-3100

**WOODS, CAROL SMITH,** private school educator; d. David E. and Margaret (Ballinger) Smith; m. William Kent Woods, Apr. 1, 1980; children: Stephen, Todd. BA, U. Iowa, Iowa City, 1967; MEd, Xavier U., 1997. Tchg. coord. Montessori Ctr. Rm., Cin., 1975—. Cons. Am. Montessori Soc., Cin., 1982—99; adj. prof. Xavier U., Cin., 1992—2000; master tchr. Scottish Rite Learning Ctr., Cin., 1998—; presenter in field. Author: Wood's Words, 2002, Early Literacy Handbook, 2003; contbr. articles to profl. jours. Mem.: Orton-Gillingham Acad. (cert. mem. 2001—), Am. Montessori Soc., Internat. Dyslexia Assn. Avocations: reading, crossword puzzles, fitness. Home: 3750 Broadview Dr Cincinnati OH 45208

**WOODS, CHERYL,** financial analyst; b. Cleve., Nov. 15, 1960; d. Virgle Lee and Mary Grace Woods; m. Danny Thomas Couch, Jan. 18, 1984 (div. Nov. 1988); m. Eddie Lee Grays, Jr., Feb. 2, 1992 (div. Mar. 1997); m. Neil Hollis Moss, July 19, 2003; children: Camille Dana Couch, Eddie Lee Grays, III. BS in Bus. Adminstrn., U. Akron, 1980—87; MBA, Cleve. State U., 1994—95, postgrad., 1997—. Letter carrier US Postal Svc., Cleve., 1979—92, customer svc. supr., 1992—93, fin. systems coord., 1993—2000, budget/fin. analyst, 2000—, mgr. budget/fin. analyst, 2001—. Deacon Eastside Christian Ref. Ch., Warrensville Hts., Ohio, 1997—2000; lay min. Christ Cmty. Fellowship Ch., Twinsburg, Ohio, 2002, dir. of christian edn., 2002. Recipient Disting. alumni, Aurora H.S., 2001; Nat. Merit scholarship 1978. Mem.: Acad. of Mgmt., Nat. Honor Soc., Mensa, Beta Gamma Sigma. Democrat. Methodist. Avocations: travel, reading, dance, cooking. Office Phone: 216-443-4104. Personal E-mail: woodsc@alltel.net.

**WOODS, DALE,** retired mathematics professor; b. Stone County, Mo., Nov. 1, 1922; s. Fielding J. Woods and N. Elizabeth Holt. BS, Mo. State U., 1943; MS, Okla. State U., 1950, EdD, 1960. Instr. ND State U., Fargo, 1946—50; geophysics rschr. Advanced Geophysics, Houston, 1950—51; asst. prof. U. So. Miss., Hattiesburg, 1951—52; rsch. asst. Halliburton, Houston, 1952—53; asst. prof. U. Memphis, 1953—57; assoc. prof. Idaho State U., Pocatello, 1957—59; prof., head divsn. math. Truman State U., Kirksville, Mo., 1959—82, prof. emeritus, 1982—; prof. U. Ctrl. Okla., 1982—93. Served with USN, 1944—45. Mem.: Am. Math. Soc., Math. Assn. Am., Masons. Democrat. Address: 2430 Holt Wood Rd Reeds Spring MO 65737

**WOODS, DAN,** information technology manager, consultant; BA in Computer Sci., U. Mich., 1982; MS in Journalism, Columbia U., 1989. Database editor The News and Observer/Nando.net, 1992—95; info. tech. cons. Time Inc. New Media, 1995—99, TheStreet.com, 1998—99; CTO CapitalThinking, 1999—2002. Mem. CTO adv. coun. InfoWorld; bd. mem. Big Star Entertainment; mem. policy adv. bd. on pub. key infrastructure Am. Bankers Assn. Author: The Education of a CTO, 2003; co-author: Developers Guide to the Java Web Server, 1999; contbr. articles to profl. jours. Home: Apt 3B 890 West End Ave New York NY 10025

**WOODS, DANIEL JAMES,** lawyer; b. Bklyn., Nov. 12, 1952; s. James J. and Elinor (Masten) W.; m. Kathryn Anne Morris, Dec. 27, 1974; children: Meghan M., Alexandra K., Shauna E. AB cum laude, U. So. Calif., 1974, JD, 1977. Bar: Calif. 1977, US Dist. Ct. (cen., ea., so. and no. dists.) Calif., US Ct. Appeals (9th cir.) 1978, US Supreme Ct. 1981. Law clk. to judge U.S. Dist. Ct. (ctrl. dist.), Calif., 1977-78; assoc. Brobeck, Phleger & Harrison, L.A., 1978-84, ptnr., 1984-96, White & Case LLP, 1996—. Vol. pro tem LA Mcpl. Ct., 1985—, LA Superior Ct., 1989—. Roman Catholic. Avocations: tennis, bicycling, travel. Office: White & Case LLP 633 W 5th St Los Angeles CA 90071-2627 Office Phone: 213-620-7700. E-mail: dwoods@whitecase.com.

**WOODS, DAVID G.,** dean; MusB, Washburn U.; MusM, Northwestern U., PhD in Philosophy; student, Aspen Inst., Copenhagen Conservatory Music. Dir. music Colo. Acad., 1966—73; chmn. div. music. edn. Iowa State U., Ames, 1974—84; dir. Sch. Music U. Ariz., 1985—91; dean Coll. Fine Arts U. Okla., 1991—97; dean Sch. Music. Ind. U., 1997—99; dean Sch. Fine Arts U. Conn., 2000—. Author: Phoebe in Her Petticoat, Congotay; co-author: Teaching Music in 21st Century, Jump Right In!; contbr. chapters to books, Handbook for Rsch. in Music Teaching & Learning, Second Handbook for Rsch. in Music Teaching & Learning. Fulbright scholar to Iceland, 1979, Fulbright scholar to Australia, 1986. Office: Office of the Dean U Conn Sch Fine Arts 830 Bolton Rd Rm 202 Unit 1128 Storrs Mansfield CT 06269 Office Phone: 860-486-3016. E-mail: david.woods@uconn.edu.

**WOODS, DAVID LYNDON,** broadcast executive, former federal agency executive, publishing executive; b. San Jose, Calif. s. Donald Mason and Lynda Rosalia (Mueller) W.; m. Barbara Sue Vacin, June 9, 1956 (div. July 1987); children: Stephanie Lynn Woods Snide, Allison Elizabeth Woods Traba, Roberta Lee, Dana Royce Woods Bruce, Meredith Mason; m. Jeanne-Renee Jones, July 5, 1998. AB, San Jose State Coll., 1952; MA, Stanford U., 1955; postgrad., U. So. Calif., 1962—63; MBA, Rollins Coll., 1965, Oxford U., 1974; PhD, Ohio State U., 1976. Dir. broadcasting Lehigh U., Bethlehem, Pa., 1953—54; project officer NARAD Briefing Reports Navy Chief of Naval Ops., 1956—59; sr. writer-editor Martin-Marietta Corp., Orlando, Fla., 1963—65; head program support br. Navy Dept. Speech Bur., Washington, 1965—70; spl. asst. to chief material Naval Material Command, Washington, 1970—84, dir. Navy sci. and tech. info. Arlington, Va., 1984—93; pres. DaleWood Enterprises, Inc., Hedgesville, W.Va., 1987—. Adj. prof. bus. and pub. adminstrn. George Washington U., 1975-86; instr. Stanford (Calif.) U.; lecturer U. Ohio State U., U. Md., U. Va., and other colls., 1953-88, 94-97; adj. prof. comm. Marshall U., 1998—; bd. correction naval records Sec. of Navy, Washington, 1980-85; commentator, on-air radio host local radio, 1995-99, 96-97; ptnr. Cap'n Dave's Flotsam and Jetsam, 1996-2005. Author: A History of Tactical Communication Techniques, 1965,

82, The Development of Visual Signals on Land and Sea, 1976, (four histories): U.S. Naval and Marine Corps Bases (2 vols.), 1986; editor: Signaling and Communicating at Sea (2 vols.), 1984; author, editor numerous fed. publs., 1966-2003; editl. columnist newspaper, 1998-2004; contbr. over 400 articles and revs. to mags. and jours. Chmn. fin. Commn. on Aging, Alexandria, 1993; bd. dirs. Middleway Hist. Conservancy, 1994-2002, The Station at Shepherdstown, W.Va., 1998-2000; vice chmn. Coun. on Aging of Jefferson County, 1995-2005, Nat. Assn. for Uniformed Svcs., 1986-91; U.S. del. NATO Congress Internat. Res. Officers, 1984-91, U.S. v.p., 1988-89. Capt. USNR, 1949-87. Recipient Navy Superior Pub. Svc. medal, 1986. Mem.: Naval Officers Assn. Can., Nat. Comm. Assn. (emeritus, chair mass comm. divsn. 1970—71), Naval Enlisted Res. Assn. (life assoc., pub. 1987—93), Naval Order of the U.S. (life; recorder-gen. 1996—97), Armed Forces Comm. and Electronics Assn. (life; author), Res. Officers Assn. (life; nat. pres. 1985—86, columnist 2000—04), Def. Edn. Forum 2002—04), Naval Res. Assn. (life; nat. pub. affairs officer 1966—72, dist. pres. 1974—75, 1993—94), U.S. Naval Inst. (life; author 1966—), Nat. Def. Indsl. Assn. (life; author 1991—92), Sons of the Revolution, Lambda Chi Alpha. Avocations: American musical comedy, bluegrass and old-time banjo music, military signals, history of technology. Office Phone: 304-754-4818. E-mail: dlwoods70@earthlink.net.

**WOODS, DEIRDRE,** information technology executive; With Wharton Sch., U. Pa., Phila., 1987—, dir., Wharton Learning Lab, chief information officer, assoc. dean, 2004—. Created a model for information technology support where information technology staff are embedded within faculty departments to provide maximum support and user satisfaction. This best practice came to be implemented by other business schools. Office: Wharton Sch U Pa 1030 Steinberg Hall Dietrich Hall Philadelphia PA 19104

**WOODS, DENNIS OLIVER,** headmaster, market and political research analyst; b. Spirit Lake, Iowa, Mar. 11, 1947; s. Peter Ashton and Edna Elizabeth Woods; m. Jane Robertson; children: Miranda, Vijay, Catherine. BS in Agrl. Journalism, Iowa State U., 1970; MEd, Oreg. State U., 1973; postgrad., Multnomah Bible Coll., 1973—74, Computer Career Inst., 1974—75. Polit. rsch. asst., vol. several polit. and social action coms., Portland, 1976—79; market/polit. rsch. analyst Bardsley & Haslacher, Portland, 1980—84; market/statis. rsch. analyst Columbia Info. Sys., Portland, 1985—90; owner Target Market Strategies LLC, Clackamas, 1991—; founder, headmaster ClassicalFree Virtual Acad., Clackamas, 2001—. Lectr. in field. Author: textbooks; contbr. articles to profl. jours. Issues and strategy cons. Multnomah County Rep. Party, Portland, 1986—90, vice chmn., 1990; bd. mem. Oreg. Mktg. Assn., Portland, 1973—74. First lt. art. U.S. Army, 1971—72. Presbyterian. Achievements include being one of the first to develop perception analyzer system for testing print and television advertising; first to blending ancient trivium methodology (grammar, dialectic, rhetoric) and classical content with internet delivery technologies. Avocation: woodworking. Office: ClassicalFree Virtual Acad PO Box 497 Clackamas OR 97015 Office Phone: 503-658-1755. Business E-Mail: headmaster@classicalfree.org. E-mail: tmarkets@netzero.net.

**WOODS, DONALD E.,** healthcare executive; b. Memphis, Nov. 1, 1946; s. John Thomas and Hazel O. (Perry) W.; m. Shirlene M. Durutta, 1978 (div. 1992); children: Donald E. Jr., Lori Ann, Ryan Christopher; m. Joan M. Turley, 1995 (div. 2000); children: Kathryn Ashley, Lauren Rose. BS in Acctg., U. So. Calif., 1972, MBA, 1976. CPA, Calif. Audit supr. Ernst and Young, L.A., 1972-76; asst. v.p. Am. Med. Internat., Beverly Hills, Calif., 1976-80; corp. contr. Safeco Title Ins. Co., Panorama City, Calif., 1980-82; sr. v.p. fin. Heritage divsn. Beverly Enterprises, Md., 1982-84; co-founder, CFO Hannover Health Care, Inc., Md., 1984-85; founder, pres., CEO Oakwood Living Ctrs., Inc., McLean, Va., 1985-91; owner, pres. HMS of Newport (R.I.), Inc., 1992—; owner, pres. Lizzie Borden Bed and Breakfast, LLC, Fall River, Mass. Sgt. USMC, 1964-68. Mem. AICPA, Newport C. of C. Avocations: sailing, skiing. Home: 173 Gideon Lawton Ln Portsmouth RI 02871 Office: HMS of Newport Inc PO Box 610 Newport RI 02840-0011

**WOODS, EMILY,** apparel executive; b. 1961; m. Cary Woods, 1991 (div.); m. Tom Scott; 1 child, Walt Scott. BA, U. Denver, 1982. Co-founder (with Arthur Cinader) J Crew, N.Y.C., 1983—; former chief designer J Crew Group Inc., N.Y.C., chmn. of bd., 1997—2003. Bd. dirs. J. Crew, Inc., Beringer Wine Estates, 1998, Yankee Candle Co., Inc. Office: J Crew Group Inc 770 Broadway New York NY 10003-9522

**WOODS, GARY V.,** professional football team executive, former professional basketball team executive, automotive executive; b. Nov. 9, 1943; BBA, So. West Tex. State; MBA, SMU. Pres. San Antonio Spurs, 1988—93; ceo, pres., chair. McCombs Enterprises, San Antonio, 1979—; pres., ceo Minnesota Vikings, Eden Prairie, 1998—. Office: Minnesota Vikings 9520 Viking Dr Eden Prairie MN 55344-3898 also: Mark B Woods 755 E Mulberry Ave Ste 600 San Antonio TX 78212-6013

**WOODS, GERALD WAYNE,** lawyer; b. Durham, N.C., Sept. 15, 1946; m. Deborah Jordan Bates, Apr. 30, 1983; children: Paul Ellis, Katherine Jordan. BS, U. N.C., 1968; JD, Emory U., 1973. Bar: Ga. 1973, U.S. Dist. Ct. (no. dist.) Ga. 1974, U.S. Supreme Ct. 1980, U.S. Dist. Ct. (so. dist.) Ga. 1987. With retail mgmt. Sears, Roebuck & Co., Atlanta, 1968-73; asst. to exec. sec. bd. regents U. Ga. System, Atlanta, 1973-76, asst. exec. sec., 1976-78; legal advisor to pres. Med. Coll. of Ga., Augusta, 1978-2000. v.p. for bus. ops., legal advisor to the pres., asst. prof. med. jurisprudence, 1990-2000; of counsel Kilpatrick Stockton LLP, 2001—. Mem. faculty Sr. Acctg. Officers Workshop Nat. Assn. of Coll. and Univ. Bus. Officers, Myrtle Beach, S.C., 1981; lectr. law seminars and med. confs. nationwide. Contbr. articles to profl. jours. Councilman City of Augusta, 1984-95; pres. YMCA of Augusta, Inc., 1987-88; bd. dirs. Leadership Augusta, 1982-85, 94-96, others; bd. dirs. Augusta Symphony, 1988-90, pres., 1990-91; trustee Augusta-Richmond County Pub. Libr., 1984-85; mem. Richmond County Dem. Exec. Com., 1983-86, Richmond County Bd. of Health, 1986-95, Augusta Symphony League, 1986—; bd. dirs. Augusta Youth Ctr., 1988-93, Southeastern Nat. Scis. Acad., 1998—, vice chair, 2005, bd. dirs. Sacred Heart Cultural Ctr., Southeastern Natural Scis. Acad. Land Trust, Inc., 2001-02, United Way of CSRA, Inc., 2004—, mem., 2004—; chmn. cultural action plan steering com. Greater Augusta Arts Coun., 1992, active, 1996-2005, pres., 1999; mem. air svc. task force Augusta C. of C., 1990-93; mem. Cmtys. in Sch. Inc. Bd., 1996-98, Southeastern Tech. of Bd., 1996-2000; trustee Historic Augusta, Inc., 1998-2004, treas., 2002-04; active Ga.-Carolina coun. Boy Scouts Am., 1999—2002; co-chair exec. forum Leadership Augusta, 1994-96, 2002; asst. scoutmaster Boy Scouts Am., 1998-2005. Mem. State Bar Ga. (medico-legal liaison and mental health coms. 1979, vice chmn. coll. and univ. com., sch. and coll. law sect. 1986-88), Augusta Bar Assn., Ga. Soc. Hosp. Attys., Nat. Assn. Coll. and Univ. Attys. (exec. bd. 1983-86, co-vice chair fin. com. 2002-05, treas. 2005-), Am. Health Lawyers Assn.(formerly Nat. Health Lawyers Assn.), Kiwanis (treas. Ansley club 1977, bd. dirs. 1977-78), Nat. Assn. Coll. and Univ. Bus. Officers, Forrest Hills Assn. (pres. 1982-85, bd. dirs. 1985-94), Met. Augusta C. of C. (co-chair govt. affairs com.), U. N.C. Alumni Assn. (v.p. Augusta chpt. 1984-90), Pinnacle Club, Augusta Country Club, Rotary (bd. dirs. Augusta 2002-, sec. 2004-05, treas. 2005-). Avocation: photography. Office Phone: 706-823-4224.

**WOODS, HARRIETT RUTH,** political organization worker, retired state official; b. Cleve., June 2, 1927; d. Armin and Ruth (Wise) Friedman; m. James B. Woods, Jan. 2, 1953; children: Christopher, Peter, Andrew. Student, U. Chgo., 1945; BA, U. Mich., 1949; LLD (hon.), Webster U., 1988, U. Missouri, 2003. Reporter Chgo. Herald-Am., 1948, St. Louis Globe-Democrat, 1949-51; prodr. Star, KPLR-TV, St. Louis, 1964-74; moderator, writer Sta. KETC-TC, St. Louis, 1962-64; council mem. University City, Mo., 1967-74; mem. Mo. Hwy. Commn., 1974, Mo. Transp. Commn., 1974-75, Mo. Senate, 1976-84; lt. gov. State of Mo., 1985-89; pres. Inst. for Policy Leadership U. Mo., St. Louis, 1989-91, lectr., 1995—; commentator KWMU Radio, 1985—. Pres. Nat. Women's Polit. Caucus, 1991-95; fellow inst. politics J.F. Kennedy Sch. Govt., Harvard U., 1988; adj. prof. U. Mo., St.

Louis, 1995—, Hunter Coll., N.Y.C., 2004—, Pace U., 2006—. Author: Stepping Up to Power: The Political Journey of American Women, 2000. Bd. dirs. LWV of Mo., 1963, Nat. League of Cities, 1972-74; Dem. nominee for U.S. Senate, 1982, 86; commr. St. Louis Regional Conf. and Sports Complex Authority, 2000—. Jewish. Office Phone: 314-863-4055. Personal E-mail: hw1781@sbcglobal.net.

**WOODS, HARRY ARTHUR, JR.,** lawyer; b. Hartford, Ark., Feb. 15, 1941; s. Harry Arthur and Viada (Young) W.; m. Carol Ann (Meschter), Jan. 21, 1967; children: Harry Arthur III, Elizabeth Ann. BA in Econs., Okla. State U., 1963; JD, NYU, 1966. Bar: Okla., 1970. Assoc. White and Case, NYC, 1966—67, Crowe and Dunlevy, Oklahoma City, 1971—75, ptnr., 1976—. Councilman City of Edmond, 1975-79; mayor pro tem, 1977-79. Capt. JAGC, U.S. Army, 1967-71. Fellow Am. Bar Found.; mem. ABA (ho. of dels. 2003-05, interim state del. 2004-05), Am. Law Inst., Internat. Assn. Def. Counsel, Okla. Bar Assn. (pres. 2004, bd. govs. 2001-05, profl. responsibility tribunal 1999-02, Outstanding Svc. award 1982, Golden Gavel award 1998, Neil Bogan Professionalism award 1998), Ruth Bader Ginsburg Inn of Ct. (pres. 1998-00), Okla. County Bar Assn. (bd. dirs. 2001-03). Democrat. Methodist. Avocations: rock climbing, flying, jogging, bicycling, photography. Office: Crowe and Dunlevy PC 1800 Mid-America Tower 20 N Broadway Ave Oklahoma City OK 73102-8273 Office Phone: 405-235-7754. Business E-mail: woodsh@crowedunlevy.com.

**WOODS, J. P.,** religious organization administrator; b. Houston, June 22, 1950; s. William Oliver and Lilly Virginia (Hetherington) W. Student, Blinn Coll., 1968—69; BA, Ft. Lewis Coll., 1971; PhD in Bus. Adminstrn. Mktg., Trinity So. U., 2003. Ordained to ministry, Life Bible Coll., 1996. V.p. sales Bon Ton, Inc., Dallas, 1977-80; regional sales mgr. John O. Butler Co., Chgo., 1980-81; sales mgr. Fox Meyer, Inc., Oklahoma City, 1981-82; sales cons. trainer Rugby Labs., Inc., N.Y.C., 1982-83; nat. dir. key accounts United Rsch. Labs., Inc., Mut. Pharm., Inc., Phila., 1983-88; v.p. Western div. Barr Labs., Pomona, NY, 1988-94; pres., CEO J. P. Woods Ministries, Inc., 1996—2006. Sr. pastor Aspen Christian World Outreach, Aspen, Colo., 1996—; elected to Tex. State Bd. Pharmacy, 1992. Author, editor: Sales and Marketing Techniques, 1984. Mem. Rep. Presdl. Task Force, Washington, 1982—, life membership honor roll; mem. Presdl. Commn., 1988; sustaining mem. Rep. Nat. Com., Washington, 1983—, cert. recognition, 1991-92; preferred mem. Nat. Conservative Polit. Action Com., Washington, 1983—; elected mem. Rep. Campaign Coun. Com., 1992—; elected del. State Tex. Rep. Party, 1992; founding mem. CBN Founders, Virginia Beach, Va., 1986—; active Christian Coalition, 1992—, Kenneth Copeland Ptnrs. Ministries, 1992. Recipient Medal of Merit, Ronald Reagan, Pres., Washington, 1985, Presdl. Commn. from Ronald Reagan, 1986, Cert. of Recognition Rep. Nat. Com., 1991-92; named to Rep. Presdl. Task Force Life Membership Honor Roll. Mem. Nat. Assn. Chain Druggists, Nat. Wholesale Drug Assn., Nat. Assn. Retail Druggists, Tex. Pharm. Assn. (com. mem. 1991-92), DAV Comdrs., U.S. Senatorial Club (founder). Mem. Full Gospel Ch. Avocations: collecting western art, golf, tennis, skiing, travel. Office Phone: 325-657-0420. Personal E-mail: TheRevJPW@aol.com, jpwminc@aol.com.

**WOODS, JACQUELINE F.,** public relations executive; BA, Muskingum Coll. Former v.p. of licensing and pricing Oracle Corp.; former pres. Ameritech Ill., Cleve., Ameritech Ohio subs. Ameritech Corp., Cleve.; sr. consultant Landau Public Relations, 2002—. Bd. dirs. Timken Co., Andersons Inc. Exec. com. mem. Greater Cleve. Sports Commn.; trustee Playhouse Square, Muskingum Coll.; chair emeritus Cleve. Chapter of Am. Red Cross; bd. mem. Great Lakes Sci. Ctr., Cleve. Found., 1998—, Kent State U., U. Hosp. Healthcare Sys., Columbus Met. Library. Office: Landau Public Relations 700 W St Clair Ave Cleveland OH 44113 Fax: 312-207-1601.*

**WOODS, JAMES,** actor; b. Vernal, Utah, Apr. 18, 1947; m. Kathryn Morrison-Pahoa, 1980 (div. 1983); m. Sarah Owen, June 2, 1989 (div. 1990). Student, MIT, 1965-69. Performances include (Broadway prodns.) Borstal Boy, Trial of the Catonsville 9, Finishing Touches, Moonchildren (Theatre World award), off-Broadway prodn. Saved (Obie award, Clarence Derwent award); actor (films) The Visitors, 1971, Hickey and Boggs, 1972, The Way We Were, 1973, The Gambler, 1974, Night Moves, 1975, Distance, 1975, Alex & the Gypsy, 1976, The Choirboys, 1977, The Onion Field, 1979 (Golden Globe award nomination), The Black Marble, 1980, Eyewitness, 1981, Split Image, 1982, Fast-Walking, 1982, Videodrome, 1983, Against All Odds, 1984, Once Upon a Time in America, 1984, Cat's Eye, 1985, Joshua Then and Now, 1985, Salvador, 1986 (Acad. award nomination, 1987), Best Seller, 1987, Cop, 1988, The Boost, 1988, True Believer, 1989, Immediate Family, 1989, The Hard Way, 1991, Straight Talk, 1992, Diggstown, 1992, Chaplin, 1992, The Getaway, 1994, The Specialist, 1994, Curse of the Starving Class, 1994, Nixon, 1995, Casino, 1995, Ghosts of Mississippi, 1996 (Acad. award nomination, Golden Globe nomination), For Better or Worse, 1996, Killer: A Journal of Murder, 1996, (voice) Hercules, 1997, Contact, 1997, Vampires, 1998, Kicked in the Head, 1998, Another Day in Paradise, 1998, True Crime, 1999, The General's Daughter, 1998, Any Given Sunday, 1999, The Virgin Suicides, 2000, Race to Space, 2001, Scary Movie 2, 2001, Riding in Cars with Boys, 2001, John Q, 2002, (voice only) Stuart Little 2, 2002, Northfork, 2003, This Girl's Life, 2003, Ark, 2005, Pretty Persuasion, 2005, Be Cool, 2005, End Game, 2006; (TV films) All the Way Home, 1971, Footsteps, 1972, A Great American Tragedy, 1972, Foster and Laurie, 1975, F. Scott Fitzgerald in Hollywood, 1976, The Disappearance of Aimee, 1976, Raid on Entebbe, 1977, The Gift of Love, 1978, And Your Name is Jonah, 1979, The Incredible Journey of Doctor Meg Laurel, 1979, Badge of the Assassin, 1985, Promise, 1986 (Emmy award, Golden Apple award, Golden Globe award), In Love and War, 1987 (Golden Globe award nomination), My Name Is Bill W. (Emmy award 1989), Women & Men: Stories of Seduction, 1990, The Boys, 1991, Citizen Cohn, HBO, 1992 (Emmy nomination, Lead Actor - Miniseries, 1993), Jane's House, 1994, Indictment: The McMartin Trial, 1995 (Emmy nomination, Cable Ace nomination), The Summer of Ben Tyler, 1996 (Golden Globe nomination), Dirty Pictures, 2000, Showtime, 2000 (Best Actor in Mini-Series of Motion Picture Made for TV award Golden Satellite 2000), (voice only) Legend of the Lost Tribe, 2002, Rudy: The Rudy Giuliani Story, 2003; (TV miniseries) Holocaust, 1978; (TV series) Shark, 2006-; (TV appearances) Kojak, 1974, The Rockford Files, 1974, Welcome Back, Kotter, 1975, The Streets of San Francisco, 1975, The Rookies, 1975, Barnaby Jones, 1976, Police Story, 1976, Young Maverick, 1979, 80, (voice) The Simpsons, 1994, Fallen Angels, 1995, Clerks, 2002, Celebrity Poker Showdown 2004, 2005, (voice only) Family Guy, 2005, ER, 2005; dir., writer (films) Falling In Love in Pongo Ponga, 2002 Recipient Daytime Emmy for Outstanding Performer Animated Program for Disney's Hercules, 2000. Mem. Acad. Motion Picture Arts and Scis., Internat. Platform Assn., Players Club, Mountaingate Country Club. Avocations: golf, photography, cooking. Office: Guttman Assocs 118 S Beverly Dr Ste 201 Beverly Hills CA 90212-3016*

**WOODS, JAMES M.,** history professor; m. Rebecca Ann Woods; children: Matthew, Theresa, Lydia. BA, Univ. Dallas, 1976; MA, Rice Univ., 1979; PhD, Tulane Univ., 1983. Prof. history Ga. So. Univ., Statesboro. Author: Rebellion and Realignment: Arkansas's Road to Secession, 1987, Mission and Memory: A History of the Catholic Church in Arkansas, 1993. Office: Dept of History-Ga Southern Univ 1122 Forest Bldg PO Box 8054 Statesboro GA 30460-8054 Office Phone: 612-681-0238. Business E-mail: jmwoods@georgiasouthern.edu.*

**WOODS, JAMES ROBERT,** lawyer; b. San Francisco, Aug. 3, 1947; AB with honors, U. Calif., Berkeley, 1969; JD, U. Calif., Davis, 1972. Bar: Calif. 1972, N.Y. 1973, U.S. Dist. Ct. (so. & ea. dists.) N.Y. 1975, U.S. Ct. Appeals (2d cir.) 1975, U.S. Dist. Ct. (no. dist.) Calif. 1984. Mng. ptnr. LeBoeuf, Lamb, Greene & MacRae LLP, San Francisco, 1983—, mng. ptnr. San Francisco office, co-chair ins. practice, mem. exec. com. Co-author: California Insurance Law and Practice; contbr. articles to profl. jours. Office: LeBoeuf Lamb Greene & MacRae LLP 1 Embarcadero Ctr Ste 400 San Francisco CA 94111-3619 Office Phone: 415-951-1100. Office Fax: 415-951-1180. Business E-Mail: jrwoods@llgm.com.

**WOODS, JAMES STERRETT,** toxicologist; b. Lewistown, Pa., Feb. 26, 1940; s. James Sterrett and Jane Smith (Parker) W.; m. Nancy Fugate, Dec. 20, 1969; 1 dau., Erin Elizabeth. AB, Princeton U., 1962; MS, U. Wash., 1968, PhD, 1970; MPH, U. N.C., 1978. Diplomate Am. Bd. Toxicology. Rsch. assoc. dept. pharmacology Yale U. Sch. Medicine, New Haven, 1970-72; staff fellow environ. toxicology. Nat. Inst. Environ. Health Scis. br. NIH, Research Triangle Park, NC, 1972-75, head biochem. toxicology sect., 1975-77; sr. rsch. leader environ.-occupational health risk evaluation Battelle Ctrs. for Pub. Health Rsch. and Evaluation, Seattle, 1978—; rsch. prof. U. Wash., Seattle, 1979—. Pres. Am. Bd. Toxicology, 1997-98. Contbr. articles to profl. jours. With USN, 1962-66. Scholar USPHS, 1966-70; Fellow Am. Cancer Soc., 1970-72. Mem. AAAS, Am. Assn. Cancer Rsch., Am. Soc. Pharmacology and Exptl. Therapeutics, Pacific NW Assn. Toxicologists (founding pres.), Soc. Epidemiology Rsch., Soc. Toxicology, Am. Coll. of Epidemiology, Am. Bd. Toxicology (pres. 1997-98). Home: 4525 E Laurel Dr NE Seattle WA 98105-3838 Office: Univ Wash Ste 100 4225 Roosevelt Way NE Seattle WA 98105 Office Phone: 206-685-3443. Business E-Mail: jwoods@u.washington.edu.

**WOODS, JEANNIE MARLIN,** theater educator; b. Shreveport, La., Oct. 6, 1947; d. Charles Raymond and Orlando Smith; m. Daniel Carl Woods, Sept. 6, 1973. BA, U. Idaho, 1970; MA, Hunter Coll., 1987; MPh, CUNY, 1988, PhD, 1989. Actress Germinal Stage, Third Eye Theatre, Denver, 1971-80; lectr. CCNY, N.Y.C., 1987, Baruch Coll., 1988; asst. prof. theatre Winthrop U., Rock Hill, SC, 1989-95, assoc. prof., 1995—2000, dir office for effective tchg., 1996—98, prof., 2000—06, assoc. dean Coll. Visual & Performing Arts, 2001—06; artistic dir. New Stage Ensemble Theatre, 1993—2006; prof. theatre Western Ill. U., Macomb, Ill., 2006—, chair dept. theatre and dance, 2006—. Author: Theatre to Change Men's Souls, The Artistry of Adrian Hall, 1993, Maureen Stapleton: A Bio-Bibliography, 1992; contbg.author: Notable Women in American Theatre, 1989; co-translator: (with Chi Mei Wang) The Bride and Her Double. Fellow, CUNY, 1988—89; Fulbright scholar, Nat Inst of Arts, Taipei, Taiwan, 1998—99. Mem. Assn. for Theatre in Higher Edn. (v.p. profl. devel. 2003—), Fulbright Assn., League Profl. Theatre Women. Office: Western Ill U Dept Theatre and Dance 2 Univ Cir Brown Hall 103 Macomb IL 61455 Office Phone: 309-298-2995. Business E-Mail: jm.woods@wiu.edu.

**WOODS, JOHN ELMER,** plastic surgeon; b. Battle Creek, Mich., July 5, 1929; m. Janet Ruth; children: Sheryl, Mark, Jeffrey, Jennifer, Judson. BA, Asbury Coll., 1949, DHL, 1999; MD, Western Res. U., 1955; PhD, U. Minn., 1966. Intern Gorgas Hosp., Panama Canal Zone, 1955-56, resident in gen. surgery, 1956-57, Mayo Grad. Sch., Rochester, Minn., 1960-65, resident in plastic surgery, 1966-67, Brigham Hosp., Boston, Mass., 1968; fellow, transplant cons. Harvard Med. Sch., Cambridge, Mass., 1969; cons. in gen. and plastic surgery Mayo Clinic, Rochester, 1969-93, vice chmn. Dept. Surgery; asst. prof. Mayo Med. Sch., Rochester, 1973-76, assoc. prof., 1976-80, prof. plastic surgery, 1980-93, Stuart W. Harrington prof. surgery. Vis. prof. Yale Sch. Medicine, New Haven, 1984, Harvard Sch. Medicine, Cambridge, 1984. Contbr. over 200 articles to profl. jours.; also 26 book chpts. and 1 film. Recipient Disting. Mayo Clinician award, 1991, Disting. Mayo Alumnus award, 1999. Mem. AMA (coun. on sci. affairs 1985-87), ACS (grad edn. com. 1985-87), Am. Bd. Med. Specialties, Am. Bd. Plastic Surgery (sec.-treas. 1985-88, chmn. 1988-89), Am. Soc. Plastic Surgeons Ednl. Fedn. (pres. 1984-85). Avocations: skiing, sailing, reading, the arts. Office: Mayo Clinic Plummer N-10 Rochester MN 55905-0001 Business E-Mail: woods.john@mayo.edu.

**WOODS, JOHN WILLIAM,** electrical, computer and systems engineering educator, consultant; b. Washington, Dec. 5, 1943; s. John Gill and Margaret (McHugh) W.; m. Harriet Hemmerich, June 17, 1972; children: Anne, Christopher. BSEE, MIT, 1965, MSEE, 1967, PhD, 1970. Sr. rsch. engr. Lawrence Livermore (Calif.) Nat. Lab., 1973-76; asst. prof. Rensselaer Poly. Inst., Troy, NY, 1976-78, assoc. prof., 1978-84, prof., 1985—. Vis. prof. Delft Tech. U., The Netherlands, 1985, Heinrich-Hertz Inst., Berlin, 2000; program dir. NSF, Washington, 1987-88; assoc. dir. Ctr. for Image Processing Rsch., 1992—; cons. Kodak, Rochester, N.Y., 1985-86, Johns Hopkins Applied Physics Lab., Laurel, Md., 1987, Calian Comms. Ltd., 1990-91; co-founder Focus Interactive Tech., Inc., 1993; assoc. dir. NSF I/U Ctr. for Next Generation Video, 1998-2001, dir. 2002-05; mem. compression com. Digital Cinema Initiatives, 2003-04. Author: Multidimensional Signal, Image, and Video Processing and Coding, 2006; co-author: Probability and Random Processes for Engineers, 1986, 3d edit., 2002; editor: Subband Image Coding, 1991; co-editor: Handbook of Visual Communications, 1995; mem. editl. bd. Graphical Models and Image Processing, 1989-93; contbg. author book chpts., articles to profl. jours. Mem. Com. Acad. Excellence, Clifton Park, N.Y., 1984. Capt. USAF, 1969-73. Grantee NSF, Army Rsch. Office, Advanced Rsch. Projects Agy., Ctr. Advanced TV Studies, 1978-2005. Fellow: IEEE (editl. bd. Trans. on Video Tech. 1990—2002, Third Millennium medal 2000); mem.: Nat. Com. for Info. Tech. Stds., Internat. Stds. Orgn. (mem. motion pictures expert group 2001—05), IEEE Signal Processing Soc. (assoc. editor jour. 1979—82, com. chmn. 1983—85, ad. com. 1986—88, ednl. com. chmn. 1987—93, 1st IEEE Internat. Conf. on Image Processing 1994, co-chmn. tech. program com., Best Paper awards 1977, 1986, Meritorious Svc. award 1989, Tech. Achievement award 1993). Roman Catholic. Home: 43 Longview Dr Clifton Park NY 12065-2318 Office: Rensselaer Poly Inst ECSE Dept Troy NY 12180-3590 Office Phone: 518-276-6079. E-mail: woods@ecse.rpi.edu.

**WOODS, JOYCELYN SUE,** alcohol/drug abuse services professional; b. Highland Park, Mich., July 13, 1946; d. William Edward Woods and Joyce Yvonne Stokes. MA, Hunter Coll., 1984. Cert. methadone advocate Nat. Alliance of Methadone Advocates. Pres. Nat. Alliance of Methadone Advocates, N.Y.C., 1999—. Mem. dir.'s coun. of pub. reps. NIH, Washington 1998—. Author: (med. textbook) Comprehensive Textbook of Substance Abuse. Pub. policy Ctr. for Substance Abuse Treatment, Rockville, Md., 1991—99. Recipient Richard Lane Internat. Advocacy Award for Achievement in Methadone Maintenance Treatment, 2001. Mem.: Baccalaureate Alumni Assn. of CUNY (life). Home: # 203 222 W 77th St New York NY 10024 Office: Nat Alliance of Methadone Advocates 435 2d Ave New York NY 10010 Office Phone: 212-595-6262. Home Fax: 702-925-8432; Office Fax: 212-595-6262. Personal E-mail: joycelyn.woods@verizon.net. E-mail: nama.president@verizon.net.

**WOODS, KRYSTYNA JANINA,** artist, pharmacist; b. Warwick, Queensland, Australia, Jan. 28, 1961; arrived in U.S., 1998; d. Jan and Janina Dzierzanowski; m. Ross Maxwell Woods, Aug. 28, 1993; children: Harrison George Maxwell, Jack Henry Alexander. BPharm, U. Queensland, Brisbane, 1980. Registered pharmacist Pharmacy Bd. Queensland. Pre-registration pharmacist, asst. mgr. Payless Chemists, Brisbane, Queensland, 1980—81; pharmacist, mgr. Benowa Pharmacy, Gold Coast, Australia, 1981—83; chief pharmacist, asst. mgr. Sorrento Pharmacy, Gold Coast, Australia, 1983—85; chief pharmacist, mgr. Moses Edward St. Pharmacy, Brisbane, 1986—88; chief pharmacist, part-time mgr. Aspley Day & Night Pharmacy, Brisbane, 1988—93; locum pharmacist mgr. Auchenflower Pharmacy, Brisbane, 1993—95, Terry White Pharmacy, Brisbane, 1993—95, Transit Ctr. Pharmacy, Brisbane, 1993—95; owner, mgr., chief pharmacist Indooroopilly Day & Night Pharmacy, Brisbane, 1995—2000. Model, actress Viviens Model Agy., Brisbane and Sydney, 1985—93; actress, model print, TV, radio and stage Margo Mott/Buckinghams, Gold Coast, 1985—93, Queensland Theatre Co., Brisbane, 1985—93, Javeenbah Little Theatre, Gold Coast, 1985—93, Gold Coast Little Theatre, 1982—84; mentor Young Australian Profls. in Am., N.Y.C., 2003; represented Queensland, Australia in Miss World Pageant, 1985; lectr. Mt. Gravatt Tech. Coll. Further Edn., Brisbane, 1989; interviewed by mags. N.J. Monthly, 2001, Australian House and Garden Mag., 1999, Sunday Mail Mag., 1998, Matters Mag., 2005. One-woman shows include Natura Gallery, Heritage Hotel, Brisbane, 1995—97, Brisbane Herbsfest, 1995—97, one-woman shows and exhbns., Wentworth Gallery, Palm Beach, 1995—96, White Plains, 1995—96, Boston, 1995—96, Chgo., 1995—96, one-woman shows include Madison Studio Gallery, 2001, The Show Gallery,

Chatham, 2002—03, Internat. Art Expo, N.Y.C., 2003, Solange Rabello Art Gallery, Miami, 2003, Australian Consulate, N.Y.C., 2003, Solange Rab Art Gallery, Miami, 2004, Arts Coun. of Morris Area, 2004, Happy Dog Gallery, Piermont, N.Y., 2005, Maplewood Open Studio Exhbn., 2005, South Orange and Maplewood Artist Studio Tour, 2005, Tori Collection Gallery, Phila., 2005, exhibitions include Village Gallery, Laguna Beach, 2003, Maplewood/So. Orange Artist Study Tour, 2004, Artists Studio Tours, 2004—05, Happy Dog Gallery, Piermont, N.Y., 2004—06, Tori Collection, Phila., 2005, Maplewood Open Studio Exhbn., 2006, executed murals, S. Orange/Maplewood, NJ, 2005. Rep. city for state visit by Queen Elizabeth II; asst. to pres. in presentation to MP regarding protection of pharmacy ownership Queensland Pharmacy Guild, Brisbane, 1997. Recipient Award of Merit for Outstanding Achievement, Manhattan Arts Internat., 1999, Art Show awards, city couns. and art assns., 1977—89, Adjudicator's Choice award, Warana Drama Festival and Arts, 1982. Mem.: Australian Am. Assn., Arts Coun. of Morris Area (invited spkr. art promotion 2002), Nat. Mus. Women in Arts, Maplewood Club, Internat. Friends Club, Catharine Lorillard Wolfe Art Club (assoc.). Episcopalian. Avocations: tennis, golf, interior decorating, reading, travel. Office: Krysia D Designs 422 Walton Rd Maplewood NJ 07040 E-mail: krysiadart@aol.com.

**WOODS, LAWRENCE MILTON,** airline company executive; b. Manderson, Wyo., Apr. 14, 1932; s. Ben Ray and Katherine (Youngman) Woods; m. Joan Frances Van Patten, June 10, 1952; 1 child, Laurie. B.Sc. with honors, U. Wyo., 1953; MA, N.Y. U., 1973, PhD, 1975; LL.D., Wagner Coll., 1973. CPA Colo., Mont.; bar: Mont. 1957. Acct. Peat, Marwick, Mitchell & Co. (C.P.A.'s), Billings, Mont., 1953; supervisory auditor Army Audit Agy., Denver, 1954-56; acct. Mobil Producing Co., Billings, Mont., 1956-59; planning analyst Socony Mobil Oil Co., N.Y.C., 1959-63, planning mgr., 1963-65; v.p. N.Am. divsn. Mobil Oil Corp., N.Y.C., 1966-67, gen. mgr. planning and econs. N.Am. divsn., 1967-69, v.p. N.Am. divsn., 1969-77, exec. v.p. N.Am. divsn., 1977-85, also dir. N.Am. divsn.; pres., CEO, dir. Centennial Airlines, Inc., 1985-87. Bd. dirs., chmn. The Heartland Funds, 2005. Author: Accounting for Capital, Construction and Maintenance Expenditures, 1967, The Wyoming Country Before Statehood, 1971, Sometimes the Books Froze, 1985, Moreton Frewen's Western Adventures, 1986, British Gentlemen in the Wild West, 1989; co-author: Takeover, 1980; editor: Wyoming Biographies, 1991, Wyoming's Big Horn Basin, 1996, Agent R, 2000, John Clay, Jr., 2001, Asa Shinn Mercer, 2003, A Material Witness, 2003, Alex Swan, 2006; contbr. Accountants' Encyclopedia, 1962; editor: Edward Shelley's Journal, 2005. With U.S. Army, 1953—55. Mem.: AICPA, ABA, Mont. Bar Assn. Republican. Lutheran. Office: High Plains Pub Co PO Box 1860 Worland WY 82401-1860

**WOODS, LINDA LEE,** chemistry professor; d. Te-Sheng and Hsin-Hsin Lee; m. Craig Robert Woods, Sept. 3, 2000. PhD in Chemistry, U. San Diego, 2001. Adj. faculty U. San Diego, 2002—05. Fellow, Scripps Inst. Oceanography, La Jolla, Calif. Mem.: Am. Chem. Soc. Office: San Diego Miramar College 10440 Black Mountain Rd San Diego CA 92126 Office Phone: 619-388-7434. E-mail: lwoods@sdccd.edu.

**WOODS, MICHAEL LEE,** lawyer; b. Denver, Colo., July 13, 1972; s. Robert Lee and Wai Chun Woods; m. Becky Turner Woods, Mar. 18, 2000; children: Fischer, Ella. BS in Mech. Engring., U. Colo., 1994; JD, George Washington U., 2002. Bar: Va. 2002, D.C. 2002, Ill. 2004. Atty. Finnegan Henderson, Washington, 2002—04, Caterpillar Inc., Peoria, Ill., 2004—. Editor: AIPLA Quarterly Jour., 2001. With USN, 1994—99. Office: Caterpillar 100 NE Adams St Peoria IL 61629 Office Phone: 309-675-4280. E-mail: woods.michael@insightbb.com.

**WOODS, NANCY FUGATE,** dean, women's health nurse, educator; BS, Wis. State U., 1968; MSN, U. Wash., 1969; PhD, U. N.C., 1978. Staff nurse Sacred Heart Hosp., Wis., 1968, Univ. Hosp., Wis., 1969-70. St. Francis Cabrini Hosp., 1970; nurse clinician Yale-New Haven Hosp., 1970-71; instr. nursing Duke U., Durham, N.C., 1971-72, from instr. to assoc. prof., 1972-78; assoc. prof. physiology U. Wash., Seattle, 1978-82, prof. physiology, 1982-84, chairperson dept. parent and child nursing, 1984-90, prof. parent and child nursing, 1990—, dean Sch. Nursing, 1998—; dir. Ctr. Women's Health Rsch., U. Wash., Seattle, 1989—. Pres. scholar U. Calif., San Francisco 1985-86. Contbr. articles to profl. jours. Fellow ANA, Am. Acad. Nursing, Inst. Medicare, N.A.S.; mem. AAUP, APHA, Am. Coll. Epidemiology, Soc. Menstrual Cycle Rsch. (v.p. 1981-82, pres. 1983-85), Soc. Advancement Women's Health Rsch. Office: U Wash Sch Nursing PO Box 357260 Seattle WA 98195-7260

**WOODS, PENDLETON,** college director, author; b. Ft. Smith, Ark., Dec. 18, 1923; s. John Powell and Mabel (Hon) W.; m. Lois Robin Freeman, Apr. 3, 1948; children: Margaret, Paul Pendleton, Nancy Cox. BA in Journalism, U. Ark., 1948; D (hon.), Okla. Christian U., 2005. Editor, asst. pub. mgr. Okla. Gas & Electric Co., Oklahoma City, 1948—69; dir. Living Legends of Okla., Okla. Christian U., Oklahoma City, 1969—82; dir. project, promotion Enterprise Sq. and Am. Citizenship Ctr., 1982—92, dir. Nat. Edn. Program and Am. Citizenship Ctr., 1992. Arbitrator BBB; leader youth seminars in field; state pub. affairs officer Employer Support Guard and Res. Author: You and Your Company Magazine, 1950, Church of Tomorrow, 1964, Myriad of Sports, 1971, This Was Oklahoma, 1979; recorded Sounds of Scouting, 1969, Born Grown, 1974 (Okla. We. Heritage award Nat. Cowboy Hall of Fame), One of a Kind, 1977, Countdown to Statehood, 1982, The Thunderbird Tradition, 1989, A Glimpse at Oklahoma, 1990, Historic Oklahoma County, 2002; editor Libertas. Vol. reader Okla. Libr. for the Blind; past pres. Okla. Assn. Epilepsy, Keep Okla. Beautiful, Okla. City Mental Health Clin.; past pres., hon. lifetime dir. Variety Health Ctr.; pub. rels. chmn. Okla. County chpt. ARC; past chmn. We. Heritage award Nat. Cowboy Hall of Fame; Am. Freedom Coun.; charter dir. Okla. Vets. Med. Rsch. Found.; cons. Exec. Svc. Corps.; ex-state comdr. Am. ex-Prisoners of War; vol. Okla. City VA Hosp.; state historian Okla. N.G.; chmn. Okla. City Independence Day Parade; exec. com. Okla. City Bicentennial Commn.; v.p. Okla. City chpt. Freedom Found.; bd. dirs. Campfire Girls Coun., Okla. Jr. Symphony, past pres.; bd. dirs. Zoo Amphitheater of Okla. City, Will Rogers Centennial Commn., Greater Okla. City Tree Bank Found., Boy Scout Am. (life); bd. dirs., co-founder Ctrl. Pk. Neighborhood Assn.; dir. Okla. for Resource Preservation; chmn. State Directional Signage Task Force. With U.S. Army, WWII and Korean War, ret. col. Named Outstanding Young Man of Yr., Oklahoma City Jr. C. of C., 1953; recipient Silver Beaver award Boy Scouts Am., 1963, Wokan award Oklahoma City Coun. Camp Fire Girls, 1968, Silver medal Advt. Fedn. Am., Disting. Cmty. Svc. award Neighborhood Devel. and Conservation Ctr., 2 Commendation awards Am. Assn. for State and Local History, 4 honor medals Freedoms Found., Jefferson Davis medal United Daus. of Confederacy, Okla. Disting. Svc. medal (2), Outstanding Contbn. to Okla. Mus., Okla. Mus. Assn., 1987, Outstanding Contbn. to Okla. Tourism award Okla. Dept. Tourism, 1989, Cmty. Svc. award U. Ark. Alumni Assn., 1992, Citizenship and Patriot awards SAR, 1992, 5 Who Care award KOCO-TV, 1993, Jefferson award Am. Inst. for Pub. Svc., 1993, Mayor's award in Beautification, 1994, George Washington award Youth Leadership Found., St. Augustine, Fla., 1993, Golden Rule award J.C. Penney Found., 1999, Lifetime Achievement award Keep Okla. Beautiful, Pres.'s Vol. Svc. award, 2005; inducted into Okla. Journalism Hall of Fame, 2001, Okla. Mil. Hall of Fame, 2002, U. Ark. Journalism Hall of Fame, 2002 Mem.: DAR (Medal of Honor 2005, Nation's Most Outstanding Ex-prisoner of War 2005), VFW, DAV, Okla. Distributive Edn., Okla. Jr. C. of C. (hon. life, past internat. dir.), Ctrl. Okla. Bus. Communicators (past pres., hon. life), Advt. Fedn. Am. (past dist. dir.), Soc. Assoc. Indsl. Editors (past v.p.), Okla. Vets. Coun. (chmn.), Okla. Heritage Assn., Okla. City Beautiful (publ. editor), Okla. Safety Coun. (publ. editor), Okla. County Hist. Soc. (dir., past pres.), 45th Inf. Divsn. Assn. (past pres.), Korean War Vets. Assn., Am. Legion, Mus. Unassigned Lands (chmn.), Mil. Order World Wars (regional comdr.), Oklahoma City comdr., Okla. State comdr., nat. staff, Gold and Silver Patrick Henry Patriotism medals), Okla. Hist. Soc. (life; publ. editor), Words of Jesus Found. (pres.), Okla. Zool. Soc. (past pres.), Okla. Geneal. Soc., Okla. County Sr. Nutrition Found. (sec., bd. dirs.), Freedom's Found. (v.p.), Nat. Eagle Scout Assn.

(Okla. chmn.), U. Ark. Alumni Assn. (charter pres. Oklahoma City chpt.), Okla. Lung Assn. (pub. rels. com.), Am. Cancer Soc. (dir. Okla. County chpt.), Okla. Travel Industries Assn., Am. Ex-Prisoners of War (state comdr.), Okla. City Hist. Preservation Commn., Okla. City Clean and Green Coalition, Lincoln Park Country Club (pres.), Oklahoma City Advt. Club (past pres., hon. life), Kappa Sigma (nat. comdr. publs.), Sigma Delta Chi. Home: 541 NW 31st St Oklahoma City OK 73118-7334 Office Phone: 405-425-5032. Personal E-mail: penwoods@cox.net.

**WOODS, PHYLLIS MICHALIK,** librarian; b. New Orleans, Sept. 12, 1937; d. Philip John and Thelma Alice (Carey) Michalik; 1 child, Tara Lynn Woods. BA, Southea. La. U., 1967. Cert. in speech and English, libr. sci., secondary edn., La. Tchr. speech, English and drama St. Charles Parish Pub. Schs., Luling, La., elem. tchr., secondary tchr. remedial reading, Chpt. I reading specialist, Wicat tchr. coord., elem. sch. libr.; media specialist Jefferson Parish Pub. Sch. System. Tchr. cons. St. Charles parish writing project La. State U. Writing Project; tchr. gifted writing students in a summer writing workshop. Author: Egbert, the Egret, Egbert's Picnic, Egbert Visits Sammy, Angel Without Wings, The Necklace and Egbert's Calf, The Hurricane, The Cleanup Day, The Rainbow, The Fair, The Tornado; songwriter; musical compositions include The Fruits of the Spirit, Father's Day Song, Mother's Day Song; contbr. articles and poems to River Parish Guide, St. Charles Herald. Sch. rep. United Fund, St. Charles Parish Reading Assn.; parish com. mem. Young Authors, Tchrs. Who Write; active 4-H leader; bd. trustees Michalik Scholarship Trust. Mem. ASCD, Internat. Platform Assn., Internat. Reading Assn., Am. Fedn. Tchrs., St. Charles Parish Reading Coun., Newspaper in Edn. (chmn., historian), La. Assn. Newspapers in Edn. (state com.), Jefferson Parish Libr. Assn., Jefferson Parish Reading Assn., Jefferson Parish Tchrs. Union.

**WOODS, REGINALD FOSTER,** management consulting executive; b. Charleston, W.Va., Sept. 25, 1939; s. Reginald Foster and Jean Lee (Hill) W.; m. Katharine Terry Norden, May 11, 1963; children: Eric Arthur, Elizabeth Terry, Tracy Lee. MBE, Cornell U., 1961, MME, 1962, MBA, 1963. Mktg. specialist Gen. Electric Co., NYC, 1963-64; dir. flight equipment and facilities planning Eastern Airlines, NYC, 1964-70; v.p. planning Butler Internat., Inc., Montvale, NJ, 1970, sr. v.p. fin., 1971-80, exec. v.p., 1980-86, pres., 1986-87; chmn. Mgmt. Resources Group, Inc., Saddle River, NJ, 1987-96; pres., CEO The Advantage Ptnrs., Chatham, NJ, 1992-94; pres. DCG Corp., 1994—2004. Bd. dirs. DCG Corp., Roseville, Calif., The Greenleaf Co., Cranford, NJ, Sement, Inc., Charlottesville, Va. Mem. Ridgewood Country Club, Glenmore Country Club, Keswick Club, Keswick Hunt Club. Home and Office: Fox Ridge Farm PO Box 490 Keswick VA 22947-0490

**WOODS, RICHARD DALE,** lawyer; b. Kans. City, Mo., May 20, 1950; s. Willard Dale and Betty Sue (Duncan) W.; m. Cecelia Ann Thompson, Aug. 11, 1973 (div. July 1996); children: Duncan Warren, Shannon Cecelia; m. Mary Linna Lash, June 6, 1999. BA with distinction, U. Kans., 1972; JD, U. Mo., 1975. Bar: Mo. 1975, Kans. 2000, U.S. Dist. Ct. (we. dist.) Mo. 1975, U.S. Tax Ct. 1999. Assoc. Shook, Hardy & Bacon L.L.P., Kansas City, Mo., 1975-79, ptnr., 1980-2000; shareholder Kirkland & Woods, P.C., Overland Park, Kans., 2001—. Gen. chmn. Estate Planning Symposium, Kansas City, 1985-86; chair Northland Coalition, 1993. Chmn. fin. com. North Woods Ch., Kansas City, 1986-88, 93-96; mem. sch. bd. N. Kansas City Sch. Dist., 1990-97, treas., 1992-97; mem. North Kansas City Ednl. Found., 1998-2002, pres., 1999-2002; mem. devel. com. Truman Med. Ctr., 1992—, chmn., 1992-98; mem. Clay County Tax Increment Fin. Commn., 1990-99; bd. dir. Heart of Am. Family Svcs., 1998-2004, sec., 2000-01, v.p. 2003-04, The Family Conservancy, 2005-, v.p., 2005, chmn. 2006—, Friends of Gilda's Kans. City, 2003—, sec., 2005—. Named to Best Lawyers in Am., Trusts and Estates, 1993—. Fellow Am. Coll. Trust and Estate Counsel; mem. ABA, Mo. Bar Assn., Kans. Bar Assn., Johnson County Bar Assn., Kansas City Met. Bar Assn., Lawyers Assn. Kans. City (sec., v.p., pres. young lawyers sect. 1981-84), Kans. City Estate Planning Soc. (bd. dirs. 1985-88, 93-95), Ea. Kans. Estate Planning Coun. Democrat. Office: Kirkland & Woods PC 6201 College Blvd Ste 250 Overland Park KS 66211 Office Phone: 913-469-0900. E-mail: rwoods@kcnet.com.

**WOODS, ROBERT EDWARD,** lawyer; b. Albert Lea, Minn., Mar. 27, 1952; s. William Fabian and Maxine Elizabeth (Schmit) W.; m. Cynthia Anne Pratt, Dec. 26, 1975; children: Laura Marie Woods, Amy Elizabeth Woods. BA, U. Minn., 1974, JD, 1977; MBA, U. Pa., 1983. Bar: Minn. 1977, U.S. Dist. Ct. Minn. 1980, U.S. Ct. Appeals (8th cir.) 1980, Calif. 2000. Assoc. Moriarty & Janzen, Mpls., 1977-81, Berger & Montague, Phila., 1982-83, Briggs and Morgan, St. Paul and Mpls., 1983-84, ptnr., 1984-99; exec. v.p., gen. counsel imsWeb Corp., Redwood City, Calif., 1999-2000; gen. counsel BORN Info. Svcs., Inc., Mpls., 2000—. Adj. prof. William Mitchell Coll. Law, St. Paul, 1985; exec. com., bd. dirs. LEX MUNDI, Ltd., Houston, 1989-93, chmn. bd. 1991-92; bd. dirs. Midwest Asia Ctr., 1993-95, chmn. bd., 1994-95. Author (with others) Business Torts, 1989; sr. contbg. editor: Evidence in America: The Federal Rules in the States, 1987. Mem. ABA, Minn. State Bar Assn., State Bar of Calif., Hennepin County Bar Assn., Ramsey County Bar Assn. (chmn. corp., banking and bus. law sect. 1985-87), Assn. Trial Lawyers Am., Wharton Club of Minn., Phi Beta Kappa. Home: 28 N Deep Lake Rd North Oaks MN 55127-6506

**WOODS, RONALD G.,** lawyer, former prosecutor; b. Moab, Utah, Jan. 1, 1938; LLB, U. Tex., 1964. Bar: Tex. 1964, US Supreme Ct. 1967, US Ct. Appeals (5th cir.) 1976, US Ct. Appeals (10th cir.), US Dist. Ct. (no., so., ea. and we. dist.) Tex. 1997. Spl. agent, legal advisor FBI, 1965-68; asst. dist. atty. Harris County Dist. Atty.'s Office, Tex., 1969—76; chief prosecutor Special Crimes Div. Tex., 1972—76; asst. US atty (so. dist.) Tex. US Dept. Justice, 1976—85, US atty., 1990—93, chief Narcotics Div., 1976—78, chief Pub. Integrity Div., 1978—80, chief Fraud Div., 1980—85, sr. litig. counsel, 1980—85; pvt. practice Houston, 1993—. Adj. faculty mem. U. Tex. Law Sch. Trial Advocacy Seminars, 1985—94, 2002; chair merit selection panel US Magistrate Judge, So. Dist. Tex., 1990. Mem.: ABA, Nat. Assn. of Former US Attys., Coll. of State Bar of Tex., Nat. Criminal Defense Lawyers Assn., Tex. Criminal Defense Lawyers Assn., State Bar Tex., Fed. Bar Assn., Houston Bar Assn. (chair Fed. Practice Sect. 1992—93). Office: 5300 Memorial, Ste 1000 Houston TX 77077 Office Phone: 713-862-9600. Office Fax: 713-964-8738. E-mail: ron@ronwoodslaw.com.*

**WOODS, SANDRA KAY,** real estate executive; b. Loveland, Colo., Oct. 11, 1944; d. Ivan H. and florence L. (Betz) Harris; m. Gary A. Woods, June 11, 1967; children: Stephanie Michelle, Michael Harris. BA, U. Colo., 1966, MA, 1967. Personnel mgmt. specialist CSC, Denver, 1967; asst. to regional dir. HEW, Denver, 1968-69; urban renewal rep. HUD, Denver, 1970-73, dir. program analysis, 1974-75, asst. regional dir. cmty. planning and devel., 1976-77, regional dir. fair housing, 1978-79; mgr. ea. facility project Adolph Coors Co., Golden, Colo., 1980, dir. real estate, 1981, v.p. chief environ. health and safety officer, 1982-96, v.p. strategic selling initiatives, 1996—2000; pres. Woods Properties LLP, Golden, 2000—. Mem. Exec. Exch., The White House, 1980. Bd. dirs. Golden Local Devel. Corp., 1981-82; fundraising dir. Coll. Arts and Scis., U. Colo., boulder, 1982-89, U. Colo.found.; mem. exec. bd. NCCJ, Denver, 1982-94; v.p. women in bus. Inc., Denver, 1982-83; mem. steering com. 1984 Yr. for All Denver Women, 1983-84; mem. 10th dist. Denver br. Fed. Res. Bd., 1990-96, chmn. bd., 1995-96; bd. dirs. Nat. Jewish Hosp., 1994—; chmn. Greater Denver Corp., 1991—. Named one of Outstanding Young Women Am., U.S. Jaycees, 1974, 78, Fifty Women to Watch, Businessweek, 1987, 92, Woman of Achievement YWCA, 1988. Mem. Indsl. Devel. Resources Coun. (bd. dirs. 1986-89), Am. Mgmt. Assn., Denver C. of C. (bd. dirs. 1988-96, Disting. Young Exec. award 1974, mem. Leadership Denver, 1976-77), Colo. Women's Forum, Nat. Assn. Office and Indsl. Park Developers (sec. 1988, treas. 1989), Committee of 200 (v.p. 1994-95), Phi Beta Kappa, Pi Alpha Alpha, PEO Club (Loveland). Republican. Presbyterian. E-mail: sandrawoods@qwest.net.

**WOODS, SHARHONDA MICHELE,** military officer; b. Jacksonville, NC, Aug. 22, 1976; d. Richard Cecil and Linda Joyce Berry; m. David Lawrence Woods, Dec. 18, 1998. BA in Criminal Justice, U. Ala., 1998. Dir. Cmty. Svc. Ctr., U. Ala., Tuscaloosa, 1997—98; commd. USAF, 1998, advanced through grades to capt., 1998; chief logistics plans 55th Logistics Support Squadron, Offutt AFB, Nebr., 2000; installation deployment officer 42d Air Base Wing, Maxwell AFB, Ala., 2000—02; exec. officer 42d Logistics Group, Maxwell AFB, 2001—02; chief plans and programs 12AF Davis-Monthan AFB, Ariz., 2002—03; chief transportation 12AF, Davis-Monthan AFB, Ariz., 2003—. Facilitator Dorothy I. Height Leadership Inst., Washington, 1998—2003; trainer Faith Cmtys. Adv. Bd./Ala. Coalition Against Domestic Violence, Montgomery, Ala., 2001—02. Vice chair Nat. Coun. Negro Women, Washington, 1999—2003; judge Shell Oil Excellence in Tchg. Award, 2001; bd. dirs. Brewster Ctr. Domestic Violence Shelter, 2003—; adv. bd. Girls First Inc., 2003—; co-chair Missy Foundation, Washington, 2002—; adv. bd. Rap the Vote, 2002. Mem.: Delta Sigma Theta, Inc. Avocations: reading, travel, volunteer work, fencing. Office: 12AF Transportation 2915 S 12th Air Force Dr Davis Monthan Afb AZ 85707 E-mail: ladywoods2003@yahoo.com

**WOODS, STUART,** writer; b. Manchester, Ga., Jan. 9, 1938; s. Stuart Franklin Lee and Dorothy Callaway Woods. BA, U. Ga., 1959. Writer, creative dir. various advt. agys., N.Y.C. and London, 1960-73; freelance writer, 1976—. Author: (memoir) Blue Water, Green Skipper, 1977, (travel book) A Romantic's Guide to the Country Inns of Britain and Ireland, 1979, 30 novels, including Chiefs (Edgar Allan Poe award 1982), Run Before the Wind, 1983, Deep Lie, 1986, Under the Lake, 1987, White Cargo, 1988, Grass Roots, 1989, Palindrome, 1991 (Edgar nomination, New York Dead, 1991, LA Times, 1993, Dead Eyes, 1994, Heat, 1994, Imperfect Strangers, 1995 (Grand Prix de Litérature Policière 1997), Choke, 1995, Dirt, 1996, Dead in the Water, 1997, Prince of Beverly Hills, 2004, Two Dollar Bill, 2005; contbr. articles to numerous pubs. including Yachting, TV Guide, NY Times. Served as airman US N.G., 1961-62. Mem. Writers Guild Am., Authors Guild, Am. PEN, N.Y. Yacht Club, Century Assn. (N.Y.C.), Royal Yacht Squadron (Eng.). Democrat. Avocations: sailing, aviation. Office: Janklow & Nesbit care Anne Sibbald 445 Park Ave New York NY 10022 Address: 88 Parker Farm Rd Mount Desert ME 04660 Home: 570 Park Ave New York NY 10021-7370 Business E-Mail: stuart@stuartwoods.com.

**WOODS, SUSANNE,** academic administrator, educator; b. Honolulu, May 12, 1943; d. Samuel Ernest and Gertrude (Cullom) W. BA in Polit. Sci., UCLA, 1964, MA in English, 1965; PhD in English and Comparative Lit., Columbia U., 1970; MA (hon.), Brown U., 1989. Institute of Educational Management Harvard U., 1993. Staff Senator Daniel K. Inouye, 1963; asst. editor Rand Corp., Calif., 1963-65; instr. Ventura Coll., Calif., 1965-66; lectr. CUNY, 1967-69; asst. prof. U. Hawaii, 1969-72; asst. prof. Fullerton State U., Providence, 1972-77, assoc. prof., 1977-83, prof., 1983-93, dir. grad. studies 1986-88, assoc. dean faculty, 1987-90; v.p., dean Franklin and Marshall Coll., Lancaster, Pa., 1991-95, prof. English, 1991—99; provost, prof. English Wheaton Coll., Norton, Mass., 1999—. Vis. assoc. prof. U. Calif., 1981-82; chair exec. bd. NEH-Brown Women Writers Project, 1988—. Author: Natural Emphasis, 1984; gen. editor: Women Writers in English, 1350-1850, 1992—; editor: The Poetry of Aemilia Lanyer, 1993; contbr. numerous articles to profl. jours. and scholarly books; reviewer for various profl. jours., including Renaissance Quar., Jour. of English and Germanic Philology; reader for PMLA Jour., SEL Jour.; also others; editorial bd. Hunting Libr. Quar., 1987-90, Ben Jonson Jour., Duquesne U. Press. Pres. Cultural Coun. of Lancaster County, 1993-95, bd. dirs., 1990-95; bd. dirs. Lancaster Gen. Hosp. Found., 1992-95; active various polit. campaigns, 1960-64, 68-76, 84, 92. Bronson fellow, 1976, Huntington Library, 1979-80, 81, Clark Library, 1981, Huntington-NEH, 1984-85, Woodrow Wilson Found., 1968-70 Mem. Am. Council Edn. (R.I. women's coord. 1988-90), MLA (chmn. div. 17th Century English lit. 1982), N.E. MLA (chmn. English Renaissance sect. 1978, Milton sect. 1983), Am. Assn. Higher Edn., Nat. Women's Studies Assn., Renaissance Soc. Am., Milton Soc. (exec. com. 1987-89), Lyrica Soc. (pres. 1987-90), Alpha Gamma Delta. Democrat. Episcopalian. Episcopalian. Achievements include Founding Director, Brown University Women Writers Project (literary recovery and text encoding). Avocations: music, travel, boating, scuba.

**WOODS, TIGER (ELDRICK WOODS),** professional golfer; b. Cypress, Calif., Dec. 30, 1975; s. Earl (died May 5, 2006) and Kultida W., m. Elin Nordegren, Oct. 5, 2004. Student, Stanford U., Calif. Winner Optimist Internat. Jr. World Championship, 1984, 1985, 1988, 1989, 1990, 1991, Ins. Youth Golf Classic (youngest ever to win), 1990, 1992, CIF-So. Calif. HS Invitational Championship, 1991, So. Calif. Jr. Championship, 1991, PING/Phoenix Jr. Championship, 1991, 1992, Edgewood Tahoe Jr. Classic, 1991, LA City Jr. Championship, 1991, Orange Bowl Jr. Internat. Championship, 1991, US Jr. Amateur Championship (youngest ever to win), 1991, US Jr. Amateur Championship, 1992, US Jr. Amateur Championship (only golfer to win three times), 1993, Nabisco Mission Hills Desert Jr. Championship, 1992, Pro Gear San Antonio Shootout, 1992, So. Calif. Jr. Best Ball Championship, 1993, US Amateur Championship (youngest ever to win, also largest comeback ever), 1994, US Amateur Championship, 1995, 1996, Western Amateur Championship, 1994, So. Calif. Golf Assn. Amateur Championship, 1994, Pacific N.W. Amateur Championship, 1994, William Tucker Invitational, 1994, Jerry Pate Invitational, 1994, Stanford Invitational, 1995, Walt Disney World/Oldsmobile Classic, 1996, Las Vegas Invitational, 1996, NCAA Championship, 1996, John A. Burns Invitational, 1996, Cleve. Golf Championship, 1996, Tri-Match Championship (Stanford U., Ariz. State U., U. Ariz.), 1996, Cougar Classic, 1996, Pac-10 Championship (shot course record 61), 1996, NCAA West Regional, 1996, Masters Tournament, 1997, 2001, 2002, 2005, Mercedes Championships, 1997, 2000, Asian Honda Classic, 1997, GTE Byron Nelson Classic, 1997, Motorola Western Open, 1997, 1999, Johnnie Walker Classic, 1998, 2000, BellSouth Classic, 1998, PGA Grand Slam, 1998, 1999, 2000, 2001, 2002, Meml. Tournament, 1999, 2000, 2001, PGA Championship, 1999, 2000, 2006, Buick Invitational, 1999, 2003, 2005, 2006, Deutsche Bank-SAP Open, 1999, 2001, 2002, WGC NEC Invitational, 1999, 2000, 2001, 2005, Nat. Car Rental Classic, 1999, Tour Championship, 1999, WGC Am. Express Championship, 1999, 2002, 2003, 2005, World Cup individual and team titles (with Mark O'Meara), 1999, AT&T Pebble Beach Pro-Am, 2000, Bay Hill Invitational, 2000, 2001, 2002, 2003, US Open Championship, 2000, 2002, Brit. Open Championship, 2000, 2005, 2006, Bell Can. Open, 2000, World Cup (with David Duval), 2000, The Players Championship, 2001, Williams World Challenge, 2001, Buick Open, 2002, 2006, WGC Accenture Match Play, 2003, Western Open, 2003, Ford Championship 2005—06, WGC Bridgestone Invitational, 2006, Deutsche Bank Championship, 2006. Mem. US Team World Amateur Team Championships, Versailles, France, 1994, Walker Cup Match, Porthcawl, Wales, 1995, Ryder Cup, 1997, 99, 2002, 04, 06, President's Cup, 1998, 2000, 03, 05, Dunhill Cup, 1998. Co-founder (with father, Earl) Tiger Woods Found. 1996-; With the Tiger Woods Foundation, initiated and supported community-based programs that promote the health, education and welfare to America's children (programs include: Tiger Woods Learning Center, Southern California, started in 2006, Start Something (partners with Target Corporation), started in 2000, Tiger Woods Foundation National Junior Golf Team, Target World Challenge (also host), Tiger Jam (AT&T-sponsored event) (also host) and various grant/scholarship programs). Named Player of Yr., Am. Jr. Golf Assn., 1991, Golf Digest, 1991, 1992, Golf World, 1993, 1994, LA Times, 1994, Orange County, 1994, So. Calif. Player of Yr., 1991, 1992, 1993, Nat. Amateur of Yr., Titleist-Golfweek, 1991, 1992, Orange County League MVP, 1994, Pac-10 Player of Yr., 1995, 1996, First Team All-Am., 1995, 1996, Sportsman of Yr., Sports Illustrated, 1996, 2000, Reuters, 2000, PGA Tour Rookie of Yr., 1996, Fred Haskins Coll. Player of Yr., 1996, Jack Nicklaus Coll. Player of Yr., 1996, Male Athlete of Yr., AP, 1997, 1999, 2000, Male Athlete of Yr. (with Ken Griffey, Jr.), ESPN, 1997, Male Athlete of Yr., 1999—2001, World Sportsman of Yr., World Sports Acad., 1999, Most Powerful Person in Sports, Sporting News, 2000, World Champion of Champions, L'Equipe, France, 2000; named to First Team Rolex Jr. All Am., 1991, 1992; recipient Dial award, 1993, Jack Nicklaus award, PGA Am., 2000, Golf Writers Assn. Am., 1997, 1999—2003, Byron Nelson award, PGA Tour, 1999—2003, Vardon Trophy, PGA of Am., 1999—2003, Mark H. McCormack award as No. 1 player on world ranking, 1999—2003, ESPY award, Best Golfer, 2006. Achievements include winning 12 maj. PGA Tour events including the Masters Tournament, 1997, 2001, 02, 05, PGA Championship, 1999, 2000, 06, US Open Championship, 2000, 02, Brit. Open Championship, 2000, 05, 06; youngest player, first African Am., first Asian Am., and having largest margin of victory (12 strokes) to win Masters Tournament, 1997; first player ever to win US Open, Brit. Open and PGA Championship in same yr., 2000; first player ever to hold all 4 maj. golf championships at the same time, 2001; ranked number 1 player in world for a record 264 consecutive weeks, 1999-2004; youngest to win 50 PGA Tour titles with victory at Buick Open, 2006; 8 time PGA Tour Player Yr. Office: PGA PO Box 109601 100 Avenue Of Champions Palm Beach Gardens FL 33418-3665*

**WOODS, WILLIE E.,** information specialist; CEO, pres. Digital Sys. Internat. Corp., Arlington, Va., 1988—. Office: DSIC 1100 N Glebe Road Arlington VA 22201

**WOODSIDE, FRANK C., III,** lawyer, educator, physician; b. Glen Ridge, NJ, Apr. 18, 1944; s. Frank C. and Dorothea (Poulin) W.; m. Julia K. Moses, Nov. 15, 1974; children: Patrick Michael, Christopher Ryan. BS, Ohio State U., 1966, JD, 1969; MD, U. Cin., 1973. Diplomate Am. Bd. Legal Medicine, Am. Bd. Forensic Medicine, Am. Bd. Profl. Liability Attys. Mem. Dinsmore & Shohl, Cin.; clin. prof. pediats. emeritus U. Cin., 1992—. Adj. prof. law U. Cin., 1973—. Editor: Drug Product Liability, 1985—. Fellow Am. Coll. Legal Medicine, Am. Coll. Forensic Examiners, Am. Soc. Hosp. Attys., Soc. Ohio Hosp. Attys.; mem. ABA, Ohio Bar Assn., Internat. Assn. Def. Counsel, Def. Rsch. Inst. (chmn. drug and med. svc. com. 1988-91), Cin. Bar Assn. Office: Dinsmore & Shohl 1900 Chemed Ctr 255 E 5th St Cincinnati OH 45202-4700 Office Phone: 513-977-8266. Business E-Mail: frank.woodside@dinslaw.com.

**WOODSIDE, LISA NICOLE,** humanities educator; b. Portland, Oreg., Sept. 7, 1944; d. Lee and Emma (Wenstrom) W. Student, Reed Coll., 1962—65; MA, U. Chgo., 1968; PhD, Bryn Mawr Coll., 1972; cert., Harvard U. Inst. Ednl. Mgmt., 1979; MA, West Chester U., 1994. Cert. tchr. ecstatic trance postures Cuyamungue Inst., N.Mex., 2003, wellness counseling, creative energy options. Mem. dean's staff Bryn Mawr Coll., 1970-72; asst. prof. Widener U., Chester, Pa., 1972-77, assoc. prof. humanities, 1978-83, asst. dean student svcs., 1972-76, assoc. dean, 1976-79, dean, 1979-83; acad. dean, prof. humanities Holy Family Coll., Phila., 1983—, v.p., dean acad. affairs, prof. humanities, 1990-98, prof. humanities, 1998—. Cons. State NJ Edn. Dept., 1990, Houghton-Mifflin for English reader, 2000; cons., reader Test of Spoken English Ednl. Testing Svc., 2002—; accreditor Commn. on Higher Edn., Mid. States Assn., 1977—83, 1994. Co-author: New Age Spirituality: An Assessment. City commr. for cmty. rels., Chester, 1980-83; mem. Adult Edn. Coun. Phila. Recipient Crasilneck award for best paper Am. Soc. Clin. Hypnosis; Am. Assn. Papyrology grantee Bryn Mawr Coll., S. Maude Kaemmerling fellow. Mem.: MLA, AAUW (univ. rep. 1975—83), APA, Pa. Coll. Tchrs. Assn., Mid. States Classics Assn., Audubon Soc., Psi Chi, Alpha Sigma Lambda, Phi Eta Sigma. Office: Humanities Dept Holy Family Univ Torresdale Philadelphia PA 19114 Office Phone: 215-637-7700. E-mail: woodside@holyfamily.edu.

**WOODSOME, EDWIN VALENTINE, JR.,** lawyer; AB summa cum laude, Holy Cross Coll., 1968; JD magna cum laude, Harvard U., 1971. Bar: Mass. 1972, Calif. 1973, D.C. 1973. Law clk. to Hon. James R. Browning US Ct. Appeals (9th cir.), 1971—72; ptnr. Orrick, Herrington & Sutcliffe LLP, LA, 2003—. Mem.: State Bar Calif., D.C. Bar, ABA (litig. sect., environ. sect., employment sect.), L.A. County Bar Assn. Office: Orrick Herrington & Sutcliffe LLP 777 S Figueroa St Ste 3200 Los Angeles CA 90017 Office Phone: 213-612-2398. Business E-Mail: ewoodsome@orrick.com.

**WOODSON, DARREN RAY,** retired professional football player; b. Phoenix, Apr. 25, 1969; Student, Ariz. State U. Safety Dallas Cowboys, 1992—2004. Named to Sporting News NFL-All-Pro Team, 1994; selected to Pro Bowl, 1994, 96. Mem. Dallas Cowboys Super Bowl XXVII Champions, 1992, Super Bowl XXVIII, 1993.

**WOODSON, GAYLE ELLEN,** otolaryngologist; b. Galveston, Tex., June 9, 1950; d. Clinton Eldon and Nancy Jean (Stephens) W.; m. Kevin Thomas Robbins; children: Nicholas, Gregory, Sarah. BA, Rice U., 1972; MD, Baylor Coll. Medicine, 1975. Diplomate Am. Bd. Otolaryngology (bd. dirs., residency rev. com. for otolaryngology, exam. chair). Fellow Baylor Coll. Medicine, Houston, 1976, Inst. Laryngology & Otology, London, 1981-82; asst. prof. Baylor Coll. Medicine, 1982-87; asst. attending Harris County Hosp. Dist., Houston, 1982-86; with courtesy staff Saint Luke's Episcopal Hosp., Houston, 1982-87; assoc. attending The Methodist Hosp., Houston, 1982-87; asst. prof. U. Calif. Med. Sch., San Diego, 1987-89; chief otolaryngology VA Med. Ctr., San Diego, 1987-92; assoc. prof. U. Calif. Sch. Med., San Diego, 1989-92; prof. otolaryngology U. Tenn., Memphis, 1993—2000, So. Ill. U., 2003—. Numerous presentations and lectures in field. Contbr. numerous articles and abstracts to med. jours., also videotapes. Recipient deRoldes award, Am. Layrngol. Assn., 2003. Fellow ACS (bd. govs.), Royal Coll. Surgeons, Soc. Univ. Otolaryngologists (past pres.), Am. Soc. Head and Neck Surgery, Am. Laryngol. Assn. (pres.-elect de Roaldes award, 2003), Triological Soc.; mem. AMA, Am. Acad. Otolaryngology-Head and Neck Surgery (bd. dirs. 1993-96), Am. Med. Women's Assn. (past pres. Memphis br.), Soc. Head and Neck Oncologists Eng., Am. Physiol. Soc., Assn. Women Surgeons, Am. Soc. Head and Neck Surgeons, Johns Hopkins Soc. Scholars, Collegium OtoRhinolaryngolicum Amicus Sacrum. Office: Southern Illinois Univ PO Box 19662 Springfield IL 62794-9662 Business E-Mail: gwoodson@siumed.edu.

**WOODSON, JACQUELINE,** writer; b. Columbus, Ohio, Feb. 12, 1964; 1 child. Fellow MacDowell Colony and the Fine Arts Work Ctr., Provincetown, Mass. Author: (book) Last Summer With Maizon, 1990, Martin Luther King Jr., and His Birthday, 1990, The Dear One, 1991, Maizon at Blue Hill, 1992, I Hadn't Meant to Tell You This, 1994, Between Madison and Palmetto, 1995, Autobiography of a Family Photo, 1995, From the Notebooks of Melanin Sun, 1995, A Way Out of No Way, 1996, The House You Pass on the Way, 1997, We Had a Picnic this Past Sunday, 1997, If You Come Softly, 1998, Lena, 1998, Miracle's Boys, 2000, Sweet, Sweet Memory, 2000, The Other Side, 2001, Hush, 2002, Our Gracie Aunt, 2002, Visiting Day, 2002, Locomotion, 2003 (Nat. Book award nominee, 2003); author: (ill. by E.B. Lewis) Coming On Home Soon, 2004 (Caldecott award, 2005, Am. Libr. Assn. Notable Book, 2005, Child Mag. Best of 2004, Booklist Editor's Choice); author: (ill. by Hudson Talbott) Show Way, 2005 (Newbery Honor Book, 2006). Recipient Coretta Scott King Honors, 2001, Kenyon Review award for lit. excellence in fiction, 3 Am. Libr. Assn. awards, 2 Jane Adams Peace award honors, 3 Lambda Lit. awards.*

**WOODSON, LEON C.,** mathematics professor; PhD, Howard U., Washington. Asst. prof. Howard U., 1988—91; assoc. prof. Morgan State U., Balt., 1991—. Mem.: Nat. Assn. Math. (assoc. mem.), Math. Assn. Am. (life). Office: Morgan State Univ 1700 E Coldspring Ln Baltimore MD 21251 Office Phone: 443-885-3776. Office Fax: 443-885-8216. Business E-Mail: woodson@morgan.edu.

**WOODSON, MIKE,** professional basketball coach; b. Indianapolis, In., Mar. 24, 1958; m. Terri Woodson; children: Alexis, Mariah. Graduated, Indiana Univ., 1980. Basketball player New York Knicks, 1980—82, New Jersey Nets, 1982, Kansas City Kings (now Sacramento Kings), 1982—86, LA Clippers, 1986—88, Houston Rockets, 1988—91, Cleve. Cavaliers, 1991; asst. coach Milw. Bucks, 1996—99, Cleve. Cavaliers, 1999—2001, Phila. 76ers, 2001—03, Detroit Pistons, 2004—05; head coach Atlanta Hawks, 2005—. Office: Atlanta Hawks Philips Arena One Philip Ave Atlanta GA 30303*

**WOODSON, RILEY DONALD,** thoracic and cardiovascular surgeon, lawyer; b. Winfield, Kans., Dec. 24, 1931; s. Riley Delma and Virginia Marie Woodson (Stepmother), Ruth Benedict Woodson; married; children: Riley David, Wade Clinton. BA, U. Kans., 1953, MD, 1956; JD, U. Toledo, 1984. Bar: OH 1984, US Dist. Ct. (no. dist. OH) 1985; Med. Licensure Kans., 1956, Calif., 1961, Ariz., 1962, OH, 1968, diplomate Am. Bd. Surgery, 1964, Am. Bd. Thoracic Surgery, 1968, Am. Bd. Cardiothoracic Surgery, 1978. Intern Parkland Meml. Hosp., Southwestern Med. Sch., Dallas, 1956—57; resident in gen. surgery U. Minn. Hosps., Mpls., 1957—63; resident in thoracic and cardiovasc. surgery U. Oreg. Med. Sch., Portland, 1965—67; asst. prof. surgery, asst. chief, thoracic and cardiovasc. surgery U. Ill. Sch. Medicine, Chgo., 1967—69; assoc. prof. surgery, chief, thoracic and cardiovasc. surgery Med. U. OH, Toledo, 1969—78, clin. assoc. prof. surgery, 1979—; pvt. practice Toledo, 1978—92, Palm Springs, Calif., 1993—99; contract med. malpractice case analyst Jacobson, Maynard, Tuschman & Kalur, LLC, Toledo, 1997—98; ptnr. Sodeman, Kirkhope & Woodson, LLP, Toledo, 2001—. Pres. OH Coll. Chest Physicians, Columbus, 1971—72; medicolegal case cons., Toledo, Port Clinton, Ohio, 1975—2001; mem. jud. and profl. rels. OH State Med. Assn., Columbus, 1986—90; bd. dirs. Palm Springs Acad. Medicine, 1994—96. Author 29 works in nat. and internat. med. and legal publs. Nat. basic and advanced CPR faculty Am. Heart Assn., 1976—83; exec. com. mem., bd. trustees sec., med. dir. Regional Emergency Med. Svcs. N.W. OH, Toledo, 1975—79; trustee N.W. OH Heart Assn., Toledo, 1976—80. Capt. USNR, 1963—88. Recipient Owl Soc., U. Kans., 1952, Sachem Cir., Omicron Delta Kappa (Pres.), 1953, Russell Hayden Outstanding Med. Student Rsch. medal, 1956, Outstanding Resident Rsch. award, Portland Surg. Soc., 1967, Ann. Outstanding Med. Writing award, N.W. Medicine, 1967, Golden Apple for Tchg. Excellence, Med. U. OH, 1972, Outstanding Physician Vol., N.W. OH Heart Assn., 1980; Summerfield scholar, U. Kans., 1949, Nat. Honor Soc. scholar, 1949, Athletic scholarship Basketball and Track, 1949. Fellow: ACS (sr.), Soc. Vascular Surgery (disting. fellow), Am. Coll. Legal Medicine (sr.), Am. Coll. Angiology (sr.), Am. Coll. Chest Physicians (sr.; gov. 1972—78), Am. Coll. Cardiology (sr.); mem.: AMA, AAUP (sr.), ABA, Am. Soc. Law and Medicine, Soc. Internat. Surgery, Undersea Med. Soc., Assn. Academic Surgery, Assn. Mil. Surgeons of US, Toledo Surg. Soc. (founding mem.), Am. Thoracic Soc. (sr.), Soc. Thoracic Surgeons (sr.), Am. Assn. Surgery of Trauma (sr.), Am. Assn. Vascular Surgery (sr.), Toledo Acad. Med., OH Med. Assn., Ottawa County Bar Assn., Toledo Bar Assn. (mem. JD/MD and continuing legal edn. commns. 1985—), OH Bar Assn., U. Kans. K Club, Shrine, Scottish Rite, Knights Templar, Phi Kappa Phi, MENSA, Beta Theta Pi (U. Kans. chpt. pres. 1953). Office: 4445-E Marin Pines Port Clinton OH 43452 Office Fax: 419-797-7311. Personal E-mail: rd_woodson2@hotmail.com.

**WOODSON-GLENN, YOLANDA,** social worker; b. L.A., July 29, 1958; d. Lewie B. and Clareece Woodson; children: James Glenn, Kimberly Glenn. BA cum laude in journalism, Bowie State, 1995; MA in counseling psychology, Bowie State U.; postgrad., Calif. Grad. Inst. Social worker Dept. Children and Family Svcs., Baltimore, MD, 1994-95; victim advocate State's Atty's Office, Annapolis, MD, 1995-96; social worker Children of the Village, Carson, CA, 1997-99, Dept. of Children and Family Svcs., Lakewood, CA, 1999—. Counselor City of Refuge Ch., Gardena, Calif., 2000—. Author: Suffering for Righteousness, 2001. Pentecostal. Avocations: cooking, crafts, museums, concerts. Home: 17125 Stark Ave Cerritos CA 90703 E-mail: ywoodsonglenn@aol.com.

**WOODSON-HOWARD, MARLENE ERDLEY,** former state legislator; b. Ford City, Pa., Mar. 8, 1937; d. James and Susie (Lettrich) Erdley; m. Francis M. Howard; children: George Woodson, Bert Woodson, Robert Woodson, Daniel Woodson, David Woodson. BS, Ind. U. of Pa., 1958; MA, U. South Fla., 1968; EdD, Nova U., 1981. Prof. math Manatee Community Coll., 1970-82, dir., Inst. Advancement, 1982-86; exec. dir. Manatee Community Coll. Foundation, 1982-86; pres. Pegasus Enterprises, Inc., 1986—; state senator Fla., 1986-90. Candidate for gov. of Fla., 1990; past pres. New Coll. Libr. Assn.; past pres. Manatee Symphony; bd. dirs. Manatee Red Cross; bd. dirs. Manatee Players, Inc., v.p.; trustee Fla. Kiwanis Found. Mem. Manatee C. of C., Sarasota C. of C., Sarasota Kiwanis (bd. dirs., v.p., pres.). Bradenton Kiwanis. Republican. Roman Catholic. Home: 12 Tidy Island Blvd Bradenton FL 34210-3301 E-mail: marlenewhoward@aol.com.

**WOODSWORTH, ANNE,** academic administrator, librarian; came to U.S., 1983; d. Thorvald Ernst and Roma Yrsa Lindner; 1 child, Yrsa Anne. BFA, U. Man., 1962; BLS, U. Toronto, 1964, MLS, 1969; PhD, U. Pitts., 1987. Edn. libr. U. Man., 1964—65; reference libr. Winnipeg Pub. Libr., 1965—67; reference libr. sci. and medicine dept. U. Toronto, 1967—68; med. libr. Toronto We. Hosp., 1969—70; rsch. asst. to chief libr. U. Toronto, 1970—71, head reference dept., 1971—74; pers. dir. Toronto Pub. Libr., 1975—78; dir. librs. York U., Toronto, 1978—83; assoc. provost for librs. U. Pitts., 1983—88, assoc. prof., 1988—91; dean Palmer Sch. Libr. and Info. Sci., L.I. U., 1991—98; dean Sch. Edn. Dowling Coll., Oakdale, NY, 1999—2000; dean sch. info. and libr. sci. Pratt Inst., Bklyn., 2000—02, acting provost, 2002—03; provost Katherine Gibbs Sch., Melville, NY, 2003; learning sys. advisor Bklyn. Pub. Libr., 2004—. Pres. Anne Lindner Ltd., 1974—83; rsch. libraries adv. coun. OCLC, 1984—87. Author: The Alternative Press in Canada, 1972, Leadership and Research Libraries, 1988, Patterns and Options for Managing Information Technology on Campus, 1990, Library Cooperation and Networks, 1991, Managing the Economics of Leasing and Contracting Out Information Services, 1993, Reinvesting in the Information Job Family, 1993, The Future of Education for Librarianship: Looking Forward from the Past, 1994. Sec., mem. bd. trustees Katharine Gibbs Sch., L.I., 2003-04; dir. Sr. Fellows Inst., 1995-98; trustee L.I. Libr. Resources Coun., 1993-96; bd. dirs. Population Rsch. Found., Toronto, 1980-83. Grantee Can. Coun., 1974, Ont. Arts Coun., 1974, Coun. on Libr. Resources, 1986, 88, 91, 93; UCLA sr. fellow, 1985. Mem. ALA (com. on accreditation 1990-94, councillor 1993-97), Can. Assn. Rsch. Librs. (pres. 1981-83), Assn. Rsch. Librs. (bd. dirs. 1981-84, v.p. 1984-85, pres. 1985-86), Assn. Coll. and Rsch. Librs. (chair K.G. Saur award com. 1991-93), Assn. for Libr. and Info. Sci. Edn. (chair honors and awards com. 1995, bd. dirs. 1998-99, v.p. 1998-99), Am. Soc. Higher Edn., Internet Soc., Am. Soc. Info. Sci. (convenor 1999-2000), Archons of Colophon. Office Phone: 718-230-2003. Personal E-mail: alwoods@intergate.com.

**WOODWARD, BOB (ROBERT UPSHUR WOODWARD),** newspaper reporter, writer; b. Geneva, Ill., Mar. 26, 1943; s. Alfred E. and Jane (Upshur) W.; m. Elsa Walsh, Nov. 25, 1989; children: Tali, Diana. BA, Yale U., 1965. Reporter Montgomery County (Md.) Sentinel, 1970-71; reporter Washington Post, 1971-78, met. editor, 1979-81, asst. mng. editor, 1981—. Author: Wired: The Short Life and Fast Times of John Belushi, 1984, Veil: The Secret Wars of the CIA, 1987, The Commanders, 1991, The Agenda: Inside the Clinton White House, 1994, The Choice, 1996, Shadow: Five Presidents and the Legacy of Watergate, 1999, Maestro: Greenspan's Fed and the American Boom, 2000, Bush At War, 2002, Plan of Attack, 2004, The Secret Man: The Story of Watergate's Deep Throat, 2005; Co-Author: (with Carl Bernstein) All the President's Men, 1974, The Final Days, 1976, (with Scott Armstrong) The Brethren, 1979. Served with USN, 1965-70. Office: Washington Post Co 1150 15th St NW Washington DC 20071-0002

**WOODWARD, CLIFFORD EDWARD,** chemical engineer; b. Richmond, Va, Jan. 17, 1941; s. Clifford Rawlings and Myrtis (Wilson) W.; m. Katherine Roberts, June 1, 1967; children: Ted, Robert, Christopher, John. BSChemE, Va. Poly. Inst. and State U., 1962, MS in Nuclear Sci. and Engr., 1963; MSChemE, U. Houston, 1975. Registered profl. engr., Tex. Devel. engr. Olin Corp., 1963-65; supervising engr. Monsanto Co., 1965-72; lead engr. Brown & Root Inc., Houston, 1972-74; process mgr. Kvaerner Process Inc., Houston, 1974-77, 1979-81, process dir., 1983-88, process mgr., 1992—2000; prin. engr. Jacobs Engring. Group, Inc., Houston, 1977-79; process mgr. M.W. Kellogg, Amsterdam, NC, 1981-83; sr. engr. mgr. Houston, 1988-89; process dept. mgr. BE&K, Houston, 1989-92; pres. Protective Environ. Engring. Svcs. Inc., Houston, 2000—. Mem. planning comm. City of Alvin, Tex., 1970-72; founder Cypress Creek Emergency Med. Svc. Assn., 1975; pres.

Klein (Tex.) Sch. Bd., 1979-90. Mem. AIChE, Engrs. Coun. of Houston (v.p., sec. 1991). Achievements include electrodeposition of polymers from latex solutions and surface kinetics and direct contact heat transfer. Home: 4114 Oxhill Rd Spring TX 77388-9705 Office Phone: 281-353-8980. E-mail: cwoodward@peesiengineering.com.

**WOODWARD, DANIEL HOLT,** librarian, researcher; b. Ft. Worth, Oct. 17, 1931; s. Enos Paul and Jesse Grider (Butts) W.; m. Mary Jane Gerra, Aug. 27, 1954; children: Jeffrey, Peter. BA, U. Colo., 1951, MA, 1955; PhD, Yale, 1958; MSLS, Cath. U. Am., 1969. Mem. faculty Mary Washington Coll. of U. Va., 1957-72, prof. English, 1966-72, librarian, 1969-72, Huntington Library, Art Collections and Bot. Gardens, San Marino, Calif., 1972-90, sr. rsch. assoc., 1990-97; ind. scholar, 1997—. Editor: The Poems and Translations of Robert Fletcher, 1970, The Ellesmere Chaucer: A New Monochromatic Facsimile, 1997, Wallace Stevens, Vassar Viewed Veraciously, 1997; co-editor: New Ellesmere Chaucer Facsimile, Ellesmere Chaucer: Essays in Interpretation, 2 vols., 1995. Bd. dirs. Friends of the Princeton U. Libr. With U.S. Army, 1952—54. Mem. Bibliog. Soc. Am., Phi Beta Kappa, Beta Phi Mu. Home: 80 Runyon Mill Rd Hopewell NJ 08525 E-mail: danielhwoodward@aol.com.

**WOODWARD, HOPE,** soil scientist, biologist; d. Edward Wells and Patricia Galloway Woodward; m. Adolfo Marin Minguillon, Mar. 5, 1985 (dec. May 18, 1993). BA in Anthropology, U. Wash., Seattle, 1986, BA in Spanish, 1986; MA in Latin Am. Studies, U. Tex., Austin, 1991; M in Pub. Health, U. Wash., Seattle, WA, 1995; BS with honors, Western N.Mex U., Silver City, NM, 2003; PhD in Wildlife Scis., Tex. Tech U., Lubbock, 2006; postgrad. in Biology, N.Mex. State U., Las Cruces, 2003—. Cert. Spanish med. and social svcs. interpreter Seattle-King County Pub. Health Dept., 2002; oiler engr. USCG, 1982, Southwestern Willow Flycatcher Surveyor U.S. Fish and Wildlife Svc., 2000, Mexican Spotted Owl Surveyor U.S. Fish and Wildlife Svc., 1998. Spanish and Portuguese med. translator Seattle-King County Pub. Health Dept., 1992—95; pub. health intern Ctrs. for Disease Control, Atlanta, 1994—95; pub. health analyst Ga. Divsn. Pub. Health, Atlanta, 1996—97; biol. technician vol. Red Rock Lakes Nat. Wildlife Refuge, Lima, Mont., 1998—2000; naturalist Mo. Dept. Conservation, Jefferson City, Mo., 2000; biol. technician Gila Nat. Forest, Silver City, N.Mex., 2000—02; supervisory biol. technician Rocky Mountain Rsch. Sta., Albuquerque, 2002; biol. technician Yukon Delta Nat. Wildlife Refuge, Bethel, Alaska, 2003; grad. biology tchg. asst. N.Mex State U., Las Cruces, 2003—04; grad. rsch. asst. Tex. Tech U., Lubbock, 2005—06; GIS spatial analyst USDA Ctrs. for Epidemiology and Animal Health, Fort Collins, Colo., 2005; soil conservationist Natural Resources Conservation Svc., Casper, Wyo., 2006—. Co-dir., founder Amazon Indian Action Network, Austin, Tex., 1989—91. Sec. Ga. Pub. Health Assn., Atlanta, 1996—97; Spanish translator Spay Neuter Assistance Program, Las Cruces, 2004—05; conservation chair Native Plant Soc. N.Mex, Gila, N.Mex., 2004—05; first aid and safety tng. Singles Outdoor Adventures, Atlanta, 1995—97. Scholar Fgn. Lang. Area Studies, U. Tex., Austin, 1988—89, 1990—91; Helen Devitt Jones Grad. fellow, Helen Devitt Trust Fund, 2006—, Bruce Hayword Biology scholar, Biology Dept., Western N.Mex U., 2003, Pub. Svc. Leaders scholar, USDA, 2005—. Mem.: N.Mex Ornithol. Soc., Native Plant Soc. N.Mex. (conservation chair 2004—05), Llano Estacado Audubon Soc., Cooper Ornithol. Soc. (Travel award 2002), Assn. Field Ornithologists, Wilson Ornithol. Soc., The Wildlife Soc. (Ariz.-N.Mex. chpt.), Southwestern Assn. Naturalists, Soc. for Conservation Biology, Am. Ornithologists' Union, Phi Kappa Phi, Sigma Xi, Phi Beta Kappa. Avocations: organic gardening, canoeing/kayaking, reading, hiking, birdwatching. Home: PO Box 342 Gila NM 88038 Office Phone: 307-261-5436 110.

**WOODWARD, JAMES HOYT,** retired academic administrator, retired engineering educator; b. Sanford, Fla., Nov. 24, 1939; s. James Hoyt and Edith Pearl (Breeden) Woodward; m. Martha Ruth Hill, Oct. 13, 1956; children: Connie, Tracey, Wade. BS in Aero. Engring. with honors, Ga. Tech. Inst., 1962, MS in Aero. Engring., 1963, PhD in Engring. Mechanics, 1967; MBA, U. Ala.-Birmingham, 1973. Asst. prof. engring. mechanics USAF Acad., Colo., 1965-67, assoc. prof. Colo., 1967-68; asst. prof. N.C. State U., 1968-69; assoc. prof. engring. U. Ala., Birmingham, 1969-70, assoc. prof., 1973-77, prof. civil engring., 1977-89, asst. v.p., 1973-78, dean engring., 1978-84, acad. v.p., 1984-89; chancellor U. N.C., Charlotte, 1989—2005. Dir. tech. devel. Rust Engring. Co., Birmingham, 1970—73; cons. in field. Contbr. articles to profl. jours. With USAF, 1965—68. Mem.: Am. Soc. Engring. Edn., Sigma Xi. Methodist. Office: U NC Chancellors Emeriti Office 9201 University City Blvd Charlotte NC 28223-0002

**WOODWARD, JOAN B.,** science association director; BS magna cum laude, U. Mo.; MS in engring. econ. systems, Stanford U.; PhD in mech. engring., U. Calif. With Sandia Nat. Labs., Albuquerque, 1974, dir., Environ. Progs. Ctr., leader material support group, nat. security and weapons progs., mgr., Neutron Generator and Explosives Component Ctr., v.p., Energy, Info., and Infrastructure Tech. Div., currently exec. v.p., dep. dir. Chair lab. mgmt. coun. for Mission and Risk Mgmt. Oversight Sandia Nat. Labs., responsible for ind. assessment of weapons' safety, security, and reliability; bd. mem. Intelligence Sci. Bd (ISB), Congl. Commn. to assess vulnerabilities of US infrastructure to Electromagnetic Pulse; mem. Army Sci. Bd (ASB) study on Force Protection, Defense Sci. Bd. (DSB) study on Homeland Security; co-chair Nat. Reconnaissance Office Bd. (NRO) for Nat. Space Security (NSS); served Nat. Acad. Study on S&T for countering Terrorism. Mem. adv. coun. Kirtland Hon. Comdrs.; mem. bd. adv. Family Security Group, Ctr. for Security Policy; bd. dirs. Bosque Sch., Greater Albuquerque C. of C. Mem.: U. N.Mex Sch. Engring. Bd. of Visitors, U. Mo.-Rolla Dean's Bd. Visitors, N.Mex Women's Forum, Soc. Women Engrs. (life), Phi Kappa Phi. Office: Sandia Nat Labs PO Box 5800, Mail Stop 0102 Albuquerque NM 87185-0102

**WOODWARD, JOANNE GIGNILLIAT,** actress; b. Thomasville, Ga., Feb. 27, 1930; d. Wade and Elinor (Trimmier) W.; m. Paul Newman, Jan. 29, 1958; children: Elinor Terese, Melissa Stewart, Clea Olivia. Student, La. State U., 1947-49; grad., Neighborhood Playhouse Dramatic Sch., N.Y.C. First TV appearance in Penny, Robert Montgomery Presents, 1952; understudy broadway play Picnic, 1953; appeared in plays Baby Want a Kiss, 1964, Candida, 1982, The Glass Menagerie, Williamstown Theatré Festival, 1985, Sweet Bird of Youth, Toronto, 1988; motion pictures include Three Faces of Eve, 1957 (Acad. award Best Actress, Nat. Bd. Rev. award, Fgn. Press award), Count Three and Pray, 1955, Long Hot Summer, 1958, No Down Payment, 1957, Sound and the Fury, 1959, A Kiss Before Dying, 1956, Rally Round the Flag Boys, 1958, The Fugitive Kind, 1960, Paris Blues, 1961, The Stripper, 1963, A New Kind of Love, 1963, A Big Hand for the Little Lady, 1965, A Fine Madness, 1965, Rachel, Rachel, 1968, Winning, 1969, WUSA, 1970, They Might Be Giants, 1971, The Effect of Gamma Rays on Man-in-the-Moon Marigolds, 1972 (Cannes Film Festival award), Summer Wishes, Winter Dreams, 1973 (N.Y. Film Critics award), The Drowning Pool, 1975, The End, 1978, Harry and Son, 1984, Glass Menagerie, 1987, Mr. & Mrs. Bridge, 1990, Philadelphia, 1993, The Age of Innocence (voice), 1993, My Knees Were Jumping: Remembering the Kindertransports, (voice) 1998; TV appearances include All the Way Home; TV-film appearances in Sybil, 1976, Come Back, Little Sheba, 1977, See How She Runs, 1978 (Emmy award), Streets of L.A., 1979, The Shadow Box, 1980, Crisis at Central High, 1981, Do You Remember Love?, 1985 (Emmy award), Blind Spot, 1993 (Emmy nomination, Lead Actress - Miniseries, 1993), Breathing Lessons, 1994 (Emmy nomination, Lead Actress - Special, 1994, Golden Globe award, Best Actress), James Dean: A Portrait, 1996; narrator film documentary Angel Dust, TV documentary on Group Theatre, 1989. Co-recipient (with Paul Newman) Kennedy Ctr. Honors for Lifetime Achievement in the Performing Arts. Democrat. Episcopalian. Office: ICM 40 W 57th St Fl 16 New York NY 10019-4098

**WOODWARD, JOHN SIMPSON, JR.,** orthopedic surgeon; b. San Pedro, Calif., Aug. 2, 1970; s. John Simpson and Frances Louisa Woodward; m. Kristin T. Woodward, June 8, 1996; 1 child, John Simpson Woodward, III. BS

magna cum laude, UCLA, 1992; MD, Tufts U., 1996. Diplomate Am. Bd. Orthopaedic Surgeons, 2004. Intern Maricopa Med. Ctr., Phoenix, 1996—97; resident Phoenix Orthop. Residency, Phoenix, 1996—2001; orthop. surgeon, ptnr. Orthop. Physicians of Colo., Englewood, 2001—. Instr. AO/ASIF, Denver, 2001—02, Denver, 2003. Contbr. articles to profl. jours. Recipient Howard P. Aidem Meml. award, Ariz. Orthop. Soc., 1998. Fellow: Am. Acad. Orthopaedic Surgeons; mem.: AMA, Arapahoe Med. Soc., Colo. Med. Soc., UCLA Alumni Assn. (scholarship 1988), Golden Key Nat. Honor Soc., Phi Beta Kappa. Republican. Avocations: basketball, mountain biking, teaching, photography. Office: Orthopaedic Physicians Colo 799 E Hampden Ste 400 Englewood CO 80110

**WOODWARD, KENNETH EMERSON,** retired mechanical engineer; b. Washington, Oct. 30, 1927; s. George Washington and Mary Josephine (Compton) W.; m. Mary Margaret Eungard, Mar. 29, 1956; children: Stephen Mark, Kristi Lynn. BME, George Washington U., 1949, M Engring. Adminstrn., 1960; MS, U. Md., 1953; PhD, Am. U., 1973. Mech. engr. Naval Rsch. Lab., Washington, 1950-54; supr. med. engring. program, chief engring. support branch, chief reliability and assessment, value engring. program mgr. Harry Diamond Labs., Washington, 1955-74; sci. adviser U.S. Army Med. Bioengring. R & D Lab., Ft. Detrick, Md., 1974-75; mech. engr. Woolcott & Co., Washington, 1975-90; ret., 1990. Author: Solar Energy Applications for the Home, 1978; contbr. over 40 articles to profl. publs. With U.S. Army, 1946-47. Recipient Dept. of the Army Decoration for Exceptional Civilian Svc., Honors Achievement award Angiology Rsch. Found., Purdue Frederick Co., Engring. Alumni Achievement award George Washington U., Washington, 1987. Mem. ASME, Am. Soc. for Artificial Internal Organs. Republican. Baptist. Achievements include 12 U.S. and 2 foreign patents, development of artifical human heart. Home: 1701 Hunts End Ct Vienna VA 22182-1833

**WOODWARD, KIRK,** theater director; b. Louisville, Nov. 22, 1947; s. Ernest and Mary Hardin (Morris) W.; m. Patricia Ann Woodward, June 23, 1984; children: Erin, Heather, Craig. BA, Washington and Lee U., 1969. Acting instr. N.Y.C. Housing Authority, 1975; dir. acting studies Pushcart Players, Verona, N.J., 1979-82; dir. New Scripts Project, N.Y.C., 1986; pres. The Attic Ensemble, Jersey City, 1982-85; programmer analyst Time Warner Inc., N.Y.C., 1985—2001; mng. dir. Stage Left, Inc., N.Y.C., 1986-95; instr. Performers Theater Workshop, West Orange, NJ, 1989—. Tech. writer Vis. Nurse Svc., NYC, 2001—; artistic dir. Throupe Vagabonds Theatre, Bloomfield, NJ, 2002—. Author: (play) Who's Who in Murder, 1990 (1st pl. award Hardin County Playwriting Competition). Elder Presbyn. Ch. Upper Montclair. 1st lt. USAR, 1970-72, Korea. Mem. Dramatists Guild Am., Delta Epsilon. Avocation: piano. Home: 25 Melrose Pl Montclair NJ 07042-2531 Office: VNSNY 5 Penn Plz New York NY 10001 Office Phone: 212-609-5509. Personal E-mail: kwdwd@aim.com.

**WOODWARD, LESTER RAY,** lawyer; b. Lincoln, Nebr., May 24, 1932; s. Wendell Smith and Mary Elizabeth (Theobald) W.; m. Marianne Martinson, Dec. 27, 1958; children: Victoria L. Woodward Eisele, Richard T., David M., Andrew E. BSBA, U. Nebr., 1953; LLB, Harvard U., 1957; LLD (hon.), Bethany Coll., 1974. Bar: Colo., 1957. Assoc. Davis, Graham & Stubbs, Denver, 1957-59, 60-62, ptnr., 1962—2004, sr. counsel, 2004—. Teaching fellow Sch. Law Harvard U., 1959-60. Bd. dirs. Bethany Coll., Lindsborg, Kans., 1966-74, 87-95, chmn., 1989-92; bd. dirs. Pub. Edn. Coalition, Denver, 1985-92, chmn., 1988-89; mem. Colo. Common. Higher Edn., Denver, 1977-86, chmn., 1979-81; mem. bd. edn. Denver Pub. Schs., 1999-2005, pres., 2003-05. Mem. ABA, Colo. Bar Assn., Am. Law Inst. Republican. Lutheran. Home: 680 Bellaire St Denver CO 80220-4935 Office Phone: 303-892-7392. Business E-Mail: les.woodward@dgslaw.com.

**WOODWARD, MARY LOU,** retired elementary school educator; b. Vandalia, Mo., Sept. 9, 1931; d. Carl Wesley and Katy Jane (Williams) Lovelace; m. A. Leon Woodward, Aug. 17, 1954; children: Charles Leon, Paul Louis, Robert Lee, William Lawrence. BA, N.E. Mo. U., 1954; MA, Washington U. St. Louis, 1980. Cert. elem. and secondary tchr. Tchr. elem. edn. Vandalia Pub. Schs., 1950-52, Berkeley (Mo.) Pub. Schs., 1954-55, St. Louis Pub. Schs., 1959-95. Mem. St. Louis tchrs. ret. com., ad hoc com. St. Louis Pub. Schs. Retirement Sys., 1988-95; cons. affective domain, presenter workshops for Title I Ctr., Insvc. Ctr., 1976-79; cons. spl. projects St. Louis Pub. Schs., 1979-82. Mem. Grand Oak Hill Neighborhood Assn., 1959—, pub. newsletter, 1960-75; block co-chmn. Operation Brightside, 1970-95; mem., spokesperson Mo. State Found., Columbia, 1990-1997; mem. Concerned Citizens Against Govt. Waste, Nat. Right to Work, Mo. Bot. Gardens, St. Louis Art Mus., St. Louis Zoo, Mo. Hist. Soc., St. Louis Sci. Ctr., St. Louis Geneal. Soc. Leader caregiver support group Oak Hill Presbyn. Ch., 1998—; pub. Caregiver Corner, 1999—. Mem. Mo. State Tchrs. Assn. (state exec. bd. 1984-90, pres. local chpt. 1992-94, pres.-elect local chpt. 1990-92, pub. newsletter 1972-92, Outstanding Educator of Yr. 1994), Ret. Tchrs. St. Louis, Am. Assn. Ret. Persons. Avocations: reading, travel, word puzzles, drama, research, computers. Home: 4158 Arsenal St Saint Louis MO 63116-3923

**WOODWARD, RALPH BARCLAY,** music educator, small business owner; b. Blackfoot, Idaho, Nov. 11, 1944; s. H. Ralph and Margaret Barclay Woodward. Student, U. Ill., Urbana, 1962—64; BS in Music Edn., Brigham Young U., Salt Lake City, 1970; student, Folkwangschule, Essen, Germany, 1968—69, student, 1971. Student Am. Wind Symphony, 1963; tchr. music Elko County Sch. Dist., Carlin, Nev., 1972; tchr. Round Valley Consol. Sch. Dist., Eagar, Ariz., 1973; French horn Rheinische Philharmonie, Koblenz, Germany, 1974—75, Städtische Orchester, Wuppertal, 1976; salesman Daynes Music and Keyboard Showcase, Salt Lake City, 1977—82; founder and dir. Salt Lake Children's Choir, 1979—; prin. and owner Cherbourne Music, 1995—. Freelance musician, 1977—; composer and arranger. Prodr.: (albums) Beside Thy Cradle, 1995, A Day in Spring, 2000; musician: (plays) Fiddler on the Roof (European prodn.), 1968, Compania d'Opera Milano Touri Orchestra, 1971, Ruhrland Orchestra, 1969, Rheinische Philharmonie, 1975, (albums) Concerto Amsterdam, 1971, Columbia Symphony Orchestra, 1983, (ballets) Ballet West Orch., 1977. Missionary LDS Ch., Brazil, 1965—66. Recipient Spl. Recognition award, Gloden Gate Internat. Children's Choir Festival, 1999. Mem.: Am. Choral Dir.'s Assn. Mem. Lds Ch. Avocations: athletics, hiking, writing, languages.

**WOODWARD, RALPH FREDERICK, JR.,** elementary school educator, consultant, education educator; b. Nouméa, New Caledonia, South Pacific, July 6, 1944; arrived in U.S., 1945; s. Ralph Frederick and Monique Madline Woodward; m. Sandy Ann Wylie, Oct. 24, 1970. BA, San José U., 1970; MS, U. So. Calif., LA, 1983; PhD, Iowa State U., 1994. Elem. tchr., Milpitas, Calif., Germany, 1971—76; sch. counselor Germany, 1977—84, 1984—88; sch. improvement, 1989—91; sch. adminstr., 1991—92; curriculum dir. Gilbert Sch. Dist., Iowa, 1994—96; co-dir. Ackerman Lab Sch., Eastern Oreg. U., La Grande, 1995—96; title I coord. La Grande Sch. Dist., Oreg., 1996—98. Ad hoc to state superintendent Oreg. State, Salem, 1995—. Sargent Army, Paratroops U.S. Army, 1963—66, Dominican Republic. Mem.: ASCD (recognition svc. 2002), First Book (treas. 1998—, appreciation award 2002), Cmty. Forestry Commn. (civic award 2000), Phi Kappa Phi. Avocations: cooking, skiing, hiking, bicycling, woodworking. Office: Eastern Oreg Univ 1 University Blvd La Grande OR 97850 Office Phone: 541-962-3413.

**WOODWARD, RALPH LEE, JR.,** historian, educator; b. New London, Conn., Dec. 2, 1934; s. Ralph Lee and Beulah Mae (Suter) W.; m. Sue Dawn McGrady, Dec. 30, 1958; children: Mark Lee, Laura Lynn, Matthew McGrady; m. Janice Chatelain, Aug. 8, 1996. AB cum laude, Central Coll., Mo., 1955; MA, Tulane U., 1959, PhD, 1962. Asst. prof. history Wichita (Kans.) U., 1961-62, U. S.W. La., Lafayette, 1962-63; asst. prof. history U. N.C., Chapel Hill, 1963-67, assoc. prof., 1967-70; prof. history Tulane U., New Orleans, 1970-99, head dept. history, 1973-75, chmn. dept. history, 1986-88; dir. Tulane Summer in C. Am., 1975-78; prof. in charge Tulane Jr. Year Abroad, Paris, 1975-76; Penrose prof. L.Am. studies Tex. Christian U., Ft. Worth, 1999—2003; ret., 2003. Fulbright lectr. U. Chile, U. Catolica de Valparaiso, Chile, 1965-66, U. del Salvador, Universidad Nacional, Buenos Aires, 1968; vis. prof. U.S. Mil. Acad., West Point, N.Y., 1989; regional liaison officer Emergency Com. to Aid Latin Am. Scholars, 1974, bd. dirs. Common Case Miss., 2004-2005. Author: Class Privilege and Economic Development, 1966, Robinson Crusoe's Island, 1969, Positivism in Latin America, 1850-1900, 1971, Central America: A Nation Divided, 1976, 3d edit., 1999, Tribute to Don Bernardo de Galvez, 1979, Belize, 1980, Nicaragua, 1983, 2d edit., 1994, El Salvador, 1988, Guatemala, 1992, Rafael Carrera and the Emergence of the Republic of Guatemala, 1993 (Alfred B. Thomas Book award), A Short History of Guatemala, 2005; editor: Central America: Historical Perspectives on the Contemporary Crises, 1988, Here and There in Mexico: The Travel Writings of Mary Ashley Townsend, 2001; assoc. editor: Revista del Pensamiento Centroamericano, 1975, Research Guide to Central America and the Caribbean, 1985, Encyclopedia of Latin American History and Culture, 1996; contbg. editor: Handbook of Latin American Studies, 1987-90; series editor: World Bibliographical Series, 1987-2000; contbr. articles to profl. jours. Capt. USMC, 1955-58. Recipient Alfred B. Thomas Book award Southeastern Coun. Latin Latin Am. Studies, 1994; Henry L. and Grace Doherty Found. fellow Tulane U., 1962; named La. Humanist of Yr. La. Endowment for Humanities, 1995. Disting. Svc. award, Conf. Latin Am. History, 2002. Mem. Am. Hist. Assn. (mem. Conf. L.Am. History, pres. 1989, mem. gen. com. 1974-76, Disting. Svc. award 2002), Southeastern Conf. L.Am. Studies (program chmn. 1975, pres. 1975-76), L.Am. Studies Assns., Com. on Andean Studies (chmn. 1972-73), Geography and History Acad. Guatemala, Common Cause Miss. (bd. dirs. 2004-05). Home: 303 N Linn St Fayette MO 65248 Office Phone: 660-248-9891. Business E-Mail: woodward@tulane.edu.

**WOODWARD, SERENA,** school psychologist; b. Brunswick, Ga., Aug. 3, 1980; d. Kenny M. and Wanda K. Woodward. BS, Ga. So. U., 2002, MEd, 2003. Edn Specialist, 2005. Cert. K-6 tchr. Ga., 2005. Child adv. Citizens Against Violence, Inc., Statesboro, Ga., 2002—04; sch. psychologist intern McDuffie County Bd. of Edn., Thomson, Ga., 2004—05; sch. psychologist Bryan County Bd. of Edn., Pembroke, Ga., 2005—. Mem.: NASP, Ga. Assn. of Sch. Psychologists. Avocations: travel, scrapbooking, music, video editing. Home: 11 Ballastone Ct Savannah GA 31410 Office: Bryan County Bd of Edn 66 S Industrial Blvd Pembroke GA 31321 Office Phone: 912-626-5085. Personal E-Mail: swoodward@bryan.k12.ga.us.

**WOODWARD, THOMAS MORGAN,** actor; b. Ft. Worth, Sept. 16, 1925; s. Valin Ridge and Francis Louise (McKinley) W.; m. Enid Anne Loftis, Nov. 18, 1950; 1 child, Enid Anne. AA, Arlington State Coll., 1948; BBA, U. Tex., 1951. Motion picture and TV actor, 1955—; numerous TV appearances include Dallas; motion pictures include The Great Locomotive Chase, 1955, Slaughter on 10th Ave., 1957, The Gun Hawk, 1962, Cool Hand Luke, 1966, The Wild Country, 1973, Which Way Is Up, 1977, Speed Trap, 1978, Battle Beyond the Stars, 1980, Girls Just Want to Have Fun, 1985, Dark Before Dawn, 1987, Gunsmoke III, 1991. With USAAF, 1944-45; to capt. USAF, 1951-53. Recipient Golden Boot award Motion Picture and TV Fund, 1988, Golden Lariat award Nat. Western Film Festival, 1988, Lifetime Achievement award in the arts Arlington Tex. Arts Coun., 1994, Lifetime Achievement award for western film acting Wild West Film Festival, 1995, Internat. Star award 1997, Silver Spur award, Hollywood, Calif., 2004, Hands Across History Western film award Sedona, Ariz., 2004, Spirit of the West award, 2006; named Disting. Alumnus of Arts U. Tex., 1969; inducted into the Walk of Western Stars William S. Hart Mus., L.A., 1990. Mem. Acad. Motion Picture Arts and Scis., SAR, Pi Kappa Alpha (Disting. Achievement award 1981, inducted into Order of West Range 1988). Office Phone: 323-876-7877.

**WOODWELL, GEORGE MASTERS,** ecologist, conservationist; b. Cambridge, Mass., Oct. 23, 1928; s. Philip McIntire and Virginia (Sellers) W.; m. Alice Katharine Rondthaler, June 23, 1955; children: Caroline Alice, Marjorie Virginia, Jane Katharine, John Christopher. AB, Dartmouth Coll., 1950; AM, Duke U., 1956, PhD, 1958; DSc (hon.), Williams Coll., 1977, Miami U., 1984, Carleton Coll., 1988, Muhlenberg Coll., 1990, Duke U., 1994, Dartmouth Coll., 1996. Mem. faculty U. Maine, 1957-61, assoc. prof. botany, 1960-61; vis. asst. ecologist, biology dept. Brookhaven Nat. Lab., Upton, NY, 1961-62, ecologist, 1965-67, sr. ecologist, 1967-75; founder, dir. Ecosystems Center, 1975-85; dep. and asst. dir. Marine Biol. Lab., Woods Hole, Mass., 1975-76; founder, pres. and dir. Woods Hole Research Ctr., 1985—2005. Founder, chmn. Conf. on Long Term Biol. Consequences of Nuclear War, 1982-83. Editor: Ecological Effects of Nuclear War, 1965, Diversity and Stability in Ecological Systems, 1969, (with E.V. Pecan) Carbon and the Biosphere, 1973, The Role of Terrestrial Vegetation in the Global Carbon Cycle: Measurement by Remote Sensing, 1984, The Earth in Transition: Patterns and Processes of Biotic Impoverishment, 1990, (with K. Ramakrishna) Forests for the Future, 1993, (with F.T. Mackenzie) Biotic Feedbacks in the Warming of the Earth, 1995, Forests In A Full World, 2001 Founding trustee Environ. Def. Fund, 1967, Natural Resources Def. Coun., 1970, vice chmn., 1974-04, World Resources Inst., 1982-96; bd. dirs. Conservation Found., 1975-77, Ctr. for Marine Conservation, 1990-98, The Ocean Conservancy, 1990-2006, World Wildlife Fund, 1970-84, chmn., 1980-84, Ruth Mott Fund, 1984-91, chmn., 1989-91; bd. trustees Inst. Environ. Rsch. in Amazon, 1996—; adv. com. TMI Pub. Health Fund, 1980-94; bd. trustees Grand Canyon Nat. Pk. Found., 1999—. Recipient Joseph Priestley award Dickinson Coll., 1993, Hutchinson medal Garden Club of Am., 1993, Disting. Svc. award Am. Inst. Biol. Scis., 1982, Heinz Environ. prize, 1996, Volvo Environ. prize, 2001. Fellow AAAS, Am. Acad. Arts and Scis.; mem. NAS, Brit. Ecol. Soc., Ecol. Soc. Am. (v.p. 1966-67, pres. 1977-78), Sea Edn. Assn. (bd. dirs. 1980-85), World Comm. on Forests and Sustainable Development, 1994-98, Sigma Xi. Achievements include rsch., pub. on structure and function of natural communities, biotic impoverishment, especially ecological effects of ionizing radiation, effects of persistent toxins, world carbon cycle and warming of the earth, sci. and internat. environ. affairs. Office: Woods Hole Research Ctr PO Box 296 Woods Hole MA 02543-0296 Office Phone: 508-540-9900 x104. Business E-Mail: gmwoodwell@whrc.org.

**WOODWORTH, RAMSEY LLOYD,** lawyer; b. Syracuse, N.Y., Dec. 26, 1941; m. Diane Elizabeth McMillion, June 12, 1971; children: Scott, Ashley, Jeffrey. AB, Brown U., 1964; LLM cum laude, George (N.Y.) U., 1967. Bar: N.Y. 1967, D.C. 1968, U.S. Ct. Appeals (D.C. cir.) 1968. Atty., advisor FCC, Washington, 1967-68; from assoc. to ptnr. Hedrick & Lane, Washington, 1968-82; prin. Wilkes, Artis, Hedrick & Lane, Chartered, Washington, 1982-99; of counsel Shook, Hardy & Bacon LLP, Washington, 1999—2003, Irwin, Campbell & Tannenwald, PC, Washington, 2003—. Convenor Peace Luth. Ch., Alexandria, 1985-86; chair Libr. Am. Broadcasting Found., Inc., 1997—. Mem. Fed. Comm. Bar Assn. (exec. com. 1986-89, chair profl. responsibility com. 1984-86, treas. 1989-90, chmn. Fed. Commn. Bar Assn. Found. 1991-93, trustee 1991-94, Univ. Club Washington, Order of Coif. Avocation: swimming. Office: Irwin Campbell & Tannenwald PC 1730 Rhode Island Ave NW Washington DC 20036 Office Phone: 202-772-0013. E-mail: rwoodworth@ictpc.com.

**WOODWORTH, STEVEN EDWARD,** history professor, writer; b. Akron, Ohio, Jan. 28, 1961; s. Ralph Leon and Erma Jean Woodworth; m. Leah Dawn Bunke, Aug. 13, 1983; children: Nathan William, Jonathan Steven, David Eric, Daniel Timothy, Anna Constance, Elizabeth Grace, Mary Faith. BA, So. Ill. U., 1982; PhD, Rice U., 1987. Assoc. prof. history Toccoa Falls (Ga.) Coll., 1989—97; prof. history Tex. Christian U., Fort Worth 1997—. Author: (history book) Jefferson Davis and His Generals (Fletcher Pratt award, 1991), While God Is Marching On, Nothing but Victory: The Army of the Tennessee, 1861-1865, Davis and Lee at War (Fletcher Pratt award, 1996), A Deep Steady Thunder, Six Armies in Tennessee, No Band of Brothers, This Grand Spectacle, Chickamauaga: A Battlefield Guide; editor: Civil War Generals in Defeat, Cultures in Conflict: The American Civil War, Grant's Lieutenants: From Cairo to Vicksburg, The American Civil War: A Handbook of Literature and Research. Fellow: Grady McWhiney Rsch. Found.; mem.: Soc. Civil War Historians, So. Hist. Assn. Office: Texas Christian University Fort Worth TX 76129 Office Phone: 817-257-6293. Office Fax: 817-257-5650. Business E-Mail: s.woodworth@tcu.edu.

**WOODY, JOHN FREDERICK,** retired secondary school educator; b. Indpls., Apr. 27, 1941; s. Ralph Edwin and Crystal Oleta (Thomas) W.; m. Nancy Ann Henry, July 7, 1963; children: Michael, Laura. BS in Secondary Sch. Teaching, Butler U., 1963, MS in Edn., 1967, adminstrn. lic., 1979, postgrad., 1991—, UCLA, 1980-82, Ind. U., 1990, U. Amsterdam, The Netherlands, 1985, Mont. State U., 1993, Purdue U., 1994. Tchr. Pub. Sch. 90, Indpls., 1963-66, Broad Ripple High Sch., Indpls., 1966-89; tchr. head social studies dept. Arlington H.S., Indpls., 1989—2003; ret., 2003. Author: (resource kits for hist. events) Cram, Inc., 1976-81, (filmstrips) Lowe Sheldrew, 1976-81; contbr. articles to profl. jours. and sch. materials. Sponsor Rep. Nat. Com., 1982—; deacon North Star Bapt. Ch., 1983—, Oak Spring Ch., 2004—; mem. U.S. Congress German Bundestag Select Com. Ind., 1986-93; vol. Arlington HS Libr., 2005-06. Fulbright scholar U.S. Info. Agy., 1985. Mem. ASCD, Nat. Coun. Social Studies, Ind. Coun. Social Studies, Arlington Acad. Com. Baptist. Avocations: reading, writing, swimming, lifting weights. Home: 7362 Woodside Dr Indianapolis IN 46260-3137

**WOODY, MARY FLORENCE,** nursing educator, academic administrator; b. Chambers County, Ala., Mar. 31, 1926; d. Hugh Ernest and May Lillie (Gilliland) W. Diploma, Charity Hosp. Sch. Nursing, 1947; BS, Columbia U., 1953, MA, 1955. Staff nurse Wheeler Hosp., Lafayette, Ala., 1947-48; polio nurse Willard Parker Hosp., NYC, 1949; staff nurse, supr. VA Hosp., Montgomery, Ala., 1950-53; faculty, field supr. nursing dept. Columbia U. Tchrs. Coll., NYC, 1955-56; asst. dir. nursing Emory U. Hosp., Atlanta, assoc. dir., DON, 1984-93; clin. asst. prof. Emory U. Sch. Nursing, Atlanta, 1956-68, interim dean, 1992-93; asst. dir., DON Grady Meml. Hosp., Atlanta, 1968-79; founding dean, prof. Auburn U. Sch. Nursing, Ala., 1979-84; disting. emeritus prof. Emory U. 2003—. Chair Ga. Statewide Master Planning Com. for Nursing and Nursing Edn., 1971-75; faculty preceptor patient care adminstrn. Sch. Public Health, U. Minn., 1977-79; bd. dirs. Wesley Woods Found. & Long Term Hosp.; chair bd. dirs. Am. Jour. Nursing Co., 1978-83. Recipient Spl. Recognition award 5th Dist. and Ga. Nurses Assn., 1978, 93, Disting. Achievement in Nursing Svc. award Columbia U. Tchrs. Coll. Alumni Assn., 1992, Jane Van de Vrede Outstanding Svc. to Citizens Ga. award Ga. League Nursing, Cert. Spl. Recognition award Ga. Nurses Assn., 1993, Internat. Founders award Sigma Theta Tau, 1999, The Marie Hippensteel award, 1999, Disting. Prof. award Emeritus Coll. Emory U., 2003; named Ga. Women Pioneer in Health Care, Ga. Commn. on Women and Ga. Womens History Month Com., 1998, Hall of Fame Nursing, Tchrs. Coll., Columbia, U., N.Y Fellow Am. Acad. Nursing (charter, Living Legend 1997); mem. Am. Nurses Assn., Nat. League Nursing, Am. Heart Assn., Emory U. Nell Hodgson Woodruff Sch. Nursing Alumni Assn. (hon.), Sigma Theta Tau (Marie Hippensteel Lingemald award for excellence in nursing 1999); mem. Nursing Tchr.'s Coll. Columbia U. of Hall of Fame (charter). Democrat. Address: 19488 Veterans Memorial Pkwy Lafayette AL 36862

**WOODY, TERESA ANN,** lawyer; b. Littlefield, Tex., Jan. 8, 1960; d. Ronald L. and Shirley A. (Yates) Woody; m. Rik N. Siro, Aug. 9, 1980; children: Alexander L. Siro, Lisa A. Siro. BA with high distinction, U. Calif., Berkeley, 1982; JD magna cum laude, U. Calif., Hastings, 1985. Bar: Mo. 1985, Calif. 1986, Kans. 1995, U.S. Ct. Internat. Trade 1998. Law clk. Hon. Ross T. Roberts, U.S. Dist. Ct. (we. dist.) Mo., Kansas City, 1985-86; assoc. Spencer Fane Britt & Browne, Kansas City, 1986-92; ptnr. Spencer Fane Britt & Browne, LLP, Kansas City, 1993—2004, chair litig. dept., 2001—04; ptnr. Stueve Siegel Hanson Woody LLP, Kansas City, 2004—. Pres., bd. dirs. Westport Ballet Theatre, Kansas City, 1988—89, Mattie Rhodes Counseling and Arts Ctr., Kansas City, 1994—95; mem. steering com. Centurions Leadership Program, Kansas City, 1992—94. Mem.: ABA (chair com. environ. litig. techs. 1996—97), Assn. Women Lawyers Greater Kansas City (pres. 1992—93), Midwest Regional Conf. Women Law (co-chair 1997—98), Nat. Conf. Women's Bar Assns. (bd. dirs. 1994—97). Office: Stueve Siegel Hanson Woody LLPLLP 330 W 47th St Ste 250 Kansas City MO 64112 Office Phone: 816-714-7127. Business E-Mail: woody@sshwlaw.com.

**WOOFTER, VIVIEN PERRINE,** interior designer, consultant; d. Orie Ray and Hazel Lucille (Bostic) Perrine; m. Perry Wilson Woofter, Oct. 5, 1952; children: James Perry, Lori Evan Hugh. BS in Home Econ., W.Va. U., 1952, LHD (hon.), 1998. Lic. interior designer Va., 2003. Interior designer GSA, Washington, 1968—76; head interior design The White Hou., 1976—77, U.S. Dept. Health & Human Services, 1977—81; sr. interior designer U.S. Dept. of State, 1981—88; dir. interiors & furnishings divsn. Overseas Buildings Ops., U.S. Dept. of State, 1988—. Mem. W.Va. U. Alumni Bd., Morgantown, 1994—; vol. mem. designer renovation W.Va. U. President's Ho. Com., 1996—2003; mem. W.Va. U. Found. Bd., 1999—; pres. Coll. Creative Arts Vis. Com., 2001—. Author: Develop. Furniture Standards- Phys. Handicap (Written up in Congl. Record, 1977); interior design Interior Design Hdqs. Bldg. for HHS (Fed. Design Coun. of Excellence, 1979), Riyadh Embassy, Paris, Buenos Aires - (Meritorious Honor & Superior Honor, 1988). Restoration work Met. Theater, Morgantown, 2003. Mem.: Internat. Interior Design Assoc. Achievements include development of Art Programs for all new embassies; Culturally Significan Program for US State Dept. Overseas Inter; a Maintenance Manual for US State Dept. Culturally Significant Building-sofp; Featured in Articles, in Architectural Digest, Southern Accents, Paris Match, Chicago Tribune, other newspapersnchi. Home: 4856 N 35th Rd Arlington VA 22207 Office: Interiors & Furnishings Div Overseas Buildings Ops US Dept State Washington DC 20520 Personal E-mail: vivienwoofter@erols.com. E-mail: wooftervp@state.gov.

**WOOKEY, JOHN,** computer software company executive; b. Seattle; married; 3 children. BA, MS, U. Calif. Berkeley. Various mgmt. positions Anderson Cons., Williams & Burrows, Inc.; v.p. devel. Ross Systmes, 1987—95; v.p. fin. applications products Oracle Corp., Redwood Shores, Calif., 1995—99, sr. v.p. fin. applications products, 1999—2000, sr. v.p. applications devel., 2000—. Office: Oracle 500 Oracle Pkwy Redwood City CA 94065*

**WOOL, ALAN D.,** mathematics educator; b. Plymouth, N.H., May 29, 1950; s. Louis Thomas and Priscilla Ann Wool; m. Sally Marie Wentworth, Aug. 26, 1972; children: Amy Rebecca, Jason Alan. BS in Math, Plymouth State Coll., 1972, EdM in Math, 1976. Cert. track ofcl. N.H. Tchr. Daniel Hand H.S., Madison, Conn., 1972—74, Gilford (N.H.) H.S. and Math, N.H., 1974—2003, Gilford H.S., 2003—05. Cross county coach. Named Girls Cross County Coach of Yr., Nat. Fedn. Interscholastic Coaches Assn., 1991; named to Gilford H.S. Hall of Fame, 1999, N.H. Coaches Assn. Hall of Fame, 1999. Mem.: NEA, N.H. Track Officials Assn. (cross county com.), N.H. Interscholastic Athletic Assn., N.H. Edn. Assn., Gilford Edn. Assn., Belknap County Sportsmen's Assn. Baptist. Avocations: hunting, fishing, jogging. Office: Gilford High Sch 88 Alvah Wilson Rd Gilford NH 03249

**WOOLAM, GERALD LYNN,** surgeon; b. Lubbock, Tex., Apr. 16, 1937; s. Rawson Harp and Christine Leta (Rampy) W.; m. Nan Kelly, Feb. 28, 1959; children— Kelly Ann, Gerald Lynn, Gregory Alan. BA, Tex. Tech U., 1958; MD, Baylor U., 1962. Diplomate Am. Bd. Surgery. Intern Parkland Meml. Hosp., Dallas, 1962-63; resident in gen. surgery Mayo Clinic and Mayo Grad. Sch. Medicine, U. Minn., Rochester, 1963-67, chief resident assoc. in surgery, 1967-68; surgeon Lubbock, 1968—; chief med. officer S.W. Life and Health/Firstcare; assoc. clin. prof. surgery Tex. Tech. U. Sch. Medicine, 1972-74, clin. prof., 1975—, prof., interim chmn. dept. surgery, 1980-81. Contbr. articles to profl. jours. Bd. dirs. Community Concert Assn. of Lubbock, 1968-71, 1st United Meth. Ch., Lubbock, 1970—, South Plains Health Systems, 1976-81; trustee West Tex. Found., 1971-74. With USNR. Recipient Outstanding Clin. Prof. award Tex. Tech. U., 1977; named Disting. Alumnus, Tex. Tech. U., 2000. Fellow ACS; mem. AAAS, Priestley Soc. (dir. 1970-73, pres. 1981-82), Lubbock Surg. Soc. (pres. 1972), AMA, Lubbock-Crosby-Garza County Med. Soc. (treas., exec. com. 1971—, pres. 1986), Osler Soc., Am. Cancer Soc. (del. 1980-88, dir. 1988—, nat. pres. 1999-2000, pres. Lubbock unit 1972-73, pres. Tex. divsn. 1978-79), Am. Heart Assn. (pres. Lubbock County divsn. 1973-74), Tex. Surg. Soc., Surg. Surgery Alimentary Tract, Soc. for Surg. Oncology, Central Assn. Dentists and

Physicians, So. Surg. Assn., Sigma Xi, Phi Chi, Alpha Omega Alpha, Phi Kappa Phi, Phi Eta Sigma, Alpha Epsilon Delta. Home: 4007 69th St Lubbock TX 79413-5945 Office: 3611 22d Pl Lubbock TX 79410 E-mail: gwoolam@lubbocksurgical.com.

**WOOLARD, CONNIE WARD,** retired art gallery manager, art director; b. Wilkes-Barre, Pa., Mar. 25, 1931; d. Harold Walton and Betty Bertha (Mandeville) Ward; m. Maurice Emmett Woolard, Oct. 25, 1952; 1 child, Karin Elise Woolard Snoots. Student, U. Md., 1949—50, Abbott Art Sch., 1951—52. Comml. artist Rex Engraving Co., Silver Spring, Md., 1953-60, art dir., 1959-60; mgr. Town Ctr. Gallery, Rockville, Md., 1978—90, Bethesda, Md., 1990—99, ret., 1999. Freelance artist, fine artist, 1965-. One-woman shows include Town Ctr. Gallery, 1984, 1986, 1989, 1991, 1993, 1996, Art Contemporary, Bethesda, 1982, Sugar & Frichtl Gallery, 1993, exhibited in group shows at Glenview Mansion Gallery, 2004. Recipient Salmagundi Non-Member award Salmagundi Club, NYC, 1983, Judges Choice award Nat. League Am. Penwomen, 1996, Juror's award Miniature Painters Sculptors and Gravers Washington, 1997, Grumbacher award 2d pl. and 3d pl. pencil drawing, 2002, 1st pl. Landscape award Cider Painters Am., 2004, Arthur M. Wagman award Peerless Rockville Hist. Preservaton Ltd., 2003, Mid Atlantic Regional award, Balt. Watercolor Soc., 1985, others. Mem.: Potomac Valley Watercolorists, Miniature Painters, Sculptors & Engravers Soc. Washington, Nat. League Am. Penwomen (past sec., pres., named Women Yr. 1984), So. Watercolor Soc. (signature mem.), Phila. Watercolor Soc. (Cert. of Merit), Washington Watercolor Assn. (past pres.), Rockville Art League (past pres.), Salmagundi Club (Maria Szerti Meml. award 2001, Nat. Soc. Painters in Casein and Acrylic award). Avocations: gardening, reading, photography. Home: 3922 Havard St Silver Spring MD 20906-4311

**WOOLARD, EDGAR S., JR.,** retired chemical company executive; b. Wash., NC, Apr. 15, 1934; s. Edgar Smith and Mamie (Boone) W.; m. Peggy Harrell, 1956; children: Annette, Lynda. BS, N.C. State U., 1956. Indsl. engr. DuPont, Kinston, NC, 1957-59, 1959-62, supr. mfg. sect., 1962-64, planning supr., 1964-65, staff asst to prodn. mgr. Wilmington, Del., 1965-66, product supr. Old Hickory, Tenn., 1966-69, engring. supt., 1969-70, asst. plant mgr. Camden, SC, 1970-71, plant mgr. Kinston, SC, 1971-73, dir. products mktg. div. Wilmington, Del., 1973-75, mng. dir. textile mktg. div., 1975-76, mgr. corp. plans dept., 1976-77, gen. dir. products and planning div., 1977-78, gen. mgr. textile fibers, 1978-81, v.p. textile fibers, 1981-83, exec. v.p., 1983-85, vice chmn., 1985-87, pres., COO, 1987-89, chmn., CEO, 1989-96, chmn., 1997—98. Bd. dirs. NC Textile Found., Citicorp, Apple Computer Inc., Dupont, 1996-2000, NY Stock Exch., 2005-2006, NYSE Group, Inc., 2006-, Telex Comms. Inc. Trustee Med. Ctr. Del., N.C. State U., Winterthur Mus. Lt. U.S. Army. Recipient Internat. Palladium medal Soc. Chimie Industrille (Am. sect.), 1995. Office: NYSE Group Inc 11 Wall St New York NY 10005 Office Phone: 212-656-3000.*

**WOOLARD, GILBERT GARLAND, JR.,** educational consultant; b. Greenville, NC, Sept. 23, 1929; s. Gilbert Garland Woolard Sr. and Elizabeth Inez (Vandyde) Woolard; m. Betty Ethel Heath, Dec. 19, 1950; children: Garland, Becky Marie, David Lee. BS in Sci. and Edn., E. Carolina U., 1950, MA in Edn. Adminstrn., 1951; postgrad., U. Calif., Berkely, 1953—54, Clemson U., 1968—69; EdD NC State U., 1973; postgrad., Ball State U., 1974—75. Prin, tchr. Bushy Fork Sch., Roxboro, NC, 1951; mgr. Woolard Furniture Co., Williamston, NC, 1956—63, Kimbrell's of Camden, SC, 1964—68; founding dir. Kershaw Co. Applied Tech. Edn. Campus, Camden, 1968—92; sr. ednl. cons. Com. for Instruction, Camden, SC, 1992—2006. Instr. U. SC, 1972—92, Chemson U., SC, 1972—92; cons. various sch. and coll., 1992—2006; presenter in field. Contbr. articles to profl. jours.; writer over 100 grants, 1984—2004. 1st lt. USAF, 1953—54, Korea, lt. col. Civil Air Patrol SC, 1965—70. Named Jr. Chamber Young Man of Yr., Williamston, 1963; recipient Silver Beaver award, 1963, SC Order of the Palmetto State award, 1992, Camden C. of C. Svc. award, 1996. Mem.: Am. Vocational Assn. (SC nominee for Pres. 1988), Kiwanis, Camden (pres. 1972, 1988), Kiwanis, Williamston (pres.). Methodist. Avocations: swimming, flying. Home: 108 Valley Ct Camden SC 29020 Office: Cons for Instruction PO Box 2556 Camden SC 29020 Office Phone: 803-432-7525. Personal E-mail: drgil3@aol.com.

**WOOLDRIDGE, PATRICE MARIE,** marketing professional, personal trainer; b. Chgo., June 3, 1954; d. Charles E. and Marlys E. Reardon; m. Patrick Wooldridge, June 27, 1981. AS, Moraine Valley Coll., 1974; BA, Govs. State U., 1976, MA, 1977; MBA, Loyola U., Chgo., 1983. Cmty. prof. Govs. State U., University Park, Ill., 1977-78; counselor, social worker Bloom Twp. HS, Chicago Heights, Ill., 1977-78; market analyst Dr. Scholl Footcare, Chgo., 1978-79; supr. consumer rsch. Unocal, Schaumburg, Ill., 1979-84; group rsch. dir. Tatham-Laird & Kudner, Chgo., 1984-87; v.p., assoc. dir. strategic planning & rsch. Bayer Bess Vanderwarker Advt., Chgo., 1987-90; v.p. dir. qualitative svcs. Goldring/MIL Rsch., 1990-91; pres. Wooldridge Assocs., Inc., Chgo., 1991—. Instr. dancing, 1969—89; instr. Arica Inst., N.Y.C., 1978—, T'ai Chi Found., N.Y.C., 1986—. Performer: Anawim Players, 1985—97. Participant White House Conf. Small Bus., 1996; treas. Karma Thegsum Choling, Chgo., 1987—97; bd. dirs. Illustrated Theatre Co., Chgo., 1987, Human Process, Chgo., 1992—2004, T'ai Chi Found., Inc., 1994—97, 2004, pres. bd. dirs., 2003—04; adv. bd. N.W. Suburban Boy Scouts Am., Schaumburg, 1984. Recipient Gold medallion, Ogilvy Awards, 2000. Mem.: Union Concerned Scietists, Qualitative Rsch. Cons. Assn., Am. Mktg. Assn., Planetary Soc. Home and Office: 1717 W Rascher Ave Chicago IL 60640-1117 Business E-Mail: patrice@wastrategy.com.

**WOOLDRIDGE, STEPHEN CRAIG,** health facility administrator; s. Stephen Edward and Kathryn Lee Wooldridge; m. Jodi Lynn Young, May 30, 1992; children: Jacqueline St. Marie, Stephen Blake, Hollyn Claire. BS in Elec. Engring., Purdue U., 1990, MS in Engring., 1992; PhD, MIT, 2001. Cert. profl. engr., Va., 1998; healthcare exec. Am. Coll. of Healthcare Execs., 2005. Engr. intern NASA Johnson Space Ctr., Houston, 1990—93, project mgr. and asst. ops. officer US Army 56th Med. Evacuation Bn., Fayetteville, NC, 1992—93; brigade engr. & project officer US Army 44th Med. Brigade, Fayetteville, NC, 1993—95; dep. dir., constrn. mgmt. US Army Health Facility Planning Agy., Falls Church, Va., 1995—97, dir., programming, analysis, and evaluation, 1997—98; dir., health facility planning Europe, US Army Europe Regional Med. Command, Heidelberg, Germany, 2001—03, exec. officer, 2003—04; comdr. US Army Health Clinic, Darmstadt, Germany, 2004—. Coach Child Youth Svcs., Darmstadt, Germany, 2002—06; mem. adv. bd. ARC, Darmstadt, Germany, 2004—06. Lt. col. US Army, 2005—06. Decorated Meritorious Svc. Medal US Army, Army Commendation Medal, Army Achievement Medal, US Army Order of Mil. Med. Merit US Army Med. Dept., Commanders Award for Excellence US Army Health Facility Planning Agy.; recipient NASA Outstanding Co-op Award, NASA. Mem.: ASCE, Am. Soc. of Healthcare Engrs., Soc. of Am. Mil. Engrs., Assn. of Mil. Surgeons of US, Healthcare Fin. Mgmt. Assn., Am. Coll. of Healthcare Execs. (regents adv. coun. 2005—), Phi Eta Sigma, Eta Kappa Nu, Omicron Delta Kappa, Sigma Xi. Office Phone: 011496151687527.

**WOOLDRIDGE, SUE ELLEN,** federal agency administrator, lawyer; b. Riverside, Calif. d. Robert and Patricia Wooldridge. BA, U. Calif. Davis, 1983; JD, Harvard U., 1987. Bar: Calif., U.S. Supreme Ct. Assoc. Diepenbrock, Wulff, Plant & Hannegan, Sacramento, 1987—; spl. asst. atty. gen. State of Calif., Sacramento, 1994—98; founding ptnr. Riegles Campos & Kenyon LLP, Sacramento, 1999—2001; gen. counsel Calif. Fair Polit. Practices Cons., 2000; dep. chief staff US Dept. Interior, Washington, DC, 2001—04, solicitor, 2004—05; asst. atty. gen. Environment & Nat. Resources Divsn. US Dept. Justice, Washington, DC, 2005—. Office: US Dept Justice 950 Pennsylvania Ave NW Rm 2141 Washington DC 20530

**WOOLDRIDGE, WILLIAM CHARLES,** lawyer; b. Miami, Fla., Feb. 24, 1943; s. Clarence Edward and Easter Marguerite (Souders) W.; m. Joyce L. Norton, June 15, 1968; children: William Charles, John Michael. BA, Harvard U., 1965; LLB, U. Va., 1969. Bar: Va. 1969. Atty. Norfolk and Western Ry. Co., 1973-82; with Norfolk So. Corp., 1982-2000, v.p. dept. law,

1996-2000. Pres. John Marshall Found., Richmond, Va., 1992-94; pres. Norfolk Hist. Soc., 1995-96; chair Friends of Chrysler Mus. Hist. Houses, 1997-99; bd. dirs. Sta. WHRO (FM and TV), 1997-00, WHRO Found., 2003-05, Libr. Va. Found. Capt. JAGC, US Army, 1969-73. Mem. Va. Bar Assn. Republican.

**WOOLER, JOHN WILLIAM,** multi-media specialist; s. William James and Moira Nesbitt Wooler; m. Rosemary Bernadette Gorman, June 20, 1980; children: Lewis James, Roxanna Susan, Carla Louise. Student, Dundee Sch. Of Tech., Scotland, 1978—79. Dep. head of a&r Virgin Records Uk, London, 1984—94; sr. v.p. Virgin Records USA, L.A., 1994—2002. Record prodr., L.A. Prodr.: (music) various (grammys, 1993). Office: Sunset Strip Inc 1201 Alta Loma Los Angeles CA 90069 Office Phone: 310-360-4055. Business E-Mail: jwooler@sunsetstrip.com.

**WOOLERY, JAMES C.,** lawyer; b. Louisville, May 8, 1969; BA cum laude, Wake Forest Univ., 1991; JD, Univ. Ky., 1994. Bar: NY 1995. Assoc. Cravath Swaine & Moore, NYC, 1994—95, 1997—2002, ptnr., corp., 2002—, assoc. London, 1995—97. Office: Cravath Swaine & Moore LLP Worldwide Plz 825 Eighth Ave New York NY 10019-7475 Office Phone: 212-474-1912. Office Fax: 212-474-3700. Business E-Mail: jwoolery@cravath.com.

**WOOLEY, GERALDINE HAMILTON,** poet, writer; b. Idlewild, Mich., Feb. 15, 1942; d. Charles Loren and Alice (Smith) Hamilton; m. David Wooley, June 11, 1961 (div. 1983); children: Vickie Wooley Houston, Monica Wooley Roberts, Deborah Wooley Williams. *Geraldine Wooley's maternal grandparents are Adam Daniel Smith, an African-American, born Selma Alabama Thirty-three Degree Mason, and Vina Gallaway Smith, an African-American/Cherokee, born Girade, Kansas, Worthy Grandmatron, Eastern Star. They lived in Girade, Kansas and Idlewild, Michigan. They bore five children: Alice (Eastern Star), Sam, James, Ernest, and Katherine. Geraldine's paternal grandparents are Rome Hamilton, an English White from Maricopa County in Phoenix, Arizona and Almetta Hogan Hamilton, an Apache/African-American from Montgomery, Alabama. They lived on a reservation in Phoenix, Arizona and bore two children: Charles Loran and Geraldine Hamilton. Charles, a carpenter, and Alice Hamilton had nine children; Charles, Vaughn, Janet, Geraldine, Van, Leonard, Lorenzo, Phillip and thirty-four grandchildren.* GED, Flint, Mich. Cosmetologist pvt. practice, Flint, Mich., 1967-70; tchr's. aide Flint Comty. Schs., 1969-71; nurse's aide Clara Barton Home, Flint, 1972; factory worker GM AC Plant, Flint, 1973-76; child care worker Beecher Cmty. Schs., Flint, 1987-89; poet, songwriter Flint, 1994—. Songwriter Hilltop Records, Hollywood, Calif., 1996—. Author: (poems) Between The Raindrops, 1995 (Editor's Choice 1995), At Water's Edge, 1995 (Editor's Choice 1995), Tapestry, 1996 (Editor's Choice 1996), Memories of Tomorrow, 1996 (Editor's Choice 1996), (poems) A Treasury of Famous Poets, 1997 (Editor's Choice award 1997). Mem. PTA Flint Sch. Dist., 1969-70. Named to Internat. Poetry Hall of Fame, 1996. Mem. Internat. Soc. Of Poets, Nat. Writers Assn., Internat. Black Writers. Democrat. Avocations: camping, playing organ, exploring old houses, writing. Home: 723 E Lansing Apt 611E Idlewild MI 49642 Office Phone: 810-423-2053. E-mail: ladyknight77@webtv.net.

**WOOLF, KENNETH HOWARD,** architect; b. NYC, Aug. 19, 1938; s. Howard Walter and Elizabeth Ann (Levy) W.; m. Elizabeth Adair Rainwater, July 3, 1965; children: Robert Gregg, Susan Adair, Jennifer Adair. BArch, Cornell U., 1961. Staff arch. Look & Morrison, Archs., Pensacola, Fla., 1965-72; pvt. practice arch. Pensacola, Fla., 1972—. Instr. architecture Pensacola Jr. Coll., part-time 1967-76; chmn. Pensacola Archtl. Rev. Bd., 1970-81; mem. Gulf Breeze Planning Bd., 1976-78; chmn. Pensacola City Bd. Adjustment and Appeals, 1995—. Prin. works include Coca-Cola Bottling Co. Plant, Pensacola, 1974, 3 profl. office bldgs. towers, Pensacola, 1976, 84, 92, Bapt. Hosp. addition, 1977, The Village, Housing for Elderly, 1978, 81, 98, Azalea Trace Ret. Cmty. Complex, 1980, 99, Northview Cmty., 1981, Coca-Cola Bottling Plant, Beaumont, Tex., 1983, Episcopal Day Sch., Pensacola, 1993. With USN, 1961-65. Named Jaycee of Yr., 1970. Mem. AIA (sec. N.W. Fla. chpt. 1976-77, 77-78, pres. 1979-81, Comml. Design Hon. award 1975), Rotary. Episcopalian. Home: 15 N Sunset Blvd Gulf Breeze FL 32561-4051 Office: 100 W Gadsden St Pensacola FL 32501-3910 Office Phone: 850-438-3653. Business E-Mail: khwarch@networktel.net.

**WOOLF, STEVEN MICHAEL,** artistic director; b. Milw., Dec. 23, 1947; s. Raleigh and Lenore (Shurman) W. BA in Theatre, U. Wis., 1968, MFA, 1971; D of Fine Arts (hon.), U. Mo., 1993. Prodn. stage mgr. The Juilliard Sch. Drama, N.Y.C., 1973-75; project prodr. Musical Theatre Lab., N.Y.C., 1974-75; prodn. stage mgr. Barter Theatre, Abingdon, Va., 1976-79; Stagewest, Springfield, Mass., 1976-79; prodn. mgr. Repertory Theatre of St. Louis, 1980-83, acting artistic dir., mng. dir., 1983-85, mng. dir., 1985-86, artistic dir., 1986—. Adj. faculty Webster U., St. Louis, 1982—; mem. nat. negotiating coms. League of Resident Theatres, N.Y.C., 1986—; on-site evaluator Nat. Endowment for the Arts, 1985. Dir. plays A Life in the Theatre, 1982, the Crucible, 1986, Company, 1987, The Voice of the Prairie, 1988, 90, The Boys Next Door, 1989, Dog Logic, 1990, Born Yesterday, 1990, Terra Nova, 1991, The Diary of Anne Frank, 1991, Other Peoples Money, 1991, Six Degrees of Separation, 1992, Sight Unseen, 1993, Lion in Winter, 1993, Death and the Maiden, 1993, The Living, 1994, Wait Until Dark, 1994, The Caine Mutiny Court Martial, 1994. The Life of Galileo, 1995, Death of a Salesman, 1995, Betrayal, 1996, As Bees in Honey Drown, 1997, Who's Afraid of Virginia Woolf, 1998, Closer, 1998, Dinner With Friends, 2000, The Dresser, 2001, The Shape of Things, 2002, Copenhagen, 2003, Two Rockin' Gents, 2003, The Goat, Or Who is Sylvia, 2003, Blue/Orange, 2004, The Crucible, 2004, The Retreat From Moscow, 2004, Henry IV & Humble Boy, 2006, others. Mem. ad hoc coms. for funding Mo. Arts Coun., St. Louis, 1988; chair citizen rev. panel Reg. Arts Commn., St. Louis, 1986; bd. dirs. Mo. Citizens for the Arts, 1990—; exec. com. League of Resident Theatres, 1990—. Recipient award Mo. Citizens for the Arts, 1992, Women's Polit. Caucus, 1993, award for Individual Excellence in the Arts, Arts Edn. Coun., 1993. Mem. AFTRA, Soc. of Stage Dirs. and Choreographers, Actors Equity Assn. Office: Repertory Theatre St Louis 130 Edgar Rd Saint Louis MO 63119-3228 Office Phone: 314-968-7340. E-mail: swoolf@repstl.org.

**WOOLF, WILLIAM BLAUVELT,** retired association executive; b. New Rochelle, N.Y., Sept. 18, 1932; s. Douglas Gordon and Katharine Hutton (Blauvelt) W. AA, John Muir Jr. Coll., 1951; student, U. Calif. at Berkeley, 1951; BA, Pomona Coll., 1953; MA, Claremont Grad. Sch., Calif., 1955; PhD, U. Mich., 1960. Instr., asst. prof., U. Wash., Seattle, 1959-68; assoc. sec., dir. adminstrn. AAUP, Washington, 1968-79; mng. editor Math. Revs., Am. Math. Soc., Ann Arbor, Mich., 1979-90, acting exec. editor, 1984-85; assoc. exec. dir. Am. Math. Soc., Providence, 1990-96. Bd. dirs. Nat. Child Rsch. Ctr., Washington, 1975-77; trustee Friends Sch. Detroit, 1985-90, treas., 1986-90; mem. Law and Justice Coun., Jefferson County, Wash., 1998—, chmn., 2001; mem. Wash. State U. Jefferson County Adv. Team, 1999-2003, chmn., 2002-2003, Jefferson County Edn. Com., 1998-2003, chmn., 1999-2001; bd. dirs. Jefferson County Farmers Market Assn., 2002-03. Fulbright Research fellow U. Helsinki, Finland, 1963-64 Fellow AAAS; mem. ACLU (life, treas. Washington 1966-68, bd. dirs. Washtenaw County and Mich. State 1989-90, bd. dirs. R.I. State 1993-95, treas. 1994-95, chmn. Jefferson County chpt. 2003-2005), Am. Math. Soc., Math. Assn. Am. Mem. Soc. Of Friends. Home: PO Box 235 Port Townsend WA 98368-0235

**WOOLFENDEN, JAMES MANNING,** nuclear medicine physician, educator; b. LA, Nov. 8, 1942; BA with distinction, Stanford U., 1964; MD, U. Wash., 1968. Diplomate Am Bd. Nuclear Medicine (chmn. credentials comm. 1993-94, vice chmn. exams. com. 1993-95, chmn. exam. com. 1995-96, sec. 1994-96, chmn. 1996-97, life mem.), Nat. Bd. Med. Examiners. Med. intern L.A. County-U. So. Calif. Med. Ctr., 1968-69; med. resident West L.A. VA Med. Ctr., 1969-70; nuclear medicine resident L.A. County-U. So. Calif. Med. Ctr., 1972-74; from asst. prof. radiology to assoc. prof. radiology U. Ariz., Tucson, 1974-84, prof. radiology, 1984—. Med. staff Univ. Med. Ctr., Tucson, 1974—; cons. VA Med. Ctr., 1974—; cons. med. staff Tucson Med. Ctr., 1975-2004, Carondelet St. Joseph's Hosp., 1974-98, St. Mary's Hosp.,

Tucson, 1976-90; mem. Nat. Cancer Inst. site visit team NIH, 1976, mem. NHLB Inst. site visit team NIH, 1976, mem. diagnostic radiology study sect., 1989-97, chmn., 1995-97; med. liaison officer network EPA, 1983-85; cons.-tchg. med. staff Kino Cmty. Hosp., 1984-94; med. officer Clin. Ctr., NIH, Bethesda, 1984-85; mem. Ariz. Cancer Ctr., U. Ariz., 1988—, sr. clin. scientist Univ. Heart Ctr., 1990—; Ariz. bd. regents U. Ariz. Presdl. Search Com., 1990-91; chmn. Ariz. Atomic Energy Commn., 1979-80, Ariz. Radiation Regulatory Hearing Bd., 1981—; bd. dirs. Calif. Radioactive Materials Mgmt. Forum, chmn., 1994-95, Western Forum Edn. in Safe Disposal of Low-Level Radioactive Waste, 1990-2000, vice chmn., 1991-92, chmn., 1992-94. Manuscript reviewer: Noninvasive Med. Imaging, 1983-84, Jour. Nuclear Medicine, 1985—, Investigative Radiology, 1989-94, Archives of Internal Medicine, 1990—; contbr. book chpts.: Diagnostic Nuclear Medicine, 2d edit., 1988, Adjuvant Therapy of Cancer, 1977, Fundamentals of Nuclear Medicine, 1988, others; contbr. articles to profl. jours. Mem. Am. Heart Assn. Coun. on Cardiovasc. Radiology. Maj. U.S. Army, 1970-72, Vietnam. Fellow Am. Coll. Nuc. Physicians (long range planning com. 1981-83, govt. affairs com. 1984-94, exec. com. 1987-91, sec. 1989-91, parliamentarian 1991-95, treas. 1996-98, publs. com. 1993-98, chmn. publs. com. 1993-94, pres.-elect 1998-99, pres. 1999-2000, others); mem. AMA (diagnostic and therapeutic tech. assessment reference panel 1982-98), Am. Nuc. Soc., Soc. Nuc. Medicine (com. on audit 1992-99, trustee 1992-96, ho. dels. 1996-2003, fin. com. 1996-99, bd. dirs. 1997-99, bronze medal for sci. exhibit 1984, bd. dirs., sec.-treas. So. Calif. chpt. 1993-95, pres.-elect 1995-96, pres. 1996-99), Assn. Univ. Radiologists, Ariz. Med. Assn., European Assn. Nuc. Medicine, Pima County Med. Soc., Radiol. Soc. N.Am., Acad. Molecular Imaging, Soc. for Molecular Imaging. Office: Ariz Health Scis Ctr Nuc Medicine 1501 N Campbell Ave Tucson AZ 85724-5068

**WOOLHANDLER, ANN,** law educator; b. Shreveport, La., 1953; BA, Yale U., 1975; JD, Harvard U., 1978. Bar: La. 1978. Atty. pvt. practice, New Orleans, 1978—85, 1988—90; Bigelow Tchg. fellow & lectr. U. Chgo., 1985—86; asst. prof. U. Cin., 1986—88; vis. asst. prof. Loyola U., New Orleans, 1990; vis. assoc. prof. Tulane U., New Orleans, 1990—91, assoc. prof., 1991—97, prof., 1997—2002; vis. prof. Boston U., 1998, Harvard U., Cambridge, Mass., 1999; vis. assoc. prof. U. Va. Sch. Law, Charlottesville, 1994—95, vis. prof., 2001, prof., 2002—, now William Minor Lile prof. law, Class of 1948 prof. scholarly rsch. law. Bd. gov. La. State Bar Assn., 1993. Office: U Va Sch Law 580 Massie Rd Charlottesville VA 22903 Office Phone: 434-924-4411. E-mail: naw2b@virginia.edu.

**WOOLHOUSE, MAUREEN ANN,** mathematics professor; b. Somerville, Mass., Sept. 28, 1944; d. James Francis and Mary Margaret (O'Brien). m. Jan Edward Woolhouse, June 24, 1973; children: Megan Short, Matthew Jason, Megan Short, Matthew Jason, Elizabeth Leslie. BA, Anna Maria Coll., Paxton, Mass, 1966; M in Edn., Worcester State Coll., Mass., 1972; M in Math., Worcester Poly. Inst., Mass., 1990. Asst. prof. math. Dean Jr. Coll., Franklin, Mass., 1988—92; prof. asst. prof. math. Middlesex C.C., Lowell, 1992—2001; prof. math. Quinsigamond C.C., Worcester, 2001—. Cmty. v.p. United Way, Worcester, 1982—84; bd. mem. Instl. Rev. Bd. U. Mass. Med. Ctr., 1978—82; chmn. Worcester Cmty. Action Coun., 1980—82. Mem.: New England Assn. Two Yr. Coll. (pres. 2000—02). Democrat. Avocations: travel, golf, gardening, baking. Home: 84 Coolidge Road Worcester MA 01602 Office: Quinsigamond Community College 670 West Boylston Street Worcester MA 01606 Personal E-mail: mwoolhouse@qcc.mass.edu.

**WOOLLAM, JOHN ARTHUR,** electrical engineering educator, physics professor; b. Kalamazoo, Mich., Aug. 10, 1939; s. Arthur Edward and Mildred Edith (Hakes) W.; children: Catherine Jane, Susan June. BA in Physics, Kenyon Coll., 1961; MS in Physics, Mich. State U., 1963, PhD in Solid State Physics, 1967; MSEE, Case Western Res. U., 1978; Doctorate (hon.), Linköping (Sweden) U., 2004. Rsch. scientist NASA Lewis Rsch. Ctr., Cleve., 1967-80; prof. U. Nebr., Lincoln, 1979—, dir. Ctr. Microelectronic and Optical Materials Rsch., 1988—2000; pres. J.A. Woollam Co., Inc., Lincoln, 1987—. Editor Jour. Applied Physics Com., 1979-94. Trustee J.A. Woollam Found. Grantee NASA, NSF, USAF, Advanced Rsch. Projects Agy. Fellow Am. Phys. Soc., Am. Vacuum Soc. (chmn. thin film divsn. 1989-91). Office: U Nebr Dept Elec Engring 209NWSEC Lincoln NE 68588-0511

**WOOLLEY, BRIAN N.,** lawyer; s. Stuart W. and Shirley S. Woolley; m. Patricia L. Martin, Oct. 26, 1985; children: Meredith, Philip. BS, Iowa State U., 1978; JD, Northwestern U., Chgo., 1982. Bar: Mo. 1982, U.S. Dist. Ct. Western Dist. Mo. 1982, Ill. 1984, No. Dist. Ill. 1984, U.S. Cts. Appeal for 7th, 8th and 10th Circuits. Assoc. Lathrop, Koontz, Kansas City, Mo., 1982—84, D'Ancona & Pflaum, Chgo., 1984—86; mem. Lathrop & Gage L.C., Kansas City, Mo., 1986—. Guest lectr. U. Mo., Kansas City, 2001—. Contbg. editor: The Developing Labor Law, 2003—06. Bd. dirs., pres. Wonderscope Children's Mus., Shawnee, Kans., 1996—2004; chmn., legal counsel com. Farmhouse Fraternity Bd. Dirs., Kansas City, Mo., 2000—; bd. dirs. Arthritis Found. of Greater Kansas City (Mo.), 2004—. Mem.: ABA, Am. Health Lawyers Assn., Soc. Human Resource Mgmt. Office: Lathrop & Gage LC 2345 Grand #2800 Kansas City MO 64108 Office Phone: 816-292-2000.

**WOOLLEY, DONNA PEARL,** lumber company executive; b. Drain, Oreg., Jan. 3, 1926; d. Chester A. and Mona B. (Cheever) Rydell; m. Harold Woolley, Dec. 27, 1952 (dec. Sept. 1970); children: Daniel, Debra, Donald. Diploma, Drain High Sch. Sec. No. Life Ins. Co., Eugene, Oreg., 1943—44; sec., bookkeeper D & W Lumber Co., Sutherlin, Oreg., 1944, Woolley Logging Co. & Earl Harris Lumber Co., Drain, 1944—70; pres. Woolley Logging Co., 1970—, Smith River Lumber Co., 1977—, Mt. Baldy Mill, 1970—81, Drain Plywood Co., 1970—81, Woolley Enterprises, Inc., Drain, 1973—, Eagle's View Mgmt. Co., Inc., Eugene, 1981—. Bd. dirs. Wildlife Safari, Winston, 1991, Oreg. Cmty. Found., Portland, 1990-99, chair, 1997-99; bd. trustees Linfield Coll., McMinnville, U. Oreg. Found., Eugene, Oreg. Trl. coun. Boy Scouts Am., 1980—, World Forestry Ctr., Portland, 1990, Umpqua C.C. Fedn., 2001. Recipient Pioneer award, U. Oreg., 1982, Pres.'s medal, 2005, Econ. and Social Devel. award, Soroptimist Club, 1991, First Citizen of Eugene award, 2000, Aubrey Watzek award, Lewis & Clark Coll., 2001, Howard Vollum award, Associated Fund Raisers in Philanthropy Oreg. chpt., 2001, Pioneer award, Umpqua C.C., 2003, Hart Pioneer award, Wildlife Safari, 2003, Pres. medal, U. Oreg., 2005, Paul Harris Fellow, Rotary, 2006. Mem. Oreg. Women's Forum, Pacific Internat. Trapshooting Assn., Amateur Trapshooting assn., Eugene C. of C. (bd. dirs. 1989-92), Arlington Club, Town Club (bd. dirs., pres.), Sunnydale Grange, Cottage Grove/Eugene Rod & Gun Club. Republican. Avocations: golf, travel. Office: Eagle's View Mgmt Co Inc 1399 Franklin Blvd Eugene OR 97403-1979 Office Phone: 541-683-0771.

**WOOLLEY, MARY ELIZABETH,** science administrator, advocate; b. Chgo., Mar. 16, 1947; John Joseph and Ellen Louise (Bakke) McEnerney; m. John Stuart Woolley, Dec. 6, 1969 (div. 1985); children: George Newsom, Nora Ellen; m. Michael Howland Campbell, Jan. 1, 1989 (div. 2004). BS, Stanford U., 1969; MA, San Francisco State U., 1972; postgrad., U. Calif., San Francisco and Berkeley, 1974-75. Assoc. dir. Inst. Epidemiology and Behavioral Medicine, San Francisco, 1979-81; adminstr. Med. Rsch. Inst. of San Francisco, 1981-82, v.p., adminstr., 1982-86, v.p., exec. dir., 1986-90; pres. Research! Am., Alexandria, Va., 1990—. Cons. in fin. and mgmt NIH, Bethesda, Md., 1984—92; adj. faculty U. Calif. Sch. Pub. Health, Berkeley, 1983—92, mem. Dean's adv. coun., 1995—2002; founding mem. Whitehead Inst. Bd. Assocs., 1995—; bd. dirs. Lovelace Inst., Respiratory Rsch. Inst., vice chmn., 1999—2004; bd. dirs. Children's Rsch. Inst., Washington, 2003—; lectr. to profl. assns.; mem. bd. visitors Harvard U. Sch. Pub. Health, Cambridge, 2002—; mem. bd. advisors Johns Hopkins Sch. of Nursing, 2002—; mem. bd. advisors IBM Life Scis., 2003—. Editor Jour. of Soc. Rsch. Adminstrs., 1986-89, mem. editl. rev. bd., 1989-95; mem. editl. bd. Jour. Women's Health, 1992-2003, Sci. Comm., 1994—; contbr. articles and editls. to profl. jours. Bd. dirs. Kensington (Calif.) Edn. Found., 1986-89, Enterprise for H.S. Students, 1990-92; mem. 'capital campaign com. Calif. Shakespeare Festival, 1989-91; bd. advisors Friends

of Cancer Rsch., 1996—; bd. dirs. Nat. Patient Safety Found., 1998-2000, Friends of Nat. Inst. of Nursing Rsch., 2001—. Recipient Silver Touchstone award Am. Hosp. Assn., 1994, Disting. Svc. award Columbia Coll. Physicians and Surgeons, 1994, Advocacy award Fedn. Am. Socs. Exptl. Biology, 1998, Advocacy award Friends Nat. Inst. Nursing Rsch., 1999, Leadership award Coun. Scientific Soc. Pres.'s, 1999, Advocacy award Friends of Dental Rsch., 2002; honored Women of Vision Am. Com. Weizmann Inst. Sci., 2004, 05. Fellow AAAS; mem. Assn. Ind. Rsch. Insts. (pres.-elect 1987-89, pres. 1989-90), Inst. Medicine (elected), Soc. Rsch. Adminstrs. (bd. dirs. 1986-90, bd. advisors 1990-93, Hartford-Nicholson Svc. award 1990, Disting. Contbn. to Rsch. Adminstrm. award, 1993), Calif. Biomed. Rsch. Assn. (bd. govs. 1986-90), Nat. Press Club. Democrat. Office: Research! Am 1101 King St Ste 520 Alexandria VA 22314-3067 Office Phone: 703-739-2577. Business E-Mail: mwoolley@researchamerica.org.

**WOOLLEY, ROGER SWIRE,** lawyer; b. Chgo., Nov. 18, 1924; s/ Anthony Walter and Agnes Louise (MacMurray) W.; m. Patricia Ann Jundt, 1951 (dec. 1978); children: Elliott Payne, Merrit Ann. BA, Coll. William & Mary, 1947; student, Exeter Coll., London, 1947-48; LLB, Columbia U., 1951. Bar: Calif., U.S. Supreme Ct. Legal counsel Solar Aircraft, San Diego, 1952-54; prin. Law Offices of Roger S. Woolley, Rancho Santa Fe, Calif., 1954—. Active Automobile Club So. Calif., L.A., dir. 1974-98, chmn. 1988-90; active Am. Automobile Assn., Falls Church, Va., Orlando, Fla., dir., 1986-97, chmn., 1991-93; founding dir., sec. Bank La Jolla, 1962-68; founding dir., sec. Rancho Santa Fe Savs. & Loan, 1972-78; founding dir., sec. Torrey Pines Bank, 1979-84; dir. Scripps Meml. Hosp. Found., La Jolla, Calif. 1984—; trustee emeritus The Endowment Assn. of Coll. William & Mary, Williamsburg, Va.; chmn., mem. Calif. State Hwy. Commn., 1958-67. Lt. jr. U.S. Navy, 1942-46, WW II. Mem. ABA, State Bar Calif., San Diego County Bar Assn., Rotary Club Rancho Santa Fe. Office: Law Offices of Roger S Woolley PO Box R 16903 Avenida de Acacias Rancho Santa Fe CA 92067 Office Phone: 858-756-1144.

**WOOLLING, KENNETH RAU,** vascular internist; b. Indpls., Mar. 6, 1918; m. Catherine Margaret McColl, Mar. 20, 1948; 2 children. BA magna cum laude, Butler U., 1939; postgrad., Harvard U., 1939-40; MD, Ind. U., 1943; MS in Medicine, U. Minn., 1951. Diplomate Nat. Bd. Med. Examiners, Am. Bd. Internal Medicine, Am. Bd. Cardiovascular Disease. Intern Indpls. City Hosp. (now Wishard Meml.), Indpls., 1943-44; resident in internal medicine Marion County Gen. Hosp., Indpls., 1947; fellow, first asst. internal medicine Mayo Found., Rochester, Minn., 1948-52; mem. med. staff, mem. tchg. staff postgrad. med. edn. Marion County Gen. Hosp. (name now Wishard Meml. Hosp.), Indpls., 1952—; founder, dir., peripheral vascular diseases clinic Indpls City & Marion County Gen. Hosp. (now Wishard Meml.), Indpls., 1952-68; pvt. practice internal medicine and cardiovascular diseases Indpls, 1952—; founder, dir. peripheral vascular diseases clinic Meth. Hosp., Indpls., 1967-72, founder, dir. vascular lab., 1970-73, mem. med. staff, tchr. staff postgrad. med. edn., 1952—. Mem. med. staff St. Vincent Hosp., St. Francis Hosp. and Winona Meml. Hosp., Indpls., 1952—; charter mem. med. staff Cmty. Hosp., Indpls., 1952—; charter mem. med. adv. com. Butler U., Indpls, 1956—. Contbr. articles to profl. jours., 1950—. Capt. Med. Corps U.S. Army, 1944-46. Fellow ACP, Am. Coll. Chest Physicians, Coun. on Cardiology Am. Heart Assn., Am. Coll. Angiology (gov. state of Ind. 1979-80); mem. AMA (50 Yr. award 1993), SAR, Internat. Union Angiology, Am. Soc. Internal Medicine, Am. Diabetes Assn., Ind. State Med. Soc., Ind. Diabetes Assn., Am. Fedn. for Clin. Rsch., N.Y. Acad. Med. Scis., North Ctrl. Clin. Soc., Mayo Cardiovascular Soc., Ind. Hist. Soc., Res. Officers Assn., Indpls. Med. Soc., Am. Legion, Shriners, Masons (Scottish Rite and Mystic Tie Lodge, 50 yr. award 1989), Contemporary Club of Indpls., Indpls. Athletic Club, Columbia Club, Highland Golf and Country Club, Phi Delta Theta (50 yr. award 1985), Phi Kappa Phi, Phi Chi. Presbyterian. Office: PO Box 80192 Indianapolis IN 46280-0192

**WOOLS, ESTHER BLANCHE,** library science educator; b. Louisville, Mar. 30, 1935; d. Arthur William and Esther Lennie (Smith) Sutton; m. Donald Paul Wools, Oct. 21, 1953 (div. Nov. 1982); 1 son. Arthur Paul AB in Fine Arts, Ind. U., 1958, MA in Libr. Sci., 1962, PhD in Libr. Sci., 1973. Elem. libr. Hammond (Ind.) Pub. Schs., 1958-65, libr. coord., 1965-67, Roswell (N.Mex.) Ind. Schs., 1967-70; prof. libr. sci. U. Pitts., 1973-97; prof., dir. Sch. Lib. and Info. Sci. San Jose (Calif.) State U., 1997—2005; consulting editor Librs. Unlimited, Glendale, Calif., 2005—. Exec. dir. Beta Phi Mu, 1981-95. Author: The School Library Media Manager, 1995, 3d edit., 2004, So You're Going to Run a Library, 1995, Ideas for School Library Media Centers, 1996, Whole School Library Handbook, 2004; co-author: Information Literacy, 1999; editor: Continuing Professional Education and IFLA: Past, Present, and a Vision for the Future, 1993, Delivering Lifelong Continuing Professional Education Across Space and Time, 2001. Fulbright scholar, 1995-96; recipient Disting. Svc. award Pa. Sch. Librs. Assn., 1993. Mem. ALA (mem. coun. 1985-89, 95—2003), Am. Assn. Sch. Librs. (bd. dirs. 1983-88, pres. 1993-94, Disting. Svc. award 1997), Pa. Learning Resources Assn. (pres. 1984-85), Internat. Assn. Sch. Librs. (pres. 1998-2001), Internat. Fedn. Libr. Assns. (mem. standing com. sch. librs. sect. 1991-99, sec. Continuing Profl. Edn. Round Table 2000—). Home: 144 S 4th St # 637 San Jose CA 95112 Office: Libraries Unlimited 2040 Verdugo Blvd Glendale CA 91208

**WOOLSEY, LYNN C.,** congresswoman; b. Seattle, Nov. 3, 1937; 4 children. BS, U. San Francisco, 1981. Mgr. human resources Harris Digital Telephone, 1969—80; owner Woolsey Personnel Svs., 1980—92; mem. U.S. Congress from 6th Calif. dist., 1993—, ranking mem. edn. reform subcom. ho. com. edn. and the workforce. Mem. Petaluma City Coun., 1984-92 Mem.: NOW, LWV, Sierra Club. Democrat. Office: US Ho Reps 2263 Rayburn Ho Office Bldg Washington DC 20515-0506 Address: Santa Rosa Dist Office Ste 200 1101 College Ave Santa Rosa CA 95404 also: San Rafael Dist Office Ste 354 1050 Northgate Dr San Rafael CA 94903*

**WOOLSEY, R. JAMES (ROBERT JAMES WOOLSEY),** lawyer, former CIA director; b. Tulsa, Sept. 21, 1941; s. Robert James and Clyde (Kirby) W.; m. Suzanne Haley, Aug. 15, 1965; children—Robert Nathaniel, Daniel James, Benjamin Haley. BA with great distinction, Stanford U., 1963; MA (Rhodes scholar), Oxford U., Eng., 1965; LLB, Yale U., 1968. Bar: Calif. bar 1969, D.C. bar 1970. Program analyst Office Sec. Def., Washington, 1968-70, NSC, Washington, 1970; gen. counsel Com. Armed Services, U.S. Senate, 1970-73; assoc. firm Shea & Gardner, Washington, 1973-77, ptnr., 1979-89; ambassador and U.S. rep. to negotiation on conventional armed forces in Europe, 1989-91; ptnr. with Shea & Gardner, 1991-93; dir. CIA, Washington, 1993-95; ptnr. Shea & Gardner, 1995—2002; v.p. Global Strategic Security Booz Allen Hamilton, McLean, Va., 2002—. Undersec. of navy, 1977-79; advisor U.S. del. SALT, Helsinki and Vienna, 1969-70 Mem. Pres.'s Commn. on Strategic Forces, 1983-84, Fed. Ethics Law Reform, 1989; Blue Ribbon Commn. on Defense Mgmt., 1985-86; del.-at-large Soviet Arms Talks, Geneva, 1983-86; mem. Rumsfeld Commn. to Assess Ballistic Missile Threat, 1998; mem. Nat. Commn. on Terrorism 1999-2000; trustee Stanford U., 1972-74, Regent Smithsonian Instution, 1989-93; bd. chmn. Freedom House; adv. bd. chmn. Clean Fuels Found., New Uses Council; vice-chmn. adv. bd. Global Options LLC; trustee Ctr. for Strategic & Internat. Studies; past mem. bd. gov. Phila. Stock Exch.; dir. Info. Sys. Lab., Linsang Ptnrs., Fibersense Tech. Corp., Invicta Networks, DIANA LLC, Agorics Inc.; mem. bd. adv. BioDefense Corp.; past bd. dir. Martin Marietta, British Aerospace, Fairchild Industries, Titan Corp., DynCorp, USF&G, Sun Healthcare Group, Inc., Yurie Systems, Inc. Served with U.S. Army, 1968-70. Mem. Council Fgn. Relations, Phi Beta Kappa. Presbyterian. Office: Booz Allen Hamilton 8283 Greensboro Dr Mc Lean VA 22102

**WOOLSEY, THOMAS ALLEN,** neuroscientist, biologist; b. Balt., Apr. 17, 1943; s. Clinton Nathan and Harriet (Runion) W.; m. Cynthia Tull Ward, June 8, 1969; children: Alix, Timothy. BS, U. Wis., 1965; MD, Johns Hopkins, 1969. Asst. prof. anatomy Washington U. Sch. Medicine, St. Louis, 1971-75, asst. prof. anatomy, neurobiology, 1975-77, assoc. prof. anatomy, neurobiology, 1977-80, assoc. prof. anatomy, neurobiology, physiology biophysics,

1980-83, coord. neurosci. program, 1980-84, sr. neuroscientist, 1982—, prof. neurology, neurological surgery, 1984—, dir. experimental neurology, neurological surgery, 1984—. Chmn., Washington U. Teaching Space Evaluation, 1989-90. Contbr. articles to profl. jours. NIH Rsch. grantee, 1970—; George H. and Ethel R. Bishop scholar, 1984—; recipient McKnight Neurosci. Devel. award, 1987-85, Jacob Javits award NIH, 1993-2000; fellow John Simon Guggenheim Found., 2004. Fellow AAAS; mem. Am. Assn. Anatomists, Am. Acad. Neurology, St. Louis Acad. Sci., Soc. Neurosci., Johns Hopkins Med. Surgical club., Cajal Club. Avocations: hiking, history, woodworking. Office: Washington U Sch Medicine 660 S Euclid Ave # 8057 Saint Louis MO 63110-1010 Office Phone: 314-362-3601. E-mail: tom63105@yahoo.com.

**WOOLSTON-CATLIN, MARIAN,** psychiatrist; b. Seattle, Jan. 20, 1931; d. Howard Brown and Katharine Nichols (Dally) Woolston; m. Randolph Catlin Jr., July 5, 1959; children: Laura Louise, Jennifer Woolston, Randolph III. *Father, Howard Brown Woolston, was a scholar, educator and author. He was a pioneer of sociology and regularly wrote for The Encyclopedia Britannica. He was a global traveler, mountain climber, raconteur and devoted family man. Mother, Katharine Nichols Dally, left journalism for social work, specializing in adoptions and juvenile court. Husband, Randolph Catlin, Jr., MD, was a flight surgeon in space medicine, hospital commander, now psychoanalyst and former chief of mental health at Harvard University-.Daughter, Laura Rogers, has two sons, Noah and Nathaniel. Daughter, Jennifer Tucker, has a daughter, Katherine, and a son, Andrew. Son, Randolph III, has two daughters, Hannah and Molly.* BA cum laude, Vassar Coll., 1951; MD, Harvard U., 1955. Diplomate Nat. Bd. Med. Examiners. Intern in pediatric medicine Children's Hosp., Boston, 1956, asst. resident in pediatric medicine, 1956; resident in psychiatry Mass. Mental Health Ctr., Boston, 1957-59; fellow in child psychiatry Tavistock Clin., London, 1960; Commonwealth fellow in child psychiatry Harvard U. at Gaebler Children's Unit, Waltham, Mass., 1975-78, clin. instr. psychiatry, 1978-79; pvt. practice Wellesley Hills, Mass., 1978-91, Medfield, Mass., 1991—. Clin. instr. psychiatry Harvard U. at Mass. Mental Health Ctr., Boston, 1957-59, 78-82, Tufts U. at Mass. Mental Health Ctr., 1957-59; mem. exec. bd. Parents' and Children's Svcs., Boston, 1983-86. Designer H.H. Hunnewell Meml. Garden for New Eng. Flower Show Mass. Hort. Soc., 1975 (Ames Cup award). Mem. exec. bd. Ext. Divsn. New Eng. Conservatory Music, 1972-75; charter mem. reuse com. Medfield State Hosp., 1992—; corporator Schepens Eye Rsch. Inst., 2005—; mem. adv. bd. Women's Eye Health Task Force, 2005—. Fellow Am. Acad. Child and Adolescent Psychiatry; mem. AMA, Am. Psychiat. Assn. (life), Mass. Psychiat. Assn., Mass. Med. Soc., New Eng. Coun. Child and Adolescent Psychiatry (hon.), Boston Vassar Club (exec. bd. 1963-75), Hills Garden Club Wellesley (exec. bd. and design chief 1973-75). Episcopalian. Avocations: landscape design, sculpting.

**WOOLWICH, MADLYN-ANN CRAWFORD,** artist, educator; b. Fall River, Mass. d. Edward Francis and Louise Anthony (Hathaway) Crawford; m. Joseph Woolwich; children: Kimberly, Stephanie, Allison. BS in Edn., Bridgewater (Mass.) Coll., 1957, MEd, 1961; postgrad., Parson's Sch. of Design, 1984, 86, Southeastern Mass. U., 1987, Nat. Acad. Design, 1988-89. Cert. tchr. Mass., Pa. Tchr. Twp. of Scituate, Mass., 1957-58, Twp. of Somerset, Mass., 1958-61, Lansdowne (Pa.) Alden System, 1975-84; instr. in painting and pastel Guild of Creative Art, Shrewsbury, N.J., 1985-981985-90, v.p. edn., 1984-90. V.p. edn. Guild Creative Art, Shrewsbury, 1984—90, instr. in painting and pastel, 1985—90; v.p. programs Monmouth Arts Gallery, Shrewsbury, 1986—99; instr. workshops, 2003; workshops Willow Wisp Workshops, 2004; judge of admissions, 1st juror N.E. Nat. Pastel Exhbn., 2005; demonstrator Monmouth Festival of the Arts, 2005, Monmouth Arts Found.; judge/juror N.E. Nat. Pastel Soc., N.Y.C.; nat. workshop tchr.; judge in nat. and internat. art shows; instr. Willow Farm Studios, 2004, Cooperville Arts Ctr., Whidby Island, Wash., 2006—. Author: Pastel Interpretations, 1993, 1995, The Art of Pastel Portraiture, 1995; contbg. editor: Pastel Jour.; contbr. articles to mags. including Pastel Jour., The Artist's Mag.; included in: books Best of Pastel I, 1997, Best of Pastel II, 1998, A Gallery of Marine Art, 1998, The Artist's Sketchbook, 2003; one-woman shows include Bridges Gallery, Shrewsbury, N.J., 2005, Evergreen Gallery, Spring Lake, N.J., Linderbridges Gallery, Shrewsbury, Guild Creative Art. Judge Am. Profl. League, 2006. Recipient Materials award, PSWC, Duane Wakeham award, Am. Artist award, N. Fla. Pastel Soc., Disting. Pastelist award, Pastel Soc. N. Fla., award of merit, Sierra Pastel Soc., 2002; scholar, Vermont Sch., Scottsdale Artist Sch. Mem.: AAUW (scholar), Am. Artists Profl. League, Knickerbocker Artists (1st v.p. nat. events coord. 1992—2003), Art Alliance Monmouth County (v.p. Red Bank, N.J. chpt. 1978—), Pastel Soc. Am. (bd. dirs., corr. sec. N.Y. chpt. 1986—97, workshop tchr., master pastelist 1985—99, mem. adj. faculty 1990), Internat. Soc. Marine Artists, Salmagundi Club. Avocations: dance, singing, athletics, aerobics, website operator. Home and Office: 473 Marvin Dr Long Branch NJ 07740-5003 Personal E-mail: mwoolwich@aol.com.

**WOOLWORTH, SUSAN VALK,** primary school educator; b. Toledo, Ohio, Apr. 24, 1954; d. Robert Earl and Alice (Melick) Valk; children: Alison Valk, Andrew Baker. BA, Pine Manor Jr. Coll., Chestnut Hill, Mass., 1974; BS, Boston U., 1976. Tchr. kindergarten Lancaster (Pa.) Country Day Sch., 1986—. Bd. dirs. YWCA, Lancaster, Pa.; past bd. dirs. Fulton Opera House, Planned Parenthood, Vis. Nurse Assn., Hands-On House. Mem.: Jr. League (sustainer), Sigma Gamma. Republican. Episcopalian. Avocations: walking, gardening, tennis, decorating.

**WOOMER, DAVID LEE,** pharmacist; b. Danville, Pa., May 23, 1957; s. Lewis Jackson and Carolyn May Woomer; m. Karen Elaine Daniel, May 24, 1980; 1 child, Peter Lewis. BS in Pharmacy, Phila. Coll. Pharmacy and Sci., 1980. Registered pharmacist Pa., Mo.; cert. anticoagulation McConnell Heart Health Ctr. Staff pharmacist Divine Providence Hosp., Williamsport, Pa., 1980—82; clin. pharmacist Cox Health, Springfield, Mo., 1982—, Cox pharmacist Cox Home Health Svc., Springfield, 1987—91, Cox Skilled Nursing Unit, Springfield, 1992—96, Cox Planetree Unit, Springfield, 1996—98, Cox Health Metabolic Support Team, Springfield, 2000—. Mem. planning and zoning commn. City of Willard, Mo., 1996—98. Recipient award, Phila. Coll. Pharmacy Alumni Assn., 1980. Mem.: Rho Chi, Ozark Soc. Health Sys. Pharmacists, Am. Soc. Health Sys. Pharmacists. Republican. Baptist. Home: 6895 W Elwood Ln Springfield MO 65802-6462 Office: Cox Health Dept Pharmacy 3801 S National Ave Springfield MO 65807 Personal E-mail: dwoomer@sbcglobal.net.

**WOOSLEY, RAYMOND,** pharmacologist, educator; b. Ky., Oct. 2, 1942; m. Julianne Buchert. BS, Western Ky. U., 1964; PhD, U. Louisville, 1967; MD, U. Miami, 1973. Intern, resident Vanderbilt U. Hosp., Nashville, 1973-76; sr. pharmacologist, dir. rsch. Meyer (GSK) Labs., Ft. Lauderdale, Fla., 1968-71; instr. dept. medicine, pharmacology Vanderbilt U., Nashville, 1976-77, asst. prof., 1977-81, assoc. prof., 1979-84, assoc. dir. clin. rsch. ctr., 1981-88, prof., 1984-88; prof. pharmacology, medicine, chmn. dept. pharmacology Georgetown U. Sch. Medicine, Washington, 1988-2000, assoc. dean clin. rsch., 2000—01, also chief divsn. clin. pharmacology 1988-94; dir. Inst. Cardiovascular Scis., Washington, 1995-2000, dean Coll. Clin. Rsch. Ctr., Washington, 1999-2001; v.p Ariz. Health Scis. Ctr., 2001—04; dean Sch. Medicine U. Ariz., 2001—02; pres. The Critical Path Inst., Tucson, 2005—. Rschr. in field. Contbr. chapters to books, articles to profl. jours. Recipient Career Devel. award in Clin. Pharmacology, Pharm. Mfrs. Assn. Found., 1977—80; fellow, Am. Coll. Clin. Pharmacology, 1974; Predoctoral fellow, NIH, 1964—67, Postdoctoral fellow, U. Louisville, 1967—68, Vanderbilt U., 1976—77, Ogden scholar, Western Ky. U., 1960—64. Fellow: ACP, Am. Coll. Clin. Pharmacology; mem.: Soc. Women's Health Rsch. (bd. dirs. 1999—2001), Assn. Med. Sch. Pharmacology (pres. 1996—98), Am. Bd. Clin. Pharmacology, Am. Soc. Clin. Pharmacology and Therapeutics (v.p. 1998—99, pres. 1999, Rawls-Palmer award 1990), Am. Fedn. Clin. Rsch., Am. Soc. Pharmacology and Exptl. Therapeutics (mem. clin. pharmacology exec. com. 1981—92, Harry Gold award 2001), Am. Heart Assn. (fellow coun. clin. cardiology 1985—). Office: The Critical Path Inst 4280 N Campbell # 214 Tucson AZ 85718 Business E-mail: RWoosley@C-Path.org.

**WOOSNAM, IAN HAROLD,** professional golfer; b. St. Martins, Shropshire, U.K., Mar. 2, 1958; s. Harold and Joan Woosnam; m. Glendryth Mervyn Pugh, Nov. 12, 1983; children: Daniel Ian, Rebecca Louise, Ami Victoria. Student, St. Martins Modern Sch. Profl. golfer, 1976—. Tournament winner News of the World under 23 match-play, 1979, Cacharel under 25 Championship, 1982, Swiss Open, 1982, Silk Cut Masters, 1983, Scandinavian Enterprise Open, 1984, Zambian Open, 1985, Lawrence Batley TPC, 1986, 555 Kenya Open, 1986, Hong Kong Open, 1987, Jersey Open, 1987, Cepsa Madrid Open, 1987, Bell's Scottish Open, 1987, 90, Lancome Trophy, 1987, 93, Suntory World Match-Play Championship, 1987, 90, World Cup (Wales) Team and Individual, 1987, Million Dollar Challenge, 1987, Welsh Pro Championship, 1988, Volvo PGA Championship, 1988, Panasonic European Open, 1988, Carrols Irish Open, 1988, 89, AmEx Med Open, 1990, Epson Grand Prix, 1990, Torras Monte Carlo Open, 1990, 91, Fujitsu Mediterranean Open, 1991, U.S. Masters, 1991, USF&G Classic, 1991, PGA Grand Slam of Golf, 1991, World Cup Individual, 1991, European Montecarlo Open, 1992, Murphy's English Open, 1993, Air France Cannes Open, 1994, Brit. Masters, 1994, Johnnie Walker Classic, 1996, Scottish Open, 1996, German Open, 1996, Heineken Classic, 1996, Volvo PGA Championship, 1997, Hyundai Motor Masters, 1997; ranked 1st Sony world rankings, 1991, Ryder Cup Team Mem., 1983, 85 (winners), 87 (winners), 89, 91, 93, 95 (winners), 97 (winners), Cisco World Match Play championship, 2001, vice-capt. Ryder Cup winners, 2001-02; capt. European Ryder Cup Team, 2006. Avocations: snooker, sports, water-skiing. Office Phone: 44 7768 862459. E-mail: dbarlow@imgworld.com.

**WOOSNAM, RICHARD EDWARD,** venture capitalist, lawyer; b. Anderson, Ind., June 27, 1942; s. Richard Wendell and Ruth (Cleveland) W.; m. Diane Dalto; children: Cynthia S., Elizabeth C. BS, Ind. U., 1964, JD, 1967, MBA, 1968. Bar. Ind. 1967, U.S. Dist. Ct. (so. dist.) Ind. 1967. Instr. bus. law Ind. U., Bloomington, 1966-68; assoc. Ferguson, Ferguson & Lloyd, Bloomington, 1967-68; dep. prosecutor Monroe County, Bloomington, 1967-68; tax acct. Price Waterhouse, Phila., 1968-69; v.p., treas. Innovest Group, Inc., Phila., 1969-82, chmn., pres., 1983—. Bd. dirs. Capital Mgmt. Corp., N.Y. Achievement, L.L.C., Innovest Talent Svcs., Inc., Ind. U. Found., Phila. Hospitality, Inc., Phila. Zoo. Pa. Acad. Fine Arts; vice chmn. World Affairs Coun. of Phila.; chmn. Walnut St. Theatre. Mem. ABA, Ind. Bar Assn., Union League of Phila., Sunday Breakfast Club, The Pa Soc. Office: 1528 Walnut St Ste 1701 Philadelphia PA 19102

**WOOSTER, KELLY C.,** lawyer; b. San Francisco, Dec. 18, 1942; AB cum laude, Stanford U., 1964; JD, U. Calif., Berkeley, 1967. Bar: Calif. 1967. Ptnr. Brobeck, Phleger & Harrison, San Francisco, 1978—2002. Note and comment editor: Calif. Law Rev., 1966-67. Mailing: PO Box 62 Copperopolis CA 95228 Office Phone: 209-785-2437.

**WOOSTER, LARRY D.,** music educator; b. Tucson, Ariz., Aug. 1, 1960; s. Arthur Wayne Wooster and Barbara A McCastle; m. Lynette M Collingwood, June 18, 1983; 1 child, Elizabeth M. AA, Concordia Coll., 1980; BS in Edn., Concordia Teachers Coll., 1982; MA, U. N.Mex, 1985; Ednl. Specialist (EdS), Nova Southeastern U., 2005, ABD, 2006. Cert. profl. tchr. N.Mex, 1982, master tchr. Iowa, 1991. Tchr./music dir. Immanuel Luth. Ch. and Sch., Albuquerque, 1982—91; tchr. St. Paul Luth. Ch. and Sch., Fort Dodge, Iowa, 1991—97; music dir./tchr. Grace Luth. Ch. and Sch., Lancaster, Calif., 1997—. Gen. electric math fellow Albuquerque Cmty. Found., 1985—86. Mem.: Music Educators Nat. Conf. Lutheran Church - Missouri Synod. Avocations: hot air balloon pilot, travel. Office: Grace Lutheran Church and School 856 West Newgrove St Lancaster CA 93534 Office Phone: 661-948-1018. Business E-mail: lwooster@gracelancaster.org.

**WOOSTER, NICHOLAS WAYNE,** band director; b. Dyersburg, Tenn., Feb. 3, 1978; s. Gary Wayne and Deborah Kay Wooster; m. Karen Elizabeth Climer, June 20, 1980. MusB in Edn. with Instrumental Music Emphasis, Ark. State U., 2001. Lic. tchr. Tenn., Ark., Mo., 2001. Dir. of bands Caruthersville Schs., Caruthersville, Mo., 2001—02; jr. high band dir. Wynne Jr. High, Wynne, Ark., 2002—03; dir. band Halls H.S., Halls, Tenn., 2003—. Music dir. Tucker St. Ch., Dyersburg, Tenn., 2003—06. Scholar Music scholar, Ark. State U. Music Dept., 5 years. Mem.: Tenn. Music Educators Assn., West Tenn. Sch. Band and Orch. Assn., Music Educators Nat. Conf., Bands of Am. (assoc.), Kappa Kappa Psi. Avocations: travel, trombone performance. Office Phone: 731-836-7691.

**WOOSTER, ROBERT,** history professor; b. Beaumont, Tex., Aug. 27, 1956; s. Ralph Ancil and Edna Lee (Jones) W.; m. Catherine Cox, 1992. BA, Lamar U., 1977, MA, 1979; PhD, U. Tex., 1985. Scholar in residence Tex. State Hist. Assn., Liberty, 1985-86; asst. prof. Tex. A&M U., Corpus Christi, 1986-90, assoc. prof., 1990-95, prof., 1995—, chmn. dept. humanities, 1997—2000, Piper prof., 1988, Frantz prof. history, 2001—04. Author: Soldiers, Sutlers and Settlers (Bates award 1987), U.S. Military and Indian Policy, 1988, History of Fort Davis, 1990, Nelson A. Miles and The Twilight of the Frontier Army, 1993, The Civil War 100, 1998, The Civil War Bookshelf, 2001, Frontier Crossroads: Fort Davis and the West, 2006; editl. adv. bd. Southwestern Hist. Quar., Austin, Tex., 1989—, Military History of the West, 1995—, Jour. of the West, 1996-2000; editor: Soldier, Surgeon, Scholar: The Memoirs of William Henry Corbusier, 2003. Dep. dir. U.S. Mil. Acad./ROTC fellowship U.S. Mil. Acad., West Point, N.Y., 1990. Fellow Tex. State Hist. Assn. (pres. 2005—06); mem. Am. Historians. Democrat. Home: 4600 Ocean Dr Apt 708 Corpus Christi TX 78412-2543 Office: Texas A&M Univ 6300 Ocean Dr Corpus Christi TX 78412-5599 Office Phone: 361-825-2402. Business E-mail: robert.wooster@tamucc.edu.

**WOOTAN, MARGO G.,** nutritionist, director; m. Gregory James McCarthy, June 23, 1998; 1 child, Camryn Wootan McCarthy. AA, Ulster County C.C., Stone Ridge, NY, 1984; BS, Cornell U., Ithaca, NY, 1986; DS, Harvard U., 1993. Dir. nutrition policy Ctr. Sci. Pub. Interest, Washington, 1993—. Dir. Nat. Alliance Nutrition and Activity, Washington, 2000—; mem. steering com. Nat. 5 A Day Partnership, 2000—; chair food and nutrition sect. legislation and pub. policy com. APHA, 2002—05; adv. com. pub. policy Soc. Nutrition Edn., 1997—2001; pres. Metro-DC Affiliate Soc. Nutrition Edn., 1997—98. Recipient award Excellence Advocacy, Assn. State and Territorial Pub. Health Nutrition Directors, 1994, 2000, Dietary Guidance award, APHA, 2000, 2005, Early Career award, Soc. Prevention Rsch., 2000, Disting. Achievement award, Assn. Ednl. Pubs., 2003, award Pub. Excellence, APEX, 2003, 5 A Day Nat. Excellence award, Produce Better Health Found., 2004. Office: Ctr Sci Public Interest 1875 Connecticut Ave NW Ste 300 Washington DC 20009 Office Phone: 202-777-8352. Office Fax: 202-265-4954. E-mail: nutritionpolicy@cspinet.org.

**WOOTEN, CAROL G.,** music educator, minister; MusB in Edn., Gordon Coll., 1987; student, Gordon-Conwell Theol. Sem., 1999. Cert. tchr. Mass. Music dir. Danvers Pub. Schs., Danvers, Mass., 1988—92; dir. of music Orange UMC, Chapel Hill, NC, 1992—96; dir. music and arts ministry Epworth United Meth. Ch., Durham, NC, 2000—05; founder and condr. Triangle Youth Music Chorus, Durham and Chapel Hill, NC, 2000; chaplain resident Hosps. U. N.C., Chapel Hill, NC, 2006—. Instr. pvt. lessons, 1976—96; adjudicator, 1998—; dir. various workshops, 1998—. Founding dir. Arts Ministry, Durham and Chapel Hill, 2002—. Recipient First Pl. award, Jubilate Choral Soc., 1987. Mem.: Am. Choral Dirs. Assn. (life), Chorister's Guild (chpt. pres. 1994—96), Worship List (advisor and chaplain 1998—2003). Independent. Avocations: outdoors, reading, travel.

**WOOTEN, CECIL AARON,** retired religious organization administrator; b. Laurel, Miss., June 3, 1924; s. Cecil A. and Alice (Cox) W.; m. Helen Moss, Apr. 4, 1947; children: Michael, Margaret, Martin, Marsha, Mark. BS in Mech. Engring., U. Ala., 1949. With CBI Industries, 1941—83, bd. dirs., 1965-83, mng. dir. CBI Constructors Ltd., London, 1957-62, mgr. Houston sales dist., 1962-64, v.p. engring., 1964-69, v.p., mgr. corp. svcs. Oak Brook, Ill., 1968-69, sr. v.p.-gen. sales mgr., 1969-78; sr. v.p. comml. devel. Chgo. Bridge & Iron Co. (subs. CBI Industries), 1978-79; sr. v.p. corp. adminstrn.

CBI Industries, Oak Brook, 1980-83; dir. devel. Christian Family Services, Gainesville, Fla., 1983-86, Denver Ch. of Christ, 1986-88, Boston Ch. of Christ, 1988-92; pres. Internat. Chs. of Christ, Inc., L.A., 1994-99; chair Internat. Chs. Christ, L.A., 1999—2000, retired, 2002. Bd. dirs. Oak Brook (Ill.) Bank. Former trustee Elmhurst (Ill.) Coll.; former bd. sponsors Good Samaritan Hosp., Downers Grove, Ill. Served to 1st lt. AUS, 1943-46. Mem. ASME, NSPE, Rotary. Personal E-mail: cecilwooten@hotmail.com.

**WOOTEN, FRANK THOMAS,** retired research facility executive; b. Fayetteville, N.C., Sept. 24, 1935; s. Frank Thomas and Katherine (McRae) Wooten; m. Linda Walker, July 14, 1962; children: Laurin Walker, Patrick Thomas, Ashley Tripp. BSEE, Duke U., 1957, PhD, 1966. Engr. Corning Glass Works, Raleigh, NC, 1966—84; from engr. to pres. Rsch. Triangle Inst., Research Triangle Park, NC, 1966—89, pres., 1989—99; ret., 1999. Bd. dirs. N.C. Biotech. Ctr., Troxler Electronics Labs., N.C. Biosci. Investment Fund. Contbr. articles on semiconductors and biomedical engring. to profl. publs.; patentee semiconductors tech. Lt. (j.g.) USN, 1957—59. Recipient Disting. Engring. Alumnus award, Duke U., 1991; fellow, Shell, 1961. Mem.: IEEE, Nat. Inst. Statis. Scis. (corp. 1990—98), Ballistic Missile Def. Orgn. (tech. application rev. panel 1990—94), Assn. for Advancement Med. Instrumentation (chmn. com. on aerospace tech. 1971—77). Baptist.

**WOOTEN, GLEN DONOVAN,** media consultant; s. Lester Lee Wooten and Veda Diloros Johnson; 1 child, Jennifer Rachel Pitts. BA in Psychology, U. Nev., Las Vegas, 2000. Ops. mgr. Procell, Las Vegas, Nev., 1992—97; technician Network, Las Vegas, Nev., 1998—. Cons., media editor Profitscape, Las Vegas, Nev., 1997—98. Contbr. articles to pubs. Mentor, tutor math., stats. Student Devel. Ctr., Las Vegas, Nev., 1998—. Mem.: Mega Soc., Top One Percent Soc., Triple Nine Soc., Intertel, Mensa, Prometheus Soc., Internat. Soc. for Philos. Enquiry, Pi Mu Epsilon, Omicron Psi, Psi Chi, Omicron Delta Epsilon, Golden Key, Phi Kappa Phi, Nat. Forensic League, Phi Sigma Tau. Achievements include development of novel relational ideas in fields of calculus and graph theory. Avocations: frisbee, working out, reading, mathematics, philosophy. Office: PO Box 70122 Las Vegas NV 89170-0122

**WOOTEN, JAMES TERRELL,** journalist; b. Detroit, July 13, 1937; s. J.R. and Clara Charlene (Richmond) W.; m. Katherine Joanne Richardson, Aug. 26, 1958 (dec. 1978); children: Karen, Kristen, Katie, Elizabeth; m. Patience Jean O'Connor, Sept. 27, 1980; 1 dau., Jacqueline DeLacie O'Connor. BA, Bethel Coll., McKenzie Tenn., 1958; B.D., Presbyn. Theol. Sem., Memphis, 1961. Reporter Huntsville Times, Ala., 1965-68, N.Y. Times, N.Y.C, 1968-73, 74-78; columnist Phila. Inquirer, 1973-74; writer Esquire mag., N.Y.C., 1978-79; nat. corr. ABC News, Washington, 1979—, now sr. corr. Author: Soldier, 1972, Dasher, 1978, We Are All the Same: A Story of a Boy's Courage and a Mother's Love, 2004 (25th Annual Robert F. Kennedy Book award, 2005). Recipient Ernie Pyle Meml. award Scripps-Howard, 1974; recipient Blue Pencil award Columbia U., 1979*

**WOOTEN, JOAN HEDRICH,** minister; b. Washington, Jan. 4, 1953; d. Albert Louis Hedrich and Maxine Keller Smith; m. David Randall Wooten, Jan. 11, 1983; children: Michael, Sarah. BA, Coll. William and Mary, 1975; MA, Bryn Mawr Coll., Mass., 1978; MDiv, Gordon-Conwell Theol. Sem., 1981; ThM, Duke U. Div. Sch., Durham, N.C., 1987. Ordained 1982. Chaplain U.S. Navy, Oak Harbor, Wash., 1982—84, Yokosuka, Japan, 1984—86, Norfolk, Va., 1987—90, res. chaplain, 1990—, capt.; pastoral counselor Episcopal Diocese of So. Va., Norfolk, 1990—93; campus min. Presbytery of Ea. Va., Portsmouth, 1993—2001; interim and stated supply pastor Presbytery Fla., 2003—. Doctoral fellow Union Theol. Sem., Richmond, 2001—. Singer Va. Symphony Chorus, Norfolk, 1992—2001. Decorated Commendation medal U.S. Navy. Presbyterian. Avocations: music, languages, cooking. Personal E-mail: joanwooten@aol.com.

**WOOTEN, JOEL ORBA,** lawyer; b. Hazlehurst, Ga., June 4, 1950; s. Joel Orba and Mary Eleanor (Whitlock) W.; m. Sybrina G. Franklin; children: Joel III, Katherine, Frank. BBA, U. Ga., 1972, JD, 1975. Bar: Ga. 1975. U.S. Dist. Ct. (mid. dist.) Ga. 1976, U.S. Ct. Appeals (11th cir.) 1981. Ptnr. Kelly, Denney, Pease & Allison, Columbus, Ga., 1975-88, Butler, Wooten, Overby & Cheeley, Columbus, Ga., 1988—. Bd. dirs. Columbus Symphony Orch., Columbus, Ga., 1983-88; bd. regents Univ. Sys. of Ga., 1999-2006, chair, 2004-05. With U.S. Army, 1972. Mem. Am. Bar Assn., Fed. Bar Assn., Ga. Trial Lawyers Assn., State Bar Ga. (chmn. gen. practice & trial sect. 1990-91), Columbus Lawyers Club (pres 1988-89), Columbus Younger Lawyers (pres. 1983-84), Assn. Trial Lawyers Am., The Roscoe Pound Found., U. Ga. Alumni Soc. (bd. dirs. 1981-83, 89-91). Office: Butler, Wooten, & Fryhofer, LLP 105 Thirteenth St Columbus GA 31901

**WOOTEN, MARC,** hospital administrator, medical educator; s. Marc and Mosie Wooten; m. Mary Wooten, July 15, 1995; children: Marc, Michael. MBA, UCLA, 1975; MD, U. of Tex. Southwestern Med. Sch., 1988. Asst. prof. of medicine Tulane U. Med. Ctr., New Orleans, 1995—97; assoc. prof. of medicine Jefferson Med. Coll., Wilmington, Del., 1997—2003; voluntary clin. assoc. prof. of medicine Ind. U. Sch. of Medicine, Ft. Wayne, Ind., 2003—; chief of staff VA No. Ind. Health Care Sys., Ft. Wayne, Ind., 2003—. Contbr. articles to med. jours. Capt. USAF, 1974—82. Decorated Air Force Commendation medal USAF; named Jr. Officer of the Quar., 1980. Fellow: ACP, Am. Coll. of Rheumatology, Am. Coll. of Physician Executives (cert. physician exec.). Office: Dept VA Affairs 2121 Lake Ave Fort Wayne IN 46805 Office Phone: 260-460-1311.

**WOOTEN, RALPH G.,** career officer; b. La Grange, N.C. Commd. officer U.S. Army, advanced through grades to maj. gen., 1996; comdg. gen. U.S. Army Chem., Mil. Police Ctrs., and Ft. McClellan, Ft. McClellan, Ala., 1996—. Address: 125 Cross Foxes Dr Fort Washington MD 20744-5566

**WOOTEN, ROBERT E.,** music educator; b. Chgo., Feb. 17, 1930; s. John and Flora (Waits) W.; m. Frances Louise Carter, Aug. 26, 1956; children: Robert Jr., Carol Lynne, John D. BMus, Chgo. Conservatory Music, 1956; M in Music Edn., Roosevelt U., 1968; D in Music Edn., Va. Seminary & Coll., 1983. Min. music Beth Eden Bapt. Ch., Chgo., 1941—; founder, dir. Wooten Choral Ensemble, 1949—; dir. music Greater Harvest Bapt. Ch., 1950-86. Music dept. chair Parker H.S., Chgo., 1957-62; staff asst., Chgo. Pub. Schs. 1962-75, dist. administr., 1976-95. Named Living Legend in Ch. Music, Hampton U. Ministers Conf. and Choir Dirs. Guild, 2005; recipient Local award, Nat. Assn. Study and Performance African Am. Music, 2005. Mem. Am. Choral Dirs., Music Educators Nat. Conf., Nat. Assn. Study Performances of African Am. Music Home: 9531 S Union Ave Chicago IL 60628-1031 Personal E-mail: maestrob1@aol.com

**WOOTEN, ROSALIE (ROSALIE O'REILLY WOOTEN),** automotive company executive; Exec. v.p. O'Reilly Automotive Inc., Springfield, Mo., also bd. dir., 1993—. Office: O'Reilly Automotive Inc 233 S Patterson Ave Springfield MO 65802-2298

**WOOTON, JOEL,** history professor, basketball coach; s. John and Joetta Wooton; m. Vicki Lynn Lillie, Aug. 1, 1981; children: Ashley, Lindsey, Whitney. BS, U. Nebr., Omaha, 1975; MS, US Sports Acad., Daphne, Ala., 1986, US Sports Acad., 1993. History instr. Scribner-Snyder HS, Nebr., 1983—89; phys. edn. chair, head men's basketball coach Iowa Wesleyan Coll., Mt. Pleasant, 1989—95, LaGrange Coll., Ga., 1995—98; history instr. Auburn HS, Nebr., 1998—2000, Red Oak HS, Iowa, 2001—04; history instr., head men's basketball coach Southeast C.C., Beatrice, Nebr., 2004—. Regional basketball rater NAIA, Kansas City, Mo., 1995—98. Named Coach of Yr., 1995. Mem.: NABC, Metro Coaches Assn., Nebr. Coaches Assn. (assoc.). Office Phone: 402-228-3468.

**WOOTTON, JOHN EDENDEN,** physiology educator; b. Penn Yan, N.Y., May 31, 1929; s. John Edenden and Margaret Eliza (Smith) W.; m. Joyce Albertine Mac Mullen, Aug. 28, 1959; children: J. Timothy, David M.,

Barbara H., Bruce C. BS, Cornell U., 1951, MS, 1953, PhD, 1960. Grad. rsch. asst. Cornell U., Ithaca, NY, 1956-60, from asst. prof. to prof. emeritus, 1962—2004, prof. emeritus, 2004—, assoc. dean Grad. Sch., 1980-83; post doctoral fellow U. Coll., London, 1960-62. Grad. faculty rep. field of physiology Cornell U., 1990-92, 93-97, chmn. dept. physiology, 1997-98, co-chmn. dept. biomed. scis., 1998-99, chmn. 1999-2000; vis. scientist MRC Molecular Biology, Cambridge, Eng., 1969-70, Nat. Inst. Med. Rsch., London, 1985-86, 92-93, 2002; temporary sr. rsch. assoc. Stanford (Calif.) U., 1977-78. Contbr. articles to profl. jours. 1st lt. USAR, 1954-56. Rsch. and Travel grantee NIH, USDA Burroughs Wellcom Fund, Med. Rsch. Coun.. Cornell Biotech. Program. Mem. AAAS, Am. Soc. Biochemistry and Molecular Biology, Am. Chem. Soc., Biophys. Soc., Protein Soc., Sigma Xi (v.p., pres. Cornell chpt.). Avocations: travel, choral singing, gardening, art, fishing. Office: Cornell U Dept Biomed Scis T8-014 Vet Rsch Tower Ithaca NY 14853-5908 Business E-Mail: jfw1@cornell.edu.

**WORAM, BRIAN J.,** lawyer; b. Perth Amboy, NJ, July 24, 1960; m. Allison M. Woram. BS cum laude, Tex. A & M U., 1981; JD, U. Tex., 1986. Gen. counsel Centex Homes (subsidiary Centex Corp.), 1998—. State Bar Tex. 1986, Tex. Law Rev., Dallas Bar Assn., ABA. Achievements include Author article "Fed. Statues of Limitation," Banking Law Jour. 7-8, 1993. Mailing: Centex Corp PO Box 199000 Dallas TX 75219-0001 Office: Centex Corp 2728 N Harwood St Dallas TX 75201-1516 Home: 3821 Colgate Ave Dallas TX 75225-5224

**WORBOYS, ROGER DICK,** retired communications executive; b. Syracuse, N.Y., Sept. 1, 1947; s. Carl Stape and Dorothy Elsa (Dick) W.; m. Mary Lee Tasker, Nov. 27, 1971; children: Thomas, Elizabeth. Bachelors degree, Alfred U., 1969; M in Bus., U. N.H., 1971. Asst. dir. residences U. N.H., Durham, 1971; mgr.- regional mgr. Continental Cablevision, Boston, 1974-86; v.p. ops. Simmons Comm., Stamford, Conn., 1986-88, Insight Comm., Glasgow, Scotland, N.Y.C., 1988-95, Bresnan Comms., White Plains, N.Y., 1996-98, sr. v.p., 1999-2000; ret., 2001; mem. eCoast Angels Investor, 2005—. Chair Pub. Sch. Tech. Adv, Dover, NH, bd. trustees Mill Pond Ctr. Arts. Mem.: Rotary Internat. (bd. dirs., exec. com bd. dirs. great bay svcs.), Portsmouth N.H. C. of C. (pres.). Roman Catholic.

**WORCESTER, HOWARD LESTER,** internist; b. Kansas City, Mo., Jan. 3, 1945; s. Howard Elmer and Alma Jane (Evans) W. div.; m. Tammy Worcester; children: Tiffany, Chase. BS, U. Oregon, 1967, MD, 1971. Diplomate Am. Bd. Internal Medicine, Am. Bd. Forensic Pathology. Intern Harbor Gen. Hosp. UCLA, 1971-72; med. officer U.S. Army, West Germany, 1972-75; resident U. Calif., Irvine, 1975-77, chief med. resident, 1977-78; pvt. practice internal medicine Meml. Hosp., Long Beach, Calif., 1978—. Dir. utilization rev. Long Beach Meml. Hosp., 1983—, trustee, 1983—, also bd. dirs.; cons. Sultanate of Oman, Muscat, Oman, 1984—. Patron L.A. County Mus. Major U.S. Army, 1972-75. Recipient Merck scholarship U. Oreg. Med. Sch., 1969 Mem. Long Beach Meml. Hosp. Med. Group (pres. 1983—), Long Beach Meml. Med. Svc. Orgn. (pres. 1993-96), Phi Beta Kappa, Alpha Omega Alpha. Episcopalian. Avocations: cooking, wine collecting, travel, sports. Home: 11042 Skyline Dr Santa Ana CA 92705-2473 Office: Meml Med Group 2650 Elm Ave Ste 309 Long Beach CA 90806-1600 Office Phone: 562-595-8549. Personal E-mail: rworcester@cox.net.

**WORDEN, KATHARINE COLE,** sculptor; b. NYC, May 4, 1925; d. Philip Gillette and Katharine (Pyle) Cole; m. Frederic G. Worden, Jan. 8, 1944; children: Fred, Dwight, Philip, Barbara, Katharine. Student, Potters Ch., Tucson, 1940-42, Sarah Lawrence Coll., 1942-44. Exhibited in group shows at Royce Galleries, Galerie Francoise Besnard, Paris, Cooling Gallery, London, Galerie Schumacher, Munich, Selected Artists Gallery, N.Y.C., Art Inst. Boston, Reid Gallery, Nashville, Weiner Gallery, N.Y.C., Boston Athanaeum, House of Humor and Satire, Gabrovo, Bulgaria, 1983, Newport Bay Club, 1984; pvt. collections Grand Palais, Paris, Dakar and Bathurst, Africa. Occupl. therapist psychopathic ward L.A. County Gen. Hosp., 1953-57; Headstart vol., Watts, Calif., 1965-67; tchr. sculpture Watts Towers Art Ctr., 1967-69; participant White House Women Doers Luncheon meeting, 1968; dir. Cambridgeport Problem Ctr., Cambridge, Mass., 1969-71; mem. Jud. Nominating Commn., 1976-79; bd. overseers Boston Mus. Fine Arts, 1980-83; bd. govs. Newport Seamens Ch. Inst., 1989-91; tustee Comm. Rsch., Miami, Fla., 1960-69, chmn. bd., 1966-69; trustee Newport Art Mus., 1984-86, 92-94, Jamestown Cmty. Theatre, 1994-97, 99-2005, 06—, Newport Health Found., 1986-91, Hawthorne Sea Fund, 1990-93; bd. dirs. Boston Ctr. for Arts, 1976-80, Child and Family Svcs. Newport County, 1983-97, 99-2005, 2006—. Mem. Common Cause (Mass adv. bd. 1971-72, dir. 1974-75), Mass. Civil Liberties Union (exec. bd. 1973-74, dir. 1976-77). Home: 9 Meadow Ln Jamestown RI 02835 Office Phone: 401-423-1758.

**WORDSWORTH, JERRY L.,** wholesale distribution executive; b. Charlotte, NC, Sept. 22, 1945; BS, N.C. State U., 1963. With MBM, Rocky Mount, NC, 1966—, CEO, pres. & chmn. Co-owner Carolina Panthers. Office: MBM 2641 Mountainbrook Rd Rocky Mount NC 27802 Home: PO Box 800 Rocky Mount NC 27802-0800 Office Fax: 252-985-7241.*

**WORELL, JUDITH P.,** psychologist, educator; b. NYC. d. Moses and Dorothy Goldfarb; m. Leonard Worell, Aug. 11, 1947 (div.); children: Amy, Beth, Wendy; m. H.A. Smith, Mar. 23, 1985 BS magna cum laude, Queens Coll., 1950; MA, Ohio State U., 1952; PhD in Clin. Psychology, 1954; DHL (hon.), Colby-Sawyer Coll., 1993. Research assoc Iowa Psychopathic Hosp., Iowa City, 1957-59; research assoc. Okla. State U., 1960-66; asst. prof. U. Ky., Lexington, 1969-71, assoc. prof., 1971-75, prof. ednl. and counseling psychology, 1976—, dir. counseling psychology tng. program, 1980-93, chairperson dept. ednl. and counseling psychology, 1993-97, prof. emerita, 1999—. Author: (with C.M. Nelson) Managing Instructional Problems, 1974; (with W.E. Stilwell) Psychology for Teachers and Students, 1981; Psychological Development in the Elementary Years, 1982; (with Fred Danner) The Adolescent as Decision-maker: Applications to Development and Education, 1989; (with Pam Remer) Feminist Perspectives in Therapy: An Empowerment Model for Women, 1992; (with N. Johnson) Shaping the Future of Feminist Psychology: Education, Research, and Practice, 1997, (with Norine Johnson & Michael Roberts) Beyond Appearance: A New Look at Adolescent Girls, 1999, Encyclopedia of Women and Gender: Sex Similarities and Differences and the Impact of Society on Gender, 2001, (with Pam Remer) Feminist Perspectives in Therapy: Empowering Diverse Women, 2003, (with Carol Goodheart) Oxford Handbook of Girls' and Women's Psychological Health, 2006; assoc. editor Jour. Cons. and Clin. Psychology, 1976-79, mem. editl. bd., 1984-89; assoc. editor Psychol. Women Quar., 1984-89, editor, 1989-95; mem. editorial bd. Sex Roles, 1984-2000, Psychol. Assessment, 1991-97, Clin. Psychology Rev., 1991-97, Women and Therapy, 1992-2000; cons., reviewer 10 jours.; contbr. articles to profl. jours. Named U. Ky. Campus Woman of Yr., 1976, Outstanding Univ. Grad. prof., 1991, Disting. Ky. psychologist, 1990; USPHS fellow, 1953; NIMH rsch. grantee, 1962-69. Fellow APA (pres. Clin. Psychology of Women 1986-88, chmn. com. state assn. rels. 1982-83, fellow selection divsn. 35 com. 1983-84, policy and planning bd. 1989-92, publs. and comm. bd. 1992-99, chair 1996-98, chair jours. com., pres. divsn. psychology of women 1997-98, Disting. Leader for Women in Psychology 1990, Carolyn Wood Sherif award, 2001, Psychology of Women Heritage award 2004, coun. rep. 2000-02, chair women's caucus 2002) Soc. Psychol. Study of Social Issues (chmn. fellow com. 2005-), Ky. Psychol. Assn. (pres. 1981-82, rep. at large 1995-97), Southeastern Psychol. Assn. (exec. coun. mem.-at-large, pres.-elect 1993-94 pres. 1994-95), Am. Women in Psychology, Phi Beta Kappa. Home: 3892 Gloucester Dr Lexington KY 40510-9729 Office: U Ky Dept Ednl and Counseling Psychology 245 Dickey Hl Lexington KY 40506-0017 E-mail: jworell@alltel.net.

**WORENKLEIN, JACOB JOSHUA,** lawyer; b. NYC, Oct. 1, 1948; s. Abraham and Cela (Zyskind) W.; divorced; children: David, Daniel, Laura; m. Cindy Sternkler, Feb. 26, 1995; 1 child, Sacha Anne. BA, Columbia U., 1969; MBA, JD, NYU, 1974. Bar: N.Y. 1974. From assoc. to ptnr. Milbank, Tweed, Hadley & McCloy, N.Y.C., 1973-93, chmn. firm planning com., 1988-90, exec. com., 1990-93, sr. advisor to exec. com., 1993-94; mng. dir.,

group head of global project fin. group Lehman Bros., N.Y.C., 1993-96; mng. dir., head project fin, commodity fin., export fin. Soc. Gen., N.Y.C., 1996-98, mng. dir., global head project and sector fin. Paris and N.Y.C., 1998—2003; pres., CEO U.S. Power Generating Co., N.Y.C., 2003—. Mem. investment banking mgmt. com. Lehman Bros., 1993-96; mem. adv. coun. Amoco Power Resources Corp., 1995-97; adj. prof. fin. NYU Stern Sch. of Bus.; bd. dirs., mem. audit com. CDC Globeleq, 2004—, Ormat Techs., Inc., 2004—. Mem. editl. bd. Jour. Structured and Project Fin., 1996—; contbr. articles to profl. jours. Chmn. bd. Old Broadway Synagogue, N.Y.C., 2001-, pres. 1978-2001; trustee Fedn. Jewish Philanthropies, N.Y.C., 1984-86; bd. overseers United Jewish Appeal-Fedn. Jewish Philanthropies, 1987, chmn. lawyers divsn. major gifts, 1989-91, chmn. lawyers divsn., 1991-93, bd. dirs., 1991-97; trustee Jewish Cmty. Rels. Coun., N.Y., 1995-98, Com. for Econ. Devel. 2001-. Mem. Coun. on Fgn. Rels. Office Phone: 212-223-8240. Business E-Mail: jworenklein@uspowergen.com

**WORK, BRUCE VAN SYOC,** small business owner, consultant; b. Monmouth, Ill., Mar. 20, 1942; s. Robert M. and Evelyn (Ruskin) W.; m. Janet Kay Brown, Nov. 12, 1966; children: Bruce, Terra. BA, Monmouth Coll., 1964; BS, U. Mo.-Rolla, 1966; postgrad., U. Chgo., 1978-79. Registered profl. engr., Ill. Various mgmt. positions Midcon Corp. (and subs.), 1966-79; pres. Indsl. Fuels Corp., Troy, Mich., 1979-85, Costain Coal Inc., Troy, Mich., 1985-89; pvt. practice small bus. cons., 1989-92; bus. cons. Wallis Oil Co., 1992-2000; small bus. cons., 2000—. Mem. various coms. Cuba United Meth. Ch. Mem. Detroit Athletic Club, Blue Key. Office: 2280 Hwy DD Cuba MO 65453-9684 Office Phone: 573-885-4724. *People are the key to our success. Treat each individual as you would like to be treated.*

**WORK, CHARLES ROBERT,** lawyer; b. Glendale, Calif., June 21, 1940; s. Raymond P. and Minna M. (Fricke) W.; m. Linda S. Smith, Oct. 4, 1965 (div.); children: Matthew Keehn, Mary Lucila Landis, Benjamin Reed; m. Veronica A. Haggart, Apr., 1985, 1 child, Andrew Haggart. BA, Wesleyan U., 1962; JD, U. Chgo., 1965; LLM, Georgetown U., 1966. Bar: D.C. 1965, Utah 1965. Asst. U.S. atty. D.C., 1966-73; dep. adminstr. law enforcement assistance adminstrn., U.S. Dept. Justice, 1973-75; ptnr. Peabody, Lambert & Meyers, Washington, 1975-82, McDermott, Will & Emery, Washington, 1982—. Recipient Rockefeller Pub. Service award 1978. Mem. D.C. Bar (pres. 1976-77). Office: McDermott Will & Emery 600 13th St NW Fl 12-8 Washington DC 20005-3005 Office Phone: 202-756-8030. E-mail: cwork@mwe.com.

**WORK, GEORGE PAUL,** cellist; b. Lincoln, Nebr., June 20, 1957; s. George Arthur Work, Carol Puckett Work; m. Dawn Elizabeth Work MaKinne. Cert. in performance, Eastman Sch. Music, 1979, B in Music Performance, 1979, M in Music Performance, 1981. Founder, dir. Iowa State Summer Chamber Music Workshop, Ames, Iowa, 1993—2000; prof. cello Iowa State U., Ames, 1981—. Cellist Ames Piano Quartet, Ames, 1981—; artist faculty mem. Luth. Music Program, Mpls., 1984—97; Bravo! Summer String Inst., Mpls., 1994; adj. prof. cello Drake U., Des Moines, 1997—98; artist faculty mem. Brevard (N.C.) Music Ctr., 1998—. Musician: (recording) Piano Quartets by Chausson and Saint-Saens, 1989, Dvorak: The Two Piano Quartets, 1990, Faure: The Two Piano Quartets, 1991, Piano Quartets by Strauss and Widor, 1993, Piano Quartets of Schumann and Brahms, 1994, Piano Quartets of Brahms, 1995, The Russian Piano Quartet, 2000, Dorian Sampler, Volume 2, 1989, Gemini, 2001, (chamber music performances) over 300 concerts throughout N.Am., also France, Austria, Taiwan, and Mex. Mem. Amnesty Internat., Iowa; case coord. Amnesty Internat, Ames, 1986—91. Grantee Grants for Ames Quartet concerts and workshops, Affiliated Arts Agencies of Upper Midwest, 1985—87, 1989—91, Grant for Ames Quartet concerts and workshops, Nat. Endowment for Arts, 1982—83. Mem.: Am. String Tchrs. Assn. (Studio Tchr. of Yr. award, Iowa 1991). Avocations: astronomy, travel. Office: Iowa State U Ames IA 50011 Office Phone: 515-294-4013. Business E-Mail: gwork@iastate.edu.

**WORK, HENRY HARCUS,** psychiatrist, educator; b. Buffalo, Nov. 11, 1911; s. Henry Harcus and Jeannette (Harcus) W.; m. Virginia Codington, Oct. 20, 1945 (dec. Nov. 1991); children: Henry Harcus III, David Codington, William Bruce, Stuart Runyon. AB, Hamilton Coll., Clinton, N.Y., 1933; MD, Harvard, 1937. Intern, resident Boston Children's Hosp., 1937-40, Emma P. Bradley Home Providence, 1940, Buffalo Children's Hosp., 1940-42, N.Y. Hosp., 1945-47; psychiat. services adviser, chief U.S. Children's Bur., Washington, 1948-49; assoc. prof. pediatrics U. Louisville, 1949-55; mem. faculty UCLA, 1955-72, prof. psychiatry and pub. health, 1966-72; chief profl. svcs. Am. Psychiat. Assn., Washington, 1972-83; clin. prof. George Washington U., Georgetown U., Uniformed Svcs. U. of Health Scis., U. Md., 1973—. Author: A Guide to Preventive Child Psychiatry, 1965, Minimal Brain Dysfunction: A Medical Challenge, 1967, Psychiatric Emergencies in Childhood, 1967, Crisis in Child Psychiatry, 1975, also articles. Served to capt. AUS, 1942-45. Recipient Simon Wile Award, Amer. Acad. of Child and Adolescent Psychiatry, 1994. Mem. So. Calif. Psychiat. Assn. (pres. 1966-67), Am. Orthopsychiat. Assn. (v.p. 1968-69), Am. Coll. Psychiatry (sec.-gen. 1979-93), Group for Advancement of Psychiatry (pres. 1982-85) Home: 4986 Sentinel Dr Apt 504 Bethesda MD 20816-3581

**WORK, JANE ALLEN,** psychologist; b. Phila., May 17, 1916; d. Robert Louis and Lois (McKinney) Allen; m. Homer R. Allen (dec. 1943); children: Robert M., Emily Allen Berg, Homer G.; m. William McClean Work, 1979. BA, Westminster Coll., 1965; MA, Case Western Res. U., 1967, PhD, 1973. Lic. psychologist, Penn. Sch. psychologist City of Cleve., 1968-70; psychologist adv. edn. dist. Lake County, Ill., 1970-73, Coop. Ednl. Svc. Agy. 18, Burlington, Wis., 1974-76; dir. psychol. svcs. Marion (Ohio) Area Counseling Ctr., 1976-78; pvt. practice psychology Pitts., 1979—99; freelance writer Pittsburgh, 1987—. Instr. Loyola U., Chgo., Roosevelt U., Chgo., 1973-74, Nat. Sch. Edn., Evanston, Ill., 1974. Mem. Pa. Task Force for Women, Harrisburg, 1986. Mem. APA, Pa. Psychol. Assn., NOW (pres. South Hills chpt. 1987-88, membership dir. 1992-94), Soc. for the Sci. Study of Sexuality, Alumni Coun. Case Western Res. U., Sylvania Hills Hound and Hunt Club, Entre Nous Club. Democrat. Presbyterian. Home: Apt B305 1290 Boyce Rd Pittsburgh PA 15241-3933

**WORKMAN, GEORGE HENRY,** structural engineering consultant; b. Muskegon, Mich., Sept. 18, 1939; s. Harvey Merton and Bettie Jane (Meyers) W.; m. Vicki Sue Hanish, June 17, 1967; children: Mark, Larry. AS, Muskegon C.C., 1960; BS in Engring., MS in Engring., U. Mich., 1966, PhD, 1969. Registered profl. engr., Ohio. Prin. engr. Battelle Meml. Inst., Columbus, Ohio, 1969-76; pres. Applied Mechanics Inc., Longboat Key, Fla., 1976—. Instr. dept. civil engring. Ohio State U., 1973, 82. Contbr. tech. papers to nat. and internat. confs. With USN, 1961-64. Mem. ASME, Am. Acad. Mechanics, Sigma Xi, Chi Epsilon, Phi Kappa Phi, Phi Thea Kappa. Congregationalist. Home and Office: 3431 Bayou Ct Longboat Key FL 34228-3028 Office Phone: 941-383-0721. Business E-Mail: workman@appliedmechanicsincorporated.com.

**WORKMAN, JEROME JAMES, JR.,** chemist; b. Northfield, Minn., Aug. 6, 1952; s. Jerome James and Louise Mae (Sladek) W.; m. Rebecca Marie Zittel, Aug. 3, 1974; children: Cristina Louise, Stephannie Michelle, Daniel Jerome, Sara Marie, Michael Timothy. BA with honors, St. Mary's U., Winona, Minn., 1976, MA with distinction, 1980; PhD, Columbia Pacific U., San Rafael, Calif., 1984; grad. in Sr. Exec. Program, Columbia U., 2004, CBE, 2006; postgrad., MIT, 2001—, Columbia U., 2004—06. Prin. Workman & Assocs., Mankato, Minn., 1980-82; pres. Biochem. Cons., Mankato, Minn., 1982-84; sr. chemist Technicon Instruments, Tarrytown, NY, 1984-87; supervising scientist Bran & Luebbe/Technicon, Tarrytown, 1987; sr. scientist Hitachi Instruments, Danbury, Conn., 1987-89; mgr. tech. support NIR Systems/Perstorp Analytical, Silver Spring, Md., 1989-90; mgr. mktg., 1990-92, dir. mktg., 1992-93; assoc. advisor Inst. Textile Tech., Charlottesville, Va., 1992—; prin. scientist Perkin Elmer Corp., Norwalk, Conn., 1993-96; sr. tech. fellow Kimberly-Clark Corp., Analytical and Measurement Tech., Neenah, Wis., 1996—2002; chief tech. officer, v.p. rsch. and engring. Argose, Inc., Waltham, Mass., 2002—04; dir. rsch. and tech. Thermo Electron

Corp., Madison, Wis., 2004—. Instr. Fedn. Analytical Chemistry and Spectroscopy Socs.; external examiner U. Guelph, Ont., Can., 1993-94, chair rep. indsl. adv. bd. Ctr. for Process Analytical Chemistry 1993—2002; apptd. mem. subcom. on process analytical techs. U.S. FDA, 2002, vis. prof. 2002; mem. NRC panel U.S. Nat. Acads., 2003—. Author: Handbook of Organic Compounds: NIR, IR, Raman, and UV-Vis Spectra Featuring Polymers and Surfactants, 3 vols., 2000; co-author: Statistics in Spectroscopy, 1991, 2003, (series) Chemometrics in Spectroscopy, UV-Vis Spectroscopy, 1993, Near-Infrared Spectroscopy in Agr., 2003; editor: The Process Pages for NIRnews, Internat. Com. for Near Infrared Spectroscopy, 1993—97; co-editor: Applied Spectroscopy: A Compact Reference for Practitioners, 1998, Near-Infrared Reflectance Spectroscopy in Analysis of Agricultural Products, 2003, Spectroscopy Letters 1996-2002, 2003; contbg. editor: Spectroscopy Mag.; mem. adv. editl. bd. Spectroscopy, 1995—, assoc. editor Wiley-Intersci. Series in Lab. Automation, 1993, Applied Spectroscopy Reviews, 1995—2000, Lab. Robotics and Automation, 1995—98, process editor Jour. Near Infrared Spectroscopy, 1995—97; contbr. articles. Recipient Heart of Gold award Minn. affiliate Am. Heart Assn., 1984, Ea. Analytical Symposium award, 2002; Am. Heart Assn. H.N. and H.B. Shapira scholar, 1971-72; NSF grantee, 1977-78. Fellow: ASTM (exec. com., chair main com. on molecular spectroscopy, Award of Merit 2002, Appreciations award 2000, 2005), Am. Inst. Chemists, Royal Soc. Chemistry U.K. (chartered chemist, chartered scientist); mem.: Coblentz Soc. (bd. mgrs. 2002—), Joint Com. Atomic and Molecular Phys. Data (chmn. UV-VIS, exec. coun.), Coun. Near-Infrared Spectroscopy (pres.), Soc. for Applied Spectroscopy (Nat. Tour spkr. 2006), Am. Chem. Soc. (instr. course on Practical Near-IR Analysis), Nat. Honor Soc., Sigma Xi, Delta Epsilon Sigma. Achievements include research in molecular spectroscopy, statistics and chemometrics; development and applications of spectroscopic methods and sensors to consumer products and processes; U.S. and international patents for analytical systems. Office: Thermo Electron Corp 5225 Verona Rd Madison WI 53711 Office Phone: 608-276-5626. E-mail: jerry.workman@thermo.com.

**WORKMAN, JOHN MITCHELL,** chemist; b. Uniontown, Pa., Oct. 25, 1949; s. Hugh Lawrence and Mary Louise (Mitchell) W.; m. Gayle Sue Zappin, Nov. 20, 1987. BA in Psychology, Miami U., Oxford, Ohio, 1971; MS in Edn., Kans. State U., 1976; MS in Chemistry, U. Cin., 1985, PhD in Chemistry, 1987; MBA in Fin., Wright State U., 1995. Tchg. and rsch. asst. dept. chemistry Wright State U., Dayton, Ohio, 1977—81; grad. tchg. asst. U. Cin., 1982—83, grad. rsch. asst., 1983—86; sr. scientist Chemsys Inc., Fairborn, Ohio, 1986—89, dir. elemental analysis, 1989—, lab. dir., 1994—. Contbr. articles to jours. Analytical Chemistry, Applied Spectroscopy. With U.S. Army, 1972-75. Mem.: Soc. for Applied Spectroscopy, Am. Phys. Soc., Am. Chem. Soc., Sigma Iota Epsilon, Sigma Pi Sigma, Sigma Xi. Episcopalian. Personal E-mail: tacitfalcon@woh.rr.com.

**WORKMAN, JOHN P., JR.,** marketing professor; b. Wilmington, NC, Sept. 26, 1958; s. John P. and Elinor A. Workman; m. Jeanne Marie Bertch, June 19, 1993; children: Justina Suzanne, Juliana Leigh. BS, NC State U., 1980; MBA, U. Va., 1984; PhD, MIT, 1991. Product mktg. engr. Tex. Instruments, Johnson City, Tenn., 1980—82, field sales engr. Fairfax, Va., 1984—85; asst. prof. mktg. U. NC, Chapel Hill, 1991—98; assoc. prof. mktg. Creighton U., Omaha, 1998—2002, prof. mktg., 2003—. Expert witness Kutak Rock, Omaha, 2000—02; vis. fellow Jesuit Inst. at Boston Coll., 2005—06. Music min. St. Stephen the Martyr Ch., Omaha, 1998—; bd. dirs. Colleagues in SJ Bus. Edn., 2002—04. Recipient Best Paper award in mktg. strategy track, Am. Mktg. Assn., 1997, Best Paper of Yr. award, Jour. of Acad. Sci., 2000, Teacher of Yr., Creighton U. Coll. Bus., 2002, Outstanding Faculty award, 2003; Rsch. grant, Mktg. Sci. Inst., 1995, 1998. Mem.: Acad. Mgmt., Acad. Mktg. Sci., Am. Mktg. Assn. (mem. academic coun. 2000—02). Roman Catholic. Office Fax: 402-280-5565. Business E-Mail: workman@creighton.edu.

**WORKMAN, MICHAEL,** editor-in-chief, publishing executive, art critic; Bachelor's Degree, Northwestern U., 2001. Dir. Bridge NFP, Chgo.; pub., editor-in-chief Bridge Magazine, Chgo. Lectr. Sch. Art Inst. Chgo., Northwestern U.; presenter Chgo. Mus. Contemporary Art, Chgo. Humanities Festival. Writer (column on visual art) Eye Exam, NewCity, (catalog essays) Chgo. Cultural Ctr., Chgo. corr. Flash Art, art critic and commentator WBEZ-FM; contbr. fiction, journalism and critical writing appeared in New Art Examiner, Chgo. Reader, zingmagazine, TenbyTen, Contemporary Mag. Mem.: Chgo. Art Critics Assn. Office: c/o Bridge Magazine 119 N Peoria #3D Chicago IL 60607 Office Phone: 312-421-2227. Business E-Mail: mworkman@bridgemagazine.org.

**WORKMAN, NORMAN ALLAN,** accountant, management consultant; b. Boston, Apr. 20, 1918; s. William Horace and Estelle Emily (Hanlon) W.; m. Harriet Patricia Banfield, Aug. 1, 1946; children: Stephen, Mark, Brian, Patricia. Student, Coll. William and Mary, 1938-39; BS in Econs. magna cum laude, Bowdoin Coll., 1941. CPA, Oreg. Staff acct. Lybrand Ross Bros. & Montgomery, Boston, 1941-43, Whitfield Stratford & Co., Portland, Oreg., 1946-51; ptnr. Workman, Shephard & Co., CPAs, Portland, 1951-60; sole practitioner Portland, 1961-96; ret. Dir. Iron Fireman Mfg. Co., 1953—56, Electronic Specialty Co., 1956—65. Newsletter columnist Good Impressions, 1993-98. Chmn. bd. Sylvan Fire Bd., 1953-55, Sylvan Sch., Portland, 1956-57; pres. Doernbecher Children's Hosp. Found., Portland, 1963-85, Bowdoin Club Oreg., Portland, 1963—; trustee Oreg. Episcopal Schs., Portland, 1974-76. Lt. (j.g.) Supply Corps, USNR, 1944-46. Named Mr. Doernbecher, Doernbecher Children's Hosp. Found., 2002. Mem. AICPA, Inst. Mgmt. Accts. (pres. Portland chpt. 1954-55), Oreg. Soc. CPA's, Pacific Printing and Imaging Assn., Arlington Club, Multnomah Athletic Club, Phi Beta Kappa. Avocations: bird hunting, fishing, horticulture. Home: 4381 SW Fairview Blvd Portland OR 97221-2709

**WORKMAN, SHARON JOY,** journalist; b. Louisa, Ky., May 20, 1930; d. Charlie B. Workman and Jessie Virginia Beaire; children: Patrick Corsiglia, Joan Corsiglia, James Corsiglia, Cynthia Corsiglia. BA, Marshall Coll., 1952; MA in Lit., Oxford U., Eng., 1990; MA in Creative Writing, Dartmouth Coll., 1992. Feature writer The Herald-Advertiser, Huntington, W.Va., 1951—52; mil. intelligence analyst Hdqrs. US Armed Forces Far East, Psychol. Warfare Sect., Japan, 1952—54; reporter Life Mag., NYC, 1954—59, People Mag., NYC, 1974—88. Mem.: DAR, TIME-LIFE Alumni Assn., Dartmouth Club, Overseas Press Club, The Coll. Club of Boston, The Tokeneke Club. Republican. Meth. Avocations: travel, swimming, opera, museums, concerts. Home: 9 Hale Ln Darien CT 06820 Personal E-mail: sharonworkman@aol.com.

**WORKMAN, WILLARD ALLYN,** association executive; b. Milford, Del., Oct. 30, 1946; s. Willard Harold and Louise Elizabeth Workman; 1 child, Amanda. BA in Polit. Sci., L.I. U., 1969. Spl. negotiator internat. trade controls Dept. State, Washington, 1987-88; v.p., gen. mgr. internat. U.S.C. of C., Washington, 1988-2001, sr. v.p. Internat. Affairs, 2001—. V.p. Ctr. Internat. Pvt. Enterprise, Washington, 1992; trustee U.S. Coun. for Internat. Bus., N.Y.C., 1993-2001. With USN, 1969-73. Mem. Univ. Club. E-mail: wworkman@uschamber.com.

**WORLEY, APRIL COLE,** artist, grant writer; b. Santa Barbara, Calif., Dec. 17, 1976; d. John E. Colgan and Susan Valerie Geoghegan; m. Peter Ryan Worley, June 10, 2001. BA in Humanities, New Coll. Calif., 2001. Grant writer Nimbus Grants, San Luis Obispo, Calif., 2004—. Editor: COLD mag.; contbr. articles to profl. jours.; contbg. writer Violet Mag., 2005, Ctrl. Coast Mag., 2006; author: Road, 2002, The Underling, 2003, Women and Their Bikes, 2005. Avocations: riding motorcycles, photography, silk screening, hiking, dancing. E-mail: apemayhem@hotmail.com.

**WORLEY, DEBERE,** educational consultant; b. Toledo, Apr. 22, 1953; d. Thomas Daniel and Dorothy Mae Worley. BS in Edn., Bowling Green State U., 1976; MS in Edn., U. Toledo, 1990. Cert. tchr. Ohio. Tchr. Toledo Pub.

Schs., 1977—; rehab. technician Lucas County, Toledo, summers 83-85; ednl. cons. State Tchrs. Ret. Sys., Columbus, Ohio, 96-98, 99—; mem. pres.'s coun. Avon Products, Inc., Atlanta, 1997-98. Grad. asst. U. Toledo, 1988—89, Bowling Green State U., 1995—96. Actor: Godmother: The Late Dr. Ella P. Stewart, Goodwill Ambassador United States of America 1950-60, (poems) Dreams Really Do Come Tru, 1999. Scholar, U. Toledo, 1988—89, Bowling Green State U., 1995—96. Avocations: crafts, home decorating, gardening, home repair, collecting collectibles and restoring antiques. Office Phone: 419-917-2380. E-mail: dlworley@buckeyeexpress.com.

**WORLEY, DONALD LEE,** quality assurance professional; b. Bristol, Tenn., Oct. 28, 1973; s. Douglas Melvin and Wilma Sue Worley; m. Melissa Kaye Lewis, Apr. 7, 2001; 1 child, Jackson Robert. BS in Indsl. Tech., Tenn. Technol. U., 1998. Quality mgr. Moll Industries, Inc., Morristown, Tenn., 1999—99, P & S Engineered Plastics, Inc., Knoxville, 1999—2001, Techni-mark, Inc., Fayetteville, NC, 2002—03, Kamco Plastics, Inc., Florence, SC, 2003—. Mem.: Am. Soc. Quality (sr.), Tau Kappa Epsilon (life; bd. advisors Mu Omicron Chpt 1993—2001, chpt. advisor 2001—02). Democrat. Avocations: woodworking, remodeling homes, mentoring college students, collecting and restoring antique / classic automobiles. Office Phone: 843-679-0347. Personal E-mail: donaldleeworley@hotmail.com.

**WORLEY, LLOYD DOUGLAS,** language educator; b. Lafayette, La., Sept. 11, 1946; s. Albert Stiles and Doris (Christy) W.; m. Maydean Ann Mouton, Apr. 4, 1966; children: Erin Shawn, Albert Stiles II. BA, U. SW La., 1968, MA, 1972; PhD, So. Ill. U., 1979. Ordained priest, Liberal Cath. Ch., 1977, consecrated aux. bishop, 2005. Tchr. Lafayette H.S., 1969-74; vis. asst. prof. dept. English So. Ill. U., Carbondale, 1979-80; asst. prof. dept. English Pa. State U., DuBois, 1980-87; assoc. prof., assoc. dir. composition dept. English U. No. Colo., Greeley, 1987-88, prof. dept. English, 1988—, chair dept. English, 1988—90. Acting dir. Writing Component Ctr. Basic Skills, So. Ill. U., 1980. Editor: Ruthven Literary Bull., 1988-92; contbr. book chpts., articles. Rector Parish of St. Albertus Magnus The Liberal Cath. Ch., 1987-2001, sec-treas. Am. Province; provost Am. Clerical Synod Chpt. The Liberal Cath. Ch., 1991-2001; Sovereign Grand Master, Order of Holy Sepulchre, 1982-; vicar-gen. Decorated Knight Bachelor, 1996, Hereditary Knight of San Luigi, 1996, Knight Cmdr. Order of Merit St. Angilbert, 1993, Prelate Comdr. Order of Noble Companions of Swan, 1993, Grand Chamberlain, 1995, Knight Order of Guadalupe, 1995, Knight Comdr. Justice Sovereign Order St. John, Knight Grand Cross of Bear of Alabona, 1995, Knight Grand Cross Order St. Stanislaus, 1998, Knight Comp. Crown of Alabona, 1998, Knight Grand Cross Order St. John, 1998, Knight Grand Cross Order Sts. Constantine the Great and Helen, Knight Grand Cross of Justice Ordine dei Cavalieri Lauretani, Grand Cross with Collar of Order of Noble Companion of Swan, 2000 Grand Cross of Justice, Sovrano Ordine Militare ed Ospitaliero di S.Maria di Gerusalemme Teutonico di Svevia; created hereditary Baron, Royal and Serene House of Alabona-Ostrogojsk et de Garama, HRSH Prince William I, created Count Palatine of Maxalla, 1996, created Hereditary Duke of Maxalla, 2000. Fellow Philalethes Soc.; mem. ASCD, Internat. Assn. for Fantastic in Arts (divsn. head Am. Lit. 1987-93), Lord Ruthven Assembly (pres. 1988-94, founding pres. emeritus 1994), Conf. Coll. Composition and Commn., Nat. Coun. Tchrs. English, Am. Conf. Irish Studies, Sigma Tau Delta (bd. dirs. 1990-96, high plains regent various states 1992-96, 10-Yr. Outstanding Advisor award 1997), Masons (century lodge #190), Order of DeMolay (chevalier, cross of honor, legion of honor), Knights Holy Sepulchre (Sov. Grand Master), Rose Croix Martinist Order (pres. premier nat. coun.). Democrat. Office: 3620 W 10th B-150 Greeley CO 80634-9655 Office Phone: 970-357-2942. Office Fax: 266-350-2268. Business E-Mail: prof@profw.com.

**WORLEY, MICHELLE LYNN,** music educator; b. Fairmont, W.Va., Jan. 11, 1975; d. Kenneth Eugene and Susan Kay (King) Conrad; m. Paul DeWayne Worley. BA in Music Edn., Fairmont (W.Va.) State Coll., 1998. Tchr. gen. and choral music Hallsboro Middle Sch., Hallsboro, NC, 1999—2003; tchr. gen. and choral music Acme-Delco Middle Sch., Delco, NC, 1999—2003; gen. music tchr. Benson (NC) Elem. Sch., 2003—. Private tchr. piano, Whiteville, NC, 1999—2003. Mem. Ctrl. Baptist Ch., Dunn, NC, 2003—; mem. ch. music com. Christian and Missionary Alliance Ch., Whiteville, NC, 1999—2003. Named New Student Orientation Counselor, Fairmont State Coll., 1994-1997. Mem.: N.C. Assn. Educators, N.C. Music Educators Assn., Music Educators' Nat. Conf., Sigma Alpha Iota (life; v.p. rituals 1994—97). Avocations: piano, reading.

**WORLEY, NANCY L.,** state official; b. Madison County, Ala., Nov. 7, 1951; d. Leonard O. and Lillian (Smith) W. BA magna cum laude, U. Montevallo, Ala., 1973; MA, Jacksonville (Ala.) State U., 1974; postgrad., U. Ala., Tuscaloosa and Huntsville, 1974, U. Edinburgh, Scotland, 1975. Cert. English, speech and Latin tchr., Ala. Instr. English, NE State Jr. Coll., Rainsville, Ala., Calhoun Community Coll., Decatur, Ala.; tchr. lang. arts Decatur City Schs.; sec. of state State of Ala., Montgomery, 2003—. Former mem. Governor's Task Force on Welfare Reform, Governor's Task Force on Education Reform. Contbr. articles to profl. jours. Named Ala.'s Outstanding Young Educator, Dist. Tchr. of Yr., Decatur City Schs.; grantee grantee UN. Mem. NEA, Ala. Edn. Assn. (pres., 1983-84, 95-97, legis. com.), Ala. Fgn. Lang. Tchrs. Assn. (past pres.), Ala. Classroom Tchrs. Assn. (past pres., bd. dirs.), Sigma Tau Delta, Kappa Delta Pi, Lambda Sigma Chi, Omicron Delta Kappa. Office: Office of Sec of State State House 600 Dexter Ave Montgomery AL 36104 Office Phone: 334-242-7205. Office Fax: 334-242-4993. E-mail: nworley@sos.al.gov.*

**WORLEY, RICHARD ALAN,** music educator; b. Hanover, Pa., Jan. 16, 1967; s. William Jacob and Charlotte Ruth (Bubb) Worley; m. Amy Marie Schnetzler, Dec. 16, 1989; children: Keegan Scott, Seth Patrick. MusB, U. Cin., 1990; MS, Towson U., 1999. Profl. tchg. II cert. Pa. Dept. Edn. Music dir. Archbishop Muhluhulm N.J., Cin., 1991—92 ; local dir. asst. band dir. Three Rivers Local Sch. Dist., Cin., 1992—93; band dir. West York (Pa.) Area Sch. Dist., 1993—2003, Ctrl. York Area Sch. Dist., 2003—. Freelance percussionist, musician, Pa., 1993—; percussionist, extra Harrisburg (Pa.) Symphony Orch., 1993—98; percussionist York Symphony Orch., 1996—2004. Coach, instr., site dir. Tennis for Kids, York, 2001—04; coach Spring Grove (Pa.) Youth Baseball, 2005—; den leader pack 92 Cub Scouts, Thomasville, Pa., 2003—06. Profl. Growth grantee, Ctrl. York Sch. Dist., 2005. Mem.: NEA, Pa. Music Edn. Assn. (guest condr. Dist. 7 Elem. Band Fest 1998), Music Educators Nat. Conf. Avocations: tennis, camping, hiking. Home: 233 Melinda Dr York PA 17404 Office: Ctrl York Middle Sch 1950 N Hills Rd York PA 17402 Business E-Mail: rworley@cysd.k12.pa.us.

**WORLEY, RICHARD B.,** financial consultant; b. 1945; m. Leslie Anne Miller. Grad., U. Tenn. Chmn. Miller Anderson & Sherrerd; CEO, chief investment officer Morgan Stanley Investment Mgmt.; now mng. dir. Permit Capital Group LLC, 2002—. Bd. trustees Putnam Investments, 2004—. Trustee Med. Ctr. of U. Pa., Colonial Williamsburg Found., The Robert Wood Johnson Found., Princeton, NJ, 2000—; mem. investment com. Phila. Orchestra. Office: Permit Capital Group LLC 100 Front St West Conshohocken PA 19428*

**WORLEY, ROBERT BRUCE, JR.,** lawyer; b. Mobile, Ala., Mar. 9, 1960; s. Robert Bruce and Linda (Edgar) Worley; m. Catherine Anna Steck, Nov. 14, 1987; children: Nancy Jane, Catherine Turner. BBA with honors and distinction, U. Tex., 1982; JD, Tulane U., 1985. Bar: La. 1985, Tex. 2003, U.S. Dist. Ct. (ea. dist. La.) 1985, U.S. Dist. Ct. (mid. dist. La.) 1986, U.S. Dist. Ct. (we. dist. La.) 1988, U.S. Dist. Ct. (ea. dist. Ark.) 1996, U.S. Dist. Ct. (we. dist. Ark.) 1996, U.S. Dist. Ct. (ea. dist. Ill.) 1997, U.S. Dist. Ct. (so. dist. Tex.) 2001, U.S. Dist. Ct. (ea. dist. Tex.) 2001, U.S. Ct. Appeals (5th cir.) 1990, U.S. Ct. Appeals (4th cir.) 1990, U.S. Ct. Appeals (6th cir.) 1996, U.S. Ct. Appeals (7th cir.) 1997, U.S. Ct. Appeals (11th cir.) 1998, U.S. Ct. Appeals (8th cir.) 1999, U.S. Supreme Ct. 1997. Assoc. Gelpi, Sullivan, Carroll and Laborde, New Orleans, 1985—88; ptnr. Kullman Firm, New Orleans, 1988—99, Jones, Walker, Waechter, Poitevent, Carrere & Denegre, New Orleans, 1999—. Chmn. profl. employment com. Jones Walker et al, New

Orleans, 2001—04, chmn. United Way, 2000—. Mem., pres. New Orleans Area Habitat for Humanity Bd.; co-chair lawyers com. New Orleans United Way Campaign, 2003; chmn. La. Jr. Tennis Coun.; bd. dirs. La. Tennis Assn.; pres. ch. coun. Rayne Meml. United Meth. Ch. Named One of Best Labor and Employment Lawyers, New Orleans Mag., 2005; recipient, 2006, Leadership in Law award, City Business, 2006. Mem.: ABA, Am. Inns Ct., Coll. Master Adv. and Barristers, New Orleans Bar Assn., La. State Bar Assn. Avocations: tennis, swimming, fishing. Office: Jones Walker et al 201 St Charles Ave New Orleans LA 70170-5100 Office Phone: 504-582-8192. Office Fax: 504-589-8192. Business E-Mail: rworley@joneswalker.com.

**WORLEY, ROBERT MICHAEL,** criminologist, educator; b. Dallas, Tex., Jan. 6, 1976; s. Bob Worley and Linda Irene Gisi. BA in Gov., U. Tex., Austin, 1996; MA, Sam Houston State U., Huntsville, 2001, PhD in Criminal Justice, 2006. Correctional officer Tex. Dept. Criminal Justice, Huntsville, Tex., 1998—2005; lectr. criminal justice Sam Houston State U., Huntsville, 2003—06; asst. prof. criminal justice U. Tex. of Permian Basin, Odessa, 2006—. Contbr. articles various prof. jours. Pub. com. Am. Soc. Criminology, 2006; beto chair Grad. Student Orgn., Huntsville, 2004—05, social coord., 2005—06. Recipient Student Rsch. Paper Competition award, Southwestern Assn. Criminal Justice, 2004, Outstanding Leadership award, 2005, 2006; Grad. scholarship, 2004, Timothy Flanagan scholarship, 2000. Mem.: Southwestern Assn. Criminal Justice (assoc.), Acad. Criminal Justice Scis. (assoc.), Am. Soc. Criminology (assoc.). Avocations: travel, exercise, outdoors, writing, music. Office: U Tex of Permian Basin Dept Behavioral Sci 4901 E University Odessa TX 79762 Office Phone: 936-577-0973. Business E-Mail: stdrmw11@shsu.edu.

**WORLEY, ROBERT WILLIAM, JR.,** retired lawyer; b. Anderson, Ind., June 13, 1935; s. Robert William and Dorothy Mayhew (Hayler) W.; m. Diana Lynn Matthews, Aug. 22, 1959; children: Nathanael, Hope Hillegas. BS in Chem. Engring., Lehigh U., 1956; LLB, Harvard U., 1960. Bar: Conn. 1960, U.S. Supreme Ct. 1966, Fla. 1977. Assoc. then ptnr. Cummings & Lockwood, Stamford, Conn., 1960-91; gen. counsel Consol. Asset Recover Corp. sub. Chase Manhattan Corp., Bridgeport, Conn., 1991-94; v.p., asst. gen. counsel The Chase Manhattan Bank, N.Y.C., 1994-2001; ret., 2001. Trustees com. on bequests and trusts Lehigh U., 1979—; mem. Conn. Legis. Task Force on Probate Court Sys., 1991-93; chmn. Greenwich Arts Coun., 1981-82; v.p., bd. dirs. Greenwich Choral Soc., 1962-77, 80; bd. dirs. Greenwich Ctr. for Chamber Music, 1981-85, Greenwich Symphony, 1986-89; commr. Greenwich Housing Authority, 1972-77; bldg. com. for sr. ctr. Greenwich Bd. Selectman, 1980-81. Capt. JAGC, AUS, 1965. Mem. Conn. Bar Assn. (exec. com. probate sect. 1980), Sippican Choral Soc., Harvard Club Boston. Christian Scientist. Home: PO Box 1055 Marion MA 02738-0019

**WORMAN, HOWARD JAY,** internist, educator; b. Paterson, NJ, May 21, 1959; s. Louis and Dora (Rubin) W. BA, Cornell U., 1981; MD, U. Chgo., 1985. Diplomate Am. Bd. Internal Medicine. Intern NY Hosp., NYC, 1985—86, resident, 1986—87; guest investigator Rockefeller U., NYC, 1987—90; asst. prof. Mt. Sinai Sch. Medicine, NYC, 1990—94; asst. attending physician Mt. Sinai Hosp., NYC, 1990—94; asst. prof. Columbia U. Coll. Physicians and Surgeons, NYC, 1995—98, assoc. prof., 1998—; asst. attending physician NY Presbyn. Hosp., Columbia-U. Med. Ctr., NYC, 1995—98, assoc. attending physician, 1998—; dir. divsn. digestive and liver diseases Presbyn. Hosp., NYC, 1999—2002. Mem. med. adv. com. Muscular Dystrophy Assn., 2000—05. Mem. editl. bd. Hepatology, Frontiers in Biosci., World Jour. Gastroenterology, Biomed. Ctrl. Cell Biology, Molecular Biology of the Cell; mem. bd. reviewing editors Molecular Biology of the Cell; contbr. articles to profl. jours. Recipient Physician-Scientist award NIH, 1987-92; Charles E. Culpeper scholar in Med. Scis., 1994-95, Irma T. Hirschl scholar, 1997-2002. Mem. AAAS, ACP, Am. Chem. Soc., Am. Fedn. Med. Rsch. (Trainee award in clin. rsch. 1989, Henry Christian award 1990), Am. Soc. Cell Biology, Am. Assn. Study of Liver Diseases, Am. Gastroent. Assn., Am. Soc. Clin. Investigation, N.Y. Acad. Scis. (vice chmn. biol. scis. sect. 1992-93, chmn. 1993-94), Am. Diabetes Assn., Hon. Order Ky. Cols., Phi Beta Kappa. Democrat. Jewish. Avocations: music, reading. Office: Columbia U Coll Physicians-Surgeons 630 W 168th St New York NY 10032-3795 Business E-Mail: hjwl4@columbia.edu.

**WORMER, THOMAS ANDREW,** surgeon; b. Buffalo, Dec. 3, 1956; s. Donald Andrew and Elinor Ann (Bliss) W.; m. Melissa Jane Ertell, Apr. 11, 1988; children: Matthew Thomas, Margaret Elizabeth, Samuel James, Sarah Jane. BS, Allegheny Coll., 1978; MD, Albany Med. Coll., 1984. Diplomate Am. Bd. Surgery. Intern Millard Fillmore Hosp., Buffalo, 1984—85, resident in gen. surgery, 1985—89; attending surgeon F.F. Thompson Hosp., Canandaigua, NY, 1989—95, chief surgery, 1994—99. Fellow ACS; mem. Canandaigua Med. Soc. (pres. 1994), N.Y. State Med. Soc. Presbyterian. Office: Canandaigua Medical Group 335 Parrish St Canandaigua NY 14424-1794 E-mail: twormer@rochester.rr.com.

**WORMHOUDT, PEARL SHINN,** voice educator, writer; b. Knoxville, Iowa, Oct. 27, 1915; d. Joda Horace and Marie (vander Beek) Shinn; m. Arthur Louis Wormhoudt, Nov. 24, 1948; 1 child, Joda. BA, Cen. Coll., 1936; studies with Douglas Stanley, N.Y.C., 1942-48, MA, Columbia U., 1945; studies with Paola Novikova, N.Y.C., 1965-67. Dir. girls work Garibaldi Inst., Chgo., 1936-37; sec. to dir. weekday religious edn. Protestant Council, N.Y.C., 1937-43; recreational program worker N.Y.C. YWCAs, 1943-49; assoc. prof. fine arts William Penn Coll., Oskaloosa, Iowa, 1958-81, prof. emeritus, 1981, adj. prof. voice, 1985-92; pvt. voice tchr., 1992—. Condr. master classes in univs. various colls. and univs., Iowa, Ohio and Minn.; lectr. 1991; curator William Penn Coll. Mid-East Art Gallery, 1976-97. Author: Building the Voice as an Instrument, 1981, With a Song in My Psyche, On the Psychology of Singing and Teaching Singing, 2002; contbr. articles to profl. jours. Grantee Schepp Found., 1943-45. Mem AAUW (corp. rep, 1960-84), Nat. Assn. Tchrs. of Singing (hon., life, gov. Iowa 1986-88), internat. Congress Voice Tchrs. (program chmn. 1987), Am. Acad. Tchrs. Singing, Delta Kappa Gamma. Democrat. Avocations: studying psychology, reading, walking, opera, dance. Home: 1 Pennsylvania Pl Apt 1 Ottumwa IA 52501-2173 Office Phone: 641-684-8795. Personal E-mail: psw102@hotmail.com.

**WORMSER, SHERRI LYNNE,** pediatric physical therapist; b. Cleve., Apr. 23, 1968; d. Samuel J. and Mary Ann (Lee) W. BS in Phys. Therapy, NYU, 1992. Lic. phys. therapist, Ariz. Pediat. phys. therapist N.Y.C. Pub. Schs., 1992-93, Tuba City (Ariz.) Unified Sch. Dist., 1993—, Indian Health Svc., Tuba City, 1995—; phys. therapist Chinle (Ariz.) Comprehensive Health Care Facility, 1993-95. Lt. (j.g.) USPHS, 1993-95. Navajo Nation grantee, 1996. Avocations: hiking, camping, biking, climbing, outdoor activities.

**WORNALL, ILAH RUTH (RUTHIE),** publishing executive, educator; b. Harrison, Ark., Dec. 29, 1941; d. William Curtis and Velora Delia (Copeland) Davis; m. James Frederick Wornall, Nov. 23, 1974; children: Desirée Blythe, John Bristow V. BS in Edn., Central Mo. State U., 1963, MS in Edn., 1971, cert. edn. specialist, 1976. Tchr. Consolidated Sch. Dist #2, Raytown, Mo., 1963—80; owner Wornall Publ. Co., Overland Park, Kans., 1988—. ESOL tchr. Emmanuel Bapt. Ch., 1999—2000, 2002—03. Author: Three Ingredient Cookbook, Vol. I, 1988, Three Ingredient Cookbook, Vol. II, 1990; columnist Weston Chronicle News, 1991—; author: Three Ingredient Cookbook, Vol. III, 1991, Three Ingredient Low Cholesterol Cookbook, 1991, Three Ingredient Party Cookbook, 1992, Three Ingredient Main Dish Cookbook, 1993, Two Ingredient Cookbook, 1994, Three Ingredient Low Fat Cookbook, 1995, Three Ingredient Low Sugar Cookbook, 1996, Best of the Three Ingredient Cookbooks, 1996, The Three Ingredient Dieters Cookbook, 1997, (novels) Murder in San Miguel, 1998, Murder in Guanajuato, 1998, Murder at the University of Guanajuato, 1999, Microwave Three Ingredient Cookbook, 2001, The Best of Cooking with 3 ingredients, 2002, 3 - Ingredient Recipes for College Students, 2005; contbr. articles to profl. jours., local newspapers. Vol. at nursing homes, 1986—. Mem.: DAR, Ret. Raytown Tchrs. Club, Mystery Lovers Bookclub, Rainbow Connection. Republican. Baptist. Avo-

cations: horseback riding, reading, writing, singing, interior decorating. Office: Wornall Publ Co 9800 W 104th St Overland Park KS 66212 Office Phone: 913-888-1530. Personal E-mail: wornall3@aol.com.

**WORNER, THERESA MARIE,** internist, educator; b. Breckenridge, Minn., Feb. 19, 1948; d. William Daniel and Elizabeth (Stelten) W.; m. Martin Herbst, Mar. 24, 1979. AB, St. Theresa Coll., 1970; MD, U. Minn., 1974. Diplomate Am. Bd. Internal Medicine. Rotating intern Kings County Hosp., Bklyn., 1974-75, resident medicine, 1975-77; fellow VA Med. Ctr., Bronx, NY, 1977-78, chief med. sect. Alcoholism treatment program, 1978-87; asst. prof. medicine Mt. Sinai Sch. Medicine, N.Y.C., 1984-87; mem. faculty Postgrad. Ctr., 1985-90; physician in charge alcoholism svcs. L.I. Coll. Hosp., Bklyn., 1987-92; assoc. prof. clin. medicine SUNY, Health Sci. Ctr., Bklyn., 1988—; dir. rsch. 32BJ Health Fund, 1992-99; clin. assoc. prof. Pub. Health Cornell U. Med. Coll., 1996—; pres. Menachem Publ., Bethlehem, NH, 1999—. Pres./founder Alcohol, Info. 1995-97; advisor Patient Care Mag., 1984—; cons. REA, 1996—. Referee Hepatology, 1986, Jour. Study Alcohol, 1984—, Substance Abuse, 1992—, Alcoholism: Clinical and Exptl. Rsch., 1992—, Drug and Alcohol Dependence, 1993—, Drug Therapy, 1994—, Addiction, 1996—; contbr. numerous articles to profl. jours. Active Israel Mus., Israeli Opera, Israel Symphony. Grantee Child Welfare Adminstrn., 1991, 92, 93; recipient Physicians Recognition award AMA, 1984, 89, 91, 96, Cert. of Merit Govt. Employees Ins. Co., 1986, PACT Intern Site award, 1991, 92. Fellow ACP, N.Y. Acad. Medicine; mem. AAAS, Am. Med. Soc. on Alcoholism and Other Drug Dependence, Am. Soc. Internal Medicine, Am. Assn. for Study Liver Diseases (Travel award 1978), N.Y. Acad. Scis., Rsch. Soc. on Alcoholism, Internat. Soc. Biologic Rsch. in Alcoholism.

**WORONOFF, ISRAEL,** former psychology educator; b. Bklyn., Dec. 30, 1926; s. Samuel and Lena (Silberman) W.; m. Fay Goldberg, Feb. 11, 1950; 1 child, Gary. AB in Psychology, U. Mich., 1949, MA in Sociology, 1952, PhD in Edn., 1954. Lic. psychologist, Mich. Instr. Flint (Mich.) Jr. Coll., 1953-54; asst. prof. St. Cloud (Minn.) State Coll., 1954-56, Ea. Mich. U., Ypsilanti, 1956-59, assoc. prof., 1959-62, prof., 1962-92, prof. emeritus. Cons. psychologist Midwest Mental Health Clinic, Dearborn, Mich., 1978-83, Orchard Hills Psychiat. Ctr., Novi, Mich., 1983—; mem. Bd. Jewish Fedn. Washtenaw Cmty., 1997-2003; co-chair Bd. Jewish Family Svc. of Ann Arbor, 1997. Author: Educator's Guide to Stress Management, 1986. Mem. bd. Jewish Family Svc. of Ann Arbor, 1996—; mem. cmty. rels. com. Jewish Cmty. Assn., Ann Arbor, Mich., 1990-92; v.p. edn. Beth Israel Congregation, Ann Arbor, 1985-87; mem. adv. bd. Mich. Anti-Defamation League of B'nai B'rith, 1958—. Mem. APA, Mich. Psychol. Assn. Democrat. Home: 2519 Londonderry Rd Ann Arbor MI 48104-4017

**WORONOV, MARY PETER,** actress; b. Bklyn., Dec. 8, 1946; d. Victor D. and Carol W.; m. Ted Gershuny, 1969 (div.); m. Ted Whitehead, 1979. Student, Cornell Univ., 1964—68. Actor: (films) The Chelsea Girls, 1967, Death Race 2000, 1975, Rock 'n' Roll High School, 1979, Eating Raoul, 1982, Black Widow, 1987, Warlock, 1989, Good Girls Don't, 1995, The Munster's Scary Little Christmas, 1996, Invisible Mom II, 1999, New Women, 2001; (TV series) Logan's Run, 1977, Sledge Hammer!, 1987; (TV films) Challenge of a Lifetime, 1985, (TV spl.) Cheech and Chong's Get Out of My Room, 1985, (stage prodns.) Kitchenette, 1968, Boom Boom Room, 1974; author: Wake for the Angels: Paintings and Stories, 1994, Swimming Underground: My Years in the Warhol Factory, 1995, Snake, 2000, Niagara, 2002, Eyewitness to Warhol, 2002, Blind Love, 2004; dir.: (TV show) Little Vampire, Blind Love, The Gigolo. Avocation: painting.

**WORRALL, JOHN DENNIS,** economics professor, consultant, writer; b. Wildwood, N.J., July 29, 1942; s. John and Adele Veronica (McKenna) W.; m. Suzanne Elizabeth Hopkins; children: Heather, John; m. Janet Priscilla Moran; 1 child, Kevin. BA, Rutgers U., 1969, MA, 1972, PhD, 1978. Asst. dir. Rutgers Bur. Econ. Rsch., New Brunswick, NJ, 1974-77; dir. rsch. Nat. Ctr. for Employment Handicapped-Human Resources Ctr., L.I., NY, 1977-78; v.p., dir. econ. rsch. NCCI, N.Y.C., 1979-83; prof. econs. Rutgers U., Camden, NJ, 1983—; asst. dir. Bur. Econ. Rsch. New Brunswick, NJ, 1983—. Advisor Courier Post newspaper, Camden, 1994-97; John R. Commons lectr. U. Wis. Bus. Sch., Madison, 1991. Co-author: An Evaluation of Policy Related Rehabilitation Research, 1975; co-editor: Placement in Rehabilitation, 1979, Benefit Issues in Workers' Compensation, 1985; editor: Safety and the Workforce, 1983; assoc. editor Jour. Risk and Ins., 1990-2000, Jour. Risk and Ins., 1992—. Del. White House Conf. on Handicapped, Washington, 1977; pres. South Jersey Irish Am. Unity Conf., Fedn. Irish Am. Socs., Phila., 1996-98; bd. dirs. St. Patrick's Day Observance Com., Phila., 1996-98, Phila. Immigration Resource Ctr., 1999-2001. Sgt. U.S. Army, 1960-66. Named Outstanding Faculty Mem. Rutgers U. Alumni Assn., 1991; honoree Gaelic Ball, Ladies Ancient Order Hibernians, Phila., 1998. Fellow Risk Theory Soc. (sec. 1990, pres. 1991); mem. Nat. Acad. Social Ins., Am. Econs. Assn., Am. Risk and Ins. Assn. (Robert I. Mehr award 2001), Commodore John Barry Soc. (pres. 1996-98). Roman Catholic. Avocations: golf, fishing. Office: Rutgers U Armitage Hall Camden NJ 08102 Office Phone: 856-225-6290. Business E-Mail: jworrall@crab.rutgers.edu.

**WORRELL, CYNTHIA LEE,** bank executive; b. Moncton, N.B., Can., May 27, 1957; came to U.S., 1979; d. Ronald William and Audrey Helen (Crothers) Jones; m. Geoffrey H. Worrell, Sept. 1, 1979; children: Lindsay Andrea, Geoffrey Andrew, Ashley Taylor. Student, U. New Brunswick, Fredericton, 1979. Lic. real estate broker, Mass., Pa., Calif. Instr. New Brunswick C.C., Fredericton, N.B., Canada, 1978-79, Massasoit C.C., Brockton, Mass., 1981-82, Brockton Cmty. Schs., 1981-82; regional mgr. and instr. Worldwide Ednl. Svcs., Clifton, NJ, program dir. Taunton, Mass., 1995; procedures and documentation analyst Capital Blue Cross, Harrisburg, Pa., 1985; v.p., sr. mgr. Comfed Mortgage Co. Inc. Mass., 1985-90; sr. residential loan officer Bank of Am., Santa Clara, Calif., 1990-92; regional sales mgr., v.p. Shearson Lehman Mortgage, San Jose, Calif., 1992-93; br. mgr. Cypress Fin., San Jose, 1993-94, PNC Mortgage Corp. Am., San Jose, 1994—; program dir. worldwide Ednl. Svcs., Taunton, Mass., 1995; area prodn. mgr. Plymouth Mortgage Co., Foxborough, Mass., 1995-96, Ameriquest Mortgage, Hingham, Mass., 1996-97; br. mgr. Bank United of Tex. Commonwealth United Mortgage, West Bridgewater, Mass., 1996—; br. mgr. Nat. City Mortgage-Commonwealth United Mortgage, 1997-98, Family Choice Mortgage, West Bridgewater, 1998—2000, Orchard Mortgage, Raynham, Mass., 2000—06; asst. v.p., br. mgr. Sallie Mae Home Loans, West Wareham, Mass., 2006—. Guest spkr. numerous trade shows, real estate bd. seminars, cmty. workshops, stress mgmt. personal profiles, motivational speaking and workshops; instr. mortgage banking Calif. State U., Hayward, 1994—; mem. adv. bd., instr. outside cons. Calif. State U. Ext. divsn., 1993-95; cert. trainer Carlson Learning Co., 1993—; trainer in diversity, conflict resolution, sexual harassment, and time mgmt.; cmty. trainer WCR, BPW, Old Colony Vocat. Schs., Wareham H.S., Wareham Mid. and Elem. Schs., Wareham Supts. Office, Fall River Sch. Dist., Old Rochester Jr. and Sr. H.S., Bristol County Tng. Consortium, and Transitional Assistance, Bridgewater Cmty., Wareham Foster Parents, Wareham Decas Sch., 1996—. Mem. editl. bd. Mortgage Originator, 1995; contbr. articles to profl. jours. Vol. Handi Kids, Bridgewater, Mass., 1985—90, Fremont/Newark YMCA youth basketball and soccer; active Forest Park PTA, Self-Def. Inst. Tau Kwon Do Club; donor Berwick Boys Club; mem. adv. com. Wareham H.S.; mem. coun.; alumni dir. U. New Brunswick, 1998—; bd. dirs. Wareham Childcare; trustee Le Lycee Internat. de la Nouvelle Angleterre, Inc., Boston, 1997; trustee, chair Tabor Acad., Marion, Mass. Named to IBC 200 Women of Achievement, 1991-92, ABI 2000 Notable Women, 1991-92,ABI Personalities of Am., 1992, Internat. Order of Merit, 1992, The World Found. of Successful Women, 1992, Outstanding Young Women in Am., 1984, 88. Mem. NAFE, Mass. Mortgage Bankers Assn., Data Entry Mgmt. Assn., Middleboro C. of C., Chief Exec. Officer Club Boston, Wareham Bus. and Profl. Women's Club (v.p. program dir.), Taunton Area C. of C., Toastmasters, Plymouth Bd. Realtors, Bristol County Bd. Realtors, Women's Coun. of Realtors, Bristol County C. of C. Republican. Avocations: swimming, golf, horseback riding, curling. Home: 2 Peter Cooper Dr Wareham MA 02571-2209 Office: Sallie Mae Home Loans 2360 Cranberry Hwy PO Box 237 West Wareham MA 02570 Office Phone: 508-930-1792, 508-930-1792. E-mail: clworrell@aol.com.

**WORRELL, FRANCIS TOUSSAINT,** retired physics professor; b. Hartford, Conn., Apr. 19, 1915; s. William Hoyt and Maria Toussaint Worrell; m. Ruthanna Powell Winchell, 1948 (div. 1972); children: William Winchell, Edwin Lloyd Francis; m. Marjorie M. Petheram, Sept. 3, 1972. BS in Engring. Physics, U. Mich., 1936; MS in Physics, U. Pitts., 1940, PhD in Physics, 1941. Mem. staff Physicsts Rsch. Co., Ann Arbor, Mich., 1936—37; tchg. asst. U. Pitts., 1937—41; instr. U. Tenn., Knoxville, 1941—42; staff mem. MIT Radiation Lab., Cambridge, 1942—46; rsch. assoc. Inst. Metals, U. Chgo., 1946—47; asst. prof. Rensselaer Poly. Inst., Troy, NY, 1947—55; assoc. prof. DePauw U., Greencastle, Ind., 1955—58, Beloit (Wis.) Coll., 1959—60; staff mem. MIT Lincoln Lab., Cambridge, 1960—63; prof. physics Lowell (Mass.) Tech. Inst. (later U. Mass. Lowell), 1963—80; ret. Summer vis. lectr. U. Ill., Bloomington, 1956, Bloomington, 57, Wesleyan U., Middletown, Conn., 1958; Fulbright lectr. Al Hikma U., Baghdad, Iraq, 1958—59; summer vis. lectr. Tufts U., Boston, 1964, Boston, 66, Boston, 67. Chmn. Trail Com., Harwich, Mass., 2004—; mem. Real Estate and Open Space Com., Harwich, Mass., 2001—. Mem.: Country Dance Soc., Appalachian Mountain Club (life). Avocations: hiking, folk dancing, local history, conservation. Home: 26 Pleasant Lake Ave #15 Harwich MA 02645

**WORRELL, RICHARD VERNON,** orthopedic surgeon, dean; b. Bklyn., June 4, 1931; s. John Elmer and Elaine (Callender) Worrell; m. Audrey Frances Martiny, June 14, 1958; children: Philip Vernon, Amy Elizabeth. BA, NYU, 1952; MD, Meharry Med. Coll., 1958. Diplomate Am. Bd. Orthop. Surgery, Nat. Bd. Med. Examiners. Intern Meharry Med. Coll., Nashville, 1958—59; resident in gen. surgery Mercy-Douglass Hosp., Phila., 1960—61; resident in orthop. surgery State U. N.Y. Buffalo Sch. Medicine Affiliated Hosps., 1961—64; resident in orthop. pathology Temple U. Med. Ctr., Phila., 1966—67; pvt. practice orthop. surgery Phila., 1967—68; asst. prof. acting head divsn. orthop. surgery U. Conn. Sch. Medicine, 1968—70; attending orthop. surgeon E.J. Meyer Meml. Hosp., Buffalo, Millard Fillmore Hosp., Buffalo, VA Hosp., Buffalo, Buffalo State Hosp.; clin. instr. orthop. surgery SUNY, Buffalo, 1970—74; chief orthop. surgery VA Hosp., Newington, Conn., 1974—80; asst. prof. surgery (orthop.) U. Conn. Sch. Medicine, 1974—77, assoc. prof., 1977—83, asst. dean student affairs, 1980—83; prof. clin. surgery SUNY Downstate Med. Ctr., Bklyn., 1983—86; dir. orthop. surgery Brookdale Hosp. Med. Ctr., Bklyn., 1983—86; prof. orthop. U. N.Mex. Sch. Medicine, 1986—97, prof., vice chmn. dept. orthop., 1997—99, prof. emeritus, 1999—; dir. orthop. oncology U. N.Mex. Health Scis. Ctr., 1987—99; mem. med. staff U. N.Mex. Cancer Ctr., 1987—99; chief orthop. surgery VA Med. Ctr., Albuquerque, 1987—97. Cons. in orthop. surgery Newington (Conn.) Children's Hosp., 1968—70; mem. sickle cell disease adv. com. NIH, 1982—86. Bd. dirs. Big Bros. Greater Hartford. Served to capt. M.C. USAR, 1962—69. Fellow: ACS, Royal Soc. Medicine, London, Am. Acad. Orthop. Surgeons; mem.: AMA, N.Mex. Soc. Clin. Oncology, Internat. Soc. Orthop. Surgery and Traumatology, Orthop. Rsch. Soc., Internat. Fedn. Surg. Colls. (assoc.), Am. Soc. Clin. Oncology, Am. Soc. Clin. Pathologists, Am. Orthop. Assn., Alpha Omega Alpha. Personal E-mail: rworrellmd@aol.com. Business E-Mail: rworrell@salud.unm.edu.

**WORRELL, SHARYN DIANNE,** volunteer, retired flight attendant; b. Lynn, Mass., Feb. 23, 1948; d. Richard Allen Kelley and Norma Lovett (Gregory); m. Blaine Patten Worrell, Feb. 15, 1979 (div. Dec. 20, 1985); 1 child, Ryan Richard. Flight attendant United Airlines, Chgo., 1966—2002. Spkr. and co-founder Speakers' Bur. LA-based Flight Attendants. Author: (book) Ancestral Lines of Joseph Browne of Essex County, Massachusetts and Mary Brown (Joseph's wife) of Kensington, New Hampshire with Related Brown Lines, From Stewardess to Flight Attendant-The Changing Years, When You Were A Boy; co-author: The History of the Auxiliary of Good Shepherd Hospital, Barrington, Illinois; compiler (book) Illinois Court, National Society Women Descendants of the Ancient and Honorable Artillery Company, Celebrating 60 Years, (books) A Few of My Favorite E-Mails. Co-founder Young Women's League for Muscular Dystrophy Assn., LA, 1975; asst. supt. of Sunday sch.; summer Sunday sch. supt.; sch. bd. Immanuel Luth. Ch. and Sch., Palatine, Ill., 1990—93, pub. rels. chair, 1992—2002, bd. of human care ministry com. mem., 1999—2001, pres's. vol. svc. award chmn., 2000—04, bd. of trustees, sec. of congregation, 2001—03; bd. mem. Aux. Good Shepherd Hosp., Barrington, Ill., 2000—, pres., 2006—, mem. chair, 2000—02, chef fest bd. mem., 2003—06; founding mem. Immanuel Luth. Sch. Edn. Found., Palatine, 1998—2003; program chair Art in the Barn; reach for the stars event chairperson Immanuel Luth. Sch. Edn. Found., Palatine, Ill., 1998—2003. Recipient Vol. Recognition, YMCA, 1988, Servant of Youth award, Boy Scouts Am., Merit award (3), United Air Lines, Pres.'s Vol. Svc. Lifetime award, George W. Bush, 2006. Mem.: Clipped Wings (ways and means com. 2002—), others, Continental Soc. Daus. Indian Wars (charter mem., cradle roll), Nat. Soc. U.S. Daus. 1812, Nat. Soc. Daus. of Union (#2 tent), Nat. Soc. Sons and Daus. Pilgrims (organizing gov. Ill. br.), Daus. Am. Colonists (state libr.), Ill. State Soc. Dames Ct. of Honor (parliamentarian), Nat. Soc. Colonial Dames XVII Century (charter mem. lac des Ill. chpt., historian lac des Ill. chpt., state chaplain, pres. lac des Ill. chpt., libr. lac des Ill. chpt., chaplain lac des Ill. chpt., state chair heraldry and court arms), Order Descs. Colonial Physicians and Chirugiens (life), Order First Families of Maine (life; corres. sec. gen., charter mem.), Family of Bruce Soc. Am. (life), Guild Colonial Artists and Tradesmen (life; charter mem.), Sons and Daus. Colonial and Antebellum Bench and Bar (life), Hereditary Order Descs. Loyalists and Patriots Am. Revolution (life), Order First Families Conn. (life; founding mem.), Nat. Soc. Descs. Early Quakers (life), Hereditary Order First Families Mass. (life; primary), Soc. Mayflower Descs. State of Ill. (life; chmn. jr. membership, elder), Soc. Descs. of Colonial Clergy (life), Nat. Soc. Women Descs. Ancient and Hon. Arty. Co. (life; first v.p., treas., hospitality chmn.), Assn. Daus. Early Am. Witches (life; nat. corr. sec. gen.), Daus. Union Vets. of Civil War 1861-1865 (life; chaplain), Nat. Sons and Daus. Antebellum Planters (life), Presdl. Families Am. (life), Order Crown of Charlemagne in U.S.A. (life), Sovereign Soc. Ams. Royal Descent (life), Huguenot Soc. Ill. (registrar, dir.), Nat. Soc. Magna Carta Dames and Barons, Order First Families R.I. and Providence Plantations, N.H. Hist. Soc., New Eng. Historic Geneal. Soc., Essex Soc. Genealogists, Flagon and Trencher (life), Nat. Soc. New Eng. Women (life; 1st v.p. 2006, program spkr., Vol. Cmty. Svc. award 1995), Ill. Cameo Soc. (life), Piscataqua Pioneers (life). Lutheran. Achievements include Lobbied 3 years for exoneration of 6 women executed in 1692 as Salem witches during the Witch Hysteria. Acting Gov. Jane Swift signed the Bill on October 31, 2001 exonerating all 6. Avocations: genealogy, volunteering. Home: 269 Bluff Ct Barrington IL 60010-7312 Personal E-mail: sdworrell@aol.com.

**WORSHAM, HAL GLENN,** marketing professional; b. Ypsilanti, Mich., July 12, 1955; s. Francis Glenn and Priscilla June Worsham; m. Pamela Jean Wusthoff, Oct. 8, 1977; children: Aimee Laurel, Kimberly Victoria. BBA, U. Mich., 1977; MBA, Case Western Res. U., 1981. Mktg. and product mgr. BF Goodrich, Akron, Ohio, 1977—84, advt. mgr., 1977—84; product and mktg. mgr. Dunlop Tire Corp., Buffalo, 1984—87; brand mgr. Fisher Price divsn. Quaker Oats, East Aurora, NY, 1987—91; dir. internat. mktg. Hanna-Barbera Studios, Hollywood, Calif., 1991—92; dir. of licensing and pub. rels. Converse Inc., North Andover, Mass., 1992—2000; sr. v.p. of global licensing Everlast Worldwide Inc., N.Y.C., 2000—. Solicitor Cleve. Orch., 1983; chmn. of bd. of deacons Westminster Presbyn. Ch., Akron, 1983; mem. music com. United Ch. of Christ, South Ch., Andover, Mass., 1999; publicity chmn. Am. Mktg. Assoc., Chgo., 1983—84; bd. dirs. WYDACA Sch., Akron, 1983—84. Scholar, U. of Chgo., 1973. Mem.: Mensa (assoc.). Democrat. Home: 260 Summer St North Andover MA 01845-4819 Office: Everlast Worldwide Inc 1350 Broadway 23d Fl New York NY 10018 Office Phone: 978-258-3834. E-mail: halw@everlast.com.

**WORSLEY, JAMES RANDOLPH, JR.,** lawyer; b. Rocky Mount, N.C., July 28, 1924; s. James Randolph and Helen Marie (Killian) W.; m. Cornelia Cheston, Feb. 11, 1956; children: Cornelia Worsley Newell, Julia Worsley Neilson, Charlotte Cheston Worsley. BS, E. Carolina U., 1944; postgrad., Harvard U., 1944-45, LLB, 1949. Bar: N.C. 1949, D.C. 1949. Assoc. Klagsbrunn, Hanes & Irwin, Washington, 1949-54; ptnr. Ober, Kaler, Grimes & Shriver (and predecessor firm), Washington, 1955-94, coun., 1995—. Chmn. Md. Potomac Water Authority, 1969-71, Montgomery County (Md.) Charter Revision Commn., 1967; mem. pastoral coun. Archdiocese of Washington, 1975-78; bd. dirs. Madeira Sch., McLean, Va., 1975-81. Fellow Am. Bar Found.; mem. Chevy Chase Club, Met. Club, Knights of Malta. Democrat. Roman Catholic. Avocations: sailing, tennis. Home: 11 Quincy St Chevy Chase MD 20815-4226 Office: Ober Kaler Grimes & Shriver 1401 H St NW Ste 500 Washington DC 20005-2175 Office Phone: 202-408-8400.

**WORSTER, ANN MARTIN,** historian; b. Brulington, Vt., Apr. 24, 1937; d. Raymond George and Lucille Worster; m. David Alden Concepcion, Dec. 3, 1960 (dec.); children: Leslie M. Mayns, David W. Concepcion. BA, Colby Coll., 1959. Asst. archivist Libr. Congress, Washington, 1959—61; tchr. Am. History, Swansboro H.S., NC, 1961—62; chairperson Berkeley Landmarks Commn., Calif., 1975—78; dir. pub. programs San Francisco Maritime Mus., 1986—89; intern coord. Maine Hist. Soc., Portland, 1998—2000. Sec. Berkeley Archtl. Assn., Calif., 1970—75; tchr. continuing edn. U. So. Maine, Portland, 2003; bd. mgr. Tate House Mus., Portland, Maine, 2005—. Co-editor: Ruby. An Ordinary Woman, 1995. Vol. Berkeley Archtl. Heritage, Calif., 1972—80; docent Victoria Mansion, Portland, Maine, 1998—99; del. Dem. State Convention, Portland, Maine, 2004. Mem.: Nat. Trust, Am. Assn. Museums, Colonial Dames (chair hist. activities 2005). Democrat. United Ch. Of Christ. Avocation: antiques.

**WORTH, GARY JAMES,** communications executive; b. Berkeley Township, N.J., Dec. 13, 1940; s. Melvin Raymond and Viola Vista (Landis) W. Student, Trenton State Coll., 1964, Palm Beach Jr. Coll., 1958-59. Dir. sta. relations MBS, Inc., N.Y.C., 1972, v.p. sta. relations, 1972, exec. v.p. Washington, 1972-79, mem. exec. com., 1978-79; v.p. Mut. Reports, Inc., Washington, 1972-79, dir., 1972-79; v.p.; dir. WCFL, Inc., Chgo., 1979, Mut. Radio N.Y., N.Y.C., 1979; pres., dir. Robert Wold Co. Inc. and subs. Wold Communications, Inc., L.A., 1980-85; pres., chief exec. officer, dir. WesternWorld Inc. and subs. WesternWorld TV, L.A., 1986-93, The Video Tape Co., North Hollywood, Calif., 1987-93; sec. dir. WesternWorld Video Inc., L.A., 1986-87; CEO Starcom Television Svcs., Inc., 1993—96; chmn., CEO Starcom Entertainment, Inc., 1993—; CEO Starcom Mgmt. Svcs. Inc., 1993—, New Age Conversions, Inc., 1996—. Producer, dir.: USAF movie Assignment McGuire. Served to capt. USAF, 1960-66, Vietnam. Decorated Air Force Commendation medal, Armed Forces Expeditionary medal; recipient Chief Herbert H. Almers Meml. award Bergen County (N.J.) Police Acad., 1972 Mem. Nat. Assn. Broadcasters, Nat. Assn. TV Program Execs., Nat. Infomercial Mktg. Assn. Methodist. Personal E-mail: star2874@msn.com.

**WORTH, GEORGE JOHN,** retired English literature educator; b. Vienna, June 11, 1929; arrived in U.S., 1940, naturalized, 1945; s. Adolph and Theresa (Schmerzler) W.; m. Carol Laverne Dinsdale, Mar. 17, 1951; children: Theresa Jean (Wilkinson), Paul Dinsdale. AB, U. Chgo., 1948, MA, 1951; PhD, U. Ill., 1954. Instr. English U. Ill., Urbana, 1954-55; faculty U. Kans., Lawrence, 1955—, assoc. prof., 1962-65, prof. English lit., 1965-95; prof. emeritus English, 1995—; asst. chmn. dept. U. Kans., Lawrence, 1961-62, assoc. chmn., 1962-63, acting chmn., 1963-64, chmn., 1964-79. Author: James Hannay: His Life and Work, 1964, William Harrison Ainsworth, 1972, Dickensian Melodrama, 1978, Thomas Hughes, 1984, Great Expectations: An Annotated Bibliography, 1986, (book) Macmillan's Magazine, 1859-1907, 2003; editor: (with Harold Orel) Six Studies in Nineteenth Century English Literature and Thought, 1962, The Nineteenth Century Writer and His Audience, 1969, (with Edwin Eigner) Victorian Criticism of the Novel, 1985. Mem. MLA, Dickens Fellowship, Dickens Soc., Midwest Victorian Studies Assn., Rsch. Soc. for Victorian Periodicals. Office: U Kans Dept English Wescoe Hall Lawrence KS 66045-7590 E-mail: GJWorth@aol.com.

**WORTH, KATHERINE MARIE,** retired vocalist; b. Pleasantville, N.J., Dec. 26, 1925; d. Thedore John Philippi and Anna Gladys Weber; m. Melvin R. Worth, June 23, 1952 (dec.). Grad. H.S., Pleasantville, N.J. Profl. vocalist, Atlantic City, 1945—75; ret. Past mem., pres. Red Cedar Twig Cmty. Med. Ctr.; educator Elder Hostle Stockton Coll., ATlantic County; hon. mem. Antique Seekers Ocean County ARea, 1st pres., 1962; bd. mem. Red Cross, Toms River, NJ, 1958—61; v.p., program chair Ocean County Hist. Soc., 1962—97, pres., 1995—97; dir., curator Berkeley Hist. Mus., Bayville, NJ, 1982—92; historian Berkeley Twp., Bayville, 1982—94; bd. mem. Former N.J. State Police Edn. Fund, 1967—. Recipient Outstanding Civic Contbn. award, Berkely Twp., 1975, Berkeley Twp. Hidden Heroine award, 1989. Mem.: Am. Contract Bridge League. Avocations: antiques, bridge, golf, singing, travel. Home: 8 Sloop Creek Rd Box 7 Bayville NJ 08721

**WORTH, MARY PAGE,** mayor; b. Balt., Jan. 23, 1924; d. Christian Allen and Margaret Pennington (Holben) Schwarzwaelder; m. William James Worth, Nov. 4, 1947 (dec. May 1986); children: Margaret Page, William Allen, John David III. Student, Ladychff Coll., Highland Falls, N.Y., 1941-42, Abbott Sch. Art, Washington, 1942-44; grad., Packer Coll. Inst., Brooklyn. Selectman Town of Searsport, Maine, 1973-75; mayor City of Belfast, Maine, 1986-2000. Recreation chmn. Town of Searsport, 1970-72. Del. Rep. State Conv., Maine, 1970-94; pres. Searsport Reps., 1974-76; active ARC Overseas Assn., 1976—; pres. Searsport C. of C., 1976-79; mem. exec. bd. Waldo County Com. for Social Action, Belfast, 1986—; mem. Abnacki coun. Girl Scouts U.S.; tutor Literacy Vols. Am.; recreation specialist ARC, Camp Haugen, Japan, 1946-47; bd. dirs. RSVP-Waldo County, Heat Start Waldo County; vol. tchr. Sch. for Blind, Cholon, Republic Vietnam, 1959-61, Am. Sch. at Saigon, Republic Vietnam, 1959-61; club dir. USAF Spl. Svcs., Ft. Meyer, Va., 1962-63, U.S. Army Spl. Svcs., Ft. Belvoir, Va., 1963-64; mem. Congresswoman Olympia Snow's Mpcl. Adv. Bd.; town chair Rep. Party; mem. adv. Belfast History Project. Mem. Gibson Island Club, 1938-73, mem. DAR (officer Maine 1986—), Internat. Platform Assn., Ret. Officers Assn. (life), 11th Airborne Assn./511th Parachute Infantry Regiment Korea War Vets. Assn., Waldo County Humane Soc. (pres. 1990—), Waldo County Law Enforcement (v.p. 1990—), VFW Aux., Am. Legion Aux., Belfast Garden Club (parliamentarian 1984—), Rotary (dist. govs. com. Maine St. '90), ARC Overseas Assoc. Avocations: great dane breeding, antiques. Office: City of Belfast Mayor's Office 71 Church St Belfast ME 04915-6208 Home: 10 Shoreland Dr Apt 306 Belfast ME 04915-6062

**WORTHAM, JAMES CALVIN,** retired mathematics educator; b. Oconee County, Ga., Sept. 12, 1928; s. James Notley and Effie (Cross) W.; m. Mary Helena Shelley, Dec. 23, 1953; children: Sharon Elaine, Marilyn Kay, Deborah Louise, James Donald. BA, U. Akron, 1957; MA (NSF Scholar), Ohio State U., 1969. Tchr. jr. H.S. Akron Pub. Schs., 1956-62, tchr. sr. H.S. 1962-66; math. curriculum specialist Akron (Ohio) Pub. Schs., 1966-90; instr. math. U. Akron, 1966-90; ret., 1990. Served with USAF, 1951-55. Mem. NEA, Ohio Edn. Assn., Math. Assn. Am., Nat., Ohio couns. tchrs. of Math. Nat. Coun. Suprs. of Math., Greater Akron Math. Educators Soc. (pres. 1984-86), Pi Mu Epsilon. Republican. Mem. Ch. of Nazarene. Home: 229 Sand Run Rd Akron OH 44313-5364

**WORTHAM, THOMAS RICHARD,** literature and language professor; b. Liberal, Kans., Dec. 5, 1943; s. Tom and Ruth (Cavanaugh) W. AB, Marquette U., 1965; PhD, Ind. U., 1970. From asst. prof. to assoc. prof. UCLA, 1970-82, prof., 1982—, vice-chmn. and dir. undergrad. studies, 1993-97, chmn. dept., 1997—. Vis. prof. Am. lit. U. Warsaw, Poland, 1976-77; sr. rsch. fellow Am. Coun. of Learned Socs., 1983-84. Editor: James Russell Lowell's The Biglow Papers: A Critical Edition, 1977, Letters of W. D. Howells, vol. 4, 1892-1901, 1983, The Early Prose Writings of William Dean Howells, 1853-1861, 1990, William Dean Howells' My Mark Twain, 1996, Mark Twain's Chapters From My Autobiography, 1999; asst. editor Nineteenth-Century Fiction, 1971-75,

mem. adv. bd., 1976-83, co-editor, 1983-86; co-editor Nineteenth-Century Literature, 1986-95, editor, 1995—; mem. editl. bd. The Collected Works of Ralph Waldo Emerson, 1996—, Am. Documentary Heritage Edn., 1999—. Regent's faculty fellow in the humanities U. Calif., 1971; travel grantee Nat. Endowment for the Humanities, 1985-86, 88-89; grants-in-aid of rsch. Am. Philos. Soc., 1976, 81. Mem. MLA Am. (Norman Foerster prize com. of Am. Lit. sect. 1973, chmn. Pacific coast region, com. on manuscript holdings of Am. Lit. sect. 1972-78, mem. Hubbell prize com. of Am. Lit. sect. 1989-91), Am. Studies Assn., Ralph Waldo Emerson Soc. (bd. dirs. 1992-95), Assn. for Document Editing, Internat. Assn. Univ. Profs. English, Soc. Textual Scholarship. Lutheran. Office: U Calif Dept English 405 Hilgard Ave Los Angeles CA 90095-1530 Office Phone: 310-825-4459. Business E-Mail: wortham@humnet.ucla.edu.

**WORTHEN, KEVIN,** dean, law educator; AS, Coll. Ea. Utah, 1978; BA summa cum laude, Brigham Young U., 1979, JD summa cum laude, 1982. Law clerk for Judge Malcolm R. Wilkey U.S. Ct. Appeals, Columbia Cir., 1982—83; Judge Byron R. White U.S. Supreme Ct., 1984; atty. Jennings, Strouss & Salmon, Phoenix, 1984—87; Fullbright scholar U. Chile Law Sch., 1994; prof. law Brigham Young U., J. Ruben Clark Law Sch., 1987—, assoc. dean, 1999—2004, dean, 2004—. Chmn. Utah State Constl. Revision Commn. Contbr. articles to law jours. Order of Coif. Mem.: Ariz. State Bar Assn. Office: Brigham Young U J Reuben Clark Sch Law 340 JRCB Provo UT 84602 Office Phone: 801-422-2619. E-mail: worthenk@lawgate.byu.edu.

**WORTHEN, VAUGHN EUGENE,** psychologist, educator; b. Salt Lake City, Feb. 6, 1956; children: Caleb Vaughn, Seth Eugene. PhD, U. Kans., 2001. Lic. psychologist Utah, 1988. Psychology trainee Iowa State U., Ames, Iowa, 1990—91; prof. Brigham Young U., Provo, Utah, 1991—, psychologist, 1991—. Counselor Brigham Young U., 1991—. Eccles. leader LDS Ch., Orem, Utah, 2000—05. Mem.: APA (licentiate). Office: Brigham Young University 2529 Wsc Provo UT 84602-7906 Office Phone: 801-422-6865. Business E-Mail: vaughn_worthen@byu.edu.

**WORTHING, CAROL MARIE,** retired minister; b. Duluth, Minn., Dec. 27, 1934; d. Truman James and Helga Maria (Bolander) W.; children: Gregory Alan Beatty, Graydon Ernest Beatty. BS, U. Minn., 1965; MDiv, Northwestern Theol. Seminary, 1982; DMin, Grad. Theol. Found., Notre Dame, Ind., 1988; MBA in Ch. Mgmt., Grad. Theol. Found., Donaldson, Ind., 1993; cert., Austin Presbyn. Theol. Sem., 2001; PhD, Grad. Theol. Found., 2002. Cert. Episcopal Diocese of Tex., 2003. Secondary educator Ind. (Minn.) Sch. Dist., 1965-78; teaching fellow U. Minn., 1968-70; contract counselor Luth. Social Svc., Duluth, 1976-78; media cons. Luth. Media Svcs., St. Paul, 1978-80; asst. pastor Messiah Luth. Ch., Fargo, ND, 1982-83, vice pastor, 1983-84; assoc. editor Luth. Ch. Am. Ptnrs., Phila., 1982-84; editorial assoc. Luth. Ptnrs. Evang. Luth. Ch. Am., Phila. and Mpls., 1984—2004; parish pastor Resurrection Luth. Ch., Pierre, SD, 1984-89; assoc. pastor Bethlehem Luth. Ch., Cedar Falls, Iowa, 1989-90; exec. dir. Ill. Conf. Chs., Springfield, 1990-96, Tex. Conf. of Chs., 1996—2003; ret., 2003. Asst. pastor Messiah Luth. Ch., Fargo, N.D., 1982-84; mem. pub. rels. and interpretation com. Red River Valley Synod, Fargo, 1984-86, mem. ch. devel., Pierre, 1986-87; mem. mgmt. com. office comm. Luth. Ch. in Am., N.Y.C., Phila., 1984-88; mem. mission ptnrs. S.D. Synod, 1988, chmn. assembly resolutions com., 1988; mem. pre-assembly planning com., ecumenics com., chmn. resolutions com. N.E. Iowa Synod, 1989-90; mem. ch. and society com., 1990-96; ecumenical com., 1995-96; Luth. Ecumenical Rep. Network, 1995—2003; mem. Cen. and So. Ill. Synod, 1996; mem. S.W. Tex. Synod, 1996—2003, mem. ecumenical com., 1998-2001; mem. ecumenical com. Mpls. Area synod and St. Paul Area synod ELCA, 2004—; nat. edn. cons. Am. Film Inst., Washington, 1967-70; chaplain state legis. bodies, Pierre, 1984-89; mem. exec. bd. Luth. Ecumenical Rep. Network for Region 4, Evang. Luth. Ch. in Am., 2002-03; preacher Nat. Cathedral, Washington, 2002. Author: Cinematics and English, 1967, Peer Counseling, 1977, Tischrede Lexegete, 1986, 88, 90, Way of the Cross, Way of Justice Walk, 1987, Introducing Collaboration as a Leadership Stance and Style in an Established Statewide Conference of Churches, 1993, The Anointing of Jesus--A Christological Necessity, 2001. Co-facilitator Parents of Retarded Children, 1985; bd. dirs. Countryside Hospice, 1985; cons. to adminstrv. bd. Mo. Shores Women's Ctr., 1986. Named John Macquarrie fellow, Grad. Theol. Found., 2002, homilist, Tex. Day, Washington Nat. Cathedral, 2002. Mem. NAFE, Nat. Assn. Ecumenical Staff (chair of site selection com. 1991-92, chair of scholarship com. 1993-94, mem. profl. devel. com. 1993-94, chair program planning com. 1996, bd. dirs 1995-96), Pierre-Ft. Pierre Ministerium (v.p. 1986-87, pres. 1987-88). Democrat. Avocations: writing prose and poetry, concerts, theater, art, photography. Home: 5555 Dewey Hill Rd # 106 Edina MN 55439 Personal E-mail: cworthi@winternet.com. Ecumenism is, I believe, about full coherence between our ecclesiology and our ethics. The Spirit of God calls the church to come together for a compassionate purpose: to respond to all who suffer, so that the world might be transformed into God's own vision of peace, justice, and love.

**WORTHING, LOUIE FABIAN, III,** plastic surgeon; b. Wharton, Tex., Feb. 28, 1947; s. Louie Fabian Jr. and Imogene (Cogburn) W. BA in Biology, Baylor U., Waco, Tex., 1969; MD, U. Tex., Galveston, 1973. Diplomate Am. Bd. Plastic and Reconstructive Surgery. Owner Aesthetic Biotherapy Ctr., Houston, 1993-95, L. Fabian Worthing III MD PA, Houston, 1980—. Bd. trustees, pres. bd. Pallen Corp., Houston. Bd. trustees Houston Grand Opera, 1988-96. Fellow ACS; mem. AMA, Texas Medical Assn., Am. Bd. Plastic Surg., Am. Soc. Plastic and Reconstructive Surgeons, Am. Soc. Aesthetic Plastic Surgeons, Champions Gold Club, Bentwater Golf Club, Houstonian Club, Univ. Club. Office: 17070 Red Oak Dr Ste 307 Houston TX 77090-2616 Office Phone: 281-440-7797.

**WORTHINGTON, BRUCE R.,** lawyer; b. 1949; BA in economics cum laude, Claremont McKenna Coll.; JD, U. Calif at Davis. Bar: Calif. 1974. Joined law dept. Pacific Gas and Electric Co., 1974, sr. counsel, chief counsel corp., 1991—94, v.p., gen. counsel, 1994—95, sr. v.p., gen. counsel, 1995—97, PG&E Corp., San Francisco, 1997—. corp. rep. Calif. Minority Counsel Program. Mem.: ABA (vice chair Sect. Pub. Utility, Comm., and Transp. Law), Calif. Bar Assn., San Francisco Bar Assn. Office: PG&E Corp One Market Spear Tower Ste 2400 San Francisco CA 94105

**WORTHINGTON, CAROLE YARD LYNCH,** lawyer; b. Knoxville, Tenn., Aug. 29, 1951; d. Charles R. and Alma (Allred) Yard; m. Robert F. Worthington Jr., Sept. 14, 1996; 1 child, Cassandra Kathleen. BA, U. Tenn., 1972, JD, 1977. Bar: Tenn. 1977, Ga. 1982. Assoc. Thomas, Leitner, Mann, Warner & Owens, Chattanooga, 1977-78; Thomas, Mann & Gossett, Chattanooga, 1978-81, ptnr., v.p., 1981-86; ptnr. Grant, Konvalinka & Harrison, P.C., Chattanooga, 1987-96, Carole Lynch Worthington, Atty. at Law, Knoxville, 1996—. Sec. Nat. Transp. Rsch. Inc., 1991—2005. Author: Estate Planning Tennessee Practice, 1992; asst. editor Tenn. Law Rev., 1976-77. Vice chmn. allocations United Way of Chattanooga, 1985, pilot campaign, 1986; active Jr. League of Chattanooga, 1981-92; mem. alumnae adv. coun. U. Tenn. Coll. Law, 1983-92, dean's ci., 1983-92. Mental Health Assn. Chattanooga Inc., 1986-92, 1st v.p., 1988-89, sec., 1989-92; trustee St. Nicholas Sch., 1992-95, East Tenn. Opera Guild, 2001—04. Recipient Alumni Leadership award, U. Tenn. Coll. Law, 1988, 1992. Fellow Am. Bar Found., Tenn. Bar Found., Chattanooga Bar Found.; mem. ABA (del. at large 1991-97, 98-2001), com. on legal aid and indigent defendants 1994-95, select com. of house 1994-96, standing com. on charter and by laws 1999-2000, standing com. on credentials and admissions 1999-2000, standing com. on credentials and admissions 1999-2000, mem. on client rels. 1999-2002), Chattanooga Bar Assn. (bd. govs. 1982-89, sec.-treas. 1985-86, pres. 1987-88), Knoxville Bar Assn. (chair pro bono com. 2002), Tenn. Bar Assn. (vice chair comml. law, banking and bankruptcy 1988-90, unified bar study com. 1990-91, chair bar leadership conf. 1990, editl. bd. Tenn. Bar Jour. 1991-94, Tenn. Bar Assn. long range planning com. 1992-95, 97-99, bd. govs. 1994-96, chair long range planning com. 1995-96, future of bar com. 1998-2001), Ga. Bar Assn., Nat. Conf. Lawyers and Realtors (ABA del. 1990-92), Nat. Conf. Bar Pres.'s (exec. coun. 1989-92, treas. 1992-93, sec.

1993-94, pres.-elect 1994-95, pres. 1995-96), Tenn. Bd. Profl. Responsibility, Phi Alpha Delta, East Tenn. Opera Guild Bd., 2001-02. Office: 861 Ebenezer Rd Knoxville TN 37923 Office Phone: 865-540-4400. Business E-Mail: cworthington@clw-law.com.

**WORTHINGTON, GEORGE RHODES,** retired naval officer; b. Louisville, July 11, 1937; s. William Bowman and Elizabeth (Frost) W.; m. Sydna Anne Alexander, Mar. 28, 1981 (div. Oct. 1990); children: Rhodes Ballard, Graham Rankins, Greer Anne. BS, U.S. Naval Acad., 1961; postgrad., USMC, Quantico, Va., 1975-76, Nat. War Coll., 1978-79. Commd. ensign USN, 1961, advanced through grades to rear adm., 1989, communications officer USS Halsey Powell San Diego, 1961-63, flag lt., aide comdr. cruiser-destroyer Flotilla Seven, 1963-65, exec. officer Underwater Demolition Team Eleven Coronado, Calif., 1965-68, ops. officer USS Strong Charleston, S.C., 1969-71, exec. officer Naval Spl. Warfare Group Saigon, Vietnam, 1971-72, comdg. officer SEAL Team One Coronado, 1972-74, naval attache Def. Attache Office Phnom Penh, Cambodia, 1974-75, comdg. officer Undersea Warfare Group One Coronado, 1976-78, program sponsor Office of Chief of Naval Ops. Washington, 1979-85; comdr. Naval Spl. Warfare Group One, Coronado, 1985-87; chief of staff Spl. Ops. Command Europe USN, Stuttgart, Fed. Republic Germany, 1987-88; dep. asst. sec. of def. (spl. ops.) Def. Dept., Washington, 1988-89; comdr. Naval Spl. Warfare Command, Coronado, 1989-92; mktg. agent, cons. PIDEAC Inc., Coronado, 1992-96. Naval adv. IFG Ltd.; with Burdeshaw Assoc., Inc.; former v.p. govt. rels. WarRoom Rsch., Inc.; bd. dirs. ZODIAC N.Am., WESCAM-Sonoma, Inc., Spl. Ops. Warrior Found. Decorated D.S.M., Legion of Merit (2), Def. Superior Svc. medal, Meritorious Svc. medal. Mem. Res. Officers Assn. (past chpt. pres.), U.S. Parachute Assn., Underwater Demolition Team-Seal Assn. (life), Mayflower Soc. D.C. (life), Naval Acad. Alumni Assn., Naval Inst., Navy League San Diego, Nat. Def. Indsl. Assn. (life), Army-Navy Club, Army-Navy Country Club. Republican. Episcopalian. Avocations: masters swimming, skiing, sport parachuting. Address: 1118 Pacifica Ave Chula Vista CA 91913-1550 Fax: 619-216-1712. E-mail: grw7@cox.net.

**WORTHINGTON, MELVIN LEROY,** minister, writer; b. Greenville, N.C., June 17, 1937; s. Wilbur Leroy and Alma Lee (Braxton) W.; m. Anne Katherine Wilson, Sept. 12, 1959; children: Daniel Edward, Lydia Anne. Diploma, Imperial Detective Acad., Cin., 1965; B.Bibl.Edn., Columbia Bible Coll., S.C., 1959; B.Th., Luther Rice Sem., Jacksonville, Fla., 1967, B.Div., 1969, M.Th., 1970, D.Th., 1974; M.Ed., Ga. State U.-Atlanta, 1979; EdD, Vanderbilt U., 1998. Ordained to ministry, Central Conf. Free Will Baptists, 1957. Pastor Union Chapel Free Will Bapt. Ch., Chocowinity, NC, 1959-62, Palmetto Free Will Bapt. Ch., Vanceboro, NC, 1959-62, First Free Will Bapt. Ch., Darlington, SC, 1962-66, Wesconnett Free Will Bapt. Ch., Jacksonville, Fla., 1967, First Free Will Bapt. Ch., Amory, Miss., 1967-72, Albany, Ga., 1972-79; exec. sec. Nat. Assn. Free Will Bapt., Inc., Antioch, 1979-2002, chmn. Sunday Sch. bd., 1975-77, asst. moderator, 1977-79, chmn. grad. study com., 1976-77, exec. sec. emeritus, 2002—; pastor Liberty Free Will Bapt. Ch., Ayden, NC, 2003—. Clk. S.C. State Assn. Free Will Bapt., Florence, 1966-67; asst. moderator Ga. State Assn. Free Will Bapt., Moultrie, 1973-74, moderator, 1975-79; pres. Ga. Bible Inst., Albany, 1978 Editor in chief: Contact mag., 1979—2002, author editorial, 1980—2002; contbr. articles to profl. jours. Adv. bd. Nat. Fedn. Decency, 1985; nat. bd. dirs. Christian Leaders for Responsible TV, 1986 Mem. Evang. Press Assn., Religious Conf. Mgmt. Assn. (dir. 1983, v.p. 1986, pres. 1989-92), Nashville C. of C., Future Farmers Am. (N.C. Farmer degree 1955, Am. Farmer degree 1957). Democrat. Mem. Free Will Baptist Ch. Office: Nat Assn Free Will Bapt Inc 5233 Mount View Rd Antioch TN 37013-2306 Office Phone: 252-746-3132. *The basic principle which has guided, governed and guarded my life has been a burning desire to find, follow and finish the will of God.*

**WORTHINGTON, NANCY G.,** sculptor, multi-media artist; b. Norfolk, Va., July 20, 1947; life ptnr. J T Fein. BA, James Madison U., 1965—69; MFA, Pa. State U., 1970—72. Profl. visual artist Nancy Worthington Fine Arts Studios, San Francisco, 1975—90, Sebastopol, Calif., 1990—. Kinetic construction/assemblage artworks, Fantasy/Social/Political Artworks (Gold Medal Winner Stockholm Sweden, 1996), permanent in permanent collections College National Museum of Women in the Arts, Washington, D.C., exhibitions include U.S. Biennial, Sao Palo, Brazil, 1985, U.S. State Dept., Majlis Cultura Ctr., Bombay, India, 2004, GSU Catalog, 2006. Mem.: Coll. Art Assn., Ylem (Artists Using Sci. & Tech.). Achievements include artwork represented at US-Biennial Sao Paolo, Brazil, Art in Embassies Program, World Social Forum, Majlis Cultural Center, Bombay, GSU. Avocations: tennis, gardening, hiking. Home: PO Box 2558 Sebastopol CA 95473 Office: Nancy Worthington Fine Arts Studios PO Box 2558 Sebastopol CA 95473 Office Phone: 707-823-3581.

**WORTHINGTON, ROBERT FLETCHER,** lawyer; b. Knoxville, Tenn., July 17, 1931; s. Robert Fletcher Worthington and Rachel Ann Boggs; m. Carole Lynch Worthington; 1 child, Cassandra Lynch; children: Julia Elizabeth Worthington Farry, Katherine Louisa Worthington Kinnard. LLD, U. Tenn., 1957. Bar: Tenn. 1957, DC 1977. Assoc. Baker & Baker, Knoxville, 1957—59; ptnr. Baker, Young, Young & Baker, Knoxville, 1959—63, Baker Worthington, Knoxville, 1963—94; of counsel Baker, Donelson, Bearman, Caldwell & Berkowitz, Knoxville, 1994—. Gen. counsel Tenn. Valley indsl. com. Tenn. Gas Assn. and NeWire, Inc. Mem. past pres. coun. Tenn. Bus. Roundtable; past vice chmn. Tenn. Higher Edn. Commn.; gen. counsel World's Fair, Knoxville, 1982; mem. adv. bd. Cumberland trail conf. Cumberland Trail State Pk.; mem. adv. bd. Florence Crittenton Agy., Inc. Devel. Coun., Cmty. Sch. Arts; chmn. bd. govs. Club LeConte; bd. dirs. East Tenn. Intermodal Transp. Commerce Ctr., Inc., Boathouse Benevolent Soc., Inc., Knoxville Zool. Soc., East Tenn. Hist. Soc. 1st lt. inf. U.S. Army, 1953—60. Named to Dean's Cir., U. Tenn. Coll. Law-, Best Lawyers in Am., 1991—. Mem.: ABA, D.C. Bar Assn., Knoxville Bar Assn., Tenn. Bar Assn., Phi Delta Phi. Office: Baker Donelson Bearman Caldwell & Berkowitz Ste 2200 900 S Gay St Knoxville TN 37902 Office Phone: 865-549-7700 Office Fax: 865-633-7200. Business E-Mail: rworthington@bakerdonelson.com.

**WORTHINGTON, WILLIAM ALBERT, III,** lawyer; b. June 26, 1950; s. William Albert Jr. and Patricia Lou (Reynolds) W.; children: Elizabeth Clark, Emily Robin, Katherine Anne, William Jackson. BS, U. Utah, 1972; JD, Washington and Lee U., 1976. Bar: Tex. 1976, U.S. Dist. Ct. (so. dist.) Tex. 1977, U.S. Ct. Appeals (5th cir.) 1977, U.S. Ct. Appeals (11th cir.) 1981, U.S. Supreme Ct. 1981, U.S. Dist. Ct. (we. dist.) Tex. 1982, U.S. Dist. Ct. (ea. dist.) Tex. 1986, U.S. Dist. Ct. (no. dist.) Tex. 1993. Assoc. Sewell & Riggs, Houston, 1976—82, ptnr., 1982—89, shareholder, 1990—94; ptnr. Strasburger & Price, LLP, Houston, 1994—. Exec. editor Washington and Lee Law Rev., 1976; contbr. articles to law jours. Active Houston YMCA, Amnesty Internat. USA, ARC; del. state bar of Tex. to Rep. Cuba, 2001. Mem. Am. Law Inst., Def. Rsch. Inst., Product Liability Adv. Coun., Houston Bar Found., Tex. Bd. Legal Specialization (cert. civil trial lawyer, personal injury trial lawyer), U.S. Cycling Fedn., Sierra Club. Office: Strasburger & Price LLP 1401 Mckinney Ste 2200 Houston TX 77010-3033 Office Phone: 713-951-5600. Business E-Mail: william.worthington@strasburger.com.

**WORTHLEY, HAROLD FIELD,** retired minister, educator; b. Brewer, Maine, Nov. 3, 1928; s. Herbert Morrison and Aline May (Field) W.; m. Barbara Louise Bent, June 25, 1955; children: Susan Louise Field, Laura May, David Bruce. AB, Boston U., 1950, MA, 1951; STB, Harvard Div. Sch., 1954, STM, 1956, ThD, 1970. Ordained to ministry United Ch. of Christ, 1954. Min. Congl. chs., Maine, N.H. and Mass., 1952-62; assoc. prof. religion, chaplain Wheaton Coll., Norton, Mass., 1963-77; exec. sec., archivist Congl. Christian Hist. Soc., Boston, 1971—2004; exec. dir. Am. Congl. Assn., 1999—2004; libr. Congl. Libr., 1977—2004, libr. emeritus, 2004—. Editor Bull. of Congl. Library, 1976—2004, Hist. Intelligencer, 1980-86. Author: Inventory of the Records of the Particular Churches of Massachusetts, 1620-1805, 1970; contbr. articles to profl. jours. Mem. Hist. Coun. United Ch. of Christ. Fellow Pilgrim Soc., Congl. Christian Hist. Soc. Home: 14 Mansfield Ave Norton MA 02766-2212 E-mail: blwhfw@msn.com.

**WORTHY, K(ENNETH) MARTIN,** retired lawyer; b. Dawson, Georgia, Sept. 24, 1920; s. Kenneth Spencer and Jeffrie Pruett (Martin) W.; m. Eleanor Vreeland (Blewett), Feb. 15, 1947 (dec. July 26, 1981); children: Jeffrie Martin, William Blewett; m. Katherine Teasley (Jackson), June 17, 1983. Attended, The Citadel, 1937-39; PhB, Emory U., 1941; MBA cum laude, Harvard Univ., 1943 (cum laude, Emory U., 1947. Bar: Ga., 1947; D.C., 1948. Assoc. Foley and Lardner (formerly Hopkins, Sutter, Hamel, and Park), Washington, 1948-51, ptnr., 1952-69, 72-90, sr. counsel, 1991—; chief counsel IRS, 1969—72; asst. gen. counsel Treasury Dept., 1969—72. Mem. Nat. Coun. Organized Crime, 1970-72; cons. Justice Dept., 1972-74. Co-author: (with John M. Appleman) Basic Estate Planning, 1957; contbg. articles to profl. jour. Del. Montgomery County Civic Fedn., 1951—61, D.C. Area Health and Welfare Coun., 1960—61; pres. Sea Island Property Owners Assn., 2004—05; chmn. dept. fin., mem. diocesan coun. Episc. Diocese, Washington, 1969—70; trustee Associated Marine Inst. Found. 1999—2002, Ga. Wilderness Inst. 1997—2003, emeritus, 2003—; trustee St. Simons Island Libr. Found., 2000—, chmn., 2001—05; fellow Aspen Inst., 1982—92; trustee St. John's Coll., Annapolis and Santa Fe, 1987—93, 1995—2001, Sherman Found., Newport Beach, Calif., 1991—; mem. coun. Emory U. Law Sch., 1976—2001, chmn., 1993—95, emeritus, 2001—; bd. dirs. Assn. Citadel Men, 1964—68; trustee Chelsea Sch., 1981—2001, trustee emeritus, 2001—. Capt. U.S. Army, 1943—46, 1951—52. Recipient Army Commendation Ribbon, 1945; Treasury Exceptional Svc. Award and medal, 1972; IRS Commr. Award, 1972; Disting. Alumnus Award, Emory U., 1992. Fellow Am. Bar Found., Am. Coll. Tax Counsel (bd. regents 1980-88, chmn. 1985-87), Atlantic Coun. (counselor 1989-99); mem. ABA (coun. taxation sect. 1965-69, 72-75, chmn. 1973-74, del. Nat. Conf. Lawyers and CPAs 1981-87, ho. of dels. 1983-89, chmn. audit com. 1985-90; Disting. Svc. award taxation sect. 2004), Fed. Bar Assn. (nat. coun. 1969-74, 77-79), Ga. Bar Assn., D.C. Bar, Am. Law Inst., Am. Tax Policy Inst. (trustee 1989-98), Rotary, Chevy Chase Club, Met. Club, Sea Island Club, Ivy League Club (pres. 2002-03), Harvard Club N.Y.C., Phi Delta Theta, Phi Delta Phi, Omicron Delta Kappa. Office: Foley and Lardner 3000 K St NW Ste 500 Washington DC 20007-5143 Home: PO Box 30264 234 W 18th St Sea Island GA 31561 Personal E-mail: kmartinworthy@aol.com. Business E-Mail: kworthy@foley.com.

**WORTHY, PATRICIA MORRIS,** lawyer, educator; b. Fort Benning, Ga., May 28, 1944; d. Walter and Ruby Mae (Lovett) Morris. AA, Queensborough C.C., 1964; BA, Bklyn. Coll., 1966; JD, Howard U., 1969. Bar: DC 1971. Trial atty. NLRB, Washington, 1969—71; dep. gen. counsel ACTION, Washington, 1971—74; assoc. Dolphin, Branton, Stafford & Webber, Washington, 1977—80; dep. asst. sec. for regulatory functions HUD, Washington, 1977—80; adj. prof. Howard U. Sch. Law, 1979—82; chmn. D.C. Pub. Svc. Commn., 1980—91, Washington Met. Area Transit Commn., 1980—91; chief of staff Office of Mayor Sharon Pratt Kelly, Washington, 1991—92; prof. law Howard U., Washington, 1992—2001; dean acad. affairs Howard U. Law Sch., Washington, 2001—02, 2003—04, interim dean, 2002—03; prof. law Howard U., Washington, 2004—. Chmn. D.C. Jud. Nomination Commn., 1992-2005, mem., 2005—. Bd. dirs. Nat. Black Child Devel. Inst., 1975-80, Anacostia Econ. Devel. Corp., 1970-74; chmn. Occupl. Safety and Health Bd., Washington, 1979-80; trustee WETA-TV Channel 26, 1984-94. Mem. ABA, Nat. Conf. Black Lawyers, Nat. Conf. Bar Examiners (multistate profl. responsibility cqm. 1986-89), World Peace Through Law (chairperson young lawyers sect. 1973-75). Office: Howard U Sch Law Van Ness & Connecticut Ave NW Washington DC 20001 Office Phone: 202-806-8061.

**WORTIS, AVI See AVI**

**WORTLEY, GEORGE CORNELIUS,** congressman, consultant; b. Syracuse, N.Y., Dec. 8, 1926; s. George C. and Arlene (Hirsh) W.; m. Barbara Jane Hennessy, May 13, 1950; children: George C. IV, Ann Wortley Lavin, Elizabeth Wortley Ring. BS, Syracuse U., 1948. Newspaper pub., pres. Manlius Pub. Corp., Fayetteville, NY, 1950-92; pres. Nat. Editorial Found., 1968-73; mem. 97th-100th Congresses from 27th N.Y. Dist., 1981-89, mem. Banking, Fin. and Urban Affairs com., mem. Select Com. on Aging, Select Com. on Children, Youth and Family; pvt. bus. cons.; investor Washington, 1989—. Pres. Am. Newspapers Reps., 1966—68; bd. dirs. Dierman, Wortley, Zola & Assocs., Washington Solutions. Pres. Hiawatha coun. Boy Scouts Am., 1972-75; mem. Nat. Commn. on Hist. Publs. and Records, 1977-80. Fayetteville Sr. Citizen Housing Commn., 1977-80; mem. allocations com. United Way of Ctrl. N.Y., 1979-81; mem. pub. rels. com. St. Camillus Health Care Ctr., 1971-78; mem. fed. legis. com. Am. Lung Assn., 1974-77; bd. dirs. Crouse-Irving Meml. Hosp. Found., 1975-87, pres. 1979-81; bd. dirs. Am. Heart Assn., Upstate N.Y., 1960-80, chmn. pub. rels. com., 1970-74, chmn. legis. com. 1977, mem. fund raising adv. com., 1974-79; trustee Cazenovia Coll., 1981-94; bd. dirs. Onondaga Hist. Assn., 1980-90; dir. Global Leadership Inst., 1987-2001. Served with MMR, USNR, WWII. Recipient Silver Beaver award Boy Scouts Am., 1973, Silver Antelope award, 1981 Mem. Nat. Newspaper Assn. (legis. com. 1976-80), Greater Syracuse C. of C. (dir. 1979-81), Upstate Coun. Indsl. Editors, LeMoyne Coll. Pres.'s Assocs., Syracuse U. Alumni Assn. (nat. treas. 1973-77), Former Mems. of U.S. Congress Assn., Navy League of U.S., Cosmos Club, Georgetown Club, Coral Ridge Yacht Club, Union, KC, Kappa Sigma (pres. 1957-59). Republican. Roman Catholic. Office: 1750 K St NW Ste 325 Washington DC 20006-2326

**WORTLEY, MICHAEL D.,** lawyer; b. Tulsa, Olka., June 9, 1947; BA with highest honors, So. Meth. U., 1970, JD with honors, 1978; MRP, U. NC 1973. Bar: Tex. 1978. Shareholder Johnson & Wortley PC, 1985—93, mng. dir., 1993—93; ptnr., co-head Corp. Fin. & Securities Sect. Vinson & Elkins LLP, Dallas, 1993—. Mem.: ABA, Dallas Bar Assn. Office: Vinson & Elkins LLP Trammell Crow Center 2001 Ross Ave, Ste 3700 Dallas TX 75201 Office Phone: 214-220-7732. E-mail: mwortley@velaw.com.

**WORTMAN, MARLENE STEIN,** historian; b. Vienna; d. Leon and Pauline (Lindenbuam) Stein; m. Richard S. Wortman, June 14, 1960; 1 child, Leonie. AB, Syracuse U., 1958; PhD, U. Chgo., 1966; postgrad. in law, Bklyn. Law Sch., 1988-92. Asst. prof. in Am. history Ill. Inst. Tech., Chgo., 1969-77; ind. scholar Inst. for Rsch. in History, N.Y.C., 1977-81, Princeton (N.J.) Rsch. Forum, 1981-87. Pres., v.p. Princeton Rsch. Forum, 1981-85; grants officer Inst. for Rsch. in History, N.Y.C., 1980; coord. Chgo. Met. Area Women's History Group, 1974-76. Editor: (book) Women in American Law, 1985; co-author: The Roads They Made: Women in Illinois History, 1977; contbr. articles to profl. jours; editor: (newsletter) Conf. Group in Women's History, 1975-79. Vice pres. ACLU, N.J., 1982-84, co-chair Women's Rights Com., 1983-87. Conf. grantee on housing N.J. Com. for Humanities, Princeton, 1983; grantee NEH, 1979-81; recipient travel fellowship Am. Philos. Soc., 1975, rsch. fellowship III Inst. Tech., 1974. Mem. NOW, Planned Parenthood. Avocation: hiking. Home: 410 Riverside Dr Apt 91 New York NY 10025-7924

**WORTMAN, RICHARD S.,** historian, educator; b. NYC, Mar. 24, 1938; s. Joseph R. and Ruth (Nacht) W.; m. Marlene Stein, June 14, 1960; 1 child, Leonie. BA, Cornell U., 1958; MA, U. Chgo., 1960, PhD, 1964. Instr. history U. Chgo., 1963-64, asst. prof., 1964-69, asso. prof., 1969-76, prof., 1976-77; prof. history Princeton U., 1977-88, dir. Russian studies, 1982-88; prof. history Columbia U., 1988—; Bryce prof. history, 2001—. Trustee Nat. Coun. for Soviet and Ea. European Rsch., 1983-89; sr. fellow Harriman Inst., 1985-86; bd. dirs. Soc. Ct. Studies, London, 2005; mem. adv. bd. Kennan Inst., 2005—, Soc.Court Studies, Washington, 2002—. Author: The Crisis of Russian Populism, 1967, The Development of a Russian Legal Consciousness, 1976, (with Leopold Haimson and Ziva Gallili) The Making of Three Russian Revolutionaries: Voices from the Menshevik Past, 1987, Scenarios of Power: Myth and Ceremony in Russian Monarchy, vol. I, 1995, vol. II (George L. Mosse prize Am. Hist. Assn., Efim Etkind prize), 2000. Social Sci. Rsch. Coun. grantee, 1975-76; Guggenheim fellow. Mem. Am. Assn. Advancement Slavic Studies (pres. Mid-Atlantic Slavic Conf. 1982-83), AAUP, Am. Hist. Assn., Soc. for Court Studies. Home: 410 Riverside Dr Apt 91 New York NY 10025-7924 Business E-Mail: rsw3@columbia.edu.

**WOSNITZER, MOREY,** urologist; b. Passaic, N.J., Sept. 4, 1944; s. Morris and Ethel (Saltzman) W.; m. Nancy Joell Coplin, Sept. 18, 1978; children: Matthew, Brian. BS, Rutgers U., 1951, MS, 1952; MD, Columbia U., 1956. Diplomate Am. Bd. Urology, Am. Bd. Sexology. Intern in surgery Mt. Sinai Med. Ctr., N.Y.C., 1956-57, asst. resident in surgery, 1957-58; asst. resident in urology Columbia Presbyn. Med. Ctr., N.Y.C., 1958-59, Mass. Gen. Hosp., Boston, 1959-60; resident in urology Peter Bent Brigham Hosp., Boston, 1962-63; pvt. practice Springfield, N.J., 1964—. Assoc. in Clin. Urology Columbia U., N.Y.C., 1975—; clin. instr. in Urology Cornell U., N.Y.C., 1989—. Lt. Comdr. USN, 1960-62. Fellow ACS, Internat. Coll. Surgeons, Soc. Urology and Engring., Am. Assn. Clin. Sexologists. Avocations: gardening, reading, music, horticulture, computers, hurling. Office: 420 Morris Ave Springfield NJ 07081-1149

**WOSTAL, HOLLY ANN,** music educator; b. New Braunfels, Tex., Dec. 22, 1960; d. Samuel Joseph and June Marie Wostal; 1 child, Richard Ross. BA in Music Edn., Houston Bapt. U., 1986; M.Applied Music in Conducting, U. of Houston, 1990. Cert. all level music tchr. Tex., 1986, Mo., 2005. Asst. h.s. dir. Alief Ind. Sch. Dist., Alief, Tex., 1986—88; asst. choral condr. Houston Symphony, 1988—90; elem. music tchr. Sheldon Ind. Sch. Dist., Houston, 1991—92, Pasadena Ind. Sch. Dist., Pasadena, Tex., 1992—93; head h.s. choral dir. Bastrop Ind. Sch. Dist., Bastrop, Tex., 1998—2004; jr./sr. h.s. choral dir. Carl Junction R-1 Sch. Dist., Carl Junction, Mo., 2004—06. Music coord. and condr. City of Baytown, Tex., 1992—93; choir dir. First United Meth., Bastrop, 2001—02, First Christian Ch., Ruidoso, N.Mex., 1997—98, St. John's United Meth., Baytown, 1992—93. Scholar Grad. scholar, MD Anderson, 1988, Dept. of Music scholar, Houston Bapt. U., 1984—86. Mem.: Mo. Choral Dirs. Assn. Avocations: travel, hiking, crossword puzzles, cooking. Home: 1709 Dogwood Dr Joplin MO 64801 Office: Carl Junction R-1 School District PO Box 4 Carl Junction MO 64834 Office Phone: 417-649-7246. E-mail: hwostal.cj.k12.mo.us.

**WOTEKI, CATHERINE ELLEN,** nutritionist; b. Fort Leavenworth, Kans., Oct. 7, 1947; d. Joseph Jeremiah and Catherine (Costello) O'Connor; m. Thomas Henry Woteki, June 7, 1969. BS, Mary Washington Coll., 1969; MS, Va. Poly. Inst. and State U., 1971, PhD, 1973. Registered dietitian. Asst. prof. Drexel U., Phila., 1975-77; project dir. Congl. Office of Tech. Assessment, Washington, 1977-80; group leader USDA, Washington, 1980-83; dep. dir. Nat. Ctr. for Health Statis., Washington, 1983-90; dir. Food and Nutrition Bd., Washington, 1990-93; dep. assoc. dir. for sci. Office of Sci. and Tech. Policy, Washington, 1994-95; undersec. food safety USDA Office of Food Safety, Washington, 1996—2001; dean agrl. Iowa State U., 2002—05; global dir. sci. affairs Macs, Inc., 2005—. Contbr. articles to profl. jours. Named Outstanding alumna Va. Poly. Inst. and State U., 1987; recipient Elijah White award Nat. Ctr. for Health Statis., 1987, Spl. Recognition award USPHS, 1987, Staff Achievement award Inst. of Medicine, 1991. Mem. Am. Inst. Nutrition, Am. Dietetic Assn. Coun. on Rsch., Inst. Food Technologists, Am. Pub. Health Assn., Inst. Medicine Office Phone: 703-821-4900.

**WOTIPKA, CHRISTINE MIN,** education educator; BA in Internat. Rels. and French, U. Minn., Twin Cities, 1993; MA in Sociology, Stanford U., 1999, PhD in Internat. Comparative Edn., 2001. Vol. U.S. Peace Corps, Thailand, 1993—95; econ. rschr., English editor 1st Econ. Rsch. Inst., 1995—96; rsch. asst. Comparative Sociology Workshop, 1996—2001; cons. MentorNet, 2001; asst. prof. edn., dir. master's program in internat. and comparative edn. Stanford (Calif.) U., 2001—03; global fellow, vis. asst. prof. internat. inst. UCLA, 2003—04; vis. scholar, acting asst. prof., sch. edn. Stanford Univ., 2004—. Faculty affiliate Expansion and Impact of World Human Rights Regime project, 2002—; MacArthur Consortium affiliate Ctr. for Internat. Security and Coop., 2000—; mem. adv. bd. sci. and tech. TV Digital Turbulence, 2002—. Office: Stanford U Sch Edn 485 Lasuen Mall Stanford CA 94305-3096

**WOTT, JOHN ARTHUR,** arboretum and botanical garden executive, horticulture educator; b. Fremont, Ohio, Apr. 10, 1939; s. Arthur Otto Louis and Esther Wilhelmina (Werth) W.; children: Christopher, Timothy, Holly. BS, Ohio State U., 1961; MS, Cornell U., 1966, PhD, 1968. Mem. staff Ohio State Coop. Extension Svc., Bowling Green, 1961-64; rsch. asst. Cornell U., Ithaca, NY, 1964-68; prof. Purdue U., West Lafayette, Ind., 1968-81; prof. Ctr. Urban Horticulture U. Wash., Seattle, 1981—; assoc. dir. Ctr. Urban Horticulture U. Wash., Seattle, 1990-93, acting dir., 2004—05; dir. arboreta Washington Park Arboretum, Seattle, 1993—2005. Writer columns for Nursery Mgmt. Profession, Balls and Burlap, Am. Nurseryman, The Arboretum Found.; contbr. articles to profl. jours. and papers including Nursery Mgr. Profl., Balls and Burlap, Arboreteum Found. Bull., Am. Nurseryman. Mem. Am. Soc. Hort. Sci. (com. chmn. 1967-82), Am. Assn. Bot. Gardens and Arboreta, Internat. Plant Propagators Soc. (internat. pres. 1984, internat. sec.-treas. 1985—). Avocations: music, antiques. Office: Internat Plant Box 354115 U Wash Seattle WA 98195 Office Phone: 206-543-8602. Personal E-mail: jwott10623@aol.com. Business E-Mail: jwott@u.washington.edu.

**WOUK, HERMAN,** writer; b. NYC, May 27, 1915; s. Abraham Isaac and Esther (Levine) W.; m. Betty Sarah Brown, Dec. 9, 1945; children: Abraham Isaac (dec.), Nathaniel, Joseph. AB with gen. honors, Columbia U., 1934; LHD (hon.), Yeshiva U., 1954; LLD (hon.), Clark U., 1960; LittD (hon.), Am. Internat. Coll., 1979; PhD (hon.), Bar-Ilan U., 1990, Hebrew U., 1997; DLitt (hon), George Washington U., 2001, Trinity Coll., 1998. Writer radio programs for various comedians, N.Y.C., 1935; asst. writer weekly radio scripts comedian Fred Allen, 1936-41. Presdl. cons. to U.S. Treasury, 1941; vis. prof. English Yeshiva U., 1952-57; scholar-in-residence Aspen Inst. Humanistic Studies, 1973-74 Author: (novels) Aurora Dawn, 1947, The City Boy, 1948, Slattery's Hurricane, 1949, The Caine Mutiny, 1951 (Pulitzer Prize award for fiction, 1952), Marjorie Morningstar, 1955, Youngblood Hawke, 1962, Don't Stop the Carnival, 1965, The Winds of War, 1971, War und Remembrance, 1978, Inside, Outside, 1985 (Washington Book award, 1986), The Hope, 1993, The Glory, 1994, A Hole in Texas, 2004, (dramas) The Traitor, 1949, The Caine Mutiny Court-Martial, 1953, (comedy) Nature's Way, 1957, (non-fiction) This is My God, 1959, The Will to Live On, 2000, (screenplays for TV serials) The Winds of War, 1983, War and Remembrance, 1986. Trustee Coll. of V.I., 1961-69; bd. dirs. Washington Nat. Symphony, 1969-71, Kennedy Ctr. Prodns., 1974-75. Exec. officer U.S.S. Southard USNR, 1942-46, PTO. Recipient Richard H. Fox prize, 1934, Columbia U. medal for Excellence, 1952, Alexander Hamilton medal, 1980, U. Calif.-Berkeley medal, 1984, Golden Plate award Am. Acad. Achievement, 1986, USN Meml. Found. 'Lone Sailor' award, 1987, Yad Vashem KaZetnik award, 1990, Bar Ilan U. Guardian of Zion award, 1998, USCD medal U. Calif.-San Diego, 1998. Mem. Naval Res. Assn., Dramatists Guild, Authors Guild, Internat. Platform Assn. (Ralph Waldo Emerson award 1981), PEN Clubs: Bohemian (San Francisco); Cosmos, Metropolitan (Washington); Century Assn. (N.Y.C.). Jewish. Office: care BSW Literary Agy 303 Crestview Dr Palm Springs CA 92264

**WOVSANIKER, ALAN,** lawyer, educator; b. Newark, Mar. 19, 1953; s. Harold and Sally (Gooen) Wovsaniker. AB, Brown U., 1974; JD, Harvard U., 1977. Bar: N.J. 1977. Law clk. to presiding judge U.S. Dist. Ct. N.J., Camden, 1977-78; ptnr. Lowenstein Sandler PC, Roseland, NJ, 1979—. Adj. prof. Seton Hall Law Sch., 1988—91, Rutgers U. Law Sch., 1989—95; chmn. dist. ethics com. Supreme Ct. Contbr. articles to profl. jours. Mem.: Essex County Bar Assn. (trustee 1996—99, chmn. banking law com. 1994—97, chmn. corp. law com. 1999—2003). Office: Lowenstein Sandler PC 65 Livingston Ave Roseland NJ 07068-1791 E-mail: awovsaniker@lowenstein.com.

**WOYCZYNSKI, WOJBOR ANDRZEJ,** mathematician, educator; b. Czestochowa, Poland, Oct. 24, 1943; came to U.S., 1970; s. Eugeniusz and Otylia Sabina (Borkiewicz) W.; m. Elizabeth W. Holbrook; children: Lauren Pike, Gregory Holbrook, Martin Wojbor. MSEE, Wroclaw Poly., 1966; PhD in Math., Wroclaw U., 1968. Asst. prof. Inst. Math. Wroclaw U., 1968-72, assoc. prof., 1972-77; prof. dept. math. Cleve. State U., 1977-82; prof., chmn. dept. math. and stats. Case Western Res. U., Cleve., 1982-91, dir. Ctr. for

Stochastic and Chaotic Processes in Sci. and Tech., 1989—, chmn. dept. stats., 2002. Rsch. fellow Inst. Math. Polish Acad. Scis., Warsaw, 1969-76; postdoctoral fellow Carnegie-Mellon U., Pitts., 1970-72; vis. assoc. prof. Northwestern U., Evanston, Ill., 1976-77; vis. prof. Aarhus (Denmark) U., 1972, U. Wis., Madison, 1976, U. S.C., 1979, U. N.C., Chapel Hill, 1983-84, Gottingen (Germany) U., 1985, 91, 96, U. NSW, Sydney, Australia, 1988, Nagoya (Japan) U., 1992, 93, 94, U. Minn., Mpls., 1994, Tokyo U., 1997, Princeton U., 1998, U. Paris 6, 2003. Dep. editor in chief: Annals of the Polish Math. Soc., 1973-77; assoc. editor Chemometrics Jour., 1987-94, Probability and Math. Stats., 1988—, Annals of Applied Probability, 1989-96, Stochastic Processes and Their Applications, 1993-99; co-editor: Martingale Theory and Harmonic Analysis in Banach Spaces, 1982, Probability Theory and Harmonic Analysis, 1986, Nonlinear Waves and Weak Turbulence, 1993, Nonlinear Stochastic PDE's: Hydrodynamic Limit and Burgers' Turbulence, 1995, In a Reporter's Eye: The Life of Stefan Banach, 1996, Stochastic Models in Geosystems, 1997; author: (monograph) Martingales and Geometry in Banach Spaces 1, 1975, part II, 1978, Burgers-KPZ Turbulence: Göttingen Lectures, 1998; co-author: Random Series and Stochastic Integrals: Single and Multiple, 1992, Distributions in the Physical and Engineering Sciences, vol. 1: Distributional and Fractal Calculus, Integral Transforms and Wavelets, 1997, Introductory Statistics and Random Phenomena: Uncertainty, Complexity and Chaotic Behavior in Engineering and Science, 1998, A First Course in Statistics for Signal Analysis, 2005. Rsch. grantee NSF, 1970, 71, 76, 77, 81, 87—, Office of Naval Rsch., 1985-96. Fellow Inst. Math. Stats.; mem. Am. Math. Soc., Am. Statis. Assn., Polish Math. Soc. (Gt. prize 1972), Polish Inst. Arts and Scis., Racquet Club East. Roman Catholic. Avocations: tennis, music, skiing, sailing, rare books collecting. Home: 3296 Grenway Rd Cleveland OH 44122-3412 Office: Case Western Res U Dept Statistics Cleveland OH 44106 E-mail: waw@po.cwru.edu.

**WOYSKI, MARGARET SKILLMAN,** retired geology educator; b. West Chester, Pa., July 26, 1921; d. Willis Rowland and Clara Louise (Howson) Skillman; m. Mark M. Woyski, June 19, 1948; children: Nancy Elizabeth, William Bruno, Ronald David, Wendelin Jane. BA in Chemistry, Wellesley (Mass.) Coll., 1943; MS in Geology, U. Minn., 1945, PhD in Geology, 1946. Geologist Mo. Geol. Survey and Water Resources, Rolla, 1946-48; instr. U. Wis., Madison, 1948-52; lectr. Calif. State U., Long Beach, 1963-67, lectr. to prof. Fullerton, 1966-91, assoc. dean Sch. Natural Sci. and Math., 1981-91, emeritus prof., 1991—. Contbr. articles to profl. jours.; author lab. manuals; editor guidebooks. Fellow Geol. Soc. Am. (program chmn. 1982); mem. South Coast Geol. Soc. (hon. pres. 1974), Mineral Soc. Am. Home: 880 Morningside Dr Apt M-320 Fullerton CA 92835-3577

**WOZENCRAFT-ORNELLAS, (BETTY) JEAN,** singer, music educator; b. Alamogordo, N.Mex., Oct. 24, 1957; d. John George and Betty Jean Wozencraft; m. Jerry Ornellas, Nov. 1, 1991. MusB in Vocal Performance, Oberlin Coll., 1979; MusM in Vocal Performance, Bowling Green State U., 1981; MusD in Vocal Performance, Fla. State U., 1987. Free lance singer, Portales, N.Mex., 1979—; prof. voice Ea. N.Mex U., Portales, 1984—. Profl. debut: Cleve. Opera, 1979; singer: (songs) various venues internationally. Recipient 2d pl. award, Hemphill-Wells Sorantin Young Artists, 1987, W.Va. Symphony, 1979; regional finalist, winner, Met. Opera Auditions, 1986, 1988. Mem.: Rotary. Office: Eastern New Mexico University Station 16 Portales NM 88130 Business E-Mail: jean.ornellas@enmu.edu.

**WOZNIAK, JUDITH T.,** pastor; b. Passaic, N.J., Dec. 23, 1948; d. Edward Wozniak and Edna Basalyga. BA, Caldwell Coll., 1970; MA, Seton Hall U., 1971; MDiv, Lutheran Theol. Seminary, Phila., 1988; PhD, SUNY, Buffalo, 1995. Tchr. h.s. N.J. Pub. Schs., 1972-75; adminstrv. asst. Ann Smith Real Estate, 1976-77; personnel adminstr. Child Guidance Toys, Bronx, 1977-79; pastor ELCA, N.Y., Ohio, 1988—. Asst. prof. Cleve. State U., 1994—. Author: A Time for Peace, 1996; editor: Western Civilization, 1995; contbr. articles to profl. jours. Mem. Am. Hist. Assn., Renaissance Soc., Am. Soc. Ch. Historians, Erasmus & Rotterdam Soc., Phi Alpha Theta. Democrat. Lutheran. Avocations: running, cross-country, theater, music. Office: Grace Lutheran Ch 146 High St Wadsworth OH 44281-1859

**WOZNIAK, RICHARD ANTHONY,** computer engineer; b. Buffalo, Aug. 24, 1959; s. Richard Anthony and Julia Marie (Cefaratti) W. BA, U. Buffalo, 1981, MS, 1983. Software engr. Sierra Rsch., Buffalo, 1983-85; sr. analyst HSB Bank U.S.A., Buffalo, 1985-91, project mgr., 1991-93, tech. specialist, 1993—2000, IT mgr., 2001—. Pres. South Cheektowaga Baseball Assn., Cheektowaga, N.Y., 1984—. Recipient award Cheektowaga C. of C., 1992. Home: 33 Grand Prix Dr Cheektowaga NY 14227-3613

**WOZNIAK, STEPHEN GARY,** computer scientist, philanthropist; b. San Jose, Calif., Aug. 11, 1950; s. Jerry; m. Alice Robertson, 1980 (div.); m. Candice Clark, 1987 (div.); 3 children; m. Suzanne Mulkern, 1990. BS in computer sci. and elec. engring., U. Calif., Berkeley, 1987; DSc (hon.), NC State U., 2004. Designer calculator chips Hewlett-Packard Co., 1976; co-founder Apple Computer, Inc., 1976, v.p. R&D, 1976—81, designer, 1979—81, re-joined as principal engr., 1983—85, cons., 1985—; founder CL9 - Remote Control Co., US Festivals, San Bernardino, Calif., 1983; co-chmn. Axlon, Inc., Sunnyvale, Calif., 1986—; founder, chmn., CEO Wheels of Zeus (wOz), 2001—. Bd. dirs. Jacent, Danger, Inc.; Dem. convention del. (Hart), 1984; former tchr. Co-author (with Gina Smith): iWoz: Computer Geek to Cult Icon-Getting to the Core of Apple's Inventor, 2006. Founder Elec. Frontier Found.; founding sponsor Tech Museum, Silicon Valley Ballet, Children's Discovery Museum, San Jose, Calif. Named to Nat. Inventor's Hall of Fame, 2000, Consumer Electronics Hall of Fame, 2004; recipient Grace Murray Hopper award, Assn. Computing Machinery, 1979, Nat. Medal Tech., presented by Pres. Ronald Reagan, 1985, Fellow award, Computer History Mus., 1997, Heinz Award for Tech., 2000, numerous awards from tech. and cmty. groups. Mem.: Fremason, Charity Lodge (life). Achievements include invention of the first line of Apple products - the Apple I and II computers; influenced the popular Macintosh computer; supports the Los Gatos School Dist., providing students and teachers with hands-on teaching and donations of state-of-the-art tech. equip; sponsored computers for schs. in USSR through US/USSR Iniative, 1990; youngest Fortune 500 man in 1982 at age 27; involved in charitable activities in field of education. Avocation: pets (dogs). Office Phone: 408-358-6030.*

**WRAASE, DENNIS RICHARD,** utilities executive, accountant; b. Washington, Mar. 15, 1944; s. Richard Harold and Esther Morelle (Cowan) W.; m. Cecilia Anne Kirby, Dec. 30, 1987; children: Richard Reid, Elisabeth Kirby. BS, U. Md., 1966; MS, George Washington U., 1975. CPA, Md. Acct: Exxon Corp., Balt., 1966-70, fin. analyst Houston, 1970-74; mgr. fin. systems Potomac Electric Power Co., Washington, 1974-78, asst. comptr., 1978-81, dir. computer and gen. svcs., 1981-83, comptr., 1983-92, v.p., 1986-89, sr. v.p., 1989—, CFO, 1996—; exec. v.p. Potomac Capital Investment, Washington, 1999, pres., COO, 2000—; pres., CEO Pepco Holding Inc., 2002—, chmn., 2004—. Pres. Olney Jaycees, Md., 1978; bd. dirs., v.p. Nat. Capital area Boy Scouts Am., Washington, 1987—, Washington Bd. Trade, Federal City Coun., 2001—; bd. dirs. Washington Performing Arts Soc., 2002—, Washington Hosp. Ctr., 2002-, U. Md. Found., 2003-. With USAR, 1967-73; US C. of C., 2004. Mem. AICPA, Fin. Execs. Inst. Democrat. Lutheran. Office: Potomac Electric Power Co 701 Ninth St NW Ste 1000 Washington DC 20068 E-mail: drwraase@pepco.com.

**WRAGA, WILLIAM GERARD,** education educator; b. Teaneck, N.J., Mar. 21, 1957; s. William Francis and Maryjane M. (Conlon) W.; m. Amy Jeanne Schneider, June 26, 1982; children: William Frederic, Ian Thomas. AB, Rutgers U., 1979; MAT, U. Chgo., 1980; EdD, Rutgers U., 1991. Tchr. Hillsborough H.S., Belle Mead, N.J., 1980-81, Green Brook (N.J.) H.S., 1981-84, Mendham (N.J.) H.S., 1984-86; dept. supr. Freehold (N.J.) Twp. H.S., 1986-87; dist. supr. K-12 Bernards Twp. Pub. Schs., Basking Ridge, N.J., 1987-94; adj. asst. prof. Rider U., Lawrenceville, 1994; assist. prof. dept. edn. leadership U. Ga., Athens, 1995-99, assoc. prof., 1999—2004, interim founding head dept. ednl. adminstrn. and policy, 2002—04, prof. dept. ednl.

adminstrn. and policy, 2004—05, prof. dept. lifelong edn., adminstrn. and policy, 2005—. Chmn. civics com. N.J. State Dept. Edn., 1988—90, mem. social studies core course proficiencies panel, 1989—91; bd. dirs. N.J. Coun. for Social Studies, 1988—90, chmn. publ. com., 1988—89; mem. exec. bd. N.J. ASCD, 1992—93; mem. adv. com. N.J. Vietnam Vets. Meml. Ednl. Ctr., 1993—94; cons. La. Bd. Regents, 2004—06, Coll. Edn., U. Iowa; presenter in field. Author: Democracy's High School, 1994; contbg. author: Readings in Middle School Curriculum, 1993, Curriculum Issues and the New Century, 1995, Handbook on Teaching Social Issues, 1996, We Gain More Than We Give, 1997, Historical Dictionary of American Education, 1999, Encyclopedia of Education, 2003, Explorations in Curriculum History, 2005, Experiencing Dewey, 2005; exec. editor Focus on Edn. Jour., N.J. ASCD, 1993; co-editor: Rsch. Rev. for Sch. Leaders, 1996, 1998, 2000; guest co-editor Social Edn., 1990, mem. editl. bd. History of Edn. Quar., 2004—, former mem. editl. bd. Jour. Curriculum and Supervision, The Ednl. Forum; contbr. articles and book revs. to profl. jours. Grad. Merit scholar Rutgers U., 1984-85, 85-86; recipient Excellence in Dissertation award Rutgers Grad. Sch. Edn. Alumni Assn., 1992. Fellow John Dewey Soc. (bd. dirs. 2000-02); mem. Am. Ednl. Rsch. Assn., Profs. of Curriculum (Factotum 1998-99), Soc. Study Curriculum History (pres. 2001—03), Soc. Profs. Edn. (exec. bd. 2003—05), Phi Delta Kappa, Pi Lambda Theta, Kappa Delta Pi. Office: U Ga Coll Edn Dept Lifelong Adminstrn and Policy 850 College Station Rd Athens GA 30602-4808 Business E-Mail: wraga@uga.edu.

**WRANCHER, ELIZABETH ANN,** music educator, opera singer; b. Indpls., Oct. 19, 1930; d. Charles Edwin and Evelyn Louise (Helck) W. MusB, Ind. U., 1955. Opera singer, Europe, 1955-68; asst. prof. music U. South Fla., Tampa, 1968-74; pvt. practice Winter Park, Fla., 1974—; assoc. prof. music U. Ctrl. Fla., Orlando, 1974—2003. Cons. Disney World, Orlando, 1987—; summer tchr. Music Theatre Bavaria, Oberandorf, Germany, 2001. Actress in 3 German movies, 1964-87; opera concert singer, 1968-91; recorded music of Thomas Beversdorf. Past bd. dirs., adv. bd. Orlando Opera Co. Recipient Life Achievement award, 1993, T.I.P. award U. Ctrl. Fla., 1996; Fulbright scholar, Germany, 1955; U. Ctrl. Fla. grantee, 1987. Mem.: Fla. State Music Tchrs. Assn., Fla. Vocal Assn., Nat. Assn. Tchrs. Singing (pres. Ctrl. Fla. chpt. 1996—), Nat. Arts and Letters, Nat. Federated Music Clubs (life), Wed. Music Club (1st v.p. 2004—05, pres. 2005—), Phi Kappa Lambda, Mu Phi Epsilon (life). Republican. Baptist. Achievements include concert recordings in Mozart Deim Archives, Salzburg, Austria, Augsburg Archives. Avocations: art, pastels, philosophy, religions. Home: 2630 Amsden Rd Winter Park FL 32792-3513 Office Phone: 407-678-1916. Personal E-mail: ewrancher@yahoo.com.

**WRATHALL, JAMES R.,** lawyer; b. Sept. 14, 1962; BS cum laude, Tulane Univ., 1984; JD cum laude, Georgetown Univ., 1987. Bar: Md. 1987, DC 1990. Ptnr., vice chmn. Bankruptcy & Comml. dept. Wilmer Cutler Pickering Hale & Dorr, Washington. Editor (articles): Georgetown Law Jour. Named one of Top Lawyers in Washington, Washingtonian mag., 2004. Mem.: ABA, Am. Bankruptcy Inst. Office: Wilmer Cutler Pickering Hale & Dorr Willard Office Bldg 1445 Pennsylvania Ave NW Washington DC 20004 Office Phone: 202-663-6895. Office Fax: 202-942-8484. Business E-Mail: james.wrathall@wilmerhale.com.

**WRAY, BETTY BEASLEY,** allergist, immunologist, pediatrician; b. Ga., 1935; MD, Med Coll. Ga., 1960. Diplomate Am. Bd. Allergy and Immunology, Am. Bd. Clin. Lab. Immunology. Intern Talmadge Meml. Hosp., Augusta, Ga., 1960-61, resident in pediatrics, 1962, 64-65, fellow in pediatric allergy, 1966-68; staff mem. Med. Coll. Ga., Augusta, 1979—, prof. pediat. medicine, interim dean Sch. Medicine, v.p. clin. activities, 2000—02, prof. emeritus, 2002—. Mem. Am. Coll. Allergy, Asthma and Immunology, Am. Acad. Pediat., Am. Acad. Allergy and Immunology, Am. Pediatric Soc. Office: Med Coll Georgia BG 1009 Augusta GA 30912 Office Phone: 706-721-3531. E-mail: bettyw@mail.mcg.edu.

**WRAY, CECIL, JR.,** lawyer; b. Memphis, Nov. 19, 1934; s. Thomas Cecil and Margaret (Malone) W.; m. Gilda Gates, Sept. 11, 1964; children: Christopher A., Kathleen Wray Baughman. Student, U. Va., 1952-53; BA magna cum laude, Vanderbilt U., 1956; LLB, Yale U., 1959. Bar: Tenn. 1959, N.Y. 1961, U.S. Supreme Ct. 1964. Registered counseil juridique, France, 1978-82. Law clk. to justice Tom C. Clark U.S. Supreme Ct., Washington, 1959-60; assoc. Debevoise & Plimpton, N.Y.C., 1960-67, ptnr., 1968-96, of counsel, 1997-99, resident ptnr. Paris, 1976-79. Adj. prof. N.Y. Law Sch., 1997-2001. Co-author: Innovative Corporate Financing Techniques, 1986. Bd. dirs. Search & Care, Inc., N.Y.C., pres., 1981-87; bd. dirs. Episcopal Charities, N.Y., pres., 1995-2002; vestryman St. James' Ch., N.Y.C., 1982-87, warden, 1988-94; trustee Fondation des Etats-Unis, Paris, 1976-79, Ch. Pension Fund; bd. dirs. East Side Comty. Ctr., Inc.; bd. fgn. parishes Episcopal Ch., 1995—; bd. dirs. Hudson Highlands Land Trust; commr. Adirondack Park Agy.; chmn. bd. Ch. Ins. Co. Fellow Am. Coll. Investment Counsel (trustee 1981-86, pres. 1983-84); mem. Am. Law Inst., Assn. Bar City N.Y., Coun. Fgn. Rels., Audubon Club (St. Huberts, N.Y.), Union Club, Century Club, Order of Coif, Phi Beta Kappa. Episcopalian. Home: 47 E 88th St New York NY 10128-1152 Office: Debevoise & Plimpton 919 3rd Ave New York NY 10022-3902

**WRAY, CHRISTOPHER ASHER,** lawyer, former federal agency administrator; b. Dec. 1966; Grad. cum laude, Yale U., 1989, JD, 1989. Law clk. to Hon. J. Michael Luttig U.S. Ct. Appeals (4th Cir.), 1992—93; atty. King & Spaulding, LLP, Atlanta, 1993—97; asst. U.S. atty. criminal divsn. (No. dist.) Ga. US Dept. Justice, Atlanta, 1997—2001, assoc. dep. atty. gen. Washington, 2001, prin. assoc. atty. gen. criminal divsn., 2001—03, acting asst. atty. gen. criminal divsn., 2003, asst. atty. gen. criminal divsn., 2003—07; ptnr. King & Spalding LLP, Washington, 2005—. Office: King & Spalding LLP 1700 Pennsylvania Ave NW Washington DC 20006 E-mail: cwray@kslaw.com.

**WRAY, KENT,** academic administrator; m. Wanda Wray. BS in Physics, Washburn U.; BS in Civil Engring., Kans. State U.; MS in Civil Engring., Air Force Inst. Tech.; PhD in Civil Engring., Tex. A&M U. Engr. Kans. Hwy. Dept.; chmn. dept. civil engring. Tex. Tech. U.; dean engring. and tech. Ohio U.; provost and sr. v.p. for acad. and student affairs Mich. Technol. U., Houghton, 2000—. Chair Ohio Engring. Deans Coun., 1990. Contbr. articles to profl. jours. Recipient Coll.-level Halliburton Outstanding Rsch. award, Halliburton Outstanding Tchr. award. Fellow: ASCE. Office: Mich Technol Univ Rm 503A Adminstrn Bldg 1500 Townsend Dr Houghton MI 49931-1295

**WRAY, PETER,** theater educator; s. John David and Audrey Wray; m. Robin Neuhauser, Aug. 21, 1982; 1 child, Kyle. BFA in Theatre Arts, U. N.Mex, Albuquerque, 1982; MFA in Theatre Arts, Pa. State U., University Park, 1999. Freelance theater dir., actor, Phila., 1984—90; resident dir. Gretna Theatre, Mount Gretna, Pa., 1990—95; mktg. coord. Ctr. for the Arts, Pa. State U., University Park, 1999—2001; asst. prof. dept. theater arts Towson U., Md., 2001—. Co-founder Mum Puppettheatre, Phila., Gretna Theatre Sch., Mt. Gretna. Named one of Towson Elite, Towson U., 2004—05; recipient Coll. of Fine Arts Most Disting. Sr. award, U. N.Mex; grantee Pa. State Arts Coun.; Graham fellow, Pa. State U., Nadine Blackburn scholar, U. N.Mex. Mem.: Theatre Comm. Group, Assn. Theatre in Higher Edn., Actors Equity Assn., NCR Trl. Snails Running Club. Office Phone: 410-704-2785.

**WRAY, ROBERT,** lawyer; s. George and Ann (Moriarty) W.; m. Lila Keogh (dec.); children: Jennifer, Edward, Hillary. BS, Loyola U., 1957; JD, U. Mich., 1960. Bar: DC, Ill. 1960. Assoc. Hopkins & Sutter, Chgo., 1964—69; gen. counsel Agy. for Internat. Devel., 1969—71; sr. counsel TRW, Inc., 1972—73, Export-Import Bank of the U.S., 1974—79; prin. Robert Wray Assocs., 1979—86; internat. ptnr. Pierson, Ball & Dowd, 1986—87; prin. Robert Wray Assocs., 1988—; spec. counsel Graham & James, 1988—97; ptnr. Holland & Knight, Washington, 1997—2003; mng. mem. Robert Wray

PLLC, Washington, 2003—. Recipient medal of superior honor Dept. of State. Mem.: Chevy Chase Club, Annapolis Yacht Club, Talbot Country Club, Met. Club, Bretton Woods Com. Office: 1150 Connecticut Ave NW Ste 350 Washington DC 20036

**WRAY, ROBERT THEODORE,** music educator; b. Santa Monica, Calif., Aug. 12, 1977; s. George Brown and Dianne Mae Wray; m. Natalie Kay Miller, Nov. 6, 2004. BA, The Ohio State U., 2001. Cert. basketball referee Ohio, 2000. Tchr. vocal music Westlake H.S., Waldorf, Md., 2001—. Coach various sports Westlake H.S., 2001—. Singer: Ohio State U. Chorale, Ohio State U. Men's Glee Club, Ohio State U. Symphonic Choir. Asst. coach baseball Westerville (Ohio) Youth Baseball and Softball League, 2000—01. Mem.: Md. Chorale Educators Assn. (mem. exec. bd. 2002—05), Music Educators Nat. Conf., Am. Chorale Dirs. Assn. (mem. men's hon. choir 1998), Md. Music Educators Assn. (presenter 2004). Home: 5304 Aberdeen Ave Apt 105 Lubbock TX 79414-1846 Office: Graduate Asst Choral Dept Texas Tech Univ Lubbock TX 79414

**WRAY, THOMAS JEFFERSON,** lawyer; b. Nashville, July 17, 1949; s. William Esker and Imogene (Cushman) W.; m. Susan Elizabeth Wells, Aug. 19, 1972; children: William Clark, Caroline Kell. BA, Emory U., 1971; JD, U. Va., 1974. Bar: Tex. 1974, U.S. Dist. Ct. (so., no. and ea. dists.) Tex. 1976, U.S. Ct. Appeals (5th and 11th cirs.) 1976, U.S. Supreme Ct. 1987. Assoc. Fulbright & Jaworski, L.L.P., Houston, 1974-82; ptnr. Fulbright & Jaworski, Houston, 1982—. Mem. ABA, Coll. Labor and Employment Lawyers, Houston Bar Assn., Houston Mgmt. Lawyers Forum (chmn. 1981-82), Briar Club, Phi Beta Kappa. Republican. Episcopalian. Home: 3662 Ella Lee Ln Houston TX 77027-4105 Office: Fulbright & Jaworski 1301 Mckinney St Ste 5100 Houston TX 77010-3095 Office Phone: 713-651-5585. Business E-Mail: tjwray@fulbright.com.

**WREGGLESWORTH, KYMBERLI APRIL,** social studies educator; d. Eugene John Barrette and Faye Louse McDonald; m. Keith Ray Wregglesworth, Oct. 16, 1999. BA, Alma Coll., Mich., 1998; MA in Edn., Mich. State U., Lansing, 2003. Tchr. h.s. social studies Onaway Area Cmty. Schs., Mich., 1999—. Varsity competitive cheer coach Onaway H.S., Mich., 2000—; choreographer Miss Onaway Scholarship Pageant, 2003—04, exec. dir. 2005—. Grantee, John M. Ashbrook Ctr. Pub. Affairs, Ashland U., 2006; Global Svc. Fellow, Alma Coll., 1996—97. Mem.: Mich. Cheer Judges Assn., Competitive Cheer Coaches Assn. Mich., Mich. Cheerleading Coaches Assn., Am. Mensa. Avocations: travel, bicycling, camping, reading, gardening. Office: Onaway Area Community Schools PO Box 307 4549 M-33 South Onaway MI 49765 Office Phone: 989-733-2700. Personal E-mail: ohscheercoach@i2k.net. Business E-Mail: kwregglesworth@oacsd.com.

**WREN, GAYDEN,** playwright, theater director; b. N.Y.C., May 24, 1961; s. Gayden and Mary Alice Wren; m. Sara Holliday, July 7, 2001. BA, Oberlin Coll., 1983. Entertainment editor NY Times Syndicate, N.Y.C., 1995—. Author: (book) A Most Ingenious Paradox: The Art of Gilbert & Sullivan, (theater) As If, Baseball, Sex and Other Facts of Life, Ernest, An Evening with Gilbert & Sullivan, A Gilbert & Sullivan Christmas Carol, ID, Moonlight and Midnight, A Night on the Tomb, Swords & Frenchmen, Tales from the Bible, Two for the Show, Very Truly Yours, Gilbert & Sullivan, The World According to Gilbert & Sullivan; dir.: (opera) The Sorcerer, HMS Pinafore, The Pirates of Penzance, Patience, Iolanthe, Princess Ida, The Mikade, Ruddigore, The Gondoliers, Utopia, Limited. Dir. The Gilbert & Sullivan Light Opera Co. of LI, Merrick, NY, 1984—; artistic dir. The New Punctuation Army Inc., N.Y.C., 1984—; chmn. Citizens for Classic Movies, N.Y.C., 1992—; artistic dir. Troupers Light Opera, New Canaan, Conn., 2002—03. Home: 19-92 78th St East Elmhurst NY 11370 Office: The New York Times News Svcs 609 Greenwich St New York NY 10014-3610 E-mail: wreng@nytimes.com.

**WREN, JOHN D.,** advertising executive; married; 2 children. BA, MBA, Adelphi U., 1975. Mgmt. cons. Arthur Anderson & Co.; with Norton Simon Inc., Needham Harper Worldwide; joined Diversified Agency Services (subs. Omnicom Group, Inc.), 1986, CFO, pres. 1990—93, chmn., CEO 1993—95; pres. Omnicom Group, Inc., NYC, 1995—97, pres., CEO 1997—. Office: Omnicom Group Inc 437 Madison Ave Fl 9 New York NY 10022-7001*

**WREN, JONATHAN DANIEL,** research scientist; b. Tallahassee, Oct. 12, 1968; s. Daniel A. and Karen Wren; m. Thanya Del Valle Santos, Mar. 21, 1998; children: Karen Nicole, Ethan Daniel. BBA, U. Okla., Norman, 1986—91, BS, 1994—96; PhD, U. Tex. Southwestern Med. Ctr., Dallas, 1996—2002. Rschr. in bioinformatics U. Tex. S.W. Med. Ctr., 1996—2003; rsch. scientist U. Okla., Norman, 2003—. Mem.: Okla. Bioinformatics Soc. (pres. 2004). Achievements include invention of an automated literature-based inference system; patents pending for an automated literature-based inference system; discovery of the epigenetic connection to Type II Diabetes; patents for medical biomarkers for human genetic variation. Office: Univ Okla 101 David L Boren Blvd Norman OK 73019 Office Phone: 405-325-3415. Office Fax: 405-325-3442. E-mail: jonathan.wren@ou.edu.

**WREN, ROBERT JAMES,** aerospace engineering manager; b. Moline, Ill., May 12, 1935; m. Jordis Wren; children: James, Patrick, Kiley. BSCE, U. Tex., 1956; MSCE, U. Tex. 1956; doctoral candidate, U. Houston. Registered profl. engr. Tex. Engring. aide Ctrl. Power and Light Co., Corpus Christi, 1954; sta. clk. City of Austin (Tex.) Power Plant, 1954-55; assoc. engr., hydraulic engr. U.S. Bur. of Reclamation, Austin, 1955-57; structural test engr. Gen. Dynamics, Ft. Worth, 1957-62; sr. structural dynamics engr., mgr. vibration and acoustic test facility NASA-Manned Spacecraft Ctr., Houston, 1962-63, 63-64, head exptl. dynamics sect., 1965-70; mgr. Apollo Spacecraft 2TV-1 CSM Test Program, 1966-68, Apollo Lunar Module-2 Drop Test Program, 1968-70; mgr. structural design space sta., space base, lunar base, mars mission NASA-Manned Spacecraft Ctr., Houston, 1970-73; mgr. structural design and devel., space shuttle carrier aircraft-747 NASA Johnson Space Ctr., Houston, 1973-74, mgr. structural divsn. space shuttle payload systems, 1974-84; mgr. directorate for space shuttle payload safety NASA-Johnson Space Ctr., Houston, 1984-94, mem. space shuttle payload safety rev. panel, 1984-2000, alternate chmn. space shuttle payload safety review panel, 1994-2000, mgr. engring. dir. vehicle and payload flight sys. safety, 1994-2000. Mem. NASA Internat. Space Sta. Flight sys. safety panel, 1994-2000; dir. safety and mission assurance Internat. Space Sta. Program Office, United Space Alliance Hdqs., Houston, 2000—. Pres. Friendswood Little League Baseball, 1980-83; bd. dirs. Bay Area YMCA, Houston, 1982—, chmn., 1983-84. Recipient Sustained Superior Performance award NASA, Personal Letter of Commendation, George Low NASA Apollo Program, Outstanding Svc. award NASA, Group Achievement awards NASA; Paul Harris fellow Rotary. Mem. Space Ctr. Rotary (dir., treas., sec., v.p. 1979-85, pres. 1985-86, Rotary dist. 5890/govt. rep. 1986-87, area coord. 1987-89, zone leader 1988-89, gov.'s aide 1989-90, chmn. dist. assembly 1989-90, 93-94, fin. com. 1989-91, Rotary Nat. award for Space Achievement Found./co-founder, bd. dirs. 1984—), Rotary World Health Found. Plastic Surgery for Children (bd. dirs. 1985—), Rotary Space Meml. Found. (co-founder, bd. dirs. 1986—, co-founder, bd. dirs. Rotary Space Rotary Endowment Found., 1987—). Methodist. Avocations: snow and water skiing, running, scuba diving, tennis, sailing. Home: PO Box 1466 Friendswood TX 77549-1466 Office: United Space Alliance Hdqrs 1150 Gemini Houston TX 77058 E-mail: robert.j.wren@ush.unitedspacealliance.com

**WRENN, CHRISTOPHER JAY,** physician; b. Margarita, Panama Canal Zone, July 16, 1947; s. Earl Walton and Maxine Elizabeth (Luther) W.; m. Nancy Margaret Bowie, June 27, 1970; children: Kristina Elizabeth, Courtney Bowie. BS, Baylor U., 1969; MD, U. Nebr., 1973. Diplomate Am. Bd. Pediatrics, Am. Bd. Allergy and Immunology. Intern pediatrics Children's Med. Ctr., Dallas, 1973-74, resident pediatrics, 1974-76, chief resident pediatrics, 1976-77; staff pediatrician Los Barrios Unidos Community Clinic, Dallas, 1977-78; fellow allergy and immunology Med. Br. U. Tex., Galveston, Tex., 1978-80; practice medicine specializing in allergy Graves-Gilbert

Clinic, Bowling Green, Ky., 1980-83, Wichita Clinic, 1983-84, Allergy Clinic, Tyler, Tex., 1984—. Staff pediatrician Dallas County Children's Shelter, 1975-78, Dallas County Juvenile Detention Ctr., 1975-78, Buckner Bapt. Children's Home, 1977-78. Author (chpt. of book) Pediatrics by Self Instruction, 1982. Fellow Am. Acad. Pediatrics, Am. Coll. Allergists; mem. Am. Acad. Allergy and Immunology. Presbyterian. Avocation: writing fiction and poetry. Office: Allergy Clinic PA 1128 Medical Dr Tyler TX 75701 Office Phone: 903-593-8273.

**WRIGGERS, WILLY RUDOLF,** science educator; Degree, U. Regensburg, Germany, 1992; PhD, U. Ill., 1998. Rsch. assoc. U. Calif., San Diego, 1997—99; asst. prof. Scripps Rsch. Inst., La Jolla, Calif., 1999—2003; from asst. to assoc. prof. U. Tex. Sch. Health Info. Sci., Houston, 2003—. Recipient John P. McGovern Outstanding Tchr. Award, U. Tex. Health Sci. Ctr. Houston, 2004, Paper of Yr. award, Jour. Structural Biology, 2001; Predoctoral fellow, Friedrich Ebert Found., Germany, 1991—94, Internat. Vis. scholar, German Acad. Exch. Svc., 1992—93, Postdoctoral fellow, Burroughs Wellcome Fund, 1998—99, Rsch. grantee, NIH, 2001—06, 2006—, Human Frontier Sci. Program, 2003—, Computational and Evolutionary Molecular Biology fellow, Alfred P. Sloan Found., 2003—. Mem.: Am. Chem. Soc., Microscopy Soc. Am., Am. Crystallographic Assn., IEEE Computer Soc., Biophys. Soc., U. Ill. Alumni Assn. (life). Achievements include research in multi-scale molecular modeling. Office: U Texas Sch Health Info Sci 7000 Fannin St Ste 600 Houston TX 77030 Office Phone: 713-500-3961.

**WRIGHT, ADAM,** information technology executive; b. Berkeley, Calif., Oct. 3, 1981; s. Harold and Diane Wright. BS with hons., Stanford U., Calif., 2004. Pres. HappyLand Software Corp., Portland, Oreg., 1996—; engr. Intel Corp., Hillsboro, Oreg., 1998—2004; fellow Oreg. Health & Sci. U., Portland, 2004—; vis. fellow Office Nat. Coord. for Health Info. Tech., Washington. Chmn. bd. dirs. Chapel Courtyard, Lake Oswego, Oreg., 2000—05. Recipient Presdl. Academic Excellence award, Stanford U.; fellow, Nat. Libr. Medicine, 2004—; scholar, Nat. Merit Scholarship Corp. Mem.: Health Info. Mgmt. Sys. Soc. (state bd. dirs. 2004—), Am. Med. Informatics Assn., Phi Beta Kappa, Tau Beta Pi. Achievements include research in assistive and rehabilitative technology for Alzheimer's patients; development of strategies for deploying ambulatory electronic health records; first to data mining techniques for large patient data warehouses; development of standards for automatic defibrillator deployment. Avocations: golf, swimming, basketball. Home: 7 Westminster Dr Lake Oswego OR 97034 Office: Oregon Health & Science University 3181 Sam Jackson Park Rd Portland OR 97239

**WRIGHT, ALAN,** lawyer; b. Ft. Worth, Tex., May 17, 1956; BA with high honors, U. Tex., 1978, MPA, 1982, JD with honors, 1982. Bar: N.Mex. 1982, Tex. 1985, admitted to practice: US Ct. Appeals (10th Cir.) 1982, US Dist. Ct. (Dist. N.Mex.) 1983, US Dist. Ct. (No. Dist.) Tex. 1984, US Ct. Appeals (5th Cir.) 1984, US Dist. Ct. (We. Dist.) Tex. 1986, US Supreme Ct. 1987, US Dist. Ct. (So. Dist.) Tex. 1992, US Dist. Ct. (Ea. Dist.) Tex. 1992, US Ct. Appeals (3rd Cir.) 1992, US Ct. Appeals (11rd Cir.) 1992, US Ct. Appeals (6th Cir.) 1993, US Ct. Appeals (8th Cir.) 1993, US Ct. Appeals (Fed. Cir.) 2005. Ptnr., appellate law Haynes and Boone LLP, Dallas. Mem.: Dallas Bar Found., Dallas Bar Assn., ABA, State Bar N. Mex., Phi Beta Kappa. Office: Haynes and Boone LLP 901 Main St Ste 3100 Dallas TX 75202-3789 Office Phone: 214-651-5575. Office Fax: 214-200-0614. Business E-Mail: alan.wright@haynesboone.com.

**WRIGHT, ANDREW,** English literature educator; b. Columbus, Ohio, June 28, 1923; s. Francis Joseph and Katharine (Timberman) W.; m. Virginia Rosemary Banks, June 27, 1952; children: Matthew Leslie Francis, Emma Stanbery. AB, Harvard U., 1947; MA, Ohio State U., 1948, PhD, 1951. Prof. English lit. U. Calif., San Diego, 1963—, chmn. dept. lit., 1971-74; dir. U. Calif. Study Center, U.K. and Ireland, 1980-82. Vis. prof. U. Queensland, Australia, 1984, Colegio de la Frontera Norte, San Antonio del Mar, Baja, Calif., 1991-92. Author: Jane Austen's Novels: A Study In Structure, 1953, Joyce Cary: A Preface to His Novels, 1958, Henry Fielding: Mask and Feast, 1965, Blake's Job: A Commentary, 1972, Anthony Trollope: Dream and Art, 1983; Fictional Discourse and Historical Space, 1987; contbg. author numerous books, articles to profl. jours., numerous short stories to lit. mags.; editorial bd. Nineteenth Century Fiction, 1964-86. Bd. dirs. Calif. Coun. Humanities, 1983-87. Guggenheim fellow, 1960, 70; Fulbright Sr. Research fellow, 1960-61 Fellow Royal Soc. Lit.; mem. MLA, Jane Austen Soc., Athenaeum (London), Trollope Soc., Santayana Soc., Phi Beta Kappa. Home: 7227 Olivetas Ave La Jolla CA 92037-5335 Office: U Calif San Diego Dept Lit La Jolla CA 92093-0410 Business E-Mail: ahwright@ucsd.edu.

**WRIGHT, BAGLEY,** venture capitalist, entrepreneur, art collector; m. Virginia Bloedel; children: Merrill, Charles, Robin. BA, Princeton U., 1946. With Daily Mirror, Newsweek; real estate developer Pentagram Corp., Harbor Properties; chmn Physio Control Corp., 1968—80. Developer Space Needle, Seattle. Named one of Top 200 Collectors, ARTnews Mag., 2004, 2006. Avocation: Collector of Contemporary Art; Japanese Art. Office: 407 Dexter Ave Seattle WA 98109*

**WRIGHT, BARBARA CLARE,** business librarian; b. Mt. Holly, N.J., Dec. 6, 1943; d. Charles Hodge and Charlotte Elizabeth (Brown) W. BA, Temple U., 1966; MS, Drexel U., 1972; MA, Temple U., 1985. Circulation asst. Temple U., Phila., 1967-72, asst. to dir., 1972-75, asst. to dir. of pub. svcs., 1975-77, reference libr., 1977-80, bus. libr., 1980—. Mem. ALA, Pa. Libr. Assn., Spl. Librs. Assn., Assn. Coll. and Rsch. Librs., Drexel U. Libr. Sch. Alumni Assn. Democrat. Office: Temple U Paley Libr 1210 W Berks St Philadelphia PA 19122 Office Phone: 215-204-3189. Business E-Mail: bwright@temple.edu.

**WRIGHT, BETTY REN,** children's book writer; b. Wakefield, Mich., June 15, 1927; d. William and Revena Evelyn (Trezise) W.; m. George Albert Frederiksen, Oct. 9, 1976. BA, Milw.-Downer Coll., 1949. With Western Pub. Co., Inc., 1949-78, mng. editor Racine Editl., 1967-78. Author: The Doll House Murders, 1983, Christina's Ghost, 1985, The Summer of Mrs. MacGregor, 1986, A Ghost in the Window, 1987, The Pike River Phantom, 1988, Rosie and the Dance of the Dinosaurs, 1989, The Ghost of Ernie P., 1990, A Ghost in the House, 1991, The Scariest Night, 1991, The Ghosts of Mercy Manor, The Ghost of Popcorn Hill, 1993, The Ghost Witch, 1993, A Ghost Comes Calling, 1994, Out of the Dark, 1995, Haunted Summer, 1996, Too Many Secrets, 1997, The Ghost in Room 11, 1998, A Ghost in the Family, 1998, Pet Detectives, 1999, The Moonlight Man, 2000, The Wish Master, 2000, Crandalls' Castle, 2003, The Blizzard, 2003, Princess for a Week, 2006; contbr. articles to mags. Recipient Alumni Svc. award Lawrence U., 1973, Lynde and Harry Bradley Maj. Achievement award, 1997, numerous awards for books including Mo. Mark Twain award, 1986, 96, Tex. Bluebonnet award, 1986, 88, Young Readers award Pacific N.W. Libr. Assn., 1986, Reviewer's Choice Booklist, Ala. Young Readers award, 1987, Ga. Children's Choice award, 1988, Ind. Young Hoosier Book award, 1989, 96, Children's Choice Book/Internat. Reading Assn.—CBC, 1984, S.C. Children's Choice award, 1995, Okla. Sequoyah Children's Choice award, 1988, 95, award Fla. Sunshine State, 2001. Mem.: Coun. Wis. Authors (Juvenile Book award 1985, 1996), Allied Authors, Phi Beta Kappa. Avocations: reading, travel. Home and Office: 6223 Hilltop Dr Racine WI 53406-3479

**WRIGHT, BOB (ROBERT C. WRIGHT),** broadcast executive; b. Rockville Center, N.Y., Apr. 23, 1943; m. Suzanne Werner, Aug. 26, 1967; children: Kate, Christopher, Maggie. AB in History, Coll. Holy Cross, 1965; LLB, U. Va., 1968. Bar: N.Y. 1968, Va. 1968, Mass. 1970, N.J. 1971. With GE Co., 1969—70, 1973—80, gen. mgr. plastics sales dept., 1978—80; law sec. to chief judge US Dist. Ct., N.J., 1970—73; pres. Cox Cable Comm., Atlanta, 1980—83; exec. v.p. Cox Comm., 1980—83; v.p., gen. mgr. housewares, audio and cable TV ops. GE, 1983—84; pres., CEO GE Fin. Svcs. Inc., 1984—86; vice chmn., exec. officer GE, 2000—; pres., CEO NBC, N.Y.C., 1986—2001, chmn., CEO, 2001—04, NBC Universal, 2004—. Bd.

dirs. GE, 2000—, Motion Picture & Television Fund Corp., Damon Runyon Cancer Res. Found.; bd. trustees Am. Film Inst., Mus. Television & Radio; hon. trustee Found. Am. Women in Radio & Television; bd. governors New York - Presbyterian Hosp.; mem. Soc. N.Y. Hosp. Inc.; trustee Coll. Holy Cross. Recipient Steven J. Ross Humanitarian of Yr. award, UJA Fedn. NY. Office: NBC 30 Rockefeller Plz New York NY 10112-0002

**WRIGHT, BONNIE H.,** elementary school educator; b. Raleigh, NC, Sept. 30, 1960; d. William T. and Secunda P. Huxster; m. Tony T. Wright, Aug. 8, 1989 (dec.); 1 child, Josh Gordon. BA in Early Childhood Edn., U. NC, Charlotte, 1982, BA in Intermediate Edn., 1984, BA in Intermediate Edn., 2002. Cert. mentor N.C., 1989. 6th & 7th grade mid. sch. math tchr. Scotland County Schs., Laurinburg, NC, 1988—89, 6th grade elem. tchr. Charlotte-Mecklenburg Schs., NC, 1988—89, 6th grade elem. tchr., 1989—90; 7th grade mid. sch. math tchr. Wake County Pub. Schs., Raleigh, NC, 1991—92; elem. and mid. sch. math tchr. Charlotte-Mecklenburg Schs., NC, 1992—2000; 7th and 8th grade mid. sch. sci. tchr. Charlotte Christian Sch., NC, 2000—. Migrant edn. instr. Scotland County Schs., Laurinburg, NC, 1984—85, math/sci. fair coord., 1984—85, math dept. head, 1985—86, so. assn. creditation for schools, 1985—86, math field day coord., 1986—87, grade level chairperson, 1986—87, mid. sch. tv teen scene, 1987—88, refugee tutorial program, 1987—88; assistance and intervention team Charlotte-Mecklenburg Schs., NC, 1988—91; math counts coord. Wake County Pub. Schs., Raleigh, NC, 1991—92, Beta Club sponsor, 1991—92, sch. improvement com., 1991—92, staff devel. com., 1991—92, math dept. head, 1991—92, team leader, 1991—92; grade level chairperson Charlotte-Mecklenburg Schs., NC, 1992—2000, mentor, 1992—2000, math field day coord., 1992—93, pre-algebra acad. instr., 1993—95, minority achievement com., 1995—98, sci. fair coord., 1995—98, right moves coord., 1998—99; sci. dept. com. Charlotte Christian Sch., NC, 2000—04, grade chairperson/team leader, 2000—05, initially lic. tchr. (ILT) coord., 2000—06, math tutor, 2000—06, 8th grade trip coord., 2000—06. Summer sch. instr. Charlotte-Mecklenburg Schs., NC, 1988—98, Scotland County Schs., Laurinburg, NC, 1985—88, Wake County Pub. Schs., Raleigh, NC, 1991—92; vol. Operation Christmas Child, Charlotte Christian Schs., NC, 2000—06; Bible svc. project Charlotte Christian Sch., 2002—03; Sunday sch. tchr. U. City United Meth. Ch., Charlotte, 1994—98; partnership of mid. sch. students with pre-k students as mentors and to incorporate literacy Charlotte Christian Sch., NC, 2005—06. Finalist Joint Engring. Societies Award for Outstanding Math & Sci. Tchr., Engrs. of Am., 1993, Harris Y award, First Union Bank, 1995; recipient Tchr. of the Yr. award, Sycamore Ln. Mid. Sch. in Scotland County, 1987, Tchr. of the Yr. 1st Runner-up in Scotland County, Scotland County Schs., 1987, Unsung Am. Heroes award, ING, 2005. Fellow: N.C. Assn. of Educators (assoc.), Internat. Reading Assn. (assoc.), Parent, Tchr., Student Assn. (assoc.), Career Devel. Program (assoc.), PTO (assoc.), Assn. of Christian Schs. (assoc.), Assn. of Christian Schs. (assoc.); mem.: Parent Tchr. Fellowship (assoc.), PTA (assoc.), N.C. Coun. of Tchg. Math. (assoc.), N.C. Sci. Tchrs. Assn. (assoc.), Delta Zeta (life). Dc Statehood Party. Methodist. Avocations: travel, coin collector, piano, cross-stitching, scrapbooking. Home: 2845 Sharon View Rd Charlotte NC 28210 Office: Charlotte Christian Sch 7301 Sardis Rd Charlotte NC 28270 Office Phone: 704-366-5657. Office Fax: 704-366-5678. Business E-Mail: bonnie.wright@charchrist.com.

**WRIGHT, BONNIE SHANKLE,** assistant principal, choir director; b. Jan. 16, 1960; d. Preston and Adeline Luttrell Shankle; m. James Barry Wright, June 9, 1984; children: Preston, David. B in Music Edn., Ind. U., 1983; MA in Tchg., Bethel Coll., 1990. Cert. ednl. specialist Union U., 2005. Tchr. Covington Elem., Tenn., 1986—99; chorus, drama tchr. Covington HS, 1999—2003; asst. prin. Covington Integrated Arts Acad., 2003—05. Instr. Red Cross, 1983—2004; pianist, bell choir dir. First United Methodist Ch., Covington, 1997—2005, choir dir., 2003—05. Mem.: Alpha Delta Kappa (pres. 2003). Republican. Methodist. Office: Covington Integrated Arts Acad 760 Bert Johnston Covington TN 38019

**WRIGHT, BRADLEY ABBOTT,** lawyer; b. Des Moines, Nov. 24, 1964; s. James Bradley and Carolyn (Abbott) W.; m. Alisa Labut, Aug. 24, 1993; children: Hannah, Alexandra. BA, Miami U., Oxford, Ohio, 1987; JD, Ohio State U., 1990. Bar: Ohio 1990. Assoc. Roetzel & Andress, Akron, Ohio, 1990-97, ptnr., 1997—. Grad. Leadership Akron, 1998; active Big Bros. and Big Sisters, Inc., Akron, United Way of Summit County, Akron. Mem. Akron Bar Assn. (vice chmn./social chmn.), Transp. Lawyers Assn., Def. Rsch. Inst., Assn. for Transp. Law Logistics and Policy, Am. Trucking Assn., Nat. Assn. R.R. Trial Counsel. Home: 91 N Hayden Pkwy Hudson OH 44236-3157 Office: Roetzel & Andress 222 S Main St Akron OH 44308-1533 E-mail: bwright@ralaw.com.

**WRIGHT, BURTON,** sociologist; b. Detroit, Jan. 31, 1917; s. Burton and Hazel Marie (Thomas) Wright; m. Marie Fidelis Gallivan, Jan. 26, 1942; children: Burton III(dec.), Catherine Margaret(dec.). AA, C.Z. Coll., 1944; BA, U. Wash., 1947, MA, 1949; PhD, Fla. State U., 1972. Enlisted USN, 1937, commd. and advanced through grades to comdr., 1957; dir. Naval Res. Recruiting, 1960-64; ret., 1964; mem. faculty U. Wash., 1947-49, George Washington U., Washington, 1954-60, Rollins Coll., Winter Park, Fla., 1966-69; prof. dept. sociology U. Ctrl. Fla., Orlando, 1972-82, prof. emeritus, 1982-89; ret., 1989; prof. sociology Troy State U., 1991—. Cons. Ford Found., 1951, Dept. Air Force, 1955, U.S. Army Chem. Corps, 1956; mem. faculty Northwestern U., summers 1956-59; vis. prof. sociology Troy U., Dothon; dir. Am. Sociol. Assn. Nat. Honors Program, 1981-89. Author: (with J.P. Weiss and C.M. Unkovic) Perspective: An Introduction to Sociology, 1975, (with V. Fox) Criminal Justice and the Social Sciences, 1978, (with J.P. Weiss) Social Problems, 1980; contbr. articles to pubs. Decorated Navy Commendation medal. Fellow Am. Anthrop. Assn.; mem. AAUP, Am. Sociol. Assn. (membership com. 1983-86), Soc. Psychol. Study Social Problems. Am. Avnd. Arts and Scis., Soc. Study Social Problems So. Sociol. Soc., North Ctrl. Sociol. Soc., Univ. Club (Winter Park). Roman Catholic. Home: 502 Dunleith Blvd Dothan AL 36303-2936 Personal E-Mail: bw7626@ala.net.

**WRIGHT, C. T. ENUS,** former academic administrator; b. Social Circle, Ga., Oct. 4, 1942; s. George and Carrie Mae (Enus) W.; m. Mary Stephens, Aug. 9, 1974. BS, Fort Valley State U., Ga., 1964; MA, Atlanta U., 1967; PhD, Boston U., 1977; LHD, Mary Holmes Coll., 2000. Tchr. Ga. Pub. Schs., Social Circle, 1965-67; mem. faculty Morris Brown Coll., Atlanta, 1967-73, divsn. chmn., 1973-77; program dir., asst. provost Eastern Wash. U., Cheney, 1977-81; v.p. acad. affairs Talladega Coll. (Ala.), 1981-82; pres. Cheyney U. Pa., Cheyney, 1982-85; v.p. and provost Fla. Meml. Coll., 1985-89; pres. Internat. Found. and Coord. African-African Am. Summit, 1989-2001; chmn., founder The Light of Hope Inst., 2000—; pres., CEO IFESH, 2001—04; pres. AZ Africa, 2004—. Cons. and lectr. in field; bd. dirs. Internat. Found. for Edn. and Self Help, England, Leow Sullivan Trdst, South-Africa, People's Investment Fund for Africa; chmn. adv. com. AMI Consultants, 1982—. Author: (booklet) The History of Black Historical Mythology, 1980; contbr. articles to profl. jours. Commr. Wash. Pub. Broadcasting, Olympia, 1980—84; exec. com. Boy Scouts Am., Phila., 1982—; Goodwill Amb. State of Ga., 1997—; chmn. com. World Children Relief, 2002—. Human Rels. scholar, 1969, Nat. Tchg. fellow, Boston U., 1971. Mem. Am. Assn. Colls. and Univs. (coms. 1982—), Am. Hist. Assn. (coms. 1970—), Assn. Study Afro-Am. Life & History (coms. 1965—), Nat. Assn. Equal Opportunity in Higher Edn. (coms. 1982—), NEA (coms. 1965—), Am. Baptist. Clubs: Lions (Cheyney, Wash. (v.p. 1979-81), Tuscan, Fountain Hills Times, Atlanta Constitution. Address: 17420 E Dull Knife Dr Fountain Hills AZ 85268 Office Phone: 480-837-5534. E-mail: ctwright31@cox.net.

**WRIGHT, CARLTON JEFFERY,** music educator, conductor; b. Montgomery, Ala., Mar. 28, 1962; s. James Arthur and Adeline Wright; m. Jocelyn Payton, Apr. 11, 1963; children: Walter Joseph Payton, Carmen Catrice, Jaylen Janae. BS, Ala. A&M U., 1986; MA, Hampton U., Va., 1993. Ala. State Dept. Edn., Ala., 1987. Dir. of bands Fairfield H.S., Ala., 1987—91, Fairfield High Prep. Sch., 1993—2001, George Wash. Carver H.S. Band, Montgomery, Ala., 2001—03; asst. dir. of bands Minor H.S., Adamsville,

Ala., 2003—. Instr. Lawson State CC, Brimingham, 2005—; dir. bands Minor HS, Adamsville, 2005—. Capt. USAR, 1987—91, Hoover, Ala. Recipient Tchr. Yr., Fairfield H.S., Fairfield Bd. Edn., 1996, 1998. Mem.: NEA (life), Jefferson County Edn. Assn. (life), Ala. Music Educators Assn. (life), Music Educators Nat. Conf. (life), Ala. Edn. Assn. (life). Baptist. Achievements include Marching and Jazz band arrangements. Avocations: music, travel, exercise, gardening. Office: Minor High Sch 2285 Minor Pky Adamsville AL 35005 Office Phone: 205-796-2263. Personal E-Mail: cwright@bham.rr.com or cbanddirector@yahoo.com.

**WRIGHT, CAROLYN D. (C.D. WRIGHT),** language educator, poet; b. Mountain Home, Ark., 1949; BA, U. Memphis, 1971; MFA, U. Ark., 1976. Lectr. poetry San Francisco State U., 1979—81; prof. English Brown U., Providence, 1983—. Vis. faculty Burren Sch. Art., Ireland, 1996, U. Iowa., 1997, U. Cin., 2004. Author: Terrorism, 1979, Translations of the Gospel Back into Tongues, 1981, Further Adventures With You, 1986, String Light, 1991 (Poetry Ctr. Book award), Just Whistle, 1993, The Lost Roads Project: A Walk-in Book of Arkansas, 1994, The Reader's Map of Arkansas, 1994, Tremble, 1996, Deepstep Come Shining, 1998, Steal Away: Selected and New Poems, 2002, One Big Self, 2003, Cooling Time: An American Poetry Vigil, 2005, numerous poems. Named State Poet RI, 1994—99; recipient Witter Bynner prize for poetry, 1986, Whiting Writers award, 1989, Gov. Award for Arts, RI, 1990, Lila Wallace award, 1992; fellow, Nat. Endowment for Arts, 1981, 1987; Guggenheim fellow, 1987, MacArthur Fellow, 2004. Fellow: Am. Acad. Arts and Scis. Office: Brown U Box 1923 Providence RI 02912 Business E-Mail: Carolyn_Wright@Brown.edu.

**WRIGHT, C(ARROLL) LEE, JR.,** architecture educator; m. Beverly Ann Carroll, 1980; children: Benjamin Carroll, Alexander Lee. BArch, U. Tex., 1963, MArch, 1969. With Hirsch and Cassetti, Elmira, NY, 1964—65, Claude Pendley, Austin, Brook, Barr, Graeber and White, Austin, Pierce/Lacey Assocs., Dallas, 1965; mem. faculty U. Tex., Arlington, 1968—, assoc. prof. arch., 1972—, assoc. dean, 1975—77, dir. arch. program, 1978—79, undergrad. advisor, 1989—99, interim dean Sch. Arch., 1999—2001, assoc. dean Sch. Arch., 1993—99, dir. arch., 2002—04; pvt. practice Lee Wright Assocs., 1968—. Mem. univ. curriculum com. U. Tex., Arlington; bd. dirs. Dallas Arch. Found., 1999—2002; acad. and career counselor Sch. Arch., 2004—. Named Outstanding Advisor, U. Tex. Arlington, 1993. Office: Univ Tex Arlington Sch Arch Rm 203 Box 19108 701 S Nedderman Dr Arlington TX 76019-0108

**WRIGHT, CHARLES PENZEL, JR.,** language educator; b. Pickwick Dam, Tenn., Aug. 25, 1935; s. Charles Penzel and Mary Castleman (Winter) Wright; m. Holly McIntire, Apr. 6, 1969; 1 child, Luke Savin Herrick. BA, Davidson Coll., 1957; MFA, U. Iowa, 1963; postgrad., U. Rome, 1963—64. Mem. faculty U. Calif., Irvine, Calif., 1966—83, prof. English, 1976—83; mem. faculty U. Va., Charlottesville, Va., 1983—. Vis. prof. N.Am. Lit. U., Padua, Italy, 1968—69; disting. vis. prof. U. Degli Studi, Florence, Italy, 1992. Translator: The Storm and Other Poems (Eugenio Montale), 1978, Orphic Songs (Dino Campana), 1984. With AUS, 1957—61. Recipient Pen Transl. prize, 1979, Nat Book award for Poetry, 1983, citation in poetry, Brandeis U. Creative Arts Awards, 1987, L.A. Times Book prize, 1997, award, Nat. Book Critics Circle, 1997, Pulitzer Prize, 1998, Ambassador Book award, 1998; fellow Guggeheim fellow, 1976, Ingram Merrill fellow, 1980, 1993; scholar, Fulbright Found., 1963—65. Mem.: Acad. Am. Poets (chancellor), Am. Acad. Arts and Sci., Am. Acad. Arts and Letters, Fellowship of So. Writers. Home: 940 Locust Ave Charlottesville VA 22901-4030 Office: English Dept Univ Va Charlottesville VA 22901

**WRIGHT, CHATT GRANDISON,** academic administrator; b. San Mateo, Calif., Sept. 17, 1941; s. Virgil Tandy and Louise (Jeschien) W.; children from previous marriage: Stephen Brook, Jon David, Shelley Adams; m. Janice Teply, Nov. 28, 1993. Student, U. Calif., Berkeley, 1960-62; BA in Polit. Sci., U. Calif., Davis, 1964; MA in Econs., U. Hawaii, 1968. Instr. econs. U. Hawaii, Honolulu, 1968-70; mgr. corp. planning Telecheck Internat., Inc., Honolulu, 1969—70; economist State of Hawaii, Honolulu, 1970—71; adminstr. manpower City & County of Honolulu, 1971-72; bus. adminstr., dean. Hawaii Pacific U., Honolulu, 1972-74, v.p., 1974-76, pres., 1976—. Mem. City and County of Honolulu Manpower Area Planning Commn., 1976—82; mem. Mayor's Salary Commn. City and County of Honolulu, 1977—80; mem. Honolulu City Ethics Commn., 1978—84, City and County of Honolulu Labor Market Adv. Coun., 1982—84; bd. dirs. Hawaii Econ. Devel. Corp., 1980—84; trustee Queen's Med. Ctr., Honolulu, 1986—92, Honolulu Armed Svcs. YMCA, 1984—86, Hawaii Maritime Ctr., 1990—92; chmn. bd. trustees Hist. Hawaii Found., 1995—96, trustee, 1990—96; mem. adv. bd. Cancer Rsch. Ctr. Hawaii, 1987; trustee St. Andrew's Priory Sch., 1994—98; bd. dirs. Hawaii Visitors Bur., 1995—97; bd. dir. Downtown Improvement Assn., 1988—96; bd. dirs. Outrigger Duke Kahanamoku Found., 1996—98, Hawaii Opera Theatre, 1997—99; bd. govs. Hawaii Coun. on Econ. Edn., 1998—; trustee Oceanic Inst., 1998—, chmn., 2003—; mem. Hawaii Execs. Coun., 1996—, chmn., 2002, Hawaii Exec. Conf., 2002; bd. govs. Hawaii Med. Libr., 1989—92; mem. adv. bd. Aloha coun. Boy Scouts Am., 1991—2002; trustee Molokai Gen. Hosp., 1991—92; mem. Pacific Asian Affairs Coun., 1990—2001; steering com. Asian Devel. Bank, 2000—. With USN, 1968—70. Recipient Pioneer award Pioneer Fed. Savs. Bank, 1982, Stephen J. Jackstadt award, Hawaii Coun. Econ. Edn., 1998; named Sales Person of Yr., Sales and Mktg. Execs. of Honolulu, 1998; Paul Harris fellow Rotary, 1986. Mem.: Hawaii Assn. Ind. Colls. and Univs. (chmn. 1986), Western Coll. Assn. (exec. com. 1989—92), Hawaii Joint Coun. Econ. Edn. (bd. dirs. 1982—88), Nat. Assn. Intercollegiate Athletics (mem. 1985—98, vice chair NAIA coun. of pres. 1994), Assn. Governing Bds. Univs. and Colls., Am. Assn. Higher Edn., Soc. Sci. Assn. (mem. 1994—99), Japan-Am. Soc. Honolulu, Waialae Country Club, Plaza Club (bd. govs. 1992—97), Pacific Club (Honolulu), Outrigger Canoe Club. Republican. Episcopalian. Avocations: hunting, fishing, reading, travel. Office: Hawaii Pacific U Office of Pres 1166 Fort Street Mall Honolulu HI 96013-2700 E-mail: president@hpu.edu.

**WRIGHT, CHELY,** country singer; b. Kans. City, Mo., Oct. 25, 1970; Founder Reading, Writing and Rhythm Found. Singer: (songs) He's a Good Ole Boy, 1994, Love That We Lost, 1996, Shut Up and Drive, 1997, Jezebel, 2001, Bumper of My S.U.V., 2004, (albums) Woman in the Moon, 1994, Right in the Middle of It, 1996, Let Me In, 1997, Single White Female, 1991, Never Love You Enough, 2001; actor: (films) Max Keeble's Big Movie, 2001, (TV appearance) Another World, 1999. Recipient Top New Female Vocalist award, Acad. Country Music, 1994. Mailing: PO Box 627 Mokena IL 60448

**WRIGHT, CLARK PHILLIPS,** computer systems specialist; b. Orange, Tex., Aug. 30, 1942; s. Madison Brown and Mary Elizabeth (Phillips) W.; m. Stacy Charlotte Klutz, June 5, 1965 (div. Oct. 1979); m. Cora Lou Alexandria Schelling, Oct. 31, 1979; 1 child, Isaac Schelling. BA, U. Tex., 1965. Computer programmer Lockheed Electronics Co., Houston, 1965-67; prin. analyst Control Data Corp., St. Paul, 1967-76; computer scientist DBA Systems, Inc., Lanham, Md., 1976-79; engring. specialist Ford Aerospace Corp., Houston, 1979-90, Loral Aerospace Corp., 1990-97, Lockheed Martin Space Mission, 1997—. Precinct chmn. Rep. Party of Tex., 1982-86. Mem. IEEE, Math. Assn. Am., Assn. Computing Machinery, SAR (chartered, sec., treas.), Sons Republic Tex., Info. Sys. Security Assn., Masons, Rotary. Avocations: travel, photography. Home: 5000 Park Ave Dickinson TX 77539-7013 Office: Lockheed Martin Space Ops PO Box 58487 Houston TX 77258-8487 Personal E-Mail: cpwright@ghg.net. Business E-Mail: clark.p.wright@lmco.com.

**WRIGHT, CONSTANCE MOHR,** retired elementary school educator; b. N.Y.C., Oct. 28, 1934; d. Conrad Franz Josef and Olga Maria (Kuttner) Mohr; children: Melani Mohr, Bradley Edward. B in Music Edn., Westminster Coll., 1956; MEd, Fla. Atlantic U., 1980; EdS, Nova U., 1983. Tchr. Waldwick (N.J.) Schs., 1956-58, East Orange (N.J.) Schs., 1958-59, Ramsey (N.J.) Schs., 1959-64, Palm Beach County Schs., West Palm Beach, Fla., 1978—2000, tchr. vocat. edn., exceptional student edn. coord., 1986—2000, ret., 2000. Child care cert. trainer HRS, Palm Beach County, 1986; adj. prof. Palm Beach. C.C. and Nova U.; assoc. Master Tchr., Fla.; presenter Nat. Assn. for Gifted Children. Corr. sec. Greenacres (Fla.) PTA, 1986-87; deacon First Presbyn. Ch., Delray Beach, Fla.; vice chair water events SunFest. Ednl. grantee Edn. Found. Palm Beach County, 1986. Mem. Nat. Assn. for Gifted Children (presenter), Fla. Assn. for Gifted (area VII coord.), Zeta Tau Alpha, Phi Delta Kappa. Republican. Presbyterian. Avocation: antiques. Home: 5146 Donnelly Dr Se Olympia WA 98501-5012 Address: 1776 Mariners Walk Fernandina Beach FL 32034 Personal E-mail: cmwright@ispwest.com.

**WRIGHT, CONSTANCE STOREY,** retired humanities educator; b. Boston, Mar. 3, 1928; d. Samuel Lame and Dorothy Storey Wright. BA, Scripps Coll., 1950; MA, U. Calif., Berkeley, 1959, PhD, 1965. Instr. English Grinnell Coll., Iowa, 1952—65; asst. prof. U. Colo., Boulder, 1965—69, assoc. prof., 1969—92, prof. emeritus, 1992—; ret., 1992. Adv. bd. Genders, Boulder, 1985—89, Medieval Assn., Rocky Mountain, Tempe, Ariz., 1987—92; rschr. Monterey (Calif.) Mus. Art, 1996—. Editor: Equally in God's Image, 1990; asst. editor: English Lang. Notes, 1965—2003; author (editor): Tales within Tales: Apuleius through Time, 2000. Sec., bd. dirs. Residents Assn., Carmel, Calif., 1993—2000, Preservation Found., Carmel, 2002—. Mem.: MLA, Dante Soc. Am., New Chaucer Soc. Avocations: Asian art, Asian antiques, Latin literature. Home: PO Box 2331 Carmel CA 93921

**WRIGHT, CREIGHTON BOLTER,** cardiovascular surgeon, educator; b. Washington, Jan. 29, 1939; s. Benjamin Washington and Catherine Adele (Bolter) W.; m. Carolyn Eleanor Craver, Jan. 29, 1966; children: Creighton Bolter, Benson, Kathryn, Elizabeth. BA, Duke U., 1961, MD, 1965; MBA, Xavier U., Cin., 1995. Diplomate Am. Bd. Surgery, Am. Bd. Thoracic Surgery, Am. Bd. Gen. Vascular Surgery. Intern Duke U., Durham, NC, 1965—66; resident in surgery U. Va., Charlottesville, 1966—71; asst. prof., then assoc. prof. George Washington U., Washington, 1974—76; assoc. prof., then prof. surgery U. Iowa, Iowa City, 1976—81; prof. clin. surgery, assoc. dean U. Cin., 1982—; prof. clin. surgery Uniformed Svcs. U., 1982—; dir. dept. surgery Jewish Hosp., Cin., 1989—2003; med. dir. cardiovasc. svcs. Health Alliance Cin., 1999—2003; chief of staff VA Med. Ctr., Cin., 2003—. Councilor Acad. Medicine, 2003—. Editor: Vascular Grafting, 1983, (with others) Venous Trauma, 1983; contbr. articles to med. jours., chpts. to books. Col. USAR, 1966-93. Decorated Bronze Star; recipient Kindred Resident Tchr. award, 1967, Golden Apple Tchg. award, 1975, Tchg. award Jewish Hosp., 2001. Mem.: Greater Cin. Vascular Soc. (pres. 1997—98), Cin. Surgery Soc. (pres. 1996), Midwestern Vascular Surgery Soc., So. Thoracic Surgery Assn., Muller Surg. Soc. (pres. 1985—87), Am. Heart Assn. S.W. Ohio (v.p. 1998—, pres. 2000, Kaplan award 1999, award of excellence 2003), Internat. Soc. Cardiovasc. Surgery, Ctrl. Surg. Assn., Soc. Thoracic Surgery, Am. Assn. Thoracic Surgery, Soc. Vascular Surgery, Soc. Univ. Surgeons, Assn. Acad. Surgery (pres. 1980), Comml. Club, Sigma Chi (Significant Sig award 1993, Hall of Fame 2005), Alpha Omega Alpha. Home: 312 E 2d St Covington KY 41011-1704 Office: Cardiovascular Vascular & Thoracic Surgeons 4030 Smith Rd Ste 300 Norwood OH 45209 Office Phone: 513-421-3494. Personal E-mail: cbw@one.net.

**WRIGHT, DANIEL V.,** judge, carrer military officer; b. Birmingham, Ala., July 4, 1951; married; 4 children. Grad., U.S. Mil Acad., 1973; JD, U. Miami, 1980; grad., Army War Coll., Army Command and Gen. Staff Coll. Bar: Fla. Advanced through ranks to maj. gen. U.S. Army, 2005, with 25th infantry divsn. Schofield Barracks, Hawaii, prosecutor Ft. Dix., NJ, 1980—82, chief adminstrv. law, 1982—85, regimental judge advocate 75th ranger regiment Ft. Benning, Ga., 1985—88, tchr. mil. law br. ctr. for army leadership Command and Gen. Staff Coll. Ft. Leavenworth, Kans., 1988—90, br. chief, 1990—92, dep. staff judge advocate XVIII Airborne Corps Ft. Bragg, 1992—93, legal advisor joint spl. ops. command, 1993—96, staff judge advocate so. European task force Vicenza, Italy, 1996—98, staff judge advocate XVIII airborne corps. Ft. Bragg, 1999—2001, comdr. legal svcs. agency, chief judge ct. criminal appeals, 2001—03, asst. JAG mil. law and ops., 2003—. Decorated Def. Superior Svc. Medal, Legion of Merit, Army Meritorious Svc. Medal, Joint Svc. Commendation Medal, Army Commendation Medal, Army Achievement Medal, Armed Forces Expeditionary Medal, Humanitarian Svc. Medal, Expert Infantryman's Badge, Master Parachutist Badge, Ranger Tab. Office: JAGC US Army Pentagon Washington DC 20310-1500

**WRIGHT, DARCY LAUREEN,** leadership educator, writer; b. Berkeley, Calif., Apr. 15, 1959; d. Larry Edward Mobraaten and Natalie Paula Wells; m. Kirby Michael Wright, Dec. 28, 1991. MBA, San Diego State U., 2003. Assoc. prodr. Golden Films, Menlo Park, Calif., 1995—2000; sr. prodr. Holiday Channel, San Jose, 2000—01; dir. profl. mentor program Tri-City Med. Ctr., Oceanside, Calif., 2004—. Founder SAT Success, Redwood City, Calif., 1998—2000. Recipient Best Feature award, Santa Clarita Internat. Film Festival, 1998. Democrat-Npl. Avocations: jogging, swimming, writing, travel, gardening. Home: 1604 Marbella Dr Vista CA 92081-5463 Office: Tri-City Medical Center 4002 Vista Way Oceanside CA 92056 Office Phone: 760-940-3170. Personal E-mail: wrightdl@tcmc.com. E-mail: dlwright@tcmc.com.

**WRIGHT, DAVID,** professional baseball player; b. Norfolk, Va., Dec. 20, 1982; Third baseman NY Mets, 2004—. Endorsements Hickey Freeman, Nike spikes and batting gloves, Vitamin Water, Wilson David Wright signature glove. Founder David Wright Found., 2005—. Named to NL All-Star Team, MLB, 2006; recipient Defensive Play Yr., This Year in Baseball awards, 2005. Office: Shea Stadium 123-01 Roosevelt Ave Flushing NY 11368*

**WRIGHT, DAVID BURTON,** retired newspaper publishing company executive; b. Fowler, Ind., Aug. 29, 1933; s. Claude Matthew and Rose Ellen (Lavelle) Wright; m. Geraldine F. Gray, May 9, 1964; children: David Andrew, Anne Kathleen. AB, Wabash Coll., 1955. CPA Ind. Audit staff George S. Olive Co. C.P.A.s, Indpls., 1958-63, mgmt. cons., 1963-65; controller Herff Jones Co., 1965-69, corp. controller, asst. sec., 1970-71; asst. bus. mgr. Indpls. Newspapers Inc., 1971-77; asst. sec., treas. Central Newspapers Inc., 1975-79, Muncie Newspapers Inc., 1975-93, Indpls. Newspapers Inc., 1975-93, bus. mgr., 1977-93; sec., treas. Central Newspapers Inc., 1979-89; v.p. Indpls. Newspapers Inc., 1982-93. Mem. St. Francis Hosp. Adv. Bd., Indpls., 1983—99. Sec. St. Francis Hosp. adv. Bd., Indpls., 1986—87, v.p., 1987—91, pres., 1991—93. Served U.S. Army, 1956—58. Mem.: Ind. Assn. CPAs, Knights Columbus, Indpls. Econ. Club. Roman Cath. Home: 6713 Forrest Commons Blvd Indianapolis IN 46227-2396 E-mail: daviddavegerry@aol.com.

**WRIGHT, DAVID L.,** food and beverage company executive; b. Wenatchee, Wash., Mar. 12, 1949; s. Franklin Sven and Mary Elizabeth (Collins) W.; m. Karen Sue Rice, Mar. 28, 1981; children: Kara, Erin, Jonathan, Anna Catherine. BA, U. Calif., Davis, 1971. Chief of rsch. dept. of benefit payments State of Calif., Sacramento, 1972-75; profl. staff mem. com. on agr. U.S. Ho. Reps., Washington, 1975-77; adminstrv. asst., chief of staff Rep. William C. Wampler, Washington, 1977-81; spl. asst. for legis. affairs to Pres. The White House, Washington, 1981-84; dir. govt. affairs PepsiCo Inc., Purchase, NY, 1984-87, v.p. worldwide govt. affairs, 1987—2005; ret. Mem. exec. com. U.S. Coun. for Internat. Bus., 1997-2005; bd. dirs. U.S. C. of C.; vice chair Harvard Ctr. on Media and Child Health, 2004-06. Capt. USAR, 1971-79. Mem Capitol Hill Club.

**WRIGHT, DEBORAH C.,** bank executive; b. Bennetsville, SC, Jan. 30, 1958; BA, Radcliffe, 1980; MBA, JD, Harvard U., 1984. Assoc. corp. fin. First Boston Bank, 1984; dir. mktg. NYC Partnership, Harlem, 1987; apptd. Housing Authority Bd. NYC, 1992, commr., 1994—96; dir. Upper Manhattan Zone Devel. Corp., 1996—99; pres, CEO Carver Bancorp, Harlem, 1999—, chmn., 2005—. Bd. dirs. Carver Bancorp, Inc., Kraft Foods, Time Warner, 2005—; Bd. dirs. Harvard U., Meml. Sloan-Kettering Cancer Ctr., Partnership

NYC, Ministers and Missionaries Benefit Bd. Am. Baptist Churches; founding mem. Lower Manhattan Develop. Corp. Named Community Banker of the Year, The Am. Banker, 2003. Office: Carver Bancorp 75 W 125th St New York NY 10027*

**WRIGHT, DEIL SPENCER,** political science professor; b. Three Rivers, Mich., June 18, 1930; s. William Henry and Gertrude Louise (Buck) W.; m. Patricia Mae Jaffke, Aug. 22, 1953; children: David C., Mark W., Matthew D., Lois L. BA, U. Mich., 1952, M in Pub. Adminstrn., 1954, PhD, 1957. Asst. prof. polit. sci. Wayne State U., Detroit, 1956-59; from asst. to assoc. prof. U. Iowa, Iowa City, 1959-67; assoc. prof. U. Calif., Berkeley, 1965-66; prof. U. N.C., Chapel Hill, 1967-83, alumni disting. prof., 1983—; Carl Hatch vis. prof. U. N.Mex., Albuquerque, 1987. Lectr. USIA, Washington, various dates; cons. Office Mgmt. and Budget, Washington, 1979-80. Author: Understanding Intergovernmental Relations, 3d edit., 1988; editor: Federalism and Intergovernmental Relations, 1984, Globalization and Decentralization, 1996; contbr. over 100 articles to various polit. sci. and pub. adminstrn. jours. Mem. dir's. adv. com. NIH, Bethesda, Md., 1970-74, N.C. Coun. on State Goals and Policies, Raleigh, 1973-77, N.C. State Internship Coun., Raleigh, 1985-93. Internat. Inst. Mgmt. research fellow, Berlin, 1977. Fellow Nat. Acad. Pub. Adminstrn.; mem. AAAS, Am. Polit. Sci. Assn., Am. Soc. Pub. Adminstrn. (Waldo Lifetime Career Achievement award), Midwest Polit. Sci. Assn., Policy Studies Orgn., So. Polit. Sci. Assn. (pres. 1981-82). Lodges: Rotary (bd. dirs. Chapel Hill club 1981, 84, 90, v.p. 2000-01, pres. 2001-02). Republican. Methodist. Home: 204 Velma Rd Chapel Hill NC 27514-7641 Office: U North Carolina Dept Polit Sci CB 3265 Chapel Hill NC 27599-3265 Office Phone: 919-962-0414.

**WRIGHT, DELL,** residential care and treatment facility executive; b. Greenville, S.C., Aug. 29, 1944; s. Thomas C. and Marie (Tate) W.; m. Ines R. Teran, Oct 22, 1977; children: Anthony, Andre, Fionna, Al-Jonn. Diploma in computer tech., Control Data Inst., 1969. Electronic tester RCA, Marlboro, Mass., 1970-71; customer svc. rep. Honeywell Info. Systems, Inc., Waltham, Mass., 1971-75; sr. field engr. Ford Aerospace and Comm. Corp., Palo Alto, Calif., 1975-78; sr. field engr. Ford Aerospace and Comm. Corp., Palo Alto, Calif., 1978-79; systems integration engr. Kentron Internat./NASA/JPL, Pasadena, Calif., 1979-83; sr. fabrication technician Rockwell Internat., Anaheim, Calif., 1983-84; computer engr. Al-Johi Internat., Dhahran, Saudi Arabia, 1984-85; sr. test engr. Gen. Dynamics, San Diego, 1985-88; owner Wrights Food Vending Svc., 1988—90; pres., founder Residential Care and Treatment Facility for Youth, 1991—. Author: Inspirational, 1995, My Life's Journey, 2005; inventor mechanical multiple picture frame. Chair, utilities commr. City of Colton, Calif., 1996—. With U.S. Army, 1962-65. Democrat. Avocations: rv camping, fishing, motorcycling.

**WRIGHT, DIXIE LEE,** special needs persons consultant; b. Winslow, Ind. d. Edward Franklin and Ann Berenece Corne; m. Lendon L. Wright; children: Kevin, LeAnn, Michael. BS in Edn., Ind. U.; postgrad., U. No. Colo., 1980. Self employed workshop developer for schs. and agys.; career coord. postsecondary sch. Colo.; ind. contractor Colo. State Rehab. and other govtl. and ind. agys. working with spl. needs persons. Cons., job assessor for special need persons, Colo.; presenter in field. Author: Know How is the Key, 1997, Job Survival: How to Adjust and Keep Your Job, 2000, 2d edit., 2005, Stuff You Need to Know to Teach Job Retention, 2000, Job Smarts, 2004. Bd. dirs. Littleton C. of C. Mem.: AARP (state coord. works program), Bus. Profl. Women (state program chair, adv. bd. pres. Littleton chpt.). Avocations: art, drawing, writing. E-mail: dixiecolorado@cs.com.

**WRIGHT, DOUGLAS,** playwright; b. Dallas, 1962; BA, Yale U., 1985; MFA, Tisch Sch. Arts, NYU, 1987. Author: (plays) The Stonewater Rapture, 1987, Buzzsaw Berkeley, 1989, Watbanaland, 1994, Quills, 1995 (OBIE award for Playwriting, 1996), I Am My Own Wife, 2003 (Pulitzer prize for Drama, 2004, Tony award best play, 2004, Drama Desk award best play, 2004), The Little Mermaid, 2005, Interrogating the Nude; author, dir.: Unwrap Your Candy, 2001 (Paul Selvin award, Writers Guild Am., 2001); author: (screenplays) Quills, 2000 (Golden Satellite for Best Motion Picture Screenplay, 2000, Phoenix Film Critics Soc. award for Best Screenplay, 2000). Office: Lyceum Theatre 149 W 45th St New York NY 10036

**WRIGHT, DOUGLAS TYNDALL,** former university administrator; b. Toronto, Ont., Can., Oct. 4, 1927; s. George C. and Etta (Tyndall) W. BASc. with honors in Civil Engring, U. Toronto, 1949; MS in Structural Engring, U. Ill., 1952; PhD in Engring, U. Cambridge, 1954; D.Eng. (hon.), Carleton U., 1967; LLD (hon.), Brock U., 1967, Concordia U., 1982; DSc (hon.), Meml. U. Nfld., 1969; DHL (hon.), Northeastern U., 1985, U. Waterloo, 1995; DUniv (hon.), Strathclyde U., Glasgow, 1989; D de L'Université, Compiegne U., France, 1991; D Univ. (hon.), Université de Sherbrooke, 1992; DSc, McMaster U., 1993, Queen's U., 1993; LLD (hon.), U. Waterloo, 1995; LLD, U. Toronto, Can., 2005. Lectr. dept. civil engring. Queen's U., 1954-55, asst. prof., 1955-58, assoc. prof., 1958; prof. civil engring. U. Waterloo, 1958-67, chmn. dept. civil engring., 1958-63, dean engring., 1959-66; chmn. Ont. Com. on Univ. Affairs Govt. of Ont., 1967-72, Ont. Comm. Post-Secondary Edn., Toronto, 1969-72, dep. provincial sec. for social devel., 1972-79; dep. minister culture and recreation, 1979-80; pres. U. Waterloo, Ont., 1981-93, prof. engring. Ont., 1981—, pres. emeritus Ont., 1995—. Vis. prof. U. Autónoma Mex., 1964, 66, U. Sherbrooke, 1966-67; cons. engr. Netherlands and Mexican Pavillions Expo, 1967, Olympic Sports Palace, Mexico City, 1968, Ont. Place Dome and Forum, 1971; tech. advisor Toronto Skydome, 1984—92; bd. dirs. Com Dev Ltd., Geometrica Inc., RIM Ltd., Perimeter Inst. for Theoretical Physics, RDM Corp.; mem. Premier's Coun. on Sci. and Tech., Ont., 1985—91; Can. rep. Coun. Internat. Inst. Applied Sys. Analysis, Laxenburg, Austria, 1986—97; prime min.'s personal rep. to Coun. Misn. of Edn., 1990—91. Contbr. articles to profl. jours. Bd. govs. Stratford Shakesperean Festival, 1984—86, mem. senate, 1987; bd. dirs. African Students Found., Toronto, 1961—66, Ont. Curriculum Inst., 1964—67, Ont. R&D Challenge Fund, 1998—2004, NB Innovation Found., 2001—05. Decorated Officer Order of Can., chevalier Ordre National du Mérite (France); recipient Gold medal Ont. Profl. Engrs., 1990, Gold Medal award Can. Coun. Profl. Engrs., 1992, Sir John Kennedy Medal award Engring. Inst. Can., 1995, Can. Entrepreneur of Yr. award, 1997; Athlone fellow, 1952-54. Fellow ASCE, Can. Acad. Engring., Engring. Inst. Can. (del. Engrs. Coun. Profl. Devel., N.Y.C. 1961-70); mem. Assn. Profl. Engrs. Province Ont., Internat. Assn. Bridge and Structural Engring., Internat. Assn. Shell Structures, Royal Can. Yacht Club, Univ. Club (Toronto). Office: U Waterloo Waterloo ON Canada N2L 3G1 Personal E-mail: dtwright@uwaterloo.ca.

**WRIGHT, DOUGLASS BROWNELL,** retired judge, lawyer; b. Hartford, Conn., May 30, 1912; s. Arthur Brownell and Sylvia (Stephens) W.; m. Jane Hamersley, Sept. 24, 1938 (dec. Feb. 1997); children: Jane C., Douglass B. Hamersley S., Elizabeth B. Arthur W.; m. Ann Hallowell Ferguson, Nov., 1999. AB, Yale U., 1933; LL.B., Hartford Coll. Law, 1937. Bar: Conn. 1937. Legal dept. Aetna Life Ins. Co., 1937-39; partner Davis, Lee, Howard & Wright, Hartford, 1939—; lectr. law U. Conn., 1945—; asst. state's atty. Conn., 1952-59; judge Conn. Circuit Court, 1959-65, Conn. Superior Ct., 1965—98; ret., 1998. Leader orch. Judge Wright and the Four Wrongs Author: Connecticut Law of Torts, 1956, Connecticut Legal Forms, 5 vols., 1958, Connecticut Jury Instructions, 3 vols., 1960, 76. Sec., dir. Captioned Films for the Deaf, Inc.; bd. dirs. Am. Sch. for Deaf, 1942—; trustee Hartt Mus. Found., 1949—, Good Will Boys Club Hartford, 1950—; regent U. Hartford; bd. dirs. Vis. Nurse Assn., Newington Home for Crippled Children, Hartford Times Farm, Loomis Sch.; incorporator Conn. Inst. for Blind. Served as lt. USNR, 1942-45. Mem. Phi Beta Kappa, Psi Upsilon. Clubs: University (Hartford), Hartford Golf (Hartford), Hartford Tennis (Hartford), 20th Century (Hartford); Coral Beach and Tennis (Bermuda); Hillsboro (Pompano Beach, Fla.). Congregationalist. Home: 20 Loeffler Rd Apt T519 Bloomfield CT 06002-2273 Office: 95 Washington St Hartford CT 06106-4431

**WRIGHT, EDWARD THOMAS, JR.,** elementary school educator; b. Macon, Ga., Sept. 6, 1949; s. Edward Thomas and Susan Rehr Wright; m. Joanne Sivier, Mar. 2, 1996; children: June, Melissa, Eddie, Jackson, Elliot. BA in Polit. Sci., Principia Coll., Ill., 1971; JD, U. Mo., Columbia, 1975. Lawyer Wright & Wright, Brentwood, Mo., 1975—80; property mgr. St Louis, 1980—91; tchr. Clayton Sch. Dist., Mo., 1991—2004, Brentwood Sch. Dist., 2004—. Mem.: NEA (pres. Brentwood chpt. 2005—, bd. dirs. Mo. chpt. 2002—05, pres. Clayton chpt. 2000—02). Avocations: writing, poetry.

**WRIGHT, ELEASE,** insurance company executive; BS in education, Univ. of Conn. Sr. v.p. human resources Aetna Inc., Hartford, Conn., 1999—. Mem.: advisory bd., Cornell Univ. Center for Advanced Human Resource Studies, bd. of advisors, Univ. Conn. School of Bus., Exec. Leadership Council. Office: 151 Farmington Ave Hartford CT 06156-0001

**WRIGHT, ELIZABETHADA AMANDA,** communications educator; b. Boston, July 19, 1960; d. David Edwin Wright and Ada Louise Smith-Wright; m. Scott Howard Segee, Aug. 21, 1993; children: George Howard Segee-Wright, Jamie Scott Segee-Wright. PhD, Rensselaer Poly. Inst., Troy, NY, 1997. Vis. asst. prof. U. Albany, NY, 1996—99; assoc. prof. Rivier Coll., Nashua, NH, 1999—. Co-author: (plays) The Night the Men Landed on the Moon; contbr. numerous jours. and articles on commn. rhetoric. Co-anchor WSCA-FM LP, Portsmouth, NH, 2005—06; chair LWV, Portsmouth, NH, 2003—04. Mem.: Rhetoric Soc. Am. (life). Episcopalian. Office: Rivier College 420 S Main St Nashua NH 03060 Office Phone: 603-897-8283. Business E-Mail: ewright@rivier.edu.

**WRIGHT, ELLEN,** writing educator; d. Alexander and Anne Faber; m. John Henry Wright, June 16, 1962; children: Jennifer Sarah, Emily Anna. Part BA, Swarthmore Coll., Swarthmore, PA, 1961—62; BA summa cum laude, Ind. U., Bloomington, 1964, MA, 1966, PhD, 1975. Instr. English Kendall Coll., Evanston, Ill., 1976—77; lectr. writing program Northwestern U., Evanston, 1977—94, sr. lectr. writing program, 1995—97, coll. lectr. writing program, 1998—. Editor Arts & Scis. mag. Coll. Arts and Scis. Northwestern U., Evanston, 1985—88; editl. cons. for novel, poetry, and academic writing. Author: (biography) Pressing On: The Story of Roni Stoneman; musician: (CD) I Shook Hand With Eleanor Roosevelt (Played on over 150 stations internationally); contbr. articles to profl. jours. Named to Primary Listing of Non-Southern Bluegrass Musicians Who've Got It, Bgrass-I, 2002; recipient Charles Deering McCormick U. Disting. lecturership, Northwestern U., 2005—06. Mem.: Phi Beta Kappa, Eta Sigma Phi. Office: Northwestern Univ 1860 Campus Dr Evanston IL 60208 Office Phone: 847-491-7414.

**WRIGHT, ERNEST MARSHALL,** physiologist, consultant; b. Belfast, Ireland, June 8, 1940; came to U.S., 1965; BSc, U. London, 1961, DSc, 1978; PhD, U. Sheffield, Eng., 1964. Research fellow Harvard U., Boston, 1965-66; from asst. prof. to full prof. physiology UCLA Med. Sch., 1967—, chmn. dept. physiology, 1987—2000. Cons. NIH, Bethesda, Md., 1982—, Senator Jacob K. Javits neurosci. investigator, 1985. Fellow: Royal Soc., Biophysical Soc. Office: UCLA Sch Med Dept Physiology 10833 Le Conte Ave Los Angeles CA 90095-1751

**WRIGHT, EVELYN LOUISE,** artist; b. Odessa, Mo., Aug. 2, 1913; d. Elmer Clarence and Anna Bell (Ford) Adams; m. Douglas P. Wright, July 19, 1934 (dec. Dec. 27, 1986); children: Annetta Louise, Judith Elaine, Duane Douglas. Student, Stockton Coll., Calif., 1958—60, U. of Pacific, Stockton, 1960—61, Merced Coll., Calif., 1962—64, Columbia Coll., 1962—64. Graphic artist, Independence, Mo., 1928—34; asst. mgr., bookkeeper Wrights, Stockton, 1945—86; owner, instr. Evelyn's Art Classes and Workshops, Stockton, 1980—; instr. Stockton Sch. Sys., 1945—, Ripona Sch. Calif., 1992—94. Recipient Best of Show award, Richard Yip Art Co., 1980, award, Sonora Nat. Festival, 1982, 1984, Lodi Grape Festival, 1986. Avocation: travel. Home and Studio: 508 W Morada Ln Stockton CA 95210

**WRIGHT, FAITH-DORIAN,** artist; b. Bklyn., Feb. 9, 1934; d. Abraham and Molly (Janoff) J.; children: Jordan Merritt, Igrid-beth. BS, NYU, 1955, MA, 1958; postgrad., Pratt and Parsons Sch. of Design. Works exhibited in Kathryn Markel Gallery, N.Y.C., 1981, 92, Cumberland Gallery, Nashville, 1981, 92, Barbara Gillman Gallery, Miami, 1982, Hand and Hand Gallery, 1985, 86, Suzanne Gross, Phila., 1986, 87, Gallery Four, Alexandria, Va., 1986, 87, 88, Henri Gallery, Washington, 1986, 87, 88, 89. 90. 91. 92. 93. 94, Benton Gallery, Southampton, 1986, 87, 88, 89, 91, 92, 93, King Stephen Mus., Hungary, 1987, Nat. Gallery Women in the Arts, 1987, 88, 90, 91, 92, Ruth Volid Gallery, Chgo., 1990, James Gallery, Pitts., 1990, Aart Vark Gallery, Phila., 1990, Merrill Chase Gallery, Chgo., 1990, 91, 92, Guild Hall Mus., East Hampton, N.Y., 1991, Joy Berman Gallery, Phila., 1992, Ctr. for Book Arts, N.Y.C., 1992, Barnard-Biederman Fine Arts, N.Y.C., 1994, Arlene Bujese Gallery, East Hampton, 1994, 95, 96, Stoney Brook U., 1994, Harper Collins Exhbn. Space, 1995, Ctr. for Book Arts, 1996, arlene bujese, 1997, Galerie Cargo, Paris, 1997, N.Y. State Mus., Albany, 1997, U. Mont., Missoula, 2002, Nat. Mus. Women in Arts, Washington, 2002, Arlene Bujese, East Hampton, N.Y., 1997-03, Seton Hall U., NJ, 2003, Arlene Bujese Gallery, East Hampton, N.Y. 2003—, Gayle Wilson Gallery, Southampton, N.Y., 2004-2005; permanent collections Nat. Postal Art Mus., Ottawa, Can., Nat. Inst. Design, Ahmedabad, India, Fine Arts Acad., New Delhi, India, Mus. Modern Art, N.Y.C., Nat. Mus. Women in the Arts, Washington, D.C., Israel Mus., Jerusalem, Brenau Coll., Grainsville, Ga. Blue Cross, Blue Shield, Phila., Mc Donald's, Oakbrook, Ill., The Hyatt Collection, Chgo., Guild Hall Mus., Saul, Ewing, Reineck & Saul, Phila., Shevick, Ravich, Koster, Tobin, Clark, N.J., Sidley & Austin, L.A., Catalano & Sparber, N.Y., Islip (N.Y.) Mus. of Art, NY Pet Rescue Orgn., Larchmont, Islip (NY) Mus.; contbr. critical essays to various periodicals. Mem. Women in Arts, Women's Caucus for Arts, Artists Equity, Visitation Bd. of Met. Mus.-Rockefeller Connection. Address: 300 E 74th St New York NY 10021-3712

**WRIGHT, FELIX E.,** manufacturing executive; b. 1935; married Student, East Tex. State U., 1958. With Leggett & Platt, Inc., Carthage, Mo., 1959—, sr. v.p., from 1976, chief operating officer, exec. v.p., 1979 pres., COO, 1985-2000, vice chmn., 1999—2002, pres., CEO, 2000—02, CEO, 2002—06, chmn., 2002—. Office: Leggett & Platt Inc 1 Leggett Rd Carthage MO 64836-9649*

**WRIGHT, FRANZ PAUL,** poet, writer, translator; b. Vienna, 1953; s. James Wright and Liberty Kardulis. Grad., Oberlin College, 1977; studied postgrad., U. Va. Translator, author of introduction Rainer Maria Rilke, The Unknown Rilke, 1990; translator modern and contemporary French and German poets; author: (poems) Tapping the White Cane of Solitude, 1976, The Earth Without You, 1980, Eight Poems, 1981, The One Whose Eyes Open When You Close Your Eyes, 1982, No Siege Is Absolute, 1983, Going North in Winter, 1986, Entry in an Unknown Hand, 1989, Midnight Postscript, 1990, And Still the Hand Will Sleep in Its Glass Ship, 1990, Rorschach Test, 1995, The Night World and the Word Night, 1993, Knell, 1998, ILL LIT: Selected and New Poems, 1998, The Beforelife, 2001, Walking to Martha's Vineyard, 2003 (Pulitzer Prize for poetry, 2004); represented in anthologies; contbr. articles to profl. publs. Recipient Witter Bynner prize for Poetry, 1995, PEN/Voelcker award, 1996, Pulitzer prize in Poetry, 2004; NEA fellow, 1985, 92, Guggenheim fellow, 1989, Whiting fellow, 1991. Office Phone: 781-788-0540. E-mail: franzwright@earthlink.net.

**WRIGHT, FREDERICK LEWIS, II,** lawyer; b. Roanoke, Va., Sept. 17, 1951; s. Frederick Lewis and Dorothy Marie (Trent) W.; m. Margaret Suzanne Rey, Oct. 16, 1982; children: Lauren Elizabeth, Emily Trent. BA, Ga. State U., 1978; JD, U. Ga., 1981. Bar: Ga. 1982, U.S. Dist. Ct. (no. dist.) Ga. 1984, U.S. Ct. Appeals (11th, 8th and 4th cirs.) 1984, U.S. Supreme Ct. 1990. Law clk. to presiding justice U.S. Ct. Appeals, Atlanta, 1981-82; ptnr. Smith, Currie and Hancock, Atlanta, 1982-96, Vaughn, Wright and Boyer, Atlanta, 1997—. Articles editor Ga. Law Rev., 1980—81. Mem.: ABA (forum com.

constrn. industry), Ga. Def. Lawyers Assn., Fed. Bar Assn., Def. Rsch. Inst., Order of Coif. Methodist. Office: One Paces West Ste 1740 2727 Paces Ferry Rd Atlanta GA 30339 Office Phone: 770-805-9889. Personal E-mail: fwright@mindspring.com.

**WRIGHT, G. TODD,** lab administrator, director; s. William Houghton and Betty Ritenour Wright; m. Colleen Rae Lebrum, June 22, 1974; children: Chris, Kellie, Matthew. BSME, Va. Poly. Inst. and State U., Blacksburg, VA, 1974, MSME, 1976, PhD, 1979. Lab. dir. Savannah River Nat Lab., Aiken, SC, 2003—; rsch. mgr. River Protection Project, Hanford, Wash., 2001—02; dep. dir. Savannah River Tech. Ctr., Aiken, SC, 1997—2000; mgr., ops. Westinghouse Savannah River Site, Aiken, SC, 1989—97; rsch. mgr. E. I. duPont Savannah River Lab, Aiken, SC, 1983—89. Office: Savannah River Nat Lab Building 773-A A221 Aiken SC 29808 Office Phone: 803-725-3994. Home Fax:; Office Fax: 803-725-1660. Personal E-mail: n/a. E-mail: todd.wright@srnl.doe.gov.

**WRIGHT, GLADYS STONE,** music educator, writer, composer; b. Wasco, Oreg., Mar. 8, 1925; d. Murvel Stuart and Daisy Violet (Warren) Stone; m. Alfred George Wright, June 28, 1953. BS, U. Oreg., 1948, MS, 1953. Dir. bands Elmira (Oreg.) U-4 H.S., 1948-53, Otterbein (Ind.) H.S., 1954-61, Klondike H.S., West Lafayette, Ind., 1962-70, Harrison H.S., West Lafayette, 1970-84. Organizer, condr. Musical Friendship Tours, Ctrl. Am., 1967-79; v.p., condr. U.S. Collegiate Wind Band, 1975—; bd. dirs. John Philip Sousa Found., 1984—; chmn. Sudler Cup, 1986—, Sudler Flag, 1982; pres. Internat. Music Tours, 1984—, Key to the City, Taxco, Mex., 1975. Editor: Woman Conductor, 1986—; composer: marches Big Bowl and Trumpets and Tabards, 1987; contbg. editor: Informusica (Spain). Recipient Medal of the order John Philip Sousa Found., 1988, Star of Order, 1991, Internat. Contbrn. to Music award Phi Beta Mu, 2000; 1st woman guest condr. U.S. Navy Band, Washington, 1961, Goldman Band, NYC, 1958, Kneller Hall Band, London, 1975, Tri-State Music Festival Massed Orch., Band, Choir, 1985; elected to Women Bd. Dirs. Hall of Fame of Disting. Women Condrs., 1994; inductee Hall of Fame Disting. Condrs., Nat. Band Assn., 1999; named Ind.'s Sagamore of the Wabash, 2004. Mem. Am. Bandmasters Assn. (bd. dirs. 1993, 1st woman mem.), Women Band Dirs. Nat. Assn. (founding pres. 1967, sec. 1985, recipient Silver Baton 1974, Golden Rose 1990, Hall of Fame 1995), Am. Sch. Band Dirs. Assn., Nat. Band Assn. (Citation excellence 1970), Tippecanoe Arts Fedn. (bd. dirs. 1986-90), Tippecanoe Fife and Drum Corps. (bd. dirs. 1984), DAR, Col. Dames-Pre Quitanen Chpt., New Eng. Women, Tau Beta Sigma (Outstanding Svc. to Music award 1970), Phi Beta Mu (1st hon. woman mem. 1972), N.Am. Wildlife Park (Battleground, Ind., bd dirs. 1985, 1990—). Avocation: history.

**WRIGHT, GORDON BROOKS,** musician, conductor, educator; b. Bklyn., Dec. 31, 1934; s. Harry Wesley and Helen Philomena (Brooks) W.; m. Inga-Lisa Myrin Wright, June 13, 1958 (div. 1979); children: Karin-Ellen Sturla, Charles-Eric, Daniel Brooks. MusB, Coll. Wooster, 1957; MA, U. Wis., 1961; postgrad., Salzburg Mozarteum, 1972, Loma Linda U., 1979; studied with, René Leibowitz, Carl Melles, Wilfred Pelletier, Herbert Blomstedt, Hans Swarowsky. Founder, music dir. Wis. Chamber Orch., 1960-69; music dir. Fairbanks (Alaska) Symphony Orch., 1969-89; prof. music Univ. Alaska, Fairbanks, 1969-89, prof. emeritus, 1989—; founder, music dir. Arctic Chamber Orch., Fairbanks, 1970-89; exec. dir. The Reznicek Soc., Indian, Alaska, 1982—. Prin. guest condr. Fla. Keys Chambor Orch., 2003—. Guest condr. Philharmonia Hungarica, Philomusica London, Norwegian Radio Orch., Orch. St. Luke's, Anchorage Symphony Orch., Musashino Orch., Tokyo, Tohoku Orch., Sendai, Japan; prin. guest condr. Fla. Keys Chamber Orch., 2003—; composer: Suite of Netherlands Dances, 1965, Six Alaskan Tone Poems, 1974, Symphony in Ursa Major, 1979 (Legis. award 1979), 1984 Overture, Scott Joplin Suite, 1987, Toccata Festiva, 1992, Meditation for Orchestra, 2000; columnist Alaska Advocate. Founder, bd. dirs. No. Alaska Environ. Ctr., Fairbanks, 1971-78. Served as pvt. AUS. 1957-59. Mem.: Am. Fedn. Musicians, Arturo Toscanini Soc., Condr.'s Guild, Am. Symphony Orch. League, Royal Musical Assn., Am. Musicol. Soc., Ctr. for Alaskan Coastal Studies (bd. dirs. 1982—), Alaska Conservation Soc. (editor Rev. 1971—78), Audubon Soc., Wilderness Soc., Friends of Earth-Alaska (bd. dirs. 1978—), Sierra Club (chmn. Fairbanks Group 1969—71). Avocations: hiking, kayaking, collecting books, photography. Home: HC 52 Box 8899 Indian AK 99540-9604 Office Phone: 907-653-1163. Personal E-mail: turnagain@earthlink.net.

**WRIGHT, GREGORY A.,** energy executive; BBA, Ohio State Univ., 1971; MBA, Univ. Del., 1979. With Columbia Gas Systems Inc., 1972—81; positions through v.p. Valero Energy Corp., 1981—95; v.p. corp. comm. Tesoro Petroleum Corp., San Antonio, 1995—2001, sr. v.p., CFO, 2001—03, exec. v.p., CFO, 2003—. Office: Tesoro Petroleum 300 Concord Plz San Antonio TX 78216-6999*

**WRIGHT, GWENDOLYN,** writer, architecture educator, historian; b. Chgo., May 14, 1946; d. William Kemp and Mary Ruth (Brown) W.; m. Paul Rabinow, Nov. 18, 1980 (div. 1982); m. Thomas Bender, Jan. 14, 1984; children: David, Sophia. BA, NYU, 1969; MArch, U. Calif., Berkeley, 1974, PhD, 1980. Assoc. prof. Columbia U., N.Y.C., 1983—87, prof., 1988—; dir. Buell Ctr. for Study Am. Architecture, N.Y.C., 1988—92. Cons. Fulbright Scholars, Coun. Internat. Exch. Scholars, Washington, 1988-91, ArchNet, 1999—, Nat. Bldg. Mus., Washington, 2001—. Author: Building the Dream: A Social History of Housing in America, 1980, Moralism and the Model Home, 1981, The History of History in American Schools of Architecture, 1990, The Politics of Design in French Colonial Urbanism, 1991; writer N.Y. Times, 1999; presenter PBS TV series History Detectives, 2003—. Fellow, Ford Found., 1979—80, Stanford Inst. for Humanities, 1982—83, Mich. Inst. for Humanities, 1991, Getty Ctr. for History of Art and the Humanities, 1992—93, Guggenheim Found., 2004—05, Graham Found., 2004—05. Fellow; Soc. Am. Historians, NY Inst. for Humanities; mem.; Soc. Archtl. Historians, Coll. Art Assn., Am. Hist. Assn., Orgn. Am. Historians. Democrat. Home: 54 Washington Mews New York NY 10003-6608 Office: Columbia U Avery Hall New York NY 10027 Office Phone: 212-854-1587. Business E-Mail: gw8@columbia.edu.

**WRIGHT, HARRISON MORRIS,** historian, educator; b. Phila., Oct. 6, 1928; s. Sydney L. and Catharine W. (Morris) W.; m. Josephine Stearns Cole, July 20, 1957; children: Rebecca H., J. Rodman, Thomas F., Daniel H., James L. BA, Harvard, 1950, MA, 1953, PhD, 1957. Teaching fellow Harvard, 1955-57; mem. faculty Swarthmore Coll., 1957—, prof. history, 1968-87, Isaac H. Clothier prof. history and internat. relations, 1987-93, chmn. dept., 1968-79, provost, 1979-84, Clothier prof. and provost emeritus, 1993—, acting pres., 1982. Author: New Zealand, 1769-1840: Early Years of Western Contact, 1959, The Burden of the Present: Liberal-Radical Controversy over Southern African History, 1977; Editor: The New Imperialism—Analysis of Late Nineteenth-Century Expansion, 1961, 2d edit., 1976, Sir James Rose Innes: Selected Correspondence (1884-1902), 1972. Mem. Jamestown (R.I.) Harbor Commn., 2000—03. Fulbright scholar New Zealand, 1950-51; Ford Found. fgn. areas fellow Eng. and Ghana, 1961-62; grantee Am. Philos. Soc., S. Africa, 1966-67; grantee Old Dominion Fund, S. Africa, 1971-74; mem.: Hist. Soc. (coun. 1984—91, v.p. 1986—88, chmn. 1989—91, coun. emeritus 1992—), African Studies Assn., Internat. Sailing Inst. (bd. dir. 1998—), Humanities Forum R.I. (bd. dir. 1995—2000), R.I. Hist. Soc. (bd. dir. 1998—2005), Newport Hist. Soc. (bd. dir. 1973—88), Phi Beta Kappa. Home: PO Box 209 Jamestown RI 02835-0209

**WRIGHT, HARRY HERCULES,** psychiatrist; b. Charleston, S.C., Jan. 4, 1948; s. Harry Vernon and Agnes Lucile (Simmons) W. BS, U. S.C., 1970; MD, MBA, U. Pa., 1976. Resident in psychiatry Wm. S. Hall Psychiat. Inst., Columbia, SC, 1977—79; adminstrv. fellow in psychiatry NIMH, Rockville, Md., 1979; fellow in child psychiatry William S. Hall Psychiat. Inst. 1979—81, instr. child psychiatrist, 1981—; instr. dept. neuropsychiatry and behavioral sci. U. S.C. Sch. Medicine, 1981—82, asst. prof. 1982—86, assoc. prof., 1986—90, prof., 1990—. Contbr. articles to profl. jours. Bd. dirs. Carolina Children's Home, 1992—, Zero to Three, 1997—; bd. trustees, First

---

Steps to Sch. Readiness, 1999-2003; mem. landmarks commn. City of Columbia, 1986-98. Recipient Freed award, Hall Psychiat. Inst., 1978, Outstanding Svc. award, Sickle Cell Found., Clin. Sci. Rsch. award, 1998, America's Top Doctors award, 2001—05, Rsch. Advancement award, 2002, 2004; grantee Falk fellow, 1977—79, Laughlin fellow, 1979. Mem.: AAAS, Am. Coll. Psychiatrists, Am. Soc. Human Genetics, Soc. Study Psychiatry and Culture, Acad. Orgnl. and Occupl. Psychiatry, So. Med. Assn., Am. Soc. Adolescent Psychiatry, World Assn. Infant Mental Health, World Psychiat. Assn., Am. Acad. Child Psychiatry, Autism Soc. Am., Riverbank Zool. Soc., Sigma Xi, Omicron Delta Kappa. Methodist. Home: PO Box 12474 Columbia SC 29211-2474 Office: 3555 Harden St Ext Ste 104 Columbia SC 29203-6894 Office Phone: 803-434-4250.

**WRIGHT, HERBERT E(DGAR), JR.,** geologist; b. Malden, Mass., Sept. 13, 1917; s. Herbert E. and Annie M. (Richardson) W.; m. Rhea Jane Hahn, June 21, 1943; children: Richard, Jonathan, Stephen, Andrew, Jeffrey. AB, Harvard U., 1939, MA, 1941, PhD, 1943; DSc (hon.), Trinity Coll., Dublin, Ireland, 1966, U. Minn., 1996; PhD (hon.), Lund U., Sweden, 1987. Instr. Brown U., 1946-47; asst. prof. geology U. Minn., Mpls., 1947-51, asso. prof., 1951-59, prof., 1959-74, Regents' prof. geology, ecology and botany, 1974-88, Regents' prof. geology, ecology & botany emeritus, 1988—; dir. Limnological Research Center, 1963-90. Served to maj. USAAF, 1942-45. Decorated D.F.C., Air medal with 6 oak leaf clusters; recipient Pomerance award Archeol. Inst. Am., 1985, Ann. award Sci. Mus. Minn., 1990, Guggenheim fellow, 1954-55, Wenner-Gren fellow, 1954-55. Fellow AAAS, Geol. Soc. Am. (Ann. award archeol. divsn. 1989, Disting. Career award geology and geomorphology divsn. 1992), Soc. Am. Archeology (Fryxell award 1993); mem. NAS, Ecol. Soc. Am., Internat. Quaternary Assn. (hon. pres. 16th Congress 2003), Am. Quaternary Assn. (Career award 1996). Achievements include research on Quaternary geology, paleoecology, paleolimnology and environ. archaeology in Minn., Wyo., Sweden, Yukon, Labrador, Peru, eastern Mediterranean. Home: 1426 Hythe St Saint Paul MN 55108-1423 Office: U of Minn 310 Pillsbury Dr SE Minneapolis MN 55455-0219 Business E-Mail: hew@umn.edu.

**WRIGHT, J. CLAYTON,** music educator; b. NYC, July 1, 1956; s. Robert Brown and Katherine Green Wright; m. Marsha Elyn Jurca, Dec. 14, 1991; 1 child, Tyler Anton. B of Music Edn., U. So. Calif., 1979, M of Music Edn., 1984. Dir. choral music Palos Verdes High Sch., Palos Verdes Estates, Calif., 1981—82; tchr. music, math. Rolling Hills Prep. Sch., 1982—87; tchr. music, dir. choir Brentwood Sch., L.A., 1987—90; tchr. music Pilgrim Sch., 1990—91; dir. choral music Leuzinger High Sch., Lawndale, 1992—2002, Garden City C.C., Kans., 2002—. Dir. youth choir Neighborhood Ch., Palos Verdes Estates, 1977—86. Composer: (songs) The Lord's Prayer, 1978. Dir. music Rolling Hills United Meth. Ch., Rolling Hills Estates, 1987—2002. Recipient Univ. Chorus award, U. So. Calif., L.A., 1986. Mem.: Kans. Music Educators Assn., Music Educators Nat. Conf., Am. Choral Dirs. Assn. Avocations: fly fishing, travel, golf, motorcycling. Office: Garden City CC 801 Campus Dr Garden City KS 67846 E-mail: clay.wright@gcccks.edu.

**WRIGHT, JAMES DAVID,** social studies educator, writer; b. Logansport, Ind., Nov. 6, 1947; s. James Farrell and Helen Loretta (Moon) W.; m. Christine Ellen Stewart, July 25, 1987; children: Matthew James, Derek William. BA, Purdue U., 1969; MS, U. Wis., 1970, PhD, 1973. Cert. specialist social policy and evaluation rsch. Asst. prof. sociology U. Mass., Amherst, 1973-76, assoc. prof., 1976-79, prof., 1979-88; Favrot prof. human rels. Tulane U., New Orleans, 1988-2001; prof. sociology U. Ctrl. Fla., Orlando, 2001—. Author, co-author: The Dissent of the Governed, 1976, Under the Gun, 1983, The State of the Masses, 1986, Homelessness and Health, 1987 (commendation Nat. Press Club 1988), Address Unknown: Homeless in America, 1989, The Greatest of Evils: Urban Poverty and the Urban Underclass, 1993, Beside the Golden Door, 1998, Fixin' to Git: One Fan's Love Affair with NASCAR, 2002, Social Sci. Rsch. Jour., 1978—; contbr. numerous articles, essays, book chpts. to profl. publs. Mem. Am. Sociol. Assn. Democrat. Avocations: cooking, gardening, travel. Office Fax: 407-823-6738. E-mail: jwright@mail.ucf.edu.

**WRIGHT, JAMES DORSEY,** lawyer; b. Easton, Md., July 11, 1944; s. M. Dorsey and Dorothy (Booker) W.; m. Christine Ulrich, May 17, 1980. BA, U. Del., 1966; JD, Harvard U., 1969. Bar: Md. 1969. Law clk. to presiding judge Frank A. Kaufman, U.S. Dist. Ct. (Md.) U.S. Dist. Ct. Md., Balt., 1969-70; assoc. Venable, Baetjer & Howard (now Venable LLP), Balt., 1970-75, ptnr., Real Estate practice, 1976—. Mem. ABA, Am. Coll. Real Estate Lawyers, Md. State Bar Assn., Bar Assn. Balt. City, Md. Club (Balt.). Office: Venable LLP 1800 Merc Bank & Trust Bldg 2 Hopkins Plz Baltimore MD 21201 Office Phone: 410-244-7422. Office Fax: 410-244-7742. Business E-Mail: jdwright@venable.com.

**WRIGHT, JAMES EDWARD,** judge; b. Arlington, Tex., Jan. 15, 1921; s. James Robert and Clairete (Smith) W.; m. Eberta Adelaide Slataper, June 25, 1946; 1 child, Patricia Diane Wright Rogers. JD, U. Tex., 1949. Bar: Tex. 1949. Practice in, Ft. Worth, 1949-69; city atty. Arlington, 1951-61; judge 141st Dist. Ct., Ft. Worth, 1970-88, sr. dist. judge, 1988—. Served with USAAF, World War II. Paul Harris fellow, 1981; named Disting. Alumnus U. Tex.-Arlington, 1982; named to Mil. Sci. Dept. Hall of Honor, U. Tex.-Arlington, 1985 Fellow Tex. Bar Found. (life); mem. ABA, Ft. Worth-Tarrant County Bar Assn. (pres. 1958-59), Tex. Bar Assn., Sons of the Rep. of Tex., Rotary (pres. Downtown Ft. Worth club 1966-67), Masons (32 degree), Shriners, Jesters (life), Phi Alpha Delta. Methodist. Home: 717 Briarwood Blvd Arlington TX 76013-1502 Personal E-mail: bewright@sbcglobal.net.

**WRIGHT, JAMES EDWARD,** academic administrator, historian, educator; b. Madison, Wis., Aug. 16, 1939; s. Donald J. and Myrtle (Hendricks) Wright; m. Joan Bussan, Sept. 3, 1962 (div.); children: James J., Ann Marie, Michael J.; m. Susan DeBevoise, Aug. 18, 1984. BS, Wis. State U., 1964; MS, U. Wis., 1966, PhD, 1969; MA (hon.), Dartmouth Coll., 1980. From asst. prof. to assoc. prof. history Dartmouth Coll., Hanover, NH, 1969—80, prof. history, 1980—, assoc. dean faculty, 1981—85, dean faculty, 1989—97, acting pres., 1995, provost, 1997—98, pres., 1998—. Sr. historian U. Mid Am., Lincoln, Nebr., 1976—77; humanist-in-residence Colo. Humanities Coun., Georgetown, 1975. Author: Galena Lead District, 1966, Politics of Populism, 1974, Progressive Yankees, 1987; author: (co-editor) Great Plains Experience, 1978. Trustee Kimball Union Acad., Meriden, NH, 1990—94; dir. Sherman Fairchild Found., Greenwich, Conn., 1991—; chair Hanover Dem. Town Com., 1970—74; bd. dirs. Divsn. 1 NCAA, 2001—03. Cpl. USMC, 1957—60. Danforth fellow, 1964—69, Guggenheim fellow, 1973—74, Charles Warren fellow, Harvard U., 1980—81. Fellow: Am. Acad. Arts and Scis.; mem.: Western History Assn. (chair Caughey prize 1986—87), The Century Assn., Orgn. Am. Historians (chair film, media com. 1983—85), Phi Beta Kappa. Home: 1 Tuck Dr Hanover NH 03755-3575 Office: Dartmouth Coll Office of the President 207 Parkhurst Hall Hanover NH 03755 Office Phone: 603-646-2223. Business E-Mail: james.wright@dartmouth.edu.

**WRIGHT, JAMES F.,** agricultural products executive; Sr. level positions K-Mart Corp., 1974—88, Western Auto Supply Co., 1988—96; pres., CEO Tire Kingdom, 1997—2000; COO, pres. Tractor Supply, Brentwood, Tenn., 2000—, CEO, 2004—. Mem.: Automotive Parts and Accessories Assn. (past chmn.). Office: Tractor Supply Co 200 Powell Pl Brentwood TN 37027

**WRIGHT, JAMES NASH,** healthcare educator, psychologist; b. Roanoke, Va., Mar. 7, 1952; s. Ralph Ross and Kathleen Maphis Wright; m. Wanda Huffman Huffman, June 16, 1973; children: James Michael, Matthew Ross. BS, Va. Tech, Blacksburg, 1974, MS, 1981. Registered clin. exercise psychologist Am. Coll. of Sports Medicine, 1999, exercise test technologist Am. Coll. Sports Medicine, 1981, cert. advanced cardiac life support Am. Heart Assn., 2000, instr. and instr. trainer for CPR, First Aid and CPR profls. ARC; cert. fitness specialist Nat. YMCA, 1974, instr. and instr. trainer of water safety and lifeguarding ARC. Svc. coord. Cosmopolitan Spa, Roanoke, Va., 1978—79; phys. dir. Roanoke Ctrl. YMCA, 1974—78; instr. of phys.

---

edn., dir. of aquatics, track, indoor track, and cross country coach Bridgewater Coll., Va., 1981—83; dir. wellness Roanoke Meml. Hosp., Roanoke Athletic Club, 1983—85; dir. Lancerlot Family Fitness Ctr., Vinton, Va., 1985; dir. wellness svcs. Carilion Health Care Sys., Radford, Va., 1986—97; adj. instr. New River CC, Dublin, Va., 1986—2005; instr., exercise physiology, dir. therapeutic exercise and cmty. health ctr. Va. Tech, Blacksburg, VA, Va., 1998—2000, program dir., 1998; project devel. coord. Floyd County Health Ctr., Va., 2000—01; dir. New River Fitness Ctr., Radford, 2001—02, Twin County Regional Wellness Ctr., Galax, Va., 2002—05; instr. Blue Ridge CC, Weyers Cave, Va., 2005—. Cons. for fitness ctr. devel. Wytheville CC, Rowes Furniture, Shenandoah Life Ins., Blue Cross Blue Shield, Twin County Cmty. Hosp., S.W. Va. Areas, 1978—2003; spkr. and presenter in field. Corp. team leader Mar. of Dimes, Dublin, Va., 1986—94; adult leader Boy Scouts and Cub Scouts, Blacksburg, 1990—95; ann. fund dir., chair Am. Heart Assn., Radford, 1991—97, chair, 1991—97; ann. fund dir. United Way, Radford, Va., 1988—89, chair, 1988—89, bd. mem., 1988—89. Recipient Top Fundraiser award, Am. Heart Assn., 1991—97, Top Individual Fund Raiser award, Mar. of Dimes, 1988—94, Gold medal, Va. State Commonwealth Games, 2001—02. Mem.: Am. Coll. Sports Medicine. Achievements include development of numerous innovative programs, especially comprehensive therapeutic exercise and community health center at virginia tech and community fitness and walking programs in Radford, Virginia. Avocations: endurance bicycler, swimming, canoeing, fishing. Office: Blue Ridge CC PO Box 80 Weyers Cave VA 24486 Office Phone: 540-234-9261.

**WRIGHT, JAMES RALPH,** lawyer; b. Pitts., Jan. 18, 1944; s. Paul J. and Gertrude M. (Stienecker) W.; m. Harriett Ann Howard, Sept. 7, 1968; children: Karen, Cathy. BS, Ohio State U., 1966; JD, George Washington U., 1969. Bar: D.C. 1973, U.S. Dist. Ct. D.C. 1975, U.S. Ct. Appeals (D.C. cir.) 1981. Dir. legal affairs Airport Operators Coun., Internat., Washington, 1969-70; with NAS, Washington, 1970—, staff officer, counsel com. on motor vehicles, 1973-74, staff counsel, 1974-80, gen. counsel, 1980—. Exec. dir. Nat. Academies' Corp., a Calif. nonprofit pub. benefit corp., 1986—. Editor, pub. newsletter, 1985-90. Mem. ABA. Office: NAS 2101 Constitution Ave NW Washington DC 20418-0007

**WRIGHT, JAN CAROL,** indexer; b. Camden, N.J., June 19, 1954; d. Harry Gilbert and Dorothy Wright; m. A. Christopher James, Aug. 14, 1988. BA with honors, Rutgers U., 1976; MLS, U. Ariz., 1980. Prodn. trainer/archivist Aldus Corp., Seattle, 1987—91; pres. Wright Info., Sandia Park, N.Mex., 1991—. Head libr. Navajo Nation Libr. Sys., Window Rock, Ariz., 1980—83; libr. Colo. Mountain Coll., Steamboat Springs, 1983—86. Editor: (jour.) A to Z: The Newsletter of STC's Indexing SIG (Merit Award for Soc. Newsletters, 2002); contbr. articles to profl. jours. Vol. Rio Grande Libr. Sys., Albuquerque, 1999—2006. Mem.: Am. Soc. of Indexers (webmaster 1989—91), Soc. for Tech. Comm. (numerous awards 1991—2003). Avocations: kayaking, photography, xeriscape landscaping, birdwatching, beadwork. Personal E-mail: jancw@wrightinformation.com.

**WRIGHT, JANE COOKE,** oncologist, educator, consultant; b. N.Y.C., Nov. 30, 1919; d. Louis T. and Corinne (Cooke) W.; m. David D. Jones. AB, Smith Coll., 1942; MD with honors, N.Y. Med. Coll., 1945; D in Med. Scis., Women's Med. Coll. Pa., 1965; ScD, Denison U., 1971. Intern Bellevue Hosp., N.Y.C., 1945-46, resident, 1946, mem. staff, 1955-67; resident Harlem Hosp., 1947, chief resident, 1948; clin. Cancer Rsch. Found., Harlem Hosp., 1949-52; dir., 1952-55; mem. staff Harlem Hosp., 1949-55; practice medicine specializing in clin. cancer chemotherapy N.Y.C.; mem. faculty dept. surgery Med. Ctr., N.Y. U., N.Y.C., 1955-67, adj. assoc. prof., 1961-67, also dir. cancer chemotherapy services research, 1955-67; prof. surgery N.Y. Med. Coll., N.Y.C., 1967-87, prof. surgery emeritus, 1987—, assoc. dean, 1967-75; mem. staff Manhattan VA Hosp., 1955-67, Midtown, Met., Bird S. Color, Flower-Fifth Ave. Hosps., all N.Y.C., 1967-79, Westchester County Med. Center, Valhalla, NY, 1971-87, Lincoln Hosp., Bronx, NY, 1979-87. Cons. Health Ins. Plan of Greater N.Y., 1962—94, Blvd. Hosp., 1963—, St. Luke's Hosp., Newburgh, NY, 1964—; pelvic malignancy rev. com. N.Y. Gynecol. Soc., 1965—66, St. Vincent's Hosp., N.Y.C., 1966—, Dept. Health, Edn. and Welfare, 1968—70, Wyckoff Heights Hosp., N.Y.C., 1969—, NIH, 1971—, others; adv. bd. Skin Cancer Found. Contbr. articles to profl. jours. Mem. Manhattan coun. State Commn. Human Rights, 1949—, Pres.'s Commn. Heart Disease, Cancer and Stroke, 1964-65, Nat. Adv. Cancer Coun. NIH, 1966-70, N.Y. State Women's Coun., 1970-72; bd. dirs. Medico-CARE, Health Svcs. Improvement Fund Inc.; trustee Smith Coll., Northampton, Mass., 1970-80. Recipient numerous awards, including: Mademoiselle mag. award, 1952; Lady Year award Harriet Beecher Stowe Jr. High Sch., 1958; Spirit Achievement award Albert Einstein Sch. Medicine, 1965; certificate Honor award George Gershwin Jr. High Sch., 1967; Myrtle Wreath award Hadassah, 1967; Smith medal Smith Coll., 1968; Outstanding Am. Women award Am. Mothers Com. Inc., 1970; honored as one of 150 Am. Women Physicians at exhbn. Changing the Face of Medicine at the Nat. LIbr. Medicine, NIH, 2003; Golden Plate award Am. Acad. Achievement, 1971; Exceptional Black Scientists Poster Ciba Geigy, 1980. Fellow N.Y. Acad. Medicine; mem. Nat. Med. Assn. (edit. bd. jours.), Manhattan Ctrl. Med. Soc., N.Y. County Med. Soc. (nominating com.), AMA, AAAS, Am. Assn. Cancer Rsch. (dir. Rsch. Salute 1971-74, established Jane Cooke Wright lectureship 2006), N.Y. Acad. Scis., N.Y. Cancer Soc., Internat. Med. and Rsch. Found. (v.p.), Am. Cancer Soc. (dir. div.), N.Y. Cancer Soc. (pres. 1970-71), Am. Soc. Clin. Oncology (sec. treas. 1964-67, Spl. Appreciation award as a founding mem. 2004), Contin Soc., Sigma Xi, Lambda Kappa Mu, Alpha Omega Alpha. Clubs: The 400 (N.Y. Med. Coll.). Address: 7002 Kennedy Blvd East Apt 9C Guttenberg NJ 07093

**WRIGHT, JASON CHASE,** history educator; s. Donn David and Barbara Townsend Chase Wright; m. Deborah Lynn Cole, Dec. 21, 1987; children: Samantha Elizabeth, Erin Nicole. BA, U. Maine, Orono, 1986; MEd, Argosy U., Tampa, Fla., 2002. Dir. of admissions Hoosac Sch., Hoosick, NY, 1990—92, tchr., 1990—95; master tchr. The Canterbury Sch. of Fla., St. Petersburg, 1995—. Mem.: ASCD, Nat. Coun. Social Studies, The History Channel Club (life). Avocations: writing, golf, boating, juggling. Office Phone: 727-525-1419, 813-269-2750. E-mail: jcwfla@earthlink.net.

**WRIGHT, JASON HOWARD SEBASTIAN,** communications executive; b. Waterbury, Conn., Nov. 2, 1960; s. Joseph Thomas and Lyda (Hawkins) W. AB, Georgetown U., 1982. With Aetna Life & Casualty Co., Hartford, Conn., 1982—87, mgr. corp. pub. rels., 1987-88, dir. corp. comms., 1988—90; v.p. comm. RJR Nabisco, 1990—93; sr. v.p. Nabisco Group Holdings Corp. (formerly RJR Nabisco), 1993—2000; prin. Geer Mountain Holdings, LLC, 2000—03; sr. v.p. comm. and pub. affairs Merrill Lynch & Co. Inc., 2003—. Bd. dirs. CCW Holdings Corp. Trustee Mus. for African Art, N.Y., Cooper Union for the Advancement of Sci. and Art, James Beard Found. Democrat. Avocation: tennis. Office: Merrill Lynch & Co Inc 4 World Fin Ctr New York NY 10080 Office Phone: 212-449-3535. E-mail: jason_wright@ml.com.

**WRIGHT, JAY,** men's college basketball coach; b. Dec. 24, 1961; m. Patricia Reilly; children: Taylor, Colin, Reilly. Graduated with degrees in economics and sociology, Bucknell Univ., 1983. Adminstrv. asst. Phila. Stars Football, 1983; began career in coaching U. Rochester, 1984: various assignments including scouting, on-court coaching and recruiting, 1987—92; aide Drexel Univ., 1984, asst. coach, 1986—87, Villanova Univ., 1987—92, UNLV, 1992—94; head coach Univ. Rochester, 1984—86, Hofstra Univ., 1994—2001, Villanova Univ., 2001—. Asst. coach U.S.A. Basketball World Championship for Young Men Qualifying Team, 2000; head coach U.S.A. Basketball, 2005. Involved with Phila. Chpt. Coaches vs Cancer. Named Phila. Big Five Eastern College Coach of Yr., 2004—05. Office: Villanova Univ Dept Athletics 800 Lancaster Ln Villanova PA 19085-1603*

**WRIGHT, JEFFREY,** actor; b. Washington, D.C., Dec. 7, 1965; m. Carmen Ejogo, Aug. 2000; 1 child, Elijah. BA in polit. sci., Amherst Coll., 1987, degree (hon.), 2004. Actor: (plays) Les Blancs, 1989, She Stoops to Conquer, 1990—91, Juno and the Paycock, Search and Destroy, 1990—91, Playboy of the West Indies, Daylight in the Exile, Othello (NY Shakespeare Fest.),

Angels in America: Millennium Approaches, 1993—94, Angels in America: Perestroika, 1993—94 (Outer Critics Circle award best sup. actor, 1994, Drama Desk award for featured actor, 1994, Tony award for featured actor, 1994), Bring in da Noise, Bring in da Funk, 1996, King Lear, 1996, This Is How It Goes, 2005; (films) Presumed Innocent, 1990, Jumpin' at the Boneyard, 1991, Basquiat, 1996, Critical Care, 1997, Celebrity, 1998, Ride With the Devil, 1999, Cement, 1999, Sin's Kitchen, 2000, Crime and Punishment in Suburbia, 2000, Hamlet, 2000, Shaft, 2000 (Toronto Film Critics Assoc. award for best sup. actor, 2000), Boycott, 2001, Ali, 2000, Eye See You, 2001, Intolerable Cruelty, 2002, The Manchurian Candidate, 2004, Broken Flowers, 2005, Syriana, 2005, Lady in the Water, 2006; (TV films) Angels in America, 2003 (Golden Globe for best supporting actor in a miniseries, 2004, Emmy award Outstanding Supporting Actor in a Miniseries or a Movie, 2004). Office: Creative Artists Agency 9830 Wilshire Blvd Beverly Hills CA 90211*

**WRIGHT, JESSE HARTZELL,** psychiatrist, educator; b. Altoona, Pa., Sept. 21, 1943; s. Jesse H. and Marion (Stone) W.; m. Susanne Judy Wright, July 9, 1967; children: Andrew, Laura. BS, Juniata Coll., 1965; MD, Jefferson Med. Coll., 1969; PhD, U. Louisville, 1976. Diplomate Am. Bd. Psychiatry and Neurology, Am. Bd. Med. Examiners; lic. psychiatrist, Ky. Asst. prof. U. Louisville, 1975-79, assoc. prof., 1979-87, prof., 1987—; clin. dir. Norton Psychiat. Clinic, Louisville, 1975-83, med. dir., 1983—; chief adult psychiatry U. Louisville, 2000—; resident in psychiatry U. Mich., Ann Arbor, 1970-73. Author: first multimedia computer program for psychotherapy, Good Days Ahead, chpts. to books; contbr. articles to prof. jours; author: (self help book for depression) Getting Your Life Back, (textbook with DVD) Learning Cognitive-Behavior Therapy, others. Fellow Am.Psychiat. Assn.; Am. Coll. Psychiatry; mem. Ky. Psychiat. Assn. (sec. 1979-80, v.p. 1980-81, pres. 1982-83), Acad. Cognitive Therapy (founding pres.), Alpha Omega Alpha. Avocations: gardening, running, theater, skiing. Home: 15 Indian Hills Trl Louisville KY 40207-1532 Office: Norton Psychiat Clinic 200 E Chestnut St Louisville KY 40202-1822

**WRIGHT, JO ANNE,** priest; b. Wichita, Kans., May 31, 1935; d. Everett Joseph and Agnes Josephine (Ketcham) Steinheimer; m. John Cook Wright, June 25, 1955 (div. June 1976); children: Elizabeth, Jennifer, Melanie, Kennedy Weston. AB, Oberlin Coll., 1955; MDiv, Ch. Divinity Sch. of Pacific, Berkeley, Calif., 1987. Ordained deacon Episcopal Ch., 1987, ordained priest, 1987. Pre-sch. tchr. Children's Hour Headstart, Lawrence, Kans., 1977-79; reference libr. Lawrence (Kans.) Pub. Libr., 1979-84; rector St. Luke's Episcopal Ch., Wamego, Kans., 1987-98, St. John's Episcopal Ch., Vinita, Okla., 1999—2005; mem. diocesan coun. Diocese of Okla., 2000—01, dean NE region, 2001—05; ret. Youth officer Diocese of Kans., Topeka, 1987-92, rural missioner, 1992-98, mem. standing com., mem. diocesan coun., 1997-98; pres. Vinita Minsterial Alliance, 2001, sec., 2003. Writer monthly column Plenteous Harvest, 1987-92. Chair Wamego Coun. Chs., 1998, CROP walk organizer, 1988, 92, 95; tour leader Ednl. Opportunities, Israel, 1998; mem. bishop search com. Diocese Okla., 2005—. Roanridge grantee Episcopal Ch. U.S.A., 1995. Mem. Phi Beta Kappa. Democrat. Avocations: reading, travel. Home: 821 N Foreman Apt 222 Vinita OK 74301-1432 E-mail: jowright@junct.com.

**WRIGHT, JOAN L.,** artist; d. William Henry and Elsie Christina (Motzer) Harrison; m. Barry Duane Wright; children: Stephen Craig, Michael Alan, Jeffrey Lynn. Student, Art League LA, 1964-68, Valley Coll., 1966-69. Designer, sculpture, glazer Al Hardy, Burbank, Calif., 1951-53; budget coord. Los Angeles County, North Hollywood, Calif., 1953; writer Intermountain Contractor, Salt Lake City, 1954-56; artist, instr. Art League LA, Van Nuys, Calif., 1966—, Sylmar, Calif., 1966—. Rep. for State of Calif. Presdl. Arts Program, Washington. Contbr. articles to art publs.; films, children's books, album covers; featured in many books and publs. western art; collector plates, Danbury Mint, Norwalk, Conn., 1995—, other pub. cos., installations of murals worldwide, exhibitions include Gene Autry Western Heritage Mus., LA, Lancaster Mus. Art, Ronald Reagan Libr., Simi, Calif., Las Vegas (Nev.) Art Mus., Learnin' Tree, Boulder, Colo., Scafa, other cos. Mem.: Wildlife Waystation, Oil Painters Am., Internat. Art and Culture Assn., Women Artists of West (bd. dirs. 1971—73, pres. 1974—77, v.p. 1978—). Avocations: birdwatching, environmental activities, sports, stained glass, stamp collecting/philately. Personal E-mail: jwartist1@aol.com.

**WRIGHT, JOHN,** classics educator; b. N.Y.C., Mar. 9, 1941; s. Henry and Dorothy (Chaya) W.; m. Ellen Faber, June 16, 1962; children: Jennifer, Emily. BA, Swarthmore Coll., 1962; MA, Ind. U., 1964, PhD, 1971. Instr. classics U. Rochester, 1968-72, asst. prof., 1972-75; assoc. prof. Northwestern U., Evanston, Ill., 1975-77, prof., 1977-83, John Evans prof. Latin lang. and lit., 1983-2001, chmn. dept., 1978-97, 00-01, prof. emeritus in class, 2002—. Author: The Play of Antichrist, 1967, Dancing in Chains: The Stylistic Unity of the Comoedia Palliata, 1974, The Life of Cola di Rienzo, 1975, Essays on the Iliad: Selected Modern Criticism, 1978, Plautus: Curculio, Introduction and Notes, 1981, rev. edit., 1993, Ralph Stanley and the Clinch Mountain Boys: A Discography, 1983, The Five-String Banjo Stanley Style, 1984, rev. edit. (Clyde Pharr) Homeric Greek: A Book for Beginners, 1985, It's the Hardest Music in the World to Play: The Ralph Stanley Story in His Own Words, 1987, Traveling the High Way Home: Ralph Stanley and the World of Traditional Bluegrass Music, 1993; albums Everything She Asks For, 1993, Traveling the High Way Home, 1995, Promises, 1996, Ellen and John Wright 1, Ellen and John Wright 2, 1998, I Should Hands with Eleanor Roosevelt, 2004; contbr. articles to profl. jours. Fellow Am. Acad. Rome, 1966-68; Nat. Endowment Humanities Younger humanist fellow, 1973-74; named to Honorable Order of Ky. Colonels; recipient songwriting prize Santa Fe Bluegrass and Old Time Music Festival, 1996. Mem.: Am. Fedn. of Musicians, Local 1000, BMI, Nat. Acad. Recording Arts and Scis., Am. Acad. in Rome Soc. of Fellows, Internat. Bluegrass Music Assn. (Print Media Personality of Yr. 1994), Chgo. Area Bluegrass Assn. Home: 1137 Noyes St Evanston IL 60201-2633 Office: Northwestern U Dept Classics Evanston IL 60208-2200 Office Phone: 847-491-8039. Business E-Mail: jhwright@northwestern.edu.

**WRIGHT, JOHN COLLINS,** retired chemistry professor; b. Oak Hill, W.Va., Aug. 5, 1927; s. John C. and Irene (Collins) W.; m. Margaret Ann Cyphers, Sept. 11, 1949; children: Jeffrey Cyphers, John Timothy, Curtis Scott, Keith Alexander. BS, W.Va. Wesleyan Coll., 1948, LLD, 1974; PhD, U. Ill., 1951; DSc (hon.), U. Ala., 1979, W.Va. Inst. Tech., 1979. Research chemist Hercules, Inc., 1951-57; mem. faculty W.Va. Wesleyan Coll., 1957-64; asst. program dir. NSF, 1964-65; dean Coll. Arts and Scis., No. Ariz. U., 1966-70, W.Va. U., Morgantown, 1970-74; vice chancellor W.Va. Bd. Regents, Charleston, 1974-78; pres. U. Ala., Huntsville, 1978-88, prof. chemistry, 1988-95, prof. emeritus, 1995—; interim pres. W.Va. Coll. Grad. Studies, Institute, 1975-76. Hon. rsch. assoc. Univ. Coll. London, 1962-63; cons. NSF, 1965—, Army Sci. Bd., U.S. Army, 1979-82, Nat. Sci. Resources Ctr. Served with USNR, 1945-46. Mich. fellow Center Study Higher Edn., U. Mich., 1965-66 Mem. AAAS, NSTA. Office: 2312 Carlton Cove Blvd Huntsville AL 35802 Office Phone: 256-883-2272. E-mail: johnhasp@aol.com.

**WRIGHT, JOHN COTTON,** archivist, consultant; b. Sharon, Mass., July 27, 1928; s. George Carroll and Dorothy (Cotton) Wright; m. VerlieAnn Kapule Malina, May 23, 1978. Degree in philosophy, U. Hawaii, 1955, MLS, 1987. Cert. archivist Acad. Archivists. Editl. asst. U. Hawaii Press, Honolulu, 1953—55; self employed Kona, Hawaii, 1956—57; administrv. asst. Oahu Rwy. and Land Co., Honolulu, 1958—61; asst. to chmn. Dillingham Corp., Honolulu, 1962—66; historian, archivist Bernice Pauahi Bishop Mus., Honolulu, 1966—81; pres. Wright Cons., Kailua, Hawaii, 1982—; prodn. editor Mechas Press, LLC, Honolulu, 1998—. Cons. Mariners Mus., Newport News, Va., 1967, JDR 3rd Fund, NYC, 1975, NYC, 77, Asia Found., San Francisco, 1979, San Francisco, 81. Mem.: Internat. Coun. Archives (hon.). Office: Wright Cons 361 Kaimake Loop Kailua HI 96734-2018

**WRIGHT, JOHN DANIEL,** minister; b. Middletown, Ohio, July 30, 1984; s. Hargie and Ilene Wright. Dr. Letters (hon.), Christian Ministry Inst. Tex.; DD (hon.), St. Luke Evang. Sch. Biblical Studies. Ordained minister 2001, lic. to preach 2003, evangelist 2003. Sr. pastor Mt. Sterling Evang. Christian Ch., Ky., 2003—. Recipient Ky. Col., The Hon. Paul E. Patton, Gov. Ky., 2002. Democrat. Protestant (Pentecostal). Home: 707 Four Mile Rd Apt 12 Richmond KY 40475-8876

**WRIGHT, JOHN F.,** state supreme court justice; BS, U. Nebr., 1967, JD, 1970. Atty. Wright & Simmons, 1970-84, Wright, Sorensen & Brower, 1984-91; mem., coord. Commn. on Post Secondary Edn., 1991-92; judge Nebr. Ct. Appeals, 1992-94; assoc. justice Nebr. Supreme Ct., 1994—. Chmn. bd. dirs. Panhandle Legal Svcs., 1970. Mem. Scottsbluff Bd. Edn., 1980-87, pres., 1984, 86. Served with U.S. Army, 1970, Nebr. N.G., 1970-76. Recipient Friend of Edn. award Scottsbluff Edn. Assn., 1992. Office: Nebr Supreme Ct 2207 State Capitol PO Box 98910 Lincoln NE 68509-8910*

**WRIGHT, JOHN ROBERT,** pathologist, educator; b. Winnipeg, Man., Can., Aug. 18, 1935; came to U.S., 1961, naturalized, 1968; s. Ross Grant and Anna Marie (Crispin) W.; m. Deanna Pauline Johnson, June 25, 1960 (dec. May 24, 2004); children— Carolyn Deanna, David John. MD with honors, U. Man., 1959. Diplomate: Am. Bd. Pathology. Intern Winnipeg Gen. Hosp., 1959-60, resident, 1960-61, Balt. City Hosp., 1961-63, Buffalo Gen. Hosp., 1963-64; teaching fellow in medicine U. Man., 1960-61; instr. in pathology, Buswell fellow SUNY-Buffalo, 1965-67, prof. pathology, chmn. dept. pathology, 1974-96, interim dean medicine, v.p. clin. affairs, 1997-98, dean medicine, 1998—2001; asst. chief pathology Balt. City Hosps. and asst. prof. Johns Hopkins U., 1967-74; cons. Roswell Park Meml. Inst., 1975—, bd. visitors, 1981-97, interim dir., 1985-86, chmn. bd. visitors, 1987-97. Recipient Louis A. and Ruth Siegel Disting. Teaching award SUNY-Buffalo, 1977, 78, 88, Deans award SUNY, 1987. Fellow Mass. Pathology Chairs (sr., pres. 1994-96); mem. AMA, AAAS, Coll. Am. Pathologists, Am. Soc. Investigative Pathologists, Am. Soc. Clin. Pathologists, U.S. and Can. Acad. Pathology, Alpha Omega Alpha. Achievements include research in amyloidosis and aging. Home: 46 Wynngate Ln Williamsville NY 14221-1840 Office: 204 Farber Hall SUNY Buffalo NY 14214 Personal E-mail: jrwright@buffalo.edu.

**WRIGHT, JOHN WILLIAM,** psychology educator; b. Seattle, June 12, 1944; m. Donna Elene W.; children: Timothy William, Shonna Ann. BA, We. Wash. U., 1966, MS, 1968; PhD, Mich. State U. Asst. prof. psychology Fordham U., N.Y.C., 1972-75, Wash. State U., Pullman, 1975-78, assoc. prof. psychology, 1978-83, prof. psychology, 1983—, chair psychology dept., 1994-99, dir. neurosci. program, 1998—. Pres. Pacific Northwest Biotech., Pullman, 1994—. Co-author: Hypertension and Blood Pressure, 1988; contbr. over 150 articles to profl. jours. Cmty. aide, Pullman Disaster Response, 1996—. Mem. Soc. Neurosci., Am. Heart Assn., Am. Psychol. Soc., Internat. Behavioral Neurosci. Soc. Office: Wash State U Dept Psychology Pullman WA 99164-0001 E-mail: wrightjw@wsu.edu.

**WRIGHT, JOSEPH ROBERT, JR.,** corportate executive; b. Tulsa, Sept. 24, 1938; s. Joe Robert and Ann Helen (Cech) W. BS, Colo. Sch. Mines, 1961; M.I.A., Yale U., 1964. Vice pres. Booz, Allen & Hamilton, 1965-71; dep. dir. Bur. Census, Dept. Commerce, 1971-72; dep. administr. Social and Econ. Statis. Adminstrn., 1972-73, acting asst. sec. econ. affairs, 1973; asst. sec. administr. Dept. Agr., 1973-76; pres. Citicorp Retail Inc. and Retail Consumer Services Inc., N.Y.C.; v.p. Citicorp, Inc., 1976-81; dep. sec. Dept. Commerce, Washington, 1981-82; dep. dir. Office Mgmt. and Budget, Washington, 1982-89; chmn. Pres.'s Council on Integrity and Efficiency, 1982-89; chmn. Pres.'s Coun on Mgmt. Improvement, 1984-89; dir. Office Mgmt. and Budget, 1988-89; exec. v.p., vice chmn., bd. dirs. W.R. Grace & Co., N.Y.C., 1989-94; chmn. Grace Energy, Inc., 1989—94, Grace Environ., Inc., 1989—94; chmn., CEO, dir. AmTec, Inc., N.Y.C., 1994—. Chmn. GRC Internat., 1997-2000; co-chmn. Baker & Taylor, 1996—; chmn. Jefferson Consulting, 1998—; vice-chmn. Terremark Worldwide, 2000—; bd. dirs. Pan Am. Sat, Inc., Fusion Tech., Inc., Bion Enviorn. Tech.; fed. co-chmn. Coastal Plains Regional Commn., 1981-82, Four Corners Regional Commn., 1981-82, New Eng. Regional Commn., 1981-82, Old West Regional Commn., 1981-82, Pacific N.W. Regional Commn., 1981-82, S.W. Border Regional Commn., 1981-82. Mem. Pres. Export Coun., 1989-93, adv. bd. Coun. for Excellence in Govt., 1988-96; trustee Hampton U., 1990-98; mem. Pres.'s Commn. on Postal Reform; mem. Pres.'s Nat. Security Telecomm. Adv. Coun.; mem. FCC Network REliability and Interoperability Coun. 1st lt. AUS. 1963-65. Recipient Pres.'s Citizens award and medal, 1989; named Govt. Exec. of Yr., Govt. Computer News Mag., 1988, medal disting. achievement Colo. Sch. Mines, 1985. Mem. Nat. Acad. Pub. Adminstrn. (com. for responsible fed. budget), Colo. Sch. Mines Alumni Assn., Chief Execs. Orgn., World Bus. Coun., Coun. on Fgn. Rels., Reagan Alumni Assn., Hampton Hills Golf Club (N.Y.), Banyon Country Club (Fla.), Sky Club (N.Y.C.), N.Y. Econ. Club (N.Y.C.), The Bridge Golf Club (N.Y.), Lost Tree Country Club (Fla.). Address: 10 Gracie Sq # 7G New York NY 10028-8031 Office: Pan Am Sat 20 Westport Rd Wilton CT 06897 Office Phone: 203-210-8606. Business E-Mail: jwright@panamsat.com.

**WRIGHT, JOSEPHINE ROSA BEATRICE,** musicologist; b. Detroit, Sept. 5, 1942; d. Joseph Le Vander and Eva Lee Garrison W.; Mus.B., U. Mo., Columbia, 1963, M.A., 1967; Mus.M., Pius XII Acad., Florence, Italy, 1964; Ph.D., N.Y.U., 1975. Instr. music York Coll., CUNY, 1972-75, asst. prof., 1975; asst. prof. Afro-Am. studies in musicology Harvard U., Cambridge, Mass., 1976-81; assoc. dir. integration of Afro-Am. folk arts with music project, Nat. Endowment Humanities, 1979-82; assoc. prof. music and Black studies Coll. of Wooster, 1981-90, prof. music and Black studies, 1991-2000, prof. Music and the Josephine Lincoln Morris prof. Black studies, 2000, prof. music and African studies, 2005—; panelist, cons. on music Mass. Coun. of Arts and Humanities, 1978-80; cons. Nat. Endowment Humanities, 1982-83, 87, 89, 90, Ohio Humanities Coun., 1986; apptd. mem. Nat. Artistic Directorate, Am. Classical Music Hall of Fame, Cin. Author: Ignatius Sancho (1729-1780), An Early African Composer in England: The Collected Edition of His Music in Facsimile, 1981; editor: Am. Music, 1993-97, Journal American Music, 1994-1994, Music in African Am. Culture series, 1995—2000; editor of new music: The Black Perspective in Music, 1979-91, (with Sam Floyd) New Perspectives on Music: Essays in Honor of Eileen Southern, 1992; co-editor: The Bicentennial Issue of The Black Perspective in Music, 1976, (with Eileen Southern) African-American Traditions in Song, Sermon, Tale and Dance, 1991, (with Eileen Southern) Images: Iconography of Music in African-American Culture, 2000; mem. editl. bd. Jour. Am. Musicol. Soc., 2003, Am. Music, 2004; contbr. articles to profl. jours. Mem. Am. Musicol. Soc. (dir.-at-large 1998-2000), Soc. Am. Music (bd. dirs.), Nat. Coun. for black studies. U. Mo. Faculty of Arts and Sci. Alumni Assn. (trustee 1982-85), Pi Kappa Lambda. Democrat. Anglican. Office Phone: 330-263-2044. Business E-Mail: jwright@wooster.edu.

**WRIGHT, JUDITH ANN,** elementary school educator; d. Harold Eugene Donzé and Glenna Mae Van Hise; m. Kurt Ornell Wright, Sept. 4, 1965 (dec.); children: Tyson, Karin Paul, Jennifer. BA, Calif. State U., Northridge, 1964, MA in Spl. Edn., 1995. Spl. edn. tchr., Malabar St. Elem. Sch. L.A. Unified Sch. Dist., 1988—93; spl. edn. tchr., Leo Politi Elem. Sch., 1993—97, resource specialist tchr., 1997—. Office: Sylvan Park Elem Sch 6238 Noble Ave Van Nuys CA 91411 Office Phone: 818-988-9816. Personal E-mail: jwright916@aol.com.

**WRIGHT, JUDITH MARGARET,** law librarian, educator, dean; b. Jackson, Tenn., Aug. 16, 1944; d. Joseph Clarence and Mary Catherine (Key) Wright; m. Mark A. Johnson, Apr. 17, 1976; children: Paul, Michael. BS, U. Memphis, 1966; MA, U. Chgo., 1971; JD, DePaul U., 1980. Bar: Ill. 1980. Librarian Oceanway Sch., Jacksonville, Fla., 1966-67; program dir. ARC, South Vietnam, 1967-68; documents and reference librarian D'Angelo Law Library, U. Chgo., 1970-74, reference librarian 1974-77, dir., lectr. in law, 1980—2000, law libr., assoc. dean for libr. and info. svcs., lectr. in law, 2000—. Mem. adv. bd. Legal Reference Svcs. Quar., 1981—. Mem.: Chgo. Assn. Law Libraries, Am. Assn. Law Libraries, ABA. Democrat. Methodist.

Office: U Chgo Law Sch D'Angelo Law Libr 1111 E 60th St Chicago IL 60637-2745 Office Phone: 773-702-9616. Office Fax: 773-702-2889. Business E-Mail: jm-wright@uchicago.edu.

**WRIGHT, JULIANNE CLEMMONS,** psychologist; b. Murphysboro, Ill., Mar. 27, 1967; d. J.D. and Barbara Sharon Clemmons; m. K. Mitchell Wright, Feb. 6, 1967; children: Eleanore Marie, Nathan Mitchell. BA, U. Ill., 1989; MA, U. Notre Dame, 1994; PhD, U. Denver, 1999. Lic. psychologist Colo. 2002. Lt. comdr., psychologist USNR, 1997—2001. Mem.: Psychol. Soc. (treas. 2005—06). Republican.

**WRIGHT, KATIE HARPER,** educational administrator, journalist; b. Crawfordsville, Ark., Oct. 5, 1923; d. James Hale and Connie Mary (Locke) Harper; m. Marvin Wright, Mar. 21, 1952; 1 child, Virginia K. Jordan. BA, U. Ill., 1944, MEd, 1959; EdD, St. Louis U., 1979. Elem. and spl. edn. tchr. East St. Louis (Ill.) Pub. Schs., 1944-65, dir. Dist. 189 Instrnl. Materials Program, 1965-71, dir. spl. edn. Dists. 188, 189, 189 Instrnl., asst. supt. programs, 1977-79; interim supt. East St. Louis Sch. Dist. 189, 1993-94. Adj. faculty Harris/Stowe State Coll., 1980, adj. prof. edn. emeritus; mem. staff St. Louis U., 1989—; interim supt. Dist. 189 Schs., 1994—; mem. Pres.'s Commn. on Excellence in Spl. Edn. Author: Delta Sigma Theta/East St. Louis Chapter History, 1992; contbr. articles to profl. jours.; feature writer St. Louis Argus Newspaper, 1979—. Mem. Ill. Commn. on Children, 1973-85, East St. Louis Bd. Election Comms., East St. Louis Fin. Adv. Authority, 1999—; pres. bd. dirs. St. Clair County Mental Health Ctr., 1970-72, 87—; bd. dirs. River Bluff coun. Girl Scouts USA, 1979—, nat. bd. dirs., 1981-84; bd. dirs. Jackie Joyner-Kersee Youth Ctr. Found., 1991—, United Way, 1979—, Urban League, 1979— Provident Counseling Ctr., 1995-98; pres. bd. trustees East St. Louis Pub. Libr., 1992—; pres., bd. dirs. St. Clair County Mental Health Ctrs., 1987; mem. adv. bd. Magna Bank; charter mem. Coalition of 100 Black Women; mem. coord. coun. ethnic affairs Synod of Mid-Am., Presbyn. Ch. U.S.A.; mem. Ill. Dept. Corrections Sch. Bd., 1995—; charter mem. North East Links Group, Gateway chpt. The Links, Inc.; mem. Ill. Minority/Female Bus. Coun., 1991—; mem. Pres.'s Commn. on Excellence in Spl. Edn., 2001--. Recipient of more than 150 awards including Lamp of Learning award East St. Louis Jr. Wednesday Club, 1965, Outstanding Working Woman award Downtown St. Louis, Inc., 1967, Ill. State citation for ednl. document Love is Not Enough, 1974, Delta Sigma Theta citation for document Good Works, 1979, Girl Scout Thanks badge, 1982, award Nat. Coun. Negro Women, 1983, Cmty. Svc. award Met. East Bar Assn., 1983, Journalist award Sigma Gamma Rho, Spelman Coll. Alumni award, 1990, A World of Difference award, 1990, 92, Edn. award St. Louis, YWCA, 1991, SIU-E-Kimmel award, 1991, St. Clair County Mental Health award, 1992, Gateway East Met. Ministry Dr. M.L. King award, 1993, Nat. Coun. Negro Women Black Leader of Yr., 1995, Disting. Alumni award U. Ill., 1996, Pioneer award Mosque 28B, 2000, Tri Del Globe award, 2001, Urban League Merit award, 2002, Ill. Office of Edn. award, 2002, Eugene B. Redmond Writers Club award, 2002, NFPW Quest award, 2004, Liberty Bell award St. Clair County Bar Assocs., 2005, St. Clair County Bar Assn. award, 2005; named Woman of Achievement, St. Louis Globe Democrat, 1974, Outstanding Adminstr. So. Region III Office Edn., 1975, Woman of Yr. in Edn. St. Clair County YWCA, 1987, Nat. Top Lady of Yr., 1988, Disting. Alumnus U. Ill., 1996, Citizen Amb., South Africa, 1996, sch. named after her East St. Louis Sch., 2005; named to Vashon H.S. Hall of Fame, 1989, Sr. Illinoisan Hall of Fame, 1997; East St. Louis Elem. Sch. named for Dr. Katie Harper Wright, 2005. Mem. Am. Clubs. Trustees Assn. (regional v.p 1978-79, 92, nat. sec. 1979-80), Ill. Commn. on Children, Mensa, Coun. for Exceptional Children (mem. pres.'s commn. excellence spl. edn.), Top Ladies of Distinction (pres. 1987-91, nat. editor 1991—), Journalism award 1992, Media award 1992), Delta Sigma Theta (chpt. pres. 1960-62, Letters award 2000), Kappa Delta Pi (pres. So. Ill. U. chpt. 1973-74), Phi Delta Kappa (Svc. Key award 1984, chpt. pres. 1984-85), Iota Phi Lambda, Phi Lambda Theta (chpt. pres. 1985-87), East St. Louis Women's Club (pres. 1973-75). Republican. Home: 733 N 40th St East Saint Louis IL 62205-2138

**WRIGHT, KENNETH BROOKS,** lawyer; b. Whittier, Calif., June 5, 1934; s. Albert Harold and Marian (Schwey) W.; m. Sandra Beryl Smith, June 20, 1959; children: Margo Teresa, Daniel Brooks, John Waugh. BA cum laude, Pomona Coll., 1956; JD, Stanford U., 1960. Bar: Calif. 1961, U.S. Supreme Ct. 1979. Assoc. then ptnr. Lawler, Felix & Hall, 1961—77; ptnr. Morgan, Lewis & Bockius, L.A., 1978—99, counsel, 1999—2003, ret. ptnr., 2004. Tchg. team leader Nat. Inst. Trial Advocacy, 1978-87; governing com. Calif. Continuing Edn. Bar, 1973-77, chmn., 1975-76; nat. panel arbitrators Am. Arbitration Assn., 1970-91; lectr. ABA Sect. Litig. Nat. Inst., 1979-86; bd. dirs. L.A. Internat. Comml. Arbitration Ctr. Chmn. bd. editors: Am. Bar Jour, 1977-81. Pres. Pomona Coll. Alumni Assn., 1970-71; pres. parent tchr. coun. Campbell Hall Sch., 1973-74, bd. dirs., vice chmn., 1994—; counsel Vol. League San Fernando Valley, 1979-81; chmn. sect. adminstrn. justice Town Hall of Calif., 1970-71; sr. warden Episcopal Ch., 1973-74. Served with U.S. Army, 1956-57. Mem. ABA (dir. programs litig. sect. 1977-81, coun. 1982-88, standing com on comm. 1978-88, chmn. 1987-88, chmn. sect. book pub. com. 1986-89, pres. fellows young lawyers 1985-86, bd. dirs. 1980-89), Internat. Bar Assn., Assn. Bus. Trial Lawyers (chair com. alt. dispute resolution 1991-93, bd. dirs. 1993-96), Am. Law Inst., Am. Bar Found., State Bar Calif. (gov. com. continuing edn. bar 1972-77, chmn. 1975-76), Conf. Barristers (exec. com. 1966-69, 1st v.p. 1969), L.A. County Bar Assn. (conf. judiciary 1981-83, chmn. CLE adv. com. 1989-91, vice-chmn. CLE com. 1991-93, bd. dirs. L.A. Lawyers 1989-94), L.A. County Bar Found. (bd. dirs., trustee 1993-99, exec. com. internat. sect. 1996-99), Jonathan Club, Phi Beta Kappa. Republican. Avocations: skiing, tennis. Home: 3610 Longridge Ave Sherman Oaks CA 91423-4918 Office: Morgan Lewis & Bockius 300 S Grand Ave Los Angeles CA 90071-3109

**WRIGHT, KIRBY MICHAEL,** writer, editor; b. Honolulu, Sept. 1, 1955; s. Harold Stanley and June Gertrude (McCormack) W.; m. Darcy Laureen Mobraaten, Dec. 28, 1991. BA, U. Calif., San Diego, 1983; MFA, San Francisco State U., 1994. Pub. rels. dir. Winners Circle Resorts, Carlsbad, Calif., 1987-90; instr. Palo Alto (Calif.) Adult Sch., 1994-95; writer GT Prodn. Co., Palo Alto, 1995-96, editor, 1997—. Author: The Rainbow Warrior, 1998; (screenplay) Gordon & Al, 1996; (dramatic monologue) Blue Mesa Review, 1994 (1st pl. award Browning Soc. 1993, 94); (play) Houdini, 1999; (novel) Ulua Lines, 2000, Punahou Blues, 2005; (poetry) Before the City, 2003. Rschr. Ctr. for Auto Safety, Washington, 1980; advisor SAT Success, Palo Alto, 1998. Recipient Poetry prize Ann Fields Trust, San Francisco, 1993, 1st pl. Poets award Acad. Am. Poets, San Francisco, 1993, 1st pl. San Diego Book awards, 2002. Fellow Arts Coun. Santa Clara County, Arts Coun. Silicon Valley. Democrat. Roman Catholic. Avocations: boxing, surfing, gourmet cooking. Home: 1604 Marbella Dr Vista CA 92081 Office: GT Prodn Co 3259 Alma St Palo Alto CA 94306-2925 E-mail: kirby33@earthlink.net.

**WRIGHT, KRISTOPHER,** biology professor; b. St. Paul; m. Angela Schaefer, Sept. 6, 1998; 1 child, Caleb. PhD, Oreg. State U. Prof. biology U. Wis., Platteville, 2001—. Pres. Platteville Cmty. Arboretum, 2005—06. Office Phone: 608-342-1689.

**WRIGHT, LAURA L.,** air transportation executive; m. Randy Wright; children: Lindsay, Jeffrey. BSA, MSA, Univ. No. Tex., 1982. CPA Tex. Tax mgr. Arthur Young & Co. Dallas; dir. corp. taxation Southwest Airlines, Dallas, 1988—90, dir. corp. fin., 1990—95, asst. treas., 1995—98, treas. 1998—2001, v.p. fin. & treas., 2001—04, sr. v.p. fin. & CFO, 2004—. Named one of 50 Women to Watch, Wall St. Journal, 2005. Office: Southwest Airlines 2702 Love Field Dr PO Box 36611 Dallas TX 75235-1611 Office Phone: 214-792-7784. Office Fax: 214-792-4011.*

**WRIGHT, LAUREN NOELLE,** elementary school educator, music educator; d. Steven Vincent and Rita Cuningham Wright. BS in Music Edn., U. Ala., 2004. Tchr. music Elem. Sch. Pell City (Ala.) Sch. Sys., 2004—, instr. color guard H.S. 2006—. Mem. Aspera Winterguard, Atlanta, 2004—05;

mem. color guard Alliance Drum and Bugle Corps. Grantee, Eden Elem. Sch., 2005; Whacker grantee, 2004. Mem.: Music Educators Nat. Conf. Office: Eden Elem Sch 412 Wolf Creek Rd North Pell City AL 35125 E-mail: edenmusicwright@yahoo.com.

**WRIGHT, LAWRENCE GEORGE,** writer; b. Oklahoma City, Aug. 2, 1947; s. John Donald and Dorothy (Peacock) W.; m. Roberta Murphy, Jan. 22, 1970; children: Gordon, Caroline. BA, Tulane U., 1969; MA in Linguistics, Am. U., Cairo, 1971. English tchr. Am. U., Cairo; writer Southern Voices, So. Regional Coun., Atlanta, 1973—80, Texas Monthly Mag., Austin, 1980; founder Tex. Writers' Month. Mem. Coun. on Fgn. Rels. Author: Saints & Sinners, 1993, Remembering Satan, 1994, Twins: Genes, Environment, and the Mystery of Identity, 1997, (novels) God's Favorite, 2000, (children's books) City Children, Country Summer, 1979, (memoir) In the New World, 1988, (screenplays) Noriega: God's Favorite, 2000, (with Ed Zwick, Menno Meyjes) The Siege, 1998, (plays) Sonny's Last Shot; contributing writer, The New Yorker, 1992-. Recipient NYU Olive Branch award for internat. reporting, Nat. Magazine award for reporting, John Bartlow Martin award for Public Interest Magazine Journalism, Overseas Press Club's Ed Cunningham award for best magazine reporting, O'Henry award for Best Work of Magazine Journalism, Tex. Inst. Letters, 2005. Fluent in Arabic.

**WRIGHT, LORI DUNKLE,** music educator, musician; b. Kettering, Ohio, Sept. 17, 1967; d. Robert Kean and Elaine Mary Dunkle; m. Douglas Allan Wright, Aug. 1, 1992; 1 child, Rebecca Ann. MusB in Edn., Ohio State U., 1989, MA, 2001. Tchg. Cert., K12 Music Ohio Dept. of Edn., 1989. Orch. dir. Kent City Schs., Ohio, 1990—91, Worthington City Schs.: Columbus, Ohio, 1991—. Clinician Ministry of Edn., Santiago, Chile, 2002; cellist, asst. prin. Springfield Symphony Orch., Ohio, 1991—; state treas. Ohio Music Edn. Assn., 2004—. Mem.: NEA (assoc.), Am. Fedn. of Musicians (assoc.), Music Edn. Nat. Conf. (assoc.; treas., state of ohio 2004—), Am. String Tchrs. Assn. (assoc.), Ohio State U. Alumni Assn. (life), Phi Kappa Phi (life), Delta Omicron (life). Conservative-R. Christian. Avocations: travel, golf, camping, hiking, backpacking.

**WRIGHT, MARGARET TAYLOR,** marketing consultant, publisher; b. Wilmington, N.C., Nov. 8, 1949; d. Thomas Henry and Margaret (Taylor) W. BA, U. N.C., 1972; MBA, Wake Forest U., 1978. Child advocacy specialist Child Advocacy Council Dept. Human Resources, Raleigh, NC, 1973-74; region dir. N.C. Office for Children Dept. Human Resources, Winston-Salem, 1974-76; product mgr. food div. Am. Home Products, N.Y.C., 1978-80; account exec. Ted Bates Advt., N.Y.C., 1981; product mgr. C.F. Mueller div. McKesson, Inc., Jersey City, 1981-83; mgr. new products Popsicle div. Sara Lee Corp., Englewood, NJ, 1983-86; pres. Wright Mktg. Blueprint, Old Chatham, NY, 1987—; chmn. Equatorial Group, Ltd., Old Chatham, NY, 1994—; pub. Grey Play Round Table Mag. on African Grey Parrots, Old Chatham, NY, 1994—, Nature's Corner Mag., 2005—. Author: African Grey Parrots, A Complete Owner's Manual, 2001; co-author: (pamphlets) Children--Helping Them Grow, 1973; pub.: Grey Play Round Table mag., 1994—; pub., creator Nature's Corner Mag., 2005. Youth coord. Jim Holshouser Gubernatorial Campaign, New Hanover County, N.C., 1972; mem. Jr. League, N.Y. and N.C., 1972-84. Episcopalian. Avocations: tennis, sailing, golf, travel. Home: # 9-609 13835 N Tatum Blvd Phoenix AZ 85032 Personal E-mail: merlin@africangreys.com.

**WRIGHT, MARK A.,** lawyer; b. Manchester, N.H., Oct. 23, 1965; s. Laurence Gary Wright and Sophia Mary Abuod; m. Paula M. Venne; children: Michael, Matthew. BS, U. N.H., 1987; JD, 1991, MS in Intellectual Property, 1997. Bar: N.H. 1991, Mass. 1998. Ptnr. McLane, Graf, Anderson & Middleton, Manchester, NH, 1991—. Named one of Best Lawyers in Am., 2003, 2004, 2005, N.H.'s Forty Under 40, Manchester (N.H.) Union Leader, 2005. Mem.: ABA, Internat. Trademark Assn., N.H. Bar Assn. (chmn. corp. bus. and banking sect.). Office: McLane Law Firm 900 Elm St Manchester NH 03101

**WRIGHT, MARSHALL,** manufacturing executive, diplomat; b. El Dorado, Ark., July 14, 1926; s. John Harvey and Helen Vaughan (Williams) W.; m. Mable Olean Johnson, Sept. 12, 1950 (dec. June 1989); children: William Marshall, Jefferson Vaughan; m. Lind Groseclose Vaughan, Mar. 31, 1990. Student, U. Ark., 1946-48, Cornell U., 1957-58; BS in Fgn. Service, Georgetown U., 1951. Joined U.S. Fgn. Service, 1953; vice consul Egypt, 1953-55; adminstrv. officer Laos., 1956; econ. officer Burma, 1958-60; polit. officer Thailand, 1966-67; spokesman for State Dept., 1964-66; country dir. for Philippines, 1969; sr. mem. NSC, 1967-68, dir. long range planning, 1970-72; asst. sec. state for congl. relations, 1972-74; sr. fellow Nat. War Coll., 1969-70; v.p. govt. affairs Eaton Corp., 1974-76, v.p. pub. affairs, 1976-80, v.p. corp. affairs, 1980-91. Chmn. Cleve. ARC; trustee Cleve. Orch., Cleve. Inst. Music; chmn. Cleve. Com. Fgn. Rels.; vice chmn. Govtl. Rsch. Inst.; mem. Conf. Bd. Pub. Affairs Rsch. Coun., MAPI, Pub. Affairs Coun.; bd. dirs. Cleveland Town Hall, Bus. Industry Polit. action Com. With USMC, 1944-46. Recipient Meritorious Service award State Dept., 1966, Distinguished Service award, 1972 Mem. Am. Fgn. Svc. Assn., Met. Club, Dacor, Mayfield Country, Union, Moss Creek Golf Club, Berkeley Hall Golf Club. Home: 22 Cedar Ln Hilton Head Island SC 29926-1025 Office Phone: 843-837-7474.

**WRIGHT, MARY ELLEN,** theater educator; b. Commerce, Tex. d. Joseph Perry and Ora Berniece Gentry; m. James Hatfield; children: Christopher Collin, Sarah Allison Wright Metzger. BA summa cum laude, U. Tex., Tyler, 1988, MAIS, 1991—91; PhD, Tex. Tech U., Lubbock, 2001. Lectr. U. Tex. at Tyler, 1994—95, 1996—2001, asst. prof., 2002—. Adjudicator Tex. U. Interscholastic League, 1993—, St. Gregory's Sch., Tyler, 1999—; conf. planner Assn. for Theatre in Higher Edn., 1994—98; presenter in field. Costume designer (musical) Annie, (play) The Mandrake; dir.: (play) A Small Family Business, Bloomsymary; costume designer (play) Oleanna (Citation for Excellence in Costume Design, 1992); author: (play) Maggie and Mac; author: (presenter) (workshop) Creative Drama in the Classroom; costume designer (play) Othello; dir.: (play) The King Stag; costume designer (musical) The Fantasticks; dir.: (play) Art; costume designer (musical) Sound of Music, (play) Comic Potential (Citation of Excellence for Costume Design, 2001); dir.: (play) Beauty Queen of Leenane, Pygmalion; contbr. articles to profl. publs. Recipient award, Assn. for Theatre in Higher Edn., 2002, Citation of Excellence for Festival Hosting, Kennedy Ctr./Am. Coll. Theatre Festival, 1999—2000; grantee Adrian Hall Del. Project, Tex. Commn. on the Arts, 2003. Mem.: Tex. Ednl. Theatre Assn., Assn. for Theatre in Higher Edn. (conf. planner 1994—98), Alpha Chi, Phi Kappa Phi, Alpha Psi Omega (advisor 1996—2003), Gamma Phi Beta (life). Home: 5404 Briar Cove Dr Tyler TX 75703 Office: U Tex at Tyler 3900 University Blvd Tyler TX 75799 E-mail: mwright@mail.uttyl.edu.

**WRIGHT, MARY JAMES,** senior education consultant; b. Charlottesville, Va., Aug. 20, 1946; d. Harry Beech and Virginia Allen (Root) James; m. Paul Sims Wright, July 26, 1969; children: Christopher Brennan, Keith Allen. BA summa cum laude, Mary Washington Coll., 1968; MA, Northwestern U., 1969. Instr. drama and speech Mary Washington Coll., Fredericksburg, Va., 1969-71, Charles County Community Coll., La Plata, Md., 1973-79; arts and media coord. Charles County Arts Coun., La Plata, 1973-82, Gen. Smallwood Mid. Sch., Indian Head, Md., 1980-82, No. Va. Community Coll., Annandale, 1982-84; computer-based learning specialist USDA Grad. Sch., Washington, 1984-85, U.S. Army Engr. Sch., Ft. Belvoir, Va., 1985-87, Battelle Meml. Inst., Columbus, Ohio, 1987-88; videodisc designer Kendrick & Co., Washington, 1988-90; instrnl. design mgr. The Discovery Channel, Bethesda, Md., 1990-93; instnl. design mgr., writer Edunetics Corp., Arlington, Va., 1994-97. Project mgr., instl. designer Toby Levine Comms., Inc., 1997-99; mng. editor Time-Life Edn., Alexandria, Va., 1997-99, sr. edn. cons. ThinkNet, 1999—. Author, dir.: Story-Theatre for Children, 1979; contbr. articles to profl. jours.; pub. children's books, videos, videodiscs, CD-ROMS, Web sites, multimedia kits and classroom guides for Time Life, PBS, Discovery Channel, Nat. Geographic Soc., Edunetics/Steck Vaughn. Pres. Am. Christian Television System of No. Va., Action for Women, Charles County AAUW; sign lang.

interpreter Deaf Ministry; ministry vol. Sports and Rec Plus. Nat. Danforth fellow 1969; recipient Achievement award Dept. of Army, 1986, Kendrick & Co., 1989; recipient Outstanding Arts Programming award Md. Dept. Parks and Recreation, 1980, Silver and Bronze Cindy awards (Cinema in Industry and Edn.), 1992, Red Ribbon Am. Film & Video Assn. Festival, Special Gold Jury award Houston Internat. Film Festival, 1992, Gold award Nebr. Interactive Media, 1993, award for Excellence, Time Life, Inc. 1999. Mem. Internat. Interactive Courseware Soc. (Mark of Excellence award 1992), Assn. for Devel. Computer-Based Instrn. Systems (coord. spl. interest groups D.C. chpt. 1989-90), Mortar Bd., Alpha Psi Omega, Alpha Phi Sigma. E-mail: writght1mj@aol.com.

**WRIGHT, MARY P.,** counselor; b. NC; AAS with honors, Ctrl. Carolina CC, Sanford, NC, 1992; BAS, Campbell U., Buies Creek, NC, 1994; MA, Campbell U., 1999. Dep. clk. of ct. Adminstrv. Office of the Cts., Raleigh, NC, 1978-83; computer lab. asst., news reporter Campbell U., 1992-94, asst. to curriculum materials coord., 1994-95; tutorial coord. Ctrl. Carolina CC, 1995-96; data entry staff N.C. Dept. Environ. Health, Raleigh, 1997; counseling intern North Harnett Elem. Sch., Angier, NC, 1997-98. Interviewer, counselor Employment Security Commn., 1998-2000; admissions counselor Campbell U., 2000-01, sch. counselor, 2001—. Mem. Cape Fear Friends of the Fine Arts, Buies Creek, 1996—. Recipient All Am. Scholar award, award, U.S. Achievement Acad. Mem. Omicron Delta Kappa, Delta Kappa Pi. Democrat. Baptist. Avocations: reading, singing, horseback riding, photography, computers. Home: PO Box 234 Buies Creek NC 27506-0234 Personal E-mail: wright_m03@yahoo.com.

**WRIGHT, MICHELLE DENISE,** elementary school principal; b. Caro, Mich., Oct. 21, 1956; d. Roger James Frank; children: Joshua Roger, Valerie Leigh. BA in Elem. Edn., Saginaw Valley State U., 1988, MA, 1999, MEd in Ednl. Leadership, 2005. Cert. tchr. Mich. Ednl. sec. Highland Pines Sch., Caro, Mich., 1978—87; preschool instr. Akron-Fairgrove Coop. Preschool, 1988—89; fifth grade tchr. Akron-Fairgrove Elem. Sch., Mich., 1990—2005; prin. Lakeland Elem. Sch., Coldwater, Mich., 2005—. Girls jr. high volleyball coach Akron-Fairgrove Schools, 1992—2000; young authors coord. Akron-Fairgrove Elem. Sch., 1995—2004, mentor tchr., 2002—05. Named Akron-Fairgrove Elem Employee of the Yr., 2000. Mem.: ASCD, NAESP, Mich. Edn. Assn., Akron-Fairgrove Edn. Assn. (pres. 1997—2004), Mich. Elem. and Mid. Sch. Prins. Assn. Office: Akron-Fairgrove Elem Sch 4335 Lynn St Akron MI 48701 E-mail: MWright@coldwater.k12.mi.us.

**WRIGHT, MINTURN TATUM, III,** retired lawyer; b. Phila., Aug. 7, 1925; s. Minturn T. and Anna (Moss) Wright; m. Nonya R. Stevens, May 11, 1957; children: Minturn T., Richard S., Robert M., Marianne F. BA, Yale U., 1949; LLB, U. Pa., 1952. Bar: Pa. 1953, U.S. Ct. Appeals (3d cir.) 1953, U.S. Supreme Ct. 1962. Law clk. US Ct. Appeals (3d cir.), 1952-53; assoc. Dechert LLP, Phila., 1953-61, ptnr., 1961-95, chmn., 1982-84; ret. Vis. prof. U. Pa. Law Sch., 1965—69, 1993—97; bd. dirs Cotiga Devel. Co. Contbr. articles to profl. jours. Trustee Acad. Natural Scis., Phila., 1958—, chmn., 1976—81; trustee Marshall-Reynolds Found., Hawk Mountain Sanctuary Assn., chmn. bd. dirs., 1992—97. With U.S. Army, 1943—46. Mem.: ABA, Phila. Bar Assn., Pa. Bar Assn., Milldam Club. Episcopalian. Office: Dechert LLP Cira Ctr 2929 Arch St Philadelphia PA 19104-2808 Office Phone: 215-994-2689.

**WRIGHT, NANNIE BELL,** retired secondary school educator; b. Laing, W.Va., May 7, 1934; d. Samuel Thomas and Edna (Irving) W. BS in Edn. magna cum laude, W.Va. State Coll., 1956; MA, U. Chgo., 1960; postgrad., NYU, 1966, L.I. U., 1990. Tchr. social studies, math., and English Wiley H. Bates Jr. H.S., Annapolis, Md., 1956-63; English tchr. Copiague (N.Y.) Jr. H.S., 1963—95. Resource tchr. Copiague Jr. High Sch., 1970-75. Chmn. edn. com. AAUW, Annapolis, 1960; pres. women's aux. Crownsville Hosp., 1960—61. Mem.: NAACP (v.p.Long Island br. 1992—), Nat. Coun. English Tchrs., Inst.Gen. Semantics, Noetic Scis., U. Chgo. Alumni Assn., Copiague Retired Tchrs. Assn., Delta Sigma Theta (v.p. Annapolis alumnae chpt. 1961), Pi Lambda Theta, Alpha Kappa Mu. Republican. Roman Catholic. Avocations: reading, travel, energy healing, poetry, attending plays and concerts. Home: 27 Wellington Pl Amityville NY 11701-3030 E-mail: nanbwlucky@aol.com.

**WRIGHT, PAMELA ANN,** surgeon; b. Silver Spring, S.D., Mar. 6, 1964; d. Harold Bell and Geogeann Wright; m. John George Menkart, Oct. 8, 1994; children: Nicole, Matthew, Danielle. BS, U. Md., Coll. Pk., Md., 1985; MS, U. Md., Balt., 1988, MD, 1992. Diplomate Am. Bd. Surgery. Intern U. Md. Med. Ctr., Balt., 1992—93, resident, 1993—99; trauma rsch. fellow NIH, 1994—96; surgeon Horizon Surg. Group, Rockville, Md., 1999—2003; pvt. practice surgeon Bethesda, Md., 2003—. Assoc. med. dir. breast programs Suburban Hosp., Bethesda, 2006. Fellow: ACS; mem.: Am. Soc. Breast Surgeons, Alpha Omega Alpha. Office: 6420 Rockledge Dr Ste 3700 Bethesda MD 20817 Office Phone: 301-530-5151.

**WRIGHT, PAUL KENNETH,** mechanical engineering educator; b. Watford, Eng., Aug. 24, 1947; came to U.S., 1979; s. Kenneth Browett and Violet Anne (Woodland) W.; m. Frances June Ody, Oct. 24, 1970 (div. June 1984); children: Samuel, Joseph, Thomas; m. Terry Lee Naylor Schuster, Jan. 1, 1996; stepchildren: Jesse, Jennifer. BSc, U. Birmingham, Eng., 1968, MSc, 1970, PhD, 1971. Engr. dept. sci. and indsl. rsch. U. Auckland, New Zealand, 1972-75, sr. lectr., 1975-78; rsch. assoc. Cambridge (Eng.) U., 1978; prof. Carnegie Mellon U., Pitts., 1979-87, NYU, N.Y.C., 1987-91, U. Calif., Berkeley, 1991—. A Martin Berlin Chair in Mech. Engring., assoc. dean coll. engring. Dir., prin. Berkeley (Calif.) Mfg. Group, 1991—; mem. mfg. studies bd. Nat. Rsch. Coun., Washington, 1988—, mem. com. on info. tech. mfg., 1991—. Author: Manufacturing Intelligence, 1988, contbr. articles to profl. jours. Recipient Bursary award Royal Soc., London, 1978. Mem. ASME (Blackall award 1984), N.Am. Mfg. Rsch. Inst., Am. Computing Mem. Ch. of England. Avocations: singing jazz, skiing, sports. Office: UC Berkeley 5133 Etcheverry Hall Berkeley CA 94720-1740

**WRIGHT, PEGGY SUE ESPY,** elementary school educator; b. Chattanooga, Dec. 27, 1929; d. Lavada Pilgrim Espy Newell; m. John Lawton Wright, Nov. 27, 1959; children: John Lawton III, Stephen Martin. BA, U. Chattanooga, 1951, MEd, 1976; spl. cert., Emory U., 1957. Cert. elem. tchr., K-12 reading tchr., adminstrv., supr., music tchr., Tenn. Tchr. Bright Sch., Chattanooga; tchr. summer reading program McCallie Sch., Chattanooga; tchr. Chpt. I reading Chattanooga Pub. Schs. Adj. prof. Chattanooga State Tech. C.C.; workshop leader; presenter in field. Violinist Chattanooga Symphony; active local ch.; pres. Chattanooga Sister City; chmn. Tenn. Literacy Com. Mem. NEA, Internat. Reading Assn., Tenn. Reading Assn. (pres.), Tenn. Edn. Assn., Chattanooga Edn. Assn., MCCAC (past pres.), Delta Kappa Gamma, Alpha Xi. Presbyterian.

**WRIGHT, PETER MELDRIM,** lawyer; b. Charlottesville, Va., Apr. 10, 1946; s. David McCord and Caroline Wallace (Jones) W.; m. Astrid Gabriella Mercedes Sandberg, June 4, 1972; children: David Habersham, Christian Langdon. AB, U. Ga., 1967, JD, 1972. Bar: Ga. 1972, U.S. Dist. Ct. (no. dist.) Ga. 1972. Assoc. Jones, Bird & Howell, Atlanta, 1972-77, ptnr., 1977-82, Alston & Bird, Atlanta, 1982-2001; gen. counsel Resource Healthcare of Am., Inc., 2001—. Soc. chmn. blue sky laws and legal investment law coms. Soc. Colonial Wars in Ga., 1985-88, dep. gov., 1989-91, mem. coun. 2003—; mem. Soc. Cin. Ga., Savannah, historian 1996—, v.p. 1998-2004, pres. 2004—. Mem. Ga. Bar Assn., Nat. Assn. Bond Lawyers (chmn. blue sky laws and legal investment law coms. 1982-85, bd. dirs 1985-86), Ga. Hist. Soc. (bd. curators 1993-2000, sec. 1994-98; v.p. Atlanta chpt. 1996-2000), Skidway Health and Living Svs., Inc. (pres., dir. 2003-), Oglethorpe Club (Savannah, Ga.), St. Andrew's Soc. Savannah. Office: Resource Healthcare Am One Buckhead Plz Ste 900 3060 Peachtree Rd NW Atlanta GA 30305

**WRIGHT, PHILIP B.,** lawyer; BS, U. Mo., Columbia, 1979; JD, Georgetown U., 1982; LLM, NYU, 1985. Ptnr., group co-leader Tax Advice and Controversy Bryan Cave LLP, St. Louis. Office: Bryan Cave LLP One Metropolitan Square 211 N Broadway, Ste 3600 Saint Louis MO 63102 Office Phone: 314-259-2499. Business E-Mail: pbwright@bryancave.com.

**WRIGHT, RANDOLPH EARLE,** retired petroleum company executive; b. Brownsville, Tex., Dec. 22, 1920; s. William Randolph and Nelle Mae (Earle) W.; m. Elaine Marie Harris, May 9, 1943; 1 son, Randolph Earle. BS, U. Tex., 1942. With Texaco Inc., 1946-82, mgr. gas div. Houston, 1968-70, gen. mgr. producing dept., 1970-71, v.p. gas dept., 1971-82, v.p., sr. officer Houston, 1972-80; past dirs., dir. Sabine Pipe Line Co.; v.p., asst. to pres. Texaco U.S.A., 1980-82, ret., 1982; past v.p. Texaco Mineral Co. Past chmn. engring. found. adv. council U. Tex., Austin. Past mem. exec. bd. Sam Houston Area coun. Boy Scouts Am.; past bd. dirs., past pres. Jr. Achievement S.E. Tex.; past bd. dirs. Houston Symphony Soc., Tex. Research League, Houston C. of C.; past trustee U. St. Thomas, S.W. Rsch. Inst. Served with USNR, World War II. E-mail: rewright49@aol.com.

**WRIGHT, RANDY S.,** management consultant; m. Kathy A. Brackin, Feb. 2, 1991; 1 child, Randall (Scotty) S. II. Mcse Microsoft, 2001, Mcp+I Microsoft, 2001, Mcp Microsoft, 2001. Spl. fin. mgr. Town & Country Ford, Nashville, 1995—97; fin. mgr. Reddell Mazda, 1997—98; sr. tech. support analyst Covance, 1998—2003, sys. adminstr., 2003—04; sys. mgmt. profl. IBM, 2004—. Asst. scoutmaster Troop 87, Boy Scouts Am., Nashville, 2005—05; instr. Fin. Peace U., 2000—02; vol. Nashville Sports Coun., Loaves & Fishes, 1995—2005, Holy Rosary Acad., 1999—2002, St. Ann Cath. Sch., 2002—05; com. mem. Boy Scouts Am. Troop 87, 2004—05; eucharistic min. St. Ann Cath. Ch., 2002—04, Holy Rosary Cath Ch., 1996—2002. Staff sgt. USAF, 1983—94. Recipient award Distinction, IBM On Demand Cmty., 2005, Pres.' Vol. Svc. award, 2005. Mem.: IEEE, Phi Theta Kappa. Democrat. Roman Catholic. Avocations: scouting, travel, music. Office: IBM c/o Covance 150 4th Ave North Ste 600 Nashville TN 37219 Office Phone: 615-313-6753. Personal E-mail: ntninja@bellsouth.net. E-mail: wrightr@us.ibm.com.

**WRIGHT, RAYFIELD,** professional football player; b. Griffin, Georgia, Aug. 23, 1945; Attended, Fort Valley St. Univ. Offensive tackle Dallas Cowboys, 1967—79. Named to NFL All-Decade Team, 1970s, NFL Pro Football Hall of Fame, 2006; recipient Dallas Cowboys Ring of Honor. Achievements include six NFL Pro-Bowl appearances; being member two-time Super Bowl Champions. Office: Pro Football Hall of Fame 2121 George Halas Dr NW Canton OH 44708 Office Phone: 330-456-8207.*

**WRIGHT, RICHARD NEWPORT, III,** retired engineering executive, engineering educator; b. Syracuse, NY, May 17, 1932; s. Richard Newport and Carolyn (Baker) Wright; m. Teresa Rios, Aug. 23, 1959; children: John Stannard, Carolyn Maria, Maria, Elizabeth Rebecca, Edward Newport. BCE, Syracuse U., 1953, MCE (Parcel fellow), 1955; PhD, U. Ill., 1962. Jr. engr. Pa. R.R., Phila., 1953-55; instr. civil engring. U. Ill., Urbana, 1957-62, asst. prof., 1962-65, assoc. prof., 1965-70, prof., 1970-74, adj. prof., 1974-79; chief structures sect. Bldg. Rsch. divsn. U.S. Bur. Stds., Washington, 1971—72; dep. dir. Ctr. Bldg. Tech., 1972—73, dir., 1974—91; dir. Bldg. and Fire Rsch. Lab. Nat. Inst. Stds. and Tech., 1991—99; chmn. Bd. Infrastructure and Constructed Environment, 1999—2002; ret. 2002. Pres. Internat. Coun. Bldg. Rsch., Studies and Documentation, 1983—86. Contbr. articles to profl. jours. Govt. ofcl., Gaithersburg, Md., 1971—99; pres. Montgomery Village Found., 1989—90, 2001—03, bd. dirs., 1985—. With AUS, 1955—57. Named Fed. Engr. of the Yr., Nat. Soc. Profl. Engrs.; recipient Henry L. Michel award Industry Advancement Rsch., Civil Engring. Rsch. Found., 1999, Internat. Award, Japan Soc. Civil Engrs., 2003. Fellow: AAAS; mem.: NAE, ASCE (hon.). Home: 20081 Doolittle St Montgomery Village MD 20886-1354 Office: Dept of Commerce Nat Inst Standards & Tech Bldg And Fire Research Labs Gaithersburg MD 20899-0001 Personal E-mail: richard.n.wright@verizon.net.

**WRIGHT, RICHARD OSCAR, III,** pathologist, educator, clinical ethicist; b. La Junta, Colo., Aug. 9, 1944; s. Richard O. Jr. and Frances R. (Curtiss) W.; m. Bernale Trout, May 31, 1969; children: Lauren Diane, Richard O. IV. BS in Biology, Midwestern State U., 1966; MS in Biology, U. Houston, 1968; DO, U. Health Sci., 1972; MA in Bioethics, Midwestern U., 2001. Cert. anatomic pathology and lab. medicine Am. Osteo. Bd. Pathology. Sr. attending pathologist Normandy Met. Hosps., St. Louis, 1977-81, Phoenix (Ariz.) Gen. Hosps., 1981-97, dir. med. edn., 1989-92, 96—; clin. asst. prof. pathology Coll. Osteo. Medicine, Western U., Pomona, Calif., 1985—; dir. labs., chmn. dept. John C. Lincoln Hosp., Deer Valley, 1997—, dir. med. edn., dir. labs., 1997—; v.p. Osteo. Postdoctoral Tng. Inst., Kirksville, Mo., 1998—. Clin. instr. pathology Ohio U. Coll. Osteo. Medicine, Athens, 1976—77; clin. prof. pathology Kirksville Coll. Osteo. Medicine, 1985—; vis. lectr. pathology New Eng. Coll. Osteo. Medicine, Biddeford, Maine, 1989—92; clin. asst. prof. pathology Midwestern U. Ariz. Coll. Osteo. Medicine, 1997—; cons. pathologist Phoenix Indian Med. Ctr., 1992—94; adv. bd. Inter Soc. Clin. Pathology, Chgo., 1992—; sec. med. staff John C. Lincoln Hosp.-Deer Valley, 1997—99, v.p. med. staff, 2000—03, pres. med. staff, 2004—; dir. John C Lincoln Health Network Bd., 2001—. Active Ariz. Rep. Party, Phoenix, Rep. Nat. Coun., Washington; precinctman Dist. 18 Maricopa County, Ariz., 1996-98, Madison Heights Precinct, 1996-98; dir. John C. Lincoln Healthcare Network, 2001—; chmn. bd. trustees Phoenix (Ariz.) Gen. Hosp., 1994-95; ex-officio, trustee, 1995-97; dir. John C. Lincoln Health Network Guild, 1997—; v.p. found. adv. coun. Lincoln Health Found.-Phoenix Gen. Hosp. Osteo. Endowment Fund. Recipient Meade-Johnson award, Mat. Osteo. Assn., 1973. Fellow Am. Osteo. Coll. Pathologists (disting., pres. 1989-90, bd. govs. 1984-91), Coll. Pathologists, Coll. Am. Pathologists, Am. Soc. Clin. Pathologists; mem. Ariz. Osteo. Med. Assn. (del. dist. 2 ho. of dels. 1998), Century Club Alumni Assn., AAAS, Alpha Phi Omega, Rho Sigma Chi, Phi Sigma Alpha. Presbyterian. Office: Anatomic Pathology Assoc 19829 N 27th Ave Phoenix AZ 85027-4001 Office Phone: 623-879-5500. E-mail: rwrigh@jcl.com.

**WRIGHT, ROBERT JOSEPH,** lawyer; b. Rome, Ga., Dec. 13, 1949; s. Arthur Arley and Maude T. (Lacey) W.; m. Donna Ruth Bishop, Feb. 18, 1972; children: Cynthia Ashley, Laura Christine. BA cum laude, Ga. State U., 1979; JD cum laude, U. Ga., 1983. Bar: Ga. 1983, U.S. Dist. Ct. (no. dist.) Ga. 1983, U.S. Dist. Ct. (mid. dist.) Ga. 1985. Assoc. Craig & Gainer, Covington, Ga., 1983-84, Heard, Leverett & Adams, Elberton, 1984-86; gen. counsel Group Underwriters, Inc., 1987—2002; legal cons. Health Plan Select, Athens, 2001—. Mem. editl. staff Ga. Jour. Internat. and Comparative Law, 1981-82. Mem. State Bar Ga. (sec. legal econs. sect. 1987-88, chmn. legal econs. sect. 1988-90), Order of Coif, Masons, Phi Alpha Delta. Baptist. Home: 1030 E Canyon Creek Ct Watkinsville GA 30677-1500 Personal E-mail: rjw30677@bellsouth.net.

**WRIGHT, ROBERT PAYTON,** lawyer; b. Beaumont, Tex., Feb. 15, 1951; s. Vernon Gerald and Huberta Read (Nunn) W.; m. Sallie Chesnutt Smith, July 16, 1977; children: Payton Cullen, Elizabeth Risher. AB, Princeton U., 1972; JD, Columbia U., 1975. Bar: Tex. 1975. Ptnr. Baker Botts L.L.P., Houston, 1975—. Author: The Texas Homebuyer's Manual, 1986. Mem. Am. Coll. Real Estate Lawyers (bd. govs. 2002—), State Bar Tex. (chmn. coun. real estate, probate, trust law sect. 1994-95), Houston Bar Assn. (chmn. real estate sect. 1989-90), Tex. Coll. Real Estate Lawyers, Houston Real Estate Lawyers Coun., Houston Club. Episcopalian. Office Phone: 713-229-1237.

**WRIGHT, SANDRA,** science administrator; B in Acctg., Calif. State U., Long Beach. V.p., contr. Aerojet; with Litton; corp. v.p., contr. Northrop Grumman Corp., LA, 2001—. Office: Northrop Grumman Corp 1840 Century Park E Los Angeles CA 90067-2199

**WRIGHT, SARAH ELIZABETH,** writer, poet; b. Wetipquin, Md., Dec. 9, 1928; d. Willis Charles and Mary Amelia (Moore) Wright; m. Joseph Gilbert Kaye, June 17, 1960; children: Michael, Shelley. Student, Howard U., 1945—49, Pa. State Tchrs. Coll., 1952—56, New Sch. Social Rsch., L.I. U.; BS, SUNY, Albany. MacDowell Colony fellow MacDowell Colony, Peterborough, NH, 1973; writer-in-residence Finkelstein Meml. Libr., Spring Valley, NY, 1978, 1979, 1980. Pres. Pen & Brush, Inc., N.Y.C., 1992—93, cons., prodr. Black History Month celebration and commemoration; cons. for creative artists pub. svc. program N.Y. State Coun. on the Arts. Co-author (with L. Smith): Give Me A Child, 1955; author: (novels) This Child's Gonna Live, 1969, A. Philip Randolph, 1990 (N.Y. Pub. Libr. award, 1990). Recipient Disting. Writer award, Middle Atlantic Writers Assn., 1988, The Sarah E. Wright Best Grad. Paper award, Salisburg State U., 1997, Outstanding Contbn. to Am. Lit. award, Zora Neale Hurston Assn., U. Md. Ea. Shore, Princess Anne, Md., 1999. Mem.: Pen Am. Ctr. (events com.), Authors Guild, Inc. (coun. mem. 1980—90), Harlem Writers Guild, Inc. (v.p., pres. 1958—65, award enduring commitment 1998), Nat. Assn. for Poetry Therapy (cert. poetry therapist). Home: 780 West End Ave New York NY 10025

**WRIGHT, SCOTT OLIN,** federal judge; b. Haigler, Nebr., Jan. 15, 1923; s. Jesse H. and Martha I. Wright; m. Shirley Frances Young, Aug. 25, 1972. Student, Central Coll., Fayette, Mo., 1940-42; LLB, U. Mo., Columbia, 1950. Bar: Mo. 1950. City atty., Columbia, 1951-53; pros. atty. Boone County, Mo., 1954-58; practice of law Columbia, 1958-79; U.S. dist. judge Western Dist. Mo., Kansas City, from 1979. Pres. Young Democrats Boone County, 1950, United Fund Columbia, 1965. Served with USN, 1942-43; as aviator USMC, 1943-46. Decorated Air medal. Mem. ABA, Am. Trial Lawyers Assn., Mo. Bar Assn., Mo. Trial Lawyers Assn., Boone County Bar Assn. Clubs: Rockhill Tennis, Woodside Racquet. Lodges: Rotary (pres. Columbia 1965). Unitarian Universalist. Office: Charles E Whitaker Courthouse 400 E 9th St Ste 8662 Kansas City MO 64106-2684 Office Phone: 816-512-5700.

**WRIGHT, SHANNON MARIE,** psychotherapist, counselor; b. Syracuse, N.Y., Aug. 5, 1978; d. Steven Rae and Cindy Lou Phillips; m. Samuel Benjamin Wright, Apr. 7, 2002; children: Jayden Rain, Balyn Wind, Skylah Marie. MS Counseling and Psychology, Troy U., Fort Walton Beach, Fla., 2005. Registered Mental Health Counselor Intern Fla., 2005. Neuropsychometrist Pensacola Psychol. Clinic, Pensacola, Fla., 2004—; mental hearlth counselor intern Pattison Profl. Counseling Ctr., Fort Walton Beach, Fla., 2005—. Advanced aftercare counselor U. W. Fla., Pensacola, Fla., 2003. Grantee Academic Award for single mothers, U. W. Fla., 2000-2002. Mem.: APA (cert.). Liberal. Native American. Office: Pensacola Psychol Clinic PA 3 W Garden St Ste 370 Pensacola FL 32501 Home: 1771 E Mallory St Pensacola FL 32503 Office Phone: 850-433-1656. Office Fax: 850-433-1656. Personal E-mail: sswright1@earthlink.net.

**WRIGHT, STEVEN,** comedian; b. N.Y.C., Dec. 6, 1955; s. Dolly Wright. Bachelor's, Emerson Coll., 1978. Ind. standup comedian, 1979—. First appearance on The Tonight Show with Johnny Carson, 1982, numerous appearances since then, also Late Night with David Letterman, An Evening at the Improv, various HBO comedy spls. including starring role in On Location; film debut in Desperately Seeking Susan, 1985, other films include So I Married an Axe Murderer, 1993, Speechless, 1994, Natural Born Killers, 1994, Mixed Nuts, 1994, Canadian Bacon, 1994, (voice) Reservoir Dogs, 1992, (voice) The Swan Princess, 1994, For Better or Worse, 1996, Half Baked, 1998, (voice) Babe: Pig in the City, 1998, The Muse, 1999, Loser, 2000, Coffee and Cigarettes, 2003; appeared in TV series Mad About You, 1993; TV series The Downer Channel, 2001; rec. artist (album) I Have a Pony, 1985; standup comedian numerous concerts in clubs, colls. and univs.

**WRIGHT, STUART I.,** materials scientist, materials engineer; b. Murray, Utah, Sept. 22, 1962; BS, Brigham Young U., Provo, Utah, 1987, MS, 1988; PhD, Yale U., New Haven, 1992. Staff mem. Los Alamos Nat. Lab., N.Mex., 1992—95; scientist EDAX-TSL, Draper, Utah, 1995—. Mem.: ASM Internat. (Henry Marion Howe medal 1994), Microscopy Soc. Am., Minerals, Metals and Materials Soc. Achievements include development of fully automated electron backscatter diffraction system. Office: EDAX-TSL Ste H 392 E 12300 S Draper UT 84020 Office Phone: 801-495-2750.

**WRIGHT, SUSAN WEBBER,** federal judge; b. Texarkana, Ark., Aug. 22, 1948; d. Thomas Edward and Betty Jane (Gary) Webber; m. Robert Ross Wright, III, May 21, 1983; 1 child, Robin Elizabeth. BA, Randolph-Macon Woman's Coll., 1970; MPA, U. Ark., 1972, JD with high honors, 1975. Bar: Ark. 1975. Law clk. U.S. Ct. Appeals (8th Cir.), 1975-76; from asst. prof. to assoc. prof. law U. Ark., Little Rock, 1976—83, prof., 1983-90, asst. dean, 1976-78; dist. judge U.S. Dist. Ct. (ea. dist.) Ark., Little Rock, 1990—, chief judge, 1998—2005. Vis. assoc. prof. Ohio State U., Columbus, 1981, La. State U., Baton Rouge, 1982—83; mem. adv. com. U.S. Ct. Appeals (8th cir.), St. Louis, 1983—88. Author (with R. Wright): Land Use in a Nutshell, 1978, Land Use in a Nutshell, 2d edit., 1985; editor-in-chief: Ark. Law Rev., 1975; contbr. articles to profl. jours. Mem.: Am. Law Inst., Pulaski County Bar Assn., Ark. Bar Assn., Am. Judicature Soc., Ark. Women's Forum. Anglican. Office: US District Court 600 W Capitol Ave Ste 522 Little Rock AR 72201-3329 Office Phone: 501-604-5100. Business E-mail: susan_wright@ared.uscourts.gov.

**WRIGHT, SYLVIA,** government agency administrator; b. Balt. BA, Temple U., 1963, MA, 1965. Group leader Sch. Improvement Program Office U.S. Dept. Edn., Washington, dir. Sch. Support and Tech. Programs, Office Elementary and Secondary Edn., 2001—. Office: US Dept Edn FB6 Rm 3E121 400 Maryland Ave SW Washington DC 20202

**WRIGHT, TAMI LADONNA,** pre-school educator; d. Joseph Edward and Eva LaVerne Wright; 1 child, William Marcus Reynolds. MusB, Bethany Coll., 1984; BS in Family & Child Devel., U. Cntl. Okla., 2000, MS in Family & Child Svcs., 2002; MS in Reading, Okla. State U., 2004. Literacy mentor New Zealand Presch. Project, Auckland, 1986—90; lab. tchr. U. Va., Charlottesville, Va., 1990—92; lead tchr. Kinder Care, Okla. City, 1994; head start head tchr. Cmty. Action Program, Okla. City, 1994—2001; head start dir. CDI Temp. Grantee, Denver, 2002—03, Ponca Tribe Okla., 2003—05; child care tchr. Independence CC, Kans.; pre-sch. asst. St. Andrew's Catholic Sch., Independence, Kans. Mem.: Success By Early Childhood Coun., Ponca City, 2003—; N.W. rep. Spirits Hope Domestic Violence Coalition, Okla. City, 2005—. Contbr. articles to profl. jours. Mem. troop coun. Boy Scout Am., Independence, 2006—. Mem.: Tri-State Indian Head Start Dirs. Assn., Nat. Assn. Edn. Young Children, Early Childhood Assn. Okla. (conf. co-chair 2000), Phi Kappa Phi. Democrat. Catholic. Avocations: cross stitch, reading. Home: 725 N 13th St Independence KS 67301-2740 Personal E-mail: ecteacher1@yahoo.com.

**WRIGHT, TAMMY SUE (MARSHALL),** language educator, comedian; b. Norfolk, Nebr., Sept. 13, 1968; d. Ronald James and Lois Ann (Filsinger) Marshall; m. Phillip Frederick Wright, July 14, 1990; children: Trevor Marshall, Samantha Nicole. MS, Wayne State Coll., 1997; BA, U. Nebr. 1990. Cert. tchr. Nebr. Tchr. Newman Grove (Nebr.) Pub. Schs., Neligh (Nebr.)-Oakdale Pub. Schs., 1992—. Play dir. Neligh-Oakdale Pub. Schs., 1992—, one-act and speech coach, 1995—. Actor: cmty. plays. Master ceremony fund raising. Mem.: NEA. Avocations: travel, reading, writing, swimming, hosting exchange students. Home: 203 Weeping Willow Ln Neligh NE 68756

**WRIGHT, THEODORE OTIS,** forensic engineer; b. Gillette, Wyo., Jan. 17, 1921; s. James Otis and Gladys Mary (Marquiss) Wright; m. Phyllis Mae Reeves, June 21, 1942 (div. 1968); children: Mary Suzanne, Theodore Otis Jr., Barbara Joan; m. Edith Marjorie Jewett, May 22, 1968; children: Marjorie Jane, Elizabeth Carter. BSEE, U. Ill., 1951, MS in Engring., 1952; postgrad., Air Command and Staff Coll., 1956—57, UCLA, 1958. Registered profl. engr., Wash. Commd. 2d lt. USAF, 1942-65, advanced through grades to lt. col., 1957, ret., 1965; dep. for engring. Titan SPO, USAF Sys. Command,

L.A., 1957-65; rsch. engr. Boeing Co., Seattle, 1965-81; pres. Pretzelwich, Inc., Seattle, 1981—2002; cons., forensic engr. in pvt. practice Bellevue, Wash., 1988—. Adj. prof. U. Wash., 1967—68, Greenriver Jr. Coll., 1967—68; internat. presenter in field. Contbr. articles to profl. jours. Decorated Purple Heart, Air medal. Fellow: NSPE (life; v.p. western region 1985—87); mem.: ASTM (mem. com. E-43 metric practice 1988—, chmn. 2004—), Am. Nat. Metric Coun. (bd. dirs. 1978—94), Wash. Soc. Profl. Engrs. (state pres. 1981—82, Disting. Svc. award 1980, Engr. of the Yr. 1996, Columbia award 1996), Nat. Coun. Weights and Measures, U.S. Metric Assn. (life cert. advanced metrication specialist), Air Force Assn. (life; state pres. 1974—76, 1990—91, Jimmy Doolittle fellow 1975), Order of Daedalians (life), Tau Beta Pi, Pi Mu Epsilon, Eta Kappa Nu. Democrat. Presbyterian. Avocations: flying, photography, classical music, archaeology. Home: 22975 SE Black Nugget Rd Apt 453 Issaquah WA 98029 Personal E-mail: towright1969@msn.com.

**WRIGHT, THEODORE PAUL, JR.,** political science professor; b. Pt. Washington, N.Y., Apr. 12, 1926; s. Theodore Paul and Margaret (McCarl) W.; m. Susan Jane Standfast, Feb. 18, 1967; children: Henry Sewall, Margaret Standfast, Catherine Berrian (Mrs. Matthew H. Smith). BA magna cum laude, Swarthmore Coll., 1949; MA, Yale U., 1951, PhD, 1957. Instr. govt. Bates Coll., Lewiston, Maine, 1955-57; asst. prof., 1957-64; assoc. prof., 1964-65; assoc. prof. polit. sci. Grad. Sch. Public Affairs, SUNY, Albany, 1965-71, prof., 1971-95; prof. emeritus SUNY, Albany, 1995—. Mem. Columbia U. Faculty seminar on South Asia, 1967—. Author: American Support of Free Elections Abroad, 1964; contbr. chapters to books, articles to profl. jours. Trustee Am. Inst. Pakistan Studies, 1973-82; bd. dirs. Am. Coun. Study of Islamic Societies, 1998—, European Conf. on Modern South Asian Studies, 1974-. Served with USNR, 1944-46. Carnegie intern Indian civilization U. Chgo., 1961-62; Fulbright rsch. prof. India, 1963-64; Am. Inst. Indian Studies rsch. fellow India, 1969-70; Am. Coun. Learned Socs. grantee on South Asia in London, 1974-75; Am. Inst. Pakistan Studies/Fulbright rsch. fellow, Pakistan, 1983-84, Fulbright lectr., 1990-91. Mem. South Asian Muslim Studies Assn. (pres. 1988-2000), Assn. Asian Studies (chmn. N.Y. Conf. on Asian Studies 1988-89), Coun. for Study of Islam and Democracy, Dutch Settlers Soc. of Albany (pres. 1988-90, 98-2001, 1st v.p. 2002-), The New Netherland Inst. (bd. dirs. 2000-), Adirondack Mountain Club, Phi Beta Kappa (chpt. pres. 1992-93), Phi Delta Theta. Unitarian Universalist. Home: 17 Wellington Way Niskayuna NY 12309 Personal E-mail: wright15@juno.com.

**WRIGHT, THEODORE ROBERT FAIRBANK,** biologist, educator; b. Kodaikanal, Tamil Nadu, India, Apr. 10, 1928; s. Horace Kepler and Adelaide Caskey (Fairbank) Wright; m. Eileen Marie Yongen, Jan. 6, 1951 (dec. Jan. 2002). AB in Biology, Princeton U., 1949; MA in Biology, Wesleyan U., 1954; PhD in Zoology, Yale U., 1959. Asst. professor biology Johns Hopkins U., Balt., 1959-65; assoc. professor biology U. Va., Charlottesville, 1965-75, prof. biology, 1975-95; prof. emeritus, 1995—. Vis. scientist Max Planck Inst. for Biology, Tubingen, 1975-76, Devel. Biology Ctr., U. Calif., Irvine, 1982. Editor: The Genetics and Biology of Drosophila, vol. 2a-c, 1978, vol. 2d, 1980, Genetic Regulatory Hierarchies in Development, 1990; co-editor: Advances in Genetics, 1988-92. With U.S. Army, 1950-52. NIH postdoctoral fellow Max Planck Inst. for Biology, Tubingen, Fed. Republic Germany, 1958-59; NSF grantee, 1967-72, 90-93; NIH grantee, 1972-93; Am. Cancer Soc. grantee, 1988-90. Fellow AAAS; mem. AAUP, Genetics Soc. Am., Soc. for Devel. Biology, Va. Acad. Sci., Sigma Xi.

**WRIGHT, THOMAS PARKER,** artist; b. Springfield, Mo., July 3, 1924; s. James Lewis and Vesta Marie (Parker) Wright; m. Elizabeth Jane Smith; children from previous marriage: Jeffrey, Kathleen, Thomas, Ramona, Karen. BA in Math., Henderson State U., 1948; MA in Math., La. State U., 1962. Math., sci. tchr. Hondo (N.Mex.) Union H.S., 1950-53; prin. Westridge (Ark.) H.S., 1954-55; math. tchr. Santa Ana (Calif.) Unified Sch. Dist., 1955-63; math., computer instr. Santa Ana Coll., 1963-71; adminstrv. dean Rancho Santiago CC., Santa Ana, 1971-79; art gallery mgr. Lahaina (Hawaii) Galleries, Inc., 1979-80; pres. Maui Fine Arts, Inc., Kihei, 1981—2006; computer sci. instr. Maui C.C., Kahului, Hawaii, 1983-94. Multi-media and internet software developer NSF. One-man shows include Maui C.C., 1989, exhibited in group shows at Art Maui, 1984, 1986, 1989. Pres. Santa Ana Tchrs. Assn., 1960, Santa Ana Coll. Faculty Assn., 1965. 2d lt. USMCR, 1944—46, 1st lt. USMCR, 1950—52. Mem.: NEA, U. Hawaii Profl. Assembly. Republican. Presbyterian. Avocations: painting, computer art, ocean fishing, photography. Home: 902 Wilshire Ct Mc Kinney TX 75070 Business E-mail: wrightt@hawaii.edu. E-mail: liztomw@netscape.net.

**WRIGHT, TONY,** advertising executive; b. London, United Kingdom; Student, l'universite Paris-Sorbonne, Freie Universitat Berlin. With Saatchi & Saatchi, London, Chiat/Day, LA & Toronto; co-founder McElligott Wright Morrison White (sold to Omnicom), Mpls., 1989; founding ptnr. (with Omnicom) Berlin Wright Cameron, NYC; worldwide chief strategy officer Ogilvy & Mather, 1995—2004; CEO, pres. Lowe Worldwide (divsn. Interpublic), NYC, 2004—06, chmn., 2006—. Named to Advt. Hall of Fame, Am. Advt. Fedn., 2001. Office: Lowe Worldwide 150 East 42nd St New York NY 10017 Office Phone: 212-605-8000.*

**WRIGHT, VERNON HUGH CARROLL,** bank executive; b. Bronxville, N.Y., Sept. 24, 1942; s. Dudley Hugh and Helen Margurite (Carroll) W. m. Lucy Hiss Babb, June 7, 1966; children: Dudley Hugh II, Katherine Babb. BS in acctg., U. Balt., 1969. Sr. v.p. Maryland Nat. Bank, Balt., 1969—91, MNC Fin., Balt., 1990—91; chief corp. fin. officer MBNA Am. Bank N.A., Wilmington, Del., 1992—; sr. vice chmn. MBNA Am. Bank, N.A., 2001—; CFO MBNA Corp., Wilmington, Del., 2003—. Bd. dirs. MBNA Am. Bank, Wilmington, Del. Exec. v.p., chief corp. fin. officer MBNA Corp. With USN, 1962-66. Avocations: farming, teaching. Office: MBNA Am Bank 1100 N King St Wilmington DE 19884-0151 Business E-mail: vernon.wright@mbna.com.

**WRIGHT, VIRGINIA,** art collector, curator; m. Bagley Wright; children: Merrill, Charles, Robin, Bing. BA, Barnard Coll., 1951. Asst. Sidney Janis Gallery; trustee Virginia Wright Fund, Seattle Art Mus. Curator Color Field Paintings and Related Abstractions, 2005. Named one of Top 200 Collectors, ARTnews Mag., 2004, 2006. Avocation: Collector of Contemporary Art; Japanese Art.*

**WRIGHT, WAYNE E.,** education educator; b. Bellflower, Calif., May 1, 1967; s. James L. and Janet Wright; m. Phal Mao Wright, May 28, 1994; children: Jeffrey Sovan, Michael Sopat, Catherine Sophaline. BA in Liberal Studies, Calif. State U., Long Beach, 1992, MA in Lang., Literacy and Learning, 1998; PhD in Ednl. Leadership and Policy Studies, Ariz. State U., 2004. Humanitarian vol. Cambodian Am. Nat. Devel. Orgn., Phnom Penh, 1993—94; tchr. bilingual Khmer (Cambodian) Long Beach (Calif.) Unified Sch. Dist., 1994—2000; rschr. Lang. Policy Rsch. Unit Edn. Policy Studies Lab., Tempe, Ariz., 2000—04; asst. prof. U. of Tex., San Antonio, 2004—. Co-dir. Lang. Policy Rsch. Unit Edn. Policy Studies Lab., Tempe, 2004—; book rev. editor Internat. Multilingual Rsch. Jour., Washington, 2006—. Co-editor: Ebonics in the Urban Education Debate; contbr. articles to profl. jours. Preparing Future Faculty fellow, Ariz. State U., 2001—04, Grad. Scholars Program scholar, 2000—04, Noel Chadwick Gray fellow, 2001, dean's fellow, 2003, dissertation grantee, Grad. Student Assn., Ariz. State U., 2002. Mem.: TESOL, Nat. Assn. for the Edn. and Advancement of Cambodian, Laotian, and Vietnamese Ams. (v.p. for public 2003—), Am. Assn. for Applied Linguistics, Nat. Assn. for Bilingual Edn. (co-chair lang. policy spl. interest group 2002—06), Am. Edn. Rsch. Assn. Mormon. Avocation: music. Office: U Tex San Antonio One UTSA Cir San Antonio TX 78249 Office Phone: 210-458-2024. Office Fax: 210-458-5962. Business E-mail: wayne.wright@utsa.edu.

**WRIGHT, WAYNE KENNETH,** federal agency statistician; b. Chelsea, Mass., Jan. 26, 1944; s. Wayne K. and Louise Annette (Olson) W.; m. Sharon Kay Brown, Aug. 30, 1964 (div. 1974); 1 child, Trent Edward; m. Linda Susan Berkel, Mar. 15, 1975 (div. 1979); 1 child, Stacey Danielle; m. Bonnie Sue Oberhelman, Apr. 3, 1982; 1 child, Forrest Kenneth. BS in Sociology, U. Iowa, 1971; postgrad., U. North Iowa, 1971-72; cert. in marketing, Atlanta U., 1988. Survey asst. Shive-Hall-Hattery Engring., Cedar Rapids, Iowa, 1962-66; chem. lab technician Wilson Packing Plant, Cedar Rapids, 1966-71; grad. rsch. asst. U. No. Iowa, Cedar Falls, 1971-72, grad. tchng. asst., demographic and econ. stats., 1972-73; survey statistician U.S. Bur. Census, Kansas City, Kans., 1973-74, info. specialist, 1974-83, Charlotte, NC, 1983—; data specialist U.S. Bur. of Census, Charlotte, NC, 1991—. Named Ky. Col., 1987; named Hon. Citizen, City of Beloit (Wis.), 1974. Fellow Alpha Kappa Delta. Lutheran. Avocations: fishing, camping, hiking, alpine skiing and racing. Home: 1417 Morrocroft Trl Gastonia NC 28054-6499 Office: US Bur Census 901 Center Park Dr Ste 106 Charlotte NC 28217-2935 Office Phone: 704-424-6430. Personal E-mail: wrghtgmp@aol.com. Business E-mail: w.kenneth.wright@census.gov.

**WRIGHT, WILEY REED, JR.,** lawyer, retired judge, mediator; b. Seattle, Jan. 31, 1932; s. Wiley Reed and Gertrude Ellen (Datson) W.; m. Sally Harrison Clarke, 1955 (div. 1963); children: Wiley III, Margaret, Andrew; m. Roberta Hostinsky, Oct. 18, 1963; children: Cathryn, Amy, Susan. BS in Commerce, Washington and Lee U., 1954, LLB, 1956. Bar: Va. 1956, U.S. Dist. Ct. (ea. dist.) Va. 1956, U.S. Ct. Appeals (4th cir.) 1956, U.S. Supreme Ct. 1993. Law clk. to hon. judge U.S. Dist. Ct., Alexandria, Va., 1958-59; ptnr. Clarke, Richard, Moncure & Whitehead, Alexandria, 1959-68; judge corp. and cir. cts. Alexandria, 1968-79; chief judge cir. ct., 1979-84; ptnr. Hazel & Thomas P.C., Alexandria, 1984-96; mediator McCammon Mediation Group Ltd., Richmond, Va., 1996—. Mem. at large Va. State Bar Coun., 1984-90; mem. Jud. Coun. Va., 1982-84, vice chmn. jud. conf. Va., 1980-82. Assoc. editor: Virginia Circuit Judges Benchbook, 1987. Legal counsel to Alexandria C. of C., 1984-88. 1st lt. U.S. Army, 1956-58. Fellow: Va. Law Found., Am. Bar Found.; mem.: Va. Bar Assn., Omicron Delta Kappa, Phi Delta Phi. Avocations: boating, fishing. Home: 579 Lovers Ln Lancaster VA 22503 Office: McCammon Group Bank of Am Ctr 1111 E Main St Ste 1700 Richmond VA 23219 Office Phone: 804-343-0922. Business E-mail: wwright@rivnet.net.

**WRIGHT, WILLIAM COOK,** archivist, director; b. Jersey City, July 11, 1939; s. Harry Cook and Edna Marguerite Tompkins) W. BA, Gettysburg Coll., 1961; MA, U. Del., 1965, PhD, 1971. Tchr. William J. High Sch., 1961-65; adj. instr. U. Del., Newark, 1968-70; assoc. dir. N.J. Hist. Commn., Trenton, 1970-76; head Bur. Archives and History N.J. State Libr., Trenton, 1976-83; dir. Div. Archives and Records Mgmt., N.J. State Dept., Trenton, 1983-85; chief Bur. Records Mgmt., Trenton, 1985-89, ret., 1989. Coord. state hist. records adv. bd. Nat. Hist. Publs. and Records Commn. 1976-87; mem. adv. com. for papers of William Livingston; sec. N.J. State Records Com., 1976-85, chmn., 1985; mem. adv. bd. dirs. N.J. Archives Series, 1971-86; mem. region 2 adv. coun. Nat. Archives and Records Svc., 1976-77; mem. adv. com. N.J. Newspaper Project, 1983-85, state rev. com. for hist. sites, 1976-79; mem. implementation and planning com. N.J. Supreme Ct., 1982 Author monograph: The Secession Movement in the Middle Atlantic States, 1972; compiler Directory of N.J. Newspapers, 1765-1970; contbr. articles and book revs to profl. jours. Mem. Lawrence Twp. Cultural and Heritage Adv. Com., 1989-92, chmn., 1991. Recipient Award of Recognition N.J. Hist. Commn., 1992. Mem. Acad. Cert. Achivists (cert.). Home: 7 Redwood Ct Glassboro NJ 08028-2934 Personal E-mail: wcwright@comcast.net.

**WRIGHT, WILLIAM EVAN,** physician, consultant; b. NYC, Aug. 1, 1946; s. Samuel and Frances Elnora (Perpente) W.; m. Diana Claire Dryer, Aug. 15, 1970; children: Jason William, Elizabeth Garland, Edwin Samuel. BA in Music, U. Rochester, 1968; MD, U. Pa., 1972; MSPH, U. Utah, 1979; MS in Physiology, Harvard U., 1980. Diplomate Am. Bd Internal Medicine, Am. Bd. Preventive Medicine, Occupl. Medicine, Am. Bd. Ind. Med. Examiners; ACOEM cert. med. rev. officer; cert. FAA med. examiner. Intern LDS Hosp., Salt Lake City, 1972-73, resident, 1973-75, U. Utah Med. Ctr., Salt Lake City, 1978-79, Harvard Sch. Pub. Health, Boston, 1979-80; asst. med. dir. U. So. Calif., L.A., 1980-86; med. dir. US DEA, Arlington, Va., 1986-96; program mgr. site med. dir. DynCorp, Reston, Va., 1991-96; med. dir. Md. Office, CORE, Inc., Irvine, Calif., 1996—2003; cons. Office of Worker Advocacy, US Dept. Energy, Washington, 2003—05; pres. WorkWright, Inc., 2005—. Cons. Westwood Group, 2003—05; dist. med. cons. U.S. Dept. Labor, 2006—. Contbr. articles to profl. jours. Maj. M.C., U.S. Army, 1975-77. Fellow ACP, Am. Coll. Occupl. and Environ. Medicine, mem. Cosmos Club (Washington), Alpha Omega Alpha. Avocation: music. Home: 6801 Wemberly Way Mc Lean VA 22101-1532 Office Phone: 703-556-0092. E-mail: ww4ohs@cox.net.

**WRIGHT CARRIER, J. T.,** business owner; b. McKenzie, Tenn., July 31, 1952; d. Gilbert M. and Mildred B. Wright; m. William W. Carrier III, July 28, 1973; 1 child, Morgan Bailey. BA in Psychology cum laude, Memphis State U., 1974, MA in Ednl. Counseling, Pers. Svcs., 1976, EdD, 1992. Sales rep. API Inc., Memphis, 1980—; casting dir. Theatrics Etc., Memphis, 1980—. Profl. model; casting dir., crew svcs. staff for nat. feature and advt. accts. including Warner Bros., Disney, Phillips 66, Exxon, KC Masterpiece BBQ Sauce, Northwest Airlines; scriptwriter for corp. videos, including Fed. Express, Memphis Bus. Jour.; developer Careers 2000 ednl. video series for adolescents. Pub. Crisis Intervention Studies for Memphis Police Dept.; crew svcs. for U.S. Def. Dept. tng. videos. Co-founder Memphis and Shelby County Film, Tape and Music Commn. Named Miss Memphis, 1972, Top Casting Co. Adweek Mag., 1986. Avocations: environmentalism, ballet, modern dance, theater. Office: Theatrics Etc PO Box 11862 Memphis TN 38111-0862 Office Phone: 901-278-7454.

**WRIGHTON, MARK STEPHEN,** academic administrator, chemistry professor; b. Jacksonville, Fla., June 11, 1949; s. Robert D. and Doris (Cutler) Wrighton; children: James Joseph, Rebecca Ann. BS, Fla. State U., 1969; PhD, Calif. Inst. Tech., 1972; DSc (hon.), U. West Fla., 1983. From asst. prof. chemistry to provost MIT, Cambridge, 1972—90, Frederick G. Keys prof in chemistry, 1981, head dept. chemistry, 1987—90, provost, 1990—95; prof., chancellor Washington U., St. Louis, 1995—. Bd. dirs. A.G. Edwards, Inc., Brooks Automation, Danforth Plant Sci. Ctr., Nidus Ctr. for Sci. Enterprise, Barnes Jewish Hosp., BJC HealthCare, Assn. Am. Univs., St. Louis Regional Chamber and Growth Assn., Bus. Higher Edn. Forum., Univs. Rsch. Assn., Global Climate and Energy Project, Cabot Corp. Author: Organometallic Photochemistry, 1979. Trustee St. Louis Art Mus., Mo. Bot. Garden, St. Louis Symphony Orch., St. Louis Sci. Ctr.; bd. dirs. United Way Greater St. Louis; trustee St. Louis Sci. Ctr. Recipient Herbert Newby McCoy award, Calif. Inst. Tech., 1972, Disting. Alumni award, 1992, E.O. Lawrence award, Dept. Energy, 1983, Halpern award in photochemistry, N.Y. Acad. Scis., 1983, Fresenius award, Phi Lambda Upsilon, 1984, Dreyfus tchr.-scholar, 1975—80; fellow, Alfred P. Sloan, 1974—76, MacArthur fellow, 1983—88. Fellow: AAAS; mem.: Acad. of Sci. of St. Louis, Electrochem. Soc., Am. Chem. Soc. (award in pure chemistry 1981, award in inorganic chemistry 1988), Am. Philos. Soc., Am. Acad. Arts and Scis., Sigma Xi. Office: Washington Univ Office of Chancellor One Brookings Dr Campus Box 1192 Saint Louis MO 63130-4899 Office Phone: 314-935-5100. Business E-mail: wrighton@wustl.edu.

**WRIGHT PENN, ROBIN,** actress; b. Dallas, Apr. 8, 1966; d. Fred Wright; m. Sean Penn, Apr. 27, 1996; children: Dylan Frances, Hopper Jack. Television appearances include The Yellow Rose, 1983-84, Santa Barbara, 1984-87 (Emmy awards Best Ingenue in a Daytime Drama series 1985-87); films include Hollywood Vice Squad, 1986, The Princess Bride, 1987, State of Grace, 1990, Denial, 1991, The Playboys, 1992, Toys, 1992, Forrest Gump, 1994, The Crossing Guard, 1995, Moll Flanders, 1995, Loved, 1996, She's so Lovely, 1997, Loved, 1997 (Seattle Film Festival Award for best actress, 1997), Hurly-Burly, 1998, Just to Be Together, 1999, Message in a Bottle,

1999, Unbreakable, 2000, The Pledge, 2001, The Last Castle, 2001, White Oleander, 2002, The Singing Detective, 2003, A Home at the End of the World, 2004, Nine Lives, 2005, Sorry Haters, 2005; actor, exec. prodr. (films) Virgin, 2003; (TV miniseries) Empire Falls, 2005. Office: United Talent Agy 9560 Wilshire Blvd Beverly Hills CA 90212

**WRIGHT-RIGGINS, AIDSAND F., III,** religious organization executive; b. Oct. 31; m. Betty Wright-Riggins; 3 children. BA in Comparative Religions, Calif State Univ., Fullerton; MDiv, Am. Bapt. Sem., W. Berkeley, Calif.; postgrad. and doctoral studies, Sch. Theology, Claremont, Calif.; PhD in Ministry, Va. Union Univ., Richmond, Va.; LHD (hon.), Benedict Coll., Columbia, SC. Lic. Gospel Min. 1960, Ordained Bapt. Ch., 1975. Pastor Macedonia Bapt. Ch., LA; dir.; Peace with Justice Ministry So. Christian Leadership Conf. of Greater LA, Calif.; pastor Garden of Gethsemane Bapt. Ch., LA; dean Ecumenical Ctr. for Black Ch. Studies, LA; commd. Am. Bapt. home missionary, 1991; exec. dir. ABCUSA Bd. of Nat. Ministries, Valley Forge, Pa., 1991. Adj. prof. philosophy and preaching Univ. La Verne, Calif. Office: ABC Bd of Nat Ministries PO Box 851 Valley Forge PA 19482-0851

**WRIGLEY, BRENDA JEAN,** communications educator; b. Sidney, NY, Aug. 4, 1954; d. Keith Allen Wrigley and Marjorie Blanche Corby. BS in Broadcast Journalism, U. Mo., Columbia, 1975; MS in Pub. Rels., Syracuse U., N.Y., 1996, PhD in Mass Comm., 1999. Radio and TV advt. exec., Binghamton, NY, 1975—90; mktg. comm. mgr. The Raymond Corp., Greene, NY, 1990—96; asst. prof. Mich. State U., East Lansing, 1999—2004; assoc. prof. Syracuse U., 2004—. Co-author: The Gender Challenge to Media, 2001; contbr. articles various profl. jours. Mem.: Assn. for Edn. in Journalism and Mass Comm., Internat. Comm. Assn. Rep. Rels. Soc. Am. Office: S I Newhouse Sch of Pub Syracuse U 215 U Pl Syracuse NY 13244 Office Phone: 315-443-1911. Office Fax: 315-443-3946. Business E-Mail: brwrigle@syr.edu.

**WRIGLEY, DREW H.,** prosecutor, lawyer; b. Fargo, ND, Oct. 1965; BA, U. N.D., 1988; JD, Am. U., 1991. Pros. atty. City of Fargo, 1992—93; asst. dist. atty. Phila. Dist. Atty.'s Office, 1993—98; gen. counsel for pub. policy N.D. Workers Compensation Bur., 1998—99; exec. dir., legal counsel ND Rep. Party, 1999—2000; dep. chief of staff Office of Gov. of ND, 2000—01; US atty. ND US Dept. Justice, 2001—. Office: US Attys Office 655 First Ave N Ste 250 Fargo ND 58102*

**WRIGLEY, WILLIAM, JR.,** candy company executive; b. 1964; Asst. to pres. William Wrigley Jr. Co., Chgo., 1985—92, dir., 1988— v.p., 1991—98, sr. v.p., 1999, pres., CEO, 1999—, chmn., 2004—. Named one of Forbes' Richest Americans, 2006; recipient Hunt-Scanlon Human Capitol Advantage award, 2003. Office: William Wrigley Jr Inc 410 N Michigan Ave Chicago IL 60611*

**WRINKLE, JOHN NEWTON,** lawyer; b. Chattanooga, July 31, 1929; s. John Stuart and Anne (Ownbey) W.; m. Louise Rucker Agee, Feb. 1, 1958; children: Anne Blair, Margaret Rucker. BA, Vanderbilt U., 1951; LLB, Yale U., 1955. Bar: Ala. 1955, U.S. Dist. Ct. (no. dist.) Ala. 1956, U.S. Ct. Appeals (5th cir.) 1958, U.S. Ct. Appeals (11th cir.) 1981, U.S. Tax Ct. 1957. Assoc. White, Bradley, Arant, All & Rose, Birmingham, Ala., 1955-63; ptnr. Bradley Arant Rose & White LLP, 1963-92, counsel, 1993—. Coord. pre-law students Birmingham So. Coll., 1989—. Trustee Birmingham Symphony Assn., 1970-79, 80-83, Episcopal Found. Jefferson County, 1994-2000; mem. bd. advisors St. Andrew's Sewanee Sch., 1985—; bd. dirs. Yale Law Sch. Fund, 2005—. With USAF, 1951-52. Disting. fellow Birmingham-Southern Coll., 1995—. Fellow Am. Coll. Trust and Estate Counsel; mem. ABA, So. Employee Benefits Conf. (steering com. 1970-73), Birmingham Bar Assn., Assn. of Bar of City of N.Y., Birmingham Com. Fgn. Rels., Redstone Club, Mountain Brook Club, Summit Club, Knickerbocker Club (N.Y.C.), Yale Club (N.Y.C.), Phi Beta Kappa, Phi Alpha Delta. Episcopalian. Home: 2 Beechwood Rd Birmingham AL 35213-3914 Office: Bradley Arant Rose & White LLP 1819 5 Ave N Birmingham AL 35203 Office Phone: 205-521-8000. Business E-Mail: jwrinkle@bradleyarant.com.

**WRISTEN, EDWARD L.,** health facility administrator; BA, Kettering U.; MBA, Ohio State U. Cons., 1976; from mem. staff to pres. First Health Group Corp., Downers Grove, Ill., 1990—2001, pres., 2001—, CEO, 2002—. Exec. com. bd. dirs. Coun. Affordable Quality Healthcare, co-chmn. quality care and patient safety com., 2003—. Office: First Health Group Corp 3200 Highland Ave Downers Grove IL 60515

**WROBBEL, KAREN,** education educator, consultant; b. Phila., Nov. 14, 1956; d. Raymond and Lillian Sauter; m. Paul H Wrobbel, Aug. 20, 1977; children: Elizabeth Gorden, Rebekah Stathakis. BA, Biola U., 1981; MA, Wheaton Coll., 1988; EdD, U. Minn., 2005. Cert. elem. tchr. Assn. Christian Schs. Internat., 2003, Bible specialist Assn. Christian Schs. Internat., 2003. Tchr. Christiansen Acad., Rubio, Venezuela, 1982—83; asst. head and tchr. Evang. Christian Acad., Madrid 1983—97; children's edn. coord. Evang. Alliance Mission, Wheaton, Ill., 1997—2003; asst. prof. Trinity Internat. U., Deerfield, Ill., 2003—; sch. bd. mem. Hinkson Christian Acad., Moscow, co-chair Intermission Missionary Kid Edn. Consultation, Colorado Springs, Colo., 1999—2001. Contbg. editor (newsletter) World Pulse, 2002—04; contbr. articles to profl. jours. Recipient Mary LeBar award in Christian Edn., Wheaton Coll., 1988. Mem.: ASCD, Nat. Coun. Tchrs. Math., Am. Ednl. Rsch. Assn., Phi Delta Kappa. Evangelical Christian. Office: Trinity Internat Univ 2065 Half Day Rd Deerfield IL 60015 Office Phone: 847-317-7178. Office Fax: 847-317-4786. Business E-Mail: kwrobbel@tiu.edu.

**WROBEL, BRUCE J.,** energy and utilities company executive; Degree in [illegible] and mgmt. sci., MIT, 1980. Co founder US power co. (acquired by Sithe Energies Inc., 1986), 1981; exec. v.p. worldwide bus. devel. and fin. Sithe Energies Inc., 1986—99; founder EnCom, Japan, 1999, Guinea Aluminum Products Corp. (GAPCO); CEO, pres. Herakles Capital Corp., NYC; CEO Sithe Energies Inc., NYC, 2003—. Office: Sithe Energies Inc 335 Madison Ave 28th Fl New York NY 10017

**WROBLESKI, JEANNE PAULINE,** lawyer; b. Phila., Feb. 14, 1942; d. Edward Joseph and Pauline (Popelak) Wrobleski; m. Robert J. Klein, Dec. 3, 1979. BA, Immaculata Coll., 1964; MA, U. Pa., 1966; JD, Temple U., 1975. Bar: Pa. 1975. Pvt. practice law, Phila., 1975—; pres., shareholder Jeanne Wrobleski & Assocs., LLC, Phila., 1999—. Lectr. Bus. Law Wharton Sch., Phila.; mem. Commn. on Women and the Legal Profession, 1986—89; v.p. Ctr. City Residents' Assn.; Eisenhower Citizen Amb. del. Soviet Union; judge Pro Tem Phila. Ct. Common Pleas; chmn. bd. dirs. Charlotte Cushman Found. Bd. dirs., mem. exec. com. Temple Law Alumni; del. Moscow Conf. on Law and Econ. Coop., 1990; del. to jud. conf. 3d Cir. US Ct. Appeals, 1991; mediator US Dist. Ct. (ea. dist.) Pa., 1996; sec. bd. trustees Phila. Prisons; bd. dirs. South St. Dance Co., Women in Transition; bd. dirs. vice chair The Wilma Theater; chmn. Charlotte Cushman Found. Rhea Liebman scholar, 1974. Mem.: ABA, AAUW, Jagiellonian Law Soc. (exec. com.), Am. Judicature Soc., Phila. Bar Assn. (chmn. women's rights com. 1986, com. on jud. selection and retention 1986—87, chmn. appellate cts. com. 1992, bus. cts. task force, com. on bus. litig.), Pa. Bar Assn., Phila. Art Alliance, Nat. Mus. Women in the Arts, Pa. Acad. Fine Arts, The Athenaeum of Phila., Penn Club, Founders Club, Lawyers Club, Cosmopolitan Club, Franklin Inn Club, Union League Phila., Lambda Iota Tau, Alpha Psi Omega. Democrat. Office: Jeanne Wrobleski & Assocs LLC 1845 Walnut St Fl 24 Philadelphia PA 19103-4708 Office Phone: 215-814-9320. Business E-Mail: jwrobleski@wwdlaw.com.

**WROE, THOMAS, JR.,** semiconductor company executive; BS in engring., U. RI, 1972. Mfg. engr. materials and controls Tex. Instruments Inc., Attleboro, Mass., 1972—95, pres. materials and controls, 1995—98, sr. v.p., 1998—, pres. sensors and controls, 2000—. Mem. exec. com. Mass. Bus. Roundtable; mem. bd. advisors Carroll Sch. Mgmt., Boston Coll.; chmn. bd.

United Way Greater Attleboro/Taunton, gen. campaign chmn., 1997; vice chmn. Assoc. Industries Mass., mem. bd.; mem. bd. trustees Mass. Taxpayers Found.; mem. bd. dirs. Cape Cod Healthcare. Office: Tex Instruments 34 Forest St Attleboro MA 02703 also: Tex Instruments Inc 12500 TI Blvd Dallas TX 75243 Office Phone: 972-995-2011. Office Fax: 972-995-4360.

**WRONG, DENNIS HUME,** retired sociologist, educator; b. Toronto, Nov. 22, 1923; s. Humphrey Hume and Mary Joyce (Hutton) W.; m. Elaine L. Gale, Nov. 24, 1949 (div. Oct. 1965); 1 child, Terence Hume; m. Jacqueline Conrath, Mar. 26, 1966; stepchildren: Jaya, Sheila. BA, U. Toronto, 1945; PhD, Columbia U., 1956. Tchr. Princeton U., 1949-50, Rutgers U., 1950-51, U. Toronto, 1954-56, Brown U., 1956-61; mem. grad. faculty New Sch. Social Research, 1961-63; prof. sociology, chmn. dept. Univ. Coll., NYU, 1963-65; prof. sociology NYU, 1966-94, prof. emeritus, 1994—; retired. Vis. prof. U. Nev., 1965-66; vis. fellow Oxford (Eng.) U., 1978, European U. Inst., 1996-97; Simon vis. prof. U. Manchester, Eng., 1978. Author: American and Canadian Viewpoints, 1955, Population, 1956, 59, Population and Society, 1961, 67, 77, Skeptical Sociology, 1976, Power: Its Forms, Bases and Uses, 1979, 88, 95, Class Fertility Trends in Western Nations, 1980, The Problem of Order: What Unites and Divides Society, 1994, 95, The Modern Condition: Essays at Century's End, 1998, The Oversocialized Conception of Man (reissue of Skeptical Sociology), 1999, Reflections on a Politically Skeptical Era, 2003, 2d edit. 2005, The Persistence of the Particular, 2005; editor: Social Research, 1961-64, (with Harry L Gracy)Readings in Introductory Sociology, 1967, 72, 77, Contemporary Sociology: A Journal of Reviews, 1972-74, Max Weber, 1970; mem. editl. bd. Dissent, 1966—; contbg. editor Partisan Rev., 1981-87. Guggenheim fellow, 1984-85, Woodrow Wilson Internat. Ctr. for Scholars fellow, 1991-92. Mem.: Soc. for Advancement of Socio Econs., Eastern Sociol. Soc., Am. Sociol. Assn. Personal E-mail: dhwrong@voicenet.com.

**WROTH, JAMES MELVIN,** retired military officer; b. Lincoln, Nebr., Feb. 2, 1929; s. Charles M. and Reba (Sharp) Wroth; m. Donna Mae Benson, June 4, 1951 (dec.); children: Mark, David S., Mary E. Bannon; m. Molly B. Mullan, June 15, 1975; stepchildren: Edward H. Mullan(dec.), Philip C. Mullan. BS, U. Nebr., 1951; MBA, Syracuse U., 1963; postgrad., F.A. Sch., 1957, Command and Gen. Staff Coll., 1962, Armed Forces Staff Coll., 1967, Army War Coll., 1968, Harvard U., 1972. Commd. 2d lt. U.S. Army, 1951, advanced through grades to brig. gen., 1973, 40th inf. divsn. Republic of Korea, 1952-53; instr. A.A.A. Sch., Ft. Bliss, Tex., 1954-56; with 3d Inf. Div., Ft. Benning, Ga., also Germany, 1957-61; with Office Chief of Staff U.S. Army, 1963-66; comdg. officer 1st Bn. 31st Arty., Republic of Korea, 1967; exec. asst. to asst. sec. Army U.S. Army, 1968-70; exec. officer I Field Force Vietnam Arty., 1970; comdg. officer 52d Arty. Group, Vietnam, 1971; with Office Dep. Chief Staff for Personnel, Dept. Army, 1972-75; comdg. gen. VII Corps Arty. and Augsburg Germany Mil. Community, 1975-77; comdr. 2d ROTC region, Ft. Knox, Ky., 1977-79; ret., 1979; v.p. dir. mgmt. scis. ops. Gen. Research Corp., McLean, Va., 1979-82; group v.p Info. Systems & Network Corp., Bethesda, Md., 1982-93. Trustee Washington Adventist Hosp. Found., 1989—93. Decorated D.S.M., Legion of Merit, Bronze Star, Air Medal with V device, Army Commendation medal, Vietnamese Gallantry Cross with palm; recipient F. A. Assn. award, 1950, John J. Pershing award, 1951, 40 and 8 award, 1951. Mem.: U.S. Coast Guard Aux. (past flotilla comdr.), Ret. Officers Assn. (past chpt. pres.), Nat Soc. Pershing Rifles (past nat. comdr.), Indian Creek Yacht and Country Club (dir. 2000—03), Indian Creek Yacht Club (past commodore), Beta Gamma Sigma, Alpha Kappa Psi. Home: 286 Breezy Pt White Stone VA 22578-2400 E-mail: jim@wroth.us.

**WROTH, L(AWRENCE) KINVIN,** law educator; b. Providence, July 9, 1932; s. Lawrence Counselman and Barbara (Pease) W.; m. Susan Collins, May 2, 1958 (div. 1972); children: Ann K., Caroline D., Eliza H.; m. Deborah Bethell, Aug. 10, 1972; 1 dau., Katharine L.; stepchildren— John H., David H., Elizabeth T. and Sarah B. Zobel. BA, Yale U., 1954; LLB, Harvard U., 1960. Bar: Mass. 1960, Maine 1974. Teaching fellow, asst. prof. law Dickinson Sch. Law, 1960-62; rsch. assoc. Harvard U., 1962-64; assoc. prof. law U. Maine Sch. Law, Portland, 1964-66, prof., 1966-76, dir. grad. studies Sch. Law U. Maine, 1977-78, acting dean, 1978-80, dean, 1980-90; prof. Vt. Law Sch., 1996—, dean, 1996—2004, pres., 2003—04. Rsch. fellow Charles Warren Center Studies in Am. History, Harvard U., 1968-74; cons. civil and probate procedure, profl. and jud. responsibility, and ct.-bar rels. Maine Supreme Jud. Ct., 1967-96; cons. civil, probate, family ct. and criminal procedure and evidence Vt. Supreme Ct., 1969— Author: (with R.H. Field and V.L. McKusick) Maine Civil Practice, 2d edit. 1970; editor-in-chief: Province in Rebellion, 1975; editor: (with H.B. Zobel) Legal papers of John Adams, 1965; reporter: Vermont Rules of Civil Procedure, 1971, Vermont Rules of Criminal Procedure, 1974, Vermont Rules of Probate Procedure, 1980, (with J. Dooley) Vermont Rules of Evidence, 1982, Maine Code of Judicial Conduct, 1993, Vermont Code of Judicial Conduct, 1994. Pres. Greater Portland Landmarks, Inc., 1966—69, adv. trustee, 1969—85; adv. coun. Nat. Trust Hist. Preservation, 1967—70; mem. Maine Commn. on Legal Needs, 1989—90, Commn. to Study Future of Maine's Cts., 1991—93, Commn. on Future of Vt.'s Judiciary, 1998—99, Vt. Bus. Roundtable, 1998—2004; bd. dirs. Maine Bar Found., 1983—89, sec., 1983—86, v.p., 1987, pres., 1988, fellow, 1991; bd. dirs. Pine Tree Legal Assistance Inc., 1985—96, Nat. Adv. Commn. IOLTA Programs, Inc., 1988—90, Portland Symphony Orch., 1990—98, v.p. ops. and resources, 1991—95, pres., 1995—96. Recipient Littleton-Griswold prize Am. Hist. Assn., 1966, Howard H. Dana award Maine Bar Found., 1991, Justice Louis Scolnik award Maine Civil Liberties Union, 1992, Herbert Harley award Am. Judicature Soc., 1994. Fellow Am. Bar Found.; mem. ABA, Maine Bar Assn. (Disting. Svc. award 1990), Am. Law Inst., Vermont Bar Assn., Colonial Soc. Mass., Mass. Hist. Soc. Office: Vt Law Sch PO Box 96 South Royalton VT 05068-0096 Office Phone: 802-831-1268. E-mail: kwroth@vermontlaw.edu.

**WROTTEN, MARYLEAN,** medical coordinator, counselor; d. Evelyn Saxton and Perry Elmore; 1 child, Evelyn DeShawn Wroten. Student, Audrey Cohn Coll., 1984. Approved med. authorized pers. Fedn. Puerto Rican Orgns., 1991; strategist crisis intervention pers. Fedn. Puerto Rican Orgns., 1991, cert. CPR-First Aid Fedn. Puerto Rican Orgns., 2004. Resident therapist Audrey Cohen Coll., 1991—; med. coord. Agy. Fedn. Multicultural Orgns., NY, 1991—. Author: (poetry) I Love God (Editor's Choice award, 2004), Hope, 2004. Youth coord. Jackson Dem. Club, Bronx, 1995—99; Sunday sch. tchr. Praying Band of Faith, Bronx, 1985—89; proposal rev. com. Neighborhood Adv. Bd., Bronx, 1995—96; del. 1199 Nat. Health & Human Employees Union, NYC, 1996—2004. Mem.: Internat. Soc. Poets (disting.). Democrat. Pentecostal. Avocations: hiking, reading, volunteering, singing. Home: 1291 Union Ave Bronx NY 10459 Office: Federation Multicultural Organization 2 VanSinderen Ave Brooklyn NY 11207 Office Phone: 212-234-2268. Personal E-mail: Lynnmary10@yahoo.com.

**WRUBLE, BERNHARDT KARP,** lawyer; b. Wilkes-Barre, Pennsylvania, Mar. 21, 1942; s. Maurice and Ruth Yvonne (Karp) W.; m. Judith Marilyn (Eyges), Nov. 16, 1968 (div. 1987); children: Justine, Vanessa, Alexis; m. Jill (Diamond), Nov. 24, 1990; children: Mattia, Austin. BA in Polit. Sci., Williams Coll., Williamstown, Mass., 1963; JD, U. Pa., 1966; postgrad., N.Y. Univ., 1972—74, Harvard U., 1978. Bar: Conn., 2003, U.S. Dist. Ct. (so. dist.) N.Y., 1969, U.S. Dist. Ct. (ea. dist.) N.Y., 1972, U.S. Ct. Appeals (2d cir.), 1972, U.S. Supreme Ct., 1972, U.S. Ct. Appeals (7th cir.), 1974, U.S. Ct. Appeals (D.C. and 4th cir.), 1984, U.S. Ct. Appeals (5th cir.), 1985, U.S. Ct. Appeals (11th cir.) 1986. Law clk. to presiding judge U.S. Ct. Appeals (3d cir.), 1966—67; assoc. Simpson, Thacher, and Bartlet, N.Y.C., 1968—73, ptnr., 1973—79; prin. dep. gen. counsel U.S. Dept. Army, Washington, 1977—79; dir. Office Govt. Ethics, Washington, 1979; exec. asst. to sec. and dep. sec. U.S. Dept. Energy, Washington, 1979—81; dir. President's Interagy. Coal Export Task Force, Washington, 1980—81; ptnr. Verner, Liipfert, Bernhard, McPherson, and Hand, Washington, 1981—99; sr. v.p. legal affairs N.W. Airlines, St. Paul, 1999—2001. Bd. dir. Epilepsy Found. Am., 1983, chmn., 1991. Hartford County Pro Bono Award, 2004. Mem. ABA, D.C. Bar

Assn., N.Y. State Bar Assn., Williams Coll. Alumni Assn. (pres. Washington chpt. 1986-91), Williams Coll. Soc. Alumni Assn. (exec. com. 1988-91). Democrat. Office Phone: 860-521-3543. Personal E-mail: bkwruble@yahoo.com.

**WRUBLE, BRIAN FREDERICK,** investor; b. Kalamazoo, Apr. 18, 1943; s. Milton and Rose Muriel (Nathanson) W.; m. Susan Roberta Shifrin, June 23, 1968 (div. Oct. 1984); children: Amy Carolyn, Jordan Todd; m. Kathleen Wilson Bratton, Apr. 20, 1985; 1 child, Henrietta Zane Bratton. BEE, Cornell U., 1965, MEE, 1966; MBA with distinction, NYU, 1976. Field engr. Sperry Gyroscope Corp., Lake Success, NY, 1966—70; v.p. Alliance One Instl. Svcs., Inc., N.Y.C., 1970—76, H. C. Wainwright and Co., Inc., N.Y.C., 1976-77, Wainwright Securities, Inc., N.Y.C., 1977; v.p., co-mgr. fundamental equities rsch. Smith Barney, Harris Upham & Co., N.Y.C., 1977-79; exec. v.p. chief fin. ops. Equitable Life Assurance Soc. U.S., N.Y.C., 1979-92; chmn., pres., CEO Equitable Capital Mgmt. Corp., N.Y.C., 1985-92; chief investment officer Equitable Life Assurance Soc. U.S., N.Y.C., 1991-92; pres., COO, dir. Delaware Mgmt. Holdings, Inc., 1992-95; pres., CEO The Delaware Group, 1992-95; pres., COO Delaware Mgmt. Co., 1992-95; chmn. Delaware Distributors, Inc., 1992-95; chmn., CEO Delaware Svc. Co., Inc., 1992-95; gen. ptnr. Odyssey Ptnrs., L.P., N.Y.C., 1995—; mng. prin. Odyssey Investment Ptnrs., LLC, NYC, 1997—98, spl. ltd. ptnr., 1999—2004; pvt. investor, 2004—. Chmn., pres. Equitable Realty Assets Corp., Atlanta, 1983—92; v.p., dir. TELMARI, Inc., N.Y.C., 1982—83, Equitable Variable Life Ins. Co., 1987—92; chmn. Equico Capital Corp., N.Y.C., 1984—92; CEO Equitable Gen. of Okla., Oklahoma City, 1985—86; trustee Equitable Retirement Plans, N.Y.C., 1980—86, Oppenheimer Funds, 2001—; pres. Hudson River Trust, 1991—92, Equitable Funds, 1991—92; mem. investment adv. bd. Zurich Fin. Svc. Group, 2004—; dir. Spl. Value Opportunities Fund LLC, 2004—. Vice-chmn. Boys Choir of Harlem, N.Y.C., 1984 92; vice chmn. Corp. Ptnrs. Phila. Art Mus., 1993—95; bd. govs. Jerome Levy Econ. Inst., 1990—2001; bd. dirs. Harlem Youth Devel. Found., 1989—92, Corp. Ptnrs. Phila. Art Mus., 1992—95. The Jackson Lab., Inc., 1990—. Inst. for Advanced Study, 1992—, treas., 2006—. Recipient Heroes award Boys Choir Harlem, 1990, Founders award, 1993. Mem.: IEEE, Phila. C. of C. (bd. dirs. 1992—95, mem. exec. com. 1993—95), Inst. CFAs (CFA, bd. trustees 1992—98, vice chmn. 1993—94, chmn. 1994—95, bd. trustees rsch. found. 1994—95, 2000—02, assoc. editor CFA Digest 1983—), N.Y. Soc. Security Analysts, Assn. Investment Mgmt. and Rsch. (gov. 1992—98, C. Steward Sheppard award 2000). Republican. Jewish. Avocations: skiing, amateur radio.

**WRUCKE-NELSON, ANN C.,** elementary school educator; b. Mankato, Minn., Nov. 5, 1939; d. G.F. and Dorothy (Thomas) Wrucke; children: Chris, Dor-Ella. BS, Mankato State U., 1961; MLA, So. Meth. U., 1974; postgrad., U. Minn., 1963, Tex. Woman's U., EdD in Early Childhood Edn., 1992. Cert. elem., kindergarten, ESL, history tchr., Tex., adminstrn., 2000. Tchr. Rochester (Minn.) Pub. Schs., Christ the King Sch., Dallas; dir., tchr. Norway Christian Presch., Dallas; Every Student Learns Lang. program kindergarten tchr. Dallas Ind. Sch. Dist., 1971—. Tchr. summer session Tex. Woman's U., 1991; tchr. PreK Rosemont Primary, 2005—; presenter in field. Producer: (video) A Year of Language Learning, 1990. Sunday sch. tchr. Holy Trinity Ch. Recipient Tchr. of Yr. award, 1989; Tex. TESOL scholar, 1994; Bill Martin Literacy Conf. scholar; named ESL Tchr. of Yr., 1991. Mem. TESOL, Kindergarten Tchrs. Tex., Phi Delta Kappa. Mailing: Rosemont 1919 Steven Forest Dr Dallas TX 75208

**WU, ALBERT W.,** medical educator; b. N.Y.C., July 27, 1957; s. Ray J. and Christina (Chan) W BA, Cornell U., Ithaca, N.Y., 1980; MD, Cornell U., Ithaca, 1984; MPH, U. Calif. Berkeley, 1990. Resident medicine Mt. Sinai Hosp., N.Y.C., 1984—86, U. Calif. San Diego, 1986—87, clin. instr., 1987—88; Robert Wood Johnson scholar U. Calif. San Francisco, 1988—90; asst. prof. Johns Hopkins U., Balt., 1990—96, assoc. prof., 1996—2005, prof., 2006—. Pres. Internat. Soc. for Quality of Life Rsch., 2003—. Office: Johns Hopkins U 624 N Broadway Baltimore MD 21205-1900 E-mail: awu@jhsph.edu.*

**WU, BAOLIN,** statistician; b. Jingmen, China, Oct. 27, 1977; s. Zhongde Wu and Xinxiu Chen. PhD, Yale U., 2004. Asst. prof. U. Minn., Mpls., 2004—. Achievements include research in bioinformatics. Office: University of Minnesota 420 Delaware St SE Minneapolis MN 55455 Office Phone: 612-624-0647.

**WU, BENJAMIN H.,** federal agency administrator, lawyer; BA, NYU, 1985; JD, U. Pittsburgh, 1988. Former counsel Office of Congresswoman Constance A. Morella; former counsel, sci. com. US Ho. of Reps., mem., investigations and oversight subcom., 1993—94, mem., tech. subcom., 1995—2001; dep. under sec. for tech. US Dept. Commerce, Washington, 2001—04, exec. sec., NSTC com. on tech., asst. sec. for tech. policy, 2004—. Office: US Dept Commerce Tech Admin 1401 Constitution Ave NW Washington DC 20230

**WU, CARL,** medical researcher; PhD, Harvard U., 1979. Postdoctoral fellow Harvard U., 1979—82; joined Lab. Biochemistry Nat. Cancer Inst., 1982; chief Lab. Molecular Cell Biology Ctr. Cancer Rsch., Nat. Cancer Inst., 1996—, also head Chromosome Structure and Gene Regulation Sect., Lab. Molecular Cell Biology. Contbr. articles to sci. jours. Recipient Outstanding Young Scientist Award, Md. Acad. Sciences, 1987, Young Investigator Award, Am. Soc. Biochemistry and Molecular Biology, 1992. Mem.: NAS, Am. Acad. Arts and Sciences. Office: Lab Molecular Cell Biology Nat Cancer Inst Ctr Cancer Rsch 37 Convent Dr Bldg 37 Rm 6068 Bethesda MD 20892-4255 Office Phone: 301-496-3029. Office Fax: 301-435-3697. E-mail: carlwu@helix.nih.gov.*

**WU, CHAI WAH,** research scientist; b. Hong Kong, China; BS in Computer Engring., Lehigh U., 1990. BA in Cognitive Sci., 1990; MSEE, U. Calif., Berkeley, 1991, MA in Math., 1994, PhD in Elec. Engring., 1995. Rschr. U. Calif., Berkeley, 1996; postdoc IBM, Yorktown Heights, NY, 1996—97, rsch. staff mem., 1997—. Author: (book) Synchronization in Coupled Chaotic Circuits and Systems, 2002. Fellow: IEEE (assoc. editor 1997—99, 2002—, Fellow 2001); mem.: Am. Math. Soc. Achievements include invention of several inventions in field. Office: IBM T J Watson Rsch Ctr PO Box 218 Yorktown Heights NY 10598

**WU, CHIN H.,** engineering educator; b. Chow-Fei Wu. PhD, MIT, Cambridge, 1994—99. Asst. prof. U. Wis. Madison, 1999—2005, assoc. prof., 2005—. Recipient Tchg. award, U. Wis. Mem.: AGU. Office: Univ Wis Civil & Environ Engring Madison WI 53706 Office Fax: 608-262-5199. Business E-Mail: chinwu@engr.wisc.edu.

**WU, DANIEL,** actor; b. San Francisco, Sept. 30, 1974; BA in Achitecture, U. Oreg., 1997. Vocalist Alive, Hong Kong. Founder, instructor Wushu Club, U. Oreg. Actor: (films) Young & Dangerous: The Prequel, 1998, Bishonen, 1998, City of Glass, 1998, Gorgeous, 1999, Gen-X Cops, 1999, Purple Storm, 1999, 2000 AD, 2000, Headlines, 2001, Hit Team, 2001, Peony Pavilion, 2001, Cop on a Mission, 2001, Born Wild, 2001, Beijing Rocks, 2001, The Peeping, 2002, Beauty and the Breast, 2002, Princess D, 2002, Love Undercover, 2002, Devil Face, Angel Heart, 2002, Naked Weapon, 2002, Love Undercover 2, 2003, Hidden Track, 2003, Miss Du Shi Niang, 2003, Magic Kitchen, 2004, Enter the Phoenix, 2004, One Night in Mongkok, 2004, Around the World in 80 Days, 2004, The Huadu Chronicles: Blade of the Rose, 2004, New Police Story, 2004 (Best Supporting Actor award, Golden Horse Awards, 2004), Beyond Our Ken, 2004, House of Fury, 2005, Divergence, 2005, Chin bai but dzui, 2005, Everlasting Regret, 2005, (voice) Dragon Blade, 2005; actor, prodr.: (films) Night Corridor, 2003; actor(guest appearance): (TV series) MTV Whatever Things, 2003, Getaway, 2005.; (documentaries) Hong Kong Superstars, 2001. Avocations: Kung Fu, travel, photography, swimming, wakeboarding, fitness. Office: c/o The JC Grp 145 Waterloo Rd Kowloon Hong Kong*

**WU, DAVID,** congressman; b. Taiwan, Apr. 8, 1955; came to US, 1961; m. Michelle Wu; children: Matthew, Sarah. BS, Stanford U., Calif., 1977; student, Harvard Med. Sch.; JD, Yale U., New Haven, 1982. Clk. to fed. judge, Portland, Oreg.; ptnr. Cohen & Wu, Oreg., 1988-98; mem. US Congress from 1st Oreg. dist., 1999—, mem. edn. and the workforce com., mem. sci. com., ranking minority mem. environment, tech. and standards subcommittee, mem. exec. bd. Congl. Asian Pacific Am. Caucus, mem. New Dem. Coalition. Democrat. Office: US Ho Reps 1023 Longworth Ho Office Bldg Washington DC 20515 Office Phone: 202-225-0855.*

**WU, DE TING,** mathematics professor, researcher, writer; b. Shanghai, Jan. 9, 1938; came to U.S., 1981; s. Bing Huo and Wei Fen (Zhang) W.; m. Pei Hua Zhang, July 16, 1974; 1 child, Yin. BA, Peking (China) U., 1962; MA, U. Ga., 1983, PhD, 1988. Instr. Shanghai Textile Coll., 1963-71; worker Shanghai # 12 Textile Factory, 1971-78; sr. lectr. Shanghai Textile Coll., 1978-81; tchg. asst. U. Ga., Athens, 1981-88; assoc. prof. Morehouse Coll., Atlanta, 1989—. Editor: Selected Problems from Theoretical Mechanics, 1981. Bd. dirs. Orgn. Chinese Ams., 1992-96, Asian-Pacific Ams. of Coun. of Ga., 1994. Mem. AAUP, Shanghai Mechanics Assn., Am. Math. Soc., Math. Assn. Avocations: photography, travel, playing contract bridge. Office: Morehouse Coll Dept Math 830 Westview Dr SW Dept Math Atlanta GA 30314-3773 Office Phone: 404-681-2800 2459. E-mail: dtwu@morehouse.edu.

**WU, FRANK H.,** law educator, journalist; b. Cleve., Aug. 20, 1967; s. Hai and Grace (Ma) Wu. BA, Johns Hopkins U., 1988; JD, U. Mich., 1991. Bar: Calif. 1992, DC 1995. Law clerk to Honorable Frank Battisti, Cleve., 1991—92; assoc. Morrison & Foerster, San Francisco, 1992-94; fellow Stanford U. Law Sch., Palo Alto, Calif., 1994-95; asst. prof. Howard U. Law Sch., Washington, 1995—98, assoc. prof. 1998—2001, prof., 2002—04, clinic dir., 2000—02; dean, prof. law Wayne State U. Law Sch., Detroit, 2004—. Scholar-in-residence Deep Springs Coll., 2001—03; vis. prof. U. Mich., 2002—03; adj. prof. Columbia U., 2002—04. Co-author: (book) Beyond Self Interest, 1996, Race, Rights and Reparation: Law and the Japanese American Internment, 2001; contbg. author: book The Affirmative Action Debate, 1996, Illegal Immigration Viewpoints, 1996; author: Yellow: Race in Amercia Beyond Black and White, 2001. Chmn. DC Human Rights Commn., 2001—03, DC Ct. Appeals Bd. Profl. Responsibility, 2003—04; bd. dirs. Leadership Conf. on Civil Rights Edn. Fund, 2004—; trustee Gallaudet U., 2000—. Named one of Best Lawyers Under 40, Nat. Asian Pacific Am. Bar Assn., 2004. Fellow: Am. Bar Found.; mem.: Com. of 100, Am. Law Inst., Asian Pacific ABA (dir. ednl. fund 1995—98). Office: Wayne State Univ Law Sch 471 W Palmer St Detroit MI 48202 Office Phone: 313-577-3933. Business E-Mail: frankhwu@wayne.edu.

**WU, FUMING,** computer science educator; s. L. Wu and H. Shen; m. Y. Fang, June 11, 1992; 1 child, Wenbo. PhD in Math. and Theoretical Computer Sci., U. Haifa, Isreal, 1998. Sr. mem. sci. staff Nortel Networks, Richardson, Tex., 2000; rsch. scientist Alcatel USA Resources, Inc., Plano, Tex., 2001—06; asst. prof. of computer sci. Tex. A&M Internat. U., Laredo, 2006—. Contbr. scientific papers to profl. jours. Mem.: ACM, IEEE (sr.). Achievements include patents pending for. Office: Tex A&M Internat U CH302C 5201 University Blvd Laredo TX 78041-1900 Office Phone: 956-326-2600. Personal E-mail: fwu@ieee.org. Business E-Mail: fwu@tamiu.edu.

**WU, GEORGE YUNG-HSING,** medical educator, gastroenterologist; b. N.Y.C., Nov. 10, 1948; s. Te Leng and Carol (Lee) W.; m. Catherine H. Chang, Feb. 23, 1975; children: Jonathan, David, Victoria. BS in Chemistry magna cum laude, U. Rochester, 1970; MD, PhD in Medicine and Biochemistry, Albert Einstein Coll. Medicine, 1976. Diplomate Am. Bd. Internat. Medicine, Nat. Bd. Med. Examiners. Intern in medicine Harlem Hosp. Ctr.-Columbia U. Coll. Physicians and Surgeons, N.Y.C., 1976-77, resident, 1977-79; fellow in gastroenterology and liver disease Albert Einstein Coll. Medicine, Bronx, N.Y., 1979-81, asst. prof. medicine, 1982-83, U. Conn. Sch. Medicine, Farmington, 1983-87, assoc. prof. depts. medicine and physiology, 1987-92, prof. dept. medicine, 1992—, chief divsn. gastroenterology and hepatology, 1989—, dir. endoscopic svcs., 1996—, Herman Lopata chair hepatitis rsch., 1992—. Mem. gastrointestinal adv. bd. U. Chgo.; mem. adv. bd. liver rsch. unit Yale U., New Haven. Author: Liver Diseases: Diagnosis and Therapy Using Specific Receptors and Ligands, 1991, Diseases of the Liver and Bile Ducts: Diagnosis and Treatment, 1997; contbr. over 100 articles and abstracts to med. jours., including Jour. Biol. Chemistry, Hepatology, Jour. Clin. Investigation, Gastroenterology, Human Gene Therapy, Nature Medicine, also numerous chpts. to books. Recipient rsch. prize Am. Liver Found., 1982, rsch. career devel. award NIH, 1986-91, Young Scientist award gastroenterology rsch. group Am. Gastroenterol. Assn., 1990, sci. award Chinese Am. Med. Soc., 1992; NIH fellow Albert Einstein Coll. Medicine, 1970-76, fellow Gail I. Zuckerman Found., 1979, postdoctoral fellow Am. Liver Found., 1980-81; grantee Nat. Inst. Arthritis, Metabolism and Digestive Diseases, 1980-81; industry rsch. scholar Am. Gastroenterol. Assn., 1985-88. Mem. Am. Soc. Clin. Investigation (Young Turks 1989), Assn. Am. Physicians (Old Turks 1995), Phi Beta Kappa. Achievements include patents for method of enhancing and/or prolonging expression of a gene introduction into cells and carrier system and method for introduction of genes into mammalian cells (U.S.), for targeting viruses and cells for selective internalization by cells and targeted protection from cytotoxins (Australia), targeted delivery of genes encoding immunogenic proteins (Europe). Home: 52 Ridgebury Rd Avon CT 06001-3825 E-mail: wu@nso.uchc.edu.

**WU, GUOFA FELIX,** computer company executive; b. Nanchang, Jiangxi, China, Oct. 19, 1945; s. Luxing Wu and Guande Xiong; m. Juan Liu, Jan. 1987; 1 child, Libby; m. Youming Zhong, June 1971 (div. Nov. 1985); 1 child, Zhehui. M in Engring., Tsinghua U., Beijing, China, 1984; MS, 1993, PhD in Info. Sci., 1995. Pres. Global Internet Corp., Boston, 1999—. Tech. specialist Nat. Transp. Systems Ctr. of U.S. Dept. Transp., Cambridge, Mass., 1997—99; guest prof. Xi'an Jiaotong U., 2001—, Harbin Inst. Tech., China, 2002—. Honor chair U.S. House Majority Trust, 2004—; pres. Pacific Rev. Monthly, Hong Kong, 2005—. Fellow: North Am. Soc.Experts and Entrepreneurs (pres. 2001—); mem.: Pres. Bus. Commn. Home: 36 Parsons St Boston MA 02135 Business E-Mail: felixwu@email.com.

**WU, HARRY PAO-TUNG,** retired librarian; b. Jinan, Shandong, China, May 1, 1932; arrived in U.S., 1960; s. James Ching-Mei and Elizabeth Hsiao (Lu) Wu; m. Irene I-Len Sun, June 23, 1961; children: Eva Pei-Chen, Walter Pei-Liang. BA, Nat. Taiwan U., Taipei, 1959; student, Ohio State U., 1962; MLS, Kent State U., 1966. Archive and libr. asst. Taiwan Handicraft Promotion Ctr., Taipei, 1959-60; student asst. Kent State U. Libr., 1960-61; reference libr. Massillon (Ohio) Pub. Libr., 1964-65, acting asst. dir., 1965, asst. dir., head adult svcs., 1966; dir. Flesh Pub. Libr., Piqua, Ohio, 1966-68, St. Clair County Libr. Sys., Port Huron, Mich., 1968-96; founder, dir. Blue Water Libr. Fedn., Port Huron, 1974-96; ret., 1996. Pres. Mich. Libr. Film Cir., Lansing, 1977—79; mem. St. Clair County Literacy Project Com., 1986—96. Cmty. mem. editl. bd. Times Herald, 1998—99. Bd. dirs Mich. Waterways Coun. Girl Scouts U.S., Port Huron, 1985—86, Blue Water Reading Coun., 1987—88, United Way St. Clair County, Mich., 1990—91; trustee Libr. Mich., 1992—95; mem. sister city com. City of Port Huron, 2002—04. Mem.: ALA, Chinese-Am. Librs. Assn., Detroit Suburban Librs. Roundtable, Assn. Ednl. Comm. and Tech., Am. Mgmt. Assn., Mich. Libr. Assn., Port Huron Internat. Club (pres. 1988), Rotary (dir. 1972—74, 1988—90, grand marshall Internat. Day Parade 2005, Paul Harris fellow 1988). Home: 1518 Holland Ave Port Huron MI 48060-1511

**WU, HONG,** pathologist; arrived in U.S., 1988; d. Xing-Yu Wu and Xu-Zhi Xu; m. Lance Mark Wiseman, Nov. 24, 1999. MD, Peking Union Med. Coll. Beijing, 1986; PhD, U. Va., 1992. Diplomate in surg. and clin. pathology and in dermatopathology Am. Bd. Pathology. Rsch. asst. dept. med. genetics Inst. Basic Med. Scis., Chinese Acad. Med. Scis., Beijing, 1987—88; rsch. assoc. dept. microbiology U. Va. Sch. Medicine, Charlottesville, 1993—94; resident dept. pathology and lab. medicne U. Pa., 1994—99, fellow dept. dermatology,

1999—2000; assoc. mem., staff pathologist dept. pathology Fox Chase Cancer Ctr., Phila., 2000—. Contbr. articles to profl. jours. Mem.: Am. Soc. Clin. Pathologists, Coll. Am. Pathologists, Am. Soc. Dermatopathology. Office: Fox Chase Cancer Ctr 7701 Burholme Ave Philadelphia PA 19111 Office Phone: 215-728-6900. E-mail: hong.wu@fccc.edu.

**WU, HSIU KWANG,** economist, educator; b. Hankow, China, Dec. 14, 1935; came to U.S., 1952, naturalized, 1963; s. Kao Cheng and Edith (Huang) W.; m. Kathleen Gibbs Johnson, Aug. 17, 1968. Grad., Lawrenceville Sch., 1954; AB, Princeton U., 1958; MBA, U. Pa., 1960, PhD, 1963. Prof., group coordinator fin., econs. and internat. bus. Kao Cheng and Edith (Huang) fin., econs. and legal studies faculty U. Ala., 1972-81, Lee Bidgood prof. fin. and econs., 1978-97, Ala. Banker Edn. Found. Banking Chair prof., 1973-78, prof. emeritus fin., 1997—; econ. adviser Office of Comptroller of Currency, U.S. Treasury, 1966-69, 75-80; dir. Ala. Fed., 1984-88, SECOR Bank FSB, 1988-93, chmn. bd., 1992-93. Cons. instl. investor study SEC, 1969-70; mem. com. examiners undergrad. program for counseling and evaluation test in bus. Ednl. Testing Service, 1971, 77 Co-editor: Elements of Investments, 2d rev. edit, 1972; Contbr. articles to law and econ. jours. Sloan Faculty fellow Sloan Sch. Mgmt., Mass. Inst. Tech., 1965-66 Mem. Am. Fin. Assn., Fin. Mgmt. Assn. Home: 3201 Old Barn Ct Ponte Vedra Beach FL 32082-3713

**WU, HUAN-TER,** statistician; arrived in USA, 1971, naturalized, 1978; s. Chin-mu and Lin-lun Wu; m. Ling-Ling Wu, July 18, 1976; 1 child, Joy. BS (hon.), Nat. Chung Hsing U, Taichung, Taiwan, 1964; MS, Va. Poly. Inst. & State U, Blacksburg, Va., 1975, PhD, 1979. Cons. Statis. Cons. Lab., Va. Poly. Inst. & State U, Blacksburg, Va., 1973—79; asst. prof. statis. State U of NY, Oneonta, NY, 1980—82; prin. Biostatis. R.W. Johnson Pharm. Rsch. Inst. Raritan, NJ, 1982—95; statis. cons. Bristol-Myers Squibb Pharm. Rsch. Inst. Princeton, NJ, 1995—96; asst. dir. of Biometrics Ohmeda Inc./Baxter Healthcare Corp., Liberty Corner, NJ, 1996—98; VP Sinney Assoc., Princeton Jct., NJ, 1998—. Cons. Bristol-Myers Squibb Pharm. Rsch. Inst., Princeton, NJ, 1995—96, Baxtor Healthcare Corp., New Providence, NJ, 1999—2005. Mem.: Am. Statis. Assoc. (assoc.). Avocations: movies, music, fishing, picnics. Home: 6 Baylor Place Princeton Junction NJ 08550 Office: Sinney Associates Inc 6 Baylor Place Princeton Junction NJ 08550 Office Phone: 609-799-6749. Personal E-mail: htwu03@yahoo.com.

**WU, JAMES CHEN-YUAN,** aerospace engineering educator; b. Nanking, China, Oct. 5, 1931; came to U.S., 1953, naturalized, 1963; s. Chien Lieh and Cheng-Ling Wu; m. Mei-Ying Chang, Sept. 7, 1957; children—Stephanie, Yee-Hwa, Norbert Mao-Hwa. Student. Nat. Taiwan U., 1949-52; BS, Gonzaga U., 1954; postgrad., Columbia U., 1954; MS (univ. fellow), U. Ill., 1955, PhD, 1957. Engr. Wah Chang Corp., N.Y.C., 1954; researcher Mass. Inst. Tech. at Cambridge, 1957; asst. prof. Gonzaga U., Spokane, Wash., 1957-59; research specialist Douglas Aircraft Co., 1959-65, group leader, 1960-61, supr., 1961-62, br. chief, 1963-65; prof. aerospace engring. Ga. Inst. Tech., 1965-96; pres. Applied Aero, LLC, 1996—. Cons. N.Am. Aviation Co., Geophys. Tech. Corp., European Atomic Energy Commn., Ispra, Italy, European Atomic Energy Commn. (research center), U.S. Army Research Office, Durham, S.C. Contbr. articles to profl. jours. Chmn. bd. dirs. Chinese-Am. Inst. Recipient profl. achievement award Douglas Aricraft Co., 1963, Outstanding Tchrs. award Gonzaga U., 1959; Assoc. fellow Am. Inst. Aeros. and Astronautics Mem. Am. Soc. Engring. Sci. (founding), Soc. Indsl. and Applied Math. (vice-chmn. Pacific N.W. 1958-59), Am. Astron. Soc. (sr.), Am. Phys. Soc., Nat. Assn. Chinese Ams. (pres. Atlanta chpt.), Sigma Xi, Tau Beta Pi, Sigma Alpha Nu. Office: Sch Aerospace Engring Georgia Inst Tech 48365 Avalon Heights Ter Fremont CA 94539-8005

**WU, JEREMY S.,** federal official; b. Hong Kong; m. Deanie Pin. BA in Mathematical Statistics, MA in Mathematical Statistics, PhD in Mathematical Statistics, George Washington U. Chief, statistics branch Agriculture Mktg Svc., US Dept. of Agriculture, Washington, 1982—96; dep. dir., office of civil rights US Dept. of Agriculture, Washington, 1997—2000; nat. ombudsman US Dept. of Energy, Washington, 2000—02; dir., civil rights office US Dept. of Transportation, Washington, 2002—. Adjunct prof. statistics George Washington U., 1978—. Chair Asian Am. Govt. Executives Network.

**WU, JIA HAO,** transportation executive, researcher, consultant; PhD, U of Montreal, Montreal, Que., Can., 1988—91; MS engring., Shanghai U of Sci. and Tech., Shanghai, 1982—88, B engring., 1978—82. Pres. Traffic Moves, Pleasanton, Calif., 2002—; dir. of its TJKM Transp. Consultants, Pleasanton, Calif., 2000—. Mng. dir. INRO Solutions, Montreal, Que., Canada, 1999—2000; project mgr. INRO Consultants, Montreal, Montreal, Canada, 1991—99; invited rschr. U of Montreal CRT, Montreal, Que., Canada, 1994—2000, rsch. assoc., 1988—91; asst. prof. Shanghai U of Sci. and Tech. Shanghai, 1983—91. Contbr. transportation system modeling Transport. Modeling and Math. Programming (Natural Sciences and Engring. Rsch. Coun. of Can., 1994), transportation system modeling Transport. Modeling and GIS (Natural Sciences and Engring. Rsch. Coun. of Can., 1997); author: (book transportation and network analysis) A multi-class multi-mode variable demand network equilibrium model with hierarchical logitimate structures, (transportation research b) Two improved numerical algorithms for continuous dynamic network loading problem, On the equivalence between stationary link flow patterns and traffic network equilibria, (transportation science) Advances in the dynamic network loading problem, (transportation research b) A continuous dynamic network loading problem and its math. formulations, (mathematical programming) A gen. descent framework for the monotone variational inequality, (transportation science) Transit equilibrium assignment study: model and algorithm. Recipient Third Prize, Shanghai City, 1988, Machine Bldg. Commn. of China, 1988, Adv. Prof., Shanghai U. of Sci. and Tech. of China, 2000, Invited Prof., The Gan Su U of Tech. of China, 1999; scholar PhD Study, 10. Can. Internat. Devel. Agy. Fellowship, 1990, U of Montreal, 1988. Mem.: Math. Programming Soc. (Internat.), Inst. of Ops. Rsch. and the Mgmt. Sci. (INFORMS, Internat.), Transp. Rsch. Bd. (TRB, Internat.), Inst. of Transp. Engineers (ITE, Internat.) (assoc.). Achievements include first to Transit Network Optimization in Shanghai. Office: TJKM Transport Cons 5960 Inglewood Dr Suite 100 Pleasanton CA 94588 Office Phone: 925-463-0611. Personal E-mail: wu_jia_hao@hotmail.com. E-mail: jhwu@tjkm.com.

**WU, JIE,** electronics engineer, educator; d. Fu Chen Wu and Zheng Chen Yu; life ptnr. Michael Heinz Stoiber. B in Engring., Hefei U. Tech., Hefei, Anhui Prov., China, 1993; MS in Engring., Hefei U. Tech., 1996; PhD, Chinese Acad. of Scis., Shanghai, P.R. China, 1999, U. Notre Dame, Notre Dame, Ind., 2004. Rsch. assoc. U. Notre Dame, Ind., 2003—04; asst. prof. U. Tenn., Knoxville, 2004—. Contbr. articles to profl. jour. Recipient Faculty Early Career Devel. Award, NSF, 2005, Ralph E. Powe Jr. Faculty Award, Oak Ridge Associated Univ., 2006; grantee Rate-Based Sensor Devel. for Advancing Heat Transfer Measurements, NSF. Achievements include patents pending for Method and apparatus for AC micropump; Method and apparatus for enhancing microbial detection. Office: U Tenn 1508 Middle Dr Knoxville TN 37996 Office Phone: 865-974-5494. Office Fax: 865-974-5483.

**WU, JINGCHUN,** research scientist; b. Maanshang, China, Nov. 25, 1962; s. Guang-Long Wu and Yulan Wang; m. Youju Cao, Jan. 28, 1989; 1 child, Yang. PhD, Nagoya U., Furo-cho, Chikusa-ku, Nagoya, Japan, 1998. Engr. The Yangtze Water Conservancy Com., Wuhan, China, 1983—85; asst. prof. U. Shanghai For Sci. and Tech., Shanghai, 1988—94; lead rsch. scientist Hitachi Ltd., Hitachi, Japan, 1998—2001; sr. rsch. scientist LaunchPoint Tech., Inc., Goleta, Calif., 2001—; rsch. engr. Computational Dynamics, Ltd., London, 2001. Editl. bd. mem. ASAIO Jour. Fellow Japanese Govt. Scholarship, Japanese Govt., 4 years. Fellow: Artificial Organs (editl. bd. mem. 2006). Achievements include patents for Pediatric ventricular assist device. Home: 290 Mathilda Dr Goleta CA 93117 Office: LaunchPoint Tech 5735 Hollister Ave Ste B Goleta CA 93117 Office Phone: 805-683-9659. Home Fax: 805-683-9671; Office Fax: 805-683-9671. Business E-Mail: jwu@launchpnt.com.

**WU, KATHLEEN J.,** lawyer; b. Great Neck, NY, 1960; BA, Columbia U., 1982; JD, George Washington U., 1985. Bar: NY 1986, Conn. 1986, Tex. 1987. Ptnr., Real Estate, Fin., Bus. Transactions Andrews Kurth LLP, Dallas, mem. mgmt. com. Contbr. articles to profl. jour.; lectr. in field. Mem. Dallas Assembly; bd. dir. Women's Leadership Exchange (Southwest), Tex. Cultural Trust Coun.; adv. bd. Turtle Creek Manor; bd. trustees Greenhill Sch. Named a Texas "super lawyer", Tex. Monthly Mag., 2003, 2004; named one of top 6 "go to" real estate lawyers in Tex., Tex. Lawyer Mag., 2003, best lawyers in Dallas, DMagazine, 2003. Mem.: Attys. Serving Cmty. (co-hon. chmn. 2003), Nat. Asian Pacific ABA, State Bar Tex., ABA, Conn. Bar Assn., NY State Bar Assn., Dallas Bar Assn. Office: Andrews Kurth LLP 1717 Main St Ste 3700 Dallas TX 75201 Office Phone: 214-659-4448. Office Fax: 214-659-4401. Business E-Mail: kwu@andrewskurth.com.

**WU, LAWRENCE MG HLA MYIN,** physician; b. Rangoon, Burma, May 12, 1937; arrived in U.S., 1964; s. John and Maria (Wong) W.; m. Margaret Perez, June 1968. MBBS, U. Rangoon, Burma, 1961. Internship Knickerbocker Hosp., N.Y.C., residency, chief residency; house phys. (fell.) St. Mary's Hosp., Bklyn.; surgeon Harrison Cmty. Hosp., Cadiz, Ohio, Harris Walker Clin., S. Williamsoms, Ky.; priv. prac. Boenger Clin., Edgerton, Ohio. Med. dir., Boenger Clin., Edgerton, Ohio, 1991—; bd. govs., Community Meml. Hosp., Hicksville, Ohio, 1996—. Mem. C. of C., Edgerton, Ohio. Fellow Am. Coll. Emergency Medicine (life, charter); mem. AMA, Am. Coll. Gen. Practice (life, charter), Ohio St. Med. Assn., Williams Co. Med. Assn., Am. Coll. Internal Phys., Midwest Burma Med. Assn. Republican. Roman Catholic. Home: 3804 Lake Rd Edgerton OH 43517-9536 Office: 104 N West St Edgerton OH 43517-9697

**WU, LISA MARIA,** psychologist; b. Wellington, New Zealand, June 4, 1972; d. Robin and Barbara Ann Wu. B in Commerce and Adminstrn., Victoria U., 1992; BSc with First Class Honors in Psychology, Victoria U., New Zealand, 1994; PhD in Clin. Psychology, Columbia U., 2004. Lic. Psychology NY State Edn. Dept. Asst. lang. tchr. Iwanuma City (Japan) Bd. Edn., 1995—96; editl. asst., rsch. assist. Jour. Cognitive Psychotherapy, Am. Inst. for Cognitive Therapy, N.Y.C., 1999—2000; rsch. coord. Mt Sinai Sch. Medicine, N.Y.C., 1999—2000, psychology extern, 2000—01, project mgr., 2001—02; psychology intern Rusk Inst. Rehab. Medicine, NYU Med. Ctr., N.Y.C., 2002—03, cognitive remediation specialist, 2003—04, resident psychologist, 2004—05, staff psychologist, 2005—06; clin. psychology Massey U., Wellington, New Zealand, 2006—. Clin. supr. Tchrs. Coll., Columbia U., N.Y.C., 2004—05. Recipient G. Schweislinger award, Tchrs. Coll., Columbia U., 1997; Gen. scholarship, 1999-2000. Mem.: APA, NY State Psychol. Assn. Home: 85 Pk Rd Wellington Miramar 6003 New Zealand Office: Massey Univ Wellington Campus Psychology Clinic Bldg K1 24 King St Wellington New Zealand Office Phone: 64-4-8015799. Business E-Mail: l.m.wu@massey.ac.nz.

**WU, LI-TZY,** alcohol/drug abuse services professional, researcher; d. Yu-Tsai and Yu-Chi Wu; m. Hsin-Hsong Tseng, Apr. 20, 1992; children: Jonathan Tseng, Harrison Tseng. DSc, Johns Hopkins U., 1998. RN N.J., 1993. Psychiat. epidemiologist RTI Internat., Research Triangle Park, NC, 1999—2005; asst. rsch. prof. Sch. Medicine Duke U., Durham, NC, 2005—. Recipient Nat. Inst. on Drug Abuse Women and Gender Jr. Investigator Travel award, 2001; fellow, NIH, 1997—99; grantee, Nat. Inst. Drug Abuse, 2000—02, 2003—06, Nat. Inst. Alcohol Abuse and Alcoholism, 2001—03. Mem.: APHA, Coll. on Problems of Drug Dependence, Delta Omega (Alpha chpt.). Office: Duke Univ Med Ctr DCRI 2400 Pratt St Durham NC 27705 Office Phone: 919-668-8576. Personal E-mail: litzywu@yahoo.com.

**WU, MIN,** cell biologist, researcher, educator; b. Qixian, China, Oct. 4, 1958; s. Han Zhang Wu and Su Bi Cheng; m. Yun Zeng, July 12, 1985; 1 child, Lu-shen. BSc in Medicine, Luzhou (China) Med. U., 1983; MD, Shanghai Second Med. U., 1988; PhD, Leeds (Eng.) U., 1997. Lectr. Luzhou (China) Med. Sch., 1988-91, assoc. prof., 1992—, rsch. asst., 1993-94; rsch. officer Leeds (Eng.) U., 1994-97; rsch. assoc. pulmonary Ind. U./Purdue U., Indpls., 1998-2001, asst. scientist, 2001—. Sr. scientist Synvirion, Ltd., Leeds, 1988—; hon. prof. Tsinghua U., Beijing, 1988—; vis. scientist Peking U., Beijing, 1994-95, Tohoku U., Sendai, Japan, 1991-92; mem adv. coun., GM Cancer Rsch. Found. Author: Medical Microbiology, 1990; contbr. articles to profl. jours. Mem. Life Sci. Soc. for Chinese Bioscientists in U.K. (v.p. 1995-96, pres. 1996-97), Drug Delivery System Soc., chinese Immunology Soc., Biochem. Soc., Chinese Scholars Assn. (exec. mem. 1993-94), Leeds Chinese Scholars Assn. (pres. 1994-95). Avocations: football, painting, singing. Office: Res Asso Pulmonary Divsn IUPU 1 1001 W 10th St #425 Indianapolis IN 46202-2859

**WU, MIN,** computer and electrical engineer; b. China; BA in Econs., Tshinghua U., 1996; BSE in Elec. Engring., Tsinghua U., 1996; MA in Elec. Engring., Princeton U., 1998, PhD in Elec. Engring., 2001. Asst. prof. dept. elec. and computer engring. U. Md., 2001—06, assoc. prof., 2006—. Author: Multimedia Fingerprinting Forensics for Traitor Tracing, 2005; co-author: Multimedia Data Hiding, 2003; contbr. articles to profl. jour. Named one of Top 100 Young Innovators, MIT Tech. Review, 2004; recipient Career award, NSF, 2002, Young Investigator award, US Dept. Defense, Office Naval Rsch., 2005, Best Paper award, IEEE, European Signal Processing Soc. Achievements include co-holder of 5 US patents. Business E-Mail: minwu@eng.umd.edu.

**WU, SING-YUNG,** physician, researcher; b. China, 1939; MB, Nat. Taiwan U., 1963; PhD, U. Wash., 1969; MD, Johns Hopkins U. 1971. Staff physician VA Med. Ctr., Long Beach, Calif., 1977—; asst. prof. U. Calif., Irvine, 1977—84, assoc. prof., 1985—90, prof. dept. radiol. scis. and medicine, 1990—. Editor: Thyroid Hormone Metabolism, 1991, 1994. Office: Thyroid Rsch Lab 5901 E 7th St Long Beach CA 90822 Office Phone: 562-826-5808. Business E-Mail: sing.wu@va.gov.

**WU, TAI TE,** biological sciences and engineering educator; b. Shanghai, Aug. 2, 1935; m. Anna Fang, Apr. 16, 1966; 1 child, Richard. MB, BS, U. Hong Kong, 1956; BS in Mech. Engring, U. Ill., Urbana, 1958; SM in Applied Physics, Harvard U., Cambridge, Mass., 1959; PhD in Engring. (Gordon McKay fellow), Harvard U., 1961. Rsch. fellow in structural mechanics Harvard U., 1961-63; rsch. assoc., 1965-66; rsch. scientist Hydronautics, Inc., Rockville, Md., 1962; asst. prof. engring. Brown U., Providence, 1963-65; asst. prof. biomath. Grad. Sch. Med. Scis., Cornell U. Med. Coll., N.Y.C., 1967-68, assoc. prof., 1968-70; assoc. prof. physics and engring. scis. Northwestern U., Evanston, Ill., 1970-73, prof., 1973-74, prof. biochemistry and molecular biology and engring. scis., 1973-85, acting chmn. dept. engring. scis., 1974, prof. biochem., molecular biology, cell biology and biomed. engring., engring. scis., applied math., 1985-94, profl. biochemistry, molecular biology, cell biology, biomed. engring.; author: (with E.A. Kabat and others): Variable Regions of Immunoglobulin Chains, 1976, Sequences of Immunoglobulin Chains, 1979, Sequences of Proteins of Immunological Importance, 1983, Sequences of Proteins of Immunological Interest, 1987, 5th edit., 1991; editor: New Methodologies in Studies of Protein Configuration, 1985, Analytical Molecular Biology, 2001, Best Scientific Discovery or Worst Scientific Fraud of the 20th Century, 2006; contbr. articles to profl. jours. Recipient Progress award Chinese Engrs. and Scientists Assn. So. Calif., LA, 1971, Rsch. Career Devel. award NIH, 1974-79; C.T. Loo scholar, 1959-60. Mem. Am. Soc. Biochem. and Molecular Biology, Sigma Xi, Tau Beta Pi, Pi Mu Epsilon Office: Northwestern U Dept Biochem Molecular and Cell Biology Evanston IL 60208-3500 Office Phone: 847-491-7849. Business E-Mail: t-wu@northwestern.edu.

**WU, TAI TSUN,** physicist, researcher; b. Shanghai, Dec. 1, 1933; came to U.S., 1950, naturalized, 1964; s. King Ching and Wei Van (Tsang) W.; m. Sau Lan Yu, June 18, 1967. BS, U. Minn., 1953; S.M., Harvard U., 1954, PhD, 1956. Jr. fellow Soc. Fellows Harvard U., 1956-59, asst. prof., 1959-63, assoc. prof., 1963-66, Gordon McKay prof. applied physics, 1966—, prof.

physics, 1994—. Mem. Inst. Advanced Study, Princeton, 1958-59, 60-61, 62-63; vis. prof. Rockefeller U., 1966-67; sci. assoc. Deutsches Elektronen-Synchrotron, Hamburg, Ger., 1970-71, 82-83; Kramers prof. U. Utrecht, Netherlands, 1977-78; sci. assoc. CERN, Geneva, Switzerland, 1977-78, 86—. Author: (with Ronold W.P. King) Scattering and Diffraction of Waves, 1959, (with Barry M. McCoy) Two-Dimensional Ising Model, 1973, (with Ronold W.P. King, Glenn S. Smith and Margaret Owens) Antennas in Matter: Fundamentals, Theory and Applications, 1981, (with Hung Cheng) Expanding Protons: Scattering at High Energies, 1987, (with Raymond Gastmans) The Ubiquitous Photon: Helicity Method for QED and QCD, 1990, (with Ronold W.P. King and Margaret Owens) Lateral Electromagnetic Waves: Theory and Applications to Communications, Geophysical Exploration, and Remote Sensing, 1992. Putnam scholar, 1953; fellow A.P. Sloan Found., 1960-66, NSF, 1966-67, Guggenheim Found., 1970-71; recipient Alexander von Humboldt award, 1985, Dannie Heineman prize math. physics, Am. Inst. Physics, 1999. Mem. Am. Acad. Arts and Sci., Sigma Xi, Eta Kappa Nu, Tau Beta Pi. Home: 35 Robinson St Cambridge MA 02138-1403 Office: Harvard U 204B Pierce Hall Cambridge MA 02138-2901 *A person's strength is, simultaneously, his weakness.*

**WU, TSE CHENG,** chemist, researcher; b. Hong Kong, Aug. 21, 1923; came to U.S., 1947, naturalized, 1962; s. Shau Chuan and Shui (Chan) W.; m. Janet Ling, June 14, 1963; children: Alan, Anna, Bernard. BS, Yenching U., 1946; MS, U. Ill., 1948; PhD, Iowa State U., 1952. Prodn. chemist Yungli Industries, Tangku, China, 1946-47; rsch. assoc. Iowa State U., Ames, 1952-53; rsch. chemist duPont Co., Waynesboro, Va., 1953-60, GE, Waterford, NY, 1960-71; sr. rsch. chemist Abcor, Inc., Wilmington, Mass., 1971-77; rsch. assoc. Allied-Signal, Inc., Morristown, NJ, 1977-88; cons., 1989—. Contbr. articles to profl. jours; patentee in polymer chemistry and organosilicon chemistry. Mem. Troy Arts Guild, 1968-71, Morris County Art Assn., 1981, Rossmoor Art Assn., 1999. Recipient Gold medallion award for inventions GE, 1967; Allied Corp. patent award, 1983; Eastman Kodak Rsch. fellow, 1951-52. Mem. Am. Chem. Soc., Sigma Xi, Phi Kappa Phi, Phi Lambda Upsilon, Alpha Chi Sigma. Home: 601 Red Wing Ct Walnut Creek CA 94595-3927

**WU, TUNG,** curator, artist, art historian, educator; b. Fuzhou, Fukien, China, Dec. 10, 1940; came to U.S., 1965; s. Chin-Wen and Jingrong (Chen) W.; m. Ying Chin, July 16, 1974. BA, Normal U., Taipei, Taiwan, 1962; postgrad., U. Mich., 1967-70, Harvard U., 1979—. Rsch. asst. Nat. Palace Mus., Taichung, Taiwan, 1962-65; with visual art archive U. Mich., 1966-68; rsch. asst. Cleve. Mus. Art, 1968; Ford Found. curatorial intern Nelson-Atkins Mus. Art, Kansas City, Mo., 1969; rsch. fellow Mus. Fine Arts, Boston, 1971-79, asst. curator, 1980-84, assoc. curator, 1984—85, curator Asian art, 1985—91, Matsutaro Shoriki curator Asian art, 1992—2004, emeritus Matsutaro Shoriki curator Asian art, 2005—, head dept. art of Asia, Oceania and Africa, 1999—2004. Guest rsch. fellow The Palace Mus., Beijing; tchg. asst. U. Kans., Lawrence, 1969, Harvard U., 1978, vis. lectr., 75, Emmanuel Coll., Boston, 1992; assoc. prof. Simmons Coll., Boston, 1993; advisor Chinese Inst. Am., N.Y.C., 1985—, Chinese Cultural Found., San Francisco, 1985—87, Nat. Mus. History, Taipei, 1984—; cons. Project Emperor-One, Boston, 1983—86; panelist mus. program NEA, 1995; panelist Korea Found. Workshop on Korean painting, Seoul, 2000, Workshop Korean Buddhist art, Gyoengju, Republic of Korea, 2002, Workshop Korean crafts, 2003, Workshop Korean archaeology, 2004, Korean architecture, Gyoengju, 2005. Mem. Nat. Com. on U.S.-China Rels., Washington, 1985—, Nat. Devel. Seminar Taipei, 1989, 92, Nat. Edn. Reform, Taipei, 1994; The Ink Soc. of Hong Kong (advisor 2003—), dept. Asian trade art Peabody Mus., Salem. Mass., 1991—; trustee W.A. Compton Found. Oriental Arts, 1988-2004 Grantee Freer Found. U. Mich., 1968, Ford Found., Kansas City, 1969, Smithsonian Instn., Washington, 1978; recipient Outstanding Alumnus award Taiwan Normal U., 1997, Best Exhibition Catalogue, Independent Publ. Assn, 1997 Mem. Taoist Soc. Japan, Soc. Chinese Kunqu Opera, Soc. Chinese Calligraphy. Office: Mus Fine Arts Asiatic Dept 465 Huntington Ave Boston MA 02115-5597 Office Phone: 617-492-1829. Personal E-mail: wutungart@yahoo.com.

**WU, WAYNE WEN-YAU,** artist; b. Tachia, Taiwan, Republic of China, Oct. 5, 1935; s. K. C. Kau and Chin-Fong (Chen) Wu; m. Amy Hsueh, Dec. 25, 1961; children: Ingrid, Judy, David. BA in Fine Arts, Taiwan Normal U., 1959. Supr. art edn. ctr. Taichung (Taiwan) Libr., 1970-74; instr. fine arts dept. Taiwan Normal U., Taipei, 1973-74; instr. paintings Hunter Mus. of Art, Chatanooga, Tenn., 1980-92; artist, painting instr. Wayne Wu's Art Studio, Atlanta, 1994-2000, San Jose, Calif., 2000, Salinas, Calif., 2000—04, Gilroy, Calif., 2004—. One-man shows include Taiwan Mus. Art, 1995, Hunter Mus. Am. Art, 1980, 1998, Taipei Internat. Art Fair, 2001, 2004, Korea Internat. Art Fair, 2004, Taichung Seaport Art Ctr., 2006, others, over 100 group shows. Mem.: Am. Watercolor Soc. Home: 7440 Carnoustie Ct Gilroy CA 95020

**WU, XIANREN,** anesthesiologist, researcher; s. Chenglai and An Wu; m. Ling Li, Jan. 1990; 1 child, Jieshen. MD, Second Mil. Med. U., China, 1986; M in Medicine, Second Mil. Med. U., 1989; MD, U. Basel, Switzerland, 1998. Cert. Completion of USMLE ECFMG. Resident Second Mil. Med. U., Shanghai, 1989—92, attending anesthesiologist, 1992—96; rsch. fellow Safar Ctr. Resuscitation Rsch., Basel, Switzerland, 1995—2005, U. Basel, Switzerland, 1996—99, U. Pitts., 1999—, resident, 2005—. Reviewer Critical Care Medicine, 2001. Recipient Young Investigator award, U.S. Soc. Critical Care Medicine, 2005; Nancy Caroline fellow, Safar Ctr., U. Pitts., 2004. Mem.: Am. Soc. Anesthesiologist, Soc. Critical Care Medicine. Achievements include patents pending for cerebral preservation for delayed resuscitation; patents for novel equipments for tracheotomy; intrathoracic heart presser. Office: Safar Ctr Resuscitation Rsch 3434 Fifth Ave Pittsburgh PA 15260

**WU, XIN,** electrical engineer, researcher, educator; s. Jizhou Wu and Lingling Liu. B of Engring., Tsinghua U., Beijing, 1996; MS, Chinese Acad. Scin., Beijing, 1999, PhD, U. of Engring., Johns Hopkins U., Balt., 2001; PhD, U. Md., College Park, 2004. Rsch. asst Johns Hopkins, Balt., 1999—2001, U. Md., College Park, 2001—03; rsch. engr. Etenna Corp, Laurel, Md., 2003—04; spl. operation engr. Fluent Inc., Austin, Tex., 2004—05, product mgr., 2005—. Contbr. articles to profl. jours. Scholarship, Tsinghua U., 1998, Chinese Acad. Scis., 1998, Johns Hopkins U., 1999, U. Md., 2001—03. Mem.: IEEE. Independent Thinkers. Achievements include patents pending for mesh fencing technique for PCB edge radiated emission suppression; research in computational electromagnetics, radiated EMI noise reduction technologies, electromagnetic bandgap materials, high-speed eletronic packaging performance and signal integrity analysis, electromagnetic modeling and EMC. Avocations: travel, soccer, reading, photography, history.

**WU, YI,** mechanical engineer; b. Chongqing, China; PhD, U. of Va., Charlottesville, 2004. Electromech. engr. China Aerospace Corp., Beijing, 1995—99; rsch. asst. U. of Va. Charlottesville, 1999—2004; asst. prof. Pa. State U. - Erie, 2004—. Fellow Biomedical Engring. Student fellow, Am. Soc. of Artificial Internal Organs, 2003, U. of Va., 2002—04; grantee Rsch. Incentive grantee, Pa. State U. - Erie, 2005, Student Travel grantee, Am. Control Conf., 2004, 2003, IEEE/EMBS' 02 Conf., 2002. Mem.: IEEE, ASME, ASEE, Am. Soc. of Artificial Internal Organs. Achievements include research in development of innovative adaptive control algorithm for permanent artificial heart pump to meet the varying body requirement in different physiological loading situations. Office: Pennsylvania State Univ 5101 Jordan Rd Erie PA 16563 Office Phone: 814-898-6559.

**WU, YIDER,** research scientist; b. Taipei, Taiwan, Jan. 11, 1968; arrived in U.S., 1992; s. Jui-han and Hsiu-yu Wu, M. Nat. Tsing-Hua U., Taiwan, 1990; MS, U. Mass., Lowell, 1994; PhD, N.C. State, Raleigh, 1999. Rsch. asst. N.C. State, Raleigh, 1994—99; mem. of tech. staff Advanced Micro Devices, Sunnyvale, Calif., 1999—; dept. mgr. Macronix, 2004—. Patent adv. Advanced Micro Devices, Sunnyvale, Calif., 2000—; presenter at profl. confs. Contbr. scientific papers, articles to profl. jours. (introductory invited paper, 2000). Mem. Taiwanese Assn. of N.C., Raleigh, 1995—98; v.p. Taiwanese Student Assn., N.C. State, Raleigh, 1995—96. Scholar Outstanding Rschr., Semiconductor Rsch. Corp., 1998. Mem.: IEEE, Semiconductor Rsch. Corp.

Achievements include patents in field. Avocations: jogging, swimming, travel, hiking. Office: Advanced Micro Devices One AMD Pl PO BOX 3453 M/S 177 Sunnyvale CA 94088 Personal E-mail: yider_wu@yahoo.com.

**WU, YING,** telecommunications industry executive; b. Beijing, 1961; BS in Engring., Beijing Indsl. U., 1982; MS, NJ Inst. Tech., 1987. Rschr. Bell Labs and Bellcore Lab, 1987—91; founder, pres. Starcom Inc., 1991—95; pres. UTStarcom China Co., Ltd., 1995—; vice-chmn., exec. v.p. UTStarcom Inc., 1995—. Office: UTStarcom 10th Fl 2d Bldg Oriental Trading City Oriental Sq No 1 E Chang An St Beijing 100738 China Office Phone: 86-10-85205588. Office Fax: 86-10-85205599.

**WU, YUSEN (JOHN WOO),** film director; b. Guangzhou, Canton, China, May 1, 1946; Asst. dir. Shaw Bros. Studios, 1969. Dir. (films) A Better Tomorrow, 1986, The Killer, 1989, Bullet in the Head, Hard Boiled, Hard Target, 1993, Broken Arrow, 1996, Face/Off, 1997 (Acad. Sci. Fiction, Horror and Fantasy Films Saturn award Best Dir.), Black Jack, 1998, Kings Ransom, 1998, Hong Kong Face-Off, 1998, Mission Impossible 2, 1999, Windtalkers, 2002, Hire: The Hostage, 2002, Paycheck, 2003, The Red Circle, 2006; writer, prodr., dir. (TV) Once a Thief: Brother Against Brother, 1996; exec. prodr. The Replacement Killers, 1998. Recipient CineAsia Lifetime Achievement award, 1996. Office: William Morris Agency c/o Mike Simpson 151 S El Camino Dr Beverly Hills CA 90212-2775*

**WU, ZHENG Y.,** hydroinformatics engineer, hydrologist, consultant; b. Tongzi, Guizhou, China, Aug. 21, 1963; arrived in U.S., 2000; s. Xian C. Wu and Yue Q. Yang; m. Feng Hua Zhang, Aug. 22, 1963; children: Shelley X., Annie X. BSc in Civil Engring. (hon.), Guizhou Inst. Tech., 1983; MSc in Hydroinformatics, Internat. Inst. for Infrastructural, Hydraulic and Environ Engring., Delft, Netherlands, 1994; PhD in CIvil and Environ. Engring., U. Adelaide, South Australia, 1998. Sr. lectr. Guizhou Inst. Tech., Guiyang, 1986—92; hydroinformatics rsch. scholar Danish Hydraulics Inst., Horsholm, Copenhagen, 1993—94; sr. project engr. Sembawang Project Engring., Singapore, 1994—95; sr. engr. Sinclair Knight Merz Pty. Ltd., Sydney, NSW, Australia, 1996—97; hydroinformatics specialist Montgomery Watson Australia, Melbourne, Victoria, 1998—2000; supervising profl. software engr. Montgomery Watson Am., Pasadena, Calif., 2000—01; chief hydroinformatics engr. Haestad Methods, Bentley Systems Inc., Waterbury, Conn., 2001—. Contbr. scientific papers to profl. jours. Netherlands fellow, 1992, Rsch. fellow, Danish Hydraulics Inst., 1993, Overseas Rsch. fellow, Australia, 1995, Frank Perry scholar, U. Adelaide, South Australia, 1995. Mem.: ASCE, Am. Water Works Assn. (Best Paper award 2002), Am. Assn. Artificial Intelligence. Achievements include patents pending for Method and System for Automatic Water Distribution Model Calibration; first to Competent Genetic Algorithm Optimization of water Distribution System; development of Rehabilitation of water distribution system using genetic algorithm; research in Evaluation of Critical Transient Loading for Optimal Design of Water Distribution Systems; Verification of Hydrological and Hydrodynamic Models Calibrated by Genetic Algorithms; first to Optimal operation of urban sewer system by using genetic algorithm and expert system; patents pending for Method and System for Optimal Design and Rehabilitation of Water Distribution System; Method and System for Reduction of a Network Topology-based System Having Automated Optimization Features; first to Automatic Model Calibration by Simulating Evolution; research in Messy Genetic Algorithm for Optimization of water Distribution System Including Water Hammer; Self-adaptive boundary search of genetic algorithms and application to water distribution systems; development of An Efficient Genetic Algorithms Approach to an Intelligent Decision Support System for Water Distribution Networks; Calibrating Water Distribution Model Via Genetic Algorithms; research in Optimal Capacity of Water Distribution Systems; development of Mining Water consumption and GIS Data for Loading Water Distribution Model, rsch. in Integrating Water Quality Analysis and GIS Spatial Sys. for Water Security Modeling. Avocations: swimming, travel, reading. Office Phone: 203-805-0562. Business E-Mail: zheng.wu@bentley.com.

**WUBBENA, JAN HELMUT,** music professor; b. Dover, Del., July 11, 1947; s. Wyatt Jan and Erika Luise Wubbena; m. Teresa Lee Roper, May 17, 1980; children: Robert, Mary. BA, Lebanon Valley Coll., Annville, Pa., 1969; MusM, U. Colo., Boulder, 1970, D of Mus. Arts, 1975. Asst. prof. music Ferrum Coll., Va., 1975—77; prof. music John Brown U., Siloam Springs, Ark., 1977—. Organist, choirmaster Grace Episcopal Ch., Siloam Springs, 1977—. Composer: (choral work) With Every Power for Good, 1980, There is a Land of Pure Delight, 1999, Eagle Us Waking Lord, 2002. Fellow Am. Guild Organists (assoc.; chpt. dean 1982—84, coord. for edn. in Region VII 1984—88, chair nat. com. on ednl. resources 1988—90); mem.: Assn. Anglican Musicians. Episcopalian. Home: 410 E Jefferson St Siloam Springs AR 72761 Office: John Brown Univ 2000 W University Ave Siloam Springs AR 72761 Office Phone: 479-524-7159. Personal E-mail: wubbenark@cox.net. Business E-Mail: jwubbena@jbu.edu.

**WUCKER, MICHELE,** educational association administrator, writer; d. Edward V. and Danielle J. Wucker. BA in French and Policy Studies, Rice U., 1989; M of Internat. Affairs, Columbia U., 1993. Reporter Milw. Sentinel, 1990—91, Dow Jones Emerging Markets Report, Jersey City, 1993—94; analyst Thomson Fin., N.Y.C., 1994—96; mng. editor Latin Am. Info. Svcs., N.Y.C., 1996—2000; Latin Am. bur. chief Internat. Financing Rev., N.Y.C., 2000—01; sr. fellow World Policy Inst., N.Y.C., 2001—. Author: (book (nonfiction) Why the Cocks Fight: Dominicans, Haitians, and the Struggle for Hispaniola, Lockout: Why America Keeps Getting Immigration Wrong When Our Prosperity Depends on Getting It Right. Adviser Batey Relief Alliance, N.Y.C.; vol. Adopt A Boxer Rescue, N.Y.C.; adviser Dominican Republic Edn. and Mentoring Project, Cabarete, Puerto Plata. Recipient Paul F Bobb Award for Journalism, Rice U., 1989; scholarship, Scripps Howard, 1991, 1992, Summer Rsch. grant, Tinker Found., 1992. Mem.: Immigration and Ethnic History Soc., Authors Guild. Office: World Policy Inst 66 Fifth Ave 9th Fl New York NY 10011 Office Phone: 212-229-5808 4270. Home Fax: 775-435-4517. Business E-Mail: wuckerm@newschool.edu.

**WUDKA, JOSE,** physics professor; b. Mexico City, Feb. 26, 1958; PhD, MIT, Boston, 1986. Postdoctoral fellow U. Mich., Ann Arbor, 1986—88, U. Calif., Davis, 1988—90, prof. Riverside, 1990—. Fellow SSC fellow, SSC Lab., 1991—92. Mem.: Am. Physics Soc. Office: Univ California Riverside Physics Department Riverside CA 92521-0413 Office Phone: 951-827-4296. Office Fax: 951-827-4529. Business E-Mail: jose.wudka@ucr.edu.

**WUDL, FRED,** chemistry professor; b. Cochabamba, Bolivia, Jan. 8, 1941; came to U.S., 1958; s. Robert and Bertha (Schorr) W.; m. Linda Raimondo, Sept. 2, 1967. BS, UCLA, 1964, PhD, 1967; PhD (hon.), U. Complutense, Madrid, 2004. Postdoctoral rsch. fellow Harvard U., 1967-68; asst. prof. dept. chemistry SUNY, Buffalo, 1968-72; mem. tech. staff AT&T Bell Labs., Murray Hill, NJ, 1972-82; prof. chemistry and materials U. Calif., Santa Barbara, 1982-97; Dean M. Willard prof. Chemistry and Materials (formerly Courtaulds prof.) UCLA, 1997—. Peter A. Leermakers lectr., 1988; vis. scientist C.N.R.S. Postes Rouge Orsay, France, 1992; 3M lectr. U. B.C., 1992; Peter A. Leermakers lectr., 92; Karcher lectr. U. Okla., 1992; Clapp lectr. Brown U., 1994; Bayer lectr. Cornell U., 1996. Hon. fellow Coun. of Chem. Rsch. Soc., 2005; recipient Arthur C. Cope scholar award Am. Chem. Soc., 1993, Arthur D. Little award Boston U., 1993, Stouffer award U. So. Calif., 1993, Award for Chemistry of Materials, 1996, Giulio Natta medal Italian Chem. Soc., 1994, Wheland medal U. Chgo., 1994, Herbert Newby McCoy award UCLA, 2001. Fellow AAAS, Am. Acad. Arts and Scis. Office: UCLA Dept Chemistry and Biochem 607 Charles E Young Dr E Los Angeles CA 90095-1569 E-mail: wudl@chem.ucla.edu.

**WUDUNN, SHERYL,** journalist, correspondent; b. NYC, Nov. 16, 1959; d. David and Alice (Mark) WuDunn; m. Nicholas D. Kristof, Oct. 8, 1988. BA, Cornell U., Ithaca, N.Y., 1981; MBA, Harvard U., 1986; MPA, Princeton U., 1988. Lending officer Bankers Trust Co., NYC, 1981—84; intern reporter

Wall St. Jour., LA, 1986; bus. reporter South China Morning Post, Hong Kong, 1987; corr. NY Times, Beijing, 1989—93, Tokyo, 1995—99, exec. dir. Nexgen group NYC, 1999—; anchor, prin. writer PAGE ONE Discovery Times Channel, 2003. Co-author: China Wakes, 1994, Thunder From the East, 2000. Recipient Pulitzer Prize for fgn. reporting, 1990, George Polk award, L.I. U., N.Y., 1990, Hal Boyle award, Overseas Press Club, 1990. Avocations: aerobics, singing. Office: NY Times 229 W 43rd St New York NY 10036*

**WUEBBLING, DONALD J.,** lawyer, insurance company executive; Sr. v.p. & gen. counsel Western & Southern Fin. Group, Cincinnati.

**WUEBKER, COLLEEN MARIE,** retired librarian; b. LaCrosse, Wis., June 22, 1943; d. Harris M. and Mary Frances (Collins) Gruber; m. William Joseph Wuebker, Aug. 14, 1965; children: Jon Paul, Timothy William, Maree Jean. BA, Mt. Mercy Coll., 1965; MS, Mankato State U., 1975. Cert. permanent profl. media specialist, tchr. Iowa. Secondary tchr. Luverne Cmty. Sch., Minn., 1965-66; tchr. St. Mary's Sch., Larchwood, Iowa, 1966; secondary tchr. SEMCO Community Sch., Gilman, Iowa, 1966-67; substitute tchr. West Bend-Mallard (Iowa) Cmty. Schs., 1968-74, sch. media specialist, 1974—2002, 1975—2002; ret., 2002. Mem. selection com. Lakeland Area Edn. Agy., Cylinder, Iowa, 1977—; mem. Gov.'s Sch. Efficiency Task Force, West Bend, 1987; mem. sch. evaluation team Dept. Pub. Instrn., Des Moines, 1986. Spkr. Marriage Encounter Movement, Sioux City Diocese, 1985—; Pre-Cana Workshops, Emmetsburg, 1985—; mem., liturgy and music coord., song leader Sts. Peter and Paul Parish Coun., West Bend, 1987—; chmn. Parish Liturgy Com., West Bend, 1987—. Mem.: Iowa Ednl. Media Assn., Cath. Daus. Am. (past v.p. West Bend). Roman Catholic. Avocations: genealogy, music. Home: Box 426 11 1st Ave NE West Bend IA 50597-0426

**WUENSCH, BERNHARDT JOHN,** ceramic engineering educator; b. Paterson, NJ, Sept. 17, 1933; s. Bernhardt and Ruth Hannah (Slack) W.; m. Mary Jane Harriman, June 4, 1960; children: Stefan Raymond, Katrina Ruth. SB in Physics, MIT, 1955, SM in Physics, 1957, PhD in Crystallography, 1963; DEng (hon.), Hanyang U., Seoul, 2003. Rsch. fellow U. Bern, Switzerland, 1963-64; asst. prof. ceramics MIT, Cambridge, 1964-69, assoc. prof. ceramics, 1969-74, prof., 1974—, TDK chair materials sci. and engring., 1985-90, dir. Ctr. Materials Sci. and Engring., 1988-93, acting dept. head dept. materials sci. and engring., 1980. Vis. prof. Crystallographic Inst., U. Saarland, Fed. Republic Germany, 1973; physicist Max Planck Institut für Festkorperforschung, Stuttgart, Fed. Republic Germany, 1981; mem. US nat. com. for crystallography NRC, NAS, 1980-82, 89-94; mem. NE regional com. for selection of Marshall Scholars, 1970-73, chmn., 1974-80. Co-editor: Modulated Structures, 1979, Neutron Scattering in Materials Science, 1995; adv. editor: Physics and Chemistry of Minerals, 1976—85; assoc. editor Can. Mineralogist, 1978—80; editor: Zeitschrift fuer Kristallographie, 1981—88, Jour. Ceramic Processing Rsch., 2000—. Ford Found. postdoctoral fellow, 1964-66. Fellow Am. Ceramic Soc. (Outstanding Educator award 1987), Mineral. Soc. Am.; mem. AAAS, Am. Crystallographic Assn., Mineral. Assn. Can., Materials Rsch. Soc. Episcopalian. Home: 190 Southfield Rd Concord MA 01742-3432 Office: MIT 77 Massachusetts Ave Rm 13-4037 Cambridge MA 02139-4307 Office Phone: 617-253-6889. Business E-Mail: wuensch@mit.edu.

**WUENSCHE, VERNON EDGAR,** construction company executive; b. Elgin, Tex., Nov. 25, 1945; s. Harry Edwin Jacob and Emma Martha (Dube) W. BBA, U. Tex., 1967, MBA, 1968. CPA, Tex. Audit asst. Arthur Andersen & Co., Houston, 1968-70; tax cons. Peat Marwick Mitchell & Co., Houston, 1970; cost acct. Bemis Bros. Bag Co., Houston, 1970-71; asst. controller Prodn. Systems Internat., Inc., Houston, 1971-72; controller Am. Housing Guild, Inc., Houston, 1972-73, Wood Bros. Homes, Inc., Houston, Dallas, 1973-74, Oklahoma City, 1975; pres., founder, custom home builder Woodmark Homes, Inc., Houston, Dallas, Austin, Tex., 1975—; founder, kitchen and bath renovator Woodmark Kitchen & Bath, Inc., 1994—. Election judge Harris County, Houston, 1978, Rep. state del., Tex., 1978, 80, 94, 96, 98, 2000, 02, 04, 06; elder Meml. Luth. Ch., Houston, 1982-2002, elder emeritus, 2003; founder Texans for Efficiency in Govt., 1991, Bus. Consensus, 1999, Legal Reform Now, 2004; bd. dirs. Houston Entrepreneurs Forum with USAR, 1968—74. Recipient Builder of Tex. Design award Tex. Arch. Mag., 1994. Mem. Alley Theater Guild, Tex. Wendish Heritage Soc., U. Tex. Ex-Students Assn., Rice Design Alliance, Mus. of Fine Arts, Arts Symposium of Houston, Phi Kappa Phi, Beta Gamma Sigma. Avocation: running. Home: 14211 Swiss Hill Dr Houston TX 77077-1029 Office Phone: 713-468-3300. Business E-Mail: vern@woodmarkkitchens.com, vern@legalreform-now.org.

**WUERL, DONALD WILLIAM,** archbishop; b. Pittsburgh, Nov. 12, 1940; s. Francis J. and Mary A. (Schiffhauer) W. BA, Cath. U. Am., 1962; MA, Cath. U. Am., Rome, 1963; ThM, Pontifical Gregorian U., Rome, 1967; ThD, Pontifical U. St. Thomas, Rome, 1974; DD (hon.), Duquesne U., 1989, Washington and Jefferson Coll., 1990; HLD (hon.), La Roche Coll., 1990; LHD (hon.), St. Vincent Coll., 1992. Ordained priest Roman Cath. Ch., 1966. Asst. pastor, parochial vicar St. Rosalia Ch., Pitts., 1967-69; sec. to Cardinal John Wright Congregation for Clergy, Rome, 1969-79; vice-rector St. Paul Sem., Pitts., 1980-81, rector, 1981-85; apptd. aux. bishop Archdiocese of Seattle, Wash., 1985, aux. bishop Wash., 1985—87; apptd. titular bishop of Rossmarkaeum, 1985; titular bishop of Rossmarkaeum, 1986—87; apptd. bishop Diocese of Pitts., Pa., 1988, bishop Pa., 1988—2006; archbishop Archdiocese of Washington, Washington, 2006—. Sec. to Bishop of Pitts., 1967-69; lectr. Duquesne U., Pitts., 1968-69, 80-85, Pontifical U. St. Thomas, 1975-79; lectr. adult theology program Diocese of Pitts., 1967-69. Continuing Edn. for Priests, 1982-84, assoc. gen. sec., 1985; ofcl. Congregation for Clergy, Rome, 1969-79; mem. alumni bd. govs. Cath. U. Am., 1977-84, vice-pres. for religious, 1981-82; exec. sec. to Papal rep. for Study of Sems. in U.S., 1982-85. Author: The Forty Martyrs, 1971, Fathers of the Church 1975 The Catholic Priesthood Today, 1976, A Visit to the Vatican, 1981, The Church and Her Sacraments: Making Christ Visible, 1990, co-author: The Teaching of Christ: A Catholic Catechism for Adults, 1976, rev., 1984, 91, abridged, 1979, study guide, 1977, A Catholic Catechism, 1986; contbg. author: New Catholic Ency.; contbr. articles to religion publs.; author religious cassette programs. Recipient Disting. Pennsylvanian award Gannon U., 1989, Brotherhood award NCCJ, 1991, Treee of Life award Jewish Nat. Fund, 1992, Disting. Alumni award Cath. U. Am., 1992; named Vectors/Pitts. Man of Yr. in religion, 1988. Mem. Am. Cath. Hist. Assn., Cath. Theol. Soc. Am., Fellowship Cath. Scholars, Acad. Romana Universale, Phi Kappa Theta (Man of Achievement award 1988). Office: Archdiocesan Pastoral Ctr 5001 Eastern Ave Hyattsville MD 20782-3447 Mailing: PO Box 29260 Washington DC 20017-0260*

**WUETIG, JOYCE LINDA,** realtor; b. Little Rock, Feb. 11, 1938; d. John Clifford and Viva Emily (Summerhill) Dilbeck; m. James Russell McKinney, Aug. 30, 1958 (div. Sept. 1981); children: Melissa Ellen, James Blake; m. Frederick Lewis Wuetig, June 1, 1985. BA, Hendrix Coll., 1959; postgrad., Incarnate Word Coll., 1970-072. Cert. residential specialist; lic. real estate broker, Tex., Ark. Tchr. Little Rock Sch. Dist., 1959-62; fashion cons. Doncaster, Inc., San Antonio, 1958-; tchr. Edgewood Ind. Sch. Dist., San Antonio, 1982-83; sales assoc. Dijon Plaza Realtors, San Antonio, 1978-83; relocation specialist HEB Grocery Co., San Antonio, 1981-82; asst. v.p. Independence Fed. Bank, Little Rock, 1984-85; sales assoc. Agar Realtors, Little Rock, 1986-89; broker assoc., residential specialist McKay & Co. Residential Realtors, Little Rock, 1989—98; accredited buyer rep. Ebby Halliday Realtors, Colleyville and Southlake, Tex., 1998—2002, DFW Keller Williams Realty, Southlake, 2002—. mem. own. Southwest Found. Forum, San Antonio, 1975-81; chmn. San Antonio Kitchen Tour, 1977-80; host mother, area activities chmn. Am. Field Svc., San Antonio, 1975-76, 77-78; life mem. Tex. PTA. Mem.: DAR, AAUW, Southlake C. of C. (leadership ambassador com.), Ebby Halliday Realtors Platinum Plateau, Little Rock Realtors Assn., N.E. Tarrant County Bd. Realtors, Tex. Realtors Assn., Ark. Realtors Assn., Nat. Assn. Realtors, Little Rock Realtors Million Dollar Club (licentiate). Methodist. Home: 1310 Regency Ct Southlake TX 76092-9516 Office Phone: 817-410-9990. Personal E-mail: jfwuetig@earthlink.net.

**WUHL, CHARLES MICHAEL,** psychiatrist; b. N.Y.C., Sept. 24, 1943; s. Isadore and Sali (Ackner) W.; m. Gail; children— Elise, Amy. M.D., U. Bologna, 1973. Diplomate Am. Bd. Psychiatry and Neurology. Intern, N.Y. Med. Coll., 1975-76, resident in psychiatry, 1976-77; fellow in child psychiatry Columbia Presbyn. Med. Center, 1977-78; practice medicine specializing in psychiatry and child psychiatry, Englewood, N.J., 1978—; attending staff, mem. faculty N.Y. Med. Coll.; psychiatrist NYU, also asst. clin. prof. psychiatry NYU Sch. Medicine. Contbr. to Psychosocial Aspects of Pediatric Care, 1978, World Book Ency., 1980—. Mem. Am. Psychiat Assn., AMA, Am. Acad. Child Psychiatry. Office: 163 Engle St Englewood NJ 07631-2530 Office Phone: 201-569-2228. E-mail: cw3@nyu.edu.

**WUHL, ROBERT,** actor; b. Union, N.J., Oct. 9, 1951; Student, U. Houston. Actor: (films) The Hollywood Knights, 1980, Flashdance, 1983, Good Morning, Vietnam, 1987, Ray's Male Heterosexual Dance Hall, 1987, Bull Durham, 1988, Batman, 1989, Blaze, 1989, Wedding Band, 1990, Missing Pieces, 1991, Mistress, 1992, The Bodyguard, 1992, Sandman, 1993, Blue Chips, 1994, Cobb, 1994, Dr. Jekyll and Ms. Hyde, 1995, Good Burger, 1997; actor, writer: Open Season, 1996; actor: (TV films) Percy and Thunder, 1993, A Kiss Goodnight, 1994; (TV miniseries) The Last Don, 1997, The Last Don II, 1998; writer, actor, exec. prodr., dir. (TV series) Arliss, 1996—2002.

**WUJCIK, THEO FRANK,** artist; b. Detroit, Jan. 29, 1936; s. Stanley Wujcik and Anna Wujcok; children: Anna, Kathryn Tenney, Frankie. Diploma, Ctr. for Creative Studies, Detroit, 1962; Master Printer, Tamarind Inst. Lithography, L.A., 1968. Instr. printmaking Ctr. for Creative Studies, Detroit, 1962—70; shop dir. graphic studio U. South Fla., Tampa, 1970—72, assoc. prof., 1972—2003, prof. emeritus, 2003—. Exhibitions include Gulf Coast Mus. Art, Largo, Fla., 2000, Lowe Art Mus., U. Miami, Coral Gables, Fla., 2001, Polk Mus. Art, Lakeland, Fla., 2001—02, Tampa Mus. Art, 2006—07, Represented in permanent collections Mus. Modern Art, N.Y., Whitney Mus. Am. Art, Bklyn. Mus., L.A. County Mus. Art, Yale U. Art Gallery, New Haven, Conn., Mus. Fine Arts, Boston, Chgo. Inst. Art, Detroit Inst. Arts, Pasadena Art Mus., Calif., Libr. Congress, Washington. With U.S. Army, 1954—56. Printmakingfellowship, Nat. Endowment for Arts, 1977—78, Ind. Artist fellowship, Fla. Dept. State, Cultural Affairs, 2001—02, fellowship, Edwin Austin Abbey Meml. Fund for Mural Painting in Am., 2004. Home: 1507 E Ninth Ave Tampa FL 33605-3711 Office Phone: 813-242-8241.

**WUKOVITS, JOHN FRANCIS,** secondary school educator, writer; b. Akron, Ohio, Nov. 3, 1944; s. Thomas William and Grace Annette Wukovits; children: Amy Dickerman, Julie, Karen. BA in History, U. Notre Dame, 1967; M in Am. History, Mich. State U., 1968. Cert. secondary tchr. Mich. Tchr. St. Timothy Sch., Trenton, Mich., 1968—71, Trenton Pub. Schools, 1971—73, St. Joseph Sch., Trenton, 1981—91, Trenton Pub. Schools, 1991—. Author: (book) Devotion to Duty: A Biography of Admiral Clifton A. F. Sprague, 1995, Barry Sanders, 1995; contbg. author: book Men of War: Great Naval Leaders of World War II, 1992, Reference Guide to United States Military History, 1995, Quarterdeck & Bridge: Two Centuries of American Naval Leaders, 1997,: book The Great Admirals: Command at Sea, 1587-1945, 1997; author: Jesse James, 1997, The Gunslingers, 1997, Vince Lombardi, 1997, Wyatt Earp, 1997, Annie Oakley, 1997, The Black Cowboys, 1997, Butch Cassidy, 1997; Scientists & Inventors, 1998; author: John Stockton, 1998, Jack Nicklaus, 1998, Tim Allen, 1998, The Composite Guide to Auto Racing, 1998, The Composite Guide to Soccer, 1998, Anne Frank, 1998, Martin Luther King, Jr., 1998, Stephen King, 1999, Jim Carrey, 1999, Life of an American Soldier in Europe, 2000, Life As A POW, 2000, Colin Powell, 2000, The 1910s, 2000, The 1920s, 2000, George Bush, 2000 (NY Pub. Library's "Books for the Teen Age List", 2001), Bill Gates, 2000, The Encyclopedia of World Sports, 2001, The Persian Gulf War: Leaders and Generals, 2001, History of Sports: Hockey, 2001, The Spanish-American War, 2001, Strategic Battles of World War I, 2001, World War I Flying Aces, 2002, The Encyclopedia of The Winter Olympics, 2002, Michael J. Fox, 2002, Oskar Schindler, 2003, Pacific Alamo: The Battle for Wake Island, 2003; contbg. author: book Book of Days, 1988, Best Little Stories from World War II, 1989, Best of the Wild West, 1996. Mem.: Orgn. Am. Historians, The Golf Writers Assn. Am., Soc. for Mil. History. Roman Catholic. Avocations: golf, reading. Home: 1235 Harbour # 22 Trenton MI 48183 Office: Trenton Pub Schs 4000 Marian Dr Trenton MI 48183 Personal E-mail: johnwukovits@comcast.net.

**WULBERT, DANIEL ELIOT,** mathematician, educator; b. Chgo., Dec. 17, 1941; s. Morris and Anna (Greenberg) W.; children: Kera, Noah. BA, Knox Coll., 1963; MA, U. Tex., Austin, 1964, PhD, 1966. Rsch. assoc. U. Lund, Sweden, 1966-67; asst. prof. U. Wash., Seattle, 1967-73; prof. U. Calif.-San Diego, La Jolla, 1973—; provost Revelle Coll., 2003—. Vis. prof. Northwestern U., Evanston, Ill., 1977. Contbr. articles in field. Office: Provost Bldg Revelle Coll 0321 U Calif San Diego La Jolla CA 92093-0321 Business E-Mail: dwulbert@ucsd.edu.

**WULF, WILLIAM ALLAN,** foundation administrator, information scientist, educator; b. Chgo., Dec. 8, 1939; s. Otto H. and Helen W. (Westermeier) Wulf; m. Anita K. Jones, July 1, 1977; children: Karin, Ellen. BS, U. Ill., 1961, MSEE, 1963; PhD in Computer Sci., U. Va., 1968. Prof. computer sci. Carnegie-Mellon Univ., Pitts., 1968—81; chmn., CEO Tartan Labs, Pitts., 1981—87; AT&T prof. computer sci. U. Va., Charlottesville, Va., 1988—. Bd. dir. Charles Strak Draper Labs., Cambridge, Mass., Nat. Action Coun. Minorities Engring., Inst. Women and Tech., Biblioteque Alexandrina; asst. dir. NSF, Washington, 1988—90; vice-chair NRC, Washington; cons. various computer mfr. Author: Fundamental Structures of Computer Science, 1981. Bd. dirs. Pitts. High Tech. Coun., 1982—88. Fellow: AAAS, IEEE, Assn. Women in Sci., Assn. Computing Machinery; mem.: NAE (pres. 1996—), Nat. Rsch. Coun., Chinese Acad. Engring., Japanese Acad. Engring., Russian Acad. Sci., Spanish Acad. Engring., Am. Acad. Arts and Sci. Avocations: woodworking, photography. Office: Nat Acad Engring 2101 Constitution Ave NW Washington DC 20418-0007 Office Phone: 202-334-3201.

**WULFF, LOIS YVONNE,** librarian; b. Seattle, Nov. 23, 1940; d. Arthur Ray and Audrey June (Carpenter) Roark; B.S., Washington State U., 1962; M.L.S., U. Wash., 1963; postgrad. Syracuse U., 1969-70; m. Barry Kahn, Dec. 18, 1971 (dec. 1982). Intern, then head documents div. Ohio State U., 1963-67; spl. project investigator U. Wash., 1968-69; staff asst., head search unit Johns Hopkins Med. Instns., 1971-72; project coordinator, asst. to dir., coordinator health sci. libraries U. Minn., 1973-77; head librarian Alfred Taubman Med. Library, U. Mich., 1977-87, coordinator Med. and Sci./Tech. Libraries, 1981-87, asst. dir. for collection mgmt. Gaylord fellow, 1969-70. Mem. City Coun., Yachats, Oreg., 2002—. Mem. AAAS, Med. Library Assn., ALA, Mich. Library Assn., Assn. Coll. and Rsch. Libraries.

**WULKER, LAURENCE JOSEPH,** portfolio manager, educator, financial planner; b. Cin., Apr. 6, 1945; s. Joseph Laurence and Dorothea Clare (Link) W. BS, Xavier U., Cin., 1967, MA, 1971; cert. fin. planner, Coll. Fin. Planner, 1985. Instr. Lloyd High Sch., Erlanger, Ky., 1967-68, Elder High Sch., Cin., 1968-73, Peoples High Sch., Cin., 1973-74, Regina High Sch., Cin. Tech. U., Cin., 1974-75; stockbroker Harrison-Bache, Cin., 1976-78; portfolio mgr., fin. planner, v.p. investments UBS, Cin., 1978—; formed Wulker/Cummins Group Paine Webber, Cin., 1997; instr. U. Cin., 1981-98, Nat. Inst. Fin., South Plainfield, N.J., 1986-88; systems operator, Fin. Planning Forum Tristate Online, Cin., 1991—93. Speaker at numerous seminars 1984—; systems operator Investor Forum, Compuserve, 1985-86. Author column Japanese-Am. League Newsletter, 1985-96; contbr. articles to Cin. Enquirer, Cin. Post, Cin. Bus. Courier. Bd. dirs., v.p., pres. No. Ky. Symphony, 1993-99; treas. Friends of Findlay Market, Findlay Market Assn., 1999—; bd. dirs. Riverwinds Condo Assn., Behringer- Crawford Mus., 2003—. Named one of the best stockbrokers in the country Money Mag., 1987; Fulbright scholar HEW, 1972. Mem. Internat. Assn. Fin. Planners (bd. dirs. Cin. chpt. 1980-87), Fulbright Soc., Order Ky. Cols. Roman Catholic. Avocations: computers, tennis, golf, volleyball, reading. Home: Riverwinds Condos 558 Davenport Ave No 11 Cincinnati OH 45204-1362 Fax: 513-369-4020. Office Phone: 513-369-4181. Business E-Mail: laurence.wulker@ubs.com.

**WUNDER, CHARLES C(OOPER),** physiologist, biophysicist, educator; b. Pitts., Oct. 2, 1928; s. Edgar Douglas and Annabel (Cooper) W.; m. Marcia Lynn Barnes, Apr. 4, 1962; children: E(dgar) Douglas, David Barnes, Donald Charles. AB in Biology, Washington and Jefferson Coll., 1949; MS in Biophysics, U. Pitts., 1952, PhD in Biophysics, 1954. Assoc. U. Iowa, Iowa City, 1954-56, asst. prof. physiology and biophysics, 1956-63, assoc. prof. physiology and biophysics, 1963-71, prof. physiology and biophysics, 1971-98, prof. emeritus, 1998—. Cons. for biol. simulation of weightlessness U.S. Air Force, 1964; vis. scientist Mayo Found., Rochester, Minn., 1966-67. Author: Life into Space: An Introduction to Space Biology, 1966; also chpts., numerous articles, abstracts Recipient Research Career Devel. award NIH, 1961-66; AEC predoctoral fellow U. Pitts., 1951-53; NIH spl. fellow, 1966-67; grantee NIH, NASA Mem. Am. Physiol. Soc., The Biophys. Soc. (charter); Aerospace Med. Assn., Iowa Acad. Sci. (chmn. physiology sect. 1971-72, 83-84, 96-97), Am. Soc. Biomechanics (founding), Aerospace Physiologist Soc., Iowa Physiol. Soc. (pres. 1996-97), Am. Soc. for Gravitational and Space Biology (Founders award 2000). Presbyterian. Achievements include the establishment of chronic centrifugation as an approach for investigating gravity's role as a biological determinant. Home: 702 W Park Rd Iowa City IA 52246-2425 Office: U Iowa BSB Iowa City IA 52242 Business E-Mail: charles-wunder@uiowa.edu.

**WUNDERLICH, ALFRED LEON,** artist, art educator; b. Salem, Oreg., June 26, 1939; s. Joseph Anthony and Anna Margaret (Meyer) W.; children: Annelise, Jonathan Resor. Cert., Cooper Union, 1961; BFA, Yale U., 1962, MFA, 1968. Dir. visual studies program Hopkins Ctr., Dartmouth Coll., Hanover, NH, 1965-66; asst. prof. art Hopkins Ctr., Darmouth Coll., Hanover, NH, 1966-74; assoc. prof. R.I. Sch. of Design, Providence, 1983-94; prof. R.I. Sch. of Design, Providence, 1994—2005, prof. emeritus, 2005—. Adj. lectr. Hunter Coll. CUNY, 1973, adj. prof., vis. artist Pahlavi U., Shiraz Iran, 1978, vis. artist U. Edinburgh, Scotland, Edinburgh Internat. Arts Festival, 1973, Kansas City Art Inst., Art Inst. Chgo., Ohio State U., 1986, Carnegie Mellon U., 1987, Moscow State U., 1991, Ariz. State U., 1995; fine arts advisor Inst. for Internat. Edn.; mem. US Art in Space team, met with Soviet Artists Union team, Moscow, 1990; owner, artistic dir. GAS-523 project to fly aboard NASA Space Shuttle; executor first bacteria based living paintings, Rich Biology Labs. M.I.T., 2001. Solo shows Dartmouth Coll., 1969, Kyoto, Japan, 1969, Pahlavi U., 1978, Kwanghow Mus., Canton, China, 1979, Chang-tu Mus., Szechwan, China, 1978, MIT, 1981, Swarthmore Coll., 1985, Knoerdler Gallery, NYC, 1995, 97, Alfonz Ver Gallery, San Francisco, 1997, 98; group exhbns. Harvard U. 1995, MIT 1996, also numerous other group exhbns.; represented in permanent collections Mus. Modern Art, NYC, Art Inst. Chgo., Yale U. Art Gallery, Nat. Gallery Scotland, 1st Nat. Bank Boston, Dartmouth Coll., Smithsonian-Cooper Hewitt Mus., Stanford U. Art Mus., also others. Recipient Bocour Color award, 1960; Yale ALumni fellow, 1962-63; Yaddo fellow, 1973; Dartmouth Faculty fellow, 1968; Fulbright grantee to India, 1963-64; Dartmouth Coll. research grantee, 1970-72; SUNY research grantee, 1983 Home: 1850 Big Ridge Rd Healdsburg CA 95448

**WUNDERLICH, BERNHARD,** physical chemistry professor; b. Brandenburg, Germany, May 28, 1931; came to U.S., 1954, naturalized, 1960; s. Richard O. and Johanne (Wohlgefahrt) W.; m. Adelheid Felix, Dec. 28, 1953; children: Caryn Cornelia, Brent Bernhard. Student, Humboldt U., Berlin, Germany, 1949-53, Goethe U., Frankfurt, Germany, 1953-54, Hastings Coll., 1954-55; PhD, Northwestern U., 1957. Instr. chemistry Northwestern U., Evanston, Ill., 1957-58, Cornell U., Ithaca, NY, 1958-60, asst. prof., 1960-63; assoc. prof. phys. chemistry Rensselaer Poly. Inst., Troy, NY, 1963-65, prof. phys. chemistry 1965-88, prof. emeritus, 1988—; prof. chemistry U. Tenn., Knoxville, 1988-2001; prof. emeritus, 2001—; Disting. scientist div. chemistry Oak Ridge Nat. Lab., 1988-2001. Cons. E.I. duPont de Nemours Co., 1963-88; dir. Lab. for Advanced Thermal Analysis; rsch. in solid state of linear high polymers and thermal analysis, 1980-2001. Author: Macromolecular Physics, Vol. 1, 1973, Vol. 2, 1976, Vol. 3, 1980, Thermal Analysis, 1990, Thermal Analysis of Polymeric Materials, 2005; author computer and audio courses on Crystals of Linear Macromolecules, and Thermal Analysis of Materials; contbr. over 500 articles to profl. jours.; mem. editl. bd. Chemistry, 1965-68, Makromolekulare Chemie, 1966-96; mem. editl. bd. Jour. Thermal Analysis and Calorimetry, 1963-2001, mem. hon. bd., 2004—; mem. adv. bd. Jour. Polymer Sci., 1963-2001, Macromolecules, 1984-88, Polymers for Advanced Tech., 1988-2001, Macromolecular Sci. and Physics, 1995-2001, Thermochim. Acta, 1996-2001. Recipient Humboldt award, 1987-88, award for applied chem. thermodynamics Swiss Soc. for Thermal Analysis and Calorimetry, 1993, TA Instruments award Internat. Conf. Thermal Analysis and Calorimetry, 1996. Fellow Am. Phys. Soc., N.Am., Thermal Analysis Soc. (Mettler award in thermal analysis 1971, Disting. Svc. award 2002); mem. Am. Chem. Soc. Home: 200 Baltusrol Rd Knoxville TN 37934-3707 Personal E-Mail: wunderlich@chartertn.net.

**WUNDERLICH, DOROTHY ANASTASIA,** superintendent; b. Evergreen Pk., Ill., Apr. 30, 1952; d. Raymond William and Dorothy Patricia Gavin; m. Russell Jay Wunderlich, June 15, 1974; children: Colleen Wunderlich Ciarlette, Meghan Gavin. BA, U. St. Francis, 1973; MEd, Ill. State U., 1991; MA, Lewis U., 1998. Tchr. Joliet Township Dist., Ill., 1985—96; tchr., curriculum dir. Will County Sch. Dist., Lockport, Ill., 1997—2002; curriculum dir. Cicero Pub. Sch. Dist., 2002—05; asst. superintendent Berwyn North Sch. Dist., Berwyn, Ill., 2005—. Tchr. Power Luncheon, 2001. Mem. pres. coun. Purdue U.; mem. ednl. found. Berwyn Dist. Mem.: Purdue Music Org. Home: 1040 N Lakeshore Dr Apt 20B Chicago IL 60611 Office: Berwyn North Sch Dist 98 6633 W 16th St Berwyn IL 60402

**WUNDERLICH, GOOLOO S.,** demographer, statistician, policy analyst; b. Bombay, Aug. 21, 1930; d. Hormusji and Shirin Sahiar; m. Gene Lee Wunderlich, Mar. 19, 1957; children: Karl Arthur, Roshna Evelyn. BA, U. of Bombay, 1949, MA, 1951, PhD, 1955; postgrad., U. of Minn., 1956, U. of Chgo., 1957. Statistician USPHS, Washington, 1958—66, demographer, 1967—74; statistician U.S. Bur. of Census, Suitland, Md., 1966; demographer Pres. Nat. Adv. Commn. on Rural Poverty, Washington, 1966—67, Pres. Com. on Population and Family Planning, Washington, 1968; dir. divsn. of data policy U.S. Health and Human Svcs., Washington, 1974—88; sr. program officer NRC and Inst. Medicine, Washington, 1990—. Editor (and author): Towards A National Health Care Survey: A Data System for the 21st Century, 1992, Nursing Staff in Hospitals and Nursing Homes: Is it Adequate?, 1996, The Social Security Administration's Disability Decision Process: A Framework for Research, 1998, Measuring Functional Capacity and Work Requirements: Summary of a Workshop, 1999, Survey Measurement of Work Disability, 2000, Improving the Quality of Long Term Care, 2001, Dynamics of Disability: Measuring and Monitoring Disability for Social Security Programs, 2002, Food Insecurity and Hunger In the United States: An Assessment of the Measure, 2006. Recipient Pub. Health Svc. Superior Svc., USPHS, 1981, Commendation of Asst. Sec. of Health, 1988, Cecil Medal for disting. service, Inst. of Medicine, Nat. Acad. Sci., 2001, Significant Contbns. award, Am. Pub. Health Assn., 2004, Outstand Contributions award, Inst. Medicine, 1998, Staff Achievement award, 2000, cert. Appreciation, 2000; fellow Internat. fellow, Population Coun. of Am., 1955—57; scholar Internat. scholar, AAUW, 1955—56. Mem.: Nat. Acad. Social Ins., Indian Sociol. Soc. (founding mem.), Indian Fedn. of U. Women, Am. Sociol. Assn., APHA, Am. Statis. Assn., Population Assn. of Am. Office: Nat Acad Sci Com Nat Statistics 500 Fifth St NW Washington DC 20001 Personal E-Mail: gooloow@rcn.com.

**WUNDERMAN, JAN DARCOURT,** artist; b. Winnipeg, Man., Can., Jan. 22, 1921; d. Rene Paul and Georgette Marie (Guionet) Darcourt; m. Frank Joseph Malina, 1938 (div. 1945); m. Lester Wunderman (div. 1967); children: Marc, Geroge, Karen Renee. BFA, Otis Art Inst., L.A., 1942. One man shows include Easthampton Guild Hall, L.I., 1977, Denise Bibro Fine Art Gallery, N.Y.C., 1996-98, 2002, Roko Gallery, 1963, 66, 68, 71, 73, 76; represented in numerous permanent pub., corp. and pvt. collections including Zimmerli Mus., NYU Loeb Collection, Norfolk Mus., Health and Sci. Ctr., Salt Lake City, Alfred Kouri Collection, Skidmore Coll. Print Collection, Nat. Assn. of Women Artists, Rutgers U., 1994, Albright Knox Mus., 1998-99, Daimler Chrysler Coll., Germany, 2002, Northwest Airlines, Detroit, 2003, abstract-nonrepresentational. Recipient Ohashi award Pan Pacific Exhbn., Tokyo and Osaka, 1962, Emily Lowe award 1965, J.J. Akston Found. prize, 1965, Canaday Meml. prize, 1979, Marian De Solo Mendes prize, 1981, Charles Horman Meml. prize, 1983, Amelia Peabody award Nat. Assn. Women, 1991, Grumbacher Gold medal of honor, 1992, Doris Kreindler award 1992. Mem. Nat. Assn. Women Artists (medal of honor 1966, Marcia Brady Tucker award 1965, E. Holzinger prize 1966, Jane C. Stanley prize 1977, Marge Greenblatt award 1990, Amelia Peabody award 1991, Solveig Stomsoe Palmer prize 1997), Am. Soc. Contemporary Artists (corr. sec. 1977-78, Bocour award 1980, Elizabeth Erlanger Meml. award 1990, Kreindler award 1992, N. Ransom award 2002), Contemporary Artists Guild (Irwin Zlowe Meml. award 1998). Avocations: history, travel. Studio: 41 Union Sq W Rm 516 New York NY 10003-3208 Address: Denise Bibro Fine Art Gallery 529 West 20th St New York NY 10011

**WUNNICKE, BROOKE,** lawyer; b. Dallas, May 9, 1918; d. Rudolph von Falkenstein and Lulu Lenore Brooke; m. James M. Wunnicke, Apr. 11, 1940; (dec. 1977); 1 child, Diane B. BA, Stanford U., 1939; JD, U. Colo., 1945. Bar: Wyo. 1946, Colo. 1969, U.S. Dist. Ct. Wyo. 1947, U.S. Dist. Ct. Colo. 1970, U.S. Supreme Ct. 1958, U.S. Ct. Appeals (10th cir.) 1958. Pvt. practice law, 1946—56; ptnr. Williams & Wunnicke, Cheyenne, Wyo., 1956—69; counsel Calkins, Kramer, Grimshaw & Harring, Denver, 1969—73; chief appellate dep. atty. Dist. Atty's Office, Denver, 1973—86; counsel Hall & Evans L.L.C., Denver, 1986—. Adj. prof. law U. Denver Coll. Law, 1978-97, 1st Frank H. Ricketeen Jr. adj. prof., 2003; lectr. Internat. Practicum Inst. Denver, 1978-2003 Author: Ethics Compliance for Business Lawyers, 1987; co-author: Standby Letters of Credit, 1989, Corporate Financial Risk Management, 1992, UCP 500 and Standby Letters of Credit-Special Report, 1994, Standby and Commercial Letters of Credit, 2000, 2006, Legal Opinion Letters Formbook, 2002, 2006; contbr. articles to profl. jours. Pres. Laramie County Bar Assn., Cheyenne, 1967-68; Dir. Cheyenne C. of C., 1965-68 Recipient Outstanding Svc. award, Colo. Dist. Attys. Coun., 1979, 1982, 1986, Disting. Alumni awards, U. Colo. Sch. Law, 1986, 1993, William Lee Knous award, 1997, Lathrop Trailblazer award, Colo. Women's Bar Assn., 1992, Eleanor P. Williams award for Disting. Svc. to Legal Profession, 1997, Potter Lifetime Profl. Svc. award, 1999, Nat. award, Def. Rsch. Inst., 1999, Law Star award, Denver Coll. Law, 2003. Fellow Colo. Bar Found. (hon.), Am. Bar Found.; mem. ABA, Wyo. State Bar, Denver Bar Assn. (hon. life; trustee 1977-80, award of merit 2004), Colo. Bar Assn. (hon., life, Merit award 1999), Am. Arbitration Assn. (comml. panel), William E. Doyle Inn of Ct. (hon.), Order of Coif, Phi Beta Kappa. Republican. Avocations: reading, writing. Office: Hall & Evans LLC 1125 17th St Ste 600 Denver CO 80202-2037 Office Phone: 303-628-3300. Business E-Mail: wunnickeb@hallevans.com.

**WUNSCH, JAMES STEVENSON,** political science professor; b. Detroit, Sept. 27, 1946; s. Richard Ellis and Jane Rolston (Kershaw) W.; m. Lillian C. Richards, Mar. 29, 1969 (div. Feb. 1983), 1 child, Kathryn; m. Mary Gayle Gundlach, Aug. 19, 1983; children: Hallie, Hannah. BA, Duke U., 1968; MA, Ind. U., 1971, PhD, 1974. Rsch. fellow U. Ghana, Accra, 1971-72; asst. prof. Creighton U., Omaha, 1974-78, assoc. prof., 1978-86, prof. polit. sci., 1986—, chmn. dept., 1983-93, 96—, dir. African studies program, 1998—. Social sci. analyst and cons., Ghana, Liberia, Kenya, Sudan, Thailand, Philippines, Joint African Inst., African Devel. Bank, USAID, Washington, 1978-80; vis. assoc. prof. Ind. U., Bloomington, 1985-86; sr. project mgr. Assocs. in Rural Devel., Burlington, Vt., 1987-88, cons., Bangladesh, Zambia, Nigeria, South Africa, Swaziland, Botswana, Uganda, 1985—; USIA Disting. lectr., South Africa, 1993. Author: The Failure of the Centralized State, 1990, Local Governance in Africa, 2004 (monograph) Rural Development, Decentralization and Administrative Reform, 1988; mem. bd. editors Pub. Adminstrn. and Devel., 1998—; contbr. more than 40 articles to profl. jours., chpts. to books. Bd. dirs. Omaha Symphony Chorus, 1977-78, Nebr. Choral Arts Soc., 1982-96, Voices of Omaha, 1982-85, Trinity Cathedral, Omaha, 1980-83; participant Leadership Omaha, 1982-83; mem. Omaha Com. Fgn. Rels., 1975-95; mem. govt. affairs com. Greater Omaha C. of C., 1980-85; mem. issues and interests com. Nebr. Rep. party, 1984-88. Recipient R.F. Kennedy Quality Tchg. award Creighton U., 1985, Burlington No. award, 1992, Dean's award for excellence in tchg., 1994, Dean's award for excellence in scholarship, 2000, Dean's award for excellence insvc., 2006, Student Senate award for excellence in advising, 1989; rsch. award NSF, NEH, USAID, Am. Philos. Soc.; Fulbright-Hays fellow in Ghana, 1971-72, Internat. Affairs fellow N.Y. Coun. Fgn. Rels., 1978-79. Mem. Am. Polit. Sci. Assn., Midwest Polit. Sci. Assn., African Studies Assn., Internat. Studies Assn., Phi Beta Kappa, Pi Sigma Alpha, Phi Beta Delta. Episcopalian. Avocations: vocal music, camping, cross country skiing, bicycling. Home: 1631 N 53rd St Omaha NE 68104-4947 Office: Creighton U Dept Polit Sci 30th And California Omaha NE 68178-0001 Office Phone: 402-280-2568. Business E-Mail: jwunsch@creighton.edu.

**WUORINEN, CHARLES PETER,** composer; b. NYC, June 9, 1938; s. John Henry and Alfhild (Kalijarvi) W. BA, Columbia U., 1961, MA, 1963; DMus (hon.), Jersey City State Coll. 1971. Lectr. Columbia U., 1964-65, instr., 1965-69, asst. prof., 1969-71, co-dir. Group Contemporary Music, 1962—; prof. music Rutgers U., 1984—2005. Vis. lectr. Princeton U., 1967-68, New England Conservatory, 1968-71, Yale U., 1983; adj. lectr. U. South Fla., 1972; faculty Manhattan Sch. Music, 1972-79, U. So. Calif., 1981; artistic dir., chmn. Am. Composers Orch., 1973-87; composer-in-residence Ojai Festival, 1975, Santa Fe Chamber Music Festival, 1993, 2001, Tanglewood Music Festival, 2001; San Francisco Symphony, 1984-89; condr. Cleve. Orch., 1976, Finnish Radio Orch., 1979, Helsinki Philharm., 1979; disting. prof. Rutgers U., 1984—; vis. prof. SUNY, Buffalo, 1989-94, NYU, 1990 Author: Simple Composition; mem. editorial bd. Perspectives of New Music; bd. mem. Composers Recs. Inc., 1962-89; composer numerous works including Music for Orchestra, 1956, Be Mery All That Be Present, mixed chorus, 1957, Concert for Four Trombones, 1960, Madrigale Spirituale, 1960, Turetzky Pieces, 1960, Evolutio: organ, 1961, Evolution Transcripta for chamber orch., 1961, Tiento Sobre Cabezon, 1961, Concert for Double Bass Alone, 1961, Trio No. 1 for flute, cello and piano, 1961, Invention for percussion quintet, 1962, Octet, 1962, Duuiensela for cello and piano, 1962, Bearbeitungen über das Glogauer Liederbuch, 1962, The Prayer of Jonah, 1962, 2d Flute Trio: Piece for Stefan Wolpe, 1962, Chamber Concerto for cello and 10 players, 1963, Piano Variations, 1963, Flute Variations, 1963, Composition for violin and 10 instruments, 1964, Chamber Concerto for flute and 10 players, 1964, Orchestral and Electronic Exchanges, 1965, Composition for oboe and piano, 1965, Chamber Concerto for oboe and 10 players, 1965, Super Salutem for male voices and instruments, 1964, Piano Concerto, 1966, The Bells for carillon, 1966 (revised 1997), Bicinium, 2 oboes, 1966, Janissary Music for 1 percussionist, 1966, Harpsichord Divisions, 1966, Making Ends Meet for piano four-hands, 1966, John Bull: Salve Regina Versus Septem, 1966, Duo for violin and piano, 1967, The Politics of Harmony: A Masque, 1967, String Trio, 1968, Flute Variations II, 1968, Time's Encomium (electronic), 1969, Adapting to the Times for cello and piano, 1969, The Long and the Short for violin, 1969, Nature's Concord trumpet and piano, 1969, Piano Sonata, 1969, Ringing Changes for percussion, 1970, A Song, 1970, Tuba Concerto, 1970, A Message to Denmark Hill, 1970, Cello Variations, 1970, String Quartet, 1971, Canzona for 12 instruments, 1971, Grand Bamboula for string orch., 1971, Amplified Violin Concerto, 1972, Harp Variations, 1972, Bassoon Variations, 1972, Violin Variations, 1972, On Alligators for 8 instruments, 1972, Speculum Speculi for 6 players, 1972, Third Trio for flute, cello and piano, 1973, 12 Short Pieces for piano, 1973, Grand Union for cello and drums, 1973, Arabia Felix for 6 Instruments, 1973, Second Piano Concerto, 1974, Fantasia for violin and piano, 1974, The W. of Babylon (opera), 1975, TASHI, 1975, Hyperion for 12 instruments, 1975, Cello Variations 2, 1975, 2d Piano Sonata, 1976, Percussion Symphony, 1976, The Winds, 1977, Fast Fantasy for cello and piano, 1977, Archangel for trombone and string quartet, 1977, Six Pieces for violin and piano, 1977, Six Songs for two voices, Wind Quintet, Self Similar Waltz for piano, Ancestors for chamber ensemble, 1978, Two-Part Symphony, 1978, Archaeopteryx for bass trombone and chamber ensemble, 1978, The Magic

Art, A Masque for chamber orch., 1979, Fortune for 4 instruments, 1979, 2d String Quartet, 1979, The Celestial Sphere for chorus and orch., 1979, Psalm 39 for baritone and guitar, 1979, Percussion Duo, 1979, Joan's for 5 instruments, 1979, Blue Bamboula for piano, 1980, Capriccio for piano, 1981, Horn Trio, 1981, Trio for bass instruments, 1981, New York Notes for 6 players, 1982, Mass, 1982, Divertimento, 1982 (string quartet), Divertimento for alto sax and piano, 1982, Spinoff for violin, double bass and congas, 1983, Trio for violin, cello and piano, 1983, Third Piano Concerto, 1983, Rhapsody for violin and orch., 1984, Concertino, 1984, Natural Fantasy for organ, 1985, Horn Trio Continued, 1985, Trombone Trio, 1985, Prelude to Kullervo for tuba and orch., 1985, Double Solo for Horn Trio, 1985, Fanfare for the Houston Symphony, 1986, The Golden Dance for orch., 1986, Third Piano Sonata, 1986, Third String Quartet, 1987, Galliard for chamber orch., 1987, Bamboula Beach for orch., 1987, FIVE: Concerto for amplified cello and orch., 1987, Sonata for violin and piano, 1988; (piano) Bagatelle, 1988, Ave Christe, 1988; Contrafactum, 1969 (orch.), Reliquary for Igor Stravinsky, 1975, Short Suite, 1981, Crossfire, 1984, Movers and Shakers, 1984, Bamboula Squared, 1984, Another Happy Birthday, 1988, Machault Mon Chou, 1988, String Sextet, 1989, A Solis Ortu, 1989, Astra, 1990, Delight of the Muses, 1991, Missa Brevis, 1991, The Mission of Virgil, 1993; (soprano and piano) Twang, 1989; Genesis, 1989 (chorus and orch.), A Winter's Tale for Soprano and Six Instruments, 1992, Microsymphony, 1992, Missa Renovata, 1992, Saxophone Quartet, 1992, Concerto for Saxophone Quartet and Orch., 1993, Percussion Quartet, 1994, Piano Quintet, 1994, Christes Crosse, 1994, Lightenings VIII, 1994, Guitar Variations, 1994, Sonata for Guitar and Piano, 1995, The Great Procession, 1995, Katz Fugue for piano, 1995, Windfall for band, 1994, Schoenberg Op. 31 Variations, 1996 (remade for two pianos), The River of Light, 1996 (string orch. and percussion), Epithalamium, 1997 (two instruments), Symphony Seven, 1997, Fenton Songs, 1997, Cello Variations III, 1997, Lepton trio for celeste, piano and harp, 1998; An Orbicle of Jasp, 1999 (cello and piano); Brass Quintet, 2000, Fourth String Quartet, 2000; Cyclops 2000 (chamber orch.); Haroun and the Sea of Stories, 1997-2001 (opera); Stanzas Before Time, 2001 (tenor and harp); Buttons and Bows, 2001 (cello and accordion); Alap, 2001, Josquiniana, 2001; Two Machine Portraits, September 11, 2001, 2001 (tenor and piano); Fifty Fifty, 2001 (two pianos); The Haroun Songbook, 2002 (4 vocal soloists and piano); Hexadactyl, 2002 (guitar); Pentecost, 2002 (tenor and harp), 4th Piano Concerto, 2003, Fenton Songs II (soprano and piano trio), 2002, The Long Boat (mezzo, English horn), 2003, The Haroun Piano Book (solo piano), 2003, Dodecadactyl (two guitars), 2003, Visible (mezzo and violin), 2004, Ashberyana (baritone and ensemble), 2004, Duo Sonata (flute, piano), 2004, Theologoumenon (orchestra), 2005, Flying to Kahani (piano and orchestra), 2005, Heart Shadow (piano), 2005, Praegustatum (piano), 2006, (bass-bariton and tuba) Never Again the Same, 2006, (for violin and 18 players) Spin 5, 2006, Eighth Symphony, 2006. Recipient Philharmonic Young Composers award, 1954; Bennington Composers Conf. scholar, 1956-60; Bearns prize, 1958-59, 61; MacDowell Colony fellow, 1958; Alice M. Ditson fellow, 1959; Arthur Rose teaching fellow, 1960; Broadcast Music-Student Composers award, 1959, 61, 62, 63; Lili Boulanger Meml. award, 1963; Festival fellow Santa Fe Opera, 1962; Festival fellow World's Fair Music and Sound, 1962; commd. by Koussevitzky Found., 1964, Berkshire Music Center, 1963, Fromm Found., 1963-71, Ford Found., 1962, Orch. of Am., 1958, Columbia U., 1956, Washington and Lee U., 1964, Fine Arts Quartet, 1969, Naumberg Found., 1971, U. South Fla., 1972, Nat. Opera Inst., 1973, Light Fantastic Players, 1973, N.Y. State Council on the Arts, 1974, N.Y. Philharm., 1974, Balt. Chamber Music Soc., 1974, Buffalo Philharm., 1974, Ojai Festival, 1974, Contemporary Chamber Ensemble, 1974, TASHI, 1974, Beethoven Festival, Bonn, 1978, Albany Symphony, 1981, San Francisco Symphony, 1984, 86, 88, 89, Cleve. Orch., 1984, Balt. Symphony, 1984, Houston Symphony, 1986, N.Y.C. Ballet, 1987, 90, Libr. of Congress, 1988, New World Symphony, 1987, Chamber Music Soc. Lincoln Ctr., 1989, 92, Am./ Soviet Youth Orch., 1990, Phila. Orch., 1992, Beethorenhalle Orch., Bonn Mönchengladbach und Ludwig Forum, Germany; grantee Nat. Inst. Arts and Letters, 1967, Nat. Endowment Arts, 1974, 76; Guggenheim fellow, 1968, 72; Ingraham Merrill fellow, 1972, Rockefeller Found. fellow, 1979, 80, 81, John D. and Catherine T. MacArthur fellow, 1986-91; recipient Pulitzer prize, 1970, Brandeis U. creative arts award, 1970, Creative Artists Pub. Svc. award, 1976; Arts and Letters award Finlandia Found., 1976, Koussevitzky Internat. Rec. award, 1970, 72. Mem. AAAS, AAAL, Am. Soc. Univ. Composers, Am. Composers Alliance (former bd. dirs.), Am. Music Ctr. (bd. dirs.), Internat. Soc. Contemporary Music (bd. dirs.), Am. Acad. Arts and Scis., Phi Beta Kappa. Office: care Howard Stokar Mgmt 870 W End Ave New York NY 10025-4918 Office Phone: 212-866-5798. Business E-Mail: hstokar@stokar.com.

**WURDEMAN, LEW EDWARD,** Internet company executive, consultant; b. Colorado Springs, Colo., Oct. 31, 1949; s. Robert Martin and Shirley Gladys (Reetz) W. Student, U. Tex., 1967-69, U. Minn., 1969-72. Adminstr. Control Data Corp., Bloomington, Minn., 1969-81; product splst., 1981-83; sys. mgr., 1983-84; cons., 1984-89; mgr. The Roach Orgn., Inc., Mpls., 1989-90; computer cons. Wurdeman Enterprises, Inc., Farmington, Minn., 1991-93; sr. cons. Norstan Consulting, Minnetonka, Minn., 1993-2001; photographer Vividere Glamour Photography, 1996—; tree farm owner Golden Pond Farm, 2003—. Freelance photographer; virtual tour photographer 360 Minn., 2003—. Commr. Parks and Recreation Dept., City of Farmington, Minn. 2001-03. Mem. Internat. Freelance Photographers Orgn., Internat. Glamour Photographers Assn., Photog. Soc. Am. Profl. Photographers Am., German Shepherd Dog Club Mpls., German Shepherd Dog Club Am. Republican. Lutheran. Avocations: dog breeding and training, computers, photography. Office: Link Up Hosting PO Box 332 Farmington MN 55024-0332 Office Phone: 612-327-6178. E-mail: lew@linkuphosting.com.

**WURGLER, TIMOTHY RAYMOND,** music educator; b. Monroe, Wis., Jan. 8, 1961; s. Raymond Mathias and Ruth Ella Wurgler; m. Kristen Marie Arnold, June 3, 2000. B of Music, U. Wis., 1984. Tchr. Laekview Elem. Sch., Twin Lakes, Wis., 1981-89, Wilmot High Sch., 1989-2002; tchr. St. Francis Schs., 2002—. Dir. Milw. Liederkranz, 2001—, Milw. Damen Choir, 2002—. Author: The History of CSJA, 2000. Mem.: Ctrl. States Judges Assn. (asst. dir. 1997—98), Am. Choral Dirs. Assn., Wis. Music Educators Assn. Independent. Methodist. Avocations: scuba diving, bicycling, camping, hiking, baking. Home: 8534 S Rebecca Ct Oak Creek WI 53154 Office: Deer Creek Elem Sch 3680 S Kinic Kinic Ave Saint Francis WI 53235 Business E-Mail: twurgler@stfrancisschools.org.

**WURMFELD, SANFORD,** artist, educator; b. NYC, Dec. 6, 1942; s. Charles Jacob and Esther (Witzling) W.; m. Rella Stuart-Hunt, Dec. 11, 1971; children: Jeremy Philip, Treva. BA in Art with honors, Dartmouth Coll., 1964; ind. study, Rome, 1964—65. Lectr. Hunter Coll., NYC, 1967—72, asst. prof., 1972—77, assoc. prof., 1977—80, chmn. dept. art, 1978—2006, prof. art, 1980—, Caroff prof., 2000—. Vis. artist lectr. Calif. State Coll., Hayward, Cooper Union, NY, Bare Coll., Anondale-on-Hudson, NY, Drexel U., Phila. 1970, SUNY, Fredonia, 1971, Livingston Coll., New Brunswick, NJ, 1973, Whitney Mus., 1982, Met. Mus. Art, 1987, 87, Princeton U., 1990, The Slade Sch. U. Coll., London, 1991, Chelsea Coll. Art, London, 1991, Whitney Mus., 1992, Hochschule der Kunst, Berlin, 1995, Simon Fraser U., Vancouver, 1996, U. Victoria, B.C., 1996, Acad. Minerva, The Netherlands, Glasgow Sch. of Art, Scotland, 1997, external examiner, 1999—2003. One-man shows include Talbot Rice Gallery, Edinburgh, 2004, Altötting, Germany, 2003, Karl Ernst Osthaus Mus., Hagen, Germany 2000, Susan Caldwell Gallery, N.Y., 1978, Bard Coll. Invitational Exhibit, 1977, Susan Caldwell Gallery, 1976-77, Galarie Denise Rene, 1974, Rockefeller Meml. Gallery, Fredonia, N.Y., 1971, Tibor de Nagy Gallery, 1968, Bryant Park, N.Y., Fischbach Gallery, 1969; group shows include Mus. Modern Art, N.Y., 1968, Grank Palais, Paris, 1968, Kunsthaus, Zurich, 1968, Tate Gallery, London, 1968, Ft. Worth Art Ctr., 1969, Galerie de Gestlo, Kunstfair, Basel Switzerland, 1970, 72, Columbia Film Festival, 1973, Galerie Denise Rene, 1974, Hopkins Ctr. Galleries, 1974, Lehigh U., 1976, Susan Caldwell Gallery, 1977-79, Toni Birckhard Gallery, Cin., 1980, Carnegie Internat., 1983, Shanghai Exhbn. Hall Shanghai, China, 1986, Long Beach Mus. of Art, Calif., 1989, William Paterson Coll. of N.J., 1990, Hallwells Contemporary Arts Ctr., Buffalo, 1991, Louis Stern Fine Arts,

L.A., 1995, Andre Zarre Gallery, N.Y., 1996, 2003, Condeso-Lawcer Gallery, N.Y., 1997, Karl Ost Haus-Mus., Hagen, Germany, Mucsarnok, Budapest, 1999, 02, Am. Acad. Arts and Letters, 2000, Muscarnok, 2002, Hunter Coll. Times Sq. Gallery, 2003, 04, Panorama Mesdag, The Hague, 2006; represented in permanent collections at Espace de l'Art Conret, Mouans-Sartoux, France, Karl Ernst Osthaus Mus., Hagen, Germany, Met. Mus. Art, N.Y., Guggenheim Mus., N.Y., SUNY, Fredonia, Ctrl. Trust Co., Cin., AT&T, N.Y., Baxter Travenol Labs., Deerfield, Ill., GE Corp., Fairfield, Conn., Sprengler Mus., Hannover, Germany, City of Hannover, Shreve, Lamb & Harmon Corp., N.Y., Silkscreeners Guild, Germany, Warner Nat. Corp., Cin., U. N.C., William Hayes Ackland Meml. Art Ctr., Chapel Hill, others; contbr. articles to profl. jour. Recipient Ames award Dartmouth Coll., 1964; fellow Guggenheim Found., 1974, Nat. Endowments for the Arts Individual Artist's, 1987-88; CUNY faculty rsch. grantee. Home: 18 Warren St New York NY 10007-1066 Office: Hunter Coll Dept Art 695 Park Ave New York NY 10021-5024 Office Phone: 212-772-5051. Business E-Mail: sanford.wurmfeld@hunter.cuny.edu.

**WÜRSIG, BERND GERHARD,** marine biology educator; b. Barsinghausen, Germany, Nov. 9, 1948; s. Gerhard Paul and Charlotte Annemarie (Yorkowski) Würsig; m. Melany Anne Carballeira, Nov. 19, 1969; children: Kim Carballeira, Paul Carballeira. BS, Ohio State U., 1971; PhD, SUNY, Stony Brook, 1978. Postdoctoral researcher U. Calif., Santa Cruz, 1978-81; prof. Moss Landing (Calif.) Marine Labs., 1981-89; prof. marine biology, dir. Marine Mammal Lab. Tex. A&M U., Galveston, 1989—, dir. The Inst. of Marine Life Scis., 1996—. Govt. cons. Minerals Mgmt. Svc., Washington, 1980—. Contbr. articles to profl. jours., 7-part miniseries to TV on lives of dolphins, dolphin problems induced by humans, also Discovery Channel show on Life of B Würsig; co-author: The Hawaiian Spinner Dolphin, 1994, Whales, Dolphins and Porpoises, 1995; sr. advisor (IMAX film) Dolphins, 2000 (nominee Acad. award best spl. category nature movie), sr. author The Marine Mammals of the Gulf of Mexico, 2000; co-editor: The Encyclopedia of Marine Mammals, 2002. Recipient Chmn.'s award for rsch. and exploration, Nat. Geog. Soc., 1998, Alban-Heiser award for excellence in Tex. conservation rsch., Zool. Soc. Houston, 1991; Fulbright Found. scholar, 2001—03. Mem. Marine Mammal Soc. (pres. 1991-93), N.Y. Acad. Scis., Soc. Cryptozoology, Am. Behavior Soc., Am. Mus. Natural History, Soc. Archimedes. Clubs: Explorers (N.Y.C.) (fellow of research). Avocations: photography, diving, airplane piloting, skiing, hiking. Home: 2402 Creekridge Pearland TX 77581- also: 2402 Creekridge Dr Pearland TX 77581-5728 Office Phone: 409-740-4413. E-mail: wursigb@tamug.edu.

**WURSTER, ABIGAIL MICHELLE,** theater educator, costume designer; b. St. Louis, Nov. 1, 1977; d. David and Ruth Wurster. BA, Valparaiso U., Ind., 1999; MFA, Ill. State U., Normal, 2003. Theatre costume designer Francis Marion U., Florence, SC, 2003—; prof. theatre, 2003—. Mem.choir St. Luke Luth. Ch., Florence, 2006. Scholar, Traditional Theatre Tng., Kyoto, Japan, 2005. Mem.: U.S. Inst. Theatre Tech., SC Theatre Assn., Alpha Psi Omega. Office: Francis Marion Univ 4822 E Palmetto St Florence SC 29506 Office Phone: 843-661-1685. Business E-Mail: awurster@fmarion.edu.

**WURSTER, CHARLES FREDERICK,** environmental scientist, educator; b. Phila., Aug. 1, 1930; s. Charles Frederick and Helen B. Wurster; children: Steven Hadley, Nina F., Erik Frederick. SB, Haverford Coll., 1952; MS, U. Del., 1954; PhD, Stanford U., 1957. Tchg. asst. U. Del., 1952-54; rsch. asst. Stanford U., 1954-57; Fulbright fellow Innsbruck, Austria, 1957-58; rsch. chemist Monsanto Rsch. Corp., 1959-62; rsch. assoc. biol. scis. Dartmouth Coll., 1962-65; asst. prof. biol. scis. SUNY, Stony Brook, 1965-70; assoc. prof. environ. scis. Marine Scis. Rsch. Ctr., 1970-94, prof. emeritus, 1994—. Founding trustee, sec., mem. exec. com. Environ. Def., 1967—; vis. prof. Macquarie U., Sydney, Australia, 1988; mem. adminstr.'s pesticide policy adv. com. EPA, 1975—78; leader ecol. tours worldwide. Contbr. articles to profl. publs. Scholar, U. Wash., Seattle. Fellow: AAAS; mem.: Nat. Pks. Conservation Assn. (trustee 1970—79), Defenders Wildlife (dir. 1975—84, 1987—96). Achievements include research on DDT, PCBs, other chlorinated hydrocarbon effects on phytoplankton, birds; relationship between environmental sciences and public policy; seabird protection; instrumental in banning several insecticides, including DDT, Dieldrin and Aldrin. Address: 644 Hillside Dr E Seattle WA 98112 Office Phone: 206-325-3665. E-mail: cfwurster@yahoo.com.

**WURSTER, DALE ERWIN,** pharmacist, educator, retired dean; b. Sparta, Wis., Apr. 10, 1918; s. Edward Emil and Emma Sophia (Steingraeber) W.; m. June Margaret Peterson, June 16, 1944; children: Dale Eric, Susan Gay. BS, U. Wis., 1942, PhD, 1947. U. Wis. Sch. Pharmacy, Madison, 1938-71, mem. faculty, 1947-71; prof., dean N.D. State U. Coll. Pharmacy, 1971-72; prof. Dale E. Wurster Ctr. Pharm. Tech., Iowa City, 2003, dean, 1972-84, dean emeritus, 1984—. George B. Kaufman Meml. lectr. Ohio State U., 1968; Hancher Finkbine Medallion prof. U. Iowa, 1984; Joseph V. Swintosky disting. lectr. U. Ky., 2000; cons. in field; phys. sci. adminstr. USN, 1960-63; sci. advisor U.S. Army, Munition Rsch. Found., 1968-72; mem. revision com. U.S. Pharmacopoeia, 1961-70; mem. pharmacy rev. com. USPHS, 1966-72; mem. tech. adv. com. contraceptive R&D program Ea. Va. Med. Sch., 1987-2002, rsch., U. Wis. Contbr. articles to profl. jours., chpts. to books; patentee in field. With USNR, 1944-46. Recipient Superior Achievement citation Navy Dept., 1964, merit citation U. Wis., 1976, Disting. Alumni award U. Wis. Sch. Pharmacy, 1984; Dale E. Wurster Ctr. Pharm. Tech. at U. Iowa named in his honor. Fellow Am. Assn. Pharm. Scientists (founder, sponsor Dale E. Wurster rsch. award 1990—, Disting. Pharm. Scientist award 1991); mem. Am. Assn. Colls. Pharmacy (exec. com. 1964-66, chmn. conf. tchrs. 1960-61, vis. scientist 1963-70, Disting. Educator award 1983), Acad. Pharm. Scis. (exec. com. 1967-70, chmn. basic pharmaceutics sect. 1965-67, pres. 1975, Indsl. Pharm. Tech. award 1980), Am. Pharm. Assn. (chmn. sci. sect. 1964-65, rsch. achievement award 1965, Wis. Disting. Svc. award 1971), Iowa Pharmacists Assn. (Robert G. Gibbs award 1983), Wis. Acad. Scis., Arts and Letters, Soc. Investigative Dermatology, Rumanian Soc. Med. Sci. (hon.). Roman Catholic. Pharm. Edn. (bd. grants 1987-92), Sigma Xi, Kappa Psi (past officer), Rho Chi, Phi Lambda Upsilon, Phi Sigma. Home: 16 Brickwood Cir NE Iowa City IA 52240-9129 Office Phone: 319-335-8799.

**WURTELE, CHRISTOPHER ANGUS,** paint and coatings company executive; b. Mpls., August 25, 1934; Valentine and Charlotte (Lindley) W.; m. Heather Campbell (div. Feb. 1977); children: Christopher, Andrew, Heidi; m. Margaret Von Blon, Aug. 21, 1977. BA, Yale U., 1956; MBA, Stanford U., 1961. V.p. Minn. Paints, Inc., Mpls., 1962—65; exec. v.p. Minn. Paints, Inc. (merged with Valspar Corp. 1970), Mpls., 1965—73, pres., CEO, 1973-96, chmn., 1973-98. With USN, 1956—59. Mem.: Mpls. Club. Episcopalian. Home: 2970 Gale Rd Wayzata MN 55391 Office: 4900 IDS Ctr 80 S 8th St Minneapolis MN 55402

**WURTH, MONTY,** information technology manager; BS in Indsl. Engring., U. Iowa, 1992; MS in Computer Info. Systems, U. Phoenix, 2004. Regional ops. sr. mgr. MCI, Chandler, Ariz., 1999—. Master: Toastmasters (pres. 2005—06). Office Phone: 480-567-1294.

**WURTMAN, RICHARD JAY,** neuroscientist, educator; b. Phila., Mar. 9, 1936; s. Samuel Richard and Hilda (Schreiber) W.; m. Judith Joy Hirschhorn, Nov. 15, 1959; children: Rachael Elisabeth, David Franklin. AB, U. Pa., 1956; MD, Harvard U., 1960. Intern Mass. Gen. Hosp., 1960-61, resident, 1961-62, fellow medicine, 1965-66, clin. assoc. in medicine, 1985—; research assoc., med. research officer NIMH, 1962-67; mem. faculty MIT, Cambridge, 1967—, prof. endocrinology and metabolism, 1970-80, prof. neuroendocrine regulation, 1980-94, Cecil H. Green disting. prof., 1994—; dir. Clin. Rsch. Ctr., MIT, Cambridge, 1985—2005; prof. neurosci. MIT, 1984-94. Lectr. medicine Harvard Med. Sch., 1969—; prof. Harvard-MIT Divsn. Health Scis. and Tech., 1978—; Smithies lectr. Oxford U., 2002; sci. dir. Ctr. for Brain Scis. and Metabolism Charitable Trust, 1981—; invited prof. U. Geneva, 1981; Sterling vis. prof. Boston U., 1981; vis. fellow Balliol Coll., Oxford U., 1997; mem. small grants study sect. NIMH, 1967-69, preclin. psychopharmacology study sect., 1971-75; behavioral biology adv. panel NASA, 1969-72; coun. basic sci. Am. Heart Assn., 1969-74; rsch. adv. bd. Parkin-

son's Disease Found., 1972-80, Am. Parkinson's Disease Assn., 1978—; com. phototherapy in newborns NRC-Nat. Acad. Scis., 1972-74, com. nutrition, brain devel. and behavior, 1976, mem. space applications bd., 1976-82; mem. task force on drug devel. Muscular Dystrophy Assn., 1980-87; chmn. life scis. adv. com. NASA, 1979-82; chmn. adv. bd. Alzheimer's Disease Assn., 1981-84; assoc. neuroscis. rsch. program MIT, 1974-82; chmn. life scis. adv. bd. USAF, 1985—94; founder, chmn. sci. adv. bd. Interneuron Pharms., Inc., 1989-99; co-founder Wurtco, 1999, Back Bay Sci., 1999. Author: Catecholamines, 1966; (with others) The Pineal, 1968; editor: (with Judith Wurtman) Nutrition and the Brain, Vols. I and II, 1977, Vols. III, IV, V., 1979, Vol. VI, 1983, Vol. VII, 1986, Vol. VIII, 1990, also some 1000 other articles and books; mem. various editl. bds. Mem. bd. overseers Boston Symphony Orch., 1997—; bd. dirs. Fenway Cmty. Health Ctr., Boston, 1998—2003, Provincetown Art Assn. and Mus., 2000—, pres., 2005—. Recipient various awards and lectureships. Mem. Endocrine Soc. (Ernst Oppenheim award 1972), Am. Physiol. Soc., Am. Soc. Biol. Chemists, Am. Soc. Pharmacology and Exptl. Therapeutics (John Jacob Abel award 1968), Am. Soc. Neurochemistry, Soc. Neuroscis., Am. Soc. Clin. Nutrition, Am. Inst. Nutrition (Osborne & Mendel award 1982), Harvard Club (Boston). Achievements include some 80 U.S. patents on new treatments for diseases and conditions; invention of melatonin for promoting sleep, of dexfenfluramine for treating obesity, of citicoline for treating stroke and of Sarafem for the treatment of premenstrual syndrome. Home: 300 Boylston St Boston MA 02116-3923 Office: Mass Inst Tech 77 Massachusetts Ave, 46-5023 Cambridge MA 02139-1323 Office Phone: 617-253-6731. Business E-Mail: dick@mit.edu.

**WURZBACH, LINDA,** educational consultant; b. San Antonio, Jan. 21, 1954; d. Delmar Earl Wurzbach, Dorothy Lang Wurzbach; m. Mark Allison Tatom. BS, U. Tex., 1975, MEd, 1978. Lic. tchr. Tex. Tchr. Austin Ind. Sch. Dist., Tex., 1976—81; project mgr. Tex. Sch. for the Blind and Visually Impaired, Austin, 1981—82, tchr., 1982—89; project dir. The Psychol. Corp., San Antonio, 1989—90; planner Tex. Edn. Agy., Austin, 1990—96; sr. project assoc. Coun. Chief State Sch. Officers, Washington, 1996—98; pres. Resources for Learning, LLC, Austin, 1998—. Cons. in field. Editor: TxBESS Toolkit, 2005, TxBESS Activity Profile, 2001, Fine Arts Curriculum Frameworks, 2000; author: Works in Progress, 1997, Portfolio Assessment for Beginning Teachers, 1999, Performance Assessment System, 2000; prodr.: (video) If You Love It, Teach It., 2000, Express Yourself, 2001, Fine Arts for All Students, 2003, Beginning Teacher Induction Toolkit: A Systems Approach, 2004; contbr. articles to profl. jours. Mem.: ASCD, Women Pres.' Orgn., U.S. Women's C. of C., Nat. Coun. Measurement in Edn., Am. Ednl. Rsch. Assn., Nat. Staff Devel. Coun. Home: 4504 Moose Dr Austin TX 78749 Personal E-Mail: lindaw@resourcesforlearning.net.

**WURZEL, LEONARD,** retired candy manufacturing company executive; b. Phila., Feb. 4, 1918; s. Maurice L. and Dora (Goldberg) W.; m. Elaine Cohen, Aug. 18, 1949; children — Mark L., Lawrence J. BS, Washington and Jefferson Coll.; 1939; MBA, Harvard, 1941. With Loft Candy Corp., Long Island City, NY, 1946-64, v.p., 1949-56, exec. v.p., 1956-57, pres., 1957-64, dir., 1949-64; chmn., dir. Calico Cottage Candies, Inc., 1964-94; ret., 1994; mayor Village of Sands Point, NY, 1989—. Capt. U.S. Army, 1941—46. Decorated Bronze Star. Mem. Assn. Mfrs. Confectionery and Chocolate (bd. dirs., past pres., chmn.), Candy Chocolate and Confectionery Inst. (bd. dirs., treas.), Retail Confectioners Internat. (bd. dirs., past pres.) Home: 25 Woodland Dr Sands Point NY 11050-1136 Office: 26 Tibbits Ln Sands Point NY 11050-1135

**WUSINICH, JOSEPH F., III,** lawyer, educator; b. Phila., Pa., Oct. 30, 1946; s. Joseph F. Wusinich Jr. and Mary M. (Madden) Wusinich; m. Catherine T. Consalvi, Sept. 7, 1968; children: Nicole, Lisa, Dana, Maria, Christa, Joanna, Catherine. BSc in Mgmt. Mktg., St. Joseph's U., Phila., 1968; JD, DePaul U., Chgo., 1974; LLM in Trial Advocacy, Temple U., Phila., 1995. Bar: Pa. 1974, U.S. Dist. Ct. (ea. dist.) Pa. 1976, U.S. Circuit Ct. Appeals Third Circuit 1976, U.S. Supreme Ct. 1984. Assoc. house counsel Liberty Mut. Ins. Co., Phila., 1974—76; law ptnr. Landis & Wusinich, West Chester, Pa., 1976—80, Wusinich & McCarthy, West Chester, Pa., 1980—85, Wusinich & Brogan, West Chester, Pa., 1993—2000, Wusinich, Brogan & Stanzione, Downington, Pa., 2000—; sr., mng. atty. Law Offices Joseph F. Wusinich, III, West Chester, Pa., 1985—93. Pres. coun., bd. trustees Immaculata U., Pa., 1997—; chair, vice chair med. health related issues PA. Bar Assn., Harrisburg, 2000—. Contbr. bull. and articles in field. Lt., chief tng. ops. officer, combat engr. U.S. Army, 1968—71, Vietnam. Decorated Army Commendation medal US Army, Bronze Star medal; recipient Defender of Life award, Pro-Life of Chester County, West Chester, Pa., 1998, St. Thomas More award, Pro-Life Union of S.E. Pa., Phila., 2002. Master: Hon. John E. Stively, Jr. Am. Inn Ct. (pres. elect 2002—03, pres. 2003—06); mem.: KC, Downington Pa. chpt. (3rd degree Knight 1987—). Republican. Roman Catholic. Avocation: basketball. Office: Wusinich Brogan Stanzione 537 W Uwchlan Ave Ste 200 Downingtown PA 19335 Office Phone: 610-594-1600. Office Fax: 610-594-6518. Business E-Mail: info@wusinichbrogan.com.

**WUSSLER, ROBERT JOSEPH,** broadcast executive, media consultant; b. Newark, Sept. 8, 1936; s. William and Anna (MacDonald) Wussler; children: Robert Joseph, Rosemary, Sally, Stefanie, Christopher, Jeanne. BA in Communication Arts, Seton Hall U., 1957, LLD (hon.), 1976, Emerson Coll., 1976. With CBS News, N.Y.C., 1957-72; v.p., gen. mgr. Sta. WBBM-TV, Chgo., 1972-74; v.p. CBS Sports, N.Y.C., 1974-76, pres., 1977-78, Sta. CBS-TV, N.Y.C., 1976-77, Pyramid Enterprises Ltd., N.Y.C., 1979—80; exec. v.p. Turner Broadcasting System Inc., Atlanta, 1979—89, sr. exec. v.p., from 1987, bd. dirs. pres. Atlanta Sports Teams, Inc., 1981-87; pres., chief exec. officer COMSAT Video Enterprises, Inc., Washington, 1989-92; pres. Wussler Group, 1992—. Chmn. bd. dirs. NATAS, 1980—84, 1986—90; co-owner Denver Nuggets, 1989—92; bd. dirs. Atlanta Hawks Ltd., Atlanta Braves Nat. League Baseball Club, Inc. Trustee Marymount Manhattan Coll. 1977—81; bd. regents Seton Hall U., 1978—84. Recipient Emmy awards, numerous other nat. and internat. news and sports awards. Mem.: European Broadcasting Union, Nat. Cable TV Assn. (mem. satellite network com.), Cable Advt. Bur., Ariz. Heart Inst., Internat. Radio and TV Soc., Dirs. Guild Am. Roman Catholic. Home and Office: Unit 4630 75 Fourteenth St Atlanta GA 30309 Office Phone: 301-469-0203. Personal E-Mail: rjwtv@aol.com.

**WÜTHRICH, KURT,** molecular biologist, biophysicist, educator; b. Oct. 4, 1938; MS in Chemistry, Physics and Maths., U. Bern, Switzerland, 1962; Eidgenössisches Turn-und Sportlehrerdiplom, U. Basel, Switzerland, 1964, PhD in Chemistry, 1964; D in Chemistry (hon.), U. Siena, Italy, 1997; PhD (hon.), U. Zürich, Switzerland, 1997, École Polytechnique Federale, Lausanne, Switzerland, 2001, U. Sheffield, Eng., 2004, U. Valencia, Spain, 2004, King George's Med. U., Lucknow, India, 2005, U. Pecs, Hungary, 2005. Postdoctoral tng. U. Basel, U. Calif., Berkeley, Bell Telephone Labs., Murray Hill, N.J., 1964-69; prof. biophysics Swiss Fed. Inst. Tech., Zürich, 1972—, chmn. dept. biology, 1995-2000; prof. structural biology The Scripps Rsch Inst., La Jolla, 2001—. Mem. coun. Internat. Union Pure and Applied Biophysics, 1975-78, 87-90, sec. gen., 1978-84, v.p., 1984-87; mem. gen. com. Internat. Coun. Sci. Unions, 1980-86, standing com. on free circulation of scientists, 1982-90. Editor Jour. Biomolecular NMR, Quar. Rev. Biophysics, Macromolecular Structures; contbr. articles to profl. jours. Recipient Friedrich Miescher prize Schweizerische Biochemische Gesellschaft, 1974, shield of faculty of medicine Tokyo U., 1983, P. Bruylants medal Cath. U. Louvain, 1986, Stein and Moore award Protein Soc., U.S., 1990, Louisa Gross Horwitz prize Columbia U., 1991, Gilbert N. Lewis medal U. Calif., Berkeley, 1991, Marcel Benoist prize Swiss Confederation, 1992, Disting. Svc. award Miami Winter Symposia, 1992, Prix Louis Jeantet de Médecine, Geneva, 1993, Kaj Linderstrøm-Lang prize Kaj Linderstrøm-Lang Found., Copenhagen, 1996, Eminent Scientist of RIKEN (Tokyo), 1997, Kyoto prize in Advanced Tech., 1998, Guenther Laukien prize Exptl. Nuclear Magnetic Resonance Conf., 1999, Otto Warburg medal Soc. for Biochemistry and Molecular Biology, Germany, 1999, World award M. Gorbatschow Found., 2002, Nobel Prize in Chemistry, 2002; Swiss award, 2002; Fgn. fellow Indian Nat. Sci. Acad.; hon. fellow NAS India. Fellow: AAAS; mem.: U.S. Nat.

Acad., World Innovation Found., Schweizerische Akademie der Medizinischen Wissenschaften, Schweizerische Akademie der Technischen Wissenschaften, Acad. Scis. Inst. France, Academia Europea, European Molecular Biology Orgn., Deutsche Akad. der Naturforscher Leopoldina, Indian Biophys. Soc. (hon.), Nuc. Magnetic Resonance Soc. Japan (hon.), Groupement Ampère (hon.), Latvian Acad. Sci. (hon.), European Soc. Scis. and Arts (hon.), Hungarian Acad. Sci. (hon.), Internat. Soc. Magnetic Resonance in Medicine (hon.), Royal Soc. Edinburgh (hon.), Royal Soc. Chemistry (hon.), Swiss Chem. Soc. (hon.), Nat. Magnetic Resonance Soc. India (hon.), Japanese Biochem. Soc. (hon.), Am. Acad. Arts and Scis. (hon.). Office: Inst Molecular Biology Biophysics 8093 Zurich Switzerland also: Scripps Rsch Inst Dept Molecular Biology 10550 N Torrey Pines Rd La Jolla CA 92037 Office Phone: +41-44-633-2473.

**WUZOR, GEOFFREY ONYEMA,** psychotherapist; b. Port Harcourt, Nigeria, Dec. 22, 1954; s. Amadioha and Epelle Grace Wuzor; m. Florence E. Wuzor, Oct. 29, 2004; children: Beatrice, Chelem, Ugwechi, Sunday, Prince stepchildren: Imani, Ikpoki, Ologhi. BS, U. England, Oxford, 1982, Southeastern U., 1986, MBA, 1988, AS, 1990; postgrad, Howard U., 1993—96; PhD, La Salle U., 1998. Adminstrv. asst. to dean Howard U., Sch. Divinity, Washington, 1991—96; asst. tchr. behavior mgmt. Edgemead-Raymond A. Rogers Jr. Sch., Upper Marlboro, Md., 1997—98; residential counselor Cmty. Residences - Queen Elizabeth Ho., Annandale, Va., 1997—98; adminstrv. asst. Md.-Nat. Capital Pk. and Planning Commn., Upper Marlboro, 1998—2001; program coord. Psychotherapeutic Outreach Svcs., Washington, 2000—03, program mgr., 2002—03; cons., cmty. support counselor Life Stride, Inc., 2004—05; residential program counselor Loudoun County Govt., Dept. Mental Health/Mental Retardation and Substance Abuse, Leesburg, Va., 2005—. Author: Essential Assessments in Behavioral Psychology, 2001, Management Pyramid, 1995. Gen. sec. Ogbakor Ikwerre USA, Wash., DC, pres. Mem.: Am. Psychological Assn. Democrat. Avocations: tennis, sports. Home: 6630 Ga Ave NW 204 Washington DC 20012 Office: Primary Care Support Svc PO Box 56698 Washington DC 20040 Office Phone: 202-251-5606. Office Fax: 202-723-9144. E-mail: geowuzor1@juno.com.

**WWGIACOMINI, GARY T.,** lawyer; BA, St. Mary's Coll., Calif., 1962; JD, U. Calif. Hastings Coll. of Law, 1965. Ptnr. Hanson Bridgett Marcus Vlahos Rudy LLP. Mem. Marin County Bd. of Supervisors, 1972—96; bd. dirs. Golden Gate Bridge, Highway and Transportation Dist.; coastal commsr., Calif.; mem. San Francisco Bay Conservation and Develop. Commn., Northwest Pacific Railroad Authority, Assn. of Bay Area Govt. Bd. and Local Agy. Formation Commn., Marin Agricultural Land Trust. Bd. dirs. Marconi Conference Ctr. Bd., North Bay Council, Marin Cmty. Found., 2003. Mem.: Marin County Bar Assn., Bar Assn. of San Francisco. Office: Hanson Bridgett 425 Market St San Francisco CA 94105*

**WYANT, CLYDE W., JR.,** manufacturing executive; b. Ada, Okla., Sept. 20, 1938; s. Clyde W. and Geneva Pauline (George) W.; m. Anne L. Edgerton, Nov. 23, 1984; children: Lynn, John, James, Markham, Carolyn BA in History, Stanford U., 1960; MBA, Harvard U., 1965. Asst. to pres. Helmerich & Payne, Inc., Tulsa, 1965-68, fin. v.p., 1968-85; exec. v.p., chief fin. officer Purolator Products Co. (formerly Facet Enterprises, Inc.), Tulsa, 1985-90; exec. v.p., CFO, treas. Lennox Internat., Inc., 1990-2001. Dir. Am. Nursery Products, Tahlequah, Okla., Hawkins Energy Co., Tulsa. Vice pres., trustee Holland Hall Sch., Tulsa, 1978-86; trustee Hillcrest Med. Ctr., Tulsa; vice chmn. admissions com. Tulsa Area United Way, 1978-86, chmn. allocations com., 1987, pres.-elect 1989, pres., 1990; fin. com. chmn. Community Network for Public Edn., Tulsa, 1983-85, Okla. Profl. Achievement Trust, 1989—; pres., treas., dir. Jr. Achievement of Greater Tulsa, 1978-86; community advisor Jr. League of Tulsa, 1979-82. Served to lt. U.S. Army, 1960-62 Recipient Bronze Leadership award Jr. Achievement, 1983 Mem. Fin. Execs. Inst. (pres. 1979-80), Am. Petroleum Inst., Mid-Continent Harvard Bus. Sch. Assn. (pres. 1980-82) Clubs: Tulsa Tennis (pres. 1985). Avocations: fishing, cooking, tennis. Office: Lennox Internat Inc PO Box 799900 Dallas TX 75379-9900 also: Two Warren Pl E 61st St Ste 1100 Tulsa OK 74136-0523 Home: 2140 Lake Park Blvd Richardson TX 75080-2252

**WYANT, JAMES CLAIR,** engineering company executive, educator; b. Morenci, Mich., July 31, 1943; s. Clair William and Idah May (Burroughs) W.; m. Louise Doherty, Nov. 20, 1971; 1 child, Clair Frederick. BS, Case Western Reserve, 1965; MS, U. Rochester, 1967, PhD, 1968. Engr. Itek Corp., Lexington, Mass., 1968-74; instr. Lowell (Mass.) Tech. Inst., 1969-74; prof. U. Ariz., Tucson, 1974—; 1984pres. WYKO Corp., Tucson, 1984—97; dir. optical sci. ctr. U. Ariz., 1999—2005, dean Coll. Optical Scis., 2005—. Chmn. Gordon Conf. on Holography Plymouth (N.H.) State Coll., 1984; vis. prof. U. Rochester, N.Y., 1983. Editor: Applied Optics and Optical Engineering, vols. VII-X, 1979-80, 83, 87. Recipient of Joseph Fraunhofer-Robert M. Burley Prize, 1992, Optical Soc. Am. Mem. Optical Soc. Am. (bd. dirs. 1979-81, Tech. Achievement award 1988, Joseph Fraunhofer award 1992, R&D 100 award 1993, Gold medal 2003), Soc. Photo-Optical Instrumentation Engring. (pres. 1986, Gold medal 2003). Home: 1881 N King St Tucson AZ 85749-9367 Office: Univ Ariz Optical Scis Ctr Tucson AZ 85721-0001 Business E-Mail: jcwyant@optics.arizona.edu.

**WYARD, VICKI SHAW,** investment and insurance company executive; b. LA, Oct. 29, 1945; d. Clinton Gilbert and Lois (Griswold) Shaw; m. Gary Edwin Wyard, July 1, 1966; children: Brett, Lori, Lisa. Student, Carleton Coll., 1963-65; BS, U. Minn., 1967. Cert. fin. planner. Systems analyst Univac Fed. Systems Div., Mpls., 1967-69, Internat. Timesharing Corp., Chaska, Minn., 1973-76; dir. Minnetonka Bd. of Edn., Excelsior, Minn., 1978-81, vice chairperson, 1981-84; fin. planner IDS Fin. Svcs., Mpls., 1986-89, trainer of planners, 1988-89; fin. planner, rep. Fin. Network Investment Corp., Torrance, Calif., 1989-91, Multi-Fin. Securities Corp., Mpls., 1991—2005. Bd. dirs. Westerlund Products Corp., Homescape Systems; seminar presenter in field. Contbr. articles to profl. jours. Trustee Washburn Child Guidance Ctr., Mpls., 1986-89; bd. dirs. Perspectives, Inc., St. Louis Park, Minn., 1988-2005, pres. bd., 1989-96; chmn. stewardship campaign Wayzata Cmty. Ch., 1996-98, pers. com., 1999-2005 Mem. Internat. Assn. Fin. Planners, Fin. Profls. Assn. (bd. dir., v.p. legis. and regulatory task force Mpls. chpt. 1990-92). Avocations: skiing, writing, reading, music, golf. Home and Office: 3630 Northome Rd Wayzata MN 55391-3021 Business E-Mail: vswyard@aol.com.

**WYATT, EDWARD AVERY, V,** city manager; b. Petersburg, Va., Nov. 1, 1941; s. Edward Avery IV and Martha Vaughan (Seabury) W.; m. Regina Helen Stec, Aug. 23, 1969; children: Edward Avery VI, Stephen Alexander, Kent Seabury. AS in Bus., Bluefield Coll.; BS in Bus., Pub. Adminstrn., Va. Poly. Inst. and State U., 1964; M.Commerce, U. Richmond, 1969; MA in Polit. Sci., Appalachian State U., 1977. Chief gen. svc. City of Petersburg, Va., 1966-67; asst. to city mgr. Va., 1967-70; city mgr. City of Washington, NC, 1970-73, City of Morganton, NC, 1973-78, City of Greenville, NC, 1978-82, City of Fairfax, Va., 1982-91; ncity mgr. City of Wilson, NC, 1991—2004. Adj. lectr. George E. Mason U. Bus. Sch., 1985-86, 1995-2003; bd. dir. Electricities of NC, sec. 2000; comunt. NC Ea. Mcpl. Power Agy., 1996-2004. Contbr. numerous articles to profl. jour. and newsletters. Chmn. NC Code Ofcl. Qualification Bd., 1980-82; mem. adv. bd. Wilson Salvation Army, 1992—; chmn. adv. coun. Wilson Boys and Girls Club; bd. dirs Flynn Home, Diversified Opportunites, Wilson United Way; chmn. Wilson Bd. Elections; festry. St. Timothy's Episc. Ch., clk., 2005. Served with USNG and USAR, 1964-70. Paul Harris fellow Rotary Internat.; Dennis Duffey Meml. award Fairfax Police Neut Club; named GEM of Yr., Wilson Downtown Devel. Corp., 2004; Wilson Hot Stove chpt. Red Barrett Spl. Achievement award Fairfax Police Youth Club, 2004. Internat. City Mgmt. Assn. (endowment com. 1985-2000, chair 1991-92, city mgr. plan task force 1993-94), Va. Local Govt. Mgmt. Assn. (pres. 1989-90), NC City/County Mgmt. Assn. (pres.2000-2001). Soc. Cincinnati in Va., Descendants of Francis Epes of Va., 2000-2003 (pres.), Wilson Hist. Assn., Rotary (asst. dist. gov. 2003—). Home: 1307 Waverly Rd NW Wilson NC 27896-1483

**WYATT, GERARD ROBERT,** biology professor, researcher; b. Palo Alto, Calif., Sept. 3, 1925; came to Can., 1935; s. Horace Graham and Mary Aimee (Strickland) W.; m. Sarah Silver Morton, Dec. 19, 1951 (dec. Mar. 1981); children— Eve Morton, Graham Strickland, Diana Silver; m. Mary Evelyn Rogers, Mar. 16, 1985 BA, U. B.C., Can., 1945; postgrad., U. Calif.-Berkeley, 1946-47; PhD, Cambridge U., 1950. Research scientist Can. Dept. Agr., Sault Ste. Marie, Ont., 1950-54; asst. prof. biochemistry Yale U., New Haven, 1954-60, assoc. prof., prof. biology, 1960-73; prof. biology Queen's U., Kingston, Ont., 1973-94, prof. emeritus, 1994—; sci. dir. Insect Biotech Can., 1990-93. Contbr. articles to profl. jours. Guggenheim fellow, 1956; Killam Research fellow, 1985 Fellow Royal Soc. Can. Avocation: natural history. Home: 114 Earl St Kingston ON Canada K7L 2H1 E-mail: wyatt@biology.queensu.ca.

**WYATT, HELEN J.,** special education educator; b. Fayette, Miss., Jan. 1, 1948; d. Milton Louis and Hazel James; m. Dewitt Wyatt, Aug. 26, 1973; children: Derrick Dewayne, Carla Amaris. BS in Bus. Edn., Alcorn A & M Coll., Lorman, Miss., 1969; MS in Spl. Edn., Alcorn State U., Miss., 1979, MEd in Adminstrn and Supervision, 1994; EdD in Spl. Svcs. and Exceptional Edn., Nova Southeastern U., 2000. Lic. bus. edn. tchr. Miss. State Dept. Edn., spl. edn. tchr. La. Dept. Edn., child search coord. La. Dept. Edn., parish or city sch. supr. instrn. La. Dept. Edn., parish or city sch. supr.dir. spl. edn. La. Dept. Edn., supr. student tchg. La. Dept. Edn. Tchr. St. Joachim Cath. Elem. Sch., Chgo., 1970—71; counselor, employment and tng. instr. Fayette Pub. Svc. Careers Program, 1971—74; exec. sec. Alcorn State Admission Office, Lorman, 1975—78; spl. edn. tchr. Tensas Parish Sch. Dist., St. Joseph, La., 1978—86, Concordia Parish Sch. Dist., Vidalia, La., 1987—89, facilitator individual edn. plan, 1989—2000; asst. prof., dir. Am. Reads-Miss. Alcorn State U., 2000—. Parish monitor Concordia Parish Spl. Edn. Dept., Vidalia, 1989—2000; state monitor La. State Dept. of Edn., Baton Rouge, 1995—2000; cons. automated individual edn. plan Region 6 parishes, Alexandria, La., 1998—2000; presenter for spl. edn. tngs. Concordia Spl. Edn. Dept., Vidalia, 1989—2000; adminstr. Alcorn State U., 2000—; trainer Americorps members Am. Reads-Miss., Alcorn State, 2000—; workshop presenter Multi-State Cross Program Tng. Conf., Nashville, 2005. Author: (practicum) Assisting Newly Hired Special Education Teachers to Function More Effectively Through Inservice Training and Mentoring; contbr. a, workshop presenter: 10th Nat. Svc. Orientation Life After AmeriCorps (Commendation, Gov. of Miss., 2003); writer (handbook) Guidebook for New Special Education Teachers (Commendation, Spl. Edn. Supr., 2000). Mentor for youth Zion Hill #1 Bapt. Ch., Natchez, Miss., 1995—2005. Recipient Cmty.-Based Tutorial Program grant, La. Dept. of Edn., 2000—06, Commendations for participating and moderating at several confs., Miss. Commn. for Vol. Svc., 2000—06, Commendation for judging reading and sci. fairs, Natchez-Adams Sch. Dist., 2001—04, Cert. of Excellence, S.W. Miss. Ctr. for Ednl. Tech., 2003, Read Across Am. Appreciation cert., NEA, 2006. Mem.: NAACP, CEC (assoc.), Alcorn Alumni Assn. (life), Phi Delta Kappa (assoc.; historian 1996—97, Cert. Appreciation 1997), Delta Sigma Theta (pres., v.p., treas. Vidalia Alumnae chpt. 1966—2006, Pres.'s award Vidalia Alumnae chpt. 2006). Democrat. Baptist. Avocations: travel, reading, completing puzzles, playing computer games. Home: 401 S Spruce St Vidalia LA 71373 Office: Alcorn State U 1000 ASU Dr 480 Alcorn State MS 39096 Office Phone: 601-877-6215. Office Fax: 601-877-6213. Personal E-mail: hjwyatt@bellsouth.net. E-mail: hwyatt@lorman.alcorn.edu.

**WYATT, JAMES FRANK, JR.,** lawyer; b. Talladega, Ala., Dec. 1, 1922; s. James Frank and Nannie Lee (Heaslett) W.; m. Rosemary Barbara Slone, Dec. 21, 1951; children: Martha Lee, James Frank III. BS, Auburn U., 1943; JD, Georgetown U., 1949, postgrad., 1950. Bar: D.C. 1949, Ala. 1950, Ill. 1953, U.S. Supreme Ct 1953. Atty. Office Chief Counsel, IRS, 1949-51; tax counsel Universal Oil Products Co., Des Plaines, Ill., 1951-63, asst. treas., 1963-66, v.p. fin., treas., 1966-75; treas. CF Industries, Inc., Long Grove, Ill., 1976-78, v.p. fin., treas., 1978-82; assoc. Tenney & Bentley, 1983-85, Arnstein, Gluck, Lehr, Barron & Milligan, 1985-88; pvt. practice, 1989—. Dir. 1st Nat. Bank, Des Plaines. Village trustee, Barrington, Ill., 1963-75; bd. dirs. Buehler YMCA, Barrington Twp. Republican Orgn., 1963—; pres. Barrington Area Rep. Workshops, 1962-63. Served to capt., Judge Adv. Gen. Corps AUS, 1944-47. Mem. Tax Execs. Inst. (v.p. 1965-66, chpt. pres. 1961-62), Fed., Am., Chgo. bar assns., Barrington Home Owners Assn. (pres. 1960-61), Newcomen Sco., Assn. U.S. Army, Scabbard and Blade, Phi Delta Phi, Sigma Chi. Clubs: Barrington Hills Country; Economics, University (Chgo.). Episcopalian. Home: 625 Concord Pl Barrington IL 60010-4508 Office: 200 Applebee St Barrington IL 60010-3063

**WYATT, JAMES LUTHER,** drapery hardware company executive; b. Williamsburg, Ky., May 13, 1924; s. Jesse Luther and Grace Edwina (Little) W.; m. Barbara Christman, Aug. 28, 1946; children— Linda Lou, William Charles Christman (dec.). BS, U. Ky., 1947, MS, 1948; Sc.D., Mass. Inst. Tech., 1952. Registered profl. engr., Ohio, Pa. Devel. engr. titanium div. Nat. Lead Co., Sayreville, NJ, 1948-50; tech. mgr., head, dept. metall. engring., mgr. new products Horizons, Inc., Cleve., 1953-57; cons., assoc. Booz, Allen & Hamilton, N.Y.C., 1957-61; v.p. program devel. Armour Research Found., Chgo., 1961-63; v.p. new product devel. Joy Mfg. Co., Pitts., 1963-67; v.p. corp. devel. Nat. Gypsum Co., Buffalo, 1967-69, Max Factor & Co., Hollywood, Calif., 1969-71; pres. Wyatt & Co., 1971—, Jimbabs, Inc., 1983—, Ambassador Industries, Inc., Los Angeles, 1988—. U.S. del. 1st World Metall. Congress. Contbr. tech., mgmt. papers to profl. lit.; patentee in field. Mem. Pompano Beach Power Squadron, adminstr. officer, 1991, exec. officer, 1992, comdr., 1993; chmn. bd. trustees Meth. Ch., 1992, mem. fin. com., 1993, mem. adminstrv. bd.; chmn. bd. trustees 1st United Meth. Ch., Boca Raton; bd. dirs., v.p. Golden Harbour Homeowners Assn., 1997—. Lt. col. USAAF, 1942-46. Elected to U. Ky. Hall of Distinction, 2001. Mem. AIME, Am. Soc. Metals, Econ. Club (Chgo.), Execs. Club (Chgo.), Univ. Club (N.Y.C.), Calif. Yacht Club, Pompano Beach Power Squadron (comdr.), Sigma Phi Epsilon, Alpha Chi Sigma. Clubs: Econs. (Chgo.), Execs. (Chgo.); Univ. (N.Y.C.); Calif. Yacht. Home: 510 Golden Harbour Dr Boca Raton FL 33432-2942 Office: 510 Golden Harbour Dr Boca Raton FL 33432-2942 Office Phone: 561-395-9148. Personal E-mail: jim_wyatt@juno.com.

**WYATT, JOSEPH LUCIAN, JR.,** lawyer, writer; b. Chgo., Feb. 21, 1924; s. Joseph Lucian and Cecile Gertrude (Zadico) W.; m. Marjorie Kathryn Simmons, Apr. 9, 1954; children: Daniel, Linn, Jonathan. AB in English Lit. with honors, Northwestern U., 1947; LLB, Harvard U., 1949. Bar: Calif. 1950, U.S. Dist. Ct. (cen. dist.) Calif. 1950, U.S. Ct. Appeals (9th cir.) 1950, U.S. Tax Ct., U.S. Supreme Ct. 1965. Assoc. firm Brady, Nossaman & Walker, Los Angeles, 1950-58, ptnr. L.A., 1958-61; pvt. practice L.A., 1961-71; sr. mem. Cooper, Wyatt, Tepper & Plant, P.C., L.A., 1971-79; of counsel Beardsley, Hufstedler & Kemble, L.A., 1979-81; ptnr. Hufstedler & Kaus, L.A., 1981-95; sr. of counsel Morrison & Foerster, L.A., 1995—. Mem. faculty Pacific Coast Banking Sch., Seattle, 1963-92, Southwestern Grad. Sch. Banking, 1988-89; advisor Restatement, Trusts 3d, 1988—. Author: Trust Administration and Taxation, 4 vols., 1964—; editor: Trusts and Estates, 1962-74. Lectr. continuing legal edn. programs, Calif. and Tex.; trustee Pacific Oaks Coll. and Children's Sch., 1969-97; counsel, parliamentarian Calif. Democratic party and presdl. conv. dels., 1971—; mem. Calif. State Personnel Bd., 1961-71, v.p., 1963-65, pres., 1965-67; bd trustees Calif. Pub. Employees Retirement System, 1963-71. 1st sgt. USAAF, 1943-45. Fellow Am. Coll. of Trust and Estate Counsel; mem. ABA, Internat. Acad. Estate and Trust Law (treas. 1990-96), Am. Law Inst., Calif. State Bar Assn. (del. state conf. 1956, 62-67), L.A. Bar Assn. (trustee 1956). Democrat. Christian Scientist. Avocations: fishing, composing doggerel. Home: 1119 Armada Dr Pasadena CA 91103-2805 Office Phone: 213-892-5200. E-mail: jwyatt@mofo.com, jwyatt3@charter.net.

**WYATT, LANCE B.,** pharmaceutical executive; married. BChemE, U. Ala. Registered profl. engr. Mgr. process/project engring. Abbott Labs., Rocky Mount, NC, 1976—81, various positions hosp. products divsn., 1981—84, plant quality assurance mgr., 1984—90, dir., divisional v.p. quality assurance hosp. products divsn. Abbott Park, Ill., 1990—91, divisional v.p. quality assurance and regulatory affairs pharm. products divsn., 1991—95, corp. officer, v.p. corp. engring. divsn., 1995—2000, sr. v.p., pres. specialty products divsn., 2000—02, sr. v.p. specialty products, 2002—. Lt. U.S. Army C.E.

**WYATT, LENORE,** civic worker; b. N.Y.C., June 12, 1929; d. Benedict S. Rosenfeld and Ora (Copel) Kanner; m. Bernard D. Copeland, May 17, 1953 (dec. March 1968); children: Harry (dec.), Robert (dec.); m. C. Wyatt Unger, Mar. 26, 1969 (dec. Feb. 1992); 1 child, Amy Unger; m. F. Lowry Wyatt, Sept. 12, 1992 (dec. Nov. 1996). Student, Mills Coll., 1946-48; BA, Stanford U., 1950, MA, 1952; postgrad., NYU, 1952-53. Instr. Stanford U., Palo Alto, Calif., 1952, Hunter Coll., N.Y.C., 1952-53, Calif. State U., Sacramento, 1956-60, U. Calif., Davis, 1965-69; property mgr. Unger, Demas & Markakis, Sacramento, 1974-83. Former actress and model; fin. com. Charles Wright Acad.; fin. mgr. several trusts. Pres. Sacramento Opera Assn., 1972—73; treas. Sacramento Children's Home, 1990—92, v.p., 1992—; former mem. bd. dirs. Sutter Hosp. Aux., Sutter Hosp. Med. Rsch. Found., Sacramento Symphony League, Temple B'nai Israel Sisterhood, Sacramento chpt. Hadassah, Sacramento Children's Home Guild; formerly active Sacramento Opera Assn., Crocker Soc. of Crocker Art Gallery, Sacramento Symphony Assn., Sacramento Repertory Theater Assn.; founding mem. Tacoma Cmtys. Art Sch.; past mem. bd. dirs. Charles Wright Acad.; past mem., bd. dirs. Tacoma Art Mus. Mem.: Century Orthop. Guild (pres. 2006—), Pathfinders of Palm Springs, Stanford U. Alumni Assn. (past bd. dirs. Sacramento), Am. Contract Bridge League, Sacramento Pioneer Assn., Del Paso Country Club (past capt. women's golf group, Sacramento), Thunderbird Country Club, Tacoma Club, Wash. Athletic Club, Maui Country Club, Tacoma Country and Golf Club, Sutter Club. Republican. Jewish. Avocations: golf, duplicate bridge, sculpting. Home: 70551 Placerville Rd Rancho Mirage CA 92270

**WYATT, OSCAR SHERMAN, JR.,** energy company executive; b. Beaumont, Tex., July 11, 1924; s. Oscar Sherman Sr. and Eva (Codey) Wyatt; m. Lynn Sakowitz; children: Steven, Douglas, Oscar Sherman III, Brad. BS in Mech. Engring., Tex. A&M U., 1949. With Kerr-McGee Co., 1949, Reed Roller Bit Co., 1949—51; ptnr. Wymore Oil Co., 1951—55; founder Coastal Corp., Corpus Christi, Tex., 1955—2001, chmn. exec. com. Houston. Trustee DeBakey Med. Found., 1987—; founding mem., bd. stewards Tex. Aviation Hall of Fame, 1997—. With USAF, WWII. Office: 3355 W Alabama Ste 500 Houston TX 77098 Office Phone: 713-877-6700. E-mail: ow@nucoastal.com.

**WYATT, RICHARD L., JR.,** lawyer; b. Andalusia, Ala., 1953; BA, Auburn Univ., 1975; JD, Emory Univ., 1979. Bar: Ga. 1979, DC 1990. Outside counsel Texas Air, Continental Airlines, Eastern Airlines, 1983—91; now ptnr., chair advocacy dept., labor and employment practice group Akin Gump Strauss Hauer & Feld LLP, Washington; and mem. mgmt. com., 1998—. Named one of Top Employment/Labor Lawyers, National Law Journal, 1997. Office: Akin Gump Strauss Hauer & Feld LLP Robert S Strauss Bldg 1333 New Hampshire Ave NW Washington DC 20036-1564 Office Phone: 202-887-4048. Office Fax: 202-955-7618. Business E-Mail: rwyatt@akingump.com.

**WYATT, ROBERT LEE, IV,** lawyer; s. Robert Lee III and Louise Carole (Bard) W.; m. Vicki Harris Wyatt. BS, Southeastern Okla. State U., 1986; JD, U. Okla., 1989. Bar: Okla. 1989, U.S. Dist. Ct. (we. dist.) Okla. 1990, U.S. Ct. Appeals (10th cir.) 1990, U.S. Dist. Ct. (no. dist.) Okla. 1991, U.S. Ct. Appeals (8th cir.) 1991, U.S. Supreme Ct. 1993, U.S. Dist. Ct. (Ea. Dist.) 2004. Intern Okla. State Bur. Investigation, Oklahoma City, 1988-89, guest lectr., 1989; dep. spl. counsel Gov. of Okla., 1995; atty. Jones & Wyatt, Enid, Okla., 1989-2000. Criminal justice panel atty. We. Dist. Okla., Wyatt Law Office, 2000—. Contbr. Vernon's Forms Oklahoma, Criminal Law and Procedure, 1999. Counsel to Fire Civil Svc. Commn. City of Enid, 1998-2000. Mem. ABA (mem. criminal and litigation sects.), Okla. Bar Assn. (mem. ins., mem. criminal law com., guest lectr. 2003-05), Oklahoma County Bar Assn., Okla. Criminal Def. Lawyers Assn. (Internet Champion of Liberty award, 2003), Nat. Inst. for Trial Advocacy, Nat. Assn. Criminal Defense Lawyers (life mem.), Luther Bohanon Am. Inn of Ct. (barrister), Phi Delta Phi, Alpha Chi. Democrat. Baptist. Office Phone: 405-234-5500. E-mail: bobwyatt@wyattlaw.com.

**WYATT, ROBERT ODELL,** journalism educator; b. Jackson, Tenn., Feb. 7, 1946; s. Odell and Sera Mae (Mebane) Wyatt. BA, U. of the South, 1968; MA, Northwestern U., 1970, PhD, 1973; MS, U. Tenn., 1977; Cert. in Theology, Seabury-Western Theol. Sem., 2002; MTS, Vanderbilt U., 2004. Ordained priest Episcopal Ch., 2004. From asst. to assoc. prof. U. Tenn., Nashville, 1973-79; assoc. prof. Mid. Tenn. State U., Murfreesboro, 1979-84, prof., 1984—. Office Comm. Rsch., 1989—. Vis. prof. comm. U. Caen, France, 1994; cons. in comm.; mem. Pulitzer Prize Jury, 1980, 85, 91, 93, 99, chair jury, 1985, 91, 93, 99; bd. trustees Seabury-Western Theol. Sem., Evanston, Ill., 1996-2001. Author: Free Expression and the American Public, 1991 (Sigma Delta Chi award for rsch. on journalism 1992); co-author, Free Expression in 5 Cultures, 2004; editor book sect. The Nashville Tennessean, 1978-93; contbr. articles to profl. jours. Worcester prize World Assn. for Pub. Opinion Rsch., 1996, Vanderbilt U. Founder's medal, 2004. Mem. Assn. for Edn. in Journalism and Mass Comm., Internat. Comm. Assn., Am. Assn. Pub. Opinion Rsch. Democrat. Episcopalian. Home: 3526 Maple Ave Berwyn IL 60402 Office: St Helena's Episcopal Ch Burr Ridge IL 60527 Office Phone: 708-662-5660.

**WYATT, ROLAND GRATTS,** music educator, voice educator, consultant; b. Ft. Worth, Tex., June 23, 1932; s. Charles Henry Robinson and Marguerite Collins Pennybacker; m. Deborah Kay West, Nov. 28, 1987 (div. Dec. 22, 2001). MusB in edn., Lincoln U., Jefferson, Mo., 1954; MA, San Jose State U., Calif. 1968. Instr. Yankton Coll., SD, 1967—68; asst. prof. Seattle U., 1968—70, U. Wis., Eau Claire, 1970—71; vis. prof. Humboldt State U., Arcata, Calif., 1971—72; prof. Mannes Sch. of Music, NYC, 1972—74; lectr. San Francisco State U., 1974—76; voice coach Manhattan Transfer, LA, 1974—95; vis. prof. SUNY, 1986—87; cons., therapist, tchr. Roland Wyatt Voice Studio, LA, San Francisco and San Diego, 1987—. Dir. Inst. of Self Directed Learning, Pitts. and San Diego, 1991—. Performer: (recording) Voice Lessons with Manhattan Transfer, 1989; co-author with Dr. Hans von Leden (book) A Handbook for Correcting Vocal Problems, 2003. Recipient Robert Shaw award, 1958, Mack Harrel scholarship at Aspen Music Sch., Am. Choral Soc. Conducting award, 1969, 1972. Office: Roland Wyatt Voice Studio Seminars 3306 E Glenn St Tucson AZ 85716-2240 E-mail: wyattvoice-studio@sbcglobal.com.

**WYATT, WILSON WATKINS, JR.,** communications executive, public affairs executive, writer; b. Louisville, Dec. 3, 1943; s. Wilson Watkins Sr. and Anne (Duncan) W.; m. Jane Clay, Aug. 15, 1964 (dec. 1975); children: Carol, Wilson III, Sarah Wyatt; m. Kathleen Valonis, June 14, 1998. Student, U. of the South, 1961-65. Reporter The Courier-Jour., Louisville, 1965-67; pub. rels. account exec. Doe-Anderson Advt., Louisville, 1967-68; account exec. Zimmer-McClaskey-Lewis (McCann-Ericksn Advtsg.), Louisville, 1968-70; ptnr. Bennett & Wyatt Pub. Rels., Louisville, 1970-71; state rep., vice chair appropriations and revenue com. Ky. Gen. Assembly, Frankfort, 1969-71; exec. dir. Louisville Cen. Area Inc., 1971-77; dir. corp. affairs and communications Brown & Williamson Tobacco Corp., Louisville, 1977-82; v.p. pub. policy BATUS Inc., Washington, 1982-86, v.p. corp. affairs Louisville, 1986-90; sr. v.p. corp. affairs PNC Fin. Corp., Pitts., 1990-92; sr. v.p. corp. comm. and govt. rels. The Travelers Cos., Hartford, 1992-94; exec. dir., CEO Am. Acad. of Actuaries, Washington, 1995-98; CEO Wyatt Comm. Cons., 1998—. Lead U.S. def. pub. rels. activities against hostile takeover for B.A.T. Industries, U.K., 1989-90; chmn. Travelers Found., 1991-94; moderator Working Writers Forum, Md., 2006-. Mem. youth adv. com. Atlantic Inst., 1967-68; del. North Atlantic Treaty Assn. Young Leaders Conf., 1967; chmn. Leadership Effort for All Dems., Ky., 1967-68; regional campaign coord. for Robert F. Kennedy, Ky.-Ind., 1968; mem. Pres.'s Forum, Washington, 1988-91; trustee Conn. Policy Econ. Commn., 1992-95; mem. exec. com. Hartford Downtown Coun., 1992-94; mem. adv. bd. Dem. Leadership Coun., Washington; mem. Am. Savings Edn. Campaign U.S. Dept. Labor, 1996.

Named one of Outstanding Young Men in Am., Ky. Jaycees, 1973. Mem. The Pres.'s Forum, Pub. Affairs Rsch. Coun. (conf. bd. 1986-95), Forum I, Assn. Chief Execs. Coun., Pub. Affairs Coun. (bd. dirs. 1982—, exec. com. 1982-86), Speakers Club (Washington), Greater Hartford C. of C. (exec. com. 1992-94), Hartford Stage (bd. dirs. 1993-95), Md. Writers Assn., Eastern Shore Writers Assn. (v.p. 2006—), Working Writers Forum (moderator). Avocations: boating, photography, writing. Home and Office: PO Box 298 Bozman MD 21612 Personal E-mail: wwwtwo@earthlink.net.

**WYCHE, CYRIL THOMAS,** lawyer; b. Greenville, S.C., Jan. 28, 1926; C. Granville and Mary (Wheeler) W.; m. Harriet Smith, June 19, 1948; children: Sara McCall, Bradford Wheeler, Mary Frances. BE, Yale U., 1946; LLB, U. Va., 1949; LLD (hon.), Clemson U., 1997, Furman U., 1997; HLD (hon.), Wofford Coll. Bar: S.C. 1948, U.S. Dist. Ct. S.C. 1950, U.S. Ct. Appeals (4th cir.) 1952, U.S. Ct. Claims 1964, U.S. Supreme Ct. 1970. Ptnr. Wyche, Burgess, Freeman & Parham, P.A., Greenville, SC, 1948—. Pres., bd. dirs. YMCA, Greenville, 1960; pres Greenville Little Theatre, 1965, Arts Festival Assn., Greenville, 1970, Greenville Community Corp., 1976—; bd. dirs. Greater Greenville C. of C., 1980. Served with USN, 1943-46. Named Environmentalist of Yr. State of S.C., 1979; recipient Conservation award Gulf Oil Corp., 1983, Alexander Calder award, 1996, Garden Clubs Am., 1999, Oak Leaf award The Nature Conservancy, 1996, Order of the Palmetto award S.C. Gov., 1996. Mem. ABA (Environ. award 2002), S.C. Bar Assn., Greenville County Bar Assn., Am. Judicature Soc., Nat. Wildlife Fedn. (Spl. Conservation Achievement award 2003). Presbyterian. Avocations: skiing, scuba diving, piano, tennis, white water canoeing. Office: Wyche Burgess Freeman & Parham 44 E Camperdown Way PO Box 728 Greenville SC 29602-0728 Office Phone: 864-242-8213. E-mail: twyche@wyche.com.

**WYCHE, JAMES RAMAGE,** lawyer; s. Madison Baker Wyche III and Marguerite Ramage Wyche; m. Sally B. Hubbard. BS magna cum laude in Fin., Clemson U., 2000; JD cum laude, Duke U., 2003. Intern Sen. J. Strom Thurmond, 1997; atty. Kennedy Covington Lobdell & Hickman, Charlotte, NC, 2003—. Scholar, Wachovia Bank Nat. Assn., 1998—2000. Mem.: Phi Kappa Phi, Beta Gamma Sigma, Omicron Delta Kappa. Office: Kennedy Covington 214 N Tryon St 47th Flr Charlotte NC 28202 Office Phone: 704-331-7400.

**WYCHE, MADISON BAKER, III,** lawyer; b. Albany, Ga., Aug. 11, 1947; s. Madison Baker Jr. and Merle (McKemie) W.; m. Marguerite Jernigan Ramage, Aug. 7, 1971; children: Madison Baker IV, James Ramage. BA, Vanderbilt U., 1969, JD, 1972. Bar: Ga. 1972, U.S. Dist. Ct. (mid. dist.) Ga. 1972, U.S. Ct. Appeals (5th cir.) 1973, S.C. 1976, U.S. Dist. Ct. S.C. 1977, U.S. Ct. Appeals (4th cir.) 1977, U.S. Supreme Ct. 1980, U.S. Ct. Appeals (11th cir.) 1981, U.S. Dist. Ct. (no. dist.) Ga. 1995. Assoc. Perry, Walters, Lippitt & Custer, Albany, 1972-76, Thompson, Ogletree & Deakins, Greenville, SC, 1976-77, Ogletree, Deakins, Smoak & Stewart, Greenville, 1977-80; shareholder Ogletree, Deakins, Nash, Smoak & Stewart P.C., Greenville, 1980—. Bd. dirs. Happy Ho., Inc., Albany. Co-editor Labor and Employment Law for South Carolina Lawyers, 1999. Co-incorporator, sec. State of Tenn. Intercollegiate State Legislature, Nashville, 1967-69; mem. employer and employee rels. com., legal issues & workplace policy com. N.C. Citizens for Bus. and Industry, Raleigh, 1984—; mem. Greenville C. of C., gen. counsel, 2003— bd. dirs.; mem. Advantage Greenville, United Way Greenville; bd. dirs. Palmetto Soc. of the United Way, 1992-2004; mem. vestry Christ Episcopal Ch., Greenville, 1981-85; treas. All Saints Episcopal Ch., Linville, NC 2001-05; mem. bd. visitors Clemson U. 1998-2001, mem. continuing/distance edn. advancement bd., 2003—; bd. dirs. Blue Ridge coun. Boy Scouts Am., 1999-2000; bd. dirs. Internat. Arts Festival, ARTISPHERE, Greenville, 2003—. Capt. U.S. Army, 1969-77. Recipient Eagle Scouts award Boy Scouts Am., 1961, God and Country award, 1961. Mem. ABA, Coll. of Labor and Employment Lawyers, S.C. Bar Assn. (unauthorized practice of law com. 1977-95, chmn. 1982-92, ho. of dels. 1991-98, 2004—, nominating com. 1992-95, CLE divsn., chmn., 1997-98, exec. com. 1995-99, chmn. seminars subcom. 1995-97), Ga. Bar Assn., Atlanta Bar Assn., S.C. Def. Trial Lawyers Assn., St. Andrews Soc. Upper S.C. (bd. dirs. 1979-81, v.p. 1986-87, pres. 1988-90, scholarship chmn. 1998—), Vanderbilt U. Alumni Assn. (pres. S.C. chpt. 1990-95, bd. dirs. 1994—), The Poinsett Club (v.p., bd. dirs.) (Greenville, S.C.), Rotary (bd. dirs. 1982-84, Paul Harris fellow 1986), Commerce Club of Greenville (bd. dirs. 1990—), Phi Delta Phi. Office: Ogletree Deakins Nash Smoak & Stewart PO Box 2757 Greenville SC 29602-2757 Office Phone: 864-271-1300.

**WYCHE, RUTH SKYLER,** rehabilitation contractor, researcher; b. Houston, Aug. 10, 1955; d. Malcolm Joseph and Dorothy Earlene (King) LeGrande; 1 child: Patricia Ann. BS, Sam Houston State U., 1977, lic. min., 1996; cert., Inst. Child Lit., 1988; postgrad., San Jacinto Coll., 1993, Sam Houston State U., 1996-2000. Cert.elem. tchr., Tex., 1977. Med. records Green Acres Convalescent Home, Huntsville, Tex., 1979-80, 81-82; tchr. Magnolia (Tex.) High Sch., 1980-81; sec. Harris Engring., Huntsville, 1982-83; artist M&M Design, Huntsville, 1983-84; fin. sec. First United Meth. Ch., Huntsville, 1984-87; nursery sch. coord., 1986-87; contractor Tex. Rehabilation Commn., Huntsville, 1986-87, Pasadena, Tex., 1990-92; counselor Houston Substance Abuse Clinic, Pasadena and Houston, 1992-93, Lake Charles Substance Abuse Clinic, 1992-93; administrt. Johnson Glass & Mirror, Pasadena, 1993-96; contractor Tex. Rehab. Commn., Pasadena, 1996-97. Author poetry, 1985. Ballot counter Voting Polling places, Huntsville, 1977, 78, 79. Recipient Lady Kentiggerma Soc. Creative Anachronism, 1986, Sable Comet, 1986. Mem. NAFE, Tex. Acad. Sci., Phi Beta Chi. Republican. Avocations: biology, mathematics, writing, crochet, driving.

**WYCKOFF, E. LISK, JR.,** lawyer; b. Middletown, NJ, Jan. 29, 1934; m. Elizabeth Ann Kuphal; children: Jenny Adele, Edward Lisk III, Elizabeth Hannah Longstreet. BA. Duke U., 1955; JD, U. Mich., 1960. Bar: N.Y. 1961, U.S. Dist. Ct. (so. and ea. dists.) N.Y. 1962, U.S. Ct. Appeals (2d cir. 1963), U.S. Tax Ct. 1974. Ptnr. Trubin Sillcocks, 1975—79, Kelley Drye & Warren, 1979—93, Kramer, Levin, N.Y., N.Y., 1993—2001. Lectr. Practising Law Inst., 1970—, various profl. and bus. orgns. in U.S. and abroad; spl. counsel N.Y. Bankers Assn., 1974-98; counsel N.Y. State Senate Com. Housing and Urban Renewal, 1969-71, N.Y. State Senate Com. Judiciary, 1963-64, Com. Affairs of the City of N.Y., 1962; mem. N.Y.C. Mayor's Taxi Study Commn., 1967 Directing editor, author West's McKinney's Forms on Estates and Trusts, 1974—; commentator McKinney's Not-For-Profit Corp. law, 1995—; contbr. articles to profl. jours. Trustee Inner-City Scholarship Fund., Inc., 1993—2004; chmn., bd. dirs. 1652 Wyckoff House and Assn., Inc., 1982—; trustee Goodspeed Opera Co., 1996—, Florence Griswold Mus., 1997—; trustee emeritus Wildlife Conservation Soc., 1993—; elector Wadsworth Atheneum; trustee, pres. Homeland Found., 1988—; mem. Concilium Socialium to Vatican Mus., 1991—; trustee emeritus NY Geneal. and Biographic Soc., 2002—. Named papal hon. Knight Commdr., Order of St. Gregory the Great, 1998; recipient Star, 2002. Fellow: Am. Bar Found., Am. Coll. Trust and Estate Counsel; mem.: ABA, St. Nicholas Soc., Holland Soc., Assn. of Bar of City of N.Y., N.Y. State Bar Assn., Internat. Bar Assn., Internat. Fiscal Assn., Old Lyme Country Club, N.Y. Yacht Club, Essex Yacht Club (Conn.), Mashomack Fish and Game Preserve Club (Pine Plains, N.Y.), Racquet and Tennis Club (N.Y.C.), Knickerbocker Club. Avocations: tennis, sailing.

**WYCKOFF, SYLVIA SPENCER,** art educator, artist; b. Pitts., Nov. 14, 1915; d. Lynn Boyd Wyckoff and Bess Jeannete Hohes. BFA, Syracuse U., NY, 1937, MFA, 1944. Cert. art tchr. NY, 1987. Art tchr. various pub. schs., Homer and Cobleskill, NY, 1937—42; instr. Coll. Visual Arts, Syracuse U., 1942—81, asst. to full prof., chmn. freshman core program, 1971—72, chmn. London art program; ret., 1981. Adj. art instr. Cazenovia Coll.; judge arts recognition and talent search Nat. Found. Arts, Princeton, NJ, 1983. Exhibited in group shows, Cortland, NY, 1938, Syracuse Regional Show, 1942—45 (1st prize for watercolor, 1943) with Rick Wolff, Oneida, NY, exhibitions include Nat. League Am. Pen Women, NYC and Washington, DC, 1968 (1st prize for watercolor, 1945), Chancellor's Office, Syracuse U., 1976, St. Lawrence U., Munson William Proctor Mus. Art, Utica, NY, 1980—81, Cazenovia Watercolor Soc., 1981—95, Core Faculty-Wells Coll., one-woman shows include

Coleman Hall, Cazenovia, NY, 1975, New Coll. Art Bldg., Cazenovia Coll. 2004. Dispatcher CAVAC (Cazenovia Area Vol. Corps., NY, 1974—91; vol. Stone Quarry Art Pk. Recipient 1st prize for watercolor, Onondaga Hist. Soc., 1945, Gordon Steele award for painting, Assoc. Artists of Syracuse, 1968, spl. award, NY State Tchrs. Assn., 1981. Mem.: Nat. Mus. Women in Arts (charter mem.), Stone Quarry Art Pk., Manson Williams Proctor Mus., Cazenovia Watercolor Soc. (founder 1976; first recipient Priscilla Hancock award 1992), Sigma Chi Alpha, Eta Phi Upsilon (hon.), Alpha Xi Delta (award to 10% Top Alumnae 1967). Presbyterian. Achievements include first woman on athletic bd., Syracuse U., 1974; named in honor of Spl. Sylvia Wyckoff Book award, Alpha Sigma Lambda, U. Coll. Syracuse, NY, 1981. Avocations: painting, drawing, bridge, knitting. Home: 4 Liberty St Cazenovia NY 13035

**WYCOFF, CHARLES COLEMAN,** writer, retired anesthesiologist; b. Glazier, Tex., Sept. 2, 1918; s. James Garfield and Ada Sharpe (Braden) W.; m. Gene Marie Henry, May 16, 1942 (dec.); children: Michelle, Geoffrey, Brian, Roger, Daniel, Norman, Irene, Teresa. AB, U. Calif., Berkeley, 1941; MD, U. Calif., San Francisco, 1943; postgrad., U. London, 1954-55. Diplomate Am. Bd. Anesthesiology. Intern San Francisco County Hosp., 1943-44; resident in anesthesiology U. Calif. Hosp., San Francisco, 1944-45; tng. in anesthesiology Walter Reed Gen. Hosp., 1945; founder The Wycoff Group of Anesthesiology, San Francisco, 1947-53; chief of anesthesia St. Joseph's Hosp., San Francisco, 1947-52, organizer residency tng. program in anesthesiology, 1950, San Francisco County Hosp., 1954, chief anesthesia, 1953-54; tchr. practice anesthesiology Presbyn. Med. Ctr., NYC, 1955-63; asst. prof. anesthesiology Columbia U., NYC, 1955-63; clin. practice anesthesiology St. Francis Meml. Hosp., San Francisco, 1963-84. Prodr., dir. films on regional anesthesia; contbr. articles to sci. jours. Scoutmaster Boy Scouts Am., San Francisco, 1953-55. Capt. M.C., U.S. Army, 1945-47. Mem. Alumni Faculty Assn. Sch. Medicine U. Calif.-San Francisco (councilor at-large 1979-80). Democrat. Avocations: researching origins of human behavior, writing, gardening. Home: 3875 Castro Valley Blvd Spc 55 Castro Valley CA 94546-4584

**WYCOFF, WILLIAM MORTIMER,** lawyer; b. Pitts., Jan. 1, 1941; s. William Clyde and Margaret (Shaffer) W.; m. Deborah Seyl, Jan. 25, 1963; children: Ann Richardson, Pieter Claesen. AB, Cornell U., 1963; JD, Northwestern U., 1966. Bar: Pa. 1967, U.S. Ct. Appeals (3d cir.) 1967), U.S. Dist. Ct. (we. dist.) Pa. 1967. Assoc., now ptnr. Thorp Reed and Armstrong, Pitts., 1966—. Pres. Children's Home Pitts-78, 86-88, 2004-; pres. Pressley Ridge Schs., Pitts., 1988-90, now bd. dirs.; pres Pressley Ridge Found., 1998-2004, no bd. dirs.; pres. bd. dirs. Pitts. Dance Coun., 1991-94; trustee Pitts. Cultural Trust, 1991-94. Fellow Internat. Acad. Trial Lawyers, Am. Coll. Trial Lawyers; mem. Acad. Trial Lawyers Allegheny County. Avocations: photography, skiing, biking, hiking, golf. Office: Thorp Reed & Armstrong LLP One Oxford Ctr 14th Fl 301 Grant St Pittsburgh PA 15219 Office Phone: 412-394-7782. Business E-Mail: wwycoff@thorpreed.com.

**WYDEN, RON (RONALD LEE WYDEN),** senator; b. Wichita, Kans., May 3, 1949; s. Peter and Edith W.; m. Laurie Oseran, Sept. 5, 1978 (div. 1999); 2 children: m. Nancy Bass, Sept. 2005. Student, U. Santa Barbara, 1967-69 AB in Polit. Sci., with distinction, Stanford U., 1971; JD, U. Oreg., 1974. Bar: Oreg. 1975. Campaign aide Senator Wayne Morse, 1972, 74; co-founder, co-dir. Oreg. Gray Panthers, 1974-80; dir. Oreg. Legal Services for Elderly, 1977-79; instr. gerontology U. Oreg., 1976, U. Portland, 1980, Portland State U., 1979; mem. 97th-104th Congresses from 3d Oreg. dist., Washington, 1981-96; US Senator form Oreg., 1996—. Mem. com. fin. US Senate, com. intelligence, com. energy and natural resources, com. budget, spl. com. on aging. Contbr. articles to profl. journals. Mem. Oreg. Environmental Coun. Recipient Service to Oreg. Consumers award Oreg. Consumers League, 1978, Citizen of Yr. award Oreg. Assn. Social Workers, 1979, Significant Service award Multnomah County Area Agy. on Aging, 1980, Philip A. Hart Pubilc Svc. award Consumer Fedn. Am., 1999, Champion of Sci. award, U. Oreg./The Sci. Coalition, 2003; named Young Man of Yr. Oreg. Jr. C. of C., 1980, Senator of Yr. Nat. Assn. Police Orgn., 1997, People of Yr. (with Rep. Christopher Cox) PC Computing mag., 1999, Legis. of Yr. Info. Tech. Coun., 2000; named to Legis. Hall of Fame Am. Electronics Assn. Mem. ABA, Iowa Bar Assn., Oreg. Bar Assn. Democrat. Jewish. Office: US Senate 230 Dirksen Senate Office Bldg Washington DC 20510-0001 also: District Office Ste 585 1220 SW 3rd Ave Portland OR 97204 Office Phone: 202-224-5244, 503-326-7525. Office Fax: 202-228-2717.*

**WYDICK, RICHARD CREWS,** lawyer, educator; b. Pueblo, Colo., Nov. 1, 1937; s. Charles Richard and Alice Wydick; m. Judith Brandli James, 1961; children: William Bruce, Derrick Cameron. BA, Williams Coll., 1959; LL.B. Stanford U., 1962. Bar: Calif. bar 1962. Asso. firm Brobeck, Phleger & Harrison, San Francisco, 1966-71; mem. faculty U. Calif. Law Sch., Davis 1971—, prof. law, 1975—2003, dean, 1978-80, prof. emeritus, 2003—. Author: Plain English for Lawyers, 5th edit., 2005 Served to capt. USAR, 1962-66. Office: Sch Law U Calif Davis CA 95616

**WYDRA, FRANK THOMAS,** healthcare executive; b. Republic, Pa., May 11, 1939; s. Frank T. and Anne M. (Kois) W.; m. Karen Branch, June 24, 1961; children: Denise Lee, Sheryl Lynn, Frank Thomas III. BS in Mgmt., U. Ill., 1961. V.p. Allied Supermarkets, Inc., Detroit, 1967-75; sr. v.p. HGH Health System, Detroit, 1975-85; pres. Radius Health Care Sysytems, Inc., Detroit, 1983-85; cons. Birmingham, Mich., 1985-88; exec. v.p. The Chi Group, Ann Arbor, Mich., 1988-91; mng. ptnr., CEO, owner IRI, Mgmt. Cons., Detroit, 1991—. Lectr. various profl. groups; bd. dirs. Mich. Health Systems Inc., Saber-Salisbury Assocs. Inc., Midwestern Health Ctr., Multi-Care Med. Inc., RHS Inc. Author: Learner Controlled Instruction, 1980, (with others) Hospital Survival Guide, 1984, The Cure, 1992; creator 2 mgmt. games Performulations, 1978, The Dynamics of Power and Authority, 1981; contbr. articles to profl. jours. Personnel program advisor Mich. State U. Sch. Labor Relations, 1979-83; chmn. new program Wayne County Community Coll., Detroit, 1979-80; bd. dirs. Detroit Metro Youth Found., 1980-83, State Mich. Health Occupations Council, Lansing, 1982-85. Capt. U.S. Army, 1961-63. Recipient numerous awards ASTD, Nat. Soc. Performance and Instrm., Mich. SOc. Instructional Tech., Supermarket Inst. Mem. Am. Hosp. Assn., Planning Soc. of Am. Hosp. Assn., Hosp. Personnel Adminstrs. Assn. (pres. 1981-82, numerous awards), Am. Mgmt. Assn., Am. Soc. Hosp. Pers.Adminstrs. (bd. dirs. 1981-83), Mich. Soc. Instrnl. Tech. (life, pres. 1973-74), Mich. Hosp. Assn., Employers Assn. Detroit (bd. dirs. 1982-85), Detroit Athletic Club. Avocations: writing, sailing. Home: 8945 Reese Rd Clarkston MI 48348

**WYETH, ANDREW NEWELL,** artist; b. Chadds Ford, Pa., July 12, 1917; s. Newell Converse and Carolyn (Bockius) W.; m. Betsy Merle James, May 15, 1940; children: Nicholas, James Browning. Educated pvt. tutors; DFA (hon.), Colby Coll., Maine, 1954, Harvard U., 1955, Dickinson Coll., 1958, Swarthmore Coll., 1958, Nasson Coll., 1963, U. Md., U. Del. Northeastern U., Temple U., 1964; LHD (hon.), Tufts U., 1963; DFA (hon.), Princeton U., 1965; LHD (hon.), Franklin and Marshall Coll., 1965, Lincoln U., 1966, Amherst Coll., 1967; DFA (hon.), Bowdoin Coll., 1970; LHD (hon.), Ursinus Coll., 1971; DFA (hon.), U. Pa., 1972; LHD (hon.), West Chester U., 1984; DFA (hon.), Dartmouth Coll., 1984, Bates Coll., 1987; LHD (hon.), U. Vt., 1988. Artist, landscape painter, 1936—; first one-man show William Macbeth Gallery, N.Y., 1937; first solo exhbn. ever held in White House, 1970, first exhbn. by living Am. artist Royal Acad. Arts, London, 1980; exhibited Doll & Richards, Boston, 1938, 40, 42, 44, Cornell U., 1938, Macbeth Gallery, 1938, 41, first tempera show, 1943, 45, Currier Gallery, Manchester, N.H., 1939, room of watercolors, Art Inst. Chgo., 1941; room at Realist and Magic Realist show, Mus. Modern Art, N.Y.C., 1943; one-man exhbn., M. Knoedler & Co., N.Y.C., 1953, 58, Mass. Inst. Tech., Cambridge, 1960, Fogg Art Mus., William Farnsworth Library and Mus., 1963, Helga Pictures at numerous art museums, other univs. and museums; also exhbns. Arnot Mus., Elmira, N.Y., 1986, Seibu-Pisa, Tokyo, 1986, Kenesaw (Ga.) Mus. Art, 1986, Thomasville (Ga.) Art Ctr., 1987, Acad. of the Arts of USSR, Leningrad, 1987, Acad. of the Arts USSR, Moscow, 1987, Nat. Gallery of Art, Washington, 1987, Corcoran Gallery Art, Washington, 1987, An American Vision: Three Generations of

Wyeth Art, various mus., 1987, Dallas Mus. Art, 1987, Mus. Fine Arts, Boston, 1988, Terra Mus. Am. Art, Chgo., 1988, Mus. Fine Arts, Houston, 1988, Setagaya Art Mus., Tokyo, 1988, L.A. County Mus. Art, L.A., 1988, Palazzo Reale, Milan, Italy, 1988, Fitzwilliam Mus., Cambridge, Eng., 1988, Fine Arts Mus. San Francisco, 1988, Brandywine River Mus., Chadds Ford, Pa., 1988, Detroit Inst. Arts, 1989, Sezon Mus. Art, Tokyo, 1991, Heckscher Mus., Huntington, N.Y., 1989, Gilcrease Mus., Tulsa, 1989, Portland (Maine) Mus. Art, 1989, Nukaga Gallery, Japan, 1990, Marcelle Fine Art Inc., N.Y.C. 1990, Takuji Kato Modern Art Mus., Tokyo, 1991, Takuji Kato Modern Art Mus., Chichibu City, Japan, 1991, Jacksonville (Fla.) Art Mus., 1992, Portland (Maine) Mus. Art, 1993, Farnsworth Art Mus., Rockland, Maine, 1994, San Francisco Mus. Modern Art, 1995, Charles and Emma Frye Art Mus., 1995, William King Regional Arts Center, Va., 1996, Butler Inst.Am.Art, Ohio, 1997, Whitney Mus. Am. Art, 1998, Self Family Art Center, Hilton Head Island, SC, 2000, Greenville County Mus. Art, 2001, Telfair Mus. Art, Savannah, Ga., 2001; Cin. Art Mus., 2002, Creekwood Mus. Art, Nashville, 2002, Frye Art Mus. Collection, Seattle, 2003, Addison Gallery Am. Art, Mass., 2004; (represented in permanent collections Met. Mus. Art, Nat. Gallery Art. Awarded 1st prize Wilmington Soc. Fine Arts, 1939, Obrig prize Am. Watercolor Soc., 1945, award of Merit, Am. Acad. Arts and Letters and Nat. Inst. Arts and Letters, 1947, 1st prize in watercolor Nat. Acad., 1946, Gold medal Nat. Inst. Arts and Letters, 1965, George Walter Dawson Meml. medal Phila. Watercolor Club, 1957, Mellon Gold medal of Achievement Pa. Artists Exhibit, Ligonier Valley, Pa., 1958, Arts Festival award and Citation for bringing dignity to Am. art Phila. Mus. Art, 1959, Percy M. Owens Meml. award Fellowship of Pa. Acad. Fine Arts, Phila., 1960, Presdl. Medal of Freedom, 1963, citation LaSalle Coll., Phila., 1965, Gold medal of honor Pa. Acad. Fine Arts, 1966, Carnegie Inst. award, award for excellence 1st award recognize outstanding performance in arts, Washington Coll., Chestertown, Md., 1976; Gold medal Nat. Arts Club, 1978, first Am. artist awarded Presdl. award Gold Congl. medal, 1988. Mem. Am. Watercolor Soc. (certificate of merit 1962), Nat. Inst. Arts and Letters, Soviet Acad. Arts (hon.), Academie des Beaux-Arts, Chester County Art Assn. (dir.), Audubon Soc. (dir.), N.Y. Watercolor Soc., Wilmington Soc. Fine Arts, Phila. Watercolor Club (dir.), Washington Watercolor Club (dir.), Balt. Watercolor Club (dir.), Am. Acad. Arts and Letters, NAD (Academician elect May 1945, Gold medal preeminence in painting 1965), Am. Acad. Arts and Scis., Royal Soc. Painters and Watercolours (London).

**WYETH, JAMES BROWNING,** artist; b. Wilmington, Del., July 6, 1946; s. Andrew and Betsy (James) W.; m. Phyllis Overton Mills, Dec. 12, 1968. Privately tutored. One-man shows include M. Knoedler & Co., N.Y.C., 1966, William A. Farnsworth Mus., Rockland, Maine, 1969, 1992, 1995, Coe Kerr Gallery, N.Y.C., 1974, 1990, Brandywine River Mus., Chadds Ford, Pa., 1974, 1994, 1995, 1999, Joslyn Art Mus., Omaha, 1976, Pa. Acad. Fine Arts, 1980, Greenville County Art Mus., Greenville, N.C., 1981, Amon Carter Mus., Ft. Worth, 1981, Anchorage Fine Arts Mus., 1983, James Graham and Sons, N.Y.C., 1993, 1995, 1999, 2000, Decatur House, 1995, Double Door Gallery, Isleboro, Maine, 1996, Butler Art Inst., Youngstown, Ohio, 1999, Russell Rotunda, Washington, 2000, Ringling Mus. Art, Sarasota, Fla., New Britain (Conn.) Mus. Am. Art, one-man shows include touring exhibn. An American Vision: Three Generations of Wyeth Art, various mus. worldwide, 1987—, Farnsworth Art Mus., 1988—2000, Terra Mus. Am. Art, Chgo., 1997—, (illustrator) childrens books, The Stray, 1979, Cabbages and Kings, 1997. Mem. NEA, 1972; mem. stamp adv. com. U.S. Postal Svc., 1969; bd. govs. Nat. Space Inst., 1975. With Del. Air N.G., 1966—71. Mem.: NAD (assoc. 1969—80, academician 1980—). Office: care Priscilla Vail Caldwell James Graham & Sons 1014 Madison Ave New York NY 10021-0103 Fax: (212) 794-2454. E-mail: jgsgal@aol.com.

**WYGANT, FOSTER LAURANCE,** art educator; b. Dayton, Ohio, Oct. 30, 1920; s. Harold F. and M. Esther (Weber) W.; m. Rae E. Hoyt, 1 child, Nancy Laura Profl. diploma, Juilliard Sch. Music, 1942; BA, Columbia U., 1949, MA, 1956, Ed.D., 1959; postgrad., Am. Art Sch., Art Students League, 1951-53. Clarinetist Dallas Symphony and free-lance clarinetist, N.Y.C., 1945-47; publicity, fund-raising positions, and free-lance artist, 1952-56; tchr. art, pub. schs., 1956-59; asst. prof. Montclair State Coll., NJ, 1959-63, assoc. prof. NJ, 1963-68; prof. art edn. U. Cin., 1968-87, chmn. dept., 1968-84, dir. Sch. Art Edn. and Art History, 1984-86, emeritus prof., 1987—. Pub., owner Interwood Press, 1987—; vis. sr. lectr. Leeds Coll. Art, Eng., 1966; regional chmn. Scholastic Awards Program, 1968-84; chmn. Action for Arts in Ohio Schs., 1974-75. Author: Art in American Schools in the Nineteenth Century, 1983, School Art in American Culture 1820-1970, 1993, School Art in American Culture Supplement: 1900-1915, 1997; editor, prin. author: Standards for Art Teacher Preparation Programs, 1979, Principles, Purposes and Standards for School Art Programs, 1982; contbr. numerous articles to profl. jours. Pres. Tri-State Chamber Players, Inc., 2002—. With U.S. Army, 1941—45. N.Y. State and Juilliard Sch. Music scholar, 1939-41; Kellogg Found. fellow Columbia U., 1955-56 Nat. Art Edn. Assn. (V. Pres., nat. dir. higher edn. divsn. 1975-79, Recognition award 1980, Disting. Svc. award 1982, Disting. fellow 1995), Ohio Art Edn. Assn. (pres. 1972-74, Disting. fellow 2000), Seminar for Rsch. in Art Edn., Coun. for Policy Studies in Art Edn., Am. Fedn. Musicians, Phi Beta Kappa. Home: 3562 Interwood Ave Cincinnati OH 45220-1824 Office Phone: 513-751-5239. Business E-Mail: wygantfl@ucmail.uc.edu.

**WYGANT, PATRICIA BRYANS,** artist; b. Marion, Ohio, Nov. 10, 1926; d. Ralph Armond and Frances Annetta (Kilbury) Bryans. BFA, Syracuse U., 1950. Resident Millay Colony for Arts, Austerlitz, N.Y., 1979. Exhibited in 62 nat. juried exhbns. including Watercolor USA, Nat. Watercolor Soc., Watercolor Workshop Greek Islands Sifnos Amorgos, Paros, 1988; paintings publ. in A Gallery of Marine Art, 1988, 98, The Best of Watercolor, 1995 (1st Pl. award). Recipient Winsor Newton award Rochester Art Club, 1994. Mem. Am. Artists Profl. League, Ga. Watercolor Soc. (signature mem.), Niagara Frontier Watercolor Soc. (signature mem.). Avocation: travel. Office: Anderson Alley Artists 250 N Goodman St Rochester NY 14607

**WYKER, KENNETH E.,** lawyer; b. N.Y.C., Apr. 1, 1961; s. Robert Harris and Elin Barbara (Eisner) W. BA, Trinity Coll., 1983; JD, George Washington U., 1986. Bar: D.C. 1988. Staff atty. Securities & Exch. Commn., Washington, 1986-87; assoc. gen. counsel Infotech., Fairfax, Va., 1988-90; sr. v.p. legal affairs Clear Channel Comms., San Antonio, 1993—; corp. counsel Greater Media, East Brunswick, N.J., 1990-93; gen. counsel Clear Channel Comms., 2001—. Bd. charitable giving Children;s Shelter, San Antonio, 1993-95. Mem. Am. Corp. Coun. Assn. (bd. dirs. San Antonio chpt. 1998—). Office: Clear Channel Comms 200 E Basse Rd San Antonio TX 78209-8328

**WYKLE, MAY L.,** dean, educator, researcher; BSN, Case Western Res. U., 1956, MSN Psychiat. Nursing, PhD Edn. Dean, Cellar prof. gerontological nursing Frances Payne Bolton Sch. Nursing, Ohio, 1988—; dean, dir. u. ctr. aging and health Case Western Res. U. Established ednl. programs, Europe, Africa, Asia; vis. prof. U. Mich., U. Tex.-Houston, U. Zimbabwe-Africa; del., served on planning com. White Ho. Conf. on Aging, 1993. Contbr. articles, chapters to books; author: Decision Making in Long-Term Care, Practicing Rehabilitation with Geriatric Clients, Stress and Health Among the Elderly, Family Caregiving Across the Lifespan, Service Minority Elders in the 21st Century (AJN Book of Yr. award, 2000). Dir. Robert Wood Johnson Tchg. Nursing Home Project; project dir. several tng. grants; cons. nursing homes, psychiat. hosps.; mem. bd. dirs. numerous cmty. orgns., nursing homes, profl. assns. Named first Pope Eminent scholar, Rosalynn Carter Inst. Human Devel. Southwestern State U., Americus, Ga., Outstanding Rschr. in State of Ohio, Ohio Rsch. Coun. on Aging, Ohio Network Edn. Cons. in field of Aging, 1992; recipient Humanitarian award, Outstanding Contbns. to Nursing Profession, 1999, Acad. award, NIMH Geriatric Mental Health, Merit award, Cleve. Coun. Black Nurses, Gerontological Doris Schwartz Nursing Rsch., award, Gerontological Soc. Am., Belle Sherwin award, Cleve. Vis. Nurse Assn., Leadership award excellence in geriatric care, Midwest Alliance in Nursing, Disting. nurse-scholar lectr. award, Nat. Coun. Nursing Rsch., Nursing Educator award, New Cleve. Woman mag. Fellow: Gerontological

Soc. Am., Am. Acad. Nursing; mem.: NIA, NIMH, NINR, Vets Adminstrn. (geriatric/gerontology adv. com.), Sigma Theta Tau Internat. (pres.-elect 1999). Office: 10900 Euclid Ave Cleveland OH 44106*

**WYLAN, BARBARA,** artist; b. Providence, 1933; divorced; children: Andrea, Brock. BFA, R.I. Sch. of Design, Providence, 1955; studied with Donald Stoltenberg, Claude Croney, Murray Wentworth, Ruth Wynn, Charles Movalli, Dong Kingman. Tchr. watercolor workshops; juror various exhbns. One-woman shows include Sturgis Libr., Mass., 1974, 77, 83, Falmouth Artists' Guild, Mass., 1977, Skylight Gallery, Colo., 1979, Market Barn Gallery, Falmouth, Mass., 1981, 89, 91, Dom's Restaurant, Mass., 1981, Spectrum Am. Artists and Craftsmen, Brewster, Mass., 1983-88, 90, 92-93, 95, 2000, 03, Cape Cod Conservatory, Mass., 1984, 86, Cape Cod Mus. Nat. History, Brewster, Mass., 1987, Old Selectmens' Gallery, West Barnstable, Mass., 1995, Cahoon Mus. Am. Art, Cotuit, Mass., 1998; exhibited in group shows at Watercolor USA (Springfield award 1982), Nat. Soc. Painters in Casein and Acrylic 38th Ann., Nat. Arts club, NYC (Dr. David Soloway award 1991), Cahoon Mus. Am. Art, Coteit, Mass., 1991, 97, 2003, 04, 06, Cape Cod Mus. Art, Dennis, Mass., 2002, 06; represented in permanent and pvt. collections Mobile (Ala.) Mus. Art, Cahoon Mus. Am. Art, Cotuit, Mass., Cape Cod Mus. of Art, Dennis, Mass., Springfield, Mo. Art Mus. Mem. Nat. Soc. Painters in Casein and Acrylic, Watercolor USA Honor Soc., New Eng. Watercolor Soc., Copley Soc. Art, and Twenty-one in Truro.

**WYLAND, MARK,** state official; b. Escondido, Calif. 1 child, Nicole. BA in Internat. Rels., Pomona Coll.; MA in Polit. sci., Columbia U. Co-owner family bus.; state assembly mem. Dist. 74 Calif. State Assembly, 2000—. Mem. bus. and professions com.; mem.com.; mem. govtl. orgn. com.; vice-chair revenue and taxation com.; mem. VA com.; mem. Escondido Union Sch. Bd.; trustee Pomona Coll. Mem.: YMCA, Encinitis. Republican. Mailing: Rm 4130 PO Box 942849 Sacramento CA 94249 Home: 1800 Thibodo Rd Ste 300 Vista CA 92081-7515

**WYLDE, KATHRYN S.,** business organization executive; BA, St. Olaf Coll., 1968. With Lutheran Med. Ctr., 1968—79; pres., CEO, N.Y.C. Housing Partnership, 1982—96; founding pres., CEO, N.Y.C. Investment Fund, 1996—; pres., CEO Partnership for N.Y.C., 2000—. Chair Luth. Med. Ctr., Bklyn.; mem. bus. adv. bd. CUNY; bd. dirs. NYC Econ. Devel. Corp., Biomed. Rsch. Alliance N.Y., NYC Leadership Acad., Manhattan Inst. Policy Rsch. Recipient HBSCNY Bus. Statesman award. Office: Partnership for NYC One Battery Pk Plz 5th Fl New York NY 10004 Business E-Mail: kwylde@nycp.org.

**WYLE, FREDERICK S.,** lawyer; b. Berlin, May 9, 1928; came to U.S., 1939, naturalized, 1944; s. Norbert and Malwina (Mauer) W.; m. Katinka Franz, June 29, 1969; children: Susan Kim, Christopher Anthony, Katherine Anne. BA magna cum laude, Harvard U., 1951, LL.B., 1954. Bar: Mass. 1954, Calif. 1955, N.Y. 1958. Teaching fellow Harvard Law Sch., 1954-55; law clk. U.S. Dist. Ct., No. Dist. Calif., 1955-57; assoc. firm Paul, Weiss, Rifkind, Wharton & Garrison, NYC, 1957-58; pvt. practice San Francisco, 1958-62; spl. asst. def. rep. U.S. del. to NATO, Paris, 1962-63; mem. Policy Planning Council, Dept. State, Washington, 1963-65; dep. asst. sec. def. for European and NATO affairs Dept. Def., Washington, 1966-69; v.p. devel., gen. counsel Schroders, Inc., NYC, 1969-71, atty., cons., 1971-72; chief exec. officer Saturday Rev. Industries, Inc., San Francisco, 1972-76; individual practice law San Francisco, 1976—82. Internat. counsel to Fed. States Micronesia, 1974-82; cons. Rand Corp., Dept. Def., Nuclear Regulatory Commn. Contbr. to: Encyc. Brit, 1972, also articles in profl. publs., newspapers. Trustee US Interest Bicycle Club Casino, 1996-99; trustee in bankruptcy Garden City, Inc., 2000-; liquidating trustee Synthetic Industries, 2000—; Biosurg. Industries, 2000—; negotiator for Gov. of Calif. with Indian tribes re gambling, 2003. Served with AUS, 1946-47. Mem. Internat. Inst. Strategic Studies, Phi Beta Kappa. Office: 23 Embarcadero Ctr Fl 7 San Francisco CA 94111-4065 Personal E-mail: fwyle@earthlink.net.

**WYLE, NOAH,** actor; b. Hollywood, Calif., June 4, 1971; m. Tracy Warbin, 2000; children: Owen Strausser, Auden. Artistic prodr. The Blank Theatre Co., LA. Actor: (films) Crooked Hearts, 1991, A Few Good Men, 1992, Swing Kids, 1993, There Goes My Baby, 1994, The Myth of Fingerprints, 1997, Can't Stop Dancing, 1999, Scenes of the Crime, 2001, Enough, 2002, White Oleander, 2002, The Californians, 2004; (TV films) Blind Faith, 1990, Guinevere, 1994, Pirates of Silicon Valley, 1999, Fail Safe, 2000, The Librarian: Quest for the Spear, 2004; (TV series) ER, 1994—2005 (SAG award for outstanding performance by ensemble in drama series, 1998, 1999, TV Guide award for supporting actor of yr. in drama series, 2001); assoc. prodr. Myth of Fingerprints, 1997. Office: The Blank Theatre Co 1301 Lucile Ave Los Angeles CA 90026*

**WYLIE, GUY STEPHEN,** psychologist, educator; s. Henry John and Shirley Elizabeth Wylie; m. Janiese Arends, May 17, 1981. BA, Bucknell U., Lewisburg, Pa., 1973; MS, Kans. State Coll. at Pittsburg, 1976; PhD in Counseling, Kans. State U., 1989. Cert. counselor Nat. Bd. for Cert. Counselors, Inc., 1983. Human svc. program coord./psychology instr. Western Nebr. C.C., Scottsbluff, Nebr., 1977—. bd. mem. Panhandle Partnership for Health and Human Svcs., Panhandle of Nebraska, Nebr., 1997—2003; chmn. region i behavioral health adv. bd. Panhandle Mental Health Ctr., Scottsbluff, Nebr., 1985—; co-chairperson State of Nebr. Substance Abuse Adv. Bd., Lincoln, Nebr., 1994—96; bd. mem. Nebr. State Mental Health Adv. Bd., Lincoln, 1986—90. Pottery and sculpture. Pres. and dir. Scottsbluff-Gering Duplicate Bridge Club, Scottsbluff, Nebr., 1990—2006. Recipient Excellence in Tchg. award, WNCC Phi Theta Kappa, 1999—2000, Outstanding Faculty Mem. award, 1981—82, UNMC Coll. of Nursing Tchr. award, U. of Nebr. Med. Ctr. Coll. of Nursing, 1991. Mem.: Nat. Orgn. for Human Svcs. Edn., APA, ACA, Am. Contract Bridge League (unit bd. mem. 1990—2006, Bronze Life Master 2003), Elks (scholarship com. chmn. 1988—2006, Elk of the Yr. 2001-2002). Avocations: potter, bridge. Office: Western Nebraska Community College 1601 East 27th St Scottsbluff NE 69361 Office Phone: 308-635-6129. Office Fax: 308-635-6100. Personal E-mail: gwylie@wncc.net.

**WYLIE, JAMES MALCOLM,** adult education educator; b. N.Y.C., Mar. 16, 1938; s. James M. and Nancy Beatrice (Worthy) Wylie. BS, Boston U., 1960. Columnist Mexico City Times, 1964; prof. Cooper Union Coll., N.Y.C., 1986—. Author: The Lost Rebellion, 1971, The Homestead Grays, 1977, The Sign of Dawn, 1981; participant Spoleto Festival U.S.A., 2001. Office: 51 Astor Pl New York NY 10003-7132

**WYLIE, PAUL RICHTER, JR.,** lawyer; b. Dec. 25, 1936; s. Paul Richter and Alice (Dredge) W.; m. Arlene Marie Klem, Mar. 6, 1982; children: Lynne Catherine, John Michael, Thomas Robert. BSChemE, Mont. State U., 1959; JD, Am. U., 1965. Bar: Utah 1978, Calif. 1970, U.S. Supreme Ct. 1971. Mont. 1990. Patent examiner U.S. Patent and Trademark Office, Washington, 1962-64; asst. gen. patent counsel Dart Industries Inc., L.A., 1967-81; pvt. practice L.A., 1981-86, Pacific Palisades, Calif., 1986-90, Bozeman, Mont., 1990—. Mem. ABA, AIChE, Am. Intellectual Property Law Assn., L.a. Intellectual Property Law Assn., Am. Chem. Soc., Licensing Execs. Soc., Tech. Transfer Soc. Home: 106 Silverwood Dr Bozeman MT 59715-9255 Office: 1805 W Dickerson St Ste 3 Bozeman MT 59715-4131

**WYLLIE, STANLEY CLARKE,** retired librarian; b. Clearwater, Fla., Nov. 19, 1935; s. Stanley Clarke and Euginia Lee (Tison) W.; m. Martha Ann Thomason, June 14, 1963; children: Stanley Clarke Jr., Susan Lynne DeHerder, Patricia Anne. BS in History and Social Scis., Fla. So. Coll., 1958; MS in Libr. Sci., Fla. State U., 1963. Tchr. civics and English Lakeland (Fla.) Jr. H.S., 1960-61; libr. I Tampa (Fla.) Pub. Libr., 1962; dir. Chestatee Reg. Libr. Sys., Gainesville, Ga., 1963-64; ind. and sci. ref. libr. Dayton and Montgomery County Pub. Libr., Dayton, Ohio, 1964-66, collection libr., 1967-73, social scis. and genealogy ref. libr., 1973-90; ret. Adv. bd. Sinclair C.C. Srs., recording sec., 2005—. Editor Mad River Currents newsletter,

1996-97, Bits, 1964-66. Corr. sec. Montgomery County Geneal. Soc., 1990-91, rec. sec., 1997-98; pres. Men's Rep. Club, Lakeland, 1960-61; mem. TV cable commn. City of Riverside, Ohio, 1997-98; presiding judge Riverside, Montgomery County Bd. Elections, 1992—; mem. exec. com. Montgomery County Rep. Party, 2004—, ctrl. com., 2004—. Recipient Edward M. Selby award Ohio Lodge Rsch., 1991-92, R. Marion Snyder award Ohio chpt. Rsch., 2005, Alumnus Disting. svc. award Fla. So. Coll., 1991; Knight York Cross of Honor, Ohio Priory #18, KYCH, 1983; named Ky. Col. Mem.: AARP (dist. coord. 1997—99), Dayton and Montgomery County Pub. Libr. Staff Assn. (pres. retiree chpt. 2004—), Mensa, Pub. Employee Retirees Inc. (chpt. pres. 1998, dist. 3 rep. 1999—2002), Am. Fedn. State, County, Mcpl. Employees (v.p. 2004—05, 2006—), United Ancient Order of Druids (noble arch Franklin Grove #2), Fla. State Geneal. Soc., SAR (pres. Richard Montgomery chpt. 1990—91, Silver Good Citizenship medal 1997), Dayton High Twelve (pres. 1994) Odd Fellows (Noble Grand Steuben Rebekah Lodge 1997, chief patriarch Mad River Encampment # 16 1998—99, grand lodge rep. 1998—2000, Noble grand 1998—2001, Noble Grand Steuben Rebekah Lodge 2000, pres. S.W. Boosters Assn. 2001—, pres. S.W. Promotional Assn. 2001—, grand lodge rep. 2002—, Marion lodge #18 Noble Grand 2003—04, grand patriarch Grand Encampment Ohio 2003—04, maj. occidental Canton patriarchs militant 2003—), Grand Monarch, El Aliman Sanctorum, Ancient Mystic Order of Samaritans, Toastmasters (area 3 gov. 1995, v.p. edn. 1997), Audubon Soc., Order of DeMolay (adv. bd. 3d dist. 1996—2002, Cross of Honor, Legion of Honor), Order Rainbow for Girls (Grand Cross of Color), Far Hills High Twelve Club, Fla. Geneal. Soc., Pres.'s Club of Dayton (pres. 2000—01), Knights of Khorassan, United Ancient Order of Druids (grand grove midwest chpt. 2004—05, grand herald, grand dir. ceremonies nat. grand grove chpt.), Lions (pres. 1996—97, zone chmn. 1996—98, Pres. Excellence award 1997), Jr. Order Mechanics (counsellor 2005—), Grange, Marion Lodge, Orange Order (worthy master Gideons Hope 802 2002—03), Improved Order of Redmen (Sachem Lone Eagle Lodge 2004—05), Elks (Exalted ruler 2005—06), KP (chancellor comdr. Red Star Lodge 2000—01, Grand Lodge rep. 2002—06, dist. dep. 2004—06), Shriners, Masons. Anglican Catholic. Avocations: reading, stamp collecting/philately. Home: 4960 Franlou Ave Dayton OH 45432-3120 Personal E-mail: scwyllie@msn.com. E-mail: s.wyllie@sbcglobal.net.

**WYLLY, BARBARA BENTLEY,** performing arts association administrator; b. Bala-Cynwyd, Pa., June 10, 1924; d. William Henry and Virginia (Barclay) Bentley; m. William Beck Wylly, Apr. 26, 1947; children: Virginia Wylly Johnson, Barbara Wylly Klausman, Thomas C. II. A, Briarcliff Jr. Coll., 1943. Pres. bd. dirs. Hillside Hosp. Inc., Atlanta, 1982, mem. adv. coun., 1982—; pres. Atlanta Symphony Assocs., 1975-76, mem. adv. bd., 1976—; chmn. bd. dirs. Ctr. for Puppetry Arts, Atlanta, 1988-2004, mem. exec. com., 1988—. Bd. dirs. Mountain Conservation Trust, Atlanta Opera Guild, 1999—; mem. bd. sponsors Georgian Chamber Players, 2000— Republican. Episcopalian. Avocations: walking, reading, music. Home: 940 Foxcroft Rd NW Atlanta GA 30327-2622 Office: Ctr Puppetry Arts 1404 Spring St NW Atlanta GA 30309-2820

**WYLY, CHARLES JOSEPH, JR.,** retail executive; b. Lake Providence, La., Oct. 13, 1933; s. Charles Joseph and Flora (Evans) W.; m. Caroline Denmon; children: Martha, Charles Joseph III, Emily, Jennifer. BS, La. Tech. U., 1956. Sales rep. IBM Service Bur. Corp., 1956-64; v.p. Wyly Corp., Dallas, 1964-65, exec. v.p., 1965-69, pres., 1969-73, chmn. exec. com., 1973-76, dir., 1964-76; chmn. bd. Earth Resources Co., 1968-80. Vice chmn. bd. dirs. USACafes, Inc. (Bonanza Internat., Inc.), 1968-89, Sterling Software, Inc.; chmn. Tex. High-Speed Rail Authority, 1990-91, Maverick Capital, 1990-96, Michaels Stores, Inc. Mem. Pres.'s Advisory Council on Mgmt. Improvement, 1970-73; vice-chmn. Devel. Council So. Methodist U. Found. Sci. and Engring., 1970-71; Mem. Republican Nat. Fin. Com., 1970—; Bd. dirs. Dallas County United Way Fund; pres. Dallas Theater Center., 1972-79. Mem. Am. Mgmt. Assn., Pi Kappa Alpha, Omicron Delta Kappa, Delta Sigma Pi, Beta Gamma Sigma. Clubs: City, Crescent, Park City, Brookhollow (Dallas). Office: Ste 1000 300 Crescent Ct Dallas TX 75201-7852

**WYLY, SAMUEL E.,** retail executive; Founder Univ. Computing Co., 1963-79; co-owner, chmn. Bonanza Steakhouse, 1967-89; founder Datran, Inc., 1968; co-founder, mem. exec. com. Earth Resources Co., 1968-80; co-founder, chmn. Sterling Software, Inc., 1981—; chmn. Michaels Stores Inc., Irving, Tex., 1984—. Named one of Forbes' Richest Americans, 2006. Office: Michaels Stores Inc 8000 Bent Branch Dr Irving TX 75063*

**WYMAN, DAVID SWORD,** retired historian, educator; b. Weymouth, Mass., Mar. 6, 1929; s. Hollis Judson and Ruth (Sword) W.; m. Mildred Louise Smith, Sept. 13, 1950; children: James Nayler, Teresa Carol. AB, Boston U., 1951; DHM, Plymouth State Coll., 1961; AM, Harvard U., 1962, PhD, 1966; DHL (hon.), Hebrew Union Coll. Jewish Inst. Religion, 1986, Yeshiva U., 1988. Various positions, 1951-57; tchr. pub. schs. Tilton, NH, 1957-60; tchr. pub. high sch. Penacook, NH, 1960-61; prof. history U. Mass., Amherst, 1966-91, Josiah DuBois prof. history, 1986-91, Josiah DuBois prof. emeritus, 1991—, chmn. Judaic Studies Program, 1977-78, 82-84, chmn. David S. Wyman Inst. for Holocaust Studies, 2003—. Acad. advisor Simon Wiesenthal Ctr., L.A., 1983—; nat. coun. Nat. Christian Leadership Conf. for Israel, 1986, numerous radio and TV appearances; historian advisor to films. Author: Paper Walls: America and the Refugee Crisis, 1938-41, 1968, The Abandonment of the Jews: America and the Holocaust 1941-45, 1984 (Anisfield-Wolf award 1984, Stuart Bernath award 1984, Theodore Saloutos book award 1984, Present Tense Lit. award 1984, Boston Hadassah Myrtle Wreath award 1985, Nat. Jewish Book award 1985), new edit., 1998; co-author: A Race Against Death: Peter Bergson, America, and the Holocaust, 2002; editor: America and the Holocaust, 13 vols. documents, 1989-90, The World Reacts to the Holocaust, 1996; contbr. articles to profl. jours., chpts. to books. Recipient Chancellor's medal, U. Mass., 1986, Achievement award Isaac M. Wise Temple, Cin. 1986, Humanitarian award Bklyn. Holocaust Meml. Com., 1986, Herbert Katzki award Am. Jewish Joint Distbn. Com., 1999; elected to Boston U. Collegium Disting. Alumni, 1986; Woodrow Wilson fellow, 1961-62, 65-66; grantee Social Sci. Rsch. Coun., 1969-70, Am. Coun. Learned Socs., 1969-70, Charles Warren Ctr. at Harvard U., 1969-70. Mem. Soc. for Am. Baseball Rsch., N.H. Hist. Soc., Friends Hist. Assn., Phi Beta Kappa. Avocations: baseball, local history. Home: 61 Columbia Dr Amherst MA 01002-3105

**WYMAN, JAMES VERNON,** retired publishing executive; b. Brockton, Mass., Nov. 17, 1923; s. George Dewey and Christine Laverne (Skinner) W.; m. Viola Marie Bousquet, June 24, 1950; children: Vernon, Douglas Phillip, Carolyn Anne. Student, Northeastern U., Boston, 1946—48; BS in Journalism, Boston U., 1951. From staff to dep. exec. editor Providence Jour.-Bull., 1951-88, v.p., exec. editor, 1989-95, ret., 1995. Mem. dean's adv. bd. Boston U. Coll. Comm. Served with AUS, 1942-46, PTO. Recipient Yankee Quill award, 1989. Disting. Alumni award Boston U. Coll. of Comm. Alumni Bd., 1996; named to R.I. Journalism Hall of Fame, 1999. Mem. New Eng. AP News Execs. Assn. (past pres.), AP Mng. Editors Assn., New Eng. Soc. Newspaper Editors, Acad. New Eng. Journalists (past dir.), New Eng. Newspaper Assn., Sigma Delta Chi (past pres. New Eng. chpt.). Roman Catholic. Home: 44 Starflower Ct Wakefield RI 02879-5475 Personal E-mail: foxtango44@cox.net.

**WYMAN, JANE (SARAH JANE FULKS),** actress; b. St. Joseph, Mo., Jan. 4, 1914; d. R. D. and Emme (Reise) Fulks; m. Myron Futterman, 1937; m. Ronald Reagan, 1940 (div. 1948); children: Maureen Reagan Revell, Michael; m. Fred Karger (div.). Student, U. Mo., 1935. Formerly radio singer, chorus girl in movie musicals; actress. Chorus girl: Gold Diggers of 1937; actress: (featured roles) films My Man Godfrey, 1936, Brother Rat, 1938, Lost Weekend, 1945 (Acad. award nomination), The Yearling, 1946 (Acad. award nomination), Johnny Belinda, 1948 (Acad. award winner), Stage Fright, 1950, The Glass Menagerie, 1950, The Blue Veil, 1951 (Acad. award nomination), Magnificent Obsession, 1954 (Acad. award nomination), All That Heaven Allows, 1956, Miracle in the Rain, 1956, Holiday for Lovers, 1959,

Pollyanna, 1960, Bon Voyage, 1962, How to Commit Marriage, 1969; TV shows Fireside Theater, 1955, Jane Wyman Theater, Falcon Crest, 1981-90 (recipient Golden Globe awardBest Actress in Series-Drama, 1984).*

**WYMAN, RALPH MARK,** security firm executive, healthcare company executive; b. Usti, Czechoslovakia, Feb. 7, 1926; arrived in U.S., 1941, naturalized, 1946; s. Hans and Stella (Parnas) Wyman; m. Lotte Ann Novak, Oct. 25, 1947; 1 child, Leslie Andrea Wyman Cooper. Student, Upper Can. Coll., 1942, Bucknell U., 1942-43; BSBA, NYU, 1945; postgrad., Columbia U., 1945-46. Asst. mgr. export dept. Liebermann Waelchi & Co., Inc., N.Y.C., 1946-47; trainee White Weld Co., 1947-48; v.p. H. O. Canfield Co., 1948-65, vice chmn. bd. dirs., 1965-79, bd. dirs., 1953-79, Pantasote Inc., 1960-89, vice chmn. bd. dirs., 1967-89; mng. partner United Eagle Mgmt. Co., Eagle Mgmt. Co., 1960-95; pres. Veritas, ING, 1960—2005; bd. dirs., chmn. Eagle Capital Internat. LLC, 1985—; bd. dirs., vice chmn. Affiliate Artists, Inc., 1971-88; chmn. AMA Eagle LLC, 2003—. Pres. Panwy Found.; bd. dirs. United Way Greenwich, Conn., 1980—86, Kids in Crisis, Greenwich, 1993—2001, sec., 1995—2001; trustee Greenwich Acad., 1963—71, chmn., 1968—70; elder, trustee Synod New Eng., 1974—76; trustee Princeton Theol. Sem., 1976—2001, vice chmn., 1997—2001, trustee emeritus, 2001—; trustee Ctr. Theol. Inquiry, 1997—. Mem.: Indian Harbor Yacht Club, Greenwich Country Club, Lambda Chi Alpha. Home: 34 Baldwin Farms N Greenwich CT 06831-3307 Office: # 4 Greenwich Office Park IV Greenwich CT 06831-5246 Office Phone: 203-661-6616. Business E-Mail: ralph.wyman@amaglobal.com.

**WYMAN, RICHARD THOMAS,** information technology manager, researcher; b. Wilmington, Del., June 4, 1951; s. William Harper and Marian Kathryn (Bode) W.; Pa. State U., 1969-71, Def. Language Inst., 1974-75, Control Data Inst., Dallas, 1979. Enlisted U.S. Army, 1971, served to staff sgt., 1979; data ctr. mgr. thrift svcs. divsn. ADP Inc., Dallas, 1979-80; support mgr. Electronic Data Sys., Inc., Dallas, 1980-85, info. modeling analyst, 1985-90; pres. Strategic InfoSource, Plano, Tex., 1991-93; sr. cons. The SABRE Group, Ft. Worth, 1993-97; assoc. Perot Sys. Corp., Richardson, Tex., 1997-98; info. architect The Technical Resource Connection, Inc., Tampa, Fla., 1998—2005; enterprise architect Perot Sys. Corp., Plano, Tex., 2005—. Rep. 101st Airborne Divsn. Nat. Conf. Skill Maintenance, Ft. Meade, Md., 1977. Author: (spl. course) U.S. Army Intelligence, 1978-79. Co-chmn. sub-com. City Bond Referendum Com., Plano, 1990; mem. City of Plano Historic Landmark Com., 1993-97, vice chmn. 1996, chmn. 1996-97. Recipient Army Commendation medal, 1978, 79, Vol. Svc. award, Office of Mayor, Plano, 1990. Achievements include patents pending for computer system and process for aiding in an outsourcing environment. Home: 3608 Trailview Dr Plano TX 75074 Office: Perot Systems Corp 2300 W Plano Pkwy Plano TX 75075 Business E-Mail: richard.wyman@ps.net.

**WYMAN, RICHARD VAUGHN,** engineering educator, engineering company executive; b. Painesville, Ohio, Feb. 22, 1927; s. Vaughn Ely and Melinda (Ward) W.; m. Anne Fenton, Dec. 27, 1947; 1 son, William Fenton. BS, Case Western Res. U., 1948; MS, U. Mich., 1949; PhD, U. Ariz., 1974. Registered profl. engr., Nev., Ariz.; registered geologist, Ariz., Calif.; lic. water right surveyor, Nev. Geologist N.J. Zinc Co., 1949, 52-53, Cerro de Pasco Corp., 1950-52; chief geologist Western Gold & Uranium, Inc., St. George, Utah, 1953-55, gen. supt., 1955-57, v.p., 1957-59; pres. Intermountain Exploration Co., Boulder City, Nev., 1959-93; tunnel supt. Reynolds Electric & Engring. Co., 1961-63, mining engr., 1965-67; asst. mgr. ops. Reynolds Electric and & Engring. Co., 1967-69; constrn. supt. engr. Sunshine Mining Co., 1963-65; lectr. U. Nev., Las Vegas, 1969-73, assoc. prof., 1973-80, dept. chmn., 1976-80, prof., 1980-92, prof. emeritus, 1992—, chmn. dept. civil and mech. engring., 1984-90, chmn. dept. civil and environ. engring., 1990-91. Mineral rep. Ariz. Strip Adv. Bd., 1976-80, U.S.B.L.M.; mem. peer rev. com. Nuclear Waste Site, Dept. Energy, Las Vegas, 1978-82; pres. Ariz. Juno Resources, Boulder City, 1980-87, v.p., 1990-97; pres. Wyman Engring. Cons., 1987—; cons. Corp. Andina de Fomento, Caracas, Venezuela, 1977-78; v.p. Comstock Gold, Inc., 1984-93; program evaluator Accreditation Bd. for Engring. and Tech., 1995-2001. Contbr. articles to profl. jours. Sec. Washington County Republican Party, Utah, 1958-60; del. Utah Rep. Conv., 1958-60; scoutmaster Boy Scouts Am., 1959-69; mem. citizens adv. com., tech. adv. com. Clark County Regional Flood Control Dist., 1998-2004. Served with USN, 1944-46. Recipient Order of Engr. award, 2000. Fellow ASCE (life; edn. divsn. 1990, local rep. nat. conv. Las Vegas), Soc. Econ. Geologists (life); mem. AIME/SME (life, chmn. So. Nev. sect. 1971-72, dist. 1968-2002, sec.-treas. 1974-92, chmn. Pacific S.W. Minerals Conf. 1972, gen. chmn. nat. conv. 1980, Disting. Mem. award 1989, Legion of Honor 1999), Assn. Engring. Geologists (dir. S.W. sect. 1989-91), Am. Inst. Minerals Appraisers, Am. Water Works Assn., Nev. Mining Assn. (assoc.), Northwest Mining Assn., Geological Soc. Nev., Assn. Ground Water Scientists and Engrs., Arctic Inst. N.Am. (life), Am. Soc. Engring. Edn., Soc. for History of Discoveries, Am. Philatelic Soc., SAR, Am. Legion, Sigma Xi (pres. Las Vegas sect. 1986-91), Phi Kappa Phi (pres. U. Nev. Las Vegas chpt. 100 1982-83), Sigma Gamma Epsilon, Tau Beta Pi. Congregationalist. Home: 610 Bryant Ct Boulder City NV 89005-3017 Office: Wyman Engring PO Box 60473 Boulder City NV 89006-0473 Office Phone: 702-293-1098.

**WYMER, DOUGLAS A.,** environmental scientist, educator, ecologist; b. Troy, Ohio, Sept. 13, 1971; s. Larry Lee and Mary Ann (Dufresne) Wymer; m. Mary C. Clark, Aug. 12, 1995; 1 child, Matthew Nicholas. BS, Shorter Coll., 1994; MS, Clemson U., 1997. Asst. prof. environ. sci., program dir. U. West Ala., Livingston, 2002—; univ. liaison Black Belt Regional Mus., Livingston, 2004—. Adj. prof. biology Cumberland U., Lebanon, Tenn., 2000—02. Unit coord. Cath. Engaged Encounter, 2005—. Recipient Campus Ecology Recognition award, Nat. Wildlife Fedn., 2006; Rsch. grant, U. West Ala., 2004—05. Mem.: Soc. for Ecol. Restoration, Sigma Xi, Phi Kappa Phi (sec. 2005—). Roman Catholic. Avocations: canoeing, fishing. Office: Univ West Ala Station 07 Livingston AL 35470

**WYNALDA, ERIC,** professional soccer player; b. Fullerton, June 9, 1969; m. Amy. Student, San Diego State U. Forward FC Saarbruecken, Vfl Bochum Football Club, San Jose Clash, Calif., 1996-99; with U.S. Nat. Team, 1990—2002; forward Miami Fusion, 1999—2003; soccer analyst, World Cup commentator ESPN, 2006. Named to All-Copa Am. Team, 1995; named U.S. Soccer Male Athlete of Yr., 1996. Achievements include being all-time leading scorer on US World Cup Soccer team. Office: ESPN ESPN Plz 935 Middle St Bristol CT 06010*

**WYNAR, BOHDAN STEPHEN,** retired librarian, writer, editor; b. Lviv, Ukraine, Sept. 7, 1926; came to U.S., 1950, naturalized, 1957; s. John I. and Euphrosina (Doryk) W.; children: Taras, Michael, Roxolana. Diplom-Volkswirt Econs., U. Munich, Germany, 1949, PhD, 1950; MA, U. Denver, 1958. Methods analyst, statistician Tramco Corp., Cleve., 1951-53; freelance journalist Soviet Econs., Cleve., 1954-56; assoc. prof. Sch. Librarianship, U. Denver, 1962-66; dir. div. libr. edn. State U. Coll., Geneseo, NY, 1966-67, dean Sch. Libr. Sci., prof., 1967-69; pres. Libraries Unlimited Inc., 1969—2002. Author: Soviet Light Industry, 1956, Economic Colonialism, 1958, Ukrainian Industry, 1964, Introduction to Bibliography and Reference Work, 4th edit, 1967, Introduction to Cataloging and Classification, 8th edit, 1992, Major Writings on Soviet Economy, 1966, Library Acquisitions, 2d edit, 1971, Research Methods in Library Science, 1971, Economic Thought in Kievan Rus', 1974; co-author: Comprehensive Bibliography of Cataloging and Classification, 2 vols., 1973, Ukraine: A Bibliographic Guide to English Language Publications, 1990, Independent Ukraine: A Bibliographic Guide to English Language Publications, 1999-99, 2000, Wynar's Introduction to Cataloging and Classification, 2000; editor Ukrainian Quar., 1953-58, Preliminary Checklist of Colorado Bibliography, 1963, Studies in Librarianship, 1963-66, Research Studies in Library Science, 1970—, Best Reference Books, 3d edit., 1985, 4th edit., 1992, Colorado Bibliography, 1980; gen. editor: American Reference Books Ann., 1969-2001; editor: ARBA Guide to Subject Encyclopedias and Dictionaries, 1985, ARBA Guide To Biographical Dictionaries, Reference Books in Paperback, An Annotated Guide, 2d edit.,

1976, 3rd edit., 1991, Dictionary of Am. Library Biography, 1978, Ukraine-A Bibliographic Guide to English-Language Publications, 1990, 99, International Writings of Bohdan S. Wynar 1949-1992, 1993, Independent Ukraine, Bibliographic Guide, 2000, My Life-Memoirs-, 2003, Recommended Reference Books for Medium-Sized and Small Libraries, 1981-2001; co-editor, contbr. Ency. Ukraine, 1955—; editor Library Sci. Ann., 1984-90, 98, Libr. Info. Sci. Annual 1984-90, 98—. Bd. dirs., mem. exec. bd. ZAREVO, Inc. Mem. ALA (pres. Ukrainian Congress com. br., Denver 1976), Colo. Library Assn., N.Y. Library Assn.. Am. Assn. Advancement Slavic Studies (pres. Ukrainian Research Found. 1976-90), AAUP, Ukranian Hist. Assn. (exec. bd.), Sevčenko Societe Scientifique (Paris), Ukrainian Acad. Arts and Scis. (N.Y.C.).

**WYNDRUM, RALPH WILLIAM, JR.,** communications consultant; b. N.Y.C., Apr. 20, 1937; s. Ralph W. and Virginia M. (Woolley) W.; m. Meta Schmidt, Apr. 23, 1960; children: Dorothy, Jeanne, Ralph, Joan BS, Columbia U., 1959, MSEE, 1960, MS Bus. Administrn., 1978; DSc, NYU, 1963. Mem. tech. staff Bell Labs., Murray Hill, NJ, 1963—65, supr. exploratory circuit design, 1965—69, head loop transmission tech. dept. Holmdel and Whippany, NJ, 1969—79, head advanced loop transmission sys. dept. Whippany, 1979—87, head internat. loop sys. dept., 1987, dir. sys. analysis ctr., 1987—90, dir. quality process ctr., 1990—92, dir. quality, engring., software and techs., 1993—94; v.p. AT&T World Svcs., 1994—, dir. process engr. ctr., 1995—96; tech. v.p. AT&T Labs., 1996—99, v.p. program mgmt., 1999—2000, exec. cons., 2000—; CEO Exec. Engring. Cons., 2000—; staff exec. SmartOrg, Inc., Menlo Park, Calif., 2001—04. Adj. prof. N.J. Inst. Tech., 1965, Rutgers U., 2004—; Stevens Inst. Tech., 1980—88, mem. industry adv. bd., 2000—. Contbr. articles to profl. jours.; patentee in field Fellow: IEEE (bd. dirs. 1988—90, v.p. publs. 1990—91 bd. dirs 2000—01, v.p. tech. activities 2003—04, bd. dirs. 2003—04, bd. dirs., exec. com. 2004, Pres.'s Leadership award 1991); mem.: IEEE-USA (v.p. tech. policy 2002—03, bd. dirs. 2002—04, pres. 2006), IEEE Components, Packaging and Mfg. Tech. Soc. (pres. 1992—95), IEEE Comm. Soc. (chmn. conf. bd. 1981—87), Shrewsbury River Yacht Club, Sigma Xi, Beta Gamma Sigma, Eta Kappa Nu. Republican. Roman Catholic. Office: 35 Cooney Ter Fair Haven NJ 07704-3001 Office Phone: 732-219-0005. E-mail: rwyndrum@comcast.net, rww@monmouth.com.

**WYNER, YEHUDI,** composer, educator, pianist, conductor; b. Calgary, Alta., Can., June 1, 1929; s. Lazar and Sarah Naomi (Shumiatcher) Weiner; m. Nancy Joan Braverman, Sept. 16, 1951 (div. 1967); children: Isaiah, Adam, Cassia; m. Susan M. Davenny, June 15, 1967. Diploma, Juilliard Sch. Music, 1946; AB, Yale U., 1950, B.Mus., 1951, M.Mus., 1953; MA, Harvard U., 1952. Vis. assoc. prof. Hofstra Coll., 1959; lectr. Queens Coll., N.Y.C., 1959-60; instr. Hebrew Union Coll., N.Y.C., 1957-59; music dir. Westchester Reform Temple, N.Y.C., 1959-68; asst. prof. Yeshiva Univ. U., 1963-69, assoc. prof. theory, 1969-73; chmn. composition dept., 1969-73; prof. music SUNY, Purchase, 1978-89, dean music, 1978-82. Faculty Tanglewood Music Ctr. (formerly Berkshire Music Ctr.), 1975-97; vis. prof. composition Cornell U., 1987, Ziskind vis. prof. composition Brandeis U., 1987-88, Walter Naumburg prof. composition, dir. contemporary ensemble, 1989-2005, prof. emeritus, 2005—; vis. prof. Harvard U., 1991-93, 96-98, 2003-04; Mary Duke Biddle Disting. composer Duke U., 1995; master composer Atlantic Ctr. for the Arts, 2005. Mus. dir. Turnau Opera Assn., 1961—64, New Haven Opera Soc., 1968—77, mem. Bach Aria group, 1968—, composer, condr. Tanglewood, 1961, composer-in-residence Santa Fe Chamber Music Festival, 1982, Am. Acad. Rome, 1991; composer-in-residence: Atlantic Ctr. Arts, 2005; composer: Easy Suite for Piano, 1949, Songs, 1950—2004, Two Chorale Preludes for Organ, 1951, Partita for piano, 1952, Dance Variations for wind octet, 1953, rev., 1959, Psalm 143, chorus, 1952, Sonata for piano, 1954, Concert Duo for violin and piano, 1955—57, Dedication Anthem, 1957, Serenade for Seven Instruments, 1958, Passover Offering for Flute, Clarinet, Cello and Trombone, 1959, Three Informal Pieces for violin and piano, 1961, Friday Evening Service for Cantor, Chorus, Organ, 1963, orchestrated, 1992, (incidental music for play) The Old Glory, 1964, Torah Service with Instruments, 1966, Da Camera for piano and orch., 1967, Cadenza! for clarinet and harpsichord (or piano), 1969, De Novo for cello and small ensemble, 1971, Liturgical Fragments for the High Holidays, 1971, Three Short Fantasies for piano, 1963—71, Canto Cantabile for soprano and concert band, 1972, (music for play) The Mirror, 1972—73, Memorial Music for soprano and 3 flutes, 1971—73, Intermedio for soprano and string orchestra, 1974, Wedding Music, 1976, Dances of Atonement for violin and piano, 1976, Fragments from Antiquity: 5 songs for soprano and symphony orch., 1978, Romances for Piano Quartet, 1980, All the Rage for flute and piano, 1980, Processionals and Marches, 1979, 1980, Tanz and Maissele for clarinet, violin, cello, piano, 1981, On This Most Voluptuous Night for soprano and 7 instruments, 1982, Wind Quintet, 1984, String Quartet, 1985, Composition for Viola and piano, 1987, Toward the Center for piano, 1988, Sweet Consort for flute and piano, 1988, Leonardo Vincitore for 2 sopranos, string bass and piano, 1988, O To Be a Dragon, four songs for women's chorus and piano, 1989, Trapunto Junction for brass trio and percussion, 1991, Changing Time for small ensemble, 1991, New Fantasies for piano, 1991, Amadeus' Billiard for small ensemble, 1991, Il Cane Minore for 2 clarinets and bassoon, 1992, Wedding Dances: From the Notebook of Suzanne de Venné, 1993, Post Fantasies for piano, 1993, Prologue and Narrative for cello and orch., 1994, Song Cycle for soprano, baritone and piano: Restaurants, Wines-Bistros, Shrines, 1994, More Fantasies for piano, 1994—2002, Lyric Harmony for orch., 1995, Praise Ye the Lord for soprano and ensemble, 1996, Brandeis Sunday for string quartet, 1996, A Mad Tea Party for soprano, 2 baritones, flute, violin, cello and piano, 1996, Epilogue for orch., 1996, Horntrio, 1997, Madrigal for string quartet, 1999, The Second Madrigal: Voices of Women for soprano and eleven players, 1999, Quartet for oboe and string trio, 1999, Commedia for clarinet and piano, 2002, Tuscan Triptych: Echoes of Hannibal (string orch. version of String Quartet 1985), 2002, (piano concerto) Chiavi in mano, 2004 (Pulitzer Prize for music, 2006), (commn.) Yale U., 1950, Mus. U., 1959, Fromm Found., 1960, Koussevitzky Found. at Lib. Congress, 1960, 1991, Ford Found., 1971, Yale Band, Yale Repertory Theater, Cantilena Chamber Players, Aeolian Chamber Players, Santa Fe Chamber Music Festival, Collage of Boston, N.Y. Woodwind Quintet, Frank Taplin project, NEA Consortium, Boston Symphony Chamber Players, Atlantic Symphonietta, Carnegie Hall Am. Composers Orch., RNCM Manchester Internat. Cello Festival, Boston Symphony; pub. Associated Music Pub., Inc.; recs.: Bridge, New World, Albany, Naxos, Pro Arte & Columbia Records. Recipient Elise Stoeger prize, Lincoln Ctr. Chamber Music Soc., 1998; Rome Prize fellow, 1953—56, Alfred E. Hertz fellow, U. Calif., 1953—54, Guggenheim fellow, 1960, 1977, Rockefeller Found. fellow, Bellagio, 1998, Inst. Arts and Letters grant, 1961, grantee, NEA, 1976. Mem. Am. Music Center, Am. Acad. Arts and Letters (elected). Office: Music Dept Brandeis U Waltham MA 02454

**WYNGAARDEN, JAMES BARNES,** retired physician; b. East Grand Rapids, Mich., Oct. 19, 1924; s. Martin Jacob and Johanna (Kempers) W.; m. Ethel Vredevoogd, June 20, 1946 (div. 1977); children: Patricia Wyngaarden Fitzpatrick, Joanna Wyngaarden Gandy, Martha Wyngaarden Krauss, Lisa Wyngaarden, James Barnes Jr. Student, Calvin Coll., 1942—43, Western Mich. U., 1943—44; MD, U. Mich., 1948; DSc (hon.), U. Mich., Med. Coll. of Ohio, 1984, U. Ill., 1985, George Washington U., 1986, U. SC, West Mich. U., 1989, Duke U., 2006; PhD (hon.), Tel Aviv U., 1987. Diplomate Am. Bd. Internal Medicine. Intern Mass. Gen. Hosp., Boston, 1948-49, resident, 1949-51; vis. investigator Pub. Health Rsch. Inst., N.Y.C., 1952-53; investigator NIH, USPHS, Bethesda, Md., 1953-56; assoc. prof. medicine and biochemistry Duke U. Med. Sch., 1956-61, 1961-65; vis. scientist Inst. Biologie-Physiochemique, Paris, 1963-61; prof., chmn. U. Pa. Med. Sch., 1965-67; physician-in-chief Med. Svc. Hosp. U. PA., Phila., 1965-67; Frederic M. Hanes prof., chmn. dept. medicine Duke U. Sch. of Medicine, Durham, NC, 1967-82; physician-in-chief Med. Svc. Duke U. Hosp., Durham, 1967-82; chief of staff Duke U. Hosp., Durham, 1981-82; dir. NIH, Bethesda, MD, 1982-89; assoc. dir. life scis. Office of Sci. and Tech. Policy, Exec. Office of Pres., The White House, Washington, 1989-90; dir. Human Genome Orgn., 1990-91; fgn. sec. NAS, 1990-94; prof. medicine, assoc. vice chancellor for health affairs Duke U., Durham, NC, 1990-94, ret., 1994; mem. staff VA,

Durham County Hosps.; sr. assoc. dean internat. med. programs U. Pa., Phila., 1995-97. Cons. Office Sci. and Tech. Exec. Office of Pres., 1966-72; Mem. Pres.'s Sci. Adv. Com., 1972-73; mem. Pres.'s Com. for Nat. Medal of Sci., 1977-80; mem. adv. com. biology and medicine AEC, 1966-68; mem. bd. sci. counselors NIH, 1971-74; mem. adv. bd. Howard Hughes Med. Inst., 1969-82; mem. adv. council Life Ins. Med. Research Fund, 1967-70; adv. bd. Sci. Yr., 1977-81; vice-chmn. Com. on Study Nat. Needs for Biomed. and Behavioral Rsch. Personnel, NRC, 1977-81; bd. dirs. Idera Pharm., Genaera Pharm., Van Andel Rsch. Inst.; prin. Wash. Adv. Group, 1995-02. Author: (with W.N. Kelley) Gout and Hyperuricemia, 1976; mem. editorial bd. Jour. Biol. Chemistry, 1971-74, Arthritis and Rheumatism, 1959-66, Jour. Clin. Investigation, 1962-66, Ann. Internal Medicine, 1964-74, Medicine, 1963-90; editor: (with J.B. Stanbury, D.S. Fredrickson) The Metabolic Basis of Inherited Disease, 1960, 66, 72, 78, 83, (with O. Sperling and A. DeVries) Purine Metabolism in Man, 1974, (with L.H. Smith, Jr.) Cecil Textbook of Medicine, 16th edit., 1982, 19th edit., 1992. Bd. dirs. Royal Soc. Medicine Found., 1971-76, The Robert Wood Johnson Found. Clin. Scholar Program, 1973-78. Ensign USNR, 1943-46; sr. surgeon USPHS, 1951-56, rear adm. USPHS, 1982-90. Recipient Borden Undergrad. Research award, U. Mich., 1948, NC Gov.'s award for sci., 1974, Disting. Alumnus award We. Mich. U., 1984, Robert Williams award Assn. Profs. Medicine, 1985, Dalton scholar in medicine, Mass. Gen. Hosp., 1950, Richard Schweiker Excellence in Govt. award, 1985, Fedn. of Am. Socs. of Exptl. Biology Pub. Svc. award, 1989, Humanitarian award Nat. Orgn. for Rare Diseases, 1990; Royal Coll. Physicians fellow, 1984. Mem. Am. Rheumatism Assn., Am. Fedn. Clin. Rsch., Soc. Soc. Clin. Investigation (pres. 1974, founder's medal 1978), ACP (John Phillips Meml. award 1980), Am. Soc. Clin. Investigation, AAAS, Am. Soc. Biol. Chemists, Assn. Am. Physicians (councillor 1973-77, pres. 1978, Kober medal 1991), Endocrine Soc., Nat. Acad. Scis., Royal Acad. Scis. Sweden, Am. Acad. Arts and Sci., Inst. Medicine, Sigma Xi Clubs: Interurban Clinical (Balt.). Democrat. Presbyterian. Avocations: tennis, skiing, painting. Office Phone: 919-383-0921. Personal E-mail: jwyngaarden@nc.rr.com.

**WYN-JONES, ALUN (WILLIAM WYN-JONES),** software developer, mathematician; b. Tremadoc, Gwynedd, Great Britain, Aug. 15, 1946; arrived in U.S., 1976; s. Goronwy Wyn and Mai Jones; m. Jocelyn Ripley, July 29, 1977; 1 stepchild, Electra Truman BSc honors, U. Manchester, U.K., 1968; MSc, U. Coll. London, 1970. Rsch. engr. Marconi-Elliott Computer Labs., Borehamwood, England, 1970—71; asst. tutor math. Poly. North London, 1971—72; programmer CRC Info. Sys., Ltd., London, 1972—76; mgr. devel. Warner Computer (now Warner Ins.), N.Y.C., 1976—80; pres., owner, developer Wallsoft Sys., Inc., N.Y.C., 1982—92, Integrity Sys. Corp., N.Y.C., 1980—94. Cons. investment banking divsn. Goldman, Sachs & Co., N.Y.C., 1994-2000, FirstRain, Inc., N.Y.C., 2000-02, Thomson Fin., 2002-04; invited spkr. profl. confs Author, co-author computer software Recipient Byte Award Distinction Byte Editors and Columnists, 1988, Readers Choice award Data Based Advisor Readers, 1990, 91 Mem. AAAS, Am. Math. Soc., Math. Assn. Am Achievements include development of template programming in automatic code generation. Home: 3241 Enola Rd Carlisle PA 17015 E-mail: awynjones@comcast.net.

**WYNN, ALBERT RUSSELL,** congressman; b. Phila., Sept. 10, 1951; m. Jessie Jackson, Jan. 14, 1994 (sep.); 1 child, Gabrielle; m. Gaines Clore Wynn. BS, U. Pitts., 1973; student, Howard U.; JD, Georgetown U., 1977. Intern African Regional Affairs, U.S. State Dept., 1972-73; exec. dir. consumer protection divsn. Prince George's County, 1977-81; mem. Md. Ho. of Dels., 1983-86; lawyer Albert R. Wynn & Assocs., 1982-86; mem. Md. State Senate from Dist. 25, 1987-92, U.S. Congress from 4th Md. Dist., Washington, 1993—; dep. Dem. whip; mem. commerce com. Mem. banking & fin. svcs com., internat. rels. com., Patuxent Inst. reform task force, 1988-92, joint com. econ. devel. strategy, 1989-92; del. Dem. Nat. Conv. 1984, 88,96; pres. Metro. Washington coun. consumer agenices. Mem. NAACP legal assistance program, coalition on black affairs, voter registration, edn. coalition, gov.'s task force drunk & drugged driving; 1st vice chmn. legis. black caucus; chmn. Prince George's County black elected officials alliance. Recipient 100 Most Influential Black Americans, Ebony mag., 2006. Mem. J. Franklin Bourne Bar Assn., Kappa Alpha Psi (past pres.). Democrat. Baptist. Office: US Ho of Reps 434 Cannon House Ofc Bldg Washington DC 20515-0001 Office Phone: 202-225-8699.*

**WYNN, BOBBYE FAYE,** music educator; b. Morton, Miss., Nov. 11, 1950; d. Albert Wilson and Lucy Bob Winstead; m. Daniel Arthur Wynn; children: Daniel Ashley, Melody Joy. BS in Edn., Miss. Coll., 1977. Cert. tchr. Miss. Tchr. Powell Elem. Sch., Jackson, Miss., 1979, Woodville Heights Elem. Sch., Jackson, 1979—80; 6th grade tchr. West Elem. Sch., Natchez, Miss., 1981—84; tchr. West Primary Sch., Natchez, 1984—86, music tchr., 1990—; tchr. Northside Elem. Sch., Natchez, 1987—89; elem. music tchr. Northside Primary Sch., Natchez, Miss., 1989—90. Named Tchr. of Yr., Natchez-Adams Sch. Dist., 1997; grantee Internat. Paper Co., 2000, Entergy, 2003—05. Mem.: Miss. Music Educators Assn. (dist. chmn. 1989—90, pres. elect 1990—91, pres. elem. divsn. 1991—92, past pres. elem. divsn. 1992—93, honor choir chmn. 1992—95, bd. mem. 2002—05), Music Educators Nat. Assn. Baptist. Office: West Primary Sch 161 Lewis Dr Natchez MS 39120 Fax: 601-445-3010. Office Phone: 601-445-2891. E-mail: cidom@natchez.k12.ms.us.

**WYNN, JOHN CHARLES,** clergyman, retired theology studies educator; b. Akron, Ohio, Apr. 11, 1920; s. John Francis and Martha Esther (Griffith) W.; m. Rachel Linnell, Aug. 27, 1943; children: Mark Edward, Martha Lois Borland, Maryan Kay Ainsworth. BA, Coll. Wooster, 1941; BD, Yale U., 1944; MA, Columbia U., 1963, EdD, 1965; DD, Davis and Elkins Coll., 1958. Ordained to ministry Presbyn. Ch. (U.S.A.), 1944. Student asst. pastor Trinity Luth. Ch., New Haven, 1943-44; assoc. minister First Presbyn. Ch., Evanston, Ill., 1944 47; pastor Presbyn. Ch. El Dorado, Kans., 1947-50; dir family edn. and research United Presbyn. Bd. Christian Edn., Phila., 1950-59; prof. Colgate Rochester/Bexley Hall/Crozer Divinity Sch., 1959-85; prof. emeritus Colgate Rochester/Bexley Hall/Crozer Theol. Sem., 1985—; pvt. practice family therapy; vis. prof. U. Rochester, San Francisco Theol. Sem., St. Bernard's Sem., Wesley Theol. Sem., Hartford Theol. Found.; postdoctoral fellow Cornell U., 1973-74, St. John's U., 1980. Mem. summer faculty Union Theol. Sem., N.Y.C., San Francisco Theol. sem.; del. study conf. World Coun. Chs., 1953, 57, 64, 65, 67, 75, 80; lectr. 5 univs., Republic of South Africa, 1968; chmn. com. on sexuality in human cmty. U.P. Ch.; vol. mem. chaplaincy staff Charlestown Care Ctr., Balt. Author: How Christian Parents Face Family Problems, 1955, Pastoral Ministry to Families, 1957, Families in the Church, A Protestant Survey, 1961, Christian Education for Liberation and Other Upsetting Ideas, 1977, Family Therapy in Pastoral Ministry, 1982 (rev. and expanded as Family Therapy in Pastoral Ministry: Counseling for the Nineties, 1991), The Family Therapist, 1987; Editor: Sermons on Marriage and Family Life, 1956, Sex, Family and Society in Theological Focus, 1966, Sexual Ethics and Christian Responsibility, 1970; Contbr. articles to mags. and religious jours. Bd. dir. Presbyn. Life, Planned Parenthood League Rochester and Monroe County, Family Service Rochester, Samaritan Pastoral Counseling Ctr. Fellow Am. Assn. Marriage and Family Therapy (approved supr.); mem. Religious Edn. Assn., Nat. Coun. Chs. of Christ in U.S.A. (chmn. com. family life 1957-60), Nat. Coun. Family Rels., Family Svc. Assn. Am., Rochester Coun. Chs. (dir.) Address: 717 Maiden Choice Ln Apt 523 Catonsville MD 21228-6173 E-mail: rlwynn1@verizon.net.

**WYNN, JOHN THOMAS,** retired academic administrator, farming executive, economic consultant, oil and gas producer; b. Corsicana, Tex., May 4, 1938; s. Sam Grady and Marjorie (Reese) W.; m. Sally Ruth Adams, Mar. 19, 1958 (div. 1975); children: Martha Maria, Catherine Clarissa, Lorraine Lemae; m. Myra Louise Alexander, Oct. 30, 1976; 1 child, John Thomas. AA, Wharton County Jr. Coll., 1960; BBA in Gen. Bus., Agrl. and Mech. Coll. Tex., 1962; MBA, Tex. A&M U., 1965; PhD in Higher Edn. Mgmt., U. So. Miss., 1973. Asst. registrar, then instr. Tex. A&M U., College Station, 1962—67; exec. dean Delgado C.C., New Orleans, 1967—74, program dir.,

1977—78; asst. exec. sec. So. Assn. Colls and Schs., Atlanta, 1974—77; pres. emeritus Williamsburg Tech. Coll., Kingstree, SC, 1978—94; pres., CEO econ. cons. M&W Farm & Ranch, Egypt, Tex., 1994—. Cons. AID, Dominican Republic, 1966; bd. govs. Coastal Edn. Consortium, Conway, S.C., 1982-90; mem. exec. com. pres.'s coun. S.C. Tech. Edn. Coll., Columbia, 1985-86. Vestryman St. Thomas Episc. Ch., College Station, 1962-67, St. George Episc. Ch., New Orleans, 1969-72; vestryman St. Thomas' Episc. Ch., Wharton, Tex., 1998-2001, 06—, sr. warden, 1999-2000; Rep. precinct 2 chmn., Wharton County, Tex., 1998-2000. Served as sgt. USAR, 1955-62. Recipient Order of the Palmetto S.C. Gen. Assembly, 1994; named Hon. Order of Ky. Cols.; col. Aide-de-Camp, La., col. Aide-de-Camp, Ala.; col. Aide-de-Camp, N.Mex. Mem. Future Farmers Assn. (hon.), S.C. Tech. Edn. Assn. (bd. dirs. 1985-88), Kingstree C. of C. (bd. dirs 1981-84), Kiwanis, Masons (32 degree), Shriners (hon.), Phi Delta Kappa, Kappa Delta Pi. Avocations: chess, camping, music composition, reading. Home and Office: PO Box 307 Egypt TX 77436 Personal E-mail: johnwynn@agristar.net. Business E-mail: egypt@agristar.net.

**WYNN, KAREN,** psychologist, educator, researcher; b. Austin, Tex., Dec. 18, 1962; d. Lucy Shombert and William "Buddy" Wynn; m. Paul Bloom; children: Max Bloom, Zachary Bloom. BA, McGill U., Montreal, Que., Can., 1985; PhD, MIT, 1990. Asst. prof. psychology, asst. rsch. scientist in cognitive sci. U. Ariz., Tucson, 1990—96, assoc. prof. psychology, assoc. rsch. scientist in cognitive sci., dir. developmental psychology program, 1996—99; prof. psychology and cognitive sci. Yale U., New Haven, 1999—. Vis. assoc. rsch scientist, med. scientist rsch. coun. cognitive develop. unit U. Coll. London, 1997—98; lectr. in field. Contbr. articles to profl. jours. and newspapers; participated in radio interviews. Recipient James McKeen Cattell Found. Sabbatical award, 1997, Disting. Sci. award for Early Career Contbn. to Psychology, APA, 2000, Troland Rsch. award, NAS, 2001; grantee, NIH, NSF, 1987—90. Mem.: Cognition (editl. bd. mem. 1993), Trends in Cognitive Scis. (adv. editl. bd. mem. 1998), Soc. for Rsch. in Child Devel., Internat. Soc. Infant Studies. Avocation: dressage. Office: 2 Hillhouse Ave Yale Univ Dept Psychology Box 208205 New Haven CT 06520-8205 Office Phone: 203-436-1406. Office Fax: 203-436-1915. Business E-mail: karen.wynn@yale.edu.

**WYNN, KEVIN D.,** secondary school educator, coach; b. Council Bluffs, Iowa, July 21, 1962; s. Joyce Sikora; m. Jane Renee Corson, May 24, 1985; children: Zachary B., Sara J. BA in Secondary Edn., U. Nebr., Lincoln, 1984; MS in Secondary Edn., U. Nebr., Omaha, 1991. Tchr. Papillion/ LaVista Pub. Schs., Nebr., 1985—; baseball coach Skutt Cath. H.S., Omaha, 1995—2001. Baseball coach East-West Ambassadors, N.Y., 1994, Patroit Youth Baseball, Omaha, 1996—2002. Recipient Nebr. Youth Coach of Yr., 2002. Mem.: Papillion/LaVista Edn. Assn., Nebr. State Edn. Assn., NEA. Achievements include national champions in National Baseball Congress 14 year olds, 2002; State Junior League Champion, 2001. Avocations: reading, birdwatching, fishing, hunting, hiking. Office: Papillion Jr HS P23 S Washington Papillion NE 68046 Business E-mail: kwynn@paplu.esus.org.

**WYNN, ROBERT E.,** electronics executive, retired military officer; b. Dallas, Jan. 31, 1942; s. Wendell W. and Thelma (Smart) W.; m. Lavenia K. Davis, Mar. 25, 1972; children: Leslie, Lauren. Bachelors degree, West Point Mil. Acad., 1964; MEE, U. Tenn., 1971. Commd. 2d lt. U.S. Army, 1964, advanced through grades to commdg. gen., 1990; chief comm. Ops. Divsn. 5th Signal Command, Heidelberg, Germany, 1979-81, chief of staff Worms, Germany, 1984-85; chief plans and programs, dep. chief staff Ops. and Plans DCS for OPS and PLANS, Washington, 1981-84; comdr. 2d Signal Brigade, Mannheim, Germany, 1986-88, U.S. Army Info. Systems Command/Tng. Doctrine Command, Ft. Monroe, Va., 1988-90; commdg. gen. 7th Signal Command, Ft. Ritchie, Md., 1990-92, U.S. Army Info. Systems Engring. Command, Ft. Huachuca, Ariz., 1992-95; ret., 1995; mgr. C3 sys. Raytheon E-Systems Inc., Richardson, Tex., 1995-97; v.p. Harris Corp., Alexandria, Va., 1997—. Decorated Bronze Star, Legion of Merit, Silver Order of Mercury. Mem. Assn. U.S. Army Assn. Grads. (life), Armed Forces Comm. and Electronics Assn. (life, bd. dirs.), Sky Soldier (life, 173d airborne brigade), Signal Corps Regiment (life). Avocations: golf, tennis. Office: Harris Corp 1201 E Abingdon Dr Ste 300 Alexandria VA 22314-1487 Home: 355 Baytree Dr Melbourne FL 32940-2106

**WYNN, STEPHEN A.,** hotel and entertainment facility executive; b. 1942; m. Elaine Paschal, 1963; children: Kevin, Gillian. BA, U. Pa, 1963. Pres., chief exec. officer Best Brands, Inc., 1969-72; chmn. bd. dirs., pres., CEO Mirage Resorts Inc. (formerly Golden Nugget Inc.), 1973—2000; mng. mem. Valvino Lamore, LLC, 2000—02; chmn., CEO Wynn Resorts Ltd., 2002—. Named one of Top 200 Collectors, ARTnews Mag., 2004, 2006, 100 Most Influential People, Time Mag., 2006, Forbes' Richest Americans, 2006. Avocation: Collector of French Impressionism; Modern and Contemporary Art. Office: Wynn Resorts Ltd 3145 Las Vegas Blvd S Las Vegas NV 89109*

**WYNN, THOMAS JOSEPH,** judge, educator; b. Chgo., Aug. 30, 1918; s. Phillip H. and Delia B (Madden) W.; m. Bernadette L. Lavelle, Apr. 17, 1948; children: Thomas Joseph, John P. AB, DePaul U., 1941, JD, 1944. Bar: Ill. 1942. Spl. investigator Phoenix & Murphy, Chgo., 1942; pvt. practice law Chgo., 1946-59; ptnr. Wynn & Ryan, Chgo., 1959-79; assoc. judge Cir. Ct. Cook County, Ill., 1979-83, judge chancery div. mechanic's lien sect. Ill., 1983-96, retired Ill., 1996. Lectr. bus. law Latin Am. Inst., Chgo., 1946-47; mem. faculty Coll. Commerce, DePaul U., Chgo., 1947-98, assoc. dean Evening div., 1957-73, prof., 1972-79, part-time faculty, 1979-83, adj. prof. bus. law, 1983-98; asst. atty. Am. Bar Assn., 1957-58; bd. dirs., gen. counsel Suburbanite Bowl, Inc., 1958-79; gen. legal counsel Chgo. Consortium Colls. and Univs., GM Tool Corp.; pres., bd. dirs. Metroplex Leasing and Financing, Inc. Candidate for alderman Chgo. City Coun., 1931; candidaw for judge Mcpl. Ct. Chgo., 1956; mem. adv. bd. dirs. Ill. Good Govt. Assn. 1958-79; mem. adv. bd. to dean Coll Law DePaul U., 1992—. Ensign-lt. (S.G.) USNR, 1942-46. Mem. Ill. Bar Assn., Chgo. Bar Assn. (mem. arbitration and alternative dispute resolution com., civil practice coms., mem. internat. law com., mem. judiciary com., mem. cir. ct. com.), Ill. Judges Assn. (com. mandatory arbitration alt. dispute resolution, com. pubs.), Assn. Univ. Evening Colls. (past chmn.), Am. Bus. Law Assn. (pres. 1972-73), Am. Real Estate and Urban Econs. Assn., Chgo. Area Evening Deans and Dirs. Assn., U.S. Adult Edn. Assn., Ill. Adult Edn. Assn., Am. Right-of-Way Assn. (advisor chmn., nat. advisor com. 1963-64), St. Vincent DePaul Soc., DePaul Law Alumni Assn. (past pres.), Smithsonian Inst., Pres.'s Club, (DePaul U. 1986—), Blue Key, Lambda Psi, Beta Gamma Sigma, Delta Mu Delta. Home: 27592 W Cuba Rd Barrington IL 60010-2770

**WYNN, TRACY KEENAN,** screenwriter; b. Hollywood, Calif., Feb. 28, 1945; s. Frank Keenan Wynn and Eve (Kimmel) Johnson; m. Kerstin Helena Wassgren, Aug. 28, 1977; children: Aidan, Amanda, Brendan. Student, UCLA, 1964-67. Ind. screenwriter, 1967—. Screenwriter: (TV series) The Net, 1988-89, (TV films) Tribes, 1970 (Emmy award), The Glass House, 1972, The Autobiography of Miss Jane Pittman, 1974 (Emmy award), The Quest: The Longest Drive, 1976, In the Line of Duty: The FBI Murders, 1988 (also co-prodr.), The Revenge of Al Capone, 1989 (also co-prodr.), Carolina Skeletons, 1991 (also co-prodr.), (films) The Longest Yard, 1974, The Drowning Pool, 1975 (Poe Mystery award), The Deep, 1977, Robinson Crusoe, 1997, Mean Machine, 2001, The Longest Yard, 2005; dir.: (TV films) Hit Lady, 1974. Mem. Writers Guild Am. (mem. exec. bd. 1975-77), Dirs. Guild Am. Episcopalian. Avocations: skiing, Karate.

**WYNN, WILL,** mayor; b. Beaumont, Tex. m. Anne Elizabeth Wynn 1992; 2 children. B in Environ. Design cum laude, Tex. A&M U., 1984. Founder CIVITAS Investments, Inc., 1997; mayor City of Austin, Tex., 2003—. With Hill Country Conservancy, St. David's Found., Women and their Work, KLRU, Blanton Mus., Austin Poetry Slam, Austin Film Soc.; chmn. Downtown Austin Alliance; dir. Children's Mus. and Heritage Soc. Named

Austinite of Yr., Austin Under Forty; recipient Scenic Hero award, Scenic Austin. Mem.: Urban Land Inst. Avocations: listening to music, canoeing, bicycling. Mailing: PO Box 1088 Austin TX 78767 Office: Mcpl Bldg 124 West 8th St #103 Austin TX 78701*

**WYNNE, BENJAMIN RAY,** history professor; b. Jackson, Miss., Apr. 22, 1961; s. George Ervin Wynne and Patricia Dear Mullican. BBA, Millsaps Coll., 1984; MA, Miss. Coll., 1995; PhD, U. Miss., 2000. Hist. instr. U. Miss., Oxford, Miss., 1998—2002; vis. asst. prof. Fla. State U., Tallahassee, 2002—04; adj. prof. Valdosta (Ga.) State U., 2005; asst. prof. hist. Gainesville State Coll., Watkinsville, Ga., 2005—. Organizer Grad. Conf. So. Hist., U. Miss., 2000; manuscript evaluator U. Nebr., Lincoln, Nebr., 2003. Author: A Hard Trip: A History of the 15th Mississippi Infantry, (book introduction) Recollections and Letters of Robert E. Lee, Mosby's Memoirs, Stonewall Jackson and the American Civil War; contbr. chapters to books. Mem.: Miss. Hist. Soc., Ga. Hist. Soc., So. Hist. Assn., Am. Hist. Assn., Phi Alpha Theta, Pi Kappa Alpha. Office Phone: 706-310-2230. Business E-Mail: bwynne@gsc.edu.

**WYNNE, BRIAN JAMES,** retired professional society administrator; b. N.Y.C., Dec. 2, 1950; s. Bernard and Dolores (Doyle) W. Student, Institute des Sciences Politiques, Paris, 1970-71; BA, Coll. Holy Cross, 1972; MA, U. So. Calif., 1974. Staff Exec. Cons., Inc., McLean, Va., 1974-76; prin., 1976-78; exec. dir. Indsl. Designers Soc. Am., Washington, 1978-88. Cons. to various non-profit orgns.; dir. Worldesign 85, founder Worldesign Found. Mem. Am. Soc. Assn. Execs., Indsl. Designers Soc. Am. (hon.), Phi Sigma Iota. Home: 5200 N Ocean Blvd Apt 1004 Lauderdale By The Sea FL 33308-3019

**WYNNE, J. JUDSON,** research scientist, ecologist; b. Mineral Wells, Tex., Jan. 25, 1969; s. Judson Holmes Wynne and Melanie Wynne Gregory. Postgrad. Cert. in Ecotech., Free U. of Brussels, Belgium, 1998; MS in Environ. Sci. and Policy, No. Ariz. U., Flagstaff, 2003; postgrad. in Biol. Scis., No. Ariz. U., Flagstaff, AZ, 2005. Wildlife ecologist US Forest Svc. - Rocky Mountain Rsch. Sta., Flagstaff, Ariz., 2000—03; wildlife ecologist/cave rsch. scientist USGS-Southwest Biol. Sci. Ctr., Flagstaff, Ariz., 2002—. Presenter to local schools on importance of cave and bat conservation, Flagstaff, Ariz., 2002—06. Grantee, NASA, 2005-2006. Mem.: Soc. of Conservation Biology (assoc.; Colo. Plateau chpt.), Ariz. Bat Resource Group (assoc.), Nat. Speleological Soc. (assoc.), Karst Conservancy (assoc.), Western Bat Working Group (assoc.), Cousteau Soc. (assoc.), Union of Concerned Scientists (assoc.), Bat Conservation Internat. (assoc.) Achievements include discovery of new cricket genus. Office: USGS SW Biol Sci Ctr 2255 N Gemini Dr Flagstaff AZ 86011 Office Phone: 928-556-7466 238.

**WYNNE, JAMES J.,** research scientist; B Physics, M Physics, PhD Physics, Harvard U. Mgr. Laser Physics and Chemistry Group IBM T.J. Watson Rsch. Ctr.; rsch. scientist IBM Watson Rsch. Ctr., 1971—. Contbr. articles, scientific papers. Co-recipient R.W. Wood prize, Optical Soc. Am., 2004; named one of Inventors of the Yr., Ea. NY Intellectual Property Law Assn., 2001; named to National Inventors Hall of Fame, 2002. Achievements include patents in field; development of Lasik eye surgery. Office: Watson Rsch Ctr 1101 Kithawan Rd Ste 134 Yorktown Heights NY 10598*

**WYNNE, JOHN CARLTON,** lawyer; b. Oklahoma City, 1961; BS in Economics, magna cum laude, U. Okla., 1983, JD cum laude, 1986. Bar: Tex. 1986. Ptnr., Banking /Fin. Andrews Kurth LLP, Houston, chmn. pro bono com. Mem.: Fifth Cir. Bar Assn., State Bar Tex., Houston Bar Assn., Phi Beta Kappa. Office: Andrews Kurth LLP 600 Travis St Ste 4200 Houston TX 77002-3090 Office Phone: 713-220-4088. Office Fax: 713-238-7234. Business E-Mail: jwynne@andrewskurth.com.

**WYNNE, JOHNNY CALVIN,** dean, plant pathologist, researcher; b. Williamston, N.C., May 17, 1943; s. James Harry and Rachel Loraine (Ayers) Wynne; m. Diane Louise Sawyer, June 1961 (div. Feb. 1989); m. Jacqueline Crawford Creech. Nov. 25, 1989; children: Debbie Ann, Donna Carol, John Christopher, James Alexander. BS, N.C. State U., 1965, MS, 1968, PhD, 1974. Instr. crop sci. dept. N.C. State U., Raleigh, 1968-74, from asst. prof. to assoc. prof., 1974—83, prof., 1983-91, acting tchg. adminstr., 1987-89, head dept., 1984-91, dir. N.C. agr. rsch. svc., 1992—2003, dean, exec. dir. Coll. Agr. & Life Scis., 2003—. Recipient Rsch. award, Nat. Peanut Coun., 1992. Fellow: AAAS, Am. Soc. Agron, Crop Sci. Soc. Am., Am. Peanut Rsch. and Edn. Soc. (pres. 1990, Bailey award 1977); mem.: So. Assn. Exptl. Sta. Dirs. (chmn. 1994), Coun. Agrl. Sci. and Tech., Sigma Iota Rho. Office: NC State Univ PO Box 7643 Raleigh NC 27695-0001 E-mail: johnny_wynne@ncsu.edu.

**WYNNE, LYMAN CARROLL,** psychiatrist; b. Lake Benton, Minn., Sept. 17, 1923; s. Nels Wind and Ella C. (Pultz) W.; m. Adele Rogerson, Dec. 22, 1947; children: Christine, Randall, Sara, Barry, Jonathan. War certificate, Harvard, 1943, MD, 1947, PhD in Social Psychology, 1958; MD (hon.), Oulu U., Finland, 1989. Med. intern Peter Bent Brigham Hosp., Boston, 1947-48; grad. fellow social relations dept. Harvard, 1948-49; resident neurology Queen Square Hosp., London, Eng., 1950; resident psychiatry Mass. Gen. Hosp., Boston, 1951-54; psychoanalytic tng. Washington Psychoanalytic Inst., 1954-60, teaching analyst, 1965-72. Cons., investigator WHO, 1965—; staff NIMH, 1954-57, chief sect. family studies, 1957-61, chief adult psychiatry br., 1961-72; mem. faculty Washington Sch. Psychiatry, 1956-72; prof. U. Rochester Sch. Medicine and Dentistry, 1971-98, chmn. dept. psychiatry, 1971-77, dir. div. family programs, 1971-83; psychiatrist-in-chief Strong Meml. Hosp., Rochester, N.Y., 1971-77, prof. emeritus psychiatry, 1998—; vis. lectr. Am. U., Beirut, Lebanon, 1963-64 Bd. dirs. Family Process, 1969-97; mem. editl. adv. bd. Jour. Nervous and Mental Diseases; sr. editor: The Nature of Schizophrenia, 1978; editor: The State of the Art in Family Therapy Research; co-editor: Psychosocial Intervention in Schizophrenia, 1983, Children at Risk for Schizophrenia, 1984, The Language of Family Therapy, 1985; sr. editor Systems Consultation, 1986 Chmn. AAMFT Rsch. & Edn. Found., 1992-94. Med. dir. USPHS, 1961-72; mem. NRC, 1969-72. Recipient Commendation medal USPHS, 1965; Hofheimer prize Am. Psychiat. Assn., 1966; Frieda Fromm-Reichmann award Am. Acad. Psychoanalysis, 1966; Meritorious Service medal USPHS, 1966; Stanley Dean award Am. Coll. Psychiatrists, 1976; McAlpin Research Achievement award, 1977, Disting. Achievement in Family Therapy Research, Am. Family Therapy Assn., 1981; Disting. Research Achievement award Assn. Marriage and Family Therapy, 1982, Disting. Profl. Contbn. award Am. Assn. for Marriage and Family Therapy, 1985, Disting. Contbn. to Family Therapy award Am. Family Therapy Assn., 1989. Fellow: Am. Acad. Psychoanalysis, Am. Psychiat. Assn. (life); mem.: Soc. for Rsch. in Psychopathology, Nat. Coun. for Family Relations, Assn. for Clin. Psychosocial Rsch. (coun. 1984—91), Am. Psychoanalytic Assn., Am. Assn. for Marriage and Family therapy (bd. dirs. 1992—94), Am. Family Therapy Acad. (pres. 1986—87), Am. Coll. Psychoanalysts, Western N.Y. Psychoanalytic Soc. (pres. 1986—87), Psychiat. Rsch. Soc. Office: Strong Meml Hosp Rochester NY 14642-8409 Home: 1 Sinclair Dr Apt 117 Pittsford NY 14534-1735 E-mail: lcwynne@rochester.rr.com.

**WYNNE, MICHAEL WALTER,** civilian military employee; b. Hillsborough County, Fla., Sept. 4, 1944; s. Edward P. and Dorothy T. Wynne; m. Barbara Ann Hill, July 23, 1966; children: Lisa, Collene, Karen, Laura. BS in Gen. Engring., U.S. Mil. Acad., 1966; MSEE, Air Force Inst. Tech., 1970; MBA in Fin., U. Colo. 1975. Commd. lt. USAF, 1966, advanced through grades to capt., 1969; project engr. Electronics Systems Div., Bedford, Mass., 1966-68; asst. prof. astronautics USAF Acad., Colorado Springs, 1970-73; sec.-treas., v.p. R.A.D. Inc., Colorado Springs, 1973-75; mgr. estimating dept. Ft. Worth div. Gen. Dynamics, 1975-78, mgr. pricing. corp. hdqrs., St. Louis, 1978-82; v.p. contracts, estimating Land Systems div. Gen. Dynamics, Sterling Heights, Mich., 1982-87, v.p. bus. devel., 1987-91; corp.v.p., gen. mgr. Space Systems Div. Gen. Dynamics, San Diego, 1991-92, pres., corp. v.p. Space Systems Div., 1992—94; v.p., gen. mgr. space launch systems

Lockheed Martin Astronautics, 1994—97; sr. v.p. for internat. planning & bus. devel. Gen. Dynamics, 1997—99; prin. under sec. acquisition, tech. & logistics US Dept. Def., Washington, 2001—05, under sec. for acquisition, tech. & logistics, 2005, sec. USAF, 2005—. Fellow Nat. Contract Mgmt. Assn. (pres. Detroit chpt. 1983-86), Assn. U.S. Army (pres. Detroit chpt. 1987-89), Am. Def. Preparedness Assn. (pres. Mich. chpt. 1986-87). Roman Catholic. Avocations: golf, skiing. Office: USAF 1670 Air Force Pentagon Washington DC 20330*

**WYNNE, WILLIAM FRANCIS,** lawyer; b. N.Y.C., Sept. 21, 1952; s. William F. and Catherine Wynne; m. Barbara Brizzi Wynne; children: William, Andrew, Emily. AB in Econs., Rutgers U., 1973; JD, U. Pa., 1976. Bar: N.Y. 1977. From assoc. to ptnr. White & Case LLP, N.Y.C., 1976—. Law chmn. mgmt. bd. White & Case LLP, N.Y.C., 2004—. Office: White & Case LLP 1155 Avenue of the Americas New York NY 10036-2787 Business E-Mail: wwynne@whitecase.com.

**WYNNE-EDWARDS, HUGH ROBERT,** geologist, educator, entrepreneur; b. Montreal, Que., Can., Jan. 19, 1934; s. Vero Copner and Jeannie Campbell (Morris) W.-E.; married Janet Elizabeth McGregor; children from previous marriages: Robin Alexander, Katherine Elizabeth, Renée Elizabeth Lortie, Krista Smyth, Jeannie Elizabeth, Alexander Vernon. BSc with 1st class honors, U. Aberdeen, Scotland, 1955; MA, Queen's U., Kingston, Ont., Can., 1957, PhD, 1959; DSc (hon.), Meml. U., 1975. Registered profl. engr., B.C., 1995. With Geol. Survey Can., 1958-59; lectr. Queen's U., 1968-72, asst. prof., then assoc. prof., 1961-68, prof., head dept. geol. scis., 1968-72; prof., then Cominco prof., head dept. geol. scis. U. B.C., Vancouver, Canada, 1972-77; asst. sec. univ. for Ministry of State for Sci. and Tech., Ottawa, Canada, 1977-79; sci. dir. Alcan Internat. Ltd., Montreal, 1979-80, v.p. R & D, chief sci. officer, 1980-89; CEO Moli Energy Ltd., Vancouver, 1989-90; pres. Terracy Inc., Vancouver, 1989—; sci. advisor Teck Corp., Vancouver, 1989-91; pres., CEO B.C. Rsch. Inc., Vancouver, 1993-97, exec. chmn., pres., 1997-2000. Chmn. Silvagen Inc., 1996-99; advisor Directorate Mining and Geology, Uttar Pradesh, India, 1964, Grenville project Que. Dept. Natural Resources, 1968-72; vis. prof. U. Aberdeen, 1965-66, U. Witwatersrand, Johannesburg, South Africa, 1972; UN cons., India, 1974; pres. SCITEC, 1977-78; mem. sci. adv. com. CBC, 1980-84; mem. Sci. Coun. Can., 1983-89, Nat. Adv. Bd. on Sci. and Tech., 1987-90 indsl. liaison com. UN Ctr. for Sci. and Tech. in Devel., 1982-84; vice chmn. rsch. adv. group Bus. Coun. for Sustainable Devel., Geneva, 1991; mem. Nat. Biotech. Adv. Coun., 1995-98; chmn. Neurosci. Can. Partnership, 1999-2003, Azure Dynamics Inc., 2000-01; pres. Silvagen Holdings Inc., 1999-2000; bd. dirs. Welichem Biotech Inc., chmn., 2000-; bd. dirs. Photon Control Inc. Bd. dirs. Royal Victoria Hosp., Montreal, 1984-89. Decorated officer Order of Can., 1991; recipient Spendiarov prize 24th Internat. Geol. Congress, Montreal, 1972. Fellow Can. Acad. Engring., Royal Soc. Can., World Acad. Arts and Scis.; mem. Can. Rsch. Mgmt. Assn. (vice chmn. 1982-84, chmn. 1984-85, Assn. medal 1987), Univ. Club (Montreal). Mem. United Ch. Canada. Avocations: tennis, skiing, carpentry. Office: Terracy Inc 2030 27th St West Vancouver BC Canada V7V 4L4 Office Phone: 604-926-1191. Business E-Mail: hughwynn@terracy.com.

**WYRICK, JERMAINE ALBERT,** lawyer; b. Detroit, Oct. 19, 1971; s. Albert and Loretta Wyrick. BA in Polit. Sci., U. Mich., 1993; JD, Wayne State U., 1996. Bar: Mich., US Dist. Ct. (ea. dist.) Mich., 1997, US Ct. Appeals (6th cir.), 1997, US Supreme Ct., 2001. Pvt. practice, Detroit, 1997—. Bd. dirs. Coalition Affirmative Action Preservation NAACP, Legal Redress, Detroit; lectr. in field. Bd. dirs. Coleman A. Young Scholarship Found.; with Angels Night Wayne County Juvenile Ct., 1998. Coun. on Legal Edu. Opportunity fellow, Ohio, 1993; recipient Achievement award Coleman A. Young Found., 1989-92, Disting. Grad. award, 1993, Pro Bono Project award FBA ea. dist. Mich., 1997, Fed Bar Assn. award, 1997, 2001, Trailblazer award Jordan Ednl. Svcs., 2004, Civil Rights and Law School U.S. Attys. Office, 2005, Five Under Ten award U. Mich. African Am. Alumni Coun. Mem. ABA, ATLA, Nat. Bar Assn. (region IV bd. dirs.), Mich. Trial Lawyers Assn., Wolverine Bar Assn.(bd. dirs.). Democrat. Mem. Hartford Meml. Bapt. Ch. Avocations: basketball, golf. Home: PO Box 44646 Detroit MI 48244 Office: Law Offices Jermaine A Wyrick P L C Ste 1610 615 Griswold Detroit MI 48226-3319 Office Phone: 313-964-8950. E-mail: attyjaw1@ameritech.net.

**WYRSCH, CAROLYN IRWIN,** historian, educator; b. Gilbert Raymond Irwin, Sr. and Eleanor Womsley Irwin; m. Edward J. Wyrsch, Dec. 29, 1973; children: Elizabeth Mary, Kathleen Mary, Matthew Gilbert. BA in History, Caldwell Coll., NJ, 1968; MA in History, Rutgers U., Newark, NJ, 1970; MA, Montclair State U., NJ, 1974. Instr. history instr., admissions officer Caldwell Coll., NJ, 1969—76; tchr. history, dept. chair Wakefield Sch., The Plains, Va., 1994—. AP exam reader U.S. history Ednl. Testing Svc., Princeton, NJ, 2005—; cons. African Am. Hist. Assn., The Plains, Va., 1998—; adj. instr. history No. Va. C.C., Manassas, 1987—. Author: (historical booklet) History of Gainesville School: 1935-1985. Leader Girl Scouts and Boy Scouts, Haymarket, Va., 1984—95; mem. Med. Missionaries, Manassas, 1998—2006. Grantee, Va. Hist. Assn., 2004, Japan Fulbright Meml. Fund, 2005. Mem.: Va. Assn. Ind. Schs., Nat. Coun. History Edn. Achievements include research in creating the lesson plans on slavery in Fauquier County, Virginia; development of identity to unnamed slaves in official records by examining primary journals from the 19th century. Avocations: travel, antiques, reading. Office Phone: 540-253-5393 427.

**WYRSCH, JAMES ROBERT,** lawyer, educator, writer; b. Springfield, Mo., Feb. 23, 1942; s. Louis Joseph and Jane Elizabeth (Welsh) W.; m. B. Darlene Wyrsch, Oct. 18, 1975; children: Scott, Keith, Mark, Brian, Marcia. BA, U. Notre Dame, 1963; JD, Georgetown U., 1966; LLM, U. Mo., Kansas City, 1972. Bar: Mo. 1966, U.S. Ct. Appeals (8th cir.) 1971, U.S. Ct. Appeals (10th cir.) 1974, U.S. Ct. Appeals (5th cir.) 1974, U.S. Ct. Appeals (6th cir.) 1982, U.S. Ct. Appeals (11th cir.) 1984, U.S. Ct. Appeals (7th cir.) 1986, U.S. Ct. Appeals (4th cir.) 1990, U.S. Ct. Appeals (9th cir.) 1998, U.S. Ct. Mil. Appeals 1978, U.S. Tax Ct. 1983, U.S. Supreme Ct. 1972. Assoc. Wyrsch, Hobbs & Mirakian P.C., Kansas City, 1970-71, of counsel, 1972-77, ptnr., 1978—, pres., shareholder, 1988—; adj. prof. U. Mo., 1981—. Mem. Mo. Supreme Ct. Procedures Com., 1983—; mem. adv. coun. legal assts. program U. Mo. at Kansas City, 1985-88; mem. cir. ct. adv. com. Jackson County, Mo., 1998—; mem. jud. selection com. U.S. Magistrate U.S. Dist. Ct. Mo., 1985; mem. fed. practice com. U.S. Dist. Ct. Mo., 1985-88; mem. subcom. to draft model criminal instrns.for dist. cts. of 8th cir., 1986—; bd. dirs. Kansas City Bar Found.; Mo. membership co-chmn., 2002-06; vice chair U.S. Supreme Ct. Hist. Soc., 2006—. Contbr. articles to profl. jours.; co-author: Missouri Criminal Trial Practice, 1994. Capt. U.S. Army, 1966-69. Recipient Joint Svcs. Commendation medal, 1969, U. Mo. Kansas City Svc. award Law Found., 1991-92, Lawyer of Yr. award Mo. Lawyers Weekly, 2001, Practitioner of Yr. award U. Mo. Kans. City Law Sch. Alumni Assn., 2002; named Best of the Bar, Kansas City Bus. Jour., 2002-05, Dean of Trial Bar award Kans. City Met. Bar Assn., 2002, Lifetime Achievement award Kansas City Bar Assn., 2004, Charles Shaw Trial Advocacy award Mo. Assn. Crminal Def. Lawyers, 2004; named a KC Legal Leader of Yr., Daily Record, 2005. Fellow: Mo. Bar Found., Am. Coll. Trial Lawyers (access to justice com. 2002—, Mo. State chair 2004—06), Am. Bar Found. (life); mem.: ATLA, ABA, Nat. Lawyers Assn. (chmn. criminal law com. 2003), Coll. Master Advs. and Barristers (sr. counsel), Mo. Assn. Criminal Def. Attys. (dir. 1978, sec. 1982), Nat. Assn. Criminal Def. Attys., Am. Bd. Trial Advs. (adv.), Kansas City Met. Bar Assn. (chmn. anti-trust com. 1981, chmn. bus. tort, anti-trust franchise com. 1998), Mo. Bar Assn. (vice chmn. criminal law com. 1978—79), Am. Arbitration Assn. (panel arbitrators 1976—2000), Country Club of Blue Springs, Kansas City Club, Phi Delta Phi. Democrat. Roman Catholic. Home: 1501 NE Sunny Creek Ln Blue Springs MO 64014-2044 Office: Wyrsch Hobbs & Mirakian PC 1000 Walnut St Ste 1600 Kansas City MO 64106-2140 Office Phone: 816-221-0080. Business E-Mail: jimwyrsch@whmlaw.net.

**WYRSCH, MARTHA B.,** lawyer, energy executive; b. Laramie, Wyo., 1958; m. Gerry Wyrsch; 2 children. BA in Lit., U. Wyo., 1980; JD, George Washington U., 1986; graduate, Harvard Bus. Sch. Advanced Mgmt. Pro-

gram, 2002. Legis. asst. to Sen. Alan K. Simpson of Wyo., 1980—83; assoc. Davis, Graham & Stubbs, 1986—91; v.p., gen. counsel and sec. KN Energy Inc. (now Kinder Morgan, Inc.), 1991—99; sr. v.p., gen. counsel, sec., Duke Energy Field Svcs. Duke Energy Corp., Charlotte, NC, 1999—2001, sr. v.p., gen. counsel, energy transmission and distribn., 2001—03, sr. v.p., legal affairs, 2003—04, group v.p., gen. counsel, sec., 2004—05; pres., CEO Duke Energy Gas Transmission, Houston, 2005—. Bd. advisors George Washington Law Sch.; bd. dirs. Inst. and Sch. for Environ. and Natural Resources, U. Wyo. Mem.: ABA (vice chair, pub. utility, comm. and transp. law sect.), Interstate Natural Gas Assn. Am., Edison Elec. Inst., Am. Gas Assn., Am. Corp. Counsel Assn., Colo. Bar Assn. Office: Duke Energy Gas Transmission 5400 Westheimer Ct Houston TX 77056

**WYRTKI, KLAUS,** oceanography educator; b. Tarnowitz, Germany, Feb. 7, 1925; came to U.S., 1961; s. Wilhelm and Margarete (Pacharzina) W.; m. Helga Kocher, June 6, 1954 (div. 1970); children: Undine, Oliver; m. Erika Maassen. PhD magna cum laude, U. Kiel, Germany, 1950. With German Hydrographic Inst., Hamburg, 1950-51; German Rsch. Coun. postdoctoral rsch. fellow U. Kiel, 1951-54; head Inst. Marine Rsch., Djakarta, Indonesia, 1954-57; sr. rsch. officer, then prin. rsch. officer div. fisheries and oceanography Commonwealth Sci. and Indsl. Rsch. Orgn., Sydney, Australia, 1958-61; assoc. rsch. oceanographer, then rsch. oceanographer Scripps Instn. Oceanography, U. Calif., 1961-64; prof. oceanography U. Hawaii, Honolulu, 1964—, prof. emeritus, 1993. Chmn. North Pacific Expt., 1974-80, com. on climate changes and ocean Internat. Assn. Phys. Scis. of the Oceans; mem. Spl. Com. on Ocean Rsch. Working Group on Prediction of El Nino, Sci. Working Group on Topography Expt., panel on climate and global change NOAA. Author: El Nino—The Dynamic Response of the Equatorial Pacific Ocean to Atmospheric Forcing, 1975; editor: Oceanographic Atlas of the International Indian Ocean Expedition, 1971; mem. editl. bd. Jour. Phys. Oceanography, 1971-79. Recipient Excellence in Rsch. award U. Hawaii, 1980, Rosenstiel award U. Miami, 1981, Prince Albert I medal Internat. Assn. Phys. Scis. Ocean, 2003, Alexander Agassiz medal NAS, 2004 Fellow Am. Geophys. Union (Maurice Ewing medal 1989), Am. Meteorol. Soc. (Harald Ulrick Sverdrup Gold medal 1991), Deutsche Meteorologische Gesellschaft (Albert Defant medal 1992). E-mail: wyrtki@aloha.net.

**WYSCHOGROD, EDITH,** philosophy educator; b. N.Y.C. d. Morris and Selma Shurer; m. Michael Wyschogrod, Mar. 6, 1955; children: Daniel, Tamar. AB, Hunter Coll., 1957; PhD, Columbia U., 1970. Prof. philosophy Queens Coll., Flushing, NY, 1967-92; J. Newton Rayzor prof. philosophy and religious thought Rice U., Houston, 1992—2003, emerita, 2003—. Vis. prof. philosophy Villanova U. 2003; Croghan vis. prof. religion Williams Coll. 2004. Author: Emmanuel Levinas: The Problem of Ethical Metaphysics, 1974, 2d edit., 2000, Spirit in Ashes, 1985, Saints and Postmodernism, 1990, An Ethics of Remembering: History, Heterology and the Nameless Others; co-editor: Lacan and Theological Discourse, 1989, The Enigma of Gift and Sacrifice, 2002, The Ethical, 2003, Crossover Queries: Dwelling with Negatives, 'Embodying Philosophy's Others, 2006. Nat. Humanities Ctr. fellow, 1981, Woodrow Wilson Ctr. fellow, 1987-88, Guggenheim fellow, 1995-96. Fellow Am. Acad. Arts and Scis.; mem. Am. Acad. Religion (pres. 1992-93). Home: Apt 9C 522 West End Ave New York NY 10024 E-mail: stedith@rice.edu.

**WYSE, JASON LAMAR,** music educator, director; b. Bellefonaine, Ohio, Sept. 20, 1978; s. LaMar LaRay and Karon Eve Wyse; m. Julie Marie Unkefer, Nov. 6, 2004. MusB, Grove City Coll., Pa., 2001; MusM, The Ohio State U., Columbus, 2003. Dir. bands Punxsutawney (Pa.) Area H.S., 2003—; asst. dir. bands Brecksville-Broadview Heights H.S., 2006—. Mem.: Ohio Music Educators Assn.

**WYSE, LOIS,** advertising executive, writer; b. Cleve. d. Roy B. Wohlgemuth and Rose (Schwartz) Weisman; m. Marc Wyse (div. 1980); m. Lee Guber (dec. 1988). Pres. Wyse Advt. Inc., 1951—. Author: 60 books; syndicated columnist: Wyse Words; contbg. editor: (mag.) Good Housekeeping, 1983—98. Mem. bd. overseers Beth Israel Med. Ctr. Ctr. for Comms., N.Y.C.; trustees East Hampton Hist. Soc. Mem. Woman's Forum, PEN, Author's Guild, League of Profl. Theater Women. Office Phone: 631-324-3448. E-mail: lolowy@fastmail.fm.

**WYSE, ROGER EARL,** physiologist, department chairman; b. Wauseon, Ohio, Apr. 22, 1943; BS in Agr., Ohio State U., 1965; MS, Mich. State U., 1967, PhD in Crop Sci., 1969. Fellow Mich. State U., 1969-70; plant physiologist Agr. Rsch. Svc. USDA, 1970-86; dean of rsch. Cook Coll. Rutgers U., 1986-92; dean, dir. Coll. Agr. and Life Sci. U. Wis., Madison, 1992-98; mng. dir. Burrill & Co., San Francisco, 1998—. Recipient Arthur Flemming award, 1982. Fellow Am. Soc. Agronomy, Crop Sci. Soc. Am.; mem. AAAS, Am. Soc. Plant Physiol. Office: Burrill & Co 1 Embarcadero Ctr Ste 2700 San Francisco CA 94111-3744

**WYSHOCK, MICHAEL THOMAS,** artist, educator; BFA, U. of Del.; MFA, Fla. State U. 2002. Asst. prof. Nicholls State U., Thibodaux, 2002—05; lectr. SUNY, Oneonta, NY, 2006—. Digital video, Lacuum, Vegetables, 020102. Office: SUNY Oneonta Dept Art Oneonta NY 13820 Office Phone: 607-436-3718. Business E-Mail: wyshocmt@oneonta.edu.

**WYSK, RICHARD A.,** engineering educator, researcher; b. Holyoke, Mass., Sept. 22, 1948; s. Stanley and Sophia Dorothy (Mazurowski) W.; m. Caryl Lynne Ray, Jan. 18, 1969; children: Richard Patrick, Rebecca Jeanne, Robyn Caryl. BS in Indsl. Engring. & Ops. Rsch., U. Mass., 1972, MS in Indsl. Engring. & Ops. Rsch., 1973; PhD in Indsl. Engring., Purdue U., 1977. Prodn. control mgr. Gen. Electric, Erie, Pa., 1973-75; rsch. analyst Caterpillar Tractor, Inc., Peoria, Ill., 1975-76; assoc. prof. Va. Polytechnic Inst., Blacksburg, 1977-83; prof. Pa. State U., State College, 1983-90, William Lionhard chair in engring., 1995—; dir. Inst. Mfg. Systems, College Station, 1990-94; Royce Wisenbaker chair Tex. A&M U., College Station, 1990-94; William Lionhard chair in engring. William Leonhard chair in engring., State College, 1995—. Co-author: A Study Guide for the P.E. in I.E., 1982, An Intro to Automated Proc. Plan., 1985, Modern Manufacturing Process Engineering, 1989, Computer-aided Manufacturing, 1991 (Book-of-the-Yr. award Inst. Indsl. Engrs. 1992, E. Eugene Merchant Mfg. Textbook award Soc. Mfg. Engrs. 1992). Pks. commr. Montgomery County Pks. & Recreation, Blacksburg, 1982-83; adv. mem. Inst. Systems Rsch. U. Md., 1991-95. With U.S. Army, 1969-71, Vietnam. Decorated Army Commendation medal with 2 oak leaf clusters. Fellow Inst. Indsl. Engrs. (chpt. pres. 1990—, Region III Award of Excellence 1982, D. Baker award 1993), Soc. Mfg. Engrs. (sr., Outstanding Young Mfg. Engr. 1981), Engring. Accreditation Commn. (commr. 1990-92), Sigma Xi. Avocations: racquetball, basketball. Office: Pa State U 310 Leonard Bldg University Park PA 16802 Office Phone: 814-863-1001. Business E-Mail: rwysk@psu.edu.

**WYSONG, EARL EDWARD,** sociologist, educator; b. Kokomo, Ind., June 25, 1944; s. Earl Wysong and June Maxine Talbert; m. Janet Sue Myers, Aug. 30, 1966; children: Kristi Lynn, Heather Sue. BS in Edn., Ind. U., 1968; MA in Sociology, Ball State U., 1971; PhD in Sociology, Purdue U., 1990. Cert. secondary edn. Ind. Dept. Pub. Instrn., 1968. Asst. prof. sociology Ind. U., Kokomo, 1991—95, assoc. prof. sociology, 1995—98, prof. sociology, 1998—. Author: (book) High Risk and High Stakes: Health Professionals, Politics, and Policy, 1992; co-author: The New Class Society, 1999, The New Class Society, 3d edit., Goodbye American Dream?, 2007; mem. editl. bd.: Jour. Contemporary Sociology, 2001—05; contbr. chapters to books, articles to profl. jours. Doctoral Dissertation Improvement grantee, NSF, 1990, Faculty Fellowship Rsch. grantee, Ind. U. Kokomo, 1992. Mem.: Am. Fedn. Tchrs., Am. Sociol. Assn., Ind. Acad. Social Scis. (dir. sociology and anthropology 1993—96, exec. v.p. 1997—98, pres. 1998—99), North Ctrl. Sociol. Assn., Midwest Sociol. Soc., Soc. for the Study Social Problems (program co-chair 1999—2000). Home: 2850 East Southway Blvd Kokomo IN 46902 Office: Ind Univ Kokomo 2300 South Washington St Kokomo IN 46904-9003 Office Phone: 765-455-9394. E-mail: ewysong@iuk.edu.

**WYSS, DAVID ALEN,** diversified financial services company executive; b. Ft. Wayne, Ind., Nov. 14, 1944; s. Alen G. and Anne W. (Winicker) W.; m. Grace H. Hawes, June 11, 1966; children: Sarah J., Alen D. BS, MIT, 1966; PhD, Harvard U., 1971. Economist Fed. Res., Washington, 1970-74, sr. economist, 1975-77; advisor Bank Eng., London, 1974-75; sr. staff economist Council Econ. Advisers, Washington, 1977-79; v.p. DRI Ltd., London, 1979-83; rsch. dir. DRI/McGraw Hill, Lexington, Mass., 1983-97; chief economist Std. & Poor's/DRI, Lexington, 1997-99, Std. & Poor's, N.Y.C., 1999—. Dir. Nat. Assn. for Bus. Econ., N.Y. Collegium. Contbr. numerous articles to profl. jours. Mem. Am. Econ. Assn., Nat. Assn. Bus. Office: Standard & Poors 55 Water St Ste 39th Fl New York NY 10041-0003 Office Phone: 212-438-4952. Business E-Mail: david_wyss@sandp.com.

**WYSS, JOHN BENEDICT,** lawyer; b. Evanston, Ill., Nov. 23, 1947; s. Walther Erwin and Caroline Nettie (Benedict) W.; m. Joanne P. Comstock, Oct. 22, 1994; children: John Christian, Kirsten Dunlop. BS in Physics summa cum laude, Stanford U., 1969; JD, Yale U., 1972. Bar: Calif. 1972, D.C. 1974, U.S. Supreme Ct. 1976. Trial atty. antitrust div. U.S. Dept. Justice, Washington, 1972-74; assoc. Kirkland & Ellis, Washington, 1974-78, ptnr., 1978-83, Wiley, Rein & Fielding, Washington, 1983—. Mem. ABA, Phi Beta Kappa. Office: Wiley Rein & Fielding 1776 K St NW Washington DC 20006-2304 Office Phone: 202-719-7038. Business E-Mail: jwyss@wrf.com.

**WYSZYNSKI, DIEGO FEDERICO,** epidemiologist, educator; b. Buenos Aires, May 19, 1967; m. Caroline Panhuysen, Sept. 7, 1963; children: Shoshana Basia, Sara Yentl, Daniel Yehoshua, Rena Michal. MD, U. Buenos Aires Sch. of Medicine, Argentina, 1991; MHS, Johns Hopkins Sch. of Pub. Health, 1994, PhD, 1996. MD Min. of Health, Argentina, 1991. Asst. prof. medicine and epidemiology Boston U. Sch. Medicine, 1999—. Editor: (reference books) Cleft Lip and Palate: From Origin to Treatment, Neural Tube Defects: From Origin to Treatment; genetics sect. editor: Cleft Palata-Craniofacial Jour. Recipient NIH FARE fellow, NIH, 2000, Rsch. award, Cleft Palate Found., 2002. Achievements include research in the etiology of birth defects; patent pending for use of genetic markers for the identification of metabolic syndrome. Office: Boston Univ Sch of Medicine 715 Albany Str L-320 Boston MA 02118 E-mail: dfw@bu.edu.

**WYZNER, EUGENIUSZ,** diplomat; s. Henryk and Janina Wyzner; m. Elzbieta Laudanska, June 27, 1961; 1 child, Jaroslaw. LLM, U. Warsaw, 1954; postgrad., Hague Acad. Internat. Law, Netherlands, 1958. Mem. staff Ministry Fgn. Affairs, 1956—71, dir. legal dept., 1971—73; ambassador to Geneva, 1973-78; dir. dept. internat. orgns. Ministry Fgn. Affairs, Warsaw, 1978-81; chmn. UN Disarmament Commn., 1982; undersec. gen. conf. services and spl. assignments UN, N.Y.C., 1982-92, undersec. gen. pub. info., 1992-94; dep. min. for fgn. affairs Republic of Poland, Warsaw, 1994-95, 1st dep. min. for fgn. affairs, sec. of state, 1996-97; permanent rep. amb. to UN N.Y.C., 1998-99; vice-chmn. Internat. Civil Svc. Commn., N.Y.C., 1999—. Vice-chmn. preparatory com. Internat. Conf. on Human Rights, chmn. com. on periodic reports on human rights, 1965-68; chmn. sub-com. of UN Com. on Peaceful Uses of Outer Space, 1967-82; pres. Rev. Conf. of Parties to Treaty on Prohibition of Nuclear Weapons, 1977; mem. Polish del. of UN Gen. Assembly, UN Programme Planing and Budgeting Bd., 1984-93; chmn. UN Publs. Bd., 1982-93; chmn. com. for 2000 review conf. of the parties to the treaty on the non-proliferation of nuclear weapons, 1998-99. Decorated Cross of Polonia Restituta Polish Council of State, 1969, 77, Golden Cross of Merit, 1964, Comdr.'s Cross with a star Order of Polonia Restituta, 1996, Comdr. of the Legion d'Honneur, Pres. of France and Grand Comdr.'s Cross of the Order of the Phoenix, Pres. of Greece, 1996. Mem. Internat. Inst. Outer Space Law (bd. dirs. 1974—, Citation 1977), Internat. Peace Acad. (bd. dirs. 1983-91), Internat. Congress Inst. (bd. dirs. 1987-90), Internat. Congress Acad. (mem. senate 1990-95). Office: Internat Civil Svc Commn Rm 1050 2 United Nations Plz New York NY 10017-4403 Business E-Mail: wyzner@un.org.

**XI, CECILIA Q.,** research scientist; PhD, Northwestern U., 2003. Cert. NASPExAM Testamur Heart Rhythm Soc. Contbr. articles to profl. jours. Recipient 2d prize poster contest, 2003, Jos. Willems Young Investigator award, Jour. Electrocardiology, 2003; fellow, Northwestern U., 2000; Ou Yangzao scholar, Nanjing U., 1994, People scholar, 1995, Wu Jianxiong and Yuan Jialiu scholar, 1995, Bao Gang scholar, 1996. Achievements include patents pending for method to monitor progression of atrial fibrillation; methods and devices for determining exercise compliance diagnostics; research in new features for modern pacemakers and ICDs; development of remote monitoring system for patients sith heart diseases; design of protocols to evaluate new features/products; invention of methods and improvement for existing algorithms for pacemakers and ICDs. Office Phone: 408-522-6619.

**XI, LEI,** medical educator; b. Chengdu, China, Dec. 4, 1962; arrived in US, 1990; s. Ning Xi and Meiling Zhao; m. Thuy Nguyen Ho; children: Lillian Shee, Luke Shee. MD, Chengdu Inst. of Phys. Culture, China, 1983; postgrad., U. of Geneva, Switzerland, 1990; postdoctoral, U. of Wis., Madison, 1992, Va. Commonwealth U., Richmond, 2000. Team physician Chinese Nat. Athletes Tng. Ctr., Beijing, 1983—87; instr. of medicine Va. Commonwealth U., Richmond, 2000—05, asst. prof. of medicine, 2005—. Contbr. articles to biomed. jours.; reviewer: sci. jours. Mem.: Am. Heart Assn. (Scientist Devel. grant 2005—08), Am. Physiol. Soc. (Rsch. Career Enhancement award 2002). Office: Va Commonwealth Univ Rm 7042 1101 E Marshall St Richmond VA 23298-0281 Office Phone: 804-475-9589. Business E-Mail: lxi@vcu.edu.

**XIA, GUOHUA,** scientist, psychiatrist, psychologist; married; 1 child, M-Y. MB in Clinical Medicine, Beijing Med. U., 1986; PhD in Psychology, U. Nebr., Lincoln, 2002. Physician The 2nd Hosp. of Hebei Med. U., Shijiazhuang, China, 1986—93; tchr. ZhongGuanCun Software Coll., Beijing, 1993—95; counselor Counseling and Psychotherapy Ctr. Peking U., Beijing, 1993—95; database analyst, info. specialist and grad. asst. U. Nebr., Lincoln, 1995—2001; physician U. Texas, Houston, 2001—02, U. Tex. Southwestern Med. Ctr., Dallas, 2002—05; asst. prof. Case Western Reserve U., 2005—; head, Transcranial Magnetic Stimulation program, 2005—. Sec. Hebei Mental Health Orgn., Shijiazhuang, 1990—93. Contbr. articles to profl. jours., chapters to books. Recipient Young Investigator award, Nat. Alliance for Rsch. on Schizophrenia and Depression, 2005, NCDEU New Investigator award, NIMH, 2006. Mem.: Am. Psychology Assn., Psychol. Assn. China, Chinese Med. Assn. (Excellent Acad. Paper award 1993), Chinese Mental Health Assn., Am. Psychiatry Assn., Kappa Omicron Nu.

**XIA, TONGSHENG,** electrical engineer; s. Daorong Xia and Fenyang Que. BS, U. Sci. and Tech. of China, 1997, MS, 2000; PhD, U. Tex., 2005. Rsch. asst. U. Sci. & Tech. of China, AnHui, 1997—2000, U. Tex., Austin, 2000—. Fellow Legend Computer Group of China, 1997, Chinese Acad. Sci., 2000. Mem.: IEEE. Achievements include discovery of a totally new concept, the complex band structure effect, for nano-transistors, which is important for the realization of IC inlcuding novel structure/ materials, such as carbon nanotubes; new radiation spectrum form for electron radiation in a curved magnetic field, which helps explain a lot of lab results puzzling people. Home: 228 Crittenden Way Apt 2 Rochester NY 14623-2245 Office: 1999 Lake Ave Rochester NY 14650 Business E-Mail: xiats@mail.utexas.edu.

**XIA, YUNI,** information scientist, educator; PhD, Purdue U., 2005. Rsch. asst. Purdue U., West Lafayette, Ind., 1999—2005; rsch. intern IBM T.J. Watson Rsch. Ctr., Hawthorn, NY, 2003; asst. prof. Ind. U. Purdue U., Indpls., 2005—. Recipient Leading light Award for Women in HiTech, State of Ind., Grace Hopper/Anita Borg scholar, IBM Rsch., 2004. Office Phone: 317-274-9738.

**XIAO, SHUYI,** finance company executive; b. Aug. 1, 1966; m. Bing Shi; 1 child, eMing. MBA, Pace U., 1996—98. Prin. Option123, Purchase, NY, 1999—. Author: (accounting software) Option123, (reference book) Black-Scholes Option Valuation Factor Table @ $1, (software) E-Model of Stock Historical Volatility Calculation. Mem.: The Nat. Assn. of Cert. Valuation Analysts, NY Soc. of Security Analysts. Achievements include patents pending for. Office: Option123 PO Box 603 Purchase NY 10577 E-mail: sxiao@option123.com.

**XIAO, YANAN,** physicist, researcher; b. Miyun, China, Oct. 12, 1964; s. Qisen Xiao and Xiuying Ma; m. Xiao Meiqin, Aug. 24, 2002; children: Ji, Giana Shuge, Shirley You. PhD, U. Tokyo, 1999. Rsch. assoc. Beijing Synchrotron Radiation Facility, 1990—95; postdoctoral fellow So. Ill. U., 1999—2002; postdoctoral appointee Argonne (Ill.) Nat. Lab., 2002—06. Achievements include development of powder spectro-diffractometry based on in-advance simulation; x-ray nanodiffraction technique; software package for standardless x-ray fluoresence analysis; software for powder spectro-diffractometry. Home: 1859 Slippery Rock Rd Naperville IL 60565 Personal E-mail: xiaoyanan@yahoo.com.

**XIE, GANQUAN,** mathematician, computational geophysical scientist, educator; b. Changsha, Hunan, People's Republic of China, July 2, 1943; s. Shuming Xie and Sumen Liu; m. Jianhua Li, Sept. 29, 1969; children: Feng, Lee. BCS, Hunan U., ChangSha City, 1966; PhD, SUNY, 1984; postdoctoral rsch., Courant Inst. Math., 1984-86. Asst. prof. Hunan Computer Research Inst., 1967-80; vice-chmn. Soc. Computational Math., Hunan, 1979-81; postdoctoral research Courant Inst. Math., N.Y.C., 1984—; prof., dir. Hunan Computer Rsch. Tech. Inst., 1987-88; staff scientist Lawrence Berkely Nat. Lab., 1991—. Chmn. Chinese Computational Math. Soc., 1986-88; vis. rscher SUNY, 1989; vis. prof. KSU, 1990. Mem. editorial com. Jour. Computational Math., Beijing, 1987-88; inventor in field; contbr. to profl. jours. Nat. Sci. Found. grantee, 1986-87, recipient Chinese Scientific prize, 1978. Mem. N.Y. Acad. Scis., Soc. Indsl. Applied Math., Soc. of Exploration Geophysicists, Am. Geophys. Union. Home: 1413 Glendale Ave Berkeley CA 94708-2027 Office: Lawrence Berkeley Nat Lab Bldg 90 MS 90-1116 Earth Scis Divsn Berkeley CA 94720 E-mail: g_xie@lbl.gov.

**XIE, HUIKAI,** engineering educator; s. Chengmai Xie and Fuqing Du; m. Yuxiao Tong, Sept. 19, 1968; children: Yutong, Brian. PhD, Carnegie Mellon U., Pitts., 2002. Dir. engring. Akustica, Inc., Pitts., 2002—02; asst. prof. U. Fla., Gainesville, 2002—. Tech. cons. Robert Bosch Corp., Palo Alto, Calif., 2000—02; presenter and com. mem. tech. confs. Contbr. chapters to books (Best paper of the yr., 1996). Recipient Excellent Tchg. award, Tsinghua U., 1996; grantee, NSF, 2004, 2006. Mem.: IEEE (v.p. Gainesville chpt. 2005—). Achievements include patents for vertical displacement device; method of fabricating microstructures and devices made therefrom. Office: University of Florida 221 Benton Hall Gainesville FL 32611 Office Phone: 352-846-0441. Business E-Mail: hkx@ufl.edu.

**XIE, JEFF ZHENGQUAN,** lawyer; b. Hubei, China, Mar. 18, 1963; m. Bin Wu; 1 child, Maylene. JD, Ga. State U., 1999. Bar: Ga. 2000, U.S. Dist. Ct. (no. dist.) Ga. 2000, U.S. Ct. Internat. Trade 2001. Asst. counsel Ga. Dept. Corrections, Atlanta, 1999—2000; mng. mem. Xie Law Offices, LLC, Norcross, Ga., 2000—. Mem.: ABA, Am. Immigration Lawyers Assn. Office: Xie Law Offices Llc 1770 Indian Trail Lilburn Rd Ste 450 Norcross GA 30093-2676 Office Phone: 678-421-9668. Business E-Mail: jeffxie@uslawnet.com.

**XIE, KEN,** software company executive; b. China; BS, MS Computer Sci., Tsinghua U.; MEE, U. Stanford. Founder, CEO, pres. NetScreen, 1997—2004, Stanford Infosystems, Fortinet Inc., 2000—. Mng. partner Jedi Venture; security architect Healtheon. Named a Technology Pioneer, World Econ. Forum, 2006; recipient Top 15 Technology Innovator, Computer Reseller News magazine, 2004, Northern California Entrepreneur of the Year, Ernst & Young, 2006. Office: Fortinet Inc 1090 Kifer Rd Sunnyvale CA 94086 Office Phone: +1-408-235-7700. Office Fax: +1-408-235-7737.*

**XIE, LAI-HUA,** physiologist; b. China; BSc, MSc, Nankai U., Tianjin, China, 1989; PhD, Kyoto U., Japan, 1999. Asst. rsch. scientist U. Calif., L.A., 2002—06, adj. asst. prof., 2006—. Contbr. articles to profl. jours. Office: University of California at Los Angeles 675 Young Drive South MRL 3645 Los Angeles CA 90095 Office Phone: 1-310-825-6713.

**XIE, MINGE,** statistician, educator; PhD in Stats., U. Ill., Champaign-Urbana, 1996. Assoc. prof. stats. Rutgers U., Piscatawy, NJ, 1997—. Grantee, NSF, NIH. Office Phone: 743-445-2546.

**XIE, SHAOCHENG,** atmospheric scientist; arrived in US, 1993, permanent resident, 2000; s. Guoxing Xie and Taoyuan Xu; m. Jing Sun; children: Anna, Edward. BS. Najing Inst. Meteorology, China, 1985; MS, Chinese Acad. Meteorol. Scis., Beijing; PhD, SUNY, Stony Brook, 1998. Rsch. meteorologist/sr. rsch. meteorologist Nat. Meteorol. Ctr., Beijing, 1988—93; atmospheric scientist Lawrence Livermore Nat. Lab., Calif., 1998—. Presenter in field. Contbr. articles to profl. jours. Recipient Young Meteorol. Excellent Rsch. award, Chinese Nat. Meteorol. Ctr., 1988, Outstanding Achievement award, Atmospheric Sciences and Tech., Chinese Meteorol. Adminstrn., 1993, Energy and Environment Directorate Program award, Lawrence Livermore Nat. Lab., 2004. Mem.: Am. Geophys. Union, Am. Meteorol. Soc. Achievements include development of a new convective triggering function for NCAR CAM2 to improve the predicted precipitation over land; second-generation of the medium-range weather forecast model for National Meteorological Center (China); positive-definite advection scheme to improve the moisture prediction in numerical weather prediction models. Office: L-103/ASD Lawrence Livermore Nat'l Lab 7000 East Ave Livermore CA 94550 Office Phone: 925-422-6023. Business E-Mail: xie2@llnl.gov.

**XIE, SONG,** musician, educator; b. Nanning, China, Oct. 25, 1963; arrived in U.S., 1991; s. Shun-Feng Xie and Shu-Nan Yang; m. Renee Chen, July 25, 1991; 1 child, David. BA, Guangxi Inst. Art, 1987, MusM, La. State U., 1995. Mem. violin faculty Guangxi Inst. Arts, Nanning, China, 1987—91; prin. 2d violin Miss. Symphony Orch., Jackson, 1997—; string dir. Belhaven Coll., 1998—. Concertmaster Met. Chamber Orch., 1999—; asst. concert master Lyric Mountain Festival, Pitts., 1998; adj. prof. Millsaps Coll., Jackson State U., 1998—; Miss. Coll. Named winner, La. State U. Symphony Concerto Competition, 1991, 1994; recipient Excellent Performance award, Chinese Arts/Culture Ministry, 1984. Mem.: Nat. Sch. Orch. Assn., Am. String Tchr. Assn. (pres. elect Miss. chpt.), Music Tchrs. Nat. Assn., Miss. Music Tchrs. Assn., Coll. Music Soc., Am. Fedn. Musicians. Office: 601-974-6149. Personal E-mail: songxie66@hotmail.com.

**XIE, XIAOLIANG SUNNEY,** chemist, educator; arrived in U.S., 1985; PhD in Chemistry, U. Calif., 1990. Postdoctoral fellow U. Chgo., 1990—92; sr. rsch. scientist Environ. Molecular Scis. Lab. Pacific N.W. Nat. Lab., Richland, Wash., 1992—95, chief scientist Environ. Molecular Scis. Lab., 1995—98; prof. chemistry Harvard U., Cambridge, Mass., 1999—. Recipient Coblentz award, Coblentz Soc., 1996, Raymond and Beverly Sackler Prize in Phys. Scis., Israel, 2003, Pioneer award, NIH, 2004. Mem.: Biophysical Soc., Optical Soc. Am., Am. Chem. Soc. Achievements include research in single molecule spectroscopy at room temperature, single molecule enzymology, conformational dynamics of proteins, and near-field optical microscopy; patents for Coherent Anti-Stokes Raman Scattering Microscopy, a noninvasive method for imaging live cells and tissues. Office: Harvard Univ Chemistry & Chem Biology Dept 12 Oxford St M026 Cambridge MA 02138 Office Phone: 617-496-6501.

**XIE, YU,** adult education educator; b. Zhenjiang, Jiangsu, China, Oct. 12, 1959; s. Liangyao Xie and Huazhen Zhao; m. Yijun Helen Gu, Dec. 1985; children: Raissa, Kevin. BA in Metallurgical Engring., Shanghai U. of Tech., China, 1982; MA in History of Sci., MS in Sociology, U. Wis., Madison, 1984, PhD in Sociology, 1989. From asst. to assoc. prof. U. Mich., Ann Arbor, 1989-96, John Stephenson Perrin prof. sociology, 1996, now Frederick G.L. Huetwell prof. sociology. Mem. adv. panel sociology program NSF, 1995-97; bd. dirs. Bd. Overseers of Gen. Social Survey, Dep. editor Am. Sociol. Review, 1996—; mem. editl. bd. Sociol. Methods and Rsch. 1989—, Jour. Sociology, 1994-96, Sociol. Methodology, 1994-97; presenter in field; contbr. articles to profl. jours. Spencer fellow Nat. Acad. Edn., 1991-92; recipient Young Investigator award NSF, 1992-97, Faculty Scholar award William T. Grant Found., 1994-99. Fellow: Am. Acad. Arts & Sci. Mem. Am. Stat. Assn., Am. Sociol. Assn., Sociol. Rsch. Assn. (elected mem.), Population Assn. of Am. Office: U Mich Population Studies Ctr 426 Thompson St Ann Arbor MI 48104-2321 Fax: 734-998-7415. E-mail: yuxie@umich.edu.

**XIN, JACK,** mathematician, educator; BS in Math., Peking U., 1985; MS in Math., NYU, 1988, PhD in Math., 1990. Postdoctoral fellow Math. Scis. Rsch. Inst., Berkeley, Calif., 1990—91, Inst. for Advanced Study, Princeton, NJ, 1991—92; asst. prof. math. U. Ariz., 1991—97, assoc. prof., 1997—99; prof. math. U. Tex., Austin, 1999—. Invited prof. Math. Inst. Stuttgart (Germany) U., 1998; invited prof. Multimedia Lab. Hokkaido (Japan) U., 2000; invited prof. Inst. de Henri Poincaré, Paris, 2002. Contbr. articles to profl. jours. Fellow, John Simon Guggenheim Meml. Found., 2003; grantee, NSF, 1993—96, 1996—99, Army Rsch. Office, 1999—2000, 2000—02, 2002—03, Info. Tech. Rsch., NSF, 2002—; NFR Rsch. fellow, Swedish Natural Sci. Rsch. Coun., Inst. Mittag-Leffler, Sweden, 1994. Office: Dept Math Univ Tex Austin Austin TX 78712 Office Phone: 512-471-3149.

**XING, GUANGMING,** engineering educator; BS, Nanksi U., Tianjin, China, 1996; PhD, U. Ga., Athens, 2001. Asst. prof. Western Ky. U., Bowling Green, Ky., 2002—. Grantee, Ky. Sci. and Engring. Found., 2005. Mem.: ACM. Office: Western Ky U 1906 College Heights Blvd Bowling Green KY 42101

**XING, GUANG-QIAN,** aerospace scientist; b. Nai Ling, Ah Hui Province, China, Nov. 19, 1938; m. Ming Zhu, Feb. 5, 1978; children: Lei Zhu, Neil, Meng Chen. Equivalent Master, Peking U., Beijing, China, 1957—63. Graduated Certification, Peking U., China, 1963. Engr. Beijing Inst. of Control Engring., Chinese Acad. of Space Tech., 1963—86; sr. rsch. assoc. Howard U., Inst. of Large Flexible Space Structure, Howard U., NASA, 1986—95; prin. scientist Space Products and Applications, Inc., Fairfax, Va., 1996—. Author: (profl. jours.) Jour. Guidance, Control, and Dynamics; Acta Astronautica; The Jour. of the Astronautical Sciences; ASME Traction: Journal of Dynamic System, Measurement and Control;Book Chapter:Control and Dynamics System Advance, Volum 79. Recipient The first class Citation of Merit due to successfully Design and implementation of the Chinese First Communication satellite, Chinese Ministry of Astronautics, 1984, The Nat. Prize(Super Class) for Promoting Progress of Sciences and Technologies., The State Sci. and Tech. Commn. of China, 1985. Achievements include patents for The first patent is used for Autonomous Spacecraft Constellation Control Using GPS; The second patent is used for the Autonomous Orbit/Attitude Unified Control for Spacecraft Formation Flying Usng GPS. Home: 8515 Pelham Rd Bethesda MD 20817 Office: Space Products and Applications(SPA)Inc 3900 Jermantown Rd Ste 300 Fairfax VA 22030 Personal E-mail: xingspa@erols.com.

**XING, YIPING,** electrical engineer, researcher; PhD, Stevens Inst. Tech., Hoboken, NJ, 2006. Sys. engr. China Unicom, Chengdu, 2001—02; rsch. asst. dept. elec. and computer engring. Stevens Inst. Tech., 2002—. Contbr. articles to profl. jours. Named Outstanding Rsch. Asst. dept. elec. and computer engring., Stevens Inst. Tech., 2005; recipient Grad. Fellowship award Sch. Engring., 2005, Best Ph.D thesis award in elec. engring., 2006. Mem.: IEEE (CCNC Best Student Paper award 2006, DySPAN Student Travel Grant award 2005). Achievements include research in next generation wireless communication networks. Office: Stevens Inst Tech Dept Elec and Computer Engring 1 Castle Point Hoboken NJ 07030 Office Phone: 201-216-8312. Personal E-mail: yipingxing@gmail.com. E-mail: yxing@stevens.edu.

**XIONG, NING,** computer scientist, researcher; b. Shanghai, Nov. 11, 1964; arrived in Sweden, 2000; s. Dezheng and Guiling (Li) Xiong; m. Xiaoyu Wang, Oct. 10, 1968. BS, Dong Hua U., Shanghai, 1986, MS, 1989; PhD with Excellent Distinction, U. Kaiserslautern, Germany, 2000. Asst. lectr. Dong Hua U., Shanghai, 1989—92, lectr., 1992—95; rsch. asst. U. Kaiserslautern, Germany, 1996—2000; guest rscher. Swedish Defence Rsch. Agy., Stockholm, 2000—01; rscher. Royal Inst. Tech., Stockholm, 2001—02; sr. lectr. Mid Sweden U., 2003—04; sr. rscher., lectr. dept. computer sci. and electronics Mälardalen U., 2004—. Project leader in intelligent robotics Dong Hua U., Shanghai, 1990—95; key rscher. in fuzzy systems U. Kaiserslautern, Kaiserslautern, Germany, 1996—2000; cons. feature selection Schott Glass Co., Mainz, Germany, 2000; prin. investigator in sensor management Swedish Defence Rsch. Agy., Stockholm, 2000—01; co-chair Swedish Artificial Intelligence and Learning Sys. Conf., 2005. Author: (book) Designing Compact and Comprehensible Fuzzy Controllers Usng Genetic Algorithms., 2001, (book chpt.) Identifying flexible structured premises for mining concise fuzzy knowledge. in "Interpretability Issues in Fuzzy Modeling", 2002; contbr. articles to profl. jours, papers to sci. confs. and convs., 2000. Named an Outstanding Young Tchr., Dong Hua U., 1993; recipient Outstanding Paper award, Sci. and Tech. Com., Shanghai, 1995; grantee Doctoral Fellowship, German Academic Exchange Service, 1995-2000. Mem.: IEEE. Avocations: travel, ping pong/table tennis. Office: Mälardalen U Dept Computer Science and Electronics SE-721 23 Västerås Sweden Office Phone: 4621151716. Personal E-mail: n.xiong@ieee.org. Business E-Mail: ning.xiong@mdh.se.

**XIONG, TOUSU SAYDANGNMVANG,** minister, theology studies educator; b. Hmong Long Chieng, June 23, 1966; arrived in U.S. 1976, naturalized, 1996; s. Nhialue Saydang and May (Vang) X.; m. Zoua Pahoua Moua, Sept. 14, 1993; children: Chivkeeb Genesis Toupa, Nasamonnas Ruth, Nujsimloob Hebrews, Nkaujzuapaaj Esther. BA in Bibl. Studies, Simpson Coll., San Francisco, 1989; MA in Theology, Mennonite Brethren Bibl. Sem., Fresno, Calif., 1991, AS in Computerized Acctg., Phillips Jr. Coll., Fresno, Calif., 1993. Ordained to ministry Christian and Missionary Alliance, 1991. Assoc. min. Hmong San Raphael (Calif.) Bapt. Ch., 1986-88; youth min. Hmong Alliance Ch. of Santa Barbara, Goleta, Calif., 1984-85, Hmong Alliance Ch. of Fresno, 1989—; med. record acct. Dr. Suchat Jariprassert Med. Clinic, Fresno, Calif., 1993—96; assoc. shareholder Wal-Mart Stores, Inc., Bentonville, Ark., 1998—. Scoutmaster Boy Scouts Am., 1984—85. Eagle Scout, 1983; mission coun. Santa Barbara, Calif. Avocations: hiking, camping, computers. Office: Hmong Alliance Ch Fresno 8234 E Belmont Ave Fresno CA 93727-9725 Home: PO Box 1903 Mount Dora FL 32756-1903 E-mail: xteagle76@wmconnect.com. *In my life as I have experienced both the world of the Hmong Animistic Religion in the East and the Christian faith from the West, I have come to realize that Jesus Christ is superior, for Jesus is the way, the truth and the life pointing us towards the Supreme and Creator Being.*

**XIONG, ZIXIANG,** engineering educator, researcher; PhD, U. Ill., 1995. Prof. Tex. A&M U., College Station, 1999—. Recipient Career award, NSF, 1999, Young Investigator award Army Rsch. Office, 2000, Office Naval Rsch. Mem.: IEEE. Office: Texas A&M U Dept Elec and Computer Engring College Station TX 77843 Office Phone: 979-862-8683.

**XIU, LIMING,** electrical engineer; m. Zhihong You; children: Katherine, Helen. BS, TsingHua U., Beijing, 1981—86, MS, 1986—88; MS in Elec. Engring., Tex. A&M U., College Station, 1993—95. Project mgr. China Radiation Tech. Corp., Beijing, 1989—90; rsch. scientist U. Houston, 1990—93; sr. mem. tech. staff Tex. Instruments Inc., Dallas, 1995—. Contbr. articles to profl. jours. Mem.: IEEE (mem. chair, circuit and sys. soc., Dallas chpt. 2003—04, vice chair 2004—), Cir. and Sys. Soc. (gen. chmn. Dallas chpt. 2006). Achievements include patents for precision frequency and phase synthesis; scalable high-speed precision frequency and phase synthesis; patents pending for precision jitter-free frequency synthesis; scalable high-speed precision frequency and phase synthesis; flying-adder frequency synthesizer-based digital-controlled oscillator and video decoder including the same. Avocations: soccer, tennis, travel. Office: Texas Instruments Inc 12500 TI Blvd Dallas TX 75243 Office Phone: 214-480-4930.

**XU, CHONG-WEI,** computer scientist, educator; arrived in US, 1987, naturalized, 1995; s. Zongjia Xu and Yuhua Weng; m. Lili Hu, 1994; children: Leslie Linglei, Daniel Nan; m. Yongkang Gu Xu, 1971 (dec. 1992). BEE, Hefai Indsl. Engring. U., China, 1963; MS in Computer Sci., U. Wis., Madison, 1981; PhD in Computer Sci., Mich. State U., East Lansing, 1981—86. Asst. prof. So. Ill. U., Edwardsville, 1986—92; assoc. prof. Ga. So. U., Statesboro, 1993—2001; prof. Kennesaw State U., Ga., 2001—. Contbr. articles to profl. jours. Mem.: IEEE, Assn. Computing Machinery. Home: 3185 Country Club Ct Kennesaw GA 30144 Office: Kennesaw State Univ 1000 Chastain Rd #1101 Kennesaw GA 30144

**XU, JINCHAO,** mathematics professor; m. Jenny Li; children: Lillian, Melissa. BA, Xiangtan U., Xiangtan, Hunan, China, 1982; MA, Peking U., Beijing, 1984; PhD, Cornell U., Ithaca, NY, 1988. Asst. prof. Pa. State U., State College, 1989—91, assoc. prof., 1991—95, prof., 1995—, dir. Ctr. Computational Math. and Applications, 1997—; dir. Inst. Computational and Applied Math., Xiangtan U., Hunan, China, 1996—. Co-editor: Numerical Methods in Applied Sciences, 1996; mem. editl. bd.: SIAM Jour. Numerical Analysis, 1993—2002, Jour. Computational Math., 1993—, Jour. Computational Methods Applied Scis. and Engring., 2000—, Advances Computational Math., 2000—, Math. Computation, 2001—, Math. Modeling and Numerical Analysis, 2002—, Numerische Mathematik, 2003—, Chinese Jour. Computational Physics, 2003—, Internat. Jour. Numerical Analysis & Modeling, 2003—, Math. Models and Methods Applied Sci., 2004—; contbr. articles to profl. jours. Recipient Liu Meml. award, Cornell U., 1988, Natural Sci. award, Academia Sinica, 1989, Leslie Fox prize, Scotland, UK, 1991, Schlumberger Found. award, 1993, First Feng Kang prize Sci. Computing, 1995, Outstanding Achievement award, Xiangtan U., China, 1995, Rsch. award Nat. Outstanding Youth (Class B) 2005; fellow, Chinese Ministry Edn., Peking U. 1999—2004, Hunan Province China, Xiangtan U., 2003—; grantee, NSF, 2000—03, 2002—05, 2002—04, Indsl. funds, Honda, 2003—04, NSF, 2005—06, Pa. State U., 2006. Mem.: Am. Math. Soc. (assoc.), Soc. Indsl. and Applied Math. (assoc.) Office: Department of Mathematics Penn State University Park State College PA 16802 Business E-Mail: xu@math.psu.edu.

**XU, JINSHENG,** computer scientist, educator; s. Guangnan Xu and Shunai Gui; m. Jinghua Zhang, 1999; 1 child, Haiming Eric. PhD, Mich. State U., East Lansing, 2002. Assoc. prof. N.C. A&T State U., Greensboro, 2003—. Antai Fellowship, Beijing U., 1995. Achievements include research in Overhead Reducing Technique for Time Warp. Office: North Carolina A&T State University 1601 E Market Street Greensboro NC 27411 Office Phone: 336-334-7245. Office Fax: 336-334-7244. E-mail: jxu@ncat.edu.

**XU, PING,** chemist; b. Shanghai, Apr. 29, 1957; came to U.S., 1985; s. Yuan Xu and Changfu Zhu; m. Shuhong Wang, Feb. 17, 1987; children: Helen W., Olivia W. BS, East China U. Chem. Tech., Shanghai, 1982, MS, 1984, U. Cin., 1987, PhD, 1991. Asst. prof. East China U. Chem. Tech., 1984-85; Paul J. Flory meml. fellow U. Cin., 1990-92; sr. rsch. chemist Quantum Chem. Corp., Cin., 1991-94; polymer scientist W.L. Gore & Assocs., Inc., Elkton, Md., 1994—. Vis. scientist Oak Ridge (Tenn.) Nat. Lab., 1998—; vis. scientist Nat. Inst. Stds. and Tech., Gaithersburg, Md., 1999—. Contbr. numerous articles to sci. jours. Mem. AAAS, Am. Chem. Soc., Material Rsch. Soc. Achievements include research in engineering, rubber elasticity, polymer morphology and polymer physics. Home: 22 Piersons Rdg Hockessin DE 19707-9291 Office: WL Gore & Assocs Inc 2401 Singerly Rd Elkton MD 21921-2733 E-mail: pxu@aol.com.

**XU, SHAOHUA,** biochemist, researcher; m. Jianqing Jeny Yu, June 2, 1986; children: Haoxuan Anna, Haochen Frank. PhD, Purdue U., West Lafayette, Indiana, 1989. Dir./rsch. prof. Fla. Space Rsch. Inst./Fla. Inst. of Tech., Kennedy Space Ctr., Fla., 2004—. Post doctoral fellow U. Calif., San Diego, 1990—91; rsch. asst. prof. U. Chgo., Chgo., 1992—2001; sr. rsch. investigor U. Pa., Phila., 2002—03. Scholar CUSBEA Scholar, China and US Biochemistry Exam. Application Com., 1984. Mem.: Biophysical Soc. Achievements include discovery of Four configurations for lipoprotein(A); Amyloid fiber formation to be a special case of colloidal aggregation; patents for functionalization of atomic force microscopy for biomolecular recognition; discovery of Low-density lipoprotein aggregation pathway; Configurations for lipoprotein (a); Pathway for low-density lipoprotein aggregation. Office Phone: 321-861-2899. Personal E-mail: shaohuaxu8@yahoo.com.

**XU, XIAOWEI,** education educator, researcher; b. Jiao-Zhou, China, June 27, 1962; arrived in U.S., 2002; s. Fu-Hai Xu and Ying-Qi Kang; m. Mei Song, Mar. 11, 1988; children: Yeqian, Anni. BS in Math., Nan-Kai U., China, 1983; MS in Computer Sci., Chinese Acad. Sci., 1987; PhD in Computer Sci., U. Munich, 1998. Rsch. scientist Chinese Acad. Scis., Shenyang, China, 1983—92; vis. scholar U. of Hildesheim (Germany), 1992—93; tchg. and rsch. asst. U Munich (Germany), 1993—98; sr. rsch. scientist Siemens AG, Munich, 1998—2002; assoc. prof. U. Ark., Little Rock, 2002—. Cons. Microsoft Rsch., Beijing, 2000, Siemens AG, Munich, 2003—04, Axciom, Little Rock, 2003—. Leader Chinese Christian Ch., Little Rock, 2003—. Rsch. grant, Axciom, 2003—06, NIH, 2005—06, FDA, 2006—. Mem.: Assn. for Computing Machinery. Avocations: swimming, travel, classical music. Office: Univ Ark 2801 S Univ Ave Little Rock AR 72204 Business E-mail: xwxu@ualr.edu.

**XU, XIPING,** adult education educator, director; b. Anhui, China, Aug. 1, 1956; m. Xiaobin Wang; children: Benjamin, Richard. MS, HSPH, 1982; PhD, U. Tsukuba, Japan, 1988; MD, Anhui Med. U., 1996. Dir., program for population genetics Harvard Sch. of Pub. Health, Harvard U., Boston, 1994—. Instr., guest lectr. on modern genetic epidemiology and gene mapping Harvard U., Boston, 1998—. Author over 130 articles regarding genetic rsch. Pres. Chinese Prof. in Biomedicine, Boston, 1998—2002. Office: Harvard Sch Pub Health 665 Huntington Ave Boston MA 02115 Home: 2611 Laurel Ln Wilmette IL 60091-2231 E-mail: xu@hsph.harvard.edu.

**XU, YIFANG,** engineer, researcher; d. Derun Xu and Fuzhen Miao; m. Hongtao Mu, May 21, 2004. PhD, Duke U., Durham, NC, 2004. Fellow Duke U., Durham, NC, 2000—01, rsch. asst., 2000—04; sr. clin. and rsch. engr. Gallaudet U., Washington, 2004—. Contbr. articles to profl. jours. Mem.: IEEE, Am. Audiology Soc., Assn. for Rsch. in Otolaryngology.

**XUE, DONG CYNTHIA,** research scientist, consultant; b. Wuhan, Hubei, China, Oct. 27, 1977; d. ZhongChuan Xue and XianPing Cheng. PhD, U. Tex., Austin, 2005. Rsch. scientist U. Tex. Austin, 2005—; scientist Houston Tech. Ctr., 2005—. Cons. Baker Atlas, Houston, 2005—. Contbr. articles to profl. jours. Recipient First pl. poster competition, Nat. Partnership Advanced Computational Infrastructure and San Diego Super Computer Ctr., 2003; fellow, Internat. Fedn. U. Women, 1999, in Computational Mechanics, 7th U.S. Nat. Congress on Computational Mechanics, 2003, 6th World Congress on Computational Mechanics, 2004. Mem.: Soc. Petroleum Engrs. (corr.), Soc. Exploration Geophysicists (corr.), Soc. Profl. Well Log Analysts (hon.). Achievements include patents for correction of multi-component measurements for the tool eccentricity in deviated wells. Home: 2350 Bagby Houston TX 77006 Office: Baker Hughes 2001 Rankin Rd Houston TX 77073 Office Phone: 713-625-5757. Home Fax: 713-625-6795; Office Fax: 713-625-6795. E-mail: cynthia.xue@bakerhughes.com.

**XUE, RUI-DE,** entomologist; s. Youcai Xue and Qingye Shao; m. Minjin Hao; 1 child, Hui. PhD, Chinese Acad. of Med. Sciences, Beijing, 1986—89. Asst. prof. Shanxi Med. U., Taiyuan, China, 1981—85; assoc. prof. Beijing Inst. of Microbiology and Epidemiology, Beijing, 1989—91; vis. scientist U. of Mass., Ahmerst; vis. scientist U. of Fla., IFAS, Mid. Fla. Rsch. and Edn. Ctr., Apopka, Fla., 1993—99; rsch. entomologist USDA, ARS, Ctr. for Med., Agrl. and Vet. Entomology, Gainesville, Fla., 1993—2003, Anastasia Mosquito Control Dist., St. Augustine, Fla., 2003—. Author (reviewers) co-editor, Chinese jour. of pest control. Worldwide com. mem. Am. Mosquito Control

Assn., Eatontown, NJ, 1995—98. Mem.: Fla. Mosquito Control Assn., Soc. for Vector Ecologists. Am. Mosquito Control Assn., Entomol. Soc. of Am. Achievements include discovery of new oviposition repellents, mosquito larvicides. Office: Anastasia Mosquito Control Dist 500 Old Beach Rd Saint Augustine FL 32085 Home: 2022 SW 75th Ter Gainesville FL 32607-3478 Office Phone: 904-471-3107. Home Fax: 352-332-4088; Office Fax: 904-471-3189. Business E-Mail: xueamcd@bellsouth.net.

**XUE, YONGKANG,** science educator; m. Su Q. Liu, Jan. 10, 1973; children: Fransis, Cathleen. PhD, U. Utah, 1987. Rsch. scientist Ctr. for Oean-Land-Atmosphre Studies, Bletsville, Md., 1993—97, U. Md., College Park, 1997—99; assoc. prof. UCLA, 1999—2003, prof., 2003—. Mem.: Am. Assn. Geography, Am. Geophys. Union, Am. Meteorol. Soc. Office: UCLA 1255 Bunche Hall Los Angeles CA 90094-1524 Business E-Mail: yxue@geog.ucla.edu.

**XUE, YUAN,** engineering educator; d. Li Xue and Xiuying Sun; m. Yi Cui. BS, Nankai U., 1998; MS, U. Ill., Urbana-Champaign, 2002, PhD, 2005. Rsch. asst. U. Ill., Urbana-Champaign, 2000—05; asst. prof. Vanderbilt U., Nashville, 2005—. Contbr. articles to profl. jours. Vodafone fellow, Vodafone-U.S. Found., 2003, 2004. Achievements include research in resource management in wireless networks.

**YABLON, HEATHER D.,** lawyer; b. LI, Jan. 14, 1970; BA, U. Mich., 1992; JD, St. John's U., 1995. Bar: NY 1996. Ptnr. Wilson, Elser, Moskowitz, Edelman & Dicker LLP, NYC. Mem.: Assn. of the Bar of the City of NY, NY State Bar Assn. Office: Wilson Elser Moskowitz Edelman & Dicker LLP 150 E 42nd St 23rd Fl New York NY 10017-5639 Office Phone: 212-490-3000 ext. 2578. Office Fax: 212-490-3038. Business E-Mail: yablonh@wemed.com.

**YABLON, JEFFERY LEE,** lawyer; b. Chgo., June 28, 1948; s. Robert R. and Faye I. (Goldberg) Y.; m. Jean C. LaPrade, Apr. 17, 1983. BA with honors, U. Wis., 1970; JD, Stanford U., 1973. Bar: Calif. 1974, D.C. 1975. Law clk. to Judge Cynthia Holcomb Hall U.S. Tax Ct., Washington, 1973-75; Fulbright scholar U. Florence, Italy, 1975-76; assoc. Covington & Burling, Washington, 1976-80, Lee, Toomey & Kent, Washington, 1980-82, Pillsbury Winthrop Shaw Pittman LLP, Washington, 1982-84, ptnr., 1984—. Mem. bd. advisors Taxation of Exempts Jour., 1998—. Contbr. articles to legal jours.; editl. adv. bd. Moment Mag., 2000—. Mem. ABA, State Bar Calif., D.C. Bar, Cosmos Club. Jewish. Office: Pillsbury Winthrop Shaw Pittman LLP 2300 N St NW Washington DC 20037-1172 Office Phone: 202-663-8441. Business E-Mail: jeffery.yablon@pillsburylaw.com.

**YABLON, LEONARD HAROLD,** publishing executive; b. N.Y.C., June 3, 1929; s. Philip A. and Sarah (Herman) Y.; m. Carolyn Sydney Torgan (dec. Aug. 1995); children: Scott Richard, Bonnie Michelle; m. Pamela Gallin; children: Laura, Abigail, Hilary, Peter. BS, L.I. U., 1950; MBA, CCNY, 1969. CPA, N.Y. Acct., 1950-63; emeritus dir. Forbes Inc., N.Y.C.; chmn. emeritus Forbes Family Holdings Inc.; pres. Sangre de Cristo Ranches; pres. emeritus Fiji Forbes; v.p. emeritus Forbes Investors Adv. Inst.; pres. emeritus Forbes Trinchera, Forbes Europe. Sec.-treas. Forbes Found.; dir. Yablon Found., Mack Goldner Found. Home and Office: 2 Fargo Ln Irvington NY 10533-1202 Office Phone: 914-591-8387. Business E-Mail: lyablon@forbes.com.

**YABLONOVITCH, ELI,** electrical engineering educator; b. Puch, Austria, Dec. 15, 1946; BSc, McGill U., 1967; AM, Harvard U., 1969, PhD in Applied Physics, 1972. Tchg. fellow Harvard U., 1971—72, asst. prof. applied physics, 1974-76, assoc. prof. applied physics, 1976-79; mem. tech. staff Bell Labs., 1972-74; assoc. rsch. assoc., group head Exxon Rsch. Ctr., 1979-84; mem. tech. staff Bellcore, 1984-90, disting. mem. staff, 1990-93, dir. solid state physics rsch., 1991-93; prof. elec. engring. UCLA, 1993—. Chmn. Gordon Conf. on Nonlinear Optics and Lasers, 1979; founder W/PECS Series of Photonic Crystal Internat. Workshops, 1999; Clifford Paterson lectr. Royal Soc. London, 2000; Edison lectr. Notre Dame U., 2004; Anson L. Clark Meml. lectr. U. Tex., 2004; Morris Loeb lectr. Harvard U., 2005. A.P. Sloan fellow, 1978-79; recipient Julius Springer prize in applied physics, 2001. Fellow: IEEE (W. Streifer Sci. Achievement award 1993), Optical Soc. Am. (Adolph Lomb medal 1978, R.W. Wood prize 1996), Am. Physics Soc.; mem.: NAS, NAE. Achievements include research in solar cells, strained-semiconductor lasers, photonic band structure. Office: UCLA Dept Elec Engring 66-147K Engring Bldg IV Los Angeles CA 90095-1594 Business E-Mail: eliy@ee.ucla.edu.

**YABUKI, JEFFREY W.,** data processing company executive, former accounting company executive; BBA, Calif. State U. Cert. CPA Calif., Minn., lic. Nat. Assn. Securities Dealers. With Am. Express Co., 1987—99; v.p., mergers & acquisitions Am. Express Tax Bus. Svcs., Mpls., 1996—98, pres., CEO N.Y.C., 1998—99; pres. H&R Block Internat., 1999—2002; exec. v.p., COO H&R Block Inc., Kans. City, 2002—05; pres., CEO Fiserv, Inc., Brookfield, Wis., 2005—. Bd. dir. PetSmart, Inc., 2004—, Fiserv Inc., 2005—, MBIA. Former mem. Minn. Bd. Accountancy. Office: Fiserv Inc 255 Fiserv Dr Brookfield WI 53045*

**YACANTE, MARIA LUCY,** music educator, researcher; b. San Juan, Argentina, July 4, 1941; arrived in U.S., 1978; d. Carlos Alberto Yacante and Maria Elena Cuello. Maestra Normal Nacional, Sarmiento Normal Sch., San Juan, Argentina, 1966; MusB in piano, Tex. Wesleyan U., Ft. Worth, 1982; MusM in piano pedagogy, Tex. Christian U., Ft. Worth, 1984; post grad., Tex. Christian U., 1989. Prof. of music Sarmiento Normal Sch., San Juan, Argentina, 1975—76, Nat. U. of San Juan, Argentina, 1975—78; piano accompanist Tex. Wesleyan U., 1978—82; piano instr. piano prep. divsn. Tex. Christian U., 1983—88; piano tchr. Our Lady of Victory, Ft. Worth, 1985—86, Ft. Worth Music and Arts Sch., 1986—87, piano studio, Ft. Worth, 1983—. Piano tchr. Inst. Superior de Artes, San Juan, Argentina, 1963—64; adjudicator piano festivals, 1989, 92, 2000; spkr. Reflections on Learning and Tchng., 2001—; student in tchrs. program Plano Tex. Internat. Acad. and Festival (formerly Tex. Christian U./Cliburn Piano Inst.), 2005, 06. Performer solo recitals. Mem.: Ind. Piano Tchrs. Forum (chair 2002—), Tex. Fedn. of Music Clubs, Tex. Music Tchrs. Assn., Music Teachers Nat. Assn., Ft. Worth Piano Tchrs. Forum (first v.p., piano recitals 2004—), Ft. Worth Music Tchrs. Assn. Forum (chair 2002—06), Ft. Worth Music Tchrs. Assn. (chmn. Sunday piano rcitals 2001—), Pi Kappa Lambda. Avocations: reading, writing, drawing. Home: PO Box 100912 Fort Worth TX 76185-0912

**YACK, PATRICK ASHLEY,** editor; b. Little Rock, Oct. 25, 1951; s. Leo Patrick and Sarah Ann (Dew) Y.; m. Suzanne (Burnett) Y.; children: Alexander Ryan, Kendall Elizabeth. BFA, So. Meth. U., 1974. Staff asst. U.S. Rep. Alan Steelman, Washington, 1975-76; press aide U.S. Senator Charles Percy, Chgo., 1977-78; reporter Fla. Times-Union, Jacksonville, 1979-80, regional reporter Atlanta, 1981-82; reporter The Denver Post, 1983-85, Washington bur. chief, 1985-87; nat. editor Atlanta Constitution, 1987-89; mng. editor The Register-Guard, Eugene, Oreg., 1989-94; editor News & Record, Greensboro, NC, 1994-98, Fla. Times-Union, Jacksonville, 1998—. Journalism coun. So. Meth. U.; journalism adv. coun. U. Fla., Gainesville, 2003—; mem. com. protect journalists Investigative Reporters and Editors; bd. dirs. First Amendment Found. Mem. news/editl. adv. bd. Am. Press Inst.; active First Amendment Found.; bd. dirs. Leadership Jacksonville, 2004—05; co-chair Freedom of Info. Com. Mem.: Am. Soc. Newspaper Editors (past membership com. chair, co-chair Freedom of Info.), Fla. Soc. Newspaper Editors (former pres., bd. dirs.).

**YACKEL, JAMES WILLIAM,** mathematician, academic administrator; b. Sanborn, Minn., Mar. 6, 1936; s. Ewald W. and Marie E. (Heydlauff) Y.; m. Erna Beth Seecamp, Aug. 20, 1960; children: Jonathan, Juliet, Carolyn. BA, U. Minn., 1958, MA, 1960, PhD, 1964. Rsch. instr. dept. math. Dartmouth Coll., Hanover, NH, 1964-66; asst. prof. dept. stats. Purdue U., West Lafayette, Ind., 1966-69, from assoc. prof. to prof., 1969-76, assoc. dean sci., 1976-87; vice chancellor acad. affairs Purdue U. Calumet, Hammond, Ind.,

1987-90, chancellor, 1990-2001, chancellor emeritus, 2001—. Rsch. mathematician Inst. Def. Analysis, Washington, 1969. Author: Applicable Finite Mathematics, 1974; editor Statistical Decision Theory, 1971; contbr. articles to profl. jours. Fellow AAAS; mem. Am. Math. Soc., Math. Assn. Am., Inst. Math. Stats. Achievements include research on Ramsey's theorem and finite graphs. E-mail: yackelj@calumet.Purdue.edu.

**YACKIRA, MICHAEL WILLIAM,** electric power industry executive; b. N.Y.C., Aug. 14, 1951; s. Alan Israel and Lillian (Landau) Y.; m. Roberta Guido, July 24, 1977; children: Steven, Andrew. BS in Acctg., Herbert H. Lehman Coll., CUNY, 1972. Sr. acct. Arthur Andersen, N.Y.C., 1972-75; v.p. St. Joe Petroleum, Houston, 1975-83; mgr. fin. analysis US Industries, Stamford, Conn., 1983-84; dir. bus. analysis and research GTE Svc. Corp., Stamford, 1984-85, dir. bus. devel. and analysis, 1985-86, asst. controller budget planning and analysis, 1986-87; v.p. fin. and revenues GTE Fla., Tampa, 1987-88; v.p. fin. and info. mgmt. GTE Info. Svcs., Tampa, 1988-89; v.p. corp. devel. and planning FPL Group, Inc., Juno Beach, Fla., 1989-91; chief planning officer Fla. Power and Light Co., 1991-97; sr. v.p. market and regulatory svcs. Fla. Power & Light Co., Juno Beach, 1991—. Bd. dirs. Ctr. for Family Svcs., West Palm Beach, Fla.

**YACKTMAN, STEPHEN,** investment company executive; BS in Econs., Brigham Young U.; MBA in Fin., Brigham Young Y., 1993. Co-mgr. funds Yacktman Asset Mgmt. Co., Buffalo Grove, Ill., 1993—. Bd. dir. 1-800 CONTACTS. Office: Yacktmay Asset Management 6300 Bridge Point Pkwy # 320 Austin TX 78730-5016

**YACOUB, IGNATIUS I.,** dean; b. Dwar Taha, Syria, Jan. 5, 1937; came to U.S. 1978; s. Immanuel and Martha (Khanna) Y.; m. Mary Haddad, Sept. 14, 1961; children: Hilda, Lena, Emile. AB, Mid. East Coll., Beirut, Lebanon, 1960; MA, Pacific Union Coll., Angwin, Calif., 1964; PhD, Claremont Grad. Sch., Calif., 1976. Dean studies Mid. East Coll., Beirut, 1967-73, 75-78; dir. dept. edn. Afro-Mideast divsn. Seventh-Day Adventist Ch., 1970-73, dir. dept. pub. affairs, 1975-78; prof., chmn. dept. bus. econs. Southwestern Union Coll., Keene, Tex., 1978-80; prof., chmn. dept. bus. and econs. Loma Linda U., Riverside, Calif., 1980-86, founding dean Sch. of Bus. and Mgmt., 1986-90, prof. mgmt., 1995—; founding dean Sch. Bus. and Mgmt., La Sierra U., Riverside, 1990—95; prof. adminstrn. and mgmt. Loma Linda U., Loma Linda, Calif., 1995—. Bd. dirs. Riverside Nat. Bank; bd. advisors City Nat. Bank, 1997—2003. Mem. Exec. 2000 Coun. Riverside Cmty. Hosp. Found., 1991-95. Recipient Gov.'s Appreciation award, Lions Club, Lions Club award, Beirut, cert. Appreciation Exec. 2000 Coun., 1994, 95, Cert. of Appreciation Claremont Grad. Sch. Alumni Coun., 1996, Mentemoreles Univ. Mex., 1992, 94. Mem. Am. Mgmt. Assn., Acad. Mgmt., Soc. for Advancement Mgmt., Greater Riverside C. of C. (Svc. award 1995), Corona C. of C. Seventh-Day Adventist. Home: 2722 Litchfield Dr Riverside CA 92503-6213 Office Phone: 909-558-7148. Personal E-mail: iyacoub@charter.net. Business E-Mail: iyacoub@univ.llu.edu.

**YACOWITZ, HAROLD,** biochemist, nutritionist; b. NYC, Feb. 17, 1922; s. Louis and Clara (Kurtzberg) Y.; m. Ann Ruth Barnett, Dec. 31, 1941; children: Caryn R., Richard S., Suzanne Yacowitz Dragan. BS, Cornell U., Ithaca, N.Y., 1948, M in Nutritional Sci., 1948, PhD, 1950. Rsch. biochemist Parke-Davis Inc., Detroit, 1950-51; assoc. prof. Ohio State U., Columbus, 1951-55; head nutrition rsch. dept. Squibb Inst. for Med. Rsch., New Brunswick, NJ, 1955-59; dir. rsch. Nopco Chem. Co. Inc., Harrison, NJ, 1959-61, Amburgo Co. Inc., Phila., 1961-80; rsch. assoc. Fairleigh Dickinson U., Madison, NJ, 1961-80; pres., dir. rsch. Dr. H. Yacowitz & Co., Piscataway, NJ, 1961—, Animal Identification & Marking Systems Inc., Piscataway, 1982-97. Pres. Peninsula Investment & Devel. Inc., Cambridge, Md., 1961—; pres., bd. dirs. rsch. Drug Delivery Devices Inc., Piscataway, 1991—. Contbr. articles to profl. jours.; patentee in field. Leader Boy Scouts Am., Ithaca, N.Y., 1946-50, Piscataway, 1955-59. With U.S. Army, 1943-46, ETO, PTO. Grange League Fedn. fellow Cornell U., 1947-48, Robert Gould rsch. fellow, Cornell U., 1949-50, Coun. on Arteriosclerosis fellow Am. Heart Assn., 1970. Fellow N.Y. Acad. Scis. (chmn. sect. biology and medicine 1972-76); mem. Am. Chem. Soc., Am. Inst. Nutrition, Am. Assn. Lab. Animal Scientists, Exptl. Biology. Jewish. Avocations: gardening, sailing, fishing, swimming. Office: Drug Delivery Devices Inc 221 2nd Ave Piscataway NJ 08854-3519 Office Phone: 732-356-9366. Personal E-mail: halyacowitz@webtv.net.

**YADAV, HARI OM,** research scientist; b. Farida Barouli, India, Jan. 10, 1964; s. Bodam Singh and Ram Beti; m. Sangita Yadav, July 22, 1957; children: Mayank H., Shubham h, Rajat H. MS, Agra U., India; PhD, U. Bombay, India. From jr. rschr. to sr. rschr. U. Bombay, Mumbai, India, 1986—91; vis. rschr. U. Dhaka, Bangladesh, 1992—93; sci. officer Indian Inst. Tech., New Delhi, 1993—95; sr. lectr. U. Agra, Agra, India, 1995—2001; sr. vis. rschr. ETL, Tsukuba, Japan, 1995—96; scientist CSIR, New Delhi, 2001—. Scientist Coun. Sci. and Indsl. Rsch., New Delhi, 2001—. Contbr. over 38 articles to profl. jours. Mem.: Japanese Phys. Soc., IPA (life), IAPT (life). Avocations: cricket, reading, information technology. Office: Coun Sci and Indsl Rsch 2 Rafi Marg New Delhi 110001 India Office Phone: +91-11-23715258. Office Fax: +91-11 23736842. E-mail: hoy@csir.res.in.

**YADAV, OM PRAKASH,** reliability engineer, educator; b. Naghore, India, July 7, 1964; s. Matadeen and Chiriya Yadav; m. Uma Yadav, Dec. 15, 2005. B of Engring., U. Rajasthan, Jaiper, India, 1986; MS, Nat. Inst. Indian Engring., Bombay, 1992; PhD, Wayne State U., Detroit, Mich., 2002. Asst. prof. M.R. Engring. Coll., Jaiper, India, 1987—96, assoc. prof., 1996—99; grad.-rsch. asst. Wayne State U., Detroit, 1999—2002; reliability engr. Rapid Global Solution Inc. (based at Ford Motor Co.), Detroit, 2002—04; asst. prof. N.D. State U., Fargo, 2004—. Contbr. articles to profl. jours. Founding mem. (non-govtl. orgn.) Sahyog-Rashms, India, 1992—. Mem.: Am. Soc. Quality, Inst. Indsl. Engrs., Soc. Mfg. Engrs. Office: ND State Univ GECIE 202 1410 14th Ave N Fargo ND 58105 Office Phone: 701-231-7285. Office Fax: 701-231-7195. E-mail: Om.Yadav@ndsu.edu.

**YADAV, PRASHANT,** finance educator; s. Surendra and Usha Yadav. PhD, U. Ala., Tuscaloosa, 2004. Prof. supply chain mngmt. MIT, Spain, 2004—. Office: MIT-Zaragoza International Logistics Pro Avenida Gomez Laguna 25 Zaragoza 50009 Spain Office Phone: + 34 976077615.

**YADEKA, THEOPHILUS ADENIYI,** hospital administrator; b. Ibadan, Nigeria, Apr. 16, 1939; came to U.S. 1971; s. Joshua A. and Alice (Opawole) Y.; m. Julianah M., Aug. 23, 1965; children: Olatunde, Mofoluke, Ayoola, Mobolaji, Adedoja. Diploma, S.D.A Nursing Sch., 1965, SUNY, 1972; BS in Healthcare Adminstrn., St. Francis Coll., 1976; MS in Healthcare & Hosp. Adminstrn., L.I. U., 1977. Lic. pvt. sch. tchr. clin. instr. Charge and staff nurse Met. City Hosp., N.Y.C., 1971—74, Barnabas Hosps., N.Y.C., 1974—77; prin. hosp. adminstr. Ministry of Health/State Hosp. Mgmt. Bd., Ibadan, Nigeria, 1978-85, asst. DON Lincoln Hosp., State Hosps. Mgmt. Bd., Ibadan, Nigeria, 1985-89; asst. DON Lincoln Hosp., Bronx, NY, 1977—78, 1989-90; asst. dir. Bronx Lebanon Hosp. Ctr., 1990—95; clin. instr., healthcare cons., 1999—. Fellow Internat. Biog. Ctr. Eng.; mem. Am. Coll. Hosp. Adminstrs., Am. Coll. Nursing Home Adminstrs., Inst. Health Svc. Adminstrs. Nigeria. Home: Bronx GPO 496 Bronx NY 10451 Office: Calibe Training Inst 500 Seventh Ave New York NY 10018 Office Phone: 212-564-0500, 212-564-0500.

**YADRICK, ROBERT MARTIN,** occupational analyst; b. Kansas City, Mo., Oct. 24, 1949; s. John George and Joanne Jean Yadrick; m. Patricia Eileen (Koelzer), May 30, 1986 (div. 2004); children: Lauren Nicole, John Nicholas. BA, Rockhurst Coll., 1971; MA, U. Mo., 1973, PhD, 1975. Cert. profl. ergonomist Bd. Certification in Profl. Ergonomics, Inc. Asst. prof. psychology Columbia (Mo.) Coll., 1975-78; rsch. assoc. U. Mo., Columbia, 1978-79; sr. rsch. assoc. Ctrl.-N.E. Colo. Health Sys. Agy., Inc., Denver, 1979-82; sr. human factors engr. McDonnell Douglas Corp., St. Louis, 1982-90; rsch.

scientist Metrica, Inc., San Antonio, 1991; pers. rsch. psychologist USAF Rsch. Lab., Brooks AFB, Tex., 1991-99; occupl. analyst USAF, Randolph AFB, Tex., 1999—, quality assurance mgr., 2001—. Adj. lectr. U. Tex. San Antonio, Our Lady of the Lake U., St. Mary's U., Wayland Bapt. Univ.; editor newsletter Insight, Human Factors and Ergonomics Soc., Santa Monica, Calif., 1994-96, reviewer visual performance tech. group, 1995-97; reviewer jour. Behavior Rsch. Methods, Instruments and Computers, 1996. Contbr. articles to profl. jours. Mentor, tutor Judson Sch. Dist., San Antonio, 1999—. Recipient Lab. Dir.'s award Armstrong Lab., 1996. Mem.: Sigma Xi. Avocations: flying, hiking, water sports. Personal E-mail: sloper52@aol.com. Business E-Mail: robert.yadrick@randolph.af.mil.

**YAEGER, DOUGLAS HARRISON,** gas industry executive; b. St. Louis, Mar. 3, 1949; s. Walter Earl and Mary Eloise (Drinkwater) Y.; m. Lynn Mary Halloran, June 24, 1951; children: Lauren Harrison, Drew Halloran. BS, Miami U., Oxford, Ohio, 1971; MBA, St. Louis U., 1976. Sales asst. Miss. River Transmission Corp., St. Louis, 1974-75, coordinator mktg. and regulatory supply, 1975-78, coordinator mktg. and supply, 1978, mgr. mktg. and supply coordination, 1978-81, asst. v.p. mktg., 1981-82, v.p. mktg., 1982-86, sr. v.p. mktg., 1986-88, exec. v.p., 1988-90; v.p. Laclede Gas Co., St. Louis, 1990—97, pres., 1997—2000, chmn., CEO, 1999—2000; chmn., pres., CEO Laclede Group Inc., St. Louis, 2000—. Bd. dir. Am. Gas Assn., First Banks Inc., St. Louis. Dir Barnes Jewish Hosp., St. Louis; bd. commr. St. Louis Sci. Ctr. Mem. Am. Gas Assn., So. Gass Assn., Interstate Natural Gas Assn., Assn. Corp. Growth, Sunset Country, Media, Strathalbyn Farm, The Planning Forum, St. Louis Club. Avocations: golf, fishing, hunting. Office: LACLEDE GAS COMPANY 720 Olive St Saint Louis MO 63101*

**YAFFA, ANDREW BRYAN,** lawyer; b. Richmond, Va., May 26, 1966; s Jack Ber and Phyllis P. Yaffa; m. Romy J. Yaffa, Aug. 17, 1991; children: Ryan, Garrett, Hailey. BA, U. Richmond, 1988; JD, U. Miami, 1991. Bar: Fla. 1991, U.S. Dist. Ct. (so. dist.) Fla. 1992. Atty. Grossman, Roth, Olin, Meadow, Cohen, Yaffa, Pennekamp & Cohen, P.A., Miami, 1991—. Mem. ABA, Acad. Fla. Trial Lawyers. Avocations: sports, fishing. Office: Grossman Roth Olin Madow Cohen Yaffa Pennekamp & Cohen PA 925 South Federal Hwy Ste 775 Boca Raton FL 33432

**YAFFE, BARBARA MARLENE,** journalist; b. Montreal, Que., Can., Mar. 4, 1953; d. Allan and Anne (Freedman) Yaffe; m. Wilson E. Russell, Aug. 30, 1985. Student, McGill U., 1970-73; BA, U. Toronto, 1974; B.A. in Journalism, Carleton U., 1975. Reporter Montreal Gazette, 1975-76, Toronto Globe and Mail, 1976-79, reporter, columnist Halifax, N.S., 1979-81; chief nat. TV news bur. CBC, St. Johns, Nfld., Canada, 1981-84, Edmonton, Alta., Canada, 1983; reporter Toronto Globe and Mail, St. John's, 1984-86; editor Sunday Express, St. John's, 1987-88, Vancouver Sun, 1988-93, columnist, edit. bd. adv., 1993—. Recipient Gov. Gen.'s award, Roland Michener Found., 1977, Commentary award, Jack Webster Found., 2004, Animal Action award, Internat. Fund for Animal Welfare, 2004. Office: c/o Vancouver Sun Ste 1 200 Granville St Vancouver BC Canada V6C 3N3 Office Phone: 604-605-2189. E-mail: byaffe@png.canwest.com.

**YAFFE, JAMES,** writer; b. Chgo., Mar. 31, 1927; s. Samuel and Florence (Scheinman) Y.; m. Elaine Gordon, Mar. 1, 1964; children: Deborah Ann, Rebecca Elizabeth, Gideon Daniel. Grad., Fieldston Sch., 1944; BA summa cum laude, Yale U., 1948. Prof. Colo. Coll., Colo. Springs, 1968—2002, prof. emeritus, 2002—. Author: Poor Cousin Evelyn, 1951, The Good-for-Nothing, 1953, What's the Big Hurry?, 1954, Nothing But the Night, 1959, Mister Margolies, 1962, Nobody Does You Any Favors, 1966, The American Jews, 1968, The Voyage of the Franz Joseph, 1970, So Sue Me!, 1972, Saul and Morris, Worlds Apart, 1982, A Nice Murder for Mom, 1988, Mom Meets Her Maker, 1990, Mom Doth Murder Sleep, 1991, Mom Among the Liars, 1992, My Mother the Detective, 1997; play The Deadly Game, 1960, (with Jerome Weidman) Ivory Tower, 1967, Cliffhanger, 1985; also TV plays, stories, essays, revs. Served with USNR, 1945-46. Recipient Nat. Arts Found award, 1968 Mem. P.E.N., Authors League, Writers Guild of Am., Dramatists Guild, A.A.U.P., Mystery Writers of Am., Phi Beta Kappa. Clubs: Elizabethan (Yale). Jewish. Avocations: music, bridge, movies. Home: 12 W 72 St New York NY 10023

**YAFFE, STUART ALLEN,** physician; b. Springfield, Ill., July 6, 1927; m. Natalie, 1952; children: Scott, Kim Yaffe Schoenburg. BS cum laude, U. Alaska, 1951; MD, St. Louis U., 1956. Diplomate Am. Bd. Family Practice. Intern St. Louis CIty Hosp., 1956-57, resident, 1957-58; physician pvt. practice, 1958—; clin. assoc. prof. So. Ill. U. Sch. Medicine., Springfield, 1971—; ptnr. Springfield Clinic, 1989—. With U.S. Army, 1945-47. Mem. AMA, Am. Acad. Family Physicians, Ill. Acad. Family Physicians, Ill. State Med. Soc., Sangamon County Med. Soc. Office: 1100 Centre West Dr Springfield IL 62704-2100 Office Phone: 217-793-9960. E-mail: yaffe62704@yahoo.com.

**YAFFE, SUMNER JASON,** pediatrician, educator, science administrator; b. Boston, May 9, 1923; s. Henry H. and Ida E. (Fisher) Yaffe; children: Steven, Kris, Jason, Noah, Ian, Zachary. AB, Harvard U., 1945, MA, 1950; MD, U. Vt., 1954. Diplomate Am. Bd. Pediatrics. Rsch. fellow in pharmacology U Vt. Coll. Medicine, Burlington, 1950—52; intern in pediat. Children's Hosp., Boston, 1954—55, resident, 1955-56; resident in pediatrics St. Mary's Hosp., London, 1956-57; instr. pediatrics Stanford U., Palo Alto, Calif., 1959-60, asst. prof., 1960-63; assoc. prof. pediatrics SUNY-Buffalo, 1963-66, prof., 1966-75, adj. prof. biochem. pharmacology, 1968-75, acting chmn. dept. pediatrics, 1974-75; clin. prof. pediatrics and pharmacology U. Pa., Phila., 1975-81; clin. prof. pediat. UCLA Sch. Medicine, 2001—06; cons. prof. Stanford Med. Ctr., 2006—. Vis. prof. pharmacology Karolinska Inst., Stockholm, 1969—70; dir. Dyline Renal Clinic, Stanford Mod. Ctr., 1960—63; dir. newborn nursery svc. Palo Alto-Stanford Hosp., 1960—63, program dir. Clin. Rsch. Ctr. for Premature Infants, 1962—63; dir. Clin. Rsch. Ctr. for Children Children's Hosp., Buffalo, 1963—70, dir. Poison Control Ctr., 1967—75, dir. divsn. clin. pharmacology, Phila., 1975—81; dir. Ctr. for Rsch. for Mothers and Children Nat. Inst. Child Health and Human Devel., NIH, 1981—2001, program cons., 1963—71, mem. tng. grant com., 1963—65, mem. reproductive biology com., 1965—67; mem. adv. panel on maternal and child health WHO, Geneva, 1970—; liaison rep. drug rsch. bd. NRC, 1971—75, com. on drug dependence, 1972—75, mem. com. on problems of drug safety, 1972—75; mem. adv. panel in pediat. U.S. Pharmacopeia, 1970—, mem. adv. panel in toxicology, 1974—75; cons. Am. Found. for Maternal and Child Health, Inc., 1973—; pres. Maternal and Child Health Rsch. Found., Children's Hosp., 1974—75; Wall Meml. lectr. Children's Hosp., Washington, 1968—; Dr. W.E. Upjohn lectr. Can. Med. Assn., 1974; Louisville pediat. lectr. Sch. Medicine U. Louisville, 1974; William N. Creasy vis. prof. clin. pharmacology SUNY, 1976; advisor Internat. Childbirth Assn. Greater Phila., 1979—83; guest lectr. dept. pediat. Georgetown U. Hosp., Washington, 1988—2001; lectr. in pediat. Johns Hopkins Sch. Medicine, Balt., 1988—2001; mem. Roundtable on Drug Devel., Inst. of Medicine. Author: (book) Clinics in Perinatology, 1974, Drug Assessment: Criteria and Methods, 1979, Pediatric Pharmacology, 1980, Pediatric Pharmacology, 2d edit., 1992; author: (with R. Galinsky) Clinical Therapeutics, 1978; editor (with R. H. Schwartz): Drug and Chemical Risks to the Fetus and Newborn, 1980; editor: (with G. G. Briggs, T. w. Bodendorfer, R. K. Freeman) Drugs in Pregnancy and Lactatin, A Reference Guide to Fetal and Neonatal Risk, 1983, Drugs in Pregnancy and Lactatin, A Reference Guide to Fetal and Neonatal Risk, 2d, edit., 1986, Drugs in Pregnancy and Lactatin, A Reference Guide to Fetal and Neonatal Risk, 3d edit., 1990, Drugs in Pregnancy and Lactatin, A Reference Guide to Fetal and Neonatal Risk, 4th edit., 1994, Drugs in Pregnancy and Lactatin, A Reference Guide to Fetal and Neonatal Risk, 5th edit., 1998; editor: (with J. V. Aranda) Pediatric Phyarmacology, 2d edit., 1993, Neonatal and Pediatric Phyarmacology, 3d edit., 2004; mem. editl. bd.: Pediatric Alert, 1977—, Pharmacology, 1977—, Devel. Pharmacology and Therapeutics, 1979—95, mem. editl. adv. bd.: Drug Therapy, 1979—, cons. editor: Clin. Pharacokinetics, 1977; co-editor: Developmental Pharmacology, 1979—94; contbr. articles to profl. jours. With U.S. Army, 1943—44. Recipient Oscar Hunter award, ASCPT, 2002, Sumner J. Yaffe award, PPAG, 2002; scholar Fulbright, 1956—57. Fellow: Acad.

Pharm. Scis.; mem.: AAUP, AMA (com. on drugs 1963—68), Soc. Pediat. Rsch., Perinatal Rsch. Soc., Fedn. Am. Socs. Exptl. Biology, Am. Soc. Pharmacology and Exptl. Therapeutics, Am. Soc. Clin. Pharmacology and Therapeutics (chmn. sect. pediatric pharmacology 1977—83), Am. Pub. Health Assn.; Soc. Maternal Fetal Medicine (hon.), Am. Pharmaceutics Assn., Am. Pediat. Soc., Am. Fedn. for Clin. Rsch., Am. Coll. Clin. Pharmacology and Chemotherapy, Am. Acad. Pediat. (chmn. com. drugs 1967—76), Alpha Omega Alpha, Sigma Xi. Office Phone: 310-435-4210. Personal E-mail: sjyatla@yahoo.com.

**YAGAHASHI, TAKASHI,** chef; C. chef Tribute, Farmington Hills, Mich., 1996—. Named Best Restaurant in Detroit, NY Times; named one of America's Best Restaurants, Gourmet mag.; recipient award, James Beard Found., 2001. Office: Tribute 31425 W 12 Mile Rd Farmington Hills MI 48334

**YAGAMI, KAZUO,** historian; s. Iko and Tomeko Yagami; m. Frances Tay; children: Michelle, Michael. BA in English, Daito Bunka U., Tokyo, 1981; PhD, Fla. State U., 2002. Vis. asst. prof. U. North Fla., Jacksonville, 2002—03; lectr. U. No. Colo., Greeley, 2004—. Author: Konoe Fumimaro and the Failure of Peace in Japan, 1931-1941: A Critical Appraisal of Three-time Prime Minister. Faculty and Rsch. and Publ. grantee, U. No. Colo., 2004, Japan-United States Friendship Commn. grantee, NE Asia Coun., Assn. Asian Studies, Inc., 2000, dissertation rsch. grantee, Fla. State U. Mem.: Am. Hist. Assn. (assoc.). Home: 2748 Oak Park Ct Tallahassee FL 32308 Office: U No Colo Ross Hall 3270 Greeley CO 80639 Office Phone: 970-351-2114. Personal E-mail: kazuoyagami@yahoo.com. Business E-Mail: kazuo.yagami@unco.edu.

**YAGER, JOSEPH ARTHUR, JR.,** economist, consultant; b. Owensville, Ind., Apr. 14, 1916; s. Joseph Arthur and Edna (Pratt) Y.; m. Virginia Estella Beroset, Sept. 2, 1938; children: Thomas, Martha. AB, U. Mich., 1937, JD, 1939, MA, 1940; grad., Nat. War Coll., 1955. Economist OPA, 1942-44; economist State Dept., 1946-47, chief China research br., 1949-50, chief div. rsch. for Far East, 1952—57; attaché U.S. consulate gen., Canton, China, 1947-48, consul Hong Kong, 1950-51; econ. counselor Taipei, 1957-59; dep. chief of mission, 1959-61; dir. Office Chinese Affairs, 1961, Office East Asian Affairs, 1961-63; mem. Policy Planning Council, 1963-66, vice chmn., 1966-68; dep. dir. internat. and social studies div. Inst. Def. Analyses, 1968-72; sr. fellow Brookings Instn., 1972-83, guest scholar, 1983-86; resident cons. Sci. Applications Internat. Corp., 1986-89, sr. fellow, 1989-96; cons., 1996—. Author: Transforming Agriculture in Taiwan, 1988, Prospects for Nuclear Weapons Proliferation in a Changing Europe, 1992; co-author: Energy and U.S. Foreign Policy, 1974, New Means of Financing International Needs, 1978, Military Equation in Northeast Asia, 1979, Nonproliferation and U.S. Foreign Policy, 1980, International Cooperation in Nuclear Energy, 1981, Energy Balance in Northeast Asia, 1984, Energy Policy Experience of Asian Countries, 1987. Served in AUS, 1944-45. Mem. Phi Delta Phi, Delta Tau Delta. Home: 10450 Lottsford Rd #5109 Bowie MD 20721 Office Phone: 301-541-5094. Personal E-mail: hoosierjoe@earthlink.net.

**YAGER, THOMAS C.,** retired judge; b. LA, Feb. 16, 1918; s. Thomas C. and May M. (McGowan) Yager; m. Antonia M. Gussenhoven, Nov. 2, 2000. AB in pol. sci., UCLA, 1939, gen. secondary lifetime tchg. credential, 1940; JD, USC, 1948; LLD, Western State U., Calif., 1972. Reader UCLA Philosophy Dept., 1940; atty., 1949-57; legal advisor Gov. Calif., 1957, 58; superior ct. sr. judge Calif., 1959-78; founder Cmty. Betterment Svc., LA. Author: numerous legal and religious books; contbr. articles to profl. jours. Founder Judge Thomas F. Found., LA, Antonia M. Yager Found. Maj. U.S. Army, 1942—46. Office: The Cmty Betterment Svc 108 N Gower St Los Angeles CA 90004-3828 Personal E-mail: pvtsecty@aol.com, tonilsngls@aol.com.

**YAGER, VINCENT COOK,** retired bank executive; b. Chgo., June 15, 1928; s. James Vincent and Juanita (Cook) Yager; m. Dorothy Marie Gallagher, Sept. 28, 1957; children: Susan Marie, Sheila Ann. BA, Grinnell Coll., 1951. V.p. commnl. loan dept. Madison Bank & Trust, Chgo., 1963-68; v.p. fin. Cor-Plex Internat. Corp., Chgo., 1968-70; pres., CEO, dir. First Nat. Bank Blue Island, Ill., 1970-89; pres., CEO Great Lakes Fin. Resources, Inc., Matteson, Ill., 1982-96, bd. dirs.; ret. With U.S. Army, 1951—53, ETO. Mem.: Econ. Club Chgo., Bankers Club Chgo., Robert Morris Assocs. (pres. chpt. 1981—82), Midlothian Country Club, Rotary. Home: 1032 S Rand Rd Villa Park IL 60181-3145 Office: Great Lakes Bank Blue Island 13057 S Western Ave Blue Island IL 60406-2418

**YAGHMAI, DINA,** dermatologist, educator; d. Naser and Fataneh Yaghmai; m. Sasan Payvar, Apr. 11, 1997; children: Kayla Payvar, Kyle Payvar. BS suma cum laude, U. Calif., Irvine, 1993; MD, Stanford U., 1997, Northwestern U., 2001. Diplomate Am. Bd. Dermatology. Chief resident Northwestern U., Chgo., 2001; dermatologist Physicians Laser and Dermatology, Chgo., 2001—; assoc. Northwestern Meml. Hosp., Chgo., 2001—. Instr. Northwestern U., Chgo., 2001—. Author: (book chpt.) Gynecology and Obstetrics, 2000, Textbook of Facial Rejuvenation, 2000; contbr. articles to profl. jours. Fellow: Am. Acad. Dermatology, Am. Soc. Laser Medicine and Surgery, Am. Soc. Dermalogic Surgery; mem.: Chgo. Dermatol. Soc. Office: Physicians Laser and Dermatology 150 E Huron Ste 910 Chicago IL 60611 Office Phone: 312-280-0890. Office Fax: 312-280-9615. Business E-Mail: d-yaghmai@northwestern.edu.

**YAGUDIN, ALEXEI,** Olympic athlete, ice skater; b. St. Petersburg, Russia, Mar. 18, 1980; s. Zoya. Attended. Acad. Sports and Physical Culture, 2001. Winner World Jr. Skating Championships, World Championships, 1999, 2001, 2002, Olympic Championship (Mens), 2002, European Figure Skating Champion (Mens), 2002, Tour with Smucker's Stars on Ice, Can HBSC Stars on Ice. Finalist Athlete Yr., ABC Wide World Sports, 1999. Achievements include second youngest men's world champion in history; first Russian man to win world championship. Avocations: tennis, bowling, fishing, travel, computers, soccer, golf. Office: c/o Internat Skating Ctr Conn PO Box 577 Simsbury CT 06070

**YAKIMOVICH, VLADIMIR,** chemist, director; b. Kiselevo, Belarus, Jan. 1, 1950; s. Nikifor Fedorovich and Anna Artemovna Yakimovich; m. Anna Dmitrievna Chernish, Apr. 23, 1971; children: Sergei, Dmitry. MS in Chemistry, Byelorussian State U., Belarus, 1972, PhD in Chemistry, 1983. Scientist Inst. of Solid State Physics and Semiconductors, Minsk, Belarus, 1972—95, sr. scientist, 1995—98, head scientist, 1998—99, head of lab., 1999—2001; dir. of crystal growth rsch and devel. Internat. Crystal Labs., Garfield, 2001—. Contbr. articles various prof. jours. Recipient Inventor of USSR medal, Nat. Com. of the USSR on Inventions and Discoveries, 1982. Mem.: Am. Assn. for Crystal Growth. Avocations: chess, skiing. Home: 389 President St Saddle Brook NJ 07663 Office: Internat Crystal Labs 11 Erie St Garfield NJ 07026 Office Phone: 973-478-8944. Personal E-mail: iclcrystalgrow@optonline.net.

**YAKOVLEV, ALEXANDER B.,** electrical engineer, educator; b. Krivoy Rog, Dnepropetrovsk Region, Ukraine, June 5, 1964; s. Boris N. Yakovlev and Nina V. Yakovleva; m. Natalie V. Tukalova, May 16, 1992; 1 child, Anastasia A. Yakovleva. MSEE (hon.), Dnepropetrovsk State U., Dnepropetrovsk, Ukraine, 1986, PhD in Radio Physics, 1992; PhD Elec. Engring., U. Wis., Milw., 1997. Rsch. scientist Dnepropetrovsk State U., Ukraine, 1986—91, asst. prof., 1992—93; rsch. asst. U. Wis., Milw., 1994—95, tchg. asst., 1995—97; engr. R&D Ansoft Corp., Pitts., 1997—98; rsch. assoc. NC State U., Raleigh, 1998—2000; asst. prof. U. Miss., University, 2000—04, assoc. prof., 2004—. Co-author (with George W. Hanson): (book) Operator Theory for Electromagnetics: An Introduction. Recipient Young Scientist award, IEEE Electromagnetic Theory Symposium, Sydney, Australia, 1992, Internat. Symposium Antennas and Propagation, Chiba, Japan, 1996, Jr. Faculty Rsch. award, U. Miss., 2003. Mem.: IEEE, Miss. Acad. Scis., Antennas and Propagation, Microwave Theory and Techniques, Internat.

Union Radio Sci., Sigma Xi, Eta Kappa Nu. Office: U Miss Dept Elec Engring Anderson Hall Rm 306 University MS 38677-1848 Office Phone: 662-915-7196. E-mail: yakovlev@olemiss.edu.

**YAKU, TAKEO T.,** computer scientist, educator; b. Tokyo, Oct. 21, 1947; s. Masao and Teru (Nagashima) Yaku. BSc, Jiyu Gakuen Coll., Tokyo, 1970; MSc, Waseda U., Tokyo, 1972, DSc, 1977. Vis. lectr. Tokai U., Hiratsuka, Japan, 1975-76, 85-90, asst. prof., 1976-79, assoc. prof., 1979-85; IBM travel fellow, 1978; vis. lectr. Waseda U., 1979-92; assoc. prof. Tokyo Denki U., Hatoyama, Japan, 1985-92; prof. Nihon U., Setagaya-Tokyo, 1992—. Vis. lectr. Toyo U., Kawagoe, Japan, 1991—94; chmn. curriculum bd. Sch. Sci. & Engring. Tokyo Denki U., 1991—92; vis. lectr. Tokyo Denki U., 1992—94; Tsuru U., Japan, 1994—95, Hitotsubashi U., 1995—96, Nigata U., Japan, 1996, Musashino Art U., 1996—, Niigata U., 1998, Shimane U., 2002; vice dir. Inst. Info. Sci. Coll. Humanities and Scis. Nihon U. Setagaya-Tokyo, 1994—98, chmn. dept. applied math., 1997—98, advisor of the dean for students' job placement, 1998—2001, vice advisor dean rsch. activities, 2004—05, vice advisor of the dean for job placement, 2005—; chmn. earth info. math. scis. Grad. Sch. Integrated Basic Scis., Nihon U., 2004—05. Author: (with others) Micro Computer Handbook, 1985, (with others) Structured Editors, 1987; editorial bd. mem: Transac. Inst. Electronics, Information and Communication Engrs., 1993-98; contbr. articles to profl. jours. Mem. examination com. Nat. Pers. Authority, Japan, 1994-96; trustee Japan Assn. Devel. Info. Edn., 2005-. Fellow Tokau U. Ski Alpine Club; mem. Am. Math. Soc., Assn. Computing Machinery, Japan Soc. Computer Assisted Instrn. (mem. com. 1987—). Home: 3-4-4-405 Sagawa Nishi-Tokyo 202-0022 Japan Office: Nihon U 3-25-40 Sakura-Josui Setagaya Tokyo 156-8550 Japan Business E-Mail: yaku@cs.chs.nihon-u.ac.jp.

**YALAM, ARNOLD ROBERT,** allergist, immunologist, consultant; b. NYC, Apr. 11, 1940; s. Herman and Sylvia (Taber) Y.; m. Carol Ann Strocker, June 16, 1964; children: John, Matthew. AB, Johns Hopkins U., 1960; MD, U. Md., Balt., 1964. Diplomate Am. Bd. Internal Medicine, Am. Bd. Allergy and Immunology. Intern Jackson Meml. Hosp., Miami, Fla., 1964-65; resident in internal medicine SUNY Downstate Med. Ctr., Bklyn., 1965-67; fellow Scripps Clinic and Rsch. Found., La Jolla, Calif., 1967-68; cons. allergist and immunologist San Diego, 1970—. Maj. U.S. Army, 1968—70. Fellow Am. Acad. Allergy and Immunoloy; mem. Am. Soc. Addiction Medicine (cert.), San Diego Allergy Soc.

**YALAVARTHI, RAMARAJA,** physician; MD, Guntur Med. Coll., India, 1975. Diplomate Am. Bd. Internal Medicine, Am. Bd. Gerontology. Intern Govt. Gen. Hosp., 1974—75, India Ellis Hosp., 1975—76; resident psychiatry SUNY, Stony Brook, 1976—78; resident internal medicine Weiss Meml. Hosp., Chgo., 1978—80; chmn. dept. medicine, pres. med. staff St. James Hosp. and Health Ctrs., Chgo. Heights and Olympia Fields, 2004—05; chmn. quality improvement com. South Suburban Hosp.; physician WellGroup Health Partners, Chgo. Heights. Recipient Leadership award (Internat. Med. Grad. Physician), AMA Assn., 2005. Mem.: IAMA, AAPI, AMA. Office: WellGroup Health Partners 333 Dixie Hwy Chicago Heights IL 60411 E-mail: rajayakavarth@pol.net.

**YALDEN, MAXWELL FREEMAN,** Canadian diplomat; b. Toronto, Ont., Can., Apr. 12, 1930; s. Frederick and Marie (Smith) Y.; m. Janice Shaw, Jan. 28, 1952; children: Robert, Cicely (dec.). BA, Victoria Coll., U. Toronto, 1952; MA, U. Mich., PhD, 1956; D.U. (hon.), U. Ottawa; LLD (hon.), Carleton U. With Can. Dept. External Affairs, 1956-69, asst. undersec. state, 1969-73, dep. minister communications, 1973-77, commr. ofcl. langs., 1977-84; Can. amb. to Belgium and Luxembourg, 1984-87; chief commr. Can. Human Rights Comms., Ottawa, 1987—96; mem. UN Human Rights Com., 1996—2004. Decorated companion Order of Can. Office: 201 31 Durham Pvt Ottawa ON Canada K1M 2J1

**YALE, JOHN PAUL,** computer systems developer; b. Uhrichsville, Ohio, Sept. 4, 1945; s. Vernon Elna and Joan (Papworth) Y.; m. Mary Anne Hinkley, Feb. 9, 1966; children: John Vernon, Eric Kendall. AAS, Orange County C.C., 1968; BS, Ohio U., 1971; MS in Engring., U. New Haven, 2006. Dir. Pub. Broadcasting, Athens, Ohio, 1969-71; freelance prodr./dir. GGT, Niantic, Conn., 1971-79; dir. media svcs. L & M Hosps., New London, Conn., 1979-96; dir. sys. devel. C&E group MPTN, Ledyard, Conn., 1996—. Mem. Internat. TV Assn., Internat. Teleconf. Assn., Assn. fo Multimedia Internat. Toastmasters Internat., Project Mgmt. Inst. Home: Westgate Farm 299 Pond Hill Rd Chatham NY 12037 Office: 110 Pequot Trail PO Box 3180 Mashantucket CT 06339-3180 Business E-Mail: john@jpyale.net.

**YALE (YELEYENIDE-YALE), MELPOMENE FOTINE,** researcher, anthropologist, archaeologist, art historian, conservator; b. NYC, Mar. 31, 1963; d. John P. and Serina Yale (Yeleyenide-Yale). *Father John, a businessman, was one of the first to aid in the rebuilding of Europe after WWII sending medical relief to Greece without economic recompense. Mother Serina, born in 1924, in Moudros Lemnos, Greece to Adam Chiros is a philanthropist who served as president on various charity organizations and as NGO representative to the UN in 1992. One of first awarded the highest title of Archon of the Knights of St. Andrew from Patriarch Athenagoras for decades of selfless, important humanitarian work. Her name is inscribed in the rolls of the Knights of St. Andrew at the Patriarchate in Constantinople. She was awarded the Archdiocesan Medal of Saint Paul by Archbishop Iakovos.* BA in Art History, Columbia U., 1985, MA in Art History and Arch., 1998, MA in Anthropology, 2001; studied lithics and flint knapping with Prof. William Parry, CUNY Grad. Ctr., 2001; studied, Art Students League N.Y., 1987; studied fine art, Nat. Acad. Sch. Fine Arts, 1997—98; studied art history, painting, drawing, inorganic and organic chemistry, Lehman Coll., 1980—81, studied, 1987—88, studied, 1995, studied, 1996, Hunter Coll., 1983; studied with renowned iconographer Constantine Youssis, 1996—98. Sci. asst. dept. anthropology The Am. Mus. Natural History NYC, 1987—89, collections mgmt. asst. dept. anthropology, 1989—90; fieldwork archeologist (excavations) Brit. Sch. Arch., Palaikastro, Crete, 1990, 1991; fieldwork archeologist Fordham U., Rose Hill Excavations, NY, 2000; conservator The Benaki Mus., Athens, Greece, 1991, 1992, The Monastery of St. John the Theologian, Patmos, Greece, 1992, The Hispanic Soc., Am., N.Y.C., 1989—93, Brit. Sch. Archeol. Excavations, Palaikastro, Crete, 1990, 1991, Nat. Acad., 1997, Lilly Hollander Conservation Studio, NY, 1998—99, N.Y. Acad. Medicine, NY, 1999, Sherman Fairchild Ctr. Objects Conservation, Met. Mus. Art, NY, 2000; pvt. conservator, 1993—; rsch. asst. Ani project Columbia U.-World Monuments Found., NY, 1997; curatorial asst. Nat. Acad. N.Y., 1997; rsch. asst. to prof. emeritus Ralph Solecki and Dr. Rose Solecki Shanidar project Columbia U., 2001—03, coord. Ralph Holloway Endocast collection preservation and rsch. project, 2002—04, prehistoric collection, 2003—. Designer (group fashion show) Chinese New Yr. Festival, Columbia Univ., 1984. Vol. Greek Orthodox Clergy Laity Congress, Greek Orthodox Archdiocese N.Am. and S.Am., NYC, 1984, NY Convocation for Peace in the Middle East, US Interreligious Com. for Peace in the Middle East, 1990. Recipient Cert. of merit Bd. Edn. Art Exhbn., N.Y. Daily News, Lever Bros. N.Y.C., 1981, Cert. of Achievement, N.Y. Acad. Medicine, 1999, Mcpl. hon., Moudros Lemnos Greece, 2004, Mcpl. award, 2005. Mem.: N.Y. State Archaeol. Assn., Archeol. Inst. Am., Registered Profl. Archaeologists, Am. Inst. Conservation (prof.); Am. Anthrop. Assn., The Prehistoric Soc. Achievements include research in emergence of human cognition in the Palaeolithic as indicated by stone tools and art; research on brain casting techniques; independent research towards a PhD on emergence of human cognition in Palaeolithic Period of Greece and Aegean based on Palaeontological-Palaeoanthropological data, stone tools, art, & their relation; to and their influence throughout the Palaeoanthropogeographic region of Europe and the World. Avocations: flintknapping, mosaics, painting, collecting art, archel. material, and stone tools for study. Personal E-mail: mfy2@columbia.edu.

**YALE (YELEYENIDE-YALE), SERINA,** philanthropist, apparel designer; b. Moudros, Lémnos, Greece, Oct. 16, 1924; d. Adam and Fotika Chiros; m. John P. Yale (Yeleyenide-Yale); children: Mary Anne, Andrew Chris, Melpomene Fotine. *Daughter of Fotika and Adam Chiros, both of whom were the* *earliest expatriate Greeks to settle in the US in the beginning of the 20th century. Fotika was known for her rich work in the preservation of Greek and Byzantine culture and the Orthodox faith. Adam, one of the first Greek sea captains of modern day Greece and a WWI US veteran, was the son of Captain Christodoulos Chiros who aided in the freedom of Greece. Wife of businessman John P. Yale (Yelenides-Yale), was one of the first to aide in the rebuilding of Europe after WWII especially sending medical aide to Greece without economic recompense.* Grad., Washington Irving HS, NYC, 1941. Draper haute couture dept. Henri Bendel, NYC, 1941—46, Bergdorf Goodman, NYC, 1946—53; asst. designer R&K Originals, NYC, 1953—56. Pres., mem. bd. dirs. Jr. Philoptochos Philanthropic Soc., Ch. of Holy Trinity, Greek Orthodox Cath. Ch. NYC, 1942—49, mem. bd., 1949—91; pres. bd. dirs Philoptochos Philanthropic Soc., Ch. St. Spyridon, NYC, 1971—72, 1977—78; chair supervisory com. St. Michael's Home for the Aged, Yonkers, NY, 1982—84; hospitality chair 27th Greek Orthodox Clergy Laity Congress, Greek Orthodox Archdiocese N.Am. and S.Am., NYC, 1984; pres. NY Diocese Philptochos Philanthropic Soc., Greek Orthodox Archdiocese of North and South Am., NYC, 1986—88; Greek sec., mem. exec. bd. Nat. Philoptochos Philanthropic Soc., NYC, 1986—88, cardiac chmn., 1986—88; coord. benefit luncheon Greek Children's Fund, Meml. Hosp. Sloan-Kettering Cancer Ctr., NYC, 1988—90; mem. organizing com. NY Convocation for Peace in the Mid. East, US Interreligious Com. for Peace in the Mid. East, 1990, del. Ch. Women United, 1990; treas., bd. dirs. Ch. St. Spyridon, NYC, 1990—91; hon. amb. of hospitality and goodwill Greek Orthodox Archdiocese of N. and S.Am., 1933—54, Greek war relief organizer, 1941—54; hon. amb. hospitality and goodwill Consulate Gen. Greece, NYC, 1944—54; Sunday sch. tchr. Ch. of Holy Trinity, Greek Orthodox Cath. of NYC, 1938—54; asst. treas., bd. dirs. Ch. Women United, NYC, 1986—92, NGO rep. UN, 1991—92. Recipient Mcpl. honor, Moudros Lemnos Greece, 2004, Mcpl. award, 2005, Title of Archon, Order of St. Andrew of Ecumenical Patriarchate in Constantinople, 1966, Archdiocesan Medal of St. Paul, Archbishop Iakovos of N.Am. and S.Am., 1972. Home: 4555 Henry Hudson Pky Riverdale NY 10471

**YALE, SEYMOUR HERSHEL,** dental radiologist, educator, gerontologist, dean; b. Chgo., Nov. 27, 1920; s. Henry and Dorothy (Kulwin) Y.; m. Muriel Jane Cohen, Nov. 6, 1943; children: Russell Steven, Patricia Ruth. BS, U. Ill., 1944, D.D.S., 1945, postgrad., 1947-48, Spertus Inst. Jewish Studies, 1995—. Pvt. practice of dentistry, 1945-54, 56—; asst. clin. dentistry U. Ill., 1948-49, instr. clin. dentistry, 1949-53, asst. prof. clin. dentistry, 1953-54, assoc. prof. dept. radiology Coll. Dentistry, 1956, prof., head dept. Coll. Dentistry, 1957-65, adminstrv. asst. to dean Coll. Dentistry, 1961-63, asst. dean Coll. Dentistry, 1963-64, acting dean Coll. Dentistry, 1964-65, dean, 1965-87, dean emeritus, 1987—, also mem. grad. faculty dept. radiology Coll. Medicine Chgo., prof. dentistry and health resources mgmt. Sch. Pub. Health, 1987—. Sr. dental dir. Dental Care Plus Mgmt. Corp., Chgo.; pres., dir. dental edn. Dental Care Plus Mgmt. Ednl. Svcs., Ltd.; health care facilities planner; dir. tng. Dental Technicians Sch., U.S. Naval Tng. Ctr., Bainbridge, md., 1954-56; mem. subcom. 16 Nat. Com. on Radiation Protection; mem. Radiation Protection Adv. Bd., State of Ill., 1971, City of Chgo. Health Sys. Agy.; founder Ctr. for Rsch. in Periodontal Disease and Oral Molecular Biology, 1977; organizer, chmn. Nat. Conf. on Hepatitis-B in Dentistry, 1982; organizer, dir. Univ. Taskforce Primary Health Care Project, U. Ill., Chgo.; chmn. U. Ill.-U. Stockholm-U. Gothenberg Conf. on Geriatrics, 1985; dir. planning AMVETS/UIC Tchg. Nursing Home Project, 1987-91; co-sponsor 1st Egyptian Dental Congress, 1984; adj. prof. Ctr. for Exercise Sci. and Cardiovasc. Rsch., Northeastern Ill. U., Chgo., 1991, Northwestern U. Sch. Dentistry Divsn. Behavioural Scis., Evanston, Ill., 1996—. Editor-in-chief Dental Care Plus Mgmt. Digest, 1995—. Bd. dirs., co-benefactor (with wife) World Heritage Mus., U. Ill., Urbana, 1985; mem. Hillel Bd., U. Ill.-Chgo.; life mem. (with wife) Bronze Circle of Coll. Liberal Arts, U. Ill., Urbana; mem. (with wife) Pres.' Council, U. Ill. Recipient centennial research award Chgo. Dental Soc., 1959; Distinguished Alumnus award U. Ill., 1973; Harry Sicher Meml. Lecture award Am. Coll. Stomologic Surgeons, 1983 Fellow Acad. Gen. Dentistry (hon.), Am. Coll. Dentists; mem. Ill. Dental Soc. (mem. com. on radiology), Chgo. Dental Soc., Internat. Assn. Dental Rsch., Am. Acad. Oral Roentgenology, Am. Dental Assn., Odontographic Soc. Chgo. (Award of Merit 1982), Council Dental Deans State Ill. (chmn.), N.Y. Acad. Scis., Gerontol. Soc. Am., Pierre Fauchard Acad. (Man of Yr. award Ill. sect. 1988), Am. Pub. Health Assn., Gerontol. Soc. Am., Omicron Kappa Upsilon, Sigma Xi, Alpha Omega (hon.) Achievements include established (with wife) collection of Coins of Ottoman Empire and Related Mohammedan States and supplemental antique map collection at World Heritage Mus., U of Ill.; established Muriel C. Yale Collection, antique maps of Holy Land collection at Spertus Inst. Jewish Studies. Home: 155 N Harbor Dr Chicago IL 60601-7364 Office: 30 N Michigan Ave Chicago IL 60602-3402 E-mail: ddssy@uic.edu.

**YALEN, GARY N.,** retired insurance company executive; b. NYC, May 17, 1942; s. Sidney Leo and Mildred (Epstein) Y.; m. Rena Lynn Gear, Nov. 3, 1968; children: Robert, Lesley BEE, Rensselaer Poly. Inst., 1964; MBA, U. Mich., 1965. Chartered fin. analyst. Mktg. engr. N.Y. Telephone Co., N.Y.C., 1965-69; security analyst Merrill Lynch, N.Y.C., 1969-74; from security analyst to exec. v.p. Irving Trust Co., NYC, 1974—89; exec. v.p. Bank of N.Y., 1989-90; chief investment officer, exec. v.p. Fortis Asset Mgmt. (formerly Amev), 1990-95; pres., chief investment officer Fortis Advisers, 1995-2001, Fortis Asset Mgmt., 2001—02; ret., 2002. Served with U.S. Army, 1966-68, Vietnam. Mem.: Beta Gamma Sigma. Avocations: chess, golf, bridge. Home: 360 E 88th St Apt 36B New York NY 10128

**YALMAN, ANN,** judge, lawyer; b. Boston, June 9, 1948; d. Richard George and Joan (Osterman) Yalman. BA, Antioch Coll., 1970; JD, NYU. 1973. Trial atty. Fla. Rural Legal Svcs., Immokalee, Fla., 1973-74; staff atty. EEO, Atlanta, 1974-76; pvt. practice Santa Fe, 1976—2005; probate judge Santa Fe County, 1999—2005; mcpl. judge Santa Fe, 2006—. Part time U.S. magistrate, N.Mex., 1988—96. Commr. Met. Water Bd., Santa Fe, 1986-88. Mem. N.Mex. Bar Assn. (commr. Santa Fe chpt. 1983-86). Home: 441 Calle La Paz Santa Fe NM 87505-2821 Office: 2511 Camino Entrada Santa Fe NM 87507 Office Phone: 505-955-5133. Business E-Mail: ayalman@santaferm.edu.

**YALOW, ROSALYN SUSSMAN,** biophysicist; b. NYC, July 19, 1921; d. Simon and Clara (Zipper) Sussman; m. Aaron Yalow, June 6, 1943; children: Benjamin, Elanna. AB, Hunter Coll., 1941; MS, U. Ill., Urbana, 1942, PhD, 1945; DSc (hon.), U. Ill., Chgo., 1974, Phila. Coll. Pharmacy and Sci., 1976, NY Med. Coll., 1976, Med. Coll. Wis., Milw., 1977, Yeshiva U., 1977, Southampton Coll., NY, 1978, Bucknell U., 1978, Princeton U., 1978, Jersey City State Coll., 1979, Med. Coll. Pa., 1979, Manhattan Coll., 1979, U. Vt., 1980, U. Hartford, 1980, Rutgers U., 1980, Rensselaer Poly. Inst., 1980, Colgate U., 1981, U. So. Calif., 1981, Clarkson Coll., 1982, U. Miami, 1983, Washington U., St. Louis, 1983, Adelphi U., 1983, U. Alta., 1983, SUNY, 1984, Tel Aviv U., 1985, Claremont U., Calif., 1986, Mills Coll., Oakland, Calif., 1986, Cedar Crest Coll., Allentown, Pa., 1988, Drew U., Madison, NJ, 1988, Lehigh U., 1988; LHD (hon.), Hunter Coll., 1978; DSc (hon.), San Francisco State U., 1989, Technion-Israel Inst. Tech., Haifa, 1989, Med. Coll. Ohio Toledo, 1991; LHD (hon.), Sacred Heart U., Conn., 1978, St. Michael's Coll., Winooski Park, Vt., 1979, Johns Hopkins U., 1979, Coll. St. Rose, 1988, Spertus Coll. Judaica, Chgo., 1988; DHC (hon.), U. Rosario, Argentina, 1980, U. Ghent, Belgium, 1984; D. Humanities and Letters (hon.), Columbia U., 1984; DSc (hon.), Fairleigh Dickinson U., 1992, Conn. Coll., 1992, Smith Coll., Northampton, Mass., 1994, Union Coll., Schenectady, 1994. Diplomate Am. Bd. Scis. Lectr., asst. prof. physics Hunter Coll., 1946-50; physicist, asst. chief radioisotope service VA Med. Ctr., Bronx, NY, 1950-70, chief nuclear medicine, 1970-80, acting chief radioisotope service, 1968-70, sr. med. investigator emeritus; research prof. Mt. Sinai Sch. Med., CUNY, 1968-74, Disting. Service prof., 1974-79, Solomon A. Berson Disting. prof.-at-large, 1986—; chmn. dept. clin. scis. Montefiore Med. Ctr., Bronx, 1980-85; Disting. prof.-at-large Albert Einstein Coll. Medicine, Yeshiva U., 1979-85, prof. emeritus, 1986. Cons. Lenox Hill Hosp., NYC, 1956—62, WHO, Bombay, 1978; sec. U.S. Nat. Com. on Med. Physics, 1963—67; mem. nat. com. Radiation Protection, subcom. 13, 1957, Pres.'s Study Group on Careers for

Women, 1966—72; sr. med. investigator VA, 1972—92, sr. med. investigator emeritus, 1992—. Co-editor: Hormone and Metabolic Research, 1973—79; editl. adv. coun. Acta Diabetologica Latina, 1975—77, Ency. Universalis, 1978—, editl. bd. Mt. Sinai Jour. Medicine, 1976—79, Diabetes, 1976, Endocrinology, 1967—72, contbr. numerous articles to profl. jours. Bd. dirs. NY Diabetes Assn., 1974. Recipient VA William S. Middleton Med. Rsch. award, 1960, Eli Lilly award, Am. Diabetes Assn., 1961, Van Slyke award, NY met. sect. Am. Assn. Clin. Chemists, 1968, ACP award, 1971, Dickson prize, U. Pitts., 1971, Howard Taylor Ricketts award, U. Chgo., 1971, Gairdner Found. Internat. award, 1971, Commemorative medallion, Am. Diabetes Assn., 1972, Bernstein award, Med. Soc. State NY, 1974, Boehringer-Mannheim Corp. award, Am. Assn. Clin. Chemists, 1975, Sci. achievement award, AMA, 1975, Exceptional Svc. award, VA, 1975, A. Cressy Morrison award, NY Acad. Scis., 1975, sustaining membership award, Am. Mil. Surgeons, 1975, Disting. Achievement award, Modern Medicine, 1976, Albert Lasker Basic Med. Rsch. award, 1976, La Madonnina Internat. prize, Milan, 1977, Golden Plate award, Am. Acad. Achievement, 1977, Nobel prize in physiology or medicine, 1977, citation of esteem, St. John's U., 1979, G. von Hevesy medal, 1978, Rosalyn S. Yalow R&D award established, Am. Diabetes Assn., 1978, Banting medal, 1978, Torch of Learning award, Am. Friends Hebrew U., 1978, Virchow Gold medal, Virchow-Pirquet Med. Soc., 1978, Gratum Genus Humanum Gold medal, World Fedn. Nuc. Medicine or Biology, 1978, Jacobi medallion, Assoc. Alumni Mt. Sinai Sch. Med., 1978, Jubilee medal, Coll. of New Rochelle, 1978, VA Exceptional Svc. award, 1978, Fed. Woman's award, 1961, Harvey lectr., 1966, Am. Gastroenterol. Assn. Meml. lectr., 1972, Joslin lectr., New Eng. Diabetes Assn., 1972, 1st Hagedorn Meml. lectr., Acta Endocrinologica Congress, 1973, Franklin I. Harris Meml. lectr., 1973, Sarasota Med. award for achievement and excellence, 1979, Gold medal, Phi Lambda Kappa, 1980, Achievement in Life award, Ency. Britannica, 1980, Theobald Smith award, 1982, Pres.'s Cabinet award, U. Detroit, 1982, John and Samuel Bard award in med. and sci., Bard Coll., 1982, Disting. Rsch. award, Dallas Assn. Retarded Citizens, 1982, Nat. medal of Sci., 1988, Abram L. Sachar Silver medallion, Brandeis U., 1989, Disting. Scientist of Yr. award, ARCS, NYC, 1989, Golden Scroll award, The Jewish Advocate, Boston, 1989, spl. award, Clin. Ligand Assay Soc., Washington, 1988, numerous others. Fellow: Clin. Soc. N.Y. Diabetes Assn., Am. Coll. Radiology (assoc. in physics), N.Y. Acad. Scis. (chmn. biophysics divsn 1964—65); mem.: NAS, Am. Physiol. Soc., Endocrine Soc. (pres. 1978, Kocn award 1972), Soc. Nuc. Medicine, Soc. Nuc. Medicine (hon.), Am. Gastroenterol. Assn. (hon.), Am. Coll. Nuc. Physicians (hon.), Harvey soc. (hon.), Med. Assn. Argentina (hon.), Diabetes Soc. Argentina (hon.), The N.Y. Acad. Medicine (hon.), N.Y. Roentgen Soc. (hon.), Biophys. Soc., Am. Assn. Physicists in Medicine, Radiation Rsch. Soc., Am. Phys. Soc., Am. Acad. Arts and Scis., Tau Beta Pi, Sigma Delta Epsilon, Pi Mu Epsilon, Sigma Pi Sigma, Sigma Xi, Phi Beta Kappa. Office: Vet Affairs Med Ctr 130 W Kingsbridge Rd Bronx NY 10468-3904*

**YAMADA, KENNETH MANAO,** cell biologist; b. Mpls., Sept. 18, 1944; s. Paul Manao and Masaye (Uriu) Yamada; m. Susan Jane Sleeper, July 1, 1973. BA in Biol. Scis., Stanford U., 1966, PhD in Biol. Scis., 1971, MD, 1972. Intern Mary's Help Hosp./Seton Med. Ctr., Daly City, Calif., 1972-73; commd. lt. USPHS, 1974, advanced through grades to capt., 1982—2003, ret., 2003; sect. chief Nat. Cancer Inst., Bethesda, Md., 1980-90; lab. chief Nat. Inst. Dental and Craniofacial Rsch., NIH, Bethesda, 1990-96, br. chief 1996—. Mem. Cell Biology Study sect. NIH, 1979—83; mem. external adv. com. Cancer Rsch. Ctr. Howard U., 1979—88; co-chmn. Gordon Conf. on Fibronectin, 1982; Stadtler lectr. U. Tex. Sys. Cancer Ctr. M.D. Anderson Hosp., 1988; Swerling lectr. Dana-Farber Cancer Inst. Harvard Med. Sch., 1988; Retzius lectr. Karolinska Inst., 2005. Editor: Jour. Cell Biology, 1999—; contbr. more than 350 publs. to biomed. lit. Recipient Eli Luke and Jacob David Rsch. award, 1972, Sr. Lectureship award, Am. Soc. Matrix Bio., 2004. Fellow: AAAS; mem.: Soc. Devel. Biology, Southeastern Cancer Rsch. Assn. (bd. dirs. 1980—83), Am. Soc. Matrix Biology (coun. 2003—), Internat. Soc. Matrix Biology (coun. 1994—2006), Am. Soc. Biochemistry and Molecular Biology, Am. Soc. Cell Biology (coun. 1992—95), Sigma Xi, Phi Beta Kappa (Undergrad. rsch. award). Office: Nat Inst of Dental and Craniofacial Rsch 30 Convent Dr Bldg 30 Rm 426 Bethesda MD 20892-4370 Office Phone: 301-496-9124. Business E-Mail: kenneth.yamada@nih.gov.

**YAMADA, TETSUJI,** health economist, educator; M of Internat. Affairs, Columbia U., 1978; MPhil, Grad. Ctr. of CUNY, 1983, PhD in Econs., 1987. Instr. CUNY, N.Y.C., 1982—86; postdoctoral fellow Grad. Ctr. of CUNY, N.Y.C., 1987; assoc. prof. dept. econs. Rutgers U., Camden, NJ, 1987—91; rsch. fellow NBER, 1987-90, rsch. assoc., 1991-94, Ctr. Pacific Basin Fed. Res. Bank, San Francisco, 1990—; assoc. prof. Ritsumeikan U., Kyoto, 1991-92; health economist Internat. Leadership Ctr. Longevity and Soc., 1993-94; assoc. prof. Rutgers U., 1993—2002, chair dept. econs., 1996-99, prof., 2003—, assoc. mem. Inst Health, Health Care Policy and Aging Rsch., 2004—; exec. bd. China East Inst. Soc. Ins., China, 1998—2004; vis. rsch. scholar dept. health econs. and mgmt. Peking U. Sch. Mgmt., China, 2005. Rep. Japan Econ. Fedn., Ditchley, Oxford, England, 1994; vis. rsch. scholar Inst. Policy and Planning Scis., Tsukuba U., Japan, 1997—2005; temp. adviser WHO, 1999, 2005—06; faculty assoc. Walter Rand Inst., 1999—; ctr. assoc. Ctr. for Children and Childhood Studies, 2000—; cons. Japan Found., 2001, 2005—06; reviewer and referee profl. jours., books and rsch. grants; mem. editl. bd. Internat. Jour. Applied Econs., 2004—; adviser Japanese Am. Assn. N.Y., 2006—. Contbr. articles to profl. jours. Grantee, Ministry Edn., Japan, 1991, Iryo Kagaku Kenkyu Jo, Japan, 1991—92, Pfizer Health Rsch. Found., 1992—93, 21st Century Cultural Rsch. Found., 1993, Ministry Health and Welfare, Japan, 1993—94, Nomura Found., Japan, 1995—96, Iryo Kagaku Kenkyu Jo, Japan, 1996—97, Iryo Keizai Kenkyu Kiko, Japan, 1997—98, Ctr. for Children and Childhood Studies, 2000—01, Ministry of Edn., Sci., Sports and Culture of Japan, 2002—03, Pfizer Health Rsch. Found., 2003—05, Inst. Statis. Rsch., Labor Marjet Rsch. Com., 2003—04; ORSP grant, Rutgers U., 1992—. Dialogues grant, 2002—03. Internat. Health Econ. Rsch. grant, Eli Lilly, 2005. Mem. Am. Econ. Assn., Internat. Health Econs. Assn., So. Econs. Assn., We. Econ. Assn., Am. Soc. Health Econs. (sci. com. 2005-2006), Internat. Soc. for Pharmacoeconomics and Outcome Rsch. (mem. rev. com. 2005-2006), Japan Econ. Sem., Inst. Statis. Rsch. (labor market rsch. com. 2003-04), Omicron Delta Epsilon (award). Home: 300 East 40th St #4M New York NY 10016 Office: Dept Econs-CCAS Rutgers Univ State Univ NJ Camden NJ 08102 Office Phone: 856-225-6136 and 856-225-6025. Home Fax: 212-297-0192. Business E-Mail: tyamada@crab.rutgers.edu. E-mail: ytetsuji@aol.com.

**YAMADA, TOHRU,** biologist, educator, researcher, director; b. Hadano, Kanagawa, Japan, June 30, 1975; s. Yoshio and Tamiko Yamada; m. Kaori Horiguchi, May 7, 2005. Bachelor's degree, Tokyo Inst. Tech., 1999, Master's degree, 2001, PhD, 2003. Post-doctoral fellow dept. microbiology/immunology U. Ill. Coll. Medicine, Chgo., 2003—04, vis. rsch. asst. prof. dept. surg. oncology, 2004—06; dir drug devel. CDG Therapeutics Inc., 2006—. Contbr. articles to profl. jours. First Class scholar, Japan Student Svcs. Orgn., 1999. Mem.: Soc. Microbiology. Office: U Ill Coll Medicine Chgo 840 South Wood St Chicago IL 60612 Office Phone: 312-996-0459. Personal E-Mail: tohru630@gmail.com. Business E-Mail: tohru@uic.edu.

**YAMADA-FELLS, MIZUE,** music educator; b. Yokohama, Japan, Nov. 7, 1954; arrived in US, 1977; d. Fumio and Yoko Yamada; 1 child, JR Fells. BA magna cum laude, Musashino Music conservatory, Japan, 1977, Northwest Coll., 1979; MusM, U. Wash., 1982. Pvt. instr., Seattle, 1973—99, Japan, 1973—99; adj. faculty Northwest Coll., Kirkland, Wash., 1985—2000; asst. faculty Northwest U., Kirkland, 2000—. Choir dir. Woodinville Cmty. Ch., Woodinville, Wash., 2002—; tchg. assistantship U. Wash., 1980—83. Publisher (CD) Faculty Piano Recital, 2003, 2005. Recipient Performance Competition award, Sigma Alpha Iota. Mem.: Delta Epsilon Chi. Office: Northwest U 5520 108th Ave NE Kirkland WA 98033 Office Phone: 425-889-7807. Office Fax: 425-889-5740. E-mail: mizue.fells@northwestu.edu.

**YAMAGUCHI, KRISTI TSUYA,** ice skater; b. Hayward, Calif., July 12, 1971; d. Jim and Carole (Doi) Y.; m. Bret Hedican, July 8, 2000; children: Keara Kiyomi, Emma Yoshiko. Gold medalist, Figure Skating Albertville Olympic Games, 1992; U.S. Skating champion, 1992; World Skating champion, 1991, 1992; World Junior champion, 1988; world profl. figure skating champion, 1994. Founder Always Dream Found., 1996—; goodwill amb. Winter Olympics, Salt Lake City, 2002. Named Skater of the Yr., 1996, Favorite Female Athlete, Nickelodeon's Kid's Choice Awards, 1996—98, Athlete of the Yr. for figure skating, US Olympic Com., 1989; named to World Figure Skating Hall of Fame, 1999, US Figure Skating Hall of Fame, 1998; recipient Women First award, YWCA, 1993, Make a Wish grantor recognition for the yr. award, 1999. Avocations: tennis, rollerblading, reading, dance.

**YAMAGUCHI, MASAYA,** musician, educator; b. Japan, July 18, 1970; s. Shigenori and Mieko Yamaguchi. BA in English, Meikai U., 1994; MA in Jazz Performance, CCNY, 1999. Author: The Complete Thesaurus of Musical Scales, 1999, Symmetrical Scales for Jazz Improvisation, 2001, Pentatonicism in Jazz: Creative Aspects & Practice, 2002:; 2d edit., 2006, John Coltrane Plays Coltrane Changes, 2003, A Creative Approach to Multi-Tonic Changes: Beyond Coltrane's Harmonic Formula, 2004, Charlie Parker "Yardbird" Originals, 2005; contbr. articles to profl. jours. Home: 321 W 54th St Apt 305 New York NY 10019 Personal E-mail: masayayamaguchi@hotmail.com.

**YAMAGUCHI, YURIKO FUJITA,** artist; b. Japan, Jan. 25, 1948; came to the U.S., 1971; d. Alexander and Michi (Hirose) Fujita; m. Hiroyuki Yamaguchi, Mar. 25, 1975; children: Seiji, Mariko. BA, U. Calif., Berkeley, 1975; MFA, U. Md., 1979. Instr. U. Md., College Park, 1988—97; adj. faculty Corcoran Sch. Art, Washington, 1988-97; asst. prof. George Washington U., 2003—. Vis. artist Md. Inst. Art, Balt., 1991, Balt., 95, Mass. Coll. Art, Boston, 1994. One-woman shows include Columbia U., NY, Howard Scott Gallery, N.Y.C., 2005, Mus. Contemporary Art, Ise, Japan, 2005, exhibited in group shows at Hirshhorn Mus., 1984, L.A. County Mus., 1987, Koplin Gallery, L.A., 1991, 1994, 1996, 1999, 2002, Gallery Emon, Japan, 1997, 2000, Numark Gallery, 1999, 2003, Del. Ctr. for Contemporary Arts, 2001, Suyama Space, Seattle, 2002, Mus. Modern Art, Kanagawa, Japan, 2004, commd. wall mural, Atlanta Internat. Airport, 1998, Represented in permanent collections Hirshhorn Mus., Nat. Mus. Women in Arts, Nat. Mus. Am. Art, Smith Coll. Art Mus., Corcoran Gallery of Art. Recipient Benesse award, 2005, Joan Mitchell award, 2005; Va. Mus. Fine Arts fellow, 1988, 85, 2001; Mid-Atlantic Found. fellow, 1995; Va. Commn. Arts grantee, 1994, 2000, Salzburg Kunstlerhaus Residency grantee, 1993; Franz and Virginia Bauer grantee, 2004. Home: 1517 Snughill Ct Vienna VA 22182-1724 E-mail: yuriko414@aol.com.

**YAMAKOV, VESSELIN IVANOV,** aerospace scientist, researcher; b. Sofia, Bulgaria, Sept. 1, 1965; arrived in U.S., 1999; s. Ivan Yakov and Anna Borisova Yamakov; m. Milena Momcheva Marinova, Dec. 20, 2002; children: Ioan Vesselinov, Miroslava Marinova Marinova. PhD, Inst. Phys. Chemistry, Sofia, 1999. Rsch. scientist Argonne Nat. Lab., Ill. Rsch. scientist Inst. of Applied Mineralogy, Bulgarian Acad. of Scis., Sofia, 1991—95, Inst. for Phys. Chemistry, Bulgarian Acad. of Scis., Sofia, 1995—99, Argonne Nat. Lab., 1999—2003; staff scientist Nat. Inst. of Aerospace, Hampton, Va., 2003—. Office: Nat Inst of Aerospace 100 Exploration Way Hampton VA 23666 Office Phone: 757-864-2850. Personal E-mail: vyamakov@mail.com. Business E-Mail: yamakov@nianet.org.

**YAMAMOTO, AKIMASA,** transportation executive; m. Kyoko Yamamoto; children: Maki, Ayami. Degree in Law, Keio U., 1972. Lawyer Toyota Motor Corp., Toyota Aichi, Japan, 1972—74; treas. Toyota Deutschland, Germany, 1994—97; from gen. mgr. Dept. Fin. Reporting to sr. v.p. and treas. Toyota Motor Corp., Toyota Aichi, Japan, 1998—2001; sr. v.p. and treas. Toyota Motor Sales, USA, Inc, Torrance, Calif., 2001—. Office: Toyota Motor Sales USA Inc 19001 South Western Ave Torrance CA 90509

**YAMAMOTO, ALICE M.,** secondary school educator; b. Phoenix, Sept. 8, 1958; d. Frank and Kumiko Yamamoto. BA in Journalism, U Ariz., 1981; MEd in Curiculum and Instrn., Ariz. State U., 1997. Cert. cmty. coll. tchr. Ariz. English tchr. Mountain Pointe H.S., Phoenix, 1993—96, Desert Vista H.S., Phoenix, 1996—99, 1999—; tchr. Rio Salado Coll., Tempe, 1999—. Acad. decathlon coach Desert Vista H.S., Phoenix, 1996—2001, Asian Student Union co-sponsor, 1999—. Recipient Most Improved Coach award, Acad. Decathlon, 1999. Mem.: MLA (assoc.), NEA (assoc.). Home: 779 E Park Ave Chandler AZ 85225-1757 Office: Desert Vista HS 16440 S 32nd St Phoenix AZ 85048-7807

**YAMAMOTO, JANET KAZUKO,** science educator; d. Shunta and Chizuko Catherine Yamamoto. BA, U. Calif., Davis, 1976; PhD, U. Tex. Med. Br., 1981. Rsch. assoc. scientist Okla. Med. Rsch. Found., Oklahoma City, 1982—83; rschr. U. Calif., Davis, 1983—85; asst. rsch. immunologist U. Calif. Sch. Vet. Medicine, Gainesville, 1985—91, adj. assoc. prof., 1991—93; assoc. prof. U. Fla. Coll. Vet. Medicine, Gainesville, 1993—2001, prof., 2001—. Cons. Ft. Dodge Animal Health, Iowa, 2000—. Bd. dirs. Creating Hope Internat. (Afghanistan Projects), Mich., 1996—. Recipient Pfizer Animal Health award, U. Fla., 1996; fellow, U. Tex. Med. Br., Galveston, 1979—81, U. Calif., San Diego, 1981—82. Mem.: Clin. Immunology Soc., Internat. AIDS Soc., Am. Assn. Immunologists, Phi Zeta Upsilon. Achievements include discovery of FIV (feline immunodeficiency virus) and vaccine. Avocation: music. Office: U Fla Coll Vet Medicine PO Box 110880 Gainesville FL 32611 E-mail: yamamotoj@mail.vetmed.ufl.edu.

**YAMAMOTO, JOE,** retired psychiatrist, educator; b. LA, Apr. 18, 1924; s. Zenzaburo and Tomie (Yamada) Y.; m. Maria Fujitomi, Sept. 5, 1947; children: Eric Robert, Andrew Jolyon. Student, Los Angeles City Coll., 1941-42, Hamline U., 1943-45; BS, U. Minn., 1946, MB, 1948, MD, 1949. Asst. prof. dept. psychiatry, neurology, behavioral sci. U. Okla. Med. Center, 1955-58, asst. prof., 1958-60; assoc. prof. dept. psychiatry U. So. Calif. Sch. Medicine, Los Angeles, 1961-69, prof., 1969-77, co-dir. grad. edn. psychiatry, 1963-70; prof. UCLA, 1977-94, emeritus prof., 1994—; dir. Psychiat. Outpatient Clinic, Los Angeles County-U. So. Calif. Med. Center, 1958-77; dir. adult ambulatory care services UCLA Neuropsychiat. Inst., 1977-88, chief Lab. for Cross Cultural Studies; ret. Contbr. articles in field to profl. jours. Served to capt., M.C. U.S. Army, 1953-55. Fellow Am. Psychiat. Assn. (life), Pacific Rim Coll. Psychiatrists, Am. Acad. Psychoanalysis (trustee, mem. exec. com., 1978-79), Am. Coll. Psychiatrists, Am. Orthopsychiat. Assn. (pres.-elect 1993-94, pres. 1994-95, past pres.), Am. Assn. for Social Psychiatry (trustee 1981-84, v.p. 1984-86); mem. So. Calif. Psychoanalytic Inst. and Soc. (pres. 1972-73), Soc. for Study of Culture and Psychiatry, Group for Advancement Psychiatry (bd. dirs. 1992-94), Kappa Phi, Alpha Omega Alpha. *Learning about the diverse peoples of America, I have been fascinated with how we can be Asian, Hispanic, Black, European, and Native American and still identify with our national values. We value our freedom, individual rights and our ability to be someone different but equal. In mental health also there is a need for recognition of cultural differences and the need of treatment response to the individual.*

**YAMAMOTO, KAORU,** retired psychology professor; b. Tokyo, Mar. 28, 1932; arrived in U.S., 1959; s. Saburo and Hideko (Watanabe) Y.; m. Etsuko Hamazaki, Apr. 6, 1959 (div. 1986); m. Carol-Lynne Moore, Oct. 4, 1986; children: Keita Carey Moore, Kiyomi Lynne Moore. BS in Engring., U. Tokyo, 1953; MA, U. Minn., 1960, PhD, 1962. Mng. Engr. Toppan Printing Co. Tokyo, 1953; engr., rsch. chemist Japan Oxygen Co., Tokyo, 1954-57, 58-59; asst. prof. Kent (Ohio) State U., 1962-65; from asst. to assoc. prof. U. Iowa, Iowa City, 1965-68; prof. Pa. State U., University Park, 1968-72, Ariz. State U., Tempe, 1972-87, U. Colo., Denver, 1987-99, prof. emeritus, 1999—. Vis. prof. U. Minn., Mpls., 1974, Simon Fraser U., Burnaby, B.C., Can., 1984, U.Victoria, B.C., 1985, 86, U. Wash., Seattle, 1987, Zhejiang Normal U., Jinhua, China, 1991; Fulbright lectr. U. Iceland, 1985. Author: The Child and

His Image, 1972, Their World, Our World, 1993; author, editor 7 books, including Children and Stress, 2001; co-author: Beyond Words, 1988; editor Am. Ednl. Rsch. Jour., 1972-75, Ednl. Forum, 1984-92; contbr. chpts. to books and articles to profl. jours. Recipient Disting. Tchr. award Ariz. State U., 1980; Landsdowne scholar U. Victoria, 1985, Ctr. scholar Ctr. for Rsch. on Ethics and Values Azusa Pacific U., 1998-2000. Fellow: APA; mem.: Motus Humanus. Avocations: winter sports, travel, classical music, reading. Office: 13651 W 54th Ave Arvada CO 80002

**YAMAMOTO, KEITH ROBERT,** molecular biologist, educator; b. Des Moines, Feb. 4, 1946; BS, Iowa State U., 1968; PhD, Princeton U., 1973. Asst. prof. biochemistry U. Calif., San Francisco, 1976-79, assoc. prof., 1979-83, prof. biochemistry, 1983—2003, vice chmn. dept. biochemistry & biophysics, 1985—94, dir. biochemistry and molecular biology program, 1988—2001, chmn. dept. cellular & molecular pharmacology, 1994—2003, prof. dept. cellular & molecular pharmacology, 1994—; vice dean for rsch. UCSF Sch. Medicine, 2002—03, exec. vice dean, 2002—. Co-author: Gene Wars: Military Control Over the New Genetic Technologies, 1988; co-editor: Transcriptional Regulation, 1992; assoc. editor: Jour. Molecular Biology, 1988—2001; editor: Molecular Biology of the Cell, 1991—2001; editor-in-chief:, 2002—. Testifier hearings on biol. warfare com. on govtl. affairs U.S. Senate, Washington, 1989. Recipient Career Devel. award, NIH, 1977-82, UCSF Disting. Teaching award, 1979-80, Dreyfus Teacher-Scholar award, 1982-86, Gregory Pincus medal Worchester Found. for Exptl. Biology, 1990, Vanderbilt U. Medal of Merit, 1999. Fellow: AAAS; mem.: IOM (elected 2003), NAS, Am. Acad. Arts & Sciences, Am. Acad. Microbiology. Office: UCSF Box 2280 San Francisco CA 94143-2280 Office Phone: 415-476-3128. Office Fax: 415-476-6129. E-mail: yamamoto@cgl.ucsf.edu.*

**YAMAMOTO, MASAKO,** music educator; b. Okayama, Japan, Oct. 22, 1956; d. Yoshio and Satoko Ogawa (Stepmother); m. Tadashi Yamamoto, Nov. 23, 1985; children: Ayae, Yoshie. MusB, Elisabeth U. Music, Japan, 1979; MS, U. Ill., 1997, EdD, 2002. Cert. tchr. Music for Young Children, Can., Harmony Rd., Oreg., tchr. Yamaguchi prefecture Bd. Edn., Japan. Music educator Bd. Edn., Japan, 1979—89; japanese lang., culture tchr. Urbana (Ill.) Sch. Dist., 1994—95; tchr. Little Angels Japanese Preschool, San Francisco, 2003—04; music educator Melody Acad. Music, San Jose, Calif., 2003—. Brass band dir. Kumage (Japan) Mid. Sch., 1983—84; dance club dir. Tabuse (Japan) Spl. Edn. Sch., 1980—83, rsch. dir., 1981—83. Singer: Italian Opera. Recipient Verdell Frazier Young awards, U. Ill., 2001, 2002; Marilyn Pflederer Zimmerman Music Edn. Doctoral fellowship, 1998. Mem.: Am. Coll. of Musicians (assoc.), Kappa Delta Pi (assoc.), Pi Kappa Lambda (assoc.). Achievements include research in multicultural music edn. Home: 41089 Bairo Ct Fremont CA 94539 Office Phone: 510-565-6230. Home Fax: 510-657-5348. Personal E-mail: myamamot3000@sbcglobal.net.

**YAMAN, CEVAT,** environmental engineer, educator; b. Tokat, Turkey, May 1, 1969; s. Hasan and Asiye Yaman. BSc, Istanbul Tech. U., Turkey, 1992; MSc, Drexel U., Phila., 1996, PhD, 2003. Environ./geotechnical engr. Melick-Tully and Assocs., Mt. Laurel, NJ, 2001—02; staff engr. Roux Assocs., West Deptford, NJ, 2002; rsch. and tchg. asst. Drexel U., Phila., 1998—2003; asst. prof. Fatih U., Istanbul, 2005—. Cons. engr. Tech. Roller Inc., Istanbul, 2005—. Contbr. articles to profl. jours. Democrat. Achievements include research in wastewater treatment using geotextile biofilters; wastewater treatment with biomass attached to porous geotextile baffles; effects of wastewater filtration on geotextile permeability; use of layered geotextiles to provide a substrate for biomass development in treatment of septic tank effluent prior to ground infiltration. Personal E-mail: cevatyaman@yahoo.com.

**YAMANOUCHI, MIDORI,** social sciences educator; b. Osaka City, Japan, Jan. 8, 1928; arrived in US, 1950, naturalized, 1961; d. Shin'ichi and Fumiko (Urai) Yamanouchi; m. Edward J. Rynn, Oct. 10, 1975 (dec. July 29, 1987). Diploma, Tokyo Kasai U., 1948; student, U. Tampa, 1950—51; AB, Sophia U. Internat. Divsn., 1956; MA, Mich. State U., 1958, PhD, 1972; MA in LS, U. Mich., 1959. Chief rsch. assoc. Internat. Divsn. Sophia U., Tokyo, 1952—56; libr., bibliographer Mich. State U., East Lansing, 1959—63, 1964—67; asst. dir. R&D Sperry & Hutchinson Co., N.Y.C., 1963—64; asst. prof. sociology and anthropology Marshall U., Huntington, W.Va., 1967—70, Fisk U., Nashville, 1970—72; assoc. prof. Livingston Coll., Salisbury, NC, 1972—74; vis. prof. Frostburg State U., 1974—75; prof. U. Scranton, Pa., 1975—2006; v.p. acad. affairs Lackawanna Coll., 2006—. Translator: Listen to the Voices from the Sea, 2000, In The Far Away Mountains and Rivers, 2005; editor: Sociol. Viewpoint, 1989—91, 2004—05; assoc. editor Comparative Civilizations Rev., 1996—2001. Trustee Lacawac Sanctuary, Lake Ariel, Pa., 1993—, Lackawanna Coll., 1995—2001, 2002—06, Tokyo Kasai U., 1997—; mem. pres. coun. Cedar Crest Coll., 1996—2002; mem. adv. bd. Northeastern Intermediate Unit Sch. Bd., Scranton, Pa., 1998—, Diversity Inst. Coll. Misericordia, Dallas, Pa., 1999—; bd. mem. Northeastern Pa. Philharmonic, 2006—, Everhart Mus., 2003—. Recipient Seeley Svc. medal, Lackawanna Coll., 2001, Ednl. Svc. award, Wilkes Barre (Pa.) Bd. Edn. 2002. Mem.: Assn. for Gen. and Liberal Studies (mem. exec. bd. 1975—78), Internat. Orgn. for Unification of Terminological Neologisms (del. UN, non-govt. orgn. 1995—, Disting. Contbn. award 2000), Internat. Soc. for Comparative Study of Civilizations (mem. exec. bd. 1978—2005, editor newsletter 1990—93), Pa. Sociol. Soc. (editor newsletter 1986—89, pres. 1990—91). Home: 220 Salem Pk Ln Lake Ariel PA 18436 Office: Lackawanna Coll 501 Vine St Scranton PA 18509 Business E-Mail: yamanouchi@lackawanna.edu.

**YAMAOKA, YOSHIO,** gastroenterologist, researcher; b. Otsu, Japan, Jan. 3, 1961; s. Susumu and Setsuko Yamaoka; m. Naoko Nishikawa, June 4, 1995. BS, Kyoto U., Japan, 1983; MD, Kyoto Prefectural U. Medicine, Japan, 1990, PhD, 1997. From rech. assoc. to assoc. prof. Baylor Coll. Medicine, Houston, 1997—2002; assoc. prof., 2002—, dir. Molecular Pathogenesis Lab., 2002—. Vis. prof. Shaheed Beheshti of Med. U., Tehran, Iran, 2006—. Editor: Molecular Genetics of Helicobacter. Grantee, NIH, 2004—. Office: Baylor College of Medicine VAMC (111D) 2002 Holcombe Blvd Houston TX 77030 Office Phone: 713-794-7597. Business E-Mail: yyamaoka@bcm.tmc.edu.

**YAMASHINA, TADASHI (GEORGE),** transportation executive; arrived in U.S., 1993; m. Hiromi Yamashina; children: Kae, Kaki. BME, Waseda U., 1977. From engr. to project mgr. Toyota Motor Corp., Aichi, Japan, 1977—93; from exec. coord. to pres. Toyota Tech. Ctr., Ann Arbor, Mich., 1993—2001, pres., 2001—. Office: Toyota Technical Ctr USA Inc 1555 Woodridge Ave RR 7 Ann Arbor MI 48105

**YAMAUCHI, PAUL STEVEN,** dermatologist, researcher; PhD, MD, Case We. Res. U., 1991. Med. dir. Clin. Rsch. Specialists, Santa Monica, Calif., 2000—; exec. med. dir. Dermatology Inst. & Skin Care Ctr., Santa Monica, 2004—. Med. lectr., cons. Clin. Rsch. Specialists, Santa Monica, 2000—. Contbr. articles to profl. jours. Recipient Bill Reed Award Lectureship, European Soc. Dermatol. Rsch., 1999, Everett C. Fox Residents and Fellows Award, Am. Acad. Dermatology, 1999, Ronald M. Reisner Award, UCLA Sch. of Medicine, 1998, Paul H. Curtiss, Jr. Musculoskeletal Award, Case We. Res. U., 1993. Fellow: Am. Acad. Dermatologists; mem.: Nat. Psoriasis Found. (corr.). Achievements include research in Clinical research in the development of biologic agents in the treatment of psoriasis and psoriatic arthritis. Key opinion leader in the subject of psoriatic disease; Clinical research in the development of cosmetic procedures for facial rejuvenation. Office: 2001 Santa Monica Blvd Ste 490W Los Angeles CA 90049 Office Phone: 310-829-4104. Office Fax: 310-829-4150. Business E-Mail: dermatology@earthlink.net.

**YAMBRUSIC, EDWARD SLAVKO,** lawyer, consultant; b. Conway, Pa., Mar. 9, 1933; s. Michael Misko and Slavica Sylvia (Yambrusic) Y.; m. Natalie Visniak, 1990. BA, Duquesne U., 1957; postgrad., Georgetown U. Law Ctr., 1959-61; JD, U. Balt., 1966; cert., The Hague Acad. Internat. Law, Nether-

lands, 1967, 69; diploma, Ctr. Study and Rsch. Internat. Law and Internat. Rels., 1970; PhD in Pub. Internat. Law, Cath. U. Am., 1984. Bar: Md. 1969, U.S. Ct. Customs and Patent Appeals 1972, U.S. Supreme Ct. 1972, U.S. Ct. Internat. Trade 1988. Copyright examiner U.S. Copyright Office, Libr. of Congress, Washington, 1960-69; atty. adviser Office Register of Copyrights, 1969-98; pvt. practice internat. and immigration law, 1969—. Legal counsel Nat. Ethnic Studies Assembly, 1976—, Soc. Fed. Linguists, 1980; pres. AMCRO Internat. Consulting, Inc., 1995—. Author: Treat Interpretation: Theory and Reality, 1987, The Trade-Based Approaches to the Protection of Intellectual Property, 1990; contbr. articles to ofcl. newsletter Nat. Confedn. Am. Ethnic Groups, also legal jours. Pres. Nat. Confedn. Am. Ethnic Groups, Washington; nat. chmn. Croatian-Am. Bicentennial Com. nat. chmn. Nat. Pilgrimage of Croatian-Ams. to Nat. Shrine of Immaculate Conception, Washington; v.p. Croatian Acad. Am. Served to capt. U.S. Army, 1957-59. Duquesne U. Tamburitzans scholar, 1953-57; Hague Acad. Internat. Law fellow, 1970. Mem. ABA, Md. Bar Assn., Internat. Law Assn., Internat. Fiscal Assn., Am. Soc. Internat. Law, Croatian Cath. Union Am., Croatian Frat. Union Am. Republican. Roman Catholic. Certificate issued by the Librarian of Congress in recognition of 40 years of distinguished service to the people of the United States of America, 1957-98. Home and Office: 4720 Massachusetts Ave NW Washington DC 20016-2346 Office Phone: 202-368-7104.

**YAMIN, MICHAEL GEOFFREY,** lawyer; b. NYC, Nov. 10, 1931; s. Michael and Ethel Yamin; m. Martina Schaap, Apr. 16, 1961; children: Michael Jeremy, Katrina. AB magna cum laude, Harvard U., 1953, LLB, 1958. Bar: NY 1959, U.S. Dist. Ct. (so. and ea. dists.) NY, U.S. Ct. Appeals (2d cir.) 1966, U.S. Supreme Ct. 1967. Assoc. Weil, Gotshal & Manges, NYC, 1958-65; sr. ptnr. Colton, Hartnick, Yamin & Sheresky, NYC, 1966-93, Kaufmann, Feiner, Yamin, Gildin & Robbins, LLP, NYC, 1993—. Trustee Gov.'s Com. Scholastic Achievement, 1976—; mem: Manhattan Cmty. Bd. 6, 1974—88, Manhattan Borough Bd., 1986—88; trustee Project Sail, Inc., 2005—. Mem.: ABA, Internat. Bar Assn., Soc. de Legis. Comparee, Internat. Law Assn., Am. Fgn. Law Assn. (Am. br.), Fed. Bar Coun., Assn. Bar City of NY, NY State Bar Assn., Harvard Alumni Assn. (bd. dirs. 1995—98, 2005—), Harvard Club of NYC (sub-chmn. schs. and scholarships com. 1972—93, trustee NY Found. 1981—, bd. mgrs. 1985—88, chair ho. com. 1992—95, bd. mgrs. 1993—98, v.p. 1995—98, chair comm. com. 1997—99, chair membership svcs. com. 1999—2000, pres. 1999—2006, chair cmty. svc. com. 2006—), Harvard Faculty Club (Cambridge, Mass.). Office: Kaufmann Feiner Yamin Gildin & Robbins LLP 777 3rd Ave New York NY 10017-1401 Office Phone: 212-755-3100. Business E-Mail: myamin@kaufmannfeiner.com.

**YAMIN, ROBERT JOSEPH,** lawyer; b. Waterbury, Conn., May 31, 1949; s. Joseph George and Elizabeth Mary (Bouharoun) Y.; m. Dianne Elizabeth Yamin, Sept. 3, 1988; children: Samantha Blythe, Rebecca Anne. Student, Yale U., 1978; AB summa cum laude, Western Conn. State U., Danbury, 1979; JD, Harvard U., 1982. Bar: Conn. 1982, U.S. Dist. Ct. Conn. 1983, U.S. Tax Ct. 1983, N.Y. 1984, U.S. Supreme Ct. 1986. Mng. ptnr. Yamin & Yamin LLP, Danbury, Conn., 1990—. Conferee Am. Soc. Writers on Legal Subjects, 1985. Bd. editors Conn. Bar Jour., 1991—. Pres. Greater Danbury Young Republicans, 1973-75; del. White House Conf. on Libr. and Info. Svcs., 1978; mem. state ctrl. com. Conn. Rep. party, 1992—; councilman, minority leader Danbury City Coun., 1993—; corp. counsel, chief legal officer City of Danbury, 2002—. Fellow Acad. Continuing Legal Edn., 1985. Mem. ABA (mem. forum com. on health law 1986—), Fed. Bar Assn., N.Y. Bar Assn., Danbury Bar Assn., Conn. Bar Assn. (profl. discipline com. 1983-93, chmn. young lawyers com. on corp. and bus. law 1985-86), Conn. Health Lawyers Assn., Lions Club of Danbury (dir. 1993-94), Phi Alpha Delta. Roman Catholic. Avocations: political consultant, outdoor activities, travel. Home: 66 Barnum Rd Danbury CT 06811-2938 Office: Yamin & Yamin LLP 4 Moss Ave Danbury CT 06810-6818 Office Phone: 203-744-7090. Personal E-mail: ryamin5567@aol.com. Business E-Mail: lawyers@yaminlaw.com.

**YAMIN, SONYA,** music educator, voice educator; b. San Antonio, Feb. 4, 1970; d. Robert Rangel Ochoa and Maria Martha Garcia; m. Leslie Neil Yamin, Jan. 14, 1995; children: Joshua Ochoa, Kaisar Jonas. Grad., John Marshall H.S., San Antonio, Texas, 1984—88; student in Vocal Performance, U. Tex., 1988—94. Co. mem. Little Opera Co., San Antonio, 1993—94; voice faculty John Marshall H.S., San Antonio, 1998—, Earl Warren H.S., San Antonio, 2004—, William Taft H.S., San Antonio, 2005—, Ronald Reagan H.S., San Antonio, 2005—. Vocal cons./coach Guadalupe Cultural Arts Theater, San Antonio, 2003—04. Singer (vocalist/instrumentalist): (CD) Ancient Echoes:Music from the time of Jesus and the second temple (#2 in NPR's New Sounds Ann. Listener's Poll, 2002), La Noche Buena (NPR's Weekend Edit. Best Year's Music by Ned Wharton, 2005). Named one of Outstanding Coll. Students of Am., 1989; Music scholarship, U. Tex., 1988-1992. Mem.: Tex. Music Educators Assn., Nat. Assn. of Tchrs. of Singing (1st place winner Sophomore divsn. 1989, 1st place winner Jr. divsn. 1990, 1st place winner Sr. divsn. 1991), Golden Key Nat. Honor Soc., Sigma Alpha Iota. Achievements include Role: 1st Spirit in The Magic Flute with the San Antonio Music Festival 1991; Vocalist/SAVAE-representing the USA at the International Baroque Music Festival of Bolivia; Vocalist/SAVAE has been featured on national radio shows including NPR's Performance Today, Sound & Spirit, Latino USA, The Savvy Traveler, and Weekend Edition; Vocalist/SAVAE-Director Ridley Scott included a track from that recording in his 2005 feature film, The Kingdom of Heaven; Vocalist/SAVAE-the groups music is required listening in many university music programs; Role: Maria in West Side Story at the the Josephine Theater 1999; Role: Rizzo in Grease at the Josephine Theater 1999; Role: Consuela in World Premiere of Liberty at the Josephine Theater 1999; Role: Maid in The Devil take Her with the University of Texas at San Antonio Opera Department 1990; vocalist for Internationally known aujewish only music group, SAVAE's Virgen de los Indios CD charted #11 in Billboard Charts World Music in 1999; Vocalist/SAVAE-recorded original compositions for PBS Award Winning Documentary Discovering Dominga by Academy Award Winning Composer Todd Boekelheide. Avocations: vocal recording, performing in musical theater, ballet. Home: 11844 Bandera Rd #206 Helotes TX 78023 Office: Sonya Yamin's Voice Studio 11844 Bandera Rd # 206 Helotes TX 78023 Office Phone: 210-639-4736. Personal E-mail: s_yamin@hotmail.com.

**YAMMINE, RIAD NASSIF,** retired oil industry executive; b. Hammana, Lebanon, Apr. 12, 1934; came to U.S., 1952, naturalized, 1963; s. Nassib Nassif and Emilie (Daou) Y.; m. Beverly Ann Hosack, Sept. 14, 1957; children: Kathleen Yammine Gross, Cynthia Yammine Rotman, Michael. BS in Petroleum Engring., Pa. State U., 1956; postgrad. advanced mgmt. program, Harvard U., 1977. Registered profl. engr., Ohio. Engr. Trans-Arabian Pipe Line Co., Saudia Arabia, 1956-61; with Marathon Pipe Line Co., 1961-75, mgr. we. divsn. Casper, Wyo., 1971-74, mgr. Ea. divsn. Martinsville, Ill., 1974-75; mktg. ops. divsn. mgr. Marathon Oil Co., 1975-83, pres., 1983-84; v.p. supply and transp. Marathon Petroleum Co., 1984-88, dir. 1984-90; pres. EMRO Mktg. Co., 1988-98; exec. v.p. Marathon Ashland Petroleum, 1998-99; ret. Bd. dirs. Marathon Oil Co.; chmn. bd. Findlay Devel. LLC. Patentee in field. Past trustee Wright State U. Found., Fisk U; bd. dirs. Findlay C. of C., bd. mgrs. Findlay Devel. LLC. Mem. ASME, Am. Petroleum Inst. (bd. dir.), Springfield and Clark C. of C. (bd. dirs.), Findlay C. of C. (bd. dirs.), Findlay Country Club. Republican. Home: 200 Penbrooke Dr Findlay OH 45840-8301

**YAMNER, MORRIS,** lawyer; b. Passaic, N.J., Sept. 5, 1938; s. Sam and Edna (Halpern) Y.; 1 child, Laura; m. Gail Garber, Oct. 23, 1975; children: Amy, Lisa. BS in Bus., Ohio State U., 1959; JD, Georgetown U. 1962. Bar: NJ. 1962, N.Y. 1983. Law sec. Superior Ct., Somerville, NJ, 1962-63; dep. atty. gen. Atty. Gen. Office, Trenton, NJ, 1963-66; ptnr. Cole, Yamner & Bray, Paterson, NJ, 1966-90. Sills, Cummis, Newark, 1990—. Bd. dirs. Jewish Fedn., Clifton, N.J., 1985—, YM/YMHA, 1980—. Mem. Daus. of Miriam (bd. dirs. 1985—), Preakness Hills Country Club (bd. dirs. 1992—). Office: Sills Cummis 1 Riverfront Plz Fl 10 Newark NJ 07102-5401

**YAMPOLSKY, PHYLLIS,** artist; b. Phila. d. Louis Jacob Yampolsky and Bassia Yampolsky Green; m. Peter Forakis, June 12, 1959 (div. 1964); children: Gia, Jozeph Peter. Student, Phila. Mus. Sch. Arts, 1950-52, Inst. Allende, San Miguel de Allende, Mex., 1954-55, Ecole Beaux Arts, Fontainbleau, France, 1956, Hans Hofmann Atelier, N.Y.C., 1956-58. Founder, dir., tchr. Workshop Yampolsky, NYC, 1956-66; art instr. 92d St. YMHA, NYC, 1958-60; founder, dir. Hall of Issues, NYC, 1960-61; 1st artist-in-residence NYC, 1966-67; creator, dir. Portrait of Ten Towns NY State Coun. Arts, 1967-70; founder, officer Northeast Windham Coun. Arts, Vt., 1978-79; instr. Vt. Acad., Saxton's River, 1979-81, Vt. C.C., Springfield, 1979-81; co-founder, instr. New Vt. Sch. Arts, 1981; founder, pres. Ind. Friends McCarren Pk., Inc., NYC, 1988—. Creator, dir., prodr. Hoving Happenings, 1966, 67; cons. Model Cities, Columbus, Ohio, 1968, Province Ont. Coun. Arts, 1968-70, Phila. Bicentennial Commn., Smithsonian Inst. Bicentennial Travelling Festival Kit; cons., panelist, performance artists Arcosanti, Ariz., 1977-78, 80, 81; facilitator NEA, 1970-75; cons., organizer, program dir. Habitat II CBO Host Com., NYC, 1995-96; spl. events dir. Youth Pavilion, World's Fair, San Antonio, 1968; writer, dir. art curriculum Marylerose Acad., Albany, 1969, Bennett Coll., 1970; presenter Habitat II, UN conf., Istanbul, Turkey, 1996. One-woman shows include Phila. Art Alliance, 1953, Judson Gallery, NYC, 1960, 62, Walker Gallery, NYC, 1974, Kulicke Gallery, NYC, 1975, Graham Gallery, NYC, 1977, O.K. Harris and Susan Caldwell Galleries, NYC, 1978, Stryke Gallery, NYC, Windam Coll., Vt., 1978, Marlboro Coll., Vt., 1981, A Place Apart, NYC, 1984, City Bank Gallery, Bklyn., 1986, Loft Lawyers, NYC, 1987, 479 Gallery, NYC, 1996, Stephan Gang, 1999, The Cave, 2000; exhibited in group shows at Park Place Gallery, NYC, Brata Gallery, Cornell U., Dallas Mus. Fine Arts, Mus. Erotic Art, San Francisco, Mus. Erotic Art, Stockholm, Whitney Mus., Weisner Gallery, NYC, City Without Walls Gallery, Newark, Green Gallery, NYC, Leo Castelli Gallery, NYC, Allan Stone Gallery, NYC, Franklin Furnace, NYC, Dorsky Gallery, NYC, Bklyn. Terminal Show, NYC, Food Stamp Gallery, NYC, ABC No Rio, NYC, Blue Mountain Gallery, NYC, Boriqua Coll., NYC, Phila. Mus. Art, Holland-Goldowsky, Chgo., Peter David, Mpls., Mc Nay Inst., San Antonio, Tex., Stephen Gang Gallery, NYC, The Cave, Bklyn., Brewery; represented in permenant collections Am. Town Hall Wall Sys. used in Robert Kennedy Presdl. Primary, 1968, Clinton Presdl. Campaign and Inaugural Festivities, 1993, 97, UN Women's Conf., Beijing, 1995, UN 50th Celebration, NYC, 1995, V.P. Gore's Reinvention Revolution Conf., Washington, 1996-97, March Against Cancer, Washington, 1998, W.A.F.E. Festival/Conf. on the Environment, Bklyn., 1998, The Hague (The Netherlands) Appeal Peace Conf., 1999, Main St. Millennium, Washington, Dallas Mus. Fine Arts, Mus. Erotic Art, Pres. Clinton Libr.; contbr. articles to profl. jours. Recipient Cue Mag., 1967, Betsy Barlow Rogers award Ind. Friends McCarren Pk., 1995; Ecole Beaux Arts scholar, Hans Hofmann Atelier scholar; grantee Ind. Friends McCarren Pk., J.M. Kaplan Fund, Andy Warhol Found., NY Found., Vincent Astor Found., Citizen's Com. NYC Inc., 1990—. Personal E-mail: partage@earthlink.net.

**YAN, MARTIN,** celebrity chef; b. Guangzhou, China, 1948; m. Susan Yan; 2 children. Grad., Overseas Inst. Cookery, Hong Kong; BS Food Sci., MS Food Sci., U. Calif., Davis; PhD Culinary Arts (hon.), Johnson & Wales U.; PhD Humane Letters (hon.), Colo. Inst. Art. Product mgr. canning corp., Hong Kong, 1976; mgr. head chef Lee's Garden Restaurant, Alberta, 1977; tchr., Chinese Cooking U. Calif.; founder Yan Can Cook Inc., 1997—, Yan Can Internat. Cooking School, San Francisco. Guest chef-instr. Calif. Culinary Acad., Johnson & Wales U., Culinary Inst. Am., U. San Francisco. Host (TV series) Yan Can Cook, 1978—, Martin Yan's Chinatowns, 2002—, Martin Yan Quick & Easy, 2004—; author: Yan Can Cookbook, 1981, The Joy of Wokking, 1982, Martin Yan, the Chinese Chef, 1985, A Wok For All Seasons, 1988, Everybody's Wokking, 1991, The Well-Seasoned Wok, 1992, Simply Delicious, 1993, A Simple Guide to Chinese Ingredients, 1994, Martin Yan's Culinary Journey Through China, 1995, Martin Yan's Asia, 1997, Martin Yan's Feast, 1998, Chinese Cooking for Dummies, 2000, Martin Yan's Invitation to Chinese Cooking, 2000, Martin Yan's Asian Favorites, 2001, Martin Yan's Chinatown Cooking, 2002, Martin Yan's Quick and Easy, 2004; guest appearances (TV series) The Today Show, The Rosie Show, A&E: Top Ten Television Chefs, Cooking Live with Sara Moulton, The Tonight Show, Good Morning America, Q&A Asia, Lo & Co., Howie Mandell Show, Donnie & Marie Show, Mornings on Two, Live with Regis and Kelly, The Dennis Miller Show, The Late Show with David Letterman, Late Night with Conan O'Brien, The Martin Short Show. Named Culinary Diplomat, Am. Culinary Fedn.; recipient Best TV Cooking Show, James Beard Found., 1994, Best TV Food Journalism award, 1996, D'Artagnan Cervena Who's Who of Food and Beverage award, 2001, Single Camera Photography award, Daytime Emmy Awards, 1998, Antonin Careme award, Chef's Assoc. of the Pacific Coast, Courvoisier Leadership award. Achievements include design of cookware and kitchen tools; owner of several pan-Asian restaurants. Office: Yan Can Cook Inc PO Box 4755 Foster City CA 94404*

**YAN, QING,** bioinformatics scientist; d. Chongli Yan and Shaoshan Zhang; m. Donglei Hu, June 23, 2002. MD in Internal Medicine, Nanjing U. of TCM, Nanjing, China, 1993; MS in Microbiology, Immunology, U. of Ariz., 1998; PhD in Biol. and Med. Informatics, U. of Calif. San Francisco, 2001. Diplomate in Chinese Herbology Nat. Certification Commn. for Acupuncture and Oriental Medicine, 2000. Bioinformatics scientist MedImmune, Inc., Mountain View, Calif., 2001—. Editor: (author: (scientific book) Membrane Transporters: Methods and Protocols; author (scientific publ.): (article in book) Hypertension: Methods and Protocols, (article in jour.) AAPS Pharm Sci., Drug Information Jour., Biochemical and Biophysical Rsch. Comm. Mem.: AAAS, Am. Chem. Soc., Drug Info. Assn. Achievements include first to design and develop the human membrane transporter relational database for drug discovery and pharmacogenomics studies; design and develop web portal and the first influenza mutation database for viral vaccine studies; research in bioinformatics and drug information; pharmacogenomics; cancer rsch. Office: MedImmune Inc 297 N Bernardo Ave Mountain View CA 94043 Business E-Mail: yanq@medimmune.com, qyan@itsa.ucsf.edu.

**YAN, SU,** mechanical engineer, researcher; d. Zhenwu Yan and Guifu Cui; m. Side Zhao, Sept. 15, 1971; 1 child, Leonard Zhao. Doctorate, U. Hawaii, 2001. Registered mech. engr., Henan, China, 1996. Mech. engr. Tech. Ctr., China Yituo Group Co. Ltd., Luoyang, Henan, China, 1994—96, 1999—2000; rsch. asst. Jilin U. of Tech., Changchun, Jilin, China, 1996—99, U. Hawaii, Honolulu, 2001—. Recipient Bili scholarship, Jilin U. of Tech., 1996. Mem.: ASME (assoc.), Soc. for Advancement of Material and Process Engring. (assoc.), Internat. Soc. for Optical Engring. (assoc.). Office Phone: 808-956-7435.

**YAN, YING,** statistician, researcher; b. Beijing, Feb. 9, 1960; arrived in U.S., 1985; d. Youguang Yan and Jinzhong Du; married; children: Alice Y. Wang, Carolyn Y. Wang. MA in Math., U. Wyo., 1990, MS in Stats., 1991, PhD in Stats., 1994. Rschr. Radian Corp., Research Triangle Park, NC, 1992—94, PPD, Inc., Cary, NC, 1994—96, Astra Zeneca, Del., 1996—97, Glaxo-Smith Kline, King of Prussia, Pa., 1997—. Mem.: Drug Info. Assn., Am. Statis. Assn. Office: 2301 Renaissance Blvd King Of Prussia PA 19406

**YANAI, SHUNJI,** former diplomat; b. Tokyo, Jan. 15, 1937; Grad., U. Tokyo, 1961. Joined Ministry Fgn. Affairs Japan, 1961, dir. internat. convs. divsn. Treaties Bur., 1976, cabinet councilor Prime Mins. Office, 1977, dir. legal affairs divsn. Treaties Bur., 1977, dir. treaties divsn. Treaties Bur., 1978, french interpreter Imperial Household Agy., 1980, amb. Embassy of Japan Republic Korea, counselor min., 1981, dep. dir.-gen. Asian Affairs Bur., 1984, dep. dir.-gen. Treaties Bur., 1987, consul-gen. Japan San Francisco, 1987, dir.-gen. Treaties Bur., 1990, exec. sec. Internat. Peace Cooperation Hdqrs. Prime Mins., 1992, dir.-gen. Fgn. Policy Bur., 1993, dep. min. fgn. affairs, 1995, vice-min. fgn. affairs, 1997; amb. E.& P. U.S., 1999. Office: Embassy of Japan 2520 Massachusetts Ave NW Washington DC 20008-2869 Fax: 202-328-2187.

**YANAR, MARIA LUISA (TITA),** director; d. Graciela and Victor Medina (Stepfather); m. Victor Antonio Yanar, June 23, 1971; children: Soraya, Victor Omar. BS in Secondary Edn., U. Tex., 1971, MEd in Curriculum and Instrn., 1975. Tchr. Spanish, English and reading Bassett Mid. Sch., El Paso, Tex., 1971—77; assoc. dir. Ctrl. Am. Peace Scholarship Program, 1991—92; assoc. dir. Mother-Daughter Program U. Tex., 1992—95, from curriculum coord. to asst. dir. Upward Bound program, 1995—2005, dir. Upward Bound program, 2005—. Dir. Nat. Hispanic Insts. El Paso Programs, 1990—2000. Ednl. programs com. Nat. Hispanic Inst., Maxwell, Tex., 1992—2000; bd. dirs. Internat. Hispanic Cultural Inst., El Paso, 2004—; outreach com. co-chair Women's Fund of El Paso, 2005—. Mem.: S.W. Assn. Student Assistance Programs (assoc.), Golden Key Nat. Honor Soc. (life), Sigma Delta Pi (assoc.). Roman Catholic. Avocations: community service, travel, health and wellness. Office: U Tex 500 W Univ Graham Hall 208 El Paso TX 79968 Office Phone: 915-747-5149. Personal E-mail: tyanar@utep.edu.

**YANAS, JOHN JOSEPH,** lawyer; b. Albany, N.Y., July 18, 1929; m. Mary Faith Casey; children: John J., Joseph J., Kathleen Ann, Mary Patricia. Student Russell Sage Coll., 1947-50; LLB, Albany Law Sch., 1953, LLD, 1989. Bar: N.Y. 1954, U.S. Ct. Appeals (2d cir.) 1962. Assoc. Casey, Honikel and Wisely, Albany, 1954-60; ptnr. Dugan, Casey, Burke & Lyons, Albany, 1960-69; ptnr. Casey, Yanas, Mitchell & Amerling, Albany, 1969-84, Casey, Yanas, Clyne, Mitchell & Amerling, Albany, 1984-88; ptnr. Degraff, Foy, Kunz & Devine LLP, 1989—; counsel Albany County Pub. Welfare Dist., 1959-60; mem. Albany City CSC, 1970-73, Albany County CSC, 1970-73; justice Albany City Ct., 1973-77; Bank. Trustee Christian Bros. Acad., Albany, 1972-2002, chair, 1992, Albany Law Sch., 1975-2001, chair, 1993. Fellow Am. Bar Found., N.Y. Bar Found., AAJ; mem. Am. Coll. Real Estate Lawyers, N.Y. State Bar Assn. (chmn. real property law sect. 1974-75, chmn. com. to confer with N.Y. State Realty Bd. 1975-77, chmn. com. continuing legal edn. 1977-80, treas. 1980-86, chmn. fin. com. 1987, pres.-elect 1988, pres. 1989), Albany County Bar Assn. (pres. 1978). Office: 90 State St Albany NY 12207

**YANCEY, ASA GREENWOOD, SR.,** physician, educator; b. Atlanta, Aug. 19, 1916; s. Arthur H. and Daisy L. (Sherard) Yancey; m. Carolyn E. Dunbar, Dec. 28, 1944; children: Arthur H. II, Carolyn L., Caren L., Asa Greenwood Jr. BS, Morehouse Coll., 1937, ScD (hon.), 1991; MD, U. Mich., 1941; ScD (hon.), Howard U., 1991. Diplomate Am. Bd. Surgery. Intern City Hosp., Cleve., 1941-42; resident Freedmen's Hosp., Washington, 1942-45, U.S. Marine Hosp., Boston, 1945; instr. surgery Meharry Med. Coll., 1946-48; chief surgery VA Hosp., Tuskegee, Ala., 1948-58; chief surgery of Hughes Spalding Pavilion, 1958-72; pvt. practice specializing in surgery Atlanta, 1958-86; from asst. prof. to assoc. prof. surgery Emory U., 1958—75, prof., 1975-86, prof. emeritus, 1986—; assoc. dean Sch. Medicine, 1972-89; med. dir. Grady Meml. Hosp., Atlanta, 1972-89, trustee, 1989—93; clin. prof. surgery Morehouse Sch. Medicine, 1985—; mem. staff Hughes Spalding Hosp., St. Joseph Hosp., Emory U. Hosp., 1986—88. Contbr. articles to profl. jours. Mem. Atlanta Bd. Edn., 1967—77, Fulton-De Kalb Hosp. Authority. 1st lt. M.C. U.S. Army, 1942. Fellow: ACS, Am. Surg. Assn.; mem.: So. Surg. Assn., Inst. Medicine of NAS, Nat. Med. Assn. (1st v.p. 1988—89, trustee 1960—66, mem. editl. bd. jour. 1964—80). Baptist. Home and Office: 2845 Engle Rd NW Atlanta GA 30318-7216 Office Phone: 404-799-5045.

**YANCEY, CAROLYN DUNBAR,** academic administrator; b. Detroit, Feb. 10, 1921; d. Henry Steward and Annie Louise (Dye) Dunbar; m. Asa Greenwood Yancey, Sr., Dec. 28, 1944; children: Arthur H. II, Carolyn L., Caren L., Asa Greenwood Jr. BA, Wayne State U., Detroit, 1941. Cert. tchr. Mich. Mem. Bd. Edn. Atlanta Pub. Schs., 1982-97, v.p. Bd. Edn., 1993. Mem. bd. regents Univ. Sys. Ga., 1985—92; trustee Spellman Coll., Atlanta, 1972—2001; bd. dirs. Women's C of C, Atlanta, 1972—74. Pres. PTA Frank L. Stanton Sch., Atlanta, 1960; active voter registration Atlanta Voters League, 1963. Recipient Leadership award, NAACP, 1981, Achievement award, Atlanta Med. Assn., 1982, Daniel James Gen. Edn. award, Tuskegee Airmen, Inc., 1993. Mem.: Links Inc. (pres. 1968), Delta Sigma Theta. Congregationalist. Avocations: sewing, homemaking. Home: 2845 Engle Rd NW Atlanta GA 30318-7216 Office Phone: 404-799-5045.

**YANCEY, KIM BRUCE,** dermatology researcher; b. Atlanta, Nov. 25, 1952; s. Andrew Jackson and Edrie (Johnson) Yancey. BS, U. Ga., Athens, 1974; MD, Med. Coll. Ga., 1978. Diplomate Am. Bd. Dermatology. Intern dept. internal medicine Med. Coll. Ga., Augusta, 1978-79, resident dept. dermatology, 1979-81; med. staff fellow dermatology br. NIH, Bethesda, Md., 1981-84, sr. staff fellow dermatology br., 1984-85, sr. investigator dermatology br., 1993—2000; assoc. prof. dept. dermatology Uniformed Svcs. U. Health Scis., Bethesda, 1985-87, assoc. prof. dept. dermatology, 1987-93, acting chmn. dept. dermatology, 1990-93; prof., chair dept. dermatology Med. Coll. Wis., Milw., 2001—. Cons. Walter Reed Army Med. Ctr., Washington, 1985—2000. Author monographs and sci. manuscripts; mem. various editl. bds.; contbr. articles to profl. jours. Grantee NIH, 1986—, NATO, 1988-93. Fellow: Am. Acad. Dermatology (editl. bd. 1986—93, 2004—); mem.: AMA, Med. Coll. Physicians (mem. exec. com. 2004—, chmn. 2004—05), Assn. Profs. Dermatology (chmn. program com. 2004), Wis. Dermatol. Assn., Dermatology Found., Am. Fedn. Med. Rsch., Soc. Investigative Dermatology (bd. dirs. 1982—84, co-chmn. ea. region 1990—92, co-chmn. cons. 2004, bd. dir. 2004—), Am. Dermatol. Assn. (Young Leadership award 1986), Am. Bd. Dermatology (v.p. 2005), Am. Soc. Clin. Investigation. Methodist. Office: Med Coll Wis Dept Dermatology 8701 Watertown Plank Rd Milwaukee WI 53226 Office Phone: 414-456-4081. Business E-mail: kyancey@mcw.edu.

**YANCEY, RICHARD CHARLES,** investment banker; b. Spokane, Wash., May 28, 1926; s. George R. and M. Ruth (Yenney) Y.; m. Mary Anne Shaffer, Feb. 5, 1956; children: Leslie, Jennifer, Richard C. Jr. BA in Econs., Whitman Coll., Walla Walla, Wash., 1949; MBA with distinction, Harvard U., 1952. Assoc. Dillon, Read & Co. Inc., N.Y.C. 1952—63; v.p. Dillon, Read & Co., Inc., N.Y.C., 1963-75, mng. dir., 1975-89, dir., 1990; sr. adv., 1992; ret. Dillon, Read & Co., Inc., N.Y.C., 1992. Trustee, chmn. W.M. Group of Funds, Seattle; mng. dir. Ad Media Ptnrs., Inc., N.Y.C.; vice chmn., dir. Czech and Slovak Am. Enterprise Fund, Massapequa, N.Y.; former mem. partnership bd. Whittle Comms. L.P., Knoxville, Tenn. Former bd. overseers Whitman Coll.; former trustee, former pres. Plymouth Ch. of Pilgrims, Bklyn.; former trustee N.Y. Infirmary-Beekman Downtown Hosp. Served with USNR, 1944-46, PTO. Mem. N.Y. Soc. Security Analysts, Assn. for Investment Mgmt. and Rsch., Harvard Club, Met. Club, N.Y.C., Pilgrims of the U.S. Republican. Home: 42 Monroe Pl Brooklyn NY 11201-2603 Office: Ad Media Ptnrs Inc 19th Fl 444 Madison Ave Fl 19 New York NY 10022-6903 Office Phone: 212-759-1870. Personal E-mail: rc1yancey@earthlink.net. Business E-mail: ryancey@admediapartners.com.

**YANCEY, ROBERT EARL, JR.,** retired oil industry executive; b. Ashland, Ky., June 16, 1945; s. Robert E. Sr. and Estelline (Tackett) Y.; m. Nina McGee, June 16, 1962; children: Rob, Yvonne, Elizabeth. BS in Chem. Engring., Cornell U., 1969. Sr. v.p., group operating officer; supt. Catlettsburg (Ky.) Refinery, 1976-79; exec. asst. Ashland (Ky.) Petroleum Co., 1979-80, group v.p., 1980-81, sr. v.p., 1981-86, pres., 1986—; sr. v.p., group operating officer Ashland Inc., 1988-97; ret. Republican. Avocations: golf, hunting, fishing. Home: 504 Amanda Furnace Dr Ashland KY 41101-2193

**YANCEY-JONES, FLORISTINE DARLENE,** artist, educator; b. Pocahontas, Va., Dec. 24, 1945; d. Viola Phyllis Yancey-Carter; m. Richard C. Jones, Mar. 28; children: Mark, Brian, Todd. Student, Capital U. Lectr., tchr. Christopher Program, Columbus, 1993; artist, tchr. Children of the Future, Franklin U., Columbus, 1995; art exhbn. artist Columbus Mus. Art, 1996; lectr. Ohio State U. Coll. Art, Columbus, 1999; lectr. Black history Ohio State U., Columbus, 2000; artist in-sch. program Greater Columbus Arts Coun., 1992—2002; lectr., tchr. My Brothers Who Are We, Columbus, 1992—2003; visual artist, clothes designer. Adv. bd. mem. Ace and Acme Art Gallery, Columbus, 1993—95. Author: (poetry) A Black Woman's Soul, 1973. Pres. Somerset Civic Assn., Columbus, Ohio,

1974—76; dir. food pantry New Hope Ch. of God, Columbus, 1992—95; coun. woman Pocahontas (Va.) Town Coun., 1984—86. Recipient commendation, Ohio Ho. of Reps., Columbus, 1992, Ednl. Coun. award, Franklin U., Columbus, 1993, Ednl. Svc. award, Fed. Govt. Am., Washington, 1995, Hon. Mention, Ace 25th Anniversary Art Exhbn., 2004. Mem.: Children of the Future (tchr.), Greater Columbus Arts Coun. (artist, tchr.), Ace Art Gallery. Jewish. Avocations: guitar, interior decorating, painting, gardening, reading. Home: 1637 Liv-moor Ct Columbus OH 43227

**YANCIK, JOSEPH JOHN,** retired government official; b. Mt. Olive, Ill., Dec. 1, 1930; s. Joseph John and Anna (Gubach) Y.; m. Rosemary Panich, Feb. 19, 1955; children— Geri Anne, Ellen Marie. BS, U. Ill., 1954; MS in Mining Engring., Mo. Sch. Mines, 1956; PhD, U. Mo., Rolla, 1960. Mining research engr. St. Joe Lead Co., Bonne Terre, Mo., 1955-58; mgr. research and devel. Monsanto Co., St. Louis, 1960-70; asst. dir. mining U.S. Bur. Mines, Washington, 1970-77; v.p. research Nat. Coal Assn., Washington, 1977-82; pres. Bituminous Coal Research, Inc., Washington, 1980-82; dir. Coal Export Office U.S. Dept. Commerce, Washington, 1982-84; dir. Office of Energy Internat. Trade Adminstrn., Washington, 1984-95; pvt. practice Mc Lean, Va., 1995—2003; ret., 2003. Cons. energy in internat. trade and investment; dir. energy affairs U.S.-Russia Bus. Coun., Washington, 1996—2002. Contbr. articles to profl. jours. Served with C.E. U.S. Army, 1950-52. Recipient Alumni Achievement award U. Mo.-Rolla, 1975, Silver Medal award U.S. Dept. Commerce, 1986, Gold Medal award Dept. Commerce, 1992. Roman Catholic. Home and Office: 1703 James Payne Cir Mc Lean VA 22101-4223 E-mail: joeyan12@msn.com.

**YANCOPOULOS, GEORGE D.,** pharmaceutical executive; BA, Columbia U., 1980, PhD in Biochemistry and Molecular Biophysics, 1986, MD, 1987. Sr. staff scientist Regeneron Labs., Tarrytown, NY, 1989—91, head of discovery, 1991—92, v.p. discovery, 1992—97, chief scientific officer, 1998—, sr. v.p. rsch., 1997—2000; exec. v.p., pres. Regeneron Rsch. Labs., Regeneron Pharm., 2000—. Adj. prof. Columbia U., 1990—; bd. dirs. The Planetary Soc. Recipient Univ. medal for excellence, Columbia U., 2002; Howard Hughes Medical fellow, 1987, Lucille P. Markey scholar, 1988—89. Fellow: Am. Acad. Arts & Sciences; mem.: NAS. Office: Regeneron Labs 777 Old Saw Mill River Rd Tarrytown NY 10591*

**YANCY, DOROTHY COWSER,** college president; 1 child. BA in History and Social Sci., Johnson C Smith U.; MA in History, U. Mass.; PhD in Polit. Sci., Atlanta U. Cert. MNGT, Harvard U. Tchr. Albany State Coll., Hampton U., Evanston (Ill.) Twp. H.S.; dir. Afro-Am. studies program Barat Coll., Lake Forest, Ill.; prof. Sch. History, Sch. Mgmt. Ga. Inst. Tech., Atlanta, 1972-94. Lectr. Acad. Pub. Adminstrn. and Social Studies of Small Hural and Ulan Bator, Mongolia, 1991; apptd. spl. master Fla. Pub. Employee Rels. Commn.; mem. labor del. to Soviet Union and Europe, 1988, 90; cons. to govt. agys., unions and cos., including GM, AT&T Bell Labs; arbitrator fed. mediation and conciliation svs. Am. Arbitration Assn. Contbr. over 40 articles to profl. jours. Bd. advisor USAR Historically Black Colls. and Univs./Minority Instn.; bd. dirs. College Fund/UNCF; past mem. N.C. Post-Secondary Eligibility Commn.; former bd. dirs. Opera Carolina, Charlotte Urban League, Charlotte C. of C. Fulbright scholar; named one of Six Best Tchrs. in U.S., Newsweek on Campus, 1988. Mem. Assn. Social and Behavioral Scientists (past pres., Torchbearer award, Belle Ringer Image award), Indsl. Rels. Rsch. Assn. (past pres. Atlanta chpt.), Ctrl. Intercollegiate Athletic Assn. (past pres.), Links, Inc. (past mem. exec coun.), Coun. Ind. Colls. (former mem. governing bd.), Assn. for Study of African-Am. Life and History (exec. coun.), Omega Psi Phi, Phi Kappa Phi, Alpha Kappa Mu, Sigma Rho Sigma, Omicron Delta Kappa, Phi Beta Kappa (mem. Delta Ga. chpt.). Episcopalian. Office: 100 Beatties Ford Rd Charlotte NC 28216-5302 Office Phone: 704-378-1007. Business E-mail: dcyancy@jcsu.edu.

**YANDELL, CATHY MARLEEN,** language educator; b. Anadarko, Okla., Dec. 27, 1949; d. Lloyd O. and Maurine (Dunn) Y.; m. Mark S. McNeil, Sept. 7, 1974; children: Elizabeth Yandell McNeil, Laura Yandell McNeil. Student, Inst. des Professeurs de Français à l'Etranger U. Sorbonne, Paris, 1970; BA, U. N.Mex., 1971; MA, U. Calif., Berkeley, 1973, PhD, 1977. Tchg. asst. U. Calif., Berkeley, 1971, acting instr., 1976—77; asst. prof. Carleton Coll., Northfield, Minn., 1977—83, assoc. prof., 1983—89, prof. French, 1989—. Chair commn. on the status of women Carleton Coll., Northfield, 1983-85, ednl. policy com., 1985-86, 96-97, romance langs. and lits., 1990-94, chair faculty affairs com., 2000-02, pres. of faculty, 1991-94, Bryn-Jones disting. tchg. prof. humanities, 1996-99, mentor to jr. faculty, 1996—, W.I. and Hulda F. Daniell prof. French lit., lang. and culture, 1999—; dir. Paris French Studies Program, 1998, 2004. Author: Carpe Corpus: Time and Gender in Early Modern France, 2000; co-author: Vagabondages: Initiation à la litt. d'expression française, 1996; contbr. to Art & Argumentation: The Sixteenth Century Dialogue, 1993, French Texts/American Contexts: French Women Writers, 1994, Montaigne: A Collection of Essays, Vol. 4, Language and Meaning, 1995, Reflexivity in Women Writers of the Ancien Régime, 1998, High Anxiety, 2002, Ronsard, figure de la variété, 2002, Lectrices d'Ancien Régime, 2003, Reflections on Teaching, 2004, Ecriture courante: Critical Perspectives on French and Francophone Women, 2005; editor: Pontus de Tyard's Solitaire Second, ou prose de la musique, 1980; contbr. articles to profl. jours. Active exec. com., then mem. Amnesty Internat., Northfield, 1980—. Grantee Faculty Devel., Carleton Coll., 1988, 1991; Regents' Travelling fellow, U. Calif. Berkeley, 1975—76, NEH Rsch. fellow., 1994—95, Mellon Faculty fellow, 2003, Mellon New Directions grantee, 2006. Mem.: MLA (del. 1989—92, chair exec. com. French 16th Century lit. 2001—), Phi Beta Kappa (pres. 2004—05). Democrat. Home: 514 5th St E Northfield MN 55057-2220 Office: Carleton College 1 N College St Northfield MN 55057-4044 Office Phone: 507-646-4245. Business E-mail: cyandell@carleton.edu.

**YANDERS, ARMON FREDERICK,** biological sciences educator, science administrator; b. Lincoln, Nebr., Apr. 12, 1928; s. Fred W. and Beatrice (Pate) Y.; m. Evelyn Louise Gatz, Aug. 1, 1948; children: Mark Frederick, Kent Michael. AB, Nebr. State Coll., Peru, 1948; MS, U. Nebr., 1950; PhD, 1953. Rsch. asso. Oak Ridge Nat. Lab. and Northwestern U., 1953-54; biophysicist U.S. Naval Radiol. Def. Lab., San Francisco, 1955-58; asso. geneticist Argonne (Ill.) Nat. Lab., 1958-59; with dept. zoology Mich. State U., 1959-69; prof., asst. dean Mich. State U. (Coll. Natural Sci.), 1963-69; prof. biol. scis. U. Mo., Columbia, 1969—, dean Coll. Arts and Scis., 1969-82, rsch. prof., dir. Environ. Trace Substances Rsch. Ctr., 1983-93, dir. Alzheimer's Disease and Related Disorders Program, 1994—, dir. Spinal Cord Injury Rsch. Program, 2002—, rsch. prof., dir. Environ. Trace Substances Rsch. Ctr. and Sinclair Comparative Medicine Rsch. Farm, 1984-94, prof. emeritus, 1994—. Trustee Argonne Univs. Assn., 1965-77, v.p., 1969-73, pres., 1973, 76-77, chmn. bd., 1973-75; bd. dirs. Coun. Colls. Arts and Scis., 1981-82; mem. adv. com. environ. hazards VA, Washington, 1985-2002, chmn. sci. coun., 1988-2000, chmn. of com., 1990-2002. Contbr. articles to profl. jours. Trustee Peru State Coll., 1992-2001. Served from ensign to lt. USNR, 1954-58. Recipient Disting. Svc. award Peru State Coll., 1989. Fellow AAAS; mem. AAUP (Robert W. Martin acad. freedom award 1971), Environ. Mutagen Soc., Genetics Soc. Am., Radiation Rsch. Soc., Environ. Toxicology and Chemistry. Home: 1204 Castle Bay Pl Columbia MO 65203-6257 Office: U of Mo 521 Clark Hall Columbia MO 65211-4420 Office Phone: 573-882-1640. Business E-mail: YandersA@umsystem.edu.

**YANDLE, STEPHEN THOMAS,** dean; b. Oakland, Calif., Mar. 7, 1947; s. Clyde Thomas and Jane Walker (Hess) Y.; m. Martha Anne Welch, June 26, 1971. BA, U. Va., 1969, JD, 1972. Bar: Va. 1972. Asst. dir. admissions U. Va. Law Sch., Charlottesville, 1972-76; from asst. to assoc. dean Northwestern U. Sch. Law, Chgo., 1976-85; assoc. dean Yale U. Law Sch., New Haven, 1985—2002; exec. dir. Housing Authority of New Haven, 2002—04; dep. cons. on legal edn. ABA, 2004—. Bd. dirs. The Access Group, 1996-2004; lectr. in law Yale Law Sch., 2002-04. Commr. New Haven Housing Authority, 1998-02; trustee Nat. Assoc. for Law Placement Found. for Rsch. and Edn., 2000-04. Capt. U.S. Army, 1972. Mem. Law Sch. Admission Coun. (programs, edn. and prelaw com. 1978-84), Assn. Am. Law Schs. (chmn. legal

edn. and admissions sect. 1979, nominations com. 1987, chmn. adminstrn. of law schs. sect. 1991), Nat. Assn. for Law Placement (pres. 1984-85, co-chmn. Joint Nat. Assn. com. on placement 1986-88), New Haven Legal Assistance Assn. (bd. dirs., treas. 1992-98). Office: Am Bar Assn Sect on Legal Edn and Admissions to Bar 321 N Clark St Chicago IL 60610-4714 Office Phone: 312-988-6743. Business E-mail: yandles@staff.abanet.org.

**YANEY, GEORGE,** retired history professor; b. Teaneck, N.J., Oct. 30, 1930; s. Arthur J. and Frances (Levings) Y.; m. Ann Hinrichs, June 7, 1952; children: Brian, Dale, Carolyn, Tara. B in Mgmt. Engring., Rensselaer Poly. Inst., 1952; MA in History, U. Colo., 1956; PhD, Princeton U., 1961. Instr. Coll. Wooster, Ohio, 1957-58; prof. history U. Md., College Park, 1960-92, prof. emeritus, 1992—; ret., 1992. Author: Systematization of Russian Government, 1973, Urge to Mobilize, 1982, World of the Manager, 1994. Served to capt. USMC, 1952-54. Rsch. fellow Harvard U., 1969-70, fellow Slavic Rsch. Ctr., U. Hokkaido, Japan, 1990-91; Fulbright grantee, 1975, 77, 85, Internat. Rsch. Exchanges Bd. grantee 1965, 75, 77, 85, 89. Home: 1831 Pine Mesa Grove Colorado Springs CO 80918 Personal E-mail: georgeyaney@msn.com.

**YANG, BING-SHIANG,** biomedical engineer; BS, MS, Nat. Taiwan U.; PhD, U. Mich., 2004. Refrigeration and Air-Conditioning Professional Engineer, ROC, 1995. Rsch. asst. Nat. Taiwan U., Taipei, 1993—96; engr. Tenkey Refrigeration MFG. Co. Ltd., Taipei, 1994; lectr. Tjing-Ling Indsl. Rsch. Ctr., Taipei, 1995—96; tchg. asst. Nat. Taiwan U., 1998—99; rsch. asst. U. Mich., 1999—2004; rsch. assoc. Rehab. Inst. of Chgo., 2005—; postdoctoral fellow Northwestern U., Chgo., 2005—. Mem. com. internat. Conf. on Rehab. Robotics, Chgo., 2005; invited spkr. Nat. Taiwan U., 2006, Nat. Chiao-Tung U., Taiwan, 2006, Nat. Cheng-Kung U., 2006, Rehab. Inst. of Chgo., 2005, Kessler Med. and Rehab. Rsch. Ctr., West Orange, NJ, 2004, Marquette U., Milw., 2004; invited spl. session chair and organizer Innovative Strategy for Rehab. Following Neurol. Injuries, 15th Internat. Conf. on Mechanics in Medicine and Biology, Singapore, 2006. Contbr. articles. Second lt. Armor, Army, 1996—98, Taiwan. Decorated ROC Army Award - ranked 1st/250 second lt. ROC Army Armor Officer Tng. Ctr., ROC Army Award for Best Trainee ROC Army Pre-Mil. Tng. Ctr.; recipient Academic, Personal, Profl., and Leadership Devel. Cert., U. Mich., 2004, Sarah Baskin Award for Excellence in Rsch., Rehab. Inst. Chgo., 2006; Mich. Tchg. Fellow, U. Mich., 2004, Advanced Rehab. Rsch. Tng. Postdoctoral fellowship, US Nat. Inst. on Disability and Rehab. Rsch., 2005—; Travel grant, Neural Control of Movement Soc. and Nat. Inst. on Disability and Rehab. Rsch., 2006, U of Mich. Internat. Inst., 2002, U of Mich. Rackham Grad. Sch., 2002, 2003, 2004. Mem.: Soc. for Neurosci., Soc. for Neural Control of Movement, Internat. Soc. of Biomechanics, Am. Soc. of Biomechanics, Am. Soc. for Mech. Engineers. Achievements include patents for self-guided drill jig for equal-distance holes, ROC utility model; research in simulation study of human balance control on raised rigid structures; experimental study of age and gender differences on stepping and balancing behavior on laterally-compliant raised structures; modelling of human balance control on raised structures with lateral structural compliance; sensory input-enhanced stroke rehabilitation; task-specific modulation arm/hand posture and stiffness. Office Phone: 312-238-1404. Business E-mail: bsyang@umich.edu.

**YANG, CHARLES QI-XIANG,** chemistry educator, researcher, consultant; b. Sanchang, Jiangsu, China, Jan. 30, 1944; came to U.S., 1982; s. Weizhu and Zhiyin (Zhou) Yang; 1 child, Chen. BS, Peking U., China, 1969; MS, Nanking U., China, 1981; PhD, Kans. State U., 1987. Rsch. scientist Henan Rsch. Inst. of Chemistry, Zhenzhou, Honan, China, 1975-78, 82; lab. scientist Perkin-Elmer Corp., Eden Prairie, Minn., 1986; asst. prof. Marshall U., Huntington, W.Va., 1987-90; assoc. prof. U. Ga., Athens, 1990-95, prof., 1995—. Contbg. author: Adhesion Science, 1984, The Structures of Cellulose, 1987, Adhesives, Sealants, and Coatings for Space and Harsh Environment, 1988, Structure-Property Relations in Polymers, 1993; contbr. articles to profl. jours. Mem. Am. Chem. Soc. (treas. Cen. Ohio Valley sect. 1989, chmn.-elect Cen. Ohio Valley sect. 1990, chmn-elect N.E. Ga. sect. 1991, chmn. N.E. Ga. sect. 1992), Am. Assn. Textile Chemists and Colorists, Fiber Soc. Achievements include patents in field. Avocations: swimming, hiking, classical music. Home: 189 Elderberry Cir Athens GA 30605-4954 Office: U Ga 305 Dawson Hall Athens GA 30602 Office Phone: 706-542-4912. Business E-Mail: cyang@fcs.uga.edu.

**YANG, CHAU-JYE (JAY),** management consultant; b. Taipei, Taiwan; MS in Bus. Adminstrn., U. So. Calif., L.A., Calif., 1998, MS in Indsl. and Sys. Engring., 1998. Competency leader, indsl. supply chain strategy IBM Global Bus. Svcs., San Francisco, 2000—. Mem.: IEEE, Alpha Mu Epsilon (life). Achievements include patents pending for reverse supply chain management.

**YANG, CHEN NING FRANKLIN,** physicist, educator; b. Hofei, Anhui, Anhwei, China, Oct. 1, 1922; naturalized, 1964; s. Ke Chuan and Meng Hwa Loh Yang; m. Chih Li Tu, Aug. 26, 1950 (dec. 2003); children: Franklin, Gilbert, Eulee; m. Weng Fan Yang, 2005. BSC, Nat. SW Associated U., Kunming, China, 1942; MSc, Tsinghua U., 1944; PhD, U. Chgo., 1948; DSc (hon.), Princeton U., 1958, Bklyn. Polytechnic Inst., 1965, U. Wroclaw, Poland, 1974, Gustavus Adolphus Coll., Minn., 1975, U. Md., 1979, U. Durham, Eng., 1979, Fudan U., China, 1984, Eidg. Technische Hochschule, Switzerland, 1987, Moscow State U., 1992, Drexel U., 1995, Tsinghua U., Taiwan, 1996, Chiao Tung U., 1996, Chinese U., Hong Kong, 1997, U. Mich., 1998, SUNY, Stony Brook, 1999, Washington Coll., 1999, Baptist U., Hong Kong, 1999, Chung-Cheng U., Taiwan, 2000, U. Sci. and Tech., Hong Kong, 2002, Ecole Normale Superieoure, Paris, France, 2003. Instr. U. Chgo., 1948—49; postdoctoral position Inst. Adv. Study, Princeton, NJ, 1949—53, prof., 1955—66; position at Brookhaven Lab., 1953—54; Albert Einstein prof. physics SUNY, Stony Brook, 1966—99, prof. emeritus, 1999—; dir. Inst. Theoretical Physics, 1966—99; dir. emeritus C.N. Yang Inst. Theoretical Physics; disting. prof.-at-large Chinese U. Hong Kong, 1986—; prof. Tsinghua U., Beijing, 1998, Ji-Bei Hoang and Kai-Qun Lu prof., 2005—. Chmn., divsn. particles and fields Internat. Union Pure and Applied Physics, 1972—76; chmn. Fachbeirat, Max Planck Inst. Physics, 1980—83; established the found. Ctr. for Advanced Rsch., Zhongshan U., 1983, chmn.; organized a theoretical physics divsn. Nankai Inst. Math., 1986; coun. mem. Shaw Prize, mem. bd. adjudicators, 2005—; invited lectr. Contbr. articles to profl. jours.; author: Elementary Particles: a short history of some discoveries in atomic physics, 1961. Mem. governing coun. Courant Inst. Math. Sci., 1963—; mem. sci. adv. com. IBM, 1966—71; mem. High Energy Physics Adv. Panel, 1968—70; bd. trustee Rockefeller U., 1970—76, Stony Brook Found., 1981—99, Salk Inst., 1978—89, Ben Gurion U., 1981—; Brookhaven Sci. Associates, 1998—99; mem. Woods Hole Oceanographic Institution, 1962—78; mem. coun. scholars The Libr. Congress, 1990—; bd. dir. Neuroscience Inst. 1983—88, Scientific American Inc., 1983—90. Co-recipient Nobel Prize in Physics, 1957; recipient Albert Einstein Commemorative award, 1957, Rumford prize, 1980, US Nat. Medal Sci., 1986, Benjamin Franklin medal, 1993, Bower award, 1994, N. Bogoliubov prize, 1996, Lars Onsager prize, 1999, King Faisal prize, 2001. Fellow: Am. Phys. Soc. (chmn., divsn. particles and fields 1970—71), Academia Sinica (Taiwan); mem.: AAAS (bd. dir. 1975—79), Brazilian Acad. Sciences, Asia Pacific Ctr. Theoretical Physics (pres. 1996), Assn. Asia Pacific Phys. Societies (pres. 1989—94), Nat. Assn. Chinese Americans (pres. 1977—80), Pontifical Acad. Sciences, Korean Acad. Sci. and Tech., Royal Spanish Acad. Sci., Polish Acad. Sciences, Venezuelan Acad. Sciences, Am. Philos. Soc., Russian Acad. Sciences, Royal Soc. London (fgn. mem.), NAS (chmn. panel of theoretical physics, physics survey com. 1965), Chinese Acad. Sciences. Achievements include being best known for the Yang-Mills Theory, the Yang-Baxter equation, and work with Tsung-dao Lee on parity nonconservation in weak interactions. Office: Tsinghua U Ctr for Advanced Study 1 Qinghuayuan Beijing 100084 China*

**YANG, DAGANG,** mathematician, educator; PhD, SUNY, Stony Brook, 1986; BS, Zhe Jiang U., 1982. Vis. asst. prof. Purdue U., West Lafayette, Ind., 1987—89; assoc. prof. Tulane U., New Orleans, 1989—. Contbr. articles to profl. publs. Fellow, Sloan Found., 1984—85; grantee, NSF, 1987—. Mem.: Am. Math. Soc. Achievements include research in differential geometry, Einstein Manifolds. Office: Tulane U Dept Math New Orleans LA 70118 E-mail: dgy@tulane.edu.

**YANG, DEBRA WONG,** prosecutor; b. LA; 3 children. B, Pitzer Coll., 1981; JD, Boston Coll., 1985. Assoc. Haight Dickson Brown & Bonesteel, Santa Monica, Calif., 1985—87; Wildman Harrold Allen & Dixon, Chgo., 1987; law clk. to Dist. Judge Ronald Lew LA, 1988—89; atty. Greenberg Glusker, 1989; judge L.A. Mcpl. Ct., 1997—2000, L.A. Superior Ct., 2000—02; US atty. (ctrl. dist.) Calif. US Dept. Justice, L.A. 2002—. Adj. prof. U. So. Calif. Law Sch. Mem.: Asian Pacific Bar Assn. (Pub. Svc. award 2003), Asian Am. Bar Assn., So. Calif. Chinese Lawyer Assn. Republican. Office: US Attys Office US Courthouse Rm 1200 312 N Spring St Los Angeles CA 90012*

**YANG, DIHUA,** architecture educator, researcher; d. Weili Yang and Fanglan Zhang; m. Ming Tang, Aug. 1, 2000. MArch, U. Md., College Park, 2001. Arch. Andi Archtl. Design & Consultation Co., Ltd, Beijing, 1997—2000; jr. arch. HOK Group, Inc, Washington, 2002—04; prof. Savannah (Ga.) Coll. Art and Design, 2004—. Prin. works include Bloom architecture (2nd Pl., 2004). Fellow, U. Md., 2000. Mem.: Am. Inst. Architects. Office: Savannah Coll Art and Design 22 E Lathrop Ave Savannah GA 31415 Office Phone: 912-525-6883. Office Fax: 912-525-6904. Business E-Mail: dyang@scad.edu.

**YANG, EDMUND YI-BIN,** biomedical researcher, pediatric surgeon; b. Syracuse, N.Y., May 29, 1962; s. George and Stringner Yang; m. Laurie Hauber, Sept. 3, 2000; children: Aiden Wen-Yan, Kyman Wen-Jie. AB, Cornell U., 1984; MD, PhD, Vanderbilt U., 1993. Diplomate Am. Bd. of Surgery, 2002. Resident in gen. surgery U. of Calif., San Francisco, 1993—2001; postdoctoral rsch. fellow Children's Hosp. of Phila., 1995—98; pediatric surgery fellow Boston Children's Hosp., 2001—03; asst. prof. of surgery Vanderbilt Children's Hosp., Nashville, 2003—. Author: (research publication) Fetal Gene Therapy: Efficacy, Toxicity, and Immunologic Effects of Early Gestation Recombinant Adenovirus. (Brit. Assn. of Pediatric Surgeons Prize, 1998). Mgmt. of Myelomeningocele Study grant, NIH, 2001 to 2008. Office: Vanderbilt Children's Hosp 2200 Children's Way DOT 4150 Nashville TN 37232-9870 Office Phone: 615-936-1050. Office Fax: 615-936-1046. E-mail: edmund.yang@vanderbilt.edu.

**YANG, FAN,** electrical engineer, researcher; b. Wuhan, Hubei Province, China, 1975; s. Zhixi Yang, Weidong Zhou; m. Jianxia Xue. Ph. D, UCLA, Los Angeles, 1999—2002; MS, Tsinghua University, Beijing, 1997—99, BS, 1992—97, MS, 1997—99, BS, 1992—97. Research scientist UCLA electrical engineering, Los Angeles, CA, 2002—02; Graduate student researcher UCLA electrical engineering Dept., Los Angeles, CA, 1999—2002; research assistant State key laboratory of microwave and digital communication, Beijing, CA, China, 1995—99; teaching assistant Tsinghua University, Beijing, CA, China, 1996—99; Research assistant State key laboratory of Microwave and Digital Communication, Beijing, CA, China, 1994—99. Publicity officer IEEE AP society, Los Angeles Chapter, Los Angeles, CA, 2002—02; Session chair 2001 IEEE AP-s International Symposium Committee, Boston, 2001—01; reviewer IEEE Transactions on Antenna and Propagation, Piscataway, NJ, 2001—01. Author: (jounal articles) IEEE Transactions on antenna and propagations, 2001 (Honorable mention of IEEE APS student paper competition, 2000), (journal papers) microwave and optical technology letters, 2001, electronic letters, 2001, microwave and wireless components letters, 2002, (papers and presentations) in various international symosium from 1997 to present. Vice president Chinese student and scholar association at UCLA, Los Angeles, CA, 2001—02. Mem.: IEEE. Office: UCLA Electrical Engineering Dept 420 Westwood Plaza Los Angeles CA 90095 Office Phone: (310)206-4801. Office Fax: (310)206-8495. Business E-Mail: ygfn@ee.ucla.edu.

**YANG, GRACE H.,** lawyer; d. Tai-cheng and Alice Yang; m. James T. Huang, Nov. 15, 1997; 2 children; 2 children. BA, Yale U., New Haven, Conn., 1994; JD, Cornell Law Sch., Ithaca, NY, 1997. Bar: Fla. Bar 1997, DC Bar 1997. Assoc. Holland & Knight LLP, Tampa, Fla., 1997—2005; shareholder GrayRobinson, P.A., Tampa, 2005—. Bd. mem. Yale Club of Tampa Bay, 2001—06; steering com. mem. Bay Area Legal Services, Tampa; v.p. membership Hillsborough Assn. for Women Lawyers, Tampa, 2004—06. Home: 319 Columbia Dr Tampa FL 33606-3724 Office: GrayRobinson PA 201 N Franklin St Ste 2200 Tampa FL 33602 Office Phone: 813-273-5043. E-mail: gyang@gray-robinson.com.

**YANG, GUANGBIN,** engineer; s. Xitan and Meirong Y.; m. Ling Jin, Nov. 19, 1991; children: Benjamin, Laurence. BS, Hangzhou Inst. Elec. Engring., China, 1986, M of Engring., 1989; MS, Wayne State U., Detroit, 1998, DPhil, 2000. Engr., team leader China Elec. Product Reliability & Environ. Testing, Guangzhou, China, 1989-95; rsch. asst. Wayne State U., Detroit, 1995-96; rschr. Ford Motor Co., Dearborn, Mich., 1996-98; reliability engr. Yazaki N.Am., Inc., Canton, Mich., 1998-2000; Ford Motor Co., Dearborn, Mich., 2000—. Mem. tech. com. Fault-Tolerance Computation Soc., Beijing, 1994-95; cons. in field. Contbr. articles to profl. jours.; referee various tech. jours. and internat. confs. Recipient Engr. of Yr. award, IEEE Reliability Soc., 2002. Mem. IEEE (sr.), Internat. Soc. Sci. and Applied Tech. (organizer and chair invited sessions, mem. program com. Internat. Conf. on Reliability and Quality in Design), Am. Soc. Quality (sr.), IEEE Reliability Soc. (chair automotive sys. com., internat. program com., Engr. of the Yr. award 2002), Reliability Conf. France. Avocations: poetry, classical music. Office: Ford Motor Co 21500 Oakwood Blvd MD 71 Dearborn MI 48121 Business E-Mail: gyang@peoplepc.com.

**YANG, GUANGRONG,** physicist, researcher, educator; b. Pi County, Sichuan, China, Feb. 25, 1941; arrived in US, 1988; s. Guangyuan and Kaide (Liu) Y.; m. Shiyi Tong, Jan. 12, 1968; children: Bizhou, Tingzhou. BS, U. Sci. and Tech. China, Beijing, 1964. Rsch. assoc. prof. Inst. Semiconductors, Chinese Acad. Scis., Beijing, 1964-85; vis. prof. U. Western Ont., London, Ont., Can., 1985-88; vis. scholar, rsch. assoc. Rensselaer Poly. Inst., Troy, NY, 1988—2003; concurrent prof. Xian (China) U. Tech., 1993—. Translator, editor: VLSI Electronics, 1986. Mem. Materials Rsch. Soc. Achievements include patent for Vapor Deposition of Parylene-F using 1, 4-bis Trifluoromethyl Benzene; increase of deposition rate of vapor deposited polymer by electric field; invention (with others) of thermoelectric semiconductor refrigerator, amorphous chalcogenide read mostly memory and dual low energy ion beam epitaxy equipment. Office: 127 Xin Wen Hua St Beijing 100031 China Personal E-mail: gryang2003@yahoo.com.

**YANG, HENRY T.Y.,** chancellor, educator; b. Chungking, China, Nov. 29, 1940; s. Chen Pei and Wei Gen Yang; m. Dilling Tsui, Sept. 2, 1966; children: Maria, Martha. BS, Nat. Taiwan U., 1962, D, 2000; MS, W.Va. U., 1965; PhD, Cornell U., 1968; D (hon.), Purdue U., 1996, Hong Kong U. Sci. and Tech., 2002, City U. Hong Kong, 2005. Structural engr. Gilbert Assocs., Reading, Pa., 1968—69; asst. prof. Sch. Aeros. and Astronautics, Purdue U., West Lafayette, Ind., 1969, assoc. prof., 1972, prof., 1976—94, Neil A Armstrong Disting. prof. aero. and astronautical engring., 1988—94, sch. head, 1979—84; dean engring. Purdue U., 1984—94; chancellor U. Calif., Santa Barbara, 1994—. Mem. sci. adv. bd. USAF, 1985—89, mem. sci. adv. group aero. sys. divsn., 1986—89; mem. aero. adv. com. NASA, 1985—89; mem. engring. adv. com. NSF, 1988—91; def. sci. bd. DoD (merged with Def. Mfg. Bd.), 1988—91, mem. def. mfg. bd., 1998—99; mem. mechanics bd. vis. ONR, 1990—93; mem. tech. adv. com. Pratt & Whitney, 1993—95; mem. Naval Rsch. Adv. Com., 1996—98; bd. mem. AlliedSignal, 1996—99. Calif. Coun. Sci. and Technology, 1997—2004; rschr. in field. Contbr. over 160 articles in engring. to profl. jours. Bd. trustees Univs. Rsch. Assn., 2002—; bd. dirs. Axle and Mfg., 2004—. Named Hon. alumnus, U. Calif. Santa Barbara, 2001, Exec. of Yr., South Coast Bus. and Tech. Awards Dinner, 2004; recipient Twelve Outstanding Tchg. awards, Purdue U.,

1970—94, Outstanding Aerospace Engr. award, 1999, Educator of Yr. award, Goleta C. of C., 2002, Pierre Claeyssens award disting. svc., Emmaus Santa Barbara, 2004. Fellow: AIAA, Am. Soc. Engring. Edn. (Centennial medal 1993, Benjamin Garver Lamme award, Gold medal 1998); mem.: ASCE, NAE (mem. acad. adv. bd. 1991—94), ASME, Univs. Rsch. Assn., Academia Sinica, Tau Beta Pi. Office: U Calif Santa Barbara Chancellors Office 5221 Cheadle Hall Santa Barbara CA 93106-2030

**YANG, JERRY,** Internet company executive; b. Taiwan, Nov. 6, 1968; married; 1 child. BSEE, MSEE, Stanford U., 1990, PhD studies in Elec. Engring. Co-creator Yahoo! Navigational Guide to the Internet, 1994; co-founder Yahoo!, Inc., Calif., 1995—, chief Yahoo!, bd. dirs. Calif., 1996—. Bd. dirs. Cisco Systems, Inc., 2000—. Co-author (with David Filo, Karen Heyman): (books) Yahoo! Unplugged: your Discovery Guide to the Web, 1995; co-author: (with David Filo, Richard Raucci, Elizabeth Crane) Yahooligans!: Way Cool Web Sites, 1996. Named one of 400 Richest Ams., Forbes mag., 2004, 2005, 2006. Mem.: Com. 100, Phi Kappa Psi. Named company YAHOO!(acronym for Yet Another Hierarchical Officious Oracle). Office: Yahoo! Inc 701 First Ave Sunnyvale CA 94089-1019*

**YANG, JIDONG,** transportation engineer; PhD, U. S. Fla., Tampa, 2000—04. Profl. Engr., Fla. Bd. Profl. Engrs., 2006. Sr. transp. engr. Tindale Oliver and Associates, Inc., Tampa, 2002—. Contbr. papers to profl. jours. and pubs. Bd. mem. Chinese Am. Assn. Tampa Bay, 2001—02; pres. Friendship Assn. Chinese Students & Scholars, U. S. Fla., 2001—02. Mem.: ASCE, Inst. Transp. Engrs. (assoc.). Achievements include research in deveopment of new methodologies. Office Phone: 813-224-8862.

**YANG, JINBO,** biomedical researcher; b. Rongcheng, China, Nov. 22, 1969; m. Qing Ge, Aug. 6, 1997. PhD, Peking U., Beijing, China, 1998. Rsch. asst. prof. U. Mo., Rolla, Mo., 2000—06, rsch. assoc. prof., 2006—. Contbr. articles to profl. jours. Fellow, Alexander von Humboldt Found., 1998. Office: University of Missouri Rolla 1870 Miner Circle Rolla MO 65409 Office Phone: 573-241-6165. Home Fax: 573-341-2071. Personal E-mail: y_jinbo@hotmail.com.

**YANG, JINGZHOU,** engineer, educator; BS, Jilin U., Changchun, China, 1989, MS, 1992; M in Computer Sci., U. Iowa, 2003, PhD, 2003. Asst. prof. Tsinghua U., Beijing, 1992—97; rsch. engr. Nat. U. Singapore, 1997—98; post doctoral assoc. U. Iowa, Iowa City, 2003—04, rsch. engr., adj. asst. prof., 2004—. Guest prof. Huazhong U. Sci. and Tech., Wuhan, Hubei, China, 2004—. Author: (novels) Towards Understanding the Workspace of The Upper Extremities (Arch T. Colwell Merit award, 2001), Digital Humans and Virtual Reality for Future Combat Systems; assoc. editor: Internat. Jour. Robotics and Automation, mem. editl. bd.: Internat. Jour. Human Factors Modelling and Simulation. Recipient Outstanding Paper award, ASME, 2004. Mem.: AIAA (corr.), Soc. Automotive Engrs. Office: Univ Iowa Ctr for Computer Aided Design Iowa City IA 52242 Office Phone: 319-353-2249. Office Fax: 319-384-0542. E-mail: jyang@engineering.uiowa.edu.

**YANG, JIONG,** education educator; b. Shanghai, PR China, Aug. 28, 1972; PhD, UCLA, 1995—99. Vis. asst. prof. U. Ill., Urbana Champaign, 2002—04; schroeder asst. prof. Case Western Res. U., Cleve., Ohio, 2004—. Office Phone: 216-368-6197.

**YANG, JOSEPH,** lawyer; s. Tony Tien-Sheng and Hsiu-Ying Tsai Yang; m. Roxana H. Hwu, 1999; children: Jacqueline O., Russell A. BS, Calif. Inst. Tech., 1986, MS, 1987, PhD, 1991; JD, Stanford U., 1996. Bar: U.S. Patent and Trademark Office 1996, Calif. 1996, U.S. Ct. Appeals (Fed. Cir.) 2002. Engr. TRW Corp., Redondo Beach, Calif., 1986—87; Office Naval Rsch. fellow Calif. Inst. Tech., Pasadena, Calif., 1987—91; rsch. engr. Shell Devel. Co., Houston, 1991—93; tech. advisor Weil, Gotshal & Manges LLP, Menlo Park, Calif., 1994—95; atty. McCutchen, Doyle, Brown & Enersen LLP, Palo Alto, 1995—98; counsel Skadden, Arps, Slate, Meagher & Flom LLP, Palo Alto, 1998—2005; v.p., gen. counsel Cryptography Rsch. Inc., San Francisco, 2005—; founding ptnr. PatentEsque Law Group, LLP, Menlo Park, 2005—. Adj. prof. Calif. Law Calif., Berkeley, 1998—99; program chair Practicing Law Inst., NY, 2002—; co-founder intellectual property transactions practice Skadden Arps LLP, Palo Alto; spkr. on intellectual property law. Contbr. chapters to books; editor: Advanced Licensing Agreements, 2003—; author: (jour. article) IP Litigator, 2003; contbr. articles to jours. including The Practical Lawyer, The Licensing Jour., others. Named Outstanding Student in Engring. at Caltech, Inst. for Advancement of Engring., 1986; GM scholar, 1983—86. Mem.: Licensing Execs. Soc., Am. Intellectual Property Law Assn., Calif. Inst. Tech. Alumni Assn. (dir. 1999—2003), Caltech Alumni Assn. (pres. San Francisco chptr. 1998—99). Office: PatentEsque Law Group LLP 2460 Sand Hill Rd Ste 101 Menlo Park CA 94025 Office Phone: 650-233-0822. Business E-Mail: joe@patentesque.com.

**YANG, KEY PAIK,** librarian, archivist; b. Naju, Chollo Namdo, Korea, Jan. 8, 1919; s. Yunmuk and Yunhui Yang; m. Hazel K. Yang; children: Won Kyung, A Kyung, Mal Kyung. Diploma, Song Sil Acad., Pyongyang, Korea, 1939; diploma in Commerce, Nihon U., Tokyo, 1943; BA in Polit. Sci., Monmouth Coll., 1949; MA in Pub. Adminstrn., Am. U., 1958; MSLS, Cath. U. Am., 1960; PhD (hon.), Dongguk U., Seoul, Korea, 1975. With Chosen Kinyu Kumiai, Seoul, 1939, Chosen Kinsoku Butshi Eidan, Seoul, 1943—45; chief Property Custodian Office, Seoul, 1945—46; head of sect. Pub. Works Divsn., Seoul, Kyonggi Province, 1947—48, Pub. Info., Seoul, 1948—49; head Korean sect. Libr. of Congress, Washington, 1950—94, chief, Asian divsn., 1994—95; advisor Korean Embassy Archives, Washington. Mem. panel Bd. of U.S. Civil Svc. Examiners, 1955—57; chmn. Subcom. on East Asian Librs., 1980—80. Author: Physiology of Korean Culture, Art and Civilization, Introduction to Koreanology; co-author: The School of Yi Confucianism, contbr. articles to profl. jours.; author: Quotations to Ponder Medley of Quotations on Traditional Society of Korea, China and Japan. Recipient Meritorious award, The Libr. of Congress, 1984; U.S. State Dept. sr. fellow, Korea, 1965. Fulbright Lectr., Korean U., Seoul, 1983, Harvard U. grantee in Korean Ecology, 1960. Mem.: Assn. of Asian Studies. Democrat-Npl. Home: 5104 Marlyn Drive Bethesda MD 20816

**YANG, LI,** computer scientist, educator; b. Hexe, Shandong, China, Sept. 20, 1966; arrived in U.S., 2000; s. Mu Yang and Yunxia Dong; m. Xiaojie Wang, Dec. 8, 1995; children: Chang, Ann. BS, Shandong U., 1985; M in Engring., U. Sci. and Tech. China, 1988, PhD, 1992; postgrad., Chinese Acad. Scis., Beijing, 1994. Lectr. U. Sci. and Tech. China, Hefei, 1992; vis. scientist Nat. U. Singapore, 1994—95; tech. staff Inst. High Performance Computing, Singapore, 1995—99; asst. prof. U. We. Mich. U., Kalamazoo, 2000—02, assoc. prof., 2002—. Mem.: IEEE (sr.), Assn. for Computing Machinery. Office: Western Mich Univ Dept Computer Sci 1903 W Michigan Ave Kalamazoo MI 49008 Business E-Mail: li.yang@wmich.edu.

**YANG, LIANXIANG,** optical engineer, educator; b. Shaoxing, Zhejiang, China, Nov. 27, 1959; s. Huiyuan Yang and Furong Cai; m. Yang Hu, July 26, 1959; 1 child, Yang Jia. PhD, U. Kassel, Germany, 1996. Lectr. and assoc. prof. Hefei (China) U. of Tech., 1986—91; rschr. and sr. rsch. fellow U. of Kassel, Hessen, Germany, 1991—98; sr. engr. Dr. Ettemeyer GmbH, Neu Ulm, Bavaria, Germany, 1998—2000; r&d scientist JDS-Uniphase Corp., Ottawa, Ontaria, Canada, 2000—01; assoc. prof. Oakland U., Rochester, Mich., 2001—. Cons. Ettemeyer LLC, Tucker, Ga., 2001—, Ettemeyer AG, Elchingen, Bavaria, Germany, 2001—. Co-author: Digital Shearography. Recipient The Silver Medal award, The Chinese Nat. Com., 1987, 1st prize, Assn. of German Engrs., 1998; fellow Rsch. fellowship, Otto-Braun Found. of Germany 1993—94, DaimlerChrysler, 2003, Oakland U., 2003; grantee, German Nat. Rsch. Found., 1995—98; scholar, The Chinese Nat. Edn. Ministry, 1992. Fellow: The Soc. of Chinese Physicists (chmn. 1996); mem.: The Am. Soc. of Nondestructive Testing (corr.), The Internat. Soc. of Optical Engring. (corr.). Achievements include patents in field; patents pending for field. Office: Oakland University Department of Mechanical Engineering Rochester MI 48309 E-mail: yang2@oakland.edu.

**YANG, LIJIAN,** educator; s. Zhenchuan Yang and Qiaoyun Yan; m. Yuliya Zyryanova, Dec. 27, 2002. BS, Peking U., Beijing, 1987; MS, U. NC, Chapel Hill, 1993, PhD, 1995. Asst. prof. Mich. State U., East Lansing, 1997—2001, assoc. prof., 2001—06, prof., 2006—. Judith C. & William G. Bollinger vis. prof. U. Pa., Phila., 2001—02; vis. professor Peking U., 2004; vis. assoc. prof. Nat. U. Singapore, 2005. Assoc. editor: Computational Stats., 2000—06. Fellow: Royal Statis. Soc.; mem.: Inst. Math. Stats., Am. Statis. Assn. (fellow 2003—04). Office: Michigan State University Department of Statistics and Probability East Lansing MI 48824 Office Phone: 517-353-6369.

**YANG, MICHAEL VINCENT,** literature and language professor, researcher; b. Kunming, China, Dec. 28, 1948; s. Chien-fa Yang and Shu-chin Mei; m. Suzanne Marie Imler, Apr. 1, 1964; children: James Michael, David William, Christopher Graham, April Elizabeth, Paul Joseph, Sarah Marie. PhD, Rutgers U., 1985. Chinese instr. Coll. William and Mary, Williamsburg, Va., 1983—85; asst. prof. comparative lit. and Chinese Pa. State U., State College, 1985—91; prof. English, dept. head Nat. Chung Cheng U., Minhsiung, Taiwan, 1991—93, prof. English, dir., rsch. ctr. langs. and lit., 1991—95; assoc. prof. Baylor U., Waco, Tex., 1996—. Author: (book) Nature and Self, The Life and Works of Ralph Waldo Emerson, The Autobiography of William Carlos Williams, John Locke's View of Language and Literature; contbr. articles to profl. jours. in field. Recipient Disting. Rsch. award, 1994; fellow, Ministry of Edn., Taiwan, 1991-93; grantee, Pacific Cultural Found. 1989, Nat. Sci. Coun., Taiwan, 1994-95. Home: 324 Will Boleman Dr Hewitt TX 76643 Office: Baylor Univ S 5th St Waco TX 76798 Office Phone: 254-710-3799. Business E-mail: vincent_yang@baylor.edu.

**YANG, MING-HSUAN,** research scientist; PhD, U. Ill., Urbana-Champaign, 2000. Sr. rsch. scientist Honda Rsch. Inst., Mountain View, Calif , 2000—. Ray Ozzie Fellowship, U. Ill., 1999. Mem.: IEEE. Office: Honda Rsch Inst 800 California St Sunnyvale CA 94086 Office Phone: 650-314-0418.

**YANG, PEIDONG,** material science researcher; b. Suchow, Jiangsu, China, Aug. 22, 1971; came to U.S., 1993; s. Xueli and Amei Yang; m. Mei Wang, May 15, 1996. BS, U. Sci. and Tech. of China, Anhui, 1993; MS, Harvard U., 1995, PhD, 1997. Rsch. asst. U. Sci. and Tech. of China, 1989-93, Harvard U., Cambridge, Mass., 1993—99; postdoctoral fellow U. Calif., Santa Barbara, 1997—99, assoc. prof. chemistry Berkeley, 1999—. Mem. Tech. Rev. TR 100 MIT, 2003; chmn. chemistry Chevron Texaco, 2003. Recipient Presdl. prize U. Sci. and Tech. of China, 1993, Zhongzhi Zhang prize, 1992, Career award, NSF, 2001, Beckman Young Investigator award, 2002, MRS Outstanding Young Investigator award, 2004. Mem. Am. Chem. Soc. (chmn. nanosci. subdivsn., 2003, ExxonMobil Solid State Chemistry award, 2001, award in Chemistry, 2005), Materials Rsch. Soc., Am. Phys. Soc. Achievements include invention of metal oxide nanorods and their incorporation into the high temperature superconductor, thus enhancing the critical current density. Office: Univ Calif Berkeley B68 Hildebrand Berkeley CA 94720-1460 Office Phone: 510-643-1545. Office Fax: 510-642-7301. Business E-Mail: p_yang@berkeley.edu.

**YANG, PHILIP Q.,** social sciences educator; arrived in US, 1986; m. Jianling Li, Dec. 20, 1984; children: Ming, William Zeus. PhB, Zhongshan U., Guangzhou, China, 1982; MA, UCLA, 1988, PhD, 1993. Assoc. prof. Zhongshan U., Guangzhou, 1982—86; lectr. UCLA, 1994—95; asst. prof. Calif. Poly. State U., San Luis Obispo, 1995—99; from assoc. prof. to prof. Tex. Woman's U., Denton, 1999—. Author: Post-1965 Immigration to the United States: Structural Determinants, 1995, Ethnic Studies: Issues and Approaches, 2000; editor: Introduction to Ethnic Studies: A Reader, 1999; contbr. articles to profl. jours., chapters to books. Fellow, UN, 1986—87; grantee, NSF, 2002—04; Chancellor's Rsch. fellow, Tex. Woman's U., 2001—02, 2002—03. Mem.: Population Assn. Am., N.Am. Chinese Sociologists' Assn. (bd. dirs. 2001—03), Nat. Assn. for Ethnic Studies, Assn. for Asian Am. Studies (bd. dirs. 2001—03), Southwestern Social Sci. Assn., Assn. Chinese Profs. Social Scis. in the US, Am. Sociol. Assn. (Book award Internat. Migration Sect. 1998). Office: Texas Womans Univ PO Box 425887 Denton TX 76204 Office Phone: 940-898-2054. Office Fax: 940-898-2067. Business E-Mail: pyang@mail.twu.edu.

**YANG, ROXANA HWU,** lawyer, investor; d. Sen-Yao and Guey-Dan Liaw Hwu; m. Joseph Yang; children: Jacqueline, Russell. BSEE, U. Calif., LA, 0199; JD, U. Calif., Berkeley, 1997. Bar: Calif., US Patent and Trademark Office, US Dist. Ct. (no dist.) Calif., US Ct. Appeals (fed. cir.); lic. real estate broker Calif. Atty. Pennie & Edmonds, LLP, Palo Alto, Calif., 1997—2001; prin. Law Office Roxana H. Yang, Los Altos, 2001—05; mng. ptnr. PatentEsque Law Group, LLP, 2005—. Faculty Practising Law Inst., San Francisco, 2002—. Contbr. articles to profl. jours. Ednl. patron Assocs. Calif. Inst. Tech., Pasadena, 1999—2006. Recipient Am. Jury award Torts, Pepperdine U. Sch. Law, Am. Jury award Real Property. Office: PatentEsque Law Group LLP PO Box 400 Los Altos CA 94023 Office Phone: 650-948-0822. Office Fax: 650-948-0833. E-mail: roxana@patentesque.com.

**YANG, SHU,** materials scientist; b. China; BS in material sci., Fudan U., 1992; MS in chemistry and chemical biology, Cornell U., 1997, PhD in chemistry and chemical biology, 1999. Skirkanich asst. prof. in materials sci. and engring. U. Pa. Contbr. articles to profl. jour. Named one of Top 100 Young Innovators, MIT Tech. Review, 2004; recipient ICI award in applied polymer sci., ACS, 1999, Unilever award in polymer sci. and enring., 2001. Office: U Pa Dept Materials Sci and Engring 203 LRSM 3231 Walnut St Philadelphia PA 19104-6272

**YANG, SONG-YU,** biochemist; b. Wu-Xi, Jiangsu, China, Oct. 27, 1938; came to U.S., 1981; s. Rong-Geng Zhong and Su-Fei Yang; m. Xue-Ying He, Jan. 1965; children: Ying-Zi, Yu-Xiao. MD, Beijing U. Med. Ctr., 1960; MS, CCNY, 1963; PhD, CUNY, 1984. Diplomate Beijing U. Med. Ctr. Instr. Peking Med. Coll./Beijing U. Med. Ctr., 1960—75; asst. prof. Shanghai Inst. Biochem. and Cell Biology, Acad. Sci., 1975—80; tchg. asst. CCNY, 1981—84; rsch. assoc. Rsch. Found. CUNY, 1984—88; rsch. scientist N.Y. State OMRDD, 1988—; head med. biochem. lab. Inst. for Basic Rsch. in Devel. Disabilities, 1994—. Contbr. chpts. to books and numerous articles to profl. jours. Investigator Am. Heart Assn., N.Y.C., 1991-94. Recipient L.J. Curtman prize CCNY, 1984, Wall Street Run Fellowship award, 1991, NIH Rsch. award, 1994, Alzheimer's Assn. Rsch. award, 1999. Mem. AAAS, Am. Chemistry Soc., Am. Soc. Biochemistry and Molecular Biology, N.Y. Acad. Scis., Sigma Xi. Research contribution to the fatty acid oxidation and the steroid hormone metabolism, neurological disorders; enzymes and related genes. Office: NYS Inst Basic Rsch Devel Disabilities Dept Neurochemistry 1050 Forest Hill Rd Staten Island NY 10314-6356 Personal E-mail: yang_songyu@yahoo.com

**YANG, STEPHEN C.,** thoracic surgeon; b. Beaumont, Tex., Sept. 15, 1959; s. H. H. and M. T. Yang; m. Maria Victoria Guillem, June 9, 1984; children: Kristin M., Andrew J. MD, Med. Coll. Va., 1984. Cert. Am. Bd. Surgery, 1995, Am. Bd. Thoracic Surgery, 1996. Chief thoracic surgery Johns Hopkins Med. Instns., Balt., 2001—, prof. surgery. Dir. thoracic oncology program Johns Hopkins Med. Instns. Author: Current Therapy of Thoracic and Cardiovascular Surgery (Alumni of Yr., 2004). Office: Johns Hopkins Med Instns 600 NWolfe St Blalock 240 Baltimore MD 21287-5674 Office Phone: 410-614-3891. Office Fax: 410-614-9428.

**YANG, TIANYU,** electrical engineer, educator; arrived in U.S., 2001; s. Jian Yang and Bingjie Tang. BSEE, Zhejiang U., Hangzhou, China, 2001; PhD, U. Ctrl. Fla., 2004. Asst. prof. Embry Riddle Aero. U., Daytona Beach, Fla., 2005—. Grad. rsch. asst. Dept. of ECE, U. Ctrl. Fla., Orlando, 2001—04; adj. faculty 2003—03; reviewer IEE Electronics Letters, IEE Procs. on Vision, Image and Signal Processing, Eurasip Jour. on Wireless Comms. and Networking. Contbr. articles to profl. jours. Provost fellow, U. Ctrl. Fla., 2001—02. Mem.: IEEE, Phi Kappa Phi, Eta Kappa Nu. Achievements include development of novel image rejection technique for single branch BPSK receivers; novel independent component analysis algorithm (OBA/ICA). Office Phone: 386-226-7098. E-mail: yang482@erau.edu.

**YANG, TSONG-TOH (T.T.),** pharmacist, researcher; b. Taiwan, Mar. 1, 1949; s. Yen-Leng and Chhai-Shia Lin Yang; m. Lee-Ju Wu Yang, Aug. 26, 1951; children: Benson Pin-Sheng, Steven Shih-E. BS in Pharmacy, Kaohsiung Med. Coll., Taiwan, 1971; MS in Pharmacy, U. R.I., 1979; PhD in Pharm. Sci., U. So. Calif., 1984. Registered pharmacist Taiwan, 1971. Med. supply officer Chinese Army in Taiwan, 1971—73; prodn. supr. Sterling Products Internat. Inc., Taiwan, Taipei, 1973—77; tchg. asst. U. R.I., Kingston, 1977—79, U. So. Calif., L.A., 1979—81; U. N.C., Chapel Hill, 1982—83; rsch. pharmacist Am. Cyanamid Co., Pearl River, NY, 1984—85; devel. fellow Schering-Plough Rsch. Inst., Kenilworth, NJ, 1985—. Recipient Pres.'s award for Devel., Schering-Plough Rsch. Inst., 1994, 2002, 2005, DuPont Gold award for dry powder inhaler, 1998, Thomas Alva Edison Patent award, R&D Coun. NJ, 2005. Mem.: Am. Chinese Pharm. Assn., Controlled Release Soc., Am. Assn. for Pharm. Scientists. Achievements include patents for Preparation of powder agglomerates; inhaler for powdered medications; invention of Twisthaler dry powder inhaler- device and formulation. Home: 9 Old Farm Rd Warren NJ 07059 Office: Schering-Plough Research Institute 2000 Galloping Hill Rd K-11-2-J4 Kenilworth NJ 07033 Personal E-mail: ttyangphd@yahoo.com. Business E-Mail: tsong-toh.yang@spcorp.com.

**YANG, WEN-CHING,** chemical engineer; b. Taipei, Taiwan, Nov. 11, 1939; came to U.S., 1964; s. Ting-Lien and Ho (Lee) Y.; m. Rae Tien, Aug. 24, 1968; children: Evonne R., Peter T. BSChemE, Nat. Taiwan U., Taipei, 1962; MSChemE, U. Calif., Berkeley, 1965; PhD in Chem. Engring., Carnegie Mellon U., 1968. Sr. engr. rsch. and devel. ctr. Westinghouse Electric Co., Pitts., 1968-76, fellow engr., 1976-93, adv. engr. sci. and tech. ctr., 1993-98, Siemens Westinghouse Power Corp., Pitts., 1998—. Instr. U. Pitts., 1980, 83; cons., adj. prof., 2004—; chmn. rsch. rev. panel Office Fossil Energy, Dept. Energy, Washington, 1990; hon. guest prof. Tsinghua U., Beijing, 1996—; co-chair 10th Internat. Conf. on Fluidization, Beijing, 2001. Author: (with others) Encyclopedia of Fluid Mechanics, 1986, 92; editor spl. vol. Powder Tech. jour., 1987, 98; editor: Fluidization, Solids Handling, and Processing, 1999, Handbook of Fluidization and Fluid-Particle Systems, 2003; contbr. over 100 papers to sci. jours. Lt. Army Tank Corp., 1962-63. Fellow AIChE (programming chair and sec. group 3, editor 9 symposium series vols. 1987-88, 92-93, sec. particle tech. forum 1993—, Fluidized Processes Recognition award 1993, George Westinghouse Signature award of excellence 1995. Fluidization Lectureship award 2000); mem. Am. Chem. Soc., Chinese Am. Chem. Soc. (pres. Pitts. chpt. 1994), Orgn. Chinese Am. Achievements include patents in field; development of widely-used correlations and design equations in pneumatic transport and fluidization areas. Home: 3117 Treeline Dr Murrysville PA 15668-1569 E-mail: yangwc@adelphia.net.

**YANG, XIAOJUN,** education educator; PhD, U. Ga., Athens, 2000. Asst. prof. U. West Fla., Pensacola, 2000—03, Fla. State U., Tallahassee, 2003—. Recipient Best Paper By Young Authors award, Internat. Soc. for Photogrammetry and Remote Sensing, 1996. Mem.: AAAS. Office: Florida State Univ Dept Geography Tallahassee FL 32306 Office Phone: 850-644-8379. Office Fax: 850-644-5913. Business E-Mail: xjyangusa@gmail.com.

**YANG, YUNG Y.,** economics professor, consultant; arrived in U.S., 1970; s. Hoe W. Yang and Soon I. Song; m. Choongja Jane Kim, Dec. 16, 1944; children: Eugene W., Benjamin E., Laura E. PhD, U. of Oreg., 1974. Prof. econs. Calif. State U., Sacramento, 1974—. Mem.: Am. Econ. Assn., Korea Am. Econ. Assn. (pres. 2001—02). Achievements include research in international economic problems, particulary in the East Asian countries. Office: Calif State U - Sacramento 6000 J Street Sacramento CA 95819

**YANG, YUNZHI,** biomedical engineer; PhD, Sichuan U., China, 1997. Rsch. asst. prof. U. Tenn. Health Sci. Ctr., Memphis, 2004—05, asst. prof., 2006—. Contbr. articles to profl. jours. Mem.: Orthop. Rsch. Soc., Biomed. Engring. Soc., Am. Rsch. For Dental Rsch., Soc. For Biomaterials. Office: Univ Tenn HSC 920 Madison Ave Ste 1005 Memphis TN 38163 Office Phone: 901-448-1742.

**YANG, ZHI-QIANG,** chemist; s. Liduan and Xiurong Yang; m. Miao Wang, July 14, 1991; children: Mira Muxi, Jason Michael. PhD, U. Wis., Madison, 1996—2001. Rsch. fellow Sloan-Ketering Inst. Cancer Rsch., NYC, 2002—04; sr. scientist Merck Rsch. Labs., West Point, Pa., 2004—. Mem.: Am. Chem. Soc. Achievements include patents pending for preparation of spiropiperidine compounds as b-secretase inhibitors for the treatment of Alzheimer's disease; preparation of aigialomycin D, radicicol and monocillin I and their macrocyclic analogs for use in pharmaceutical compositions as antitumor agents; research in a concise route to benzofused macrolactones via ynolides: cycloproparadicicol; trophoblast L-Selection-mediated adhesion at the maternal-fetal interface; simplified synthetic TMC-95A/B analogues retain the potency of proteasome inhibitory activity. Office: Merck Rsch Labs WP14-3 770 Sumneytown Pike West Point PA 19486

**YANJUN, YAN,** electrical engineer, statistician; M in Engring., Harbin Inst. Tech., China, 2001. Rschr. Osaka Kyoiku U., Japan, 2000—02, Syracuse U., NY, 2002—. Fellow, Syracuse U., 2002—05. Office: Syracuse U Link Hall 335 Syracuse NY 13210 Office Phone: 315-443-3366.

**YANKWITT, GEORGE B(RUCE),** lawyer; b. Bklyn. Feb. 4, 1943; s. Irvin and Roslyn (Smith) Y.; m. Adrienne G. Schwartz, Nov. 24, 1966; children—Ian, Russell, Craig. B.S., N.Y. State Sch. Indsl. and Labor Relations, Cornell U., 1964, LL.B. with distinction, 1967. Bar: N.Y. 1967, U.S. Dist. Ct. (so. and ea. dists.) N.Y. 1968, U.S. Tax Ct. 1982, U.S. Ct. Appeals (2d cir.) 1968. Assoc. law clk. to judge U.S. Ct. Appeals (2d cir.), 1967-68; assoc. Graubard, Moskovitz, McGoldrick, Dannett & Horowitz, N.Y.C., 1968-72; assoc. Finley, Kumble, Heine, Underberg & Grutman, N.Y.C., 1972-74; assoc. Robinson, Silverman, Pearce, Aronsohn & Berman, N.Y.C., 1974-76, ptnr., 1976, ptnr., group co-head Comml. Litig., Bryan Cave LLP. Mem. Bar Council (treas., chmn. com. on 2d cir. cts.), ABA, N.Y. State Bar Assn., N.Y. State Trial Lawyers Assn., N.Y. County Lawyers Assn., Order of Coif. Editor, Cornell Law Rev. Office: Bryan Cave LLP 1290 Ave of the Americas New York NY 10104 Office Phone: 212-541-2220. E-mail: gbyankwitt@bryancave.com.

**YANNALFO, BRETT CONLON,** bank executive; b. Lawrence, Mass., Jan. 20, 1969; MBA, So. N.H. U., Salem, N.H., 1998. Treas., COO Merrimac Savs. Bank, Mass., 1999—2001; br. adminstr. Stoneham Savs. Bank, Stoneham, Mass., 2001—02; v.p. ops. The Atlas Group, LLC, Andover, Mass. 2002—. Fin. officer Norther Essex C.C., Haverhill, Mass., 2004—05. Home: 53 Lowell Street Andover MA 01810 Office: The Atlas Group LLC PO Box 819 Andover MA 01810 Office Phone: 978-804-2492. Office Fax: 978-824-2352. Personal E-mail: byannalfo@comcast.net. Business E-Mail: byannalfo@theatlasgroup.com.

**YANNAS, IOANNIS VASSILIOS,** polymer science educator; b. Athens, Apr. 14, 1935; s. Vassilios Pavlos and Thalia (Sarafoglou) Yannas; m. Stamatia Frondistou (div. Oct. 1984); children: Tania, Alexis. AB, Harvard U., 1957; SM, MIT, 1959; MS, Princeton U., 1965, PhD, 1966. Asst. prof. mech. engring. MIT, Cambridge, 1966-68, duPont asst. prof., 1968-69, assoc. prof., 1969-78, prof. polymer sci. and engring. dept. mech. engring., 1978—, prof. dept. materials sci. and engring., 1983—; prof. Harvard-MIT Div. Health Scis. and Tech., Cambridge, 1978—. Vis. prof. Royal Inst. Tech., Stockholm, 1974. Author: Tissue and Organ Regeneration in Adults, 2001; editor: Regenerative Medicine, 2 vols., 2005; mem. editl. bd. Jour. Biomed. Materials Rsch., 1986—, Jour. Materials Sci. Materials Medicine, 1990—, Tissue Engring., 1994—, Interface, 2004; contbr. articles to profl. jours. Recipient Founders award, Soc. Biomaterials, 1982, Clemson award, 1992, Fred O. Conley award, Soc. Plastics Engrs., 1982, award in medicine and

---

genetics, Sci. Digest/Cutty Sark, 1982, Doolittle award, Am. Chem. Soc., 1988; fellow, Shriners Burns Inst., Mass. Gen. Hosp., 1980—81; Pub. Health Svc. fellow, Princeton U., 1963. Fellow: Biomaterials Sci. and Engring., Am. Inst. Med. and Biol. Engrs. (founding mem.), Am. Inst. Chemists; mem.: Inst. Medicine Nat. Acad Scis. Achievements include patents in field. Office: MIT Bldg 3-332 77 Mass Ave Cambridge MA 02139-4307

**YANNELLA, DONALD,** literature and language professor; b. N.Y.C., May 12, 1934; s. Donald Joseph and Johanna (Meehan) Y.; m. Kathleen Malone, May 23, 1959; children: Susan Y. Harrigan, Katherine Y. Jennings, Donald III, Christopher, Clare. BS, Fordham U., 1956, MA, 1963, PhD, 1971. Teaching asst. dept. English Auburn U., 1956-57; prof. dept. English U. So. Miss., 1981-83, Rowan U. (formerly Glassboro State Coll.), 1964-81, 83-91, prof. emeritus, 1991—; prof. dept. English Barat Coll., 1991-94, disting prof. Am. lit., 1995—2000. Dir. grad. studies English Rowan U., 1973-81, co-dir. Am. studies program, 1974-81; chair dept. English U. So. Miss., 1981-83; v.p. acad. affairs, dean coll. Barat Coll., 1991-94; cons. in field. Author: American Prose to 1820, 1979, Ralph Waldo Emerson, 1982, The Perfect Prodigy: Melville on the Birth of Malcolm, 1986, Herman Melville's Malcolm Letter: "Man's Final Lore", 1992, New Essays on Billy Budd, 2002; contbr. articles to profl. jours. With U.S. Army, 1957-58. Recipient Merit awards Rowan U., 1979-80, 85-86; NEH fellow, 1978-79. Mem. AAUP (chpt. pres. 1968-69, mem. cons. group Coll. and Univ. Govt. 1969, v.p. N.J. State Conf. 1969-71, founding editor N.J. Conf. newsletter 1969-71, nat. spl. com. non-tenured faculty 1971-72, chair 1973-79), Modern Lang. Assn. (Am. lit. sect., sec.-treas. 1982-85, exec. com. 1982-86, 88, adv. coun. 1986-88, nominating com. 1987-89, chair 1989, award 1988), Melville Soc. (program chair 1972-73, acting sec.-treas. 1973-74, acting editor 1973-74, sec.-treas. 1975-89, editor 1976-89, pres. 1990), Nat. Project Ctr. Film & Humanities (adv. com. 1974-75). Office Phone: 609-978-6443. E-mail: yannellakd@aol.com.

**YANNEY, PATRICK STEVEN,** human resources specialist; b. Denver, Sept. 9, 1952; s. Merle Philip and Madeline Veronica Yanney; m. Stephanie Ann Robinson, Aug. 15, 1981; children: Mark Phillip, Luke Steven. BA, Colo. State U., 1974. Gatekeeper Glen Eyrie Conf. Ctr., 1974—76, reception ctr./bookstore mgr., 1977—78; adminstrv. asst. to dir. of adminstrv. svcs. The Navigators, 1978—79, pers. and facilities mgr., 1980—82, dir. adminstrv. svcs., 1983—91, pers. svcs. dir., 1992—2006, corp. human resources dir., 2000—. Chmn. supervisory com. Mountain Bell Credit Un ion, Colorado Springs, 1984—86; guest lectr. Webster U., Colorado Springs, 2003—04. Editor: ASTD newsletter, 1988—89; contbr. articles to profl. jours.; actor: (TV). Vol. mediator BBB, Colorado Springs, 1995—, 4th Jud. Dist. Small Claims Ct., Colorado Springs, 1997—. Named Outstanding Young Bus. and Profl. Person, Rotary Internat., 1986. Mem.: ASTD, Toastmasters (area gov. 1988—89). Avocations: Porsche racing, aviation, photography, camping, commercial acting. Office: The Navigators 3820 N 30th St Colorado Springs CO 80904 Office Phone: 719-594-2362. E-mail: pat.yanney@navigators.org.

**YANNI, JOHN MICHAEL,** pharmacologist; b. St. Mary's, Pa., Nov. 3, 1952; s. John Paul and Regina (Emmert) Y.; m. Nancy Jane Reedy, Sept. 22, 1979; children: Susan Elizabeth, Jennifer Ruth, Steven Reedy. BS, Allegheny Coll., 1974; MS, Va. Commonwealth U., 1979, PhD, 1982; AMP, Harvard U., 2000. Biologist A.H. Robins Co., Richmond, Va., 1980-82; sr. rsch. biologist, 1982-86, rsch. assoc., 1986-88; group leader Eastman Kodak Co., Rochester, N.Y., 1988-90; asst. dir. Alcon Labs., Inc., Ft. Worth, 1990-92, dir., 1992-93, sr. dir., 1993-2000, v.p. pharm rsch. R & D, 2001—. Contbr. articles to profl. jours.; patentee in field. Alden scholar Allegheny Coll., 1974. Mem. Am. Soc. Pharmacology and Exptl. Therapeutics, N.Y. Acad. Sci., Assn. for Rsch. in Vision and Ophthalmology, Soc. for Leukocyte Biology, Am. Acad. Allergy, Asthma and Immunology. Achievements include patents in area of allergy; description of thromboxane A2's muco-secretory effect; identification of antiallergic potential of Arylalkly-heterocyclic amines; discovery of drugs Patanol and Emadine for treatment of ocular allergy; description of secretory response of human conjunctival and choroidal mast cells; discovery of drug Nevanac for inflammation and pain. Office: Alcon Labs Inc 6201 South Fwy Fort Worth TX 76134-2099 Business E-Mail: john.yanni@alconlabs.com.

**YANNONE, RONALD MATTHEW,** systems engineer, researcher; b. Fanny Kalamira Yannone. BSEE, Stevens Inst. Tech., 1976; MSEE, Syracuse U., 1979. Elec. engr. GE, Utica, NY, 1976—91; math tutor Asbury Pk. Mid. Sch., NJ, 1992—95, Brookdale CC, 1992—95; engring. fellow BAE Elec. & Integrated Solutions, Nashua, NH, 1996—. Contbr. articles to profl. jours.; editor: BAE Systems Fellows Periodical, 2004—05. Med. missionary Missionary, Edn. Evangelistic Tng., Huntingdon, Tenn., 1992—95; math problem developer Am. Math. Competitions, Lincoln, Nebr., 1994—. Named to Electronic Warfare Tech. Hall of Fame, 2005. Mem.: Internat. Acad. Sci., Assn. of Old Crows, Mensa Soc. (editor Noesis 2004) Achievements include patents for passive 360-degree target ranging; Commander's Decision Aid (CDA) for U.S. Army ground combat vehicles; passive single-aircraft air-to-air ranging; passive missile time-to-go estimation; patents pending in field. Avocations: reading, puzzles, swimming, rowing, exercise. Home: 189 Ash St #2 Nashua NH 03060 Office: BAE Sys Info and Elec Warfare Sys 95 Canal St Nashua NH 03064 Office Phone: 603-885-0454. Office Fax: 603-885-0698. Business E-Mail: ronald.m.yannone@baesystems.com.

**YANNUCCI, THOMAS DAVID,** lawyer; b. Springfield, Ohio, Mar. 30, 1950; s. David Marion and Patricia (Wilson) Y.; m. Lisa Marie Copeland, June 30, 1972; children: Teresa, Andrea, Thomas D. Jr. AB summa cum laude, U. Notre Dame, 1972, JD cum laude, 1975. Bar: Ohio 1977, U.S. Ct. Appeals (D.C., 1st, 2d, 3d, 4th, 5th, 6th, 7th, 8th, 11th and 10th cirs.) 1980, U.S. Supreme Ct. 1980, D.C. 1981. Law clk. to judge Joseph P. Kinneary US Ct. Appeals (DC cir.), Washington, 1976-77; trial atty. US Dept. Justice, 1977-80; ptnr. Kirkland & Ellis, 1980—, chair firm mgmt. com., 2001—. Editor-in-chief U. Notre Dame Law Rev., 1975-76. Roman Catholic. Office: Kirkland & Ellis LLP 655 15th St NW Ste 1200 Washington DC 20005-5793 Office Phone: 202-879-5000. Office Fax: 202-879-5200. Business E-Mail: tyannucci@kirkland.com.

**YANO, ELIZABETH MARTIN,** epidemiologist, researcher; d. William Oliver Martin and Marjorie Ann Turner; m. Grant Akira Yano, May 3, 1986; children: Michael, David, Steven. BS in Psychobiology, UCLA, 1983, MSPH in Epidemiology, 1986, PhD in Epidemiology, 1995. Rsch. analyst med. outcomes study RAND Corp., Santa Monica, Calif., 1984—86, rsch. epidemiologist, 1986—95; project mgr. dept. medicine UCLA, 1986—88, assoc. prof. health svcs. Sch. Pub. Health, 1997—; sr. assoc. Arlene Fink Assocs., Inc., Pacific Palisades, Calif., 1986—95; assoc. chief pace evaluation Sepulveda (Calif.) VA Med. Ctr., 1989—94, assoc. chief evaluation and decision support, 1994—97; rsch. health scientist VA Health Svcs. R & D Ctr. Excellence, Sepulveda, 1993—97, asst. dir., 1997—99, assoc. dir., 1999—2002, sr. social scientist, 2002—, co-dir. VA associated health postdoctoral trg. program, 2002—04, deputy dir., 2004—. Mem. sci. rev. bd. VA Greater LA Healthcare Sys., 2002—; exec. com. mem. colorectal cancer quality enhancement rsch. initiative Ctr. for Chronic Disease Outcomes Rsch., Mpls., 2001—; mem. nat. ethics task force on gender disparities Dept. Vets., Washington, 2001—; presenter in field. Contbr. articles to profl. jours. Chair VA Women's Health Rsch. Agenda Conf., 2004. Recipient Achievement awards, UCLA Alumni Assn., 1980, 1981, Nat. Psychology Honors award, Psi Chi, 1982; grantee, VA HSR&D Svc., 1997—99, 1998—2002, VHA Survey of Women Veterans Health Programs and Practices, Dept. Vets. Affairs, 2001; Regents scholar, UCLA, 1979—83; Alumni scholar, UCLA Alumni Assn., 1979—83, UCLA Coll. Honors Meeker scholar, UCLA Coll. Honors Program, 1981—82, UCLA Marhoefer Med. scholar, UCLA, 1982—83, Health Policy fellow, RAND-UCLA, Inst. Medicine, Pew Meml. Trusts, 1986—89. Mem.: Acad. Health, Soc. for Gen. Internal Medicine. Office: VA Health Svcs R&D Ctr Excellence 16111 Plummer St 152 Sepulveda CA 91343 Business E-Mail: elizabeth.yano@va.gov.

**YANOFF, MYRON,** ophthalmologist; b. Phila., Dec. 21, 1936; s. Jacob and Lillian S. (Fishman) Yanoff; m. Karin Michelle Lindblad, Aug. 8, 1980; 1 child, Alexis A.;children from previous marriage: Steven L., David A., Joanne

---

M. AB, U. Pa., 1957, MD, 1961. Prof. ophthalmology and pathology U. Pa. Med. Sch., Phila.; William F. Norris and George E. de Schweinitz prof. ophthalmology, chmn. dept., dir. Scheie Eye Inst., 1977-86; chmn., prof. ophthalmology Drexel U., Phila., 1988—. 1st exch. vis. prof. U. Vienna, 1992. Author: Ocular Pathology, Textbook of Ophthalmology; contbr. articles to profl. jours. Served to maj. M.C. USAR. Recipient Humboldt award, 1988. Mem.: Am. Acad. Ophthalmology (Sr. Honor award 1995), Am. Ophthalmic Soc., Verhoeff Soc. Office: 219 N Broad St Fl 3 Philadelphia PA 19107 Office Phone: 215-762-3937. Business E-Mail: myanoff@drexelmed.edu

**YANOFSKY, CHARLES,** retired biology professor; b. NYC, Apr. 17, 1925; s. Frank and Jennie (Kopatz) Y.; m. Carol Cohen, June 19, 1949, (dec. Dec. 1990); children: Stephen David, Robert Howard, Martin Fred; m. Edna Crawford, Jan. 4, 1992. BS, CCNY, 1948; MS, Yale U., 1950, PhD, 1951, DSc (hon.), 1981, U. Chgo., 1980. Rsch. asst. Yale U., 1951-54; asst. prof. microbiology Western Res. U. Med. Sch., 1954-57; mem. faculty Stanford U., 1958—2000, prof. biology, 1961—2000, Herzstein prof. biology, 1966—2000, prof. emeritus, 2000—; ret. Career investigator Am. Heart Assn., 1969-95. Served with AUS, 1944-46. Recipient Lederle Med. Faculty award, 1957, Eli Lilly award bacteriology, 1959, U.S. Steel Co. award molecular biology, 1964, Howard Taylor Ricketts award U. Chgo., 1966, Albert and Mary Lasker award, 1971, Townsend Harris medal Coll. City N.Y., 1973, Louisa Gross Horwitz prize in biology and biochemistry Columbia U., 1976, V.D. Mattia award Roche Inst., 1982, medal Genetics Soc. Am., 1983, Internat. award Gairdner Found., 1985, named Passano Laureate, Passano Found., 1992; recipient William C. Rose award in biochemistry and molecular biology, 1997, Abbott Lifetime Achievement award Am. Soc. Microbiology, 1998, Nat. medal of Sci., 2003. Mem. NAS (Selman A. Waksman award in microbiology 1972), Am. Acad. Arts and Scis., Genetics Soc. Am. (pres. 1969, Thomas Hunt Morgan medal 1990), Am. Soc. Biol. Chemists (pres. 1984), Royal Soc. (fgn. mem.), Japanese Biochem. Soc. (hon.) Home: 725 Mayfield Ave Stanford CA 94305-1016 Office: Stanford U Dept Of Biological Sci Stanford CA 94305

**YANSOUNI, CYRIL J.,** computer company executive; BSEE, U. Louvian, Belgium; MSEE, Stanford U. Various tech. and mgmt. positions including v.p., gen. mgr. Hewlett-Packard Co., 1967-86; pres. Convergent Techs. (now Unisys Corp.), 1986-88; various sr. mgmt. positions including exec. v.p. Unisys Corp., 1988-91; CEO, chmn. Read-Rite, Milpitas, Calif., 1997-2000, chmn., 2000—. Dir. Informix Software, Inc., PeopleSoft, Inc., Raychem Corp., ActiveCard, Inc.

**YANTIS, STEVEN GEORGE,** psychology educator; b. Oct. 24, 1955; BS in Psychology with honors, U. Wash., 1978; PhD in Exptl. Psychology, U. Mich., 1985. Postdoctoral fellow dept. psychology Stanford U., 1985-86; asst. prof. psychology Johns Hopkins U., Balt., 1986-92, assoc. prof. psychology and cognitive sci., 1992-95, prof. psychology, cognitive sci., 1995—. Mem. perception and cognition rsch. rev. com. NIMH, 1993-97, chair, 1996-97, spl. reviewer psychobiology and behavior rsch. rev. com. Mem. editl. bd. Jour. Exptl. Psychology: Human Perception and Performance, 1991—, Perception & Psychophysics, 1991—, Psychol. Bull., 1994-1999, Psychological Science, 1999-2003, Psychonomic Bulletin & Review, 2006-; contbr. articles to profl. jours. Recipient Troland Rsch. award NAS, 1996; NSF grad. fellow, 1981-84; Rackham Dissertation fellow, 1984-85. Mem. APA (Disting. Sci. award for Early Career Contbn. to Psychology 1994), Am. Psychol. Soc., Ea. Psychol. Assn., Psychonomic Soc. Office: Dept Psychology Ames 139 Johns Hopkins Univ Baltimore MD 21218-2686

**YAO, ANDREW CHI-CHIH,** engineering educator; b. Shanghai, Dec. 24, 1946; BS in Physics, Nat. Taiwan U., 1967; AM in Physics, Harvard U., 1969, PhD in Physics, 1972; PhD in Computer Sci., U. Ill., 1975; DSc (hon.), City U. Hong Kong, 2003; DEng (hon.), Hong Kong U. Sci. and Tech., 2004. Rsch. assoc. physics dept. U. Calif., Santa Barbara, 1972—73; asst. prof. math. MIT, 1975—76; asst. prof. computer sci. Stanford U., 1976—81, prof., 1982—86, U. Calif., Berkeley, 1981—82; William and Edna Macaleer prof. engring. and applied sci. Princeton U., 1986—2004; prof. Ctr. Advanced Study Tsinghua U., 2004—; disting. prof.-at-large Chinese U. Hong Kong, 2005—. Vis. scientist IBM Rsch. Ctr., Yorktown Heights, NY, 1975, San Jose, Calif., 1980—81, San Jose, 1982—83, Bell Labs., Murray Hill, NJ, 1978, Xerox Palo Alto Rsch. Ctr., Calif., 1979; cons. DEC Systems Rsch. Ctr., Palo Alto, Calif., 1986, AT&T Bell Labs., Murray Hill, NJ, 1991, Microsoft Rsch. Asia, Beijing, 2003—04. Contbr. articles to profl. jours.; mem. editl. bd.: Jour. Algorithms, 1980—91, SIAM Jour. Computing, 1981—87, mng. editor:, 1989—91, mem. editl. bd.: Jour. Assn. Computing Machinery, 1982—83, Info. and Control, 1982—85, Algorithmica, 1985—, Random Structures & Algorithms, 1990—2002, Jour. Cryptology, 1991—96, mem. adv. bd.: Internat. Jour. Founds. of Computer Sci., 1994—, adv. editor: Jour. Combinatorial Optimization, 1997—, assoc. editor-in-chief: Jour. Software, 2001—. 2nd lt. Taiwan Air Force, 1967—68. Recipient Donald E. Knuth Prize, 1996, Pan Weh-Yuan Rsch. award, 2003. Fellow: AAAS; mem. Soc. Indsl. and Applied Math. (George Polya prize 1987), IEEE, Assn. Computing Machinery (A.M. Turing award 2000), Am. Math Soc., Chinese Acad. Scis. (fgn. mem.), Am. Acad. Arts and Scis., Academia Sinica, NAS. Office: Ctr Advanced Study Tsinghua U Beijing 100084 China E-mail: yao@cs.princeton.edu.*

**YAO, BIN,** mechanical engineering educator; b. Shaanxi, China, Dec. 23, 1968; came to U.S., 1992; s. Weikuan Yao and Qingrong Liu; m. Ying Xie, July 14, 1999 (div. 2003). PhD, U. Calif., Berkeley, 1996. Postdoctoral rschr. mech. engring. dept. U. Calif., Berkeley, 1996; asst. prof. Sch. Mech. Engring. Purdue U., West Lafayette, Ind., 1996—2002, assoc. prof. Sch. Mech. Engring., 2002—. Summer faculty sabbatical leave Advanced Hydraulics Group, Joliet (Ill.) plant, Caterpillar Inc., 1997. Contbr. numerous tech. articles to profl. publs. (NSF Career award 1998). Recipient O. Hugo Schuck Best Paper award Am. Automatic Control Coun., 2004; Regents fellow U. Calif., 1992. Mem. IEEE, ASME. Avocations: sports, travel, art, music. Office: Purdue U Sch Mech Engring West Lafayette IN 47907 Office Phone: 765-494-7746. Office Fax: 765-494-0539. Business E-Mail: byao@ieee.org.

**YAO, DAVID DA-WEI,** engineering educator; b. Shanghai, July 14, 1950; came to U.S., 1983, naturalized, 1990; s. William Kang-Fu and Nancy Yun-Lan (Lu) Y.; m. Helen Zhi-Heng Chen. Jan. 31, 1979; children: Henry, John. MASc, U. Toronto, Ont., Can., 1981, PhD, 1983. Assoc. prof. systems engring. Harvard U., Cambridge, Mass., 1986-88; asst. prof. indsl. engring. and ops. rsch. Columbia U., N.Y.C., 1983-86, prof., 1988—, Thomas Alva Edison prof., 1992—. Acad. visitor AT&T Bell Labs., Holmdel, N.J., 1989, T.J. Watson Rsch. Ctr., IBM, Yorktown, N.Y., 1990—. Co-author: Monotone Structure in Discrete-Event Systems, 1994, Fundamentals of Queueing Networks, 2001, Dynamic Control of Quality in Production-Inventory Systems, 2002; contbr. over 160 articles to profl. jours. including Maths. Ops. Rsch., Jour. of Assn. Computing Machinery, Advances in Applied Probability. Recipient Presdl. Young Investigator award NSF, Washington, 1987-92, Guggenheim fellow John Simon Guggenheim Meml. Found., N.Y.C., 1991-92. Fellow IEEE; mem. Soc. Indsl. and Applied Math. (Outstanding Paper prize 2003), Ops. Rsch. Soc. Am. (George Nicholson prize 1983, Franz Edelman award 1999). Achievements include development of theory of algebraic structures in discrete-event systems, theory of stochastic convexity and its applications in queuing networks, stochastic network models for manufacturing systems and supply chains, methodologies in the optimization and control of stochastic discrete-event systems. Home: 1261 Underhill Ave Yorktown Heights NY 10598-5718 Office: Columbia U IEOR Dept 302 Mudd Bldg New York NY 10027-6699 Business E-Mail: yao@columbia.edu.

**YAO, DONG-QING,** research scientist, educator; b. Suzhou, JiangSu, China, Sept. 23, 1969; s. GuangRui Yao and Meihe Wu; m. Jin Xu, Aug. 25, 1998; children: Anthony, Kathy. PhD, U. Wis., Milw., 2002. Prof. Towson U., Md., 2001—. Mem.: INFORMS. Home: 301 Burke Ave # C Towson MD 21286 Office: Towson U 8000 York Rd Towson MD 21252 Office Phone: 410-704-6185. Business E-Mail: dyao@towson.edu.

**YAO, JIANAN JOHNNY,** research scientist, consultant; MD, Henan Med. U., Zhengzhou, China, 1982; MD, PhD, Beijing Med. U., 1990. Assoc. rsch. prof. Columbia U., NYC, 1991—2003; head ion channel pharmacology, study dir. Quintiles, Inc, Kansas City, Mo., 2003—06; prin. rsch. scientist Wyeth Rsch., Pearl River, NY, 2006—. Program project cons. Columbia U., NYC; reviewer Jour. Cardiovasc. Pharmacology, Jour. Molecular Pharmacology. Personal E-mail: jy18@yahoo.com.

**YAO, JOHN SEN,** physician; b. Honolulu, Aug. 28, 1954; s. Hsin-Hung and Dorothy W. Yao; m. Pauline A. Mysliwiec, Oct. 16, 1993. MPH, Columbia U., 1978, MD, 1983; MBA, UCLA, 1998; MPA, Harvard U., 1999. Diplomate Am. Bd. Internal Medicine, Nat. Bd. Med. Examiners. Resident in internal medicine U. Calif.-San Francisco Med. Ctr., 1983-86, asst. clin. prof., 1988-94; chief med. officer USPHS, Calif., 1990-98; med. dir. Cigna Healthcare, inc., 1997-98; fellow in policy studies Harvard U., Cambridge, Mass., 1998—. Mem. exec. com. State of Calif. TB Control, 1994—; mem. steering com. Breast and Cervical Cancer Prevention, Stte of Calif., 1991-94; med. advisor State of Calif. Medicaid Reform com., 1994-95. Contbr. articles to profl. jours. Med. advisor Gov.'s Coun. on Exercise and Health, Calif., 19945; mem. Calif. HIV-AIDS Commn., 1990-93. Fellow ACP. Avocations: golf, tennis, skiing, classical music, opera. Office: PO Box 191202 San Francisco CA 94119 E-mail: jyaomd@jyaomd.com.

**YAO, MIKE,** otolaryngologist; b. Marietta, Ga., Sept. 20, 1968; s. Lun-Shin Yao and Susan Boyd; m. Pamela Hao Nguyen, Aug. 14, 2004. MD, Yale U., New Haven, Conn., 1994. Asst. prof. U. of Ill., Chgo., 2001—. Organizer Yul Brenner Cancer Screening, Chgo., 2006. Recipient Triologic soc. rsch. grant, Triologic Soc., 1996—97. Mem.: Chgo. Larynogologic Soc. (life; coun. of seven 2004—05). Office: U Ill M/C 648 1855 W Taylor St Chicago IL 60612 Office Phone: 312 413 4240. Office Fax: 312-996-4910. E-mail: myao@uic.edu.

**YAO, MINGZHONG,** medical researcher, educator; arrived in U.S., 2002; M of Medicine, Shanghai U. of Traditional Chinese Medicine, 1995, PhD, 2000. From asst. instr. to instr. Danyang Med. Sch., Jiangsu, China, 1982—92; asst. prof. Shanghai U. of Traditional Chinese Medicine, 1995—98, assoc. prof., 1999—2000; postdoctoral rschr., assoc. prof. Inst. Biochemistry and Cell Biology, Chinese Acad. Scis., Shanghai, 2000—02; rschr. U. So. Calif., L.A., 2002—. Contbr. articles to profl. jours., chapters to books in field. Recipient Basic Sci. Rsch. award, State Adminstrn. Traditional Chinese Medicine, 1998, Sci. Achievement award, Shanghai Sci. and Tech. Com., 1997, 1st Prize natural sci. thesis contest, China Gene Net, 2002. Mem.: Am. Soc. Neurosci., Internat. Soc. Interferon and Cytokine Rsch., Sigma Xi. Achievements include patents for method for treating chronic ache using interleukin-2 gene therapy and construction of related vectors; testing method in application of interleukin-2 and its gene to morphine withdrawal syndrome. Office: U So Calif 3715 McClintock Ave Los Angeles CA 90089 E-mail: myao@usc.edu.

**YAO, TESSA LORIEN,** portfolio manager; arrived in U.S., 1991; m. H. C. Yao; 1 child, Stella. BA in Econs., U. Calif., L.A., 1995; MBA, Woodbury U., Burbank, Calif., 2003. Sr. account exec. Fleishman Hillard, L.A., 1999—2003. Fin. writer Glendale News-Press, Glendale, Calif. Contbr. columns in newspapers. Named Intramural Tennis Champion, U. Calif., L.A., 1992; scholar, Shaw Found., 1990. Mem.: Soc. Prevention Cruelty to Animals, Mensa, Delta Mu Delta. Avocations: tennis, horseback riding, snowboarding, travel.

**YAO, TITO GO,** pediatrician; b. Manila, May 30, 1943; arrived in U.S., 1970, naturalized, 1984; s. Vincente and Sin Keng (Go) Yao; m. Lilia Ytem, July 3, 1976; children: Robert, James, Richard. MD, Far Eastern U., Manila, 1969. Diplomate Am. Bd. Pediatrics, Am. Bd. Quality Assurance. Intern Evang. Deaconess Hosp., Milw., 1970-71; resident in pediatrics T.C. Thompson Children's Hosp., Chattanooga, 1971-72, Meth. Hosp., Bklyn., 1972-73; fellow St. Christopher Hosp. Children, Phila., 1973-74, Cook County Children's Hosp., Chgo., 1974-75; dir. GSK Med. Ctr., Chgo., 1976—; preceptor Rush Med. Coll., 2003—. Chmn. dept. pediat. St. Anne's Hosp., Chgo., 1986—88, Loretto Hosp., Chgo., 1988—; dir. RJ Med. Ctr., Chgo., 1980—; mem. staff Norwegian Am. Hosp., St. Anthony's Hosp., St. Mary Nazareth Hosp. Fellow: Am. Coll. Utilization Rev. Physicians, Am. Acad. Pediat. (life) mem.: AMA (life Physician Recognition award 1973—), Chgo. Pediatric Soc., Chgo. Med. Soc., Am. Assn. Individual Investors, Ill. Med. Assn., Assn. Philippine Physicians Practicing in Am. Home: 5140 W Chicago Ave Chicago IL 60651-2903 Office Phone: 773-287-0751. Personal E-mail: titogyao@aol.com.

**YAO, YONGXUE,** immunologist; b. Hengshui, China, Oct. 23, 1971; s. Yusheng Yao and Shuhui Wang; m. Zhuo Wang, Aug. 30, 1997; 1 child, Daniel. MD, China Med. U., Shenyang, 1996; PhD, Fukui Med. U., Japan, 2003. Diplomate China Med. U., Shenyang, 1996. Resident China Med. U., Shenyang, China, 1996—97; postdoctoral fellow U. Sch. of Medicine, Indpls., 2003—05, rsch. assoc. Grantee Postdoctoral Fellowship, AHA, 2004, 2005—06; Monbosho Scholarship, Japanese Gov., 1997—2003. Communist. Achievements include research in role of interleukine-4 indendritic cell-mediated immunity. Avocations: swimming, reading. Home: 3735 Wishbone Blvd Indianapolis IN 46268 Office: Indiana Univ Sch of Medicine 950 W Walnut St Indianapolis IN 46202 Office Phone: 317-274-7517. Business E-Mail: yonyao@iupui.edu.

**YAO, YU-DONG,** electrical engineer, educator, electrical engineer, researcher; PhD, SE U., Nanjing, China, 1988. Rsch. assoc. Carleton U., Ottawa, Ont., Canada, 1989—90; mem. tech. staff, sr. mem. tech. staff Spar Aerospace Ltd., Montreal, Que., Canada, 1990—94; sr. engr., staff engr. Qualcomm, Inc., San Diego, Calif., 2000; assoc. prof. Stevens Inst. Tech., Hoboken, NJ, 2000—. Mem. IEEE. Achievements include patents in field. Office: Stevens Institute Technology Castle Point on Hudson Hoboken NJ 07030 Office Phone: 201-216-5264.

**YAPLE, HENRY MACK,** librarian; b. Vicksburg, Mich., May 30, 1940; s. Henry J. and Pauline B. (Spencer) Y.; m. Marilyn Lou Bales, Dec. 31, 1971; children: Sean H., Kendra S. BA in English with hons., Kalamazoo Coll., 1963; MA, U. Idaho, 1966; postgrad., U. d'Aix-Marseille, France, 1965-66, U. Toronto, 1966-69; MLS, W. Mich. U., 1972. Order libr. Mich. State U., E. Lansing, 1972-74, humanities bibliographer, 1974-78; acquisitions libr. U. Wyo., Laramie, 1978-87; coll. libr. Whitman Coll., Walla Walla, Wash., 1987—. mem. Wyo. Coun. for the Humanities, 1982-86. Author: Spartan Poets: A Preliminary Checklist, 1955-1978, 1978, Programmed Instruction in Librarianship: A Classified Bibliography 1960-74, 1976, Ski Bibliography, 1890-2002, 2004. U. Toronto scholar, 1966-69; Rotary fellow, 1965, 66; U. Wyo. rsch. grantee, 1982, 86. Mem. ALA, Wyo. Libr. Assn. (pres. 1984-85), Nat. Ski Patrol System (sr. patroller 1978-95, nat. #6946 1988), Wash. Libr. Assn., Northwest Assn. of Pvt. Colls. and U. Librs. (pres. 1987-88, 94-95), Beta Phi Mu. Avocations: book collecting, skiing, kayaking. Home: 1889 Fern St Walla Walla WA 99362-9393 Office: Whitman Coll Penrose Libr 345 Boyer Ave Walla Walla WA 99362-2067 E-mail: yaple@whitman.edu.

**YARAGUDRI, VINOD K.,** neuroscientist, researcher; b. Belgaum, Karanataka, India, July 11, 1973; s. Kallappa V. and Ratna K. Yaragudri; m. Shilpa Sulebhavi, Apr. 3, 2003; 1 child, Nathan. BS, Karanatak U., Dharwad, India, 1994, MS, 1996; PhD, NIMH and Neuroscience, Bangalore, India, 2002. Rsch. scholar NIMH and Neuroscis., Banaglore, India, 1996—97, sr. rsch. scholar, 1997—2001; rsch. project mgr. Nathan S. Kline Inst. Psychiat. Rsch., Orangeburg, NY, 2002—03, asst. rsch. scientist, 2003—05, assoc. rsch. scientist, 2005—; rsch. project mgr. N.Y. State Psychiat. Inst., N.Y., 2002—03, asst. rsch. scientist, 2003—05, assoc. rsch. scientist, 2005—. Contbr. articles to profl. jours. Founder Narayana Rural Devel. Soc., Mudhol, India, 2003. Recipient Academic Excellence Gold medal, Karnatak U., Dharwad, India, 1997, Burswood Rsch. Poster award, Asian Pacific Congress Clin. Biochemistry, 2003; fellow, Lady Tata Meml. Trust, India, 1998, Indian

Coun. Med. Rsch., 1999—2001, Internat. Brain Rsch. Orgn., 2001, Rsch. Found. Mental Hygeine, 2002—; grantee, Am. Found. Suicide Prevention, 2004—06; scholar, Karnataka State Tchr.'s Assn., Bangalore, India, 1991, Jindal Aluminium Trust, Bangalore, India, 1994—96. Mem.: Am. Found. Suicide Prevention (hon.), Soc. Biol. Psychiatry (assoc.), Internat. Cannabinoid Rsch. Soc. (assoc.), Rsch. Soc. Alcoholism (assoc.), Schizophrenia Rsch. Forum (life), Indian Acad. Neurosci. (life), Internat. Brain Rsch. Orgn. (life). Achievements include research in the implication of the role of the brain endocannabinoid system in major depressive disorder and suicide. Home: 120 Nottingham Ct Montvale NJ 07645 Office: Nathan Kline Inst 140 Old Orangeburg Rd Orangeburg NY 10962 Office Phone: 845-398-5454. Office Fax: 845-398-5451. Personal E-mail: ky_vinod@yahoo.com. Business E-Mail: vyaragudri@nki.rfmh.org.

**YARASHESKI, KEVIN EDWARD,** medical educator; s. Edward and Elsie Yarasheski; m. Jill Andrea Campbell, July 7, 1995; 1 child, Curtis Alexander. PhD, Kent State U., 1986. Grantee, NIH, 1989—. Mem.: Am. Physiol. Soc. (assoc.). Achievements include research in Pathogenesis and treatments for metabolic syndromes. Office: Washington U Sch Medicine 660 S Euclid Ave Metabolism Box 8127 Saint Louis MO 63110 Office Phone: 314-362-8173.

**YARBOROUGH, CLINTON JOSEPH,** lawyer; b. Ft. Leavenworth, Kans., Dec. 28, 1969; s. William Glenn and Betsy Yarborough; m. Patsy Lee, Aug. 16, 1997; child, CJ. BS, Coll. Charleston, 1991; JD, U. S.C., 1993. Bar: S.C. 1994, Ga. 1995, U.S. Dist. Ct. (so. dist.) S.C. 1995, U.S. Supreme Ct. 2000. Title abstractor Woodward, Leventis, Unger, Daves, Herndon & Cothran, Columbia, S.C., 1992-94; forclosure atty. Ronald C. Scott, P.A., Columbia, 1994-95; asst. pub. defender Defender Corp Aiken County, Aiken, S.C., 1995-98; asst. dist. atty. Toombs Judicial Cir., Thomson, Ga., 1998-99; assoc. Jackson R. Massey & Assocs., P.C., Augusta, Ga., 1999-2000, Rogers, Townsend & Thomas, P.C., Columbia, SC, 2000—02; v.p. underwriting and claims counsel Atlantic Title Ins. Co., Columbia, 2002—03; assoc. state counsel First Am. Title Ins. Co., Columbia, 2003—. Mem. ABA, Sigma Chi, Rotary Internat. Roman Catholic. Avocations: archaeology, reading, anthropology, forestry. Office: PO Box 1462 Columbia SC 29202 Office Phone: 803-731-4409. Business E-Mail: cjyarborough@firstam.com.

**YARBOROUGH, WILLIAM GLENN, JR.,** military officer, forester; b. June 21, 1940; s. William Glenn and Bessie (Rainsford) Y.; m. Betsy Gibson, Jan. 24, 1969; children: Bill, Clinton, Frank, Elizabeth. BS, U. S.C., 1961, MBA, 1969; postgrad., Command and Gen. Staff Coll., 1970, Naval War Coll., 1979, U. Va., 1983. Commd. to U.S. Army, advanced through grades to col., 1980, co. and troop comdr., squadron staff officer Vietnam and Europe, 1961-71, strategist Washington, 1971-73; chief of assignments Office Pers. Mgmt. Mil. Pers. Ctr., Washington, 1973-76; comdr. 1st Squadron 1st Cavalry, Europe, 1976-78; chief of staff, spl. asst. to chief of staff 1st Armored Divsn., Europe, 1978; br. chief Office of Chief of Staff, Washington, 1979-80; exec. to dep. comdg. gen. Material Devel. and Readiness Command, Washington, 1980-81; mil. dep. for asst. sec. for rsch., devel. and acquisition Washington, 1981-85; dir. ops. Ford Aerospace, Washington, 1986—89; army mktg. dir. Grumman Corp., Bethpage, NY, 1990-93; pres., CEO Allied Rsch. Corp., Vienna, Va., 1993—2001; founder & prin. WGY & Assocs. Bd. dirs. Carleton Techs., Eads N.Am. Def. Co., Am. Conversion Corp., Old Dominion Corp. Trustee Patton Mus.; bd. dirs. So Others Might Eat (Some), Easter Seals; bd. dirs. Moore Sch. Bus. U. S.C. Decorated Silver Star, Bronze Star medal with 4 oak leaf clusters and V device, Purple Heart, Legion of Merit. Mem. VFW, SAR, Assn. U.S. Army (George Washington chpt., v.p. membership), Am. Legion, Armed Forces Comms. and Electronics Assn., U.S. Army Armor Assn., Nat. Def. Indsl. Assn. (bd. dirs. N.Y. chpt.), Rotary Internat., Mil. Order of the World Wars, N.G. Assn., Res. Officers Assn., Soc. of the Purple Heart, Army-Navy Club, Army Navy Country Club, Belle-Meade Country Club, Tower Club. Home: Box 115 Thomson GA 30824-0115 Office: Box 828 Mc Lean VA 22101 Office Phone: 703-748-1717. Personal E-mail: wgyarc@aol.com.

**YARBROUGH, ALLYSON DEBRA,** electrical engineer; b. Peterborough, England, Feb. 14, 1958; d. Freddy Dekhoma and Rosalind Mavis Y.; m. John Russell Scarpulla, May. 8, 1990. BSEE, N.Mex. State U., 1979; MSEE, Cornell U., 1985, PhD in Elec. Engring., 1988. Rsch. asst. Nat. Atmospheric and Ionospheric Ctr., Arecibo, P.R., 1979; microwave applications engr. Hewlett-Packard Co., Santa Rosa, Calif., 1979-82; assoc. prof. Calif. State U., L.A., 1988-89; tech. staff Aerospace Corp., El Segundo, Calif., 1989-93, sect. mgr., 1993-99, dept. dir., 1999—. Mem. IEEE, Microwave Theory and Techniques Soc., Alpha Kappa Alpha, Eta Kappa Nu. Democrat. Roman Catholic. Avocations: woodworking, sewing, collecting vintage radios. Home: 26821 Grays Lake Rd Palos Verdes Estates CA 90275 Office Phone: 310-375-9695. Personal E-mail: blue.onyx@verizon.net.

**YARBROUGH, FRANCES CAROLE,** music educator; b. Memphis, Aug. 28, 1938; d. Frank Chester Masserano and Iris Marcella Viehe; m. William Hugh Yarbrough Sr., Apr. 16; children: William Hugh Jr., Darrell Craig. B in Music Edn., McNeese State U., 1983; M in Sacred Music, Logos Grad. Sch., 2000. Music evangelist, Memphis, 1959—68, Christian Assemblies of God, Sherwood, Ark., 1968—76, Lake Area Worship Ctr., Westlake, La., 1979—2004, pastor; music tchr., music evangelist, 2004—. Mem.: Lake Charles Piano Tchrs. Assn., Nat. Music Tchrs. Assn., Sigma Alpha Iota. Address: PO Box 154 Westlake LA 70669 Office Phone: 337-912-9530.

**YARBROUGH, KATHRYN DAVIS,** public health nurse; b. Montrose, Colo., Aug. 31, 1947; d. L.O. and V. Jean (Dunn) Davis; m. James H. Yarbrough, Aug. 8, 1970; children: James, Jason. Diploma, Good Samaritan Hosp. Sch. Nursing, Phoenix, 1971; BSN, Kennesaw State Coll., 1996. RN, Ga.; cert. NAACOG. Supr. Cherokee County Health Dept., Canton, Ga., 1976-97. Den mother Boy Scouts Am., Canton, 1986-87; bd. dirs. Cancer soc., Canton, 1987—, Cherokee County Violence Ctr., 1990, First Steps Bd., 1993-97, Cherokee County Advocacy Ctr., 1994-97; HIV cons. ARC, Canton, 1988—, disaster vol., Cherokee County, 1993-99; co-chair Early Intervention Coun., Canton, 1991-93; mem. Leadership Cherokee, 1994, Literacy Coun., 1994; mem. Blue Ridge Jud. Cir. Domestic Violence Task Force, 1995. Mem.: ANA, Ga. Nurses Assn., Svc. League Cherokee County (hon.). Methodist. E-mail: Kyarbro216@aol.com.

**YARBROUGH, MARTHA CORNELIA,** music educator; b. Waycross, Ga., Feb. 8, 1940; d. Henry Elliott and Jessie (Sirmans) Y. BME, Stetson U., 1962; MME, Fla. State U., 1968, PhD, 1973. Choral dir. Ware County H.S., Waycross, 1962-64, Glynn Acad., Brunswick, Ga., 1964—70; asst. choral dir. Fla. State U., 1970-72; cons. in music Muscogee County Sch. Dist., Columbus, Ga., 1972-73; cons. in tchr. edn. Psycho-Edno. Cons., Inc., Tallahassee, 1972-73; asst. prof. music edn., dir. choruses and oratorio socs. Syracuse (NY) U., 1973-76; assoc. prof. music edn. Syracuse U., 1976-83, prof., 1983-86; acting asst. dean Coll. Visual and Performing Arts, 1980-82, acting dir. Sch. Music, 1980-82, chmn. music edn., 1982-86; prof. music La. State U., Baton Rouge, 1986—; coord. music edn., 1986—2000, Haymon prof. of music, 1995—, disting. rsch. master arts, humanities, social scis., 2004. Artist-in-residence Sch. Music U. Ala., Tuscaloosa, 1989-90, 98, 2002; chair exec. com. Music Edn. Rsch. Coun., 1992-94. Co-author: Competency-Based Music Education, 1980; mem. editl. com.: Jour. Rsch. in Music Edn., editor-in-chief:, 2000—; contbr. chapters to books, articles to profl. jours. Recipient Disting. Rsch. Master of Arts, Humanities and Social Scis. award, La. State U., 2004. Mem. Music Educators Nat. Conf. (Sr. Rschr. award 1996), La. State Music Assn., Am. Ednl. Rsch. Assn., Soc. Rsch. Music Edn. (mem. exec. com. 1988-90, program chair 1990-92, chair 1992-94), AAUP, Coll. Music Soc., Pi Kappa Lambda, Phi Beta, Kappa Delta Pi. Office: Sch Music La State U Baton Rouge LA 70803-2504 Office Phone: 225-578-2481. Business E-Mail: cyarbro@lsu.edu.

**YARCHOAN, ROBERT,** clinical immunologist, researcher; b. N.Y.C., July 21, 1950; s. Zachary and Anne Mae (Veneroso) Y.; m. Giovana Tosato; children: Mark, John. BA magna cum laude, Amherst Coll., 1971; MD, U. Pa., 1975. Diplomate Am. Bd. Internal Medicine, Am. Bd. Allergy and Immunology. Resident in medicine U. Minn. Hosps., Mpls., 1975-78; clin. assoc. metabolism br. Nat. Cancer Inst., Bethesda, Md., 1978-80, investigator metabolism br., 1980-83, investigator clin. oncology program, 1983-87, sr. investigator clin. oncology program, 1988-91, chief retroviral diseases sect. medicine br., 1991-96, chief HIV and AIDS malignancy br., 1996—. Co-author: (chpt.) Cecil Textbook of Medicine, 1992, 95, 99; assoc. editor Jour. Immunology, 1985-89, AIDS Rsch. and Human Retroviruses, 1986-2004, AIDS, 1990-00, Jour. AIDS, 2000-06, Jour. Human Virology, 2002-04, Infectious Agents and Cancer, 2006-; sect. editor Thymus, 1992-97; contbr. articles to sci. jours.; patentee in field. Capt. USPHS, 1978—. Recipient Commendation medal USPHS, 1991, Asst. Sec. Health award U.S. govt. Dept. Health & Human Svcs., 1989, Inventors award U.S. Dept. Commerce, 1986, 87, Fed. Tech. Transfer Act award, 1999, 2000, 01, Outstanding Svc. medal USPHS, 2002. Fellow AAAS; mem. Am. Soc. Hematology, Am. Assn. Immunologists, Clin. Immunology Soc., Am. Soc. for Clin. Investigation, Internat. AIDS Soc. Achievements include co-inventor of therapies for AIDS and AIDS malignancies including ddI (didanosine) and ddC (zalcitabine) for AIDS and IL-12 for Kaposi's sarcoma; co-developer of therapies for AIDS and AIDS malignancies including AZT (zidovudine) for AIDS and paclitaxel for Kaposi's sarcoma; research in interactions between viruses and the immune system, therapy of AIDS and virally induced tumors; pathogenesis of AIDS and viral-induced tumors.

**YARDE, RICHARD FOSTER,** art educator; b. Boston, Oct. 29, 1939; s. Edgar St. Clair and Enid (Foster) Y.; m. Susan Donovan, July 8, 1967; children: Marcus, Owen. BFA in Painting cum laude, Boston U., 1962, MFA, 1964; DFA (hon., Mass. Coll. Art, 2002. Asst. prof. art Boston U., 1965-71; assoc. prof. art Wellesley Coll., 1971-76; vis. assoc. prof. Amherst Coll., 1976-77, Mt. Holyoke Coll., 1980-81; vis. artist Mass. Coll. Art, 1977-80; prof. art U. Mass., Boston, 1981-90, Amherst, 1990—. Visual arts panelist Mass. Coun. Art and Humanities, 1976-78; bd. overseers Inst. Contemporary Art, Boston, 1991-2003; panelist Painting Mass. Cultural Coun. One-man shows include Studio Mus. in Harlem, San Diego Mus., Balt. Mus., Smith Coll. Mus. Art, Northampton, Mass., 1977, Mass. Coll. Art, 1996—99, Worcester Mus. Art, 2003, exhibited in group shows at Newport (RI) Art Mus., Nat. Acad. Design, N.Y.C. and Mass., Smithsonian Inst., Washington, 1999, New Mus. Contemporary Art, N.Y.C., 1999, Mus. Fine Arts, Boston, 1999, Master Drawings from the Smith Coll. Art Mus., Lacaixa and Madrid, 2002, DeCordova Mus., Lincoln, Mass., 2002, Inst. Contemporary Art, Boston, 2003, Heckscher Mus. Art, Huntington, NY, 2003, NAS, Washington, 2004—05, Sheldon Meml. Art Gallery U. Nebr., Lincoln, Nat. Acad. Design, 2005, Boston U. Art Gallery, 2005—06, Danforth Mus. Art, Framingham, Mass., 2005. Recipient Alumni award for disting. contbn. to arts Boston U., 1987, Chancellor's award disting. scholarship U. Mass., Boston, 1984, Acad. award in art Am. Acad. Arts and Letters, 1995, Disting. Tchg. award U. Mass. Amherst, 1997, Works on Paper award New Eng. Found. Arts, Boston, 1998, honoree Studio Mus. in Harlem Gala, N.Y.C., 2001; Nat. Endowment Arts fellow, 1976, Samuel F. Conti faculty fellow U. Mass., 2000, When the Spirit Moves Group Exhib., Spelman Coll. Mus., 2000, Charles Wright Mus., 2000, Commonwealth Award, Artist Category, Mass. Cultural Council, 2001, William P. and Gertrude Schweitzer prize Nat. Acad. Design, N.Y., Amherst, Mass.; NAD (academician 1994—). Office: U Mass Amherst Fine Arts Ctr Dept Art and Art History 151 Pres Dr Office1 Amherst MA 01003-4330 E-mail: rfyarde@art.u.mass.edu.

**YARDLEY, BILL,** journalist; Reporter New York Times. Office: The New York Times Hartfor Bur 210 Capitol Ave Rm 409 A Hartford CT 06106*

**YARDLEY, JIM,** journalist; b. NYC, June 18, 1964; married; 3 children. BA in hist., U. NC at Chapel Hill, 1986. With Times Cmty. Newspapers, Fairfax County, Va., Anniston Star, Ala.; nat. desk reporter Atlanta Journal-Constitution, 1990—97; met. reporter NY Times, NYC, 1997—99, bur. chief Houston, 1999—2003, fgn. corr. Beijing, 2003—. Recipient Pulitzer Prize for internat. reporting (with James Kahn), 2006. Office: NY Times 229 W 43rd St New York NY 10036*

**YARDLEY, JONATHAN,** journalist; b. Pitts., Oct. 27, 1939; s. William Woolsey and Helen (Gregory) Y.; m. Rosemary Roberts, June 14, 1961 (div. 1975); children: James Barrett, William W. II.; m. Susan L. Hartt, Mar. 23, 1975 (div. 1998); m. Marie Arana, Mar. 22, 1999. AB, U. N.C., 1961; DHL (hon.), George Washington U., 1987. Writer N.Y. Times, 1961—64; editl. writer, book editor Greensboro (N.C.) Daily News, 1964—74; book editor Miami (Fla.) Herald, 1974—78, Washington Star, 1978—81; book critic Washington Post, 1981—. Author: Ring: A Biography of Ring Lardner, 1977, Our Kind of People: The Story of an American Family, 1989, Out of Step: Notes from a Purple Decade, 1991, States of Mind: A Personal Journey Through the Mid-Atlantic, 1993, Misfit: The Strange Life of Frederick Exley, 1997, Monday Morning Quarterback, 1998; editor: My Life as Author and Editor (H.L. Mencken), 1993, Selected Stories (Ring Lardner), 1997. Recipient Pulitzer prize for criticism, 1981, Disting. Alumnus award U. N.C., 1989; Nieman fellow in journalism Harvard U., 1968-69. Address: Malecon de la Reserva 801 Miaflores Lima 18 Peru Office: Washington Post 1150 15th St NW Washington DC 20071-0001 Home: 1500 Vermont Ave NW 1 Washington DC 20005 Office Phone: 202-544-7779. E-mail: yardleyj@washpost.com.

**YARES, RIVA,** art dealer, writer, publishing executive; b. Tel-Aviv, Aug. 17, 1940; d. Fishel and Sala (Singer) Kilstok; single; children: Dennis, Shelli Yares Poulos. BA in Art and Psychology, U. Jerusalem. Art dealer Riva Yares Gallery, Scottsdale, Ariz., 1964—, Santa Fe, 1990—, Riva Yares Sculpture Pk., Ariz., 1985—. Pres. Pueblo Arts & Real Estate, Scottsdale, Ariz., 1970—. Author various books on artists. Recipient Archtl. award City of Scottsdale, 1972. Mem. Charter 100. Avocations: animals, dogs. Office: Riva Yares Gallery 3625 N Bishop Ln Scottsdale AZ 85251-5511

**YARGER, JAMES RICHARD,** protective services official, director; b. Hastings, Mich., Aug. 26, 1961; m. Dana Drummond-Rittenberg, Dec. 29, 2005; children: Michael James, Briana, Max Rittenberg, Mason Rittenberg. Fire chief Freeport Rural Fire Assn., Mich., 1996—; dir. Barry County Emergency Mgmt. Dept., Hastings, Mich., 2004—. Coun. mem. Village of Freeport, Mich., 1996—2000; vol. firefighter Freeport Area Vol. Fire Dept., Mich., 1979—96. Mem.: Nat. Fire Protection Assn., Emergency Mgmt. Dirs. Assn. of Mich., Internat. Assn. of Fire Chiefs. Home: 1451 Session Rd Freeport MI 49325 Office: Barry County Emergency Mgmt Dept 220 W State St Hastings MI 49058 Office Phone: 269-945-1412. Office Fax: 269-948-4884. Personal E-mail: chiefywiefy820@yahoo.com. E-mail: jyarger@barrycounty.org.

**YARI, BOB,** film company executive, film producer; Diploma in Cinematography. Owner El Camino Pictures, Bull's Eye Entertainment, Syndicate Films Internat., Bob Yari Prodns., Stratus Film Co., LA. Dir., exec. prodr.: (films) Mind Games, 1989; prodr.: Perfect Fit, 1999, Where the Red Fern Grows, 2003, Employee of the Month, 2004, Agent Cody Banks 2: Destination London, 2004, House of D, 2004, A Love Song for Bobby Long, 2004, Crash, 2004 (Best First Feature, Independent Spirit award, 2006), Haven, 2004, Hostage, 2005; prodr.: Agent Cody Banks, 2003, Devil's Pond, 2003, Sueno, 2004, In Enemy Hands, 2004, Laws of Attraction, 2004, Around the Bend, 2004, Thumbsucker, 2005, The Matador, 2005, The Chumscrubber, 2005, The LA Riot Spectacular, 2005. Named one of 50 Most Powerful People in Hollywood, Premiere mag. 2005. Office: Stratus Film Co 10850 Wilshire Blvd 6th Fl Los Angeles CA 90024 Office Phone: 310-234-8970. Office Fax: 310-234-8975.

**YARINGTON, CHARLES THOMAS, JR.,** surgeon, educator, health facility administrator; b. Sayre, Pa., Apr. 26, 1934; s. C.T. and Florence (Hutchinson) Yarington; m. Barbara Taylor Johnson, Sept. 28, 1963; children:

Leslie Anne, Jennifer Lynne, Barbara Jane. AB, Princeton U., 1956; MD, Hahnemann Med. Coll., 1960; grad., Army Command and Gen. Staff Coll., 1969, Air War Coll., 1973, Indsl. Coll. Armed Forces, 1974. Intern Rochester Gen. Hosp., NY, 1960-61; resident Dartmouth Hosp., 1961-62, U. Rochester Strong Meml. Hosp., 1962-65; instr. otolaryngology U. Rochester Sch. Medicine, 1962-65; chief ENT US Army Hosp., Ft. Carson, Colo., 1965—67; asst. prof. surgery W.Va. U. Sch. Medicine, 1967-68; assoc. prof., chmn. dept. otorhinolaryngology U. Nebr. Med. Ctr., 1968-69, prof., chmn. dept. otorhinolaryngology, 1969-74; clin. prof. otolaryngology U. Wash., Seattle, 1974—; clin. prof. surgery Uniformed Svcs. U. Health Scis., Bethesda, Md., 1985—; chief otolaryngology Virginia Mason Med. Ctr., Seattle, 1978-88, 92-95, chief dept. surgery, 1988-91; surgeon Mason Clinic, Seattle, 1974-97. Cons. Surg. Gen. USAF, Hunter Group Med. Mgmt. Cons., 1996-98, Seattle Multispecialty Panel, 1998—; pres. Virginia Mason Rsch. Ctr., Seattle, 1983-85; trustee Mason Clinic, 1988-91; adv. coun. Nat. Inst. Neurol. Diseases, Communicative Diseases, Stroke of NIH, Bethesda, Md., 1986-90; bd. dirs. Virginia Mason Hosp., Virginia Mason Med. Ctr., bd. govs., 1989-98; mem. bd. regents Uniformed Svcs. U. Health Scis., Bethesda. Mem. editl. bd. Aviation, Space, Environ. Med. Jour., Otol. Clinics of N.Am., Mil. Medicine, Otolaryngology-Head and Neck Surgery; contbr. articles to profl. jours. Trustee Seattle Opera Assn., 1983-89. Served to lt. col. USAR, 56-70, to brig. gen. USAF, 1970-86. Decorated D.S.M., Legion of Merit, comdr. Venerable Order St. John (Gt. Britain), companion with star Order Orthodox Hospitallers (Republic of Cypress), knight grand cross Mil. and Hospitaller Order of St. Lazarus; recipient Sir Henry Wellcome medal, 1984. Fellow ACS, Royal Soc. Medicine, Am. Acad. Otolaryngology (Barraquer Meml. award 1968, mem. standing com., bd. govs. 1982-88, Honor award 1974); mem. AMA, Am. Broncho-Esophagological Assn. (coun., treas. 1982-86, pres. 1987-88), Am. Laryngol. Assn., Pacific Coast Soc. Ophthalmology and Otolaryngology (coun., pres. 1987-88), Soc. Med. Cons. to Armed Forces, Am. Soc. Head and Neck Surgery, N.W. Acad. Head and Neck Surgery (pres. 1984-86), Am. Soc. Otology, Rhinology and Laryngology (v.p. 1992-93, coun. 1997-2000), Res. Officers Assn. (past pres. Seattle chpt., nat. officer), Soc. Colonial Wars, Sons Revolution (pres. Wash. 1985-87), Internat. Power Boat Assn. (comdr. 1999-2000), Seattle Yacht Club (trustee 2001-05), Princeton Quadrangle Club, Broadmoor Golf Club, RAF Club (London), Sigma Xi. Home and Office: 2136 38th Ave E Seattle WA 98112

YARIV, AMNON, electrical engineering educator, research scientist; b. Tel Aviv, Apr. 13, 1930; arrived in U.S., 1951, naturalized, 1964; s. Shraga and Henya (Davidson) Y.; m. Frances Pokras, Apr. 10, 1972; children: Elizabeth, Dana, Gabriela. BS, U. Calif., Berkeley, 1954, MS, 1956, PhD, 1958. Mem. tech. staff Bell Telephone Labs., 1959-63; dir. laser research Watkins-Johnson Co., 1963-64; mem. faculty Calif. Inst. Tech., 1964—, Martin Summerfield prof. applied physics, 1966—. Co-founder Xponent, Orbits Corp., Teleris Corp., Inc. Author: Quantum Electronics, 1967, 75, 85, Introduction to Optical Electronics, 1971, 77, 89, Theory and Applications of Quantum Mechanics, Propagation of Light in Crystals. With Israeli Army, 1948—50. Recipient Pender award U. Pa., Harvey prize Technion, Israel, 1992. Fellow IEEE (Quantum Electronics award 1980), Am. Optical Soc. (Ives medal 1986, Esther Beller medal 1998), Am. Acad. Arts and Scis.; mem. NAS, NAE, Am. Phys. Soc. Office: 1201 E California Blvd Pasadena CA 91125-0001 Business E-Mail: ziemer@eas.uccs.edu.

YARKONY, GARY MICHAEL, physician, researcher; b. N.Y.C., May 22, 1953; m. Kirsten Kohlmeyer; children: Judith, Rachel, Seth, Lauren. BA in Biology, SUNY, Buffalo, 1974; MD, SUNY, Syracuse, 1978; Master in Mgmt., Northwestern U., 1994. Intern, then resident in physical medicine, rehab. Northwestern U., Chgo., 1978—81, chief resident dept. rehab. medicine, 1980; asst. dir. head trauma program Rehab. Inc. Chgo., 1981—84, attending staff, 1981—94; chief of rehab. svcs. U. Chgo. Hosps. Rehab. Ctr., 1994—2000; clin. prof. sect. orthopaedic surgery and rehab. medicine U. Chgo. Med. Ctr., 1995—2000, clin. prof. dept. surgery and neurology, 1995—2000; clin. prof. dept. rehab. medicine Chgo. Med. Sch., 2000—. Attending physician Northwestern Meml. Hosp., Chgo., 1984-94, Provera St. Joseph's Hosp., Elgin, Ill., 2000—; assoc. prof. dept. rehab. medicine Northwestern U. Med. Sch., 1985-94; adj. prof. Pritzker Inst. for Med. Engring., Ill. Inst. Tech., 1991-97; dir. rehab. Midwest Regional Spinal Cord Injury Care Sys., Chgo., 1984-94; dir. rsch. Schwab Rehab. Hosp., 1997-2000. Contbr. articles to profl. jours. and chpts. to book. Fellow Am. Acad. Physical Medicine and Rehab.; mem. Assn. Academic Physiatrists, Am. Spinal Injury Assn., Internat. Med. Soc. Paraplegia, Internal Rehab. Medicine Assn., Phi Beta Kappa, Phi Eta Sigma. Office: Rehabilitation Medicine Spec 1990 Larkin Ave Ste 3 Elgin IL 60123-5827

YARNELL, MICHAEL ALLAN, lawyer; b. Chgo., Sept. 10, 1944; s. Howard Winfred and Mary Elizabeth (Card) Y.; m. Karen Alice Hockenyos, June 12, 1971 (div. Mar. 1994); children: Sarah Munro, Jacob Rainey; m. Kristina Louise Renshaw, July 17, 1996. BS, Ariz. State U., 1967; JD with honors, U. Ill., 1971. Bar: Ariz. 1971. Ptnr. Streich, Lang, Weeks & Cardon, Phoenix, 1971-91, also bd. dirs.; mem. Myers, Barnes & Jenkins, Phoenix, 1991; judge Maricopa County Superior Ct., Phoenix, 1991—2005, mediator, arbitrator, spl. master, 2005—; mem. faculty U. Phoenix; adj. prof. U. Canberra Law Sch., Australia, 2004—; asst. clin. prof. law Phoenix Sch. Law, 2006—. Author: Ins and Outs of Foreclosure, 1981, 12th edit., 2005; projects editor Law Rev. U. Ill. Law Forum, 1970; contbr. articles to profl. jours. Chairperson Phoenix Children's Theatre, 1987; vol. Habitat for Humanity, Adopt-a-Home sponsor; chmn. Legal Cmty. Builds, 1999. 1st lt. U.S. Army, 1971-72, Korea. Fellow Ariz. Bar Found.; mem. ABA, Am. Arbitration Assn. (Roster Neutrals, Comml. Panel), Maricopa Bar Assn., State Bar Ariz. (Outstanding Contbn. to Continuing Legal Edn. award 1988, Com. on Profl. Conduct award 2000), Order of Coif, Lorna Lockwood Inn of Ct. (co-pres. 2000-01), Ariz. Yacht Club (vice comdr. 2000, comdr. 2001-02, staff comdr. 2002-03), Phi Kappa Phi. Republican. Avocations: computers, sailing, whitewater rafting. Office: Esplanade Ctr 2415 E Camelback Rd Ste 700 Phoenix AZ 85016 Office Phone: 602-553-1010. Personal E-mail: michael@michaelyarnell.com.

YARNO, WENDY, pharmaceutical executive; BS, Portland State U., 1982; MBA, Temple U., 1988. Profl. rep. U.S. Human Health, 1983—85, mktg. analyst, 1985—87, product mgr. pediatric vaccines, 1988, assoc. dir. econ. affaris, 1989, sr. dir. mktg. planning, 1990—91, nat. account exec., 1991, sr. dir. managed health care affairs, 1992, project leader for U.S. Health Care Reform, 1992—93; v.p. ctrl. region Merck-Medco, 1994; v.p. hypertension and heart failure therapeutic bus. group U.S. Human Health, 1994—97; v.p. Ortho McNeil Pharm., Johnson & Johnson, 1997—98; v.p. worldwide human health Merck & Co., Inc., Whitehouse Station, NJ, 1999; v.p. human resources, 1999, sr. v.p. human resources, 2000—, exec. v.p. worldwide human health mktg., 2003—. Bd. dirs. St. Jude Med. Ctr.; pres. bd. trustees Women's Health and Counseling Ctr., Somerville. Office: Merck and Co Inc One Merck Dr Whitehouse Station NJ 08889-0100 Office Phone: 908-423-6525.

YAROS, CONSTANCE GREENBERG, painter, sculptor; b. Phila., Aug. 03; d. Harry William and Dorothy (Hofberg) Greenberg; m. Irvin Yaros June 17, 1950 (dec. Nov. 1983); children: Michael J., James E. Student, Nancy S. Student, Temple U., Tyler Sch. of Art, Phila., 1957—60, Blai Studio, 1976—81, Pa. Acad. Fine Arts, 1987, student, 1978—79, Schuler Sch. of Art, 1990. One-woman shows include Tyler Alumni Gallery, 1992; exhibited in group shows icluding History Mus., Phila., 1984-88, Woodmere Art Mus., Phila., 1995, Am. Artists Profl. League, N.Y., 1993, Oil Painters Am., 1994, Art at the Armory, Phila., 1990-92, Artists Equity Assn. Triennial, 1984, 88, 91, Allied Artists of Am., 1988, Catherine Loriliard Wolfe Art Club, 1988, Salmagundi Art Club, 1988, Tyler Alumni Gallery-Diamond Club, Temple U., 1988-92, Phila. Sketch Club, 1987, Old York Rd. Art Guild, 1975; public collections at Temple U., Jefferson Park Hosp., Bd. City Trusts, Fed. Dist. Ct. House, Bd. City Trusts; numerous pvt. collections. Mem. Portrait Soc. Am., Am. Technion Assn., Greenpeace, Phila. Mus. Art, Allied Artists Am., Soc. Classical Realism, Am. Soc. Portrait Artists, Am. Artist Profl. League, Pa. Acad. Fine Arts, Oil Painters Am., Artists Equity Assn., Woodmere Art

Mus., Phila. Art Alliance, Archives of Women's Mus. of Art, Alumni Pa. Acad. Fine Arts, Alumni Tyler Sch. Art., Plastic Art Club. Avocations: music, ballet, exercise, photography. Home and Office: 2401 Pennsylvania Ave Ste 4a5 Philadelphia PA 19130-3002

YAROSLAVSKY, ANNA, biophysicist, educator; b. Saratov, Russia, Sept. 11, 1968; arrived in U.S., 1998; d. Nikita Petrovich Mityashin and Lubov Mikhailovna Mityashina; m. Ilya Vladimirovich Yaroslavsky, Oct. 23, 1987; 1 child, Anatasia Ilinichna. MS in Physics summa cum laude, Saratov State U., Russia, 1990, PhD in Physics, 1999. Engr. Russian Acad. Sci., Saratov, 1989—90, rsch. fellow, 1990—91, U. Twente, Enschede, Netherlands, 1992—93; scientist Heinrich Heine U., Dusseldorf, Germany, 1994—98; rsch. assoc. La. State U., Shreveport, La., 1998—2000; asst. physicist Wellman Ctr. Photomedicine, Boston, 2000—, instr., 2000—05; asst. prof. dept. dermatology Harvard Med. Sch., 2005—. Reviewer NIH, Bethesda, Md., 2004—, Optics Letters, Lasers in Surgery & Medicine; presenter in field. Co-author: Optics of Blood, 2002; contbr. articles to profl. jours. Fellow: Am. Soc. Lasers in Medicine and Surgery; mem.: Optical Soc. Am., Internat. Soc. Optical Engring., Animal Rescue League Boston. Avocations: music, history, art, sports. Home: 12 Farnum St North Andover MA 01845 Office: Wellman Ctr Photomedicine BHX 314B 55 Fruit St Boston MA 02114 Office Phone: 617-726-1590. Business E-Mail: yaroslav@helix.mgh.harvard.edu.

YAROWS, STEVEN ALLEN, internist; BS, U. Mich.; MD, Wayne State U., 1977. Diplomate Am. Bd. of Medicine, 1980, cert. specialist in hypertension Am. Soc. of Hypertension, 1999. Intern, resident Henry Ford Hosp., Detroit, 1977—81; dir. ICU Chelsea (Mich.) Cmty. Hosp., 1985, chief of medicine, 1988—. Bd. dir. Purple Rose Theater, Chelsea, 1990—2002, Huron Valley Ambulance, Ann Arbor, Mich., 1990—97. Named one of Best Doctors in Am., Woodward White, 1999—2005. Fellow: ACP; mem.: Am. Heart Assn. (bd. dir. 2002). Office: Chelsea Internal Medicine 128 Van Buren Chelsea MI 48118 Office Phone: 734-475-8677. E-mail: syarows@cimmd.com.

YARRIGLE, CHARLENE SANDRA SHUEY, realtor, investment advisor; b. Redlands, Calif., July 25, 1940; d. Troy Frank and Anna (Miskew) Shuey; m. Robert Charles Yarrigle, Oct. 16, 1965 (div. July 1985); children: Stephanie Ann, Steven Charles. AA, San Bernardino (Calif.) Coll., 1965; student, Ariz. State U., 1965-66; BS, No.Mich. U., 1976; postgrad., No. Mich. U., 1976-77. Clk. Bungalow Grocery, Redlands, 1957-59; operator Pacific Tel. Co., San Bernardino, 1958-61; svc. rep. So. Calif. Gas, San Bernardino, 1961-66; tchr. bus. Gwinn (Mich.) HS, 1976-78; realtor, investment counselor Remax Gold West, Calif., 1978—; broker, 1990—. Tchr. Project 100,000, Sheppard AFB, Wichita Falls, Tex., 1966—70. Vol. Easter Seal Soc., Humane Soc., Coventry Ho.; adv. mentally ill; tchr. family-to-family classes Nat. Alliance Mentally Ill., 1999—; mem. steering com., adv. bd. Sacramento Bd. Realtors, 1981—. Recipient Hall of Fame award, Remax Internat., 2005. Mem.: NAFE, Sacramento Assn. Realtors, Calif. Assn. Realtors (Outstanding Life Mem.), Nat. Assn. Realtors (lic.), Nat. Alliance Female Execs., Calif. Alliance Mentally Ill (adv.), Nat. Alliance Mentally Ill (adv.), Masters Club. Republican. Avocations: financial planning for seniors, physical fitness, stock market, gardening. Office: Remax Gold Internat 983 Reserve Dr Roseville CA 95678 Office Phone: 916-367-5133. Personal E-mail: charrigle@aol.com.

YARROW, PETER, folksinger; b. N.Y.C., May 31, 1938; BA, Cornell U.; D (hon.), Nat. Lewis U., 2002, San Francisco State U., 2003. Mem. group: Peter, Paul and Mary, 1962—, also solo performer, recording artist, Warner Bros.: albums with Peter, Paul, and Mary include: Peter, Paul, and Mary, Moving, In the Wind, In Concert, A Song Will Rise, See What Tomorrow Brings, Peter, Paul, and Mary Album, Album 1700, Late Again, Peter, Paul & Mommy, 10 Years Together: The Best Of, Reunion, Peter, Paul & Mommy, Too (Emmy nominee 1993), No Easy Walk to Freedom, Lifelines, Songs of Concience and Concern, In These Times, Carry It On; solo album: Peter, 1972, That's Enough for Me, 1973, Hard Times, 1975, Love Songs, 1975; on Broadway appearance: Peter, Paul, and Mary "From Bleecker to Broadway", 1986; TV spls. include: Reunion, Holiday Concert, Peter, Paul & Mommy, Too, Lifelines (PBS). Bd. dirs. Newport Folk Festival Found., Kerrville (Tex.) Folk Festival, 1971, Ctr. for Global Edn., Augsberg Coll.; chmn. bd. trustees Telluride Inst., 1997; founder, co-chair Oper. Respect, "Don't Laugh At Me", 1999 Recipient Emmy nominee for "Puff the Magic Dragon", 1979, Citizen Action Leadership award, Vista, 1979, Alfred Lowenstein award, 1982, Hospice Care of R.I. award, 1987, Nat. Emergency Civil Liberties Com. award, 1988, Interlochen Disting. Alumnus Arts award, 1992, Conn. Hospice award, 1993, Grammy award for prodr. Peter Paul & Mommy, Too, 1994, Kate Wolf Meml. award for the World Folk Music Assn., 1994, Tikkum Plam award, Ctrl. Synogogue, 1995, People for th Am. Way Defenders Democracy award, 1999, Ctrl. Sunagogue Shofar awartd, 1999, Spirit Crazy Horse award, 2000, AASC Sch. Counselor of Yr. award, 2001, Gandhi World Peace Flame, 2001,Rescuer of Humanity award, 2001, Starr Commonwealth Bd. Trustees Child Advocacy award, 2001, Good Neighbor award, 2002, N.Y. STate ASCS Educator of Yr. award, 2002; Congressional hon., 1999.

YARUSS, HOWARD SETH, lawyer; b. NYC, Aug. 12, 1958; s. Ben and Bernice (Saltzman) Y. BS magna cumlaude, Brown U., 1980; student, London Sch. Econs., 1978-79; JD, U. Pa., 1983. Bar: N.Y. 1984, Pa. Assoc. Willkie, Farr & Gallagher, N.Y.C., 1983-84, Baker & McKenzie, 1984-90; v.p. asst. gen. counsel Capital Reinsurance Co., N.Y.C., 1991—97; exec. v.p., gen. counsel, sec. Radian Group Inc., 1997—. NY State Dem. Committeeman for 80th Assembly Dist. Office: Radian Group 1601 Market St Philadelphia PA 19103 Office Phone: 215-231-1388.

YARVIS, JEFFREY SCOTT, military officer, social worker; b. Morristown, N.J., Oct. 9, 1965; s. Stephen Harlen Yarvis and Arlene Haskin; m. Laura Suzanne Gabrielle Yarvis, Aug. 31, 1997; children: Jacob, Olivia. BA, Ind. U., 1988; MEd, Cambridge Coll., 1992; MSW, Boston Coll., 1994; PhD, U. Ga., 2004. Clin. social work diplomate Am. Bd. Examiners in Clin. Social Work, 1997, diplomate psychotherapy Am. Psychotherapy Assn., 1997, domestic violence counseling CDV-III ABFE, 1997, cert. sch. social work N.J., 1994, lic. master social worker-advanced clin. practitioner Tex., 1996, Acad. Cert. Social Workers NASW, 1996. With U.S. Army; occupl. social worker 85th Med. Detachment, Fort Hood, Tex., 1994—97; chief social work and family advocacy Dewitt Army Cmty. Hosp., Fort Belvoir, Va., 1997—99; instr. U.S. Army Med. Dept. Ctr. & Sch., Fort Sam Houston, Tex., 1999—2001; chief mental health 30th Med. Brigade, Heidelberg, Germany, 2004—05; deputy chief of staff G-S, Civil Mil. Operations Office, TF 30th Med. Brigade Camp Victory, Iraq, 2005—. Tank platoon leader 1/63 Armor Bn., Fort Irwin, 1989—91; prevention team leader 47th Field Hosp., Port-au-Prince, Haiti, 1994—95, 85th Med. Detachment, Eagle Base, Bosnia-Herzegovina, 1997. Contbr. articles to profl. jours. Critical incident stress debriefing Bell-Coryell County Chpt. of ICISF, Killeen, 1994—97. Decorated 26 military decorations and badges; recipient Mental Health Profl. Yr. award, Internat. Critical Incidence Stress Found., Tex., 1997, Social Policy Grad. assistantship, Boston Coll. Grad. Sch. of Social Work, 1993—94. Mem.: Am. Soc. of Clin. Hypnosis, Assn. of Mil. Surgeons of the U.S., 5th U.S. Cavalry Assn., Nat. Guild of Hypnotists, Soc. for Social Work and Research, Assn. of U.S. Army, Nat. Assn. of Social Workers, Am. Legion. Democrat. Avocations: running, boating. Home: CMR 442 Box 726 APO AE 09042 Office: 30th Med Brigade APO AE 09014 Heidelburg Germany Office Phone: 01104906221-2416. Personal E-mail: yarvis831@aol.com. Business E-Mail: jeffrey.yarvis@us.army.mil.

YARWOOD, BRUCE, health science association administrator; b. Sacramento, Calif. 2 children; 2 stepchildren. Mgr. MediCal program Calif. Dept. Health; exec. v.p. Calif. Assn. Health Facilities; CEO Crestwood Hospitals, Inc.; legis. counsel Am. Health Care Assn., Washington, acting pres., CEO, 2005, pres., 2005—. Office: Am Health Care Assn 1201 L St NW Washington DC 20005-4014 Office Phone: 202-842-4444. Office Fax: 202-842-3860. E-mail: byarwood@ahca.org.*

YASHER, MICHAEL, retired accountant; b. United, Pa., Aug. 17, 1928; s. Michael and Mary (Sasik) Y.; m. Margaret Jean Wallace, June 23, 1956 (dec. July 12, 1987); 1 child, Michael. BS, Pa. State U., 1956; diploma, Air Command & Staff Coll., 1972, Nat. Defense U., 1977; MA, Central Mich. U., Mt. Pleasant, 1983. CPA, D.C.; cert. profl. contract mgr., D.C. Enlisted USAF, 1948—52; commd. 1st lt. U.S. GAO, Washington, 1956—83, advanced through grades to col., 1982; officer USAF, 1961—88, ret., 1988; mem. appropriations com. U.S. House of Reps., 1978-79; acct. to the comptroller U.S. Air Materials Command, 1979-83; acct., cons. E. K. Williams Co., Silver Spring, Md., 1985-98. Contbr. numerous papers and articles to profl. publs. Treas. Boy Scouts Am., Rockville, Md., 1970; bd. dirs. Sr. Softball Assn., Montgomery County, Md., 1993—94, Montgomery County Sr. Sports Assn., 1999—2001; pres. Leisure World (Md.) Billiards Club, 1994—96, treas., 1997, 1999; commr., organizer Sr. Softball League, Montgomery County, 1994; participant Nat. Sr. Olympics, 1995—2006; news corr. Billiards Club-Leisure World, 2000—. Decorated with 14 mil. decorations; recipient Bronze medal softball, Md. Sr. Olympics, 1992—93, 1996—98, Silver medal softball, 1995, 2000—02, 2003, Gold medal softball, 1994, 1998—99, 2004, 2005, Bronze medal volleyball, 1993, 1995—97, 2005, Silver medal volleyball, 1998, 2000, 2002—03, Gold medal volleyball, 1999, 2005, 2001, Bronze medal Billards, 1998, Bronze medal softball, Nat. Sr. Olympics, 1999, 2005, Gold medal Billiards, 2000, 2005, Meritorious Svc. award, U.S.G.A.O., 1975, USAF Outstanding Officer, Data Sys. Design Ctr., 1978, Silver medal 10 pin bowling doubles, 2003. Mem. AICPA, Nat. Capital Area Bowling Assn., Res. Officers Assn., Disabled Am. Vets. Comdrs. Club, Leisure World Billiards Club, Nat. Sr. Games Assn. (charter mem.), Montgomery County Sr. Sports Assn., Am. Legion, VFW. Democrat. Roman Catholic. Avocations: coin collecting/numismatics, sports. Home: 15107 Interlachen Dr Apt 318 Silver Spring MD 20906-5629

YASHIN, ALEXEI, professional hockey player; b. Sverdlovsk, Russia, Nov. 5, 1973; Profl. hockey player Ottawa Senators, 1992—2001, NY Islanders, 2001—. Player CIS Jr. Team, 1992, World Jr. Championships, Russia Jr. Team, 1993, Russia Team World Championships, 1994, 96, NHL All-Star Game, 1994.

YASHON, DAVID, neurosurgeon, educator; b. Chgo., May 13, 1935; s. Samuel and Dorothy (Cutler) Y.; children— Jaclyn, Lisa, Steven. BS in Medicine, U. Ill., 1958, MD, 1960. Diplomate Am. Bd. Neurol. Surgery. Intern U. Ill., 1961, resident, 1961-64, asst. in neuroanatomy, 1960; clin. instr. neurosurgery U. Chgo., 1965-66; asst. prof. neurosurgery Case Western Res U., Cleve., 1966-69; assoc. prof. neurosurgery Ohio State U., Columbus, 1969-74, prof., 1974-89, prof. emeritus, 1989—; mem. staff St. Ann's Hosp., Children's Hosp., Grant Med. Ctr., Ohio State U. East Med. Ctr. Cons. Med. Research and Devel. Command, U.S. Army; mem. Neurology B Study Sect NIH. Author: Spinal Injury; contbr. articles to med. jours. Served as capt. U.S. Army, 1960-68. Fellow Royal Coll. Surgeons Can. (cert.), A.C.S.; mem. AMA, Am. Physiol. Soc., Congress Neurol. Surgeons, Am. Assn. Anatomists, Canadian, Ohio neurosurg. socs., Am. Assn. Neurol. Surgeons, Research Soc. Neurol. Surgeons, Acad. Medicine Columbus and Franklin County, Soc. for Neurosci., Soc. Univ. Surgeons, Am. Acad. Neurology, Assn. for Acad. Surgery, Am. Acad. Neurol. Surgery, Am. Assn. for Surgery of Trauma, Central Surg. Soc., Ohio Med. Soc., Columbus Surg. Soc., Sigma Xi, Alpha Omega Alpha. Address: 500 Columbia Pl Bexley OH 43209-1677 E-mail: dyashon@columbus.rr.com.

YASHRUTI, SALAH HADI, retired surgeon; b. Acre, Palestine, Sept. 2, 1930; arrived in U.S., 1953; s. Hadi Ibrahim and Fatima Yashruti; m. Liljana Atanas Kolarovski, Nov. 2, 1973; children: Fadi, Nenad. BA, Am. U. Beirut, 1951, MPH, 1953; MD, U. La., 1959; degree in gen. surgery, U. Wis.-Madison, 1965. Chief hematology Toledo Gen. Hosp., Ohio, 1954—64; gen. surgeon Lebanon Hosp., Beirut, 1964—66, Kitsap County Med. Ctr., Port Orchard, Wash., 1966—84; cons. Skopjk Therapy Hosp., Macedonia, 1984—87; chief profl. svcs. U.S. Air Force Reserve, McChord AFB, Wash., 1988—96; ret. Lt. col. Med. USAAF, 1988—96. Recipient award for Outstanding Contbns., 446th Airlift Wing Joint ORI, Superior Performance, Sheppard Tech. Tng. Ctr., Meritorious Svc. medal, Robins AFB, 1992 Achievement medal, 1995. Fellow: Internat. Coll. Surgeons. Avocations: tennis, camping, writing, navigation. Home: 1970 Harvard Ave E #2 Seattle WA 98102 Personal E-mail: imfadi@aol.com.

YASNYI, ALLAN DAVID, communications company executive; b. New Orleans, June 22, 1942; s. Ben Z. and Bertha R. (Michalove) Y.; m. Susan K. Manders; children: Benjamin Charles, Evelyn Judith, Brian Mallut. BBA, Tulane U., 1964. Free-lance exec. producer, producer, writer, actor, designer TV, motion picture and theatre, 1961-73; producer, performer the Second City; dir. fin. and adminstrn. Quinn Martin Prodns., Hollywood, Calif., 1973-76, v.p. fin., 1976-77, exec. v.p. fin. & corp. planning, 1977; vice chmn., CEO QM Prodn., Beverly Hills, Calif., 1977-78, chmn. bd., CEO, 1978-80; exec. dir. Susan Manders Fine Art, 2002—; pres., CEO The Synapse Comm. Group, Inc., 1981—, ASI Entertainment, 1998-99. Mng. dir. Susan Mandears Fine Art, 2001—; exec. dir., adj. prof. U. So. Calif. Entertainment Tech. Ctr., 1994-99, exec. dir. emeritus, 1999—; participant IC IS Forum, 1990-95; exec. prodr. first live broadcast combining Intelsat, Intersputnik, The Voice of Am., and The Moscow World Radio Svc., 1990; resource guest Aspen Inst. Exec. Seminars, 1990; chmn. bd. dirs. Found. of Global Broadcasting, Washington, 1987-93; nat. adv. bd. DeSantis Ctr. Fla. Atlantic U., 1998-. Trustee Hollywood Arts Coun., 1980-83; exec. v.p., trustee Hollywood Hist. Trust, 1981-91; bd. dirs. Internat. Ctr. Intergative Studies, N.Y.C, 1988-92; bd. dirs. Asthma and Allergy Found. Am., 1981-85. With US Army, 1964-66, Vietnam. Named to Tulane U. Hall of Fame. Mem. Acad. TV Arts and Sci., Inst. Noetic Sci., Hollywood Radio and TV Soc., Hollywood C. of C. (dir., vice chmn. 1978-93), Screen Actors Guild, Assn. Transpersonal Psychology (keynote spkr. 1988). Office: 4132 Fulton Ave Sherman Oaks CA 91423-4340 Office Phone: 818-995-0009. Personal E-mail: yasnyi@aol.com.

YASSIN, ROBERT ALAN, museum director, curator; b. Malden, Mass., May 22, 1941; s. Harold Benjamin and Florence Gertrude (Homburg) Y.; m. Marilyn Kramer, June 9, 1963; children: Fredric Giles, Aaron David. BA, Dartmouth Coll., 1962; postgrad., Boston U., 1962—63; MA, U. Mich., 1965, postgrad., 1968—70, PhD candidate, 1970; postgrad., Yale U., 1966—68. Asst. to dir. Mus. Art U. Mich., 1965-66, asst. dir., 1970-72, assoc. dir., 1972-73, acting dir., 1973, instr. dept. history of art, 1970-73; co-dir. Joint Program in Mus. Tng., 1970-73; chief curator Indpls. Mus. Art, 1973-75, 87-89, acting dir., 1975, dir., 1975-89; exec. dir. Tucson Mus. Art, 1990—2001, Palos Verdes (Calif.) Art Ctr., 2002—. Adj. prof. Herron Sch. Art Ind. U./Purdue U., 1975-89. Contbr. to mus. publs. Rufus Choate scholar, 1962, Samuel H. Kress Found. fellow, 1968—70, Ford Found. fellow, 1966—68. Mem.: Calif. Assn. Museums, Western Mus. Assn., Nat. Trust Hist. Preservation, Coll. Art Assn. Am., Am. Assn. Museums (bd. dirs. Internat. Coun. Mus. 1986—89). Jewish. Office: Palos Verdes Art Ctr 5504 W Crestridge Rd Rancho Palos Verdes CA 90275 Home: 7321 Marina Pacifica Dr N Long Beach CA 90803-3808 Office Phone: 310-541-2479. Personal E-mail: rayassin@charter.net.

YASTE, CHRISTIAN, dentist; DDS, U. Mich. Resident in oral medicine, Charlotte, NC; co-founder Ballantyne Ctr. for Dentistry; clin. instr. Carolinas Med. Ctr. Dept. Dentistry. Mem.: Am. Acad. Cosmetic Dentistry, Charlotte Dental Soc., NC Dental Soc., Am. Dental Assn. Office: Ballantyne Ctr for Dentistry Ste K 15105 John J Delaney Dr Charlotte NC 28277 Office Phone: 704-540-2255. E-mail: drdiaz@ballantynedentistry.com.

YASTINE, BARBARA A., diversified financial services company executive; BA in Journalism, NYU, 1981, MBA in Finance, 1987. Various communications and investor-relations positions W.R. Grace & Co.; dir. investor relations, Primerica Citigroup, 1987—91, v.p. investor relations and fin. planning & analysis, Traveler's Group, 1991, exec. v.p. fin. and insurance, CitiFinancial, chief admin. officer, global consumer group, 1998, chief auditor, CFO, global corp. and investment bank, 2000—02; CFO Credit Suisse First Boston, 2002—. Office: Credit Suisse First Boston 11 Madison Ave New York NY 10010-3629 Office Phone: 212-325-2000. Office Fax: 212-325-6665.

**YATES, ALLISON A.,** medical association administrator; BS, MS, Univ. of Calif.; PhD, Univ. of Calif. at Berkley, 1974. Dean Univ. of Southern Miss., 1988—97; dir. emeritus food and nutrition bd. Washington, 1997—2003; sr. prog. officer food and nutrition bd. Inst. of Medicine, Washington; dir. nutritional sciences Environ Found., Arlington, Va.; dir. Beltsville (Md.) Human Nutrition Rsch. Ctr. US Dept. Agr. Office: Environ Ste 300 4350 N Fairfax Dr Arlington VA 22203 also: Beltsville Human Nutrition Rsch Ctr Bldg 307-C Barc-East 10300 Baltimore Ave Beltsville MD 20705-2350 Office Phone: 703-516-2349. Office Fax: 703-516-2304. E-mail: yatesa@ba.ars.usda.gov.

**YATES, BRENDA H. CARROLL,** secondary school educator; b. Carrolltown, Ga., Sept. 16, 1949; d. Buford Bledsoe and Lovie Beatrice (Thaxton) Holmes; m. Kenneth Wayne Carroll, Aug. 23, 1969 (div. Aug. 1984); children: Kenneth W. Jr., Samuel Mark; m. Gwendolyn Ray Yates, Dec. 10, 1987. BA in Secondary Edn. Social Studies, West Ga. Coll., 1970, MEd in Secondary Edn. English, 1974, EdS in Secondary Edn. English, 1988. Cert. tchr., Ga. Social studies and lang. arts tchr. Rockmart (Ga.) H.S., 1970-78; lang. arts tchr., dept. head Douglas County Comprehensive H.S., Douglasville, Ga., 1978—. Adj. instr. Mercer U., Lithia Springs, Ga., 1990—. Named Star Tchr., State of Ga., 1994. Mem. NEA, Ga. Assn. Educators. Democrat. Baptist. Avocation: reading. Home: 4978 Pebblebrook Dr Douglasville GA 30135-4520 Office: Douglas County Comp HS 8705 Campbellton St Douglasville GA 30134-2202

**YATES, DAVID JOHN C.,** chemist, researcher; b. Stoke-on-Trent, Staffordshire, Eng., Feb. 13, 1927; arrived in US, 1958; s. Eric John and Beatrice Victoria Y.; m. Natalie Chmelnitsky, June 22, 1983 BS with honors, U. Birmingham, U.K., 1949; PhD, U. Cambridge, Eng., 1955, Sc.D., 1968. Rsch. physicist Kodak Labs., Wealdstone, London, 1949-50; rsch. chemist Brit. Ceramic Rsch. Assn., Stoke-on-Trent, 1950-51; rsch. assoc. dept. colloid sci. U. Cambridge, 1951-58; lectr. Sch. Mines and dept. chemistry Columbia U., N.Y.C., 1958-60; sr. rsch. fellow Nat. Phys. Lab., Teddington, England, 1960-61; rsch. assoc. corp. labs. Exxon Rsch. and Engring., Annandale, NJ, 1961-86; rsch. prof. dept. of chem. engring. Lafayette Coll., Easton, Pa., 1986-87; rsch. prof. dept. materials sci. Rutgers U., Piscataway, NJ, 1987-88; cons. San Diego, 1988—. Contbr. over 70 articles to profl. jours., chpts. to books; 13 U.S. patents, numerous fgn. patents. Fellow Inst. of Physics (U.K.), Royal Soc. Chemistry (U.K.), N.Y. Catalysis Club (chmn. 1966-67). Clubs: N.Y. Catalysis (chmn. 1965-66). Avocations: photography, bicycling, gliding, travel, sports cars.

**YATES, ELLA GAINES,** librarian, consultant; b. Atlanta, June 14, 1927; d. Fred Douglas and Laura (Moore) Gaines; m. Joseph L. Sydnor (dec.); 1 child, Jerri Gaines Sydnor Lee; m. Clayton R. Yates (dec.). AB, Spelman Coll., Atlanta, 1949; MS in L.S. Atlanta U., 1951; JD, Atlanta Law Sch., 1979. 1954Asst. br. librarian Bklyn. Pub. Library, 1951; head children's dept. Orange (N.J.) Pub. Library, 1956—59; br. librarian East Orange (N.J.) Pub. Library, 1960—69; med. librarian Orange Meml. Hosp., 1967—69; asst. dir. Montclair (N.J.) Pub. Library, 1970—72, Atlanta-Fulton Pub. Library, 1972—76, dir., 1976—81; dir. learning resource ctr. Seattle Opportunities Industrialization Ctr., 1982—84; asst. dir. adminstrn. Friendship Force, Atlanta, 1984—86; state librarian Commonwealth of Va., 1986—90; library cons. Price Waterhouse, 1991; adv. bd. Library of Congress Center for the Book, 1977—85; interim dir. Atlanta-Fulton Pub. Libr., 1998—99; cons., dir. Woodruff Libr., Atlanta, 2000—02. Cons. in field; vis. lectr. U. Wash., Seattle, 1981-83; mem. Va. Records Adv. Bd., 1986-90; mem. Niagara Exec. Bd., 1987-91. Contbr. to profl. jours. Vice chmn. N.J. Women's Coun. on Human Rels., 1957-59; chmn. Friends Fulton County Jail, 1973-81; bd. dirs. United Cerebral Palsy Greater Atlanta, Inc., 1979-81 Coalition Against Censorship, Washington, 1981-84, YMCA Met. Atlanta, 1979-81, Exec. Women's Network, 1979-82, Freedom To Read Found., 1979-85, Va. Black History Mus., Richmond, 1990-91; sec., exec. dir. Va. Libr. Found. Bd., 1986-90; founder Coretta Scott King Book Award, Ala., 1968—. Recipient meritorious svc. award Atlanta U., 1977, Phoenix award City of Atlanta, 1980, Serwa award Nat. Coalition 100 Black Women, 1989, Black Caucus award, 1989, disting. svc. award Clark-Atlanta U., 1991, ednl. support svc. award Tuskegee Airmen, 1993, Alumnae Achievement award Spelman Coll., 1998, Annie McPheters award Atlanta-Fulton Pub. Libr., 1998, Disting. Alumnae award Clark Atlanta U., 2001; named profl. woman of yr. NAACP N.J., 1972, outstanding chum of yr., 1976; named outstanding alumni Spelman Coll., 1977, named to alumni hall of fame, 1995. Mem. ALA (exec. bd. 1977-83, commn. freedom of access to info., founder Coretta Scott King Book Award 1968), NAACP, Southeastern Libr. Assn., Nat. Assn. Govt. Archives and Records Adminstrn. (exec. bd. 1987-91), Delta Sigma Theta (Pinnacle leadership award 2001). Baptist. Home and Office: 1171 Oriole Dr SW Atlanta GA 30311-2424 E-mail: ellayates4@aol.com.

**YATES, GARY L.,** marriage and family therapist; b. Washington, Aug. 16, 1944; s. Lewis Edward and Norma Jean (Andruss) Y.; m. Cynthia Ann Pagay, Aug. 16, 1974; children: David, Jonathan, Daniel, Matthew, Nathan. BA, Am. U., 1967; MA, U. No. Colo., 1978. Tchr. St. Anthony's, Kailua, Hawaii, 1970-74, Acad. of Pacific, Honolulu, 1974-79; adminstr. Dept. Pub. Health, San Bernardino, Calif., 1979-81, Charles Drew Sch. of Medicine, L.A., 1981-82; assoc. dir. Divsn. of Adolescent Medicine/Children's Hosp., L.A., 1982-92; sr. program officer Calif. Wellness Found., Woodland Hills, Calif., 1992-93, program dir., 1993-94, pres., CEO, 1995—. Asst. clin. prof. U. So. Calif., 1988—; bd. dirs. Calif. Wellness Found., Grantmaker in Health, Hispanics in Philanthropy, So. Calif. Assn. Philanthropy, Coun. Found. Contbr. articles to profl. jours., contbg. author; Multi Agency System of Care, 1990. Mem. L.A. Roundtable for Children, 1988-92, United Way Task Force on AIDS, L.A., 1988-92, San Bernardino Comm. Coun., 1980-82; chmn. Hawaii Sch. Counseling Assn., Honolulu, 1978-79. S(sgt.) U.S. Army, 1968-70. Recipient NACO Achievement award Nat. Assn. U.S. Counties, 1980, 3rd Century award Hollywood Coord. Coun., 1989, Gov.'s Victim's Svc. award Gov. of Calif., 1990, Commendation award Calif. State Senate, 1992, Hispanic Health Leadership award, 1999, L.A. Free Clinic Lenny Somberg award, 1998. Mem. Am. Assn. Humanistic Psychologists, Soc. for Adolescent Medicine, Calif. Assn. Marriage and Family Therapists, Am. Pub. Health Assn. Democrat. Methodist. Avocations: reading, walking. Office: Calif Wellness Found 6320 Canoga Ave Ste 1700 Woodland Hills CA 91367-2565*

**YATES, JAMES ARTHUR,** plastic surgeon; b. Butler, Pa., June 5, 1935; s. Adolph Walter and Laura Marie (De Foggie) Y.; m. Debra Lynne Stringer, June 19, 1983; 1 child, Jamie Dale Yates Reynolds. BA, Cornell U., 1956; MD, U. Md., 1960. Diplomate Am. Bd. Plastic Surgery, Nat. Bd. Med. Examiners, Am. Bd. Surgery; lic. physician, Pa., Ohio, R.I. Intern Cleve. Clinic Hosp., 1960—61, resident in gen. surgery, 1960—61, resident in gen. surgery, U. Pitts. Med. Ctr., 1963—65; resident in plastic surgery R.I. Hosp., 1966—67, chief resident, 1967—68; pvt. practice Plastic Surgery Ctr Ltd., Camp Hill, Pa., 1968—; med. dir. Grandview Surgery Ctr., Camp Hill, Pa. Tchg. fellow gen. surgery U. Pitts. Med. Ctr., 1963-65, instr. gen. surgery, 1965-66; clin. instr. plastic surgery Milton S. Hershey (Pa.) Med. Ctr., 1968—; staff maxillofacial and plastic surgery dept. Harrisburg (Pa.) Hosp., 1968—; chief plastic and aesthetic surgery dept. Holy Spirit Hosp., Camp Hill, 1968—; staff Mechanicsburg Rehab. Hosp., Carlisle (Pa.) Hosp., Pinnacle Health Sys. Hosps.; med. dir. Grandview Surgery and Laser Ctr., Camp Hill; cons. Harrisburg State Hosp.; physician surveyor Am. Assn. Ambulatory Health Care; physician trainer plastic surgery residency program Am. Coll. Osteo. Surgery; bd. dirs., pres. Am. Assn. Accreditation of Ambulatory Surgery Facilities. Contbr. articles to profl. jours.; adv. bd. Town and Country Mag. Police commr. West Shore Regional Police Dept.; pres. Boro Coun. Lemoyne Boro; mem. credentialling com. Keystone Health Plan; mem. task force on ambulatory surgery Pa. Dept. Health; mem. coun. Lemoyne (Pa.) Borough Coun., pres.;

credentialing officer Freedom Health Care HMO; commr. West Shore Regional Police. Fellow ACS; mem. AMA, Pa. Med. Soc., Am. Burn Assn., Am. Soc. Plastic and Reconstructive Surgeons, Am. Burn Victim Found., Am. Soc. Aesthetic Plastic Surgery, Vail Cosmetic Surgery Soc., Pa. Plastic Surgery Soc. (past pres.), Am. Soc. Automobile Medicine, Northeastern Soc. Plastic Surgeons, Royal Soc. Medicine, Lipolysis Soc. N.Am., Internat. Soc. Clin. Plastic Surgeons, South Ctrl. Pa. Regional Med. Dirs., Am. Coll. Physician Execs. Republican. Roman Catholic. Avocations: bicycling, skiing, model building, sports cars. Home: 833 Kiehl Dr Lemoyne PA 17043-1201 Office: Plastic Surgery Ctr Ltd 205 Grandview Ave Camp Hill PA 17011-1708 Office Phone: 717-763-7814. Personal E-mail: jay5plas@msn.com.

**YATES, JEROME WILLIAM,** medical association administrator; b. Rockford, Ill., Nov. 9, 1936; s. Frank and Eily Yates; m. Mary Elizabeth McAuley, June 1, 1979; children: Elizabeth Ann, Sarah Eily. AB, Lawrence U., Appleton, Wis., 1961; MD, U. Ill., Chgo., 1965; MPH, Harvard Sch. of Pub. Health, Boston, 1981. Diplomate Nat. Bd. of Med. Examiners, 1966, Am. Coll. of Med. Executives, 2002. Rsch. scientist ii Roswell Pk. Cancer Inst., Buffalo, 1970—74; prof. of medicine U. Vt., Burlington, Vt., 1974—82; assoc. dir. for centers and cmty. oncology Nat. Cancer Inst., Bethesda, Md., 1982—87; sr. v.p. for clin. affairs Roswell Pk. Cancer Inst., Buffalo, 1987—2001; nat. v.p., rsch. Am. Cancer Soc., Atlanta, 2002—. Dir. Sheehan Meml. Hosp., Buffalo, 2003—; intermittent cons. and reviewer Nat. Cancer Inst., Bethesda, NY, 1971—. Contbr. scientific papers. Cancer ctr. adv. com. NCI Designated Cancer Ctr., 1982—2006; dir. Sheehan Meml. Hosp., Buffalo, 2003—06. Sp4 AMEDS U.S. Army, 1955—57, Landstuhl, Germany. Recipient Outstanding Leadership and Svc. award, Assn. of Am. Cancer Ctr., 2002, Award of Merit, NIH, 1983, Outstanding Work Performance award, Nat. Cancer Inst., 1983, 1984, 1985. Mem.: Assn. of Am. Cancer Inst (assoc.; pres. 1991—92). Independent. Achievements include research in leukemia treatment, standard for 30 years; initiated community clinical oncology program. Avocations: aviation, golf. Home: 240 Independence Dr Orchard Park NY 14127 Office: Am Cancer Soc 1599 Clifton Rd Atlanta GA 30333 Office Phone: 404-929-6850.

**YATES, JOHN MELVIN,** retired ambassador; b. Superior, Mont., Nov. 25, 1939; s. Leon Glen and Violet May (McPheeters) Y.; m. Peggy Maureen Simpson, Mar. 26, 1961 (dec. Apr. 1986); children: Catherine Diener, John Simpson, Maureen Cole, Paul Marion, Leon Gregory; m. Mary Barbara Carlin, Jan. 30, 1988. AB, Stanford U., 1961; MA, Fletcher Sch. Law and Diplomacy, 1962, MALD, 1963, PhD, 1972. Fgn. service officer US Dept. State, Washington 1964—2002, Algiers, Algeria, 1964-66, Blantyre, Malawi, 1967-68, Bamako, Mali, 1969-71, New Delhi, 1973-75, Ankara, Turkey, 1975-77, Libreville, Gabon, 1977-80, Washington, 1971-73, 80-82; amb. to Republic of Cape Verde, Am. Embassy, 1983-86, counselor for polit. affairs Manila, 1986-89, dep. chief of mission Lagos, Nigeria, 1989-91, Kinshasa, Zaire, 1991-93, chief of mission, 1993-95, amb. to Republic of Benin, Cotonou, 1995-98, amb. to Republic of Cameroon and Republic Equatorial Guinea, Yaounde, 1998—2001, ret., 2001; sr. US advisor Somalia Reconciliation Talks, 2004; sr. advisor Darfur (Sudan) Polit. Negotiations, 2005—06. Recipient Presdl. award for sustained superior accomplishment in conduct of fgn. policy. Mem. Am. Fgn. Service Assn. Home: CMR 480 Box 2317 APO AE 09128 Personal E-mail: johnnymontana@gmail.com.

**YATES, JOHN ROBERT, JR.,** civil engineering educator; b. Boston, Feb. 9, 1930; s. John Robert and Rosemary Natalie (Logue) Y.; m. Virginia Dianne Finocchio, July 3, 1954 (dec. Feb. 1988); children: Deborah A., John Robert, Thomas F., Catherine I.; m. Barbara Marandola, Dec. 28, 1990. AB, Northeastern U., 1954. Commd. 2d lt. USMC, 1954, advanced through grades to lt. col., 1970; action officer, constrn. team, joint logistics rev. bd. Office Sec. Def., 1969-70; engr. III Marine Amphibious Force, Fleet Marine Force, Okinawa, 1970-71; comdg. officer, marine barracks U.S. Naval Base, Boston, 1971-74, ret., 1974. Dir. engring. Soldiers' Home, Chelsea, Mass., 1974-85; energy conservation coord. Exec. Office of Human Svcs., Commonwealth of Mass.; faculty Energy Mgmt. in Healthcare Instns., HEW, 1977. Mem. exec. bd. USO Coun. New Eng., 1971-84, pres., 1988-94; trustee Charlestown YMCA, 1974—, pres. 1988-94, vice chmn., 1977-79, chmn., 1980-82. Decorated Joint Svc. Commendation medal, Navy Commendation medal, Army Commendation medal. Mem. Soc. Am. Mil. Engrs. (dir. Boston post), Am., New Eng. hosp. engrs. socs., Navy League U.S. (v.p. Mass. Bay coun.), Am. Legion, VFW, Bostonian Soc., Wardroom Club (Boston), Army-Navy Club (Washington). Roman Catholic.

**YATES, JOHN THOMAS, JR.,** chemistry professor, research scientist; b. Winchester, Va., Aug. 3, 1935; s. John Thomas and Kathryn (Barnett) Y.; m. Kerin Joyce Narbut, Oct. 18, 1958; children: Geoffrey, Nathan. BS, Juniata Coll., 1956; PhD, MIT, 1960. Asst. prof. chemistry Antioch Coll., Yellow Springs, Ohio, 1960-63; NRC fellow, rsch. chemist Nat. Bur. Standards, Washington, 1963-82; R.K. Mellon prof. chemistry U. Pitts., 1982—, dir. Surface Sci. Ctr., 1982—. Co-dir. materials rsch. ctr. U. Pitts., 1994, R.K. Mellon prof. chemistry and physics, 1994—; Gwathmey vis. prof. U. Va., 2002-03 Author: Experimental Innovations in Surface Science, 1997; co-author: The Surface Scientist's Guide to Organometallic Chemistry, 1987; co-editor: Vibrational Spectroscopy of Molecules on Surfaces, 1987, Chemical Perspectives of Microelectronic Materials, Vol. 131; assoc. editor: Studies in Surface Science and Catalysis, 1986; series editor: Methods of Surface Characterization, 1987; bd. editors Ann. Rev. Phys. Chemistry 1983-85, Jour. Phys. Chemistry, 1983-88, Jour. Chem. Physics, 1984-87, Jour. Catalysis, 1987-91, Chem. Revs., Langmuir, Surface Sci., Applications of Surface Sci., Accounts Chem. Rsch., Chem. Phys. letters, 1997—; assoc. editor Langmuir, 1991-98; contbr. revs. and articles to profl. jours.; inventor desorption spectrometer, 1981. Sherman Fairchild Disting. scholar Calif. Inst. Tech., 1977-78; recipient Silver medal Dept. Commerce-Nat. Bur. Stds., 1973, Superior award, 1981, Gold medal Dept. Commerce-Nat. Bur. Stds., 1981, Pres.'s Disting. Rsch. award U. Pitts., 1989, Procter & Gamble award, 1989, Alexander von Humboldt Sr. Rsch. award, 1995, 1997, Linnett lectr. Cambridge U., 2000, Outstanding Alumnus Juniata Coll., 2000, named Among 100 Most Highly Cited Chemists in World 1984—, G.N. Lewis lectr. U. Calif.-Berkeley, 2002, lectr. Sidney Sussex Coll., 2000, Japan Soc. Promotion of Sci., 2002, Inst. Physics, 2004 Fellow Am. Phys. Soc. (bd. dirs. divsn. chem. physics 1991—, chmn. divsn. chem. physics 1989), Am. Vacuum Soc. (chmn. surface sci. divsn. 1973, 92, trustee 1975, bd. dirs. 1982-85, M.W. Welch award 1994, fellow 1994); mem. NAS, Am. Chem. Soc. (chmn. divsn. colloid and surface chemistry, Langmuir lectr. 1979, Kendall award in colloid of surface chemistry 1986, Morley prize Cleve. chpt. 1990, Peter Debye lectr. Cornell U. 1993, Pitts. award 1998, A.W. Adamson award 1999), Pitts.-Cleve. Catalysis Soc. Office: U Pitts Surface Sci Ctr Dept Chemistry Pittsburgh PA 15260 E-mail: jyates@pitt.edu.

**YATES, LEIGHTON DELEVAN, JR.,** lawyer; b. Atlanta, Sept. 4, 1946; s. Leighton Delevan and Stella Louise (Hill) Y.; m. Phyllis Jeanne Hummer, Dec. 22, 1968; children: Leighton Delevan III, Lauren Jeanne. BA, Hampden-Sydney Coll., Va., 1968; JD with high honors, U. Fla., 1973. Bar: Fla. 1974, U.S. Dist. Ct. (middle dist.) Fla. 1975. Assoc. Maguire, Voorhis & Wells, P.A., Orlando, Fla., 1974-77, shareholder, 1978-98, dept. chmn., 1985-90; ptnr. Holland & Knight LLP, Orlando, Fla., 1998—, nat. practice group leader, 2005—. Bd. dirs. Hubbard Constrn. Co., Winter Park, Fla., 1985—2004, Blythe Constrn., Inc. Charlotte, NC, 1998—2004; adminstrv. dir. SunTrust Bank, Orlando, Fla., 1990—. Exec. editor U. Fla. Law Rev., 1973. Mem. Fla. Bd. Bar Examiners, 1992-97, 2002-05, vice chmn., 1995-96, chmn. 1996-97; chmn. Fla.'s Blood Ctrs., 1995—, vice chmn., 1980-95; chmn. Orlando Opera Co., 1994, pres., 1993. Fellow Am. Bar Found.; mem. ABA, Fla. Bar Assn., Orange County Bar Assn., Univ. Club of Orlando, Country Club of Orlando, Order of the Coif, Omicron Delta Kappa, Phi Kappa Phi. Republican. Presbyterian. Avocations: scuba diving, bicycling, music, reading. Home: 3218 S Osceola Ave Orlando FL 32806-6251 Office: Holland & Knight LLP 200 S Orange Ave Ste 2600 Orlando FL 32801-3453 Office Phone: 407-425-8500. Personal E-mail: lyates@cfl.rr.com. Business E-mail: leighton.yates@hklaw.com.

**YATES, MARY CARLIN,** former ambassador; b. Portland, Oreg., Dec. 1946; m. John Melvin Yates. BA in English, Oreg. State U.; M in Comparative East West Humanities, NYU, postgrad. Joined fgn. svc., 1980; press attaché for Amb. Pamela Harriman US Dept. State, sr. cultural attaché Am. Embassy Paris, U.S. amb. to Burundi Washington, 1999—2002, U.S. amb. to Ghana, 2002—05.

**YATES, MICHAEL FRANCIS,** management consultant; b. N.Y.C., Feb. 9, 1946; s. John Berchmans and Jane Ann (Gretz) Y.; m. Christine Mary Dallos, Jan. 14, 1967; children: Erik Michael, Alison. BA, U. Buffalo, 1968. Mgmt. trainee, dept. mgr. Sears, Roebuck & Co., Buffalo, 1968-69; cons. Rothman & D'Alessandro, Inc., N.Y.C., 1969-71; sr. cons. Martin & Segal & Co., Inc., N.Y.C., 1971-75, A.S. Hansen, Inc., N.Y.C., 1975-78; exec. v.p. A.M. D'Alessandro & Co., Inc., North Haledon, NJ, 1978-81; mng. dir. Alexander & Alexander Cons. Group, Inc., Lyndhurst, NJ, 1981-97; pres. Michael F. Yates & Co., Inc., Hampton, NJ, 1997—. Bd dirs. Am. Intercon, Inc. Host of Your Human Resources Resource, WALE AM, 2001—. Pres. Lincoln Sch. PTA, 1975-77, Bethlehem Twp. Rep. Club. mem. Hunterdon County com.; chmn. Bethlehem Twp. Econ. and Indsl. Devel. Bd., 1980-83; active Rep. Nat. Com. Mem. Am. Mgmt. Assn., Am. Compensation Assn., Soc. Human Resource Mgmt., Adminstrv. Mgmt. Soc., Aircraft Owners and Pilots Assn. Home: 519 Lannon Ln Glen Gardner NJ 08826-3817 Office: 2 Manor Dr Hampton NJ 08827-5409

**YATES, NORRIS WILLIAM, JR.,** lawyer; b. Alamo Heights, Tex., July 6, 1926; s. Norris William and Maggie Barkley (Curry) Y.; m. Mary Hutchings Spencer, Dec. 30, 1947 (div. Aug. 1969); 1 child, William Spencer; m. Jimmie Carolyn Cook, Sept. 17, 1955; children: Victoria Carolyn Marullo (dec.), Rebecca Elizabeth Yates Bird. BA in Econs., Tex. A&M U., 1950; JD, U. Tex., 1957. Bar: U.S. Ct. of Military Appeals, 1963, U.S. Supreme Ct., 1964, Tex., 1957. Asst. to mgr. rates and tariffs Slick Airways, Inc., San Antonio 1950; assoc. Beckmann, Stanard, Wood, Barrow & Vance, San Antonio, 1957-60; pvt. practice San Antonio, 1960-67, 83—; asst. criminal dist. atty., chief civil sect. Bexar County Dist. Atty.'s Office, San Antonio, 1967-82. Mcpl. ct. judge City of San Antonio, 1966-67. Editor The Subpoena, 1958-59. Exec. com. Bexar County Dem. Party, San Antonio. Cpl. U.S. Army, Airborne Infantry, 1944-46, ETO; 1st lt. USAF, 1951-55, B-29 Bomber Pilot, Korea, JAG lt. col. USAFR, ret. 1978. Decorated Bronze Star medal, combat infantry badge, glider badge, pilot's wings, three battle stars; Eagle Scout. Mem. Daedalians, Mil. Officer Assn. Am. (sec. Alamo chpt.), USAF Pilot Class 52-George Assn. (recording sec.), 307th Bomb Group/Wing Inc. (past pres.), Toastmasters (past pres., Disting. Dist. Gov. 1969-70, Disting. Toastmaster 1984, Presdl. citation 1992), Masons (past master, 32 degree), San Antonio A&M Club (dir.), Oak Pk. Neighborhood Assn. (dir., past pres.), Sam Houston Club (mem. coun.) Democrat. Presbyterian. Avocations: travel, photography. Home: 2118 Kenilworth Blvd San Antonio TX 78209-2329 Personal E-mail: nyates@satx.rr.com.

**YATES, RONALD EUGENE,** newspaper editor, educator, author, journalist; b. Kansas City, Mo., Feb. 19, 1941; s. Guy Raymond and Willadene (Peterson) Y.; m. Ingeborg Zoelss, May 7, 1966; children: Jennifer Christina, Nicole Brigitte. BS (Gannett Newspapers scholar 1968-69, Angelo C. Scott Meml. scholar 1969), U. Kans., 1969. Reporter Kansas City (Kans.) Star, 1968; editor Univ. Daily Kansan, 1969; reporter, asst. city editor, fgn. corr. Chgo. Tribune, Chgo. and Tokyo, 1969-76, Asia and Latin Am. corr., 1976-82, met. editor, 1983—, nat. editor, 1984—, chief Asia corr., 1985—, sr. writer, 1992—; prof., chmn. dept. journalism U. Ill., Champaign, 1997—, dean Coll. Comms., 2003—. Contbr. articles to mags. Served with U.S. Army Intelligence, 1962-66. Recipient award for excellence in staff leadership William Allen White Sch. Journalism, 1968, Edward Scott Beck award for best fgn. reporting, 1975, 87, 89, Inter-Am. Press Assn. award for reporting on Latin Am., 1979, Peter Lisagor award for bus. and fin. reporting, 1993; named Outstanding Sr. U. Kans., 1969 Mem. Fgn. Corrs. Club of Japan (v.p. 1989—), Los Angeles Press, Sigma Delta Chi. Lutheran. Office Phone: 217-333-2350. Business E-Mail: ryates@uiuc.edu.

**YATES, SHARON,** artist; b. Rochester, NY, 1942; BFA, Syracuse Univ. Sch. Art, 1964; MFA, Tulane Univ. 1966. Faculty Md. Inst. Coll. Art, Balt., 1968—. One-woman shows include Fishbach Gallery, NYC, 1976, Univ. Maine, Macias, 1991, 1997, Maine Coast Artists Exec. Gallery, Rockport, 1993, exhibited in group shows at Turtle Gallery, Deer Isle, Maine, 1997, NAD Mus., NYC, 1997, Maine Coast Artists Gallery, Rockport, 1999, Va. Hist. Soc., Richmond, 2000, Bates Coll. Mus. Art, Maine, 2000, L.C. Bates Mus., Hinkley, Maine, 2000, Represented in permanent collections NAD, NYC, Bates Coll. Art, United Technologies, Conn., Lucent Technologies, Univ. Louisville, Okla. City Art Mus. Recipient Prix de Rome, 1972—74; grantee Ingram-Merrill Found. fellowship, France, 1977—78, Ludwig Vogelstein Found., 1996. Mem.: NAD (academician 1995—, Shatalow award). Office: Painting Drawing Found MICA 1300 Mount Royal Ave Baltimore MD 21217 Office Phone: 410-669-9200.

**YATES, STEVEN A.,** curator, artist; b. Chgo., Nov. 14, 1949; s. Thomas A. and Phyllis E. (Wilson) Y.; m. Lynne A. Smith, Aug. 5, 1972; children: Kelsey Victoria, Mackenzie Phyllis. BFA, U. Nebr., 1972; MA, U. N.Mex., 1975, MFA, 1978. Curatorial asst. Sheldon Meml. Art Gallery, 1972-73, U. Art Mus., U. N.Mex., 1973-75; faculty dept. art Claremont (Calif.) Colls. and Pomona, 1976; part-time faculty U. N.Mex., Albuquerque, 1976—, assoc. adj. prof. dept. art and art history, 1994—; curator prints, drawings and photographs Mus. of N.Mex., Santa Fe, 1980-84; curator of photography Mus. Fine Arts, 1985—. Vis. prof. 19th and 20th century photography Santa Fe C.C., 1998-02; vis. specialist in field; instr. U. N.Mex., 1975-78; frequent lectr. and essayist on contemporary and early modern history of photography and rsch. internationally; guest artist Tamarind Inst., Albuquerque, 1988; vis. instr. Pomona Coll., Claremont Coll., Calif., 1976, U. Calif. LA, 1976; lectr., rschr. curator exhbns. internationally. One-man shows include Sheldon Meml. Art Gallery, Lincoln, Nebr., 1978, Gallery A-3, Moscow, 1996, Up and Down Gallery, Kharkov, Ukraine, 1997, U. Nebr., 1997, Mus. Photography, Riga, Latvia, 1998, Gallery A-3 Moscow, 2002; collaborative installation Ctr. for Contemprary Arts, Irving, Tex., 2000; group shows include San Francisco Mus. Modern Art, 1980, 81, 84, 86, 96, Cinema Ctr., Moscow, 1991, St. Petersburg, Russia, 1997, Photographic Icons: Film Form and Montage, A homage to Sergei Eisenstein adn Gustav Klucis, Latvia, 1998, Empires: Russia Past and Present, 1998; represented in permanent collections San Francisco Mus. Modern Art, Sheldon Art Gallery, Mint Mus., Art Mus. U. N.Mex., Ctr. for Creative Photography, Tucson; editor: The Essential Landscape, The New Mexico Photographic Survey, 1985; guest editor spl. issue Contemporary Photography, 1987, El Palacio, 1987, Poetics of Space: A Critical Photographic Anthology, 1995, Betty Hahn: Photography or Maybe Not, 1995, Theatre as Memory: L. Millet, 1999, The Avant-garde Document: A. Macijauskas, 2001, Idea Photographic: After Modernism, 2002, Poéticas del espacia, 2002, Alexander Rodchenko, Modern Photography, Film, and Photomontage, 2003; contbr. essays in field; numerous mus. catalogs and pubs. nationally and internationally. Ford Found. fellow, 1977, Nat. Endowment Arts fellow, 1980; recipient Vreeland award U. Nebr., 1972, Outstanding Alumni Achievement award U. Nebr., 1994; Sr. Fulbright Scholars award USSR, 1991, Russian Fedn., 1995. E-mail: steve.yates@state.nm.us.

**YATES, WILLARD ROSS,** retired humanities educator; b. Oreg. s. Willard W. and Phoebe Mae Yates; m. Catharine M. Gleason. B.A., U. Oreg., 1948, MA, 1949; PhD, Yale U., 1956; LLD (hon.), Moravian Coll., 1977; LHD (hon.), Lehigh U., 1993. Instr. Kenyon Coll., Gambier, Ohio, 1952—53, U. Vt., Burlington, 1953—55; from asst. prof. to prof. Lehigh U., Bethlehem, Pa., 1955—63, 1972—86, dean Coll. Arts & Sci., 1963—72, prof. govt. emeritus, 1986—. Author: Joseph Wharton, Quaker Industrial Pioneer, 1987, Lehigh University, A History of Education in Engineering, Business and the Human Condition, 1992; contbr. editor: Bethlehem of Pennsylvania, Vols. 1 and 2, 1968, 1976. Trustee Bethlehem Bach Choir, Mary Immaculate

Seminary of the Vincentian Fathers, Northampton, Pa. Sgt. AUS, 1943—46. Fulbright scholar, 1951—52. Mem.: Phi Beta Kappa. Roman Catholic. Avocation: writing. Home: Hillside Manor 900 N Hill Rd Mcminnville OR 97128

**YATES, WILLIAM TENNYSON, II,** educational consultant, management consultant; b. Tuskegee, Ala., Mar. 26, 1944; s. William Tennyson Yates, Sr. and Dorothea Jordan Yates; m. Sue Wilson, Aug. 4, 1984. BS, Temple U., 1968; MS, Troy State U., 1975; PhD, St. Louis U., 1987. Commd. lt. USAF, 1969, advanced through grades to lt. col., 1985, ret., 1989; program dir., grant writer Woodrow Wilson Nat. Fellowship Found., Princeton, NJ, 1990—92; asst. v.p. Temple U., Phila., 1993—96; founding exec. dir. Moore Multi-Cultural Ctr., Cocoa, Fla., 1996—99; mgmt. cons. Phoenix Orgn., Indialantic, Fla., 1999—2001; regional v.p. Hire Golden, Inc., Valley Forge, Pa., 2001—. Mem. Civilian/Mil. Affairs Com., Melbourne, Fla., 1997—2002; v.p. Hosts of Brevard, Inc., Melbourne, 1999, pres., 2000—. Decorated Def. Meritorious Svc. medal, Air Force Meritorious Svc. medals (4), Air Force Commendetion Medal. Mem.: Rotary. Republican. Avocations: music, martial arts, computers, writing, photography.

**YATES-RILEY, VERONICA A.,** mathematics educator; b. Orlando, Fla., Aug. 27, 1963; d. James (Stepfather) and Elease Montgomery Marshall; children: Koltan E. Riley II, Kertesha B. Riley, Krystal V. Riley. BS, U. Fla., Gainesville, 1988; MS, Nova Southeastern U., Ft. Lauderdale, Fla., 2000. Cert. tchr. Nat. Bd. Profl. Tchg. Stds., 2001. Math. tchr. Orange County Pub. Schs., Orlando, 1989—. Adj. prof. Valencia C.C., Orlando, Fla., 2001—. Mem.: Mentor Area Coun. (assoc.), Nat. Coun. Tchrs. Math. (assoc.), Am. Assn. Women C.C. (assoc.), Pi Mu Epsilon (assoc.), Gamma Phi Delta (life; chmn. 2005—06).

**YATSENKO, YURI PETROVICH,** economics professor, mathematician; b. Kiev, Ukraine, Oct. 15, 1955; arrived in US, 2000, permanent resident, 2001; s. Petr Yatsenko and Nadiya Betina; m. Natali Hritonenko; children: Oleg, Victoria, Olga. BS in Physics, Kiev State U., Ukraine, 1977, MS, 1977, PhD, 1981; DSc, Presidium Acad. Scis. USSR, 1988. Lic. prof. Edn. Ministry Ukraine, 1995. Sr. rschr., dept. head Cybernetics Inst. Ukrainian Acad. Scis., Kiev, 1983—90; prof. Kiev State U., 1991—93, Acad. Tech. & Agr., Bydgoszcz, Poland, 1993—95; sr. analyst Electric Submersible Pumps, Inc., Okla. City, Okla., 1997—99; adj. prof. U. Alta., Edmonton, Alberta, Canada, 1999—99; sr. sys. analyst Netherland, Sewell & Assoc., Inc., Dallas, 2000—01; prof. Houston Bapt. U., 2002—. Owner Cybernetics Cons. Inc., Edmonton, Alberta, Canada, 1996—2000; lectr. in field; mem. editl. bd. Internat. Jour. Applications and Applied Maths., United States, 2005—, Internat. Jour. Ecology and Devel., India, 2006—, Jour. Computational and Applied Maths., Ukraine, 2006—; assoc. editor Internat. Jour. Ecological Econs. and Stats., India, 2006—; mem. program & organizing coms. at confs. in field. Author: (monograph) Integral Dynamical Models and Optimal Control Problems, 1985, Integral Models of Systems with Controllable Memory, 1991;: Modeling and Optimization of the Lifetime of Technologies, 1996, Mathematical Modeling in Economics, Ecology and the Environment, 1999, 2006, Applied Mathematical Modeling of Engineering Problems, 2003; contbr. scientific papers. Rsch. grants, Sorros Internat. Sci. Found. & Edn. Ministry Ukraine, 1992—95, Rsch. grant, NATO, 2006—. Russian Orthodox. Achievements include discovery of new results in mathematical modeling and optimization of economic and industrial development, technological change, innovation processes, and technology replacement. Home: 15434 Tysor Park Ln Houston TX 77095 Office: Houston Bapt Univ 7502 Fondren Houston TX 77074 Office Fax: 281-649-3436. Business E-mail: yyatsenko@hbu.edu.

**YAU, SHING-TUNG,** mathematics professor; b. Swatow, China, Apr. 4, 1949; arrived in US, 1969; m. Yu-Yun Kuo; children: Isaac, Michael. PhD, U. Calif., Berkeley, 1971; PhD (hon.), Chinese U. Hong Kong 1980, Harvard U., 1987, Chao Tung U., 1997, Nat. Tsing Hua U., 2000, Macau U., 2002. Mem. Inst. Advanced Study, Princeton, NJ, 1971-72; asst. prof. math. SUNY, Stony Brook, 1972-73; prof. math. Stanford U. Ark., 1974-79; hon. prof. Chinese Acad. Scis, 1983; prof. math. Inst. Advanced Study, Princeton, 1979-84, U.Calif.-San Diego, La Jolla, 1984-87; hon. prof. Hangzhou U., 1987—, Tsinghau U., 1987—; prof. math. Harvard U., Cambridge, Mass., 1987—; William Casper Graustein Prof., 2000—; Fairchild Disting. Scholar Caltech, 1990; disting. vis. prof. SUNY, Stony Brook, 1990; hon. prof. Nankai U., 1993—; Higgins Prof., 1997—2000; hon. prof. Beijing U., 1998—, U. Sci. & Tech., China, 1999—, Zhejian U., 2002—; disting. prof.-at-large Chinese U. of Hong Kong, 2003. Vis. prof., chair math. dept. U. Tex., Austin, 1986; spl. chair Nat. Tsing Hua U., Hsinchu, Taiwan, 1991—92; Wilson T.S. Wang Disting. Vis. prof. Chinese U., Hong Kong, 1991—92; adj. prof. math. Chinese U. of Hong Kong, 1994—2003, dir. Inst. Math. Scis., 1994—. Contbr. articles to profl. publs. Named Honorable prof., Fudan U. China, Academia Sinica China, Sci. Digest, Am. 100 brightest scientists under 40, 1984; recipient Calif. Scientist of Yr., 1979, Sr. Scientist award, Humboldt Found. fellow, 1985, Crafoord prize, 1994, Veblen prize, 1981, Fields medal, 1982, Certy prize, 1980, Nat. Medal Sci. (USA), 1997, China International Sci. and Tech. Cooperation award, 2003; grantee Sloan Fellow, 1975—76, Guggenheim Fellowship, 1982, MacArthur Fellow, 1985. Fellow: Russian Acad. Scis. (fgn. mem.); mem.: AAAS, Nat. Acad. Scis. (bd. mem. math. scis.), Scientific Adv. Coun., Chinese Acad. Sci. (hon. mem. academic com. 1980—, fgn. mem.), Acad. Sinica (Taiwan), Soc. Indsl. Applied Math., Am. Phys. Soc., Am. Math. Soc. Achievements include research in differential geometry. Office: Harvard U Dept Math 3d Fl Sci Ctr 1 Oxford St Cambridge MA 02138-2901 also: Inst Math Scis Chinese U Hong Kong Unit 601, 6/F Academic Bldg #1 Shatin Hong Kong E-mail: yau@math.harvard.edu, yau@ims.cuhk.edu.hk.*

**YAU, SIU-TUNG,** physics professor; BS, U. So. Calif., 1983; PhD, U. Ill. Urbana-Champaign, 1990. Assoc. prof. physics Hunter Coll. CUNY, N.Y.C., 2001—. Prodr.: (classical music CD) Haydn Mozart Beethoven. Mem.: Am. Chem. Soc. Achievements include discovery of the first sequence of molecular-scale images of the very earliest stages of crystal growth; invention of the first prototype field-effect transistor using protein as the active material. Business E-Mail: syau@hunter.cuny.edu.

**YAU, STEPHEN SIK-SANG,** computer scientist, information scientist, educator; b. Wusei, Kiangsu, China, Aug. 6, 1935; arrived in U.S., 1958, naturalized, 1968; s. Pen-Chi and Wen-Chum (Shum) Y.; m. Vickie Liu, June 14, 1964; children: Andrew, Philip. BSEE, Nat. Taiwan U., Taipei, 1958; MSEE, U. Ill., Urbana, 1959, PhD, 1961. Asst. prof. elec. engring. Northwestern U., Evanston, Ill., 1961-64, assoc. prof., 1964-68, prof., 1968-88, prof. computer scis., 1970-88, Walter P. Murphy prof. Elec. Engring. and Computer Sci., 1986-88, also chmn. dept. computer scis., 1972-77, chmn. dept. elec. engring. and computer sci., 1977-88; prof. computer and info. sci., 1988-94; chmn. dept. U. Fla., Gainesville, 1988-94; prof. computer sci. and engring. Ariz. State U.; Tempe, 1994—, chmn. dept. computer sci. and engring., 1994—2001. Conf. chmn. IEEE Computer Conf. Chgo., 1967; gen. chmn. Nat. Computer Conf., Chgo., 1974, First Internat. Computer Software and Applications Conf., Chgo., 1977; Trustee Nat. Electronics Conf., Inc., 1965-68; chmn. organizing com. 11th World Computer Congress, Internat. Fedn. Info. Processing, San Francisco, 1989; gen. co-chmn. Internat. Symposium on Autonomous Decentralized Systems, Japan, 1993; gen. chmn., Phoenix, 1995; conf. co-chair 24th Ann. Internat. Computer Software and Applications Conf., Taipei, 2000. Editor-in-chief Computer mag.: 1981-84; assoc. editor Jour. Info. Sci., 1983-99; editor IEEE Trans. on Software Engring., 1988-91; contbr. numerous articles on software engring., distributed and parallel processing systems, computer sci., elec. engring. and related fields to profl. publs.; patentee in field. Recipient Louis E. Levy medal Franklin Inst., 1963, Golden Plate award Am. Acad. Achievement, 1964, The Silver Core award Internat. Fedn. Info. Processing, 1989, Spl. award, 1989. Fellow IEEE (mem. governing bd. Computer Soc. 1967-76, pres. 1974-75, dir. Inst. 1976-77, chmn. awards com., 1996-97; Richard E. Merwin award Computer Soc. 1981, Centennial medal 1984, Extraordinary Achievement award 1985, Outstanding Contbn. award Computer Sci. Soc. 1985, The Third Millennium medal 2000, Tsutomu Kanai award 2002), AAAS, Franklin Inst.;

mem. Assn. for Computing Machinery, Am. Fedn. Info.-Processing Soc. (mem. exec. com. 1974-76, 79-82, dir. 1972-82, chmn. awards com. 1979-82, v.p. 1982-84, pres. 1984-86; chmn. Nat. Computer Conf. Bd. 1982-83, spl. award 1990), Am. Soc. Engring. Edn., Sigma Xi, Tau Beta Pi, Eta Kappa Nu, Pi Mu Epsilon. Office: Ariz State U PO Box 878809 Tempe AZ 85287-8809 Business E-Mail: yau@asu.edu.

**YAVARI, ARASH,** engineering educator; b. Tehran, Iran; s. Mansour Yavari and Batoul Mahmoudi. BS in civil engring., Sharif U. Tech., Iran, 1997; MS in mech. engring., George Wash. U., 2000; PhD in mech. engring., Calif. Inst. Tech., Calif. 2004. Grad. asst. George Washington U., 1998—2000, Calif. Inst. Tech., 2000—04; asst. prof. Georgia Inst. Tech., Atlanta, 2005—. Author over 25 jour. papers, (jour. article) Engring. Fracture Mechanics, Internat. Jour. Fracture, 2002. Office: Georgia Inst Tech 790 Atlantic Dr Atlanta GA 30332 Office Phone: 404-294-2436.

**YAVARKOVSKY, JEROME HAROLD,** library director; b. NYC, May 12, 1940; B Mech. Engring., Rensselaer Poly. Inst., 1960; MS in Mgmt., MIT, 1962; M Libr. Sci., Columbia U., 1971. Lic. pub. libr. Adminstrv. specialist Bell Labs., Murray Hill, NJ, 1963-64; systems analyst J.C. Penney Co., NYC, 1965-67; tech. cons. Auerbach Assocs., NYC, 1967-68; head programming Columbia U., NYC, 1969-71, chief systems, 1971-72, asst. univ. libr., 1972-83; dean librs. Adelphi U., Garden City, NY, 1983-85; dir. NY State Libr., Albany, 1985-95; univ. libr. Boston Coll., Chestnut Hill, 1995—. Office: Thomas P O'Neill Libr Boston Coll Chestnut Hill MA 02467

**YAVORNIK, BARBARA ANN,** pre-school educator; b. Olympia, Wash., July 12, 1957; d. Eugene Earl and Betty Ann Brown; m. Edward J. Yavornik, II, Jan. 11, 1980. BA, Cen. Wash. U., Ellensburg, 1981; MEd, West Tex. A&M U., 1990. Cert. adminstrn. Dir., tchr. Fifth Ave. Pres-Sch., Ellensburg, 1981—82; tchr. Coronado Acad., Albuquerque, 1985—86, N.W. Primary, Hereford, Tex., 1987—. Presenter I-Teach K West Tex. A&M U. Sci. Conf., 2000, 01, 05; presenter HISD Sci. Inservice, 2005. Greeter coord. St. Anthony's Parish Coun., 2004—, eucharistic minister, 2004—; bd. dirs. Campfire, Hereford, 1988—90. Named Tchr. of Yr., N.W. Primary, 2002; recipient Excel in Sci. Tchg. award, Tex. Sci. Assn., 2001, Golden Apple award, Hereford Ind. Sch. Dist., 2004. Mem.: Hereford C. of C. (v.p. women's divsn. 1987—89), Delta Kappa Gamma (pres. 2002—04, v.p., Achievement award 1999—2004). Republican. Roman Catholic. Avocations: gardening, reading, collecting bears, travel. Home: 201 N Texas Ave Hereford TX 79045 Office: NW Primary Sch 400 Moreman Ave Hereford TX 79045 Office Phone: 806-363-7660. E-mail: barbarayavornik@herefordisd.net.

**YAVORSKY, WILLIAM D.,** semiconductor company executive; BS in Bus. Adminstrn., Bowling Green State U.; postgrad., Stanford U., U. Va. With Xerox Corp., Genicom, Tektronix; dir. internat. sales InFocus Corp., 1993—96, v.p. worldwide sales, 1996—2000, sr. v.p., gen. mgr., 2000—03; v.p. worldwide sales Pixelworks, Inc., Tualatin, Oreg., 2004—. Office: Pixelworks Inc 8100 SW Nyberg Rd Tualatin OR 97062 Personal E-Mail: billy@pixelworks.com.

**YAVUZ, DENIZ DERVIS,** electrical engineer, researcher; b. Omerli, Turkey, Sept. 25, 1975; s. Sehmus and Fehime Yavuz; m. Sunduz Keles, Sept. 16, 2004. PhD, Stanford (Calif.) U., 2003. Registered profl. engr., Calif., 2003. Rsch. asst. Stanford (Calif.) U., 1997—2003; postdoctoral rschr. U. Wis., Madison, Wis., 2004—. Achievements include research in generation of the shortest laser pulses in the world. Home: 25 University Houses Apt C Madison WI 53705 Office: University of Wisconsin 1150 University Avenue Chamberlin Hall Madison WI 53706 Office Phone: 608-265-7894. Business E-Mail: yavuz@wisc.edu.

**YAWITZ, RICHARD A.,** lawyer; b. St. Louis, May 22, 1954; s. Aubrey and Juanita Yawitz; 1 child, Kathryn R. BBA in Acctg., U. Mich., 1976; JD, U. Mo., Kansas City, 1982. CPA Mo., 1978; bar: Mo. 1982. Prin. Ziercher & Hocker, PC, St. Louis, 1989—99; mem. Gallop, Johnson & Neuman, LC, St. Louis, 1999—. Mem.: ABA, Bar Assn. Met. St. Louis, Mo. Bar, Order of Bench and Robe. Office: Gallop Johnson & Neuman LC 101 S Hanley Ste 1700 Saint Louis MO 63105 Office Fax: 314-615-6001. Business E-Mail: rayawitz@gjn.com.

**YAWNEY, TRENT,** professional hockey coach, retired professional hockey player; b. Hudson Bay, Sask., Can., Sept. 29, 1965; m. Charlane Yawney; children: Ashley, Conor. Defenceman Can. Nat. Team, 1985—88, Chgo. Blackhawks, 1987—91, 1997—99, Calgary Flames, 1991—96, St. Louis Blues, 1996—97; asst. coach Chgo. Blackhawks, 1999—2000, head coach, 2005—, Norfolk Admirals, 2000—05. Mem. Team Can., Olympic Games, Calgary, 1988. Named Minor Pro Coach of Yr., The Hockey News, 2003—04. Office: Chgo Blackhawk Hockey Team 1901 W Madison St Chicago IL 60612*

**YAWORSKI, JAMES JOHN, III,** elementary school educator; b. Conn., July 20, 1960; s. James John Yaworski, Jr. and Joyce Graham; m. Jeanette Anne Kotowski, July 28, 1990; children: Jordan Taylor, Blake Frances, Hunter James, Bo Michael. BS in Edn., U. Conn., Storrs, 1982; MEd, Ea. Conn. State U., Willimantia, 1989. Middle sch. math and history tchr. Canterbury Bd. Edn., 1983—. Girls soccer coach Baldwin Middle Sch., Canterbury, 1983—94, girls softball coach, 1984—94, mem. social studies curriculum com., 2002—06. Umpire Little League Baseball Canterbury Athletic Assn., 1978—94, soccer referee, 1990—94; instr. Ams. Game Baseball Camp, Norwich, Conn., 2006. Recipient 20th Yr. Tchg. award, Canterbury Bd. Edn., 2003. Mem.: Canterbury Edn. Assn. Office: Canterbury Bd Edn 45 Westminster Rd Canterbury CT 06331

**YAWORSKY, BOHDAN,** law educator; s. Dmytro and Cornelia Yaworsky; m. Tedra L. Buckmaster, Sept. 19, 2000; children: Amy Gravett, Samantha Wall. BA, Rutgers U., New Brunswick, 1969; MA, Rutgers U., Newark, 1981, PhD, 1994. Drug counselor U.S. Army, Long Binh, Vietnam, 1970—71; tng. coord. Middlesex County Probation Dept., New Brunswick, 1973—78; dir. criminal justice planning Union County, Elizabeth, NJ, 1978—80, acting dir. dept. pub. safety, 1980, asst. county adminstr., 1980—81; prof., chair dept. criminal justice New Jersey City U., Jersey City, 1981—. Disting. faculty mem. Nat. Coun. Juvenile & Family Ct. Judges, Reno; sr. cons. Office Internat. Criminal Justice, Chgo., Rutgers Ctr. Mgmt. Devel., Piscataway, NJ; cons., Hamburg, NJ, 1978—, Nat. Inst. Corrections, Longmont, Colo.; charter mem. N.J. Supreme Ct. Mcpl. Ct. Certification Bd., Trenton; charter mem. exec. com. N.J. Supreme Ct. State Adv. Bd. for Probation, Trenton; charter mem. N.J. Juvenile Intensive Supervision Program Adv. Bd., Trenton. Author: 100 criminal justice studies. Mem.: Am. Correctional Assn., Am. Probation and Parole Assn. (cons.), Acad. Criminal Justice Scis. Office: New Jersey City U Dept Criminal Justice Jersey City NJ 07305

**YAZDANPANAH, MEHDI MOHAMMAD,** physicist, researcher; arrived in U.S., 2001; s. Mohammad Hossein Yazdanpanah and Baygom Rezaie; m. Romaneh Jalilian. Grad., Sharif U. Tech., Teheran, 1991; MS, U. Beheshti, Tehran, 2001; PhD with honors, U. Louisville, 2006. Rsch. asst. U. Louisville, 2001—. Contbr. articles to profl. jours. Recipient Outstanding grad. student for U. of Louisville, 2005, Promotional Sect. Second Pl. award, Internat. Material Nanotechnology Workshop, 2004. Mem.: Am. Phys. Soc. (assoc.). Achievements include discovery of room temperature self-assembly of metal alloy nanostructures via Ga reaction with metal; invention of selective growth of Ag2Ga nanoneedles on AFM tips. Home: 3143 Doreen way Louisville KY 40220 Office: University of Louisville Room 253 BRB University of Louisville Louisville KY Office Phone: 502-852-1551. Personal E-mail: mmyazd01@gwise.louisville.edu. E-mail: yazdaanpanah@yahoo.com.

**YAZDI, AHMAD,** computer scientist, researcher; b. Tehran, Iran, Apr. 8, 1978; s. Kazem Yazdi and Minoo Mapar. BS, Sharif U. of Tech., Tehran, 2000; MS, U. So. Calif., 2003; postgrad., U. Calif., Irvine, 2003—. Rsch. asst. U. Calif., Irvine, 2003—. Contbr. articles to profl. jours., confs. Fellow Ctr. for Pervasive Comm. and Computing, 2003—05. Mem.: IEEE, Eta Kappa Nu. Achievements include patents for a novel silicon-based differential non-uniform downsized distributed amplifier; ultra-wideband CMOS distributed mixer. Home: 2233 Martin Apt 314 Irvine CA 92612 Office: U Calif Irvine Dept Elec Engring and Computer Sci ET 521 Irvine CA 92697-2625 Personal E-mail: yazdi75a@yahoo.com. E-mail: yazdia@uci.edu.

**YAZZIE, AARON FRANKLIN,** events laborer; b. Ft. Defiance, Az., Apr. 30, 1962; s. Robert Franklin Yazzie Sr. and Sadie Mildred (Williams) Yazzie; life ptnr. Linda James, Jan. 20, 1965 (dec.). Mechanic Ft. Sill, Lawton, Okla., 1985—87; parts washer Embassy Suites, Phoenix, 1996—98; staff rug racker Baker Bros., Super Floors, Phoenix, 1997—99; events set up crew Ariz. State U., West Phoenix, 2002—04. V.p. Native Am. Student Orgn., Phoenix, 2002—03, pres., Phoenix. — Pvt. U.S. Army, Korea. Recipient Mil. Svc. award, Dept. of Def., 1987. Mem.: Nat. Scholars Honor Soc. Democrat. Avocations: painting, bicycling, naturalist, pow wows. Home: Rancho Santa fe Apts #2134 10201N 44th D Glendale AZ 85302 Personal E-mail: aaronfyazzie62@hotmail.com. Business E-Mail: aaronfyazzie@asu.edu.

**YBABEN, MARC A.,** psychologist, consultant; m. Rose Saverino, May 21, 1995; children: Conner, Carina. BA, U. Pacific, 1987; MA, No. Ill. U., 1989, PhD, 1996. Lic. psychologist Calif. Dir. The Leadership Devel. Ctr., Seal Beach, Calif., 1999—; psychologist Newport Psychology Group, Newport Beach, Calif., 2001—. Adj. prof. Argosy U., Santa Ana, Calif., 1999—, U. Phoenix, Costa Mesa, Calif., 2000—. Musician: (albums) Keep Me in Mind (Best Jazz Artist - Orange County Music Awards, 2005). Mem. Leadership Tomorrow, Newport Beach, 2002—04. Maj. USAF, 1994—99. Named Tchr. of Yr., U. Phoenix So. Calif. Campus. Mem.: APA, Orange County Psychol. Assn. (pres. 2006—).

**YE, HUA,** electronics engineer; b. Chengdu, China, Sept. 4, 1972; s. Naishu Ye and Xiuzhen Wang; m. Jingxia Ni. PhD, SUNY, Buffalo, 2004. Rsch. asst. Electronic Packaging Lab., SUNY, Buffalo, 1999—2004, postdoctoral assoc. Coll. Nanoscale Sci. and Engring., Albany, 2004—. Mem.: IEEE, CPMT Soc., Internat. Microelectronics and Packaging Soc. (founding pres. SUNY student chpt. 2003—04, Sidney J. Stein Ednl. Found. grant 2001—02).

**YE, RICK W.,** microbiologist; s. Rongtao Ye and Xiuqiong Li; 1 child, Victor M. MS. Mich. State U., East Lansing, 1986, PhD, 1992. Prin. investigator DuPont Ctrl. R & D, Wilmington, Del., 1995—. Recipient Accomplishments award, DuPont Ctrl. Rsch.; fellow, Cystic Fibrosis Found., 1992, UI. Ill., Chgo., 1992—95; scholar, Office Higher Edn. China, 1983—85. Mem.: Am. Soc. Microbiologist. Achievements include patents in field. Personal E-Mail: yer@verizon.net.

**YEAGER, ANSON ANDERS,** writer, retired editor, retired columnist; b. Salt Lake City, June 5, 1919; s. Charles Franklin and Elise Marie (Thingelstad) Yeager; m. Ada May Bidwell, Sept. 10, 1944; children: Karen Ann, Anson Anders, Harry H., Terry Douglas, Ellen Elise. BS, S.D. State U., Brookings, 1947; LLD (hon.), Dakota State Coll., Madison, S.D., 1972; DPub.Svc. (hon.), S.D. State U., Brookings, 1991. Commd. lt. U.S. Army, 1942, advanced through grades to lt. col., 1961, ret., 1979; printer's devil, linotype operator Faith Ind. and Gazette (S.D.), 1935-38; printer S.D. State U., 1940-41; staff writer Argus Leader, Sioux Falls, SD, 1947-55, Sunday editor, 1955-60, exec. editor, 1961-77, assoc. editor, 1977—84, editor editl. page, 1961-84, columnist, 1984-98, author travel articles and commentary. Lectr. dept. journalism S.D., 1953—55. Contbr. to World Book Ency., 1966—84; author: Anson Yeager's Stories, 2000. Bd. dirs. Sioux Falls Area C. of C., 1964—70, Sioux Falls Devel. Found., 1967, Boys Club of Sioux Falls, 1966—68, S.D. State U. Found., 1987—99, chmn., 1988—89; bd. dirs. Sioux Coun., Boy Scouts Am., Sioux Falls, 1967—72, v.p., 1970—72; coun. mem. Ctr. for We. Studies, 2002—. Lt. col. S.D. Army N.G., 1961—64. Named Newsman of Yr., 1978; named to S.D. Newspaper Hall of Fame, 1994, S.D. Hall of Fame, 1998; recipient S.D. Sigma Delta Chi award, 1956, Editl. Excellence award, William Allen White Found., 1976, Disting. Alumni award, S.D. State U., 1980, Friend of Augustana Coll. award, 1980, Ralph D. Casey Minn. award for disting. svc. in journalism, U. Minn., 1981, Eminent Svc. award, East River Elec. Power Coop., 1984, Mass. Comms. award, S.D. State U., 1984, Les Helgeland Cmty. Svc. award, S.D. AP Mng. Editors, 1985, Disting. Svc. award, S.D. Press Assn., 1988, A.H. Pankow award, 1995, Jerome J. Lohr award, S.D. State U. Found., Western Am. award, Ctr. for Western Studies, Augustana Coll., 2000.

**YEAGER, BOBBI ANN,** visual arts educator, artist; b. Defiance, Ohio, Aug. 26, 1967; d. Robert Lee Clyburn and Shirley Ann Shew; m. Gregory Allen Yeager, Oct. 19, 1991. BS, The Defiance Coll., 1989, MEd, 2003; postgrad., Bowling Green State U., Ohio, 1987—88. Substitute tchr. Defiance City Schs., 1989—90; art instr. Triad HS, North Lewisburg, Ohio, 1990—92, Delphos (Ohio) Jr. High, 1992—94, Ayersville Local Sch., Defiance, 1994—. Instr. sch. in-svcs., Defiance, 1995—96; chair for sch. in-svcs. for tchrs., 1996. Exhibited in group shows at St. Francis U., Ft. Wayne, Ind., 2000, Toledo (Ohio) Mus. Art, 2003. Supr. Ayersville Art Club, Defiance, 1995—. Mem.: Triad Edn. Assn. (v.p. 1991), Ohio Edn. Assn., Ayersville Edn. Assn. (pres. 1996—98), Ohio Arts Edn. Assn. (regional dir. 2000—04, Outstanding Art Tchr. 2003), NW Ohio Kayak Club. Avocations: art, kayaking, reading, gardening. Home: 600 Downs St Defiance OH 43512 Office: Ayersville Local Schs 28046 Watson Rd Defiance OH 43512 Office Phone: 419-395-1111. E-mail: ayr_aca_ry@nwoca.org.

**YEAGER, CAROLINE HALE,** writer, retired radiologist, consultant; b. Little Rock, Sept. 5, 1946; d. George Glenn and Crenor Burnelle (Hale) Y.; m. William Berg Singer, July 8, 1978; children: Adina Atkinson Singer, Sarah Rose Singer. BA, Ind. U., Bloomington, 1968; MD, Ind. U., Indpls., 1971. Diplomate Am. Bd. Radiology; med. lic. State of Calif. Intern Good Samaritan Hosp., Los Angeles, 1971-72; resident in radiology King Drew Med. Ctr. UCLA, Los Angeles, 1972-76; dir. radiology Hubert Humphrey Health Ctr., Los Angeles, 1976-77; asst. prof. radiology UCLA, Los Angeles, 1977-84, King Drew Med. Ctr. UCLA, Los Angeles, 1977-85, dir. ultrasound, 1977-84; ptnr. pvt. practice Beverly Breast Ctr., Beverly Hills, Calif., 1984-87; cons. Clarity Communications, Pasadena, Calif., 1981—; pvt. practice radiology Claude Humphrey Health Ctr., 1991-93; dir. sonograms and mammograms Rancho Los Amigos Med. Ctr., 1993-94, ret., 1994. Trustee Assn. Teaching Physicians, L.A., 1976-81; cons. King Drew Med. Ctr., 1984, Gibraltar Savs., 1987, Cal Fed. Inc., 1986, Medical Faculty At Home Professions, 1989—, Mobil Diagnostics, 1991-92, Xerox Corp., 1990-91, Frozen Leopard, Inc., 1990-91; writer gen. med. answers pub. on internet, 1994-. Author: (others) Infectious Disease, 1978, Anatomy and Physiology for Medical Transcriptionists, 1992; contbr. articles to profl. jours. Trustee U. Synagogue, Los Angeles, 1975-79; mem. Friends of Pasadena Playhouse, 1987-90. Grantee for innovative tng. Nat. Fund for Med. Edn., 1980-81. Mem. Am. Inst. Ultrasound in Medicine, L.A. Radiology Soc. (ultrasound sect.), Nat. Soc. Performance and Instrn. (chmn. conf. Database 1991, publs. L.A. chpt. 1990, info. systems L.A. chpt. 1991, dir. adminstrn. L.A. chpt. 1992, Outstanding Achievement in Performance Improvement award L.A. chpt. 1990, bd. dirs. 1990-93, Pres. award for Outstanding Chpt. 1992, v.p. programs 1993), Stanford Profl. Women L.A. Jewish. Avocations: writing, humor, design. Home and office: 3520 Yorkshire Rd Pasadena CA 91107-5440 Personal E-mail: doccarrie@earthlink.net.

**YEAGER, DAVID P.,** transportation executive; b. 1953; BA, U. Dayton, 1975; MBA, Univ. Chgo., 1987. With affiliated cos. Hub Group, Inc., 1975—, vice chmn. Hub Group, Inc., LLC, 1992—, CEO, 1995—. Bd. dir. SPR Inc., Thrall Car Mfg. Co. Bd. dir. Children's Memorial Hospital-Chgo., Fenwick High School; mem. adv. council Univ. Dayton. Office: Hub Group 3050 Highland Pkwy Downers Grove IL 60515*

**YEAGER, DEBRA LYN,** science educator; b. St. Paul, Mar. 20, 1957; d. Lyle Milton and Grace Jeanette (Mitchell) Yeager, adopted d. Wilma Mitchell; life ptnr. Christopher Charles Pfannes. AS in Computer Sci., Mesa C.C., Ariz., 1982; student, Scottsdale C.C., Ariz., 1979—80. Ordained minister Order of Melchizedek, 1991. Investigator - profiler Elk River Sheriff's Dept., Minn., 1992—94; sensor sci. tchr. Open U. of Minn., Mpls., 1994—99; sensory sci. tchr. Yeager Consulting / Into the Mystic, Minnetonka, Minn., 1998—2005, Wis. Indianhead Tech. Coll., New Richmond, 2003—, West Ctrl. Ctenan Symposium, Willmar, Minn., 2003, U. Alaska-Sitka, 2003—, U. Manitoba, 2004—, U. Coll. Dublin, Ireland, 2004—, Queens U.-Belfast, Ireland, 2004—; on the air talent, lectr. Kare 11 - NBC TV Mpls, 2002—03, WCCO 4 - CBS TV. Mpls., 2002, NW Mag. Cable Show, New Hope, Minn., 1996; sensory sci. specialist, prof. spirituality Park Hill, Okla., 2005—. Criminologist and profiler Crema Law Offices, Mpls., 1999—. Author: (novel) Encounters with the Sixth Dimension (Book in print), Intervention across time, Medium, Rare - the Bio of Debra Yeager, Karman from MU. Mem.: Delta Zeta (hon.). Achievements include research in Metaphysical Studies; development of Programs of Metaphysical Studies. Avocations: motorcycling, designing jewelry, horse training, running, travel. Home and Office: PO Box 310 Park Hill OK 74451 Personal E-mail: century30@aol.com.

**YEAGER, EVAN TODD,** academic administrator, small business owner; b. Shaddock, Okla., Apr. 15, 1960; s. Clay Arnold and Serieta Nadine Yeager; m. Joleen Louise Deibert, Apr. 28, 1956; children: Victoria Gabriele, Nathaniel William Arnold. AS, Cooke County Coll., 1982; BS, East Tex. State U., 1985, MS, 1991; EdD, Tex. A&M U., Commerce, Tex., 1999. Cert. tchr. Tex., 1985, secondary prin. Va., 1992. Tchr. Rains Ind. Sch. Dist., Emory, Tex., 1986—91, Norfolk (Va.) Christian Schs., 1991—92; prin., owner The Yeager Group, Commerce, 1992—; tex. Trail Dust Cycling, Commerce, 1992—; prin., tech. dir., instr. math Benjamin (Tex.) Ind. Sch. Dist., 1994—96; co-dir. pre-school children's ministries Ch. on the Rock, Quitman, Tex., 1996—97; chief tech. officer Trenton (Tex.) Ind. Sch. Dist., 1997—. Cons. Boles (Tex.) Ind. Sch. Dist., 1993; spkr. in field; presenter in field. Author: A Study of Cooperation between Home Schools and Public and Private, K-12, A Christian Educator's Thoughts on Home Education; musician: Wing and a Prayer Christian Rock Band, Bois d' Arc Dixieland Jazz Band; author: (curriculum) Parenting with Purpose. Leader Boy Scouts Am., Commerce, 2003—06; co-commdr. Awana, Commerce, 2001—06; tchr. Sparrow's Nest Ministry, Greenville, Tex., 2001—06; musician First Bapt. Ch., Commerce, Tex. Mem.: NRA, Consortium Sch. Networking, Tex. CTO Coun., Christian Motorcyclists Assn., Phi Theta Kappa (v.p. Cooke County Coll. chpt. 1981—82), Alpha Chi (mem. coun. East Tex. State U. chpt. 1984—85), Kappa Delta Pi, Phi Delta Kappa, Mensa. Republican. Avocations: bass, bicycling, model railroading, auto restoration, photography. Office: Trenton ISD 300 Ballentine Street Trenton TX 75490 Office Phone: 903-989-2242. Office Fax: 903-989-5173. E-mail: etyeager@ednet10.net.

**YEAGER, JEANA,** aviator; b. Fort Worth, Tex., May 18, 1952; Aviator Scaled Composites Inc., Mojave, Calif. Recipient Presdl. Citizen Medal of Honor, 1986, Collier Trophy, Nat. Aeronautic Assn., 1986, Ivan C. Kincheloe award, Soc. of Exptl. Test Pilots, 1987, Nat. Air and Space Mus. Trophy, 1987. Achievements include flying the Voyager aircraft around the world non-stop without refueling; set four separate speed records in the Rutan EZ planes.

**YEAGER, KURT ERIC,** research and development company executive; b. Cleve., Sept. 11, 1939; s. Joseph Ellsworth and Karolyn Kristine (Pedersen) Y.; m. Rosalie Ann McMillan, Feb. 5, 1960; children: Geoffrey, Phillip; m. Regina Ursula Querfurt, May 12, 1970; 1 dau., Victoria. BA in Chemistry, Kenyon Coll., 1961; postgrad., Ohio State U., 1961-62; MS in Physics, U. Calif., Davis, 1964; MS Wharton Sch. Bus., U. Pa., 1995. Tchg. asst. Ohio State U., 1961-62; officer, program mgr. Air Force Tech. Applications Ctr., Alexandria, Va., 1962-68; assoc. dept. dir. Mitre Corp., McLean, Va., 1968-72; dir. energy rsch. and devel. planning EPA, Washington, 1972-74; dir. fossil power plants dept. Electric Power Rsch. Inst., Palo Alto, Calif., 1974-79, dir. coal combustion systems, 1979-83, v.p. coal combustion systems, 1983-88, v.p. generation and storage, 1988-96, pres., CEO, 1996—2004; founder, pres., CEO, Keyworks, Aptos, Calif., 2004—. Chmn. World Energy Coun. Climate Change Study; dir. Galvin Elec. Initiative; Oak Ridge fossil energy adv. bd. Nat. Acad. Engring.; mem. exec. bd. Nat. Coal Coun.; bd. dir. nat. coalition advanced mfg. U.S. Energy Assn. Contbr. articles to profl. jours. Pres. No. Va. Youth Football Assn., 1973-74. Capt. USAF, 1962-68. Decorated Air Force Commendation medals (2); recipient Outstanding Svc. award EPA, 1974; named Energy Policy Leader, Sci. Am., 2003. Fellow ASME (rsch. policy bd., trustee com. econ. devel.); mem. AAAS, Am. Chem. Soc., Palo Alto C. of C. Republican. Episcopalian. Office Phone: 831-786-9832. Business E-mail: KYeager@EPRI.com.

**YEAGER, MARK,** real estate company executive; Degree, Lehigh U.; MBA in Mktg., Fairleigh Dickinson U. From v.p. to pres., CIO The Gale Co. Real Estate Investment Svcs. (formerly Sammis then Gale & Wentworth), Florham Pk., NJ, 1991; pres. The Gale Co. Real Estate Investment Svcs., CIO. Mem. Regional Bus. Partnership; mem. exec. com. Tri-County Scholarship Fund. Mem.: Nat. Assn. Indsl. and Office Properties (bd. dirs.). Office: The Gale Co Rela Estate Investment Services 100 Campus Drive Ste 200 Florham Park NJ 07932

**YEAGER, MARK LEONARD,** lawyer; b. Chgo., Apr. 7, 1950; BA, U. Mich., 1972; JD, Northwestern U., 1975. Bar: Ill. 1975, Fla. 1985. Ptnr. McDermott, Will & Emery, Chgo., 1975—. Mem. ABA.

**YEAGER, PETER CLEARY,** sociologist, educator; b. Terre Haute, Ind., Nov. 29, 1949; s. Ralph Oscar and Dorothy (Cleary) Y.; m. Kathy Ellen Kram, Aug. 9, 1981; 1 child, Jason Kram Yeager. BA in Journalism, U. Minn., 1971; MS in Sociology, U. Wis., 1976, PhD in Sociology, 1981. Writer, photographer Sun Newspapers, Mpls., 1971-72; from lectr. to asst. prof. sociology Yale U., New Haven, 1979-82; from asst. to assoc. prof. sociology Boston U., 1982—. Rsch. fellow ethics and the professions program Harvard U., Cambridge, Mass., 1989-90. Co-author: Illegal Corporate Behavior, 1979, Corporate Crime, 1980 (named one of Choice's outstanding acad. books 1981), republished 2006; author: The Limits of Law, 1991. Bd. assessors 1st Parish in Framingham, Mass., 1992-94. Managerial Ethics Rsch. grantee Amsterdam Found., 1989-92, Human Resources Policy Inst. Boston U., 1986-87, 93-94. Mem. Am. Sociol. Assn., Am. Soc. Criminology, Law and Soc. Assn., Soc. for Study of Social Problems, US Office of Rsch. Integrity (rsch. integrity adv. com., 1999—), Phi Beta Kappa, Kappa Tau Alpha. Avocations: hiking, reading, creative writing, tennis, travel. Office: Dept Sociology Boston U 96-100 Cummington St Boston MA 02215 Office Phone: 617-358-0635. Business E-mail: pcyeager@bu.edu.

**YEAGER, PHILLIP CHARLES,** transportation company exeuctive; b. Bellevue, Ky., Nov. 15, 1927; s. Ferd A. and Helen (Koehler) Y.; m. Joyce E. Ruebusch, June 2, 1951; children: David P., Debra A. Yeager Jensen, Mark A. BA, U. Cin., 1951. Warehouse mgr. Pure Carbonic Co., Cin., 1950-52; trace clk., rate clk., asst. office mgr. Pa. R.R., Chgo., 1952-56, salesman Kansas City, Mo., 1956-59, asst. dir. Trailvan Phila., 1959-65, div. sales mgr. Milw., 1965-68; dir. Trailvan Penn-Ctrl. R.R., N.Y.C., 1968-71; pres. Hub City Terminals, Chgo., 1971-85; chmn. The Hub Group, Chgo., 1985—; also bd. dirs. Bd. dirs. 30 Hubcity terminals. Cpl. U.S. Army, 1946-47. Recipient Achievement award Intermodal Transp. Assn., 1991, Harry E. Salzberg medallion for outstanding achievement in transp.; named Chgo. Transp. Man of Yr., Chgo. Transp. Assn., 1990. Mem. N.Y. Traffic Club, Chgo. Traffic Club. Republican. Lutheran. Avocations: golf, biking, swimming.

**YEAGER, WILLIAM ROBERT,** musician, educator; b. Seattle, Oct. 1, 1952; s. Robert Frederick and Prisilla May Yeager; m. Chutaphin Chanlongbutr, Jan. 16, 1996. MusM, U. N.Tex., Denton, 1970—76. Profl. musician of studio, jazz & classical pvt., San Diego, 1965—, LA, 1965—; dir. instrumen-

tal music Grove Sch. Music, LA, 1976—78; founder, dir. LA Jazz Workshop, 1978—87; dir. jazz studies San Diego State U., 1985—; trombonist Westwind Brass, San Diego, 2002—, North Atlantic Jazz Alliance, LA, 2005—, Berlin, 2005—.

**YEAMANS, GEORGE THOMAS,** librarian, educator; b. Nov. 7, 1929; s. James Norman and Dolphine Sophia (Manhart) Yeamans; m. Mary Ann Seng, Feb. 1, 1958; children: Debra, Susan, Julia. AB, U. Va., 1950; MLS, U. Ky., 1955; EdD, Ind. U., 1965. Asst. audio-visual dir. Ind. State U., Terre Haute, 1957—58; asst. film libr. Ball State U., Muncie, Ind., 1958—61, film libr., 1961—69, assoc. prof. libr. sci., 1969—72, prof., 1972—95, prof. emeritus, 1995—. Cons. Pendleton (Ind.) Sch. Corp., 1962, 67, Captioned Films for the Deaf Workshop, Muncie, 1963—65, Decatur (Ind.) Sch. Sys., 1978; adjudicator Ind. Media Fair, 1979—93, David Letterman Scholarship Program, 1993. Author: Projectionists' Programmed Primer, 1969, rev. edit., 1982, Mounting and Preserving Pictorial Materials, 1976, Tape Recording, 1978, Transparency Making, 1977, Photographic Principles, 1981, Computer Literacy — A Programmed Primer, 1985, Designing Dynamic Media Presentations, 1996, Robert F. Kennedy Archival Project, 1968—2004, Building Effective Creative Project Teams, 2000, Building Effective Creative Project Teams, rev. ed., 2005; songwriter: Branson Bound, 1996; contbr. articles to profl. jours. Campaign worker Wilson for Mayor, Muncie, 1979. With USMC, 1950—52. Recipient Citations of Achievement, Internat. Biog. Assn., Cambridge, Eng., 1973, Am. Biog. Assn., 1976, Mayor James P. Carey award for achievement for disting. contbns. to Ball State U. and City of Muncie, 1988; Video Info. Sys. grant, Ball State U., 1993. Mem.: ALA, NEA (del. assembly dept. audiovisual instrn. 1967), Audio-Visual Instrn. Dirs. Ind. (exec. bd. 1962—68, pres. 1966—67), Thomas Jefferson Soc. Alumni U. Va., Ind. Pub. Libr. Assn., Ind. Acad. Libr. Assn., Ind. Corp. and Network Libr. Assn., Ind. Libr. Fedn., Assn. Ednl. Comm. and Tech., Autisim Soc. Am., Assn. Ind. Media Educators (chmn. auditing com. 1979—81), Ind. Assn. Ednl. Comms. and Tech. (dist. dir. 1972—76), Am. Assn. Sch. Librs., Phi Delta Kappa. Republican. Unitarian-Universalist. Avocations: photography, stamp collecting/philately, coin collecting/numismatics, genealogy. Home: 4507 W Burton Dr Muncie IN 47304-3575

**YEARGAN, MICHAEL,** scenic designer; MFA, Yale U., 1973. Assoc. prof. design Yale Sch. Drama, New Haven; resident designer Yale Repertory Theatre. Scenic designer Becket, London's West End, Cyrano de Bergerac, Napoleon, Present Laughter, Stratford Festival, Can., Noises Off!, (Operas) Otello, Met. Opera, Ariadne auf Naxos, Cosi Fan Tutti, Don Giovanni, Susanna, The Great Gatsby, Norma, NYC Opera, Madama Butterfly, Tosca, La Finta, Giardiniera, Central Park, Previn's A Streetcar Named Desire, San Francisco Opera, Luisa Miller, Dead Man Walking, Simon Boccanegra, Cold Sassy Tree, Houston Grand Opera, Royal Opera House, London, Australian Opera, La Scala, Staatsoper, Vienna, The Nutcracker, San Francisco Ballet, The Rainmaker, 2006, (Off-Broadway) Dinah Was, Juvenalia, (Broadway Shows) Terrence McNally's The Ritz, Bad Habits, Hay Fever, Ah, Wilderness!, Athol Fugard's A Lesson From Aloes, The Light in the Piazza, Lincoln Ctr. Theater, 2005— (Tony Award for best scenic design of a musical, 2005, Drama Desk award outstanding set design of a musical, 2005), Awake and Sing!, 2006 (Drama Desk award outstanding set design of a play, 2006). Office: Yale Sch Drama PO Box 208325 New Haven CT 06520 also: Lincoln Ctr Theater 150 W 65th St New York NY 10023*

**YEARLEY, BARBARA ELLEN,** music educator; b. Lorain, Ohio, May 5, 1950; d. Quentin Fred and June Louise Linger; m. Craig E. Yearley, Apr. 19, 1978; children: Eric Jason, Jay Alan. BSc in Edn., OH State U., 1973; student, Cleve. State U., 1989—90; M in Curriculum and Instrn., Ashland U., 2008. Cert. Elem. Music Tchr. (grades one through eight) Ohio, 1985, Elem. Edn. Tchr. Ohio, 1975. Music tchr. St. Mary Elem. Sch., Vermilion, Ohio, 1985—2000, St. Jude Sch., Elyria, Ohio, 1990—2000, Copopa Elem. Sch., Columbia Station, Ohio, 2000—. Reading tutor Columbia Station Sch. Dist., Ohio, 2000—04, music program prodr., 2000—, mentor, 2004—. Author, prodr.: music program Ohio Sings, 2003, Scientific Music, 2004. Organist First Bapt. Ch., Lorain, 1995—. Recipient Pursuit of Excellence award, Columbia Schs. Bd. Edn., 2001, Most Valuable Educator, Applebees Restaurant, Strongsville, OH, 2003. Mem.: Music Educators Nat. Conf., Ohio Edn. Assn., Nat. Educators Assn., Ohio Music Edn. Assn., Firelands Lions Club (publicity chmn. 2003—04, v.p. 2005—). Avocations: skiing, boating, gardening. Home: 8038 Claus Rd Amherst OH 44001 Office: Copopa Elem Sch 14168 SW River Columbia Station OH 44028

**YEARWOOD, TRISHA,** country music singer, songwriter; b. Monticello, Ga., 1964; m. Chris Latham (div.); m. Robert Reynolds, May 21, 1994 (div.); m. Garth Brooks, Dec. 10, 2005. Degree in Music Bus., Belmont U. Intern MTM Records, demo singer, commercial jingles singer; recording artist MCA Records. Albums include Trisha Yearwood, 1991 (double platinum), Hearts in Armor, 1992 (Grammy nomination: Best Country Female Vocal, 1994 for "Walkaway Joe"), The Song Remembers When, 1993, Thinkin' About You, 1995, Everybody Knows, 1996, (songbook) A Collection of Hits, 1997, Where Your Road Leads, 1998, Real Live Woman, 2000, Inside Out, 2001, Jasper County, 2005; back-up vocalist Garth Brooks albums; opening act Garth Brooks Tour, 1991; TV appearances on TNN American Music Shop, The Tonight Show, Late Night with David Letterman, Good Morning America, A&E Live By Request, 1998 Academy Awards, 1996 Summer Olympic Closing Ceremonies. Named Best New Country Artist by Am. Music Awards, 1992, Top New Female Vocalist by Acad. Country Music, Mus. Assn., 1997, 98; first female in country music history to have debut single reach #1 on charts with She's in Love with the Love, 1991; recipient Grammy awards for best female country vocal, 1998, best country vocal collaboration (with Aaron Neville) 1994, (with Garth Brooks), 1998.

**YEARY, SHERIDAN TODD,** pastor, educator; b. Augusta, Ga., Sept. 26, 1966; s. Aaron Vaughn Yeary and Marjorie Gordon Barbee; m. Sarah Adams, July 2, 1994 (div. June 0, 2002); children: Robert Aaron, Simone Kathlene. BA, National-Louis U., Wheaton, Ill., 1991—93; MDiv, Garrett-Evangelical Theol. Sem., Evanston, Ill., 1993—96; PhD, Northwestern U., Evanston, 1996—2006. Asst. dir. No. Ill. U., DeKalb, 2000—; sr. pastor Logan St. Bapt. Ch., Batavia, Ill., 2001—. Mem., bd. christian edn. & publ. Prog. Nat. Bapt. Conv., Inc., 2004—; nat. moderator African Am. Male Empowerment Summit, East Orange, NJ, 2000—02; founder Cmty. Excellence & Empowerment Devel. Corp., Batavia, 2004; mem. Two Rivers Head Start, Aurora, Ill., 2004—. Sgt. Army Res., 1985—92, Aurora. Grantee Hartmann fellow, Garrett-Evangelical Theol. Sem., 1996—98, SPS Devel. grant, No. Ill. U., 2005—06. Fellow: Oxford Round Table; mem.: Am. Sociol. Assn., Free and Accepted Mason, PHA, Phi Beta Delta Internat. Honor Soc., Alpha Phi Alpha Frat., Inc. (life). Avocations: travel, golf, music, public speaking. Home: 2301 Independence Dr Aurora IL 60506 Office: Logan Street Baptist Ch 908 N River St Batavia IL 60510 Home Fax: 630-879-7209; Office Fax: 630-879-7209. Personal E-mail: stoddyeary@loganstreet.net.

**YEATES, MARIE R.,** lawyer; b. New Orleans, Feb. 24, 1956; BS summa cum laude, La. State U., 1977, JD, 1980. Bar: La. 1980, U.S. Ct. Appeals (5th cir.) 1981, U.S. Ct. Appeals (11th cir.) 1981, Tex. 1982, Tex. Supreme Ct. 1982, U.S. Dist. Ct. (so. dist.) Tex. 1985, U.S. Supreme Ct. 1986, U.S. Ct. Appeals (9th cir.) 1998, U.S. Dist. Ct. (no. dist.) Tex. 2001, U.S. Ct. Appeals (10th cir.) 2002, U.S. Ct. Appeals (7th cir.) 2004. Ptnr., co-head Appellate Sect. Vinson & Elkins LLP, Houston, 1990—. Office: Vinson & Elkins LLP First City Tower 1001 Fannin St, Ste 2300 Houston TX 77002 Office Phone: 713-758-4576. E-mail: myeates@velaw.com.

**YEATMAN, HARRY CLAY,** biologist, educator; b. Ashwood, Tenn., June 22, 1916; s. Trezevant Player and Mary (Wharton) Y.; m. Jean Hansford Anderson, Nov. 24, 1949; children — Henry Clay, Jean Hansford. AB, U. N.C., Chapel Hill, 1939, MA, 1942, PhD, 1953; student, Cornell U., summer 1937. Asst. prof. biology U. of South, Sewanee, Tenn., 1950-54, asso. prof., 1954-60, prof., 1960—, Kenan prof., 1980—, chmn. dept., 1972-76, elderhostel tchr., 1987-88. Vis. prof. marine biology Va. Inst. Marine Sci.,

Gloucester Point, summer 1967; cons. Smithsonian Instn., Sci. Applications, Inc., La Jolla, Calif., Ctrs. for Disease Control, Atlanta, WHO, Ecol. Analysts, Inc., Balt., Duke Power Co., Charlotte, N.C., Helminthic Disease Branch. Contbr. articles to profl. jours. Served with AUS, 1942-46. Gen. Edn. Bd. fellow, 1941-42; Brown Found. fellow, 1984 Fellow AAAS; mem. Soc. Systematic Biology (charter), Soc. Limnology and Oceanography (charter), Soc. Ichthyology and Herpetology, Tenn. Acad. Sci., Am. Micros. Soc., Am. Ornithologists Union, Tenn. Ornithol. Soc., Tenn. Archeol. Soc., Nat. Speleological Soc., Blue Key, Phi Beta Kappa, Sigma Xi, Omicron Delta Kappa, Sigma Nu. Republican. Episcopalian. Home: PO Box 356 Jumpoff Rd Sewanee TN 37375 Office: 735 University Ave Sewanee TN 37383-1000 Office Phone: 931-598-5367. Office Fax: 931-598-1145.

**YEATMAN, HENRY CLAY,** mechanical engineer; b. Sewanee, Tenn., July 13, 1957; s. Harry and Jean Yeatman; m. Paula Ann Hess, Oct. 7, 2000. BA in Math., U. South, Sewanee, Tenn., 1976—79; B of Mech. Engring., Ga. Inst. Tech., Atlanta, 1979—81. Tire devel. engr. B. F. Goodrich, Akron, Ohio, 1981—85; rsch. engr. Honda R&D Americas, Torrance, Calif., 1985—89; sr. engr. Am. Honda, Alpharetta, Ga., 1989—. Mem.: Soc. Automotive Entrs., Sports Car Club Am. Unitarian. Office: American Honda 4900 Marconi Dr Alpharetta GA 30005 Office Phone: 678-339-2567.

**YEATS, ROBERT SHEPPARD,** geologist, educator; b. Miami, Fla., Mar. 30, 1931; s. Robert Sheppard and Carolyn Elizabeth (Rountree) Y.; m. Lillian Eugenia Bowie, Dec. 30, 1952 (dec. Apr. 1991); children: Robert Bowie, David Claude, Stephen Paul, Kenneth James, Sara Elizabeth; m. Angela M. Hayes, Jan. 7, 1993. BA, U. Fla., 1952; MS, U. Wash., 1956, PhD, 1958. Registered geologist, Oreg., Calif., Wash. Geologist, petroleum exploration and prodn. Shell Oil Co., Ventura and L.A., Calif., 1958-67, Shell Devel. Co., Houston, 1967; assoc. prof. geology Ohio U., Athens, 1967-70, prof., 1970-77; prof. geology Oreg. State U., Corvallis, 1977-97, prof. oceanography, 1991-97, prof. emeritus, 1997—, chmn. dept., 1977-85; geologist U.S. Geol. Survey, 1968, 69, 75, Glomar Challenger scientist, 1971, co-chief scientist, 1973-74, 78; mem. Oreg. Bd. Geologist Examiners, 1981-83; chmn. Working Group 1 Internat. Lithosphere Program, 1987-90, chmn. task force group on paleoseismology, 1990-98; chmn. subcom. on Himalayan active faults Internat. Geol. Correlation Program, Project 206, 1984-92; mem. geophysics study com. NRC, 1987-94. Rschr. on Cenozoic tectonics of So. Calif., Oreg., Wash., New Zealand and Himalaya; active faults of Calif. Transverse Ranges, deep-sea drilling in Ea. Pacific; vis. scientist New Zealand Geol. Survey, 1983-84, 99, Geol. Survey of Japan, 1992, Inst. de Phys. du Globe de Paris, 1993, So. Calif. Earthquake Ctr.; sr. cons. Earth Cons. Internat., 1997—, ptnr., 2001—. Author: The Geology of Earthquakes, 1997, Living with Earthquakes in the Pacific Northwest, 1998, 2d edit., 2004, Living with Earthquakes in California-A Survivor's Guide, 2001. Mem. Ojai (Calif.) City Planning Commn., 1961-62, Ojai City Coun., 1962-65. 1st lt. U.S. Army, 1952-54. Named Richard H. Jahns Disting. Lectr. in Engring. Geology, 1995; Ohio U. rsch. fellow, 1973-74; grantee NSF, U.S. Geol. Survey. Fellow AAAS, Geol. Soc. Am. (chmn. structural geology and tectonics divsn. 1984-85, Cordilleran sect. 1988-89, assoc. editor bull. 1987-89); mem. Am. Assn. Petroleum Geologists (Outstanding Educator award Pacific sect. 1991, Michel T. Halbouty human needs award 1998), Am. Geophys. Union, Seismol. Soc. Am., Earthquake Engring. Rsch. Inst. Home: 1654 NW Crest Pl Corvallis OR 97330-1812 Office: Oreg State U Dept Geoscis Corvallis OR 97331-5506 Office Phone: 541-737-1226. E-mail: yeatsr@geo.oregonstate.edu.

**YEAZELL, CAROL D.,** language educator; b. Cin., Aug. 26, 1948; MA in English, Xavier U., Cin., 1988. English tchr. Seton HS, Cin., 1971—72, St. Antonitus Elem., Cin., 1972—73, McAuley HS, Cin., 1973—77, Mother of Mercy HS, Cin., 1980—88, St. Ursula Acad., Cin., 1988—96, McAuley HS, 1996—. Office: McAuley HS 6000 Oakwood Ave Cincinnati OH 45224 Office Phone: 513-681-1800. Business E-mail: yeazellc@mcavlyhs.net.

**YEAZELL, RUTH BERNARD,** English language educator; b. NYC, Apr. 4, 1947; d. Walter and Annabelle (Reich) Bernard; m. Stephen C. Yeazell, Aug. 14, 1969 (div. 1980). BA with high honors, Swarthmore Coll., 1967; MPhil, Yale U., 1970, PhD, 1971. Asst. prof. English Boston U., 1971-74, UCLA, 1975-77, assoc. prof., 1977-80, prof., 1980-91, Yale U., New Haven, 1991—; dir. grad. studies, 1993-98, Chace family prof., 1995—, chair, 2000—05. Author: Language and Knowledge in the Late Novels of Henry James, 1976, Death and Letters of Alice James, 1981, Fictions of Modesty: Women and Courtship in the English Novel, 1991, Harems of the Mind: Passages of Western Art and Literature, 2000; assoc. editor Nineteenth-Century Fiction, 1977-80; editor: Sex, Politics and Science in the 19th Century Novel, 1986, Henry James: A Collection of Critical Essays, 1994. Dir. Lewis Walpole Libr., 1996—. Woodrow Wilson fellow, 1967-68, Guggenheim fellow, 1979-80, NEH fellow, 1988-89, Pres.'s rsch. fellow U. Calif., 1988-89, Getty scholar, 2003-04 (declined), Bellagio Ctr. Residency scholar, 2005. Mem. MLA (exec. coun. 1985-88), English Inst. (supervising com. 1983-86). Office: Yale U Dept English New Haven CT 06520-8302 Office Phone: 203-432-2239.

**YECKE, CHERI PIERSON,** educational researcher, administrator, columnist, writer; b. St. Paul, Feb. 5, 1955; d. Leo Sylvester and Marceline Mae (Intihar) Pierson; m. Dennis Joseph Yecke. Dec. 22, 1973; children: Anastasia, Tiffany. BA, U. Hawaii, 1975; MST, U. Wis., River Falls, 1984; PhD, U. Va., 2001. Apptd. mem. State Bd. Edn., State of Va., 1995—98, dep. sec. edn., 1998—2001, sec. edn., 2001—02; dir. tchr. quality and pub. sch. choice US Dept. Edn., 2002—03; sr. adv. to White House on USA Freedom Corps., 2003; commr. edn. State of Minn., 2003—04; disting. sr. fellow for edn. and social policy Ctr. of the Am. Experiment, 2004—05; chancellor for K-12 edn. State of Fla., Tallahassee, 2005—. Author: The War Against Excellence: The Rising Tide of Mediocrity in America's Middle Schools, 2003, Mayhem in the Middle: How Middle Schools Have Failed America and How to Make Them Work, 2005. Mem.: Am. Coun. Trustees & Alumni, Nat. Assn. Scholars. Republican. Home: 1315 Peacefield Pl Tallahassee FL 32308-0844 Office Phone: 850-245-0509.

**YEDIDSION, MEIRA,** computer artist, sculptor; b. Tehran, Iran, Oct. 29, 1955; arrived in U.S., 1988, naturalized, 1999; d. Moshe Moussa Yedidsion and Ester Ashraf Lavi. MFA, U. Tehran, 1976, Acad. Fine Arts Rome, 1983. Painter, sculptor, installation artist, multimedia artist FIFA World Cup Korea Japan, Republic of Korea, 2002—. Exhibitions include Seville Universal Expo, Spain, 1992, prin. works include a 9/11 Meml. Monument, Levantine Cultural Ctr., LA, 2002, exhibitions include The 34th Festival of Two Worlds of Spoleto, Italy, 1991, over 240 solo and group shows, Represented in permanent collections The Israel Mus., Jerusalem, Skirball Mus., LA, Mus. Modern Art. N.Y.C., Detroit's Musem of New Art, Mus. of Catujia, Seville, Spain, Fuller Mus., Mass.; contbr. articles to mags. and websites; one-man shows include Italian Cultural Inst., L.A., Calif., 1998, Bank of Am. Main, Beverly Hills, Calif., 2002—06, Mus. Ducal Palace of Mantua, Italy, 1996, numerous others, exhibited in group shows at Balt. Mus. Art, 2002, Venice Film Festival, Italy, 2003, exhibitions include Balt. Mus. Art, 2002, Detroit Mus. New Art, 2001—02, Museo Nazionale Di Villa Pisani, 1996, Palazzo Valentini, Rome, 1986, Galleria Civica dell Arte Contemporanea, Termoli, Italy, 1992, Museo de la Ciudad, Mex., 2002, Mus. Chung HakDae, Ansung-si, Korea, 2002, Mus. Nat. Ctr. African Am. Artists, Mass., 1992, prin. works include The Suspended Room, Italian Cultural Inst. Italy in L.A. (Proclamation of City of L.A., 1998), exhibitions include Inner Mongolia Mus. Fine Arts, China, 2002, Castle Aragonese, Otranto, Italy, 1987, Chgo. Cultural Ctr., 2002. Recipient Medal for Americas award, Dir. Dep. Gen., 2003; scholar, U. Fine Arts Tehran, 1972—76. Jewish. Home and Office: 411 North Palm Drive Suite 6 Beverly Hills CA 90210 Office Phone: 310-283-7503. Home Fax: 310-275-7540; Office Fax: 310-275-7540. E-mail: meirayedidsion@aol.com.

**YEE, ALBERT HOY,** educator, retired psychologist; educator; b. Santa Barbara, Calif., June 14, 1929; children: Lisa Diane, Hoyt Brian. BA, U. Calif., Berkeley, 1952; MA, San Francisco State U., 1959; EdD, Stanford U., 1965. Post-doctoral research fellow U. Oreg., Eugene, 1966-67; assoc. prof.

edn. U. Wis., Madison, 1967-70, prof., 1970-73; prof. ednl. psychology, dean grad. studies and research Calif. State U., Long Beach, 1973-79, originating founder Grad. Ctr., 1974; prof. edn. U. Mont., 1979-83, dean Sch. Edn. 1979-82; sr. lectr. psychology Chinese U. of Hong Kong, 1985-89; dean, prof. psychology Am. Coll., Singapore; sr. lectr. psychology Nat. U., Singapore, 1989-90; dir. program U. Md., Hongkong, 1990; disting. vis. prof. ednl. psychology spl. adviser coll. grad. studies and internat. programs Marist Coll., 1990-92; prof. ednl. psychology Fla. Internat. U., Miami, 1992-94, rsch. scholar, 1994-95. Chmn. 1st Fed. Adv. Com. for Asian and Pacific Island Ams., Bur. Census, 1976-81; bd. dirs. Sino-Judaie Inst., 2004-. Author: Man, Society and the World, 1968; co-author: Comprehensive Spelling Instruction: Theory, Research and Application, 1971; editor: Social Interaction in Educational Settings, 1971, Perspectives on Management Systems Approaches to Education: A Symposium, 1973, Search for Meaning, 1984, A Study on Possible Future Developments for Hong Kong: Strategic Planning and Innovations, 1985, A People Misruled: Hong Kong and the Chinese Stepping-Stone Syndrome, 1989, 2d edit., 1992; editor: East Asian Higher Education: Traditions and Transformations, 1994, Whither Hong Kong: China's Shadow or Visionary Gleam?, 1999, Yeee-Hah!: Remembrances and Longing, 2005. With AUS, 1952-55, Korea, Japan. Recipient Civic Commendation Madison, 1973; sr. Fulbright lectr. Tokyo and Tamagawa Univs., Japan; also 1st Fulbright scholar to People's Republic China, 1972. Fellow AAAS, Nat. Conf. Research in English, Am. Psychol. Assn., Am. Psychol. Soc.; mem. Calif. Coll. and Univ. Faculty Assn. (founder 1961), Chinese Hist. Soc. Am. and Orgn. of Chinese Americans (Bicentennial speaker), Asian-Am. Psychol. Assn. (pres. 1979-82, jour. editor 1981-82), Western Mont. Stanford Alumni Club (founding pres. 1997—). Home: 3822 Lincoln Rd Missoula MT 59802-3039 E-mail: alyee@montana.com.

**YEE, KEITH PHILIP,** finance company executive, accountant; b. Luton, Eng., Apr. 26, 1958; came to the U.S., 1985; m. Ginny Sung, Feb. 9, 1985; children: Ashley, Brittany. BA in Acctg. with honors, Exeter U., 1979. CPA, Calif. Sr. audit Ernst & Whinney, London, 1979—83, supr. investigation Hong Kong, 1983—85, audit mgr. Memphis, 1985—86; audit sr. mgr. Ernst & Young, San Francisco, 1986—91, internat. resident, 1991—93, audit sr. mgr. San Francisco, 1993—95, Price Waterhouse, San Jose, Calif., 1995—97, Adaptec, Milpitas, Calif., 1997—98, Synnex Info. Tech., Fremont, Calif., 1998—2000, Tripath Tech., Inc., Santa Clara, Calif., 2000—05, Atheros Comm., Inc., Santa Clara, 2005—. Vice chmn. adv. coun. for svcs. to srs. Salvation Army, San Francisco, 1989. Grad. leadership San Francisco program San Francisco C. of C., 1990. Fellow Inst. Chartered Accts. in Eng. and Wales; mem. AICPA, Asian Am. CPAs (mem. adv. bd. 1994-95), Calif. Soc. CPAs, Inst. for Internat. Edn. (student programs com. 1990-95), San Francisco C. of C. (internat. bus. devel. com. 1993-95), Palo Alto Tennis Club. Avocations: international travel, music, sports. Office: Atheros Comm Inc 5480 Great America Pkwy Santa Clara CA 95054 E-mail: xyee@athoos.com.

**YEE, KENTON K.,** educator; MS, Calif. Inst. of Tech., Pasadena, 1985; JD, Stanford U., Palo Alto, 2000; PhD, Stanford U., Palo Alto, Calif., 2001. Asst. prof. Columbia U., N.Y.C., 2001—. Mem. adv. bd. HedgeStreet, Inc., San Mateo, Calif., 2004. Office: Columbia U 615 Uris Hall 3022 Broadway New York NY 10027 Office Phone: 212-854-4495. Office Fax: columbia.edu/kky2001/.

**YEE, LELAND Y.,** state legislator; b. China; four children. Grad. U. Calif., Berkeley; MA, San Francisco State U.; PhD in Child Psychology, U. Hawaii. Pres. Bd. Edn. City of San Francisco, 1988-96, mem. Bd. Suprs., 1996—2002; mem. Calif. State Assembly, 2002—, speaker pro tempore, 2004—, chair children's phys. and mental well-being in diverse Calif. comtys. subcom. Pres. Nat. Asian Pacific Am. Caucus of State Legislators, 2004—. Mem. San Francisco Bay Conservation and Devel. Commn., Calif. Performance Rev. Commn. on Runaway Prodn. Office: State Capitol PO Box 942849 Sacramento CA 94249 Address: San Francisco Stae Bldg 455 Golden Gate Ave Ste 14600 San Francisco CA 94102 Office Phone: 916-319-2012. E-mail: Assemblymember.Yee@assembly.ca.gov.

**YEE, ROBERT DONALD,** ophthalmologist; b. Beijing, Feb. 21, 1945; came to U.S., 1947, naturalized, 1947; s. James and Mary Y.M. (Li) Y.; m. Linda Margaret Neil, June 28, 1968; children: Jillian Neil, Allison Betram. AB in biology summa cum laude, Harvard U., 1966; MD in medicine cum laude, Harvard Med. Sch., 1970. Diplomate Am. Bd. Ophthalmology. Fullbright scholar, 1966; intern in internal medicine U. Rochester, NY, 1970-71; resident in ophthalmology Jules Stein Eye Inst. UCLA, 1971-74; fellow in neuro-ophthalmology Nat. Eye Inst., NIH, Bethesda, Md., 1974-76; chief ophthalmology Harbor-UCLA Med. Ctr., Torrance, Calif., 1976-78; asst. prof. ophthalmology Sch. Medicine UCLA, 1976-78, assoc. prof., 1978-82, prof., 1982-87; prof., dept. chmn. ophthalmology Ind. U. Sch. Medicine, Indpls., 1987—. Mem. residency rev. com. for ophthalmology Accrediation Coun. for Grad. Med. Edn., 1995-2002, vice-chmn., 1998-2000, chmn., 2000-2002. Mem. editorial bd. Investigative Ophthalmology and Visual Sci., 1982—, von Graefe's Archives of Ophthalmology, 1983-89; Feldman endowed chair ophthalmology UCLA, 1984-87; Grayson endowed chair ophthalmology Ind. U., 2003—. Author numerous med. research papers. Lt. comdr. USPHS, 1974—76. Grantee, NIH, 1976—84; scholar Dolly Green Rsch. scholar, 1984—86. Fellow: ACS, Am. Acad. Ophthalmology; mem.: AMA, Accreditation Cou. for Grad. Med. Edn. (residency rev. com., chair 2000—02), Indpls. Ophthal. Soc., Ind. Med. Soc., Chinese Am. Ophthal. Soc. (pres. 1996—98), Ind. Acad. Ophthalmology, Am. Ophthal Soc., Assn. Rsch. in Vision and Ophthalmology (chmn. eye movement sect. 1981, 1987, trustee 1996—2001, v.p. 2000—01), Phi Beta Kappa, Alpha Omega Alpha. Office: Ind U Med Ctr 702 Rotary Cir Indianapolis IN 46202-5133 Office Phone: 317-274-7101. E-mail: ryee@iupui.edu.

**YEE, SANDRA GAYLE BROWN,** librarian; b. Benzonia, Mich., July 17, 1949; d. Al Powell and Maxine G. (Wallace) Brown; m. D. Johnny Yee, June 29, 1974; 1 child, Melissa Ann. BA, Western Mich. U., 1970, MLS, 1973; EdD, U. Mich., 1979. Libr., coord. libr. svcs. Muskegon C.C., Mich., 1973—82; coord. access svcs. Univ. Libr., Ea. Mich. U., Ypsilanti, 1982—90, assoc. dean for learning resources and tech., 1990—2001; dean univ. libr. sys. Wayne State U., Detroit, 2001—. Author: (with M. Boone and R. Bullard) Training Student Library Assistants, 1991. Mem. ALA, Assn. Coll. and Rsch. Librs. (past chair univ. libr. section 2005—), Mich. Libr. Assn. (treas. 1989-91, pres.-elect 1992-93, pres. 1993-94, past pres. 1994-95, Mich. libr. consortium bd. chair 1997-98, OCLC mem. coun. v.p., pres.-elect, 2006—). Office: Wayne State U Detroit MI 48202 Home: 46355 Wesford Ct Plymouth MI 48170-3059 Office Phone: 313-577-4020. Business E-Mail: sandra.yee@wayne.edu.

**YEE, SIENHO,** law educator; b. Zhanjiang, Guangdong, China, July 9, 1965; BA, Brandeis U., 1989; JD, Columbia U. 1993. Bar: U.S. Ct. Appeals (3rd cir.) 1994, N.Y. 1994, U.S. Supreme Ct. 2004. Law clk. Judge Robert Cowen U.S. Ct. Appeals (3rd cir.), Trenton, NJ 1993—94; law clk. Appeals Chamber, UN Internat. Criminal Tribunal for the Former Yugoslavia, The Hague, Netherlands, 1995—96; counsel legal dept. Internat. Monetary Fund, Washington, 1996—97; tutor in internat. law St Hugh's Coll., Oxford (Eng.) U., 1999—2000; vis. asst. prof. Northwestern U. Law Sch., Chgo., 2000—00; lectr. law Queen Mary, U. London, 2001—01; assoc. prof. law U. Colo. Law Sch., Boulder, 2001—; assoc. Sullivan & Cromwell, N.Y.C. Author: Towards an International Law of Co-progressiveness, 2004; editor-in-chief: Chinese Jour. Internat. Law, 2003; editor: International Law in the Post-Cold War World, 2001, International Crime and Punishment, vol. 1, 2003, International Crime and Punishment, vol. 2, 2004; contbr. articles to profl. jours. Wien Internat. scholar, Brandeis U., 1987—89, Harlan Fiske Stone scholar, Columbia Law Sch., 1990—92. Mem.: Phi Beta Kappa. Office: Univ Colo Law School 401 UCB Boulder CO 80309-0401 Office Phone: 303-735-0205. Home Fax: 707-788-4178; Office Fax: 707-788-4178. Personal E-mail: yee@sienhoyee.org.

**YEEND, FRANCES,** soprano, music educator; b. Vancouver, Wash., Jan. 28, 1913; d. Warren DeWitt and Grace Johnson Lynch; m. Kenneth Yeend (div.); 1 child, Warren; m. James William Benner, May 9, 1951. LHD (hon.), W.Va. U., 1996; DMus (hon.), Shenandoah Conservatory, 2000; studied, Wash. State U. Prof. W.Va. U., Morgantown, 1966—78; ret., 1978. Soprano (Operas) The Merry Widow, 1943, Carmen, 1944, Boston Symphony Orch., 1946, Peter Grimes, Tanglewood Music Festival, Bel Canto Trio, La Traviata, NYC Ctr. Opera, 1948, Amelia Goes to the Ball, The Marriage of Figaro, Faust, Die Meistersinger, Carmen, The Four Ruffians, Aida, Pagliacci, Tosca and Turandot, La Boheme, The Tales of Hoffman, La Traviata, Vienna Staatsoper, 1953, La Boheme, Covent Garden, London, Turandot, Arena di Verona, Italy, 1958, Elektra, 1961, Philharmonic, Chgo. Symphony, Phil. Orch., Boston Symphony.

**YEGGE, ROBERT BERNARD,** law educator, retired dean; b. Denver, June 17, 1934; s. Ronald Van Kirk and Fairy (Hill) Y. AB magna cum laude, Princeton U., 1956; MA in Sociology, U. Denver, 1958, JD, 1959. Bar: Colo. 1959, D.C. 1978. Ptnr. Yegge, Hall and Evans, Denver, 1959-78; with Harding Shultz & Downs successor to Nelson and Harding, 1979—; prof. U. Denver Coll. Law, 1965—, dean, 1965-77, 97-98, dean emeritus, 1977—; asst. to pres. Denver Post, 1971-75; v.p., exec. dir. Nat. Ctr. Preventive Law, 1986-91. Author: Colorado Negotiable Instruments Law, 1960, Some Goals; Some Tasks, 1965, The American Lawyer: 1976, 1966, New Careers in Law, 1969, The Law Graduate, 1972, Tomorrow's Lawyer: A Shortage and Challenge, 1974, Declaration of Independence for Legal Education, 1976, Principles of Law Office Management, 2004. Mng. trustee Denver Ctr. for Performing Arts, 1972-75; chmn. Colo. Dumb Friends League, 1992—, chmn. 2000—, Met. Denver Legal Aid Soc., 1994-99, Colo. Legal Svcs., 2000—, Colo. Acad.; chmn. Colo. Prevention Ctr., 2000—; trustee, vice chmn. Nat. Assembly State Arts Agys.; vice chmn. Mexican-Am. Legal Edn. and Def. Fund, 1970-76. Recipient Disting. Svc. award Denver Jr. C. of C., 1965; Harrison Tweed award Am. Assn. Continuing Edn. Adminstrs., 1985, Alumni Faculty award U. Denver, 1993. Mem. ABA (chmn. lawyers conf. 1987-88, chmn. accreditation comm. for legal asst. programs 1980-90, standing com. legal assts. 1987-92, 98-2001, standing com. delivery legal svcs. 1992-95, 2001-04, com. on Gavel award 1995-98, del. to jud. adminstrn. coun. 1989-95, Robert B. Yegge award 1996), Law and Soc. Assn. (life, pres. 1965-70), Colo. Bar Assn. (bd. govs. 1965-77, 97-98), Denver Bar Assn., D.C. Bar Assn., Am. Law Inst. (life), Am. Judicature Soc. (bd. dirs. 1968-72, 75-85, Herbert Harley award 1985), Assn. Am. Law Schs., Order St. Ives, Phi Beta Kappa, Phi Delta Phi, Alpha Kappa Keta, Omicron Delta Kappa. Home: 3472 S Race St Englewood CO 80113-3138 Office: U Denver Coll Law 2255 E Evans Ave Denver CO 80208 Office Phone: 303-871-6294. Business E-Mail: ryegge@law.du.edu.

**YEGULALP, TUNCEL M.,** mining engineer, educator; b. Konya, Turkey, Nov. 5, 1937; came to U.S., 1963; s. Faik Suleyman and Selma Safiye (Karatay) Y.; m. Sevinc Guneri, July 5, 1963; children: Ali, Serdar. BS, Tech. U., Istanbul, 1961; DEngring. Sci., Columbia U., 1968. Mining engr. M.T.A., Ankara, Turkey, 1961-63, chief feasibility studies group, 1971; rsch. engr. Mobil Rsch., Paulsboro, NJ, 1967-69; chief sys. cons. Sisag Ltd., Ankara, 1971-72; asst. prof. Columbia U., N.Y.C., 1972-75; assoc. prof. Henry Krumb Sch. Mines, 1975-85, prof., 1985—. Dir. N.Y. Mining and Mineral Resources Inst. Rsch., 1987—; elected permanent mem. U.S. del. World Mining Congress, 1993. Author articles in field. Served to 2d lt. C.E. Turkish Army, 1969-71. Internat. AEC fellow, Vienna, 1963; Krumb fellow, Columbia U., 1964, Campbell fellow, 1965. Mem. AIME, Internat. Higher Edn. Acad. Scis., Turkish Studies Assn., Inst. for Ops. Rsch. and the Mgmt. Scis., Sigma Chi. Moslem. Office: Columbia U 924 SWM MC4711 500 W 120th St New York NY 10027 Office Phone: 212-854-2984. E-mail: yegulalp@columbia.edu.

**YEH, CHIA-CHOU,** electrical engineer, researcher; b. Taipei, Taiwan, Oct. 10, 1978; arrived in U.S., 1996; s. Kuo Xsing and Hsu Pao Chai Yeh. BSEE with hons., Marquette U., Milw., Wis., 2000, MSEE, 2003, student in Elec. Engring., 2003—. Registered profl. engr., Dept. of Regulation and Licensing, Wis., 2000. Elec. engr. R. R. Donnelley & Sons Co., Dwight, Ill., 1998—99; power electronics engr. (intern) Eaton Corp., Milw., 2003—; grad. rsch. asst. Marquette U., 2003—. Contbr. articles to profl. jours. Fellow, U.S. Dept. Edn., 2000—01; grantee, NSF, 2003—; scholar, Marquette U., 2001—02. Mem.: IEEE, Sigma Xi, Phi Mu Epsilon, Eta Kappa Nu, Tau Beta Pi. Avocations: travel, computer, music, movies. Home: 610 N 17th Street 309 Milwaukee WI 53233 Office: Marquette University 1515 W Wisconsin Ave Milwaukee WI 53233 Office Phone: 414-288-1593. Office Fax: 414-288-5579. Personal E-mail: chiachouyeh@hotmail.com. Business E-Mail: chiachou.yeh@marquette.edu.

**YEH, KUO HSING,** bank executive; b. Taipei, Taiwan, Republic of China, Feb. 1, 1932; m. Hsiu-Mei Yeh Tsang. BA, Nat. Taiwan U., 1954. Exec. v.p. Hwa Nan Comml. Bank, Ltd., Taiwan, 1955-81; pres. Banking Inst. Republic China, 1981-88; CEO Fin. Info. System Group Ministery Fin., Taiwan, 1984-88; pres. Chang Hwa Comml. Bank Ltd., Taiwan, 1988-94; chmn. Taipeibank, Taipei, 1994-97, Taiwan First Investment & Trust Co Ltd, Taipei, 1998, Cathay United Bank Co Ltd., Tapei, Taiwan, 1998—. Author: Theory and Practice of Lending Management, 1980; editor: Practice of Bank's Consumer Loan, 1983. Recipient Disting. Fin. Staffer award Ministry Fin., Taipei, 1974. Mem. Banker's Assn. Taiwan (chmn. 1988-92), Banker's Assn. Taipei (chmn. 1992-97), Taiwan U. Alumni Assn. (mng. dir. Taipei chpt. 1994), Taiwan U. Alumni Club, Taipei Yuen-Shan Club. Home: 3 Fl No 432 Chi Lin Rd Taipei 104 Taiwan Office: Cathay United Bank Co Ltd 218 Sec 2 Tun Hwa S Rd Taipei 104 Taiwan

**YEH, RAYMOND WEI-HWA,** architect, educator; b. Shanghai, Feb. 25, 1942; came to U.S., 1958, naturalized, 1976; s. Herbert Hwan-Ching and Joyce Bo-Ding (Kwan) Y.; m. Hsiao-Yen Chen, Sept. 16, 1967; children: Bryant Po Yung, Clement Chung-Yung, Emily Su-Yung. BA, U. Oreg., 1965, B.Arch., 1967; M.Arch., U. Minn., 1969. Cert. Nat. Coun. Archtl. Registration Bds.; registered architect, Tex., Okla., Calif., Hawaii. Draftsman, designer various archtl. firms, 1965-68; design architect Ellerbe Architects, St. Paul, 1968-70; v.p., dir. design Sorey Hill, Binnicker, Oklahoma City, 1973-74; prin. architect Raymond W.H. Yeh & Assos., Norman, Okla., 1974-80; asst. prof. to prof. U. Okla., Norman, 1970-79; head dept. architecture, prof. Calif. Poly. State U., San Luis Obispo, 1979-83; dean Coll. Architecture U. Okla., Norman, 1983-92; prin. architect W.H. Raymond Yeh, Norman, 1983-93; dean sch. architecture U. Hawaii at Manoa, Honolulu, 1993—. Profl. adviser Neighborhood Conservation and Devel. Center, Oklahoma City, 1977 79 Works include: St. Thomas More U. Parish and Student Center, Norman, Summit Ridge Center Retirement Community, Harrah, Okla., (recipient Nat. Design award Guild Religious Architecture 1978). Nat. Endowment for Arts fellow, 1978-79 Fellow AIA (dir., pres. Okla. chpt. 1986, design awards, nat. com. chmn. 1989); mem. Calif. Coun. Archtl. Edn. (dir., pres. 1982-83), Okla. Found. for Architecture (founding chair bd. 1989-90), Asian Soc. Okla. (award of Excellence 1992), Asia Pacific Ctr. for Arch. (founding bd. dirs. 1996). Presbyterian. Office: U Hawaii Manoa Sch Architecture Honolulu HI 96822 E-mail: yeh@hawaii.edu.

**YEH, SANG-WOOK,** research scientist; b. Deagu, Republic of Korea, Jan. 6, 1970; arrived in U.S., 2002; s. Young-Hea Yeh and Bong-Eui Kang. BA, Seoul Nat. U., 1992, MA, 1994, PhD, 2001. Rsch. scientist Ctr. Ocean-Land-Atmosphere Studies, Calverton, Md., 2002—05; sr. rsch. scientist Korea Ocean Rsch. & Devel. Inst., Ansan, Republic of Korea, 2005—. Achievements include research in climate variability and change. Home: Ansan Sa2 Dong 1270 Ansan 426-744 Republic of Korea Office: Kordi 1270 Sa2 Dong Ansan 426-744 Republic of Korea Office Phone: 82-31-400-7605. Home Fax: 82-31-408-5829. Personal E-mail: swyeh@kordi.re.kr.

**YEH, SHING-SHING,** geriatrician, researcher, internist; arrived in U.S., 1977; d. Yeh. BS, Nat. Taiwan Normal U., 1976; PhD, MD, Miami Med. Sch., Fla. Assoc. prof. SUNY, Stony Brook, NY, 2000—. Grantee VACOOP, VA rsch. Achievements include research in nutrition; cytokine and geriatric nutrition. Office: Vamc 79 Middleville Rd Northport NY 11768 Office Phone: 631-261-4400.

**YEH, YING-YU EMILY,** music educator; permanent resident, 2004; d. Jing-Chao Yeh and Show-Chu Chu; m. Joseph Sanford Myers, July 26, 2003. MusB, Shenandoah U., 1998; MusM, U. Mo., 2001; MA, Ctrl. Bapt. Theol. Sem., 2004. Cert. tchr. Musikgarten, S.C., 2004. Pianist Eagle Heights Presbyn. Ch., Winchester, Va., 1997—98; dir. music, accompanist United Campus Ministry, Kansas City, Mo., 1999—2002; organist, accompanist Wornall Rd. Bapt. Ch., Kansas City, 2002—03; tchr. piano Toon Shop Sch. Music, Overland Pk., Kans., 2003—; instr. musikgarten Schmitt Music Ctr., Overland Pk., 2005—; accompanyist Bristol Hill United Meth. Ch., Kans. City, 2004—. Grantee, U. Mo., 1999—2002; scholar, Ctrl. Bapt. Theol. Sem., 2002—03, U. Mo., 2001—02; Rudolph C. Evans Piano scholarship, 1997. Mem.: Am. Coll. Musicians (named to Nat. Honor Roll Guild Tchrs. 2004, 2005), Music Tchr. Nat. Assn. Personal E-mail: musicblossom@yahoo.com.

**YEHUDA, SIMONE NAOMI,** education educator; d. Walter and Renee Molino Juda; m. Barry Michael Shapiro, Oct. 9, 1999; children: Corinna Nicole Press, Valerie Gabriella Press. Certificat d'Etudes Francaises, Universite de Lausanne, 1962; BA in Am. Lit., Bennington Coll., 1965; MA in English and Comparative Lit., Columbia U., 1967; PhD in Comparative Lit. and Creative Writing, Union Inst., 1998. English prof. Siena Heights U., Adrian, Mich., 1973—; artistic dir. Ann Arbor Repertory Theatre, Mich., 1986—90. Artistic dir. Young People's Theater, Ann Arbor, Mich., 1985—88. Author: (book of poetry) Thaw. Co-dir., interfaith seder Temple Beth Emeth, Ann Arbor, Mich., 2004—06; co-dir., women's seder The Jewish Fedn., Ann Arbor, Mich., 2000—03. Recipient Cir. of Scholars, Union Inst., 1998, Creative Artist award, Mich. Coun. for the Arts, 1982—83; Summer Seminar fellow, Nat. Endowment for the Humanities, 1994. Mem.: Screenwriters Guild West (assoc.), Dramatists Guild (assoc.), MLA (assoc.). D-Liberal. Jew. Avocations: swimming, gardening, quilting, pilates, walking. Office: Siena Heights U 1247 E Siena Hts Dr Adrian MI 49221 Office Phone: 517-264-7675. Office Fax: 517-264-7710. Personal E-mail: syehuda@sienahts, edu. E-mail: syehuda@sienahts, edu.

**YELENICK, MARY THERESE,** lawyer; b. Denver, May 17, 1954; d. John Andrew and Maesel Joyce (Reed) Y. B.A. magna cum laude, Colo. Coll., 1976; J.D. cum laude, Georgetown U., 1979. Bar: D.C. 1979, U.S. Dist. Ct. D.C. 1980, U.S. Ct. Appeals (D.C. cir.) 1981, N.Y. 1982, U.S. Dist. Ct. (so. and ea. dists.), N.Y. 1982, U.S. Supreme Ct. 1992, U.S. Ct. Appeals (5th cir.) 1995. Law clk. to presiding justices Superior Ct. D.C., 1979-81; ptnr. Chadbourne & Parke, LLP, N.Y.C., 1981—. Editor Jour. of Law and Policy Internat. Bus., 1978-79.; mem. NETWORK, The Nat. Cath. Soc. Justice Lobby (bd. dirs., 2004—) Mem. Phi Beta Kappa. Democrat. Roman Catholic. Home: 310 E 46th St New York NY 10017-3002 Office: Chadbourne & Parke LLP 30 Rockefeller Plz Fl 31 Ste 3550 New York NY 10112-0129

**YELICH, LOUIS JAMES,** engineering executive; b. Ironwood, Mich., July 20, 1928; s. Louis and Ann Catherine (Miller) Yelich; m. Barbara Catherine Den Dooven, Feb. 22, 1952; children: Louis J., Ann M., Mary B., Thomas E. BBA, U. Minn., 1954; MBA, No. Ill. U., 1963. Cost acctg. and data processing mgr. Badger Meter Mfg. Co., Milw., 1955—60; contr. Elgin (Ill.) Nat. Watch Co., 1960—65, Cleco Air Tools, Houston, 1966—69; v.p., contr. Hycel, Inc., Houston, 1970—71; pres. Modular Bldg. Sys., Inc., Houston, 1972—73; v.p. fin. NSW Corp., Houston, 1974—83; founder, pres. Hydro Pump & Equipment, Inc., Houston, 1983—. Established Perpetuity Ann. Scholarship Gogebic CC, Ironwood. Staff sgt. USAF, 1946—51. Recipient cert., Jr. Achievement, Milw., 1959, U. Minn. Found. plaque, 1999. Mem.: Assn. Chem. Industry Tex., Soc. Naval Arch. & Engrs., Rotary. Republican. Roman Catholic. Avocations: golf, skiing, coin collecting/numismatics. Home: PO Box 40294 Houston TX 77240 Office: Hydro Pump & Equipment PO Box 40294 Houston TX 77240 Office Phone: 281-232-8960. Business E-Mail: hydropump@msn.com.

**YELICH, LYNNE,** member of parliament; b. Mar. 24, 1953; m. Matt Yelich; 2 children. Grad., Kenaston HS, 1971. Farmer, Kenaston; mem. House of Commons, Ottawa, Ont., Canada, ofcl. opposition critic for status of women and families and caregivers. Address: Unit #71 Market Mall 2325 Preston Ave Saskatoon SK S7J 2G2 Canada Office: House of Commons Confederation Bldg Rm 622 Ottawa ON K1A 0A6 Canada Business E-Mail: yelicl@parl.gc.ca.

**YELLAND, MARY VIRGINIA,** artist; b. Mason City, Iowa, Apr. 16, 1916; d. George Curtis and Gladys Adele (Richardson) Y. Student, Stephens Coll., 1935, U. Minn., 1936-37, Mills. Acad., 1938. Chief draftsman Northwest Airlines, St. Paul, 1941-45; drafting bus. owner Newport, Minn., 1947-85. Author: Unique Legacy of Red Rock and Newport, 1989; creator logo for Newport Centennial, 1989. Bd. dirs. Newport Pub. Libr., 1955-80, 89—; chair Centennial Celebration, Newport, 1989; mem. Newport Hist. Preservation Commn., 1992—. Republican. Presbyterian. Avocation: photography. Home: 480 2nd Ave Newport MN 55055-1401

**YELLEN, JANET LOUISE,** bank executive; b. Bklyn., Aug. 13, 1946; d. Julius and Anna Ruth (Blumenthal) Y.; m. George Arthur Akerlof, July 8, 1978; 1 child, Robert Joseph. BA in Econs. summa cum laude, Brown U., 1967; PhD, Yale U., 1971; LLD (hon.), Brown U., 1998; LHD (hon.), Bard Coll., 2000. Asst. prof. econs. Harvard U., Cambridge, Mass., 1971-76; lectr. London Sch. Econs. and Polit. Sci., Washington, 1978-80; asst. prof. econs. Sch. Bus. Adminstrn., U. Calif., Berkeley, 1980-82, assoc. prof., 1982-85, prof. Haas Sch. Bus., 1985—, Bernard T. Rocca Jr. prof. internat. bus. and trade, 1992—, Eugene E. and Catherine M. Trefethem prof. bus., 1999—; cons. div. internat. fin., Fed. Res. Sys., Washington, 1974-75, economist trade and fin. studies sect., 1977-78, mem., 1994-97; chair, Coun. Econ. Advisors Exec. Office of the Pres., Washington, 1997-99; pres., CEO Fed. Res. Bank San Francisco, 2004—. Mem. adv. panel in economics NSF, 1977—78, 1991—92, cons. visitors, economics program, 1996, 2004; adv. bd. Women's Econ. Round Table, 1999—, Ctr. Internat. Polit. Economy, 1999—, Jerome Levy Economics Inst., 2002—; Calif. Assembly Select Com. on Asian Trade, 2003; bd. dirs. Economists Allied for Arms Reduction, 2002—, Delta Dental of Calif., 2003—; mem. amb. adv. coun. for Marshall Scholarships, 1996—; OECD, High-Level Sustainable Devel. Group, 1999—2001, NAS Panel, Ensuring Best Presidential Sci. and Tech. Appointments, 2000; chair Pres. Interagency Com. on Women's Bus. Enterprise, 1997—99, Econ. Policy Com. Orgn. for Econ. Coop. and Devel., 1997—99; rsch. fellow MIT, Cambridge, 1974; cons. Congl. Budget Office, 1975—76, mem. panel econ. advisers, 1993—94; rsch. affiliate Yale U., 1976; fellow Yale Corp., 2000—; rsch. assoc. Nat. Bureau Econ. Rsch., 1999—; prin. investigator Russell Sage Found. Grant on Sustainable Employment, 2000; sr. adviser Macroeconomic Advisers, 2003—; mem. Brookings Panel on Econ. Activity, 1987—88, 1990—91, sr. adviser, 1989—94, adv. bd., 1999—; Yrjö Jahnsson Found. lectr. on macroecon. theory, Helsinki, 1977—78; mem. Coun. on Fgn. Rels, 1976—81. Author: (monograph) (with Arrow and Shavell) The Limits of the Market in Resource Allocation, 1992; assoc. editor Jour. Econ. Perspectives, 1987-91; contbr. articles to profl. jours. Hon. Woodrow Wilson fellow, 1967, grad. fellow NSF, 1967-71, Guggenheim fellow, 1986-87, rsch. assoc. Am. Academy Arts and Sciences, 2001; grantee NSF, 1975-77, 90-94; Maria and Sidney Rolfe award for Nat. Econ. Svc., Women's Econ. Round Table, 1997, Wilbur Lucius Cross Medal, Yale U., 1997; named one of 50 Women to Watch, Wall St. Journal, 2005. Mem. Am. Econ. Assn. (adv. com. to Pres. 1986-87, nominating com. 1988-90, v.p. 2004-), Western Econ. Assn. (pres. 2003-04), Phi Beta Kappa. Office: Fed Res Bank San Francisco 101 Market St San Francisco CA 94105-1579*

**YELLON, ROBERT FORREST,** surgeon, medical educator; b. N.Y.C., N.Y., June 26, 1956; s. Pauline Yellon; m. Keely Ann Cofano, June 24, 2003; children: Jeremy Marc, Nathaniel Benjamin. AB in Biology, Princeton U., N.J., 1978; MD, SUNY Stony Brook, 1986. Diplomate Am. Bd. of Otolaryngolgoy, 1993. Dir. of clin. svcs. dept. otolaryngology Children's Hosp. of Pitts., 1997—; assoc. prof. dept. otolaryngology U. Pitts., 2000—. Dir. pediat. ear ctr. Children's Hosp. of Pitts., 2006—. Editor: (textbook) Pediatric Otolaryngology. Named to Best Doctors in Am., 2006. Fellow: Am. Soc. of Pediat. Otolaryngology, Am. Acad. of Otolaryngology Head and Neck Surgery; mem.: Alpha Omega Alpha. Achievements include microtia surgery, aural atresia surgery, laryngotracheal reconstruction. Office: Children's Hospital of Pittsburgh 3705 5th Ave Pittsburgh PA 15213 Office Phone: 412-692-5902. Home Fax: 412-692-6974; Office Fax: 412-692-6074. E-mail: yellra@chp.edu.

**YEMENIDJIAN, ALEX,** former film company executive; b. Buenos Aires; arrived in Boston, 1968; married; 2 children. BA in acctg., Calif. State U., Northridge; M in bus. taxation, U. So. Calif. Mng. ptnr. Parks, Palmer, Turner & Yemenidjian; with MGM Grand Inc. (now MGM Mirage), Las Vegas, 1990—2005, pres., COO, 1995-99; chmn., CEO Metro-Goldwyn-Mayer Inc., Santa Monica, Calif., 1999—2005. Bd. dirs. MGM Grand Inc. (formerly MGM Grand Inc.), 1989-2005, Regal Entertainment Group, 2005-. Chmn. United Armenian Fund; bd. dirs. Kirk Kerkorian's Lincy Found.

**YEN, BING CHENG,** retired civil engineer, retired engineering educator; arrived in U.S., 1959; s. Ding Y. and Shu J. Yen; m. Ann Margret Nielsen, June 21, 1964; children: Annette, Brigitte, Pei, Charlotte, Dagmarette. BS, Nat. Taiwan U., Taipei, 1956; PhD, U. Utah, Salt Lake City, 1963. Cert. civil engr., Calif., 1966, geotech. engr., Calif., 1994. Asst. prof. civil engring. U. Utah, Salt Lake City, 1963—64; asst. prof. to prof. civil engring. Calif. State U., Long Beach, 1964—89; pres. Bing Yen & Associates, Irvine, Calif., 1989—98. Cons. engring. dept. L.A. County, 1966—69; cons. Woodward Clyde Cons., 1970—79; ind. cons. U.S. and Europe, 1979—89. Contbr. articles to profl. jours., scientific papers. Recipient Outstanding Educator of Am., AAUP, 1972; grantee rsch., Nat. Sci. Found., 1980, U.S. Navy, 1979—88, State of Calif., 1979—88. Achievements include research in long term slope stability analyses under static and seismic loadings, holding capacity, soil-pipe interaction in soil mechanics.

**YEN, HENRY CHIN-YUAN,** computer systems programmer, software engineer, consulting company executive; b. Mpls., Apr. 18, 1958; s. James and Elizabeth Y.; m. Michele Calen, Oct. 8, 1988; children: Andrew, Matthew. Sr. systems programmer Grumman Data Systems Corp., Bethpage, N.Y., 1978-83; mgr. Data Ctr. On-Line Software Internat., Inc., Ft. Lee, N.J., 1983-85, lead systems programmer, 1985-88; v.p. The Galamery Co., Inc., Del., 1988—, Aegis Info. Systems, Inc., Del., 1989—. Bd. dirs. Personal Computer Systems Corp. Bd. trustees Syosset Pub. Libr., NY, 2001—05. Mem. IEEE, Assn. Computing Machinery, Network and Sys. Profls. Assn., Mensa (bd. dirs. greater N.Y. chpt. 2002-), Intertel. Avocations: bicycling, profl. musician. Home: PO Box 1 Hicksville NY 11802-0001 Office: Aegis Info Systems Inc PO Box 730 Hicksville NY 11802-0730 Business E-Mail: henry@AegisInfoSys.com.

**YEN, SAMUEL S(HOW)-C(HIH),** obstetrician, gynecologist, educator, endocrinologist; b. Beijing, Feb. 22, 1927; divorced; children: Carol Amanda, Dolores Amelia, Margaret Rae. BS, Cheeloo U., China, 1949; MD, U. Hong Kong, 1954, DSc, 1980. Diplomate Am. Bd. Ob-Gyn, Am. Bd. Reproductive Endocrinology. Intern Queen Mary Hosp., Hong Kong, 1954—55; resident Johns Hopkins U., Balt., 1956—60; fellow reproductive endocrinology Harvard Med. Sch., Boston, 1960—62; assoc. prof. reproductive biology Case Western Res. U., Cleve., 1967—70; prof. ob-gyn U. Calif., San Diego, 1972—83, chmn. dept. reproductive medicine, 1972—83, prof. reproductive medicine, 1983—; dir. reproductive endocrinology U. Calif. Med. Ctr., San Diego, 1983—98, W.R. Persons chair, 1987. Assoc. dir. obstetrics Univ. Hosp., Cleve., 1968—70; DeGroof lectr., 1987; Van Campenhaut lectr. Can. Fertility and Andrology Soc., 1995; bd. examiners Am. Bd. Ob-Gyn., 1973—78, Am. Bd. Reproductive Endocrinology, 1976—82; 1st Marilyn and John Huffman Meml. lectr. XII World Congress Adolescent Gynecology, Helsinki, 1998; James M. Cuaseo Meml. lectr. U. Pa., 1998; A. Marsh Panloon Jr. lectr. U. Utah, 2001; plenary lectr. 4th Internat. Congress Reproductive Endocrinology, Beijing, 2001, 9th World Congress Gynecol. Endocrinology, Hong Kong, 2001. Editor: Reproductive Endocrinology Physiology, Pathophysiology and Clinical Management, 1978, 1999, 2003; mem. editl. bd. Endocrine Revs., 1984—. Named to Soc. of Scholars, Johns Hopkins U., 1992; recipient Axel Munthe Found. award, 1982, Simpson medal, U. Edinburgh, Scotland, 1996; fellow, Oglebay, 1968—69. Fellow: Royal Coll. Ob-Gyn. (ad eundem, London); mem.: Am. Fertility Soc., Endocrine Soc. (Rorer Clin. Investigator award 1992, Disting. Scientist award 1992), Soc. Gynecol. Investigation (pres. 1981, Disting. Scientist award 1992), Assn. Am. Physicians, NAS Inst. Medicine. Office: U Calif San Diego Reproductive Medicine # 0633 La Jolla CA 92093 E-mail: syen@san.rr.com.

**YEN, STEPHEN L.,** orthodontist, researcher; m. Christine Kuida; children: Leia, Daniel, Lauren. DMD, Harvard U., Boston, 1985. Resident in orthodontics U. So. Calif., LA, 1993—97, asst. prof. Div. Craniofacial Molecular Biology, 1997—. Contbr. articles to profl. jours. Achievements include research in Treatment Of Facial Birth Defects. Office: Childrens Hosp LA MS 116 4650 Sunset Blvd Los Angeles CA 90027 Office Phone: 323-669-2130. Office Fax: 323-667-2093. E-mail: syen@usc.edu.

**YEN, TEH FU,** civil and environmental engineering educator; b. Kun-Ming, China, Jan. 9, 1927; came to U.S., 1949; s. Kwang Pu and Ren (Liu) Y.; m. Shiao-Ping Siao, May 30, 1959 BS, Cen. China U., 1947; MS, W.Va. U., 1953; PhD, Va. Poly. Inst. and State U., 1956; PhD (hon.), Pepperdine U., 1982, Internat. U. Dubna, Russia, 1996, All Russian Petroleum Exploration Inst., St. Petersburg, Russia, 1999. Sr. research chemist Good Yr. Tire & Rubber Co., Akron, 1955-59; fellow Mellon Inst., Pitts., 1959-65; sr. fellow Carnegie-Mellon U., Pitts., 1965-68; assoc. prof. Calif. State U., Los Angeles, 1968-69, U. So. Calif., 1969-80, prof. civil engring. and environ. engring., 1980—. Hon. prof. Shanghai U. Sci. and Tech., 1986, U. Petroleum, Beijing, 1987, Daqing Petroleum Inst., 1992; cons. Universal Oil Products, 1968-76, Chevron Oil Field Rsch. Co., 1968-75, Finnigan Corp., 1976-77, GE, 1977-80, United Techs., 1978-79, TRW Inc., 1982-83, Exxon, 1981-82, DuPont, 1985-88, Min. Petroleum, Beijing, 1982—, Biogas Rsch. Inst.-UN, Chengdu, 1991. Author: numerous tech. books; contbr. articles to profl. jours. Recipient Disting. Svc. award Tau Beta Pi, 1974, Imperial Crown Gold medal, Iran, 1976, Achievement award Chinese Engring. and Sci. Assocs. So. Calif., 1977, award Phi Kappa Phi, 1982, Outstanding Contbn. honor Pi Epsilon Tau, 1984, Svc. award Republic of Honduras, 1989, award in Petroleum Chem. Am. Chem. Soc., 1994, Kapitsa Gold medal Russian Fedn., 1995. Fellow Chem. Soc., Inst. Petroleum, Am. Inst. Chemists; mem. Am. Chem. Soc. (bd. dirs. 1993, councillor, founder and chmn. geochemistry divsn. 1979-81, Chinese Acad. Scis. (standing com.), Acad. Scis. Russian Fedn. (academician, fgn. mem.). Office: U So Calif KAP 224A Viterby Sch Engring 3620 S Vermont Ave Los Angeles CA 90089-2531 Office Phone: 213-740-0586. Business E-Mail: tfyen@usc.edu.

**YEN, WEN-HSIUNG,** language and music professional, educator; b. Tainan, Taiwan, June 26, 1934; came to U.S., 1969; m. Yuan-yuan Yen, Jan. 6, 1961; children: Tin-ju, Tin-jen, Tin-Tao. BA, Nat. Taiwan Normal U., 1960; MA, UCLA, 1971; PhD in Music, World U., 1988; Candidate Philosophy in Ethnomusicology, UCLA, 1995; cultural doctorate philosophy of music, The World Univ., 1988. Instr. Nat. Taichung Tchr. Coll., 1961-62; prof. Chinese Culture U., Taipei, 1964-69; lectr. West L.A. C.C., 1978-82; founder Chinese Culture Sch. L.A., 1976—. Grad. tchng. assoc. U. Md., 1982-83; instr. L.A. City Coll., 1983—; Calif. State U. L.A., 1984—; Pasadena City Coll., 1989—; prof. Chinese Santa Monica (Calif.) Coll., 1984—. Calif. State U. Northridge, 1986—; founder Wen Yen Piano Studio, 1972—; founder, dir. Chinese Mus. Orch. So. Calif., 1974—; founder, pres. Chinese- Amer. Musicians Assn. of So. Calif., 1990—; co-chair Conf. Students of Chinese Lang. and Culture;

Chinese lang. instrn. course designer, instr. All Seasons Children's Learning Ctr., 2001—; music dir. Soc. Confucian Studies Am., 2004—; dir. bd. Chinese Studies Ctr., Calif. State U., LA. Musician: musical compositions include Collection of Works by Mr. Yen, 1969, (recordings) Art Songs and Chinese Folk Songs, 1982, Ode To My Home Land, 1992, Mother Earth-Found-Season: Spring, Summer, Autumn and Winter, 1997, Song of 911; author: Taiwan Folk Songs, 1967, vol. 2, 1969, A Collection of Wen-hsiung Yen's Songs, 1968, vol. 2, 1987, vol. 3, 2000 (award Fedn. Overseas Assns., 2000, 2002); translator: Achievement and Methodology for Comparative Musicology, 1968, Chinese Musical Culture and Folk Songs, 1989, Silk and Bamboo Expresses Emotion and Meaning, 2000, Ethnomusicology Series, 2002; composer: 100 songs and instrumental music; exhibitor traditional Chinese musical instruments and publs., Chinese Culture Ctr., 1995, 1996, Arcadia Pub. Libr., 1999; musician: East and West Music Concert, 2004, Concert for Traditional Music and New Performing Arts, 2006; organizer concerts, contbr. articles to profl. jours. Bd. dirs. So. Calif. Coun. Chinese Sch., 1998—; bd. dirs. Chinese Studies Ctr., Calif. State U., L.A., 1990—; conductor Chinese Music Orch. So. Calif., 1974-; producer Chinese Art and Culture Festival, 1990-2003. Mem.: Chinese Writers Assn. So. Calif. (v.p. 2000), Fedn. Overseas Chinese Assns. (bd. dirs. (hon.) 2002), So. Calif. Coun. Chinese Schs. (v.p. 2000—), chmn. exec. com.), Chinese Am. PTA So. Calif. (supr. 1985—), Taiwan Benevloent Assn. Calif. (v.p. 1986, pres. 1987—89, bd. dirs.), Taiwan Benevolent Assn. Am. (bd. dirs.), Alumni Assn. Chinese Culture U. So. Calif., Soc. Asian Music (founder, pres.), Internat. Coun. Traditional Music, Coll. Music Soc., Soc. Ethnomusicology, Chinese Performing Arts Assn. of Am. (bd. dirs.), Chinese Choral Soc. So. Calif. (music dir.), Chinese-Am. Musicians Assn. So Calif. (pres.). Avocations: walking, ping pong/table tennis, tai chi chuan. Office: Chinese Culture Sch 615 Las Tunas Dr Ste B Arcadia CA 91007-8469 Office Phone: 626-447-3823. Personal E-mail: wenhyen2000@yahoo.com.

**YEN, WILLIAM MAO-SHUNG,** physicist, consultant; b. Nanking, Kiangsu, China, Apr. 5, 1935; came to U.S., 1952; s. Wanli and Jane Hsanlin (King) Y.; m. Delane Robinson, Aug. 16, 1968 (div. May 1974); m. Laurel Frances Curtis, Aug. 18, 1978; 1 child, Jane Luhsan Bess. BS, U. Redlands, 1956; PhD, Washington U., 1962. Rsch. assoc. Stanford (Calif.) U., 1962-65; asst. prof. U. Wis., Madison, 1965-68, assoc. prof., 1968-72, prof., 1972-90, ret., 1990; Graham Perdue prof. U. Ga., Athens, 1986—. Edwin T. Jaynes vis. prof. Washington U., 2004; affiliated rsch. prof. U. Hawaii, Manoa, 2005; cons. Lawrence Livermore Nat. Labs., Calif., 1975—84, Argonne Nat. Labs., Ill., 1976—82, Rosemount Corp., Eden Prairie, Minn., 1988—95, Chromonix LLD, Beverly Hills, Mich., 1995—99. Editor: Laser Spectroscopy of Solids I, 1981, II, 1988, Dynamical Processes in Disordered Solids, 1989, Phosphor Handbook, 1998, Inorganic Phosphors, 2004; contbr. more than 230 articles to scholarly and profl. jours. Named hon. prof., U. St. Antonio de Abad, Cusco, Peru, 1983, Inst. Physics, Acad. Sinica, 1995, Washington U., 2004, Beijing Jiaotone U., 2005; recipient Sr. U.S. Scientist award, A.V. Humboldt Found., 1985, 1990, Lamar Dodd award, U. Ga., 2005, IOL prize for luminescence rsch., 2005; Washington U. fellow, 1960, J.S. Guggenheim Found. fellow, 1979, Fulbright Sr. fellow, 1995. Fellow AAAS, Am. Physical Soc., Optical Soc. Am., Electro Chem. Soc.; mem. Materials Rsch. Soc., Ceramics Soc. Am., Sigma Xi. Achievements include pioneering establishment of laser spectroscopy as a tool to study optical properties of solids. Home: 180 River Oak Way Athens GA 30605-2677 Office: U Ga Dept Physics and Astronomy Athens GA 30602-3451 Office Phone: 706-542-2491. E-mail: wyen@physast.uga.edu.

**YENKIN, BERNARD KALMAN,** coatings and resins company executive; b. Columbus, Ohio, Dec. 2, 1930; s. Abe I. and Eleanore G. Yenkin; m. Miriam Schottenstein, Mar. 31, 1957; children: Leslie Mara, Jonathan, Allison Katsev, Amy. BA, Yale U., 1952; MBA, Harvard U., 1954. V.p. Yenkin-Majestic Paint Corp., Columbus, 1968-77, pres., 1977-85, chmn. bd., 1985—. Pres. Columbus Jewish Fedn., 1980-82, Pro Musica Chamber Orch., Columbus, 1983-85, Columbus Torah Acad., 1977-79; bd. v.p. Jewish Ednl. Svc. N.Am., N.Y.C., 1991-95. Recipient Mayor's award for Vol. Svc. City of Columbus, 1984, Young Leadership award Columbus Jewish Fedn., 1965. Mem. Yale Club of Cen. Ohio (pres. 1979-81), Yale Club of N.Y., Athletic Club (Columbus). Office: Yenkin-Majestic Industries 1920 Leonard Ave Columbus OH 43219-2514

**YEO, KIM ENG,** artist; b. Singapore, Apr. 24, 1947; came to U.S., 1978; d. Cheng Chye and Seok Kim (Chew) Lee; m. Bock Cheng Yeo; children: Beng Lin, Beng Jene. Student, Nanyang Acad. Fine Arts, Singapore, 1963; BSc with honors, U. Singapore, 1968. Watercolor demonstrator Flushing Art League, N.Y.C., 1980-84; art instr. Poppenhusen Inst., N.Y.C., 1984; substitute art lectr. UN Internat. Sch., N.Y.C., 1984-85; freelance paper product designer, 1981-87; textile designer J. Brown Designs, N.Y.C., 1987-91; tchg. artist Flushing (N.Y.) Town Hall, 1995—2002; artist-in-residence Pub. Sch. 214, 165, Francis Lewis H.S., Flushing, 1997-2001. Art cons. Corp. Art Directions, N.Y.C.; visual arts panelist, Flushing Coun., 1985-87, Queen's Coun., 1998-99, 2001-04. One person shows at Alliance Francais, 1975-77, Bhirasri Inst. Modern Art, Bangkok, Thailand, 1975-77, Flushing Coun. on Arts, 1995, 2000, Adirondack Lakes Ctr. for the Arts, N.Y., 2005, Synagogue For Arts Gallery, NY, 2006; exhibited Mallette Gallery, L.I., N.Y., 1998, 99, Artfolio Gallery, Singapore, 2000, Langston Hughes Cmty. Libr. and Cultural Ctr., N.Y., 2004; exhibited in group shows at Womanart Gallery, N.Y.C., 1979-80, Nat. Art League, Douglastown, N.Y., 1979-86, Flushing Coun. on Arts, 1984-88, 96-2004, Postcrypt Art Gallery, N.Y.C., 1997, Singapore Watercolor Soc., 1997-99, 2001-03; represented in corp. and pvt. collections; artist greeting cards UNICEF, 1997-98; featured on QPATV Artists Series, 1993, QPTV Queens Jour., 2000; featured in Watercolor Mag., 1997, Internat. Mag., 2004. Benefit show UN Devel. Fund for Women Singapore, 1999. Mem. Flushing Art League (bd. dirs., treas. 1979-85, award 1986), Flushing Coun. on Arts. Buddhist. Avocations: gardening, bookmaking. Home: 16202 77th Ave Flushing NY 11366-1022 Fax: (718) 591-8483 E-mail: artist@kmengyeo.com.

**YEO, RON,** architect; b. LA, June 17, 1933; s. Clayton Erik and Rose G. (Westman) Y.; m. Birgitta S. Bergkvist, Sept. 29, 1962; children: Erik Elov, Katarina Kristina. B.Arch., U. So. Calif., 1959. Draftsman Montierth & Strickland (Architects), Long Beach, Calif., 1958-61; designer Gosta Edberg S.A.R. Arkitekt, Stockholm, 1962; partner Strickland & Yeo, Architects, Garden Grove, Calif., 1962-63; pres. Ron Yeo, Architect, Inc., Corona del Mar, Calif., 1963—. Cons., lectr. in field. Archtl. works include Garden Grove Civic and Cmty. Ctr., 1966, Hall Sculpture Studio, 1966, Garden Grove Cultural Ctr., 1978, Gem Theater, 1979, Festival Amphitheatre, 1983, Los Coyotes Paleontol. Interpretive Ctr., 1986, Calif. State U. Fullerton Alumni House, 1997, O'Neill Regional Pk. Nature Ctr., 1998, Upper Newport Bay Interpretive Ctr., 2000, Stough Canyon Nature Ctr., 2000, Quon residence, 2005. Mem. Orange County Planning Commn., 1972-73, 1975-79; chmn. Housing and Community Devel. Task Force, 1978, Orange County Fire Protection Planning Task Force, City of Newport Beach City Arts Commn., 1970-72; pres. Orange County Arts Alliance, 1980-81; gen. plan advisory com. Newport Beach, 2002-06. Fellow AIA; mem. Green Bldg. Coun., Internat. Conf. Bldg. Ofcls., Nat. Assn. for Interpretation (founding), Constrn. Specification Inst. Democrat. Office: Ron Yeo FAIA Architect Inc 500 Jasmine Ave Corona Del Mar CA 92625-2308

**YEOMAN, LYNN CHALMERS,** medical educator; b. Evanston, Ill., May 17, 1943; m. Carol J. Yeoman; children: Caroline, Christopher, Sarah. BA, DePauw U., 1965; PhD, U. Ill., 1970. Instr. Baylor Coll. Medicine, Houston, 1972-73, asst. prof., 1973-76, assoc. prof., 1976-84, prof., 1984—; assoc. dir. Bristol-Baylor Lab, Houston, 1989-90; assoc. dir. anti-cancer drug discovery and cell and molecular biology Bristol-Myers Co., Wallingford, Conn., 1989—90; dir. curriculum database program Baylor Coll. Medicine, Houston, 1995—; dir. integrated problem solving program, 1997—, dir. ednl. resource ctr., 2001—, sr. dir. acad. computing, 2004—. Cons. Litton Bionetics, Ft. Detrick, Md., 1977-78, Colon Cancer Working Group, Houston, 1985-86, Oncos, Ltd., Houston, 1985-87, Bristol-Myers Co., Wallingford, Conn., 1985-89, Ubiquitex Techs. Corp., 1995-96, U. Tex. Med. Br., Galveston,

1998, Feedback Techs., Inc., 2004-; mem. com. revision U.S. Pharmacopeial Conv., 1985-90, 1995—, chmn. expert com. on biols. and biotech.: proteins and polysaccharides, 2000—, com. of experts exec. com., 2004—. Editor: Methods in Cancer Research, Vols. 19 and 20, 1982; mem. editl. bd. Frontiers in Biosci., Med. Edn. Online; contbr. articles to profl. jours. V.p. Marilyn Estates Assn., Houston, 2004-2005, chapel organist, St. Luke's United Meth. Ch., Houston, 1996-. NCI grantee, 1987-2003. Mem. Am. Chem. Soc., Am. Soc. Biochem. and Molecular Biology, Group on Ednl. Affairs. Methodist. Achievements include patent for detection of antigen gp650 in sera and other specimens from cancer patients with anti-gp650 monoclonal antibody. Home: 5434 Rutherglenn Dr Houston TX 77096-4032 Office: 1 Baylor Plz Houston TX 77030-3411 Office Phone: 713-798-7336. Business E-Mail: lyeoman@bcm.edu.

**YEOMANS, DONALD KEITH,** astronomer; b. Rochester, NY, May 3, 1942; s. George E. and Jessie Y.; m. Laurie Robyn Ernst, June 20, 1970; children: Sarah, Keith. BA, Middlebury (Vt.) Coll., 1964; MS, U. Md., 1967, PhD, 1970. Supr. Computer Scis. Corp., Silver Spring, Md., 1973-76; sr. rsch. astronomer Jet Propulsion Lab., Pasadena, Calif., 1976-92, supr., 1992—. Discipline specialist Internat. Halley Watch, 1982-89; sci. investigator NASA Comet Mission, 1987-91, Near-Earth Asteroid Rendezvous Mission, 1994-2001, Multi-Comet Flyby Mission, 1997-2002, Comet Impact Mission, 1999—; project scientist for asteroid sample return mission, 1998—; mgr. NASA Near-Earth Object Program Office, 1998-. Author: Comet Halley: Once in a Lifetime, 1985, The Distant Planets, 1989, Comets: A Chronological History of Observation, Science, Myth, and Folklore, 1991. Recipient Space Achievement award AIAA, 1985, Exceptional Svc. medal NASA, 1986, Achievement award Middlebury Coll. Alumni, 1987; named NASA/JPL Sr. Rsch. Scientist, 1993. Mem.: Am. Astron. Soc. (chair divsn. planetary scis. 1999—2000, chair hist. astronomy divsn. 2005—06). Democrat. Presbyterian. Avocations: tennis, history of astronomy. Office: Jet Propulsion Lab #301-150 4800 Oak Grove Dr Pasadena CA 91109-8001 Office Phone: 818-354-2127. Business E-Mail: donald.k.yeomans@jpl.nasa.gov.

**YEOMANS, DONALD RALPH,** Canadian government official, consultant; b. Toronto, Ont., Can., Mar. 25, 1925; s. Ralph and Louise (Weismiller) Y.; m. Catherine Simpson Williams, May 13, 1950; children: Patricia Ann, Nancy Louise, Jane Elizabeth. BASc, U. Toronto, 1947. Registered profl. engr., Ont., cert. mgmt. acct. Mem. Bur. of Govt. Orgns., Ottawa, Ont., 1962-64; dep. sec. Treasury Bd., Ottawa, 1964-69; asst. dep. minister Dept. Supply and Services, Ottawa, 1969-75; assoc. sec. dir. Anti-Inflation Bd., Ottawa, 1975-76; asst. dep. minister Dept. Nat. Health-Welfare, Ottawa, 1976-77; commr. Correctional Services of Can., Ottawa, 1977-85; chmn. Tariff Bd., 1985-89; spl. advisor Can. Jud. Centre, 1989-92; mem. bd. govs. Carleton U., 1980-93, chmn., 1989-91. Spl. advisor Royal Com. Govt. Orgns., 1961, Royal Com. Fin. Accountability, 1977; assoc. Cons. and Audit Can., 1992-97; exec. counsellor Pub. Svc. Commn., 1990-95; cons. to govt. and industry, 1990-97, bd. dirs. Corrections Corp. Can.; mem. bd. govs. Can. Comprehensive Audit Found., 1989-94; mem. ind. adv. com. Auditor Gen. Can., 1989-95; chmn. Coun. Adminstrv. Tribunals, 1986; chmn. Coun. Chairs Ont. Univs., 1991-93; mem. Expert Com. on AIDS in Prisons, 1992-94; chmn. awards com. Am. Correctional Assn., 1992-97; bd. dirs. Corrections Corp. Can., Baker Group Internat., Inc. Recipient Centennial medal Govt. Can., 1967, Jubilee medal Govt. Can., 1977, E.R. Cass award Am. Corr. Assn., 1991, Corr. Svc. of Can. Exemplary Svc. medal, 2000, Founder's award Carleton U., 2000; Australian Commonwealth fellow, 1985. Fellow: Soc. Mgmt. Accts. Can. (pres. 1977); mem.: Fed. Superannuates Nat. Assn. (pres. Ottawa br. 1998—2000, bd. dirs., nat. regional dir. 2002—), Inst. Pub. Adminstrn. Can. (pres. 1974), Assn. State Correctional Adminstrs. (pres. 1983, Spl. Founders award 2006), Ottawa Heart Inst. Alumni Assn. (v.p.), Five Lakes (pres. 1975); Canadian (Ottawa, pres. 1978), Canadian Club (Ottawa), Five Lakes Club (pres. 1975). Home and Office: 205-211 Second Ave Ottawa ON Canada K1S 2H8 Fax: 613-231-4557. Office Phone: 613-232-5022. E-mail: kdyeom@cyberus.ca.

**YEONAS, GEORGE C.,** real estate executive; m. Marjorie Yeonas; children: Christina, Constance. Grad., Georgetown U.; MBA, U. Pa. Divsn. ptnr. Trammel Crow; v.p. devel. NVR; v.p., gen. mgr. South Fla. divsn. The Arvida Co.; pres., COO, The Fortress Group, Inc., McClean, Va., 1996-99, CEO 1999—.

**YEOSOCK, JOHN JOHN,** military officer; b. Wilkes-Barre, Pa., 1937; s. John A. and Elizabeth B. Yeosock; m. Betta Lynn Hoffner; children— John John, Elizabeth John BS in Indsl. Engring., Pa. State U., 1959; MS in Ops. Rsch., U.S. Naval Postgrad. Sch., Monterey, Calif., 1969; postgrad., Nat. War Coll., 1976. Commd. officer U.S. Army, 1959, advanced through grades to lt. gen.; brigade comdr. 194th Armored Brigade, Ft Knox, Ky., 1978-80; chief of staff 1st Cavalry div. U.S. Army, Ft. Hood, Tex., 1980-81, asst. div. comdr., 1983-84; project mgr. Saudi N.G., Riyadh, Saudi Arabia, 1981-83; dep. chief of staff ops. Forces Command, Atlanta, 1984-86; comdr. 1st Cavalry Div., Ft. Hood, 1986-88; asst. dep. chief of staff for ops. The Pentagon, Washington, 1988-89; comdr. 3d Army and dep. comdg. gen. Forces Command, Ft. McPherson, Ga., 1989—&; comdr. U.S., U.K., French Army Forces, Kuwaiti Theater Ops., Desert Storm, Saudi Arabia, 1990-91; internat. cons., 1993—. Decorated D.S.M. (3), Legion of Merit (2), Bronze Star with v (2), French Legion of Honor, King Faisal award Class II, King Abdul Aziz medal Class II (Saudi Arabia), Combat Infantryman badge; recipient Nat. Vets. award, 1994, AUSA Inspiration award Atlanta, 1992; named Outstanding Engring. Alumnus, Pa. State U., 1990, Disting. Alumni, 1992, Disting. Alumnus, Valley Forge Mil. Acad., 1994; named to Pi Kappa Phi Hall of Fame. Mem. Wilkes-Barre C.C. (hon., Achievement award 1991).

**YEOSOCK, MICHAEL MICHAEL,** funeral director, civil engineer; b. Wilkes-Barre, Pa., July 28, 1961; s. Michael J. and Patricia A. (Sauerwein) Y.; m. Mary Jacqueline Clemente; children: Adriana Grace, Christopher Michael. Student, Pa. State U., 1980-82; BS, W.Va. U., 1984; diploma in mortuary sci., New Eng. Inst., 1985; MS in Environ. Engring., U. New Haven, 1993. Cert. engr.-in-tng.; lic. profl. engr., Pa., Conn., N.Y. Project mgr. M.J. Pasonick, Jr., Inc., Wilkes-Barre, 1986-89; asst. civil engr. in tng. City of Norwalk (Conn.) Dept. of Pub. Works, 1989—, sr. engr., 1994—; supr. Jan Fabian Funeral Chapel, Hanover, Pa., 1990-91. Bd. dirs. Norwalk (Conn.) Tree Alliance. Mem. IEEE, AIME, ASCE, Soc. Mining Engrs., Can. Mining and Metallurgy, N.Y. Acad. Scis., Am. Rock Mechanics Assn., Internat. Soc. Rock Mechanics, Geospatial Info. and Tech. Assn., Inst. Traffic Engrs., Internat. Mcpl. Signal Assn. Republican. Russian Orthodox. Avocations: flying, white-water rafting. Home: 5 Country Club Dr White Plains NY 10607 Office: City of Norwalk 125 East Ave Norwalk CT 06851-5702 Office Phone: 203-854-7791. Personal E-mail: mmyeosock@optonline.net.

**YEP, LAURENCE MICHAEL,** author; b. San Francisco, June 14, 1948; s. Thomas Kim and Franche (Lee) Yep; m. Joanne Ryder, 1984. BA, U. Calif., Santa Cruz, 1970; PhD, SUNY, Buffalo, 1975. Tchr. San Jose (Calif.) City Coll., part-time 1975-76, Foothill Coll., Mountain View, Calif., 1975, U. Calif., Berkeley, 1987-89, writer in residence Santa Barbara, 1990. Book-of-the-Month writing fellow, 1970; teaching fellow SUNY, Buffalo, 1970-73, research fellow, 1973-74 Author sci. fiction stories, children's stories, 1968—: Sweetwater, 1973, reissue, 2004, Dragonwings (Newbery Honor Book award ALA 1976, Children's Book award Internat. Reading Assn. 1976), (Carter G. Woodson award Nat. Coun. Social Studies 1976), 1975, Child of the Owl, 1977, Seadreamos, 1977, Sea Glass, (Commonwealth Club lit. award 1979), 1979, Kind Hearts and Gentle Monsters, 1982, The Mark Twain Murders, 1982, Dragon of the Lost Sea, 1982, Liar, Liar, 1983, Tom Sawyer Fires, 1984, Dragon Steel, 1985, Mountain Light, 1985, Shadow Lord, 1985, Monster Makers, Inc., 1986, Curse of the Squirrel, 1987, The Rainbow People, 1989; author one-act plays Pay the Chinaman, 1987, FairyBones, 1987, Dragon Cauldron, 1991, The Lost Garden, 1991, The Star Fisher, 1991 (Christopher award 1992, W.Va. Literary award 1995), Tongues of Jade, 1991, Lion Dance, 1998, Cook's Family, 1998, The Imp Ate My Homework, 1998, Firecrackers, 1999, Amah, 1999, Cockroach Cooties,

2000,Dream Soul, 2000, Diary of Wong Ming Chin, 2000, The Magic Paintbrush, 2000, Angel Fish, 2000, The Diary of the Lady of Chiao Kuo, 2002, The Tiger's Apprentice, 2003, Tiger's Blood, 2005; theatrical adaption of Dragonwings, 1991, Dragon War, 1992, American Dragons, 1992, also editor, Butterfly Boy, 1993, Dragon's Gate, (Newbery Honor Book award ALA 1994), 1993, The Ghost Fox, 1993, The Man Who Tricked a Ghost, 1993 (Am. Book award 1995), The Shell Woman and the King, 1993, The Boy Who Swallowed Snakes, 1994, The Junior Thunder Lord, 1994, The Tiger Woman, 1994, Thief of Hearts, 1995, Ribbons, 1996, Goblin Pearls, 1996, The Khan's Daughter, 1996, The Traitor: Golden Mountain Chronicles: 1885, 2003. Literature fellow Nat. Endowment for Arts, 1990; recipient, Laura Ingalls Wilder award for contribution to children's literature, 2005. Mailing: 244 Crocker Ave Pacific Grove CA 93950

**YERG, BEVERLY JOHNSON,** physical education educator, researcher; b. Warren, Pa., Nov. 11, 1938; d. C. Walter and Emma Josephine Erickson Johnson; m. Robert Robison Yerg. June 24, 1961; 1 child, David Robert. BS, Temple U., 1960, EdM, 1973; PhD, U. Pitts., 1977. Tchr., coach Manheim Ctrl. Schs., Pa., 1961—64; tchr. Lancaster City Schs., 1960—61; substitute and homebound tchr. Warren Area Schs., 1964—73; lectr. LaRoche Coll., 1973—74; tchg. fellow U. Pitts., 1974—77; asst. prof. Fla. State U., Tallahassee, 1977—82, assoc. prof., 1982—2001, dept. head, 1982—85, dir. acad. support programs student athletes, 1986—93, chair pres.'s com. intercollegiate athletics; ret. Editl. bd., reviewer Jour. Tchg. Physical Edn., Nat. Assn. Athletic Acad. Advisors Jour., reviewer Rsch. Quar. Exercise and Sport, Merrill Pub. Co., Mosby Book Co.; contbr. chapters to books, articles to profl. jours. Bd. dirs. Neighborhood Health Clinic, Tallahassee, 1986—88; bd. mem. North Fla. Fellow Christian Athletes, 1987—90; chair Fla. Cabinet for Campus Ministry, Presbyn. Ch. USA, Fla., 1996—; treas., interim bd. of dirs. Presbyn. Assn. for Collegiate and Higher Edn. Ministries, 2004—06, treas., bd. dirs., 2006—; leadership team Higher Edn. Ministries Presbyn. Ch. USA, Louisville, 2001—; mem., pres., com. chair Presbyn. U. Ctr., 1984—2000; elder Fellowship Presbyn. Ch., 1987—90, Christ Presbyn. Ch, 1994—97; permanent jud. commn. Fla. Presbyn., Panama City, Fla., 2002—05, com. on preparation for ministry, 1991—97; bd. mem. YWCA, Warren, Pa., 1965—67. Recipient Peter W. Everett Honor award, Fla. Assn. for Health, Phys. Edn., Recreation, and Dance, 2002; Rsch. Consortium fellow, Am. Alliance for Health, Phys. Edn., Recreation, and Dance, 1986 to present. Mem.: Am. Ednl. Rsch. Assn., Fla. Assn. for Health, Phys. Edn., Recreation, and Dance, Am. Alliance for Health, Phys. Edn., Recreation, and Dance (life), Delta Psi Kappa (life; pres. 1984—86, bd. dirs.). Presbyterian. Avocations: reading, handwork, gardening, woodworking. Home: 4121 Tralee Rd Tallahassee FL 32309-2822 Personal E-mail: yerg@coe.fsu.edu.

**YERGIN, DANIEL HOWARD,** writer, consultant; b. Los Angeles, Feb. 6, 1947; s. Irving H. and Naomi Y.; m. Angela Stent, Aug. 10, 1975; children: Alexander George, Rebecca Isabella. BA, Yale U., Eng., 1970, PhD, 1974; PhD (hon.), U. Mo., 1980, U. Houston, 1994. Contbg. editor New York mag., 1968-70; research fellow Harvard U., Cambridge, Mass., 1974-76, lectr. bus. sch., 1976-79, lectr. Kennedy Sch. Govt., 1979-83, research assoc. Cambridge, 1983-90; chmn. Cambridge Energy Research Assoc., Cambridge, 1982-98, also chmn., sec. energy task force on strategic energy R&D, 1998—. Mem. policy adv. com. Program on U.S.-Japan Rels., Harvard U.; mem. bd. energy experts Dallas Morning News; mem. internat. panel advisors Asia-Pacific Petroleum Conf.; fellow World Econ. Forum, Davos. Author: Shattered Peace: The Origins of the Cold War and the National Security State, 1977, rev. edit., 1990, The Prize: Epic Quest for Oil, Money and Power, 1991 (Pulitzer Prize for non-fiction 1992, Eccle prize 1992); co-author: Cold War, 1977, Energy Future, 1979, Global Insecurity, 1982, Future of Oil Prices: Perils of Prophecy, 1984, Russia 2010: And What It Means for the World, 1993, The Commanding Heights, 1998; contbg. editor Atlantic Monthly, 1977-83. Mem. adv. bd. Solar Energy Rsch. Inst., Golden, Colo., 1979-81; sec. Energy Adv. Bd. Fellow Univ. Consortium for World Order Studies, 1974-75, Rockefeller Found., 1975-79, German Marshall Fund, 1980-81, Harvard U., Ctr. for Bus. and Govt., 1997—; Marshall scholar Cambridge U., 1974; recipient U.S. Energy award, 1997. Mem. PEN, Coun. on Fgn. Rels. (com. on studies), Nat. Petroleum Coun., Internat. Assn. for Energy Econs., Am. Hist. Assn., Am. Polit. Assn., Royal Inst. Internat. Affairs, Assn. Marshall Scholars (bd. dirs. 1988-91), U.S. Energy Assn. (bd. dirs.), Nat. Petroleum Coun., Yale Club (N.Y.C.), Harvard Club (N.Y.C.). Office: Cambridge Energy Research Assoc 55 Cambridge Pkwy Cambridge MA 02142-1234

**YERIC, GREG,** electronics executive; b. Columbus, Ohio, July 13, 1965; s. Jerry and Peggy Yeric. BSEE, U. Tex., Austin, 1987, PhD, 1993. Sr. engr. process integration Freescale Semiconductor Advanced Products R & D Labs., Austin, Tex., 1993-97; chief technologist HPL TestChip Techs., 1997—2005; sr. dir. mktg. Synopsys, 2005—. Tech. chmn. IEEE Internat. Conf. Microelectronic Test Structures, Austin, Tex., 2006—. Fellow, Semiconductor Rsch. Assn., 1987—93. Mem.: IEEE. Avocations: golf, volleyball. Office Phone: 512-372-7680. Personal E-mail: gyeric@yahoo.com.

**YERKAN, ROBERT R.,** educational consultant; b. Chgo., Nov. 23, 1960; s. Milan and Rita A. Jerkan; m. Jamile M. Shammo, June 9, 1991; children: Nikola R., Alexander M., Michael K. BA, Loyola U., Chgo., 1980, MA, Governors State U., 1990. Social studies tchr. Thornridge HS, Dolton, Ill., 1984—93; counselor Rolling Meadows (Ill.) HS, 1993—95, ESL counselor, 1995—2001, coll. cons., 2001—. mem.: Ill. Assn. Coll. Admission Counseling, Nat. Assn. Coll. Admission Counseling. Serbian Orthodox. Avocations: coin collecting/numismatics, gardening, model railroading. Home: 43 Cedar St Park Ridge IL 60068 Office: Rolling Meadows HS 2901 Central Rd Rolling Meadows IL 60008

**YERKES, DAVID NORTON,** architect; b. Cambridge, Mass., Nov. 5, 1911; s. Robert Mearns and Ada (Watterson) Y.; m. Catharine Noyes, Oct. 7, 1939 (dec. 1969); 1 dau., Catharine; m. Sarah Hitchcock Satterlee, July 9, 1972. BA, Harvard U., 1933; M.F.A., Yale U., 1935. Draftsman, designer, Chgo. and Washington, 1937-39, Deigert & Yerkes and Assos., Washington, 1945—65, David N. Yerkes & Assos., Washington, 1965—69, Yerkes, Pappas and Parker, 1980-83. Mem. panel archtl. advisers Nat. Commn. Fine Arts, 1961-63, 79-82; vice chmn. Presdl. Inaugural Parade Com., 1965 Prin. works include Voice of America Studios, Washington, 1958, Nat. Arboretum Hdqrs. Bldg. Am. Embassy, Somalia, also Madeira Sch. Auditorium, 1969; 4 stas. Washington subway sys., 1971-81, hdqrs., Nat. Trust Historic Preservation, Washington, 1977, suite, Time, Inc., Washington, 1980, also various schs., labs; paintings exhibited in New Eng. and Washington. Served to capt. AUS, 1943-45. Firm recipient numerous regional and nat. awards; recipient Kemper award AIA, 1972 Fellow AIA (bd. dirs. 1965-68, v.p. 1968-69, chmn. nat. honor awards jury 1966, chmn. Reynolds Meml. award jury 1969, pres. found. 1974-76) Home: 3050 Military Rd NW #449 Washington DC 20015

**YERMAN, FREDRIC WARREN,** lawyer; b. NYC, Jan. 8, 1943; s. Nat W. and Tina (Barotz) Y.; m. Ann R. Rochlin, May 31, 1965; children: Emily, Deborah. BA, CUNY, 1963; LLB, Columbia U., 1966. Bar: N.Y. 1967. Assoc. Kaye Scholer LLP, NYC, 1966-74, prnr., 1974—, chmn. exec. com., 1990—92. Bd. dirs. United Way Tri-State, Jewish Bd. Family and Children Svcs., N.Y.C. Fellow Am. Coll. Trial Lawyers. Home: 31 Sheridan Rd Scarsdale NY 10583-1523 Office: Kaye Scholer LLP 425 Park Ave New York NY 10022-3506 Business E-Mail: fyerman@kayescholer.com.

**YERRICK, RANDY KREGG,** science educator; b. Owosso, Mich., Feb. 19, 1963; s. Rand Lee Yerrick and Sally Vernon; m. Metra Lynn Moghadam, June 6, 1986; children: Taylor James, Jackson David. PhD, Mich. State U., 1993. Tchr. Calif., Mich., 1985, 1992. Assoc. prof. East Carolina U., Greenville, NC, 1993—99; prof. San Diego State U., 1999—. Disting. educator Apple, Cupertino, Calif., 1999— Vol. Poway Unified Sch. Dist., San Diego, 1999—2005, Green Valley Ch., San Diego, 1999—2005. Recipient John Keating Award, Omicron Delta Kappa, 1998—99, Coll. Edn. Outstanding Faculty Award, San Diego State U., 2002—03, U. President's Top 25, 2003—04; NPACI Edn. Supercomputing fellow, Nat. Partnership for Ad-

vanced Computational Infrastructure, San Diego Supercomputer Ctr., 2001—02, Tchr. Scholar fellow, Ctr. for Tchg. and Learning, San Diego State U., 2002. Mem.: Nat. Assn. for Rsch. in Sci. Tchg. (life; leadership team 1994—2005). Republican. Protestant. Avocations: computers, tennis. Office Phone: 619-594-5090.

**YERRID, C. STEVEN,** lawyer; b. Charleston, W.Va., Sept. 30, 1949; s. Charles Gerard and Audrey Faye Yerrid; m. Sharon Wainman, Feb. 13, 2000. BA in History and Polit. Sci., La. State U., 1971; JD, Georgetown U., 1975. Bar: Fla. 1975, Va. 1975, U.S. Supreme Ct. 1979, D.C. 1984; cert. civil trial advocate Nat. Bd. Trial Advocacy. Aide U.S. Senator Ellender, Washington, 1971-73; prtnr. Holland & Knight, Tampa, Fla., 1975-86; pres. Stagg, Hardy & Yerrid, Tampa, 1986-89, Yerrid, Knopik & Krieger PA, Tampa, 1990-2000, The Yerrid Law Firm, Tampa, 2000—. Mediator and Cir. Ct. arbitrator Fla. and Fed. Cts. Mem. ABA, Va. Bar Assn., D.C. Bar Assn., Fla. Bar Assn. (chmn. admiralty law com. 1984-85, bd. cert. com. 1988-91, vice chmn. 1990-91, chmn. 1994-95, bd. cert. civil trial lawyer), Southeastern Admiralty Law Inst., Am. Judicature Soc., ATLA (sustaining), Am. Bd. Trial Advocates (advocate), Maritime Law Assn. (proctor), Tex. Trial Lawyers Assn., Acad. Fla. Trial Lawyer (designated continuing legal edn. speaker 1982—, bd. dirs. 1989-97, 2000-01), Inner Cir. Advocates, Internat. Soc. Barristers, Am. Inns of Ct. (supporting fellow), Cousteau Soc., Centre Club, Tampa Club, Univ. Club, Grand Havana Club, Old Memorial Golf Club. Democrat. Avocations: fishing, tennis, boxing. Office: The Yerrid Law Firm Bank of America Plz Ste 3910 101 E Kennedy Blvd Tampa FL 33602-5192 Office Phone: 813-222-8222. E-mail: syerrid@yerridlaw.com

**YERSHOV, ANDREI R.,** computer scientist; b. Irkutsk, Russia, Oct. 29, 1963; s. Rudolf Yershov and Alla Yershova; m. Mariya S. Nechaeva, Feb. 6, 2003; children: Nikita, Olga Yershova, Oleg. MSEE, BSCS, Irkutsk State Tech. U., 1991. Prin. engr. Rules Power Inc., Burlington, Mass., 2004—05; software engring. mgr. Fair Isaac Corp., San Rafael, Calif., 2005—. Rschr. Inst. Energy Systems, Russian Acad. Scis., Irkutsk, 1992—. Mem.: IEEE (assoc.), Assn. Computing Machinery (assoc.). Achievements include research in static analysis of hybrid knowledge bases. Personal E-mail: ayershov@acm.org.

**YERSIZ, HASAN,** medical educator; b. Ankara, Turkey, Aug. 30, 1957; s. Hamdi and Mediha Yersiz; m. Sehnaz Alansatan, Mar. 18, 1983; 1 child, Melike. MD, Istanbul U., Turkey, 1981. Asst. prof. UCLA, 1998—2004, assoc. prof., 2004—. Dir. organ procurement UCLA Liver/Pancreas Transplant Ctr., 1995—. Mem. adv. bd. OneLegacy, LA. Scholar, Am. Field Svc., 1974—75. Mem.: Am. Soc. Transplant Surgeons (mem. of membership commitee 2003—). Achievements include development of In-Situ Split Liver Transplantation. Office: UCLA 10833 LeConte Ave Los Angeles CA 90095 Office Phone: 1-310-825-5318. Home Fax: 1-310-267-0392; Office Fax: 1-310-267-0392. Personal E-mail: hyersiz@ucla.edu.

**YERUSHALMI, YOSEF HAYIM,** historian, educator; b. NYC, May 20, 1932; s. Leon and Eva (Kaplan) Y.; m. Ophra Pearly, Jan. 4, 1959; 1 child, Ariel. BA, Yeshiva U., 1953; M in Hebrew Lit., Jewish Theol. Sem. Am., 1957; MA, Columbia U., 1961, PhD, 1966; MA (hon.), Harvard, 1970; DHL (hon.), Jewish Theol. Sem. Am., 1987; LHD (hon.), Hebrew Union Coll. 1996; PhD (hon.), U. Haifa, 1997, Ludwig Maximilians U., Munich, 1997; DHL (hon.), Spertus Inst., 2002; PhD (hon.), Ecole Pratique des Hautes Etudes Sorbonne Paris, 2003. Instr. Jewish history Rutgers U., New Brunswick, NJ, 1963-66; asst. prof. Hebrew and Jewish history Harvard U., 1966-70, prof., 1970-78, Jacob E. Safra prof. Jewish history and Sephardic civilization, 1978-80, Salo Wittmayer Baron Prof. of Jewish History, Culture, Soc.; dir. Columbia U. Inst. Israel and Jewish Studies, N.Y.C., 1980—. Author: From Spanish Court to Italian Ghetto: Isaac Cardoso, A Study in Seventeenth-Century Marranism and Jewish Apologetics, 1971, Haggadah and History, 1975, The Lisbon Massacre of 1506, 1976, Zakhor: Jewish History and Jewish Memory, 1982, Freud's Moses: Judaism Terminable and Interminable, 1991, A Field in Anatot: Essays on Jewish History (in German), 1993, Servants of Kings and Not Servants of Servants: Some Aspects of the Political History of the Jews (in German), 1995, Sefardica: Essays on the History of the Jews, Marranos and New Christians of Hispano-Portuguese Origin (in French), 1998; author (in Hebrew): Spinoza on the Survival of the Jews, 1983; contbr. articles to profl. publs. com. publs. com. Jewish Publ. Soc., 1972-84; pres. Leo Baeck Inst., 1986-91. Bd. dirs. Conf. Jewish Social Studies, Psycho analytic Research and Devel. Found. Editorial Bd., History and Memory. Recipient Newman medal CUNY, 1975, Nat. Jewish Book award, 1983, 92, Ansley award Columbia U. Press, 1968, Achievement medal Nat. Found. Jewish Culture, 1995, Leopold Lucas prize U. Tübingen, Germany, 2005; Kent fellow, 1963, Nat. Found. Jewish Culture, 1964, NEH, 1976-77, Rockefeller Found., 1983-84, Guggenheim Found., 1989-90, Carl Friedrich von Siemens Stiftung fellow, 1996-97, fellow Inst. Advanced Studies Tel Aviv U., 2004. Fellow Am. Acad. Jewish Research, Am. Acad. Arts and Scis., Acad. Portuguesa da História Lisbon (hon.), Acad. Sci. Lisboa (hon.). Office: Columbia U 511 Fayerweather Hall 1180 Amsterdam Ave New York NY 10027-7039

**YERVES, KEN,** information technology executive; B, Dowling Coll., NY; MBA, Jacksonville Univ., Fla. With Todd Travel Promotions, Micro Cons. Co. Inc.: asst. v.p. remarketing applications devel. JM Family Enterprises, Deerfield Beach, Fla., asst. v.p., tech. arch., planning and control, v.p. tech. delivery, 2001, v.p. & chief info. officer. Office: SVP & CIO JM Family Enterp 100 Jim Moran Blvd Deerfield Beach FL 33442*

**YESAIR, DAVID WAYNE,** biochemist; b. Newbury, Mass., Sept. 9, 1932; s. Wayne and Roma Jackson (Arlin) Y.; m. Ruth Elizabeth Avery, June 6, 1954; children: Karen, Catherine, Peter. BS in Chemistry, U. Mass., 1954; PhD in Biochemistry, Cornell U., 1958. NSF postdoctoral fellow Nat. Inst. for Rsch., Shinfield, England, 1961-62; sr. scientist biochemistry group Arthur D. Little, Inc., Cambridge, Mass., 1962-66, head biochemistry/biomed. and pharmacology group, 1966-71, 72-77, mgr. biomolecular scis. sect., 1977-82, v.p., 1978-84; pres. BioMolecular Products, Inc., 1984—; founder, pres. Lym-Med Nutritional Products LLC, 2000, Lym-Drug Products, LLC, 2000. NIH sabbatical fellow L'Inst. de Chemie des Substances Naturelle, CNRS, Gif-Sur-Yvette, France, 1971-72; drug metabolism chmn. Gordon Rsch. Conf., 1983; mem. biotech. adv. bd. U. Conn., 1986-94; guest lectr. toxicology curriculum MIT, 1972-82. Contbr. numerous articles to profl. jours. and chpts. to books; holder more than 50 worldwide patents. Active Newbury Hist. Soc., Newburyport Maritime Mus., Sons and Daus. First Settlers of Newbury, pres., 1975, 76; active Newburyport Choral Soc.; class agt., Mass. capital fund chairperson Gov. Dummer Acad. Fellow Leukemia Soc. Am., NSF, NIH. Fellow Am. Inst. Chemists; mem. N.Y. Acad. Scis., Internat. Lecithin and Phospholipid Soc., AAAS, Am. Chem. Soc., Mass. Inst. Chemists, Am. Assn. for Cancer Rsch., Am. Soc. Toxicology, Am. Soc. Pharmacology Exptl. Therapeutics, Internat. Soc. for Studying Xenobiotics, Sigma Xi. Avocations: woodworking, antique furniture restoration, creative landscape gardening, choral singing, swimming. Office: BioMolecular Products Inc PO Box 929 Byfield MA 01922-0929 Office Phone: 978-462-2224. E-mail: lymxsorb@comcast.net.

**YESAWICH, PETER CHARLES,** advertising executive; b. Ithaca, N.Y., Oct. 28, 1950; s. Paul Joseph Jr. and Elizabeth (Larkin) Y.; m. Paris Pyne; children: Peter Charles, Paul Christopher, Logan Baker. BS, Cornell U., 1972, MS, 1974, PhD, 1976; AMP, Yale U., 1994. Dir. rsch. Robinsons, Inc., Orlando, Fla., 1976-78, v.p., 1978-81, exec. v.p., 1981-83; pres., CEO Yesawich, Pepperdine, Brown & Russell, Orlando, 1983—. Vis. assoc. prof. Cornell U., Ithaca, 1977—, U. Ctrl. Fla., Orlando, 1988—; chmn. Pope Tourism Inst., Orlando, 1988-90. Co-author: Marketing, Leadership in Hospital Life, 2006; contbr. articles to profl. jours. Recipient World Travel award Am. Assn. Travel Editors, 1985, Silver Medal award Am. Assn. Advt. Agys., 1992, Adrian award Hospitality Sales and Mktg. Assn. Internat., 1993; named Author of Yr. Cornell Quar., 1986. Mem. Cornell Hotel Soc., Am.

Hotel & Motel Assn., Caribbean Hotel Assn., Hotel Sales Mktg. Assn., Am. Mktg. Assn. Avocations: jogging, writing. Office: Yesawich Pepperdine Brown and Russell 423 S Keller Rd # 100 Orlando FL 32810-6102 Office Phone: 407-875-1111. E-mail: peter_yesawich@ypbr.com.

**YESILADA, BIROL ALI,** political science professor; b. Nicosia, Cyprus, Aug. 12, 1956; came to U.S., 1971; s. Ali and Sermin (Mustafa) Y.; m. Susan Diana Lesea, Aug. 20, 1980; children: Sermin, Selin. AB, U. Calif., Berkeley, 1977; MA, San Francisco State U., 1979; PhD, U. Mich., 1984. Vis. asst. prof. U. Mo., Columbia, 1984-85, asst. prof., 1985-91; vis. asst. prof. Middle East Tech. U., Ankara, Turkey, 1987-88; vis. rsch. specialist State Planning Orgn., Ankara, Turkey, 1987-88; assoc. prof. U. Mo., Columbia, 1991-98, chair dept. polit. sci., 1994-98; pres. Oceania Corp., 1992-98; prof. Portland (Oreg.) State U., 1998—, endowed chair Contemporary Turkish Studies, 1998—; exec. dir. Northwest Am. Turkish Rsch. Inst., 1999—; ptnr. BCM Internat., LLC, 2000—04. Cons. State Planning Orgn., Ankara, 1987-88, Libr. of Congress, Washington, 1988-92, Coun. on Fgn. Rels., N.Y.C., 1990-91, U.S. State Dept. Fgn. Svc. Inst., 1995-99, Nat. Intelligence Coun., Washington, 1996-97, 99—, Rand Corp., 2003, U.S. Inst. Peace, 1996, U.S. State Dept., 1995—; chair internat. studies adv. com. U. Mo., Columbia, 1992-94; adv. coun. Inst. Turkish Studies Georgetown U., 2000—; adv. bd. Istanbul Strategic Rsch. Ctr. Bahcesehir U., 2000—. Author, co-editor: Agrarian Reform in Reverse: The Food Crisis in the Third World, 1987, The Political and Socioeconomic Transformation of Turkey, 1993; co-author: The Emerging European Union, 1996, 2001, 03; editor Comparative Polit. Parties and Party ELites, 1999; mem. editl. bd. Cyprus Rev. Jour., 1987-98, New Perspectives on Turkey, 1987-95; assoc. editor: MESA Bull., 2000—; pub. rev. com., Istanbul Stock Exchange Publ., 1999—; mem. editl. rev. bd. Istanbul Stock Exchange pubs.; co-editor: Internat. Studies Perspectives, 2004—; contbr. articles to profl. jours. Bd. dirs. U. Mo. Peace Studies, Columbia, 1988-92; adv. bd. Constl. Studies Found. Mo., 1996-98. Rsch. fellow Am. Coun. Learned Socs. and Social Sci. Rsch. Coun., 1987, Fulbright-Hays, 1982, Turkish Econ. and Social Studies Found. of Eczacibasi Holding, 1995, William T. Kemper fellow for tchng. excellence U. Mo. and Commerce Bank, 1996; recipient Purple Chalk Tchg. Excellence award U. Mo., Columbia Arts and Scis. Coll., 1991; rsch. bd. grantee U. Mo., 1996. Mem. Internat. Studies Assn., Am. Polit. Sci. Assn., European Union Studies Assn., Middle East Studies Assn., Rotary (Tigard, Oreg.), Golden Key Honor Soc. Moslem. Avocations: jogging, swimming, camping, fly fishing, ballroom dancing. Home: 12556 SW 114th Ter Tigard OR 97223-4061 Office Phone: 503-725-3257. Business E-Mail: yesilada@pdx.edu.

**YESSMAN, TIMOTHY,** insurance company executive; b. 1959; Bachelor's Degree, Seton Hall U.; JD, Villanova U. Joined Travelers Ins., 1984, sr. v.p. spl. liability group, 1997—2001; exec. v.p. claims St. Paul Co., Inc., 2001—. Office: St Paul Cos Inc 385 Washington St Saint Paul MN 55102

**YETERIAN, EDWARD HARRY,** psychologist, educator, administrator; b. New Britain, Conn., 1948; s. Arthur and Mary Yeterian; m. Margaret Emily Wellock; children— Robert, Julie. BS, Trinity Coll., 1970; MA, U. Conn., 1974, PhD, 1975. Rsch. fellow Harvard Med. Sch., Boston, 1975-78, postdoctoral fellow, 1975-78; cons. Maine State Bur. Mental Retardation, Augusta, 1982—88; v.p. for acad. affairs, dean of faculty, dept. psychology Colby Coll., Waterville, Maine. Author book chpts.; contbr. articles to profl. jours. Mem. bd. fellows Trinity Coll., Hartford, Conn., 1986—93. NIMH fellow, 1977-78. Mem. Soc. for Neurosci., Eastern Psychol. Assn., Nat. Assn. for Armenian Studies and Rsch. Achievements include: automobile repair and rebuilding; short-wave radio. Home: 86 Lake Ridge Dr Sidney ME 04330-2103 Office: VP Acad Affairs Dept Psychology Colby Coll Waterville ME 04901

**YETMAN, GARY,** investment company executive; BBA, Adelphi Univ.; JD, Bklyn. Law Sch.; completed advanced study in taxation, NYU Law Sch. Bar: NY State 1975. Mgr., tax dept. Oppenheim, Appel, Dixon & Co.; pres., COO Wagner Stott Clearing Corp., N.Y.C.; pres., chmn. Merrill Lynch Prof. Clearing.; joined Merrill Lynch Prof. Clearing, 1980—; pres., CEO Merrill Lynch Clearing Corp., New York, 1997—; mng. dir., co-head, global equity fin., global markets & investment banking divsn. Merrill Lynch. Bd. dir. Options Clearing Corp., Merrill Lynch. Mem.: Wall Street Tax Assn. (mem. 1983—93), Phila. Stock Exchange Option Com. (mem. 1986—88). Office: Merrill Lynch Pro 222 Broadway 6 New York NY 10038-2510

**YETMAN, RANDALL JOHN,** plastic surgeon; b. Casper, Wyo., Nov. 1, 1948; s. Jack Eugene and Mary Yetman; m. Nancy Lynn Devins, Apr. 29, 1969; children: Koren Dodson, Jamie Finnicum. Degree, SUNY, Buffalo, 1970; MD, U. Miami, 1975. Diplomate Am. Bd. Plastic Surgery, 1984. Intern in gen. surgery Albert Einstein Sch. Medicine, 1975—79, residency in gen. surgery, 1975—79; residency in plastic surgery Cornell Sch. Medicine, NYC, 1979—81, asst. prof. surgery, 1981—83; staff surgeon Cleve. Clinic, 1983—. Residency program dir. in plastic surgery Cleve. Clinic, 1995—. Fellow: ACS; mem.: Am. Soc. Plastic Surgeons, Am. Assn. Plastic Surgeons. Republican. Roman Catholic. Avocations: golf, fly fishing. Home: 2603 Fairmount Blvd Cleveland Heights OH 44106 Office: Cleveland Clinic 9500 Euclid Ave Cleveland OH 44106 Office Phone: 216-444-6908. Business E-Mail: yetmanr@ccf.org.

**YETT, SALLY PUGH,** art educator, consultant; b. St. Louis, Feb. 15, 1935; d. John D. and Esther Ruth Pugh; m. Donald Edward Yett, June 19, 1964; children: Stephen Edward, John Harold. BFA, Washington U., St. Louis, 1956; tchg. credential, Calif. State U., L.A., 1989. Cert. gen. clear multiple subject and art supplementary Calif. Dept. Edn. Recreation therapist ARC, San Antonio, 1956-58; dir. recreation therapy dept. Jewish Hosp., St. Louis, 1958-64; tchr. art-gifted class Juan Cabrillo Elem., Malibu, Calif., 1975-78; educator pre-kindergarten Malibu Meth. Pre-Sch., 1979-81; spl. edn. educator grades 9-12 Santa Monica Sch. Dist., Calif., 1981-89; educator grades 1-6 art L.A. Unified Sch. Dist.-Visual and Performing Arts Magnet, 1990—2006; resource tchr., art edn. advisor Calif. State U., L.A., 2001—04, master tchr. Dominguez Hills, 2003—05. Judge Making History, L.A., 1998—2005; participant UCLA Tchrs. and Scholars Symposium, 1999—2003, 2005; state judge History Day in Calif., 2003; mem. art start curriculum com. Mus. Contemporary Art, 2005. Exhibitions include Malibu Art Festival, 1976 (3rd place award), Malibu Art Assn. Show, 1984 (3rd place award), Roberts Art Gallery, 1989, CAEA State Conv.-Calif. State Bakersfield Exhibit, 2001; contbr. articles to profl. jours. PTA pres. Juan Cabrillo Elem., Malibu, 1976—78, Malibu Park Jr. HS; pres. Santa Monica Jr. Programs, 1979—81; 2d, 3d, and 4th v.p. Santa Monica/Malibu PTA Coun., 1982—85; pres. Malibu Art Assn., 1992—93. Nominee Teacher of Yr., Walt Disney Co.; recipient Honoree Bravo award, L.A. Music Ctr.; grantee, Calif. Cmty. Found., 2003. Mem.: Internat. Studies Overseas Program, Gene Autrey Mus., Calif. Art Edn. Assn., Soc. Calligraphy (pub. rels. 1987—91, bd. dirs.), Nat. Art Edn. Assn., Art Mus. Long Beach, Shakespeare Festival/L.A., S.W. Mus., UCLA Fowler Mus. Cultural History, LA. County Art Mus., Mus. Contemporary Art (mem. curriculum com. 2005), Craft and Folk Mus., Mus. L.Am. Art, People to People Internat. (Indigenous Art del. to New Zealand, Australia 1998), Metro. Mus. Art, Kappa Alpha Theta. Avocations: travel, reading, calligraphy, hiking, gardening. Home: 2042 Hanscom Dr South Pasadena CA 91030-4012

**YETTER, R PAUL,** lawyer; b. Milw., Aug. 5, 1958; s. Richard and Lobelia (Gutierrez) Y.; m. Patricia D. Yetter, May 6, 1983; children: Chris, Mark, Michael, Joseph, Thomas, Andrew, Daniel. BA, U. Tex., El Paso, 1980; JD, Columbia U., 1983. Bar: Tex. 1983, U.S. Dist. Ct. (so., ea., no. and we. dists.) Tex., U.S. Ct. Appeals (5th cir.); bd. cert. in civil trial and personal injury trial law Tex. Bd. Legal Specialization. Law clk. to Hon. John R. Brown U.S. Ct. Appeals (5th cir.), Houston, 1983-84; assoc. Baker & Botts, L.L.P., Houston, 1984-89, prtnr., 1990-97, Yetter & Warden, L.L.P., Houston, 1997—. Chair state judiciary rels. com. State Bar, 1995-96; mem. Funding Parity Task Force, 1995-97; mem. ex officio Jud. Selection Task Force, 1995-97; chair Alliance for Jud. Funding, Inc., 1996—; mem. ex officio contbns. com. Tex. Ctr. for the Judiciary, mem. com. on admissions, So. Dist. Tex., 2000—. Contbr. articles to profl. jours. Recipient Presdl. citation State Bar Tex., 1996; rsch. fellow Southwestern Legal Found.; named one of Top Ten Winning

Attys., Nat. Law Jour., 2004, Tex. Super Lawyer Bus. Litigation, Tex. Monthly, 2003, 2004, 2005, 2006, One of Best Lawyers, H Tex. Mag., 2005, 2006. Fellow Tex. Bar Foun., Houston Bar Found. Office: Yetter & Warden LLP 909 Fannin Ste 3600 Houston TX 77010- Office Phone: 713-632-8000. Business E-Mail: pyetter@yetterwarden.com.

**YEUDALL, WILLIAM ANDREW,** biochemist, molecular oncologist; BSc with honors, U. Glasgow, Scotland, 1983; BDS, U. Glasgow, 1986, PhD, 1990. Rsch. fellow Beatson Inst. Cancer Rsch., Glasgow, 1987—90; lectr. U. Bristol, England, 1990—93; vis. assoc. Nat. Inst. Dental and Craniofacial Rsch., Bethesda, Md., 1993—97; vis. lectr. Eastman Dental Inst., London, 1995—98; clin. sr. lectr. King's Coll. London, 1999—2002; assoc. prof. Va. Commonwealth U., Richmond, 2002—. Mem. editl. bd. Oral Oncology, 1996—. Fellow: Internat. Acad. Oral Oncology (founding); mem.: Internat. Assn. Dental Rsch. Office: Va Commonwealth U 521 N 11th St Richmond VA 23298 Office Phone: 804-828-6415.

**YEUN, PAUL LORENZO,** clergy member; b. Hong Kong, Apr. 14, 1944; came to U.S., 1960; s. Kaki Yeun and Carmen (Flores) Pio; m. Elisabeth Wendy Chan, June 19, 1971; children: Evangeline, Abigail. BA, Azusa Pacific U., 1968; MDiv, Asbury Sem., 1971, MA, 1974; DMin, Lexington Sem., 1977. Ordained to ministry United Meth. Ch., 1973; lic. marriage and family therapist; lic. profl. counselor; cert. mental health clergy, profl. chaplain, parish pastor, Ohio, 1971-1981. Parish pastor Aberdeen (Ohio) United Meth. Ch., 1971-72, Morrow (Ohio) United Meth. Ch., 1972-76, Albany (Ohio) United Meth. Ch., 1976-78, Oakland Park United Meth. Ch., Columbus, Ohio, 1978-81; reserve chaplain USAF, Rickenbacker AFB, Ohio, 1980-81, protestant chaplain George Air Force Base, Calif., 1981-84, installation chaplain Clark Air Base, Philippines, 1984-87; sr. protestant chaplain USAF, Davis Monthan AFB, Tucson, 1987—92; sr. chaplain Lajas Field, Azorc, Portugal, 1992—94; chief edn. and tng. Wilford Hall Medical Ctr. Tex. 1994—97; sr. regional chaplain Ramsrein AB, Germany, 1997—99; dir. pastoral svcs. Chambersburg Hosp., Pa., 1999—. Bd. dirs. Ariz. Marriage and Family Therapy, Tucson Met. Ministries, v.p. Letterkenny chapel com. Author: Dealing with the Psychological Needs of Aged, 1985, Meaning of our Membership Vows, 1987. Mem. Mil. Officers Assn., 2002. Chaplain USAF, 1980—87, maj. USAF, 1987—94, lt. col. USAF, 1994—, served in Operation Desert Shield, served in Operation So. Watch, Saudi Arabia, served in Operation Allied Force, Europe, served in NATO exercise, Greece. Decorated Air Force Commendation medal with 3 oak leaf clusters, Air Force Meritorious Svc. medal with 4 oak leaf clusters, Air Force Outstanding Unit award with 4 oak leaf clusters, SW Asia medal, Expeditionary medal, Nat. Defense medal; named to Ky. Col., 1978; recipient Air Force Best Sermons, 1985, Man of Achievement award, 1989, Achievement award, Hosp. & Health Sys. Assn. Pa., 2003. Mem.: Assn. Profl. Chaplains (nominating com. 2003), Am. Legion (mem. state chaplain mental health task force 2004). Democrat. Office: 128 Buckingham Dr Chambersburg PA 17201 Office Phone: 717-267-7749. Business E-Mail: pyeun@summithealth.org. *Mutual respect is the basis for solving world's conflicts.*

**YEUNG, BERNARD YIN,** finance educator; b. Hong Kong, Sept. 29, 1953; s. Kwai Din and Kin Ling Yeung; m. Jean Jun Wei, Aug. 19, 1982; children: Michael B., Anne Y. BBA, U. B.C., Can., 1979; MBA, U. Chgo., 1981, PhD, 1984. Asst., assoc. prof. Bus. Sch. U. Alta., Edmondson, Canada, 1983—88; asst., assoc., prof. Sch. Bus. U. Mich., Ann Arbor, 1988—99; Abraham Kozimoff prof. NYU, 1999—. Fellow: Acad. Internat. Bus. (v.p. 2000—02); mem.: Acad. Mgmt., Am. Econ. Assn. Home: Apt 11-O 1 Washington Sq Village New York NY 10012 Office: NYU Stern Bus Sch 7-87 44 W 4th St New York NY 10012

**YEUNG, EDWARD SZESHING,** chemist; b. Hong Kong, Feb. 17, 1948; arrived in U.S., 1965; s. King Mai Luk and Yu Long Yeung; m. Anna Kunkwok Seto, Sept. 18, 1971; children: Rebecca Tze-Mai, Amanda Tze-Wen AB magna cum laude, Cornell U., 1968; PhD, U. Calif., Berkeley, 1972. Instr. chemistry Iowa State U., Ames, 1972-74, asst prof., 1974-77, assoc. prof, 1977-81, prof. chemistry, 1981-89, disting. prof., 1989—. Contbr. articles to profl. jours. Alfred P. Sloan fellow, 1974-76; recipient Am. Chem Soc. award in Analytical Chemistry, 1994. Fellow AAAS; mem. Soc. Applied Spectrosci. (Lester Strock award 1990), Am. Chem. Soc. (award in chem. instrumentation 1987, award in analytical chemistry 1994, award in chromatography 2002). Home: 1005 Jarrett Cir Ames IA 50014-3937 Office: Iowa State U Gilman Hall Ames IA 50011

**YEUNG, KAI S.,** engineering educator; BSc in Engring., U. Hong Kong, 1970; Dipl.-Ing., U. Karlsruhe, Germany, 1974, PhD, 1977. Design engr. Hong Kong Electric Co., 1970—71; lectr. Chinese U. Hong Kong, 1977—83; prof. U. Tex., Arlington, 1983—. Vis. prof. Drexel U., Phila., 1981—82; spkr. in field. Tchr. Arlington Chinese Ch., 1984—2006. Recipient Excellence in Engring. Tchg., Lockheed Martin Aero. Co. 2004; DAAD scholar, German Academic Exch. Svc., 1971—77. Mem.: IEEE. Office: U Tex Arlington Dept Elec Engring Box 19016 Arlington TX 76019 Office Phone: 817-272-3467. Office Fax: 817-272-2253. Business E-Mail: yeung@uta.edu.

**YEUNG, RONALD WAI-CHUN,** engineering educator, researcher; s. Foo and Pui Fong Yeung; m. Grace Y. Chow, Sept. 5, 1970; 1 child, Brian H. BSME, U. Calif., Berkeley, 1968, MS Naval Architecture, 1970, PhD Engring., 1973. Naval arch. Advanced Marine Tech. Divsn., Litton Ship Sys., Culver City, Calif., 1970—71; instr. U. Calif. L.A. ext., Long Beach Naval Shipyard, 1970—71; asst., assoc. prof. MIT, Cambridge, 1974—82; prof. hydromechanics & ocean engring. U. Calif., Berkeley, 1982—, chair dept. naval architecture & offshore engring., 1989—96, prof. disting. rank, 1994—. Prin. R. W. Yeung - Consulting Naval Architect & Ocean Engr., Moraga, Calif., 1976—; Humboldt prof. U. Hamburg, Germany, 1988, Mercator U., Duisburg, Germany, 1998—99. Editor: Ocean Mechanics, 1999; assoc. editor: Jour Ship Rsch., 1975—95, Jour. Computers & Fluids, 1983—; Jour. Engring. Math., 1986—; contbr. articles to profl. jours. Recipient Gold medal, U. Calif., 1968, Disting. Scientist award, Alexander von Humboldt Found., 1988, Best Paper award, ASME, Offshore Mechanics and Arctic Engring., 1991, ASME, Offshore Mech. and Arctic Engring., 2002, Georg Weinblum lectr., Naval Studies Bd., Soc. Naval Architects and Marine Engrs. and Schiffbautechnische Gesellschaft, 2002—03, Kenneth Davidson medal, Soc. Naval Architects and Marine Engrs., 2004; scholar Fulbright-Hayes Sr. scholar, U. Adelaide, Australian-Am. Edn. Found., 1981. Fellow: Soc. Naval Architects & Marine Engrs. (No. Calif. exec. com. and acad. liaison); mem.: Japanese Soc. Naval Architects, Am. Soc. Engring. Edn., Internat. Soc. Offshore and Polar Engrs. (chair hydrodynamics com. 2002—03), Phi Beta Kappa, Pi Tau Sigma, Tau Beta Pi. Home: 27 Indian Wells Moraga CA 94556-1020 Office: U Calif 6135 Etcheverry Hall Berkeley CA 94720-1740 Office Phone: 510-642-8347. E-mail: rwyeung@berkeley.edu.

**YGLESIAS, HELEN BASSINE,** author, educator; b. N.Y.C., Mar. 29, 1915; d. Solomon and Kate (Goldstein) Bassine; m. Bernard Cole, 1938 (div. 1950); children: Tamar Cole, Lewis Cole; m. Jose Yglesias, Aug. 19, 1950 (div. 1992); 1 child, Rafael. Student pub. schs., LHD (hon.), U. Maine, 1996. Literary editor Nation Mag., 1965-70; adj. assoc. prof. writing Columbia Sch. Arts, N.Y.C., 1973—. Vis. prof. creative writing Writers Workshop, U. Iowa, Iowa City, 1980. Author: (novels) How She Died (Houghton Mifflin award), 1972, Family Feeling, 1976, Sweetsir, 1981, The Saviors, 1987, The Girls, 1999, (non-fiction) Starting: Early, Anew, Over and Late, 1978, Isabel Bishop, 1989. Home: Apt 1303 1261 5th Ave New York NY 10029-3866

**YGLESIAS, KENNETH DALE,** college president; b. Tampa, Fla. s. Jose and Julia Yglesias; m. Donna Carmen Belli, Nov., 1977. BA, U. South Fla., 1969; MA, Western Carolina U., 1973; EdD, U. So. Calif., 1977. Cert. tchr., Calif., Fla. Tchr., coach pub. schs., Tampa, 1969-73; tchr., dept. chmn. Am. Sch. Madrid, 1973-76; fgn. svc. officer USIA, Washington and Tel Aviv, 1977-79; assoc. prof. Pepperdine U., L.A., 1979-83; prof., dir. El Camino Coll., Torrance, Calif., 1981-83; adminstrv. dean Coastline Coll., Fountain Valley, Calif., 1983-88; v.p. Coast C.C. Dist., Costa Mesa, Calif., 1988-95;

pres. Golden West Coll., Huntington Beach, Calif., 1995—2004; chancellor Coast Cmty. Coll. Dist., Costa Mesa, Calif., 2004—. Contbr. articles to profl. jours. Bd. dirs. C.C.'s for Internat. Devel., 1988-94, Orange County Marine Inst., Costa Mesa, 1990-93, United Way Orange County, Santa Ana, Calif., 1991-94. Mem. Am. Assn. for Higher Edn. (Hispanic caucus), Assn. Calif. C.C. Adminstrs., Phi Delta Kappa. Democrat. Roman Catholic. Avocations: basketball fan, walking. Office: Golden West Coll PO Box 2748 Huntington Beach CA 92647-0748

**YGLESIAS, RAFAEL JOSE,** novelist; b. N.Y.C., May 12, 1954; s. Jose and Helen (Bassine) Y.; m. Margaret Joskow, Oct. 15, 1977 (dec. June. 2004); children: Matthew, Nicholas. Author: Dr. Neruda's Cure for Evil, 1996, The Murderer Next Door, 1990, Only Children, 1988; screenwriter, author (film) Fearless, 1993; screenwriter (films) Death and the Maiden, 1995, Les Miserables, 1998, From Hell, 2001, Dark Water, 2005. Mem. The Author's Guild, Writer's Guild of Am., Acad. Motion Picture Arts and Scis.

**YI, MYONGHO,** library and information scientist; b. Seoul, July 15, 1970; s. Sungsoo Yi and Imsoon Yoo; m. Jungeun Oh, Sept. 8, 2001; 1 child, Hannah. BA, U. North Tex., 1995, MS, 1996; PhD, Fla. State U., 2003. Adj. faculty Myongj Coll., Seoul, Republic of Korea, 2002—03; asst. prof. U. Okla., Norman, 2003—. Cons. SecureSoft, Seoul, 2000—02, IBM Korea, 2002—03. Webmaster Tallahasse Bapt. Ch., Fla., 2003. Recipient 1st Place Rsch. Poster, Fla. State U., 2004. Mem.: Am. Libr. and Info. Sci. Edn., Am. Soc. for Info. Sci. Office: U Okla 401 West Brooks Rm 120 Norman OK 73019 Office Phone: 405-325-3921. E-mail: josephmyi@gmail.com.

**YI, TAEIL,** mathematician, educator; b. Seoul, Dec. 16, 1962; s. Beomyoung and Bongwol Yi; m. Moonsil Kim, Nov. 20, 1962; children: Hanyong David, Changyong Peter. BS, Dankook U., Seoul, 1988, MS, 1990, U. Ill., 1994, MEd, U. Fla., 1997, PhD, 2000. Math. tchr. Yongmoon H.S., Seoul, South Korea, 1988—90; instr. U. Fla., Gainesville, 2000—01; asst. prof. U. Tex., Brownsville, 2001—. Advisor math. honor club U. Tex., Brownsville, 2002—. Prod.: (instructional video) Name That Move (Jim Harbin Award / Fla. Assn. for Media in Edn., 1995); contbr. articles to profl. jours. Condr. choir Korean Ch., Urbana/Champaign, Ill., 1993—94; chief editor Korean Bapt. Ch., Gainesville, Fla., 1996—2001, dir. gen. affair, 1997—2000; leader youth group Open Door Ch., Brownsville, Tex., 2001, sec. bd., 2002. Recipient Jim Harbin award, Fla. Assn. Media Edn., 1995. Mem.: Scientific Rsch. Soc., Soc. Indsl. and Applied Math., Math. Assn. Am., Am. Math. Soc., Sigma Xi, Phi Kappa Phi (life), Phi Mu Epsilon. Achievements include development of an automated stereotactic radiosurgery algorithm for brain tumor treatment planning, which has been developed by a software company for broad usage. Avocations: golf, studying theology. Home: 5 Deer Haven Ct Brownsville TX 78520 Office: Univ Tex Brownsville 80 Fort Brown Brownsville TX 78520 Office Phone: 956-882-6621. E-mail: Taeil.Yi@utb.edu.

**YI, WEI,** physicist; PhD, Harvard U., Cambridge, Mass., 2005. Rsch. asst. Inst. Physics, Chinese Acad. Scis., Beijing, 1996—99; rsch. asst. divsn. engring. and applied scis. Harvard U., Cambridge, 1999—2005, postdoctoral fellow divsn. engring. and applied scis., 2005—. Recipient Wei Hua Sci. & Tech. award, Inst. Physics, Chinese Acad. Scis., 1999; fellow, Harvard U., 1999—2000. Mem.: Materials Rsch. Soc. & Am. Physical Soc. Achievements include development of 3-Omega method for specific heat and thermal conductivity measurements of a filament-like specimen, and measured those thermal quantities of carbon nanotube bundles with only nanogram in mass; avalanche spin-valve transistor; research in measured temperature dependence of thermoelectric power in multiwalled carbon nanotubes; coulomb blockade and fano resonance are found in the tunneling spectroscopy measurements of single tunnel junctions between multiwalled carbon nanotubes and a normal metal; electron diffraction characterizations of spinel iron-oxide nanocrystals grown on Fe whiskers; ballistic electron emission luminescence spectroscopy measurements of an InAs quantum dot heterostructure; vertically integrated optics for ballistic electron emission luminescence microscopy; demonstrate the potential of using a dual-probe scanning tunneling microscope to study nanoscale metal-semiconductor interfaces without the requirement of a continuous metal thin film. Office: Harvard University 9 Oxford St Cambridge MA 02138 Office Phone: 617-496-5471.

**YI, XIAOBIN,** anesthesiologist, pain management specialist; arrived in US, 1993, naturalized, 2001; MD, Hunan Med. U., Changsha, China, 1985; PhD, Chinese Acad. Med. Scis., Beijing, China, 1990. Diplomate Am. Bd. Anesthesiology, 2004, Am. Bd. Pain Medicine, 2005. Medicine resident, 5th clinical coll. Beijing U., 1990—93; GI fellow, rsch. assoc. Sch. Medicine, U. Va., 1993—96, anesthesiology rsch. fellow, 1996—99; intern Wayne State U., Detroit Med. Ctr., 1999—2000; resident, anesthesiology SUNY Health Sci. Ctr., Syracuse, 2003—04; asst. prof. Sch. Medicine Wash. U., St. Louis, 2004—. Mem.: Biophysical Soc., Am. Soc. Regional Anesthesia and Pain Medicine, Am. Soc. Anesthesiologists. Office: Washington University School of Medicine Campus Box 8054 660 S Euclid Ave Saint Louis MO 63110 Office Phone: 314-362-1630. Home Fax: 314-286-2675. Personal E-mail: yix@wustl.edu.

**YIELDING, K. LEMONE,** physician; b. Auburn, Ala., Mar. 25, 1931; s. Riley Lafayette and Bertie (Dees) Y.; m. Lerena Wade Hauge, Dec. 7, 1973; children: K. Lemone, Michael Lafon, Teresa Louise, Riley Lafayette, Katrina Elizabeth, Elaine Louise Blodgett, Laura Carlen Blodgett. BS, Ala. Poly. Inst., 1949; MS, U. Ala., 1952, MD, 1954. Intern U. Ala. Med. Center, 1954-55; clin. assoc. Nat. Inst. Arthritis and Metabolic Diseases, NIH, 1955-57, sr. investigator, 1958-64; resident med. service USPHS Hosp., Balt., 1957-58; physician in practice of oncology and emergency medicine, 1977—. Adj. asst. prof. medicine Georgetown U. Med. Sch., 1958-64; cons. USPHS, 1964-68, 75—; prof. biochemistry, assoc. prof. medicine, chief lab. molecular biology U. Ala. Med. Ctr., Birmingham, 1964-80; prof., chmn. dept. anatomy, prof. medicine U. So. Ala. Coll. Medicine, Mobile, 1980-87; dean grad. sch. U. Tex. Med. Br., Galveston, 1987-95, dean emeritus, 1995—, v.p. for rsch., 1987-94; cons. Am. Heart Assn., Arthritis Found., NIH, NASA. Contbr. to profl. jours., books. Served with USPHS, 1955-64. Grantee USPHS, Am. Cancer Soc., Nat. Found.-March of Dimes, U.S. Army, Am. Inst. Cancer Research. Mem. Am. Soc. Biol. Chemistry, Am. Assn. Cancer Research, Am. Assn. Photobiology, Assn. Research Vision and Ophthalmology, Soc. Exptl. Biology and Medicine, Am. Soc. Pharm. and Exptl. Therapeutics, Am. Assn. Pathologists, So. Soc. Clin. Investigation, Am. Assn. Anatomy, Soc. Toxicology, Sigma Xi. Personal E-mail: lemoneyielding@hughes.net. E-mail: yielding@hiwaay.net.

**YIH, MAE DUNN,** state legislator; b. Shanghai, May 24, 1928; d. Chung Woo and Fung Wen (Feng) Dunn; m. Stephen W.H. Yih, 1953; children: Donald, Daniel. BA, Barnard Coll., 1951; postgrad., Columbia U., 1951-52. Asst. to bursar Barnard Coll., N.Y.C., 1952-54; mem. Oreg. Ho. Reps. from 36th dist., 1977-83, Oreg. Senate from 19th dist., 1983—. Mem. Clover Ridge Elem. Sch. Bd., Albany, Oreg., 1969-78, Albany Union H.S. Bd., 1975-79; mem. Joint Legis. Ways and Means Com., Senate Transp. Com., 1999, Senate pres. pro-tempore, 1993. Episcopalian. Home: 34465 Yih Ln NE Albany OR 97322-9557 Office: Oreg Senate S 307 State Capitol Salem OR 97310-0001

**YIIN, LIH-MING,** educator; arrived in U.S., 1993; s. Hsiang-Hour Yiin and Suh-Kuei Lee; m. Ming-Chi Lin, Sept. 25, 1997; children: Fan-Shiuan, Fan-Yu. Degree in Chemistry, Nat. Taiwan U., 1989; MS in Environ. Sci., Rutgers U., 1995, PhD, 1999. Rsch. tchg. specialist U. Medicine and Dentistry N.J, Piscataway, 1999—2001, asst. prof. exposure assessment Sch. Pub. Health, 2001—04; assoc. prof. Dept. Public Health Tzu-Chi U., Hualien, Taiwan, 2004—, With Taiwan Mil., 1989—91. Recipient Health Homes and Lead Tech. Studies award, U.S. Dept. Housing and Urban Devel., 2002. Mem.: APHA, AAUP (UMDNJ-Coun. of Chpts.), AAAS, N.J. Pub. Health

Assn., Am. Chem. Soc., Internat. Soc. Exposure Analysis (Student award 1997). Office: Tzu Chi U 701 Chung Yang Rd Sec 3 Hualien Taiwan 970 Office Phone: 886-38565301 x7216. Business E-Mail: lmyiin@mail.tcu.edu.tw.

**YILMAZ, BILGE,** chemical engineer, researcher; s. Cengiz and Ilham Yilmaz. BSChemE, Mid. East Tech. U., Ankara, Turkey, 2001; MSChE, postgrad., Northeastern U., 2003—. Edn. Abroad Program U. of Calif. Intern engr. Egyptian Iron and Steel Co., Cairo, 2000; rsch. asst. CE-CERT U. of Calif., Riverside, 2000—01; rsch. asst. CAMMP - Northeastern U., Boston, 2001—. Contbr. articles to profl. jours. Recipient 2006 Spring Mass. Space Grant fellowship, MA Space Grant Consortium, 2006. Mem.: AIChE, Internat. Zeolite Assn., Internat. Materials Info. Soc., Minerals, Metals and Materials Soc., Internat. Union of Pure and Applied Chemistry, Materials Rsch. Soc., Am. Chem. Soc., Epsilon Eta Sigma, Phi Kappa Phi. Achievements include patents pending for Production of Synthetic Transportation Fuels From Carbonaceous Materials Using Self-Sustained Hydro-Gasification, World International Property Organization. Personal E-mail: bilge@coe.neu.edu.

**YIM, KANG SUB,** engineer; PhD, Stanford U., 2000. Engr. Applied Materials, Santa Clara, Calif., 2000—.

**YIM, MAN BIN,** neurosurgeon, educator; b. Hong Seung, Chung Nam, Republic of Korea, Feb. 29, 1948; s. Byung Soon Yim and Jeung Ok Kang; m. In Sook Kim, Dec. 4, 1974; children: Chang Ok, Chang Baek. PhD, KyungPook Nat. U., Daegu, Republic of Korea, 1988. Lic. med. practitioner Ministry Health and Welfare, Republic of Korea, 1973, cert. Korean Bd. of Neurosurgery, 1981. Instr. Keimyung U. Sch. of Medicine, Daegu, Republic of Korea, 1981—83, asst. prof., 1983—87, assoc. prof., 1988—93, head neurosurgery Dong San Med. Ctr., 1991—99, chmn. neurosurgery, 1993—99, prof. neurosurgery, 1993—; dir. brain rsch. inst. Keimyung U., 2000—05; dean Keimjung U. Sch. Medicine, 2005—. Sec. gen. 5th Japanese and Korean Friendship Conf. on Surgery for Cerebral Stroke, Cheju, Republic of Korea, 1996—99; v.p. 7th Japanese and Korean Friendship Conf. on Surgery for Cerebral Stroke, KyungJu, 2002—; sci. trustee The Korean Soc. of Cerebrovascular Surgery, Seoul, 1996—98, sec. gen., 1998—, mem. arrangement com. 6th internat. workshop, 2000, pres., 2003—04. Author: Text Book of Neurosurgery; contbr. articles to profl. jours. including Jour. Korean Neurosurg. Soc. (Best Sci. Article, Korean Soc. of Cerebrovascular Surgery, 2003, Best Sci. Article, Korean Soc. of Neurosurgery, 2003). Capt. Army, 1973—76, Republic of Korea. Named Best Dr. in Cerebrovascular Disease, Shin Dong Ah monthly mag., 1999, Best Dr. in Cerebrovascular Disease, Dong Ah Daily News, 2003; recipient Encouragement award of Han-Mi Essay Lit., The Korean Doctors' Weekly, 2003. Mem.: Korean Neurosurgical Soc. (licentiate; bd. trustees 1995—99, pres. (Daegu and Kyung Pook local chapt.) 1996—97, mem. bd. exam. com. 1996—99, mem. scientific com. 2000—02, bd. trustees 2003—), Korean Med. Assn. (licentiate), World Fedn. of Neurosurgical Societies (assoc.). Avocations: tennis, essay writing. Home: 1502 202 Dong ManChon WooBang 2 Cha Ap Daegu 706-759 Republic of Korea Office: Neurosurgery Keimyung Univ 194 DongSan Dong Jung-Gu Daegu 700-712 Republic of Korea Office Phone: 82-53-250-7700. Office Fax: 82-53-250-7356. Business E-Mail: y760111@dsmc.or.kr.

**YINGLING, JOHN A.,** military officer; b. Alexandria, Va. BA, Wake Forest U., 1975. Commd. U.S. Army, 1974, advanced through grades to brig. gen.; firing platoon comdr. Weapons Support Detachment, 3d Bn., 81st Field Artillery; from battery exec. officer to comdr. A Battery, 3d Bn., 6th Field Artillery U.S. Army, comdr. C Battery, 1st Bn., 76th Field Artillery Germany, bn. ops. officer; field artillery assignment officer Mil. Pers. Ctr., 1984—86; 1st corps officer ps. mgr., fire support officer 1st Brigade, 9th Inf. Divsn., Ft. Lewis, 1987—91; staff officer Joint Staff, Nat. Mil. Command Systems, Pentagon, 1991—93; comdr. 7th Bn., 8th Field Artillery, Red Dragons, 25th Inf. Divsn., 1993—95, 3d Inf. Divsn. Artillery, 1996—98; dir. Fire Support and Combined Ops. Dept., Ft. Sill, 1998—99; asst. divsn. comdr. 2d Inf. Divsn., 1999; chief of staff USAR Command, Ft. McPherson, Ga.; comdr. Joint Task Force, 2002—04. Decorated Legion of Merit with one oak leaf cluster, Meritorious Svc. medal with 4 oak leaf clusters, Joint Commendation medal, Army Commendation medal with 2 oak leaf clusters, many others.

**YINGLING, PHYLLIS STUCKEY,** writer; b. Martinsburg, W.Va., May 22, 1931; d. Carlton Bennett and Virginia DeHaven Stuckey; m. Lewis Carroll Yingling, Jr., June 26, 1954; children: Deborah Beth, Lewis Carroll III. BA in Edn., Shepherd Coll. (now Shepherd U.), Shepherdstown, W.Va., 1952; MEd in Edn. of Deaf, Western Md. Coll., Westminster, 1979. Cert. tchr. of deaf State of Md., 1979. Tchr. of the deaf and hard of hearing Prince George's County Pub. Schools, Oxen Hill, Md., 1971—73, Balt. City Pub. Schs., 1973—86, Parkville, Md., 1986—92; ret., 1992. Author: (children's book) My Best Friend, Elena Pappas, 1986, My Best Friend, Tony Santos, 1988; co-author: (children's book for dyslexic learners) Adventures of Dan and Sam, 1997, The Fantastic Fan and 7 More Fantastic Stories, 1999, Dan and Sam and the RV Trip, 2000; contbr. articles and stories to mags. (Best Story Award, 1984). Docent Md. Hist. Soc. Mus.; pres. Women's Internat. League for Peace and Freedom, U.S. Sect., Phila., 1999—2002; co-chair Women's Internat. League for Peace and Freedom, Catonsville, Md., 1995—99. Mem.: United Meth. Women. United Methodist. Avocations: watercolor and oil painting, travel, hiking, poetry.

**YIOTIS, GAYLE,** archivist, researcher, anthropologist, writer; d. Pedro and Margarette Rionda; m. Christos Fotios Yiotis; children: Fotios Christos, Peter Wesley. MA, George Washington U., Washington, 1992. Mus. specialist anthropology Smithsonian Instn., Washington, 1995—2003; archivist Nat. Mus. of Am. Indian, 2003—. Student career alumni network Marquette U., Milw., 2000—; presenter in field. Contbr. articles to profl. jours. Mem.: Acad. Certified Archivists, Soc. of Am. Archivists. Avocations: historical research, writing, martial arts, collecting.

**YIOTIS, KRISTIN,** librarian, educator; d. Florence Alonso and Constantine John Yiotis; life ptnr. Douglas S. Ronald. BA, SUNY, Albany, 1970—75; MA, San Francisco State U., Calif., 1986—88, MA, 1992—96; MLS, San Jose State U., Calif., 2004—. Writing instr. San Jose City Coll., San Jose, Calif., 1999—2000; reading instr. De Anza Coll., Cupertino, Calif., 2001—05. Author: (jour. article) Information Technology and Libraries (LITA/Endeavor Student Writing award, 2005). Recipient Jo Ann Clifton Student Writing award, Spl. Libr. Assn., 2005; grantee scholarship, Friends of the Mountain View Libr., 2003—06, San Jose Equity fellowship, San Jose State U., 2005—. Mem.: ALA (chair, student chpt., San Jose State U. 2006—), Calif. Academic and Rsch. Libraries, Calif. Libr. Assn. Mem. Christian Science Ch. Avocations: lap swimming, road biking. Home: 539 Dawn Dr Sunnyvale CA 94087 Office: Sch Library and Info Science San Jose State One Washington Sq San Jose CA 95192-0029 Office Phone: 408-924-2490. Personal E-mail: kyiotis@yahoo.com. Business E-Mail: kyiotis@gmail.com.

**YIP, KWOK LEUNG,** physicist, researcher; b. Canton, People's Republic China, Sept. 23, 1944; came to U.S., 1968; s. Tong and Ho (Mok) Y.; m. Gee-Ying Chao, Mar. 25, 1972; children: Nora Loey, Dana Tsing. BS, Chinese U. Hong Kong, 1965; MS, Providence Coll., 1970; PhD, Lehigh U., 1973. Rsch. assoc. U. Ill., Urbana, 1973-75; sr. tech. specialist, project mgr. Xerox Corp., Webster, NY, 1975-84; sr. prin. scientist Eastman Kodak Co., Rochester, NY, 1984—. Contbr. articles to profl. jours. Mem. Am. Phys. Soc., Soc. for Imaging Sci. and Tech., Internat. Soc. for Optical Engring. Achievements include patents in digital printing and medical imaging technologies. Home: 1112 Everwild Vw Webster NY 14580-8740 Office: Eastman Kodak Co Kodak Park # 82 Rochester NY 14650 Office Phone: 585-722-7150. Business E-Mail: kwok.yip@kodak.com.

**YIP, WINNIE,** health economics educator; arrived in U.S., 1984; BA, U. Calif., Berkeley, 1988; PhD, MIT, 1994. Asst. prof. econs., Sch. Pub. Health Harvard U., Cambridge, Mass., 1994—2001, assoc. prof. internat. health econs., Sch. Pub. Health, 2001—. Cons. World Bank, Washington, 1995—96, Washington, 1999—2000, Govt. Hong Kong, 1997—99. Mem.: Internat. Health Econs. Assn., Am. Econ Assn., Phi Beta Kappa. Office: Harvard Sch Pub Health 124 Mt Auburn St Ste 410 S Cambridge MA 02138 E-mail: wyip@hsph.harvard.edu.

**YISHAN, ZHANG,** ambassador; b. Tainjin, China, Apr. 1946; Diploma, Beijing Fgn. Studies U., 1972; vis. scholar in Pub. and Internat. Affairs, Columbia U., 1982—83; Midcareer Parven fellow Woodrow Wilson Sch. Pub. and Internat. Affairs, Princeton U., 1983—84. Staff mem. Permanent Mission China UN, NYC, 1972—79; staff mem. dept. internat. orgns. and conf. Min. Fgn. Affairs, China, 1979—82, deputy dir. then dir. dept. internat. orgns. and confs., 1984—88; 1st sec. then counsellor permanent mission China UN, Geneva, 1988—92; counsellor dept. inernat. orgns. and confs. Min. Fgn. Affairs, 1992—94, deputy dir.-gen. dept. intrnat. orgns. and confs., 1994—97; Chinese amb. UN, Vienna, 1997—2002, NYC, 2002—. Office: UN 350 E 35th St New York NY 10016 also: Apt 54B 845 United Nations Plz New York NY 10017

**YIU, FANG,** structural engineer, researcher; b. Shanghai, Apr. 21, 1972; d. Baixian Yiu and Jingfang Hua. BS, Tongji U., 1993; MS, Tongji U., Shanghai, 1997; PhD, Cornell U., 2004. Structural engr. Shanghai Posts & Telecoms. Design Inst., 1993-95; sr. staff tech. profl. Mustang Engring., L.P., 2002—. Asst. engring. mgr. Shanghai Designing INst. Telecomms., Shanghai, 1993—95; peer advisor dept. civil and environ. engring. Cornell U., Ithaca, 1999—2000, engring. grad. student assn. rep., 2000—02. Referee: for profl. jours. Mem. civil engring. del. People to People Amb., Spokane, Wash., 2000—; treas. Chinese Students and Scholars Assn. Ithaca, 1998—99. Mem.: ASCE, Soc. Woman Engrs., Earthquake Engring. Rsch. Inst. (treas. 2000—), Sigma Xi.

**YLANG, LENORE SCHULMAN,** visual artist; b. NYC, Nov. 23, 1927; d. Samuel Woolf and Rose (Horowitz) Rosenberg; m. Jerome Lewis Schulman, June 12, 1948 (div. Oct. 1973); 1 child, Ellen Frances; m. Fred Fulton Lang, Jan. 28, 1975 (dec. Nov. 1991); children: Ellen Frances, Martha Sue; m. Carl Abraham Auerbach, June 22, 1993. BFA, Pratt Inst., Bklyn., 1948; student, Balt. Mus. Art, 1953-54, IIT Sch. Design, Chgo., 1966-67. Designer Norcross, Inc., NYC, 1948-50; tchr. printmaking No. Shore Art League, Winnetka, Ill., 1971-73. Juror Art Inst. Chgo., Chgo., 1985—87. One-woman shows include U. Ill. Med. Ctr., Chgo., 1971, Fed. Jewish Orgn., 1972, Mishkenot Sha'ananim, Jerusalem, 1974, Unicorn Gallery, NYC, 1975, Botanic Gardens, Glencoe, Ill., 1977, Evanston Pub. Libr., Ill., 1982, Ill. Ctr. Bldg. lobby, Gruen Gallery, Chgo., 1985, Wacker Dr. bldg. lobby, Gruen Gallery, 1986, East, West Gallery, Mpls., 1988, Gallery 416, 1995, 1997, exhibited in group shows at Art Inst., Chgo., 1978—79, Peace Mus., 1981, Northwestern U., Evanston, 1982, WFMT, Chgo. Mag., 1983, Evanston Art Ctr., 1985, NAB Gallery, Chgo., 1986, Art Inst., 1987, Suburban Fine Arts Ctr., Highland Park, Ill., 1988, Spertus Mus., Chgo., 1988, Countryside Gallery, Arlington Heights, Ill., 1989, Chgo. Post Gallery, 1989, Evanston Art Ctr., 1989, State of Ill. Bldg., Chgo., 1989, Artemisia Gallery, 1990, Sabbeth Gallery, Glen Cove, NY, 1990, Arts Club, Chgo., 1991, exhibitions include SCAN Exhibit, 1991, exhibited in group shows at Chgo. Cultural Ctr., 1992, Riggs Gallery, La Jolla, Calif., 1992, Beancon St. Gallery, Chgo., 1994, Triangle Gallery, 1995, Ill. State Mus., Springfield, 1995, Mus. Sci. Industry, Chgo., 1995, Athaneum Music Art Libr., La Jolla, Calif., 1995, Loyola U., Chgo., 1995, Gallery 416, Mpls., 1995—97, Ancient Traditions Gallery, 1996, Judy A. Saslow Gallery, Chgo., 1997, Chgo. Cultural Ctr., 1998, exhibitions include So. Calif. Reg. Exhibit, 1998, exhibited in group shows at Sch. Chgo. Art Inst., 1998, San Diego Art Inst., 1999. Mem.: Cliff Dweller's Club (profl. mem.), Chgo. Artists Coalition, Arts Club Chgo. (profl. mem.). Avocations: shell, fossil and rock hunting, concerts, theater, reading, travel. Home: 939 Coast Blvd Unit 8C La Jolla CA 92037-4116

**YLVISAKER, JAMES WILLIAM,** insurance executive; b. Mpls., Minn., Feb. 26, 1938; s. Johannas Wilhelm and Lucille Elizabeth (Torgeson) Y.; m. Judith Diane Stevens, May 19, 1943 (div. Aug. 1980). BA, Luther Coll., 1960. Assoc. actuary North Am. Life & Casualty, Mpls., 1961-76; actuary IDS Life Ins. Co., Mpls., 1976-80; exec. v.p., chief operating officer Cologne Life Reinsurance Co., Stamford, Conn., 1980-89; pres., chief exec. officer IdeaLife Ins. Co., Stamford, 1989-90, also bd. dirs.; pres., COO, Horizons LLC, Hartford, Conn., 1997-99, U.S. Living Benefits, LLC, Hartford, Conn., 1999—. Bd. dirs. Reassurance Corp. of Del., Stamford, Stamford Life Ins. Co., 1983-90, cons. actuary, 1991—. Dist. chmn. United Way of Mpls., 1966; regional coord. Carlson for Mayor Campaign, Mpls., 1968; state chmn. Head for Gov. Campaign, Mpls., 1970; mem. bd. regents Luther Coll., Decorah, Iowa, 1990. Fellow Soc. Actuaries; mem. Am. Acad. Actuaries, Internat. Actuarial Assn. Avocations: reading, music, golf, travel. Home and Office: 40 Prides Crossing 312 Elm St New Canaan CT 06840-5305 Office Phone: 203-966-5154. E-mail: jimuslb@optonline.net.

**YNGVE, DAVID A.,** orthopedist, surgeon; b. Chgo., June 7, 1949; BA, Antioch Coll., 1972; MD, Ind. U., 1976. Intern St. Vincent Hosp., Indpls., 1977—81; resident Ind. U., Indpls., 1981—82; fellow La. State U., 1982; from instr. to asst. prof. U. Tex. Med. Br., Galveston, 1981—88, assoc. prof., 1988—, child orthopedics. pediatric orthopaedics & scoliosis, 1999—. Office: U Tex Med Br 301 University Blvd Galveston TX 77555-0353 Office Fax: 409-772-3497. Business E-Mail: dvngve@utmb.edu.

**YOAKAM, DWIGHT,** country western musician; b. Pikeville, Ky., Oct. 23, 1956; PhD (hon.), Ohio Valley Coll., 2005. Albums include Guitars, Cadillacs, Etc. Etc., 1985, Hillbilly Deluxe, 1987, Buenas Noches From A Lonely Room, 1988, Just Lookin' for a Hit, 1989, If There Was a Way, 1990, This Time, 1993, Dwight Live, 1995, Gone, 1996; duet with Buck Owens Streets of Bakersfield, 1988 (No. 1 single); co-prodr. stage appearance Southern Rapture, 1993; appeared in Roswell, Showtime cable feature, 1994, Sling Blade, feature film, 1996, (films) Painted Hero aka Shadow of the Past, 1996, The Newton Boys, 1998, Ozzie and Harriet: The Adventures of America's Favorite Family, 1998, The Minus Man, 1999, South of Heaven, West of Hell, 2000, Panic Room, 2002, Hollywood Homicide, 2003, 3-Way, 2004, The Three Burials of Melquiades Estrada, 2005, Wedding Crashers, 2005, Bandidas, 2006, Crank, 2006, (TV) When Trumpets Fade, 1998; discs include Under the Covers, 1997, Come on Christmas, 1997, A Long Way Home, 1998, Last Chance Greatest Hits from the 90's, 1999, Dwightyoakam.m-net (Justguitar@dogbone), 2000. Named Top Male Vocalist by Acad. Country Music, 1986; recipient Grammy award for best country vocal performance by male for Ain't That Lonely Yet, 1993, 41st ann. Grammy award for best country collaboration with vocals for Same Old Train, 1998, also 14 nominations; Premiere Performance acting award Motion Picture Club, 1996. Address: Dwight Yoakam Tours 7920 W Sunset Blvd Ste 460 Los Angeles CA 90046-3300*

**YOAKAM, LYNN KELLY,** harpist, educator; b. Little Rock, Ark., July 5, 1957; d. Vance Leonard and Donna Jo (Criner) Broadway; m. Robert William Yoakam, Aug. 11, 1979; children: Amy Louise, Ryan William. BA, Harding U, 1979; A in Applied Music summa cum laude, Lansing Cmty. Coll., 2004. Tchr. of arts East Lansing Cmty. Edn., Holt Cmty. Edn., East Lansing, Mich., 1989—95; sec. The Bug Man Pest Control, Mason, 1987—; music tchr. pvt. practice, Mason, Mich., 1990—; tai chi instr. Lansing (Mich.) Cmty. Coll., 2002—. Cert. in Duchess Lace Jusith de Kreijer, Etten Leur, Netherlands, 1999. CD, Shantih-Lost in Time, 1995, Shantih-Winds of Change, 2004. Fellow, Mich. State U., 2005. Master: English Lace Music Tchrs. Assn. (chmn.dist. ensemble 2000—); mem.: Music Nat. Tchrs. Assn., Am. String Tchrs. Assn., Mich. Music Tchrs. Assn. (state cchmn. non-competitive activities), Capitol Area Lace Makers (pres. 1992—97), Phi Theta Kappa. Christian. Office: Ms Yoakam 120 W Sycamore Street Mason MI 48854 Business E-Mail: kyoakam@sbcglobal.net.

**YOCAM, DELBERT WAYNE,** retired software products company executive; b. Long Beach, Calif., Dec. 24, 1943; s. Royal Delbert and Mary Rose (Gross) Y.; m. Janet McVeigh, June 13, 1965; children— Eric Wayne, Christian Jeremy, Elizabeth Janelle. BA in Bus. Adminstrn., Calif. State U.-Fullerton, 1966; MBA, Calif. State U., Long Beach, 1971. Mktg.-supply changeover coordinator Automotive Assembly div. Ford Motor Co., Dearborn, Mich., 1966-72; prodn. control mgr. Control Data Corp., Hawthorne, Calif., 1972-74; prodn. and material control mgr. Bourns Inc., Riverside, Calif., 1974-76; corp. material mgr. Computer Automation Inc., Irvine, Calif., 1976-78; prodn. planning mgr. central staff Cannon Electric div. ITT, World hdqrs., Santa Ana, Calif., 1978-79; exec. v.p., COO Apple Computer, Inc., Cupertino, Calif., 1979-91; pres., COO, dir. Textronix Inc., Wilsonville, Oreg., 1992-95; chmn., CEO Borland Internat., Inc./Inprise Corp., Scotts Valley, Calif., 1996-2000, ret., 2000. Mem. faculty Cypress Coll., Calif., 1972-79; bd. dirs. Adobe Sys Inc., San Jose, Calif., Softricity, Inc., Boston; vice chmn. Tech. Ctr. Innovation, San Jose, Calif., 1989-90. Mem. Am. Electronics Assn. (nat. bd. dirs. 1989-90), Control Data Corp. Mgmt. Assn. (co-founder 1974), L.A. County Heart Assn. (active 1966). E-mail: yocam@aol.com.

**YOCAM, ERIC WAYNE,** engineer; b. Garden Grove, Calif., Aug. 23, 1966; s. Delbert Wayne and Janet Yocam; m. Siu Kuen Annie Choi, Nov. 5, 2000; children: Hailey Jasmine, Nathan Connor. BS in Computer Engring., U. Pacific, Stockton, Calif., 1990; MBA, U. San Diego, 1997; MS in Fin., Seattle U., 2002; MS in Computer Sci., Calif. State U., Chico, 2004. Cert. software devel. profl., IEEE-Computer Soc., 2002, project mgmt. profl., PMI, 2002, E-commerce cons., tech. specialist, ICECC, 2002. Mem. of tech. staff Apple Computer/Claris Corp., Santa Clara, Calif., 1991—93, Media Vision Corp., Fremont, Calif., 1993—94; tech. mgr. Ray Dream Corp., Mountain View, Calif., 1994—96, Hewlett-Packard Co., Cupertino, Calif., 1997—97; data ctr. project mgr. Intuit Corp., San Diego, 1998—99; sr. program mgr. Microsoft Corp., Redmond, Wash., 1999—. Grad. fellowship, U. San Diego, 1997. Mem.: Sigma Xi. R-Consevative. Methodist. Avocations: private pilot, scuba diving, golf, skiing, surfing. Home: 213 259th Ave NE Sammamish WA 98074 Office Phone: 425-705-3390. Personal E-mail: eyocam@hotmail.com.

**YOCHELSON, ELLIS L(EON),** paleontologist; b. Washington, Nov. 14, 1928; s. Morris Wolf and Fannie (Botkin) Y.; m. Sally Witt, June 10, 1950; children: Jeffrey, Abby, Charles. BS, U. Kans., Lawrence, 1949, MS, 1950; PhD, Columbia U., N.Y.C., 1955. Paleontologist U.S. Geol. Survey, 1952-85, scientist emeritus, 1991—; biostratigrapher, specializing in Paleozoic gastropods and minor classes of extinct mollusks; lectr. night sch. George Washington U., 1962-65; lectr. Univ. Coll. U. Md., 1966-74; rsch. assoc. Smithsonian Instn., Washington, 1967—; lectr. U. Del., 1981; vis. prof. U. Md., 1986-87; organizer N.Am. Paleontol. Conv., 1969, 1996, editor proc., 1970-71. Co-editor: Essays in Paleontology and Stratigraphy, 1967; editor: Scientific Ideas of G.K. Gilbert, 1980; editorial bd. Nat. Geog. Rsch. and Exploration; contbr. numerous articles to profl. jours.; sec. Internat. Congress Carb. Stratigraphy, 1979. Author: Charles Doolittle Walcott, Paleontologist, 1998, Smithsonian Institution Secretary Charles Doolittle Walcott, 2001. Fellow AAAS (chmn. sect. E 1971), Geol. Soc. Am. (History Geology Divsn. award 2003); mem. Soc. Systematic Zoology (sec. 1961-66, councilor 1973), Internat. Paleontol. Assn. (treas. 1972-76), Paleontol. Soc. (pres. 1976, Centennial fellow 2006), History of Earth Sci. Soc. (hon. life; sec.-treas. 1982-85, sec. 1986-87, pres. 1989), N.Am. Paleontol. Conv. (hon. life; sec.), Smithsonian Instn. (150th Anniversary com.), Sigma Xi. Office: Smithsonian Instn E-305A Mus Natural History Washington DC 20013-7012 Office Phone: 202-633-1363. Business E-Mail: yochelse@si.edu.

**YOCHES, EDWARD ROBERT,** lawyer; b. Denver, Jan. 23, 1953; s. Marvin and Ruth Devorah (Spiegleman) Y.; m. Karen Ruth Droller, Aug. 20, 1978; children: Aaron Stuart, Meryl Laura. BEE in Computer Sci., U. Colo., 1974; JD, U. Pa., 1980. Bar: D.C. 1980. Engr. Goddard Space Flight Ctr. NASA, Greenbelt, Md., 1974-77; assoc. Finnegan, Henderson, Farabow, Garrett & Dunner, Washington, 1980-88, ptnr., 1988—. Named one of best lawyers in intellectual property law, Best Lawyers in Am., 2005—06. Mem. ABA (chmn. computer law subcom. on trade secrets and internat. protection 1982-86), D.C. Bar Assn. (vice chmn. computer law div. 1985, chmn. 1986-87), Am. Intellectual Property Assn. Office: Finnegan Henderson Farabow Garrett & Dunner LLP 901 New York Ave NW Washington DC 20001-3315 Office Phone: 202-408-4000. Office Fax: 202-408-4400. Business E-Mail: bob.yoches@finnegan.com.

**YOCHIM, JOSEPH ADOLPH,** lawyer; b. Erie, Pa., May 8, 1947; s. Adolph F. and Marian E. (Hahn) Y.; m. Dianne L. Werner, June 22, 1974; children: Joseph A. Jr., Julie J. BA in History, St. Vincent Coll., Latrobe, Pa., 1969; JD, Duquesne U., 1972. Bar: Pa. 1972, U.S. Dist. Ct. (we. dist.) Pa. 1972, U.S. Supreme Ct. 1979, U.S. Ct. Appeals (3rd cir.) 1983. Fed. law clk. U.S. Dist. Ct. (we. dist.) Pa., Erie and Pitts., 1972-74; assoc. Quinn, Gent, Buseck & Leemhuis, Erie, 1974-75; ptnr. Ambrose, Nedell & Yochim, Erie, 1975-78, Colussi, Yochim, Skiba & Moore, Erie, 1979-87, Yochim, Skiba, Moore & Nash, Erie, 1987—; Yochim, Skiba, Johnson & Nash, Erie, 1999—. Solicitor Girard (Pa.) Borough, 1992—, Fairview (Pa.) Borough, 1994-97. Mem. Pa. Bar Assn., Pa. Trial Lawyers, Erie County Bar Assn. Avocations: genealogy, sailing. Home: 2806 Colonial Ave Erie PA 16506-1832 Office: Yochim Skiba Johnson & Nash 345 W 6th Street Erie PA 16507-1244 Office Phone: 814-454-6345. Business E-Mail: jyochim@yochim.com.

**YOCKIM, JAMES CRAIG,** foundation administrator; b. Williston, N.D., Feb. 13, 1953; s. Daniel and Doris (Erickson) Y.; children: Jenna, Ericka. BSW, Pacific Luth. U., 1975; MSW, San Diego State U., 1979. Caseworker Dyslin Boys Ranch, Tacoma, 1975-77, head caseworker, program dir., 1979-80; landman Fayette Oil & Gas, Williston, 1980-82; owner Hy-Plains Energy, Williston, 1982-87; city fin. commr. City of Williston, 1984—88, 1998—2002; therapist Williston, 1983; senator N.D. State Senate, 1986-98; owner James C. Yockim Resources, Williston, 1987—. Dir. Bethel Luth. Found., 1993—; del. N.D. Dem. Conv., 1984, 86, 88, 90, 92, 94, 96, 98, 2000, 02, 04; dist. chmn. Dem. Party, Williston, 1988; caucus chmn. Dem. Caucus N.D. State Senate; mem. N.D. Legis. Coun., 1997-98; coun. pres. 1st Luth. Ch. Recipient Ruth Meiers award N.D. Mental Health Assn., 1989, Legislator of Yr. award N.D. Children's Caucus, 1989; named Outstanding Young North Dakotan N.D. Jaycees, 1988. Mem. NASW. Avocations: racquetball, golf. Home: 1123 2nd Ave E Williston ND 58801-4302 Office: PO Box 2344 Williston ND 58802-2344 Business E-Mail: JamesYoc@dia.net

**YOCUM, HARRISON GERALD,** horticulturist, botanist, educator, researcher; b. Bethlehem, Pa., Apr. 2, 1923; s. Harrison and Bertha May (Meckes) Y. BS, Pa. State U., 1955; MS, Rutgers U., 1961. Horticulture instr. U. Tenn., Martin, 1957-59; biology tchr., libr. asst. high schs., El Paso, Tex., 1959-60; rsch. asst. geochronology lab. U. Ariz., Tucson, 1960-67, rsch. asst. environ. rsch. lab., 1969-76; landscaping supt. Tucson Airport Authority, 1976-82; instr. Pima C.C., Tucson, 1976—. Contbr. articles to profl. jours. Founder Tucson Bot. Gardens, 1964. Recipient 1st Unique Gardener award Gardeners Am. Mem. Am. Hort. Soc., Nat. Trust Historic Preservation, Ariz. Preservation Found., Men's Garden Club Tucson (pres. 1991), Tucson Cactus & Succulent Soc. (pres. 1991, 92), Internat. Palm Soc. (charter), El Paso Cactus and Rock Club (life), Tucson Gem and Mineral Soc., Old Pueblo Lapidary Club, Deming Mineral Soc., Nat. Geog. Soc., Ariz.-Sonora Desert Mus., Huachuca Vigilantes, Penn State Alumni Assn. (life), Pa. Club Tucson, Nature Conservancy, N.Am. Hunting Club (life), Boyce-Thompson Arboretum, Shriners, Masons, Scottish Rite (life). Lutheran. Home: 1628 N Jefferson Ave Tucson AZ 85712-4204

**YODAIKEN, RALPH E.,** pathologist, occupational health physician, educator; b. Johannesburg, 1928; BS, U. Witwatersrand, Republic of South Africa, 1956; MPH, Johns Hopkins U., 1976. Diplomate Am. Bd. Pathology, Am. Bd. Forensic Medicine. Intern Coronation Hosp., Johannesburg, 1956-57; resident U. Witwatersrand Med. Ctr., 1957-58, Johannesburg Gen. Hosp., 1958; assoc. pathologist Buffalo Gen. Hosp., 1965-67; mem. staff Cin. Gen. Hosp., 1968-71; rsch. assoc. Johns Hopkins U. Sch. Hygiene and Pub. Health,

Balt., 1976—; sr. staff mem. Nat. Inst. Occupational Safety and Health, Washington, 1977—, chmn. sr. adv. staff, 1983; dir. office occupational medicine Occupational Safety and Health Adminstrn., U.S. Dept. Labor, Washington, 1983-91; sr. med. advisor, 1991—98; clin. prof. preventive medicine U. Health Scis., Washington, 1983—. Lectr. U. Witwatersrand, 1958-63; asst. prof. pathology, SUNY Buffalo, 1963-67; assoc. prof. pathology U. Cin., 1968-71; prof. pathology, assoc. prof. medicine Emory U., Atlanta, 1971-75; adj. clin. prof. George Washington U., 1975—; sr. assoc. Johns Hopkins Sch. Hygiene and Pub. Health; clin. prof. preventive medicine uniformed svcs. U. Health Scis. Served to lt. Israeli Army, 1948-50. Fellow Coll. Am. Pathologists, Am. Coll. Occupl. and Environ. Health, Am. Coll. Forensic Medicine. Office Phone: 301-728-4041. Personal E-mail: ryodaiken@aol.com.

**YODER, BRUCE ALAN,** chemist; b. Seward, Nebr., Apr. 29, 1962; s. Elwood John and Elda Raye (Stutzman) Y. BS in Chemistry, Wayne State Coll., 1983. Lab. technician Wayne (Nebr.) State Coll., 1982-83, Harris Labs., Lincoln, Nebr., 1984, chemist, 1984; scientist Dorsey Labs., Lincoln, 1984-86, scientist A, 1986-88; product stability analyst Sandoz Pharms., Lincoln, 1988-89, Sandoz Rsch. Inst., Lincoln, 1989-91; mgr. lab. computer ops. Sandoz Pharms., Lincoln, 1991-97; pres., CEO Data Mgmt. Svcs., Inc., Lincoln, 1997—. Active Lancaster County Young Reps., Lincoln, 1988—, co-chmn., 1990-91, pres., 1991-93; mem. Nebr. Fedn. Young Reps., 1988—, exec. com., 1990—, exec. com. Lancaster County Rep. Party, 1990-97; mem. Def. Adv. Com. Lancaster County, 1992-00; active Lincoln Mayor's Cmty. Cabinet, 1992-93, Lincoln City Charter Revision Commn., 1994-2002, co-chmn., 1998-2000, chmn., 2000-2002; trustee Wayne State Coll. Found., 1991—; advisor Jr. Achievement, 1993-97; bd. dirs. Lincoln Meadows Assn., 1998-99. Recipient Dwight M. Frost, MD award for overcoming a phys. disability Immanuel Rehab. Ctr., 1993, Verdi Smith Outstanding Voluntary Contbns. award Lancaster County Rep. Party, 1995-96, First Dist. Outstanding Vol. award Nebr. Reps., 1996-97, Daniel D. Fahrnbruch Leadership award Lancaster County GOP, 2000. Mem. Internat. Soc. for Pharm. Engrs., Am. Inst. Chemists, Am. Chem. Soc., Am. Assn. Pharm. Scientists, Lincoln Ind. Bus. Assn., Jaycees, Elephant Club. Mennonite. Achievements include design of a sample holder for solid dosage forms when using a hunter color instrument, design of a new computer system for Sandoz Pharmaceuticals laboratory computer operations, design of a new computer system for Novartis Consumer Health, Inc. Home and Office: 2240 Winding Way Lincoln NE 68506-2846 Office Phone: 402-483-1532. Personal E-mail: YoderB@aol.com.

**YODER, DALE ROY,** history educator; b. Sturgis, Mich., Dec. 20, 1955; s. Ernest Roy and Willa Mae (Parker) Yoder; m. Denise Kathleen Sivits, Apr. 12, 1985; 1 child, Daniel Parker. BS, Grand Valley State Coll., Allendale Mich., 1978, BS, 1981; MA, Western Mich. U., Kalamazoo, 1983. Head athletic trainer Holland Pub. Schs., Mich., 1981—82; tchr. and athletic trainer South Dade H.S., Homestead, Fla., 1984—87; athletic trainer U. Mich. Medsport, Ann Arbor, 1987—90, Ypsilanti H.S., 1991—92; soc. studies tchr. Benton Harbor Area Schs., 1992—. Baseball umpire Mich. H.S. Athletic Assn., 1992—; vol. Midwest Boston Terrier Rescue, 2000—. Mem.: Amateur Baseball Umpires Assn., Fruitbelt Officials Assn., Nat. Coun. Social Studies. Office: Benton Harbor HS 870 Colfax Benton Harbor MI 49022

**YODER, EDGAR PAUL,** education educator; b. Millersburg, Ohio, June 20, 1946; s. Albert Daniel Yoder and Ella Marie (Bontrager) Erb; m. Deborah Jean Barnhart, June 12, 1971; children: Scott, Suzan. BSA, Ohio State U., 1968, MS, 1972, PhD, 1976. Cert. tchr., counselor, prin., Ohio. Va. Tchr. agr. and sci. Conotton Valley Schs., Bowerston, Ohio, 1968-69, East Holmes Schs., Berlin, Ohio, 1969-72; curriculum specialist Ohio State U., Columbus, 1972-74, project dir., 1974-76; asst. prin. Montgomery County Schs., Blacksburg, Va., 1976-77; asst. prof. Va. Poly. Inst. and State U., Blacksburg, 1977-78, Pa. State U., University Park, 1978-84, assoc. prof. tchr. edn., 1984-94, prof., 1994—, interim dept. head, 1995-98. Cons. Poland Ministry Edn., Warsaw, 1994, Swaziland Ministry Agr., Mbane, 1985, 87, U. Peredenyia, Kandy, Sri Lanka, 1984. Author text: Ag Supplies and Services, 1974; (with others) Undergraduate Education in Agriculture, 1989; also chpt. to book. Chmn. community svc. Sertoma Internat., Columbus, 1975; asst. dir. Va. HSA Assn., Blacksburg, 1978; sect. chmn. Am. Heart Assn., State College, Va., 1981; pres. Ferguson Twp. PTO, State College, 1983-84; bd. dirs. RAFT Drug Rehab. Ctr., Radford, 1976-78, Nat. Future Farmers Am., Alexandria, Va., 1981-83. Recipient hon. degree, Nat. Future Farmers Am. 1983. Mem. Nat. Assn. Coll. Tchrs. Agr. (pres., teacher fellow 1987, Regional Outstanding Teaching award 1992), Am. Assn. Edn. Rsch. Assn., Am. Vocat. Edn. Rsch. Assn., Am. Assn. Internat. Agr. and Extension Edn., Phi Delta Kappa, Gamma Sigma Delta (Teaching award of Merit 1987). Avocations: collecting sports memorabilia, restoring antiques, classic cars. Office: Penn State U Rm 323 Ag Adminstrn Coll Agricultural Scis University Park PA 16802

**YODER, EDWIN MILTON, JR.,** columnist, educator, editor, writer; b. Greensboro, N.C., July 18, 1934; s. Edwin M. and Mytrice M. (Logue) Y.; m. Mary Jane Warwick, Nov. 1, 1958; children: Anne Daphne, Edwin Warwick. BA, U. N.C., 1956; BA, MA (Rhodes scholar), Oxford U., Eng., 1958; D.H.L. (hon.), Grinnell Coll., 1980, Elon Coll., 1986; DLitt (hon.), U. N.C., 1993, Richmond Coll., London. Editorial writer Charlotte (N.C.) News, 1958-61; editorial writer Greensboro Daily News, 1961-64, assoc. editor, 1965-75; asst. prof. history U. N.C., Greensboro, 1964-65; editorial page editor Washington Star, 1975-81; syndicated columnist Washington Post Writers Group, 1982-97; prof. journalism and humanities Washington and Lee U., 1992—2002, prof. emeritus, 2002—. Hon. fellow Jesus Coll., Oxford, Eng., 1998—. Author: Night of the Old South Ball, 1984, The Unmaking of a Whig, 1990, Joe Alsop's Cold War, 1995, The Historical Present, 1997, Telling Others What to Think: Recollections of a Pundit, 2004; contbr. articles to periodicals. Trustee Inst. for Early Am. History and Culture, Nat. Humanities Ctr., 1991-97. Recipient awards editorial writing N.C. Press Assn., 1958, 61, 66, Walker Stone award Scripps-Howard Found., 1978, Pulitzer prize editorial writing, 1979; Disting. Alumnus award U. N.C., Chapel Hill, 1980 Mem. Nat. Conf. Editorial Writers, Am. Soc. Newspaper Editors. Democrat. Episcopalian. Home: 4001 Harris Pl Alexandria VA 22304-1720 Office Phone: 703-751-9022. E-mail: yoderem@aol.com.

**YODER, JAMES DALE,** adult education educator; b. Souderton, Pa., May 21, 1935; s. Lloyd Rickert and Viola Sell Yoder; m. Nicole Donnay Yoder, Sept. 8, 1957; children: Michelle, Beckie, Laurie. BA, Albright Coll., 1957; MA, Lehigh U., 1959, PhD, 1969. Tchr. Palisades H.S., Bethlehem, Pa., 1957—60; prof. Del. Valley Coll., Doylestown, Pa., 1963—65, Albright Coll., Reading, Pa., 1966—. Grad. asst. Lehigh U., Bethleham, Pa., 1961—62. Author: Pearl Buck's Living Legacy, 1999. Tennis coach Albright Coll., Reading, 1971—. Named Tennis Coach of Yr., Middle Atlantic Conf., 1997. Mem.: Orgn. Am. Historians. Home: 206 Neversink Rd Reading PA 19606 E-mail: dyoder6221@aol.com.

**YODER, JEFFREY L.,** music educator; b. Phoenix, Ariz., Oct. 10, 1960; s. Willis Howard Yoder and Margaret Joan Foutts; m. Elizabeth Ann Langdon; children: LeeAnn, Katherine, Daniel. BS in Music Edn., Grand Canyon U., Phoenix, Ariz., 1986; MusM in Choral, Ariz. State U., Tempe, Ariz., 1990. Cert. tchr. Ariz. Dept. Edn. Tchr. music Glendale (Ariz.) H.S., 1986—94; tchr. vocal music Greenway H.S., Phoenix, 1994—. Dir. music Trinity United Meth. Ch., Phoenix, 1984—94, Sun City (Ariz.) Christian Ch., 1999—2003, Ch. Litchfield Pk., Ariz., 2005—06. Recipient Achievement Above award, Greenway H.S., 2004. Mem.: Ariz. Music Educators Assn. (O.M. Martsell award 2004).

**YODER, JONATHAN PAUL,** secondary school educator; b. Lebanon, Oreg., Aug. 19, 1955; s. Paul Emmons and Flossie Yoder; m. Joyce Yvonne Bontrager, Aug. 2, 1975; children: Mary, Nathan, Leah. BS in Health and Phys. Edn., Ea. Mennonite U., Harrisonburg, Va., 1978; cert. in biology edn., Oreg. State U., Corvallis, 1983; MA in Tchg., Western Oreg. U., Monmouth, 1988. Health and phys. edn. tchr. Freeman (SD) Jr. Coll. and Acad.,

1977—81; sci. tchr. Detroit (Oreg.) HS, 1983—84, North Salem (Oreg.) HS, 1984—, Mill Creek coord., 1990—. Secondary edn. coord. NW Ctr. for Sustainable Resources, Salem, 1995—; coord. Straub Environ. Learning Ctr., Salem, 1997—; presenter in field. Author: Educators Guide to Program Development, 1999, Community as a Context for Learning, 2001, American Indian Perspectives, 2004. Coach Sister City Soccer Tour, Salem, 1989; founder, coord. Friends of Straub Environ. Learning Ctr., Salem, 1997—; mem. environ. commn. City of Salem, 2002—04. Named Oreg. Tchr. of Yr., Oreg. Assn. Conservation Dists., 2005; recipient Disting. Svc. award, Environ. Edn. Assn. Oreg., 2001. Mem.: Environ. Edn. Assn. Oreg. (past pres.), Nat. Assn. Biology Tchrs., Nat. Sci. Tchrs. Assn. (Oreg. Biology Tchr. of Yr. 2002). Office: North Salem HS 765 14th St NE Salem OR 97301

**YODER, PATRICIA DOHERTY,** public relations executive; b. Pitts., Oct. 30, 1939; d. John Addison and Camella Grace (Conti) Doherty; children: Shari Lynn, Wendy Ann; m. James Ronald Wolfe, Oct. 30, 1999. BA, Duquesne U., 1961. Press sec. U.S. Ho. of Reps., 1965-69; dir. Office of Pub. Info., City of Ft. Wayne, 1973-76; asst. mgr. pub. and corp. comm. Mellon Bank N.A., Pitts., 1977-79; v.p. pub. affairs Am. Waterways Operators Inc., Washington, 1980-83, sr. v.p., gen. mgr., 1983-86, exec. v.p., dir. banking, 1989-91; exec. v.p., dir. internat. banking Hill and Knowlton Inc., Pitts.; sr. v.p. corp. and pub. affairs PNC Fin. Svcs. Group, Pitts., 1987-89; v.p., corp. pub. rels. and advt. GE Capital Svcs. Corp., Stamford, Conn., 1991-95; corp. v.p. pub. affairs and comm. GTE Corp., Stamford, 1995-96; sr. v.p. corp. comm. Avis Group Holdings, Garden City, NY, 1996-99; prin. PDY Assocs., 1999—. Trustee, exec. com. Duquesne U., Shadyside Hosp., Pressley Ridge Sch., Pitts., Ellis Sch.; bd. dirs. Children's Mus., Civic Light Opera, Pitts. Ballet Theatre, Jr. League of City of N.Y. Recipient Outstanding Woman Bus. and Industry, 1988, Disting. Alumni award Duquesne U., 1996. Mem. Pitts. Field Club, Duquesne Club, Indian Harbor Yacht Club, Boca Raton (Fla.) Resort and Country Club, Fox Hill Golf and Country Club. Roman Catholic. Home and Office: 500 SE 5th Ave Apt 601 Boca Raton FL 33432-5510 Address: 23 Wireless Way Southampton NY 10028 Personal E-mail: pdyoder@att.net.

**YODER, RANDALL D.,** music educator; b. Lancaster, Pa., Jan. 21, 1949; s. David J. and Mary Lou Yoder; m. Leslee Ann Brenneman, Jan. 24, 1992; stepchildren: Dustin M. Kemper, Jelee Elizabeth Kemper. BS in Music Edn., Susquehanna U., 1971; MusM in Choral Conducting, Westminster Choir Coll., 1978. Tchr., choral dir. Northeastern Sch. Dist., Manchester Twp., 1971—88, York (Pa.) City Schs., 1997—. Dir. York County Honors Choir, 1998—; choral dir. Pa. Ambs. of Music, European Concert Tour, 2001; choral dir. European concert tour Sound of Am. Honor Choir, 2002, 04, 06. Composer: (original music for documentary) Historic Pennsylvania, 1996 (Emmy award, 1997), Hershey Park Memories, 1998, (CD) Christmas Rose, 2000, April Rose, 2004. Mem.: Music Educators Nat. Conf., Am. Choral Dirs. Assn. Avocation: travel.

**YODER, RONNIE A.,** judge; b. Knoxville, Tenn., July 10, 1937; s. Raymond Abraham and Veryl Hope (Hostetler) Y.; m. Shirley Mae Grimes, June 28, 1961; children: Susan Elizabeth Torres, Mary Amanda Anderson, Elizabeth Anne Lee, John Anthony Gerhard. BA in Polit. Sci. with honors, U. Va., 1958, JD, 1961. Bar: Va. 1961, N.Y. 1963, D.C. 1965, U.S. Dist. Ct. D.C. 1965, U.S. Dist. Ct. (so. dist.) N.Y. 1969, U.S. Ct. Claims 1964, U.S. Supreme Ct. 1968. Assoc. Mudge Rose Guthrie & Alexander, N.Y.C. and Washington, 1962-70; of counsel Zuckert Scoutt & Rasenberger, Washington, 1970-72, ptnr., 1972-75; adminstrv. law judge U.S. Dept. Labor, Washington, 1976, CAB, Washington, 1976-84, U.S. Dept. Transp., Washington, 1985-98, acting chief adminstrv. law judge, 1999-2001, chief adminstrv. law judge, 2001—. Adminstrv. law judge Nat. Transp. Safety Bd., 1979-80, Maritime Adminstrn., 1983, 86-88, FDIC, 1982-83, SBA, 1983, FAA, 1985—, Fed. Hwy. Adminstrn., 1985-2000, Fed. R.R. Adminstrn., 1993-95, Rsch. and Spl. Programs Adminstrn., 1991-2005, Surface Transp. Bd., 1996-97, Fed. Motor Carrier Safety Adminstrn., 2000—, Fed. Transp. Security Adminstrn., 2002-04, Pipeline and Hazardous Materials Safety Adminstrn., 2005—; mem. Adminstrv. Conf. of U.S., 1994-95. Mem. editorial bd. U. Va. Law Rev., 1959-61; contbr. articles to profl. jours. Sec., co-counsel Capital Headstart, 1966-68; narrator Lincoln Commn., 1985, 86; mem. permanent jud. commn. Nat. Capital Presbytery, 1985-91. Rockefeller fellow Yale Divinity Sch., 1961-62. Fellow: Fed. Bar Found., Am. Bar Found.; mem.: SAR, FBA (jud. divsn. leadership coun. 1999—, bd. dirs. D.C. chpt. 1999—, pres. D.C. chpt. 2003—05), ABA (sec. 1991—92, vice chmn. 1992—93, chmn.-elect 1993—94, jud. divsn. coun. 1994—95, chmn. 1994—95, vice chmn. social security com. sr. lawyers sect. 1996—2000, exec. com. nat. conf. adminstrv. law judges 1997—2001, judges adv. com. on ethics and profl. responsibility 2001—04, parliamentarian exec. com. nat. conf. adminstrv. law judges 2002—04, parliamentarian, adminstrv. law sect., sect. officers chmn. task force participation profl. assns, pub. contract law sect., litig. sect.), Prettyman Levanthal Am. Inn of Ct., Am. Guild Musical Artists, D.C. Bar Assn., Va. Bar Assn., Nat. Assn. Adminstrv. Law Judges (jour. bd. advisors 2004—), Fed. Adminstrv. Law Judges Conf. (exec. com. 1976—81, 1985, 1987, 1999—), Am. Judicature Soc. (nat. adv. coun. 2005—), Phi Eta Sigma, Phi Beta Kappa. Home: 1400 Summit Ave Alexandria VA 22302-2735 Office: Dept Transp Rm 5411 400 7th St SW Washington DC 20590-0001 Office Phone: 202-366-2137. Business E-Mail: ronnie.yoder@dot.gov. E-mail: honron@aol.com.

**YODER, STEPHEN ALAN,** lawyer; b. Wilmington, Del., Aug. 9, 1953; s. Richard Esser and Jane Frances (Whitby) Y.; m. Louise Lea Whitney, Sept. 3, 1977; children: Salle Lea, Katharine Anne, Caroline Whitney. AB, Duke U., 1975; JD, Northwestern U., 1978. Bar: Pa. 1978, Calif. 1983. Assoc. Reed Smith Shaw McClay, Pitts., 1978-83, Pettit & Martin, San Francisco, 1983-84, Reed Smith, Pitts., 1984-86, ptnr., 1987-90; mng. counsel Mellon Bank, Pitts., 1990-92, asst. gen. counsel, 1992-95; gen. counsel Am. South Bancorp., Birmingham, Ala., 1995—2002, sr. exec. v.p., gen. counsel, 2002 . Trustee Birmingham Hist Fn., 1997—, Ala. Eye Inst., Birmingham, 1996—. Office: Am South Bancorp 1901 6th Ave N Birmingham AL 35203-2618

**YODER-WISE, PATRICIA SNYDER,** nursing educator; d. Belford Grant and Leona Cora (Mohler) Snyder; m. Robert Thomas Wise, Feb. 17, 1973; children: Doreen Ellen Wise, Deborah Ann Wise. BSN, Ohio State U., 1963; MSN, Wayne State U., 1968; EdD, Tex. Tech. U., 1984. RN Tex., CNAA. Interim assoc. dean practice program Tex. Tech. U. Health Sci. Ctr. Sch. Nursing, Lubbock, 1979—, interim dean, prof., 1991-93, dean, prof., 1993-2000; clin. prof. U. Tex. Health Sci. Ctr., San Antonio, 1993—2000; prof. Tex. Woman's U., 2004—. Mem. rev. panel Nursing Outlook, 1993—; mem. adv. com. GlaxoWellcome, 1996—2000; mem. Nat. Quality Forum Health Profls. Provide and Health Plans Panel, 2001—06. Author, editor: Leading and Managing in Nursing, 1994 (Book of Yr. award, 1996, 2003), 1998, 2002; co-author: Beyond Leading and Managing, 2006; peer reviewer Jour. Profl. Nursing, 1984—2003, mem. editl. bd. Jour. Continuing Edn. Nursing, 1978—; editor: Jour. Continuing Edn. Nursing, 1988—. Mem. Leadership Am., 1999—2000; participant Leadership Tex.-Found. Women's Resources, 1997—98; mem. Leadership Tex., 1998—99. Recipient Women of Excellence in Medicine, YWCA, Lubbock, 1996, Woman of Excellence in Medicine, 1996, Nurse of Yr. Fellow: Am. Acad. Nursing (chair Inst. for Nursing Leadership 1999—2002, mem. planning com. 2004); mem.: ANCC (pres. 2005—), ANA (del. 1995—2000, chair constituent assembly 1998—2000, sec. 2000—02, 1st v.p. 2002—05), Wise Group (pres.), Tex. Nurses Assn. (pres. 1995—99). Home: 7309 93d St Lubbock TX 79424 Office Phone: 806-866-9403. Personal E-mail: psywrn@aol.com.

**YODOWITZ, EDWARD JAY,** lawyer; b. NYC, 1943; BS, LI U., 1965; JD, U. Balt., 1969. Bar: NY 1972. With Skadden, Arps, Slate, Meagher & Flom LLP, NYC, 1969—, now sr. ptnr. securities and bus. fraud and accountants' liability. Co-chmn., Practising Law Inst. Seminars, "Securities Litigation: Current Strategies and Developments", 1985-95. Contbr. articles in publs.; co-author several publs.; co-editor: Securities Class Actions: Abuses and Remedies, Nat. Legal Ctr. for the Pub. Interest, 1994. Bd. trustee LI U.,

1990—99. Mem.: ABA. Home: 105 Ocean Ave Lawrence NY 11559-2006 Office: Skadden Arps Slate Meagher & Flom LLP Four Times Sq New York NY 10036 Office Phone: 212-735-3450. Office Fax: 917-777-3450. Business E-Mail: eyodowit@skadden.com.

**YOFFA, ELLEN J.,** information technology executive; BS, PhD, MIT. Tech. asst. to dir. IBM Rsch. Divsn.; with IBM Microelectronics Divsn.; dir., emerging sys. technologies IBM T.J. Watson Rsch. Ctr., Hawthorne, NY, dir., next generation web. Gen. chair IEEE/Assn. Computing Machinery Design Automation Conf., 1997. Mem. external adv. bd. U. So. Calif. Electrical Engring. Dept., U. Mass Electrical and Computer Engring. Dept. Recipient Marie R. Pistilli Women in Electronic Design Automation award, Design Automation Conf., 2006. Fellow: IEEE (pres., circuits and systems soc. 2006—, mem. exec. com. and bd. gov., circuits and systems soc., editl. adv. bd., Spectrum mag.); mem.: Assn. for Computing Machinery, Sigma Xi, Phi Beta Kappa. Office: IBM TJ Watson Rsch Ctr Room 3N-C26 19 Skyline Dr Hawthorne NY 10532 Office Phone: 914-784-5222. Office Fax: 914-784-6324. Business E-Mail: yoffa@us.ibm.com.*

**YOFFIE, ERICH H.,** religious organization administrator; m. Amy Jacobson; 2 children. Grad., Brandeis U., Hebrew Union Coll., NYC, 1974. Ordained rabbi 74. Rabbi, Lynbrook, NJ; rabbi Durham, NC; dir. Midwest Coun. Union Am. Hebrew Congregations, NYC, 1980—92, v.p., dir. Commn. on Social Action, 1992—96, pres., 1996—; exec. dir. Assn. Reform Zionists of Am., 1983—. Exec. editor: Reform Judaism mag., 1992—96; contbr. articles to profl. jours. Religious leader Million Mom March, 2000; regional pres., nat. v.p. NAm. Fedn. Temple Youth; bd. dirs. many Jewish orgns. including Mazon: A Jewish Response to Hunger and the Jewish Agy. for Israel. Named to "Top Fifty List of Leadership", Forward Annual. Office: UAHC Hdqs 633 3rd Ave New York NY 10017-6706

**YOGANATHAN, AJIT PRITHIVIRAJ,** biomedical engineer, educator; b. Colombo, Sri Lanka, Dec. 6, 1951; came to U.S., 1973; s. Ponniah and Mangay (Navaratnam) Y.; m. Tripti Yoganathan. BSChemE with honors, Univ. Coll., U. London, 1973; PhDChemE, Calif. Inst. Tech., 1978. Engring. asst. Shell Oil Refinery, Stanlow, Eng., 1972; tchg. asst. Calif. Inst. Tech., 1973-74, 1976, rsch. fellow, 1977-79; asst. prof. Ga. Inst. Tech., 1979-83, assoc. prof., 1983-88, chmn. bioengring. com., 1984-88, prof. chem. engring., 1988-94, dir. Bioengring. Ctr., 1989—, prof. mech. engring., 1989-94, co-dir. Emory U.-Ga. Tech. Biomed. Tech. Ctr., 1992—, Regents prof., 1994—, assoc. chair biomed. engring., 1998—; Wallace H. Coulter disting. faculty chair, 2004—. Adj. assoc. prof. U. Ala., 1985. Founding fellow Am. Inst. Med. & Biol. Engring., 1992; recipient Edwin Walker prize Brit. Inst. Mech. Engrs., 1988, Humboldt fellowship, 1985, Am. Heart Assn.-Ga. Affiliate Rsch. Investigatorship award, 1980-83, Calif. Inst. Tech. fellowship, 1973-77, Goldsmid Medal and prize Univ. Coll., 1972-73, Brit. Coun. scholarship, 1971-73, Sigma Xi Rsch. award, 1995, HR Lissner award, ASME, 1997. Mem. AIChE, ASME (Bioengring. div., H.R. Lissner award 1997), Biomed. Engring. Soc., Am. Soc. Echocardiography (dir. 1987-91). Office: Sch Biomed Engring Ga Tech/Emory Atlanta GA 30332-0535 E-mail: ajit.yoganathan@bme.gatech.edu.*

**YOGESWARAN, PARARAJASINGAM,** physician; b. Jaffna, Sri Lanka, Dec. 6, 1963; arrived in U.S., 2000; s. Pararajasingam and Ahilandeswary Vallipurum; m. Anitha Yogeswaran, June 9, 1990; children: Vidhushei, Shaiesh. MD, Southampton (Eng.) Med. Sch., 1994. House officer in medicine and surgery Southampton (Eng.) Gen. Hosp., Southampton, England, 1994—94; sr. house officer in emergency medicine Bromley Hosp., Kent, England, 1996; sr. house officer medicine and gerontology Hillingdon Hosp., Uxbridge, England, 1996—96; registrar internal medicine Queen Elizabeth Hosp. II, Welwyngarden City, 1996—98; registrar radiology St. Mary's Hosp., Paddington, London, 1998—2000; resident internal medicine Coney Island Hosp., Bklyn., 2000—. Mem.: Royal Coll. Physicians (London). Home: 2610 Olean Pkwy #2B Brooklyn NY 11235 Office: Coney Island Hosp 2601 Ocean Pkwy Brooklyn NY 11235

**YOH, WILLIAM HARRY, JR.,** music educator; b. Reading, Pa., June 10, 1964; s. William Harry Yoh Sr. and Sylvia Mae (Boyer) Yoh; m. Colleen Mary Ryan, June 11, 1994; 1 child, Olivia Elaine. B of Music Edn., U. Mich., 1986. Educator band, chorus Millington Cmty. Schs., Mich., 1986—88, Glades County Schs., Moore Haven, Fla., 1988—89; educator, orch., band, chorus Madison Mid. Sch., Titusville, 1989—2000, Robert Louis Stevenson Elem. Sch. Arts, Merritt Osland, 2000—. Lead tchr. arts dept. Stevenson Elem. Sch., 2000—, mem. sch. adv. coun., 2002—04. Contbr. articles to profl. jours.; performer: (trombonist, music dir.) Historic Coca Village Playhouse, 1997—, (trombonist) Keystone Band, 1982—88, Perserverance Band, 1985—87, 76ers, 1983—84. Mem.: Fla. Music Educators Assn. (editl. com. 1997—99), Music Educators Nat. Conf., Windjammers Initd. (trustee 1989—, trombonist, condr.). Republican. Mem. United Ch. Christ. Avocations: stamp collecting/philately, travel, theater. Home: 1112 Brumpton Pl Rockledge FL 32955 Office: Robert Louis Stevenson Elem Sch 1450 Martin Blvd Merritt Island FL 32952

**YOHALEM, HARRY MORTON,** lawyer; b. Phila., Jan. 21, 1943; s. Morton Eugene and Florence (Mishnun) Y.; m. Martha Caroline Remy, June 9, 1967; children: Seth, Mark. BA with honors, U. Wis., 1965; JD cum laude, Columbia U., 1969, M in Internat. Affairs, 1969. Bar: NY 1969, DC 1981, Calif. 1992, U.S. Supreme Ct. 1985. Assoc. Shearman & Sterling, NYC, 1969-71; asst. counsel to gov. State of NY, Albany, 1971-73, counsel office planning svcs., 1973-75; asst. gen. counsel FEA, Washington, 1975-77; mem. staff White House Energy Policy and Planning Office, Washington, 1977; dep. gen. counsel for legal svcs. Dept. Energy, Washington, 1978-80, dep. under sec., 1980-81; ptnr. Rogers & Wells, Washington, 1981-91; gen. counsel Calif. Inst. Tech., Pasadena, 1991—. Editor comments Columbia Jour. Transnat. Law, 1967-68, rsch. editor, 1968-69. Phi. Coun. for Excellence in Govt., Washington, 1990—; pres. Opera Bel Canto, Washington, 1984-87; mem. Lawyers Com. for Arts, Washington, 1981-88; bd. visitors dept. English U. Wis., 1999—. Harlan Fiske Stone scholar Columbia U., 1967, 69. Mem.: Athenaeum, Phi Kappa Phi. Home: 702 E California Blvd Pasadena CA 91106 Office: Calif Inst Tech Mail Code 109-31 1200 E California Blvd Pasadena CA 91125 Business E-Mail: harry.yohalem@caltech.edu.

**YOHAY, STEVEN JACOB,** healthcare company executive, consultant; b. N.Y.C., N.Y., Nov. 28, 1950; s. Nathan and Natalie (Modlinger) Y.; children: Charlotte, Paige. BS in Psychology, SUNY-Empire State Coll., Saratoga Springs, N.Y., 1977. Cert. addiction specialist, alcoholism and substance abuse counselor. Staff counselor-trainee AREBA Casriel Inst., N.Y.C., 1971-72, asst. resident dir., 1972-73, resident dir., 1973-75, exec. dir., 1975-82, pres., chief exec. officer, 1982—. Cons. Long Lane Sch., Middletown Conn., Brookside Acad., Mt. Freedom, N.J., The Key, Ghent, Belgium, New Ctr. for Psychotherapies, Boston, Psychiat. Engring. Standards Assn.; investor in broadway shows and real estate. Contbr. articles to profl. jours. Bd. dirs. N.Y. Regional Therapeutic Communities of Am. Recipient Community Svc. award Bronx Borough Pres.'s Office, 1986; Regents scholar N.Y. State Bd. Regents, 1966. Fellow Am. Soc. New Identity Process; mem. Am. Coll. of Addiction Treatment Adminstrs., Am. Coll. Healthcare Adminstrs., Nat. Assn. Alcoholism and Drug Abuse Counselors, Alcohol and Drug Problems Assn. N.Am., Nat. Assn. Addiction Treatment Providers, N.Y. State Assn. Practicing Psychotherapists. Jewish. Avocations: motorboating, sailing, tennis, scuba diving, mountain biking. Home: 78 Hawser Dr Oak Beach NY 11702 Office: AREBA Casriel Inc 500 W 57th St New York NY 10019-2902

**YOHN, WILLIAM H(ENDRICKS), JR.,** federal judge; b. Pottstown, Pa., Nov. 20, 1935; s. William H. and Dorothy C. (Cornelius) Y.; m. Jean Louise Kochel, Mar. 16, 1963; children: William H. III, Bradley G., Elizabeth Y. Lemmon. AB, Princeton U., 1957; JD, Yale U., 1960. Bar: Pa. 1961, U.S. Dist. Ct. D.C. 1961. Ptnr. Wells Campbell Reynier & Yohn, Pottstown, 1961-71; mem., chmn. coms. Pa. House of Reps., Harrisburg, 1968-80; ptnr. Binder Yohn & Kalis, Pottstown, 1971-81; judge Montgomery County Ct. of

Common Pleas, Norristown, Pa., 1981-91, U.S. Dist. Ct. (ea. dist.), Pa., 1991—. Asst. dist. atty., Montgomery County Dist. Atty. Office, 1962-65; instr. Am. Inst. of Banking, 1963-66; bd. dirs. Fed. Jud. Ctr., 1999-2003; chair Third Cir. Com. on Model Criminal Jury Instrns, 2004-. Bd. dirs. Greater Pottstown Drug Abuse Prevention Program, 1970-76, Pottstown Meml. Med. Ctr., 1974-95, chmn., 1984-95; mem. exec. com. Yale Law Sch. Alumni Assn., 1998—. Cpl. USMCR, 1960-66. Mem. Pa. Bar Assn., Montgomery Bar Assn. (bd. dirs. 1967-70), Fed. Judge Assn. Republican. Office: US Dist Ct 14613 US Courthouse 601 Market St Philadelphia PA 19106-1713 Office Phone: 215-597-4361.

**YOKEN, MEL B(ARTON),** language educator, writer, radio personality; b. Fall River, Mass., June 25, 1939; s. Albert Benjamin and Sylvia Sarah (White) Y.; m. Cynthia Stein, June 20, 1976; children: Andrew Brett, David Ryan, Jonathan Barry. BA, U. Mass., 1960; MAT, Brown U., 1961, PhD, 1972. Instr. French U. Mass., Dartmouth, 1966-72, asst. prof., 1976-81, prof., 1981—2000, chancellor prof., 2000. Dir. French summer study program French Inst., 1981-88; radio commentator Am. Field Svc., 1971—, pres., 1984-86, v.p., 2001—; vis. prof. Wheaton Coll., 1987, U. of Montreal, 1981-88; translator New Bedford Superior Ct., New Bedford, Mass., 1985—; reader, cons. AP Exams in French, 1997—; nominating com. Nobel Prize for Lit., 1972—; Acad. Am. Poets, 1999—. Author: Claude Tillier, 1976, Speech is Plurality, 1978, Claude Tillier (1801-44): Fame and Fortune in His Novelistic Work, 1978, Entretiens Quebecois I, 1986, Entretiens Quebecois II, 1989, Letters of Robert Molloy, 1989, Festschrift in Honor of Stowell Goding, 1993, Entretiens Quebecois III, 1999; contbr. articles to profl. jours. Pres. Friends of Fall River Pub. Libr., 1972-80, pres., bd. dirs., 1972-80; pres. New Bedford Pub. Libr., 1980-82; bd. dirs. Am. Field Svc., 1980—, pres., 1984-86, v.p., 2001—; v.p. Friends of U. Mass. Libr., 1998—, pres., 1999—; dir. Boivin Ctr., 1999—. Decorated officier Ordre des Palmes académiques, Acad. Française, 2001, Order Nat. du Que., 2005; recipient Disting. Svc. award City Fall River, 1974, 80, Excellence in Tchg. French award, 1984-85, Gov.'s citation, 1986, Nat. Disting. Leadership award, 1990, Dist. Svc. award Mass. Fgn. Lang. Assn., 1992, Medaille de Vermeil du Rayonnement de la Langue Française, L'Academie Française, 1993, Outstanding Cmty. Svc. award, 1997, Disting. Alumni award, Durfee H.S., 1998, Golden Apple award Fall River Herald News, 1998; Govt. of Que. grantee, 1981-85, 87-89, Can. Embassy grantee, 1986, 87, Southeastern Mass. U. grantee, 1985, 89, 90; named Hon. Life Mem., Fall River Pub. Libr., 2003; named Mel Yoken Day in his honor by Mayor of New Bedford, 1990; named Real Hero in Edn., ARC, 2005. Mem. MLA (life), Am. Assn. Tchrs. French (life, hon. 2005), Am. Coun. Tchrs. Fgn. Langs., Middlebury Amicale (life), N.E. MLA (coord. 1987-91), New Eng. Fgn. Lang. Assn., Mass. Fgn. Lang. Assn. (bd. dirs. 1985-90, disting. svc. award 1992), N.Y. State Assn. Tchrs. Fgn. Langs., Internat. Platform Assn., Francophone Assn. (v.p. 1990-98), Assn. Literary Scholars and Critics, Fall River C. of C., Brown U. Alumni Assn. (rep.), Richelieu Internat., Universal Manuscript Soc. (v.p. 1993-95). Avocations: travel, languages, baseball, postcards, meteorology. Home: 261 Carroll St New Bedford MA 02740-1412 Office: U Mass Dartmouth Lang Dept Old Westport Rd North Dartmouth MA 02747-2512 Business E-Mail: myoken@umassd.edu.

**YOKUBAITIS, ROGER T.,** lawyer; b. Wharton, Tex., Jan. 9, 1945; Student, St. Louis U.; BA, JD, U. Houston, 1969. Bar: Tex. 1969, U.S. Dist. Ct. (so., we., ea. and no. dists.) Tex., U.S. Ct. Appeals (5th, 9th, 11 cirs.), U.S. Supreme Ct. Ptnr. Carmody & Yokubaitis, L.L.P., Houston, 1995—2000; prin. Roger T. Yokubaitis, P.L.L.C., Houston, 2000—. Mem. ABA, Houston Bar Assn., State Bar of Tex., Houston Bankruptcy Bar Assn., Am. Bankruptcy Inst., Fed. Bar Assn., Federalist Soc. Office: Roger T Yokubaitis PLLC 1177 W Loop S Ste 1650 Houston TX 77027-9034 Office Phone: 713-227-9000. Personal E-Mail: Yokubaitis@msn.com.

**YOLDAS, BULENT ERTURK,** materials scientist, educator; b. Isaparta, Turkey, Feb. 19, 1938; arrived in U.S., 1958, naturalized; s. Mustafa and Hatice Yoldas; m. Lubomyra Anne Ivanycky; children: Erol, Kim. BS in Ceramic Engring, Ohio State U., 1963, MS, 1964, PhD, 1966. Sr. engr. Owens Ill. Tech. Ctr., Toledo, 1966—74; fellow scientist Westinghouse Rsch. Ctr., Pitts., 1974—84, PPG Industries R&D Ctr., Pitts., 1984—96; adj. prof. Carnegie Mellon U., Pitts., 1996—99. Mem. editl. bd. Jour. of Sol-gel Sci. of Tech., 2000—. Contbr. articles to profl. jours. Named one of top 100 Internat. Innovators, Tech. Mag. (pemier issue), 1981. Fellow: Am. Ceramic Soc.; mem.: AAAS, Materials Rsch. Soc. Achievements include invention of a radical glass forming method, 1980; image transfer technology, 1999; research in ceramic and glass formation by chemical polymerization; optical coatings and advanced materials; 75 patents in field; development of chemical process of forming transparent microporous aluminas and other oxides known as Yoldas Process. Avocations: gardening, hiking, music, poetry. Home: 16728 Adrienne Way Ramona CA 92065 Office Phone: 760-787-1786. E-mail: yoldas@sbcglobal.net.

**YOLEN, JANE,** writer; b. NYC, Feb. 11, 1939; d. Will Hyatt and Isabelle (Berlin) Y.; m. David Wilber Stemple, Sept. 2, 1962; children: Heidi Elisabet, Adam Douglas, Jason Frederic. BA, Smith Coll., 1960; EdM, U. Mass., 1978, LLD (hon.), 2006, Coll. Our Lady of Elms, 1980, Smith Coll., Baypath Coll., Keene State Coll. Asst. editor This Week mag., 1960; mem. staff Saturday Rev., 1960; asst. editor Gold Medal Books, 1961, Rutledge Press, 1961—63; asst. juvenile editor A.A. Knopf, Inc., 1963—65; freelance writer, 1965—; lectr. dept. edn. Smith Coll., 1979—84; editor Jane Yolen books, imprint Harcourt Brace Jovanovich, 1988—97. Tchr. writers confs. Centrum, Cape Cod Writers Conf., Soc. Children's Book Writers, U. Mass.; mem. Mass. Coun. on Arts, 1974. Author: Pirates in Petticoats, 1963, The Witch Who Wasn't, 1964, The Emperor and the Kite, 1968, Writing Books for Children, 1973, The Girl Who Cried Flowers, 1974, The Hundredth Dove, 1978, The Dream Weaver, 1979, Commander Toad in Space, 1980, The Gift of Sarah Barker, 1981, Tam Lin Magic, 1981, Dragon's Blood, 1982, Tales of Wonder, 1983, Heart's Blood, 1984, Cards of Grief, 1984, Dragonfield, 1985, Merlin's Booke, 1986, The Lullabye Songbook, 1986, Ring of Earth, 1986, Favorite Folktales From Around the World, 1986, Piggins, 1987, Owl Moon, 1987, Three Bears, 1987, A Sending of Dragons, 1987, The Devil's Arithmetic, 1988, Sister Light/Sister Dark, 1988, White Jenna, 1989, Dove Isabeau, 1989, Baby Bear's Bedtime Book, 1990, Tam Lin, 1990, Bird Watch, 1990, Sky Dogs, 1990, Wizard's Hall, 1991, All those Secrets of the World, 1991, Wings, 1991, Hark! A Christmas Sampler, 1991, Encounter, 1992, Briar Rose, 1992, Letting Swift River Go, 1992, What Rhymes with Moon, 1993, Welcome to the Greenhouse, 1993, Honkers, 1993, Here There Be Dragons, 1993, Grandad Bill's Song, 1994, Good Griselle, 1994, The Girl in the Golden Bower, 1994, Old Dame Counterpane, 1994, Old Macdonald's Songbook, 1994, Here There Be Unicorns, 1994, Beneath the Ghost Moon, 1994, The Wild Hunt, 1995, Ballad of the Pirate Queens, 1995, And Twelve Chinese Acrobats, 1995, Water Music, 1995, Among Angels, 1995, Here They Be Witches, 1995, O. Jerusalem, 1996, Welcome to the Sea of Sand, 1996, Passager, 1996, Hobby, 1996, Sacred Places, 1996, Here There Be Angels, 1996, Milk and Honey, 1996, Meet The Monsters, 1996, Once Upon Ice, 1997, Merlin, 1997, Child of Faerie, 1997, Twelve Impossible Things Before Breakfast, 1997, Miz Berlin Walks, 1997, Nocturne, 1997, Armageddon Summer, 1998, House/House, 1998, Prince of Egypt, 1998, Raising Yoder's Barn, 1998, The Wizard's Map, 1999, The Pictish Child, 1999, The Fairies' Ring, 1999, Moonball, 1999, Gray Heroes: Elder Tales From Around the World, 1999, How Does a Dinosaur Say Goodnight, 2000, Off We Go, 2000, Queen's Own Fool, Not One Damsel in Distress, 2000, Mirror/Mirror, 2000, Color Me a Rhyme, 2000, Welcome to the River of Grass, 2001, The Fish Prince and Other Merman Stories, 2001, Odysseus in the Serpent's Maze, 2001, Dear Mother/Dear Daughter, 2001, Hippolyta and the Curse of the Amazons, 2002, Wild Wings, 2002, Firebird, 2002, Horizons, 2002, Animal Train, 2002, Harvest Home, 2002, Girl in a Cage, 2002, Sword of the Rightful King, 2003, How Do Dinosaurs Get Well Soon, 2003, Take Joy, 2003, My Brothers' Flying Machine, 2003, Hoptoad, 2003, Mightier than the Sword, 2003, The Radiation Sonnets, 2003, The Flying Witch, 2003, Jason and the Gorgon's Blood, 2004, How Do Dinosaurs Clean their Rooms?, 2004, The Barefoot Book of Ballet Stories, 2004, Prince Across the Water, 2004,

Grandma's Hurrying Child, 2005, Perfect Wizard, 2005, Apple for the Teacher, 2005, Meow, 2005, How Do Dinosaurs Eat Their Food?, 2005, Fairy Tale Feast, 2006, Troll Bridge, 2006, This Little Piggy, 2006, Dimity Duck, 2006, Baby Bear's Books, 2006, Count Me a Rhyme, 2006, over 200 others. Mass. del. Dem. Nat. Conv., 1972; town coord. Robert Drinan's campaign, 1970; chmn. bd. trustees Hatfield (Mass.) Libr., 1978-83. Mem. Soc. Children's Book Writers (bd. dirs. 1974—), Children's Lit. Assn. (bd. dirs. 1977-79), Sci. Fiction Writers Am. (pres. 1986-88), Mystery Writers Am., Authors Guild. Democrat. Jewish/Quaker. Home: PO Box 27 Hatfield MA 01038-0027 E-mail: janeyolen@aol.com.

YOLLICK, BERNARD LAWRENCE, otolaryngologist, surgeon; b. Toronto, Mar. 24, 1922; came to U.S., 1949; s. Samuel and Beatrice (Roth) Y.; m. Liny L. Pajgin, 1947; children: Ingrid, Eric Lyf. Sr. Matriculation, Harbord Collegiate Inst., Toronto, 1939; MD, U. Toronto, 1945. Diplomate Am. Bd. Surgery, Am. Bd. Otolaryngology. Intern Sunnybrook Hosp., Toronto, 1945-46; resident D.C. Gen. Hosp., Washington, 1950, St. Louis County Hosp., Clayton, Mo., 1952-53; Am. Cancer Soc. fellow M.D. Anderson Cancer Hosp., Houston, 1953-54; resident in pathology Cook County Hosp., Chgo., 1949; surgeon Houston, 1953-59; fellowship in otolaryngology VA Hosp., Dallas, 1960-63; asst. prof. anatomy Baylor Med. Sch., Houston, 1953-59; assoc. prof. anatomy U. Tex. Dental Sch., Houston, 1953-59, Baylor Coll. Dentistry, Dallas, 1987-90; mem. staff Children's Med. Ctr., Dallas, 1990—; mem. staff, chief dept. otolaryngology St. Paul Med. Ctr., Dallas, 1990-98. Cons. Tex. Workers Compensation Ins. Fund, 1996—; Dept. Defense, Dallas, 1997—; mem. otolaryngology staff Vets. Adminstrn. Hosp., Dallas, 1990—. Contbr. articles to profl. jours. Served to capt. Royal Can. Army Med. Corps, 1942-45. Recipient fellowship Am. Cancer Soc., 1953. Fellow Am. Coll. Surgeons; mem. Tex. Otolaryn. Assn. (pres. 1979). Personal E-mail: yollick@aol.net.

YONCHAK, MICHAEL STEPHEN, music educator; b. Sharon, Pa., Mar. 16, 1978; s. Gary Stephen and Katherine Mary Yonchak. MusB in Edn., Youngstown State U., 2000, MusM in Performance, 2003. Lic. Ohio Dept. Edn., 2004. Mid. sch. dir. bands Campbell City Schs., Ohio, 2001—02; dir. bands Crestview H.S., Columbiana, 2002—. Music dir. Buhl Pk. Cmty. Concert Band, Hermitage, Pa., 2005—; big band drummer Don Burns Orch., Youngstown, 2005—. Mem.: Phi Mu Alpha (hon.). Eastern Orthodox. Avocations: golf, reading, cooking. Home: 214 E Chestnut St Lisbon OH 44432

YONDA, ALFRED WILLIAM, mathematician; b. Cambridge, Mass., Aug. 10, 1919; s. Walter and Theophelia (Naruscewicz) Y.; m. Mary Jane McManus, Dec. 19, 1949 (dec.); children: Nancy, Kathryn, Elizabeth, John; m. Peggy A. Terrel, June 22, 1975. BS, U. Ala., 1952, MA in Math., 1954. Registered profl. engr. Mathematician rocket rsch. Redstone Arsenal, Huntsville, Ala., 1953, U.S. Army Ballistic Rsch. Labs., Aberdeen, Md., 1954-56; instr. math. U. Ala., Tuscaloosa, 1954, Temple U., Phila., 1956-57; assoc. scientist, rsch. & devel. divsn. Avco Corp., Wilmington, Mass., 1957-59; sr. mem. tech. staff RCA, Camden, NJ, 1959-66; mgr. computer analysis and programming dept. Raytheon Co. Space and Info. Systems Divsn., Sudbury, Mass., 1966-70; mgr. software systems lab., 1969-70, prin. engr. missiles systems divsn., 1970-73; mgr. sys. analysis & programming GTE Govt. Systems Corp., 1973-77, mgr. software engring. Atlantic ops., 1977-82, sr. mem. tech. staff Command Control & Comm. Sector, 1983-91; software systems engr. Yonda Software Systems Cos., 1991—. Contbr. articles to profl. jours. Pres. Milford Area Assn. Retarded Children, 1970-74, vice chmn. fin. com. Town of Medway, 1973; bd. dirs. Blackstone Valley Mental Health and Retardation Area, 1970-76; trustee Medway Librs., 1973-82, chmn., 1974-81. With USAAF, 1943-46. Hon. fellow Advanced Level Telecomm. Tng. Ctr., Ghaziabad, India, 1981. Mem. AAAS, IEEE, Math. Assn. Am., N.Y. Acad. Scis., Sigma Xi, Phi Eta Sigma, Pi Mu Epsilon (pres. Ala. chpt. 1953-54), Sigma Pi Sigma. Office: Cordiss Mills 65 Canal St Apt 122 Millbury MA 01527-3270 E-mail: awyonda@aol.com.

YONETANI, AYAKO, music educator, entertainer; d. Mitsuya and Yuko Yonetani. Mus B, Juilliard Sch., 1986; MusM, Julliard Sch., 1987, MusD, 1993. Asst. prof. of violin/viola U. of Ctrl. Fla., Orlando, 1993—98, assoc. prof. of violin, 1998—; asst. faculty Aspen Music Festival and Sch., Aspen, Colo., 1989—2002. Concertmaster Aspen Music Festival and Sch., Colo., 2001—02. Translator: (book) Teaching Genius: Dorothy DeLay and the Making of a Musician. Avocations: opera, classical music. Office: U of Ctrl Fla Music P O Box 161354 Orlando FL 32816-1354 E-mail: yonetani@mail.ucf.edu.

YONG, RAYMOND NEN-YIU, civil engineering educator; b. Singapore, Apr. 10, 1929; naturalized, 1966; s. Ngim Djin and Lucy (Loh) Y.; m. Florence Lechensky, July 8, 1961; children: Raymond T.M., Christopher T.K. BA in Math. and Physics, Washington and Jefferson Coll., 1950; BS, MIT, 1952; MS, Purdue U., 1954; MEngring., McGill U., Montreal, Que., Can., 1958, PhD, 1960. Mem. faculty McGill U., 1959-95, prof. civil engring., 1965-72, William Scott prof. civil engring. and applied mechanics, 1972-95; dir. Geotech Rsch. Ctr., 1973-95; assoc. mem. Ctr. for Medicine, Ethics and Law McGill U., 1991-95. Adj. prof. civil engring. U. Fla., Gainesville, 1984—; adj. rsch. prof. civil engring. Carleton U., Ottawa, 1990; disting. rsch. prof. U. Wales, Cardiff, 1995-2002, emeritus prof., sr. sci. advisor, 2002-04; sr. sci. dir. Geoenviron. Engring. Rsch. Ctr., Cardiff Sch. Engring., U. Wales, 1995, prof. emeritus, 2002—. Author: Soil Properties and Behavior, 1975 (Japanese edit. 1977), Introduction to Soil Behavior, 1966 (Japanese edit. 1974), Vehicle Traction Mechanics, 1985, Principles of Contaminant Transport in Soils, 1992 (Japanese edit. 1995), Geoenvironmental Engineering: Contaminated Soils, Pollutant Fate and Mitigation, 2001, Natural Attenuation of Contaminants in Soils, 2004, Microstructure of Smectite Clays and Engineering Performance, 2006, Geoenvironmental Sustainability, 2006. Decorated chevalier Ordre National du Que.; recipient Killam prize Can. Coun., 1985, ASTM Charles B. Dudley award, 1988, Can. Environ. Achievement award, Lifetime Achievement Environment Can., 1991. Fellow Royal Soc. Can., Engring. Inst. Can., Can. Soc. for Civil Engring.; mem. ASCE, ASTM (Charles B. Dudley award 1988), Inst. Civil Engrs., Soc. Rheology, Clay Minerals Soc., Internat. Soc. Terrain-Vehicle Systems (pres. 1993—), Can. Geotech. Soc. (R.F. Legget award 1993). Office Phone: 250-655-3787. E-mail: r.nyong@shaw.ca.

YONKMAN, FREDRICK ALBERS, lawyer, management consultant; b. Holland, Mich., Aug. 22, 1930; s. Fredrick Francis and Janet Dorothy (Albers) Y.; m. Kathleen VerMeulen, June 9, 1953 (div. Sept. 22, 1980); children: Sara, Margriet, Nina.; m. Barbara Anne Sullivan, Aug. 22, 1981 (div. Mar. 31, 1994); 1 child, Fredrick Ryan; m. Jewel Marie Humphrey, July 4, 1998. BA, Hope Coll., Holland, 1952; JD, U. Chgo., 1957. Bar: NY 1958, Mass. 1968, DC 1984. With Winthrop, Stimson, Putnam & Roberts, NYC, 1957-64; sec., gen. counsel Reuben H. Donnelley Corp., NYC, 1964-66, Dun & Bradstreet, Inc., NYC, 1966-68; ptnr. Sullivan & Worcester, Boston, 1968-72; gen. counsel Am. Express Co., NYC, 1972-78, exec. v.p., 1975-80; pres. Buck Cons., NYC, 1980-81; mgmt. cons., psychoanalyst, 1981—; counsel Peabody, Lambert & Myers, Washington, 1983-84; exec. dir. Asian Bus. Ctr., Rutgers U. Bus. Sch., Piscataway, NJ, 2003—05. Mem. bd., chmn. audit com. Kennecott Corp., 1978—81; adj. prof. law Georgetown U., 1976—78; chmn. Georgetown Internat. Law Inst., 1980—81; vis. com. U. Chgo. Law Sch., 1980—82; mem. exec. com. Warner-Amex, 1978—80; bd. dirs. and advisors Sageworks Inc., Raleigh, NC, 1998—2004. Chmn. Outward Bound, Inc., Garrison, NY, 1980—81; mem. nat. adv. bd., 2005—; bd. dirs. Washington Campus Program, 1976—81, Young Audiences, 1978—83. With CIC U.S. Army, 1952—54. Recipient Silver Anniversary award NCAA, 1977. Mem.: ABA, NY State Bar Assn. Methodist. Home and Office: 5200 No Ocean Blvd Apt 1410 Lauderdale By The Sea FL 33308 Office Phone: 203-253-4703. Personal E-mail: fyonkman@optonline.net.

YONKMAN, MARK WILLIAM, lawyer; b. Traverse City, Mich., Sept. 22, 1960; s. Harry William and Thelma (Hoadly) Y. BA, Kalamazoo Coll., 1982; JD cum laude, Wayne State U., 1985. Bar: Mich. 1985, U.S. Dist. Ct. (we. and

ea. dists.) Mich. 1986, U.S. Ct. Appeals (6th cir.) 1986. Assoc. Pepper, Hamilton & Scheetz, Detroit, 1984-88, Phila., 1988—; sr. v.p., asst. gen. counsel, asst. sec. Comerica Inc.; now sr. v.p., gen. counsel M&T Bank Corp., Buffalo. Mem. Mich. Bar Assn., Fed. Bar Assn., Detroit Bar Assn., Order of the Coif. Avocations: French and Portuguese langs., skiing, tennis, rowing. Office: M&T Bank Corp 1 M&T Plaza Buffalo NY 14203

YONTOSH, SHARLENE MARY, principal; m. A. Thomas Yontosh; children: Kevin T., Krista M. BS in Elem. Edn., Pa. State U., 1991, MEd in Ednl. Leadership, 2000, postgrad. Cert. elem. and secondary prin. Pa., elem. tchr., early childhood nursery tchr. Tchr. West Branch Sch. Dist., Morrisdale, Pa., 1991—2000, curriculum dir., 2000—05, elem. prin., 2005—. Office: West Branch Area Sch Dist 356 Allport Cutoff Morrisdale PA 16858 Office Phone: 814-345-5627. E-mail: syontosh@westbranch.org.

YONTZ, KENNETH FREDRIC, medical and chemical company executive; b. Sandusky, Ohio, July 21, 1944; s. Kenneth Willard and Dorothy (Kromer) Y.; m. Jean Ann Marshall, July 21, 1962 (div. Aug. 1982); children: Terri, Christine, Michael, Jennifer; m. Karen Glojek, July 7, 1984 (wid. Dec. 1994); m. Karen Mc Diarmid, Jan. 10, 1997. BSBA, Bowling Green State U., 1971; MBA, Eastern Mich. U., 1979. Fin. planning mgr. Ford Motor Co., Rawsonville, Mich., 1970-74; fin. mgr. Chemetron Corp., Chgo., 1974-76, pres. fire systems div., 1976-80; pres. electronics div. Allen Bradley Co., Milw., 1980-83, group. pres. electronics, 1983-85, exec. v.p., 1985-86; chmn. bd. Apogent Techs., Milw., 1986—, Sybron Dental Specialities, Milw., 1986—. Bd. dirs. Rockwell Int., Milw. Founder Karen Yontz Womens Cardiac Awareness Ctr.; bd. dirs Am. Healthcare. Mem. Muirfield Village Golf Club, Vintage Club (Indian Wells, Calif.), Tradition Golf Club (La Quinta, Calif.), Chenequa Country Club (Hartford, Wis.), Flint Hills Country Club (Wichita), Oconomowoc Golf Club Roman Catholic. Positive results are seldom achieved from negative thoughts.

YOO, GEORGE H., otolaryngologist, medical educator; Assoc. prof. Wayne State U., Detroit, 1996—. Named Top Dr., Hour Detroit Mag., 2005; named one of The Best Dr. in Am., Best Doctors, 2005—06. Office: Wayne State University 4201 St Antoine 5E UHC Detroit MI 48201 Office Phone: 313-745-4336.

YOO, JOHN CHOON, law educator, former federal agency administrator; b. Seoul, South Korea, June 10, 1967; s. John H. and Sook (Hee) Y. BA in History, Harvard U., 1989; JD, Yale U., 1992. Bar: Pa. 1993, U.S. Dist. Ct. (9th cir.) 1997. Law clk. to Judge Laurence Silberman US Ct. Appeals (D.C. cir.), Washington, 1992-93; law clk. to Justice Clarence Thomas US Supreme Ct., Washington, 1994-95; gen. counsel US Senate Judiciary Com., Washington, 1995-96; prof. law Boalt Hall Sch. Law, Berkeley, Calif., 1993-94, 96—, dir., Internat Legal Studies Program, 1999—2001; dep. assist. atty. gen., Office of Legal Counsel US Dept. Justice, Washington, 2001—03. Visiting prof. U. Chgo., Free U. of Amsterdam; 1998; visiting scholar Am. Enterprise Inst.; chair, section on scholarship Assn. of Am. Law Schools, 2000. Author: The Powers of War and Peace: The Constitution and Foreign Affairs After 9/11, 2005. Recipient Paul M. Bator award, Federalist Soc. for Law & Pub. Policy. Office: Boalt Hall Sch Law U Calif Berkeley 890 Simon Hall Berkeley CA 94720-0001 E-mail: yoo@law.berkeley.edu

YOO, VAK YEONG, health facility administrator; b. Seoul, Republic of Korea, June 28, 1947; d. Jang Mun Yoo and So Ran Choi. MA, Ewha Women's U., Seoul, 1974, MD, 1980. Med. diplomate internal medicine. Founder pvt. med. exam. ctr., Seoul, 1981—; dir. Yoovakyeong Internal Medicine, Seoul, 1981-92; head Med. Exam. Ctr., Seoul, 1981—; dir. Cheong-Vak P.B. Hosp., Seoul, 1992—; head Women's Health Dx & Climacteric, Seoul, 1992—. Mem. menopause and osteoporosis unit, 1992—, YVY-QOL Inst., 1997, YVY-QOL osteoporosis leader NOF-PPN, 1997; mem. sci. com. Koran Soc. Menopause, 1997-99; creator, organizer YVY-QOL support group for meno/osteoporosis Nat. Osteoporosis Found., 1997. Author: Phytoestrogens, 1995, Quality of Midbeyond Womens Life, 1996, Aging and Gender Specific Quality of Life, 1997; editor Jour. Meno/Osteoporosis, 1998—; co-editor Jour. Menopause Soc. Korea, 1999—; inventor in field. Mem. N.Am. Menopause Soc., Internat. Menopause Soc., Korean Soc. Endoscopy, Christian Med. Assn. (planning dir. 1993-96), Am. Assn. Clin. Endocrinologists, AAAS, Am. Soc. for Microbiology, Korean Soc. Endocrinology, Korean Diabetes Assn., Korean Soc. Menopause (sci. com. 1996-98, editing com. 1999—), Korean Soc. Circulation, The Endocrine Soc., NY Acad. Scis., NOF-Profl. Ptnr. Network, Am. Soc. Bone and Mineral Rsch. Avocations: travel, listening to music, opera music. Home: 138-60 Yongdu Dong Dongdaemun Ku Seoul 130-072 Republic of Korea Office: Cheongvak Antiaging Hosp 582 Shinsa Dong Kangnam Ku Seoul 135-120 Republic of Korea

YOOD, HAROLD STANLEY, retired internist; b. Plainfield, N.J., Feb. 23, 1920; s. Raphael and Netta (Newcorn) Y.; m. Helen H. Hull, Nov. 8, 1941; children: Pamela, Patricia Yood Herskovitz, Paula Yood Peterson, Andrew H. BA, U. Va., 1940, MD, 1943. Intern Syracuse (N.Y.) U. Med. Ctr., 1943; pvt. practice Plainfield, N.J., 1946-91; med. dir. Cen. Jersey Individual Physicians Assn., 1987-2000; ret. Staff dept. medicine Muhlenberg Hosp., 1946—, pres. staff, 1980-86, cons., 1991-95, emeritus, 1995—. Contbr. articles to Jour. Med. Soc. N.J., Communication for Ciba, others. Pres. vol. med. staff Raritan Valley Hosp., Greenbrook, N.J., 1968; bd. govs. Muhlenberg Regional Med. Ctr., 1980-86, exec. com.; trustee, v.p. United Way Plainfield/Fanwood, 1975-81; bd. dirs. United Way Union County, 1978-81; pres. Jewish Community Ctr., Plainfield, 1970-71; v.p. Jewish Fedn. Cen. N.J., 1971-73, Cen. N.J. Jewish Home for Aged, 1973-80. Capt. M.C. AUS, 1944-45. ETO. Decorated Purple Heart, Combat Med. badge, Combat Glider badge. Fellow Am. Coll. Gastroenterology (sr.), Am. Coll. Angiology (ret.), Internat. Coll. Angiology (ret.); mem. AMA, Med. Soc. N.J. (governing coun. hosp. med. staff sect. 1983-94, chmn. 1988-90; trustee 1989-90), Union County Med. Soc., Lions (life). Enjoyment in my profession, pleasure in relationship with patients, a belief in the necessity for civic and community volunteer involvement, a commitment to support causes that aid the unfortunate and do no harm to individuals.

YOOD, JAMES W., art critic, historian, educator, writer; Asst. prof. art history Sch. Art Inst. Chgo.; vis. art prof. Northwestern U., Evanston, Ill., 1992, prof. contemporary art theory and crticism, 1995—, lect. and asst. chairperson, dept. art theory and practice, 2003—. Guest curator Miss. Invitational, Miss. Mus. Art, 1999; lectr. Biennial Exhbn., Fort Wayne Mus. Art, 2000; lectr. in field. Art critic New Art Examiner, Art Historian, Art Forum, teme celeste, GLASS; author: Feasting: A Celebration of Food in Art: Paintings from the Art Institute of Chicago, 1992; author: (with essays by Mark Pascale & David Mickenberg) Second Sight: Printmaking in Chicago 1935-1995, 1996; co-author: (with Refco Group, Eleanor Heartney, Anne Rorimer, Adam Brooks, and Sue Taylor) The Refco Collection, 1990; co-author: (with Art Institute of Chgo.) Feasting: A Celebration of Food in Art, 1992; co-author: (with Patty Carroll(photographer) & Debora Duez Donato) Spirited Visions: Portraits of Chicago Artists, 1991; co-author: (with Whitney Halsted (preface) Gladys Nilsson, 1993; co-author: (with Hollis Sigler) Hollis Sigler's Breast Cancer Journal, 1999; co-author: (with Robert Vinnedge(photographer) & Amy Herd (photographer) William Morris: Animal/Artifact, 2000; co-author: (with Blake Edgar, William Morris, and Robert Vinnedge) William Morris: Man Adorned, 2002; co-author: (with Jack H. Bloom) The Rabbi as Symbolic Exemplar: By the Power Vested in Me, 2002; editor: Ray Yoshida: A Retrospective, 1968-1998, 1998, Mississippi Invitational, Mississippi Mus. Art, 1999; cons. in modern and contemporary art Encyclopaedia Britannica. Mem.: Chgo. Art Critics Assn.

YOON, E. YUL, retired career officer; b. Pyungyang, Korea, Feb. 10, 1927; s. Jung Soon and Jung Duk (Lee) Y.; m. Sun Sam Lee Yoon, Nov. 29, 1931; children: Kyung Ran, Kyung Im, Kwang Ho. Grad., Mil. Acad. Seoul, 1948; BS in Politics and Fgn. Policy, Dangook U., Seoul, Korea, 1955; grad., U.S. Air U., Montgomery, Ala., 1957. Squadron comdr. The 12th Fighter SQ F-51,

Korea, 1952-53; armed force attache Korean Embassy, Paris, 1959-61; wing comdr. The 1st Combat Wing, The 10th Fighter Wing, Seoul, 1961-63; pres. Korean Air Force Coll., Seoul, 1963-64; supt. Korean Air Acad., Seoul, 1964-66; commanding gen. Combat Air Command, Korea, 1968-70; minister plenipotentiary Korean Embassy, France, Mexico, 1966-68; vice minister for def. devel. Ministry of Def., Seoul, 1970-73; pres., CEO Korea Tacoma Shipbuilding Indsl. Co., Korea, 1973-76, Buyeon Co., Ltd. Seoul, 1976-86; cons. United Tech./Martin Marieta, 1976-85. Mem. Korean Heavy Industrialization Com., Seoul, 1970-73. Recipient Eulchi and two Gold Stars, Chungmoo Meritorious Svc. medals, Korea, 1952, 53, Korean Disting. Svc. medal, 1955; decorated U.S. Disting. Flying Cross, U.S. Air medal, Repub. of China Disting. Svc. medal. Mem. The Disting. Flying Cross Soc. (life), Ministry of Nat. Def. of Korea (rsch. assoc.). Avocations: photography, art collecting, golf. Personal E-mail: yulyoon@hotmail.com.

YOON, HYUNG-DOO, publisher, educator; b. Kobe, Japan, Dec. 27, 1935; s. Min-sik Yoon and Cheo-rye Kim; m. Shin Young-sook; three children. Grad., Grad. Sch. Mass. Comms., Seoul, 1984, Grad. Sch. Bus. Adminstrn., 1975; LLM, Dongkuk U., 1963, PhD in Pub. Sci., 2002. Pres. Bumwoo Publ. co., Seoul, 1966—. Vis. prof. Grad. Sch. Mass. Comm., 1991—. Author: Passing By, Passing It Away, 1979, At the Seashore of Vastitude, 1987, The Theory of Publishing Currency, 1989, The Way of Book and Mine, 1994, The Deceit and Truth of Korean Publication, 2002, Love of Mountains, Books and Country; editor: The History of Books In a Glance, 1997. Mem. Korean Publ. Assn. (bd. dirs. 1978—, v.p. 1992-94), Publ. Sci. Soc. (pres. 1989-95, 1999-2003), Korean Publ. Sci. Soc. (adv. 1996—), Korean Soc. Journalism & Comm. Studies (bd. dirs. 1990-92). Office: Bumwoo Publ Co 21-1 Gusu-dong Mapo-gu 121-130 Seoul Republic of Korea

YOON, JAY MYOUNG, oncologist, hematologist, internist; b. Korea, Sept. 30, 1946; married. BA Coll. Liberal Arts & Sci. summa cum laude, Seoul Nat. U., 1967, MD summa cum laude, 1971. Diplomate Am. Bd. Internal Medicine, 1978, Am. Bd. Oncology, 1979, Am. Bd. Hematology, 1980. Intern Bklyn. Hosp. Ctr-Cornell U., N.Y.C., 1974—75; resident in medicine Bronx-Lebanon Hosp.-Albert Einstein Coll. Medicine, N.Y.C., 1975—76; fellow in hemat. oncology Baystate Med. Ctr. Tufts U. Sch. Medicine, Springfield, Mass., 1976—78; fellow in oncology Roswell Park Cancer Inst. SUNY, Buffalo, 1978—79, rsch. clinician in oncology dept. Roswell Park Cancer Inst., 1979—80, rsch. instr. medicine, 1978—80; attending physician, med. oncologist St. Francis Hosp. and Health Ctr., Clarian Health Ptnrs., Beech Grove and Indpls., 1980—98; rsch. instr. medicine SUNY 1978—80; prof. medicine Ulsan U. Med. Sch., 1997—98; CEO, pres. Yoon Clinic, P.C., Edmonds, Wash., 1999—; mem. med. staff Stevens Meml. Hosp., Edmonds, 1999—, Northwest Hosp., Seattle, 1999—, Swedish Med. Ctr., Seattle, 2000. Contbr. articles to profl. jours. Mem. AAAS, AMA, ADA, AACR, Am. Assn. Blood Banks, Am. Soc. Clin. Oncology, Am. Soc. Hematology, N.Y. Acad. Sci. Home: 11901 59th Ave W Mukilteo WA 98275-5569 Office: Yoon Clinic PC Edmonds Med and Profl Ctr 7631 212th St SW Ste 106 B Edmonds WA 98026-7565 Office Phone: 425-778-5551. Office Fax: 425-697-6222. Personal E-mail: yoonclinic@comcast.net.

YOON, WONYONG, computer scientist, researcher; b. Busan, Republic of Korea, Sept. 7, 1971; s. Chul Yoon and Myogeum Shin; m. Eunsil Choi, June 29, 2003; 1 child, Emily. Bachelor, Seoul Nat. U., 1996, Master, 1998; PhD, Info. and Comm. U., Daejon, Republic of Korea, 2002. Sr. rschr. Samsung Electronics, Kiheung, Republic of Korea, 2002—04; rsch. assoc. U. of Ill. at Urbana-Champaign, 2004—. Voting mem. IEEE 802.15 Working Group, 2003—04. Author jour. articles and conf. papers. Tchg. disabled people, Sungnam, Kyunggi, 2002; helping area devastated by typhoon Youngdong, Choongnam, 2002; sci. classes with elem. sch. students Yongin, Kyunggi, 2003. Recipient The 1st Inside Edge Paper Contest Bronze award, Samsung Electromechanics, 2005; scholar, Info. and Comm. U., 1998; Entrance Distinction Scholarship, Seoul Nat. U., 1990, Rsch. Fellowship, Ministry of Info. and Comm., Republic of Korea, 2004—06. Achievements include development of Bluetooth scatternet; patents for Wireless Communication System and Method; Adaptive Tree-Based Recovery Method for Reliable Multicast; development of Many-To-Many Reliable Multicast Protocol; Conflict avoidance and resolution for distributed MBOA MAC; Power save for distributed MBOA MAC; Associated Devices Information Element and Faster Association; MAC Enhancement Considerations for Multimedia Streaming; Application-aware Channel Time Allocation for High Rate WPAN; patents for Method of Reservation of Multicast Slots in Wireless Networks; Method of Power Save in Reservation Slots in Wireless Networks; Method of Reservation Conflict Avoidance and Resolution in Wireless Networks; Spatial Reuse of Channel Resource in Wireless Personal Area Networks; Channel Time Allocation Method in Wpan; Wireless Communication Method Adapting Priority for Transmitting Packets in Wpan; Channel Time Allocation Method in High Rate Wpan; Short-Range Wireless Communication System and a Handoff Processing Method Therefor. Avocation: walking. Home: 1022 E Kerr Ave #301 Urbana IL 61802 Office: Univ of Illinois Urbana-Champaign 1308 E Main St Urbana IL 61801 Office Phone: 217-244-5791. Personal E-mail: wyyoon@crhc.uiuc.edu.

YOON, YOUNG-SUP, medical educator; Asst. prof. Sch. Medicine Tufts U., Boston, 2003—. Contbr. articles to profl. jours. Grantee, NIH, 2004, 2005. Mem.: Am. Heart Assn. (Young Investigator's award 2004). Achievements include patents in field. Office: Caritas St Elizabeth's Medical Center 736 Cambridge Street Boston MA 02135 Office Phone: 617-562-7523. Office Fax: 617-789-3111. Business E-Mail: young.yoon@tufts.edu.

YOPCONKA, NATALIE ANN CATHERINE, executive secretary, computer specialist, educator, entrepreneur, small business owner; b. Taylor, Pa., July 21, 1942; d. Michael Joseph and Natalie Ann Lucille (Panek) Y. BS in Bus. Adminstrn., Pers. and Indsl. Rels. with high honors, U. Md., 1965; MBA, George Washington U., 1976, MA in Edn. and Human Devel., 1988; postgrad. in venture capital and entrepreneurship, U. Md., 1990—96. Mgmt. analyst, adminstrv. trainee, computer programmer U.S. Dept. Commerce, Maritime Adminstrn., Washington, 1965-67; computer programmer, computer specialist U.S. Dept. Labor, Washington, 1967-78; instr. computer sci. Assn. for Computing Machinery, Washington, 1978; instr. computer sci. and mgmt. tech. Montgomery Coll., Takoma Park and Rockville, Md., 1979; sr. programmer analyst Dynamic Data Processing, Inc., Silver Spring, Md., 1979; instr. Nat. Bus. Sch., Inc., Alexandria, Va., 1980; cons. McLeod Corp., Washington, 1980; lectr. computer sci., coop. coord. U. Md., College Park, 1980-81; sr. adminstrv. applications analyst programmer Data Transformation Corp., Washington, 1981; sr. sys. analyst Singer Link Simulation Sys. Divsn., Silver Spring, 1981-82; accessory designer Transart Corp., 1982-83; market rschr. Washington Fin. Svc., 1982-83; lectr. computer info. and sys. sci. U. D.C., Rockville, Md. 1983; prof. computer programming and mgmt. info. sys. Benjamin Franklin U., Washington, 1983; rschr. info. U.S.A., Potomac, Md., 1983-85; admissions rep. Brook-Wein Bus. Washington, 1985; pvt. distbr. Hyattsville, Md., 1979—86; distbr. AMWAY Corp., 1979—93. Course developer, instr. Grad. Sch. USDA, Balt., 1986-87; field interviewer Nat. Drug Abuse Bur., 1989-90; chmn. Cert. for Computing Profs. Exam. Review Course for Balt. Washington, D.C. corridor, 1994-95; agent Kivex, Inc., 1996-97, 3COM Corp., 1997-99, Information Builders, Inc., 1997-2000; bus. owner, cons., computer specialist, application developer, educator, salesperson Sys. and Edn. Enterprises, 1979—. Mem. Takoma Park Disability Com., Mayor's Com. on Energy, Housing and Planning, 1980-81; mem. Vision 2030 Balt./Howard County, 2002-2003; mem. Missionary Oblates of Immaculate Mary; choir Our Lady of Sorrows Cath. Ch., 1977-82, St. John the Evangelist Cath. Ch., eucharistic min. 1990-2003, internet com., 1996-97, lector, 2003-05; mem. Balt. Wash. Corridor E Com.1996-97, citizens adv. com. to Bd. Edn. Howard County, 1991-92, computer adv. com., 1993-95; chair Leukemia Soc. Md., 1996; active Suburban Md. High Tech. Coun. Chgo., Howard County High Tech. Coun., 1994-95; sec., mem. T.R.I.A.D./S.A.L.T. for Howard County; mem. Howard County Council for the Arts, Leukemia Soc. of Md., 1996. Mem. AARP, NAFE, IEEE (Balt. sect., earlier Washington sect., computer soc., commn. soc., tech. com. on software engring., stds. coms. and groups, software standards assn.),

ASCD, ASTD, IEEE, IEEE Computer Soc. (tech. com. on software engring., software engring. stds. coms. and groups), Software Stds. Assn., Info. Sys. Audit and Control Assn., Assn. Computing Machinery (DC chpt., edn. com., instr. 1978-79, edn. com. 1980-81, profl. devel. com. 1982-83), Data Processing Mgmt. Assn. (chmn. cert. for computing profls. exam. rev. course for Balt.-Washington corridor 1994-95), Balt. Washington Info. Sys. Educators (consortium com. 1984-85, program com. for 1986 regional tng. conf. 1985-86, vendor com. 1988-89), Fed. Automatic Data Processing Users Group (com. mem. 1976-1983), Armed Forces Comm. and Electronics Assn., Balt. Coun. Fgn. Affairs, Nat. Active and Ret. Fed. Employees Assn. (sec. Howard County chpt.), Nat. Bus. Edn. Assn., U. Md. Howard County Alumni Club (scholarship com. 1989), Columbia (Md.) Assn., Phi Delta Gamma (scholarship com. 1977-78, social com. 1980-81, hospitality com. 1982-83, sec. 1989-90). Achievements include first to write software engineering standards.

**YORIKAWA, HIROHARU,** physicist, researcher; b. Hyogo, Japan, Aug. 4, 1958; s. Mineo and Yaeko (Kobayashi) Y. BS, Sci. U. Tokyo, 1983, MS, 1985, DSc, 1989. Rsch. asst. Utsunomiya (Japan) U., 1989—. Contbr. articles to Phys. Rev. B, Solid State Comms., Synthetic Metals, Appl. Phys. Lett., others. Mem. Phys. Soc. Japan. Avocation: painting. Office: Utsunomiya U Faculty of Engring 7-1-2 Youtou Utsunomiya 321-8585 Japan E-mail: yorikawa@cc.utsunomiya-u.ac.jp.

**YORK, CANDACE A.,** marketing professional, writer; b. Lubbock, Tex., Mar. 7, 1954; d. Billy John and Francis Ann York; m. James R. Callahan, Feb. 23, 1947. BFA in Art History, U. Tex., 1976. Archival asst. S.W. collection Tex. Tech. U., Lubbock, 1976—77; claims analyst Met. Life, Austin, Tex., 1977—78; mktg. software engr., info. devel. IBM Corp., Austin, Tex., 1978—. Author: 155 Tips to Protect Your Home and Wealth From Fire, 2003, numerous poems, short stories; contbr. articles to profl. jours. Vol. Austin (Tex.) Cmty. Gardens, 2003—04, Tex. Sch. Blind, 2003. Named Internat. Poet of Merit, Internat. Libr. Poetry, 2001; recipient Excellence award, Soc. Tech. Comm., 1980, Honorable Mention award, Iliad Press, 2001, 1st pl. poetry in motion competition, 2001, 2nd place, Sol poet laureate competition, 2002. Mem.: Assn. Interactive Media, Pub. Rels. Soc. Am. (programs com. Austin chpt. 2003), Acad. Am. Poets, Internat. High IQ Soc. Avocations: poetry, photography, guitar, painting, tai chi. Home: 8210 Bent Tree Rd #213 Austin TX 78759 Personal E-mail: canyork@aol.com.

**YORK, DAVID P.,** prosecutor; b. 1963; m. Annie York; 3 children. BA, Birmingham So. Coll.; JD, Samford U. Asst. dist. atty. Douglas Jud. Cir., 1990—91; assoc. atty. Johnston, Wilkins, Druhan & Holz, 1991—92; asst. dist. atty. 13th Jud. Cir., 1992—97; atty. Pierce, Ledyard, Latta, Wasden & Bowron, Mobile; U.S. atty. (so. dist.) Ala. US Dept. Justice, 2001—05. Office: River View Plz 63 S Royal St Mobile AL 36602*

**YORK, DAVID PIERCE,** music educator, composer, performing company executive; b. Oklahoma City, July 13, 1958; s. Joseph and Lena May Pierce; life ptnr. Chris Korsgaard. B of Music, Oklahoma City U., 1981; MS in Tchg., Portland State U., 1985; PhD, U. Oreg., 2002. Artistic dir. Concord Cmty. of Choirs, Portland, 1992—2001; asst. coord. Oreg. Bach Festival Composer Symposium, Eugene, 1995; dir. music Living Enrichment Ctr., Wilsonville, 1999—2004; artistic dir. Portland Boys Choir, 2003—; dir. music New Thought Ministires Oreg., 2004—05. Composer, dir. David York Ensemble, Portland, 2000—; conductor, arranger Portland Choral Consortium, 1985; dir. Portland Symphonic Boys Choir, 2001—02. Composer: (ballets) Apollo & Hyacinth, 1998, (choral music) Millenium Mosaic, 1999, (Operas) Jonathan & David, 2002, (women's chorus) Dreamers, (men's chorus) Requiem. Named 1st pl. winner, Oklahoma City U., 1981; scholar, U. Oreg., Eugene, 2000. Mem.: Internat. Fedn. Choral Musicians, Am. Choral Dirs. Assn., Chorus Am. Office: David York Ensemble PO Box 2636 Portland OR 97208 Business E-Mail: davidyork@davidyorkensemble.org.

**YORK, DOUGLAS ARTHUR,** manufacturing and construction company executive; b. Centralia, Ill., June 5, 1940; s. Harry Bernice and Violet Alvera (Johnstone) Y.; m. Linda Kay McIntosh, Sept. 13, 1958; children: deborah Ann, Darren Anthony. Student, San Diego Jr. Coll., 1957. With Meredith & Simpson Constrn. Co./DBA Pressure Cool Co., Indio, Calif., 1958—, v.p., 1968—, sec., gen. mgr., 1976-82, pres., 1982—. Mem. Bldg. and Housing Appeals Bd., City of Indio, City of Coachella, Calif.; bd. dirs. Coachella Valley Wild Bird Ctr., Coachella Valley Mus.; mem. adv. com. Coachella Valley Enterprise Zone; trustee Eisenhower Med. Ctr., Rancho Mirage, Calif. Mem. ASHRAE, Internat. Conf. Bldg. Ofcls. Republican. Office: 83-801 Ave 45 Indio CA 92201

**YORK, E. TRAVIS,** retired academic administrator; b. Mentone, Ala., July 4, 1922; s. E.T. and Leila (Hixon) Y.; m. Vermelle Cardwell, Dec. 26, 1946; children: Lisa Carol, Travis Loften. BS, Auburn U., 1942, MS, 1946, DSc (hon.), 1982; PhD, Cornell U., 1949; postgrad., George Washington U., 1957-59; DSc (hon.), U. Fla., 1984, Ohio State U., 1996, NC State U., 2003. Rsch. fellow Cornell U., Ithaca, 1946-49; Assoc. prof. N.C. State Coll., 1949-52, prof., 1952-56, head dept. agronomy, 1953-56; Eastern dir. Am. Potash Inst., 1956-59; dir. Ala. Extension Service, Auburn U., 1959-61; adminstr. Fed. Extension Service, U.S. Dept. Agr., 1961-63; provost for agr. U. Fla., 1963-67, v.p. agrl. affairs, 1967-73, exec. v.p., interim pres., 1973-74, Disting. Svc. prof., 1988-96. Chancellor State U. System of Fla., 1975—80, chancellor emeritus, 1980—. Mem. Am. Food for Peace Coun., 1961-62, Freedom from Hunger Com., 1961-62, Pres.'s Panel Vocat. Edn., 1961-62; chmn. coun. grad. edn. in agrl. scis. So. Regional Edn. Bd., 1964-66, mem., 1975-80, exec. com., 1978-80, mem. pres. coun., Pres.' Sci. Adv. Coun. Task Force on World Food Problems, 1966-67; senate, exec. com. Nat. Assn. State Univs. and Land Grant Colls., 1967-70; mem. Edn. Commn. of States, 1975-79, steering com., 1977-79, treas., exec. com., 1978-79; bd. dirs. Nat. 4-H Svc. Com., 1963-75, AV Med. Corp., Santa Fe, 1987-96; trustee, bd. dirs Hlth Improvement Inc mem., 1996-98, exec. com. Nat. 4-H Found., 1968-73; mem.-at-large nat. coun. Boy Scouts Am., 1962-75; dir., pres. Alpha Gamma Rho Edn. Found., 1965-72; bd. dirs. Nat. Ctr. for Voluntary Action, 1970-74; mem. Bd. for Internat. Food and Agrl. Devel., 1980-86, chmn., 1983-86; trustee Escuela Agrícola Panamericana, 1980-88, Found. for Agronomic Rsch., 1980-92; tech. adv. com., cons. Group for Internat. Agrl. Rsch., 1983-89; trustee Agronomic Sci. Found., 1989-92; chmn. bd. Internat. Fertilizer Devel. Ctr., 1999-2004. Officer AUS, 1943-45. Recipient B.B. Comer award excellence natural sci. Auburn U., 1942; disting. svc. award Fla. Vet. Med. Assn., 1966; Nat. 4-H Alumni award, 1967; George Washington honor medal award Freedoms Found., 1967; nat. ptnr. in 4-H award, 1970; disting. faculty award U. Fla., Fla. Blue Key, 1972; E.T. York, Jr. disting. svc. award U. Fla., 1973; honors medal U. Fla. Acad. Scis., 1974; E.T. York svc. award Fla. Bd. Regents, 1983, disting. svc. award Am. Farm Bur., 1991, Svc. Above Self award Rotary Internat., 1994, Medal of Honor, DAR, 1998, Lifetime Achievement award Auburn U., 2006; named to Fla. Agrl. Hall of Fame, 1990, Ala. Agrl. Hall of Honor, 1995, Internat. Adult and Continuing Edn. Hall of Fame, 1996; designated as great Floridian, Fla. History Mus., 1997. Fellow AAAS, Am. Soc. Agronomy, Soil Sci. Soc. Am., AM. Crop Sci. Soc.; mem. Am. Soc. Hort. Sci. (hon.), Assn. So. Agrl. Scientists (pres. 1968), Blue Key, Rotary (dist. gov. 1981-82), Sigma Xi, Phi Kappa Phi, Alpha Zeta, Gamma Sigma Delta (Internat. Disting. Svc. award 1973), Omicron Delta Kappa, Phi Delta Kappa, Epsilon Sigma Phi, Alpha Gamma Rho (named to Hall of Fame 1982). Methodist. Home: 5200 SW 25th Blvd # 4216 Gainesville FL 32608-8925 Business E-Mail: etyork@ufl.edu.

**YORK, GARY ALAN,** lawyer; b. Glendale, Calif., Aug. 29, 1943; m. Lois York, 1987; 1 child, Jonathan Alan. BA, Pomona Coll., 1965; LLB, Stanford U., 1968. Bar: Calif. 1968. Ptnr. Dewey Ballantine, L.A., 1985-95, Buchalter, Nemer, Fields & Younger, L.A., 1995-98, Le Boeuf, Lamb, Greene & MacRae, L.A., 1998—2002. Mem. ABA (chmn. real estate fin. com., real property probate and trust sect. 1987-89, chmn. usury com. 1992-93), L.A. County Bar Assn. (chmn. real estate fin. sect. 1993-96, exec. com. 1995—),

State Bar of Calif., Am. Coll. Real Estate Lawyers, Am. Coll. Mortgage Attys. Office: Baker & Hostetler LLP 333 S Grand Ave Ste 1800 Los Angeles CA 90071 E-mail: GYork@Bakerlaw.com.

**YORK, HERBERT FRANK,** physics professor; b. Rochester, NY, Nov. 24, 1921; s. Herbert Frank and Nellie Elizabeth (Lang) Y.; m. Sybil Dunford, Sept. 28, 1947; children: David Winters, Rachel, Cynthia. AB, U. Rochester, 1942, MS, 1943; PhD, U. Calif., Berkeley, 1949; DSc (hon.), Case Inst. Tech.; 1960; LL.D., U. San Diego, 1964, Claremont Grad. Sch., 1974. Physicist Radiation Lab., U. Calif., Berkeley, 1943-58, assoc. dir., 1954-58; asst. prof. physics dept. U. Calif., Berkeley, 1951-54, assoc. prof., 1954-59, prof., 1959-61; dir. Lawrence Radiation Lab., Livermore, 1952-58; chief scientist Advanced Rsch. Project Agy., U.S. Dept. Def., 1958; dir. advanced rsch. projects divsns Inst. for Def. Analyses, 1958; dir. def. rsch. and engring. Office Sec. Def., 1958-61; chancellor U. Calif.-San Diego, 1961—64, acting chancellor, 1970—72, prof. physics, 1964—88, prof. emeritus, 1988—; chmn. dept. physics, 1968-69, dean grad. studies, 1969-70, dir. program on sci., tech. and pub. affairs, 1972-88; dir. Inst. Global Conflict and Cooperation, 1983-88, dir. emeritus, 1988—. Amb. Comprehensive Test Ban Negotiations, 1979-81; trustee Aerospace Corp., Inglewood, Calif., 1961-87; mem. Pres.'s Sci. Adv. Com., 1957-58, 64-68, vice chmn., 1965-67; trustee Inst. def. Analysis, 1963-96; gen. adv. com. ACDA, 1962-69; mem. Def. Sci. Bd., 1977-81; spl. rep. of sec. def. at space arms control talks, 1978-79; mem. task force future nat. labs. Sec. Emergy, 1994-95; cons Stockholm Internat. Peach Rsch. Inst.; rschr. in application atomic energy to nat. def. problems of arms control and disarmament, elem. particles. Author: Race to Oblivion, 1970, Arms Control, 1973, The Advisors, 1976, Making Weapons, Talking Peace, 1987, Does Strategic Defense Breed Offense?, 1987, (with Sanford Lakoff) A Shield in the Sky, 1989, Arms and the Physicist, 1994; also numerous articles on arms or disarmament; bd. dirs. Bull. Atomic Scientists. Trustee Bishop's Sch., La Jolla, Calif., 1963-65. Recipient E.O. Lawrence award AEC, 1962, Vannevan Bush award, 2000, Clark Kerr award, 2000, Enrico Fermi award, 2000; Guggenheim fellow, 1972. Fellow AAAS, Am. Phys. Soc. (forum on physics and soc. award 1976, Leo Szilard award 1994), Am. Acad. Arts and Sci.; mem. Fedn. Am. Scientists (chmn. 1970-71, exec. com. 1969-76, 95-2000, pub. svc. award 1992), Pugwash Movement 1969—, Phi Beta Kappa, Sigma Xi. Office Phone: 858-459-1776. Business E-Mail: hyork@uscd.edu.

**YORK, JAMES ORISON,** real estate executive; b. Brush, Colo., June 27, 1927; s. M. Orison and Marie L. (Kibble) Y.; m. Janice Marie Sjoberg, Aug. 1, 1959; children: Douglas James, Robert Orison. Student, U. Calif. at Berkeley, 1945-46; BA cum laude, U. Wash., 1949. Tchg. fellow U. Wash., Seattle, 1950-52; econ. rsch. analyst Larry Smith & Co. Real Estate, Seattle, 1953-60, ptrn., 1960-66, pres. San Francisco, 1966-71; pres., chief exec. officer R.H. Macy Properties, N.Y.C., also sr. v.p. planning and devel. dir. R.H. Macy & Co., Inc., 1971-88; chmn. James York Assocs. (real estate and venture capital), 1988—. Dir. emeritus UBP Properties, Inc.; chmn., N.Y.C. retail div. Am. Cancer Soc. Contbg. author: Shopping Towns-USA, 1960. Trustee ICSC Ednl. and Rsch. Found. With USNR, 1945-47. Recipient Disting. Alumnus award Econs. U. Wash., 1989. Fellow Phi Beta Kappa; mem. Am. Soc. Real Estate Counselors, Urban Land Inst., Internat. Real Estate Fedn., Internat. Council Shopping Centers, Lambda Alpha. Clubs: Olympic (San Francisco); American Yacht (Rye, N.Y.); Corinthian Yacht (Seattle); Union League (N.Y.C.); Knights of Malta, Order St. John, Washington Athletic (Seattle), Royal Victoria (B.C.) Yacht. Episcopalian. Home and Office: 4 Riverstone Laguna Niguel CA 92677-5309 also: Sunrise Country Club 6 Malaga Dr Rancho Mirage CA 92270-3820 Personal E-mail: jysail@aol.com.

**YORK, JAMES WESLEY, JR.,** theoretical physicist, educator; b. Raleigh, NC, July 3, 1939; s. James Wesley and Mary Smedes (Poyner) York; children: Virginia York Setzer, Guilford Mattern. BS with high honors in Physics, N.C. State U., Raleigh, 1962, PhD in Physics, 1966. Asst. prof. N.C. State U. Raleigh, 1965-68; rsch. assoc. Princeton U., 1968-69, lectr., 1969-70, asst. prof., 1970-73; assoc. prof. U. N.C., Chapel Hill, 1973-77, prof. dept. physics, 1977-89, Agnew H. Bahnson, Jr. disting. prof. physics, 1989—2001, dir. Inst. Field Physics, 1984-90; vis. asst. prof. U. Md., College Park, 1972; prof. associe U. Paris, 1976; vis. scientist ctr. astrophysics Harvard, Smithsonian, Cambridge, 1977; vis. prof. U. Tex., Austin, 1979, 87; prof. physics Cornell U., 2002—. Spkr. Internat. Symposium on Methods of Differential Geometry in Physics and Mechanics, Warsaw, 1976; spr. in field; Alfred Schild Meml. lectr. U. Tex., 1979; del. Seventh Internat. Congress on Math. Physics, Boulder, Colo., 1983, Tex. Symposium on Relativistic Astrophysics, Jerusalem, 1984, Marcel Grossman Meeting, Rome, 1985, Jerusalem, 97, Rio de Janeiro, 2003, NATO Advanced Study Inst., Les Houches, France, 1982, Huelva, Spain, 92, Paris, 92, Banff, Canada, 92, other internat. and nat. meetings; co-organizer sci. meetings including Neutron stars and pulsars, Princeton, 1969; Spacetime dynamics Aspen Ctr. for Theoretical Physics, 1981, Classical Problems in Gravitation, 1990, Cosmic Censorship, 1992; coord. lectr. Inst. Theoretical Physics U. Calif., Santa Barbara, 2000; mem. com. of visitors physics divsn NSF, 1991; plenary lectr. Fifth Can. Conf. on Gen. Relativity and Astrophysics, Waterloo, 1993, Directions in Gen. Relativity, College Park, Md., 1993, Pacific Coast Gravity Mtg., Salt Lake City, 1996, 2d Samos meeting, Greece, 1998; plenary lectr. 50 Years of the Cauchy Problem, Cargese, Corsica, 2002; hon. physics chmn. Cornelius Lanczos Internat. Centenary, Raleigh, NC, 1993; vis. prof. dept. physics N.C. State U., 1998—99, Inter-Instl. Disting. prof. physics, 2001—02. Mem. editl. bd. Jour. Math. Physics, 1989-92; contbr. chpts. to books, articles to sci. jours. Decorated Companion of St. Patrick; 1960; Ford Found. fellow, 1962-65, NSF postdoctoral fellow, 1969-70; Battelle Found. grantee, 1967, Nat. Rsch. Com. France grantee, 1976, NSF grantee, 1974— travel grantee, 1971, 76, 83, 84; U.S.A.-Israel Binat. Sci. Found. grantee, 1987-90, 90-93, Kenan Found. grantee, 1990, W.N. Reynolds Found. grantee, 1998; recipient Disting. Alumnus award, 1997, Marcel Grossmann prize, Rio de Janeiro, 2003; co-winner Dannie Heineman prize for math. physics Am. Phys. Soc., 2003. Fellow Am. Phys. Soc.; mem. AAAS, Internat. Soc. Gen. Relativity and Gravitation, Phi Beta Kappa, Sigma Xi, Phi Kappa Phi, Tau Beta Pi, Sigma Pi Sigma, Pi Mu Epsilon, Phi Eta Sigma. Avocations: literature, reading. Office: Cornell U 604 Space Scis Dept Physics Ithaca NY 14853 Business E-Mail: york@astro.cornell.edu E-mail: jaswyork1@mac.com.

**YORK, JEFFREY MICHAEL,** school psychologist; b. N.Y., 1969; s. Gerald and Karole York; m. Therese Mary Carbone, June 14, 2003; children: Anthony Carbone, Alexander. MA, Cleve. State U., 1996. Lic. sch. psychologist State Bd. of Psychology, Ohio, State of Ohio Dept. of Psychology. Sch. psychologist Summit County Ednl. Svc. Ctr., Cuyahoga Falls, Ohio, 1996—98, Akron (Ohio) Pub. Schs., 1998—. Mem.: NASP (assoc.), Ohio Sch. Psychologists Assn. (assoc. F. Peter Gross Best Practice award 2002). Office: Akron Pub Schs 785 Carnegie Ave Akron OH 44314 Office Phone: 330-848-2069. Office Fax: 330-848-2568.

**YORK, JEROME B.,** investment company executive, former computer retail executive; b. Memphis, June 22, 1938; BS, U.S. Mil. Acad., 1960; MS, MIT, 1961; MBA, U. Mich., 1966. Various engring. positions GM Corp., Pontiac, Mich., 1962-67; dir. strategic planning RCA Corp., Hertz Corp. (subs.), 1970-72, v.p., 1972-75; group v.p. Baker Industries, Inc., Parsippany, NJ, 1976-78; pres. Delta Truck Body Co., Inc., Montgomeryville, Pa., 1978-79; asst. contr. Chrysler de Mex. Chrysler Corp., Highland Park, Mich., 1979-82, mng. dir. Chrysler de Mex., 1982-85, v.p., gen. mgr. Dodge divsn., 1986-90, v.p., contr. 1989-90, exec. v.p., CFO, 1990-93; sr. v.p., CFO IBM Corp., Armonk, NY, 1993—95; vice chmn. Tracinda Corp., 1995—99; also bd. dirs. IBM Corp., Armonk, NY; chmn., pres., CEO Micro Warehouse, Inc., Norwalk, 2000—03; founder, CEO Harwinton Capital Corp., 2000—. Bd. dirs. Apple Computer, Inc., 1997—, Tyco Internat. Ltd., 2002—, Exide Technologies, 2005—, Metro Goldwyn Mayer, Inc., GM Corp., 2006—.*

**YORK, MICHAEL (MICHAEL YORK-JOHNSON),** actor; b. Fulmer, Eng., Mar. 27, 1942; s. Joseph Gwynne and Florence Edith (Chown) Johnson; m. Patricia McCallum, Mar. 27, 1968. MA, Oxford U., Eng., 1964; DFA (hon.), U. SC. Profl. debut with Dundee Repertory Theatre, Scotland, 1964; mem. Nat. Theatre Co., London, 1965-66; TV film or miniseries appearances include: Much Ado About Nothing, The Forsyte Saga, Rebel in the Grave, True Patriot, Jesus of Nazareth, 1977, A Man Called Intrepid, 1979, The Phantom of the Opera, 1983, The Master of Ballantrae, 1984, Space, 1985, The Far Country, 1985, Are You My Mother, 1986, Ponce de Leon, 1987, Till We Meet Again, 1989, The Road to Avonlea, 1991, Gardens of the World, 1993; The Four Minute Mile, The Lady and the Highway Man, 1988, The Heat of the Day, 1988, The Hunt for Stolen War Treasure, 1989, The Night of the Fox, 1990, The Magic Paintbrush, 1993, David Copperfield's Christmas, 1994, Teklab, 1994, Fall From Grace, 1994, Not of This Earth, 1995, Duel of Hearts, September, 1995, A Young Connecticut Yankee in King Arthur's Court, 1995, A Knight in Camelot, (TV series) Knots Landing, 1987, SeaQuest, 1995, The Naked Truth, 1995, Babylon 5, 1995, The Ring, 1996, Un Coup De Baguette Magique, True Women, 1997, Sliders, 1997, The Magnificat, 1997, the Long way home, 1997, A Christmas Carol, 1997, The Search for Nazi Gold, 1998, The Ripper 1998, Dead Man's Gun, 1998, Perfect Little Angels, 1998, The Haunting of Hell House, 2000, The Lot, 2000, Founding Fathers, 2002, Liberty's Kids, 2002, Curb Your Enthusiasm, 2002, Founding Brothers, 2002, La Femme Musketeer, 2004, Icon, 2005, The Simpsons, 2006, Law and Order: Criminal Intent, 2006; stage appearances include: Any Just Cause, 1967, Hamlet, 1970, Broadway prodns. of Outcry, 1973, Ring Round the Moon, 1975, Bent, 1980, Cyrano de Bergerac, 1981, Whisper in the Mind, 1990, The Crucible, 1991, Someone Who'll Watch Over Me, 1993, Nora, 1993, Ira Gershwin at 100, 1996, Enoch Arden, 2003, Russian David...Soviet Goliath, 2004, Peer Gynt, 2005, Shadows and Voices, 2005, Camelot, 2006; appeared in motion pictures including: The Taming of the Shrew, 1966, Accident, 1966, Red and Blue, 1967, Smashing Time, 1967, Romeo and Juliet, 1967, The Strange Affair, 1967, The Guru, 1968, Alfred the Great, 1968, Justine, 1969, Something for Everyone, 1969, Zeppelin, 1970, La Poudre D'Escampette, 1971, Cabaret, 1971, England Made Me, 1971, Lost Horizon, 1972, The Three Musketeers, 1973, Murder on the Orient Express, 1974, Great Expectations, 1974, Conduct Unbecoming, 1974, The Four Musketeers, 1975, Logan's Run, 1976, Seven Nights in Japan, The Last Remake of Beau Geste, 1977, The Island of Dr. Moreau, 1977, Fedora, 1977, The Riddle of the Sands, 1978, Final Assignment, 1980, The White Lions, Success is the Best Revenge, Perfect Little Angels, 1998, Dawn, 1985, Vengeance, 1986, The Secret of the Sahara, 1987, Imbalances, 1987, Lethal Obsession, 1987, Midnight Cop, 1988, The Return of the Musketeers, 1989, The Long Shadow, 1991, Eline Vere, 1991, Wide Sargasso Sea, 1991, Rochade, 1991, Discretion Assured, Shadow of a Kiss, 1993, Gospa, 1994, Goodbye America, Austin Powers, Dark Planet, The Treat, 1997, Wrongfully Accused, 1998, One Hell of a Guy, 1998, Lovers of Liars, 1998, The Ghostly Rental, 1999, Austin Powers: The Spy Who Shagged Me, 1999, The Omega Code, 1999, Borstal Boy, 2000, Megiddo, 2001, Austin Powers in Goldmember, 2002, Moscow Heat, 2004; radio performances The Dark Tower, 1977, (Peabody award), A Matter of Honor, 1986, Babbitt, 1987, The Crucible, 1988, Are You Now, UTZ, 1989, McTeague, 1992, Make and Break, 1993; recs. include: Mere Christianity, 1982, Anna Karenina, 1985, Don Quixote, 1986, The King Must Die, 1988, British Rock: The First Wave, UTZ, 1989, The Modigliani Scandal, 1989, The Mummy, 1989, Candide, 1989, The Vampire Lestat, 1989, The Berlin Stories, 1990, The Remains of the Day, 1990, City of Joy, 1991, Beyond Love, 1991, Memories, Dreams, Reflections, 1991, A Poet's Bible, 1992, Einstein's Dreams, 1993, Accidentally on Purpose, 1993, The English Patient, 1993, Fortune's Favorite, 1993, The Three Musketeers, 1993, Paradise Lost, 1993, The Book of Psalms, 1994, The Book of Virtues, 1994, The MagicPaw-Paw, 1994; (recs.) The Rubaiyat of Omar Khayyam, 1995, Aesop's Fables, 1995, The Poetry of Edgar Allen Poe, 1995, The Hunting of the Snark, Caesar's Women, 1996, Treasure Island, 1996, (Grammy nomination) The Wind in the Willows, 1996, Rose, 1996, Daily Word, 1997, Les Miserables, 1998, Caesar, 1998, Brave New World, 1998, Titanic Hearings, 1998, The Fencing Master, 1999 (Audie award), Rikki Tikki Tavi, 1999, King Rat, 1999, Going Home: Jesus and Buddha, 2000, The Lion, The Witch and The Wardrobe, 2000, A Shakespearean Actor Prepares, 2002, The Theory of Everything, 2003, Creating True Peace, 2003, The Bounty, 2003, Goodbye to Berlin, 2004, The Final Solution, 2004, For the Time Being: Advent, 2005, Jane Goodall's Message of Peace, How Do I Love Thee?, 2006; author: The Courage of Conviction, 1985, Voices of Survival, 1987; author: Accidentally on Purpose, 1992, A Shakespearean Actor Prepares, 2000, Dispatches From Armageddon, 2002, Are My Blinkers Showing?, 2005. Chmn. Calif. Youth Theatre. Decorated officer Order Brit. Empire, chevalier Nat. Order Arts and Letters (France). Avocations: travel, music, art. Office: Metropolitan Talent Agency 4500 Wilshire Blvd Fl 2 Los Angeles CA 90010-3858 Office Phone: 323-857-4500.

**YORK, RICHARD,** sociologist, educator; b. May 6, 1971; m. Theresa Koford, June 21, 1997. PhD, Wash. State U., Pullman, Wash., 2002. Asst. prof. of sociology U. Oreg., Eugene, 2002—. Mem. bd. Siskiyou Project, Grants Pass, Oreg., 2005—06. Recipient Outstanding Publ. award, Environment and Tech. Sect. of the Am. Sociol. Assn., 2004. Mem.: Am. Sociol. Assn. Atheist. Avocations: hiking, camping. Office: Univ of Oreg 1291 Univ of Oregon Eugene OR 97403-1291 E-mail: rfyork@uoregon.edu.

**YORK, TINA,** painter; b. Germany, Feb. 9, 1951; Student, Sch. Mus. Fine Arts, Boston, 1967-71; studied with, George Dergalis, Wayland, Mass., 1967-75; BA cum laude, Brandeis U., 1978; postgrad., N.Y. Med. Coll., 1980-83. Contbr. works to numerous publs., 1987-2003; one woman shows include Gallery Contemporary Art, Provincetown, Mass., 1969, Springfield (Mass.) Art Assn., 1971, Copley Soc., Boston, 1972-73, Boston U., 1974, Mendler Gallery, Rockport, Mass., 1974, Cambridge (Mass.) Art Assn., 1975, Ames Gallery, N.Y.C., 1976, Gallery Seven, Boston, 1977, Brandeis U., Waltham, Mass., 1978, Rue Oker Gallery of Art, Sturbridge, Mass., 1979, Art Collection Gallery, N.Y.C., 1981, 133 Gallery, Inc., N.Y.C., 1982, Creative Concepts, L.A., 1984, Alpha Contemporary Exhibits, L.A., 1985, Darraby Gallery, L.A., 1986, 8th St. Gallery, L.A., 1986, Koplin Gallery, L.A., 1987, Galerie Beverly Hills, Calif., 1988, Conv. Ctr., Rome, 1988, Merck, Sharpe & Dohme, Rahway, N.J., 1988, Erlangen Kultur Borse, Germany, 1989, Arwell Gallery, Laguna, Calif., 1989, Deutsch-Amerikanisches Inst., Regensburg, Germany, 1990, Art in Pub. Bldgs., Nuremberg, Germany, 1990, Art Expo, N.Y.C., 1990, Amerikahaus, Nuremberg, 1990, Art 5, Nuremberg, 1990, Dresdner Bank, Nuremberg, 1990, Amer. Hosp. Assn., Washington, 1990, So. Med. Assn., Nashville, 1990, 94-95, Studio Gallery, North Hollywood, Calif., 1991-92, Galerie Lehman, Germany, Galerie Sud, Studio la Citta, Italy, Studio Gallery, Calif., 1991 La Foire Internat. d'Art Contemporain, Paris, 1992, 94, Med. Heritage Gall., Waco, Tex., 1991, Herbstmesse, Frankfurt, Germany, 1992-93, Kunstforum Internat., Aachen, Germany, 1993, Kunstlerhaus, Germany, 1993, Ambiente, Frankfurt, 1993-98, 2000-03, ART/LA, 1993-95, Internat. Art Fair, Czechoslovakia, 1993-2003, Art Fair, Seattle, 1993-94, Art Expo, Chgo., 1993-94, Frankfurter Buchmesse, Frankfurt, Germany, 1993, Art Expo, N.Y.C., 1993-96, Chgo. Trade Show, 1993, 95, 97, Toronto Trade Show, 1993, Art Cologne, Germany, 1993-94, 96, Centre d'Art Contemporain, Switzerland, Dresdner Bank, Germany, Galerie Littmann, Switzerland, Galerie Fischer, 1994, Art Asia, Hong Kong, 1994-96, Art Expo, Calif., 1994, 96, PPFA Toronto Trade Show, 1994-95, Limited Edit. Expo, New Orleans, 1994-95, Frankfurt Book Fair, 1994, 97-98, 2000, 03, Internat. Spring Fair, Birmingham, Eng., 1994, 95, Art Miami, 1994-95, Exposition of Art, Sydney, Australia, 1993, Art Taipei, Taiwan, 1993, 94, 95, Art Santa Fe, 1993-95, NASA Ames Rsch. Ctr., Moffett Field, Calif., 1994, NASA Johnson Space Ctr., Houston, 1995, Galerie Rudelko, Germany, Scheffler Galerie, Germany, 1995, Studio Gall., Ariz., 1996, Jahns House, Germany, 1996, Internat. Contemporary Art Fair, Madrid, 1995, West Valley Mus. Art, Phoenix, 1998, Las Vegas Art Mus., 2000, Paul Joseph Galleries, Las Vegas, 2002, Rio Decor, 2003, Tina York Studio, Naples, Fla., 2003, Marco Island Art Assn., Fla. 2004, Studio Gallery, Naples, 2004, 06, Area Arts Gallery, Naples, Fla., 2005, I.C. Fine Art 2000 Gallery, Las Vegas, 2005; group shows include Area Arts Gallery, Naples, NASA Art Programs, Washington, Mus. Fine Arts, Salt Lake City, Mus. Art, Las Vegas, Regional Mus. Art, Bautzen, Germany, Mus. Art, Downey, Calif., Carter Ctr., Atlanta; represented in permanent collections, Paul Joseph Galleries, Las Vegas, Rio Decor, Mus. of Art, Las Vegas, Downey (Calif.) Mus. Art, Mus. Fine Arts, Salt Lake City, Mcpl. Art Mus., Osaka, Japan, Regional Mus. Art, Bautzen, Germany, Carter Ctr., Atlanta, Kennedy Space Ctr., Fla., New Zealand Space Adminstrn., Auckland, NASA, Internat. Peace Acad., NY, USIA, BBC (Brit. Broadcasting Co.), Lagan Jute, Ltd., India, NIH, Universitet Kliment Orchridski, Bulgaria, Hiatt Internat., Beverly Hills, Calif., Paris, Gallery Dmovrosek, Yugoslavia, Columbia U., Nat. Cancer Inst., Md., Kulturamt der Stadt Nurnberg, Germany, Planetary Soc., Calif., Mayo Clin., Ariz., Nat. Air and Space Mus., Washington, Nat. Air and Space Mus., others; represented on Artrain USA; pub. NASA/Exploration of Space, 2004. First prize painting Arts Fest., Scituate, MA, 1969, Internatl. Show, Fall River, MA, 1971; third prize mixed media painting, De Cordova Mus., Lincoln, MA, 1972; second prize painting, Amer. Artists in Paris, Paris, 1975; first prize mixed media painting Inst. Contemporary Art, 1979; Gold medal painting, Spring Arts Fest., LA, 1985; first prize mixed media painting, One Fifty Three Gall., Inc., 1987. Mem.: Internat. High IQ Soc. Studio: Tina York Studio 754 Waterloo Ct Naples FL 34120 Office Phone: 239-659-2941. E-mail: tinayorkstudio@aol.com.

YORK, VERMELLE CARDWELL, retired real estate broker and developer; b. Evergreen, Ala., Jan. 30, 1925; d. Frederick Lofton and Emmie Mildred (Pitts) Cardwell; m. E. Travis York, Jr., Dec. 26, 1946; children: Lisa, Travis. BS, Auburn U., 1946. Pres. Tralisa Corp., Gainesville, Fla., 1966—87, sec., treas., 1988—94, Caret Corp., Gainesville, Fla., 1979—86, pres., 1987—2004; ret., 2004. Mem. devel. com. Harn Mus., Gainesville, 1990-96, Hospice House, Gainesville, 1992-96; co-chair March of Dimes, Gainesville, 1995, Red Ribbon Campaign, 1989, 90; bd. dirs. Keep Alachua County Beautiful, Phillips Ctr. Performing Arts U. Fla.; bd. Gainesville Cmty. Found. Recipient President's Medallion, U. Fla., 1980; named Woman of Distinction, Santa Fe (N.Mex.) C. C., 1989, Van York Theatre at Gainesville Cmty. Playhouse 05 dedicated in her honor; named one of Women Who Make a Difference, Girl Scouts Am., 2005 Mem. Gainesville Builders Assn. (bd. dirs. 1997—), The Heritage Club (mem. amb. com. 1991-96), P.E.O. (pres. 1989-90), Surfside N. Club, (dir. 1988-91), Gainesville Women's Forum (membership chair 1994-96), Altrusa, Rotary, DAR, Phi Kappa Phi. Avocation: genealogy. Home: 5200 SW 25th Blvd #4216 Gainesville FL 32608-8925

YORKE, JAMES ALAN, mathematician, educator; b. Plainfield, N.J., Aug. 3, 1941; married; three children. AB in Math., Columbia U., 1963; PhD in Math., U. Md., 1966. Mem. faculty U. Md., College Park, 1963—, rsch. assoc., Inst. for Physical Sci. & Tech., 1966—67, asst. prof., 1967—69, assoc. prof., 1969—73, prof., 1973—, acting dir. Inst. for Phys. Sci. and Tech. College Park, 1985—88, dir. Inst. for Phys. Sci. and Tech., 1988—2001. Guggenheim fellow, 1980—81. Mem.: AAAS, Soc. Indsl. and Applied Math. Math. Assn. Am., Am. Phys. Soc., Am. Math. Soc. Office: U Md Inst For Phys Sci And Tech College Park MD 20742-2431

YORKE, JOHN BUNDY, lawyer; b. Rock Hill, S.C., Aug. 5, 1954; s. N. Felix and Lane Knox Yorke; children: H. Spencer, N. Greer. BA, Wofford Coll., 1976; JD, Wake Forest U., 1979. Bar: N.C. 1979, S.C. 1987. Assoc. Wardlow, Knox, Knox, Freeman & Scofield, Charlotte, NC, 1979—87; v.p., gen. counsel World Way Corp., 1987—96; gen. counsel Integon Corp., Winston-Salem, NC, 1996—98; mem. Helms Mulliss & Wicker, PLLC, Charlotte, NC, 1998—. Dir. New South Pizza, Inc, Charlotte, NC. Trustee Thompson Child & Family Focus, Charlotte, NC, 2001. Mem.: Wake Forest Law Alumni Bd., N.C. Bar Assn. (bus. corp. counsel sect. 1991—92), ABA, Wofford Coll. Nat. Alumni Assn. (pres. 2001), Phi Beta Kappa. Avocation: golf. Office: Helms Mulliss & Wicker PLLC 201 North Tryon Street Suite 3000 Charlotte NC 28202 Office Phone: 704-343-2167. Office Fax: 704-343-2000. Business E-Mail: john.yorke@hmw.com.

YORKE, MARIANNE, lawyer, real estate executive; b. Nov. 4, 1948; d. Joseph George and Catherine Veronica (Friel) Y. BA, West Chester U., 1971; JD, Temple U., 1980; MS in Ognl. Dynamics, U. Pa., 1987; M in Corp. Real Estate, Internat. Assn. Corp. Real Estate Execs., 1996. Bar: Pa. 1981, N.Y. 1992. Mgr. CIGNA Corp., Phila., 1982-85, asst. dir., 1985-90; v.p. Chase Manhattan Bank, NYC, 1990-92; real estate dir. Johnson & Johnson, 1992—. Real estate atty. Garfinkel & Volpicelli, Phila., 1981—prin., mng. prnr. Yorke/Eisenman, Real Estate, Phila., 1976-89, prin., mng. ptnr. Yorke/Mac Lachlin Real Estate, Phila., 1989-02; lectr. Women in the Arts, 1982-90; guest spkr. Wharton Sch. Bus. Class of 1989, U. Pa., grad. sch. arts and sci. Class of 1988; asst. prof. bus. law Rider U. Grad Sch., 2002 (eve.), asst. prof. real estate law Rutgers U. Grad. Sch., 2003—. Contbr. articles to profl. jours. Solicitor Pa. Ballet, Phila., 1983-90, United Way, Phila., 1983-90; mem. steering com. U. Pa., 1986-90, dir. alumni assn., 1987-90; mem. adv. com. for econ. devel. Luth. Settlement House Adv., 1986-88; mem. Ctr. Adv. Bd., 2000—; bd. dirs. Hamilton Townhouse Assn., Phila., 1988-90, chmn. ins. com., 1989-90, 718 Broadway Inc., NYC, 1990-94, Johnson Health Care Svcs. Recipient Live for Life Mgmt., Johnson Health Mgmt., 1995, Pres. Quality Process Excellence award, EthiconEndo Surgery, 2000, Process Excellence award, Ethicon, Inc., 2001. Mem. ABA (forum on constrn. 1982-90), Pa. Bar Assn. (condominium and zoning com. 1982-90), Assn. of Bar of City of NY (sects. on internat. law and real property law 1992-94), Phila. Bar Assn., Phila. Women Real Estate Atty., CORENET, Nat. Assoc. Corp. Real Estate Exec. (internat. coun. 1984-2002, comml. coun. 1984-2002), Internat. Atty., Roundtable, Women's Law Caucus, Phi Alpha Delta. Independent. Roman Catholic. Home: The Admiralty 55 Ocean Ave Monmouth Beach NJ 07750-1366 Office: Johnson & Johnson W H 7135 1 Johnson & Johnson Plz New Brunswick NJ 08933-0002 Office Phone: 732-524-3881. Business E-Mail: myorke@corus.jnj.com.

YORKE, THOMAS EDWARD, musician, vocalist; b. Wellingborough, England, Oct. 7, 1968; children: Noah, Agnes. Student in English and Art, Exeter U., Eng. Guitarist Flickernoise; orderly; vocalist, guitarist Radiohead, 1992—. Musician & vocalist (Radiohead albums) Pablo Honey, 1993, The Bends, 1995, Ok Computer, 1997 (Grammy award, Best Alternative Music Performance, 1998), Kid A, 2000 (Grammy award, Best Alternative Music Performance, 2001), Amnesiac, 2001, I Might Be Wrong: Live Recordings, 2001, Hail to the Thief, 2003, (solo albums) The Eraser, 2006. Office: Capital Records 1750 North Vine St 10th Floor Hollywood CA 90028 also: Chrysalis Music Group The Chrysalis Building Bramley Rd London W10 6SP England*

YORKE-VINEY, SALLY ANNE, elementary school educator; b. Williamsport, Pa., Dec. 8, 1953; d. H. Allen and Mary Ellen Yearick; m. Malcolm Christopher Stanley Viney, Nov. 26, 1988; 1 child, Colin Patrick Allen Viney. BS in Edn., Shippensburg U., 1975; MEd, East Stroudsburg U., 1993; postgrad., Marywood U., 2002—. Tchr. elem. sch. Selinsgrove Sch. Dist., Pa., 1975—76, Shikellamy Sch. Dist., Sunbury, 1976—82; tech. editor Lambda Techs., N.Y.C., 1983—85; singer/actress AFTRA, SAG Actor's Equity, 1978—85; profl. singer/cabaret artist various Cruise Lines, 1985—91; tchr. elem. sch. East Stroudsburg Sch. Dist., Pa., 1991—2005. Adj. prof. East Stroudsburg U., 1999—2005; chair Arts in Edn. Com., 2003—04. Dir. choir Luth. Ch. of Savior, Mt. Pocono, Pa., 1989—99. Mem.: ASCD, Internat. Reading Assn., Phi Delta Kappa. Avocations: singing, theater. Home: HC89 Box 831 Pocono Summit PA 18346

YORSZ, STANLEY, lawyer; b. Norwich, Conn., June 5, 1953; s. Stanley and Helen (Chimilewski) Y.; m. Margaret A. McLean, June 14, 1986. BA, Colgate U., 1975; JD, Dickinson U., 1978. Bar: Pa. 1978, U.S. Dist. Ct. (we. dist.) Pa. 1978, U.S. Ct. Appeals (3d cir.) 1980, U.S. Supreme Ct. 1980. Law clk. to judge Pa. Superior Ct., Pitts., 1978-80; assoc. Buchanan Ingersoll P.C., Pitts., 1980-86, ptnr., 1986—. Editor comments Dickinson Law Rev., 1978. Mem. ABA, Allegheny County Bar Assn., Pa. Bar Assn., Rivers Club. Roman Catholic. Avocations: tennis, squash, golf. Office: Buchanan Ingersoll & Rooney PC 1 Oxford Ct Pittsburgh PA 15219-1407 Office Phone: 412-562-8841. Business E-Mail: stanley.yorsz@bipc.com.

YOSELOFF, JULIEN DAVID, publishing company executive; b. N.Y.C., June 25, 1941; s. Thomas and Sara (Rothfuss) Y.; m. Darlene Starr Carbone, Aug. 6, 1967; children: Michael Ian, Anthony Alexander. BA, U. Pa., 1962; student, London Sch. Econs., 1962—63; MA, Rutgers U., 1994. With A.S. Barnes and Co., Inc., Cranbury, NJ, 1963-80; dir. Associated Univ. Presses, Inc., 1966—; pres. Rosemont Pub. and Printing Corp., 1980—. Served with AUS, 1964. Mem. Phi Beta Kappa Assocs., Phi Beta Kappa, Pi Sigma Alpha. Avocations: amateur radio, photography, bicycling. Office: 2010 Eastpark Blvd Cranbury NJ 08512-3518 Office Phone: 609-655-4770.

YOSELOFF, THOMAS, publisher; b. Sioux City, Iowa, Sept. 8, 1913; s. Morris and Sarah (Rabinowitz) Y.; m. Sara Rothfuss, Apr. 30, 1938 (div. 1964); children: Julien David, Mark Laurence; m. Lauretta Sellitti, Apr. 23, 1964; 1 dau., Tamar Rachel. AB, U. Iowa, 1934; LittD (hon.), Bucknell U., 1982; LHD (hon.), Fairleigh Dickinson U., 1982. Chmn. Rosemont Pub. & Printing Corp., 1969—, Associated Univ. Presses, 1969, Golden Cockerel Press, London, 1979—. Author: A Fellow of Infinite Jest, 1946, (with Lillian Stuckey) Merry Adventures of Till Eulenspiegel, 1944, Further Adventures of Till Eulenspiegel, 1957, The Time of My Life, 1979; Editor: Seven Poets in Search of an Answer, 1944, Voyage to America, 1961, Comic Almanac, 1963, The Man from the Mercury, 1986. Pres. Ctr. for War/Peace Studies, 1977-91. Recipient award of merit Bucknell U., 1975, award of merit U. Del., 1987. Mem. Phi Beta Kappa, Sigma Delta Chi, Delta Sigma Rho. Home: 27 Globeflower Ln West Windsor NJ 08550 Personal E-mail: lissie21@aol.com, lissie21@verizon.net.

YOSHIDA, AKIRA, biochemist; b. Okayama, Japan, May 10, 1924; arrived in US, 1961; s. Isao and Etsu (Kagawa) Y.; m. Michiko Suzuki, Nov. 10, 1954; 1 child, Emmy. MSc, U. Tokyo, 1947, DSc, 1954. Assoc. prof. U. Tokyo, 1952-60; sr. rsch. fellow U. Pa., Phila., 1960-63; rsch. scientist NIH, Bethesda, Md., 1963-65; rsch. prof. U. Wash., Seattle, 1965-72; dir. dept. biochem. genetics City of Hope Med. Ctr., Duarte, Calif., 1972—98, emeritus prof., 1998—. Contbr. more than 300 articles to profl. jours. Scholar Rockefeller Found., 1955-56; recipient Merit award Japanese Soc. Human Genetics, 1980, Achievement award City of Hope, 1981, Merit Grant award NIH, 1988. Mem. AAAS, Am. Soc. Biol. Chemists, Am. Soc. Human Genetics (assoc. editor), Am. Soc. Hematology, NY Acad. Scis. Home: 2140 Pinecrest Dr Altadena CA 91001-2121 Office: City Hope Beckman Inst Helford Bldg 1450 E Duarte Rd Duarte CA 91010-3011 E-mail: ma3024@earthlink.net.

YOSHIDA, HIROYUKI, mathematician, computer scientist, educator, medical science educator; b. Yokote, Akita, Japan, Mar. 16, 1961; s. Tadashi Yoshida; m. Shinobu Muto. PhD, U. Tokyo, 1989. Asst. prof. Tokyo Inst. Polytechnics, Atsugi, Kanagawa, Japan, 1989—93; from vis. rsch. assoc. to asst. prof. U. Chgo., 1993—97, asst. prof., assoc. prof., 1997—2005; assoc. prof. Harvard Med. Sch., Boston, 2005—. Author: Windows Magic, 1992, The Best Guide to NeXT Computers, 1992; editor: Introduction to the BASIC Programming Language, 1992, Essential LAN Terminology 100, 1993, The Best Guide to the World Wide Web, 1996, Essential Network Terminology 100, 1997, The Internet Dictionary, 1997; contbr. (chpt.) Practical Applications of Soft Computing Techniques, 2001; contbr.: chpt. Wavelets in Signal and Image Analysis, 2001, Atlas of Virtual Colonoscopy, 2002; contbr. articles to profl. jours., Practical Applications of Soft Computing. Recipient Cum Laude award Edn. Exhibit, Radiol. Soc. N.Am., 2000, Cert. Merit award Edn. Exhibit, 2004, Excellence in Design award Edn. Exhibit, 2002, Hon. Mention award, Internat. Soc. Optical Engring., 2002; grantee, Whitaker Found., 1995, Lewis Block Fund grant, U. Chgo., 1999, Am. Cancer Soc., 2000, 2005, NIH, 2000, Cancer Rsch. Found. Am., 2001, 2005, Nat. Cancer Inst., 2003. Mem.: IEEE, Assn. for Computing Machinery, Inst. Electronics, Info. and Comm. Engrs., Info. Processing Soc. Japan, Internat. Soc.Optical Engring., Am. Assn. Physicists Medicine. Office: Mass Gen Hosp Harvard Med Sch Dept Radiology 75 Blossom Ct Boston MA 02114 Home: 4 Summit Rd Watertown MA 02472-3537 Office Phone: 617-643-2326. Business E-Mail: Yoshida.hiro@mgh.harvard.edu.

YOSHIMURA, YOSHIKO, librarian; b. Tokyo, Oct. 21, 1933; arrived in U.S., 1958; d. Shigeru and Jun Yoshimura. BA, Tsuda Coll., Tokyo, Japan, 1956; MSLS, Syracuse U., 1961; AM, Harvard U., 1971. Libr. asst. Toyo Bunko Libr., Tokyo, 1956—58; cadet, intern Syacuse (NY) U Libr., 1958—61; sr. cataloger Harvard-Yenching Libr., Cambridge, Mass., 1961—71; sr. Japanese cataloger Libr. of Congress, Washington, 1971—81, area specialist Japan, 1981—98. Author (compiler): Japanese Govt. Documents and Censored Pub., 1992, Censored Japanese Serials of the Pre-1946 Period, 1994, Pre 1956 Japanese Documents and Censored Materials, 2002—06. Home: 2311 Pimmit Dr No 1215 Falls Church VA 22043

YOSHIUCHI, ELLEN HAVEN, healthcare educator, clinical counselor; b. Newark, Apr. 15, 1949; d. Michael Joseph and Adeline V. (Lindblom) Haven; m. Takeshi Yoshiuchi, Dec. 1, 1973; children: Teri Takumi, Niki Noboru. BA summa cum laude, CUNY, 1980; M Profl. Studies in Human Rels., N.Y. Inst. Tech., 1991. Cert. bereavement svcs. counselor, cert. kidney early evaluation program. Pvt. practice childbirth edn., 1983—89; program asst. parent/family edn. St. Luke's/Roosevelt Hosp. Ctr., N.Y.C., 1989—93, mem. faculty parent/family edn. program, 1990—2002; mem. faculty Family Ctr. at Riverdale Neighborhood House, Bronx, 1991—96; faculty mem. The Center N.Y. March of Dimes, N.Y.C., 1996—2001; mgr. patient svcs. N.Y.C. chpt. The Leukemia and Lymphoma Soc., 1998—2004; program dir. Nat. Kidney Found. of Greater N.Y., 2004—. Mem perinatal bereavement com. St. Luke's/Roosevelt Hosp. Ctr., N.Y.C., 1989-95. Editor ASPO/N.Y.C. News, 1983-86; contbr. articles to profl. jours. Trustee Pan Asian Repertory Theatre, N.Y.C., 1996-2001. Fellow: Am. Coll. Childbirth Educators; mem.: NY Citizens' Com. on Health Care Decisions, Coun. Nephrology Social Workers, C.G. Jung Found. for Analytical Psychology, Lamaze Internat. (cert. tchr., pres. N.Y.C. chpt. 1987—91, nominating com. 1987—91, certn. inddl. program 1991—93). Office: 30 E 33rd St New York NY 10016-6901 Office Phone: 212-889-2210. Personal E-mail: eenadoone@verizon.net.

YOSHIZUMI, DONALD TETSURO, dentist; b. Honolulu, Feb. 18, 1930; s. Richard Kiyoshi and Hatsue (Tanouye) Yoshizumi; m. Barbara Fujiko Iwashita, June 25, 1955 (dec. Feb. 1998); children: Beth Ann E., Cara Leigh S., Erin Yuri. BS, U. Hawaii, 1952; DDS, U. Mo., 1960, grad. cert. prosthodontics, 1962, MS, 1963. Clin. instr. U. Mo. Sch. Dentistry, Kansas City, 1960—63; pvt. practice Santa Clara, Calif., 1963—70, San Jose, Calif., 1970—. Contbr. articles to profl. jours. With USAF, 1952—56. Mem.: ADA, Santa Clara County Dental Soc., Calif. Dental Assn., Delta Sigma Delta, Omicron Kappa Upsilon. Home: 5054 Parkfield Ave San Jose CA 95129-3225 Office: 2011 Forest Ave Ste 1 San Jose CA 95128-4813

YOSKIN, JON WILLIAM, II, insurance company executive; b. Phila., Oct. 16, 1939; s. Lewis William and Louise (Houck) Y.; m. Dorothea James, Sept. 25, 1961 (div. Mar. 1992); children: Nicholas, Dorothea, Maurice P.; m. Elizabeth Anne Groves, Sept 26, 1992. Pvt. practice, Phila., 1959-74; sr. v.p. Mid. Atlantic Gen. Investment Co., Phila., 1974-80; exec. v.p. Transatlantic Life Assurance Co., Phila., 1980-85, Meritor Life Ins. Co., Phila., 1985-88; owner, CEO Tri-Arc Fin. Svcs., Phila., 1988—; chmn., CEO Magellan Ins. Co. Ltd., Bermuda, 1996—. Bd. dirs. Concerto Soloist, Phila., 1990-92, Nat. Media Corp., 1994-98, Phila. Commn. to End Homelessness, 1995—; mem. Spl. Olympics Adv. Com. Mem. Nat. Assn. Life Underwriters, Coun. Ins. Agts. and Brokers (bd. dirs.), Profl. Assn. Ins. Agts., Sons of Am. Revolution, Mil. Order Loyal Legion of U.S. Republican. Avocation: big game hunting. Office: Tri-Arc Fin Svcs 983 Old Eagle School Rd Ste 616 Wayne PA 19087-1711 Home: 1 Brightview Ave Hobe Sound FL 33455-2123 E-mail: jyoskin@triarcfs.com.

YOSKOWITZ, IRVING BENJAMIN, lawyer, merchant banker; b. Bklyn., Dec. 2, 1945; s. Rubin and Jennie Y.; m. Carol L. Magil, Feb. 11, 1973; children: Stephen M., Robert J. BBA, CCNY, 1966; JD, Harvard U., 1969; postgrad., London Sch. Econs., 1971—72. Bar: N.Y. 1970, D.C. 1972, Conn.

1982. Programmer IBM, East Fishkill, NY, 1966; sys. analyst Office Sec. Def., Washington, 1969—71; assoc. Arnold & Porter, Washington, 1972—73; atty. IBM, 1973—79, regional counsel Bethesda, Md., 1979; dep. gen. counsel United Technologies Corp., Hartford, Conn., 1979—81, v.p. and gen. counsel, 1981—86, sr. v.p., gen. counsel, 1986—90, exec. v.p., gen. counsel, 1990—98; sr. ptnr. Global Tech. Ptnrs., L.L.C., Washington, 1998—2005; sr. counsel Crowell & Moring, Washington, 2001—05; exec. v.p. & gen. counsel Constellation Energy, Balt., 2005—. Bd. dirs. Wyle Corp. Mem. editorial bd. Harvard Law Rev., 1968-69. With U.S. Army, 1969-71. Knox fellow, 1971-72 Mem. ABA, Am. Corp. Counsel Assn. (bd. dirs. 1982-85), Assn. Gen. Counsel. Office: Constellation Energy 750 E Pratt St Baltimore MD 21202

YOST, EMERY JOSEPH, music industry producer, educator; b. Chgo., May 1, 1964; s. Thomas Joseph and Jean Ann (Kawa) Yost. BA in Music, Columbia Coll., 1988; MA, DePaul U., 2003. Cert. tchr. Ill. Music instr. Chgo. Pk. Dist., Chgo., 1989—; music tchr. Immaculate Heart of Mary Sch., Chgo., 1994—95; internat. recording and performance artist Smash/Polygram Records, Chgo., 1995—97; CEO Spl. Music by Spl. People Inc., Chgo., 1998—; cons. music programming Little City, Palatine, Ill., 1999—2000; pres., dir. House of Song, Chgo., 2000—; prodr. House of Song Records Records/Media Products, Chgo., 2001—. Prodr. (Garifuna drum trg. DVD's and guitar method DVD's) Belize World Music Pub. and belizedrums.com. Finalist Osterman awards, 1996, 1998; named Stan Greanias scholar, Spl. Childrens Charities, 1997, Anne Burke scholar, 1998. Mem.: Music Educators Nat. Conf., Nat. Acad. Recording Arts and Scis. Democrat. Office: Chgo Pk Dist 3420 N Long Chicago IL Home: 1909 N Kedzie Ave #2 Chicago IL 60647-3723 Office Phone: 312-742-7511. Personal E-mail: joe@specialmusic.org.

YOST, GERALD B., lawyer; b. Harvey, Ill., Dec. 21, 1954; s. Richard Dennis and Marilyn Patricia (Moore) Y.; m. Kay Lynn Benton, Apr. 16, 1977; children: Matthew Brian, Benjamin Gerald, Andrew Richard. BA in Journalism, Drake U., 1976; student, Purdue U., 1975; JD, Hamline U., 1980. Bar: Minn. 1980, U.S. Dist. Ct. Minn. 1980, Wis. 1987. Assoc. Bergman, Street & Ulmen, Mpls., 1980—84; ptnr. Wasserman and Baill, Mpls., 1984—90, Yost, Stephenson & Sanford, Mpls., 1990—95, Yost & Baill LLP, Mpls., 1996—, Milw., 2005—. Editor: Student Osteo. Med. Assn. Publ. mag., 1976; mem. Law Review Hamline U., 1978-80. Active YMCA, St. Paul. Recipient Am. Jurisprudence award, Lawyers Coop. Pub. Co., St. Paul, 1979. Mem. ABA, Minn. State Bar Assn., Wis. Bar Assn., Phi Alpha Delta, Sigma Delta Chi. Avocations: tennis, racquetball, boating and water skiing, jogging. Home: 422 Mt Curve Blvd Saint Paul MN 55105 Office: Yost & Baill LLP 2050 US Bank Plaza South 220 S 6th St Minneapolis MN 55402-1803 also: Yost & Baill LLP 2300 N Mayfair Rd Ste 290 Milwaukee WI 53206 Office Phone: 612-338-6000, 414-259-0600. Business E-Mail: gyost@yostbaill.com.

YOST, JAMES A., manufacturing executive; BSc in Computer Sci., Johns Hopkins U., 1971; MBA in Fin., U. Chgo. Controller Autolatina; various positions Ford Europe; v.p. corp. strategy Ford Motor Co.; v.p. fin. Hayes Lemmerz, Northville, Mich., 2002—, CFO, 2002—. Office: Hayes Lemmerz 15300 Centennial Drive Northville MI 48167

YOST, NED, professional baseball player; b. Eureka, Calif., Aug. 19, 1954; m. Deborah Yost; children: Jenny, Ned, Josh, Andrew. Attended, Chabot Jr. Coll. With Milwaukee Brewers, 1980—83, Tex. Rangers, 1984, Montreal Expos, 1985; mgr. Milwaukee Brewers, 2003—; coaching staff Atlanta Braves, 1991—2002. Office: Miller Park 46th St Milwaukee WI 53214-3691*

YOST, NICHOLAS CHURCHILL, lawyer; b. Washington, Aug. 15, 1938; s. Charles Woodruff and Irene Ravitch (Oldakowska) Yost; m. Sandra Moore Rennie; children: Robert, Scott, Daniel. AB in Pub. & Internat. Affairs, Princeton U., 1960; LLB, U. Calif., Berkeley, 1963. Bar: Calif., 1964, US Supreme Ct., 1972, DC, 1978. Dep. atty. gen. adminstry. law Calif. Dept. Justice, 1965-69; counsel Calif. State Environ. Quality Study Coun., 1969-71; dep. atty. gen. in charge environ. unit Calif. Dept. Justice, 1971-77; gen. counsel Coun. Environ. Quality, Exec. Office of Pres., Washington, 1977-81; vis. scholar Environ. Law Inst., Washington, 1981-82; sr. atty. Ctr. for Law in Pub. Interest, Washington, 1982-85; ptnr. Dickstein, Shapiro & Morin, Washington, 1985-94, Sonnenschein Nath & Rosenthal, San Francisco, 1994—. US dir. Law and Adminstrn. Project under US-USSR environ. agreement, 1977—81; dir. Pres.'s Task Force on Global Resources and Environment, 1980—81; mem US Del. to UN Conf. on Environment and Devel., Rio de Janeiro, 1992; mem. & subcom. chair Calif. EPA Blue Ribbon Commn. on a Unified Environ. Statute, 1994; NEPA counsel Presidio Trust. Contbr. articles to profl. journals Capt. U.S. Army, 1963—65. Recipient Nat. Environ. Quality Award, Natural Resources Coun. Am., 1996. Mem. ABA (chmn. standing com. on environ. law 1989-91), State Bar Calif. (chmn. com. on environ. 1975-76), DC Bar Assn. (co-chmn. environ., energy and natural resources sect. 1985-86, 88-89), Environ. Law Inst. (bd. dirs. 1986-92), UN Assn. LA (v.p. 1969-71), UN Assn. Wash. (bd. dirs. 1987-93). Office: Sonnenschein Nath & Rosenthal LLP 26th Fl 525 Market St San Francisco CA 94105 Office Phone: 415-882-2440. Office Fax: 415-543-5472. Business E-Mail: nyost@sonnenschein.com.

YOST, PAUL ALEXANDER, JR., foundation executive, retired military officer; b. Phila., Jan. 3, 1929; s. Paul Alexander Sr. and Jeanne Moore (Bailey) Y.; m. Jan Worth, June 2, 1951; children: Linda L., Paul Alexander III, David J., Lisa L., Christopher J. BS, USCG Acad., 1951; MS, U. Conn., 1959; MA, George Washington U., 1964; grad., Naval War Coll., 1964. Commd. ensign USCG, 1951, advanced through grades to adm., 1986, comdr. 8th dist. New Orleans, 1978-81, chief staff hdqrs. Washington, 1981-84, comdr. 3d dist., maritime Atlantic def. zone, and Atlantic area N.Y.C., 1984-86, commandant Washington, 1986-90, ret., 1990; pres. James Madison Found., Washington 1990—. Decorated D.S.M. with gold star, Silver Star, Legion of Merit combat "V" with gold star, Meritorious Service Medal. Office: James Madison Meml Fellowship Found 2000 K St NW Washington DC 20006-1809

YOST, R. DAVID (DAVID YOST), pharmaceutical executive; b. 1947; married. BS, USAF Acad., 1969; MBA, UCLA, 1970. From v.p. to pres. Kauffman-Lattimer Co., Columbus, Ohio, 1969-74; from group v.p. to group pres. cen. region Alco Health Systems Corp., Malvern, Pa., 1989-97; pres., CEO, chmn. AmeriSource Health Corp., Malvern, Pa., 1997—2001; pres. Amerisource Bergen Corp., 2001—02, CEO, dir., 2002—. Capt. USAF, 1969—74. Office: AmerisourceBergen Corp 1300 Morris Dr Ste 100 Wayne PA 19087-5594

YOST, WILLIAM ALBERT, psychology professor; b. Dallas, Sept. 21, 1944; s. William Jacque and Gladys (Funk) Y.; m. Lee Prater, June 15, 1969; children: Kelley Ann, Alyson Leigh BA, Colo. Coll., 1966, DSc (hon.), 1997; PhD, Ind. U., 1970. Assoc. prof. psychology U. Fla., Gainesville, 1971-77; dir. sensory physiology and perception program NSF, Washington, 1982-83; prof. psychology Loyola U., Chgo., 1979—, dir. Parmly Hearing Inst., 1977—2001, dir. interdisciplinary neurosci. minor, 1977—2001, prof. hearing scis., 1990—. Prof. psychology, adj. prof. otolaryngology Loyola U., Chgo., 1990—, acting v.p. rsch., 1999—2001, assoc. v.p. rsch., dean Grad. Sch., 2001—04; individual expert bio-acoustics Am. Nat. Stds. Inst., 1983—; mem. study sect. Nat. Inst. Deafness and Other Communication Disorders, 1990—94; chair hearing bioacoustics and biomechanics com. NRC, 1992—2001, mem. bd. on behavioral cognitive and sensory scis., 1998—2004. Author: Fundamentals of Hearing, 1977, 4th edit., 2000; editor (with others) New Directions in Hearing Science, 1985, Directional Hearing, 1987, Auditory Processing of Complex Sounds, 1987, Classification of Complex Sounds, 1989, Psychoacoustics, 1993; assoc. editor Auditory Neurosci., 1994-97; ad hoc reviewer NSF, Air Force Office Sci. Rsch., Office Naval Rsch., 1971—; contbr. chpts. to books, articles to profl. jours. Pres. Evanston Tennis Assn., Ill., 1984, 90. Grantee NSF, 1974—, NIH, 1975—, AFOSR, 1983—, ONR, 1989-90. Fellow AAAS, Am. Phys. Soc., Acoustical Soc. Am. (assoc. editor jour. 1984-91, chair tech. com. 1990-94, exec. com.

1999—, v.p. 2002-04, pres. 2004—, Silver medal 2006), Am. Speech-Lang.-Hearing Assn.; mem. NAS (exec. com. on hearing bioacoustics, biomechanics 1981-87, chmn. 1993-97), Assn. Rsch. in Otolaryngology (sec.-treas. 1984-87, pres.-elect 1987-88, pres. 1988-89), Nat. Inst. Deafness and Other Comm. Disorders (task force, rev. panel 1990-94, chmn. 1994), Am. Auditory Soc. (exec. bd. 1993-98). Office Phone: 773-508-2713. Business E-Mail: wyost@luc.edu. *I am fortunate that I am in an occupation that is so much fun. Teaching and research are very enjoyable. Most days for me are fun.*

**YOU, HARRY L.,** consulting company executive, former computer software company executive; BA in Econs., Harvard Coll.; MA in Econs., Yale U. Advisor to the bd. dirs. Lucky-Goldstar Internat.; Seoul, Republic of Korea; economist, asst. to the dir. Internat. Monetary Fund; fed. reserve liaison U.S. Dept. Treasury; v.p. Salomon Bros., Inc.; sr. v.p. gen. indsl. group Lehman Bros.; mng. dir., computer and bus. svcs. group Morgan Stanley, 1996—2001; CFO Accenture Ltd., Bermuda, 2001—04; exec. v.p., CFO Oracle Corp., Redwood City, Calif., 2004—05; CEO BearingPoint Inc., McLean, Va., 2005—. Office: BearingPoint LLC 1676 International Dr Mc Lean VA 22102

**YOU, YALI,** music educator; b. Xian, Shaanxi Province, China, July 31, 1962; d. Damin You and Fang Lin; m. Paul Steven Knuth, Aug. 9, 2002. D of Musical Arts, U. of Cin., Cin., Ohio, 1989—96; MusM, Northwestern U., Evanston, Ill., 1986—87; BA, Shanghai Conservatory of Music, Shanghai, China, 1980—84. Cert. cello performance Northwestern U., 1988. Assoc. prof. of music Hamline U., St. Paul, Minn., 1996—; adj. prof. of music Concordia U., St. Paul, Minn., 1997—2001. Musician concert performances in various venues. Recipient Excellent Performance, 4th Chinese Nat. Chamber Music competition, 1985. Mem.: Am. Assoc. of Univ. Professors. Buddhism. Avocations: folk dancing, gardening, travel. Office: Hamline Univ 1536 Hewitt Ave Saint Paul MN 55104 Office Phone: 651-523-2439. Personal E-mail: yaliyou@hamline.edu. E-mail: yyou@gw.hamline.edu.

**YOU, ZHANPING,** civil engineer, educator; s. Jiamin You and Laiqin Ren; m. Qingli Dai. BCE, Chang'an U., China, 1995, MCE, 1998; PhD in Civil Engring., U. Ill., 2003. Registered profl. engr., Ohio. Dwight David Eisenhower grad. fellow rsch. asst. U. Ill., Urbana, Ill., 1999—2003; prof. Tex. A&M U., Kingsville, Tex., 2004—05, Mich. Technol. U., Houghton, 2005—. Dwight David Eisenhower Faculty fellow, Fed. Hwy. Adminstrn., US Dept. Transp., 2004—05. Mem.: ASCE (corr.; granular materials com., environ. issue com., hwy. pavement com., airfield pavement com., local rds. and sts. com., geometric design com., Transp. and Devel. Inst.), N.Am. China Overseas Transp. Assn. (bd. dirs. 2005—06), Assn. Asphalt Paving Technologists, U.S. Assn. for Computational Mechanics, Am. Soc. for Engring. Edn. Achievements include research in Asphalt Pavements and Concrete Pavements; Transportation Materials - Asphalt, Aggregate, Asphalt Concrete, and Cement Concrete; Roadway Infrastructure, Pavement Management; Micromechanical Modeling. Office: Mich Tech Univ Dept Civil and Environ Engring 1400 Townsend Dr Houghton MI 49931-1295 Office Phone: 906-487-1619. Office Fax: 906-487-1620. Personal E-mail: zhanpingyou@yahoo.com.

**YOUKER, JAMES EDWARD,** radiologist; b. Cooperstown, N.Y., Nov. 13, 1928; s. Bliss Jacob and Marian (Ostrander) Y.; children— Elizabeth Ann, James David. AB, Colgate U., 1950; MD, U. Buffalo, 1954. Diplomate: Am. Bd. Radiology. Intern U. Minn., Mpls., 1954-55, resident in radiology, 1955-56, 58-60; resident in pathology Georgetown U., Washington, 1958; pvt. practice medicine, specializing in radiology Corpus Christi, Tex., 1956-58; asst. prof. radiology Med. Coll. Va., Richmond, 1961-63; research fellow U. Lund, Malmo, Sweden, 1963-64; asst. prof. radiology U. Calif., San Francisco, 1964-67; asso. prof. U. Clif., 1967-68; prof., chmn. dept radiology Med. Coll. Wis., Milw., 1968—; bd. dept. radiology Milwaukee County Gen. Hosp., Milw., 1968-96; chmn. dept. radiology Froedtert Meml. Luth. Hosp., 1979—. Served with Project Hope, Indonesia, 1961; cons./lectr. VA Hosp., Richmond, 1961-63, San Francisco 1964-68, Martinez, Calif., 1964-68; cons./lectr. Letterman Army Med. Center, San Francisco, 1964-68, Oakknoll Naval Hosp., Oakladn, Calif., 1964-68, VA Hosp., Milwaukee, Wis., 1968—; vis. prof. U. Calif. Sch. Medicine, San Francisco, 1974, Stanford U. Sch. Medicine, Palo Alto, Calif., 1976; vis. physician dept. cardiology St. Vincent's Hosp., Melbourne, Australia, 1974-75; mem. com. diagnosis breast cancer task force NIH, 1975-79; Head Physicians for Ford; chmn. health and med. sci. tech. com. for program planning com. North Div. High Sch., 1979; bd. dirs. Med. Coll. Wis., 1986-88, mem. residency rev. commn. for radiology, 1985-90. Contbr. numerous articles to profl. jours. Served with M.C. USN, 1956-58. N.Y. State Regents scholar, 1946; Buffalo Found. scholar, 1952; grantee USPHS; grantee Squibb Pharms.; grantee Nat. Cancer Inst.; grantee others. Fellow Am. Coll. Radiology (bd. chancellors 1978—84, vice-chmn. commn. on cancer 1972-74, chmn./mem. numerous coms., v.p. 1983-84); mem. Am. Bd. Med. Specialties (pres. 2000), AMA, Am. Roentgen Ray Soc. (adv. com. research and edn.), Assn. Univ. Radiologists (chmn. govt. affairs com. 1978-79), Med. Soc. Milwaukee County (hosp. med. staff liaison com. 1978-79), Milw. Acad. Medicine, Milw. Roentgen Ray Soc., Soc. Chairmen Acad. Radiology Depts. (pres. 1972, coms.), Vail Creative Concepts Conf. (co-founder), Wis. Med. Soc., Wis. Radiol. Soc., Clubs: Univ. (Milw.); Chenequa Country. Republican. Office: Froedtert Meml Luth Hosp 9200 W Wisconsin Ave Milwaukee WI 53226-3522 E-mail: jyouker@mcw.edu.

**YOUM, GUNWOONG,** food scientist; b. Seoul, Republic of Korea, Apr. 1, 1972; s. Younho Youm and Sunja Kim; m. Gunwoong Youm, June 23, 2001; 1 child, Jeehyun. BS, Konkuk U., 1997, MS, 1999, U. Ark., 2003. Grad. asst. U. Ark., 2001—03, rsch. specialist, 1999—2003; quality control mgr. LM Foods LLC, Carteret, NJ, 2005—. Contbr. jourl. publ. (Travel grant, 2001). Mission chair Open door Bapt. Ch., Rogers, Ark., 2000. Sgt. South Korean Army, 1992—94, Seoul. Mem.: Inst. Food Technologists (assoc.). Avocations: swimming, golf, football. Home: 57 Maple Ct Highland Park NJ 08904 Office Phone: 732-735-9041. Personal E-mail: woongku@yahoo.com.

**YOUM, THOMAS,** orthopedist; surgeon; b. New York, Nebr., Nov. 24, 1973; s. Kwang-Youl and Chung Ok Youm; m. Janet Kaye Han, Mar. 18, 2006. BA in History, Yale U., New Haven, 1995; MD, NYU Sch. Medicine, NYC, 1999. Clin. asst. prof. NYU Hosp. Joint Diseases, NYC, 2005—. Fellow: Alpha Omega Alpha; mem.: Am. Orthopaedic Soc. Sports Medicine, Arthroscopy Assn. N.Am., Am. Acad. Orthopaedic Surgeons. Office: Enrique Ergas MD PC 1056 Fifth Ave New York NY 10028 Office Phone: 212-348-3636.

**YOUMANS, JULIAN RAY,** neurosurgeon, educator; b. Baxley, Ga., Jan. 2, 1928; s. John Edward and Jennie Lou (Milton) Y.; children— Reed Nesbit, John Edward, Julian Milton. BS, Emory U., 1949, MD, 1952; MS, U. Mich., 1955, PhD, 1957. Diplomate: Am. Bd. Neurol. Surgery. Intern U. Mich. Hosp., Ann Arbor, 1952-53, resident in neurol. surgery, 1953-55, 56-58; fellow in neurology U. London, 1955-56; asst. prof. neurosurgery U. Miss., 1959-62, assoc. prof., 1962-63, Med. U. S.C., 1963-65, prof., 1965-67, chief div. neurosurgery, 1963-67; prof. U. Calif., Davis, 1967-91; prof. emeritus, 1991—; chmn. dept. neurosurgery U. Calif., 1967-82. Cons. USAF, U.S. VA, NRC. Editor: Neurological Surgery, 1973; contbr. articles to profl. jours. No. vice chmn. Republican State Central Com. of Calif., 1979-81. Served with U.S. Navy, 1944-46. Mem. ACS (bd. govs. 1972-78), Congress of Neurol. Surgeons (exec. com. 1967-70), Am. Acad. Neurology, Am. Assn. Neurol. Surgeons, Am. Assn. Surgery of Trauma, Pan-Pacific Surg. Assn., Western Neurosurg. Soc., Neurosurg. Soc. Am., Soc. Neurol. Surgeons, Soc. Univ. Neurosurgeons, N. Pacific Soc. Neurology and Psychiatry, Royal Soc. Medicine, Am. Trauma Soc., U.S. C. of C., Bohemian Club, Sutter Club, Rotary. Republican. Episcopalian. Office Phone: 530-756-6018.

**YOUNATHAN, EZZAT SAAD,** retired biochemistry educator; b. Deirut, Egypt, Aug. 25, 1922; came to U.S., 1950; m. Margaret Tims, Aug. 11, 1958; children: Janet Nadya, Carol Miriam. BSc in Chemistry with honors, Cairo U., 1944; MS in Chemistry, Fla. State U., 1953, PhD in Chemistry, 1955. Chemist Govt. Labs., Cairo, 1944-50; postdoctoral rsch. assoc. Coll. Medi-

cine U. Ill., Chgo., 1955-57; asst. prof. Fla. State U., Tallahassee, 1957-59; asst. prof. Sch. Medicine U. Ark., Little Rock, 1959-63, assoc. prof., 1963-68, acting head, 1963-66; prof. biochemistry La. State U., Baton Rouge, 1968—98; ret. Vis. prof. U. Wis., Madison, 1966-67, U. Calif., Berkeley, 1978; chair rsch. grant adv. com. So. U., Baton Rouge, 1993-96. Contbg. author: (book) The Regulation of Carbohydrate Formation and Utilization in Mammals, 1981; contbr. 75 articles to profl. jours. Seagrams Internat. fellow Seagrams Co., Inc., 1950-51, Sr. Rsch. fellow NIH, 1966-67. Mem. AMA, Am. Soc. Biochemistry and Molecular Biology, Am. Chem. Soc., Soc. Exptl. Biol. Medicine. Mem. First Christian Ch. Achievements include discovery of new class of oral hypoglycemic agents; research in metabolism and chemistry of carbohydrates. Home: 1048 Castle Kirk Dr Baton Rouge LA 70808-6023 Personal E-mail: euounat@aol.com.

**YOUNG, AARON,** conceptual artist; BFA, San Francisco Art Inst., 2001; MFA, Yale Univ., New Haven, Conn., 2004. Represented in permanent collections Mus. Contemporary Art, Kansas City, Kans., Mus. Modern Art, NYC, one-man shows include Tender Buttons, Midway Contemporary Art, Minneapolis, Minn., 2004, exhibited in group shows at Paladar, 7th Havana Bienal, Havana, Cuba, 2000, Strictly Ballroom, Stanford University Museum, Palo Alto, CA, 2001, New Orleans Performance Festival, 2001, Circus, 8th Havana Bienal, 2002, From Here On, Guild & Greyshkul Gallery, NYC, 2003, Miami Heat, Miami Pacemaker Gallery, Miami, Fla., 2004, Let the Bullshit Run a Marathon, Nicole Klagsbrun Gallery NYC, 2004, Some Exhaust, Lehmann Maupin Gallery, NYC, 2004, Curatorial Choices: Drawing, Univ. Minn. Mus., 2005, Mus. Modern Art, NYC, 2005, Absolute Summer Show, Kirkhoff Contemporary Art, 2005, Day LABOR, P.S.1/MOMA, Long Island City, 2005, Whitney Biennial, Whitney Mus. Art, NYC, 2006. Office: c/o PS1 Contemporary Art Ctr 22-25 Jackson Ave Long Island City NY 11101*

**YOUNG, ALBERT FREDERICK ANTONIO,** director; b. Kingston, Jamaica, Oct. 30, 1948; s. Naphtali and Enid Hyacinth Young; m. Monica Verona Christie, Dec. 30, 1970 (div. July 1999); children: Yvonne McKenzie, Albert Jr., Maree Gordon, Yvette; m. Lorna Romona Young, Oct. 1, 2000. MEd, Cambridge Coll., 1995; PhD, Columbus U., 2000. Lic. alcohol and drug counselor; cert., internat. cert. alcohol and drug counselor, cert. domestic violence counselor III. Substance abuse counselor Cmty. Health Svcs. Inc., Hartford, Conn., 1992—95; dir. chem. dependency program Cmty. Health Svcs., Hartford, Conn., 1995—2002; grants coord. and program mgr. Waterbury (Conn.) Hosp., 2002—. Mem. exec. com. Conn. HIV/AIDS Cmty. Planning Group, Hartford, 1999—2001. Mem. Ct. Common Coun. Mayor of Hartford Commn. on Alcohol and Drug Abuse, 1997—99. Mem.: Am. Coll. Profl. Mental Health Practitioners (diplomate), Nat. Assn. Forensic Counselors (cert.), ACA (cert.). Democrat. Seventh Day Adventist. Avocations: breeding and training German shepherd dogs, movies, walking. Home: 9 Ledyard Ave Bloomfield CT 06002-3353

**YOUNG, ALICE,** lawyer; b. Washington, Apr. 7, 1950; d. John and Elizabeth (Jen) Y.; m. Thomas L. Shortall, Sept. 22, 1984; children: Amanda, Stephen. AB magna cum laude, Yale U., 1971; JD, Harvard U., 1974. Bar: N.Y. 1975. Assoc. Coudert Bros., NYC, 1974-81; mng. ptnr. Graham & James, NYC, 1981-87; ptnr. Milbank, Tweed, Hadley & McCloy, NYC, 1987-93; ptnr., chair Asia Pacific Practice Kaye, Scholer LLP, NYC, 1994—. Bd. dirs. Mizuho Trust and Banking Co., mem. examining com., 2003—; spkr. Traphagen Distinguished Alumni Speakers Forum, Harvard Law Sch., 2004; bd. dirs. Deloitte & Touche, adv. bd. diversity, 2005—. Contbr. articles to profl. jours. Bus. com. Nat. Com. on U.S.-China Rels., 1993—, U.S.-China Bus. Coun., 1993—, Com. of 100, 1993—, vice-chmn., 1999—; bd. overseers visitation com. to Law Sch. Harvard U., 1994—99, chair subcomm. on grad. program, 1996; trustee Lingnan Found., NYC, 1984—91, Pan-Asian Repertory Theatre, NYC, 1987—90, Japan Inst., Colo., 1988—, Am. Assembly, 2000—; bus. com. Met. Mus. Art, NYC, 1994—; active Coun. on Fgn. Rels., 1977—, Women's Forum, 2000—; trustee Asia Found., 2002—. Named one of Top 100 Minority Leaders, 1998, one of 40 Under 40 Crain's Bus., NYC, 1989; Bates fellow Yale U., 1970, NDFL fellow Harvard U., 1967-68; recipient Star award NY Women's Agenda, 1992, Justice in Action award, Asia Am. Legal Defense and Edn. Fund, 2004. Mem. ABA, NY State Bar Assn. (fgn. investment com.), Assn. Bar City NY (spl. com. on rels. with Japanese bar, Union Internat. des Avocats), Nat. Asian Pacific Am. Bar Assn., Asian Am. Bar Assn. NY, Harvard Law Sch. Assn. NYC (trustee 1990-94), Japan Soc. (sec. 1989-97), Asia Soc. (pres.'s coun. 1984-2002). Office: Kaye Scholer LLP 425 Park Ave New York NY 10022-3506 Office Phone: 212-836-8047. Business E-Mail: ayoung@kayescholer.com

**YOUNG, AMY Y.,** librarian; d. Sung-Ling Kwong and Daisy L Fung; m. Kenneth Young, Dec. 26, 1970; 1 child, Kenneth Scott. BS, Okla. Bapt. U., 1969; MLS, U. Calif., Berkeley, 1970. Cert. pub. librn. N.Y. State Edn. Dept., 1972, health scis. libr. Med. Libr. Assn. Acad. of Health Info. Profl., 1994. Corp. libr. Chem. Systems, Inc., N.Y.C., 1971; editor, revisor com. catalog, cataloger Queensborough Pub. Libr., Jamaica, N.Y., 1972—87; head dept. cataloging Health Scis. Libr., SUNY, Stony Brook, 1989—95, head serials dept. Thomas D. Greenley Libr. Farmingdale, 1995—97; catalog librr. N.Y. Inst. Tech., Old Westbury, 1997—. Mem. univ. residential appeals bd. SUNY, Stony Brook, 1990—91, libr. pers. policy com., 1991—92, faculty senate, senator-at-large, 1991—92, mentor program, 1991—95, budget com., Farmingdale, 1995—97, libr. pers. policies com., 1996—97; libr. pers. evaluation com. N.Y. Inst. of Tech., Old Westbury, 2001—. Editor (compiler): Best of Nursing Humor, vol. 1, vol. 2, Bedlam among the Bedpans, 2006. Christmas Fair organizer Presbyn. Ch. of Glen Cove, NY, 1990—92. Rsch. Fund grant, AAUP/N.Y. Inst. of Tech., 1997. Libr. Study Leave grant, N.Y. State United Univ. Professions, 1993-1994. Mem.: ALA, Nassau Libr. Assn. (exec. bd. and continuing edn. 1995), Med. Libr. Assn.

**YOUNG, ANDRE See DR. DRE**

**YOUNG, ANDREW JACKSON, JR.,** civil rights leader, pastor, retired mayor, ambassador, retired congressman; b. New Orleans, Mar. 12, 1932; s. Andrew J. and Daisy (Fuller) Y.; m. Jean Childs, June 7, 1954 (dec. 1994); children—Andrea, Lisa Dru, Paula Jean, Andrew J. III; m. Carolyn M. 1996. Student, Dillard U., 1947-48; BS, Howard U., 1951; B.D., Hartford Theol. Sem., 1955; D.D. (hon.), Wesleyan U., 1970, United Theol. Sem. Twin Cities, 1970; LL.D. (hon.), Wilberforce U., 1971, Clark Coll., 1973, Yale U., 1973, Swarthmore Coll., Atlanta U., Dartmouth U., 2005; numerous other hon. degrees. Ordained to ministry Congl. Ch., 1955; pastor Thomasville, Ga. 1955-57; assoc. dir. dept. youth work Nat. Council Chs., 1957-61; mem. staff So. Christian Leadership Conf., 1961-70, adminstr. citizen edn. program, 1961-64, exec. dir., 1964-70, exec. v.p., 1967-70; mem. US Congress from 5th Ga. Dist., 1973—77; permanent US rep. UN, NYC, 1977-79; mayor City of Atlanta, 1982—90; co-chmn. Atlanta Com. for the Olympic Games, 1996; prof. pub. affairs Ga. State U., Atlanta. Pres. Nat. Coun. Churches, 2000—01; chmn. nat. steering com. Working Families for Wal-Mart, 2006. Author: A Way Out of No Way: The Spiritual Memoirs of Andrew Young, 1994, An Easy Burden: The Civil Rights Movement and the Transformation of America, 1996. Chmn. Atlanta Community Relations Commn., 1970-72; chmn. bd. Delta Ministry of Miss.; bd. dirs. Martin Luther King, Jr. Center for Social Change, Robert F. Kennedy Meml. Found., Field Found., So. Christian Leadership Conf. Recipient Pax-Christi award St. John's U., 1970; Springarn medal.; Presdl. Medal of Freedom, 1980, French Legion of Honor medal, 1982; co-recipient, Martin Luther King, Jr., Award for Public Svc. (Ebony mag.), 1990. Mem. Ams. Dem. Action, Alpha Phi Alpha*

**YOUNG, ANNE B.,** neurologist, educator; AB, Vassar Coll., 1969; MD, Johns Hopkins U., 1973, PhD in Pharmacology, 1974. From asst. prof. to prof. chemistry Dept. Neurology, U. Mich., 1978-91; Julieanne Dorn prof. neurology Harvard Med. Sch., 1991—; chief neurology Mass. Gen. Hosp., 1991— Fellow Scottish Rite Found., Lexington, 1973; med. intern Mt. Zion Hosp. & Med. Ctr., San Francisco; neurological resident Dept. Neurology U. Calif., San Francisco; David Segal vis. prof. Columbia U., 1996; presdl. lectr. Am. Acad. Neurology, 1996. Contbr. numerous articles to profl. jours.

Recipient Tchr./Investor Devel. award NIH, 1979-84, Facility Devel. award Merck, 1987-89, Milton Wexler award for Huntington's Rsch. Huntington's Dis. Soc. Am., 1989, Weinstein-Goldenson award United Cerebral Palsy Assn., Inc., 1990. Mem. Inst. Medicine-Nat. Acad. Science. Office: Dept Neurology Mass Gen 15 Parkman St Ste 835 Boston MA 02114-3117

**YOUNG, ARTHUR PRICE,** librarian, educator; b. Boston, July 29, 1940; s. Arthur Price and Marion (Freeman) Y.; m. Patricia Dorothy Foss, June 26, 1965; children: John Marshall, Christopher Price. BA, Tufts U., 1962; MA in Tchg., U. Mass., 1964; MSLS, Syracuse U., 1969; PhD, U. Ill., 1976. Head reader svcs., social sci. bibliographer SUNY-Cortland, 1969-72; rsch. assoc. U. Ill. Libr. Rsch. Ctr., Urbana, 1972-75; asst. dean pub. svcs., assoc. prof. U. Ala., Tuscaloosa, 1976-81; dean librs., prof. U. R.I., Kingston, 1981-89; dir. Thomas Cooper Libr., U. S.C., Columbia, 1989-93; sr. fellow UCLA, 1991; dean librs., mem. adj. faculty dept. history No. Ill. U., DeKalb, 1993—. Mem. adj. faculty Syracuse (N.Y.) U., 1970-71, Dominican U., River Forest, Ill., 1994-96; pres. Consortium R.I. Acad. and Rsch. Librs., 1983-85; mem. bd. govs. Univ. Press New England, 1987-89; mem. exec. bd. Ill. Libr. Computer Sys. Orgn., 1995-99; chair Coun. Dirs. State Univ. Librs., 1994-95, 2001—; sr. fellow UCLA, 1991; pres. Ill. Libr. Assn., 2002. Author: Books for Sammies: American Library Association and World War I, 1981, American Library History: A Bibliography of Dissertations and Theses, 1988, Higher Education in American Life, 1636-1986: A Bibliography of Dissertations and Theses, 1988, Cities and Towns in American History: A Bibliography of Doctoral Dissertations, 1989, Academic Libraries: Research Perspectives, 1990, Religion and the American Experience, 1620-1900: A Bibliography of Doctoral Dissertations, 1992, Religion and the American Experience, the Twentieth Century: A Bibliography of Doctoral Dissertations, 1994; The Next Library Leadership: Attributes of Academic and Public Library Directors, 2003; editl. bd. various jours. Chair Coun. of Dirs. Ill. State Univ. Librs., 1994-95, 2001-02. Served to capt. USAF, 1964-68. Recipient Berner Nash award U. Ill., 1976. Mem. ALA (chmn. editl. bd., chair Libr. Rsch. Seminar I, 1996), Assn. Coll. and Rsch. Librs. (publs. in librarianship 1982-88, chmn. Jesse H. Shera Endowment Fund com. 1991-94), Ill. Libr. Assn., S.C. Libr. Assn. (chmn. libr. adminstrn. sect. 1991-92), Assn. Rsch. Librs. (scholarly commn. com. 1991-93), Orgn. Am. Historians, Am. Hist. Assn., Horatio Alger Soc. (pres. 1999-2000), Caxton Club (Chgo.), Phi Kappa Phi, Beta Phi Mu, Phi Delta Kappa. Episcopalian. Home: 9 Sandy Brook Dr Durham NH 03824-3137 Office Phone: 815-753-9801. Business E-Mail: ayoung@niu.edu.

**YOUNG, BARBARA,** psychiatrist, psychotherapist, educator, photographer; b. Chgo., Oct. 27, 1920; d. William Harvey and Blanche (DeBra) Y. AB, Knox Coll., 1942; MD, Johns Hopkins U., 1945; grad., Balt. Psychoanalytic Inst., 1953. Intern Univ. Hosps., Iowa City, 1945-46, asst. resident in neurology, 1946—47; asst. resident in psychiatry Phipps Clinic, Johns Hopkins U. Hosp., Balt., 1947-49; staff psychiatrist Perry Point (Md.) VA Hosp., 1949-51; practice medicine specializing in psychiatry/psychoanalysis Balt., 1951—; instr. Johns Hopkins U., 1953-69, asst. psychiatry, 1969—, prof. emeritus, 1997—; freelance photographer, 1958—. Lectr. psychiatry Johns Hopkins U.; lectr. Lucy Daniels Found., Carey, N.C., dept. humanities Yale U. Med. Sch., Boston Inst. for Psychotherapy, local psychiat. and social orgns. Works represented in Mus. Modern Art, N.Y.C., Balt. Mus. Art, Santa Barbara (Calif.) Mus. Art, Eastman House, Rochester, N.Y., Yale U. Gallery of Art; photographer: The Plop-A-Lop Tree, 1995, Tales of Courage: Recovering LIfe After Catastrophe, 2003; contbr. articles to profl. jours. Mem.: Am. Psychoanlytic Assn., Am. Psychiat. Assn., Balt.-Washington Ctr. for Psychoanalysis. Democrat. Address: 5307 Herring Run Dr Baltimore MD 21214-1937 Office Phone: 410-426-3583.

**YOUNG, BARNEY THORNTON,** lawyer; b. Chillicothe, Tex., Aug. 10, 1934; s. Bayne and Helen Irene (Thornton) Y.; m. Sarah Elizabeth Taylor, Aug. 31, 1957; children: Jay Thornton, Sarah Elizabeth, Serena Taylor. BA, Yale U., 1955; LLB, U. Tex., 1958. Bar: Tex. 1958. Assoc. Thompson, Knight, Wright & Simmons, Dallas, 1958-65; ptnr. Rain, Harrell, Emery, Young & Doke, Dallas, 1965-87; mem. firm Locke Purnell Rain Harrell (A Profl. Corp.), 1987-98; of counsel Locke, Liddell & Sapp LLP, 1999—. Mem. adv. coun. Dallas Cmty. Chest Trust Fund, Inc., 1964-66; bd. dirs. Mental Health Assn. Dallas County, Inc., 1969-72, Trammell Crow Family Found., 1984-87; trustee Hockaday Sch., Dallas, 1971-77, 90—, chmn., 1994-96, Dallas Zool. Soc., 1986-92, Lamplighter Sch., Dallas, 1976-99, chmn., 1983-86, St. Mark's Sch., Dallas, 1970—, pres., 1976-78, The Found. for Callier Ctr. and Comm. Disorders, 1988-99, Friends of Ctr. for Human Nutrition, 1988-2005, Dallas Hist. Soc., 1993-2001; bd. dirs. Susan G. Komen Breast Cancer Found., 2000-06, Nat. Assn. Ind. Schs., 2000-04; mem. Yale Devel. Bd., 1984-91, 98—. Fellow Tex. Bar Found., Dallas Bar Found.; mem. ABA, Tex. Bar Assn., Dallas Bar Assn., Am. Judicature Soc., Order of Coif, Phi Beta Kappa, Pi Sigma Alpha, Phi Gamma Delta, Phi Delta Phi, Dallas Country Club., Petroleum Club (Dallas), Yale Club (Dallas, N.Y.C.). Office: Locke Liddell & Sapp LLP 2200 Ross Ave Ste 2200 Dallas TX 75201-6776 Office Phone: 214-740-8402. Business E-Mail: byoung3@mindspring.com.

**YOUNG, BARRY HARRISON,** retired mathematician, mechanical engineer; b. Dallas, Dec. 9, 1948; s. Philip Haine and Dorothy Belle Young. BSME, So. Meth. U., Dallas, Tex., 1971; MS in Math., N.Mex. State U., Las Cruces, N.Mex., 1982. Mech. engr. Safsea, White Sands Missile Range, N.Mex., 1972—73; from mech. engr. to mathematician Calibration Lab. Instrumentation Directorate, White Sands Missile Range, 1973—2005, mathematician, 1986—2005, ret., 2005.

**YOUNG, BETTE ANN,** writer; b. Columbus, Ohio, Jan. 9, 1937; d. Richard Jack Abel and Gussie Ruth Dean Seiden; m. robert David Roth Mar. 17, 1957 (div. Dec. 1980); children: Deborah Anne Fay, Diane Hope Helbig, Robert David Roth Jr.; m. Sheldon Mike Young, Nov. 11, 1988. BA in Sociology, Oakland U., 1971; MA in Am. Culture, U. Mich., 1974, postgrad., 1977. Dir. libr. Jewish Cmty. Ctr., Detroit, 1980-82; edn. dir. Jewish Parents' Inst., Detroit, 1980-82; lectr. Adult Coll. Jewish Studies, Columbus, Ohio, 1985-87; adminstrv. sec. Nat. Coun. Jewish Women, Columbus, 1985-90; cons., membership dir., grant writer Columbus Jewish Hist. Soc., Columbus, 1987-90, oral historian 1990—. Author: Congregation Shaarey Zedek, 1981, The History of the Association of Jewish Community Organization Personnel, 1969-87, 1987, The Columbus Jewish Foundation, 1994, Emma Lazarus in Her World, 1995; book critic Jewish News, 1980-82, Ohio Jewish Chronicle, 1991—, Columbus Dispatch, 1992—. Cmty. cons. Anti-Defamation League, Detroit, 1982-83. Democrat. Home: 4776 Smoketalk Ln Westerville OH 43081-7838

**YOUNG, BILL (CHARLES WILLIAM YOUNG),** congressman; b. Harmarville, Pa., Dec. 16, 1930; m. Beverly Young; children: Robert, Billy, Patrick. Mem. Fla. State Senate, 1961—71, minority leader, 1967—71; mem. US Congress from 10th dist. Fla., 1971—; former chmn. ho. appropriations/intelligence coms.; mem. Fla. Constn. Revision Commn., 1965-67; chmn. So. Hwy. Policy Com., 1966-68; mem. Electoral Coll., 1968. Appropriations com., chmn. subcom. Def., Labor, HHS and Edn. Fla. Legislature. With Nat. Guard USAR, 1948—57. Named Most Valuable Senator, Capitol Press Corps, 1969. Republican. Methodist. Office: US Ho Reps 2407 Rayburn Ho Office Bldg Washington DC 20515-0910 E-mail: bill.young@mail.house.gov.

**YOUNG, BRIAN A.,** academic administrator; BA, Franklin & Marshall Coll.; MPA in mgmt. info. systems, U. Dayton. Chief technologist, dir. ednl. tech. initiatives U. Dayton, 1995—2000; v.p. info. tech., chief info. officer Hobart and William Smith Colleges, 2000—03; v.p. info. tech. Creighton U., 2003—. Named one of Premier 100 IT Leaders, Computerworld, 2005. Office: Creighton Pharmacy 1000 N Main St Findlay OH 45840-3653 Office Phone: 402-280-2202. Office Fax: 402-280-2573. E-mail: BrianYoung@creighton.edu.*

**YOUNG, BRUCE KENNETH,** obstetrician, gynecologist, educator; b. N.Y.C., Aug. 11, 1938; s. Morton David and Cecile Barbara (Lebenson) Y.; m. Phyllis Ann Lipsius, Dec. 16, 1962; children: Kathryn Rachel, Caroline Sue. AB, Princeton U., 1959; MD, NYU, 1963. Diplomate Nat. Bd. Med. Examiners, Am. Bd. Ob-gyn.; cert. spl. competence in maternal-fetal medicine Am. Bd. Ob-gyn. Intern Montefiore Hosp., Bronx, NY, 1963-64; resident ob-gyn. Bellevue Hosp. Ctr., N.Y.C., 1964-68, NYU Hosp., 1964-68, rsch. fellow reproductive endocrinology, 1966—67; chief obstetrics Bellevue Hosp., N.Y.C., 1970-95; dir. obstet. svcs. NYU Hosps. Network, 1995—2005. Cons. N.J. Health Sys. Agy., Hoffman LaRoche Co., Kimberly Clark, Litton Ind., Revlon Corp., 1975—; dir. maternal and fetal medicine NYU Sch. Medicine Med. Ctr., N.Y.C., 1975—2005; prof. ob-gyn. NYU Sch. Medicine, 1980—, Silverman prof. ob-gyn., 1996—. Editor: Perinatal Medicine Today, 1980, Problems in Perinatal Medicine, 1986, Jour. Maternal-Fetal Neonatal Medicine; mem. editl. bd. Diagnostic Gynecology and Obstetrics, Jour. Perinatal Medicine; contbr. chpts. to books and articles to profl. jours. Bd. dirs. N.Y. State Prenatal Diagnostic Ctr., N.Y.C., 1977-87; chair health professions bd. Greater N.Y. March of Dimes, N.Y.C., 1995—2005, v.p., dir., 1995-2005. Recipient Disting. Svc. in Med. Edn. award March of Dimes, 1985, Voluntary Svc. award March of Dimes, 1990, Program Excellence award March of Dimes, 1991, Outstanding Achievement award, Solomon A. Berson Med. Alumni Achievement award, NYU, 2005. Fellow ACOG, Am. Fertility Soc., Am. Gynecol. and Obstet. Soc., Am. Assn. Gynecol. Laparoscopists, Soc. Laparoendoscopic Surgeons, N.Y. Perinatal Soc. (pres. 1997-99), N.Y. Obstet. Soc. (pres. 2001-02); mem. AMA, Soc. Maternal-Fetal Medicine, NYU Sch. Medicine Alumni Assn. (pres. 1995-96, citation 1996), Mar-a-Lago Club. Home: 530 1st Ave, Ste 5G New York NY 10016-6402 Office Phone: 212-263-6359. E-mail: youngbo1@nyumc.org.

**YOUNG, BRUCE KENNETH,** film director; b. Reno, Dec. 1, 1960; s. Kenneth Evans and Mae Wittenmyer Y.; m. Jennifer Law, Aug. 7, 1993; child Catherine Louise BA, Washington and Lee U., 1982. Dir. (documentary film) Stolen Years, 1999 (Capital Region emmy, 1999). Mem. Nat. Press Club, White House News Photographers' Assn., Nat. Press Photographers Assn Office: Evans-McCan Group PO Box 763 Lexington VA 24450 Office Phone: 540-464-9050. E-mail: bruce@evans-mccan.org.

**YOUNG, BRUCE WILSON,** language educator; b. Roosevelt, Utah, Nov. 3, 1950; s. Daren Curtis and Ruth Wilson Young; m. Margaret Blair Young, May 17, 1985; children: Kaila Corinne Lifferth, Robert Daren, Julia Ruth, Michael Bruce. BA summa cum laude, Brigham Young U., Provo, Utah, 1975; MA, Columbia U., N.Y.C., 1975; PhD, Harvard U., Cambridge, Mass., 1983. Tchg. fellow Harvard U., 1978—81, instr., 1981—83; asst. prof. Brigham Young U., 1983—88, assoc. prof., 1988—. Dramaturg prodn. winter's tale Brigham Young U. Theatre and Media Arts Dept., 1989—90; assoc. dir. Brigham Young U., London Centre, London, 1996. Assoc. editor: Jour. Rocky Mountain Medieval and Renaissance Assn., 1986; contbr. chapters to books, articles to profl. jours. Various positions Ch. of Jesus Christ of Latter-Day Saints, 1958—2006. Recipient Parley A. Christensen scholar, Brigham Young U., 1975, Miron Cristo-Loveanu prize, Columbia U., 1976; fellow, Harvard U., 1980; Alcuin fellow, Brigham Young U., 2002—04, RMMLA-Huntington Libr. fellow, Rocky Mountain MLA, 1990. Mem.: Internat. Shakespeare Assn., Shakespeare Assn. Am. Avocations: travel, languages, music. Home: 561 N 700 W Provo UT 84601 Office: Brigham Young Univ English Depart Provo UT 84602 Office Phone: 801-422-2977. Office Fax: 801-422-0221. E-mail: bruce_young@byu.edu.

**YOUNG, BRYANT LLEWELLYN,** lawyer; b. Rockford, Ill., Mar. 9, 1948; s. Llewellyn Anker and Florence Ruth Y. AB, Cornell U., 1970; JD, Stanford U., 1974. Bar: Calif. 1974, Nev. 1975, D.C. 1979. Law clk. U.S. Dist. Ct. (no. dist.) Calif., San Francisco, 1974-75; assoc. Dinkelspiel, Pelavin, Steefel & Levitt, San Francisco, 1975-77; White House fellow, spl. asst. to sec. HUD, Washington, 1977-78, spl. asst. to sec., 1978-79; gen. mgr. to acting gen. mgr. New Cmty. Devel. Corp., 1979-80; mgmt. cons. AVCO Corp., 1980; spl. asst. to chmn. bd., CEO U.S. Synthetic Fuels Corp., Washington, 1980-81, project dir., 1981; pres. Trident Mgmt. Corp., San Francisco, 1981-87; of counsel Pelavin, Norberg, Harlick & Beck, San Francisco, 1981-82, 1982-87; mng. ptnr. bus. sect. Carroll, Burdick & McDonough, San Francisco, 1987-90; founding ptnr. Young, Vogl & Harlick, San Francisco, 1990-93, Young, Vogl, Harlick, Wilson & Simpson, LLP, San Francisco, 1993-99; pres. Young Enterprises, Inc., 1995—2004; mgr. SRY Industries LLC, 1997—, KML Hospitality Industries LLC, 1997—, Nev. Nugget LLC, 2004—; prin. Young Vogl LLP, 1999—2001; prin. Law Offices of Bryant L. Young, 2002—. Dir. The Whitman Inst. Pub. affairs com. San Francisco Aid Retarded Citizens, inc., 1977; U.S. co-chmn. New Towns Working Group, U.S.-USSR Agreement on Cooperation in Field of Housing and Urban Environment, 1979-80; treas., bd. dirs. White House Fellows Found., 1980-84; prin. Coun. Excellence in Govt., Washington, 1986-94; adv. com. Nat. Multi-Housing Coun., 1987-92; mem. Ross Sch. Found., 1994-97, sec., 1995-97; bd. dirs. Marin AIDS Project, 1996-97, sec., 1997; trustee Ross Sch., 1997-2003, pres. 2002-2003. Mem. ABA (real property, trust and probate law sects. 1975-96), White House Fellows Assn. (chmn. ann. meeting 1979, del. China 1980), Marin County Sch. Bds. Assn., Am. Field Svc. Returnees Assn., Can.-Am. C. of C. No. Calif. (v.p., bd. dirs. 1992), Chile-Calif. Found. (exec. com., bd. dirs. 1993-96). Office: 44 Montgomery St ste 4020 San Francisco CA 94104-4602 Office Phone: 415-291-1970. E-mail: bly@ebzlaw.net.

**YOUNG, BURT,** actor; b. N.Y.C., Apr. 30, 1940; s. Michael and Josephine Y.; m. May 20, 1961 (dec.); children: Richard (dec.), Anne Susan. Student public, pvt. schs., N.Y.C. Pres. White Crown Carpet Cleaners, 1964-67, Aurura Carpet Installation Co., 1966-69; owner, operator Burts Blues Tapes-Records, 1978. Author: book Uncle Joe Shanon, 1978; films include The Gang That Couldn't Shoot Straight, 1971, Acrosss 110th Street, 1972, Cinderella Liberty, 1973, Chinatown, 1973, The Gambler, 1974, The Killer Elite, 1975, Harry and Walter Go To New York, 1976, Chinatown, Rocky, 1976 (Acad. award nominee best supporting actor), Twilight's Last Gleaming, 1977, The Choirboys, 1977, Convoy, 1978, Rocky II, 1979, Blood Beach, 1980, All the Marbles, 1981, Rocky III, 1982, Lookin' to Get Out, 1982, Amittyville: The Possession, 1982, Once Upon a Time in America, 1984, Over the Brooklyn Bridge, 1984, The Pope of Greenwich Village, 1984, Rocky IV, 1985, Back to School, 1986, Last Exit to Brooklyn, 1990, Tashunga, 1995, Red Blooded American Girl, 1995, Kicked in the Head, 1997, Heaven Before I Die, 1997, The Undertaker's Wedding, 1997, She's So Lovely, 1997, Firehouse, 1997, The Deli, 1997, The Mouse, 1997, Mickey Blue Eyes, 1999, Terra bruciata, 1999, Table One, 2000, Never Look Back, 2000, Blue Moon, 2000, The Day the Ponies Come Back, 2000, Cugini, 2001, The Boys of Sunset Ridge, 2001, Plan B, 2001, And She Was, 2002, Checkout, 2002, The Adventures of Pluto Nash, 2002, Kiss the Bride, 2002, Crooked Lines, 2003, Shut Up and Kiss Me!, 2004, The Wager, 2004, Land of Plenty, 2004, Downtown: A Street Tale, 2004, Transamerica, 2005, Nicky's Game, 2005; author and star of films: Daddy, I Don't Like It Like This, CBS-TV, 1977, Uncle Joe Shanon, 1978; TV films The Great Niagara, 1974, Hustling, 1975, Serpico: The Deadly Game, 1976, Murder Can Hurt You, 1980, Before Women Had Wings, 1997, Firehouse, 1997, Greener Fields, 1998, Gioco di specchi, 2000, (TV series) You and Me Kid, 1983, Roomies, 1987, Alternate Realities, 2002; dir., Sunshine Film Co. Served with USMC, 1957-59. Mem. Acad. Motion Picture Arts and Scis., Writers Guild Am., Hole in the Wall Gang of Corona. Roman Catholic.*

**YOUNG, C. CLIFTON,** former state supreme court justice; b. Nov. 7, 1922; m. Jane Young. BA, U. Nev., 1943; LLB, Harvard U., 1949. Bar: Nev. 1949, US Dist. Ct. Nev. 1950, US Supreme Ct. 1955. Public adminstr. Washoe County, 1950—52; US Repr. from Nev. US Congress, Wash., DC, 1953—57; state senator Nev. State Senate, 1966—80; justice Nev. Supreme Ct., Carson City, Nev., 1985—2003, chief justice, 1989—94. State pres. Young Republicans Nev., 1952; del. RNC, 1950—. Served One Hundred and Third Infantry Div. U.S. Army, 1943—46, European Theater. Mem.: Nat. Wildlife Fedn. (pres. 1981—83). Republican.

**YOUNG, CARON L,** county official; b. Montgomery, Ala., July 13, 1960; d. Willie Lee and Eugene Lewis; m. Willie H. Young, Nov. 10, 1991; children: Trameka Jevert Rowell, Karen Jevert, Sharon Denise. Remote clk. Montgomery County Probate Office, Montgomery, Ala., 1982—. Dir. Youth Dept., Montgomery, Ala., 2000—02. Home: 1135 Birdwood Ct Montgomery AL 36111 Office: Montgomery County Probate Office 3032 Woodley Rd Montgomery AL Office Phone: 334-281-9999. Personal E-mail: tayika03@hotmail.com.

**YOUNG, CHARLES EDWARD,** former academic administrator; b. San Bernardino, Calif., Dec. 30, 1931; s. Clayton Charles and Eula May (Walters) Young. AA, San Bernardino Coll., 1954; AB, U. Calif., Riverside, 1955; MA, UCLA, 1957, PhD, 1960; DHL (hon.), U. Judaism, L.A., 1969; DHL (hon.), Occidental Coll., L.A., 1997. Congl. fellow, Washington, 1958—59; adminstrv. analyst Office of the Pres., U. Calif., Berkeley, 1959—60; asst. prof. polit. sci. U. Calif., Davis, 1960, UCLA, 1960—66, assoc. prof., 1966—69, prof., 1969—97, asst. to chancellor, 1960—62, asst. chancellor, 1962—63, vice chancellor, adminstrv., 1963—68, chancellor, 1968—97, chancellor emeritus, 1997—; pres. U. Fla., Gainesville, 1999—2004. Bd. dirs. Intel Corp., Acad. TV Arts and Sci. Found., L.A. Met. Project; cons. Peace Corps., 1961—62, Ford Found. on Latin Am. Activities, 1964—66. Mem. Nat. Com. on U.S.-China Rels.; adminstrv. bd. Internat. Assn. Univs; mem. Knight Found. Commn. on Intercollegiate Athletics, Calif. Coun. on Sci. and Tech., Town Hall of Calif., Carnegie Comm. Task Force on Sci. and Tech. and the States, Pacific Coun. on Internat. Policy, NCAA Pres.'s Commn., Coun. for Govt.-Univ.-Industry Rsch. Roundtable and the Nat. Rsch. Coun. Adv. Bd.-Issues in Sci. and Tech.; chancellor's assocs. UCLA; coun. trustees L.A. Ednl. Alliance for Restructuring Now; past chair. Assn. Am. Univs., Nat. Assn. State Univs. and Land-Grant Colls.; past co-chair Calif. Campus Compact; trustee UCLA Found.; bd. dirs. Found. Internat. Exchange Sci. and Cultural Info. by Telecom., L.A. Internat. Visitors Coun., Greater L.A. Energy Coalition, L.A. World Affairs Coun. With USAF, 1951—52. Named Young Man of Year, Westwood Jr. C. of C., 1962; recipient Inter-Am. U. Cooperation award, Inter-Am. Orgn. Higher Edn., Neil H. Jacoby Internat. award, UCLA Student Ctr., 1987, Edward A. Dickson Alumnus of Yr. award, UCLA Alumni Assn., 1994, Disting. Svc. award, U. Calif. Riverside Alumni Assn., 1996, Treasure of L.A. award, L.A. Ctrl. City Assn., 1996, Albert Schweitzer Leadership award, Hugh O'Brien Youth Found., 1996; fellow, UCLA Coll. Letters and Sci., 1996. Fellow: AAAS; mem.: Nat. Collegiate Athletic Assn. Pres. Commn.

**YOUNG, CHRISTOPHER C.,** anesthesiologist; s. John J. and Mirella A. Young; m. Gerry P. Pope, Nov. 27, 1994; children: Caroline, Christopher. MD, NY Med. Coll., Valhalla, 1987. Diplomate Am. Bd. Anesthesiology, Critical Care Medicine. Assoc. prof. anesthesiology Duke U. Sch. Medicine, Durham, NC, 1992—, chief, divsn. critical care medicine dept. anesthesiology, 1996—. Fellowship dir. Critical Care Medicine, Durham, 1996—. Fellow: Am. Coll. Critical Care Medicine. Office: Duke U Med Ctr Dept Anesthesiology Durham NC 27710 Office Phone: 919-668-3400.

**YOUNG, DAVID,** publishing executive; b. 1951; m. Elizabeth Noble; 2 children. With Thorsons, 1970; joined Time Warner Book Group, 1996; CEO Time Warner Book Group- UK, London, 2000—05; chmn., CEO Time Warner Book Group, NYC, 2005—. Chmn. World Book Day, London, 2004. Office: Time Warner Books Group 1271 Ave of Americas New York NY 10020-1300*

**YOUNG, DAVID,** anesthesiologist, educator; b. Miami, Fla. MD, U. Miami Sch. Medicine, Fla., 1990—94. Maj., anesthesiologist U.S. Army, Fort Hood, Tex., 1999—2002; pediatric anesthesiologist Baylor Coll. Medicine, Houston, 2002—06. Maj. US Army, 1999—2002, Fort Hood, TX. Office: Tex Children's Hosp 6621 Fannin St Ste A-200 Houston TX 77030 Office Phone: 832-824-5800. Office Fax: 832-825-5801.

**YOUNG, DAVID MICHAEL,** biochemist, molecular biologist, internist, educator; b. Bluffton, Ind., Oct. 11, 1935; s. Eli and Ruth (Comer) Y.; m. Diane Tangeman, Dec. 28, 1957 (div. 1971); children: Peter Michael, Amy Katherine; m. Lucia Virginia Pratt, Sept. 2, 1972; children: David Michael II, Allison Amelia. BS, Duke U., 1957, MD, 1959. Diplomate: Nat. Bd. Med. Examiners. Intern pediatrics dept. Duke U. Med. Ctr., Durham, NC, 1958-60; staff scientist Lab Cellular Physiology and Metabolism Nat. Heart Inst., NIH, 1960-62; vis. scientist McCollum-Pratt Inst., Johns Hopkins U., Balt., 1962-63, asst. prof. biology, 1963-64; asst. prof. Harvard U. Med. Sch., Boston, 1965-72, assoc. prof. Biol. chemistry, 1972-79, visit biochem. scis., 1966-76, mem. grad. program for advanced study in immunology, 1971-76, assoc. chmn. div. med. scis., chmn. program for cell biology, 1972-76; head Lab Phys. Biochemistry Mass. Gen. Hosp., Boston, 1965-79; prof. biochemistry U. Fla. Coll. Medicine, Gainesville, 1979—, prof. medicine, 1979-86, chmn. dept. biochemistry and molecular biology, 1979-81, prof. molecular biology, 1981-86, prof. pediatrics, 1986—. Mem. cell physiology study sect. NIH, Bethesda, Md., 1978-82, sect. chmn., 1980; acad. assoc. Nichols Inst., San Juan Capistrano, Calif., 1976—; vis. prof. biology Johns Hopkins U., 1994, 95. Editor-in-chief: Jour. Molecular and Cellular Biochemistry, 1983—; patentee nerve growth factor, nerve growth factor antibody. Served to sr. surgeon USPHS, 1959-63. USPHS spl. fellow, 1962; recipient career devel. award USPHS, 1967-72; NIHresearch grantee, 1964—; grantee John A. Hartford Found., 1968-73 Fellow AAAS; mem. Am. Soc. Biol. Chemists, Am. Chem. Soc., Biophys. Soc., Am. Soc. Cell Biology, Alpha Omega Alpha Home: 29 Tenney Hl Blue Hill ME 04614-5948

**YOUNG, DAVID NELSON,** media and communications consultant; b. Baton Rouge, Nov. 12, 1953; s. Nelson Joseph and Agnes (LeBlanc) Young; m. Michéle Marie-Therese Bedél, May 7, 1979; children: Jason, Jessica. Student, La. State U., 1972, U. SW La., 1975. News editor Gonzales Weekly, La., 1976—77. Organizer Soviet/Am. Culinary Exch., 1989, Soviet/Am. HS Basketball Excha., 1990; cons. in field. Host, Ascension Jour. TV Show. Bd. dirs. Ascension Cancer/Leukemia Soc., Gonzales, 1978—; organizer Soviet/Am. High Sch. Basketball Exch.; nat. conmmitteeman La. Dem. Ctrl. Com., 1996-2000. Recipient Best-in-Depth Reporting award La. Newspaper Assn., 1984, Appreciation award USIA, 1988, Sovincentr Medal Honor, Moscow World Trade Ctr., 1988. Mem. East Ascension Genealogical Soc. (pres. 1980-81), East Ascension Sportsman League. Roman Catholic. Avocations: reading, computers, cooking. E-mail: dnyoung@eatel.net.

**YOUNG, DAVID P.,** physics professor; Asst. prof. Dept. Physics La. State U., Baton Rouge. Contbr. articles to profl. jours. Recipient CAREER Award, NSF, 2005. Office: Dept Physics La State U Baton Rouge LA 70803 Office Phone: 225-578-2490. Office Fax: 225-578-5855. E-mail: dyoung1@lsu.edu.

**YOUNG, DAVID WILLIAM,** management educator; b. LA, Feb. 8, 1942; s. William Albert and Hilda Mary (Cook) Y.; m. Ernestine M.L. Van Schaik, Oct. 4, 1968 (div. 1976); m. Francesca Michela Larson, Jan. 28, 1984; children: Christian William, Anthony Edwin. BA, Occidental Coll., 1963; MA, UCLA, 1966; D in Bus. Adminstrn., Harvard U., 1977. Systems engr. IBM, Glendale, Calif., 1963-64; asst. to pres. Lundberg Survey, Inc., Hollywood, Calif., 1964-66; program economist U.S. AID, El Salvador, 1966-69; cons. Thomas Goldsmith & Assoc., Cambridge, Mass., 1969-71; mng. dir. Commonwealth Mgmt. Sys., Cambridge, 1971—; assoc. prof. mgmt. Harvard U. Sch. Pub. Health, Boston, 1976-85, adj. faculty mem., 1985—; prof. mgmt. Boston U. Sch. Mgmt., 1985—2006, chmn. dept. acctg., 1986-91, dir. acctg. MBA program, 1989-93, dir. exec. acctg. rsch. and edn., 1989-93, dir. health care mgmt. program, 1991-94, prof. emeritus, 2006—; prin. The Crimson Group, Cambridge, 1994—. Vis. prof. mgmt. control Instituto de Estudios Superiores de la Empresa, Barcelona, Spain, 1984, 2004. Author: The Managerial Process in Human Service Agencies, 1979, Financial Control in Health Care, 1984, The Hospital Power Equilibrium, 1985, Management Control in Nonprofit Organizations, 1984, 7th edit., 2003, Introduction to Financial and Management Accounting: A User Perspective, 1994, Primer on Financial Accounting, 1998, Primer on Management Accounting, 1999, Managing Integrated Delivery Systems: A Framework for Action, 1999, The Manager's Guide to Creative Cost Cutting: 181 Ways to Build the Bottom Line, 2003, Techniques of Management Accounting,: An Essential Guide for Managers and Financial Professionals 2003, Management Accounting in Health Care Organizations, 2003; contbr. articles to profl. jours. Trustee Roxbury Comprehensive Cmty. Health Ctr., 1983-86, Art Inst., Boston, 1990-96, Mass. Eye and Ear Infirmary, Boston, 1990-92, Symmes Hosp., Arlington, 1993-94, The Atrium Sch., 1995-97, Youville Hosp., 1997-2000, Coolidge Corner Theatre Found., 2000—, Spaulding Rehab. Hosp., 2001-05; commr., chair Mass. Hosp. Payment Sys., 1992-95. Milton Fund fellow Harvard Med. Sch., 1984. Mem.: Am. Acctg. Assn. Democrat. Office: Boston U Sch Mgmt 595 Commonwealth Ave Boston MA 02215-1704 Office Phone: 781-648-8417. E-mail: dwy204@cs.com.

**YOUNG, DELANO VICTOR,** pharmaceutical scientist, biochemist; b. Honolulu, Nov. 17, 1945; s. Lum Fai and Gladys Sau Pung (Wong) Y.; m. Chin-Yi Caroline Yang, Jan. 31, 1970; 1 child, Heather Tien. BS, Stanford U., 1967; PhD, Columbia U., 1973. Postdoctoral fellow Salk Inst. for Biol. Studies, San Diego, 1973-75; asst. prof. dept. chemistry Boston U., 1975-83; asst. dir. Bioassay Systems Rsch. Corp., Woburn, Mass., 1984-86; sr. scientist Damon Biotech, Inc., Needham Heights, Mass., 1986-88, dir., 1988-90; head cell biology Abbott Biotech, Inc. (formerly Damon Biotech, Inc.), Needham Heights, 1990-92; group leader tissue culture Transkaryotic Therapies, Inc., Cambridge, Mass., 1992-94; sect. head, cell culture NitroMed, Inc., Boston, 1994—2006; cons. to pharm. industry Boston, 2006—. Cons. D. Van Nostrand Pub., Boston, 1975-83, Allyn and Bacon Pub., Boston, 1975-83; vis. scholar in biochemistry and molecular biology Harvard U., 1982-83; reviewer Sci. Jour. in Biochemistry, 1973—; initial scientist several biotech. start-up cos., Boston area. Author: (chpt.) Inverted Microcarriers: Using Microencapsulation to Grow Anchorage-Dependent Cells, 1992, Culture of Anchorage Dependent Cells, 1999; contbr. over 30 articles to profl. jours. Eugene Higgins fellow Columbia U., 1967-68, Jane Coffin Childs fellow Salk Inst., 1973-75; GM scholar Stanford U., 1963-67. Mem. AAAS, Am. Soc. Cell Biology, Sigma Xi, Phi Beta Kappa, Phi Lambda Upsilon. Roman Catholic. Achievements include significant contributions to understanding of the nutritional requirements of cancer cells, to devel. of recombinant protein prodn. in biotechnology and cultivation of anchorage dependent cells and to nitric oxide pharmaceuticals. Home: 12 Dennis Rd Wellesley MA 02481 Personal E-mail: delyoung@verizon.net.

**YOUNG, DONA DAVIS GAGLIANO,** insurance company executive, lawyer; b. Bklyn., Jan. 8, 1954; BA and MA in Polit. Sci., Drew U., 1976; JD, U. Conn., 1980. Bar: Conn. 1980, U.S. Dist. Ct. Conn. 1980. Joined The Phoenix Cos., Hartford, Conn., 1980, asst. counsel, 1981—83, assoc. counsel, 1983, dir. reinsurance adminstrn., 1983—84, dir. and asst. v.p. reinsurance adminstrn., 1984—85, 2nd v.p., ins. counsel, 1985-87, v.p., asst. gen. counsel, 1987-89, sr. v.p. individual sales and mktg., gen. counsel, 1989-94, exec. v.p., gen. counsel, 1994—2000, pres., COO, 2000—02, pres., CEO, chmn., 2003—. Bd. dirs. Sonoco Products Co., 1995—, Wachovia Corp., 2000—, Foot Locker Inc. Chair United Way Capital Area Campaign, 2003; bd. dirs. Hartford Hosp.; bd. trustees Goodspeed Opera House Found. Inc. Named Laura A. Johnson Woman of Yr., Hartford Coll. for Women, 2002; recipient Leadership Award for Women in Bus., New England Coun., 1994, Antoinette Bascetta Women's Career Devel. Award, Trust House, Hartford, Conn., 2000, Outstanding Alumni Award, Drew U., 2001, Disting. Grad. Award, U. Conn. Sch. Law, 2002, Human Rels. Award, Nat. Conf. Cmty. and Justice, 2002. Mem. ABA, Hartford County Bar Assn., Conn. Bar Assn., N.Y. Bar Assn. Office: The Phoenix Cos Inc 1 American Row Hartford CT 06102*

**YOUNG, DONALD ALAN,** federal agency administrator; b. Oakland, Calif., Feb. 8, 1939; s. Leo Alan and Pearl Anita (Walker) Y.; children: Jennifer, Karen BA, U. Calif., Berkeley, 1960, MD, 1964. Diplomate Am. Bd. Internal Medicine. Intern, then resident in internal medicine U. Calif. Hosp., San Francisco, 1964-66; resident in internal medicine Parkland Hosp., Dallas, 1966-67; fellow chest diseases U. Calif. Hosp., San Francisco, 1967-68; mem. staff Palo Alto (Calif.) Med. Clinic, 1970-75; med. dir. Am. Lung Assn., 1975-77; scholar adminstrv. scholars program VA, Washington, 1977-80; dep. dir. policy Bur. Program Policy Health Care Financing Adminstrn., HHS, Washington, 1980—84; exec. dir. Prospective Payment Assessment Commn., Washington, 1984—97; sr. v.p. Am. Assn. Health Plans, 1997—99; COO, med. dir. pres. Health Ins. Associates Am., 1999—2003; now acting asst. sec. planning and evaluation HHS, Washington. Clin. instr. U. Calif. Med. Sch., San Francisco, 1968—70, Stanford U. Med. Sch., 1970—75. Bd. visitors Ind. U. Served with MC AUS, 1968-70. Decorated Commendation medal; Recipient Borden award, 1964 Home: 6109 Trotter Ridge Ct Columbia MD 21044-4919 Office: Ste 500 1201 F St NW Washington DC 20004

**YOUNG, DONALD E.,** congressman; b. Meridian, Calif., June 9, 1933; m. Lula Fredson; children: Joni, Dawn. AA, Yuba Jr. Coll., 1952; BA., Chico State Coll., Calif., 1958. Former educator, river boat capt.; mem. Fort Yukon City Council, 6 years, mayor, 4 years; mem. Alaska Ho. of Reps., 1966-70, Alaska Senate, 1970-73, U.S. Congress from Alaska, 1973—; now ranking mem. transp. & infrastructure com.; chmn. resources com., steering com., homeland sec. com. Served in 41st Tank bn. U.S. Army, 1955—57. Republican. Episcopalian. Office: US Ho Reps 2111 Rayburn Ho Office Bldg Washington DC 20515 Office Phone: 202-225-5765. Office Fax: 202-225-0425.*

**YOUNG, DONALD STIRLING,** clinical pathology educator; b. Belfast, N. Ireland, Dec. 17, 1933; s. John Stirling and Ruth Muir (Whipple) Y.; m. Silja Meret; children: Gordon, Robert, Peter. MB, ChB, U. Aberdeen, Scotland, 1957; PhD in Chem. Pathology, U. London, 1962. Terminable lectr. materia medica U. Aberdeen, 1958-59; fellow Postgrad. Med. Sch., U. London, 1959-62, registrar, 1962-64; vis. scientist NIH, Bethesda, Md., 1965-66, chief clin. chemistry service, 1966-77; head clin. chemistry sect. Mayo Clinic, Rochester, Minn., 1977-84; prof. pathology and lab. medicine U Pa., 1984—, vice chmn. lab. medicine dept. pathology and lab. medicine, 1994—; dir. William Pepper Lab. Hosp. of U. Pa., 1984—. Past bd. dirs. Nat. Com. Clin. Lab. Standards. Co-editor: Drug Interference and Drug Metabolism in Clinical Chemistry, 1976, Clinician and Chemist, 1979, Chemical Diagnosis of Disease, 1979, Drug Measurement and Drug Effects in Laboratory Health Science, 1980, Interpretation of Clinical Laboratory Tests, 1985, Effects of Preanalytical Variables on Clinical Laboratory Tests, 1997, Effects of Drugs on Clinical Laboratory Tests, 2000, Effects of Disease on Clinical Laboratory Tests, 2001. Recipient Dir.'s award NIH, 1977, Gerard B. Lambert award, 1974-75, MDS Health Group award Can. Soc. Clin. Chemists, 1978; Roman lectr. Australian Assn. Clin. Biochemists, 1979; Jendrassik award Hungarian Soc. Clin. Pathologists, 1985, ATB award Italian Soc. Clin. Biochemistry, 1987. Mem. Am. Soc. Clin. Chemistry (J.H. Roe award Capital sect. 1973, Bernard Gerulat award N.J. sect. 1977, Ames award 1977, Van Slyke award N.Y. met. sect. 1985, J.G. Reinhold award Phila. sect. 1993, past pres.), Internat. Fedn. Clin. Chemists (past pres.), Acad. Clin. Lab. Physicians and Scientists (past exec. com.), Assn. Clin. Biochemists (Ciba-Corning lectr. 1985). Achievements include research in clinical chemistry, optimized use of the clinical laboratory. Office: Hosp U Pa 3400 Spruce St Philadelphia PA 19104-4283 Business E-Mail: donaldyo@mail.med.upenn.edu.

**YOUNG, DOUGLAS REA,** lawyer; b. LA, July 21, 1948; s. James Douglas and Dorothy Belle (Rea) Y.; m. Terry Forrest, Jan. 19, 1974; 1 child, Megann Forrest BA cum laude, Yale U., 1971; JD, U. Calif., Berkeley, 1976. Bar: Calif., 1976, U.S. Dist. Ct. (no. dist.) Calif. 1976, U.S. Ct. Appeals (6th and 9th cirs.) 1977, U.S. Dist. Ct. (ctrl. dist.) Calif. 1979, U.S. Dist. Ct. Hawaii, U.S. Dist. Ct. (so. dist.) Calif., U.S. Supreme Ct. 1982; cert. specialist in appellate law. Law clk. U.S. Dist. Ct. (no. dist.) Calif., San Francisco, 1976—77; assoc. Farella, Braun & Martel LLP, San Francisco, 1977—82, ptnr., 1983—. Spl. master U.S. Dist. Ct. (no. dist.) Calif., 1977-78, 88, 96, 2000; mem. Criminal Justice Act Def. Panel no. dist. Calif.; mem. faculty Calif. Continuing Edn. of Bar, Berkeley, 1982—, Nat. Inst. Trial Advocacy, Berkeley, 1984—, Practicing Law Inst., 1988—; adj. prof. Hastings Coll.

Advocacy, 1985—; vis. lectr. law Boalt Hall/U. Calif., Berkeley, 1986; judge pro tem San Francisco Mcpl. Ct., 1984—, San Francisco Superior Ct., 1990—Author: (with Purver and Davis) California Trial Handbook, ed edit., (with Hon. Richard Byrne, Purver and Davis), 3d edit., (with Purver, Davis and Kerper) The Trial Lawyers Book, (with Hon. Eugene Lynch, Taylor, Purver and Davis) California Negotiation and Settlement Handbook; contbr. articles to profl. jours Bd. dirs. Berkeley Law Found., 1977-78, chmn., 1978-79; bd. dirs. San Francisco Legal Aid Soc., pres., 1993—; bd. dirs. Pub. Interest Clearinghouse, San Francisco, chmn., 1987—, treas., 1988—; chmn. Attys. Task Force for Children, Legal Svcs. for Children, 1987—; mem. State Bar Appellate Law Adv. Commn., 1994— Recipient award of appreciation Berkeley Law Found., 1983, Criminal Justice Achievement award Criminal Trial Lawyers Assn. of No. Calif., 2002; named a No. Calif. Super Lawyer San Francisco mag., 2004, 05, Top Ten Super Lawyer San Francisco mag., 2005. Fellow Am. Coll. Trial Lawyers, Am. Acad. Appellate Lawyers; mem. ABA (Pro Bono Pub. award 1992), San Francisco Bar Assn. (founding chmn. litigation sect. 1988-89, award of appreciation 1989, bd. dirs. 1990-91, pres. 2001), Calif. Acad. Appellate Lawyers, McFetridge Am. Inn of Ct. (master), Lawyers Club San Francisco Democrat. Office: Farella Braun & Martel 235 Montgomery St Ste 3000 San Francisco CA 94104-2902 Office Phone: 415-954-4438. Business E-Mail: dyoung@fbm.com.

**YOUNG, EDWIN HAROLD,** chemical and metallurgical engineering educator; b. Detroit, Nov. 4, 1918; s. William George and Alice Pearl (Hicks) Y.; m. Ida Signe Soma, June 25, 1944; children: David Harold, Barbara Ellen. BS in Chem. Engring. U. Detroit, 1942; MS in Chem. Engring. U. Mich., 1949, MS in Metall. Engring. 1952. Chem. engr. Wright Air Devel. Center, Dayton, Ohio, 1942-43; instr. U. Mich., Ann Arbor, 1946-52, asst. prof. 1952-56, assoc. prof., 1956-59, prof. chem. and metall. engring., 1959-89, prof. emeritus chem. and metall. engring 1989— Mem Mich Bd Registration for Profl. Engrs., 1963-78, chmn., 1969-70, 72-73, 75-76; mem. Mich. Bd. Registration for Architects, 1963-78 Author: (with L.E. Brownell) Process Equipment Design, 1959; contbr. articles to profl. jours. Dist. commr. Boy Scouts Am., 1961-64; mem. Wolverine coun., 1965-68. With USNR, 1943-46, to capt. Res. ret., 1978. Fellow ASME, ASHRAE, AIChE (Donald Q Kern award 1979), Am. Inst. Chemists, Engring. Soc. Detroit; mem. Am. Chem. Soc., Am. Soc. Engring. Edn., Nat. Soc. Profl. Engrs. (pres. 1968-69, award 1977), Mich. Soc. Profl. Engrs. (pres. 1962-63, Engr. of Year award 1976), Mich. Assn. of Professions (pres. 1966, Distinguished award 1970), Nat. Council Engring. Examiners, Naval Res. Assn., Res. Officers Assn., Sigma Xi, Tau Beta Pi, Phi Kappa Phi, Phi Lambda Upsilon, Alpha Chi Sigma. Republican. Baptist. Home: 609 Dartmoor Rd Ann Arbor MI 48103-4513 Personal E-mail: ehyoung@engin.umich.edu.

**YOUNG, EDWIN S. W.,** federal agency official; b. Honolulu, Nov. 13, 1943; s. Hoon Kwan and Clara (Lee) Y.; m. Joan Tay, May 19, 1978. BA, U. Hawaii, 1966; MBA, U. Utah, Salt Lake City, 1975; MS, U. So. Calif., 1983. Asst. gen. mgr. Royal Men's Shops, Inc., Honolulu, 1973-75; mgmt. analyst U.S. Gen. Acctg. Office, Denver and Honolulu, 1976-83; audit mgr. USAF Audit Agy., L.A., 1983-84, 87-90; fgn. svc. officer Dept. State, 1984-87; with Office of Insp. Gen., Office Policy & Program Rev., Washington, 1984-87; divsn. dir., asst. dir., dir. prodn. Naval Audit Svc. Western Region, Vallejo, Calif., 1990-95; desk officer, planning and policy dir. Naval Audit Svc., Washington, 1995; regional inspector gen. for auditing, audit mgr. U.S. Small Bus. Adminstrn., L.A., 1995-2000; dir. internal audit Calif. State U., Fullerton, 2000—01; dep. city auditor City of Palo Alto, Calif., 2001—. U.S. govt rep. Pacific and Asian Affairs Coun., Honolulu, 1978—83; USN audit svc. rep. World Affairs Coun. No. Calif., 1990—95; exec. dir. The Asian-Am. Found. Phoenix, 1990—; SBA rep. World Affairs Coun. So. Calif., 1995-2000; Calif. State Fullerton rep. World Affairs Coun., 2000—01; City of Palo Alto rep. World Affairs Coun. No. Calif., 2001—. Community coord. Kailua Neighborhood Bd., Honolulu, 1978-83; area rep. Urban Mass Transit Authority, Honolulu, 1978-83. Capt. USAF, 1966-72. Recipient Commendation awards U.S. Gen. Acctg. Office, 1980, USAF Audit Agy., 1983, 88, 90, USAF Acctg. and Fin. Ctr., 1984, U.S. Naval Audit Svc. award 1992, 94, 95, Nat. Assn. Local Auditors award/winner nat. award for best audit, 2004, 05. Mem. Assn. Govt. Accts., Inst. Internal Auditors, Chinese C. of C., World Affairs Coun. Roman Catholic. Avocations: photography, skiing, swimming, tennis, snorkeling. E-mail: eswyoung@aol.com.

**YOUNG, ELIZABETH BELL,** organization consultant; b. Franklinton, N.C., July 2, 1929; d. Joseph H. and Eulalia V. Bell; m. Charles A. Young, Nov. 27, 1964. BA, N.C. Cen. U., 1948, MA, 1950; PhD, Ohio State U., 1959. Cert. speech pathologist; cert. audiologist. Chairperson dept. English Barber Scotia Coll., Concord, NC, 1949-52; dir. speech area, prof. Talladega (Ala.) Coll., 1954-56; dir. speech clinic, prof. Va. State U., Petersburg, 1956-57; prof. Fla. A&M U., Tallahassee, 1959; chmn. dept. English Fayetteville (N.C.) State U., 1959-63; speech pathologist, rsch. assoc. Howard U. Sch. Dentistry, Washington, 1963-64; prof., chairperson dept. English U. Md.-East Shore, Princess Anne, Md., 1965-66; prof., supr. Speech Clinic Cath. U. Am., Washington, 1966-79; congl. staff aide U.S. Ho. of Reps., Washington, 1981-82, 88-90; prof. speech U. D.C., Washington, 1983-84; cons. nat. and local orgns. Washington, 1985-88, 90—. Lectr. over 250 speeches, seminars and workshops; speechwriter, cons. Nat. Assn. Equal Opportunity in Higher Edn., Washington, 1990. Contbr. articles to profl. jours. Fundraiser, pub. rels. polit. candidates, 1963-90; bd. dirs. United Negro Coll. Fund, 1970-80, D.C. Gen. Hosp. Handicapped Intervention Program, 1970-91. Recipient Citations and Certs. of Achievement community and nat. orgns., 1959-90. Fellow Am. Speech-Lang.-Hearing Assn.; mem. Pub. Mems. Assn. (bd. mem. 1980-91, 97-2003, 2003-04), Ohio State U. Alumni Assn., N.C. Cen. U. Alumni Assn. Democrat. Baptist. Avocations: reading, collecting sculpture of foreign countries, travel, writing, public speaking.

**YOUNG, ESTELLE IRENE,** dermatologist, educator; b. N.Y.C., Nov. 2, 1945; d. Sidney D. and Blanche (Krosney) Young. BA magna cum laude, Mt. Holyoke Coll., 1967. MD, Downstate Med. Ctr., 1971. Intern Lenox Hill Hosp., N.Y.C., 1971—72, resident in medicine, 1972—73; resident in dermatology Columbia Presbyn. Hosp., 1973—74, NYU Hosp., 1974—75, Boston U. Hosp., 1975—76; asst. dermatologist Harvard U. Health Svcs., Cambridge, 1975—76; assoc. staff mem. dermatology Boston U. Med. Ctr., 1975—76, 1976—97; pvt. practice medicine specializing in dermatology Petersburg, Va., 1976—97; mem. staff Poplar Springs Hosp., 1976—2002, Southside Regional Med. Ctr. (formerly Petersburg Gen. Hosp.), 1976—2002, Ctrl. State Hosp., 1984—. Clin. instr. dept. dermatology Med. Coll. Va., 1976-87, asst. clinic prof., 1988-94, assoc. clin. prof., 1994-2002; sec. med. staff Petersburg Gen. Hosp., 1982; dermatology cons. Cerebral Palsy Assn. N.Y. State, 1999-2005. Author: Visions of Mauna Kea; contbr. articles to profl. jours. Fellow: Am. Acad. Dermatology; mem.: Hawaii Dermatology Soc., Tidewater Dermatology Soc. (pres. 1982—83), Va. Dermatology Soc., Tidewater Physicians Social Responsibility (pres. 1990), Internat. Physicians Prevention of Nuclear War, Physicians Social Responsibility Soc., Sigma Xi. Home and Office: PO Box 20182 New York NY 10021-0063 Office Fax: 212-249-5948. Personal E-mail: eiy112@aol.com.

**YOUNG, FRANK EDWARD,** retired federal agency administrator, religious organization administrator; b. Mineola, NY, Sept. 1, 1931; s. Frank E. and Erma F. Y.; m. Leanne Hutchinson, Oct. 20, 1956; children: Lorrie, Debora, Peggy, Frank, Jonathan. MD, SUNY, 1956; PhD, Case Western Res. U., 1962; DSc (hon.), Roberts Wesleyan Coll., 1983, Houghton Coll., 1984, SUNY, 1986, L.I. U., 1986, Western Bapt. Coll., 1988. Asst. prof. pathology Western Res. U., Cleve., 1962-65; assoc. mem. microbiology Scripps Clinic & Rsch. Found., LaJolla, Calif., 1965-68; assoc. prof. biology U. Calif. San Diego, 1967-70; mem. microbiology & exptl. pathology Scripps Clinic & Rsch. Found., LaJolla, 1968-70; prof. microbiology and chmn. dept., prof. pathology and radiation biology and biophysics U. Rochester, N.Y., 1970-79, dir. Med. Ctr., 1979-81; dean Sch. Medicine and Dentistry, N.Y., 1979-84, v.p. for health affairs N.Y., 1981-84; commr. FDA, Rockville, Md., 1984-89, dep. asst. sec. for health sci. and environ., 1989-93; dir. office emergency preparedness, 1993-96; pastor adult ministries 4th Presbyn. Ch., Bethesda, Md., 1996—2002; exec. dir. Reformed Theol. Sem. Met. Wash-

ington, Bethesda, 1996-99; v.p. Reformed Theol. Sem., Bethesda, Md., 1999—; chmn., CEO, Cosmos Alliance, 2002—; ptnr. Essex Woodlands Health Ventures, 2006—. U.S. rep. WHO exec. bd., Geneva, 1985-88; bd. dirs. High Tech., Rochester, N.Y., 1983-84. Contbr. numerous articles on cloning, gene mapping, gene shuttle vectors, 1970-84; initiator Fed. Regulations rules to increase access to exptl. drugs to desperately ill, 1987-88. Lectr. Christian orgns., 1970—; mem. United Way, Rochester, N.Y., 1982-84, N.Y. State Statutory Adv. Com. on DNA, Albany, N.Y., 1978. Recipient sec.'s spl. citation Dept. Health and Human Svcs., 1989, Surgeon Gen.'s Exemplary Svc. medal, 1988, Disting. Svc. medal Pub. Health Svc., 1986, Edward Mott award, 1985, Surgeon Gen.'s Medallion, 1992. Mem. Inst. Medicine of NAS, AAAS, Am. Acad. Microbiology (bd. govs.). Avocations: fishing, boating. Office Phone: 301-908-3182. Personal E-mail: FrankCosmos@aol.com.

**YOUNG, FREDERIC HISGEN,** information systems executive, data processing consultant; b. Boston, Sept. 7, 1936; s. Ralph Randel Jr. and Wilhelmina Amalia (Imberger) Y.; m. Carol Joan Costello, Sept. 7, 1963 (div. Dec. 197l); children: Tracy Jean, Jodi Ann; m. Kathleen Paula Thorne, Dec. l, 1984. BBA, U. Mass., 1961; JD, Suffolk U., 1966; AAS in Acctg., Ivy Tech. State Coll., 2005. Mgr. systems and programs Matrix Corp., Burlington, Mass., 1968-69; sr. cons. Programming Dimensions, Inc., Burlington, 1969-70; bus. mgr. JTB Rehab. Ctr., North Reding, Mass., 1970-75; regional bus. mgr. Mass. Dept. Mental Health, Waltham, 1975-78, dir. personnel mgmt. Boston, 1978-81; prin. cons. Lafayette Assocs., Chelsea, Mass., 1980-81; asst. regional dir. Corp. for Applied Systems, Indpls., 1982-84; v.p. cons. svcs. HAS, Inc., Carmel, Ind., 1984-88; v.p. info. svcs. Ind. Fed. Credit Union, Anderson, Ind., 1988-95; sys. cons. AIC, Inc., Indpls., 1995-96; sr. cons. Whittman-Hart, Inc., 1996-98; pres. FHY Assoc., Inc., Rio Rancho, N.Mex., 1999-2000; sr. cons. MarchFIRST, Spencer, Ind., 2000-01; divsn. mgr. PACE 2001—. With USN, 1954-56. Republican. Avocation: woodworking. Home: 1840 Carmichael Ln Spencer IN 47460 Personal E-mail: fredericyoung@earthlink.net.

**YOUNG, GAIL DIANE,** secondary school educator; d. Melvin D Maze and Dorothy L (Evers) Maze; m. Kurt W. Young, Oct. 2, 1982; children: Amy, Kaylynn. BS in family and consumer sci., Miami U., 1982; MS in edn., U. of Dayton, 1999. Family and consumer sci. tchr. West Carrollton Sr. High, Ohio, 1982—. Family and consumer sci. dept. chair West Carrollton Sr. High, Ohio, 1997—; career tech. planning dist. tchr. liaison to the miami valley career tech. ctr. West Carrollton Sr. H.S., Ohio, 2002—; bldg. lead mentor - entry yr. tchg. program West Carrollton Sr. High, 2001—02; career devel. course mentor Miamisburg Sr. H.S., Ohio, 1999, Fairborn Sr. H.S., Ohio, 2000; career devel. adv. mem. Miami Valley Career Tech. Ctr., Clayton, Ohio, 2004—; owner/moderator - fcs work&family list serve The first nationwide E-mail group list for FCS teachers 1997—. Co-founder, former v.p. Milton-Union Early Childhood Ctr., Inc. (non-profit), West Milton, Ohio, 2003; 4-h advisor Miami County 4H Program, Troy, Ohio, 2000. Recipient I Dare You award for Qualities of Leadership, William H. Danforth Found., 1978, Significant Educator award, West Carrollton Edn. Recognition Assn., 1987—, Dickinson T. Guiler award for excellence in edn., 2005. Mem.: NEA, West Carrollton Fellowship Educators, Phi Upsilon Omicron, Kappa Delta Pi. Avocations: travel, boating, gardening, painting. Office Phone: 937-859-5121.

**YOUNG, GENEVIEVE LEMAN,** publishing executive, editor; b. Geneva, Sept. 25, 1930; came to U.S., 1945, naturalized, 1968; d. Clarence Kuangson and Juliana Helen (Yen) Y.; m. Cedric Sun, 1955 (div. 1972); m. Gordon Parks, Aug. 26, 1973 (div. 1979). BA (Wellesley Coll. scholar), Wellesley Coll., 1952. Asst. editor Harper & Row (pubs.), N.Y.C., 1960-62, editor, 1962-64, asst. mng. editor, 1964-66, mng. editor, 1966-70; exec. editor J.B. Lippincott Co., N.Y.C., 1970-77, v.p., 1972-77; sr. editor Little, Brown & Co., N.Y.C., 1977-85; editor-in-chief Lit. Guild Am., N.Y.C., 1985-88; v.p., editorial dir. Bantam Books, N.Y.C., 1988-92. Alumna trustee Phillips Acad., Andover, Mass., 1975-78, class agt., 1979-85; mem. Wellesley Bus. Leadership Coun., 1989-98; mem. Youth Counseling League, 1986-98, pres., 1989-96, mem. com. of 100, 1991-93; mem. Literacy Ptnrs., Inc., N.Y.C., 1992-2001, sec., 1996-2001; mem. Andover Devel. Bd., 1993-98; trustee Jewish Bd. Family and Children's Svcs., 1996-98. Recipient Alumna Achievement award Wellesley Coll., 1982, Matrix award, 1988. Mem. Assn. Am. Pubs. (exec. coun. gen. pub. div. 1975-78, 85-87, freedom to read com. 1972-75), Women's Media Group (pres. 1981-82, 2d v.p. 1994-95), Century Assn. Home: 30 Park Ave New York NY 10016-3801

**YOUNG, GEORGE CRESSLER,** federal judge; b. Cin., Aug. 4, 1916; s. George Philip and Gladys (Cressler) Y.; m. Iris June Hart, Oct. 6, 1951; children: George Cressler, Barbara Ann. AB, U. Fla., 1938, LLB, 1940 postgrad., Harvard Law Sch., 1947. Bar: Fla. 1940. Practice in, Winter Haven, 1940-41; asso. firm Smathers, Thompson, Maxwell & Dyer, Miami, 1947; adminstrv., legislative asst. to Senator Smathers of Fla., 1948-52; asst. U.S. atty. Jacksonville, 1952; partner firm Knight, Kincaid, Young & Harris, Jacksonville, 1953-61; U.S. dist. judge No., Middle and So. dists. Fla., 1961-73; chief judge Middle Dist., 1973-81, sr. judge, 1981—. Mem. com. on adminstrn. fed. magistrates system Jud. Conf. U.S., 1973-80 Bd. dirs. Jacksonville United Cerebral Palsy Assn., 1953-60. Served to lt. (s.g.) USNR, 1942-46. Mem. Rollins Coll. Alumni Assn. (pres. 1968-69), ABA (spl. com. for adminstrn. criminal justice), Fla. Bar Assn. (gov. 1960-61), Jacksonville Bar Assn. (past pres.), Order of Coif, Fla. Blue Key, Phi Beta Kappa, Phi Kappa Phi, Phi Delta Phi, Sigma Alpha Epsilon. Home: 2424 Shrewsbury Rd Orlando FL 32803-1334 Office: George C Young US Courthouse and Fed Bldg 80 N Hughey Ave Orlando FL 32801-2278

**YOUNG, GEORGE HAYWOOD, III,** investment banker; b. Washington, Feb. 10, 1959; s. George H. Jr. and Jeanne Marie (Collins) Y.; m. Adina Chouequet, Oct. 12, 1996; children: Nathalie Haywood, George Haywood IV. BA in Internat. Rels. with honors, Brown U., 1982; MPhil in Internat. Rels., Magdalene Coll., U. Cambridge, Eng., 1983; M in Pub. and Pvt. Mgmt., Yale U., 1987. Assoc. cons. Bain & Co., Boston, 1983-85; assoc. mergers and acquisitions dept. CS First Boston, N.Y.C., 1987-90, v.p., 1990-91, dir., 1992-94; White House fellow U.S. Dept. Treasury, Washington, 1991-92; sr. v.p. Lehman Bros., N.Y.C., 1994-96, mng. dir., 1996—, head global comms. group, 2000—. Chmn. sr. client coun. Lehman Bros., N.Y.C., N.Y., 2004—, mem. global investment banking exec. com., 2004—, mem. firm strategy com., 2005—; spkr. in field Application reader White House Fellows Commn., N.Y.C., 1993—; mem. alumni coun. exec. com. Phillips Acad., Andover, Mass., 1994—98, vis. mem. fin. and investment com. bd. trustees, 1998—2004; mem. regional selection panel White House Fellows Commn., N.Y.C., 2002—04; vol. Ch. of the Holy Trinity, N.Y.C., 1996—97. Mem. Coun. Fgn. Rels. (term membership selection com.), Assn. U.S. Army, Harrow Sch. Assn., Army and Navy Club (Washington, D.C.), Yale Golf Club, Union Club N.Y.C., Metedeconk Nat. Golf Club. Roman Catholic. Home: 115 E 78th St New York NY 10021 Office: Lehman Bros 745 7th Ave New York NY 10019-0001 Business E-Mail: gyoung@lehman.com.

**YOUNG, GILBERT JOHN, JR.,** systems administrator; b. Queens, NY, July 10, 1967; s. Gilbert and Marie Young; m. Julie Bender, June 11, 1994; children: Lindsey, Lauren. BS in Computer Engring., U. Ctrl. Fla., Orlando, 1992. EIT Fla., 1992. Network adminstr. Coleman Rsch. Corp., Orlando, 1993—2000; dir. info. tech. Maxcess, Inc, Orlando, 2000—01; network mgr. SyColeman Corp., Orlando, Fla., 2001—. Cons. in field, 1992—2006. Mem. tech. com. St. Luke's United Meth. Ch., Orlando, 2000—01, St. Lukes United Meth. Ch., Orlando, 2000—01; 2nd v.p. bd. dirs. Montpelier Village, Orlando, 2005—06; voting bd. mem. Williamsburg Homeowners Assn., Orlando, 2005—06. Avocations: ham radio, target shooting, stock market. Home: 5512 Memorial Dr Orlando FL 32821 Office: SyColeman Corp 5885 Lakehurst Dr Orlando FL 32819 Office Phone: 407-354-0047. Personal E-mail: gjy@gjy.us. E-mail: gil.young@l-3com.com.

**YOUNG, GWYNNE A.,** lawyer; b. Durham, N.C., 1950; AB, Duke U., 1971; JD, U. Fla., 1974. Bar: Fla. 1974. Asst. state atty. 13th Judicial Cir., Fla.; mem. Carlton, Fields P.A., Tampa, Fla. Instr. U. Fla. Coll. Law, 1974. Exec. editor U. Fla. Law Review, 1973-74. Pres. Jr. League Tampa, Inc.,

1985-86; bd. dirs. Assn. Jr. Leagues, Inc., 1987-89, Duke U. Nat. Alumni Assn., 1993—, pres., 1999-2000; trustee Duke U., 1999—2001, Tampa Bar Performing Arts Ctr. Fellow: Am. Bar Found.; mem.: U. Fla. Law Ctr. Assn. (trustee), Fla. Bar (bd. govs.). Office: Carlton Fields Corp Ctr Three at Internat Plaza 4221 W Boy Scout Blvd Tampa FL 33607-5736 Business E-Mail: gyoung@carltonfields.com.

**YOUNG, HENRY E.,** tissue engineering medical educator; b. Dayton, Ohio, Dec. 5, 1951; s. Henry O. and Lucille M. Y.; m. Valerie E. Achorn, May 16, 1976; 1 child, Katherine. BS in Biology, Ohio State U., 1974; MS in Zoology, U. Ark., 1977; PhD, Tex. Tech. U., 1983. Instr.biochemistry Rush-Presbyn.-St. Luke's Med. Ctr., Chgo., 1987—88; asst. prof. anatomy Mercer U. Sch. Medicine, Macon, Ga., 1988—95, asst. prof. surgery, 1988—94, assoc. prof. anatomy, pediat., 1995—2004, prof. anatomy, pediat., 2004—. Inventor in field. Recipient Hooding award for excellence in tchg. and rsch., Mercer U. Med. Sch., 1993, 1994, Gender Equity award, Am. Med. Women's Assn., 1997, Humanism in Medicine award, Arnold P. Gold Found., 2005; NIH Postdoctoral fellow in biochemistry, Case We. Res. U., Cleve., 1983—85, postdoctoral fellow, Muscular Dystrophy Assn., 1985—87. Mem.: Am. Soc. Cell Biology, Stem Cells and Regen Medicine, Tissue Culture Soc., Am. Assn. Anatomists, Arnold P. Gold Found., Humanism Hon. Soc. Achievements include discovery of adult germ layer lineage stem cells, adult pluripotent stem cells, and adult near totipotent stem cells; invention of muscle morphogenetic protein and scar inhibitory factor. Avocation: reading. Office: Mercer U Sch Medicine 1550 College St Macon GA 31207-1500 Office Phone: 478-301-4034. Business E-Mail: young_he@mercer.edu.

**YOUNG, HOWARD J.,** lawyer; b. Derby, Conn., Aug. 19, 1967; BA in Polit. Sci., magna cum laude, Tufts U., 1989; JD, Duke U., 1993. Bar: DC 1993, DC 1994. Sr. counsel Office of Counsel to the Insp. Gen., US Dept HHS, 1997—99, dep. chief civil recoveries branch, 1999—2002; ptnr., health care practice group Sonnenschein Nath & Rosenthal LLP, Washington. Mem.: ABA, Gerson Lehrman Coun. Advisors, DC Bar Assn., Health Care Compliance Assn., Am. Health Lawyers Assn. Office: Sonnenschein Nath & Rosenthal LLP Ste 600, E Tower 1301 K St NW Washington DC 20015 Office Phone: 202-408-9210. Office Fax: 202-408-6993. Business E-Mail: hyoung@sonnenschein.com.

**YOUNG, HUGH DAVID,** physics professor, writer; b. Ames, Iowa, Nov. 3, 1930; s. Hugh Surber and Nellie Sibella (Peters) Y.; m. Alice Carroll, June 25, 1960; children: Gretchen Carroll, Rebecca Susan BS in Physics, Carnegie-Mellon U., 1952, MS in Physics, 1953, PhD in Physics, 1959, BFA in Music, 1972. From instr. to assoc. prof. physics Carnegie-Mellon U., Pitts., 1956-77, prof., 1977—; head dept. natural scis. Margaret Morrison Carnegie Coll. Carnegie-Mellon U., 1962-67, acad. coordinator, lectr. modern engring. mgrs. program, 1966-82. Vis. assoc. prof. physics U. Calif., Berkeley, 1967-68, vis. prof. physics, 1974; asst. organist St. Paul's Cathedral, Pitts., 1978-82 Author: Statistical Treatment of Experimental Data, 1962, Fundamentals of Mechanics and Heat, 2d edit., 1974, Fundamentals of Optics and Modern Physics, 2d edit., 1976; (with Sears and Zemansky) College Physics, 7th edit., 1990, University Physics, 9th edit., 1996. Bd. dirs. Renaissance and Baroque Soc., 1980-86. Recipient Ryan Tchg. award Carnegie Inst. Tech., 1965, Doherty award for excellence in edn. Carnegie Mellon U., 1997. Mem. Am. Assn. Physics Tchrs., Am. Phys. Soc., Am. Guild Organists (assoc.) Democrat. Avocations: organ, rock climbing. Home: 5746 Aylesboro Ave Pittsburgh PA 15217-1412 Office: Carnegie-Mellon Univ Dept Physics Pittsburgh PA 15213 Office Phone: 412-268-2759. Business E-Mail: hdy@andrew.cmu.edu.

**YOUNG, J. WARREN,** magazine publisher; Pub. Boys' Life and Scouting Mag., Irving, Tex. Office: Boys' Life PO Box 152079 Irving TX 75015-2079

**YOUNG, JACK ALLISON,** financial executive; b. Aurora, Ill., Dec. 31, 1931; s. Neal A. and Gladys Young; m. Virginia Dawson, Jan. 24, 1959; children: Amy D., Andrew A. BS in Journalism, U. Ill., 1954. CLU; chartered fin. cons.; registered security rep. Advt. writer Caterpillar Tractor Co., 1956-58; inst. agent Equitable Life Assurance Soc., St. Geneva, Ill., 1958—, ins. broker, 1972—; pres. Jack A. Young and Assocs., 1978—, Creative Brokerage, Inc., 1982-95. Past pres., gen. securities prin. Chartered Planning, Ltd., 1984-2000; past trustee Equitable CLU Assn.; past chmn. Equitable Nat. Agents Forum. Bd. dirs. Tri-City Famiy Services, 1975-83, pres., 1979-81; trustee Delnor-Community Health System, 1985-97, chmn., 1988-91; bd. dirs. St. Charles Ctr. Phys. Rehab., 1991-97; chmn., pres. Delnor-Cmty. Health Care Found., 1986-88; dir. Kane County Bar Found., Inc., 1997-2000. Lt. (j.g.) USN, 1956. Named to Equitable Hall of Fame, 1978. Mem. Million Dollar Round Table (life), Am. Soc. C.L.U.s, Am. Coll. C.L.U. Golden Key Soc., Fox Valley Estate Planning Council, Internat. Assn. for Fin. Planning, Inc., Aurora Assn. Life Underwriters (past pres., nat. committeeman), Nat. Assn. Securities Dealers (registered prin.), Geneva Golf Club (pres. 1994). Home: 18 Campbell St Geneva IL 60134-2732 Office: 28 N Bennett St Geneva IL 60134-2207 Office Phone: 630-232-4141. Personal E-mail: jayassoc@aol.com. Business E-Mail: yjackayoung@aol.com.

**YOUNG, JACQUELINE EURN HAI,** former state legislator, consultant; b. Honolulu, May 20, 1934; d. Paul Bai and Martha (Cho) Y.; m. Harry Valentine Daniels, Dec. 25, 1954 (div. 1978); children: Paula, Harry, Nani, Laura; m. Daniel Anderson, Sept. 25, 1978 (div. 1984); m. Everett Kleinjans, Sept. 4, 1988 (div. 1998). BS in Speech Pathology, Audiology, U. Hawaii, 1969; MS in Edn., Spl. Edn., Old Dominion U., 1972; advanced cert., Loyola Coll., 1977; PhD in Communication, Internat. Women's Studies, Union Inst., 1989. Dir. dept. speech and hearing Md. Sch. for the Blind, Balt., 1975-77; dir. deaf-blind project Easter Seal Soc. Oahu, Hawaii, 1977-78; project dir. equal ednl. opportunity programs Hawaii State Dept. Edn., Honolulu, 1978-85, state ednl. specialist, 1978-90; state rep. dist. 20 Hawaii State Legislature, Honolulu, 1990-92, state rep. dist. 51, 1992-94; vice-speaker Hawaii Ho. of Reps., Honolulu. Apptd. to U.S. Dept. Def. Adv. Commn. on Women in the five cons. spl. edn. U.S. Dept. Edn., dept. edn. Guam, Am. Samoa, Ponape, Palau, Marshall Islands, 1977-85; cons. to orgns. on issues relating to workplace diversity; adj. prof. commn., anthropology, mgmt. Hawaii Pacific U.; chief staff officer Am. Cancer Soc. Hawaii Pacific, 2004—. TV writer, host, producer, 1992—. 1st v.p. Nat. Women's Polit. Caucus, 1988-90; chair Hawaii Women's Polit. Caucus, 1987-89; bd. dirs. YWCA Oahu, Kalihi Palama Immigrant Svc. Ctr., Hawaii Dem. Movement, Family Peace Ctr.; appointee Honolulu County Com. on the Status of Women, 1986-87; founding bd. dirs. Windward Spouse Abuse Shelter, 1993—; campaign dir. Protect Our Constn., 1998; trustee St. Louis Sch., 1997-99; mem. nat. adv. coun. ACLU, 2004; nat. bd. dirs. Hawaiian Am. Coalition; mem. Asian and Pacific Islander Am. Health Assn.; mem. Hawaii State Adv. Com. on Civil Rights. Recipient Outstanding Woman Leader award YWCA of Oahu, 1994, Pres.'s award Union Inst., 1993, Fellow of the Pacific award Hawaii-Pacific U., 1993, Headliner award Honolulu chpt. Women in Commn., 1993, Korean Am. Alliance Washington Spl. Recognition award, 1998, Hawaii Women Lawyers Disting. Svc. award, 1999, Disting. Equity Adv. award Hawaii chpt. Nat. Coalition for Sex Equity in Edn., 1998, NEA Mary Hatwood Futrell for advancing women's rights award, 1999, Friend of Social Work award Hawaii chpt. NASW, 1998, Allan Saunders award Hawaii chpt. ACLU, 1999, Light of the Orient award Korean Am. Found., 2006; named one of Extraordinary Women Hawaii, Found. Hawaii Women's History, 2001. Home: 212 Luika Pl Kailua HI 96734-3237 Office Phone: 808-432-9142.

**YOUNG, JAMES E.,** real estate executive, consultant, engineer; b. Celina, Ohio, Sept. 1, 1941; s. Thomas D. and Margaret E. (Flora) Y.; m. Patricia C. Teare, June 13, 1964; children: Kathleen M., Peter C. BSME, Rose-Hulman Inst. Tech., 1963; MBA, Ind. U., 1965; EdS, Ind. State U., 1998. V.p. Citicorp, N.Y.C., 1965-73; pres. James E. Young & Assoc., Inc., Indpls., 1974-91, The Young Group, Naples, Fla., 1991—. Vis. prof. guest lectr. Purdue U., Lafayette, Ind., 1986—; adv. bd. Purdue-Anderson, Inc., 1985—, Rsch. Inst. for Devel. of Interactive Learning Sys., Terre Haute, Ind., 1986—; pres. Remote Equipment Corp., Indpls., 1988-90; pres. Forum for Internat. Profl. Svcs., Inc., 1988-91, bd. dirs.; chmn. bd. WKJM, Inc., 1989-90; chmn. World Competitiveness Conf., 1990—; pres. G & G Angola,

Inc., 1991-98, Ramco of Ind., 1992-98, Jaymer, Inc., 1996—. Author: Industrial Communications Networks, 1987, Load Rating Analysis For Steel Manhole Covers, 1995; Load Rating Analysis for Composite Manhole Covers, 1996, What Makes Steel Manhole Covers Unsafe?, 1999; Smart Choices for Composite Manhole Covers, 2000; patentee in field. Co-founder, chmn. bd. Ind. Amateur Baseball Assn., Inc., 1982—; mktg. chmn. Ind. Major League Baseball Commn., Indpls., 1982-86. Mem. ASME, Soc. Mfg. Engrs., Bus. Modernization and Tech. Corp. (chmn. telecom. 1984—), Rotary, Beta Gamma Sigma. Avocations: reading, boating, golf.

**YOUNG, JAMES E.,** banker; BS in Bus. Adminstrn., Tenn. State U., 1971. Mgmt. trainee Chase Manhttan Bank, N.Y.C., 1971-72, lending officer, from 1972, various lending positions corporate banking dept., v.p., team mgr. credit audit divsn., human resource specialist in charge EEO programs, until 1989; v.p., chief comml. loan officer City Nat. Bank N.J., 1989-90, sr. v.p. gen. adminstrn. and comml. loans, 1990-93; pres., CEO, bd. dirs. 1st So. Bancshares, Atlanta, from 1993, pres., CEO, bd. dirs. 1st So. Bank subs., from 1993; pres., CEO Citizens Trust Bank, Atlanta, also bd. dirs. Mem. regional adv. bd. Fannie Mae; pres., CEO, bd. dirs. Citizens Bancshare Corp., Atlanta, Citizens Trust Bank Mortgage Svcs., Inc., Atlanta. Bd. dirs. Metro tlanta YMCA, Atlanta Neighborhood Devel. Partnership, DeKalb Conv. and Visitors Bur. Mem. Nat. Bankers Assn., DeKalb C. of C. Office: Citizens Trust Bank 75 Piedmont Ave Atlanta GA 30303

**YOUNG, JAMES EDWARD,** lawyer; b. Painesville, Ohio, Apr. 20, 1946; s. James M. and Isabel P. (Rogers) Y. BBA, Ohio U., 1968; JD, Ohio State U., 1972. Bar: Ohio 1972. Law clk. to chief judge U.S. Ct. Appeals, Nashville, 1972-73; chief counsel City of Cleve., 1980-81, law dir., 1981-82; assoc. Jones, Day, Reavis & Pogue (now Jones Day), Cleve., 1973—79, ptnr., 1983—. Office: Jones Day 901 Lakeside Ave E Cleveland OH 44114-1190 Home: 8965 Red Tail Ln Kirtland OH 44094 Office Phone: 216-586-7259. Business E-Mail: jameseyoung@jonesday.com.

**YOUNG, JAMES JULIUS,** academic administrator, retired military officer; b. Fort Ringgold, Tex., Nov. 28, 1926; s. John Cooper and Violet Thelma (Ohl) Y.; m. June Agnes Hillstead, Dec. 17, 1948; children: Robert Michael, Steven Andrew, Patrick James, Mary Frances. BS, U. Md., 1960; M.H.A., Baylor U., 1962; PhD in Hosp. and Health Adminstrn., U. Iowa, 1969. Commd. 2d lt. U.S. Army, 1947, advanced through grades to brig. gen., 1977, comdr., med. ops. officer, dir. tng. field med. units in European Command, 1949-53; comdr. Mil. Med. Leadership Sch., 1953-54; med. advisor (Nationalist Army of China), 1955-57; asst. administr. Fitzsimons Army Med. Center, 1957-60; med. plans and ops. officer (US Forces), Korea, 1962-63; sr. field med. instr., chief field med. service Med. Field Service Sch., 1963-66; dir. health care orgn. and mgmt. analysis Office of Surgeon Gen., 1969-71; dir. med. plans and ops. directorate Office of the Surgeon, Military Assistance Command, Vietnam, 1971-72; exec. officer, chief adminstrv. services Silas Hays Army Hosp., 1973-74; military health analyst, military health care study OMB, Exec. Office of Pres., 1974-76; dep. dir. resources mgmt. and cons. for health care adminstrn. Office of Surgeon Gen., 1976-77; chief med. svcs. corps U.S. Army, 1977-81; dir. ressources mgmt. Office of Surgeon Gen., 1977-81; ret., 1981; instr. U. Iowa, 1967-69; asst. prof., preceptor Baylor U., 1973-74; vice chancellor for health affairs W.Va. Bd. Regents, Charleston, 1982-87; dean sch. of allied health scis. U. Tex. Health Sci. Ctr., San Antonio, 1987-90, interim dean Sch. Medicine, 1988-89, dean Sch. Medicine, 1989—, dean emeritus, 2000—. Cons. to Min. of Health, Republic of Vietnam, 1971-72, 1989-2000; adj. prof. Baylor U., 1977-81, George Washington U., 1975-76, W.Va. U., 1986; prof. U. Tex. health Sci. Ctr., San Antonio, 1989-2000. Contbr. articles to profl. jours. Decorated D.S.M., Legion of Merit, Meritorious Service medal, others; recipient Walter Reed medal, 1981; Army Med. Dept. medal for contbn. to health service, 1981, Order of Mil. Med. Merit, 1981, U. Tex. Health Scis. Ctr. Home medallion Fountains of Progress, 2000; recipient Humanism in Medicine award Health Care Foun. N.J., 2000. Mem. APHA, Coun. Deans, Assn. of Am. Med. Colls., Bexar Cty. Med. Soc., Tex. Med. Assn., Assn. Mil. Surgeons (chmn. med. svc. sect. 1978), Assn. U.S. Army, Interagy. Inst. Fed. Health Execs., Gold Humanism Honor Soc., Phi Kappa Tau. Roman Catholic. Home: 1610 Anchor Dr San Antonio TX 78213-1943 Personal E-mail: jyoung51@satx.rr.com.

**YOUNG, JAMES MARION,** lawyer; b. Winston-Salem, N.C., Nov. 15, 1930; s. William Rector and Celia Marie (Pasley) Young; m. Barbara Marie Pultz, Feb. 2, 1957; children: Deborah Marie, Rebecca Anne, Catherine Arline, Cynthia Louise. BA, U. Va., 1953, LLB, 1957. Bar: Va. Assoc. M.S. McChung, Salem, Va., 1957—58, A. Tracy Loyd, Roanoke, Va., 1958—64, Dodson, Pence & Coulter, Roanoke, 1964—66; ptnr. Dodson Pence Vlar Young and Woodrum, Roanoke and Salem, 1966—. Pres. Roanoke County Coun. PTA, 1970; mem. exec. bd. Blue Ridge Mountains coun. Boy Scouts Am., 1960—, pres. Blue Ridge Mountains coun., 1975—77; chmn. Electoral Bd. City of Salem, 1968—83. Lt. col. (ret.) USAR. Recipient Disting. Svc. award, Salem Jaycees, 1964, Silver Beaver award, Boy Scouts Am., 1976. Fellow: Va. Law Found.; mem.: ABA, Roanoke County Bar Assn. (pres. 1970), Va. Bar Assn. (life), Salem-Roanoke County C. o C. (pres. 1972), Salem Kiwanis (pres. 1981—82). Democrat. Presbyterian. Home: 412 N Shank St Salem VA 24153-2655 Office: 723 College Ave Salem VA 24153-3846

**YOUNG, JAMES MORNINGSTAR,** internist, military officer; b. Massillon, Ohio, Oct. 28, 1929; s. Ralph Louis and Pauline Louise (Morningstar) Y.; m. Bettylu Jones, July 3, 1952; children: Anne Christine, Mark Andrew, Patricia Jane, Elizabeth Lynne, Judith Pamela, Claudia Dianne; m. Mariette M. Aubuchon, Oct. 11, 1970; children: Gretchen Camille, Jason Paul. AB, Duke U., 1951, MD, 1955. Diplomate Am. Bd. Internal Medicine. Intern Bethesda Naval Hosp., 1955-56, asst. dir. tissue bank, 1956-58, resident, 1958-61; commd. lt. (j.g.) USN, 1955, advanced through grades to lt. comdr., 1961, promoted to temporary rank capt., 1963; White House physician to Presidents Kennedy and Johnson, Washington, 1963-66. Asst. chief medicine and dir. of interns, Oakland (Calif.) Naval Hosp., 1966-69; chief medicine Naval Hosp. Boston, Chelsea, Mass., 1969-74; med. officer Naval Air Sta., South Weymouth, Mass., 1974-75; assoc. clin. prof. medicine Boston U. Sch. Medicine, 1969-75; v.p. med. affairs Mass. Blue Shield/Blue Cross, 1975-87; lectr. Harvard Sch. Pub. Health, 1987-90; sr. advisor Beijing Coll. Traditional Chinese Medicine, 1987-88; med. advisor U.S.-China People's Friendship Assn., Washington, 1988-90; cons. USPHS, Office Asst. Sec. for Health, Nat. Ctr. for Health Svcs., Rsch. and Health Care Tech. Assessment, HHS, 1985-90; v.p. for med. affairs Greenery Rehab. Group, Inc., 1988-90; assoc. med. dir. New. Eng. Rehab. Hosp., 1992-95, chief medicine, 1992-95. Contbr. articles to med. publs. Decorated knight comdr. with star Equestrian Order of the Holy Sepulchre of Jerusalem; named Disting. Citizen of Washington H.S., Massillon, Ohio, 1993. Fellow ACP, AMA, Alpha Omega Alpha, Omicron Delta Kappa, Beta Omega Sigma, Sigma Alpha Epsilon. Home: 77 Harvey Mill Rd Lee NH 03824-6302 Personal E-mail: jmyoung9@hotmail.com.

**YOUNG, JAMES R.,** railroad transportation executive; Grad., U. Nebraska. With Union Pacific Corp., 1978—, mgmt. fin. and ops., asst. v.p., re-engineering, Union Pacific R.R. Co., 1994—95, former v.p., fin. & quality, former sr. v.p. fin., exec. v.p., CFO, 1999—2004, pres., Union Pacific R.R. Co., 2004—. Office: Union Pacific Railroad 1400 Douglas St Omaha NE 68179-1001

**YOUNG, JANET MARIE,** secondary school educator; b. West Point, Nebr., Aug. 24, 1957; d. Leland August John and Mary Ann Margaret (Fullner) Liibbe; m. Greg Kent Young, June 16, 1979; children: Heidi Jo, Ryne Kent. BS, Morningside Coll., 1979; MA, U.S.D., 1984. Instr. math. Jefferson H.S., SD, 1979—87, West H.S., Sioux City, Iowa, 1987—. Coach, volley ball, Jefferson H.S., 1979-87, student coun. advisor, West H.S., 1987—Family life commn. 1st United Meth. Ch., Sioux City, 2001—03, mem. worship com., 2005—. Mem. Nat. Coun. Tchrs. Math., Nat. Assn. Student Couns. (mem. exec. bd.), Iowa Coun. Tchrs. Math., Sioux City Edn. Assn., Phi Delta Kappa. Avocation: sports. Home: 3300 Idlewood St Sioux City IA 51104-2321 Office: West High Sch 2001 Casselman St Sioux City IA 51103-1635

**YOUNG, JAY ALFRED,** chemical safety and health consultant, editor, writer; b. Huntington, Ind., Sept. 8, 1920; s. Jacob Phillip and Marie (Skully) Y.; m. Anne Elizabeth Neff, June 29, 1942 (dec. June 1962); children: John, Paul, Cecelia, Michael, Joseph, Andrea, Therese, Gregory, Thomas, Lucy, Margaret, Antonia; m. Mary Ann Owens, Aug. 15, 1962; children: James, Laurence; 4 stepchildren. BS, Ind. U., 1939; AM, Oberlin Coll., 1940; PhD, U. Notre Dame, l950. Chief chemist Asbestos Mfg. Co., Huntington, Ind., 1941-42; ordnance engr. U.S. War Dept., Washington, 1942-44; from instr. to prof. chemistry King's Coll., Wilkes-Barre, Pa., 1949-69; vis. prof. Carleton U., Ottawa, Ont., Canada, 1969-70, Fla. State U., Tallahassee, 1975-77; Hudson prof. Auburn (Ala.) U., 1970-75; mgr. tech. publs. Chem. Mfrs. Assn., Washington, 1977-80; chem. safety and health cons. Silver Spring, Md., 1980— Pro bono cons. OSHA, EPA, Consumer Product Safety Commn., Washington, 1980—; invited lectr. chem. edn. and chem. health and safety U.S., Can., Mex., Brazil, Argentina, Chile, Great Britain, Norway, France, Italy, India, Indonesia, Australia, New Zealand, Japan, 1963—. Author: Practice in Thinking, 1958, Elements of General Chemistry, 1960, Chemical Concepts, 1963, Selected Principles of Chemistry, 1963, Arithmetic for Students of Science, 1968, Instructor's Guide for Chemistry, a Cultural Approach, 1971, Study Guide for General Chemistry, 1974, Fire!, 1977, Actions and Reactions, 1978, Chemistry, A Human Concern, 1978, Kitchen Chemistry, 1980, Electron Microscopy Safety Handbook, 1985, Chemical Laboratory Information Profiles, 2001-, Introduction to Toxicology, 2004; co-author: Study Guide for Continental Classroom Chemistry, NBC/TV, vols. I and II, 1959, 60, Keys to Chemistry, 1973, Chemistry Preparation Laboratory, 1973, Keys to Oxidation-Reduction, 1974, Things that Last, 1977, Principles of Laboratory Safety (with videotape), 1980, OSHA Hazard Communication Regulations, 1984, Chemical Safety Manual for Small Businesses, 1st edit., 1989, 2d edit., 1992, Developing a Chemical Hygiene Plan, 1990; editor: Guidelines and Recommendations for the Preparation and Continuing Education of Secondary School Teachers of Chemistry, 1977, Improving Safety in the Chemical Laboratory: A Practical Guide, 1st edit., 1989, 2d edit., 1992 (also contbr.), Safety in Academic Chemistry Laboratories, Vols. 1 and 2, 7th edit., 2002, Chemical Safety for Teachers and Their Supervisors, Grades 7-12, 2001; co-editor: Heath Chemistry Laboratory Experiments, 1987, Handbook of Chemical Health and Safety, 2001 (also contbr.); contbr. and cons. numerous books; contbr. Encyclopedia Britannica, and over 100 articles to profl. jours. Tech. resource person to media and expert witness regarding chem. hazards, precautions, transp. incidents involving chems.; mem. NSF Coll. Chemistry Commn., 1962-68. Lt. USNR, 1944-46. Recipient Disting. Chemistry Alumnus award U. Notre Dame, 1968, Excellence in Chemistry Tchg. award Mfg. Chemists Assn., 1970. Fellow AAAS; mem. Am. Chem. Soc. (councilor 1963-87, policy com. 1970-81, sec. divsn. chem. edn. 1969-78, chmn. divsn. chem. health and safety 1979-80, mem. chem. safety com. 1982-2003, Chem. Health and Safety award 1991, Outstanding Svc. award 2003). Roman Catholic. Avocations: wood and metalworking, gardening. Home and Office: 12916 Allerton Ln Silver Spring MD 20904-3105 Office Phone: 301-384-1768. Personal E-mail: chemcon@juno.com.

**YOUNG, JAY MAITLAND,** health products executive, consultant; b. Louisville, Nov. 26, 1944; s. Clyde Dudley and Olive May (Tyas) Y. BA in Chemistry and Math. magna cum laude, Vanderbilt U., 1966; MS in Biochemistry, Yale U., 1967, MPhil in Phys. Chemistry, 1968, PhD in Chemistry, 1971. Cert. Am. Med. Writers Assn. Multi-disciplinary Core, 1999. Asst. prof. chemistry Bryn Mawr (Pa.) Coll., 1970-76; rsch. biochemist Abbott Labs., Ill., 1977-78, project mgr. physiol. diagnostics Abbott Park, 1978-80, project mgr. cancer product devel., 1980-82, internat. clin. specialist sci. affairs, 1982-85, clin. project mgr. physiol. diagnostic quality and sci. support, 1986-90, staff quality assurance and sci. support, 1990-93, fertility, pregnancy, thyroid mgr., quality and sci. support, 1993-95, fertility, pregnancy, thyroid, cancer mgr., product quality assurance, 1995-97, staff noninfectious disease diagnostics sci. affairs, 1997—2001; cons. and med. writer pharm. and diagnostic areas, 2002—. Cons. Inst. for Cancer Rsch., Fox Chase, Phila., 1974, vis. scientist, 1975-76; honors examiner Swarthmore Coll., 1973, 74, mem. vis. evaluation com., 1975; presenter to med. groups on cancer markers, viral hepatitis and epidemiology of AIDS, 1982-84. Contbr. articles to profl. jours.; patentee in field. Vol. Episcopal Ch. Outreach Commn. Named to Hon. Order Ky. Cols.; predoctoral fellow NSF, Yale U., 1966-70; postdoctoral fellow, NIH, U. Oxford, 1971-72; travel grantee NATO, 1974. Mem. Am. Med. Writers Assn. (Del. Valley chpt. program chair 2002-03, treas. 2003—, cert mem. Multi-disciplinary Core 1999). Office Phone: 610-322-4444. E-mail: maitland@mailbug.com.

**YOUNG, JEFFREY THOMAS,** economics professor; b. Madison, Wis., Apr. 21, 1948; s. William Henry and Sara Elizabeth (Reish) Y.; m. Cheryl Eileen Merrifield, Aug. 23, 1969; children: Christopher, Janet. BA, U. Maine, Orono, 1971; PhD, U. Colo., Boulder, 1975. Vis. asst. prof. U. Colo., Denver, 1975-76; asst. prof. Marshall U., Huntington, W.Va., 1976-80; asst. prof. econs. St. Lawrence U., Canton, N.Y., 1980-85, assoc. prof., 1985-91, prof., 1991—. Vis. prof. Newcastle U., 1993—94; hon. rsch. fellow U. Glasgow, Scotland, 2001. Author: Classical Theories of Value, 1978, Economics as a Moral Science: The Political Economy of Adam Smith, 1997; contbr. articles to profl. jours. Deacon Calvary Bapt. Ch., Canton, 1984-86, Christian Fellowship Ctr., Madrid, N.Y., 1991—. Mem. Am. Econs. Assn., History of Econs. Soc., Assn. of Christian Economists, Internat. Adam Smith Soc., European Soc. History of Econ. Thought. Avocations: reading, cross country skiing, basketball. Office: St Lawrence U Dept Econs Canton NY 13617 Business E-Mail: jyoung@stlawu.edu.

**YOUNG, JENNIFER BAXENDELL,** former federal agency administrator; b. Bellevue, Ohio; m. J. T. Young. BA magna cum laude, Georgetown U. Exec. asst. Ohio Human Services Dept.; dir. health legis. Nat. Governors' Assn.; sr. adv. to Chmn. William V. Roth Senate Fin. Com.; sr. adv. on health care issues to Chmn. William Thomas House Com. on Ways and Means; exec. dir. pub. programs Am. Assn. Health Plans, 2002; dep. asst. sec. for legis. US Dept. Health & Human Services, Washington, asst. sec. for legis., 2003—05, acting sr. counselor for health policy, 2005; ptnr. Tarplin, Downs & Young LLC, 2006—.*

**YOUNG, JESS RAY,** retired internist; b. Fairfield, Ill., Feb. 4, 1928; s. Edgar S. and Clara B. (Musgrave) Y.; m. Gloria Wynn, July 10, 1953; children—James C., Patricia A. BS, Franciscan U., 1951; MD, St. Louis U., 1955. Intern Highland Alameda County Hosp., Oakland, Calif., 1955-56; resident in internal medicine Cleve. Clinic Hosp., 1956-59, mem. staff dept. vascular medicine, 1959-97, chmn. dept., 1976-97; ret., 1998. Co-author: Leg Ulcer, 1975, Peripheral Vascular Diseases, 1991, 1996; contbr. articles to profl. jours., chpts. to books. Served with AUS, 1946-47. Mem. AMA, Am. Heart Assn. (stroke council), AMA, Coll. Cardiology, Internat. Cardiovascular Soc., ACP, Am. Fedn. Clic. Research, Ohio Soc. Internal Medicine, Soc. for Vascular Medicine and Rsch., Inter-Urban Club. Methodist. Home: 1503 Burlington Rd Cleveland OH 44118-1216 Personal E-mail: jesyoung@adelphia.net.

**YOUNG, JESSICA S.E.,** secondary school educator; b. Phila., Apr. 5, 1951; d. Frank Henry and Shirley Ruth (Rosen) Edelman; m. Michael Andrew Young, Dec. 19, 1971; children: Shana Claire, Paula Ruth, Henry David. AB, U. Chgo., 1971; MA, Columbia U., N.Y.C., 1973, MPhil, 1975, PhD, 1988. Tchr. The Harvard Sch., Chgo., 1990—94, Oak Park (Ill.) and River Forest H.S., Home: AP European History Exam., 1997—. Co-author: (book) The New Teacher's Guide to AP European History, 2005. Mem. AP European History Test Devel. Com., Princeton, NJ, 2003—. Finalist Golden Apple award, Golden Apple Found., 2001. Mem.: Nat. Coun. Social Studies, Am. Hist. Assn. (Beveridge Family Tchg. Prize 2001), World History Assn. (Nat. Tchg. Prize 2002, 2001, 2003). Office: Oak Park & River Forest HS 201 N Scoville Ave Oak Park IL 60302 Office Phone: 708-383-0700 ext. 3360. Business E-Mail: jyoung@oprfhs.org.

**YOUNG, JOHN EDWARD,** lawyer; b. Tulsa, July 11, 1935; s. Russell Edward and Frances Lucille (Wetmore) Y.; m. Mary Moore Nason, Dec. 27, 1966; children: Cynthia Nason Eberstadt, Abigail Brackett Moses. BS with honors, Calif. Inst. Tech., 1956; LLB magna cum laude, Harvard U., 1959. Bar: N.Y. 1961, U.S. Dist. Ct. (so. dist.) N.Y. 1973. Assoc. Cravath, Swaine & Moore LLP, N.Y.C., 1960-67, ptnr., 1968-95, resident ptnr. Paris, 1971-73, London, 1990-95, sr. counsel, 1996—. Editor Harvard Law Rev., 1958-59. Trustee Internat. Sculpture Ctr., 1997-2005, vice chmn., 2000—04; trustee Royal Oak Found., 1997-2002, chmn., 1999-2002; gov. Am. Crafts Mus., 1997-2000; trustee Nat. Found. for Advancement of the Arts, 2003—. Sheldon Traveling fellow, Harvard U., 1959—60. Mem. Assn. Bar City N.Y., Century Assn., Harvard Club of N.Y.C., N.Y. Yacht Club, Key Biscayne Yacht Club. Democrat. Episcopal. Home: 1088 Park Ave New York NY 10128-1132 also: 548 S Mashta Dr Key Biscayne FL 33149 Office: Cravath Swaine and Moore LLP 825 Eighth Ave New York NY 10019 E-mail: jeyoung@attglobal.net.

**YOUNG, JOHN HARDIN,** lawyer; b. Washington, Apr. 25, 1948; s. John D. and Laura Virginia (Gwathmey) Y.; m. Mary Frances (Farley) Crosby. JD, U. Va., 1973; BCL, Oxford U., Eng., 1976. Bar: Va. 1973, DC 1974, Pa. 1979, U.S. Dist. Ct. Va. 1974, U.S. Dist. Ct. DC 1974, U.S. Dist. Ct. Md. 1989, U.S. Ct. Fed. Claims 1974, U.S. Ct. Appeals (4th, 5th, Fed. and DC cirs.), Internat. Trade Ct. 1974, U.S. Supreme Ct. 1977. Ptnr., counsel Porter Wright Morris & Arthur, Washington, 1988—99; with Exec. Office of the Pres., Washington, 2000; ptnr., counsel Sandler, Reiff & Young, PC, 2001—; exec. v.p. external affairs SECORIX, Inc., Washington, 2004—. Adv. bd. Antitrust Bull., 1980-1994; mem. U.S. Sec. State's adv. com. Pvt. internat. Law, 1987-95; chmn. Va. Retirement Sys. Rev. Bd., 1990-94; asst. atty. gen. Commonwealth of Va., 1976-78; mem. Delmarva Interstate Compact, 2004-06; moderator Alexandria Forum, 1993-98, Fedn. Forum/TV Channel 10, 1989-91; sr. v.p., gen. counsel various tech. cos.; adj. faculty George Mason U. Sch. Law, 2003—05 Author: Young's Federal Rules of Evidence, Mastering Written Discovery; contbr. articles to profl. jours. Spl. counsel Dem. Nat. Com., 1998—99, chair nat. lawyers coun., 1998—2004; lead recount counsel for V.P. Gore Fla., 2000. Fellow: Am. Bar Found. (life); mem.: ABA (chmn. adminstrv. law and regulatory practice sect. 1999—2000, standing com. on continuing edn. of the bar 2002—04, standing com. on election law 2005—, fellow adminstrv. law 2001—), Am. Inns of Ct. Found. (trustee 2004—), Temple Bar Found. (bd. dirs., founder), Comml. Bar Assn. U.K. (overseas 1991—2002), George Mason Am. Inn of Ct. (master 1990—, pres. 2002—03, Best Spl. Projects award 2003), Am. Law Inst. (life), Phi Alpha Theta (history honors). Episcopalian. Office Phone: 202-479-1111. Business E-Mail: young@sandlerreiff.com.

**YOUNG, JOHN JACOB, JR.,** federal agency administrator; b. Moreland, Ga., May 29, 1962; s. John Jacob and Gloria Jewell (Wheelus) Y.; m. Barbara Joan Schleihauf, Oct. 22, 1988; children: Nathan Jacob, William Joseph. BS in Aerospace Engring., Ga. Inst. Tech., 1985; MS in Aeronautics and Astronautics, Stanford U., 1987. Engr. in Tng., Ga. Senate intern U.S. Senator Sam Nunn Intern Program, Washington, 1984; engring. coop. Gen. Dynamics Ft. Worth Div., 1980-84; mem. tech. staff The BDM Corp., Huntsville, Ala., 1985-86, Rockwell Internat. Missile Systems Div., Duluth, Ga., 1987-88, Sandia Nat. Labs., Albuquerque, 1988-93; AIAA Congl. fellow prof. staff U.S. Senate Appropriations Com., Subcommittee on Def., Washington, 1991-93; profl. staff subcom. on def., U.S. Senate Appropriations Com.; asst. sec. rsch. devel. & acquisition, USN U.S. Dept. Def., Washington, 2001—05, dir. def. rsch. & engring., 2005—. Organizer, coach BDM Co-ed. Softball team, Huntsville, Ala., 1986; big brother Big Bros., Big Sisters, Huntsville, Ala., 1986; tutor El Dorado High Sch., Albuquerque, N.Mex., 1989-90. Recipient AIAA Gen. Dynamics scholarship, 1984; fellow Coll. Engring. Stanford U., 1985; named Outstanding Young Engr., AIAA Atlanta Section, 1988. Mem. Am. Inst. of Aeronautics and Astronautics, Briaerean Soc., Phi Kappa Phi, Tau Beta Pi, Sigma Gamma Tau, Phi Eta Sigma. Presbyterian. Office: US Dept Def 3030 Def Pentagon Rm 3C638 Washington DC 20301*

**YOUNG, JOHN LLOYD,** actor; b. July 04; BA in Drama, Brown U. Actor: (Broadway plays) Jersey Boys, 2005 (Theatre World award, 2006, Outer Critics Cir. award, outstanding actor in musical, 2006, Drama Desk award outstanding actor in a musical, 2006, Tony award, best performance by leading actor in a musical, 2006), (Off-Broadway) Spring Awakening, 2000, The Five Hysterical Girls Theorem, 2001, Sarah, Plain & Tall, 2002, The Summer of the Swans, 2003, (regional theatre) A Christmas Carol, Ferdinand, 2002, Spare Change, 2004, The Chosen, 2004 (named best featured actor in a play, NJ Star-Ledger, 2004), A Bronx Tale, 2005, The Drawer Boy, 2005; (TV series) Law & Order, 2002; (films) The Belligerents, The Roman Soldier, 2001, Moon River, 2001. Adv. bd. William Inge Festival. Mailing: c/o Nina Shreiber ACME NY 875 Avenue of the Americas New York NY 10001 Office Phone: 212-328-0386. Office Fax: 646-472-5203. E-mail: jlynyc@johnlloydyoung.com.*

**YOUNG, JOHN SACRET,** writer, film director, film producer; b. Glen Ridge, N.J., May 24, 1947; s. William Clements and Margaret Eugenia (Klotz) Y. BA, Princeton U., 1969. Pres. Sacret, Inc., L.A., 1977—, Samobet, Inc., L.A., 1990—. Writer/producer (TV movies) Champions: A Love Story, 1979, Fire on The Mountain, 1981; creator/writer/exec. producer/dir. (TV series) China Beach (2 Emmy nominations, 2 WGA nominations, recipient best drama show, Golden Globe award, People's Choice award, among others), writer: West Wing, 1999 (Writer's Guild award nominee); writer/dir., Level 9, 1000; writer (mini-series) A Rumor of War, 1980, Testament, 1983; writer/exec. producer Romero, 1989; author (novel) The Weather Tomorrow, 1982, Black Rainbow, 2002, (memoir) Remains: Non-Viewable, 2005. Recipient Humanitas Prize Human Family Ednl. Cultural Inst., 1978, 89, Kennedy Found. award, 1978, Christopher award The Christopher Soc., 1983, 89, Peabody award Coll. Journalism and Communication U. Ga., 1989, Jane Pauley Media award NACHR, 1989, Crecen 7th annual award Crecen Soc., 1990, Am. Women in Radio and TV commendation, 1990. Mem. Writers Guild Am. (recipient award, 1980), Dir. Guild Am. Avocations: hockey, art, islands. Mailing: c/oAuthor Mail Farrar, Straus & Giroux 19 Union Sq West New York NY 10003

**YOUNG, JOHN WATTS,** retired astronaut; b. San Francisco, Sept. 24, 1930; s. William H. Y.; m. Susy Feldman; children by previous marriage: Sandra, John. BS in Aero. Engring. Ga. Inst. Tech., 1952; LLD (hon.), Western State U., 1969; D Applied Sci. (hon.), Fla. Technol. U., 1970; DSc (hon.), U.S.C., 1981, Brown U., 1983; DEng (hon.), Glasgow U., 2001; PhD (hon.), Ga. Tech. U., 2003. Joined USN, 1952, advanced through grades to capt.; test pilot, program mgr. F4 weapons systems projects, 1959-62; then maintenance officer Fighter Squadron 143, Naval Air Sta., Miramar, Calif.; chief astronaut office Flight Ops. Directorate NASA, 1974-87, spl. asst. dir. JSC for engring. ops., safety, 1987-96, assoc. dir. (tech.) JSC, 1996—2004; ret., 2004. Cons. NASA. Decorated DFC (3), D.S.M. (2); recipient NASA Disting. Svc. medal (4), NASA Exceptional Svc. medal (2), NASA Engring. Achievement medal, 1988, NASA Outstanding Leadership medal, 1992, NASA Outstanding Achievement medal, 1994, AIAA Goddard Astronautics award, 2000, Congl. Space medal of honor, 1981; named Disting. Young Alumni Svc. award Ga. Tech. Acad. Disting. Engrs., 1994; named to Nat. Aviation Hall of Fame, 1988, Ga. Aviation Hall of Fame, 1998, Tex. Aviation Hall of Fame, 2003, Ga. Tech. Engring. Hall of Fame, 2005. Fellow Am. Astronautical Soc. (Flight Achievement award 1972, 81, 83, Space Flight award 1993), Soc. Exptl. Test Pilots (Iven Kincheloe award 1972, 81), AIAA (Haley Astronautics award 1973, 82, 84, NASA Disting. Exec. 1998, 2001, Rotary Space Trophy 2000, Houston Hall of Fame 2002); mem. Sigma Chi. Achievements include being an astronaut NASA, made 1st two-man orbit flight, Gemini 3, Mar. 1965, Gemini 10 3 day flight, 1966, Apollo 10 8-day flight lunar landing dress rehearsal, 1969, Apollo 16 11 day lunar landing and surface exploration, 1972; comdr. 54 hour, 36 orbit 1st flight of Space Shuttle, 1981, and 10-day orbital flight 1st flight Space Lab, 1983; dir. space shuttle br., astronaut office, 1973-75.

**YOUNG, JON NATHAN,** archaeologist; b. Hibbing, Minn., May 30, 1938; s. Robert Nathan Young and Mary Elizabeth (Barrows) Roy; m. Karen Sue Johnson, June 5, 1961 (div. May 1980); children: Shawn Nathan, Kevin Leigh; m. Tucker Heitman, June 18, 1988 (div. Apr. 1996). BA magna cum laude, U. Ariz., 1960, PhD, 1967; MA, U. Ky., 1962. Archeologist Nat. Park Svc. Southwest Archeol. Ctr., Globe and Tucson, Ariz., 1967-75; exec., camp dir. YMCA of Metro. Tucson, 1976-77; asst. dir. Kit Carson Meml. Found., Taos, N.Mex., 1978; co-dir. Las Palomas de Taos, 1979; archeologist Nat. Forest Svc., Carson Nat. Forest, Taos, 1980-99, Taos Ski Valley, 2000—05. Exec. order coms. U.S. Sec. Interior, 1973-75. Author: The Salado Culture in Southwestern Prehistory, 1967; co-author: Excavation of Mound 7, 1981, First-Day Road Log in Tectonic Development of the Southern Sangre de Cristo Mountains, 1990, The Gila Pueblo Salado, 1997. Active YMCA White Rag Soc. Grantee NEH, 1978; Ariz. Wilson Found., NSF, Ky. Rsch. Found. fellow, 1960-62; Baird Found., Bausch and Lomb, Elks; recipient cert. merit USDA, 1987, 89. Fellow AAAS, Am. Anthrop. Assn., Explorers Club, Royal Anthrop. Inst.; mem. Am. Com. for Preservation of Archaeological Collection, Current Anthropology Ariz. Archaeol. and Hist. Soc., Ariz. Hist. Soc., Ctr. Anthropol. Studies, Coun. on Am.'s Mil. Past, Friends of Taos Pub. Libr., Friends of Taos Land Trust, New Mex. Heritage Preservation Alliance, Soc. Hist. Archaeology, Soc. Am. Archaeology, Southwest Forest Svc. Amigos, Harwood Found., Millicent Rogers Mus., Pimal County Hist. Soc. (life), Taos Archaeol. Soc., San Juan County Mus. Assn., Taos County Hist. Soc. (bd. dirs.), Taos Hist. Mus., Sigma Xi, Phi Beta Kappa, Alpha Kappa Delta, Phi Kappa Phi, Delta Chi. Home: HCR 74 Box 24826 El Prado NM 87529-9549

**YOUNG, JONATHAN,** lawyer; BA in govt. magna cum laude, U. Va., 1979; JD, Georgetown U., 1983. Law clk. to Hon. Caleb M. Wright US Dist. Ct. of Del.; trial atty. civil divsn. US Dept. Justice, Washington; atty. Anderson Kill & Olick PC, Shea & Gould, 1994—98; ptnr. Reed Smith LLP, NYC, 1998—, mem. exec. com. Office: Reed Smith 599 Lexington Ave 29th Fl New York NY 10022 Fax: 212-521-5450. Office Phone: 212-521-5414. Business E-Mail: jyoung@reedsmith.com.

**YOUNG, JOY W.,** gifted and talented educator; b. Birmingham, Eng., May 17, 1944; arrived in U.S., 1972; d. Robert and Bessie Warne; Cert. in biology and gifted edn., City Birmingham Coll. Edn., 1965; BS in Biology, Va. Commonwealth U., 1973, MS in Biology, 1975. Lic. in biology and gifted edn. Sci. tchr. Fentham H.S., Birmingham, 1965—69; sci. tchr. dept. chair sci. Boldmere H.S., Warwickshire, England, 1969—72; instr. biology Va. Commonwealth U., Richmond, 1972—76; earth sci. tchr. Mapp Jr. High, Portsmouth, Va., 1976—77; life health environ. sci. dept. chair I.C. Norcom H.S., 1977—81; bus. owner, 1981—85; life sci. tchr. Ruffner M.S., Norfolk, 1985—89; instr. gifted program Divsn. Experiments and Rsch. Norfolk Pub. Schs., 1989—2004; adj. prof. biology Tidewater Ctr. St. Leo Coll., 1992-2005. Presenter in field. Editor: An Introduction to Life Processes, 1974; contbr. articles to profl. jours. Com. mem. Va. Stds. Learning, Richmond, 1979; vol. charitable work feeding hungry various orgns., Portsmouth, 1979—2004. Named Tchr. of Yr., All City Tchg. Team Norfolk Pub. Schs., 1986; recipient Sch. Bell awards outstanding contbns. sch. sys., Norfolk Pub. Schs., 1989—2004, 1st Robotics award, Ford Motor Co., 2001—04; grantee, MIT U., Boston, 2004. Mem.: Chesapeake Bay Found. Episcopalian. Avocations: gardening, guitar, crafts, poetry, writing. Office: NORSTAR/NTVC 1330 N Military Hwy Norfolk VA 23502-2230 Office Phone: 757-892-3303 ext. 8. Office Fax: 757-892-3299. Personal E-mail: joyyoungnetmail@netscape.net.

**YOUNG, JOYCE L.,** chemicals executive; Chief info. officer, v.p. info. tech. CP Kelco, 2003—. Named one of Premier 100 IT Leaders, Computerworld, 2005. Office: CP Kelco Ste 1000 1000 Parkwood Cir Atlanta GA 30339 Office Phone: 678-247-7300.*

**YOUNG, JUDITH ANNE,** animal conservationist; b. LA, Feb. 11, 1953; d. John Mahlstedt Young and Cynthia Sheilds Tunnicciff. CEO Otter Conservation Ctr., Statesboro, Ga., 1983—. Copyright U.S. Govt., 1995. Avocations: gardening, agriculture. Office Phone: 912-839-2100. Personal E-mail: judy@g-net.net.

**YOUNG, KENNETH WAYNE,** environmental health specialist; b. Woodstock, Va., Feb. 12, 1947; s. Kenneth Woodrow and Florence Eleanor (Schmidt) Young; m. Sandra Lynn Sweet (div.); 1 child, James Ira. BS, East Tenn. State U., 1969. Social worker Surry County Social Svcs., Surry, Va., 1972—73; sanitarian Richmond City Health Dept., Richmond, Va., 1974—84, Caroline County Health Dept., Bowling Green, Va., 1984—86; sr. environ. health specialist Chesterfield (Va) Health Dept., 1986—. Editor: (Newsletter) Coalition Report, 1976—92. Comm. dir. Richmond Human Rights, Richmond, Va., 1973—93; pres. RHRC Found., Inc., Richmond, 1978—84. With U.S. Army, 1970. Recipient Human Rights award, Richmond Human Rights Coalition, 1986. Mem.: ACLU, Va. Organizing Project, Richmond Peace Ctr., Richmond Friends Mtg. Democrat. Achievements include founder of Va. Ctrl. Am. Network, 1982. Home: 1942 N Junalaska Dr Richmond VA 23225-2322 Office: Chesterfield Health Dept PO Box 100 Chesterfield VA 23832 Office Phone: 804-751-4456. Office Fax: 804-717-6106. Business E-Mail: Wayne.Young@vdh.virginia.gov.

**YOUNG, LAI-SANG,** mathematician, educator; b. Hong Kong, 1952; BS, U. Wisconsin, 1973; MA, U. Berkeley, 1976, PhD, 1978. Prof. Northwestern U., 1978, U. Warwick, England, 1979—80, Michigan State U., 1980; prof. math. UCLA, 1981; visiting prof. Math. Sci. Rsch. Inst., Berkeley, 1983—84, U. Bielefeld, Germany, 1985—86, Inst. Advanced Study, Princeton, 1989; prof. math. NYU, Courant Inst. Math. Sci., NYC. Recipient Ruth Lyttle Math. prize Am. Math. Soc., 1993, Guggenheim Fellowship, 1997-98. Fellow: Am. Acad. Arts & Sci.

**YOUNG, LAURA,** dance educator, choreographer; b. Boston, Aug. 5, 1947; d. James Vincent and Adelaide Janet Young; m. Anthony Charles Catanzaro, Sept. 26, 1970 (div. Nov. 1981); m. Christopher Edward Mehl, Aug. 23, 1987. Grad. H.S., Cohasset, Mass. Dancer Met. Opera Ballet, N.Y.C., 1971-73, Boston Ballet Co., 1963-65, prin. dancer, 1965-71, 73-89, ballet mistress, 1989-91. Guest tchr. Dance Tchrs. Club Boston, 1978—82, Dance Masters Assn., 1979, 90, 92, 93, Walnut Hill Sch., Natick, Mass., 1984—87, Natick, 1990—91, Granite State Ballet, 1993, Portland Ballet, Maine, Nat. Dance Theatre Bermuda, 1993, Worcester Performing Arts Sch., Mass., 1994, Alwin Sch. Dance Summer Intensive, Albuquerque, 1994—95, Ashland Youth Ballet, Ky., 1995, N.E. Regional Festival, 1996, Okla. Summer Arts Inst., 2000, Pitts. Ballet Theater Summer Program, 2000; asst. dir. Boston Ballet II, 1984—86, tchr., dir., 1986—96, dir. Summer Dance Program, 1986—94; dir. DanceLab, 2001—; 1st hon. mem. Dance Masters Assn., Chpt. 5, 1992; mem. faculty Boston Conservatory, 1990—94, Boston Ballet Sch., 2004—, prin., 1993—2004. Choreographer (ballets) Occasional Waltzes, 1984, Albinoni Suite, 1986, Champ Dances, 1987, A Place of Sound and Mind, 1988, Deadlock, 1989, Rumpelstiltskin, 1989. Recipient Leadership award Greater Boston C. of C., 1987; named Disting. Bostonian Boston's 350th Jubilee Com., 1980. Mem. Am. Guild Mus. Artists, Dance Masters Am. (hon.). Office: Boston Ballet Co 19 Clarendon St Boston MA 02116-6100 Office Phone: 617-456-6250. Business E-Mail: lyoung@bostonballet.org.

**YOUNG, LAURA ELIZABETH,** artist; b. Glen Ridge, N.J., Apr. 1, 1941; d. Thomas Edward and Charlotte Elizabeth (Post) Y.; m. James Andrew Murphy, Jun. 15, 1963 (div. 1985); children: Kevin Thomas, Timothy James.; m. Thomas Raymond Aprile, May 20, 1995. BA, Skidmore Coll., 1963; MA, Montclair State Coll., 1978; MFA, Rutgers U., 1983. Cert. Fine Arts and English, K-12 tchr., N.J. Adj. faculty Fine Arts Dept. Kean Coll., Union, N.J., 1983-84, Montclair (N.J.) State Coll., 1983-92, Long Island U., Bklyn., 1994; cons., workshop leader The Lincoln Ctr. Inst., N.Y.C., 1983—; Lectr. Mus. Modern Art, N.Y.C., 1990-96; visual arts cons., workshop leader The Nashville Inst. for the Arts, 1992-98—; Lincoln Ctr. Inst.; adj. faculty Fine Arts Dept. U. Iowa, 1996—' artist in residence Tyron Guthrie Ctr., Ireland, 2006. One person shows include: Interior Space Design, N.Y.C., 1991,

Manhattenville Coll., N.Y., 1993, Cedar Rapids (Iowa) Mus. Art, 1998, Monmouth (Ill.) Coll., 2001; group shows Colgate U., Hamilton, N.Y., 1995, Vincennes (Ind.) U., 2003. Grantee fellow in painting N.J. State Coun. on the Arts, Trenton, 1985, Iowa Arts Coun., 1997, 2001, Va. Ctr. Creative Arts, Sweet Briar, Va., 1985, 86, 2001, 2002-03, 2004, Intermedia Performance grantee Sch. Fine and Performing Arts, Montclair, 1992, Pollock Krasner Found. grantee, 1994, fellow Tyrone Guthrie Ctr., Monaghan County, Ireland, 2006. Democrat. Avocations: nature walks, collecting folk art. Home: 50 Lakeview Pl NE Iowa City IA 52240-9162 E-mail: lauraelizabethyo@aol.com.

**YOUNG, LAUREN SUE JONES,** education educator; b. San Diego, July 21, 1947; d. Warren Calvin and Lola Esther Jones; 1 child, Forest McRay Young. AB, Occidental Coll., 1969; MS, San Diego State U., 1971; EdM, Harvard U., 1979, EdD, 1984. Adminstrv. asst. Child Devel. Research Unit, Nairobi, Kenya, 1969-70; asst. prof. San Diego State U., 1974—78, assoc. dir. Tchr. Corps., 1971—78; co-chmn. and mem. Harvard Ednl. Review, Cambridge, Mass., 1979-81; research assoc. The Huron Inst., Cambridge, 1980-82, Atari Cambridge Research Lab., Cambridge, 1982-84; policy analyst N.Y. State Dept. Social Services, Albany, 1984-85, spl. asst. to commr., 1985-87; assoc. prof. Mich. State U., East Lansing, 1987-2001; sr. program officer, dir. The Spencer Found., Chgo., 1998—; bd. dirs. Josephinum Acad., 1999—, bd. chair, 2005—. Cons. Am. Insts. for Rsch., Cambridge, 1980, Tchr. Corps, Boston area, 1978-80, instr., Pago Pago, Am. Samoa, 1979; rsch. assoc. A Study of H.S.'s, Cambridge, 1980-82; disting. visitor John D. and Catherine T. MacArthur Found., 1995-96. Co-editor: Too Little, Too Late, 1988; mem. editorial bd. Evaluation Rev. Jour., L.A., 1984-88, Jour. Negro Edn. Team mem. Operation Crossroads Africa, Morogoro, Tanzania, 1968; mem. program adv. bd. Spencer Found., 1992. Recipient Danforth Found. fellow, St. Louis, 1978-84, tchr. scholar award, M.S.U., 1993. Mem. Am. Ednl. Research Assn. Office: The Spencer Foundation 625 N Michigan Ave Ste 1600 Chicago IL 60611-3109

**YOUNG, LAURENCE R.,** biomedical researcher, biomedical engineer, aeronautical engineer, aerospace engineer; AB, Amherst Coll., 1957; Cert. in Applied Math., Sorbonne, Paris, 1958; MSEE, MIT, ScD in Instrumentation, 1962. With Sperry Gyroscope Co., 1957—58; rsch. staff MIT, Cambridge, 1958—62, faculty, 1962—, Apollo prof. astronautics, 1995—, prof. health scis. and tech., 2003, Harvard - MIT, 2003—; dir. Nat. Space Biomed. Rsch. Inst., Houston, 1997—2001. Rschr. in eye movement St. Medicine, U. P.R., 1961; payload specialist Spacelab Life Scis. 2, NASA, alt. payload specialist, 1993; chmn. Harvard-MIT Com. on Biomed. Engring. and Physics and Interdeptl. PhD Program in Biomed. Engring.; vis. prof. Swiss Fed. Inst. Tech., 1972—73, Zurich Kantonsspital, 1972—73, Conservatoire des Arts et Metiers, Paris, College de France, Paris, 2002; vis. scientist NASA Ames Rsch. Ctr., 1987—88; vis. prof. elec. engring. Stanford U.; lectr. Harvard Med. Sch., Boston; chmn. airlift panel Air Force Sci. Adv. Bd.; mem. space medicine and biology com. NAS; mem. life sci. adv. com. NASA; mem. tng. com. on biomed. engring. NIH; mem. numerous coms. NRC. Contbr. over 200 articles to profl. jours. Recipient Air Force Decoration for Exceptional Civilian Svc., Dryden Lectureship in Rsch., AIAA, 1982, Jeffries award, 1992, Paul Hansen award, Aerospace Human Factors Assn., 1995, Pub. Svc. Group Achievement award, NASA, Award of Merit, U.S. Ski Assn., Best Rsch. Paper award, Am. Acad. Otolaryngol.-Head and Neck Surg. Biol. Engring., IEEE; mem.: ASTM (chair ski injury statistics subcom., com. on snow skiing chmn.), Internat. Soc. for Skiing Safety (dir.), Biomed. Engring. Soc., Aerospace Med. Assn., Human Factors Assn., Barany Soc. (pres. 1979, Alza Lectr. 1984), Nat. Acad. Engring., Inst. of Medicine of NAS, Explorers Club. Achievements include research in instrumentation and basic and applied research in field of vestibular function; psychophysical work on semicircular canal and otolith function led to models which are applied to flight simulator motion control and are being extended to include visually-induced motion effects; ski injurys. Home: 217 Thorndike St Apt 108 Cambridge MA 02141 Office: MIT Rm 37-219 77 Massachusettes Ave Cambridge MA 02139-4307

**YOUNG, LAURENCE RETMAN,** biomedical engineer, educator; b. NYC, Dec. 19, 1935; s. Benjamin and Bess (Retman) Y.; m. Joan Marie Fisher, June 12, 1960; children— Eliot Fisher, Leslie Ann, Robert Retman. AB, Amherst Coll., 1957; SB, MIT, 1957, SM, 1959, ScD, 1962; Certificat de License (French Govt. fellow), Faculty of Sci. U. of Paris, France, 1958. Registered profl. engr., Mass. Engr. Sperry Gyroscope Co., Great Neck, NY, 1957; engr. NASA Instrumentation Lab., MIT, 1958-60, asst. prof. aero. and astronautics, 1962-67, assoc. prof., 1967-70, prof., 1970—, payload specialist spacelab life sci., 1991-93; prof. Baylor Coll. Medicine, Houston, 1996—2003; prof. of health sci. and tech. Harvard MIT, 2003—. Dir. Nat. Space Biomed. Rsch. Inst., 1997-01; summer lectr. U. Ala., Huntsville, 1966-68; lectr. Med. Sch. Harvard U., 1970-78; mem. tng. com. biomed. engring. NIH, 1971-73; mem. com. space medicine and biology Space Sci. Bd., NAS, 1974-77, chmn. vestibular panel summer study of life scis. in space, 1977; mem. com. engring. and clin. care NAE, 1970; mem. Air Force Sci. Adv. Bd., 1979-85; mem. Air Force Studies Bd., NRC, 1982, Aeros. and Space Engrs. Bd., 1982-87; mem. NRC Com. on Space Sta., 1987, 1991—, Com. on Human Exploration Space, 1990, Com. on Human Factors, 1990—; CHABA coun. NASA Task Force on Sci. Uses of Space Sta., 1982-85; vis. prof. Swiss Fed. Inst. Tech., Zurich, 1972-73, Conservatoire Nationale des Arts and Metiers, Paris, 1972-73, Stanford U., 1987-88; vis. scientist Kantonsspital Zurich, 1972-73; prin. investigator vestibular expts. on Spacelabs— 1, SLS-1, 2 and D-1, 1977—; cons. Applied Sci. Lab., NASA, Gulf & Western, Link div. Singer Co., Boeing, Lockheed, others; payload specialist Space Shuttle STS-58 (Spacelab SLS-2), NASA Johnson Space Ctr., 1992—; vis. prof. Coll. de France, Paris, 2003. Contbg. author: chpt. on vestibular system Medical Physiology, 1974, Handbook of Physiology, 1983, Encyclopedia of Neuroscience, 1987; editorial bd. chpt. on vestibular system Internat. Jour. Man-Machine Studies, 1966-75, Neurosci., 1976-92; contbr. numerous articles to profl. jours. Recipient Pub. Svc. Group Achievement award NASA, 1984, Exceptional Civilian Svc. award USAR, 1985, Koetser Found. prize, 1998. Fellow IEEE (Franklin V. Taylor award 1963, First Am. Space Life Sci. lectr. 1990), AIAA (Dryden lectr. 1981), Aerospace Medical Assn. (Jeffries Medical Rsch. award 1992), Aerospace Human Factor Assn. (Paul Hensen award 1995), Am. Inst. for Med. and Biol. Engring., US Ski Assn. (award of merit 1976), Explorers Club; mem. NAE, Inst. Medicine, Am. Physiol. Soc. (1st lectr. in aerospace life scis. 1990), Biomed. Engring. Soc. (founding/charter mem. dir. 1972-75, pres. 1979-80, Alza lectr. 1984), Aerospace Med. Assn., ASTM (com. on snow skiing 1975—, chmn. 1988-93), Internat. Soc. Skiing Safety (bd. dirs. 1977-85), AIAA (working group for simulator facilities 1976-80), Nat. Acad. Engrs., Inst. Medicine, Internat. Acad. Astronautics (corr.), Barany Soc., Cosmos Club, Tau Beta Pi. Home: 217 Thorndike St Apt 108 Cambridge MA 02141-1504 Office: MIT Man-Vehicle Lab Rm 37-219 Cambridge MA 02139 Business E-Mail: lry@mit.edu.

**YOUNG, LAWRENCE,** electrical engineering educator; b. Hull, Eng., July 5, 1925; arrived in Can., 1955; naturalized, 1972; s. Herbert and Dora Y.; m. Margaret Elisabeth Jane, Jan. 5, 1951. BA, Cambridge U., Eng., 1946, PhD, 1950, DSc, 1963. Asst. lectr. Imperial Coll., London, 1952-55; mem. research staff B.C. Research Council, 1955-63; assoc. prof. U. B.C., Vancouver, 1963-65, prof. dept. elec. engring., 1965-90, prof. emeritus, 1990—. Author: Anodic Oxide Films, 1961; contbr. articles to profl. jours. Recipient Callinan award Dielectrics div. Electrochemical Soc., 1983, Can. Electrochem. Gold medal, 1990. Fellow IEEE, Royal Soc. Can., Electrochem. Soc. Office: U BC Dept Elec Engring Vancouver BC Canada V6T 1W5 Business E-Mail: youngl@interchange.ubc.ca.

**YOUNG, LEROY,** plastic surgeon; b. Oneida, Ky., Oct. 14, 1945; BS, U. Ky., Lexington, 1966, MD, 1970. Cert. in Surgery 1978, in Plastic Surgery 1981. Intern U. Ky. Med. Ctr., Lexington, 1970—71, resident, gen. surgery, 1973—77; resident, plastic surgery Barnes Hosp., Washington U., St. Louis, 1977—79; attending physician surgery Barnes Hosp., St. Louis, 1979—, St.

Louis Children's Hosp., 1979—, Barnes-Jewish West County Hosp., St. Louis, 1990—; prof., plastic reconstructive surgery Washington U. Sch. Medicine, St. Louis, 1990—. Mem.: Am. Soc. for Aesthetic Plastic Surgery (chair, nonsurg. procedures com., co-chair, breast surgery com.), Am. Bd. Plastic Surgery (examiner), Plastic Surgery Edn. Found. (chair, silicone implant rsch. com.), Am. Soc. Plastic Surgeons (bd. dirs.). Address: Ste 17424 One Barnes Hosp Plz Saint Louis MO 63110

**YOUNG, LOWELL SUNG-YI,** health facility administrator, medical educator; b. Honolulu, Dec. 5, 1938; AB, Princeton U., 1960; MD, Harvard U., 1964. Di;omate Am. Bd. Internal Medicine with subspecialty in infectious diseases. Intern, jr. asst. resident, sr. asst. resident med. divsn. Bellevue Hosp. and Meml. Hosp., N.Y.C., 1964-67; fellow in medicine Cornell U. Med. Coll., 1965-67; epidemic intelligence officer bacterial diseases br. Nat. Communicable Disease Ctr., Atlanta, 1967-69, chief spl. pathogens sect., 1968-69; spl. postdoctoral rsch. fellow Nat. Inst. Allergy and Infectious Diseases, 1969-70; rsch. fellow in medicine Meml. Hosp./Cornell U. Med. Coll., 1969-70; clin. asst. physicisn infectious disease svc. dept. medicine Meml. Hosp., 1970-72, assoc. dir. microbiology lab., 1971-72; instr. in medicine Cornell U. Med. Coll., 1970-72; chief divsn. infectious disease Calif. Pacific Med. Ctr., San Francisco, 1985-99; asst. clinician Sloan-Kettering Inst. for Cancer Rsch., 1971-72; dir. Kuzell Inst., San Francisco, 1985—; asst., assoc. prof. med. UCLA, 1972—85. Adj. prof. pharmacy U. of Pacific, San Francisco, 1989-95; mem. microbiology and invectious diseases adv. com. Nat. Inst. Allergy and Infectious Diseases, 1981-85, mem. allergy and immunology rsch. com., 1975-79; mem. adv. coun. Nat. Infectious diseases, 1996-2000; mem. staff Calif. Pacific Med. Ctr., mem. Zion Hosp. and Med. Ctr., U. Calif., San Francisco. Mem. editl. bd. Antomicrobial Agts. and Chemotherapy, Infection and Immunity; contbr. numerous articles to profl. jours., chpts. to books. Recipient Alexander D. Langmuir prize Epidemic Intelligence Svc., 1970, Garrod medal Brit. Soc., 1992. Fellow ACP (mem. med. self-assessment com.), Infectious Diseases Soc. Am. (councillor 1983-85); mem. Am. Soc. for Clin. Investigation, Am. Fedn. for Clin. Rsch., Am. Soc. for Microbiology, Western Soc. for Clin. Rsch., Internat. Immunocompromised Host Soc., Brit. Soc. Antimicrobial Chemotherapy. Office: Kuzell Inst 2200 Webster St Ste 305 San Francisco CA 94115-1821 Office Phone: 415-600-1734. Business E-Mail: younglx@sutterhealth.org.

**YOUNG, LUCY CLEAVER,** retired physician; b. Aug. 8, 1943; d. Oliver B. and Ada (Smith) Cleaver; m. Lynn H. Young, Feb. 4, 1968 (div. 1977); m. Lynn H. Young, Apr. 2, 1986; 1 child, Clinton Oliver. BS in Chemistry, Wheaton Coll., Ill., 1965; MD, Ohio State U., 1969. Diplomate Am. Bd. Family Practice, Bd. Ins. Medicine. Rotating intern Riverside Meth. Hosp., Columbus, Ohio, 1969-70; resident Trumbull Meml. Hosp., Warren, Ohio, 1970—71; practice medicine specializing in family practice West Chicago, Ill., 1971—73, Paw Paw and Mendota, Ill., 1973—78; co-founder, med. dir. Wholistic Health Ctr. of Mendota, 1976—78; asst. med. dir. Gt. Lakes head office Met. Life Ins. Co., Aurora, Ill., 1979—80; med. dir. Commonwealth Life Ins. Co., Louisville, 1980—85; locum tenens family practice Kron Med. Corp. of Chapel Hill, NC, 1986—89; physician Red Bird Mission & Med. Ctr., Beverly, Ky., 1989—90; family practice floater Ochsner Clinic satellites, New Orleans, 1990—2006; ret. Assoc. prof. U. Ill. Abraham Lincoln Sch. Medicine, 1976-79; faculty monitor MacNeal Meml. Hosp. Family Practice Ctr. (Ill.), 1979-80; faculty preceptor U. Louisville Family Practice Dept., 1981-85; clin. faculty preceptor La. State U. Sch. Medicine, 1992-2006; mem. staffs Ctrl. DuPage Hosp., Winfield, Ill., 1971-73, Mendota Cmty. Hosp., 1973-80, Ochsner Found. Hosp., New Orleans, 1991-2006; musician La. Via de Cristo, 2003-05. Vol. Red Bird Med. Ctr., 1985—; part-time worship coord. Hosanna Luth. Ch., Mandeville, La., 1996-97; musician, lay preacher, nursing home visitor, 1990—. Fellow Am. Acad. Family Practice; mem. Christian Med. and Dental Assns. (del. to Ho. 1995-2000). Lutheran. Home: PO Box 0730 Madisonville LA 70447-0730

**YOUNG, M. DENDY,** finance company executive; Pres., CEO Falcon, 1989-94; prin., cons. The Exeter Group, 1994-95; pres., CEO Govt. Tech. Svcs., Inc., Chantilly, Va., 1995-98, CEO, dir., 1995—, chmn. bd. dirs., 1998—. Office: Govt Tech Svcs Inc 3901 Stonecroft Blvd Chantilly VA 20151-1032

**YOUNG, MARILYN VIRGINIA,** elementary school educator; b. Searcy, Ark., Sept. 16, 1949; d. Russell Uel and Mary Eunice Watkins; m. William Wayne Young, Jan. 23, 1971; children: William Wayne Jr., David Russell. BS in Elem. Edn., Ark. State U., 1971. Tchg. Cert. Ark. Tchr. Osceola Sch. Dist., Ark., 1971—73, Ark., 1989—, El Dorado Sch. Dist., Ark., 1973—76; bookkeeper accounts receivable Coleman's Office Sch. Products, Conway, Ark., 1976—88; tchr. East Poinsett County Sch., Tyronza, Ark., 1988—89. Named Progressive Club Tchr. of Yr., Greater Fedn. of Women's Clubs, 2005. Episcopal. Avocations: gardening, sewing. Home: 606 W Quinn Ave Osceola AR 72370 Office: West Elem 138 Franklin Osceola AR 72370 Personal E-mail: marilyn@arkansas.net.

**YOUNG, MARVIN OSCAR,** lawyer; b. Union, Mo., Apr. 4, 1929; s. Otto Christopher and Irene Adelheide (Barlage) Y.; m. Sue Carol Mathews, Aug. 23, 1952; children: Victoria Leigh, Kendall Marvin. AB, Westminster Coll., 1951; JD, U. Mich., 1954, LLD, 1989. Bar: Mo. 1954. Practice law firm Thompson, Mitchell, Thompson Douglas, St. Louis, 1954-55, 57-58; atty. Mo. Farmers Assn., Columbia, 1958-67; exec. v.p. First Mo. Corp., Columbia, 1965-68; v.p. ops. MFA-Central Coop., Columbia, 1967-68; gen. counsel, sec. Peabody Coal Co., St. Louis, 1968-82; gen. counsel Peabody Holding Co., Inc., St. Louis, 1983-85; also dir., sec. subs. and affiliates Peabody Coal Co.; ptnr. Gallop, Johnson & Neuman, St. Louis, 1986—, chmn. corp. dept., 1988-90, chmn. energy dept., 1990—. City atty., Warson Woods, Mo., 1990—; spkr. in field. Contbr. articles to profl. jours. Pres. Warson Woods PTA, 1974-75; trustee Met. Sewer Dist. St. Louis, 1974-80, chmn. 1978-80; mem. Mo. Energy Coun., 1977-77, Mo. Environ. Improvement and Energy Resources Authority, 1983-87, vice-chmn. 1986-87; trustee Eastern Mineral Law Found., 1983-98; pres. Alumni Assn. Westminster Coll., Fulton, Mo., 1978-80, trustee coll., 1977—, exec. com., 1978-2003, chmn. 1986-90, chmn. investment com., 1998-2002; chmn. Churchill Meml. and Libr., Fulton, 1992-2000; mem. chancellor's coun. adv. bd. U. Mo., St. Louis, 1992—; trustee Stages—St. Louis, 2001—; lawyers adv. coun. Gt. Plains Legal Found., Kansas City, Mo., 1976-84; mem. Rep. Com. Boone County, Mo., 1962-68, chmn. legis. dist. com., 1962-64, 66-68; alt. del. Rep. Nat. Conv., 1968; pres. Clayton Twp. Rep. Club, 1973-77; mem. St. Lucas United Ch. of Christ, 2004—. Capt. USAF, 1955-57. Churchill fellow Churchill Meml. and Libr., Fulton, Mo.; recipient Alumni Merit award Westminster Coll., 1972; named Coal Lawyer of Yr. Nat. Coal Assn., 1994 Mem. ABA, Mo. Bar Assn., Bar Assn. Met. St. Louis, Round Table Club St. Louis, John Marshall Rep. Lawyers Club (pres. 1977), Mo. Athletic Club, Shamrock Club St. Louis County, Rotary (bd. dirs. St. Louis club 1993-95), Barristers Soc. (life), Order of Coif (life), Masons, Shriners. Home: 555 Flanders Dr Saint Louis MO 63122-1617 Office: Gallop Johnson & Neuman LC 101 S Hanley Rd Ste 1700 Saint Louis MO 63105-3489 Office Phone: 314-615-6210. E-mail: moyoung@gjn.com.

**YOUNG, MARY ELIZABETH,** history professor; b. Utica, N.Y., Dec. 16, 1929; d. Clarence Whitford and Mary Tippit Y. BA, Oberlin Coll., 1950; PhD, Cornell U., 1955. Instr. dept. history Ohio State U., Columbus, 1955-58, asst. prof., 1958-63, assoc. prof., 1963-69, prof., 1969-73; prof. history U. Rochester, NY, 1973—2000, prof. emeritus, 2000—. Cons. in field. Author: Redskins, Ruffleshirts, and Rednecks: Indian Allotments in Alabama and Mississippi, 1830-1860, 1961; co-editor, contbr.: The Frontier in American Development: Essays in Honor of Paul Wallace Gates, 1969. Recipient Pelzer award Miss. Valley Hist. Assn., 1955, award Am. Studies Assn., 1982, Ray A. Billington award, 1982; Shalkenbach Found. grantee, 1951-55, Social Sci. Rsch. Coun. grantee, 1968-69; Ezra Cornell fellow Cornell U., 1951-55. Mem. Am. Hist. Assn., Orgn. Am. Historians, Soc. for Historians of the Early Am. Republic, Am. Antiquarian Soc. Home: 2230 Clover St Rochester NY 14618-4124 Office: U Rochester Dept History Rochester NY 14627 Office Phone: 585-275-2054. Business E-Mail: yngm@mail.rochester.edu.

**YOUNG, MELODIE S.,** adult nurse practitioner; b. Sikeston, Mo., July 27, 1962; d. Joe D. and Mary Rose Smith; m. Gary P. Young, Nov. 21, 1987; children: Carder J., Chaney T. BSN, William Jewell Coll., Liberty, Mo., 1985; MSN, U.Tex., 1999. Adult Nurse Practitioner, NY, 1999; Geriatric Nurse Practitioner, NY, 2000, Dermatology Nurse Certified, NJ, 1999. Dir. Baylor Psoriasis Ctr., Dallas; nurse practitioner Tex. Dermatology Assoc., Dallas, 1999—2005, Modern Dermatology, Dallas, 2006—. Med. adv. bd. Nat. Psoriasis Found., Portland, Oreg., 2003—; bd. dirs. Internat. Psoriasis Coun., Dallas, 2004—; pres. Dermatology Nurses' Assn., Dallas, 2006—. Contbr. articles to profl. jours. Adv. coun. First Bapt. Acad., Dallas, 2003—05. Mem.: Dermatology Nurses' Assn. (treas., pres. 1995—2006). Achievements include research in national psoriasis tissue bank. Office: Modern Dermatology 9101 N Central Expressway Ste 150 Dallas TX 75231 Office Phone: 214-265-1818. Office Fax: 214-265-1806.

**YOUNG, MERWIN CRAWFORD,** political science professor; b. Phila., Nov. 7, 1931; s. Ralph Aubrey and Louise (Merwin) Y.; m. Rebecca Conrad, Aug. 17, 1957; children: Eva Colcord, Louise Conrad, Estelle Merwin, Emily Harriet. BA, U. Mich., 1953; postgrad., Inst. Hist. Rsch. U. London, 1955-56, Inst d'Etudes Politiques, U. Paris, 1956-57; PhD, Harvard U., 1964; DSc (hon.), Fla. Internat. U., 1998. Asst. prof. polit. sci. U. Wis., Madison, 1963-66, assoc. prof., 1966-69, prof., 1969—2001, emeritus, 2001—, Rupert Emerson prof., 1983; H. Edwin Young prof., 1994; chmn. African Studies Program U. Wis., Madison, 1964-68, chmn. dept. polit. sci., 1969-72, 84-87, assoc. dean Grad. Sch., 1968-71, acting dean Coll. Letters and Sci., 1992-93. Vis. prof. Makerere U. Coll., Kampala, Uganda, 1965-66; dean Faculty of Social Sci. Nat. U., Lubumbashi, Zaire, 1973-75; Fulbright prof. U. Dakar, Senegal, 1987-88. Author: Politics in the Congo, 1965, The Politics of Cultural Pluralism, 1976 (Herskovits prize 1977, Ralph Bunche prize 1979), Ideology and Development in Africa, 1982, The African Colonial State in Comparative Perspective, 1994 (Gregory Luebbert prize 1995); co-author: Cooperatives and Development, 1981, The Rise and Decline of the Zairian State, 1985; editor: The Rising Tide of Cultural Pluralism: The Nation-State at Bay?, 1993, Ethnic Diversity and Public Policy, 1998, The Accommodation of Cultural Diversity, 1999; co-editor: Dilemmas of Democracy in Nigeria, 1995, Beyond State Crisis? Postcolonial Africa and Post-Soviet Eurasia in Comparative Perspective, 2002. Served to 1st lt. U.S. Army, 1953-55. Fellow Woodrow Wilson Internat. Ctr. for Scholars, 1983—84; Social Sci. Rsch. fellow, 1967—68, Ford Faculty fellow, 1972—73, Guggenheim Found. fellow, 1977—78, vis. fellow, Inst. for Advanced Study, Princeton, 1980—81. Mem. AAAS, Am. Acad. Arts and Scis., Am. Polit. Sci. Assn., African Studies Assn. (pres. 1982-83, Disting. Africanist award 1991), Coun. Fgn. Rels. Home: 639 Crandall St Madison WI 53711-1836 Office: U Wis Dept Polit Sci North Hall 1050 Bascom Mall Madison WI 53706-1389 Business E-Mail: young@polisci.wisc.edu.

**YOUNG, MICHAEL,** professional baseball player; b. Covina, Calif., Oct. 19, 1976; Second baseman, shortstop Tex. Rangers, 2000—. Second baseman World Baseball Classic, 2006. Recipient MLB All-Star Game MVP, 2006. Achievements include winning batting title, Am. League of Major League Baseball, 2005. Office: Texas Rangers Baseball Club 1000 Ballpark Way Arlington TX 76011*

**YOUNG, MICHAEL CHUNG-EN,** allergist, immunologist, pediatrician; b. Chgo., July 10, 1953; s. Koon C. and Siu Fun (Hui) Y.; m. Karen Lee Young, Apr. 7, 1979; 1 child, Liane. AB cum laude, Harvard Coll., 1975; MD, Yale U., 1979. Diplomate Am. Bd. Allergy and Immunology, Am. Bd. Pediatrics, Nat. Bd. Med. Examiners. Resident pediat. Children's Hosp., Boston, 1979—82, fellow in allergy and immunology, 1982—84, asst. in medicine (immunology), attending physician, 1984—; clin. instr. pediat. Harvard Med. Sch., Boston, 1985—2001, asst. clin. prof. pediat., 2002—. Mem. active staff South Shore Hosp., South Weymouth, Mass., 1985—. Author: Peanut Allergy Answer Book, 2001, 2d edit., 2006; contbr. articles to profl. jours. Named physician honoree, Asthma and Allergy Found. Am., 2001; named to Guide to Top Doctors, Ctr. for the Study of Svcs.; recipient Nat. Rsch. Svc. award, NIH, 1982—84, Mariel C. Furlong award for Making a Difference, Food Allergy & Anaphylaxis Network, 2005. Fellow Am. Coll. Allergy and Immunology (Parke Davis Allergy Fellows award 1983), Am. Acad. Allergy and Immunology, Am. Coll. Chest Physicians, Am. Acad. Pediatrics; mem. New Eng. Soc. Allergy, Mass. Allergy Soc. (pres. 1992-94), Mass. Med. Soc. Office: South Shore Allergy & Asthma Specialists 851 Main St South Weymouth MA 02190-1612

**YOUNG, MICHAEL KENT,** academic administrator, law educator; b. Sacramento, Nov. 4, 1949; s. Vance Lynn and Ethelyn M. (Sowards) Young; m. Suzan Kay Stewart, June 1, 1972; children: Stewart, Kathryn, Andrew. BA summa cum laude, Brigham Young U., 1973; JD magna cum laude, Harvard U., 1976. Bar: Calif. 1976, N.Y. 1985. Law clk. to Justice Benjamin Kaplan, Supreme Jud. Ct. Mass., Boston, 1976—77; law clk. to Justice William H. Rehnquist U.S. Supreme Ct., Washington, 1977—78; assoc. prof., prof., Fuyo prof. Japanese law Columbia U., NYC, 1978—98; dir. Program Internat. Human Rights and Religious Liberties, 1995—98; dir. Ctr. Japanese Legal Studies Ctr. for Korean Legal Studies, NYC, 1985—98; dean, Lobingier prof. comparative law and jurisprudence George Washington U. Sch. of Law, Washington, 1999—2004; dep. legal advisor U.S. Dept. State, Washington, 1989—91, dep. under sec. for econ. affairs, 1991—93, amb. for trade and environ. affairs, 1992—93; pres. U. Utah, Salt Lake City, 2004—. Mem. U.S. Commn. on Internat. Religious Freedom, 1998—2005, chair, 2001—02, 2002—03, vice chair, 2002—03; vis. scholar law faculty U. Tokyo, 1978—80, 1983; vis. prof. Waseda U., 1989; chmn. bd. advisors Japan Soc., 1996—98; counsel select subcom. on arms transfers to Bosnia U.S. Ho. of Reps., 1996; mem. steering com. Law Profs. for Dole, 1996; mem. com. on internat. jud. rels. U.S. Jud. Conf., 1999—2005; mem. Brown v. Bd. Edn. 50th Anniversary Commemoration Com.; chair NAFTA labor agreement adv. com. Dept. of Labor; mem. trade and environ. policy adv. com. U.S. Trade Rep. Office, 2003—. Author: Fundamentals of U.S. Trade Law, 2001, Japanese Law in Context, 2001. Bd. visitors USAF Acad., 2000—02; bd. dirs. Salt Lake C. of C., Envision Utah, Alliance for Unity. Named Communicator of Yr., Publs. Soc. Am. and Internat. Assn. Bus. Communicators; recipient Disting. Contbns. to Human Rights award, Ctr. for Internat. Religious Freedom, Brigham Young U., 2004, Excellence in Edn. award, Utah Hispanic C. of C., Excellence in Ethics award, Utah Valley State U., Internat. Humanitarian award, Pub. Affairs Office, LDS Ch., 2006;, POSCO Rsch. Inst. fellow, 1995—98, Japan Found. fellow, 1979—80, Fulbright fellow, 1983—84. Fellow Am. Bar Found.; mem.: Coun. Fgn. Rels. Mem. U.S. Ch. Avocations: skiing, scuba diving, photography. Home: 1480 Military Way Salt Lake City UT 84103 Office: U Utah 201 S President's Cir Rm 203 Salt Lake City UT 84112 Office Phone: 801-581-5701. Business E-Mail: president@utah.edu.

**YOUNG, MICHAEL KENT,** physics professor; b. Arcadia, Calif., Aug. 12, 1965; s. Howard Kent and Barbara Loiuse Young; m. Renee Ann Ellison, July 22, 1989; children: Ryan Michael, Tyler Kent, Dylan Lee. BS, Point Loma Nazarene U., San Diego, 1987; MS, UCLA, 1989, PhD, 1993. Engr. McDonnell Douglas Corp., Monrovia, Calif., 1984—87; prof. physics Antelope Valley Coll., Lancaster, Calif., 1991—95, Pasadena City Coll., Calif., 1992—95, Santa Barbara City Coll., Calif., 1995—. Advisor Natural Philosophers, Santa Barbara, 1995—99, Gaming Club, Santa Barbara, 2003—; chair Instrnl. Tech., Santa Barbara, 1997—99; senator Santa Barbara City Coll., Calif., 1997—2000. Mem.: AAPT (assoc.). Office: Santa Barbara City Coll 721 Cliff Dr Santa Barbara CA 93109 Business E-Mail: young@sbcc.edu.

**YOUNG, MICHAEL PHILLIP,** orthopedist, surgeon; b. Oak Park, Ill., Jan. 14, 1952; s. James William and Irene Olea Young; m. Kristine Marie Curran, Sept. 7, 1974; children: Vanessa, Stephen, Allison Elizabeth. BS cum laude, U. Ill., 1974, MD, 1978. Diplomate Am. Bd. Orthop. Surgery, 1985. Intern Loyola U. Med. Ctr., Maywood, Ill., 1978—79, orthop. surgery resident, 1979—83; clin. instr. Hines Veterans Adminstr., 1983—85; ptnr. Lake Cook Orthop. Assoc., Barrington, Ill., 1983—. Bd. dirs. Tricounty Physicians Assn., Barrington, 1996—2000; gov. coun. Good Shepherd Hosp., Barrington,

1992—2002. Adult leadership Boy Scouts of Am., 1992—94; coach Barrington Youth Soccer, 1994—95. Fellow: Am. Acad. Orthop. Surgery, Am. Coll. Surgeons. Office: Lake Cook Orthop Assoc 27401 W Highway 22 3125 Barrington IL 60010 Office Phone: 847-381-0388.

**YOUNG, MICHAEL WARREN,** geneticist, educator; b. Miami, Fla., Mar. 28, 1949; s. Lloyd George and Mildred (Tillery) Y.; m. Laurel Ann Eckhardt, Dec. 27, 1978; children: Natalie, Arissa. BA, U. Tex., 1971, PhD, 1975. NIH postdoctoral fellow Stanford (Calif.) U. Med. Sch., 1975-77; asst. prof. genetics Rockefeller U., N.Y.C., 1976—83, assoc. prof., 1984—88, prof., 1988—, Richard and Jeanne Fisher prof., 1988—. Investigator Howard Hughes Med. Inst., N.Y.C., 1987-96; adv. panel on genetic biology NSF, Washington, 1983-87; spl. advisor Am. Cancer Soc., N.Y.C., 1985—; spl. reviewer genetics study sect. NIH, Bethesda, Md., 1990—, cell biology study sect., 1993-97; head Rockefeller unit NSF Sci. and Tech. Ctr. Biol. Timing, 1991-2001; dir. Levy/White Ctr. Mind, Brain and Behavioral Studies Rockefeller U., N.Y.C., 2000-2002, v.p. academic affairs, 2004-. Contbr. articles to profl. jours. Meyer Found. fellow, N.Y.C., 1978-83. Fellow N.Y. Soc. Fellows; mem. AAAS, Genetics Soc. Am., Am. Soc. Microbiologists, N.Y. Acad. Scis., Harvey Soc. (treas. 2001-04). Achievements include research on transposable DNA elements, molecular genetics of nerve and muscle development, biological clocks, molecular control of circadian rhythms. Home: 51 Greenwoods Rd Old Tappan NJ 07675-7018 Office: The Rockefeller Univ 1230 York Ave New York NY 10021-6399

**YOUNG, NANCY,** lawyer; b. Washington, Dec. 3, 1954; d. John Young and Byounghye Chang; m. Paul Brendan Ford, Jr., May 28, 1983; children: Paul Brendan III, Ian A., Hunter Chang Young, Jade Augustine Young. BA, Yale U., 1975, MA, 1976; JD, Columbia U., 1979. Bar: N.Y. 1981. Assoc. Simpson Thacher & Bartlett, N.Y.C., 1979-82, Richards O'Neil & Allegaert, N.Y.C., 1982-86; ptnr., chair internat. practice group Richards & O'Neil, N.Y.C., 1986-2001, Bingham McCutchen LLP, N.Y.C. Lectr. Am. corp. and securities law Tokyo U. Faculty of Law, 1992. Author: Basic Business Japanese, 1998; contbr. articles to legal publs. Named Internat. Woman of Yr., 1992-93. Mem. ABA (co-chmn. conf. minority ptnrs in corp. majority law firms 1992), Asian-Am. Bar Assn., Assn. Bar of City of N.Y., Am. Fgn. Law Assn., Coun. on Fgn. Rels., Fgn. Policy Assn. (bd. govs. 1995-2001), Yale U. Alumni Assn. (bd. govs. 1989-92), Columbia U. Law Sch. Assn. (bd. dirs. 1991-92), Columbia U. Alumni Assn. (bd. dirs. 1991-92), Yale Club N.Y. (bd. dirs. 1996-98), Asia Soc. Office: Bingham McCutchen LLP 399 Park Avenue New York NY 10022 Business E-Mail: nancy.young@bingham.com.

**YOUNG, NANCY MAYER,** retired secondary school educator, artist; b. Pensacola, Fla., May 24, 1933; d. Mark Bodenheimer Mayer and Elsie Nobles; m. Richard S. Young, June 7, 1955 (dec. Oct. 1996); children: Deeann, Sandra, Mark. BS, Fla. State U., 1955. Tchr. pub. schs., Athens, Ala., 1955—56; artist Sunnyvale, Calif., 1961—67; tchr. pub. schs., Arlington, Va., 1968—70; piano tchr. McLean, Va., 1968—75; salesperson art and pottery McLean and Annapolis, Md., 1975—81; salesperson Dee Real Estate, Bronxville, NY, 1981—83; travel agt. Travco, McLean, 1984—87. Mem. Beautification Bd., Cape Canaveral, Fla., 1989—96, Libr. Bd., Cape Canaveral, 1984—96. Avocation: watercolor painting. Home: 673 Heatherstone Dr Merritt Island FL 32953

**YOUNG, NEIL,** musician, songwriter; b. Toronto, Ont., Can., Nov. 12, 1945; m. Pegi Young; children: Ben, Amber, Young (with Carrie Snodgrass), Zeke. Formed rock group Buffalo Springfield (with Stephen Stills), with group until 1968; solo performer, also joined group Crosby, Stills & Nash (became Crosby, Stills, Nash & Young), 1969-70, 74-75; as solo artist and with band Crazy Horse, 1968-69, 70—. Albums include (with Crosby, Stills, Nash & Young) Déja Vu, 1970, Four-Way Street, 1971, So Far, 1974, American Dream, 1988; (solo albums) Neil Young, 1969, After the Goldrush, 1970, Harvest, 1972, Journey Through the Past, 1972, Time Fades Away, 1973, On the Beach, 1974, Zuma, 1975, American Stars 'n' Bars, 1977, Decade, 1977, Comes a Time, 1978, Hawks and Doves, 1980, Reactor, 1981, Trans, 1983, Neil and The Shocking Pink: Everybody's Rocking, 1983, Old Ways, 1985, Landing on Water, 1986, Freedom, 1989, Harvest Moon, 1992 (4 Grammy nominations), Lucky Thirteen, 1993, Unplugged, 1993; (with Crazy Horse) Everybody Knows This is Nowhere, 1969, Tonight's the Night, 1975, Rust Never Sleeps, 1979, Live Rust, 1979, Life, 1987, Ragged Glory, 1990, Weld, 1991, Arc, 1991, Arc Weld, 1991, Sleeps With Angels, 1994, Mirror Ball, 1995, Broken Arrow, 1996, Dead Man, 1996, Year of the Horse (live), 1997, Silver & Gold, 2000, Are You Passionate?, 2002, Greendale, 2003, Greatest Hits, 2004; (with Buffalo Springfield) Buffalo Springfield Again, 1967, Last Time Around, 1968, Retrospective, 1969; (with the Bluenotes) This Note's For You, 1988; (with Stills-Young Band) Long May You Run, 1976; (with The Stray Gators) Time Fade Away; Tony and Susan Alamo christian Foundation Orchestra and Chorus, 1995; (with others) Mirror Ball, 1995, Journey Through the Past, 1995, Old Ways; composed film soundtrack Journey Through the Past, 1973, Where the Buffalo Roam, 1980, Human Highway, 1982; writer, dir., performer film Rust Never Sleeps. Academy award nominee, Best Original Song, 1993 (for "Philadelphia" from Philadelphia). Office: Warner Bros Reprise Records 3300 Warner Blvd Burbank CA 91505-4694

**YOUNG, OLIVIA KNOWLES,** retired librarian; b. Benton, Ark., Sept. 3, 1922; d. Wesley Taylor and Med Belle (Crawford) Knowles; m. Calvin B. Young, Oct. 6, 1951; 1 child, Brigham Taylor. BA, Tenn. Tech. U., 1942, BS in Libr. Sci., 1946. Head periodicals and documents dept. Peabody Coll. Library, Nashville, 1946-49; area libr. U.S. Army, Austria, 1949-51; libr. Cairo Pub. Libr., Ga., 1955-57, Caney Fork Regional Libr., Sparta, Tenn., 1957-58; chief libr. Ft. Stewart (Ga.) U.S. Army, 1959-63; dir. Watauga Regional Libr., Johnson City, Tenn., 1963-70; dir. devel. and extension Tenn. State Libr. and Archives, Nashville, 1971-82, state libr. and archivist, 1982-85; ret., 1985. Mem. Tenn. Library Assn. (treas. 1970, Honor award 1985), Southeastern Library Assn., ALA, Boone Tree Library Assn. (pres. 1968), Altrusa Club (sec. 1967). Methodist. Home: 203 E Everett St Sparta TN 38583

**YOUNG, PATRICIA ANNE,** secondary school educator, writer; b. Missoula, Mont., Oct. 3, 1920; d. Dwight Newcomb and Lillian Rook Mason; m. William B. Burke (dec.); children: John Burke, Elizabeth Burke, Sean Burke; m. Willis Frederick Young, Aug. 13, 1997. BA, Ft. Lewis Coll., Durango, Colo.; MA, N.Mex. State U., 1972. Tchr. Farmington (N.Mex.) H.S. 1971—85, San Juan Coll. Founder, pres. S.W. Christian Writers Assn., 1979—2003. Author: Adventures from God's Word, 1983, The Big Missionary, 1997, China My Love, 1999. Recipient Appreciation Svc. plaque, S.W. Christian Writers Assn., 2003. Home and Office: 3204 N Coronado Ave Farmington NM 87401

**YOUNG, PATRICIA JANEAN,** speech pathology/audiology services professional; b. San Diego, Nov. 30, 1953; d. Bernarr E. and Janean Romig Young. AA, Palomar C.C., San Marcos, Calif., 1974; BA, Calif. State U., Chico, 1976; MA, Calif. State U., Long Beach, 1981. Cert. clin. competence Am. Speech-Lang.-Hearing Assn., lic. speech pathologist Calif., cert. tchr. Calif. Mgmt. trainee Robinson's Dept. Store, LA, 1976—78; speech and hearing screening coord. Riverview Hearing, Speech, Lang. Ctrs., Long Beach, 1978—81; speech pathologist, 1981—84; speech pathologist, dir. Speech Pathology Svcs., Carlsbad and Temecula, Calif., 1984—; speech pathologist, augmentative comm. coord. Lake Elsinore (Calif.) Unified Sch. Dist., 1998—. Prodr. TV shows on comm. disorders Long Beach Cable TV, 1983; coord. pub. svc. announcement and interviewee for Disabilities Awareness Week ABC TV, San Diego, 1986, San Diego, 88. Game inventor: Match This!, 1995; author: (children's book) Bird Boy, 2006; contbr. articles to lit. publs.; author. Named to Outstanding Young Women Am. Mem.: Calif. Speech-Lang-Hearing Assn. (region rep., Outstanding Achievement award 1987), Am. Speech-Lang-Hearing Assn., Zeta Tau Alpha. Avocations: writing, theater, decorating. Home: 31935 Calle Espinoza Temecula CA 92592 Office: Lake Elsinore Unified Sch Dist 545 Chaney St Lake Elsinore CA 92530 Office Phone: 951-253-7000 x5390. E-mail: pjyoung2000@aol.com.

**YOUNG, PATRICK,** editor, writer; b. Ladysmith, Wis., Oct. 19, 1937; s. Rodney and Janice (Wolf) Y.; m. Leah Ruth Figelman, Oct. 8, 1966; 1 child, Justine Young Gottshall. BA, U. Colo., 1960. Reporter UPI, Washington, 1961-62; journalist USN, 1963-64; staff writer Nat. Observer, Silver Spring, Md., 1965-77; free-lance writer Laurel, Md., 1977-79; mem. sr. staff Pres.'s Commn. on the Accident at Three Mile Island, Washington, 1979; chief sci. and med. writer Newhouse News Svc., Washington, 1980-88; editor Sci. News, Washington, 1988-95; ind. writer, editor, cons., 1995—. Sci. writer in residence U. Wis., 1986. Author: Asthma and Allergies, 1980, Drugs and Pregnancy, 1987, Schizophrenia, 1988; co-author: Keeping Young Athletes Healthy, 1991. With USN, 1963-64. Recipient Howard W. Blakeslee award Am. Heart Assn., 1971, Sci. Writing award in physics and astronomy Am. Inst. Physics, 1974, James T. Grady award Am. Chem. Soc., 1977. Mem. Nat. Assn. Sci. Writers, Nat. Press Club, Am. Assn. Adv. Sci. Office Phone: 301-498-4251. E-mail: young@nasw.org.

**YOUNG, PAUL,** graphic designer, edcator; m. Bonnie K. Burgund. BFA in Graphic Design, U. Ill., Urbana, 1983, EdM in Curriculum and Instrn., 2006. Art dir. Advt. Studios Inc, Milw., 1983—86; graphic designer Arnell Bickford Assoc, NYC, 1986—87; art dir. Muscular Dystrophy Assoc, NYC, 1987—90, The Creative Black Book, NYC, 1990—93; pub. The Octopus, Champaign, Ill., 1994—98; assoc. professor Parkland Coll., Champaign, 1998—; ptnr. Electric Pictures, Champaign, 1992—. Mem.: Ad Club Champaign-Urbana (pub. mem. 2002—05). Office: Parkland College 2400 W Bradley Ave Champaign IL 61821 Office Phone: 217-351-2403, 217-398-1923. Business E-Mail: pyoung@parkland.edu, paul@electric-pictures.com

**YOUNG, PAUL ANDREW,** anatomist; b. St. Louis, Oct. 3, 1926; s. Nicholas A. and Olive A. (Langford) Y.; m. Catherine Ann Hofmeister, May 14, 1949; children: Paul, Robert, David, Ann, Carol, Richard, James, Steven, Kevin, Michael. BS, St. Louis U., 1947, MS, 1953; PhD, U. Buffalo, 1957. Asst. in anatomy U. Buffalo, 1953, instr. anatomy, 1957; asst. prof. anatomy St. Louis U., 1957, assoc. prof., 1966, prof., 1972—, chmn. dept., 1973—2004. Author: (with B.D. Bhagat and D.E. Biggerstaff) Fundamentals of Visceral Innervation, 1977, (with P.H. Young) Basic Clinical Neuroanatomy, 1996, also computer assisted neurological anatomy tutorials; contbr. articles to profl. publs. Recipient Golden Apple award, Student AMA, 1974, 2000, Tchg. award, Acad. Sci. St. Louis, 1993, Emerson Excellence in Tchg. award, 2001. Mem. Am. Assn. Anatomists, Am. Assn. Clin. Anatomists, Soc. Neurosci., Sigma Xi, Alpha Omega Alpha. Office: St Louis U Ctr for Anatomical Sci and Edn 1402 S Grand Blvd Saint Louis MO 63104-1004 Office Phone: 314-977-8025. Personal E-mail: payoun5@aol.com. Business E-Mail: youngpa@slu.edu.

**YOUNG, PAUL RAY,** medical association administrator, physician; b. Fairfield, Nebr., June 27, 1932; s. Earl Edward and Louisa May (Saunders) Young; m. Irene Marie Gray (div. 1971); children: Michael, Susan, Jean, James; m. Faye Elizabeth Hall, Oct. 28, 1972. BA, U. Nebr., Lincoln, 1953; MD, U. Nebr., Omaha, 1958. Diplomate Am. Bd. Family Practice. Intern Rsch. Hosp., Kansas City, Mo., 1958—59, dir. continuing med. edn., 1967—71; pvt. practice Raytown, Mo., 1961—67; assoc. prof. family practice U. Mo. Coll. Medicine, Columbia, 1971—73; chmn. dept. U. Nebr. Coll. Medicine, 1975—80, U. Tex. Med. Br., Galveston, 1980—88; dep. dir. Am. Bd. Family Practice, Lexington, Ky., 1988—90, exec. dir., 1990—97, sr. exec., 1998—2003, emeritus exec. dir., 2003—. Chmn. RRC for Family Practice, Chgo., 1979—87. Founding editor: Family Practice Recert, 1979, Jour. Am. Bd. Family Practice, 1987. Pres. Nicholas J. Piscano Meml. Found., 1990—97. Capt. M.C. USAF, 1959—61. Fellow: Am. Acad. Family Physicians; mem.: Soc. Tchrs. Family Medicine (bd. dirs. 1970—72), Alpha Omega Alpha. Office: Am Bd Family Medicine Inc 2228 Young Dr Lexington KY 40505-4219 Office Phone: 859-269-5626. Business E-Mail: pyoung@theabfm.org.

**YOUNG, PAULA EVA,** animal shelter director; b. Caracas, Venezuela, May 11, 1958; arrived in U.S., 1962; d. James Francis and Fulvia (Guzzaloni) Y.; 1 child, Jonas Borra. Cert., Am. Acad. Dramatic Arts, N.Y.C., 1979; BA, CUNY, 1997. Lobbyist, facilitator East Bronx Coun. on Aging, N.Y.C., 1989—90; journalist N.Y. Newsday, N.Y.C., 1990—94; mng. editor, journalist City News, N.Y.C., 1994—95; dir. Office Comm. N.Y.C. Dept. Citywide Adminstrv. Svcs., 1995—98; asst. commr. pub. affairs N.Y.C. Dept. Sanitation, 1998—2001; owner, mgr. Between the Lines Restaurant, Westchester County, NY, 2001—03; dir. Mt. Vernon (NY) Animal Shelter, 2003—. Mem. animal cruelty task force Office of Dist. Atty., Westchester County, 2005—; bd. dirs. NY State Wildlife Rehab. Coun. Democrat. Associate: wildlife and animal rescue. Office: 600 Garden Ave Mount Vernon NY 10550 Home: 28 Colabaugh Pond Rd Croton On Hudson NY 10520-3313 Office Phone: 914-522-5945.

**YOUNG, PHILIP HOWARD,** library director; b. Ithaca, N.Y., Oct. 7, 1953; s. Charles Robert and Betty Irene (Osborne) Young; m. Nancy Ann Stutsman, Aug. 18, 1979. BA, U. Va., 1975; PhD, U. Pa., 1980; MLS, Ind. U., 1983. Asst. prof. history Appalachian State U., Boone, NC, 1980-82; reference asst. Lilly Libr. Ind. U., Bloomington, 1982-83; adminstr., info. specialist Ind. Corp. Sci. & Tech., Indpls., 1983-85; dir. Krannert Meml. Libr. U. Indpls., 1985—. Mem.: Archeol. Inst. Am., Am. Libr. Assn., Phi Beta Kappa, Beta Phi Mu, Phi Alpha Theta. Democrat. Home: 4332 Silver Springs Dr Greenwood IN 46142-9623 Office: U Indpls Krannert Meml Libr 1400 E Hanna Ave Indianapolis IN 46227-3630 Office Phone: 317-788-3399. E-mail: pyoung@uindy.edu.

**YOUNG, PHYLLIS CASSELMAN,** music educator; b. Milan, Kans., Oct. 20, 1925; d. Phillip James and Velma (Stewart) Casselman; m. James M. Young, July 14, 1945 (dec. Sept. 1991). MusB with high honors, U. Tex., 1949, MusM, 1950. Tchr. string instruments Kansas City (Kans.) Pub. Schs., 1951-52; prof. cello and string pedagogy U. Tex., Austin, 1953—; dir. U. Tex. String Project, Austin, 1958-93; Parker C. Fielder Regents prof. music U. Tex., Austin, 1991—. Presenter numerous workshops and master classes, 1976—. Author: Playing the String Game, 1978, The String Play, 1986; also articles. Mem. Am. String Tchrs. Assn. (state pres. 1972-74, nat. pres. 1978-80, Nat. citation 1974, 82, Disting. Svc. award 1984, Paul Rolland Lifetime Achievement award 2002), European String Tchrs. Assn. (hon. mem. Brit. br.), Music Educators Nat. Conf., Suzuki Assn. Ams., Tex. Music Educators Assn. Home: 7304 W Rim Dr Austin TX 78731-2043 Office: Sch Music Univ Tex Austin TX 78712 Business E-Mail: phyllis@mail.utexas.edu.

**YOUNG, RAYMOND HENRY,** lawyer; b. Brockton, Mass., Sept. 28, 1927; s. Raymond H. and Clara Elms (Oakman) Y.; m. Louisa Breda, Sept. 1, 1951; children: Christopher, Pamela, Amy. AB, Yale U., 1947, LLB, 1950. Bar: Mass. 1951. Assoc. Warner, Stackpole, Stetson & Bradlee, Boston, 1950-52; pvt. practice Boston, 1952-64; ptnr. Young & Bayle, Boston, 1964—. Mem. ABA (past sec. real property, probate and trust law, mem. commn. legal problems of the elderly), Am. Coll. Trust and Estate Counsel (mem. joint editorial bd. for trust and estate acts), Am. Law Inst. (advisor for restatement property 3d donative transfers, cons. restatement trusts 3d), Nat. Commn. on Nat. Probate Ct. Standards, Internat. Acad. Trust and Estate Law (past pres.), Mass. Bar Assn., Boston Bar Assn. (past pres.), Boston Estate Planning Coun. (past pres., Estate Planner of Yr. award 1991), Boston Probate and Estate Planning Forum. Home: 122 Garfield St Watertown MA 02472-4916 Office: Young & Bayle 150 Federal St Boston MA 02110-1713

**YOUNG, RAYMOND JAMES,** retired education educator; b. Howard, Kans., Nov. 2, 1922; s. Raymond Everett and Ethel Belle Young; m. Blenda E. Thompson, Nov. 14, 1942 (dec. 1980); children: Judy Rae, Dwight Paul; m. Ruby I. Wright, Aug. 24, 1962; children: Runell A., Raven J. BS, Kans. State Tchrs. Coll., 1948, MS, 1949; EdD, U. Colo., 1950; postgrad., U. Idaho, 1986. Cert. tchr. Kans. Tchr., prin. Elk County Sch. Dist., Howard, Kans., 1941-42; asst. prof. Okla. State U., Stillwater, 1950-54; assoc. prof. U. Okla., Norman, 1954-55, U. Ill., Champaign, 1955-59; prof. U. Mich., Ann Arbor, 1959-69, Wash. State U., Pullman, 1976-89; ret., 1990; sr. cons. edn. Arthur

D. Little, Inc., Cambridge, Mass., 1969-75; prin. assoc. McMannis Assocs., Inc., Washington, 1975-76. Co-author: The School and The Community, 1955, Summer Sessions in Colleges and University, 1991; contbr. over 150 articles to profl. jours. Editor, historian 602nd Tank Destroyer Battalion Assn., Inc., 1986-2005, pres., 2000-2005. Sgt. U.S. Army, 1943-45, ETO. Mem. Am. Legion (post commdr. 1997-2000, dist. commdr. 1998-99), Coun. Study Comty. Colls., VFW, DAV, NEA, Elks, Ind. Order Odd Fellows, Nat. WWII Tank Destroyer Soc. (v.p.), Phi Delta Kappa. Achievements include development of citizens participatory process for starting new 2-yr. colls., and holds record for the number started in the U.S; dir. major study projects in Algeria, Greece, and Holland. Avocations: fishing, golf, hunting, boating. Home: PO Box 4573 East Lansing MI 48826-4573 Office Phone: 517-420-1517.

**YOUNG, REBECCA MARY CONRAD,** retired state legislator; b. Clairton, Pa., Feb. 28, 1934; d. Walter Emerson and Harriet Averill (Colcord) Conrad; m. Merwin Crawford Young, Aug. 17, 1957; children: Eve, Louise, Estelle, Emily. BA, U. Mich., 1955; MA in Teaching, Harvard U., 1963; JD, U. Wis., 1983. Bar: Wis. 1983. Commr. State Hwy. Commn., Madison, Wis., 1974-76; dep. sec. Wis. Dept. of Adminstrn., Madison, 1976-77; assoc. Wadsack, Julian & Lawton, Madison, 1983-84; elected rep. Wis. State Assembly, Madison, 1985-99. Translator: Katanga Secession, 1966. Supr. Dane County Bd., Madison, 1970-74; mem. Madison Sch. Bd., 1979-85. Recipient Wis. NOW Feminist of Yr. award, 1996, Eunice Zoghlin Edgar Lifetime Achievement award ACLU, 1997, Outstanding Legislator award Wis. Counties Assn., 1998, Voice for Choice award Planned Parenthood Wis., 1998, Luan Gilbert award for outstanding activities in domestic violence intervention and prevention Domestic Violence Intervention Svc., 1998. Mem. LWV. Democrat. Avocations: board games, hiking. Home: 639 Crandall St Madison WI 53711-1836

**YOUNG, RICHARD ALAN,** association executive; b. Oak Park, Ill., Mar. 17, 1935; m. Carol Ann Schellinger, June 28, 1958; children: Steven, Karen, Christopher. BA, U. Iowa, 1958; MS, PhD, Western State U., 2000. Chief engr. Cardox Corp., Chgo., 1958-61; asst. chief engr. Goodman Mfg. Co., Chgo., 1961-63; plant and environ. engr. Signode Corp., Glenview, Ill., 1963-68; editor Pollution Engring. Tech. Pub. Co., Barrington, Ill., 1968-81; exec. dir. Nat. Registry of Environ. Profls., 1988—; pub. Cahners Pub. Co., Des Plaines, Ill., 1990-95; exec. dir. Office Infrastructure Preparedness, 2004—. Adj. prof. George Williams Coll., Ea. Ky. U., 2004-; mcpl. pollution control adviser and enforcement officer for 24 cities and state govts; ofcl rep. and pollution control expert U.S. Govt. at tech. transfer meetings; exec. dir. Internat. Certification Accreditation Bd., 1999—, Office of Infrastructure Preparedness, 2004—, Nat. Assn. Environ. Risk Auditors, 2004-; African Inst. Environ. Profl., 2005. Editor 26 books on environ. engring.; pollution engring.; series editor, Marcel Dekker Inc., N.Y.C.; contbr. articles to profl. jours.; patentee in field. Recipient Jesse H. Neal certificate for outstanding editorial writing Am. Bus. Press, Inc., 1971, Outstanding Service award Western Soc. Engrs., Charles Ellet award as Most Outstanding Engr. of Yr. 1970; Environ. Quality award EPA, 1976 Mem. Internat. Assn. for Pollution Control (dir.), Am. Soc. Bus. Press Editors (Editl. Excellence award 1980, Design Excellence award 1982), Am. Inst. Plant Engrs. (past nat. chmn. environ. quality), Internat. Congress Environ. Profls. (mng. dir.), Nat. Inst. Hazardous Materials Mgmts. (dir. 1984-88, cert. hazardous materials mgr.).

**YOUNG, RICHARD WILLIAM,** chemicals executive; b. Ridgewood, N.Y., Oct. 17, 1926; s. Charles Michael and Louise Margaret (Baust) Y.; m. Sheila deLisser, Sept. 11, 1949; children: Christine, Noreen, Brian, Eileen. AB, Dartmouth Coll., 1946, A.M., 1947; PhD, Columbia U., 1950; DSc (hon.), Regis Coll., 2002. Sr. rsch. chemist Chemotherapy div. Am. Cyanamid Co., Conn., 1950-56, group leader pesticide chems. Agrl. div. Conn., 1956-58, dir. chem. Agrl. div. Conn., 1958-60, dir. chem. rsch. div. Conn., 1960-62; asst. dir. rsch. Polaroid Corp., Cambridge, Mass., 1962-69, v.p., 1963-69, sr. v.p. rsch. and devel., 1969-72, sr. v.p., pres. Internat. div., 1972-80, exec. v.p., dir. worldwide mktg., 1980-82; pres. Houghton Mifflin Co., Boston, 1982-85; chmn., CEO Mentor O & O, Inc., Norwell, Mass., 1985-92. Bd. dirs. Bay State Milling Co., Quincy, Mass., Instron Corp., Canton, Mass., Oceantrawl Inc., Seattle, Mentor Corp., Santa Barbara, Calif. Patentee in field. Chmn. bd. trustees Regis Coll., Weston, Mass.; trustee Mass. Eye and Ear Infirmary, Boston, 1963-90, Trinitas Found., Quincy; mem. corp. Northeastern U., Boston, 1960-92; bd. dirs. Martin Meml. Hosp. Found., 2002—. Mem. Am. Chem. Soc. Home: 4 Scotch Pine Cir Wellesley Hills MA 02481-1222 Office: Trinitas Found 100 Congress St Quincy MA 02169-0906 E-mail: rwy1926@aol.com.

**YOUNG, RICK (RICHARD ALLEN YOUNG),** molecular biologist, educator; b. Pitts., Mar. 12, 1954; s. Allen Young and Jane (Moore) Stockhausen. BS in Biol. Sci., U., 1975; PhD in Molecular Biology, Biochemistry, Yale U., 1979. Postdoctoral fellow Swiss Inst. Exptl. Cancer Research, Lausanne, Switzerland, 1979-80, Stanford (Calif.) U., 1981-84; assoc. prof. biology MIT, Cambridge, 1984—, now prof.; mem. Whitehead Inst. Biomed. Research, Cambridge, 1984—, now prin. investigator. Cons., com. mem. WHO, Geneva, Switzerland, 1983-89, chmn. biology subcom., 1987-90. Grantee WHO, NIH, 1984—; recipient Molecular Parasitology award Burroughs Wellcome Co., 1987, Chiron Corp. Biotechnology award Am. Society for Microbiology, 1994 Fellow Molecular Medicine Soc. (charter); mem. AAAS, Am. Acad. Microbiology, Genetics Soc. Am. Avocations: skiing, mountain climbing. Office: Whitehead Inst Biomed Research 9 Cambridge Ctr Cambridge MA 02142-1479 E-mail: young@wi.mit.edu.

**YOUNG, ROBERT A., III,** freight systems executive; b. Ft. Smith, Ark., Sept. 23, 1940; s. Robert A. and Vivian (Curtis) Y.; m. Mary Carleton McRae; children: Tracy, Christy, Robert A. IV (dec.), Stephen BA in Econs., Washington and Lee U., 1963. Supr. terminal ops. Ark. Best Freight, Ft. Smith, 1964-65; pres. Data-Tronics Inc, Ft. Smith, 1965-67; sr. v.p. Nat. Bank of Commerce, Dallas, 1967-70; v.p. fin. Ark. Best Corp., Ft. Smith, 1970-73, exec. v.p., 1973, chief operating officer, 1973-88, pres., 1973—2004, chief exec. officer, 1988—, chmn., 2004—; pres. ABF Freight Systems, Inc., Ft. Smith, 1979-94. Bd. dirs. First Nat. Bank, Ft. Smith. Pres. United Way, Ft. Smith, 1981; bd. dirs. ATA Found., Inc., Ft. Smith Boys and Girls Club; chmn. bd. trustees Lyon Coll., Sparks Regional Med. Ctr., Ft. Smith, 1995-2004. Recipient Silver Beaver award Boy Scouts Am. Mem. Am. Trucking Assn. (v.p. at large), Phi Delta Theta. Presbyterian. Office: Ark Best Corp PO Box 10048 Fort Smith AR 72917-0048 also: Arkansas Best Corp PO Box 10048 Fort Smith AR 72917-0048

**YOUNG, ROBERT BOND,** lawyer; b. Phila., May 18, 1943; s. Robert A. and Anna Battelle (Bond) Y.; m. Karen Alexander, June 17, 1966; children: Jeffrey A., Randall C. BA, Denison U., 1965; JD, Ohio State U., 1969. Bar: Ohio 1969, U.S. Dist. Ct. (so. dist.) Ohio 1970, Del. 1975, U.S. Dist. Ct. Del. 1976, U.S. Supreme Ct. 1978, U.S. Ct. Appeals (3d cir.) 1986. Assoc. Young & Alexander, Dayton, Ohio, 1969-72, ptnr., 1973-75; pvt. practice Dover, Del., 1975-84; sr. ptnr. Young & Alexander, Dover, 1985-92; atty. pvt. practice, Dover, 1992—. Adj. prof. bus. law Del. Community Coll., Dover, 1975-79; adj. prof. ins. law Wesley Coll., Dover, 1993—; pres. Overseas Fiber Export Corp., Dover, 1978—. Author: (light verse/text book) Grappling With Grammar, 1974, (musical comedies) To The Revolution, 1976, MacBeth: A Family Musical, 1977, O, 1978, Swarthmore Fight Song, 1989, Calibants Rage. Mgr. Dover Little League, 1978-87, Sr. League All-Star mgr., 1984, 86, bd. dirs. 1982, 84; bd. dirs. Del. Soc. Prevention Cruelty to Animals, 1980. Mem. ABA, Am. Bd. Trial Lawyers (Del. chpt. pres. elect 1991-93, pres. 1993-95), Def. Rsch. Inst., Del. State Bar Assn. (pres. 2004), Assn. Def. Trial Advocates, Terry Carey Am. Inn of Ct. (master 1991—, counselor 1994-95). Avocations: youth sports, creative writing. Office: Young & Young 300 S State St PO Box 1191 Dover DE 19901-6730

**YOUNG, ROBERT CRABILL,** medical researcher, science administrator, internist; b. Columbus, Ohio, 1940; BS in zoology, Ohio State U., 1960; MD, Cornell U., 1965. Diplomate Am. Bd. Internal Medicine, subspecialty bds. hematology and med. oncology. Intern N.Y. Hosp., N.Y.C., 1965-66, resident, 1966-67; sr. resident Yale-New Haven Med. Ctr., 1969-70; sr. investigator, attending physician med. br. Nat. Cancer Inst., Bethesda, Md., 1971—, chief

med. br., 1974-88; pres. Fox Chase Cancer Ctr., Phila., 1988—. Clin. prof. medicine Georgetown U., from 1974, assoc. prof., 1976-84; clin. prof. medicine George Washington U., 1984—; bd. Sci. Advisors, Nat. Cancer Inst., 1996—; bd. Nat. Cancer Policy, 1997-99; chmn. bd. Nat. Comprehensive Cancer Network. Assoc. editor Jour. Clin. Oncology; chmn. editl. bd. Oncology Times. Sr. surgeon USPHS, 1967-69. Fellow ACP; mem. Am. Soc. Hematology, Am. Assn. Cancer Rsch., Am. Soc. Clin. Oncology (pres. 1990), Am. Cancer Soc. (bd. dir. 1995-99, 1st v.p. 1999-2000, pres. 2002), Internat. Gynecol. Cancer Soc. (pres.-elect 1998, pres. 2000). Office: Fox Chase Cancer Ctr 333 Cottman Ave Philadelphia PA 19111*

**YOUNG, ROBERT CRAIG,** banker; b. NYC, Mar. 15, 1960; s. Robert J. and Gloria L. (Sandhop) Y.; m. Anke Ott, Dec. 2, 2000. BS cum laude, NYU, 1982, MBA, 1985. Asst. v.p. Chem. Bank, N.Y.C., 1982-86; project mgr. GE Credit Corp., Stamford, Conn., 1986-87; dir. Merrill Lynch & Co., N.Y.C., 1987-94; sr. v.p. Greenwich (Conn.) Capital Markets, Inc., 1994-97; mng. dir. Nomura Securities, N.Y.C., 1997-2001; divsn. dir. Macquarie, N.Y.C., 2001—. Home: 98 Revere Rd Manhasset NY 11030-2733 Office: Macquarie 125 W 55th St New York NY 10019 Office Phone: 212-231-1707. E-mail: rcyoung@optonline.net.

**YOUNG, ROBERT P., JR.,** state supreme court justice; Bachelor's degree cum laude, Harvard Coll., 1974; JD, Harvard U., 1977. Atty. Dickinson, Wright, Moon, Van Dusen & Freeman, 1977-1992; v.p., corp. sec., gen. counsel AAA Mich., 1992; judge Mich. Ct. Appeals 1st Dist., 1995—98; justice Mich. Supreme Ct., 1999—. Mem. Mich. Civil Svc. Commn.; bd. trustees Cen. Mich. U. Mem.: ABA, Mich. State Bar Assn., Mich. Supreme Ct. Historical Soc. Office: Mich Supreme Ct PO Box 30052 Lansing MI 48909-7552*

**YOUNG, RONALD FARIS,** commodities trader; b. Schenectady, Dec. 17, 1939; s. James Vernon and Dorothy (Girod) Y.; m. Anne Randolph Kendig, Feb. 23, 1963; children: Margaret Randolph Reynolds, Anne Corbin. BA, U. Va., 1962; MBA, Harvard U., 1966. Grain trader Continental Grain Co., 1966-70; pres. Conti-Commodities, Chgo., 1970; v.p. commodity sales DuPont, Glore Forgan, Chgo., 1971-72; self-employed commodity trader Chgo. Bd. Trade, 1972-78; ind. trader Va. Trading Co., 1978-90, pres., 1978-84, dep. chmn., 1984-89; pres. Randolph Ptnrs., Ltd., 1983-91. Chmn. bd. Chgo. Bd. Trade, 1978, dir., 1975—77, 1980, 2003. Bd. dirs. Princeton Fund, 1981-82, Lake Forest Hosp., 1981-84, Lake Forest Country Day Sch., 1981-86. Served with USMCR, 1959-65. Mem. Racquet Club (bd. dirs. 1989-97), Onwentsia Club (Lake Forest, Ill., bd. dirs. 1981-90, pres. 1991-93), Everglades Cub (Palm Beach, Fla.), Bath and Tennis Club of Palm Beach (bd. dirs. 2006). Republican. Episcopalian. Home: 531 N Mayflower Rd Lake Forest IL 60045

**YOUNG, ROY ALTON,** university administrator, educator; b. McAlister, N.Mex., Mar. 1, 1921; s. John Arthur and Etta Julia (Sprinkle) Y.; m. Marilyn Ruth Sandman, May 22, 1950; children: Janet Elizabeth, Randall Owen. BS, N.Mex. A&M Coll., 1941; MS, Iowa State U., 1942, PhD, 1948; LLD (hon.), N.Mex. State U., 1978. Tchg. fellow Iowa State U., 1941-42, instr., 1946-47, Indsl. fellow, 1947-48; asst. prof. Oreg. State U., 1948-50, assoc. prof., 1950-53, prof., 1953—, head dept. botany and plant pathology, 1958-66, dean rsch., 1966-70, acting pres., 1969-70, v.p. rsch. and grad. studies, 1970-76, dir. Office for Natural Resources Policy, 1986-90; chancellor U. Nebr. Lincoln, 1976-80; mng. dir., pres. Boyce Thompson Inst. Plant Rsch., Cornell U., Ithaca, NY, 1980-86. Mem. Commn. on Undergrad. Edn. in Biol. Scis., 1963-68; mem. Gov.'s Sci. Coun., 1987-90; cons. State Exptl. Stas. USDA; chmn. subcom. plant pathogens, agriculture bd. NAS-NRC, 1965-68; mem. exec. com. study on problems of pest control, 1972-75; mem. exec. com. Nat. Govs.' Coun. on Sci. and Tech., 1970-74; mem. U.S. com. man and biosphere UNESCO, 1973-82; mem. com. to rev. U.S. component Internat. Biol. Program, NAS, 1974-76; mem. adv. panel on postdoctoral fellowships in environ. sci. Rockefeller Found., 1974-78; bd. dirs. Pacific Power & Light Co., 1974-91, PacifiCorp., 1984-91, Boyce Thompson Inst. for Plant Rsch., 1975-93, Boyce Thompson Southwestern Arboretum, 1981-92, Oreg. Grad. Inst., 1987-94; mem. adv. com. Directorate for Engring. and Applied Sci., NSF, 1977-81; mem. sea grant adv. panel, 1978-80; mem. policy adv. com. Office of Grants, USDA, 1985-86. Trustee Ithaca Coll., 1982-89. Lt. USNR, 1943-46. Recipient Disting. Svc. award Oreg. State U., 1978. Fellow AAAS (exec. com. Pacific div. 1963-67, pres. div. 1971), Am. Phytopathology Soc. (pres. Pacific div. 1957, chmn. spl. com. to develop plans for endowment 1984-86, bd. dirs. 1986-88); mem. Oreg. Acad. Sci. Nat. Assn. State Univs. and Land Grant Colls. (chmn. coun. for rsch. policy and adminstrn. 1970, chmn. standing com. on environment and energy 1974-82, chmn. com. on environment 1984-86), Sigma Xi, Phi Kappa Phi, Phi Sigma, Sigma Alpha Epsilon. Home: 3605 NW Van Büren Ave Corvallis OR 97330-4950

**YOUNG, RUSSELL DAWSON,** physicist, consultant; b. Huntington, NY, Aug. 17, 1923; s. C. Halsey and Edna (Dawson) Young; m. Carol Vaughn Jones, Aug. 14, 1954; children: Bessmarie, Gale, Janet, Shari. BS in Physics, Rensselaer Poly. Inst., Troy, NY, 1953; PhD in Physics, Pa. State U., 1959. Rsch. assoc. Pa. State U., State College, 1959-61; project leader Nat. Bur. Stds., Gaithersburg, Md., 1961-73, chief optics and micrometrology, 1973-78, chief mech. processing div., 1975-80, ind. sys. div. chief, 1980-81, chief mech. prodn. div., 1980-81; pres. R.D. Young Cons., Pasadena, Md., 1981—. Contbr. articles to profl. jours.; inventor in field of instrumentation. 1st lt. Signal Corps, U.S. Army, 1943-46. Recipient Edward V. Condon award Dept. Commerce, 1974, Silver medal 1979, Gaede-Langmuir award 1994, Presdl. citation 1986, Washington Acad. Scis. award 1988. Fellow Internat. Inst. Prodn. Engring. Rsch., Nat. Inst. Standards and Tech. Avocation: boating. Home: 608A Main St Gaithersburg MD 20878 Personal E-mail: cryoung2@aol.com.

**YOUNG, RUTH BROOKS,** retired elementary school educator; b. Balt., Aug. 30, 1933; d. Benjamin Franklin and Ora Estelle Brooks; m. David Donald Young Sr., 1952; children: David Donald Jr. (dec.), Gerard Brooks Sr., Mark Douglas (dec.), Elizabeth Allyson Mack. BS, Coppin State Tchrs. Coll., 1958; MS, Morgan State Coll., 1975. Cert. tchr. W. Va. Tchr. Balt. City Pub. Schs., 1958-98, supervising tchr., 1968-72, sch. test coord., 1990-96; ret., 1998. Mem. Phi Delta Kappa. Democrat. Lutheran.

**YOUNG, S. SUSAN,** electrical engineer, researcher; BS, South China U. Tech., Guangzhou, 1984, MS, 1987; PhD, SUNY at Buffalo, Amherst, 1995. Asst. prof. South China U. Tech., 1987—89; rsch. assoc. Kyushu U., Japan, 1989—90; instr. asst. Wayne State U., Detroit, 1990—91, rsch. asst., 1991, SUNY at Buffalo, Amherst, 1991—94, tchg. assist., 1994—95; postdoctoral fellow Roswell Pk. Cancer Inst., Buffalo, 1995—96; sr. rsch. scientist Health Imaging Rsch. Lab., Eastman Kodak Co., Rochester, 1996—2002; electronics engr. Army Rsch. Lab., Adelphi, Md., 2002—. Rep. Digital Imaging and Comm. in Medicine, Washington, 2000—01; reviewer Army Rsch. Office, Research Triangle Park, NC, 2003—. Contbr. articles to profl. jours. Recipient Best Demonstration Ribbon award, Radiol. Soc. N.Am., 1998. Mem.: IEEE, Assn. for Women in Sci. Achievements include patents for image analysis enhancing image visualization from low-cost sensors and low quality images that encounter in medical, consumer, and defense fields; method for improving breast cancer diagnosis using mountain-view and contrast-enhancement presentation of mammography; method for contrast-enhancement of digital portal images; method for automatically locating an image pattern in digital images; method for statistically lossless compression of digital projection radiographic images; patents pending for method of super-resolving images. Avocations: music, tennis, reading. Office: Army Research Lab 2800 Powder Mill Rd Adelphi MD 20783 Office Phone: 301-394-0230.

**YOUNG, SANDRA COOPER,** retired librarian; b. Schenectady, NY, Jan. 18, 1939; d. John Remington and Esther May (Carl) Cooper; m. Charles William Young Jr.; children: Charles W. III, Kimberly Anderson, Kathryn Whalen, Karen. BA in Anthropology, Syracuse U., 1961; MSLS, U. Ky., 1980. Info. resources asst. Council of State Govts., Lexington, Ky., 1981-82;

sr. tech. info. rsch. analyst Ashland Oil Co., Lexington, 1983—94; ret., 1994. Co-author: Directory of Special Libraries in the Bluegrass, 1991. Chmn. libr. com. LWV, Lexington, 1985, bd. dirs., 1990; vol. KET Telefund, 1990; bd. dirs. Friends Lexington Pub. Libr., 1998—; RSVP vol. Lexington in Bloom, 2002, judge; active Mayor's Tree Bd., 2003—. Named to Hon. Order of Ky. Cols., 1979. Mem. AAUW (pres. 1980-82), ALA, Spl. Librs. Assn. (pres. Ky. chpt. 1987), Cen. Ky. Online User's Group, Ky. Libr. Assn., Evergreen Garden Club (pres. 1989-91), Lexington Coun. Garden Club (v.p., sec.), Kappa Kappa Gamma. Democrat. Roman Catholic. Avocations: reading, golf, needlecrafts. Home: 209 Clinton Rd Lexington KY 40502-1923

**YOUNG, SCOTT CHRISTOPHER,** music educator, musician; s. Michael Gordon and Sherry Lee Young; m. Leigh Ann Perry, May 27, 2000; children: Emily Michelle, Rebecca Grace. MusB, Clayton State U., 1993; M in Music Edn., Valdosta State U., 1997. Music tchr. Echols County Pub. Sch., Statenville, Ga., 1996—97; hornist Valdosta (Ga.) Symphony, Albany Symphony Orch., 2001—; head fine arts dept. Deerfield-Windsor Sch., Albany, 2003—. Composer: Gloria in Excelcis, 2004, Symphonetta for Strings, 2005; arranger Be Thou My Vision, 2005. Sunday sch. tchr. 1st Meth. Ch., Albany, 2001—. Sgt. USMC, 1997—2002. Recipient Navy Commendation medal, USMC, 2002. Mem.: Internat. Horn Soc. Avocation: reading. Office: Deerfield-Windsor Sch 2500 Nottingham Way Albany GA 31707-1799 Office Phone: 229-435-1301 ext 334. E-mail: scott.young@deerfield.windsor.com.

**YOUNG, SCOTT THOMAS,** business management educator; b. Oak Park, Ill., Dec. 28, 1949; s. Thomas Menzies and Grace (Butler) Y.; children: Reginald, Galen; m. Luciana Pagotto. BA, U. Ga., 1974; MBA, Ga. Coll., 1982; PhD, Ga. State U., 1987. Prof. U. Utah, Salt Lake City, 1987—2003, chmn. mgmt. dept., 1994-97, assoc. dean David Eccles Sch. Bus., 1997-99; prof. and chair dept. mgmt. DePaul U., Chgo., 2003—. Mgmt. cons. to numerous orgns.; lectr., speaker, cons. on ops., quality and project mgmt. Author: Managing Global Operations, 1996; contbr. numerous articles to profl. jours. With U.S. Army, 1971-73. Decorated Commendation medal; grantee Nat. Assn. Purchasing Mgmt., 1986. Mem. Decision Sci. Inst., Acad. Mgmt., Prodn. and Ops. Mgmt. Soc. Avocation: marathon running. Office: DePaul U Coll Commerce 1 E Jackson Blvd Chicago IL 60604 Office Phone: 312-362-6289. Business E-mail: syoung16@depaul.edu.

**YOUNG, SHELDON MIKE,** lawyer, author; b. Cleve., Aug. 27, 1926; s. Jack and Ray Y.; m. Margery Ann Polster, Dec. 25, 1948 (div. 1988); children: Jeffrey, Martin, Janet; m. Bette Abel Roth, Nov. 11, 1988. BA, Ohio State U., 1948, JD, 1951; LLM, Case Western Res. U., 1962. Bar: Ohio 1951, U.S. Dist. Ct. (no. dist.) Ohio. Gen. counsel Eugene M. Klein & Assocs., Actuaries, Cleve., 1952-72; assoc. Shapiro, Persky & Marken, Cleve., 1972-74; counsel pension tech. svcs. dept. CNA Ins., Chgo., 1974-76; ptnr. Weiss & Young, Cleve., 1976; of counsel Arter & Hadden, Cleve., 1977-85, Squire, Sanders & Dempsey, Cleve., 1985-87; pvt. practice Columbus 1987-91; of counsel Schwartz, Kelm, Warren & Rubenstein, Columbus, 1991—93, Walter & Haverfield, Columbus, 1993—. Instr. Case Western Res. U. Law Sch., 1962-82, 85, U. Akron Law Sch., 1984, 88. Author: Pension and Profit Sharing Plans, 7 vols., 1977-93, (novel) Toledoth-City of Generations, 2003; freelance writer for newspapers and mags.; contbr. articles to pension jours. Served with USN, WWII. Recipient award Nathan Burkan Meml. Copyright Competition, 1951. Fellow Am. Coll. Employee Benefits Counsel (charter); mem. ABA (chair obsolete pension rev. rule task force), Cleve. Bar Assn., Columbus Bar Assn., Masons. Jewish. Home and Office: Walter Haverfield 4776 Smoketalk Ln Westerville OH 43081-7838 Office Phone: 614-898-1096. Office Fax: 614-898-7190. Business E-mail: yomike@asacomp.com.

**YOUNG, SHERILYN BURNETT,** lawyer; b. Providence, Nov. 7, 1953; d. Archie C. III and Hope (Westcott) Burnett; m. Gary Richard Young. Oct. 9, 1977; children: Garrett, Alanna, Valerie. BA, Cornell U., Ithaca, N.Y., 1975; JD, Franklin Pierce Law Ctr., 1982. Bar: N.H. 1982, U.S. Dist. Ct. N.H. 1982, U.S. Tax Ct. 1983. Assoc. Orr & Reno, P.A., Concord, N.H., 1982-87; ptnr. Rath, Young and Pignatelli, P.C., Concord, 1987—. Trustee U. Sys. N.H., Concord Hosp., 1991-98, N.H. Hist. Soc., 2001-, Franklin Pierce Law Ctr., 2005-; legis. counsel to Gov. Gregg, Concord, 1989-90; mem. adv. coun. to ins. commr., 1989-93; spkr. in field. Legal counsel Rudman for U.S. Senate campaign, Concord, 1984-93; bd. dirs. Concord chpt. ARC, 1988-91; mem. N.H. adv. bd. New Eng. Legal Found., 1991-97; pres. Concord Hosp. Assn., 1991-97, bd. dirs. Mem. ABA, N.H. Bar Assn., New Eng. Coun., Concord C. of C. (bd. dirs. 1988-91), Bus. and Industry Assn., Cornell Club N.H. Republican. Avocations: skiing, tennis. Office: One Capital Plz Concord NH 03302-1500 Office Phone: 603-226-2600.

**YOUNG, STEPHANIE ANGEL,** counseling administrator; b. St. Albans, W. Va., Mar. 6, 1976; d. Claude Eddie and Carolyn Sue Childers; m. Jeffrey Allen Young, May 19, 2001; 1 child, Parker Reid. BA, U. Charleston; MA, EdS, Marshall U. Grad. Coll. Cert. sch. psychol. W. Va. Counselor YWCA Child Enrichment Ctr., Charleston, W.Va., 1998; after sch. worker Sacred Heart Day Care, Charleston, 1999; day car worker Forrest Burkette United Meth. Ch., Hurricane, W.Va., 1999—2001; grad. rsch. asst. Marshall U. Rsch. Corp., Harrington, W.Va., 2000—02; sub. tchr. Knowlon County Schs., Charleston, 2001—03; sch. psychol. intern Logan (W.Va.) County Schs., 2003—05; cert. sch. psychol. RESA III, Dunbar, W.Va., 2005—. Mem.: NASP, W. Va. Assn. Sch. Psychol. Avocations: swimming, outdoors. Office: RESA III 501 22nd St Dunbar WV 25064

**YOUNG, STEPHEN BERNARD,** urogynecologist, surgeon; b. Bklyn., Apr. 21, 1943; s. Alice Dora and Louis Wolf Young; m. Martha Anne Abeles, June 25, 1995. BA, Columbia U., NYC, 1964; MD, George Washington U., 1968. Diplomate Nat. Bd. Med. Examiners. Fellow vaginal surgery Women and Infants Hosp., Brown U., Providence, 1986—89; prof., ob-gyn., chief urogynecology and reconstructive pelvic surgery U. Mass. Med. Sch., Worcester, 1990—. Tchr. in field, Guatemala, 1994, Beijing, 2005, Chennai, India, 06. Contbr. articles to profl. jours. Mem.: ACOG, Internat. Urogynecology and Reconstructive Pelvic Surgery, Soc. Gynecologic Surgeons (pres.-elect 2006—), Am. Urogynecologic Soc. (pres. 2004—05, Prize Paper award 2000). Office: Univ Mass 119 Belmont St Worcester MA 01605 Office Phone: 508-334-9842.

**YOUNG, STEPHEN K.,** dean, academic administrator; DDS, U. Mo., 1971; MS in oral pathology, U. Mich., 1974. Diplomate Am. Bd. Oral Pathology. Asst. prof., oral and maxillofacial surgery U. Okla. Coll. Dentistry, David Ross Boyd prof., adj. prof., pathology, assoc. dean, dean, 1990—. Contbr. articles to profl. jours. Chair Nat. Cancer Inst.'s Ad Hoc Cancer Edn. Grant Review Com. Decorated Meritorious award, Okla. Dental Assn., 1988. Office: 1001 Stanton L Young Blvd Rm 507 Oklahoma City OK 73190 Office Phone: 405-271-5444. Home Fax: 405-271-3423. Business E-mail: stephen-young@ouhsc.edu.*

**YOUNG, STEVE G.,** former labor union administrator; Student, Berklee Coll. Music. Pres. Local 9-535, Boston, 1987; mem. exec. bd. Am. Fedn. Musicians U.S. and Can., 1989-91, v.p., 1991-95, pres. N.Y.C., 1995—2001. Mem. faculty Berklee Coll. Music, Boston. Plays bassoon, sax, clarinet, flute; performed with Boston Ballet, Opera Co. Boston, Boston Symphony and Pops; performer Marlboro Music Festival.

**YOUNG, STEVEN,** retired professional football player; b. Salt Lake City, Oct. 11, 1961; JD, Brigham Young, 1993. With L.A. Express, USFL, 1984—85, Tampa Bay Buccaneers, 1985—87; quarterback San Francisco 49ers, 1987—2000; panelist ESPN Sunday NFL Countdown, 2001—. Founder, mgr. Forever Young Found. benefitting Bay Area and Utah youth-oriented charities, 1993—. Named MVP, NFL, 1992, Player of Yr., 1994, All-Am. team quarterback, The Sporting News, 1983, Top-rated quarterback, NFL, 1991, NFL MVP, The Sporting News, 1992, NFL All-Pro team quarterback, 1992, Bay Area Sports Hall of Fame Profl. Athlete of Yr., 1992, Superbowl MVP, 1994; recipient Davey O'Brien award, 1983. Achievements include played in Pro Bowl, 1992, 93; highest rate passer NFL, 1991-93; inducted to the Pro Football Hall of Fame, 2005. Mailing: Forever Young Foundation PO Box 527 Park City UT 84060

**YOUNG, STEVEN L.,** lawyer; b. Bklyn., Mar. 8, 1954; BA, SUNY, Binghamton, 1975; JD, St. John's U., 1978. Bar: NY 1979, US Dist. Ct. So. Dist. NY, US Dist. Ct. Ea. Dist. NY, US Dist. Ct. No. Dist. NY. Ptnr. Wilson, Elser, Moskowitz, Edelman & Dicker LLP, White Plains, NYC. Mem.: ABA, Westchester County Bar Assn., NY State Bar Assn. Office: Wilson Elser Moskowitz Edelman & Dicker LLP 3 Gannett Dr White Plains NY 10604 Office Phone: 914-323-7000 ext. 4252. Office Fax: 914-323-7001. Business E-Mail: youngs@wemed.com.

**YOUNG, TERESA GAIL HILGER,** retired adult education educator; b. Modesto, Calif., Mar. 4, 1948; d. Richard George and Jessie Dennie (Dennis) Long; m. Charles Ray Young, June 22, 1974; 1 child, Gregory Paul. BS in Edn., Abilene (Tex.) Christian U., 1970; MEd in Curriculum, Tarleton State U., Stephenville, Tex., 1976; postgrad., Tex. Tech U., 1990-92. Cert. supr., mid-mgmt., supt., Tex. Tchr. sci. Tex. Youth Coun., Gatesville, 1970-73, Gatesville Ind. Sch. Dist., 1973-81; coord. Edn. and Tng. Ctr., Cen. Tex. Coll., Gatesville, 1983; tchr. Tex. Dept. of Criminal Justice-ID, 1984—2002; ret., 2003. Conf. presenter. Trustee Jonesboro (Tex.) Ind. Sch. Dist., 1988-96. Teacher of the Year for Region II of Tex. Dept. of Criminal Justice, 1997-98. Mem. Am. Fedn. Tchrs., Assn. Tex. Profl. Educators. E-mail: tyoung@htcomp.net.

**YOUNG, TERRI L.,** ophthalmologist; b. Sacramento, 1959; AB in Bio-Chemistry and Sociology, Bowdoin Coll., Brunswick, Maine, 1981; MD in Medicine, Harvard U., 1986. Postdoctoral in pediat. Children's Hosp. Boston, 1986—87; resident in ophthalmology U. Ill., Chgo., 1987—90; clin. instr. ophthalmology U. Ill. Sch. Medicine, Chgo., 1989—90; extern in strabismus and adult motility disorders U. Iowa, 1991; fellow in pediatric ophthalmology, strabismus and adult motility disorders U. Pa. and Children's Hosp. Phila., 1990—92; clin. instr. opthalmology U. Pa., 1990—92; instr. neurobiology and ophthalmology Harvard Med. Sch., 1992—94; asst. prof. ophthalmology U. Minn., 1994—2000, assoc. prof. pediat., 1998—2000, assoc. prof. pediat., 2000—; dir.Ophthalmic Genetics Rsch. Ctr., Children's Hosp. Phila. 2000—; assoc. prof. ophthalmology and pediat. U. Pa. 2001—. Recipient Surdna Undergrad. Rsch. fellowship, Bowdoin Coll., 1980—81, Stanley J. Sarnoff Soc. Cardiovascular rsch. award and fellowship, Harvard Med. Sch., 1983—84, Commonwealth Fund Rsch. fellowship, 1985, George and Mary Knox Harvaard Med. Grad. award, 1984, Grad. Kaiser Merit award, Nat. Med. Fellowship, 1986, Keeshin Prize Rsch. award, Inst. Medicine Chgo., 1990, Honor award, Am. Acad. Ophthalmology, 1998, Robert Wood Johnson Faculty Devel. award, 1992—97, Honor award, Am. Acad. Ophthalmology, 1998, Am. Assn. Pediatric Ophthalmology and Strabismus, 2002; selected as part of NIH's "Changing the Face of Medicine" exhbn., 2003. Fellow: Am. Ophthalmol. Soc. Office: Duke U Eye Ctr Box 3082 2351 Erwin Rd Durham NC 27705 Business E-Mail: terri.young@duke.edu.

**YOUNG, THOMAS LEE,** lawyer; b. Los Angeles, Feb. 21, 1944; s. J. Donald and Nancy M. Young; m. Kathleen Grace Jacob, Sept. 10, 1967; children: Barbara, Deborah, Amy. Student, Marquette U., 1963; BA, St. John's Coll., 1966; JD, Notre Dame U., 1972; postgrad., Harvard U., 1984—85. Bar: Ohio 1972. Assoc. Fuller, Henry, Hodge & Snyder, Toledo, 1972—75; assoc. counsel Scott Paper Co., Phila., 1975—76; joined legal dept. Owens-Ill., Inc., Toledo, 1976—, asst. gen. counsel, 1983—88, v.p., gen. counsel oper., 1988—90, gen. counsel, sec., 1990—93, exec. v.p., admin & genl. counsel, 1993—2003, chief fin. officer, 2003—05. Bd. dirs. Manor Care Inc., Rocky Mountain Bottle Co., Gen. Chem. Ptnrs., GMP Employers Retirement Trust, Owens-Ill., Inc., Franklin Electric Co. Inc. 1st lt. U.S. Army, 1966—69, Vietnam. Mem.: ABA, Toledo Bar Assn., Ohio State Bar Assn. Roman Catholic. Avocation: tennis.*

**YOUNG, TOMMIE MORTON,** psychology professor, writer; b. Nashville; BA cum laude, Tenn. State U., 1951; MA, Peabody Vanderbilt U., 1955; PhD, Duke U., 1977; postgrad., U. Chicago, 1967, U. Nebr., 1968. Coord. Young Adult Program Lucy Thurman br. YWCA, 1951-52; instr. edn. Tenn. State U., Nashville, 1956-59; instr. coord. media program Prairie View Coll. (Tex.), 1959-61; asst. prof. edn., assoc. prof. English, dir. IMC Ctr. U. Ark., Pine Bluff, 1965-69; asst. prof. English and dir. learning lab N.C. Central U., Durham, 1969-74; prof., dir./chairperson libr. /dir. Afro-Am. Family Project, prof. philosophy sociol. found. N.C. Agrl. and Tech. State U., Greensboro, 1975—92; adj. prof. langs., lit. and philosophy, dir. schs. history project Tenn. State U., Nashville, 1994—. Dir. workshops, grants; pres., dir. Elman Svcs.; owner Historic Black Nashville Tours. Author: Afro-Am. Genealogy Sourcebook, 1987, Oral Histories of Former All-Black Public Schs., 1991, After School Program for At-Risk Youth and Their Families, 1997, Sable Scenes, 1996, Genealogist's Guide to Discovering Your African Ancestors, 1997, A Sister Speaks, 1998, Nashville, Tennessee, 2000, Fabulous You: Women Celebrating the Fabulous Self, 2005; contbr. poem to Poetry: American Heritage; contbr. rsch. papers, articles to profl. jours. Nat. chmn. Com. to Re-Elect the Pres.; past sec. Fedn. Colored Women's Clubs; bd. dirs. Southwestern div. ARC, Nashville area, 1994-, dir. Volun-Teens; chairperson schs. div. Durham County Unit Am. Cancer Soc.; past mem. adv. bd., bd. dirs. YMCA, Atlanta; chair Guilford County Commn. on Needs of Children; bd. advisors NIH, N.C. Dept. of the Arts; mem. Guilford County Involvement Coun.; chmn. N.C. adv. com. U.S. Civil Rights Com.; mem. exec. planning com. Greensboro; hon. staff mem. 54th Legis. Dist., Nashville, 1996; pres. Davidson County Dem. Women, 2003-04; chgt. Dist. I exec. com. Davidson County Dem. Party; chair resolutions com. Nat. Fedn. Dem. Women. Recipient awards ARC, 1968, 73, NAACP, 1973, HEW, 1978, U.S. Commn. on Civil Rights, 1982, cert. of Accomplishment Contributing to Youth Devel. Bus. and Profl. Women, 2000, others; named Disting. Alumni Tenn. State U., 1994, Peabody Colls. Gift to the World. Mem. AAUW (honor award 1983, pres. Greensboro br., chairperson internat. rels. com.), ALA (divsn. coll. and rsch. librs., past chair), NAACP (life, 1st v.p. Durham br., exec. bd. Greensboro br. dir. parent edn./child advocacy program, chair exec. com. Nashville, Woman of Yr. 1992), NEA, LWV (bd. dirs. Nashville), Assn. Childhood Ednl. Internat., Comperative and Internat. Edn. Assn., Archives Assoc., Internat. Platform Assn., Nat. Hist. Soc., Greenboro Jr. League (community adv. bd. 1991—), African Am. Gen. Soc. Tenn. (founder 1994), Zeta Phi Beta (chairperson polit. action com. eastern region, nat. grammateus, Polit. and Civic Svc. award 1974, Outstanding Social-Polit. Svc. award 1982, Woman of Yr. 1977), Comm. on Status of Women (Woman of Achievement 1991), Phi Kappa Phi (Disting. Alumni award Tenn. State U. 1994, Disting. Alumni NAFEO award, 1995, Carl Rowan-Oprah Winfrey lectr. Tenn. State U., 1995, Excellence in Journlism award SPJ, 1995, Tenn. Outstanding Achievement award, 1997), 100 Black Women, Steering Com., Tenn. Trust for Historic Preservation, 1999 (named Woman of Distinction Top Ladies, 2001, named Peabody/Vanderbilt Jnin Great, 2005, nominee Athena award 2005). Home: PO Box 281613 Nashville TN 37228-8506

**YOUNG, TZAY Y.,** electrical and computer engineering educator; b. Shanghai, Jan. 11, 1933; came to U.S. 1958; s. Chao-Hsiung and Chiu-Ming (Chu) Y.; m. Lily Liu, Dec. 27, 1965; children: Debbie Chia-Pei, Arthur Chia-Kai. BS, Nat. Taiwan U., Taipei, 1955; MS, U. Vt., 1959; DEng, Johns Hopkins U., 1962. Rsch. assoc. Johns Hopkins U., Balt., 1962-63; mem. tech. staff Bell Labs., Murray Hill, NJ, 1963-64; asst. prof. Carnegie-Mellon U., Pitts., 1964-68, assoc. prof., 1968-74; prof. elec. and computer enging. U. Miami, Coral Gables, Fla., 1974—2003, acting chmn. dept., 1988-91, chmn. dept., 1991-2000, prof. emeritus, 2004—. Sr. postdoctoral rsch. assoc. NSA, NASA, Goddard Space Flight Ctr., Md., 1972-73. Author: (with T.W. Calvert) Classification, Estimation and Pattern Recognition, 1974; editor: (with K.S. Fu) Handbook of Pattern Recognition and Image Processing, 1986; editor: Handbook of Pattern Recognition and Image Processing, vol. 2, Computer Vision, 1994; also numerous articles. Rsch. grantee NSF, NASA, FHTIC, also

indsl. grants. Fellow IEEE (assoc. editor Trans. Computers 1974-76; editorial bd. Trans. Pattern Analysis and Machine Intelligence 1979-84, adv. bd. 1984-90); mem. Sigma Xi, Eta Kappa Nu, Omicron Delta Kappa. E-mail: tyoung@miami.edu.

**YOUNG, VERNON LEWIS,** retired lawyer; b. Seaman, Ohio, Oct. 13, 1919; s. Ezra S. and Anna (Bloom) Y.; m. Eileen Humble, 1941; children: Robert, Loretta, Bettie Jo, Jon W., Denise L. Student, Albert Holbrook Coll., Manchester, Ohio, 1938—39; JD, Ohio No. U., Ada, 1942. Bar: Ohio 1942. Employee War Dept., 1942; sole practice West Union, Ohio, 1942-50, 78-81; ptnr. Young & Young, West Union, 1959—78, Young & Caldwell, 1978—81, 1995—2003, ret., 2003; ptnr. Young-Caldwell & BUBP, West Union, 1981-95; ret. Spl. counsel Office of Atty. Gen., State of Ohio, West Union, solicitor Cities of Jamestown, Seaman, Winchester, Manchester, Ohio; pros. atty. Adams County, Ohio, 1952-56, acting county judge, 1968-79. Mayor City of Seaman, 1944-46; mem. Adams County Health Bd., West Union, 1968-75; chmn. membership com. Eastern Shore Inst. Lifelong Learning, Fairhope, Ala., 1983-84; mem. Rep. Presdl. Task Force, 1980-94. Mem.: Adams County Bar Assn. (former pres.), Jr. Bar (pres. Ohio No. U. 1941—42), Ohio State Bar Assn., Ohio No. Univ., Lions (pres. 1950—51, dist. gov. 1951—52), Masons (32 degrees), Sigma Delta Kappa (chancellor 1940). Avocations: fishing, hunting, gardening. Home: 10 Hickory Dr Seaman OH 45679-9762

**YOUNG, VICTORIA E.,** occupational health nurse, lawyer; b. Concord, Mich., Apr. 20, 1933; d. Arthur Raymond and Edith Louise (Hands) Y. Diploma, Mercy Sch. Nursing, Jackson, Mich., 1954; BSN, UCLA, 1960, MPH in Adminstrn., 1966; JD, U. West LA, Culver City, 1973. Bar: Calif., U.S. Dist. Ct., Calif.; RN, Calif.; cert. pub. health nurse, pediatric nurse practitioner. Pub. health nurse L.A. City and Los Angeles County Health Dept.; exec. dir. Santa Monica (Calif.) Vis. Nurse Assn.; sch. nurse practitioner L.A. Unified Schs.; relief nurse L.A. Times. Vol. Moorpark City Hall, Moorpark Sr. Ctr; mem. Disaster Assistance Response Team, Moorpark. Ret. capt. USNR, Desert Storm. Mem. Nat. Assn. Pediatric Nurse Assocs. and Practitioners, Calif. Bar Assn., Fleet Res. Assn., Moorpark Woman's Fortnightly Club (treas. 1998-99). Home: 4359 Brookdale Ln Moorpark CA 93021-2302

**YOUNG, VINCE PAUL, JR.,** professional football player; b. Houston, Tx, June 18, 1983; Student, U. Tex., 2002—06. Quarterback U. Tex. Longhorns, Austin, 2003—06, Tenn. Titans, Nashville, 2006—. Named MVP, Rose Bowl, 2005, 2006, ESPY award, Best Male Coll. Athlete, 2006; recipient Davey O'Brien Nat. Quarterback Award, 2005, Manning award, 2006. Achievements include being the quarterback in NCAA div.1 National Champion for Texas Longhorns, 2006; being the only player in NCAA div. 1 history to pass for 2,500 yards and rush for 1,000 yards in the same season, 2005; the third overall selection in the 2006 NFL Draft. Office: Tenn Titans One Titans Way Nashville TN 37213*

**YOUNG, VIRGIL MONROE,** education educator; b. Santa Rosa, Calif., Sept. 24, 1936; s. Virgil M. and Vesta May (Huyett) Williams; stepson Louis H. Young; m. Katherine Ann Young, Dec. 20, 1964; 1 child, Susan Annette. BS, U. Idaho, 1958, EdD, 1967. Cert. advanced secondary edn. educator, sch. supt., Idaho. Tchr. Moscow (Idaho) Sch. Dist., 1959-63; adminstrv. asst. to supt. Coeur d'Alene (Idaho) Sch. Dist., 1965-67; prof. edn. Boise (Idaho) State U., 1967-96, head dept. edn., 1989-96, prof. emeritus, 1996—. Author: (elem. textbook) The Story of Idaho, 4 edits.; co-author: The Story of the Idaho Guide and Resource Book, 1993; author: (with others) Year 2000 Grolier Multimedia Encyclopedia, 2000; designer, author ednl. and comml. internet websites, 1999—. Capt. USAR. Mem. N.W. Assn. Tchr. Educators (past pres.), Idaho Assn. Colls. Tchr. Edn. (past pres.), Phi Delta Kappa (past pres.).

**YOUNG, WILLIAM BENJAMIN,** retired special education educator; b. Wichita, Kans., Jan. 30, 1929; s. Ernest William and Florence Belle (McCann) Y.; m. La Vona P., Feb., 1949 (div. 1973); children: Lynda, David, Timothy; m. Patricia Sue Reber, Aug., 1974. Student, Southwestern Coll., Winfield, Kans., 1947-48; B in Gen. Edn., U. Omaha, 1961; MS in Pers. Counseling, Miami U., Oxford, Ohio, 1965; PhD in Exceptional Edn., Adminstrn. and Counseling, Ohio State U., 1972. Cert. elem. and secondary adminstr., tchr., counselor, psychologist, psychometrist, spl. edn., mental retardation, learning disabled/behavior disordered, emotionally handicapped, Ind.; cert. K-12 guidance counselor and edn. leadership, Fla.; lic sexologist, flight instr.; lic. Coast Guard capt. Enlisted USAF, 1948, commd. 2nd lt., 1955, advanced through grades to capt., 1960, ret., 1966; numerous teaching and counseling positions as civilian, 1966-91; co-owner, instr. Ft. Wayne (Ind.) Ground Schs., 1984-88; marriage and family counselor, pvt. practice, 1966-91; tchr., counselor, behavior specialist Broward County Schs., Ft. Lauderdale, Fla., 1989-99; ret., 1999. Cons., internat. presenter/lectr. learning and behavior problems. Vol. instr. AARP Safe Driving Course; vol. support group leader for dementia caregivers support. Mem. ACA, Coun. for Exceptional Children, Coun. Behavior Disorders, Fla. Counseling Assn., 32 degree Masons. Avocations: travel, golf, swimming. Home and Office: 1101 SW 70th Ter Plantation FL 33317-4135 E-mail: wby130@aol.com.

**YOUNG, WILLIAM D.,** lawyer; b. Aug. 26, 1960; BBA, U. Miss., 1982, JD, 1984. Bar: Tex. 1985. Ptnr. Vinson & Elkins LLP, Dallas, 1998—, co-head Bus. & Internat. Sect. Mem.: ABA. Office: Vinson & Elkins Trammell Crow Ctr 2001 Ross Ave, Ste 3700 Dallas TX 75201 Office Phone: 214-220-7994. E-mail: byoung@velaw.com.

**YOUNG, WILLIAM GLOVER,** federal judge; b. Huntington, NY, Sept. 23, 1940; s. Woodhull Benjamin and Margaret Jean (Wilkes) Young; m. Beverly June Bigelow, Aug. 5, 1967; children: Mark Edward, Jeffrey Woodhull, Todd Russell. AB, Harvard U., 1962, LLB, 1967; LLD, New Eng. Sch. Law, 2001. Bar: Mass. 1967, admitted to practice: US Supreme Ct. 1970. Law clk. to chief justice Supreme Jud. Ct., Mass., 1967-68; spl. asst. atty. gen. Mass., 1969-72; chief legal counsel to gov. Mass., 1972-74; assoc. Bingham, Dana and Gould, Boston, 1968-72, ptnr., 1975-78; assoc. justice Superior Ct., Commonwealth of Mass., Boston, 1978-85; judge US Dist. Ct. Mass., Boston, 1985—, chief judge, 1999—2005. Mem. budget com. US Jud. Conf., 1987—2001, chmn. economy subcom., 1991—2001; lectr. Boston Coll. Law Sch., 1966—90, Boston U. Law Sch., 1979—; Harvard Law Sch., 1979—90. Author: Massachusetts Evidentiary Standards, Evidence, Massachusetts Practice Series; co-author: Daubert's Gatekeeper: The Role of the District Judge in Admitting Expert Testimony. Capt. U.S. Army, 1962—64. Mem.: Boston Bar Assn., Mass. Bar Assn., Am. Law Inst., Harvard Alumni (pres. 1976—77). Office: US Courthouse Rm 5710 Boston MA 02210 Office Phone: 617-748-9138. Personal E-mail: bjbg2y3@earthlink.net. Business E-Mail: william_young@mad.uscourts.gov.

**YOUNG, WILLIAM H.,** labor union administrator; b. 1947; m. Debbie Young; 4 children. Mem., Ctrl. Calif. Coast Br. 52 Nat. Assn. Letter Carriers, San Luis Obispo, 1965, pres., Ctrl. Calif. Coast Br. 52, 1971—78, regional adminstrv. asst., 1978—86, nat. bus. agent San Francisco region, 1986—90, asst. sec.-treas. Washington, 1990—94, dir. city devel., v.p., 1994—98, exec. v.p., 1998—2002, nat. pres., 2002—. Officer Calif. State Assn., 1972—; v.p. Am. Fedn. Labor, Coun. Indsl. Orgn. (AFL-CIO). Nat. v.p. Muscular Dystrophy Assn. (MDA); mem. adv. bd. Walter P. Reuther Libr. Labor and Urban Affairs, Wayne State U., Detroit. Served with U.S. Army. Office: Nat Assn Letter Carriers 100 Ind Ave NW Washington DC 20001-2144 Office Phone: 202-393-4695.*

**YOUNG, WILLIAM HENRY,** education educator, writer, consultant; b. Barnesboro, Pa., Feb. 8, 1943; m. Brenda Gallagher Young; 1 child, Douglas Bryan. EdD, Pa. State U., 1976. Permanent tchg. cert. Pa. Asst. dean Coll. Medicine, U. Ill., Peoria, 1976—79; dir. continuing edn. and pub. svc. U. Ill. at the Med. Ctr., Chgo., 1979—84; dean coll. of continuing edn. No. Ill. U., DeKalb, 1984—90, prof., 1990—99, U. South Fla., Tampa, 1999—. Author: Managing and Developing People in the Virtual Organization (runner up

Book of Yr., Acad. Human Resource Devel., 2003), Continuing Professional Education in Transition. Mem.: Assn. Clin. Pastoral Edn. (chair profl. adv. com.), Internat. Soc. Performance Improvement (mktg. com.). Home: 18003 Avalon Ln Tampa FL 33647 Office Phone: 813-974-1861. Office Fax: 813-974-3355. E-mail: wyoung@coedu.usf.edu.

**YOUNG, WILLIAM WEBB,** military officer, aire warfare specialist; poet; b. St. Louis, Aug. 4, 1967; s. Raymond Andrew and Betty Rosella (Myers) Young; children: Jamie Elizabeth, Christen Lee, Sara Rayan. Commd. ensign USN, 1987; Persian Gulf War/Cold War vet. Svc. officer Three Rivers Serenity Group, Poplar Bluff, Mo., 1989—2002, dist. 8 spl. needs com. chmn., 2001—. Author numerous poems. Local stream team coord. Mo. Dept. Conservation, Butler County, Mo., 1997—2002, frontiers program leader, 1998—2002; water quality monitoring vol. Mo. Dept. Natural Resources, Butler County, Mo., 1999—2002. Decorated Battle "E" Award Persian Excursion US Navy, Order of the Spanish Main, Joint Meritorious Unit award, Nat. Def. Medal, Overseas Deployment Ribbon, Good Conduct Medal, Kuwait Liberation Medal, Saudi Arabia Liberation Medal, Disting. Expert Pistol Medal, Expert Rifle Medal, Meritorious Unit Commendation for Bravery and Heroism, Russian Cold War Star, Navy Achievement Medal, Silver Life Saving Medal; recipient Iliad Lit. award, Internat. Poet of Merit, 1996, Editors Choice award, 1996, Americanism award, Grande Voiture of N.J. Navy, 1990, Loyalty Day award, VFW, 1990. Fellow: K.C. (1st degree crusader, Altar Server award 1981); mem.: Internat. Soc. Poets, Disabled Am. Vets. (life Golden Anchor award 1988), Amherst Soc., Iraqi Desert Yacht Club, Gulf of Oman Yacht Club, Gulf of Sidra Yacht Club, Persian Gulf Yacht Club, Persian Gulf Health Club (life; adminstr.), Am. Legion (honor guard). Roman Catholic. Avocation: art. Home: 201 W Lexington Ave Poplar Bluff MO 63901

**YOUNGBLOOD, BETTY J.,** academic administrator; b. Detroit; m. Ralph P. Youngblood; 1 child. BA in Political Sci., Oakland U., Rochester, Mich.; MA in South Asian Studies, U. Minn., PhD in Political Sci. Formerly mem. faculty State U. West Ga., Tex. Tech. U.; various adminstrv. positions Kennesaw State U., Marietta, Ga.; v.p. acad. affairs MacMurray Coll., Jacksonville, Ill., Wesley Coll., Dover, Del.; vice chancellor acad. affairs, dean faculty, prof. polit. sci. U. Wis.-Superior, 1990-91, acting chancellor, 1991-92, chancellor, 1992—95; pres. We. Oreg. U., 1995—2002, Lake Superior State U., Mich., 2002—. Cons., evaluator North Ctrl. Assn. Colls. and Schs. Contbr. articles to profl. jours. Bd. dirs. United Way, Sault Ste. Marie. Rsch. grantee for study in N.W. India. Mem. Sault Ste. Marie C. of C., War Meml. Hosp., Rotary. Office: Lake Superior State Univ 650 W Easterday Ave Sault Sainte Marie MI 49783

**YOUNGBLOOD, DEBORAH SUE,** lawyer, speech pathology/audiology services professional; b. Fairview, Okla., July 29, 1954; d. G. Dean and Beatrice J. (Hiebert) White. BS with honors, Okla. State U., 1976, MA with honors, 1979; JD cum laude, Boston Coll. Law Sch., 1991; MPH in Health Care Mgmt., Harvard U., 1992. Bar: Colo., U.S. Ct. Appeals (10th cir.). Jud. law clk. Colo. Supreme Ct., 1992-94; assoc. atty. Patton Boggs, L.L.P., Denver, 1994—97; sr. assoc. atty. Vaglica & Meinhold, L.L.C., Colorado Springs, 1997-99; pvt. practice speech-lang. pathologist North Conway, NH, 1999—2001, Sun Valley, Idaho, 2001—. Mem. leadership coun. Harvard Sch. Pub. Health, 2003—. Mem. leadership coun. Harvard Sch. Pub. Health, 2003—. Recipient LEXIS Legal Rsch. and Writing Award, Boston Coll. Law Sch. Mem.: Harvard Sch. Pub. Health Leadership (coun. 2003—), Minoru Yasui Am. Inns of Ct. (exec. coun. 1995—97), Colo. Bar Assn., Sun Valley Edn. Found. (bd. dirs.), Phi Kappa Phi. Office: 118 W Bullion St Hailey ID 83333 E-mail: youngblood@peoplepc.com.

**YOUNGBLOOD, JUDY ANN,** artist, educator; b. El Paso, Dec. 12, 1948; d. Curtis Nolan and Ruth Marie (Marck) Y. BS, U. Wis., 1971, MFA, 1974. Emeritus prof. art U. North Tex., Denton, 1977—98. Vis. lectr. art U. Wis., Madison, 1982; conducted workshops Blackhills Print Symposium, U. Tulsa, Ariz. State U., Auston Coll., U. Tex., U. B.C., Okla. State U. Collections included in Modern Mus. Art., Ft. Worth, Bklyn. Mus., Huntington Art Gallery, Weismann Art Mus., Elvehjem Mus. Art, Madison, Wis., Belo Corp., Dallas, Portland Mus. Art; one-woman shows include Art Mus. Southeast Tex., William Campbell Contemporary Art, Ft. Worth, Edith Baker Gallery, Dallas, Cidnee Patrick Gallery, Dallas. Fulbright-Hays grantee, Paris, 1979; MacDowell Colony fellow, 1982, 89. Mem. So. Graphics Coun. (bd. dirs. 1996-99), Coll. Art Assn.

**YOUNG-CAMPBELL, LAURA L.,** speech pathology/audiology services professional; b. Alaska; d. Ken and Alice Young; m. Donald Campbell; 1 child, Jennifer. BE in Comm. Disorders & Spl. Edn., Gonzaga U., Spokane, Wash., 1979—83; MS in Speech & Hearing Scis., U. Ariz., Tucson, 1990—93. Cert. spl. svcs. in speech pathology Alaska Dept. Edn., 1983, cert. of clin. competence and speech pathology Am. Speech-Hearing Assn., 1994, advanced cert. speech pathology Alaska Dept. Edn., 2002. Speech-lang. pathologist Matanuska-Susitna Borough Sch. Dist., Palmer, Alaska, 1983—. Mem. editl. bd. Perpspectives on Sch. Based Issues, Am. Speech-Hearing Assn., Md. Del., amb. to China People to People Internat., 2006—; vol. Alaska Health Fair, 1998—; healthy hearing vol. Spl. Olympics, Alaska, 2002—. Recipient award for continuing edn., Am. Speech-Hearing Assn., 1994—2006, Friend of Assn. award, Alaska Speech-Hearing Assn., 2004. Mem.: Mat-Su Speech-Hearing Assn., Coun. Exceptional Children, Alaska Speech Hearing Assn. (exec. bd. 1995—2006), Am. Speech-Hearing Assn. (licentiate; legislative councilor 2005—), Mat-Su Alaska Edn. Assn. (life; del. assembly 1999—2006). Avocations: travel, gardening, reading, movies. Office: Matanuska-Susitna Borough Schs 501 N Gulkana St Palmer AK 99645

**YOUNGDAHL, PAUL FREDERICK,** mechanical engineer; b. Brockway, Pa., Oct. 8, 1921; s. Harry Ludwig and Esther Marie (Carlson) Y.; m. Elinor Louise Jensen, Nov. 27, 1943; children: Mark Erik, Marcia Linnea, Melinda Louise. Student Pa. State U., 1938-40; BS in Engring., U. Mich., 1942, MS in Engring., 1949, PhD, 1962. Indsl. and devel. engr. DuPont, Bridgeport, Conn., 1942-43, Carneys Point, N.J., 1946-48; dir. research Mech. Handling Systems, Detroit, 1953-62; prof. U. Mich., Ann Arbor, 1962-74; cons. mech. engr., Palo Alto, Calif., 1974—; dir. Liquid Drive Corp., Holly, Mich. Contbr. articles to profl. jours. With USNR, 1943-46. Mem. Mich. Soc. Profl. Engrs., Nat. Soc. Profl. Engrs., ASME, Am. Soc. Engring. Edn., Mich. Assn. Professions, Sigma Xi, Tau Beta Pi, Phi Kappa Phi, Pi Tau Sigma. Methodist. Address: 151 Del Mesa Carmel Carmel CA 93923 Office Phone: 831-622-9965.

**YOUNGER, JARRED WAYNE,** research scientist; b. Dyersburg, Tenn., Feb. 7, 1976; s. Marissa Kim and Rick Martin Younger. PhD, U. Tenn., 2003. Rsch. asst. State U., Tempe, 2003—05, asst. rsch. scientist, 2005—. Fellow, Arthritis Found., 2005—06; grantee, NIH, 2004—06; scholar, Bonner Found., 1994—98. Mem.: APA (student coun. rep. 2003—06), Soc. Clin. and Exptl. Hypnosis (Crasilneck Award for Young Scientist 2000), Soc. Behavioral Medicine. Home: 4691 W Oakland St Chandler AZ 85226 Office: Ariz State Univ 950 S McAllister Dr Tempe AZ 85287-1104 Office Phone: 480-965-8458. Office Fax: 480-727-8203. Personal E-mail: jarredyngr@aol.com.

**YOUNGER, JENNIFER A.,** university librarian; BA in history, U. Wis.-Madison, MLA, PhD in info. studies. Various positions in libr. sys. U. Wis.-Madison, 1977—91; asst. dir. acctg. svc. Ohio State U. libr., 1991-97; Edward H. Arnold dir. libraries U. Notre Dame, 1997—. Editor: (jour.) Library Resources & Technical Services. Mem.: ALA, Assn. Libr. Collections & Tech. Svc. (pres. 1993—94), Beta Phi Mu. Office: 221 Hesburgh Libr U Notre Dame Notre Dame IN 46556 Office Phone: 574-631-7790. Office Fax: 574-631-6772. E-mail: Jennifer.A.Younger@nd.edu.*

**YOUNGER, JUDITH TESS,** law educator; b. N.Y.C., Dec. 20, 1933; d. Sidney and Kate (Greenbaum) Weintraub; m. Irving Younger, Jan. 21, 1955; children: Rebecca, Abigail M. BS, Cornell U., 1954; JD, NYU, 1958; LLD (hon.), Hofstra U., 1974. Bar: N.Y. 1958, U.S. Supreme Ct 1962, D.C. 1983, Minn. 1985. Law clk. to judge U.S. Dist. Ct., 1958-60; assoc. firm Chadbourne, Parke, Whiteside & Wolff, N.Y.C., 1960-62; mem. firm Younger and Younger, and (successors), 1962-67; adj. asst. prof. NYU Sch. Law, 1967-69; asst. atty. gen. State of N.Y., 1969-70; assoc. prof. Hofstra U. Sch. Law, 1970-72, prof., assoc. dean, 1972-74; dean, prof. Syracuse Coll. Law, 1974-75; dep. dean, prof. law Cornell Law Sch., 1975-78, prof. law, 1975-85; vis. prof. U. Minn. Law Sch., Mpls., 1984-85, prof., 1985-91, Joseph E. Wargo Anoka County Bar assn. prof. family law, 1991—. Of counsel Popham, Haik, Schnobrich & Kaufman, Ltd., Mpls., 1989-95; cons. NOW, 1972-74, Suffolk County for Revision of Its Real Property Tax Act, 1972-73; mem. N.Y. Gov.'s Panel To Screen Candidates of Ct. of Claims Judges, 1973-74; mem. Minn. Lawyers' Profl. Responsibility Bd., 1991-93. Contbr. articles to profl. jours. Trustee Cornell U., 1973-78. Mem.: AAUP (v.p. Cornell U. chpt. 1978—79), ABA (council legal edn. 1975—79), Minn. Bar Assn., Assn. of Bar of City of N.Y., Am. Law Inst. (adv. restatement property 1982—84). Home: 3520 W Calhoun Pkwy Minneapolis MN 55416-4657 Office: U Minn Law Sch Minneapolis MN 55455 Office Phone: 612-625-5844. Business E-Mail: young001@umn.edu.

**YOUNGER, KIRSTEN JEANNE,** painting restoration specialist; b. Schenectady, N.Y. d. Daniel Haven and Phyllis Jeanne Younger. BA in Art History/Fine Art, Oberlin Coll., 1989; MA in Art History and diploma in conservation, NYU, 1997. Intern in paintings conservation Met. Mus. Art, N.Y.C., 1996—97, Williamstown (Mass.) Art Conservation Ctr., 1997—98, J. Paul Getty Mus., L.A., 1998—99; paintings conservator Nancy Krieg, N.Y.C., 1999 . Mem.: Am. Inst. for Conservation of Historic and Artistic Works. Avocation: oil painting. Home: 193 Eldridge St # 5 New York NY 10002 E-mail: kyounger@nyc.rr.com.

**YOUNGER, LAURIE,** broadcast executive; BA in Comm., Queens Coll., MBA, UCLA, 1983. Former dir. bus. affairs 20th Century Fox; dir. bus. affairs network TV divsn. The Walt Disney Co., 1985—86, v.p. bus. affairs, 1986—90; sr. v.p. bus. affairs and adminstrn. Walt Disney TV and Telecomm.; sr. v.p. ABC, Inc., 1996—98, sr. v.p., CFO, 1998—2003, exec. v.p., CFO, 2003—; exec. v.p. ABC TV Distbn., 2000—03; pres. Buena Vista Worldwide TV, 2003—. Named one of 100 Most Powerful Women in Hollywood, Hollywood Reporter, 2003, 2004, 2005. Office: ABC Inc 500 S Buena Vista St Burbank CA 91521-4775*

**YOUNG III, HARMON GRIFFITH,** music educator; b. Charleston, W.Va. July 29, 1951; s. Harmon Griffith Young II and Phyllis Hall Young. BS, W.Va. Wesleyan Coll., 1973; MA, W.Va. U., 1974, MA, 1980; PhD, U. Fla. Gainesville, FL, 1995; postgrad., Westminster Choir Coll., Ohio U. Prof. music W.Va. U., Parkersburg, W.Va., 1975—. W.Va pres. Am. Choral Directors Assn., W.Va., 1993—95; pres. W.Va. Coun. Cultural Coordinators, W.Va., 1995—99; project dir., condr. Continental Harmony, W.Va., 1999—2000, W.Va., 2002—03; coll. chorale condr. W.Va. U., Parkersburg, 1975—, artistic dir. disting. performance series, 1980—. Finalist Prof. of Yr., Faculty Merit Found. W.Va., 2000;, W.Va. Humanities Coun. fellow, 2006—. Mem.: Internat. Fedn. Choral Music, Soc. Am. Music, Am. Choral Directors Assn. (life W.Va. chpt. Disting. Svc. award 2004), Pi Kappa Lambda, Phi Kappa Phi, Omicron Delta Kappa. United Methodist. Achievements include Commissioned and conducted premieres of choral works by eight American composers; Prepared choruses for numerous performances including collaborations with Robert Shaw and Dave Brubeck. Home: 75 Reamer Road Clendenin WV 25045 Office: West Virginia University Parkersburg 300 Campus Drive Parkersburg WV 26104 Office Phone: 304-424-8248. E-mail: hg.young@mail.wvu.edu.

**YOUNGJOHNS, ROBERT H.,** information technology executive; MA in physics and philosophy with honors, Oriel Coll. Various engring. and mgmt. roles IBM, 1980—95; v.p. Sun Microsystems, England, 1995—98, Sun Microsystems Europe Middle East and Africa, 1998—2002; exec. v.p. global sales ops. Sun Microsystems, 2002—04, exec. v.p. strategic devel. and Sun financing Santa Clara, Calif., 2004—.

**YOUNGLOVE, GEORGIA A.,** agricultural studies educator; d. Bill Olan and Helen Carolyn (Person) Younglove; 1 child, Brooke Lynn Howard. BS, Okla. State U., Stillwater, 1991; MS, Tex. A&M U., College Station, 1993; PhD, U. Wyo., Laramie, 1998. Grad. asst. U. Wyo. Laramie, 1994—98; assoc. prof. agr. Chadron State Coll., Chadron, Nebr., 1998—. Contbr. articles to profl. jours. Nat. adv. Am. Pre-Vet Med. Assn., 2005—06; youth dir. Colo. Pinto Horse Assn., 2006; treas. Whitney (Nebr.) Sch. Bd., 2001—04. Named Outstanding Prof., Chadron State Coll. Sch. Profl. Studies, 2003—04. Mem.: Midwest Soc. Animal Scientists (quadrathlon com. 2004—), Am. Soc. Animal Scientists, Soc. for Range Mgmt. (assoc.), Am. Paint Horse Assn., Am. Pinto Horse Assn. (life). Office: Chadron State Coll 1000 Main Chadron NE 69337 Office Phone: 308-432-6237. Office Fax: 308-432-6369. Business E-Mail: gyounglove@csc.edu.

**YOUNGMAN, LUANN L.,** minister; b. Dennison, Ohio, Dec. 1, 1953; d. Wilbert L. and Emma E. Kail; m. James R. McIntosh, Jan. 16, 1971 (div. June 1990); children: Robert J. McIntosh, Monica L. McIntosh; m. Neil A. Youngman, Sept. 12, 1998. AA, Kent Branch U.; postgrad., Garrett Evang. Sem.; BA with honors, Mt. Union Coll. Ordained min. United Meth. Ch. Sales rep. Harrison News Herald, Cadiz, Ohio, 1988—90; min. United Meth. Ch., East Ohio Conf., Canton, Ohio, 1990—. Composer Christian song. Recipient Hon. scholarship, Kent Branch, 1996. Methodist. E-mail: nyoungman@verizon.net.

**YOUNGMAN, OWEN RALPH,** newspaper executive; b. Chgo., Apr. 24, 1953; s. Ralph Elmer and Charlotte Eardline (Ottoson) Y.; m. Linda Ann Erlandson, Aug. 24, 1975. DSc, LHD, North Park U., 2005. Sportswriter Ashtabula (Ohio) Star-Beacon, 1969-71; office clk. Chgo. Tribune, 1971-73, transcriber, 1973-75, copy editor, slotman, 1976-79, copy chief, news editor, 1979-83, dep. sports editor, 1984-86, assoc. met. editor, 1986-88, assoc. features editor, 1988-90, dep. fin. editor, 1990-91, assoc. mng. editor, 1991-93, features editor, 1993-95, mng. editor, features, 1995, dir. interactive media, 1996-99, dir. planning and devel., 1999, v.p. devel., 2000—. Bd. dirs. Swedish Covenant Hosp., Lage.com Named to Ashtabula HS Alumni Hall of Fame, Ohio, 2005. Mem. Newspaper Assn. Am. New Media Fedn., Am. Soc. Newspaper Editors, Presidents Club of North Park U., Arts Club of Chgo. Avocation: vocal and instrumental music. Home: 40 Kenmore Ave Deerfield IL 60015-4750 Office: Chicago Tribune 435 N Michigan Ave Chicago IL 60611-4066 Office Phone: 312-222-4179. Business E-Mail: oyoungman@tribune.com.

**YOUNG-POHLMAN, COLETTE LISA,** music educator; b. Honolulu, July 20, 1952; d. Richard Ah On and Winifred Oi Chin Chang Young; m. Kurt I. Pohlman, Oct. 5, 1985; 1 child, Vinson Sterling Pohlman. EdB, U. Hawaii-Manoa, Honolulu, 1974, postgrad., 1975. Part-time tchr. dept. edn. Kalani High, Honolulu, 1978—79; chpt. 1 reading tchr. McKinley High, Honolulu, 1979—80, basic skills tchr., 1980—81; part-time tchg. asst. pvt. preschs., Honolulu, 1981—82; part-time tchr. dept. edn., chpt. 1 reading Ala Wai Elem. and Palolo Elem., 1982—83; classroom tchr. Heeia Elem., Kaneohe, Hawaii, 1990; part-time tchr. dept. edn. Wailupe Valley Elem., Honolulu, 1990—91; instrnl. resource augmentation tchr. Maemae Elem., Honolulu, 1991—92; project tchr. Title I reading Washington Intermediate, Honolulu, 1992—94; instrnl. resource augmentation tchr. Accelerated Gifted & Talented Performing Arts, Kailua, Hawaii, 1994—97; classroom tchr. Mokapu Elem., Kailua, 1997—2002, instrnl. resource augmentation music tchr., 2002—; Ann. Winter Concert and Talent Showcase, 2002—. Dir., choreographer, scripting/editing of musical play productions in elem. settings Windward Dist., Kalaheo Complex. Dir.(choreographer, writer): (multicultural musical plays) Little Firefly, the Rough-face Girl, Double Happiness, Souled Out; composer:

There's Something About a Pet, 1998 (2d Pl. award, 1998); composer: (choreographer) (new sch. song dance) Enchantment of Mokapu, 2000, Reading Rap, 2003, (music video) Enchantment of Mokapu, 2006; prodr. (dir.): (weekly TV program Olelo Cablevision) Na Keiki Hauoli o Mokapu, The Happy Children of Mokapu. Mem., tchr. Boy Scouts Am. Troop 113, 1999—. Mem.: Hawaii State Tchrs. Assn., Hawaii Music Educators Assn., Hawaii Orff Schulwerk Assn. (bd. dirs. 2005—), Am. Orff Schulwerk Assn., Music Educators Nat. Conf., Nat. Educators Assn. Avocations: composing songs, poetry, singing, keyboard, storytelling. Home: 45-427 Loli'i St Kaneohe HI 96744-5911 Office Phone: 808-254-7964. Business E-Mail: colette-youngpohlman@notes.k12.hi.us.

**YOUNGQUIST, WALTER LEWELLYN,** geologist, consultant; b. Mpls., May 5, 1921; s. Walter Raymond and Selma Regina (Knock) Y.; m. Elizabeth Salome Pearson, Dec. 11, 1943; children: John, Karen, Louise, Robert. BA, Gustavus Adolphus Coll., St. Peter, Minn., 1942; MSc, U. Iowa, 1943, PhD, 1948. Registered profl. geologist, Oreg. Jr. geologist U.S. Geol. Survey, 1943-44; rsch. assoc. U. Iowa, Iowa City, 1945-48; asst. prof. geology U. Idaho, Moscow, 1948-51; sr. geologist Internat. Petroleum Co., Talara, Peru, 1951-54; prof. geology U. Kans., Lawrence, 1954-57, U. Oreg., Eugene, 1957-66; cons. geologist Minerals dept. Exxon Corp., Houston, 1968-73; geothermal cons. Eugene Water & Electric Bd., 1973-92; ind. cons. Eugene, 1992—. Author: Investing in Natural Resources, 1980, Mineral Resources and the Destinies of Nations, 1990, GeoDestinies, 1997; co-author: Ordovician Cephalopod Fauna of Baffin Island, 1954. Ensign, USNR, 1944-45. Recipient Lowden Prize in Geology, U. Iowa, 1943, Journalist award, Am. Assn. Petroleum Geology, 2000, Disting. Alumni award Gustavus Adolphus Coll., 2002. Fellow AAAS, Geol. Soc. Am.; mem. Am. Assn. Petroleum Geologists, Internat. Assn Math. Geology, Soc. Exploration Geophysicists, Geothermal Resources Coun., N.W. Energy Assn., N.Y. Acad. Scis., Sigma Xi. Lutheran. Avocations: fly-tying, photography, fishing. Office: PO Box 5501 Eugene OR 97405-0501

**YOUNGREN, DELVANA HOPE,** secondary school educator; b. L.A., Apr. 13, 1941; d. Herman Melvin and Betty Floy (England) Ferguson; m. Allan Morse Youngren, June 17, 1961; children: Erik Allan, Deanna Marie. BA, Calif. State Coll., Long Beach, 1963; MA, Calif. State Coll., 1968. Cert. secondary tchr., Calif. Tchr. Long Beach (Calif.) Unified Sch. Dist., 1963-70, Faith Christian Acad., Pasadena, Tex., 1975-80, Cherry Valley (Calif.) Brethren Christian Sch., 1980-86, Arrowhead Christian Acad., Redlands, Calif., 1984—87, New Life Christian Acad., San Bernardino, Calif., 1987-90, Mt. View Jr. H.S., Beaumont, Calif., 1990—2002, Mt. View Mid. Sch., Beaumont, 2002—. Chmn. GATE, Gifted and Talented, Calif.; educator Drug, Alcohol & Tobacco Edn.; tech. computer tchr. On-Line Learning, Novanet. Head computer dept. San Gorgonio Pass Geneal. Soc., Banning, Calif., 1992-95; mem. Yucaipa Geneal. Soc., 1992-95. Mem. NEA, Calif. Tchrs. Assn., Beaumont Tchrs. Assn., Calif. Inland Area Math. Project, Soroptomists (Beaumont chpt.). Republican. Avocations: sports, cats. Home: 10640 Jonathan Ave Cherry Valley CA 92223-4974 Office: Beaumont United Sch Dist PO Box 187 Beaumont CA 92223-0187 Office Phone: 951-845-1627. E-mail: delvana@aol.com.

**YOUNGS, DIANE CAMPFIELD,** learning disabilities specialist, educator; b. Margaretville, NY, Feb. 16, 1954; d. Richard Maxwell and Charlotte June (Rickard) Campfield; m. William H. Youngs, June 30, 1984. BS in Edn., SUNY, Geneseo, 1976, MS in Edn., 1977. Professionally recognized spl. educator. Tchr. educable mentally retarded Tompkins-Seneca-Tioga Bd. Coop. Ednl. Svcs., Ithaca, NY, 1978-80; tchr. learning disabled Joint Svc. for Spl. Edn., Mishawaka, Ind., 1980-87; assoc. faculty Ind. U. South Bend Grad. Sch. Edn., 1996-98. Vis. lectr. dept. edn. Ind. U., South Bend, 1998-2002, lectr., 2002—; mem. Task Force for Reorgn. Spl. Edn., Mishawaka, 1990-91; coord. Tiny Talkers Summer Speech/Lang. Camp, 1994—. Recipient Tchg. award, Ind. U. Trustees, 2005, 2006. Mem. AAUP, Coun. for Exceptional Children, Learning Disabilities Assn., Coun. for Learning Disabilities, Ind. Prof. Reading, Internat. Reading Assn., Nat. Coun. Tchrs. English, Kappa Delta Pi. E-mail: dyoungs@iusb.edu.

**YOUNGS, JACK MARVIN,** cost engineer; b. Bklyn., May 2, 1941; s. Jack William and Virginia May (Clark) Y.; m. Alexandra Marie Robertson, Oct. 31, 1964; 1 child, Christine Marie. B in Engring., CCNY, 1964; MBA, San Diego State U., 1973. Mass properties engr. Gen. Dynamics Corp., San Diego, 1964-68, rsch. engr., 1968-69, sr. rsch. engr., 1969-80, sr. cost devel. engr., 1980-81, cost devel. engring. specialist, 1981-95; prin. estimator Martin Marietta Astronautics, 1995-96; estimating adminstr. Lockheed Martin Astronautics, 1995-96; prin., owner Youngs Group, 1996—. Dist. dir. Scripps Ranch Civic Assn. 1976-79; pres. Scripps Ranch Swim Team, 1980-82, dir., 1986-87; judge Greater San Diego Sci. and Engring. Fair, 1981-98, sweepstakes judge, 1999; mem. Princeton U. Parents Assn. Recipient 5th pl. award World Body Surfing Championships, 1987, 6th pl. award, 1988, 2d pl. award, 1999. Mem. AIAA, N.Y. Acad. Scis., Alumni assn., CUNY, Bklyn. Tech. H.S. Alumni Assn., Inst. Cost Analysis (cert., charter, treas. Greater San Diego chpt. 1986-90), Soc. Cost Estimating and Analysis (cert. cost estimator/analyst, pres. San Diego chpt. 1990-91), Internat. Soc. Parametric Analysts (bd. dirs. San Diego chpt. 1987-90), Nat. Mgmt. Assn. (space sys. divsn. charter 1988), Award of Honor Convair chpt. 1975), Assn. MBA Execs., San Diego State U. Bus. Alumni assn. (charter 1986), Convair Alumni Assn., Scripps Ranch Swim and Racquet Club (dir. 1977-80, treas. 1978-79, pres. 1979-80), Beta Gamma Sigma, Chi Epsilon, Sigma Iota Epsilon. Lutheran. Achievements include research in life cycle costing and econ. analysis. Office: 11461 Tribuna Ave San Diego CA 92131-1907 Personal E-Mail: youngsgroup@hotmail.com.

**YOUNGS, MICHAEL THERON, JR.,** non commissioned officer; b. Binghamton, N.Y., Nov. 30, 1973; s. Michael Theron Youngs, Sr. and Diane Marie Sykes; m. Marianne Viren, Apr. 17, 1992; children: Mychelle Leigh, Lauren Nicole, Michael Theron III. Student, Ctrl. Tex. Coll., 2003. Enlisted US Army, 1992, advanced through grades to sgt. first class, 2003, gens. enlisted aide Ft. Drum, NY, 1997—98, 2001—03, asst. dining facility mgr. Ft. Drum, NY, 2003—05. Task force mayor U.S Army, Iraq, 2004—05. Fellow: 1000 Islands 700 Club. Avocations: bowling, softball, golf. Home: 9116 B General Pike Loop Fort Drum NY 13603 Office: E Company 210th BSB Bldg 10182 4th Armored Divsn Fort Drum NY 13602 Business E-Mail: michael.youngs@us.army.mil.

**YOUNGS, WILLIAM ELLIS,** photographer, electronics engineer; b. Miami, Fla., Apr. 30, 1916; s. Edward Ray and Maude Myrtle (Burd) Y.; m. Mary Helen Still, Aug. 28, 1948; 1 child, Renee Helen. Student, Nat. Radio Inst., 1952. Film technician Washington Motion Picture Co., 1934-35, U.S. Dept. State, Washington, 1948-53; night service mgr. MGM Film Exchange, Washington, 1936-41; mgr., projectionist Calvert Theatre, Prince Frederick, Md., 1941-42; research asst. Exec. Office of the President, Washington, 1942; photo lab technician Office War Info., Washington, 1942-43; br. chief, advisor film and equipment USIA, Washington, 1953-78; photographer, projectionist Motion Picture Assn. Am., Washington, 1979-94; photographer, chaplain Vets. Commn., Falls Church, Va., 1997—. Advisor Stephens Coll., Columbia, Mo., 1973-75. Columnist Falls Church (Va.) Sun-Echo, 1953-55. Pres. Greenway Downs Civic Assn., Falls Church, 1953-54; pres. Second (Indian Head) Div. Assn. D.C. br., 1953-57; hon. recruiter USN, 1984; chaplain, photographer Vets. Common., U.S.A., Arlington/Falls Church, Va., 1997—. With U.S. Army, 1943-45, ETO. Fellow Soc. Motion Picture and TV Engrs. (life; nat. membership chmn. 1969, Outstanding Svc. award 1979); mem. Washington Film and Video Coun. (life; pres. 1967-68), Univ. Film and Video Assn., SAR (pres. Fairfax Resolves 1991-92, chaplain emeritus 2002, Va. ofcl. photographer, nat. mem. mag. adv. com. SAR/DAR liaison com. 1990—, historian 1993-94, editor 1994—, Meritorious Svc. medal 1991, Va. medal, 1994, Pres. Gen.'s citation for Disting. Svc. and Silver Good Citizenship medal 1994, Patriot medal 1996), Presbyterian. Avocations: photography, historical and technical writing. Home: 1436 Mayflower Dr Mc Lean VA 22101-5614

**YOUNGSTROM, PAUL CLARENCE,** anesthesiologist; b. Cedar Rapids, Iowa, Dec. 4, 1950; s. Clarence Swan and Hilda (Konga) Y.; m. Karen Jane Daykin, Aug. 18, 1973; children: Erica, Christiane, Andrew. BA in Econs., Yale U., 1972; MD, McGill U., 1976. Cert. anesthesiology. Intern U. Hosps., Cleve., 1976-77, resident in anesthesiology, 1977-79; staff anesthesiologist Cleve. Clinic, 1993—. Cons. Agy. for Health Care Policy and Rsch., Washington, 1993-94. Author: Operative Obstetrics, Common and Uncommon Obstetric Syndromes and Conditions. Elder St. Peter's Luth. Ch., Shaker Heights, 1994—. Lt. col. M.C., USAFR. Mem. Am. Soc. Anesthesiologists, Am. Soc. for Regional Anesthesia, Internat. Anesthesia Rsch. Soc., Soc. Obstetric Anesthesia and Perinatology. Business E-Mail: paul.youngstrom.es.72@aya.yale.edu.

**YOUNGWOOD, ALFRED DONALD,** lawyer; b. NYC, Apr. 27, 1938; s. Milton and Lillian (Ginsburg) Y.; m. Judith Goldfarb, June 24, 1963; children: Jonathan David, Stephen Michael. BA magna cum laude, Yale U., 1959; LLB magna cum laude, Harvard U., 1962. Bar: NY 1962, DC 1970, US Tax Ct. 1964, US Ct. Appeals (2d cir.) 1969. Law clk. to judge US Dist. Ct. NY, NY, 1962-63; assoc. Paul, Weiss, Rifkind, Wharton & Garrison LLP, NYC, 1964-70, ptnr., 1970—, pres. Ctrl. Synagogue, NYC, 2003—; bd. dirs. The Legal Aid Soc., NYC. Fulbright scholar, London, 1963-64. Fellow Am. Coll. Tax Counsel; mem. ABA, NY State Bar Assn. (chmn. tax sect. 1978-79, exec. com. 1971—, ho. of dels. 1979-80), Assn. of Bar of City of NY, Coun. on Fgn. Rels. Home: 1125 Park Ave New York NY 10128-1243 Office: Paul Weiss Rifkind Wharton & Garrison LLP 1285 Avenue Of The Americas New York NY 10019-6064 Business E-Mail: ayoungwood@paulweiss.com.

**YOUNKER, KATHLEEN TEUBER,** pianist, music educator; b. St. Cloud, Minn., Jan. 22, 1947; d. Hans Richard and Philomena (Hortsch) T.; m. Daniel William Younker, July 19, 1968; children: Laura, Jonathan. BA in History and Philosophy, St. Cloud State U., 1968; ARCT in Piano Performance, Royal Conservatory Toronto, Ont., Can., 1983; BA in Music, Bishop's U., Lennoxville, Que., Can., 1984; pvt. piano student, Rose Goldblatt, Montreal, 1985-95; MA in Spl. Studies, St. Cloud State U., 2002. Self-employed piano tchr., Lennoxville, 1978—97, St. Cloud, 1997—; sch. music tchr. Eastern Twps. Regional Sch. Bd., Lennoxville, 1982-86; ch. organist Peace United Ch. of Christ, St. Cloud, 1998-99; accompanist Sauk Rapids (Minn.) Rice HS, 1999—2000. Mem Music Tchrs. Nat Assn., Nat. Guild Piano Tchrs., Can. Fedn. Music Tchrs. Assns. (com. mem., ex officio nat. conv. 1997), Minn. Music Tchrs. Assn. (com. mem. state conv. 1999-01, com. mem. piano exam devel. com. 2002—), Eastern Twps. Music Tchrs. Assn. (pres. 1989-91), Que. Music Tchrs. Assn. (pres. provincial coun. 1993-97). Avocations: home restoration, pets, reading, gardening, cooking, entertaining.

**YOUNT, GEORGE STUART,** paper company executive; b. L.A., Mar. 4, 1949; s. Stanley George and Agnes (Pratt) Y.; m. Geraldine Marie Silvio, July 18, 1970; children: Trisha Marie, Christopher George. Postgrad., Harvard U., 1983-86. Mgmt. trainee Fortifiber Corp., L.A., 1969-71, asst. to v.p. ops., 1971-75, adminstrv. v.p., treas., sec., 1975-85, exec. v.p., sec., CFO, bd. dirs., 1985-90, chmn., CEO, 1991—; pres., dir. Fonzia Corp., 1993—. Bd. dirs. Stanwall Corp., pres., 1989—, Thompson & Co. Ins. Svcs., Pasadena, Calif., 1996—, Parasol Found., 1999—, Tracerton Enterprises, Inc., 2001-2004; past pres. Hollister Ranch Cattle Coop., Gaviota, Calif., 1986-88; trustee Sierra Nev. Coll., 1999-2002,(vice Chair, 2002); adv. bd. Med. Tech. Internat., Inc., 2004-. Team leader L.A. United Way, 1981-86; bd. dirs. Big Bros. Greater L.A., 1984-87, L.A. coun. Boy Scouts Am., 1992—; mem. Young Pres. Orgn., 1991, forum moderator, 1993-95, 2005—, chpt. forum officer, 1997-99; presdl. appointee Tahoe Regional Planning Agy. Governing Bd., 2002—; mem. adv. bd. Incline Village Cmty. Hosp., 2005-06. Named Humanitarian of Yr., Incline Village, Nev., 2003. Mem.: Am. Paper Inst. (dir. 1993—95, splty. coaters and extrusion sect. 1990—2000), Washoe County Hon. Chief Dep. Sheriff's Assn., Newcomen Soc. (life), Conferie des Chevaliers du Tastevin Wine and Food Soc., Wine and Food Soc., Chaine des Rotisseurs Food and Wine Soc., Internat. Wine and Food Soc., Rotary (bd. dirs. LA club 1992—94), Jonathan Club (LA), U. Nev. Alumni Assn. (life), USN League Club (life). Avocations: scuba diving, electronics, cattle ranching, computers. Office: Fortifiber Corp 1001 Tahoe Blvd Incline Village NV 89451-9309

**YOUNT, GWENDOLYN AUDREY,** humanities educator; b. Indpls., July 24, 1957; d. August de Alba and Hena Yount; 1 child, Clark. AA, L.A. City Coll., 1977; BA, UCLA, 1979, MA, 1982, Candidate in Philosophy, 1987. Cert. C.C. lifetime credential Calif., bilingual cert. competence. Ednl. aide Alexander Hamilton H.S., L.A., 1975—76; tchg. fellow UCLA, 1981—88; instr. L.A. Unified Sch. Dist., 1982—90; prof. Institut Franco-Americain de Mgmt., Paris, 1983—84; instr. Santa Monica Coll., Calif., 1987—88; lectr. U. Calif., Riverside, 1988—91; instr. Beverly Hills Adult Sch., Calif., 1986—88; assoc. prof. Riverside C.C., Calif., 1990—. Dir. RCC Study Abroad Program in Spain, Salamanca, Spain, 1998—2002, RCC Study Abroad Program in Costa Rica, San Jose, Costa Rica, 1993, UCLA Spanish Program in Mex., Guadalajara, Mexico, 1987. Dancer (ballet performance) Celebrate Dance, 2000; actor: (mus. theater) La Cage Aux Folles, 1998; singer: (vocal performance) Montreux Jazz Festival, 1993. Adminstr. G. Yount scholarship Riverside County Found., 1998—2003; sen. Acad. Senate, Riverside, 1997—2003; mem. Spanish lang. steering com. Riverside Pub. Libr., 1989—91; charter mem. Mus. of Tolerance, L.A., 1994—2003. Named Most Influential Instr., RCC Disabled Student Svcs., 1993, 1998, Tchr. of Distinction, LDS Ch., 1998, 2000, 2001, 2002, Tchr. of the Yr., Riverside C.C., 1999—2000, 2000—01, 2002—03; grantee Univ. grantee for grad. study, UCLA, 1979. Mem.: Philol Soc. of the Pacific Coast, Assn. for Tchrs. of Spanish, Sigma Tau Sigma, Alpha Mu Gamma, pres. 1977—78), Sigma Delta Pi (v.p. 1985—86). Liberal. Avocations: travel, reading, studying. Office: Riverside C C 4800 Magnolia Ave Riverside CA 92506 Business E-Mail: gwen.yount@rcc.edu.

**YOURIST, SHELDON ERIC,** product designer; b. Toledo, Ohio, Aug. 15, 1958; s. Isadore and Pearl Yourist, Charles Jaffe (Stepfather); m. Laurie Elizabeth Thomson, July 18, 1981; children: Adam Bryce, Cameron Everett, Sara Elizabeth. BFA with hons., Ind. U., 1981. Sculptor The Bronze Bear, Simi Valley, Calif., 1981; sculptor., mgr. Pietro Studios, Northridge and Hollywood, Calif., 1981—83; designer, sculptor Teleflora, INC, L.A., 1983—87; sr. designer The Pfaltzgraff Co., York, Pa., 1988—96; sr. mgr., global design services Graham Packaging Co., LLP, York, Pa., 1996—. Past pres. Jewish Family Svcs., York, 1996. Dinnerware and pantryware, Best New Product for Mickey and Company (Mickey award, 1995). Bd. mem. Leadership York. Recipient World Star for packaging designs, 2000, Ameristar for packaging designs, 2001, Silver award for packaging designs, 2003. Mem.: Indsl. Designer's Soc. of Am. (assoc.). Democrat. Jewish. Achievements include 38 U.S. patents, various foreign patents held. Home: 350 Wire Road York PA 17402 Office: Graham Packaging Company LLP 2401 Pleasant Valley Road York PA 17402 Office Phone: 717-849-8767. Personal E-mail: yourist@suscom.net. E-mail: sheldon.yourist@grahampackaging.com.

**YOURZAK, ROBERT JOSEPH,** management consultant, educator, engineer; b. Mpls., Aug. 27, 1947; s. Ruth Phyllis Sorenson. BCE, U. Minn., 1969; MSCE, U. Wash., 1971, MBA, 1975. Registered profl. engr., Wash., Minn. Surveyor N.C. Hoium & Assocs., Mpls., 1965-68, Lot Surveys Co., Mpls., 1968-69; site layout engr. Sheehy Constrn. Co., St. Paul, 1968; structural engring. aide Dunham Assocs., Mpls., 1969; aircraft and aerospace structural engr., program rep. Boeing Co., Seattle, 1969-75; engr., estimator Howard S. Wright Constrn. Co., Seattle, 1976-77; dir. project devel. and adminstrn. DeLeuw Cather & Co., Seattle, 1977-78; sr. mgmt. cons. Alexander Grant & Co., Mpls., 1978-79; mgr. project sys. dept., project mgr. Hennington, Durham & Richardson, Mpls., 1979-80; dir. project mgmt., regional offices Ellerbe Assocs., Inc., Mpls., 1980-81; pres. Robert Yourzak & Assocs., Inc., Mpls., 1982—. Lectr. engring. mgmt. U. Wash., 1977-78; lectr.-adj. asst. prof. dept. civil and mineral engring. and mech./indsl. engring. Ctr. for Devel. of Tech. Leadership, Inst. Tech. mem. U. Minn., 1979-90; bd. adv. inst. tech., 1989-93; founding mem., membership com., mem. U. of Minn. com.

Minn. High Tech. Coun., 1983-95; instr. principles mgmt. dept. bus. and pub. policy Concordia U., 1997, instr. constrn. mgmt., constrn. estimating and scheduling, bldg. orgn. and tech., project mgmt. and planning skills, project mgmt. software, supervision and applied leadership, and supervisory techniques for bus. Inver Hills C.C., 1998—; instr. introduction to engring. and design, statics, mechanics of materials, ops. mgmt. North Hennepin C.C., 2002—; adj. instr. ops. mgmt. Hamline U., St. Paul, 2001; spkr. in field. Author: Project Management and Motivating and Managing the Project Team, 1984, (with others) Field Guide to Project Management, 1998, 2004 (sec. edition). Chmn. regional art group experience Seattle Art Mus., 1975-78; mem. Pacific N.W. Arts Coun., 1977-78, ex-officio adviser Mus. Week, 1976; bd. dirs. Friends of the Rep. Seattle Repertory Theatre, 1973-77; mem. Symphonics Seattle Symphony Orch., 1975-78. Named Outstanding Young Man of Am., U.S. Jaycees, 1978; scholar Boeing Co., 1967-68, Sheehy Constrn. Co., summer 1967. Fellow ASCE (chmn. continuing edn. subcom. Seattle chpt. 1976-79, chmn. program com. 1978, mem. transp. and urban planning tech. group 1978, Edmund Friedman Young Engr. award 1979, chmn. continuing edn. subcom. 1979-80, chmn. energy com. Minn. chpt. 1980-81, bd. dirs. 1981-89, sec. 1981-83, v.p. profl. svcs. 1983-84, v.p. info. svcs. 1984-85, pres. 1986-87, past pres. 1987-89, spkr.), PMI Project Mgmt. Inst. (cert. project mgmt. prof., spkr., founding pres. 1985, chmn., adv. com. 1987-89, bd. dirs. 1984-86, program com. chmn. and organizing com. mem. Minn. chpt. 1984, spkr., project mgr. internat. mktg. program 1985-86, chmn. internat. mktg. standing com. 1986, long range and strategic planning com. 1988-93, chmn. 1992, v.p. pub. rels. 1987-88, ex-officio dir. 1989, 92, internat. pres. 1990, chmn. bd. 1991, ex-officio chmn. 1992, internat. bd. dirs., chmn. nominating com. 1992, PMI fellow 1995, chmn. exec. dir. selection com. 1996-97, Robert J. Yourzak Scholarship Award established Minn. chpt. 1998—), Inst. Indsl. Engrs. (pres. Twin Cities chpt. 1985-86, chmn. program com. 1983-84, bd. dirs. 1985-88, awards com., chmn. 1984-89, fellow 1999, spkr.); mem. ASTD (So. Minn. chpt.), Am. Cons. Engrs. Coun. (peer reviewer 1986-89), Am. Arbitration Assn. (mem. Mpls. panel of constrn. arbitrators), Minn. Surveyors and Engrs. Soc., Cons. Engrs. Coun. Minn. (chmn. pub. rels. com. 1983-85, vice chmn. 1988, chmn. 1989, program com. chmn. Midwest engrs. conf. and exposition 1985-90, spkr., Honor award 1992), Inst. Mgmt. Cons. (cert. mgmt. cons.), Mpls. Soc. Fine Arts, Internat. Facility Mgmt. Assn., Am. Soc. Engring. Edn., Rainer Club (co-chmn. Oktoberfest), Sierra club, Chowder Soc., Mountaineers, North Star Ski Touring, Chi Epsilon (life). Office: 7320 Gallagher Dr Ste 325 Minneapolis MN 55435-4510

**YOUSEF, FATHI SALAAMA,** communications educator, management consultant; b. Cairo, Jan. 2, 1934; arrived in U.S., 1968, naturalized, 1973; s. Salaama and Rose (Salaama) Yousef; m. Marjan Lowies El-Faizy, June 24, 1994. BA, Ain Shams U., Cairo, 1955; MA, U. Minn., 1970, PhD, 1972. Svc. ctr. supt. Shell Oil Co., Cairo, 1955-61; indsl., mgmt. tng. instr. ARAMCO, Dhahran, Saudi Arabia, 1961-68; tchg. assoc. U. Minn., Mpls., 1968-72; comm. studies prof. emeritus Calif. State U., Long Beach, 1972—. With orgn. and indsl. engring. dept. ARAMCO, 1978—80. Co-author: An Introduction to Intercultural Communication, 1975, 1985; contbr. Grantee, NSF, 1981, 1982, 1983. Mem.: Assn. Egyptian Am. Scholars. Democrat. Office: Calif State U Dept Comm Studies Long Beach CA 90840-2407 Business E-mail: fyousef@csulb.edu.

**YOUST, DAVID BENNETT,** career development educator; b. May 14, 1938; s. Howard Page and Agnes (Bennett) Y.; m. Faye Phillips; children: Stacy Sillen, Shawna Sannier, Liesl Berger, Genny Phillips, Elizabeth Curley. BS, SUNY-Albany, 1959; MS, Syracuse U., NY, 1961; PhD, Mich. State U., 1969. Cert. career counselor Nat. Bd. Counselor Cert. Tchr. sci. North Syracuse schs., 1959-61; administr. student pers. Mich. State U., 1961-63; counselor, prin., program dir. Rochester (N.Y.) schs., 1963-70; sr. rsch. technologist Eastman Kodak Co., Rochester, 1970-72; asst. dean Nat. Tech. Inst. for the Deaf, Rochester Inst. Tech., 1972-74; mem. faculty Empire State Coll., SUNY, Rochester, 1974-78; exec. dir. Career Devel. Coun., Corning, N.Y., 1978-84; mgr. engring. tng. Corning Inc., N.Y., 1984-90; ptnr. Phillips Tng. Sys., Inc., 1989—. Former adj. faculty Corning C.C., Elmira Coll., C.W. Post Coll.; mediator cmty. dispute resolution, former bd. dirs. Cmty. Dispute Resolution Ctr., Ithaca, NY; instr. MSF motorcycle safety; EEO mediator U.S. Postal Svc. Author guide, articles in field; former mem. editl. bd. Career Devel. Quar. Former bd. dirs. 171 Cedar Arts Ctr. Mem. ACA, Nat. Career Devel. Assn. (Merit award 1970, 84), Am. Ednl. Rsch. Assn., Assn. Measurement and Evaluation in Guidance. Republican. E-mail: youst@empacc.net.

**YOUTCHEFF, JOHN SHELDON,** physicist; b. Newark, Apr. 16, 1925; s. Slav Joseph and Florence Catherine (Davidson) Y.; m. Elsie Marianne, June 17, 1950; children: Karen Janette, John Sheldon, Mark Allen, Heidi Mary Anne, Lisa Ellen AB, Columbia U., 1949, BS, 1950; PhD, UCLA, 1953. Registered profl. engr., Calif., DC. Ops. analyst GE Co., Ithaca, NY, 1953—56, cons., engr. missile & space divsn. Phila., 1956—64, mgr. advanced reliability programs, 1964—72; mgr. reliability and maintainability Litton Industries, College Park, Md., 1972—73; program mgr. U.S. Postal Svc. Hdqrs., Washington, 1973—. Instr. U. Pa., 1965-66, Villanova U., 1957— Lt. USAAF, 1943-46; to comdr. USNR, 1946— Fellow AAAS, Br. Interplanetary Soc., AIAA, Explorers Club; mem. IEEE (sr.), Ops. Rsch. Soc., Rsch. Soc. Am., Am. Math. Soc., Am. Physics Soc., Am. Chem. Soc., Am. Astron. Soc., Am. Geol. Soc., NSPE, Engring. and Tech. Socs., Coun. Del. Valley (spkrs. bur.), USCG Aux. (flotilla comdr.), Res. Officers Assn., Am. Legion, Optimists Internat. (pres. Valley Forge chpt. 1970-71) Roman Catholic. Home: 1400 S Joyce St Apt 1406 Arlington VA 22202-1852 Office: L'Enfant Plz Washington DC 20260

**YOVANOF, SILVANA,** physician; b. Lubojno, Macedonia, Jan. 14, 1956; came to U.S., 1961; d. Peter and Nuna Yovanof. BS in Biology and Psychology, Loyola U., Chgo., 1978; MS, U. Ill., 1982; MD, Am. U. Caribbean, Montserrat, 1985. Diplomate Am. Bd. Internal Medicine. Intern Deaconess Hosp., St. Louis, 1986-87; resident in internal medicine St. Joseph Mercy Hosp., Pontiac, Mich., 1987-89; chief resident in medicine, 1989-90; fellow U. Ill. Med. Ctr., Chgo., 1990-92; chmn. dept. medicine Monongahela Valley Hosp., 2002—. Mem. adv. panel Internal Medicine for the Specialist, 1988—; affiliated with hosps. Jefferson Hosp., Pitts., 1991, MonValley Hosp., Monongahela, Pa., 1993, Mercy Hosp., Pitts., 1995. Contbr. articles to profl. jours. including Neurosci. Letters. Mem.: ACP, Am. Assn. Clin. Endocrinologists, Allegheny County Med. Soc. (med. legal com. 1996—), Pa. State Med. Soc., Am. Diabetes Assn. Office: Med and Endocrinology Assoc 420 W Main St Monongahela PA 15063-2552 Office Phone: 724-258-8680. E-mail: syovanof@peoplepc.com.

**YOVICH, DANIEL JOHN,** chemist, educator; b. Chgo., Mar. 5, 1930; s. Milan D. and Sophie (Dorociak) Y.; m. Anita Barbara Moreland, Feb. 7, 1959; children: Daniel, Amy, David, Julie Ann. Ph.B., DePaul U., 1952; MA, Governors State U., 1975, MS, 1976. Cert. reality therapist, profl. mgr. Formulator Nat. Lead Co., 1950-52, 56-59; researcher Montgomery Ward, Chgo., 1959-62; instr. dir. Riley Bros., Inc., Burlington, Iowa, 1962-66, Mortell Co., Kankakee, Ill., 1966-70; exec. dir. Dan Yovich Assos., 1970-79; asst. prof. Purdue U., Hammond, Ind., 1979-84, assoc. prof., 1984-90, prof., 1990-2000, prof. emeritus, 2000—. Instr. Army Security Agy. Sch., 1954—56, Napoleon Hill Acad., 1965—66; cons. Learning House, 1964—; assoc. Hill, Zediker & Assocs. Psychologists, Kankakee, 1975—79; mem. adv. bd. Nat. Congress Inventor Orgns., 1984; vis. prof. Grand Valley State U., 2000—, Northwood U., 2001—. Author: Applied Creativity; prdr., moderator: (program) Careers Unlimited, Sta. WCIU-TV, Chgo., 1967; contbr. articles to profl. jours.; patentee game Krypto, coating sanitane. Mem. cmty. adv. coun. Governors State U., 1978; mem. Hammond (Ind.) Hist. Soc. Served to 1st lt. AUS, 1952-56. Recipient Outstanding Citizen Award News Pub. Co. Am., 1971, Outstanding Tchr. award Purdue U., 1980, 82, 83, Faculty Service award Nat. U. Continuing Edn. Assn., 1984, Disting. Service award Purdue U.-Calumet Alumni Assn., 1988, Arthur Young award Venture Mag., 1988, Entrepreneurial Edn. award Inc. Mag., 1990, Indiana Spirit of Innovation award, 1996. Mem. World Future Soc., Am. Soc. Profl. Supervision (exec. sec. 1986), Inventors and Entrepreneurs Soc. Am. (founder, exec.

dir. 1984, prodr. Salute Vet. Recognition Programs 1999—), Global Intuition Network, Internat. Creativity Network, Infantry Officer Cand. Sch. Alumni Assn. (life), Napoleon Hill Found., Inst. Reality Therapy, Inst. Contemporary Living, Soc. Am. Inventors (life), Am. Legion, Vets. of the Battle of the Bulge (historian), Army and Navy Club of Grand Rapids Home: 3527 Whispering Brook Dr SE Kentwood MI 49508-3733 Personal E-mail: danyovich@aol.com.

**YOVITS, MARSHALL CLINTON,** information scientist, educator, dean; b. Bklyn., May 16, 1923; s. Louis Frederick and Rebecca (Gerber) Y.; m. Anita S. Friedman, Aug. 2, 1952; children: Bruce J., Mara F., Steven. BS, Union Coll., Schenectady, 1944, MS, 1948, Yale U., 1949, PhD, 1951. Sr. physicist Johns Hopkins U., 1951—56; physicist electronics br. Office Naval Rsch., Washington, 1956, head info. sys. br., 1956—62; dir. Naval Analysis Group, 1962—66; prof., chmn. dept. computer and info. sci. Ohio State U., 1966—78, prof., 1978—79; prof. computer and info. sci. Sch. of Sci., Ind. U., Purdue U., Indpls., 1980—, dean, 1980—88; prof. emeritus Ind. U., Purdue U., Indpls., 1993—. Gen. chmn. Computer Sci. Conf. NSF, 1973. Editor: (with Scott Cameron) Self-Organizing Systems, Proc. Interdisciplinary Conf., 1960, Large-Capacity Memory Techniques for Computing Systems, 1961 (with George T. Jacobi, Gordon D. Goldstein) Self-Organizing Systems, 1962, (with D.M. Gilford, R.H. Wilcox, S. Staveley, H.D. Lerner) Research Program Effectiveness, 1966, Advances in Computers, Vol. 11, 1971; editor: series Advances in Computers, Vols. 13-40; contbr. rsch. articles to profl. jours. Recipient Superior Civilian Svc. award, U.S. Navy, 1964, Outstanding Performance award, 1961; fellow AEC fellow, 1950—51, Indpls. Ctr. Advanced Rsch., 1988—89. Fellow AAAS (chmn. coun. sect. T 1985-88, chmn. 1996-98), IEEE (computer soc. chmn. awards com. 1989, bd. govs. 1988-89, computer pioneer award 1990), Assn. for Computing Machinery (coun., gen. chmn. computer sci. conf. 1982), EDUCOM (nominating com.), Sigma Xi. Home: 9016 Dewberry Ct Indianapolis IN 46260-1527 Office Phone: 317-274-9737. E-mail: myovits@iupui.edu.

**YRIGOYEN, CHARLES, JR.,** retired church denomination executive; b. Phila., Dec. 9, 1937; s. Charles and Erma Mae (Suters) Y.; m. Jeanette Alice Brittingham, Dec. 13, 1958; children: Debra Jean, Charles III. BS in Econs., U. Pa., 1959; BD, Lancaster (Pa.) Theol. Sem., 1962; ThM, Ea. Bapt. Theol. Sem., Phila., 1964; PhD, Temple U., 1973; DD (hon.), Albright Coll., 1987. Ordained to ministry United Meth. Ch., 1960. Pastor various chs. Meth. Ch., Pa., 1958-66, campus min. Phila., 1966-68; chaplain, prof. religion Albright Coll., Reading, Pa., 1968-82; gen. sec. Gen. Com. on Archives and History, United Meth. Ch., Madison, NJ, 1982—2005; ret., 2006. Vis. scholar Union Theol. Sem. N.Y.C., 1980, adj. prof., 1982-93, 2000-02; adj. prof. ch. history Drew U., Madison, 1982-2005; adj. prof. Moravian Theol. Sem., Bethlehem, Pa., 1994-02; exec. com. World Meth. Coun., 1986-2006; bd. dirs. Wesley Works Editl. Project, 1982—; adj. prof. Luth. Theol. Sem., Phila., 1999. Author: Acts for Our Time, 1987, John Wesley: Holiness of Heart and Life, 1996, Belief Matters: United Methodism's Doctrinal Standards, 2001; editor: Reformed and Catholic, 1978, Catholic and Reformed, 1979, Historical Dictionary of Methodism, 1996, 2d edit., 2005, The Global Impact of the Wesleyan Traditions and Their Related Movements, 2002, Praising The God of Grace: The Theology of Charles Westey's Hymns, 2005; editor History Jour., 1982-2006. Mem. alumni coun. Lancaster Theol. Sem., 2002—. Masland fellow Union Theol. Sem., 1975, 80. Mem. World Meth. Hist. Soc. (gen. sec. 1987-2006), Wesley Hist. Soc., Wesleyan Theol. Soc., Am. Soc. Ch. History, Charles Wesley Soc., Oxford Inst. Meth. Theol. Studies, Mercersburg Soc. (bd. dirs.), United Meth. Hist. Soc. Republican. Methodist. Home: I 106 950 Willow Valley Lakes Dr Willow Street PA 17584-9663 E-mail: cyrigoyen@evangelical.edu, jyrigoyen@cs.com.

**YSASI-DIAZ, GLORIA,** wholesale distribution executive; BS in Chem. Engring., Univ. Rochester; MBA, Coll. William & Mary. Ops. positions GE Co., 1978—84; ops. positions to sr. v.p., process mgmt. R.R. Donnelley, Chgo., 1984—2005; v.p. operational excellence, US branch-based businesses WW Grainger Co., Chgo., 2005—. Named one of 50 Most Important Hispanics in Tech., Bus., Hispanic Engineer and Info. Tech. mag., 2005. Office: 100 Grainger Pkwy Lake Forest IL 60045-5201 Office Phone: 847-535-1000. Office Fax: 847-535-0878.

**YSSELDYKE, JAMES EDWARD,** psychology professor; b. Grand Rapids, Mich., Jan. 1, 1944; 2 children. Student in psychology, Calvin Coll., 1962-65; BA in Psychology and Biology, Western Mich. U., 1966; MA in Sch. Psychology, U. Ill., 1968, PhD, 1971. Lic. cons. psychologist, Minn. Tchr. spl. edn. Kent County Juvenile Ct. Ctr., Grand Rapids, 1966-67; rsch. assist. U. Ill. Inst. Rsch. on Exceptional Children, 1969-70, tchg. asst. dept. ednl. psychology, 1970; sch. psychology intern Oakland County Schs., Pontiac, Mich., 1970-71; asst. prof. sch. psychology Pa. State U., 1971-75, assoc. prof., 1975, U. Minn., Mpls., 1975-79, prof., 1979-91, dir. Rsch. on Learning Disabilities, 1977-83, dir. Nat. Sch. Psychology Insvc. Tng. Network, 1977-83, dir. sch. psychology program, 1987-93, dir. Nat. Ctr. on Ednl. Outcomes, 1991-99, assoc. dean for rsch., 2000—. Emma Birkmaier endowed prof. U. Minn., 1998-2000; advisor, cons. and researcher in field. Author: (with J. Salvia) Assessment in Special and Remedial Education, 2007, 10th edit., (with B. Algozzine and M. Thurlow) Critical Issues in Special and Remedial Education, 1992, 3d edit., 2000, Strategies and Tactics for Effective Instruction, 1997, (with S.L. Christenson) Functional Assessment of Academic Behavior, 2003, (with B. Algozzine) Every Teachers Guide to Special Education, 2007; editor: Exceptional Children, 1984-90; assoc. editor: The School Psychologist, 1972-75, mem. editorial bd., cons. editor numerous jours.; contbr. chpts. to books and articles to jours. Recipient Disting. Tchg. award U. Minn., 1988, Disting. Alumni award U. Ill. Coll. Edn., 1998; fellow NIMH, 1967-69; grantee in field. Fellow APA (Lightner Witmer award 1973); mem. APA, NASP, Am. Ednl. Rsch. Assn., Coun. for Exceptional Children (Rsch. award 1995), Coun. for Ednl. Diagnostic Svcs. Office: Univ Minn Coll Edn Human Devel 350 Elliott Hall 75 E River Rd Minneapolis MN 55455-0296 Business E-Mail: jim@umn.edu.

**YSURSA, BEN T.,** state official; b. Boise, Idaho, June 10, 1949; m. Penny Ysursa; children: Shawn Del, Matthew, Andrew. BA, Gonzaga U., 1971; JD, St. Louis U. Law Sch., 1974. Bar: Idaho 1974. Dep. sec. state State of Idaho, Boise, 1974—76, chief dep., 1976—2002, sec. of state, 2002—. Mem. Basque Ctr., St. John's Parish; pres. Adh County Lincoln Day, 1990. Recipient Boyd Martin Award, Assn. of Idaho Cities, Outstanding Administr., Idaho Rep. Party, 1992. Mem.: Reagan-Bush Idaho Com. (treas. 1984), NHSS (secs. state 2003), Idaho State Bar Assn. Republican. Roman Catholic. Office: Office Sec of State Rm 203 700 W Jefferson Boise ID 83720-0080 Office Phone: 208-334-2300. Office Fax: 208-334-2282. E-mail: bysursa@idsos.state.id.us.*

**YU, ANDREW,** minister; b. Fu-Yang, Chekian, China, Feb. 28, 1927; came to the U.S., 1972; s. Kung-Chu Yu and Mei-Chen Liu; m. Julie Yu, July 13, 1957; children: Peter, Ruth. BTh, Taiwan Bapt. Theol. Sem., Taipei, 1957; postgrad., Tanghai U., Taichung, Taiwan, 1965; MA in Ministry Studies, Moody Bible Inst., 1991; postgrad., Bibl. Archaeology Sch., 1993, Fuller Theol. Sem., 1996, Fuqua Internat. Sch. Christian Comm., 1998. Cert. pastoral counseling. Jour. clk. Bankers Trust Co., N.Y.C., 1972-80; pastoral coounselor Am. Assn. Christian Counseling, Forest, Va., 1991—; minister Manhattan Chinese Bapt. Ch., N.Y.C., 1980—, sr. pastor, 1986—. Author: Rekinling the Fires of Revial, 1993, A Master Piece of Spirituality, 1995, The Poem of Draw Wings, 2001; editor Chinese Christian Workers, 1999—; editor: Chinese Newsletter, N.Y., 1999-2002. Mem. positive thinking divsn. Guideposts Norman Vincent Peal Ctr. for Positive Thinking, Paulling, NY, 2003; mem. Bapt. World Alliance 100th Anniversary Congress, Bermingham, England, 2005. Recipient Lifetime Royal Patronage status Kevin, Prince Regent Princepality of Hutt River Province, Australia, 1994, Cert. of Appreciation, Ronald Reagan Presdl. Found., 2003. Mem.: Poetry Soc. Am. Avocations: reading, writing, music, travel, collecting. Home: Apt 20E 675 Water St New York NY 10002 Office: Manhattan Chinese Bapt Ch 236 W 72nd St New York NY 10023 Office Phone: 212-496-1486.

**YU, ANTHONY C.,** religion and literature educator; b. Hong Kong, Oct. 6, 1938; came to U.S., 1956, naturalized, 1976; s. P.C. and Norma (Au) Y.; m. Priscilla Tang, Sept. 18, 1963; 1 son, Christopher Dietrich. BA, Houghton Coll., 1960; STB, Fuller Theol. Sem., 1963; PhD, U. Chgo., 1969, DLitt, 1996. Instr. U. Ill., Chgo., 1967-68; asst. prof. U. Chgo., 1968-74, assoc. prof., 1974-78, prof., 1978—2005, prof. emeritus, 2005—. Assoc. vis. prof. Ind. U., Bloomington, 1975; Whitney J. Oates short-term vis. fellow Princeton U., 1986; disting. vis. prof. Faculty of Arts, U. Alta., Can., 1992; mem. joint com. on study Chinese civilization Am. Coun. Learned Socs., 1980-86, bd. dirs., 1986-94; regional chmn. Mellon Fellowship in Humanities, 1982-92; bd. dirs. Ill. Humanities Coun., 1995-97; vis. prof. dept. religion Chinese U. Hong Kong, 1997; mem. com. social thought U. Chgo., 2004—. Asst. editor Jour. Asian Studies, 1975-78; co-editor Jour. Religion, 1980—; author, editor: Parnassus Revisited, 1973; editor, translator: The Journey to the West, 4 vols., 1977-83, Essays on The Journey to the West and Other Studies (in Chinese), 1989, The MOnkey and the Monk, An Abridgment of the Journey to the West, 2006; co-editor (with Mary Gerhart) Morphologies of Faith: Essays on Religion and Culture in Honor of Nathan A. Scott, Jr., 1990, Rereading the Stone: Desire and the Making of Fiction in Dream of the Red Chamber, 1997, State and Religion in China: Historical and Textual Perspectives, 2005. Recipient Gordon J. Laing prize, 1983; Danforth fellow, 1960-67; Guggenheim fellow, 1976-77; NEH translation grantee, 1977-82; Am. Coun. Learned Socs. sr. fellow, 1986-87; Masterworks Study grant NEH Seminar for Pub. Sch. Tchrs., 1992; elected academician Academia Sinica, 1998; Phi Beta Kappa vis. scholar 2001-02. Fellow Am. Acad. Arts and Scis.; mem. MLA (exec. coun. 1998—2001), Assn. for Asian Studies, Am. Acad. Religion (bd. dirs. 1995-97), Am. Comparative Lit. Assn., Milton Soc. Am., Arts Club. Home: 950 N Clark St Unit G Chicago IL 60610-8702 Office: U Chicago 1025 E 58th St Chicago IL 60637-1509 Office Phone: 773-702-8245. Business E-Mail: acyu@midway.uchicago.edu.

**YU, BING,** researcher; s. Zhicheng Yu and Guilin Wang; m. Xuerong Liu, Sept. 28, 1998; 1 child, Ruthie. BS, U. Electronic Sci. & Tech. China, Chengdu, 1985—89, MS, 1991—94; PhD in Elec. Engring., Va. Tech, Blacksburg, 2000—05. Rsch. engr. Chinese Acad. Engring. Physics, Mianyang, Sichuan, China, 1989—91; lectr. U. Electronic Sci. & Tech. China, Chengdu, 1994—99; engr. Chang Tong Mobile Telecomm. Eng. Co., Ltd., Chengdu, 1995—97; engring. supr. Alcatel Telecomm. Sys. Co., Ltd., Chengdu, 1997—98; rsch. asst. Nanyang Technol. U. Singapore, 1999—2000, Va. Tech, 2000—05; postdoctoral rsch. assoc. Duke U., Durham, 2005—; scientist Endls Optics Corp., Raleigh, NC, 2006—. Contbr. articles to profl. jours. and patent disclosures. Recipient Excellent Young Rschr. award, Chinese Acad. Engring Physics, 1991, Travel Fund, Grad. Student Assn., Va. Tech, 2003—04, Super Grad. Rsch. Asst. award, Va. Tech, Ctr. Photonics Tech., 2005; fellowship, U. Louisville, 2006. Mem.: Optical Soc. Am. Achievements include research in minimally invasive optical technology to monitor tumor oxygenation and vascularity for breast cancer diagnostics and miniature imaging system for tumor margin assessment; invention of thermally tunable extrinsic fabry—pérot filter; tunable optical filter based white light interferometry; development of grating-assisted demodulation of interferometric sensors; fiber fabry—perot sensors for detection of partial discharges in power transformers. Avocations: soccer, ping pong/table tennis, fishing. Office: Duke Univ 136 Hudson Hall Box 90281 Durham NC 27708 Office Phone: 919-660-5032. Office Fax: 919-684-4488. Business E-Mail: bing.yu@duke.edu.

**YU, CHACK YUNG,** pediatrics educator, molecular biologist; b. Guangdong, People Republic of China, Dec. 24, 1957; s. Hung Ho and Shui-Wo (Kwok) Y.; m. Lai-Chu, Apr. 23, 1987; children: Gayang Heidi, Gakit Richard. BS, Chinese U. Hong Kong, 1981, MPhil, 1983; DPhil, Oxford U., England, 1988. Asst. prof. Ohio State U., Columbus, 1990-96, assoc. prof., 1996—. Contbr. articles to profl. jours. Grantee NIH, Bethesda, Md., 1994—, March of Dimes, 1992-94; postdoctoral fellow Med. Rsch. Coun. Lab. Molecular Biology, Cambridge, England, 1987-90. Mem. AAAS, Am. Assn. Immunologists, Am. Soc. Human Genetics, Am. Soc. Microbiology, Am. Soc. Biochemistry and Molecular Biology, Soc. for Pediat. Rsch. Office: Children's Rsch Inst 700 Childrens Dr Columbus OH 43205-2664 E-mail: cyu@chi.osu.edu.

**YU, CHUANZHAO,** electrical engineer, researcher; b. Shuangcheng, China, Apr. 30, 1975; s. Zhifu Yu and Lizhi Wang; m. Yanhua Chen, Sept. 23, 1999; 1 child, Savannah J. PhD, U. Ctrl. Fla., 2006. Rsch. asst. Tsinghua U., Beijing, 1997—2000; engr. Huawei Technologies, Beijing, 2000—03; rsch. asst. Chip Design and Reliability Lab. U. Ctrl. Fla., Orlando, Fla., 2003—; intern engr. Advanced Micro Devices, Sunnyvale, Calif., 2005. Author: IEEE Transactions on Electron Devices, IEEE Trans. Dev. and Mater. Rel., Microelectronics Reliability. Recipient Self-funded Student award, China Govt., 2006; fellow Travel fellowship, Univ. Ctrl. Fla., 2006; Provost fellowship, 2003, Merit fellowship, 2004. Mem.: Phi Kappa Phi (hon.) Achievements include research in improved models and extraction method for nanoscale MOSFETs; reliability of novel MOSFETs (nanoscale devices, high-k dielectrics, silicon-on-insulator devices, and 1 nm ultra-thin oxide) for microelectronic applications - from device level to circuit level; equivalent circuit models for predicting the reliability of performance for new silicon transistor designs was developed; development of a methodology to predict the reliability effects on the RFIC with these novel devices, which provides guidance for the reliability consideration of the circuit design; research in interface circuit design for MEMS sensors; design of CMOS voltage-control oscillator (VCO), power amplifier (PA), low noise amplifier (LNA), mixer, output buffer and PLL: Analysis of circuit performance; Equivalent circuit modeling for devices; development of board support packet (BSP) system and low-layer drivers for router NetEngine16/NetEngine08. Office: Chip Design and Reliability Lab Research Park Univ of Central Florida Orlando FL 32816 Office Phone: 407-207-4941.

**YU, FEI,** internist; b. Beijing, Mar. 12, 1956; came to U.S., 1990; d. Longshan and Dan (Zheng) Y.; m. Xiangqun Fu, Jan. 7, 1984; 1 child, Danni. MD, Beijing Med. U., 1982; PhD in Med. Sci., Beijing Union Med. Coll., 1989. Diplomate Am. Bd. Internal Medicine, Am. Bd. Med. Acupuncture. Intern The People's Hosp., Beijing Med. U., 1981-82; resident in internal medicine Jishuitan Hosp., Beijing, 1983-84, Beijing Union Med. Coll. Hosp., 1984-87; clin. fellow hematology dept. internal medicine Beijing Union Med. Coll., Chinese Acad. Med. Scis., 1987-89; rsch. fellow dept. devel. cell biology Sloan-Ketterng Inst. Cancer Rsch., N.Y.C., 1991-93; rsch. fellow dept. internal medicine Columbia U. Coll. Physicians and Surgeons, N.Y.C., 1993—95; resident in medicine N.Y. Meth. Hosp., Bklyn., 1996-99; physician Regal Med. PC, Clifton, NJ, 2000—02, Clifton Med. & Rehab. Ctr., 2003; pvt. practice Englewood Cliffs, NJ, 2003—. Contbr. articles to profl. jours. Mem. AMA. Avocations: music, swimming, novel reading, travel, stamp collecting/philately. Office: 385 Sylvan Ave 25 Englewood Cliffs NJ 07632 Office Phone: 201-567-0686. Personal E-mail: dnffy@aol.com.

**YU, GEORGE TZUCHIAO,** political science professor; b. London, May 16, 1931; s. Wangteh and Ying (Ho) Y.; m. Priscilla Chang, Aug. 11, 1957; children: Anthony, Phillip. AB, U. Calif., Berkeley, 1954, MA, 1957, PhD, 1961. Asst. prof. polit. sci. U. N.C., Chapel Hill, 1961-65; assoc. prof. polit. sci. U. Ill., Urbana, 1965-70, prof., 1970—, head dept., 1987-92, dir. Ctr. for East Asian and Pacific Studies, 1992—, dir. grad. studies, 1981-85, chair Asian Am. studies com., 1997—2002. Vis. sr. lectr. polit. sci. Univ. Coll., Nairobi, 1968. Author: The Chinese Anarchist Movement, 1961, 65, Party Politics in Republican China, 1966, China and Tanzania, 1970, China's African Policy, 1975, Intra-Asian International Relations, 1977, Modern China and Its Revolutionary Process, 1985, American Studies in China, 1993, China in Transition, 1994, Asia's New World Order, 1997, Mongolia and Northeast Asia, 1999. Grantee, Social Sci. Rsch. Coun., 1967—68, 1970—71, NEH, 1978—81, 1984—86, Earhart Found., 1976—77, 1981—83, 1988, Ford Found., 1985—87, 1989, 1992, Freeman Found., 1996, 1997, 1999, 2001—03. Mem. Assn. Asian Studies. Office: 702 S Wright St Urbana IL 61801-3631 Business E-Mail: g-yu@uiuc.edu.

**YU, GUOLIANG,** mathematician, educator; PhD, SUNY, Stony Brook, 1991. Asst. prof. U. Colo., Boulder, Colo., 1991—98, assoc. prof., 1998—2000; prof. Vanderbilt U., Nashville, 2000—. Spkr. in field. Editor: Jour. Noncommutative Geometry. Achievements include research in the Novikov conjecture and coarse embeddings into Hilbert spaces. Office: Vanderbilt University Dept of Math 1326 Stevenson Center Nashville TN 37240 Office Phone: 615-322-2021.

**YU, HENGYONG,** research scientist; b. Tengzhou, Shandong, China, Aug. 15, 1975; s. Daohong Yu and Chuanxiu Chen; m. Ren Song. BS, Xi'an Jiaotong U., China, 1998, PhD, 2003. Instr., assoc. prof. Hangzhou Dianzi U., Zhejiang, China, 2003—04; rsch. fellow U. Iowa, Iowa City, 2004—06, assoc. rsch. scientist, 2006—. Mem.: IEEE. Office Phone: 319-384-5546.

**YU, HYUK,** chemist, educator; b. Kapsan, Korea, Jan. 20, 1933; s. Namjik and Keedong (Shin) Y.; m. Gail Emmens, Jan. 20, 1964; children: Jeffrey, Steven, Douglas. BSChemE, Seoul Nat. U., 1955; MS in Organic Chemistry, U. So. Calif., 1958; PhD in Phys. Chemistry, Princeton U., 1962. Rsch. assoc. Dartmouth Coll., Hanover, NH, 1962-63; rsch. chemist Nat. Inst. Sci. and Tech., Washington, 1963-67; asst. prof. U. Wis., Madison, 1967-69, assoc. prof., 1969-78, prof. chemistry, 1978—, Evan P. Helfaer chair chemistry, 1991—95, Eastman-Kodak prof. emeritus, W.H. Stockmayer prof. emeritus. Fulbright-Hays lectr. Inha U., Inchon, Korea,1972; chmn. Gordon Rsch. Conf. Polymer Physics, 1986, 93; cons. LG Chem., Daejeon. Contbr. articles to profl. jours. John Simon Guggenheim Found. fellow, 1984; recipient Alexander von Humboldt award Humboldt Found., 1992. Fellow Am. Phys. Soc. (High-Polymer Physics prize, 1994); mem. Am. Chem. Soc. (exec. com. polymer chemistry divsn., editorial ad. bd. 1988-91, Ho-Am Basic Sci. prize, 1997, Colloid and Surface Chemistry Langmuir Lectr. award 1999), N.Y. Acad. Scis., Biophys. Soc., Materials Rsch. Soc., Korean Chem. Soc. (life), Polymer Soc. Korea (life), Sigma Xi (chpt. pres. 1987-88). Office: Univ Wis 1101 University Ave Madison WI 53706-1396 Business E-Mail: yu@chem.wisc.edu.

**YU, JEAN,** apparel designer; b. Korea, 1968; arrived in US, 1990; Grad., Fashion Inst. of Tech. Former intern & studio asst. Ronaldus Shamask; owner, designer Jean Yu Collection, 1992—; opened first retail store, 2001. Work featured in Vogue, Vogue Paris, Vogue Italia, L'uomo Vogue, Vogue Nippon, W Magazine, NY Mag.,Town and Country, V Mag., 10, Numero, Flair. Recipient Innovator Design award, Cotton Inc. Office: Jean Yu Studio 115 Bowery St New York NY 10002*

**YU, JEN,** medical educator; b. Taipei, Taiwan, Jan. 23, 1943; came to U.S., 1969; s. Chin Chuan and Shiu Lan (Lin) Y.; m. Janet Chen, June 16, 1973; children: Benjamin, Christopher. MD, Nat. Taiwan U., 1968; PhD in Physiology, U. Pa., 1972. Diplomate Am. Bd. Phys. Medicine and Rehab. Intern Phila. Gen. Hosp., 1972-73; resident in phys. medicine and rehab. Hosps. of U. Pa., 1973-75; asst. prof. dept. phys. medicine and rehab. U. Pa. Sch. Medicine, Phila., 1975-76, U. Tex. Health Sci. Ctr., San Antonio, 1976-79, assoc. prof., 1979-81; prof. dept. phys. medicine and rehab. U. Calif. Irvine Coll. Medicine, 1981-82, prof., emeritus. Contbr. articles to profl. jours. Mem. Am. Acad. Phys. Medicine and Rehab., Am. Congress Rehab. Medicine, Assn. Acad. Physiatrists, Am. Assn. Anatomists, Soc. for Neurosci. Office: U Calif Irvine Med Ctr Dept Phys Medicine & Rehab 101 The City Dr Orange CA 92868-3201 Office Phone: 714-456-6504. Business E-Mail: jyu@uci.edu.

**YU, JESSICA,** director, producer, writer, editor; b. 1966; BA in English with honors, Yale U. Bd. dirs. Internat. Documentary Assn. Prodr.(dir.): Home Base: A Chinatown Callen Heinlenville, Sour Death Balls, 1992, Breathing Lessons: The Life and Work of Mark O'Brien, 1996 (Acad. award for best documentary short subject, 1997), Better Late, 1997, In the Realms of the Unreal, 2004; (TV films) Men of Re-enaction, 1998; dir.: The Cake Eaters, 2005; (documentaries, feature) The Living Museum, 1998; contbr. articles. Recipient Edward R. Murrow award, Skeptics Soc., 1995, 24 film festival awards. Fellow: Yaddo, MacDowell Colony; mem.: Phi Beta Kappa.

**YU, JIE,** communications engineer; s. Gang Yu and Benying Tao. B Engring., Tsinghua U., Beijing, China, 1999, M Engring., 2001; PhD, Drexel U., Phila., 2005. Rsch. assist. Drexel U., 2002—05; comm. engr. US&S Inc., Pitts., 2005—. George Hill Jr. fellow, Coll. Engring., Drexel U., 2004. Mem.: IEEE (corr.). Home: 6230 5th Ave Apt 323E Pittsburgh PA 15232 Office: 1000 Technology Dr Pittsburgh PA 15219

**YU, JUN,** biologist; s. Guofan Yu and Qingzhen Xu; m. Cong Xu; children: Yuezhou, Yueyang. PhD, NYU, 1990. Rsch. asst. prof. N.Y. U., 1990—93; sr. fellow U. Wash., 1993—98; assoc. dir. Beijing Genomics Inst. Chinese Acad. Scis., 1998—. Named Rsch. Leader of the Yr., Sci. Am., 2002. E-mail: junyu@genomics.org.cn.

**YU, JURONG,** chemist; b. Suzhou, Jiangsu, China, Aug. 15, 1963; arrived in U.S., 1990; s. Jingrong and Zhenzhu Yu; m. Huilei Shi, Aug. 14, 1986; children: Christina H., Timmy C. BSc, Xuzhou Normal U., China, 1984; PhD, Shanghai Inst. Materia Medica, Chinese Acad. Scis., 1988. Rsch. asst. prof. Shanghai Inst. Materia Medica, Chinese Acad. Scis., 1988—90; postdoctoral rsch. fellow U. Tex. Southwestern Med. Ctr., Dallas, 1990—96; sr. rsch. investigator Bristol-Myers Squibb Co., New Brunswick, NJ, 1997—. Contbr. articles to profl. jours. Recipient Presdl. Young Investigator award, Chinese Acad. Scis., 1989, Excellent Grad. Student award, Shanghai Inst. Materia Medica, Chinese Acad. Scis., 1988, Triumph award, Devel. Operating Com. Bristol-Myers Squibb Co., 2003. Mem.: Am. Chem. Soc. Achievements include patents for pharmaceutical development: research in total synthesis of complex antifungal agent FR-900848; invention of intramolecular mitsunobu displacement with carbon nucleophiles: preparation of a-Nitrocyclopropanes; synthesis of Alkyl Nitronates via Mitsunobu Condensation; stereospecific Dehydrative Alkylation of Bis-Sulfones: Synthesis of a Lessor Tea Tortrix Pheromone; Total Synthesis of Polycyclopropyl Antibiotic FR-900848; Synthesis of Camptothecin Using Nitrone Cycloaddition to Construct the CDE Ring Moiety; One-pot Synthesis of Cyclic Enecarbamates from Lactam Carbamates. Home: 15 Scenic Dr Dayton NJ 08810 Office: Bristol-Myers Squibb Company One Squibb Dr New Brunswick NJ 08903 Office Phone: 732-227-7485. Home Fax: 732-438-0678; Office Fax: 732-227-3938. Business E-Mail: jurong.yu@bms.com. E-mail: jurongyu@yahoo.com.

**YU, LINDA,** newswoman, television anchorwoman; b. Xian, China, Dec. 1, 1946; BA in Journalism, U. So. Calif., 1968. With Sta. KTLA-TV, Los Angeles, Sta. KABC-TV, Los Angeles; news anchor, reporter Sta. KATU-TV, Portland, Oreg.; gen. assignment reporter Sta. KGO-TV, San Francisco; with Sta. WMAQ-TV, Chgo., 1979-84, gen. assignment reporter, weekend anchor, 1979-80, co-anchor Monday-Friday edit. NEWSCENTER5, 4:30 PM, 1980-81, co-anchor NEWSCENTER5, 10:00 PM, 1981-84; co-anchor Eyewitness News, WLS-TV, Chgo., 1984—; spl.: Linda Yu in Chinatown; anchor WLS-TV, Chgo., 1984—. Recipient Chgo. Emmy award, 1981, 82, 87. Office: Sta WLS-TV 190 N State St Chicago IL 60601-3302

**YU, MAY HUANG,** librarian, educator; b. Chengdu, Sichuan, China, June 24; came to the U.S., 1989; s. Dazhou Huang and Jiangzhen Yu; m. Lixin Yu; 1 child, Michael. Student, Beijing U., 1988; LLB, State Normal U. Sichuan, Chengdu, 1982; MLS, SUNY, Albany, 1996. Cert. pub. libr., N.Y. Tchr. Fuxing H.S., Qingcheng, Sichuan, China, 1975-78; asst. prof. State Normal U. Sichuan, Chengdu, 1982-89; libr., instr. Alcorn State (Miss.) U., 1996—97; web developer, metadata libr. Fla. State U., Tallahassee, 1998—2000; head media dept. Alcorn State (Miss.) U., media libr., prof., 2000—. Spl. corr. Jour. Ethics, Chengdu, 1985-89; gen. sec. Sichuan State Ethics Assn., Chengdu, 1985-89; sec. Alcorn State U. Faculty Assembly, 2005—. Editor: The Dictionary of Ethics, 1987. Named Outstanding Rschr., Assn. Philosophy

and Social Scis. Sichuan State, 1987. Mem. ALA, World Libr. and Info. Congress Avocations: ping pong/table tennis, movies, travel. Office: JD Boyd Libr 1000 ASU Dr Alcorn State MS 39096-7510 Business E-Mail: mhyu@lorman.alcorn.edu.

**YU, MENGJIAO,** petroleum engineer, educator; m. Ye Feng. PhD, The U. Tex., 2002. Asst. prof. The U. Tulsa, Okla., 2002—, assoc. dir. Drilling Rsch. Projects, 2003. Office: The University of Tulsa S 600 College Ave Tulsa OK 74104 Office Phone: 918-631-2695. Office Fax: 918-631-5009. Business E-Mail: mengjiao-yu@utulsa.edu.

**YU, MING,** engineering educator, researcher; s. Chongguang Yu and Zhongying Su; m. Tian Xing, Aug. 28, 1992; children: Ellen Tian, Karen Tian. BEE, Hubei Inst. Auto Tech., 1984; MEE, Huazhong U. Sci. and Tech., 1987; D of Engring., Tsinghua U., China, 1991; PhD, Rutgers U., New Brunswick, NJ, 2002. Sr. tech. staff mem. AT&T Labs, Middletown, NJ, 1997—2000; asst. prof. SUNY, Binghamton, NY, 2000—. Sr. software engr. Jedai Broadband Networks, Red Bank, 2000; sys. engr. AT&T Labs, Middletown, 2002—03. Contbr. articles to profl. jours. Fin. chair IEEE Iwat, NYC, 2005—; cyber trust panelist NSF, Washington, 2004—05, it rsch. panelist, 2004; tech. program com. IEEE Wireless Comm. and Network Conf., Piscataway, NJ, 2005—, Internat. Workshop on Antennas Tech., 2005, Internat. Conf. Networking Sensing and Control, 2005, Internat. Conf. Circuits and Systems, 2003, Systems Man and Cybernetics Sys. Assurance, 2005; reviewer IEEE Trans on Comm., Antennas and Propagations, Piscataway, 2005—; guest editor Int. J. of Wireless and Mobile Computing, Piscataway, 2003—. Recipient Third Millenium medal, IEEE, 2000. Achievements include development of novel routing protocols and traffic models. Home: 294 Cardiff Dr Morganville NJ 07751 Office: Dept of ECE SUNY Binghamton NY 13902 Office Phone: 607-777-6133. Office Fax: 607-777-4464. Personal E-mail: mingyu@ieee.org. E-mail: mingyu@binghamton.edu.

**YU, OLIVER SHUKIANG,** corporate executive, educator, technology strategist; b. Chendu, Sichuan, China, July 8, 1939; arrived in U.S., 1961; s. Cecil S. and Susan S. Yu; m. Joanna S. Chu, June 1, 1985; children: Amy S., Christopher S., Hamilton S. MS, Ga. Inst. of Tech., 1963, Stanford U., 1967, PhD, 1972. Mgr. planning analysis Electric Power Rsch. Inst., Palo Alto, Calif., 1974—89; dir. energy and tech. strategies SRI Internat., Menlo Park, Calif., 1989—2000; pres., CEO The STARS Group, Los Altos, Calif., 2000—. Dir. Silicon Valley bus. stars program San Jose State U., 2002—; cons. assoc. prof. Stanford U., 1984—86; sr. tech. advisor Taiwan Power Co., Taipei, 1979—. Author: (book) Introduction to Technology Management, 1998. With Taiwanese Navy, 1959—61. Named Hon. Fellow, East-West Ctr., 1981; recipient Fulbright fellowship. U.S. State Dept., 1961. Mem.: IEEE, Inst. for Ops. Rsch. and Mgmt. Sci. (coun. mem., chair meeting com. 1985—91) Achievements include research in Technology Portfolio Planning and Management Methodology. Office: The STARS Group 470 Santa Barbara Dr Los Altos CA 94022 E-mail: oliveryu@starstrategygroup.com.

**YU, PAUL,** academic administrator; m. Ellen Yu; children: Gregory, Nicholas. BA in Philosophy, U. Mich., 1965, MA in Philosophy, 1967, PhD in Philosophy, 1973. Mem. faculty philosophy Ctrl. Mich. U., 1969—80, chair philosophy, 1981—87, assoc. dean Coll. Arts and Scis., 1987—89; dean Coll. Liberal Arts and Scis. Butler U., 1989—91, v.p. acad. affairs, 1991—92, provost, sr. v.p. acad. affairs, 1992—97; pres. SUNY, Brockport, 1997—2004, San Jose (Calif.) State U., 2004—. Fulbright lectr. philosophy Nat. Taiwan U., 1980—81; vis. scholar Chinese Acad. Social Scis., Beijing, 1990; bd. dirs. Am. Assn. Univ. Adminstrs., 1998—2001; mem. exec. com. Commn. on the Liberal Arts Agenda Am. Assn. State Colls. and Univs., 1998—2001, co-chair Forum on the Liberal Arts Agenda, 2001—02; mem. Commn. on Internat. Edn. Am. Coun. on Edn., 2000—02. Recipient Disting. Faculty award, Mich. Assn. Governing Bds., 1982, Disting. Hoosier award Office of Evan Bayn, Gov. Ind., 1990. Mem.: Am. Philos. Assn. Office: San Jose State Univ Office of the Pres Tower Hall 206A One Washington Sq San Jose CA 95192-0002

**YU, PAULINE RUTH,** former dean, educational association administrator; b. Rochester, NY, Mar. 5, 1949; d. Paul N. and Irene (Tang) Y.; m. Theodore D. Huters, Aug. 23, 1975 (div. Feb. 2000); children: Emily Elizabeth, Matthew Charles, Alexander David. BA in History and Lit. magna cum laude, Harvard U., 1971; MA in Comparative Lit., Stanford U., 1973, PhD in Comparative Lit., 1976. Asst. prof., then assoc. prof. U. Minn., Mpls., 1976-85; assoc. prof., then prof. Columbia U., N.Y.C., 1985-89; prof., founding chair dept. East Asian langs. and lit. U. Calif., Irvine, 1989-94; dean humanities UCLA, 1994—2003, prof. East Asian langs. and culture, 1994—2003; pres. Am. Coun. Learned Socs., N.Y.C., 2003—. Author: The Poetry of Wang Wei, 1980, The Reading of Imagery in the Chinese Poetic Tradition, 1987; editor and contbg. author: Voices of the Song Lyric in China, 1994, Culture and State in Chinese History: Conventions, Accommodations, and Critiques, 1997, Ways with Words: Writing about Reading Texts from Early China, 2000; editor, contbr.: The Longman Anthology of World Literature; mem. editl. bd. Tang Studies, Chinese Lit., Comparative Lit. Studies, 1993—. Mem. nat. adv. bd. Woodrow Wilson Found., 2004—; mem. internat. adv. bd. Asia Rsch. Inst., Nat. U. Singapore, 2002—; mem. western ctr. exec. coun. Am. Acad. Arts and Scis., 2000—03; bd. dirs. Am. Coun. Learned Soc., 1998—; trustee Nat. Humanities Ctr., 2000—, Asian Cultural Coun., 2006—; bd. dirs. The Teagle Found., 2003—; mem. adv. coun. dept. East Asian studies Princeton U., 2003—; bd. overseers Harvard U., 2003—; mem. adv. bd. Coun. for Internat. Exch. of Scholars, 2001—05. Guggenheim fellow, 1983-84, ACLS fellow, 1983-84; recipient Profl. Achievement award U. Calif. at Irvine Alumni Assn., 1993. Fellow Am. Acad. Arts and Scis.; mem. MLA, Assn. Asian Studies (mem. China and Inner Asia coun. 1982-85), Am. Comparative Lit. Assn., Am. Oriental Soc., Phi Beta Kappa Soc. (senator 1997—, exec. com. 2001—). Office: Am Coun Learned Societies 633 Third Ave New York NY 10017-6795 Office Phone: 212-697-1505 x 121. E-mail: paulineyu@acls.org.

**YU, ROBERT KUAN-JEN,** biochemistry professor; b. Chungking, China, Jan. 27, 1938; came to U.S., 1962; m. Helen Chow, July 1, 1972; children: David S., Jennifer S. BS, Tunghai U., Taiwan, 1960; PhD, U. Ill., 1967; Med.ScD. (hon.), Tokyo, 1980; MA (hon.), Yale U., 1983. assoc., instr. Albert Einstein Coll. Medicine, Bronx, 1967-72; asst. prof. Yale U., New Haven, 1973-75, assoc. prof., 1975-82, prof., 1983-88; prof. biochemistry, chmn. dept. Med. Coll. Va. Commonwealth U., Richmond, 1988-2000; dir. Inst. Mol. Med. Genetics Med. Coll., Augusta, Ga., 2000—; dir. Inst. Neurosci. Med. Coll. Ga., Augusta, 2005—. Mem. study sect. NIH, Washington, 1980-84, 96—; mem. Bd. Lab. Svcs., Va., 1994-98. Editor: Gangioside Structure Function and Biomedical Potential, 1984, New Trends in Ganglioside Research, 1988; contbr. over 500 articles to profl. publs. Josiah Macy scholar, 1979; grantee NIH, 1975—, 84-91; recipient Va. Gangioside Scientist of Yr. award, 1995, Alexander von Humboldt award, 1990, GRA Eminent scholar, 2000, Disting. Alumnus award Tunghai U., 2003, Achievement award Chinese Assn. Engrs. and Scientists So. Calif., 2004, Outstanding Faculty award Med. Coll. Ga., 2006. Mem. AAAS, Am. Soc. Cell Biology, Am. Soc. Neurochemistry (mem. coun. 1983-86, 91-95, pres. 2001-03), Internat. Soc. Neurochemistry, Soc. Neurosci., Am. Soc. Biochemistry and Molecular Biology, Am. Chem. Soc., N.Y. Acad. Sci., Academia Sinica (academician). Home: 821 River Bluff Rd North Augusta SC 29841-6056 Office: IMMAG Med Coll Ga 1120 15th St Augusta GA 30912-0004 Office Phone: 706-721-0699. Business E-Mail: ryu@mcg.edu.

**YU, SHAN,** artist; b. Fuzhou, Fujian, China, Oct. 24, 1949; came to the U.S., 1986; s. Yiqiang Chen and Juan Yue Yu; m. Hui Ling Du, Oct. 5, 1980; 1 child, Han. BA, Fujian Art Inst., Fuzhou, 1980; postgrad., Shanghai Theater Acad., 1985-86; MFA, Boston U., 1989. Art tchr. Fujian Art Sch., Fuzhou, 1980-85; chief set designer Visual Design Assn., Cambridge, Mass., 1989-92; sr. set designer V.D.A. Inc., Somerville, Mass., 1992-99; pres. Ea. Decor & Art, Somerville, 1993—. Dir. Watercolor Soc., Fuzhou, 1984-85. One-man shows include Hong Kong Art Ctr., 1989. The Market Barn Gallery, Falmouth, Mass, 1989, CCI Gallery, Boston, 1993, 1998, Fuzhou Art Acad. Gallery, China, 2003, Hong Kong Art and Design Gallery, 2003, exhibited in

group shows at The East and West Gallery, Chgo., 1990, Creative Arts Workshop Gallery, New Haven, 1992, Hewlett-Packard Co., Andover, Mass, 1994, Kane Gallery, Boston, 1995, Wilson Gallery, 1997, Am. Watercolor Soc., N.Y.C., 1999, Fuzhou Art Acad. Gallery, China, 2003, Hong Kong Art & Design Gallery, 2003, executed murals, Children's Mus., Boston, 1995, Mus. Sci., 1998—2000, The Children's Mus. at Mus. Ctr., Cin., 1998, Angel Mounds Historic Stie Mus., Evansville, Ind., 2000, Ind. State Mus., Indpls., 2001, Dinosaurs Exhibit Nat. tour, 2002, Royal BC Mus., 2003, Nat. Great Rivers Mus., Alton, Ill., 2003, Seacoast Sci. Ctr., Rye, NH, 2004, World of Dinosaur Mus. proposal, Media, Pa., 2005, art work/set decoration for Disney film, Pirates of the Caribbean 2 & 3, Burbank, Calif., 2005, three murals for Chinasaurs spl. exhibit, Sci. Mus. Minn., St. Paul, 2005, lobby design, Sheraton Xiamen Hotel, China, 2005; author: Liaoning Art Press, 1997, Landscape Paintings by Yu Shan, 1997. Fellow Asian Culture Coun., N.Y.C., 1986-89; internat. scholar Boston U., 1989. Mem. Internat. Soc., Nat. Soc. Mural Painters. Avocations: music, drama, film, photography, video. Home: 45 Robinson St Apt Decor & Art Studio B 45 Robinson St Somerville MA 02145 E-mail: yushannet1@aol.com.

**YU, SHAN PING,** neuroscientist, educator; s. Yong-niang Yu; m. Ling Wei; 1 child, Steven S. MS, Inst. of Pharmacology and Toxicology, Beijing, China, 1982; MD, Capital Inst. of Medicine, Bejing, China, 1982; PhD, SUNY, 1990. Rsch. asst. neuropharmacology Inst. Pharmacology and Toxicology, Beijing, 1982—84; vis. rschr. Lund U., Sweden, 1985—86; postdoctoral rschr. Howard Hughes Med. Inst., Stony Brook, NY, 1990—92; asst. prof. Wash. U., St. Louis, 1992—98, assoc. prof., 1998—2002, Med. U. S.C., Charleston, 2002—. Contbr. articles to profl. jours. Recipient Grant-in-Aid award, Am. Heart Assn., 1999, Am. Heart Assn. and Bugher award, 2001; Oversea fellow, WHO, 1985, Rsch. grantee, NSF, 1999, NIH, 2001. Mem.: Soc. for Neuroscience. Achievements include discovery of Potassium channel regulation in neuronal apoptosis and novel regulations of glutamate receptors. Home: 1214 Waterfront Dr Mount Pleasant SC 29464 Office: Med Univ of SC 280 Calhoun St Charleston SC 29425 Office Phone: 843-792-2992. Personal E-mail: yusp@musc.edu.

**YU, SHAOCAI,** research scientist; s. Zhimei Yu and Guangxin Liao; m. Lifen Chen. BS, Peking U., 1985, MS, 1988; PhD, NC State U., 1999. Rsch. assoc. Duke U., Durham, NC, 1999—2001; vis. scientist US EPA, NC, 2001—04, sr. scientist NC, 2004. Co-convener for the session of volatile organic compounds and organic aerosols in the atmosphere EGS-AGU-EUG Joint Assembly, Nice, France, 06 - 11 April 2003. Contbr. articles to profl. jours. Chmn. Peking U. Alumni Assn. of NC, 2006. Global Change scholarship, Am. Meteorol. Soc., 1999. Mem.: China Environ. Sci. Soc., Am. Meteorol. Soc., Am. Assn. for Aerosol Rsch., Am. Geophys. Union. Office Phone: 919-541-0362. Business E-Mail: yu.shaocai@epa.gov.

**YU, SHIAO-LING S.,** humanities educator; d. Yueh Sheng and Mei-ying Ching; m. Yun S. Yu, Apr. 17, 1960; children: Lawrence H., Michael H., Mark H., David H. BA, Caldwell Coll., 1958; MA, U. Kans., 1977; PhD, U. Wis., Madison 1983. Asst. prof. Oreg. State U., Corvallis, 1987—91, assoc. prof., 1991—. Vis. asst. prof. Ohio State U., Columbus, 1983—84, U. Kans., Lawrence, 1984—86. Author: Chinese Drama After the Cultural Revolution (Nat. Endowment for the Arts Fellowship, 1994); contbr. articles to profl. jours., chapters to books. Mem. So. Poverty Law Ctr., Montgomery, Ala., 2002—. Charlotte W. Newcombe Dissertation fellow, Woodrow Wilson Nat. Fellowship Found., 1982. Mem.: MLA (mem. del. assembly 2003—05), Assn. Asian Performance (vice chair and coun. planner 1998—2001), Assn. Asian Studies. Office: Oregon State Univ Corvallis OR 97331 Office Phone: 541-737-3943. Business E-Mail: syu@oregonstate.edu.

**YU, SIMON SHYI-JIAN,** entomologist, educator; b. Ilan, Taiwan, Republic of China, Sept. 11, 1935; arrived in Can. 1963, U.S. in 1968; s. Son-Wei and Ah-So (Liao) Yu; m. Rachel R.C. Yeh, Sept. 16, 1967; children: Robert Yu, Edmund Yu. BS, Nat. Taiwan U., 1959; MS, McGill U., Montreal, Can., 1965, PhD, 1968; postdoctoral, Cornell U. and Oreg. State U., 1968-74. Rsch. entomologist Taiwan Sugar Co., Kuohsiung, Taiwan, 1961-62; rsch. asst. McGill U., Montreal, 1963-68; postdoctoral fellow Cornell U., Ithaca, N.Y., 1968-69; rsch. assoc. Oreg. State U., Corvallis, 1969-74, asst. prof., 1974-79; asst. prof. U. Fla., Gainesville, 1980-82, assoc. prof., 1982-86, prof., 1986—. Author numerous scientific papers and book chpts. 2nd lt. Chinese infantry, 1959-61. Rsch. grantee NIH, 1979, USDA, 1980, 82, 85, 90, 91, EPA, 1981, NSF, 1988, 90. Mem. Entomol. Soc. Am., AAAS, Am. Chem. Soc., The Soc. Sigma Xi, Fla. Entomol. Soc. Avocations: classical music, fishing, bicycling. Office: U Fla Dept Entomology and NE Gainesville FL 32611 Home: 5205 NW 43rd Rd Gainesville FL 32606-4323 Office Phone: 352-392-1901. E-mail: yusj@ufl.edu.

**YU, TIAN-EN,** musician, music educator; d. Hong Liang Yu and Junyia Xu; m. Nicholas Stephen Isaacs, July 26, 1990. Student, Shanghai Conservatory, 1961—69; Artist Diploma, Oberlin Conservatory, 1989. Pianist Shanghai Ballet, 1970—80, Shanghai Philharmonic, 1980—86; accompanist Oberlin Conservatory, Ohio, 1988—89; instr. Cmty. Sch. Music and Arts, Mountain View, Calif., 1990—95; lectr. in piano Santa Clara U., Calif., 1993—; tutor, accompanist Interlochen (Mich.) Music Camp, 1987. Judge U.S. Open Piano Competition, 1993, 96, 99, 2004—06. Musician: Shanghai Philharmonic, Santa Clara U. Orch., Oberlin Conservatory. Scholar, Oberlin Conservatory, 1986—88. Mem.: Am. Coll. Musicians. Avocations: knitting, sewing, flower arranging, cats. Personal E-mail: tianenyuxu77@yahoo.com.

**YU, WEI,** economist, researcher; s. Guoxing Yu and Lixin Zhu; m. Li Fan, Aug. 9, 1952; 1 child, Yifan F. BSEE, East China U., Shanghai, 1982; MA in Econs., Clemson U., S.C., 1988, PhD in Applied Econs., 1992. Instr. dept. econs. Clemson U., 1988—92, asst. prof. applied econs., 1992—94; postdoctoral fellow Nat. Inst. Aging Boston U., 1994—96; asst. prof. Boston U. Sch. Medicine 1996—2000; health economist dept. vet. affairs Health Econs. Resource Ctr., Menlo Park, Calif., 2000—; fellow Ctr. for Health Policy, Stanford U., Calif., 2000—. Dir. expert com. for the expt. of cmty. based healthcare sys. Ministry of Health China, Beijing, 1996—2000; chair fin. com. Chinese Economist Soc., Ann Arbor, Mich., 1998—2005, dir. bd. Gregory Chow Fund, 2002—05; lectr. UN Devel. Programme, N.Y.C., 1994; mem. sci. rev. and evaluation bd. dept. vet. affairs Health Svcs. R & D, Washington, 2001—05, mem. adv. com. for evaluating cmty.-based outpatient clinics in the vets. health sys. dept. vet. affairs, 2002—05; assoc. dir. China-U.S. postdoctoral tng. program Ctrs. for Health Policy and for Primary Care and Outcomes Rsch., Stanford U., 2003—; mem. of steering coun. Ctr. for Patient Healthcare Behavior, VA Tenn. Valley Health Care Sys., Nashville, 2003—; mem. adv. com. dept. vet. affairs Info. Resource Ctr., Hines, Ill., 2003—; mem. Medicare data rev. bd. dept. vet. affairs, 2004—; mem. data safety and monitoring bd. for a clin. trial Vets. Health Adminstrn. Coop. Study Program, Perry Point, NJ, 2004—; mem. steering coun. Ctr. of Patient Healthcare Behavior. Named from 80 articles on health care, public financing, and econs. in peer-reviewed jours., books, and confs. Recipient Internat. Study award, China Ministry of Edn., 1986—88; fellow, Nat. Inst. on Aging, 1994—96. Mem.: Internat. Health Econs. Assn. Office Phone: 650-493-5000 23157. Office Fax: 650-617-2639. Business E-Mail: wyu2@stanford.edu.

**YU, WEI-WEN,** retired engineering educator; b. Shandong, China, July 10, 1924; arrived in U.S., 1954; s. Chi-tung and Mong-shih Yu; m. Yueh-hsin Wang, Sept. 6, 1953; children: Julie H.H., Dorothy H.L., Gordon H.I. BS, Nat. Taiwan U., 1950; MS, Okla. State U., 1955; PhD, Cornell U., 1960. Registered profl. engr., Mo. Structural engr. T.H. McKaig & Assocs., Buffalo, 1955—56, 1959—60; rsch. engr. Am. Iron and Steel Inst., N.Y.C., 1960—67; staff engr. TRW Sys., Redondo Beach, Calif., 1967—68; assoc. prof. U. Mo. Rolla, 1968—72, prof., 1972—82, Curator's prof., 1982—92, Curator's prof. emeritus, 1992—. Dir. Ctr. for Cold-Formed Steel Structures, Rolla, 1990—2000; founding dir. Wei-Wen Yu Ctr. for Cold-Formed Steel Structures, Rolla, 2000—. Author: Cold-Formed Steel Structures, 1973, Cold-Formed Steel Design, 1985, 1991, 2000; guest editor: Spl. Issue on Recent Devels. in Thin-Walled Structures, 1998; editor (and co-editor): Recent Rsch.

and Devel. in Cold-Formed Steel Design and Constrn., 1971—; guest editor Spl. issue on Cold-Formed Steel Structures, 1993. Recipient Alumni Merit award, U. Mo. Sch. of Mines and Metallurgy/U. Mo.-Rolla Alumni Assn., 1979, Arch T. Colwell Merit award, Soc. Automotive Engrs., 1988. Fellow: ASCE (Shortridge Hardesty award 2001); mem.: U. Mo.-Rolla Acad. Civil Engrs. (hon.), Chi-Epsilon (chpt. honor). Achievements include research in Cold-formed steel structures. Avocations: reading, gardening. Office: U Mo Rolla Dept Civil Engring Rolla MO 65409

**YU, YI-HAO,** endocrinologist, educator, physician, research scientist; s. Shi-Qing Yu, Hui-Ling Gan; m. Yiying Zhang; 1 child, Irene. BS, Fudan U., Shanghai, China; MS, PhD, MD, NYU. Diplomate Am. Bd. Internal Medicine. Rsch. asst. prof. NYU Sch. Medicine, N.Y.C.; resident physician Columbia Presbyn. Hosp., N.Y.C., 1996—98, physician, endocrine fellow, 1998—2001; Markey rsch. fellow Columbia U. Coll. Physicians and Surgeons, N.Y.C., 1998—2001; staff physician Columbia Presbyn. Med. Ctr., 2001—, dir. adult nutrition and TPN svc.; asst. prof. medicine Columbia U. Coll. Physicians and Surgeons. Cons. Physicians Cons. Network, Mt. Arlington, NJ; mem. com. Nat. Bd. Nutrition Support Certification, Inc., CNSP. Contbr. articles, sci. papers, books in field. Fellow, China-U.S. Biochemistry Exam. and Application/Ray Wu Soc., in Atherosclerosis, NIH, 1998—2001; grantee NIH, 2001—, Pfizer, 2002—; rsch. grantee, Endocrine Fellows Found., 1999. Fellow: Am. Coll. Endocrinology; mem.: ACP, AAAS, AMA, Am. Soc. Parenteral and Enteral Nutrition, Am.-Chinese Med. Assn. (med. cons. 2001—), Am. Assn. Clin. Endocrinologists, Am. Soc. Cell Biology, N.Y. U. Alumni, Fudan Alumnin U.S. Avocations: Chinese calligraphy, travel, hiking, swimming. Office: Columbia Univ P&S 630 West 168th St PH10-305J New York NY 10032 Office Fax: 212-305-3213. Business E-Mail: yy102@columbia.edu.

**YUAN, BO,** computer scientist, educator; s. Qixiang Yuan and Chanlang Huang; m. Yin Pan, Aug. 8, 1988; children: Kyle children: Jie. PhD, SUNY, Binghamton, 1996. Cert. wireless security profl. Planet3 Wireless, Geogia, 2005. Staff scientist Manning & Napier Info. Svcs., Rochester, NY, 1997—2003; asst. prof. Rochester Inst. Tech., Rochester, 2003—. Author: (book) Fuzzy Sets and Fuzzy Logic: Theory and Applications. Mem.: ACM, IEEE. Achievements include patents for trainable semantic vectors. Office: Rochester Inst Tech 102 Lomb Memorial Dr Rochester NY 14923 Office Phone: 585-475-4468.

**YUAN, CHUN,** physicist, educator; b. Beijing, Aug. 23, 1957; s. Zhenwu Yuan and Shunying Cheng; m. Tong Zhu, Dec. 17, 1987; children: Eric, Isabella. BSc, Beijing Normal U., China, 1982; PhD, U. Utah, 1988. Sr. sys. analyst GE Med. Sys., Waukesha, Wis., 1988—91; asst. prof. U. Wash., Seattle, 1991—97, assoc. prof., 1997—2001, prof., 2001—. Adv. bd. Vulnerable Plaque Orgn., Houston, 2001—; vis. prof. The Post Grad. Med. Coll. of People's Liberation Army, Beijing, 2001—. Contbr. articles to profl. jours. Recipient Rsch. Career Develop. award, NIH, 1996—2000, RO1 award, 1998—. Mem.: AAAS, Am. Asn. Physicists in Medicine, Soc. Cardiovasc. Magnetic Resonance (Best Presentation Award 1999), Internat. Soc. Magnetic Resonance in Medicine (student stipend com. 1997—2000). Avocations: skiing, tennis, hiking, bicycling, music. Office: Univ Wash PO Box 357115 1959 Pacific Ave N Seattle WA 98195 Office Phone: 206-685-3536. Office Fax: 206-543-3495. Business E-Mail: cyuan@u.washington.edu.

**YUAN, JUNYING,** medical educator, researcher; b. Shanghai; BS, Fudan U., Shanghai, 1982; PhD in Neuroscience, Harvard U., 1989. Postdoctoral trainee in devel. biology MIT, 1989—90; instr. medicine Harvard U., 1990—91, asst. prof. medicine and program in neuroscience, 1992—96, asst. prof. cell biology and program in neuroscience, 1996—2000, prof., 2000—; asst. geneticist Cardiovasc. Rsch. Ctr. Mass. Gen. Hosp., 1990—96. Mem. editl. bd.: Current Biology, 1996, ad hoc reviewer: NIH Human Embryology and Devel. 2 Study Sect., 1995, regular reviewer:, 1996—; patentee in field, —; contbr. articles to profl. jours.; presenter in field, —. Recipient Wilson S. Stone Meml. award, MD Anderson Cancer Ctr. U. Tex., 1994, Established Investigator award, Am. Heart Assn., 1996—, Dir.'s Pioneer Award, NIH, 2005; fellow Ryan, Harvard Med. Sch., 1985—89. Office: Harvard Med Sch Dept Cell Biology 240 Longwood Ave Boston MA 02115-5701 Office Phone: 617-432-4170. Office Fax: 617-432-4177. E-mail: jyuan@hms.harvard.edu.*

**YUAN, NANCI,** pediatrician, pulmonologist, educator; MD, Hahnemann U., 1996. Diplomate Am. Bd. Pediat., 1999, Am. Bd. Sleep Medicine, 2005. Clin. asst. prof. LPCH Stanford, Palo Alto, Calif., 2003—. Home and Office: LPCH Stanford 710 Welch Road 3328-A Palo Alto CA 94304-5786 Office Phone: 650-723-5191.

**YUAN, NICOLE PATRICIA,** healthcare educator; m. Jerel Eric Slaughter. BA, Oberlin Coll., 1995; PhD, Bowling Green State U., 2002. Psychology lic. Ariz. Bd. Psychologist Examiners. Dir. substance abuse rsch. Mel and Enid Zuckerman Coll. Pub. Health U. Ariz., Tucson, 2002—06, asst. prof., 2006—. Mem.: APHA, APA, Internat. Soc. Traumatic Stress Studies, Soc. Cmty. Rsch. and Action, Ariz. Psychol. Assn., So. Ariz. Psychol. Assn. (chair profl. outreach com. 2006—). Office: U Ariz Bldg 202 1295 N Martin Ave Tucson AZ 85724 Office Phone: 520-626-7215. Office Fax: 520-626-8716. Business E-Mail: nyuan@email.arizona.edu.

**YUAN, YONGHUI,** chemist, researcher; PhD, U. Del., Newark. Rsch. scientist Unilever Rsch., Edgewater, NJ, 2000—04; sr. rsch. scientist II Wyeth Rsch., Pearl River, NY, 2004—. Mem.: Am. Chem. Soc. Achievements include research in Creative work on inorigatic sunscreens. Research on skin material science and development work on bioproducts purification. Office: Wyeth Research 401 N Middletown Rd B211 Pearl River NY 10965 Office Phone: 845-602-3304.

**YUAN, ZENG-GUANG,** mechanical engineer, researcher; s. Shu-Chi Yuan and Chui-Fan Wei; m. Gui-Fang Zhang, July 28, 1945; children: Sarah Qing, James Jie. BS, Qinghua U., 1963, MS, 1966, U. Calif., 1988, PhD, 1990. Registered profl. engr., Calif., 1993. Sr. reservoir engr. Offshore Oil Exploration China, Shanghai, 1978—86; sr. rsch. engr. Dept. Mech. Engring. U. Calif., Berkeley, Calif.; staff scientist Nat. Ctr. for Microgravity Rsch. NASA Glenn, Cleve., 1998—. Cons. Calif. EPA, Berkeley, Calif., 1993—94; advanced math. instr. Shanghai Tele-U., Shanghai 1983—86; cons. Ministry of Geology China, Beijing, 1984—86. Co-author: Thermal properties and temperature-related behavior of rock/fluid systems; contbr. articles to profl. jours. Recipient China Nat. Sci. Tech. award, Sci. and Tech. Commn. China, 1982, Silver Snoopy award, NASA, 2004; fellow Jane Lewis fellowship, U. Calif., Berkeley, 1986—88. Mem.: AIAA, ASME, Combustion Inst., Soc.Petroleum Engrs. Achievements include discovery of new phenomenon of electric effects on flames. Office Phone: 216-433-2838.

**YUAN, ZHAOXU,** ophthalmologist, researcher; BA in Clin. Medicine, Tianjin Med. U., China, 1993, PhD in Ophthalmology, 1999; MS in Vision Sci., SUNY, 2003. Resident, rschr. Internat. Intraocular Implant Tng. Ctr., Tianjin, 1993—97; rschr. dept. ophthalmology Inst. Edith Cavell, Brussels, 1997—98; rsch. asst., U. Mo., NYC, 2001—03; attending dr., rschr. Tianjin Med. U. Eye Ctr., 1998—2001; instr. ophthalmology Tianjin Med. U., 2001; post doctoral fellow Scott & White Hosp., Temple, Tex., 2003—. Contbr. articles to profl. jours. Recipient Excellence award, Tianjin Health Bur. Continual Edn. Program, 1999, 1st award rsch. presentation, Tianjin Med. U., 1999, New Tech. award, Tianjin Med. & Health Application, 1998, Minnie Flaura Turner Fund for Impaired Vision award, 2003, Fight for Sight Rsch. award, 2003. Mem.: China Med. Assn., Vision Scis. Soc., Assn. for Rsch. and Vision in Ophthalmology. Achievements include research in ophthalmology and vision science. Business E-Mail: zyuan@tamu.edu.

**YUDKOWSKY, RACHEL,** medical educator; b. N.Y., 1955; m. Moshe Yudkowsky; children: Eliezer, Channah. MD, Northwestern U., Evanston, Ill., 1979. Cert. psychiatry Am. Bd. Psychiatry and Neurology. Faculty Dept. Psychiatry Evanston Northwestern Healthcare, Evanston, Ill., 1985—99,

Dept Med. Edn. Coll. Medicine U. Ill. at Chgo. Clerkship dir., residency program dir. and dir. edn. Dept. Psychiatry Evanston Northwestern Healthcare, Chgo.; dir. clin. performance ctr. Coll. Medicine U. Ill. at Chgo. Office: U Ill Chgo Coll Medicine Dept Med Edn MC 591 808 S Wood St Chicago IL 60612

**YUDOF, MARK GEORGE,** academic administrator, law educator, federal agency administrator; b. Phila., Oct. 30, 1944; s. Jack and Eleanor (Parris) Y.; m. Judith Lynn Gomel, July 11, 1965; children: Seth Adam, Samara Lisa. BA, U. Pa., 1965, LLB, 1968. Bar: Pa. 1970, U.S. Supreme Ct. 1974, U.S. Dist. Ct. (we. dist.) Tex. 1975, U.S. Ct. Appeals (5th cir.) 1976, Tex. 1980. Law clk. to judge US Ct. Appeals (5th cir.), 1968-69; assoc. gen. counsel to ABA study FTC, 1969; rsch. assoc. Harvard Ctr. Law and Edn., 1969-70, sr. staff atty., 1970-71; lectr. Harvard Grad. Sch. Edn., 1970-71; asst. prof. U. Tex., Austin, 1971-74, prof., 1974—97, 2002—, assoc. dean, 1979-84, James A. Elkins Cent. chair in law, 1983-97, dean, 1984-94, exec. v.p., provost, 1994-97, John Jeffers rsch. chair in law, 1991-94; pres. U. Minn., 1997—2002; chancellor U. Tex. Sys., 2002—, Jamail regents chair higher edn. leadership, 2002—, Wright chair fed. courts, 2002—. Of counsel Pennzoil vs. Texaco, 1987. Author: When Government Speaks, 1983 (Scribes Book award 1983, cert. merit ABA 1983), (with others) Educational Policy and the Law, 1992, (with others) Gender Justice, 1986. Mem. Tex. Gov.'s Task Force on Sch. Fin., 1989-90, Tex. Gov.'s Select Com. on Edn., 1988; bd. dirs. Freedom to Read Found., 1989-91; mem. Austin Cable Commn., 1981-84, chmn., 1982; mem. nat. panel on sch. desegregation rsch. Ford Found., 1977-80; mem. state exec. com. Univ. Interscholastic League, 1983-86; bd. dirs. Jewish Children's Regional Svc., 1980-86; mem. Gov.'s Select Task Force on Pub. Edn., 1995; mem. Telecomms. Infrastructure Fund Bd., State of Tex., 1995-97; adv. bd. Nat. Inst. for Literacy, 2002-06, Pres. Coun. on Svc. and Civic Participation, 2006—. Recipient Tchg. Excellence award, 1975, Most Meritorious Book award Scribes, 1983, Humanitarian award Austin region NCCJ, 1988, Antidefamation League Jurisprudence award, 1991, James Wilson award U. Pa. Law Sch., 2004; hon. fellow Queen Mary and Westfield Coll., U. London. Fellow: Am. Acad. Arts & Sci., Am. Bar Found., Tex. Bar Found.; mem.: Edn. Testing Svc. (mem. bd. dirs. 2000—02), Am. Coun. Edn. (mem. com. on leadership and instl. effectiveness 2000), Assn. Am. Law Schs. (chmn. law and edn. sect. 1983—84, exec. com. 1988—90), Tex. Bar Found., Am. Law Inst. Avocation: collecting antique maps. Office: U Texas System 601 Colorado St Austin TX 78701-2904 Office Phone: 512-499-4201. E-mail: myudof@utsystem.edu.

**YUE, AGNES KAU-WAH,** otolaryngologist; b. Shanghai, Peoples Republic China, Dec. 1, 1947; arrived in US, 1967; d. Chen Kia and Nee Yuen; m. Gerald Kumata, Sept. 25, 1982; children: Julie, Allison, Benjamin. BA, Wellesley Coll., 1970; MD, Med. Coll. Pa., 1974; postgrad., Yale U., 1974-78. Intern Yale-New Haven Hosp., 1974-75, resident 1975-78; fellow U. Tex. M.D. Anderson Cancer Ctr., Houston, 1978-79; asst. prof. U. Wash., Seattle, 1979-82; physician Pacific Med. Ctr., Seattle, 1979-90; pvt. practice Seattle, 1991—. Fellow Am. Acad. Otolaryngology; mem. Northwest Acad. Otolaryngology. Avocations: sailing, opera, cooking. Office: 1801 NW Market St Ste 410 Seattle WA 98107-3909 Office Phone: 206-782-1090.

**YUE, ALFRED SHUI-CHOH,** metallurgical engineer, consultant; b. China, Nov. 12, 1920; s. Choy Noon-woo and Sze Man-hun (Tom) Yue; m. Virginia Chin-wen Tang, May 21, 1944; children: Mary, Raymond Yuan, John, Ling Tsao, David, Nancy Chang. BS, Chao-tung U., 1942; MS, Ill. Inst. Tech., 1950; PhD, Purdue U., 1956. Assoc. engr. Taiwan Aluminum Co., 1942-47; instr. Purdue U., 1952-56; research engr. Dow Chem. Co., Midland, Mich., 1956-62; sr. mem. Lockheed, Palo Alto Calif., 1962-69; from prof. engring. and applied sci. to cons. UCLA, LA, 1969—. Hon. prof. Xian Jiao-tong U., China, 1980. Sec.-gen. Chinese Culture Assn. U.S., 1967; bd. dirs. Chinese scholar to U.S. Fellow: AIAA (assoc.); mem.: AIME, Materials Rsch. Soc., Am. Soc. Metals, Sigma Xi, Phi Tau Phi (pres. 1978—82), Tau Beta Pia, Sigma Pi Sigma. Personal E-Mail: asyue@yahoo.com.

**YUE, MENG,** electrical engineer; PhD, Mich. State U., East Lansing, 2002. Elec. engr. Brookhaven Nat. Lab., Upton, NY, 2004.

**YUE, WUSI,** computer engineer, researcher; arrived in US, 1999; s. Xianjin Yue and Congying Hu; m. Yuhong Zhao, May 1993. BS in Engring, Huazhong U. Sci. and Tech., Wuhan, Hubei Province, People's Republic of China, 1988; PhD, U. Iowa, Iowa City, 2003. Asst. rsch. engr. Beijing Inst. of Applied Physics and Computational Math., 1992—98; postdoctoral fellow Johns Hopkins U., Balt., 2003—. Mem.: ASME, APS. Achievements include development of Computational Method For Simulating Turbulent Free Surface Flows; Numerical Model For Plant Canopy To Study Structures Of Turbulence Within And Above Canopies. Office: Johns Hopkins Univ 313 Ames Hall 3400 N Charles St Baltimore MD 21218 Office Phone: 410-516-6042. Personal E-Mail: wusiyue@gmail.com.

**YUECHIMING, ROGER YUE YUEN SHING,** mathematics professor; b. Mauritius, Feb. 25, 1937; s. James and Marie Yuechiming; m. Renée Bethery, Nov. 9, 1963; children: Françoise, Marianne, Isabelle. BSc with 1st class honours, U. Manchester, Eng., 1964, PhD, 1967. Asst. U. Strasbourg, France, 1967-69; lectr. math. U. Paris VII, 1970—. Participant math. confs. and seminars in numerous countries; referee various math. jours. Contbr. over 100 articles to profl. jours. Mem. French Math. Soc., Am. Math. Soc., London Math. Soc., Belgian Math. Soc., Japan Math. Soc. Achievements include introduction of concept of p-injective modules and the more generalized notion of YJ-injectivity, new approaches in ring and module theory leading to a better understanding of von Neumann regular rings, V-rings, self-injective rings and generalizations. Home: 38 rue du Surmelin 75020 Paris France Office: U Paris VII Unité Mixte de Rsch 9994 CNRS 2 Pl Jussieu 75251 Paris France

**YUEN, BENSON BOLDEN,** air transportation executive, consultant, software executive; b. Hong Kong, Nov. 20, 1960; arrived in US, 1968; s. Eugene Howard and Janet Yuen. BSBA in Fin. summa cum laude, U. Cen. Fla., 1983. Mgr. market planning and automation Fla. Express, Inc., Orlando, 1983-85, dir. pricing, 1986-87; dir. customer svc. Seabrook Mktg., Inc., Houston, 1988-91, v.p. customer svc., 1992-94; v.p. market devel. svcs. PROS Strategic Solutions, Inc., Houston, 1994-96, sr. v.p. mktg. and consulting svcs., 1996-99; sr. v.p. PROS Revenue Mgmt., Inc., Houston, 2000, pres. travel and transp., 2000—. Cons. airline revenue mgmt., mktg. automation, bus. mgmt., sys. devel. and bus. process engring. to more than 100 transp. cos. worldwide; pres. travel and transp. divsn. PROS Revenue Mgmt. Inc., 2000—. Designer (software) Passenger Revenue Forecast and Optimization System, 1989, Group Revenue Optimization and Management System Version 3, 1990-94, Version 4, 1995—, Holiday Mgmt. Module, Network Pricing Analysis Sys., Hub Complex Optimization; mem. editl. bd. Jour. Revenue and Pricing Mgmt.; contbr. articles to profl. jours. Avocations: travel, music. Office: PROS Revenue Mgmt Inc 3100 Main St Ste 900 Houston TX 77002-9312 Office Phone: 713-335-5202.

**YUFEROV, VADIM,** research scientist; b. Ivanovo city, Russia, Jan. 9, 1938; s. Petr Yuferov and Anna Yuferova; m. Svetlana Shteynberg, Sept. 7, 1939; children: Anna Tolstikova, Anastasia Yuferova. DSc in Biology, Russian Acad. of Med. Sci., Moscow, 1992. Rsch. fellow Ivanovsky Inst. of Virology, Moscow, 1968—92; WHO fellow Nat. Inst. for Med. Rsch., London, 1972—73; guest rsch. fellow Karolinska Inst., Stockholm, 1992; sr. rsch. assoc. Rockefeller U. N.Y.C., 1993—. Author: (research) Pharmacogenetics; author (research) Synapse; author: (research) Addiction Biology. Recipient award, State Coun. of Ministries, Moscow, 1986. Mem.: Soc. for Neurosci. Achievements include development of Technology for production of reverse transcriptase in commercial scale. Home: 2942 W 5th St Apt 7L Brooklyn NY 11224 Office: Rockefeller Univ 1230 York Ave New York NY 10021 Office Phone: 212-327-8234. Business E-Mail: yuferov@rracefeller.edu.

**YUILL, BARBARA KREBS,** lawyer; b. Tucson, Jan. 12, 1954; d. Gordon Earl and Marianne C. Whitley; m. William A. Yuill, Aug. 3, 1985; children: Sean Elliott, Brendon Charles. BS Metall. Engring., U. Ariz., Tucson, 1976, MS Metall., 1981; PhD Chem. Engring., U. Okla., Norman, 1995; JD cum laude, Oklahoma City Coll., 2002. Bar: Okla. 2002, U.S. Patent and Trademark Office Registration. Engr. rsch. ARCO, Calif. and Ariz.; sr. engr. TechRad, Oklahoma City; sr. staff engr. Kerr-McGee, Oklahoma City; adj. prof. physics U. Ctrl. Okla., Edmond; tchr. physics Putnam City W; assoc. McAfee & Taft, Oklahoma City; counsel Resides & Resides, PLLC, Oklahoma City. Staff editor: Oklahoma City U. Law Rev. Mem.: ABA, Oklahoma County Bar Assn., Oklahoma City Traditional Music Assn. Methodist. Achievements include patents for inventions. Avocations: guitar, hammered dulcimer, china painting. Home: 7021 NW 222 Edmond OK 73003 Office: Resides & Resides PLLC 114 NW 6th St Ste 203 Oklahoma City OK 73102

**YUKNIS, CHRISTINA MARIE,** special education educator; MS, Gallaudet U., 2002. Auditory tchr. Montgomery County Pub. Schs., Rockville, Md., 2002—. Mem.: NEA (Md. rep.), Coun. for Exceptional Children. Personal E-mail: clougen@yahoo.com.

**YUKSEL, MURAT,** computer scientist, researcher; arrived in U.S., 1998; s. Ali and Zeynep Yuksel; m. Bahar Sumbul; children: Abdullah Yusuf, Meryem. BS, Ege U., 1996; MS, Rensselaer Poly. Inst., 1999, PhD, 2002. Instr., sys. adminstr. Internat. Turkmen Turkish U., Ashgabat, Turkmenistan, 1996—98; grad. tchg. and rsch. asst. Rensselaer Poly. Inst., Troy, NY, 1999—2002, postdoctoral rsch. assoc., 2002—. Sr. rsch. engr. Omega Advanced Solutions, Inc., Troy, 2002—. Contbr. articles to profl. jours. Recipient Achievement award, Sun Microsystems Labs, Burlington, MA, 2001; scholar, Turkish Govt., 1998. Mem.: IEEE (nominated Best Paper award 2003, grantee 2002), IEEE Computer Soc., Sigma Xi. Moslem. Achievements include patents pending for calculation of layered routes in a distributed manner; method of optimizing network capacity and fault tolerance in deadlock-free routing; efficient system and method of node and link insertion for deadlock-free routing on arbitrary topologies. Office Phone: 518-276-6823.

**YULE, CAROLL JANE,** real estate broker; b. Owatonna, Minn., Feb. 19, 1948; d. Leland R and Jean L Heiden; m. Dennis F Yule, June 6, 1969; 1 child, Tara K. Attended, Macalester Coll., 1966—68, U. Minn., 1968—69. Broker Calif., 1996. Owner All-U-Med, Temple, Tex., 1994—96; broker owner Shear Realty, Apple Valley, Calif., 1996—. Dir. Victor Valley Assn. of Realtors, Victorville, Calif., 2004—, Desert Cmty. Bank. Contbr. monthly column. Program com. Rotary Internat., Victorville, Calif., 2000—05; pres. Victorville C. of C., 2003—04; chmn. for ann. fundraiser Victor Valley Coll. Found., 2000—05; mem. chmn. Victor Valley Bd. of Realtors, 2004—05. Recipient Realtor of the Yr., Victor Valley Assn. of Realtors, 2003, Dir. of the Yr., Victorville C. of C., 2000—01, 2002—03. Avocations: golf, book club. Home: 13253 Country Club Dr Spring Valley Lake CA 92395 Office: Shear Realty 18564 Highway 18 Ste 205 Apple Valley CA 92307 Office Phone: 760-243-3803. Home Fax: 760-243-3804; Office Fax: 760-243-3804. Personal E-Mail: cyule@mscomm.com.

**YULE, JOE See ROONEY, MICKEY**

**YULISH, CHARLES BARRY,** retired public relations executive; b. Cleve., Oct. 24, 1936; s. Isadore and Shirley Yulish; m. Barbara Pearlman, Aug. 22, 1973 (div. 1995); 1 child, Alexi Jules-Nicholas; m. Cynthia Brown Fleek, Oct. 28, 1995. AA in Govt., U. Fla., 1957; BS in Polit. Sci., Kent State U., 1959; MPA, Maxwell Sch., Syracuse U., 1963; postgrad., NYU, 1961-63, New Sch. Social Rsch., 1963-64. Spl. projects officer U.S. AEC, Washington and N.Y.C., 1961-63; pub. affairs mgr. Atomic Indsl. Forum, N.Y.C., 1963-66; pres., chief exec. officer Charles Yulish Assocs., Inc., N.Y.C., 1966-83; exec. v.p. Wesley, Brown & Bartle Inc., N.Y.C., 1983-87; vice chmn., pres. Holt, Ross & Yulish, Edison, NJ, 1988-92; exec. v.p., mng. dir. E. Bruce Harrison Co., Washington, 1993-95; v.p. corp. comm. USEC Inc., Bethesda, Md., 1995—2005; ret., 2005. Writer, dir. (film) Energy: We Have the Choices, 1978 (Golden Eagle award); editor: Hard vs. Soft Energy Paths, 1980; author over 60 articles on classical music. Founder, bd. dirs. Serge Koussevitsky Archives Soc., N.Y.C., 1977; bd. dirs. Imperial Russia Hist. Soc., 1986, U.K. and U.S. Friends of Benjamin Franklin. Maxwell fellow Syracuse U., 1960. Mem. Internat. Assn. Pub. Participation Practitioners, Soc. Profl. Mgmt. Cons. (cert.). Home: 1438 Q St NW Washington DC 20009-3808

**YULMETYEV, RENAT MUZIPOVICH,** physicist, educator; b. Kazan, Tatarstan, USSR, Dec. 14, 1940; s. Muzip Garipovich and Zainab Khairullovna (Davletshina) Yulmetyev; m. Dinara Gabidullovna Bulgakova, Oct. 30, 1965; 1 child, Timur. MS, Kazan State U., 1962, PhD, 1967; D in Physics, Ukranian Inst. Physics, Kyiv, 1981. Theoretical physicist. Sr. lectr. Kazan State Pedagog. Inst., 1965-70; assoc. prof. Kazan State Pedagog. U., 1970-83, prof., 1983—, dean phys.-math. faculty, 1971-72, 78-86, mem. faculty, 1978—, head chair theoretical physics, physicist 1984—94, leading scientific collaborator, dept. physics, 1994—. Soros prof., 1994—. Author: An Introduction to Statistical Physics of Liquids, 1972; contbr. articles to internat. profl. jours. Named Honored Scientist, Tatarstan Republic and Russian Fedn., 1990, Russian Fedn., 1990, Hon. Man of Higher Prof. Edn., 2001—; grantee, Internat. Soros Sci. Edn. Programme Fund, 1993—, Russian Fund Fundamental Rsch., 1996—94, 2002—, Russian Humanitarian Sci. Found., 1997—2005, DAAD, 1999—2000, NOIKR Found. Tatarstan Republic, 2000—, Ministry Higher Edn. and Sci., 2005; Competitive Ctr. Fundamental Rsch. grantee, St. Petersburg U., 1992—98. Mem.: NY Acad. Scis., Acad. Nature Russian Fedn. (academician). Avocations: painting, classical music, travel, literature. Office: Kazan State Pedagog U Mezhlauk St 1 420021 Kazan Russia Fax: 7 8432 92 42 69. Business E-Mail: rmy@theory.kazan-spu.ru.

**YUN, DANIEL DUWHAN,** physician, foundation administrator; b. Chinjoo, Korea, Jan. 20, 1933; came to U.S., 1959; naturalized, 1972; s. Kapryong and Woo Im Yun; m. Rebecca Sungja Choi, Apr. 13, 1959; children: Samuel, Lois, Caroline, Judith. BS Coll. Sci. and Engring., Yon-Sei U., 1954, MD, 1958; student, U. Pa., 1963; PhD, Barrington U., 1995. Intern Quincy (Mass.) City Hosp., 1960; resident and fellow Presbyn.-U. Pa. Med. Ctr., Phila., 1961-65; med. dir. Paddon Meml. Hosp., Newfoundland, Labrador, Can., 1965-66; dir. spl. care unit Elkins Park (Pa.) Hosp., 1967-79; founder, pres. Philip Jaisohn Meml. Found., Inc., Elkins Park, Pa., 1975-85, also med. dir., trustee. Clin. prof. medicine U. Xochicalco, 1978; faculty Allegheny U. Health Scis., Phila.; bd. dirs. Elkins Park Hosp. Mem. Asian Studies Found., U.S. Senatorial Bus. Adv. Bd.; mem. home safety com. Mayor's Commn. on Svcs. to Aging, Phila.; trustee United Way of Southeastern Pa., co-founder Rep. Presdl. Task Force; mem. U.S. Congl. Adv. Bd.; cons. on Korean affairs Phila. City Coun.; founder, bd. dirs., adv. coun. Peaceful Unification Policy of Korea; trustee Albright Coll., Reading, Pa., 1997—; chmn. bd. Korean-Am. Christian Broadcasting of Phila.; mem. Phila. Korean-Am. Svc. Coord. Com.; commr. Pa. Human Rels. Commn., 1991—; founder, pres. Korean Heritage Found., 1991—; amb. City of Phila., 1991. Recipient Phila. award Human Rights award, 1981, Disting. Cmty. Svc. award Phila. Dist. Atty., 1981, medal of Merit Presdl. Task Force, 1981, Medal of Nat. Order, Republic of Korea, 1984, Nat. Dong Baek medal Republic of Korea, 1987, award City Coun. Phila., 1987, Gov.'s Pa. Heritage awards, 1990, commendation award Pa. Senate, 1991, award Asian Law Ctr., 1991, Rep. Senatorial Medal of Freedom, 1994; named to Legion of Honor, The Chapel of Four Chaplains; named Amb. City of Phila., 1991. Mem. AMA, Am. Soc. Internal Medicine, Am. Coll. Cardiology, Am. Heart Assn. (mem. coun. on clin. cardiology), Pa. Med. Soc., Phila. County Med. Soc., Phila. Korean Soc. Health, Am. Coll. Internat. Physicians, World Med. Assn., Fedn. State Med. Bds., Am. Law Enforcement Officers' Assn., Am. Fedn. Police, Internat. Culture Soc. Korea (hon.), Am. Soc. Contemporary Medicine and Surgery. Home: 3903 Somers Dr Huntingdon Valley PA 19006-1913 Office: 60 Township Line Rd Elkins Park PA 19027-2220

**YUN, JAMES KYOON,** electrical engineer; b. Andong, South Korea, Oct. 26, 1965; came to U.S., 1973; s. Joh Kyong and Karen Suk (Kim) Y. BSEE, U. Ill., 1987, MSEE, 1989. System engr. GE Co., Syracuse, NY, 1989-91, software engr., 1991-93, Martin Marietta Corp., Syracuse, 1993-95; sr. mem. engring. staff Lockheed Martin Corp., Moorestown, NJ, 1995—. Cons. Silver Knight Co., Liverpool, N.Y., 1994—. Inventor seal indicator. Mem. IEEE, Assn. for Computing Machinery, Tau Beta Pi, Eta Kappa Nu.

**YUN, LIANG,** marine engineer, educator; b. Shanghai, July 15, 1932; s. KunLin and Yun Ya (Sun) Y.; m. Li-Hui Qiu, Jan. 1, 1962; children: Gang, Xiao. Grad., Dalian U. Tech., China, 1953. Asst. prof. Mil. Engring. Acad. China, Harbin, 1953-56, lectr., 1956-66, Harbin Shipbldg. Engring. Inst., 1966-73; dir. air cushion vehicle divsn. Marine Design & Rsch. Inst. China, Shanghai, 1973-85, dep. chief engr., prof., sr. engr., cons., 1980—; tech. dir. China Air Cushion Tech. Corp., Shanghai, 1984-86, Flying Dragon Sci. and Tech. Ltd., Hong Kong, 2000—, Prof. Harbin Shipbldg. Engring. U., 1988—, Wu Han Transport Engring. U., China, 1990—; dir. Advanced Marine Vessel, Internat. Advanced Vehicles Assocs., Inc. Author: Theory and Design of Air Cushion Vehicle (in Chinese), 1990, 2000, (in English), 1993, 98. Recipient 2nd class nat. award nat. Def. Com. China, Beijing, 1980, 2nd class nat. award China State Shipbldg. Corp., Beijing, 1992, 1st class nat. award Kwang-Hua Sci. & Tech. Found., Beijing, 1994., 1st class nat. award China State Shipbuilding Corp., 2002. Fellow Royal Instn. Naval Architects; mem. China Soc. Naval Architects and Marine Engrs. (standing dir. 1993-97, chmn. high performance vehicle subcom. 1984—), vice chmn. cons. ship design com. 1992-2002, cons. ship design com. 2002—). Home: 439 Huan Long R Bldg 7 Apt 1401 Shanghai 200127 China Office: Marine Design & Rsch Inst 1688 Xi Zang Nan Rd 200011 Shanghai China Office Phone: 0086-21-62809900-807. Personal E-mail: liangyunb@yahoo.com.

**YUNDT, BETTY BRANDENBURG,** elementary school educator; b. Corydon, Ind., Sept. 23, 1957; d. Melvin Marion and Lena Beatrice (Blake) Brandenburg; m. Randall Gene Yundt, Apr. 2, 1978; 1 child, Cameron Blake. BS, Ind. U. SE, New Albany, 1981, MS with highest distinction, 1989. Cert. elem. tchr. Rank I, Ind., Ky. Tchr. pre-kindergarten Keneseth Israel Sch., Louisville; tchr. Dept. Def. Dependent Sch., Goppingen, Fed. Republic Germany; curriculum coord. Iroquois and West End Child Devel. Ctr., Louisville; elem. tchr. Ft. Knox (Ky.) Sch. Dist. KERA Fellows II cohort. Named Tchr. of Yr., Ft. Knox, Ky., 2003; named to, USA Today All Star Tchr. Team, 2003; recipient Campbellsville Coll. Excellence in Edn. award, 2003. Mem. NEA, ASCD, Internat. Reading Assn., Ind. Coun. Tchrs. Math., Louisville Assn. for Children Under Six, Kappa Delta Pi, Phi Lambda Theta, Alpha Chi. Home: 40 Springdale Rd Guston KY 40142-7151 Office Phone: 502-624-7835. Business E-Mail: betty.yundt@am.dodea.edu. E-mail: teechyundt@bbtel.com.

**YUNG, WAI KWAN ALFRED,** neurology and neuro-oncology educator; b. Hong Kong; BS, U. Minn., 1971; MD, U. Chgo., 1975. Intern in neurology U. Calif., San Diego, 1975—76; asst. resident neurology UCSD, 1976—78, chief resident neurology, 1978, MSKCC, 1978—79, fellow neurology, 1978—81; clin. fellow neurology NY Hosp., 1979—81; prof. neuorology Dept. Neurology. U. Tex. Med. Sch., Houston, 1992—; prof. of tumor biology dept. tumor biology M.D. Anderson Cancer Ctr., Houston, 1992—; prof. neurology dept. of neuro-oncology, 1992—, chmn. dept. neuro-oncology, 1999—. Florence M. Thomas prof. of cancer rsch. M.D. Anderson Cancer Ctr., Houston, 1996-2002, chmn. Margaret and Ben Love chair in clin. cancer care, 2002—. Office: MD Anderson Cancer Ctr Box 431 1515 Holcombe Blvd Houston TX 77030-4009 Office Phone: 713-794-1285.

**YUNIS, JORGE JOSE,** anatomy, pathology, and microbiology educator; b. Sincelejo, Colombia, Oct. 5, 1933; s. José and Victoria (Turbay) Yunis. MD, Complutense U., Madrid, 1956, PhD, 1957; D (hon.), UCLA, 1997. Gen. practice medicine, Barranquilla, Colombia, 1957-59; resident in clin. pathology U. Minn., Mpls., 1959-62, resident in anat. pathology, 1962-64, mem. faculty, 1965-89, prof., 1969-89, dir. grad. studies of lab. medicine, 1969-74, dir. grad. studies of pathology, 1972-74, chmn. human genetics com. for health scis., 1972-77; mem. faculty Hahnemann U., Phila., 1989-92, prof. dept. neoplastic diseases, 1989-92, vis. prof., assoc. dir. Inst. for Cancer and Blood Diseases, 1989-92, dir. Human Genetics and Molecular Biology Div., 1989-92, prof. dept. pathology, 1991-92; prof. depts. anatomy, pathology, microbiology & immunology Thomas Jefferson U. Med. Coll., Phila., 1993—; dir. cancer biol., dept. anatomy, pathology, cell biology Thomas Jefferson U. Med. Coll., Phila., 1993—. Vis. prof. numerous univs. Author: Human Chromosome Method, 1965, 1975, Biochemical Methods in Red Cell Genetics, 1969, Molecular Pathology, 1975, New Chromosomal Syndromes, 1977, Molecular Structure Human Chromosomes, 1995, Esencia Humana, 1995, Así es la Vida, 1997, The Myth of God, 2002; contbr. more than 250 articles to profl. jours. Named Clin. Prof. of Yr. Harvard Med. Sch., 1987; honored by Colombian Parliament, Bogota, 1986, 93, Colombian Med. Schs. Assn., 1993. Mem. Leukemia Soc. Am. (trustee 1983-88), Colombian Acad. Medicine. Avocations: poetry, literature, photography. Office Phone: 305-858-7684. Personal E-mail: jorgeyunis@aol.com.

**YURACKO, KIMBERLY,** law educator; BA with distinction, Stanford U., 1991, PhD in Polit. Sci., 1997, JD with distinction, 1998. Lectr. polit. sci. U. Calif., Irvine, 1999; vis. asst. prof. law Northwestern U. Sch. Law, Chgo., 2001—02, asst. prof., 2002—04, prof. law, 2005—. Law clk. to Hon. Gary L. Taylor US Dist. Ct. (ctrl. dist.) Calif., 1998—99; to Hon. Stanley Marcus US Ct. Appeals (11th cir.), 1999—2000; assoc. Paul, Hastings, Janofsky & Walker, LA, 2001. Author: Perfectionism and Contemporary Feminist Values, 2003; contbr. articles to profl. jours. Office: Northwestern U Sch Law 357 E Chicago Ave Chicago IL 60611 Office Phone: 312-503-3466. E-mail: k-yuracko@law.northwestern.edu.

**YURCHENCO, HENRIETTA WEISS,** musicologist, writer; b. New Haven, Mar. 22, 1916; d. Edward and Rebecca (Bernblum) Weiss; m. Basil Yurchenco, June 1936 (div. 1955); 1 child, Peter; m. Irving Levine, 1965 (div. 1979). Student, Yale U., 1935-36; student piano scholarship, Mannes Coll. Music, 1936-38. Radio prodr. Sta. WNYC, Sta. WBAI, others, 1939-69; writer, critic, tchr., folk music editor Am. Record Guide and Musical Am., 1959-70; radio prodr. Air Am., 2006. Prof. music CCNY, 1962—86, Bklyn. Coll., 1966—69, New Sch. Social Rsch., 1961—68; co-dir. project study women in music Grad. Ctr. CUNY; mem. exec. com. Panamerican Musical Rsch. Arts. Author: A Fiesta of Folk Songs from Spain and Latin America, 1967, A Mighty Hard Road: A Biography of Woody Guthrie, 1970, Hablamos! Puerto Ricans Speak, 1971, Around the World in 80 Years: A Memoir, 2003, in Spanish, 2004; contbr. articles to profl. jours.; field recs. issued by Libr. Congress, Folkways, Nonesuch, Folkways/Smithsonian, Global Village, Rounder Records, collections in Libr. Congress, Discoteca Hebrew U., Jerusalem, Arias Montana Inst., Madrid, Inst. Nacional Indigenista, Mexico City, Am. Sephardic Found., Instituto Cervantes (Spanish Cultural Inst.). Recipient award, Nat. Inst. Fine Arts, Mex., 2003; grants-in-aid, Am. Philos. Soc., 1954, 1956, 1957, 1965, 1967, 1989, CUNY Faculty Rsch. Fund, 1970, 1983, 1987, NEH grantee, 1964. Mem.: Am. Musicologists Soc., Internat. Assn. Study Popular Music, Soc. Am. Music, Soc. Asian Music, Soc. Ethnomusicology, Internat. Coun. Traditional Music. Avocations (no women's studies). Home: 360 W 22d St New York NY 10011-2600 Office: 139th St And Convent Ave New York NY 10031 Personal E-mail: hyurchenco@verizon.net.

**YURCHUCK, ROGER ALEXANDER,** retired lawyer; b. Amityville, NY, June 9, 1938; s. Alexander and Ella Marie (Munley) Y.; m. Sally Read, Apr. 14, 1961 (div. 1972); children: Scott, Lauren; m. Susan Holland, June 1, 1985 (div. 2005). AB cum laude, Northwestern U., 1959; LLB, Harvard U., 1962. Bar: Ohio 1962. Assoc. Vorys, Sater Seymour and Pease, Columbus, Ohio, 1962-68, ptnr., 1969—71, 1973—2002, ptnr. Cin. office, 1984—2002; v.p., gen. counsel Fed. Home Loan Mortgage Corp., Washington, 1971-73. Vice chmn., bd. dirs. Securities Investors Protection Corp., Washington, 1982-88.

Del. Rep. Nat. Conv., 1980, 84. Mem. Ohio Bar Assn., Queen City Club (Cin.), Phi Beta Kappa. Republican. Episcopalian. Office Phone: 202-467-8805. Business E-Mail: rayurchuck@vssp.com.

**YURECHKO, JOHN JOSEPH,** federal agency administrator, director; b. Hazleton, Pa., Apr. 12, 1948; s. Andrew Joseph and Helen Theresa Yurechko; m. Jane Teresa Haltmaier, Sept. 25, 1982; children: Christine, Alice, Janie. BA in History, Wesleyan U., Middletown, Conn., 1970; MA, U. Calif., Berkeley, 1973, PhD in History, 1980. Intelligence analyst Def. Intelligence Agy. (DIA), Washington, 1981—88, senior analyst, command, control, comm. program mgr., 1988—96, spl. planning office chief, 1994—96, info. warfare office chief, 1996—98, def. intelligence sr. level officer (DISL), def. intelligence officer (DIO), 1998—2004; nat. counterintelligence officer for sci. and tech, dir. strategy and policy Nat. Counterintelligence Exec. (NCIX), Washington, 2004; dir. analysis and collection, sr. exec. svc. NCIX, 2005. Adj. prof. nat. security studies program Georgetown U., Washington, 1986—92. Author, editor: poetry jour. Gallery Works, 1972—80; contbr. articles to jours. and books in field. Recipient Nat. Intelligence Achievement award, Dir. Central Intelligence, Washington, 1992. Avocations: poetry, martial arts, swimming, weightlifting.

**YURIKO, (YURIKO KIKUCHI),** dancer, choreographer; b. San Jose, Calif., 1920; m. Charles Kikuchi, 1946. Student, UCLA, Martha Graham Sch. Mem. Martha Graham Dance Co., 1944-67; dance tchr. N.Y.C., 1945—; tchr., founder Yuriko Dance Co., 1960—78; assoc. artistic dir. Martha Graham Dance Co., 1991—. Artistic dir. dance company Time and Talents Club, Bombay, 1974; organizer Modern Dance Sch., Ctr. Internat. de la Danse, Paris, 1975; resident guest tchr., modern dance cons. Ballet Nacional de Cuba, 1976; ind. modern dance choreographer Warsaw Weiklki Classic Ballet Co., 1977, 78, Australian Dance Theater's Concert at Adelaide Festival of the Arts, 1978; guest tchr., choreographer Akar Modern Dance Co., Switzerland, 1981; guest tchr. Nat. U. Costa Rica, Nat. Ballet of Mexico, Martha Graham Sch. Contemporary Dance; guest artist and tchr. various cities including London, Paris, Mexico City, Zurich, Tokyo and Cologne, Germany; founder & dir. The Arigato Project; founder Martha Graham Ensemble, 1983. Dancer premiere prodns. Appalachian Spring, Cave of the Heart, Dark Meadow, Embattled Garden, Clytemnestra; appeared on Broadway as Eliza in The King and I, 1951; performed feature role The Small House of Uncle Thomas, Sandhog, Flower Drug Song; dir., re-staged Broadway prodn. of The King and I, 1977, London prodn., 1979, dir. Toyko prodn., 1978; dir. Madame Butterfly. Recipient Bessie award NY Dance and Performance, 1991; Tribute NY/Japan Soc., 2004; Honor Saeko Ichinohe Dance Co. 2005; grantee NY State Arts Coun., Nat. Endowment for the Arts; Guggenheim fellow for choreography, 1968; commissioned to choreograph and perform Judith Symphony.

**YURIST, SVETLAN JOSEPH,** mechanical engineer; b. Kharkov, USSR, Nov. 20, 1931; came to U.S., 1979, naturalized, 1985; s. Joseph A. and Rosalia S. (Zoilman) Y.; m. Emma Lea Erlikh, Oct. 11, 1960; 1 child, Eugene. MSME with honors, Poly, Inst. Odessa, USSR, 1954. Engr., designer Welding Equipment Plant, Novaya Utka, USSR, 1954-56; sr. tech. engr. Heavy Duty Automotive Crane Plant, Odessa, USSR, 1956-60, asst. chief metallurgist, 1971-78; supr. rsch. lab. Inst. Spl. Methods in Foundry Industry, Odessa, 1960-66, project engr. sci. rsch., 1966-70; engr. designer Teledyne Cast Product, Pomona, Calif., 1979-81; sr. mech. engr. Walt Elliot Disney Enterprises, Glendale, Calif., 1981-83; foundry liaison engr. Pacific Pumps divsn. Dresser Industries, Inc., Huntington Park, Calif., 1984-86; casting engr. Superior Industries Internat. Inc., Van Nuys, Calif., 1986-89; mech. engr. TAMCO Steel, Ramcho Cucamonga, Calif., 1989-96. Contbr. articles to profl. jours. Recipient award for design of automatic lines for casting electric motor parts USSR Ministry Machine Bldg. and Handtools Mfr., 1966, for equipment for permanent mold casting All Union Exhbn. of Nat. Econ. Achievements, 1966-70. Achievements include patents for permanent mold casting. Home: 1718 Downs St Oceanside CA 92054-6191 Personal E-mail: siyurist@netzero.com.

**YUROW, MICHAEL JAY,** lawyer; b. Washington, July 11, 1954; s. John Jesse and Bette Hilary (Troshinsky) Y.; m. Rita B. Abraham, Jan. 11, 1987; children: Mathew, Samuel, Sarah Elizabeth. BA, U. Calif., Santa Cruz, 1976; M in Regional Planning, Cornell U., 1980; JD, Tulane U., 1985. Bar: Va. 1986, U.S. Ct. Appeals (4th cir.) 1986, D.C. 1993. Ptnr., Real Estate practice Venable LLP, Vienna, Va., 1997—, ptnr. in charge, No. Va. Office, 2004—. Cornell U. fellow, 1978-80, HUD fellow, 1978-80. Mem. ABA, Va. Bar Assn., D.C. Bar Assn. Office: Venable LLP Suite 300 8010 Towers Crescent Dr Vienna VA 22182 Office Phone: 703-760-1640. Office Fax: 703-821-8949. Business E-Mail: mjyurow@venable.com.

**YURT, ROGER WILLIAM,** surgeon, educator; b. Louisville, June 8, 1945; s. Albert William and Mary Louise (McGrath) Y.; m. Joan A. Terry, Sept. 3, 1971; children: Jennifer, Daniel, Gregory. BS in Biology, Loyola U., New Orleans, 1967; MS, U. Miami, 1972. Diplomate Nat. Bd. Med. Examiners. Intern. Parkland Meml. Hosp.-Southwestern Med. Sch., U. Tex., Dallas, 1972-73, resident, 1973-74; postdoctoral trainee NIH, 1975-77; resident, chief resident N.Y. Hosp.-Cornell Med. Ctr., N.Y.C., 1977-79, acting dir. Burn Ctr., dir. rsch., 1982-83, dir. Trauma Ctr., 1992-99, prof. surgery, 1982-92, 92—, The Johnson & Johnson disting. prof. surgery, 1995—; vice chmn. dept. surgery Cornell U. Med. Coll., N.Y.C., 1987—, acting chmn., 1991-93, dir. Burn Ctr., 1995—. Acting surgeon-in-chief The N.Y. Hosp., 1991-93; clin. asst. prof. surgery Uniformed Svcs. U. Health Sci., Bethesda, Md., 1980-82; clin. assoc. prof. gen. surgery Health Sci. Ctr., U. Tex., San Antonio, 1981-82; chmn. burn com., Regional Emer. Med. Svcs. N.Y., 1982-84, mem. trauma ctr. adv. com., 1984-89, chmn., 1995-98, mem. burn ctr. adv. com., chmn., 1996-2000, mem. sp. ref. ctr. com., 1996-98, N.Y. Bklyn. ACS Com. Trauma, 1994-96; dir. Mulhearn Rsch.Lab., N.Y.C., 1982—. Editor: Infections in Surgery, 1981-88; contbr. articles to med. jours. Maj. M.C., U.S. Army, 1979-82. Recipient Hewitt award, Royal Soc. medicine, 2003, Irma Hirschl Trust Career Scientist award, 1984-88; grantee United Health Found., 1968-69, NIH, 1984-87; fellow Sch. Medicine, U. Miami, summer, 1969-71, USPHS, 1973-75, postdoctoral fellow medicine Robert B. Brigham Hosp.-Harvard U. Med. Sch., Boston, 1974-77. Mem. Am. Surg. Infection Soc. (charter, chmn. membership com., sec. 1987-90, pres. 1991-92), Am. Surg. Assn., Assn. Acad. Surgery, Soc. U. Surgeons, Internat. Surg. Soc., Am. Assn. Surgery Trauma, Alpha Omega Alpha, Omicron Delta Kappa. Roman Catholic. Office: NY Hosp Cornell Med Ctr Dir The Burn Ctr 525 E 68th St Rm L-706 New York NY 10021-4885

**YUSPA, STUART HOWARD,** oncologist; b. Balt., July 19, 1941; BS, Johns Hopkins U., 1962; MD, U. Md., 1966. Diplomate Am. Bd. Internal Medicine. Intern Hosp. of U. Pa., Phila., 1966-67, resident in internal medicine, 1970-72; rsch. assoc. Nat. Cancer Inst., Bethesda, Md., 1967-70, sr. investigator, 1972—, chief Lab. Cellular Carcinogenesis and Tumor Promotion, 1981—. Assoc. editor Cancer Rsch., 1983—96; editor-in-chief Molecular Carcinogenesis, 1987—92. Recipient Lila Gruber Cancer Rsch. award, Am. Acad. Dermatology, 1989, Disting. Svc. Medal, USPHS. Fellow AAAS; mem. Am. Assn. Cancer Rsch. (G.H.A. Clowes Meml. Award 1993), Am. Soc. Cell Biology, Soc. Investigative Dermatology, USPHS Commd. Officers Assn. Achievements include research in determining mechanisms whereby chemicals initiate or promote malignant transformation of epithelial cells. Office: Lab Cellular Carcinogenesis and Tumor Promotion Ctr Cancer Rsch Bldg 37 Rm 4068A1 37 Convent Dr Bethesda MD 20892 Office Phone: 301-496-2162. Office Fax: 301-496-8709. E-mail: sy12j@nih.gov.

**YUSPEH, ALAN RALPH,** lawyer, health company executive; b. New Orleans, June 13, 1949; s. Michel and Rose Fay (Rabenovitz) Y.; m. Janet Horn, June 8, 1975. BA, Yale U., 1971; MBA, Harvard U., 1973; JD, Georgetown U., 1978. Bar: DC 1978. Mgmt. cons. McKinsey & Co., Washington, 1973-74; adminstrv. asst. legis. asst. Office of U.S. Senator J. Bennett Johnston, Washington, 1974-78; atty. Shaw, Pittman, Potts & Trowbridge, Washington, 1978-79, Ginsburg, Feldman, Weil and Bress, Washington, 1979-82; gen. counsel Com. on Armed Svcs.-U.S. Senate,

Washington, 1982-85; ptnr. Preston, Thorgrimson, Ellis & Holman, Washington, 1985-88, Miller & Chevalier, Washington, 1988-91, Howrey & Simon, Washington, 1991-97; sr. v.p. ethics, compliance and corp. responsibility HCA, Nashville, 1997—. Coord. Def. Industry Initiative on Bus., Ethics and Conduct, 1987-97; pres. Health Care Compliance Assn., 2002. Editor Law and Policy in Internat. Bus. Jour., 1978-79, Nat. Contract Mgmt. Jour., 1988-92; assoc. editor Pub. Contract Law Jour., 1987-91. Chmn. bd. ethics, City of Balt., 1988-96, planning commn., 1996-97; chmn. bd. dirs. Tenn. Repertory Theater, 2002-05; bd. dirs. Balt. Housing Authority, 1996-97, Ethics Officer Assn., 2001-04, YMCA Mid. Tenn. Camp, 2002-, Tenn. Performing Arts Ctr., 2003-, Nashville Pub. Libr. Found., 2005-. 1st lt. USAR, 1971-77. Office: HCA One Park Plaza Nashville TN 37203 Home: 126 Third Ave N Franklin TN 37064 Office Phone: 615-344-1005. Business E-Mail: alan.yuspeh@hcahealthcare.com.

**YUSSUF IZZUDDIM, SHAH GHAFRAULLAH SULTAN,** Sultan of Perak; b. Batu Gajah, Perak, Malaysia, Apr. 19, 1928; s. Sultan Yussuff Izzuddin Shah; m. Tuanku Bainun binti Mohd. Ali, 1955; children: Raja Nazrin, Raja Azureen, Raja Ashman, Raja Eleen, Raja Yong Sofia. Student, Malay Coll., Nottingham U. and Lincoln Inn.; DLitt (hon.), U. Malaya, 1979, U. Sains Malaysia, 1980. Bar: Eng. 1954. Asst. sec. state, Perak, 1954-55; magistrate Kuala Lumpur, 1955-56; session court pres., 1957-59; fed. counsel and Dy pub. prosecutor Perak, 1959; state legal advisor Perak, 1959-62; registrar high ct. Kuala Lumpur, Malaysia, 1962-63; chief registrar Fed. Ct., Kuala Lumpur, 1963-65, high ct. judge, 1965, fed. judge, 1973, chief justice, 1979; Lord Pres., 1982-83; 34th Sultan of Perak, 1984—; named King of Malaysia, 1989-94. Author: The Role of Constitutional Rulers. Co-chancellor U. Sains Malaysia, 1971, chancellor U. Malay, 1986—; chmn. Higher Edn. Adv. Council, 1974; v.p. Olympic Coun., Malayisa. Decorated PMN, 1979, SSM, 1983. Mem. Internat. Hockey Fedn., Malaysian Hockey Fedn. (pres.). Office: Istama Iskandarish 33000 Kuala Kangsar Perak Malaysia

**YUSTER-FREEMAN, LEIGH CAROL,** broadcast executive; b. Trenton, N.J., July 23, 1949; d. Leon Carl and Helen Loretta (Wisniewski) Markiewicz; m. Charles Yuster (div. Apr. 1985); stepchildren: Sarah, Elizabeth, Jared, Alexandra; m. Richard N. Freeman; 1 child, Jessica Lee Freeman. Profl. dancer, 1967—71; editor R.R. Bowker, N.Y.C., 1971—72, from ISBN agy. editl. coord. to dir. prod. devel., 1972—89, dir. product devel., pub. Ulrich's Database, 1989—90, assoc. pub. Bowker Bus. Rsch., A&I Pub. New Providence, NJ, 1990—91, also pub. Ulrich's Database, 1990—91, pub. Broadcasting & Cable Yearbook, 1991—97; mng. dir. Reed Reference Pub., New Providence, 1992—94, v.p. bibliographies, 1994—96, v.p. directories, 1996; v.p. Database Pub. R.R. Bowker, New Providence, 1996—99, sr. mng. dir. prodn., 1999—2000; project mgr. workforce devel. NJN Pub. TV, Trenton, NJ, 2000—. Ptnr. Eagle Bakery, Trenton, NJ, 1991—92. Recipient Climate of Excellence award, Cahners Pub. Co., Newton, Mass., 1987, cert. of Appreciation, Consortium of Univ. Film Ctrs., Kent, Ohio, 1986. Mem.: Actors Equity Assn. Jewish. Avocations: gardening, dance, music. Home: 19 Theodora Dr Hillsborough NJ 08844-4723 E-mail: lfreeman@njn.org.

**YUSUFI, AFIFA,** psychologist; d. Mohammed Nabi and Tabserra Yusufi. Psychology, CUNY, Queens, 2001. Project mgr. WWLR, Rumford, Maine, 2005—. Dir., vol. after sch. program Cmty. Outreach; bd. mem. WAW, Flushing, NY, 2002—05. Conservative. Islam. Avocations: travel, poetry, politics, sightseeing. Personal E-mail: afifa923@aol.com.

**YZAGUIRRE, RAUL HUMBERTO,** civil rights leader; b. San Juan, Tex., July 22, 1939; s. Ruben Antonio and Eva Linda (Morin) Y.; m. Audrey H. Bristow, Jan. 2, 1965; children: Regina Dolores, Raul Humberto, Elisa Almalinda, Roberto Hayse, Rebecca Morin, Benjamin Ruben. Student, U. Md., 1963-64; BS, George Washington U., 1968. Registered med. technologist. Student and community activist, 1963-65; active War on Poverty, 1969-74; founder, exec. dir. Interstate Research Assocs (Hispanic cons. firm), Washington, 1969-73; v.p. Center for Community Change, Washington, 1974; community organizer in S.Tex., 1974; pres. Nat. Council of La Raza, Washington, 1974—2004. Lectr. Harvard U., U. Notre Dame, U. Tex., others.; commr. U.S. Nat. Commn. for UNESCO, 1993—; chmn. bd. dirs. Associated SW Investors, 1976—. Co-chmn. Nat. Urban Coalition, 1975-83; co-chmn. Working Com. on Concerns of Hispanics and Blacks, 1979—, sec. ind. sector, 1983-84; sec., chmn. Forum of Nat. Hispanic Orgns., 1976-79; chmn. adv. com. I.N.S.; former trustee Common Cause; co-founder, chmn. Nat. Neighborhood Coalition, 1977—; immediate past chair Ind. Sector; bd. dirs. Enterprise Found., Nat. Dem. Insts. Served with USAF, 1959-62. Recipient Rockefeller Public Service award, 1979, Common Cause Pub. Service award, 1986; fellow Inst. Politics John F. Kennedy Sch. Govt. Mem. Am. GI Forum, Hispanic Assn. Corp. Responsibility (co-founder, chmn. bd. dirs.). Democrat. Roman Catholic. *The civil rights struggle of the 80's will be the transformation of America to a truly pluralistic society where cultural differences will not only be tolerated, but indeed valued.*

**YZERMAN, STEVE (STEPHEN GREGORY YZERMAN),** professional sports team executive, retired professional hockey player; b. Cranbrook, BC, Can., May 9, 1965; married; 3 children. Center Detroit Red Wings, 1983—2006, captain, 1986—2006, v.p., 2006—. Player NHL All-Star Game, 1984, 1988—93, 1997, 1990, 2000; mem. Team Can., Olympic Games, Nagano, Japan, 1998, Salt Lake City, 2002. Named Sporting News NHL Rookie of Yr. 1984; named to All-Rookie Team, NHL, 1984, First All-Star Team, 2000; recipient Lester B. Pearson award, 1989, Conn Smythe Trophy, 1998, Frank J. Selke Trophy, 2000, Bill Masterton Trophy, 2003. Achievements include being the youngest person ever to play in the NHL All-Star game, 1984; being a member of Stanley Cup Champion Detroit Red Wings, 1997, 1998, 2002; being a member of gold medal Canadian Hockey team, Salt Lake City Olympic Games, 2002; being the longest serving captain in NHL history. Office: Detroit Red Wings Joe Louis Arena 600 Civic Center Dr Detroit MI 48226-4419*

**ZABECKI, DAVID TADEUSZ,** engineer, educator, military historian, military officer; b. Springfield, Mass., Aug. 8, 1947; s. Julian Tadeusz and Virginia Charlotte (Luthgren) Z.; m. Marlies Schweigler, 1991; children: Konrad Josef, Jonathan Tadeusz. BA, Xavier U., 1972, MA, 1973; MS, Fla. Inst. Tech., 1976; PhD in Engring., Calif. Coast U., 1987; diploma, U.S. Army War Coll., 1995; PhD in Mil. Sci., Royal Mil. Coll. Sci., 2004. Patrolman Xavier U. Campus Police, Cin., 1972—74; quality assurance specialist Rock Island (Ill.) Arsenal, 1974—77; quality engr. Deere & Co., Moline, Ill., 1977—84, Zweibruechen, Germany, 1985—93; adj. instr. Fla. Inst. Tech., Fla., 1977—79; adj. lectr. European program City Colls. Chgo., 1986—89; asst. prof. Am. Mil. U., 1993—2003; dep. chief of staff for ops. 7th Army Res. Command, Schwetzingen, Germany, 1997—99, chief of staff, 1998—2000; dep. chief USAR, Washington, 2000—02; comdg. gen. 7th Army Res. Command, Schwetzineen, Germany, 2002—03; dep. chief of staff for mobilization and res. affairs U.S. Army Europe, 2003—; sr. security advisor U.S. Coord. and Monitoring Mission (Roadmap to Peace in the Mid. East), 2003. Comdr. Task Force Normandy-60, U.S. Army Europe, 2004; exec. dir. Europe, Dept. Def. World War II 60th Anniversary Observance Com. 2004—05; comdg. gdn. US So. Europe Task Force Rear Airborne, 2005-06; lectr. in field. Author: Karl Doenitz: A Defense, 1972, Field Artillery in the 1980's, 1983, Steel Wind: Colonel Georg Bruchmueller and The Birth of Modern Artillery, 1994, The German 1918 Offensives: A Case Study in the Operational Level of War, 2006; editor in chief: WWII in Europe: An Ency., 1998, translator, editor: On the German Art of War: Truppenfuhrung, 2001, contbg. editor: Mil. History mag., 1987—99, World War II mag., 1987—99; editor: Vietnam mag., 2000—; series editor: The Art of War, 2000—03; editor: Vietnam: A Reader, 2002; book reviewer: Mil. Rev., Jour. of Royal Arty., —; developer contbn. margin differential concept of quality cost analysis, —. Served to maj. gen. U.S. Army, 1966—69, 1990-97, 2003—, USAR, 1969—. Decorated Combat Infantryman's Badge, Bronze Star, Army Commendation medal, Meritorious Svc. medal with 5 oak leaf clusters, Legion of Merit with 2 oak leaf clusters, Def. Superior Svc. medal, German Army Proficiency badge in gold; Knight Comdr. Order St. John Jerusalem, Knight Sovereign Mil. Order Temple Jerusalem, Knight Comdr. Order of St.

Michael of the Wing (Portugal), Gen. John J. Pershing award U.S. Army Command and Staff Coll., 1988, George Washington Honor medal Freedoms Found., 1988, Wm. Hornaday Dist. Svc. in Conservation award, 1963, Knowlton award Mil. Intelligence Corps Assn. Fellow: The Ermine Soc.; mem.: Soc. 173d Airborne Brigade, Polish Inst. Arts and Scis. in Am., Assn. U.S. Army, N.Y. Acad. Scis., Royal Arty. Assn., Co. Mil. Historians, German Philatelic Socs., Res. Officers Assn., Ancient Order of St. Barbara, U.S. Field Arty. Assn., Am. Soc. Quality Control (cert. quality engr., cert. reliability engr.), VFW, Nat. Eagle Scouts Assn., Army and Navy Club Washington, Nat. Sojourners, York Rite, Scottish Rite, Masons, Alpha Sigma Nu. Address: Guenterstal Strasse 86 79100 Freiberg Germany Office Phone: 011-49-761-75782. E-mail: david.zabecki@gmx.de.

**ZABEL, DIANE MARION,** school librarian; b. Antigo, Wis., Mar. 20, 1957; d. Frank and Nina Wilcenski; m. Craig Robert Zabel, May 17, 1980; 1 child, Zachary. BS, U. Wis., 1978; MA, M.U. Ill., Urbana-Champaign, 1980, MS, 1982. Libr., dir. Fluvanna County Libr., Palmyra, Va., 1983—84; cataloger Bosler Free Libr., Carlisle, Pa., 1984—85; asst. libr. Pa. State U., Univeristy Park, 1985—86, social sci. ref. libr., 1986—98, bus. libr., 1998—2000, endowed libr. for bus., 2001—. Co-editor: Bridging the Gap: Examining Polarity in America, 1995, The Quality Management Sourcebook, 1994, The Flexible Workplace: A Sourcebook of Information and Research, 2001; editor: Reference and User Svcs. Quar., 2006—. Mem.: ALA (chair collection devel. and evaluation sect. 1999—2000), Reference and User Svcs. Assn. (pres. 2005—06), Internat. Coun. Hotel, Restaurant and Internat. Edn., Assn. Coll. and Rsch. Librs. (sec. instrn. sect. 1995—96). Avocations: reading, travel. Office: Schreyer Bus Libr Pa State Univ 309 Paterno Libr University Park PA 16802-1810 Office Phone: 814-865-1013. E-mail: dxz2@psu.edu.

**ZABEL, DIANNE DONNELLY,** retired elementary school educator; b. Woodburn, Oreg., Jan. 11, 1944; d. Joseph Emmett Donnelly and Beatrice Anna Bailey, Walter Eugene Bailey (Stepfather); m. Alfred Anthony Zabel, June 11, 1972; children: Shane Allen, Jill Anne. BA in Elem. Edn., Mt. Marty Coll., Yankton, S.D., 1966. Cert. elem. edn. tchr. Fla., Mentally Handicapped (0-21 years) Fla. Tchr. 3d grade St. Joseph Sch., Pierre, SD, 1967—68, St. Anthony Parish, Tigard, Oreg., 1968—70; tchr. 2d gade Mohave County Sch. Dist., Peach Springs, Ariz., 1970—71; tchr. varying exceptionalities Brevard County Sch. Sys., Melbourne, Fla., 1986—2005. Editor: (exceptional children's cookbook) Cooking With Class (Achievement Excellence award, 2001). Vol. Habitat For Humanity, Melbourne, 2000—05. Mem.: Coun. Exceptional Children. Roman Catholic. Avocations: travel, crocheting. Home: 7730 Pine Lake Dr Melbourne FL 32904 Office: Croton Elem Sch 1449 Croton Rd Melbourne FL 32935 Personal E-mail: ajsz5260@earthlink.net.

**ZABEL, SHELDON ALTER,** lawyer, law educator; b. Omaha, Apr. 25, 1941; s. Louis Julius and Anne (Rothenberg) Z.; m. Roberta Jean Butz, May 10, 1975; children: Andrew Louis, Douglas Patrick, Robert Stewart Warren. AB cum laude, Princeton U., 1963; JD cum laude, Northwestern U., 1966. Bar: Ill. 1966, U.S. Supreme Ct. 1976. Law clk. to presiding justice Ill. Supreme Ct., 1966-67; assoc. Schiff, Hardin LLP, Chgo., 1967-73, ptnr., 1973—. Instr. environ. law Loyola U., Chgo. Mem. ABA, Chgo. Bar Assn., Chgo. Coun. Lawyers, Order of Coif, Union League Club, Met. Club (Chgo.) Jewish. Avocations: skiing, bicycling. Office: Schiff Hardin LLP Sears Tower 233 S Wacker Dr Ste 6600 Chicago IL 60606-6473 Office Phone: 312-258-5540. Business E-mail: szabel@schiffhardin.com.

**ZABEL, WILLIAM DAVID,** lawyer; b. Omaha, Dec. 14, 1936; s. Louis J. and Anne I. Z.; m. Deborah M. Miller, Oct. 31, 1979; children by previous marriage: Richard, David. AB summa cum laude, Princeton U., 1958; LLB cum laude, Harvard U., 1961. Bar: N.Y. 1961, U.S. Supreme Ct. 1966, Fla. 1975. Ptnr. Schulte Roth & Zabel, NYC, 1969—. Lectr. Cornell Law Sch. So. Fed. Tax Inst., U. Miami Inst. Estate Planning, Great Plains Tax Inst., Assn. of Bar of City of N.Y., Practising Law Inst., profl. orgns.; N.Y. State adv. com. U.S. Civil Rights Commn., 1969-73; vol. civil rights litigator Lawyers Constl. Def. Com., Miss., summer 1965; bd. dirs. Del. Mgmt. Holdings Inc.; chmn. Human Rights First, 2000- Author: Estate Planning for the Large Estate, 1976, Domicile, Wills and Tax Problems of Migrating Clients Transplanted to Florida, 1976, Income, Estate and Gift Tax Consequences of Marital Settlements, 1979, Estate Planning for Interests in a Closely Held Business, 1981, Use of Trusts in Connection with Marital Dissolutions, 1983, Thy Will Be Done?, 1991, The Rich Die Richer -- and You Can Too, 1995; Am. editor: The Lawyer, Eng., 1963-66; mem. editl. adv. bd. Trusts and Estates Mag.; contbr. articles to profl. jours. Pres. Merlin Found.; mem. Lymphoma Found., Soros Founds. (Newly Ind. States and the Baltic Republics, Hungary, Romania, Bulgaria and Ctrl. European U.), Open Soc. Fund, Inc., Human Rights Watch/Helsinki, Doctors of World, Winston Found. World Peace, Ottinger Found., David H. Cogan Found., The Picower Med. Rsch. Inst., Lawson Valentine Found., Am. Friends of the Israel Mus., Am. Com. for Weizmann Inst. Sci.; legal counsel Internat. Confedn. Art Dealers; bd. dirs. Tauber Inst., Sakharov Archives, Brandeis U., Population Action Internat., 1996-2004, Lincoln Ctr. Theater, 1996-, Acad. Am. Poets, 1977-; trustee The New Sch. for Social Rsch., 1994—; adv. bd. Project on Death in Am.; chmn. Princeton U. Planned Giving Com., 1991—. Recipient Disting. Cmty. Svc. award Brandeis U., 1986, U.S. Masters Squash Team Bronze medal 14th Maccabiah Games, 1993, Disting. Svc award, New Sch. U., Extraordinary Leader award, Lawyers Com. for Human Rights, 2003, Lifetime Achievement award, Am. Lawyer mag., 2006; fellow Brandeis U., 1987—. Fellow Am. Coll. Trust and Estate Coun., Internat. Acad. Estate and Trust Law, N.Y. Bar Found., Am. Bar Found.; mem. ABA, Am. Law Inst., N.Y. State Bar Assn., Assn. of Bar of City of N.Y. (internat. human rights com.), Human Rights First (formerly Lawyers Com. for Human Rights) (bd. dirs., chmn., 2005), Vol. Lawyers for Arts (bd. dirs.), Estate Planning Coun. N.Y.C. (bd. dirs. 1975-79), Fla. Bar Assn., Harmonie Club (pres. 1989-91), Phi Beta Kappa. Office: Schulte Roth & Zabel 919 Third Ave New York NY 10022-4774 also: Phillips Point W Tower 10th Fl 777 S Flagler Dr West Palm Beach FL 33401-6161 Office Phone: 212-758-2351. Office Fax: 212-592-5955. Business E-Mail: william.zabel@srz.com.*

**ZABEL-DURHAM, MARTHA L.,** retired secondary school educator; b. Delhi, La., May 10, 1925; d. George Erwin and Gertrude Vera (Martin) LeFevre; children: Martha Jean, Karen Lynn, Kathy Louise. AA, Santa Ana Coll., 1960; BA, U. Calif., Fullerton, 1962, MA, 1965. Cert. edn. secondary tchr. Tchr. Anaheim H.S., 1966-74; Katella H.S., 1966—68, Los Alamitos (Calif.) Unified Sch. Dist., 1968—94; ret., 1994. Co-sponsor CSF; mem. NDEA Program Devel. Inst., NDEA Inst. in English Advanced Placement English, CATE Ad hoc Com. on Evaluation of English Tchrs., English Coun. Calif. State Colls. Recipient PTA Hon. Svc. award; named one of Outstanding Secondary Educators of Am., 1974, 75, Orange County Tchr. of Yr., 1979, Calif. Tchr. of Yr. finalist, 1979. Mem. LAEA, Nat. Coun. Tchrs. English, Calif. Assn. Tchrs. English, Calif. Tchrs. Assn., Phi Theta Kappa, Phi Kappa Phi. Home: 10400 Trinity Way Stanton CA 90680-1528

**ZABILKA, IVAN L.,** secondary school educator; b. Oskaloosa, Iowa, Aug. 14, 1939; s. J. Harvey and Marion (Pooley) Z.; m. Virginia Marcus, June 9, 1962 (div. Oct. 1990); children: Eric John, Laura Lynne; m. Carol Lindsay, May 21, 1992. AB, Asbury Coll., 1961; MDiv & ThM, Asbury Theol. Sem., 1965, 68; MA, U. Ky., 1976, PhD, 1980. Cert. secondary tchr., history, math., physics. Instr. math Asbury Coll., Wilmore, Ky., 1966-68, registrar, dir. admissions, 1968-71; registrar, asst. dean Asbury Theol. Sem., Wilmore, 1971-74; tchr. secondary sch. Jessamine County (Ky.) and Johnson County (ind.), 1977-80; asst. registrar U. No., Columbia, 1980-87; instr., math. Bryan Sta. Mid. Sch., Lexington, Ky., 1987—99; program cons. Ky. Dept. Edn., 1999—2002; policy analyst The Family Found. of Ky., 2002—; instr. math Lexington Christian Acad., Lexington, Ky., 2003—05. Presenter in field. Author: Scientific Malpractice, 1992, The Lottery Lie, 1998, Corporations Without Conscience, 2005; contbr. over 20 articles to profl. jours. Mem. Jessamine County Sch. Bd., 1971-74; del. Rep. State Conv., 1972. Methodist. Avocation: hiking. Personal E-mail: iczabilka@alltel.net.

**ZABLE, BARBARA A.,** manufacturing executive; b. Bklyn., Mar. 11, 1942; d. Isidore and Broda Lipton; m. Jack L. Zable, Dec. 22, 1963; children: Brian, Ilyse, Robert. BEd, Bklyn. Coll., 1963; M in Computer Sci., Binghamton U., 1982. Elem. sch. tchr. Attica Sch. Sys., Ind., 1963—64, Johnson City Sch. Sys., NY, 1964—65; staff programmer IBM, 1982—95; pres. Flatirons Disc Co., 1996—. Bd. dirs. Binghamton Youth Symphony; pres. Riverside Dr. Nursery Sch. Mem.: Temple Concord Sisterhood, Hadassah, B'nai Brith. Avocations: hiking, bridge, mahjong, travel, reading. Address: 6798 Snead St Longmont CO 80503 Office Phone: 303-442-5586.

**ZABLE, JACK LOUIS,** mechanical engineer, educator; b. Bklyn., Feb. 24, 1942; s. Phillip David and Gertrude Zable; m. Barbara Zable; children: Brian, Ilyse, Robert. BSME, CCNY, 1963; MSME, Purdue U., 1965, PhD, 1969. Sr. tech. staff IBM, Endicott, N.Y. and Boulder, Colo., 1964—97; prof. attendant, dept. mech. engring. U. Colo., Boulder, 1997—. Dir. Industry/Univ. Coop. Projects Ctr. U. Colo., Boulder, 1999—; mem. IBM Acad. Tech., Armonk, NY, 1990—97. Contbr. chapters to books, articles to profl. jours. Pres. Temple Concord, Binghamton, NY, 1982—84; bd. mem. Temple Feadon, Binghamton, NY, 1984—88. Fellow: ASME; mem.: Sigma Xi, Pi Tau Sigma. Republican. Jewish. Achievements include patents in field of printer technologies. Avocations: hiking, reading, golf, bridge. Home: 6798 Snead Ct Niwot CO 80503 Office: U Colo ME Dept Campus Box 427 Boulder CO 80309 E-mail: zable@spot.colorado.edu.

**ZABORSZKY, LASZLO,** neuroscientist; b. Budapest, Hungary, Oct. 9, 1944; s. Ilona Hegedus and Geza Zaborszky; 1 child, Sarah. MD, Semmelweis Med. Sch., Budapest, Hungary, 1969, PhD, 1981, DSc, 1999. Assoc. prof. U. Va., Charlottesville, 1981—93; prof. Rutgers U., Newark, 1993—. Author: (monograph) Afferent Connection of the Medial Basal Hypothalamus, 1982; editor: (text book) Neuroanatomical Tract-Tracing Methods 2: Plenum, 1989, Neuroanatomical Tract-Tracing 3: Molecules-Neurons-Systems, 2005. Grantee, NIH/NINDS, 1986—. Mem.: Soc. for Neurosci. Achievements include research in Basal Forebrain. Home: 2 Green Acres Dr Verona NJ 07044 Office: Rutgers Univ 197 University Ave Newark NJ 07102 Office Phone: 973-353-1080. Business E-Mail: zaborszky@axon.rutgers.edu.

**ZABREK, ALBERT SAMUEL,** architect; b. Wash., DC, July 12, 1933; s. Louis and Dora Zabrek; life ptnr. Anne Leona Goldman; children: Robin Lynn Olson, Scott M. Cert. Architectural Draftsman Columbia Tech. Inst., 1955. Chmn., CEO Imperial Tempra Corp. Est., 1966; founder I.T. Rsch. Found., 1972; dedicated Arts Scis. and Humanities, Montgomery Village, Md., 1972—2003; design, engr., cons., product rsch. ZBK/Imperial, Montgomery Village, Md., 2003—. Candidate for pres. South Village Bd. Dirs., Montgomery Village. Seaman US Coast Guard, 1950—53. Recipient Recognition for Contributing to the Advancement of Am. Architecture, 1978. Achievements include patents for Triune Energy Sys., that create indep. electric power on demand; energy sys. program for peace through econ., 1972-2003. Avocations: pvt. pilot, golf, gourmet health food, exercise. Home and Office: Imperial Tempra 18755 Walkers Choice Rd Montgomery Village MD 20886 E-mail: zbk.imperial@comcast.net.

**ZABRISKIE, JOHN L.,** healthcare and agricultural products manufacturing company executive; b. 1940; With Merck & Co., Inc., Whitehouse Station, NJ, 1965-93, past exec. v.p., past pres. mfg. divsn.; chmn., CEO Upjohn Co., Kalamazoo, 1993-95, also bd. dirs.; pres., CEO Pharmacia & Upjohn, Inc., Windsor, U.K., 1995-97, NEN Life Science Product Inc, Boston, 1997-99, chmn., 1999—.

**ZACCHINO, NARDA,** newspaper editor; b. San Diego, 1947; BA in english lit., UCLA. Assoc. editor L.A. Times, Calif. Office: Los Angeles Times Times Mirror Sq Los Angeles CA 90053

**ZACCONE, SUZANNE MARIA,** sales executive; b. Chgo., Oct. 23, 1957; d. Dominic Robert and Lorretta F. (Urban) Zaccone. Sales sec. Brookeridge Realty, Downers Grove, 1975-76; sales cons. Kafka Estates Inc., Downers Grove, 1975-76; adminstrv. asst. Chem. Dist., Inc., Oak Brook, Ill., 1976-77; sales rep., mgr. Anographics Corp., Burr Ridge, Ill., 1977-85; pres., owner Graphic Solutions, Inc., Burr Ridge, 1985—. Bd. dirs. Di Trolio Flexigraphic Inst. Curriculum adv. bd. mem. Sch. Dist. 99, 1997, 1998, 1999, 2000, 2001. Named Supplier of Yr. Through Preferred Supplied, Gen. Binding Corp., 1988—99; recipient Supplier Mem. award, Internat. Bottled Water Assn., 1987—88, Supplier award, SBA, 1990, Top Performer Supplier award, Cutler Hammer Westinghouse Divsn., 1993—99, Blue Chip Enterprise Initiative award, 1994. Mem.: NAFE, Ditrolio Flexographic Inst. (bd. dirs.), World Label Assn. (1st pl. in World Championship 1994—96, 2002—04), Women in Packaging (exec. bd.), Inst. Packaging Profls., Women Entrepreneurs DuPage County (past pres.), Tag and Label Mfrs. Inst. (chmn. pub. rels. and mktg. com., bd. dirs., pres. 1998—2000, Best Managed Co. award 1992, 1st place award in U.S. for Screen Printing 1994—97, 1999—2001, Best Managed Co. award 2001—03). Avocations: reading, sailing, cooking, needlepoint, scuba diving. Office: Graphic Solutions Inc 311 Shore Dr Burr Ridge IL 60521-5859 Office Phone: 630-325-8181. Business E-Mail: suzanne.zaccone@graphicsolutionsinc.com

**ZACEK, JOSEPH FREDERICK,** historian, educator; b. Stickney, Ill., Dec. 18, 1930; s. Joseph and Emilie (Dvorak) Z.; m. Judith Ellen Cohen (div. 1975); 1 child, Natalie Ann; m. Jane Perlberg Shapiro; stepchildren: Leslie Helen, Peter Carl. BA summa cum laude, U. Ill., Champaign-Urbana, 1952, MA in History, 1953, PhD in History, 1962; cert., Columbia U. Inst. on East Cen. Europe, 1962. Asst. prof. history Occidental Coll., L.A., 1962-65; asst. prof., dir. Russian & East European Programs UCLA, 1965-68; assoc. prof. SUNY at Albany, 1968-71, dir. Russian and East European Programs, 1968-77, 91-92, prof., 1971—2001, chair dept. history, 1974-77, prof. emeritus, 2001—. Selection com. for East Europe Internat. Rsch. and Exch. Bd., Princeton, NJ, 1978-81; nat. bd. cons. NEH, Washington, 1975—; vis. scholar IREX Comenius U., Bratislava, and Charles U., Prague, Czechoslovakia, 1973, Columbia U., 1977-78, U. Ill, Champaign-Urbana, 1987. Author: Palacky: The Historian as Scholar and Nationalist, 1970; editor, co-author: Frantisek Palacky, 1798-1876: A Centennial Appreciation, 1981, The Enlightenment and the National Revivals in Eastern Europe, 1983, The Intimate Palacky, 1984; also numerous periodical articles and chpts. in multi-authored books. With M.I., U.S. Army, 1954-57. Fgn. Area Tng. fellow Ford Found., Columbia U., 1960-62, Sr. Humanities fellow Rockefeller Found., 1977-78, fellow Russian Rsch. Ctr. Harvard U., 1986-91; Rsch. grantee Am. Coun. Learned Soc./Soc. Sci. Rsch. Coun., 1965, Am. Philos. Soc., 1968; recipient Comenius medal Govt. of Czech and Slovak Fed. Republic, 1992, Medal of Comenius Pedagogical Inst. in Prague, 1992, Josef Hlávka medal of Czechoslovak Acad. of Scis. in Prague, 1992, others. Mem. Am. Hist. Assn., Am. Assn. for Advancement Slavic Studies, Western Slavic Conf., Czechoslovak History Conf., Slovak Studies Assn., Consortium on Revolutionary Europe, Assn. for Study of Ethnicity and Nationalism, Phi Beta Kappa. Avocations: travel, gardening, music. Home: 22 Sandhurst Dr Slingerlands NY 12159-9418 Office Phone: 518-482-7478. Business E-Mail: zacekj@union.edu.

**ZACHARIAH, EMMANUEL SELVANAYAGAM,** science educator, researcher; s. Zachariah Davenesan and Rajam Paulraj; m. Parvatha Vathani David, July 5, 1996; children: Evangeline Emmanuel, Hephzibah Emmanuel. PhD, U. of Madras, Chennai, 1996. Rsch. assoc. Indian Inst. of Sci., Bangalore, India, 1996; rsch. fellow Nat. U. of Singapore, 1996—2001; rsch. staff mem. Princeton U., NJ, 2001; asst. prof. U. Medicine and Dentistry N.J., Robert Wood Johnson Med. Sch., New Brunswick, NJ, 2006—, rsch. tchg. specialist, instr., 2001—06. Cons. SiMEMS, Singapore, 2004, Northridge, Warren, NJ, 2003. Sci. advisor SiMEMS, Singapore, Singapore, 2004. Recipient postdoctoral fellowship, Inst. of Microelectronics, Nat. U. Singapore, 1997—2001, Microararys and MicroPCR grant, 1997—2001. Fellow: Indian Chem. Soc. (life). Achievements include patents for Micro-fabricated PCR chip; development of diagnostic test for the detection of 4 common Indian snake venoms; ISFET immunosensors; first to Prediction of

therapeutic response in cancer patients. Office: U Medicine Dentistry NJ-Robert Wood Johnson Med Sch Cab 7050 125 Paterson St New Brunswick NJ 08903 Office Phone: 732-235-6426. Office Fax: 732-235-6325. E-mail: zsemmanuel@aol.com.

**ZACHARIAS, AJIT,** economist; arrived in US, 1988; s. Karingada Thomas Zacharias and Annie George; m. Gowri Parameswaran, Jan. 30, 1988; children: Adityan Gowri Ajit, Ananathan Gowri Ajit. MA in Econ., U. Bombay, India, 1986; BA in Econ., U. Kerala, Trivandrum, India, 1984; PhD, New Sch. U., NYC, 1998. Rsch. scholar Levy Economics Inst., Bard Coll., Annandale-on-Hudson, NY, 2001—05, sr. scholar, 2006—. Referee Cambridge Jour. Econs., Rev. Income and Wealth, Jour. Income Distbn. Contbr. articles to profl. jours. Grantee, Alfred P. Sloan Found. Mem.: Union Radical Polit. Econ., Ea. Econ. Assn., Am. Econ. Assn. Achievements include development of unique measure of economic well-being called the Levy Institute Measure of Economic Well-Being. Avocations: travel, hiking, chess. Office: Levy Economics Inst of Bard Coll Blithewood Ave Annandale On Hudson NY 12561 Office Phone: 845-758-7734. Office Fax: 845-758-1149. Business E-Mail: zacharia@levy.org.

**ZACHARIAS, ATHOS,** artist; b. Marlborough, Mass., June 17, 1927; s. Nicholas and Anastasia (Zoethes) Z.; children: Rena, Denis. BFA, R.I. Sch. Design, 1952; MFA, Cranbrook Acad., Bloomfield Hills, Mich., 1953. One-man shows include Eileen Michels Gallery, Woodmere, L.I., Nabi Gallery, Sagharbor, N.Y., Galerie Kwartijn, Amsterdam, The Netherlands, 1986-87, Bologna Landi Gallery, East Hampton, N.J., 1982, 86-87, Mat Gallery, Amsterdam, 1987, La Foret Mus., Tokyo, 1987, Elaine Benson Gallery, Bridgehampton, N.Y., 1992; exhibited in group shows at Nat. Acad. Design, N.Y.C., 1986, Kwartijn Gallery, 1987, Internat. Conf. Ctr., Rotterdam, 1988, Hempstead (N.Y.) Mus., 1986. With USAF. Home: 463 West St Apt B 946 New York NY 10014-2039 Personal E-mail: zackartsplus@aol.com.

**ZACHARIAS, DONALD WAYNE,** retired academic administrator; b. Salem, Ind., Sept. 28, 1935; s. William Otto and Estelle Mae (Newlon) Z.; m. Tommie Kline Dekle, Aug. 16, 1959; children: Alan, Eric, Leslie. BA, Georgetown Coll., Ky., 1957, LLD (hon.), 1983; MA, Ind. U., 1959, PhD, 1963. Asst. prof. communication and theatre Ind. U., 1963-69; assoc. prof. U. Tex., Austin, 1969-72, prof., 1972-89; asst. to pres., 1974-77; exec. asst. to chancellor U. Tex. System, 1978-79; pres. Western Ky. U., 1979-85, Miss. State U., Starkville, 1985-97, pres. emeritus, 1998—. Bd. dirs. First Fed. Savs. & Loan Assn., Bowling Green, Ky., Inst. for Tech. Devel., Sanderson Farms, Inc., Miss. Econ. Coun.; dir. John Grisham Libr., Starkville, 1998-2003. Author: In Pursuit of Peace: Speeches of the Sixties, 1970. Bd. dirs. Greenview Hosp.; pres. Southeastern Conf., 1989-91. With U.S. Army, 1959-60. Named Mississippian of Yr. Data Processing Mgmt. Assn.; recipient Teaching award Ind. U. Found., 1963, Cactus Teaching award U. Tex., 1971, Justin Smith Morrill award U.S. Dept. Agriculture, 1992, Disting. Teaching award Honors Program, 2000. Mem. Inst. Tech. Devel. (bd. dirs. 1985-92), Nat. Assn. State Univs. and Land-Grant Colls. (exec. com. 1990-92), Phi Kappa Phi (pres. 1978). Democrat. Episcopalian.

**ZACHARIAS, NIKOLAOS MARIOS,** obstetrician, gynecologist; b. Athens, Greece; s. Marios Nikolaos and Constantoula Marios Zacharias; m. Ioanna Dimitrios Athanassaki, May 12, 2000. MD, Nat. and Kapodistrian U., Athens, 1995. Gen. prescription Greek Nat. Health Svc., Vassiliki, Greece, 1996-97; gen. surgery intern Laikon Gen. Hosp., Athens, 1997-98; chief resident ob-gyn. Baylor Coll. Medicine, Houston, 1998—2002; fellow in maternal-fetal medicine U. Tex. Med. Br., Galveston, 2002—05; asst. prof. ob-gyn Baylor Coll. Medicine, Houston, 2005—; program dir. dist. prenatal ultrasound maternal fetal medicine Harris County Hosp., Houston, 2005—. Undergrad. Ann. scholar Found. State Scholarships, 1990-94; Papadakis grantee Nat. and Kapodistrian U. Athens, 1990-95, Kontoleon grantee, 1998-2002, Acad. fellow U. Tex. Med. Br., 2002-. Fellow ACOG; mem. Athens Med. Assn., Gen. Med. Coun., Tex. Med. Assn., Soc. for Maternal-Fetal Medicine. Avocations: swimming, basketball, travel. Home: 6011 Saint Andrews Dr Pasadena TX 77505-4803 Office: Baylor Coll Medicine 1504 Taub Loop Rm 3LD 620-01 Houston TX 77030 Office Phone: 713-236-7192. Business E-Mail: nmz@bcm.edu, zachan@hchd.tmc.edu.

**ZACHARIAS, NORBERT,** astronomer; b. Beckum, Westfalen, Germany, June 7, 1957; arrived in U.S., 1993; s. Wilhelm and Maria Zacharias; m. Marion Ingrid Eichler, June 23, 1983. BA in Physics, U. Kiel, Germany, 1979; MS in Physics, U. Hamburg, Germany, 1982, PhD in Physics and Astronomy, 1987. Cert. postgrad. studies Inst. Astronomy, Cambridge, Eng., 1983. Chief cataloging and requirements divsn. U.S. Naval Obs., Washington, 2005—. Recipient Newcomb award, U.S. Naval Obs., 2005. Mem.: Astronomische Gesellschaft, Astron. Soc. of the Pacific, Am. Astron. Soc., Internat. Astron. Union, Sierra Club (life). Independent. Achievements include research in first astrometric all-sky survey with electronic detector. Avocations: sailing, travel, bicycling. Office: US Naval Observatory 3450 Mass Ave NW Washington DC 20392 Office Phone: 202-762-1423. Office Fax: 202-762-1516. Business E-Mail: nz@usno.navy.mil.

**ZACHAROULIS, DIMITRIS,** surgeon, researcher; b. Larisa, Greece, Nov. 8, 1967; s. Christos Zacharoulis and Anastasia Tsita. Grad. Diploma (hon.), 5th Gen. Lyceum, Greece, 1985; PhD, U. Athens, 2000. Cert. Ptychion Iatrikes Aristotelian U. Thessaloniki, Greece, 1991, Gen. Surgery Boards Com., 2000. Rsch. fellow U. Athens 1991—97; surgery intern Greek Army, Alexandroupolis, Greece, 1992—93; gen. practitioner Greek Ministry of Health, Larisa, Greece, 1993—94; rsch. fellow Harvard Med., Boston, 1994—95; resident gen. surgery SUNY, Syracuse, 1995—2000; clin. fellow, registrar, cons. of hpb surgery Hammersmith Hosp., London, 2000—03; sr. lectr. U. of Thessaly, Larisa, Greece, 2003—06. Mem. Med. Assn. of LARISA, Larisa, Greece, 2005—06, Greek Med. Assn., 2005—06. Mil. dr. U.S. Army, 1992—93, Greece. Achievements include research in Investigation of New Technology in Liver Surgery. The use of Radiofrequency Energy in bloodless resection of solid organs and endoscopy. Home: Kalliarhou Larisa 41221 Greece Office: Univ of Thessaly Univ Hosp Larisa 41222 Greece Office Phone: +1030-2410-682-730. Home Fax: +1030-2410-670-100; Office Fax: +1030-2410-670-100. Personal E-mail: zachadim@yahoo.com.

**ZACHARY, JE'QUITA YVETTE,** elementary school educator, singer; b. Jesse B. and Sharon Yvonne Zachary. AA in Music, Gordon Coll., 1997; BA in Music & Bus., Clayton Coll. and State U., 2000. Tchr. music Victory Charter Sch., East Point, Ga., 2002—04; music promoter Atlanta Internation Records, Atlanta, 1999—2001; tchr. Odyssey Charter Sch., Newnan, 2004—05; tchr. 5th grade reading UT. KIPP WAYS Acad., New Birth South, Ga., 2004—05. Tchr. after sch. chorus Odyssey Charter Sch., Newnan, Ga., 2005—; children's choir helper New Birth South, New Birth South, Jonesboro, 2005—. Singer: (songs, plays and dances) Martin's Dream and Mine and Songs from His Heart. Ch. mem. New Birth South, New Birth South, 2004. Personal E-Mail: jequitaz@yahoo.com.

**ZACHARY, LOUIS GEORGE,** chemical company consultant; b. Aug. 14, 1927; s. George E. and Angelike (Hantsis) Zacharakis; m. Lillie Vletas, Apr. 20, 1955; children: Leslie A., Louis George. Prodn. supr. Dewey & Almy Co., Acton, Mass., 1951-52; salesman chem. divsn. Union Camp Corp., Wayne, NJ, 1952-59, sales mgr. chem. divsn., 1959-62, gen. mgr. chem. ops., 1962-66, gen. mgr. chem. divsn., 1970-78, v.p., 1974-78, Drake Mgmt. Co., NYC, 1966-70; sr. v.p. GAF Corp., NYC, 1978-82, mem. office of chmn., 1981-82; cons., 1983-84; chmn., CEO Universal Die Casting, Inc., Saline, Mich., 1984-90; acting pres. chem. divsn. Church & Dwight Inc., 1990-91; v.p. Nat. Exec. Svc. Corp., NYC, 1993-96. Mem. vis. com. chem. engring. dept. Johns Hopkins U., Balt., 1981-83. Co-editor: Tall Oil and Its Uses, 1965. With USN, 1945-46. Mem. Chem. Mfrs. Assn. (dir. 1979-83), Synthetic

Organic Chem. Mfrs. Assn., Soc. Chem. Industry, Harvard Club NJ (exec. com.; trustee 2000—). Home: 227 Oak Ridge Ave Summit NJ 07901-3258 Personal E-mail: louiszachary@aol.com.

**ZACHEM, TYLER,** investment company executive; BA magna cum laude, U. Rochester; MBA first yr. honors, Harvard Bus. Sch. Cons. McKinsey & Co.; with McDonald & Co., Cleveland; ptnr. McCown De Leeuw & Co.; mng. dir. DB Capital Ptnrs.; ptnr. MidOcean Ptnrs. Bd. dirs. Infocrossing, Inc., Newroads, Inc. Mem.: Phi Beta Kappa. Office: MidOcean Ptnrs 320 Park Ave Ste 1700 New York NY 10022 Office Phone: 212-497-1400.

**ZACHER, IRMAGENE,** elementary school educator; b. Lynden, Wash., Dec. 16, 1941; d. Elmer Spencer and Amy Ellen (Ritchey) Kulp; m. Donald A. Zacher, Dec. 28, 1963; children: Kimberly, Kenneth, Kippy. AA, Columbia Basin Coll., Pasco, Wash., 1979; BA in Edn., Ea. Wash. U., 1981, 5th yr. cert., 1983, MS in Curriculum, 1989. Elem. tchr. 1st grade Kennewick (Wash.) Sch. Dist., tchr. kindergarten; sci. facilitator Vista Sch. Mem.-primary rep. Kennewick Sch. Dist. Sci. Com.; condr. sci. program field test Silver Burdett Pubs., 1989; mem. Sci. Alive II team. Book reviewer Spokane (Wash.) Regional Libr.; Wash. State Centennial chmn. Vista Sch. Recipient Sally Mae award, 1985. Mem. NEA, Wash. Edn. Assn., Kennewick Edn. Assn. (Vista staff rep. 1988-91, 93-95), Internat. Reading Assn., Wash. Sci. Tchrs. Assn., Nat. Sci. Tchrs. Assn. Home: 3617 W Wernett Rd Pasco WA 99301-2555

**ZACHERT, MARTHA JANE,** retired librarian; b. York, Pa., Feb. 7, 1920; d. Paul Rodes and Elizabeth Agnes (Lau) Koontz; m. Edward G. Zachert, Aug. 25, 1946; 1 child, Lillian Elizabeth. AB, Lebanon Valley Coll., 1941; MLS, Emory U., 1953; DLS, Columbia U., 1968. Asst. Enoch Pratt Free Library, Balt., 1941-46; head librarian Wood Research Inst., Atlanta, 1947; sch. librarian DeKalb (Ga.) County Schs., 1950-52; head librarian, prof. history of pharmacy So. Coll. Pharmacy, Mercer U., Atlanta, 1952-63; mem. faculty Library Sch., Fla. State U., 1963-78, prof., 1973-78, Coll. Librarianship U. S.C., Columbia, 1973-74, 78-84. Vis. fellow Brit. Library, 1980; cons. So. Regional Med. Library, Emory U., 1976-77, Nat. Library Medicine, 1977, others. Author: Fine Printing in Georgia, 1959-1990, 1994; assoc. editor Jour. Libr. History, 1966-71, 73-76; mng. editor, 1971-73; cons. editor Jour. Libr. Adminstrn., 1979-86; contbr. numerous articles to profl. jours. Fellow Med. Libr. Assn. (named among 100 Most Notables 1998); mem. ALA, Spl. Librs. Assn. (past pres. Fla. chpt., spl. citation 1977, Hall of Fame 1985), Am. Printing History Assn., Beta Phi Mu (pres. 1974-75). Home and office: 4436 Meandering Way #108AG Tallahassee FL 32308-8705

**ZACHERT, VIRGINIA,** retired psychologist; b. Jacksonville, Ala., Mar. 1, 1920; d. R.E. and Cora H. (Massee) Z. Student, Norman Jr. Coll., 1937; AB, Ga. State Woman's Coll., 1940; MA, Emory U., 1947; PhD, Purdue U., 1949. Diplomate Am. Bd. Profl. Psychologists. Statistician Davison-Paxon Co., Atlanta, 1941-44; research psychologist Mil. Contracts, Auburn Research Found., Ala. Poly. Inst.; indsl. and research psychologist Sturm & O'Brien (cons. engrs.), 1958-59; research project dir. Western Design, Biloxi, Miss., 1960-61; self-employed cons. psychologist Norman Park, Ga., 1961-71, Good Hope, Ga., 1971-99; ret. Rsch. assoc. med. edn. Med. Coll. Ga., Augusta, 1963-65, assoc. prof., 1965-70, rsch. prof., 1970-84, rsch. prof. emeritus, 1984—, chief learning materials divsn., 1973-84, faculty senate, 1976-84, acad. coun., 1978-82; pres. acad. coun., 1983, sec., 1978; mem. Ga. Bd. Examiners Psychologists, 1974-79, v.p., 1977, pres. 1978; adv. bd. Comdr. Gen. ATC USAF, 1967-70; cons. Ga. Silver Haired Legislature, 1980-86, senator, 1987-93, pres. protem, 1987-88, pres., 1989-93, rep., spkr. protem, 1993-96, spkr., 1997-98, Nat. Silver-Haired Congress rep., 1995—, spkr. 1997-99; govs. appointee White House Coun. on Aging, 1971, 96, Ga. Coun. on Aging, 1988-96; U.S. Senate mem. Fed. Coun. on the Aging, 1990-93; senator appointee White House Conf. on Aging, 1995; Ga. Health Decision's appointee to Ga. Coalition for Health, 1996-98. Author: (with P.L. Wilds) Essentials of Gynecology-Oncology, 1967, Applications of Gynecology-Oncology, 1967. Del. White House Conf. on Aging, 1981, 95. Served as aerologist USN, 1944-46; aviation psychologist USAF, 1949-54. Recipient Jane Kennedy Excellence Aging award, 1999. Fellow AAAS, Am. Psychol. Assn.; mem. AAUP (chpt. pres. 1977-80), Sigma Xi. (chpt. pres. 1980-81) Baptist. Home: 4275 Owens Rd # 403 Evans GA 30809 *It's really quite simple-I find, if I wish to be understood or heard, that simplicity is necessary but not ever easy. Simplicity is basic, essential and always the major factor in my search for truth.*

**ZACHMANN, WILLIAM FRANCIS,** computer and communications industry market research company executive; b. Cleve., Oct. 19, 1942; s. Kurt Wilhelm and Jean (O'Konski) Z.; m. Elizabeth Ann Loftus, June 7, 1980. BA, Harvard U., 1966. Programmer, analyst Cambridge (Mass.) Computer Assocs., 1967-69; sys. rsch. officer 1st Nat. Bank, Boston, 1969-74; dir. rsch. Forum Corp., Boston, 1974-75; coord. personnel adminstrn. Harvard U., Cambridge, 1976-77; mgr. tech. support CallData Sys., Boston, 1977-79; v.p. tech. assessment Internat. Data Corp., Framingham, Mass., 1979-83, v.p. corp. rsch., 1983-87, sr. v.p., 1987-88; pres. Canopus Rsch., Duxbury, Mass., 1988—, editor, pub. Canopus report, 1992—; host Canopus rsch. forum, 1992-99; v.p. Meta Group, Stamford, Conn., 2000—02; chmn., CEO Canopus Rsch. Inc., Duxbury, 2002—; pres., CEO Agylity, 2004—. Mem. Harvard (Boston), Harvard Faculty (Cambridge), Compuserve. Author: Keys to Application Development Productivity, 1981; contbg. editor Computer Industry Report, 1982-88, Communications and Distributed Resources Report, 1983-87, PC World mag., 1987-88; columnist On Communications mag., 1984-86, Software News mag., 1984-86, Computerworld mag., 1986-88, Infoworld mag., 1987-88, Micromarketworld mag., 1985-87, PC Mag., 1988-92, PC Week mag., 1988-92, MacUser mag., 1988-89, Windows World, 1992-95, Ad Week's Marketing Computers, 1993-95, Computing Pro, 1996-99, CIO mag., 1999-2002; columnist, sr. contbg. editor OS/2 Professional, 1992-94, Real Estate Jour. 2004— Duxbury Clipper, 2004— Mem. City Mgrs. Adv. Com. on Cable TV, Cambridge, 1979-93; mem. Duxbury Econ. Devel. Com., 1992-95, 2004—; mem. Planning Bd., Duxbury, 1995-2001, vice chmn., 1996-2000. Home: 160 Standish St Duxbury MA 02332-5065 Office: Canopus Rsch Inc PO Box 2805 Duxbury MA 02331-2805 Office Phone: 781-934-9800. E-mail: wfz@canopusresearch.com.

**ZACK, ARNOLD MARSHALL,** lawyer, mediator, arbitrator, judge; b. Lynn, Mass., Oct. 7, 1931; s. Samuel George and Bess Ethel (Freedman) Z.; m. Norma Eta Wilner, Aug. 10, 1969; children: Jonathan Samuel, Rachel Ann. AB, Tufts Coll., 1953; LLB, Yale U., 1956; MPA, Harvard U., 1961. Asst. to Saul Wallen (arbitrator), 1956-63; cons. govt. South Africa UN Mission to Congo, 1960; cons. U.S. Peace Corps, 1961-63, Labor Dept., 1962-79, Pres.'s Study Commn. on Nat. Service Corps, 1962-63, U.S. AID, 1963—, Friedrich Ebert Stiftung, 1963-64, Nat. Center for Dispute Settlement, 1968-76; judge Asian Development Bank Adminstrn. Tribunal, 2004—. Cons. IMF, 2000—02, Govt. Italy, 2002—, Internat. Labor Orgn., 1961—; mem. steering com. Permanent Ct. Arbitration, 2002—; vis. Fulbright lectr. Haile Selassie U., Addis Ababa, Ethiopia, 1963—64; referee Nat. R.R. Adjustment Bd., 1964—; mem. faculty Labor and Worklife Program Harvard Law Sch., 1985—; full time mediator/arbitrator, Boston, 1968—; bd. dirs. Ctr. for Socio-Legal Studies faculty of law U. Natal, South Africa, 1986—92; mem. Fgn. Svc. Labor Rels. Bd., 1982—84, Presdl. Emergency Bds. 221 and 222; chair Presdl. Emergency Bd. 232, 234; chmn. Essential Industries Dispute Settlement Bd. Bermuda, 1993—2000; chair Essential Svcs. Dispute Settlement Bd. Bermuda, 1996—2000; vis. lectr. Yale Law Sch., 1995—96; permanent arbitrator Am. Airlines & APA, IRS & NTEU, Commonwealth Mass., Overseas Rsch. Author: Dispute Settlement: Labor Training in Developing Countries, 1964, Ethiopia's High Level Manpower-Analysis and Projections, 1964, Handbook on Grievance Arbitration in the Public Sector, 1974, Handbook on Fact Finding and Arbitration in the Public Sector, 1974, Grievance Arbitration, A Practical Guide, 1977; (with R. Bloch) Arbitration of Discipline and Discharge Cases, 1979, (with R. Bloch) The Agreement in Negotiation and Arbitration, 1983, 2d edition, 1995, Arbitration in Practice, 1984, Mediation in the Public Sector, 1985, Grievance Arbitration: Cases on the Merits in Discipline Discharge and Contract Interpretation, 1989, Hand-

book on Grievance Arbitration: Issues on Procedure and Ethics, 1992, (with J. Dunlop) Mediation and Arbitration of Employment Disputes, 1997, Arbitration Discipline and Discharge Cases, 2000; contbr. articles to profl. jours. Bd. visitors Harvard U. Recipient Whitney North Seymour medal for oustanding contbn. to arbitration, 1980, Cushing Gavin award, 1986, Mildred Spaulding award, 1987, Disting. Svc. award for arbitration of labor-mgmt. disputes, 1989, Pioneer award Assn. Conflict Resolution, 2003, Willoughby Abner award, Assn. for Conflict Resolution, 2004; Wertheim fellow Harvard U., 1996-97. Fellow: African Studies Assn.; mem.: ABA (mem. coun. labor and employment law sect. 2000—), Coll. Labor and Employment Lawyers, Internat. Soc. for Labor Law and Social Security (bd. dirs.), Indsl. Rels. Rsch. Assn. (bd. dirs.), Am. Arbitration Assn. (dir. Labor-Mgmt. Inst. 1966—68), Nat. Acad. Arbitrators (treas. 1972—75, bd. govs. 1977—79, v.p. 1980—82, pres. Rsch. and Edn. Found. 1989—91, pres. 1994—95), Yale Law Sch. Assn., Yale Club (N.Y.C.), Harvard Club ((Boston)). Address: 170 W Canton St Boston MA 02118-1216

**ZACK, DANIEL GERARD,** library consultant; b. Waukegan, Ill., Oct. 1, 1943; s. Raymond Gerard and Rosanna Marie (Atkinson) Z.; m. Mary Frances Anthony, Aug. 25, 1966; children: Jennifer Lee, Rebecca Jane. BA in Psychology, Western Ill. U., 1967; MS in Libr. Sci., U. Ill., 1975. Editor IBM Corp., Rochester, Minn., 1968-70, Memorex Corp., Mpls., 1970-74; rsch. assoc. Libr. Rsch. Ctr. U. Ill., Urbana, 1974-75; asst. dir. Portage County Pub. Libr., Stevens Point, Wis., 1976-78; dir. Burlington Pub. Libr., Iowa, 1978-87, Gail Borden Pub. Libr. Elgin, Ill., 1987—2004; with. Libr. Cons. Svcs., 2004—. Trustee Batavia Pub. Libr., Ill., 1997-2003; founder Friends of Ill. Libr., 1990, bd. dirs. 1990-97. Mem. ALA, ACLU, Ill. Libr. Assn. (mgr. pub. libr. forum 1991-92, 2002-03, exec. bd. dirs. 1992-95, pub. policy com. 1995-98), Pub. Libr. Assn. (intellectual freedom com. 1993-96), Kiwanis.

**ZACK, GEORGE J.,** conductor; b. Pine Bluff, Ark., July 8, 1936; s. George Peter and Eugenia (Paschal) Z.; m. Kerry Sheehan, Oct. 4, 1970; children: Katherine Eugenia, Melissa Sheehan. Student, Am. Conservatory Music, Chgo., 1957, 58; MusB cum laude in Music Theory and Composition, Wichita State U., 1958; MusM in Music Theory and Viola, U. Mich., 1960; PhD in Music Theory, Fla. State U., 1972; studies with Dr. Richard Lert, Stella Roberts, Gustav Meier. Instr. music U. Mich., Ann Arbor, 1962-64; assoc. prof. Hiram (Ohio) Coll., 1964-72; music dir. Music Theater Soc., Lexington, Ky., 1972-75, Lexington Philharm., 1972—, Wooster (Ohio) Symphony, 1973-75, Warren (Ohio) Chamber Orch., 1967—99. Artist-in-residence Ea. U., James Madison U.; guest condr. State Orch. Salonika, Greece, 1981, 83-84, 84-85, Louisville Orch., 1978; condr. N.E. Ohio All State Orch., 1969, Men and Boy's Choir Festival, 1975, 76, N.Y. All-State Orch., 1975, Ky. All-State Orch., 1974, 76, South Bend, Ind.; Youngstown, Ohio, Albuquerque Chamber Orch., Monterey County Symphony, Calif., Amarillo, Tex., Bridgeport, Conn., Santa Cruz, Calif., Stockton, Calif., Charleston, S.C., Modesto, Calif., Las Vegas, Nev.; guest speaker various civic orgns. Dir. (radio program) George Zack's Enhancement of Music, Sta. WEKU-FM, 1975—; dir., producer (radio program) The Enhancement of Music, Sta. WBKY-FM, 1973-75, (TV program) Form in Music, NBC, 1965; co-host (TV program) Ky. Morning, 1979. Commr. Picnic with The Pops, Lexington, 1982—. Named Gov. Artist of Yr., State of Ky., 1994, Ky. Star, Downtown Lexington Corp.; recipient Orpheus award, Phi Mu Alpha, 1976, Hellenic award, 1993, Humanitarian award, Nat. Conf., 1994, Optimist Cup, 1999, Ky. Star, Downtown Lexington Corp., 2004. Mem. Am. Symphony Orch. League, Condr.'s Guild, Am. Fedn. Musicians (hon. mem. condr. 554-635 local 118), Cen. Ky. Youth Music Soc. (bd. dirs., condr.), NCCJ (bd. dirs., co-chmn.) Greek Orthodox. Home: 237 Woodspoint Rd Lexington KY 40502-1905 Office: Lexington Philharm Artsplace 161 N Mill St Lexington KY 40507-1125

**ZACK, STEPHEN NEAL,** lawyer; b. Detroit, Dec. 2, 1947; s. Benn Zack and Anita (Rabinovich) Petluck; children: Jason, Tracey. BA, U. Fla., 1969, JD, 1971. Bar: Fla. 1972, N.Y. 1982, D.C. 1986, U.S. Dist. Ct. (no. and so. dists.) Fla. 1986, U.S. Ct. Appeals (5th and 11th cirs.)1986. Sr. ptnr. Floyd, Pearson, Richman, Greer, Weil, Zack & Brumbaugh P.A., Miami, Fla., 1972-91, Zack, Hanzman & Ponce P.A., Miami, 1991—95, Zack Kosnitzky P.A., 1995—2002, Boies, Schiller & Flexner LLP, Miami, 2002—. Legis. aide to Congressman Claude Pepper, 1971-72; chmn. environ. rev. bd. City of Miami, 1978-79, Fla. law ctr. coun. U. Fla., 1982; mem. Speakers Adv. Com. on Future, Jud. Nomination Commn. for 11th Cir.; spl. counsel to Gov. Bob Graham, 1986; bd. dirs. Jewish Family Services, 1984-; chmn. State Fla. Ethics Comm.; former pres. Nat. Conf. Bar Presidents. Named to Hall of Fame, U. Fla. Mem. ABA (life fellow, chmn. House Del. 2004—, mem. bd. govs.), ALTA, Fla. Bar Assn. (pres. young lawyers sect. 1975-76, bd. govs. 1977-88, chmn. internat. law sect. 1981-82, pres. 1989-90), Acad. Fla. Trial Lawyers (bd. dirs. 1982-86), Dade County Bar Assn. (bd. dirs. & pres. young lawyers sect. 1975-76), Cuban-Am. Lawyers Assn., Federacion Interamericana de Abogados, Blue Key (pres. Fla. chpt.), Omicron Delta Kappa. Office: Boies Schiller & Flexner LLP Bank of Amer Tower 100 SE 2nd St Ste 2800 Miami FL 33131-2115 Office Phone: 305-539-8400. E-mail: szack@bsfllp.com.

**ZACKHEIM, MICHELE,** artist; b. Reno, May 5, 1941; d. Samuel and Elizabeth (Kamenetzky) Z.; m. Charles Ramsburg, May 29, 1980; children: Benjamin, Maggie. Student, U. Calif., Santa Barbara, 1959-60, Art Students League, 1960-62, New Sch. Social Rsch., 1963-64. Graphic designer NBC, N.Y.C., 1960-63; art dir. Metromedia, N.Y.C., 1963-65; creative dir. Advt. Design Assocs., N.Y.C., 1965-69; free-lance artist N.Y., N.Mex., 1969—. Artist-conceptor The Tent of Meeting, traveling exhibit of art and music, 1985—; one woman shows include Hill's Gallery of Contemporary Art, Santa Fe, 1980, Judah L. Magnes Meml. Mus., Berkeley, Calif., 1980, Bronfman Mus., Montreal, Can., 1981, Sarah Lawrence Coll., Bronxville, N.Y., 1985, Bryn Mawr Coll. Pa., 1981, 83, 85, N.Mex. Mus. Fine Arts, Santa Fe, 1985, Cathedral of St John the Divine, 1985, Yale U., 1985, Mus. of Am. Jewish History, Phila., 1985, Art Mus. South Tex., Corpus Christi, 1986, Ufundi Gallery, Ottawa, Can., 1986, Landmark Ctr., St. Paul, Minn., 1986, Scottsdale (Ariz.) Ctr. for Arts, 1987, Bade Mus., Berkeley, Calif., 1988, St. Mary's Cathedral, San Francisco, 1988, City of Ottawa, 1986; exhibited in group shows Carlsbad Mus. Fine Arts, N.Mex., 1981, U. Calif.-Irvine Gallery, 1982, U. Toronto, 1983, Hebrew Union Coll. Skirball Mus., 1984; represented in numerous permanent collections; author: Violette's Embrace, 1996; Einstein's Daughter: The Search for Lieserl, 1999; contbr. articles in field. Recipient art awards Am. Inst. Graphic Arts, 1965, Art Dirs. Club N.Y., 1966, N.Mex. Advt. Assn., 1981, Graphic Arts/Printing Industries, 1967. Jewish. Home: 282 W 4th St New York NY 10014-2401 Personal E-mail: mszack447@aol.com.

**ZACKHEOS, H.E. SOTIRIOS,** ambassador; b. Nicosia, Cyprus, Jan. 24, 1950; 2 children. BA in Law, U. Athens, 1972, BA in Econs. and Polit. Sci., 1976; MA in Polit. Sci., Stanford U., 1977. Corp. leader, credit control mgr. N.P. Lanitis Group of Cos.; attache in econ. divsn. and protocol dept. Ministry Fgn. Affairs, 1977-79, dir.-Dir.-Gens. Office, 1975—76, sec. polit. affairs divsn., 1977—79, clk. Cyprus Embassy in Moscow, 1979—85, agrl. dir. econ. and cultural dept., 1985—87, dir. dept. coordination, enlightenment and planning, 1987—89, first Cyprus resident amb. to China with concurrent accreditations to Japan, Pakistan, Philippines and Mongolia, 1989—93, dir. econ. affairs divsn., non-resident amb. of Cyprus to Lebanon, 1993, dir. polit. affairs divsn., 1995, permanent rep. to UN Office Geneva, 1996—97, NYC, 1997—. Office: 13 E 40th St New York NY 10016

**ZACKS, SHELEMYAHU,** mathematical sciences educator; b. Tel Aviv, Oct. 15, 1932; came to U.S., 1965; s. Yechezkiel and Devora (Kolomoitzev) Z.; m. Hanna Bilik; children: Yuval Joseph, David Noam. BA, Hebrew U., Jerusalem, Israel, 1956; MSc, Technion Israel Inst. Tech., Haifa, 1960; PhD, Columbia U., 1962; PhD (hon.), U. Haifa, 2005. Prof. stats. Kans. State U., Manhattan, 1965-68; prof. math-stats. U N. Mex., Albuquerque, 1968-70; prof. math-stats. Cse Western Reserve U., Cleve., 1970-79; prof. stats. Va. Polytech. U., Blacksburg, 1979-80; prof. math. scis. SUNY, Binghamton, 1980—. Chmn. dept. math. scis., SUNY, Binghamton, 1983-, dir. Ctr. Stats.

Quality Control and Design, SUNY, Binghamton, 1983— Author: (books) The Theory of Statistical Inference, 1971, Parametric Statistical Inference: Basic Theory and Modern Approaches, 1981, Inroduction to Reliability Analysis: Probability Models and Statistical Methods, 1992, Prediction Theory for Finite Populations, 1992, Stochastic Visibility in Random Fields, 1994, Modern Industrial Statistics: Design and Control of Quality and Reliability, 1998; contbr. over 160 articles and papers to profl. jours.; assoc. editor Jour. Am. Stats. Assn., 1971-72, 86-89, Annals of Math. Stats., 1972-74, Comm. in Stats. 1973-89, Naval Rsch. Logist. Qtrlyl, 1977-87, Sequential Analysis, 1986—; joint chief editor Jour. Stats., Planning and Inference, 1981-83, coordinating editor, 1983-91, adv. editor, 1991-98, exec. editor, 1998-2000. Grantee: NSF, Washington, 1966-70, Office Naval Rsch. Washington, 1970-82, Army Rsch. Office, Durham, N.C., 1982-90. Fellow AAAS, Am. Stats. Assn., Inst. Math. Stats.; mem. Internat. Stats. Assn. Avocation: viola player Binghamton Comty. Orch. Office: SUNY Binghamton Dept Math Scis Binghamton NY 13902-6000 Office Phone: 607-777-6035. Business E-mail: shelly@math.binghamton.edu.

**ZADEH, JAVAD HAMADANI,** mathematics professor; b. Kerman, Iran, Oct. 2, 1940; arrived in U.S., 1964; s. Bagher Hamadani Zadeh and Fatemeh Asadi; children: Neda, Mina. BA, The Am. U. Beirut, Lebanon, 1963; MS, Purdue U., West Lafayette, Ind., 1966; PhD, MPhil, Columbia U., N.Y., 1976. Cert. tchr. Ga. Profl. Standards Commn., 1988. Instr. math. Shiraz (Iran) U., 1963—64, Ctrl. Coll. Ky., Danville, Ky., 1966—67, Bowling Green (Ohio) State U., 1969—70; from instr. to assoc. prof. Sharif U. Tech., Tekraa, Iran, 1970—82, assoc. prof., 1982—86, chmn. Dept. Math. and Computer Sci., 1979—81; tchr. math. Ga. Pub. Schs., Atlanta, 1987—92; asst. prof. math Mid. Ga. Coll., Cochran, Ga., 1992—93; assoc. prof. Brewton-Parker Coll., Mt. Vernon, Ga., 1993—97, prof., 1997—; asst. prof. math. Dalton State Coll., Ga., 2006. Author: Shenidi Che-Gaft, 1970, 2d edit., 2000; editor: Bull. Iranian Math. Soc., 1979—81; contbr. articles to profl. jours. Fellow, U.S. Agy. Internat. Devel., 1959—63; scholar, Sharif U. Tech., 1974—77. Avocations: painting, photography, tennis. Home: 8740 Roswell Rd 9D Atlanta GA 30350

**ZAENTZ, SAUL,** film producer, former record company executive; b. Passaic, NJ, Feb. 28, 1921; Owner Fantasy Records, 1975—2005. Founder Saul Zaentz Film Ctr., 1980. Producer films: One Flew Over the Cuckoo's Nest, 1975 (Oscar for Best Picture, 1975), Three Warriors, 1977, Lord of the Rings, 1978, Amadeus, 1984 (Oscar for Best Picture, 1984), The Unbearable Lightness of Being, 1988, At Play in the Fields of the Lord, 1991, The English Patient, 1996 (Academy Award for Producer Best Picture, Irving G. Thalberg award, 1996); exec. producer The Mosquito Coast, 1986. Recipient Prod. of Yr. Award, Nat. Bd. Review, 2005; fellow Acad. Fellowship, British Acad. Film Award (BAFTA), 2003. Office: Saul Zaentz Co 2600 10th St Berkeley CA 94710-2522*

**ZAFERSON, WILLIAM S.,** philosophy educator, publisher; b. Kalavrita, Greece, Feb. 10, 1925; came to U.S., 1953; s. Steven A. and Katharine (Michael) Z.; m. Toni Adelgunde Humberg, Oct. 15, 1955. BA in Lit. cum laude, U. Athens, Greece, 1952; MA in Classical Lang. and Lit., U. Chgo., 1965; DPhil magna cum laude, U. Athens, 1976; postgrad., Truman Coll., 2000; Internat. Scholar in Tr origin. classical texts. Asst. prof. U. Upper Iowa, Fayette, 1966-68, Marymount Coll., Salina, Kans., 1968-70; prof. philosophy St. Mary's U., San Antonio, Tex., 1970-72. Internat. scholar translating original classical texts. Author: The Meaning of Metempsychosis, 1965, The Universe, Its Elements and Justice, 1974, A Hymn to Health, 1975, The Platonic View of Moral Law and the Influence of the Tragedians on Plato's Thoughts, 1976, The Perfect Family, 1986, The Heraclitean Logos, 1996; author, pub.: The Songs of the Muses for Gods and Men, 1999, (70 philos. poems set to music) Hephaestus, 2000, (poem set to music) Hermes to King Odysseus, 2001, (lyrics and music) Mother Gaea's Reprobation, 2001, (lyrics and music) Pluto and Persephone (A Look into the Elusinian Mysteries Verifying Every Soul's Immortality), 2002, (poem set to music) Hymn to the Earth: Mother of All, 2002, (music) The Throne of Virtue, 2002, The Titans (War of Ideologies). Vice versus Virtue, words & music), 2003, The Virtuous Woman, 2006, others. A. Daniel L. Shorey fellow, U. Chgo., 1955. Mem. NRTA, AAUP, Am. Philos. Assn. (ctrl. divsn. emeritus), U. Chgo. Alumni Assn., Am. Assn. Learned Socs., Goethe-Institut Chgo., Nat. Assn. Scholars, Am.-Swedish Cultural Assn., Chgo. Avocations: poetry, classical music, opera, hiking, swimming.

**ZAFFIRINI, JUDITH,** state legislator, small business owner; b. Laredo, Tex., Feb. 13, 1946; d. George and Nieves Pappas; m. Carlos Zaffirini, 1965; 1 child, Carlos Jr. BS, U. Tex., 1967, MA, 1970, PhD, 1978. Committeewoman Tex. State Dem. Exec. Com., 1978-84; mem. Tex. State Senate, 1987—, pres. pro tempore, 1997; owner Zaffirini Comms., Laredo, 1998—. Del. Dem. Nat. Conv., 1980, 84. Recipient Medal of Excellence Nat. League United Latin Am. Citizens, 1987, Jose Maria Morelos y Pavon Medal of Merit for leadership in strengthening U.S.-Mex. rels., 1987; named Woman of Achievement Tex. Press Women, 1980, Gov. of Tex. for a Day, Apr. 19, 1997, Ten Best Legislators Tex. Monthly Mag., 1997, 2001, Disting. Alumnus U. Tex., 2003; inductee Nat. Hispanic Hall of Fame, 1987. Democrat. Roman Catholic. Home: PO Box 627 Laredo TX 78042-0627 Office: 1407 Washington St Laredo TX 78040-4411 Office Phone: 956-724-8379. E-mail: judith.zaffirini@senate.state.tx.us.

**ZAFFRAM, ROBERT,** finance educator; b. Buffalo, Nov. 18, 1956; s. Louis and Betty Zaffram; m. Helen Ferraro; children: Peter children: Kimberly. MBA, Canisius Coll., 1984. Prof. Erie C C., Buffalo, 1986—. Democrat. Office: Erie C C 6205 Main St Buffalo NY 14221 Office Phone: 716-851-1525. Business E-Mail: zaffram@ecc.edu.

**ZAFIROPOULO, ARTHUR,** electronics executive; Pres. Rayca, v.p. lab. elecs., founder, pres. Drytek; pres. internat. ops. Gen. Signal Semiconductor Equipment Groups; CEO, pres., chmn. Ultratech Stepper, San Jose, Calif., 1990—. Patentee in field. Office: 3050 Zanker Rd San Jose CA 95134-2126

**ZAGAJEWSKI, ADAM,** poet, writer; b. Lwów (now Soviet Ukraine), June 1945; Grad., Jagiellonian U. Vis. assoc. prof., creative writing U. Houston, 1988—. Co-editor of Zeszyty Literackie (Literary Review), Paris; collections are: Pragnienie, 1999; Ziemia ognista, 1994; Jechac do Lwowa, 1985, Sklepy miesne, 1975, Komunikat, 1972; (books of poetry in English) Mysticism for Beginners (Farrar, Straus & Giroux, 1997. Translated by Clare Cavanaugh), Tremor (1985, translated by Renata Gorczyński), Canvas 1991 (translated by Renata Gorczyński, B. Ivry, and C. K. Williams); author (memoir) Another Beauty (2000, translated by Clare Cavanagh) and the prose collections, Two Cities (1995, translated by Lillian Vallee) and Solitude and Solidarity (1990, translated by Lillian Vallee). Recipient Kurt Tucholsky prize, Prix de la Liberté, Neustadt Internat. prize, 2004; Berliner Kunstlerprogramm Fellowship, Guggenheim Fellowship. One of the leading poets of the Generation of '68' or the Polish New Wave; one of Poland's most famous contemporary poets.

**ZAGANO, PHYLLIS,** religious studies educator; BA in English, Marymount Coll., Tarrytown, NY, 1969; MS in Pub. Rels., Boston U., 1970; MA in English, L.I.U., 1972; PhD in English, SUNY, Stony Brook, 1979; MA in Theology, St. John's U., Jamaica, N.Y., 1990. Program officer Nat. Humanities Ctr., N.Y.C., 1979—80; asst. prof. comms. Fordham U., Bronx, NY, 1980—84; rschr. Archdiocese of N.Y., 1984—86; ind. rschr. N.Y.C., 1986—88; assoc. prof. comm. Boston U., Comm. Theology Dem. Com., 1988—98; adj. assoc. prof. theology Boston U., 1988—98, dir. inst. for democratic comm., 1988—98; sr. rsch. assoc. in residence, spl. assoc. prof. religious studies Hofstra U., Hempstead, NY, 2002—. Vis. assoc. prof. Cath. studies Yale Div. Sch., 2005; vis. Aquinas chair St. Thomas Aquinas Coll., 2004. Author: Religion and Public Affairs, 1987, Social Impact of the Mass Media, 1991, Woman to Woman, 1993, On Prayer, 1994, Ita Ford: Missionary Martyr, 1996, Twentieth Century Apostles, 1999, Things New and Old, 1999, Holy Saturday: An Argument for the Restoration of the Formale Diaconate in the Catholic Church, 2000 (Book award Catholic Press Assn. 2001, Coll. Theology Soc. 2002), Dorothy Day: In My Own Words, 2003, Called to Serve: A Spirituality for Deacons, 2004, The Dominican Tradition, 2006, Acerca de la Oracion: Una Carta a Mi Amijado (Book award Cath. Press Assn. 2003); monthly radio host Boston U. World of Ideas, 1992-97 Lector, lay min. Ch. St. Vincent Ferrer, N.Y.C., 1980—92, Our Lady of the Miraculous Medal Ch., 1996—, Newman Ctr., Boston U., 1992—96. Comdr. USNR, 1976—. Faculty Rsch. grantee Fordham U., 1983, Rsch. grantee Nat. Inst. Peace, 1989, Rsch. grantee Wabash Ctr., 2003; Coolidge fellow Episcopal Divinity Sch., 1987; recipient citation for heroism Nassau County (N.Y.) Fire Commn., 1995. Mem. Am. Acad. Religion (co-chair Roman Cath. Studies, 1995-2001), Am. Cath. Philos. Assn., Coll. Theology Soc., Cath. Theol. Soc. Am., Naval Res. Assn., Soc. for Study of Christian Spirituality. Roman Catholic. Office: 115 Hofstra Univ Hempstead NY 11549 Office Phone: 516-463-5612. Business E-Mail: phyllis.zagano@hofstra.edu.

**ZAGAR, ROBERT JOHN,** psychologist, researcher; b. Great Lakes, Ill., Nov. 26, 1948; s. Anthony John and Helen Gertrude (Kurzynowski) Z.; m. Agata. MS in Psychology, Ill. Inst. Tech., Chgo., 1975; PhD in Psychology, Northwestern U., 1981; MPH in Pub. Health, U. Ill. Med. Ctr., Chgo., 1982; postgrad., DePaul U., 1982-83, Barry U., 1984-85. Clin. psychologist, Ill.; sch. psychologist, Ill. Sch. psychologist Chgo. Pub. Schs., 1991-93; asst. prof. Nat. Louis U., Evanston, Ill., 1991-93; psychologist Juvenile Divsn. Cir. Ct., Chgo., 1985-91; economist Ill. Dept. Labor, 1986-87; pvt. practice Chgo., 1992—. Cons. psychologist But. Disability Determination, Chgo., 1992—; Dept. Children and Family Svcs., 1992—, Juvenile Divsn. Cir. Ct., 1992—; asst. prof. Ill. Sch. Profl. Psychology, 1989—91; sch. psychologist Aurora Pub. Schs., Ill., 1989—91; asst. prof. Forest Sch. Profl. Psychology, Wheeling, 1988—89; sch. psychology Chgo. Pub. Schs., 1999—, Woodstock, 2000—01; invited spkr. Nat. Summit Youth Violence, U.S. Dept. Dept. Corrections, others; asst prof. Lewis U., 1998—. Contbr. articles to profl. jours. in field of neuropsychol. tests, forensic exams. and aggress. Mem. APA, APHA, Am. Psychol. Soc., Fla. Psychol. Assn., Ill. Psychol. Assn., Nat. Assn. Sch. Psychologists. Roman Catholic. Office Phone: 312-266-3411. Personal E-mail: drzagar@hotmail.com.

**ZAGARIS, BRUCE,** lawyer; b. Modesto, Calif., Sept. 4, 1947; s. Nickolas M. and Dorothy (Chicoine) Zagaris. BA, George Washington U., 1969; JD, 1972, LLM, 1973, Stockholm U., 1975; student, Free U., Brussels, 1976. Bar: Oreg. 1973, Idaho 1976, Calif. 1978, US Ct. Appeals (10th cir.) 1978, US Ct. Appeals (4th cir.) 1979, US Supreme Ct. 1982. Law clk. US Dist. Ct., Charleston, W.Va., 1972—73; asst. atty. gen. State of Idaho, Boise, 1973—74; atty., cons. Ada Coun. Govt., Boise, 1974; assoc. Nordic Law Cons., Brussels and Stockholm, 1974—76, Glad Tuttle & White, San Francisco, 1976—77; lectr. U. W.I., Bridgetown, Barbados, 1977—78; ptnr Berliner & Maloney, Washington, 1978—90; adj. prof. Antioch Sch. Law, Washington, 1983—84; counsel Oppenheimer, Wolff & Donnelly, 1990—92; adj. prof. Fordham U. Sch. law, 1990—; assoc. Cameron & Hombostel, 1992—; cons. 13 nat. govt. UN; adj. prof. Washington Coll. Sch. Law Am. U., 1993, U. Montana Law Sch., 2004—06; editor in chief, reporter Internat. Enforcement Law; editor Internat. Criminal Law Casebook, 2006. Author: (book) Internat. Tax Law, 1978, Fgn. Investment in US, 1980; editor: Internat. Hanbook on Drug Control, 1992. Mem.: Internat. Penal Law Assn. (rep. to orgn. of Am. states), Internat. Fiscal Assn., Washington Fgn. Law Soc. (pres. 1990—91), Am. Soc. Internat. Law (exec. coun. 1990—92), ABA (chmn. com. internat. tax law, sect. internat. tax law 1989—92, chmn. com. internat. criminal law, criminal justice sect. 1990—93, Union Internationales des Avocats, coordinating com. immigration), Epsilon Housing Trust (mem. Washington 1984), Sigma Chi. Office: Berliner Corcoran & Rowe LLP 1101 Seventeenth St NW Ste 1100 Washington DC 20036 Office Phone: 202-293-5555.

**ZAGASKI, CHESTER ANTHONY, JR.,** writer, researcher, consultant; b. Manchester, Conn., Mar. 28, 1949; s. Chester Anthony Sr. and Lenora M.; m. Suzanne M. Celata, Apr. 1979 (div. Apr. 1989); children: Jason Paul, Brian Matthew. BA, U. S.C., 1971; postgrad., Northeastern U. Sch. Law, Wilbraham, Mass., 1971-72, U. Conn., 1973-75. Career trainee Hartford (Conn.) Ins. Co., 1971; spl. agt. Am. Group, Worcester, Mass., 1973-76; supr. underwriter Interstate Nat./Chgo. Ins., Boston, underwriting mgr. Phila., 1977-79; reins. mgr. N.Am. Reins. (Swiss Re), Phila., 1979-80; asst. v.p. Falcon Ins. Co./Comml. Union Group, Boston 1980-82; acct. exec. Frank B. Hall & Co., Boston, 1982-84; surplus lines broker Stewart Smith East (USA), Boston, 1984-86; sr. underwriting cons. CNA Ins. Co., Quincy, Mass., 1986-89. Former med. ins. and risk mgmt. cons. to several prominent firms and groups; organizational cons. Omnium Capital, Montreal, 1st Physicians Ins. Co. Vt., 1995, 96; instr., lectr. Inst. Libr. Assn. Boston, Tufts U., 1984-88; former advisor govt. and bus. groups, 1982-90, including New Eng. Coun., Inc., SBA New Eng., Commonwealth of Mass., Dept. Environ. Protection, Joint Ins. Com. of Mass. Legis., U.S. Congl. Subcom., U.S. SEC; lead organizer, cons. A Spl. Purpose Ins. Co., 1983; provider expert testimony before state and fed. legis. coms., among others; workshop and seminar leader. Author: Environmental Risk and Insurance, 1992; contbr. profl. bus. mags. and jours. (40 plus); involved in prodn. (films) A Civil Action, 1997. Mem. Quincy City Rep. Com., 1989-91; del. State Conv., Boston, 1990; advisor nat. Bush/Quayle Campaigns, 1989, 92; charter mem., sponsor WWII Meml., Washington, 1997. Recipient Citation of Merit Mass. Legis. Spl. Commn. Liability Release Hazardous Materials Rep. Emmett Hayes, 1986. Mem. Harvard Sq. Script Writers, Cape Cod Writers Ctr. Roman Catholic. Achievements include discovery of Royal Crown artifacts and British East India Tea Co. and Mass. Bay Co. pieces from 1620 with exceptions; and collection of the full lost dark masterpiece in cameo The Adoration of the Shepherd by Giorgionine.

**ZAGAT, NINA,** publishing executive; m. Tim Zagat, 1965; children: Ted, John. AB, Vassar Coll., 1963; LLB, Yale U.; attended, Le Cordon Bleu Ecole de Cuisine. Atty. Sherman and Sterling, N.Y.C., 1966—90; co-founder, co-pub. Zagat Survey, N.Y.C., 1979—; co-chair, co-founder Zagat.com, 1999—. Served on White House Conference on Travel and Tourism; mem. Who's Who of Food and Beverage in Am.; mem. of the corp. Culinary Institute of Am., 1994—; established lecture series, 2001. Office: Zagat Survey 4 Columbus Circle New York NY 10019

**ZAGAT, TIM,** publishing executive; m. Nina Zagat, 1965; children: Ted, John. BA, Harvard U., 1961; LLB, Yale U., 1966. Assoc. Hughes, Hubbard & Reed; ptnr. Pomerantz, Levy, Haudek & Block, 1976—82; chief litigation counsel Gulf & Western Industries Inc., 1980—87; co-founder, publisher Zagat Survey, 1979—. Office: Zagat Survey 4 Columbus Circle New York NY 10019

**ZAGEL, JAMES BLOCK,** federal judge; b. Chgo., Mar. 4, 1941; s. Samuel and Ethel (Samuels) Z.; m. Margaret Maxwell, May 27, 1979. BA, U. Chgo., 1962, MA in Philosophy, 1962; JD, Harvard U., 1965. Bar: Ill. 1965, U.S. Dist. Ct. (no. dist.) Ill. 1965, U.S. Supreme Ct. 1970, U.S. Ct. Appeals (7th cir.) 1972. Asst. state atty. Cook County, 1965—69; asst. atty. gen. criminal justice divsn. State of Ill., Springfield, 1970-77; chief prosecuting atty. Ill. Jud. Inquiry Bd., Springfield, 1973-75; exec. dir. Ill. Law Enforcement Commn., Springfield, 1977-79; dir. Ill. Dept. Revenue, Springfield, 1979-80, Ill. Dept. State Police, Springfield, 1980-87; judge U.S. Dist. Ct. (no. dist.) Ill., Chgo., 1987—. Co-author: Criminal Law and Its Administration, 1989, Cases and Comments on Criminal Procedure, 1992, Author's Money to Burn, 2002. Named Outstanding Young Citizen, Chgo. Jaycees, 1977; recipient Disting. Soc. Merit award Assn. Commerce and Industry, 1983. Mem. Chgo. Bar Assn., Jud. Coun. of U.S. (codes of conduct com. 1987-92). Office: US Dist Ct 219 S Dearborn Ste 2588 Chicago IL 60604-1801

**ZAGEL, MARGARET MAXWELL,** lawyer; b. Centralia, Ill., Jan. 17, 1949; d. Francis Edgar and Joan (Beckmeyer) Maxwell; m. James Block Zagel, May 27, 1979. BA, Tulane U., 1970; JD, U. Ill., 1973. Bar: Ill. 1973, U.S. Ct. Appeals (7th cir.), U.S. Supreme Ct. Atty. Ill. Appellate Defender's Office, Chgo., 1973-75, law clk. to Hon. Seymour Simon, 1975-76; assoc., then ptnr. Schuyler Roche & Zwirner, Chgo., 1976-84; gen. counsel Grant

Thornton LLP, Chgo., 1984-98, mng. prin. risk, regulatory & legal affairs, gen counsel, 2003; v.p., gen. counsel Tellabs, Inc., Lisle, Ill., 1998—99; sr. v.p., chief legal and admin. officer Organic, Inc., San Francisco, 1999—2001; spec. coun. litigation transactions Arthur Andersen LLP, 2002; practice lead, corp. governance, risk and crisis mgmt., co-gen. coun. Altheimer & Gray, 2002—03. Mem. planning com. Securities Inst. Northwestern U., Chgo., 1993—, mem. corp. counsel planning com., 1994-2000; mem. civil justice reform adv. com. U.S. Cir. Ct. (no. dist.) Ill., Chgo., 1994-95; mem. Ill. Commn. Regulatory Issues, mem. ACCA 1986, Nat. Assoc. Corp. Dir., 2002-2004, Economic Club Chgo. 2003-, Women Corp. Dirs. 2003-; mem. vis. com. Coll. Law U. Ill., 1997-2001.; bd. dirs Atrion Corp. 2002-2003. Office: Grant Thornton LLP 175 W Jackson 20th Fl Chicago IL 60604 Office Phone: 312-602-8413.

**ZAGER, BERNARD SOLOMON,** physician, consultant; b. Detroit, Nov. 3, 1926; s. Philip and Lena Zager; m. Denise Acheson, Sept. 11, 1953; children: Robert, Gerald, Martin. BA with distinction, Wayne State U., 1946; MD, Northwestern U., 1950. Diplomate Am. Bd. Preventive Medicine and Occpl. Medicine. Intern Detroit Grace Hosp., 1949-50, resident in surgery, 1952-56; chief physician AAD Ford Motor Co., Utica, Mich., 1964-68; med. dir. Nuc. Energy Divsn. GE, San Jose, Calif., 1968-87; occupl. medicine cons. Reno, 1987—. Capt. U.S. Army, 1950—51, Korea. Mem.: Alpha Omega Alpha. Home and Office: 1210 Bridlewood Way Reno NV 89509-7116 Office Phone: 775-329-8940. E-mail: bernzag@aol.com.

**ZAGER, RICHARD A.,** medical educator, researcher; s. Max and Ruth Zager; m. Brenda K. Burger, Apr. 15, 1973; children: David, Michael, Amy. BS, Northwestern U., 1965, MD, 1969. Diplomate Am. Bd. of Internal Medicine, 1974. Asst. chief of medicine VA, Roxbury, Mass., 1976—80; assoc. prof. of medicine Ohio State U., Columbus, 1980—85; chief of nephrology Harborview Med. Ctr., Seattle, 1985—2000; head of nephrology Fred Hutchinson Cancer Rsch. Ctr., Seattle, 1990—. Cons. Abbott Labs., Chgo., 1995—; mem. NIH Study Sect., Bethesda, Md., 2002—. Contbr. over 130 articles to profl. jours.; reviewer: articles in 20 profl. jours.; contbr. chapters to books; mem. editl. bd.; Kidney Internat., 1992, Jour. of Am. Soc. of Nephrology, 1996—2002. Lt. comdr. USPHS, 1971—73. Named Hon. Chmn., US Congress, State of Wash. Physicians, 2002; recipient Merit award, 2002; grantee, NIH, 2000. Mem.: Internat. Soc. of Nephrology, Am. Soc. of Nephrology. Avocations: skiing, fishing, gardening, piano. Office: Fred Hutchinson Cancer Research Center 1100 Fairview Ave N PO Box 19024 Seattle WA 98109-1024

**ZAGER, RONALD I.,** chemist, consultant; b. N.Y.C., Dec. 27, 1934; s. Joseph and Theodora Zager; m. Judith Ellen Bilt, Dec. 24, 1961 (div. July 1975); children: Scott Lawrence, Joseph Daniel; m. Anne Coykendall Chase, 1995. BS, Bklyn. Coll., 1955; MS in Chemistry, Stevens Inst. Tech., 1969. Chemist Charles Pfizer & Co., N.Y.C., 1956-58, Halocarbon Products, Hackensack, N.J., 1958-66; devel. chemist Tenneco Chems., Garfield, N.J., 1966-71; sr. chemist Givaudan Corp., Clifton, N.J., 1971-77; tech. dir. Internat. Flavors and Fragrances, Union Beach, N.J., 1977-88; cons. Highlands, N.J., 1988-92, Glen, N.H., 1993—; pres. Ronald Zager Assocs LLC. Overseas tech. cons. Unistar Program, UN, 1992. Mem. Am. Chem. Soc., Assn. Cons. Chemists and Chem. Engrs. (v.p. 1990-92, pres. 1993-94). Achievements include research in aroma chemicals and organic fluorocarbons. Office: Ronald Zager Assocs LLC Box 1200 85 Glen Ledge Rd Glen NH 03838 E-mail: rzager@chemconsultants.com.

**ZAGHLOUL, NORANN AMIR,** geneticist, research scientist; b. Kitchener-Waterloo, Ontario, Canada, Jan. 20, 1978; d. Amir Ibrahim and Mona Elwakked Zaghloul; m. Mohamed Tamer Abdelrahman Refaei, Jan. 2, 2003. BA, Johns Hopkins U., Balt.; MS, PhD, George Wash. U., DC. Grad. tchg. asst. George Wash. U., 2000—03, rsch. asst., 2000—06; postdoctoral fellow Johns Hopkins U., 2006—. Fellow Presdl. Merit Fellowship, George Wash. U., 2003. Mem.: Egyptian Am. Cultural Assn. (v.p. 2000), Soc. Devel. Biology. Achievements include research in genetic control of retinal development.

**ZAGON, IAN STUART,** neuroscience and anatomy educator, researcher, inventor; s. Benjamin and Beatrice (Shaffer) Z.; m. Eileen Kostel, Nov. 26, 1964. BS, U. Wis., 1965; MS, U. Ill., 1969; PhD, U. Colo., 1972. Asst. prof. biol. structure U. Miami, Fla., 1972-74; asst. prof. anatomy Pa. State U., Hershey, 1974-78, prof. genetics, 1975—, assoc. prof., 1978-85, prof., 1985-91, prof. cell and molecular biology and neurosci., 1984—, prof. neurosci. and anatomy, 1991—2003, prof. neural and behavioral scis., 2003—, Disting. educator, 2002—, program dir. on edn. in human studies, 2005—, disting. prof., 2005—. Cons. Nat. Inst. on Drug Abuse, Rockville, Md., 1980—; cons., reviewer NIH, Bethesda, Md., 1984—; grant reviewer Am. Heart Assn. of Pa., 1985—, mem. rsch. com., 1988—, bd. dirs., 1992-97, v.p., 1993-96; founder ZoeGenics LLC. Author: Maternal Substance Abuse and the Developing Nervous System, 1992, Receptors in the Developing Nervous System, 1993; mem. editl. bd. Brain Rsch. Bull., 1980—, sect. editor, 1994—; mem. editl. bd. Physiology and Behavior, 1987-97, Pharmacology, Biochemistry and Behavior, 1989—, Internat. Jour. Oncology, 1998—, Advances in Neuroimmunology, 1990, Internat. Jour. Devel. Neurosci., 1987-89, Brain Rsch., 1992—, Devel. Brain Rsch., 1992—, Internat. Jour. Oncology, 1999—, Cancer Therapy, 2003—, Exptl. Biology and Medicine, 2006—; contbr. numerous articles to med. and profl. jours.; patentee on growth factors and devel. cancer. Recipient Entrepreneurial Achievement award, Kutztown U.; grantee NIH, Am. Cancer Soc., Nat. Inst. Drug Abuse, Philip Morris. Mem.: Am. Assn. Cancer Rsch., Am. Diabetes Assn., Assn. for Rsch. in Vision and Ophthalmology, Soc. for Neurosci., Am. Soc. Cell Biology. Achievements include discovery of low-dose naltrexone and opioid growth factor therapies, non-erythroid spectrin CCK-C receptor. Office: Pa State U Coll Medicine PO Box 850 H109 500 University Dr Hershey PA 17033-0850 E-mail: isz1@psu.edu.

**ZAGORIA, SAM D(AVID),** reporter, educator, federal agency administrator; b. Somerville, N.J., Apr. 9, 1919; s. Nathan and Rebecca (Shapiro) Z.; m. Sylvia Bomse, Dec. 21, 1941; children: Paul, Marjorie Zagoria Isacks, Ronald. BL in Journalism, Rutgers U., 1941. With New Brunswick (N.J.) Daily Home News, 1940-41, N.J. Def. Coun., Trenton, 1941-42, Fed. Office Govt. Reports, Newark, 1942; reporter Washington Post, 1946-55; adminstrv. asst. to Senator Clifford P. Case, Washington, 1955-65; pres. Washington Newspaper Guild, 1953; mem. NLRB, Washington, 1965-69; dir. Labor-Mgmt. Rels. Svc. U.S. Conf. of Mayors, Washington, 1970-78; mem. U.S. Consumer Product Safety Commn., 1978-84; ombudsman Washington Post, 1984-86; arbitrator, 1986—. Fulbright lectr., Copenhagen, 1987; vis. prof. Fla. Atlantic U., Boca Raton, 1988—91; adj. prof. Wake Forest U., Winston-Salem, NC, 1993—2001. Author: Public Workers, Public Unions, 1972, The Ombudsman: How Good Governments Handle Citizens' Grievances, 1988. Campaign mgr. reelection Senator Case, 1960; campaign mgr. race for gov., former Sec. of Labor James P. Mitchell, 1961. With USAAF, 1942-45. Nieman fellow Harvard U., 1954. Mem. Common Cause, Nat. Consumers League, Rutgers U. Alumni Assn. Jewish. also: 2864 Wynfield Crossing Ln Winston Salem NC 27103-6597 Address: 3101 S Ocean Blvd 622 Boca Raton FL 33487 Office Phone: 561-274-6376.

**ZAGORIN, JANET SUSAN,** legal firm administrator, marketing professional; b. Lakewood, NJ; d. Irving C. and Dorothy (Tarshish) Zagorin. BA, Douglass Coll., 1975; MLS, Rutgers U., 1977. Asst. law libr. N.J. Atty. Gen., Trenton, 1977-78; head of reference sect. Cardozo U. Law Sch., NYC, 1978-79; law and legis. svcs. libr. FTC, Washington, 1979-81; dir. of reference Paul Weiss Rifkind, NYC, 1981-82; libr. dir. Riker Danzig Scherer & Hyland, Morristown, NJ, 1982; libr., profl. devel. dir. Baker & McKenzie, NYC, 1982-96; dir. practice devel. info. svcs. Stroock & Stroock & Lavan LLP, NYC, 1996-98; dir. practice devel. Cadwalader, Wickersham & Taft, NYC, 1998-99; Gibson, Dunn & Crutcher, NYC, 1999—2001; dir. mktg. Sidley Austin Brown & Wood, NYC, 2001—04; dir. practice devel. Sidley Austin LLP, NYC, 2004—. Bd. dirs N.Y. Cares, 1998—. Mem.: ABA (vice chmn. standing com. Law Libr. Congress 1995—96, chmn.

1996—2001, law 2000 steering com. Libr. Congress), Am. Assn. Law Librs. (chair fgn. comparative internat. law com. 1990—91, vice chair pvt. law librs. 1990—91, chair com. on recruitment 1991, chair 1991—), Fin. Women's Assn. (bd. dirs. 1993—95, 1999—), Hadassah. Office: Sidley Austin LLP 787 Seventh Ave New York NY 10019-6018 Office Phone: 212-839-8797. Business E-Mail: jzagorin@sidley.com.

**ZAGORIN, PEREZ,** historian, educator; b. Chgo., May 29, 1920; s. Solomon Novitz and Mildred (Ginsburg) Z.; m. Honoré Desmond Sharrer, May 29, 1947; 1 son, Adam. AB, U. Chgo., 1941; A.M., Harvard U., 1947, PhD, 1952. Various positions OWI, U.S. Govt., U.P. Syndicate, CIO, 1942-46; instr. Amherst Coll., 1947-49; lectr. Vassar Coll., 1951-53; from asst. prof. to prof. history McGill U., 1955-65; prof. U. Rochester, 1965—, Joseph C. Wilson prof. history, 1982-90, Joseph C. Wilson prof. history emeritus, 1990—, chmn. dept., 1968-69, acting chmn. dept., 1988-89; vis. prof. Johns Hopkins, 1964-65; Amundsen vis. prof. U. Pitts., 1964; William Andrews Clark Meml. Library prof. UCLA, 1975-76. Thompson lectr. history Vassar Coll., 1987. Author: A History of Political Thought in the English Revolution, 1954, 2d edit., 2000, The Court and the Country, 1969, Culture and Politics from Puritanism to the Enlightenment, 1980, Rebels and Rulers 1500-1660, 2 vols., 1982, 2d edit., 2003, Ways of Lying: Dissimulation, Persecution, and Conformity in Early Modern Europe, 1990, Milton Aristocrat and Rebel: The Poet and His Politics, 1992, Francis Bacon, 1998, The English Revolution: Politics, Events, Ideas, 1998, How the Idea of Religious Toleration Came to the West, 2003, Thycydides: An Introduction for the Common Reader, 2005; co-editor: Philosophy Science and Religion in England 1640-1700, 1991, Guide to Historical Literature, 1994; contbr. numerous articles to hist. jours.; mem. editl. bd. Jour. of the History of Ideas. Sheldon travel fellow Harvard U., 1949-50, Fulbright fellow 1949-50, faculty rsch. fellow Social Sci. Coun., 1958-59, 61-62, sr. rsch. fellow Folger Shakespeare Libr., 1964-65, fellow Inst. Advanced Study, Princeton, N.J., 1972-73, sr. fellow Nat. Humanities Ctr., 1978-79, fellow Ctr. Advanced Study in Behavioral Scis., 1983-84, Guggenheim fellow, 1983-84, Edgar F. Shannon Ctr. for Advanced Studies fellow U. Va., 1994—, Fellow Royal Hist. Soc., Am. Acad. Arts and Scis.; mem. Am. Hist. Assn. (chmn. Gershoy and Schuyler prize com. 1982-84). Home: 2990 Beaumont Farm Rd Charlottesville VA 22901-8717 Office: U Rochester Dept History Rochester NY 14627

**ZAGURSKY, ROBERT,** microbiologist, researcher; PhD, U. Md., 1982. Postdoctoral fellow Frederick (Md.) Rsch. Cancer Inst., 1982—84; rschr. DuPont, Wilmington, Del., 1984—90, DuPont Merck Pharm., Wilmington, 1990—94; rsch. fellow Am. Home Products/Wyeth-Ayerst, West Henrietta, NY, 1994—2003, Wyeth Vaccines, Pearl River, NY, 2003—. Third world missionary work Found. For Peace (www.foundationforpeace.org), 2005—06. Recipient Wyeth Team of the Year award; fellow, NIH, 1982—84. Mem.: N.Y. Acad. Scis. (microbiology coun. mem. 2005—06). Achievements include patents for NucA protein from Haemophilus Influenza; method for sequencing DNA; patents pending for recombinant Pilin vaccines against Neisseria Gonorrhoeae or Neisseria Meningitidis; Chlamydia Trachomatis Genomic sequence; Chlamydia Pneumonia Genomic sequence; surface proteins of Streptoccoccus Pyogenes; novel immunogeneic compositions for the prevention of Meningococcal disease; Alloiococcus Otitidis open reading frames; novel Streptococcus Pneumoniae open reading frames; research in use of bioinformatics for vaccine discovery. Office: Wyeth Vaccine Rsch 401 N Middletown Rd Pearl River NY 10965 Office Phone: 845-602-3014. Business E-Mail: zagursrj@wyeth.com.

**ZAHEDI, SINA,** electrical engineer, researcher; b. Tehran, Tehran, Iran, July 8, 1976; s. Masoud Zahedi and Parivash Abedian. BS, Sharif U. Tech. Tehran, Iran, 1998, MS, 2000; postgrad. in PhD program, Stanford U., 2000—. Rsch. asst. Sharif U. Tech., Tehran, 1997—2000, Stanford U., Stanford, Calif., 2000—. Pres. Persian Student Assn., Stanford U., Stanford, Calif., 2002—03. Mem.: IEEE (sec. student br., Sharif U. Tech. 1997—98, chmn. comm. student br. 1998—99). Office: Stanford University Packard Bldg 257 Stanford CA 94305 E-mail: szahedi@stanford.edu.

**ZAHLER, NOEL BARRY,** composer, music educator; b. NYC, May 10, 1951; s. Murray Gustav Zahler and Marion Horowitz; m. Clara Tatar, Aug. 24, 1975; children: Mathieu Pierce, Metisse Petra. BA, MA, CUNY Queens Coll., 1970—74; MFA, Princeton U., 1974—76; Certificato di Perfezionamento, L'Accademia Musicale Chigiana, 1976—77; D of musical arts, Columbia U., 1982—88. Preceptor Columbia U., NYC, 1984—86; asst. prof. music Conn. Coll., New London, 1984—90, assoc. prof. music, 1990—94, prof. music, 1994—2000, Sylvia Pasternack Marx prof. music, 2000—04; prof., dir. Sch. Music U. Minn., Mpls./St. Paul, 2004—. Dir. Cummings Electronic and Digital Sound Studios, New London, 1984—; founding dir. Ammerman Ctr. Arts and Tech., New London; v.p. Am. Composers Alliance, New York, Conn., 2002—. Composer: (concerto) Concerto for clarinet, chamber orchestra and interactive computer, (string quartet) String Quartet I, (fanfare) Olin Fanfare, (flute and interactive computer) Within The Dome Of Time, (solo guitar) reCollections, (solo piano) Piano Etudes, (video soundtrack) Sculler's dream, (orchestral) Symphony, (video soundtrack) Gothic Tempest (Silver Medal, Swiss Internat. Video Competition, 1988), (chamber opera) Automata, (piano trio) Trio (NEA Consortium Commn., 1984), (chamber orchestra) Agarttha (Aaron Copland Found. Grant for rec., 2000), (electronic) Electronic Study No. 4, (song with mixed ensemble) All Night, (solo violoncello) Rhapsody for violoncello alone, (chamber orchestra) Harlequin (NYSCA Rec. Award, 1981), (mixed ensemble) Charms, (solo violin) Tableau, (song cycle) Four Songs of Departure (NYSCA rec. grant, 1980), (solo piano) Regions I (NYSCA rec. grant, 1980), (song cycle) Three Yeats Songs for soprano and chamber orchestra, (electronic) Electronic Study No. 3, (song) Tears, (electronic) Computer Syudy No. 2, (flute and piano) Sonatina for flute and piano, (electronic) Kriss Kross, Computer Study No. I, (duo for violin and cello) Study for violin and cello, (interactive music for dance) Au Volant, (documentary soundtrack) Movement and Magic (CPTV Award for Best Documentary Yr., 1999), (song cycle) Songs from Salamandra, (solo clarinet) For clarinet alone, (virtual reality soundscape) Cézanne Set. Elected mem. Waterford Bd. Edn., Conn., 1995—99; dir. Laban/Bartenieff Inst. Movement Studies, Inc., NYC, 1987—89, TechConn, Groton, Conn., 1992—94, Thames Valley Music Sch., Conn., 1992—2000. Recipient Best Documentary Yr., Conn. Pub. TV, 2000, Best Soundtrack for exptl. video, Conn. Public TV/Conn. Commn. Arts, 1988, Individual Artists Award, State Conn. Commn. Arts, 1985; fellow Fullbright-Hays Full Grant, US Congress, 1976-1977, Residency, Composers Conf., 1976, Atlantic Ctr. Arts, 1997, Associated Kyoto Program, 1990, MacDowell Colony, 1983 and 1979; grantee Rsch. Grant at CNUCE, Italian NRC, 1977, Consortium Commn., Nat. Endowment arts, 1983-1984, Composers Grant, Meet the Composer, 1978 to date; scholar Summer Electronic Music Conf. at Dartmouth Coll. and U. NH, Nat. Endowment Arts, 1972; Grant for Rec., NY State Coun. Arts, 1981. Mem.: Conn. Composers, Inc. (corr.; pres. 1987—89), Composers Guild (corr.; dir. 1996—2000), Soc. Composers, Inc. (corr.; regional chair 1997—2000), Am. Composers Alliance (corr.; v.p. 2002—), Soc. Electro Acoustic Music US (assoc.), Internat. Computer Music Assn. (assoc.), Coll. Music Soc. (assoc.), Broadcast Music, Inc. (assoc.). Achievements include research in Score Follow, a computer program that listens to and follows a live performer, achieving accompaniment or spatialization of sound. Office: Univ Minn Sch Music 2106 Fourth St S Minneapolis MN 55455 Office Phone: 612-624-5740. Business E-Mail: nbz2@umn.edu.

**ZAHN, CARL FREDERICK,** museum program director, photographer, graphics designer; b. Louisville, Mar. 9, 1928; s. Fred Joseph and Myrtle (Fulks) Z.; m. Betty Jane Woodrow, Nov. 18, 1950 (div. July 1977); children: Lisa, Karen, Richard; m. Felicitas Magdalena Fuhlrott, July 30, 1979 (dec. Mar. 1999). BA, Harvard U., 1948. Asst. in conservation Fogg Art Mus., Cambridge, Mass., 1949-50; with art dept. Benton & Bowles Inc., N.Y.C., 1950-51; design asst. Inst. Contemporary Art, Boston, 1951-56; dir. publs. Mus. Fine Arts, Boston, 1956—; also dir. exhbns., 1995-96; ret., 1997; co-founder Mus. Pub. Ptnrs., 2000. Exhibitions include: Addison Gallery Am. Art, Andover, Mass., 1959, Am. Inst. Graphic Arts, N.Y.C., 1960—, Rose Art Mus. Brandeis U., Waltham, Mass., 1969; author: Introduction to Hermann

Zapf and His Design Philosophy, 1987, Books and Such Designed by Carl Zahn at the Museum of Fine Arts, Boston, 1956-97, 1997; co-author Weston's Westons: Portraits and Nudes, 1989; co-editor: Eye of the Beholder: Masterpieces from the Isabella Stewart Gardner Museum, 2003. Mem. Soc. Printers, Bund Deutscher Buchkünstler, East Chop Tennis Club (bd. dirs. 1970-72), Longwood Cricket Club. also: 1808 Par Pl Sarasota FL 34240-9689 E-mail: czbird@comcast.net.

**ZAHN, DONALD JACK,** lawyer; b. Oct. 24, 1941; s. Jerome and Clara (Zinsher) Z.; m. Laurie R. Hyman, Aug. 19, 1966; children: Lawrence, Melissa. AB, NYU, 1963; LLB, Union U., 1966; LLM in Taxation, NYU, 1967. Bar: N.Y. 1966, U.S. Dist. Ct. (no. dist.) N.Y. 1966, U.S. Tax Ct. 1969, U.S. Ct. Appeals (2d cir. 1970), Tex. 1972, U.S. Ct. Appeals (5th and 11th cirs.). Assoc. Bond, Schoeneck and King, Syracuse, NY, 1967-71; ptnr. Haynes and Boone, Dallas, 1971-82, Akin, Gump, Strauss, Hauer & Feld, Dallas, 1982-92; assoc. prof. income taxation, entities taxation, business associations Tex. Wesleyan Sch. Law, Ft. Worth, 1992-99. Vis. prof. fed. income taxation Baylor U. Sch. Law, 1995, prof. fed. income taxation and bus. orgns. II, 2000; grad. taxation program U. San Diego Sch. Law, 1996—98, fed. income taxation, corp. taxation, current income tax problems, tax ethics; adj. prof. Sch. Law So. Meth U., Dallas, 1972—87, 1990—91. Trustee, sec. mem. exec. and fin. com., nominating com. Greenhill Sch., Addison, Tex., 1980-90; trustee, chmn. budget com., mem. fin. com. Jewish Fedn. Greater Dallas, 1978-89; trustee, chmn. Found. Jewish Fedn., Dallas, 1980-89; trustee, v.p., pres. Dallas chpt. Am. Jewish Com., 1980-92; mem. Tex. World Trade Coun., 1986-87, Dallas Mayor's Internat. Com. Mem. State Bar Tex. (sec. 1982-83, chmn. tax sect. 1984-85, newsletter taxation sect. editor 1980-81), Internat. Bar Assn., Internat. Comte (N.Tex. commn.), Ctr. for Am. and Internat. Law (adv. bd., treas. Internat. and Comparative Law Ctr., lectr. Acad. in Internat. Law), N.Y. State Bar Assn. Address: 11218 Hillcrest Rd Dallas TX 75230-3501 Office Phone: 214-769-9712. Office Fax: 214-368-5301. E-mail: donzahn@flash.net.

**ZAHN, PAULA,** newscaster; b. Omaha, Feb. 24, 1956; m. Richard Cohen; children: Haley Brynne, Jared Brandon, Austin Bryce. BA in journalism, Stephens Coll., Columbia, Mo., 1978. With Sta. WFAA-TV, Dallas, 1978, Sta. KFMB-TV, San Diego, 1979—81, Sta. KPRC-TV, Houston, 1981—83, Sta. WHDH-TV, Boston, 1983—85; anchor, reporter Sta. KCBS-TV, L.A., 1985—87; anchor The Health Show ABC News, N.Y.C., 1987—88, co-anchor World News This Morning, 1988—90; co-anchor CBS This Morning CBS News, N.Y.C., 1990—96, anchor CBS Evening News Sat. edit., 1996—99; anchor The Fox Report with Paula Zahn Fox News Network, N.Y.C., 1999, anchor The Edge with Paula Zahn, 1999—2001; co-anchor American Morning CNN, 2001—03, co-anchor People in the News, 2002—, anchor Paula Zahn Now, 2003—. Primetime co-host Olympic Winter Games, Albertville, France, 1992; co-anchor Olympic Winter Games, Lillehammer, Norway, 94. Musician (Cellist): Carnegie Hall Debut, 1992. Named Newscaster of Yr., Am. Women in Radio and TV, 1983; recipient Broadcasting Award, Nat. Commn. Working Women, 1982, Spirit Achievement Award, Albert Einstein Coll. Medicine, 1993, Cancer Awareness Award, Congl. Families Action for Cancer Awareness, 1994, Emmy award for outstanding coverage of a continuing news story, 1994, Spirit of Life Award, City of Hope Cancer Ctr., 2003. Office: CNN 820 1st St NE Washington DC 20002-4243

**ZAHN, RICHARD GREGORY,** construction executive; s. Richard John and Maria Jose Zahn; m. Marnie Blake Resnick, Sept. 25, 2002; children: Richard Gregory Jr., Codie Thomas, Madison Ann Marie. BA in Mktg., Regis U., 1991, MBA in Mgmt., 2001, PhD in Bus. Mgmt., 2003. Lic. gen. contractor Fla., cert. mold remediator. With psychol. ops. SOCOM Spl. Ops. Command U.S. Army, Ft. Bragg, NC, 1985—97; sheriff's dep. Cumberland County Sheriff's Office, Fayetteville, NC, 1990—91; mgr. Glidden Paint Co., Fayetteville, 1991—95; regional mgr. Jones Blair Paint, Dallas, 1995—97; dir. ops. Hersh Reconstrn., Inc., Longwood, Fla., 1997—99, exec. v.p., 1999—2001, CEO, owner, 2001—. Mem. air quality bd. ADG Apt. Group, Miami, Fla., 2002—; mold cons. IAQA, Longwood, 2002—. Comdr. Civil Air Patrol, Myrtle Beach, SC, 1986; active DeBary (Fla.) Art League, 2001. Staff sgt. U.S. Army, 1985—97. Decorated Commendation medal with valor U.S. Army; recipient Tampa Bay (Fla.) Renovator of Yr. award, Tampa Apt. Assn., 2000, Renovation of Yr. award, Nat. Apt. Assn., Atlanta, 2001. Mem.: Strategic Mgmt. Soc., Am. Mgmt. Soc. Republican. Avocations: boating, scuba diving, golf, mountain biking. Office: Hersh Reconstrn Inc 688 Florida Ctrl Pky Longwood FL 32750 Home: 214 Sweet Gum Way Longwood FL 32779-4923

**ZAHND, RICHARD H.,** sports association executive, lawyer; b. N.Y.C., July 22, 1946; s. Hugo and Rose (Genovese) Z.; m. Phyllis Beth Workman, Aug. 13, 1978; children: Andrew Richard, Melissa Dawn. AB, NYU, 1968, JD, 1971. Bar: N.Y. 1972. Assoc. Paul, Weiss, Rifkind, Wharton & Garrison, N.Y.C., 1971-74; staff atty. Madison Square Garden Corp., N.Y.C., 1974-75; v.p. legal affairs Madison Square Garden Center, Inc., N.Y.C., 1975-79; v.p., gen. counsel Madison Square Garden Corp., N.Y.C., 1979-86; v.p. N.Y. Knickerbockers Basketball Club, N.Y.C., 1979-86, N.Y. Rangers Hockey Club, N.Y.C., 1979-86; pmr. Morrison & Foerster, N.Y.C., 1986-91; exec. v.p., gen. counsel NHL Enterprises, L.P., N.Y.C., 1992—. Served to capt. U.S. Army, 1972. John Norton Pomeroy scholar NYU Law Sch., 1969; Mortimer Bishop scholar NYU Law Sch., 1969; Judge Jacob Markowitz scholar NYU Law Sch., 1970; recipient Am. Jurisprudence prize NYU Law Sch., 1969 Episcopalian. Office: NHL Enterprises LP Fl 46 1251 Ave of the Americas New York NY 10020-1104 Office Phone: 212-789-2023. Business E-Mail: rzahnd@nhl.com.

**ZAHNER, MARY ANNE,** art educator; b. Dover, Ohio, Mar. 30, 1938; d. Alfred James and Anna Elizabeth (Stewart) Riggle; m. Gordon Dean Zahner, Aug. 27, 1960 (dec. Mar. 1967); 1 child, Anne Colette Krach; m. John Charles Opala, Aug. 21, 1982. BFA, Ohio U., 1960, MA, 1969; PhD, Ohio State U., 1987. Lic. tchr. Ohio. Instr. art Springfield Twp. Schs., Akron, Ohio, 1960-61, Logan H.S., Ohio, 1961-62, Dover H.S., 1967-68, chair art dept., 1969-71; teaching asst. Ohio State U., Columbus, 1980-82; from instr. art edn. to asst. prof. U. Dayton, 1971-74, asst. prof., 1974-91, assoc. prof., 1991-2000, prof., 2000—. Mem. faculty rights, governance and svc. com. U. Dayton, 1992—93, mem. arts series com., 1995—98; reviewer Harcourt, Brace, 1993—98, Prentice Hall, Inc., 1996—98; mem. higher edn. steering com. Ohio Dept. Edn., 1995, mem. adv. com., tchr. preparation programs, 97; exec. bd. Western Regional Profl. Devel. Ctr., 1996—2004. Author: Barkan, 2003; contbr. chapters to books; Exhibited in group shows at Westbeth Gallery, N.Y., 1995. Mem. Kettering (Ohio) Arts Coun., 1988—93, sec., 1990; mem. discretionary support com. Miami Valley Arts Coun., Dayton, 1992; coord. 3d congl. art contest sponsored by Tony P. Hall Dayton, 1993—95; mem.-at-large edn. com. Culture Works: Arts and Culture Alliance Miami Valley, 1996. Recipient Best of Show award, Canton Art Inst., 1969, Inst. Faculty award, Ohio Partnership for Visual Arts, 1989. Fellow: Ohio Art Edn. Assn. (mem. editl. bd. Ohio Art Edn. Jour. 1986—2005, editor newsletter Artline 1988, workshop coord. 1992, cons. tchr. insvc. for Dayton Pub. Schs. 1995, workshop coord. 1997, Outstanding Art Tchr. we. dist. 1992), mem.: ASCD, Univ. Coun. Art Edn., Ohio Alliance Arts Edu., Assn. Tchr. Educators, Nat. Art Edn. Assn., Phi Kappa Phi, Phi Delta Kappa. Democrat. Avocations: music, theater, physical fitness. Office: U Dayton 300 College Park Dayton OH 45469-0001 Office Phone: 937-229-3207. Business E-Mail: mary.zahner@notes.udayton.edu.

**ZAHNER-KRACH, ANNE COLETTE,** preschool educator; b. Mansfield, Ohio, May 15, 1962; d. Gordon Dean and Mary Anne (Riggle) Zahner; m. David Krach, 2001; 1 child, Sarah Rose Krach. BS in Journalism, Ohio U., 1984; MS in Tchg., U. Dayton, 1992. Staff writer Huber Heights (Ohio) Courier, 1984-87, editor, 1987; preschool tchr. Cath. Social Svcs., Dayton, Ohio, 1993-97, Butler County Bd. Mental Retardation, Fairfield, Ohio, 1997—. Reporter Athens Mag., 1983, Athena Yearbook, 1983. Sec. Local Profl. Devel. Com., 2003—. Mem. Sigma Delta Chi, Alpha Gamma Delta (house chair 1983-84, corr. sec. 1982-83, newsletter editor 1997). Democrat.

Roman Catholic. Avocations: travel, photography, exercise. Office: Butler County Bd Mental Retardation Janet Clemmons Ctr 282 N Fair Ave Hamilton OH 45011-4222 Home: 5967 Kensington T Liberty Township OH 45044-8652

**ZAHNER KRAEFT, DOROTHY SIMKIN,** elementary school educator, school librarian; b. Chengdu, Szechuan, China, May 1, 1926; arrived in US, 1931; d. Robert Louis and Margaret Isadore (Timberlake) Simkin; m. Henry Zahner (div.); children: Mary De Avilan, Robert Louis; m. Norman John Kraeft, May 28, 2005. BA in Sociology, Whittier Coll., 1948; MLS, U. So. Calif., LA, 1952. Cert. tchr. Calif., Ariz. Tchr. LA and Pasadena Sch., Calif., 1969-93; dir., owner Betty Ingram Sch., North Hollywood, Calif., 1976-79; dir. Foothill Nursery Sch., La Crescenta, Calif., 1970s; tchr. L.A. Unified Sch. Dist.; guest tchr. Washington Unified Sch. Dist., Phoenix, 1994-97; ret., 2002. Guest tchr. Osborn Sch. Dist., 1998-2000, Madison Sch. Dist., Phoenix, 1999-2001. Author: poems pub. in U.S., Europe and China. Bd. dirs. Ariz. Tenants Assn., Phoenix, 1994, 95; vol. Am. Friends Svc. Com., Phila., Calif., 1985-, Common Cause, LA, 1990, Internat. Rescue Com.; domestic violence vol., Phoeniz, 1999-2000; vol. Dem. candidates, LA and Phoenix; poll marshall Election Bd., Phoenix. Recipient cert. appreciation, Project Hope, 2005. Mem.: Ariz. State Poetry Soc. (pres. 2002—, chmn. 2004), Alameda Writers Group, Phoenix Poetry Soc. (pres. 1998, anthology editl. co. 2001, featured reader 2005, com. mem., Poet of Yr. 2000, poetry awards 1995, 2000), Am. Assn. Ret. Persons, Phoenix Writers Club (sec. 1998). Democrat. Avocations: theater, films, music, swimming, reading.

**ZAHORCHAK, GERALD LEE,** school system administrator, executive secretary; b. Johnstown, Pa., June 12, 1957; s. John Cyril and Ruth (Cale) Z. BS, St. Francis Coll., 1980; MEd, Ind. U. of Pa., 1987; EdD, Pa. State U. Cert. elem. and secondary prin., reading specialist, supt. Elem. tchr., asst. football coach Greater Johnstown Sch. Dist., Pa., 1980-83, parent coord., reading specialist, 1989; instr. middle sch. reading, head football coach North Star Sch. Dist., Boswell, Pa., 1985-89; prin. Stonycreek Sch. Dist., Shanksville, Pa., 1989-92, North Star Sch. Dist., Boswell, Pa., 1992; dist. supt., programs coord. Greater Johnstown, Pa.; dep. sec. for elem. edn. Pa. Dept. Edn., 2003—05, sec., 2005—. Study skills cons., Mass., 1989—; presenter to univ. couns. Author: Footreading, 1986, Transition to a Middle School, 1994. Chmn. Greater Johnstown Vo-Tech Bd., 1986-89; mem. Greater Johnstown Sch. Bd., 1986-89, Johnstown City Coun., dep. mayor. Named one of Outstanding Young Men in Am., 1988-89, Outstanding Young Citizen of Greater Johnstown Area, 1990, Pa.'s Outstanding Young Citizen, 1990; recipient Humanitarian Svc. award United Cerebral Palsy, 1982. Mem. Nat. Assn. Secondary Sch. Prins., Assn. for Supervision and Curriculum Devel., NEA, Johnstown Jaycees, Johnstown Oldtimers Baseball (bd. dirs.), K.C. (4th degree), Pa. Assn. of Secondary Sch. Prins. Democrat. Roman Catholic. Avocations: strength tng., reading. Home: 2000 Young St Johnstown PA 15902-3365 Office: Pa Dept Edn 333 Market St Harrisburg PA 17126-5820 Office Phone: 717-787-5820.

**ZAHRAN, MOHAMED MOSTAFA,** electrical engineer, educator; b. Cairo; BS in Computer Engring., Cairo U., 1997, MS in Computer Engring., 1999; PhD, U. Md., College Park, 2003. Rsch. scientist George Washington U., Washington, 2003—04; asst. prof. CUNY, NYC, 2004—. Recipient Best Talk award, Grad. Rsch. Interaction Day, U. Md., College Park, 2002, Best Sci. Talk award, Elec. and Computer Engring. Grad. Student Assn., U. Md., College Park, 2002, Best Paper award, Internat. Conf. on Computer Design, 2003; grantee, Assn. Computing Machinery, 2003, 2004; PSC-CUNY Fund grantee, CUNY, 2005—06, Collaborative Rsch Experience for Undergraduates fund grantee, Computer Rsch. Assn., 2006—. Mem.: IEEE, Assn. Computing Machinery, Sigma Xi. Achievements include research in computer architecture. Office Phone: 212-650-7310.

**ZAIDAN, RAOUF GEORGE,** music educator; b. Cairo, Mar. 7, 1952; s. George Youssef Zaidan and Gwendolyn Ralph Hutchings. BA, Am. U., Egypt, 1974; MusM, U. North Tex., 1987; MusD, U. Colo., 1995. Cert. assoc. Royal Coll. Music, London, fellow Trinity Coll. Music, England. Choir dir., tchr. Rocky Mountain Musical Arts, Lafayette, Colo., 2004—05; asst. prof. music No. State U., Aberdeen, SD, 2005—. Opera singer Cairo Opera, Lyric Opera North Mich., Denton Light Opera, Abilene Opera, Boulder Opera, Alexandria Opera, Varna Opera, 1982; singer, vocal coach Opera in Arabic, Cairo, 1987—2002; choir dir. Cairo Opera Ho., 1989—92; prof. music Am. U., Cairo, 1997—2002. Musician: (recordings) Cosi fan tutte, Le nozze di Figaro, Don Giovanni; editor (musical critic): The Middle East Times; co-editor: The Wagner Society. Mem.: Nat. Assn. Tchrs. Singing (life; tchr. 1985). Home: 1104 S Kline St Aberdeen SD 57401 Office: N State U 1200 S Jay St Aberdeen SD 57401 Office Phone: 605-626-7754. Personal E-mail: raoufzdn@abe.midco.net. Business E-Mail: raouf.zaidan@northern.edu.

**ZAIDI, EMILY LOUISE,** retired elementary school educator; b. Hoquiam, Wash., Apr. 20, 1924; d. Burdick Newton and Emily Caroline (Williams) Johnston; m. M. Baqar Abbas Zaidi, June 12, 1949 (dec. Dec. 1983). BA in Edn. and Social Studies, Ea. Wash. State U., 1948; MEd, U. Wash., 1964, EdD, 1974. Tchr. 4th grade Hoquiam Schs., 1948—49; tchr. grades 5-6 Lake Washington Sch. Dist., Kirkland, Wash., 1949—51; tchr. grades 2-3 Port Angeles Schs., Wash., 1951—54; tchr. grade 2 Seattle Schs., 1954—55; tchr., reading specialist Northshore Sch. Dist., Bothell, Wash., 1955—69, Sacramento City Schs., 1969—87; ret., 1987. Mem. Calif. State Instrnl. Materials Panel, Sacramento, 1975. Mem. Sacramento Opera Assn., 1986—, Sacramento Ballet Assn., 1987—2000. Fulbright Commn. Exch. Tchr., 1961—62. Democrat. Avocations: writing, children's literature, reading, travel. Home: 4230 N River Way Sacramento CA 95864-6055 Personal E-mail: louisezaidi@comcast.net.

**ZAIDI, IQBAL MEHDI,** biochemist, research scientist; b. Bijnor, India, June 30, 1957; s. Iqbal Haider and Habib (Zohra) Z.; m. Nuzhat Shikoh, Jan. 2, 1993; 1 child, Shan Zehra. BS in Chemistry with honors, Aligarh Med. U., 1976, MS in Biochemistry, 1978, PhD in Biochemistry, 1984. Cert. in radiation. Rsch. fellow Indsl. Toxicology Rsch. Ctr., Lucknow, India, 1979-83; rsch. affiliate NY State Health Dept., Albany, 1984-91; scientist Applied Biosystems, Applera Corp., Foster City, Calif., 1991—. Contbr. articles to profl. jours. Mem. AAAS, Am. Chem. Soc. (biochem. tech. divsn. 1992—), Shia Assn. Bay Area, NY Acad. Scis. Avocations: photography, swimming, travel, natural history. Office: Applied Biosystems 850 Lincoln Centre Dr Foster City CA 94404-1128 Personal E-mail: zaidins22@yahoo.com.

**ZAIKOW, LARRY J. JAMES,** painter; b. Red Lake, Ont., Can., Dec. 25, 1951; s. Jim DeMetor and Alice Helen (Dutka) Z. Grad., Red Lake H.S. With Poetry Co., Sacramento, Calif., 1987-92. Author: Who's in Poetry, 1992. Avocation: writing poetry and songs. Home: 334 Howey St Red Lake ON Canada

**ZAIMAN, K(OICHI) ROBERT,** dentist; b. Cin., Oct. 19, 1944; s. Noboru Gary and Toshiko (Matsuyama) Zaiman; m. Kimberly Ann Sass, Nov. 6, 1976; children: Kara Jean, Matthew Robert. Student, Creighton U., Omaha, 1962-64, DDS, 1968. Asst. prof. Creighton U. Sch. Dentistry, Omaha, 1971-73, assoc. prof., 1973-75; pvt. practice dentistry Omaha, 1971—. Dir. Chicano and Native-Am. Free Clinic Creighton U., Omaha, 1970—75. Mem. bd. elders King of Kings Luth. Ch., 1990—95, deacon, 1995—; past v.p., bd. dirs. Japanese-Am. Citizens League, Omaha, 1977—86. Fellow: Internat. Coll. Dentistry, Acad. Continuing Edn., Acad. Gen. Dentistry (nat. del. 1971—76, pres. 1976—77), Pierre Fauchard Internat. Hon. Acad.; mem.: ADA, Omaha Dental Study Club (pres. 1999—2001), Nebr. Dental Assn. (del. 1971—94), Omaha Dist. Dental Soc. (dir. 1968, treas. 1980—85, peer rev. 1996—), Delta Sigma Delta (pres. 1973—74). Office: 10841 Q St Ste 109 Omaha NE 68137-3741 Office Phone: 402-339-4999.

**ZAIS, MITCHELL M.,** career military officer; b. Ft. Bragg, N.C. Grad. in engring., US Mil. Acad., West Point, NY; MS, PhD, U. Wash. Commd. infantry U.S. Army, advanced through grades to brigadier gen.; infantry svc.

airborne, air assault, mechanized, ceremonial standard, Bradley, light infantry, other, Vietnam, Korea, U.S.; comdr. 2 rifle cos., infantry battalion, light infantry brigade; chief war plans Chmn. Joint Chiefs of Staff; social aide The White House, Washington; exec. officer to comdr. in chief U.S. So. Command, Panama; commanding gen. Coalition Joint Task Force, Kuwait, Joint Task Force Provide Refuge for Kosovar Refugees in U.S.; dep. comdg. gen. maneuvers Ft. Riley, Kans.; chief of staff USAR Command, Ft. McPherson, Ga. Asst. prof. U.S. Mil. Acad.

**ZAISER, KENT AMES,** lawyer; b. St. Petersburg, Fla., June 10, 1945; s. Robert Alan and Marion (Brown) Z. AB, Duke U., 1967; postgrad., U. Calif., Berkeley, 1971; JD, U. Fla., 1972. Bar: Fla. 1973, U.S. Dist. Ct. (no. dist.) Fla. 1974, U.S. Supreme Ct. 1978, U.S. Dist. Ct. (so. dist.) Fla. 1980, U.S. Dist. Ct. (mid. dist.) Fla. 1981, U.S. Ct. Appeals (11th cir.) 1981. Rsch. aide Fla. Supreme Ct., Tallahassee, 1973-75, administrv. asst. to chief justice, 1975-76; asst. gen. counsel Fla. Dept. Natural Resources, Tallahassee, 1976-80; asst. atty. gen. Fla. Dept. Legal Affairs, Tallahassee, 1980-85; dep. gen. counsel S.W. Fla. Water Mgmt. Dist., Brooksville, 1985-89; asst. gen. counsel, 1989-92; ptnr. Foley and Lardner, Tallahassee, 1992-93; prin. Kent A. Zaiser, P.A., Tallahassee, 1994—. Cons. Fla. State Cts. Administr., Tallahassee, 1975; mem. Fla. New Motor Vehicle Arbitration Bd., 1998-99. Contbg. author: Environmental Regulation and Litigation in Florida, 1980-84. Campaign chmn. Vince Fechtel for State Rep. of Fla., Leesburg, 1972. Mem. Jefferson County Bar Assn., Govs. Club. Democrat. Episcopalian. Home: 3286 Longleaf Rd Tallahassee FL 32310-6406 Office: PO Box 6045 Tallahassee FL 32314-6045 Office Phone: 850-576-7600.

**ZAITZEFF, ROGER MICHAEL,** lawyer; b. Detroit, June 25, 1940; s. Peter and Mary (Fedchenia) Z.; children: Zachary, Natasha, Zoe, Peter. BA with high honors and high distinction, U. Mich., 1962; MA with distinction, U. Calif., Berkeley, 1963, JD, 1969. Bar: NY 1970, US Dist. Ct. (so. dist.) NY 1975, US Ct. Appeals (2d cir.) 1975, DC 1985. Assoc. Seward & Kissel, NYC, 1969-77, ptnr., 1977-94, Latham & Watkins, NYC, 1994-2000, LeBoeuf Lamb Greene & MacRae, NYC, 2000—02, Swidler Berlin LLP, NYC, 2002—05, Sheppard Mullin Richter & Hampton LLP, NYC, 2005—. Contbr. articles to profl. jours. Mem. Tribar Opinion Com., 1990-93. Heller grantee U. Mich., 1962; recipient William Jennings Bryan Prize. Fellow: Am. Bar Found. (life); mem.: Phi Beta Kappa Assocs. Office: Sheppard Mullin Richter & Hampton LLP 30 Rockefeller Plz 24th Fl New York NY 10112 Office Phone: 212-332-3837.

**ZAJAC, JOHN,** semiconductor equipment company executive; b. NYC, July 21, 1946; s. John Andrew and Catherine (Canepa) Z.; m. Vera Barbagallo, Jan. 13, 1973; children: Jennifer, Michelle. AAS, NYU, 1966; BEE, U. Ky., Lawrence, 1968. Project engr. B.C.D. Computing, N.Y.C., 1968-70; v.p. Beacon Systems, Commack, N.Y., 1970-73, E.T. Systems, Santa Clara, Calif., 1973-77; v.p. research and devel. Eaton Corp., Sunnyvale, Calif., 1977-81; pres. Semitech/Gen. Signal, Los Gatos, Calif., 1981-83; mgr. advanced product div. Tegal/Motorola Inc., Novato, Calif., 1983-86; v.p. research and devel. U.S. Alcohol Inc., San Jose, Calif., 1986—2002; staff scientist Mattson Tech., Fremont, Calif., 1994—2002; dir. R&D Silicon Etch Tech., 2003—04; v.p. R&D Zajac Optimum Output Motors, Inc., San Jose, 2004—. Author: The Delicate Balance, 1988, A Thief's Way to Heaven, 1999, Pyramids, Prophecy and 666, 2000; guest TV and radio. Achievements include patents in field.

**ZAJICEK, JERONYM,** retired music educator; b. Krasne, Brezno, Czechoslovakia, Nov. 10, 1926; came to U.S., 1952; s. Frantisek Zajicek and Emilie (Lauterkranz) Zajickova. Studied with, Otakar Jeremias, Prague, Czechoslovakia, 1946—49; student, Charles U., Prague, Czechoslovakia, 1946-49; MusB, Roosevelt U., 1957, MusM, 1958; studied with, K.B. Jirak, Paul A. Pisk; PhD, Charles U., Prague, 1990. Music program dir. for Czechoslovak sect. Radio Free Europe, Munich, 1950-52; prof. theory and composition Loop Coll., Chgo., 1964-96; ret. Composer Clarinet Sonata, 1958, Sinfonietta for large orch., 1958, Cello Sonata, 1975; recorded Concertino for flute and string orch., 1973, Willie Schwegler Flute and Cologne Radio Orch., String Quartet, 1963, Sonatina for flute, clarinet and bassoon, 1966, Pater Noster for mixed chorus, 1990, Twenty Czech Carols, 2001, Twenty Moravian Carols for four part children chorus, 2002, Twenty Carols From Slovakia, 2004. Oliver Ditson fellow, 1956, 57; 1st prize Violin Sonata Internat. Soc. for Contemporary Music (Chgo. chpt. 1964); named hon. citizen Hrochuv Tynec, Czech Republic, 1998. Roman Catholic. Home: 4230 Prescott Ave Lyons IL 60534-1537 Office: Harold Washington Coll 30 E Lake St Chicago IL 60601-2403

**ZAK, IMAD,** radiologist, educator; b. Amman, Jordan, Nov. 8, 1962; s. Talib and Fatima Zak; life ptnr. Huweida Arikat, Oct. 2, 1987; children: Amro, Farrah. MB BChir, U. of Jordan, Amman, 1987. Am. Bd. of Radiology, cert. added qualification in neuroradiology Am. Bd. of Radiology. Asst. prof. of radiology Wayne State U., Detroit, 2000—06, dir. neuroradiology program, 2002—, assoc. prof. of radiology, 2006—. Cons. neuroradiologist Detroit Med. Ctr.; dir. neuroradiology tng. program Wayne State U., Detroit, 2000—; clinician educator One on One Edn. and Lectr. Contbr. articles to profl. jours. (Rsch. award U. of Iowa, 1995). Recipient King Hussein Scholarship award, Royal Jordanian Ct., 1981, Best Rsch. award, U. of Iowa, 1995, Wayne State U., 2003, 2005. Mem.: Am. Soc. of Neuroradiology (sr.). Achievements include improved neuroradiology educational program. Avocation: chess. Office: Wayne State U Dept Radiology DRH 3L-8 4201 St Antoine Detroit MI 48201 Office Phone: 313-745-3433. Office Fax: 313-577-8600. Business E-Mail: izak@med.wayne.edu.

**ZAK, ROBERT JOSEPH,** lawyer; b. Steubenville, Ohio, July 29, 1946; s. Joseph and Pearl (Munyas) Zak; m. Kristy Hubbard Winkler, Sept. 13, 1980; children: Elizabeth Adele, Elizabeth Jo, Barbara Ann. BS, W.Va. U., 1968, JD, 1975. Bar: WVa 1975, US Dist Ct (so dist) WVa 1975, US Dist Ct (no dist) WVa 1989, US Ct Appeals (4th cir) 1990. Staff atty. Pub. Svc. Commn. of W.Va., Charleston, 1975-76; assoc. Preiser & Wilson L.C., Charleston, 1976-81, ptnr., 1981-85; sr. ptnr. Zak & Assocs., Charleston, 1985—. Hearing examiner W.Va. Bd. Regents, Charleston, 1987—90; spl. asst. atty. gen. State of W.Va., 1987—90; mem. Workers Compensation Appeals Bd., 1991—97, 2001—04. Chmn. West Va. Support Enforcement Commn., 2003—. With U.S. Army, 1969—71, Vietnam. Fellow: Am Acad Matrimonial Lawyers; mem.: Order Barristers. Republican. Presbyterian. Office: Zak & Assocs 607 Ohio Ave Charleston WV 25302-2228 Office Phone: 304-345-0745. E-mail: zakslaw@hotmail.com.

**ZAK, STEPHANIE B.,** music educator; d. Igor and Cecelia Burdikoff; m. Jeffrey Michael Zak, Aug. 16, 1998; 1 child, Catherine Rose. AS in Music, Schenectady County CC, NY, 1991; BS, Coll. St. Rose, 1993, MS in Music Edn., 1998. Cert. tchr., pre-k-12 music NY Dept. Edn., Mass. Dept. Edn., Conn. Dept. Edn., Yamaha MIE lab. cert. Vocal tchr. Richard O'Rourke Mid. Sch., Burnt Hills-Ballston Lake, NY, 1994—98, Washington Mid. Sch., Meriden, Conn., 1998—. Pvt. piano & voice tchr.; music vocal dir. Platt HS, Meriden, Conn. Recipient Music award, Thursday Musical Club, Schenectady County CC, 1989. Mem.: Music Educator's Nat. Conf., Alpha Delta Kappa. Russian Orthodox. Avocations: reading, skiing. Office: Washington Mid Sch 1225 N Broad St Meriden CT 06450 Office Phone: 203-235-6606. Business E-Mail: stephanie.zak@meriden.k12.ct.us.

**ZAKALUZNY, IHOR ANDREW,** surgeon; b. Toronto, July 14, 1954; came to U.S., 1997; m. Sandra Ghadiali, Nov. 25, 1977. BS, U. Toronto, 1977; MD, U. Calgary, 1983. Diplomate Am. Bd. Surgery. Intern Victoria Gen. Hosp., Can., 1983-84; resident McGill U. Affiliated Hosps., Montreal, Can., 1984-88; with Garrett County Meml. Hosp., Oakland, Md.; pvt. practice gen. surgery Windsor, Ont., Canada, 1989-97, Oakland, Md., 1997—. Fellow Am. Coll. Surgeons, Royal Coll. Physicians Can.; mem. Soc. Laparoendoscopic Surgeons, Soc. Surgery of the Alimentary Tract, Soc. Am. Gastrointestinal Endoscopic Surgeons, Am. Hernia Soc., Am. Soc. Gen. Surgeons, Canadian

Assn. Gen. Surgeons, Internat. Coll. Surgeons, Am. Soc. Breast Surgeons Office: 255 N 4th St Ste 2 Oakland MD 21550 Office Phone: 301-533-4400. Personal E-mail: hammerzdl@hotmail.com. E-mail: iazakaluzny@gmail.com.

**ZAKANITCH, ROBERT RAHWAY,** artist; b. Elizabeth, NJ; s. Andrew and Mary Z. Student, Newark Sch. Fine and Indsl. Art, NJ, 1954-57. Vis. artist, lectr. Sch. Art Inst. Chgo., 1976, U. Calif., San Diego, 1974; lectr. in field. One-man shows include Henri Gallery, Alexandria, Va., 1965, Reese Palley Gallery, N.Y.C., 1970—71, Cunningham Ward, 1973—74, Holly Solomon Gallery, 1977, Robert Miller Gallery, 1978—79, 1981, 1984—85, 1988, Galerie Liatowitsch, Basel, Switzerland, 1978, Galerie Rudolf Zwirner, Cologne, Germany, 1979, Daniel Templon Gallery, N.Y.C., 1980, Bruno Bischofberger Gallery, Zurich, 1980, James Mayor Gallery, London, 1981, Marcus Gallery, 1984, Inst. Contemporary Art, Phila., 1981, Akira Ikeda Gallery, Nagoya, Japan, 1981, Daniel Templon Gallery, Paris, 1982, 1987, 1991, McIntosh-Drysdale Gallery, Washington, 1983, Harcus Gallery, Boston, 1984, 1987, 1989, Delahunty Gallery, Dallas, 1984, Helander/Rubinstein Gallery, Palm Beach, Fla., 1985, 1989, Asher Faure Gallery, L.A., 1985, Yares Gallery, Scottsdale, Ariz., 1987, Sidney Janis Gallery, N.Y.C., 1990, Jason McCoy Gallery, 1994—95, Guild Hall, East Hampton, N.Y., 1995, Hirschl & Adler, N.Y.C., 1995, Patricia Faure Gallery, L.A., 1997, Santa Monica, Calif., 2003, Locks Gallery, Phila., 1997, 1999, Patricia Faure Gallery, L.A., 2003, Spike Gallery, N.Y.C., 2003, 2005, 2006, exhibited in group shows at Franklin Gallery, Cornell U., 1978, Va. Mus. Fine Arts, 1979, Palais des Beaux-Arts, Brussels, 1979, Inst. Contemporary Art, U. Pa., 1979, New Mus., N.Y., 1979, Galerie Daniel Templon, Paris, 1980, Nat. Gallery Art, Washington, 1980, Indpls. Mus. Art, 1980, San Francisco Art Inst., 1980, Whitney Mus. Am. Art, N.Y.C., 1981, Jacksonville Art Mus., 1981, Galeria Civica, Italy, 1982, Mus. Fine Arts, Boston, 1982, Fay Gold Gallery, Atlanta, 1982, High Mus. Art, 1983, Meml. Art Gallery, Rochester, N.Y., 1983, Kunstmuseum, Luzern, 1983. With U.S. Army, 1958-60. John Simon Guggenheim fellow, 1995. Studio: 119 N 11th St Brooklyn NY 11211-1163 Office Phone: 718-486-7735. Personal E-mail: robertraw@earthlink.net. E-mail: robert@zakanitch.com.

**ZAKHEIM, DOV SOLOMON,** economist, government official; b. Dec. 18, 1948; s. Zvi Hirsh and Bella (Rabinowitz) Zakheim; m. Barbara Jane Portnoi, Aug. 20, 1972 (div. 1990); children: Keith Samuel, Roger Israel, Scott Elisha; m. Deborah Bing Lowy, May 26, 1991. Student, London Sch. Econs., 1968-69; BA summa cum laude, Columbia U., 1970; DPhil, Oxford U., 1974. Rsch. fellow St. Antony's Coll. Oxford U., 1974; asst. to mng. dir. U.K. br. Internat. Credit Bank Geneva, 1974-75; assoc. analyst Nat. Security and Internat. Affairs Congl. Budget Office, Washington, 1975-78, prin. analyst, 1978-81; spl. asst. to secy. def. (internat. security policy) Dept. Def., Washington, 1981-82, spl. asst. to under sec. def., 1982-83, asst. under sec. def. (policy and resources), 1983-85, dep. under sec. def. for planning and resources, 1985-87; exec. v.p. Sys. Planning Corp., Arlington, Va., 1987-90, corp. v.p., 1990-2001; CEO SPC Int Inc, 1998—2001; under-sec. def. (comptr. and CFO) U.S. Govt., 2001—04; v.p. Booz Allen Hamilton, McLean, Va., 2004—. Cons. to sec. def. and undersec. def., 1987—2000, 2004—; adj. prof. Nat. Def. U., 1992, Columbia U., 1995—96, Yeshiva U., 1995—96; adj prof., presdl. fellow Trinity Coll., Conn., 1998; guest lectr. War Coll. Author: (book) Flight of the Lavi; contbr. articles to profl. jours. Mem US Comn Preservation Am's Heritage Abroad, 1991—95; mem bd visitors Dept Def Overseas Regulatory Ctrs, 1998; mem Secy Def Task Force Def Reform; mem bd deps Brit Jews, 1971—72; mem Chief Rabbi's Chaplaincy Bd, England, 1971—72; bd dirs Friends of Jewish Chapel, US Naval Acad, 1997—. Fellow, NSF, 1970—73, Kellet, Columbia Col, 1974. Mem.: Royal Inst Int Affairs (UK), Int Inst Strategic Studies, Coun Foreign Relations, Cosmos Club, Columbia Club, United Oxford and Cambridge Univ Club, Phi Beta Kappa. Home: 817 Lamberton Dr Silver Spring MD 20902-3038 Office: Booz Allen Hamilton 8283 Greensboro Dr Mc Lean VA 22102 Office Phone: 703-902-7000. Business E-mail: zakheim-dov@bah.com.

**ZAKIM, DAVID,** biochemist; b. Paterson, N.J., July 10, 1935; s. Sam and Ruth (Sorokin) Zakim; m. Nancy Jane Levine, June 12, 1957 (div. 1976); children: Michael, Eric, Thomas; m. Dagmar Aurelia Stanke, July 30, 1978; children: Tamara, Robert. AB in Chemistry, Cornell U., 1956; MD summa cum laude, SUNY, Bklyn., 1961. Diplomate Am Bd Internal Med. Intern N.Y. Hosp., N.Y.C., 1961-62, asst. resident, 1962-63, fellow, 1963-65; asst. prof. to prof. medicine and pharmacology U. Calif., San Francisco, 1968-83; Vincent Astor Disting. prof. medicine Cornell U. Med. Coll., N.Y.C., 1983-2000; prof. biochemistry Cornell U. Grad. Sch. Med. Sci., N.Y.C., 1983-2000; prof. emeritus, 2000—; chief scientist, chmn. Zmedix Corp., San Francisco. Editor: (book) Hepatology: A Textbook of Liver Disease, 1982, Hepatology: A Textbook of Liver Disease, 4th edit., 2002, Disorders of Acid Secretion, 1991, (series) Current Topics in Gastroenterology, 1985, Gastroenterology Medicine Today, 1992—95; contbr. articles to profl. jours. Capt US Army, 1965—68. Named Distinguished Alumnus, SUNY-Brooklyn, 1986. Mem.: Am. Soc. Clin. Investigation, Am. Soc. Biol. Chemists, Am. Assn. Physicians. Office Phone: 415-595-8820. Personal E-mail: dzakim@pacbell.net, david@zmedix.net.

**ZAKIM, TOM EDWARD,** history professor; s. David and Nancy Zakim; m. Jill Diane Foley; 1 child, Arielle Maia. PhD, U. So. Calif., 2004. Lectr. U. Calif., San Diego, 2003—04; vis. scholar Berkeley, Calif., 2004—. Mem.: Am. Hist. Assn. Achievements include patents pending for medical diagnosis software.

**ZAKIN, JACQUES LOUIS,** chemical engineering educator; b. NYC, Jan. 28, 1927; s. Mordecai and Ada Davies (Fishbein) Z.; m. Laura Pienkny, June 11, 1950; children: Richard Joseph, David Fredric, Barbara Ellen, Emily Anne, Susan Beth. BSChemE, Cornell U., 1949; MChemE, Columbia U., 1950; DEng. Sci., NYU, 1959. Chem. engr. Flintkote Research Labs., Whippany, NJ, 1950-51; research technologist, research dept. Socony-Mobil, Bklyn., 1951-53; sr. research technologist, 1953-56, supervising technologist, 1959-62; assoc. prof. chem. engring. U. Mo., Rolla, 1962-65, prof., 1965-77, dir. minority engring. program, 1974-77, dir. women in engring. program, 1975-77; chmn. dept. chem. engring. Ohio State U., Columbus, 1977-94, Helen C. Kurtz prof. chem. engring., 1994-2000, Helen C. Kurtz prof. emeritus, 2000—. Chmn. sci. manpower and resources com. Coun. Chem. Rsch., 1984-86, governing bd., 1988-89; exec. com., 1988-89; adv. bd. State of Ohio Alternative Fuels, 1992-93; vis. prof. Technion, 1968-69, 94-95, Hebrew U., 1987; disting. vis. prof. Mex. Acad. Scis. and Mex.-USA Found. for Scis., 1999. Co-editor: Proc. Turbulence Symposium, 1969, 71, 73, 75, 77, 79, 81, 83; contbr. articles to profl. jours Bd. dirs. Rolla Cmty. Concert Assn., 1966-77, 2d v.p., 1975-77; bd. dirs. Ozark Mental Health Assn., 1976-77; trustee Ohio State Hillel Found., 1981-84, treas., 1984-89, pres., 1989-92; trustee Congregation Beth Tikvah, 1983; bd. trustees Columbus Jewish Fedn., 1989-92; co-chmn. Academics and Scientists for Soviet Refuseniks. With USNR, 1945-46. Recipient Outstanding Rsch. award U. Mo., 1970, Dept Hlavka Meml. medal Czechoslovakian Acad. Sci., 1992, Clara M. and Peter L. Scott Faculty award, 1996, Rsch. award Japanese Govt., 2001; named Outstanding Educator of Yr., Ohio Soc. Profl. Engrs., 1994, Tech. Person of Yr., Columbus Tech. Coun., 1987; Am. Chem. Soc. Petroleum Rsch. Fund Internat. fellow, 1968-69, Socony-Mobil Employee Incentive fellow NYU, 1956-59, Sr. Fulbright Rsch. fellow Technion, 1994-95. Fellow Am. Inst. Chem. Engrs.; mem. Am. Chem. Soc., Soc. of Rheology, Am. Soc. Engring. Edn., Sigma Xi, Phi Lambda Upsilon, Phi Eta Sigma, Alpha Chi Sigma, Tau Beta Pi, Phi Kappa Phi. Jewish. Achievements include patents in field. Office: Ohio State U 140 W 19th Ave Columbus OH 43210-1110 Business E-mail: zakin.1@osu.edu.

**ZALAVRAS, CHARALAMPOS,** orthopedic surgeon; arrived in U.S., 2000; s. Georgios Zalavras and Maria Zalavra. Attended, Aristoteleion U. Med. Sch., Greece, 1991; PhD, U. Ioannina, Greece, 2000. Cert. orthop. surgeon Ministry of Health, Greece, European Union, physician's cert. of registration Med. Bd. Calif. Resident dept. orthop. surgery U. Ioannina, Ioannina, Greece, 1996—2000; from clin. rsch. fellow to assoc. prof. Dept. Orthop. Surgery U.

So. Calif., LA, 2000—06, assoc. prof. Dept. Orthop. Surgery, 2006—. Recipient Best Scientific Work award, Balkan Congress Orthops., 1997, Best Resident, Fellow Paper award, Arthroscopy Assn. No. Am., 2002, Marshall Urist Young Investigator award, Assn. Bone and Joint Surgeons, 2003. Mem.: Hellenic Soc. for Reconstructive Microsurgery, Hellenic Soc. for Surgery of Hand, Hellenic Assn. Orthop. Surgery and Traumatology, European Soc. Sports Traumatology, Knee Surgery and Arthroscopy, Western Orthop. Assn. Office: USC Med Ctr 1200 N State St GNH 3900 Los Angeles CA 90033 Office Phone: 323-226-7346. Office Fax: 323-226-4051. Business E-mail: zalavras@usc.edu.

**ZALAZNICK, LAUREN,** broadcast executive; married; 3 children. Grad., Brown U. With MTV Networks, USA Cable; sr. v.p. original programming & devel. VH1; exec. v.p. network enterprises NBC Universal Television Networks, pres. Trio Networks, 2002—05, pres. Bravo Network, 2004—. Office: NBC Universal Television Group 30 Rockefeller Plz New York NY 10112 Office Phone: 212-664-4444. Office Fax: 212-664-3720.*

**ZALAZNICK, SHELDON,** retired editor, journalist; b. Bronx, Aug. 6, 1928; s. Samuel and Esther Leah (Schneiderman) Z.; m. Vera Altobelli, Apr. 4, 1953; 1 dau., Andrea. BA, NYU, 1948; MA, Tchrs. Coll. Columbia, 1950. Tchr. English Benjamin Franklin H.S., NYC, 1950-52; assoc. editor Newsweek mag., 1952-56; v.p. Manning Pub. Relations Co., 1956-59; sr. editor Forbes mag., 1959-63, mng. editor, 1976-89; founding editor New York mag. sect. NY Herald Tribune, NYC, 1963-64; Sunday editor NY Herald Tribune, 1964-66; staff writer Gen. Learning Corp., 1966-67; assoc. editor Fortune mag., 1967-69; v.p., editl. dir. New York mag., 1969-76. Home: 458 W 246th St Bronx NY 10471-3330 E-mail: zalaznick@optonline.net.

**ZALDARRIAGA, MATIAS,** cosmologist, physics professor; b. Buenos Aires, 1971; Degree in Phys. Sci., U. Buenos Aires, 1994; PhD., MIT, 1998. Keck vis. prof. Inst. Adv. Study, Princeton, NJ, 2001—02; asst. prof. NYU, 2001—02; assoc. prof. Dept. Physics, Harvard U., 2003, prof.; assoc. prof. Dept. Astronomy, Harvard U., 2003; prof. Packard Fellow, David and Lucile Packard Found., 2001, MacArthur Fellow, John D. and Catherine T. MacArthur Found, 2006. Achievements include design of CMBFAST computer software tool for astronomy research. Office: Harvard-Smithsonian Center for Astrophysics 60 Garden St MS 51 Cambridge MA 02138 Office Phone: 617-384-9665. Office Fax: 617-495-7093.*

**ZALESKE, DAVID JOSEPH,** surgeon, research scientist, health facility administrator; b. Feb. 9, 1950; BS, Yale U., 1971; MD, Harvard U., 1975. Diplomate Nat. Bd. Med. Examiners, Am. Bd. Orthop. Surgery. Intern, resident Mass. Gen. Hosp., Boston, 1975-77; orthop. resident Combined Harvard Orthop. Program, Boston, 1977-81; chief pediat. orthopedics Mass. Gen. Hosp., Boston, 1981—2001; assoc. prof. orthopedics Harvard Med. Sch., Boston, 1981—2001; prof. orthopedics George Washington U./Children's Nat. Med. Ctr., Washington, 2001—04; surg. dir. orthop. Children's Hosp. and Clinics, 2004—. Grantee, NIH, 1998—2001. Office: Childrens Hosp and Clinics of Minn 2525 Chicago Ave S Minneapolis MN 55404

**ZALESKI, GARY GEORGE,** federal agency administrator, accountant; s. Edward George and Helen Lee Zaleski; m. Kathy Rita Metcalf, May 17, 1975; children: Nathaniel Gavin, Camilla Anne. BS in Accty., Fla. State U., 1974; MPA, Harvard U., 1987. Cert. fraud examiner. Auditor Naval Audit Svc., Washington, 1984—90; planner Dept. of Treasury, Washington, 1990—94; dir., planning Office of Comptr. of Currency, Washington, 1994—99; asst. commr. planning Immigration and Naturalization Svc., Washington, 1999—2002; asst. commr. planning and performance measurement Immigration and Customs Enforcement, Washington, 2002—. Chmn. performance com. Office Mgmt. and Budget, Washington, 1994—96; spkr. in field. V.p. Home Owners Assn., Stafford, Va., 1995—98. Sgt. USAF, 1967—70. Recipient Peer award for public service to other government agencies, US Dept Treasury, 1995; fellow, Sec. of Navy, 1986. Mem.: Nat. Assn. Pub. Administrs. (assoc.). Roman Catholic. Avocations: Karate, hiking, fishing. Home: 3001 Aquia Dr Stafford VA 22554 Office: Dept Citizenship and Immigration Svcs 20 Massachusetts Ave Washington DC 20529 Office Phone: 202-272-1478. Office Fax: 202-272-1480.

**ZALESKI, JAN FRANCISZEK,** biochemist; b. Bytom, Poland, Feb. 3, 1949; came to U.S., 1979; s. Stanislaw and Maria (Fliska) Z.; m. Margaret M. Toczkowska, Dec. 28, 1971; children: Marta, Monika. MS in Biochemistry, U. Warsaw, Poland, 1971, PhD in Biochemistry, 1978. Rsch. assoc., asst. prof., assoc. prof. U. Warsaw Inst. Biochemistry, 1971-82; vis. scientist Roswell Park Meml. Inst., Buffalo, 1979-82; assoc. scientist Okla. Med. Rsch. Found., Oklahoma City, 1982-85; rsch. assoc. U. Pa. Med. Sch., Phila., 1985-88; vis. scientist Great Lakes Lab., Buffalo, 1988; rsch. assoc. Rutgers U. Sch. Pharmacy, New Brunswick, NJ, 1989-97. Cons. J.A. Haley Vets. Hosp., Tampa, 1985, Great Lakes Lab., Buffalo, 1988, Wyeth-Ayerst Rsch., Princeton, 1994. Contbr. articles to profl. jours., chpts. to books. Mem. Am. Soc. Biochemistry and Molecular Biology. Avocations: antique and modern prints collecting, interior decorating, gardening, photography, basketball. Personal E-mail: jmzaleski@comcast.net.

**ZALESKI, JEAN,** artist; b. Birkirkara, Malta; d. John M. and Carolina (Micallef) Busuttil; children: Jeffrey, Philip, Susan. Student, Art Students League, N.Y.C., 1955—58, New Sch., 1967—69, Moore Coll. Art, Phila., 1970—71, Parsons Sch. Design, N.Y.C., 1974—75, Pratt Inst., 1976—77. Dir. art studio 733, Great Neck, NY, 1963-67; sr. art instr. Hussian Coll. Art, Phila., 1970-71; dir. Naples (Italy) Art Studio, 1972-74; corp. sec. Women in The Arts, N.Y.C., 1974-75, exec. coord., 1976-78. Adj. lectr. Bklyn. Coll., 1974-75, Hofstra U., 1977-82, Cooper Union, 1996—. One-woman shows include Neikrug Gallery, N.Y.C., 1970, Wallnuts Gallery, Phila., 1971, Il Gabbiano Gallery, Naples, Italy, 1973, Adelphi U., Garden City, N.Y., 1975, Women in Arts Gallery, N.Y.C., 1975, Alonzo Gallery, 1979—80, Va. Ctr. for Creative Arts, Sweet Briar, 1981, Hodgell Galleries, Sarasota, Fla., 1982—83, Elaine Starkman Gallery, N.Y.C., 1986, Romano Gallery, Barnegat Light, N.J., 1987—88, Citicorp Ctr., N.Y.C., 1988—89, Z Gallery, 1991, Sweet Briar Coll., Va., 1993, Trinity Coll., Hartford, Conn., 1996, Myungsook Lee Gallery, N.Y.C., 1997—98, Slater Mus., Norwich, Conn., Four Decades of Painting, Retrospective Westbeth Gallery, N.Y.C., 2000, St. James Cavalier Contemporary Art Ctr., Valletta, Malta, 2002, exhibited in group shows at Art U.S.A., N.Y.C., 1969, Internat. Art Exhbn., Cannes, France, 1969, Frick Mus., Pitts., 1970, NAD, N.Y.C., 1970—71, Phila. Mus. Art, 1971, Am. Women Artists, Palazzo Vecchio, Florence, Italy, 1972, Internat. Women's Arts Festival, Milan, 1973 (Gold medal), Bklyn. Mus., 1975, Sweet Briar Coll., Va., 1977, CUNY, 1978, Va. Ctr., 1988, Mus. Hudson Highlands, 1982, Pace U. Gallery, N.Y.C., 1982, Bayly Mus., Charlottesville, Va., 1986, Allbright Knox Mus., Buffalo, 1986, E. Starkman Gallery, N.Y.C., 1987, Nabisco, 1989, Queens Coll., N.Y., 1991—92, Mus. City of N.Y., 1993, Nat. Mus. Fine Arts, Malta, 2000, Mediterranean Conf. Ctr., 2001, Westbeth Gallery, NYC, 2002—06, Represented in permanent collections N.Y. Pub. Libr., Met. Mus. Art, N.Y.C., Va. Ctr. for Creative Arts, Nat. Mus. Women in Arts, Mus. City of N.Y., Nat. Mus. Malta; author: Winged Spirits, 1995; co-author: COW/LINES, 1983. Recipient Susan B. Anthony award NOW, 1986; MacDowell fellow, 1971—, Ragdale fellow, 1986—, Va. Ctr. for Creative Arts fellow, 1976—, Tyrone Guthrie Ctr. fellow, 1991; grantee NEA/Brown U., 1982, Artists Space, 1988; invited to White House by Pres. Carter, 1977. Mem. Artists Equity, Women in the Arts. Democrat. Roman Catholic. Achievements include represented Malta in UN art exhibition celebrating entry of 25 countries to E.U. 2004. Avocations: music, opera, writing. Personal E-mail: zaleskijean@aol.com.

**ZALESKI-VEGAZO, ILENE,** librarian; b. Worcester, Mass., Sept. 26, 1946; d. John Dominic and Emily Viola (Jarvais) Z. BS in Zoology cum laude, Boston U., 1968; MLS, U. R.I., 1973. Biology tchr. Northampton (Mass.) Sch. for Girls, 1968-69; asst. circulation libr. U. R.I. Libr., Kingston, 1972-73, audiovisual cataloger computerized cataloging libr., 1973-75; asst.

editor Deep Sea Rsch/Oceanographic Abstracts and Bibliography, Woods Hole, Mass., 1977; scientific book reviewer Small Press Rev., Vt., 1977-78; assoc. editor Oceanographic Lit. Rev., Woods Hole, 1978-83; cons. editor RP Record in Natural Resources and Environ. Mgmt., Woods Hole, 1983-84; sr. editor Woods Hole Data Base, 1983-84; asst. to dir. North Miami Pub. Libr., 1984—2002, dir., 2002—06. Ofcl. del. Gov.'s Conf. on Librs. and Info. Svcs., 1990; judge Benjamin Franklin Awards Competition, 1996-2006. Named Vol. of Yr. Learn to Read Vols. of Miami, 1989; Ilene Zaleski Day named in City of North Miami, 1991, 94, 2006; recipient Key to City of North Miami, 2006. Mem. ALA, Fla. Pub. Libr. Assn. (dir.-at large 1994—, sec. 1993, Libr. Employee of Yr. 1989-90), North Miami Woman's Club (pres. 1993-95, v.p. 1991-93, treas. 1989-91), Fla. Libr. Assn. (chair awards com. 2005-06), Dade County Libr. Assn. (scholarship chair 2004-05), Assn. Fla. Laubach Orgns. (pres. 1990-91), Train Collectors Assn. Avocations: reading, bicycling, aerobics, travel, toy trains. Office: North Miami Pub Libr 835 NE 132nd St Miami FL 33161-4116 Office Phone: 305-891-5535. Business E-mail: izbabycar@aol.com.

**ZALEWSKA, ANNA,** economist, researcher; d. Lucjan Staniskaw Zalewski and Wieslawa Zofia Antonik; 1 child, Tomasz. MA in Econs., U. Leicester, Eng., 1995; MS in Math., Maria Curie-Sklodowska U., Lublin, Poland, 1989; PhD in Math., Polish Acad. Scis., Warsaw, 1998; PhD in Econs., London Bus. Sch., Eng., 1998. Tchng. and rsch. asst. math. Maria Curie-Sklodowska U., Lublin, Poland, 1988—93; rsch. officer London Bus. Scho., 1997—98; lectr. in econs. U. Bristol, England, 1998—2000; asst. prof. fin. Maastricht U., England, 2000—05; prof. fin. Sch. Mgmt., U. Bath, Bath, England, 2005—. Acad. cons. Nat. Econ. Rsch. Assoc., London, 2002—, London, 2003—. Contbr. articles to profl. jours. Mem.: Ctr. for Market and Pub. Orgn. Office: Univ Bath Sch Mgmt Bath BA2 7AY England Office Phone: 44 1825 384354. Office Fax: 441885 33 6473. E-mail: a.zalewska@bath.ac.uk.

**ZALEZNIK, ABRAHAM,** psychoanalyst, management specialist, educator; b. Phila., Jan. 30, 1924; s. Isadore and Anna (Appelbaum) Z.; m. Elizabeth Ann Aron, June 24, 1945; children: Dori Faith, Ira Harry. AB in Econs., Alma Coll., 1945, DLitt (hon.), 1992; MBA, Harvard U., 1947, DCS, 1951; grad., Boston Psychoanalytic Soc. and Inst., 1965; D (hon.), U. Montreal, 1999; prof. (hon.), Haute Etude Commercial, France, 2001. Research asst. Harvard U. Grad. Sch. Bus. Adminstrn., 1947-48, instr., 1948-51, asst. prof., 1951-56, assoc. prof., 1956-61, prof., 1961—, Cahners-Rabb prof. social psychology of mgmt., 1967-83, Konosuke Matsushita prof. leadership, 1983-90, Konosuke Matsushita prof. leadership emeritus, 1990—; research fellow Boston Psychoanalytic Soc. and Inst., 1965-68, mem. faculty, 1972—; pvt. practice psychoanalysis Boston, 1968—. Cons. in field. Author: Human Dilemmas of Leadership, 1966, (with Manfred F.R. Kets de Vries) Power and the Corporate Mind, 1975, The Managerial Mystique, 1989, An Executive Guide to Motivating People, 1990, Learning Leadership, 1992; contbr. articles to profl. jours. Bd. overseers Beth Israel Hosp., Boston, 1968—. Served with USN, 1942-46. Mem. Boston Psychoanalytic Soc., Am. Psychoanalytic Assn. (cert.), Am. Sociol. Assn., Tavern Club (Boston), Belmont Country Club (Mass.). Home: 170 N Ocean Blvd Palm Beach FL 33480-3946 Office: Harvard University Business School Boston MA 02163 Office Phone: 617-495-6285. E-mail: azaleznik@hbs.edu.

**ZALIAPIN, ILYA,** geophysical statistician; b. Chelyabinsk, Russia, Mar. 6, 1973; s. Vladimir Zalyapin and Nelly Zalyapina; m. Elena Tchigriaeva, Apr. 30, 1999; 1 child, Vladimir. MSc, Lomonosov Moscow State U., 1995; PhD, Russian Acad. Sci., 1999. Russian Acad. Sci. Rsch. scientist MITPAN, Russian Acad. Sci., Moscow, 1994—2001; postdoctoral fellow U. Calif. Inst. Geophys. and Planet. Phys., L.A., 1999—2001, rschr., 2001—06; asst. prof. dept. math. and stats. U. Nev., Reno, 2006—. Mem.: Calif. Earthquake Ctr., Inst. of Math. Stats., Am. Geophys. Union. Office: U Nevada Dept Math and Stat 084 Reno NV 89557 Office Phone: 775-784-6077. Personal E-mail: zal@unr.edu.

**ZALK, ROBERT H.,** retired lawyer; b. Albert Lea, Minn., Dec. 1, 1944; s. Donald B. and Jacqueline (Carleton) Z.; m. Ann Lee Anderson, June 21, 1969; children: Amy, Jenna. BA, Carleton Coll., 1966; JD, U. Minn., 1969. Bar: Minn. 1969, U.S. Dist. Ct. Minn. 1969. Assoc. Popham, Haik, Schnobrich, Kaufman & Doty, Mpls., 1969-72; atty. No. States Power Co., Mpls., 1972-73, Wright, West & Diessner, Mpls., 1973-84, Fredrikson & Byron P.A., Mpls., 1984-94, Zalk & Assocs., Mpls., 1994-95; ptnr. Zalk & Eayrs, Mpls., 1995-98, Zalk & Wood, Mpls., 1999, Zalk & Bryant, Mpls., 2000—06, ret., 2006. Fellow Am. Acad. Matrimonial Lawyers (pres. Minn. chpt. 2000-01), Minn. Bar Assn. (co-chmn. maintenance guideline com. 1991-94), Hennepin County Bar Assn. (co-chmn. family law sect. 1990-91). Office: Zalk & Bryant 5861 Cedar Lake Rd Minneapolis MN 55416-1481 Office Phone: 952-545-3392. Business E-mail: rzalk@zalkbryant.com.

**ZALL, PAUL MAXWELL,** language educator, consultant; b. Lowell, Mass., Aug. 3, 1922; m. Elisabeth Weisz, June 21, 1948; children: Jonathan, Barnaby, Andrew. BA, Swarthmore Coll., 1948; AM, Harvard U., 1950, PhD, 1951. Teaching fellow Harvard U., 1950-51; instr. Cornell U., 1951-55, U. Oreg., 1955-56; research editor Boeing Co., 1956-57; asst. prof. Calif. State Coll., Los Angeles, 1957-61, assoc. prof., 1961-64, prof. English, 1964-86; research scholar, cons. to library docents Huntington Library, San Marino, Calif., 1986-96; acting chmn. dept. Calif. State Coll., 1969-71. Cons. in report writing, proposal preparation and brochures to industry and govt. agys., 1957-99. Author: Elements of Technical Report Writing, 1962, Hundred Merry Tales, 1963, Nest of Ninnies, 1970, Weakly Blast, 1960-85, Literary Criticism of William Wordsworth, 1966, (with John Durham) Plain Style, 1967, Simple Cobler of Aggawam in America, 1969; (with J.R. Trevor) Proverb to Poem, 1970, Selected Satires of Peter Pindar, 1971, Comical Spirit of Seventy Six, 1976, (with Leonard Franzo) Practical Writing, 1978, Ben Franklin Laughing, 1980; (with J.A.L. Lemay) Autobiography of Benjamin Franklin, 1981; Norton Critical Edition of Franklin's Autobiography, 1986, Abe Lincoln Laughing, 1983, 95; (with E. Birdsall) Descriptive Sketches, 1984, Mark Twain Laughing, 1985, Being Here, 1987, George Washington Laughing, 1989, Franklin's Autobiography: Model Life, 1989, Founding Mothers, 1991, Becoming American, 1993, 98, Lincoln's Legacy, 1994, Wit and Wisdom of the Founding Fathers, 1996, Blue and Gray Laughing, 1996, Lincoln on Lincoln, 1999, 2003, Dolley Madison, 2001, Franklin in Franklin, 2001, Jefferson on Jefferson, 2002, Washington on Washington, 2003, Adams on Adams, 2004, Benjamin Franklin's Humor, 2005. Pres. Friends of South Pasadena Library, 1967-70. Served with USAAF, 1942-45, ETO. Recipient Outstanding Prof. award, 1965; fellow, Am. Philos. Soc., 1964, 1966, Huntington Libr., 1993; grantee, John Carter Brown Libr., Huntington Libr., 1993. Home: 2040 Amherst Dr South Pasadena CA 91030-3906 Office: Huntington Libr San Marino CA 91108 Fax: 626-449-5720. E-mail: pzall9@hotmail.com.

**ZALLEN, HAROLD,** academic administrator, chemist; b. Boston, Apr. 7, 1926; s. Joseph and Lillian L. (Stahl) Z.; m. Eugenia Malone, Aug. 23, 1959. BS in Pharmacy, Northeastern U., Boston, 1951; EdM in Sci. and Math., Boston U., 1954; MS in Organic Synthetic Medicinal Chemistry and Biochemistry, Purdue U., West Lafayette, Ind., 1959; PhD in Analytical Medicinal Chemistry and Nucleonics, Purdue U., 1960. Registered pharmacist, Mass., Ind. With USAAF, 1943-46, combat flier, sgt. 487th bomb group H, 839th bomb squadron; commd. 1st lt. U.S. Army, 1955, advanced through grades to col., Phila. mgr. Shoppers World Pharmacy, Inc., Framingham, Mass., 1951-53; asst. prof. phys. sci. Portia Law Sch. Calvin Coolidge Coll., Boston, 1952-54; tchr. physics and chemistry Natick (Mass.) High Sch., 1955-56; asst. prof. microbiology Lowell Gen. Hosp. Sch. Nursing, Mass., 1955-56; grad. instr., asst. radiol. control officer Purdue U., West Lafayette, Ind., 1957-58; assoc. prof. chemistry Coll. Pharmacy Mercer U., Atlanta, 1960-61; assoc. prof. to prof. head dept. radiol. scis., dir. Office Radiol. Safety Auburn U., Ala., 1961-66; specialist phys. sci. chem. div. higher edn. rsch. Bur. Rsch., U.S. Office Edn., 1966-67, head curriculum higher edn. rsch., 1967; head instructional sci. equipment program, assoc. chmn. prior, then dir. spl. projects program NSF, Washington, 1967-72; asst. dean, dir. rsch. and grad. studies Okla. State U., Stillwater, 1972-73, prof. chemistry, 1972-73, rsch. prof. biochemistry and molecular biology, 1973-75; assoc. v.p.

for adminstrn. and fin., CEO Health Scis. Ctr. Campus U. Okla., Oklahoma City and Tulsa, 1973-75, assoc. v.p. for systems planning, procedure devel. and spl. projects, cen. adminstrn. Norman, 1975—; exec. v.p. Acad. World Inc., 1975—; pres., CEO Malone, Zallen & Assocs. div. AcaWorld Corp., Greenville, NC; v.p.; dir. nuclear divsn. Vachon, Nix & Assocs., Atlanta; pres., CEO Computer Profis. Inc., Computer Distbrs. Corp., Malone Group Internat., Columbus, Ga.; sci. advisor Litton Corp./Army Rsch. Inst., 1991, Omega Tng. Group Inc./GIAT Industries, France, 1992—, Wetzel Internat., Inc., 1994—; chmn. bd. dirs. Cons. Unltd., Columbus, Ga. Asst. dean, dir. rsch. and grad. studies Okla. State U., Stillwater, 1972-73; analytical chemist Communicable Diseases Ctr. USPHS, Atlanta, 1962; spl. lectr. NSF Radiobiology Inst., Tuskegee U., 1963-64, head instrnl. sci. equipment program, assoc. program dir., dir. spl. projects program, 1967-72; pres. Pres.'s Sci. and Technol. Adv. Commn., Washington; v.p. Okla. Coll. Osteo. Medicine and Surgery, Tulsa; Gov. N.C. primary alt. to So. States Energy Bd., 1984-90, exec. com. bd., 1986; bd. vis. Tex. Christian U., Ft. Worth, 1993-76; adv. coun. Coll. Sci. and Math. Auburn U., 2003—; cons. in field. Editor, pub. Jour. Internat 6800 Computer Ctr.; contbr. articles to profl. jours. Hon. chmn. bus. adv. coun., Ala., 2003; rep. candidate NC Gen. Assembly, 1986; mem. nat. rep. congl. com. Recipient Mayoralty cert. of merit for outstanding svc. and Key to City, City of New Orleans, 1973, Most Outstanding Alumni award Northeastern U., 1996, Comdg. Gen. award U.S Army Inf. Ctr., 1998; GE sci. fellow Union U., Schenectady, NY., 1955, fellow Purdue Rsch. Found., 1958, Elks Cancer Soc., 1959, Am. Cancer Soc., 1960. Mem. Am. Chem. Soc. (bd. dirs., chmn. Auburn sect. 1966), Am. Soc. Engring. Edn. (long range planning com.), Nat. Coun. Univ. Adminstrs., Soc. Rsch. Adminstrs. (pres. So. sect. from 1974, chmn. publs. com.), Health Physics Soc., Greenville (NC) Area C of C. (chmn. rsch.), Columbus Club, Rotary (chmn. bull. com. Auburn 1963, bd. dirs. Auburn 1964, bd. dirs. Stillwater 1972-73, Greenville 1981-86, charter pres. Greenville, N.C. Morning Club 1986, 91, 94, Paul Harris fellow, R.I. Svc. Above Self award 1986), Masons (32 degree), Shriners, Sigma Xi, Phi Lambda Upsilon, Rho Chi, Phi Delta Kappa, Delta Sigma Theta, Beta Phi (past nat. sec.) Baptist. Office: Malone Group Internat PO Box 3682 Auburn AL 36831-3682 Office Phone: 334-887-2085. Personal E-mail: zallen1780@hotmail.com.

**ZALOZNIK, ARLENE JOYCE,** retired oncologist, retired military officer; b. Pitts., Jan. 30, 1948; d. Ernest and Frances Elizabeth (Augustin) Z. BS, Carlow Coll., 1969; MS, Duquesne U., 1972; MD, Med. Coll. Pa., 1976. Diplomate Am. Bd. Internal Medicine, Am. Bd. Oncology. Commd. U.S Army, 1976, advanced through grades to col.; intern then resident in internal medicine Madigan Army Med. Ctr., Tacoma, 1976-77; fellow in hematology and oncology Fitzsimons Army Med. Ctr., Aurora, Colo., 1979-81, staff oncology, 1981-82, asst. chief med. oncology, 1982-84, chief hematology and oncology, 1984-86, Brooke Army Med. Ctr., Ft. Sam Houston, Tex., 1986-90; assoc. prof., chief divsn. hematology/oncology divsn. Tex. Tech. U. Health Scis., El Paso, 1997—. Clin. instr. dept. medicine U. Colo. Health Scis. Ctr., 1982-86. Contbr. articles to books and profl. jours. Active profl. edn. com. Aurora-Adams Unit Am. Cancer Soc., 1983-86, pres., 1983-86, active Colo. divsn., 1984-86. Fellow ACP; mem. AMA, Am. Soc. Clin. Oncology. Home: 324 Sharondale Dr El Paso TX 79912-4250 Office Phone: 915-545-6619. E-mail: arlene.zaloznik@ttuhsc.edu.

**ZALTA, EDWARD,** otolaryngologist, physician; b. Houston, Mar. 2, 1930; s. Nouri Louis and Marie Zahde (Lizmi) Zalta; m. Carolyn Mary Gordon, Oct. 8, 1971; 1 child, Ryan David;children from previous marriage: Nouri Allan, Lori Ann, Barry Thomas, Marci Louise. BS, Tulane U., 1952, MD, 1956. Diplomate Am. Bd. Quality Assurance and Utilization Rev. Physicians. Intern Brooke Army Hosp., San Antonio, 1956—57; resident otolaryngology U.S Army Hosp., Ft. Campbell, Ky., 1957—60; practice medicine specializing in otolaryngology Glendora, West Covina and San Dimas, Calif., 1960—82. ENT cons. City of Hope Med. Ctr., 1961—76; mem. staff Foothill Presbyn.; past pres. L.A. Found. Cmty. Svc., L.A. Poison Info. Ctr., So. Calif. Physicians Coun., Inc.; founder, chmn. bd. dirs., CEO Health Solutions Internat.; founder, chmn. bd. dirs CAPP CARE, Inc.; founder Inter-Hosp. Coun. Continuing Med. Edn.; trustee U.S. Pharmacopeial Conv., Inc.; mem. adv. bd. Global Health Sys., Inc. Author (with others): Medicine and Your Money; mem. editl. staff Jour. Assn. Managed Healthcare Orgns., Managed Care Interface, Mng. Employee Health Benefits, mem. editl. adv. bd. Inside Medicaid Managed Care, Disease Mgmt. News, Managed Care Outlook; contbr. articles to profl. jours. Pres. bd. govs. Glendora Unified Sch. Dist., 1965—71; mem. Calif. Cancer Adv. Coun., 1967—71, Commn. Californians, Los Angeles County Common. Economy and Efficiency. Served to capt. Med. Corps U.S. Army, 1957—60. Recipient award of Merit, Order St. Lazarus, 1981. Mem.: AMA, Los Angeles County Med. Assn., Am. Coll. Med. Quality, Am. Assn. Preferred Provider Orgns., Am. Coun. Otolaryngology, Am. Acad. Otolaryngology, Calif. Med. Assn., Pacific Golf Club (San Juan Capistrano), Glendora Country Club, Ctr. Club (Costa Mesa, Calif.), Sea Bluff Beach and Racquet Club, Centurion Club, Phi Delta Epsilon, Kappa Nu. Republican. Jewish. Home: 3 Morning Dove Laguna Niguel CA 92677 Office: Ste 1123 27136 B Paseo Espada San Juan Capistrano CA 92675 Office Phone: 949-292-1951. Personal E-mail: edzalta@cox.net.

**ZALTMAN, MARK ALLEN,** federal agency administrator; b. Revere, Mass., Apr. 27, 1948; s. Isadore and Ethel Zaltman; m. Donna Jean Matthews, Jan. 13, 1974; 1 child, Rebecca. BA magna cum laude, U. Mass., 1970; MA, Binghamton U., 1974, PhD, 1995. Claims examiner Social Security Adminstrn., Chgo., 1974-90; labor rels. specialist Dept. Housing Urban Devel., Chgo., 1990-98, Region V human resources coord., 1998—. Tchg. asst. U. Wis., Milw., 1971-72, Binghamton (N.Y.) U., 1972-74; del. Milw. County Labor Coun., 1971-72. Author: Suburban/Rural Conflict in Late 19th Century Chicago, 1998; contbr. articles to profl. jours. Chief steward Am. Fedn. Govt. Employees Local 1395, Chgo., 1974—75, v.p., 1975—79, exec. v.p., 1979—83; mem. adv. bd. fed. sector labor rels. and labor law program Chgo.-Kent Coll. Law, 1998—; bd. dirs. Temple Menorah, Chgo., 2000—. Recipient Achievement award Am. Fedn. Govt. Employees Local 1395, 1976. Mem. Phi Beta Kappa, Phi Eta Sigma. Avocations: reading, travel. Office Phone: 312-353-5950 x2557. Business E-Mail: mark_zaltman@hud.gov.

**ZALUTSKY, MORTON HERMAN,** lawyer; b. Schenectady, Mar. 8, 1935; s. Albert and Gertrude (Daffner) Z.; m. Audrey Englebardt, June 16, 1957; children: Jane, Diane, Samuel BA, Yale U., 1957; JD, U. Chgo., 1960. Bar: Oreg. 1961. Law clk. to presiding judge Oreg. Supreme Ct., 1960-61; assoc. Hart, Davidson, Veazie & Hanlon, 1961-63, Veatch & Lovett, 1963-64, Morrison, Bailey, Dunn, Cohen & Miller, 1964-69; prin. Morton H. Zalutsky, P.C., 1970-76; ptnr. Dahl, Zalutsky, Nichols & Hinson, 1977-79, Zalutsky & Klarquist, P.C., Portland, Oreg., 1980-85, Zalutsky, Klarquist & Johnson, Inc., Portland, 1985-94; Zalutsky & Klarquist, P.C., Portland, 1994—. Instr. Portland State U., 1961-64, Northwestern Sch. of Law, 1969-70; assoc. prof. U. Miami Law Sch.; lectr. Practising Law Inst., 1971—, Oreg. State Bar Continuing Legal Edn. Program, 1970, Am. Law Inst.-ABA Continuing Legal Edn. Program, 1973—, 34th, 37th NYU ann. insts. fed. taxation, So. Fed. Tax Inst., U. Miami Inst. Estate Planning, Southwestern Legal Found., Internat. Foun. Employee Benefit Plans, others; dir. A-E-F-C Pension Plan, 1994-99, chmn., 1989-99. Author: (with others) The Professional Corporation in Oregon, 1970, 82; contbg. author: The Dentist and the Law, 3d edit.; editor-in-chief: Matthew Bender's Federal Tax Service, 1987-90; contbr. articles to profl. jours. Mem. vis. com. U. Chgo. Law Sch., 1986-88. Mem. ABA (vice chair profl. svcs. 1987-89, mem. coun. tax sect. 1985-87, spl. coord. 1980-85), Am. Law Inst., Am. Bar Retirement Assn. (trustee, bd. dirs., vice chair 1990-91, chair 1991-92), Am. Coll. Employee Benefits Coun. (charter mem.), Am. Coll. Tax Coun. (charter mem.), Multnomah County Bar Assn., Am. Tax Lawyers (charter mem.), Oreg. Estate Planning Coun. Jewish. Home: 3118 SW Fairmount Blvd Portland OR 97201-1466 Office: 215 SW Washington St Fl 3 Portland OR 97204-2636 Office Phone: 503-248-0300. E-mail: mort@erisalaw.com.

**ZAMANKHAN, PARSA,** mechanical engineer; arrived in U.S., 2001; s. Esfaniar Zamankhan and Firoozdokht Feridooni. BSME, U. Tehran, Iran, 1993; MSME, Shiraz U., Iran, 1997; DSc in Energy, Lappeenranta U. Tech.,

Finland, 2004; PhD in Mech. Engring., Clarkson U., Potsdam, N.Y., 2006. Rsch. scholar Lappeenranta U. Tech., Lappeenranta, Finland, 1999—2001; rsch. scientist Iranian Ctr. Energy Studies, Tehran, Iran, 1996—99; post doctoral rsch. Clarkson U., Potsdam, NY, 2006—. Reviewer Jour. Physics D-Applied Physics, Jour. Micromechanics and Microengineering, IEEE Transactions in Plasma Sci. Contbr. scientific papers, articles to profl. jours. Grantee, Finnish Acad., 1999—2003, Nat. Inst. Occupl. Safety and Health, 2003—06, Xerox Found., 2004—06. Mem.: ASME, Am. Assn. Aerosol Rsch. Achievements include development of Iranian national standards for energy consumption in room air conditioners; research in Iranian national standards for centrifugal pumps. Office: Clarkson U Dept Mech Potsdam NY 13699-0001 Office Phone: 315-268-4400.

**ZAMARIN, RONALD GEORGE,** lawyer; b. NYC, May 2, 1946; s. Leonard Leon and Laura Aileen (Gargus) Z.; m. Kathleen Veronica Durkin, July 20, 1968; children: Ryan, Chad, Jennifer. BA, UCLA, 1969, JD, 1972. Bar: Ill. 1972, U.S. Ct. Appeals (7th cir.) 1972, Fed. Trial Bar. Assoc. Isham, Lincoln & Beale, Chgo., 1972-79, ptnr., 1980-88; pvt. practice Des Plaines, Ill., 1988—2003, Palatine, Ill., 2003—. Coop. atty. ACLU, Chgo., 1982—; litigating mem. Lawyers Com. for Civil Rights under Law, Chgo., 1974-78. Co-author: Media Law Handbook, 1982. Trustee, treas. Palatine Pub. Libr. Dist. (Ill.), 1980-89; co-chair Citizens Com. for the Palatine Libr., 1990-95, Citizens Com. for the Palatine Park Dist., 1994—; co-founder Palatine Pub. Libr. Found.; mem. Palatine Adv. Bd., 1978-79; mem. bd. commrs. Palatine Boys' Baseball, 1983-98, sec., 1986-98. Mem.: ABA (forum on comm. law), First Amendment Lawyers Assn. Office: Suite 700 800 E Northwest Hwy Palatine IL 60074 Home: 200 White Branch Ct Buffalo Grove IL 60089 Office Phone: 847-705-3895. Personal E-mail: rgzlaw@comcast.net.

**ZAMARRA, GALEN,** chef; b. Switzerland, Grad., Culinary Inst. Am. Garde mgr. Bouley, NYC; cook Michel Bras, France, Georges Blanc, France, L'Arpege, France, Union Pacific, NYC; chef de cuisine Bouley Bakery, NYC, 2000—01; co-owner, chef Mas (farmhouse), NYC, 2004—. Named Grey Poupon Rising Star Chef of Yr., James Beard Found., 2001, Best New Restaurant, NYC, Esquire Mag., 2004; named one of NYC's Rising Stars, StarChefs.com, 2006. Office: Mas (farmhouse) 39 Downing St New York NY 10014 Office Phone: 212-255-1790.*

**ZAMARRIPA, VICTOR MANUEL,** sound recording engineer, purchasing agent; b. Matamoros, Tamaulipas, Mexico, Sept. 27, 1959; s. Preston Lee Jobe and Elidia Zamarripa Jobe. Grad., C.E. Vail H.S., La Feria, Texas, 1977. Cert. audio rec. engr., Tex., 2000. Mem. com. La Fiesta De La Feria, Tex., 1999—; chief audio engr. Valley Internat. Christian Ctr., San Benito, Tex., 1999—2005. Cons., installer, engr. Missing Lynck Prodns., La Feria, Tex., 1974—. Prodr.(rec. and mixing engr.): rec. studios. Leader Valley Internat. Christian Ctr., San Benito, Tex., 1999—2005. Recipient Tejano award, Tex. Conjunto Assn., 2002. Home: Box 6906 1008 S Chelo Dr La Feria TX 78559 Office: Missing Lynck Prodns 1008 S Chelo Dr La Feria TX 78559 Office Phone: 956-797-4718. Personal E-mail: vzamarripa@aol.com.

**ZAMBIE, ALLAN JOHN,** lawyer; b. Cleve., June 9, 1935; s. Anton J. and Martha (Adamski) Z.; m. Nancy Hall, Sept. 22, 1973. Student, Ohio U., 1953-54; BA, Denison U., 1957; LL.B., Western Res. U. (now Case Western Res. U.), 1960. Bar: Ohio 1960. Asso. firm Hribar and Conway, Euclid, Ohio, 1961-63; staff atty. The Higbee Co., Cleve., 1963-67, asst. sec., 1967-69, sec., 1969-74, v.p.-sec., 1974-88, gen. counsel, 1978-88; v.p., sec., gen. counsel The Lamson & Sessions Co., Cleve., 1989-94; of counsel Conway, Marken, Wyner, Kurant & Kern Co., LPA, Cleve., 1994-95; v.p.-sec. John P. Murphy Found., Cleve., 1996-2000, exec. v.p., 2001—. V.p.-sec. Kulas Found., 2001—. Trustee Cleve. Music Sch. Settlement, pres. bd. trustees, 1980—82, treas., 1996—2001; trustee N.E. Ohio affiliate Am. Heart Assn., 1989—96. With U.S. Army, 1960—61. Mem.: Am. Soc. Corporate Secs. (nat. v.p 1977—), Cleve. Bar Assn., Ohio Bar Assn. Office: 50 Pub Sq Ste 924 Cleveland OH 44113-2203 Home: 25243 Bryden Rd Beachwood OH 44122 Office Phone: 216-623-4772. Business E-Mail: azambie@murphykulas.org.

**ZAMBONE, ALANA MARIA,** special education educator, consultant; b. Vineland, NJ, Sept. 17, 1952; d. L. Alan and Joyce (Bernero) Z. AB in Spl. Edn. and Elem. Edn., U. N.C., Chapel Hill, 1974; MS in Human Devel. Liaison, George Peabody Coll. Tchrs., 1978; PhD in Spl. Edn., Vanderbilt U., 1984. Cert. spl. edn., elem. edn., visual impairments, mental retardation, N.C. Tchr., counselor Orange County Assn. for Retarded Citizens, Chapel Hill, N.C., 1973-74; lead tchr. Shelbyville-Bedford (Tenn.) County Adult Svc. Ctr., 1974; program coord. Dickson (Tenn.) County Adult Svcs., 1974-75; dept. head, habilitative svcs. CloverBottom Devel. Ctr., Nashville, Tenn., 1975-76; exec. dir. Waves, Inc. Adult Svcs., Fairview, Tenn., 1976-77; from vocat. cons. to liaison, Peabody Tchrs. Coll. Vanderbilt U., 1977-80; chairperson, bd. dirs. Residential Svcs., Inc., Nashville, 1976-80; asst. prof., coord., dept. curriculum N.C. State U., Raleigh, N.C., 1981-84; coord. and asst. prof., div. spl. edn. Minot (N.D.) State U., 1984-86; coord. internat. outreach svcs. Hilton-Perkins Internat. Program Perkins Sch. for the Blind, Watertown, Mass., 1989-94; assoc. prof., dir. Inst. for Visually Impaired Pa. Coll. Optometry, Phila., 1994—. Co-founder, sr. rsch. fellow Walker-Wheelock Inst. for Equity in Edn.; sr. project dir. exceptional needs assessment devel. lab. Edn. Devel. Corp., Newton, Mass., 1998—; co-coord. grad. program tchrs. of students with spl. needs, grad. faculty infant toddler program evaluator Danforth cmty. devel. project Wheelock Coll., 1995-98; nat. cons. Am. Found. for the Blind, NYC, 1986-89; adj. mem. of. div. spl. edn. Columbia U., 1987—; co-dir. model infant/toddler program, sch. medicine, U. N.C., Chapel Hill, 1983-84; project dir., mem. grad. faculty severe and multiple disabilities Simmons Coll., 1990—; bd. dirs. ND Coun. for the Arts, Specialized Svcs. for Children, Inc.; adv. bd. Blind Babies Found.; adv. coun. Robert E. Miller, Inc., Community Residential Svcs. for Disabled Children; sch. edn. rep. to fac. N.C. State U., sch. edn. fac. senate, others; dir. visual impairment tng programs N.C. Ctrl. U., 2002 05; affiliate dept. curriculum and instrn. East Carolina U. Greenville, N.C. Grantee Busch Found., N.D. Coun. Arts, Nat. Coun. on the Arts, Dean's Grant Program, Burlington/No. Found., Kate B. Reynolds Found., Nat. Rural Spl. Edn. Consortium, U.S. Office Human Devel. Svcs., U.S. Office of Spl. Edn. Mem. Coun. for Exceptional Children (past dir. div. visual handicaps), Assn. for Retarded Citizens, Assn. for Persons with Severe Handicaps, Am. Assn. Mental Deficiency, Am. Assn. for Applied Behavior Analysis, Nat. Assn. for Parents of the Visually Impaired, Internat. Assn. for the Edn. of the Deaf-Blind, Assn. for the Edn. and Rehab. of the Blind and Visually Impaired (pre-sch. div., multihandicaps div., chairperson multiple disabilities div.), Internat. Coun. Educators of Children and Youth Who Are Blinded or Visually Impaired (co-coord. functions curriculum devel. project 1993—) Avocation: scuba diving. Office: Inst for Equity in Schs Affiliate Walker Home & Sch 1968 Central Ave Needham MA 02492-1410 also: Edn Devel Corp 35 Chapel St Newton MA 02458-1010 also: East Carolina Univ Sch Edn 307 Speight Hall Greenville NC 27858 Office Phone: 919-530-5346. Personal E-mail: azambone@earthlink.net.

**ZAMBRANO, EDUARDO VICENTE,** pathologist, researcher; b. Guayaquil, Guayas, Ecuador, Sept. 13, 1965; arrived in U.S., 1997; s. Jose Vicente Zambrano and Ana Julia Tola. MD, Cath. U., Guayaquil, 1992; MS, Vrije U., Brussels, 1994; grad. profl. cert., U. New Haven, 2001. Prof. of biology Sch. of Medicine, Universidad Catolica, Guayaquil, Guayas, Ecuador, 1995—97; resident in anat. and clin. pathology Yale-New Haven Hosp., Yale U., New Haven, 1997—2002, attending pathologist, 2003; clin. fellow in pathology Children's Hosp., Harvard U., Boston, 2002—03. Rschr. Ctr. for Human Genetics, U. of Louvain, Leuven, Belgium, 1993—95; acting dir. Inst. of Tropical Molecular Biology, Cath. U., Guayaquil, 1995—97; instr. of lab. courses Yale U. Sch. of Medicine, New Haven, 2000—; lectr., tutorial group leader Yale U. Sch. Medicine, 2003—. Author: (textbook) Introducción a la Biología Molecular; contbr. articles, sci. papers, abstracts, poster presentations; editl. bd. mem. Pediat. and Developmental Pathology Jour. Vol. support and cmty. programs for the Hispanic population Hispanos Unidos, New Haven, 2000—01. Named Disting. Guest, Mayoralty of the City of Managua, Nicaragua, 2001; recipient

Clin. fellowship in pathology, Harvard Med. Sch., 2002—03. Mem.: AMA, Ecuadorian Coll. of Surgeons, Latin Am. Pathology Found. (chair of admissions com. 2000—), Soc. for Pediat. Pathology, U.S. and Can. Acad. of Pathology, Coll. of Am. Pathologists (inspector 2001). Achievements include one of first to develop human molecular genetics in Ecuador. Avocations: travel, reading, hiking, soccer, running. E-mail: eduardo.zambrano@yale.edu.

**ZAMDBORG, YURY,** internist; b. Kiev, USSR, Jan. 25, 1956; came to U.S., 1989; s. Leonid and Riva (Keselman) Z.; m. Ninel Reznik, Mar. 19, 1982; children: Leonid, Rebecca. MD, Ivano-Frankovsk Med. Sch., 1979; PhD in Med. Scis., U. Kiev, 1984. Diplomate Am. Bd. Internal Medicine. Intern United Hosps. Med. Ctr., Newark, 1991-92, resident, 1992-95; attending physician N.Y. Cmty. Hosp., 1997, N.Y. Meth. Hosp., Bklyn., 1997—; pvt. practice Bklyn. Author: Medical Ethics, 1988; contbr. articles to med. jours. Office: 2005 Ocean Ave Brooklyn NY 11230-6872 Office Phone: 718-375-8052.

**ZAME, WILLIAM R.,** mathematician, educator; b. Long Beach, NY, Nov. 4, 1945; s. Herbert and Miriam Zame; m. Linda Susan Goettina, Nov. 24, 1997; m. Elaine Bennett, 1989 (dec. 1995). BS, Calif. Inst. Tech., Pasadena, 1965; MS, Tulane U., 1967, PhD, 1970. Instr. Rice U., Houston, 1970—72; asst prof. math. SUNY, Buffalo, 1972—76; assoc. prof. math. Tulane U., New Orleans, 1975—78, SUNY, Buffalo, 1976—81, prof. math., 1981—91; prof. math. and econs. Johns Hopkins U., Balt., 1991—94, UCLA, 1994—. Assoc. editor Jour. Math. Econs., 1988—, Jour. Econ. Theory, 1990—, Econometrica, 1998—; mem. com. on status of women in the econs. profn., 1997—99; co-organizer profl. confs., including Exptl. Econs., Calif. Inst. Tech./UCLA, 1999; vis. prof. Inst. Advanced Study, U. Wash., Inst. Math. and its Applications, Math. Scis. Rsch. Inst., Inst. Mittag-Leffler, U. Copenhagen, Va. Poly. Inst., U. Calif., Berkeley. Contbr. articles to profl. jours., chapters to books. Grantee NSF, 1970—88, 1988—. Fellow: Econometric Soc. (program com. summer mtgs. 1991, 1997, program co-chair summer mtgs. 2002). Office: UCLA Dept Econs 405 Hilgard Ave Los Angeles CA 90095-9000

**ZAMECNIK, PAUL CHARLES,** oncologist, medical researcher; b. Cleve., Nov. 22, 1912; married; 3 children. AB, Dartmouth Coll., 1933; MD, Harvard U., 1936; DSc (hon.), U. Utrecht, 1966, Columbia U., 1971, Harvard U., 1982, Roger Williams Coll., 1983, Dartmouth Coll., 1988, U. Mass., 1994. Resident Huntington Meml. Hosp. Harvard U., Boston, 1936—37; intern U. Hosps., Cleve., 1938—39; Moseley traveling fellow Carlsberg Labs. Harvard U., Copenhagen, 1939—40; Finney-Howell fellow Rockefeller Inst. 1941—42; instr., assoc. prof. medicine Harvard U., 1942—56, Collis P. Huntington prof. oncologic medicine, 1956—79; dir. J.C. Warren Labs., 1956—79; chmn. exec. com. Dept. Medicine Harvard U., 1956—61; emeritus prof. oncological medicine Sch. Medicine, 1979—; prin. sci. Worcester Found. Experimental Biology, 1979—97; physician Mass. Gen. Hosp., 1956—79, hon. physician, 1979—, sr. scientist, 1998—. Vis. fellow dept. chemistry Calif. Tech. U., 1952; vis. Commonwealth scholar in chemistry U. Cambridge, 1962. Recipient Warren Triennial prize, Mass. Gen. Hosp., 1946, 1950, 1999, James Ewing award, 1962, Borden award, 1965, Am. Cancer Soc. Nat. award, 1968, Passano award, 1970, Nat. medal of sci., NSF, 1991, Hudson Hoagland award, 1992, City of Medicine award, Durham, N.C., 1995, Enterprize 2000 award, City of Worcester, Mass., 1996, Lasker award for Special Achievement in Medicine, Lasker Found., 1996, Lifetime Achievement award, Inst. Human Virology, 2004. Mem.: NAS, Am. Philosophy Soc., Am. Soc. Experimental Biologists (Merck award 1997), Mass. Med. Soc. (annual lectr. 1998, Amn. Orator 1998), Nat. Acad. Medicine, Assn. Am. Physicians, Am. Assn. Cancer Rsch. (pres. 1964—65), Am. Soc. Biol. Chemists, Am. Acad. Arts and Scis., Interurban Club. Office: Mass Gen Hosp Charlestown 149 13th St Rm 1494005 Charlestown MA 02129-2020 Office Fax: 671-724-9627.

**ZAMFIR, NICOLAE VICTOR,** physicist, researcher; b. Brasov, Romania, Mar. 24, 1952; arrived in U.S., 1992; s. Nicolae Zamfir, Livia Zamfir; m. Ecaterina Edita Petre; children: Radu Bogdan, Ioana Livia. Masters Degree (magna cum laude), U. Bucharest, Romania, 1976; PhD, Ctrl. Inst. Physics, Bucharest, Romania, 1984. Physicist Inst. Physics and Nuc. Engring., Magurele, Bucharest, Romania, 1978—84, sr. rschr. Bucharest, 1984—; physicist Brookhaven Nat. Lab., Upton, NY, 1994—97; sr. rsch. scientist Yale U., New Haven, 1997—2004; dir. Nat. Inst. Physics and Nuc. Engring., Bucharest, 2004—; plenipotentiary rep. Romania Joint Inst. Nuc. Rsch., Dubna. Cons. Clark U., Worcester, Mass., 1992—2003; mem. adv. com. 7 Internat. Confs. Contbr. over 160 articles to profl. jours.; co-editor 7 internat. conf. proceedings. Recipient Hurmuzescu award in physics, Romanian Acad., 1984. Mem.: AAAS, Am. Phys. Soc. Achievements include research in evolution of nuclear collectivity, phase/shape transition and phase co-existence in nuclei, octupole collectivity in nuclear structure. Office: Nat Inst Physics and Nuc Engring PO Box MG6 Bucharest Romania Office Phone: 40-21-4042301. Business E-Mail: zamfir@tandem.nipne.ro.

**ZAMKA, GEORGE D.,** astronaut; b. Jersey City, N.J., June 29, 1962; s. Conrad P. and Sofia Zamka; m. Elisa P. Walker; 2 children. BS in Math., U.S. Naval Acad., 1984; MS in Engring. Mgmt., Fla. Inst. Tech., 1997. Commd. 2d lt. USMC, 1984, advanced through grades to lt. col.; with Navy Attack Squadron, Marine All Weather Attacki Squadron, VMA, El Toro, Calif.; squadron weapons and tactics instr.; with Marine All Weather Fighter Attack Squadron VMFA, El Toro; forward air contr. 1st Bn, 5th Marines, Camp Pendleton, Calif.; with 31st Marine Expeditionary Unit, USS Belleau Wood, Western Pacific; test pilot/project officer Naval Strike Aircraft Test Squadron; aircraft maintenance officer VMFA, 1998; astronaut (pilot) NASA, Houston, 1998—, various duties with Astronaut Office. Pilot STS-120 Mission to Internat. Space Station, 2006. Decorated 6 Navy Strike Air medals, Navy Commendation medal with Combat V. Mem.: Soc. Exptl. Test Pilots, Marine Corps Assn., U.S. Naval Acad. Alumni Assn. Achievements include logged over 3,000 flight hours in over 30 different aircraft Avocations: sky diving, running, bicycling, scuba diving, boating. Office: Astronaut Office /CB NASA Johnson Space Ctr Houston TX 77058*

**ZAMMIT, JOSEPH PAUL,** lawyer; b. N.Y.C., May 19, 1948; s. John and Farla (Rudolph) Z.; m. Dorothy Therese O'Neill, June 6, 1970; children: Michael, Paul, Brian. AB, Fordham U., 1968; JD, Harvard U., 1971; LLM, NYU, 1974. Bar: N.Y. 1972, U.S. Dist. Ct. (so. and ea. dists.) N.Y. 1973, U.S. Dist. Ct. (no. dist.) Ala. 1989, U.S. Dist. Ct. (we. dist.) N.Y., 1991, U.S. Ct. Appeals (2d cir.) 1973, U.S. Supreme Ct. 1978, U.S. Dist. Ct. (no. dist.) N.Y. 1983, U.S. Ct. Appeals (11th cir.) 1987, U.S. Ct. Appeals (fed. cir.) 1995. Assoc. Reavis & McGrath, N.Y.C., 1971-74; asst. prof. law St. John's U., Jamaica, NY, 1974-76, assoc. prof. 1976-78; assoc. Reavis & McGrath, N.Y.C., 1978-79, ptnr., 1979-88, Fulbright & Jaworski L.L.P. (formerly Fulbright Jaworski & Reavis McGrath), N.Y.C., 1989—. Adj. assoc. prof. St. John's U., Jamaica, 1979-83, adj. prof., 1984—; mem. panel comml. arbitrators tech. panel Am. Arbitration Assn., N.Y.C., 1977—. Bd. editors E-commerce Law and Strategy, 1987—; contbr. articles to profl. jours. Mem.: ABA, Computer Law Assn., Assn. Bar City of N.Y. (tech. comml. liability subcom. 1981—87, chmn. com. computer law 1995—98, fgn. ct. comml. cons. 1998—2001, info. tech. law com. 2004—06), N.Y. State Bar Assn., Phi Beta Kappa. Office: Fulbright & Jaworski LLP 666 5th Ave Fl 31 New York NY 10103-0001 Office Phone: 212-318-3000. Personal E-mail: jzammit@fulbright.com.

**ZAMORA, MARJORIE DIXON,** retired political science professor; b. Farm Randolph, N.Y., Nov. 8, 1933; d. Wendell Hadley and Jessie (Mercer) Dixon; m. Cornelio Raul Zamora, Dec. 20, 1969; 1 child, Daniel Cornelio. BA, Earlham Coll., 1956; MA, U. Ill., 1968; postgrad., U. Ill., Chgo., 1989—. Tchr. Ridge, Sch., Godsman Sch., Stenson Sch., various cities, 1956-62; with U.S. Peace Corps, tchr. Palmares High Sch., Costa Rica, 1963-64; reporter Lerner Newspaper, Chgo., 1965; dormitory counselor U. Ill., Urbana, 1966-68, 86; instr. Chgo. City Coll., 1968-69; prof. polit. sci. Moraine Valley C.C., Palos Hills, Ill., 1969-94, prof. emerita. Rschr. in U.S.A., Chgo. 1985-88. Author short stories; contbr. articles on Costa Rican polit. bus. cycle and economy, land reform to publs. in U.S., Cen. Am.; contbr. short stories to mags. Dir., founder Dept. of Peace Coalition, 2000—05; rep. Beijing Plus Five Regional Steering Com., 1999; appointed to planning com. for a dept. of peace bill Rep. D. Kucinich; pub. speaker Dept. of Peace and Nonviolence & Peace in Space Bills in Congress, 2005—06; active Peace Alliance Orgn. Mem. AAUW (Western Spring area chpt. 1999, Ill. congressional liaison 2000—), Western Springs Band and Orch. Assn. (pres. 1990-91), Am. Assn. Ret. Persons, State Cmty. Coll. Retirees Assn. Mem. Soc. Of Friends. Avocations: skiing, swimming, writing fiction, nonfiction and filmscripts, symphonic music, scuba. Home: 3820 Lawn Ave Western Springs IL 60558-1141 Office Phone: 708-246-7363. E-mail: marjoriez@aol.com.

**ZAMVIL, LINDA SUSAN,** psychiatrist, educator; d. Louis and Stella Savage Zamvil; m. John Mott-Smith; m. John McNeil Angier II, Aug. 26, 1990; children: Lucas Angier, Robin Tucker Angier stepchildren: Katrina Meadville Angier, Judith Tegan Angier, John McNeil Angier III. BA cum laude, U. Calif., Berkeley, 1973; MD, U. Cinn., 1983. Lic. Mass., 1984, Calif., 1988, NH, 1990, Nat. Bd. Examiners, 1984, Am. Soc. Addiction Medicine, 1992, diplomate Am. Bd. of Psychiatry and Neurology, 1988, Am. Bd. of Psychiatry and Neurology, 1991, Am. Bd. Child and Adolescent Psychiatry, 1991, Am. Bd. of Adult Psychiatry. Counselor, med. asst. Santa Cruz Women's Health Ctr., Calif., 1977—78, Yolo County Rape Crisis and Womankind Health Ctr., Santa Cruz, 1978—79; clin. fellow in pediat. Harvard Med. Sch., 1983—84, clin. fellow in psychiatry, 1984—90, clin. instr. in psychiatry, 1990—98, asst. clin. prof. psychiatry, 1999—; intern, resident, psychiatrist Mass. Gen. Hosp., 1983—, intern in pediat., 1983—84, intern, resident Chelsea, 1983—85, resident in psychiatry Dept. Psychiatry, 1984—87, psychiatrist Revere Health Ctr. Mass., 1985—86, mem. women's com. Dept. Psychiatry, 1986—90, resident in child psychiatry, 1987—90, clin. assoc. in psychiatry, 1990—, psychiatrist, 2001; intern Med. Sch. Harvard U., Boston, 1983—84, resident Med. Sch. 1984—87, fellow child and adolescent psychiatry Med. Sch., 1987—90; with Pembroke Hosp., Mass., 1985—90, Westwood Lodge, Mass., 1985—90, Lynn and Union Hosps., Mass., 1988—90, The Cambridge (Mass.) Hosp., 1988—90, psychiatrist, 1988—90, 1997—, psychiatrist Ctr. St. Clinic Somerville, 1999—2002, dir. mental health and addictions, 1999—2000; with New Eng. Meml., Stoneham, Mass., 1989—90; staff psychiatrist Cath. Med. Ctr., Manchester, NH, 1990—94, with, 1990—95; staff psychiatrist Meml. Hosp., Nashua, 1990—94, with, 1990—96, McLean Hosp., Belmont, Mass., 1993—, attending child psychiatrist Child and Adolescent Program Dept. Psychiatry, 2002—; with Sts. Meml. Med. Ctr., Lowell, Mass., 1996—99, psychiatrist Teen Health/Pediatric Counseling Svcs., 1997—99; with St. Joseph Hosp., Nashua, 1997—99, Somerville Hosp., Mass., 1997—, Mt. Auburn Hosp., Cambridge, 1997—; med. dir. adolescent chem. dependency svcs. Brookside Hosp., Nashua, 1990—91, med. dir. child and adolescent psychiatry, 1990—94, mem. instnl. rev. bd. N.E. Psychiat. Assocs., 1990—94, mem. med. record and rev./utilization rev. com., 1990—94, with, 1990—99, med. dir. child and adolescent program svcs., 1991—94; intern, resident Chelsea Health Ctr., 1983—85, psychiatrist, 2001; psychiat. cons. STRAIGHT, Outpatient Adolescent Substance Abuse Treatment, Stoughton, Mass., 1986—87, McLean Hosp., Belmont, Mass., 1992—; psychiatrist Human Resource Inst., Malden and Franklin, Mass., 1986—87, Family Svc. Assn., Boston, 1988—90, Ctr. Mental Health and Retardation Svcs., Waltham, Mass., 1989—90, Stoneybrook Counseling Ctr., Chelmsford, Mass., 1989—90; staff psychiatrist Lahey Hitchcock Clinic, Nashua, 1994—96; med. dir. Northeast Psychiat. Assoc., Lowell, Mass., 1996—99, Charter Behavioral Health Sys. Brookside/New Eng., Lowell, 1996—99, Cambridge Psychiat. Svcs., Inc., Psychiat. Recruitment and Placement Svcs. (sub. North Charles, Inc.-affiliation with Harvard Med. Sch. Dept. Psychiatry Cambridge Hosp.), 1996—2000, Mass. Behavioral Health Partnership, Boston, 2000—01; dir. Ambulatory Psychiatry Svcs. The Cambridge Health Alliance, 1999—2000, Somerville, 1999—2000; mem. instnl. rev. bd. Dept. Psychiatry The Cambridge Health Alliance Cambridge Hosp., 1999—2000; dir. Child and Adolescent Psychiatry, Advs., Inc., Framingham, 2001—, Framingham/Marlborough, Mass., 2002—. Bd. dirs. New Eng. Coun. Psychiatrists, Waltham; mem. com. youth and children NH Coun. Child and Adolescent Psychiatry, 1992—94; mem. Psychiat. Adv. Panel Patient Care Assessment Com. Bd. Registration in Medicine Commonwealth Mass., 1997—; with New Eng. States Partnership Divsn. Med. Assistance Pediatric Psychoactive Medication Prescribing Workgroup Commonwealth Mass., 2001—; mem. adv. bd. Families Depression Awareness, Waltham, 2004—; invited spkr. in field; rschr. in field. Expert reviewer Bipolar Disorder and Depression, 1999; contbr. chapters to books, monographs in books, articles in newsletters. Organizer continuing edn. Ednl. Programs, N.E.; chair N.E. coms. Calif. Gov.'s scholar, Gov. Ronald Reagan, 1969. Mem.: Internat. Soc. Bipolar Disorders, Am. Soc. Addiction Medicine (spkr.), Am. Acad. Psychiatrists Alcoholism and Addictions, Am. Acad. Child and Adolescent Psychiatry, Mass. Med. Soc., Mass. Psychiat. Assn., New Eng. Coun. Child and Adolescent Psychiatry (mental health task force 2001—, mem. consortium New Eng. Coun. Child Psychiatry 2001—, mass. chpt. acad. pediat. com. access to mental health 2001—, mem. bd. 2002—05, spkr.), Am. Acad. Child and Adolescent Psychiatry (presenter 1992), Am. Psychiat. Assn. (mem. nat. com. psychiatrists 1985—86, leader pub. mental health programs 1985—86, spkr. 1986, 1991, Mead Johnson fellow 1985—86). Achievements include worked with Depakote/Valproate as both a principal investigator and as a co-investigator studying the effects of lithium on Bipolar Mood Disorder in adults, adolescents and children; contributed to neuroimaging studies with children and adolescents on the mood stabilizer lithium. Office: Advs Inc 27 Hollis St Framingham MA 01702 Office Phone: 508-935-0769.

**ZAMZOW, JILL PATRICIA,** biologist, consultant; b. Mountain View, Calif., Feb. 4, 1972; d. Henry and Ann Marie Zamzow. BA, U. Calif., Santa Cruz, 1993; MS, U. Hawaii, Manoa, 1999; PhD, U. Hawaii, 2003. Grad. rsch. asst. U. Hawaii Manoa, Honolulu, 1999—2003; jr. rschr. Hawaii Inst. Marine Biology, Kaneohe, 2003—04; marine biologist Rsch. Corp. U. Hawaii, Kailua-Kona, 2004—05; Sir Keith Murdoch fellow Am. Australian Assn., Brisbane, 2005—06; rsch. coord. State of Hawaii, Honolulu, 2006—. Contbr. articles to profl. jours. Hair donor Locks of Love, Fla., 2005; blood donor ARC, Honolulu, 1995—2006; mentor Hawaii State Sci. Fair, Honolulu, 2002; vol. Hawaii Humane Soc., Honolulu, 2006. Named U. Hawaii Scholar of Yr., ARCS, Inc., 2002, Top Tchg. Asst. Biology dept., U. Hawaii, 2003; recipient Lerner-Gray Fund award, Am. Mus. Natural History, 1997, 2003, Arts & Scis. Adv. Coun. award, U. Hawaii, 2002, 2003; Pulley scholar for zoology, ARCS, Inc., 2002, Rsch. grant, Sigma Xi, 2002, Women's Internat. Sci. Collaboration grantee, NSF-AAAS, 2003, Vis. Postdoctoral Scientist grantee, Smithsonian T. R. I., Panama, 2003, New Investigator Travel grantee, NSF, 2004, Polar Programs Travel grantee, 2005, Antarctic Biology Course scholar, 2006. Mem.: Am. Soc. Ichthyologists and Herpetologists (travel award 2002). Avocations: sailing, marathon running, surfing, travel, scuba diving. Home: 2051 Young St Honolulu HI 96826 Office: NWHI CRER 6600 Kalaniana'ole Hwy Ste 300 Honolulu HI 96825 Office Phone: 808-397-2660. E-mail: jzamzow@gmail.com.

**ZANARDELLI, JOHN JOSEPH,** healthcare organization executive; b. Monongahela, Pa., July 27, 1950; s. John and Linda (Lazzari) Z.; m. Suzanne King, Jan. 29, 1972; children: Brandon John, Stephen William, Robyn Lynn. Student, Davis & Elkins Coll., 1968; AA, C.C. Allegheny Cty, Pitts., 1970; AS in Acctg., C.C. Allegheny Cty., Pitts., 1991; BS in Edn., California State Coll. Pa., 1972; MPH, U. Pitts., 1979, cert. acct. 1994; cert. non-profit mgmt., Harvard U., 1998; cert. gen. mgmt., Carnegie Mellon U., 1999. Rsch. asst. grad. sch. pub. health U. Pitts., 1973-78; adminstrv. resident Ctrl. Med. Ctr. and Hosp., Pitts., 1978-79; vice-chmn., exec. dir. Allegheny Mountain Health Enterprises Inc., Oil City, Pa., 1985-88; exec. v.p. Oil City Area Health Ctr., Inc., 1979-88; exec. v.p., COO Grane Healthcare, Inc., Pitts., 1988-90; adminstr., COO Southwood Hosp. Inc., Pitts., 1990-91; exec. dir. Allegheny divsn. Presbyn. Sr.Care Pitts., Pa., 1991-92; exec. dir., CEO United Meth. Svcs. for Aging, 1993—. Preceptor, mentor health adminstrn. program U. Pitts. Grad. Sch. Pub. Health, 1980—; vis. faculty, 1997—98; adj. asst. prof. health svcs. adminstrn. Grad. Sch. Pub. Health, 1998—2001, adj. assoc. prof. health policy and mgmt., 2001—05, adj. assoc. prof. behavioral and cmty. health scis., 2005—; pres. HCCP, Inc., Pitts., 1983—; bd. dirs.

Faith-Based Network, Inc., 1998—; co-chair pub. rels. and mktg. com. Davis and Elkins Coll., 2000—02; co-chair exec.-in-residence com. U. Pitts. Grad. Sch. Pub. Health, 2001—02, exec. in residence, health adminstrn. program, 2001—03, fellow evaluation sci., dept. behavioral and cmty. health scis., 2004—; preceptor, Initiative on Social Enterprise, Harvard Bus. Sch., 2001—; mem. planning com. and faculty for longterm care program U. Pitts. Inst. on Aging, 2002—. Fellow: Am. Coll. Healthcare Execs.; mem.: Delta Omega (Omicron chpt., pres. 2000—01). Home: 2997 Greenwald Rd Bethel Park PA 15102-1615 Office: Asbury Heights 700 Bower Hill Rd Pittsburgh PA 15243-2040 Office Phone: 412-571-5134. Business E-Mail: johnzan@alumni.pitt.edu, jzanardelli@asburyheights.org.

**ZAND, DALE EZRA,** business management educator; b. NYC, July 22, 1926; m. Charlotte Edith Rosenfeld, Oct. 16, 1949; children: Fern, Mark, Karen, Jonathan, Matthew. BEE, Cooper Union, 1945; MBA, NYU, 1949, PhD, 1954. Asst. to v.p. Spectator Bags, 1947-49; v.p. Glo-Cold Co., 1949-50; mem. faculty Stern Sch. Bus., NYU, N.Y.C., 1950—, prof. mgmt., 1963—, chmn. dept., 1968—, sr. faculty fellow, Press., cons. to industry, 1951—; bd. dirs. Newfield Exploration Co., Inst. Applied Behavioral Sci. Author: Information, Organization, and Power, 1981, The Leadership Triad, 1997, also articles. Served with USNR, 1945. Ford Found. fellow, 1959-60 Mem. Am. Psychol. Soc., Inst. Mgmt. Sci., Acad. Mgmt., Internat. Assn. Applied Social Scientists. Office: NYU 40 W 4th St KMC890 New York NY 10012-0157

**ZANDER, EDWARD J.,** communications executive; b. Brooklyn, NY, Jan. 12, 1947; m. Mona Zander; 2 children. BSEE, Rensselaer Poly. Inst., 1968; MBA, Boston U., 1975. Formerly with Apollo Computer, Data Gen., Raytheon; with Sun Microsystems Inc., Palo Alto, Calif., 1987—2002, COO, 1998—2002, pres., COO, 1999—2002; mng. dir. Silver Lake Ptnrs., 2002—03; chmn., CEO Motorola Inc., Schaumburg, Ill., 2004—. Bd. dirs. Documentum, Inc., Portal Software, Inc., Rhythms Netconnections, inc., Seagate Tech. Mem. sci. adv. bd. Rensselaer Poly. Inst., Troy, NY, presdl. advisor; mem. dean's adv. bd., sch. of mgmt. Boston U.; bd. dirs. Jason Found. for Edn.; mem. Economics Club Chgo., Exec. Club Chgo.; mem. civic com. Comml. Club Chgo. Office: Motorola Inc 1303 E Algonquin Rd Schaumburg IL 60196*

**ZANDER, GAILLIENNE GLASHOW,** psychologist; b. Bklyn., Apr. 7, 1932; d. Saul and Anna (Karasik) G.; m. A.J. Zander, Aug. 5, 1952; children: Elizabeth L., Caroline M., Catherine A. MusB, U. Wis., 1953, MS, 1970; PhD, Marquette U., 1984. Diplomate Am. Bd. Forensic Examiners, Am. Acad. Pain Mgmt.; cert. Am. Soc. Clin. Hypnosis. Music tchr. Wis. Sch. Systems, 1953-65; psychol. asst. Vernon Psychol. Labs., Chgo., 1965-70; psychologist Milw. Pub. Schs., 1970-92, CESA 19, Kenosha, Wis., 1977-78; pvt. practice psychology Milw., 1980—. Fellow Am. Orthopsychiat. Assn.; mem. APA, Wis. Psychol. Assn. Home: 13750 Carson Ct Brookfield WI 53005-4989 also: A Healing Ctr 20860 Watertown Rd Waukesha WI 53186-1872 Office Phone: 262-821-6117. E-mail: zanderga@aol.com.

**ZANDER, JEANNE MARIE,** healthcare educator; b. Temple, Tex., Dec. 21, 1962; d. James Smith and Ann Marie Rainer; m. Philip Ray Zander, May 5, 1990; 1 child, Julie Ann. Bachelors, Tex. A&M U., 1985. Cert. med. technologist Am. Soc. Clin. Pathology. Health sci. edn. tchr. Brenham (Tex.) H.S., 1994—. Advisor Health Occupations Students Am. Office: Brenham HS 525 A H Dr Brenham TX 77833 Office Phone: 979-277-6570.

**ZANDMAN, FELIX,** electronics executive; b. Grodno, Poland, 1928; MS, U. Nancy, France, 1953; PhD, U. Paris The Sorbonne; doctorate (hon.), Univ. Beer Sheva, Israel Inst. Tech. (Technion). With French Nat. Ctr. Sci. Rsch., Paris, 1950-53; with engring. and consulting SNECMA, 1953-57; dir. basic rsch. Tatnall Measuring Systems Co., Phoenixville, Pa., 1957-62; founder, dir., chmn. bd. Vishay Intertechnology, Malvern, Pa., 1962—, pres., 1962—98, CEO, 1962—2004, chief tech. officer, 2004—. Author: Never the Last Journey, 3 textbooks in electronics; contbr. articles to profl. jours. Recipient Medal of Honor, Electronic Industries Alliance, 2001. Achievements include 39 patents in electronics. Office: Vishay Intertechology 63 Lincoln Hwy Malvern PA 19355

**ZANDMAN-ZEMAN, RONALD EDWIN,** elementary school educator, minister; s. Marshall B. and Dorothy Zeman; m. Sharon Lee Zandman-Zeman, Mar. 21, 1995; children: Ari M. Schuhmann, Adam Zane. BA in Liberal Arts, San Jose State U., Calif., 1970, BA in Radio and TV, 1971; tchg. cert., U. Alaska, Anchorage, 1981; MA in Edn., Towson State U., Md., 1993. Reverend Universal Life Ch., San Jose; tchr. 3rd grade traditional/5th grade slingerland Northwood Elem., Anchorage, 1983—88; tchr. 4-5-6 grade optional edn. Susitna Elem., Anchorage, 1988—97; tchr. 7th grade lang. arts regular/gifted Goldenview Middle Sch., Anchorage, 1997—2001, tchr. 7th grade social studies regular/gifted, 2001—. Mentor tchr. and coach Anchorage Sch. Dist., basketball, volleyball and track coach; head social studies dept. Goldenview Middle Sch., Anchorage; adj. prof. Alaska Pacific U., 2002, U. Alaska, Anchorage, 2004; presenter in field. Nominee Nat. Disney award, 2000; named BP Tchr. of Excellence, BP Exploration, 1997, Tchr. of Week, KGOT Radio, 1999; recipient Disting. Tchr. award, Nat. Coun. for Geog. Edn., 1991. Avocations: river rafting, fishing, hiking, bicycling, cabin building. Office: Goldenview Middle Sch 15800 Golden View Dr Anchorage AK 99516-4924

**ZANDVAKILI, KATAYOON,** writer; b. Tehran, Iran, Oct. 7, 1967; came to U.S., 1976; d. Amir Hossein and Nahid (Farazian) Z. BA, U. Calif., Berkeley, 1988; MFA, Sarah Lawrence Coll., 1992. Editl./oral history asst. McKinsey & Co., San Francisco, 1994-97; West Coast assoc. Pubs. Weekly, Woodacre, Calif., 1997-98. Contbr. work to Five Fingers Rev., Hawai'i Rev., Mass. Rev.; author of poems. Home: 6055 Fairlane Dr Oakland CA 94611-1849 Personal E-mail: kzawriter@mindspring.com.

**ZANE, BILLY,** actor; b. Chgo., Feb. 24, 1966; m. Lisa Collins, 1988 (div. 1995). Appeared in films Back To The Future, 1985, Critters, 1986, Dead Calm, 1989, The Case of the Hillside Strangler, 1989, Back To The Future Part II, 1989, Memphis Belle, 1990, Blood and Concrete I.R.S., 1991, Orlando, 1992, Sniper, 1993, Tombstone, 1993, Only You, 1994, Tales From The Crypt Presents Demon Knight, 1995, Danger Zone, 1995, Head Above Water, 1996, The Phantom, 1996, Titanic, 1997, Susan's Plan, 1998, (voice) Pocahontas II: Journey to a New World, 1998, Taxman, 1999, Morgan's Ferry, 1999, The Believer, 2001, CQ, 2001, Landspeed, 2001, Claim, 2002, Starving Hysterical Naked, 2003, Imaginary Grace, 2003, Vlad, 2003, Three, 2004, Dead Fish, 2004, Silver City, 2004, The Pleasure Drivers, 2005, The Last Drop, 2005, BloodRayne, 2005, Mem-o-re, 2005, (TV miniseries) Cleopatra, 1999, Sole Survivor, 2000, (TV movies) Hendrix, 2000, The Diamond of Jeru, 2001, Invincible, 2001, Bet Your Life, 2004; actor, prodr.: I Woke Up Early the Day I Died, 1998, Sea Devils, 2002; actor, exec. prodr.: This World, Then the Fireworks, 1997; actor, exec. prodr., dir.: Big Kiss, 2004; dir.: (TV series) Stop for a Minute, 2001; appeared in Broadway prodn.: Chicago, 2002. Office: Creative Artists Agy 9830 Wilshire Blvd Beverly Hills CA 90212-1825*

**ZANE, PHILLIP CRAIG,** lawyer; b. N.Y.C., Sept. 25, 1961; s. Martin I.L. and Rosalind Carol (Siegler) Z.; m. Denise Janine Wydra; 1 child, Christopher Abelard. BA, Pomona Coll., 1983; postgrad., U. Mich., 1985-88; JD cum laude, NYU, 1991. Bar: Ill. 1991, D.C. 1996, U.S. Dist. Ct. (no. dist.) Ill. 1991, U.S. Ct. Appeals (7th cir.) 1994, U.S. Ct. Appeals (8th cir.) 1993, U.S. Ct. Appeals (9th cir.) 1996, U.S. Fed. Cir. Ct. 1994, U.S. Dist. Ct. D.C. 2000, U.S. Supreme Ct. 2004. Assoc. Mayer, Brown & Platt, Chgo., 1991-93; judicial law clerk to Hon. Morris S. Arnold 8th Cir. Ct. Appeals, Little Rock, 1993-94; assoc. Mayer, Brown & Platt, Chgo., 1994-95, Morgan, Lewis & Bockius, Washington, 1996—2000, of counsel, 2000—04; solo practice, 2004—05; of counsel Baker, Donelson, Bearman, Caldwell & Berkowitz, PC, 2005— Staff editor NYU Rev. of Law and Social Change, 1989-90, critical legal studies editor, 1990-91; editor Sherman Act Almanac, 1998; contbr.

articles to profl. jours. Sec. gen. coun. Arthur F. Burns Fellowship Program, Inc., 1998—. Fellow Thomas J. Watson Found., 1983-84; fgn. lang. area studies fellow U. Mich., Ann Arbor, 1986, 87-88. Mem. ABA (vice chair Sherman Act sect. one com. 1999-2001, chair antitrust oral history task force 2005—), Ill. State Bar Assn. (spl. com. on Law Day in Moscow and Kiev 1992). Democrat. Avocation: legal history. Office: Baker Donelson Bearman Caldwell & Berkowitz PC 555 11th St NW Fl 6 Washington DC 20004-1314 Office Phone: 202-508-3490. E-mail: pzane@bakerdonelson.com.

**ZANGEN, ABRAHAM,** neuroscience researcher, consultant; s. Menachem and Miriam Zangen; m. Rachel Grinberg, Mar. 15, 1994; children: Elyashiv, Maayan, Yair, Idit. BSc in pharmacy, Med. Sch., Hebrew U., 1988—92; MSc, Bar-Ilan U., 1995—96, PhD, 1995—99. Rsch. and tchg. asst. Bar-Ilan U., Ramat-Gan, Israel, 1995—99; postdoctoral fellowship Nat. Inst. of Health, Nat. Inst. on Drug Abuse, Balt., 1999—. Cons. Brainsway Technologies, 2003—. Author: (neuroscience research) The role of the endogenous opioid, endomorphin-1, in brain reward circuitry, (neuroscience research) Psychophysiological aspects in the etiology of depression and the mode of action of antidepressant drugs mode of action of, (neuroscience research) Depressive behavior correlates with absence of serotonin-dopamine interaction. Recipient The Israeli Soc. for Biol. Psychiatry Ann.prize, 1999, Fulbright Postdoctoral fellowship, 2000, Fellows award for Rsch. Excellence, Nat. Inst. of Health, 2002; Fogarty Post-doctoral fellowship, Fogarty Found., 1999—2003, Fulbright Post-doctoral fellowship, Fulbright Found., 2000. Mem.: NIDA fellows com. (assoc.), Soc. for Biol. Psychiatry (assoc.), Israeli Soc. for Neuroscience (assoc.), Soc. for Neuroscience (assoc.). Achievements include invention of a coil for transcranial magnetic stimulation of deep brain regions. Personal E-mail: azangen@intra.nida.nih.gov.

**ZANGWILL, STEVEN,** pediatrician, cardiologist; Asst. prof. Pa. State Childrens Hosp., Hershey, Pa., 1995—2002, Children's Hosp. Wisc., Milw., 2002—, 2002—. Med. dir. cardiac transplantation Children's Hosp Wis. Office Phone: 414-266-2380.

**ZANI, FREDERICK CAESAR,** retired financial consultant; b. Medford, Mass., June 9, 1929; s. John and Catherine (Voluletti) Zani; m. Dorothy Ann Menezes, Feb. 20, 1960; children: Gregory Robert, Elizabeth Ruth. BS, Salem State Coll., 1954; M.Ed., Boston U., 1959, cert. in advanced grad. studies, 1967; PhD (hon.), World U., 1986. Lic. sch. psychologist. Tchr., 1954—60; tchr. pub. schs. Gloucester, Mass., 1960—65; guidance counselor Attleboro, Mass. public schs., 1965—90; ret. Former owner, exec. dir. Zani Group Internat. Consulting Co., 1990—. Contbr. articles to profl. jours. Recipient Outstanding Svc. award, Bristol County Tchrs. Assn. Mem.: Ret. State, County and Mcpl. Employees Assn., Boston Children's Hosp. Med. Center Parent Orgn. for Exceptional Children, Mass. Sch. Psychologists Assn., Mass. Ret. Tchrs. Assn., Mass. Tchrs. Assn., Attleboro Tchrs. Assn., Mass. Assn. Children with Learning Disabilities (v.p. Attleboro chpt. 1969—70), Ret. Nat. Educators Assn., Christian Edn. Assn., Internat. Platform Assn. Mem. Assembly Of God. Ch. Home: 45 Washington St Unit 210 Plainville MA 02762-2686 E-mail: fcz1@aol.com.

**ZANJACOMO, PAULO REGIS,** engineering executive; s. Expedicto and Alzira Zanjacomo; m. Hilda Hortensia Valero Tonone, Mar. 27, 1999. BSc in Computer Scis., U. Sao Paulo, 1990, MSc in Applied Math., 1992; PhD in Indsl. Engring., Ga. Inst. Tech., 1998. Asst. prof. U. Sao Paulo, 1992—94; sr. engr. for rsch. and product design Energy Imperium, Atlanta, 1999—99; dir. rsch. and design Altra Energy Technologies, Houston, 1999—2000; chief tech. officer Delfin Energy, Atlanta, 2000—04, Stats. and Research Autom. Trading Desk Charleston, SC, 2002—. Contbr. articles to profl. jours. Mem.: INFORMS.

**ZANK, VIRGINIA,** literature and language professor; b. Plainview, Ark., Apr. 29, 1942; d. Hayes Dale and Imogene Bridges; m. Martin J. Kugel (dec.); children: Cynthia Gail Kugel, Melissa Gene Kugel-Couch; m. Dale M. Zank, Nov. 25, 1995. BS in Secondary Edn., John Brown U., 1963; MA in English, Ctrl. Mo. State U., 1978. Lifetime cert. tchr. English Mo. Tchr. Higbee (Mo.) H.S., 1963—64; tchr. English Hallsville (Mo.) H.S., 1964—67, Marshall (Mo.) H.S., 1967—93; assoc. prof. English Mo. Valley Coll., Marshall, 1993—. Named Disting. Educator, Optimist Club, Marshall, 1997; recipient Gov.'s award for tchg. excellence, State of Mo., 1996. Mem.: Mo. State Tchrs. Assn., Nat. Coun. Tchrs. English, Mo. Assn. Tchrs. English (pres.). Home: PO Box 658 Marshall MO 65340 Office: Mo Valley Coll 500 E College Marshall MO 65340 Business E-Mail: zankv@moval.edu.

**ZANNA, MARTIN THOMAS,** physician; b. Mpls., Apr. 2, 1947; s. Peter J. and Mary L. (Peck) Z. AB, Harvard U., 1969, MPH, 1976; MD, U. Minn., 1973. Diplomate Am. Bd. Preventive Medicine. Resident in pub. health N.J. State Dept. Health, 1974-77, acting dir. chronic disease svcs., 1976-79, dir. chronic disease svcs., 1979-81; med. adminstr. Fla. Dept. Health and Rehab. Svcs., Tallahassee, 1981-82; med. cons. N.J. Medicaid, Trenton, 1982—, chief med. cons., 1990-96; med. cons. N.J. State Dept. Health and Sr. Svcs., 1996—. Mem. Fla. Cancer Coun., 1981-82, Fla. Bd. Med. Examiners, 1982, N.J. Hypertension Study Group, 1977-81; chmn. grad. med. edn. com. N.J. State Dept. Health & Sr. Svcs., 1993—; diabetes adv. coun. exec. com. N.J. Dept. Health, 2001—. Contbr. articles to profl. jours. Participant Fla. Gov.'s Mission to Haiti, 1982; mem. divsn. profl. edn. Am. Cancer Soc., 1976-81. Fellow Am. Coll. Preventive Medicine; mem. APHA, Harvard Club (Boston), Harvard Faculty Club (Cambridge), Harvard Club (Washington). Home: # 11 201 Salem Ct Apt 11 Princeton NJ 08540-7039 Office: NJ State Dept Health & Sr Svcs PO Box 807 Trenton NJ 08625-0722

**ZANNIERI, NINA,** museum director; b. Summit, N.J., Feb. 1, 1955; d. Angelo Joseph and Louise Mary (Brumm) Z.; m. Douglas M. Vogel, Oct. 29, 1994. BA, Boston Coll., 1977; postgrad., Coll. of William & Mary, 1977-78; MA, Brown U., 1980. Curatorial asst. R.I. Hist. Soc., Providence, 1980-81, asst. curator, 1981-83, curator, 1983-86; dir. Paul Revere Meml. Assn., Boston, 1986—. Gen. editor: (exhbn. catalog) Paul Revere: The Man Behind the Myth, 1988; collaborator: A Most Magnificent Mansion; project dir.: (exhbn. catalog) Let Virtue Be A Guide To Thee, 1983 Mem. Am. Assn. Mus.'s (bd. dirs. 1999-02, vice-chair 2002-03), New Eng. Mus. Assn. (pres. 1998-02), Am. Assn. State and Local History (gov. coun. 2004-), Phi Beta Kappa. Office: Paul Revere Meml Assn The Paul Revere House 19 North Sq Boston MA 02113-2405

**ZANNINO, RICHARD F.,** publishing executive; b. Oct. 26, 1958; m. Anna Zannino; 4 children. BS, Bentley Coll., 1980; MBA, Pace U., 1983. With Continental Group, Inc., Stamford, Conn.; various fin. positions Emery Worldwide, 1984—86, Peter Kiewit Sons, Inc., 1986—91, JWP, 1992; v.p., CFO Saks Fifth Ave., 1993—98; CFO Gen. Signal Corp., 1998; various sr. level positions including exec. v.p. Liz Claiborne, Inc., 1998—2001; CFO Dow Jones & Co., NYC, 2001—02, exec. v.p., COO, 2002—06, CEO, 2006—. Vice chmn. Advt. Edn. Found.; mem. dean's adv. coun.coll. commerce and fin. Villanova U.; mem. Columbia Bus. Sch. Media Forum. Office: Dow Jones & Co 1 World Fin Ctr 200 Liberty St New York NY 10281 Office Phone: 212-416-2000.*

**ZANOT, CRAIG ALLEN,** lawyer; b. Wyandotte, Mich., Nov. 15, 1955; s. Thomas and Faye Blanch (Sperry) Zanot. AB with distinction, U. Mich., 1977; JD cum laude, Ind. U., 1980. U.S. Ct. Appeals (6th cir.) 1985, U.S. Dist. Ct. (ea. dist.) Mich. 1987, U.S. Dist. Ct. (we. dist.) Mich. 1990. Law clk. to presiding justice Allen County Superior Ct, Ft. Wayne, 1980-81; ptnr. Davidson, Breen & Doud P.C., Saginaw, Mich., 1981—. Mem.: ABA, Genesee County Bar Assn., Bay County Bar Assn., Saginaw County Bar Assn., Mich. Bar Assn. Roman Catholic. Home: 547 S Linwood Beach Rd Linwood MI 48634-9432 Office: Davidson Breen & Doud PC 1121 N Michigan Ave Saginaw MI 48602-4762 Office Phone: 989-752-9595. E-mail: umchiphi@aol.com.

**ZANUCK, LILI FINI,** film director, producer; b. Leominster, Mass., Apr. 2, 1954; m. Richard Zanuck, Sept. 23, 1978. Rsch. asst. World Bank, Washington, 1970-78; office mgr. Carnation Co., L.A., 1977-78; rsch. and devel. Zanuck-Brown Co., 1978-89; co-founder, co-owner Zanuck Co., 1989—. Prodr. films Cocoon, 1985, Cocoon: The Return, 1988, Driving Miss Daisy, 1989 (Acad. award 1989), Rich in Love, 1993, Clean Slate, 1994, Wild Bill, 1995, Dvojnik, 1995, Mulholland Falls, 1996, True Crime, 1999, Reign of Fire, 2002; dir. film Rush, 1991, TV miniseries From the Earth to the Moon (Part 3), 1998. Mem.: Calif. Film Commn. Office: The Zanuck Company 9465 Wilshire Blvd Beverly Hills CA 90212-2612

**ZANUCK, RICHARD DARRYL,** motion picture company executive; b. Beverly Hills, Calif., Dec. 13, 1934; s. Darryl F. and Virginia (Fox) Z.; m. Lili Gentle; children: Virginia, Janet; m. Linda Harrison, Oct. 26, 1969; children: Harrison Richard, Dean Francis; m. Lili Fini, Sept. 23, 1978. Grad., Harvard Mil. Acad., 1952; BA, Stanford, 1956. Story, prodn. asst. Darryl F. Zanuck Prodns., 1956, v.p., 1956-62; president's prodn. rep. 20th Century-Fox Studios, Beverly Hills, 1962-63, v.p. charge prodn., 1963-69, pres., 1969-71, dir., 1966-71; founder, pres., owner Zanuck Co., Beverly Hills, 1989—. Chmn. 20th Century-Fox Television, Inc.; sr. exec. v.p. Warner Bros., Inc., 1971-72; co-founder, pres. Zanuck/Brown Co., 1972-88. Producer: The Sting, 1973 (Acad. award), The Sugarland Express, 1974, Jaws, 1975, Jaws 2, 1978, The Island, 1980, Neighbors, 1982, The Verdict, 1983, Cocoon, 1985, Cocoon, the Return, 1988, Driving Miss Daisy, 1989 (Acad. award, Irving G. Thalberg award 1991), Rush, 1991, Rich in Love, 1992, Mulholland Falls, 1996, Deep Impact, 1998, True Crime, 1999, Rules of Engagement, 1999, Planet of the Apes, 2000, Road to Perdition, 2001, Big Fish, 2003; prodr. Acad. Award Show, 2000. Nat. chmn. Fibrosis Assn., 1966-68; mem. organizing com. 1984 Olympics; trustee Harvard Sch. 2d lt. U.S. Army. Named Producer of Yr., Nat. Assn. Theatre Owners, 1974, '85, Producers Guild Am., 1989; recipient Irving Thalberg award, 1991, Lifetime Achievement award, Producers Guild Am., 1993. Mem. Acad. Motion Picture Arts and Scis. (bd. govs.), Screen Producers Guild, Phi Gamma Delta. Office: Zanuck Co 9465 Wilshire Blvd Ste 930 Beverly Hills CA 90212-2608

**ZAPEL, ARTHUR LEWIS,** book publishing executive; b. Chgo., 1921; m. Janet Michel (dec.); children: Linda (dec.), Mark, Theodore, Michelle; m. Cynthia Rogers Pisor, 1986; stepchildren: Dawn, Anthony. BA in English, U. Wis., 1946. Writer, prodr. Westinghouse Radio Stas.; film writer Galbreath Studios, Ft. Wayne; creative dir. Kling Studios, Chgo., 1952-54; writer, prodr. TV commls. J. Walter Thompson Advt., Chgo., 1954-73, v.p. TV and radio prodn., 1954-73; founder, pres. Arthur Meriwether, Inc., 1973-83; pres. Meriwether Pub. Ltd., 1969-90, chmn., 1990-97. Pres. Westcliffe (Colo.) Ctr. for the Arts. Author: Sweet Uncertainty, 2001; illustrator: 'Twas the Night Before, The Jabberwock mystery; created game A Can of Squirms; wrote plays and musical comedy scripts for ednl. use in schs. and chs.; supr. editing and prodn. 2500 plays and musicals, 1970-99; exec. editor 210 books on theater skills for secular and religious use. Founding pres. Art Students League of Colorado Springs, 1992; past pres. Colo. Springs Symphony Coun.; past bd. dirs. Colorado Springs Opera Festival. Recipient numerous awards Freedoms Found., Valley Forge, Art Dirs. Club N.Y., Art Dirs. Chgo., Hollywood Advt., 1960-67, Gold Records Radio Ad Bur., 1959-60, XV Festival Internat. Du Film Publicitaire Venise, 1968, Gold Camera award U.S. Indsl. Film Festival, 1983, Dukane award, 1983, Gold award Houston Internat. Film Festival, 1984, 2d pl. award Best New Fiction, Colo. Ind. Publishers Assoc., 2002. Office: Meriwether Pub Ltd 885 Elkton Dr Colorado Springs CO 80907-3576

**ZAPF, HERMANN,** book and type designer; b. Nuremberg, Germany, Nov. 8, 1918; s. Hermann and Magdalene (Schlamp) Zapf; m. Gudrun von Hesse, Aug. 18, 1951; 1 child, Christian Ludwig. D in Fine Arts (hon.), U. Ill., 2003. Freelance designer, 1938—; type dir. D. Stempel AG, type foundry, Frankfurt, Fed. Republic of Germany, 1947-56; design cons. Mergenthaler Linotype Co. (NYC and Frankfurt), 1957-74; cons. Hallmark Internat., Kansas City, Mo., 1966-73; v.p. Design Processing Internat. Inc., NYC, 1977-86; prof. typographic computer programs Rochester (N.Y.) Inst. Tech., 1977-87; chmn. Zapf, Burns & Co., NYC, 1987-91. Instr. lettering Werkkunstschule, Offenbach, Fed. Republic Germany, 1948-50; prof. graphic design Carnegie Inst. Tech., 1960; instr. typography Technische Hochschule, Darmstadt, Fed. Republic Germany, 1972-81. Author: William Morris, 1948, Pen and Graver, 1952, Manuale Typographicum, 1954, 1968, About Alphabets, 1960, 1970, Typographic Variations, 1964, Orbis Typographicus, 1980, Hora fugit/Carpe diem, 1984, Hermann Zapf and His Design Philosophy, 1987, ABC-XYZapf, 1989, Poetry Through Typography, 1993, August Rosenberger, 1996, (film) The Art of Hermann Zapf, German version Die Welt der Buchstaben von Hermann Zapf, (CD-ROM) The World of Alphabets, 2001; designer types Palatino, Melior, Optima, ITC Zapf Chancery, ITC Zapf Internat., Digiset Marconi, Digiset Edison, Digiset Aurelia, Pan-Nigerian, URW-Roman and San Serif, Renaissance Roman, Linotype Zapfifo, Zapfino Extra, ITC Dingbats, Zapf Essentials, Palatino Sans, Palatino Arabic. Hon. mem. Edward Johnston Found., Ditchling, Eng.; hon. curator Computer Mus., Boston. Named hon. citizen, State of Tex., 1970, hon. Royal Designer for Industry, London, 1985; recipient Silver medal, Brussels, 1962, 1st prize typography, Biennale Brno, Czechoslovakia, 1966, Gold medal, Type Dirs. Club, N.Y., Frederic W. Goudy award, Inst. Tech. Rochester, 1969, Silver medal, Internat. Book Exhbn., Leipzig, 1971, Gold medal, 1989, Johannes Gutenberg prize, Mainz, Fed. German Republic, 1974, Gold medal, Museo Bodoniano, Parma, Italy, 1975, J.H. Merck award, Darmstadt, 1978, Robert Hunter Middleton award, 1987, Euro Design award, 1994, Wadim Lazursky award, Acad. of Graphic Arts, Moscow, 1996, SOTA Typography award, 2003. Mem. Royal Soc. Arts, Am. Math. Soc., Alliance Graphique Internationale, Bund Deutscher Grafik Designer, Internat. Gutenberg Gesellschaft; hon. mem Type Dirs. Club NYC, Soc. Typographique de France, Soc. Typographic Arts, Double Crown Club, Soc. Scribes and Illuminators, Friends of Calligraphy, Soc. Printers, Soc. Graphic Designers Can., Bund Deutscher Buchkünstler, Grafiska Inst., Typophiles, Alpha Beta Club (Hong Kong), Soc. of Calligraphy, Wynkyn de Worde Soc., Letter Exchange, Caxton Club, Monterey Calligrapher's Guild, Washington Calligraphers Guild, Eesti Kalligraafide Koondis (Tallinn, Estonia), Chgo. Calligraphy Collective, Typographers Internat. Assn., Art Dirs. Club Kans. City, Alcuin Soc., Goudy Internat. Ctr., Brno Biennale Assn., Soc. Scribes NY, Grolier Club (hon.), Dante e.V. (German TEX Group), Gamma Epsilon Tau.

**ZAPFFE, NINA BYROM,** retired elementary school educator; b. Independence, Mo., Aug. 17, 1925; d. Richmond Douglas and Nina Belle (Howell) Byrom; m. Robert Glenn Fessler, June 25, 1946 (dec. June 1947); 1 child, Robert Glenn Fessler Zapffe; m. Fred Zapffe, July 1, 1952 (dec. Dec. 1999); children: Paul Douglas, Carl Raymond. BA, So. Meth. U., Dallas, 1946. Fin. sec. Tyler St. Meth. Ch., Dallas, 1948-49; tchr. Dallas Ind. Sch. Dist., 1949-52, Norman (Okla.) Pub. Schs., 1966-74; chief reader for GED Writing Skills Test Part II GED Testing Svc., Am. Coun. on Edn., Washington, 1990—98; ret. 1998. Adv. com. Acad. Resource Ctr. Moore-Norman Tech. Ctr., 1988-2004. Adv. bd. Norman Salvation Army, 1978-90, chmn., 1986; organizer, historian Norman Salvation Army Womens Aux., 1983-2000, pres., 1985; organizer, past pres. Norman Literacy Coun., 1976—; organizing com., past pres. Norman Interfaith Coun., 1974-93; organizing com., past treas. Friends of the Norman Libr., 1979—; mem. McFarlin Meml. United Meth. Ch., historian 2-in-1 Sunday Sch. class, 1990-2002, lay leader, 1980-81, adminstrv. bd., 2001-2004. Named Woman of Yr., Norman Bus. and Profl. Women, 1999; named to Literacy Hall of Fame, Pioneer Libr. Sys., Norman, 1995; recipient medal of appreciation, SAR, 2002. Mem. DAR (regent Black Beaver chpt. 1998-2000, state literacy chmn. 2000-02, chpt. sec. 2003—), Nat. Soc. Daus. 1812 (pres. 1889er chpt. 1991-93, state pres. 1996-2000, chpt. sec. 2002—), Old Regime Study Club (pres. 1998-99), Coterie Club (pres. 1996, 2002), Delta Delta Delta Alumnae. Independent. Avocation: genealogy. Home: 2717 Walnut Rd Norman OK 73072-6940

**ZAPPA, GAIL,** record producer; m. Frank Zappa (dec.); children: Moon, Dweezil, Ahmet, Diva. Recipient (with Frank Zappa) Best Recording Package-Boxed Grammy award for Frank Zappa's Civilization, Phaze III, 1996.

**ZAPPALA, STEPHEN A.,** state supreme court justice; b. 1932; s. Frank and Josephine Zappala. BA, Duquesne U.; LL.B., Georgetown U., 1958. Bar: Pa. 1958. Solicitor Allegheny County, Pitts., 1974-76; judge Ct. of Common Pleas-Allegheny County, 1980-82; assoc. justice Pa. Supreme Ct., 1982—2003, judge. Served with U.S. Army. Office: Gladys Zappa LLC 14 McKelvey Ave Pittsburgh PA 15218-1454

**ZAPPE, JOHN PAUL,** city editor, educator, newspaper executive; b. NYC, July 30, 1952; s. John Paul and Carolyn (Pikor) Z. BA, Marist Coll., 1978; JD, Syracuse (N.Y.) U., 1978. Reporter Poughkeepsie Jour., 1973-75, Nev. State Jour., Reno, 1979-80; prin. Am. Media Bold (Ariz./Calif.), 1983-88; reporter Press-Telegram, Long Beach, Calif., 1983-88, city editor, 1988-97, webmaster PT Connect, 1995-97, mng. new media, 1997-98; dir. new media Riverside (Calif.) Press-Enterprise, 1998-2000; v.p. new media L.A. Newspaper Group, Woodland Hills, Calif., 2000—03; prin. Zappe Media Svcs., 2003—; prin., dir. bus. devel. Classified Intelligence. Tchr. journalism U. 1976-78, Calif. State U., 1985-87, U. So. Calif., 2003—04; cons. Am. Media Bold, 1981-83. Chmn. Local 69 Newspaper Guild, Long Beach, 1984-87. Mem. Investigative Editors and Reporters, NAA New Media Fedn. Office Phone: 562-252-0686. Business E-Mail: jzappe@classifiedintelligence.com.

**ZAR, JUDITH L. (MICKEY MCBRIDE),** writer; b. Evanston, Wyo., May 12, 1942; d. Jack LaDoy and Cecile Marie McBride; m. James Courtney Zar, May 14, 1977; children: Richelle, Jack Richard, Chet Edward. Hosp. ward clk., 1981. Substitute tchr. St. Peter's Tuller Sch., San Pedro, Calif., 1967—74, kindergarten tchr., 1974—77; tchr. Adult Phonics Reading, Torrance, Calif., 1985—86; asst. Paine Webber, Palos Verdes, Calif., 1986—87; journalist San Pedro (Calif.) Weekly, 1987—88; novelist, 1988—. Author (as Mickey McBride): (plays) The Phone Call, 1998, (novels) Two Kinds of Miracles, 2001, Command Performance, 2002, Scream Once for Help--A San Pedro Mystery, 2003, Art to Die For--A Harry Calle Mystery, 2003, Stealer of Wishes--A Harry Calle Mystery, 2004. Chmn. March of Dimes, San Pedro, Calif., 1966; mem. Jr. C. of C., San Pedro, Calif., 1966. Avocations: horticulture, knitting, painting, gourmet cooking. Home: 1843 Jaybrook Dr Rancho Palos Verdes CA 90275 Personal E-mail: jjzar@juno.com.

**ZARATE, JUAN CARLOS,** federal official; b. Santa Ana, Calif., 1971; AB magna cum laude, Harvard U., JD cum laude. Bar: 1997. Law clerk US Dist. Ct. (So. dist.) Calif.; atty. appellate sect. criminal divsn. U.S. Dept. Justice, Washington, prosecutor terrorism and violent crime sect.; asst. sec. treas. counter-terrorist financing U.S. Dept. Treasury, Washington, 2004—05; dep. asst. to the Pres. The White House, Washington, 2005—; dep. nat. security advisor for combating terrorism NSC, Washington, 2005—. Head Fin. Crimes Enforcement Network (FinCEN), Office Fgn. Assets Control (OFAC), Tri-Border conf., Brazil, U.S. delegation to UAE; head treas. delegation G-8 Counter-Terrorism conf., Florence, Italy; policy advisor criminal investigation divsn. IRS; policy advisor Fin. Action Task Force (FATF). Author: (book) Forging Democracy, 1994; contbr. articles to profl. jours. Rotary internat. fellow, U. Salamanca, Spain. Mem.: Calif. Bar Assn. Office: Net Security Coun 1600 Pennsylvania Ave Washington DC 20500

**ZARB, FRANK GUSTAVE,** investment company executive; b. NYC, Feb. 17, 1935; s. Gustave and Rosemary (Antinoro) Z.; m. Patricia Koster, Mar. 31, 1957; children: Krista Anne, Frank, Jr. BBA, Hofstra U., 1957, MBA, 1962, L.H.D., 1975. Trainee Cities Service Oil Co., N.Y.C., 1957-62; gen. partner Goodbody & Co., N.Y.C., 1962-69; exec. v.p. CBWL-Hayden Stone, Inc. (investment banking), N.Y.C., 1969-71; asst. sec. US Dept. Labor, Washington, 1971-72; exec. v.p. Hayden Stone, Inc., N.Y.C., 1972-73; assoc. dir., Office Mgmt. & Budget Exec. Office of the Pres., Washington, 1973-74; asst. to Pres. for Energy Affairs The White House, Washington, 1974-77; adminstr. Fed. Energy Adminstrn., Washington, 1974-77; adv. U.S. Congress, 1977-78; gen. ptnr. Lazard Freres & Co. N.Y.C., 1977-88; chmn., pres. chief exec. officer Smith, Barney, Harris, Upham & Co., Inc., 1988-93; vice chmn., group chief exec. The Travelers Inc., N.Y.C., 1993-94; chmn., pres., CEO, Alexander & Alexander Svcs. Inc., N.Y.C., 1994-97; pres. Nat. Assn. Securities Dealers, 1997-98, chmn., CEO, 1997—2000, Nasdaq Stock Market, Inc, 1997—2001; chmn. Frank Zarb Associates; sr. advisor, mng. dir. Hellman & Friedman LLC, San Francisco, 2002—; interim chmn. Am. Internat. Group (AIG), NYC, 2005—. Bd. dirs. CS First Boston, Inc., Coun. on Fgn. Rels., FPL Group, Inc., 2002-; chmn. L.I. Power Authority, 1996-97; bd. dirs., mem. exec. com. Am. Internat. Group (AIG), 2001-; co-chair, Promontory Fin. Group, 2006- Author: The Stockmarket Handbook, 1969, Handbook of Financial Markets, The Municipal Bond Handbook Mem. bd. trustees Gerald R. Ford Found.; mem. and former chmn. bd. trustees Hofstra U, bd. dirs. Lower Manhattan Develop. Corp. Recipient Disting. Scholar award Hofstra U., 1974; bus. sch. named in his honor Hofstra U. Mem. Coun. Fgn. Rels.*

**ZARE, RICHARD NEIL,** chemistry professor; b. Cleveland, Nov. 19, 1939; s. Milton and Dorothy (Amdur) Zare; m. Susan Leigh (Shively), Apr. 20, 1963; children: Bethany Jean, Bonnie Sue, Rachel Amdur. BA, Harvard U., 1961, PhD (hon.), 1964; postgrad., U. Calif., Berkeley, 1961—63; DS (hon.), U. Ariz., 1990, Northwestern U., 1993, ETH, Zürich, 1993, Columbia U., 2000, State U. West Ga., 2001; DP (hon.), Uppsala U., Sweden, 2000; PhD (hon.), U. York, 2001, Hunan U., 2002, U. Paul Sabatier, 2003. Postdoctoral fellow Harvard U., 1964; rsch. assoc. Joint Inst. for Lab. Astrophysics, 1964—65; asst. prof., chemistry MIT, 1965—66; asst. prof., dept. physics and astrophysics U. Colo., 1966—68, assoc. prof. physics, astrophysics, chemistry, 1968—69; prof. chemistry Columbia U., 1969—77, Higgins prof. natural sci., 1975—77; prof. Stanford U., 1977—, Shell, disting. prof. chemistry, 1980—85, Marguerite Blake Wilbur prof., natural sci., 1987—, prof., physics, 1992—. Cons. Aeronomy Lab, NOAA, 1966—77; radio standards physics divsn. Nat. Bur. Std., 1968—77, Lawrence Livermore Lab. U. Calif., 1974—, SRI, Internat., 1974—, Los Alamos Sci. Lab., U. Calif., 1975—; fellow adj. Joint Inst. Lab. Astrophysics, U. Colo.: sci. adv. com. IBM, 1977—92; chmn. commn. on phys., scis., and math applications Nat. Rsch. Coun., 1992—95; chmn. bd. dir. Ann. Rev., Inc., 1995—. Contbr. articles to profl. jour.; editor: Chem. Physics Letters, 1982—85. Named Calif. Scientist of Yr., 1997; recipient Fresenius Award, Phi Lambda Upsilon, 1974, Michael Polanyi Medal, 1979, Nat. Medal Sci., 1983, Spectroscopy Soc. Pitts. Award, 1983, Michelson-Morley Award, Case Inst. Tech., Case We. Res. U., 1986, ISCO Award for significant contbn. to instrumentation for biochemical separations, 1990, Bing Fellowship Tchg. Award, 1996, Ea. Analytical Symposium Award, 1997, Exceptional Sci. Achievement Award, NASA, 1997, Space award Aviation Week and Space Tech., 1997, Disting. Svc. Award, Nat. Sci. Bd., 1998, Centennial Medal, Harvard U., The Welch Award, 1999, Faraday Medal, Royal Soc. Chemistry, 2001, Wolf prize in chemistry, Wolf Found., Israel, 2005; fellow Alfred P. Sloan fellow, 1967—69, Non-resident fellow, Joint Inst. for Lab. Astrophysics, 1974—, Christensen fellow, St. Catherine's Coll. Oxford U., 1982, Stanford U., 1984—86. Fellow: AAAS, Inst. of Physics, Royal Soc. Chemistry (hon.), Calif. Acad. Sci. (hon.); mem.: NAS (coun. mem., Chem. Sci. Award 1991), European Acad. Scis., Chinese Acad. Scis. (fgn.), Swedish Acad. Engring. Sci. (fgn.), Royal Soc. London, Chem. Soc. London, World Jewish Acad. Scis. (hon.), Am. Philos. Soc., Am. Chem. Soc. (Harrison Howe Award 1985, Remsen Award 1985, Kirkwood Award 1986, Willard Gibbs Medal 1990, Peter Debye Award in phys. chemistry 1991, Linus Pauling Medal 1993, Dannie-Heineman Prize 1993, The Harvey Prize 1993, Analytical Chemistry Divsn. Award in chem. instrumentation 1995, Analytical Chemistry Award 1998, G.M. Kosalapoff Award 1998, E. Bright Wilson award in spectroscopy 1999, Nobel Laureate Signature Award 2000, Charles Lathrop Parsons award 2001, Madison Marshall award 2001, James Flack Norris award for outstanding achievement in the tchg. of chemistry 2004, Nichols medal NY sect. 2005), Am. Phys. Soc. (Earle K. Plyler prize 1981, Irving Langmuir Prize 1985, Arthur L. Schawlow prize in

laser sci. 2000), Am. Acad. Arts and Scis., Phi Beta Delta. Achievements include research in laser chemistry and chem. physics. Office: Stanford U Dept Chemistry Stanford CA 94305-5080 Office Phone: 650-723-3062. Business E-Mail: zare@stanford.edu.

**ZARELLA, PETER T.,** state supreme court justice; b. Boston; BS, Northeastern U., 1972; JD, Suffolk U., 1975. Bar: Mass. 1975, Conn. 1977, U.S. Dist. Ct. Mass. 1976, U.S. Dist. Ct. Conn. 1977, U.S. Supreme Ct. 1985, U.S. Ct. Appeals (2nd cir.) 1985, U.S. Dist. Ct., So. Dist. N.Y. 1990. Pvt. practice, 1977—96; ptnr. Brown, Paindiris & Zarella, Hartford, Conn., 1978—96; judge Superior Ct., 1996—99, Appellate Ct., 1999—2001; assoc. justice Conn. Supreme Ct., 2001—. Chmn. Criminal Justice Commn., 2001—; chmn. rules com. Superior Ct., 2001—. Mem.Ethics Commn., Town of West Hartford, Conn., 1992—95, mem. Charter Revision Commn., 1996. Mem.: Conn. Bar Assn. (mem. exec. com. coml. law and bankruptcy sect. 1985—90, mem. banking law com. 1990—94). Office: Conn Supreme Ct 231 Capitol Ave Hartford CT 06106*

**ZAREM, ABE MORDECAI,** management consulting executive; b. Chgo., Mar. 7, 1917; s. I.H. and Lea (Kaufman) Z.; m. Esther Mariam Moskovitz, Oct. 4, 1941; children: Janet Ruth, David Michael, Mark Charles. BS in Elec. Engring. Ill. Inst. Tech., 1939, LL.D. (hon.), 1968; MS in Elec. Engring. Calif. Inst. Tech., 1940, PhD, 1944; LL.D., U. Calif. at Santa Cruz, 1967. Design engr. very high voltage power transmission system Allis Chalmers Rsch. div., 1944; group leader Ultra Micro Time Program Manhattan Dist. Project/CalTech, 1944—45; initiator, group mgr. Microtime & Electro Optical Phys. Rsch., U.S. Naval Test Sta., 1945-48; assoc. dir., mgr. L.A. div. Stanford Rsch. Inst., 1948-56; mem. faculty UCLA, 1956-61; founder, chmn., pres. Electro-Optical Systems, Inc., Pasadena, Calif., 1956-67; v.p. Xerox Corp., L.A., 1963-67, sr. v.p., dir. corp. devel., bd. dirs., 1967-69; mgmt. and engring. cons., 1969-79; founder, chmn. Xerox Devel. Corp., L.A., 1975-80; strategic bus. planning, techno-econ. and venture capital, pres., owner Abe M. Zarem & Co., 1981—; founder, mng. dir., Frontier Assoc., 1980—. Mem. adv. com. competitive tech. program State of Calif., 1989; mem. Calif. Coun. Sci. and Tech., chmn. advanced sci. & tech. programs com., 1989-97, disting. fellow 1997—; cons., disting. vis. exec. in sci. and tech., sr. advisor on tech. transfer and commercialization and strategic planning studies Jet Propulsion Lab./Calif. Inst. of Tech., 1997—; cons., advisor, chair of sr. adv. bd. UCLA Brain Rsch. Inst., 1997—; mem. adv. bd. dept. urology UCLA, 1994—. Author: Utilization of Solar Energy, 1963. Traffic and parking commr. City of Beverly Hills, 1971-72, planning commr., 1972-73; Bd. dirs. Music Center Opera Assn., Los Angeles, 1968—; nat. trustee City of Hope; trustee Calif. Inst. Arts, 1973-76. Named Outstanding Young Elec. Engr. in U.S. Eta Kappa Nu, 1948; One of America's Ten Outstanding Young Men U.S. Jr. C. of C., 1950; recipient Albert F. Sperry medal Instrument Soc. Am., 1969 Fellow AIAA, IEEE; sci. mem. (a founder) Solar Energy Soc.; mem. Nat. Acad. Engring. Achievements include inventing World's fastest high-speed camera, automatic oscillograph. Home: 9640 Lomitas Ave Beverly Hills CA 90210-3333 Personal E-mail: azarem@mednet.ucla.edu. *I have always had a Vision, Mission & Series of Strategic Objectives - The principal one having been instilled by loving parents & family who encouraged me. I was born to identify talent and to challenge it to do more and better than it would have done if it had not met me. In stretching and challenging people, I fulfill the role of mentor and tormentor.*

**ZAREM, HARVEY ALAN,** plastic surgeon; b. Savannah, Ga., Feb. 13, 1932; s. Harry A. and Rose (Gold) Z.; m. Beth McCanghey, July 11, 1981; children: Harold, Allison, Melissa, Kathryn, Michael, Robert. BA, Yale U., 1953; MD, Columbia U., 1957. Diplomate Am. Bd. Surgery, Am. Bd. Plastic Surgery; lic. physician, Md., Ill., Calif. Intern Johns Hopkins Hosp., Balt., 1957-58, resident in plastic surgery, 1964-66; rsch. fellow Peter Bent Brigham Hosp., Boston, 1958-59, asst. resident in surgery, 1959-61; resident in surgery then chief resident Boston City Hosp., 1961-63; postdoctoral fellow NYU, N.Y.C., 1963-64; from asst. prof. to assoc. prof. surgery U. Chgo., 1966-73; prof. surgery U. Calif., L.A., 1973-87, prof. emeritus, 1987—; mem. med. staff Pacific Surgicenter, Santa Monica, Calif., 1987— Physician Sepulveda (Calif.) VA Hosp., 1974—; mem. med. staff St. Johns Hosp., Santa Monica, Calif., 1987—, Santa Monica Hosp., 1988—; vis. prof. So. Ill. U., 1983, Lackaland AFB, 1986, Creighton U., 1987, Comesa, Milan, 1989, Baylor Coll. Medicine, 1990; Kazanjian vis. prof. Mass. Gen. Hosp., 1986, 88; cons. and presenter in field; surgeon, Extreme Makeover, ABC TV, 2003-. Contbr. numerous articles to profl. jours. Grantee NIH, 1964-75, NIH, 1967-72, Sheldon and Carol Appel Family Found., 1982—, Chantal Pharms., 1983-84, Mentor Corp./Heyer-Schulte Products, 1985—, Michael Jackson Burn Found., 1986-87. Fellow ACS; mem. AMA, Am. Soc. Plastic Reconstructive Sugeons, Inc., Am. Burn Assn., Am. Cleft Palat Assn., Am. Assn. Plastic Surgeons, Am. Soc. Aesthetic Plastic Surgery, Am. Assn. Hand Surgery, Am. Assn. Surgery of Trauma, Calif. Med. Asssn., Calif. Soc. Plastic Surgeons, New Eng. Soc. Plastic Surgeons (hon.), L.A. County Med. Assn., Johns Hopkins Med. and Surg. Soc., Plastic Surgery Rsch. Coun., Soc. Head and Neck Surgeons (sr.), Soc. U. Surgeons, N.W. Soc. Plastic Surgeons (hon.), Calif. Plastic Surgeon Assn. (pres.), others; Calif. Yacht Club, Beverly Hills Country Club, bd. dirs. Office: Pacific Surgicenter 1301 20th St Ste 470 Santa Monica CA 90404-2082 Office Phone: 310-315-0222. Business E-Mail: hzarem@ucla.edu.

**ZAREMSKI, MILES JAY,** lawyer; b. Chgo., Aug. 16, 1948; s. Samuel and Ann (Levine) Z.; m. Elena Cinthia Resnik, July 19, 1970; children: Jason Lane, Lauren Devra. BS, U. Ill., 1970; JD, Case Western Res. U., 1973. Bar: Ill. 1973, Pa. 2000, Ind. 2000, U.S. Dist. Ct. (no. dist.) Ill. 1973, U.S. Dist. Ct. Nebr. 1996, U.S. Dist. Ct. (ea. dist.) Tenn. 1997, U.S. Dist. Ct. (no. dist.) Ind. 2005, U.S. Ct. Appeals (7th cir.) 1973, U.S. Ct. Appeals (8th cir.) 1988, U.S. Ct. Appeals (6th cir.) 1998, U.S. Ct. Appeals (9th cir.) 2002, U.S. Supreme Ct. 1977. Sr. asst. state's atty. Lake County, Ill., 1980-82; ptnr. Kamensky, Rubinstein, Hochman, & DeLott, Lincolnwood, Chgo., Ill., 2000—. Arbitrator, mandatory arbitration programs Cook and Lake Counties, Ill., 1990—; asst. prof. med. jurisprudence Rosalind Franklin U. Medicine and Sci., 1991—; adj. faculty U. Chgo. Law Sch., 1999—2001; advisor to congressman and staffs on patient rights, 1999—; adj. prof. Case We. Res. Law Sch., 2002—03; vis. prof. divsn. of law Macquarie U., Sydney, Australia, 2004; cons. Gerson-Lehmon, Washington, 2005—; lectr. nat. and internat. healthcare, medical jurisprudence. Editor: Medical and Hospital Negligence, 4 vols., 1988, supplement, 1993, 95-99; contbr. chpts. in books and articles to profl. jours.; author: Reengineering Healthcare Liability Litigation, 1997, supplement, 1999; mem. editl. bd. Medicine and Law, Haita, Israel, 2004—; patentee in field Oversight com. law sch. Case Western Res. U., Cleve., 1999, alumni bd. dirs., 1996-99; mem. exec. com. law sch. ctr for health care Loyola U., Chgo., 1987-89; mem. lakefront commn. City of Highland Park, Ill., 1982-84; bd. dirs., coun. officer Regional Organ Bank Ill., Chgo., 1986-91, The Lambs, Libertyville, Ill., 1982-84, Jocelyn Ctr. for Mental Health, 1994-96; field play marshall U.S. Olympics Baseball, Atlanta, 1996. Named one of Outstanding Young Men in Am. U.S. Jaycees, 1979; named Superlawyer, Health Care-Ill., 2005, 06, Leading Lawyer, 2005, 06. Fellow: Am. Bar Found., Am. Coll. Legal Medicine (assoc. in law 1973—91, editl. bd. Jour. Legal Medicine 1981—, chair legal com. 1996—98, chair Amicus com. 1997—, bd. govs., sec. 1999—2000, treas. 2000—01, pres.-elect 2001—02, pres. 2002—03); mem.: ABA (editor-in-chief Forum 1979—81, vice chmn. 1979—90, chmn. med. and law com. 1984—85, editl. bd. Forum on Health Law 1989—91, spl. com. on med. profl. liability 1991—95, 1998—, chmn. spl. com. on med. profl. liability 2000—03, chmn. std. com. med. profl. liability 2005—, chmn. med. and law com. 2005—, various coms. tort, trial and ins. practice sect.), Medicine and Law (mem. editl. bd.), Am. Arbitration Assn. (arbitrator 2002—), World Congress Med. Law (mem. editl. bd. Medicine and Law 2004—), Ill. Assn. Healthcare Attys., Quality Mgmt. Health Care (editl. bd.), Am. Soc. Writers on Legal Subjects (scribes), Am. Health Law Assn. (vice chair hosp. liability com. 1999—2001), Am. Soc. Law and Medicine (editor-in-chief 1981—83, bd. editors 1983—86), Lake County Bar Assn., Ill. Bar Assn. (1st and 3d prizes 1978—79). Jewish. Avocations: baseball, soccer, coaching athletic teams. Office: Kamensky Rubinstein Hochman DeLott 7250

N Cicero Ave Ste 200 Lincolnwood IL 60712 Office Phone: 847-568-5602. Business E-Mail: mzaremski@kr-law.com. *"Success is a journey; not a destination." "A man may make many mistakes but he isn't a failure until he starts blaming someone else." John R. Wooden.*

**ZARET, BARRY LEWIS,** cardiologist, medical educator; b. NYC, Oct. 3, 1940; s. Irving Z. and Beatrice (Fader) Zaret; m. Myrna Zimmerman, June 23, 1963; children: Adam L., Elliot C., Owen M. BS, Queens Coll., 1962; MD, NYU, 1966; MA, Yale U., 1982. Diplomate Am. Bd. Internal Medicine. Intern Bellevue Hosp., N.Y.C., 1966-67, resident, 1967-79; rsch. fellow John Hopkins U., Balt., 1969-71; asst. prof. medicine Yale U., New Haven, 1973-76, assoc. prof. medicine and diagnostic radiology, 1976, chief sect. cardiology, 1978—2004, assoc. prof. medicine and diagnostic radiology, 1980-82, prof. medicine and diagnostic radiology, 1982-84, Robert W. Berliner prof. medicine, 1984—, assoc. chair clin. affairs dept. internal medicine, 1994—2004; mem. staff Yale-New Haven Med. Ctr.; head dept. Yale-New Haven Med. Hosp. Heart Ctr., 1999—2004. Mem. cardiovasc. subsplty. bd. Am Bd. Internal Medicine, 2002—. Mem. editl. bd. Am. Jour. Cardiology, 1977—, Jour. Am. Coll. Cardiology, 1986-91, 92-97, Jour. Cardiac Imaging, 1986—, Circulation, 1993; assoc. editor: Yearbook of Nuc. Medicine, 1980-95; editor-in-chief Jour. Nuc. Cardiology, 1993-2004; contbr. articles to profl. jours. Recipient Casimir Funk award Soc. Mil. Surgeons, 1973; recipient Herrman Blumgart Pioneer award New Eng. chpt. Soc. Nuc. Medicine, 1978, Solomon Berson Alumni Achievement award in clin. sci. NYU Sch. Medicine, 1998, Ellis Island medal Honor, 2004. Fellow Am. Coll. Cardiology, Coun. Clin. Cardiology, Am. Heart Assn., Coun. Circulation, Am. Heart Assn., Am. Physiology Soc.; mem. Am. Soc. Clin. Investigation, Am. Fedn. Clin. Rsch., Assn. Am. Physicians, Soc. Nuc. Medicine, Am. Soc. Nuc. Cardiology (Disting. Svc. award 2006), Assn. Univ. Cardiologists, Assn. Profs. Cardiology (pres. 1992), Phi Beta Kappa, Alpha Omega Alpha, Interurban Clin. Club. Jewish. Home: 15 Cassway Rd Woodbridge CT 06525-1214 Office: 333 Cedar St # 3fmp New Haven CT 06520-8017 Office Phone: 203-785-4127.

**ZARGES, THOMAS H.,** engineering executive; Degree in engring., Va. Mil. Inst. V.p. bus. devel. United Engrs. & Constructors, 1990; pres., CEO power and indsl./mfg. divsns. Washington Group, 1991; sr. exec. v.p. ops. Washington Group Internat., Boise, Idaho, 2002—. Office: Washington Group Internat PO Box 73 Boise ID 83729

**ZARGHAMI, CYMA,** broadcast executive; b. Iran, 1962; d. Gorham and Catherine; m. George Obergfoll, 1990; children: Liam, Ethan. BA, U. of Vt., Burlington, 2000. Scheduling clerk, scheduling exec., programming exec. Nickelodeon, 1985—96, exec. v.p., gen. mgr., 1996—2004, pres., 2004—. Directs co. initiatives Big Help and Kids Pick the Pres. Campaign; launched Nick Jr., SNICK, Nicktoons. Office: Nickelodeon 1515 Broadway New York NY 10036*

**ZARICZNYJ, BASILIUS,** orthopedic surgeon; b. Ukraine, Aug. 31, 1924; came to U.S., 1951; m. Stefania Pidburny, Aug. 21, 1954; children: Marta, Stephanie Christine, Andrea Maria, Mark B. MD, U. Bonn, Germany, 1951; MD (hon.), Odessa State Med. U., Ukraine, 1996. Diplomate Am. Bd. Orthopedic Surgery. Resident St. Luke's Hosp., Chgo., 1954-56, Univ. Hosps., Oklahoma City, 1955-56; fellow in orthopedics Northwestern U., Chgo., 1957; asst. prof. Sch. Medicine U. Okla., Oklahoma City, 1957-58; orthopedic surgeon Springfield, Ill., 1958—; clin. prof. Sch. Medicine So. Ill. U., Springfield, Ill., 1973-85, acting chmn. divsn. orthopedic surgery, 1972-75, chief sports medicine sect., 1975-82, program chmn. sports injury symposium, 1977-79, 82, 83. Mem. sports medicine com. Ill. State Med. Soc., 1979-80; chmn. dept. orthopedic surgery St. John's and Meml. Hosps., Springfield, 1970-79; program chmn. Med. Congress of World Fedn. of Ukrainian Med. Assn., Dniepropetrovsk, 1994, Odessa, Ukraine, 1996; presenter Am. Acad. Orthopedic Surgeons, Miami, Fla., 1961, N.Y., 1969, San Francisco, 1971, Washington, 1972, Las Vegas, 1973, 77, Anaheim, Calif., 1983, Chgo. Orthopedic Soc., 1978, O'Donoghue Orthopedic Alumni Assn., Oklahoma City, 1972, 75, 78, Internat. Soc. for Orthopedic Surgery and Traumatology, XII World Congress, Tel Aviv, 1972, Copenhagen, 1975, Kyoto, Japan, 1978, So. Ill U. Sch. Medicine, Springfield, 1977, 79, 80, 82, Ill. State Orthopedic Soc., Chgo., 1978, ACS, Chgo., 1979, Am. Orthopedic Soc. for Sports Medicine, Atlanta, 1980, Big Sky, Mont., 1980, Lake Tahoe, Nev., 1981, Clin. Orthopedic Soc., Chgo., 1987, World Fedn. Ukrainian Med. Assn., Kiev, Ukraine, 1990, U. Lviv, Ukraine, 1990, 11th Congress of Orthopedic Surgeons of Ukraine, Kharkiv, 1991, Congress of World Fedn. of Ukrainian Med. Assn., Kharkiv, 1992, Dniepropetrovsk, 1994, Odessa, 1996, Ukraine, among others. Mem. editl. bd. Jour. Ukrainan Med. Assn. N.Am., 1977-95; contbr. articles to editl. jours. and med. textbooks. Fellow Am. Acad. Orthopedic Surgery; mem. AMA, Ill. Orthopedic Soc., Internat. Soc. Orthopedic Surgery and Traumatology, Am. Orthopedic Soc. for Sports Medicine, Internat. Soc. of the Knee, Mid-Am. Orthopedic Assn., Ukrainian Acad. and Profl. Assn. Pres. 1985-89), Sangamon County Med. Soc., Chgo. Orthopedic Soc. Avocations: golf, walking, chess. Home and Office: 125 Oakmont Dr Springfield IL 62704-3118

**ZARING, ALLEN G.,** homebuilding company executive; Student, Babson Coll. Founder, chmn., CEO Zaring Homes, 1964—. With U.S. Army. Recipient High Achievement award Profl. Builders Mag.; named Builder of Yr., Home Builders Assn. Greater Cin., 1995, Ams. Best Builder. Office: 625 Eden Park Dr #1250 Cincinnati OH 45202-6024 Fax: 513-247-2667.

**ZARINS, BERTRAM,** orthopedic surgeon; b. Latvia, June 22, 1942; came to U.S., 1946, naturalized, 1956; s. Richard Arthur and Maria (Rozenbergs) Z. AB in Chemistry, Lafayette Coll., 1963; MD, SUNY, Syracuse, 1967. Diplomate Am. Bd. Surgery. Clin. instr. orthop. surgery Harvard Med. Sch., Boston, 1976—, asst. clin. prof., 1982—, assoc. clin. prof., 1996—, Harvard Thorndike prof. orthopaedic surgery, 2006—; orthop. surgeon Mass. Gen. Hosp., Boston, 1982-95, chief sports medicine svc., 1982—; team physician Boston Bruins Hockey Team, 1976—. Chmn. edn. com. Sports Medicine Coun., U.S. Olympic Com., 1980-92; team physician New England Patriots football team, 1982—; head physician USA Olympic teams XIV Winter Olympic Games, Sarajevo, Yugoslavia, 1984; cons. editor for sports medicine jour. of Bone and Joint Surgery, 1999—. Contbr. articles to profl. jours. Team physician N.E. Revolution profl. soccer team, 1996—. Lt. comdr. M.C., USNR, 1973-75. Fellow ACS, Am. Acad. Orthop. Surgeons (chmn. com. on sports medicine 1993-97), Am. Coll. Sports Medicine; mem. AMA, Internat. Arthroscopy Assn. (bd. dirs. 1991-95), Arthroscopy Assn. N.Am., N.Am. Trauma Assn. (pres. 1977), Internat. Soc. of Arthroscopy, Knee Surgery and Orthopaedic Sports Medicine, Am. Shoulder and Elbow Surgeons, Herodicus Soc., Brookline (Mass.) Country Club, Somerset Club. Office: 617-726-3421. Business E-Mail: bzarins@partners.org.

**ZARINS, CHRISTOPHER KRISTAPS,** surgeon, educator; b. Tukums, Latvia, Dec. 2, 1943; came to U.S., 1946; s. Richard A. and Maria (Rozenbergs) Z.; m. Zinta Zarins, July 8, 1967; children: Daina, Sascha, Karina. BA, Lehigh U., 1964; MD, Johns Hopkins U., 1968. Surgery residency U. Mich., Ann Arbor, 1968-74; asst. prof. surgery U. Chgo., 1976-79, assoc. prof. surgery, 1979-82, prof. surgery, 1983-93, chief vascular surgery, 1978-93; prof. surgery Stanford (Calif.) U., 1993—, chmn. divsn. vascular surgery, 1993—2005, acting chmn. dept. of surgery, 1995-97. Author: Essays In Surgery, 1986, Atlas of Vascular Surgery, 1988; editor Jour. of Surg. Rsch., 1982-95; contbr. articles to profl. jours. Pres. Latvian Med. Found., Boston, 1991. Lt. comdr. USN, 1974-76. Grantee NIH, NSF. Mem. Am. Surg. Soc., Soc. for Clin. Vascular Surgery (pres. 1998-99), Internat. Soc. for Cardiovascular Surgery of Univ. Surgeons, Latvian Nat. Acad. of Scis., Latvian Vascular Surg. Soc. (pres. 1989), Soc. for Vascular Surgery (pres. 1998-99). Avocations: triathlons, skiing. Office: Stanford U Med Ctr Divsn Vascular Surgery 300 Pasteur Dr # H3642 Stanford CA 94304-2203 Office Phone: 650-725-7830.

**ZARKIN, HERBERT J.,** retail executive; Exec. vice-pres. Zayre Corp., Framingham, Mass., until 1986; pres. Zayre Corp., HomeClub subs., Framingham, Mass., 1986-88; chmn. Zayre Corp., Zayre Stores div., Framingham, Mass., 1988; pres., CEO Waban Inc. Natick, 1988-95, chmn. bd., 1997-98; chmn. BJ's Wholesale Club Inc., 1998—, HomeBase, Irvine, Calif., 1999—2001. Address: HomeBase 3345 Michelson Dr Irvine CA 92612 Office: BJs Wholesale Club Inc 1 Mercer Rd Natick MA 01760-2400*

**ZARNOCH, STANLEY JOSEPH,** research scientist, statistician; b. Newark, Jan. 5, 1950; m. Deborah Lee Herbert, Aug. 30, 1975; children: Melissa Christine, Richard Christopher. BS with high honors, Rutgers U., New Brunswick, NJ, 1971; MS, Pa. State U., University Park, Pa., 1973; PhD, Va. Tech, Blacksburg, 1976. Math. statistician USDA Forest Svc., New Orleans, 1976—77; asst. prof. Mich. State U., East Lansing, Mich., 1977—80; math. statistician USDA Forest Svc., New Orleans, 1980—85, forester Broomall, Pa., 1985—88, math. statistician Athens, Ga., 1988—96, rsch. statistician Asheville, NC, 1996—, math. statistician, 1996—. Author of over 100 sci. manuscripts. George H. Cook scholar, Rutgers U., 1971. Mem. Am. Men and Women of Sci., Biometric Soc., Xi Sigma Pi Nat. Forestry Hon. Frat. Achievements include research in forest inventory estimation; mark-recapture simulator; growth and yield modeling; forest insect and disease; global climate change; forest health monitoring; plant physiology; development of NONPAR statistical software package; design of outdoor recreation surveys. Avocations: fishing, boating, camping, woodworking, gardening. Office: USDA Forest Svc PO Box 2680 Asheville NC 28802-2680 Office Phone: 828-259-0515. Personal E-mail: stanzarnoch@aol.com. Business E-Mail: szarnoch@fs.fed.us.

**ZARO, BRAD A.,** research and development company executive, biologist; b. San Jose, Calif., Dec. 4, 1949; s. Raymond J. and Irene R. Z.; children: Amy C., Kristen E. BA in Zoology, San Jose State U., 1974, MA in Biology, 1981. Chemist, Dept. Drug Metabolism Syntex Rsch., Inc., Palo Alto, Calif., 1976-78, chemist II, Dept. Drug Metabolism, 1978-81, chemist III, Dept. Drug Metabolism, 1981-84, clin. rsch. assoc. I, Inst. of Clin. Medicine, 1984-85, clin. rsch. assoc. II, Inst. of Clin. Medicine, 1985-87, sen. clin. rsch. assoc., Inst. of Clin. Medicine, 1985-87; sen. clin. rsch. assoc. Triton Biosciences, Inc., Alameda, Calif., 1988, mgr. clin. trials, 1988; pres., CEO Clinimetrics Rsch. Assoc., Inc., San Jose, 1988—. Contbr. articles to scholarly jours. Mem. AAAS, Am. Coll. Clin. Pharmacology, Am. Soc. Pharmacognosy, Assn. Clin. Rsch. Profls., Drug Info. Assn. Democrat. Roman Catholic. Avocations: scuba diving, skiing, flying. Office: Clinimetrics Rsch Assocs 5285 Hellyer Ave San Jose CA 95138

**ZAROS, WENDY CECILIA,** soprano, educator; d. Leonard and Doris Zaros; m. Ben Harrison, July 13, 2002. BS in Music Edn., Roberts Wesleyan Coll., 1999; MusM in Vocal Performance, New England Conservatory, 2001. Lic. tchr. music N.Y., 1995, S.C., 2002. Pvt. practice voice instr., Mass., 1995—2001, NY, 2001—02; tchg. asst. music history New Eng. Conservatory, Boston, 1999, rschr., 2000—01; tchr. music Dows Lane Elem. Sch. Irvington (N.Y.) Pub. Schs., 2001—02; instr. voice Anderson (S.C.) Acad. Music, 2002—03; mem. faculty voice Clemson (S.C.) U., 2003—05. Singer numerous sh. choirs. Singer: (albums) Peaceable Kingdom, 1998, (Operas) numerous shows including most recently, NEC Opera, 1999—2001, Rome (Italy) Festival Orch., 2000, New Eng. Conservatory Opera, 2001, Spartanburg Repertory Co., 2002, 2003, Harrower Opera Studio, 2003, Crittenden Opera Studio, 2004, Brooks Performing Arts Theater, 2004, N.Y. Opera Forum, 2005, Westminster Choir Coll., 2005, Touring Concert Opera Co., 2005, 2006, Operesque Classical Concerts, 2006. Coord., dir., performer Opera in Armonk, NY, 2005; vol. Pivot Ministries, Darien, Conn., 1992—95. Finalist Miss Teen USA, 1991—94; recipient Nat. Talent award, Miss Am. Pre-teen, 1989, 3d Runner Up award, Miss Am. Teen N.Y., 1993, 1st Runner Up award, Roberts Wesleyan Coll. Concerto Competition, 1998, Achievement award, Di Capo Opera Theater, 1995, award, Palmetto Opera Competition, 2003; scholar, New Eng. Conservatory, Roberts Wesleyan Coll., Byram Hills Coll. Mem.: Nat. Assn. Tchg. Soc., Alpha Kappa Sigma, Phi Kappa Lambda. Avocations: skiing, travel.

**ZARR, MELVYN,** lawyer, educator; b. Worcester, Mass., Aug. 29, 1936; m. Gail Sclar, Aug. 29, 1971. AB, Clark U., 1958; LL.B., Harvard U., 1963. Bar: Mass. bar 1964, Maine bar 1973. Staff atty. NAACP Legal Def. & Edn. Fund, Inc., N.Y.C., 1963-69; co-dir. Mass. Law Reform Inst., Boston, 1970-73; profl. law U. Maine, 1973—; U.S. magistrate, Portland, Maine, 1977-82. Mem.: Am. Law Inst. Home: 19 Mckinley Rd Falmouth ME 04105-1913 Office: U Maine Sch Law 246 Deering Ave Portland ME 04102-2837 Office Phone: 207-780-4359. Business E-Mail: mzarr@usm.maine.edu.

**ZARRA, ERNEST JOSEPH, III,** secondary school educator, researcher; b. Montclair, N.J., Dec. 14, 1955; s. Ernest Joseph Jr. and Faith Zarra; m. Susan Sembrat, May 29, 1976; children: Elya Joelle, Jonathan Joseph. BA, Northeastern Bible Coll., 1978; MA, Simon Greenleaf U., 1981; MABS, Grace Grad. Sch., Long Beach, Calif., 1986; MEd, Calif. State U., Bakersfield, 1988; PhD, U. So. Calif., 1999. Cert. tchr., N.J., Calif. Pvt. sch. tchr., 1978-89; pastor Millington Bapt. Ch., Basking Ridge, NJ, 1994-95; tchr., GATE coord. Fruitvale Sch. Dist. Pub. Sch., Bakersfield, Calif., 1989-94, 95-00; tchr. govt. and econs. Centennial H.S., Bakersfield, Calif., 2000—; girls varsity soccer coach, 2000—. Adj. faculty Calif. State U., Bakersfield, 1998—, Pt. Loma Nazarene U.; lectr. U.Pa., Bakersfield Coll., Fresno Pacific U., U. San Diego, others; presenter in field. Author: It Should Never Happen Here, 1997; contbr. articles to profl. jours. Youth coach Am. Youth Soccer Orgn., Kern County, Calif., 1993—; youth and adults tchr. Laurelglen Bible Ch., Bakersfield, 1984—; presenter to law enforcement officers Kern County Sheriffs Dept., 1988. Named All-Am. Soccer Player Nat. Christian Coll. Athletic Assn., 1978, All-State, All Dist., All Conf.; drafted Dallas Tornado (NASL), 1978. Mem. ASCD, Am. Ednl. Rsch. Assn., Evang. Theol. Soc., Link Inst., Kappa Delta Pi (Character Edn. Partnership). Republican. Mennonite Brethren. Avocations: athletics, writing, travel, ministry, debate. Home: 400 Sinaloa Ave Bakersfield CA 93312-9334

**ZARRELLA, RONALD L.,** pharmaceutical executive; b. Waterbury, CT, 1949; BS electrical engineering, Worcester Polytechnic Institute, Worcester, MA, 1971; student, NYU Graduate School of Business. With Bristol Myers Co., Esmark Corp.; executive Bausch & Lomb, 1985—94; v.p., No. Am. Vehicle Sales General Motors, 1994—98; exec. v.p. General Motors, North America, 1998—2001; chmn., CEO Bausch & Lomb, 2001—. Bd. dir. Avaya, Inc., FIRST (For Inspiration and Recognition of Science and Technology), Univ. of Rochester Medical Center. Mem.: Rochester Institute of Technology, Comm. for Economic Development, Nat. Italian Found. Office: c/o Bausch & Lomb One Bausch & Lomb Place Rochester NY 14604

**ZARRES, SHARON L.,** marriage and family therapist, health facility administrator; b. Altadena, Calif., June 11, 1947; d. Verne Ivan and Ruth Elizabeth Hatfield; m. Michael Paul Zarres, 1977; adopted children: Rebecca, Philip, Victor, Amber, MacKenzie. BA, Azusa Pacific U., 2000, MA in Clin. Psychology, 2002, MA in Marriage and Family Therapy, 2003. Ordained to ministry Western Evang. Orgn. Dir. Jack & Jill Pre-Sch./Grade Sch., La Puente, Calif.; office mgr. World Vision Internat., Monrovia, Calif.; owner, mgr. Zarres Family Day Care, Covina, Calif., 1995—2005; adminstr., marriage and family therapist Father's Heart Ranch, Desert Hot Springs, Calif., 2003—. Mem. integration com. Azusa (Calif.) Pacific U., 2000—; tchg. and rsch. asst., 2001—02. Foster parent Koinonia Foster Homes, San Bernardino, Calif.; v.p., founder Lighthouse Prayer, Covina, lay counselor, 1980—90; bd. dirs. Prevailing Word, Azusa. Avocations: reading, travel, movies. Home and Office: 71-175 Aurora Rd Desert Hot Springs CA 92241

**ZARRO, JANICE ANNE,** lawyer; b. Newark, June 30, 1947; BA, Rutgers U., 1969; JD, IIT-Chgo.-Kent Coll. Law, 1973. Bar: Pa. 1974. Counsel jud. com. U.S. Ho. Reps., Washington, 1973-77; profl. staff mem. counsel labor and human resources com. U.S. Senate, Washington, 1977-80; dir. Avon Products, Inc., N.Y.C., 1980-81, Washington, 1982-86, v.p., 1986-90; pres.

The Novus Group, Inc., 1990-92; dir. fed. affairs Mallinckrodt Med., 1992—, v.p., 1993-94; v.p. govt. affairs Worldwide Mallinckrodt Inc., 1994-2000; exec. dir. Women's Resource Ctr. Sarasota County, 2003—. Gen. counsel Nat. Italian-Am. Found., 1989-96, chair bd. trustees, 1996-99; mem. Bus. Govt. Rels. Coun., Washington, 1987—; past chair Women's Fgn. Policy Group. Past chmn. Nat. Capital chpt. Multiple Sclerosis Soc. Recipient Leadership Recognition award Nat. Women's Econ. Alliance, 1984. Office Phone: 341-366-1700.

**ZARTMAN, DAVID LESTER,** retired zoology educator, researcher; b. Albuquerque, July 6, 1940; s. Lester Grant and Mary Elizabeth (Kitchel) Z.; m. Micheal Aline Plemmons, July 6, 1963; children: Kami Renee, Dalan Lee. BS cum laude in Dairy Husbandry, N.Mex. State U., 1962; MS in Genetics, Ohio State U., 1966, PhD in Genetics, 1968. Cert. dairy cattle specialist, Am. Registry Profl. Animal Scientists. Jr. ptnr. Marlea Guernsey Farm, Albuquerque, 1962-64; grad. rsch. assoc. Ohio State U., Columbus, 1964-68; asst. prof. dairy sci. N.Mex. State U., Las Cruces, 1968-71, assoc. prof., 1971-79, prof., 1979-84, Ohio State U., Columbus, 1984—2006, emeritus prof., 2006—. Chmn. dept. Ohio State U., Columbus, 1984-99; pres. Mary K. Zartman, Inc., Albuquerque, 1976-84; cons. Bio-Med. Electronics, Inc., San Diego, 1984-89, Zartemp, Inc., Northbrook, Ill., 1990, Recom Applied Solutions, 1993-2000, Am. Registry of Profl. Animal Scientists, 1996—, Midwest Univs. Consortium for Internat. Assistance, 2004. Contbr. articles to profl. jours.; patentee in field. Recipient State Regional Outstanding Young Farmer award Jaycees, 1963, Disting. Rsch. award N.Mex. State U. Coll. Agr. and Home Econs., 1983, Outstanding Svc. award Ohio Poultry Assn., 1999, Grazier of Yr. award Gt. Lakes Internat. Grazing Conf., 2001, hon. state degree Ohio FFA, 2000, The Jack Tucker Disting. Svc. award Ohio Forage and Grassland Coun., 2004; course acclaimed by Humane Soc. of U.S.; named one of Top 100 Agr. Alumni, N.Mex. State U. Centennial, 1987; spl. postdoctoral fellow NIH, New Zealand, 1973; Fulbright-Hayes lectr., Malaysia, 1976. Fellow AAAS; mem. Am. Dairy Sci. Assn., Am. Soc. Animal Sci., Dairy Shrine Club, Ohio Farm Bur., Sigma Xi, Gamma Sigma Delta, Alpha Gamma Rho (1st Outstanding Alumnus N.Mex. chpt. 1985), Alpha Zeta, Phi Kappa Phi. Home: 7671 Deer Creek Dr Worthington OH 43085-1551 Office: Ohio State U 2027 Coffey Rd Columbus OH 43210-1043 Office Phone: 614-292-1387. Business E-Mail: zartman.3@osu.edu.

**ZARTMAN, PATRICK JOSEPH,** secondary school educator; b. San Pedro, Calif., Mar. 12, 1942; s. Charles George and Agnes Christina Zartman; m. Charleen Therese Sharkie, July 31, 1976; children: Therese Ann, Christine Marie. BA, Loyola U., L.A., 1964, MA, 1965. Tchr., coach San Gabriel Mission HS, 1965—67, Bishop Montgomery HS, Torrance, 1967—71, Torrance HS, 1971—. Pres., CEO Spoilers Enterprizes, 1970—; coach U.S.A. Volleyball, Colorado Springs, 1970, 74, 2000—04; head coach Major League Volleyball, San Jose, 1987; Am. coach Brazilian Women's Beach Volleyball Olympic Gold medalists, 1996; coach U.S. Women's FISU Beach Volleyball Univ. World Champions & Gold Medalists, 2002. Author: (book) Youth Volleyball, 1997; contbr. articles to profl. jours.; coach/writer: instrnl. videos. Roman Catholic. Home: 37 4th St Hermosa Beach CA 90254 Office: Spoilers Enterprizes 37 4th St Hermosa Beach CA 90254

**ZARWYN, BERTHOLD,** physicist, consultant; b. Vienna, Aug. 22, 1921; came to U.S., 1949, naturalized, 1955; s. Joseph and Bronislawa Regina (Unger) Zarwyn. ME, Gliwice, Poland, 1946; ScD, UN Univ., Munich, 1947; PhD, NYU, 1954; ScD in Engring., Columbia U., 1963. Project engr. Curtiss-Wright Corp., Woodridge, NJ, 1951-55; staff scientist AMF Corp., N.Y.C., 1955-57; chief scientist Link Aviation Co., Binghamton, NY, 1957-58; head rsch. staff Am. Bosch-Arma Corp., Garden City, NY, 1958-63; corp. cons. Cutler-Hammer Corp., Deer Park, NY, 1963-65; chief engr. Bell Aerosystems Corp., Niagara Falls, NY, 1965-66; sr. cons. Mitre Corp., Bedford, Mass., 1966-68; spl. asst. to commdg. gen., acting chief engr. Hdqs. U.S. Army Materiel Command, Arlington, Va., 1968-71; chief phys. scis. br. U.S. Army Devel. and Readiness Command, Alexandria, Va., 1971-75; phys. scientist U.S. Army Harry Diamond Labs., Washington, 1975-78; chief sys. analysis br. U.S. Army Elec. Rsch. and Devel. Command, Adelphi, Md., 1978-79, chief tech. divsn., 1979-81, asst. tech. dir., 1981-85; spl. asst. to dep. chief of staff for tech. & program mgmt. U.S. Army Lab. Command, Adelphi, Md., 1985-87; pres. Pan-Tech. Corp., Delray Beach, Fla., 1987—. Adj. faculty, lectr., cons. in field; dir. Film Microelectronics Co. Inc., Burlington, Mass., 1965-67. Mem. editl. bd. Bavarian Soc. Engrs., 1947-49, transl. panel Russian Jour. Applied Math. and Mechanics with Pergamon Inst., 1956-57; inventor nuc. gyroscope, microwave holography, other items. Mem. IEEE, Am. Phys. Soc., N.Y. Acad. Scis., Sigma Xi. Home and Office: Pan-Tech Corp 7589 Mansfield Hollow Rd Delray Beach FL 33446-3314 Office Phone: 561-637-9387. Personal E-mail: zarwyn22@adelphia.net.

**ZARYCHTA, WILLIAM ALEX,** physician assistant; BS, West Chester U., 1996; AAS, Gloucester County Coll., 1999; BS, MCP, Hahnemann U., 2001; M in physician asst. studies, U. Nebr., 2002. Cert. physician asst., registered paramedic; RN, Pa. Commd. It. U.S. Army, 1990, advanced through grades to capt.; paramedic Mercy Health Sys., Darby, Pa., 1993—99; emergency dept. RN Mercy Fitzgerald Hosp., Darby, Pa., 1999—2000; emergency medicine physician asst. Brandywine Emergency Physician Assocs., Wayne, Pa., 2001—06; with U.S. Army, Afghanistan, 2004—05, USPHS, 2006—. Clin. instr. Arcadia U., Glenside, Pa., 2001—06, Drexel U., Phila., 2001—06. Contbr. articles to profl. jours. Med. screening Spl. Olympics, Phila., 2000, Mid Atlantic Powerboat Assn., Ocean City, Md., 2001. Decorated Army Commendation medal, Armed Forces Res. medal, Army Achievement medal,, Army Res. Component Achievement medal, Mil. Outstanding Vol. Svc. medal, Combat Med. badge, Bronze Star, Combat Action badge. Fellow: Pa. Soc. Physician Assts., Soc. Army Physician Assts., Soc. Emergency Medicine Physician Assts.; mem. Am. Acad. Physician Assts.; mem.: Pub. Health Svc. Acad. Physician Assts. (sec. 2006—), Am. Coll. Clinicians (charter), Phi Theta Kappa. Office: Brandywine Hosp 201 Reeceville Rd Coatesville PA 19320

**ZATSIORSKY, VLADIMIR MOISEEVICH (MICHAILOVICH),** biomechanics educator, researcher; b. Leningrad, Russia, Dec. 26, 1932; came to U.S., 1990; s. Moisey T. and Berta L. (Bardenstein) Z.; m. Rita Y. Zatsiorsky, Oct. 27, 1960; children: Betty V. Ulitsky, Michael V. PhD, Lesgaft Inst. Phys. Culture, Leningrad, 1961; DSc, Ctrl. Inst. Phys. Culture, Moscow, 1969; D honoris causa, Acad. Phys. Culture, Wroclaw, Poland, 1999, Russian State U. Phys. Culture, 2003. Asst. prof. Lvov (Ukraine) Inst. Phys. Culture, 1954—57; asst. prof., assoc. prof., prof. Ctrl. Inst. Phys. Culture, Moscow, 1959—90; vis. prof. UCLA, 1990, U. Calgary, Canada, 1991; prof. kinesiology Pa. State U., University Park, 1991—. Med. commn. Internat. Olympic Com., 1982—. Author (15 books including): Science and Practice of Strength Training, 1995—2006, Kinematics of Human Motion, 1998, Kinetics of Human Motion, 2002; editor: Biomechanics in Sport, 2000, Classics in Movement Science, 2001 (all books published in English, Russian, German, Italian, Spanish, Portuguese, Chinese, Japanese, Polish, Romanian, Czech, Serbo-Croatian & Bulgarian); contbr. over 350 rsch. papers. Recipient J. Dyson award Internat. Soc. of Sport Biomechanics, 1992. Fellow: Am. Acad. Kinesiology; mem.: Internat. Soc. Sport Kinetics (hon.). Avocations: reading, music. Office: Pa State U 39 Rec Bldg University Park PA 16802 Office Phone: 814-865-3445. Business E-Mail: vxz1@psu.edu.

**ZATZ, ARLINE,** writer, photographer; m. Joel Leon Zatz; children: Robert Jay, David Alan. BA in Journalism, Rutgers U., 1977. Asst. coord. N.J. Div. Consumer Affairs, Newark, 1972-75; writer, photographer A-Z Publs., Metuchen, N.J., 1977—. Author: 30 Bicycle Tours in New Jersey, 2003, New Jersey's Special Places, rev. edition 1994 (Best Book N.J. Press Women, Nat. Assn. Press Women), Best Hikes with Children in New Jersey, 2005, New Jersey's Great Gardens, 1999 (Best Book Nat. Travel Journalists Assn. 1999, Horsing Around in New Jersey: The Horse Lover's Guide to Everything Equine, 2004; contbr. articles to profl. jours. Bd. dirs. YMCA, Metuchen, 1984-86. Mem. Nat. Assn. Press Women, Outdoor Writers Assn. Am.

Avocations: hiking, canoeing, horseback riding, sailing, reading. Home: 77 Woodside Ave Metuchen NJ 08840-1629 Office: A-Z Publs 77 Woodside Ave Metuchen NJ 08840-1629 Office Phone: 732-494-9258. E-mail: azatz@funtravels.com.

**ZAUBLER, THOMAS SCOT,** psychiatrist, educator; b. N.Y., June 13, 1963; s. Leland and Lynn Zaubler; m. Katharine L. Sonnenberg, Sept. 11, 1993; children: William Sonnenberg, Elizabeth Dale Sonnenberg. BA, Columbia U., 1986; MD, Albert Einstein Coll. of Medicine, 1991; MPH, U. Wash., 1997. Diplomate Nat. Bd. Med. Examiners, 1992, lic. gen. psychiatry Am. Bd. Psychiatry and Neurology, 1997, cert. subspecialty in psychosomatic medicine Am. Bd. Psychiatry and Neurology, 2005. Resident gen. psychiatry Cornell Med. Ctr. N.Y. Hosp., 1991—95; fellow psychosomatic medicine U. Wash., Seattle, 1995—97; dir. residency tng., asst. prof. Dept. Psychiatry Med. Ctr. Georgetown U., Washington, 1997—2000; chmn. Dept. Psychiatry Morristown (N.J.) Meml. Hosp., 2000—, med. dir. Dept. Psychiatry, 2000—; clin. assoc. prof. Dept. Psychiatry U. of Medicine and Dentistry N.J. Med. Sch., Newark, 2002—. Contbr. chapters to books, articles to profl. jours. Named Top Psychiatrist, Consumers' Checkbook, Guide to Top Doctors, 2002—05; recipient Tchr. of the Yr. award, Dept. Psychiatry, U. of Medicine and Dentistry N.J. Med. Sch., 2002; grantee, NIH, 1995—97. Fellow: Am. Psychiat. Assn. (life); mem.: Am. Coll. Psychiatry Execs., Am. Coll. Psychiatry, Acad. Psychosomatic Medicine. Office: Morristown Meml Hosp 100 Madison Ave Morristown NJ 07960 Office Phone: 973-971-5366. Office Fax: 973-290-7166. Business E-Mail: thomas.zaubler@ahsys.org.

**ZAUCHA, JEROME J.,** lawyer; b. Uniontown, Pa. AB summa cum laude, Univ. Notre Dame, 1974; JD, Yale Univ., 1977. Bar: Pa. 1977, DC 1978. Ptnr., Internat. Trade practice Venable LLP, Washington. Mem.: Phi Beta Kappa. Office: Venable LLP 575 7th St NW Washington DC 20004 Office Phone. 202-344-4710. Office Fax: 202-344-8300. Business E-Mail: jjzaucha@venable.com.

**ZAUDERER, MARK CARL,** lawyer; b. Jan. 26, 1946; BA, Union Coll. 1967; JD, NYU, 1971. Bar: N.Y. 1972, US Dist. Ct. (So. & Ea. dist. NY) 1974, US Ct. Appeals (2d, 5th, Fed. cir.), US Supreme Ct. 1993. Law clk. U.S. Dist. Ct., Newark, 1971—72; founding ptnr. Solomon Zauderer Ellenhorn Frischer & Sharp, NYC, 1981—2003; ptnr., litigation practice DLA Piper Rudnick Gray Cary, NYC, 2003—05; ptnr. Flemming Zulack Williamson Zauderer LLP, NYC, 2005—. Faculty chmn. Practicing Law Inst. Program., Litigating Comml. Cases up to Trial, N.Y.C. and San Francisco, 1986, faculty mem. Deposition Skills Tng. Program, N.Y., 1986, 88-90; adv. com. on civil practice to Chief Adminstrn. Judge N.Y. State Ctrs., 1992—; trustee bd. advisors Union Coll., 1993—; chief Judge's Task Force on Comml. Cts., 1995—; chmn. Chief Judge's Commn. on Jury, 2003—. Author, moderator practising law inst. satellite TV program Deposition Strategy and Tactics, 1989; contbr. articles to profl. jours. Life fellow N.Y. Bar Found.; mem. ABA, N.Y. State Bar Assn. (exec. com. 1991—, chmn. exec. com. 1996-97, comml. and fed. litigation sect., chmn. complex civil litigation com.), Assn. of Bar of City of N.Y. (chmn. com. complex civil litigation, comml. and fed. litigation sect., mem. exec. com. 1991—, chair 1996-97), Fed. Bar Coun. (trustee 1998-2004, treas. 1998—, pres.-elect 2004). Office: Flemming Zulack Williamson Zauderer LLP Once Liberty Plz 35th Fl New York NY 10006-1404 Office Phone: 212-412-9562. Office Fax: 212-964-9200. Business E-Mail: mzauderer@fzw.com.

**ZAVACKY, SUSAN KLINE,** law librarian; b. Doylestown, Pa., May 5, 1953; d. Percy H. and Helen C. K.; m. Stephen C. Zavacky, Sept. 12, 1981. BS in Libr. Edn., Millersville (Pa.) U., 1971-75. Asst. libr. Legis. Reference Bureau, Harrisburg, Pa., 1975-79, libr., 1979—. Vice chair. legis. rsch. librs. staff sect. Nat. Conf. of State Legis., Denver, 1987-88, chair, 1988-89; mem. Dauphin County Libr. Sys. Mem.: Greater Phila. Law Libr. Assn., Easter Seal Soc., Chesapeake Bay Found. Office: Legis Reference Bur Main Capitol Building Rm 641 Harrisburg PA 17120-0033

**ZAVADA, BARBARA JOHANNA,** artist, educator; b. Jena, Thueringia, Germany, June 20, 1938; came to U.S., 1953; d. Paul Egon and Johanna Helene (Kuehlich) Weber; m. Gerhard Manfred Grote, Mar. 6, 1971 (div. Jan. 1975); 1 child, Erika Barbara. Student, Art Students League, NYC, 1961, student, 1970—71; cert., Trahagen Sch. Fashion, NYC, 1960; Assoc., Rochester Inst. Tech., NY, 1966; studied with Karl Bobeck, Berlin, 1962. Painter, 1960—; fashion designer H & U Schmidt, Berlin, 1961—62, Dave Goldberg, NYC, 1967—71; graphic designer Zavada Assocs., Stamford, Conn., 1974—90. One-woman shows include Mus. Art, Sci. and Industry, Bridgeport, Conn., 1974, Stamford Landmark Tower, 1985, So. Conn. State U., 1990, Colo. Arts Ctr., Grand Junction, 1998, St. John's Coll., Santa Fe N.Mex., 2005, traveling group show, Europe, 1964. Vice pres. Ind. German Lang. Sch., Westport, Conn., 1981-83; search and rescue pilot CAP, Rochester, N.Y., 1964-68, N.Y.C., 1969-70. Recipient 1st prize N.Y.C. Fashion Competition, 1960, Faber Birren Color award, Stamford, 1981. Mem.: Nat. Women's History Mus. (charter mem.). Avocations: travel, hiking, gardening, wine making. Home: HC64 Box 3001 Castle Valley UT 84532 E-mail: bjzavada@yahoo.com.

**ZAVADIL, MARTIN R.,** music educator, director, retired conductor; b. Jackson Heights, NY, Feb. 12, 1943; s. Richard and Blanche Elizabeth Zavadil; m. Sharon Lenore Silva-Zavadil, Sept. 2, 1973; children: Carrie, Matthew, Amy, Daniel. BSc in Music Edn., SUNY, Fredonia, 1965; postgrad., LI U., 1971, SUNY, Potsdam, 1972—73. Music tchr. Bd. Coop. Ednl. Svcs., Carl Place, NY, 1965—66; elem. band dir. Hauppauge Centennial Schs., NY, 1966—71; dir. bands Schalmont Centennial Schs., Rotterdam, NY, 1971—77; Susquehanna Valley Centennial Schs., Conklin, NY, 1977—87, Shenendehowa Centennial Schs., Clifton Park, NY, 1987—2002; ret., 2002. Adjudicator NY Sch. Music Assn., 1985—; condr. Schoharie Valley Concert Band, NY, 2000—, Saratoga Springs Youth Orch, Wind Ensemble, NY, 2001—; guest condr. in field. Dutch Reformed. Avocations: curling, golf, kayaking, softball, gardening. E-mail: zavamart@aol.com.

**ZAVALIN, ANDREY I.,** optics scientist, educator; Sr. rsch. assoc. Russian Acad. Scis., Moscow, 1989—99; rsch. prof. NASA Ctr. Photonic Materials and Devices, Nashville, 1999—2003, Vanderbilt U., Nashville, 2003—. Adj. prof. Conservative Optical Logic Devices Program Fisk U., Nashville, 2004—. Mem.: Soc. Sci. Exploration, Optical Soc. Am., Am. Phys. Soc. Achievements include patents for device for multipolar sound emission; development of effect of a self-assembly in one-beam optical trap; optical logic devices; ionoluminescence in nano-particles. Home: 104 Glenway Ct Nashville TN 37221-3021 Office: Vanderbilt University VU Sta B 351807 2301 Vanderbilt Pl Nashville TN 37235-1807 Office Phone: 615-397-6743. Office Fax: 615-329-8634. E-mail: andrey.zavalin@vanderbilt.edu.

**ZAVATSKY, MICHAEL JOSEPH,** lawyer; b. Wheeling, W.Va., Dec. 15, 1948; s. Mike and Mary (Mirich) Z.; m. Kathleen Hanson, May 28, 1983; children: David, Emily. BA in Internat. Studies, Ohio State U., 1970; MA in Polit. Sci., U. Hawaii, 1972; JD, U. Cin., 1980. Bar: Ohio 1980, US Dist. Ct. (so. dist.) Ohio 1981, US Ct. Appeals (6th cir.) 1985, U.S. Supreme Ct. 1989. Ptnr. Taft, Stettinius & Hollister, Cin., 1980—. Adj. prof. in trial practice and immigration law U. Cin., 1986— Trustee Internat. Visitors Ctr., Cin., 1984-86; bd. dirs. Cin. Charter Com., 1988-91; bd. dirs., mem. steering com. Leadership Cin., 1994-96. Capt. USAF, 1973-77. William Graham fellow U. Cin., 1979, East West Ctr. fellow U. Hawaii, 1970; named Best Lawyers in Am., 1995; Ohio Super Lawyers, 2003—, Cin. Leading Lawyers, 2004—. Mem ABA, Ohio Bar Assn., Cin. Bar Assn., Am. Immigration Lawyers Assn. (chmn. Ohio chpt. 1987-88, 90-93), Potter Stewart Inn of Ct., Order of Coif. Home: 3820 Eileen Dr Cincinnati OH 45209-2013 Office: 1800 US Bank Tower Cincinnati OH 45202 Office Phone: 513-357-9393.

**ZAVERI, DIMPLE JIGISH,** microbiologist, medical technician; d. Navinchandra Ranchoddas and Laxmi Navinchandra Thacker; m. Jigish Shirish Zaveri, Nov. 13, 1961; children: Alisha Jigish, Anay Jigish. BSc, Bombay U.,

Mumbai, India, 1989; BS, Morgan State U., Balt., 1997. Med. technologist U. Md. Med. Sys., Balt., 1997—99, MedStar Health - Franklin Sq. Hosp., Balt., 1999—2004; supr. stat. lab. MedStar Health-Franklin Sq. Hosp., Balt., 2004—. Mem.: Am. Soc. Clin. Pathology (assoc.; cert. med. technologist). Office: MedStar Health-Franklin Sq Hosp 9000 Franklin Sq Dr Baltimore MD 21237 Office Phone: 443-777-7226.

**ZAVERI, JIGISH SHIRISH,** chemical engineer, educator; s. Shirish Mafatlal and Vilas Shirish Zaveri; m. Dimple Jigish Zaveri, Dec. 30, 1967; children: Alisha Jigish, Anay Jigish. B.Tech in Chem. Engring., Indian Inst. Tech., Kharagpur, 1985; MSChemE, U. Ky., Lexington, 1987, PhD, 1992. Assoc. prof. Morgan State U., Baltimore, Md., 1992—. Office: Morgan State U 1700 E Cold Spring Ln Baltimore MD 21251 Office Phone: 443-885-3738.

**ZAVITSAS, ANDREAS ATHANASIOS,** chemistry professor, researcher; b. Athens, Greece, July 14, 1937; came to U.S., 1954; s. Athanasios A. and Catherine K. Zavitsas; m. Lourdes Romanacce, Apr. 17, 1959; 1 child, Athanasios. BS magna cum laude, CCNY, 1959; MS, Columbia U., N.Y.C., 1961, PhD, 1962. Rsch. assoc. Brookhaven Nat. Lab., Upton, N.Y., 1962-64; rsch. chemist Monsanto Chem. Co., Springfield, Mass., 1964-67; prof. L.I. U., Bklyn., 1967—; grad. dean, 1975-80. Cons. in field. Contbr. articles to Jour. Polymer Sci., Jour. Am. Chem. Soc., Jour. Phys. Chemistry. Chmn. sch. bd. Holy Cross Sch., Bklyn., 1980-87. Mem. Am. Chem. Soc., Phi Beta Kappa. Greek Orthodox. Office: LI U University Plz Brooklyn NY 11201 Office Phone: 718-488-1351. Business E-Mail: zavitsas@liu.edu.

**ZAVON, MITCHELL RALPH,** occupational medicine physician; b. N.Y.C., May 9, 1923; s. Irving and Claire (Gutterman) Z.; m. Betty Berthold, June 24, 1976; children by previous marriage: Peter, Dan, Juliet, Barbara. Student, Cornell U., 1940-43, Harvard U., 1943-44; MD, Boston U., 1949, postgrad., Duke U., 1951-52, U. Cin., 1956-58. Diplomate Am. Bd. Med. Examiners, Am. Bd. Preventive Medicine, Am. Bd. Indsl. Hygiene. Intern Wilson Meml. Hosp., Johnson City, NY, 1949-50; surgeon USPHS, Washington, 1950-56; from instr. to asst. clin. prof. U. Cin., 1952-74, from asst. prof. to clin. prof. indsl. medicine, 1956-71; asst. health commr. Cin. Health Dept., 1956-74; med. dir. Ethyl Corp., Baton Rouge, 1974-76; dir. health Occidental Chem. Corp., Niagara Falls, NY, 1976-86; pres., med. dir. Agatha Corp., Sarasota, Fla., 1968—. Mem., cons., del. Threshold Limits Com., 1962-87; mem., cons. Biol. Indices Com., 1982-96; pres. Place-to-Be, 1978-83; mem. cons. staff Mt. St. Mary's Hosp., 1980-94; med. dir. Buffalo Union Occupl. Health Ctr., 1996-98; mem. sci. adv. bd. Internat. Joint Commn. (U.S./Can.), 1977-80; pres. Am. Assn. Poison Control Ctrs., 1962-64. Contbr. articles to profl. jours. Bd. dirs. HART; mem. Cincinnatus Assocs., 1969-77; mem. Niagara County (N.Y.) Bd. Health, 1994-00, pres., 1997; chair Sarasota/Manatee Common Cause. Fellow APHA, Am. Coll. Occupl. and Environ. Medicine, Am. Indsl. Hygiene Assn.; mem. AMA, AAAS, N.Y. State Med. Soc., Niagara County Med. Soc., Am. Conf. Govtl. Indsl. Hygienists. Unitarian Universalist. Home and Office: 4559 Trails Dr Sarasota FL 34232-3450 Office Phone: 941-378-7015. Personal E-mail: zavonm@cs.com.

**ZAWACKI, BRUCE EDWIN,** surgeon, educator, ethicist; b. Northampton, Mass., Dec. 6, 1935; BS, Coll. of Holy Cross, 1957; MD, Harvard U., 1961; MA, U. So. Calif., 1986. Diplomate Am. Bd. Surgery. Intern in surgery Mass. Gen. Hosp., 1961—62, resident in surgery, 1962—65; vis. scholar in trauma surgery Birmingham Accident Hosp., Birmingham, England, 1966; resident in surgery Mass. Gen. Hosp., 1967; gen. surgeon So. Calif. Permanente Med. Group, Panorama City, 1969-71; dir. burn ctr. L.A. County and U. So. Calif. Med. Ctr., L.A., 1971-98; assoc. prof. surgery U. So. Calif. Sch. Medicine, L.A., 1975-98, assoc. prof. emeritus, 1998—; assoc. prof. religion U. So. Calif. Sch. Religion, L.A., 1992-98; assoc. for edn. Pacific Ctr. for Health Policy and Ethics, 1997—; adj. assoc. prof. religion U. So. Calif., 2001—02. Contbr. articles to profl. jours. Served to maj. U.S. Army, 1967-68. Mem. Am. Burn Assn. (2d v.p., bd. trustees 1992-93; Harvey Stuart Allen Disting. Svc. award 1996), Am. Soc. Bioethics and Humanities, L.A. Surg. Soc., Internat. Soc. for Burn Injuries. Achievements include first to describe the natural history of reversible burn injury, the independence of burn hypermetabolism from evaporative water loss and an autonomous role for burn patients without precedent for survival.

**ZAWADA, EDWARD THADDEUS, JR.,** physician, educator; b. Chgo., Oct. 3, 1947; s. Edward Thaddeus and Evelyn Mary (Kovarek) Z.; m. Nancy Ann Stephen, Mar. 26, 1977; children: Elizabeth, Nicholas, Victoria, Alexandra. BS summa cum laude, Loyola U., Chgo., 1969; MD summa cum laude, Loyola-Stritch Sch. Medicine, 1973. Diplomate Am. Bd. Internal Medicine, Am. Bd. Nephrology, Am. Bd. Nutrition, Am. Bd. Critical Care, Am. Bd. Geriatrics, Am. Bd. Clin. Pharm., Am. Bd. Forensic Examiners, Am. Bd. Forensic Medicine; specialist Hypertension, Am. Soc. Hypertension. Intern UCLA Hosp., 1973, resident, 1974-76; asst. prof. medicine UCLA, 1978-79, U. Utah, Salt Lake City, 1979-81; assoc. prof. medicine Med. Coll. Va., Richmond, 1981-83; assoc. prof. medicine, physiology & pharmacology U. S.D. Sch. Medicine, Sioux Falls, 1983-86, Freeman prof., chmn. dept. Internal Medicine, 1987—2002, prof. emeritus, 2002—, chief div. nephrology and hypertension, 1983-88, mem. univ. physician's practice plan, 1992—95; v.p. sci. affairs, dir. dialysis, critical care Avera Health Sys., 2002—04, dir. e-icu, 2004—. Chief renal sect. Salt Lake VA Med. Ctr., 1980-81; asst. chief med. service McGuire VA Med. Ctr., Richmond, 1981-83. Editor: Geriatric Nephrology and Urology, 1984; contbr. articles to profl. publs. Pres. Minnehaha div. Am. Heart Assn., 1984-87, pres. Dakota affiliate Am. Heart Assn., 1989-91. VA Hosp. System grantee, 1981-85, 85-88; Health and Human Svcs. grantee Pub. Health Scvs. Rsch. Adminstrn. Bureau Health Profl., 1993—. Master ACP; fellow Am. Coll. Chest Physicians, Am. Coll. Nutrition, Am. Coll. Clin. Pharmacology, Internat. Coll. Angiology, Am. Coll. Angiology, Am. Coll. Pharmacology, Am. Coll. Forensic Examiners, Royal Soc. Medicine, Soc. for Vascular Medicine and Biology, Am. Soc. Nephrology; mem. Internat. Soc. Nephrology, Am. Soc. Pharmacology and Applied Therapeutics, Am. Physiol. Soc., Am. Inst. Nutrition, Am. Soc. Clin. Nutrition, Am. Geriatric Soc., Am. Soc. Transplant Physicians, Westward Ho Country Club. Democrat. Roman Catholic. Avocations: golf, tennis, skiing, cinema, music. Home: 2908 S Duchess Ave Sioux Falls SD 57103-4826 Office: North Central Kidney Inst 1001 E 21st St Ste 300 Sioux Falls SD 57105-1017 Office Phone: 605-322-5800. E-mail: ezawada@sio.micko.net, edward.zawada@mckennan.org.

**ZAWAIDEH, SAMER K.,** orthodontist; b. Amman, Jordan, June 23, 1967; s. Kamel Michael Zawaideh and Violette M. Baqae'en; m. Salma Al-Nims, 2002. BDS, U. Jordan, Amman, 1989; DMSc, Harvard U., 1997. Tchg. and rsch. asst. orthodontic dept. U. Jordan, 1989-93; acting dir. postdoctoral orthodontic program dept. growth and devel. Harvard U. Sch. Dental Medicine, Boston, 1997-98, dir. postdoctoral orthodontics, 1998—2000, dir. grad. orthodontics dept. growth and devel., 2000—; orthodontist Harvard Dental Ctr., 1997—. Editl. advisor Orthodontic Products Mag., 1999—. Author articles, abstracts in field. Recipient Coenraad Moorrees award, Harvard Soc., 1997; scholar, Fulbright Found., 1993—95, U. Jordan, 1995—97. Mem.: ADA, NE Soc. Orthodontists, Connective Tissue Oncology Soc., Jordan Dental Assn., Am. Assn. Orthodontists, Harvard Soc. Advancement of Orthodontics. Avocations: cooking, swimming, travel. Office: Harvard Sch Dental Medicine Dept Growth and Devel 188 Longwood Ave Boston MA 02115-5819 Home: 166 Woodside Ave West Harrison NY 10604-2021 E-mail: samerzawaideh@post.harvard.edu.

**ZAWICKI, JOSEPH LEO,** science educator; b. Batavia, N.Y., Sept. 24, 1958; s. Leo Stanley Zawicki, Rita Zawicki; m. Ann Marie Hartley, July 27, 1984; children: Richard John, Erin Kathleen, Lee Joseph, Sean Michael. BA, Canisius Coll., 1980; MSEd, U. Rochester, 1989; PhD in Sci. Edn., SUNY, Buffalo, 2002. Cert. tchr. certificate N.Y. Lab technologist Strong Meml. Hosp., Rochester, NY, 1984—89; tchr., dept. chair Elba Ctl. Sch., Elba, NY, 1989—2002; asst. prof. Buffalo State Coll., Buffalo, 2002—. Lectr. Buffalo State Coll., NY, 2001—02, U. Buffalo, 2002; item writer, cons. N.Y. State Edn. Dept., Albany, 1995—; physics mentor N.Y. State Mentor Network,

Oneonta, 1996—; bd. dirs. N.Y. Sci. Edn. Leadership Assn. Developer Optic Bench Sci., 2001. Bd. dirs. Cornell Coop. Ext., Batavia, 1996—98; dir. religious edn. Our Lady of Fatima, Elba, 1999—. Recipient St. Joseph the Worker award, Diocese of Buffalo, 2001; grantee Environ. Empowerment, N.Y. State, 1998. Mem.: Nat. Assn. Rsch. in Sci. Tchg., N.Y. State Edn. Leadership Assn., Sci. Tchrs. Assn. N.Y., Am. Assn. Physics Tchrs., Am. Chem. Soc. Avocations: youth programs, reading. Home: PO Box 172 7 S Main St Elba NY 14058-0172 Office: Buffalo State Coll Sci 130 Dept Earth Scis and Sci Edn 1300 Elmwood Ave Buffalo NY 14222 Office Phone: 716-878-3800. E-mail: zawickjl@buffalostate.edu.

**ZAWISTOWSKI, STEPHEN LOUIS,** psychologist, educator; b. Lackawanna, NY, July 28, 1955; s. Louis Henry and Alice Theresa (Bartus) Z.; m. Jane Elaine Clark, May 26, 1979; 1 child, Matthew. BA, Canisius Coll., 1977; AM, U. Ill., 1979, PhD, 1983. Cert. tech. animal rescue specialist, Am. Humane Assn./Rescue 3. Vis. asst. prof. Ind. U., Bloomington, 1983-84, postdoctoral fellow, 1984-85; asst. prof. St. John's U., NYC, 1985-88; exec. sr. v.p. ASPCA, NYC, 1988—, adj. prof. U. Ill. Vet. Coll., 2004; nat. rsch. coun. panel for rev. of the nat. zoo NAS. Author: Animal Shelter Medicine for Veterinarians and Staff, 2004, co-editor, 2004; co-author: Animal Rights Handbook, 1990; editor Animal Behavior Cons. Newsletter; co-editor: For Kids Who Love Animals, 1991; contbg. editor Animal Watch Mag.; co-exec. prodr. (film) Question of Respect, 1990 (Silver Apple award 1990); writer, host ASPCA pet check segments, PBS; mem. bd. editors Psychologists for the Ethical Treatment of Animals, 1988-95; founding co-editor Jour. Applied Animal Welfare Sci.; contbg. editor, sci. advisor Animaland Mag., 1998-2000; script cons. Animal Rescue Kid, 1997; contbr. articles to profl. jours. Scoutmaster Boy Scouts Am., SI, 1988-98; asst. coach SI Youth Soccer, 1986-95; bd. dirs. Nat. Coun. on Pet Population Study and Policy, v.p., 1995-96, 99-2000, pres., 1996-97; advisor, 2004—; mem. steering com. NY State Watchable Wildlife Program; mem. Nat. Humane Dog Tng. Task Force; bd. dirs. United for Wildlife, 1999-2001, Harmony Inst. Cmty. Adv. Bd.; mem. sci. adv. com. Humane Farm Animal Care, 2003—; bd. dirs., vice chair Alliance for the Contraception of Cats and Dogs, 2005—. Recipient Stan Lesny scholarship Kosciuszki Found., 1977, U. Ill. Grad. fellowship, 1977, Postdoctoral fellowship NSF, 1984, Patrick Daley award for contbns. to edn. St. John's U.; named Psychologist of Yr., Psychologists for Ethical Treatment of Animals, 1989. Mem. NAS (mem. nat. rsch. coun. com. rev. nat. zoo 2004-05, mem. inst. lab. animal resources com. alleviation pain and distress in lab. animals 2006), World Soc. for Protection of Animals (sci. adv. panel 2003—), Animal Behavior Soc. (cert. applied animal behaviorist, chmn. bd. profl. cert. 1998—, devel. com. 1995-98, animal welfare com. 1989-95), Order of Arrow (mem. exec. bd. 1996-98), Sigma Xi. Achievements include research in genetics and animal learning, animal behavior and welfare. Office: ASPCA 110 5th Ave 2d Fl New York NY 10010 Office Phone: 212-876-7700 ext. 4401. Business E-Mail: SteveZ@aspca.org.

**ZAWODNY, LARAE JEAN,** artist, secondary school educator; b. Chgo., Feb. 9, 1949; d. Raymond William and Dorothy (Hammersmith) Koppit; m. Janusz Kazimierz Zawodny, Sept. 18, 1971; 1 child, Roman Janusz. BA magna cum laude, U. Nebr., Omaha, 1970; MFA, Claremont Grad. U., Calif., 1982. Artist Color on Edge, Vancouver, Wash., 1985—; secondary tchr. dept. visual and performing arts Vancouver Sch. Dist., 1992-99; artist, instr. Vancouver Sch. Arts and Acads., 1996-99. One-woman shows include Claremont Grad. U., 1982, U. Portland, 1984, Columbia Arts Ctr., Vancouver, 1985, City Hall, Beaverton, Oreg., 1989, Royal Durst Theatre, Vancouver, 1997, exhibited in group shows at Lang Gallery Scripps Coll., Claremont, 1978, Libra Gallery, 1981, 1982, Factory Pl., L.A., 1982, U. Calif., Irvine, 1982, Portland Ctr. Visual Arts, 1983, Elizabeth Leach Gallery, 1983, 1984, Coos Bay (Oreg.) Art Mus., 1985, Marianne Partlow Gallery, Olympia, Wash., 1986—87, Pacific N.W. Art Expo, Seattle, 1986, U. Portland, 1986, Abbot Hall Gallery, Portland, 1990, Vancouver Sch. Arts and Acads., Wash., 1997, 1998, North Bank Gallery, Vancouver, Wash., 2005, 2006, Represented in permanent collections Mercedes Benz Corp., Frankfurt, Germany, Pomona Coll., Claremont. Home: 23703 NE Margaret Rd Brush Prairie WA 98606-5602

**ZAX, LEONARD A.,** lawyer; b. Paterson, NJ, July 16, 1950; s. Harry and Shirley Jeanne (Hollander) Z.; m. Helen Kemp, May 25, 1980; children: David Hollander, Laura Alexandra. BA, U. Chgo., 1971; M of City Planning, Harvard U., 1975, JD, 1975. Bar: N.J. 1978, D.C. 1978. Spl. asst. to gen. counsel HUD, 1975-76, spl. asst. to sec., 1976-77; lectr., mem. faculty Harvard U., Cambridge, Mass., 1977-78; assoc. Fried, Frank, Harris, Shriver & Kampelman, Washington, 1977-82, ptnr., 1982-95, Latham & Watkins, Washington, 1995—, also chmn. real estate group. Co-chmn. Mayor's Downtown Housing Commn., Washington, 1986-89, D.C. Enterprise Zones Study Commn., 1986-89; D.C. Downtown Interactive Retail Task Force, 1996-98; co-chmn. Washington adv. com. Asian Real Estate Assn., Washington, 1991-92. Contbg. author Nat. Law Jour., N.Y. Times, L.A. Times, Harvard Law Bull., Real Estate Fin. Jour., Urban Land, Washington Business Jour., Washington Post; editor: Real Estate and the RTC: A Guide to Asset Purchases and Contracting, Urban Land Inst., 1990. Trustee Nat. Bldg. Mus., D.C. Preservation League, 1988-95; mem. Fannie Mae Nat. Adv. Coun., 1994-95; mem. vis. com. Harvard Design Sch., 2000—. Mem. ABA (chmn. com. on housing and urban devel. law 1986-89, steering com. representation of the Homeless Project 1988-91, governing bd. forum com. affordable housing and community devel. 1991-94), D.C. Bar Assn., Urban Land Inst., Nat. Multi Housing Coun. Home: 4511 28th St NW Washington DC 20008-1035 Office: Latham & Watkins 555 11thSt NW Ste 1000 Washington DC 20004-1304

**ZAX, MELVIN,** psychologist, educator; b. Cambridge, Mass., Apr. 14, 1928; s. Joseph and Sadie (Kirshner) Z.; m. Ruth Leah Vogel, Apr. 23, 1977; children: Jeffrey S., David B., Jonathan B. AB, Boston U., 1951, AM, 1952; PhD, U. Tenn., 1955. Clin. psychologist II Tenn. Townville, 1953-56, staff psychologist St. Elizabeths Hosp., Washington, 1956-57; asst. prof. psychology U. Rochester, NY, 1957-62, assoc. prof. psychology NY, 1962-67, prof. NY, 1967-93, prof. emeritus NY, 1993—; pvt. practice, 1973—. Chmn. exptl. and spl. tng. rev. com. NIMH, 1970-71. Author: (with G. Stricker) Patterns of Psychopathology, 1963, (with E.L. Cowen) Abnormal Psychology: Changing Conceptions, 1972, (with G.A. Specter) An Introduction to Community Psychology, 1974, (with M. Nichols) Catharsis in Psychotherapy, 1977; editor: (with Stricker) The Study of Abnormal Behavior: Selected Readings, 1964, (with Cowen and E.A. Gardner) Emergent Approaches to Mental Health Problems, 1967, (with D. Dorr and J. Bonner) The Psychology of Discipline, 1983; adv. editor Jour. Cons. and Clin. Psychology, 1965-81; contbr. articles to profl. jours. Served with NAS, 1946-47. NIMH spl. research fellow Psykologisk Inst., Copenhagen, 1966-67 Fellow Am. Psychol. Assn.; mem. Eastern Psychol. Assn., AAUP, Phi Beta Kappa, Sigma Xi, Phi Kappa Phi. Home: 27 Sky Ridge Dr Rochester NY 14625-2167 Office: 625 Panorama Trl Bldg 2 Rochester NY 14625-2432 Office Phone: 585-385-6370.

**ZAYAC, LINDA MARY,** sociologist, educator; d. Ernest F. and Barbara T. Dauplaise; m. Paul Edward Zayac, Nov. 3, 1976; children: Nicholas Alexander, Alexander Joseph. BA in Sociology and Psychology, Am. Internat. Coll., Springfield, Mass., 1972, MA in Edn., 1973. Instr. of social studies Southwick H.S., Mass., 1975—79; project dir. visual edn. lab. Southwick Pub. H.S., 1978—85; co-owner sr. cons. and svcs. Pvt. Geriatric Care Mgmt. Firm, West Springfield, Mass., 1999—2002; instr. sociology Westfield State Coll., Westfield, 1994—, assoc. dir. ctr. for instrnl. tech, 2003—06. Mem. Town Meeting, West Springfield, 1983—2002; traffic safety com. chair Town of West Springfield, 1989—2002; chair Master Plan Commn., 1994—2002; mem. Planning Bd., 1983—2002, Traffic Adv. Commn., 1989—2002, Pioneer Valley Planning Commn. Joint Study Com., West Springfield, 1990—2002, Holyyoke, Mass., 1990—2002; chair Corridor Bus. Assn., Riverdale, Mass., 1993—2002; mem. Pioneer Valley Planning Commn. Study Group, 1989—2002, Mass. Sr. Action Coun., 1989—2002. Home: Town Com., 1983—2002; lacrosse dir. Youth League, 1992—98; pres. Lacrosse Booster Club, 1998—2002; it steering com. Westfield State Coll., 2003—. Mem.: Mass. Coun. Aging Affairs, Nat. Assn. Profl. Geriatric Care Mgrs., Children

Aging Parents, Native Am. Inst., Mass. Women in Pub. Higher Edn., Mass. Coll. Online (liason 2003—06), Mass. Teachers Assn., NERCOMP (assoc.). Home: 79 Highmeadow Dr West Springfield MA 01089 Office: Westfield State Coll 577 Western Ave Westfield MA 01086 Office Phone: 413-572-8142. Office Fax: 413-572-8048. E-mail: lzayac@wsc.ma.edu.

**ZAYAS, ELINOR ABRAMS,** music educator; b. Bay Shore, N.Y., Feb. 25, 1954; d. Alfred and Rosaline Abrams; m. Robert Zayas, Jr., June 12, 1983; 1 child, Alison Rose. MusB, Manhattan Sch. Music, 1976, MusM, 1978; adv. cert. in sch. dist. adminstrn., SUNY, Stony Brook, 2003. Freelance musician, N.Y.C., 1978—85; music faculty Guitar Study Ctr., N.Y.C., 1981—83; musical dir. Gateway Playhouse, Bellport, NY, 1991—99; prof. music Five Towns Coll., Dix Hills, NY, 1994—96; adj. instr. Hofstra U., Hempstead, NY, 1996—98; music tchr. Massapequa (N.Y.) Pub. Schs., 1997—99, Sachem Ctrl. Sch. Dist., Holbrook, NY, 1999—. Artistic dir., pianist Nepenthe Chamber Ensemble, Brightwaters, NY, 1986—. Prodr.: (CD rec.) Nepenthe Chamber Ensemble, 1999. Campaign vol. Re-election Rep. Steve Israel, Hauppauge, NY, 2003; bd. mem. B'Nai Israel Reform Temple Sisterhood, Oakdale, NY, 1998. Mem.: Suffolk County Music Educators Assn., Phi Delta Kappa. Avocations: sailing, attending concerts and museums, reading, travel. Home: 480 Ackerson Blvd Brightwaters NY 11718

**ZAYAS-BAZAN, EDUARDO,** foreign language educator; b. Camagüey, Cuba, Nov. 17, 1935; came to U.S., 1962, naturalized, 1969; s. Manuel Eduardo and Aida Modesta (Loret de Mola); m. Lourdes Abascal; children: Eduardo, Elena María. Dr. en Derecho, U. Nacional José Martí, 1958; MS, Kans. State Tchrs.' Coll., 1966. Social worker Cuban Refugee Asst. Program, 1962-64; Spanish tchr. Plattsmouth High Sch., 1964-65, Topeka West High Sch., 1965-66; Spanish instr. Appalachian State U., 1966-68; asst. prof. East Tenn. State U., Johnson City, 1968-73, assoc. prof., 1973-79, prof., 1979-99, chmn. fgn. lang. dept., 1973-93, prof. emeritus, 1999—. Author (with P. Ferreiro): Cómo dominar la redacción, 1989; author: Guía de G. Fernández de la Torriente) Cómo aumentar su vocabulario 3; author: Cómo escribir cartas eficaces, 1989; author: (with N.A. Humbach and José B. Fernández) Nuestro mundo, 1990; author: (with José Fernández) ¡Arriba!, 1993, 1997; author: (with Carolyn M. Novak) No se equivoque con el inglés, 1993; author: El inglés que usted no sabe que sabe, Primera y Segunda Serie, 1993; author: (with Susan Bacon and Dulce García) Conexiones, 1999, 2002, 2006; editor (with Anthony G. Lozano): Del amor a la revolución, 1975; editor: (with L. Suárez) De aquí y de allá, 1980; editor: (with G. J. Fernández) Así somos, 1983; translator: Secret Report on Cuban Revolution, 1981; author (with Susan Bacon): ¡Arriba!, 2001, 2004. Pres. Sister Cities Internat., Johnson City, 1971-76. Recipient Disting. Faculty award E. Tenn. State U., 1978 Mem.: Cuban Cultural Heritage Assn. (bd. dirs. 2000—02, sec. 2003—06, v.p. 2006—), Nat. Assn. Cuban-Am. Educators (pres. 1991—93, chair bd. dirs. 1994—2002, pres. 2002—04, treas. 2004—), Tenn. Fgn. Lang. Teaching Assn. (pres. 1980, Jacqueline Elliott award 1989), Am. Assn. Tchrs. Spanish and Portuguese (pres. 1985, assoc. editor Hispania 1994—98), Am. Coun. Tchrs. Fgn. Langs., Municipality of Camagüey in Exile (pres. 2000—02, editor El Camagüeyano Libre 2002—), Sigma Delta Pi (Premio Martel 1984). Home: 7540 SW 52 Ct Miami FL 33143 Office Phone: 305-495-5436. E-mail: ezbazan@aol.com.

**ZAYAS-CASTRO, JOSÉ,** engineering educator, researcher; BS in Indsl. Engring., U. PR-Mayaguez, MS in Indsl. and Mgmt. Engring., Rensselaer Polytechnic Inst., MBA, PhD in Mgmt. Head indsl. engring. dept. U. PR-Mayaguez, Coll. Engring., 1987—90, co-holder, Baxter chair in mfg. engring., 1994—97, assoc. dean for academic and rsch affairs, 1995—98; tchg. and leadership positions U. Mo., Columbia, 1999—2001; prof., dept. indsl. mgmt. sys. engring. U. So. Fla., 2001—, chair, dept. indsl. mgmt. sys. engring., 2002—. Established, Learning Factory U. PR-Mayaguez; implemented, Entrepreneurial Mfg. Innovation Learning Experience Progam U. Mo., Columbia; served on the Com. Visitors and the Adv. Com., Divsn. Design, Manufacture, and Indsl. Innovation. Recipient Bernard M. Gordon prize, NAE, 2006. Fellow: Inst. Indsl. Engrs. (named Disting. Indsl. Engr. Yr., Chpt. 188, San Juan, PR 1985—86); mem.: Nat. Sci. Found. (grant reviewer 1990—). Office: U So Fla Indsl and Mgmt Sys Engring 4202 E Fowler Ave ENC 2400 Tampa FL 33620 Office Phone: 813-974-2269. Office Fax: 813-974-5953. Business E-Mail: josezaya@eng.usf.edu.

**ZAYDON, JEMILLE ANN,** language educator, communications educator; b. Peckville, Pa., Feb. 21; d. Joseph and Catherine Ann (Hazzouri) Zaydon. Student, Barry Coll. for Women, 1957—58; BS, Marywood U., 1963; MS in Edn., Wilkes U., 1978; postgrad., Temple U. Tchr. St. Hugh Elem. Sch., Coconut Grove, Fla., Allapattah Elem. Sch., Miami, Columbus Elem. Sch., Westfield, NJ; comm. instr. Keystone Job Corps, Drums, Pa.; vol. instr. Keystone Rehab. Ctr., Scranton, Pa.; curriculum cons. for mentally retarded Vienna; prof. English and reading Lackawanna Jr. Coll., Scranton, head dept. English, speech and reading, chmn. dept. arts, humanities and social studies; assoc. prof. Marywood U., Wilkes U. Adj. prof. English U. Scranton; comm. instr. Lackawanna County Vocat. Tech. Sch. Editor: Lebanese Am. Jour. Supr. recreation program, Hazleton, Pa.; founder, adviser Keystone Kourier; sec. Fedn. Youth, Willim W. Scranton; coord. annual Christmas for Mentally Retarded Keystone City Residence; supr. students Heart Fund campaign; developer program mentally retarded Allied Svcs. Handicapped Scranton; class rep. Marywood U. Fund Dr.; gen. faculty coord. Am. Cancer Soc.; active ARC, March of Dimes, Heart Fund, Leukemia and United Fund drs., Sickle Cell Anemia Found.; exec. bd. Northeastern Pa. Environ. Coun., co-chmn. pub. edn. and funding; bd. dirs. Lackawanna County Comm. for Women, 2003—06, 2d v.p., 2004—06, seminar chair, 2005; exec. bd. Lackawanna County Commr., 2004—; chmn. seminar Lackawanna County Commn.; instr. Confraternity Christian Doctrine; chairperson St. Joseph's Melkite Cath. Ch., 2003—04; bd. dirs. Michael F. Harrity Meml. Fund. Named Tchr. of the Yr., Tchr. We Will Never Forget, Dade County Allpattah Elem. Students, 1991, N.E. Woman, Scranton Sunday Times, 1993; recipient Faculty Mem. of the Yr. award, Keystone Job Corps, Humanitarian award, Outstanding Educators award, 1992, Educators award, Dade County; Svc. scholar, Barry Coll. Mem.: NEA, Pa. State Edn. Assn., Theta Chi Beta (charter pres.), Sigma Tau Delta, Beta Lambda Tau, Lambda Iota Tau (life). Home: 608 N Main Ave Scranton PA 18504-1870 Personal E-mail: jemillez@webtv.net.

**ZAYDON, THOMAS JOHN, JR.,** plastic surgeon; b. Phila., Apr. 3, 1952; s. Thomas J. and Helen (Joseph) Z. BS, Fla. State U., 1974; MD with spl. honors, Hahnemann Med. U., 1978. Cert. Am. Bd. Plastic Surgery, 1982; diplomate Am. Bd. Surgery, 1991. Intern in gen. surgery Eastern Va. Med. Sch., Norfolk, 1978—79, resident in gen. surgery, 1979—80; jr. resident in gen. surgery Monmouth Med. Ctr., Long Beach, NJ, 1980-81, sr. resident in gen. surgery, 1981-82; resident in plastic surgery La. State U., New Orleans, 1982-83, chief resident in plastic surgery, 1983-84, clin. instr.; pvt. practice surgery Cosmetic Surgery Inst., Miami, 1984—; assoc. chief plastic surgery Miami Heart Inst., Fla., 1985—; assoc. chief, plastic surgery Mercy Hosp., 2004—05; pvt. practice. Vol. clin. instr. plastic surgery U. Miami, Fla. 1986—. Author articles and book chpts. in field. Fellow ACS; mem. Dade County Med. Assn., John Rives Surg. Soc., Aesculapian Soc. Miami, Fla. Med. Assn., Fla. Soc. Plastic and Reconstructive Surgeons, Fla. Soc. Plastic Surgeons, Greater Miami Soc. Plastic Surgeons, Am. Soc. Plastic Surgeons, Am. Soc. Aesthetic Plastic Surgeons, Southeastern Soc. Plastic Surgeons. Office: Cosmetic Surgery Inst Miami Mercy Hosp Profl Bldg 3661 S Miami Ave Ste 509 Miami FL 33133-4206 also: Dadeland Med Ctr 7400 N Kendall Dr Ste 502 Miami FL 33156 Office Phone: 305-856-3030. E-mail: tzaydon@pol.net.

**ZAYHOWSKI, JOHN J.,** electrical engineer, researcher; b. Troy, N.Y., 1958; s. John J. and Carole E. J. Zayhowski; m. Lien N. Zayhowski, 1982; children: Justine A., Kimberly M. BS, MS, MIT, 1982, PhD, 1986. Engr. Tex. Instruments, Dallas, 1979-82; mem. tech. staff Lincoln Lab. MIT, Lexington, Mass., 1986—2000, sr. staff Lincoln Lab., 2000—. Chmn. bd. Advanced Concept Com., Lincoln Lab., 1998-99; vis. prof. Tufts U., Medford, Mass., 1997; chmn. various meetings in field; cons. in field. Author: (chpt.) CRC Handbook of Photonics, 1997, Encyclopedia of Applied Physics, 1994, LIA

Handbook of Laser Materials Processing, 1999, The Optics Encyclopedia, Basic Foundations and Practical Applications, 2003, Encyclopedia of Physics, 3d edit., 2005; topical editor Optics Letters, 2005—; contbr. over 70 articles to profl. jours. Pres. Sherwood Forest Homeowners Assn., 1997-98. Recipient fellowship Hertz Found., 1981, scholarship Edith Craig Reynolds, 1977, 1998 R&D 100 award R&D Magazine, commendation for Excellence in Tech. Communications Laser Focus World, 1996, 99, Appreciation cert. NBC, 2004, Team award MIT, 2002, 03, Tech. Excellence award, MIT, 2005. Mem. Optical Soc. Am., Sigma Xi, Tau Beta Pi, Eta Kappa Nu. Achievements include development of microchip laser technology resulting in four start-up companies; 16 patents in field. Office: MIT Lincoln Lab L-142 244 Wood St Lexington MA 02420-9108

**ZAZZALI, JAMES R.,** state supreme court justice; b. Newark, June 17, 1937; s. Andrew F. Zazzali; m. Eileen Fitzsimmons; children: Mara, James Jr., Robert, Courtney, Kevin. BA, Georgetown U., 1958, JD, 1962. Bar: NJ, NY, DC. Law clk. to Hon. Lawrence A. Whipple U.S. Dist. Ct. NJ, 1964—65; from asst. prosecutor to chief appellate sect. Essex County Prosecutor's Office, 1965—68; ptnr. Zazzali, Zazzali, Fagella, & Nowak, Newark; gen. counsel NJ Sports and Exposition Authority, 1973—81; atty. gen. State of NJ, 1981—82; assoc. justice NJ Supreme Ct., 2000—. Adj. prof. Seton Hall Law Sch., 1984—; commr. NJ State Commn. of Investigation, 1984—94, chmn., 1990—94; vice-chair Disciplinary Rev Bd., 1984—2000. Democrat. Office: NJ Supreme Court Hughes Justice Complex PO BOX 23 Trenton NJ 08625-0023*

**ZBAR, LLOYD IRWIN STANLEY,** otolaryngologist, educator; b. Jersey City, June 2, 1939; m. Margo Wally, Mar. 25, 1965; children: Ross I.S., Brett I.W. MD, Queen's U., Kingston, Ont., Can., 1964. Cert. otolaryngologist. Intern Beth Israel/Harvard, Boston, 1964; resident surgery French Hosp., N.Y.C., 1965—66; resident otolaryngology Bellevue Hosp. Ctr.-NYU, N.Y.C., 1966—69, fellow otolaryngology, 1969—70; chmn. med. edn. com. Mountainside Hosp., Montclair, NJ, 1979—89, dir. otolaryngology, 1990—97, 1999—. Sec. med. bd. Mountainside Hosp., Glen Ridge, N.J., 1986-90, clin. assoc. prof. otolaryngology NYU Sch. Medicine Contbr. rev. to New Eng. Jour. Medicine, 1988 Mem. exec. bd. Boy Scouts Am., Essex County, N.J., 1984-95; pres. Mountainside Physicians Scholarship Loan Fund, 1972-85 With USAF. Named a Top Dr. N.Y. Metro Area, 1998—2005. Fellow ACS, Am. Acad. Otolaryngology-Head and Neck Surgery, Royal Soc. Medicine Office: 200 Highland Ave Glen Ridge NJ 07028-1528 Office Phone: 973-744-2424. Office Fax: 973-743-3111. Personal E-mail: liszmd@yahoo.com.

**ZBORAY, MARY SARACINO,** historian; d. Angelo and Elizabeth Saracino; m. Ronald J. Zboray, Dec. 4, 1984. BA in History summa cum laude, U. Bridgeport, Conn., 1971—75; MA in Anthropology, New Sch. Social Rsch., NY, 1977—80. Cert. secondary social scis So. Conn. State Coll., 1982. Rsch. assoc. II dept. history Ga. State U., Atlanta, 1999—2001; vis. scholar in commn. U. Pitts., 2005—. Hon. vis. fellowship, Schlesinger Libr. Radcliffe Inst. Harvard U., Cambridge, Mass., 1998—99. Author (with Ronald J. Zboray): (books) Everyday Ideas: Socio-Literary Experience Among Antebellum New Englanders, Literary Dollars and Social Sense: A People's History of the Mass Market Book, A Handbook for the Study of Book History; contbr. articles to profl. jours. Recipient Clarke Covert prize in mass comm. history, Assn. Edn. Journalism and Mass Comm., 1997, Carrie Chapman Catt prize for rsch. on women and politics, Iowa State U., 2003; Charles A. Dana scholar, U. Bridgeport, 1972—74, Grad. Faculty scholar, New Sch. for Social Rsch., 1977—78, Smithsonian fellow, George Washington U., 1982—83. Mem.: MLA, Rsch. Soc. Am. Periodicals, Soc. Historians of Early Am. Republic, Am. Hist. Assn., Nat. Comm. Assn., Am. Studies Assn., Am. Antiquarian Soc. Office: Univ Pitts Dept Comm 1117 Cathedral of Learning Pittsburgh PA 15260

**ZDANIS, RICHARD ALBERT,** academic administrator; b. Balt., July 15, 1935; s. Albert Francis and Elsie (Kral) Z.; m. Barbara Rosenberger, June 5, 1955; children: Michael Richard, Carole Lynn. BA, Johns Hopkins U., 1957, PhD in Physics, 1960. Rsch. assoc. Princeton (N.J.) U., 1960-61, instr., 1961-62; asst. prof., then assoc. prof. Johns Hopkins U., Balt., 1962-69, prof., 1969-88, assoc. provost, 1975-79, v.p. for adminstrv. svcs., 1977-79, vice provost, 1979-88; provost Case Western Res. U., Cleve., 1988-2000, retired, 2000. Cons. Naval Ordnance Lab., 1967-68, 69-74. Bd. dirs. Great Lakes Mus., 1990-, Cleve. Edn. Found., 1990-96; mem. governing coun. Ohio LINK, 1994-2000; mem. Cleve. Initiative for Edn., 1999-2004. Mem.: Associated Univs. Inc. (bd. dirs.), Am. Phys. Soc.

**ZDEBLICK, MARK JAMES,** information technology executive; b. William and Mary Zdeblick; m. Melanie C. Smitt; children: Daniel, Grace. Student, U. Paris, No. III, Versailles, France, 1981—82; B of Fine and Applied Arts, Arch., U. Ill., 1982, BSCE, 1982; MS Aeronautics and Astronautics, Stanford U., 1984, PhD, 1988. Founder, dir. chief tech. officer Redwood Microsystems, Menlo Park, Calif., 1989—97; consulting prof. Stanford (Calif.) U., 1997—98; pres. Aspire Tech., Portola Valley, Calif., 1998—2000; chief tech. officer optical switch program K2 Optronics, Inc., Sunnyvale, Calif., 2000—01; entrepreneur in residence Spring Ridge Ventures, Atherton, Calif. 2001—02; CEO Vivomems, Inc., Atherton, 2001—02. Contbr. articles to profl. jours. Pres. Ladera Cmty. Assn., 1994—95; judge Santa Cruz County Sci. Fair, 2001, IEEE Sect. 6 for Intel Sci. Fair, 2001; Bd. dirs. Ladera Comty. Assn., 1992—95; bd. dirs. Palo Alto Adult Soccer League, 1990—91. Recipient Commendation for Excellence in Tech. Comms., Laser Focus World, 2001, Trip to Nixon's Inauguration Competition, Park Ridge Newspaper Svc., 1973, Sawyer Cup, Phi Gamma Delta, 1981. Mem.: IEEE, Sensors and Materials Jour. (assoc. editor 1993—2002), Phi Eta Sigma, Tau Beta Pi. Achievements include patents for integrated microminiature electric-to-fluidic valve pressure/flow regulator; method of making an integrated scanning tunneling microscope; microfabricated cantilever stylus with integrated conical tip; microfabricated microscope assembly; integrated variable focal length lens and its application; microfabricated cantilever stylus with integrated pyramidal tip; integrated scanning tunneling microscope; integrated mass storage device. Avocations: soccer, hiking, travel, swimming. Home: 300 La Mesa Dr Menlo Park CA 94028 Office: Vivomems, Inc 3351 El Camino Real Menlo Park CA 94027 Personal E-mail: mark.zdeblick@stanfordalumni.org. Business E-Mail: mzdeblick@stvc.com.

**ZDERIC, STEPHEN ANTHONY,** urologist, surgeon; b. Detroit, July 2, 1956; s. John Anthony and Marie Alice Zderic; m. Kathleen (Kate) Marie Cronan, Dec. 6, 1953; children: Olivia Cronan, Colin Cronan, Natalie Sang Me. BS Chemistry and BioChemistry, U. Calif. Riverside, 1979; MD, UCLA, 1983. Cert. Urologist Am. Bd. of Urology, 1993. Asst. prof. surgery in urology Sch. Medicine U. Pa., Phila., 1991—99; attending surgeon Children's Hosp. Phila., 1991—; assoc. prof. surgery in urology Sch. Medicine Sch. Medicine U. Pa., 1999—2006, prof. surgery in urology, 2006—. Editor: (sci. mongraph) Muscle Matrix and Bladder Function, Pediatric Gender Assignment A Critical Reappraisal; cons. reviewer Jour. Urology, Brit. Jour. Urology; contbr. articles to profl. jours. Grantee, NIH, 1993—98, 1994—95, 2003—05, 1998—; Rsch. Grant, Am. Found. Urologic Disease, 1989—90. Avocations: tennis, skiing, swimming. Office: Children's Hosp Philadelphia 34th & Civic Center Blvd Philadelphia PA 19104 Office Phone: 215-590-3766. Office Fax: 215-590-3985. Personal E-mail: zderic@email.chop.edu.

**ZEAGER, LLOYD,** librarian; b. Elizabethtown, Pa., Sept. 19, 1942; s. Russel S. and Anna Mae (Givens) Z. BA, Goshen Coll., 1976; MS, Drexel U., 1983. Sec., adminstrv. asst. Mennonite Brotherly Aid, Salunga, Pa., 1967-72; asst. libr. Lancaster (Pa.) Mennonite Hist. Soc., 1976-82, libr., 1983—. Author: A York County Givens Family, 1980, Master Alphabetical Compilation of Hymns Appearing in Mennonite Hymn Books, 1980, Mission in the City, 1997. Mem. ALA, Hymn Soc. Club of Am. Democrat. Mennonite. Avocations: hymnology, genealogy. Office: Lancaster Mennonite Hist Soc 2215 Millstream Rd Lancaster PA 17602-1429

**ZEALEY, SHARON JANINE,** lawyer; b. St. Paul, Aug. 30, 1959; d. Marion Edward and Freddie Zealey. BS, Xavier U. of La., 1981; JD, U. Cin., 1984. Bar: Ohio 1984; U.S. Dist. Ct. (so. dist.) Ohio 1985; U.S. Ct. Appeals (6th cir.) 1990; U.S. Supreme Ct. 1990. Law clk. U.S. Atty. for S. Dist. of Ohio, Cin., 1982; trust adminstr. U.S. Bank (formerly First Nat. Bank), Cin. 1984-86; atty. UAW Legal Svcs., Cin., 1986-88; assoc. Manley, Burke, Lipton & Fischer, Cin., 1988-91; mng. atty. and dep. atty. gen. Ohio Atty. Gen. Office, Cin., 1991-95; asst. U.S. atty. criminal div. for So. Dist. Ohio U.S. Attys. Office, Cin., 1995-97; United States atty. So. Dist. Ohio, Cin., 1997—2001; ptnr. Blank Rome LLP, 2001—. Adj. instr. Coll. Law U. Cin., 1997—; mem. U.S. Atty. Gen.'s Adv. Com., 1999—2001, chair civil rights subcom., 2001; mem. merit selection com. Sixth Cir. Ct. of Appeals Bankruptcy Ct., 1992—96, 2003. Mem. commn. Cin. Cmty. Action Now, 2001—; commr. Tall Stacks Commn., City of Cin., 1990—94, Mayor's Commn. on Children, City of Cin., 1992—94; mem. equal employment adv. rev. panel City of Cin., 1989—91; bd. dirs. Nat. Inst. for Law and Equity, 2002—; trustee, bd. visitors U. Cin. Coll. Law, 1992—; trustee Legal Aid Soc. Cin., 1987—92; bd. dirs. Freestore Foodbank, 2003—, Playhouse in the Park, 2002—; co-chair Greater Cin. Minority Counsel Program, 2005—; mem. exec. bd. Cin. Youth Collaborative, 2005—. Named Career Woman of Achievement, Cin. YWCA, 1988; named one of Top Ten Women Attys., Women's Bus. Cin., 2005; named to Super Lawyers, Ohio, 2006; recipient Disting. Alumni award, Friends of Women's Studies, U. Cin., 2001, Theodore M. Berry award for outstanding achievement in politics and in svc. to cmty., Cin. chpt. NACCP, 1998, Nicholas Longworth III Alumni Achievement award for disting. pub. svc., U. Cin. Coll. Law, 1997. Mem. Black Lawyers Assn. of Cin. (pres. 1989-91, round table 1988-), Legal Aid Soc. (sec. 1991-92), ABA, Fed. Bar Assn., Ohio Bar Assn., Nat. Bar Assn. (bd. govs. 1991-93), Nat. Assn. Women Yr. region VI 1990), Cin. Bar Assn. (trustee 1989-94), Cin. CAN Commn. Democrat. Episcopalian. Office: 1700 PNC Ctr 201 E 5th St Cincinnati OH 45202 Office Phone: 513-362-8700. Business E-Mail: zealey@blankRome.com.

**ZEARFOSS, HERBERT KEYSER,** retired lawyer; b. Montandon, Pa., Oct. 13, 1929; s. Dean Wilson and Susan Lesher (Keyser) Z.; m. Thelma Mary McCarthy, Dec. 19, 1953 (dec. 1984); children: Timothy McCarthy, Jonathan Andrew, Sarah Creighton; m. Suzanne VanderVeer, Nov. 14, 1992. AB, Bucknell U., 1951; postgrad., Yale U., 1951-53; JD, Am. U., 1958. Bar: Pa. 1959, U.S. Dist. Ct. (mid. dist.) Pa. 1959, U.S. Dist. Ct. (ea. dist.) Pa. 1975, U.S. Supreme Ct. 1975. Ptnr. Fetter & Zearfoss, Lewisburg, Pa., 1959-60; asst. counsel Fidelity Mut. Life Ins. Co., Phila., 1960-67, sr. v.p., gen. counsel, 1978-82; sec., mgr. Ins. Fedn. of Pa. Inc., 1967-68; ptnr. Zearfoss & Campbell, 1968-78; sr. v.p., sec., gen. counsel Provident Indemnity Life Ins. Co. and parent co. Provident Am. Corp., Norristown, Pa., 1982-87; sole practice Radnor, Pa., 1987-91; adj. faculty Cabrini Coll., 1988-90; asst. gen. counsel, asst. sec. Teleflex Inc., Limerick, Pa., 1991-2001. Author: The Life Insurance Law of Pennsylvania, 1983; book rev. editor Am. U. Law Rev., 1956-58. Rep. Pa. Gen. Assembly from 167th dist., 1968-78; justice of the Peace, Radnor Twp., Delaware County, Pa., 1966-67; v.p. Valley Forge coun. Boy Scouts Am., 1982-86; treas. Netherlands-Am. Amity Trust, Inc., 1981-86; treas. Civil War and Underground R.R. Mus. Phila., 2003—; bd. dirs. Am. Revolution Patriots Fund, 2002—. Lt. comdr. USNR, 1954-58. Decorated officer Order of Orange-Nassau (Netherlands); recipient Silver Beaver award Boy Scouts Am., 1989. Mem. ABA, Pa. Bar Assn., Assn. Life Ins. Counsel, Netherlands Soc. Phila. (pres. 1979-83), SAR (pres. Phila. Continental chpt. 1986-87), Colonial Soc. Pa. (gov. 1988-91), Del. Soc. Cin. (pres. 1996-99), Soc. Colonial Wars in the Commonwealth of Pa. (gov. 2004—), Pa. Geneal. Soc. (counsel 1987-91, pres. 1995—), Soc. War 1812 (pres. 1996-99), Mil. Order Loyal Legion U.S. (comdr. Pa. comdr. 1999-2001, judge adv.-in-chief 2001-05), Sovereign Mil. Order Temple Jerusalem (grand officer), Priory of Phila. (prior 1994-98), Yale Club Phila., Phila. Club, Penn Club, Merion Cricket Club, Omicron Delta Kappa, Phi Alpha Delta, Phi Alpha Theta, Tau Kappa Alpha, Pi Sigma Alpha. Republican. Presbyterian. Home: 532 Candace Ln Villanova PA 19085-1702 Personal E-mail: hzearfoss@aol.com.

**ZEBI, SANDRA,** artist; b. Sao Paulo, Brazil, Mar. 23, 1960; d. Fernando and Yvonne Landi (Visconti) Zeminian; children: Zebi Zeminian Birnbaum, Gabi Zeminian Birnbaum. BA, U. Mackenzie, Brazil, 1982; student in Architecture, Westminister Coll., London, Eng., 1983—84; student in Graphic Design, Santa Monica Coll. Artist Zebi Designs, L.A., 1990—. Prin. works include sculpture, Inglewood City Hall, Calif. Business E-Mail: sandrazebi@zebidesigns.com.

**ZEBROSKI, EDWIN LEOPOLD,** risk management consultant; b. Chgo., Apr. 1, 1921; s. Peter Paul and Sophie (Rydz) Z.; m. Gisela Karin Rudolph, Sept. 6, 1969; children: Lars, Zoe, Susan, Peggy. BS, U. Chgo., 1941; PhD, U. Calif., Berkeley, 1947. Registered prof. engr., Calif. Project engr. Gen. Electric Co., Schenectady, N.Y., 1947-53, mgr. devel. engring. San Jose, Calif., 1958-73; mgr. engring. SRI Internat., Menlo Park, Calif., 1954-58, dir. systems and materials dept., 1974-79; dir. nuclear safety analysis ctr. EPRI, Palo Alto, Calif., 1979-81; v.p. engring. INPO, Atlanta, 1981-83; chief nuclear scientist EPRI, 1982—88; dir. risk mgmt. svcs. APTECH Engring. Svcs., Sunnyvale, Calif., 1988-97; safety and risk mgmt. advisor DOE-Sandia Nat. Lab., 2000—04. Vis. prof. Purdue U., Lafayette, Ind., 1977-78; cons. OTA, Washington, 1980, 82-83, Dept. Energy, Washington, 1985-90, panels Nat. Rsch. Coun., 1990—, Electricite de France, 1986-87, Dept. Interior, Washington, 1987-89, EPRI, Palo Alto, 1988-98, Acad. Sci., USSR, 1987, Karlsruhe Lab., Germany, 1988; mem. commn. engring. edn. NRC, Washington, 1970-73; mem. NAS-NRC Panel on Decision-Making in Govt. Agy., 1997-98; mem. NAS-NRC Panel on High Level Waste R&D, 2001; mem. NAE Panel on Countering Terrorism, 2002—03. Contbr. chpts. to books, numerous articles to profl. jours.; patentee in field. Pres. bd. dirs. Unitarian Ch., Palo Alto, 2003—; bd. dirs. Stevenson House, Palo Alto, 2003—. Recipient Charles A. Coffin award Gen. Electric Co., Schenectady, 1954, Edward Teller award, 2002. Fellow AAAS, Am. Nuclear Soc. (bd. exec. com. 1969-71), Am. Inst. Chemists; mem. NAE (chmn. energy com. 1984-86, chmn. mem. com. 1986-87, policy com. 1995-96), Am. Phys. Soc., Soc. for Risk Analysis. Avocations: safety and risk management, public sector decision processes, music, writing. Office: ELGIS Consulting 1546 Plateau Ave Los Altos CA 94024-5320 Business E-Mail: edzeb@sbcglobal.net.

**ZECCHINO, VINCENT,** retired surgeon; b. Bklyn., N.Y., May 14, 1909; s. Michael and Rose Zecchino; 1 child, Paul Y. MD. U. Med. Sch. Bologna, Italy, 1936. Diplomate Am. Bd. Orthop. Surgery. Chief dept. orthop. surgery 48th Gen. Hosp., Burma, India, Lowell Gen. Hosp., Ft. Devens, Mass. Cons. Boston Childrens Hosp. R. I. Hosp., 1936—. Fellow: ACS; mem.: Am. Bd. Cerebral Palsy. Republican. Avocations: fishing, travel, reading. Home: 530 S Collier Blvd 202 Marco Island FL 34145

**ZECH, EDWARD R.,** cardiothoracic surgeon; b. Seattle, Mar. 25, 1953; s. Ralph K. and Helen E. Zech; m. Deborah N. Nyholm, July 16, 1977; children: Anthony E., Kathleen A., Andrew J., Daniel P., Maureen E. MD, Creighton U., 1980. Diplomate Am. Bd. Thoracic Surgery, 1994. Commd. ensign USN, 1976, advanced through grades to capt.; head dept. CT surgery Nat. Naval Med. Ctr., Bethesda, Md., 1992—2000; ret. USN, 2000; surgeon, med. dir. St. Joseph Hosp. Med. Group, Bellingham, Wash., 2000—. Founding dir. St. Joseph Hosp. Found., Bellingham, 2003. Decorated Navy Marine Corps Achievement medal U.S. Marine Corps, Navy Commendation medal with gold star USN, Meritorious Svc. medal, Legion of Merit; vis. scholar Ralph Alley fellow, Kennedy Sch. Govt., Thoracic Surgery Found., 1999; U.S. Navy Health Professions scholar, Naval Health Sci. and Edn. Command, 1976—80. Fellow: ACS, Am. Coll. Chest Physicians; mem.: Med. Group Mgmt. Assn., Soc. Thoracic Surgeons. Office: St Joseph Hosp CT Surgery Associates 2979 Squalicum Pkwy Ste 303 Bellingham WA 98225 Office Phone: 360-756-6800.

**ZEDILLO PONCE DE LEÓN, ERNESTO,** former president of Mexico; b. Mexico City, Apr. 27, 1951; s. Rodolfo Zedillo Castillo and Martha Alicia Ponce de Leon; m. Nilda Patricia Velasco Nuñez; children: Ernesto, Emiliano,

Carlos, Nild Patricia, Rodrigo. Student, Instituto Politécnico Nacional, Bradford U.; U. Colo.; MA, Yale U., 1977, PhD, 1981, LLD (hon.), 2001. With Partido Revolucionario Institucional, 1971—, Instituto de Estudios Políticos, Económicos y Sociales; econ. rschr. Dirección Gen. de Programación Económica y Social; lectr. Colegio de Mex., 1978-80; dep. mgr. finance and econ. rsch., advisor to bd. dirs. Banco de Mex.; dep. sec. for planning and budget Govt. Mex., Mexico City, 1985-88, sec. for planning and budget, 1988-92, sec. public edn., 1992-93; campaign mgr. presdl. candidate Luis Donald Colosio Partido Revolucionario Institucional, 1993-94; pres. Govt. Mex., Mexico City, 1994—2000; chair, high level panel financing for devel. UN; prof., internat. economics, politics Yale U.; dir. Yale Ctr. Study of Globalization, 2002—; co-chmn. Internat. Task Force on Global Public Goods, UN Commn. on Private Sector and Devel.; chair Global Devel. Network. Mem. Trilateral Commn.; mem. internat. adv. bd. Coun. Fgn. Rels.; bd. dirs. Internat. Economics. Recipient Wilbur Cross Medal, Yale U., 2001, Franklin D. Roosevelt Freedom from Fear award, Gold Insigne, Coun. Americas, Tribuna Americana award, Casa de America, Madrid, Berkeley medal, U. Calif. Office: Yale U Ctr Study of Globalization Betts Hall New Haven CT 06520

**ZEDROSSER, JOSEPH JOHN,** lawyer; b. Milw., Jan. 24, 1938; s. Joseph and Rose (Zollner) Z.; m. Antonina Krass, Sept. 6, 1997. AB, Marquette U., 1959; LLB, Harvard U., 1963. Bar: N.Y. 1964, U.S. Dist. Ct. (so. dist.) N.Y. 1966, U.S. Dist. Ct. (ea. dist.) N.Y. 1971, U.S. Ct. Appeals (2d cir.) 1971, U.S. Ct. Appeals (D.C. Cir.) 1975, U.S. Supreme Ct. 1975. Assoc. William G. Mulligan, N.Y.C., 1964-67, Christy, Bauman, Frey and Christy and successors, N.Y.C., 1967-71; dir. cmty. devel. unit Bedford-Stuyvesant Cmty. Legal Svcs. Corp., N.Y.C., 1971-73; assoc. atty. fed. defender svcs. unit Legal Aid Soc., N.Y.C., 1973-74; asst. atty. gen. Environ. Protection Bur., N.Y. State Dept. Law, N.Y.C., 1974 80; regional counsel EPA, N.Y.C., 1980-82, assoc. prof. St. John's U. Sch. Law, N.Y.C., 1982-86; ptnr. Rivkin, Radler, Dunne & Bayh, Uniondale, N.Y., 1986-89, Breed, Abbott & Morgan, N.Y.C., 1989-93, Whitman Breed Abbott & Morgan, N.Y.C., 1993-95; v.p. CPR Inst. for Dispute Resolution, N.Y.C., 1996; sr. investigative counsel com. on investigations, taxation, and gov. ops. N.Y. State Senate, 1998-99; asst. atty. gen. Environ. Protection Bur. N.Y. State Office Atty. Gen., N.Y.C., 1999—. Lectr., contbr. to course handbooks for courses sponsored by Practicing Law Inst. and other assns. Lt. USNR, 1965-74, USAR, 1963-65. Mem. ABA, Assn. Bar City N.Y., N.Y. State Bar Assn., Alpha Sigma Nu. Roman Catholic. Home: 1520 York Ave Apt 15B New York NY 10028-7982

**ZEE, PHYLLIS C.,** physician, educator, researcher; b. Hong Kong, June 27, 1954; came to U.S., 1973; d. William and King Di (Wong) Cheung; m. Benjamin Zee; children: David, Caroline, Alex. BA, Mills Coll., 1976; PhD, Chgo. Med. Sch., 1980, MD, 1983. Diplomate Am. Bd. Psychiatry and Neurology, Am. Bd. Med. Examiners, Am. Bd. Sleep Medicine. NIH postdoctoral fellow Northwestern U., Evanston, Ill., 1987-89, asst. prof. neurobiology and neurology Chgo., 1989-95, assoc. prof., 1996—2000, prof., 2001—; dir. Sleep Ctr. Northwestern Meml. Hosp., Chgo., 1991—. Mem. bd. advisors Jour. Biol. Rhythms, 1994—; bd. dirs. Nat. Sleep Found., 2003—; mem. NIH study sect. Contbr. articles to profl. jours. Fellow Buelher Ctr. on Aging, 1995—, Brookdale Found., 1994; grantee NIH, 1994—. Fellow: Am. Sleep Disorders Assn.; mem.: Am. Neurol. Assn., Soc. Biol. Rhythms, Soc. for Neuroscience, Am. Acad. Neurology. Office: Northwestern U 710 N Lake Shore Dr Chicago IL 60611-3006 Office Phone: 312-908-8549. Business E-mail: p-zee@northwestern.edu.

**ZEFFREN, EUGENE,** cosmetics executive; b. St. Louis, Nov. 21, 1941; s. Harry Morris and Bess (Dennis) Z.; m. Steccia Leigh Stern, Feb. 2, 1964; children: Maryl Renee, Bradley Cruvant. AB, Washington U., 1963; MS, U. Chgo., 1965, PhD, 1967. Research chemist Procter & Gamble Co., Cin., 1967-75, sect. head, 1975-77, assoc. dir., 1977-79; v.p. R & D, Helene Curtis, Inc., Chgo., 1979-95; pres. Helene Curtis USA, Chgo., 1995-96; sr. v.p. Helene Curtis bus. unit Unilever Home and Personal Care USA, Chgo., 1996-98, exec. v.p., COO hair and deodorant bus. unit, 1998-2000; sr. v.p. brand devel. Unilever Home and Personal Care N.Am., 2000—02; chmn. NFG Staff, LLC, 2002—; CEO AG Brands, Inc., 2005—. Mem. vis. com. for phys. scis. U. Chgo., 1995—; active Wash. U. Nat. Coun. for Arts and Scis., 1997—; pres. bd. dirs. River North Dance Co., 1998-2000, chmn. 2000-04. Co-author: The Study of Enzyme Mechanisms, 1973; contbr. articles to profl. jours.; patentee in field of enzymes and hair care. Bd. dirs. Goodman Theatre, 1999—, Children's Meml. Rsch. Ctr., 2002—05; trustee Spertus Inst. Jewish Studies, 2002—. Mem. AAAS, Am. Chem. Soc., Soc. Cosmetic Chemists, Cosmetic Toiletry and Fragrance Assn. (sci. adv. com. 1979-95, vice chmn. 1984-88, chmn. 1988-90, bd. dirs. 1996-02), Soap and Detergent Assn. (bd. dirs., exec. com. 2000-02), Indsl. Rsch. Inst., Omicron Delta Kappa. Republican. Jewish. Avocations: tennis, skiing, reading adventure and espionage novels.

**ZEGAS, ALAN LEE,** lawyer; b. Newark, Oct. 28, 1952; s. Norman and Harriet (Lava) Z.; m. Tina Hannah Burk, Aug. 22, 1976; children: Rachel Sarah, Leah Ariel, Joelle Shira. BS, U. Pa., 1974; MBA, Harvard U., 1978; JD, Rutgers U., 1981. Bar: N.J. 1981, U.S. Dist. Ct. N.J. 1981, N.Y. 1982, U.S. Ct. Appeals (3d cir.) 1982. Law clk. to Hon. H. Lee Sarokin U.S. Dist. Ct. N.J., Newark, 1981-83; assoc. Robinson, Wayne, Levin, Riccio & La Sala, Newark, 1983-84; pvt. practice Chatham, NJ, 1984—. Adj. prof. law Rutgers U., Newark, 1983-88; reader N.J. Bd. Bar Examiners, Trenton, 1985; pres. Assn. Criminal Def. Lawyers N.J., 1998-99. Editor-in-chief Rutgers U. Law Rev., 1980-81; editor (pamphlet) Law Tips for the Elderly, 1983. Mem. N.J. Bar Assn. (dist. rep. young lawyers div. 1983-85, vice chmn. 1985-86, trustee 1986-88, chmn. criminal law sect. 1996-97), Essex County Bar Assn. (chmn. lawyers referral service 1986—), Rutgers U. Law Sch. Alumni Assn. (rep. 1983—), U. Pa. Alumni Assn. (sec. 1986-87), Harvard U. Bus. Sch. Alumni Assn., Assn. Criminal Def. Lawyers of N.J. (pres. 1990-99). Home: 476 South St New Providence NJ 07974-2132 Office: 552 Main St Chatham NJ 07928-2120

**ZEGERS, MIRJAM M.,** cell biologist, researcher; PhD, Sch. of Medicine, Groningen, the Netherlands, 1997. Asst. prof. U. Cin., 2003—. Office: U Cin Dept Surgery 3125 Eden Ave Cincinnati OH 45267-0581 Office Phone: 513-558-1725. E-mail: zegersm@ucmail.uc.edu.

**ZEGLIS, JOHN D.,** communications executive, lawyer; BS, U. Ill., 1969; JD, Harvard U., 1972. Bar: Ill. Assoc. Sidley & Austin, 1973—78, partner, 1978—84; corporate v.p., gen. attorney AT&T, 1984—86, vice chmn., pres., 1997—99, gen. counsel, 1986—97; chmn., CEO AT&T Wireless, Redmond, Wash., 1999—. Mem. ABA (vice chmn. communications of pub. utility law sect).

**ZEGURA, STEPHEN LUKE,** biologist, anthropologist, educator; b. San Francisco, Calif., July 2, 1943; s. Dragomir Božo Zegura and Adele Eugenia-Cecilia Perelli-Minetti; m. Elizabeth Ann Chesney, Jan. 23, 1983; children: Daniel Dragomir, Krista Elise. BA, Stanford U., Calif., 1965; MS, U. Wis., Madison, PhD, 1971. Asst. prof. NYU, N.Y., 1971—72; from asst. prof. to prof. U. Ariz., Tucson, 1972—92, prof., 1992—. Contbr. articles to profl. jours., to mags.; co-editor, contg. author: Eskimos of Northwestern Alaska: A Biological Perspective, 1978. Fellow, Woodrow Wilson Found., 1965—66; grantee, Internat. Demokritos Found., 1985, NRC, 1990, IREX, 1988. Fellow: Human Biology Coun., Am. Anthrop. Assn.; mem.: Am. Assn. Phys. Anthropologists. Avocation: golf. Home: 1580 N Rachel Pl Tucson AZ 85721 Office: Dept Anthrop Dept Univ Ariz Haury 310E Tucson AZ 85721

**ZEHR, CONNIE,** sculptor, art educator; b. Ohio, 1938; BFA, Ohio State U. Artist Occidental Coll., 1977; visiting artist Calif. State U. Fullerton, 1978—80, Claremont Grad. Sch., 1981, UCLA, 1981, U. Calif. Irvine, 1981—82; prof. Claremont Grad. Sch., 1982—, chairperson dept. art. One-woman shows include Newspace, L.A., Calif., 2002, Harris Art Gallery, U. LaVerne, Calif., 1998, Weingart Gallery, Occidental Coll., 1991, Santa Monica (Calif.) Coll. Art Gallery Santa Monica (Calif.) Coll., 1989, West

Gallery, Claremont Coll. Grad. Sch., 1988, Taipei (Taiwan) Fine Arts Mus., 1987, Calif. State U., Fullerton, Calif., Barnsdall Mcpl. Art Gallery, L.A., Calif. Mural Project Claremont Cmty. Found., 1999; Transit Ctr. Art Com. City Claremont, 1992; Visual Art Com. Claremont Cmty. Found., 1991—; Art Selection Panel for Grand Hope Park Cmty. Redevel. Agency, LA, 1986; Process Oriented Design Santa Ana Calif., 1987. Grantee Individual Artist Grant, Nat. Endowment Arts, 1975, Landmark Project, Art Collaboration, 1984, Individual Artist Grant, 1986, Mentor Grant, Lorser Feitelson & Helen Lundeberg-Feitelson Arts Found., 1987. Office: Art Dept Claremont Grad U 251 East 10th St Claremont CA 91711 Office Phone: 909-607-9292.

**ZEHR, NORMAN ROBERT,** retired association administrator; b. Niagara Falls, May 19, 1930; s. George Andrew and Ina kate (Morrell) Zehr; m. Janet Hutchinson, Apr. 24, 1976; children: Jeannette Ann, Leslie. Engr. of mines, Colo. Sch. Mines, 1952, MS, 1956. Sales trainee Ingersoll-Rand Co., NYC, 1955—56, sales engr. Lima, Peru, 1956—64, regional mgr. mining and constrn. sales, 1964—68, gen. sales mgr. Latin Am. NYC, 1968—69, gen. mgr. Latin Am. ops., 1969—71, v.p., 1975—83, Ingersoll Rand Internat., Woodcliff Lake, NJ, 1971—72, pres., 1972—83; exec. dir. Colo. Sch. Mines Alumni Assn., 1984—95; ret., 1995. Mem. editl. bd. Encyclopedia of the Korean War, 2000. With U.S. Army, 1952—54. Recipient Disting. Achievement medal, Colo. Sch. Mines, 1977. Mem.: AIME, Nat. Soc. Pershing Rifles, Scabbard and Blade, Mining Club, Sigma Nu.

**ZEHRING, KAREN,** information executive; b. Washington, Dec. 5, 1945; d. Robert William Zehring and Gretchen (Lorenz) Proos; m. George Lang, 1970 (div. 1979); m. Peter Frank Davis, 1979 (div. 1995); children: Jesse, Antonia. BA, U. Denver, 1967; grad., Yale U., 1967-68. Assoc. pub. mktg. and sales Instl. Investor mag., NYC, 1968-74; co-owner, co-creator Cafe des Artistes Restaurant, NYC, 1975-79; owner, pub. The Corp. Fin. Letter, NYC, 1976-78; group dir. planning and devel. Bus. Week mag., NYC, 1977-78; owner, pub., exec. editor Corp. Fin. Sourcebook The Corp. Fin. Bluebook, NYC, 1979-84; chmn., pres., pub., editor-in-chief Corp. Fin. mag., NYC, 1986-90; cons. Karen Zehring & Assocs., Castine, Maine, 1990-94; CEO SourceCapital InterNetwork, NYC, 1998—2001; mng. ptnr. Creative Devel. Ptnrs., NYC, 1995-98, 2001—. Mem.: The Internat. Women's Forum. Unitarian Universalist.

**ZEHRING, LAWRENCE EDWARD,** music educator; b. Tulsa, Okla., Dec. 18, 1940; s. Edward Charles and Virginia Powell (Minshall) Zehring; m. Annette Lee Zehring, Dec. 31, 1965; 1 child, Jared Lee. BA, U. Ozarks, 1961; M, Tulsa U.,1964; MusD, U. Mo., Kans. City, 1985. Dir. vocal music Saranac Lake Schools, NY, 1968—77; asst. condr. Gregg Smith Singers, NYC, 1977—79; assoc. prof. choral music Bridgewater Coll., Va., 1979—80; assoc. prof. Tarkio Coll., Mo., 1980—81, Ft. Hays State U., Kans.; dir. music Roeland Park United Meth. Ch., Kans., 1981—87; First United Meth. Ch., Bella Vista, Ark., 1994—. Exec. dir. Mashburn Scholarship Found., Fayetteville, Ark., 2000—05; founder, condr. Northwest Ark. Chorale, Rogers, 1985—2006; dir. Bella Vista Women's Chorus, 1986—2006. Mem.: Coll. Music Soc. (life), Am. Choral Dir. Assn. (life). Avocations: travel, hiking, camping. Home: 4505 Cedar Brook Lane Rogers AR 72758 Office: Bella Vista United Meth Ch 20 Boyce Dr Bella Vista AR 72714

**ZEHRING, PEGGY JOHNSON,** artist; b. Hutchinson, Kans., Jan. 4, 1941; d. Phillip E. and Bernice (Ashley) Johnson; m. R David Zehring, July 27, 1963; children: Lisa, Geoff. BS, U. Kans., 1963; BA, U. Ill., 1977. Instr. Bellevue (Wash.) C.C., 1979-93, Sch. Visual Concepts, Seattle, 1985-86, Seattle Ctrl. C.C., 1987-97, North Seattle C.C., 1987-97, Coupeville (Wash.) Art Ctr., 1993—. Juror and lectr. Eastside Assn. Fine Art, Mercer Island Visual Arts League, Nat. League Am. Artists & Pen Women; lectr. Women Painters of Washington, Bellevue Art Mus., N.W. Watercolor Soc., Hutchinson Art Assn., Kans. One-woman shows include King County Arts Commn., Seattle, Blake Gallery, Seattle, Bellevue (Wash.) C.C., PACCAR, Bellevue, Pacific N.W. Bell, Seattle, U. Ill., Chgo., Hutchinson Art Assn.; exhibited in group shows at COCA Annual, Seattle, Seattle Art Mus. Sales & Rental Gallery, LewAllen Fine Art, Santa Fe, Bellevue Art Mus., Diablo Valley Coll., Elizabeth Prince Gallery, Prescott, Ariz.; represented in selected collections City of Lynnwood, Wash., Pacific NW Bell, PACCAR, Delitte, Haskins & Sells, Opti-Copy, Kansas City, Harper & Assocs., Bellevue and numerous other pvt. collections; work published in The Artistic Touch I, II and III, The Encyclopedia of Living Artists. Pres. The LaVeta (Colo.) Sch. of Arts. Recipient 1st pl. award Ariz. Internat., Snowgrass Art Inst., Cashmere, Wash., Kans. State Fair, Hutchinson, SPACe, La Veta, Colo., Honorable Mention award W. Wash. State Fair, 2d pl. award Ea. N.Mex. U., Portales, Snowgrass Art Inst., Cashmere, Wash., Merit award Mont. Inst. of the Arts, Butte; named finalist Pierce County Libr. Project, Gig Harbor, Wash., 3rd place Greeley Nat. Juried show. Home: PO Box 967 La Veta CO 81055-0967 E-mail: zehrings@rmi.net.

**ZEICHNER, HARVEY,** psychologist; b. N.Y.C., Feb. 16, 1945; s. David Zeichner and Lillie Leder; m. Helene Pavlov, Sept. 4, 1983; 1 child, Dalas. BS, Farleigh Dickinson U., 1966; MA, CCNY, 1970; JD, Cardoza Sch. Law, 1982; PsyD, Yeshiva U., 1996—79; atty. Costigan, Hyman and Hyman, Mineola, NY, 1982—85, N.Y.C., 1986—. Psychologist cons. Alzheimer Treatment Meml. Ctr., N.Y.C., 2003—; counsel N.Y.C. Dept. Parks and Recreation, 1985—96; psychologist White Plains Sch. Dist., NY, 1997—, Little Flower Children's Svcs., Bklyn., 2003—, N.Y.C., 2000—. Mem.: APA, Legal Aide Soc. (law guardian). Office: Queens Family Court 304 E 65th St Ste 36C New York NY 10021 E-mail: hzeichner@aol.com.

**ZEIDENSTEIN, GEORGE,** population educator; b. Pitts., July 29, 1929; s. Max and Sophia (Cohen) Z.; m. Sondra F. Auerbach, Jan. 25, 1953; children: Laura, Louis Peter. BA, U. Pitts., 1951; JD cum laude, Harvard U., 1954. Bar: N.Y. 1954. Pvt. practice N.Y.C. 1954—65; vol. lawyer Lawyers Conctl. Def. Com., Holly Springs, Miss., 1965; ptnr. Spear and Hill, 1962—65; country dir. Kathmandu, Nepal, Peace Corps, Nepal, 1965-68; regional dir. designate Office E. Asia and Pacific, Washington, 1968; pres. Bklyn. Linear City Devel. Corp., N.Y.C., 1968—69; sr. program officer Asia and Pacific Ford Found., 1969—71, dep. head Asia and Pacific, 1971—72, rep. Bangladesh, 1972—76; pres., trustee Population Coun., N.Y.C., 1976—93; disting. fellow Harvard Ctr. Population and Devel. Studies, Cambridge, Mass., 1993—. Chmn. Himalayas coun. Asia Soc., 1970-72; assoc. seminar tradition and change in South and S.E. Asia, Columbia U., 1971-73, assoc. seminar on tech. and pub. issues, 1981-85; coun. Overseas Devel. Coun., 1979-93; chmn. Appraisal Group Global Com. Parliamentarians on Population and Devel., 1985-86; bd. visitors Grad. Sch. Pub. Health, U. Pitts., 1988—; advisor to chair Ind. Commn. on Population and Quality of Life, 1993-95. Vice chmn. bd. trustees, chmn. program com. Save the Children Fedn., 1991-95, Internat. Ctr. Rsch. on Women, 1993—; chmn. Internat. HIV/AIDS Alliance, 1993—; bd. dirs. Electroverse, 1993-95; active Britton Woods Com., 1992—. Decorated knight comdr. Order of Lion (Finland, Senegal). Home: 795 East St N Goshen CT 06756-1130 Office: Harvard Ctr Population Devel Studies 9 Bow St Cambridge MA 02138-5103

**ZEIDMAN, PHILIP FISHER,** lawyer; b. Birmingham, Ala., May 2, 1934; s. Eugene Morris and Ida (Fisher) Z.; m. Nancy Levy, Aug. 19, 1956; children: Elizabeth Miriam, John Fisher (dec.); Jennifer Kahn. BA cum laude, Yale U., 1955; LLB, Harvard U., 1958; postgrad., Grad. Sch. Bus. Administrn., 1957-58. Bar: Ala. 1958, Fla. 1960, U.S. Supreme Ct. 1961, D.C. 1968, N.Y. 1981. Trial atty. FTC, 1960-61; staff asst. White House Com. Small Bus., 1961-63; spl. asst. to administr. SBA, 1961-63, asst. gen. counsel, 1963-65, gen. counsel, 1965-68; spl. asst. to Vice Pres. of U.S., 1968; govt. rels. mgr. Nat. Alliance Businessmen, 1968; founding prin. Brownstein & Zeidman P.C., Washington, 1968-96; sr. ptnr. Rudnick, Wolfe, Epstien & Zeidman, Washington, 1996-99; ptnr. Piper Marbury Rudnick & Wolfe, Washington, 1999—2001; ptnr., co-chmn. Franchise & Distribution practice group DLA Piper Rudnick Gray Cary, Washington, 2005—. Chmn. grants and benefits com. Administrv. Conf. U.S., 1968; chmn. food industry adv. com. Dept. Energy, 1979-81; chmn. retail food merchandising subcom. Alliance to

Save Energy, 1978; mem. Pres.'s Commn. on Exec. Exch., 1978-81; gen. counsel Internat. Franchise Assn., Am. Bus. Conf.; spl. counsel Japanese Franchise Assn.; advisor to govts. and internat. orgns.; founder EastEuropeLaw, Ltd., Budapest, Hungary. Editor, author: Survey of Laws and Regulations Affecting International Franchising, 1982, 2nd edit., 1990, Regulation of Buying and Selling a Franchise, 1983, Legal Aspects of Selling and Buying, 1983, 2nd edit., 1991; cons. editor Global Franchising Alert; assoc. editor Jour. of International Franchising Law and Distribution; contbg. editor Legal Times of Washington, 1978-85; mem. adv. bd. Antitrust and Trade Regulation Report for Bur. Nat. Affairs, 1978-85. Mem. young leadership coun. Dem. Nat. Conv.; exec. dir. Dem. platform com., 1972; adviser Nat. Presdl. Campaign of Jimmy Carter, 1976; mem. pres.'s adv. coun. John F. Kennedy Ctr. for Performing Arts, 1981; mem. adv. bd. Yale U. Sch. Mgmt.; trustee Yale-China Assn., 1983-89; dir. & mem. exec. com. Appleseed Found. 1994—; mem. adv. bd. DeWitt Wallace Ctr. for Comm., Terry Sanford Inst. Pub. Policy, Duke U., 1994-98; mem. Council for Excellence in Govt., Administrv. Conf. U.S.; gen. counsel Internat. Franchise Assn., Am. Bus. Conf.; spl. counsel Japan Franchise Assn. With USAF, 1958-60. Recipient Younger Fed. Lawyer award Fed. Bar Assn., 1965; Jonathan Davenport Oratorical award, 1954; William Houston McKim award, 1955 Mem. ABA (chmn. com. on franchising 1977-81), D.C. Bar Assn., Ala. Bar Assn., Fla. Bar Assn., Fed. Bar Assn., Bar Assn. D.C., Internat. Bar Assn. (chmn. internat. franchising com. 1986-90, mem. coun. sect. bus. law 1996—), Am. Intellectual Property Law Assn. (chmn. franchising com. 1987-90), Assn. Yale U. Alumni (class rep.). Office: DLA Piper Rudnick Gray Cary 1200 19th St NW Washington DC 20036-2412 Office Phone: 202-861-6676. Office Fax: 202-223-2085. Business E-mail: philip.zeidman@dlapiper.com.

**ZEIGER, LARRY See KING, LARRY**

**ZEIGLER-HILL, VIRGIL,** psychology professor; b. Columbus, Ind., Oct. 28, 1975; s. Arnold and Annie Hill; m. Shellie Zeigler, Aug. 22, 1999. PhD, U. Okla., Norman, 2000—04. Asst. prof. U. So. Miss., Hattiesburg, Miss., 2004—. Fellow Alumni Fellowship, U. Okla., 2000—04. Mem.: APA, Soc. Personality & Social Psychology, Internat. Soc. Self & Identity, Assn. Psychol. Sci. Independent. Avocations: reading, tennis, films. Office: Univ So Miss 118 College Dr #5025 Hattiesburg MS 39406 Business E-mail: virgil@usm.edu.

**ZEILBERGER, DORON,** mathematics professor, researcher; b. Haifa, Israel, July 2, 1950; s. Yehuda Heinz and Ruth (Alexander) Z.; m. Jane Deborah LeGrange, June 3, 1979; children: Celia, Tamar, Hadas. BS with first class hons., U. London, 1972; PhD, Weizmann Inst., Rehovot, Israel, 1976. Mem. Inst. for Advanced Study, Princeton, NJ, 1977-78, 93; vis. assot. prof. Ga. Inst. Tech., Atlanta, 1978-79; lectr. U. Ill., Urbana, 1979-80; sr. scientist Weizmann Inst., Rehovot, Israel, 1980-82; lectr. U. Pa., Phila., 1982-83; assoc. prof. Drexel U., Phila., 1983-88, prof., 1988-90, Temple U., Phila., 1990-99, Laura H. Carnell prof., 1999-2001; bd. govs. prof. Rutgers U., New Brunswick, NJ, 2001—. Mem. editl. bd. Elec. Jour. of Combinations, others, editor-in-chief Advances in Applied Math.; contbr. numerous articles to profl. jours. Mem. Am. Math. Soc. (Leroy P. Steele prize 1998), Math. Assn. Am. (Lester R. Ford award 1990). Inst. for Combinatorics and Its Applications (Euler medal, 2004). Business E-mail: zeilber@math.rutgers.edu.

**ZEILIG, NANCY MEEKS,** writer, editor; b. Nashville, Apr. 28, 1943; d. Edward Harvey and Nancy Evelyn (Self) Meeks; m. Lanny Kenneth Fielder, Aug. 20, 1964 (div. Dec. 1970); m. Charles Elliot Zeilig, Jan. 6, 1974 (div. Dec. 1989); 1 child, Sasha Rebecca. BA, Birmingham-So. Coll., 1964; postgrad., Vanderbilt U., 1971-73. Editorial asst. Reuben H. Donnelley, N.Y.C., 1969-70; asst. editor Vanderbilt U., Nashville, 1970-74; editor U. Minn., St. Paul, 1975; asst. editor McGraw-Hill Inc., Mpls., 1975-76; mng. editor Denver mag., 1976-80; editor Jour. Am. Water Works Assn., Denver, 1981—99; owner Nancy Zeilig Writing & Editing, Denver, 2000—. Editor, co-pub.: WomanSource, 1982, rev. edit., 1984; contbr. articles to trade and consumer mags. Co-chair arts adv. com. Denver Sch. Arts, 1994-96. Avocations: travel, reading, cooking. Office Phone: 303-758-7750. E-mail: nzeilig@earthlink.net.

**ZEINE, RANA RAMSEY,** neuropathologist, research professor; b. Beirut, May 13, 1962; arrived in U.S., 1998; d. Ramsey and Omayma Zeine; m. Hinhark Gan, July 1, 1989. BS in Biology, Am. U. Beirut, 1983, MD, 1987; PhD, McGill U., Montreal, Can., 1993. Rsch. fellow Ottawa (Can.) U., 1995—98; rsch. assoc. Albert Einstein Coll., NY, 1998—2000, resident in neuropathology NY, 2002—04; resident in pathology Montefiore Med. Ctr./Albert Einstein Coll. Medicine, Bronx, NY, 2000—04; rsch. scientist Ctr. for Dementia Rsch. Nathan Kline Inst., NY, 2004—05; rsch. assoc. prof. Cancer Ctr. Northwestern U., Chgo., 2006—. Presenter in field. Author numerous abstracts in neuroimmunology and neuropathology fields; contbr. articles to profl. jours. Fellow, Multiple Sclerosis Soc. Can., 1996—98. Mem.: AMA (fellow 2003—), U.S. and Can. Assn. Pathologists, Internat. Soc. Neuropathology, Coll. Am. Pathologists, NY Acad. Scis. Mem. Baha'i Faith. Avocations: ballet, piano, swimming. Office: R H Lurie Comprehensive Cancer Ctr Olson 8313 Northwestern Univ 303 E Chgo Ave Chicago IL 60611 Office Phone: 312-908-0881. E-mail: r-zeine@northwestern.edu.

**ZEISEL, STEVEN H.,** nutritionist, scientist, educator; b. N.Y.C., July 16, 1950; BS in Life Sci., MIT, 1971; MD, Harvard Med. Sch., 1975; PhD in Nutrition, MIT, 1980. Asst. in medicine Children's Hosp., Boston, 1980-81; asst. prof. pathology and pediatrics Boston U. Sch. Medicine, 1982—90, assoc. prof., 1987-90, prof., 1990; prof. dept. pediatrics U. N.C., Chapel Hill, 1990—, prof. dept. nutrition, 1990—, chair dept. nutrition, 1990—2005; chair med. edn. com. Am. Soc. Clin. Nutrition, 1995—97. Chair joint membership com AIN/ASCN, 1992 94; chmn. adv. bd. Gen. Clin. Rsch. Ctr., U. N.C., 1990-2000; mem. of Medicine panel on folate and B Vitamins, 1997-99; mem. sci. adv. bd. Monsanto Corp., 1998-2000; mem. sci. bd. Dannon Inst.; bd. dirs. Interactive Info. Editor-in-chief Jour. Nutritional Biochemistry. Mem. Internat. Soc. for Rsch. on Human Milk and Lactation, Am. Soc. Nutritional Scis., Am. Soc. Clin. Nutrition (councilor 1991-94, chmn. residency edn. and subspecialty com. 1995—), Am. Soc. Parenteral and Enteral Nutrition, Am. Coll. Nutrition, Am. Pub. Health Assn., Soc. Pediatric Rsch. Office: UNC Dept Nutrition #7461 Sch Pub Health/Sch Medicine 2115A Michael Hooker Rsch Ctr Chapel Hill NC 27599-7461 Office Phone: 919-843-4731. Office Fax: 919-843-8555. E-mail: steven_zeisel@unc.edu.

**ZEITELHACK, GLORIA JEANNE,** artist; b. San Diego, June 24, 1952; d. Leon Mathew and Claire Irene (Morel) Morissette; m. Don Roger Zeitelhack, Sept. 3, 1977. Artist, Tomahawk, Wis., Alto, N.Mex.; owner Many Moons Jewelry Gallery, Ruidoso, N.Mex. Achievements include design of mother of pearl shell landscapes (1st place award in watercolor, artis, music, dance. Home and Office: PO Box 419 Alto NM 88312-0419: Many Moons Jewelry Gallery Time Sq 2501 Sudderth Ruidoso NM 88345 Office Phone: 505-630-9201.

**ZEITLIN, EUGENIA PAWLIK,** librarian, educator, writer; b. N.Y.C., Jan. 29; d. Charles and Pauline (Klimowsz) Pawlik; m. Herbert Zakary Zeitlin, July 3, 1949; children: Mark Clyde, Joyce Therese Zeitlin Harris, Ann Victoria, Clare Katherine. BA in English, Bklyn. Coll., 1945; MA in English, NYU, N.Y.C., 1951; MALS, Rosary Coll., 1968. Teaching credential N.Y., Ariz., Calif.; Ill. English tchr., Sea Cliff, L.I., NY, 1945—47; English, math. tchr. Merrick (N.Y.) Sch. Dist., 1948—49; English tchr. Wilson Sch. Dist., Phoenix, 1949—50; counselor West Phoenix (Ariz.) High Sch., 1953—56; asst. prof. English Wright Coll., Chgo., 1965—66; asst. prof. English, asst. to v.p. curriculum and instrn. Oakton C.C., Des Plaines, Ill., 1970—76; libr. Pasadena City Coll., L.A., 1979—84, L.A. Pub. Libr., 1984—2004; ret., 2004. Contbr. articles to profl. jours. Named Northridge City Employee of Yr., 1986. Mem. AAUW (br. pres. Lancaster, Calif. 1959-60), Thoreau Soc. (life), Beta Phi Mu. Avocations: writing and editing, book collecting. Home: 20124 Phaeton Dr Woodland Hills CA 91364-5633 E-mail: epzeitlin2000@aol.com.

**ZEITLIN, HERBERT ZAKARY,** college administrator, real estate consultant, writer; b. NYC, Jan. 14; s. Leonard and Martha Josephine (Soff) Zeitlin; m. Eugenia F. Pawlik, July 3, 1949; children: Mark Clyde, Joyce Therese Zeitlin Harris, Ann Victoria, Clare Katherine. BS, NYU, 1947, MA, 1949; EdD, Stanford U., 1956. Tchr. Mepham HS, Bellmore, NY, 1946—47, Nassau County Vocat. Edn. Extension Bd., Mineola, NY; electronics instr., adj. faculty Mepham CC; tchr., counselor, dir. testing Phoenix Union HS and Coll. Dist.; dean eve. coll., prin. high sch. Antelope Valley Union HS and Coll. Dist., Lancaster, Calif.; dean instrn. Southwestern Coll., Chula Vista, Calif.; pres., supt., cons. Triton Coll., River Grove, Ill., 1964—79; dean, pres. West LA Coll., 1976-80; pres. Trident Cons., LA, mgmt. cons., 1979—; adj. faculty Ariz. State U., Flagstaff, No. Ill. U., DeKalb, U. Calif., Santa Barbara. Author: Turbulent Birth of Triton College, 2001, Corruption: How to Fight It and Win, 2004, What Makes A Teacher Great?, 2005; editor: in field. Pres. Antelope Valley Breeze & Sage, Bon Vivant Homeowners Assn.; mayor Upper Woodland Hills, Calif. With USAAF, 1942—46. Named Adminstr. of the Yr., Triton Coll. Faculty Assn., 1974, Most Influential Educator in Ill., Chgo. Sun Times; recipient Spl. commendation, Chgo. Tribune, Richard Ogilvie, former Gov. Ill., Spl. Achievement award for visionary accomplishment, Ill. Sch. Adminstrs. Assn. Mem.: Ariz. State Vocat. Assn. (pres.), Ariz. Vocat. Guidance Assn. (pres.), Maywood Ill. Rotary (pres.), Antelope Valley Rotary (pres.). Office: Paramount Properties 21031 Ventura Blvd Woodland Hills CA 91364-1845 Mailing: Trident Cons PO Box 571412 Tarzana CA 91357 Home: 20124 Phacton Dr Woodland Hills CA 91364 Office Phone: 818-999-2030. Personal E-mail: herbertzzeitlin@aol.com. *I always felt that being the president of an organization, having held many presidencies in my lifetime, was like being the quarterback on the football team. You had a choice of running with the ball and taking some bruises or passing it to someone who should score. I was lucky most of the time in selecting some very fine receivers.*

**ZEITLIN, JIDE JAMES,** investor; b. Ibadan, Nigeria; came to U.S., 1976; s. Arnold S. and Marian F. Z. BA, Amherst Coll., 1985; MBA, Harvard U., 1987. Mng. dir. Goldman, Sachs & Co., N.Y.C., 1987—2005, The Keffi Group Ltd., 2006—. Bd. dirs. Affiliated Mgr. Group. Trustee Amherst Coll., Common Ground Cmty., Milton Acad., Montefiore Med. Ctr., Playwrights Horizons, Teach for Am. Office: 767 Fifth Ave 19th Fl New York NY 10153

**ZEITLIN, LAURIE,** printing company executive, information technology executive; BA in Econs., Duke U., 1984; MBA in Fin., U. Pa., 1989. Rsch. asst. Touche Ross & Co., 1985—87; sr. mng. consulting Deloitte & Touche LLP, 1989—95; dir. info. tech., sr. mgr. application devel., v.p. info. tech. Home Depot, Inc., Atllanta, 1995—2003; sr. v.p., chief info. officer Kinko's Inc., Dallas, 2003—. Named one of Premier 100 IT Leaders, Computerworld, 2006. Office: Kinkos 13155 Noel Rd Ste 1600 Dallas TX 75240 Office Phone: 214-550-7020. E-mail: laurie.zeitlin@fedexkinkos.com.*

**ZEITLIN, LOUISE R.,** music educator; arrived in U.S., 1965; d. Gerald Leon and Aideen Natalie Zeitlin; m. James Wilfred Howsmon, Aug. 21, 1988; children: Rachel Elizabeth, Andrew Stuart. MusB, Eastman Sch. Music, 1985; MusM, Yale U., 1987. Mem. faculty Suzuki-Orff Sch., Chgo., 1995—98, Brevard (N.C.) Music Ctr., 1998—2004; tchr. Baldwin Wallace Coll., Berea, Ohio, 2004—. Faculty MacPhail Ctr. Arts, Mpls., 1990—93, Cleve. (Ohio) Inst. Music, 1994—2004, Oberlin (Ohio) Cmty. Music Sch., 2003—04; adj. faculty Carleton Coll., Northfield, Minn., 1991—93; lectr. in field. Musician: Chgo. (Ill.) String Ensemble, Chgo. (Ill.) Philharmonic, Brevard (N.C.) Music Ctr. Orch., Brevard Music Ctr., 1999—, Oberlin Coll. Cmty. Music Sch., 2003. Recipient Tchr. Recognition award, Nat. Found. Advancement Arts, 2003. Mem.: Ohio Viola Soc. (pres. 2000—02), Am. Viola Soc. (sec. 2002—04, bd. dirs. 2001—04). Avocation: figure skating. Office: Baldwin Wallace College 275 Eastland Rd Berea OH 44017

**ZEITLIN, MARILYN AUDREY,** museum director; b. Newark, July 14, 1941; d. Sidney M. and Theresa Feigenblatt) Litchfield; widowed; children: Charles C. Sweedler, Milo Sweedler. Student, Vanderbilt U., 1963-65; AB in Humanities, Harvard U., 1966, MA in Teaching of English, 1967; postgrad., Cornell U., 1971-74. Dir. Ctr. Gallery, Bucknell U., Lewisburg, Pa., 1975-78; Freedman Gallery, Albright Coll., Reading, Pa., 1978-81; Anderson Gallery, Va. Commonwealth U., Richmond, 1981-87; curator, acting co-dir. Contemporary Arts Mus., Houston, 1987-90; exec. dir. Washington Projects for the Arts, 1990-92; dir. Univ. Art Mus., Ariz. State U., Tempe, 1992—. Juror Dallas Mus. of Arts, McKnight Awards, Mpls.; grant evaluator IMS; grant evaluator, panelist NEH; lectr., cons. in field. Editor, contbr. essays to art publs. Bd. dirs. Cultural Alliance Washington; curator, commr. for U.S. for 1995 Venice Biennale. Samuel H. Kress fellow, 1972-73. Mem. Assn. Coll. and Univ. Mus. and Galleries (v.p. 1986-88), Am. Assn. Mus., Coll. Art Assn. (U.S. commr. Venice Biennale 1995). Office: Ariz State U Art Mus PO Box 872911 Tempe AZ 85287-2911

**ZEITLIN, MAURICE,** sociology educator; b. Detroit, Feb. 24, 1935; s. Albert J. and Rose (Goldberg) Zeitlin; m. Marilyn Geller, Mar. 1, 1959; children: Michelle, Carla, Erica. BA cum laude, Wayne State U., 1957; MA, U. Calif., Berkeley, 1960, PhD, 1964. Instr. anthropology and sociology Princeton (N.J.) U., 1961-64; rsch. assoc. Ctr. Internat. Studies, 1962-64; from asst. prof. to assoc. prof. sociology U. Wis., Madison, 1964—70, prof., 1970-77; dir. Ctr. Social Orgn., 1974-76; disting. prof. sociology UCLA, 1977—, rsch. assoc. Inst. Inds. Rels. Vis. prof. polit. sci. and sociology Hebrew U., Jerusalem, 1971—72. Author (with R. Scheer): Cuba: An American Tragedy, 1963, 1964, Revolutionary Politics and the Cuban Working Class, 1967, 1970, The Civil Wars in Chile, 1984; author: (with R. E. Ratcliff) Landlords and Capitalists, 1988, The Large Corporation and Contemporary Classes, 1989; author: (with J. Stepan-Norris) Talking Union, 1996, Left Out: Reds and America's Industrial Unions, 2003; Latin Am. editor: Ramparts mag., 1967—73, editor-in-chief: Political Power and Social Theory, 1980—90; mem. editl. adv. bd. Progressive mag., 1985—96; editor (with J. Petras): Latin America: Reform or Revolution?, 1968, American Society, Inc., 1970, 1977, Father Camilo Torres: Revolutionary Writings, 1972, Classes Class Conflict, and the State, 1980, How Mighty a Force?, 1983, Insurgent Workers: The Origins of Industrial Unionism, 1987. Chmn. Madison Citizens for a Vote on Vietnam, 1967—68, Am. Com. for Chile, 1973—75; mem. exec. bd. U.S. Com. Justice to Latin Am. Polit. Prisoners, 1977—84; mem. exec. com. Calif. Campaign for Econ. Democracy, 1983—86. Co-resident Inaugural Disting. Publ. award in Labor Studies, Soc. for Study Social Problems, 1996; named to Ten Best Censored Stories list, 1978; recipient Project Censored award, Top Censored Story, 1981; Ford Found. fellow, 1965—67, 1970—71, Guggenheim fellow, 1981—82, NSF grantee, 1981, 1982, 1998. Mem.: Internat. Sociol. Assn. (mem. editl. bd. 1977—81), Am. Sociol. Assn. (mem. governing coun. 1977—80, co-recipient Disting. Contbn. Scholarship award in Polit. Sociology 1992, 1996, 2002, The 2004 Max Weber award for an Outstanding Book Published Over the Past Three Years in Orgns., Occupations and Work). Democrat. Jewish. Office: UCLA Dept Sociology 264 Haines Hall Los Angeles CA 90095-1551 Office Phone: 310-825-3968. Business E-mail: zeitlin@soc.ucla.edu. *Personal philosophy: "If I am not for myself who will be? And when I am for myself, what am I?" Hillel, the Elder.*

**ZEKMAN, TERRI MARGARET,** graphic designer; b. Chgo., Sept. 13, 1950; d. Theodore Nathan and Lois (Bernstein) Z.; m. Alan Daniels, Apr. 12, 1980; children: Jesse Logan, Dakota Caitlin. BFA, Washington U., St. Louis, 1971; postgrad, Art Inst. Chgo., 1974-75. Graphic designer (on retainer) greeting cards and related products Recycled Paper Products Co., Chgo., 1970—, Jillson Roberts, Inc., Calif.; apprenticed graphic designer Helmuth, Obata & Kassabaum, St. Louis, 1970-71; graphic designer Container Corp., Chgo., 1971; graphic designer, art dir., photographer Cuerden Advt. Design, Denver, 1971-74; art dir. D'Arcy, McManus & Masius Advt., Chgo., 1975-76; freelance graphic designer Chgo., 1976-77; art dir. Garfield Linn Advt., Chgo., 1977-78; graphic designer Keiser Design Group, Van Noy & Co., Los Angeles, 1978-79; owner and operator graphic design studio Los Angeles,

1979—. Art and photography tchr. Ctr. for Early Edn., L.A., 1996—, Buckley Sch., Sherman Oaks, 1996—; 3d grade tchr. asst., 1999—. Recipient cert. of merit St. Louis Outdoor Poster Contest, 1970, Denver Art Dirs. Club, 1973 Personal E-mail: redzek50@aol.com.

**ZELANTE, THOMAS ANDREW,** lawyer; b. NYC, Nov. 30, 1954; s. Sabino and Rae Zelante; m. Maureen Connors; children: Thomas Andrew Jr., Christopher William. BA, LaSalle Coll., 1976; JD, Seton Hall U., 1979. Bar: NJ 1980. Assoc. atty. Ribis, McCluskey, Short Hills, NJ, 1982—83, Bowkley & Zelante, Randolph, NJ, 1986—. Mem. ethics com. Morris and Sussex counties Supreme Ct. of NJ Dist. X, 1996—2000; town atty. Borough of Victory Gardens, NJ, 2005—; atty. Morristown Zoning Bd. Adjustment, 2006—. Mem. govtl. affairs com. Morris County C. of C., Morristown, mem. infrastructure adv. group, 2004—06; mem. NJ Health Care Facilities Financing Authority, 2002—04; chmn. Morris County Dem. Com., Morristown, 2002—04; mem. Head Start of Morris County, 1998—2003, pres., 2003—04; trustee Ramapo Coll., Mahwah, NJ, 2004—, chmn. bd. trustees, 2005—; commr. Morris County Bd. Taxation, Morristown, 2005—. Mem.: Morris County Bar Assn. (trustee, Cmty. Svc./Pro Bono award (lifetime achievement) 2004). Avocations: golf, travel, ice hockey. Home: 7 Stoneybrook Way Morristown NJ 07960 Office: Bowkley & Zelante 390 Rte 10 West Randolph NJ 07869 Office Phone: 973-361-1500. Office Fax: 973-366-0191.

**ZELASKO, ERIC EDWARD,** music educator; b. Houma, La., Oct. 14, 1978; s. Theodore Edward Zelasko, Jr. and Janet Sue Zelasko. MusB in Edn. Northwestern State U., 2002. Cert. tchr. K-12 instrumental music La., 2005. Band dir. Mulberry Elem. and Greenwood Mid. Schs., Houma, La., 2002—04; Ellender Meml. H.S., Houma, 2004—. Condr. Houma-Terrebonne (La.) Cmty. Band, 2003—. Mem.: NEA, World Assn. Sch. Band Ensembles, Nat. Band Assn., La. Assn. Educators, La. Bandmasters Assn., La. Music Educator Assn., Dist. VII Band Dirs. Assn., Phi Mu Alpha Sinfonia (life; sec. 1997—98). Democrat. Roman Catholic. Avocations: music, theater. Personal E-mail: eric_zelasko@yahoo.com.

**ZELAZNY, CATHERINE,** elementary school educator; d. Edward and Irene R. Zelazny. BS in Edn., Edinboro U., 1971; MEd in Guidance and Counseling, Gannon U., 1974; postgrad., Pa. State U., 1985; postgrad. in Sch. Adminstrn., Edinboro U., 1987. Counselor, math. tchr. Gannondale Home for Girls, Erie, Pa., 1972; tchr. Ft. LeBoeuf Sch. Dist., Waterford, Pa., 1972—77, 1979—86, 1987—, counselor, 1977—78; spl. edn. coord. Edinboro Intermediate Unit # 5, 1978—79. Pvt. practice counselor, Erie, Pa.; mentor to educators, probationary boys, Erie. Author: Teacher Handbook and Parent Handbook, 1987. Logistics/project mgr., coord. Summer Arts Festival, Erie, 1980—85; mem. County Com. for Abuse Prevention, Erie; vice chmn. Erie County Dem. Party, Erie, 2002—06, chmn., 2006—. Recipient Project GIVE award, Pa. Dept. Edn., 1972. Mem.: NEA, Pa. Edn. Assn., Ft. LeBoeuf Edn. Assn. (treas., v.p., pres., mem. grievance com., membership com.), Erie County Hist. Soc., Phi Delta Kappa (v.p.). Avocations: antiques, piano, canoeing, rock climbing, jewelry collecting. Home: 903 W Grandview Blvd Erie PA 16509

**ZELBY, LEON WOLF,** electrical engineer, educator, consultant; b. Sosnowiec, Poland, Mar. 26, 1925; came to U.S., 1946, naturalized, 1951; s. Herszel and Helen (Wajnryb) Zylberberg; m. Rachel Kupfermintz, Dec. 28, 1954; children: Laurie Susan, Andrew Stephen. BSEE, Moore Sch. Elec. Engring., 1956; MS, Calif. Inst. Tech., 1957; PhD, U. Pa., 1961. Registered profl. engr., Pa., Okla. Mem. staff RCA, Hughes R & D Labs., Lincoln Lab., MIT, Sandia Corp., Argonne (Ill.) Nat. Labs., Inst. for Energy Analysis; mem. faculty U. Pa., 1959-67, assoc. prof., 1964-67; assoc. dir. plasma engring. Inst. Direct Energy Conversion, 1962-67; prof. U. Okla., Norman, 1967-95, dir. Sch. Elec. Engring., 1967-71, 1995. Cons. RCA, 1961-67, Moore Sch. Elec. Engring., 1967-68, also pvt. firms. Editor Tech. and Soc. mag., 1990-93; contbr. articles on energy-associated problems and issues to profl. jours. With AUS, 1946-47. Cons. Electrodynamic Corp. fellow Calif. Inst. Tech., 1957, Mpls.-Honeywell fellow U. Pa., 1957-58, Harrison fellow, 1958. Mem. IEEE, Franklin Inst., Sigma Xi, Tau Beta Pi, Eta Kappa Nu, Pi Mu Epsilon, Sigma Tau, Phi Kappa Phi. Home: 1009 Whispering Pines Dr Norman OK 73072-6912 Business E-Mail: zelby@ou.edu. *To learn as much, and to experience as much as possible, without harm to others; read, study, vary professional and recreational activities within constraints of the system.*

**ZELDES, BENJAMIN,** retired optometrist; b. New Britain, Conn., Oct. 23, 1924; m. Edith R. Zeldes. Student, U. Conn., 1945—48; BS, OD, Ill. Coll. Optometry, 1950, postgrad., 1954, Gesell Inst. Child Devel., 1961—62. Pvt. practice, Newington, Conn., 1957—2004; ret., 2004. Optometric cons. Mediplex of Newington and Mediplex of Wethersfield; cons. Hartford (Conn.) Easter Seal Rehab. Ctr., 1970—73, Continuous Progress Ednl. Consultants, 1970—73. Mem. Conn. Comprehensive Health Planning Adv. Coun., 1970—73; mem. adv. bd. Conn. Assn. Children with Perceptual Learning Disabilities, 1966—68; mem. Physicians Task Force on Mental Retardation, 1964—65; chmn. religious sch. Temple Sinai, Newington. Fellow: Am. Acad. Optometry; mem.: Nat. Eye Rsch. Found. (fellow internat. orthokeratology sect.), Hartford County Optometric Assn., Conn. Assn. Optometrists (chmn. ins. com. 1959—76, exec. coun. 1970—82, pres. 1976, commn. on personal health svcs., chmn. children's vision), New Eng. Coun. Optometrists (chmn. ins. com. 1965—84, 1986, pres.), Am. Optometric Assn. (ins. com. 1983—84, key person, polit. action com.), Lions (past pres. Newington dept., chmn. eye rsch.). Home: 107 Lake Shore Blvd Stafford Springs CT 06076

**ZELDIN, KIM S.,** lawyer; b. Springfield, Pa., Nov. 24, 1961; d. Michael Herman and Saydean Zeldin. BA with highest honors, U. Calif., Santa Cruz, 1985; JD cum laude, U. Calif. Hastings Coll. Law, San Francisco, 1988. Bar: Calif. 1988, US Dist. Ct. (no. dist. Calif.) 1988, US Dist. Ct. (ctrl. and ea. dists. Calif.) 1990, US Dist. Ct. (so. dist. Calif.) 2000, Calif. Supreme Ct. 1988. Assoc., sr. counsel Pillsbury Winthrop LLP, San Francisco, 1988—2002; ptnr. Liner Yankelevitz, Sunshine & Regenstreif LLP, 2002—. Bd. mem. San Francisco Women Lawyers, 1994—97. Bd. mem. Pets are Wonderful Support, 2001—02, Breathe Calif., 2006—. Recipient Fair Housing Leadership award, Fair Housing of Marin, Calif., 2003, No. Calif. Super Lawyers award, Super Lawyers Mag., 2004—06. Mem.: ABA, Western Pension and Benefits Conf., French-Am. C. of C., Nat. Assn. Women Bus. Owners, Assn. Trial Lawyers Am., San Francisco Bar Assn., Order of the Coif. Office: Liner Yankelevitz Sunshine Regenstreif LLP 199 Fremont St 20th Fl San Francisco CA 94105 Office Phone: 415-489-7755. Office Fax: 415-489-7701.

**ZELDIN, RICHARD PACKER,** publisher; b. Worcester, Mass., Aug. 7, 1918; s. M. and Virginia (Gealt) Z.; m. Virginia Graves, Nov. 25, 1950; children— Elizabeth Ann, Richard Shepherd. BS, West Chester U., Pa., 1942; grad. exec. program bus. adminstrn., Columbia U., 1966. Gen. mgr. profl. and reference book div. McGraw-Hill Book Co., Inc., 1948-68; v.p., publishing dir. Litton Ednl. Pub. Co., Inc., 1968-70; pres. R.R. Bowker Co., 1970-76, Xerox Coll. Pub., Xerox Individualized Pub., 1976-79; pub. John Wiley & Sons, Inc., 1976-83; v.p. Moseley Assocs. Inc., N.Y.C., 1983—. Sec.-treas. sci., tech. and med. book pubs. group Assn. Am. Pubs., 1966-70; mem. adv. com. combnl. publs. AEC, 1966-70 Author: A Tennis Guide to the USA, 1980, Business Forms on File, 1984, Personal Forms on File, 1984; contbr. Scholarly Publishing, Books, Journals, Publishers and Libraries in the 20th Century, 2002. Served to lt. USNR, 1942-46. Recipient Disting. Alumni award West Chester U., 1974. Mem. Info. Industry Assn. (sec. 1973—), IEEE, Am. Soc. Info. Sci., Soc. for Scholarly Pub. Clubs: Dutch Treat (N.Y.C.), Pubs. Lunch (N.Y.C.). Home: 20 Fairfield Dr Eatontown NJ 07724-3114 Office: Moseley Assocs Inc 342 Madison Ave Rm 1414 New York NY 10173-1423

**ZELEK, CHARLES ANDREW,** program specialist, director; b. Louisville, Ky., Nov. 19, 1970; s. Walter Andrew and Charlotte Anne Zelek. BA in Econs., OH U., 1993; MS in Resource Econs., U. Alaska, Fairbanks, 1997;

PhD in Agrl. Econs., Purdue U., West Lafayette, 2002. Rsch. asst. Purdue U., 1998—2002; state economist USDA/Nat. Resources Conservation Svc., Indpls., 2002—05; program specialist, exec. Washington, 2005—. Sub.-com. chmn. Pres.' Biomass Initiative, Washington, 2003; pres. State Office Employees Assn., Indpls., 2004; co-pres. USDA-Economist Group, Washington, 2006. Contbr. articles to profl. jours. With U.S. Army, 1993—98. Decorated Army Commendation medal. Mem.: Am. Agrl. Econs. Assn. Avocations: running, reading, martial arts, computers.

**ZELEVANSKY, LYNN,** curator; 2 children. Student in art history, NYU. Curator Mus. Modern Art, NYC, 1987—95; named assoc. curator dept. 20th century painting LA County Mus. Art, 1995, assoc. curator modern and contemporary art, curator, dept. head modern and contemporary art. Curator (exhibitions) Sense and Sensibility: Women Artists and Minimalism in the '90s, 1994, Love Forever: Yayoi Kusama 1958-68, 1998—99, Robert Therrian retrospective, 2000, Jasper Johns to Jeff Koons: Four Decades of Art from the Broad Collections, 2001, Keith Renner and Farah Fawcett, 2002, Beyond Geometry: Experiments in Form, 1940s-70s, 2004 (Award for Best Thematic Mus. Show Nationally, Internat. Assn. Art Critics/USA, 2005), many others. Office: LACMA 5905 Wilshire Blvd Los Angeles CA 90036

**ZELIKOW, PHILIP DAVID,** federal official, public policy educator; b. NYC, Sept. 21, 1954; s. Nate and Lee (Landsman) Z.; m. Paige Ellen Partain, May 30, 1982; children: Alexander, Carolyn. BA, U. Redlands, 1977; JD, U. Houston, 1981; MA, Tufts U., 1984, PhD, 1995. Bar: Tex. 1979. Briefing atty. Tex. Ct. Criminal Appeals, Austin, 1979-80; assoc. David Berg and Assocs., P.C., Houston, 1980-84; adj. prof. Naval Postgrad. Sch., Monterey, Calif., 1984-85; fgn. svc. officer US Dept. State, Washington and overseas, 1985-89; dir. European security NSC, White House, Washington, 1989-91; assoc. prof. pub. policy John F. Kennedy Sch. Govt. Harvard U., Cambridge, Mass., 1991-98; Burkett Miller prof. history U. Va., Charlottesville, 1998—, dir. Miller Ctr. Pub. Affairs, 1998—2005; counselor US Dept. State, Washington, 2005—. Mem. Presdl. Fgn. Intelligence Advisory Bd., 2001—03; exec. dir. Nat. Commn. on Terrorist Attacks Upon U.S. (The 9-11 Commn.), 2003—04. Author: Germany United and Europe Transformed, 1995, The Kennedy Tapes, 1997, Essence of Decision, 1999; editor: Why People Don't Trust Government, 1997; commentator: newspapers, TV and radio programs, 1991—. Recipient 1st Pl. in Nation award Moot Ct. Competition, ABA, 1979. Mem. Internat. Inst. for Strategic Studies, Coun. Fgn. Rels., State Bar Tex., Soc. for Historians of Am. Fgn. Rels., Am. Polit. Sci. Assn. Avocations: hiking, skiing, tennis. Office: US Department of State 2201 C Street NW Washington DC 20520

**ZELIN, JEROME,** retired retail executive; b. Bklyn., Dec. 24, 1930; s. Isidore and Ida (Roffman) Z.; m. Muriel Altsher, Dec. 18, 1955; children— Dorothy, Michael, Steven. BS magna cum laude, N.Y.U., 1952. Acct. Seymour Schwartz CPA, 1954-57; partner firm Schwartz, Zelin & Weiss CPAs, N.Y.C., 1958-61; vice chmn., pres., exec. v.p., treas., financial v.p., dir. Unishops, Inc. (retail co.), Jersey City, 1961-74; exec. v.p. Masters, Inc., Westbury, NY, 1974-97; cons. Master's, Inc., Westbury, NY, 1997-2000; ret. Served with AUS, 1952-54. Mem. N.Y. Soc. CPAs, Am. Inst. CPAs, Beta Gamma Sigma, Tau Alpha Omega. Jewish. Home: 6 Maiden Stone Lane Monroe Township NJ 08831 Personal E-mail: jzelin1000@aol.com.

**ZELINSKI, JOSEPH JOHN,** engineering educator, consultant; b. Glen Lyon, Pa., Dec. 30, 1922; s. John Joseph and Lottie Mary (Oshinski) Z.; m. Mildred G. Sirois, July 22, 1946; children: Douglas John, Peter David. BS, Pa. State U., University Park, 1944; PhD, Pa. State U., 1950. Grad. fellow Pa. State U., University Park, 1946—50; project supr. applied physics lab. Johns Hopkins U., Silver Spring, Md., 1950—58; staff scientist Space Tech. Labs. (now TRW, Inc.), Redondo Beach, Calif., 1958—60; head chem. tech. divsn. Ops. Evaluation Group MIT, Cambridge, 1960—62; prin. rsch. scientist Avco Everett Rsch. Lab., Mass., 1962—64; prof. mech. engring. Northeastern U., Boston, 1964—85, prof. emeritus, 1985—; pres. World Edn. Resources, Ltd., Tampa, Fla., 1984—. Cons. Avco Everett Rsch. Lab., 1964-71, Pratt & Whitney Aircraft, East Hartford, Conn., 1966-70, Modern Electric Products and Phys. Scis. Co., Inc., Boston, 1980-82, Morrison, Mahoney and Miller, Boston, 1984; vice-chmn., chmn. exec. com. Univ. Grad. Coun., Northeastern U., Boston, 1980-84, dir. mech. engring. grad. program, 1982-85; del. 4th World Conf. Continuing Engring. Edn., Beijing China People to People, Spokane, Wash., 1989. Contbr. articles to profl. jours. Prin. Confraternity Christian Doctrine, Andover, Mass., 1961-64; pres. Andover Edn. Coun., 1962-64; vice chmn. Dem. Town Com., Boxford, Mass., 1980-84. Lt. (j.g.) USNR, 1943-46, PTO. Mem. AAAS, ASME, Am. Chem. Soc. Democrat. Roman Catholic. Achievements include foreign and domestic patents for coal combustion system for magnetohydrodynamic power generation, for fuel-cooled combustion systems for jet engines flying at high Mach numbers; prediction of optical observables of re-entry vehicles from analysis of decomposition mechanisms of heat-shield materials; invention of high-temperature furnace for production of crystalline graphite; development of a design method for ramjet combustors, liquid fuel-oxygen combustion system for Avco Mark 5 MHD power generator, carbon-air combustion system for lasers. E-mail: jjzelin@bellsouth.net.

**ZELINSKY, DANIEL,** mathematics professor; b. Chgo., Nov. 22, 1922; s. Isaac and Ann (Ruttenberg) Z.; m. Zelda Oser, Sept. 23, 1945; children: Mara Sachs, Paul O., David. BS, U. Chgo., 1941, MS, 1943, PhD, 1946. Rsch. mathematician applied math group Columbia U., N.Y.C., 1944-45; instr. U. Chgo., 1943-44, 46-47; Nat. Rsch. Coun. fellow Inst. Advanced Study, Princeton, NJ, 1947-49; from asst. to assoc. prof. dept. math. Northwestern U., Evanston, Ill., 1949-60, prof., 1960-93, prof. emeritus, 1993—, acting chmn. math. dept., 1959-60, chmn., 1975-78. Vis. prof. U. Calif. Berkeley, 1960, Fla. State U., Tallahassee, 1963, Hebrew U., Jerusalem, 1970-71, 85, others; vis. scholar Tata Inst., 1979; mem. various coms. Northwestern U.; lectr. in field. Author: A First Course in Linear Algebra, 1968, rev. edit., 1973; contbr. articles to profl. jours. Fulbright grantee Kyoto U., 1955-56, grantee NSF, 1958-80; Guggenheim fellow Inst. Advanced Study, 1956-57, Indo-Am. fellow, 1978-79. Fellow AAAS (mem. nominating com. sect. A 1977-80, chmn. elect sect. A 1984-85, chmn. 1985-86, retiring chmn. 1986-87), Am. Math. Soc. (mem. coun. 1961-67, editor Transactions of A.M.S. 1961-67, mem. various coms., mem. editorial bd. Notices of A.M.S. 1983-86, chmn. editorial bds. coms. 1989, chmn. ad hoc com. 1991-92). Jewish. Home: 613 Hunter Rd Wilmette IL 60091-2213 Office: Northwestern U Dept Math Evanston IL 60208-0001 Personal E-mail: d.zelinsky@comcast.net. Business E-Mail: dz@northwestern.edu.

**ZELINSKY, EDWARD ALAN,** law educator; b. Moline, Ill., Nov. 11, 1950; adopted s. Harold and s. Lucille Frances Brotman Zelinsky, s. Morris Zukerman; m. Doris Dronski, June 6, 1971; children: Jacoba Zelinsky Urist, Joshua Ben Brotman, Aaron Simcha Jon, Nathaniel Avi Gideon. BA, Yale Coll., New Haven, Conn., 1972; JD, Yale Law Sch., New Haven, Conn., 1975; MA in Econs., MPhil in Econs., Yale U., New Haven, Conn., 1978. Morris and Annie Trachman prof. law Yeshiva U., Benjamin N. Cardozo Sch. of Law, NYC, 1980—2005. Alderman City New Haven, 1973—87. Home: 1366 Grasso Blvd New Haven CT 06511 Office: Benjamin N Cardozo Sch Law 55 Fifth Ave New York NY 10003 Office Phone: 212-790-0277. Home Fax: 203-787-7441; Office Fax: 212-790-0205. Personal E-mail: zelinsky@prodigy.net. E-mail: zelinsky@yu.edu.

**ZELINSKY, PAUL O.,** illustrator, artist, writer; b. Evanston, Ill., Feb. 14, 1953; s. Daniel and Zelda B. (Oser) Z.; m. Deborah M. Hallen, Dec. 31, 1981; children: Anna H., Rachel L. BA summa cum laude, Yale U., 1974; MFA in Painting, Tyler Sch. Art, 1976. Art instr. San Diego State U., 1976; freelance illustrator/author, 1977—. Illustrator: Emily Upham's Revenge, 1978, How I Hunted the Little Fellows, 1979, The History of Helpless Harry, 1980, What Amanda Saw, 1981, Ralph S. Mouse, 1982, The Song in the Walnut Grove, 1982, The Sun's Asleep Behind the Hill, 1982, Zoo Doings, 1983, Hansel and Gretel, 1984 (Caldecott Honor 1985), The Story of Mrs. Lovewright and Purrless her Cat, 1985, The Random House Book of Humor for Children, 1988, Strider, 1991, The Enchanted Castle, 1992, Dear Mr. Henshaw, 1993,

More Rootabagas, 1993, Swamp Angel, 1994 (Caldecott honor 1995), Five Children and It, 1999, Awful Ogre's Awful Day, 2001, Doodler Doodling, 2004, Toys Got Out, 2006, The Shivers in the Fridge, 2006; illustrator, adapter: The Maid and the Mouse and the Odd-shaped House, 1981, Rumpelstiltskin 1986 (Caldecott medal 1987), Rapunzel, 1997 (Caldecott medal 1998); illustrator, author: The Lion and the Stoat, 1984; illustrator, adapter, designer: The Wheels on the Bus, 1990, Knick-Knack Paddywhack!, 2002. Recipient Boston Globe/Horn Book Honor, 1994, Best Illustrated Book N.Y. Times Book Rev., 1981, 85, 94, 2001, 02, Reading Magic award Parenting Mag., 1990, 94, 2002; runner-up Bologna Ragazzi award 2005, Mazza medallion, 2006. Mem. PEN, Graphic Artists Guild, Author's Guild, Soc. Children's Book Writers and Illustrators, Phi Beta Kappa.

**ZELIS, ROBERT FELIX,** cardiologist, educator; b. Perth Amboy, NJ, Aug. 5, 1939; s. Felix Andrew and Rita Marie (Jurasz) Z.; m. Gail Ann Heelon, Sept. 10, 1960; children: Robert Felix, Kathleen, Karen, David. BS cum laude, U. Mass., 1960; MD with honors, U. Chgo., 1964. Diplomate: Am. Bd. Internal Medicine (cardiovascular disease). Intern, then asst. resident in medicine Beth Israel Hosp., Harvard U. Med. Sch., 1964-66; clin. assoc. (lt. comdr. USPHS) cardiology br. Nat. Heart Inst., NIH, Bethesda, Md., 1966-68; mem. faculty U. Calif. Med. Sch., Davis, 1968-74, asst. assoc. prof. medicine, 1972-74, chief lab. clin. physiology, 1968-74, asst. chief sect. cardiovasc. medicine, 1970-74; prof. medicine and cellular/molecular physiology Milton S. Hershey (Pa.) Med. Ctr., Pa. State U. Coll. Medicine, 1974—, chief divsn. cardiology, 1974-84, dir. cardiology rsch., 1984—. Editor: The Peripheral Circulations, 1975; co-editor: Calcium Blockers, 1982; mem. editorial bd. Annals Internal Medicine, 1976-79, Am. Jour. Physiology, 1976-79, Circulation, 1979-82, Am. Heart Jour., 1980-90, Am. Jour. Cardiology, 1983-86, Jour. Cardiovasc. Pharmacology, 1991-2001, Jour. Am. Coll. Cardiology, 1994-99; contbr. articles to profl. jours. Walter S. Barr fellow, 1960-64; recipient Borden Rsch. award, 1964, Palmer award for Faculty Mentoring Pa. State U., 1997, Disting. Educator award Pa. State U. Coll. Medicine, 2003, Disting. Svc. award U. Chgo. Med. and Biol. Scis. Alumni Assn., 2004. Fellow A.C.P., Am. Coll. Chest Physicians, Am. Coll. Cardiology (gov. Eastern Pa. 1977-80); mem. Am. Fedn. Clin. Research (pres. 1977-78), Am. Soc. Clin. Investigation (nat. council 1981-85, v.p. 1984-85), Am. Physiol. Soc., Assn. Am. Physicians, Assn. Univ. Cardiologists, Am. Soc. Pharmacology and Exptl. Therapeutics, Am. Heart Assn. (nat. fellow councils circulation, arteriosclerosis, clin. cardiology and epidemiology, v.p. for community programs 1979-81, award of merit 1983 v.p., exec. com. Pa. 1976-79, pres. Pa. affiliate 1979-80, Charles T. Mears Humanitarian award 1984), Western Soc. Clin. Research, Sigma Xi, Alpha Omega Alpha, Phi Eta Sigma. Roman Catholic. Home: 815 Verden Dr Hummelstown PA 17036-9700 Office: MS Hershey Med Ctr Cardiology Divsn HO-47 PO Box 850 Hershey PA 17033-0850

**ZELKA, SANDRA LYNN,** finance company executive; b. Albany, N.Y., Apr. 22, 1967; d. Charles Franklin Sherman and Theresa Louise Clark; m. Jeffrey M. Zelka; children: Brandon Michael Mueller, Victoria Kathryn Mueller, Taylor Ann, Nicole Mary. BBA in Acctg., Siena Coll., 1999; MBA in Mgmt. of Info. Sys., SUNY, Albany, 2003. Bookkeeper N.Y. State Troopers PBA, Albany, 1989—96; office adminstr. E. Stewart Jones PLLC, Troy, NY, 1996—2003; auditor PriceWaterhouse Coopers, Albany, 2003—04; fin. specialist Gen. Dynamics, Pittsfield, Mass., 2004—. Cons. N.Y. State Troopers PBA, Albany, 1996—97. Recipient Nat. Leadership award, Nat. Rep. Congl. Com., 2003. Mem.: NAFE, AICPA, Assn. Legal Adminstrs. (pres. Hudson Valley chpt. 2002—03). Roman Catholic. Avocations: gardening, golf, boating, fishing, running. Office: General Dynamics 100 Plastics Ave Pittsfield MA 01201 E-mail: shermmba@hotmail.com.

**ZELL, JOSEPHINE MAY,** retired language educator; b. Harwood, Lancashire, England, Apr. 26, 1934; d. Joseph Henry Howe and Emily Emma Herod; m. Robert Earl, Apr. 17, 1968 (div. Oct. 2002); children: Rosemary, Philip. BA Honors English Lang. and Lit., U. Manchester, Eng., 1955; MA in Latin, U. Wis., 1989. Chair dept. English, Milham Ford Sch., Oxford, England, 1964—68; lectr. English, U. Wis., Milw., 1968—71; tchr. English, Madison (Wis) Met. Sch. Dist., 1977—97; tchr. Latin, West H.S., Madison Sch. Dist., 1992—97. Author: (poetry) The Curtain Rises, 1993. Mem.: AAUW. Methodist. Home: 7001 Havenswood Dr Madison WI 53718

**ZELL, SAMUEL,** transportation leasing company executive; b. Chgo., Sept. 28, 1941; married. BA, U. Mich., 1963, JD, 1966. With Yates Holleb and Michelson, 1966-68; pres. Equity Fin. and Mgmt. Co., 1968—; chmn. Great Am. Mgmt. and Investment Inc., 1981—, also chief exec. officer; also co-chmn. Revco D.S.; chmn. Equity Group Investments, LLC, 1976—. Chmn. Delta Queen Steamboat Co., New Orleans, 1984—, Eagle Industries Inc.; chmn. Itel Corp., 1985—, bd. dirs. Named one of Forbes' Richest Americans, 2006.*

**ZELLER, ANCHARD FREDERIC,** retired psychologist; b. Clayton, N.Mex., Jan. 7, 1918; s. Roland Emil Zeller and Mabel Claire Hefner; m. Elizabeth Jean Uehren, July 9, 1948; children: Elizabeth, Juliana, Carolyn. BS, U. N.Mex., 1941, MA, 1942; PhD, Johns Hopkins U., 1948. Instr. U. N.Mex., Albuquerque, 1944—45; tchg. asst. The Johns Hopkins U., Balt. 1946—47; assoc. prof. U. Tulsa, Okla., 1947—52; aviation psychologist Inspector Gen.'s Office USAF, San Bernardino, Calif., 1952—84, ret., 1984. Lectr. U. So. Calif., L.A., 1953—85. Contbr. articles to profl. jours. Named to Wall of Honor, Nat. Air and Space Mus., 2003; recipient Meritorious Civilian Svc. award, USAF, 1974, Exceptional Civilian Svc. award, 1984. Fellow: Aerospace Med. Assn. (Raymond F. Longacre award 1965, Harry G. Moseley award 1979); mem.: APA, AIAA (sr.), Nat. Assn. Ret. Fed. Employees (pres. chpt. 1988—90). Home: 927 W Clifton Ave Redlands CA 92373

**ZELLER, CHRISTOPHER LEE,** preservation archaeologist; b. Northampton, Pa., Nov. 25, 1956; s. Karl Fredrich and Joan Veron (Hagenbuch) Zeller; m. Christi Joanne Wiggins, Apr. 24, 1982 (div. Mar. 11, 2004); 1 child, Kaeti Grace. BA in Anthropology, Ft. Lewis Coll., 1980. Fireline archaeologist US Forest Svc., cert. ski patroller Nat. Ski Patrol and Assn. Profl. Patrollers, EMT Colo. Preservation tech., foreman San Juan Stabilization, Mancos, Colo., 1977—81; archaeologist Bur. Land Mgmt., Durango, Colo., 1982; preservation specialist Paul Nickens and Assocs., Montrose, Colo., 1983; mil. contractor, preservation specialist Woods Canyon Archaeol. Cons., Yellow Jacket, Colo., 1985—87; mil. contractor, project dir. Four Corners Rsch. Inst., Durango, 1986—87; owner, operator Petro Graphics, Durango, 1987—. Ski patroller Durango Mountain Resort, 1974—83, patrol foreman, 1984—2002, asst. patrol dir., 2003—. Achievements include invention of toboggan platform; conducted over 70 major preservation projects involving over 60 archaeological and historic sites in American Southwest. Avocations: fine art, trout fishing, motorcycle touring. Office: Petro Graphics Po Box 745 Durango CO 81302 Office Phone: 970-799-5146.

**ZELLER, JOSEPH PAUL,** advertising executive; b. Crestline, Ohio, Mar. 19, 1940; s. Paul Edward and Grace Beatrice (Kinstle) Z.; m. Nancy Jane Schmidt, June 17, 1961; children: Laurie, Joe. BA, U. Notre Dame, 1962; MFA, Ohio U., 1963. Mgr.radio/televaion Drewrys Ltd. USA, Inc., South Bend, Ind., 1963-64; media supr. Tatham-Laird & Kudner, Chgo., 1964-67; v.p. assoc. media dir. J. Walter Thompson Co., Chgo., 1967-77; v.p. media dir, v.p. Campbell-Mithun, Chgo., 1977-80; sr. v.p., dir. media, fin., chmn. media coun. D'Arcy Masius Benton & Bowles, Chgo., 1980-96, sr. v.p., 1996-2000; pres. Fox River Trading Co., East Dundee, Ill., 2000—. Chmn. Z Prop, 1986—; dir. circle Desert Caballeros Mus., 1996-96; founder Native Am. Images web mag., 1999. Pres. Amateur Hockey Assn. Ill., 1985. Named to Ill. Hockey Hall of Fame, 2005. Mem. Broadcast Pioneers, Chgo. Advt. Club, Moose. Roman Catholic. Avocations: hockey, photography, music. Business E-Mail: trader@rivertradingpost.com. E-mail: jzeller@prodigy.net.

**ZELLER, MARILYNN KAY,** retired librarian; b. Scottsbluff, Nebr., Mar. 1, 1940; d. William Harold and Dorothy Elizabeth (Wilkins) Richards; m. Robert Jerome Zeller, May 21, 1966; children: Kevin Jerome and Renae Kay.

BS, Calvary Bible Coll., 1985; MLS, U. Mo., Columbia, 1989. Cert. libr. File clk. Waddell & Reed, Kansas City, Mo., 1962-65; payroll clk. Century Fin. Co., Kansas City, Mo., 1965-67, Percy Kent Bag Co., Independence, Mo., 1968-70; accounts receivable Swansons on the Plaza, Kansas City, 1971-73; clk. casualty ins. Mill Mutuals, Kansas City, 1977-80; registrar's asst. Calvary Bible Coll., Kansas City, 1980-85, libr. asst., 1985-88, asst. libr., 1988-89, head libr., 1990—96. Chairperson libr. com. Calvary Bible Coll., Kansas City, 1990-96; libr. rep. Friends of the Hilda Kroeker Libr., Kansas City, 1990-96. Author: History of the Christian Librarian's Association, 1989. Mem. Christian Librs. Assn. Avocations: walking, reading, crocheting, sewing, swimming. Home: 401 13th Ave N Greenwood MO 64034-9750

**ZELLER, MICHAEL EDWARD,** physicist, researcher; b. San Francisco, Oct. 8, 1939; s. Edward Michael and Marie (Eschen) Z.; m. Linda Marie Smith, June 12, 1960; children: Jeffrey, Daniel. BS, Stanford U., 1961; MS, UCLA, 1964, PhD, 1968. Rsch. assoc. UCLA, 1968-69; instr. physics Yale U., New Haven, 1969-70, asst. prof., 1970-76, assoc. prof., 1976-82, prof., 1982—, chmn., 1989-95, Henry Ford II prof., 1996—. Recipient DeVane medal Phi Beta Kappa, 1980. Fellow Am. Phys. Soc.; mem. N.Y. Acad. Sci., Sigma Xi, Sigma Pi Sigma. Democrat. Jewish. Home: 135 Newton Rd Woodbridge CT 06525-1534 Office: Yale U Physics Dept 260 Whitney Ave New Haven CT 06511-8903 Business E-Mail: michael.zeller@yale.edu.

**ZELLER, RONALD JOHN,** lawyer; b. Phila., Jan. 28, 1940; m. Lucille Bell; children: John, Kevin, Suzanne. BSBA, LaSalle Univ., 1964; JD, Ohio State U., 1967. Bar: Mich. 1968, Fla. 1971. Ptnr. Patton & Kanner, Miami, Fla., 1973-80, of counsel, 1980-89; dir., pres., CEO Norwegian Cruise Lines, 1980-86; pres. Twenty First Century Mgmt. Group, Inc., Coconut Grove, Fla., 1986-90, Miami Voice Corp., 1990 92; gen. counsel Splty. Mgmt. Co., Delray Beach, Fla., 1992-93, pres., 1994-96; ptnr. Zeller & Assocs., LLC, Palm Beach, Fla., 1996—; of counsel Koeppel Gottlieb Mesches, 2000—. Dep. chmn. Cruise Lines Internat. Assoc., NYC, 1981-85, chmn., 1986. Trustee United Way Dade County, 1981-86; pres. Cath. Charities, Archdiocese of Miami 1976-78, Broward County, 1975-76, Excalibur Devel. Ctrs., Inc., 1973-75; mem. citizens bd. U. Miami, 1980-92; mem. exec. bd. New World Sch. Arts, 1986-87; mem. centennial campaign com. Ohio State U. Coll. Law, 1982-92, also mem. nat. coun.; mem. coun. Pres.'s Assocs., LaSalle U., 1982-87; mem. Fla. Postsecondary Edn. Planning Commn., 1986-87; mem. Cmty. Assns. Inst., 1995-2000; chmn. exec. com. Maritime Inst., 1997-99; mem. utility rev. bd. Village of Wellington, 1997-98; mem. gen. counsel Palm Beach Maritime Mus., 1997-2005; mem. Fla. com. Affirm Thy Friendship Campaign, Ohio State U., 1997-2000; mem. cruise line incentive com. Port of Palm Beach, 1997-2000; mem. ecumenical rev. bd. Diocese Palm Beach, 2002—03, mem. comm. adv. bd., 2002—. Mem. ABA (sect. taxation, closely held businesses com.), Fla. Bar Assn. (lawyers and CPA's com. 2003-04, long range planning com. 2001-04), Maritime Law Assn. (proctor in admiralty), Pres.' Club Ohio State U. Office: Zeller & Assocs LLC Trump Plz Office Ctr 525 S Flagler Dr Ste 200 West Palm Beach FL 33401 Office Phone: 561-802-4480. Office Fax: 561-802-4387. Business E-Mail: rjzelleresq@bellsouth.net.

**ZELLER, TOM, JR.,** journalist; b. Cleveland, Ohio; BA in English Lit., Cleve. State U., 1997; MS in Journalism, Columbia U., 1998. Editor NY Times Week in Rev., 2000—04; bus., tech. reporter, columnist NY Times, 2004—. Office: New York Times 229 W 43rd St New York NY 10036 Office Phone: 212-556-4679.

**ZELLERBACH, WILLIAM JOSEPH,** retired paper company executive; b. San Francisco, Sept. 15, 1920; s. Harold Lionel and Doris (Joseph) Z.; m. Margery Haber, Feb. 25, 1946; children: John William, Thomas Harold, Charles Ralph, Nancy. BS, Wharton Sch., U. Pa., 1942; grad., Advanced Mgmt. Program, Harvard U., 1958. With Crown Zellerbach Corp. and subs., 1946-85; officer, dir. Crown Zellerbach Corp., Phila., 1960-85. Mem gen. adv. com. fgn. assistance programs AID, 1965-68; chmn. bd. Zellerbach Family Found. Served as lt. USNR, 1942-46. Mem. Nat. Paper trade assn. (pres. 1970) Clubs: Villa Taverna (San Francisco), Presidio Golf (San Francisco), Pacific Union (San Francisco), Commonwealth (San Francisco); Peninsula Country (San Mateo, Calif.). Office: 120 Montgomery St Ste 1960 San Francisco CA 94104-4323

**ZELLERS, ROBERT CHARLES,** materials engineer, consultant, speaker; b. Youngstown, Ohio, June 13, 1943; s. Charles Newton and Beatrice Eleanor (Snavely) Z.; m. Patricia Ann Ockerman, Nov. 27, 1965; children: Derek, Shannon, Robyn. BEng in Civil Engring., Youngstown State U., 1967. Registered profl. engr., Pa., Ohio; registered profl. land surveyor, Pa. Materials engr. Standard Slag Co., Youngstown, 1966-72; asst. chief engr. The Duquesne Slag Co., Pitts., 1972-81; exec. sec. Pa. Slag Assn., Pitts., 1972-81; v.p. engring. Forta Corp., Grove City, Pa., 1978-82, exec. v.p., 1983-97; owner, mgr. Zellers Design Group, Mercer, Pa., 1982—; owner Zellers Galleries, Mercer, 1979—; prin. IMTEK, Grove City, Pa., 1988-91; pres. ICEMS, Toledo, 1992-99; v.p. MIZEL, Crowley, Tex., 1994-97; pres. ZELLCO, Crowley, Tex., 1994-97; v.p. mktg. Fibercon Internat. Inc., 1998-99; dir. tech. and engring. Nycon, Inc., Mercer, 1999—2001, v.p. tech. and engring., 2002—. Presenter in field at confs., seminars and profl. orgn. meetings; profl. speaker; rev. tech. papers. Contbr. articles to profl. jours. Dir. pub. rels. Greenville Symphony Orch. Mem. ASCE, ASTM (various coms.), Constrn. Specifications Inst., Internat. Code Coun., Nat. Ready Mixed Concrete Assn., Fiber Reinforced Concrete Assn. (co-founder, pres. 2004-), Transp. Rsch. Bd., Am. Concrete Inst. (various coms.), Lions. Office: Nycon Inc 102 Latonka Dr Mercer PA 16137-9360 Office Phone: 724-475-3885. Personal E-mail: zzzman13@hotmail.com.

**ZELLNER, ARNOLD,** economics, econometrics and statistics professor; b. Bklyn., Jan. 2, 1927; s. Israel and Doris (Kleiman) Z.; m. Agnes Marie Sumares, June 20, 1953; children— David S., Philip A., Samuel N., Daniel A., Michael A. AB in Physics, Harvard, 1949; PhD in Econs., U. Calif. at Berkeley, 1957; PhD (hon.), Autonomous U. Madrid, 1986, Tech. U. Lisbon, 1991, U. Kiel, 1998, Erasmus U. 2006. Asst., then assoc. prof. econs. U. Wash., 1955-60; Fulbright vis. prof. Netherlands Sch. Econs., Rotterdam, 1960-61; assoc. prof., then prof. econs. U. Wis., 1961-66; H.G.B. Alexander disting. service prof. econs. and statistics U. Chgo., 1966-96, prof. emeritus, 1996—; dir. H.G.B. Alexander Rsch. Found., 1973—. Cons. Battelle Meml. Inst., 1964—71; vis. rsch. prof. U. Calif., Berkeley, 1971, vis. prof., 1997—2006, Am., Cairo, 1997, Hebrew U., 1997; trustee Nat. Opinion Rsch. Corp., 1973—80; bd. dirs. Nat. Bur. Econ. Rsch., 1980—; seminar leader NSF-NBER Seminar on Bayesian Inference in Econometrics and Stats., 1970—95. Co-author: Systems Simulation for Regional Analysis, 1969, Estimating the Parameters of the Markov Probability Model, 1970; author: Bayesian Inference in Econometrics, 1971, Basic Issues in Econometrics, 1984, Bayesian Analysis in Econometrics and Statistics: The Zellner View and Papers, 1997, Statistics, Econometrics and Forecasting, 2004; editor: Economic Statistics and Econometrics, 1968, Seasonal Analysis of Economic Time Series, 1978, Simplicity, Inference and Modelling, 2001; assoc. editor: Econometrica, 1962-68; founding co-editor: Jour. Econometrics, 1972—; co-editor Studies in Bayesian Econometrics and Statistics, 1975, The Economics of Marine Resources, 2001, The Structural Econometrics, Time Series Analysis Approach, 2004; founding editor ASA Jour. Bus. and Econ. Stats., 1983; contbr. articles to profl. jours. Pres. Leonard J. Savage Meml. Trust Fund, Chgo., 1977-2000. Served with AUS, 1951-53. Fellow AAAS, Am. Acad. Arts and Scis., Am. Econ. Assn., Internat. Inst. Forecasters, Econometric Soc., Am. Statis. Assn. (pres. elect 1990—, pres. 1991—, chmn. bus. and econs. sect. 1980, chmn. Bayesian statis. sci. sect. 1993); mem. Internat. Statis. Inst., Internat. Soc. Bayesian Analysis (co-pres. 1993, pres. 1994-96, Founders award 1998), Soc. Actuaries (trustee, rsch. found., 1994-98). Avocations: golf, tennis, travel. Home: 5 Dorchester Ave Chicago IL 60637-1722 Office: U Chgo Grad Sch Bus 5807 S Woodlawn Ave Chicago IL 60637-1511 Office Phone: 773-702-7145. Business E-Mail: arnold.zellner@chicagogsb.edu.

**ZELLNER, RYAN MATTHEW,** music educator; b. Easton, Pa., Oct. 1, 1974; s. Kenneth and Elaine Zellner; m. Sandra Nuss, Aug. 3, 1996; children: Tyler Ryan, Abigail Page. B in Music Edn., Moravian Coll., 1996; MusM, U. of Conn., 1998; MA in Classroom Tech., Wilkes U., 2005, MA in Edn. Leadership and Devel., 2006. Cert. profl. tchr. cert. Pa. Grad. asst. U. of Conn., Storrs, 1996—98; dir. of instrumental activities Tunkhannock (Pa.) Area H.S., 1998—. Mem.: Pa. State Edn. Assn. (assoc.), Pa. Music Educator Assn. (assoc.), Music Educators Nat. Conf. (assoc.), Mensa (assoc.), Omicron Delta Kappa (assoc.), Delta Omicron (assoc.). Office: Tunkhannock Area H A 120 W Tioga St Tunkhannock PA 18657 Office Phone: 570-836-8260. Personal E-mail: ryan.zellner@tasd.net.

**ZELLWEGER, RENEE,** actress; b. Katy, Tex., Apr. 25, 1969; d. Emil Erich Zellweger and Kjellfrid Irene Andreassen; m. Kenny Chesney, May 9, 2005 (annulled Dec. 20, 2005). BA in English, U. Tex., 1991. Actress feature films including Reality Bites, 1994, Love and a .45, 1994, 8 Seconds, 1994, The Low Life, 1995, Empire Records, 1995, The Whole Wide World, 1996, Jerry Maguire, 1996, Texas Chainsaw Massacre: The Next Generation, 1997, Deceiver, 1997, One True Thing, 1998, A Price Above Rubies, 1998, The Bachelor, 1999, Nurse Betty, 2000 (Golden Globe award for best actress in a comedy or musical 2000), Me, Myself & Irene, 2000, Bridget Jones's Diary, 2001 (nominee Best Actress SAG award, Broadcast Film Critics Assn. award, Brit. Acad. Award and Acad. award 2001; Golden Globe award nominee best actress in a comedy or musical, 2001), White Oleander, 2002, Chicago, 2002 (Golden Globe award for best supporting actress in a comedy or musical, 2002, SAG award for Best Actress, 2003, Academy award nominee Best Actress, 2003), Down With Love, 2003, Cold Mountain, 2003 (Golden Globe for best supporting actress, 2004, Screen Actors Guild Award for best supporting actress, 2004, Acad. Award for best supporting actress, 2004), (voice) Shark Tale, 2004, Bridget Jones: The Edge of Reason, 2004, Cinderella Man, 2005; (TV films) A Taste for Killing, 1992, Murder in the Heartland, 1993, Shake, Rattle and Rock 1994. Office: Byant Joel Creative Artists Agy 9830 Wilshire Blvd Beverly Hills CA 90212*

**ZELMAN, PATRICIA GRACE,** history educator; b. Cin., Jan. 15, 1944; d. Louis George and Althea (Moyer) Grace; m. Donald Lewis Zelman, Apr. 29, 1940; 1 child, Julie Grace. BA, U. N.C., 1966; MA, Ohio State U., 1967, PhD, 1980. Instr. Tarleton State U., Stephenville, Tex., 1979-81, asst. prof. history, 1981-88, assoc. prof. history, 1988—; prof. History, 1999—. Author: Women, Work and National Policy: The Kennedy-Johnson Years, 1981. Election judge Erath County Precinct 3, 1981-85, precinct chmn. Dem. Party, 1982-86, 97—. Named Woman of Yr. Erath County Womens Clubs, 1985; NEH fellow Yale U., summer 1989, Pres. teaching fellow Tarleton State U., 1991-92; recipient Jack and Louise Arthur Teaching Excellence award, 1992. Mem. Am. Hist. Assn., Nat. Coun. on History Edn., So. Hist. Assn., Tex. Assn. Coll. Tchrs., Tarleton Faculty Womens Forum (pres. 1987-88), Southern Assn. Women Historians. Democrat. Avocations: bicycling, yoga, gardening. Office: Tarleton State Univ Dept Social Sciences PO Box T 0660 Stephenville TX 76402-0001

**ZELMAN, SUSAN TAVE,** school system administrator; DEd, U. Mich.; D in Pub. Edn. (hon.), U. Rio Grande, Ohio; D in Humanities (hon.), Youngstown U. Assoc. prof. edn. Emmanuel Coll., Boston, chair dept. edn.; assoc commr. ednl. dept. personnel Mo. Dept. Edn., Jefferson City, 1988—94; dep. commr. Mo. Dept. Elem. and Secondary Edn., Jefferson City, 1994—99; supt. pub. instrn. Ohio Dept Edn., Columbus, 1999—. Rschr. Edn. Tech. Ctr. Harvard Grad. Sch. Edn. Recipient Nat. Sci. Rsch. Opportunity award, Columbus Tchrs. Coll. Office: Ohio Dept Edn 25 S Front St Columbus OH 43215-4183

**ZELMANOV, EFIM ISAAKOVICH,** mathematician, educator; b. USSR, Sept. 7, 1955; MS, Novosibirsk State U., 1977, PhD in Math., 1980; doctoral scientist, Leningrad U., St. Petersburg, Russia, 1985. Jr. rschr. Inst. of Math., Acad. of Scis. of USSR, Novosibirsk, 1980-85, sr. rschr., 1985-86, leading rschr., 1986-90; prof. math. U. Wis., Madison 1990-94, U. Chgo., 1994-95, Yale U., New Haven 1995—2002, U. Calif., San Diego, 2002—, Rita L. Atkinson Endowed Chair of Math. Recipient Fields medal Inst. de Matematica Pura e Aplicada, 1994, Coll. de France medal, 1992, Andre Aizenstadt prize, 1996. Mem.: Nat. Acad. Sci. (elected mem. math. dept. 2001).

**ZELMANOWITZ, JULIUS MARTIN,** mathematics professor, academic administrator; b. NYC, Feb. 20, 1941; s. Morris and Tillie (Holtz) Z.; m. Joan R. Traubel, June 24, 1962; 1 child, Dawn Michèle. AB, Harvard U., 1962; MS, U. Wis., 1963, PhD, 1966. From asst. prof. to assoc. prof. U. Calif., Santa Barbara, 1966—77, prof. maths., 1977—, assoc. vice chancellor acad. affairs, 1985-87, assoc. vice chancellor acad. personnel, 1988-98; assoc. prof. Carnegie-Mellon U., Pitts., 1970-71; interim vice provost acad. initiatives U. Calif., 1999-2000, v.p. acad. initiatives, 2000—06, sr. vice provost acad. programs, 2005; dep. dir. Math- Sci. Rsch. Inst., Berkeley, Calif., 2006—. Vis. asst. prof. UCLA, 1969-70, vis. assoc. prof. 1973-74; vis. prof. U. Rome, 1977, McGill U., Montreal, Quebec, 1982-83, 87-88, U. Munich, 1983, 88, U. Calif., Berkeley, 2006. Contbr. articles to profl. jours. Sr. rsch. grantee Italian Nat. Rsch. Coun., Rome, 1977, Palermo, 1988; named Milw. Prof. of Maths. The Technion, Haifa, Israel, 1979; Fulbright sr. fellow, Munich, 1983. Mem. Am. Math. Soc., Math. Assn. Am. Home: 2040 Franklin St # 1407 San Francisco CA 94109-2982 Office: 17 Gauss Way Berkeley CA 94720-5070 Office Phone: 510-643-6040. Business E-Mail: julius.zelmanowitz@ucop.edu. E-mail: jz@msri.org.

**ZELNAK, STEPHEN P., JR.,** construction materials company executive; BS, Ga. Inst. Tech.; M Adminstrv. Sci. and Bus. Adminstrn., U. Ala. With Martin Marietta Corp., Raleigh, NC, 1981—, head aggregates ops., 1982-92, pres. materials group, 1992-93; pres., CEO Martin Marietta Materials, Raleigh, NC, 1993—, chmn. bd. dirs., 1997—. Bd. dir. Beazer Homes USA Inc. Former chmn. NC Citizens for Bus. and Industry. Office: Martin Marietta Materials Inc 2710 Wycliff Rd Raleigh NC 27607*

**ZELNICK, CARL ROBERT,** writer, educator; b. NYC, Aug. 9, 1940; s. David Isadore and Lillian (Ostrow) Z.; m. Pamela Margaret Sharp, Dec. 30, 1967; children: Eva Michal, Dara Yael, Marni Ruth. BS, Cornell U., 1961; LLB, U. Va., 1964. Bar: NY 1965, DC 1966. Law assoc. H. Charles Ephraim, Washington, 1966-67; corr./columnist Anchorage Daily News, 1968-76; assoc. editor Environ. Law Reporter, 1971-72; spl. corr. Christian Sci. Monitor, 1973-77; corr./bur. chief Nat. Pub. Radio, Washington, 1972-76; exec. editor Frost/Nixon Interviews, Washington, 1976-77; dir. news coverage ABC-TV, Washington, 1977-81; dep. bur. chief ABC News, Washington, 1981-82, Moscow bur. chief, corr., 1982-84, Israel corr., 1984-86; ABC News Pentagon corr. Washington, 1986-94; media fellow Hoover Instn., Stanford U., 1998. Mem. Citizens Commn. on Race, 1998—2003; vis. prof. Boston U., 1998—2000, prof., 2000—; prof. dept. journalism, 2002—; rsch. fellow Hoover Instn., 2002—. Author: Backfire—A Reporter Looks at Affirmative Action, 1996, Gore—A Political Life, 1999, Winning Florida: How the Bush Team Fought the Battle, 2000, Swing Dance: Justice O'Connor and the Michigan Muddle, 2004, After Gaza, 2006; contbr. articles to newspapers and mags. Served with USMC, 1964-65. Recipient Gavel awards Am. Bar Assn., 1969, 74, Du Pont award Columbia U. Sch. Journalism, 1984, Emmy award, 1984, 92; rsch. fellow Hoover Inst., 2001—. Mem. Council on Fgn. Relations, Phi Epsilon Pi, Pi Delta Phi. Jewish. Office: Boston U Coll Comm 640 Commonwealth Ave Boston MA 02215-2422 Business E-Mail: bzelnick@bu.edu.

**ZELNICK, RONALD STUART,** surgeon; b. N.Y.C., Dec. 6, 1958; BS, George Washington U., 1980; MD, Albany Med. Coll., 1984. Diplomate Am. Bd. Surgery, Am. Bd. Colon Rectal Surgery. Resident gen. surgery L.I. Jewish Hosp., New Hyde Park, N.Y., 1984-89; fellowship colon and rectal surgery Henry Ford Hosp., Detroit, 1989-90; pvt. practice Jupiter, Fla., 1991—. Fellow ACS, Am. Soc. Colon Rectal Surgeons; mem. Fla. Surg. Soc., Fla. Colon Rectal Surgery Soc. Office: Ste 105 210 Jupiter Lakes Blvd #3105 Jupiter FL 33458

**ZELNICK, STRAUSS,** entertainment company executive; b. Boston, June 26, 1957; s. Allan Zelnick and Elsa Lee Strauss; m. Wendy Belzberg, 1990; children: Cooper, Lucas, Leigh. BA summa cum laude, Wesleyan U., Middletown, Conn., 1979; MBA, Harvard U., 1983, JD cum laude, 1983. Bar: N.Y. 1984. Founder Zelnick Media; dir. internat. TV Columbia Pictures Internat. Corp., N.Y.C., 1983-85, v.p. internat. TV, 1985-86; sr. v.p. corp. devel. Vestron Inc., Stamford, Conn., 1986-87, exec. v.p., 1987, pres., chief oper. officer, 1988-89, Twentieth Century Fox, L.A., 1989-93; pres., CEO Crystal Dynamics, Palo Alto, Calif., 1993-95; pres., CEO, BMG Entertainment N.Am., N.Y.C., 1995-98, BMG Entertainment, N.Y.C., 1998—; nonexec. dir. Reed Elsevier. Trustee Wesleyan U., 1992—; mem. contemporary arts coun. Mus. Modern Art, 1989, Young Pres. Orgn.; chmn. Covenant House Calif., 1992-95; bd. dirs. Covenant House, N.Y.C., 1995-2000. Mem. N.Y. State Bar Assn., Harvard Club, Phi Beta Kappa. Avocations: squash, sailing, skiing.

**ZELON, LAURIE DEE,** judge; b. Durham, NC, Nov. 15, 1952; d. Irving and Doris Miriam (Baker) Z.; m. David L. George, Dec. 30, 1979; children: Jeremy, Daniel. BA in English with distinction, Cornell U., 1974; JD, Harvard U., 1977. Bar: Calif. 1977, US Ct. Appeals (9th cir.) 1978, US Supreme Ct. 1989. Assoc. Beardsley, Hufstedler & Kemble, LA, 1977-81, Hufstedler, Miller, Carlson & Beardsley, LA, 1981-82, ptnr., 1983-88, Hufstedler, Miller, Kaus & Beardsley, LA, 1988-90, Hufstedler, Kaus & Ettinger, LA, 1990-91, Morrison & Foerster, LA, 1991-2000; judge LA Superior Ct., 2000—03; assoc. justice Calif. Ct. Appeal, LA, 2003—. Contbg. author: West's California Litigation Forms: Civil Procedure Before Trial, 1996; editor-in-chief Harvard Civil Rights and Civil Liberties Law Rev., 1976-77 Bd. dirs. NY Civil Liberties Union, 1973-74. Mem. ABA (chmn. young lawyers divsn. pro bono project 1981-83, delivery and pro bono projects com. 1983-85, subgrant competition-subgrant monitoring project 1985-86, chair standing com. on lawyers pub. svc. responsibility 1987-90, chair law firm pro bono project 1989-91, standing com. legal aid and indigent defendants 1991-97, chmn. 1993-97, mem. ho. dels. 1993—, state del. 1998-2006, commn. on ethics 2000 1997-2002, bd. govs. 2006—), Calif. Bar Assn. (bd. dirs. appellate project 1995-2000, chair commn. on access to justice 1997-99), LA County Bar Assn. (trustee 1989-91, v.p. 1992-93, sr. v.p. 1993-94, pres.-elect 1994-95, pres. 1995-96, fed. cts. and practices com. 1984-93, vice chmn. 1987-88, chmn. 1988-89, chmn. judiciary com. 1991-92, chmn. real estate litigation subsect. 1991-92), Women Lawyers Assn. LA, Calif. Women Lawyers Assn. Democrat. Office: Calif Ct of Appeal 2d Appellate Dist 300 S Spring St Los Angeles CA 90013 Business E-Mail: laurie.zelon@jud.ca.gov.

**ZEMANIAN, ARMEN HUMPARTSOUM,** electrical engineer, mathematician; b. Bridgewater, Mass., Apr. 16, 1925; s. Parsegh and Filor (Paparian) Z.; m. Edna Odell Williamson Zemanian, July 12, 1958; children: Peter, Thomas, Lewis, Susan. BEE, CCNY, 1947; ScD in Engring., NYU, 1953; prof. (hon.), Dubna (Russia) U., 1996. Registered profl. engr., N.Y. Tutor CCNY, 1947-48; engr. The Maintenance Co., N.Y.C., 1948-52; from asst. to assoc. prof. NYU, 1952-62; prof. SUNY, Stony Brook, 1962-83, leading prof., 1983-98, distinguished prof., 1998—. Author: Distribution Theory and Transform Analysis, 1965, Generalized Integral Transformations, 1968, Realizability Theory for Continuous Linear Systems, 1972, Infinite Electrical Networks, 1991, Transfiniteness for Graphs, Electrical Networks and Random Walks, 1996; Pristine Transfinite Graphs and Permissive Electrical Networks, 2001, Graphs and Networks: Transfinite and NonStandard, 2004; co-author: Electronics, 1961; co-founder, editor-in-chief emeritus Circuits, Systems and Signal Processing, 1982—. Sr. Faculty fellow NSF, 1975-76; recipient Sci. award Armenian Students Assns. Am., 1982. Fellow IEEE, IEEE Circuits and Systems Soc. (Golden Jubilee medal 2000), Am. Math. Soc., Russian Acad. Natural Scis. (fgn.; Kapitsa Gold medal 1996), Armenian Acad. Scis. (fgn.), Armenian Acad. Engrs. (fgn.), Sigma Xi, Tau Beta Pi, Eta Kappa Nu. Democrat. Office: SUNY Electrical Engring Dept Stony Brook NY 11794-0001 Personal E-mail: aezem@optonline.net. Business E-Mail: zeman@ee.sunysb.edu.

**ZEMECKIS, ROBERT L.,** film director; b. Chgo., May 14, 1952; m. Mary Ellen Trainor (div.), 1 child, Alexander; m. Leslie Harter, Dec. 4, 2001. Student, U. So. Calif. Cinema Sch. Co-owner ImageMovers prodn. co., DarkCastle Entertainment. Dir. (films) I Wanna Hold Your Hand (also writer), 1978, Used Cars, 1980, Romancing the Stone, 1984, Back to the Future (also writer), 1985, Who Framed Roger Rabbit?, 1988, Back to the Future Part II (also writer), 1989, Back to the Future Part III (also writer), 1990, Death Becomes Her (also prodr.), 1992, Forrest Gump, 1994 (Best Dir. Acad. award), Contact, 1996 (TV series episode) Amazing Stories; co-screenwriter 1941, 1979, Trespass (also exec. prodr.), 1992; prodr. (films) Contact, 1997, (TV series) Johnny Bago, 1993, The House on Haunted Hill, 1999, Thirteen Ghosts, 2001, Ritual, 2001, Ghost Ship, 2002, Gothika, 2003, House of Wax, 2005, The Prize Winner of Defiance, Ohio, 2005; exec. prodr. (films) The Public Eye, 1992, Tales from the Crypt Presents: Demon Knight, 1995, The Frighteners, 1996, Tales from the Crypt Presents: Bordello of Blood, 1996 (also writer), The 20th Century: The Pursuit of Happiness, 1999 (TV), Matchstick Men, 2003, Last Holiday, 2006, Monster House, 2006, (TV series) Tales from the Crypt, 1989, W.E.I.R.D. World, 1995, Perversions of Science, 1997; writer (films) 1941, 1979, Used Cars, 1980; TV guest appearances include Parker Lewis Can't Lose, 1990; prodr., dir. What Lies Beaneath, 2000, Cast Away, 2000, The Polar Express, 2004. Mem. bd. councilors U. So. Calif. Sch. Cinema-TV. Mem. Dirs. Guild Am. Office: care of Semel Rennert & Feldman 1880 Century Park E Ste 900 Los Angeles CA 90067-1609 also: Creative Artists Agy c/o Karen Sage 9830 Wilshire Blvd Beverly Hills CA 90212-1804 also: South Side Amusement Bugalow 127 100 Universal City Plz Universal City CA 91608-1002*

**ZEMLICKA, JIRI,** medical educator, researcher; b. Prague, Czech Republic, July 31, 1933; arrived in U.S., 1968; s. Vojtech Zemlicka and Otilie Zemlickova; m. Helena Zvarova, Mar. 30, 1961; children: Helena, George. MS, Charles U., Prague, 1956, Rerum Naturarum Dr., 1966; PhD, Czech Acad. Scis., Prague, 1959. Rsch. scientist Czech Acad. Scis., Prague, 1959—69; vis. scientist Mich. Cancer Found., Detroit, 1968—69, rsch. scientist, 1969—83, mem., 1983—94, Karmanos Cancer Inst., Detroit, 1994—. Assoc. prof. Wayne State U., Detroit, 1971—85, prof., 1985—; cons. Microbiotix, Inc., Worcester, Mass., 2002, Therapeutic Sys. Rsch. Labs., Inc., Ann Arbor, Mich., 2005—. Mem. editl. bd.: Nucleosides, Nucleotides & Nucleic Acids, 1982—, Antiviral Chemistry and Chemotherapy, 2000—; contbr. chapters to books, articles to profl. jours. Grantee, NIH, 1972—81, 1984—. Mem.: Internat. Soc. for Antiviral Rsch., Internat. Soc. for Nucleosides, Nucleotides and Nucleic Acids, Am. Chem. Soc. Achievements include patents in field. Home: 2025 Common Warren MI 48092 Office: Karmanos Cancer Inst 110 E Warren Ave Detroit MI 48201-1379 Business E-Mail: zemlicka@kci.wayne.edu.

**ZEMM, SANDRA PHYLLIS,** lawyer; b. Chgo., Aug. 18, 1947; d. Walter Stanley and Bernice Phyllis (Churas) Z. St. U., Ill., 1969; JD, Fla. State U., 1974. Bar: Fla. 74, Ill. 75. With fin. dept. Sinclair Oil, Chgo., 1969-70; indsl. rels. advisor Conco Inc., Mendota, Ill., 1970-72; assoc. Seyfarth, Shaw, Fairweather & Geraldson, Chgo., 1975-82, ptnr., 1982—. Mem. Art Inst. Alliance, Chgo., 1993—; bd. dirs. Chgo. Residential Ins., 1993—97, pres., 1995—97. Mem. Ill. State Bar Assn., Fla. State Bar Assn., Univ. Club Chgo. (bd. dirs. 1991-94); Nat. Coll. of Labor and Employment Lawyers. Office: Seyfarth Shaw LLP 55 E Monroe St Ste 4200 Chicago IL 60603-5863

**ZEMON, STACY J.,** disc jockey, writer, small business owner; b. Manhattan, NY, Aug. 21, 1960; d. Robert R. Zemon and Gloria B. Goodman. Dj/emcee Stacy Zemon Entertainment, Phila., 2003—; reporter Disc Jockey News Network, 2004—; ptnr. DJ Camp, Tucson, 2005—. Sales, mktg. & success cons., 1997—; DJ Times' Internat. DJ Expo DJ of Yr. competitions, Atlantic City, 1998—; spkr. Internat. DJ Expo Mobile Beat Show & Conf., Mid-America DJ Conv. Author: (books) The Mobile DJ Handbook, The DJ Sales & Marketing Handbook. Recipient Alternatives Cmty. Svc. award for contbg. to artistic & cultural life of cmty., 1991, Recognition award for producing Cabaret 1991-93, Project 100, 1993. Mem.: Am. Disc Jockey Assn.

(leadership coun. 2005—06). Achievements include originating a ground-breaking company by partnering with a national broadcasting group to form a mobile DJ entertainment division at a chain of radio stations, an industry-first. Avocations: travel, reading, music. Personal E-mail: djstacyz@aol.com.

**ZEN, E-AN,** research geologist, educator; b. Peking, China, May 31, 1928; came to U.S., 1946, naturalized, 1963; s. Hung-chun and Heng-chi'h (Chen) Z. AB, Cornell U., 1951; MA, Harvard U., 1952, PhD, 1955. Rsch. fellow Woods Hole Oceanographic Inst., 1955-56, rsch. assoc., 1956-58; asst. prof. U. N.C., 1958-59; geologist U.S. Geol. Survey, 1959-80, rsch. geologist, 1981-89, scientist emeritus, 1990—; sr. scientist Va. Mus. Natural History. Adj. prof. geology U Md., 1990—; vis. assoc. prof. Calif. Inst. Tech., 1962; Crosby vis. prof. MIT, 1973; Harry H. Hess sr. vis. fellow Princeton U., 1981; counselor 28th Internat. Geol. Congress. Mem. editl. bd. Contbr. articles to profl. jours. Recipient Maj. John Coke medal Geol. Soc. London, 1992, Outstanding Contbn. to Pub. Understanding of Geology award Am. Geol. Inst., 1994, Thomas Jefferson medal Va. Mus. Natural History Found., 1996. Fellow: AAAS, Mineral Soc. Am. (coun. 1975—77, pres. 1975—76, Roebling medal 1991), Geol. Soc. Am. (councillor 1985—88, v.p. 1991, ores. 1992, Day medal 1986), Am. Acad. Arts and Scis.; mem.: NAS, Geol. Soc. Washington (pres. 1973), Va. Mus. Natural History (sr. scientist). Office: U Md Dept Geology College Park MD 20742-0001

**ZENDLE, HOWARD MARK,** systems engineer, researcher; b. Binghamton, N.Y., June 8, 1949; s. Abraham and Evelyn (Hershowitz) Z. BA in Physics summa cum laude, SUNY, Binghamton, 1972, MA in Physics, 1976; MSEE, Syracuse U., 1987. With IBM, Owego, NY, 1974—94, staff programmer, 1978-83, mgr. microprocessor application software, 1979-81, mgr. tactical avionics software, 1981-82, adv. programmer, 1983-86, sr. programmer, 1986-94, Loral, Owego, NY, 1994-96, Lockheed Martin, Owego, NY, 1996—2005, sys. engr. sr. staff, 2005—. Mem. Fed. Sector div. Mktg. Conf. IBM, 1991. Sec. Men's Club Beth David Synagogue, Binghamton, 1984-85, v.p., 1986-88; bd. dirs. Jewish Cmty. Ctr., Binghamton, 1983-86. Mem. IEEE, Assn. Computing Machinery, Ctrl. Electric Railfan's Assn., Linklaen Assembly, Masons, Phi Beta Kappa, Sigma Pi Sigma. Republican. Avocations: railfanning, history. Home: 5 Leigh St Johnson City NY 13790-1608 Office: Lockheed Martin 1801 State Route 17C Owego NY 13827-3998 Office Phone: 607-751-2625. Personal E-mail: hzendle@stny.rr.com.

**ZENG, EDDY YONGPING,** chemist; b. Guangzhou, China, Jan. 11, 1960; came to U.S., 1986; s. Li and Qiuzhen (Zhou) Zeng. BS, U. Sci. and Tech. of China, Heifei, 1982; MS, Zhongshan U., Guangzhou, China, 1985; MA, U. So. Calif., L.A., 1989, PhD, 1991. Rsch./tchg. asst. dept. chemistry U. So. Calif., L.A., 1986-90; chemist Enviropro, Inc., Chatsworth, Calif., 1990-92; prin. scientist So. Calif. Coastal Water Rsch. Project, Westminster, 1992—. Lectr. dept. chemistry Zhongshen U., 1985-86; adj. prof. State Key Lab. of Organic Geochemistry, Guangzhou, 1998—. Contbr. articles to profl. jours. Mem. Am. Chem. Soc., So. Calif. Environ. Chemist Soc. (pres. 1997-98), Soc. of Environ. Texicology and Chemistry (bd. dirs. So. Calif. chpt. 1999—). Office: So Calif Coastal Water Rsch Project 7171 Fenwick Ln Westminster CA 92683-5218 Home: 6218 Adobe Cir Irvine CA 92617-3199 E-mail: ypzeng@yahoo.com.

**ZENG, FANXING,** chemist; arrived in U.S., 1999; d. Qingkai Zeng and Ruqin Shan; m. Yulong Li, Jan. 17, 1997; 1 child, Kevin Zeng Li. BS, Nanjing U. Sci. and Tech., 1993; PhD, Chinese Acad. Scis., 1999. Rsch. assoc. Shanghai (China) Inst. Materia Medica Chinese Acad. Scis., 1996—99; postdoc. fellow Purdue U., West Lafayette, Ind., 1999—2002, Ga. Inst. Tech., Atlanta, 2002—03; sr. rsch. assoc. Emory U., Atlanta, 2003—. Co-author: Handbook of Organopalladium Chemistry for Organic Synthesis, 2002, Encyclopedia of Reagents for Organic Synthesis, 2003; contbr. articles to profl. jours. Recipient Excellent Grad. Student award, Nanjing U. Sci. and Tech., 1996, P&G prize, Chinese Acad. Scis., 1999, Diao awards 1998, 1999, Rsch. Accomplishments award, Purdue U., 2002. Mem.: Soc. Nuclear Medicine, Am. Chemical Soc., Am. Inst. Chemists, Am. Assn. Advancement Sci., Sigma Xi. Achievements include development of general method for the synthesis of conjugated oligoenes involving Pd-catalyzed cross coupling, and completed the synthesis of Vitamin A, beta Carotene, r-Carotene, and the polyene subunits; completed the synthesis and characterization of several chain-extended bismaleimides; completed the design, synthesis and pharmacological assay of several new types of AChE inhibitors-(+)-14-Fluorohuperzine A and Huperzine A-E2020 combined compound; development and evaluation of PET imaging agents for neurodegenerative diseases. Office: Dept Radiology Emory Univ 1364 Clifton Road NE Atlanta GA 30322 Home: 11155 Thames Ln Suwanee GA 30024 Office Phone: 404-727-1365. Personal E-mail: zengfanxing1@yahoo.com. Business E-Mail: fzeng@emory.edu.

**ZENG, HONG,** audio system architect, researcher; b. Changchun, Jilin, China, Feb. 20, 1958; arrived in France, 1990; s. Peiwei Zeng and Shige Chen; m. Yuzhi Guo, Jan. 14, 1983 (div. Nov. 2000); 1 child, Yu; m. Jie Li, Aug. 8, 2001; 2 children: Aisling, Elaine. B in Elec. Engring., Changchun Coll. Geology; M in Elec. Engring., U. Pierre & Marie Curie, Paris, 1991, D in Physics, 1996. Asst. engr. Hangzhou (China) Applied Acoustics Rsch. Inst., 1982-85, rsch. engr., dir. magnetic signal processing sect., 1985-90; rsch. engr. French Nat. Sci. Rsch. Ctr., Paris, 1990-95; sys. engr. O1dB Co., Lyon, France, 1995-98; sr. software engr., project team leader ATI Technologies, Inc., Toronto, 1998-2001; audio sys. arch. ViXS Sys. Inc., Toronto, 2001—. Contbr. articles to profl. jours.; inventor in field. Recipient Sci. and Tech. award China Shipbuilding Industry Corp., Beijing, 1989. Mem. IEEE. Home: 815 Grandview Way Toronto ON Canada M2N 6V5 Office: ViXS Systems Inc 2235 Sheppard Ave E # 1705 Toronto ON Canada M2J 5B5 E-mail: hongzeng@hotmail.com.

**ZENG, HONGLIU HENRY,** geophysicist, geologist; b. Ningdu, Jiangxi, China, Jan. 5, 1957; arrived in U.S., 1989; s. Zhikang Zeng and Lianrong Chen; m. Yan Phoebe Yang, Feb. 4, 1986; children: Luying, Leo. BA, U. Petroleum, Dongying, 1982, MA, 1985; PhD, U. Tex., 1994. Advanced geoscientist Texaco Inc., New Orleans, 1994—96; rsch. scientist Bur. Econ. Geology, Jackson Sch. Geosci., U. Tex., Austin, 1997—. Lectr. U. Petroleum, Beijing, 1995—99. Contbr. articles to profl. jours. Mem.: Soc. Exploration Geophysicists, Am. Assn. Petroleum Geologists (Wallace E. Pratt Meml. award 2005). Achievements include invention of stratal slicing, a 3-D seismic data interpretation technique; Seismic frequency control on seismic stratigraphy, a seismic data interpretation theory; research in seismic sedimentology, seismic stratigraphy, reservoir characterization, and special seismic processing, as applied to petroleum prospecting. Office: Bur Econ Geology Bldg 130 10100 Burnet Rd Austin TX 78758-4445 Office Phone: 512-475-6382. Business E-Mail: hongliu.zeng@beg.utexas.edu.

**ZENG, MING,** molecular biologist, researcher; b. Dajishan, China, Sept. 8, 1968; s. Guangjun Zeng and Jinyu Liao; m. Elena O. Martsen; children: Katherine, Andrew. BS, Beijing Normal U., 1990; grad., Peking Uion Med. Coll., Beijing, 1993. Rschr. Duke U. Med. Ctr./Howard Hughes Med. Inst., NC, 1997—2001; scientist Schering Plough Rsch. Inst., Kenilworth, NJ, 2001—05, Attagene Inc., NC, 2005—. Vis. scientist Tampa Bay Rsch. Inst., Fla., 1993—96. Rschr. Beijing Normal U./Beijing Tchg. U., 1998. Achievements include research in drug target identification; nitric oxide biology. Home: 304 New Parkside Dr Chapel Hill NC 27516-1162 Office Phone: 919-313-0167. E-mail: mzen2000@hotmail.com.

**ZENGER, JOHN HANCOCK,** training company executive; b. Salt Lake City, Nov. 13, 1931; s. John H. and L. (Hancock) Z.; m. Dixie Robison, June 1, 1955 (div. 1978); children: Mark R., Robin, Todd R., Blake R., Mitchell R., Drew R.; m. Holly Olsen, June 29, 1979; stepchildren: Roger, Kirk, Lori, Michael. BS, Brigham Young U., 1955; MBA, UCLA, 1957; DBA, U. So. Calif., 1963. Asst. prof. Grad Sch. Bus. U. So. Calif., L.A., 1966—67; exec. v.p. Blanfield-Smith and Co., Pasadena, Calif., 1965—67; sr. v.p. human

resources Syntex Corp., Palo Alto, Calif., 1967—77; pres. Zenger-Miller Inc., Cupertino, Calif., 1977—92; group v.p. Times Mirror Co., San Jose, 1992—97; pres., CEO Provant, Inc.; CEO Zenger Folkman Corp., 2003—. Chmn. Palo Alto Human Rels. Coun., 1961-66; trustee Utah Valley State Coll., chmn., 2003-04; pres. Midway Boosters, Inc. Ford Found. fellow, 1962-63; recipient Disting. Svc. award Brigham Young U., 1983; named to Human Resources Devel. Hall of Fame, 1994. Mem. Brigham Young U. Alumni Assn. (pres. 1981). Independent. Mem. Lds Ch. Avocation: magic. Home: 275 Luzern Rd Midway UT 84049-1268 Office Phone: 801-705-9494. E-mail: jzenger@zfcorp.com.

**ZENKOVSKY, BETTY JEAN,** modern languages educator; b. Mankato, Minn., Mar. 6, 1927; d. William and Sarah (Cloyd) Bubbers; m. Serge A. Zenkovsky, May 10, 1952. AB in Russian, U. Mich., 1950; AM in Slavic Studies, Ind. U., 1954; postgrad., Radcliffe U., 1956—58. Instr. modern langs. Stetson U., DeLand, Fla., 1958—60, asst. prof., 1962—65; instr. fgn. langs. U. Colo., Boulder, 1960—62; vis. lectr. Russian, Vanderbilt U., Nashville, 1967—68; rsch. assoc., translator NEH, DeLand, 1978—82. Co-translator: The Nikonian Chronicle, (5 vols.), 1984, 86, 88, 89. Grace Hill fellow, Radcliffe Grad. Sch., 1957—58. Mem. AAUW (pres. DeLand chpr. 1982-84, sec. Daytona Beach chpt. 1984-86), DAR (chpt. James Ormond br, vice regent, 1988-89), Am. Assn. Advancement Slavic Studies, Am. Assn. Tchrs. Slavic and Ea. European Langs., UN Assn., So. Conf. Slavic Studies, Tiger Bay Club of Volusia County, St. Barbara's Philoptochos. Democrat. Greek Orthodox. Home: 1224 S Peninsula Dr Apt 507 Daytona Beach FL 32118-4861 Home Fax: 386-253-3540. Personal E-mail: bjzenk@aol.com.

**ZENNER, SHELDON TOBY,** lawyer; b. Chgo., Jan. 11, 1953; s. Max and Clara (Goldner) Z.; m. Ellen June Morgan, Sept. 2, 1984; children: Elie, Nathaniel. BA, Northwestern U., 1974, JD, 1978. Bar: U.S. Dist. Ct. (no. dist.) Ill. 1978. Assoc. Shadur, Krupp & Miller, Chgo., 1978-80; law clk. to judge U.S. Dist. Ct. (no. dist.) Ill., Chgo., 1980-81; asst. U.S. atty., dep. chief spl. prosecutions div. No. Dist. of Ill., Chgo., 1981-89; ptnr. Katten Muchin Rosenman LLP, Chgo., 1989—. Adj. faculty Medill Sch. Journalism, Northwestern U., 1982-89, Sch. of Law, 1986—; mem. practitioners adv. com. U.S. Sentencing Commn.; mem. editl. adv. bd. Northwestern U. Magazine. Mem. Phi Beta Kappa. Office: Katten Muchin Rosenman LLP 525 W Monroe St Chicago IL 60661-3693 Office Phone: 312-902-5476. Business E-Mail: sheldon.zenner@kattenlaw.com.

**ZENNI, ELISA ALTER,** pediatrician; m. Martin M. Zenni. MD, Tufts U., Boston, 1989. Asst. prof. pediat. Sch. Medicine Stanford U., Palo Alto, Calif., 1993—95; assoc. prof. pediat. Coll. Medicine U. Fla., Jacksonville, Fla., 1995—. Office: Univ Florida Coll Medicine Jacksonville 653-1 West 8th Street Jacksonville FL 32209 Office Phone: 904-244-3140. Office Fax: 904-244-4771.

**ZENNSTRÖM, NIKLAS,** Internet company executive, entrepreneur; married. Dual degree in Bus. Adminstrn. and MSc Engring. Physics, Computer Sci., Uppsala U., Sweden; attended, U. Mich., Ann Arbor. With Tele2, ATT-Unisource; various bus. develop. roles get2net; various bus. develop. roles, CEO everyday.com; co-founder, CEO KaZaA, 2002—; founder, CEO Joltid, 2002—; co-founder Altnet, 2002—; co-founder, CEO Skype Technologies S.A., Luxenburg, 2003—. Spkr. in field. Named one of 100 Most Influential People, Time mag., 2006. Avocations: sailing, skiing, outdoor activities and travelling. Office: Skype Technologies SA 130 Shaftesbury Ave London W1D 5EU England*

**ZENTAY, JOHN H.,** lawyer; AB cum laude, Harvard Univ., 1953, LLB, 1958. Bar: Mo. 1958, DC 1966, US Supreme Ct. 1962. Legis. asst. to U.S. Senator Stuart Symington, Mo., 1958—62; mem. legis. staff AID, U.S. Dept. of State, 1963—66; cons. Bureau of the Budget, Washington, 1967—68; ptnr. Verner Liipfert Bernhard McPherson & Hand, Washington; ptnr., chmn. Fed. Affairs & Legis. practice group DLA Piper Rudnick Gray Cary, Washington, 2002—. Mem. adv. com. on revision of rules of practice & procedure FERC, Washington, 1979—81. Bd. dir. Found. for Nat. Archives; trustee George C. Marshall Found.; chmn. fin. com. Nat. Protestant Episcopal Cathedral; bd. mem. Beauvoir Sch.; mem. long range planning com. St. Albans Sch.; mem. bd. mgr. Historical Soc. of Washington; bd. mem. Children's Hosp. Nat. Med. Ctr. Served U.S. Army, 1953—55. Office: DLA Piper Rudnick Gray Cary 1200 19th St NW Washington DC 20036-2412 Office Phone: 202-861-6449. Office Fax: 202-689-8563. Business E-Mail: john.zentay@dlapiper.com.

**ZENTZ, PATRICK JAMES,** artist, rancher; b. Cando, N.D., Jan. 22, 1947; s. Clifford Wayne and Sybil Mae (Dehrer) Z.; m. Susan Grace Hedley, Dec. 7, 1968; children: Keenan, Jesse, Tyson. BA in Biology, Westmont Coll., 1969; MFA in Sculpture, U. Mont., 1974. Juror Nev. State Coun. on the Arts Grants Program, Las Vegas, 1989, Nev. State Coun. on the Arts, Artists Fellowship Program, Reno, 1990, Wash State Commn. on the Arts, Olympia, 1992; artist adv. task force Western States Arts Fedn., Portland, 1991; del. Japan-Am. Grassroots Summit, Tokyo and Kyoto, Japan; vis. artist program U. Ill., Carbondale, 1994, Oxbow Sch., Napa, Calif., 1999, U. Idaho, Moscow, 2003; lectr. in field. Exhibited in group shows Western State Arts Found., Bklyn. Mus., 1986, No. Ariz. U., 1987, Mont. State U., 1987, Washington Project for the Arts, 1987, Curtis Ctr., Phila., 1987, Aspen Art Mus., 1988, Missoula Mus. of the Arts, 1989, Beall Park Art Ctr., Bozeman, Mont., 1989, John Michael Kohler Art Ctr., 1989, Henry Art Gallery, U. Wash., Seattle, 1989, Seattle Art Mus., 1989, The Ctr. on Contemporary Art, Seattle, 1990, Hockaday Ctr. for the Arts, Kalispell, Mont., Contemporary Arts Mus., Houston, 1990, Boulder Art Ctr., 1991, U. Mont., 1992, Beam Art Gallery, U. Nev., 1992, Internat. Sculpture Ctr., Phila., 1992, Cheney Cowles Mus., Spokane, Wash., 1994, San Antonio Mus. of Art, 1994, Rubelle & Norman Schaffer Gallery, Pratt Inst., Bklyn., 1994, Boise Art Mus., 1995, Neuberger Mus. of Art, SUNY, Purchase, 1997, Sheppard Gallery, U. Nev., Reno, 1998, Tarble Art Ctr., Ea. Ill. U., 1998, McAllen (Tex.) Internat. Mus., 1999, Yellowstone Art Mus., Billings, Mont., 1999, Miami U., Oxford, Ohio, Suyama Space, Seattle, 1999, Mont. State U. Sch. Arch., Bozeman, 2000, U. Mont. Mus. Art and Culture, Missoula, 2000, Oates Park Art Ctr., Fallon, Nev., 2001, Paris Gibson Sq. Mus., Grant Falls, Mont., 2002; represented in permanent collections U. Med. Ctr. U. Wash., Seattle, 1990, Richard Tam Alumni Ctr. U. Nev., Las Vegas, 1991, Snake River Correctional Instn., Ontario, Oreg., 1993, Yellowstone Art Mus., Billings, Mont., 1992, Western State Hosp., Ft. Steilecom, Wash., 1993, Salt Palace, Salt Lake City, 1994, TRI-MET Westside Light Rail Sys., Portland, 1995, Mus. of Fine Art, U. Mont., Missoula, 1997, FDA, College Park, Md., 1999, Edgewood Coll., Madison, Wis., 1999, Miami U., Oxford, Ohio, Reno/Sparks Conv. Ctr., Wash. State U., Spokane, Boise City Arts Commn., Idaho, U. Mont. Recreational Ctr., Missoula, 2003, Cultural Devel. Authority, King Co., Seattle, 2003, Boise City Arts Comm. Watershed Project, Idaho. Grantee Art Matters, Inc., 1988, LEF Found., 1992; fellow Nat. Endowment for the Arts, 1990, Olympic Coll., Bremerton, Wash., 2005. E-mail: patrickz@180com.net.

**ZEOLLA, KIM ANNE,** minister; b. Pitts., Jan. 21, 1961; d. Edward William Logue and Melody Joy Long; m. Allen Lee Zeolla, Sept. 8, 1984; children: April Nicole, Daniel Nicholas, Jonathan Michael. Student, Dayspring Bible Sch., 1982—84; grad., Greater Works Outreach Bible Sch., Monroeville, Pa., 2006. Min. women's groups, retreats, outreach, families, 1998—. V.p. min. develop., exec. bd. Murrysville Aglow Lighthouse, Murrysville, Pa., 2003—05; prayer chairperson Pure Freedom (abstinence retreat), 2004, Capital Stewardship Campaign, Cornerstone Ministries Pa., 2005—; coord. Cornerstone Min., Drug Awareness Seminar, Export, Pa., 2004; founder, min. Expressions of Love, Pitts., 1998—; ministry team' chair Healing and Prophetic Conf., Latter Glory Ministries, Pa., 2005—; prayer co-chair Capital Stewardship Campaign, Cornerstone Min., 2005—; team leader Murrysville Aglow Cmty. Outreach, 2004; min. Peek 'N Peak Resort Aglow Conf., N.Y.C., 2006; mem. pastors gathering Harmony Zelionople United Meth. Ch., 2005; spkr. in field; asst. to worship and drama leader Peek'N Peak Resort and Conf. Ctr., Findley Lake, NY, 2006; prophetic evangelistic leader Expressions of Love Outreach, Pitts., 2005. Judge fine arts Assemblies of God, Pa. and

Del., 2001—; deaf interpreter Our Lady of Joy C.C.D. Class, Plum Boro, Pa., 2002—04; vol. ARC, Pitts., 2004; team leader Murrysville Aglow Cmty. Outreach, 2004; vol. ARC Disaster Relief, 2004; bd. dir. Latter Glory Ministries, India and USA, 2005—; choreographer March for Jesus, Pitts., 1997—98; leadership United for Christ Marriage Ministry, Pitts., 1988—94, Dayspring Christian Ctr., Pitts., 1988—99; jr./sr. high new life bible study tchr. Pitts., 1995—2003; fin. sec. Murrysville Aglow Lighthouse, 2002—03; group leader VIP visually inspired people Cornerstone Ministries, Export, Pa., 2004, leader beginners' sign class Pa., 2004, elder lead prayer and ministry team, 2005—06, mem. women's connection ministry team, 2006—; dance ministry with Daus. of Judah, New Life Assembly Women's Conf., Pitts., 2005; evangelistic outreach Washington, Pa., 2005; active Expressions of Love Outreach Three Rivers Regatta, Pitts., 2006; active Pitts. healing crusade 1st Presbyn. Ch. Pitts., 2006—. Mem. Full Gospel Ch. Home: 128 Alcan Dr Pittsburgh PA 15239 Personal E-mail: kimmwaone@yahoo.com.

**ZEPEDA, OFELIA,** linguist, educator; b. Stanfield, Ariz., Mar. 24, 1954; BA, U. Ariz., 1980, MA, 1981, PhD, 1984. Tchr. O'odham and linguistics U. Ariz., 1979-92, assoc. prof. linguistics, 1992-98, full prof., 1998—. Tchr. O'odham and Pima, Am. Indian Lang. Devel. Inst., 1980—, co-dir., 1989—. Author: A Papago Grammar, 1983, Ocean Power: Poems From the Desert, 1995, Earth Movement, 1997; editor: Mat Hekid o Ju: When It Rains: Papago and Pima Poetry, 1982; co-editor: South Corner of Time, 1980; contbr.: Returning the Gift, 1994, Home Places, 1995; series editor Sun Tracks Fellow MacArthur, 1999—; grantee, NSF, 1986, NEH, 1992. Office: U Ariz Douglass Bldg Rm 222 Tucson AZ 85721-0001 E-mail: ofelia@u.arizona.edu.

**ZEPEDA, SUSAN GHOZEIL,** foundation administrator; b. N.Y.C., Aug. 8, 1946; d. Harry S. and Anne (Golden) Kantor; m. Isaac Ghozeil, Jan. 29, 1967 (div. Oct. 1979); children: Daniel Jacob Ghozeil, Adam Leo Ghozeil; m. Fernando Zepeda, Jan. 2, 1983 (div. Feb. 1990); children: Paloma Andrea, Sofia Elisa. BA, Brown U., 1967; MA, U. Ariz., 1971, postgrad., 1971-75; PhD, Internat. Coll., 1985. Rsch. assoc. div. bus. and econ. rsch. U. Ariz., Tucson, 1971-73, rsch. assoc. Coll. Medicine, 1975-76; assoc. dir. Pima Alcoholism Consortium, Tucson, 1976-79, exec. dir. 1979-80; dep. dir. pub. health Orange County Health Care Agy., Santa Ana, Calif., 1980-89, dir. policy, planning-1989-90; dir. pub. fin. Orange County, 1990-92; dir. San Luis Obispo County Health Agy., 1993-99; CEO Healthcare Found. Orange County, Santa Ana, Calif., 1999—2005; exec. dir. Found. for Healthy Ky., 2005—. Cons. Tucson Sch. Dist., 1973-75, U.S. Dept. Labor, Washington, 1976—79, Indian Health Svc., Rockville, Md., 1984—85; ptnr. Zepeda Assocs., Fullerton, Calif., 1987—93; presenter in field. Mem. Fullerton Planning Commn., 1984—91, chmn., 1990—91; mem. Calif. Task Force Comparable Worth, 1984—85, Calif. Dist. Appeal Bd. No. 510, LA, 1986—. Recipient Women of Achievement award, Orange County Bd. Suprs., 1988, Disting. Achievement awards, Nat. Assn. Counties, 1985—87, 1989. Mem.: APHA, Grantmakers in Health (bd. dirs. 2004—), So. Calif. Grantmakers (bd. dirs. 2002—05), County Alcohol Program Adminstrs. Assn. Calif. (v.p. 1983, pres. 1984—85), Ctrl. Coast Hosp. Coun. (chair 1996), Nat. Assn. County and City Health Ofcls. (bd. dirs.), County Health Execs. Assn. (v.p. 1998—99), Health Funders Partnership Orange County (chair 2000—02), Rotary Club (pres. 2001—02). Avocation: fiber arts. Office: Found for a Healthy Ky 9300 Shelbyville Rd Ste 1305 Louisville KY 40222 Home: 10203 Springhurst Gardens Cir Louisville KY 40241 Office Phone: 502-326-2583. Business E-Mail: szepeda@healthyky.org.

**ZEPF, THOMAS HERMAN,** retired physics professor; b. Cin., Feb. 13, 1935; s. Paul A. and Agnes J. (Schulz) Z. BS summa cum laude, Xavier U., 1957; MS, St. Louis U., 1960, PhD, 1963. Asst. prof. physics Creighton U., Omaha, 1962-67, assoc. prof., 1967-75, prof., 1975—2002, prof. emeritus, 2002—, acting chmn. dept. physics, 1963-66, chmn., 1966-73, 81-93, coord. allied health programs, 1975-76, coord. pre-health scis. advising, 1976-81. Cons. physicist VA Hosp., Omaha, 1966-71; vis. prof. physics St. Louis U., 1973-74; program evaluator Am. Coun. on Edn., 1988-2002. Contbr. articles and abstracts to Surface Sci., Bull. Am. Phys. Soc., Proceedings Nebr. Acad. Sci., The Physics Tchr. Jour., others. Recipient Cert. Recognition award, Phi Beta Kappa U. Cin. chpt., 1953. Mem. AAAS, Am. Phys. Soc., Am. Assn. Physics Tchrs. (pres. Nebr. sect. 1978), Nebr. Acad. Sci. (life, chmn. physics sect. 1985-05), Internat. Brotherhood Magicians, Soc. Am. Magicians (pres. assembly #7, 1964-65), KC, Sigma Xi (Achievement award for rsch. St. Louis chpt. 1963, pres. Omaha chpt. 1993-94), Sigma Pi Sigma. Roman Catholic. Office: Creighton U Dept Physics Omaha NE 68178-0001 Business E-Mail: thzepf@creighton.edu. *The real magic we all have at our disposal is the ability to comprehend our world, to understand how things behave. This understanding, which we gain through science, enables us to predict outcomes and exert a measure of control over nature. It's a sacred trust. It makes the scientist a kind of modern day magician.*

**ZEPHIR, JEANNE YVONNE,** artist; b. Leominster, Mass., May 23, 1935; d. Eugene Leodore and Lydia M. (Cantin) Tourigny; m. Edward W. Zephir Art tchr. Leominster (Mass.) High Sch., Adult Edn., 1960; artist Jeanne Zephir Studio, Gallery, Leominster, 1966—; art tchr. Fitchburg (Mass.) Art Museum, 1968-83. Cons. to mayor of Leominster, 1982—. Bd. dirs., Leominster Arts Council; chairperson, Conlon, Murphy Art Recipient 1st prize Fitchburg Art Mus., Conant Gallery, Lawrence Acad., Groton, Mass., 2d prize Cape Cod Art Assn., N.H. Inst. Art Juror's Choice award, Manchester; named Copley Artist, Copley Art Assn., Boston. Mem. Leominster Art Assn. (charter), Mass. Library Trustee Assn. Avocations: music, travel. Home: 146 Harvard St Leominster MA 01453-3431

**ZEPOS, NICHOLAS S.,** academic administrator; BA, U. Wis., 1976, JD, 1979. Joined faculty Vanderbilt U., Nashville, 1987, assoc. dean rsch. Law Sch., assoc. provost, 1999, vice chancellor for instnl. planning and advancement, 2000, provost, vice chancellor for acad. affairs, 2001—. Contbr. articles to publs. Office: Vanderbilt Univ 131 21st Ave South Nashville TN 37203-1181

**ZERBE, DARELL,** metal products executive; PhD in Indsl. Engring. Named an IT Inspiration, Enterprise Systems, 2001. Office: Ryerson Tull 2621 W 15th St Chicago IL 60608

**ZERBE, KATHRYN JANE,** psychiatrist; b. Harrisburg, Pa., Oct. 17, 1951; d. Grover Franklin and Ethel (Schreckengaust) Z. BS with BA equivalent cum laude, Duke U., 1973; MD, Temple U., 1978. Diplomate Am. Bd. Psychiatry. Resident Karl Menninger Sch. Psychiatry, Topeka, 1982, dean, dir. edn. and rsch., 1992-97; staff psychiatrist Menninger Found., Topeka, 1982-2001; v.p. edn. and rsch. The Menninger Clinic, Topeka, 1993-97, prof., 1997-2001, Jack Aron chair in psychiat. edn., 1997-2001, apptd. tng. and supr. analyst, 1995—; prof. psychiatry, prof. ob-gyn. Oreg. Health Scis. Univ., Portland, 2001—, dir. behavioral medicine dept. women's health, 2001—, prof. psychiatry, prof. ob-gyn., dir. behavioral medicine, women's health, chmn. psychotherapy, dir. outpatient clinic, 2003—, vice chair for psychotherapy, 2003—; tng. and supr. analyst Oreg. Psychoanalytic Ctr., 2002—. Instr. numerous seminars and programs. Author: The Body Betrayed: Women, Eating Disorders and Treatment, 1993, Women's Mental Health in Primary Care, 1999, numerous articles profl. rsch. papers; editor: Womens Mental Health: Primary Care Clinics, 2001, Bull. of Menninger Clinic, 1998—2001; assoc. editor., 1996—98, mem. editl. bd.: Eating Disorders Rev., Eating Disorders: The Jour. of Treatment and Prevention Postgrad. Medicine; editor (sect.): Current Women's Health; contbr. book revs. and articles to profl. jours. Probation officer Juvenile divsn. Dauphin County, Pa., 1973. Recipient Ann. Laughlin Merit award The Nat. Psychiat. Endowment Fund, 1982, Outstanding Paper of Profl. Programs award The Menninger Found. Alumni Assn., 1982, Writing award Topeka Inst. for Psychoanalysis, 1985, 90, Mentorship award, 1997, Women Helping Women award, 1995, Tchr. of Yr. award, 1988, 96, 99; named one of Outstanding Young Women in Am., 1986, 88; Seeley fellow, 1979-82; Hilde Bruch lectureship, 1996. Fellow Am. Psychiat. Assn.; mem. AMA, Am. Coll. Psychiatrists, Am. Med. Women's Assn., Oreg. Med. Assn., Oreg. Psychiat. Assn., Sigma Xi, Alpha Omega Alpha. Avocations:

---

writing, reading, art history, travel. Office: Oreg Health and Scis U Adult Psychiatry 3181 SW Sam Jackson Park Rd Portland OR 97239-3098 Office Phone: 503-494-1009. Business E-Mail: zerbek@ohsu.edu.

**ZERCHER, CRAIG ALLEN,** special education educator, researcher; s. Chris Robert and Barbara Eloise Zercher; m. Christine Joy Nakagawa, June 26, 1982; children: Jackie Miya, Mia Marissa, Emma Christine. BA in Psychology, U. Calif., Berkeley, 1982; MA in Spl. Edn., San Francisco State U., 1990; PhD in Spl. Edn., U. Calif. and San Francisco State U., 2003. Respite worker Cmty. Assn. for the Retarded, Palo Alto, Calif., 1977—82; profound disability specialist Assn. for Retarded Citizens, San Leandro, Calif., 1982—83; dir. therapeutic preschool program Zonta Svcs., San Jose, Calif., 1985—93; dir. resources for early assessment children's mental health, 1990—93; early childhood tchr. Santa Clara County Office, San Jose, 1993—94; rsch. assoc. San Francisco State U. Early Childhood Rsch. Inst. on Inclusion, 1994—99; lectr. spl. edn. San Francisco State U., 1997—; edn. rschr. SRI Internat., Menlo Park, Calif., 2000—. Preschool disability and behavior cons. various local sch. dists. and day care assns., San Francisco and Bay Area, 1990—. Contbr. chapters to books, articles to profl. jours. Named Non-Profit Program of the Yr., United Way Santa Clara County, 1992; Spl. Edn. Leadership scholar, San Francisco State U., 1994—98. Mem.: Coun. for Exceptional Children, Soc. for Rsch. in Child Devel., Phi Beta Kappa. Achievements include development of innovative multidisciplinary programs for the treatment of young children with behavior disorders; research in examining the peer conflicts of preschool children with problem behavior; peer culture and mixed qualitative and quantitative research methods in the study of young children with disabilities; influence of cultural and linguistic diversity in the early education of children with disabilities. Avocations: running, history, studying theology and the history of christian dogma, swimming. Office: SRI Internat 333 Ravenswood Ave Menlo Park CA 94025 Personal E-mail: jzz10@aol.com.

**ZERELLA, JOSEPH T.,** retired pediatric surgeon; b. Youngstown, Ohio, Mar. 7, 1941; s. Atilio and Ann (Capuzello) Z.; m. Diana Isabelle Talbot, Aug. 5, 1967; children: Ann, Michael, Mark. BS, Northwestern U., 1962, MD, 1966. Diplomate Am. Bd. Surgery, Am. Bd. Pediatric Surgery. Intern Med. Coll. Wis., Milw., 1966-67, resident in surgery, 1967-68, 70-73; tng. fellow in pediatric surgery Children's Hosp. Med. Ctr., Cin., 1973-75; staff pediatric surgeon Phoenix Children's Hosp., 1975—; pvt. practice medicine, specializing in pediatric surgery Phoenix, 1975—. Mem. staff Good Samaritan Hosp., Phoenix, 1975—, sect. chief pediatric surgery, 1979—; mem. staff St. Joseph's Hosp., Phoenix, 1975—, sect. chief pediatric surgery, 1980—. Contbr. articles to profl. jours. Capt. USAR, 1968—70. Fellow ACS, Am. Acad. Pediatrics, Am. Pediatric Surg. Assn., Pacific Assn. Pediatric Surgeons. Roman Catholic. Mailing: 8426 N 15th Dr Phoenix AZ 85021 E-mail: dzerella@aol.com.

**ZERHOUNI, ELIAS ADAM,** federal agency administrator; b. Algeria, Apr. 12, 1951; s. Mohamed and Yamna (Raahmouni) Z.; m. Nadia Azza, Oct. 25, 1975; children: Djillali, Yasmin, Adam. MD, U. Algiers, 1975. Diplomate Am. Bd. Radiology. Asst. dir. body CT Johns Hopkins Hospital, Balt., 1978—81; vice chmn., dir. body imaging De Paul Hospital, Norfolk, Va., 1982—85; co-dir. MRI and body CT, coord. clinical research Johns Hopkins Med. Institutions, Balt., 1985—88, dir. thoracic imaging and MRI, 1988—96; dir. Advanced Med. Imaging Inst., Norfolk, Va., 1991—92; radiologist-in-chief Johns Hopkins Hospital, Balt., 1996—; dir. NIH, Bethesda, Md., 2002—. Resident in diagnostic radiology Johns Hopkins U., Balt., 1975—79, instr., 1978—79, asst. prof. radiology, 1979—81, Ea. Va. Med. Sch., Norfolk, Va., 1981—83, assoc. prof. radiology, 1983—85; cons. Nat. Cancer Inst., NHLBI, 1985—88; assoc. prof. radiology Johns Hopkins U., Balt., 1985—92, prof. radiology, 1992; centennial lectr. Swedish Royal Acad. Radiology, Stockholm, 1994; prof. biomed. engring. Johns Hopkins U., Balt., 1995, chmn. radiology, 1996—, exec. vice dean, vice dean clinical affairs, 1996—99, vice dean research, 1999—2000, exec. vice dean, 1999—2002; assoc. editor, mem. of the editorial bd. Journal of Surgical and Radiological Anatomy, 1980—86; assoc. editor Radiology, 1983—90; mem. editorial bd. Topics in Clinical MRI, 1990—96; assoc. editor, mem. of the editorial bd. Journal of Thoracic Imaging, 1990—97. Patentee in field. Recipient Lauterbur award for MRI research, 1989, 93, Hounsfield award for CT Imaging, 1991. Mem.: Inst. of Med., NAS, Soc. for Chmn. of Academic Radiology Dept., Soc. for Cardiovascular Magnetic Resonance, N. Am. Soc. for Cardiac Imaging, Balt. City Med. Soc., Am. Assn. for the Advancement of Sci., Am. Coll. of Radiology, Am. Heart Assn., Internat. Soc. for Magnetic Resonance in Med. (bd. of trustees 1995—98), Fleischner Soc. (Fleischner Soc. medal 1997), Assn. of U. Radiologists, Soc.of Computed Body Tomography, Soc. of Thoracic Radiology (founding member), Radiological Soc. of N.Am., Am. Roentgen Ray Soc. Avocations: swimming, windsurfing, music. Office: NIH 9000 Rockville Pike Bethesda MD 20892 Office Phone: 301-496-2433. Office Fax: 301-402-2700. E-mail: ez26y@nih.gov.*

**ZERIN, STEVEN DAVID,** lawyer; b. NYC, Oct. 1, 1953; s. Stanley Robert and Cecilie Paula (Goldberg) Z.; children: Alexander James, J. Oliver. BS, Syracuse U., 1974; JD, St. Johns U., 1977. Bar: N.Y. 1978, U.S. Dist. Ct. (so. dist.) N.Y. 1985, U.S. Supreme Ct. 1986. Of coun. Sperry, Weinberg, Wels, Waldman & Rubenstein, N.Y.C., 1982-85; ptnr. Wels & Zerin, N.Y.C., 1985—. Trustee, mem. bd. govs. Daytop Village. Mem. ABA (exec. mem. and lectr. family law sect.), N.Y. State Bar Assn. (exec. com. family law sect.), Assn. of Bar of City of N.Y. Democrat. Home: 12 E 88th St New York NY 10128-0535 Office: Wels & Zerin 600 Madison Ave Fl 22 New York NY 10022-1615 Office Phone: 212-838-8608. Business E-Mail: szerin@welsandzerin.com.

**ZERMAN, MELVYN BERNARD,** retired publishing executive, writer; b. NYC, July 10, 1930; s. Abraham and Ida (Belsky) Zirman; m. Miriam Baron, Jan. 2, 1985 (dec.); children: Andrew, Jared, Lenore. BA, U. Mich., 1952; MA, Columbia U., 1953. With Oxford Book Co., N.Y.C., 1953-55; asst. editor Abelard-Schuman, Pubs., N.Y.C., 1955-57; office mgr., salesman Harper & Row, N.Y.C., 1957-61, sales rep., 1961-69, sales mgr., 1969-79, Random House, Inc., N.Y.C., 1979-83, sales cons., 1983-87; pres., pub. Limelight Edits., N.Y.C., 1983—2004. Mem. exec. com. N.Y. Is Book Country, N.Y.C., 1985-2004. Author: Call the Final Witness, 1977, Beyond a Reasonable Doubt, 1981 (Freedoms Found. medal 1981), Taking on the Press, 1986. Mem.: Phi Beta Kappa. Democrat. Avocations: book collecting, travel.

**ZERUBAVEL, EVIATAR,** sociologist, educator; BA in Sociology, Anthropology and Polit. Sci., Tel-Aviv U., 1971; MA in Sociology, U. Pa., 1973, PhD, 1976. Asst. prof. psychiatry and sociology U. Pitts., 1976—80; assoc. prof. sociology Columbia U., 1980—84, Queens College, 1984—85; prof. sociology SUNY, Stony Brook, 1985—88, Rutgers U., 1988—, dir. sociology grad. program, 1992—2001. Author: Patterns of Time in Hospital Life: A Sociological Perspective, 1979, Hidden Rhythms: Schedules and Calendars in Social Life, 1981, The Seven-Day Circle: The History and Meaning of the Week, 1985, The Fine Line: Making Distinctions in Everyday Life, 1991, 1993, Terra Cognita: The Mental Discovery of America, 1992, Social Mindscapes: An Invitation to Cognitive Sociology, 1997, 1999, The Clockwork Muse: A Practical Guide to Writing Theses, Dissertations, and Books, 1999, Time Maps: Collective Memory and the Social Shape of the Past, 2003. Fellow, John Simon Guggenheim Meml. Found., 2003. Mem.: Am. Sociol. Assn. (chair culture sect. 2000—01). Office: Rutgers Univ Dept Sociology 54 Joyce Kilmer Ave Piscataway NJ 08854

**ZERVAS, NICHOLAS THEMISTOCLES,** neurosurgeon; b. Lynn, Mass., Mar. 9, 1929; s. Themistocles and Demetra P. (Stasinopoulos) Z.; m. Thalia Poleway, Feb. 15, 1959; children: T. Nicholas, Christopher Louis, Rhea. AB, Harvard U., 1950; MD, U. Chgo., 1954. Intern N.Y. Hosp., 1955; resident in neurology Montreal Neurol. Inst., 1956; resident in neurosurgery Mass. Gen. Hosp., Boston, 1958-62, fellow in stereotaxic cerebral surgery U. Paris, 1960-61; asst. attending surgeon, asso. neurosurgery Jefferson Med. Coll., Phila., 1962-67; asso. prof. surgery Harvard U., 1971-77; also chief neurosurg. service Beth Israel Hosp., Boston, 1967-77; prof. surgery Harvard U.,

---

1977-200; also chief neurosurg. service Mass. Gen. Hosp., 1977-2000; Higgins prof. neurosurgery Harvard U., 1986-2000. Contbr. numerous articles to sci. jours. Chmn. Mass. Coun. Arts and Humanities, 1983-91; trustee Boston Symphony Orch., 1990—, vice chmn., 1993—, pres., 1994-2002; bd. dirs. Medical Edn. South African Blacks, 2004-. Capt. M.C. AUS, 1956-58, 87-2002. Fellow Am. Acad. Arts and Scis.; mem. Am. Acad. Neurol. Surgery (pres. 1990-91), Am. Assn. Neurol. Surgeons, Soc. Neurol. Surgeons, Am. Neurol. Assn., Am. Bd. Neurol. Surgery (chmn. 1990-91), Inst. Medicine Nat. Acad. Scis., Sigma Xi. Home: 100 Canton Ave Milton MA 02186-3507 Office: Mass Gen Hosp Attn Barbara Perrier 55 Fruit St Boston MA 02114-2620 Business E-Mail: nzervas@partners.org.

**ZES, TIKEY A.,** music minister; b. Long Beach, Calif., Oct. 10, 1927; s. Athanasios and Anna Zes; m. Theodore P. Chlentzos-Zes, Sept. 8, 1963; children: Athan, Evan, Anna-Matina. MusB, U. So. Calif., 1951, MusM, 1953, D in Musical Arts, 1969. Prof. music San Jose State U., 1964—91, prof. emeritus, 1991—; music minister San Francisco Greek Orth. Met., 1993—. Choir dir. Greek Orthodox, Long Beach, San Francisco, Oakland, San Jose, 1950—. Composer: A Unison Liturgy for Greek Orthodox Choirs, 1976, The Choral Music for the Liturgy of St. John Chrysostom, 1977, The Choral Music for Mixed Voices for the Divine Liturgy, 1991, A Liturgy with English Text, 1992, The Divine Liturgy in Greek and English, 2004, Memorial Service for the Orthodox Church, in English, 1996, Unison Doxology, Cherubic Hymn, propers for major feast days. Corp. U.S. Army, 1951—53, Korea. Recipient Archon, Patriarch Demetrios of Greek Orthodox Ch., San Jose, 1977, Axion award, Hellenic Am. Profl. Soc. Calif., 1989. Mem.: Nat. Forum Greek Orth. Ch. Musicians. Democrat. Greek Orthodox. Avocations: history, politics, chamber music. Home: 2503 Booksin Ave San Jose CA 95125

**ZESCH, HAL,** energy executive; BBA in Acctg., U. Tex., Austin. CPA. Audit and consulting mgr. Deloitte & Touche; various positions including v.p. best bus. practices, asst. corp. contr., contr. natural gas ops., dir. corp. acctg. Valero Energy Corpn., San Antonio, v.p. SAP systems integration, v.p., chief info. officer, 2003. Office: Valero Energy Corpn PO Box 696000 San Antonio TX 78269-6000

**ZETA-JONES, CATHERINE,** actress; b. Swansea, Wales, Sept. 25, 1969; d. Dai and Pat Jones; m. Michael Douglas, Nov. 18, 2000; children: Dylan Michael, Carys Zeta. Film appearances include Les 1001 nuits (Italy), 1990, Christopher Columbus: The Discovery, 1992, Splitting Heirs, 1993, Blue Juice, 1995, The Phantom, 1996, The Mask of Zorro, 1998, Entrapment, 1999, The Haunting, 1999, High Fidelity, 2000, Traffic, 2000, America's Sweethearts, 2001, Chicago, 2002 (Best Sup. Actress Academy award, 2003, Best Actress in Sup. Role, British Acad. Film Award (BAFTA) 2003), Sinbad: Legend of the Seven Seas (voice only), 2003, Intolerable Cruelty, 2003, The Terminal, 2004, Ocean's Twelve, 2004, The Legend of Zorro, 2005; (T.V. films) Out of the Blue, 1991, The Cinder Path, 1994, The Return of the Native, 1994, Catherine the Great, 1995, Titanic, 1996; (T.V. series) The Darling Buds of May, 1991; (T.V. appearances) The Adventures of Young Indiana Jones: Daredevils of the Desert, 1992.*

**ZETHMAYR, ELLEN LOLAKOS,** music educator, writer; b. Chgo., Dec. 1943; d. Anthony Paul Mishur, Sr. and Helen Catherine Mishur; m. David Zethmayr (div.); children: Sylvia, Nöel, Benjamin, Katrina, Miriam; m. Thomas Christ Lolakos, June 8, 2003. AA. Mt. St. Clare Coll.; BA, Marycrest Coll.; postgrad., U. Ill., Chgo., Am. Conservatory of Music. Cert. tchr. Mo., Ill. Tchr. 1st and 2d grades Sisters of St. Francis, 1967—73; tchr., rschr., dir. St. Stephens Acad., La Grange, Ill., 1986—90; tchr. programs for gifted Louis U., Wheaton, Ill., 1986—93; piano tchr. Music Makers, Western Springs, Ill., 1996—; tchr., arranger, co-composer, performer, 2003—; co-prodr. Prospect Players, 2003—. Home schooling cons. St. Stephens Acad., 1987—90; mem. staff, asst. Prospect Players, Des Plaines, Ill., 2003—05. Author: (poetry) Poems of a Dreamer, 1973; sculpture, Madonna & Child, wood mosaic, Hands on Piano Keyboard; singer Grant Park Chorus, Chgo., 1989, Opera La Traviata, Glen Ellyn, Ill., 1990. Recipient Outstanding award, 1st pl. paper divsn., Am. Jr. Acad. Sci. Mem.: Internat. Dyslexia Assn., Nat. Assn. Tchrs. of Singing, Nat. Guild Piano Tchrs. Eastern Orthodox. Avocations: art, woodcarving, writing, music. Home: 413 S 8th Ave La Grange IL 60525 Office Phone: 708-579-0787.

**ZETSCHE, DIETER,** automotive executive; b. Istanbul, Turkey; May 5, 1953; m. Gisela Zetsche. Grad., U. Karisuhe, 1971—76; DEng, Tech. U. Paderborn, 1982. Joined rsch. dept. Daimier-Benz AG, 1976—81, asst. to chief engr. comml. vehicle divsn., 1981—84, coord. comml. vehicle devel. activities, 1984—86, sr. mgr., chief engr. cross-country vehicle unit, 1986—87; head devel. dept., chief engr. Mercedes-Benz do Brazil, 1987—88, mem. mgmt., 1988—89; pres. Mercedes-Benz, Argentina, 1989—91, Freightliner Corp., Portland, Oreg., 1991—92; dep. mem. bd. mgmt. Mercedes-Benz AG, 1992, chief engr. devel. divsn. passenger cars bus. unit, 1992, mem. bd. mgmt. sales divsn., 1995, Daimier-Benz AG, 1997—98, DaimlerChrysler AG, 1998—99, mem. bd. mgmt. comml. vehicle divsn., 1999—2000, chmn. bd. mgmt., 2006—, mem. bd. mgmt., Mercedes Car Group, 2005—; mem. bd. mgmt., CEO Chrysler Group Divsn., 2000—05. Spokesperson for TV commercials DaimlerChrysler, 2006. Named one of 100 Most Influential People, Time Mag., 2006. Office: DaimlerChrysler AG Epplestrasse 225 D-70546 Stuttgart Germany Office Phone: +49-711-17-0. Office Fax: +49-711-17-94022.*

**ZETTEL, LAURA A.,** psychology professor, researcher; b. Warren, Mich., Feb. 29, 1976; d. Richard J. and Donna Zettel. BA, U. Mich., Ann Arbor, 1997; PhD, U. Calif., Irvine, 2004 Rschr. U. Mich. Ann Arbor 1997—98; instr. and rschr. U. Calif., Irvine, 1998—2005; prof. Calif. State U., Fullerton, Calif., 2005—. Tchg. asst. cons. U. Calif., Irvine, 2002—04; adj. faculty Soka U. Am., Aliso Viejo, Calif., 2004. Named Most Promising Future Faculty Mem., U. Calif. Irvine, 2004; fellow, 2004; grantee, Anthony Marchionne Found., 2003. Mem.: APA, Gerontol. Soc. Am. Avocations: travel, reading, tennis. Office: Psychology Dept CSUF PO Box 6846 Fullerton CA 92834-6846 Office Phone: 714-278-3898. Business E-Mail: lzettel@fullerton.edu.

**ZEUGNER, JOHN FINN,** historian, educator, writer; b. NYC, Oct. 7, 1938; s. Orland Kump and Ethel (Finn) Z.; m. Alice Chatfield Valentine, Sept. 7, 1968; children: Emily Valentine, Maxwell Finn, Laura Ruth. AB, Harvard U., 1959; MA, Fla. State U., 1968, PhD, 1971. Night mgr. Beach Cart, Sarasota, Fla., 1960-67; asst. prof. history Worcester Poly. Inst., Mass., 1971-74, assoc. prof., 1974-82, prof., 1982—; Fulbright lectr. Osaka U., Kobe U., Japan, 1976-78. Vis. prof. Keio U., Tokyo, 1981-83; Bryant Drake guest prof. Kobe Coll., Japan, 1994-95. Contbr. articles to profl. jours. With USCG, 1961—62. Named Paris Fletcher Disting. Prof. Humanities, Worcester Poly. Inst., 1985; grantee NEA, 1970 Mem.: Soc. Historians in Am. Found. Am. Historians. Avocations: tennis, chess. Home: 31 William St Worcester MA 01609-2313 Office: Worcester Poly Inst Humanities & Arts Dept Worcester MA 01609 Office Phone: 508-831-5215. Business E-Mail: jzeugner@wpi.edu.

**ZEUSCHNER, ERWIN ARNOLD,** brokerage house executive; b. Freiburg, Germany, Nov. 17, 1935; came to U.S., 1936; s. Reinhold Hermann and Helene Barbara (Maas) Z.; m. Christa Elfreide Ellmers, June 20, 1959 (dec. Aug., 1971); children—Peter Erwin, Suzanne Christina, Andrea Ellmers; m. Margaret Anne Finn, Mar. 25, 1972; 1 dau., Elizabeth Nora. BA in Econs., Queens Coll., 1957; MBA in Fin, NYU, 1964. Sr. v.p. Chase Manhattan Bank, N.Y.C., 1970-72; sr. v.p. dir. Chase Investors Mgmt. Corp., 1972-80; sr. v.p. Chase Manhattan Corp., 1970-80; ptnr. David J. Greene & Co. (investment advs.), N.Y.C., 1980—. Trustee Marymount Manhattan Coll., 1997. Served to capt. USAF, 1958-60. Mem. N.Y. Soc. Security Analysts (dir.) Home: 1 Middle Dr Manhasset NY 11030-1414 Office: 599 Lexington Ave New York NY 10022-6030

**ZEVON TSCHACBASOV, IRENE ANN,** artist, consultant, art historian; b. N.Y.C., Nov. 24, 1918; d. Joseph and Minnie (Saslowsky) Zivitofsky; m. Murray Barton, Apr. 28, 1943 (div. 1960); 1 child, Leonard; m. Nahum Tschacbasov, Aug. 30, 1966 (dec. 1984). Pres. Am. Archives of World Art Inc., N.Y.C., 1960—. Exhibited in group shows at Glassboro (N.J.) State Coll., Ga. Mus. Art, Athens, Calif. State Libr., Sacramento, Miss. State Coll. for Women, Columbus, Neville Pub. Mus., Green Bay, Wis., Williamantic (Conn.) State Coll., Monmouth (Ill.) Coll., Stetson U., DeLand, Fla., Columbus (Ga.) Mus. Arts and Crafts, Gulf Coast Jr. Coll., Panama City, Fla.; oil paintings on display at numerous museums and ednl. instns. Mem. Nat. Assn. Women Artists.

**ZEWAIL, AHMED HASSAN,** chemistry and physics educator, consultant, editor; b. Damanhour, Egypt, Feb. 26, 1946; arrived in U.S., 1969, 1982; s. Hassan A. Zewail and Rawhia Dar; m. Dema Zewail; children: Maha, Amani, Nabeel, Hani. BS, Alexandria U., Egypt, 1967, MS, 1969; PhD, U. Pa., 1974; MA (hon.), Oxford U., 1991; DSc (hon.), Am. U., Cairo, 1993, Katholieke U., Leuven, Belgium, U. Pa., U. Lausanne, Switzerland, 1997; DU (hon.), Swinburne U., Australia, 1999; HDA Sc (hon.), Arab Acad. for Sci. and Tech., Egypt, 1999, Alexandria U., 1999; DSc (hon.), U. New Brunswick, Canada, 2000; DHC (hon.), U. Rome, Italy, 2000, U. de Liège, Belgium, 2000. Teaching asst. U. Pa., Phila., 1969—70; IBM fellow U. Calif., Berkeley, 1974—76; asst. prof. chem. physics Calif. Inst. Tech., Pasadena, 1976—78, assoc. prof., 1978—82, prof., 1982—89, Linus Pauling prof. chem. physics, 1990—94, Linus Pauling prof. chemistry and prof. physics, 1995—, dir. NSF Lab. for Molecular Scis., 1996—. Cons. Xerox Corp., Webster, NY, 1977—80, ARCO Solar, Inc., Calif., 1978—81. Editor Laser Chemistry, 1980—85, Jour. Phys. Chemistry, 1985—90, Chem. Physics Letters, 1991—; editor: International Series Monographs on Chemistry, 1992—, Advances in Laser Spectroscopy, 1977—, 1978—, Photochemistry and Photobiology, 1983—, Ultrafast Phenomena, 1990—, 1993—, 1994—, The Chemical Bond: Structure and Dynamics, 1992, Femtochemistry-Ultrafst Dynamics of the Chemical Bond, 1994; contbr. numerous articles to sci. jours., patentee in solar energy field. Recipient Tchr.-Scholar award, Dreyfus Found., 1979—85, Alexander von Humboldt Sr. U.S. Scientist award, 1983, John Simon Guggenheim Meml. Found. award, 1987, King Faisal Internat. prize in sci., 1989, NASA award, 1991, 1st AMM Achievement award, 1991, Nobel Laureate Signature award, 1992, Carl Zeiss award, Cairo U. Medal and Shield of Honor, 1992, U. Qatar medal, 1993, Wolf prize in chemistry, Wolf Found., Israel, 1993, Niles award of honor Bonner Chemiepreis, Germany, 1994, Order of Merit first class, Egypt, 1995, Coll. de France medal Leonardo Da Vinci award of excellence, France, 1995, J.G. Kirwood medal, Yale U., 1996, Beijing U. medal, 1996, Robert A. Welch award in chemistry, 1997, Pitts. Spectroscopy award, 1997, Benjamin Franklin medal, 1999, Paul Karrer Gold medal, Zurich, 1999, Roentgen prize, Germany, 1999, E.O. Lawrence award, U.S. Govt., 1999, Merski award, U. Nebr., 1999, Nobel prize in Chemistry, 1999, Egypt Postage Stamp with portrait issued, 1999, Grand Collar of the Nile, Highest Award, 2000, Order of Zayed, United Arab Emirates, 2000, Ahmed Zewail fellow established, U. Pa., 2000, Order of Cedar, Lebanon, 2000, Order of ISESCO 1st class, Saudi Arabia, 2000, Order of merit, Tunisia, 2000, Insignia Pontifical Acad., Vatican, 2000. Mem.: NAS (Chem. Scis. award 1996), AAAS, Third World Acad. Scis., European Acad. Arts, Scis. and Humanities, Royal Danish Acad. Scis. and Letters, Pontifical Acad. Sci., Am. Phys. Soc. (Herbert P. Broida prize 1995), Am. Philos. Soc., Am. Chem. Soc. (Buck-Whitney medal 1985, Harrison-Howe award 1989, Hoechst prize 1990, Peter Debye award 1997, Linus Pauling medal 1997, 1st E.B. Wilson award 1997, William H. Nichols award 1998, Richard C. Tolman medal 1998), Am. Acad. Arts and Scis. (Royal Netherlands Acad. Arts and Scis. medal 1993), Sigma Xi (Earle K. Plyler prize 1993, Wolf prize 1993). Office: Arthur Amos Noyes Lab of Chem Physics Mail Code 127-72 Pasadena CA 91125*

**ZEX, DAMON,** artist; b. Columbus, Ohio, July 11, 1963; s. Arnold Hobart Zaner, Rhoda Lee Zaner. BA, Ohio State U., 1985, MFA, 1991. Sales rep. FAZ Art Products, Columbus, Ohio, 1984—86; dir. gallery Artreach Gallery, Columbus, 1986—87; designer Contemporary Glass, Columbus, 1987—88; comml. designer Columbus Arts & Entertainment Mag., Columbus, 1988—89, Ohio Transmission Corp., Columbus, 1989—91; videographer, tech. dir. Cmty. 21 TV, Columbus, 1992—2001; co-owner Damon Zex Ltd., Columbus, 2001—. Expert art witness U.S. Fed. Ct., Columbus, 1999. Video artist Zex Invasion, 1992—2001 (Innovation award, 2000); Zex Cards, 1991; actor: Zex TV, 1993—2001 (Comedy award, 1994, 1997, 1998). Avocations: chess, yoga, dance, astrology, weight training. Home: Apt 361A 2913 Neil Ave Columbus OH 43202-2043 Office Phone: 614-262-0274. E-mail: zex@zexart.com.

**ZEXTER, ELEANOR M.,** secondary school educator; b. Providence, R.I., Sept. 7, 1936; d. Morris and Anna Rae (Cantor) Marks; m. D. Ronald Zexter, Dec. 24, 1958; children: Francine Deborah, Judith Blair. BA, Brown U., 1958, MAT, 1962. Cert. tchr. R.I., Calif. Tchr. French and English Hope H.S., Providence, 1959—69, Nathan Bishop Mid. Sch., Providence, 1970—93; tchr. English and social studies Harkham Hillel Hebrew Acad., Beverly Hills, Calif., 1993—99. Mktg. dir. DRZ Sales; grant writer Nathan Bishop Mid. Sch., Providence, 1980-93, choral dir., 1985-93, founder Famous Authors, 1987-93; cons. substance abuse program, Brown U., 1987-93; ednl. cons. Vol. tutor Harkham Hillel Hebrew Acad., 1993-99, French club coord., Harkham Hillel Acad., 1993-99. Recipient Citizen Citation for outstanding efforts with Providence children, Mayor, 1990, McClorin award, 1991. Mem. Am. Assn. French Tchrs., Alliance Francaise, R.I. Assn. Foreign Language, Beverly Hills Country Club (tennis team capt.). Avocations: tennis, antique collecting, reading clubs, bridge, travel. Home: 8544 Burton Way Apt 401 Los Angeles CA 90048-3390

**ZFAZ, MARTIN,** medical director, treatment professional, consultant; b. Federal District, Mex., Mar. 7, 1940; Attended, Nat. U. Autonoma Mex., 1957—61; MD, 1964. Lic. Med. Coun. Can., 1972, Fla. Med. State Bd., 1977, cert. in addiction medicine Am. Med. Soc. Alcoholism and Other Drug Dependencies, 1987. Rotating intern Reg. Gen. Mex., 1962, Jewish Gen. Hosp., McGill U., Montreal, Canada, 1966—67; with social svc. Amatlan Reyes, Veracruz, Mexico, 1963; surg. fellow Drs. Hosp., Cleve., 1964—65; first yr. resident gen. surgery Jewish Hosp., Cin., 1967—68; second yr. resident in gen. surgery Jewish Gen. Hosp., Montreal, Canada, 1968—69; third yr. resident in gen. surgery Jewish Gen. Hosp. McGill U., Montreal, 1969—70, fourth yr. resident in gen. surgery, 1970—71, fifth yr. resident, chief resident in gen. surgery, 1971—72; chief surgery, prof. surgery postgrad. courses Hosp. Gen. and Centro Salu Tlaneplantia, Estado de Mex., Mexico, 1972—75; pvt. practice, 1972—75, Sarasota, Fla., 1981—83, 1994—95, 2000; house physician in surgery Hillcrest Hosp., Cleve., 1975—77; emergency dept. physician South Miami Hosp., Fla., 1977—80, Pembroke Pines Gen. Hosp., Fla., 1980; with Ridgeview Inst. Alcohol and Drug Abuse, Smyrna-Atlanta, Ga., 1980; med. dir. CareUnit Tampa, Fla., 1983—85, Glenbeigh of Tampa, 1985—91, Nat. Recovery Insts., Boca Raton, Fla., 1995—97, Pathways, 1997—, Alternatives, 2000—, Advance Recovery Ctr., 2000—, High Point, 2000—; with addiction medicine Mt. Sinai Med. Ctr., Miami Beach, Fla., with, Centurion Carrollwood, Tampa, Glenbeigh of Tampa, Tampa Gen. Hosp., U. Cmty. Hosp., South Shore Hosp., Miami Beach. Mem. Am. Brit. Cowdray Hosp., Mex., Distrito Fed., 1972—75; cons. Horizon Hosp., Clearwater, Fla., 1980—81; with Ednl. Coun. Fgn. Med. Grads.; physician, spring tng. cons. Kans. City Royals, 1983—90; pvt. practice, Fla., 1983—91; mem. bd. dirs. Alcohol Cmty. Treatment Svcs., Inc., 1984—91; expert witness State Fla. Dept. Profl. Regulations, 1987—; preferred treatment provider, cons. Triumph Unltd., 1983—95, Employee Assistance Program Toronto Blue Jays, 1983—95, Fla. Marlins, 1983—95, Cin. Reds, 1983—95, Pitts. Pirates, 1983—95, Baseball Assistance Team Commr.'s Office, 1983—95, Baran Consulting Svcs. Internat., Inc., 1983—95, Employee Assistance Program Internat. Bus. Industry Royal Bank Can., 1983—95, Physicians Recovery Network, 1983—, Physicians Nurses Program, 1983—95, State Bd. Bar Examiners, 1991—; prof. pharmacology U. Miami, 1994—2001. Rsch. fellow, McGill U., 1968—69. Mem.: AAAS, AMA, Am. Acad. Addictionology, Am. Med. Soc. Alcoholism and Other Drug Dependencies, NY Acad. Scis., Internat. Coun. Alcohol and Addictions, AMA on Alcoholism, Nat. Coun. Alcoholism, Hillsborough County Med. Assn., Interam. Coll. Physicians and Surgeons, Fla. Med. Assn. Office: 1144 Southeast Third Ave Fort Lauderdale FL 33316

**ZGALJARDIC, DENNIS JOSEPH,** clinical neuropsychologist; b. Flushing, NY, Mar. 11, 1975; s. Joseph and Maria Zgaljardic; m. Heather Ann Zgaljardic, July 13, 2002; 1 child, Isabella Jean. PhD, CUNY, 2004; degree, SUNY, Buffalo. License in Psychology NYS Licensing Bd. in Psychology, 2005. Clin. neuropsychology fellow North Shore U. Hosp., Manhasset, NY, 2003—05; clin. neuropsychologist Transitional Learning Ctr. at Galveston, Tex., 2005—. Adj. prof. Queens Coll., Flushing, NY, 1998—2005. Contbr. articles to profl. jours. Scholar, CUNY, 1998. Mem.: APA (assoc.), Internat. Neuropsychologiclal Soc. (life), Golden Key. Office Phone: 409-797-1472. Personal E-mail: neurodjz2@yahoo.com.

**ZHA, GECHENG,** engineer, educator; PhD, U. Montreal, Canada, 1994. Prof. U. Miami, Coral Gables, Fla., 2001—. Achievements include design of co-flow jet airfoil. Office Phone: 305-284-3328.

**ZHA, XUAN-FANG,** engineering educator, researcher; b. Dongzhi, Anhui, China, Oct. 17, 1965; arrived in Singapore, 1996. s. Cheng-Gen and Qiao-Lian (Lu) Z.; m. Ling-Ling Li, Feb. 1, 1993; 1 child, Jiali. BSME with honors, Wuhan (China) U. Tech., 1988; MSME, S.E. U., Nanjing, China, 1991; PhD in Mech. and Prodn. Engring., Nanyang Tech. U., 1999. Ednl. diplomate; prof. engr., China, Canada. Asst. lectr. Nanjing U. Aeronautics and Astronautics, China, 1991-92, 1992-94, assoc. prof., 1994-95, adj. assoc. prof., 1995-99; rsch. fellow Nanyang Tech. U., Singapore, 1999—. Rsch. asst. Wuhan U. of Tech., 1985-88, S.E. U. 1988-91, tchg. asst. 1989-91; sr. engr. Nanjing Tiandi Group Co., Nanjing, 1992-93; postdoctoral fellow Cambridge (Eng.) U., 2001—. Author (books): (with others) Machine and Mechanism Design, 1992, Robot Mechanics, 1994, Computer Aided Design, Engineering and Manufacturing Systems, 1999, Knowledge-Based Systems, 2000, Integrated Intelligent Systems, 2001, Computer Aided Design, 2001, Internet and World-wide Web Based Design for Microelectro-Mechanical Systems, 2001, Hybrid Intelligent Systems for Human-Machine System Design, 2001, contbr. over 80 articles to profl. jours. Rsch. fellowship Hong Kong Polytechnic U., 1995-96, Nanyang Technol. U., 1996-99, 1999-2001, 2001—, Gintic Inst. Mfg. Tech.; recipient Best Paper award Chinese Soc. Automation, 1994, Second Rank prize Jiangsu Provincial Com. Sci. and Tech., 1995. Mem. IEEE (Best Paper award, 1998), Chinese Assoc. Automation, Robotics and Automation Soc. Avocations: reading, swimming, ping pong/table tennis.

**ZHAI, YAN,** education educator, researcher; s. Zhai and Song. MS, Okla. State U., Stillwater, 2002; postgrad., U. Okla., Norman, 2003—. Design engring. Beijing Constrn. Corp., 1998—2000; rsch. asst. Okla. State U., Stillwater, 2000—02, U. Okla., Norman, 2003—. Contbr. articles to profl. jours. Mem.: IEEE (signal processing), Phi Kappa Phi, Tau Beta Pi. Achievements include development of novel signal processing algorithms. Office: Univ Okla 202 W Body St Norman OK 73071 Office Phone: 405-535-1419.

**ZHAI, YUN,** electrical engineer, researcher; s. Xuda Zhai and Yuzhen Shi. PhD in Elec. Engring., U. Ctrl. Fla., Orlando, 2001—06. Rsch. engr. U. Ctrl. Fla., 2001—. Contbr. papers to profl. jours. and pubs. Grantee scholarship, All Am. Scholar Assn., 2001. Mem.: IEEE. Achievements include research in multimedia processing, computer vision and content-based image and video retrieval. Office: Univ of Ctrl Fla 4000 Central Florida Blvd Orlando FL 32816 Office Phone: 407-823-4733.

**ZHANG, CHARLES C.,** financial planner; MA in Econs., Western Mich. U., 1991; MBA, Northwestern U., 2004. ChFC; CFP; CLU; chartered mutual fund counselor; cert. fund specialist. Sr. fin. advisor Am. Express Fin. Advisors, Inc., Kalamazoo, 1991—. Adj. prof. finance Western Mich. U. Mem. Am. Soc. CLU and ChFC, Inst. cert. Fin. Planners, Internat. Assn. Fin. Planning. Office: Am Express Fin Advisors Inc 1302 W Milham Portage MI 49024 E-mail: charles.c.zhang@aexp.com.

**ZHANG, CHUANLUN,** microbiologist, researcher; PhD, Tex. A&M U., College Station, 1994. Asst. prof. U. Mo., Columbia, 1998—2002; assoc. prof. Savannah River Ecology Lab. U. Ga., Aiken, SC, 2002—. Nomination com. Chinese scholars Internat. Profls. Advancement Chinese Earth Scis., Ann Arbor, Mich., 2003. Fellow, U. Minn., Inst. Rock Magnetism, 1998; scholar, Oak Ridge Nat. Lab., Tenn., 1994—98, Petroleum U. China, 2003. Mem.: Geol. Soc. Am. (Student Rsch. award 1992), Am. Soc. Microbiology, Am. Geophys. Union. Achievements include design of novel organisms in hot springs. Home: 4120 Heritage Ridge Evans GA 30809 Office: Savannah River Ecology Laboratory Bldg 737A Aiken SC 29802 Office Phone: 803-725-5299. Office Fax: 803-725-3309. Business E-Mail: zhang@srel.edu.

**ZHANG, CHUNLONG,** environmental scientist, engineer; b. Lanxi, Zhejiang, China, May 4, 1964; s. Yunfeng Pan and Peile Zhang; m. Shuou Zhao; 1 child, Richard. PhD, Louisiana State University, Baton Rouge, 1993—97; student, Rice U., 1998—2000. Asst. prof. U. Houston-Clear Lake, 2000—05, assoc. prof., 2005—. Environ. engring. cons. Tyndall Air Force Base, 1999. Author, co-author of original rsch. in more than 70 peer-reviewed jour. articles and conf. proceedings. Recipient Award for Outstanding Dissertation in Field of Engring. and Physical Scis., Univs. Coun. on Water Resources (UCOWR), Inc., 1997, Exceptional Leadership and Commitment in Tchg. Environ. Sci., Tex. Commn. on Environ. Quality (TCEQ), 2003; John Lee Pratt Fellowship, Va. Tech., 1991—93. Mem.: Assn. Environ. Engring. and Sci., Professors Soc. Environ. Toxicology and Chemistry. Office: Univ Houston Clear Lake 2700 Bay Area Blvd Houston TX 77058 Office Phone: 281-283-3746. Office Fax: 281-283-3709. Business E-Mail: zhang@uhcl.edu.

**ZHANG, CYNTHIA HONGBING,** lawyer; b. Linshui, Sichuan Province, China, Apr. 24, 1966; d. Xintian Zhang and Zaifeng Guo. BS, Tsinghua U., Beijing, 1987, MS, 1990—90; PhD, Ind. U., 1995; JD, U. Houston, 2001. Bar: Md. 2002, DC 2003, U.S. Patent and Trademark Office 2002, Mass. 2004. Postdoctoral rschr. Dana Farber Cancer Inst. and Harvard Med. Sch., Boston, 1995—97, Boston, U., 1998; jud. intern US Dist. Ct. (so. dist.) Tex., Houston, 2000; assoc. Shanks & Herbert, Alexandria, Va., 2001—03, Palmer & Dodge LLP, Boston, 2003—05; patent atty. Novartis Corp. Intellectual Property, Cambridge, Mass., 2005—. Mem.: Am. Intellectual Property Law Assn. Achievements include research in functional analysis of an intron 3' splice site in Caenorhabditis elegans. Office: Novartis Corp Intellectual Property Rm 105 400 Technology Sq Cambridge MA 02139 Office Phone: 617-871-3096, 617-871-3096. Office Fax: 617-871-3392.

**ZHANG, DAJUN,** biomedical engineering educator; BS, Beijing U., 1987, MS, 1990; PhD, CUNY, NYC, 1997. Postdoctoral rschr. CCNY, NYC, 1997—98; rsch. engr. U. Chgo., 2000—; assoc. prof. Rutgers, State U. NJ, Piscataway, 2000—. Dir. Bone Mechanics Lab. Rutgers State U., Piscataway, 2000—, undergrad. student rsch, supervision, 2000—06; proposal reviewer NSF, 2003—06. Reviewer: Annals Biomed. Engring. Busch Biomedical grantee, Rutgers State U. NJ, 2002, 2004. Mem.: AAAS. Achievements include design of multiple experimental setups; development of novel research on multiple interdisciplinary projects. Office: Rutgers State University of New Jersey 98 Brett Rd Piscataway NJ 08854 Office Phone: 732-445-3797.

**ZHANG, DONGXIAO,** research scientist; b. Wuning, Jiangxi, China, Mar. 15, 1967; m. Liheng Zhang, May 3, 1967; children: Benjamin Ary, Grace Danyi. MS, U. Ariz., 1992, PhD, 1993. Assoc. rsch. scientist U. Ariz., Tucson, 1994—95; sr. hydrologist Daniel B. Stephens & Assocs. Inc., Albuquerque, 1995—96; sr. rsch. scientist Los Alamos Nat. Lab., N.Mex., 1996—. Author: Stochastic Methods for Flow in Porous Media: Coping with Uncertainties; editor: Theory, Modeling and Field Investigation in Hydrogeology; assoc. editor: Water Resources Rsch., 2001—. Mem.: Soc. Petroleum Engrs. (mem. editl. bd. jour. 2002—), Geol. Soc. Am., Am. Geophys. Union. Office: Los Alamos National Lab PO Box 1663 Los Alamos NM 87545 Personal E-mail: dzhang601@msn.com. Business E-Mail: donzhang@lanl.gov.

**ZHANG, DU,** engineering educator; b. Nanjing, Jiangsu, China; arrived in U.S., 1984; s. Wen-Tang Zhang and Xue-Wen Yu; m. Meiliu Lu; 1 child, Bryan. BS, Nanjing U., 1977, MS, 1982; PhD, U. of Ill., 1987. Lectr. Nanjing U., 1977—80, 1982—84; rschr. U. of Ill., Chgo., 1984—87; asst. prof. Calif. State U., Sacramento, 1987—89, assoc. prof., 1989—93, prof., 1993—, dept. assoc. chair, 1996—97, dept. grad. coord., 1997—98, dept. chair, 2004—. Assoc. editor Internat. Jour. on Artificial Intelligence Tools, Singapore City, 2003—; program co-chair Workshop on Applications of Petri Nets to Intelligent Sys. Devel., 20th Internat. Conf. on Applications and Theory of Petri Nets, Williamsburg, Va., 1999; program chair 2nd Golden West Internat. Conf. on Intelligent Sys., Reno, 1992; mem. program com. various internat. confs., 1991—2006; mem. editl. bd. Internat. Jour. of Cognitive Informatics and Natural Intelligence, Hershey, Pa., 2005—; guest editor Software Quality Jour., Secaucus, NJ, 2005—, Internat. Jour. of Software Engring. and Knowledge Engring., Singapore City, 2004—05, Internat. Jour. on Artificial Intelligence Tools, Singapore City, 2003—04, Internat. Jour. of Computer Applications in Tech., Olney, United Kingdom, 2004—05. Editor: (book) Machine Learning Applications in Software Engineering, Advances in Machine Learning Applications in Software Engineering; contbr. articles and tech. reports, book chpts. to profl. pubs. Recipient Chancellor's Student Svc. award, U. of Ill., 1986, Student Leadership Recognition award, U. of Ill. Alumni Assn., 1987, Nat. award, U.S. Achievement Acad., 1987, Outstanding Scholar award, Coll. of Engring., Calif. State U., Sacramento, 1998, 2004, Meritorious Performance award, Calif. State U., Sacramento, 1989, 1996. Mem.: ACM, IEEE (sr.; SMC tech. com. on knowledge acquisition in intelligent sys., gen. chair 16th internat. conf. on tools with artificial intelligence 2004, program co-chair internat. conf. on info. reuse and integration 2004, internat. symposium on bioinformatics and bioengring. 2004, program chair 15th internat. conf. on tools with artificial intelligen 2003, vice program chair 6th internat. conf. on tools with artificial 1994, program co-chair internat. conf. on info. reuse and integration 2006—, 4th internat. conf. on cognitive informatics 2005, internat. conf. on info. reuse and integration 2005), IEEE Computer Soc. (tech. coun. on software engring., com. on multimedia computing), Upsilon Pi Epsilon, Phi Beta Delta. Achievements include research in A high-level Petri net model for definite clause logic programs; ZCZOS, a distributed operating system; Pr/T net model for planning; Pr/T net model for parallel query processing in deductive databases; Theory And Verification Methods For Knowledge Bases; Machine Learning Applications In Software Engineering. Avocations: travel, sports. Office: Calif State U 6000 J St Sacramento CA 95819-6021 Office Phone: 916-278-7628.

**ZHANG, GUOLONG,** immunologist, educator; b. Quanjiao, Anhui, China, Aug. 25, 1971; s. Liren Zhang and Yulan Dong; m. Yan Song, Dec. 15, 1972; children: Alex Shijie, Andrew Shixuan. BS, China Agrl. U., Beijing, 1993, MS, 1995; PhD, Kans. State U., Manhattan, 1999. Postdoctoral fellow Yale U. Sch. of Medicine, New Haven, 2000—01; asst. prof. of molecular biology Okla. State U., Stillwater, 2002—. Contbr. articles to profl. jours. (Pres.'s award China Agrl. U., 1992, Travel Fellowship Grant award for young investigators Soc. for Exptl. Biology and Medicine, 1998, Big XII Faculty Fellowship award Okla. State U., 2005). Mem.: AAAS, Conf. of Rsch. Workers in Animal Diseases, Am. Assn. of Vet. Immunologists, Am. Assn. of Immunologists. Achievements include patents pending for Fowlicidins and Methods of Their Use. Office: Okla State Univ 212 Animal Sci Bldg Stillwater OK 74078 Office Phone: 405-744-6619.

**ZHANG, GUOQIANG,** finance educator; b. Shanghai, Oct. 27, 1963; s. Lei and Lucy S. Zhang. BS, E. China Normal U., Shanghai, 1985, MS, 1987; PhD, Kent State U., 1998. Stats. sr. engr. Emery Worldwide Airline, Dayton, Ohio, 1998; asst. prof. Ga. State U., Atlanta, 1998—2003, assoc. prof., 2003—. Contbr. articles to profl. jours. Recipient Outstanding Acad. Achievement, Phi Beta Delta, 1996—98, Oustanding Paper award, Inst. Internat. Forecaster, 2002, Best Paper award, IEEE, 2004. Mem.: N.Y. Acad. Scis., Prodn. and Ops. Mgmt. Soc., Inst. Ops. Rsch. and Mgmt. Sci., Decision Sci. Inst., Sigma Xi (Doctoral award 1998). Avocations: music, reading, travel. Office: Ga State U 35 Broad St Atlanta GA 30303 Office Phone: 404-651-4065. Business E-Mail: gpzhang@gsu.edu.

**ZHANG, HONG (RICK),** design engineer, researcher; b. Hancheng, Shaanxi, China, May 28, 1961; s. Runmin Zhang and Mingzhu Ma; m. Li Qu, Apr. 1, 1995; 1 child, Chi (Jim). PhD, Beijing U. Aero & Astro, 1992. Assoc. prof. Beijing Inst. Machinery Industry, 1992—95; post doctoral rschr. U. Minn., Mpls., 1998—2001; design engr. ADC Telecomm., Inc., 2001—02; sr. design engr. Princetel, Inc., Lawrenceville, NJ, 2002—. Presenter in field. Contbr. articles to profl. jours. Fellow, Nanyang Technol. U., Singapore, 1995—97. Achievements include patents for Apparatus and method for sensing switching positions of a MEMS optical switch; Latching apparatus for a MEMS optical switch; MEMS optical switch on a single chip and method. Pub: A new type of load balancing mechanisms for planetary gearing; scanning apparatus; patents pending for optic rotary joint using rotatable fiber; anti-backlash planetary gearing for optic rotary joint; two-channel, dual-mode fiber optic rotary joint; off-axis optic slip ring. Office: 1595 Reed Rd Pennington NJ 08534 Office Fax: 609-895-9552. Personal E-mail: mr_hongzhang@yahoo.com.

**ZHANG, JIANZHI,** geneticist, educator; b. Shanghai, May 20, 1970; s. Shikang Zhang and Weiying Dai; m. Yue Zhou, Apr. 14, 1970; 1 child, Daniel T. BS, Fudan U., 1992; PhD, Pa. State U., University Park, PA, 1994—98. Asst. prof. U. Mich., Ann Arbor, Mich., 2001—; assoc. prof., 2005—. Achievements include research in Molecular and genomic evolution. Office: Univ Mich 830 North University Ave Ann Arbor MI 48109-1048 E-mail: jianzhi@umich.edu.

**ZHANG, JI-HU,** biochemist, researcher; b. Wei Xian, China, 1962; s. Lian Zhang and Li; m. Li Qin; children: James N., Amy Q. PhD, U. Ga., Athens, Ga., 1991. Prin. scientist DuPont Pharmaceuticals, Wilmington, Del., 1997—2001; sr. investigator / rsch. fellow Novartis Pharmaceuticals, Cambridge, Mass., 2002. Jour. editor The Soc. for Biomolecular Scis., 2002. Contbr. articles to profl. jour. Grant reviewer Nat. Inst. of Health, Bethesda, Md., 2005. Recipient Accomplishment Award, Soc. for Biomolecular Screening. Achievements include first to Devel. a novel statistics for assay quality evaluation and quality control in high throughput screening. Office: Novartis Pharm 250 Mass Ave Cambridge MA 02139 Office Phone: 617-871-7142. E-mail: ji-hu.zhang@novartis.com.

**ZHANG, JINSONG,** chemistry professor; PhD, U. of Mont., Missoula, 2003. Lectr. Calif. Poly. State U., San Luis Obispo, 2005—06; asst. prof. Calif. State U., Chico, 2006—. Undergrad. rsch. adviser Calif. State U., Chico, 2006—. Contbr. articles to profl. jours. Recipient Bertha-Morton Grad. Student scholarship, 2001, Lola Walsh Anacker scholarship, 1999, Stanley R. Ames scholarship, 2000, 2002. Mem.: Am. Chem. Soc. Achievements include patents for Polymer Synthesis. Office Phone: 530-898-5622.

**ZHANG, JOHN X,** medical educator; b. Jinan, China, June 1, 1960; m. Dongli Wang, Nov. 18, 1961; children: Jessica, Elena, Matthew. PhD, U. Sydney, 1987. Clinical Laboratory Director Am. Bd. of Bioanalysis, 1998. Assoc. prof. U. Calgary, Canada, 1992—98, Northwestern U. Med. Sch., Chgo., 1998—. Office: Northwestern U Med Sch 675 N Saint Clair STE 14-200 Chicago IL 60611 Office Phone: 312-695-1364. Office Fax: 312-695-4924. E-mail: jzhang@nmff.org.

**ZHANG, JUN,** finance educator; s. Zhenhao Zhang and Zhenling Yan; m. Weini Weini Tong, June 9, 1969; 1 child, Andrew Chang. PhD, Carnegie Mellon U., 2005. Asst. prof. Tulane U., New Orleans, 2002—. Mem. tech. staff Bell Labs., Lucent Techs., Holmdel, NJ, 1999—99; vis. asst. prof. Tulane

U., 2000—02. Contbr. articles to profl. jours. Recipient Outstanding Young Rschr. award, A. B. Freeman Sch. of Bus., Tulane U., 2004, Provost's award, Tulane U., 2005; fellow, Shanghai Jiao Tong U., 1984—87; William Larimer Mellon fellow, Carnegie Mellon U., 1995—98. Mem.: Prodn. and Ops. Mgmt. Soc. (assoc.), Inst. Ops. Rsch. and Ops. Mgmt. (assoc.). Office: A B Freeman Sch Bus 7 McAlister Dr New Orleans LA 70118 Office Phone: 504-865-5075. Personal E-mail: jzzk@yahoo.com.

ZHANG, KEHONG, pharmacologist, educator; b. Tumen, Jilin Province, China, Nov. 4, 1964; married. PhD, La. State U., 1997. Asst. prof. psychiatry and neurosci. Harvard Med. Sch./McLean Hosp., Belmont, Mass., 1999—. Contbr. articles to profl. jours. Recipient Branfman Found. award, Branfman Found., 2002, Livingston award, Harvard Med. Sch., 2000, Alfred Pope Young Investigator award, 2001, Travel award, Am. Coll. Neuropharmacology, 2002; fellow, Pharm. Rsch. and Mfrs. Am/ion, 1995. Mem.: ASPET, Soc. Neuroscis. Office: Harvard Med Sch McLean Hosp 115 Mill St Belmont MA 02478 Home: 346 Lincoln St Apt 3 Waltham MA 02451-2141 Office Phone: 617-855-3222. Business E-mail: kz@mclean.harvard.edu.

ZHANG, LI, engineer, researcher, educator; b. Beijing, Nov. 8, 1969; s. Qicheng Zhang and Liuying. MS in Nuclear Engring., MIT, 1996, MS in Elec. Engring and Computer Sci., 1996, PhD in Radiol. Scis. 1998. Tchg. asst. MIT, Cambridge, 1993-94, rsch. asst., 1994-98; sys. engr. Robotic Vision Sys., Inc., Hauppauge, NY, 1998; tech. mgr. Youngtech Inc., Edison, NJ, 1998—2001; project leader ADP Inc., Parsippany, NJ, 2001—03; pres. Internat. Innovative Imaging Sys., LLC, Piscataway, NJ, 2003—; mem. faculty DeVry U., Westminster, Colo., 2005—. Dir. electronics Beijing Perfect Electronics Engring. Corp., Beijing, 1992-93; project mgr. AT&T, Bedminster, N.J., 1998-99. Mem. AAAS, IEEE, SPIE, Assn. for Computing Machinery, Health Physics Soc., Am. Nuclear Soc., N.Y. Acad. Scis., Sigma Xi. Achievements include creation and research for explosive detection and nuclear medicine imaging. Avocations: hiking, travel, movies, Broadway shows, computer/internet surfing. Office Phone: 732-821-4508. E-mail: lizhang@alum.mit.edu.

ZHANG, LIBING, botanist; b. Shimian, Sichuan, China, Nov. 18, 1966; s. Binglin Zhang and Defang Chen; m. Lihong Zhang, Nov. 15, 1990; 1 child, Gechen. PhD, Johannes Gutenberg U., Mainz, Germany, 2002. Rsch. asst. Chengdu Inst. of Biology, Chinese Acad. Scis., 1990—92, asst. prof., 1992—95, assoc. prof., 1995—97; DAAD fellow Johannes Gutenberg U. Mainz, Germany, 1997—2002; postdoctoral fellow U. Mo., St. Louis, 2002—03, Colo. State U., Fort Collins, 2003—05, Brigham Young U., Provo, Utah, 2005—. Contbr. over 40 articles to books and profl. jours. (Outstanding Paper awards). Office: Brigham Young Univ Dept Integrative Biology 401 WIDB Provo UT 84602 Office Phone: 801-422-5240.

ZHANG, MING, business and management consultant; b. Jiangsu, China, 1962; arrived in U.S., 1988; m. Jiping Wu, 1993; children: Oak, Sky. BA, Nanjing U., 1983, MA, 1986; cert., Johns Hopkins U.-Nanjing U., 1987; PhD, Purdue U., 1994. Rsch. fellow Nat. Def. U., Washington, 1994—97; rsch. analyst Libr. Congress, Washington, 1995—97; cons. Carnegie Endowment, Washington, 1998—99; non-resident sr fellow Atlantic Coun. U.S., Washington, 2000—. Dir. rsch. IHS Internat., Arlington, Va., 1998—2004; pres. Crossroads Initiative LLC, Va., 2002—; spkr. in field. Author: Major Powers at a Crossroads, 1995, China's Changing Nuclear Posture, 1999, A Triad of Another Kind, 1999. Grantee Tchg. grant, Rockefeller Bros. Fund, 1991, Travel grant, Am. Polit. Sci. Assn., 1993, Rsch. grant, NDU Found., 1994—97. Avocations: basketball, travel. Office Phone: 703-264-9080. Personal E-mail: mingzhang28@aol.com.

ZHANG, NENGLI, research scientist; b. Sichuan, China, Jan. 8, 1940; arrived in US, 1989; s. Sunxian Zhang and Huirong Xiong; m. Xiaohui Sun, Jan. 29, 1968; 1 child, Chi. BS equivalent in thermophysics, Tsinghua U., Beijing, 1962; PhD equivalent in thermophysics, Tsinghua U., 1984. Rsch. asst. Tsinghua U., Beijing, 1962-78, asst. prof., 1978—80; vis. scholar U. Mich., Ann Arbor, 1981—83; assoc. prof. Tsinghua U., 1984—89; rsch. assoc. U. Mich., 1989—93; sr. rsch. assoc. NRC at NASA Lewis Rsch. Ctr., Cleve., 1994—98; sr. scientist Ohio Aerospace Inst. at NASA Glenn Rsch. Ctr., Cleve., 1998—. Concurrent deputy chief engr. Hai Hua New Tech. Devel. Ctr., Beijing, 1984—88; cons. Beijing Inst. of Rubber Industry, 1984—86, Da peng Sci.-Tech. Industry Ltd., Co., 1987—89. Author: Process System Engineering (in Chinese), 1982; contbr. articles various profl. jours. Recipient Achievements in Sci. award, Beijing Sci.-Tech. Com., 1983, Nat. Sci-Tech. Progress award, Nat. Sci.-Tech. Com., 1985, Achievement in Sci. award, China State Edn. Com., 1988, Achievement in Natural Sci. award, Nat. Sci-Tech. Com., 1989, 3 NASA Tech Innovations awards, NASA, 1998. Mem.: Am. Soc. for Advancement of Sci., Am. Soc. of Mech. Engrs. Achievements include patents for innovative heat pipe systems using new working fluids; shadowgraphic method to measure contact angles with flow visualization in a sessile drop; research in thermal instability in evaporating sessile drops; discovery of identifying the profiles near three-phase contact line through caustic-diffraction of wave; convective instability in transient evaporating thin liquid layer; catastrophe optics applying to study of spreading of liquid drops. Avocations: music, gardening, sports. Home: 34671 Plantation Pl North Ridgeville OH 44039 Office: Ohio Aerospace Inst NASA Glenn Rsch Ctr 21000 Brookpark Rd Cleveland OH 44135 Office Phone: 216-433-8750. Business E-Mail: nzhang@grc.nasa.gov.

ZHANG, QIMING, engineering educator, researcher; arrived in US, 1981; s. Hui and Baoqin (Baoqin) Zhang; m. Ailan Cheng, Nov. 17, 1963; children: Andrew, Michelle. BS, Nanjiang U., 1981; PhD, Pa. State U., 1986. Rschr. Brookhaven Nat. Lab., NY, 1988—91; faculty Pa. State U., University Park, 1991—. Mem. bd. dirs. Electropolymer Tech., Inc., Palo Alto, Calif., 1999—2002; cons. Thin Film Electronics, Linkoping, Sweden, 2000—01, Brilyue Semiconductor, Inc., Pitts., 2004; keynote spkr. in field. Editor: Electroactive Polymers, 1999. Mem. adv. com. Knowledge Found. Conf., Calif., 2000. Recipient David Rank award, Pa. State U. physics dept., 1982, Outstanding Rsch. award, Pa. State Engring. Soc., 1999. Mem.: IEEE (sr.; mem. tech. program com. internat. ultrasonic symposium 1994—, assoc. editor IEEE, ultrasounics, ferroelectrics and frequency control 2002—), Am. Phys. Soc., Materials Rsch. Soc. (organizer fall meeting symposium 2003). Achievements include patents for relaxor ferroelectric polymers; polyvinylidene fluoride/tri-fluoroethylene (PVDF-TrFE) based terpolymers. Office: Pa State U 187 MRL University Park PA 16802 Office Phone: 814-863-8994. Business E-Mail: qxz1@psu.edu.

ZHANG, QINGYU, education educator; BE in Mech. Engring., Tsinghua U., Beijing, 1993, M in Mgmt. Engring., 1995; PhD, U. Toledo, 2000. Asst. prof. Ark. State U., Jonesboro, 2000—03, assoc. prof., 2004—. Editor: (book) E-Supply Chain Technologies and Management. Recipient Disting. Paper award, Irwin-McGraw-Hill at MBAA, 1999. Fellow: APICS; mem.: Decision Sciences Inst. Office Phone: 870-680-8076.

ZHANG, RUIFENG, engineering educator; m. Lei Zhou, July 0, 1971; 1 child, Steven. PhD, Stevens Inst. of Tech., 2000. Asst. prof. Drexel U., Phila., 2000—. Recipient Best Paper award, IEEE Signal Processing Soc., 2002. Mem.: IEEE (chpt. chair 2001—06). Office: Drexel Univ 3141 Chestnut St Philadelphia PA 19104 Office Phone: 215-895-2257. Office Fax: 215-895-1695. Personal E-mail: rzhang5@gmail.com. Business E-Mail: rzhang@ece.drexel.edu.

ZHANG, SHENGLIANG, materials scientist, physicist; b. Zhangjiagang, Jiangsu Province, China, May 21, 1964; s. Xiangxing Zhang and Yongdi Wang; m. Qian Zhou, Mar. 20, 1993; 1 child, Gloria. BS, Nanjing U., 1984, MS, 1987; Ph.D. U. Rochester, 2001. Vis. rschr. Kyoto U., 1986—88; lectr. Nanjing U., 1988; sr. project engr. Xerox Corp., 1998—99. Internat. NY, 1999—2001, tech. specialist, 2001—. Contbr. articles to profl. jours.; patents in field (Xerox Inventor's awards, 2003). Japanese Govt. Monbusho scholar, 1988. Mem.: AlChe, ASM Internat., Materials Rsch. Soc. Avocations: fishing,

hiking. Home: 155 Lac Kine Dr Rochester NY 14618 Office: Xerox Corp 800 Phillips Rd Bldg 111-30N Webster NY 14580 Office Phone: 585-422-9511. Personal E-mail: johnslz@yahoo.com. E-mail: john.s.zhang@xerox.com.

ZHANG, SHU, statistician; arrived in US, 1986; d. Xiongfei Zhang and Zhunian Cui. MD, Beijing Med. Sch. Chinese Medicine, 1983; MS, U. Minn., 1988; ScD, Harvard U., 1997. Biostatistician Harvard Med. Sch., Boston, 1988—90, Trilogy Corp., Waukegan, Ill., 1990—93; sr. biostatistician Pfizer, Inc., Groton, Conn., 1997—2001; prin. biostatistician Sepracor, Inc., Marlborough, Mass., 2001—. Contbr. articles to profl. jours. and ency. Recipient Student Travel award, Internat. Biometric Soc., 1998, Presentation Award, Fourth World Conf. on Acupuncture, 1996; grantee, Nat. Inst. Environ. Health Scis., 1993—97. Mem.: Am. Statis. Assn.

ZHANG, SHUGUANG, biomedical engineer; b. Chongqing, Sichuan, China, Feb. 9, 1953; came to US, 1980; s. Zenming and Xingdi (Zhao) Z.; m. Kathleen R. Schaefer, June 12, 1982; 1 child, Niklas. BS in Biochemistry, Sichuan U., China, 1980; PhD in Genetics, Biochemistry and Molecular Biology, U. Calif., Santa Barbara, 1988. Am. Cancer Soc. postdoctoral fellow structural and molecular biology MIT, Cambridge, Mass., 1988—91, rsch. scientist dept. biology, 1992-96, prin. rsch. scientist, 1997—, assoc. dir. Ctr. Biomedical Engring., 1998—. Cons. Acorda Therapeutics, NYC, 1996; sci. adv. Mitsubishi Chem. Corpn., Tokyo, 1997; vis. prof. Qinghua U., Beijing, 1998—, Chinese Acad. Med. Sci., Beijing, China U. Petroleum, Qingdao; hon. prof., disting. Changjiang scholar Sichuan U., Chengdu, China. Contbr. articles to profl. jours. Recipient R & D 100 award, R & D Magazine, 2004, Wilhelm Exner medal, Austria, 2006; grantee, Whitaker Found., 1997, NIH, 1997, Japan Soc. for Promotion of Sci., 2003, Japan Advancement for Med. Instrument, 2005, John Simon Guggenheim fellowship, 2006. Mem.: Internat. Soc. Study of Origin of Life, NY Acad. Scis., Protein Soc., Human Genome Orgn., Am. Soc. Biochemistry and Molecular Biology, AAAS, Sigma Xi. Achievements include a patent on a discovery of self-assembling peptide systems. Office: Lab Molecular Self-Assembly MIT 77 Mass Ave Bldg 56-341 Cambridge MA 02139 E-mail: shuguang@mit.edu.*

ZHANG, WEI DAVID, finance educator; s. C. Li. PhD, Syracuse U., NY, 1997—2001. Asst. prof. fin. SUNY, Fredonia, NY, 2002—05, Ariz. State U., Phoenix, 2005. Mem.: Beta Gamma Sigma (life).

ZHANG, WEIZHEN, physiologist; b. Chaoyang, Guangdong, China, Dec. 6, 1964; s. Mingsheng and Wenshan Zhang; m. Mei Shan, Jan. 12, 1963. PhD, Beijing Med. U., 1994. Rsch. investigator U. Mich., Ann Arbor, 2000—04, rsch. asst. prof., 2004—. Contbr. articles to profl jours. Mem.: Am. Gastroent. Assn., Am. Physiol. Soc., Soc. Neurosci. Achievements include discovery of ghrelin directly regulates pancreatic exocrine secretion; ghrelin can stimulate neurogenesis; research in ghrelin inhibits adipogenesis via an unknown subtype of ghrelin receptor. Office: Univ Mich 1520B MSRB I 1150 W Med Ctr Dr Ann Arbor MI 48109 Office Phone: 734-615-0360. Office Fax: 734-763-4135. E-mail: weizhenz@umich.edu.

ZHANG, WENXIAN, librarian; b. Zhengzhou City, China, Aug. 27, 1963; came to U.S., 1988; s. Jiatai Zhang and Sufen Cao; m. Qun Du, Oct. 12, 1987; children: Michelle, Nathan. BA, Beijing U., 1985; MLS, So. Conn. State U., 1989, MS in Bus., 1993. Libr. Yellow River U., Zhengzhou, 1985-86, acting dir. libr., 1986-88; grad. asst. So. Conn. State U., New Haven, 1988-89; asst. dir. Ansonia (Conn.) Libr., 1990-91, libr. dir., 1991—95; head pub. svcs. Rollins Coll., Winter Park, Fla., 1995—2001, assoc. prof., head archives and spl. collections, 2001—. Reference libr. Conn. State U., New Britain, 1993—95. Grantee Christian Higher Edn. in Asia, N.Y., 1988-89; H. W. Wilson scholar, 1989-90. Mem. Soc. Am. Archivists, Soc. Fla. Archivists, Chinese Am. Librs. Assn., Winter Park Hist. Assn., Beta Phi Mu. Avocations: archival management, Chinese librarianship, Asian American affairs. Home: 2226 Wembley Pl Oviedo FL 32765-7360 Office: Rollins Coll Box 2768 Winter Park FL 32789 E-mail: wzhang@rollins.edu.

ZHANG, XIAN, conductor; b. Dandong, China; BA in Orchestral Conducting, Ctrl. Conservatory of Music, Beijing; MA in Orchestral Conducting, Ctrl. Conservatory Music, Beijing. Resident conductor China Opera House, Beijing; conductor JinFan Symphony Orchestra; music dir. Lucca Festival Orch., Italy, 2000; music dir. Concert Orch. Opera Theatre of Lucca, Italy, 2000—; cover conductor NY Philharmonic, 2002—04, asst. conductor, 2004—05, assoc. conductor 2005—; asst. prof. orch. conducting U. Cin. Col. - Conservatory of Music, 2000, music dir. Concert Orch., 2000. Guest conductor (Operas) La traviata, Cin. Opera, 2003, Don Giovanni, 2004, Cin. Symphony, Colo. Symphony, Minn. Opera, Auckland Philharmonia, New Zealand, London Symphony Orchestra, 2005, 2006, conductor Scherzoid, NY Philharmonic, 2005, Four Sea Interludes, 2005, Historia du Soldat, 2005, NY Philharmonic Time Warner Concerts in the Parks, Bravo! Vail Valley Music Festival, Colo., 2005. Achievements include co-winner Maazel-Vilar Conductors' Competition. Office: NY Philharmonic Avery Fisher Hall 10 Lincoln Ctr Plz New York NY 10023 Office Phone: 212-875-5900. Office Fax: 212-875-5717.*

ZHANG, XIANG YANG, psychiatrist, researcher; b. Guo-Yang, An-Hui Province, China, Nov. 19, 1967; arrived in U.S., 1999; s. Rong Ming Zhang and Zhong Xiang Ma; m. Gui Ying Wu, Dec. 1, 1992; children: Yi Kun, Yi Tang. BS, Anhui Med. U., 1988; MD, PhD, Peking U., Beijing, 1998. Diplomate Nat. Med. Assn., China, 1995. Intern Beijing HuiLong Guan Psychiat. Hosp., 1988—89, resident, 1989—92; clin. psychiatrist Beijing Psychiat. Hosp., 1995—; assoc. rsch. scientist Yale U. Sch. Medicine, New Haven, 2003—. Chief behavioral pharmacology, psychiatry Yale U. Med. Sch., New Haven, 2003—. Contbr. articles to profl. jours. Recipient Pfizer Young Investigator award, World Psychiat. Assn., China, 1996, 1st Place award for Janssen Med. award, Chinese Psychiat. Assn. 1997 Lilly Excellence In Thesis award, Chinese Jour. Psychiatry, 1999, Young Scientist award, 10th Biennial Winter Workshop on Schizophrenia, Davos, Switzerland, 2000, Young Investigator Travel award, Nat. Inst. Drug Abuse, Fla., 2003. Mem.: Soc. for Neuroscience (assoc.). Achievements include discovery of extract of Gingko biloba may increase the effectiveness of antipsychotic medications in schizophrenia, as well reduce their side effects; research in molecular genetics in schizophrenia; psychopharmacology for the treatment of tardive dyskinesia; immune dysfunction in schizophrenia; extract of Gingko biloba added to haloperidol in the treatment of chronic patients with schizophrenia. Office: Ribicoff Labs Rm S-316 CHMC 34 Park St New Haven CT 06508 Office Phone: 203-932-5711 x 4133. E-mail: zhangxy9@yahoo.com.

ZHANG, XIAOQI, education educator; PhD, U. of Cin., 1999. Asst. prof. U. of Mass., Lowell, 2002, U. of Mo., Rolla, 1999—2002. Office: Univ of Mass Lowell One University Ave Lowell MA 01854 Office Phone: 978-934-2287.

ZHANG, XINWEN, computer scientist, researcher; b. Niangxiang, China, Jan. 1, 1974; s. Qiqiu Zhang and Meizhi Xiao; m. Wei Xiong. BA, Huaxhong U. Sci. and Tech., Wuhan, China, 1993, PhD, George Mason U., Fairfax, Va., 2006. Software devel. engr. CE-Infosys Pte. Ltd., 1998—2000; rsch. asst. George Mason U., 2001—. Achievements include analysis of usage control models, application in trusted computing systems. Home: 9136 Barrick St Apt 301 Fairfax VA 22031 Office: George Mason U 4400 University Dr MSN 4A4 Fairfax VA 22030 Office Phone: 703-993-1668. Home Fax: 270-398-5872; Office Fax: 703-993-1638. Personal E-mail: xinwenzhang@hotmail.com. Business E-Mail: xzhang6@gmu.edu.

ZHANG, XUDONG, literature and language professor, department chairman; b. Beijing, Jan. 23, 1965; s. Mingyang and Liangying (Sun) Zhang; m. Jing Wang, July 4, 1987; 1 child, Xi Alexander. PhD, Duke U., Durham, NC, 1995. Lectr. lit. theory Ctrl. Conservatory of Music, Beijing, 1987—90; asst. prof. Chinese Rutgers State U., New Brunswick, NJ, 1995—99; prof. Chinese and comparative lit., chair dept. East Asian studies NYU, NYC, 1999—. Rockefeler fellow in the humanities Internat. Ctr. for Advanced Studies NYU., NYC, 1998—99; Zijiang vis. scholar prof. humanities East China

Normal U., Shanghi, 2002—. Mem.: MLA. Home: 100 Bleecker St Apt 10A New York NY 10012 Office: NY Univ 715 Broadway 3rd Fl New York NY 10003 Office Phone: 212-998-7622. Office Fax: 212-995-4682. Business E-Mail: xz3@nyu.edu.

ZHANG, YANWEN, research scientist; arrived in US, 2002, permanent resident, 2004; m. William J. Weber, May 4, 2002. MS, Beijing Normal U., 1990—93, PhD in Sci., 1993—99; PhD in Engring. Physics, Lund U., Sweden, 1995—98. Asst. prof., divsn. ion physics Uppsala U., Sweden, 2000—02; sr. rsch. scientist Pacific NW Nat. Lab., Richland, Wash., 2003—. Recipient Outstanding Young Alumnae award, Beijing Normal U., 1990, Hon. Docent award, Lund Univ., Sweden, 2004, Presdl. Early Career award for scientists & engrs., US Govt., 2006, Early Career Scientist and Engr. award, Office of Sci., DOE, 2006; grantee Fellowship, The Swedish Inst., 1995—96; Rsch. grant for overseas young scholar, Nat. Lab. Radiation Beam and Materials Engring., China, 2000, Rsch. grant, Vetenskapsradet Swedish Rsch. Coun., 2002. Mem.: Materials Rsch. Soc. Avocations: skiing, camping, hiking, hunting.

ZHANG, YAWEI, epidemiologist; m. Kaiyong Zou, May 15, 1994; 1 child, Zhihan Zou. MD, West China U., Chengdu, 1993; PhD, Yale U., New Haven, Conn., 2004. Postdoctoral fellow Nat. Cancer Inst., Rockville, Md., 2004—05; asst. prof. Yale U., 2005—. Rsch. asst. Yale U., 2001—04. Editor: Encyclopedia of Global Health. Mem.: APHA (assoc.), InterLymph (assoc.), Internat. Genetic Epidemiology Soc. (assoc.), Am. Assn. Cancer Rsch. (assoc. Scholar in Tng. award 2005). Achievements include research in personal hair dye use and risk of non-hodgkin lymphoma; genetic susceptability and risk of non-hodgkin lymphoma; PCBs and CYP1A1 and risk of breast cancer. Office: Yale Univ 60 College St New Haven CT 06520 Office Phone: 203-785-6210. Business E-Mail: yawei.zhang@yale.edu.

ZHANG, YOUXUE, geology educator; b. Huarong County, Hunan, China, Sept. 17, 1957; came to U.S., 1983; s. Zaiyi Zhang and Dezhen Wu; m. Zhengjiu Xu; children: Dan, Ray. BS in Geol. Scis., Beijing, 1982; MA in Geol. Scis., Columbia U., 1985, MPhil, 1987, PhD in Geol. Scis., 1989. Grad. rsch. asst. Columbia U., N.Y.C., 1983-88; postdoctoral fellow Calif. Inst. Tech., 1988-91; asst. prof. geology U. Mich., Ann Arbor, 1991-97, assoc. prof., 1997—2004, prof., 2004—. Contbr. articles to profl. jours. Named Young Investigator, NSF, 1994. Fellow: AAAS, Geol. Soc. Am.; mem.: Am. Geophys. Union, Geochem. Soc. (F.W. Clarke medal 1993), Mineral. Soc. Am., Sigma Xi. Office: Univ Mich Ann Arbor MI 48109-1005 E-mail: youxue@umich.edu.

ZHANG, YUWEN, mechanical engineer, researcher; b. Xiaoyi, Shanxi, China, Jan. 7, 1965; came to U.S., 1994; s. Zengwei and Linmei (Zhao) Z.; m. Jianfeng Guo, Jan. 1, 1988; children: Angela, Joanna. BS, Xi'an (China) Jiaotung U., 1985, MS, 1988, PhD, 1991. Asst. prof. Xi'an Jiaotong U., 1991-92, assoc. prof., 1992-94; rsch. assoc. Wright State U., Dayton, Ohio, 1994-95, U. Conn., Storrs, 1995-98, rsch. scientist, 1999—. Contbr. articles to profl. jours. Mem. AIAA (sr.), ASME, Chinese Assn. Engring. Thermophysics. Achievements include research on forced convection heat transfer, phase change heat transfer and heat transfer in manufacturing and materials processing. Office: U Conn 191 Auditorium Rd Unit U-139 Storrs Mansfield CT 06269-3139

ZHANG, ZHIJIAN, engineering educator; b. TongXiang, ZheJiang Province, China, July 4, 1973; s. LinHan Zhang and GuiZhen Chen; life ptnr. YiPing Ma. PhD, ZheJiang U., HangZhou, 2002. Asst. prof. ZheJiang U., HangZhou, China, 2001—01; rschr. U. Minn., Twin City, 2002—04; assoc. prof. ZheJiang U., 2004—. Grantee, Nat. Ministry Edn., China, 2005. Mem.: Nat. Watershed Mgmt. Assn. China. Socialist. Achievements include patents pending for Novel bioreactor for simultaneous removal of nitrogen and phosphrus from wastewater; invention of Paddy field can be operated to intercept phosphorus through innovated irrigation-drainage practices. Home: 20-2-604 KaiXuan 268 ZheJiang Province HangZhou 310029 China Office: Center of Eco-environment ZheJiang Unive KaiXuan 268 ZheJiang Province HangZhou 310029 China Office Phone: 133-0581-9218. Personal E-mail: zhangzhijian@zju.edu.cn, or zjzhangox@yahoo.com. E-mail: zjzhangox@yahoo.com.

ZHANG, ZHONGJIAN, research scientist; b. Zhengzhou, Henan, China, Dec. 14, 1956; s. Weimin Zhang and Guangrong Cui; m. Juan Zhang, Jan. 7, 1986; 1 child, Feipeng. MS, Xian (China) Med. U., 1986; PhD, U. Miami, 1992. Rsch. assoc. U. Miami, 1993-94; intramual rsch. tng. Award fellow NIH, Bethesda, Md., 1994-98, staff rsch. scientist, 1998—. Contbr. articles to profl. jours. Achievements include domestic and international patents.

ZHANG, ZHONGQI, chemist; arrived in U.S., 1989, naturalized, 2003; m. Rong Wang, Dec. 25, 1990; children: Justin R., Wesley S. PhD, Purdue U., 1990—95. Postdoctoral rsch. assoc. Nat. High Magnetic Field Lab., Tallahassee, 1995—97; rsch. scientist Amgen, Thousand Oaks, Calif., 1997—. Mem.: Am. Chem. Soc., Am. Soc. for Mass Spectrometry. Achievements include invention of techniques in mass spectrometry based peptide sequencing; research in quantitative prediction of peptide tandem spectrum; invention of method for gradient elution in micro-flow liquid chromatography; first to new technique for studying protein structure using hydrogen exchange and mass spectrometry; invention of new method for charge state deconvolution in electrospray mass spectrometry; development of software for automated mining of mass spectrometric data; research in peptide conformation by collision-induced dissociation. Office: Amgen One Amgen Ctr Dr Thousand Oaks CA 91320 Personal E-mail: zzhang@amgen.com.

ZHAO, FANG LI, medical researcher; b. Wugong, Shaan Xi, China, Jan. 3, 1963; s. Huoan Zhao and Yu Ling Zhou; m. Tinhu Gu, De. 19, 1989, 1 child, Guanchao. BA, Shaanxi Teachers U., China, 1984; MA, Xi'an Med. U., China, 1987, PhD, 1997. Asst. rschr. Xi'an Med. U., China, China, 1987—93, China, 1997—98; postdoctoral rschr. Ohio State U., Ohio, 1998—. Contbr. articles to profl. jours. Mem.: Am. Chemoreception Sci. Avocations: movies, science novels, political news. Office: Oral Biology College of Dentistry 3 at W 12th Avenue Columbus OH 43218-2357

ZHAO, FENG-QI, endocrinologist, educator; PhD, U. Alta., Edmonton, Can., 1993. Asst. prof. U. Vt., Burlington, 2001—. Contbr. articles to profl. jours. Mem.: Endocrine Assn. (assoc.). Office: Univ Vt 570 Main St Burlington VT 05405 Office Phone: 802-656-0786. Office Fax: 802-656-8196.

ZHAO, JIA, lawyer; b. Shanghai, Sept. 23, 1940; came to U.S., 1980; BA, Beijing Fgn. Studies U., 1963; JD, Harvard U., 1983. Bar: Ill. 1985, D.C. 1986. U.S. desk officer dept. Am. and Oceanic Affairs, Fgn. Ministry People's Republic of China, 1972; atty. Arnold & Porter, Washington, Covington & Burling, Washington, Pillsbury, Madison & Sutro, San Francisco; 1st sec. dept. treaty and law, Am. and oceanic affairs Chinese Fgn. Ministry, 1986—88; with Baker & McKenzie, Chgo., 1988—, ptnr., 1994—. Mem. ABA, D.C. Bar, Chgo. Bar Assn., Beijing Fgn. Econ. Law Assn. Office: Baker and McKenzie One Prudential Plz 130 E Randolph Dr Chicago IL 60601

ZHAO, TONG, research scientist; s. Wenliang Zhao and Zhenfang Wang; m. Jiayi Chen, Oct. 12, 2001. PhD, Chinese Acad. Sci. Rsch. staff mem. Seagate Tech., Pitts. Contbr. articles to profl. jours. Mem.: Materials Rsch. Soc., Am. Phys. Soc. Achievements include research in oxide thin films and heterostructures for electronic, magnetic, and optical devices; charge carrier mediation nature of the magnetism in oxide magnetic semiconductor which is the key to integrate a calculating and a memory device onto a single chip; CMR based ferroelectric filed effect transistor which integrate magnetic and electric control into an electronic device; observation of electrical induced antiferromagnetic domain switching in a single phase material at room temperature which enables the multiable control in a memroy device; patents in field. Office Phone: 412-918-7087.

**ZHAO, WEI (WAYNE),** materials scientist, researcher, transmission electron microscopist; s. Zuyao Zhao and Dingru Liu; m. Yi (Merry) Sun, Jan. 28, 1992; 1 child, Allen Aquila. B in Engring., Harbin Inst. Tech., 1987; M in Engring., NE Forestry U., 1989; PhD, U. Tenn., 1999. Asst. prof. Tianjin U., China, 1989—91, lectr., prin. investigator, 1992—95; postdoc. rsch. faculty U. Pa., Phila., 1999—2001; sr. TEM engr. Infineon Tech. Richmond, Sandston, Va., 2001—03; TEM analyst Internat. Sematech, Austin, Tex., 2003—04; staff scientist, supr. electron microscopy and particle physics group, project mgr. particle physics Kerr McGee Chem., LLC, Oklahoma City, 2004—. Grad. tchg. and rsch. asst. NE Forestry U., Harbin, 1987—89; grad. rsch. asst. U. Tenn., Knoxville, Tenn., 1996—99. Contbr. articles to profl. jours. Mem.: Microscopy Soc. Am., Materials Rsch. Soc. Achievements include discovery of stacking sequence effects on mechanical performance for a plain-weave Nicalon fiber-fabric reinforced SiC ceramic-matrix composite; first to computer-aided modeling on effects of lamina stacking sequence and laminate layup for plain-weave Nicalon/SiC ceramic-matrix composite; introduce SEM/XEDS linescan technique to semi-quantify fiber/matrix interfacial oxidation behavior for a Nicalon/SiC ceramic-matrix composite; discovery of fiber orientation effects on mechanical properties for a crow-foot woven Nextel fiber-fabric reinforced Blackglas low-cost ceramic-matrix composite; first to initiate combined SEM/XEDS elemental mapping, ultrasonic, and x-ray computed tomography characterization on fiber and void distributions in a crow-foot woven Nextel/Blackglas ceramic-matrix composite; research in atomic-scale high-resolution transmission electron microscopy in nanometer semiconductor wafer process development; analytical transmission electron microscopy in physical failure analysis for nanometer semiconductor wafer and device process integration; materials science issues in advanced metallization for nanometer semiconductor wafer integration; development of advanced surface coatings to nanometer titanium dioxide pigment and particle physics; first to introduce polycrystallined diamond compact and tungsten carbide composite blank onto woodworking tools in China; research in synthesis of diamond thin film by combustion flames techniques. Office Phone: 405-775-5691. Personal E-mail: wayne_zhaowei@yahoo.com.

**ZHAO, WENYI,** systems analyst; b. Zigong, Sichuan, China, Feb. 24, 1969; s. Zhili Zhao and Anrong Zhang; m. Ying Liu, Dec. 2, 1971. BA, Tsinghua U., 1990; MS, U. Va., 1995; PhD, U. Md., 2000. Mem. tech. staff Sarnoff Corp., Princeton, NJ, 2000—. Contbr. articles to profl. jours., chapters to books. Recipient Innovation award, Sarnoff Corp., 2003, Best Industry Related Paper award, Internat. Conf. Pattern Recognition, 2004. Mem.: IEEE. Office: Sarnoff Corp 201 Washington Rd Princeton NJ 08540 Business E-Mail: wyzhao@ieee.org.

**ZHAO, XIAOLIANG,** mechanical engineer, researcher; b. Qingdao, China, Nov. 21, 1973; arrived in U.S., 1999; m. Jing Zhang, July 14, 1999; 1 child, Andrew Kun. BSEE, Nanjing U., China, 1996, MS in Acoustics, 1999; PhD in Engring. Mechanics, The Pa. State U., Univ. Pk., Pa., 2003. Application engr. Krautkramer Branson, Inc., Lewistown, Pa., 2000—01; mgr. program Intelligent Automation, Inc., Rockville, Md., 2002—. Contbr. articles to profl. jours. Mem.: Acoustical Soc. Am. (assoc.). Avocations: ping pong/table tennis, swimming, rollerblading. Office: Intelligent Automation Inc 15400 Calhoun Dr Suite 400 Rockville MD 20855 Office Phone: 301-294-5232. Business E-Mail: xzhao@i-a-i.com.

**ZHAO, XUEHENG,** research scientist; s. Dishun Zhao and Shouzhen Wang; m. Tang Yarong, May 1, 1999. BE, Beijing Inst. Clothing Tech., 1994; PhD, U. Ga., Athens, 2004. Instr. Dept. Applied Chemistry, Beijing U. Chem. Tech., 1997—99; rsch. asst. U. Ga., Athens, 1999—2004; postdoctoral rsch. scientist Dept. Biology, Jackson State U., Miss., 2004—. Reviewer (jour.) Jour. of Hazardous Materials. Student Rsch. grantee, Am. Assn. of Textile Chemists and Colorists, 2001. Mem.: Am. Chem. Soc. (assoc.), Miss. Acad. of Sci. (assoc.). Office Phone: 601-979-1226. E-mail: xueheng.zhao@jsums.edu.

**ZHAO, ZHEN,** music educator; b. Tian Jin, China, Aug. 27, 1947; arrived in U.S., 1985; parents Tian Qi Zhao and Pei Ying Gong; m. Yang Zhong Zhang, Apr. 29, 1976; 1 child, William Wen Wei Zhang. *Husband Yang Zhong Zhang earned his physics PhD from the University of Texas at Austin in 1988. Son William Wen Wei Zhang received his Bachelor of Science degree in Electrical Engineering from the University of Texas at Austin in 2002. After graduating, he established a website design company under the name of Star 16 Studios. He has launched numerous websites for clients in many fields.* MusB, U. Tex., 1991, MusM, 1994. Pvt. piano tchr., Austin, Tex., 1995—. Contbr. articles to profl. jours. Mem.: Nat. Guild Piano Tchrs., Music Tchrs. Nat. Assn., Tex. Music Tchrs. Assn., Austin Dist. Music Tchrs. Assn. Achievements include established the Zhen Zhao piano studio; her students have won numerous competitions. Avocations: ping pong/table tennis, tai chi, travel, photography. Personal E-mail: zhaozhen@austin.rr.com.

**ZHAO, ZHONGSHAN,** structural engineer, researcher; b. Zhejiang Province, China, Oct. 5, 1963; s. Zongrong Zhao and Chunchai Zhang; m. Qinglin Shen Zhao, Apr. 13, 1971; 1 child, Audrey Y. B in Bridge Engring., Tongji U., China, 1985; M in Engring., U. of Tokyo, 1992; PhD, Tex. Tech U., 1997. Rsch. asst. Tongji U., Shanghai, 1985—90; structural engr. Wind Engring. Inst., Tokyo, 1992—94; rsch. assoc. Tex. Tech U., Lubbock, 1998—2000; structural engr. Mustang Engring., LP, Houston, 2000—. Contbr. articles to profl. jours. Recipient John B. Hawley award, ASCE, Tex. Sect., 1999. Achievements include patents for Cable stay aerodynamic damper band and method of use.

**ZHARIKOV, ALEXANDER NIKOLAEVICH,** trade union federation executive; b. Michailov, Rjazan, Russia, Jan. 2, 1945; s. Nikolaj Philippovich and Claudia Egorovna (Gorodnicheva) Z.; m. Eva Svachova; children: Michail, Anette. Student, Shipbldg. Inst., Leningrad, Russia, 1969. Sec. Student Orgn. Shipbldg. Inst., Leningrad, 1967-70; dir. student dept. Leningrad City Youth Orgn., Leningrad, 1970-71, sec., 1971-74; vice chmn. Com. Youth Orgns. USSR, Moscow, 1974-76; chmn. Student Coun. USSR, Moscow, 1976-78; v.p. Internat. Union Students, Prague, Czechoslovakia, 1978-84; officer Internat. Dept. Ctrl. Com. CPSU, Moscow, 1984-88; dir. internat. dept. All Union Ctrl. Coun. Trade Unions, Moscow, 1988-90; gen. sec. World Fedn. Trade Unions, Prague, 1990—. Co-author: International Union of Students, 1978. Mem. City Com. Leningrad Youth Orgn., 1970-71, sec., 1971-74; mem. Ctrl. Com. Youth Orgn. USSR, Moscow, 1978-84. Capt. Russian mil., 1962-66. Office: PO Box N80 Na Losach CP 123 14200 Prague 4 Czech Republic Office Phone: (420) 244462085. Personal E-mail: wftu@login.cz.

**ZHDANOV, BORIS,** research scientist; PhD, Moscow State U., 1975. Assoc. prof. Moscow State U., 1988—99; vis. prof. USAF Acad., Colo., 1998—2000, sr. scientist, 2004—; prin. scientist Directed Energy Solutions, Inc., Colorado Springs, 2004—04. Office Phone: 719-333-2109. Personal E-mail: zhdanovb@hotmail.com. Business E-Mail: boris.zhdanov.ctr@usafa.af.mil.

**ZHDANOV, MICHAEL SEMENOVICH,** geophysicist, educator; b. Moscow, Oct. 2, 1946; m. Olga Nikolaevna Zhdanov; 1 child, Elena. MSc in Geophysics, Moscow State Oil and Gas U., 1968; MSc in Math., Moscow State U., 1969, PhD in Physics and Math., 1970, D of Scis., 1978. From asst. to full prof. dept. geophysics Moscow Gubkin State U. of Oil and Gas, 1970—92; head of dept., dep. dir. Inst. Terrestrial Magnetism, Ionosphere and Radio Wave Propagation USSR Acad. Scis., Moscow, 1978—90; dir. Inst. Geoelectromagnetic Rsch. Russian Acad. Scis., Moscow, 1991—92; prof. dept. geology and geophysics U. Utah, Salt Lake City, 1993—. Lansdown vis. prof. U. Victoria, B.C., Canada, 1991; Gauss prof. Gettingen Acad. Scis., Gettingen, Germany; vis. prof. Colo. Sch. Mines, Golden. Author: Advanced Theory of Deep Geomagnetic Sounding, 1984, Integral Transforms in Geophysics, 1988, The Geoelectrical Methods in Geophysical Exploration, 1994, Geophysical Inverse Theory and Regularization Problems, 2002; patentee in field. Named Hon. Prof., China Nat. Ctr. of Geol. Exploration

Tech., 1997; recipient award for outstanding achievement in the devel. of sci. and tech., Russian Acad. Natural Scis., 2000. Fellow: Electromagnetics Acad, U.S.A., Acad. Natural Scis. Russia; mem.: Am. Geophys. Union, Soc. Exploration Geophysics. Office: U Utah 135 S 1460 E Rm 719 Salt Lake City UT 84112 Business E-Mail: mzhdanov@mines.utah.edu.

**ZHENG, FAWEN,** fluid mechanics engineer; BS with hons. in Engring., MS with hons. in Engring., Hohai U., Nanjing, China, 1990; MSc, UNESCO-IHE, Delft, The Netherlands, 1997; PhD, S.D. Sch. Mines and Tech., Rapid City, S.D., 2001. Cert. floodplain mgr., Assn. State Floodplain Mgr., Inc., 2005. Sr. water resources rsch. engr. Nanjing Inst. Hydrology and Water Resources, Nanjing, China, 1990—95; engr. ii PBS&J, Inc., West Palm Beach, Fla., 2002—. Contbr. articles to profl. jours. Recipient Exellent Student award, Hohai U., 1986, Best Engring. Design award, South Fla. Water Mgmt. Dist., 2003, Best Paper award, PBS&J, Inc. 2005; fellow, Netherlands Govt., 1995, S.D. Sch. Mines and Tech., 1999, 2000. Mem.: NSPE, Am. Geophical Union, Fla. Engring. Soc., Assn. State Floodplain Mgr., Inc. Office Phone: 561-698-7275.

**ZHENG, GANG,** mathematician, statistician, researcher; arrived in U.S., 1994; s. Chang-Gen Zheng; m. Liu Ling-Xian. BS in Applied Math., Fudan U., Shanghai, 1987; MS in Math., Mich. Technol. U., 1996; PhD in Stats., George Washington U., 2000. Lectr. Shanghai Second Poly. U., 1987—94; math. statistician Nat. Heart, Lung and Blood Inst., Bethesda, Md., 2000—. Contbr. articles to profl. jours. Fellow: The Royal Statis. Soc.; mem.: Internat. Statis Inst., Internat. Biometrics Soc., Internat. Indian Statis. Assn. (life), Internat. Chinese Statis. Assn. (life), Inst. Math. Stats., Am. Statis. Assn. Office: National Heart Lung and Blood Institute 6701 Rockledge Dr MSC 7938 Room 8223 Bethesda MD 20892-7938 Office Phone: 301-435-1287.

**ZHENG, JAMES,** architectural firm executive; b. 1970; BA in Arch., Univ. Ill. Chgo., 1995; MBA student, Northwestern Univ. Kellogg Sch. Bus. Assoc. prin. Goettsch Ptnrs., Chgo., 1995—2005, dir. Asian ops., 1995—, ptnr., 2005—. Named one of 40 Under Forty, Crain's Chgo. Bus., 2005. Office: Goettsch Ptnrs Inc Fl 17 224 S Michigan Ave Chicago IL 60604 Office Phone: 312-356-0600. Office Fax: 312-356-0601.*

**ZHENG, LINGYI ALBERT,** materials scientist, materials engineer, researcher; s. Cheng and Yuhe Zheng; m. Zhenwan Jennifer Xu; 1 child, Albert D. PhD, Rice U., Houston, 1999. Sr. engr. Micron Tech., Boise, Idaho, 1999—2004, Micron Tech. Inc, Manassas, Va., 2004—. Contbr. articles to profl. jours. Scholar, Rice U., 1995. Mem.: IEEE. Achievements include patents in field. Office Phone: 703-396-1452. Personal E-mail: albertzheng@yahoo.com.

**ZHENG, LU,** educator; d. Qingsheng Yong and Huijun Zheng; m. Warren Zhang, Mar. 30, 2002. PhD, Yale U., New Haven, Conn., 1999. Prof. U. of Mich., Ann Arbor, 1998—. Office Phone: 734-763-5392. E-mail: luzheng@umich.edu.

**ZHENG, QI,** statistician, biomathematician; b. Lanxi, Zhejiang, China, July 8, 1958; arrived in U.S., 1988; s. Huanming Zheng and Sulan Zhuge; m. Huiping Hu, May 12, 1987; children: Yan, Eric Hugh. BS in math., Zhejiang U., 1978—82; PhD in stats., Tex. A&M U., 1988—93, postgrad., 1993. Cert. independent Mathematica trainer. Post-doc Nat. Ctr. Toxicological Rsch., Jefferson, Ark., 1994—96, staff fellow, 1996—2002; rsch. scientist Tex. A&M U., College Station, 2002—03, assoc. prof. dept. epidemiology and biostats. Sch. Rural Pub. Health, 2003—. Contbr. articles to jour. (Commendable Svc. award, FDA, 1997.) Grantee Mathematica Vis. Scholar Grant, Wolfram Rsch. Inc., 1995, 1997. Mem.: Am. Statis. Assn., Phi Kappa Phi. Achievements include research in directed mutation hypothesis; irrelevancy of dispersion index in the molecular clock controversy; schochastic modeling of carcinogtenesis; development of first comprehensive computer software SALVADOR for estimating mutation rates using data from fluctuation experiments. Avocations: reading, mountain hiking, music. Office: Tex A&M U Sys Health Sci Ctr Sch Rural Pub Health Dept Epidemiology and Biostats College Station TX 77843 E-mail: qzheng@srph.tamhsc.edu.

**ZHENYU, KONG,** industrial engineer; PhD, U. Wis., Madison, 2004. Indsl. engr. Dimensional Control Systems, Troy, Mich. Office: Dimensional Control Systems Ste 309 580 Kirts Blvd Troy MI 48084

**ZHITNIK, ALEXEI,** professional hockey player; b. Kiev, Russia, Oct. 10, 1972; m. Luda Zhitnik. Defense L.A. Hockey Team, Buffalo Sabres, 1995—2005, N.Y. Islanders. Mem. def. team Russia World Championships, Austria, 1996, World Cup Tournament, 1996, World Championships, Italy, 1993—94; rep. Gold medal unified team Albertville Winter Olympics, France, 1992. Office: NY Islanders 1535 Old Country Rd Plainview NY 11803 Office Phone: 516-501-6700. Office Fax: 516-501-6762.

**ZHONG, DALONG,** materials scientist, consultant; m. Dashan Zhong; m. Xiaolan Zhang, Nov. 6, 1996. BS metallurgy, Ctrl. South U. Tech., Changsha, Hunan, China, 1993, MS metallurgy, 1996; PhD in materials sci., Colo. Sch. Mines, 2001. Tchg./rsch. asst. Colo. Sch. Mines, Golden, 1997—2001, lab mgr. advanced coatings & surface engring. lab., 1999—, rsch. assoc., 2001—. Pvt. cons. Protonetics Internat. Inc., Golden, Colo., 2001—, MVSystems, Inc., Golden, Colo., 2001—; referee Thin Solid Films, 2001—, Tribology Internat., 2001—, Jour. Materials Synthesis and Processing, 2001—, Jour. Applied Physics, 2002—, Surface & Coating Tech., 2002—, Acta Materialia, 2002—; presentor invited papers at confs. Contbr. articles to profl. jours. Fellow Zhao Tiancong fellow, Ctrl. South U. Tech., 1994, Li Found. fellow, Colo. Sch. Mines, 1997—2000. Mem.: Am. Vacuum Soc., Materials Rsch. Soc., The Minerals, Metals & Materials Soc. Office: Colorado Sch Mines 1500 Illinois St Golden CO 80401 Office Phone: 303-273-3178. Office Fax: 303-273-3057. Business E-Mail: dazhong@mines.edu.

**ZHONG, HAIZHEN,** research scientist, educator; s. Peichang Zhong and Honglan He; m. Ping Yang, June 27, 2000; 1 child, Joseph Shengyang. BSc, Beijing Med. U., China, 1994, MSc, 1997; PhD, U. Ga., Athens, 2001. Postdoctoral rsch. fellow U. Mich., Ann Arbor, 2001—03; rsch. scientist U. N.C., Greensboro, 2004—. Author: (rsch. on anticancer drug discovery) Jour. Molecular Graphics and Modelling. Mem.: Sigma Xi. Home: 6424 Highland Oak Dr Greensboro NC 27410 Office: Univ North Carolina 1000 Spring Garden St Greensboro NC 27402 Office Phone: 336-334-5121. Personal E-mail: haizhen_zhong@yahoo.com. Business E-Mail: h_zhong@uncg.edu.

**ZHONG, MIAO,** pharmacologist, researcher; m. Yan Gao; 1 child, Xiao-Yue. B.S., China Pharm. U., Nanjing, 1989; PhD, Peking Union Med. Coll., 1998. Rsch. asst. Nat. Pharm. Rsch. and devel., Beijing, 1989—93; rsch. assoc. Tex. A&M U., College Station, 1998—99, U. Louisville, 1999—2000; rsch. fellow U. Tex. Med. Sch., Houston, 2000—. Contbr. articles to profl. jours. Mem.: Soc. for Study of Reprodn. (assoc.). Achievements include research in identifying the anti-inflammatory effort of interleukin-6 biosynthesis inhibitor; identifying some important functional regions of cannabinoid receptor and oxytocin receptor. Office: Univ Tex Houston Med Sch 6431 Fannin St Houston TX 77030 Home: 500 W Prospect Rd #20-D Fort Collins CO 80526

**ZHONGREN, CAO,** electrical engineer, researcher; s. Chuanyi Cao; m. Yinqiu Lu. PhD, Stevens Inst. Tech., 2004. Project scientist Calif. Inst. Telecom. and Info. Tech. U. Calif., La Jolla, Calif., 2004—. Contbr. articles to profl. jours. Mem.: IEEE. Achievements include research in radio link and system enabling technology for software defined broadband wireless communication platform. Office: University of California San Diego 9500 Gilman Drive MC 0436 La Jolla CA 92093 Office Phone: 858-822-0176.

**ZHOU, BANG RONG,** physicist, researcher; b. Chengdu, Sichuan, China, Apr. 18, 1941; s. Fu Cheng and Ying Juan (Wang) Z.; m. Yong Pu Kang, Feb. 2, 1981; 1 child, Xiao Zhi. Grad., U. Sci. and Tech. China, Beijing, 1963, degree, 1966. Tchg. asst. U. Sci. and Tech. of China, Hefei, 1973-78, lectr.; 1979-85, assoc. prof. Grad. Sch., Chinese Acad. Scis., Beijing, 1985-87, 87-90, prof., 1990—. Vis. scholar Fermi Nat. Accelerator Lab., Batavia, 1981-83, Stanford Linear Accelerator Ctr., Calif., 1983; assoc. vis. prof. Internat. Centre for Theoretical Physics, Trieste, Italy, 1992, 94, 98; judging specialist Nat. Natural Sci. award of China in Physics and Astronomy, 2002—. Contbr. articles to profl. jours. including Atomic Energy, Nuclear Physics B. Physics Letters B, Phys. Rev. D, others. Recipient award Chinese Nat. Sci. Conf., 1978, Sci. Achievements award Chinese Acad. Scis., 1981, award Nat. Natural Sci. of China, 1982, Spl. Allowance Upon Contbn. to Chinese Advanced Edn. award The State Coun. of China, 1992. Mem. Chinese Assn. of High Energy Physics, Chinese Ctr. of Advanced Sci. and Tech. (assoc., Excellent Paper prize 1994, 97, 2001, 04), Western Returned Scholars' Assn. Achievements include participating in work on straton (quark) model of hadrons; creative research on asymptotic freedom in heavy quark potential, dynamical chiral and electroweak symmetry breaking, finite temperature field theory and phase transitions. Avocations: collecting stamps and coins, swimming, ping-pong, classical music, athletic competition, detective films on television. Office: Chinese Acad Scis Grad Sch Beijing 100049 China E-mail: zhoubr@163bj.com, zhoubr@gucas.ac.cn.

**ZHOU, CHENN QIAN,** mechanical engineer, department chairman; m. Harry Hou, Jan. 23, 1985; 1 child, Jia Hou. BS, Nanjing U. Aeronautics and Astronautics, 1982, MS, 1984; PhD, Carnegie Mellon U., 1991. Sr. rsch. engr. NOXSO Corp., Pitts., 1991—94; prof. Purdue U. Calumet, Hammond, Ind., 1994—, head Dept. Mech. Engring., 1994—. Recipient R&D 100 award, R&D Mag., 2004, Josef S. Kapitan award, Am. Iron and Steel Tech. Assn., 2005. Fellow: ASME. Office: Purdue University Calumet 2200 169th Street Hammond IN 46323 Office Phone: 219-989-2665. Business E-Mail: qzhou@calumet.purdue.edu.

**ZHOU, DAYONG,** research scientist; PhD, U. Okla., 2005. Rsch. asst. U. Okla., Norman, 1999—2005, postdoctoral rsch. assoc., 2005—. Author: (article) IEEE Transaction on Signal Processing (Best Dissertation Reward, 2006). Mem. com. internat. conf. ECU, 2006. Mem.: Sigma Xi. Achievements include patents pending for ANC without secondary path identification. Business E-Mail: dayong@ou.edu.

**ZHOU, DESHENG,** petroleum engineer; b. Wusheng, Sichuan, China, Nov. 1963; s. L. Zhou and H. Luong; m. Xiaoping Zhang, Sept. 1988; children: Ruoyao, Jennifer Aileen. BS, Beijing U., Aeronautics and Astronautics, China, 1985; MS, S.W. Petroleum Inst., China, 1988; D in Engring., S.W. Petroleum Inst., 1992; PhD, La. State U., 2000. Cert. petroleum engineer, China. Engr. China Nat. Petroleum Corp., Nanchong, Sichuan, China, 1988—94, vice chmn. petroleum-mech. engring. dept., 1994—96; from rsch. assoc. to rsch. asst. La. State U., Baton Rouge, 1996—2000; sr. petroleum engr. IHS Energy, Dallas, 2000—. Contbr. articles to profl. jours. Recipient 2d Class award, Tech. and Sci. Progress. Mem.: China Soc. Petroleum Engrs. (dir. Nanchong divsn. 1994—96), Nat. Petroleum Engring. Honor Soc. Achievements include patents for parabolic tooth of roller cone bit; design of three types of roller cone bits: XHP1s, XHP2s, and XHP3s; research in computer simulation of rock-bit interaction, leak-off tests in shallow marine sediments. Home: 7510 David Dr Frisco TX 75034 Office: Ihs Energy 17177 Preston Rd # 200 Dallas TX 75248-1235 Personal E-mail: deshzhou@yahoo.com. Business E-Mail: desheng.zhou@ihsenergy.com.

**ZHOU, GUOFU,** finance educator; b. Chengdu, China, May 1, 1960; s. Chicheng Zhou and Xuxiu Yang; m. Huixia Li, Nov. 23, 1994; children: Jason, Steve Guo. PhD, Duke U., Durham, N.C., 1990. Prof. of fin. Wash. U., St Louis. Contbr. articles to profl. jours. Home: 14310 Wainridge Dr Saint Louis MO 63017 Office: Washington Univ 1 Brookings Dr Saint Louis MO 63130 Office Phone: 314-935-6384. Business E-Mail: zhou@wustl.edu.

**ZHOU, HAI,** engineering educator; b. Bijie, China, Dec. 2, 1969; arrived in U.S., 1994; s. Guanghan Zhou and Yiwen Wang; m. Bozhao Jiang, Feb. 5, 1994; children: Ivana, Eric. BS, Tsinghua U., Beijing, 1992, MS, 1994; PhD, U. Tex., 1999. Sr. R&D engr. Synposys, Mountain View, Calif., 1999—2001; prof. Northwestern U., Evanston, Ill., 2001—. Cons. Cadence Design Sys., San Jose, Calif., 2005—. Author: Layout Optimization in VLSI Designs, 2001; editor: Encyclopedia of Algorithms, 2006; contbr. articles to profl. jours. Recipient Early Career award, NSF, 2003; rsch. grantee, Intel, Santa Clara, Calif., 2005, Cadence, 2005. Mem.: IEEE (sr.). Office: Northwestern U 2145 Sheridan Rd L359 Evanston IL 60208 Business E-Mail: haizhou@ece.northwestern.edu.

**ZHOU, JUHUA,** molecular biologist; b. Dongyang, Zhejiang, China, Apr. 21, 1963; arrived in U.S., 1994; s. Fude Zhou, Yuguan Shan; m. Yin Zhong; 1 child, Beibei. MS, Zhejiang U., 1988; BS, Zhejiang U., Hangzhou, China, 1983; PhD, U.La., 1999. Assoc. prof. Zhejiang U. (Formerly Hangzhou University), Hangzhou, Zhejiang, China, 1988—94; postdoctoral fellow ctr. for cell & gene therapy Baylor Coll. Medicine, Houston, 1999—. Vice dir. divsn. plant physiology Zhejiang U., Hangzhou, Zhejiang, China, 1988—94. Contbr. articles to profl. jours. Grantee, Zhejiang Provincial Natural Sci. Found., 1994, Chinese Natural Sci. Found., 1994. Mem.: AAAS, N.Y. Acad. Sci., Sigma Xi. Office: Baylor College Med Path Dept 2627 Landera Ct Pearland TX 77584-9113 Home: 1 Big Acre Sq #21 Gaithersburg MD 20878-2838 Office Phone: 7137985064. Office Fax: 7137981362. Personal E-mail: juhuaz@hotmail.com. Business E-Mail: jzhou@bcm.tmc.edu.

**ZHOU, LIMING,** environmental scientist; s. Haoting Zhou and Guiyun Liu; m. Ying Zhang, Apr. 5, 2006. BS, Tsinghua U., Beijing, China, 1998; MS, Dalian Inst. Chem. Physics, China, 2001; PhD, Clarkson U., Potsdam, NY, 2004. Rsch. asst. Clarkson U., 2001—04; environ. scientist Providence Engring., Baton Rouge, 2004—05, sr. environ. scientist Baton Rouge, 2005—. Designer (atmospheric environment) Intelligent Air Monitor System (Albert Einstein Award by Providence Engring., 2004). Chmn. Chinese Students and Scholar Assn., Potsdam, 2003. Mem.: Am. Assn. Aerosol Rsch. Achievements include development of advanced receptor model methods and cheometric tools to further our understanding of the origin and characteristics of atmospheric pollutants. Office: Providence Engring and Environ PO Box 84380 Baton Rouge LA 70884-4380 Office Phone: 225-766-7400. Office Fax: 225-766-7440. Business E-Mail: limingzhou@providenceeng.com.

**ZHOU, NAN,** finance educator; BA, Tsinghua U., Beijing 1989; M, So. Ill. U., Carbondale, 1993; PhD in Mith., Minn., Mpls., 2000. Lectr. SUNY, Binghamton, 1999—2000, asst. prof., 2000—06, assoc. prof., 2006—. Vis. scholar NYU, N.Y.C., 2005. Contbr. articles to profl. jours. and pubs. Mem.: Am. Acctg. Assn. Office: SUNY Sch Mgmt Binghamton NY 13902-6000 Office Phone: 607-777-2401. Business E-Mail: nzhou@binghamton.edu.

**ZHOU, PENG,** mechanical engineer; PhD in Mech. Engring., Stanford U., Calif., 2002. Staff hardware engr. Intel Corp. Hudson, Mass., 2002; sr. staff engr. Cooligy Inc, Mountain View, Calif., 2002—. Office: Cooligy Inc 800 Maude Ave Mountain View CA 94043 Office Phone: 650-417-0316. Personal E-mail: roczhou@yahoo.com. Business E-Mail: pzhou@cooligy.com.

**ZHOU, SHAO MAN,** chemist, researcher; arrived in US, 2000; s. Xingde Zhou and Huixiu Yi; m. Yi Huang, Mar. 1, 2000. BA, Jiangxi Normal U., 1994; PhD, Shanghai Inst. Organic Chemistry, Chinese Acad. Scis., 2000. Postdoctoral fellow Wayne State U., Detroit, 2000—03, rsch. assoc., 2003—. Recipient award, BASF, 2000, Chinese Acad. Scis., 2000. Mem.: Am. Chem. Soc. Achievements include patents for 2, 2-BIS(hydroxymethyl) cyclopropylidenemethyl -purines, -pyrimidines as antiviral agents; research in synthesis of stereodefined (chiral) cyclopropylboronic acids and their application. Personal E-mail: shaomanzhou@yahoo.com.

**ZHOU, SOPHIA HUAI,** biomedical engineering scientist; b. Huaiyin, Jiangsu, China, Dec. 6, 1953; MS, Dalhousie U., Halifax, Can., 1987, PhD, 1991. Profl. engr., Nova Scotia. Rsch. assoc. U. Alta., Edmonton, Canada, 1991-93, asst. prof., 1993-94, St. Louis U., 1994-95; engring. scientist Hewlett-Packard Co., Andover, Mass., 1995-99; prin. scientist Agilent Techs. Inc., Andover, Mass., 1999—2001; sr. rsch. mgr. Advanced Algorithm Rsch. Ctr.; prin. scientist Philips Med Sys, Thousand Oaks, Calif., 2001—. Contbr. articles to profl. jours.; editor: Jour. of Electrocardiology. Mem. editl. bd. Journ. of Electro Cardiology. Fellow Am. Coll. Cardiology; mem. NY Acad. Sci., Soc. Women Engrs., Internat. Soc. Electrocardiology, Internat. Soc. Computerized Electrocardiology, Am. Heart Assn., Assn. for Advancement of Med. Instrumentation, Internat. Electromagnetic Commn. (convener). Achievements include design of automated ECG interpretations. Office: Philips Med Sys 1525 Rancho Conejo Blvd Ste 100 Thousand Oaks CA 91320 Office Phone: 805-214-5111. Business E-Mail: sophia.zhou@philips.com.

**ZHOU, SUPING,** biologist, research scientist, educator; d. Yantian Zhou and Guilan Li; m. Qian Zhang; 1 child, Cheng Zhang. PhD, Nanjing Agrl. U., China, 1995. Post-doctoral fellowship Hebrew University, 1998—99, Tenn. State U., Nashville, rsch. asst. prof., 2000—. Recipient Outstanding Rsch. Scientist award, Inst. Agrl. & Environ. Rsch., Tenn. State U.; grantee Rsch. grant for identification of heat stress and genes from tolerant plant species, USDA-CSREES, 2003, Rsch. grant for aluminum toxicity in tomato roots, 2004. Mem.: Am. Assn. Plant Biologist. Achievements include discovery of new genes. Office: Tenn State Univ 3500 John A Merritt Blvd Nashville TN 37209

**ZHOU, WEI,** engineer, educator; b. China, Jan. 23, 1965; s. Qishun Zhang and Cuiying Zhou, m. Hui Chen. BEng, Tsinghua U., Beijing, 1980—85; PhD, U. Cambridge, 1987—91. Guest scientist Fraunhofer Inst. Mechanics of Materials, Freiburg, Germany, 1991—92; lectr. Nanyang Tech. U., 1992—97, sr. lectr., 1998—99, prof., 2000—, dir. Precision Engring. and Nanotechnology Ctr., 2005—. Cons. Def. Sci. Orgn., 1999—2003, Singapore Techs. Engring. Ltd., 1995—, Def. Materials Orgn., 1996—97; pres. Singapore Fracture Group, 1998—99; chmn. Consulting Com., Singapore Welding Soc., 1998—2001; vis. scholar in applied physics Harvard U., Cambridge, Mass., 2002—03; vis. scientist U. Mich., Ann Arbor, 2004—05. Fellow, Mech. Engring. Lab., Tsukuba, Japan, 1995; scholar The Sino-British Friendship Scholarship, The Chinese and Brit. Governments, 1987—91. Mem.: Materials Rsch. Soc., Minerals, Metals and Materials Soc. (life). Office: Nanyang Tech Univ 50 Nanyang Ave Singapore 639798 Singapore Office Fax: 6791 1859. Personal E-mail: wzhou@cantab.net. E-mail: mwzhou@ntu.edu.sg.

**ZHOU, WEI,** research scientist; BE in Polymer Materials & Composites, Beijing U.Aeronautics & Astronautics, 1996; ME in Materialogy, Tsinghua U., 1999; MS in Elec. Engring., U. So. Calif., 2004, PhD. Rsch. asst. Compound Semiconductor Lab., U. So. Calif., 2000—04; postdoctoral rschr. Calit2, U. Calif. Irvine, Calif., 2005—. Reviewer & author Jour. Crystal Growth. Recipient Outstanding Grad. scholarship, awarded among all univs. in Beijing, China, 1996; fellow Dean's Doctoral Merit Fellowship, Charles Lee Powell Found., 1999—2002, GuangHua Fellowship, Tsinghua U., China, 1998. Mem.: ASTM, Soc. for the Advancement of Material and Process Engring., IEEE, Microscopy Soc. Am., The Minerals, Metals and Materials Soc., Materials Rsch. Soc. Achievements include discovery of defect reduction method in Nanoplanar template for GaN blue LED/Laser materials; development of nanometer scale lateral epitaxy overgrowth of GaN for effective dislocation reduction employing block copolymer lithography. Office: Calit2 3400 CALIT2 Bldg Irvine CA 92697-2800 Office Phone: 949-824-0315.

**ZHOU, WEI,** surgeon; d. Jikui Zou and Jingmin Han; m. Van Chiem, July 7, 2000. MD, NY Med. Coll., Valhalla, NY, 1998. Cert. Am. Bd. Surgery, 2004, lic. Calif., 1999, Tex., 2005, Vascular Surgery Am. Bd. Surgery, 2006. Asst. prof. surgery Baylor Coll. of Medicine, Houston, 2005—; staff physician Michael E. DeBakey Med. Ctr., Houston, 2005—. Assoc. program dir. Baylor Coll. of Medicine - Vascular Surgery Fellowship, Houston, 2005—; vacular lab. dir. Michael E. DeBakey VA Med. Ctr., Houston. Recipient Molecular Surgeon Young Investigator Award, 2004, Alpha Omega Alpha Med. Honor Soc., 1998, Surg. Soc. Award, 1998, Janet M. Glasgow Meml. Achievment Citation, 1998, Provost Honor, 1992-1993; fellow Med. Student Rsch. Fellowship, 1995; grantee VA network Career Devel. Award, Basic sci. rsch. with potential clin. implication, 2006—, NIH T32 Tng. grant, Basic sci. rsch. with clin. potential, 2005—; scholar Trustee Scholarship, 1995-1997. Mem.: AMA, Assn. of Women Surgeons, Internation Soc. for Vascular Surgery, Assn. for Academic Surgeons, Peripheral Vascular Surgery Soc. Achievements include Extensive vascualr surgery-related publ. in peer-reviewed jour. and presentations in nat. and internat. meetings; research in Herbal supplement and vascular diseases. Home: 7469 Brompton St Houston TX 77025 Office: Baylor Coll of Medicine 1709 Dryden St ste 1500 Houston TX 77030 Office Phone: 713-798-8412. Office Fax: 713-798-8632. Business E-Mail: wzhou1@bcm.edu.

**ZHOU (SYUU), WEI (YI),** medical researcher, educator; s. Hideo Shuto and Yuelan Wang. PhD (hon.), Okayama U. Sch. Medicine, 2000. Asst. prof. Kyushu U. Health and Welfare, Nobeoka, Miyazaki, Japan, 2000—03; rschr. U. Calif., Irvine, 2003—. Fellow, Am. Heart Assn., Ministry Edn., Sci., Tech., and Sports of Japan. Mem.: Am. Physiology Soc., AAAS, Am. Heart Assn. Achievements include research in the neural mechanism underlying the effect of acupuncture on cardiovascular system. Office: U Calif Irvine Medical Sciences 1 C240 Irvine CA 92697 Office Phone: 949-824-861. Office Fax: 949-824-2200. Personal E-mail: syuuyi2002@yahoo.co.jp. Business E-Mail: wzhou2@uci.edu.

**ZHOU, XIAOBO,** computer scientist, educator; s. Dejun Zhou and Taihua Wang; m. Ping Wang; 1 child, Steven. BS in Computer Sci., Nanjing U., China, 1994, MS in Computer Sci., 1997, PhD, 2000. Postdoctoral rsch. assoc. U. Paderborn, Germany, 2000—01; vis. asst. prof. Wayne State U., Detroit, 2001—03; asst. prof. U. Colo., Colorado Springs, 2003—. Contbr. articles to profl. jours. Named Outstanding Graduate Student, Nanjing U., 1996, Outstanding Rschr. of Yr., Coll. Engring. and Applied Sci., U. Colo., Colorado Springs, 2005; recipient Com. on Rsch. and Creative Works award, U. Colo., Colorado Springs, 2005. Mem.: IEEE Computer Soc. Achievements include research in scalable distributed systems and Internet services, network communications, and cyber-security; founding program co-chair of IEEE International Workshop on Security in Systems and Networks. Avocations: ping pong/table tennis, tennis, golf. Office: Univ Colorado 1420 Austin Bluffs Pkwy Colorado Springs CO 80921 Office Phone: 719-262-3493. Office Fax: 719-262-3369.

**ZHOU, YIQUN,** humanities educator; b. Yongxin, China, 1971; d. Yuanbiao Zhou and Peiqiong Liu. PhD, U. Chgo. Asst. prof. humanities and East Asian studies Christ Coll., Valparaiso, Ind., 2004—. Office: Christ Coll Valparaiso Univ 1300 Chapel Dr Valparaiso IN 46383 Business E-Mail: Yiqun.Zhou@valpo.edu.

**ZHU, AIMING,** application developer; s. Wenzhi Shao; m. Lin He. PhD, U. Ky., Lexington, Ky., 2004. Rsch. scientist U. Ky., 1999—2006; staff software devel. engr. Alpha Omega Electromagnetics, Elicott City, Md., 2006—. Contbr. articles to profl. jours. Mem.: IEEE. Achievements include research in novel and fast solvers for computational electromagnetics. Home: 1970 New Rodgers Rd Apt M7 Levittown PA 19056 Personal E-mail: azhu0@uky.edu.

**ZHU, BEN-ZHAN,** education educator, researcher; PhD, The Hebrew U. of Jerusalem, Israel, 1999. Asst. prof. Oreg. State U., Corvallis, 2002—05; prof. The Chinese Acad. of Scis., Beijing, 2006—. Grantee, NIH/NIEHS; Golda Meir Fellowship, The Hebrew U. of Jerusalem, 1995. Achievements include discovery of A Novel Metal-independent Mechanism for Hydroxyl Radical Production.

**ZHU, CAROLYN WEI,** healthcare educator; d. Yu Zhu and Alice Jiang; 1 child, Andrew K. Shen. PhD, Duke U., 1999. Health economist, 2004—. Contbr. chapters to books, articles to profl. jours. Mem.: Phi Beta Kappa.

**ZHU, CHEN,** science educator, consultant; arrived in U.S., 1987; s. Mingqian Zhu and Renying Zhang; m. Lei Gong, Aug. 18, 1988; children: Agnes Qianqian, Gregory Hong. BS, Chengdu Coll. Geology, China, 1982; MS, U. Toronto, Can., 1987; MA, Johns Hopkins U., 1989, PhD, 1992. Sr. geochemist Geo Trans, Inc., Boulder, Colo., 1994—98; asst. prof. Old Dominion U., Norfolk, Va., 1998—2000, U. Pitts., 0200—2003; assoc. prof. Ind. U., Bloomington, 2004—. Cons. Nuc. Regulatory Coun., Washington, 2000—03; instr. Dept. of Energy, Pitts. 2000—04. Author: Environmental Application of Geochemical Modeling, 2002; contbr. over 20 articles to profl. jours. Recipient Sr. Associateship, NRC, 2003, Elsworth prize in mineralogy, U. Toronto, 1986, 1987; grantee, NSF, Dept. of Energy, U.S. EPA, Inst. Geophysics and Planetary Physics. Fellow: Geol. Soc. Am.; mem.: Am. Geophys. Union, Geochem. Soc. Office: Ind Univ 1001 E 10th St Bloomington IN 47405 Office Phone: 812-856-1884. Office Fax: 812-856-2223. Business E-Mail: chenzhu@indiana.edu.*

**ZHU, DONGMING,** materials scientist; b. Hefei, Anhui, China, Dec. 2, 1962; arrived in U.S., 1989; s. ZhengSe Zhu and Jingjuan Xu; m. Huixiang Deng; 1 child, Shirley. BS, Hefei U. of Tech., China, 1984, MS, 1988; PhD, U. of Minn., 1996. Sec. of rsch. inst. forecast & devel. Hefei U. Tech., Hefei, Anhui, China, 1988—90, asst. prof., 1988—90; rsch. & tchg. asst. U. Minn., Mpls., 1990—96; sr. materials scientist U.S. Army Rsch. Lab./NASA Glenn Rsch. Ctr., Cleve., 1996—. Contbr. articles to profl. jours. Bd. dir. Commonwealth Ter. Coop. U. Student Family Housing Sys. U. of Minn., Mpls., 1992—93. Rsch. Assoc. Fellowship, Nat. Rsch. Coun./Nat. Acad. Sci. & Nat. Acad. Engring., 1996. Mem.: ASM Internat., Am. Ceramic Soc. (chmn. nominating/awards com. engring. ceramic divsn. 2001—03, sec. engring. ceramic divsn. 2004, vice chair engring. ceramic divsn. 2005—06, Best Paper award 2002). Office: NASA Glenn Rsch Ctr 21000 Brookpark Road Mail Stop 24-1 Cleveland OH 44135 Home: 27671 Royal Forest Dr Westlake OH 44145 Business E-Mail: Dongming.Zhu@grc.nasa.gov.

**ZHU, HUA,** biochemist, researcher; b. Xiaogan, Hubei, China, Nov. 5, 1965; came to U.S., 1994; d. Chaoqun Zhu and Yuanying Long; married, May 7, 1997; children: Jessica Xiaoman Yao, Stephanie Xiaoru Yao. BA in Agronomy, Hua Zhong Agrl. U., Wuhan, China, 1985; M in Botany, Northwestern Agrl. U., Yang Ling, China, 1991; PhD in Botany, Chinese Acad. Sci., Beijing, 1994; M in Biochemistry, U. Okla., 1997, PhD in Biochemistry, 2001. Rsch. asst. dept. botany and microbiology U. Okla., Norman, 1994-96, rsch. asst. dept. biochemistry and chemistry, 1996—2001; rsch. scientist Advanced Ctr. for Genome Tech., U. Okla., Norman, 2001—02; rsch. assoc. Civil Aerospace Med. Inst., FAA, Oklahoma City, 2002—04; rsch. assoc. NRC, NAS FAA, Oklahoma City, 2004—; assoc. rsch. scientist cardiovasc. biology dept. Okla. Med. Rsch. Found., Oklahoma City, 2004—. V.p. Soc. Chinese Scholar and Students of U. Okla., 1996-97. Mem. AAAS, Am. Chemistry Soc., Microscopy Soc. Am., Botanic Soc. China. Avocations: bedmington, swimming, travel, music, movies. Office: Cardiovasc Biology Dept Okla Med Rsch Found 825 13th NE St Oklahoma City OK 73104 E-mail: zhuhua9863@yahoo.com.

**ZHU, HUIGUANG,** research educator; PhD in Chemistry, Zhejiang U., 2003. Rsch. asst. prof. Inst. Micromfg., LaTech, Ruston, La., 2003—06. Office: Inst Micromfg LaTech 911 Hergot Ave Ruston LA 71272 Business E-Mail: hzhu@latech.edu.

**ZHU, JIAN ZHONG,** research scientist; b. Zhengzhou, Henan, China, Oct. 25, 1955; arrived in U.S., 1991; m. Song Yu, Aug. 17, 1997; 1 child, Jiang Wei. BSc, Harbin Engring. U., China, 1978; MSc, Tianjin U., China, 1982; PhD, U. Coll. Swansea, Eng., 1987. Lectr. Harbin Engring. U., China, 1978—80, Tianjin U., China, 1983; rsch. asst. Univ. Coll. Swansea, 1986—87, sr. rsch. asst., 1987—91; sr. scientist UES-Software, Inc., Annapolis, Md., 1991—2002, Procast Inc., Columbia, Md., 2003—. Contbr. articles to profl. jours.; mem. editl. bd. Commun. Numerical Meth. Engring. Named one of Highly Cited Rschrs., ISI Thomson Scientific, 2000. Mem.: U.S. Assn. for Computational Mechanics, Internat. Assn. for Computational Mechanics, ASME. Mailing: ESI US R&D Inc Suite 140 5850 Waterloo Rd Columbia MD 21045-1941 Business E-Mail: jz.zhu@ESI-group.na.com.

**ZHU, JIANG,** materials scientist; m. Jane Sun, Sept. 1, 1997; children: Michelle, Michael. BS (hon.), Xian Jiaotong U., China, 1989; MS, Nanyang Technol. U., Singapore, 1997; PhD, U. Mo., Rolla, 2002. Chief scientist NanoRidge Materials Inc., Houston, 2004—. Contbr. articles to profl. jours. Mem.: ASME, SAMPE. Achievements include first to invent nanotube polymer composites; invention of polymer composites reinforced by functionalized nanotubes. Office: NanoRidge Materials Inc 2315 Schlumberger St Houston TX 77023 Office Phone: 713-928-6180. Office Fax: 713-928-6180. E-mail: jzhu@nanoridge.com.

**ZHU, JUNHONG,** biostatistician; s. Qianshen Zhu and Shixiu Sun; m. Weihong Fan, Jan. 16, 1990; 1 child, Olivia. B. Engring., Tsinghua U., Beijing, China, 1985; MS, NW Poly. U., Xi'an, Shaanxi, China, 1988; PhD, U. Memphis, 2002. Lectr. NW Poly. U., Xi'an, Shaanxi, China, 1988—96; biostatistician (intern) St. Jude Children's Rsch. Hosp., Memphis, 1998—2002; rsch. biostatistician Organon USA, Inc., Roseland, NJ, 2002—. Statis. cons. U. of Memphis Acad. Computing Systems, Memphis, 1997—98; rsch. fellow Chinese Acad. of Mgmt., Soft Sci. Inst., Xi'an, Shaanxi, China, 1990—96. Contbr. articles to profl. jours. Recipient Outstanding Cert., The U. of Memphis Edn. Support Sys., 1997—98, Excellent Tchg. award, NW Poly. U., 1993; grantee Young Rschr. grantee, 1989—91. Mem.: Am. Statis. Assn. (sec. 2001—02). Achievements include research in Stochastic model and analysis of cancer tumor development of statistical design and analyses in the development of new drug. Office: Organon USA Inc 56 Livingston Ave Roseland NJ 07068 Office Phone: 973-324-6977. Personal E-mail: junhong.zhu@gmail.com.

**ZHU, QIANG,** education educator; s. Tingyi Zhu and Jingqin Xu; m. Yanping Zhang; children: Han, Kayla Jie. BSc, S.E. U., China, 1978—82, MEng, 1982—84; MSc, McMaster U., Can., 1988—90; PhD, U. Waterloo, Can., 1990—95. Lectr. SE U., 1984—88; vis. scientist IBM Centre for Advanced Studies, Toronto, Canada, 1998—2005, faculty fellow, 2005—; asst. prof. U. Mich., Dearborn, 1995—2001, assoc. prof., 2001—. Assoc. editor Internat. Jour. Computers and Their Applications, 2005—; program com. mem., numerous internat. confs., 1998—2006; workshop/track/session/publicity chair, numerous internat. confs., 1985—2006. Contbr. articles to profl. jours. and pubs. Recipient 1999/2000 IBM U. Partnership Rsch. award, IBM U. Rels., 1999, Faculty award, 2003, 2004; grantee Rsch. grant, NSF, 1998, IBM Toronto Lab., 1998, 2002, NSF, 2005. Mem.: IEEE, Assn. Computing Machinery. Achievements include research in techniques for multidatabase cost modeling, multidimensional non-ordered discrete data space indexing, etc. Office: Univ Mich 4901 Evergreen Rd Dearborn MI 48128-1491

**ZHU, WEIXING,** ecologist, educator; b. China, 1965; s. Hexiang Zhu and Shiying Sheng; m. Jinfang Wei; children: Kathryn Ting, Joyce Yang. BS, Fudan U., China, 1986; PhD, Rutgers U., NJ, 1995. Rsch. assoc. Fordham U., Armonk, NY, 1996—99, Ariz. State U., Tempe, 1999—2000; prof. Binghamton U., NY, 2000—. Contbr. scientific papers. Grantee, NSF, 2004—06, USDA Nat. Rsch. Initiative, 2005—. Mem.: Sino-eco Assn., Ecol. Soc. Am. Office: Binghamton University - SUNY Dept of Biological Sciences Binghamton NY 13902 Office Phone: 1-607-777-3218. E-mail: wxzhu@binghamton.edu.

**ZHU, WEIYING,** engineering educator; b. Wuhan, Hubei, China, Mar. 8, 1974; d. Yisheng Zhu and Suzhen Leng; m. Chuan Yue, Jan. 28, 2002; 1 child, Catherine Yue. BS in Biomedical Electronic Engring., Xi'an Jiaotong U.,

**ZHU, XIANKUI,** mechanical engineer, researcher; b. Zhongxiang, Hubei, China, Aug. 29, 1962; s. Mingjing Zhu and Fengying Wu; m. Lin Zhang; children: Julia, Jesse. BS, Hohai U., Nanjing. China, 1984; MS, Hohai U., Nanjing, China, 1987; PhD, Tsinghus U., Beijing, 1995. Rsch. asst. Hohai U., 1984—87; asst. prof. Wuhan U., Hubei, China, 1987—91; rsch. asst. Tsinghua U., Beijing, 1991—95, postdoctoral rsch., 1995—96; rsch. prof. U. SC, Columbia, 1997—2001; prin. rsch. scientist Battelle, Columbus, 2002—. Contbr. Jour. of the Mechanics and Physics of Solids. Grantee, NASA, 2000, NSF, 2001, USAF, 2001, US Dept. Engring., 2001, PRCI, 2002. Mem.: ASME, ASTM, Am. Acad. Mechs. Office: Battelle 505 King Ave Columbus OH 43201 Home: 2714 Westmont Blvd Columbus OH 43221-3335 Personal E-mail: xkuizhu@yahoo.com. Business E-Mail: zhux@battelle.org.

**ZHU, YILIANG,** research scientist, educator; BSc, Shanghai U., 1982; MSc, Queen's U. Kingston, Ont., Can., 1987; PhD, U. Toronto, 1991. Rsch. scientist Environ. Health Ctr. Health Can., Ottawa, Ont., 1991—93; from assoc. prof. to prof. U. South Fla., Tampa, 1993—. Principle biostatistician Shriner's Hosps. for Children, Tampa, 1997—2000; CEO Scinfo Assocs., Tampa, 2000—; vis. scientist Nat. Ctr. for Environ. Assessment, U.S. EPA, Research Triangle Park, NC, 2000—01; mem. organ transplant adv. com. Dept. HHS, 2005—; mem. dioxin risk rev. com. Nat. Acad. Sci., 2004—05. Exec. com. mem. Asian Am. Coalition Fla., Tampa, 2001—02; founding pres. Chinese Am. Assn. Tampa Bay, 2001—02; pres. USF Asian Faculty and Staff Alliance. Tampa, 1997—98. Grantee, NSF, 2002. Mem.: Am. Statis. Assn. Office: Coll Pub Health Univ S Fla 13201 Bruce B Downs Blvd Tampa FL 33612 Office Phone: 813-974-6674. E-mail: yzhu@hsc.usf.edu.

**ZHU, YONG,** research scientist; b. Shanghai, Oct. 30, 1947; s. Shuping Chu and Zhiping Wang; m. Shaokui Wang, Apr. 22, 1977; 1 child, Shenke. B of Engr., East China Inst. Chem. Tech., Shanghai, 1981; postgrad., Tianhin Inst. Textile Engring., 1982; PhD in Organic Chemistry, U. Ill., 1992. Laborer Qingdao (China) Cigarette Manufacture, 1968-72; rsch. asst. Qingdao Inst. Light Industry, 1972-77; asst. prof., head dept. Shandong Inst. Textile Engring., China, 1983-87; vis. scientist U. Ill., Urbana, 1987-88, tchg./rsch. asst., 1988-92, postdoctoral rsch. assoc., 1992-93; scientist Procter and Gamble Far East, Kobe, Japan, 1993-95; sr. staff scientist Procter and Gamble Co., Cin., 1995—. Cons. Qingdao Manufacture of Dyeing Auxiliaries, 1983-87, Jiaonan Manufacture of Fragrances, China, 1984-87; hon. prof. Qingolao U., China, 2004. Patentee in field; contbr. chpts. to books and articles to profl. jours. Recipient Edn. scholarship Chinese Edn. Assn., 1987. Mem. Am. Chem. Soc. (vol. in pub. outreach 1991-95), Inter-Am. Photochem. Soc., Chinese Color-Optical Soc., Shandong Textile Engring. Assn. Achievements include patent in field. Avocations: volleyball, swimming, violin, travel, ballroom dancing.

**ZHUK, SERGEI IVANOVICH,** history professor, researcher; b. Vatutino, Ukraine, Dec. 18, 1958; s. Ivan Grigorovich Zhuk and Valentina Fedorovan Kochetkova; m. Irina Mikhailovna Kozintseva, Sept. 27, 1959; 1 child, Andrey Sergeievich. Kandidat istoricheskikh nauk, Inst. World History, Soviet Acad. Scis., 1987; Doktor istoricheskikh nauk, Dnipropetrovsk State U., Ukraine, 1996; PhD, Johns Hopkins U., 2002. Assoc. prof. Dnipropetrovs'k State U., Dnipropetrovs'k, 1989—97; asst. prof. Ball State U., Muncie, Ind., 2003—. Recipient Mellon Fellowship, Am. Coun. of Learnes Socs., 2003—04; fellow Kennan Inst., Woodrow Wilson Internat. Ctr. for Scholars, 2002—03; grantee IARO, IREX, 1999—2000, Bellagio Ctr., Rockefeller Found., 1996, Fulbright, U.S. Govt., 1994—95. Mem.: AHA. Home: 2530 W White River Blvd Apt 6 Muncie IN 47303 Office: Ball State Univ Department of History Muncie IN 47306 Office Phone: 765-285-8735. Home Fax: 765-285-5612; Office Fax: 765-285-5612. Personal E-mail: zhuks@mail.ru. Business E-Mail: sizhuk@bsu.edu.

**ZHUKON, TATYANA ANATOLY,** biologist, researcher; b. Kiev, Ukraine, Mar. 20, 1948; arrived in US, 1990; d. Anatoly Kirienko and Polina Golderbit; m. Boris Zhukov; 1 child, Polina Zhukov. MS, Kiev State U., 1972; PhD, Kiev State Med. Inst., 1981. Lic. clin. cytologist Fla. Rsch. fellow USSR Acad. Scis., Kiev, 1972—74; rsch. scientist dept. biochemistry Kiev Rsch. Inst., USSR Acad. Med. Scis., 1974—86; asst. prof. biophys. chemistry North-Osetian Med. Inst., Ordzhonikidze, 1986—87; sr. rsch. scientist Kiev State U., 1987—90; biochemist Molecular Tool, Inc., Balt., 1990—91; lab. mgr. Johns Hopkins U., Balt., 1993—97; rsch. assoc. H. Lee Moffitt Cancer Ctr., Tampa, Fla., 1997—2002, asst. prof., 2002—. Lectr., presenter in field. Contbr. articles to profl. jours.; patentee in field. Recipient Rsch. Coun. Faculty award, U. South Fla., 2001; grantee, 2003; rsch. grantee, NIH, 2002—. Mem.: Am. Soc. Cytopathology, Am. Assn. Cancer Rsch., Internat. Acad. Cytology, Sigma Xi. Avocation: boating. Home: 2611 Fiddlestick Cir Lutz FL 33559 Office: H Lee Moffitt Cancer Ctr 12902 Magnolia Dr MRC 3056B Tampa FL 33612 Office Phone: 813-745-1718. Fax: 813-903-6817. E-mail: zhukovta@moffitt.usf.edu.

**ZI, GOANGSEUP,** engineering educator; b. Suncheon, Jenlanam Do, Apr. 5, 1969; s. Gyu-Yul Zi and Myung-Ja Kim; m. Soo Yun Cho, Jan. 29, 1994; children: Haeun, Evelyn Hayoon, Hawon. BSc, Hanyang U., Korea, 1994, MSc, 1996; PhD, Northwestern U., 2002. 1st Grade Civil Engineer, KSCE / Seoul, Korea, 1994. Engr. Korea Infrastructure Safety and Tech. Anyang Kyungki Do, Republic of Korea, 1996—97; postdoctoral fellow Northwestern U., Evanston, Ill., 2002—04; asst. prof. Korea U., Seoul, Republic of Korea, 2004—. Rsch. edn. Korea U., Seoul, Korea (South), 2004—. V.p. Korean Student Assn., Northwestern U., Evanston, Ill., 1998—99. Sgt. Korean Army, 1989—91, South Korea. Recipient Industry Stipend of Excellence, Larfarge and EDF, 2001; Walter P. Murphy hon. fellowship, Northwestern U., McCormick Sch. Engring., 1998-1999. Presbyterian. Achievements include research in size effect of negative-positive geometries, development of constitutive models, analysis of radionuclide decontamination using microwaves, computational mechanics. Office: Korea U Anam Dong 5Ga 1 South Korea Seoul 136-701 Republic of Korea Office Phone: 82-2-3290-3324. Personal E-mail: g-zi@korea.ac.kr.

**ZI, XIAOLIN,** epidemiologist, medical researcher; b. Leiyang, Hunan, China, Nov. 20, 1964; s. Ruinan Zi and Heying Xu; m. Jun Xie, Nov. 9, 1966; children: Yujie, Jessie. MSc, McGill U., Montreal, Can., 2003; PhD, Shanghai Med. U., 1995. Rsch. assoc. Case Western Res. U., Cleve., 1996—98; asst. rschr. U. Calif. at Irvine, Orange, Calif., 2002—. Author (inventor): (cancer prevention and therapy) Cancer Research, Pnas, Jnci, Clincal Cancer Research, Bbrc, Carcinogenesis. Grantee, NIH, NCI, 2004. Mem.: Am. Assn. Cancer Rsch. (corr.). Achievements include patents pending for 1. Novel compounds (i.e. flavokawains) from kava extracts for prevention of bladder cancer. 2. Use of secreted wnt antiagonists for treatment of androgen-independent prostate cancers; research in cancer research, Pnas, Jnci, clincal cancer research, Bbrc, Carcinogenesis. Home: 2004 East Los Trancos Dr Irvine CA 92617 Office: U Calif at Irvine 101 City Dr Southy Orange CA 92868 Office Phone: 714-456-2241. Home Fax: 714-456-8350; Office Fax: 714-456-8350. Personal E-mail: xzi@uci.edu. E-mail: x_zi@hotmail.com.

**ZIBART, MICHAEL ALAN,** wholesale book company executive; b. Nashville, Mar. 12, 1947; s. Alan Walter and Joy (Hughes) Z.; m. Margaret Anne Boyd, Dec. 27, 1976; children: Emily Joy, Mary Claire. BA, Vanderbilt U., 1969. Mgmt. trainee Zibart Bros. Books, Nashville, 1961-69; property mgr. Pollack Co., Nashville, 1966-69; buyer Ingram Book Co., Nashville, 1970-75, mgr. trade dept., 1976, v.p., 1976-85, exec. v.p., 1985-88; founder, pres. ProMotion, Inc., Nashville, 1988—. Author: Almanac on Bookselling, 3d edit., 1980; pub. (monthly book review) BookPage, 1988—. Office: ProMotion Inc 2143 Belcourt Ave Nashville TN 37212-3503 Office Phone: 615-292-8926.

**ZIBELL, DONALD FREDRICK,** lawyer; b. St. Paul, Feb. 13, 1937; s. Otto Ernst and Anna Emma Zibell; m. Luella Louise Lepisto, Oct. 14, 1967; 1 child, Deanne. BA, U. Minn., 1959; JD, William Mitchell Coll. Law, 1962. Bar: Minn.; cert. public acct. Minn. Mng. tax ptnr. Boulay, Heutmaker, Zibell and Co., LLP, Mpls., 1959—90; real estate devel., 1965—; pvt. practice Roseville, Minn., 1990—. Dir. Cmty. Nat. Bank, N.A., Northfield, Minn., 1999—; dir., treas. Poly-Cam, Inc., Blaine, Minn., 1992—; dir. Roseville (Minn.) Cmty. Bank, 1983—91. Trustee, treas. North Suburban Cmty. Found., Roseville, 1982—; dir., asst. treas. Donald and Luella Zibell Family Found., Shoreview, Minn., 1999—; trustee, exec. com. William Mitchell Coll. Law, St. Paul, 2002—; mem. various other charitable bds. and adv. coms. Named one of Ten Outstanding Young Men of Minn., Minn. Jaycees, 1971, 100 Who Made a Difference, William Mitchell Coll. Law, 2001. Mem.: ABA, Roseville Rotary Club (former pres. 1970—, Paul Harris fellow 1980), Minn. Soc. CPAs and AICPA (life; former com. chair 1964—). Republican. Luth. Avocations: gardening, reading, boating, golf, spectator sports. Home: 3422 Chandler Rd Saint Paul MN 55126-3914 Office: 2233 N Hamline Ave 511 Saint Paul MN 55113

**ZICHERMAN, DAVID L.,** lawyer, educator, financial consultant; b. N.Y.C., Oct. 12, 1961; BA in Psychology magna cum laude, W.Va. U., 1984; JD, MPIA, U. Pitts., 1989. Bar: Del. 1990, Pa. 1990, D.C. 1990, cert.: Good Shepherd Mediation Program (mediator); sr. advisor Soc. Cert. St. Advisors, fin. mgr. Merrill Lynch & Coll. Fin. Planning, chartered retirement plans specialist Coll. Fin. Planning. Assoc. Richards, Layton & Finger, Wilmington, Del., 1989-92, Klehr Harrison et al, Phila., 1992-94, Kelly Grimes Pietrangelo & Vakil, P.C., Media, Pa., 1994-97; fin. cons. Merrill Lynch, 1998—2004; pvt. practice Law Offices of David L. Zicherman, Esq., 2004—. Adj. prof. Widener U. Law Ctr., Wilmington, 1993—95. Editor: State Legis. Forum newsletter, 1991—93, Delaware County Legal Jour., 1995—97; contbr. chapters to books, articles to profl. jours. Bd. dirs. Nat. Tay Sachs and Allied Diseases Assn., Delaware Valley, 1998—2001; mem. tech. com. Rose Tree Media Edn. Found., 1998—2000. Avocations: sports, photography, creative writing, travel. Office: 41 University Dr Ste 400 Newtown PA 18940 Office Phone: 267-757-8707.

**ZIDICH, JOHN M.,** publishing executive; b. San Francisco, 1954; m. Pam Zidich; children: Katie, Ali. Circulation dist. mgr. to advt. and sales mgmt. positions The Record (Gannett Newspapers), Stockton, Calif., 1977—90; retail advt. mgr. Reno Gazette-Jour., Nev., 1990—2000, pres., pub., 2000—01; exec. v.p. Ariz. Republic, Phoenix, 2001—04, pres., COO, 2004—05, CEO, pub., 2005. Bd. dir. Banner Health Found., Greater Phoenix C. of C., Phoenix Suns Charities. Mem.: Ariz. Sports Found. Avocations: cooking, golf, entertaining. Office: Arizona Republic 200 E Van Buren St PO Box 1950 Phoenix AZ 85001 Office Phone: 602-444-8000.*

**ZIEBARTH, ROBERT CHARLES,** management consultant; b. Evanston, Ill., Sept. 12, 1936; s. Charles A. and Marian (Miller) Z.; m. Patience Arnold Kirkpatrick, Aug. 28, 1971; children— Dana Kirkpatrick, Scott Kirkpatrick, Christopher, Nicholas. AB, Princeton, 1958; MBA, Harvard, 1964. With Bell & Howell Co., Chgo., 1964-73, treas., chief fin. officer, 1969-73; mgmt. cons. Ziebarth Co., 1973—. Mem. dirs. adv. bd. Arkwright Boston Ins. Co., devel. com. Nat. Assn. Ind. Schs.; bd. dirs. M.B.A. Resources, Inc., Telemedia, Inc., Corp. Resources, Inc., Nordemann Grimm Inc. Assoc. Community Renewal Soc., Citizens Coun. Gateway House; mem. Ill. Bd. Higher Edn., Ill. Joint Edn. Commn.; trustee Choate Sch.; trustee, pres. Latin Sch.Chgo., Chgo. Maternity Ctr.; bd. dirs. Harvard Bus. Sch. Fund, U.S.O., Inc., Prentice Women's Hosp., Northwestern Meml. Corp., Found. for Reproductive Rsch. and Edn., Endowments Inc., Bond Portfolio Endowments Inc. Served to lt. USNR, 1958-62. Mem. Naval Hist. Found., Art Inst. Chgo., Chgo. Hist. Soc., Mus. Modern Art. Clubs: Mid-Am. (Chgo.), Racquet (Chgo.), Saddle and Cycle (Chgo.), Economic (Chgo.), Executives (Chgo.). Presbyterian. Office: PO Box 4569 Ketchum ID 83340-4569

**ZIEGELMEIER, PATRICIA KAY,** music educator, executive secretary; b. Colby, Kans., July 14, 1944; d. Lon Elmer and Mary Marie (Saddler) Sowers; m. Carl Ernest Ziegelmeier, June 9, 1963; children: Matt, Steve, Lisa, Amy, Lori. BA in Music Edn., U. Wyo., 1967; MS in Ednl. Adminstrn., Ft. Hays State U., 1991. Tchr. music, sub. tchr. Golden Plains Schs., Rexford, Kans., 1969-72; pvt. piano instr. Gem, Kans., 1972-87; ch. organist Gem and Colby, Kans., 1968—; instr. music Colby C.C., 1988—. Cmty. leader 4-H, Gem, 1980-88, 99-2005; bd. dirs. Thomas County Fair Coun., Colby, 1986-88, 94-95. Mem. NEA, Music Tchrs. Nat. Assn., Kans. Music Tchrs. Assn. (bd. dirs. 1981—, exec. sec. 1987—, Outstanding Tchr. award 1994), Western Plains Arts Assn. (exec. dir. 1989—), Northwest Kans. Piano Assn. (clinic chair 1973—). Methodist. Avocations: reading, music listening, playing piano, walking. Office: Kans Music Tchrs Assn 2154 County Road 27 Gem KS 67734-9008 Office Phone: 785-462-3984 ext. 307. E-mail: patz@colbycc.edu.

**ZIEGENHAGEN, DAVID MACKENZIE,** retired health facility administrator, not-for-profit developer; b. Mpls., May 25, 1936; s. Elmer Herbert Ziegenhagen and Margaret Ruth (Mackenzie) Kruger; m. Mary Ange Kinsella, Nov. 26, 1966 (div. Dec. 1982); children: Marc, Eric; m. Mary Kinsella, Feb. 7, 2002. BA in Mass. Comm., Political Sci., U. Minn, 1961. Reporter WCCO-TV, Mpls., 1956—61; assoc. dir. Thailand Peace Corps, Bangkok, 1963-65, Thailand program officer Washington, 1965—67, dir. Western Samoa Apia, 1967-70; exec. dir. Mental Health Assn. Minn., 1970-76; co-founder, pres. Current Newspapers, Inc., Burnsville, Minn., 1975-84; sr. program officer The St. Paul Found., 1982—85; pres. DMZ Assocs., Cloverdale, Calif., 2000—; exec. dir. Minn. Bd. Med. Practice, St. Paul, 1985-88; CEO, pres. Stratis Health, Bloomington, Minn., 1988-2000. Democrat. Avocations: travel, international development, arts.

**ZIEGLER, ARTHUR P., JR.,** foundation executive; b. Pitts. June 20, 1937; s. Arthur P. and Vinnie (DeWinter) Ziegler. BA, U. Pitts., 1958, MA, 1959; postgrad., Union Theol. Sem., NYC, 1960, Western Res. U., 1961. Instr. Carnegie Mellon U., Pitts., 1961-64, Pa. State U., 1961-63; pres. Pitts. History, Landmarks, 1964—, Cranston Devel. Corp., 1980-87. Trustee Allegheny Found., Pitts., 1975—, Walden Trust, 1990—, Sarah Scaife Found., 2000—; trustee emeritus Nat. Trust, Washington; chmn. Allegheny County Hist. Properties Commn., Pa. Editor: (novels) A Critical Edition of Lord of the Flies, 1964; author: (book) Historic Preservation of Inner City Areas, 1971, Revolving Funds for Historic Preservation, 1975; co-author: Allegheny, 1975, Historic Preservation for Small Towns, 1980, Landmark Architecture of Allegheny County, 1987. Mem. N.E. regional, Pitts. adv. coun. Fannie Mae; advisor 10,000 Friends of Pa.; dir. Riverlife Task Force, Harbor Gardens, Pitts.; advisor, sustainable architecture program Carnegie Mellon U.; mem. bd. advisors The Waterfront Ctr.; bd. dirs. Preservation Pa., Preservation Action. Recipient Crowninshield award, Nat. Trust, Nat. Recognition award, Ptnrs. for a livable Cmty., Pvt. Sector award, Pres. of the US, Otto Haas award, Preservation, Pa., Pa. Man of Yr. in Arts award, Pitts., Jaycees, Golden Quill award, Remax Renaissance award. Mem.: Internat. Urban Devel. Assn. N.Am., HYP Club. Avocation: gardening. Office: One Station Sq Ste 450 Pittsburgh PA 15219

**ZIEGLER, DEWEY KIPER,** neurologist, educator; b. Omaha, May 31, 1920; s. Isidor and Pearl (Kiper) Z.; Mar. 30, 1954; children: Amy, Laura, Sara. BA, Harvard U., 1941, MD, 1945. Diplomate Am. Bd. Psychiatry and Neurology (bd. dirs. 1974-83, exec. com. 1978-82). Intern in medicine Boston City Hosp., 1945-46; asst. resident then chief resident in neurology N.Y. Neurol. Inst.-Columbia U. Coll. Physicians and Surgeons, 1948-51; resident in psychiatry Boston Psychopathic Hosp., 1951-53; asst. chief neurol. service Montefiore Hosp., N.Y.C.; and asst. prof. neurology Columbia U., 1953-55;

asst. prof. U. Minn., 1955-56; asso. clin. prof. U. Kans. Med. Sch., 1956-64, chief dept. neurology, 1968-85; prof. U. Kans. Med. Center, 1964-89, prof. emeritus, 1989—. Cons. Social Security Adminstrn., 1975—; mem. com. on certification and co-certification Am. Bd. Med. Specialties, 1979-82 Author: In Divided and Distinguished Worlds, 1942; Contbr. numerous articles to profl. jours. Served to j.g.; M.C. USNR, 1946-48. Fellow Am. Acad. Neurology (pres. 1979-81); mem. AMA, Am. Neurol. Assn. (v.p. 1972-73), Am. Headache Assn. Avenh. Home: 8347 Delmar Ave Shawnee Mission KS 66207-1821 Office: Kans U Med Ctr 3900 Rainbow Blvd Kansas City KS 66103-2918 Office Phone: 913-588-6922. Business E-Mail: dziegler@kumc.edu.

**ZIEGLER, DHYANA,** broadcasting educator, academic administrator; b. NYC, May 5, 1949; d. Ernest and Alberta Allie (Guy) Z. BS cum laude, CUNY, 1981; MA in Radio and TV, So. Ill. U., 1983, PhD in Higher Edn., 1985. Freelance researcher Essence Mag., NYC, 1972-75; copywriter, radio producer Rosenfeld, Sirowitz & Lawson Advt. Agy., NYC, 1974-75; exec. v.p. Patten & Guest Prodns., NYC, 1976-79; prodn. intern Sta. WNEW TV, NYC, 1979-80; upward bound counselor Seton Hall U., South Orange, NY, 1979-81; prodn. intern Sta. WCBS TV, NYC, 1980-81; asst. prof. Jackson (Miss.) State U., 1984-85; assoc. dir. Diversity Resources and Ednl. Svcs. U. Tenn., Knoxville, 1995, prof. broadcasting, pres., faculty senate; Garth C. Reeves Eminent Scholar Chair of Excellence in Journalism Fla. A&M U., 1997, asst. v.p., instructional tech., asst. v.p. academic affairs, acting v.p. sponsored rsch., mem. Innovation Park bd., dir. U. planning, 2002. Bd. dirs. Knoxville Women's Ctr., 1989-92; bd. trustees East Tenn. Discovery Ctr., Knoxville, 1989-92; adv. bd. Bethel Love Kitchen, Knoxville, 1990-93; subject matter expert Gov.'s Digital Divide Coun. Author books; contbr. articles to profl. jours.; producer, dir. (video documentary) Single Parenting, 1988 (2d Pl. award), Rape is a Reality, 1982 (UPI Outstanding Achievement award 1982). Chmn. comms. Knoxville chpt. NAACP, 1990-91, chpt. advisor U. Tenn. student chpt., 1989—, chmn. chancellor's commn. for blacks, 1990-95, pres. faculty senate, 1995—; chmn. social action com. Delta Sigma Theta, Knoxville, 1986-89, mem. commn. on arts and letters, 1990-91; bd. dirs. East Tenn. regional Am. Heart Assn., 1990—; mem. athletics bd. U. Tenn., 1990—; regional devel. edn. coord. Delta Rsch. and Ednl. Found. (chairperson Rsch. and resource com.), v.p., bd. dirs.; mem. allocations com. United Way, Knoxville, 1990-91; bd. trustee Florida Virtual HS, 2002-04, 2004-; bd. dirs. Fla. Virtual Sch. So. Scholarship Found. Named one of Top 50 African-Ams. in Tech., U.S. Black Engring. Info. Tech. Mag. and Blackmoney.com, 2002, 2003, 2004; recipient Gov.'s Outstanding Faculty Mem. of the Yr., 1987, Rsch. award, 1992, Coll. of Comms., Outstanding Faculty award, Interfraternity Coun., 1992, YWCA Finalist in Edn., 1990, Consortium of Dr.'s award, 1991; fellow Poynter Inst., 1992; grantee, FISPE, US Dept. of Edn., 1989—, Delta Rsch. & Ednl. Found., 1987, 1990; inductee U. Tenn. African Am. Hall of Fame, 1994, Leadership Devel. Initiative scholar, Grad. Sch. Edn., Mgmt. and Leadership in Edn. Inst., Harvard U., 2000, Chosen Fulbright-Hays Spl. Seminar Participant, US Dept. Edn. and the Nat. Com. on US-China Rels., China, 2004. Mem. NAFE, Women in Comm. (pres. Knoxville chpt. 1990—), Broadcast Edn. Assn. (chair multicultural div. 1989-92, chair gender divsn. 1996—), Speech Comm. Assn., Soc. Profl. Journalists (Jane Pauley task force on mass comm. edn. 1995-96, co-author Jane Pauley Task Force Report 1996), Golden Key Nat. Honor Soc., Kappa Tau Alpha, Phi Delta Kappa, Delta Sigma Theta (Post-secondary Educators award 1992, Black Achievement award 1993), Phi Kappa Phi. Office: U Tenn 295 Communications Bldg Knoxville TN 37996-0001 also: Fla A&M U Academic Affairs I&R Program FHAC 301 Tallahassee FL 32307 Office Phone: 850-599-3460, 850-599-3461. Business E-Mail: dhyz@aol.com.

**ZIEGLER, DONALD EMIL,** retired federal judge; b. Pitts., Oct. 1, 1936; s. Emil Nicholas and Elizabeth Ziegler; m. Claudia J. Chermak, May 1, 1965; 1 son, Scott Emil. BA, Duquesne U., 1958; LL.B., Georgetown U., 1961. Bar: Pa. 1962, U.S. Supreme Ct. 1967. Practice law, Pitts., 1962-74; judge Ct. of Common Pleas of Allegheny County, Pa., 1974-78, U.S. Dist. Ct. (we. dist.) Pa., Pitts., 1978—2003, chief judge, 1994-2001. Mem. Jud. Conf. U.S., 1997-2000. Treas. Big Bros. of Allegheny County, 1969-74. Mem. ABA, Pa. Bar Assn., Allegheny County Bar Assn., Am. Judicature Soc., St. Thomas More Soc. Clubs: Oakmont Country. Democrat. Roman Catholic. Office: 100 Ross St Ste 105 Pittsburgh PA 15219-2013 Office Phone: 412-281-6770. E-mail: coopzieg@aol.com.

**ZIEGLER, DONALD ROBERT,** accountant; b. Lancaster, Pa., Nov. 15, 1932; s. John Jacob and Esther Mae (McKelly) Z.; m. Suzanne Foster; children: D. Rand, Scott F., Kurt J. BS in Econ. Acctg., Franklin and Marshall Coll., 1954. CPA, Pa. Mgr., sr. staff mem. Price Waterhouse, Phila., 1954-67, ptnr., 1967-92, sr. practice ptnr., 1978-92, mng. ptnr. Mid-Atlantic area, 1985-88, vice-chmn. S.E. region, 1988-92, mem. policy bd. N.Y.C., 1980-88, mem. mgmt. com., 1989-92. Author: (with others) Managing and Accounting for Inventories, 1980; contbg. author various books in field. Trustee Franklin and Marshall Coll., 1983—, mem. alumni exec. coun., 1979—83, mem. exec. com., 1995—, chmn. audit com., 1989—2003, vice-chmn. bd. trustees, 2002—, mem. Phila. alumni coun.; trustee Pa. Ballet, 1988—92, 1994—95, mem. devel. and fin. coms., vice chmn. bd. trustees, 1989—92, chmn. exec. com., 1989—91; chmn. audit com., budget and fin. com., ethics com., bd. of adjustment Town of Dewey Beach; bd. dirs. Beebe Med. Ctr., 2000—06, Beebe Med. Found., 2001—06, So. Del. Surgery Ctr., 2003—06. With U.S. Army, 1955—57. Recipient Outstanding Soldier award U.S. Army, 1955, Disting. Svc. Alumni medal Franklin and Marshall Coll., 1991. Mem. AICPA (auditing stds. com. 1973-76, chmn. subcom. fraud 1976-80), Pa. Inst. CPAs (Phila. chpt. exec. coun.), Rehoboth Beach Country Club (bd. govs. 2000—, treas. 2003—), Phila. Aviation Club (bd. govs. and treas. 1969-90). Home: One West St Dewey Beach DE 19971 Office: PricewaterhouseCoopers LLP Two Commerce Sq 2001 Market St Ste 1700 Philadelphia PA 19103-7042 Personal E-mail: drsfzig@comcast.net.

**ZIEGLER, EKHARD ERICH,** pediatrics educator; b. Saalfelden, Austria, Apr. 12, 1940; (former: Stefan, Gabriele, Lena. MD, U. Innsbruck, Austria, 1964. Diplomate: Am. Bd. Pediatrics. Intern U. Innsbruck, 1966-67, resident in pediatrics, 1967-68 70-71, resident in pharmacology, 1964-66, asst. dept. pediatrics, 1970-73; vis. instr. pediatrics U. Iowa, Iowa City, 1968-70, asst. prof. pediatrics, 1973-76, assoc. prof., 1976-81, prof., 1981—. Mem. nutrition study sect. NIH, 1988-92. Recipient Nutrition award Am. Acad. Pediactrics, 1988. Mem. Am. Soc. Clin. Nutrition, Soc. Pediatric Research, Soc. Exptl. Biology and Medicine, N.Am. Soc. Pediatric Gastroenterology, Midwest Soc. Pediatric Research, Am. Pediatric Soc., The Nutrition Soc., N.Y. Acad. Scis., Am. Acad. Pediatrics., Am. Dietetic Assn. (hon.). Clubs: Univ. Athletic (Iowa City). Office: U Iowa Dept Pediatrics Iowa City IA 52242 Office Phone: 319-356-2836. Business E-Mail: ekhard-ziegler@uiowa.edu.

**ZIEGLER, GWENDOLYN WOODS,** minister, consultant; d. William Darnell and Catherine Anna Woods; children: Geraldine, Tonia Elaine, Faith Evangeline, Charity Elise. BTh, United Bible Coll., Orlando, Fla., 1988, EdM, 1990; DMin, Howard U., 2006. Pastoral lic. Deliverance Evangelistic Ctrs., Inc./N.J., 1970, Evangelistic lic. Deliverance Evangelistic Ctrs., Inc./N.J., 1967. Pres./cons. G. Chafto Industries, Washington, 1990—; v.p. In The Midst, Inc., Severn, Md., 1999—2002. Spl. asst. to the pres. We Can Do Ministries, Inc., Newark, 1990—97; radio broadcaster Positive Proof Ministries, Orange, NJ, 1995—97; cons./radio broadcaster Global Ministries, South Orange, NJ, 1997—98. Author: (non-fiction book) Judgment Work - A Conclusion To The Matter, 2003. Mem.: N.Am. Bookdealers Exch. Independent. Office: G Chafto Industries 7240 Talisman Lane Columbia MD 21045 Office Phone: 301-758-5386. E-mail: gwen_ziegler@hotmail.com.

**ZIEGLER, HENRY STEINWAY,** lawyer; b. Utica, NY, June 21, 1933; s. Frederick J. and Alice (Cantwell) Z.; m. Patricia Blackmore (div.); children: Frederick S., Alicia P., Timothy O.; m. Jourdan Arpelle, Apr. 6, 1991. AB, Harvard U., 1955; LLB, Columbia U., 1958. Bar: N.Y. 1961, U.S. Dist. Ct. (ea. and so. dists.) N.Y. 1962, U.S. Ct. Appeals (2d cir.) 1963, U.S. Tax Ct. 1972. Assoc. Shearman & Sterling, N.Y.C., 1958-67, ptnr., 1967-92; chmn.

CEO Deutsche Bank Trust Co., 1995-97, trust estate planning dir., 1998—99; sr. v.p. Fiduciary Trust Co. Internat., N.Y.C., 1999—2003; pres., cons., governance and transfer of family wealth HSZ Cons. LLC, 2003—06; of counsel Withers Beigman LLP, 2006—. Pres. Chamber Music Soc. of Lincoln Ctr., Inc., 1983-89, bd. dirs., 2004—; pres. Lincoln Ctr. for Performing Arts, N.Y.C., 1985-89; hon. trustee St. Lukes-Roosevelt Hosp. Ctr.; bd. regents Am. Coll. Trust Estate Counsel, 1988-94. With U.S. Army, 1958-60, 61-62. Mem. ABA (former vice chmn. internat. com. on property probate and trust law), Acad. internat. Trust and Estate Law (mem. exec. coun., v.p.), N.Y. State Bar Assn., Assn. Bar City of N.Y., Century Assn., Order St. John of Jerusalem. Clubs: Racquet and Tennis, Knickerbocker. Republican. Avocation: music. Home: 55 Liberty St Apt # 7A New York NY 10005 Office Phone: 212-848-9842. Personal E-mail: hsziegler@earthlink.net. Business E-mail: henry.ziegler@withers.us.com.

**ZIEGLER, JACK (JACK DENMORE),** cartoonist; b. NYC, July 13, 1942; s. John Denmore and Kathleen Miriam (Clark) Z.; m. Jean Ann Rice, Apr. 20, 1968 (div. 1995); children: Jessica, Benjamin, Kelli Joseph, Aug. 1996. BA in Comm. Arts, Fordham U., 1964. Free-lance cartoonist, N.Y.C., 1972—; cartoonist The New Yorker, N.Y.C., 1974—. Author: Hamburger Madness, 1978, Filthy Little Things, 1981, Marital Blitz, 1987, Celebrity Cartoons of the Rich and Famous, 1987, Worst Case Scenarios, 1990, Mr. Knocky, 1993, The Essential Jack Ziegler, 2000, How's The Squid?, 2004, Olive Or Twist?, 2005, You Had Me at Bow Wow, 2006; illustrator: (children's books) Lily of the Forest, 1987, Flying Boy, 1988, Annie's Pet, 1989, Eli and the Dimplemeyers, 1994 (adult books) Waiting Games, 1983, The Joy of Stress, 1984, That's Incurable!, 1984, Modern Superstitions, 1985, The No-Sex Handbook, 1990, There'll Be a Slight Delay, 1991, Byte Me!, 1996, Fictoids, 2005. Democrat. Personal E-mail: jkziegler@sbcglobal.net.

**ZIEGLER, JAMES L.,** marketing executive; b. Fort Benning, Ga., Sept. 10, 1965; s. Gordon L. and Kum S. Ziegler. BS, US Mil. Acad., 1989; MBA, U. Chgo., 1998. Sales Pfizer, Inc, Dallas, 1993—96; biotech. exec. Amgen, Inc., Thousand Oaks, Calif., 2000—. Bd. mem. West Point Soc. LA, 2000—03. Capt. U.S. Army, 1989—93. Decorated Army Achievement Medal U.S. Army, Army Commendation Medal; recipient Disting. Contbn., Nat. Hispanic Med. Assn., 2003, President's award, Nat. Med. Assn., 2004, Significant Achievement award, Assn. of Am. Indian Physicians, 2002. Personal E-mail: jziegle@gsb.uchicago.edu.

**ZIEGLER, JANICE H.,** lawyer; b. Bklyn., Jan. 25, 1962; m. Karl Groskaufmanis. BS in Indsl. & Labor Rels., with honors, Cornell U., 1984; JD magna cum laude, Harvard U., 1987. Bar: Mass. 1987, DC 1989. Law clk. to Hon. John H. Pratt US Dist. Ct DC; assoc. to ptnr. Shaw Pittman LLP, Washington; ptnr., health care practice group Sonnenschein Nath & Rosenthal LLP, Washington, 2003—. Mem.: ABA (health law sect.), Am. Health Lawyers Assn., DC Bar Assn. (health law sect.). Office: Sonnenschein Nath & Rosenthal LLP Ste 600, E Tower 1301 K St NW Washington DC 20015 Office Phone: 202-408-9158. Office Fax: 202-408-6399. Business E-Mail: jziegler@sonnenschein.com.

**ZIEGLER, JOHN ALAN,** historian, political scientist, educator; b. Belleville, Ill., Jan. 28, 1933; s. John Wendell and Georgia Elizabeth (Reppel) Z.; m. Carol Ruth Alcorn, June 15, 1963; children: Mimi, Robin. BS, So. Ill. U., 1955, MS, 1956; Rotary Found. fellow, St. Andrews U., Scotland, 1956-57; PhD, Syracuse U., 1970. Asst. prof. polit. sci. and social sci. Calif. State U., Hayward, 1966-72; lectr. Am. civilization Calif. State Poly. U., Pomona, 1972-74; assoc. prof. polit. sci. Hendrix Coll., Conway, Ark., 1974-84, prof., 1984-91, Harold and Lucy Cabe Disting. prof. history and politics, 1991-98, emeritus prof., 1998—; legendary lectr. 1998. Coord. and founder Hendrix-Oxford program, 1979-98, head social sci. area, 1978-82, chmn. dept. polit. sci. and history, 1974-83; guest lectr. St. Peter's Coll., Oxford U., 1983, 90, 94, Clare Coll., Cambridge U., 1988, 89, Dundee U., 1994; Churchill life fellow Westminster Coll., Fulton, Mo.; participant Wilton Pk. Confs., Wiston House Internat. Conf. Ctr., Sussex, England, 1979—. Author: Experimentalism and Institutional Change, In Search of the Special Relationship with Britain. With AUS, 1957-60. Mem. AAUP, Friends Churchill Meml. (life), Am. Friends Wilton Park, ACLU, Royal Oak Found., Soc. Sussex Downsmen (life), Dundee (Scotland) Curling Club. Mem. United Ch. of Christ. Home: PO Box 1045 Conway AR 72033-1045 Office: Hendrix Coll Conway AR 72032 E-mail: johnziegler@webtv.net.

**ZIEGLER, JOHN AUGUSTUS, JR.,** lawyer; b. Grosse Pointe, Mich., Feb. 9, 1934; s. John Augustus and Monnabell M. Ziegler; m. G. Kay Brubeck; children: John Augustus III, Laura, Lisa, Adeline. AB, U. Mich., JD, 1957. Bar: Mich. 1957. Since practiced in, Detroit; assoc. Dickinson, Wright, McKean & Cudlip, 1957-65, ptnr., 1965-68, Parsons, Tennent, Hammond, Hardig & Ziegelman, 1969-70, Ziegler, Dykhouse & Wise, 1970-77; pres., CEO Nat. Hockey League, 1977-92, chmn. bd. govs., 1976-78; of counsel Dickinson, Wright, PLLC, Bloomfield Hills, 1992—99. Office: 375 Park Ave Ste 2004 New York NY 10152-2099

**ZIEGLER, PETER F.,** lawyer; b. Aug. 31, 1945; BS in Indsl. Adminstrn. and Orgnl. Behavior, Yale Univ., 1967; JD, Univ. So. Calif., 1974. Bar: Calif. 1974. Assoc. Gibson Dunn & Crutcher LLP, LA, 1974—82, ptnr. corp. transactions and securities, 1982—, and ptnr.-in-charge LA office, 1999—. Mem. So. Calif. Law Rev., 1972—74, note and article editor, 1973—74. Bd. dir. LA Philharmonic Assn., World Affairs Coun., bd. trustees Webb Schools, Claremont, Calif. Line officer USN, 1967—71. Mem.: ABA, Calif. Bar Assn., LA County Bar Assn. (past exec. com. chair, bus. and corp. law section 1990—91), Order of Coif. Office: Gibson Dunn & Crutcher LLP 333 S Grand Ave Los Angeles CA 90071-3197 Office Phone: 213-229-7595. Office Fax: 213-229-6595. Business E-Mail: pziegler@gibsondunn.com.

**ZIEGLER, R. W., JR.,** lawyer, consultant; b. Pitts. children: Caroline, Gretchen, Jeremy, Benjamin, Phoebe, Polly. Student, Carnegie Mellon, U. Pitts.; JD, Duquesne U., 1972. Bar: Pa. 1972, Calif. 1981, U.S. Ct. Appeals (3d cir.) 1977, U.S. Dist. Ct. (we. dist.) Pa., 1977, U.S. Supreme Ct. 1977, U.S. Tax Ct. 1978, Calif. 1982, U.S. Dist. Ct. (no. dist.) Calif. 1982, U.S. Ct. Appeals (9th cir.) 1982. Ptnr. Ziegler & Ombres, 1973-79; pres. Ziegler Ross Inc., San Francisco, 1979—. Lectr. for Bar Assns. Author: Law Practice Management; editor: Law Office Guide in Computing. Mem. ABA, Am. Mgmt. Assn., Pa. State Bar Assn., Calif. State Bar Assn., Assn. of Legal Admin., Young Presidents' Org., Am. Assn. of Law Librarians, San Francisco Bar Assn. Office: 220 Montgomery St Ste 900 San Francisco CA 94104-5413 Office Phone: 415-732-0300.

**ZIEGLER, RICHARD FERDINAND,** lawyer; b. Elizabeth, NJ, Aug. 1, 1949; m. Carolyn Lewis; children: Anna B., David A., Andrew P. D-J. BA in History summa cum laude, Yale u., 1971; JD magna cum laude, Harvard U., 1975. Bar: N.Y. 1976, U.S. Dist. Ct. (so. and ea. dists.) N.Y. 1976, U.S. Dist. Ct. (ea. dist.) Mich. 1982, U.S. Supreme Ct. 1984, U.S. Dist. Ct. (no. dist.) N.Y. 1987. Law clk. to judge U.S. Dist. Ct. (so. dist.), N.Y.C., 1975-76; assoc. Paul, Weiss, Rifkind, Wharton & Garrison, N.Y.C., 1976-77; asst. U.S. atty. U.S. Dept. Justice (so. dist.) N.Y., N.Y.C., 1977-80; assoc. Cleary, Gottlieb, Steen & Hamilton, N.Y.C., 1980-83, ptnr., 1983—2002; sr. v.p. legal affairs, gen. counsel 3M Co., St. Paul, 2003—. Lectr. law Columbia Law Sch., 1997—. mem. ABA, Assn. Bar City of N.Y., Fed. Bar Coun., N.Y. State Bar Assn. (chmn. com. on profl. ethics, 1995-98). Office: 3M Ctr Bldg 220 14W 07 Saint Paul MN 55144

**ZIEGLER, RICHARD J.,** dean, educator; BS in biology, Muhlenberg Coll., 1965; PhD in microbiology, Temple U., 1970. Rsch. assoc. in microbiology Rockefeller U., 1970—71; asst. prof. microbiology U. Minn.-Duluth, 1971—77, assoc. prof. microbiology, 1977—89; prof. microbiology Sch. Medicine, U. Minn.-Duluth, 1989—, interim dean, 1997—98, dean, 1998—

Recipient James H. Sova award, Minn. Med. Found., 2000. Office: UMD Sch Medicine 1035 Univ Dr Duluth MN 55812 Office Phone: 218-726-7572. Fax: 218-726-7383. Business E-Mail: rziegler@d.umn.edu.*

**ZIEGLER, ROCHELLE ELIZABETH,** special education educator; b. Virginia Beach, Va., Dec. 21, 1974; d. Robert Herman and Elizabeth Ethiel Ziegler. BS in Interdisciplinary Studies /Mental Retardation, Norfolk State U., Norfolk, Va., 2003; M in Severe Disabilities, Norfolk State U., 2005. Tchr. asst. Southeastern Coop. Ednl. Programs, Norfolk, Va., 1995—2004; tchr. spl. edn. Portsmouth Pub. Schs., 2005—. Mentor Young Sister's In Christ, Virginia Beach, Va., 1996. Recipient Nat. Collegiate Edn. Awards, US Achievement Acad., 2000; scholar All-Am. Scholar at Large Divsn., 2000. Mem.: Coun. of Exceptional Children (assoc.). Democrat-Npl. Bapt. Avocations: reading, helping in the community/church, exercise. Home: 834 Tuition Dr Virginia Beach VA 23462 Personal E-mail: rez1221@msn.com.

**ZIEGLER, WILLIAM ALEXANDER,** lawyer; b. N.Y.C., July 15, 1924; s. William Alexander and Sally (Cootes) Z.; m. Glenn Crawley, Feb. 10, 1950; children: Richard S., Daryl A. Henning, Susan G. Barrows, W. Thomas. AB, Harvard U., 1944, JD, 1949. Bar: N.Y. 1949, U.S. Tax Ct. 1950, U.S. Dist. Ct. (so. dist.) N.Y. 1949, U.S. Dist. Ct. (ea. dist.) N.Y. 1957, U.S. Dist. Ct. (no. dist.) Ohio 1973, U.S. Dist. Ct. (ea. dist.) Mich. 1983, U.S. Ct. Apppeals (1st cir.) 1963, U.S. Ct. Appeals (2d cir.) 1957, U.S. Ct. Appeals (3d cir.) 1986, U.S. Ct. Appeals (4th cir.) 1979, U.S. Ct. Appeals (5th cir.) 1987, U.S. Ct. Appeals (6th cir.) 1984, U.S. Ct. Appeals (7th cir.) 1992, U.S. Ct. Appeals (8th cir.) 1981, U.S. Ct. Appeals (9th cir.) 1973, U.S. Ct. Appeals (10th and 11th cirs.) 1983, U.S. Ct. Appeals (D.C. cir.) 1982, U.S. Supreme Ct. 1972. Assoc. Sullivan & Cromwell, N.Y.C., 1949-56, ptnr., 1957-89. Bd. dir. Wilton (Conn.) Land Conservation Trust, Friends of Canterbury Cathedral in U.S. Mem. Assn. Bar City N.Y., Riverside Country Club (Mont.), Harvard Club of Fairfield Country (bd. dir.), Harvard Club Mont.

**ZIEHLER, TONY JOSEPH,** insurance agent; b. Anderson, Ind., June 20, 1936; s. Joseph Anthony and Julie Ann (Kette) Z.; m. Alice Mae Pattison, Apr. 2, 1956 (div. 1972); children: Susan Z. Brown, Kathryn Z. Dwyer, Jane Z. Bee, Patricia Z. Koty, Michael; m. Barbara Buys Wood, Feb. 28, 1981; stepchildren: David Wayne Wood, Brent Douglas Wood. BSBA, U. Ariz., Tucson, 1958. CLU. Prin. mng. ptnr. Ziehler Ins. Group, LLC, Tucson, 1958—. Mem. Fed. Jud. Magistrate Selection Com., 1998—. Employee edn. chmn. So. Ariz. Div. Am. Cancer Soc.; co-chmn. Medic-Alert Found., Pima County, Ariz.; chmn. Tucson Festival Soc.: mem. Salpointe High Sch. Found., others. Recipient William Wisdom award U. Ariz., Tucson, 1958. Mem. Nat. Assn. of Ins. & Fin. Advisors (pres. 1963-64, Agt. of Yr. 1975), Ariz. Nat. Assn. of Life Underwriters (pres. 1970-71, Agt. of Yr. 1980), So. Ariz. CLU Soc. (pres. 1968-69), Salvation Army (pres. adv. bd. 1984-85), Univ. of Ariz. Found. (mem. planned giving com.), Rotary, (com. chmn.), Tucson Conquistadores (pres. 1985-86), Los Charros del Desierto, Golden Key Soc., Million Dollar Round Table, Tucson Country Club, White Mountain Country Club (Pinetop, Ariz.). Republican. Avocations: travel, horseback riding, hiking, sports. Home: 4845 N Camino Escuela Tucson AZ 85718-5913 Office: 6992 E Broadway Blvd Tucson AZ 85710-2803 Office Phone: 520-747-8787. E-mail: tony-ziehler@leavitt.com.

**ZIELINSKI, PAUL BERNARD,** grant program administrator, civil engineer; b. West Allis, Wis., Sept. 9, 1932; s. Stanley Charles and Lottie Charlotte (Pliszkiewicz) Z.; m. Monica Theresa Beres, July 13, 1957; children: Daniel Paul, Gregory John, Robert Mathias, Sarah Ann. BSCE, Marquette U., 1956; MS, U. Wis., 1961, PhD, 1965. Registered profl. engr., Wis., S.C. Asst. instr. engring. mechanics Marquette U., Milw., 1956-59, asst. prof., 1964-67; instr. civil engring. U. Wis., Madison, 1959-64; from asst. prof. to prof. Clemson (S.C.) U., 1967-78, prof. environ. and systems engring., 1978-82, prof. civil engring., 1982-90, prof. emeritus, 1991—; dir. S.C. Water Resources Rsch. Inst., Clemson, 1978-90; assoc. dir. associateship grant program Nat. Rsch. Coun., Washington, 1990—2006; ret., 2006. Cons. Am. Pub. Works Assn., Chgo., 1973-76, Nat. Coun. Examiners of Engring. and Surveying, Clemson, 1973—; cons. swirl devices for storm water separation; com. on exams for profl. engrs. Author numerous publs. on hydraulics and water resources rsch. Chmn. Clemson City Planning Commn., 1971-74; ex-officio mem. S.C. Water Resources Commn., Columbia, 1978-90. Mem. ASCE, Sigma Xi. Roman Catholic. Home: 508 Shorecrest Dr Clemson SC 29631 Office Phone: 202-334-3196.

**ZIELINSKI, THOMAS C.,** lawyer; Various positions Cozen & O'Connor PC, 1982—2001; sr. v.p., gen. counsel Coventry Health Care Inc., Bethesda, Md., 2001—. Office: Coventry Health Care Inc 6705 Rockledge Dr Ste 900 Bethesda MD 20817 Office Phone: 301-581-0600. Office Fax: 301-493-0731. Business E-Mail: tielinski@cvty.com.

**ZIEMBA, KAREN,** actress; Appeared in Broadway plays A Chorus Line, Teddy & Alice, 42nd Street, Crazy for You, Chicago, Contact (Drama Desk award, Outer Critics Cir. award, Tony award, 2000), Never Gonna Dance (Tony nom. best featured actress in a play, 2004); (off-Broadway) And the World Goes 'Round (Drama Desk award) I Do! I Do!; (musical) Steel Pier (Tony award nominee), The Pajama Game, Allegro, Leading Ladies, 2005; (tour) Crazy for You (Joseph Jefferson award), Chicago (1998-99); (regional plays) Much Ado About Nothing, House and Garden, The Foreigner, Fifth of July, Curtains, 2006; (opera) The Most Happy Fella, 110 in the Shade; singer Allegro, Grand Night for Singing; (TV show) Sondheim: A Celebration at Carnegie Hall, Evening at Pops, My Favorite Broadway: The Leading Ladies, Law and Order; (film) The Devil and Daniel Webster; (albums) And the World Goes 'Round, Fifty Million Frenchmen, Lost in Boston II, Shakespeare on Broadway, 110 In The Shade, The Most Happy Fella, Ziegfeld Follies of 1936.*

**ZIEMER, JAMES L.,** motorcycle company executive; BBA, MBA, U. Wis., Milw. CPA Wis. With Harley-Davidson, Inc., Milw., 1969—, v.p., CFO, 1990—2005, pres., CEO, 2005—; pres. Harley-Davidson Found., 1993—. Bd. dirs. Harley-Davidson, Inc. Office: Harley-Davidson Inc PO Box 653 3700 W Juneau Ave Milwaukee WI 53201-0653

**ZIEMER, RODGER EDMUND,** electrical engineering educator, consultant; b. Sargeant, Minn., Aug. 22, 1937; s. Arnold Edmund and Ruth Ann (Rush) Z.; m. Sandra Lorann Person, June 23, 1960; children: Mark Edmund, Amy Lorann, Norma Jean, Sandra Lynn. BS, U. Minn., 1960, MS, 1962, PhD, 1965. Registered profl. engr., Mo. Research asst. U. Minn., Mpls., 1960-62, research assoc., 1962; prof. elec. engring. U. Mo., Rolla, 1968-83, U. Colo., Colorado Springs, 1984—, chmn. dept. elec. engring., 1984-93; program dir. comms. rsch. NSF, 1998-2001. Cons. Emerson Electric Co., St. Louis, 1972-84, Mid-Am. Regional Coun., Kansas City, Mo., 1974, Motorola, Inc., Scottsdale, Ariz., 1980-84, Martin Marietta, Orlando, 1980-81, TRW, Colorado Springs, summer, 1985, Sperry, Phoenix, 1986, Pericle Communications, summer, 1994, Motorola, Schaumburg, 1995, Scottsdale, 1996, Arlington Heights, 1997. Author: Principles of Communications, 1976, Principles of Communications, 2d edit., 1985, Principles of Communications, 3d edit., 1990, Principles of Communications, 4th edit., 1995, Principles of Communications, 5th edit., 2002, Signals and Systems, 1983, Signals and Systems, 2d edit., 1989, Signals and Systems, 3d edit., 1993, Signals and Systems, 4th edit., 1998, Digital Communications and Spread Spectrum Systems, 1985, Introduction to Digital Communication, 1992, Introduction to Digital Communication, 2d edit., 2001, Introduction to Spread Spectrum Communications, 1995, Elements of Engineering Probability and Statistics, 1997; editor: IEEE Jour. on Selected Areas in Comms., 1989, 1992, 1995, IEEE Comm. Mag., 1991. Served to capt. USAF, 1965-68. Scholar Western Electric, 1957-59; trainee NASA, 1962-65. Fellow IEEE (life; Third Millenium award 2000); mem. Am. Soc. Engring. Edn., Armed Forces Comms. and Electronics Assn., Sigma Xi, Tau Beta Pi, Eta Kappa Nu. Lutheran. Home: 8315 Glacier Ct Colorado Springs CO 80920-4412 Office: Univ Colo PO Box 7150 Colorado Springs CO 80933-7150 Office Phone: 719-262-3350. Business E-Mail: ziemer@eas.uccs.edu.

**ZIEMKE, EARL FREDERICK,** history professor, researcher; b. Milw., Dec. 16, 1922; s. Otto and Frieda Ziemke; m. Ida Mae Saltenberger; 1 child, Caroline Frieda Ziembke. BS in Edn., Milw. State Tchrs. Coll., 1948; PhD, Univ. Wis., Madison, 1952. Rschr. Columbia Univ., Alexadria, Va., 1951—55; supr. historian Dept. Army, Washington, 1955—67; rsch. prof. Univ. Ga., Athens, 1967—93. Author: The German-Soviet War 1941-45, 1968, The Red Army 1918-1941, 2004, USArmy in Occupation of Germany, 1975. Cpl. USMC, 1943—46, PTO. Decorated Purple Heart. Home: 400 Brookwood Dr Athens GA 30605-3810

**ZIENTEK, LINDA REICHWEIN,** mathematician, educator; b. Houston, Oct. 31, 1965; d. Kenneth John and Harriet Kay Reichwein; m. Gilbert Zientek, July 30, 1984; children: Jason Wayne, Jacob John, Jenna Marie. BS in Math., Sam Houston State U., 1995, MS in Math., 1997; PhD in Curriculum and Instn., Tex. A&M U., 2006. Math. instr. Blinn Coll., Brenham, Tex., 1997—. Mem.: Math Assn. of Am. (assoc.), Tex. Math. Assn. Two Yr. Colls. (pres.), Tex. C.C. Tchrs. Assn. (sec. 2002, chair math. sect. 2004). Home: 5420 Larkspur Ln Chappell Hill TX 77426 Office: Blinn College 902 College Ave Brenham TX 77833 Personal E-mail: zientek@alpha1.net. Business E-Mail: lzientek@blinn.edu.

**ZIERDT, CHARLES HENRY,** retired microbiologist; b. Pitts., Apr. 24, 1922; s. Conrad Henry and Nancy Leora (Harshberger) Zierdt; m. Margaret May Wise, June 1, 1942 (div. 1962); children: Charles Henry Jr., Carolyn, Douglas, Richard; m. Willadene Smith, Sept. 30, 1967. BS, Pa. State U., 1943; MS, U. Mich., 1945; PhD, George Washington U., 1967. Rsch. assoc. Parke-Davis & Co., Detroit, 1945—48; microbiologist Henry Ford Hosp., Detroit, 1948—53, USPHS, Detroit, 1953—56; rsch. microbiologist NIH, Bethesda, Md., 1956—93, ret., 1993. Scientist sponsor U. Md., 1975—; instr. Found. Advanced Edn. Scis., Bethesda, Md., 1978—. Author: Glucose Nonfermenting Gram Negative Bacteria in Clinical Microbiology, 1978, Non-fermentative Gram Negative Rods: Laboratory Identification and Clinical Aspects, 1985, McGraw-Hill Yearbook of Science and Technology, 1986, Diagnostic Procedures for Bacterial Infections, 1987; contbr. articles to profl. jours. Fellow: Am. Acad. Microbiology; mem.: Mensa, Avanti Owners Assn. Internat., U.S. Fedn. Culture Collections (membership chmn. 1985), Am. Soc. Microbiology (chpt. pres. 1976), Antique Auto Club Am. (pres. Sugar Loaf Mountain region 1997), Model T Ford Club Internat., Model A Ford Club Am. (Fairfax, Va. chpt. pres. 1985), Sigma Xi. Achievements include the classification and pathogenesis of Blastocystis Hominis, an intestinal protozoan parasite of man; description of non-oxidative (anaerobic) mitochondria. Avocations: gardening, antique car restoration, church historian. Home: 4100 Norbeck Rd Rockville MD 20853-1869 Office: NIH Bethesda MD 20816

**ZIERING, CRAIG L.,** osteopath; b. 1960; DO, Southeastern U. Health Scis., Miami Beach, Fla. Diplomate Am. Bd. Dermatology, Am. Bd. Hair Restoration Surgery, lic. physician Fla., N.Y., Ohio, Ill., Mich., Pa. Clin. dir. Advanced Laser Ctrs.; founder, med. dir. Ziering Med., L.A. Resident in dermatology Ohio U./Grandview Med. Ctr. Mem.: Am. Osteo. Coll. of Dermatology (exec. bd. pres. 1999), Am. Soc. Hair Transplant Surgeons (charter), Am. Soc. Phlebology, Am. Soc. for Laser Medicine and Surgery, World Hair Soc., Am. Osteo. Assn., N.Am. Acad. Cosmetic and Restorative Surgery, Am. Acad. Dermatology, Am. Acad. Facial, Plastic and Reconstructive Surgery, Am. Soc. Dermatologic Surgery, Am. Acad. Cosmetic Surgery, Internat. Soc. Hair Restoration Surgery, Am. Hair Loss Coun. Office: Ziering Medical 8500 Wilshire Blvd #1010 Los Angeles CA 90211

**ZIERING, WILLIAM MARK,** lawyer; b. New Britain, Conn., Feb. 4, 1931; s. Jacob Max and Esther (Freedman) Z.; m. Harriet Koskoff, Aug. 20, 1958 (div. Sept. 1993); 1 son, Benjamin. BA, Yale U., 1952; JD, Harvard U., 1955. Bar: Conn. 1955, Calif. 1962. Assoc. Koskoff & McMahon, Plainville, Conn., 1959-60; sr. trial atty. SEC, San Francisco, 1960-65; pvt. practice law San Francisco, 1965—; ptnr. Bremer & Ziering, 1972-77. Instr. Golden Gate U. Law Sch., San Francisco, 1968-75 Vice pres., bd. dirs. Calif. League Handicapped, 1972—. Served to comdr. USNR, 1955-58. Mem. ABA, Calif. Bar Assn., San Francisco Bar Assn. (past chmn. securities, corps. and banking), Navy League (dir.) Clubs: Commonwealth. Home: 440 Davis Ct Apt 620 San Francisco CA 94111-2418 Office Phone: 415-982-4581. Personal E-mail: wmziering@sbcglobal.net.

**ZIERLER, NEAL,** retired mathematician; b. Balt., Sept. 17, 1926; children: Robert Eugene, Joan Mariye, Ann Michie. AB, Johns Hopkins U., 1945; AM, Harvard U., 1949, PhD, 1959. Mathematician, physicist Ballistic Rsch. Labs., Aberdeen, Md., 1951; mem. tech. staff instrumentation lab. MIT, Cambridge, Mass., 1952-54, mem. tech. staff Lincoln Lab. Lexington, Mass., 1954-60; supr. info. processing group of jet propulsion lab. Calif. Inst. Tech., Pasadena, 1960-61; sr. scientist ARCON Corp., Lexington, 1961-62; head sub-dept. process analysis MITRE Corp., Bedford, Mass., 1962-65; tech. staff Ctr. for Comm. Rsch. Inst. Def. Analysis, Princeton, N.J., 1965-96. Patentee error-detecting and -correcting devices; contbr. articles to profl. jours. Lt. USN, 1944-46. Fellow IEEE; mem. Am. Math. Soc., Math. Assn. Am., Am. Physics Soc. Avocations: tennis, skiing, photography. E-mail: nzierler@ieee.org.

**ZIESE, DENNIS RUSSELL,** retired protective services official, retired military officer; b. Bklyn., Jan. 18, 1950; s. Russell Arthur and Joan Elizabeth Ziese; m. Kazuko Katashi, Apr. 23, 1971 div. June 1985); children: Diane, John, Kathy; m. Linda Nell Pohl, May 18, 1999; children: Eric Pohl, Evan Pohl. AS, Columbia Coll., 1992, BA, 1993; MA, Lincoln U., 1996. Master sgt. USMC, Washington, 1967—89, served in Vietnam, ret., 1989; functional unit mgr. Mo. Dept. Corrections, Jefferson City, 1990—2005; ret.; prof. So. Ill. U., Edwardsville, 2005—, SCCC, St. Peters, Mo., 2005—. Decorated Vietnam Cross of Galantry, Combat Action medal USMC, Naval Commendation medal with combat V, recipient Compliments, mo. medal, State of NY, 1973. Mem.: VFW, USMC League, KC. Republican. Roman Catholic. Avocations: golf, fishing, hunting, reading.

**ZIESE, NANCYLEE HANSON,** social worker; m. J. A. Ziese; 1 child, G. Graham. BA in Sociology, Morningside Coll., 1960; MSW, U. Iowa, 1982, cert. in aging studies, 1986; Edn. for Minister, U. of South, 1996. Social worker Florence Crittenton Home, Sioux City, 1960—65, L.A. County, 1965; social worker, supr. Polk County Dept. Social Welfare, Des Moines, 1966—69; social worker, cmty. liaison Tommy Dale Meml., Sioux City, 1977—79; dir. internships Briar Cliff Coll., Sioux City, 1981—83; dir. continuing edn. Coe Coll., Cedar Rapids, Iowa, 1983—85; exec. dir. Profl. Women's Network, Cedar Rapids, 1985—87; pvt. practice counselor, cons., spkr., writer Womanplace Counseling, Cedar Rapids, 1985—87, 1999—; coord. adoption Hillcrest Family Svcs., Cedar Rapids, 1987—99. Bd. dirs. Young Parent's Network M.E.L.D., Cedar Rapids, pres., 1994—96; cons. cmty. empowerment, recycling; spkr. in field; gov. apptd. mem. Iowa State Child Advocacy Bd., 2002—. Contbr. articles to newspapers. Steering bd. Iowa Women's Polit. Caucus, 1987—93, pres., 1992—93; dep. gen. conv. Episcopal Ch. USA, 1997—2006; past chair Iowa Birth Defects Inst. Adv. Com., Iowa Assn. Adoption Agys.; bd. dirs. Linn County Adolescent Pregnancy Prevention Coalition, treas., 1992—96; steering com. mem. ERA Iowa 1992, 1991—93; gov.'s com. Adoption Reform in Iowa, 1993—94; It. gov.'s com. spl. needs Adoption in Iowa, 1994; bd. dirs. pub. policy chair AAUW, 1995—2002, pres., 2000—01; co-founder, pres. Iowa Breast Cancer Action Found., 1998—2006; mem. to chmn. Cedar Rapids Civil Rights Commn., 2000—04; clinic advisor Cmty. Health Free Clinic, 2005—; bd. dirs. commn. mem. Human Needs, commn. on ministry Episcopal Diocese Iowa, 1996—99, standing com., 2000—, dep. gen. conv., 2000—06; v.p. Sioux City Sch. Bd., 1978—83; bd. dirs., pres. Friends of Iowa Pub. TV, 1978—88; bd. dirs. Family Svc. Boys and Girls Home, Sioux City, 1973—81; bd. dirs. Goodwill Industries S.E. Iowa, 2003—. Named Woman of Yr., Linn County, Cedar Rapids, 1995; recipient Outstanding Svc. awards, Sioux City C. of C., 1976, Siouxland Arts Coun., 1977, Child Advocate-Children's Voice award, 2004; Paul Harris fellow, Rotary, 2005. Mem.: Profl. Women's Network Cedar Rapids (bd. mem., Woman of Yr. 1997), NASW,

Rotary Internat. Avocations: community service, social justice advocate, reading. Home and office: 1759 Applewood Pl NE Cedar Rapids IA 52402-3321 E-mail: ziesenancylee@hotmail.com.

**ZIESMER, JERRY H.,** film director; b. 1933; married. Attended, High Sch. Inst., Northwestern Univ.; Master's, UCLA; grad. DGA Producer Ass. Dir. Training Prog. Tchr., The Craft of the Asst. Dir., UCLA Extension. Asst. dir (films): Tell Me That You Love Me, Junie Moon, 1970, The Great White Hope, 1970, Something Big, 1971, Fools' Parade, 1971, Honky, 1971, J.W. Coop, 1972, The Wrath of God, 1972, Lost Horizon, 1973, The Way We Were, 1973, Mitchell, 1975, Harry & Walter Go to New York, 1976, Black Sunday, 1977, The Bad News Bears Go to Japan, 1978, Apocalypse Now, 1979, Rocky II, 1979, 1941, 1979, History of the World: Part I, 1981, Annie, 1982, Blue Thunder, 1983, Scarface, 1983, The River, 1984, American Flyers, 1985, Jo Jo Dancer Your Life Is Calling, 1986, Short Circuit, 1985, Jumpin' Jack Flash, 1986, Some Kind of Wonderful, 1987, Illegally Yours, 1988, Midnight Run, 1988, Say Anything, 1989, Love at Large, 1990, Solar Crisis, 1990, Marked for Death, 1990, Out For Justice, 1991, Deep Cover, 1992, Singles, 1992, Jerry Maguire, 1996, Almost Famous, 2000; asst. dir. (TV): King, 1978, Life on the Mississippi, 1980, George Carlin: Playin' with Your Head, 1986, Secrets, 1992; author (autobiography): Ready When You Are, Mr. Coppola, Mr. Spielberg, Mr. Crowe. Mem.: Directors Guild Am. (Frank Capra achievement award 2006), Acad. Motion Picture Arts & Scis. Mailing: Directors Guild Am 7920 Sunset Blvd Los Angeles CA 90046*

**ZIETZ, KARYL LYNN KOPELMAN See LYNN, KARYL**

**ZIFCHAK, WILLIAM C.,** lawyer; b. 1948; BA, Harvard U., 1970; JD, Columbia U., 1973. Bar: N.Y. 1974, U.S. Ct. Appeals (2d cir.) 1975, U.S. Ct. Appeals (3d cir., D.C. cir.) 1983, U.S. Dist. Ct. (so. dist.) N.Y. 1984. Ptnr., co-chair labor and employment law dept. Kaye, Scholer, Fierman, Hays & Handler, N.Y.C. Planning com. NYU Ann. Nat. Conf. Labor, 1991-97. Contbr. articles to profl. jours. Named Super Lawyer, N.Y., 2006. Mem. ABA (sect. labor and employment law 1975—, subcom. antitrust, RICO and labor rels. law), Assn. Bar City of N.Y. (sec. com. labor and employment law 1984-87), N.Y. State Bar (comml.-fed. litig. sect. co-chair labor and employment law com. 1995-97). Office: Kaye Scholer LLP 425 Park Ave New York NY 10022-3506 Business E-Mail: wzifchak@kayescholer.com.

**ZIFF, LARZER,** literature and language professor; b. Holyoke, Mass., Oct. 2, 1927; s. Isadore Menden and Sara (Rosenbloom) Z.; m. Ruth Rosalind Geisenberger; children— Joshua, Oliver, Joel, Abigail. Student, Middlebury Coll., 1945-47; MA, U. Chgo., 1951, PhD, 1955; MA (hon.), U. Oxford, Eng., U. Pa. Prof. English U. Calif., Berkeley, 1956-73; univ. lectr. Oxford U., Eng., 1973-78; prof. English U. Pa., 1978-81; Caroline Donovan prof. English Johns Hopkins U., Balt., 1981—, chair dept., 1991-95. Dir. U. Calif. Edn. Abroad Program, U.K., Ireland, 1969-71; cons. and lectr. in field. Author: The Career of John Cotton, 1962; The American 1890's, 1968; Puritanism in America, 1973; Literary Democracy, 1981; Writing in the New Nation, 1991, Return Passages, 2000, Mark Twain: Life and Legacy, 2004; also articles, essays in profl. jours.; mem. editl. bds. including ELH, 1981—94. Recipient numerous awards for excellence in English including Christian Gauss award, the American 1890's, 1967; Fulbright fellow, 1959-60, fellow Am. Coun. Learned Socs., 1963-64, Newberry Libr., 1964, NEH, 1967-68, Guggenheim fellow, 1977-78, Woodrow Wilson Internat. Ctr. for Scholars, 1986-87; Fulbright Disting. Sr. Lectr., 1993. Fellow Am. Acad. Arts and Scis., Am. Historians; mem. MLA, Am. Antiquarian Soc. (Johns Hopkins U Dept English Baltimore MD 21218 Personal E-mail: lziff@attglobal.net.

**ZIFFREN, KENNETH,** lawyer; b. Chgo., June 24, 1940; BA, Northwestern U., 1962; JD, UCLA, 1965. Bar: Calif. 1967. Law clerk to Chief Justice Warren, 1965—66; ptnr. Ziffren, Brittenham, Branca & Fischer, L.A. Mem.: ABA, L.A. Copyright Soc., Beverly Hills Bar Assn., L.A. County Bar Assn. (pres. 1977—78), State Bar Calif. Office: Ziffren Brittenham Branca & Fischer 1801 Century Park W Los Angeles CA 90067-6406

**ZIGERELLI, LAWRENCE,** retail products company executive; Grad., Yale U., 1980. Category mgmt., consumer response specialist Procter & Gamble, 1980-99; exec. v.p. corp. devel. CVS Corp., Woonsocket, SC, 1999—2002; sr. v.p. mktg., advertising, and corp. devel. Meijer Inc., 2002, sr. v.p. merchandising, 2003, exec. v.p., 2004—05, pres., 2005—. Office: Meijer Inc 2929 Walker Ave NW Grand Rapids MI 49544*

**ZIGLAR, JAMES W.,** telecommunications industry executive, federal agency administrator, investment banker, lawyer, educator; b. Pascagoula, Miss., Dec. 8, 1945; married; 3 children. BA, George Washington U., 1968, JD, 1972. Bar: Va. 1972, D.C. 1973, N.Y. 1977. Staff asst. Senator James Eastland, Washington, 1964-71; spl. asst. Dept. of Justice, Washington, 1971-72; law clk. to assoc. justice Harry Blackmun U.S. Supreme Ct., Washington, 1972-73; assoc. Mudge, Rose, Guthrie et al, N.Y.C., 1973-77; ptnr. O'Connor, Cavanagh, Anderson et al, Phoenix, 1977-80; sr. v.p. Dillon, Read & Co., N.Y.C., 1980-84; mng. dir. UBS Fin. Svcs., N.Y.C., 1984—87, 1990—98, 2004—05; asst. sec. Dept. of Interior, Washington, 1987-88; mng. dir. Drexel Burnham Lambert Inc., N.Y.C., 1989-90; sgt. at arms U.S. Senate, Washington, 1998—2001; commr. immigration and naturalization serv. U.S. Dept. Justice, Washington, 2001—02; resident fellow Inst. of Politics Harvard U., Cambridge, Mass., 2003; pres. and CEO Cross Match Tech., Inc., Palm Beach Gardens, Fla., 2005—. Disting. vis. prof. Law Sch. George Washington U., 2003—04. Office: 3950 RCA Blvd Ste 5001 Palm Beach Gardens FL 33410 Office Phone: 561-622-1650. Business E-Mail: james.ziglar@crossmatch.com

**ZIGLER, EDWARD FRANK,** psychologist, educator; b. Kansas City, Mo., Mar. 1, 1930; s. Louis and Gertrude (Gleitman) Z.; m. Bernice Gorelick, Aug. 28, 1955; 1 child, Scott. BA, U. Mo.-Kansas City, 1954; PhD, U. Tex., 1958; MA (hon.), Yale, 1967; DSc (hon.), Boston Coll., 1985; LHD (hon.), Bank St. Coll. Edn., 1989, U. New Haven, 1991, St. Joseph Coll., 1991; PhD (hon.), U. Mo., 1993, CUNY, 1995, degree (hon.), 1995, Wheelock Coll., 2005; LLD (hon.), Gonzaga U., 1995; HHD, Park U., 2000; LHD, McGill U., 2001. Psychol. intern Worcester (Mass.) State Hosp., 1957-59; asst. prof. psychology U. Mo., 1958-59; mem. faculty Yale U., 1959—, prof. psychology and child study center, 1967—, Sterling prof., 1975—; dir. child devel. program, 1961-76, chmn. dept. psychology, 1973-74; head psychology sect. Yale Child Study Center, 1967—; dir. Bush Center in Child Devel. and Social Policy, 1977—. Chief Children's Bur. NEW, Washington, 1970-72; cons. in field, 1962—; mem. nat. steering com. Project Head Start, 1965-70, chmn. 15th anniversary Head Start com. 1980; mem. nat. adv. center Nat. Lab. Early Childhood Edn., 1967-70; nat. rsch. adv. bd. Nat. Assn. Retarded Children, 1968-73; nat. rsch. coun. Project Follow-Through, 1968-70; chmn. adv. com. Vietnamese Children's Resettlement, 1975; mem. Pres.'s Com. on Mental Retardation, 1980; joint appointee U.S. State U. Med. Medicine, 1982—, chmn. Yale Infant Care Leave Commn., 1983-85, Parents as Tchrs., 1986—; mem. adv. com. Head Start Quality and Expansion, 1993; mem. vis. com. on svcs. for families with infants and toddlers HHS, 1994; mem. 25th Anniversary hon. com. Children's Def. Found. 1997; mem. program com. Head Start's 5th Nat. Rsch. Conf., 1998—; mem. nat. adv. panel hon. chair, hist. mentor Nat. Head Start Assn.: Fulfilling the Promise 2010 Project 1998-00; mem. adv. com. Head Start Rsch. and Evaluation for Administrn. for Children and Families, 1999—, Nat. Partnership's Family Leave Income Initiative, 1999—; mem. program com. Head Start Nat. Rsch. Conf., 2005. Author, co-author, editor books and monographs; contbr. articles to profl. jours. With AUS, 1951-53. Recipient Gunnar Dybwad Disting. scholar in behavioral and social sci. award Nat. Assn. Retarded Children, 1964, 69, Social Sci. Aux. award, 1962, Alumni Achievement award U. Mo., 1965, Alumnus of Yr. award, 1972, C. Anderson Aldrich award Am. Acad. Pediatrics, 1985, Nat. Achievement award Assn. for Advancement of Psychology, 1985, Dorothea Lynde Dix Humanitarian award for svc. to handicapped Elwyn Inst., 1987, Sci. Leadership award Joseph P. Kennedy Jr. Found., 1990, Mensa Edn. and Rsch. Found. award for excellence, 1990, Nat. Head Start Assn. award, 1990

Founders award, 1995, Bldg. dedication Edward Zigler Head Start Ctr., 1990, As They Grow award in edn. Parents mag., 1990, Excellence in Edn. award Pi Lambda Theta, 1991, Friend of Edn. award Conn. Edn. Assn., 1991, Loyola-Mellon Social Sci. award 1991, Pres.'s award Conn. Assn. Human Svcs., 1991, Harold W. McGraw, Jr. prize in edn., 1992, Disting. Achievement in Rsch. award Internat. Assn. Sci. Study of Mental Deficiency, 1992, Disting. Svc. award Coun. Chief State Sch. Officers, 1993, Outstanding Fed. Leadership in Support of Head Start Rsch., Adminstrn. on Children, Youth and Families, 1993, Child and Family Advocacy award Parents as Tchrs. Nat. Ctr., 1994, Nat. Distinction award U. Pa. Edn. Alumni Assn., 1994, Disting. Fellow award So. Conn. State U. chpt. Phi Delta Kappa, 1997, Lifetime Achievement award in Applied and Preventive Psychology Am Assn. Applied and Preventive Psychology, 1998, Recognition award Coun. for Early Childhood Profls., Child Devel. Assocs., 1999, Heinz award pub. policy, 1999, Nat. Head Start Assn. award appreciation, 2000, Disting. Svc. medal Tchrs. Coll. Columbia U., 2000, Disting. Alumnus U. Tex., 2000, Key to the City, Independence, Mo., 2000, Nat. Head Start Assn. award appreciation, 2000, Disting. Svc. medal Tchrs. Coll. Columbia U., 2000, Lifetime Mentoring award, ACYF, 2000, Lifetime Contbn. psychology award CT Psychol. Assn., 2000, Lifetime Commitment to comty. svc. award Ct dept. higher edn. and CT commn. on nat. and comty. svc., 2001, Florence Halpern award disting. profl. contbns. in clin. psychology APA, 2001, Bridges Over Barrtiers awrd, Family REsources Youth Svcs. Coalition Ky., 2002, others; named Hon. Commr. Internat. Yr. of Child, 1979. Fellow Am. Orthopsychiat. Assn. (Blanche F. Ittleson award 1989, pres. 1993-94), APA (pres. divsn. 7, 1974-75, G. Stanley Hall award 1979, award for disting. contbns. to psychology in pub. interest 1982, Nicholas Hobbs award 1985, award for disting. profl. contbns. to knowledge 1986, Edgar A. Doll award 1986, award for disting. contbn. to cmty. psychology and cmty. mental health 1989, pres.-elect divsn. 37 1997, pres. 1998, past pres. 1999, Bronfenbrenner Lifetime Contbn. award divsn. 7 1998, Florence Halpern award for disting. profl. contbns. in clin. psychology divsn. 12 2001); mem. Inst. Medicine of NAS, AAAS, Am. Acad. Mental Retardation (Career Rsch. award 1982), Soc. Psychol. Study Social Issues (Kurt Lewin meml. award 1995), Zero to Three (Dolley Madison award 1995), P.R. Head Start Assn. (Outstanding Leadership award 1995, True Father of Headstart recognition award 1996, award of appreciation for lifelong support and participation 1997), Am. Psychol. Found. (gold medal for life contbn. 1997, Parents Child Care award for advocacy 1998, Heinz award in pub. policy, 1999). Home: 177 Ridgewood Ave North Haven CT 06473-4442 Office: Edward Zigler Cctr Child Devel and Social Policy 310 Prospect St New Haven CT 06511 E-mail: edward.zigler@yale.edu.

**ZIGO, PAUL EDWARD,** historian, educator; b. Newark, July 14, 1942; s. Edward and Jeannette Zigo; m. Kim Irene Schmerler; children: Paul Jr., Drew, Travis, Marc, Kristen. BA in History, Rutgers U., New Brunswick, NJ, 1964; M in Pers. and Guidance, Rider U., Lawrenceville, NJ, 1973; diploma, US Army War Coll., Carlisle Barracks, Pa., 1989; M in Recent Am. Diplomatic and Mil. History, Temple U., Phila., 2000. Lic. radio broadcaster FCC. Asst. dir. cmty. rels. Monmouth U., West Long Branch, NJ, 1966—75, dir. cmty. rels., 1975—77; dir. off campus svcs. Brookdale CC, Lincroft, NJ, 1977—2003, asst. prof. history, 2003—, dir. Ctr. World War II Studies and Conflict Resolution, 2003—. Bd. dirs. Eastern CC Social Sci. Assn., Arlington, Va.; adv. coun. Brookdale CC Internat. Ctr. Policy adv. bd. mem. NJ Profl. Devel. Ctr. Early Childhood Edn., Union, 2001—03; mem., exec. com. Monmouth U., Monmouth Jr. Sci. Symposium, West Long Branch, NJ, 1979—2005; bd. dirs. Western Monmouth C. of C., Freehold, NJ, 1999—2005; mem. adv. coun. Battleship NJ (BB 62) History Mus., Camden; mem. allocations com. Monmouth County United Way, Farmingdale; chairperson, adv. coun. Ctr. for WWII Studies and Conflict Resolution Brookdale CC; mem. Ft. Monmouth Retiree Coun., Eatontown, NJ; founder Ctr. for WWII Studies and Conflict Resolution, Brookdale CC, 2000. Col. USAR, 1964—94. Decorated Def. Meritorious Svc. medal US Dept. of Def., Legion of Merit medal US Army; named to Point Pleasant Beach HS Hall of Fame, Point Pleasant Beach Pub. Edn. Found., 2002; recipient Cert. of Recognition for Svc. to Monmouth County, Monmouth County Bd. of Chosen Freeholders, 1994, Excellence award for Outstanding Contbns. to Tchg., Leadership and Learning, Nat. Inst. for Staff and Orgnl. Devel., 2005, George Washington Honor medal, Freedoms Found. at Valley Forge, 2006. Mem.: Eastern Cmty. Colls. Social Sci. Assn. (assoc.), Brookdale CC Faculty Assn. (assoc.), Mil. History Soc. (assoc.), Assn. of US Army (assoc.), Monmouth chpt. Vets. Battle of Bulge (assoc.). Roman Catholic. Avocations: military history, overseas and national travel, photography. Home: 15 Beach Rd Neptune NJ 07753 Office: Brookdale CC 765 Newman Springs Rd Lincroft NJ 07738 Office Phone: 732-224-2029. Office Fax: 732-224-2444. Personal E-mail: pzigo@optonline.net. Business E-Mail: pzigo@brookdalecc.edu.

**ZIGWEID, RICHARD NEIL,** music educator; b. Buffalo, Wyo., May 29, 1977; s. Robert E. and Peggy J. Zigweid; m. Christy Anne Davis, June 16, 2001; 1 child, Whitney Christine. B in Music Edn., U. Wyo., 2000. Cert. tchr. Nebr. Dept. Edn., 2001. Band/choir tchr. Limon (Colo.) Pub. Schs., 2000—01; band tchr. Sidney (Nebr.) Pub. Schs., 2001—. Sponsor Nat. Jr. Honor Soc., Sidney, 2003—04. Mem.: Music Educator Nat. Conf. (assoc.). Democrat. Office: Sidney Public Schools 2103 King St Sidney NE 69162 Office Phone: 308-254-5853. Office Fax: 308-254-5992.

**ZIKMUND, BARBARA BROWN,** minister, religious organization administrator, educator; b. Ann Arbor, Mich., Oct. 16, 1939; d. Henry Daniels and Helen Langworthy Brown; m. Joseph Zikmund II, Aug. 26, 1961; 1 child, Brian Joseph. BA, Beloit Coll., 1961; BDiv, Duke U., 1964, PhD, 1969; D in Div (hon.), Doane Coll., 1984, Chgo. Theol. Sem., 1985, Ursinus Coll., 1989; LHD, U. Hartford, 1998. Ordained to ministry United Ch. of Christ, 1964. Instr. Albright Coll., Reading, Pa., 1966-67, Temple U., Phila., 1967-68, Ursinus Coll., Collegeville, Pa., 1968-69; asst. prof. religious studies Albion Coll., Mich., 1970-75; asst. prof. ch. history, dir. studies Chgo. Theol. Sem., 1975-80; dean and assoc. prof. ch. history Pacific Sch. Religion, Berkeley, Calif., 1981-85, dean and prof. ch. history, 1985-90; pres. Hartford (Conn.) Sem., 1990-2000. Prof. grad. sch. am. studies Doshisha U., Kyoto, Japan, 2000-05; vis. Life Cycle Inst. scholar Cath. U. Am., 2005—; chmn. United Ch. of Christ Hist. Coun., 1983-85, mem. coun. for ecumenism 1983-89; mem. Nat. Coun. Chs. Commn. on Faith and Order, 1979-87, World Coun. of Chs. Programme Theol. Edn., 1984-91, Nat. Coun. Chs. Working Group on Inter-Faith Rels., 1992-96, Nat. Coun. Chs. Commn. on Inter-faith Rels., 1996—, chair Commn. on Inter-faith Rels., 2000—, World Conf. Assns. for Theol. Instns., sec. treas., 1992-96, pres., 1996-2000. Author: Discovering the Church, 1983, Clergy Women: An Uphill Calling, 1998; editor: Hidden Histories in the UCC, 1984, vol. 2, 1987; (with Manschreck) American Religous Experiment, 1976; mem. editl. bd. Jour. Ecumenical Studies, 1987—, Mid-Stream, 1991—; series editor: Living Theological Heritage of the United Church of Christ, co-editor Vol. 7 United and Uniting, 2005; contbr. articles to profl. jours. Mem. City Coun., Albion, Mich., 1972-75; elector Wadsworth Atheneum, 1994-2000; corporator St. Francis Hosp., 1994-2000, Hartford Hosp. 1996-2000; pres. Greater Hartford Consortium for Higher Edn., 1994-96. Woodrow Wilson fellow, 1964-66; NEH grantee, 1974-75; vis. scholar Schlesinger Libr. Women's History, Radcliffe Coll., 1988-89, Disting. Alumna, Duke Divinity Sch., 1994; recipient Disting. Svc. Citation Beloit Coll., 1986; Antoinette Brown award, United Ch. of Christ, 2005. Mem. Assn. Theol. Schs. (v.p. 1984-86, pres. 1986-88, issues implementation grantee 1983-84, Disting. Svc. award 2004), Am. Soc. Ch. History (coun. 1983-85, pres. elect 1996-97, pres. 1997-98), Internat. Assn. Women Ministers (v.p. 1977-79), AAUW (v.p. 1977-79). Democrat. Office: Life Cycle Inst Cath U Am Washington DC 20064 Home: Apt 510 4545 Connecticut Ave NW Washington DC 20008-6016 Business E-Mail: beebeezee@verizon.net. E-mail: zikmund@cua.edu.

**ZILBER, NORMAN ALBERT,** lawyer; b. Detroit, Nov. 12, 1931; s. Israel and Bessie L. (Steir) Z.; m. Lucille Parnes, Sept. 25, 1994. BBA, U. Mich., 1953, JD, 1956. Bar: Calif. 1962, U.S. Ct. Appeals (9th cir.) 1962, U.S. Supreme Ct. 1962. Atty. Office Gen. Counsel USAF, Washington, 1956-59;

assoc. Hahn, Loeser & Parks, Cleve., 1959-61; dir. Bancroft & McAlister PC, San Francisco, 1992-99; ptnr. Bancroft & McAlister LLP, San Francisco, 1999—. Dir., sec. San Francisco Jazz Festival, 1990-03. Capt. USAF, 1956-59. Mem. ABA (negotiated acquisitions com. bus. law sect. 1988—), Internat. Assn. Jewish Vocat. Svcs. (pres. 1994-95). Avocations: hiking, biking, cultural events, travel, book clubs. Office: Bancroft & McAlister LLP 650 California St 25th Fl San Francisco CA 94108 Office Phone: 415-781-8855. Office Fax: 415-781-8855. E-mail: nzilber@bamlaw.com.

**ZILBERT, ALLEN BRUCE,** education educator, computer scientist, consultant; b. Bronx, N.Y., May 26, 1957; s. Murray and Perla Z.; m. Barbara Dale Palley, July 1, 1984; children: Heather Robynne, Jared Lee. BA in Econ., CUNY, 1978; MBA, St. Johns U., 1980, advanced profl. cert., 1982; MEd in Adminstrv. Computer Systems Edn., Columbia U., 1986, EdD, 1988; postgrad., Kennedy-Western U., 1995—. Instr. bus. computer info. systems & quantitative methods Hofstra U., Hempstead, NY, 1981-83; asst. prof. info. systems Pace U. Sch. Computer Sci. and Info. Systems, N.Y.C., 1983-89; dir. ancillary systems Advanced Med. Systems, Rockville Centre, 1989-90; asst. prof. mgmt. Long Island U. Sch. Bus., Coll. Mgmt., Brookville, 1990-94; asst. prof. mgmt. info. sys. Sy Syms Sch. Bus., David Zysman prof. of mgmt. info. sys. Yeshiva U., N.Y.C., 1994-2000; assoc. prof. math./computer sci. Molloy Coll., Rockville Centre, 2000—03, dir. computer sci. and computer info. systems programs, 2000—03; assoc. prof. computer info. sys. Briarcliffe Coll., Patchogue/ Bethpage, 2003—, chair computer info. sys. dept., 2003—04, dir. acad. portal and web sys., 2003—. Mem. acad. affairs com. Pace U. Sch. Computer Sci. and Info. Sys., 2003—; chmn. personal computer resources com. Advanced Med. Sys., 1989-90; campuswide computer com. L.I. U., 1991-94, chmn., 1993-94, chmn. scholarship awards com., 1990-91; assembly collegiate schs. bus. curriculum planning com. Coll. Mgmt., 1993-94, chmn. computer needs, usage and stds. com., 1990-93, chmn. mgmt. dept. computer com., chmn. scholar awards com., 1992-93; book and software reviewer. Contbr. articles to profl. jours. Mem. IEEE, Assn. for Computer Tng. and Support, Assn. for Computing Machinery, Assn. of Info. Tech. Profls., Internat. Assn. for Computer Info. Sys., Internat. Assn. Mgmt., Info. Resources Mgmt. Assn Business E-Mail: azilbert@bcl.edu.

**ZILIAK, STEPHEN T.,** economics professor; b. Quincy, Ill., Oct. 17, 1963; s. Lawrence O. and Barbara J. Ziliak; children: Jude L., Flora S. BA in Econs., Ind. U., Bloomington, 1986; MA in Econs., U. Iowa, Iowa City, 1993, PhD in Econs., 1996, PhD in Rhetorics of Inquiry. 1996. Caseworker Marion County Dept. Pub. Welfare, Indpls., 1987—88; rsch. analyst Ind. Dept. Employment and Tng., 1988—91; instr. U. Iowa, Iowa City, 1994; asst. prof. econs. Bowling Green State U., Ohio, 1996—2001; assoc. prof. econs. Roosevelt U., Chgo., 2003—05, prof. econs., 2006—. Vis. asst. prof. econs. Emory U., Atlanta, 1993—2003, Ga. Inst. Tech., 2000—03; cons. in field. Author: (book) Size Matters: How Some Sciences Lost Interest in Magnitude, and What to Do About It (University of Michigan Press), The Economic Conversation (Palgrave/MacMillan); editor: Measurement and Meaning in Economics: The Essential Deirdre McCloskey (Edward Elgar Ltd.); mem. editl. bd.: Jour. Econ. Methodology, 1997—, Econ Jour. Watch, 2003—; contbr. articles to profl. jours. Faculty advisor RACES, Emory U., 2001—03, Entrepreneurship Industry, Ga. Tech, 2001—03, Honors Selection Com., Ga. Tech, 2001—03. Recipient Faculty Mem. Yr., Student Govt. Assn., Ga. Tech, 2002. Achievements include research in economic history and rhetoric and philosophy of the social sciences; rhetoric of the social sciences. Office: Roosevelt U 430 S Michigan Ave Chicago IL 60605 Office Phone: 312-341-3763. Office Fax: 312-341-3762. E-mail: sziliak@roosevelt.edu.

**ZILKHA, EZRA KHEDOURI,** banker; b. Baghdad, Iraq, July 31, 1925; arrived in U.S., 1941, naturalized, 1950; s. Khedouri A. and Louise (Bashi) Z.; m. Cecile Iny, Feb. 6, 1950; children: Elias Donald, Donna, Bettina Louise. Grad., Hill Sch., Pottstown, Pa., 1943; AB, Wesleyan U., Middletown, Conn., 1947, LLD (hon.), 1987. Dir. Zilkha & Sons, Inc., NYC, 1946—, chmn., pres., 1956—. Dir. Cigna Corp., Phila., 1968—96, former chmn. investment com.; dir. Mothercare, Ltd., England, 1970—82, INA Life Ins. Co. of NY, 1973—87, Blyth Eastman Dillon & Co., 1976—79, Newhall Land & Farming Co., Calif., 1977—2004, Revlon, Inc., 1981—95, Chgo. Milw. Corp., 1981—96, Cambridge Assocs., Boston, 1988—2000; vice chmn. bd. Fortune Bancorp, 1990—94, Handy & Harman, 1969—88; chmn. bd. Fidelity Internat. Bank., 1968—79; chmn. Union Holdings, 1984—90. Trustee emeritus, former chmn. investment com. Wesleyan U.; hon. trustee, former chmn. investment com. Brookings Inst., Washington; former trustee Spence Sch., NYC, French Inst., NYC, Lycee Francais de NY; trustee Am. Soc. French Legion of Honor; former mem. exec. com., former chmn. bd. Internat. Ctr. for Disabled, NYC. Decorated comdr. Legion d'Honneur, officer Ordre Nat. du Merite (France); recipient Freedom of Human Spirit award Internat. Ctr. for Disabled, 1989, Pilier d'Or award French Inst./Alliance Francaise, 1995, Charles de Ferry de Fontnouvelle award Lycee Francais de N.Y., 2003. Mem.: Coun. Fgn. Rels., The Brook Club, Polo Club, Travellers Club, Meadow Club, Knickerbocker Club, Racquet & Tennis Club. Office Phone: 212-758-7750.

**ZILLMER, JOHN J.,** waste management administrator; MBA, Kellogg Graduate School Northwestern Univ. Mgmt. Aramark Corp., pres. food and support services group, exec. vice-pres.; chmn. bd. and CEO Allied Waste Industries, 2005—. Mem. bd. dir. United Stations Directors, Inc. Office: Allied Waste Management Ste 100 15880 N Greenway Hayden Loop Scottsdale AZ 85260 Office Phone: 480-627-2700.*

**ZILLY, THOMAS SAMUEL,** federal judge; b. Detroit, Jan. 1, 1935; s. George Samuel and Bernice M. (McWhinney) Z.; divorced; children: John, Peter, Paul, Luke; m. Jane Greller Noland, Oct. 8, 1988; stepchildren: Allison Noland, Jennifer Noland, Ba, U. Mich., 1956; LLD, Cornell U., 1962. Bar: Wash. 1962, U.S. Ct. Appeals (9th cir.) 1962, U.S. Supreme Ct. 1976. Ptnr. Lane, Powell, Moss & Miller, Seattle, 1962-88; dist. judge U.S. Dist. Ct. (we. dist.) Wash., Seattle, 1988—. Judge pro tem Seattle Mcpl. Ct., 1972-80; mem. adv. com. bankruptcy rules U.S. Judicial Conf., 1998—; chair adv. com. U.S. Jud. Conf., 2004—. Contbr. articles to profl. jours. Mem. Cen. Area Sch. Council, Seattle, 1969-70; scoutmaster Thunderbird Dist. council Boy Scouts Am. Seattle, 1976-84; bd. dirs. East Madison YMCA. Served to lt. (j.g.) USN, 1956-59. Recipient Tuahku Dist. Service to Youth award Boy Scouts Am., 1983. Mem. ABA, Wash. State Bar Assn., Seattle-King County Bar Assn. (treas. 1979-80, trustee 1980-83, sec. 1983-84, 2d v.p. 1984-85, 1st v.p. 1985-86, pres. 1986-87). Office: US Dist Ct 700 Stewart St Ste 15229 Seattle WA 98101

**ZILVETI, CARLOS BENJAMIN,** preventive medicine physician, pediatrician; b. Sucre, Bolivia, June 14, 1928; came to U.S., 1956; s. Carlos and Marina (De La Reza) Z.; m. Halina J. Daszewski, Sept. 8, 1957 (div. Sept. 1976); 1 child: Carlos Joseph III; m. Vita Palazzolo, Sept. 5, 1987. BS, Sacred Heart Coll., Sucre, Bolivia, 1946; MD, U. San Francisco Xavier, Sucre, Bolivia, 1954; MPH, Yale U., 1966. Physician in rural medicine Bolivian Power Co., La Paz, 1955; intern Hosp. Obrero Victor Paz Estenssoro, La Paz, 1956; asst. resident in pediats. St. Luke's Hosp., Meml. Cancer Ctr., Woman's Hosp., N.Y.C., 1957-58; resident and chief resident in pediats. Hosp. of St. Raphael, New Haven, 1958-59; pvt. practice New Haven and Branford, Conn., 1960-63; dir. maternal-child health New Haven Dept. Health, 1964-74; regional health officer South and Ctrl. Am. Peace Corps, Bogota, Colombia, 1975-76; regional health officer, sci. attache in West Africa U.S. Dept. of State, Liberia, Ghana, Togo, Sierra Leone, 1976-79; reserve appt. of maj., advanced to col. USAF San Antonio, 1979-91, chief environ. medicine Wilford Hall Med. Ctr., 1979-83, cons. preventive and occupl. medicine, 1983-91, cons. aerospace-preventive medicine Wilford Hall Med. Ctr. Lackland AFB, Tex., 1984-91, ret. col. 1991. Cons. FDA, HEW, Washington, 1966-75; cons. to Headstart Nat. Am. Acad. Pediats., Stanford-Norwalk, Conn., 1968-75; regional med. officer, sci. attache West Africa U.S. Dept. State. Contbr. articles to profl. jours. Chmn. gov.'s task force Conn. State Dept. Health, Hartford, 1969-75. Fellow Am. Acad. Pediats. (emeritus), Am. Coll.

Preventive Medicine (emeritus); mem. APHA, AMA, New Eng. Pub. Health Assn., Conn. Acad. Preventive Medicine, Am. Occupl. Med. Assn. Avocations: swimming, tennis, golf, travel, classical music. Home: 9222 Dover Rdg San Antonio TX 78250-3557

**ZIMAN, BARRY RUSSELL,** government relations executive; s. Arthur Ziman and Eileen Ziman Ravin. BA, SUNY, 1980—84. Legislative dir. NY State Assembly, 1988—89; dir. of legislation and commn. NY State Assemblyman Larry Seabrook, Albany, 1985—89; dir. of govt. and pub. affairs NY and NJ. Printing Industry Assn., 1989—92; dir. of strategic advocacy Consumer Splty. Products Assn., Washington, 1992—2001; dir. state affairs Coll. of Am. Pathologists, Washington, 2001—. Polit. analyst Manila Broadcasting Co., Washington, 2003—05; cons. Gerson Lehman Group, NYC, 2004. Dep. mayor's econ. adv. com., NYC, 1991—92; state student coord. NY State Dem. Com., Mondale-Ferraro Presdl. Campaign, 1984; campaign adviser State Senator Larry Seabrook For U.S. Congress, NYC, 2000—01; bd. mem. Oneonta Ancillary Services Corp., 1983—84, Binding Together Inc. (Non-Profit), NYC, 1991—92. Recipient President's award, Coll. of Am. Pathologists, 2003, 2004; scholar NY State Regents scholar, NY State Regents, 1979. Office: Coll of Am Pathologists 1350 I Street NW Ste 590 Washington DC 20005 Office Phone: 202-354-7117.

**ZIMAND, HARVEY FOLKS,** lawyer; b. NYC, Aug. 28, 1928; s. Savel and Gertrude (Folks) Z.; m. Ingeborg Rockosch, 1963 (div. 1980); children: Patricia Folks Carpenter, Stephanie Folks Plexico; m. Noel French, Apr. 30, 1983 (dec. 2006). BA, Colgate U., 1950; postgrad., Oxford U., Eng., 1950; MA, U. Chgo., 1951; postgrad., Columbia U., 1952-53; LL.B., Yale U., 1957. Bar: N.Y. 1957. Rapporteur Council for Fgn. Relations, N.Y.C., 1952-53; atty. Dept. Navy, Washington, 1956-70; ptnr. Kelley Drye & Warren, N.Y.C., 1970—. Dir. Toronto-Dominion Trust Co., N.Y.C., 1975-83. Bd. editors The Chase Jour. Bd. dirs. Virginia Day Nursery, N.Y.C., 1980-84. Served to cpl. U.S. Army, 1951-53 Named to The Best Lawyers in Am., 1996—, Best Lawyers in NY, 1996—. Fellow NY Bar Found.; Am. Coll. Trust and Estate Counsel; mem. ABA, NY State Bar Assn., Assn. Bar City of NY, Estate Planning Coun., Univ. Club, Yale Club (NYC), Randolph Mountain Club (NH). Republican. Episcopalian. Home: 120 E 81st St New York NY 10028-1428 Office: Kelley Drye & Warren LLP 101 Park Ave New York NY 10178-0002 Business E-Mail: hzimand@kelleydrye.com.

**ZIMBALIST, MICHAEL,** publishing executive; m. Melissa Zimbalist; children: Lila, Peri, Quentin. BA in Chemistry and Philosophy, Brown U., 1979. Mgmt. positions AT&T Downtown Digital; dir. production Capital Cities/ABC, 1995—97; gen. mgr., online svcs. United Media, Divsn. E.W. Scripps Co., 1997—99; exec. v.p., mktg. and bus. develop. ePod Corp. (sold to Star Media Network), 1999—2001; exec. dir. Online Publishers Assn., 2001—04, pres., 2004—06; v.p., R&D ops. NY Times Co., 2006—. Disney imagineer, wrote and produced a number of i; frequent commentator on issues affecting the online media and advertising bus.; regular spkr. at industry conf. and events. Exec. prodr. (Disney imagineer, wrote & produced): a number of interactive exhibits at Epcot Ctr. and Euro Disneyland for sponsors such as AT&T and IBM; contbr. TV shows for Hanna Barbara and interactive games for MCA/Universal Studios; guest appearances NBC News and CNN; contbr. to NY Times, Wall Street Jour., and USA Today. Office: NY Times Co 229 W 43rd St New York NY 10036*

**ZIMBARDO, PHILIP GEORGE,** psychologist, educator, writer; b. NYC, Mar. 23, 1933; s. George and Margaret (Bisicchia) Z.; m. Christina Maslach, Aug. 10, 1972; children: Zara, Tanya; 1 son by previous marriage, Adam. AB, Bklyn. Coll., 1954; MS, Yale U., 1955, PhD, 1959; D (hon.), U. Peru, 1996; LHD in Clin. Psychology, Pacific Grad. Sch. Psychology, 1996, D (hon.), 1997, Nat. U. of San Martin, 1996, Nat. U. Peru, Thessalonoki, Greece, 1997, Aristotle U., 1998. Asst. prof. psychology Yale U., New Haven, 1959-61, NYU, N.Y.C., 1961-67; vis. assoc. prof. psychology Columbia U., N.Y.C., 1967-68; prof. psychology Stanford (Calif.) U., 1968—. Pres. P.G. Zimbardo, Inc., San Francisco; sr. project advisor Exploratorium, 1993; host, writer, gen. acad. advisor PBS-TV series Discovering Psychology, 1987, 2001; cons. NBC. Author: Cognitive Control of Motivation, 1969, Canvassing for Peace, 1970, Psychology and Life, 17th edit., 2005, Shyness, What It Is, What To Do About It, 1977, Influencing Attitudes and Changing Behavior, rev. edit., 1977, The Shyness Workbook, 1979, A Parent's Guide to the Shy Child, 1981, reprinted, 1999, The Psychology of Attitude Change and Social Influence, 1991, Core Concepts in Psychology, 5th edit., 2005. Ctr. for Advanced Study of Behavioral Scis. fellow, 1971; recipient Peace medal Tokyo Police Dept., 1972, City Medal of Honor, Salamanca, Spain, Disting. Tchr. award Am. Psychol. Found., 1975, award Havel Found., 2005. Fellow APA (pres. 2002, Presdl. citation Discovery Psychology series 1994, Tchg. award 1999); mem. Am. Psychol. Soc., AAUP, Internat. Congress Psychology, Western Psychol. Assn. (pres. 1985, 2001), Ea. Psychol. Assn., Calif. Psychol. Assn. (Disting. Contbn. to Rsch. award 1978), Soc. for Psychol. Study of Social Issues, Coun. Sci. Soc. Pres. (chair 2005), Sigma Xi, Phi Beta Kappa, Psi Chi. Roman Catholic. Office: Stanford U Psychology Dept Stanford CA 94305 Office Phone: 415-776-4748. Office Fax: 415-673-2294. Business E-Mail: zim@stanford.edu. *One of the few virtues of growing up in a poor urban ghetto is the realization that people are the most important resource we have— to be used wisely, well and as often as possible. The second is the tempering of book learning by street wits. The third is to value a career that allows me to contribute to improving the quality of our lives through research and teaching.*

**ZIMET, CARL NORMAN,** psychologist, educator; b. Vienna, June 3, 1925; came to U.S., 1943, naturalized, 1945; s. Leon and Gisela (Kosser) Z.; m. Sara F. Goodman, June 4, 1950; children: Andrew, Gregory. BA, Cornell U., 1949; PhD, Syracuse U., 1953; postdoctoral fellow, Stanford U., 1953-55. Diplomate in clin. psychology Am. Bd. Professional Psychology (trustee 1966-74). Instr., then asst. prof. psychology and psychiatry Yale U., 1955-63; mem. faculty U. Colo. Med. Center, 1963—, prof. clin. psychology, 1966—, head div., 1963—. Mem. Colo. Bd. Psychol. Examiners, 1966-72, Colo. Mental Health Planning Commn., 1964-66; mem. acad. adv. com. John F. Kennedy Child Devel. Center, U. Colo., 1966-68; chmn. Council for Nat. Register of Health Service Providers in Psychology, 1975-85, pres., mem. exec. bd. div. psychotherapy, 1970-89; chair exec. com. Assn. Psychol. Internship Ctrs., 1988-91. Bd. editors: Jour. Clin. Psychology, 1962-91, Jour. Clin. and Cons. Psychology, 1964-73, Psychotherapy, 1967—, Profl. Psychology, 1969-75. With USNR, 1943-46. Recipient Disting. Service award Colo. Psychol. Assn., 1976 Fellow: APA (coun. reps. 1969—72, 1973—76, bd. dirs. 1985—88, Disting. award for profl. contbn., div. psychotherapy and div. clin. psychology 1987), Soc. Personality Assessment (pres. 1975—76, 1975—76, chair gen. psychol. svcs. 1987—97, bd. dirs.); mem.: Med. Sch. Profs. Psychology (pres. 1992—94, bd. dirs. 2004—), Denver Psychoanalytic (trustee 1968—71), Am. Acad. Clin. Psychology (pres. 1993—2001). Home: 400 E 3rd Ave # 901 Denver CO 80203 Office Phone: 303-315-8611. Business E-Mail: carl.zimet@uchsc.edu.

**ZIMET, LLOYD,** sport psychologist, health educator, program planner and administrator; b. Bklyn., 1951; s. Victor R. and Marcia Z. BA, Whittier (Calif.) Coll., 1973; MA, U. Md., 1983, PhD, 1984; MPH, NYU, 1989. Head basketball coach Aarhus (Denmark) U., 1973—78, 1980—82, 1985—86; resident dir. U. Md., College Park, 1978—80; sports supr. Montgomery County (Md.) Dept. of Recreation, 1978, 1982—84; dir. health promotion Optimal Fitness Inc., N.Y.C., 1986—91; internat. cons. cmty. and occupational health, 1984—; dir. World of Discovery Day Camp, Bklyn., 1997—2000. Dir. edn. AIDS Ctr. of Queens (N.Y.) County, 1989-90; bd. dirs. Patricia Manning Meml. Fund childhood cancer Am. Cancer Soc., Queens, 1988-95; mem. AIDS med. adv. com. N.Y.C. Bd. Edn., 1989-90; mem. adv. bd. Adolescent Health Network, Queens, 1989-90; keynote speaker NYU Health Edn. conf., May 1990, USPHS Region II Conf., 1991; prevention specialist Hillsborough County (Fla.) Sch. Dist., 2004, mem. sch. health adv. com., 2004, staff & program developer, 2005; mgr. prevention and wellness, 2005; mem. AIDS adv. com. Dept. Edn., State of Fla., 2004. Bd. govs. U.S.

Amateur Boxing Fedn., Colorado Springs, Colo., 1988-91; bd. dirs. Met. Amateur Boxing Fedn., N.Y.C., 1988-91; mem. USA Boxing Nat. Scholarship com., 1984-88. Fellow: Soc. Pub. Health Educators; mem.: AAHPERD, APHA, APA.

**ZIMILES, MURRAY,** artist, educator; b. Bklyn., Nov. 30, 1941; s. Joseph Zimiles and Eugenia Margolis; m. Martha M. Rogers, May 23, 1970; 1 child: Andrei. BFA, U. Ill., 1963; MFA, Cornell U., 1965; postgrad., Atelier Clot-Bramson, Paris, 1966. Tchg. asst. Cornell U., Ithaca, 1963-65; instr. Pratt Graphics Ctr., Bklyn., 1968-71; chmn. graphics dept., asst. prof. Silvermine Coll. Art, 1969-71; lectr. Lehman Coll. CUNY, 1972; dir. Silvermine-Lacoste Sch. Art, France, 1972; asst. prof. Coll. SUNY, New Paltz, 1972-76, prof. Coll. Purchase, 1977-98; Kempner disting. prof. Purchase Coll., 1998—. Vis. artist Brandywine Workshop, Phila., 1987. One-man shows include Stuart Levy Gallery, N.Y., 1992, Nat. Mus. Am. Jewish History, Phila., 1989, Vorpal Galleries, San Francisco, 1985, and N.Y.C., 1984, DFN Gallery, N.Y.C., 1999, BMG Gallery, Adelaide, Australia, 1998, Sydney Jewish Mus., 1996, Neuberger Mus., Purchase, N.Y., 2003, Cape Cod Mus. Art, Dennis, Mass., 2003, Houston Holocaust Mus., 2006; exhibited in group shows at Pratt Graphics Ctr., Princeton (N.J.) U., Wis. State U., numerous others; represented in permanent collections Bklyn. Mus., Jewish Mus., Mus. Modern Art., N.Y. Pub. Libr., Neuberger Mus., Purchase, Johnson Mus., Ithaca, Portland Mus. Oreg.; curator, essay author Boris Margo, 1988, retrospective traveling exhbn.; The Lithographic Workshop Around The World, 1974, Early American Mills, 1973, The Technique of Fine Art Lithography, 1970. Fellow Royal Norwegian Govt., Harriet Hale Wooley Foun. fellow, 1965-66; recipient Dutchess County Arts Coun. award, 1991; N.Y. state coun. on arts grant for artists' books fellowship, 1995-96, Smart Found. grant, 1995, 96, Dorot Found. grant, 1994, Richard Florsheim Art Fund grant, 2002. Home: 78 Charlie Hill Rd Millerton NY 12546-9721 Office: SUNY Coll Dept Art and Design Purchase NY 10577 E-mail: zimiles@taconic.net.

**ZIMMAN STETSON, NANCY See STUART, NANCY**

**ZIMMER, ANNA HELD,** social worker; b. Revere, Mass., Jan. 1, 1922; d. Morris and Sarah (Javits) Held; m. Fred Zimmer, Apr. 4, 1948; children: Harold, Sarah, Bonnie. BA, Bklyn. Coll., 1943; MSW, Smith Coll., 1944. Cert. social worker, N.Y. Caseworker New Haven Family Svc., 1944-46, Phila. Family Svc., 1946-48, United Svc. for New Ams., N.Y.C., 1948-49, Coun. Ctr. Sr. Citizens, Bklyn., 1957-69; caseworker, student supr. Community Svc. Soc. N.Y., N.Y.C., 1967-82; co-dir. Network Assocs., 1982-87; dir. media assistance to caregivers Brookdale Ctr. Aging/Hunter Coll., N.Y.C., 1985-87, dir. Inst. on Mut. Aid/Self Help in Field of Aging, 1986—. Mem. long term home health care com. Jewish Home and Hosp. for Aged; regional rep. Nat. Inst. on Community-Based Long-Term Care, Nat. Coun. on Aging, mem. adv. com. caregivers project, 1986; mem. adv. com. Ret. Sr. Vol. Program, N.Y.C. Editorial Bd. Jour. Gerontol. Social Work. Mem. NASW (Social Worker in Aging award N.Y.C. chpt. 1987, Walter Beattie award 1998), Aca.d Cert. Social Workers, Gerontol. Soc. Am., Am. Soc. Aging, N.Y. Soc. Aging. Home: 975 Massachusetts Ave Apt 305 Arlington MA 02476-4545

**ZIMMER, CONNIE WHITLOW,** librarian; b. Willow Shade, Ky., Nov. 11, 1950; d. Elmer and Carrie Mae (Lester) Whitlow; m. Steven Wilkinson Zimmer, May 29, 1971; 1 child, Charlotte Melissa. BA, We. Ky. U., 1972, MLS, 1975. Cert. sch. libr. Ky. Student asst. dept. geography and geology We. Ky. U., Bowling Green, 1968—71; ref. libr. Bowling Green Pub. Libr., 1971—72; libr. Ohio County Mid. Sch., Hartford, Ky., 1972—73, Bowling Green H.S., 1972—73; night supr. Bowling Green Pub. Libr., 1976—77; head libr. Warren East H.S., 1974—90; asst. prof. secondary edn. Ark. Tech. U., Russellville, 1990—2002, assoc. prof., 2002—. Video instr. camp for gifted and talented youth We. Ky. U., 1985—90, faculty dept. tchr edn. libr. media edn., 1988—90. Del. 3d Dist. Edn. Assn., 1982, 1984—90; sponsor 3d Dist. Beacon Builders, Bowling Green, 1974—90, Warren East Student Assts., 1974—90, Student Libr. Assts. Ky., 1983—90; vol. Firefighter Barren River Vol. Fire Dept., 1977—86; audio-visual resource person Bowling Green Presbyn. Ch., 1984—86; church libr. Ctrl. Presbyn. Ch., Russellville; bd. dirs. Pope County Libr., 2005. Mem.: NEA, ALA, Ark. Assn. Tchr. Educators, Assn. Tchr. Educators, Ark. ASCD, Am. Assn. Sch. Librs., Assn. Ednl. Comm. Tech., Ark. Assn. Sch. Libr. Media Educators (chair 2005—06), Ark. Assn. Instrl. Media (Leadership award 2002), Ark. Edn. Assn., Ark. Libr. Assn., Assn. Sch. Libr. Internat. (internat. book awards com. 1988—90, mem. Chandlie May Simon book award com. 1998—, chmn. Ark. diamond primary book award com. 2000—), Ark. Tech. U. Dames Club (rec. sec. 1991—92, dir. young author's conf. 1992, pres.-elect 1993, co-dir. 1993, cons. libr. automation on site mgmt., MARC cataloging records), Gamma Sigma Sigma. Presbyterian. Avocations: antiques, reading, walking. Office: Ark Tech U Sch Edn Crabaugh Bldg Russellville AR 72801 Office Phone: 479-968-0434. Business E-Mail: connie.zimmer@atu.edu.

**ZIMMER, DONALD WILLIAM,** former professional baseball coach, former professional baseball manager; b. Cin., Jan. 17, 1931; s. Harold Lesley and Lorraine Bertha (Ernst) Z.; m. Jean Carol Bauerle, Aug. 16, 1951; children: Thomas Jeffrey, Donna Jean. Student Pub. Schs., Cin. Baseball player Dodger Farm Clubs, 1949-54, Bklyn. Dodgers, 1954-57, L.A. Dodgers, 1958-59, 1963, Chgo. Cubs, 1960-61, N.Y. Mets, 1962, Cin. Reds, 1962, Washington Senators, 1963-65, Toei Flyers, Tokyo, 1966; mgr. Cin. Reds Farm Clubs, Knoxville and Buffalo, 1967, Indpls., 1968, San Diego Padre Farm Clubs, Key West, Fla., 1969, Padre Farm Club, Salt Lake City, 1970; coach Montreal Expos, Que., Canada, 1971; mgr. San Diego Padres, 1972-73; coach Boston Red Sox, 1974-76, 1992, mgr. 1976-80, Tex. Rangers, 1981-82; coach Chgo. Cubs, 1984, 85, 86, mgr., 1988-91; coach San Francisco Giants, 1987, Colo. Rockies, Denver, 1993-95, N.Y. Yankees, 1983, 1986, 1996—2003; sr. baseball advisor Tampa Bay Devil Rays, 2004—06. Mem. minor league All-Star Teams, Hornell, N.Y., 1950, Elmira, N.Y., 1950, Mobile, Ala., 1951, St. Paul, 1953; player World Series teams 1955, 56, 59; coach World Series teams 1975, 96, 98, 99, 2000, 01, 03; mem. adv. bd. Baseball Assistance Team. Recipient Bill Stern award NBC, 1949; named St. Paul Rookie of Yr., 1953, All Star Team Player, 1961, All Star Coach, 1978, 81, 90, 97, 99, 2000, 01, 02, 03; named Nat. League Mgr. of Yr. 1989. Mem. Profl. Baseball Players Assn. (life), Maj. League Baseball Players Alumni Assn., Old Time Ball Players Wis. Office: c/o Tampa Bay Devil Rays 1 Tropicana Drive Saint Petersburg FL 33705 Office Phone: 727-825-3137.

**ZIMMER, GEORGE A.,** men's apparel executive; b. NYC, Nov. 21, 1948; s. Robert Zimmer; m. Lorri Zimmer; 4 children. BA in Econ., Washington U., St. Louis, 1970. Founder, chmn., CEO The Men's Wearhouse Inc., Houston, 1973—. Bd. dir. Apollo Group Inc., 2006—. Bd. dirs. Inst. Noetic Sciences. Office: The Mens Wearhouse 40650 Encyclopedia Cir Fremont CA 94538-2453 also: 5803 Glenmont Dr Houston TX 77081

**ZIMMER, HANS FLORIAN,** composer; b. Frankfurt, Germany, Sept. 12, 1957; m. Suzanne Zimmer; 4 children. Former mem. The Buggles; co-founder Media Ventures LLC. Composer (with Stanley Myers): (films) (scores) Moonlighting, 1982, Success is the Best Revenge, 1984, The Wind, 1987, The Zero Boys, 1987, Taffin, 1988; composer: Terminal Exposure, 1987, Wonderland, 1988, (with Myers) The Nature of the Beast, 1988, with Luis Bonfa Prisoner of Rio, 1988, Burning Secret, 1988, (with Myers) Paperhouse, 1988, Rain Man, 1988 (Acad. award nominee best original score, 1988), A World Apart, 1988, Arcadia, 1988, Black Rain, 1989, Diamond Skulls, 1989, Driving Miss Daisy, 1989, Twister, 1989, Bird on a Wire, 1990, (with Shirley Walker) Chicago Joe and the Showgirl, 1990, Days of Thunder, 1990, Fools of Fortune, 1990, Green Card, 1990, The Neverending Story II: The Next Chapter, 1990, Pacific Heights, 1990, Backdraft, 1991, Regarding Henry, 1991, Thelma and Louise, 1991, Radio Flyer, 1991, The Power of One, 1992, A League of Their Own, 1992, (with Mark Mancina) Where Sleeping Dogs Lie, 1992, Sniper, 1993, (with Bob Telson) Younger and Younger, 1993, Point of No Return, 1993, True Romance, 1993, composer: Calendar Girl, 1993; Cool Runnings, 1993, The House of the Spirits, 1993, I'll Do Anything, 1994, Renaissance Man, 1994, The Lion

King, 1994 (Acad. award best original score, 1994), Crimson Tide, 1995; composer: Nine Months, 1995; (TV films) Wild Horses, 1985, First Born, 1989, Millennium: Tribal Wisdom and the Modern World, 1992, music prodr. The Last Emperor, 1987. Office: Gorfaine Schwartz Agency 4111 W Alameda Ave Ste 509 Burbank CA 91505-4171

**ZIMMER, JANIE LOUISE,** mathematics professor, academic administrator; b. Balt., Sept. 25, 1943; d. Joseph Max and Anna Margaret (Vogtmann) Zimmer; m. Gordon Henry Stills, Jan. 7, 1972 (div. May 1978); 1 child, Sanova Stills; m. William Broaddus Long, Jr., Nov. 17, 1984; children: W. Michael, Calvin, Travon. BA in Math., Trinity Coll., Washington, 1966; MEd, Loyola Coll., Balt., 1973; postgrad., U. Md., 1982—. Tchr. math. Norfolk (Va.) Cath. H.S., 1966-69, Balt. City Pub. Schs., 1969-73, math. specialist, 1980-83; chmn. dept. math. Edmondson H.S., Balt., 1973-80; math. supr. Howard County Pub. Schs., Ellicott City, Md., 1983-91, exec. supr. math., 1991-92, curriculum coord., 1992-2000; math. assoc. Rsch. for Better Schs., Phila., 2000—; founder, pres. Rsch.-Based Edn., LLC. Cons. Md. Math. League, 1987-2000; profl. U. Md., Balt. County, 1989-95; clown/mathemagician Md., 1981—. Columnist in math. jour., 1986-98; editor: State Functional Math Guide, 1984, IMAGES: Improving Measurement and Geometry in the Elementary Schools, 2002, 2d edit., 2004; contbr. Mathematical Connections: A Bridge to Algebra and Geometry, 1992; editor: EdThoughts: What We Know About Science Teaching and Learning, 2001, EdThoughts: What We Know About Mathematics Teaching Learning, 2002. Recipient Outstanding Math. Educator award Md. Coun. Tchrs. of Math., 1991, Outstanding Svc. award Md. Coun. Tchrs. Math., 1985, United Cerebral Palsy, 1974, Citizenship award K.C., 1961, Outstanding Alumna of Yr. award Maryvale Trinity Coll. Prep Sch., 1983. Mem. Md. Assn. Supervision and Curriculum Devel. (bd. dirs. 1999-2000), Md. Coun. Tchrs. Math (rep. 1986-94, pres. 1984-85), Nat. Coun. Tchrs. Math. (regional svcs. com. 1994-97, chair 1997-98, chair regional conf. 1991, bd. dirs. 2002—), Nat. Assn. Sci. Tchrs., Pa. Sci. Tchrs. Assn., Nat. Mid. Sch. Assn., Pa. Coun. Tchrs. Math., Pa. Coun. Suprs. Math. Math., Nat. Coun. Suprs. Math. (bd. dirs.), Md. Coun. Suprs. Math., Clowns of Am. Internat., Freestate Clown Alley, Phi Delta Kappa. Republican. Roman Catholic. Avocations: clowning, games, skiing, reading. Home: 125 N Maple St Woodbury NJ 08096-1838 Office: Rsch Based Edn LLC 125 N Maple St Woodbury NJ 08096-1838 Office Phone: 415-913-9981. Business E-Mail: zimmer.j@comcast.net.

**ZIMMER, LARRY WILLIAM, JR.,** sports announcer; b. New Orleans, La., Nov. 13, 1935; s. Lawrence W. Sr. and Theodora (Ahrens) Z.; m. Dawn M. Caillouet, June 4, 1955 (div. June 1972); children: Larry III, Tracey; m. Brigitte Bastian, Nov. 17, 1972. Student, La. State U., 1953-55; BJ, U. Mo., 1957. Sports dir. KFRU Radio, Columbia, Mo., 1960-66; asst. mgr. programming WAAM Radio, Ann Arbor, Mich., 1966-71; broadcaster football, basketball Mich., 1966-70; sportscaster, sports dir. KOA Radio, Denver, 1971—; broadcaster Denver Broncos Football, 1971-96; broadcaster football, basketball U. Colo. Buffaloes, 1971—; broadcaster Denver Rockets, 1972-74. Adj. prof. journalism U. Colo., 2001—. Author: Stadium Stories--The Denver Broncoes, 2004. Bd. mem. Colo. Ski Mus. and Hall of Fame, Vail, 1981-2000, Opera Colo., Denver, 1985—, Colo. chap. Nat. Football Found; adv. bd. Jefferson Co. Youth Advocacy Ctr. 1st lt. US Army, 1958-60. Named Colo. Sportscaster of the Yr., Nat. Sportscasters and Sportswriters Assn., Salisbury, NC, 1988, 90, 91, 2001, 02, Broadcaster of the Yr., Colo. Broadcaster's Assn., Denver, 1995; recipient Powerade award for best radio/TV sports story of yr. Nat. Sportscasters and Sportswriters Assn., 2000. Avocations: skiing, jogging, opera. Office: KOA Radio 4695 S Monaco St Denver CO 80237-3403 E-mail: larryzimmer@clearchannel.com.

**ZIMMER, MARC,** chemistry professor; b. Sasolburg, South Africa, July 26, 1961; s. Joachim and Hannele Zimmer; m. Dianne Egan, Mar. 29, 1986; children: Matthew Holden, Caitlin Egan. PhD, Worcester Poly. Inst., Eng., 1989. Barbara Zaccheo Kohn '72 prof. of chemistry Conn. Coll., New London, 2004—. Author: (nonfiction) Glowing Genes. Recipient John King Tchg. award, Conn. Coll., 2001, Nancy Batson Nisbet Rash Faculty Rsch. award, 2005. Mem.: Am. Chem. Soc. (program chair inorganic divsn. 1998—2003, Burlew Award for Contbns. to Chemistry, Conn. Valley sect. 2005—06). Office: Conn Coll 270 Mohegan Ave New London CT 06320 Office Phone: 860-439-2476.

**ZIMMER, MARKUS BERNHARD,** legal association administrator; b. Basel, Switzerland, Oct. 10, 1946; came to U.S., 1948; s. Max Bernhard and Elisabeth (Sulzmann) Z.; m. Shelley Elaine Melcomian, Jan. 5, 1976; children: Jessica, Christopher. BA in Philosophy, U. Utah, 1971, MA in Philosophy, 1975; MEd, Harvard U., 1977; EdD in Philosophy of Edn., 1980. Rsch. asst. Harvard Law Sch., Cambridge, Mass., 1977-78; teaching fellow law and ethics Harvard U., Cambridge, Mass.; asst. divsn. dir. Div. Continuing Ed. and Tng., Fed. Jud. Ctr., Washington, 1981—83, chief legal svcs. tng. br., 1983—84, chief mgmt. tng. br., 1984-87; adj. assoc. prof. mgmt. U. Md., College Park, 1985-87; clk. of ct., dist. ct. administr. U.S. Dist. Ct., Dist. Utah, Salt Lake City, 1987—. Fed. dist. ct. clks. adv. com. Adminstry. Office US Cts., 1990-96, fed. dist. ct. case mgmt. and stats. umbrella group, 1992-98, dist. ct. efficiencies task force, 1992-93, ct. adminstrn. adv. com., 1995-96, chmn. tech. panel on automation, 1999-2002; interagy. adv. group on tng. and devel. Office of Pers. Mgmt., Washington, D.C. 1984-87; ABA Cen. and East European Law Initiative ct. adminstrn. cons. Bulgarian Ministry Justice, Sofia, 1992, cons. Constnl. Ct. Bosnia and Herzegovina, 1995, legal specialist, Skopje, Macedonia, 1997, faculty, Jud. Tng. Inst., Prague, Czech Republic, 2000-01; ct. cons., Zagreb, Croatia, 1994; spkr., Workshop on US Jud. Conf., Budapest, Hungary, 1998; ct. adminstrn. sr. cons. Croatia, 1994, Macedonia, 1997, Warsaw, Poland, 1998, Romania, 1999, Slovak Republic, 2000, 2004, Azerbaijan, 2002, Kosovo, 2003, Bahrain, 2003, Jordan, 2004, Serbia, 2004, Liberia, 2005, Serbia, 2005; leader World Bank Regional Justice Sector Capacity Bldg. Program, Prague, Czech Republic, 2003-05; mem. faculty ABA Ceeli Prague Inst. Iraqi Judges, 2004; strategic planning cons. to Iraqi Judiciary, 2005, 06, faculty Internat. Seminar on Jud. Transparency, Chegdu, China, 2005; founding ptnr. and pres., Internat. Assn. Ct. Admin., 2004—, chair US Dist. Cts. Civil/Criminal User Group, 1995-98; ad hoc task force on budget allotment simplification US Cts., 1996-98; dist. clk. liaison US Jud. Conf. IT Com., 1999-2001, internat. jud. rels. com., 2002-04; adv. roundtable on law on cts. Coun. Europe, Rep. of Montenegro, 2001; jud. edn. cons., Kigali, Rwanda, 2002; cons. in field. Contbr. articles to profl. jours. Exec. bd. Utah Combined Fed. Campaign, 1989—, bd. chmn. and statewide campaign dir., 1992, 2002. Fulbright fellow, 1972-73; recipient U.S. Cts. Dir.'s award for outstanding leadership, 1994, Roy B. Gibson Freedom of Into. award Utah chpt. Soc. Profl. Journalists, 2000. Mem. ABA (CEELI ct. adminstrn. working group 1991-94, Russian jury trial working group 1993-94, African human rights subcom., 2004—), ASTD (dir. justice sys. trainers 1984-86), Fed. Ct. Clks. Assn. (exec. bd. 1991-92), Internat. Assn. for Ct. Adminstrn., 2004—. Office: U S Dist Ct 120 Frank E Moss Courthouse 350 S Main St Ste 150 Salt Lake City UT 84101-2180 Office Phone: 801-524-6120. E-mail: markus_zimmer@utd.uscourts.gov, zimmermb@gmail.com.

**ZIMMER, RICHARD ALAN,** lawyer, retired congressman; b. Newark, Aug. 16, 1944; s. William and Evelyn (Schlank Rader) Zimmer; m. Marfy Goodspeed Zimmer, Dec. 27, 1965; children: Carl William, Benjamin Goodspeed. BA, Yale U., 1966, LLB, 1969. Bar: N.Y. 1971, U.S. Dist. Cts. (so. and ea. dists.) N.Y. 1974, N.J. 1975, U.S. Dist. Ct. N.J. 1975, U.S. Supreme Ct. 1980, D.C. 2005. Assoc. Cravath, Swaine and Moore, N.Y.C., 1969—75; gen. atty. Johnson & Johnson, New Brunswick, NJ, 1976—91; mem. N.J. Gen. Assembly, 1982—87, chmn. state govt. com., 1986—87; mem. N.J. Senate, 1987—91, 102nd-104th Congresses from 12th N.J. dist., Washington, 1991—97; with Dechert, Princeton, NJ, 1997—2001; of counsel Gibson, Dunn & Crutcher, Washington, 2001—. Lectr. pub. and internat. affairs Woodrow Wilson Sch., Princeton U., 1997—2000. Chmn. Citizens for a Better N.J., 1997—2000, Study Commn. on the Implementation of the Death Penalty, 1997—98; trustee Freedom House Found., 1997—2001. Republican. Office: Gibson Dunn & Crutcher 1050 Connecticut Ave NW Washington DC 20036-5306 E-mail: rzimmer@gibsondunn.com.

**ZIMMER, ROBERT J.,** academic administrator, mathematician, educator; b. NYC, Nov. 5, 1947; s. Max S. and Harriet (Brokaw) Z.; m. Terese Schwartzman, Oct. 27, 1974; children— David, Benjamin, Alexander. AB summa cum laude, Brandeis U., 1968; PhD, Harvard U., 1975. Asst. prof. US Naval Acad., Annapolis, Md., 1975-77; instr. U. Chgo., 1977-79, assoc. prof., 1979-80, prof. math. 1980—, chmn. math dept., 1991-95, assoc. provost for rsch. & edn., 1995—98, dep. provost for rsch., 1998—2000, dep. provost, 2000—01; pres. U. Chgo, 2006—; prof. math. U. Calif.-Berkeley, 1981-83; provost, Ford Found. prof. math. Brown U., Providence, 2002—06. V.p. rsch. Argonne Nat. Lab., 2000—02. Author: Ergodic Theory and Semisimple Groups, 1984, Essential Results of Functional Analysis; contbr. articles to profl. jours. Sloan Found. fellow, 1979-83 Office: U Chgo Office of Pres 5801 S Ellis Ave Chicago IL 60637*

**ZIMMER, WILLIAM,** art critic; Undergraduate work, Columbia U.; Art History Degree, U. Tex. With The Soho News, 1977; art critic NY Times, 1981—. Lectr. in field; juried art exhbns. Office: NY Times 229 West 43rd St New York NY 10036

**ZIMMERER, KATHY LOUISE,** museum director; b. Whittier, Calif., Dec. 9, 1951; BA cum laude, U. Calif., Berkeley, 1974; MA, Williams Coll., 1976. From tour guide to curatorial asst. Sterling and Francine Clark Inst., Williamstown, Mass., 1975-76; spl. asst. dept. modern art L.A. County Mus. Art, 1976-77; mus. edn. fellow Fine Arts Mus. San Francisco, 1977-78; dir. coll. art gallery SUNY, New Paltz, 1978-80; cons. in field, 1980-81; dir. univ. art gallery Calif. State U., Dominguez Hills, 1982—. Project dir. Painted Light: California Impressionist Paintings from the Gardena H.S./L.A. Unified Sch. Dist., 1996—. Mem. Internat. Assn. Art Critics, Art Table. Office: Univ Art Gallery Calif State U 1000 E Victoria St Carson CA 90747-0001 Office Phone: 310-243-3334. E-mail: kzimmerer@csudh.edu.

**ZIMMERMAN, BERNARD,** investment banker; b. Bklyn., Dec. 7, 1932; s. Jacob and Pearl (Schechner) Z.; m. Joyce M. Singer, Dec. 24, 1960; children: Wayne Jay, Ellen Holly. BBA, CCNY, 1954; MBA, NYU, 1957. CPA NY. Fin. exec. consumer products Spartans Industries, Inc., NYC, 1961-65; sr. v.p. Scheinman, Hochstin, and Trotta, Inc., NYC, 1965-72; pres. Bernard Zimmerman and Co., Inc., Weston, Conn., 1972—; pres., CEO FCCC Inc. (formerly First Conn. Capital Corp.), Norwalk, 2003—. Pres. Beacon Hill Mgmt., Inc., Boston, 1994-97; sr. v.p. corp. fin. Gruntal & Co., Inc., N.Y.C., 1983-84; pres., chmn. bd., pres. St. Lawrence Seaway Corp., Indpls., 1985-93, fin. cons.; v.p. The Zimmerman Group, Inc., 1991-96; chmn. bd. dirs., pres. Beacon Hill Mut. Fund, Inc., Boston, 1994-97; Liquidating trustee Unity Buying Svc. Co. Liquidating Trust, Hicksville, NY; bd. dirs. Sbarro, Inc., Melville, NY; fin. cons. Beautiful Visions-U.S.A., Ltd., Bethpage, NY, Task Mgmt. Co., Ridgefield, Conn., 1998-99; pres. and CEO FCCC, Inc., Norwalk, Conn., 2003—; chmn. bd., pres. GVC Venture Corp., N.Y.C., 2004—. Bd. dirs. Inst. Cancer Rsch. and Molecular Medicine, Temple U., Phila., 1995—; trustee Sharro Family Found., Melville, 1993—; mem. Nat. Assn. Corp. Dir. Blue Ribbon Commn. on Corp. Governance-Best Practice Coun., 1997. With AUS, 1955-57. Mem.: NY State Soc. CPAs. Home and Office: 18 High Meadow Rd Weston CT 06883-2946 Office Phone: 203-226-5165.

**ZIMMERMAN, BERNARD,** judge; b. Munich, Bavaria, Fed. Republic Germany, May 31, 1946; came to U.S., 1949; s. Sam and Roza Z.; m. Grace L. Suarez, Oct. 23, 1976; children: Elizabeth, Adam, David, Dara Bylah. AB, U. Rochester, 1967; JD, U. Chgo., 1970. Bar: Calif. 1971, La. 1971, U.S. Supreme Ct. 1975, U.S. Dist. Ct. (no., ea., cen. and so. dists.) Calif., U.S. Dist. Ct. (ea. dist.) La., U.S. Ct. Appeals (9th cir.). Law. clk. chief judge U.S. Dist. Ct. (ea. dist.) La., New Orleans, 1970-71; assoc. prof. law La. State U., Baton Rouge, 1971-72; ptnr. Pillsbury, Madison & Sutro, San Francisco, 1972-95; legal cons. 3d Constnl. Conv. Commonwealth of the No. Mariana Islands, Northern Mariana Islands, 1995; U.S. magistrate judge U.S. Dist. Ct. (no dist.) Calif., 1995—. Dep. pub. defender City of San Francisco, 1975; arbitrator U.S. Dist. Ct., San Francisco, AAA; judge pro tem San Francisco Superior and Mcpl. Cts. Bd. dirs., mem. exec. com. San Francisco Lawyers' Com. on Urban Affairs, 1984-95, treas., 1987; mem. regional bd. Anti-Defamation League, 1989-95. Mem. Phi Beta Kappa. Clubs: Olympic (San Francisco). Office: 450 Golden Gate Ave San Francisco CA 94102-3661 Office Phone: 415-522-4093.

**ZIMMERMAN, BONNIE ELIZABETH,** physical education educator; b. Buffalo, Mar. 5, 1960; d. Samuel John and Carol Ann (Goltz) Z. BS, Canisius Coll, 1982; MS, SUNY, Buffalo, 1990; MS in ednl. leadership, Canisius Coll., 2005. Cert. tchr., N.Y.; cert. sch. dist. administr. Aquatics instr. Kenton YMCA, Kenmore, N.Y., 1977-81; fitness instr. Buffalo Hilton, 1980-82; rehab. specialist/athletic trainer Buffalo Phys. Therapy, Tonawanda, NY, 1987; tchr., athletic trainer Iroquois Schs., Elma, NY, 1981—93; tchr. North Tonawanda City Schs., 1985—2000, dept. coord. K-12, health and phys. edn., 2000—. Trainer Buffalo Geminis Football team, 1979-82; coach Western N.Y. Kidney Found. Transplant Team, 1983-84; instr. ARC, Buffalo, 1977—; lead regional staff N.Y. State Empire State Games. Instr. ARC Nat. Aquatic Sch., 1993, 94. Named Vol. of Yr., Kidney Found., 1984. Mem. AAHPERD, ASCD, N.Y. State Assn. Health Phys. Edn., Recreation and Dance (past pres. western zone), Coun. for Exceptional Children. Episcopalian. Home: 358 Argonne Dr Kenmore NY 14217-2418 Office: North Tonawanda Middle Sch 1500 Vanderbilt Ave North Tonawanda NY 14120-1819 Office Phone: 716-807-3700 3167. Personal E-mail: bez2828@msn.com.

**ZIMMERMAN, CONNIE ANN,** public administrator; AA, Harrisburg Area CC, 1978; BS in Pub. Policy, Pa. State U., 2002. Exec. sec. DER, 1993—95, adminstrv. asst., 1995—99; adminstrv. mgr. PennDOT Bureau of Design, Harrisburg, 1999—. V.p. Women's Legis. Exchange, 2001—; chair legis. com, Ctrl. Pa. Female Execs. 2005—; bd. dirs Ctrl Pa Women Execs. Harrisburg, Pa., 1991—2002, YWCA of Greater Harrisburg, 2002—. Recipient Sarah Wright award, YWCA, 2006. Mem.: NAFE, Am. Soc. Pub. Adminstrn., Nat. Women's History Mus. and Nat. Constl. Ctr. (charter), Hamburg Mannechor, Mitgleider Deutscher Verein, Pi Gamma Mu. Roman Catholic. Avocations: dance, music, gardening. Home: 933 Highland St Steelton PA 17113-1537

**ZIMMERMAN, DAVID CARL,** controller, corporate financial executive; b. Harrisburg, Pa., July 9, 1957; s. Raymond S. and Alice Hoke Z.; m. JoAnn G. Zimmerman. BBA, Ga. State U., 1981; MBA, Montclair State U., 2001. Field auditor Grand Union, Atlanta, 1981-89, sr. field auditor Wayne, NJ, 1989-96, acctg. mgr., 1996-99; CFO, controller Dowel Assocs., Morristown, NJ, 1999—2002; CFO Atkins Companies, West Orange, NJ, 2002—. Mem. AICPA, N.J. Soc. CPAs, Ga. CPAs, Phi Kappa Phi, Alpha Epsilon Lambda, Beta Gamma Sigma. Avocation: golf. Home: 74 Donald Pl Waldwick NJ 07463 Office: 101 Old Short Hills Rd Ste PH1 West Orange NJ 07052 Business E-Mail: davidz@atkinscompanies.com.

**ZIMMERMAN, DIANE LEENHEER,** law educator; b. Newton, N.J., Apr. 16, 1941; d. Adrian and Mildred Eleanor (Booth) Leenheer; m. Earl A. Zimmerman, Sept. 24, 1960 (div. Aug. 1982); m. Cavin P. Leeman, Feb. 18, 1984. BA, Beaver Coll., Glenside (Pa.), 1963; JD, Columbia U., 1976. Bar: N.Y. 1977, US Supreme Ct. 1983. Reporter, Newsweek mag., N.Y.C., 1963-71; spl. features writer N.Y. Daily News, NYC, 1971-73; law clk. to Hon. Jack B. Weinstein US Dist. Ct. Ea. Dist. N.Y., 1976-77; asst. prof. law N.Y.U. Sch. Law, 1977-80, assoc. prof., 1980-82, prof., 1982—; now Samuel Tilden prof. law; mem. faculty Practicing Law Inst., N.Y.C., 1979, 84, 90, 92, 94, 96-02; Disting. Lee Vis. Prof. Constl. Law Coll. William and Mary, 1994; moderator justice and the press program Aspen Inst., 1992, 99; Disting. Vis. Holser Chair Intellectual Property, DePaul Coll. Law., Chgo., 2001; lectr. 17th Ann. Marques Lectr. Intellectual Property, 2004. Recipient citation of merit Columbia U. Sch. Journalism, 1972; Kent scholar and Stone scholar, 1973-76; Mem. ABA (vice chmn. tort liability study com. tort and ins. sect. 1986-87, chair 1st amendment rights com. 1989-94), Am. Law Inst., Assn. of Bar City of N.Y. (chairperson com. civil rights 1981-83), Copyright Soc. USA (trustee 1988-91, 2004—). Office: NYU Sch Law Vanderbilt Hall Rm 332 40 Washington Sq S New York NY 10012-1099 Office Phone: 212-998-6250. Business E-Mail: zimmermd@juris.law.nyu.edu.

**ZIMMERMAN, DONALD PATRICK,** lawyer; b. Albany, N.Y., Mar. 20, 1942; s. Bernard M. and Helen M. (Eshelman) Z. Student, Lawrenceville Sch., 1960, McDonogh Sch.; BA, Rollins Coll., 1964; JD, Dickinson Sch. Law, 1967. Bar: Pa. 1968, U.S. Supreme Ct. 1971. Atty. Legal Aid, 1968-69; pub. defender Lancaster County, Pa., 1969-72; pvt. practice Lancaster, 1974—. Instr. Ct. Common Pleas for Constables, 1976-; solicitor Lancaster County Dep. Sheriff Assn., 1977-, Lancaster County Constable Assn., 1975-; sheriff solicitor Lancaster County Sheriff Office 2004-; instr. sheriff's dept. Lancaster County for Dep. Sheriffs, 1978-85; of counsel to Dep. Sheriff Assn. Pa., 1979-81; spl. counsel Pa. State Constables Assn., 1981; chmn. Bd. Arbitrators Lancaster County, 1975-81; spl. counsel Legislative Com. to Constable Assn. Pa., 1982; bd. dirs Sheriff Solicitors Assn Pa. Author: The Pennsylvania Landlord and Tenant Handbook, 1982, revised edit., 1993; editor (with J. Hatfield and A. Taylor) Pennsylvania Constable Handbook, 1998; contbr. articles to profl. jours. Mem. pastoral coun. St. Anthony's Cath. Ch., 1995-98. Recipient Ofcl. Commendation of Merit, Lancaster County Sheriff's Dept., 1979, Ofcl. Commendation of Merit, F.O.P. State Police Lodge 66, 1985, Disting. Svc. award, 1987, Cert. of Appreciation, Lancaster Crime Commn., 2003, Recognition award City of Lancaster, 2004, Recognition award Borough of Manheim, 2006; named Extraordinary Min., 2002. Mem. ABA, ATLA, Pa. Bar Assn., Acad. Family Mediators, Lancaster County Bar Assn., W. Hensel Brown Inn of Ct., Lancaster County Constables Assn. (Outstanding Leadership award 1988, Disting. Svc. award as solicitor 1998, 25 Yrs. Dedicated Svc. award 2000, Dedicated Svc. award 2004). Office: 214 E King St Lancaster PA 17602-2977 Office Phone: 717-394-6859. Business E-Mail: patrickzimm@dpzlaw.us, patrickzimm@comcast.net.

**ZIMMERMAN, EARL ABRAM,** neurologist, educator; b. Harrisburg, Pa., May 5, 1937; s. Earl Beckley and Hazel Marie (Myers) Z. BS in Chemistry, Franklin and Marshall Coll., 1959; MD, U. Pa., 1963. Diplomate Am. Bd. Psychiatry and Neurology, Am. Bd. Internal Medicine. Intern Presbyn. Hosp., N.Y.C., 1963-64, resident, 1964-65, Neurol. Inst. CPMC, N.Y.C., 1965-68, research fellow endocrinology, 1970-72; asst. prof. to prof. neurology Columbia U., N.Y.C., 1972-85; prof., chmn. dept. neurology Oreg. Health Sci. U., Portland, 1985-2000; chmn. dept. neurology Albany (N.Y.) Med. Coll., 2000—04; clin. dir. neuroscis. Advanced Imaging Rsch. Ctr. dir. Alzheimer's Ctr., Albany Med. Ctr./GE Global Rsch., 2002—. Dir. neurology Helen Hayes Hosp., Haverstraw, N.Y., 1982-83 Mem. editl. bd. Jour. Histochem. Cytochemistry, 1980-85, 87, Neuroendocrinology, 1985-88, Annals of Neurology, 1985-91, Western Jour. Medicine, 1993-98, Jour. Clin. Endocrinal Metabolism, 1995-99; contbr. numerous articles to profl. jours. Maj. USAF, 1968-70 Rsch. grantee NIH, 1977—. Mem. Am. Neurol. Assn. (program chmn. 1980-82), Am. Acad. Neurology (Wartenber lectr. 1985), Endocrine Soc. Democrat. Mem. United Ch. of Christ Avocations: woodworking, gardening, theater, music, art, skiing, tennis. Office: Albany Med Coll Dept Neurology 47 New Scotland Ave MC-65 Albany NY 12208 Office Phone: 518-262-0801. Business E-Mail: zimmere@mail.amc.edu.

**ZIMMERMAN, EDWIN MORTON,** lawyer; b. NYC, June 11, 1924; s. Benjamin and Tobie (Fuchs) Z.; m. Caroline Abbot, July 3, 1956; children: Sarah Abbot, Lyle Benjamin, Miriam Appleton. AB, Columbia U., 1944, LLB, 1949. Bar: N.Y. 1949, D.C. 1969, U.S. Supreme Ct 1969. With Hoover Commn. Reorgn. Exec. Br., 1948; law clk. to Hon. Stanley F. Reed U.S. Supreme Ct., 1950-51; law clk. to Judge Simon H. Rifkind U.S. Dist. Ct., 1949-50; pvt. practice law N.Y.C., 1951-59; prof. law Stanford U., 1959-69; with Justice Dept., 1965-69, asst. atty. gen. charge antitrust div., 1968-69; mem. Covington & Burling, Washington, 1969-94; sr. counsel, 1994—. Mem. coun. Adminstrv. Conf. U.S., 1975—78; mem. mfg. studies bd. Nat. Acad. Sci., 1983—87; adj. prof. George Washington Sch. Law, 1996—2001. Trustee Textile Mus., 1983—, pres. bd. trustees, 1987-96; mem. Folger Poetry Bd., 1990—; mem. adv. bd. Partisan Rev., 1996-2003. 1st lt. AUS, 1944-46. Mem. ABA, Assn. of Bar of City of N.Y., Am. Law Inst., Coun. Fgn. Rels., Phi Beta Kappa. Home: 1820 Kalorama Sq NW Washington DC 20008-4022 Office: Covington & Burling PO Box 7566 1201 Pennsylvania Ave NW Washington DC 20004-2401 Office Phone: 202-662-5190. Business E-Mail: ezimmerman@cov.com.

**ZIMMERMAN, ELYN,** artist; b. Phila., Dec. 16, 1945; d. Louis B. and Sylvia (Snyder) Z.; m. Kirk Varnedoe, Oct. 8, 1983. BA in Painting, UCLA, 1968, MFA in Painting, 1972. Apptd. mem. Commn. Fine Arts, 2003. One-man shows include Univ. Art Mus., Berkeley, Calif., 1974, P.S. 1, Long Island City, N.Y., 1977, Mus. Contemporary Art, Chgo., 1979, Hudson River Mus., Yonkers, N.Y., 1982, Joslyn Art Mus., Omaha, 1984, Wave Hill, Riverside, N.Y., Contemporary Art Mus. U. South Fla., Tampa, 1991, Gagosian Gallery, N.Y.C., 1993, 96, 98, 2001, 03, 04; exhibited in group shows at Whitney Mus. Am. Art, N.Y.C., 1975, Biennale of Sydney, Australia, 1976, Walker Art Ctr., Mpls., 1979, San Diego Mus. Art, 1980, Venice Biennale, USA Pavillion, Italy, 1980, Mus. Contemporary Art Chgo., 1981, Newport Harbor Art Mus., Calif., 1982, Hirshhorn Mus., Washington, 1983, San Francisco Mus. Modern Art, 1984, Socrates Sculpture Park, N.Y.C., 1996, L.A. County Mus. Art, 1996, Addison Gallery, Andover, Mass., 1998, Marlborough Gallery, N.Y.C., 1998, Chesterwood, Stockbridge, Mass., Montclair Mus., N.J., 1999, Ctr. for Photography, Woodstock, N.Y., Witherspoon Gallery Durham, N.C., 2002; sculpture commns. include Nat. Geographic Soc., Washington, O'Hare Internat. Airport Ctr., Rosemont, Ill., Dade County Justice Ctr., Miami, Fla., Moffit Rsch. Ctr./U. South Fla., Tampa, Market Plz., San Francisco, Birmingham Mus. Art, AT&T Hdqrs., N.J., World Trade Ctr. Meml., N.Y.C. Nat. Endowment for Arts grantee, 1976, 80, 83, Creative Artist Pub. Svc. grantee, 1980; NEA and Japan-U.S. Friendship Commn. fellow, 1982. Mem. Creative Time, Inc. (bd. dirs. 1984-90). Home: 140 Greene St New York NY 10012-3241 Office Phone: 212-219-3224. Business E-Mail: elynzimmerman@nyc.rr.com.

**ZIMMERMAN, GIDEON K.,** minister; b. Lehr, ND, Aug. 18, 1920; m. Eleanor Pekrul; children: Paul, Mark (dec.), Thomas. Diploma, N.Am. Baptist Sem., Rochester, NY, 1943; BA, U. ND, 1951; postgrad., Bethany Bibl. Sem., 1958—59, Chgo. Lutheran Sem., 1959—61; BD, N.Am. Bapt. Sem., Sioux Falls, SD, 1960, DD, 1971. Pastor First Bapt. Ch., Auburn, Mich., 1943-47, Grace Bapt. Ch., Grand Forks, N.D., 1947-51, Temple Bapt. Ch., Milw., 1951-55; gen. sec. dept. Christian edn. N. Am. Bapt. Conf., 1955-68, exec. sec., 1968-79, estate planning counselor, 1979-85. Home: 3721 Bardstown Rd Apt 601 Louisville KY 40218-2261 Office Phone: 502-458-2452.

**ZIMMERMAN, HAROLD SAMUEL,** retired state legislator, publishing executive, state agency administrator; b. Valley City, N.D., June 1, 1923; s. Samuel Alwin and Lulu (Wylie) Z.; m. Julianne Williams, Sept. 12, 1946; children: Karen, Steven, Judi Jean (dec.). BA, U. Wash., 1947. News editor Sedro-Woolley (Wash.) Courier-Times, 1947-50; editor, pub. Advocate, Castle Rock, Wash., 1950-57; pub. Post-Record, Camas, Wash., 1957-80; assoc. pub., columnist, dir. Eagle Publs., Camas, 1980-88. Mem. Wash. Ho. of Reps., 1967-80; mem. Wash. Senate, 1981-88, Wash. State Environ. Hearings Bd., Lacey, 1988-93. Mem. Grange, Lions, Kiwanis, Sigma Delta Chi, Sigma Chi. Republican. United Methodist. Personal E-mail: hszim@aol.com.

**ZIMMERMAN, HELENE LORETTA,** retired business educator; b. Rochester, NY, Feb. 26, 1933; d. Henry Charles and Loretta Catherine (Hobert) Z. BS, SUNY, Albany, 1953, MS, 1959; PhD, U. N.D., 1969. Cert. records mgr. Bus. tchr., chmn. bus. dept. Williamson (N.Y.) Cen. Sch., 1953-69; asst. prof. U. Ky., Lexington, 1969-70; assoc. prof. bus. Cen. Mich. U., Mt. Pleasant, 1970-74, prof., 1974-98. Author General Business, 1977; contbg. author to records mgmt. text book, 1987. Sec. Isabella County Christmas Outreach, Mt. Pleasant, 1983-2004. internat. rels. com., 2003— Mem.: AAUW (pres. 1984—86), Mich. Bus. Edn. Assn. (bd. dirs. 1985—90, pres. 1988—89, bd. dirs. 1995—97), Nat. Bus. Edn. Assn., Internat. Soc. Bus. Edn. (internat. v.p. English speaking nations 1986—88, editor Internat. Rev. 1997—2006), Inst.

Cert. Records Mgrs. (sec. 1985—89, exam. devel. com. 1993—2002), Assn. Records Mgmt. and Adminstrn., Gen. Fedn. Women's Clubs (pres. 2004—06, pres. Mt. Pleasant chpt. 2005—06), Delta Kappa Gamma (state pres. 1987—89, internat. fin. com. 1990—94, internat. ad hoc com. on tech. 1996—2000). Avocations: travel, crafts. Business E-Mail: zimme1hl@cmich.edu.

**ZIMMERMAN, HOWARD ELLIOT,** chemist, educator; b. NYC, July 5, 1926; s. Charles and May (Cohen) Zimmerman; m. Jane Kirschenheiter, June 3, 1950 (dec. Jan. 1975); children: Robert, Steven, James; m. Martha L. Bailey Kaufman, Nov. 7, 1975 (div. Oct. 1990); 1 stepchild, Peter B. Kaufman; m. Peggy J. Vick, Oct. 1991; 1 stepchild, Tanya Kaufman. BS, Yale U., 1950, PhD, 1953. NRC fellow Harvard U., 1953-54; faculty Northwestern U., 1954-60, asst. prof., 1955-60; assoc. prof. U. Wis., Madison, 1960-61, prof. chemistry, 1961—; Arthur C. Cope and Hildale prof. chemistry, 1975—. Chmn. 4th Internat. Union Pure and Applied Chemistry Symposium on Photochemistry, 1972; organizer, chmn. Organic Photochemistry Symposium at Pacifchem, Honolulu, 1972, Honolulu, 95, Honolulu, 2000, Honolulu, 05. Author: (book) Quantum Mechanics for Organic Chemists, 1975; mem. editl. bd.: Jour. Organic Chemistry, 1967—71, Molecular Photochemistry, 1969—75, Jour. Am. Chem. Soc., 1982—85, Revs. Reactive Intermediates, 1984—89; contbr. articles to profl. jours. and chpts. to profl. texts. Recipient Halpern award for photochemistry, N.Y. Acad. Scis., 1979, Chem. Pioneer award, Am. Inst. Chemists, 1986, Sr. Alexander vonHumboldt award, 1988, Hilldale award, U. Wis., 1988—89, 1990, Porter medal, IUPAC, 2006. Mem.: NAS, Inter-Am. Photochemistry Assn. (co-chmn. orgnic divsn. 1977—79, exec. com. 1979—86), German Chem. Soc., Chem. Soc. London, Am. Chem. Soc. (James Flack Norris award 1976, Arthur C. Cope Scholar award 1991, XXI IUPAC Porter medal 2006), Phi Beta Kappa, Sigma Xi. Home: 7813 Westchester Dr Middleton WI 53562-3671 Office: U Wis Chemistry Dept 1101 University Ave Madison WI 53706-1322 Business E-Mail: Zimmerman@chem.wisc.edu.

**ZIMMERMAN, JAMES M.,** retail company executive; b. 1944; Chmn. Rich's Dept. Store div. Federated Dept. Stores, 1984-88; pres., COO Federated and Allied Dept. Stores, Cin., 1988-97; CEO Federated Dept. Stores, Cin., 1997—2003, chmn., 1997—. Office: Federated Department Stores Inc 7 W 7th St Cincinnati OH 45202-2424

**ZIMMERMAN, JEAN,** lawyer; b. Berkeley, Calif., Dec. 3, 1947; d. Donald Scheel Zimmerman and Phebe Jean (Reed) Doan; m. Gilson Berryman Gray III, Nov. 25, 1982; children: Charles Donald Buffum and Catherine Elisabeth Phebe (twins); stepchildren: Alison Travis, Laura Rebecca, Gilson Berryman. BSBA, U. Md., 1970; JD, Emory U., 1975. Bar: Ga. 1975, D.C. 1976, N.Y. 1980. Asst. mgr. investments FNMA, Washington, 1970-73; assoc. counsel Fuqua Industries Inc., Atlanta, 1976-79; assoc. Sage Gray Todd & Sims, N.Y.C., 1979-84; from assoc. counsel to sr. v.p., gen. counsel, sec. IBJ Whitehall Bank & Trust Co., N.Y.C., 1984—99; sr. v.p., gen. counsel, sec., bd. dirs. IBJ Schroder Bus. Credit Corp., N.Y.C., 1996-98, Innovest Capital Mgmt., Inc., N.Y.C., 1997-99; sr. v.p., gen. counsel, sec. Innovest Corp., N.Y.C., 1997-99; from gen. counsel, sec. to exec. v.p. ops. and legal ArrowSight, Inc. (formerly ParentWatch.com), Mt. Kisco, NY, 2001—. From asst. sec. to sr. v.p., gen. counsel, sec., bd. dirs IBJ Whitehall Bus. Credit Corp., IBJ Whitehall Capital Corp., IBJ Whitehall Securities, Inc., Delphi Asset Mgmt., Inc., Innovest Asset Mgmt., Inc., N.Y.C., 1997-99; from asst. sec. to v.p., gen. counsel, sec. IBJ Schroder Internat. Bank, Miami, Fla., 1989-98; sr. v.p., gen. counsel, sec. Execution Svcs., N.Y.C., 1991-93. Founder, officer ERA Ga., Atlanta, 1977-79; bd. dirs. Ct. Apptd. Spl. Advs., 1988-94. Named one of Outstanding Atlantans, 1978-79; recipient Disting. Alumni award Emory U. Sch. Law, 1999. Mem.: ABA, LMV, Am. Soc. Corp. Secs., Inc., Ga. Assn. Women Lawyers (bd. dirs. 1977—79), Assn. Bar City N.Y., Assn. Emory Alumni (N.Y. pres. 1999—2003, bd. govs. 2001—05), DAR. E-mail: jzimmer642@aol.com, jean.zimmerman@arrowsight.com.

**ZIMMERMAN, JO ANN,** retired health science association administrator, educator, retired lieutenant governor; b. Van Buren County, Iowa, Dec. 24, 1936; d. Russell and Hazel (Ward) McIntosh; m. A. Tom Zimmerman, Aug. 26, 1956; children: Andrew, Lisa, Don and Ron (twins), Beth. Diploma, Broadlawns Sch. of Nursing, Des Moines, 1958; BA with honors, Drake U., 1973; postgrad., Iowa State U., 1973—75. RN, Iowa. Asst. head nurse maternity dept. Broadlawns Med. Ctr., Des Moines, 1958—59, weekend supr. nursing svcs., 1960—61, supr. maternity dept., 1966—68; instr. maternity nursing Broadlawns Sch. Nursing, 1968—71; health planner, community rels. assoc. Iowa Health Systems Agy., Des Moines, 1978—82; mem. Iowa Ho. Reps., 1982—86; lt. gov., pres. of Senate, State of Iowa, 1987—91; cons. health svcs., grant writing and continuing edn. Zimmerman & Assocs., Des Moines, 1991—2000; dir. patient care svcs. Nursing Svcs. Iowa, 1996—98; nurse case mgr. Olsten Health Svcs. (now Gentiva Health Svcs.), 1998—2004; founder JAZ Tours, 2002—04, ret., 2004, 2004. Ops. dir. Medlink Svcs., Inc., Des Moines, 1992-96. Contbr. articles to profl. jours. Mem. advanced registered nurse practioner task force on cert. nurse midwives Iowa Bd. Nursing, 1980-81, Waukee, Polk County, Iowa Health Edn. Coord. Coun., Iowa Women's Polit. Caucus, Dallas County Women's Polit. Caucus; chmn. Des Moines Area Maternity Nursing Conf. Group. 1969-70, task force on sch. health svcs. Iowa Dept. Health, 1982, task force health edn. Iowa Dept. Pub. Instruction, 1979, adv. com. health edn. assessment tool, 1980-81, Nat. Lt. Govs., chair com. on Agrl. and Rural Devel., 1989; Dallas County Dem. Ctrl. Com., 1972-84, 98—; bd. dirs. Waukee Cmty. Sch. Bd., 1976-79, pres. 1978-79; bd. dirs. Iowa PTA, 1979-83, chair Health Com., 1980-84; mem. steering com. ERA, Iowa, 1991-92; founder Dem. Activist Women's Network (DAWN), 1992; mem. Disciples of Christ Mission Group to El Salvador, 2003, 04; founder health ministry First Christian Ch., Des Moines, Iowa, 2004. Named to Iowa Women's Hall of Fame, 2005; recipient Woman Achievement award, YWCA Greater Des Moines, 2005. Mem. ANA, LWV (health chmn. met. Des Moines chpt.), Iowa Nurses Assn., Iowa League for Nursing (bd. dirs. 1979-83), Family Centered Childbirth Edn. Assn. (childbirth instr., advisor), Iowa Cattleman's Assn., Am. Lung Assn. (bd. dirs. Iowa 1988-92), Dem. Activist Women's Network (founder 1992). Mem. Christian Ch. Avocations: gardening, sewing, reading, bridge.

**ZIMMERMAN, JORDAN,** advertising executive, marketing professional; b. NJ; MBA, U. South Fla. Chmn. CEO Zimmerman & Ptnrs. (Omnicom group since 1999), Ft. Lauderdale, Fla., 1984—; ptnr., pres., alt. gov. Fla. Panthers hockey, 2001—. Achievements include led Just Say No marketing initiative during the Carter administration which is one of the most recognizable anit-drug campaigns to date. Office: 2200 West Commerical Blvd Fort Lauderdale FL 33309

**ZIMMERMAN, JOSEPH FRANCIS,** political scientist, educator; b. Keene, N.H., June 29, 1928; s. John Joseph and May Veronica (Gallagher) Z.; m. Margaret Bernardette Brennan, Aug. 2, 1958; 1 child, Deirdre Ann. BA, U. N.H., 1950; MA, Syracuse U., 1951, PhD, 1954. Instr. govt. Worcester Poly. Inst., 1954—55, asst. prof., 1955-57, assoc. prof., 1957-62, prof., 1962-65; lectr. Clark U., Worcester, Mass., 1957-65; prof. polit. sci. SUNY, Albany, 1965—. Staff dir. N.Y. State Joint Legis. Com. Transp., 1967-68, rsch. dir., 1968-73; rsch. dir. N.Y. State Select Legis. Com. Transp., 1977-82, Legis. Commn. on Critical Transp. Problems, 1982-95. Author: State and Local Government, 1962, The Massachusetts Town Meeting: A Tenacious Institution, 1967, The Federated City: Community Control in Large Cities, 1972, Pragmatic Federalism, The Reassignment of Functional Responsibility, 1976, (with Frank W. Prescott) The Politics of the Veto of Legislation in New York, 1980, The Government and Politics of the Empire State, 1981, Local Discretionary Authority, 1981, (with Deirdre A. Zimmerman) The Politics of Subnational Governance, 1983, State-Local Relations: A Partnership Approach, 1983, 2d edit., 1995 (CHOICE award as outstandin acad. book, 1984), Participatory Democracy: Populism Revived, 1986, Federal Preemption: The Silent Revolution, 1990, Contemporary American Federalism, 1992, (with Wilma Rule) United States Electoral System: Their Impact Upon Women and Minorities, 1992, (with Wilma Rule) Electoral Systems in Comparative Perspective: Their Impact on Women Minorities, 1994, Curbing

Unethical Behavior of Government, 1994, Interstate Relations: The Neglected Dimension of Federalism, 1996, The Recall: Tribunal of the People, 1997, The New England Town Meeting: Democracy in Action, 1999; The Initiative: Citizen Law-Making, 1999, (with Wilma Rule) The U.S. House of Representatives: Reform or Rebuild?, 2000, The Referendum: The People Decide Public Policy, 2001 Interstate Cooperation: Compacts and Administrative Agreements, 2002, Interstate Economic Relations, 2004, Congressional Preemption: Regulatory Federalism, 2005, Interstate Disputes: The U.S. Supreme Court's Original Jurisdiction, 2006; contbr. articles to profl. publs. Pres. Citizens' Plan E Assn., Worcester, 1960-62, Citizens for Neighborhood Improvement Worcester, 1957-59. Served to capt. USAF, 1951—53. Named 1 of 3 Outstanding Young Men Worcester Jr. C. of C., 1959, 61, 1 of 3 Outstanding Young Men Mass, Jr. C. of C., 1961, disting. citizen award Nat. Conf. on Govt., 1986. Mem. Am. Polit. Sci. Assn. (Outstanding Academician sect. intergovtl. adminstrn 1997), Am. Soc. Pub. Adminstrn. (Outstanding Federalism Academician 1997), Nat. Mcpl. League. Clubs: German-Am. Social. Roman Catholic. Home: 82 Greenock Rd Delmar NY 12054-4414 Office: SUNY Rockefeller College 135 Western Ave Albany NY 12222 Office Phone: 518-439-9440, 518-442-5378. E-mail: zimmer@albany.edu.

**ZIMMERMAN, LAWRENCE A.,** printing company executive; b. NY, Dec. 2, 1942; BS in Fin., NYU, 1965; MBA, Adelphi U., 1967. From dir. budgets to corp. contr. IBM Corp., 1988—94, v.p. fin. Europe, Middle East and Africa ops. Paris, 1994—96, v.p. fin. and planning server and tech. divsn., 1996—98; exec. v.p., CFO Sys. Software Assoc., Inc., Chgo., 1999; corp. sr. v.p., CFO Xerox Corp., Stamford, Conn., 2002—. Bd. dirs. Brunswick Corp., 2005—. Office: Xerox Corp 800 Long Ridge Rd Stamford CT 06904*

**ZIMMERMAN, LORETTA ELLEN,** history professor; b. Metairie, La., Sept. 14, 1935; d. Harry Peter and Hilda Katie (Brondum) Z.; m. Howard J. Kuhnle, II. BA, Newcomb Coll., 1957; MA, Tulane U., 1961, PhD, 1964. Asst. prof. William Woods Coll., Fulton, Mo., 1964-65; vis. prof. Augustana Coll., Sioux Falls, S.D., 1965-66; asst. prof. U. Tex., Arlington, 1966-67; asst. prof. history U. Portland, Oreg., 1967—2000. prof. emeritus, 2000—. Author (with C.J. Baydo and John Born) History of U.S. With Topics, vol. I and II, 1994. Mem. Phi Beta Kappa, Kappa Delta Pi, Alpha Lambda Delta, Phi Alpha Theta. Roman Catholic. Home: PO Box 431 Washougal WA 98671-0431

**ZIMMERMAN, MARLIN U., JR.,** chemical engineer; b. Akron, Ohio, Aug. 2, 1923; s. Marlin Ulrich and Helen (Nelson) Z. BChemE, Johns Hopkins U., 1944; MBA, Harvard U., 1966. Registered profl. engr., Ohio. Jr. engr. Standard Oil Co. (Ohio), Cleve., 1944-46, engr., 1946-48, sr. engr., 1948-49, process engr. Lima (Ohio) refinery, 1949-50, group engr. Cleve., 1951-55, group supr., 1956-60, supr. process sys. sect., 1961-63, head acrylonitrile task force, 1961, tech. specialist, 1964-66; mgr. long term planning Norton Co., Worcester, Mass., 1966-69; cons. John Van Der Valk & Assocs., N.Y.C., 1970-73; pvt. practice cons. chem. engr. ammonia-urea Hackensack, NJ, 1974—. Head task force to help commercialize Sohio acrylonitrile process. Contbr. articles to profl. jours. Baker scholar, 1966. Mem. AIChE, Johns Hopkins Club, Tudor and Stuart Club, Tau Beta Pi, Omicron Delta Kappa, Beta Theta Pi. Methodist. Achievements include patent for process improvement of Tosco shale process for oil recovery; patent for pig handling for gasoline blender meter testing loop, others. Avocations: travel, photography, reading, investing, computer programming.

**ZIMMERMAN, MARTIN B.,** automotive executive; b. New York City, June 19, 1946; B (hon.), Dartsmouth Coll.; D in Econ., Mass. Inst. of Tech. Faculty mem. Sloan Sch. of Mgmt., Mass. Inst. of Tech.; prof. bus. econ. dept. Univ. Mich. Grad. Sch. Bus. Admin., 1983—85, prof. and chmn. bus. econ. dept., 1985; co. chief economist Ford Motor Co., Dearborn, Mich., 1987—94, exec. dir. govtl. rels. and corp. econ., 1994—99, v.p. govtl. affairs, 1999—2001, group v.p., corp. affairs, 2001—. Sr. economist President's Coun. of Econ. Advisors, Washington, 1985—86; adv. coun. Nat. Aeronautic and Space Admin., 1988—92. Serves on bd. of the Citizens Rsch Coun. of Mich., Cmty. Found. of S.E. Mich. and Detroit Met. Visitors and Conv. Bur. Recipient Blue Chip Econ. Forecasting Award. Mem.: Citizens Rsch. Coun. of Mich., Bus. for Soc. Responsibility (bd. dir.), The Panel of Econ. Advisors to the Congl. Budget Office, Com. for Econ. Devel. (bd. of trustees), Nat. Assn. Bus. Economists, Phi Beta Kappa. Office: Ford Motor Co One American Rd Dearborn MI 48123-1899

**ZIMMERMAN, MARY ALICE,** performing arts educator; BA, MA, PhD, Northwestern U. Asst. prof. performance studies Northwestern U., Evanston, Ill.; artistic assoc. Goodman and Seattle Repertory Theater; mem. Lookingglass Theater Company, Chicago. Dir.: (plays) The Notebooks of Leonardo da Vinci, The Odyssey, Arabian Nights, Journey to the West, Metamorphoses (Tony award for best director, 2002), Secret in the Wings, Eleven Rooms of Proust, Measure for Measure, Henry VIII, A Midsummer Night's Dream, All's Well That Ends Well. Active Lookingglass Theatre Co. Recipient MacArthur Fellowship, 1998, 20 Joseph Jefferson Awards for best direction. Fellow: Am. Acad. Arts & Sci. Office: Dept Performance Studies Northwestern U 1920 Campus D Evanston IL 60208

**ZIMMERMAN, MICHAEL DAVID,** lawyer; b. Chgo., Oct. 21, 1943; s. Elizabeth Porter; m. Lynne Mariani (dec. 1994); children: Evangeline Albright, Alessandra Mariani, Morgan Elisabeth; m. Diane Hamilton, 1998. BS, U. Utah, 1966, JD, 1969, LLD (hon.), 2001. Bar: Calif. 1971, Utah 1978. Law clk. to Chief Justice Warren Earl Burger U.S. Supreme Ct., Washington, 1969-70; assoc. O'Melveny & Myers, L.A., 1970-76; assoc. prof. law U. Utah, 1976-78, adj. prof. law, 1978-84, 89-93; of counsel Kruse, Landa, Zimmerman & Maycock, Salt Lake City, 1978-80; spl. counsel Gov. of Utah, Salt Lake City, 1978-80; ptnr. Watkiss & Campbell, Salt Lake City, 1980-84; assoc. justice Supreme Ct. Utah, Salt Lake City, 1984-93, 98-00, chief justice, 1994-98; atty., mediator, arbitrator, ptnr. Snell & Wilmer, Salt Lake City, 2000—. Co-moderator Justice Svc. Program of Snowbird Inst. for Arts and Humanities, 1991, 92, 93, 94, 95, 97, 98; moderator, Tanner lecture panel dept. philosophy U. Utah, 1994; faculty Judging Svc. Program Duke U., 1992, 93; bd. dirs. Conf. of Chief Justices, 1995-98. Note editor: Utah Law Rev., 1968-69; contbr. numerous articles to legal publs. Mem. Project 2000, Coalition for Utah's Future, 1985—96; trustee Hubert and Eliza B. Michael Found., 1994—98; bd. dirs. Rowland-Hall St. Mark's Sch., 1995—2002; bd. assoc. Utah Mus. Natural History Found., 1997—; bd. dirs. Summit Inst. for Arts and Humanities, 1989—2002, chair, 2002—; bd. dirs. Hansen Planetarium, 1997—2001, Snowbird Inst. for Arts and Humanities, 1998—98, Deer Valley Inst. for Arts and Humanities, 1996—98, Kanzeon Zen Ctr., 1999—, chair, 2000—; bd. dirs. Utah Coun. on Conflict Resolution, 1999—2005, chair, 1999—2005; bd. dirs. Adjudication Ct.; mem. Duke U., 2000—02; co-dir. Registry of Ind. Sci. and Tech. Advisors, Duke U., 2000—02; chair Utah Jud. Coun. Task Force on Racial and Ethnic Fairness in the Jud. Sys., 1996—2000. Named Utah State Bar Appellate Ct. Judge of Yr., 1998; recipient Excellence in Ethics Award, Ctr. for Study of Ethics, 1994, Disting. Svc. Award Utah State Bar, 1998, Individual Achievement Award Downtown Alliance, 1997, The Peter W. Billings, Sr. American Arbitration Assoc. Outstanding Dispute Resolution Svc. Award, 1997, Humanitarian award, Nat. Conf. for Cmty. and Justice, 2005. Fellow: Am. Bar Found.; mem.: Am. Acad. Appellate Lawyers, Gov. Radiation Exposure Study Mgmt. Com., Ririe-Woodbury Dance Co. (exec. bd. 1982—84), U.S. Dept. of Energy Dose Assessment Adv. Group of the Off-Site Radiation Exposure Reconstruction Project (Utah citizen rep. 1980—84), Utah Legal Svc. Corp. (Bd. of Trustees 1985—87, 2002—), U. Utah Master of Pub. Adminstrn. Program Practitioners' Adv. Com. (mem 1985—89), U.S. Vet. Adminstrn. Adv. Com. on Environ. Hazards (e.g., agent orange, nuclear radiation 1985—89), Nat. Endowment for the Humanities Scholar in Residence at Utah Valley Cmty. Coll. (Orem, Utah 1990), Order of Coif, Am. Judicature Soc. (bd. dirs. 1995—2001), Am. Inns of Ct. VII, Utah Jud. Coun. (supreme ct. rep. 1986—91, chair 1994—98), Jud. Conf. U.S. (adv. com. civil rules 1985—91), Salt Lake County Bar Assn., Utah Bar Assn., Am. Law Inst., ABA (faculty mem. appellate judges' seminar 1993), Phi Kappa Phi. Office: Snell & Wilmer 15 West South Temple Ste 1200 Salt Lake City UT 84101 Office Phone: 801-257-1964. E-mail: mzimmerman@swlaw.com.

**ZIMMERMAN, MYRON,** information technology executive; BS in physics & math., MIT, PhD in atomic physics. Founder, chief tech. officer, pres. VenturCom, Cambridge, Mass.; co-founder, CEO Storage Matrix; chief tech. officer Certeon, Inc., Waltham, 2004—. Founder Bos/TEN. Recipient Albert M. Sargent Progress Award, Soc. Mfg. Engrs., 2002.

**ZIMMERMAN, NANCY PICCIANO,** library and information scientist, educator; b. Jeannette, Pa., July 29, 1951; d. Daniel Joseph and Helen Elizabeth (Lipinski) Picciano; m. Lee W. Zimmerman, Aug. 10, 1974; children: Matthew, Renée. BA in English, Carlow Coll., Pitts., 1973; MLS in Libr. Sci., U. Pitts., 1974; MS in Computer Edn. and Cognitive Sys., U. North Tex., 1992; PhD in Libr. and Info. Studies, Tex. Woman's U., 1992. Lic. libr. media specialist, K-12, lang. arts/English 7-12. Libr. media specialist Fairfield (Calif.)-Suisun Sch. Dist., 1976-78; reference libr. Pikes Peak Libr. Dist., Colorado Springs, Colo., 1983; libr. media specialist North Pole (Alaska) H.S., 1984-85, Prince William County Schs., Woodbridge, Va., 1985-89; dir. info. retrieval lab. Tex. Woman's U., Denton, 1989-91; adj. prof., rsch. assoc. U. North Tex., Denton, 1991-92; from asst. to assoc. prof. Sch. Info. and Libr. Studies SUNY, Buffalo, 1993-99; assoc. prof. Sch. Libr. and Info. Scis. U. S.C., Columbia, 1999—. ALISE/OCLC rsch. grantee, 1994, 2004. Mem. ALA (coun. 2000—, chair Libr. Rsch. Round Table 1995-96, com. profl. ethics, 2006-), Am. Assn. Sch. Librs. (treas. 1996-99, pres. 2002-2003, exec. bd. 1996-99, 2001-04), Internat. Assn. Sch. Librs., N.Y. Libr. Assn. (pres. 1999), Nat. Bd. for Profl. Tchg. Stds. (sch. libr. media com. 1997-2000), Phi Delta Kappa, Beta Phi Mu (nat. exec. coun. 1994-99). Office: U SC Sch Libr and Info Scis 217 Davis Coll Columbia SC 29208-0001 Office Phone: 803-777-1215. Business E-Mail: nzimmerman@gwm.sc.edu.

**ZIMMERMAN, PAUL ALBERT,** retired academic administrator, minister; b. Danville, Ill., June 25, 1918; s. Albert Carl and Hanna Marie (Haffner) Z.; m. Genevieve Emmaline Bahls, June 11, 1944; children— Karmin (Mrs. Raymond Philp), Thomas. Student, Concordia Coll., Ft. Wayne, Ind., 1936-39; BA, Concordia Sem., St. Louis, 1941, M.Div., 1944; MA, U. Ill., 1947, PhD, 1951; D.D., Concordia Sem., Springfield, Ill., 1975; LLD (hon.), Concordia Coll., Ann Arbor, Mich., 1994. Prof. theology and sci. Bethany Coll., Mankato, Minn., 1944-53; prof. Concordia Tchrs. Coll., Seward, Nebr., 1953-54, pres., 1954-61, Concordia Luth. Jr. Coll., Ann Arbor, Mich., 1961-73, Concordia Coll., River Forest, Ill., 1973-83, ret., 1983; pastor St. Luke's Luth. Ch., Harrison, Mich., 1983-88. Author and editor: Darwin, Evolution and Creation, 1959, Rock Strata and the Bible Record, 1971, Creation, Evolution and God's Word, 1972. Chmn. Washtenaw County Red Cross, 1968-70; pres. Ann Arbor Found., 1970-71; mem. Citizens Com. Study Taxation, Ann Arbor, 1972; mem. adv. bd. St. Joseph Mercy Community, 1969-72; chmn. Luth. Ch. Mo. Synod's Bd. for Mission Services, 1982-92, Mission Task Force, 1990-91, adminstrv. asst. pres. Mo. Synod, 1972-73, 93-94, mem. curriculum comm. bd. higher edn., 1963-73, mem. task force constl. revision Mo. Synod, chmn. com. adjudication procedures Mo. Synod, Mo. Synod com. on structure, 1995-98. Fellow Creation Rsch. Assn. Lutheran. Home: 2798 Princeton Dr Traverse City MI 49684-9131

**ZIMMERMAN, PHYLLIS ELAINE,** music educator, composer, director; b. Pitts., Feb. 22, 1934; d. William H. and Isabelle Anderson Zimmerman. BA in Sociology, Thiel Coll., 1956; BA in Vocal Performance, Concordia Coll., 1959; student in Voice, U. Colo., 1966; student in Choral Techniques and Voice, Meadowbrook Sch. Music, 1967; student in Music, Choral Conducting, Choral Technique & Voice, Occidental Coll., 1968—69. Dir. choral Wellsville (Ohio) H.S., 1959—63, Churchill Area H.S., Pitts., 1963—68; thr. music, dir. choral Santa Barbara (Calif.) H.S., 1969—95; founder, artistic dir. Canticle A Cappella Choir, Santa Barbara, 1995—. Dir. madrigal singers Santa Barbara H.S. Choir, 1969—95, dir. concert tours, 1972—92. Dir.(prodr.): (compact disc) Earth Chants, 1994, Canticle, 1996, My Song in the Night, 2000, O Wondrous Mystery, 2003, Phoenix (27 original compositions and arrangements), 2004, Every Time I Feel the Spirit, 2006; composer: (songs) Seasons of his Mercies, 2003, Four Songs of Concord, 2005, Four Lyrics of Sara Teasdale, 2006. Named Local Hero, Santa Barbara (Calif.) Ind. 1995; recipient Outstanding Contbn. to Cmty. award, Santa Barbara (Calif.) City Coun., 2004, Disting. Alumni award, Concordia Coll., 2006. Mem.: Am. Choral Dirs. Assn. (performer).

**ZIMMERMAN, ROBERT ALLEN See DYLAN, BOB**

**ZIMMERMAN, ROGER JOSEPH,** fishery biologist; b. Alice, Tex., Dec. 2, 1941; s. Walter George and Laura Virgie (Heine) Z.; m. Domenica Marie DeCaro, Dec. 28, 1976; children: Kathryn, Robert. BS in Biology, Tex. A&I Coll., 1966, MA in Biology and Geology, 1969; PhD in Marine Scis., U.P.R., Mayaguez, 1979. Tchg. asst. biology dept. U. South Fla., Tampa, 1971, rsch. assoc. marine sci. dept. St. Petersburg, 1971-73; rsch. assoc. P.R. Nuclear Ctr. U. P.R., 1974-75, grad. fellow, 1975-78, marine benthic ecologist Ctr. for Energy & Environ. Rsch., 1978-81; fishery ecologist fishery mgmt. divsn. NOAA/NMFS Galveston (Tex.) Lab., 1981-91, divsn. chief fishery ecology divsn., 1991-93, lab. dir., 1993—. Rsch. fellow U.S. Nat. Mus. Natural History, Smithsonian Instn., Washington and Harbor Beach, Fla., summer 1975, 76; vis. instr. marine biology dept. Tex. A&M U., Galveston, summer 1988, 89; vis. instr. biology dept. Corpus Christi (Tex.) State U., 1986; tchg. asst. biology U. South Fla., 1970; lectr.-counselor Tex. A&I U., 1969, lab. coord., tchg. asst., 1968-69; OAS and U.S. AID advisor to Instuto de Pesca de Ecuador, 1985-88; mem. com. coastal ocean estuarine habitat rsch. planning com. NOAA 1987, sci. adv. com., 1989; chair predator-prey com. S.E. Fisheries Sci. Ctr., 1990-91; coord. climate and global change ecol. sys. and dynamics work group NMFS, 1990, spl. asst. to office of sr. scientist, 1990; mem. sci. adv. com. Galveston Bay project Nat. Estuary Program, 1993-96, mgmt. com. Coastal Bend project, 1994-98; bd. dirs. Gulf of Mex. regional marine rsch. program NMFS-SEFSC, 1992-93; rep. programs on coastal fisheries and estuarine ecology SERSC, 1992-95; grad. student advisor, adj. wildlife and fisheries dept. and biology dept. Tex. A&M U., dept. biology Corpus Christi State U., dept. marine scis. La. State U., 1985-89, dept. biology U. Houston, 1983-85; presenter workshops in field. Reviewer for jours. in field, including Fishery Bull., Contbns. to Marine Sci., Marine Ecology Progress Series, Jour. Exptl. Marine Biology and Ecology, Marine Biology, Bull. Marine Sci., Jour. Wetlands Ecology and Mgmt., Estuaries, Coastal and Shelf Sci., also various proposals; editl. reviewer SEFSC Galveston Lab., 1984—; contbr. numerous articles to profl. publs.; author abstracts, revs. in field. Mem. Estuarine Rsch. Fedn., Gulf Estuarine Rsch. Soc., Crustacean Soc., Am. Fisheries Soc., Assn. Marine Labs. of the Caribbean. Office: Nat Marine Fisheries Svc SE Fisheries Sci Ctr 4700 Avenue U Galveston TX 77551-6901

**ZIMMERMAN, S(AMUEL) MORTON (MORT ZIMMERMAN),** engineering executive; b. Paterson, N.J., Mar. 18, 1927; s. Solomon Zimmerman and Miriam (Feder) Glatzer; m. Marion Patricia Boque, Sept. 15, 1951 (dec. 1993); children: Judy, Suzy, Sharon, Dan; m. Rosalie Fitzgerald, June 1, 1998. Student, Ga. Inst. Tech., 1942-44, 46-48, Oglethorpe U., 1948-51; BSEE, Pacific Internat. U., L.A., 1958. Pres. Comml. Electronics Corp., Dallas, 1954-56, Electron Corp. subs. LTV Corp., 1956-65; chmn. bd., pres. Capital Bancshares, Inc., 1965-66; chmn. bd. Capital Nat. Bank Tampa (formerly Springs Nat. Bank), Fla., 1965, Capital Nat. Bank Miami (name now Peoples Downtown Bank), Fla., 1966, Merc. Nat. Bank Miami Beach (name now Barnett Bank), Fla., 1967, Underwriters Bank & Trust Co. N.Y. (name now Banco Cen.), 1968; chmn. bd., pres. Capital Gen. Corp., 1967, Comml. Tech., Inc., 1977—, Petro Imperial Corp. and subs. DOL Resources and Tech.-Star, Dallas, 1983—; founder, chmn. bd. Atmospheric & Magnetic Tech., Inc. (now Atmospheric Water Tech., Inc.), 1997—. Chmn. bd.; pres. Trans Exchange Corp., 1965—, Electric & Gas Tech., Inc., 1985—; also chmn. 8 subs. cos.; chmn. bd. Video Sci. Tech., Inc., 1981-92, Interfed. Capital, Inc., 1990—, Dynamic Funding Inc., 2000—, Logic Metals Tech., Inc., 2002—. Patentee: TV camera video amplifier and blanking circuits, electronic thermometer, video x-ray image system and methods, video system and method for presentation and reproduction x-ray film images, electromagnetic radio frequency lighting system, laser display of electronically generated image signal; additional patents pending; U.S. copyrights on electronic atmosphere

dew point generator of pure refrigeration drinking water, 2001, hydrogen peroxide electrical power generator, 2001. Petty oficer USN, 1942-45. Recipient Interfaith award City of N.Y. Mem. IEEE, Brookhaven Country Club. Republican. Jewish. Home: 1211 Stonewall Trl Rockwall TX 75032-8959 Office: Electric Gas Technology Inc 3233 W Kingsley Rd Garland TX 75041-2205 Fax: 972 991-3265. Office Phone: 972-934-8797. E-mail: mortzim@webtv.net.

**ZIMMERMAN, SOL SHEA,** pediatrician; b. N.Y.C., June 25, 1948; s. Isaac and Estera (Berkowicz) Z.; m. Diana F. Zimmerman, Aug. 8, 1971; children: Jeffrey, Steven, Andrew. AB, Columbia U., 1968; MD, NYU, 1972. Diplomate Am. Bd. Pediats.; pediat. critical care medicine. Intern dept. pediats. NYU-Bellevue Hosp. Ctr., N.Y.C., 1972-73, resident dept. pediats., 1973-75, chief resident dept. pediats., 1977-78, asst. prof. clin. pediats., 1978-83, assoc. prof. clin. pediats., 1983—, dir. pediat. critical care medicine, 1998-98, assoc. dir. dept. pediats., 1985—; assoc. chair dept. pediats. NYU Sch. of Medicine, N.Y.C., 1997—, assoc. prof. pediat., 2002—. Pres. Pediat. Assocs. N.Y.C., P.C., 1997—; v.p. Univ. Physicians Network, 1996—; chmn. bd. mgrs. Univ. MSO, 1998—; assoc. prof. pediat. NYU-Bellevue Hosp. Ctr., 2002. Editor, author: (textbook) Critical Care Pediatrics, 1985. Chmn. com. on heart, health in the young N.Y.C. affiliate Am. Heart Assn., 1987-93. Maj. USAF MC, 1975-77. Fellow Am. Acad. Pediats., Am. Coll. Chest Physicians, Critical Care Medicine; mem. N.Y. Soc. Pediat. Critical Care Medicine (v.p. 1989-91, pres. 1991-93), Alpha Omega Alpha. Office: Pediat Assocs NYC PC 317 E 34th St New York NY 10016-4974 also: 20 Plaza St E Brooklyn NY 11238-4955

**ZIMMERMAN, STEVEN CHARLES,** chemistry professor; b. Chgo., Oct. 8, 1957; s. Howard Elliot and Jane (Kirschenheiter) Z.; m. Sharon Shavitt, Aug. 5, 1990; 2 children, Arielle Reneé, Elena Michelle. BS, U. Wis., 1979; MA, MPhil, Columbia U., PhD, 1983. Asst. prof. chemistry U. Ill., Urbana, 1985-91, assoc. prof. chemistry, 1991-94, prof. chemistry, 1994—, Roger Adams prof. chem., interim chem. dept. head; affiliate faculty mem. Beckman Inst. Mem. bioorganic natural products study sect. NIH, 1994—98. Contbr. articles to profl. publs. Presdl. Young Investigator award, NSF, 1988-93; Alfred P. Sloan fellow, 1992-93; recipient Buck-Whitney award, Am. Chem. Soc., 1995, Arthur C. Cope Scholar award, 1997. Home: 55 Chestnut Ct Champaign IL 61822-7121 Office: U Ill 345 Roger Adams Lab 600 S Mathews Ave Urbana IL 61801 E-mail: sczimmer@uiuc.edu.*

**ZIMMERMAN, WILLIAM EDWIN,** editor, writer; b. Bklyn., Feb. 2, 1941; s. George and Ruth (Edelbaum) Z.; m. Teodorina Bello, Dec. 13, 1969; 1 child, Carlota Pastora. BA, Queens Coll., 1962. Pres. Guarionex Press, Ltd., N.Y.C., 1979—; with Am. Banker, N.Y.C., 1962-82, editor, sr. v.p., 1982-89; editor in chief Banking Week, 1986-89; dep. editor Sunday Bus. sect. The N.Y. Times, 1989; spl. projects editor, editor Student Briefing Page Newsday, L.I., NY, 1989—. Author: How to Tape Instant Oral Biographies, 1979, A Book of Questions to Keep Thoughts and Feelings, 1984, Make Beliefs, 1987, Life Lines: A Book of Hope, 1990, The Little Book of Joy, 1995, Dogmas: Simple Truths from a Wise Pet, 1995, Make Beliefs for Kids of All Ages, 1996, A Book of Sunshine, 1997, Cat-e-chisms: Feline Answers to Life's Big Questions, 1997, My Life: An Open Book, 2000, Lunch Box Letters, 2000, Idea Catcher for Kids, 2000, Butterfly Wishes, 2002, My Paper Memory Quilt, 2004, 100 Things Guys Need to Know, 2005. Mem. Am. Oral History Assn., Am. Soc. Bus. Writers, Am. Soc. Bus. Press Editors, N.Y. Fin. Writers Assn., Overseas Press Club, Deadline Club, Dowtown Athletic Club, N.Y. Athletic Club, Sigma Delta Chi. Democrat. Jewish. Office: Newsday Inc 2 Park Ave New York NY 10016-5679 Office Phone: 212-724-5259. Personal E-mail: wmz@aol.com.

**ZIMMERMANN, FRANK MARTIN,** physicist, educator, research scientist; b. Karlsruhe, Germany, May 6, 1964; arrived in US, 1987, naturalized, 2004; s. Manfred Eugen and Herta Zimmermann; m. Yeong-Ah Soh, Oct. 29, 1995 (div. Sept. 2, 2003); 1 child, Ingrid Hana; m. Sophia Tsai, July 2, 2006. MS in Physics, Cornell U., 1993, PhD in Physics, 1995. Rsch. asst. solid state physics Ariz. State U., 1988-89; rsch. asst. surface sci. Cornell U., 1990-95; asst. prof. physics dept. physics and astronomy and lab. surface modification Rutgers U., Piscataway, NJ, 1995-2001, assoc. prof., 2001—. Lectr., presenter in field. Contbr. numerous articles to profl. jours. including Surface Sci. Reports and Phys. Rev. Lett. Fulbright fellow, 1987-88, Internat. Rsch. fellow Sci. and Tech. Agy., Japan, 1996, 98; Rutgers bd. trustees rsch. fellow for scholarly excellence, 2001. Mem. Am. Phys. Soc., Am. Vacuum Soc. (Grad. Rsch. award 1994, Morton M. Traum award 1995), Am. Chem. Soc. (Victor K. LaMer award 1996), Phi Kappa Phi. Achievements include elucidation of mechanisms and dynamics of thermal and photochemical desorption and adsorption using laser spectroscopy. Avocations: whitewater kayaking, downhill skiing, bicycling. Office: Rutgers U Dept Physics 136 Frelinghuysen Rd Piscataway NJ 08854-8019

**ZIMMERMANN, JEREMY GRAY,** lawyer; b. New Haven, Conn., June 21, 1941; s. Armand Lafay and Eleanor Live (Goldman) Z.; m. Darlene Linn, June 28, 1969; children: Kent Malcolm, Tad Uten. AB, Brown U., 1963; LLB, Georgetown U., 1966. Bar: Conn. 1966, U.S. Dist. Ct. Conn. 1970, U.S. Ct. Appeals (1st and 2nd cirs. 1970), U.S. Supreme Ct. 1970. Law clerk Hon. Luther Youngdahl-U.S. Dist. Ct., Washington, 1966-67; spl. atty. criminal div. U.S. Dept. Justice, Washington, 1967-70; assoc. Wiggin & Dana, New Haven, Conn., 1970-74, ptnr., 1974—. Bd. dirs. Alcohol Coun. Greater New Haven, 1971-74, John Magee House, New Haven, 1973-74; v.p. The Children's Ctr., Hamden, Conn., 1973-74; mem., treas. Dem. Town Com., Guilford, Conn., 1975-80; vol. New Haven Bd. Edn., 1977-93. Recipient Product Liability Litigation Def. award Skandia Ins. Co., Stockholm, Sweden, 1991, Spl. Master cert. of appreciation U.S. Dist. Ct., 1990-92. Mem. ABA, Conn. Bar Assn. (ho. of dels. 1984-86), Product Liability Adv. Coun., Conn. Def. Lawyers Assn., Conn. Trial Lawyers Assn., New Haven County Bar Assn. Democrat. Jewish. Avocations: tennis, juggling, reading. Office: Wiggin & Dana PO Box 1832 New Haven CT 06508-1832 Business E-Mail: jzimmermann@wiggin.com.

**ZIMMERMANN, JOERG,** biophysicist; b. Berlin, July 1, 1971; PhD, Humboldt U., 1990—96. Postdoctoral fellow UC Berkeley, Dept. of Chemistry, Berkeley, Calif., 2001—03; rsch. assoc. The Scripps Rsch. Inst., La Jolla, Calif., 2003—. Recipient Humboldt award, 2001. Mem.: Am. Chem. Soc., The Biophys. Soc., European Soc. for Photobiology. Office: Scripps Rsch Inst CVN-22 10550 N Torrey Pines Rd La Jolla CA 92037

**ZIMMERMANN, LAURA,** psychology professor, researcher; PhD in Psychology, U. N.Mex, Albuquerque, 1997. Vis. asst. prof. Hobart and William Smith Coll., Geneva, NY, 1997—98; chair, assoc. prof. psychology Shenandoah U., Winchester, Va., 1998—. Contbr. articles to profl. jours. Grantee, Shenandoah U., 2000—06, Va. Found. for Ind. Colleges, 2001. Mem.: Soc. for Rsch. in Child Devel. Office: Shenandoah Univ 1460 University Dr Winchester VA 22601 Office Phone: 540-678-4339. Business E-Mail: lzimmerm@su.edu.

**ZIMMERMANN, ROBERT LAURENCE,** marketing professional; b. Mpls., Jan. 1, 1932; s. Lawrence and Bertha Mabel (Foss) Z. BA, U. Minn., 1954, MA, 1965, PhD, 1970. Asst. prof. psychology U. Winnepeg, Man., Can., 1968-69; research assoc. psychiatry research unit U. Minn., Mpls., 1969-75; sr. scientist biometrics lab. George Washington U., Washington, 1975-76; pvt. cons. research design and data analysis Mpls., 1976-84; sr. research mgr. Maritz Market Rsch., Mpls., 1984—. Clin. asst. prof. psychiatry dept. U. Minn., Mpls., 1976-90; external rev. officer FDA, Washington, 1974-77. Contbr. numerous articles to profl. jours. Fellow NIMH, 1958, 61, 69-71; merit fellow State of Minn. Mem. AAAS, Com. on Space Rsch., Nat. Space Soc., Nat. Space Found., The Planetary Soc., ACLU, Amnesty Internat., Ctr. for Pub. Integrity, Oxfam. Democrat. Avocation: writing. Home: 1920 S 1st St Apt 1104 Minneapolis MN 55454-1048 Office: Maritz Market Rsch Inc 7701 France Ave S Minneapolis MN 55435-5288 Personal E-mail: zimmermannbobl@mn.rr.com.

**ZIMMERMANN, THOMAS CALLANDER PRICE,** retired historian, educator; b. Bryn Mawr, Pa., Aug. 22, 1934; s. R.Z. and Susan (Goodman) Z.; m. Margaret Upham Ferris. BA, Williams Coll., 1956, Oxford U., 1958, MA, 1964; AM, Harvard U., 1960, PhD, 1964. Asst. prof. Reed Coll., Portland, Oreg., 1964-67, assoc. prof., 1967-73, prof. history, 1973-77, chmn. dept. history, 1973-75; v.p. acad. affairs Davidson (N.C.) Coll., 1977-86, Charles A. Dana prof. History, 1986-99, Charles A. Dana prof. history emeritus, 1999-2000, ret., 2000. Mem. Oreg. Com. for Humanities NEH, 1971—77; mem. Region 14 selection com. Woodrow Wilson Nat. Fellowship Found., Princeton, NJ, 1967—70. Author: Paolo Giovio: The Historian and the Crisis of Sixteenth-Century Italy, 1995 (Helen and Howard R. Marraro Book prize Am. Hist. Assoc. 1996, Presdl. Book award Am. Assn. for Italian Studies 1997); co-editor of collected works of Paolo Giovio, 1985; contbr. articles to profl. jours. Pres. Am. Alpine Club, N.Y.C., 1979-82, bd. dirs., 1975-83; bd. dirs. Charlotte Opera Assn., N.C., 1980-82, N.C. Outward Bound Sch., Morgantown, 1978-81; bd. advisors Lowell Obs., 1988-93; mem. Rome Prize Jury (Post-Classical Humanistic Studies) Am. Acad. in Rome, 1993. Danforth fellow, 1956-62, Fulbright fellow, Italy, 1962-64, Villa "I Tatti" fellow Harvard U. Ctr., 1970-71; Am. Council of Learned Socs. fellow, N.Y.C., 1975-76. Mem. Renaissance Soc. Am., Sixteenth Century Studies Conf., Soc. Italian Hist. Studies, Am. Assn. Italian Studies, Phi Beta Kappa.

**ZIMMERN-REED, ANNETTE WACKS,** psychologist; b. Exeter, Va., Feb. 7, 1933; d. Samuel Cleve and Zella Edith (Nelson) Wacks; m. James Robert Reed; children: Kenneth Zimmern, Ronald Zimmern stepchildren: Susan, Kathleen. RN, Sinai Hosp. Sch. Nursing, 1954; BA, U. Md., 1969, MA, 1971, PhD, 1975. RN Md.; lic. Family-Marriage Therapist Tex. Capt., dir. substance abuse, dir. mental health divsn. USPHS, Rockville, Md., 1976—96. Asst. prof. dept. psychiatry divsn. psychology U. Tex., Dallas, 1985. Author: Violence in America, 1986. Fellow: Am. Assn. Marriage and Family Therapists; mem.: Am. Counselors Assn. Avocations: swimming, reading, writing. Address: PO Box 5116 Johnson City TN 37602-5116

**ZIMMERS, VIVIAN ELEANOR,** small business owner, consultant; b. St. Louis, Oct. 19, 1946; d. John Dominic and Aurea Genevieve (Schottel) Baron; m. John Paul Hargis, Aug. 21, 1964 (div. Mar. 1968); m. Filomeno Mariano Ramos, June 30, 1973 (dec.); children: William S. Ramos, Kiersten E. Ramos, Leilani A. Ramos; m. Ronald Franklin Zimmers, Sept. 27, 1997 (dec.). Student, St. Louis U., 1968-69, U. Hawaii, 1986-87; BA in Mgmt., Nat. Louis U., 1991. Co-founder, owner, pres. Batts Ramos and Assocs., Inc., St. Louis, 1991—. Cons. Hawaii Govtl. Affairs Com., Honolulu, 1975—76; mem. govtl. affairs com. St. Louis Assn. Realtors, 1996—97. Bd. dirs. Mo. Orthopedically Disabled, 1993—, pres., 1997—; active Assoc. Pres.'s Youth Opportunity Program, St. Louis, 1968; vol. literacy coun., rschr. Vols. in Probation and Parole. Mem.: Mililani Mchts. Assn. (pres. 1985), St. Louis Real Estate Bd., Nat. Assn. Realtors (mem. com. pub. rels. 1987), Rotary. Democrat. Roman Catholic.

**ZIMMETT, MARK PAUL,** lawyer, educator; b. Waukegan, Ill., July 4, 1950; s. Nelson H. Zimmett and Roslyn (Yastrow) Zimmett Grodzin; m. Joan Robin Urken, June 11, 1972; children: Nora Helene, Lili Eleanor. BA, Johns Hopkins U., 1972; JD, NYU, 1975. Bar: N.Y. 1976, U.S. Dist. Ct. (so. and ea. dists.) N.Y. 1976, U.S. Dist. Ct. (no. dist.) Calif. 1980, U.S. Ct. Appeals (2d cir.) 1980, U.S. Supreme Ct. 1981, U.S. Ct. Appeals (5th cir.) 1986, U.S. Ct. Appeals (9th cir.) 1988. Assoc. Shearman & Sterling, N.Y.C., 1975-83, ptnr., 1984-90; adj. assoc. prof. internat. law NYU, 1986-88; lectr. internat. comml. litig. and arbitration Practicing Law Inst., 2000—02. Author: Letters of Credit, New York Practice Guide Business and Commerical Law, 1990; contbr. articles to profl. jours. Mem. ABA (subcom. on letters of credit, com. on uniform comml. code sect. bus. law), N.Y. State Bar Assn., Assn. of the Bar of the City of NY (task force on corp. governance, com. on fed. cts., coun. on profl. and jud. ethics), NY County Lawyers Assn. (com. on bus. bankruptcy law, task force corp. governance, com. fed. cts., com. profl. and jud. ethics), Citizens Union. Democrat. Jewish. Office: 126 E 56th St New York NY 10022-3613 Office Phone: 212-755-0808.

**ZIMMIE, THOMAS FRANK,** civil engineer, educator; b. Scranton, Pa., Jan. 24, 1939; s. Thomas and Stella Josephine (Price) Z.; m. Patricia Joyce Kelly, June 8, 1962 (div. 1979); 1 child, David Thomas; m. Judith Anne Braden, July 13, 1989. BSCE, Worcester Poly. Inst., 1960; MSCE, U. Conn., 1962, PhD in Geotech. Engring., 1972. Registered profl. engr., N.Y., Conn. Staff engr. Union Carbide Corp. (Linde div.), Buffalo, 1964-68; profl. engr. Town of Mansfield, Conn., 1968-72; ptnr. Wang and Zimmie Cons., Troy, NY, 1973-80; v.p. Arch Engring. Cons., Troy, 1984-88; program dir. NSF, Washington, 1988-90; pres., CEO Civrotech Engrs., Inc., Troy, 1993—; prof., chair dept. civil engring Rensselaer Poly. Inst., Troy, 1973—, acting chair dept. civil and environ. engring., 2005—. Postdoctoral researcher Norwegian Geotech. Inst., Oslo, 1972-73; geotech. engr. N.Y. Dept. Environ. Conservation, Albany, 1983-85; town engr. Town of North Greenbush, N.Y., 1985-88. Editor: Permeability and Groundwater Contamination, 1981. 1st lt. U.S. Army, 1962—64. Fellow Am. Coll. of Forensic Examiner, fellow ASCE (cert., Outstanding Svc. award 1986, 87); mem. ASTM (Spl. Svc. award 1980, Charles Dudley award 1984), Transp. Rsch. Bd., Am. Rd. and Transp. Builders Assn. Achievements include research in environmental protection. Home: 39 Zelenke Dr Wynantskill NY 12198-8627 Office: Rensselaer Poly Inst Civil & Environ Engring Dept Soil Mechanics Lab Troy NY 12180 Office Phone: 518-276-6939. Business E-Mail: zimmit@rpi.edu.

**ZIMNY, MAX,** labor union administrator, lawyer, arbitrator; b. Bklyn., Mar. 9, 1925; s. Joseph and Rebecca (Nadelman) Z.; m. Bernice Nelson, June 25, 1948; children: Stuart, Andrew. Student, Bklyn. Coll., 1942—47, LLB cum laude, 1950; postgrad., NYU Grad. Sch. Labor Law, 1950—52. Bar: N.Y. 1950, U.S. Dist. Ct. (so. and ea. dists.) N.Y. 1951, U.S. Ct. Appeals (2nd cir.) 1955, U.S. Supreme Ct. 1958, U.S. Ct. Appeals (D.C. cir.) 1968, U.S. Ct. Appeals (4th cir.) 1969, U.S. Ct. Appeals (9th cir.) 1975, U.S. Ct. Appeals (8th cir.) 1980, U.S. Dist. Ct. (no. dist.) N.Y. 1983, U.S. Ct. Appeals (6th cir.) 1987, U.S. Ct. Appeals (7th cir.) 1988, U.S. Ct. Appeals (3rd and 5th cirs.) 1991. Mem. Zimny & Goldberg, N.Y.C., 1950—52; asst. gen. counsel Textiles Workers Union Am., N.Y.C., 1952—58, Internat. Ladies' Garment Workers' Union, N.Y.C., 1958—63, assoc. gen. counsel, 1963—72, gen. counsel, 1972—95, Union of Needletrades, Indsl. and Textile Employees, 1995—2001. Mem. Vladeck, Elias, Vladeck, Zimny and Englehart, N.Y.C., 1976-78; lectr. NYU Sch. Law, Stetson U. Sch. Law, Indsl. Rels. Rsch. Inst., Nat. Acad. Arbitrators. Editor: Labor Arbitrator Development, 1983, Arbitration: A Guide for Advocates, 1990, Arbitration Casebook, 1997. Mediator, fact finder N.Y. Pub. Employment Rels. Bd., 1968—; chmn. Consumer Adv. Coun. City of N.Y.; mem. Levittown (N.Y.) Bd. Edn.; chmn. Profls. for Histadrut, N.Y.C.; arbitrator NYS disciplinary panel; bd. dirs. Nat. Resources Ctr. for Consumers Legal Svcs., Lawyers Coord. Com. AFL-CIO; bd. dirs. Corsi Labor Mgmt. Inst.; mediator, arbitrator Am. Arbitration Assn.; labor, employment and comml. panels, arbitrator labor and mgmt. panel Fed. Mediation and Concilation Svc.; arbitrator N.Y.C. Office of Collective Bargaining, Electric Boat, Groton, Conn.; mem. nat. adv. coun., chair com. on rules and procedures, chair nat. task force on ADR in employment and due process protocol; mem. steering com. ctr. for Law and Econ. Policy Columbia U. Sch. Law; adv. com. NYU and Fordham Conf. on Labor, 1985—. With U.S. Army, 1943—46. Fellow: Coll. Labor and Employment Lawyers (chair, com. on ethics and civility); mem.: ABA (chmn. com. on arbitration 1977—81, coun. labor sect. 1989—, chair labor and employment sect., pub. rels. com.), Nassau Bar Assn., Commn. Healthcare Dispute Resolution, N.Y. State Bar Assn., Bar Assn. City of N.Y. (labor com.), B'nai B'rith Club (pres. lodge), Order of Coif. Office Phone: 516-731-4358. E-mail: maxzimny@optonline.net.

**ZIMPHER, NANCY LUSK,** academic administrator; b. Gallipolis, Ohio, Oct. 29, 1946; d. Aven Denzle and Elsie Gordon (Hammond) L.; 1 child from a previous marriage, William Fletcher Zimpher; m. Kenneth R. Howey, May 8, 1987. BS, Ohio State U., 1968, MA, 1971, PhD, 1976. Cert. K-12 Tchr., Ohio. English tchr. Montgomery County Schs., Md., 1968, Reynoldsburg (Ohio) Schs., 1970; substitute tchr. Rolla (Mo.) City Schs., 1970-71; tchr.

Phelps County Schs., Mo., 1971-72; grad. teaching assoc. Coll. Edn. Ohio State U., Columbus, 1972-73; dir. Coll. of Edn. Ohio State U., Columbus, 1973-74, grad. adminstrn. asst. to dean, 1974-76, dir. field experiences alumni rels., 1976-80, coord. undergraduate programs, 1980-84; asst. prof. Ednl. Policy and Leadership Ohio State U., 1984-86, assoc. prof., 1986-91, full prof., 1991-98, assoc. dean, 1992, dean, 1993, exec. dean, 1994; chancellor, prof. curriculum and instrn. U. Wis., Milw., 1998—2003; pres. U. Cincinnati, 2003—. Prin. investigator U.S. Office Edn. Field Devel. Grant, 1981-83, 85-88; co-principal investigator Metro. Life Found. Grant. 1989—, 1992—; cons. The Holmes Group, Lansing, Mich., 1991—. Book rev. editor: Journal of Teacher Education, 1986-89; co-author: Book Profiles of Preservice Teacher Education, 1989, RATE Profiles, 1987-92. Chair Faculty Compensation and Benefits Commn., 1989-90, Fiscal Com., 1991-92, Spousal Equivalency Com., 1990-91, Search Com., v.p. for Fin., 1992, Ohio State U; pres., chair bd. dirs Holmes Partnership, 1997; chair edn. vision coun. United Way Franklin County, 1997; chair bd. dirs. United Way Franklin County, 1998. Fellow Com. for Instnl. Coop., Acad. Leadership Program. 1989-90; recipient Disting. Rsch. award, Disting. Teacher Educator award Assn. Tchr. Educators, 1990, Adams Professorshi Coll. Edn. Ind. State U., 1990—, Alumni Disting. Tchg. award, The Ohio State U., 1992, Chief Exec. Leadership award Coun. for the Advancement and Support Edn., 2003, Career Woman of Achievement award YWCA, 2004, Profl. Achievement award Ohio State U., 2004; named YWCA Woman of Achievement, 1997. Mem. Am. Edn. Rsch. Assn., Am. Assn. Coll. Teacher Edn. Rsch. Comm., Assn. Tchr. Educators, ASCD, Phi Delta Kappa. Episcopalian. Avocations: watercolorist, golf, sewing. Office: Univ Cin 625 Univ Pavilion PO Box 210063 Cincinnati OH 45221-0063

**ZIMRING, FRANKLIN E.,** lawyer, educator; b. 1942; BA, Wayne State U., 1963; JD, U. Chgo., 1967. Bar: Calif. 1968. Asst. prof. U. Chgo., 1967-69, assoc. prof., 1969-72, prof., 1972-85; co-dir. Ctr. for Studies in Criminal Justice, 1973-75, dir., 1975-86; prof. law dir. Earl Warren Legal Inst., Univ. Calif., Berkeley, 1985—2002. Author: (with Newton) Firearms and Violence in American Life, 1969; The Changing Legal World of Adolescence, 1982; (with Hawkins): Deterrence, 1973, Capital Punishment and the American Agenda, 1986, The Scale of Imprisonment, 1991, The Search for Rational Drug Control, 1992, Crime is Not the Problem, 1997, American Youth Violence, 1998, Punishment and Democracy, 2001, The Contradictions of American Capital Punishment, 2003, An American Travesty, 2004, American Juvenile Justice, 2005. Mem. Am. Acad. Arts and Scis. Office: U Calif Earl Warren Legal Inst Boalt Hall Berkeley CA 94720 Business E-mail: zimring@law.berkeley.edu.

**ZINBARG, RICHARD EVAN,** psychologist, educator; b. N.Y.C., Dec. 18, 1960; s. Eugene David and Doris (Austrian) Z.; m. Gina Ott, Dec. 14, 1964. BA, U. Pa., Phila., 1982; PhD, Northwestern U., Evanston, Ill., 1989. Instr. Northwestern U., Evanston, 1985-88; rsch. scientist Johnson O'Connor Rsch. Found., Chgo., 1986-87; clin. psychology intern Ea. Pa. Psychiat. Inst., Phila., 1988-89; project dir. Phobia and Anxiety Disorders Clin., albany, N.Y., 1989-92; adj. asst. prof. U. Albany, SUNY, 1989-92; asst. prof. dept. psychology U. Oreg., Eugene, 1992—; dir. Oreg. Program Anxiety Study and Treatment, Eugene, 1993—. Dir. Oreg. Program for Anxiety Study and Treatment, Eugene, 1993—; co-dir. Oreg. Ctr. for Anxiety and Depression, Eugene, 1994—. Cons. editor Jour. Abnormal Psychology, 1994—; contbr. articles to profl. jours. Bd. dirs. Hillel, U. Oreg., Eugene, 1944—; mem. Citizens United Against Discrimination, Eugene, 1992—. Univ. fellow Northwestern U., Evanston, 1983-84, psychology dept. fellow, 1984-87, Nat. Rsch. Svc. award NIMH, Bethesda, Md., 1987-88. Mem. APA, Internat. Soc. for Study of Individual Differences, Assn. for Advancement of Behavior Therapy. Achievements include identification of descriptive criteria for a possible new psychiatric disorder-mixed anxiety depression; formulation of an animal model of post-traumatic stress disorder; empirical demonstration of relation between trait anxiety and sensitivity to punishment. Office: U Oreg Dept Psychology Eugene OR 97403-1227

**ZINBERG, DOROTHY SHORE,** sociologist, educator; b. Boston; m. Norman E Zinberg (dec.); children: Sarah Zinberg Mandel, Anne. BA, MA, Boston U.; PhD, Harvard U., 1966. Research chemist Lever Bros., Cambridge; sr. research assoc. Daniel Yankelovich, Inc., N.Y.C., and; Cambridge Center for Research in Behavioral Scis., 1966-68; NSF research sociologist dept. chemistry U. Coll. London, 1968-69; lectr. Harvard U., 1960—. Mem. adv. com. Office Sci. Pers. NRC, Washington, 1971—74, bd. on engring. edn., 1991; spl. adviser Aspen Inst.; cons. MacArthur Found., 1989—93; vis. scholar NAS, China, 1987, Nat. Inst. Sci. and Tech., Tokyo, 1991; vis. lectr. Inst. for Human Scis., Vienna, 1995; mem. adv. bd. Erik Erikson Inst. for Edn. and Rsch., 1996—; vis. prof. Imperial Coll., London, 2001—04; assoc. Whitehead Inst. Biomed. Rsch., MIT, 2004—; vis. sr. fellow U. Coll. London, 2006—. Columnist: London Times Higher Educ Supplement, 1993—2001, NY Times Syndication, 1994—96. Mem. internat. sci. exchs. NAS, 1994—96, mem comt int relations, 1977—80, mem comt int human resources; chmn adv coun int div NSF, 1978—81; mem coun Int Exchange Scholars, 1978—81; mem comt int exchange engrs NAE, 1987—88; mem adv panel Office Technology Assessment Educ and Employment Scientists and Engrs, 1986—88; trustee Simon's Rock Col, 1971—75; mem panel sci and tech policy NATO, 1995—99; bd. dirs. Fine Arts Workshop, Provincetown, Mass., 1997-98, Bill T. Jones Found for Dance Promotion, 1997—99; bd dirs Gen Scanning, Inc, 1998—99; bd dirs eng educ NRC, 1990—95. Fellow: AAAS (mem comt sci freedom and responsibility 1972—74, comt opportunities in sci 1973—76, comt sci, eng, and pub policy 1982—88, com. exch. scientists with Fed. Republic Germany 1987—91, 1991); mem. NAS (com. to evaluate Internat. Sci. and Tech. Ctr. Moscow 1995—97), Int Sci Policy Found (adv. bd. 1988—2004), Coun Foreign Relations, Fedn. Am. Scientists (mem. coun. 1980—85, bd. talking sci.). Home: 3 Acacia St Cambridge MA 02138-4818 Office: Harvard U 79 JF Kennedy St Cambridge MA 02138 E-mail: dorothy_zinberg@harvard.edu.

**ZINCZENKO, DAVID,** publishing executive; s. Bohdan Zinczenko and Janice Sobieski. B, Moravian Coll. Assoc. editor Men's Journal, 1991—93; editl. dir. Men's Health Internat.; editor-in-chief Men's Health Mag., 2000—; Guest expert in field. Author: The Abs Diet, 2004 (named N.Y. Times Best Seller, 2004). Nominee Nat. Mag. award, ASME, 2005; named Folio's 1999 Thirty Under 30, one of People Mag. 50 Most Eligible Bachelors, 2002; named one of Ten Best-Dressed in Media, Ad Age, 2005; recipient 6 gold medals in Folio Mag. CDMA competition, Nat. Mag. award, ASME, 2000. Office: Men's Health 733 Third Ave New York NY 10017 also: Men's Health Roadale 33 E Minor St Emmaus PA 18098*

**ZINDER, NEWTON DONALD,** investment advisor, consultant; b. N.Y.C., Aug. 12, 1927; s. Paul and Jennie (Feld) Z.; m. Clarice Katz, Dec. 26, 1954; children:— Marla, Andrea, Pamela. BA, NYU, 1948, MBA, 1957; MA, Columbia U., 1949. Securities analyst Ira Haupt & Co., N.Y.C., 1953-60; securities analyst E.F. Hutton & Co., N.Y.C., 1960-63, stock market analyst, 1963-88, Shearson Lehman Bros., N.Y.C., 1966. Securities analyst investment cons., 1993—. Served with USN, 1945-46 Mem. Market Technicians Assn. Home: 1734 Roland Ave Wantagh NY 11793-2856 E-mail: newtwiz@webtv.net.

**ZINGALE, DONALD PAUL,** academic administrator, educator; b. Bklyn., Aug. 3, 1946; s. Charles and Helen (Puglisi) Z. BS in Health, Phys. Edn., Bklyn. Coll., 1967; MS in Phys. Edn., U. Mass., 1969; PhD in Phys. Edn., Ohio State U., 1973; MSW, Calif. State U., Sacramento, 1984. Lic. clin. social worker, Calif.; lic. marriage and family counselor, Calif.; cert. health and phys. edn. instr. secondary schs., N.Y.C., N.Y.; cert. Alpine ski instr. Prof., assoc. dean health, human svcs. Calif. State U., Sacramento, 1973-93, assoc. v.p. rsch. and grad. studies, 1993-95, dean L.A., 1995—96; dean Coll. Health and Human Svcs. San Francisco State U., 1996—2004; v.p. academic affairs The Calif. Maritime Acad., 2004—. Contbr. articles to profl. jours. and publs. Mem.: APHA, Nat. Coun. U. Rsch. Adminstrs., Am. Assn. Higher Edn., Am.

Assn. Health Phys. Edn., Recreation and Dance, Profl. Ski Instrs. Am. Roman Catholic. Avocations: alpine skiing, sailing, travel, cooking, home renovation. Office: Calif Maritime Acad 200 Maritime Academy Dr Vallejo CA 94590-8181

**ZINGER, MICHAEL,** reproductive endocrinologist; BA, Brandeis U., Waltham, Mass., 1991; MD, Albert Einstein Coll. of Medicine, N.Y.C., 1995. Diplomate Am. Bd. of Obstetrics and Gynecology. Resident dept. obstetics gynecology North Shore U. Hosp., NYU Coll. of Medicine, Manhasset, 1995—99, chief resident dept. obstetics gynecology, 1998—99; clin. instr. in reproductive endocrinology and infertiilTy U. Cin. Coll. of Medicine, 1999—2002, fellow in reproductive endocrinology and inferlty, 1999—2002; dir. in vitro fertilization Charles E. Miller and Assos.: Specialists in Reproductive Health, Naperville, Ill., 2002—. Profl. adv. bd. RESOLVE, Chgo., 2003—. Spkr. at ann. symposium RESOLVE, Chgo., 2003. Recipient Merck Sr. Fellow's award, The Endocrine Soc., 2002. Fellow: Am. Coll. of Obstetrics and Gynecology; mem.: Am. Soc. of Reproductive Medicine, Soc. for Reproductive Endocrinology. Achievements include research in reproductive endocrinology. Office: Charles E Miller MD and Assocs 120 Osler Dr #100 Naperville IL 60540 Office Phone: 630-428-2229. Office Fax: 630-428-0336. E-mail: mzinger@usa.net.

**ZINGG, PAUL JOSEPH,** academic administrator; b. Newark, July 22, 1947; s. Carl William Zingg and Dolores Lucking Dulebohn. BA in History, Belmont Abbey Coll., Belmont, N.C., 1968; MA in History, U. Richmond, Va., 1969; PhD in History, U. Ga., 1974. Chair and asst. prof., dept. of history and polit. sci. St. Bernard's Coll., Cullman, Ala., 1975-77; dean, academic affairs Daniel Hale Williams U., Chgo., 1977-78; adj asst./assoc. prof., dept. of Am. civilization U. Pa., Phila., 1978—86, asst. dean, academic affairs, Coll. of Arts and Sciences, 1978—79, vice dean, undergraduate studies and admissions, Coll. of Arts and Sciences, 1979—83, Am. Coun. on Edn. Fellow in Academic Adminstrn. and spl. asst. to the pres., 1983—84, exec. asst. to pres., 1984—86; cons. U. Calif., Berkeley, 1986; dean liberal arts and prof., dept. of history Calif. Poly. State U., San Luis Obispo, Calif., 1993—2003, dean liberal arts, 1993-95, provost and acad. v.p. 1995—2003; pres. Calif. State U., Chico, 2004—. Vis. instr. history Ga. Coll., Milledgeville, 1971; cons., contbr. on exhibits Oakland Mus., 1992-94, Calif. Hist. Soc., 2004, PBS-TV documentary film Baseball, 1991-93; editorial cons. U. Nebr. Press, 1994—, U. Ill. Press, 1995-, others. Author: Pride of the Palestra, 1987, Harry Hooper, 1887-1974: An American Baseball Life, 1993, Runs, Hits and Era: The Pacific Coast League, 1903-1958, 1994, 2nd edit., 1996, A Good Round: A Journey Through the Landscapes and Memory of Golf, 1999, The Moraine Country Club 1930-2005, 2005; co-author: Through Foreign Eyes, 1982; editor, co-author: The Academic Penn, 1986; editor, contbr.: The Sporting Image: Readings in American Sport History; editor: In Search of the American National Character, 1984; contbr. numerous articles to profl. jours. Mem. Calif. Hist. Soc., 2000—; charter mem., Calif. Coun., Oakland Mus., 1995—. NEH summer fellow, 1975, summer rsch. grant, 1989, Ctr. for Internat. Study and Rsch. fellow, 1980-82, Am. Coun. on Edn. fellow, 1983-84; U. Pa. Rsch. Found. awards, 1983-85, faculty mem. of the yr., 1984, grantee St. Mary's Coll., 1987, 90, 91, 93, alumni faculty scholarship award, 1992. Mem. Orgn. Am. Historians, Soc. for History Edn., N.Am. Soc. for Study of Sport, Am. Studies Assn., Soc. for Am. Baseball Rsch., Am. Coun. on Edn., Assn. Am. Colls. and Univs., Am. Assn. Higher Edn., Nat. Assn. State Univs. and Land-Grant Colls., Rotary Club, Merion Golf Club, U. Calif. Golf Club, Butte Creek Country Club, Canyon Oaks Country Club, Phi Alpha Theta, Phi Beta Delta. Avocations: golf, labrador retrievers, baseball, hiking. Office: Calif State U 400 W First St Chico CA 95928-0155 Office Phone: 530-898-5201. E-mail: pzingg@csuchico.edu.

**ZINK, JOAN WILSON,** writer, poet, composer; b. Tulsa, Dec. 17, 1928; d. Paul Almus and Gladys Emily Wilson; m. David Daniel Zink, Feb. 5, 1948; children: Laurie Zink Menard, David Paul; m. Lawrence Eugene Dalen, June 24, 1990. BA, U. Colo., 1958. Contbg. author The Ancient Stone's Speak, 1979, The Stones of Atlantis, 1978; author: (book of poetry) The Road Less Travelled, 1980; co-author (with David Zink): (book) You Are the Mystery, 1976, You Are the Mystery, new edit., 2001; contbr. articles to profl. jours., poetry to profl. pubs. Mem.: Nat. League Am. Pen Women (hon.), SPUR. Home: 4060 NW 110th Ave Ocala FL 34482-1828

**ZINK, JOHN H., III,** lawyer; b. Balt., Feb. 14, 1945; BA, Washington & Lee U., 1967, JD, 1970. Bar: Md. 1970, US Dist. Ct. (md.), US Ct. Appeals (DC, 4th cir.), US Supreme Ct. Ptnr., Comml. Litigation practice Venable LLP, Towson, Md. Atty. Grievance Commn. Rev. Bd., 1982; mem. Gov's Jud. Nominating Commn., 1982-90. Fellow Md. Bar Found.; mem. ABA, Md. State Bar Assn. (chair ins. trust com.), Md. Def. Counsel, Def. Rsch. Inst., Baltimore County Bar Assn., Phi Delta Phi. Office: Venable LLP PO Box 5517 210 Allegheny Ave Towson MD 21204 Office Phone: 410-494-6251. Office Fax: 410-821-0147. Business E-Mail: jhzink@venable.com.

**ZINK, LEE BERKEY,** retired academic administrator, economist, educator; b. Salem, Ind., June 7, 1930; s. Otto C. and Lera (Berkey) Z.; m. Patricia Louise Patton, Aug. 16, 1964; children: Kevin Patrick, Barry Lee. BA in Econs. magna cum laude, Ind. U., 1959; PhD in Econs., Okla. State U., 1967. Field rep. GM Acceptance Corp., Louisville, Ky., 1953-54; asst. mgr. Dougherty Motor Sales, Salem, 1954-56; asst. prof. econs. Southeastern State Coll., Durant, Okla., 1964-67, spl. asst. to dir. Tech. Use Studies Ctr., 1964-65, dir., 1965-68, assoc. prof. of Econs., 1967-68; dir., prin. rsch. economist, bur. bus. and econ. rsch. U. N.Mex., Albuquerque, 1968-77; prof. bus. adminstrn. N.Mex. Highlands U., Kirtland, 1974-81; dir. Inst. Applied Rsch. Svcs. U. N.Mex., Albuquerque, 1975-2000, dir. Nat. Energy Info. Ctr. affiliate/U.S. Dept. Energy, 1978-87, assoc. v.p. rsch., bus. and govt. rels., 1988-2000; mem. Gov's adv. com. statis. standards for Okla., 1964-66, sci. and industry Okla., 1965-66, statewide planning com. implemenation of Tech. Svcs. Act, Okla., 1965-66; cons. majority leader U.S. Ho. Reps., 1964-68, So. Okla. Devel. Assn., 1965-68, Gov. Okla., 1967-68, Kiamichi Econ. Devel. Dist., 1967-68, N.Mex. Corp. Commn., 1969-74, N.Mex. State Planning Office, 1971, Ohio State U. Evaluation Ctr., 1972, others; mem. Gov.'s adv. com. N.Mex. Dept. Devel., 1971; adv. panel spl. tech. assistance program Office Econ. Opportunity, 1972-74; mem. Albuquerque adv. coun. U.S. Small Bus. Adminstrn., 1974-81, chmn. 1977-79; chmn. Gov.'s Coun. Econ. Advisors, 1975-78; sec. econ. devel. Gov.'s Cabinet, 1975-76, policy advisor, 1976-78; econ. devel. task force We. Interstate Commn. Higher Edn., 1979. Mem. edit. review bd. Review of Regional Economics and Business, 1976-85; bd. edit. contbrs. The Albuquerque Tribune, 1979-82; mem. edit. adv. bd. The Southwest Review of Management and Economics, 1981-85; contbr. articles to profl. jours. Organizing pres. Kiamichi Econ. Devel. Dist., Okla., 1966-67; active Monte Vista Christian Ch., 1968—; adv. bd. dir. N.Mex. Coun. Econ. Edn., 1969-75, chmn. operating com., 1976-86; pres. East Holiday Park Neighborhood Assn., 1978-94; adv. coun. city growth and devel. Greater Albuquerque Leadership Devel. Program, 1980-82; adv. bd. U.S. Armed Svcs., 1980-87; adv. bd. econ. devel. City of Albuquerque, 1980-84; community advisor NCAA Vols. for Youth, 1981-85; mem. Bernalillo county Human Svcs. Coalition, 1982-85; apptd. by Gov.-elect Anaya N.Mex. Jobs Task Force, 1982-83; apptd. chmn. by mayor Better Albuquerque Bond Coms., 1983-87, 93-95; trustee U. Albuquerque, 1983-86; bd. dirs. Nat. Tng. Inst. Cmty. Econ. Devel., 1979-82, Inst. Study Cmty. Econ. Devel. 1980-82, Albuquerque Conv. and Vis. Bur., 1984-87, Consumer Credit Counseling Svc. N.Mex., 1985-94, pres. 1989-90, Better Bus. Bur. N.Mex., 1992—; pres. adv. coun. UNICEF, Albuquerque, 1985-95; mem. employment and tng. needs task force City of Albuquerque, 1987-88; evaluation team Congressman Lujan's South Valley task force, 1987; apptd. chmn. by Mayor Saavedra and city coun. pub. forum com. recycling, 1991. 2d lt. U.S. Army, 1951-53, Germany; lt. col. USAR, 1951-77. Fellow Nat. Defense Edn. Act, 1959-62; grantee Nat. Aeronautics and Space Administrn., 1964-68, N.Mex. Dept. Devel., 1968-80, HEW, 1968-76, 1971-72, Bank N. Mex., 1969-77, The Albuquerque Model Cities Agy., 1969-70, Four Corners Regional Commn., 1969-80, U.S. Forest Svc., 1974-77, U.S. Dept. Commerce, 1975-79, 1976-2000, N.Mex. Energy Resources Bd., 1976-77, The

Navajo Nation, 1976-78, U.S. Army Corps. Engrs., 1976-78, U.S. Dept. Energy, 1978-87. Mem. Am. Assembly Collegiate Schs. Bus. (rsch., statis., publs. com. 1976-77, small bus. adminstrn. liasion com. 1976-78), Am. Soc. Info. Sci. (frontier chpt. exec. com. 1972-73, chmn.-elect 1972, chmn. 1973), Assn. Univ. Bus. and Econ. Rsch. (exec. com. 1971-78, v.p. 1975-76, pres. 1976-77), Mid continent Rsch. and Devel. Coun. (bd. dirs. 1965-69), Fedn. Rocky Mountain States (chmn. bus. rsch. com. 1969-75), Rocky Mountain Coun. Bus. Bus. and Econ. Rsch. (chmn. 1969-77), N.Mex. Coun. Econ. Edn. (bd. dirs. 1969-90), Am. Guild Organists (dean Albuquerque chpt. 1996-98), Greater Albuquerque C. of C. (edn. com. 1968-73, bd. dirs. 1970-76, 78-82, chmn. growth com. 1972, v.p. 1973-74, pres. 1981), U. N.Mex. Retiree Assn. (pres. 2003-05), Phi Kappa Phi, Phi Beta Kappa (alpha chpt. exec. com., sec. 1973-75), Golden Key (hon.). Democrat. Avocation: pipe organs. Home: 3741 Mount Rainier Dr NE Albuquerque NM 87111-4399 Personal E-mail: drLBZ@aol.com. Business E-Mail: leezink@unm.edu.

**ZINKE, MICHAEL DUANE,** finance and accountancy manager; b. Mendota, Ill., Oct. 13, 1954; s. Elmer H. and Barbara A. (Williams) Z.; m. Cathy L. Myers, July 22, 1978; children: Duane M., Brian M. AA cum laude, Ill. Valley C.C., 1974; BS, No. Ill. U., 1976; MBA, Ctrl. State U., 1988. Comptr. Office World, Oklahoma City, 1977—79; credit analyst C.I.T. Corp., Oklahoma City, 1979—80, sr. credit analyst, 1980—81, dist. credit mgr., 1982—84; credit mgr. Macklanburg-Duncan Co., Oklahoma City, 1984—87, mgr. credit, payroll, accounts payable, gen. acctg., 1987—90; credit mgr. N.Am. Chem. Co., Mission, Kans., 1991—92, N.Am. Salt Co. and N.Am. Chem. Co., Overland Park, Kans., 1992—98; dir. acctg. and credit IMC Salt, Inc., 1998—2001; contr. N.Am. Compass Minerals Group, Inc., Overland Park, 2001—04; v.p., contr. Compass Minerals Internat., Overland Park, 2004—. Chmn. unsecured creditors com. H.E. Leonhardt Lumber, Oklahoma City, 1989-90; mem. unsecured creditors com. O'Hommel Co., Overland Park, Kans., 1991—. Author rsch. papers. Membership drive vol. Oklahoma City C. of C., 1989; rep. Napco Constrn. to Oklahoma City C. of C., 1990-91; dist. sec.-treas. Am. Bus. Clubs, Oklahoma City, 1985-86; bearer of U.S. Olympic Festival Torch, 1989; leader Boy Scouts Am., 1994—. Mem. Nat. Assn. Credit Mgmt., Nat. Chem. Creditors Assn., Fin. Credit and Internat. Bus. Assn., Inst. Mgmt. Acctg., Internat. Trade Club Greater Kansas City. Democrat. Lutheran. Avocations: fishing, hunting, reading. Home: 8800 Candlelight Ln Lenexa KS 66215-3432 Office: Compass Minerals Group 8300 College Blvd Overland Park KS 66210-1841 E-mail: mzinke54@aol.com.

**ZINKERNAGEL, ROLF MARTIN,** immunology educator; b. Basle, Switzerland, Jan. 6, 1944; s. Robert W. and Suzanne (Staehlin) Zinkernagel; m. Kathrin G. Ludin, Mar. 11, 1968; children: Christine, Annelies, Martin. MD, U. Basel, 1968. Intern in surgery Claraspital, Basel, 1968—69; postdoctoral Inst. Biochemistry, Lausanne, 1970—72, Dept. Microbiology, ANU, Canberra, Australia, 1973—75; asst. prof. Dept. Immunopathology, Scripps U., La Jolla, Calif., 1975—80, mem., 1978—79; assoc. prof. Dept. Pathology, Div. Exptl. Pathology, U. Zurich, 1979—92; full prof. Dept. Pathology, Inst. Exptl. Immunology, U. Zurich, 1992—. Editl. bd. Exptl. Cell Biology, 1976—88, Immunogenetics, 1977—, Parasite Immunology, 1978—84, Jour. of Immunology, 1978—80, Thymus, 1979—89, Antiviral Rsch., 1980—88, Jour. of Exptl. Medicine, 1981—84, European Jour. of Immunology, 1981—, Jour. of Environ. Pathology Toxicology and Oncology, 1981—, Cellular Immunology, 1983—, Internat. Jour. of Microbiology, 1983—, and others. Co-recipient Nobel Prize for medicine, 1996; recipient Albert Lasker award for Basic Med. Rsch., 1995. Mem.: others, Deutsche Gesellschaft fur Virologie, Deutsche Gesellschaft fur Immunologie, ENI European Network of Immunol. Instns., Internat. Soc. for Antiviral Rsch., Acadmia Euopea, Swiss Soc. of Cell and Molecular Biology, Swiss Soc. of Microbiology, Swiss Soc. of Pathology, Am. Assn. of Pathologists, Am. Assn of Immunologists, Australian Soc. for Immunology, Swiss Soc. of Allergy and Immunology, Soc. Francaise d'Immunologie (hon.), Scandinavian Soc. of Immunology (hon.). Achievements include discovery of of MHC-restricted T cell recognition; of the thymus role in determining MHC-restricted T-cell specficity; NK-cell activity in virus infections, T-cell epitope escape virus mutants, tolerances to viruses; research in on role of virus-specific T-cells in causing immunopathology. Office: Univ Hosp Inst Exptl Immunology Schmelzbergstr 12 CH-8091 Zurich Switzerland Office Phone: 0041 44 255 2989. Office Fax: 41 44 255 44 20. Business E-Mail: Rolf.Zinkernagel@usz.ch.

**ZINKHAM, W. ROBERT,** lawyer; b. Balt., May 30, 1955; s. William H. and Claire A. Z.; m. Theresa McGeehan, July 7, 1985; children: Natalie Anne, Elizabeth Claire. BA, Johns Hopkins U., 1977; JD, U. Md., Balt., 1980. Law clerk to chief judge Md. Ct. Appeals, Balt., 1980-81; assoc. Venable, Baetjer and Howard, Balt., 1981-88, ptnr., 1989—. Bd. dirs. Greater Balt. Med. Ctr. Found., 1992—. Editor Md. Law Rev., 1979. Chmn. Johns Hopkins Hosp. Psychiat. Day Hosp., Balt., 1982-92; pres. Mt. Washington Hills Assn., Balt., 1984-87. Mem. ABA, Am. Health Hosp. Attys., Nat. Health Lawyers Assn., Md. Bar Assn., Balt. Bar Assn. Republican. Office: Venable 2 Hopkins Plz Ste 1800 Baltimore MD 21201-2982 E-mail: wrzinkham@venable.com.

**ZINKHAN, GEORGE MARTIN, III,** marketing educator; b. Balt., Feb. 17, 1952; s. George Martin Jr. and Mary Elizabeth (Stoner) Z.; m. Marie Bruce; children: George M. IV, Lydia F., Sam S., M. Elizabeth S., L James G. BA in English Lit., Swarthmore Coll., 1974; MBA in Ops. Rsch., U. Mich., 1979, PhD in Bus. Adminstrn., 1981. Stats. lab. counselor U. Mich., Ann Arbor, 1978-79, teaching fellow, 1979-81; asst. prof. U. Houston, 1981-86, Conn prof. mktg., 1989-93; Coca-Cola prof. mktg., dept. head U. Ga., Athens, 1994—. Vis. assoc. prof. U. Pitts., 1987-88; mem. exec. com. Faculty Senate, U. Houston, 1991-92; cons. FTC, Washington, 1992-93, San Francisco, 1994-96. Co-author: Electronic Commerce: The Strategic Perspective, 2000, Consumers, 2002, 2004; editor: Enhancing Knowledge Developments in Marketing, 1995, Advertising Research: The Internet, Consumer Behavior, and Strategy, 2002; editor Jour. Acad. of Mktg. Science, 2003-; editor Jour. Advt., Richmond, Va., 1991-95, (spl. issue) Jour. Bus. Rsch., 1996, 2d edit. 1999, book rev. editor, mem. rev. bd. Jour. of Mktg., College Station, Tex., 1991—; mem. rev. bd. Jour. Current Issues 1991—, Jour. Bus. Rsch., 1994—, Jour. MacroMarketing 1998—. Mem. Am. Mktg. Assn. (track chair 1991-96, v.p. for rsch. 1996-98, pres. advt. spl. interest group 1996-2003, acad. coun. 2005), Am. Acad. Advt. (named one of Top 12 Contbrs. to Advt. 1990, one of Top 10 Contbrs. to Svcs. Advt. 1997, one of top 5 Contbrs. to Advt. Lit., Jour. of Advt., 1998, co-chair Nat. Conf., 2001), Acad. Mktg. Sci. (track chair promotion mgmt. 1994, track chair electronic commerce 1998), Assn. Consumer Rsch. (session chair 1990, program com. 1996, 2000, Judge Peabody awards 1996—). Democrat. United Ch. of Christ. Avocations: soccer, basketball, swimming, tennis, chess. Home: 372 Chesterfield Rd Bogart GA 30622-1761 Office: Univ Ga Dept Mktg 138 Brooks Hall Athens GA 30602-6258 Business E-Mail: gzinkhan@terry.uga.edu.

**ZINMAN, DAVID JOEL,** conductor; b. N.Y.C., July 9, 1936; s. Samuel and Rachel Ilo (Samuels) Z.; m. Leslie Heyman (dec.); children: Paul Pierre, Rachel Linda; m. Mary Ingham, May 19, 1974; 1 child, Raphael. MusB, Oberlin Conservatory, Ohio, 1958; MA, U. Minn., 1961. Asst. to Pierre Monteux, 1961-64; guest condr. U.S. and Europe; music dir. Netherlands Chamber Orch., 1964-77, Rochester (N.Y.) Philharm. Orch., 1974-85; prin. guest condr. Rotterdam (Netherlands) Philharm. Orch., 1977-79; chief condr. Rotterdam Philharm. Orch., 1979-82; prin. guest condr., music dir. designate Balt. Symphony Orch., 1983-85, music dir., 1985—98, Tonhalle Orch., Zurich, Switzerland, 1995; music dir. designate Aspen (Colo.) Music Festival and Sch., 1997, music dir., 1998—; program dir. Am. Acad. Conducting, Aspen, 1998—. Adj. prof. Eastman Sch. Music, Rochester. Rec. artist Phillips, Nonesuch, Decca/London, Decca/Argo, Angel/EMI, Telarc, Sony Classical. Recipient Grand Prix du Disque, 1967, 82, Edison award, 1967, 3 Grammy awards, 1990, Grammophone best selling record award, 1993, Grammophone award, 1994, Deutschen Schallplatten prize, George Peabody medal for outstanding contbn. to music in Am., 1996. Office: PO Box 161 Millville DE 19970 Office Phone: 302-541-8087.

**ZINMEISTER, KARL,** federal official; BA, Yale U., 1981. Legis. asst. to Sen. Daniel Patrick Moynihan, 1981—82; rsch. assoc. Am. Enterprise Inst. for Pub. Policy Rsch., 1982—86, Dewitt Wallace Reader's Digest fellow, 1994—95, J.B. Fuqua fellow, 1997—; self-employed writer, rschr., 1986—94; editor-in-chief The Am. Enterprise mag., 1994—2006; asst. to Pres. for domestic policy The White House, 2006—. Weekly commentator Trend Watch Radio Am., 1985—89; rsch. dir. Working Seminar on Family and Am. Welfare Policy, 1986—87; mem. bd. advisors Nat. Fund for Improvement and Reform of Schools and Tchg., U.S. Dept. Edn., 1988—89, Found. Cmty. and Faith-Centered Enterprise, 2002—04. Author: (book) Boots on the Ground: A Month with the 82nd Airborne in the Battle for Iraq, 2003, Dawn Over Baghdad: How the U.S. Military is Using Bullets and Ballots to Remake Iraq, 2004, Combat Zone: True Tales of G.I.s in Iraq, 2005; editor: Are World Population Trends a Problem?, 1985, In Real Life: Powerful Lessons from Everyday Living, 2005; prodr.: (films) Warriors, 2007. Named Am. at a Crossroads Winne, Corp. Pub. Broadcasting; recipient Media award, 1998, Best in Media award, Nat. Coun. Children's Rights, 1990, Disting. Svc. award for reporting in Operation Iraqi Freedom, 2003. Office: The White House Eisenhower Exec Office Bldg Rm 469 Washington DC 20502*

**ZINN, KEITH MARSHALL,** ophthalmologist, educator; b. Bklyn., Oct. 15, 1940; s. Victor Zinn and Eve (Lane) Z.; m. Elaine H. Kirban, Apr. 8, 1979. Student, NYU, Bronx, 1961; MD, SUNY, Bklyn., 1965. Diplomate Am. Bd. Ophthalmology; lic. physician, NY, Calif. Intern St. Lukes Hosp., NYC, 1965-66; research assoc. NIH, Bethesda, Md., 1966-68; post-doctoral fellow Retina Found., Boston, 1968-69; post-doctoral fellow dept. ophthalmology Harvard U. Med. Sch., Boston, 1968; asst. resident chief resident dept. ophthalmology Mount Sinai Hosp., NYC, 1969-71, ednl. fellow dept. ophthalmology, 1971-72; chief clin. fellow retina service Mass. Eye & Ear Infirmary, Harvard U. Med. Sch., Boston, 1972-73, Heed fellow dept. ophthalmology, 1972-73; research assoc. dept. retina research Retina Found., Boston, 1972-73; mem. faculty Lancaster Post-Grad. Course Ophthalmology, Harvard U. Med. Sch., Boston, 1969-70; consulting mng. dir. HT Capital Advisors, LLC, 2000—. Guest faculty dept. ophthalmology Harvard U. Med. Sch., Boston, 1969-84; asst. prof. dept. ophthalmology Mt. Sinai Sch. medicine, NY, assoc. clin. prof., 1976-80, clin. prof., 1980—; attending ophthalmic surgeon NYC, 1980—; attending ophthalmic surgeon Manhattan Eye Ear & Throat Hosp., NYC, 1981—; surgeon cons. Hosp. Joint Diseases, NYC, 1975-83, Patrolmen's Benevolent Assn., NYC, 1977—; lectr. field. Author: The Pupil, 1972, Ocular Fine Structure for the Clinician, 1973, The Developing Visual System, 1975, The Retinal Pigment Epithelium, 1975; author-editor: The Retinal Epithelium, 1979, Clinical Atlas of Peripheral Retinal Disorders, 1988; numerous audio-visual teaching progs. in ophthalmology; contbg. editor Mt. Sinai Jour. Medicine, 1975—; assoc. mem. editorial bd. Ophthalmic Surgery, 1980-89; mem. faculty editorial bd. Clin. Ophthalmology Update, 1982—; inventor field. Served lt. comdr. USPHS, 1966-68. Recipient numerous awards excellence medicine, including: Joseph Globus award Mount Sinai Jour. Medicine, 1979, Abraham Kornzweig Teaching award Mount Sinai Sch. Medicine, 1982. Fellow Am. Acad. Ophthalmology, Otolaryngology, ACS, Internat. Coll. Surgeons, Internat. Eye Found., Soc. Eye Surgeons, NY Acad. Medicine, NY Diabetes Assn., NY Heart Assn., NY Soc. Clin. Ophthalmology, Soc. Heed Fellows, Retina Soc., Ophthalmic Soc. UK, Oxford Ophthal. Congress, Brit. Am. Retinal Group; mem. AMA (Physicians Recognition award 1971, 76, 81, 82, 85), Ophthalmic Laser Surg. Soc. (v.p. 1986-88, pres. 1988-90), Am. Intraocular Lens Implant Soc., NY Acad. Medicine (trustee 1989-90, sec. 1985-86, chmn. ophthalmology sect. 1987-88, David Warfield fellowship com. 1990-92), Am. Bd. Laser Surgery (bd. dir. 1987—). Home: 125 E 87th St Apt 14C New York NY 10128 Office Phone: 212-535-5030.

**ZINN, MICHAEL WALLACE,** aerospace engineer; b. Washington, Dec. 30, 1962; s. Wallace Bernard and Frances E. AA, Charles County C.C., La Plata, Md., 1983; BS, Tri-State U., Angola, Ind., 1986. Coop student Naval Ordnance Sta., Indian Head, Md., 1980-86, mine decoy engr., 1986-87, airbreathing propulsion engr., 1987-92; airbreathing propulsion engr. Air/Cruise Missile Br. Naval Surface Warfare Ctr., Indian Head, 1992—2005, quality evaluation engr., 2005—. Mem. Joint Army-Navy-NASA-Air Force (JANNAF) airbreathing com., expendable engine subcom., Laurel, Md., 1987—; mem. Internat. Tech. Coop. Program involved in pyrotechnic aging and degradation Key Tech. Area 421, 1994-98. Author several tech. papers for AIAA and JANNAF. Pres. Port Tobacco Players, Inc., La Plata, Md., 1992-93; bd. dirs. Charles County Fair, Inc. Mem. AIAA (life, sr.), Am. Def. Preparedness Assn. (life), Cruise Missile Assn., Internat. Pyrotechnics Soc., Charles County Darts Assn. (webmaster) Achievements include work on aging surveillance programs for expendable gas turbine engines, on aging properties of expendable engines and solid propellant gas generators; assisted in new predictive techniques for ordnance surveillance; assisted in design of mine clearing line charge solid propellant rocket motor. Home: 11922 Charles St La Plata MD 20646-6414 Office Phone: 301-744-1434. Business E-Mail: michael.zinn@navy.mil.

**ZINN, WILLIAM,** musician, composer; b. N.Y.C., Nov. 19, 1924; s. Philip and Anna (Miller) Z.; m. Sophia Kalish, July 11, 1948; children: Karen Louise Heau, David Benjamin. Student, SUNY, 1952-54. Violinist Balt. Symphony, 1944-45, Indpls. Symphony, 1945-46, Ft. Wayne Philharm., 1946-47, Pitts. Symphony, 1947-49, Mpls. Symphony, 1950-51; concertmaster New Britain (Conn.) Symphony, 1968-90, Queens Symphony, 1969-71, Ridgefield (Conn.) Symphony, 1973-76, Chappaqua (N.Y.) Symphony, 1976, Yonkers Philharm., 1993—. Soloist with orchs. on records, on radio, TV, and in recitals, 1993-2003; founder Masterwork Piano Trio, Masterwork Piano Quartet, Classical String Quartet, Zinn's Ragtime String Quartet, Excelsior String Quartet, Queens Festival Orch., Bayside, N.Y., 1965, Assn. Musical William Zinn, Caracas, Venezuela, 1968, Vitametrics of Am., 1976, Internat. Symphony for World Peace, 1978, Big Apple Chamber Pops, 1983, Excelsior Composer's Festival Competition, 1984; tchr. movh. drafting Mondell Inst., 1956; coach ensembles for Chamber Music Assocs., 1973-78; engr. N.Y.C. Bd. Edn., 1951-57, Bodin-Zinn Corp., 1957-58, Chem. Constrn. Corp., 1958-59; pres. Zinn Originals, Inc., 1959-68, Sparx, Inc., Trademark Hall of Fame, Inc., Nice Realty Corp., MFW Restaurant Corp.; co-founder Excelsior Music Pub. Co., Visionary Music Pub. Co., Nat. Music Promotion Agy., Telecomm. Svcs., 1982, Assoc. Sci. Publs., 1985, Barclay House Publs., 1985, Excelsior Typographers and Engravers Unltd., 1985, Empco Recs. Internat., 1985, Imperial Editions, 1986, Missing Link Publs., 1986, Krazy Klassics Kompany, 1986, New Age Publs., 1987, Krazy Klassics Komix, 1988, Zinn Pub. Group, 1989, Zinn Comm., 1989, Decca Books, 1993, Arlington House, 1993, Zinn Labs., Inc.; sec. treas Spark Industries, Inc., Music Clearing House, 1989, Innovation Records, 1991, Krazy Klassics Records, 1991, Hanover House, 1991; pres. Zinn Labs., Inc., 1994, Caramoor Press Internat. Corp., 1996, Dunhill Pub. Co., 1996, ZinnPrint Internat., Inc., 1996, Barclay Holdings Group, Inc., 1998; adj. prof. NYU, 1987—; cons. Worldwide Leisure Corp., 1997. Author: (with Edward Gordon) Themography, 1947, (with George S. Grosser) Vitametrics I, The Human Formula for Self-Evaluation, 1976, Vitametrics II, The Human Formula for Self-Improvement, 1978, The Lost Chord, 1981, To Whom It May Concern, 1995, 1,001 Original Wise Sayings of William Zinn, 1996, 2,600 Wise Sayings, 1997, 3,500 Wise Sayings, 1998, 4,100 Wise Sayings, 1999, 6,000 Wise Sayings, 2000, 6,700 wise sayings, 2001, 10,000 Wise Sayings, 2002, 11,000 Wise Sayings, 2003, 12,500 Wise Sayings, 2004, 13,500 Wise Sayings, 2005, 14,500 Wise Sayings, 2006; composer (perpetual movement for woodwinds, strings and percussion) Chromatique, 1944, Piccolo Concerto, 1948, Violin Concerto, 1950, String Quartet, 1963, (piano solo) Chopinesque, 1965, (ballet) Night Creatures, 1966, Andante for Strings, 1967, Concerto for Octahorn, 1976, The International Anthem for World Peace, 1977, String Symphony, 1977, Romance for French Horn or Viola and Piano, 1981, Concerto for Violin/Viola/Cello/Double Bass and Orch., 1985, Kol Nidrei Meml. for String Quartet or String Orchestra, 1985, six concert duos for violin and viola, 1988, 15 Leroy Anderson favorites for string quartet or string orch., 1988, also songs including Mia, 1989, Aloha Hawaii, 1989, The Willows, 1990 (winner Hawaiian Nat. Song Contest 1990), Our Song of Love, 1990, Symphony in Ragtime, 1990, In Old Hawaii, 1991, Christmas in Hawaii, 1991, A Tribute to the Masters for String Quartet or String Orchestra (14 original works in the style of Bach, Vivaldi, Mozart, Beethoven, Brahms, Rossini, Chopin, Schubert, J. Strauss, Jr., Tschaikowsky, Dvorak, Debussy, Mendelssohn, Sousa), 1991, A Stroll in a Japanese Garden for Violin, Cello, Harp trio in 24 movements, 1996; arranger numerous operatic arias for string quartet or string orch.; orginator Musiphonics, 1981, 24 Paganini Caprices for String Quartet, 1992, 10 Sousa marches for string quartet, 1992, The Merry Widow Waltz for string quartet or string orch., 1992, Mozart Symphony # 40, 1992; arranger 21 Henry Mancini songs for string quartet/string orch., 1992, 16 Duke Ellington songs for string quartet/string orch., 1993, Gold and Silver Waltz, Skater's Waltz for string quartet and string orch., 8 arias from Porgy & Bess for string quartet/string orch., 1992, A Tribute to Fritz Kreisler for violin and piano, 1994, 16 arrangements of Fritz Kreisler works for string quartet/string orch., 1994, 12 classic Jewish favorites for string quartet/string orch., 1995, 12 Jewish Songs for String Quartet/String Orch., 1995, 6 duets for violin and viola, vol. II, 1996, An elegy for Mother Teresa, 1997, concerto Hebraic for piano and string orch., Let Freedom Ring, a Tribute to Martin Luther King, Jr., for orchestra, chorus, and narrator; 24 Etudes for solo cello, 1998, Hebraic Lament of Atonement for solo cello and string quartet or string orch., 1999, A Symphonic Portrait of Yonkers, 1999, The Seven Seasons for orchestra: seven symphonic works commemorating the Jewish holidays of Rosh Hashanah, Yom Kippur, Sukkot, Hanukkah, Purim, Passover, Shavuot, 2000, Siegfried Idyll Rhapsody solo violin and orch. (original Wagner orch.), 2001, A Requiem for Jerome G. Sala for soloists, chorus and orch., 2001; 6 Bach cello solo suites converted to duets with original violin part added, 2002, Dance of the Hours Fantasy for solo violin and orch. or piano, 2002, Meditation for solo violin or flute, harp and string orch., 2002, 28 Beethoven Bagatelles arranged for string quartet or string orch., 2002, Beethoven: Pathetique Sonata, slow movement arranged for string quarter or string orch., 2002, arranged for violin and piano The Carnival of the Animals, Nutcracker Suite, 2003, In Hallowed Ground, 9/11/2001 for solo voice chorus, string orch., bass clarinet, 2003, Peter & the Wolf for violin and piano, 2004, String Trio, 2004, A Klezmer Symphony, 2004, 6 Dvorak waltzs for quartet or string orch., 2004, String Quartet No. 2, 4 Clarinet Quartet, 2004, concertino for 2 violins and strings, 2004, Elegy forsolo trumpet and strings, 2005, concertino for 2 French horns and strings, 2005, Octet Netherworld for low brass and woodwinds, 2005, solo for flute and strings, 2005, solor for clarinet and strings, 2005, solo for bisscon and strings, 2006, solo for trombone and strings, 2005, others; pioneer multi-styles of music for string quartet and string orch.; composer over 500 works; developer numerous products for home, personal, automobile, and novelty use. Chmn., bd. dirs. Let Us Remember to Remember, 1984. Recipient 41st Hawaiian Nat. Song Contest award, 1990, Mayor and City Coun. citations for Yonkers 2000, a Symphonic Portrait. Mem. ASCAP, Internat. Platform Assn., Nat. Coun. Women of U.S., Am. Fedn. Musicians, N.Y. Humanist Assn. Home: 35-19 215th Pl Bayside NY 11361-1725

**ZINNEN, ROBERT OLIVER,** management consultant, consultant; b. Racine, Wis., June 28, 1929; s. Aloys Henry and Mabel Helen (Holy) Z.; m. Darlene Mary Weyers, Aug. 25, 1956; children: Claudia Jane, Robert O. BBA, U. Wis., 1951, JD, 1956. Bar: Wis. 1956, Ill. 1959, Mass. 1982; CPA, Ill. Tax accountant Price Waterhouse, Chgo., 1956-59; mem. firm Tenney & Bentley, Chgo., 1959-64; assoc. dir. taxes Allstate Cos., Skokie, Ill., 1964-65; v.p. fin. Do-All Co., Des Plaines, Ill., 1965-67; dir. taxes Quaker Oats Co., Chgo., 1967-71; internat. atty. Am. Hosp. Supply Corp., 1971-75; fin. cons. Alexander Proudfoot Co., Chgo., 1975-76; v.p. fin. Milton Bradley Co., Springfield, Mass., 1976-82; co-owner, exec. v.p. Roadmaster Corp., Olney, Ill., 1982-88, cons., 1988—. Mem. Housing and Traffic Commns., Highland Park, Ill., 1963-66; chmn. Congl. Action Com., Springfield; bd. dirs. Assoc. Industries, Mass. Served with U.S. Army, 1951-53. Mem. Toy Mfrs. Am. (bd. dirs. 1984-88), Quail Creek Country Club, Moorings Country Club, Longmeadow Country Club. Republican. Roman Catholic. E-mail: cyberzinn@comcast.net.

**ZINNER, ERNST K.,** physics educator, earth and planetary science educator, researcher; b. Steyr, Austria, Jan. 30, 1937; MS, Tech. U., Vienna, Austria, 1960; PhD in Physics, Wash. U., Mo., 1972. Instr. physics Coll. Vet. Medicine, Vienna, 1963-64; program and calculation magnetic field distbr. Brown-Boveri Co., Switzerland, 1964-65, rsch. assoc., 1972-74, sr. rsch. scientist, 1974-89; rsch. prof. physics Wash. U., St. Louis, 1989—. Vis. scientist Max-Planck Inst. Physics, Germany, 1980, Max-Planck Inst. Chemistry, Germany, 1980, U. Pavia, Italy, 1989. Recipient J. Lawrence Smith medal NAS, 1997. Fellow Am. Physics Soc., Meteoritical Soc.; mem. AAAS, Am. Geophysics Union, Sigma Xi. Office: Wash U Campus Box 1169 1 Brookings Dr Saint Louis MO 63130-4862

**ZINNER, MICHAEL JEFFREY,** surgeon, educator; b. Miami, Fla., Apr. 2, 1945; s. Doran D. and Eve Zinner; m. Rhonda Zinner; children: Darren, Daniel. BEE, Johns Hopkins U., 1967; MD, U. Fla., 1971; postgrad., NIH Found. for Edn. in the Scis., Bethesda, Md., 1973-74. Diplomate Am. Bd. Surgery (bd. dirs. 1988-94). Intern The Johns Hopkins Hosp., Balt., 1971-72, jr. asst. resident in surgery, 1972-73, sr. asst. resident, 1976-79, asst. chief of svc. in surgery, 1979-80; registrar thoracic surgery Frenchay Hosp., Bristol, Eng., 1977; instr. The Johns Hopkins U. Sch. Medicine, Balt., 1978-80; asst. prof. surgery Downstate Med. Ctr., Bklyn., 1980-83, assoc. prof., 1983-85; assoc. dir. surg. residency program, coord. residency program The Johns Hopkins Med. Instns., Balt., 1985-88, assoc. prof., div. chmn. dept. surgery, 1985-88, prof., 1988; prof., chmn. dept. surgery UCLA Sch. Medicine, 1988-94; mem. staff Kings County Hosp., 1980-85, chief gen. surgery and oncology, 1983-85; mem. staff Balt. VA Hosp., 1985-88, Johns Hopkins Hosp., 1985-88, Wadsworth VA Hosp., L.A., 1988-94; chief of surgery UCLA Med. Ctr., 1988-94; surgeon-in-chief Brigham and Womens Hosp., Boston, 1994—; prof. Harvard Med. Sch., 1994—. Bd. dirs. Sisters of Mercy Health Sys., 1992—98, Ptnrs. Health Care Sys., 1996—2000, Brigham and Women's Hosp, 1996—. Contbr. over 200 articles to profl. jours.; lectr. in field. Maj. M.C., U.S. Army, 1973-74. Rsch. grantee NIH, 1982-86, 88—; merit rev. grantee VA, 1988-91; grantee numerous univs., founds., pharm. cos., 1978—. Fellow ACS (com. on rsch. and edn. 1988, adv. com. on gen. surgery 1988); mem. IEEE, NIH (ad hoc, study sect., surgery and biomed. engring. 1986), Am. Fedn. Clin. Rsch., Assn. Acad. Surgery (com. on issues 1980-82, recorder 1982-84, exec. coun. 1982-88, pres. 1985-86), Am. Physiol. Soc., Am. Gastroenterol. Assn., Am. Pancreatic Assn., Soc. Univ. Surgeons (com. on publs. 1984-86, com. on edn., 1986-87, exec. coun. 1986-92, pres. 1987-88), Soc. Critical Care Medicine, Surg. Biology Club, Collegium Internationale Chirugiac Digestival (bd. dirs. 1990-96), Soc. Surgery of Alimentary Tract, Soc. Clin. Surgery, Alpha Omega Alpha. Avocations: fishing, boating. Office: Brigham and Womens Hosp Dept Surgery 75 Francis St Boston MA 02115-6106

**ZINNES, HARRIET FICH,** poet, retired English educator, literary and art critic; b. Boston; d. Assir and Sarah (Goldberg) Fich; m. Irving I. Zinnes, Sept. 24, 1943 (dec. 1979); children: Clifford, Alice. BA cum laude, CUNY, 1939, MA, 1944; PhD, NYU, 1953. Editor publs. divsn. Raritan (N.J.) Arsenal, 1942-43; assoc. editor Harper's Bazaar, N.Y.C., 1944-46; tutor Hunter Coll. CUNY, N.Y.C., 1946-49; asst. prof. Queens Coll. CUNY, Flushing, 1949-53, assoc. prof., 1962-78, full prof., 1978-89, prof. emerita, 1989—; lectr. in English Rutgers U., New Brunswick, N.J., 1961-62. Vis. prof. Am. lit. U. Geneva, 1968. Author: Waiting and Other Poems, 1964, An Eye for an I, 1966, I Wanted to See Something Flying, 1976, Entropisms, 1978, Book of Ten, 1981, Lover: Short Stories, 1988, Book of Twenty, 1992, My, Haven't the Flowers Bare?, 1995, The Radiant Absurdity of Desire, 1998, Plunge, 2001, Drawing on the Wall: Poems, 2002, Whither Nonstopping, 2005; editor: Ezra Pound and the Visual Arts, 1980; translator Blood and Feathers: Selected Poems of Jacques Prevert, 1988, rev. edit., 1993; contr. editor, Hollin's Critic, Denver Quarterly; contr. writer, N.Y. Arts Mag.; author numerous poems; contbr. articles to popular mags. MacDowell Art Colony fellow, 1972-74, 77, 2004, Yaddo fellow, 1978, 81, Va. Ctr. for Creative Arts fellow, 1975-76, 81-82, 84, 86, 88-93, resident fellow, Djerassi Found., 1990, La Napoul, 2002; Am. Coun. Learned Socs. grantee, 1978, CUNY summer grantee, 1979, 81, 86. Fellow Poets Editors & Novelists, Nat. Book Critics Circle, Acad. Am. Poets, Internat. Assn. Art Critics, Poetry Soc. Am.; mem. Phi Beta Kappa. Home: 25 W 54th St New York NY 10019-5404 Office: Dept English Queens Coll Flushing NY 11367 Office Phone: 212-582-8315. Personal E-mail: hzinnes@rcm.com.

**ZINNI, ANTHONY CHARLES,** retired military officer; b. Conshohocken, Pa., Sept. 17, 1943; s. Antonio and Lilla (Disabatino) Z.; m. Dale Elaine Bathke, Nov. 19, 1966; children: Lisa, Maria, Anthony. BS in Econs., Villanova U., 1965; MA in Bus., Cen. Mich. U., 1984; MA in Internat. Rels., Salve Regina Coll., Newport, R.I., 1986; postgrad., Nat. War Coll., Washington, 1983-84. Commd. 2d lt. USMC, 1965, advanced through grades to gen., 1997, ret., 2000; comdg. officer 2d bn. 8th Marines, Camp Lejeune, N.C., 1980-81, 9th Marines, Okinawa, Japan, 1987-89; instr. Comdt. Staff Coll., Quantico, Va., 1981-83; staff ops. officer Hdqrs. USMC, Washington, 1984-86; chief naval ops. fellow Strategic Studies Group, Newport, 1986-87; chief staff Tng. and Edn. Ctr., Combat Devel. Command, Quantico, 1989-90; dep. ops. officer European Command, Stuttgart, Germany, 1990-91; chief of staff, dep. commdg. gen. Task Force Provide Comfort, 1991-92; dir. ops. Unified Task Force, Stuttgart, Somalia, 1992-93; commdg. gen. I Marine Expeditionary Force, 1994-96; dep. comdr. U.S. Ctrl. Command, 1996-97, comdr., 1997-2000; spl. envoy to the Middle East US Dept. State, 2002—03; disting. sr. advisor Ctr. for Strategic & Internat. Studies, Washington, 2000—; disting. mil. fellow Ctr. for Def. Info., Washington. Co-author (with Tom Clancy & Tony Koltz): Battle Ready, 2004; co-author: (with Michael DeLong & Noah Lukeman) Inside CentCom: The Unvarnished Truth About the Wars in Afghanistan and Iraq, 2004; co-author: (with Tony Koltz) The Battle for Peace: A Frontline Vision of America's Power and Purpose, 2006. Roman Catholic. Office: Ctr for Def Info 1779 Massachusetts Ave NW Washington DC 20036

**ZINOMAN, JASON,** theater critic; Chief Broadway and Off-Broadway critic Time Out NY Mag.; theater critic, reporter NY Times, NYC. Contbr. New Republic, Esquire, Salon, Slate. Office: NY Times Culture Desk 229 W 43rd St New York NY 10036 Office Phone: 212-556-7329. Office Fax: 212-556-1516.*

**ZINSER, ELISABETH ANN,** academic administrator; b. Meadville, Pa., Feb. 20, 1940; d. Merle and Fae Zinser. BS, Stanford U., 1964; MS, U. Calif., San Francisco, 1966, MIT, 1982; PhD, U. Calif., Berkeley, 1972. Nurse VA Hosp., Palo Alto, Calif., 1964-65, San Francisco, 1969-70; instr. Sch. Nursing U. Calif., San Francisco, 1966-69; pre-doctoral fellow Nat. Inst. Health, Edn. and Welfare, 1971-72; adminstr. Sch. Medicine U. Wash., Seattle, 1972-75, Coun. Higher Edn., State of Ky., 1975-77; prof., dean. Coll. Nursing U. N.D., Grand Forks, 1977-83; vice chancellor acad. affairs U. N.C., Greensboro, 1983-89; pres. Gallaudet U., Washington, 1988, U. Idaho, Moscow, 1989-95; chancellor U. Ky., Lexington, 1995—2001; pres. So. Oreg. Univ., Ashland, 2001—. Bd. dir. Assoc. Am. Coll. & Univ., 1999—, Am. Council Edn., Nat Assoc. State Univ. & Land Grant Coll.; bd. mem. Ctr. on Academic Integrity; past chmn. Commn. Outreach & Tech. Transfer. Primary author: (with others) Contemporary Issues in Higher Education, 1985, Higher Education Research, 1988; spkr. in field. Mem. Oreg. Women's Forum; bd. mem. Ashland C. of C., Oreg. Shakespeare Festival, Crater Lake Nat. Park Trust. Leadership fellow Bush Found., 1981-82. Office: So Oregon Univ 1250 Siskiyou Blvd Ashland OR 97520

**ZINTER, STEVEN L.,** state supreme court justice; m. Sandra Zinter; 2 children. Doctorate, Univ. So. Dakota, 1975, BS, 1972. Pvt. practice, 1978—86; state atty. Hughes County; cir. judge State of So. Dakota, 1987—97; presiding judge Sixth Judicial Cir., 1997—2002; judge SD Supreme Court, 2002—. Mem. Harry S Truman Found.; trustee So. Dakota Retirement Sys.; elect. pres. So. Dakota Corrections Commn. Mem.: ABA, S.D. Judges Assn. (past pres.), S.D. Bar Assn. Office: SD Supreme Ct 500 E Capital Ave Pierre SD 57501-5070*

**ZIOLKOWSKI, JAN MICHAEL,** medievalist educator; b. New Haven, Nov. 17, 1956; s. Theodore J. and Yetta (Goldstein) Z.; m. Elizabeth Ann Hillenius; children: Saskia Elizabeth, Ada Margaret, Yetta Joy. AB summa cum laude, Princeton U., 1977; PhD, U. Cambridge, Eng., 1982; MA (hon.), Harvard U., 1987. Asst. prof. Harvard U., Cambridge, Mass., 1981-84, John L. Loeb assoc. prof. of the humanities, 1984-87, prof. medieval Latin and comparative lit., 1987—2002, Arthur Kingsley Porter prof. medieval Latin, 2002—. Author: Alan of Lille's Grammar of Sex, 1985, Nigel of Canterbury, Miracles of the Virgin Mary, 1986, Jezebel: A Norman Latin Poem, 1989, On Philology, 1990, Talking Animals: Medieval Latin Beast Poetry, 1993, Nigel of Canterbury, The Passion of St. Lawrence, 1994, The Cambridge Songs, 1994, 98, Obscenity: Social Control and Artistic Creation in the European Middle Ages, 1998, The Medieval Craft of Memory, 2002; editor Comparative Literature Studies. Pres. Internationales Mittellateiner Komitee, 2000—. Fellow Guggenheim Found., 1987-88, ACLS, 1986, Netherlands Inst. for Advanced Study, 2005—; Rome Prize fellow Am. Acad. in Rome, 1980-81; Marshall scholar, 1977-80. Mem. Medieval Acad. Am. (councillor 1991-94), Dante Soc. Am. (councillor 2004—), Am. Philol. Assn., Phi Beta Kappa. Home: 930 Centre St Newton MA 02459-1266 Office: Harvard Univ Classics 221 Boylston Hall Cambridge MA 02138

**ZIOLKOWSKI, THEODORE JOSEPH,** literature educator; b. Birmingham, Ala., Sept. 30, 1932; s. Miecislaw and Cecilia (Jankowski) Z.; m. Yetta Bart Goldstein, Mar. 26, 1951; children: Margaret Cecilia, Jan Michael, Eric Josef. AB, Duke U., 1951, AM, 1952; student, U. Innsbruck, Austria, 1952-53; PhD, Yale U., 1957; DrPhil honoris causa (hon.), U. Greifswald, 2001. Instr., then asst. prof. Yale U., New Haven, 1956-62; assoc. prof. Columbia U., N.Y.C., 1962-64; prof. Germanic langs. and lit. Princeton (N.J.) U., 1964-69, 1973-79, Class of 1900 prof. modern langs., 1969-2001, prof. comparative lit., 1975-2001, dean Grad. Sch., 1979-92, prof. emeritus, 2001. Vis. prof. Rutgers U., 1966, Yale U., 1967, 73, CUNY, 1971, Bristol U., 1987, U. Munich, 1992; vis. scholar U. Ctr. in Va., 1971, Piedmont U. Ctr., N.C., 1971; Dancy Meml. lectr. U. Montevallo, 1973; Christopher Longest lectr. U. Miss., 1979; Patten Found. lectr. Ind. U., 1980; vis. lectr. Österreichische Akademie der Wissenschaften, 1992; vis. lectr. Korean Ministry of Edn., 1996; chmn. N.Y. State Doctoral Evaluation Program in German, 1975-80; nat. rev. panel for U.S. Nat. Grad. Fellows Program, 1985-87, 91—; chmn. overseers vis. com. on German Harvard U., 1982-88; mem. selection com. for Bennett award, 1988; with German-Am. Acad. Coun., 1993-99; chmn. N.Y. State Humanities Screening Com., 1996; chmn. bd. German-Am. Ctr. for Vis. Scholars, 1997-99; forum assembly spkr. Brigham Young U; mem. evaluation team Rosenzweig Zentrum of Hebrew U., Jerusalem, 1999; mem. search com. for chair in German, Bristol U., 1999; mem. search com. for dean Internat. U. Bremen, 1999-00. Author: Hermann Broch, 1964, The Novels of Hermann Hesse, 1965, Hermann Hesse, 1966, Dimensions of the Modern Novel, 1969, Fictional Transfigurations of Jesus, 1972 (James Russell Lowell prize MLA), Disenchanted Images, 1977, Der Schriftsteller Hermann Hesse, 1979, The Classical German Elegy, 1980, Varieties of Literary Thematics, 1983, German Romanticism and Its Institutions, 1990, Virgil and the Moderns, 1993, The Mirror of Justice, 1997 (Christian Gauss prize Phi Beta Kappa), Das Wunderjahr in Jena, 1998, The View from the Tower, 1998, The Sin of Knowledge, 2000, Berlin: Aufstieg einer Kulturmetropole um 1810, 2002, Hesitant Heroes, 2004, Clio the Romantic Muse, 2004 (Barricelli prize), Ovid and the Moderns, 2005 (Robert Motherwell award Dedalus Found.); contbr. over 160 articles and 400 revs.; editor: Hermann Hesse, Autobiographical Writings, 1972, Hermann Hesse, Stories of Five Decades, 1972, Hesse: A Collection of Critical Essays, 1972, Hermann Hesse, My Belief: Selected Essays, 1974, Hermann Hesse, Tales of Student Life, 1976, Hermann Hesse, Pictor's Metamorphoses and Other Fantasies, 1982, Hermann Hesse, Soul of the Age: Selected Letters, 1891-1962, 1991; mem. editl. bd. Germanic Rev., 1962-95, Publs. MLA, 1971-75, Arbitrium, 1983-, 17th Century Studies, 1985-2005, Germanistik, 1987-, Jahrbuch für Internat. Germanistik, 1991-, World Literature Today, 1998-, Etudes Germaniques, 1998-; Publications of the English Goethe Society, 2003-; Spectrum Lit./Comparative Studies, 2004-; mem. editl. bd. Princeton U. Press, 1972-75, trustee, 1982-95; translator (with Yetta Ziolkowski): The Poetics of Quotation

(Herman Meyer) 1968, Hermann Hesse: A Pictorial Biography, 1975. Decorated comdr.'s cross Order of Merit (Germany), 2000; recipient Howard T. Behrman award for disting. achievement in humanities, 1978, Wilbur Lucius Cross medal Yale U., 1982, Goethe Inst. gold medal, 1987, Henry Allen Moe prize in humanities, 1988, Festschrift Themes and Structures (ed. Alexander Stephan), 1997, Jakob-und-Wilhelm Grimm prize for German Studies, 1998, Humboldt Sr. Rsch. prize, 1998, 00; Mellon Emeritus Faculty fellow, 2003; Fulbright rsch. grantee, 1958-59, grantee Am. Philos. Soc., 1959, NEH grantee, 1978, Guggenheim fellow, 1964-65, Am. Coun. Learned Socs. fellow, 1972, 76; resident fellow Bellagio Study Ctr., 1993. Mem. MLA (hon. life; exec. coun. 1976-77, pres. 1985), Acad. Lit. Studies, Am. Comparative Lit. Assn., Am. Acad. Arts and Scis., Assn. Lit. Scholars and Critics, Authors Guild, Am. Assn. Tchrs. German (hon. life), Yale Grad. Sch. Assn. (pres. 1974-76), Assn. Grad. Schs. (v.p. 1989-90, pres. 1990-91), Heinrich von Kleist Gesellschaft, Goethe-Gesellschaft, Novalis-Gesellschaft, Internat. Vereinigung für Germanistik (exec. coun. 1985-95, treas. 1990-95), Am. Philos. Soc. (councillor 1991-97), Göttingen Akademie der Wissenschaften, Austrian Akademie der Wissenschaften, Deutsche Akademie für Sprache und Dichtung, Inst. Germanic and Romance Studies London, Phi Beta Kappa. Home: 36 Bainbridge St Princeton NJ 08540-3902 Personal E-mail: tjziol@aol.com.

ZIOMEK, JONATHAN S., journalist, educator; b. Newport News, Va., July 28, 1947; s. Stanley Walter and Joy Carmen (Schmidt) Z.; m. Rosalie Ziomek, Aug. 14, 1971; children: Joseph, Jennifer; 1 stepchild, Daniel. BA in Sociology, U. Ill., 1970, MS in Journalism, 1982. Reporter, labor writer, feature writer, Sun. fin. editor Chgo. Sun-Times, 1970-78; press sec. for U.S. Senate campaign, Chgo., 1979-80; asst. prof. Medill Sch. Journalism, Northwestern U., Evanston, Ill., 1983-88; dir. grad. editl. programs Medill Sch. Journalism/Northwestern U., Evanston, Ill., 1988—, asst. dean, 1994—2004, assoc. prof., 1994—. Rapporteur Aspen Inst., Journalism and Soc. Seminar, 2004, McCormick Found. Mil. and Media Conf., 2005, 06; presenter writing workshops; corp. writing cons. Contbr. articles to various mags.; editor: Chgo. Journalist Newsletter, 1991-93. Participant Internat. Visitors Ctr., Chgo., 1988—; fact-finder USIA, Bulgaria and Yugoslavia, 1990. Mem. Assn. for Edn. in Journalism and Mass Communications, Soc. Profl. Journalists, Nat. Assn. Sci. Writers, Chgo. Headline Club. Home: 2149 Hartrey Ave Evanston IL 60201-2571 Office: Northwestern Univ Medill Sch Journalism Evanston IL 60208-0001

ZION, ROGER HERSCHEL, retired management consultant, retired congressman; b. Escanba, Mich., Sept. 17, 1921; s. Herschel G. and Helen (Hutchinson) Z.; m. Marjorie Knauss, Feb. 20, 1945; children: Gayle, Scott, Randy. BA, U. Wis., 1943, postgrad., 1944-45. With Mead Johnson & Co., 1946-66, dir. tng. and profl. rels., 1965-66; internat. mktg. mgmt. cons., 1966; mem. 90th-93d congresses from 8th Dist. Ind.; chmn. Rep. Task Force on Energy and Resources; pres. Resources Devel., Inc., Washington, 1975—. Hon. chmn. GoPlus Assn. Author: Keys to Human Relations in Selling, 1963, The Hallowed Howls of Congress, 1994, The Republican Challenge, 1995, The Amazing Adventures of Congressman Zion, 2004 V.p. Buffalo Trace council Boy Scouts Am., 1961; Bd. dirs. Evansville (Ind.) chpt. ARC, 1960-65. Lt. USNR, 1943-46, PTO. Named Toastmaster, Evansville Press Gridiron dinner, 1963; recipient Citizen of Month award New Image Com. of Evansville's Future, 1962 Mem. Nat. Sales and Mktg. Execs. Assn. (pres. Evansville 1962), Wabash Valley Assn., AMVETS (life), Rotary (dir. Evansville club 1964), Evansville Country Club (dir. 1960-65), Alpha Delta Phi (pres. Wis. chpt. 1941-43) Congregationalist. Home: 7938 E Oak St Evansville IN 47715-7214

ZIOTIS, JOSEPHINE, elementary school educator, restaurant owner; b. Nyack, N.Y., Dec. 12, 1943; d. Joseph Antonio and Anna (Felice) Ramundo; m. James George Ziotis, Aug. 22, 1965; children: Smaragda Thomas, Anna Kurzrok. BS in Elem. Edn., St. Thomas Aquinas, Sparkill, N.Y., 1982; MS in Urban Edn., Iona Coll., 1986, postgrad. Cert. elem. edn. N.Y. Sec. Am. Cyanamid, Pearl River, NY, 1961—67; owner Skylark Restaurant, Nyack, 1967—; tchr. St. Gregory Barbarigo, Garnerville, NY, 1982—85, N.Y.C. Pub. Sch. #9, Bronx, 1985—93, N. Rockland Ctrl. Sch. Dist., Garnerville, 1993—. Mem. drama club Willow Grove Mid. Sch., Thiells, NY, 1994—99; mem. dist. social studies com. N. Rockland Ctrl. Sch. Dist., Garnerville, 2003—. Mem. Philopotochos Soc. Sts. Constantine, 1972—77. Recipient Schoolhouse award, Willow Grove Mid. Sch., 2000. Mem.: NY State Reading Assn., Internat. Reading Assn., Nyack C. of C. Avocations: reading, travel, walking, cooking, theater. Home: 82 Pine Dr Stony Point NY 10980 Office: Willow Grove Mid Sch Storrs Rd Thiells NY 10984

ZIPES, DOUGLAS PETER, cardiologist, researcher; b. White Plains, NY, Feb. 27, 1939; s. Robert Samuel and Josephine Helen (Weber) Z.; m. Marilyn Joan Jacobus, Feb. 18, 1961; children: Debra, Jeffrey, David. BA cum laude, Dartmouth Coll., 1961, B of Med. Sci., 1962; MD cum laude, Harvard Med. Sch., 1964. Diplomate Am. Bd. Internal Medicine, mem. subsplty. bd. cardiovasc. disease 1989-99, chmn., 1995-99, chmn. com. cert. in clin. cardiac electrophysiology 1989-96, bd. dirs. 1995-2003, exec. com. 1999-2003, chmn. bd. 2002-03. Intern, resident, fellow in cardiology Duke U. Med. Ctr., Durham, NC, 1964-68; vis. scientist Masonic Med. Rsch. Lab., Utica, NY, 1970-71; from asst. prof. medicine to disting. prof. emeritus Ind. U., Indpls., 1970—2004, disting. prof. emeritus, 2004—, Medtronic Zipes chair cardiology Sch. Medicine, 2004—, Zipes vis. prof., 2005. Bd. dirs. Inst. for Clin. Evaluation; cardiology adv. com NIH, 1991—94; mem. med. adv. bd ABCNews.com, 2000—; mem. dean's coun. Dartmouth Med. Sch., Ind. Med. Sch.; cons. in field. Author: Comprehensive Cardiac Care, 7th edit., 1991; editor: Slow Inward Current, 1980, Cardiac Electrophysiology and Arrhythmias, 1985, Nonpharmacological Therapy of Tachyarrhythmias, 1987, Cardiac Electrophysiology From Cell to Bedside, 1990, 4th edit., 2004; co-editor: Treatment of Heart Diseases, 1992, Ablation of Cardiac Arrhythmias, 1994, 2d edit., 2002, Antiarrhythmic Therapy: A Pathophysiologic Approach, 1994, Heart Disease, A Textbook of Cardiovascular Medicine, 7th edit., 2005, Thoracic Vein Arrhythmias, 2004, Sudden Cardiac Death, A Handbook for Clinical Practice, 2006; mem. editl. bd. Circulation, 1974-78, 83-, Am. Jour. Cardiology, 1979-82, 88-, Am. Jour. Medicine, 1979-90, Jour. Am. Coll. Cardiology, 1983, 2002-, Am. Heart Jour., 1977-97, PACE, 1977-, Circulation Rsch., 1983-90, Am. Jour. Noninvasive Cardiology, 1985-89, Jour. Electrophysiology, 1987-89, Cardiovasc. Drugs and Therapy, 1986-93, Japanese Heart Jour., 1989-, Jour. Cardiovasc. Pharmacology and Therapeutics, 1994-, Jour. Cardiovasc. Pharmacology, 1995—, Cardiovasc. Therapeutics, 1995, Current Clin. Trials, 1995-98, Jour. Interventional Cardiac Electrophysiology, 1996-, Am. Heart Hosp. Jour., Jour. Am. Coll. Cardiology; editor-in-chief: Progress in Cardiology, 1988-92, Cardiology in Rev., 1992-2002, Contemporary Treatments of Cardiovasc. Disease, 1996-98, Am. Coll. Cardiology Extended Learning, 1997-, Ind. Jour. Pacing and Electrophysiology Online, 2001-; founding editor Heart Rhythm, 2004—, Jour. Cardiovasc. Electrophysiology 1990-2004; contbr. articles to profl. jours.; patentee cardioverter, elec. prevention of arrhythmia, discrimination of atrial fibrillation, fixation of implantable devices, and pericardial delivery of therapeutic and diagnostic agents. Pres., bd. dirs. Indpls. Opera Co., 1983-85; mem. adv. bd. NIH, Washington, 1977-81; mem. nat. merit rev. bd. VA, 1982-85, Cardiology Adv. Com. NHLBI, 1991-98, chmn. steering com. AVID; chmn. Data and Safety Monitoring Bd. AFFIRM, 1996-2002; bd. dirs. Am. Bd. Internal Medicine Found., 2002-04; chmn. Am. Bd. Internal Medicine, 2002-03. Recipient Disting. Achievement award Am. Heart Assn., 1989, Sagamore of the Wabash award, Gov. Ind., 2001. Master Am. Coll. Cardiology (chmn. ACC/AHA subcom. to assess EP studies, chmn. young investigators award com. 1988-94, trustee 1992-97, 2002-05, chair nominating com. 2003, chmn. devel. com. 1996-2001, sci. sessions program com. 1996-98, v.p. 1999-2000, pres. 2001-02, co-chair ventricular arrythms guidelines 2003—), Bethesda (Md.) conf. guidelines for athletes with heart disease, endowed lectr. 2005, Disting. Scientist award 1996, endowed Douglas P. Zipes Disting. Young Sciedntist award 2005); fellow ACP, Am. Heart Assn. (exec. com. 1980-88, sci. sessions program 1983-86, chmn. various coms., chmn. 1995, bd. dirs. Internat. Cardiology Found. 1993-98, bd. dirs. 1994-96, chmn. emergency cardiac care com. 1995-96, Herrick award 1997, Cor Vitae award 2004); mem. Am. Soc.

Clin. Investigation, Assn. Univ. Cardiologists (v.p. 1994, pres. 1995), Assn. Am. Physicians, Am. Physiol. Soc., Cardiac Electrophysiology Soc. (pres. 1985-86), Heart Rhythm Soc. (pres. 1988-90, trustee 1990-2000, lectr. 2005, Disting. Scientist award 1995), InterAm. Soc. Cardiology (1st v.p. 1995-98), Ind. Cardiac Electrophysiology Soc. (founder). Home: 10614 Winterwood Carmel IN 46032-9688 Office: Ind U Sch Medicine 1100 W Michigan St Indianapolis IN 46202-5208 Office Phone: 317-962-0556. Business E-Mail: dzipes@iupui.edu.

ZIPF, ROBERT EUGENE, JR., legal medicine consultant, pathologist; b. Sept. 18, 1940; s. Robert Eugene and Meriam (Murr) Z.; m. Nancy J. Gaskell, Sept. 11, 1965; children: Karin Lorene, Marjorie Kristine. BA, DePauw U., 1962; MD, Ohio State U., 1966. Diplomate Am. Bd. Pathology. Intern Miami Valley Hosp., Dayton, Ohio, 1966-67; dir. forensic pathology Duke U. Med. Ctr., Durham, NC, 1967-72; dir. radioisotope pathology Riverside Meth. Hosp., Columbus, 1974-78; dep. coroner, forensic pathologist Franklin County, Columbus, 1974-78; regional forensic pathologist State of N.C., Rocky Mount, 1978—. Clin. asst. prof. East Caroline U. Med. Sch., Greenville, N.C., 1979—; adj. prof. Atlantic Christian Coll., Wilson, N.C., 1980-89, dir. Sch. Med. Tech., 1983-89; dir. clin. and diagnostic labs. Nash Gen. Hosp., Rocky Mount, 1978—2006; dir. forensic toxicology lab. Nash Health Care Sys., Rocky Mount, 1990—2000; cons. in field. Contbr. articles to profl. jours. Trustee United Fund, 1979-84; active Mayor's Com. on Drug and Substance Abuse, 1987—; bd. dirs. NC Wesleyan Coll. Found., 2005—, Nash C.C., 2005—; advisor Zipf Charitable Trust and Fund, 1999—. Maj. USAF, 1972-74. Fellow Am. Soc. Clin. Pathologist, Am. Acad. Forensic Scientists; mem. SMS (clin. adv. bd. 1988-91, lab. advisors bd. 1989-91), Assn. Clin. Scientists, Am. Coll. Nuclear Medicine, N.C. Med. Soc., N.Y. Acad. Scis. (pres. Lab. Users Group 1988-90, 92), Nash County Med. Soc. (pres. 1995). Home: 120 Newby Ct Rocky Mount NC 27804-3322 Office: Nash Gen Hosp Pathology Lab Rocky Mount NC 27804 E-mail: rezpath@email.com.

ZIPORI-BECKENSTEIN, PNINIT, business educator, researcher; b. Tel Aviv, Oct. 22, 1947; d. Shmaya and Tirza Beckenstein; m. Dov Zipori, June 1, 1971 (div. 1993); children: Sigal, Dan. MSc with honors, Tel Aviv U., 1970; PhD, Weizman Inst. Sci., Rehovot, Israel, 1976; MBA, Bar-Ilan U., Ramat-Gan, Israel, 1985; PhD (hon.), Weizman Inst. Sci., 1977. Researcher Leiden (The Netherlands) U., 1976-78; with software mktg. dept. Med. Corp., Palo Alto, Calif., 1985-87; dir. mktg. Orgenics Ltd., Yavne, Israel, 1987; health editor Globes Econs. Newspaper, Tel Aviv, 1988-90; exec. Med. Mktg., Rehovot, 1988-97; lectr. Sch. Bus. Adminstrn., Israel, 1990-97. Researcher Sheba Med. Ctr., Tel-Hashomer, Israel, 1993-97. Author: Effective Interpersonal Communication, 1996, Effective Coping with Obstacles, 1997; contbr. articles to profl. jours. Municipality com., Rehovot, 1980; leadership com. Meretz Polit. Party, Tel Aviv, 1997; legis. activist for disabled, 1993—. Mem. Biochemistry Soc. Jewish. Avocations: solo travel, swimming, painting. Home: 4 Hagra St 76310 Rehovot Israel Office: Med Mktg Ltd 23A Weizman St 76282 Rehovot Israel Office Phone: 972-8-9474789. Business E-Mail: pntzpbc@012.net.il.

ZIPP, JOEL FREDERICK, lawyer; b. Shaker Heights, Ohio, Feb. 12, 1948; s. Jack David and Eleanor Adele Zipp; m. Elizabeth Ann Frieden, Dec. 4, 1976; 1 child, Carlyn Leigh. BS, U. Wis., 1970, MS, 1972; JD, Case Western Res. U., 1975. Bar: Ohio 1975, D.C. 1976, U.S. Claims Ct., U.S. Ct. Appeals (D.C. cir.) 1976, U.S. Ct. Appeals (5th cir.) 1979, U.S. Ct. Appeals (11th cir.) 1983, U.S. Supreme Ct. 1983. Trial atty. Fed. Energy Regulation Com., Washington, 1975-79, asst. dir. office of enforcement, 1979; assoc. Morley & Caskin, Washington, 1979-80; ptnr. Morley, Caskin & Generelly, Washington, 1981-98; mng. ptnr. Cameron McKenna LLP, Washington, 1998—2003; gen. counsel, sec. Portland Natural Gas Transmission Sys., 1993-99; ptnr. Bracewell & Giuliani, Washington, 2003—. Notes editor: Energy Law Jour., 1990—98; contbr. articles to profl. jours. Bd. dirs. Westmoreland Children's Ctr., Washington, 1987—88, Found. Energy Law Jour., 1999—2001. Fellow Smithsonian, 1969. Mem.: ABA, Energy Bar Assn. (v.p. 1989—99, past com. chair ann. meeting 1992, 1993, bd. dirs. 1993—96, pres. 2000—01, bd. dirs. 2001—02, mem. nominations com. 2002—05). Jewish. Avocations: skiing, running, bicycling. Home: 9216 Burning Tree Rd Bethesda MD 20817-2251 Office: Bracewell & Giuliani 2000 K St NW Washington DC 20006-1872 Office Phone: 202-828-5811. E-mail: Joel.Zipp@bracewellgiuliani.com.

ZIPPERER, LORRI ANN, librarian, consultant; b. Chgo., Mar. 5, 1959; d. James John and Jo Anne Marie Zipperer; m. Ross Jon Vagnieres, Sept. 9, 1994. BA, So. Ill. U., 1982; MA in Libr. and Info. studies, No. Ill. U., 1991. Reference libr. Dept. of Libr. and Info. Services Am. Med. Assn., Chgo., 1990—94, info. project mgr. Health Law, 1994—96; info. projects mgr. Nat. Patient Safety Found., Chgo., 1996—2000; cybrarian Medscape, N.Y.C., 2000—01; cybrarian and prin. Zipperer Project Mgmt., Evanston, Ill., 2001—. Bd. sec. Ill. chpt. Spl. Libraries Assn., Chgo., 1998—2000, dir. Biomedical and Life Sciences divsn., Wash., 2001—03; editl. bd. mem. Jour. of Med. Libr. Assn., Chgo., 2004—; safe medicine adv. bd. mem. Inst. Safe Medication Practices, Huntingdon Valley, Pa., 2004—; patient safety leadership fellow Health Forum Nat. Patient Safety Found., Health Rsch. and Ednl. Trust, Chgo., 2004—. Author: Special Libraries: A Guide for Management, 1993, 4th edit., 1997; editor: Health Care Almanac, 3d edit., 1998 (Author award, Ill. chpt. Spl. Libraries Assn., 1997), Lessons in Patient Safety; contbr. articles to profl. jours. (HW Wilson award, 1994, 2003). Recipient Cheers award, Inst. Safe Medication Practices, 2005; grantee, Spl. Libraries Assn. Endowment Fund, 2004—05. Mem.: Med. Libr. Assn., Spl. Libr. Assn. Office: Zipperer Project Mgmt 1002 Washington #3E Evanston IL 60202 Office Phone: 847-328-5075. Office Fax: 847-857-4008. Business E-Mail: lorri@zpm1.com.

ZIPPIN, CALVIN, epidemiologist, educator; b. Albany, NY, July 17, 1926; s. Samuel and Jennie (Perkel) Z.; m. Patricia Jayne Schubert, Feb. 9, 1964; children: David Benjamin, Jennifer Dorothy. AB magna cum laude, SUNY, Albany, 1947; ScD, Johns Hopkins U., Balt., 1953. Rsch. asst. Sterling-Winthrop Rsch. Inst., Rensselaer, NY, 1947-50, Johns Hopkins U., Balt., 1950—53; instr. biostats. Sch. Pub. Health, U. Calif., Berkeley, 1953-55; asst. to full rsch. biostatistician Sch. Medicine U. Calif., San Francisco, 1955-67, asst. prof. preventive medicine, 1958-60; post doctoral fellow London Sch. Hygiene and Tropical Medicine, 1964-65; prof. epidemiology U. Calif., San Francisco, 1967-91, prof. emeritus, 1991—. Vis. assoc. prof. stats. Stanford U., 1962; adv. WHO, 1969—; vis rsch. worker Middlesex Hosp. Med. Sch., London, 1975; com. mem. Am. Cancer Soc. and Nat. Cancer Inst., 1956—; faculty adviser Regional Cancer Centre, Trivandrum, India, 1983—; cons., lectr., vis. prof. in field. Co-author book, book chpts.; author or co-author papers primarily on biometry and epidemiology of cancer; editorial advisor Jour. Stats. in Medicine, Boston, 1981-86. Mem., alt. mem. Dem. Ctrl. Com., Marin County, Calif., 1987-96. Recipient Disting. Alumnus award SUNY, Albany, 1969, Lifetime Achievement and Leadership award Nat. Cancer Inst., 2003, also awards, fellowships and grants for work in cancer biometry and epidemiology. Fellow Am. Statis. Assn., Am. Coll. Epidemiology, Royal Statis. Soc. Gt. Britain; mem. Biometric Soc. (Am. internat. coun. 1978-81, pres. Western N.Am. region 1979-80), Calif. Cancer Registrars Assn. (hon.), Internat. Assn. Cancer Registries (hon.), B'nai B'rith (pres. Golden Gate lodge 1970-71, pres. Greater San Francisco unit 21 2003-06, internat. bd. govs. 2005—), Phi Beta Kappa, Sigma Xi, Delta Omega. Office: Univ Calif Dept Epidemiology and Biostats San Francisco CA 94107 Office Phone: 415-514-8000. Business E-Mail: calvin.zippin@ucsf.edu.

ZIPSER, EDWARD J., meteorologist, educator; BS in Aero. Engring., Princeton U., NJ, 1958; MS in Meteorology, Fla. State U., 1960, PhD in Meteorology, 1965. PhD scientist Nat. Ctr. Atmospheric Rsch., Boulder, Colo., 1966—76, sr. scientist, 1976—90; prof. dept. meteorology Tex. A&M U., Coll. Sta., 1990—99; prof., chair dept. meteorology U. Utah, Salt Lake City, 1999—. Chief scientist Global Atmospheric Rsch. Prog. Nat. Ctr. Atmospheric Rsch., 1971—73; project head Global Atmospheric Rsch. Prog. Atlantic Tropical Expt., 1973—77, head mesoscale interactions sect. Convective Storms Divsn., 1981—84, dir. Convective Storms Divsn. and Cloud

Systems Divsn., 1984—87, sci. visitor Mesoscale and Microscale Divsn., 1990—98; rsch. fellow of Natural Environment Rsch. Coun. Imperial Coll., London, 1974—75; Nat. Ctr. Atmospheric Rsch. affiliate vis. prof. dept. atmospheric sci. U. Wash., 1989; head dept. meteorology Tex. A&M U., 1990—95. Contbr. articles to sci. jours.; chair editl. bd.: Bull. of Am. Meteorol. Soc., 2001—. Recipient NOAA award, Outstanding Contbns., 1975; grantee Univ. Space Rsch. Assn. Vis. fellowship, NASA Goddard Space Flight Ctr., 1996—97. Fellow: Am. Meteorol. Soc. (Editor's award 1999, Spl. award, Outstanding Contbns. award, Meisinger award 1971); mem.: Am. Geophys. Union, Sigma Xi. Office: Dept Meteorology U Utah 135 S 1460 E Rm 819 Salt Lake City UT 84112-0110 E-mail: ezipser@met.utah.edu.*

ZIRINSKY, BRUCE R., lawyer; b. NYC, Sept. 6, 1947; BS, Cornell U., 1969; JD, NYU, 1972. Bar: N.Y. 1973, U.S. Dist. Ct. (so. and ea. dists.) N.Y. 1973, U.S. Ct. Appeals (2d cir.) 1974, U.S. Ct. Appeals (1st cir.) 1980, U.S. Ct. Appeals (11th cir.) 1981, U.S. Ct. Appeals (6th cir.), 1995. Mem. Weil, Gotshal & Manges, N.Y.C., 1999; ptnr. & chmn. Fin. Restructuring dept. Cadwalader Wickersham & Taft, N.Y.C. Mem. ABA (sect. corp., banking and bus. law), N.Y. State Bar Assn. (mem. com. bankruptcy laws banking and bus. law sects. 1979—). Office: Cadwalader Wickersham & Taft LLP 1 World Fin Ctr New York NY 10281 Office Phone: 212-504-6404. Office Fax: 212-504-6666. Business E-Mail: bruce.zirinsky@cwt.com.

ZIRINSKY, SUSAN, television producer; m. Joe Peyronnin; 1 child, Zoe. Grad., Am. U. Sr. prodr. CBS Evening News, 1986-91, sr. broadcast prodr., 1991-93; sr. prodr. Eye to Eye, 1993-94, exec. prodr., 1994-95, CBS News, 48 Hours, N.Y.C., 1996—. Sr. prodr. CBS News coverage of 1992 Olympic Winter Games, Campaign '96. Co-recipient Edward R. Murrow award, Overseas Press Club, 2006. Office: CBS News 48 Hours 524 W 57th St Fl 5 New York NY 10019-2924

ZIRKIND, RALPH, physicist, educator; b. NYC, Oct. 20, 1918; s. Isaac and Zicel (Lifshitz) Z.; m. Ann Goldman, Nov. 22, 1940; children: Sheila Zirkind Knopf, Elaine Zirkind Gorman, Edward I. BS, CCNY, 1940; MS, Ill. Inst. Tech., 1945; postgrad., George Washington U., 1946-47; PhD, U. Md., 1950; D.Sc., U. R.I., 1968. Physicist Navy Dept., 1945-50, chief physicist, 1951-60; physicist Oak Ridge Nat. Lab., 1950-51, Advanced Research Project Agy., Washington, 1960-63; prof. Poly. Inst. Bklyn., 1963-70, U. R.I., Kingston, 1970-72, adj. prof., 1972—; physicist Advanced Research Projects Agy., Arlington, Va., 1972-74; cons. Advanced Rsch. Projects Agy., Arlington, Va., 1974—. Lectr. U. Md., 1947-48, 48-50, George Washington U., 1952-53, U. Mich., 1964, 66, Haifa Inst. Tech., 1971; cons. ACDA, Jet Propulsion Lab. Calif. Inst. Tech.; cons. to industry, 1974—. Contbg. author: Jet Propulsion Series, 1952, FAR Infrared Properties of Materials, 1968, NAS Study Biology and Exploration of Mars, 1966; editor: Electromagnetic Sensing of Earth, 1967, Proc. SPIE-Developments in Electronic Imaging Techniques, vol. 32, 1972; mem. editl. bd. Infrared Physics, 1963—; contbr. articles profl. jours. Recipient Meritorious Civilian Svc. award Navy Dept., 1957; Meritorious Civilian Svc. award Dept. Def., 1970; Outstanding Educator of Am. medal, 1972; Maj. Contbn. award BMDO/AIAA, 1994; Spl. Lifetime Achievement Award for Pioneering Work in Sensors, SPIE, 2002. Mem. Am. Phys. Soc., N.Y. Acad. Scis., Sigma Xi, Sigma Pi Sigma (SPIE Aerosense Lifetime Achievement award 2002), Eta Kappa Nu. Home: 820 Hillsboro Dr Silver Spring MD 20902-3202 Office: 4100 North Fairfax Dr Ste 910 Arlington VA 22203 Business E-Mail: rzirkind@stassociates.com.

ZIRKLE, WARREN E., lawyer; b. Harrisonburg, Va., 1943; BS, Va. Poly. Inst. and State U., Blacksburg, 1965; JD, U. Va., Charlottesville, 1975. Bar: Va. 1975, US Dist. Ct. Ea. & We. Districts Va. 1976, US Supreme Ct. 1980, US Ct. Appeals 11th Cir. 1987, US Ct. Appeals 4th Cir. 1989, US Ct. Appeals Fed. Cir. 1998, US Ct. Appeals 3rd Cir. 2004. Ptnr. McGuireWoods LLP, Richmond, Va., McLean, Va., 2000—, now chair firm comml. litig. dept., mem. bd. partners, 1995—2001. Adj. prof. law U. Richmond, 1993—94. Office: McGuireWoods LLP Ste 1800 1750 Tysons Blvd Mc Lean VA 22102-4215 Office Phone: 703-712-5371. Office Fax: 703-712-5262. Business E-Mail: wzirkle@mcguirewoods.com.

ZIRNHELD, JENNIFER L., engineering educator, researcher; b. Buffalo, May 12, 1969; d. Mark D. McMahon and Carolyn V. Pfeil; m. Mark J. Zirnheld, May 22, 1993. BSEE, SUNY, Buffalo, 1993, MS, 1997, PhD, 2004. Lectr. SUNY, Buffalo, 1997—2004; co-prin., investigator, dep. dir. Energy Systems Inst., 2005—. Contbr. articles to profl. jours. Recipient Milton Plesur award, U. Buffalo Student Assn., 2000—01; Bergquist Doctoral fellow, SUNY, Buffalo, 1998—2002, James Clerk Maxwell Primex doctoral fellow, 2000—01. Mem.: IEEE (treas. 2000, newsletter editor 2000—, chair 2001—02), Am. Phys. Soc., Am. Soc. Engring. Edn., Eta Kappa Nu. Office: U Buffalo 312 Bonner Hall Buffalo NY 14260 Business E-Mail: zirnheld@eng.buffalo.edu.

ZISCHKE, DOUGLAS ARTHUR, foreign service officer; b. Sioux Falls, S.D., May 24, 1929; s. Arthur Gustav and Alice Minetta (Wedeking) Z.; m. Janice Mae Kuehnemann, June 8, 1957; children: Mark Douglas, Deborah Jan, Todd Lincoln. BS in Journalism cum laude, U. Wis., 1951, MS, 1952. Joined U.S. Fgn. Svc., 1957; tech. editor Forest Svc., Madison, 1955-57; asst. info. officer USIS, Montevideo, Uruguay, 1957-58, La Paz, Bolivia, 1958-59; asst. cultural affairs officer, br. pub. affairs officer Mexico, 1960-65; info. specialist Washington, 1965-67; pub. affairs officer Tegucigalpa, Honduras, 1967-69; dep. pub. affairs officer Buenos Aires, 1969-71; pub. affairs officer Guatemala City, Guatemala, 1971—74; assigned to U.S. Army War Coll. 1974-75; dep. pub. affairs officer Am. embassy Tehran, Iran, 1975-78; cultural coord. USICA, Washington, 1979-80; internat. cons., 1980-86; fgn. affairs advisor State Dept., 1986-98. Author monograph. Bd. dirs. Boy Scouts Am; dir. Lutheran Ch. 1973-74. Served with Signal Corps, AUS, 1953-55. Mem. Diplomatic and Consular Officers Ret.

ZISCHKE, MICHAEL HERMAN, lawyer; b. Yokahama, Japan, Dec. 30, 1954; s. Peter H. and Alice Marian (Oliver) Z.; children: Julia Carol, Jessica Marian. BA magna cum laude, Dartmouth Coll., 1977; JD, U. Calif., Berkeley, 1982. Bar: Calif. 1982. Legis. asst. Congressman Bob Carr, Washington, 1977-79; assoc. Miller, Starr & Regalia, Oakland, Calif., 1982-87, McCutchen, Doyle, Brown & Enersen, Walnut Creek, Calif., 1987-91, counsel, 1991-93; ptnr. Landels Ripley & Diamond LLP, San Francisco, 1993—2000, Morrison & Foerster LLP, San Francisco, 2000—, co-chmn. land use and environ. law practice group, 2003—. Lectr. land use issues U. Calif. Extension, 1988—, U. Calif. Davis Sch. Law, 1993-2001, U. Southern Calif. Law Sch., 1995—. Co-author: Land Use Initiatives and Referenda in California, 1990, Practice Pursuant to the California Environmental Quality Act, 1993, 2d edit., 2006; contbr. articles to profl. jours. Dir. Boys & Girls Clubs Oakland, 2000—. Mem. ABA, Calif. State Bar Assn. (exec. com. environ. law sect., 1995-2004), Calif. Bldg. Industry Assn. (select com. on industry litigation), Bar Assn. San Francisco. Democrat. Episcopalian. Office: Morrison & Foerster LLP 425 Market St San Francisco CA 94105-2482 Office Phone: 415-268-6718. Office Fax: 415-276-7286. Business E-Mail: mzischke@mofo.com.

ZISKIN, LAURA, television producer, film producer; Grad., USC, 1973. Asst. to Jon Peters; co-founder Frogwood Films, 1984; founder, pres. Fox 2000, Beverly Hills, Calif., 1994—99; founder Laura Ziskin Productions, 1999—. Films include: (assoc. prodr.) Eyes of Laura Mars, 1978; (prodr.) Murphy's Romance, 1985, No Way Out, 1987, D.O.A., 1988, Everybody's An American, 1988, The Rescue, 1988, What About Bob?, 1991, The Doctor, 1991, Hero, 1992, To Die For, 1995, Spider-Man, 2002, Spider-Man 2, 2004; (exec. prodr.) Pretty Woman, 1990, As Good As it Gets, 1997; (TV) Fail Safe, 2000, Dinner with Friends, 2001, 74th Ann. Acad. awards, 2002, Tarzan, 2003, The Spaces, 2003., prodr.(TV) How I Learned to Drive, 2001. Named one of 100 Most Powerful Women in Entertainment, Hollywood Reporter, 2004, 2005. Office: Laura Ziskin Prodns 10201 W Washington Blvd Astaire Bldg Culver City CA 90232 Office Phone: 310-244-7373. Office Fax: 310-244-0073.*

ZISKIND, ANDREW A., cardiologist, medical educator, health facility administrator; b. Boston, Aug. 31, 1958; s. Alan and Barbara (Schiff) Z.; m. Geraldynn Landry, May 16, 1990; children: Katherine, Rebecca. AB, Bowdoin Coll., 1980; MD, U. Pa., 1984; MBA, Loyola Coll. Md., 1999. Diplomate Am. Bd. Cardiology, Am. Bd. Internal Medicine. Intern, resident Mass. Gen. Hosp., Boston, 1984-87, fellow in cardiology, 1987-90; asst. prof. medicine U. Md., Balt., 1990-96, assoc. prof., 1996-99, U. Washington, 1999—2005, assoc. dean clin. affairs/assoc. v.p. clin specialty program, 1999—2005; pres. Barnes-Jewish Hosp., St. Louis, 2005—; prof. Washington U. Sch. Medicine, St. Louis, Dir. cardiac catheterization lab. U. Md., 1990-95, dir. cardiac network, 1995-99, v.p. clin. svcs. Univ. Care, 1997-99. Fellow Am. Coll. Cardiology, Am. Coll. Physicians, Soc. Cardiac Angiography & Interventions; mem. Am. Coll. Physicians Execs., Am. Fedn. Clin. Rsch. Avocation: woodworking. Office: Barnes-Jewish Hosp 1 Barnes-Jewish Hosp Plaza Saint Louis MO 63110 Office Phone: 314-362-5400.

ZISMAN, BARRY STUART, lawyer; b. N.Y.C., Sept. 18, 1937; s. Harry and Florence Rita (Tucker) Z.; m. Maureen Frances Brumond, Dec. 30, 1979; children: Michael Glenn, Marlene Ann. AB, Columbia U., 1958, JD, 1961. Bar: D.C. 1962, N.Y. 1965, Tex. 1986, U.S. Dist. Ct. (ea. and so. dists.) N.Y. 1967, U.S. Ct. Appeals (D.C. cir.) 1967, U.S. Dist. Ct. (no. and so. dists.) Tex. 1986, U.S. Ct. Appeals (5th cir.) 1988, U.S. Supreme Ct. 1987. With U.S. Govt., 1962-66; pvt. practice Syosset, N.Y., 1966-71; sr. counsel CBS Inc., N.Y.C., 1972-75; asst. gen. counsel, asst. sec. M. Lowenstein & Sons, N.Y.C., 1975 79; gen. counsel Grumman Allied Indsl. Inc., Bethpage, N.Y., 1979-83; asst. gen. counsel Grumman Corp., Bethpage, 1982-83; sr. atty. FDIC, Dallas, 1984-87; of counsel Arter & Hadden, Dallas, 1987-88, ptnr., 1988, Winstead, McGuire, Sechrest & Minick, Dallas, 1988-90, Arter & Hadden, Dallas and Washington, 1990-91, Rubinstein & Perry, Dallas, 1991-93, The Zisman Law Firm, P.C., Dallas, 1993—. Advisor in field; vice-chmn. Assn. of Bank and Thrift Receivership Coun. Editor and author: Banks and Thrifts: Government Enforcement and Receivership Law, 1991. With U.S. Army, 1961-62. Home: 905 Murl Dr Irving TX 75062-4441 Office: 1412 Main St Fl 23 Dallas TX 75202 Office Phone: 972-659-0703. Personal E-mail: zislaw@aol.com.

ZISSER, MARTIN SHEPHERD, fur apparel manufacturer, investor, securities trader; b. Bklyn., Jan. 30, 1942; s. Irving and Jean (Shepherd) Z. Student, NYU, 1960-63. Wall St. invester and trader. Sec. treas. Fur Dressers Union Local 2A, N.Y.C., 1989-92; v.p. UFCW Local 174, N.Y.C., 1992—. Recipient Ofcl. Brit. Coat of Arms, Queen Elizabeth II. Mem. Internat. Soc. Philosophical Enquiry, Mensa. Republican. Jewish. Avocations: study of history, politics, world current events, economics. Home: 2801 Emmons Ave Apt 3F Brooklyn NY 11235-2210 Personal E-mail: stargate18000@aol.com.

ZITO, BARRY, professional baseball player; b. Las Vegas, Nev., May 13, 1978; Student, U. Calif., Santa Barbara, Pierce Jr. Coll., U. So. Calif. Pitcher Oakland Athletics, 2000—. Named to, Am. League All-Star team, 2002, 2003; recipient Am. League Cy Young award, 2002. Achievements include has appeared on TV shows including JAG, ArliS$, and the Chris Isaak Show; led American League in Wins, 2002. Office: Oakland Athletics Network Assocs Coliseum 7000 Coliseum Way Oakland CA 94621*

ZITO, CHRISTOPHER RICHARD, molecular biologist, biochemist; b. New Haven, CTConn., Nov. 21, 1975; s. Andrew Richard and Ann (Panico) Zito. BS in Biol. Sci., Albertus Magnus Coll., New Haven, 1997; MS in Cellular and Molecular Biology, U.of New Haven, 1998; postgrad., Wesleyan U., Middletown. Assoc. rsch. scientist Dept. Pharmacology, Yale U., New Haven, 1994—97; ind. rsch. scientist Dept. Ob-Gyn., Yale U., 1997—99; rsch. scientist, tchg. asst. Wesleyan U., Middletown, Conn., 1999—. Molecular biology cons. Yale U., New Haven, 1997—, radiation safety lab. cons., 2000—, hazardous waste lab. instr., 2000—. Contbr. articles to sci. jours. Vol. North Haven Red Cross. Election Com., North Haven, 1994—2000; bd. dirs. St. Tarsius Squire Cir., New Haven, 1994—97, Albertus Magnus Coll. Campus Min., New Haven, 1994—97; counselor K.C., Hamden, 1994—97. Recipient The June Veckerelli Mem.l Award for Academic Excellence in Sci., Albertus Magnus Coll., 1997, Annual Acad. Rsch. Assistantship award, U. of New Haven, 1997—98; fellow Annual Doctoral Acad. Rsch. fellow, Wesleyan U./NIH, 1999—2001. Mem.: K.C. (3rd Degree Member 1994—, Squire Circle Counselor of the Year Award 1996 & 1997). Roman Catholic. Avocations: basketball, classical and contemporary piano, acoustic guitar, computers. Office: Wesleyan Univ Lawn Ave Middletown CT 06459 Home: 3 Virginia Rd North Haven CT 06473-2729 Personal E-mail: crzito@iconn.net. Business E-Mail: czito@wesleyan.edu.

ZITO, FRANK R., lawyer, accountant; b. Haverhill, Mass., Mar. 14, 1946; s. Dan and Anne (Grieco) Z.; m. Carol S. Tandy, Sept. 19, 1976. BS, U. Mass., 1969; JD, Suffolk Law Sch., 1972; LLM, NYU, 1973. Bar: Mass. 1972, U.S. Supreme Ct. 1982, U.S. Tax Ct. 1984. Gen. mgr. Sun Ray Baking Co., 1973-79; atty. mem. Tofias P.C., Cambridge, Mass., 1979—. Contbr. articles to law jour. Mem. ABA (mem. forum com. 1982-84), Mass. Bar Assn., Am. Inst. CPA's, Mass Soc. CPA's. Home: 8 Livermore Rd Belmont MA 02478-4516 Office Phone: 617-761-0510. Business E-Mail: fzito@tofias.com.

ZITO, NICK, horse trainer, breeder; b. NY, Feb. 6, 1948; m. Kim Zito; 2 children from previous marriage. Former asst. trainer John Campo, LeRoy Jolley; horse trainer. Recipient C.V. Whitney Award, the New York Turf Writers Assoc., 1994, 2000. Achievements include trained winning horse Strike Gold, Kentucky Derby, 1991, Go for Gin, 1994, Louis Quatorze, Pimlico Stakes, 1996, Birdstone, Belmont Stakes, 2004; training for George Steinbrenner, Rick Pitino, Marylou Whitney; being elected to horse racing Hall of Fame, 2005. Office: NTRA 2525 Harrodsburg Rd Lexington KY 40504

ZITO, ROBERT JOHN AMADEUS, lawyer; b. N.Y.C., Sept. 11, 1956; s. Joseph J. and Phyllis A. (Esposito) Z.; m. Dana Sabin Cole, July 4, 1992. BA, Tulane U., 1978; JD, N.Y. Law Sch., 1981. Bar: N.Y. 1985, U.S. Dist. Ct. (so. and ea. dists.) N.Y. 1983, (no. dist.) 1993, U.S. Ct. Appeals (2nd Cir.) 1988, U.S. Ct. Appeals (9th Cir.) 2000, U.S. Tax Ct. 1984, U.S. Supreme Ct. 1988; ordained deacon Epis. Ch. of U.S., 2001; parish deacon, Ch. of the Incarnation, N.Y.C. Assoc. LaRossa Cooper, N.Y.C., 1981-85, Spengler Carlson, N.Y.C., 1985-90; ptnr. Zito & Assocs., N.Y.C., 1990-91, Sullivan Donovan, N.Y.C., 1991-93, Tanner Propp & Farber, N.Y.C., 1993—98, Fischbein Badillo Wagner Harding, N.Y.C., 1998—2003, Schiff Hardin, LLP, N.Y.C., 2003—. Lt. col. (ret.) N.Y. Guard, 1991-2001; editl. adv. bd., Episcopal New Yorker. Recipient Bklyn. Achievement award Bklyn. Dems., 1994; N.Y.S. Long and Faithful Svc. award, N.Y.G. Achievement Medal. Mem. ABA, N.Y. Bar Assn., Fed. Bar Coun., Columbian Coun., Ancient Chpt. RAM, Holland Lodge F & AM (past master), Knights Templar, the Most Venerable Order of the Hosp. of St. John of Jerusalem (serving brother), Royal Order Merit Ho. of Savoy (knight). Republican. Episcopalian. Avocations: musical instruments, sailing. Office: Schiff Hardin LLP 623 Fifth Ave New York NY 10022 Office Phone: 212-745-0827. Business E-Mail: rzito@schiffhardin.com.

ZITRIN, ARTHUR, physician; b. Bklyn., Apr. 10, 1918; s. William and Lillian (Elbaum) Z.; m. Charlotte Marker, Oct. 4, 1942; children— Richard Alan, Elizabeth Ann. BS, City Coll. N.Y., 1938; MS, N.Y. U., 1941, MD, 1945; certificate psychoanalytic medicine, Columbia, 1955. Diplomate: Am. Bd. Psychiatry and Neurology. Research fellow animal behavior Am. Museum Natural History, 1939-43; intern King County Hosp., 1945-46; resident psychiatry Bellevue Hosp., 1948-51; instr. physiology Hunter Coll., N.Y.C., 1948-49; mem. faculty N.Y.U. Sch. Medicine, 1949-97, prof. psychiatry, 1967-97, prof. emeritus, 1997—; mem. staff Bellevue Hosp., N.Y.C., 1951—,

dir. psychiatry, 1955-68, N.Y.C. Dept. Hosps., 1962- 64; pvt. practice, 1949—; attending psychiatrist Univ. Hosp., N.Y.C. Cons. psychiatrist Manhattan Va Hosp. Author papers in field. Served to capt. M.C. AUS, 1946- 48. Fellow Am. Psychiat. Assn. (life), N.Y. Acad. Medicine; mem. AMA, N.Y. Soc. Clin. Psychiatry (pres. 1966- 67), Am. Psychoanalytic Assn. (life), Sigma Xi, Alpha Omega Alpha. Home: 56 Ruxton Rd Great Neck NY 11023-1529 Office: 550 1st Ave New York NY 10016-6402

ZITRIN, CHARLOTTE MARKER, psychiatrist, educator, researcher; b. NYC, Sept. 30, 1918; d. Abraham and Regina (Adler) Marker; m. Arthur Zitrin, Oct. 4, 1942; children: Richard Alan, Elizabeth Ann. BA cum laude, NYU, 1939, MD, 1943. Diplomate Am. Bd. Med. Examiners. Intern Kings County Hosp., 1943-44; resident in pediatrics Bellevue Hosp., 1944-45; asst. in pediatrics NYU Bellevue Med. Ctr., 1945-46, from rsch. fellow to asst. prof. pediatrics, 1948-58; attending physician pediatrics L.I. Jewish Hosp., 1958-60; resident in psychiatry Hillside Hosp., 1960-63, clin. asst., 1964-65; supervising psychiatrist Hillside Hosp. Div. L.I. Jewish Med. Ctr., Glen Oaks, N.Y., 1965-94, dir. Behavior Therapy Clinic, 1970-89, dir. Phobia Clinic, 1972-89; retired. Asst. clin. prof. pediatrics NYU-Bellevue Med. Ctr., 1958-60; asst. prof. clin. psychiatry dept. psychiatry and Behavioral Scis. Ctr., SUNY, Stony Brook, 1973-81, clin. assoc. prof., 1982-89; assoc. prof. psychiatry Albert Einstein Coll. Medicine, 1989-94; lectr. in field. Contbr. articles to profl. jours. Fellow Am. Psychiat. Assn., Am. Psychopath. Assn., Nassau County Acad. Med.; mem. AAAS, Assn. Advancement Behavior Therapy, Nassau County Med. Soc., Nassau County Psychiat. Soc., N.Y. Acad. Scis., N.Y. State Med. Soc., Psi Chi.

ZITT, MYRON J., allergist, immunologist; b. NYC, Sept. 15, 1939; s. Arthur and Bertha (Grossman) Z.; m. Jeanne Patricia Schwartz, Oct. 9, 1966; 1 child, Jonathan. BS, Trinity Coll., 1960; MD, SUNY, Bklyn., 1965. Diplomate Am. Bd. Internal Medicine, Am. Bd. Allergy and Immunology. Intern L.I. Coll. Hosp., Bklyn., 1965-66, resident, 1966-68; chief allergy-immunology Queens L.I. Med. Group, North Babylon, NY, 1972—. Dir. adult allergy clinic Nassau County Med. Ctr., East Meadow, N.Y., 1979—; assoc. clin. prof. SUNY, Stony Brook, 1984—. Mem. editl. bd. Annals of Allergy-Asthma-Immunology, 1995—. Maj. USAF, 1969-72. Allergy-Immunology fellow Duke U., Durham, N.C., 1968-69. Fellow Am. Coll. Allergy, Asthma and Immunology (regent 1992-95, v.p. 2002-03, pres.-elect 2003-04, pres. 2004-05), Am. Acad. Allergy, Asthma and Immunology, Nassau Acad. Medicine; mem. Am. Thoracic Soc., L.I. Allergy Soc. (pres. 1989-91). Home: 9 Cypress Dr Woodbury NY 11797-1501 Office: Queens LI Med Group 300 Bay Shore Rd North Babylon NY 11703-2823 E-mail: myron.zitt@gmad.com.

ZITTEL, ANDREA, painter, sculptor; b. Escondido, Calif., 1965; BFA in Painting & Sculpture, San Diego State U., 1988; MFA in Sculpture, RI Sch. Design, 1990. Founder A-Z Adminstrv. Svcs., 1992—; co-organizer High Desert Test Sites. One-man shows include A-Z Living Units, Jack Hanley Gallery, San Francisco, 1993, A-Z Carpet Furniture, Christopher Grimes Gallery, Santa Monica, Calif., 1993, one-woman shows include Purity, Andrea Rosen Gallery, NY, 1993, Comfort, Anthony d'Offay Gallery, London, 1994, Three Living Systems, Carnegie Mus. Art, Pitts., 1994, A series of rotating installations, Andrea Rosen Gallery, NY, 1994, 1995, New Work, San Francisco Mus. Modern Art, 1995, Social Fictions, Barbara & Steven Grossman Gallery, Sch. Mus. Fine Arts, Boston, 1996, New Art 6, Cin. Art Mus., 1996, A-Z Travel Trailer Units, La. Mus. Modern Art, Humlebaek, Denmark, 1996, A-Z Escape Vehicles, Andrea Rosen Gallery, NY, 1996, RAUGH, 1998, A-Z Personal Panels, Sadie Coles HQ, London, 1999, Point of Interest, Public Art Fund, Central Park, NY, 1999, A-Z Time Trials: Free Running Rhythms, Regen Projects, LA, 2000, A-Z Sorting Trays, Susan Inglett, NY, 2001, Andrea Rosen Gallery, NY, 2002, Regen Projects, LA, 2002, Philomene Magers Projekte, Munich, Germany, 2003, Sammlung Goetz, Munich, Germany, 2003, Small Liberties, Whitney Mus. Am. Art, NYC, 2006, exhibited in group shows at Ornament: Ho Hum All Ye Faithfull, John Post Lee Gallery, NY, 1991, One Leading to Another, 303 Gallery, NY, 1992, Writing on the Wall, 1992, Radio Show, Artist's Space, NY, 1992, Add Hot Water, Sandra Gering Gallery, NY, 1993, Don't Look Now, Thread Waxing Space, NY, 1994, Sense & Sensibility, Mus. Modern Art, NY, 1994, Light for the Dark Days of Winter, A/D Gallery, NY, 1995, About Place: Recent Art of Am., Art Inst. Chgo., 1995, Whitney Biennial, Whitney Mus. Am. Art, NY, 1995, 2004, Just Past, Mus. Contemporary Art, LA, 1996, Staging Surrealism, Wexner Ctr. Arts, Ohio, 1997, Patrick Painter Editions, Lehmann-Maupin Gallery, NY, 1997, Travel & Leisure, Paula Cooper Gallery, NY, 1998, Inglenook, Feigen Contemporary, NY, 1998, Art in Pub. Places at Miami Design District, Dacra Companies, Miami Beach, 1999, Elysian Fields, Centre Georges Pompidou, Paris, 2000, Threshold: Invoking Domestic in Contemporary Art, Contemporary Art Ctr. Va., 2000, Drawings, Regen Projects, LA, 2001, Against Design, Mus. Contemporary Art, San Diego, Calif., 2001, Everything Can Be Different, Calif. Ctr. Arts, 2002, Tempo, Mus. Modern Art, NY, 2002, Just Love Me, Bergen Art Mus., 2003, Living Units, Triple Candie, Harlem, NY, 2003, and others. Recipient Distinction Art, San Diego State U., 1988, Award Excellence, RI Sch. Design, 1989, 1990, catalogue support prize, Alfried Krupp Von Bohlen und Halbach Found., 1999, Lucelia Artist Award, Smithsonian Am. Art Mus., 2005; Deutschen Akademischen Austauschdienst Grant, Berlin, Germany, 1995, Coutts Contemporary Arts Found., Zurich, Switzerland, 1996. Mailing: c/o Andrea Rosen Gallery 525 West 24th St New York NY 10011*

ZITTRAIN, JONATHAN L., law educator; b. Pitts., Dec. 24, 1969; s. Lester and Ruth Zittrain. BS, Yale U., 1991; JD, Harvard U., 1995, MPA, 1995. Bar: Pa. 1995, D.C. 1996, U. S. Ct. Appeals (D.C. cir.) 1996. Chief forum adminstr. Compuserve Info. Svcs., 1984—86; editl. columnist Computer Shopper, 1986-90; program mgr. Microsoft Corp., Redmond, Wash., 1990; with U.S. Dept. State, Washington, 1991; staff U.S. Senate Select Com. on Intelligence, Washington, 1992, 94; law clk. U.S. Ct. Appeals, Washington, 1995; exec. dir. Berkman Ctr. for Internet & Society, Harvard Law Sch., Cambridge, Mass., 1997—2000, faculty co-dir., 2000—; lectr. law Harvard Law Sch., Cambridge, Mass., 1997—99, asst. prof., 2000—, Jack N. and Lillian R. Berkman asst. prof. for entrepreneurial legal studies, 2001—; chair internet governance & regulation Oxford U., 2005—. Office: Berkman Ctr for Internet & Society Harvard Law Sch Baker House 1587 Massachusetts Ave Cambridge MA 02138 Business E-Mail: zittrain@law.harvard.edu.

ZITZEWITZ, ERIC, economics professor; s. Paul and Barbara Zitzewitz; m. Christine Foley; children: Zachary, Zoe, Alexander. BA in Econs., Harvard Coll., Cambridge, Mass., 1993; PhD, MIT, Cambridge, 2001. Econ./bus. analyst McKinsey & Co., Washington, 1993—97; asst. prof. econs. Stanford Grad. Sch. Bus., Calif., 2001—. Grad. Rsch. fellowship, NSF, 1998—2001. Office: Stanford Graduate School of Business 518 Memorial Way Stanford CA 94305 Office Phone: 650-724-1860.

ZIVIC, WILLIAM THOMAS, artist, sculptor, art gallery owner; b. Ironwood, Mich., Aug. 31, 1930; s. Stephan and Anna Louise (Herbenar) Z.; m. Carol Jean Engebretsen, July 11, 1959; children: William, John. Mcht. seaman Atlantic and Pacific Oceans, 1948; surveyor Canada-U.S. Oil pipeline, 1949; mcht. seaman Gt. Lakes; iron miner Ironwood, 1958-61; detective Tucson Police Dept., Ariz., 1961-67; now owner Trail Dust Gallery, Tucson. Art lectr. Author: Southwest Memories, 1975; painted ofcl. bicentennial painting for Ariz., 1976; work represented in Pro Rodeo Cowboy Hall of Fame. Bd. dirs. YMCA. Served in U.S. Army, 1950-52, 54-58. Decorated Bronze Star; other awards include 1st place in watercolor Huachuca Art Show, Ariz., 1973-75, Best of Show Internat. Fine Arts Exhbn., palm Springs, Calif., 1977, 1st place in oil painting Wis. Art Festival, 1978, 1st place in bronze sculpture Internat. Fine Arts Exhbn., Tucson, 1980. Mem. Ariz. Cowboy Artists, Huachuca Art Assn., Southwest Profl. Artists, Old Pueblo Artisans, League of Southwest Artists. Roman Catholic. Home: 1778 E Bishop Pl Casa Grande AZ 85222-6324 Office Phone: 520-876-4008.

ZIVIN, NORMAN H., lawyer; b. Chgo., Aug. 10, 1944; s. Alfred E. and Irene (Scher) Z.; m. Lynn F., Dec. 27, 1967; children: Allison, Stephen, Michael. E.M. in Mining Engring., Colo. Sch. Mines, 1965; JD cum laude, Columbia U., 1968. Bar: N.Y. 1968, Ill. 1970, U.S. Supreme Ct. 1975. Assoc. Cooper & Dunham LLP (and predecessor firms), N.Y.C., 1968-70, 71-75, ptnr., 1976—. Mem. Bd. Ethics New Castle (N.Y.), 1974-79. Mem. ABA, Assn. of Bar of City of N.Y., Am. Intellectual Property Law Assn., N.Y. Intellectual Property Law Assn., Soc. Mining Engrs., U.S. Trademark Assn., Fed. Bar Coun., Town Club of Newcastle (pres. 1982-84). Home: Valley Ln Chappaqua NY 10514-2002 Office: Cooper & Dunham LLP Ste 2200 1185 Avenue Of The Americas New York NY 10036-2615 Office Phone: 212-278-0400. E-mail: nzivin@cooperdunham.com.

ZIVOT, ERIC, actor, educator; MFA, Am. Conservatory Theatre, San Francisco, Calif., 1993. Dir. tng. Gymnasia Theatrica, L.A., 1996—2004; prof. theatre and dance Rollins Coll., Winter Park, Fla., 2004—. Master trainer Carolynne Barry Creative, L.A., 2001—04. Recipient award, Can. Arts Coun., 1983. Achievements include development of triune brain method for actor training. Office: Rollins College 1000 Holt Ave Winter Park FL 32789 Office Phone: 407-646-2501. Business E-Mail: ezivot@rollins.edu.

ZIZIC, THOMAS MICHAEL, physician, educator; b. Milw., Dec. 9, 1939; s. Michael Mitchell Zizic and Dorothy (Batas) Ciric; m. Karen Owens, June 15, 1962 (div. Sept. 1967); m. Martha Ann Ardos, Nov. 22, 1967; children: Lara Ann, Kristine Michelle. BS, U. Wis., 1961; MD, Johns Hopkins U., 1965. Intern Johns Hopkins Hosp., Balt., 1965-66, asst. resident, 1966-67, fellow in internal medicine, 1969-71, instr. dept. medicine, 1971-73, asst. prof. medicine, 1971-81, assoc. prof. medicine, 1981—; pres., CEO Bionicare Med. Techs., Inc., 2002—. Pvt. practice, Balt., 1988—; co-dir. Chesapeake Osteoporosis Ctr., Balt., 1988—; dir. med. affairs Murray Electronics, 1993—; v.p. med. quality care Physicians Quality Care, 1995—; pres. U.S. Osteoporosis Network, Inc., 1996—; co-founder, dir. Creative Environ. Solutions, Inc., 1996—; cons. in field. Contbr. numerous articles and abstracts to profl. jours. V.p. Md. chpt. Arthritis Found., Balt., 1976-77; chmn. Md. Commn. on Arthritis and Related Diseases, 1986-90. Fellow Am. Coll. Rheumatology, 1986; Md. Soc. Rheumatic Diseases (pres. 1975-76), D.C. Rheumatism Assn., Balt. City Med. Soc., Johns Hopkins Hosp. Med. Soc., Arthritis Found. (fellow 1971-73, v.p. 1976-77, med. and sci. com. 1977-79, chmn. profl. edn. com. 1977-78, govtl. affairs com. 1979-83), Phi Beta Kappa, Phi Kappa Phi, Phi Eta Sigma. Avocations: skiing, tennis. Office Phone: 410-472-1888. E-mail: drzizic@bionicare.com. Give 100% today. We have only the present. Plan for the future but don't live in the future. The future never comes. We have only today.

ZLAKET, THOMAS ANDREW, lawyer, former state supreme court chief justice; b. May 30, 1941; AB in Polit. Sci., U. Notre Dame, 1962; LLB, U. Ariz., 1965; LLM, U. Va., 2001. Bar: Ariz. 1965, U.S. Dist. Ct. Ariz. 1967, U.S. Ct. Appeals (9th cir.) 1969, Calif. 1976. Atty. Lesher Scruggs Rucker Kimble & Lindamood, Tucson, 1965-68, Maud & Zlaket, 1968-70, Estes Browning Maud and Zlaket, 1970-73, Slutes Estes Zlaket Sakrison & Wasley, 1973-82, Zlaket & Zlaket, 1982-92; judge pro tempore Pima County (Ariz.) Superior Ct., 1983—; justice Ariz. Supreme Ct., 1992—2002, vice chief justice, 1996—97, chief justice, 1997—2002. Fellow Am. Coll. Trial Lawyers, Am. Bar Found., Ariz. Bar Found.; mem. ABA, Pima County Bar Assn., Am. Bd. Trial Advocates, Ariz. Coll. Trial Advocacy, U. Ariz. Law Coll. Assn., Ariz. Law Rev. Assn. Office: 310 S Williams Blvd Ste 170 Tucson AZ 85711 E-mail: tazlaket@qwest.net.

ZLATEVA, MARIA, music educator; b. Stara Zagora, Bulgaria, May 30, 1970; d. Zlati Ivanov Zlatev and Lyuba Dimitorva Zlateva. D in Musical Arts, U. Tex., 2003. Violin tchr. Orpheus Acad. Music, Austin, Tex., 2003—05; violinist Asti Duo, Austin, 2004—. Dir. strings Walla Walla (Wash.) Coll., 2001—03. Named Honorable Citizen of City Riverside, La Sierra U., 1998; recipient Women's Leadership award, 1998, Outstanding Internat. Student award, U. Nev., 1999; scholar, U. Tex. at Austin, 2000-2003. Mem.: Am. String Tchrs. Assn., Coll. Music Soc., Chamber Music Am. Home: 11811 Millwright Pkwy Austin TX 78750 Office: Asti Duo 11811 Millwright Pkwy Austin TX 78750 Office Phone: 512-787-4346. Business E-Mail: mzlatevabg@yahoo.com.

ZLATOFF-MIRSKY, EVERETT IGOR, violinist; b. Evanston, Ill., Dec. 29, 1937; s. Alexander Igor and Evelyn Ola (Hill) Z.-M.; m. Janet Dalbey, Jan. 28, 1976; children from previous marriage— Tania, Laura. B.Mus., Chgo. Mus. Coll., Roosevelt U., 1960, M.Mus., 1961. Mem. faculty dept. music Roosevelt U., Chgo., 1961-66. Founding mem., violinist, violist Music of the Baroque, 1971-2003. Violinist orch. Lyric Opera of Chgo., 1974-2003; concert master, pers. mgr. 1974-2003, violinist, soloist, Contemporary Chamber Players U. Chog., 1964-82, solo violinist, Bach Soc., 1966-83; violist, violinist, Lexington String Quartet, 1966-81; rec. artist numerous recs., radio-TV and films; solo violinist appearing throughout U.S. Recipient Olive Ditson award Franklin Honor Soc., 1961 Mem. Nat. Acad. Rec. Arts and Scis. Republican. Roman Catholic. Home: 1600 Old Pecos Trail Santa Fe NM 87505 E-mail: jdzm@aol.com.

ZLATOS, CHRISTY, librarian; b. Decatur, Ill., June 4, 1956; d. Rudolph and Iva Dene Ebersole Zlatos; m. Michael Boyd Nelson, Dec. 22, 1995. AB, U. Ill., 1978, MSLS, 1979. Reference libr. U. So. Ind., Evansville, 1980-82, Auburn (Ala.) U., 1983-89, Northeastern U., Boston, 1989-91, Wash. State U., Pullman 1991-92, head edn. libr. 1992-95, head media materials svcs., 1995—. Book rev. editor Jour. Acad. Librarianship, 1995—. Editor: Coming of Age in Reference Services; A Case History of Washington State University Libraries, 1999. Mem. ALA (various coms.). Republican. Episcopalian. Avocation: collecting american pottery. Office: Wash State U Libraries New Library Rm 1 Pullman WA 99164-0001

ZLOCH, WILLIAM J., federal judge; b. Ft. Lauderdale, Fla., 1944; BA, U. Notre Dame, 1966; JD, U. Notre Dame Law Sch., 1974. Pvt. practice, Ft. Lauderdale, 1974—85; judge US Dist. Ct. (So. Dist.) Fla., Ft. Lauderdale, 1985—, chief judge. Lt. USN, 1967—69. Office: US Dist Ct 299 E Broward Blvd Fort Lauderdale FL 33301-1944

ZLOMEK, ELIZABETH A., customer service/business processes specialist; b. Upstate, NY, 1957; d. Frederick and Muriel Zlomek. BA in Polit. Sci, Secondary Edn., SUNY, Cortland, 1980. Legis. asst. U.S. Ho. Reps., Washington, 1979-80; customer svc. mgr. Jordan Kitts Music, College Park, Md., 1980-87; sales mgr. Reines R.V. Ctr., Fairfax, Va., 1987-89; dir. customer svc. Stickley Furniture, Syracuse, N.Y., 1992-2000, sr. bus. analyst, 2000—. Cons. Elanzek Svcs., Silver Spring, Md., 1987—92. Vol. Children's Miracle Network, Syracuse, 1997—. Leukemia Soc. Am., Camp Good Days and Spl. Times; vol. reader Vols. for Visually Handicapped, Montgomery County, Md., 1979-92. Mem. Jr. League of Syracuse (bd. dirs. 1993-95, fin. chair 1996, treas. 1st Annual Holiday Shoppes Fundraiser), Nat. Assn. of Customer Svc. Mgrs., NAFE, Piano Technicians Guild (assoc.), Pi Sigma Alpha. Avocations: travel, reading, music, computers, needlecrafts. Office: L & JG Stickley Furniture 1 Stickley Dr Manlius NY 13104-2484 Office Phone: 315-682-5500.

ZLOTOLOW-STAMBLER, ERNEST, real estate executive, architectural executive; come to US, 1981; m. Laura I. Chotti; children: Dan A., Vanessa E., Paul J. BAS, Buenos Aires Nat. Coll., 1960; license architecture, U. Buenos Aires, 1968. Lic. architect; registered profl. engr., Argentina. Prof. U. Buenos Aires, 1964-81; mng. ptnr. Zlotolow, Chotti & Assocs., Buenos Aires, 1968-81; pres. Imparsa Corp., Buenos Aires, 1970-86; mng. ptnr. Archeting Assocs., Buenos Aires, 1970-81; prof. U. Belgrano, Buenos Aires, 1976-80; v.p. Playa de la Gruta Corp., Montevideo, Uruguay, 1978-79; project mgr. Kravco Corp., King of Prussia, Pa., 1981-84; chmn. Zlotolow-Evantash-Reider Ltd., Southeastern, Pa., 1985—2002; pres. Meridian Real Corp., Wayne, Pa., 1985—, U.S.E.S. Corp., 1999—. Gen: ptnr., One Jenkintown (Pa.) Sta. Assoc., 1984-89. Contbr. articles to profl. publ. Paul Harris fellow,

1987, Guy Gundaker fellow, 1990, Paul Vaughan fellow, 1991. Mem. AIA (assoc.), Urban Land Inst., Nat. Trust Historic Preservation, Pa. Soc. Architects, Sociedad Ctrl. Arquitectos (Argentina), Rotary (pres. 1990-91, chmn. charitable found. 1990-91, chmn. cmty. svc. 1998-2003), Gundaker Found. (bd. dir. 1992-1999, v.p. 1996-97, pres. 1997-98); Green Hills Landowners Assn. (bd. dir. 1994-97). Avocations: macroeconomics, computer science, cmty. svc. Office: Meridian Real Corp PO Box 589 Southeastern PA 19399-0589

**ZLOTOWSKI, MARTIN,** psychologist; b. Lodz, Poland, Aug. 10, 1934; s. Pawel and Helen Zlotowski; m. Judith Ann Lifschitz, May 17, 1974; children: David, Steven, Laura. BA, NYU, 1955; MA, Mich. State U., 1958, PhD, 1960. Rsch. assoc. Grad. Sch. Pub. Health U. Pitts., 1960-61; rsch. assoc., lectr. Boston U., 1961-62; staff psychologist VA Hosp., Coatesville, Pa., 1962-65, unit chief, 1965-73; clin. dir. St. Mary Providence, 1966-70; assoc. prof. spl. edn. West Chester (Pa.) U., 1973—2003. Grad. coord., 1987-2000; dir. Counseling Assocs., Paoli, Pa., 1973-85, chief., 1985—. Pres. Chester County Family Acad., 1999-2002, bd. trustees 2002-04; v.p. Victim Witness Svcs. Chester County, 1976-79. Fellow: Phila. Psychol. Assn., Phila. Soc. Clin. Psychologists (pres. 1978—79, sec. human svcs. ctr. 1982), Am. Orthopsychiat. Assn.; mem.: APA, Pa. Fedn. Coun. Exceptional Children (pres. Pa. divsn. behavior disorders 2000—04). Democrat. Jewish. Home: 241 Torrey Pine Ct West Chester PA 19380 Office Phone: 610-647-8270. E-mail: MZlotowski@aol.com.

**ZNAMIEROWSKI, DAVID M,** investment company executive; BA, Colby Coll.; MBA, Amos Tuck Sch. of Bus., Dartmouth Coll. V.p. corp. fin. Salomon Bros., 1986—91; portfolio mgr., v.p. investment strategy and policy Aetna Life & Casulty Co., 1991—96; dir., risk mgmt. strategy Hartford Life, Conn., 1996—97, sr. v.p., dir., life investment strategy Conn., 1997—99, sr. v.p., chief investment officer Conn., 1999—2001; chief investment officer The Hartford Fin. Svcs. Group, Inc., Conn., 2001—; pres. Hartford Investment Mgmt. Co. (HIMCO), Conn., 2001—. Mem. bd. govs. Investment Co. Inst., Am. Coun. of Life Ins.; dir. pres. Hartford sponsored mutual funds. Office: Hartford Fin Svc Group Inc Hartford Plaza 690 Asylum Ave Hartford CT 06115

**ZOBEL, RYA WEICKERT,** federal judge; b. Germany, Dec. 18, 1931; AB, Radcliffe Coll., 1953; LLB, Harvard U., 1956. Bar: Mass. 1956, U.S. Dist. Ct. Mass., 1956, U.S. Ct. Appeals (1st cir.) 1967. Assoc. Hill & Barlow, Boston, 1967-73, Goodwin, Procter & Hoar, Boston, 1973-76, ptnr., 1976-79; judge U.S. Dist. Ct. Mass., Boston, 1979—; dir. Fed. Jud. Ctr., Washington, 1995-99. Mem. Boston Bar Assn., Am. Bar Found., Mass. Bar Assn., Am. Law Inst. Office: US District Ct 1 Courthouse Way Boston MA 02210-3002

**ZOBRIST, BENEDICT KARL,** library director, historian; b. Moline, Ill., Aug. 21, 1921; s. Benedict and Lila Agnas (Colson) Z.; m. Donna Mae Anderson, Oct. 23, 1948; children: Benedict Karl II, Markham Lee, Erik Christian. AB, Augustana Coll., Rock Island, Ill., 1946; postgrad., Stanford U., 1946-47; MA, Northwestern U., 1948, PhD, 1953; postgrad., U. Ill., 1961, Tunghai U., Taiwan, 1962, Columbia U., 1962-63, Fed. Exec. Inst., Charlottesville, Va., 1974, Hebrew U., Israel, 1978; LHD, Avila Coll., 1995. Manuscript specialist in recent Am. history Library of Congress, Washington, 1952-53; asst. reference librarian Newberry Library, Chgo., 1953-54; command historian Ordnance Weapons Command, Rock Island Arsenal, 1954-60; prof. history, chmn. dept. Augustana Coll., 1960-69, asst. dean faculty, 1964-69, assoc. dean. dir. grad. studies, 1969; asst. dir. Harry S. Truman Libr., Independence, Mo., 1969-71, dir., 1971-94. Exec. sec. Harry S. Truman Inst., Independence, 1971-94; mem. steering com. Harry S. Truman Statue Com., Independence, 1973-76; dir., regent Harry S. Truman Good Neighbor Award Found., 1974—; mem. Independence Truman Award Commn., 1975-94, Mo. Hist. Records Adv. Bd., 1978—; adj. prof. history U. Mo.-Kansas City, 1975-94, Ottawa U., Kansas City, 1977-94, U. Mo. St. Louis, 1987-94; chmn. Independence Commn. Bicentennial of U.S. Constitution, 1987, Uptown Independence, Inc., 1989-94; mem. adv. coun. Truman Little White House State Historic Site, Key West, Fla., 1987-94. Contbr. articles, revs. to profl. jours. Trustee Heritage League of Greater Kansas City, 1981—, Liberty Meml. Assn., Kansas City, Mo., 1990-2002, Black Archives Mid-Am., Inc., Kansas City, 1992-94; mem. Truman Nat. Centennial Com., 1982-84. Served with AUS, 1942-46. Recipient Outstanding Alumni Achievement award Augustana Coll., 1975, Bronze Good Citizenship medal Kans. SAR, 1986, People's Choice award Independence (Mo.) Neighborhood Councils, 1987, Mid-Am. Regional Council award for contbns. to met. community, 1987, Citizen Achievement award Black Archives of Mid-Am., 1988, Silver Good Citizenship medal Mo. SAR, 1988, Special Recognition award City of Independence, 1988, Outstanding Civic Leader in Independence, 1989, Gold Medal of Honor DAR, 1990, Spl. Commendation award Nat. Park Svc., 1993; named World Citizen of Yr. Kans. City Mayor's UN Day Com., 1994; named to Hall of Honor Moline (Ill.) HS, 2005. Mem. AAUP, Am. Hist. Assn., Jackson County (Mo.) Hist. Soc. (v.p. 1972-82, 93-95), Orgn. Am. Historians, Assn. Asian Studies, Am. Assn. State, Local History, Soc. Am. Archivists, U.S. Power Squadron, Am. Legion, La Societe des 40 Hommes et 8 Chevaux, VFW. Home: 71B T St Lake Lotawana MO 64086-9728

**ZOBRIST, GEORGE WINSTON,** computer scientist, educator; b. Highland, Ill., Feb. 13, 1934; s. George H. and Lillie C. (Augustin) Z.; m. Freida Groverlyn Rich, Mar. 29, 1955; children: Barbara Jayne, George William, Jean Anne. BS, U. Mo., 1958, PhD, 1965; MS, Wichita State U., 1961. Registered profl. engr., Mo., Fla. Electronic scientist U.S. Naval Ordnance Test Sta., China Lake, Calif., 1958-59; rsch. engr. Boeing Co., Wichita, 1959-60; instr. Wichita State U., 1960-61; assoc. prof. U. Mo., Columbia, 1961-69, U. So. Fla., Tampa, 1969-70; chmn. elec. engring. dept. U. Miami, Coral Gables, Fla., 1970-71; prof. U. South Fla., Tampa, 1971-72, 73-76; prof., chmn. dept. elec. engring. U. Toledo, 1976-79; dir. computer sci. and engring. Samborn, Steketee, Otis, Evans, Inc., Toledo, 1979-82; prof. computer sci. Grad. Engring. Ctr. U. Mo., St. Louis, 1982-85, prof. computer sci. Rolla, 1985-99, chmn. dept., 1994-99, prof. emeritus, 1999—. Rsch. prof. U. Edinburgh, Scotland, 1972-73; lectr. U. Western Cape, South Africa, 1995 summer; cons. Wilcox Electric Co., Bendix Corp., both Kansas City, Mo., 1966-68, ICC, Miami, 1970-71, Def. Comm. Agy., Washington, 1971, 72, U.S. Naval Rsch. Labs., Washington, 1971, Med. Svc. Bur., Miami, 1970-71, NASA, Kennedy Space Ctr., Fla., 1973-76, 88, 89, 93, 94, Prestolite Corp., Toledo, 1977-79, IBM, Lexington, Ky., 1983-86, Wright-Patterson AFB, Ohio, 1986, PAFB, Fla., 1987, McDonnell Douglas, Mo., 1989, Digital Systems Cons., Mo., 1989, Oak Ridge Nat. Labs., 1992. Author: Network Computer Analysis, 1969, Progress in Computer Aided VLSI Design, 1988-90; editor Internat. Jour. Computer Aided VLSI Design, 1989-91, Object Oriented Simulation IEEE Press, 1996, Computer Sci. and Computer Engring. Monograph series, 1989-91, Internat. Jour. Computer Simulation, 1990-96, VLSI Design, 1992-2002; editor IEEE Potentials Mag., 1996-99, 2003; assoc. editor, 1984-96, 99—; contbr. articles to profl. jours. Served with USAF, 1951-55. Named Young Engr. of Yr. ctrl. chpt. Mo. Soc. Profl. Engrs., 1967; NSF summer fellow, 1962, 64; NASA, IBM, DOE, UES/AFOSR, McDonnell Douglas rsch. grantee, 1967-88. Fellow IEEE (life, mem. IEEE Press editl. bd. 1998—); mem. Am. Legion, Rotary, Sigma Xi, Tau Beta Pi, Phi Eta Sigma, Eta Kappa Nu, Pi Mu Epsilon, Upsilon Pi Epsilon. Home: 12030 Country Club Dr Rolla MO 65401-7469 Office: U Mo Rolla Dept Compuer Sci 1870 Miner Cir Rolla MO 65409-0001 E-mail: zobrist@umr.edu.

**ZOCCHI, LOUIS JOSEPH,** product designer, game company executive; b. Chgo., Feb. 16, 1935; s. Louis Alexander and Martha (Adams) Z.; m. Elissa Lorelei Scott, June 8, 1959 (Sept. 1976); children: David, Suzanne, LaRee, Lisa; m. Sharon Annette Olson, May 25, 1985; 1 child, Heidi Elson. Cert. air traffic controller, 1955, air traffic control instr., 1964. Commd. USAF, 1954, advanced through grades to tech. sgt., air traffic contr. Offutt AFB, Nebr., 1954, Lincoln AFB, Nebr., 1955-59, Misawa AFB, Japan, 1959-63, Holloman AFB, N.Mex., 1963-64, air traffic control instr. Keesler AFB, Miss., 1964-70, air traffic contr. Mather AFB, Calif., 1970-71, Kimpo AFB, Korea, 1971-72, George AFB, Calif., 1972-73, Biloxi, Miss., 1973-75, ret., 1975; commd. 1st

lt. Miss. State Guard, 1991, advanced through grades to capt., 1993; owner Zocchi Distbrs., Victorville, Calif., 1972—; pres. Gamescience, Inc., Cedarhurst, N.Y., 1974—. Cruise dir. Europa Star cruise ship, 1988; cons. Dupuy Inst., 1995. Designer (games) Battle of Britain, 1968, Star Fleet Battle Manual, 1977 (Gamesday award 1981), Basic and Advanced Fighter Combat, 1980 (H.G. Wells award 1981); inventor Zocchihedron 100-sided dice, 1985, inventor 16 sided die, 5-sided die, 3-sided die, 14 Sided Die Major Ala. State Guard, 1997—, col., 2003. Recipient Hobbyist award Metro Detroit Gamers, 1979, Spl. Svc. award Strategists Club, 1982, Charles Roberts Adventure Gaming Hall of Fame award, 1987, Gama Honor of Svc. award 1991, George award Coastcon, 2005. Mem. Game Mfrs. Assn. (chmn. membership com. 1978-84, v.p. 1978-84, bd. dirs. 1985), Internat. Brotherhood Magicians (Order of Merlin 2000), Hobby Industry Assn. (pres. gaming div. 1981), Gulf Coast Jazz Soc. (pres.), Soc. Am. Magicians (pres.). Avocations: playing jazz music, ventriloquism, magic. Home and Office: Gamescience Inc 7604 Newton Dr Biloxi MS 39532-2830 Office Phone: 228-392-4177.

**ZOCHOWSKI, T. ROBERT, JR.,** lawyer; b. New Brunswick, NJ, 1964; BS in Fgn. Svc., Georgetown U., 1986; JD, NYU, 1989. Bar: NJ 1989, NY 1990. Assoc., project fin. group law firm, NYC, 1989—93; assoc. Shearman & Sterling LLP, NYC, 1993—99, ptnr., structured fin., hiring ptnr., 1999—2006; ptnr. Paul, Weiss, Rifkind, Wharton & Garrison LLP, NYC, 2006—. Articles editor NYU Law Rev. Office: Paul Weiss Rifkind Wharton & Garrison LLP 1285 Ave Americas New York NY 10019 E-mail: rzochowski@paulweiss.com.*

**ZOELLER, DAVID LOUIS,** lawyer; b. Indpls., Nov. 26, 1949; s. John Louis and M. Maxine (Snoderly) Z.; m. Wesley Anne Carlton, Aug. 14, 1971; children: Laura Anne, David Carlton. BA, So. Meth. U., 1971; JD, Ind. U., 1974. Bar: Ind. 1974, U.S. Dist. Ct. (so. dist.) Ind. 1974. Asst. sec., legal counsel Stokely-Van Camp Inc., 1974-83; sr. v.p., sec., gen. counsel Merchants Nat. Corp. (now Nat. City Corp.), Cleve., 1983—. Mem. Lawyers Coun. of Fin. Svcs. Roundtable; mem. ABA, Ind. Bar Assn., Indpls. Bar Assn., Ohio Bar Assn., Cleve. Bar Assn., Am. Soc. Corp. Secretaries. Republican. Presbyterian. Office: Merchants Plz Indianapolis IN 46204-3407

**ZOELLER, DONALD J.,** lawyer; b. Queens Village, N.Y., Mar. 18, 1930; s. Henry Adolph and Marion Elizabeth (Brodie) Z.; m. Susan Josephine Campisi, Sept. 3, 1955; children: Paul Joseph, Jean Marie, Diane Marie AB, Fordham Coll., 1951; LL.B., Fordham Sch. Law, N.Y.C., 1958. Bar: N.Y. 1959, D.C. 1967. Law clk. to judge U.S. Dist. Ct. (so. dist.) N.Y., N.Y.C., 1958-59; assoc. Mudge Rose Guthrie Alexander & Ferdon, N.Y.C., 1959-68, ptnr., 1968-95, exec. ptnr. 1991-95, chmn. exec. com., 1995; counsel Carter, Ledyard & Milburn, N.Y.C., 1995-96, ptnr., 1997-98, of counsel, 1999—2003, ret., 2003. Adj. prof. law Fordham U. Law Sch., 1989—; lectr. in field. Contbr. articles to legal publs. 1st lt. U.S. Army, 1951-53, Korea. Mem.: Fed. Bar Coun., Bar Assn. City of NY. Republican. Roman Catholic. Avocations: skiing, swimming, tennis, reading. Office Phone: 516-922-7205. Business E-Mail: dzoeller@optonline.net. *Notable cases include: Matsushita Electric Indsl. Co. Ltd. et al vs. Zenith Radio Corp. et al, 475 U.S. 574, 89 L. edit. 2d 538, 106, s.ct. 1438.*

**ZOELLER, JACK CARL,** finance company executive; b. Buffalo, Feb. 26, 1949; s. Ronald Carl and Margaret Lillian (Wademan) Z.; m. Kathryn Louise Helmke, Apr. 25, 1981; children: Andrew, Alexander, Charles (dec.). BS, U.S. Mil. Acad., 1970; M of Pub. Policy, Harvard U., 1972; M of Letters, Oxford (Eng.) U., 1974. Program budget officer Army Chief of Staff's Office, Pentagon, Washington, 1978-80; v.p. E.F. Hutton & Co., Inc., N.Y.C., 1982; pres. E.F. Hutton Indemnity Group, N.Y.C., 1983-85, Capital Risk Mgmt., Iselin, NJ, 1985-87; exec. v.p., bd. dirs. Comfed Mortgage Co., Lowell, Mass., 1987-88, pres., 1988-91, ComFed Savs. Bank, Lowell, 1990-91; chmn. chief exec. officer ComFed Bancorp., Cambridge, Mass., 1990-95; pres. The Zoeller Group, Washington, 1993-95. Bd. dirs. N.Am. Health Plans, Inc., Amherst, NY, 1995—99; pres. AtlantiCare Risk Mgmt. Corp., 1995—2004; chmn., CEO AtlantiCare, Inc., 1995—2004; pres. N.Am. Health & Life Ins., Barbados, 1996—; vis. rsch. prof. George Washington U., 2005—. Mem. exec. com. Lowell Devel. and Fin. Corp., 1989-91, class gift com. U.S. Mil. Acad., 1990-95; youth sports coach, 1990-96; Am. chmn. 750th Ann. Campaign Univ. Coll., Oxford, Eng., 1998-2002; parent group leader Maret Sch., Washington, 1998-2003; bd. dirs. Am. Assn. Rhodes Scholars, 2004—, Transcommunity FinCorp., Va., 2006-. Served to capt. U.S. Army, 1970—80. Decorated Meritorious Svc. medals; Rhodes scholar, Oxford U., 1972. Mem. West Point Soc. N.Y. (bd. govs. 1985-87), West Point Soc. D.C., Am. Friends Univ Coll. Oxford, Inc. (v.p. 1999—), Fed. Nat. Mortgage Assn. (N.E. regional adv. bd. 1990-91), Assn. Am. Rhodes Scholars (bd. dirs. 2004—), New Eng. Hist. Geneal. Soc., Soc. Mayflower Descs. Home: 2810 31st St NW Washington DC 20008-3523 Personal E-mail: jackzoeller@yahoo.com.

**ZOELLER, MARK L.,** lawyer, printing company executive; b. 1959; AB, U. Chgo., 1981; JD, U. Colo., 1994. Assoc. Rothgerber, Appel, Powers & Johnson, Denver; corp. counsel Mail-Well, Inc. (now Cenveo, Inc.), Englewood, Colo., 1997—2000, asst. gen. counsel, 2000—01, v.p. corp. devel., 2001—03, v.p. gen. counsel, sec., 2003—. Office: Cenveo Inc 8310 S Valley Hwy 400 Englewood CO 80112

**ZOELLICK, ROBERT BRUCE,** diversified financial services company executive, former federal agency administrator; b. Evergreen Park, Ill., July 25, 1953; s. William T. and Gladys Zoellick; m. Sherry Lynn Ferguson, June 28, 1980. BA with honors, Swarthmore Coll., 1975; M in Pub. Policy, JD magna cum laude, Harvard U., 1981; LittD (hon.), St. Joseph's Coll., 2002. Bar: DC 1981. Spl. asst. to asst. atty. gen. criminal divsn. US Dept. Justice, Washington, 1978-79; pvt. law practice, 1981-82; law clk. to Hon. Patricia M. Wald, US Ct. Appeals (DC Cir.), Washington, 1982-83; v.p., asst. to chmn. & CEO Fannie Mae, Washington, 1983-85; from sec., dep. asst. sec. for fin. instns. policy, to counselor to sec. & exec. sec. US Dept. Treasury, Washington, 1985-88; counselor with rank under sec. US Dept. State, Washington, 1989-92, under sec. for econ. & agrl. affairs, 1991-92; dep. chief of staff, asst. to Pres. The White House, Washington, 1992-93; exec. v.p. housing and law Fannie Mae, Washington, 1993-97; Olin prof. nat. security US Naval Acad., 1997-98; pres., CEO Ctr. Strategic & Internat. Studies, Washington, 1998-99; resident fellow German Marshall Fund US, Washington, 1999—2001; rsch. scholar Belfer Ctr. Sci. and Internat. Affairs Harvard U.; U.S. Trade Rep. Exec. Office of the Pres., Washington, 2001—05; dep. sec. US Dept. State, Washington, 2005—06; vice chmn. internat. The Goldman Sachs Group, Inc., NYC, 2006—. Decorated Knight Commdr.'s Cross (for work on German unification, Germany); recipient Alexander Hamilton award US Treasury Dept., 1988, Disting. Svc. award US State Dept, 1992, Disting. Pub. Svc. medal Dept. Def., 2006; fellow Luce Found., Hong Kong, 1980. Mem. DC Bar Assn., Phi Beta Kappa. Office: The Goldman Sachs Group Inc 85 Broad St New York NY 10004 Office Phone: 212-902-1871. Business E-Mail: robert.zoellick@gs.com.

**ZOFFER, H. JEROME,** business educator, dean; b. Pitts., July 23, 1930; s. William and Sarah Leah (Fisher) Z.; m. Maye Rattner, July 19, 1959; children: Gayle Risa, William Michael. BBA, U. Pitts., 1952, MA, 1953, PhD, 1956; CPCU, Am. Inst., Phila., 1954. Sales and mgmt. cons., 1952—60; instr. Sch. Bus. Adminstrn., U. Pitts., 1953—56; asst. prof. Sch. Bus. Adminstrn. U. Pitts., 1956—59, assoc. prof. Sch. Bus. Adminstrn., Grad. Sch. Bus., 1959—66, prof. Sch. Bus. Adminstrn., Grad. Sch. Bus., 1966—, chmn. dept. real estate and ins., 1958—60, dir. spl. studies, 1960—62, asst. dean acad. affairs, 1962—65, assoc. dean for adminstrn., 1965—68, dean Grad. Sch. Bus., 1968—96, dean emeritus, 1996—. Ford Found. fellow in applied math. U. Pa., Phila., 1961—62; mem. visitation com. Am. Assembly Collegiate Schs. of Bus., 1972—2000, mem. stds. com., 1974—78, mem. exec. com., 1975—87, chmn. accreditation rsch. com., 1974—84, v.p. bd. dirs., 1984—85, pres., 1985—86, chmn. Mid. State Evaluation Accrediting Teams, 1967—85. Author: The History of Automobile Liability Insurance Rating: 1900-1958, 1959; also monographs; contbr. articles to profl. jours. Bd. dirs., v.p. Leadership Inst. for Community Devel., 1968-73, Allegheny chpt. Epilepsy Found. Am., 1971-77; bd. dirs. Pitts. Dist. Export Coun., 1974-77,

Sch. Advanced Jewish Studies, 1976-79, Czech Mgmt. Ctr., 1989—2005, Travelers Aid Soc., Pitts., 2006—; bd. govs. Internat. Ins. Seminars, Inc., 1968-77; pres. Temple Sinai Congregation, 1979-81; mem. festival bd. Three Rivers Art Festival, 1988-93; mem. steering com. Leadership Pitts., 1986-91; sec. Am. Jewish Com., 1993-95; bd. dirs. Student Cons. Project, U. Pitts., 1970-96, Consortium for Coop. and Competitiveness, 1986-96, Moral Force in the Workplace, 1986-96; investment com. United Jewish Fedn., 1992-95; sec.-treas., bd. dirs. David Berg Found., 1995—. Named Man of Yr. in Edn., Vectors Pitts., 1986, Disting. Alumnus, 1989, U. Pitts. Alumni Assn. Mem. Soc. Psychol. Study Social Issues, Mid. Atlantic Assn. Colls. Bus. Adminstrn. (pres. 1972-73), Am. Assn. Univ. Adminstrs. (exec. coun. 1971-79, pres. 1975-77, bd. 1980-83, mem. found. 1983-95), Univ. Club (bd. dirs. 1988-94, sec. 1990-93, v.p. 1991-92, pres. 1992-93), Omicron Delta Gamma, Beta Gamma Sigma (pres. Beta chpt. 1964-68). Home: 220 N Bellefield Ave Ph 1201 Pittsburgh PA 15213-1468 Office: U Pitts Pitts Campus Katz Grad Sch Bus Pittsburgh PA 15260 Office Phone: 412-624-7678. Business E-Mail: zoffer@katz.pitt.edu.

**ZOGHBI, HUDA Y.,** neurologist, geneticist, educator; b. Beirut, June 29, 1955; BSc, Am. U. Beirut; MD, Meharry Med. Coll., 1979. Prof. pediat. neurology and geriatrics Baylor Coll. Medicine, Houston, 1994—; investigator Howard Hughes Med. Inst., 1996—; pediatrician Tex. Children's Hosp. and Ben Taub Gen. Hosp. Elected mem. Inst. of Medicine, 2000; sci. adv. bd. Internat. Rett Syndrome Assn.; med. rsch. adv. bd. Nat. Ataxia Found.; sci. issues com. Am. Acad. Neurology. Recipient Sidney Carter award, Acad. Neurobiology, Javits award, NIH, E. Mead Johnson award for pediat. rsch., Derek Denny-Brown Neurological Scholar award, Am. Neurol. Assn. Mem.: Am. Acad. Neurology (sci. issues com.). Inst. Medicine, NAS. Achievements include discovery (with others) of gene that causes spinocerebellar ataxia type 1; discovery of MECP2 gene that causes Rett syndrome; identifying Math1 gene that governs development of inner-ear hair cells. Office: Baylor College of Medicine T 807 1 Baylor Plz Houston TX 77030-3411 Office Phone: 713-798-6558. Office Fax: 713-798-8728. Business E-Mail: hzoghbi@bcm.tmc.edu.*

**ZOGRAFI, GEORGE,** pharmacologist, educator; b. N.Y.C., Mar. 13, 1936; married; 4 children. BS, Columbia U., 1956; MS, U. Mich., 1958, PhD in Pharm. Chemistry, 1961; DS (hon.), Columbia U., 1976. Asst. prof. pharmacology Columbia U., N.Y.C., 1961-64; from asst. prof. to assoc. prof. U. Mich., Ann Arbor, 1964-72; rsch. fellow Am. Found. Pharm. Edn., 1970-71; Pheiffer rsch. fellow Utrecht (The Netherlands), U., 1970-71; prof. pharmacology U. Wis., Madison, 1972—, dean, 1975-80. Mem. AAAS, NAS (Inst. Medicine), Am. Pharm. Assn. (Ebert prize 1984), Am. Chem. Soc., Am. Assn. Pharm. Scientists, Internat. Pharm. Fedn., Internat. Assn. Colloid and Interface Scientists, Am. Inst. Hist. Pharm., Sigma Xi.

**ZOHN, ANDREW ELIOT,** musician, educator; b. Planefield, NJ, May 18, 1970; s. Kenneth Edward and Virginia Elizabeth Zohn; m. Kristin Miller Zohn, Aug. 6, 1994. MusB, NC Sch. of the Arts, 1991; MusM, U. Tex., 1998; Mus D, Fla. State, 1997. Asst. prof. music Columbus (Ga.)State U., 1999—. Res. artist Mediterranean Guitar Festival, Cervo, Italy, 1999—, Guitare LaChine Festival, Montreal, Canada, 2001—. Composer: (12 solo guitar works) Les Productions d'Oz, 1998—, (4 solo guitar arrangements) Tuscany Pubs., 1998—; performer: (cd) A Guitar Recital, 1999. Recipient bronze medal, Guitar Found. Am. Internat. Competition, 1992, 1993, winner Nat. Collegiate Competition, Music Tchrs. Nat. Assn., 1993.

**ZOHN, MARTIN STEVEN,** lawyer; b. Denver, Oct. 22, 1947; s. William and Alice Zohn; m. Carol Falender, June 6, 1980; children: David Joseph, Daniel Robert. BA, Ind. U., 1969; JD, Harvard U., 1972. Bar: Calif. 1972, Ind. 1973, U.S. Ct. Claims 1980, U.S. Supreme Ct. 1980, U.S. Ct. Appeals (9th cir.) 1981. Assoc. Cadick, Burns, Duck & Neighbors, Indpls., 1972-77, ptnr., 1977-80, Pacht, Ross, Warne, Bernhard & Sears, Inc., L.A., 1980-86, Shea & Gould, L.A., 1986-89, Proskauer Rose LLP, L.A., 1989—. Pres. Indpls. Settlements, Inc., 1977-79. Bd. dirs. Found. Coun., 2001—, treas., 2005—. Mem. Fin. Lawyers Conf., L.A. County Bar Assn. (exec. com. prejudgment remedies sect. 1985-92, exec. com. bankruptcy sect. 2001—), Beverly Hills Bar Assn. (exec. com. bus. law sect. 1985-92, exec. com. bankruptcy sect. 2003—), Phi Beta Kappa. Office Phone: 310-284-5648. Business E-Mail: mzohn@proskauer.com

**ZOIS, CONSTANTINE NICHOLAS ATHANASIOS,** meteorologist, educator; b. Newark, Feb. 21, 1938; s. Athanasios Konstantinos and Asimina (Speros-Biekas) Zois; m. Yfikve Stein. Dec. 26, 1971; children: Jennifer, Jonathan. *Great-grandfather Haralambos Zois was a goatherd in Greece. Grandfather A. Blekas went to sea as a cabin boy at age 8. Grandfather Konstantinos Zois was a goatherd in Greece. Blekas eventually came to U.S.A. and worked on the Pennsylvania Railroad. Konstantinos remained in Greece, but his son, Athanasios, came to the U.S.A. in 1918 at age 20. Athanasios met Asimina Blekas at the Washington Florist, where they both worked. They married and had two children, Constantine N.A. Zois and K. Barbara Zois. Constantine N.A. Zois married Elyse Stein in 1971. They had two children, Jennifer and Jonathan.* BA, Rutgers U., 1961; MS, Fla. State U., 1965; PhD, Rutgers U., 1980. Draftsman Babcock and Wilcox Corp., Newark, 1956; designer Foster Wheeler Corp., Carteret, NJ, 1956; instr. Rutgers U., New Brunswick, NJ, 1961-62; grad. asst. Fla. State U., Tallahassee, 1962-65; rsch. meteorologist Nat. Weather Svc., Garden City, LI, NY, 1965-67; prof. Kean Coll. N.J., Union, 1967—. Founder meteorology program Kean Coll. N.J., Union, 1967—, chmn. all coll. promotion com., 1991—93; cons. Connell, Foley, Geiser, Roseland, NJ, 1986—88. Author, editor: Papers in Marine Science, 1971; author: Observation of the Newark NJ Nocturnal Heat Island and Its Consideration in Terms of a Physical Model, 1980, Dynamical and Physical Oceanography, 1988, Atmosphere Dynamics: Exercises and Problems, 1988, Climatology Workbook, 1988, Weather Map Folio, 1989; co-author: Outcomes Assessment at Kean College at NJ, 1992, Synoptic Meterology-Exercises and Readings, Vols. 1-3, 1995, Weather Folio, Vol. 2, NWS Map Anthology, 2003. Mem.: AAAS, N.J. Marine Scis. Consortium, N.Y. Acad. Scis. (vice chmn. atmospheric scis. sect. 1986—87, chmn. 1987—88, mem. adv. com. atmospheric sci. sect. 1988—), Am. Meteorol. Soc. (pres. N.J. chpt. 1980—81), Nat. Weather Assn., Phi Beta Kappa. Republican. Greek Orthodox. Avocations: guitar, banjo, fishing, baseball, snorkeling. Home: 2798 Carol Rd Union NJ 07083-4831 Office: Kean Coll of NJ Dept Meterology Morris Ave Union NJ 07083-7117 Office Phone: 908-737-3693. *It is water that consecrates the atmosphere as a cathedral of wonderment, as it is water that incarnates the sea as an oasis of life.*

**ZOLA, GARY PHILLIP,** rabbi, historian; b. Chgo., Feb. 17, 1952; m. Stefani Paula Rothberg; children: Amanda Roi, Jorin Benjamin, Jeremy Micah, Samantha Leigh. BA in Am. History with distinction, U. Mich., 1973; MA in Counseling Psychology, Northwestern U., 1976; PhD in Am. Jewish History, Hebrew Union Coll., Cin., 1991. Ordained rabbi, 1982. Dir. informal edn. and youth activities Temple Israel, Mpls., 1973-74; regional youth dir., asst. camp dir. Olin-Sang-Ruby Union Inst., UAHC, Chgo., 1974-77; student pulpit B'nai Israel Congregation, Williamson, W.Va., 1978-79; mem. student pulpit Anshe Sholom Congregation, Olympia Fields, Ill., 1979-80, Columbus Hebrew Congregation, Columbus, Ind., 1981-82; rabbi for high holy days Chgo. Jewish Experience, Chgo., 1982-94; nat. dir. admissions Hebrew Union Coll.-Jewish Inst. Religion, Cin., 1982-89, nat. dean admissions and student affairs, 1989-91, nat. dean admissions, student affairs and alumni rels., 1991-98; exec. dir. Jacob Rader Marcus Ctr. Am. Jewish Archives at Hebrew Union Coll., Cin., 1998—; assoc. prof. Am. Jewish Experience Hebrew Union Coll.-Jewish Inst. of Religion. Del. Emerging Leaders Conf., Am. Coun. for Internat. Leadership, 1989, 91; bd. dirs. Am. Jewish Com., Cin., 1982—, mem. exec. com., 1984—; bd. Hillel U. Cin., 1991-94, Jewish Fedn., Cin., 1993-95; pres. Greater Cin. Bd. Rabbis, 1993-95, Jewish Cmty. Rels. Coun., (bd. dir.,1994—); founding mem. Kehillah of Cin., Jewish Think Tank; pres. Martin Luther King Jr. Coalition Cin., 2003-05; chair Commn. for Commemorating 350 Years of Am. Jewish History. Author: Isaac Harby of Charleston, 1994; editor: Hebrew Union College-Jewish Institute of

Religion--A Centennial History, 1875-1975, (Michael A. Meyer), 1992, Women Rabbis: Exploration and Celebration, 1996, The Dynamics of American Jewish History, 2003, A Place of Our Own: The Rise of Reform Jewish Camping, 2006; editor: The American Jewish Archives Jour., 1998—; contbr. numerous scholarly articles to profl. jours.; mem. editl. bd. Reform Judaism. Bd. dirs. ethics com. Jewish Hosp., Cin.; life mem. N.Am. Fedn. Temple Youth; active NCCJ. Mem. Ctrl. Conf. Am. Rabbis, Orgn. Am. Historians, Assn. Jewish Studies, So. Jewish Hist. Soc., Am. Jewish Hist. Soc., N.Am. Fedn. Temple Youth (life). Office: Hebrew Union Coll Jewish Inst Religion 3101 Clifton Ave Cincinnati OH 45220-2404

**ZOLANDZ, MICHAEL E., JR.,** lawyer; BA cum laude, George Washington U., 1998, JD with high honors, 2001. Bar: DC, MD. Assoc. Arent Fox Kintner Plotkin & Kahn, Washington, 2001—02; assoc., pub. law & policy strategies group Sonnenschein Nath & Rosenthal LLP, Washington, 2002—. Office: Sonnenschein Nath & Rosenthal LLP Ste 600, E Tower 1301 K St NW Washington DC 20015 Office Phone: 202-408-9204. Office Fax: 202-408-6399. Business E-Mail: mzolandz@sonnenschein.com.

**ZOLECKI-BROWNING, DIANA M.,** middle school educator; b. Joliet, Ill., Nov. 28, 1960; d. Albert J. and Theresa M. (Sartori) Z.; m. Bruce Browning, Oct. 6, 1984; stepchildren: Matthew, Sarah. BA, Lewis U., Romeoville, Ill., 1983; M in Curriculum and Instn., Nat. Coll. of Edn., Evanston, Ill., 1989. Sci./health tchr. Reed-Custer Middle Sch., Braidwood, Ill. Office: Reed-Custer Middle Sch 407 Comet Dr Braidwood IL 60408 Office Phone: 815-458-2868.

**ZOLLAR, ALFRED,** computer company executive; M in Applied Math., U. Calif., San Diego. Sys. engr. trainee IBM, San Francisco, 1977, gen. mgr. e-network software, sr. v.p. develop. tivoli software, lab dir. software group Raleigh, NC, DB2 product mgr. Santa Teresa, Calif., gen. mgr., network software, 1996—98, gen. mgr. lotus software Cambridge, Mass., 2000—03, gen. mgr., eServer iSeries, 2003—. Bd. dirs. Chubb Corp.; mem. Leadership Coun. of Ctr. Bus. and Govt., John F. Kennedy Sch. Govt., Harvard U. Mem.: Greater Boston C. of C. (exec. com.). Office: IBM 1 Rodgers St Cambridge MA 02142 also: IBM 1133 Westchester Ave White Plains NY 10604

**ZOLLARS, WILLIAM D.,** freight company executive; b. 1948; BA, Univ. Minn., 1969. Various exec. positions with Eastman Kodak, 1970—94; sr. v.p. Ryder Integrated Logistics Ryder Sys., Inc., 1994—96; pres. Yellow Freight Sys., 1996-99; chmn., pres., CEO Yellow Roadway Corp., Overland Park, Kans., 1999—. Bd. dir. Cigna Corp., Cerner Corp., Butler Mfg. Co. Trustee ProLogis Trust, Midwest Rsch. Inst.; bd. mem. Heart of Am. United Way, Civic Council of Greater Kans. City, Carlson Sch. Mgmt., Univ. Minn., NAM. Mem.: Am. Trucking Assn. (bd. mem.), Phi Beta Kappa. Office: Yellow Corp 10990 Roe Ave Overland Park KS 66211-1213*

**ZOLLER, KAREN ANN,** library director, art gallery director; b. East Cleveland, Ohio, May 16, 1956; d. Paul John and Sonia Ann Klodor. BA in Psychology summa cum laude, Case Western Res. U., 1978, MLS in Law Librarianship, 1981. Mgr. Booksellers, Beachwood, Ohio, 1982—87; cataloger, reference libr. Clara Fritzsche Libr., Notre Dame Coll. South Euclid, Ohio, 1988—92, interim libr. dir., 1992, libr. dir., 1993—, gallery dir., 1997—. Co-founder, bd. mem. Tolerance Resource Ctr. Notre Dame Coll. South Euclid, 1997—; presenter in field; established Eastern Ch. Resource Ctr., Notre Dame Coll., South Euclid, 1999—. Editor: On The Threshold of a New Century: The City of South Euclid, 1967-1999, 1999; compiler: source book Researching Grants on the Internet: A Resource Manual, 1999, mem. editl. bd.: Notre Dame Today, 2003—. Mem. steering com. Hillcrest Cmty. Connections, South Euclid, 2003—04; founding mem. South Euclid Cmty. Partnerships, 2005—. Recipient Ameritech Partnership award, Ameritech, 1999; N.E. Ohio Network grantee, Gund Found., 1998, mini-grant, Ohio Humanities Coun., 2005. Mem.: ALA, Cleve. Area Met. Libr. Sys., Ohio Libr. Coun., Phi Beta Kappa. Roman Catholic. Avocations: reading, hiking, antiques, movies, collecting shells. Office: Clara Fritzsche Libr Notre Dame Coll 4545 College Rd South Euclid OH 44121

**ZOLLER, MICHAEL,** otolaryngologist, head and neck surgeon, educator; b. New Orleans, July 21, 1947; s. Harry and Mildred (Daitch) Z.; m. Linda Kramer, Dec. 21, 1974; children: Rebecca, Jonathan. BS, U. New Orleans, 1971; MD, Tulane U., 1972. Resident in gen. surgery Jewish Hosp., St. Louis, Washington U. Sch. Medicine, 1972—74; resident in otolaryngology Mass. Eye and Ear Infirmary, Harvard U. Med. Sch., Boston, 1974—77; pres. Ear, Nose and Throat Assocs., Savannah, Ga., 1977—; chmn. eye, ear, nose and throat dept. Candler Hosp., 1996—98. Asst. clin. prof. surgery Med. Coll. Ga., Augusta, 1982—96, assoc. clin. prof. surgery, 1996—2003; assoc. prof. surgery Mercer Med. Sch., 2000—; dir. otology otoneurology dept. St. Joseph's Hosp., Savannah, 1994—. Chmn. med. divsn. United Way, Savannah, 1990, chmn. profl. divsn., 1991, 94-2001, vice chmn. campaign, 2002, chmn. campaign, 2003, bd. dirs., 2002-05, vice chmn. bd. dirs., 2004-2005, chmn. bd. dirs., 2005-2006; mem. allocation panel, 1997-2002; bd. dirs. Am. Cancer Soc., Savannah, 1993-2000, pres. Chatham County unit, 1996-97, chmn. bd., 1997-98; bd. dirs. Savannah Country Day Sch., 1993-97, chmn. ann. campaign, 1995-96; bd. dirs. St. Joseph's Candler Found., 2001-2006; pres. Savannah Jewish Fedn., 1991-93; active Savannah Jewish Fedn. Endowment Bd., 1995-99; mem. med. adv. bd. South Coll., 1996-2000; mem. parents coun. Washington U., St. Louis, 1997-2001, Tulane U., 2002-2005, Tulane Med. Sch., 2005-06; bd. dirs. Leadership Savannah, 1996-98. Recipient Young Leadership award Savannah Jewish Fedn., 1985, Boss of Yr. award Savannah Jaycees, 1993, Celebrate Savannah award for outstanding contbns. to Savannah, Ga. Guardian, 1996; Harvard U. Med. Sch. fellow, 1976-77. Fellow: ACS; mem.: AMA, Ga. Soc. Otolaryngology (pres. bd. trustees 1997—98, editor newsletter 1998—2001, Lester Brown Lifetime Achievement award 2005), Med. Assn. Ga. (mem. ho. of dels. 1990—2003, bd. dirs. 1995—2004, editl. bd. 2001—06, Ga. Cup award 1993, Ayest-Wyeth Cmty. Svc. award 1996, Cmty. Svc. award 2001), 1st Dist. Med. Assn. (pres. 1987—88), Ga. Med. Soc. (pres. 1992, chmn. bd. trustees 1997, chmn. endowment fund 2004—), John B. Rabun Cmty. Svc. award 1995, Hero's award 2001), Am. Neurotology Soc., Am. Soc. Head and Neck Surgery, Am. Acad. Otolaryngology and Head and Neck Surgery (tonsils and adenoids com. 1996—99, sleep disorders com. 1996—2002, pediat. otolaryngology com. 2003—06, equilibrium com. 2005—). Office: Ear Nose and Throat Assocs Savannah 5201 Frederick St Savannah GA 31405-4501 Personal E-mail: MZ47ent@aol.com.

**ZOLNO, MARK S.,** lawyer; BA Polit. Sci., No. Ill. Univ., 1965; JD, John Marshall Law Sch., 1978; MA cum laude Internat. Rels., Universidad de las Américas, Mexico, 1974. Bar: Ill. 1978, U.S. Dist. Ct. (no. dist.) Ill. 1979, U.S. Ct. Internat. Trade 1979, U.S. Ct. Appeals (fed. cir.) 1979. With U.S. Customs Svc., Dept. Commerce, U.S. Trade Rep's. Office, Internat. Trade Commn., Fed. Trade Commn., FDA; ptnr. Katten, Muchin, Rosenman, Chgo., 1988—. Past chmn. Chgo. Bar Assn. Customs and U.S. Trade Law Com.; lectr. in field. Contbr. articles to profl. jours. Office: Katten Muchin Rosenman 525 W Monroe St Ste 1900 Chicago IL 60661-3693 Office Phone: 312-902-5436. Business E-Mail: mark.zolno@kattenlaw.com

**ZOLODZ, MELISSA D.,** scientist; b. Hobart, Ind., June 13, 1974; d. Stan and Jan Zolodz. PhD, Purdue U., West Lafayette, Ind., 2003. Scientist Xencor, Monrovia, Calif., 2005—; sr. scientist U. Fla. Clin. Rsch. Ctr., Gainesville. Mem.: Am. Soc. Mass Spectrometry. Office: Xencor 111 W Lemon Ave Monrovia CA 91016 Office Phone: 626-737-8159. E-mail: mzolodz@xencor.com.

**ZOLOTH, LAURIE SUSAN,** bioethicist; b. LA, June 15, 1950; d. Arthur and Helen (Cohen) Zoloth; m. Henry Levy (div. June 1980); m. Daniel Zoloth Dorfman, Aug. 17, 1986; children: Matthew, Noah, Benjamin, Joshua, Sarah. BA cum laude, U. Calif., Berkeley, 1974; BSN, SUNY, 1982; MA in English, San Francisco State U., 1991; MA, PhD in Theology and Jewish Studies,

Grad. Theol. Union, 1993. Instr. adult edn. Jewish studies Lehrhaus Judaica, 1988-93; cons. ethicist Nat. Kaiser Permanente HMO, Berkeley, Calif., 1987; prof. ethics, dir. Jewish Studies prog. San Francisco State U., 1995—2003; dir. Ctr. Bioethics, Sci. and Soc. Northwestern U., Chicago; dir. bioethics Ctr. Genetic Medicine, Ctr. Regenerative Medicine and Inst. Nanotechnology; prof. med. ethics and humanities Northwestern U. Feinberg Sch. Medicine; prof. religion, mem Jewish Studies faculty Northwestern U. Weinberg Coll. Arts and Scis. Instr. ethics Chapman Coll., 1989; lectr. clin. bioethics prog. Stanford U. Grad. Theol. Union, 1991—92, instr. bioethics prog., 1994; asst. prof. Calif. State U., Sonoma, 1994; mem. Nat. Adv. Coun. NASA, mem. Planetary Protection Adv. Com., mem. Interagency Nat. Animal Care and Use Com.; chair bioethics adv. bd. Howard Hughes Med. Inst.; mem. data safety monitoring bd. NIH Asia AIDS Vaccine Trials. Mem. editl. bd.: Am. Jour. Law, Medicine and Ethics, Jour. Clin. Ethics, Am. Jour. Bioethics; author: Health Care and The Ethics of Encounter, 1999; co-editor: Notes From a Nattow Ridge: Religion and Bioethics, Riding on Faith: Religion, Popular Culture and the World of Disney, Margin of Error: The Ethics of Mistakes in Medicine, The Human Embryonic Stem Cell Debate: Ethics, Religion and Policy. Recipient NASA Nat. Pub. Svc. award, 2005. Mem.: Am. Acad. Religion (chair sect. on women), Soc. Women's Health Rsch. (bd. mem.), Soc. Neuroethics (bd. mem.), Soc. Scriptural Reasoning (bd. mem.), Internat. Soc. Stem Cell Rsch. (bd. mem.), Am. Soc. Bioethics and Humanities (pres. 2001). Jewish. Office: Ctr Bioethics Sci and Soc Northwestern U 676 N St Clair Rm 1260 Chicago IL 60611 E-mail: lzoloth@northwestern.edu.*

**ZOMBIE, ROB (ROBERT CUMMINGS),** musician, filmmaker; b. Haverhill, Mass., Jan. 12, 1966; m. Sheri Moon, Oct. 31, 2002. Founding mem. White Zombie, 1985—96. Musician: (albums) (with White Zombie) Psycho-Head Blowout, 1986, Soul Crusher, 1987, Make Them Die Slowly, 1989, La Sexorcisto, 1992, Astro-Creep 2000, 1995, Supersexy Swingin' Sounds, 1996, (solo albums) Hellbilly Deluxe, 1998, American Made Music to Strip By, 1999, The Sinister Urge, 2001, Educated Horses, 2006; prodn. asst. (TV series) Pee-wee's Playhouse, 1986, writer, dir. (films) House of 1000 Corpses, 2003, writer, dir., prodr. The Devil's Rejects, 2005, actor Slither, 2006, writer The Haunted World of El Superbeasto, 2006. Office: c/o The Firm Ste 1026 60 Madison Ave New York NY 10010*

**ZON, LEONARD I.,** pediatrics educator, researcher; b. Hartford, Conn. BS in Chemistry and Natural Sciences, Muhlenberg Coll., Allentown, Pa., 1979; MD, Jefferson Med. Coll., 1983. Diplomate Am. Bd. Internal Medicine; lic. physician, Mass. Rsch. asst. Jefferson Med. Coll., Phila., 1980-82; intern New Eng. Deaconess Hosp., Boston, 1983-84, from jr. to sr. resident in internal medicine, 1984-86; rsch. fellow Children's Hosp., Boston, 1987-90, founder, dir. Stem Cell Rsch. Program, Grousbeck prof. hematology/oncology; instr. Harvard Med. Sch., Boston, 1989-91, asst. prof. pediatrics, 1991—, mem. faculty grad. program biol. and biomed. scis., 1994—, prof. pediat. medicine, Children's Hosp. Boston; investigator Howard Hughes Med. Inst., 1993—. Guest faculty Okla. Health Scis. Ctr., 1993; lectr. in field. Contbr. articles to Am. Jour. Physiology, Jour. Clin. Microbiology, Lancet, Am. Jour. Medicine, Br. Jour. Haematology, Nature, Proc. Biochemics, Molecular Cell Biology, Biology of Hematopoiesis, Jour. Biol. Chemistry. Recipient Hyman Menduke Rsch. award, 1983; Friends of the Farber fellow, 1987, Dana-Farber Cancer Inst. fellow, med. oncology, 1986-89; grantee NSF, 1978, NIH, 1980, 89—, Chalres H. Hood Found., 1990-92, Hoffmann-La Roche, 1991-94. Mem. AMA, AAAS, ACP, Am. Soc. Clin. Oncology, Am. Soc. Hematology, Am. Fisheries Soc., Mass. Med. Soc., Inst. Medicine., Internat. Soc. for Stem Cell Rsch. (founder, past pres.) Achievements include research in hematopoiesis, development, genetics. Office: Childrens Hosp Boston 300 Longwood Ave Karp-7 Boston MA 02115 also: Howard Hughes Med Inst New Rsch Bldg Rm 7211 1 Blackfan Cir Boston MA 02115 Office Phone: 617-919-2069. Office Fax: 617-730-0222. E-mail: zpn@enders.tch.harvard.edu.*

**ZONANA, VICTOR,** lawyer, educator; b. Zagazig, Eqypt, Aug. 28, 1940; s. Isaac A. and Fortunee (Cohen Beyda) Z.; m. Mary Linda Haynie, Aug. 22, 1964; children: David A., Nancy B. Zonana Dickinson. BS in Econs., Hofstra U., 1961; LLB, NYU, 1964, LLM, 1966. Bar: N.Y. 1965. Assoc. Kaye, Scholer, Fierman, Hays & Handler, N.Y.C., 1966-69; prof. NYU, 1969-80, adj. prof., 1981—, Charles S. Lyon vis. prof., 1994; dep. tax legis. counsel U.S. Dept. Treasury, 1975-76; cons. to asst. commr. IRS, 1975, office of chief counsel, 1994; counsel, ptnr. Kaye, Scholer, Fierman, Hays & Handler, N.Y.C., 1980-87, Arnold & Porter, N.Y.C., 1988—2001; prof. Bklyn. Law Sch., 1996—2002; prin. KPMG LLP, London, 2002—. Mem., chmn. adv. bd. NYU Tax Inst. Fellow Am. Coll. Tax Counsel; mem. ABA, N.Y. State Bar Assn. (co-chmn. com. on fgn. activities of U.S. taxpayers, chmn. com. on depreciation and investment credit, co-chmn. com. tax acctg. matters, com. tax policy). Office: KPMG LLP 8 Salisbury Sq London EC4Y 8BB England Office Phone: +44 (0)207 694 1737.

**ZONAY, THOMAS A.,** lawyer; b. 1963; BS; JD, Vt. Law Sch. Bar: Vt. 1988. Criminal def. lawyer Carrol, George & Pratt, Rutland, Vt.; ptnr. Ford & Zonay, P.C., Woodstock, Utah, 2000—. Mem.: Vt. Bar Assn. (pres. 2004—, mem. bd. mgrs.). Office: Ford & Zonay PC PO Box 388 Woodstock VT 05091-0388 Office Phone: 802-457-1000. Office Fax: 802-457-1874. E-mail: tazonay@sover.net.

**ZONIA, DHIMITRI,** artist; b. St. Louis, June 12, 1921; s. Ligori and Polixenna Zonia; m. Margaret C. Wieland, July 11, 1927; children: Margaret E., Susan C., Carolynn L., Laura E. Ind. study, Italy and Eng., 1972. Editl. cartoonist Postmark Prague, 1984—86; editl. cartoonist illustrator Cry Justice Now, St. Louis, 1998—2000; staff mem. The Scene Newspaper, 2002—05. Vis. artist Albanian Nat. Gallery, Tirane, 2005. One-man shows include Tattershall Castle, London, 1982, Nat. Gallery Art, Tirana, Albania, 2001—05, Forest Pk. CC, St. Louis, 2004—05, exhibitions include Oak Grove Mauselium, 1972, Palais de Congress, Paris, 1976, Yamaha Corp., Madison Sq Garden. NYC, 1977, Jewish Cmty. Ctr., 1978, Macdonnel Planetarium, St. Louis, 1978, Mo. Botanical Garden, 1988, Polish Bi-ennial, Warsaw, 1992, Anheuser-Bush Breweries Employees, 1992, Represented in permanent collections St. Bernadette Mus. Sacred Art, Albuquerque, Okla. Art Ctr., Oklahoma City Ark. Art Ctr., Little Rock, Albrecht Art Ctr., St. Joseph, Mo., Rapid City Art Ctr., SD, Butler Inst. Am. Art, Youngstown, Ohio, pvt. collections, Am., Europe, Japan, Australia. Bd. govs. St. Louis Artists Guild, St. Louis, 1967. Recipient 3d pl., Mo. coll. Media Assn., 2006. Mem.: Soc. Ind. Artists (life; hon.). Mailing: 4680 Karamar Dr Saint Louis MO 63128 Office Phone: 314-487-8506. Personal E-mail: weizon@aol.com.

**ZONIS, MARVIN,** political scientist, educator; b. Boston, Sept. 18, 1936; s. Leonard and Clara (Barenberg) Z.; m. Lucy Salenger, Jan. 3, 1976; children by previous marriage-Nadia E. Leah; 1 stepdaugher, Brix E. Smith. AB, Yale U., 1958; postgrad., Harvard Grad. Sch. Bus., 1958-59; PhD, M.I.T., 1968; candidate, Inst. for Psychoanalysis, Chgo., 1977-85. Mem. faculty U. Chgo., 1966—, assoc. prof. and prof. behavioral scis., 1973-89—, prof. Grad. Sch. Bus., 1989—; dir. U. Chgo. (Center for Middle Eastern Studies), 1976-79; pres. Marvin Zonis and Associates, Internat. Cons., 1991—. Cons. in field; chmn. com. on Middle East Am. Coun. Learned Socs.-Social Sci. Rsch. Coun., 1970-76; pres. Am. Inst. Iranian Studies, 1969-71; bd. dirs. CNA Fin. Corp. Author: The Political Elite of Iran, 1971, Khomeini, The Islamic Republic of Iran, and the Arab World, 1987, Majestic Failure: The Fall of the Shah, 1991, The East European Opportunity: The Complete Business Guide and Source Book, 1992; contbr. articles to profl. jours. Served with USAF, 1959-60. Recipient Quantrell award for excellence in teaching U. Chgo., 1979 Office: U Chicago 5828 S University Ave Chicago IL 60637-1515 Office Phone: 312-397-0400. *Psychoanalytic approaches to the study of political phenomena open new vistas to understanding as well as facilitating the design of U.S. policy.*

**ZOOGMAN, NICHOLAS JAY,** lawyer; b. N.Y.C., Apr. 2, 1947; s. Morris William and Hannah (Stern) Z.; m. Carla Ganz, June 7, 1970, children: Sarah Elizabeth, Peter William. BA, NYU, 1967; MA, Harvard U., 1969, JD, 1973. Bar: N.Y. 1974, U.S. Dist. Ct. (so. and ea. dists.) N.Y. 1974, U.S. Ct. Appeals (2d cir.) 1975, U.S. Supreme Ct. 1979, U.S. Dist. Ct. (ea. dist.) Mich. 1988,

U.S. Ct. Appeals (D.C. cir.) 1990, U.S. Ct. Appeals (6th cir.) 1993, U.S. Ct. Appeals (5th cir.) 1997. Assoc. Donovan Leisure Newton & Irvine, N.Y.C., 1973-75; ptnr. Anderson Kill & Olick, N.Y.C., 1976-2000; counsel Dickstein Shapiro LLP, N.Y.C., 2000—05, ptnr., 2006—. Mem. ABA, N.Y. State Bar Assn., Assn. Bar City of N.Y., Phi Beta Kappa, Pi Sigma Alpha. Office: Dickstein Shapiro LLP 1177 Avenue of Americas New York NY 10036-2714

**ZOOK, JOHN EDWIN,** physician, surgeon, missionary; b. Tabor, Iowa, Oct. 3, 1924; s. Abram Eyster Zook and Eunice (Francis) Brenneman; m. Jeanne Pierson, Sept. 7, 1952; children: Rebecca Clair, Daniel John, Paul Michael. BA, Lewis and Clark Coll., 1950; MD, U. Oreg., 1954; cert. tropical medicine Antwerp Sch. Tropical Medicine, Belgium, 1956. Diplomate Am. Bd. Surgery. Intern Emanuel Hosp., Portland, Oreg., 1954-55; resident in surgery Good Samaritan Hosp., Portland, 1965-69; ednl. missionary Unevangelized Tribes Mission, Congo, 1943-46; med. missionary Congo Inland Mission, 1955-65; dir. med. activities Africa Intermennonite Mission, Republic of Congo, 1961-65, surgeon, 1969-77; practice medicine specializing in gen. surgery, Portland, 1977—2005; chief staff Mt. Hood Med. Ctr., 1982, Woodland Park Hosp., 1989; mem. bd. dirs., 1988-91; exchange physician China Ednl. Exchange Program, Chungquin Med. Coll., 1984-90. V.p. Mennonite Men of Mennonite Ch. USA, 1982—. Fellow ACS, Internat. Coll. Surgeons (Oreg. regent 1980-84, v.p. 1985), Portland Surg. Soc. Republican. Office: E Portland Surg Clinic 25500 SE Stark St Gresham OR 97030 Personal E-mail: jeannezook123@msn.com.

**ZOON, KATHRYN CHRISTINE,** biochemist; b. Yonkers, NY, Nov. 6, 1948; d. August R. and Violet T. (Pollock) Egloff; m. Robert A. Zoon, Aug. 22, 1970; children: Christine K., Jennifer R. BS, Rensselaer Poly. Inst., 1970; PhD, Johns Hopkins U., 1976. Rsch. chemist divsn. biochem. biophys. Bur. Biologics FDA, Bethesda, Md., 1980-84, rsch. chemist divsn. virology, 1984-88, rsch. chemist divsn. cytokine biology Ctr. Biologics, 1988—92, divsn. dir., 1989-92; dir. Ctr. Biologics Evaluation and Rsch., 1992—2003; dep. dir. Ctr. for Cancer Rsch. Nat. Cancer Inst., NIH, 2003—04; dep. dir. planning and devel. divsn. intramural rsch. NIAID, NIH, 2004—06, dir. divsn. intramural rsch., 2006—. Chmn. expert com. on biol. standardization WHO, 1997-98, 99, 2000, 01; mem. adv. com. of CMR, 2000-03; dir. NIH, NIAID, DIR; lectr. in field. Contbr. articles to rsch. in biol. chemistry to sci. jours.; sect. editor Jour. Interferon and Cytokine Rsch., 1980—. Bd. dirs. Found. Advanced Edn. Scis., 1996-2004, 1st v.p., 1999-03; mem. adv. bd. Def. Advance Rsch. Projects Agy., 1998-00. Inst. Medicine Nat. Acad. Sci., 2002-. Recipient Person of the Yr. award Biopharm, 1992, Pub. Svc. and Genetic Engring. News award, 1995, Presdl. Meritorious Exec. Rank award, 1994, Grateful Patient award Nat. Assn. Cancer Patients, 1997, Rensselaer Alumni Assn. award, 1997, Sec.'s award for disting. svc. Dept. Health and Human Svcs., 2001, 03, Disting. Alumnus award Johns Hopkins U., 2003; NY State Regents fellow, 1970, Interferon rsch. fellow NIH, Bethesda, 1975-77, staff fellow, 1979-80. Mem. Am. Soc. Biochem. and Molecular Biology, Intenat. Soc. Interferon and Cytokine Rsch. (pres. elect 1998-99, pres. 2000-01), Internat. Assn. Biol. Standardization (mem. adv. coun. 2000—), Inst. of Medicine. Roman Catholic. Office: NIAID/NIH Bldg 10 Rm 4A30A 10 Center Dr Bethesda MD 20892 Office Phone: 301-496-3006. Personal E-mail: kzoon@comcast.net. Business E-Mail: kzoon@niaid.nih.gov.

**ZOPF, ERIC PAUL,** mortgage lending company executive; b. Greensboro, NC, Nov. 15, 1962; s. Paul Edward and Evelyn La Noel (Montgomery) Z. BSBA, Guilford Coll., 1994. Owner, CEO So. Estate Landscaping, Greensboro, 1981-91; asst. v.p. 1st Greensboro Home Equity, 1993-98; ptnr. Integrity Home Mortgage LLC, Roanoke, Va., 1998—. Author: Black Summer Rain, 1996. Mem. Soc. Friends. Avocations: hiking, camping, rafting, fishing, gemology. Home: 815 George White Rd Greensboro NC 27410-3317 Office: 856 W Main St Salem VA 24153-4718 Mailing: PO Box 1644 Salem VA 24153 Office Phone: 540-312-4886.

**ZOPF, EVELYN LANOEL MONTGOMERY,** retired guidance counselor; b. Laurel, Miss., July 10, 1932; d. Arthur LaNoel and Ruby Lee (Lewis) Montgomery; m. Paul Edward Zopf, Aug. 5, 1956; 1 child, Eric Paul. MusB in Edn., U. So. Miss., 1953, MA, 1954. Guidance counselor U. So. Miss., 1953—54, U. Fla., 1954—56; tchr. New Orleans City Schs., 1956—57; pub. sch. music tchr., band dir., choral dir. Putnam County Schs., Fla., 1957—59; pvt. music tchr. voice, piano, clarinet and trumpet, 1953—61; substitute tchr. Guilford County Schs., 1959—93. Mem. arts series com. Guilford Coll., 1973—77; interim choir dir. New Garden Friends Meeting, 1961, chmn. music com., 1974—76; adviser to fgn. students, 1954—56, 1959—62; mem. First Internat. Congress on Quaker Edn. Com., 1987—88, Guilford Coll.'s Sesquicentennial Com., 1985—87; spkr. various religious and art groups. Vol. ARC, Boy Scouts Am.; mem. U. Fla. Union Bd., 1955—56; vol. comm. worker NC dist. auditions Met. Opera, 1999—2001; precinct del. County Dem. Conv., 1977, 1979, precinct worker, 1980, campaign worker, 1980; bd. dirs. Greensboro Friends of Music, 1970—71; bd. dirs. Greensboro chpt. NC Symphony Bd., 1979—83; mem. feeder bd. The Guilford Coll. Friends of the Lib. Bd., 1993—94, mem. exec. bd., 1994—95. Mem.: United Soc. of Friends Women (pres. 1979—81), Internat. Fellowship Quaker Women, Guilford Coll. Cmty. Chorus, Women's Soc. (dir. 1978—82), Guilford Coll. Arts Appreciation (v.p. 1980—85, pres. 1981—82), Guilford Gourmet Club, PhD Mu. Home: 815 George White Rd Greensboro NC 27410-3317

**ZOPP, ANDREA LYNNE,** lawyer, retail executive; b. Rochester, N.Y., Jan. 25, 1957; d. Reuben K. and P. Greta (Hurst) Davis; m. William E. Zopp, Jr., Oct. 7, 1989; children: Alyssa, Kelsey, William. BA cum laude, Harvard Coll., 1978; JD, Harvard U., 1981. Bar: Ill. 1981, U.S. Dist. Ct. (no. dist.) Ill. 1981, U.S. Ct. Appeals (7th cir.) 1982. Law clk. Hon. George N. Leighton, U.S. Dist. Ct., Chgo., 1981-83; asst. U.S. atty. U.S. Atty.'s Office, Chgo., 1983-86, dep. chief OCDETF, 1986-88, dep. chief criminal ct., 1988-89; ptnr. McDermott, Will & Emery, Chgo., 1990-91; chief narcotics prosecution bur. Cook County State's Attys. Office, Chgo., 1991-92, first asst. state's atty., 1992—96; ptnr. Sonnenschein Nath & Rosenthal, 1997—2000; v.p., dep. gen. counsel Sara Lee Corp., 2000—03; sr. v.p. gen. counsel Sears, Roebuck & Co., Hoffman Estates, Ill., 2003—. Mem. Gov.'s Commn. on Capital Punishment, State of Illinois, 2000—. Bd. dirs. Aux. Bd., Art Inst. Chgo. 1987-2000; bd. dirs. Chgo. Regional Bd. of Jr. Achievement, 1991-95, Chgo. Area Project, 1992—. Fellow Leadership Greater Chgo., 1989-90; Kizzy Scholarship Fund award, 1991-92. Fellow Am. Bar Found., Am. Coll. Trial Lawyers; Mem. ABA, Chgo. Bar Assn., Chgo. Inn of Ct., Cook County Bar Assn., Black Women Lawyers Assn., Leadership Greater Chgo. (bd. dirs.). Avocations: running, music, theater. Office: Sears Roebuck & Co 3333 Beverly Rd Hoffman Estates IL 60179

**ZOPP, DUDLEY,** visual artist; d. Lewis Burton and Frances Newell Milward; children: Ursula, Frances. BA, U. Ky., Lexington, 1963, MA, 1964; postgrad., U. Louisville, Ky., 1986—91. Co-founder Circadia Project, Camden, Maine, 2002—. One-man shows include Ctr. Maine Contemporary Art, Rockport, 1997, 2004, U. Maine, Farmington, 1998, Presque Isle, 2004, U. Southern Maine, Lewiston-Auburn, 2006; co-author: (book) A Butterfly Careless, 2002., Maine Arts Commn. fellow, 2002, Good Idea grantee, Maine Arts Commn., 2003. Project grantee, Maine Cmty. Found., 2003. Personal E-mail: dzopp@dudleyzopp.com.

**ZORE, EDWARD JOHN,** financial services executive; b. Milw., July 5, 1945; s. Joseph F. and Marie A. Z.; m. Diane Widemshek, Aug. 19, 1967; children: Annemarie, Kathryn. BS, U. Wis.-Milw., 1968, MS, 1970. With Northwestern Mut., Milw., 1969—, pres., 2000—, CEO, 2001—. Republican. Roman Catholic. Office: Northwestern Mutual 720 E Wisconsin Ave Milwaukee WI 53202-4703

**ZORICK, NANCY LEE,** artist, actress; b. Chgo., July 24, 1946; d. William Russel and Wilma Beatrice (Fithian) Noble; m. Peter Michael Zorick, Aug. 8, 1980. Student, Art Inst. Chgo., 1965-67, Second City Workshop, Chgo., 1967-68, Am. Acad. Art, 1971. Comml. artist Embosograph Display Co.,

Chgo., 1964-66, Stevens-Biondi-DiCiccio, Chgo., 1966-68. Illustrator: (book) Making Weight, 1991, The Little Acorn, 1996; exhibns. include Fontana (Calif.) Arts Assn., 1988, Riverside County Art Exhibn., 1990; appeared in plays My Sweet Charlie, Chgo., 1968, Harold, Chgo., 1969, films include Medium Cool, 1968, Jackson County Jail, 1976, Outside Chance, 1978; appeared in commercial Tastee Freeze, 1969. Mem Des Arts, 1981, historian, 1983—85, parliamentarian, 1986—93, 1996—2006, pres., 1993—95, 2006—. Named to Taft Alumni Hall of Fame, Chgo., 2000; recipient 1st place in Fine Arts, Nat. Date Festival, 1983, 2d place, Riverside Nat. Date Festival, 1993, 1996, 2001, 3d place, 2004, Best of Show in Fine Arts, Des-Arts, 1988, 1st place, Des Arts, 1986, 1990, 1992—93, 1996—98, 2000—01, 2003—05, Best of Show in Fine Arts, Fontana (Calif.) Arts Assn., 1988. Avocations: teaching sunday school, ballet and art, volunteering. Home: 51-555 Monroe St #31 Indio CA 92201 Personal E-mail: noblezorick@netscape.com.

**ZORKIN, MELISSA WAGGENER,** public relations executive; b. 1954; BA Eng., Lewis & Clark Coll. With Tektronix Inc., Beaverton, Oreg., 1975-80, Regis McKenna, Portland, 1980-83; founder Waggener Edstrom, Inc., 1983—, now pres. and CEO. Named Person of Yr., Media, Inc.; named one of 100 Most Influential People of the 20th Century in Pub. Rels., 50 Most Powerful Women in the Field, PR Week, 1999; recipient Alumni award, Lewis and Clark Coll. Office: Waggener Edstrom Inc 3 Centerpointe Dr Ste 300 Lake Oswego OR 97035-8663

**ZORN, ERIC STUART,** retail executive; b. Newark, Oct. 2, 1948; s. Arthur and Evelyn (Bernstein) Z.; m. Lois Karen Green, Nov. 29, 1979. Student, Fairleigh Dickinson Coll., Wayne, N.J., Upsala Coll., East Orange, N.J. Cash ops. supr. Vornado Inc., Garfield, N.J., 1966-69; corp. auditor Mangel Stores Corp., NYC, 1969-70; sr. v.p. Jamesway Corp., Secaucus, NJ, 1970; pres. Omnia Protective Services Inc., Ft. Lee, NJ, 1979, 1530 Owners Corp. (coop. bldg.), Ft. Lee; regional v.p. Wal-Mart Stores Inc., 1993—97, v.p. realty, 1997—99, sr. v.p. realty, 1999, pres. realty, 2003—05, exec. v.p. Wal-Mart Realty, 2005—. Mem. Internat. Mass Retailing Inst. (chmn. loss prevention group 1979-82), NJ Retail Mchts. Assn. (chmn.), Internat. Soc. Stress Analysts, Soc. Strategic Planning, Internat. Coun. Shopping Centers (trustee). Republican. Jewish. Office: Wal-Mart Realty 2001 SE 10th St Bentonville AR 72712-6489*

**ZORN, JOHN,** composer, musician; b. NYC, Sept. 2, 1953; Band mem. Naked City, NYC, 1989—94; founder, mem. Masada, 1994—; founder & exec. prodr. Tzadik record label, NYC, 1995—. Numerous commissions including NY Philharm., Kronos Quartet, Am. Composers Orch., Bklyn. Philharm., Stephen Drury, Bayerische Staatsoper, WDR Orch. Köln. Major compositions include: Christabel, 1972, Conquest of Mexico, 1973, Mikhail Zoetrope, 1974, Lacrosse, 1977, Hockey, 1978, Fencing, 1978, The Book of Heads, 1978, Pool, 1979, Archery, 1979, Track & Field, 1980, Locus Solus, 1982, Sebastopol, 1983, Rugby, 1983, Cobra, 1984, Xu Feng, 1985, Godard, 1985, Spillane, 1986, Hu Die, 1986, Ruan Lingyu, 1987, Hwang Chin-ee, 1988, Cat O'Nine Tails, 1988, Quê Trân, 1988, For Your Eyes Only, 1989, Bézique, 1989, Torture Garden, 1990, Grand Guignol, 1990, Dead Man, 1990, Elegy, 1991, Leng Tch'e, 1991, Carny, 1992, Memento Mori, 1992, Kristallnacht, 1992, Absinthe, 1992, Angelus Novus, 1993, Masada, 1993-97, The Sand's Share, 1994, Redbird, 1995, Dark River, 1995, Aporias, 1995, Music for Children, 1996, Duras, 1996, Kol Nidre, 1996, Orchestra Variations, 1996, Etant Donnés, 1997, Shibboleth, 1997, Cycles du Nord, 1998, Rituals, 1998, The String Quartets, 1999, Cartoon S&M, 2000, Love, Madness & Mysticism, 2001, Hockey, 2002, Hemophiliac, 2002, Magick, 2004, Rituals, 2005, Mysterium, 2005, Moonchild, 2006; composer for films: White & Lazy, 1986, She Must Be Seeing Things, 1987, Distribution of Lead, 1988, The Golden Boat, 1990, Maohgai, 1993, Hollywood Hotel, 1994, Zigrail, 1995, The Black Glove, 1997, Trembling Before G-d, 2001, Secret Lives: Hidden Children & Their Rescuers During WWII, 2002, Shaolin Ulysses, 2003, Invitation to a Suicide, 2004, Protocols of Zion, 2005, The Treatment, 2006; appears in films: Rising Tones Cross, 1985, Put More Blood Into the Music, 1987, The Revenge of the Dead Indians, 1993, Sabbath in Paradise, 1998, A Bookshelf on Top of the Sky: 12 Stories About John Zorn, 2002, Jack Smith & the Destruction of Atlantis, 2006. MacArthur fellow, John D. & Catherine T. MacArthur Found., 2006. Office: Tzadik PMB 126 200 E 10th St New York NY 10003 E-mail: info@tzadik.com.*

**ZORN, ROBERT LYNN,** education educator; b. Youngstown, Ohio, Mar. 22, 1938; s. Robert S. and Frances L. Zorn; m. Joan M. Wilkos, Apr. 26, 1957; children: Deborah Lynn, Patricia Lynn. BS in Edn., Kent State U., 1959; MEd, Westminster Coll., 1964; PhD, U. Pitts., 1970. Tchr. West Branch (Ohio) Pub. Schs., 1961—62; H.S. unit prin. Boardman Schs., 1967—70; dir. adminstrv. svcs. Mahoning County Schs., 1970—73, asst. supt., 1973—76; elem. prin. Poland Schs., 1962—67, supt. schs., 1976—. Adj. prof. edn. Westminster Coll., 1985—; chmn. Ohio Adv. Com. State Dept. Edn., McGuffey Hist. Soc. Nat. Educator's Hall of Fame. Author: Speed Reading, 1989, rev. edit., 1997; contbr. articles to profl. jours. Chmn. Mahoning County chpt. Am. Cancer Soc.; pres. bd. trustees Poland Meth. Ch.; trustee Mahoning County chpt. Am. Heart Assn. To lt. USAF, 1959—61. Mem.: Am. Assn. Sch. Adminstrs., Doctoral Assn. Educators (life), Ohio PTA (life), Rotary, Fond-erlac County Club, Protestant Men's Club, Phi Delta Kappa. Republican. Office: 30 Riverside Dr Youngstown OH 44514-2049 Office Phone: 330-757-7000. Business E-Mail: pola-rz@access-k12.org.

**ZORNES, MILFORD,** artist; b. Camargo, Okla., Jan. 25, 1908; s. James Francis and Clara Delphine (Lindsay) Z.; m. Gloria Codd, 1935; 1 son, Franz Milford; m. Patricia Mary Palmer, Nov. 8, 1947; 1 dau., Maria Patricia. Student, Otis Art Inst., Los Angeles, 1929, Pomona Coll., 1930-34. Instr. art Pomona Coll., 1946-50; art dir. Vortox and Padua Hills Theatre, Claremont, 1954-66. Exhibited, Calif. Watercolor Soc., Met. Mus., Am. Watercolor Soc., Corcoran Gallery, Bklyn. Mus., Denver Mus., Cleve. Mus., L.A. Mus., Brooks Gallery, London, Bombay Art Assn., Chgo. Art Inst., Butler Mus., Gallery Modern Masters, Washington, Santa Barbara (Calif.) Mus., Cin. Mus., Laguna (Calif.) Art Gallery, Oklahoma City Mus., Springville (Utah) Mus., Claremont (Calif.) Fine Arts, Anderson Art Gallery, Sunset Beach, Calif.; represented in permanent collections at L.A. Mus., White House Collection, Met. Mus., Pentagon Bldg., Butler Mus., UCLA, Nat. Acad., San Diego Mus., L.A. County Fair, Home Savs. and Loan Assn., L.A., Corcoran Gallery, Washington; mem. art com., Nat. Orange Show, San Bernardino, Calif., 1963-65; author: A Journey to Nicaragua, 1977, The California Style: California Watercolor Artists, 1925-1955, 1985; subject of book by Gordon McClelland: Milford Zornes, Hillcrest Press, 1991. Served with U.S. Army, 1943-45, CBI. Recipient Paul Prescott Barrow award Pomona Coll., 1987, David Prescott Burrows award, 1991, A Most Disting. Citizen award So. Utah State Coll., 1988, Am. Artist Achievement award Am. Artist Mag., 1994; named Nat. Academician. Mem. NAD, Am. Watercolor Soc., Southwestern Watercolor Soc., Watercolor West, Nat. Watercolor Soc., Utah Watercolor Soc. Address: 2136 Brescia Ave Claremont CA 91711-1804 *It has been my effort in life to have awareness: not to have all knowledge because no one can encompass all knowledge; not to have only wealth or only success, because there is no dimension of completeness of wealth or success; not to achieve complete goodness, because goodness and right are relative; not to enjoy the epitome in taste because taste is a gratification of self alone; but rather to seek and achieve understanding of relative values and a concept of the completeness of life. With this as my effort and my inner goal, I find success within the areas of my limited abilities, my meager knowledge, and my frail grasp of the infinite.*

**ZORNOW, DAVID MERRILL,** lawyer; b. NYC, Mar. 31, 1955; s. Jack and Marion (Gilden) Z.; m. Martha Malkin, July 21, 1985; children: Samuel Morris, Hannah Jane, Ethan Lewis. AB summa cum laude, Harvard U., 1976; JD, Yale U., 1980. Bar: NY 1981, DC 1988, US Ct. Appeals (3d cir.) 1982, US Dist. Ct. (so. dist.) NY 1983, US Ct. Appeals (2d cir.) 1984, US Dist. Ct. DC 1989, US Ct. Appeals (DC cir.) 1989, US Dist. Ct. (ea. dist.) NY 1993. Law clerk to Hon. Herbert J. Stern US Dist. Ct. NJ, Newark, 1980-82; assoc. Kramer Levin Kamin Nessen & Frankel, NYC, 1982-83; asst. US atty. So.

Dist. NY US Atty.'s Office, NYC, 1983-87; assoc. ind. counsel Office Ind. Counsel-Iran/Contra Investigation, Washington, 1987-89; ptnr., head NY white collar criminal def. practice Skadden, Arps, Slate, Meagher & Flom LLP, NYC, 1989—. Chmn. NYC Civilian Complaint Rev. Bd., 1994-96; vis. faculty Trial Advocacy Workshop Harvard Law Sch., Cambridge, Mass., 1988, Benjamin N. Cardozo Sch. Law; spkr. and writer on white collar crime issues. Contbr. articles to profl. publ. Mem. Fed. Bar Coun., Assn. Bar City NY, NY Coun. Def. Lawyers., Phi Beta Kappa. Office: Skadden Arps Slate Meagher & Flom LLP 4 Times Sq Fl 39 New York NY 10036-6595 Office Phone: 212-735-2890. Office Fax: 917-777-2890. E-mail: dzornow@skadden.com.

**ZOROWSKI, CARL FRANK,** engineering educator, academic administrator; b. Pitts., July 14, 1930; s. Stanley and Mary Josephine (Kozuch) Z.; m. Sarah Jane Crossley, Aug. 7, 1954 (dec. 1983); children: Kathleen Ann, Karl Alan, Kristine Alaine; m. Louise Parrish Lockwood, Apr. 13, 1985. BSME, Carnegie Inst. Tech., 1952, MSME, 1953, PhD, 1956. Instr. Carnegie Inst. Tech., Pitts., 1952-56, asst. prof., 1956-61, assoc. prof., 1961-62; prof. dept. mech. and aero. engring. N.C. State U., Raleigh, 1964-66; R.J. Reynolds Industries prof., 1966-97; assoc. dept. head, 1964-72; dept. head, 1972-79; assoc. dean acad. affairs Sch. Engring., 1979-85; dir. Integrated Mfg. Sys. Inst., 1986-92; dept. head, 1992-93; dir. Succeed/NSF Coalition, 1993-97; assoc. dean acad. affairs, 1993-94; R.J. Reynolds Industries emeritus prof., 1997—. Contbr. articles to profl. jours.; patentee in field. 2d lt. USAR, 1952-58. Recipient Rsch. award Sigma Xi, 1967. Fellow ASME (Richards Meml. award 1975), Fellow Am. Soc. Engring. Edn. (We. Electric award 1968); mem. Fiber Soc. (Achievement award 1970). Home: 103 Windyrush Ln Cary NC 27511-9758 Office: NC State U PO Box 7901 Raleigh NC 27695-0001 Personal E-mail: zorowski@mindspring.com. Business E-Mail: zorowski@eos.ncsu.edu.

**ZORTHIAN, BARRY,** communications executive; b. Kutahia, Turkey, Oct. 8, 1920; naturalized, US, 1930; s. Herbert Peter and Annaly (Markarian) Zorthian; m. Margaret Aylaian, June 6, 1948; children: Gregory Jannig, Stephen Arnak. BA, Yale U., 1941; LLB, N.Y. U., 1953; LLD (hon.), Ind. Inst. Tech., 1970. Bar: NY 1953. Newspaper reporter, 1936-42; newspaper and radio reporter, 1947-48; news and policy editor USIA, 1948-56, program mgr. Voice of Am., 1956-61; dep. pub. affairs. officer USIS, India, 1961-64; min.-counselor for info. Am. Embassy, Vietnam, 1964-68; v.p. Time, Inc., 1969-79, v.p. govt. affairs, 1974-79; pres. Time-Life Broadcast, 1969-73, Washington/Balt. Regional Assn., 1979-81; sr. v.p. Gray and Co., Washington, 1981-84; ptnr. Alcalde & Fay, Arlington, Va., 1984—. Bd dirs Am. Univ. Armenia, Armenian Gen Benvolent Union, Internat. Rsch. and Exchs. With USMC, 1942—46, col USMCR, 1946—73. Mem.: Marine Corps Res. Officers Assn., Washington Inst. Fgn. Affairs, Am. Fgn. Svc. Assn., Coun. Fgn. Rels., Congl. Country Club (Washington), Met. Club (Washington), Burning Tree Club (Washington), Century Assn. Club (N.Y.C.). Home: 4201 Cathedral Ave NW Apt 405E Washington DC 20016-4914 Office: Alcalde & Fay 1111 Wilson Blvd Ste 850 Arlington VA 22201-3051 Office Phone: 703-841-0626. Personal E-mail: barzor2@aol.com.

**ZOSIKE, JOANIE FRITZ,** theater director, actress; b. Bklyn., July 6, 1949; d. Nathan and Gloria S. (Greenberg) Hieger; m. Godson Zosike. BA in Theatre, NYU, 1980. Actor The Living Theatre, NYC, 1990—. Co-dir. DADAnewyork; co-founder and co-dir. Action Racket Theatre, N.Y.C., 1998—; artist-in-residence Living Theatre Workshops (USA) Author: (stage prodns.) You Told Me That the Carousel Was Crystal, Frames, Inside, 12 Steps to Murder; author: (with Hanon Reznikov) And Then The Heavens Closed; actress (stage prodns.) Chisciotte, Not in My Name, Mysteries and Smaller Pieces, Utopia, Anarchia, Humanity, Body of God, I and I, Midsummer Night's Dream, Mother Courage, Resistance, (solo performances) All Right So I AM the Earth, Harpies Complex, Ereshkigal's Peg, Fritzgabriel Cabaret, Alen Mak Festival (Bulgaria), Festival des Politisches Liedes (Germany), (films) Mass and Masses, Human Flesh; vocalist (radio show) Women on the Edge of Time; contbr. Between Ourselves: Letters Between Mothers and Daughters (edited by Karen Payne), Women in American Theatre (edited by Helen Krich Chinoy and Linda Walsh Jenkins); contbr. poetry and articles to artistic jours. Bd. dirs N.Y.C. Peoples Life Fund; participating artist Theatres Against War. Mem. War Resisters League, New Yorkers Against the Death Penalty. Office: The Living Theatre 2565 Broadway 515 New York New York 10025

**ZOTOS, FREDERIC P.,** research and development company executive; BS in Mech. Engring., Northeastern U., 1987, JD, MBA, 1993, MSEE, 1994. Bar: Mass., Conn., registered; (patent atty.). Intellectual property assoc. Pepe & Hazard, Hartford, Conn., 1994—96; asst. to pres. and patent counsel Competitive Technologies, Inc., Fairfield, Conn., 1996—98; ind. patent atty., tech. lic. cons. Cohasset, Mass., 1998—99; dir. due diligence, internal legal counsel Licent Capital, LLC, Jericho, NY, 1999—2000; dir. Atlantic Tech. Ventures, Inc., N.Y.C., 1999—, pres., 2000—. Co-chair Fairfield-Westchester. Mem.: Lic. Exec. Soc. (chair N.Y.C. chpts., mem. fin. markets com.). Office: Atlantic Technology Ventures, Inc 787 7th Ave New York NY 10019-6018

**ZOTTARELLI, LISA KATHERINE,** sociologist; b. San Antonio, Mar. 16, 1970; d. Angelo Prospero Zottarelli and Martha Ann Head; life ptnr. T. S. Sunil; children: Michael Prospero, James Alexander. BS in Criminal Justice, Tex. State U., 1996; MS, U. North Tex., 1998, PhD, 2002. Tchg. fellow U. North Tex., Denton, 1999—2001; asst. prof. Idaho State U., Pocatello, 2001—03; asst. prof., grad. advisor Tex. Woman's U., Denton, 2003—. Affiliate faculty Idaho State U., Pocatello, 2003; vis. lectr. U. Tex., San Antonio, 2004. Vol. Denton County Dem. Party, 2004. Fedn. of North Tex. Area Universities Robert Toulouse Doctoral scholar, U. North Tex., 2000—01, Toulouse Sch. Grad. Studies Doctoral fellow, 1998—2001, Faculty Rsch. grantee, Idaho State U., 2002. Mem.: Southwestern Social Sci. Assn., Am. Sociol. Assn., Internat. Visual Sociology Assn., Alpha Kappa Delta, Phi Kappa Phi. Roman Catholic. Office: Texas Womans Univ Sociology Dept PO Box 425887 Denton TX 76204 Office Phone: 940-898-2062. Office Fax: 940-898-2067. Business E-Mail: lzottarelli@mail.twu.edu.

**ZOTTER, BRUCE C.,** lawyer; b. New Britain, Conn., Sept. 18, 1942; BSME, MIT, 1965, MSME, 1966; JD with honors, George Washington U., 1975. Bar: Va. 1975, DC 1976. Recipient: US Patent & Trademark Office. Ptnr. Finnegan, Henderson, Farabow, Garrett & Dunner LLP, Washington, leader, Mech. Practice Group. Mem.: Am. Intellectual Property Law Assn., ABA, Va. Bar Assn., Bar Assn. DC, DC Bar, Sigma Xi, Pi Tau Sigma. Office: Finnegan Henderson Farabow Garrett & Dunner LLP 901 New York Ave NW Washington DC 20001-315 Office Phone: 202-408-4000. Office Fax: 202-408-4400. Business E-Mail: zotterb@finnegan.com

**ZOU, CHANGPING,** research scientist, educator; arrived in U.S., 1986; d. Daming Zou and Yidi Zhao; m. Sui Zhang; children: Aaron Tan Zou-Zhang, Philip Tigar Zou-Zhang. MD, Beijing Med. Coll., 1983; MPH, U Tex., Houston, 1990; PhD, U. Tex., Houston, 1994. Postdoctoral fellow U. Tex. MD Anderson Cancer Ctr., Houston, 1994—97, instr., 1997—98, asst. prof., 1998—2003; faculty mem. Grad. Sch. Biomed, Sci. U. Tex., Houston, 1998—2003; assoc. mem. U. Ariz., Tucson, 2003—. Grantee, Ovarian Cancer Rsch. Fund, 2004—05, Cervical Cancer Rsch., 2000—01, 2002—03; Cancer Prevention Grad. fellow, NCI, 1994—95. Mem.: Internat. Soc. Cancer Chemoprevention, Am. Soc. Preventive Oncology, Am. Assn. Cancer Rsch., Peking U. Alumni Assn. (bd. dirs 2000—03). Achievements include patents pending for nutral prodcts in cancer chemoprevention; research in Vitamin A derivatives in head and neck cancer chemoprevention; Vitamin A derivatives in bladder cancer chemoprevention. Office: U Ariz 1501 N Campbell Ave Tucson AZ 05078 Office Phone: 520-626-8883. Office Fax: 520-626-9287. Personal E-mail: zou@email.arizona.edu.

**ZOU, XIAOLEI,** meteorologist, educator; b. Jiang Ying, China, May 5, 1960; d. Shixi Zou and Jingan Li; m. Yuanzheng Yao; children: Yimei (Laura) Yao, Yige (Noah) Yao. PhD in Meteorology, Acad. Sinica, Beijing, China,

1988. Fellow U. Ill. Urbana-Champaign, 1989—89, Fla. State U., Tallahassee, 1989—93; scientist Nat. Ctr. Atmospheric Rsch., Boulder, Colo., 1993—97; prof. Fla. State U., Tallahassee, 1997—. Mem.: Royal Meteorol. Soc., Am. Geophy. Union, Am. Meteorol. Soc. Office: Fla State Univ 404 Love Bldg Tallahassee FL 32306 Office Phone: 850-644-6025. Office Fax: 850-644-9642. Business E-Mail: zou@met.fsu.edu.

**ZOUBAREFF, KATHY OLGA,** administrative assistant; b. Hassalt, Belgium; d. Vladimir F. and Kataryna (Sarcov) Z. Grad. in TV acting, J.R. Powers Sch.-Model Agy.; BA in Polit. Sci., Wayne State U.; postgrad., Ann Parsley Sch. Dance, Clinton Twp., Mich., 1990-95, Mary Skiba Sch. Dance, 1995—; A in Gen. Studies, Drama, Macomb Community Coll.; fitness and nutrition cert., Internat. Corr. Schs. Ctr., Scranton, Pa.; voice studies, Ctr. for Creative Studies, Detroit, 1994—; drama studies, Wayne State U., 1994—; broadcasting studies, Macomb C.C., Warren, Mich., 2001. Acct./adminstrv. asst. Univ. Orthopaedic Assocs. Detroit, P.C., 1990-96, office mgr., 1996-98; with The Zoubareff Co., 1998—. Actress, dancer, fashion, TV comml. and photog. model/film screen extra, Hawaiian Tropic Pageants; fragrance model Coty Fragrances, Celion Dion; swimsuit model Ujena; nat. spokesperson Dryell, Physique, Pantene, Oil of O'Lay, Vidal Sassoon, Cover Girl, Coca Cola, Marlboro, Nascar, Indy 400, others; Mae West look-alike; beauty cons. Olay, Cover Girl, Rimmell, London, Lee Jeans. Mem. Renaissance Ctr. Fashion Panel, Detroit, 1989-91; rsch. bd. advisors Am. Biog. Inst.; mem. Internat. Biog. Centre Adv. Coun., 1992, St. Clair Shores Players; contbg. Am. Fam. Inst. L.A., 2006 Avocations: art, drawing, exercise. Home: 38579 Delta Dr Clinton Township MI 48036-1711 Office: Univ Orthopaedics 28800 Ryan Rd Warren MI 48092 Office Phone: 586-201-2903, 586-558-1132. Business E-Mail: kathy_zou@mclanemodels.com. E-Mail: madonna48036@yahoo.com.

**ZOURARAKIS, DEMETRIO PERIFERACHIS,** natural resource scientist; b. Buenos Aires, Argentina, Mar. 2, 1952; s. Jorge Demetrio Zourarakis and Elena Periferachis, Jorge Periferachis and Palmira Angela Comerci; m. Joyce Carol Zourakis, July 13, 1945; 1 child. Zachary Alexander. BS, Universidad Nacional de Buenos Aires, 1977; MSc, Iowa State U., Ames, 1987; PhD, U. Ky., Lexington, 1992. Geog. info. sys. processing specialist divsn. conservation Ky. Dept. Natural Resources, Frankfort, 2000—04; remote sensing and geog. info. sys. analyst divsn. geog. info. Commonwealth Office Tech., Frankfort, 2004—. Adj. prof. dept. geography and geosciences U. Louisville, 1998—. J. Fielding Reed fellow, Potash and Phosphate Inst., 1988. Fellow: Soil and Water Conservation Soc. (mem. Ky. Bluegrass chpt.); mem.: Mensa, Gamma Sigma Delta, Sigma Xi (hon.). Home: 5011 Venetian Way Versailles KY 40383 Office: Commonwealth Office Tech Divsn Geog Info 403 Wapping St Ste 340 Frankfort KY 40601 Personal E-mail: demetrio.zourarakis@gmail.com. Business E-Mail: demetrio.zourarakis@ky.gov.

**ZSCHAU, JULIUS JAMES,** lawyer; b. Peoria, Ill., Apr. 1, 1940; s. Raymond Johann Ernst and Rosamond Lillian (Malicoat) Z.; m. Leila Joan Krueger, Aug. 7, 1971; children: Kristen Elisabeth, Kimberly Erna, Kira Jamie, Karla Johanna. BS, U. Ill., Champaign, 1964, JD, 1966; LLM, John Marshall Law Sch., 1978. Bar: Ill. 1966, Fla. 1975. Atty. Ill. Central Gulf R.R. Co., Chgo., 1966-68; assoc. Coin & Sheerin, Chgo., 1968-70, Snyder, Clarke et al, Waukegan, Ill., 1970-72; counsel Ill. Ctr. Corp., Chgo., 1972-74; v.p., gen. counsel, sec. Am. Agronomics Corp., Tampa, Fla., 1974-76; pres. Sorota & Zschau, Clearwater, Fla., 1976-90; shareholder Baynard, Harrell, Ostow & Ulrich PA, 1990-94, Johnson, Blakely, Pope, Bokor, Ruppel and Burns, Clearwater, 1994—2002, Pennington Moore Wilkinson Bell & Dunbar PA, 2002—. Bd. dirs. Attys. Title Ins. Fund, Inc., chmn. bd. dirs., 1994—95; chmn. com. on land trusts Fla. Bar, chmn. Real Property, Probate and Trust Law sect., vice chair grievance com., 1985—87, chair leadership conf., 1987; chmn. Jud. Nominating Commn. of 6th Jud. Dist., 1991—94; mem. jud. nominating com. Ct. Appeals (2d dist.). Bd. dirs. Nat. Attys. Title Assurance Fund, Attys. Title Ins. Fund, Attys. Title Guaranty Fund of Colo., treas.; mem. Pinellas County Exec. Com., Tampa Regional Planning Coun., 1988-92. Served to capt. USNR, 1962-92. Fellow: Am. Bar Found. (life; mem.: ABA (chmn. standing com. lawyers title guaranty funds 1991, chmn. land trust com.), Fla. Bar Found. (chmn. jud. nominations procedures com. 1992—93, legal aid to poor com.), Fla. Coun. Bar Assn. (past pres., past chmn. vol. bar liaison com.), Clearwater Bar Assn. (past pres.), Chgo. Bar Assn., Ill. Bar Assn., Am. Coll. Real Estate Lawyers (chmn. condominium com.), Clearwater C. of C. (bd. dirs., past v.p.), Countryside Country Club. Republican. Home: 1910 Saddlehill Rd N Dunedin FL 34698-2437 Office: Julius J Zschau 1247 S Myrtle Ave Clearwater FL 33756-3469 Business E-Mail: jayz@penningtonlaw.com.

**ZSCHAU, MARILYN,** singer; b. Chgo., Feb. 9, 1944; d. Edwin Arthur Eugene and Helen Elizabeth (Kelly) Z. BA in Radio, TV and Motion Pictures, U. N.C., 1959; grad., Juilliard Sch. Music, 1965; studied opera theatre with Christopher West, studied voice with Florence Page Kimball, studied with John Lester. Toured with Met. Nat. Co., 1965-66; debut, Vienna Volksoper, in Die Tote Stadt, 1967, Vienna Staatsoper, in Ariadne auf Naxos, 1971; with N.Y.C. Opera in La Fanciulla del West, 1978; debut Royal Opera, covent Garden in La Boheme, 1982, Met. Opera, in La Boheme, 1985, La Scala, in Die Frau ohne Schatten, 1986; has toured and sung in many countries including U.S.A., Japan, and Australia. Office: 4245 Wilshire Blvd Oakland CA 94602-3549 Office Phone: 510-484-7742. E-Mail: marilynzschau@yahoo.com.

**ZSIGMOND, VILMOS,** cinematographer, film director; b. Szeged, Hungary, June 16, 1930; came to U.S., 1957, naturalized, 1962; s. Vilmos and Bozena (Illichmann) Z.; children: Julia, Susi. MA, U. Film and Theater Arts, Budapest, Hungary, 1955. Free-lance cinematographer for numerous commls., also ednl., documentary and low-budget feature films, 1965-71; now dir., cinematographer on commls. (winner several nat. and internat. awards); feature films, 1971-; films include McCabe and Mrs. Miller, 1971; Images, 1972, Deliverance, 1972, The Long Goodbye, 1973, Scarecrow, 1973, Cinderella Liberty, 1973, The Sugarland Express, 1974, Obsession, 1976, Close Encounters of the Third Kind, 1977 (Acad. award 1977), The Last Waltz, 1978, The Rose, 1978, The Deerhunter, 1978 (Acad. award nomination and Brit. Acad. award), Heavens Gate, 1979, The Border, 1980, Blow Out, 1980, Jinxed, 1981, Table for Five, 1982, The River, 1983 (Acad. award nomination), No Small Affair, 1984, Real Genius, 1985, Witches of Eastwick, 1986, Journey to Spirit Island, 1988, Fatman and Little Boy, 1989, Two Jakes, 1989, Bonfire of the Vanities, 1990, Stalin, 1991 (CableAce award, Direction of Photography and/or Lighting Direction in a Dramatic/Theatrical Special/Movie or Miniseries, ASC award, Emmy award), Sliver, 1992; dir. The Long Shadow, 1992, Intersection, 1993, Maverick, 1993, The Crossing Guard, 1994, Assassins, 1995, The Ghost and the Darkness, 1996 (ASC Award nomination), Fantasy for a New Age, 1997, Playing By Heart, 1998, The Body, 1999, The Mists of Avalon, 2000, Life as a House, 2001, (opera film) Bánk Bán, 2002, Jersey Girl, 2003, Melinda and Melinda, 2004, The Black Dahlia, 2005. Recipient lifetime achievement award Worldfest, Flagstaff, 1998. Mem. Acad. Motion Picture Arts and Scis., Dirs. Guild, Am. Soc. Cinematographers (lifetime achievement award 1998). Office Phone: 818-753-6300. Personal E-mail: vilmoszsigmond@hotmail.com. Business E-Mail: patty@themackagency.net.

**ZUBAREV, EUGENE,** chemistry professor; b. Astrakhan, Russia, May 4, 1971; s. Ludmila Zubareva and Rudolf Zubarev; m. Elena Bolonina, May 5, 1975; children: Christina Zubareva, Alex. PhD, Russian Acad. Scis., Moscow, 1996. Asst. prof. materials sci. and chemistry, Iowa State U., Ames, 2000—05; asst. prof. chemistry Rice U., Houston, 2005—. Recipient Career Devel. award, NSF, 2006—. Office: Rice U Dept Chemistry 6100 Main St MS-60 Houston TX 77005 Office Phone: 713-348-3761.

**ZUBER, MARIA T.,** geophysicist, educator; married; 2 children. BA in Astrophysics & Geology, U. Penn., 1980; SsM in Geophysics, Brown U., 1983, PhD in Geophysics, 1986. Rsch. asst. geological sciences Brown U. 1980—86; NRC rsch. assoc., Geodynamics Branch NASA/Goddard Space

Flight Ctr., 1985—86, geophysicist, Geodynamics Branch, 1986—92, sr. rsch. scientist, Lab. for Terrestrial Physics, 1994—; assoc. rsch. prof. geophysics Johns Hopkins U., 1991—92, assoc. prof. geophysics, 1991—95, prof. geophysics, 1995; cons. aerospace div. MIT Lincoln Lab., 2002—; prof. geophysics & planetary sci. MIT, 1995—98, E.A. Griswold prof. geophysics, dept. earth, atmospheric & planetary scis., 1998—, head dept. earth, atmospheric & planetary sciences, 2003—. Visiting asst. prof. geophysics Johns Hopkins U., 1990; guest investigator Woods Hole Oceanographic Institution, 1996—2004; sr. sci. fellow Radcliffe Inst. for Advanced Study, 2002—03; visiting scholar Harvard U., 2002—03; bd. dirs. Planetary Soc., 2000—; mem. advisory council Jet Propulsion Lab.; mem. Independent Status Review Bd., NASA Mars Exploration Rover, 2003—, President's Commn. on Implementation of US Space Exploration Policy, 2004. Mem. bd. reviewing editors Science, 2000—. Recipient NASA Peer award, 1988, NASA Outstanding Performance award, 1988, 1989, 1990, 1991, 1992, NASA Exceptional Scientific Achievement medal, 1995, Scientific Achievement award, Am. Inst. of Aeronautics & Astronautics, 2002, NASA Disting. Public Service medal, 2004. Fellow: Am. Acad. Arts & Sciences, Am. Geophysical Union; mem.: NAS, Am. Astronomical Soc., AAAS. Office: MIT Dept Earth Atmospheric & Planetary Scis 54-518 77 Mass Ave Cambridge MA 02139 Business E-Mail: zuber@mit.edu.*

**ZUBER, RANDOLPH CLARK,** retired urologist; b. Dallas, Apr. 4, 1941; s. Oran H. and Minnie M. (Cuthbertson) Z.; m. Billie Gayle Schumacher, June 20, 1964; children: Randolph Blake, Rustin Kurt. AAPS, Amarillo Jr. Coll., 1961; BA, U. Tex., 1963; MD, U. Tex., Galveston, 1967. Diplomate Am. Bd. Urology. Intern Kans. U. Med. Ctr., 1967—68, resident in urology, 1969—72; practice medicine specializing in urology Kerrville, Tex., 1974—2003; part-time urology practice South Tex. VA Hosp., Kerrville, Tex., 2003—06; ret., 2006; claims cons. Tex. Med. Liability Trust, 1986—. Bishop Ch. of Christ, 1983-93; mem. urologic cultural exchange to Peoples Republic of China People to People Found., 1987; bd. dirs. Tex. Med. Liability Trust, 1979-1986. Founding dir., past pres. Hill County Right to Life; chmn. steering com. Kerr County YMCA, 1990. Served to maj. USAF, 1972-74. Recipient Disting. Leadership award, cert. of excellence Leadership Kerr County, 1989. Fellow ACS; mem. Am. Urol. Assn. (Tex. rep., bd. dirs. south ctrl. sect. 1990-96), Tex. Urol. Soc. (pres. 1988-89, bd. dirs. 1996-98), Tex. Med. Assn. Office: South Tex VA Hosp Kerrville TX 78028 Office Phone: 830-896-2020.

**ZUBERI, TUKUFU,** sociologist, educator; b. Oakland, Calif., Apr. 26, 1959; s. Willie McDaniel and Annie E. Franklin. BA, San Jose State U., Calif., 1981; MA, Calif. State U., Sacramento, Calif., 1985; PhD, U. Chgo., Chgo., Ill., 1989. Author: Swing Low Sweet Chariot, 1995, Thicker Than Blood, 2001, A Demography of South Africa, 2005; co-host: (TV series) History Detectives, 2002—. Grantee, Rockefeller Found., Andrew Mellon Found., NIMH. Mem.: Internat. Union Scientific Study Population, Population Assn. Am. Avocation: photography. Office: Univ Pa 3718 Locust Walk Philadelphia PA 19104-6209 Office Phone: 215-573-5129.

**ZUBKOFF, DANIEL J.,** lawyer; b. Buffalo, May 28, 1957; AB magna cum laude, Cornell U., 1979; JD cum laude, Harvard Law Sch., 1982. Bar: NY 1983. Co-adminstr. ptnr. Cahill Gordon & Reindel LLP, NYC, ptnr., Fin. Securities & Banking Practice Group. Mem.: Phi Beta Kappa. Office: Cahill Gordon & Reindel LLP 80 Pine St New York NY 10005-1702 Office Phone: 212-701-3466. Office Fax: 212-378-2383. Business E-Mail: dzubkoff@cahill.com.

**ZUBKOFF, MICHAEL,** medical educator; b. NYC, June 2, 1944; s. Harry and Catherine (O'Brien) Z.; children: Steven, Joel, Lisa; m. Leslee Ann Michaels, 1991. BA, Am. Internat. Coll., 1965, LLD (hon.), 1981; MA, Columbia U., 1966, cert. Internat. Fellow program, 1966, PhD, 1968; MA (hon.), Dartmouth Coll., 1980. Research assoc. conservation human resources Columbia U., N.Y.C., 1966-67; assoc. prof. econs. Fisk U., Nashville, 1967-70; assoc. prof. health econs., assoc. chmn. dept. family and community health Meharry Med. Coll., Nashville, 1967-75; assoc. prof. econs. Vanderbilt U., Nashville, 1970-75; prof. econs. and mgmt. Amos Tuck Sch. Bus., prof. chmn. dept. cmty. and family medicine Med. Sch. Dartmouth Coll., Hanover, NH, 1975—. Mem. inst. medicine Nat. Acad. Scis., 1982—, mem. assembly engrs. inst. med. com. on tech. and health care, 1977-79, grad. med. ednl. nat. adv. com., 1977-81., com. on grad.-med. edn. programs for mil. services Nat. Acad. Scis., 1980-82., nat. research council commn. on human resources Nat. Acad. Scis., 1980-84, com. on aging soc. Nat. Acad. Scis., 1984-89; corr. com. human rights Nat. Acad. Scis., 1983—, nat. rsch. coun. com. computer tech. and svc. sector productivity Nat. Acad. Scis., 1991-94; instr. econs. Harvard U., Yale U., and Columbia U., 1967-68. Co-author: Urban Health Services: The Case of New York, 1971, Consumer Incentives for Health Care, 1974, Health: A Victim of Cause of Inflation, 1976, Framework for Government Intervention in the Health Sector, 1978, Hospital Cost Containment: Selected Notes for Public Policy, 1980, Problem Based Learning of Social Science & Humanities by Fourth Year Medical Students, 1986, The Medical Outcomes Study: An Application of Methods for Monitoring the Results of Medical Care, 1989, Measuring Functional Status & Well Being: The Medical Outcomes Study Approach, 1992, Health Society & The Physician: Problem Based Learning of Social Sciences & Humanities, 1993; contbr. numerous articles to profl. jours. Del.; health spokesman White House Summit on Inflation, 1974. Fellow Woodrow Wilson Found., 1964-66, Fulbright Found., 1967-68, USPHS, 1966-67. Mem. Am. Econ. Assn., Am. Pub. Health Assn. Home: RR 1 Fairlee VT 05045-9801 Office: Dartmouth Med Sch Dept Comty & Family Med HB7250 Hanover NH 03755

**ZUBOV, LYNN,** special education educator, researcher; b. Bklyn., Dec. 3, 1960; d. David P. Roche III. BS in Spl. Edn., St. John's U., Jamaica, N.Y., 1983; MS in Spl. Edn., St. John's U., 1988, EdS in Supervision and Adminstrn., 1990; PhD in Spl. Edn., Vanderbilt U., Nashville, 1996. Tchr. asst. Little Village Sch., Garden City, N.Y., 1981-82; tchr. of emotionally disturbed I.H.B. R, Jamaica, N.Y., 1983-86, Poseidon, Los Angeles, 1986-87, ednl. coord., mainstream coord. P.S. 80, Jamaica, N.Y., 1987-91; rsch. asst. Peabody Coll. Vanderbilt U., Nashville, 1991-95; asst. prof. program dir. Canisius Coll. Buffalo, 1995-99; assoc. prof., program coord. Winston-Salem State U., 1999—2005, assoc. prof., program coord., 2005—. Spl. edn. cons. Paul J. Cooper, Bklyn., 1991; mem. project Basics I.H.S. 8, Jamaica, N.Y., 1983-86; sec. Pupil-Pers. Commn., P.S. 80, Jamaica, 1987-91. Cons., instr. How To Use The Apple Computer, How to Make Inclusion Work, Developing Positive Behavioral Support Plans Through the Use of a Functional Analysis of Behavior; co-author: Handbook for the Special Education Paraprofessional, 1990. Mem. CEC, N.Y. State Coun. for Exceptional Children (past pres.). Republican. Roman Catholic. Home: 229 Engleman Ave Burlington NC 27215-4801 Office: Winston-Salem State U 601 Martin Luther King Jr CB 19360 Winston Salem NC 27157 Office Phone: 336-750-2381. E-mail: zubovl@wssu.edu.

**ZUBRITSKY, ALEXANDER NICKOLAEVICH,** pathologist; b. Severo-Kurilsk, Sakhalin, Russia, Mar. 14, 1949; s. Nickolay Alexandrovich and Kaleriya Andreevna (Chechulina) Z.; children: Vladimir, Sergey Yashin. MD in Med. Scis., Med. Inst., 1974. Hosp. attendant dept. pathology City Hosp. N21, Sverdlovsk, Russia, 1965—67; hosp. attendant Medico-Legal Morgue N1, Sverdlovsk, 1967—68; nurse Sta. of Emergencies Care N1, Sverdlovsk, 1971—72; head pathology dept. Ctrl. Regional Hosp., Neviyansk, Russia, 1975—76; chief pathology dept., head pathologist Sverdlovsk Rd. Hosp., 1976—83; lectr. pathol. anatomy Med. Sch. Sverdlovsk Rd., 1976—77; chief dept. pathology mcpl. instn. Taldom Ctrl. Regional Hosp., 1983—; pathologist City Clin. Hosp., Moscow, 2004—. Contbr. articles to profl. jours. Recipient award Am. Coll. Chest Physicians, 1990, Pathology Rsch. Practice award, Taldom-Innsbruck, 1993, Internat. Peace prize UCC, 2003, 21st Century award for Achievement Bronze Medal, IBC, 2003, Internat. Scientist Yr. Gold Medal, 2004, World Medal of Freedom for Significant Accomplishments in Field of Pathol. Anatomy, ABI, 2005, Man of Achievement award for Outstanding Contbns. to Pathol. Anatomy of Cor Pulmonale, 2005, Best People of Russia medal, 2006; named Internat. Man Yr., 1994-95, 03. Mem.: AAAS, N.Y. Acad. Sci., Internat. Soc. Diagnostic Quantitative Pathology,

Internat. Soc. Heart Rsch. (European sect.), Internat. Union Against Tb and Lung Disease, European Soc. Pathology (rsch. bd. of advisors ABI, hon. mem. adv. and rsch. coun. IBC). Avocations: music, walking. Home: Prospekt Mira 101B/79 129085 Moscow Russia Office Phone: (7-496)-20-6-02-57. Personal E-mail: alex_79zubr@yahoo.com. Business E-Mail: zubr5taldom@mail.ru.

**ZUBROFF, LEONARD SAUL,** surgeon; b. Minersville, Pa., Mar. 27, 1925; s. Abe and Fannie (Freedline) Z. BA, Wayne State U., 1945, MD, 1949. Diplomate Am. Bd. Surgery. Intern Garfield Hosp., Washington, 1949-50, resident in surgery, 1951-55, chief resident surgery, 1954-55; pvt. practice medicine specializing in surgery, 1958-76; med. dir. Chevrolet Gear and Axle Plant, Forge Plant, GM, Detroit, 1977-78; divsnl. med. dir. Detroit Diesel Allison divsn., Detroit, 1978-87; regional med. dir. GM, 1987-89; ret., 1989. Chief of surgery, chief profl. svcs. N.E. Air Command, Pepperell AFB, Newfoundland. With USAF, 1956—58. Mem.: Le Vine Found. (trustee). Home and Office: 22511 S Bellwood Dr Southfield MI 48034-2116

**ZUCARO, ALDO CHARLES,** insurance company executive; b. Grenoble, France, Apr. 2, 1939; s. Louis and Lucy Zucaro; m. Gloria J. Ward, Oct. 12, 1963; children: Lucy, Louis, Faye. BS in Acctg, Queens Coll., N.Y.C., 1962. C.P.A., N.Y., Ill. Ptnr. Coopers & Lybrand (and predecessor), Chgo. and N.Y.C., 1962-76; exec. v.p., chief fin. officer Old Republic Internat. Corp., Chgo., 1976-81, pres., 1981—, chief exec. officer, 1990—, chmn. of the bd., 1993—. Pres., bd. dirs. Old Republic Life Ins. Co., Old Republic Life of N.Y., Old Republic Ins. Co., Internat. Bus. and Merc. Reassurance Co., Republic Mortgage Ins. Co., Old Republic Nat. Title Ins. Co., Home Owners Life Ins. Co. Editor: Financial Accounting Practices of the Insurance Industry, 1975, 76. Mem. AICPAs. Roman Catholic. Office: Old Republic Internat Corp 307 N Michigan Ave Chicago IL 60601-5311

**ZUCCARELLO, MARIO,** neurosurgeon, researcher; b. Catania, Italy, Apr. 25, 1952; m. Gabriella Tempesta, May 25, 1985; 1 child, Marco. Undergrad., U. Padova, Italy, 1970-76, MD, 1976. Intern U. Hosp., Padova, Italy, 1976-80, resident in neurosurgery, 1976-80; instr. neurosurgery Padova, 1981-84; rsch. fellow U. Va., Charlottesville, 1984-85; clin. fellow neurosurgery U. Cin., 1985-88, assoc. prof. neurosurgery, 1990-99, prof., 1999—, dir. cerebrovascular surgery; asst. prof. neurosurgery Genova, Italy, 1988-90; chief neurosurgery VAMC, Cin., 1990—; vice chmn. dept. neurosurgery U. Cin., 2004—. Contbr. articles to profl. jours. Capt. Italian Army, 1981-82. Recipient U. Cin. Rsch. award, 1995; Max Plank scholar, 1977-78, NATO scholar, 1984; VA Merit Rev. grantee Veteran Adminstrn. Med. Ctr., 1991—. Roman Catholic. Avocations: soccer, classical music, skiing, history, geography. Home: 231 Bethesda Ave Cincinnati OH 45229-2827 Office: U Cin 231 Bethesda Ave Cincinnati OH 45229-2827 Office Phone: 513-475-8624. Fax: 513-558-7702. E-mail: zuccarm@uc.edu.

**ZUCK, ALFRED MILLER,** public administration educator; b. East Petersburg, Pa., Aug. 27, 1934; s. Walter Newton and Mary (Miller) Z.; m. Geraldine Connelly, July 21, 1957; children: Susan, David. BA, Franklin and Marshall Coll., 1957; MPA, Syracuse U., 1958. Dir. fed. program Presdl. Commn. on Youth Opportunities, Washington, 1967-68; dir evaluation Employment and Tng. Adminstrn., Dept. Labor, Washington, 1968-70; dir adminstrn. and mgmt., 1970-75; comptroller U.S. Dept. Labor, Washington, 1975-77; exec. dir. Commn. on Exec., Legis. and Jud. Salaries, Washington, 1980; asst. sec. Dept. Labor, Washington, 1977-83, acting sec., 1981; asst. adminstr. EPA, Washington, 1983; exec. dir. Nat. Assn. Schs. of Pub. Affairs and Adminstrn., Washington, 1983-97; disting. prof. Am. U. Washington, 1996—2005, emeritus prof., 2005—. Pres. Internat. Inst. Adminstrv. Scis., Brussels, 1989-92, Am. Consortium for Internat. Pub. Adminstrn., Washington, 1984-89; bd. dirs. Pub./Pvt. Venture, Inc., Phila., 1984-90. Recipient Presdl. Disting. Exec. award Pres. of U.S., 1980; Disting. Alumni award Franklin and Marshall Coll., 1980. Fellow Nat. Acad. Pub. Adminstrn. (trustee 1989-95, chmn. bd. trustees 1993-95); mem. Phi Beta Kappa.

**ZUCKER, ALEXANDER,** physicist, researcher; b. Zagreb, Croatia, Aug. 1, 1924; came to U.S., 1939; s. William and Bertha (Klopfer) Z.; m. Joan-Ellen Jamieson, Nov. 28, 1953; children: Rebecca, Claire, Susannah. BA, U. Vt., Burlington, 1947; MS, Yale U., New Haven, 1948, PhD, 1950. Physicist Oak Ridge Nat. Lab., Tenn., 1950-60, assoc. dir. electro-nuclear div. Tenn., 1972-75, dir. heavy ion project Tenn., 1988, assoc. dir. phys. scis. Tenn., 1973-88, acting lab. dir. Tenn., 1988, assoc. dir. for nuclear techs., 1989-93; exec. dir., environ. studies bd. NAS-NAE, Washington, 1970-72; prof. physics U. Tenn., 1996—. Mem. U.S. del. to USSR on Peaceful Uses of Atomic Energy, 1963; Ford prof. physics U. Tenn., Knoxville, 1968-73; U.S. del. to Pugwash Conf., 1971; research coordination council Gas Research Inst., Chgo., 1978-85; com. Army manpower Nat. Research Council, Washington, 1982-83; adv. panel on technologies to reduce U.S. materials import vulnerability Office of Technology Assessment, Washington, 1982-85; council on energy engring. research Dept. of Energy, Washington, 1983—; industry, nat. lab. steel initiative White House, Washington, 1984 Editor Internat. Jour. Nuclear Sci. Applications, 1980—; cons. editor Ency. and Yearbook of Sci. and Tech. McGraw-Hill Pub. Co., 1989; mem. editorial bd. Science, 1981-82; contbr. articles to profl. jours. Guggenheim fellow, 1966-67; Fulbright-Hays Research scholar, 1966-67 Fellow Am. Phys. Soc., AAAS, Sigma Xi; mem. ASME, Nat. Acad. Scis. (nuclear physics del. to People's Republic of China 1979), Internat. Union Pure and Applied Physics (mem.-at-large U.S. nat. com. 1976-78) Achievements include research in nuclear physics with heavy ions and protons; accelerators, especially cyclotrons; materials research programs, especially high-temperature materials and surfaces; nuclear power reactors, especially gas-cooled reactors; research reactor with ultra high neutron flux. Office: Oak Ridge Nat Lab PO Box 2008 Oak Ridge TN 37831-2008

**ZUCKER, ALFRED JOHN,** English and history educator, academic administrator, historian; b. Hartford, Sept. 25, 1940; s. Samuel and Rose (Zucker) Z.; m. Sallie Lea Friedheim, Dec. 25, 1966; children: Mary Anne, John James Jr., James Patrick, Patrick Jonathan, Anne-Marie Kathleen, Kathleen Mary. AA, LA Valley Coll., 1960; AB in English, UCLA, 1962, AB in Speech, MA in English, 1962, MA in Speech, 1963, PhD, 1966; postgrad., U. So. Calif., Harvard U.; MA in history, CSULB, 2000, MA in Polit. Sci., 2004. Prof. English and history, chmn. div. humanities LA SW Coll., 1968-72; prof. English El Camino Coll., 1985—, LA Valley Coll., 1989—, chmn. dept. English, honors sponsor, 1997—. Contbr. articles to profl. jours. Mem. LA Coll. Dist. Senate, 1969—. Mem. AAUP, LA Coll. Tchrs. Assn. (dir.), Calif. Jr. Coll. Assn., Calif. Tchrs. Assn., World Affairs Coun., Calif. Scholarship Fedn., Mensa, KC, Gold Key, Phi Beta Kappa, Phi Delta Kappa (pres. UCLA chpt. 1966-67, v.p. 1967-68), Tau Alpha Epsilon, Phi Theta Kappa, Phi Alpha Theta, Phi Kappa Phi, Phi Delta Gamma. Office: 5800 Fulton Ave Van Nuys CA 91401-4062 Office Phone: 818-947-2343. E-mail: zuckeraj@lavc.edu.

**ZUCKER, BARBARA,** artist, art educator, curator; b. Phila., Aug. 2, 1940; m. Louis Lionni; 1 child, Gina. BS in Design, U. Mich., 1962; MA in Sculpture, Hunter Coll., 1977; MFA equivalency, Coll. Art Assn., 1975. Instr. Fordham U., N.Y.C., 1970, Phila. Coll. Art, 1977—79; prof. U. Vt., Burlington, 1979—2000, prof. emeritus, 2000—. Vis. prof. Princeton (NJ) U., 1974, Boston Mus. Sch., 1980, Yale U., New Haven, 1987—88, numerous art instns.; co-founder A.I.R. Gallery, N.Y.C., 1972; editl. assoc. Art News Mag., N.Y.C., 1970; docent Whitney Mus. Am. Art, N.Y.C., 1970; resident Yaddo, Saratoga Springs, NY, 2002, Saratoga Springs, 04, Ucross, Wyo., 1994. Numerous one person exhbns., group exhbns.; work reviewed in numerous publs., including NY Times, Art News, Art in Am., Boston Globe, Phila. Inquirer, Village Voice, Arts Mag., others. Recipient sculpture award, Nat. Endowment for Arts, 1975; Giverny fellow, Lila Acheson Wallace Found., Giverny, France, 1990.

**ZUCKER, BARBARA J.,** artist, educator; b. Abington, Pa., Oct. 5, 1943; d. Martin J. Herbert and Jean Elizabeth (McCormick) Martin; m. F. Donald Zucker, Apr. 4, 1964. BA, Ursinus Coll. 1966; postgrad., Acad. Fine Arts,

Florence, Italy, 1968-69; MEd, Temple U., 1971. Tchr. Ursinus Coll., 1982—99; gallery dir. ViewPoint LLC Arts and Events House, Lederach, Pa. One-woman shows include Bucknell U. Lewisburg, Pa., 1975, Phila. Art Alliance, 1975, Multiple Choice Gallery, Blue Bell, Pa., 1976, Ursinus Coll., 1977, 81, 85, Muhlenberg Coll., Allentown, Pa., 1979, Gwynedd-Mercy Coll., Gwynedd Valley, Pa., 1982, Glassboro (N.J.) State Coll., 1984, Galley 1st Bapt. Ch. in am., Providence, 1985, 2000, Univ. Gallery, St. Joseph's U., Phila., 1989, The Berman Mus. Art, Collegeville, 1990,2000, Moravian Coll., Bethlehem, Pa., 1992, Phila. Mus. Art, 1993, Widener U. Mus., Chester, Pa., 1994, 2000, Ocean Wood Gallery, Birch Harbor, Maine, 1995, Gloucester County Coll., Sewell, N.J., 1996, The Plastic Club, Phila., 1998, The Hahn Gallery, Phila., 2000, Hill Sch., Pottstown, Pa., 2004, Pfenninger Gallery, Lancaster, Pa., 2005; represented in collections at Berman Mus. Art, Reading (Pa.) Pub. Mus., Woodmere Art Mus., Phila., Rosemont (Pa.) Coll. Recipient Best of Show award Perkiomen Valley Art Ctr., 1993, 95, Open House Gallery award for excellence in water color, 1994, award in memory Ethel Sokolove, 1995, Fred D. Griffiths Printing Co. award, 1998, Friends of Artists Equity award Villanova U., 1998, 1st prize Phila./Tri State Artists Equity, 2002. Mem. Artists Equity Assn. (pres. Phila. chpt. 1993-94, exhibition chair 1993—, bd. dirs. 1992—), Golden Svc. award 1994), Phila. Water Color Club, Nat. League Am. Pen Women. Home: 10 Delphi Rd Schwenksville PA 19473-1713 Office Phone: 215-256-1444. Personal E-mail: bjzfdz@aol.com.

**ZUCKER, DAVID,** film director; b. Milw., Oct. 16, 1947; s. Charlotte Zucker; m. Danielle Zucker, May 1997; 2 children. Co-founder (with Jerry Zucker and Jim Abrahams) Kentucky Fried Theatre, Madison, WI, 1969, then Los Angeles, CA, 1972. Writer, actor: Kentucky Fried Movie, 1977; actor, writer, dir., prodr.: Airplane!, 1980, Top Secret, 1984, The Naked Gun, 1988, BASEketball, 1998; actor, writer, dir.: The Naked Gun 2 1/2: The Smell of Fear, 1991; actor, writer, prodr. The Naked Gun 33 1/3: The Final Insult, 1994; writer, dir., prodr. The Naked Gun: From the Files of Police Squad, 1988 (exec. prodr.), For Goodness Sake, 1993; dir. Ruthless People, 1986, My Boss's Daughter, 2003, Scary Movie 3, 2003; prodr. A Walk in the Clouds, 1995, For Goodness Sake II, 1996, Phone Booth, 2002, Santa Claus Conquers the Martians, 2002; exec. prodr. (TV series) Absolutely True, 2000, (TV films) Our Planet Tonight, 1987; writer, exec. prodr.: (TV series) Police Squad!, 1982.

**ZUCKER, DAVID F.,** information technology executive; b. Wichita Falls, Tex., Aug. 8, 1962; s. Paul Zucker and Margaret Anne (Keating) Chisholm. BA in Econ., Princeton U., 1984; MBA, Harvard, 1988. Fin. analyst Goldman, Sachs & Co., N.Y.C., 1984-86; exec. pub. ABC, Inc., Travel Agent Mag., N.Y.C., 1988-90; mgr. current series programming ABC Entertainment, L.A., 1991; dir. programming Eurosport, London, Paris, 1992-93; v.p. programming to exec. v.p. ESPN, Inc., Bristol, Conn., 1993-94; sr. v.p., managing dir. ESPN Internat., N.Y.C., 1995—99; pres., CEO Diva Systems Corp., 1999—2000, Skillgames LLC, 2000—02; mng. dir. Walker Digital LLC, 2000—02; pres., COO Playboy Enterprises, Inc., 2002—03; pres., CEO Midway Games, Inc., 2003—. Office: Midway Games Inc 2704 W Roscoe St Chicago IL 60618*

**ZUCKER, JEFFREY,** broadcast executive; m. Caryn Zucker; children: Andrew, Elizabeth, Peter. BA in Am. History, Harvard Coll., 1986. Rschr., 1988 Olympic Games, Seoul, Korea NBC Sports, 1986—88; field prodr. NBC News, 1989; exec. prodr. Today, 1992—93, Now with Tom Brokaw and Katie Couric, NBC Nightly News with Tom Brokaw, 1993, Today, 1994—2000; pres. NBC Entertainment, 2000—03, NBC Entertainment, News and Cable Group, 2003—05; CEO NBC Universal TV, 2005—. Exec. prodr.: (news segments) Russian coup, 1991, Persian Gulf War, 1991, 1993 and 1997 presdl. inaugurations, the bombing of Centennial Olympic Pk., 1996, 1996 and 2000 polit. conventions, Decision 2000; writer: The Games of the XXIV Olympiad (Emmy award, outstanding writing, 1988); supervising prodr.: "Senator Edward Kennedy" Today (Emmy award, outstanding interview, 1991); exec. prodr.: "California Fire" Now with Tom Brokaw and Katie Couric (Emmy award, outstanding coverage of a single breaking news story, 1993), "Tragedy in Rwanda" Now with Tom Brokaw and Katie Couric (Emmy award, outstanding background/analysis of a single current story, 1994), "The Brain" Now with Tom Brokaw and Katie Couric (Emmy award, outstanding informational or cultural program, 1994). Office: NBC 3000 W Alameda Ave Burbank CA 91523-0002 also: NBC Universal 52nd Fl 30 Rockefeller Plz New York NY 10112*

**ZUCKER, JERRY,** chemical manufacturing executive; b. Tel-Aviv, Israel, Aug. 24, 1949; s. Leon and Zipora (Shlifkovitz) Z.; m. Anita Goldberg, June 21, 1970; cildren: Jonathan Michael, Andrea Michelle, Jeffrey Mark. BS, U. Fla., 1968, MEE, 1972. Electronics design engr. Vital Industries, Inc., Gainesville, Fla., 1968-71; devel. engring. group dir. Cons. Engrs., Inc., Gainesville, 1971-73; supr. process engring. and tech. svcs. Hudson Pulp & Paper Corp. (now Ga. Pacific), Palatka, Fla., 1973-78; dir. mfg. and tech. svcs. Raybestos Manhattan, Inc., North Charleston, SC, 1978-82; chmn. bd., pres., CEO InterTech Group, Inc., 1983—; chmn., CEO Polymer Group, Inc., 1996—2003. Bd. dirs. High Tech. Coatings Corp., Advanced Chem. Techs., Inc., Tighitco, Inc., Ecosys, Inc., ConX Inc., Tycon Inc., Worthington Products Inc., Aerospace Def. Inc., Technetics Group, Inc., Thantex, Inc., Global Golf, Inc., Daramic, Inc., RemGrit Corp., Polyionix, Inc.; cons. phosphate mining, pulp and paper and sugar industries. Contbr. articles to tech. hours.; patentee in electrochem., mech. and chem. fields. Bd. dirs. Trident United Way, Charleston Jewish Fedn.; pres. Hotline Inc., Hebrew Benevolent Soc., Hebrew Orphan Soc., Orgn. Rehab. Tng., S.C. Aquarium; pres. Synagogue Emanuel; trustee S.C. Rsch. Inst., U. S.C., Med. U. S.C. Rsch. Inst.; mem. exec com., incoming pres. Coastal Coun., Boy Scouts Am.; active Charleston Regional Devel. Alliance; chmn. Charleston studies adv. bd. Coll. Charleston; mem. electronics engring. tech. bd. Trident Tech. Coll.; mem. electronics tech. adv. bd. Garrett Acad. Tech. Named one of Forbes' Richest Americans, 2006. Mem. IEEE, TAPPI (nat. elec. engring. com. 1977/95), Am. Chem. Soc., Charleston Metro C. of C. (bd. dirs.). Jewish. Office: The InterTech Group Inc PO Box 5205 4838 Jenkins Ave North Charleston SC 29405-4816

**ZUCKER, ROBERT A(LPERT),** psychologist; b. NYC, Dec. 9, 1935; s. Morris and Sophie (Alpert) Z.; m. Martine Latil; children: Lisa, Alex, Eleanor; m. Kristine Ellen Freeark, Mar. 10, 1979; 1 child, Katherine. B.C.E., CCNY, 1956; postgrad., UCLA, 1956-58; PhD, Harvard U., 1966. Diplomate Am. Bd. Profl. Psychology (clin.); lic. psychologist, Mich. From instr. to asst. prof. psychology Rutgers U., 1963-68; from asst. prof. to assoc. prof. to prof. Mich. State U., 1968-94; prof. psychology in psychiatry and psychology U. Mich., 1994—; dir. Addiction Rsch. Ctr., 1994—; dir. substance abuse sect. Dept. Psychiatry, 1994—; faculty assoc. RCGD Inst. for Social Rsch., 1996—. Vis. prof. U. Tex., Austin, 1975; vis. rsch. prof. psychology in psychiatry U. Mich., 1990-91; vis. scholar Inst. Alcohol Abuse and Alcoholism, 1980; dir. clin. tng. Mich. State U., 1982-94; lectr. Nebr. Symposium on Motivation, 1986; cons. in field. Co-author, editor: Further Explorations in Personality, 1981, Personality and the Prediction of Behavior, 1984, The Emergence of Personality, 1987, Studying Persons and Lives, 1990, Personality Structure in the Life Course, 1992, The Development of Alcohol Problems: Exploring the Biopsychosocial Matrix of Risk, 1994, Alcohol Problems Among Adolescents: Current Directions in Prevention Research, 1995, Alcohol Problems and Aging, 1998, Multiproblem Youth: Intervention and Treatment, 2004; contbr. chpts. and articles to profl. publs. Bd. dirs. Nat. Coun. on Alcoholism-Mich., 1978-82; mem. Psychosocial Initial Rev. Group, Nat. Inst. Alcohol Abuse and Alcoholism, 1989-92; mem. HPRB study sect. Ctr. for Sci. Rev., NIH, 1998-2000. Recipient Fellow's award, Inst. Children Youth and Families, Mich. State U., 1993, Excellence in Clin. Rsch. award, Blue Cross-Blue Shield Mich. Found., 1997; Merit grantee, NIH, 2003—. Fellow AAAS, APA (pres. addictions divsn. 50 1997-98), APS, Am. Orthopsychiat. Assn.; mem. Midwestern Psychol. Assn., Rsch. Soc. on Alcoholism (sec., bd. dirs. 2000-03); Office: Univ Mich Addiction Rsch Ctr 2025 Traverwood Dr Ste A Bldg 3 Ann Arbor MI 48105-2194 Office Phone: 734-998-7454. Business E-Mail: zuckerra@umich.edu.

**ZUCKER, STEFAN,** tenor, writer, editor, commentator; b. NYC; BS, Columbia U., 1967; postgrad., NYU, 1967-72. Freelance tenor concerts and operas in U.S. and Europe, 1965—; philosophy lectr. Coll. Ins. N.Y.C., 1972; tenor RCA Records, N.Y.C., 1972-77; guest singer radio and TV programs U.S. and Europe, 1975—; radio producer, host WKCR-FM, N.Y.C., 1980-94; opera critic N.Y. Tribune, 1983-84; host web radio program Opera Fanatic www.belcantosociety.org, 2002—. Lectr. The Mannes Coll. Music, 2000—. Author: The Origins of Modern Tenor Singing, 1997; appeared in film Opera Fanatic: Stefan and the Divas, 1998; record producer including Rossini's Rivals: Music By Then-Famous, Now-Obscure, Italian Composers, 1984; restorer films of opera singers, 1987—; singer, producer, stage dir., adminstr. various operas, 1967—; editor Opera Fanatic mag., 1986—; commentator articles singer (TV series) Bel canto: Tenors of the 78 Era, 1996-97; contbr. articles to Internat. Dictionary of Opera, Opera News, The Opera Quar., Am. Record Guide, Opera Fanatic, Globe & Mail, News World, Professione Musica, others. Pres. Bel Canto Soc., Inc., 1985—. Named Worlds Highest Tenor by Guinness Book of World Records, 1979—; subject of record Stefan Zucker: The World's Highest Tenor, 1981. Mem. NYU Philosophy Assn. (pres. 1969-72, v.p. 1968), Music Critics Assn., Assn. Furtherment Bel Canto (pres. 1967-80). Office: Bel Canto Soc Inc 11 Riverside Dr New York NY 10023-2504

**ZUCKERBERG, MARK (MARK ELLIOT ZUCKERBERG),** Internet company executive, entrepreneur, programmer; b. Dobbs Ferry, NY, May 14, 1984; Attended, Harvard U. Co-founder Facebook.com, Palo Alto, Calif. 2004—. Achievements include development of one of the most widely used networking websites among college and high school students with over 11 million users throughout the U.S., Canada and Europe; the ninth most highly trafficked website in U.S. Office: Facebook Inc 471 Emerson Ave Palo Alto CA 94301*

**ZUCKER-FRANKLIN, DOROTHEA,** internist, educator; b. Berlin, Aug. 9, 1930; came to U.S., 1949; d. Julian J. and Gertrude Zucker; m. Edward C. Franklin (dec.); 1 child, Deborah Julie. BA, CUNY, 1952, PhD in Sci. (hon.), 1996; MD, N.Y. Med. Coll., 1956. Diplomate Am. Bd. Medicine. Intern Phila. Gen. Hosp., 1956-57; resident in internal medicine Montefiore Hosp., N.Y.C., 1957-59, postdoctoral fellow in hematology, 1959-61; postdoctoral fellow in electron microscopy NYU Sch. Medicine, N.Y.C., 1961-63, asst. prof. medicine, 1963-67, assoc. prof., 1968-74, prof. medicine, 1974—; assoc. attending physician Bellevue Hosp., 1968-74, attending physician, 1974—; Assoc. attending physician Univ. Hosp., Tisch Hosp., 1968—74, attending physician, 1974—; cons. physician Manhattan VA Hosp., 1970—; meml. editl. bd. numerous publs., including Blood, 1963—76, 1980—86, Am. Jour. Pathology, 1979—, Ultrastructure Pathology, 1979—, Blood Cells, 1980, Am. Jour. Medicine, 1981—87, Hematology Oncology, 1982—, Jour. AIDS Rsch., 1987—, Hematopathology and Molecular Hematology, 1987—, others; meml. bd. reviewing editors Jour. Lab. and Clin. Medicine, 1990—; mem. hematology panel Health Rsch. Coun. City of N.Y., 1971—74; mem. pathology tng. com. Nat. Inst. Med. Scis., 1971—74; mem. allergy and immunology rsch. com. Nat. Inst. Allergy and Infectious Diseases, 1974—81; mem. U.S.-Israel Binat. Sci. Found., 1980—; mem. ad hoc promotion com. Harvard Med. Sch., 1981, 83; mem. blood products adv. com. FDA, 1981—86; mem. sci. adv. bd. and sci. rev. panel Israel Cancer Rsch. Found., 1982—90; mem. grant rev. panel VA AIDS Rsch., 1988—89; vis. fellow Jean Claude Bernard, 1974—75. Co-author: The Physiology and Pathology of Leukocytes, 1962, Amyloidosis, 1986, Atlas of Blood Cells: Function and Pathology, 2 vols., 1981, 3d edit., 2003, Thrombopoiesis and Thrombopoietins: Molecular, Cellular, Preclinical and Clinical Biology, 1996; contbr. over 300 articles to profl. jours. Bd. dirs. Henry M. and Lillian Stratton Found., Inc., 1987-95. Named to Hall of Fame, Hunter Coll., 1977, Internat. Profl. and Bus. Women, 1994. Fellow: AAAS, N.Y. Acad. Scis.; mem.: NTLV and Related Viruses, Internat. Retrovirology Assn., N.Y. Soc. Study of Blood (chair program com. 1976—80, pres. 1981—82), N.Y. Soc. Electron Microscopists (program chair 1984, pres. 1984—85), Am. Soc. Cell Biology (program com. internat. congress 1976), Am. Soc. Exptl. Pathology, Am. Assn. Immunologists, Am. Acad. Arts and Scis., Reticuloendothelial Soc. (life; program com. 1974—76, nominating com. 1976—78, pres. 1984—85), Am. Soc. Physiology, Federated Socs. Exptl. Biology and Medicine, Am. Soc. Hematology (program com. 1973, edn. com. 1974—78, chair subcom. on leukocyte physiology 1977, chair subcom. on immunohematology 1984, com. on advanced learning resources 1986—, exec. coun. 1987—91, pres.-elect 1992, v.p. 1993, pres. 1994—95, chair adv. bd. 1996, com. on govt. affairs 2001), Am. Soc. Clin. Investigation, Am. Fedn. Clin. Rsch., Am. Assn. Physicians, Inst. Medicine NAS, Alpha Omega Alpha, Phi Beta Kappa. Office: NYU Med Ctr 550 1st Ave New York NY 10016-6402 Office Phone: 212-263-5634. Business E-Mail: dorothea.zucker-franklin@med.nyu.edu.

**ZUCKERMAN, BRIAN DAVID,** lawyer; m. Jennifer Zuckerman; children: Jake, Mason. BA, SUNY, Binghampton, N.Y., 1991; JD, Temple U., 1994. Bar: Pa., N.J. Assoc. Klehr, Harrison, Harvey, Branzburg & Ellers, Phila., 1994—97; atty. Pepper Hamilton, Phila., 1997—99; gen. counsel, sec. Pep Boys, Phila., 1999—. Office: The Pep Boys 3111 W Allegheny Ave Philadelphia PA 19132

**ZUCKERMAN, HARRIET,** sociologist, educator; b. N.Y.C., July 19, 1937; d. Harry and Anne D. (Wiener) Z; m. Robert K. Merton, 1993. AB, Vassar Coll., 1958; PhD, Columbia U., 1965. Asst. prof. sociology Columbia U., 1965-72, assoc. prof., 1972-78, prof., 1978-92, prof. emerita, 1993—; sr. rsch. scholar, 1993—; chmn. dept. Columbia U., 1978-81; v.p. Andrew W. Mellon Found., 1991-98, sr. v.p., 1998—. Vis. scholar Russell Sage Found., 1971—72, 1985—87; mem. adv. bd. Social Sci. Citation Index Assn. Sci. Info., 1972—98; dir. Ann. Revs., Inc.; trustee Am. Savs. Bank, 1978—83. Author: Scientific Elite: Nobel Laureates in the United States, 1977, rev. edit., 1996; co-editor: Toward A Metric of Science: The Advent of Science Indicators, 1978, The Outer Circle: Women in the Scientific Community, 1991; mem. editorial bd. Scientometrics, 1977-, Am. Jour. Sociology, 1972-74, 77-79, Am. Sociol. Rev, 1972-74, 87-91, Sci., 1985-86; contbr. articles to profl. jours. Bd. dir. Social Sci. Rsch. Coun., 1974-76, AAAS, 1980-84, Women's Forum, 1989-91; trustee Ctr. for Advanced Study in Behavioral Scis., 1978-88, 89-2001, 03—; mem. advl. adv. bd. John Simon Guggenheim Meml. Found., 1986-93, mem. com. on selection, 1989-91. Woodrow Wilson fellow, 1958-59; Ctr. for Advanced Study in Behavioral Scis. fellow, 1973-74; Guggenheim fellow, 1980-81; Phi Beta Kappa vis. scholar 1982-83; recipient Dean's award for Disting. Achievement Columbia U. Grad. Sch., 1998. Mem. Am. Philos. Soc. (councillor 1997-03, 2005—, v.p. 2006-,chmn. Class III membership com. 2002-05), Am. Acad. Arts and Scis. (chmn. class III membership com. 1991-94), Soc. Social Studies Sci. (pres. 1989-91), The Century Assn., Coun. on Fgn. Rels.

**ZUCKERMAN, HERBERT LAWRENCE,** lawyer; b. Newark, June 11, 1928; s. David and Adele Zuckerman; m. Janet Albert, Sept. 10, 1950; children: Julia, Elizabeth, William. BSBA, Lehigh U., 1949; JD, Rutgers U., 1953. Acct. Zuckerman & Black, Newark, 1949-56; pvt. practice law Newark, 1956-71; ptnr. Zuckerman, Aronson & Horn, Newark, 1971-81; ptnr., v.p. Sills Cummis, Newark, 1981-98, sr.counsel, 1998—. Bd. dirs. Am. Jewish Com., 1990—; vol. The Hospice, Glen Ridge, N.J., 1985-93. Fellow Coll. of Tax Counsel; mem. ABA, N.J. Bar Assn., Fed. Bar Assn., Essex County Bar Assn., Mental Health Assn. (bd. dirs. 1997-99), Mensa. Avocations: tennis, music, theater, opera, reading. Office: Sills Cummis 1 Riverfront Plz 13th Fl Newark NJ 07102-5400 Office Phone: 973-643-7000. Business E-Mail: hzuckerman@sillscummis.com.

**ZUCKERMAN, MARC ABRAHAM,** finance educator; b. N.Y.C., May 30, 1951; s. Henry and Rela (Ast) Z.; m. Sue Carol Kezurer, Dec. 6, 1981; 1 child, Sam David. BA cum laude, CUNY, Bronx, 1973; MA, Columbia U., 1974; MBA, Manhattan Coll., 1984. Cert. mgmt. acct., cash mgt., credit executive. Dir. corp. credit Clinton Swan Clothes, N.Y.C., 1978-80; dir. fin. Lord Jeff, Norwood, N.J., 1980-88; dir. corp. credit Bernard Chaus, Inc., Secaucus, N.J., 1988-89; asst. treas. Warnaco, Bridgeport, Conn., 1989; treas. Bernard Chaus, Inc., Secaucus, 1989-95; corp. contr. Precision Custom Coatings, Totowa,

N.J., 1996-99; v.p. ops., CFO Triboro Quilt Mfg. Corp., 1999—. Pres. Meadowlands Fin. Group, 1991-95; adj. prof. fin. Contbr. articles to profl. jours. Pack com. mem. Ridgewood Boy Scouts Am., 1997-2000, treas. 1997-2000. Mem. Inst. Mgmt. Accts., Treas. Mgmt. Assn., Treas. Mgmt. Assn. N.J., Nat. Assn. Credit Mgmt., N.J. Corp. Treas. Mgmt. Assn. (treas. 1996—), Nat. Apparel Mfrs. Credit Assn. (bd. dirs. 1993-95), Bergen Rockland Inst. Mgmt. Accts. (bd. dirs. 1996-97). Avocations: jogging, golf. Home: 153 Lincoln Ave Ridgewood NJ 07450-4105 Office: Triboro Quilt Mfg Corp 172 South Broadway White Plains NY 10605 E-mail: zmarc51@aol.com.

**ZUCKERMAN, MARK ALAN,** composer, consultant; b. Bklyn., July 8, 1948; s. Irving and Claire Zuckerman; m. Judith Leah Steinhardt, June 28, 1998. AB, Bard Coll., 1970; PhD, Princeton U., 1976. Vis. prof. music Rutgers U., NJ, 2006. Composer: (musical piece to accompany dance) Randabout (New Music for Dance Commn., 2005), (musical composition) Assunpink Twilight (NJ State Coun. on the Arts showcase, 2005), Menagerie (NJ State Coun. on the Arts Fellowship, 2004), Two Emily Dickinson Settings (NJ State Coun. on the Arts Fellowship, 2004). Mem. bd. govs. Am. Composers Alliance, N.Y.C., 1999—2004. Home: PO Box 578 16 Farm Ln Roosevelt NJ 08555-0578 Personal E-mail: markz@voicenet.com.

**ZUCKERMAN, MARVIN,** retired psychologist; b. Chgo., Mar. 21, 1928; s. Eli and Sophia (Pilder) Z.; children: April B. Zuckerman Schanoes, Steven H. BA, NYU, 1949, PhD, 1954. Rsch. assoc. Inst. Psychiat. Rsch., Ind. U. Med. Ctr., 1956-59; asst. prof. psychology Bklyn. Coll., 1959-62; rsch. assoc. Albert Einstein Med. Ctr., Phila., 1963-69; prof. psychology U. Del., Newark, 1969—2002, prof. emeritus, 2002—, ret., 2002. Author: (with C.D. Spielberger) Emotions and Anxiety, 1976, Sensation Seeking: Beyond the Optimal Level of Arousal, 1979, Biological Bases of Sensation Seeking, Impulsivity and Anxiety, 1983, Psychobiology of Personality, 1991, 2d edit. 2005, Behavioral Expressions and Biosocial Bases of Sensation Seeking, 1994, Vulnerability to Psychopathology, 1999. Fellow APA, Am. Psychol. Soc.; mem. Internat. Soc. Study Individual Differences (past pres.). Home: 1500 Locust St Apt 4013 Philadelphia PA 19102-4326 Office Phone: 215-732-2408. Business E-Mail: zuckerma@udel.edu.

**ZUCKERMAN, MORTIMER BENJAMIN,** editor, real estate developer; b. Montreal, June 4, 1937; arrived in US, 1961, naturalized, 1977; s. Abraham and Esther Zuckerman. BA in Econs. and Polit. Theory with 1st class honors, McGill U., Montreal, 1957, LLB with honors, 1961; MBA with distinction, U. Pa., 1962; LLM, Harvard U., 1962. Sr. v.p. Cabot, Cabot & Forbes, Boston, 1965—69; co-founder, chmn. bd. Boston Properties Co., 1970—, also dir., 1997—; pres., chmn. bd. Atlantic Monthly Co., Boston, 1980—99; chmn., editor-in-chief US News & World Report, 1984—; chmn., co-pub. NY Daily News, 1993—2004, chmn., pub., 2004—. Lectr., then assoc. prof. Harvard U. Grad. Sch. Design, 1966—74; vis. lectr. city and regional planning Yale U., 1967—69; dir., mem. exec. com. Stride Rite Corp., 1970—83; dir. Property Capital Trust Co., 1979—80, RET Income Found., 1976—79; pub. interest dir. Fed. Home Loan Bank of Boston, 1972—73; mem. JP Morgan Nat. Adv. Bd., Internat. Inst. Strategic Studies, Washington Inst. Near East Policy. Founder Zuckerman Fellowships Harvard U., 2004—; pres. bd. trustees Sidney Farber Cancer Inst., Boston, 1980; trustee Meml. Sloan-Kettering, Aspen Inst., NYU, Hole in the Wall Gang Fund, Inc., Center for Comm. Named one of Forbes' Richest Americans, 2006; recipient Commandeur De L'Ordre des Arts et des Lettres, France, Lifetime Achievement Award, Guild Hall, Gold Medal, Am. Inst. Architecture. Mem.: Coun. Fgn. Rels., Harmonie (NYC), Harvard Club (Boston and NYC). Office: New York Daily News 450 W 33rd St Fl 3 New York NY 10001-2681 also: US News & World Report 1050 Thomas Jefferson St NW Washington DC 20007-3817 also: Boston Properties 599 Lexington Ave Rm 1800 New York NY 10022-6030 Office Phone: 212-326-4013, 202-955-2000.*

**ZUCKERMAN, PAUL HERBERT,** lawyer; b. Bklyn., Mar. 7, 1935; s. Max B. and (Mindelen) Z.; m. Sara Shiffman, Aug. 25, 1963; children: David Isaac, Daniel Mark. BS in Econs., Wharton Sch., U. Pa., 1957; MBA in Corp. Fin., NYU, 1964; JD, Bklyn. Law Sch., 1967. Bar: N.Y. 1968, U.S. Dist. Ct. (so. and ea. dists.) N.Y. 1975, U.S. Tax Ct. 1977, U.S. Ct. Appeals (2d cir.) 1972, U.S. Supreme Ct. 1973. Security analyst U.S. Trust Co., N.Y.C., 1962-66; sr. security analyst CNA Mgmt. Rsch. Corp., N.Y.C., 1966-71, mgr. dept. investment rsch., 1971-73; sole practice N.Y.C., 1973—. Speaker and writer in field; radio, TV appearances. Served to lt. (j.g.) USN, 1957—60. Mem.: Wharton Bus. Sch., NYC Bar Assn. Office: 8th Fl 226 W 26th St New York NY 10001-6785 Office Phone: 212-367-1900. Business E-Mail: EstatesWillsTrus@cs.com.

**ZUCKERT, CATHERINE HELDT,** political science educator, writer, editor; b. Miami, Fla., Oct. 20, 1942; d. Henning and Agneta Dom (Christensen) Heldt; m. Michael Paul Zuckert, Sept. 11, 1965; children: Rachel, Larissa, Emily. BA, Cornell U., 1964; MA, U. Chgo., 1967, PhD, 1970. From asst. to full prof. Carleton Coll., Northfield, 1971-98; instr. St. Olaf Coll., Northfield, Minn., 1972; assoc. prof. Claremont (Calif.) McKenna Coll., 1976-77; prof. polit. sci. U. Notre Dame, Ind., 1998—, Nancy Reeves Drew prof. polit. sci., 1999. Wm. R. Kenan Jr. prof. Carleton Coll., 1997-98; vis. prof. honors edn. U. Del., Newark, 1989-90; vis. disting. prof. Fordham U., Bronx, N.Y., 1994-95; vis. prof. U. Mich., Ann Arbor, 1996; cons., panelist NEH, Washington, 1976-97; cons. Ford Found., N.Y.C., 1988-97. Author: Natural Rights and the American Imagination, 1990 (Most Oustanding Book Published in Philosophy of Religion 1990), Postmodern Platos, 1996; co-author: The Truth About Leo Strauss, 2006; editor: Understanding the Political Spirit, 1988 (Choice award 1989); editor-in-chief The Review of Politics, 2004— Named to honor roll Templeton Found., Pa., 1997. Mem. Am. Polit. Sci. Assn., N.Am. Soc. for Study of Greek Thought, Midwest Polit. Sci. Assn. Office: U Notre Dame 412 Flanner Hall 350 Decio Notre Dame IN 46556 Office Phone: 574-631-6620.

**ZUCKMAN, HARVEY LYLE,** law educator; b. Mpls., Apr. 14, 1934; s. George and Elizabeth (Polinsky) Z.; m. Charlotte Anne Snyder, Jan. 27, 1962; children: Jill Belinda, Beth Nancy, Michael Scott. AB, U. So. Calif., 1956; LL.B., NYU, 1959. Bar: Calif. 1960, D.C. 1973, U.S. Supreme Ct. 1963. Atty. civil div. appellate sect. U.S. Dept. Justice, Washington, 1963-67; prof. law St. Louis U., 1967-70; prof. law Columbus Sch. Law Cath. U. Am., 1970—2006, prof. emeritus, 2006—, dir. Inst. for Communications Law Studies Columbus Sch. Law, 1981-01; adj. prof. communications Am. U., 1976-81. Cons. Bur. Nat. Affairs., 1974—81. Producer: Am. Law Inst.-ABA Legal Edn. TV series, 1973-74; co-author: Mass Communications Law, 1977, 5th edit., 2000, Modern Communication Law, 3 vols., 1999; editor ABA newsletter Comm. Lawyer, 1981-86. Served with U.S. Army Judge Adv. Gen., 1960-63. Mem. ABA (forum com. on comm. law, co-chmn. nat. celebration of 200th anniversary of 1st amendment 1991), D.C. Bar chairperson com. on continuing legal edn. 1975-83), Fed. Comm. Bar Assn., Am. Law Inst. (life), Assn. Am. Law Schs. (sects. family law and mass comm.), Cosmos Club. Democrat. Office: Cath U Am Columbus Sch Law 3600 John Mccormick Rd NE Washington DC 20064-0001

**ZUEHLKE, RICHARD WILLIAM,** communications executive, consultant, writer; b. Milw., June 17, 1933; s. Harold Babcock and Phoebe Blanche (Frykman) Z.; m. Carol Sue Yates, Dec. 26, 1955; children: Kenneth Richard, William Woodfill, Deanne Elizabeth. BS, Lawrence Coll., 1955; PhD, U. Minn., 1960. Instr. chemistry Lawrence U., 1958-62; asst. prof., 1962-68; Eliphalet Remington prof. chemistry U. Bridgeport, 1968-79; chmn. dept., 1968-73; vis. prof. U. R.I., 1976-77, 79-80, assoc. marine scientist, 1980-85; owner, pres. The Right Connection, Inc., 1983-91; pres. TetraR Cons., Inc., 1985-88. Cons. Kimberly-Clark Corp., 1960-62, United Illuminating Co., 1969-75, Chem. Specialties Corp., 1970-73, Sperry Remington Corp., 1976-79; NSF Sci. Faculty fellow U. Pitts., 1966-67; asst. to dir. Gordon Rsch. Confs., 1990-94; cons., writer in field. Fellow Am. Inst. Chemists; mem. Am. Chem. Soc., AAAS, Rotary, Sigma Xi, Sigma Phi Epsilon. Congregationalist. Home: PO Box 52 Wilmot NH 03287-0052 E-mail: rzuehlke@tds.net.

**ZUERLEIN, DAMIAN JOSEPH,** priest; b. Norfolk, Nebr., May 28, 1955; s. Victor Damian and Elizabeth P. (Wegener) Z. BA, U. St. Thomas, St. Paul, 1977; MDiv, St. Paul Sem., 1981. Ordained priest Roman Cath. Ch., 1981. Tchr. Norfolk Cath. HS, 1981—85; asst. pastor Sacred Heart/St. Mary's Parish, Norfolk, 1981—85; assoc. pastor St. Pius X Cath. Ch., Omaha, 1985-88, Mary Our Queen Cath. Ch., Omaha, 1988-90; pastor Our Lady of Guadalupe Parish, Omaha, 1990—2004, St. Agnes Parish, Omaha, 1997—2004, St. Francis of Assisi Parish, Omaha, 2002—03, St. Columbkille Parish, Papillion, Nebr., 2004—. Cons. Archdiocesan Vocations Office, Omaha, 1985-95; chmn., co-founder Omaha Together One Cmty., 1991-95; co-founder Weaving, Women's Advocacy Group, Omaha, 1988—, co-founder IXIM Spirit of Solidarity, 2004—. Presenter (video) Loving Your Marriage, 1990, El Matrimonio: Una Jornada Para Todo Una Vida, 1995; co-author: (manual) Hispanic Pastoral Plan, 1991. Bd. dirs. United Cath. Social Svcs., Omaha, 1990-96, Chicano Awareness Ctr., Omaha, 1991-98, Omaha Food Bank, 2000—, Vis. Nurse Assn., 1996-2000, Omaha 100 Inc., 1991-96, chair, 1991-93; advisor Mayor P.J. Morgan, Omaha, 1991-95; active Gov. Nelson's Urban Adv. Task Force, 1994, Domestic Violence Coord. Coun. Gtr. Omaha, 1996—, Nat. Campaign for Human Devel. Adv. Bd., 1997-2000, Nebr. Gov.'s Task Force on Immigration, 1999-2000; founder, dir. Guadalupe-Ines Mission Sch., 1998-2004; pres. Omaha Presbyn. Coun. 2003-; del. Omaha City Charter Review Conv., 2003; pres. Greater Omaha Clergy Assn., 1987-88; bd. dirs. South Omaha Neighborhood Assn., 1992, pres. 1994-98. Mem. Pax Cristi, Amnesty Internat., Fontenelle Forest Assn. Avocations: canoeing the bwca, skiing, travel, hiking. Home and Office: 200 E 6 St Papillion NE 68046 Office Phone: 402-339-3285. Personal E-mail: damzuer@aol.com.

**ZUFRYDEN, FRED S.,** academic administrator, finance educator, researcher; b. Grenoble, France, June 13, 1943; came to U.S., 1956; s. Henri and Cecile (Frymer) Z.; m. Toby Marlene Levin, Dec. 24, 1967; 1 child, Ryan BA in Math., UCLA, 1965, MBA, 1966, PhD in Bus. Adminstrn., 1971. Rsch. engr. mil. ops. and systems analysis group N.Am. Aviation, Inc., L.A., 1966-67; rsch. assoc. resources rsch. dept. Planning Rsch. Corp., L.A., 1967-68; ops. rsch. specialist data systems div. Litton Systems, Inc., L.A., 1968-70; asst. prof. dept. mgmt. scis. Sch. Bus. and Econs., U. Calif., Northridge, 1970-71; asst. prof. dept. mktg. Grad. Sch. Bus. U. So. Calif., L.A., 1971-75, assoc. prof., 1975-82, prof., 1982—, Ernst Hahn prof. mktg., 1991—, chmn. mktg. dept., 1987-90, rsch. dir. internat. bus. econs. and rsch. Grad. Sch. Bus., 1983—. Mem. editorial bd. Jour. Advt. Rsch., 1981—, Mktg. Sci., 1979—, Jour. Mktg., 1978—; mem. cons. and planning com. Mktg. Sci. Jour., 1979; referee Jour. Mktg. Rsch., Mgmt. Sci., Decision Sci., Jour. Internat. Rsch. in Mktg.; mem. abstract writing staff International Abstracts in Operations Rsch./Mgmt. Sci., 1973; contbr. articles to profl. jours. including Jour. Mktg. Rsch., Mktg. Sci., Jour. Operational Rsch. Soc., Mgmt. Sci., Decision Scis., Jour. Mktg., Jour. Advt. Rsch., Jour. Internat. Rsch. in Mktg., Jour. Royal Statis. Soc., Interfaces, Rsch. in Mktg., Jour. of Mktg. Rsch. Soc., Jour. of Bus., others Rsch. grantee U. So. Calif., 1973, 75, 76, 77, 78, A.C. Nielsen Co., 1988-90. Mem. Am. Mktg. Assn. (cert. recognition 1974), Ops. Rsch. Soc. Am., Inst. Mgmt. Sci., Omega Rho, Beta Gamma Sigma

**ZUG, ELIZABETH E.,** concert pianist, educator; b. Phila., Oct. 8, 1907; d. Nathan Walter and Amelia Elizabeth (Nelson) Zug. BA in Music, Irving Coll., 1928. Mem. faculty Nat. Guild Piano Tchrs., 1949. Judge piano auditions Yr. in Music, Nat. Guild Piano Tchrs., 1949. Debut N.Y. Town Hall, 1938; concert pianist, S.Am. tour, 1941. Named Outstanding N.Y. Debut as Pianist, 1938, Judge of the Yr. Nat. Guild Piano Tchrs., 1949. Mem. Music Tchrs. Nat. Assn., Pa. Music Tchrs. Assn. United Ch. Christ. Avocations: writing, designing, landscaping. Studio: 12 N 4th St Reading PA 19601-3910

**ZUGAZAGOITIA, JULIAN,** museum director; b. Mexico City; arrived in U.S., 1999; Grad., l'Ecole du Louvre; PhD in Aesthetics, Sorbonne, Paris. Cons., spl. advisor to dir. Getty Conservation Inst., L.A.; dir. visual arts Spoleto Festival, Italy, 1997—99; asst. to the dir. Guggenheim Mus., N.Y.C., 1999—2002; exec. dir. El Museo del Barrio, N.Y.C., 2002—. Recipient Chevalier des Arts et des Lettres, 2004. Office: El Museo del Barrio 1230 Fifth Ave New York NY 10029 Office Phone: 212-831-7272.

**ZUGIBE, FREDERICK THOMAS,** retired pathologist, forensic specialist; b. Garnerville, NY, May 28, 1928; s. Benjamin and Anna (Zarick) Z.; m. Catherine Frances O'Leary, Apr. 7, 1951; children: Frederick T., Thomas P., Cathryn T. Blaber, Theresa A. Mandracchia, Mary E. Raleigh, Matthew M., Kevin J. BS, St. Francis Coll., 1951; MS, U. Chgo., 1959, PhD, 1960; MD, W.Va. U., 1968. Diplomate Am. Bd. Pathology-Anatomic, Am. Bd. Pathology-Forensic, Am. Bd. Family Practice. Rsch. histologist Lederle Labs., Pearl River, NY, 1950-52, rsch. chemist, 1953-55; rsch. assoc. ophthalmic rsch. Columbia U., N.Y.C., 1955-56; dir. cardiovascular rsch. U.S. VA, Pitts., 1960—65; chief med. examiner County of Rockland, Pomona, NY, 1969—2003. Adj. assoc. prof. pathology Columbia U., 1972—; bd. dirs. Hudson Techs. Inc., Hillburn, N.Y., Rockland Westchester Found. for Sudden Infant Death, White Plains, N.Y.; med. dir. Rockland County Emergency Med. Svcs. N.Y.S. Dept. Health, Pomona, 1990-2003; supervising med. officer disaster med. assistance team Nat. Disaster Med. Assistance, Pomona, 1992-2003; expert on crucifixion and Shroud of Turin. Author: Eat, Drink and Lower Your Cholesterol, 1964, Diagnostic Histochemistry, 1970, 14 Days and a Healthy Heart, 1986, The Cross and Shroud: A Medical Inquiry into Crucifixion, 1988, Dissecting Death, 2005, The Crucifixion of Jesus: A Forensic Inquiry, 2005; contbr. numerous articles to profl. jours. and chpts. to books; appeared in TV documentaries on Discovery Channel, History Channel, Learning Channel, In Search Of, Nat. Geographic, CNN, CBC, others. Named Knight by His Royal Highness Dom Duarte Pio, Duke of Braganca, Head of Royal House Portugal, 2002, Dr. Frederick T. Zugibe Forensic Unit (formerly Rockland County Med. Examiner's Office), legis. action, 2003; named one of 25 people in Rockland County, N.Y. who most influenced this region in the 20th century; recipient Disting. Citizens award, Assn. Visually Impaired, 1998, Physician Recognition awards, more than 75 law enforcement, govtl. and med. awards, 1971—, numerous others, Presdl. Tribute, 1998, Spl. Congressional Recognition award, 1998; Dr. Frederick T. Zugibe Forensic Unit named in his honor, Rockland County Med. Examiners Office, 2003. Fellow Coll. Am. Pathologists (emeritus), Am. Coll. Cardiology (emeritus); Am. Acad. Forensic Scis., N.Y. Cardiology Soc., Coun. Arteriosclerosis of Am. Heart Assn., Assn. Scientists and Scholars Internat. for the Shroud of Turin (pres., founder), Sigma Xi. Roman Catholic. Achievements include first to describe glycoprotein storage disease (Zugibe-Gilbert Syndrome), the defect in the syndrome of the sea blue histocyte and arthrodentoosteodysplasia. an acroosteolysis syndrome, a mask to eliminate odors of putrefaction, and a demummifaction technique for fingerprinting; invented ac/dc cardiopulmonary resuscitator, many others. Home and Office: 1 Angelus Dr Garnerville NY 10923-2022 Office Phone: 845-354-1333. Personal E-mail: ftzugibe@msn.com.

**ZUHDI, NAZIH,** retired surgeon, hospital administrator; b. Beirut, May 19, 1925; arrived in U.S., 1950; s. Omar and Lutfiye (Atef) Z.; children by previous marriage: Omar, Nabil; m. Annette McMichael; children: Adam, Leyla, Zachariah BA, Am. U., Beirut, 1946, MD, 1950. Diplomate Am. Bd. Surgery, Am. Bd. Thoracic Surgery. Intern St. Vincent's Hosp., SI, NY, 1950-51, Presbyn.-Columbia Med. Ctr., NYC, 1951-52; resident Kings County SUNY Med. Ctr., NYC, 1952-56; fellow SUNY Downstate Med. Ctr., Bklyn., 1953-54; resident Univ. Hosp., Mpls., 1956, Okla. City, 1957-58, practice surgery specializing in cardiovasc. and thoracic, 1958-87, adminstr., 1985-99, ret., 1999. Founder, dir. Oklahoma Transplantation Inst. (renamed Nazih Zuhdi transplant Inst., Aug., 1999) Bapt. Med. Ctr., 1984-99, chmn. dept. transplantation 1994-99; transplantation surgeon in chief Bapt. Hosp., Okla. City, 1984-99; founder, chmn. Okla. Cardiovasc. Inst., Okla. City, 1983-84, Okla. Heart Ctr., Okla. City, 1984-85 Contbg. author Cardiac Surgery, 1967, 2d edit., 1972; contbr. articles to profl. jour.; developer numerous med. devices, techniques, rsch. and publs. on cardiopulmonary bypass, internal hypothermia, assisted circulation, heart surgery and transplantation of thoracic organs; developer heart-lung machines; designer, use of exptl. plastic bypass hearts; originator use of banked citrated blood for cardiopulmonary bypass for open heart surgery, of clin. non-hemic primes of heart-lung machines producing intentional hemodilution, at present, the universally accepted principle of cardiopulmonary bypass for partial and total body perfusion; researcher in cardiovasc. studies. Founder Islamic Ctr., Inc., Oklahoma City. Named to Okla. Hall of Fame, 1994. Fellow ACS; mem. AMA, NCCJ (Humanitarian award 1996), Am. Thoracic Soc., Okla. Thoracic Soc., So. Med. Assn., Okla. Med. Assn., Internat. Coll. Angiology, Am. Coll. Chest Physicians, Oklahoma City C. of C., Oklahoma County Med. Soc., Oklahoma City Clin. Soc., Okla. Surg. Assn., Oklahoma City Surg. Soc., Southwestern Surg. Congress, Am. Coll. Cardiology, Am. Soc. Artificial Internal Organs, Soc. Thoracic Surgeons (founding mem.), Am. Assn. for Thoracic Surgery, Internat. Cardiovasc. Soc., Okla. State Heart Assn., Osler Soc., So. Thoracic Surg. Assn., Lillehei Surg. Soc., Internat. Soc. Heart Transplantation, Dwight Harken's Founder's Group Cardiac Surgery, Westaby's Pioneers in Cardiac Surgery, Internat. Soc. Cardiothoracic Surgery (Japan, founding mem.), Am. Soc. Transplant Surgeons, Milestones of Cardiology of Am. Coll. Cardiology, Okla. City Golf and Country Club, Okla. Hall of Fame. Achievements include first to use banked citrated blood for cardiopulmonary bypass for open heart surgery; invention of experimental and clinical non-hemic primes of heart-lung machines producing intentional hemodilution. Home: 7305 Lancet Ct Oklahoma City OK 73120-1430 Personal E-mail: nzmd@aol.com.

**ZUICHES, JAMES JOSEPH,** sociologist, educator; b. Eau Claire, Wis., Mar. 24, 1943; s. William Homer and Bronnie Monica (Stich) Z.; m. Carol Ann Kurilo, Aug. 19, 1967; children:; James Daniel, Joseph Kurilo. BA in Philosophy, U. Portland, 1967; MS in Sociology, U. Wis., 1969, PhD in Sociology, 1973. Instr., asst. prof., assoc. prof. sociology Mich. State U., East Lansing, 1971-82, prof., 1982; assoc. program dir. in sociology NSF, Washington, 1979-80, program dir. in sociology, 1980-82; assoc. dir. rsch. Cornell U., Ithaca, N.Y., 1982-86; assoc. dean Coll. Agr. and Home Econs., Wash. State U., Pullman, 1986-94, dir. Agrl. Rsch. Ctr., 1986-94; program dir. food sys. and rural devel. W.K. Kellogg Found., Battle Creek, Mich., 1994-96; dean Coll. Agr. and Home Econs. Wash. State U., Pullman, 1995—2003, prof. Dept. Cmty. and Rural Sociology, 1986—. Mem. adv. subcom. NSF, 1977-79; sci. adv. com. USDA Nat. Rsch. Initiative, Washington, 1992-93; com. on future land grant univ. bd. on agr., NRC, Washington, 1994-96; pub. Wash. Land and People Mag., 1987-92; mem. Bd. Natural Resources, Wash. State, 1995-2003. Co-editor: The Demography of Rural Life, 1993; contbr. articles to profl. jours. Pres., bd. dirs. Edgewood Village Children's Ctr., East Lansing, 1978-79. Recipient sustained superior performance award NSF, 1981; rsch. grantee NIMH, 1973, ERDA, 1978. Fellow AAAS; mem. Rural Sociol. Soc. (pres. 1992-93, editor 50th Anniversary Rsch. Series, 5 vols. 1988-93), Am. Sociol. Assn., Population Assn. Am. Roman Catholic. Avocations: skiing, swimming, hiking, reading. Office Phone: 509-335-8540.

**ZUICK, ERNEST RONALD, JR.,** career officer, advertising executive; b. San Bernardino, Calif., Nov. 2, 1935; s. Ernest Ronald Sr. and Catherine Louise (Leach) Z.; m. Johnnie Fern Lemons, Aug. 19, 1966. BA, Fresno State U., 1964, MA, 1968; MPA, Auburn U., 1974; postgrad., Air Command and Staff Coll., 1974, Air War Coll., 1982. Cert. tchr., Calif. Joined Calif. Air N.G., 1958, advanced through grades to col., 1984; advt. acct. exec., sports and polit. cartoonist Turlock (Calif.) Jour., 1956-62; advt. acct. exec. Fresno (Calif.) Bee, 1965-76; various assignments Calif. Mil. Dept., Sacramento, 1976-85, dir. legis., 1985-95, spl. projects dir., 1999—2001; dir. Media Svcs., 2001—04. Mem. ancillary staff Res. Forces Policy Bd., Office of Sec. of Def., 1982-95. Co-editor: Grizzly Mag., 2005—; contbr. articles to profl. jours. Mem. N.G. Assn. Calif. (pres. 1983-84). Avocations: writing, cartooning, video production.

**ZUIDEMA, GEORGE DALE,** surgeon, educator; b. Holland, Mich., Mar. 8, 1928; s. Jacob and Reka (Dalman) Z.; m. Joan K. Houtman, June 2, 1953; children: Karen Sue, David Jay, Nancy Ruth, Sarah Kay. AB, Hope Coll., 1949, D.Sc. (hon.), 1969; MD, Johns Hopkins U., 1953. Diplomate: Am. Bd. Surgery. Intern Mass. Gen. Hosp., 1953-54, asst. resident surgeon, then chief resident surgeon, 1954, 57, 58, 59; asst. prof. surgery, then assoc. prof. U. Mich. Sch. Medicine, 1960-64; prof. surgery, dir. dept. Johns Hopkins Sch. Medicine; also surgeon in chief Johns Hopkins Hosp., 1964-84; prof. surgery, vice provost med. affairs U. Mich., 1984-94. Cons. Walter Reed Army Med. Center, Sinai Hosp., Balt., Balt. City Hosp., Clin. Center of NIH; chmn. Study on Surg. Services for U.S., 1970-75 Editor: (with O.H. Gauer) Gravitational Stress in Aerospace Medicine, 1961; (with G.L. Nardi) Surgery-A Concise Guide to Clinical Practice, 1961, 4th edit., 1982; (with R.D. Judge and F. Fitzgerald) Physical Diagnosis, 1963, 6th edit., 1997; (with W.F. Ballinger and R.B. Rutherford) Management of Trauma, 1968, 4th edit., 1985; (with L. Schlossberg) Atlas of Human Functional Anatomy, 1977, 4th edit., 1997, Shackelford's Surgery of the Alimentary Tract, 5th edit., 2001; editor Jour. Surg. Rsch., 1966-72, assoc. editor, mem. editl. bd., 1972—; mem. editl. bd. Surgery Ann., 1968-75, Surgery, 1970-97, co-editor in chief, 1975-97. Bd. dirs. Md. divsn. Am. Cancer Soc., 1964-68; trustee William Beaumont Hosp., Royal Oak, Mich., 1984-94, Hope Coll., 1984-94, chmn.—. Capt. M.C., USAF, 1954-56. John and Mary R. Markle scholar academic medicine, 1961-66; recipient Henry Russell award U. Mich., 1963 Fellow ACS, Royal Coll. Surgeons Ireland (hon.); mem. Assn. Am. Med. Colls., Ctrl. Soc. Clin. Rsch., Soc. Univ. Surgeons, Am. Surg. Assn., So. Surg. Assn., Soc. Clin. Surgery, Soc. Vascular Surgery, Internat. Cardiovascular Surgery, Halsted Soc., Nat. Inst. Medicine, Assn. Acad. Surgeons (pres. 1967-69), Allen O. Whipple Soc., Coun. on Grad. Med. Edn., Phi Beta Kappa, Tri Beta, Alpha Omega Alpha. Home: 983 Willow View Ct Holland MI 49424-6615

**ZUK, CARMEN VEIGA,** psychiatrist; b. Buenos Aires, Mar. 5, 1939; arrived in U.S., 1971; d. Carlos and Carmen Villella Veiga; m. Gerald Harvey, May 7, 1974; children: Cary Elizabeth and Gabrielle Ann (twins). MD, U. Buenos Aires, 1964, cert. psychiatry, 1969. Diplomate Am. Bd. Psychiatry and Neurology. Intern Med. Coll. Pa., Phila., 1974—75; resident in psychiatry Norristown State Hosp., Norristown, Pa., 1977—79; child psychiatry fellowship Med. Coll. Pa. and Ea. Pa. Psychiat. Inst., Phila., 1979—81; dir. child and adolescent unit Hosp. of Med. Coll. Ga., Augusta, 1981—83; dir. treatment team New Orleans Adolescent Hosp., 1983—85; assoc. Psychiatry Med. Group, Calif., 1985—86; mental health psychiatrist L.A. County Dept. Mental Health San Fernando Mental Health Svcs., 1986—88; psychiatrist-ptnr. So. Calif. Permanente Med. Group, Van Nuys, 1988—98, ptnr., 1988—98; staff psychiatrist Santa Clarita Child and Family Ctr., 1999—2002; ret., 2005. Asst. clin. prof. dept. psychiatry Med. Coll. Ga., 1981-83; clin. asst. prof. dept. psychiatry and neurology Tulane U., 1983-85. Co-author: Psychology of Delusion, 2005; contbr. articles to profl. jours. Mem. AMA, Internat. Soc. for Adolescent Psychiatry. Avocations: reading, cooking, gardening, swimming, music. Home: 7620 Hollister Ave 219 Goleta CA 93117 Personal E-mail: carmenzuk@msn.com.

**ZUK, JUDITH,** retired botanist, director; b. Canandaigua, N.Y., Sept. 11, 1951; BA, Rutgers U., 1973; MS, U. Del., 1976. CEO, pres. Bklyn. Botanic Garden, 1990—2005; ret., 2005. Bd. dirs. Botanic Gardens Conservation Internat., Greenwood Cemetery; mem. regional adv. bd. JP Morgan Chase. Mem. Phi Beta Kappa.

**ZUKER, CHARLES S.,** neuroscientist, biology professor; PhD, MIT. Investigator Howard Hughes Medical Inst.; prof. biology & neurosciences U. Calif., San Diego, 1986—. Scientific advisor Avalon Ventures; scientific co-founder Aurora Biosciences, 1995, Senomyx, Inc., 1999; mem. scientific adv. bd. Ambit Biosciences, CMEA Ventures. Recipient Alcon award, AAAS, 1999, Gogan award, 2000; fellow, Jane Coffin, U. Calif. Berkeley, Whitaker Health Scis. Found., MIT. Mem.: Am. Acad. Arts and Scis., Nat. Acad. Scis.*

**ZUKERMAN, MICHAEL,** lawyer; b. Bklyn., Oct. 3, 1940; s. Charles Morris and Gertrude Ethel Zukerman; m. Claire J. Goldsmith, June 25, 1961 (div. 1986); children: Steven, Amy; m. Elaine DeMasi, Nov. 21, 1986 (div. 1999); children: Jaclyn, Laura; m. Janey Alexander, Feb. 2, 2001. BS, U. Fla., 1961; LLB, St. John's U., 1964; LLM, NYU, 1966. Bar: NY 1965, Pa. 1983,

U.S. Tax Ct. 1984. Credit analyst, loan officer Franklin Nat. Bank, 1964-66; assoc. Jaffin, Schneider, Kimmel & Galpeer, N.Y.C., 1966-67; ptnr. Zukerman, Licht & Friedman and predecessors, N.Y.C., 1967-79, Baskin & Sears, P.C., N.Y.C., 1979-85, Graubard, Moskowitz, Dannett, Horowitz & Mollen, N.Y.C., 1985-86, Gersten, Savage, Kaplowitz & Zukerman, N.Y.C., 1986-89; of counsel Olshan, Grundman, Frome & Rosenzweig, N.Y.C., 1990-95, Graham & James, N.Y.C., 1995-2000, Bryan Cave LLP, 2000—03; exec. v.p. Brookhill Group, 1986-89; of counsel Sonnenschein Nath and Rosenthal, N.Y.C., 2003—04; Warshaw Burstein Cohen Schlessinger & Kuh LLP, N.Y.C., 2004—. Pres. First Ptnrs. Credit Corp., N.Y.C., 1988—93; bd. dirs. Interjurist Ltd., Whitestone Realty Capital, LLC; mng. dir. Nat. Aspbergers Rsch. Found., 1993—, trustee, 2001—; lectr. in field. Contbr. articles to profl. jours. Trustee Temple Beth Torah, Melville, N.Y., 1972-80, YMHA Suffolk County, Hauppauge, N.Y., 1980-85; bd. dirs. Dayton Mgmt. Corp., 1974-2001, Suffolk Jewish Cmty. Planning Bd., Hauppauge, 1982-85, Congregation Bnai Elohim, 1994, 2nd v.p., 1995; co-chmn. bus. adv. coun. Town of Greenburgh, 1992. Mem.: ABA. Home: 915 Cherry Ln Valley Stream NY 11581-2722 Office: Warshaw Burstein Cohen Schlessinger & Kuh LLP 11th Fl 555 Fifth Ave New York NY 10016 Office Phone: 212-984-7836. E-mail: mzukerman@whitestonerealty.com.

**ZUKERMAN, PINCHAS,** concert violinist, violist, conductor; b. Tel Aviv, July 16, 1948; came to U.S., 1962; s. Yehuda and Miriam (Lieberman) Z.; m. Eugenia Rich, May 26, 1968 (div.); children: Natalia, Arianna; m. Tuesday Weld, 1985 (div.); m. Amanda Forsyth, Mar. 2004. Student, Juilliard Sch. Music, 1965-68; MusD (hon.), Brown U., 1989. Ind. concert violinist, 1968—. With impresario, Sol Hurok, 1967-76; condr.; soloist English Chamber Orch., 1974, Mostly Mozart Festival, N.Y.C., 1975; guest condr., soloist Los Angeles Philharm., Boston Symphony, Chgo. Symphony, Pitts. Symphony, Phila. Orch., N.Y. Philharm.; music dir. South Bank Festival, London, 1978-80, St. Paul Chamber Orch., 1980-87, Nat. Arts Ctr. Orch. 1998—; prin. festival condr. Dallas Internat. Summer Music Festival, 1990-94; prin. guest condr. Dallas Symphony, 1993-95; toured with Isaac Stern; mem. trio with Daniel Barenboim and Jacqueline du Pre; (rec. artist) CBS, EMI, Philips Classics labels, RCA Victor Red Seal, BMG Classics. Winner Internat. Levintritt Competition, 1967, Medal of Arts, 1983, Isaac Stern award Nat. Arts Awards, 2002. Office: care Kirshbaum Demler & Assoc 711 W End Ave Apt 5KN New York NY 10025-6821

**ZUKOWSKI, KAREN ANN,** art historian, educator, writer, curator; d. Richard Zukowski and Mary Constance Rapp; m. David Diamond, May 28, 1983; 1 child, Theodore Harold Diamond. PhD, CUNY, 1999; BA, Carleton Coll., Northfield, Minn. Curator Olana State Hist. Site, Hudson, NY, 1990—2000; adj. prof. NYU, N.Y.C., Cooper-Hewitt / Parsons MA Program. Author: Creating the Artful Home: The Aesthetic Movement in America. Chair, fund raising com. Pawling Free Libr., NY, 1997—2004; chair, outreach com. Pawling Cmty. Found., 2004. Mem.: Am. Assn. State and Local History, Coll. Art Assn., Victorian Soc.Am. (bd. dirs. Met. chpt.). Avocations: hiking, swimming, cooking.

**ZULACK, MARY MARSH,** law educator; BA, Smith Coll., 1965; JD, U. Mich., 1969. Clk. for Hon. Leonard H. Sandler; atty. MFY Legal Svcs., 1971—73, Bedford-Stuyvesant Cmty. Legal Svcs., Inc., 1973—80, Harlem Neighborhood Office of Legal Aid Soc., 1980—90; clin. prof. law Columbia Law Sch., 1990—. Bd. dirs. Welfare Law Ctr. Office: Columbia Law Sch 834 Jerome Greene Hall 435 W 116th St New York NY 10027 Office Phone: 212-854-8214.    Office    Fax:    212-854-3554.    E-mail: mzulack@law.columbia.edu.

**ZULAUF, MADELINE RUTH,** photographer, artist; b. Neptune, N.J., Oct. 9, 1948; d. Everett Minor and Mary Elizabeth Slocum; m. Bateston Franklin Stoddard, Jr., Apr. 2, 1967 (div. July 1972); children: Michael, Mary Beth; m. Sander William Zulauf, May 26, 1979. AA, County Coll. of Morris, 1976; BA, Montclair State U., 1978. Photographer U.S. Army Rsch., Devel. & Engring. Ctr., Picatinny Arsenal, N.J., 1979-84, TV prodr., dir., 1984-87, visual info. specialist, 1987—96, multimedia specialist, 1996—2000, visual info. mgr., 2000—. Cons. phototech. program County Coll. of Morris, Randolph, N.J., 1983-88, mem. student co-op adv. bd., 1989-94; pres. federally employed women U.S. Army Rsch., Devel. & Engring. Ctr., Picatinny Arsenal, 1984-85, chairperson fed. women's program, 1987-89. Photographer: (mags.) Horns of Plenty, 1989, Jour. of NJ Poets, 2005, (book) Above the River, 1990; photo exhbns. include Sussex City Arts Coun., 1996-97, James Wright Poetry Festival, Martins Ferry, Ohio, 1999, McKeowns Gallery, Branchville, N.J., 1997, Tiger Gallery, Westerly, RI, 2005. Photographer Jersey Battered Women's Shelter, Morristown, N.J., 1985-88; dep. diocesan convs. Episcopal Diocese Newark, N.J. Recipient Humanitarian award Equal Opportunity Office, 1984. Mem. Acad. Am. Poets, Internat. Ctr. Photography. Episcopalian. Avocations: sailing, travel, hiking. Office: US Army Rsch Devel & Engring Ctr B-176 Picatinny Arsenal NJ 07806 Business E-Mail: mszulauf@msn.com.

**ZULAUF, SANDER (SANDER WILLIAM ZULAUF),** poet, educator, editor; b. Paterson, N.J., Nov. 5, 1946; s. William Z. and Marion Ann Zulauf; m. Christianne Beresford, June 15, 1968 (div. 1976); 1 child, Scott; m. Madeline Ruth Slocum, May 26, 1979; stepchildren: Michael, Mary Beth. BA, Gettysburg Coll., 1968; MA, Ind. U., 1973. Tchr. Martin Luther King Sch., Paterson, NJ, 1968—69, Hanover Park Regional H.S., East Hanover, NJ, 1969-71; prof. County Coll. Morris, Randolph, NJ, 1973—. Editor, pub. Ars Poetica, Lake Hopatcong, N.J., 1996-99. Author: (poetry) Succasunna New Jersey, 1987, Living Waters, 2005; editor: The Poets of New Jersey: From Colonial to Contemporary, 2005, Jour. NJ Poets, 1989—; founding editor Index Am. Periodical Verse, 1971—82. Sec.-treas. Forest South Homeowners Assn., Byram Twp., 1989—94, pres., 2004—; lay eucharistic min. St. Dunstan's Episcopal Ch., Succasunna, 1974—. Named 1st Poet Laureate, Diocese of Newark, 1999—; recipient Allen Ginsberg award, Poetry Ctr., Paterson, NJ, 1993, 2001, 2002, Excellence in Print award, Jour. NJ. Poets Pub. Radio's Poet and the Poem, 2002; fellow NEH, Princeton, 1987; grantee N.J. Arts Coun., 1992—93. Mem. Acad. Am. Poets, Poetry Soc. Am., Poets House, Kenneth Burke Soc., Thoreau Soc., Associated Writing Programs, Skylands Writers & Artists Assn. (sec. treas. 1994-98, v.p. 1999-2000). Democrat. Episcopalian. Avocations: camping, boating, environmental preservation, gardening, travel. Office Phone: 973-328-5471. Personal E-mail: sanderzpoet@msn.com. Business E-Mail: szulauf@ccm.edu.

**ZULCH, JOAN CAROLYN,** retired medical publishing company executive; b. Great Neck, N.Y., Apr. 10, 1931; d. Walter Howard and Edna Ruth (Howard) Z. BS in Biology, Allegheny Coll., 1952; postgrad., Hunter Coll., 1954. Med. sec. E.R. Squibb & Sons, N.Y.C., 1952; with Macmillan Pub. Co., N.Y.C., 1952-88, editorial asst. med. dept., 1952-56, asst. editor med. dept., 1956-58, editor med. dept., 1958-61, med. editor coll. and profl. div., 1961-75, sr. editor medicine, coll. and profl. div., 1975-78, exec. editor med. books, profl. books div., 1978-79, editor-in-chief, 1979-80, asst. v.p., editor-in-chief profl. books div., 1980-82, v.p., pub. med., nursing, health sci. dept., 1982-85, v.p., pub. med. books, sci., tech., med. dept., 1985-88. Recipient Best Illustrated Med. Book award Assn. Med. Illustrators, 1977, Outstanding Book in Health Sci. award Am. Pubs., 1983. Mem. AAAS, Post Libr. Assn., L.I.U. (rec. sec. 1990-93, exec. coun. 1990—), Friends of Locust Valley Libr. (pres. 1991-93, 94-96, 98-2000, 2004—, treas. 1993-94, 96-98, 2000-02, 1st v.p. 2002-04), Locust Valley C. of C. (bd. dirs. 1997—), Alpha Gamma Delta, Delta Sigma Rho. Republican. Home: 36 Wood Ln Lattingtown PO Box 547 Locust Valley NY 11560-0547

**ZULKER, CHARLES BATES,** broadcasting company executive; b. Pleasantville, N.J., Dec. 20, 1926; s. William John and Virginia (Carr) Z.; m. Virginia Wright, June 24, 1949; children: Connie Lee, Timothy Scott Charles. Adminstrv. officer Princeton (N.J.) U., 1950-60; asst. mgr. Sta. WPEL, Montrose, Pa., 1960-65; gen. mgr. Sta. WCHR, Trenton, NJ, 1965 . Trustee Princeton Evang. Fellowship, 1973-83; bd. council Word of Life Internat., Schroon Lake, N.Y., 1974-82; mem. exec. bd. Upper Makefield Community Assn., 1972-79; deacon Westerly Rd. Ch., Princeton, 1999-2002. With U.S.

Army, 1945-46. Mem. Wooden Canoe Heritage Assn. Am., Nat. Religious Broadcasters, Nat. Assn. Broadcasters, Squam Lakes Assn. (Holdemess, N.H.). Office: 119 Locktown Rd Flemington NJ 08822-4715 Office Phone: 215-493-4252. E-mail: czulker@nassaubroadcasting.com.

**ZULKOWSKI, KAREN,** nursing educator, researcher; d. Samuel and Eileen Sethman; m. John Zulkowski. BSN, U. of Akron, 1972; MSN, Kent State U., Ohio, 1989; DNS, SUNY, Buffalo, 1998. RN Mont. Bd. of Nursing. Pres. KM Olivo and Assocs., Akron, 1989—94; assoc. prof. Mont. State U., Bozeman, 1998—. Bd. dirs. Nat. Pressure Ulcer Adv. Panel, Washington DC; rsch. cons. Deaconess Billings Clinic, Billings, Mont., 2000—05; assoc. dir. program for the advancement of chronoc wound care Yale U., New Haven, 2002—03; adj. prof. Oreg. Health and Sci. U., Portland, 1998—; mem. editl. bd. Ostomy/Wound Mgmt., Pa. Author ostomy/wound management; editor: (book) Chapter Editor On Wounds; contbr. articles to profl. jours. Fundraiser Beartooth Nature Ctr., Red Lodge, Mont., 2005—06. Recipient Chronic Pain in Crow Indians grant, NIH/NINR, Rural Nutrition grant, USDA, Deep Tissue Injury in Nursing Home Residents grant, Longport Med. Inc. Mem.: AAWC, STTI, Am. Acad. Wound Mgmt. (cert. woundcare specialist), Mont. Nurses Assoc. Office: Mont State U MSU Billings Campus Box 574 Billings MT 59101 Office Phone: 406-657-1739. Personal E-mail: karenz@montana.edu.

**ZUMBRUN, ALVIN JOHN THOMAS,** law and criminology educator; s. Orrell Sylvester Tilton and Mary Kathryn (Sprinkle) Z.; m. Marianne Jane Nolan; children: Mary Susan, Alvin J.T. Jr., Steven M., Diane, MaryAnn, Mary Kathleen. BA, U. Md., 1952, MA, 1956; MEd in Spl. Edn., Coppin State U., 1972, MEd in Adminstrn., 1974; JD, U. Balt., 1970. Probation officer Supreme Bench of Balt., 1950-52; budget and program dir. Cmty. Chest, Balt., 1953-55; mng. dir. Criminal Justice Commn., Balt., 1956-59; exec. dir., criminologist Md. Crime Investigating Com., Balt., 1960—93; dept. chmn., prof. criminal justice Catonsville (Md.) C.C., 1968-94, dept. chmn., dir. grad. program, prof. criminal justice U. Balt., 1974-76. Adj. prof. criminal justice U. Md., Hood Coll., Coppin State U., Md. State Police Acad., Balt. County Police Acad., 1969—; mem. adv. bd. U. Balt. Criminal Justice Program, 1976-94; cons. Am. Edn. Assn., Washington, 1980-1985; mem. senate Catonsville C.C., 1970-83; mem. Nat. Disaster Med. System, 1993—; mem. acad. stds. senate com. U. Md., College Park, 1997-99. Author: Maryland Crime Report, 5 vols., 1959-94, Directory of Criminal Justice Agencies, 22 vols., 1962-94, Civil Disturbance Riots of 1968, 69, also rsch. in field. Scholarship com. Md. Troopers Assn., Pikesville, 1990-93; adv. bd. articulation com. U. Md., College Park, 1977-94; lay pres., mem. coun. Salem Luth. Ch., Catonsville, 1956-59, 65-68; pres. Maplewoods Home Owners Assn., 1996-97. Lt. (j.g.) USN Recipient Superior Pub. Svc. award Afro Am. Newspaper, 1962, Excellence in Tchg. award Md. State Bd. C.C.s, 1987, Superior Ednl. Svcs. award Balt. County Police Chief, 1994, Gov.'s citation for ednl. achievements Gov. of Md., 1994, Hon. Trooper 25.Yrs. Acad. Tchg. Md. State Police, 1995. Mem. VFW (life), Am. Legion (life), Md. Acad. Criminal Justice Profs. (pres. 1971-94), Internat. Soc. Criminology, Nat. Dist. Attys. Assn., Internat. Assn. Chiefs of Police, Maplewoods Homeowners Assn. (pres. 1995-96). Avocations: walking, bicycling, travel. Home and Office: 438 Maple Forest Rd Catonsville MD 21228-1783 Personal E-mail: azumbrun@comcast.net.

**ZUMBRUNNEN, DAVID ARNOLD,** mechanical engineering and materials science educator, consultant; b. Salt Lake City, Sept. 3, 1955; m. Elizabeth Buck. B in Mech. Engring., U. Minn., 1977; MS in Mech. Engring., Purdue U., 1984, PhD in Mech. Engring., 1988. Registered profl. engr., Ind., S.C. Co-founder NSF Ctr. for Advanced Engring. Fibers and Films. Lt. USN, 1977—82. Presdl. Faculty Fellow The White House/NSF, 1992-97. Mem.: AAAS, ASME, Polymer Processing Soc., Material Rsch. Soc., SPE, Am. Chem. Soc., AIChemE. Achievements include invention of structured materials formed by chaotic advection and smart blending technology. Office: Clemson U Dept Mech Engring Clemson SC 29634-0921 Office Phone: 864-656-5625. E-mail: zdavid@ces.clemson.edu.

**ZUMPELLA, THOMAS JOSEPH,** music educator; b. New Castle, Pa., Apr. 7, 1949; s. Ernest Albert Zumpella and Barbara DeVivo; m. Anna Maria Bullano, May 19, 1973; children: Gina Marie Zumpella Anetakis, Thomas Ernest. BME, Youngstown State U., Ohio, 1971; MusM, Youngstown State U., 1975; PhD, Kent State U., Ohio, 1993. Band dir. New Castle H.S., Pa., 1978—; supr. music edn. New Castle Area Schs., 2000—. Dir. The Red Coat Cmty. Band, New Castle, 1985—. Bd. dirs. New Castle Playhouse, 1985—. Mem.: Music Educators Nat. Conf. (dist. 5 pres. 1992—93). Roman Catholic. Avocation: golf. Home: 423 E Northview Ave New Castle PA 16105 Office Phone: 724-651-7523.

**ZUMWALDE, BARRY,** music educator; b. St. Paul, Aug. 5, 1977; s. Robert and Coralee Zumwalde; m. Elizabeth Hamberg, June 16, 2001. MusB, U. Minn., 2000. Dir. bands North Branch H.S., Minn., 2000—. Mem.: Minn. Band Dirs. Assn. (membership chair 2004—05, pres.-elect 2005—), Music Educators Nat. Conf., Minn. Music Educators Assn. (jazz edn. chair 2004—06). Office: North Branch HS 38175 Grand Ave North Branch MN 55056 Office Phone: 651-674-1566. Office Fax: 651-674-1510. E-mail: bzumwald@northbranch.k12.mn.us.

**ZUMWALT, RICHARD DOWLING,** flour mill executive; b. Amarillo, Tex., Dec. 1, 1912; s. Richard Dowling and Cora Bell (Patey) Z.; m. Florine Anita Nelson, Oct. 23, 1938; 1 dau., Alexandra Anita (Mrs. Klaus Schwabe). Student, Met. Bus. Coll., 1930; est. student, Tex. Tech. Coll., 1931, Dallas Coll., 1949. With Pearlstone Mill & Elevator Co., summers 1929/30, J. C. Crouch Grain Co., 1931-44, Burrus Mills, Inc., Dallas, 1944-83, exec. v.p. Regla, Cuba plant, 1952, pres., 1964-83; sec.-treas. Zumwalt Inc., 1973—; ret. gen. mgr. Burrus milling dept. Cargill, Inc. Past pres. Bulgur Assos., Washington, Dallas Grain Exch. Mem. Methodist. Soc. Tex. Mfrs. Assn. (past dir.) Home: 7353 Blairview Dr Dallas TX 75230-5416 Personal E-mail: ddzumwalt@aol.com.

**ZUMWALT, ROGER CARL,** hospital administrator; b. Eugene, Oreg., Oct. 26, 1943; s. Robert Walter and Jean Elaine (Adams) Z.; children: Kathryn Nicole Zumwalt DeWeber, Timothy Robert. Student, Boise State U., 1963—65; BA, We. Oreg. U., 1969; postgrad., U. Iowa, 1969—71; MA cum laude, Oreg. State U., 1973. Adminstr. Coulee Cmty. Hosp., Grand Coulee, Wash., 1973-75, Eastmoreland Hosp., Portland, Oreg., 1975-81; exec. dir. Cmty. Hosp., Grand Junction, Colo., 1981-97; pres., healthcare cons. accreditation Zumwalt Consulting, Salem, Oreg., 1997—; dir. adminstrv. svcs. dir. SAIF Corp., Salem, 1998—. Chmn., bd. dirs. Alphabet House Pediat. Rehab. and Edn., 1998—2000, Castle Rock Med. Group, Inc., Denver, 1998—2003; part owner, chmn. bd. dirs. Castle Rock Med. Ctr., Colo., 1998—. N.W. Okla. Regional Med. Ctr. Cherokee, 2000; spkr. numerous local and nat. presentations, subjects including healthcare, hosp. mktg./success/costs, 1981—97; guest lectr. Mesa State Coll., 1992—98, Colo. Christian Coll., 1996—98. Newspaper columnist, 1973-75; contbr. articles, presentations to profl. publs. Commr. Multnomah County Health Care Commn., Portland, 1978-81; health cons. Grant County Housing Auth., Grand Coulee, 1974-75; mem. pk. bd. City of Tigard, Oreg., 1976-78; caucus rep. Mesa County Rep. Party, Grand Junction, 1988; mem. adv. com., pres.'s office Mesa State Coll., Grand Junction, 1989; bd. dirs. Hospice of Grand Valley, Grand Junction, 1992-97, mem. devel. com., 1993-97, vice chmn. bd. dirs. 1996-97. Grand Valley Hospice, 1992-97; com. mem. Salem Coalition on Youth Literacy, 2000—. Fellow Coll. Osteo. Healthcare Execs. (bd. dirs. 1985-88, pres. 1987, examiner 1989—), Disting. Svc. award 1989); mem. Am. Osteo. Healthcare Assn. (bd. dirs. 1987-98, treas. 1992-93, 1st v.p. 1994-95, 2d v.p. 1993-94, vice chairperson 1994-95, chmn. 1996-97, chairperson 1997-98, past chmn. 1998), Am. Osteo. Assn. (ex-officio mem. bd. dirs. 1996), Bur. Healthcare Facilities Accreditation (v.p. 1994, advisor 1995-98, accreditation Commn. 1995—, accreditation surveyor 1978—, accreditation survey instr. 1994—), Joint Commn. on Am. Healthcare Orgn. (task force on small and rural hosps. 1994-97), Colo. Hosp. Assn. (bd. dirs. 1987-92), Mountain States Vol. Hosp. Assn. (bd. dirs. 1984-98, exec. com. 1991-98, v.p. 1993, vice chmn. bd. dirs. 1992-98), We. Coll. Ind. Practice Assn. (Medicine Mauls Measles com., fin.

com. 1991-92), We. Colo. Health Care Alliance (bd. dirs. 1989-94, v.p. 1992, chmn. bd. dirs. 1993), Mesa County Mental Health Assn. (bd. dirs. 1988-89, 91-92), Grand Junction C. of C. (bd. dirs. 1991-93), Rotary (Grand Coolee, Wash. 1973-75, Portland 1975-81, Grand Junction 1981-98, Salem 1998—, chmn. fund raising com. 2000-01, bd. dirs. 2001-02), WEstern Oreg. U. Alumni Assn. (bd. dirs. 2006—), Masons, Shriners (pres. Grand Junction club 1989, bd. dirs. El Jebel 1986-90, 1st v.p. Western Colo. club 1989), KC. Republican. Roman Catholic. Avocations: golf, camping, fishing, hunting. Home: 592 Meadowbrook Ln Stayton OR 97383 Office: SAIF Corp 440 Church St SE PWB 2 Salem OR 97312-2000 Fax: 503-315-3086. E-mail: rogzum@netzero.com, rogzum@netzero.net.

**ZUMWALT, ROSS EUGENE,** forensic pathologist, educator; b. Goodrich, Mich., July 18, 1943; s. Paul Lawrence and Lila Ann (Birky) Z.; m. Theresa Ann Schar, Sept. 12, 1970 (div. Apr. 1988); children: Christopher Todd, Tenley Ann; m. Cheryl Lynn Willman, Sept. 4, 1988; 1 child, David Willman Zumwalt. BA, Wabash Coll., 1967; MD, U. Ill., 1971. Diplomate in anat. and forensic pathology Am. Bd. Pathology. Intern, resident in pathology Mary Bassett Hosp., Cooperstown, NY, 1971-73; resident in anat. and forensic pathology Southwestern Med. Sch., Dallas, 1973-76; asst. med. examiner Dallas County, Dallas, 1974-76; staff pathologist, dir. labs. Naval Regional Med. Ctr., Camp Lejeune, NC, 1976-78; dep. coroner Cuyahoga County, Cleve., 1978-80, Hamilton County, Cin., 1980-86; assoc. prof. pathology U. Cin. Sch. Medicine, 1980-86; prof. pathology U. N.Mex. Sch. Medicine, Albuquerque, 1987—; chief med. investigator Office of Med. Investigator, Albuquerque, 1991—; pres. Am. Bd. of Pathology, Tampa, 2000—01. Trustee Am. Bd. Pathology, Tampa, Fla., 1993—. Lt. comdr. USN, 1976-78. Fellow Am. Acad. Forensic Scis., Coll. Am. Pathologists; mem. AMA, Nat. Assn. Med. Examiners (bd. dirs. 1984-96, pres. 1995-96), Am. Soc. Clin. Pathologists, Am. and Can. Acad. Pathologists. Avocation: golf. Office Phone: 505-272-0710. Business E-Mail: rzumwalt@salud.unm.edu.

**ZUNG, THOMAS TSE-KWAI,** architect; b. Shanghai, Feb. 8, 1933; came to the U.S., 1937, naturalized, 1954; 1 child, Thomas Bates. Student, Drew U., 1950-51, Va. Poly. Inst., 1951-53, Columbia U., 1955-57; BArch, U. Mich., 1960; MS in Design Sci., Columbia U., 1982. Project arch. Edward Durell Stone, Arch., N.Y.C., 1958, 60-65; arch. Cleve., 1967—. Pres. Buckminster Fuller, Sadao and Zung, Archs., 1979—; disting. sr. fellow Stanford U. Librs.; John Denver Windstar Found. Symposium spkr., Aspen, Colo., 2004. Author-editor: Buckminster Fuller, Anthology for the New Millennium; prin. works include City Cleve. Pub. Utilities Bldg., Cleve. State U. Geodesic Elongated Dome, Mayfran, Inc., Sawmill Creek Lodge, U. Akron Guzzetta Hall, Music, Speech and Theater Arts Ctr., Alumni Ctr. Bowling Green State U., U. Akron Master Plan-West, City of East Cleveland, Superior Euclid beautification plan, student recreation ctr. Bowling Green State U., Glenville Pub. Libr., campus bldg. Tex. Wesleyan Coll., recreation, health and phys. edn. bldg. Wittenberg U., Medina Res. Park Office, arena, health, phys. edn. complex U. Akron, Dyke Coll., Lima State Prison, Cleve. Children's Christian Home, State of Ohio Pre-Release Ctr. Cleve., Lorain-Grafton State Prison, Mayfield H.S., Asian Village Project, Cleve. Metroparks Tropical Rainforest Bldg., Student Union Wittenberg U., YWCA, Salem, Ohio, China Internat. Trade Ctr., People's Rep. China, additions to Cleve. Hopkins Internat. Airport, Ohio State U. Coll. of Dentistry-Postle Hall and Hist. Costume and Textile Mus., Master Plan Schreiner Coll. and Cailloux Student Ctr., Griffin Welcome Ctr., Master Plan Walsh Univ., Walsh Student Union, Columbus, Western Res. Psychiat. Hosp., Ohio, Trumbull State Prison, Ohio Dept. Transp. Prototypical Rest Stop Design; patentee in field. Trustee Pace Assn., 1970-73, Karamu House, 1974-80, Cleve. Inst. Music, 1979-86, Chinese Cultural Assn., 1980-84, Ohio Arts Coun., 1982-84; task force chmn. Greater Cleve. Growth Assn., 1970; mem. Coun. Human Rels., 1972, Leadership Cleve. Class '77; cubmaster local Boy Scouts Am., 1977-79; vestryman St. Christopher-by-River, 1980-83; bd. dirs. Buckminster Fuller Inst., 1989—, Pearl S. Buck Found., 1989-98, cons. arch. hist. house com.; mem. Adv. Coun. Aging, State of Ohio, 1997—; founder, pres. Bratenahl 100, 2006-. With Signal Corps, U.S. Army, 1953-55. Decorated 5 medals; recipient Pub. Works award, State of Ohio, 1971, Design award, Korean Inst. Constrn. Tech., 1984, Ohio Valley ABC Design Excellence award, Wittenberg U. Student Union, 1989, Synergeticists N.E. Corridor award, 2005, Buckminster Fuller SNEC award, 2005, others; Disting. sr. fellow, Stanford U. Librs. Mem. AIA (dir. Cleve. chpt. 1980, Design award Cleve. chpt. 1972, Design award 1989), Am. Soc. Planning Ofcls., English Speaking Union (trustee 1972-75), Ohio Soc. Archs., Ohio Assn. Minority Archs. and Engrs. (trustee 1982-90), Hermit Club, City Club (dir. 1972-74, v.p. 1974), Rotary. Office: Buckminster Fuller Sadao & Zung 1 Bratenahl Pl Cleveland OH 44108-1181

**ZUNGOLO, EILEEN H.,** dean; BS, MEd, EdD, Columbia U. Prof., dean Sch. Nursing Northeastern U., Boston, assoc. dean Bouve Coll. Health Scis. Office: Northeastern Univ Sch Nursing 360 Huntington Ave Boston MA 02115-5000 E-mail: ezungolo@lynx.dac.neu.edu.

**ZUNZ, OLIVIER JEAN,** history professor; b. Paris, July 19, 1946; s. Jean R. and Monique M. (Blin) Z.; m. Christine M. Crommen, July 3, 1970; children: Emmanuel, Sophie. Licence in history and geography, U. Paris X, 1968, M in History, 1969; Doctorat-ès-Lettres, U. Paris I, Panthéon-Sorbonne, 1982. Scientist Ctr. Nat. de la Recherche Scientifique, Paris, 1976-78; asst. prof. dept. history U. Va., Charlottesville, 1978-83, assoc. prof., 1983-88, prof., 1988-99 Commonwealth prof., 1999—. Vis. prof. Ecole des Hautes Etudes en Scis., Sociales, Paris, 1985—, Coll. France, 1997; dir. seminar for Coll. Tchrs. NEH, 1989, 92. Author: The Changing Face of Inequality: Urbanization, Industrial Development, and Immigrants in Detroit, 1880-1920, 1982, Making America Corporate, 1870-1920, 1990, Why the American Century?, 1998; editor, co-author: Reliving the Past: The Worlds of Social History, 1985; editor: Alexis de Tocqueville, Democracy in America (transl. A. Goldhammer), 2004; co-editor: (with David Ward) The Landscape of Modernity: Essays on New York City, 1900-1940, 1992, (with Leonard Schoppa and Nobuhiro Hiwatari): Social Contracts under Stress: The Middle Classes of America, Europe, and Japan at the Turn of the Century, 2002, (with Alan S. Kahan): The Tocqueville Reader: A Life in Letters and Politics, 2002; mem. editl. bd. Revs. in Am. History, 1990-98; contbr. articles, book revs. to profl. jours. Jr. fellow Mich. Soc. Fellows, 1973-76, John Simon Guggenheim Meml. Found. fellow, 1986-87; grantee U. Mich.-Ford Found. Population Devel. Fund, 1974-76, NSF, 1976-78, NEH, 1979-81, 84-87, Ford Found., 2004—; also recipient numerous rsch. grants. Mem. Am. Hist. Assn., Orgn. Am. Historians, The Tocqueville Soc. (pres. 2001—). Home: 1368 Hilltop Rd Charlottesville VA 22903-1225 Office: U Va Corcoran Dept of History PO Box 400180 Randall Hall Charlottesville VA 22904-4180 Business E-Mail: oz@virginia.edu.

**ZUO, MING JIAN,** industrial engineering educator; BSc, Shandong (China) Inst. Tech., 1982; MSc, Iowa State U., 1986, PhD, 1989. Asst. prof. indsl. engring. U. Windsor, Ont., Can., 1989-90; prof. U. Alta., Edmonton, Can., 1990—; assoc. editor. City U. of Hong Kong, China, 1996-98. Guest editor spl. issue Jour. IIE Transactions on Quality and Reliability Engring., 1997; author: Contemporary Engineering Economics: A Canadian Perspective, 1995, 2001, Optimal Reliability Modeling: Principles and Applications, 2002; assoc. editor IEEE Transactions on Reliability, 2002—. Mem. IEEE (sr.), Inst. Indsl. Engrs. Avocations: basketball, badminton, travel. Home: 3006-105A St Edmonton AB Canada T6J3A5 Office: U Alberta Dept Mech Engring Edmonton AB Canada T6G2G8

**ZUPAN, MARK A.,** dean, business professor; b. Rochester, NY, July 28, 1959; s. Janez and Maria (Močnik) Zupak; m. Carol Shuherk; children: Will, Walker. BA in economics, Harvard U., 1981; PhD in economics, MIT, 1987. Teaching fellow dept. economics Harvard U., Cambridge, 1983-86; asst. prof. to prof. economics Marshall Sch. Bus., U. So. Calif., 1987—97, assoc. dean masters programs; dean, prof. economics Eller Coll. Bus. and Pub. Administrn., U. Ariz., 1997—2004; dean Simon Grad Sch. Bus., U. Rochester, NY, 2004—, prof. economics and pub. policy. Vis. prof. Amos Tuck Sch. Bus. Administrn., Dartmouth Coll.; mem. editl. bd. Pub. Choice, Jour. Bus.

Economics, Rsch. in Law and Economics. Co-author: (with E.K. Browning) Microeconomic Theory and Applications, (with T. W. Gilligan, A. M. Marino) Microeconomic Cases and Applications; Contbr. articles to profl. journals. Mem. Phi Beta Kappa. Lodges: Rotary. Office: William E Simon Grad Sch Bus Adminstrn U Rochester CS-2202H Carol Simon Hall Rochester NY 14627-0107 Office Phone: 585-275-3316. Business E-Mail: zupan@simon.rochester.edu.

**ZUPSIC, MATTHEW MICHAEL,** insurance company executive; b. Pitts., Aug. 30, 1950; s. Joseph Matthew and Antoinette (Brisic) Z.; children: Tina Elizabeth, Matthew Quay. BA, Marietta Coll., 1972. Mktg. rep. Hartford Ins., Pitts., 1972-76; ins. agt. Githens Ins. Ctr., Belle Vernon, Pa., 1976-77; v.p., ptnr. Burchill Ins. Agy., Inc., Pitts., 1977-88; pres. Harte, Hawke & Zupsic Ins. Agy., Pitts., 1989—. Mem. Pa. Assn. Ind. Ins. Agts. (bd. dirs. 1980-88), Ind. Ins. Agts. Pitts. (treas. 1983, 1st v.p. 1984-86, pres. 1986-88), B&S Investment Club (pres 1985-87). Democrat. Roman Catholic. Avocations: sailing, skiing, boating, gardening. Office Phone: 724-940-7540. Business E-Mail: mzupsic@nauticom.net.

**ZURAITIS, MARITA,** insurance company executive; V.p. ceded-reins. USF&G Comml. Ins. Group, br. v.p., regional v.p., sr. v.p.; sr. v.p. U.S. ins. ops. The St. Paul Co., Inc., St. Paul, 1998—2001, exec. v.p. Comml. Lines Group, 2001—02, CEO Comml. Lines Group, 2003—. Office: The Saint Paul Cos Inc 385 Washington St Saint Paul MN 55102

**ZURAKOWSKI, TAMARA LEE,** gerontological nurse practitioner, nursing educator; b. Akron, Ohio, July 24, 1956; d. Morris and June Elizabeth Zurakowski; life ptnr. Shirley Marie Repta, Oct. 29, 1989; 1 child, SarahElizabeth Zurakowski Repta. BS, NYU, NY, 1978; MA, NYU, NY, 1980; cert., U. Conn., Storrs, Conn., 1997; PhD, Case We. Res. U., Cleve. Ohio, 1990. Registered Am. Nurses' Credentialing Ctr., Wash., D.C., 1997. Pub. health nurse Vis. Nurse Svc. NY, NYC, 1978—79; grad. student NYU, 1979—80; grad. student, nurse Wayne State U., Detroit, 1980—82; rsch. and tchg. asst. Case Western Res. U., Cleve., 1982—85, instr., 1986—89; asst. nurse Dept. Pub. Health, Cleve., 1985—86; staff nurse Univ. Hosps. Cleve., 1989—90; postdoctoral fellow Elderly Care Rsch. Ctr., Cleve., 1990—92; dir. rsch. Judson Pk., Cleve., 1992—94; asst. prof. U. Akron, Ohio, 1994—95; asst. clin. prof. U. Mass., Amherst, Mass., 1995—98; asst. prof. La Salle U., Phila., 1999—2004; practice asst. prof. U. Pa., Phila., 2004—; gerontol. nurse practitioner Penn LIFE, Phila., 2005—. Post-doctoral fellow Elderly Care Rsch. Ctr., Cleve., 1990—92; peer reviewer Divsn. Nursing, Health Svcs. and Resource Administrn., Pockville, Ohio, 2000—; cons. Neumann Coll., Aston, Pa., 1998—99. Vestry mem. St. John's Ch., Huntingdon Valley, Pa., 2003—. Fellow, Wayne State U., 1979—80; grantee, Nat. Inst. Aging, 1992—94, Am. Assn. Colls. Nursing andThe John A. Hartford Found., 2001—04; scholar, Divsn. Nursing, Health Svcs. and Resources Adminstrn., 1979—80, Nat. Inst. Aging and Brookdale Found., 1991. Mem.: Gerontol. Soc. Am. (co-convener nursing spl. interest group 1997—2000), Girl Scouts USA (life; leader Southeastern Pa. chpt. 1998—2006), Sigma Theta Tau Internat. (faculty counselor 2005—). Democrat. Episcopalian. Avocations: knitting, music. Home: 2121 Valley Road Huntingdon Valley PA 19006 Office: University of Pennsylvania 420 Guardian Drive Philadelphia PA 19104 Office Phone: 215-573-6297. Office Fax: 215-573-7496. Personal E-mail: tamaraz@comcast.net. Business E-Mail: zurakows@nursing.upenn.edu.

**ZURBENKO, IGOR GEORG,** science educator; s. George and Leokadia Zurbenko; m. Laura M. Close, June 1, 1991. MSC, Moscow State U., 1978, PhD, 1981. Chair nat. statis. lab. Moscow U., 1980—90; prof. biostatistics U. Albany, 1991—. Author: Spectral Analysis of Time Series. Mem.: Am. Statis. Assn. Liberal. Roman Catholic. Achievements include research in New Computer Algorithms In Spectral Analysis. Avocations: travel, hiking, swimming. Home: One Univ Pl 141 Rensselaer NY 12144 Office: RPI 110 Eighteen St Troy NY 12180 Office Phone: 518-276-6452. Home Fax: 518-402-0381. Business E-Mail: izurbenko@uamail.albany.edu.

**ZURBUCHEN, JOHN FREDERIC,** principal; b. Madison, Wis., July 16, 1958; s. Harold Arthur and Betty Jane Zurbuchen; m. Ann Marie Schmitt; children: Rudi Ann, Ellie Marie. MEd, Mont. State U., 1991. Cert. tchr. Wis., Utah. Prin. Davis County Schs., Farmington, Utah, 1990—2000, Cochrane-Fountain City (Wis.) Sch. Dist., Fountain City, Wis., 2000—. Coord. Cochrane-Fountain City PTO, 2004—06. Utah Principals Acad. fellow, Utah Office Edn., 1998. Mem.: AWSA (assoc.), NAESP (assoc.), NASSP (assoc.). Home: 760 E Mill St Fountain City WI 54629 Office: Cochrane-Fountain City Sch Dist S2770 State Highway 35 Fountain City WI 54629 Office Phone: 608-687-4391. Home Fax: 608-687-4422; Office Fax: 608-687-4422.

**ZURCHER, ZEAN WILLIAM,** retired music educator, musician; s. Harvey George Sheldon and Audrey Phyllis (Jones) Zurcher; m. Kay Alice Kneip, Sept. 1, 1955; children: Robert William, Linda Kay Pedersen. MusB Edn., Morningside Coll. Conservatory of Music, Sioux City, Iowa, 1956; MA, Columbia U., NYC, 1959, profl. diploma, 1960, EdD, 1973. Cert. tchr. of music NY State, 1960, sch. administr. and supervision NY State, 1973. Vocal and instrumental music tchr. (part time) Homer Pub. Schools, Homer, Nebr., 1955—58, Winnebago Pub. Schools, Winnebago, 1956—58; asst. in music edn. Teachers Coll., Columbia U., NYC, 1959—60; instrumental music tchr. Middletown Pub. Schools, 1960—63, Baldwin Pub. Schools, NY, 1960—96; ret. Music tchr. Nat. Symposium on Rsch. in Music Behavior, 1975—87; rsch. lectr., panelist NY State Sch. Music Assn., 1975—88; mem. Columbia U. Consortium on Competency-Based Tchr. Edn., NYC, 1977—78; presenter in field. Co-author: Applications of Research in Music Behavior: The Alabama Project (Music, Society and Education in America) (named Nationally-Recognized Rschr., 1987), Design for Music Learning, Research in Music Behavior: Modifying Music Behavior in the Classroom; performer: Newport Jazz Festival Nat. Tour, Tommy Vig Trio, The Roland Wiggins Quintet, Don Glasser Band, Ernie Rudy Band, Am. Opera Soc. Orch., Little Orch. Soc., Russian State Symphony. With 21st Army Band, 1954—55, Ft. Lewis, Wash. Named to All-American Bandmasters Band, Am. Bandmasters Assn., Chgo., 1957; recipient Hon. Life Membership, NY State Congress of Parents and Tchrs., 1966, Plaque for Outstanding Contbns., Badwin Band and Orch. Mothers' Club, 1969, PTA Plaque in appreciation for 20 yrs. of dedication to the students of Baldwin Harbor Jr. HS, Parent Tchrs. Assn., 1983. Mem.: NY State Sch. Music Assn. (recognized for 30 yrs. of dedicated svc. 1993), Baldwin Teachers Assn. (v.p. 1986—2000), NY State United Tchrs. (del. 1986—2000), Am. Fedn. Tchrs. (del. 1986—2000, recognized for 30 yrs. of dedicated svc.), Music Educators Nat. Conf., Phi Mu Alpha Sinfonia Music Frat. (life; pres. of Beta Gamma chpt. 1959—60). Christian Science. Achievements include music rsch. cited in numerous publ. including Achieving Ednl. Excellence by Sulzer-Azaroff and Mayer. Avocations: concerts, opera, theater, travel. Home: 81 Lester Ave Freeport NY 11520-5912 Personal E-mail: wzurcher@aol.com.

**ZURHEIDE, CHARLES HENRY,** consulting electrical engineer; b. St. Louis, May 9, 1923; s. Charles Henry and Ollie C. Z.; m. Ruth M. Plueck, June 25, 1949; children: Barbara Anne, Pamela S BS in Elec. Engring, U. Mo., Columbia, 1944. Registered profl. engr., Mo. Distbn. engr. Laclede Power & Light Co., St. Louis, 1945-51; sub-sta. engr., chief engr. Union Electric Co., St. Louis, 1945-51; chief elec. engr. Fruin-Colnon Contracting Co., St. Louis, 1951-54; a founder, treas., v.p. Smith-Zurheide, Inc., St. Louis, 1954-65; pres. Zurheide-Herrmann, Inc., St. Louis, 1965—, chmn. bd., 1988—2002; ret. Chmn. Elec. Code Rev. Commn. St. Louis, 1965-, Mo. Bd. Profl. Engrs. 1977-82, St. Louis Indsl. Devel. Commn., 1965-67; mem. adv. panel region 6 GSA, 1977—; plan commn., City of Ferguson, Mo., 1968-73; tech. adv. com. St. Louis C. of C., 1977; mem. Mo. Pub. Svc. Commn. Task Force on Retail Wheeling of Electricity, 1998 Recipient Dist. Svc. in Engring. award, U. Mo., 1976. Fellow Am. Cons. Engrs. Council; mem. Mo. Soc. Profl. Engrs. (Engr. of Year award 1970), Cons. Engrs. Council Mo., IEEE, Illuminating Engring. Soc., Engrs. Club St. Louis (Achievement award 2003),

Tau Alpha Pi. Clubs: Norwood Hills Country, Mo. Athletic Home: 14336 Spyglass Rdg Chesterfield MO 63017-2140 Office: Zurheide-Herrmann Inc 4333 Clayton Ave Saint Louis MO 63110-1684 Business E-Mail: czurheide@zhideas.com.

**ZURICK, JACK,** electrical engineer, consultant; b. Bklyn., May 28, 1952; s. Joseph and Edelgard (Wendland) Z.; m. Nenita Cardinal, Apr. 28, 1990. Pre-engring student, Queensborough Community Coll., 1969-71, AAS, 1971-73. Cert. Resource Engring. Technician. Elec. designer Ebasco Svcs., Inc., N.Y.C., 1973-76; design engr. Gibbs & Cox, Inc., N.Y.C., 1976-78; elec. designer Sci. Design Co., Inc., N.Y.C., 1978-85; design engr. Vikonics, Inc., Secaucus, N.J., 1985-87; sr. elec. designer H-R Internat., Inc., Edison, N.J., 1988-93; sr. elec. engr. Kleinknecht Elec. Co. of N.J., Maplewood, N.J., 1993-94; cons. Rotator Svcs., Inc., East Brunswick, N.J., 1994-95; elec. design engr. ICF Kaiser Engrs., Inc., Iselin, N.J., 1995-97; sr. elec. designer Fluor Daniel, Inc., Marlton, N.J., 1997, Orbital Engring. Inc., Bensalem, Pa., 1997; design mgr. Automated Control Concepts, Inc., Neptune, N.J., 1998—. Cons. Sherman Svcs., Inc., Somerset, N.J., 1988, Gen. Indsl. Techs., Inc., Valleystream, N.Y., 1987-88, Allied Resources Tech. Cons., Inc., 1997. Mem. Nat. Inst. for Cert. Engring. Technols. (assoc. engring. technician), Tau Alpha Pi (v.p. 1972-73). Avocations: golf, guitar, electronics, scuba diving. Home: 59 Pheasant Run Freehold NJ 07728-7767 Office: Automated Control Concepts 3535 Rte 66 Neptune NJ 07753-2622 Office Phone: 732-922-6611 ext. 130. Personal E-mail: jzurick@optonline.net. Business E-Mail: jzurick@automated-control.com.

**ZURICK, JOHN,** consultant, former dance company director; MFA in Theatre Arts, Brandeis U. Acting v.p. mktg. InterLearn, Inc.; creator Power of Once; regional mgr./full-time cons. Mills/James Prodns.; cofounder/pres./COO Finis; ptnr. Y&Z Mgmt., Boston; dir. mktg. Cin. Symphony Orch., 1983-88; instr. ESI Internat., Arlington, Va.; founder, past pres. MillennialMinds, Cin.; exec. dir. Cin. Ballet, 1998—2001; consultant Ballet Internationale, Ind., 2001—. Vol. v.p. mktg. Greater Cin. Arts & Edn. Ctr.

**ZURIER, ROBERT BURTON,** rheumatology educator; b. Passaic, N.J., Feb. 19, 1934; s. Milton and Lillian (Matzner) Z.; m. Catherine Elizabeth Miers, June 3, 1962; 1 child, Adam Wheaton. BS, Rutgers U., 1955; MD, U. Tex. Southwestern Med. Sch., Dallas, 1962; MA (hon.), U. Pa., 1981. Intern, then resident in medicine Boston City Hosp., 1962-64; fellow in rheumatology NYU, 1970-73; pvt. practice internal medicine Holden, Mass., 1967-70; asst. prof. medicine U. Conn., Farmington, 1973-76, assoc. prof., 1976-80; prof., chief. rheumatology U. Pa., Phila., 1980-91; prof. medicine, dir. rheumatology div. U. Mass. Med. Ctr., Worcester, 1991—. Served to capt. USAR, 1956-68. Guggenheim Found. fellow, 1986. Mem. AAAS, Am. Coll. Rheumatology (master), Am. Soc. Clin. Investigation, Interurban Clin. Club (pres. 1989-90). Office: U Mass Med Ctr 55 Lake Ave N Worcester MA 01655-0002 Office Phone: 508-856-6246. Business E-Mail: robert.zurier@umassmed.edu.

**ZUR MUEHLEN, MICHAEL,** information systems educator, researcher; b. Hameln, Germany, Mar. 1, 1972; s. Heinrich and Helga zur Mühlen; m. Nersel Buyukbay, May 7, 2005. MSc in Info. Sys., U. Muenster, Germany, 1997, PhD in Info. Sys., 2002. Rsch. asst., lectr. U. Muenster, 1997—2002; asst. prof. info. sys. Stevens Inst. Tech., Hoboken, NJ, 2002—. Process analyst German Telecom Facility Mgmt., Muenster, 1997—98; workflow tech. analyst Pub. Utility Duesseldorf, 1997—98; working group chair Workflow Mgmt. Coalition, Lighthouse Point, Fla., 1998—; vis. faculty U. Tartu, Estonia, 1998—2001; workflow analyst Anneliese Concrete Manufacturer AG, Ennigerloh, Germany, 1999—99; ins. project lead Westfaelische Provinzial Versicherungen AG, Muenster, 1999—2002; workflow project analyst Morgan Stanley Dean Witter, San Francisco, 2000—02; product strategy advisor Carnot AG, Frankfurt, Germany, 2000—02; dir. spl. interest group process automation and mgmt. Assn. Info. Sys., Atlanta, 2002—; tech. cons. Canon USA Inc., Lake Success, NY, 2004—05. Author: (monograph) Workflow-based Process Controlling, 2004; contbr. papers in field. Pvt. 1st class 1st Air Def. Rgt. German Army, 1991—92. Nominee Best Paper award, Hawaii Internat. Conf. Sys. Scis., 1999; recipient. Info. Sys. Educators Conf., 2003, Australasian Conf. info. Sys., 2005; fellow, Workflow Mgmt. Coalition, 2004; grantee Curriculum Devel. grant, SAP U. Alliance, 2000—01, U.S. Army, 2004—05; vis. scholar Rsch. grant, SAP Rsch., 2003; Industy Linkage Rsch. grant, Australian Rsch. Coun., 2005. Fellow: Workflow Mgmt. Coalition (life; working group chair 1998); mem.: IEEE (assoc.), Assn. Info. Sys. (assoc.; dir. spl. interest group 2002—), AlumniUM (corr.; regional chpt. head 2003—). Avocations: piano, travel. Office: Stevens Inst Tech Castle Point on Hudson Hoboken NJ 07030-5906 Office Phone: 201-216-8293. Office Fax: 201-216-5385. Business E-Mail: mzurmuehlen@stevens.edu.

**ZUTAUT, STEVEN ERIC,** systems analyst, application developer; s. James and Magdalena Zutaut. BS in Computer Sci./Chemistry, U. Ala., Huntsville, 1984, PhD in Materials Sci., 1993. Journeyman knowledge-based applications developer Minn., cert. internet application developer Oracle Corp., solution developer.net Microsoft Corp., developer for JavaTM 2 Platform Sun Microsystems, Inc. Assoc. systems analyst Unisys, Montgomery, Ala., 1984—87; knowledge engr. PEAKSolutions Corp., Bloomington, Minn., 1987—89; rsch. assoc. U. Ala., Huntsville, 1993—96; rsch. scientist Nichols Rsch. Corp., Huntsville, 1996—99; sr. cons. Computer Scis. Corp., Huntsville, 1999—2001; software developer (cons.) AEROTEK, Huntsville, 2001—02; sr. systems analyst III Teledyne Solutions, Inc., Huntsville, 2002—04; software developer (cons.) TEKSystems, Huntsville, 2005—06; software engr. Westar Aerospace and Def. Group, 2006—. Contbr. articles to profl. jours. Mem.: IEEE, Assn. Computing Machinery. Home: 7801 Regent Pl SW Apt 6 Huntsville AL 35802-1471 Personal E-mail: sezutaut@msn.com.

**ZVACEK, BRET,** music educator; MusB inPerformance, U. of Iowa, 1983; MusM in Jazz Studies, U. of North Tex., Denton, 1986. Instr. jazz studies U. of North Tex., Denton, 1986—87; prof. of music, dir. of jazz studies SUNY, Potsdam, NY, 1987—. Mus. dir. Cen. N.Y. Jazz Orch., Syracuse; part-time asst. prof. music McGill U., Montreal, Que., Canada 1991—94. Composer, prodr.: rec. Bret Zvacek Quintet/Day In May. Mem.: Internat. Assn. for Jazz Edn. (pres. N.Y. unit). Office Phone: 315-267-2423.

**ZVIJAC, JOHN E.,** orthopedist; b. Buffalo, Ny, Mar. 22, 1960; s. John and Ann Zvijac; m. Gail Zvijac. MD, SUNY Buffalo Sch. of Medicine, 1986. Cert. Am. Bd. of Orthop. Surgeons, 1994. Orthop. surgeon UHZ Sports Medicine Inst., Coral Gables, Fla., 1992—; prof. U. of Miami Sch. of Edn., Dept. of Exercise Sci. & Sports Medicine, Fla., 1992—2006; mem., athletic tng. educatin adv. bd. Fla. Internat. U., Miami, 1992—, courtesy prof. in exercise and sports sci., 2005—. Chief of staff Doctors Hosp., Coral Gables, 2004—; team physician Tampa Bay Buccaneers, Fla., 1998—, Fla. Internat. U., Miami, 1992—, Chaminade-Madonna Coll. Prep. Sch., Hollywood, 2002—. Contbr. chapters to books. Mem. Doctors Hosp., Coral Gables, Fla., 2004—. Fellow: Arthroscopy Assn. of N.Am., Am. Orthop. Soc. for Sports Medicine, Am. Acad. of Orthop. Surgeons; mem.: Fla. Orthop. Soc., NFL Physicians Soc., Internat. Soc. of Arthroscopy, Knee Surgery & Orthop. Sports Medicine. Office: UHZ Sports Medicine Inst 1150 Campo Sano Ave Ste 200 Coral Gables FL 33146 Office Phone: 305-669-3320. Office Fax: 305-669-3353. E-mail: jzvijac@uhzsmi.com.

**ZWANGER, JEROME,** physician; b. N.Y.C., Apr. 4, 1923; m. Bernice E. Lomazov, May 22, 1955; children: Susan, Roberta (dec.), Melissa, Betsy. AB, U. Pa., 1943; MD, Chgo. Med. Sch., 1947. Diplomate Am. Bd. Radiology. Intern Wyckoff Heights Hosp., Bklyn., 1947-49; resident L.I. Coll. Hosp. Bklyn., 1949-52; practice medicine specializing in radiology; asst. dir. dept. radiology L.I. Coll. Hosp., N.Y.C., 1953-54; radiologist L.I. Jewish Hosp., 1955-60; dir. radiology North Shore U. Hosp., Plainview, NY, 1961—, also bd. dirs. Asst. prof. clin. radiology SUNY, Stony Brook, 1974-80; governing bd. Nassau-Suffolk Health Systems Agy.; mem. N.Y. State Bd. Medicine, Bd. Profl. Med. Conduct N.Y. State Dept. Health. Mem. vis. com. Met. Mus. Art, Phila. Art Mus.; bd. overseers Sch. Arts and Scis., U. Pa. Fellow: Nassau

Acad. Medicine (founding fellow, past pres.), Am. Coll. Radiology (councilor 1975—); mem.: AMA, Soc. for Breast Imaging, Am. Inst. Ultrasound in Medicine, L.I. Radiol. Soc. (past pres.), N.Y. State Radiol. Soc. (pres. 1986—87), Radiol. Soc. N.Am., Nassau County Med. Soc. (pres.), Med. Soc. N.Y., U. Pa. Alumni Assn. (bd. overseers 1997). Office: 126 Hicksville Rd Massapequa NY 11758-5822

**ZWANZIG, ROBERT WALTER,** chemist, physical science educator; b. Bklyn., Apr. 9, 1928; s. Walter and Bertha (Weil) Z.; m. H. Frances Ryder, June 6, 1953; children: Elizabeth Ann, Carl Philip. BS, Poly. Inst. Bklyn., 1948; MS, U. So. Calif., 1950; PhD, Calif. Inst. Tech., 1952. Rsch. assoc. Yale, 1951-54; asst. prof. Johns Hopkins, 1954-58; phys. chemist Nat. Bur. Standards, 1958-66; rsch. prof. U. Md., College Park, 1966—, disting. prof. phys. sci., 1980-88, disting. prof. emeritus, 1988—; rsch. chemist NIH, Bethesda, Md., 1988—. Assoc. editor: Jour. of Chem. Physics, 1965-67, Jour. of Math. Physics, 1968-70, Transport Theory and Statistical Physics, 1970, Chem. Physics, 1973—. Contbr. articles to profl. jours. Dept. Commerce Silver medal, 1965 Fellow Am. Phys. Soc., Am. Acad. Arts and Scis., AAAS; mem. Nat. Acad. Scis., Am. Chem. Soc. (Peter Debye award in phys. chemistry 1976, Irving Langmuir award 1984, Joel H. Hildebrand award 1994). Home: 5314 Sangamore Rd Bethesda MD 20816-2355 Office: NIH Nat Inst Digestive and Diabetes and Kidney Diseases Bethesda MD 20892-0001

**ZWASS, VLADIMIR,** computer science and information systems educator; b. Lvov, USSR, Feb. 3, 1946; came to U.S., 1970, naturalized, 1979; s. Adam and Friderike (Getzler) Z.; m. Alicia Kogut, Apr. 24, 1977; 1 child, Joshua Jonathan MS, Moscow Inst. Energetics, 1969; MPhil, Columbia U., 1974, PhD, 1975. Mem. profl. staff IAEA, Vienna, 1970; asst. prof. computer sci. Fairleigh Dickinson U., Teaneck, NJ, 1975-79, assoc. prof., 1979-84, prof., 1984—, prof. computer sci. and mgmt. info. sys., 1990—, disting. prof. computer sci. and mgmt. info. sys., 1999—, chmn. com. computer sci., 1976—. Cons. U.S. Govt., Met. Life Ins. Co., Citibank, Diebold Group; seminar assoc. Columbia U., 1986—; speaker nat. and internat. meetings. Author: Introduction to Computer Science, 1981, Programming in Fortran, 1981, Programming in Pascal, 1985, Programming in Basic, 1986, Management Information Systems, 1992, Foundations of Information Systems, 1998; editor-in-chief: Jour. Mgmt. Info. Sys., 1983—, Internat. Jour. Electronic Commerce, 1996—, Advances in Mgmt. Info. Systems, —; contbr. articles to profl. jours. and publs., Ency. Britannica, N.Y. Times, chpts. to books. Columbia U. fellow, 1970-71; Helena Rubinstein Found. scholar, 1971-75; grantee USN, other agys. Mem. IEEE, Assn. Computer Machinery, Assn. for Info. Sys., Sigma Xi, Eta Kappa Nu. Home: 19 Warewoods Rd Saddle River NJ 07458-2712 Office: Sch Computer Sci and Info Sys Fairleigh Dickinson U Teaneck NJ 07666 Office Phone: 201-327-9239. Personal E-mail: zwass@fdu.edu.

**ZWEBACK, STANLEY,** psychologist, educator; s. Harry and Belle Zweback; m. Dianne Barbara Fain, Dec. 24, 1964; children: Franklin Edward, Jessica Ellen. PhD, U. Md., 1972; BA, Coll. N.J., 1964. Diplomate Am. Bd. Profl. Disability Consultants. Assoc. prof. psychology Towson U., Md., 1970—; dir. svcs. Pers. Screening Sys., Severna Park, Md., 1985—. Cons. Balt. City Pub. Sch. Sys., 1999—2003; dir. svcs. Drs. Zweback, Driscoll and Assocs., Severna Park, 1989—98; psychol. cons. Arthur Slade Regional Sch., Glen Burnie, Md., 1973—. Contbr. articles to profl. jours. Pres. Bello Machre, Inc., Pasadena, Md., 1987—96. Experienced Tchr. fellow in sch. psychology, U.S. Office Edn., 1967—68. Mem.: APA (continuing edn. com. 1989—90). Office: Towson U 8000 York Rd Towson MD 21252 Office Phone: 410-704-3210. Personal E-mail: stanzwe@yahoo.com. E-mail: zweback@towson.edu.

**ZWEBEN, STUART HARVEY,** information scientist, educator, dean; b. Bronx, NY, Apr. 21, 1948; s. Max D. and Ruth (Schwartz) Z.; m. Rochelle T. Small, June 13, 1971; 1 child, Naomi. BS, CUNY, 1968; MS, Purdue U., 1971, PhD, 1974. Sys. analyst IBM Corp., Kingston, NY, 1969-70; asst. prof. Ohio State U., Columbus, 1974-80, from vice chmn. to acting chmn. computer sci. dept., 1982-84, assoc. prof., 1980-92, prof., 1992—, chmn., 1994—2005, assoc. dean academic affairs and adminstrn. Coll. Engring., 2006—. Pres. Computing Scis. Accreditation Bd., Stamford, Conn., 1989-91, v.p. 1987-89, sec., treas. 1986-87, exec. com.; computing accreditation commn., 2001-, vice chmn. ops., 2005-06; sec., treas. Fedn. on Computing in the U.S., Washington, 1992. Contbr. articles to profl. jours. Rsch. grantee NSF, 1981-83, 88-97, 2005-06, Army Rsch. Office, 1980-83, Dept. Edn., 1983-85, Applied Info. Tech. Rsch. Ctr., 1990-91, Honda R&D, 1998—; Equipment grant AT&T Bell Labs, 1984, 86-88. Fellow ABET, Assn. for Computing Machinery (pres. 1994-96, v.p. 1992-94, coun. mem. 1982-88, chpt. bd. chmn. 1982-85, publications bd. 1988-92, fin. com. 1990-92, nominating com. chmn. 1999-2000, fellows com. chmn. 2003, constn. and bylaws chmn. 1988-92, Recognition of Svc. award 1980, 85, 87-88, Outstanding Contbn. award 1997); mem. AAUP, IEEE Computer Soc. (assoc. editor 1990-98, Computing Rsch. Assn. (bd. dirs. 1997-2004, Spl. Svc. award 2006), Coun. Scis. Soc. Presidents (sec. 1998), Columbus Tech. Coun. (Tech. Person of Yr. award 2000). Avocations: sports, stamp collecting/philately. Office: Ohio State U Computer Scis 2015 Neil Ave Columbus OH 43210-1210 Office Phone: 614-292-9526. Business E-Mail: zweben@cse.ohio-state.edu.

**ZWECKER, WILLIAM RENE, JR., (BILL ZWECKER),** newspaper columnist, television reporter; b. Chgo., Dec. 25, 1948; s. William Rene and Margaret Richnel (Bushee) Z.; m. Deborah Rashid Bunn Alley, Sept. 1, 1973 (div. July 1977); 1 child, Brayton. AB in History cum laude, Princeton U., 1971. Legis. asst. U.S. Senator Charles Percy, Washington, 1971-73; asst. officer First Nat. Bank of Chgo., 1973-75; adminstrv. v.p. Krancer & Frank, Inc., Chgo., 1975-77; pres. Animal Accents, Inc., Chgo., 1977-83; mgr. Saks Fifth Ave, Chgo. and Oak Brook, Ill., 1983-86; regional v.p. BMW (N) Holding Corp., Chgo., 1986-87; assoc. editor, columnist Lerner Newspapers, Chgo., 1987-92; columnist Chgo Sun-Times, 1992—; corr. The Joan Rivers Show, N.Y.C., 1990-94. Host, producer Cast of Characters, Group W Cable TV, Chgo., 1988-90; entertainment reporter, film critic WMAQ-TV, NBC, Chgo., 1994-2000, WPNT-FM Radio, Chgo., 1993-95, WTMX-FM Radio, Chgo., 1999—2005; entertainment reporter WFLD-TV (Fox), Chgo., 2000-03, WBBM-TV (CBS), Chgo., 2003—. Author numerous articles on lifestyle, fashion, travel in Chgo. Daily News, Crain's Chgo. Bus., Town and Country, Chgo., others. Bd. dirs. Greater N. Michigan Ave. Assn., Chgo., 1980-85, Mental Health Assn. Greater Chgo., 1983-88; founding bd. dirs. Aux. bd. Lincoln Park Zoo, Chgo., 1979-89; trustee Chgo. Acad. Arts, 2004-. Recipient Tradition of Excellence alumni awrd Oak Park-River Forest H.S., 1995, Peter Lisagor award in journalism, 1991, 99; named Man of Vision Midwest Eye-Banks, 2000, Lifetime Achievement award Israel Film Festival, 2003; nominee Publicists Guild Am. Press award, 2006, Chgo. Midwest Emmy award, 2005, 05. Mem. Soc. Profl. Journalists (bd. dirs. 1992-94), Chgo. Film Critics Assn., Broadcast Film Critics Assn., North Dearborn Assn. (bd. dirs. 1993-97), Arts Club Chgo. Episcopalian. Office: Chgo Sun-Times 350 N Orleans Chicago IL 60654 Office Phone: 312-321-2820. E-mail: bzwecker@cbs.com.

**ZWEIBEL, JOEL BURTON,** retired lawyer; b. NYC, Feb. 7, 1935; s. Jacob and Ruth (Fleischner) Z.; m. Lynn Herzog (dec. Nov. 1984); children: Jane, Emily; m. Chrystine Marie Trichter. BBA magna cum laude, CCNY, Baruch Coll., 1955; LLB, Yale Law, 1958. Bar: NY 1959. Ptnr. Kaye, Scholer, Fierman, Hays & Handler, NYC, 1969-79, Gelberg & Kronovet, NYC, 1979-81, Kramer, Levin, Nessen, Kamin & Frankel, NYC, 1981-90, O'Melveny & Myers, NYC, 1990—2001, ptnr. in-charge N.Y. office, 1998—2000. Lectr. 2d Ann. Uniform Comml. Code Law Inst., 1968, Practicing Law Inst. Sr. Workout Officers Roundtable. Author: Creditors' Rights Handbook, 1980; co-author: Herzog's Bankruptcy, Forms and Practice, 6th edit., 1980; contbr. articles to profl. jours. Recipient award Bankruptcy and Reorgn. Divsn. Fedn. United Jewish Appeal, 1989. Mem. ABA, Assn. Dar City NY (chmn. com. on bankruptcy and corp. reorgn. 1981-84), Nat. Bankruptcy Conf. (chmn. com. on avoiding powers 1983-2000, mem. exec. com., treas. 1991-2000), Yale Law Sch. Alumni Assn. (bd. dirs. 2004-), Am. Coll. Bankruptcy (dir., regent 2d cir.), (co-founder, mem. steering com.

execs. on campus program, Baruch Coll., CUNY, advisor prelaw soc. 2002-). Avocations: art, theater, music, photography, tin whistle. Office: 570 Park Ave New York NY 10021 Office Phone: 212-326-2140. Personal E-mail: jbzweibel@aol.com.

**ZWEIFEL, DAVID ALAN,** newspaper editor; b. Monroe, Wis., May 19, 1940; s. Cloyence John and Uva Lorraine (Skinner) Z.; m. Sandra Louise Holz, Sept. 7, 1968; children: Daniel Mark, Kristina Marie. BJ, U. Wis., 1962. Reporter The Capital Times, Madison, Wis., 1962-71, city editor, 1971-78, mng. editor, 1978-83, editor, 1983—. V.p. Simpson St. Free Press, 2001—; bd. dirs. Swiss Am. Ctr., Friends of Monona Terrace, Capital Times Co., Madison Newspapers Inc., William T. Evjue Charitable Trust. V.p. Alliance for Children and Youth, Madison, 1983—; bd. dirs. United Cerebral Palsy Dane County, Madison, 1984-91. Lt. U.S. Army, 1963-65; col. USNG, ret. Named Investigative Reporter of Yr. Madison Press Club, 1972; Disting. Journalism grad. U. Wis., 2003 Mem.: Soc. Profl. Journalists (Spl. Achievement award 1992, 1996), Wis. Freedom of Info. Coun. (pres. 1986—2000), Wis. AP (pres. 1987—88), Am. Soc. Newspaper Editors (com. freedom of info., Pulitzer Prize juror 2000, 2001), U. Wis. Alumni Assn., Wis. N.G. Assn. (trustee 1975—81), Elks. Avocations: running, bowling, book collecting. Home: 5714 Tecumseh Ave Monona WI 53716-2964 Office: The Capital Times PO Box 8060 Madison WI 53708-8060

**ZWEIFEL, DONALD EDWIN,** editor, lobbyist, consultant; b. LA, Nov. 30, 1940; s. Robert Fredrick and Eugenia Bedford (White) Z.; m. Donna Jean Croslin; 1 son, Phillip Matthew. Student, Orange Coast Coll., 1963-67, 90-92, U. Calif., Irvine, 1968-70, Western State U. Coll. Law, 1973, Irvine U. Coll. Law, 1974-75, Rancho Santiago Jr. Coll., 1988, Chapman U., 1993—97; grad., Aviation Ground Sch., 1990; student, USAF Air U., 1994—95, USAF Air. U., 2000—01. Cert. student pilot, registered lobbyist Calif. State Legislature. Devel. tech. Hughes Aircraft, Newport Beach, Calif., 1963-64; co-founder, station mgr. Sta. KUCI-FM, Irvine, Calif., 1970; owner, mgr. Zweifel Jaguar Car Sales and Svc., Santa Ana, Calif., 1975-76; pres. Zweifel & Assocs., Inc., Santa Ana, 1977-86, Zweifel South Coast Exotic Cars, Orange, Calif., 1987-96, ret., 1996; assoc. editor, cons. Compliance News Pub. Co., Long Beach, Calif., 1998—. Mem. small bus. coun. CalTrans, 2000—; mem. legis. com., small bus. adv. coun. Calif. Dept. Gen. Svcs., 2005—. Co-author: Challenge 2000, Regaining the America's Cup, 1996; editor: (coll. textbook) The Dream Is Alive, Space Flight and Operations In Earth Orbit. Vol. emergency coord. emergency mgmt. divsn. Orange County Fire Authority, 1985-87, Navy Relief Soc., 1993, 1st. lt. CAP Squadron 88 Group VII, 1993-95, sr. programs officer, 1993-94, asst. transp. officer Calif. Wing Hdqrs., 1994-95, Group VII Facilities officer, 1994-95, 2000-02, squadron pers. officer, 1993-95, 2000-02, Calif. wing rep. to Orange County Vol. Orgns. Active in Disaster, ARC, 1994-95, Calif. wing vol. Office Emergency Svcs., Calif., 1994-96, 2000-21, grad. Squadron Leadership Sch., 1993, Wing Supply Officers Sch., 1995, squadron safety officer, pub. affairs officer, asst. aerospace edn. officer, 1998-2001; program coord. Young Astronaut Coun., 1989-90; cadet CAP, USAF aux., Long Beach, Calif., 1953-59; mem. Orange County Homeless Issues Taskforce, 1994-95, 1997-2000, Orange County Homeless Svc. Providers for the Reuse of Marine Corps Air Sta., Tustin, Calif., 1994-95; mem. legis. com. Orange County Vets. Adv. Coun., 1998—; chmn. tech. rev. subcom. Marine Corps Air Sta., El Toro, Calif., 1998-2001; apptd. to CalEPA DTSC Adv. Group Mil. Base Closure, 1995-99, CalEPA Dept. Toxic Substances Control Adv. Group pro-bono cons., Orange County Citizen's Adv. Commn. and El Toro Local Redevel. Authority, 1996-2001; vol. mediator Victim-Offender Reconciliation program, 1995-96; restoration adv. bd. MCAS Tustin, 1994—, co-chair, 2003—; mem. restoration adv. bd. MCAS, El Toro, Calif., 1994—; mem. Freedom Com. of Orange County, Cmty. ER Response Team for City of Placentia, 2003—; mem. homeless vets. com. United Vets. Orgn. Orange County; fed. advocate for Disabled Veteran Bus. Enterprise, 2004; dir. Orange County Walk of honor, 1998 With U.S. Army Nat. Guard, 1958—59. Recipient 6 certs. achievement Fed. Emergency Mgmt. Agy., 1989-96; 2 certs. appreciation CAP, 2 certs commendation, 1994, cert. appreciation Southwest Divsn. Naval Facilities Engring. Commd., 2000, Meritorious Svc. award, Calif. State Assembly Restoration Adv. Bd. Assemblyman John Campbell, 2001. Mem. Air Force Assn. (vice-chmn. civilian recruitment Calif. state membership com. 1988-89, 90-91, chair gov. rels. Calif. 2005—), v.p. membership, Gen. Doolittle chpt. bd. dirs. 1987-89, 90-92, chair Gen. Jimmy Doolittle chpt. 2005—), Exceptional Svc. award Gen. Jimmy Doolittle chpt. 1988, 91, Calif. Meritorious Svc. award 1988, v.p. membership Gen. Curtis E. LeMay Orange County chpt. 2000-02, 2004-), Calif. Assn. for Aerospace Edn. (fellow), Marine Corps Hist. Found. (life), Aerospace Edn. Found. (Gen. Jimmy Doolittle fellow 1988, Gen. Ira Eaker fellow 1989, Pres.'s award 1988), U.S. Naval Inst., AIAA (Cert. of Appreciation 1989, L.A. chpt. hist. com. 1989), Gulf & Vietnam Vets. Strategic Studies Archives (cons., co-founder 1983—, dir.), Marine Corps League (assoc., capt. Heinsey detachment 2000-02), Confederate Air Force (col.1989), AmVets (nat. jr. vice comdr. Calif. jr. coord. 2003-04, 2d vice comdr. Dist. II, Dept. Calif 2003-04, 1st vice comdr. dist. 2004-05), Masons, Saddleback Master Chorale of Orange County. Avocations: sailing, travel, flying. Home: 386 Hawaii Way Placentia CA 92870-6036 Personal E-mail: dzweifel@sbcglobal.net.

**ZWEIFEL, PAUL FREDERICK,** retired physics professor; b. N.Y.C., June 21, 1929; s. Fritz and Dorothy Mary Zweifel; m. Kathleen Anne McKay, Nov. 13, 1967; children: Christen Anne Whitten, Frederick Feza, Evan Rudolph, Kathryn Clements. BS, Carnegie Inst. of Tech., Pitts., Pa., 1948; PhD, Duke Univ., Durham, NC, 1949. Rsch. assoc., mgr. theoretical physics, consulting physicist GE Knolls Atomic Power Lab., Schenectady, NY, 1953—58; from assoc. prof. to prof. of nuc. engring. U. Mich., Ann Arbor, 1958—68; from prof. to univ. disting. prof. Va. Poly. Inst. and State U., Blacksburg, 1968—96; univ. disting. prof. emeritus Va. Poly. Inst. and State Univ., Blacksburg, 1996—. Cons. numerous orgns. including U.S. AEC, Oak Ridge, Argonne and Los Alamos Nat. Labs., 1958-88; vis. prof. numerous univs. including both U.S. and fgn. in Italy, Germany, Slovenia, Turkey, mem. numerous editl. bds. Translator opera supertitles; contbr. music articles, including opera program notes. Recipient E.O. Lawrence medal, US Govt. (Atomic Energy Commn.), 1972; Guggenheim fellowship, John Simon Guggenheim Found., 1974-75. Fellow: Am. Phys. Soc.; mem.: Fed. Am. Scientists (sec. 1956—59), Am. Math. Soc. Episcopalian. Avocations: music, travel, bridge, flight instructor, sportswriter. Home and Office: 6820 Sahalee Cir Radford VA 24141 Office Phone: 540-639-1295. Personal E-mail: zweifel@alumni.duke.edu.

**ZWEIFEL, RICHARD GEORGE,** curator; b. L.A., Nov. 5, 1926; s. Harold Charles and Kathleen Marguerite (Garland) Z.; m. Frances Ann Wimsatt, July 30, 1956; children: Matthew Karl, Kenneth Paul, Ellen Katrina. BA, UCLA, 1950; PhD, U. Calif. at Berkeley, 1954. Mem. staff Am. Mus. Natural History, N.Y.C., 1954-89, chmn. curator dept. herpetology, 1968-80, curator emeritus, 1989—; sci. attaché Gondwana, 1974-75. Served with AUS, 1945-46. Mem. Soc. Study Amphibious and Reptiles, Am. Soc. Ichthyologists and Herpetologists. Home: PO Box 16354 Portal AZ 85632-1354

**ZWEIG, JANET,** artist; BA, Cornell U., 1971; MFA, SUNY, Rochester, 1981. Faculty RISD, 1982—; asst. prof. Boston U., 1983-84. Resident Nexus Press, Atlanta, 1981, Jacob's Pillow Dance Festival, 1986, Macdowell Colony, Peterborough, NH, 1989, Peterborough, 90, Peterborough, 93, Peterborough, 94; resident Nat. Studio program PS1 Mus., Long Island, NY, 1990—91; resident Blue Mountain Ctr., 1997, Djerassi Resident Artists Program, 1998; guest lectr. numerous instns. MIT, Sch. Mus. Fine Arts, Boston U., Wesleyan U., Worcester Art Mus., Hartford Atheneum, NYU, Harvard U., U. Mass., Folger Shakespeare Libr., Brown U., Sarah Lawrence Coll., SUNY, Purchase, Temple U. Rome, Bard Coll., Photog. Resource Ctr., Boston, Moore Coll. Art, Phila., 1980—; adj. faculty Cooper Union, Anderson Ranch Art Ctr., Emerson Coll., Mass. Coll. Art, Sch. Mus. Fine Arts, Boston, Visual Studies Workshop Summer Inst., 1982 ; juror Cultural Edn. Collaborative, Boston, 1986, Ill. State Coun. on the Arts Visual Arts Fellowships, 1987; juror The Bunting Inst. Radcliffe Coll., 1992; juror Am. Acad. Rome, 1995; vis. critic Yale U., 1991. Prin. works include sculptures at

List Visual Art Ctr. MIT, Cambridge, Mass., The Art Gallery U. Md., 1989, 1990, PS 1 Mus., Inst. Contemporary Art, Long Island, 1990, 1991, Wallace Gallery SUNY, Old Westbury, 1991, The Artists Mus., Lodz, Poland, 1992, The Ulrich Mus. Wichita State U., 1992, Diverse Works, Houston, 1992, Sala 1, Rome, 1993, Huntington Gallery Mass. Coll. Art, 1993, RISD Mus., Providence, 1994, DeCordova Mus., Lincoln, Mass., Computer Mus., Boston, 1994, Big Orbit Gallery, Buffalo, N.Y., 1995, Anderson Gallery, Buffalo, 1995, Motel Fine Arts, N.Y.C., 1997, 1997, Snug Harbor Cultural Ctr., S.I., N.Y., 1995, Eighth Floor Gallery, N.Y.C., 1997, Cooper Union and the Coll. Art Assn., 1997, The Rotunda Gallery, Bklyn., 1998, Neuberger Mus. Art, Purchase, 1998, Represented in permanent collections Mus. Modern Art, Whitney Mus., Boston Mus. Fine Arts, Internat. Ctr. Photography, Calif. Inst. Arts, The Houghton Libr. Harvard, Cleve. Art Inst., Wellesley Coll. Libr., Visual Studies Workshop, Mus. Contemporary Art, Chgo., Art Inst. Chgo., Walker Art Ctr., Pompidou Ctr., RISD. Recipient Englehard award, Englehard Found. Inst. Contemporary Art, Boston, 1991; fellow in new genres category, Mass. Artists Found., 1985, visual arts fellow, NEA, 1985, 1994, The Rome Prize fellow, Am. Acad. Rome, 1991—92, grantee, Art Matters, Inc., 1986—90, Faculty Devel. Fund grantee, RISD, 1987, 1990, Individual Artists grantee, Artists Space, N.Y., 1990, grantee, Arts Internat., N.Y., 1992. Home: 54 Willow St Apt 4A Brooklyn NY 11201-6955 E-mail: jzweig@quicklink.com.

**ZWEIG, STEVEN FREDERICK,** statistician; s. Sammuel and Shirley Zweig. BS in Animal Sci., U. of Ga., 1979; MA in Econ., Va. Commonwealth U., 1985; MS in Biostatistics, Med. Coll. of Va., 1993. Retail mgr. Pk. Drug Store, Petersburg, Va., 1980—91; cons. InfoStat Cons., Columbus, 1994—96; statis. Covance, Inc., Princeton, NJ, 1996—2000; sr. statistician Target Rsch. Associates, New Providence, NJ, 2000—01; mgr. of biostatistics MDS Pharma Services, King of Prussia, Pa., 2001—03, SFBCI/New Drug Svcs. MNGR Biostats., Kennett Sq, Pa., 2003—04; cons. biostatistician Premier Rsch., Phila., 2004—05; cons. biostatistician Bristol-Myers Squibb, NJ, 2005—06, cons. sr. biostatistician NJ, 2006—. Sec. Columbus Jaycees, Columbus, Ohio, 1994—96. Recipient Dan O'Kane award, Columbus Jaycees, 1996. Mem.: Drug Info. Assn., Am. Statis. Assn. Home: 10 Sunflower Lane Yardville NJ 08620-3002 Personal E-mail: stevenfzweig@netscape.net.

**ZWEIMAN, BURTON,** allergist, immunologist, educator; b. N.Y.C., June 7, 1931; s. Charles and Gertrude (Levine) Z.; m. Claire Traig, Dec. 30, 1962; children: Amy Beth, Diane Susan. AB, U. Pa., 1952, MD, 1956. Diplomate Am. Bd. Internal Medicine, Am. Bd. Allergy & Immunology. Intern Mt. Sinai Hosp., N.Y.C.; Hosp. U. Pa., Bellevue Hosp. Ctr. Hosp. U. Pa., Bellevue Hosp. Center, 1957-60; fellow NYU Sch. Medicine, 1960-61; mem. faculty dept. medicine U. Pa. Sch. Medicine, Phila., 1963—, prof. medicine, chief allergy and immunology divsn., 1975-98. Cons. U.S. Army, NIH; co-chmn. Am. Bd. Allergy and Immunology, 1979-81. Editor Jour. Allergy Clin. Immunology, 1988-93; editor Allergy and Asthma: Disease Management Center, 1998—, now med. editor; contbr. articles to med. jours. Served with M.C., USNR, 1961-63. Allergy Found. Am. fellow, 1959-61 Fellow ACP, Am. Acad. Allergy, Asthma and Immunology (past pres.); mem. Am. Assn. Immunologists, Am. Fedn. Clin. Rsch., Phi Beta Kappa, Alpha Omega Alpha. Office: Hosp U Pa 527 Maloney Bldg 34th & Spruce St Philadelphia PA 19104 Business E-Mail: bzweiman@mail.med.upenn.edu.

**ZWERDLING, ALEX,** language educator; b. Breslau, Germany, June 21, 1932; came to U.S., 1941, naturalized, 1946; s. Norbert and Fanni (Alt) Z.; m. Florence Goldberg, Mar. 23, 1969; 1 son, Antony Daniel. BA, Cornell U., 1953; postgrad. (Fulbright scholar), U. Munich, Germany, 1953-54; MA, Princeton U., 1956, PhD, 1960. Instr. English Swarthmore Coll., 1957-61; asst. prof. English U. Calif., Berkeley, 1961-67, assoc. prof., 1967-73, prof., 1973-86, prof. English Berkeley, 1988—, emeritus grad. studies, 1985-86; univ. prof. George Washington U., 1986-88. Vis. prof. Northwestern U., 1977; dir. edn. abroad program U. Calif., London, 1996-98; mem. advanced placement exam. com. Ednl. Testing Svc., 1975-79; mem. fellowship panel Nat. Endowment for Humanities, 1977-82, 84-87, Nat. Humanities Ctr., 1989-90; fellow Ctr. for Advanced Study in Behavioral Scis., 1964-65. Author: Yeats and the Heroic Ideal, 1965, Orwell and the Left, 1974, Virginia Woolf and the Real World, 1986, Improvised Europeans: American Literary Expatriates and the Siege of London, 1998; mem. adv. com. PMLA, 1978-82. Am. Coun. Learned Socs. fellow, 1964-65; NEH fellow, 1973-74; Guggenheim fellow, 1977-78; Woodrow Wilson Ctr. fellow, 1991-92, fellow Nat. Humanities Ctr., 1992-93. Mem. MLA (chmn. 20th Century Brit. lit. div. 1969-70, 85-86, Berkeley Citation, 2003). Office: U Calif Dept English Berkeley CA 94720-1030

**ZWERLING, GARY LESLIE,** retired investment company executive; b. N.Y.C., Aug. 6, 1949; s. Seymour Joseph and Evelyn Rhoda (Posner) Z.; m. Marierose Miraglia, Aug. 25, 1974; children: Cara Marisa, Craig Harris. BEngring., SUNY, Stony Brook, 1970; MBA, SUNY, Albany, 1972. V.p. Chase Manhattan Bank, N.Y.C., 1972-78; ptnr. Goldman, Sachs & Co. N.Y.C., 1978-96; ret., 1996. Trustee Babson Coll., Jewish Appeal Fedn. No. NJ; bd. dirs. Am. Fedn. Aging Rsch.; bd. overseers Mus. Jewish Heritage-A Living Meml. to the Holocaust; bd. govs. NY chpt. Arthritis Found. Mem. Thoroughbred Owners and Breeders Assn., Nat. Thoroughbred Racing Assn. Jewish.

**ZWERLING, LEONARD JOSEPH,** physician, educator; b. Bklyn., May 15, 1944; s. David Louis and Ray (Mooney) Z.; m. Holly Gail Margolin, June 4, 1972; children: Jared, Margo. BA, Columbia Coll., 1965; MD cum laude, Boston U., 1969. Diplomate Am. Bd. Internal Medicine, Am. Bd. Cardiovasc. Disease, Bd. Nuclear Cardiology. Intern Mt. Sinai Hosp., N.Y.C., 1969-70, resident, 1970-72; fellow cardiology Beth Israel Hosp., Boston, 1972-73, Mass. Gen. Hosp., Boston, 1975-76; pvt. practice Cardiovasc. Medicine Assocs., I.A., Miami, Fla., 1976—; clinical fellow medicine Harvard, 1972-76. Staff assoc. medicine MIT Arteriosclerosis Ctr., 1975-76; clin. asst. prof. medicine U. Miami Med. Sch., 1976-83, clin. assoc. prof., 1983-91, clin. prof., 1991—; med. dir. home health care svcs. Bapt. Health; active staff Bapt. Hosp., South Miami Hosp. Author: (chpt.) Recent Advances in Studies on Cardiac Structure and metabolism, Vol. 5, Basic Functions of Cations in Mycardial Activity, 1975, The Care of the Post MI Patient, 1986. Lt. USNR, 1973-75. Recipient Boston Women's Club award, 1969, Maimonides award Boston Med. Soc., 1969, Univ. Hosp. award, 1969. Fellow ACP, Am. Coll. Cardiology, Am. Heart Assn. (coun. clin. cardiology); mem. Am. Soc. Echocardiography and Nuclear Cardiology, Alpha Omega Alpha. Home: 8300 Cheryl Ln Miami FL 33143-8610 Office: Cardiovasc Medicine Assocs 6200 SW 73d St Ste 210 Miami FL 33143 Office Phone: 305-666-4633. Business E-Mail: leonardz@baptisthealth.net.

**ZWERN, ARTHUR LOUIS,** computer company executive; b. N.Y.C., Mar. 29, 1960; s. Simon and Blanche (Rubin) Z. BS in Applied Physics, Ga. Inst. Tech., Atlanta, 1981; MBA, Harvard U., 1985. Sys. engr. Hughes Aircraft Co., El Segundo, Calif., 1981-83; group leader mfg. engring. KLA Instruments, Santa Clara, Calif., 1985-88, mfg. mgr., 1988-89, product mktg. mgr., 1990-91, mktg. mgr., 1991-92; pres. Voice Innovation, San Jose, Calif., 1992-94, Gen. Reality Co., San Jose, 1994—. Cons. Chryschem, Riverside, Calif., 1987-88. Patentee in field. Bd. dirs. Big Bros., Big Sisters, Santa Clara, 1990-96, pres. bd. dirs. 1993-96. Avocations: skiing, scuba, travel, music. Home: 2226 Coastland Ave San Jose CA 95125-2611

**ZWICK, ROBERT A.,** music educator, conductor; b. Columbus, Ohio, Oct. 29, 1948; s. Herman L. and Mary C. Zwick; m. Sandra E. Zwick, Sept. 22, 1979; children: Todd Stanley, Aaron Stanley. B of Music Edn., Ea. Ky. U., 1970; M of Music Edn., U. North Tex., 1975, PhD, 1987. Band dir. Richbourg Jr. H.S., Crestview, Fla., 1970—74; grad. asst. U. North Tex., Denton, 1974 76; inst. music instr. San Jacinto Coll., Pasadena, Tex., 1976—81; prof. music Houston Bapt. U., 1981—95; band dir. Montgomery (Tex.) H.S., 1995—98; orch. dir. Coney Creek H.S., Conroe, Tex., 1998—. Mus. dir., condr. Conroe Symphony Orch., Conroe, 1999—; pres. Star Custom Homes,

Montgomery, 1999—; condr. Pasadena Mcpl. Band, 1976—96. Mem.: Tex. Music Educators Assn. Home: 14067 Teel Rd Montgomery TX 77356 Office: Conroe Symphony Orch # 8 304 N Main Conroe TX 77301

**ZWICKLER, ALLEN,** investment advisor, educator; b. N.Y.C., Mar. 18, 1958; s. Seymour Zwickler and Sandra Lewin; m. Ellen Karen Pikitch; children: Scott Emlen, Adam, Randi. BS Mgmt., SUNY, Binghamton, 1979; MBA, NYU, 1986. Registered rep. N.Y. Stock Exch., 1979. Rsch. analyst Ladenburg Thalmann, N.Y.C., 1981—89; investment advisor First Manhattan, N.Y.C., 1989—. Lectr. NYU Sch. Continuing Edn., N.Y.C., 2000—05. Trustee Phil Zwickler Charitable and Meml. Found., N.Y.C., 1992—; bd. dirs. Metro Club Sch. Mgmt. SUNY, Binghamton. Avocations: scuba diving, basketball. Home: 420 E 72 St Apt 12-L New York NY 10021 Office: First Manhattan Co 437 Madison Ave New York NY 10022-7001

**ZWIENER, DAVID K.,** insurance company executive; Bachelor's Degree, Duke U.; MBA in Fin. and Mktg., Northwestern U. Asst. treas. internat. ops. Kimberly Clark; sr. v.p., treas. Heller Internat. Corp., exec. v.p. capital markets; CFO, exec. v.p ITT Fin.; pres., CFO, Hartford Fin. Svcs. Group, 1995—. Office: Hartford Plaza 690 Asylum Ave Hartford CT 06105-3845

**ZWIFKA, DAVID ALAN,** not for profit executive, consultant; b. Rochester, NY, May 15, 1955; s. David L. Zwifka and Eleanor Jozwiak; life ptnr. Kenneth J. Suter, Oct. 11, 2003. BA, Houghton Coll., 1977; MA in Theology, Christ the King Sem., 1980; D, Cath. U. Am., 1997. Ordination to Priesthood Diocese of Buffalo, 1980. Lectr. Niagara U., Lewiston, NY, 1989—93; assoc. pastor St. Benedict Ch., Buffalo, 1981—85; assoc. prof. pastoral studies Christ the King Sem., East Aurora, NY, 1990—2000; lectr. Cath. U. of Am., Washington, 1999—2000; pastor St. George Ch., West Falls, NY, 1999—2000; exec. dir. Hist. Harrisburg Assn., Pa., 2003—; lic. sales agt. Jack Gaughen Realtor-ERA, Harrisburg, Pa., 2003—. Cons. Swift Assoc., Harrisburg, Pa., 2000—. Fellow Ctr. for Prog. Leadership, Washington 2006; mem. Friends of the State Mus., Harrisburg, Pa., 2006; v.p. Buffalo Area Met. Ministries, 1988—91; mem. Mt. St. Mary's Sch., Tonawanda, NY, 1988—90. Mem.: Bus. Assn. of Gays and Lesbians (treas. 2006), Am. Acad. of Religion, Nat. Assn. of Realtors. Episcopal. Avocations: travel, reading, wine. Office: Hist Harrisburg Assoc 1230 North Third St Harrisburg PA 17102 Office Phone: 717-233-4646. Home Fax: 717-233-3848; Office Fax: 717-233-0635. Personal E-mail: dazwifka@comcast.net. E-mail: historicharrisburg@choiceonemail.com.

**ZWIKELMAIER, KURT E.,** pharmaceutical executive; b. Dallas, Dec. 5, 1954; s. Robert and Pearl Zwikelmaier; m. Madeline Axum; children: Virginia, Elise. BS in Chemistry, U. Mo., 1976; MBA, U. New Orleans, 1984. Cert. mgmt. acct. Rsch. chemist Monsanto Co., St. Louis, 1976—79, budget analyst, 1980—81. Cost acct. Monsanto Co., New Orleans, 1981—84, payroll acct., St. Louis, 1985—94, HRIT specialist, 1994—96, mgr. Ctr. for Employee Svcs., 1996—97, HRIT specialist - Europe/Africa, Brussels, 1998—99; sr. mgr. HRIT ops. Pharmacia Corp., St. Louis, 1999—. Sr. warden St. Timothy's Episcopal Ch., St. Louis, 2002. Mem.: Phi Beta Kappa. Episcopalian. Avocations: travel, foreign languages. Home: 11970 Greenwalk Saint Louis MO 63146

**ZWILICH, ELLEN TAAFFE,** composer; b. Miami, Fla., Apr. 30, 1939; d. Edward Porter and Ruth (Howard) Taaffe; m. Joseph Zwilich, June 22, 1969 (dec. June 1979). MusB, Fla. State U., 1960, MusM, 1962; D Mus. Arts, Juilliard Sch., 1975; studies with Roger Sessions and Elliott Carter; MusD (hon.), Oberlin Coll., 1987, Converse Coll., 1994; LHD (hon.), Manhattanville Coll., 1991, Marymount Manhattan Coll., 1994, N.Y. New Sch., Mannes, 1995, Mich. State U., 2006. Francis Eppes disting. prof. Fla. State U., Tallahassee, 1999—. Composer in residence Santa Fe Chamber Music Festival, 1990, Am. Acad. Rome, 1990; first Composer's Chair, Carnegie Hall, 1995-99, Saratoga Chamber Music Festival, 2004. Premiere, Symposium for Orch., Pierre Boulez, N.Y.C., 1975, Chamber Symphony and Passages, Boston Musica Viva, Richard Pittman, 1979, 82. Symphony 1, Gunther Schuller, Am. Composers Orch., 1982; violinist Am. Symphony, N.Y.C., 1965-73; composer: Sonata in Three Movements, 1973-74; String Quartet, 1974; Clarino Quartet, 1977; Chamber Symphony, 1979; Passages (for Soprano and Chamber Ensemble), 1981; String Trio, 1982; Symphony 1:3 Movements for Orch., 1982 (Grammy nomination New World Records, 1987); Divertimento, 1983; Einsame Nacht, 1971; Emlekezet, 1978; Im Nebel, 1972; Passages for Soprano and Orch., 1982; Trompeten, 1974; Fantasy for Harpsichord, 1983; Intrada, 1983; Prologue and Variations, 1983, Double Quartet for Strings, Chamber Music Soc. of Lincoln Ctr., 1984; Celebration for Orch., Indpls. Symphony, John Nelson, 1984; Symphony #2 (Cello Symphony) San Francisco Symphony, Edo De Waart, 1985, Symphony #2 Louisville Orch. recording. L.L. Smith (Grammy nomination 1991); Concerto Grosso 1985, Handel Festival Orch., Steven Simon, 1986; Concerto for Piano and Orch., Detroit Symphony, Gunther Herbig, Marc-André Hamelin, 1986; Images for 2 Pianos and Orch., Nat. Symphony Orch., F. Machetti, 1987; Tanzspiel, Peter Martins N.Y.C. Ballet, 1987; Praeludium Boston chpt. AGO, 1987; Trio for piano, violin and cello; Kalichstein, Laredo, Robinson trio 1987; Symbolon, Zubin Mehta and the N.Y. Philharm., Leningrad and Moscow (USSR), 1987, (Koussevitsky Internat. Rec. award nominee 1990), 1988; concerto for trombone and orch. J. Friedman, Sir Georg Solti, Chgo. Symphony, 1989, concerto for trombone and orch. Christian Lindberg, James De Priest, Malmö Symphony, concerto for flute and orch. D.A. Dwyer, Seija Ozawa, Boston Symphony, 1990, quintet for clarinet and string quartet David Schiffrin, Chamber Music N.W., Lincoln Ctr. Chamber Mus. Soc., 1990; concerto for oboe and orch. John Mack, Christoph von Dohnanyi, Cleve. Orch., 1991; concerto for bass trombone strings, timpani and cymbals Chgo. Symphony Orch. Ch. Vernon, Daniel Barenboim, 1991; concerto for violin, violoncello and orch. Jaime Laredo, Sharon Robinson, Louisville Orch. L. Smith 1991; Immigrant Voices Peter Leonard, St. Lukes Orch., N.Y. Internat. Festival at the Arts Chorus, Ellis Island, 1991, concerto for flute and orch, D.A. Dwyer, J. Sedares, London Symphony Orch., 1992, Symphony # 3 (Grammy nominee 1993), J. Ling, N.Y. Philharmonic, 1993, concerto for bassoon and orch., Nancy Goeres, Lorin Maazel, Pitts. Symphony, 1993, concerto for horn and string Orch., JoAnn Falletta, Long Beach Symphony Orch., 1994, American Concerto Doc Severinsen, J. Falletta San Diego Symphony, 1994, A Simple Magnificat, 1994, Triple Concerto Kali-

chstein, Laredo, Robinson Trio Zdenek Macal, Minn. Orch., 1995, for piano and orch., Peanuts Gallery, 1996, violin concerto, Pamela Frank, H. Wolff, 1997; String Quartet # 2, 1998, Emerson Quartet; Upbeat! 1998, Nat. Symphony Orch., conducted by Anthony Aibel, Symphony # 4 (orch., chorus, children's chorus) Mich. State U., L. Gregorian 2000, Lament for solo piano Carnegie Hall, 2000, Millenium Fantasy for Piano & Orch., J. Biegel, J. Cobos-Lopez, Cin. Symphony, 2000, Lament for Cello & Piano, Met. Mus., N.Y.C., 2000, Partita for Violin & String Orch., Carnegie Hall, 2001, One Nation, 2002, Openings for Orch., 2002 JoAnn Falletta Va. Symphony, Clarinet Concerto, D. Shifrin, Chamber Music Soc. of Lincoln Ctr., Buffalo Philharm, 2002, Episodes for Violin & Piano, Itzhak Perlman, 2003, Quartet for Oboe & Strings, Saratoga Festival, 2004, Rituals for 5 Percussionists and Orchestra, Iris Orchestra, Nexus, 2004, LUVN BLM, Calif. Ear Unit, 2005, Naxos Am. Classics, Violin Concerto and Rituals, M.Stern, Frank, 2005; New World Records: Music By Ellen Taaffe Zwilich; N.Y. Philharm. conducted by Zubin Mehta. Bd. dir. Copland Fund. Named Martha Baird Rockefeller Fund rec. grantee, 1977, 1979, 1982, Guggenheim fellow, 1981; named to, Fla. Artists Hall of Fame, 1994; recipient Elizabeth Sprague Coolidge Chamber Music prize, 1974, Gold medal, G.B. Viotti, Vercelli, Italy, 1975, citation, Ernst von Dohnanyi, 1981, Pulitzer prize for music, 1983, Composers award, Lancaster Symphony Orch., Arturo Toscanini Music Critics award, 1987, Alfred I. DuPont award, 1991, Performing Arts award, Miami Ctr. Performing Arts, 2000, named, Musical Am. Composer of Yr., 1999, Key to the City Cinn., 2001. Fellow: Am. Acad. Arts & Sci.; mem.: AAAL (Acad. award 1984), Guggenheim Found. (bd. dirs.), MacDowell Colony (bd. dirs.), Am. Fedn. Musicians (hon.; life), BMI Found. (bd. dirs.), Am. Music Ctr. (v.p. 1982—84, bd. dirs.). Office: Coll Music Fla State Univ Tallahassee FL 32306-1180 Office Phone: 850-644-4744. Office Fax: 850-644-2033.

**ZWILLING, MARK C.,** music director; b. Albuquerque, Apr. 5, 1960; s. Daniel Zwilling and June Byles Housiaux. MusB, Ea. N.Mex. U., 1982, B in Music Edn., 1982; MusM, DePaul U., 1990. Tchr. Las Lunas (N.Mex.) Schs., 1982—85; music dir. First Presbyn. Ch., Roswell, N.Mex., 1985—87, Trinity-First United Meth. Ch. El Paso, 1987—90, First Presbyn. Ch., Las Vegas, Nev., 1990—99, Cathedral of Hope, Dallas, 1999—2000, St. Andrew United Meth. Ch., Littleton, Colo., 2000—. Music dir. MGM Grand Hotel, Las Vegas, 1994—98; Presbyn. Assn. Musicians exec. nat. bd. mem. Presbyn. Ch. USA, Louisville, 1996—99. Mem.: Music Tchrs., Am. Choral Dirs., Am. Guild Organists. Democrat. Home: 758 Monroe St Denver CO 80206 Office: St Andrew United Methodist 3350 White Bay Dr Littleton CO 80126-5070

**ZWILLINGER, MARC J.,** lawyer; b. NYC; BA in Polit. Sci., magna cum laude, Tufts U., 1991; JD magna cum laude, Harvard U., 1994. Bar: Ill. 1994, DC 1996; Cert. Info. Systems Security Profl. Law clk. to Judge Mark L. Wolf US Dist. Ct. Mass., 1994—95; assoc. Kirkland & Ellis, Chgo., 1995—97; trial atty. computer crime & intellectual property sect., criminal divsn. US Dept. Justice, 1997—2000; ptnr. Kirkland & Ellis, Washington, 2000—03, head cyberlaw & info. security group, 2001—03; ptnr. Sonnenschein Nath & Rosenthal LLP, Washington, 2003—, chair firm info. security & internet enforcement practice group, 2003—. Office: Sonnenschein Nath & Rosenthal LLP Ste 600, E Tower 1301 K St NW Washington DC 20015 Office Phone: 202-408-9171. Office Fax: 202-408-6399. Business E-Mail: mzwillinger@sonnenschein.com

**ZWINGE, RANDALL JAMES HAMILTON See RANDI, JAMES**

**ZWISLOCKI, JOZEF JOHN,** neuroscience educator, researcher; b. Lwow, Poland, Mar. 19, 1922; arrived in U.S., 1951; s. Tadeusz and Helena (Moscicki) Z.; m. Ruth Gerber, Oct. 29, 1945 (div. May 1954); m. Sylvia Claire Goldman, July 11, 1954 (dec. July 17, 1992); m. Jadwiga M. Morrison, Dec. 2, 1993. Diploma, Fed. Tech. Inst., Zurich, Switzerland, 1944, ScD, 1948; D honoris causa, U. Adam Mickiewicz, Poznán, Poland, 1991, Syracuse U., NY, 2004. Head electroacoustic lab. dept. otolaryngology U. Basel, Basel, Switzerland, 1945-51; rsch. fellow psychoacoustic lab. Harvard U., Cambridge, Mass., 1951-57; dir. Bioacoustic Lab. Syracuse U., 1958-63, founder, dir. Lab. of Sensory Communication, 1963-73, founder dir. Inst. for Sensory Rsch., 1973—84, prof. neurosci., 1984—88, disting. prof. neurosci., 1988—92, disting. prof. emeritus, 1992—; prof. communicative disorders dept. spl. edn. Syracuse U. Sch. Edn., 1982—92; rsch. prof. SUNY Health Sci. Ctr., Syracuse, 1967—. Affiliate prof. bioengring. U. State Coll. Engring., Syracuse U., 1986-92; Carhart Meml. lectr. Am. Auditory Soc., 1992; Richard C. Heyser Meml. lectr. Audio Engring. Soc., 2005; mem. exec. coun. Com. Hearing, Bioacoustics and Biomechanics, NRC, Washington, 1965-68, chmn., 1967-68; mem. rev. panel on communicative scis. NIH, Bethesda, Md., 1966-70, chmn., 1969-70; mem. Communicative Disorders Program Project rev. com. NIH, Bethesda, 1971-75; chmn. Bd. Sci. Advs. Ctr. Health Scis., U. Wis., Madison, 1975-78. Inventor acoustic ear simulator, acoustic bridge, several types of ear defenders; contbr. articles to profl. jours.; author: Auditory Sound Transmission: An Autobiographical Perspective, 2002. Recipient Faculty Rsch. award Syracuse chpt. Sigma Xi, 1973, Internat. Ctr. Ricerche e Studi Amplifon prize, 1976, Javits Neurosci. Investigator award NIH, 1984, Kwiek medal Acoustics Inst., A. Mickiewicz U., Poland, 1991, medal Acoustical Soc. Poland, 1991, Hugh Knowles prize Northwestern U., 1992. Fellow Acoustical Soc. Am. (chmn. tech. com. on psychol. and physiol. acoustics 1962, 63, exec. coun. 1982-85, recipient 1st Bekesy medal 1985, chmn. long-range planning com. 1983-86, nominating com. 1986-87, mem. com. on tutorials 1988-91, com. on meetings 1988-91, chmn. spring meeting, 1989), Am. Speech and Hearing Assn., The Polish Inst. of Arts and Scis. of Am.; mem. NAS, Polish Acad. Scis., Internat. Soc. Audiology (v.p. 1967-72), Internat. Union of Physiol. Scis. (commn. on auditory physiology 1982-89), Internat. Union Pure and Applied Physics (Commn. on Acoustics 1982-89), Collegium Oto Rhino Laryngologicum Amicitiae Sacrum, Assn. for Rsch. in Otolaryngology (award of merit 1988), Am. Otol. Soc. (assoc.), Hearing Rsch. (editl. bd.). Avocations: skiing, tennis, trout fishing, inventions. Office Phone: 315-443-9718. Business E-Mail: joe_zwislocki@isr.syr.edu.

**ZWOYER, EUGENE MILTON,** retired consulting engineering executive; b. Plainfield, NJ, Sept. 8, 1926; s. Paul Ellsworth and Marie Susan (Britt) Z.; m. Dorothy Lucille Seward, Feb. 23, 1946; children: Gregory, Jeffrey, Douglas. Student, U. Notre Dame, 1944, Mo. Valley Coll., 1944-45; BS, U. N.Mex., 1947; MS, Ill. Inst. Tech., 1949; PhD, U. Ill., 1953. Mem. faculty U. N.Mex., Albuquerque, 1948-71, prof. civil engring., dir. Eric Wang Civil

Engring. Rsch. Facility, 1961-70; rsch. assoc. U. Ill., Urbana, 1951-53; owner, cons. engr. Eugene Zwoyer & Assocs., Albuquerque, 1954-72; exec. dir., sec. ASCE, N.Y.C., 1972-82; pres. Am. Assn. Engring. Socs., N.Y.C., 1982-84; exec. v.p. T.Y. Lin Internat., San Francisco, 1984-86, pres., 1986-89; owner Eugene Zwoyer Cons. Engrs., 1989—2002; COO, treas. Polar Molecular Corp., Saginaw, Mich., 1990, exec. v.p., 1991-92; ret., 2002. Trustee Small Bus. Research Corp., 1976-80; trustee Engring. Info., Inc., 1981-84; internat. trustee People-to-People Internat. 1974-86; v.p. World Fedn. Engring. Orgns., 1982-85. Served to lt. (j.g.) USN, 1944-46. Named Outstanding Engr. of Yr. Albuquerque chpt. N.Mex Soc. Profl. Engrs., 1969, One Who Served the Best Interests of the Constrn. Industry, Engring. News Record, 1980; recipient Disting. Alumnus award the Civil Engring. Alumni Assn. at U. Ill., 1979, Disting. Alumnus award Engring. Coll. Alumni Assn., U. N.Mex., 1982, Can.-Am. Civil Engring. Amity award Am. Soc. Civil Engrs., 1988, Award for Outstanding Profl. Contbns. and Leadership Coll. Engring. U. N.Mex., 1989 Mem. AAAS, ASCE (dist. bd. dirs. 1968-71), NSPE, AFTRA, Am. Soc. Engring. Edn., Nat. Acad. Code Adminstrn. (trustee, mem. exec. com. 1973-79), Engrs. Joint Coun. (bd. dirs. 1978-79), Engring. Soc. Commn. on Energy (bd. dirs. 1977-82), Sigma Xi, Sigma Tau, Chi Epsilon. Home: 6363 Christie Ave Apt 1326 Emeryville CA 94608-1940 E-mail: eugenezwoyer@comcast.net.

**ZYCHICK, JOEL DAVID,** lawyer; b. Cleve., June 23, 1954; s. Eugene K. and Myra (Rotblatt) Z. BBA, George Washington U., 1976; JD, Case We. Res. U., 1979; LLM in Taxation, NYU, 1979. Bar: Ohio 1979, N.Y. 1985, D.C. 1985, U.S. Tax Ct. 1980, U.S. Ct. Claims 1980, U.S. Ct. Appeals (fed. cir.) 1982. Assoc. Jones, Day, Reavis & Pogue, Cleve., 1980-83, Milbank, Tweed, Hadley & McCloy, N.Y.C., 1983-85; ptnr. Hertzog, Calamari & Gleason, N.Y.C., 1986-98; pres. Zcounsel LLC; pres., CEO, GETKO Group, Inc., Westbury, NY, 1998—2001. Former gen. counsel, dir. The Egg Factory, LLC, Va. Contbr. articles to profl. jours. Dir., treas. Northside Ctr. for Child Devel., N.Y.C. Mem. ABA (past sec., dir. coun. tax sect., nominating com., former chmn. sales and fin. trans. com., past vice chmn. regulations com. govt. submissions), Am. Coll. Tax Counsel, N.Y. State Bar Assn. Avocations: hiking, music, travel. Home: PO Box 1097 Amagansett NY 11930-1097 Office Phone: 516-680-2715. E-mail: JZ@Zcounsel.com

**ZYGOCKI, RHONDA I.,** oil industry executive; b. St. John's, Nfld., July 1957; B.Civil Engring., Meml. U. of Nfld., 1980. Petroleum engr. Chevron Can. Resources, Calgary, Canada, gen. mgr. strategic bus. svcs., 1993—94; profit ctr. mgr. Chevron U.S.A. Prodn. Co., Houston, 1994—97; CFO Chevron Can. Resources, Calgary, 1997—99; mgr. strategic planning Chevron Corp., San Ramon, Calif., 1999—2000, advisor to chmn. bd., 2000—01; mng. dir. ChevronTexaco Australia Pty. Ltd., Perth, Australia, 2001—03; v.p. health, environment and safety Chevron Texaco Corp., San Ramon, 2003—. Mem.: Engrs. Without Borders (bd. dirs.), Internat. Petroleum Industry Environ. Conservation Assn. (bd. dirs.), Internat. Assn. Oil and Gas Prodrs. (bd. dirs.). Office: Chevron Texaco Corp 6001 Bollinger Canyon Rd San Ramon CA 94583-2324

**ZYLSTRA, ALEXANDRIA,** lawyer; b. Ill. LLM, U. Mo., 2001. Bar: Mo. 1997. Asst. prof. legal studies Stephens Coll., Columbia, Mo., 2002—. Contbr. articles to profl. jours. Mem.: Mo. Bar Assn. Office: Stephens Coll Legal Studies Dept 1200 East Broadway Columbia MO 65215 Office Phone: 513-876-7147. Business E-Mail: azylstra@stephens.edu.

**ZYROFF, ELLEN SLOTOROFF,** information scientist, classicist, educator; b. Atlantic City, N.J., Aug. 1, 1946; d. Joseph George and Sylvia Beverly (Roth) Slotoroff; m. Jack Zyroff, June 21, 1970; children: Dena Rachel, David Aaron. AB, Barnard Coll., 1968; MA, The Johns Hopkins U., 1969, PhD, 1971; MS, Columbia U., 1973. Instr. The Johns Hopkins U., Balt., 1970-71, Yeshiva U., N.Y.C., 1971-72, Bklyn Coll., 1971-72; libr. instr. U. Calif., 1979, 81, 91, San Diego State U., 1981-85, 94; prof. San Diego Mesa Coll., 1981-95; dir. The Reference Desk Rsch. Svcs., La Jolla, Calif., 1983—; prin. libr. San Diego County Libr., 1985—. V.p. Archaeol. Soc. Am., Balt., 1970-71. Author: The Author's Apostrophe in Epic from Homer Through Lucan, 1971, Cooperative Library Instruction for Maximum Benefit, 1989; contbr. articles to profl. jours. Pres. Women's Am. ORT, San Diego, 1979-81, Zionist Orgn. of Am., San Diego dist., 1997-2000; mem. adv. bd. With Israel Now. Mem.: ALA (chair divsn. and roundtable coms. 1982—, coun. 2003—), Libr. Congress Cataloging in Publs. Adv. Group, Assn. Jewish Librs., Am. Classical League, Calif. Libr. Assn. (assembly 1993—99, editor Calif. Librs. 1997—99, pres. mgmt. sect. 2000—01), Am. Philol. Assn., Toastmasters, Beta Phi Mu. E-mail: eszyroff@hotmail.com.

**ZYSMAN, JOHN ADLER,** political scientist, educator; b. Omaha, Mar. 23, 1946; s. Evelyn Zysman; m. Victoria Rehn; 1 child, Lara. PhD of Polit. Sci., MIT, Boston, MA, 1973; BA, Harvard Coll., 1968. Lectr. Dept. Polit. Sci. MIT, Boston, 1973—74; asst. prof. Dept. Polit. Sci. U. Calif.-Berkeley, 1974—82, assoc. prof. Dept. Polit. Sci., 1982—87, prof. Dept. Polit. Sci., 1987—; co-dir. Berkeley Roundtable on Internat. Economy, 1982—. Office: BRIE / Univ of California 2234 Piedmont Avenue Berkeley CA 94720-2322 Office Phone: (510) 642 3067. Office Fax: (510) 643 6617. Business E-Mail: johnz@socrates.berkeley.edu.*

**ZYWICKI, ROBERT ALBERT,** retired electric power industry executive; b. Chgo., Mar. 23, 1930; s. Martin Albert and Margaret Irene (Mackowski) Z.; m. Barbara Joan Hagerty; children: Robert, Cheryl, Cindy, Carrie. B in Commerce, Northwestern U., 1966. Teller Chgo. Title and Trust Bank, Chgo., 1949-50; painter Getz Molding Co., Chgo., 1950-51; purchasing agt. Woodworker's Tool Works, Chgo., 1953-54; serviceman Addressograph Multigraph, Chgo., 1954-55; mem. Chgo. Fire Dept., 1955-62; v.p. Anixter Bros. Inc., Skokie, Ill., 1955-87; co-owner A-Z Industries, Northbrook, Ill., 1987—2003; ret., 2003. Served as cpl. U.S. Army, 1951-53. Mem. Am. Legion (comdr.). Republican. Roman Catholic. Avocations: thoroughbred horse racing, classical music, baseball card collecting, tennis. Home: 1330 Sprucewood Ln Deerfield IL 60015-4771 Personal E-mail: peter1330@comcast.net. *Love your family, respect your friends and co-workers, value your customers and suppliers. Always keep each in its proper perspective. Most of all, remember - love, value and respect are all two-way streets.*

# Geographic Index

**Cullman**
Ivey, Mona Kay *secondary school educator, educational association administrator, consultant*
Little, Phyllis A. *protective services official*
Morris, Sylvia June Burbank *retired physician*

**Daleville**
Nichols, Mark A. *music educator*

**Daphne**
Curreri, Peter William *health facility administrator, consultant*
Hamilton, Virginia Van der Veer *historian, educator*
Jeffreys, Elystan Geoffrey *petroleum consultant*

**Decatur**
Julich, Nancy C. *secondary school educator*
Mardis, Elizabeth Williams *occupational health nurse*
Michelini, Sylvia Hamilton *auditor*
Smith, Trina *academic administrator*
Smith, Troy Alvin *aerospace research engineer*
Talley, Richard Woodrow *accountant*

**Demopolis**
Bonds, Philippe Dale *music educator*
Lloyd, Hugh Adams *lawyer*
Reynolds, Louise Webb *retired volunteer, director*

**Dothan**
Cotter, Melanie K. *psychologist, consultant*
Cross, Steven Jasper *finance educator*
Dean, Bobby Frank *real estate agent*
Fleming, Jennie M *retired education educator*
Flowers, V. Anne *retired academic administrator*
Glanton, Jeraline Cain *retired language educator*
Malugen, J.T. (Joe Thomas) *retail executive*
Mocker, Hans Walter *physicist*
Pearson, Deborah Faye *newscaster*
Peterson, Roger *community bank executive, retired international investment banker, retired manufacturing executive, retired air force officer*
Phillips, Kenneth Edward *history educator, writer*
Wright, Burton *sociologist*

**Duncanville**
Prescott, Perry Don *psychology professor, counselor*

**Elberta**
Kauffman, Carl Herbert *music educator*
Wilkinson, Edward Anderson, Jr. *retired military officer, manufacturing executive*

**Enterprise**
Garrett, Thomas W. *retired career officer*
Parker, Ellis D. *retired military officer*

**Eufaula**
Bush, Billie Faye *mathematics educator*
Conniff, Alexandra Acosta *secondary school educator*

**Eutaw**
Merritt, Edith Bradford *elementary school educator*

**Fairfield**
McCaslin, LaTanya *art educator*

**Fairhope**
Gwin, John Michael *retired education educator, consultant*
Mozer, Martha K. *music educator*
Mozley, Paul David *retired obstetrics and gynecology educator*

**Florence**
Badger, Phillip Charles *agricultural engineer*
Cale, William Graham, Jr. *environmental sciences educator, university administrator, researcher*
Chanin, Natalie *costume designer, apparel designer*
Dolmatov, Valeriy Konstantinovich *physicist, researcher*
Foote, Avon Edward *web developer/producer, communications educator*
Foote, Dorothy Gargis *nursing educator*
Hansen, Vagn Keith *political science educator, college administrator*
Johnson, Johnny Ray *retired mathematics professor*
Knight, Karen Anne McGee *artist, educator, educational research administrator*
Lee, Soojeong *music educator, soprano*
Marone-Cinzano, Enrico *apparel designer*
Williams, Joyce Hall *secondary school educator*

**Foley**
Pearce, Stephen Ferron *music educator*
St. John, Henry Sewell, Jr. *utility company executive*

**Fort Payne**
Cook, Jeffrey Alan *musician*
Curington, Thomas Franklin III *photographer, writer*

**Gadsden**
Gagliardo, Michael Robert *music educator, conductor*
Grimm, James R. (Ronald Grimm) *management consultant*

**Gardendale**
McKay, Marie Conyers *librarian, writer*

**Grand Bay**
Taylor, Anne Wilkerson *elementary school educator*

**Grant**
Segler, Lynn Cchandler *elementary school educator*

**Greensboro**
Massey, James Earl *retired clergyman, retired educator*

**Gulf Shores**
Wallace, John Loys *retired aviation services executive*

**Guntersville**
Burroughs, Julie M. *elementary school educator*
Jones, Valerie Marie *art educator*

**Hartselle**
Slate, Joe Hutson *psychologist, educator*

**Hayden**
King, Vickie Ruth *minister, shop owner*

**Headland**
Taylor, John Paul *music educator, minister*

**Homewood**
Tucker, Rhonda Reneé *music educator*

**Hueytown**
Nelson, Susan Rhodes *media specialist, educator*

**Huntsville**
Allan, Barry David *research chemist, government official*
Ashrafi, Ashkan *electrical engineer*
Baldaia, Peter *curator*
Bearden, Thomas Eugene *research scientist, researcher*
Bendickson, Marcus J. *engineering company executive*
Brandon, Walter Wiley, Jr. *retired physicist, retired aerospace engineer*
Burko, Lior M. *physics educator*
Conran, Michael Artemus *voice educator, director*
Contreras, Frank R. *musician*
Costes, Nicholas Constantine *aerospace scientist, educator, retired government agency administrator*
Dahm, Werner K. *aerodynamicist*
Dasher, Glenn *art educator, department chairman*
Daussman, Grover Frederick *electrical engineer, consultant*
Dimmock, John Oliver *physicist, educator*
Dunegan, Deason C. *plastic surgeon*
Foster, Deborah Simmons *elementary school educator*
Franz, Frank Andrew *academic administrator, physicist, educator*
Freas, George Wilson, II, *computer scientist, consultant*
Gillani, Noor Velshi *atmospheric scientist, researcher, educator*
Graves, Benjamin Barnes *business administration educator*
Hall, Doris Spooner *music educator*
Hawley, Harold Patrick *educational consultant*
Huber, Donald Simon *physician*
Huckaby, Gary Carlton *lawyer*
Hunter, Herbert Erwin *aerospace engineer*
Ingram, Shirley Jean *social worker*
Johnson, John D., Jr. *neurosurgeon*
King, David A. *aerospace engineer*
Krueger, Kathleen Susan *special education administrator*
Lang, Sharon *historian*
Lundquist, Charles Arthur *academic administrator*
Lyles, Brian M. *music educator*
McIntyre-Ivy, Joan Carol *data processing executive*
Moore, Ann Roy *school system administrator*
Morgan, Beverly Hammersley *elementary school educator, artist*
Morgan, John Derald *electrical engineer*
Norman, Ralph Louis *retired physicist, consultant*
Nuessle, William Raymond *surgeon*
Oluseyi, Hakeem Muata *astrophysicist, educator*
Ooi, Teng Keong *aerospace engineer, mechanical engineer*
Paciesas, William Simon *astrophysicist, educator*
Parnell, Thomas Alfred *physicist*
Pittman, William Claude *electrical engineer*
Pruitt, Alice Fay *mathematician, engineer*
Ratchford Merchant, Betty Jo *retired elementary school educator*
Richardson-Weninegar, Loretta Lynne *biologist, educator*
Roe, Fred Davis, Jr. *electronics engineer, director*
Ryan, L. Thomas, Jr. *lawyer*
Sackheim, Robert Lewis *aerospace engineer, educator*
Schumann, J. Paul *retired federal agency administrator*
Slone, Wesley Shaun *network engineer*
Smith, Robert Earl *space scientist*
Stephenson, Arthur G. *aerospace engineer*
Stewart, Verlindsey Laquetta *accounting educator*
Stuhlinger, Ernst *physicist*
Tietke, Wilhelm *gastroenterologist, educator*
Vaughan, William Walton *atmospheric scientist*
Watson, Raymond Coke, Jr. *engineering executive, academic administrator*
Watson, S.A. *lawyer, retired judge*
Williamson, Donald Ray *retired career Army officer*
Wright, John Collins *retired chemistry professor*
Zutaut, Steven Eric *systems analyst, application developer*

**Hurtsboro**
Bouilliant-Linet, Francis Jacques *global management consultant*

**Jacksonville**
Blair, Benjie G. *biology professor*
Carter, Robert Eugene, Jr. *forester, educator*
Dunaway, Carolyn Bennett *retired sociology professor*
Dunaway, William Preston *retired school system administrator*
Gossett, Jeffrey David *music educator*
Hubbard, William James *library director*
McAbee, Sonja Louise *library administrator*
Merrill, Martha *library and information scientist*
Spector, Daniel Earl *historian, educator*
Wang, Hanrong *law librarian, educator, library and information scientist*

**Jasper**
Lloyd, Karen D. *French language educator*

**Gulf Shores** *(continued — middle column)*

Morgan, Holly Guthrie *elementary school educator*
Rowland, David Jack *retired academic administrator*
Sparkman, Brandon Buster *secondary school educator, consultant, writer*

**Kinston**
Sumblin, Anne Stone *lawyer*

**Laceys Spring**
Rock, Janice C. *electronics engineer*

**Lafayette**
Woody, Mary Florence *nursing educator, academic administrator*

**Leeds**
Smith, Robert K. *music educator, director*
Wilson, Maggie Isabelle Lovell *secondary school educator, literature educator*

**Lillian**
Burnette, Ollen Lawrence, Jr. *historian*
Moyer, Kenneth Evan *psychologist, educator*

**Livingston**
Green, Asa Norman *university president*
Padgett, Christine Elizabeth King *education educator*
Smith, Louis Roycraft, Jr. *guidance and counseling educator, administrator*
Wymer, Douglas A. *environmental scientist, educator, ecologist*

**Loachapoka**
Schafer, Elizabeth Diane *historian, writer*
Schafer, Robert Louis *agricultural engineer, researcher*

**Madison**
Brannan, Eulie Ross *educational consultant*
Dannenberg, Konrad K. *aeronautical engineer*
Emerson, William Kary *engineering company executive*
Gibson, John Thomas *academic administrator, consultant*
Jones, Christine Regina *secondary school educator*
Parlier, Greg H. *military officer, engineer, research scientist*
Vo, Hieu N. *architect*

**Marion**
Bauer, David Woodfin *history professor*
Cleveland, Willie Mae *elementary school educator*
Price, Ray Hampton *mathematics professor*
Street, Deborra Lynn *fine arts director*

**Maylene**
Copes, Marvin Lee *academic administrator*

**Mc Calla**
Kes, Vicki *museum director*

**Mentone**
Herndon, Mark Joel *musician*

**Millbrook**
Boartfield, Ernest William *music educator*

**Millport**
Fowler, William Ralph *music educator*

**Mobile**
Armbrecht, William Henry III *retired lawyer*
Atkinson, William James, Jr. *retired cardiologist*
Bostwick, Robert Otis *government agency administrator*
Braswell, Louis Erskine *lawyer*
Brogdon, Byron Gilliam *radiologist, educator*
Bullard, Bettie Catherine Posey *adult education educator*
Butler, Charles Randolph, Jr. *federal judge*
Clark, Hattie Giles *real estate broker, real estate appraiser*
Clark, Jack *retired health facility administrator*
Clarke, Ulma Leverna *retired elementary school educator*
Clausell, Deborah Deloris *artist*
Conlon, James Edward *retired art educator, sculptor*
Cox, Emmett Ripley *federal judge*
Cunningham, Julian Antonia *retired protective services official*
DeBakey, Ernest George *physician, surgeon*
Edwards, Jack *congressman, lawyer*
French, Elizabeth Irene *biology professor, musician*
Gandy, Maurice Edward *language educator, writer*
Graddick, Charles Allen *judge*
Granade, Callie Virginia Smith *federal judge*
Hain, Thomas Franz *computer scientist, educator*
Hamid, Michael *electrical engineering educator, consultant*
Hariadi, John Wesley *otolaryngologist, surgeon*
Harris, Benjamin Harte, Jr. *lawyer*
Hart, Eric Mullins *consumer products company executive*
Helmsing, Frederick George *lawyer*
Holland, Lyman Faith, Jr. *lawyer*
Holmes, Broox Garrett *lawyer*
Howard, Alex T., Jr. *federal judge*
Hsiao, Kuang-Ting *mechanical engineer, educator, researcher*
Johnstone, Douglas Inge *retired state supreme court justice, lawyer*
Jones, Joseph Seymour *small business owner, poet*
Kargleder, Charles Leonard *language educator*
Lipscomb, Oscar Hugh *archbishop*
Littleton, Jesse Talbot III *radiology educator*
McCleery, Winston Theodore *information technology educator*
Milling, Bert William, Jr. *judge*
Murchison, David Roderick *lawyer*
Parden, Cindy Maria *elementary school educator*
Peebles, E(mory) B(ush) III *lawyer*
Phan, Anh-Vu *adult education educator, researcher*
Pittman, Virgil *federal judge*

**Montgomery** *(right column)*

Rewak, William John *retired academic administrator, clergyman*
Rhodes, Deborah J. *prosecutor*
Richelson, Paul William *curator*
Roby, Jasper *bishop*
Rodning, Charles Bernard *surgeon*
Roedder, William Chapman, Jr. *lawyer*
Rummel, Harold Edwin *travel company executive, retail executive*
Scantlebury, Velma Patricia *surgeon*
Smith, Jesse Graham, Jr. *dermatologist, educator*
Steadman, John Marcellus III *retired language educator*
Suess, James Francis *retired clinical psychologist*
Sumlin, Margaret Brown *special education educator*
Wertelecki, Wladimir *pediatrician, educator*
White, Richard Dean *art conservator*
Wisner, Pamela L. *social worker*
York, David P. *prosecutor*

**Montevallo**
McChesney, Robert Michael, Sr. *academic administrator*
Staik, Irene McVay *psychology professor*

**Montgomery**
Adams, Robert Barry *pathologist*
Baker, Jimmy H. *former state finance administrator*
Baxley, Lucy *lieutenant governor*
Bibb, Kartz E. *biology professor*
Black, Robert Coleman *judge, lawyer*
Blount, Winton Malcolm III *investment executive*
Bolin, Michael F. *state supreme court justice*
Boncek, John James *mathematics professor*
Brown, Jean Williams *former state supreme court justice*
Byars, Walter Ryland, Jr. *lawyer*
Campbell, Maria Bouchelle *lawyer, consultant*
Canary, Leura Garrett *prosecutor*
Carnes, Edward E. *federal judge*
Cassels, Martha Beasley *realtor, real estate developer*
Clark, Daniel Curtis *psychologist*
Copeland, Jacqueline Turner *music educator*
Cornett, Lloyd Harvey, Jr. *retired historian*
Daniell, Steven J. *language educator, department chairman*
Dean, Wendy Brown *outreach coordinator*
Dees, Morris Seligman, Jr. *lawyer*
Dixon, Larry Dean *state legislator*
Dubina, Joel Fredrick *federal judge*
Ely, Robert Eugene *lawyer, author, educator*
Foguel, Tuval Shmuel *mathematician, department chairman*
Frazer, David Hugh, Jr. *allergist*
Godbold, John Cooper *federal judge*
Gravatt, Lincoln Edmund *history educator*
Greenhaw, Wayne (Harold Wayne Greenhaw) *writer*
Hamner, Reginald Turner *lawyer*
Harwood, Robert Bernard, Jr. *state supreme court justice*
Hester, Douglas Benjamin *lawyer*
Hobbs, Truman McGill *federal judge*
Hoffman, Richard William *retired banker*
Holifield, Leonard Cleve *security firm executive, educator*
Ivey, Kay Ellen *state official*
Johnson, Mark Matthew *museum administrator*
Kim, Ki Hang *mathematician*
King, Andrea S. *secondary school educator*
King, Troy *state attorney general*
Kloess, Lawrence Herman, Jr. *retired lawyer*
Langford, Charles Douglas *lawyer*
Laurie, Robin Garrett *lawyer*
Lawson, Thomas Seay, Jr. *lawyer, actor*
Leslie, Henry Arthur *lawyer, retired bank executive*
Lewis, Joseph Brady (Jay Lewis) *lawyer*
Luna, Patricia Adele *marketing executive*
Maddox, Alva Hugh *retired state supreme court justice*
Mandry, Christine M. *public information officer*
May, Cecil Richard, Jr. *academic administrator*
McElvy, James Douglas *lawyer*
McFadden, Frank Hampton *lawyer, former judge*
McPherson, Vanzetta Penn *magistrate judge*
Methvin, Thomas James *lawyer*
Morton, Joseph *school system administrator*
Murkett, Philip Tillotson *human resource executive*
Myers, Ira Lee *physician*
Nabers, Drayton, Jr. *state supreme court chief justice, retired insurance company executive*
Napier, Cameron Mayson Freeman *historic preservationist*
Pan, Chai-Fu *engineering educator*
Parker, Tom *state supreme court justice, lawyer*
Petty, Willie Clifford *musician, composer, educator*
Riley, Bob (Robert Renfroe Riley) *governor*
Salmon, Joseph Thaddeus *lawyer*
Sass, Neil Leslie *toxicologist*
See, Harold Frend *state supreme court justice*
Segall, Robert D. *lawyer*
Shepard, Judith Bethea *librarian*
Smiley, Virginia A. *elementary school educator*
Smith, Larry Steven *financial analyst, accountant, farmer*
Smith, Patricia M. (Patti Smith) *state supreme court justice*
Steele, Rodney Redfearn *judge*
Stevenson, Bryan Allen *lawyer*
Stuart, Jacquelyn L. *state supreme court justice*
Taylor, Watson Robbins *construction company executive*
Taylor, Watson Robbins, Jr. *investment banker*
Tennimon, Dannie Earl *academic administrator, educator*
Turley, Susan Lynn Welker *military officer*
Uzzell-Baggett, Karon Lynette *career officer*
Volz, Charles Harvie, Jr. *lawyer*
Wells, Wyatt Clinton *historian*
Wendzel, Robert Leroy *political science professor*
Westhauser, Karl E. *historian*
Williamson, Donald Ellis *public health service officer, state agency administrator*
Woodall, Thomas A. *state supreme court justice*
Worley, Nancy L. *state official*
Young, Caron L *county official*

## Chandler

Barnard, Annette Williamson *educational association administrator*
Basha, Edward N., Jr. *grocery chain owner*
Braunisch, Henning *electronics engineer, researcher*
Brunello-McCay, Rosanne *sales executive*
Carpenter, Ron D. *music educator*
Casteel, Camille *school system administrator*
Faust, Donny D. *music educator*
Fons, Margaret E. *elementary school educator*
Fordemwalt, James Newton *microelectronics engineering educator, consultant*
Goyer, Robert Stanton *retired communications educator and administrator*
Graham, Anita Louise *correctional and legal nurse consultant, community health nurse*
Kim, James Joo-Jin *electronics company executive*
Meieran, Eugene Stuart *materials scientist*
Miller, Patricia Ann *secondary school educator*
Murtagian, Gregorio Roberto *mechanical engineer*
Owen, Robert H. *electronics executive*
Rossi, Mark Antony *political consultant, writer*
Rowe, Ernest Ras *education educator, academic administrator*
Simon, Diane Rose *music educator, writer, poet*
Vakanas, George P. *process engineer, research scientist, consultant, entrepreneur*
Wang, Jinlin *chemical engineer*
Williams, James Eugene *management consultant*
Willis, Edward Oliver *management consultant, state agency administrator*

## Chinle

Coor, Caren Barbara *art educator*

## Chino Valley

Norton, Douglas Ray *former auditor general*

## Clarkdale

Eide, Joel Sylvester *art consultant, appraiser*

## Davis Monthan Afb

Miller, Charles Wallace *historian, environmental geologist, educator*
Woods, Sharhonda Michele *military officer*

## Douglas

Nicodemus, Karen A. *college president*

## Duncan

Ouzts, Eugene Thomas *minister, secondary education educator*

## Eloy

O'Leary, Thomas Michael *lawyer*

## Flagstaff

Abrams, Jesse B. *forester, researcher*
Aspey, Frederick Morris (Fritz Aspey) *lawyer*
Baron, Patricia Burrell *university director*
Bolin, Richard Luddington *industrial development specialist, consultant*
Cortner, Hanna Joan *retired research scientist, political scientist*
Ellis, Cathryn G. *theater educator, costume designer*
Everett, Judith *merchandising educator*
Haeger, John Denis *academic administrator*
Hammond, Howard David *retired botanist, editor*
Hanson, Lloyd William *music educator*
Herkenhoff, Kenneth Edward *geologist, researcher*
Lapsley, James Norvell, Jr. *minister, educator*
McDonald, Craydon Dean *psychologist*
Millis, Robert Lowell *astronomer, science observatory director*
Moore, Kent Ross *music educator*
Pavlik, William Bruce *psychologist, educator*
Poen, Kathryn Louise *music educator, performing arts association administrator*
Poff, Boris *medical technician*
Riddle, Douglas S *music educator*
Shoemaker, Carolyn Spellman *planetary astronomer*
Sisk, Thomas Daniel *ecologist, educator*
Wynne, J. Judson *research scientist, ecologist*

## Fort Huachuca

Jackson II, Ralph G. *curator*

## Fort Mohave

Roy, Christopher Marvin *elementary school educator*

## Fountain Hills

Israel, Robert Allan *statistician*
Jan, George Pokung *political science professor*
Lacy, Herman Edgar *management consultant*
Sorenson, Gretchen Hartley *elementary school educator*
Tyl, Noel Jan *retired vocalist, astrologer, writer*
Wright, C. T. Enus *former academic administrator*

## Gila Bend

Barnes, William Wayne *geographer, writer*

## Gilbert

Crandall, Sharon *elementary school educator*
Kenney, Thomas Frederick *broadcast executive*
Metcalf, Virgil Alonzo *economics professor*

## Glendale

Barnett, Michael *professional sports team executive*
Cota, Lisa Foley *secondary school educator*
Cotton, Sally Jean *retired music educator*
Doan, Shane *professional hockey player*
Fuhr, Grant *professional hockey player*
Gergus, Erik *biology professor*
Gretzky, Wayne Douglas *retired professional hockey player, professional hockey coach*
Kleissle, Karyn *chemistry educator, biology educator*
Mahoney, Jill Elizabeth *music educator*
Manhold, John Henry *dental educator, consultant*
Nolan, Owen *professional hockey player*
Pang, Darren *hockey analyst, retired professional hockey player*
Roenick, Jeremy *professional hockey player*

Staczek, John Joseph *academic administrator, consultant*
Wise, John Macgregor *speech educator*
Yazzie, Aaron Franklin *events laborer*

## Goodyear

Borton, George Robert *retired airline captain*
Carlson, Norman A. *retired federal agency administrator*
Eppen, Gary Dean *business educator*
Molina, Tanya E. *school librarian*

## Grand Canyon

Bryant, Leland Marshal *business and nonprofit executive*

## Green Valley

Bennett, Bradley Frederick *retired military officer, science association director*
Brewington, Arthur William *retired English language educator*
de Soto, Ernest Frank *artist, writer*
Fuer-Davis, Beverly Jean *retired elementary school educator*
Johnson, Charles Foreman *architectural firm executive*
Lusk, Harlan Gilbert *national park superintendent, business executive*
Moser, Robert Harlan *internist, educator, writer*
Pike, George Harold, Jr. *religious organization administrator, clergyman*
Ragan, James Thomas *communications executive*
Ramette, Richard Wales *chemistry professor*
Smith, Raymond Lloyd *former university president, consultant*

## Hereford

Hirth, John Price *metallurgical engineering educator*
Schenk, Quentin Frederick *retired social work educator, psychologist, mayor*
Seeland, Arthur David *bishop*

## Holbrook

Schoeing, Benjamin Samuel *music educator, conductor*

## Kingman

Stephens, Anne Catherine *special education educator*

## Lake Montezuma

Burkee, Irvin *artist*
Loveland, John Bigelow *editor, writer*

## Lakeside

Mack, Ina Leah *secondary school educator, pre-school administrator*
Seely, Dennis M. *secondary school educator*

## Litchfield Park

McKeighen, Ronald Eugene *physicist*

## Marana

Augello, William Joseph *lawyer*
Steckler, Larry *publishing executive, writer*

## Maricopa

Kimball, Bruce Arnold *soil scientist*

## Mesa

Ahearn, Geraldine *medical/surgical nurse, writer, poet*
Boyd, Leona Potter *retired social worker*
Cooley, Jack Crain *surgeon, cardiologist*
David, Susan Holcombe *child and family therapist*
de Masi, Kenneth Forrest *secondary school educator*
DeRosa, Francis Dominic *chemical company executive*
Dillenberg, Jack *dean*
Duvall, Debra *school system administrator*
Ewing, Ann Tway *psychology professor*
Gottry, Steven Roger *communications executive, scriptwriter*
Hagen, Nicholas Stewart *medical educator, consultant*
Hawker, Keno *mayor, trucking company executive*
Hudkins, John W. *lawyer*
Johnson, Doug *advertising executive, public relations executive*
Kim, Kai Y. *art educator, artist*
Linxwiler, Louis Major, Jr. *retired finance company executive*
Luth, William Clair *retired research manager*
Molina-Walters, Debi Ann *education educator*
Murphy, Edward Francis *sales executive*
Philbrick, Douglas Robert *principal, librarian, educator, mental health professional*
Powelson, John Jay *music educator*
Pullenza, Patricia *English educator, writer, designer*
Ramirez, Janice L. *assistant school superintendent*
Rummel, Robert Wiland *aeronautical engineer, writer*
St. Cyr, Margaret Ann (Peggy St. Cyr) *writer*
Singhal, Avinash Chandra *engineering administrator, educator*
Skoldberg, Phyllis Linnea *music educator, musician*
Stroble-Thompson, Colette Mary Houle *construction company executive*
Tindle, Charles Dwight Wood *broadcast executive*
Winkler, Sheldon *dentist, educator*

## Nogales

Cochran, James Randall *music educator*

## Oracle

Rush, Andrew Wilson *artist*

## Oro Valley

Meredith, Keith Edward *retired academic administrator, educator*

## Palo Verde

Aldridge, Robert *principal*

## Paradise Valley

Burkholder, Peter Miller *retired physician, educator*

Chrisman, William Herring *tax specialist, consultant*
Hale, Harry William *retired surgeon, educator*
Lorenzen, Robert Frederick *ophthalmologist*
McCall, Robert The *artist*
Quinn, Brian Grant *art educator, sculptor*
Ratkowski, Donald J. *mechanical engineer, consultant*
Russell, Paul Edgar *electrical engineering educator*
Salmon, Matt *former congressman, communications company executive*
Targovnik, Selma E. Kaplan *retired dermatologist*
Tubman, William Charles *lawyer*
Tyner, Neal Edward *retired insurance company executive*
Unruh, James Arlen *bank executive*

## Parker

Cravath, Jay Lewis *cultural educator*
Grazier, Diana Lynn *community health nurse, medical/surgical nurse, writer*

## Patagonia

La Noue, Terence David *artist, educator*

## Payson

Hegarty, Christopher Joseph *management and financial consultant*
Hershberger, Robert Glen *architect, educator*
Lasys, Joan *medical/surgical nurse, educator*

## Peoria

Bailey, Claudia Jean *retired librarian, artist*
Black, Melissa J. *small business owner*
Cook, Mary Margaret *steamfitter, educator*
Falk, Eugene Henry *artist*
Gould, Dorothy Mae *executive secretary, soprano*
Nelson, Mary Kathryn *bilingual counselor, small business owner, real estate agent, artist, singer*
Schindler, William Stanley *retired public relations executive*

## Phoenix

Allen, Robert Eugene Barton *lawyer*
Alsentzer, William James, Jr. *lawyer*
Ammon, John Richard *anesthesiologist*
Andersen, Ib *performing company executive*
Anderson, Gary Gene *music educator*
Anderson, Lawrence Ohaco *United States magistrate judge, educator*
Anderson, Vicki *retired librarian*
Armstrong, Nelson William, Jr. *gaming company executive*
Bain, C. Randall *lawyer*
Baker, William Dunlap *lawyer*
Bakker, Thomas Gordon *lawyer*
Baldasano, Laura May *music educator, director*
Bales, W. Scott *state supreme court justice*
Ballinger, James K. *art museum executive*
Beabeau, Olivier Andre *prosecutor*
Beams, Christian C. *lawyer*
Begam, Robert George *lawyer*
Berch, Rebecca White *state supreme court justice, lawyer*
Bidwill, William V. *professional football executive*
Birk, David R. *lawyer*
Blanchard, Charles Alan *lawyer, retired state senator*
Boldin, Anquan *professional football player*
Bouma, John Jacob *lawyer*
Brewer, Janice Kay *state official*
Broomfield, Robert Cameron *federal judge*
Brown, Benjamin F., IV, *charitable foundation executive*
Brown, Denny L. *utilities executive*
Brown, Jack A. *state representative, rancher, real estate broker*
Burke, Timothy John *lawyer*
Bushee, Ward III *newspaper editor*
Canby, William Cameron, Jr. *federal judge*
Carroll, Earl Hamblin *federal judge*
Carter, Ronald Martin, Sr. *pharmaceutical executive*
Chanen, Steven Robert *lawyer*
Charlton, John Kipp *pediatrician*
Charlton, Paul K. *prosecutor, lawyer*
Chavez, Nelba *state agency administrator, former federal agency administrator*
Chen, George *lawyer*
Clark, John *corporate financial executive*
Colangelo, Jerry John *professional sports team executive*
Cole, George Thomas *lawyer*
Cole, John *controller*
Colton, Sterling David (David Colton) *lawyer*
Comus, Louis Francis, Jr. *lawyer*
Condo, James Robert *lawyer*
Cooledge, Richard Calvin *lawyer*
Cooper, Alice (Vincent Damon Furnier) *popular musician*
Coor, Lattie Finch *university president*
Coppersmith, Sam *lawyer*
Corella, John C., Jr. *telecommunications industry executive*
Coyle, Linda Marie *elementary school educator*
Crozier, Scott A. *lawyer*
Culnon, Sharon Darlene *special education educator, reading specialist*
Cunningham, Robert W. *trucking executive*
Curcio, Christopher Frank *deputy director*
D'Antoni, Mike *professional basketball player*
Davies, David George *lawyer, educator*
Dawson, John Joseph *lawyer*
Day, Sharon Hoelscher *healthcare educator*
DeBerry, Dennis Charles *lawyer*
De Michele, O. Mark *real estate company executive*
Derdenger, Patrick *lawyer*
Derouin, James Gilbert *lawyer*
Dewane, John Richard *retired manufacturing executive, small business owner*
Dickey, Robert J. *publishing executive*
Dobronski, Mark William *judge, justice of the peace*
Doss, Sylvia M. *psychologist, educator*
Doto, Irene Louise *statistician*
Drain, Albert Sterling *business management consultant*
Drnjevic, Jonathan Mark *language educator*
Dunipace, Ian Douglas *lawyer*

Edens, Gary Denton *broadcast executive*
Edwards, Vicki Ann *director*
Ehmann, Anthony Valentine *lawyer*
Ellison, Cyril Lee *literary agent, retired publishing executive*
Elmore, James Walter *architect, educator, retired dean*
Enzor, Gary R. *trucking executive*
Erwin, Barbara F. *school system administrator*
Everett, James Joseph *lawyer*
Everett, Paul Marvin *physicist*
Everroad, John David *lawyer*
Feinstein, Allen Lewis *lawyer*
Feldberg, Harley *marketing professional*
Fenzl, Terry Earle *lawyer*
Fine, Charles Leon *lawyer*
Fitzgerald, Larry *professional football player*
Fleenor, Geneva Lucille *retired elementary school educator*
Francis, Philip L. *retail executive*
Franke, William Augustus *investor*
Freyermuth, Clifford L. *structural engineering consultant*
Friedman, Shelly Arnold *cosmetic surgeon*
Fullmer, Steven Mark *engineering executive*
Gaffney, Donald Lee *lawyer*
Gaines, Francis Pendleton III *judge*
Gallagher, Michael L. *lawyer*
Gallagher, Philip *electronics executive*
Garagiola, Joe, Jr. *baseball team executive*
Genrich, Mark L. *corporate communications director*
Giedt, Bruce Alan *paper company executive*
Gilberg, Mark Richardson *environmental scientist, director*
Gilbert, Donald Roy *lawyer*
Gillette, Robert J. *aerospace transportation executive*
Gillom, Jennifer *professional basketball player*
Goddard, Terry *state attorney general*
Goldstein, Stuart Wolf *lawyer*
Golio, John Michael *technologist, engineering executive, writer*
Gomez, David Frederick *lawyer*
Gordon, Philip Bruce *mayor*
Grant, Brian Wade *professional basketball player*
Grant, Merwin Darwin *lawyer*
Green, Dennis *professional football coach*
Green, Shawn *professional baseball player*
Griller, Gordon Moore *legal association administrator, consultant*
Grimwood, Helen Perry *lawyer*
Grinell, Sheila *museum director*
Guerra, Aldo Benjamin *plastic surgeon, cosmetic surgeon*
Gwozdz, Kim Elizabeth *interior designer, furniture designer*
Haga, David L. *lawyer*
Halpern, Barry David *lawyer*
Hamada, Richard *computer company executive*
Hammond, Larry Austin *lawyer*
Hanley, Fred William *librarian, educator*
Hanneman, LeRoy C., Jr. *real estate executive*
Harris, Jack F. *police chief*
Harrison, Mark Isaac *lawyer*
Hawkins, Jasper Stillwell, Jr. *architect*
Hawkins, Michael Daly *federal judge*
Hayden, William Robert *lawyer*
Hayward, Kevin Andrew *music educator, director*
Hendin, Barry Allen *physician*
Hicks, William Albert III *lawyer*
Hochuli, Edward G. *lawyer*
Hoecker, Thomas Ralph *lawyer*
Holden, Michael John *lawyer*
Hooper, Daniel Lee *music educator, composer*
Houseworth, Richard Court *retired state agency administrator*
Hovis, John *corporate financial executive*
Howard, William Matthew *arbitrator, writer, lawyer*
Hoxie, Joel P. *lawyer*
Huelster, Jeffery James *social studies educator*
Hunt, Linda *hospital administrator*
Huntwork, James Roden *lawyer*
Hurwitz, Andrew D. *state supreme court justice*
Jakubczyk, John Joseph *lawyer*
James, Charles E., Jr. *lawyer*
James, Edgerrin Tyree *professional football player*
Jenkins, Maynard L., Jr. *automotive executive*
Jirauch, Charles W. *lawyer*
Johnson, Christopher D. *lawyer*
Johnson, Elizabeth Misner *health services executive*
Johnson, Robert D. *aerospace transportation executive*
Jones, Charles E. *retired state supreme court chief justice*
Joseph, Gregory Nelson *media critic, writer, actor, advocate*
Jungbluth, Connie Carlson *banker*
Kamins, Edward *information technology executive*
Kant, Robert S. *lawyer*
Karnas, Fred G., Jr. *urban policy advisor*
Khan, Mohammed Yousuf *physician, consultant*
King, Robert L. *foundation administrator, former academic administrator*
Kirkland, Joseph *voice educator*
Kivlahan, Coleen *public health officer*
Klahr, Gary Peter *retired lawyer*
Klausner, Jack Daniel *lawyer*
Klein, R. Kent *lawyer*
Klepinger, John William *trailer manufacturing company executive*
Knoller, Guy David *lawyer*
Kunkel, Joe Carroll *finance company executive*
Kurn, Neal *lawyer*
Kuzma, George Martin *retired bishop*
Kyl, Jon Llewellyn *senator*
LaPointe, Gregory Vincent *psychologist*
Laufer, Nathan *cardiologist*
Leach, John F. *editor, director, journalist, educator*
Lee, Barbara S. *special education educator*
Leinart, Matt *professional football player*
Lemieux, Claude *former professional hockey player, professional sports team executive*
Lemon, Leslie Gene *retired diversified financial services company executive, lawyer*
Levetown, Robert Alexander *lawyer*
Lewis, Orme, Jr. *real estate company executive, land use adviser*
Logvin, Marshall Paul *biologist, educator*

Long, Michael Alan *musician, writer*
Lovely, Randy *editor*
Lovett, William Lee *surgeon*
Lubin, Stanley *lawyer*
Magyar, Kim S. *lawyer*
Marion, Shawn *professional basketball player*
Martensen, Barbara *electronics executive*
Martone, Frederick J. *judge*
Martori, Joseph Peter *lawyer*
Masters, Jonathan Edward *clinical psychologist*
May, Bruce Barnett *lawyer*
McConnell, Albert Lynn *director*
McGregor, Ruth Van Roekel *state supreme court justice*
McKee, Roger A. *lawyer*
McNamee, Stephen M. *federal judge*
McRae, Hamilton Eugene III *lawyer*
Meeks, Jacquelynn *city health department administrator*
Melvin, Bob *professional baseball player*
Merritt, Nancy-Jo *lawyer*
Miller, Robert J. *lawyer*
Mireles, Jesse *architecture educator, department chairman, academic administrator*
Mitchell, Wayne Lee *retired health facility administrator*
Modny, Cynthia Jean *dermatologist*
Motsenbocker, Rex Alan *construction company executive*
Moulton Reger, Sara Jonene *global management executive*
Moyer, Alan Dean *retired newspaper editor*
Moyes, Jerry C. *transportation executive*
Mulheron, MariLynn *family practice nurse practitioner*
Mulholland, Terence John (Terry Mulholland) *professional baseball player*
Mullen, Daniel Robert *finance company executive*
Myers, Robert David *judge*
Napolitano, Janet Ann *governor*
Nash, Steve *professional basketball player*
Newman, Donald Lynn *psychologist, consultant*
Nijinsky, Tamara *actress, puppeteer, author, librarian, educator*
Noone, Laura Palmer *academic administrator, lawyer*
Norris, John Steven *healthcare company executive*
Olmsted, Thomas James *archbishop*
Olsen, Alfred Jon *lawyer*
Papp, Harry *science association administrator*
Peralta, Everett Figueroa *social sciences educator*
Peters, Mary E. *former federal agency administrator*
Pietzsch, Michael Edward *lawyer*
Pillalamarri, Seshasayi *computer scientist and engineer, researcher*
Placenti, Frank Michael *lawyer*
Platt, Warren E. *lawyer*
Post, William Joseph *utility executive*
Pritchard Wood, Grace Ruth *elementary school educator*
Pyle, Thomas Alton *broadcast executive*
Quddus, Mohammed Tanvir *electrical engineer, researcher*
Ralston, Barbara Jo *bank executive*
Reed, Wallace Allison *anesthesiologist*
Refo, Patricia Lee *lawyer*
Richardson, Judy McEwen *investment banker, consultant, cartoonist*
Rister, Gene Arnold *humanities educator*
Rivera, Jose de Jesus *lawyer*
Roberts, Christopher Wayne *psychologist, educational consultant*
Roof, Sally Jean-Marie *library and information scientist, educator*
Rose, Scott A. *lawyer*
Rosenfeld, Lawrence J. (Larry) *lawyer*
Ross, Richard Frederick *lawyer*
Rudolph, Gilbert Lawrence *lawyer*
Ryan, Michael D. *state supreme court justice*
Sage, Webster LeGene, Jr. *ophthalmologist*
Saggio, Joseph John *dean*
Sanders, Barry R. *lawyer*
Schaefer, Gregory Lauren *music professor*
Schenkel, Barbara Ann *minister, nurse, social worker*
Schiffner, Charles Robert *architect*
Schneider, Elizabeth Kelley *law librarian*
Schroeder, Mary Murphy *federal judge*
Sertich, Kelli Ann *land use planner*
Sherk, Kenneth John *lawyer*
Silver, Roslyn Olson *federal judge*
Silverman, Alan Henry *lawyer*
Silverman, Barry G. *federal judge*
Singer, Jeffrey Alan *surgeon*
Smith, Emmitt J. III *retired professional football player*
Smith, George *marketing professional*
Smock, Timothy Robert *lawyer*
Snider, Timothy R. *mining executive*
Sperling, John Glen *education company executive, educator*
Steckler, Phyllis Betty *publishing consultant*
Stegmayer, Joseph Henry *housing industry executive*
Stern, Richard David *investment company executive*
Stern, Stanley *psychiatrist*
Stone, Hazel Anne Decker *artist*
Storey, Norman C. *lawyer*
Stoudemire, Amare Carsares *professional basketball player*
Strand, Roger Gordon *federal judge*
Sucato, Robert Alan *filmmaker, director*
Swartz, Jack *retired chamber of commerce executive*
Taurasi, Diana *college basketball player*
Taylor, Amanda Deanne *elementary school educator*
Taylor, Elizabeth Jane *investment advisor, real estate company executive, marketing executive*
Teague, Robert Cole *physician*
Tennen, Leslie Irwin *lawyer, consultant*
Thiel, Peter *social sciences educator*
Thomas, Jim Gus *music educator*
Thompson, Terence William *lawyer*
Thumma, Samuel Anderson *lawyer*
Tsang, Raymond *electronics executive*
Turi, Louis *publishing executive*
Udall, Vesta Hammond *special education executive*
Ulrich, Paul Graham *lawyer, writer, editor*

Underwood, Paul Lester *cardiologist*
Upson, Donald V. *retired corporate financial executive*
Vallee, Roy A. *electronics executive*
Van Fleet, David Dominic *management educator*
Vaughn, Richard P. *mathematics professor*
Verbin, Jeffrey Harold *lawyer*
Von Hoff, Daniel Douglas *oncologist*
Walker, Richard K. *lawyer*
Walker, Thomas Carlton *music educator*
Ward, Charlie *professional basketball player*
Weisenburger, Theodore Maurice *retired judge, poet, educator*
Wells, GladysAnn *library director*
Werner, Leo C. *music educator, consultant*
Wheaton, Marilyn *musician*
Whisler, James Steven *mining executive, lawyer, rancher*
White, Edward Allen *electronics executive*
Williams, Quinn Patrick *lawyer*
Willocks, Robert Max *retired librarian*
Winthrop, Lawrence Fredrick *judge*
Wirken, Charles William *lawyer*
Wolf, G. Van Velsor, Jr. *lawyer*
Wright, Margaret Taylor *marketing consultant, publisher*
Wright, Richard Oscar III *pathologist, educator, clinical ethicist*
Yamamoto, Alice M. *secondary school educator*
Yarnell, Michael Allan *lawyer*
Zerella, Joseph T. *retired pediatric surgeon*
Zidich, John M. *publishing executive*

### Pinetop
Gilbert-Tiegs, Marion Ann *gifted and talented educator, consultant*

### Portal
Williams, Jeanne *writer*
Zweifel, Richard George *curator*

### Prescott
Anderson, Parker Lynn *columnist, playwright*
Bieniawski, Zdzislaw Tadeusz Richard *engineering educator, writer, consultant*
Chesson, Eugene *retired civil engineering educator, consultant, volunteer*
Garcia-Buñuel, Luis *neurologist*
Kahne, Stephen James *systems engineering educator, engineering company executive, academic administrator*
Madden, Paul Robert *lawyer, director*
Masotti, Louis Henry *real estate educator, consultant*
Parkhurst, Charles Lloyd *electronics executive*
Roberts, Deborah Marie *historian, consultant*
Semon, Warren Lloyd *information scientist, educator*
Waldock, William David *aerospace transportation executive*
Waterer, Bonnie Clausing *retired secondary school educator*

### Prescott Valley
Beck, Doris Olson *retired library media director*
Shelley, Bonnie J. *voice educator*

### Rio Rico
Lowell, J(ames) David *geological consultant, cattle rancher*

### Rio Verde
Culligan, John Austin *thoracic surgeon*
Harding, John Hibbard *retired insurance company executive*
Ramsey, David Selmer *retired health facility administrator*
Scott, Louis Edward *advertising executive*
Vanselow, Neal Arthur *retired academic administrator, retired internist*

### Sacaton
Stephenson, Larry Kirk *geography educator, financial planner*

### Safford
Kaliher, Michael Dennis *historian, librarian*

### Sahuarita
Albertson, Paulette Smith *music educator*

### San Carlos
DJangi, Ahmad Reza *health facility administrator*

### Scottsdale
Alsary, Cyrus *artist*
Allen, A. William, III, (Bill Allen) *food service executive*
Baack, Paula D. *music educator*
Baker, Edward Martin *engineering and industrial psychologist*
Ballinger, Charles William *sanitary engineer, consultant*
Behrens, Robert Chadwick *real estate company executive*
Berman, Gizel *sculptor*
Birkelbach, Albert Ottmar *retired oil industry executive*
Blinder, Martin S. *management consultant, art dealer*
Brown, Frederick Lee *health facility administrator*
Brown, Shirley Margaret Kern (Peggy Brown) *interior designer*
Bullerdick, Kim H. *lawyer, petroleum executive*
Burg, Jeffrey Howard *technology company executive*
Buri, Charles Edward *lawyer*
Burley, John M. *music educator*
Calise, Nicholas James *lawyer*
Chaurasia, Vishal *physician, writer*
Chikly, Bruno Jacques *osteopath physician*
Como, Ed *theater educator, set designer*
Coutts, Lawrence Robert *publisher*
Crawford, Robert F. *lawyer*
Dahl, Mark Victor *dermatologist, educator*
Daniel, William Walter, Jr. *radiologist*
Doede, John Henry *investment company executive*
Doglione, Arthur George *data processing executive*
Dorrance, Bennett *real estate company executive*

Drake, Albert Estern *retired statistics educator, farming administrator*
Evans, Tommy Nicholas *obstetrician, gynecologist, educator*
Faig, Harold *information technology executive*
Farley, James Newton *retired manufacturing executive, electrical engineer*
Farney, Charlotte Eugenia *musician, educator*
Ferree, John Newton, Jr. *fundraising specialist, consultant*
Freedman, Stanley Marvin *manufacturing executive*
Gans, Eugene Howard *cosmetic and pharmaceutical company executive, consultant*
Garfield, Ernest *bank executive, consultant*
Getz, Bert Atwater *investment company executive*
Gibney, John *plastic surgeon, consultant, medical researcher*
Gookin, Thomas Allen Jaudon *civil engineer*
Gregory, Robert Erb *surgeon*
Grenell, James Henry *retired manufacturing company executive*
Grier, James Edward *hotel executive, lawyer*
Gwinn, Mary Dolores *liberal studies organization administrator, writer*
Hadder, Donald Everett, Sr. *urban planner*
Hansen, Donald W. *diversified financial services company executive, consultant*
Harrison, Nedra Joyce *surgeon*
Hecht, Frederick *pediatrician, medical geneticist, researcher, consultant, writer, editor*
Heilman, Raymond L. *health facility administrator*
Helm, Steven M *lawyer*
Heppell, Jacques Philippe *surgeon, educator*
Hermann, Robert John *lawyer*
Highet, Mac *travel company executive*
Hill, Louis Allen, Jr. *retired dean, civil engineer, consultant*
Holliger, Frederic Lee *oil industry executive*
Howard, William Gates, Jr. *electronics company executive*
Hutchison, Stanley Philip *retired lawyer*
Jacobson, Frank Joel *cultural organization administrator*
Jarman, Beth S. *writer, educational consultant*
Jesky, T. J. *pharmaceutical products executive*
Johnson, Micah William *television newscaster, director*
Kinney, Carolyn *physician*
Kinsinger, Jack Burl *chemist, educator*
Krane, Susan *museum director, curator*
Krupp, Clarence William *lawyer, health facility administrator*
Kumar, Kv *management consultant*
L'Allier, James Joseph *training services executive, educator*
Land, George A. *philosopher, consultant, writer*
Lavenson, Susan Barker *hotel corporate executive, consultant*
Leighton, William D. *plastic and reconstructive surgeon*
Leonard, George Edmund *bank executive, credit manager, marketing professional*
Levidow, Debra *psychologist*
Levin, Warren Mayer *family practice physician*
Lewis, John Christopher *allergist*
Lillestol, Jane Brush *educational consultant*
Lindgren, D. Kenneth, Jr., (Derbin Kenneth Lindgren Jr.) *retired lawyer*
Lloyd, Eugene Walter *retired construction company executive*
Lowry, Edward Francis, Jr. *lawyer*
Maggard, Woodrow Wilson, Jr. *management consultant*
Marks, Merton Eleazer *lawyer, international arbitrator, mediator, consultant*
Meyers, Marlene O. *retired hospital administrator*
Mohraz, Judy Jolley *foundation administrator*
Morrison, Donald Nick *surgeon*
Newman, Ursula Irene *music educator*
Nielsen, Greg Ross *lawyer*
Northey, William Thomas *microbiologist, educator*
O'Meara, Sara *non-profit organization executive*
Orford, Robert Raymond *physician, consultant*
Overgaard, Cordell Jersild *lawyer, rancher, director*
Parish, James Michael *medical educator*
Patel, Naresh Pratap *medical educator, physician, consultant*
Pelham, Judith *health system administrator*
Peterson, John Willard *composer, publishing executive*
Phillips, Wanda Charity *secondary school educator, writer*
Quayle, Dan (James Danforth Quayle) *former vice president United States*
Quayle, Marilyn Tucker *wife of former United States vice president, lawyer*
Redden, Persefini Kore Anne *protective services official*
Rethore, Bernard Gabriel *retired manufacturing and mining company executive*
Reznick, Richard Howard *pediatrician*
Roarke, Michael Charles *medical educator, nuclear medicine physician*
Robb, Cameron *wireless communications company executive*
Roberts, Catherine C. *radiologist, educator*
Sanderson, David R. *physician*
Schutzky, Marilyn Horsley *artist*
Shors, Clayton Marion *retired cardiologist*
Shower, Robert Wesley *corporate financial executive*
Slager, Donald W. *waste management executive*
Smith, David Burnell *lawyer, state legislator*
Smith, Patrick W. (Rick Smith) *manufacturing executive*
Smith, Thomas P. *manufacturing executive*
Steier, Jeffrey David *neurologist*
Stone, Alan Jay *retired academic administrator*
Stott, Brian *software company executive, consultant*
Strock, James Martin *communications executive, writer, entrepreneur*
Summerhill, Ronald Raymond *psychotherapist, psychologist*
Sydnor, Douglas Bryan *architect, educator*
Taylor, James C. *writer*
Tazelaar, Henry Dale *physician, educator*
Thompson, Bradford *chef*
Timmons, Evelyn Deering *pharmacist*

Travers, Paul *company executive*
Trimble, Thomas James *retired utilities executive, lawyer*
Vairo, Robert John *insurance company executive*
Van Brunt, Gary T. *tire dealer company executive*
Walsh, Edward Joseph *food products executive, cosmetics executive*
Washburn, Jerry Martin *accountant, corporate executive*
Weaver, Linda Marie *pharmacist, education educator*
Weil, Louis Arthur III *retired newspaper publishing executive*
Westmoreland, Preston *radio personality*
Williams, Margaret M. (Meg Williams) *insurance company executive*
Williams-De Silva, Lisa Annette *small business owner, adult nurse practitioner*
Wojcik, Martin Henry *not-for-profit executive*
Wong, Joe Bing *retired architect*
Yares, Riva *art dealer, writer, publishing executive*
Zillmer, John J. *waste management administrator*

### Sedona
Bays, Theresa *music director, liturgist*
Briney, Allan King *retired radiologist*
Coleman, M.L. (Michael Lee) *artist*
Connor, Nancy L. *small business owner*
Copeland, Suzanne Johnson *real estate company executive*
Dansby, John Walter *retired oil industry executive*
Gore, Willma Clarice *writer, educator*
Hawkins, David Ramon *psychiatrist, writer, researcher, spiritual teacher*
Metzner, Richard Joel *psychiatrist, psychopharmacologist, educator*
Sasmor, James Cecil *publishing representative, educator*

### Sells
Juan-Saunders, Vivian *Native American tribal leader*
Steere, Peter Lawson *archaeologist, historian*

### Show Low
Pershing, Robert George *retired telecommunications industry executive*

### Sierra Vista
Boughan, Zanetta Louise *music educator*
Bowen, Harry Ernest *management consultant*
Ponder, Herman *geologist*
Sizemore, Nicky Lee *computer scientist*

### Sonoita
Cook, William Howard *architect*

### Sun City
Blanchet, Jeanne Ellene Maxant *artist, educator, performer*
Chokshi, Parag H. *gastroenterologist, internist*
Coffman, Harold Emerson *retired agricultural products supplier, retail merchant*
Cooper, Vivian M. *minister, writer*
Crisman, Mary Frances Borden *librarian*
Davies, Percy (Pete) Charles *mechanical engineer*
Hamilton, Ronald Ray *minister*
Joyce, Jeffrey *research scientist, consultant*
Keesling, Karen Ruth *lawyer*
Nicchi, Vincent, Jr. *cardiologist*
Oppenheimer, Max, Jr. *foreign language educator, consultant*
Randall, Claire *retired religious organization administrator*
Reynolds, John Francis *insurance company executive*
Tijmann, Willem Bert *civil engineer, consultant*
Treece, James Lyle *retired lawyer*
Williams, William Harrison *retired librarian*

### Sun City West
Berkenkamp, Fred Julius *management consultant*
Brown, Ruth Geisler *engineer*
Forti, Lenore Steimle *business consultant*
Holloway, Diane Elaine *psychotherapist, consultant, writer*
Schrag, Adele Frisbie *business education educator*
Stevens, George Richard *business consultant, public information officer*

### Sun Lakes
Sharpless, Joseph Benjamin *retired county official*
Thompson, Loring Moore *retired college administrator, writer*

### Surprise
Bradford, Mariah *elementary school educator, consultant*
Brahms, Katheryn Ann *early childhood educator*
Clark, Lloyd *historian, writer, educator*
Eastman, Donna Kelly *composer*
Fennelly, Jane Corey *lawyer*
Koessel, Donald Ray *retired bank executive*
Lazar, Max Seymour *retired pharmaceutical company executive*
Miller, James Rumrill III *finance educator*
Neuman, Isabel *mathematics educator*
Stevenson, Norma Ann *elementary school educator, real estate agent, property manager*
Uhlmann, Elenore Arlene *interior designer, writer*
Veigel, Jon Michael *science administrator*

### Tempe
Aaen, Peter Harald *electrical engineer*
Abedinpour, Siamak *electrical engineer*
Adelson, Roger Dean *history professor, historian, editor*
Aist, Gregory S. *computer scientist, linguist*
Anand, Suresh Chandra *physician*
Ariaratnam, Samuel T. *engineering educator*
Balanis, Constantine Apostle *electrical engineering educator*
Barker, David *actor, educator*
Barnhill, Robert E. *university administrator, educator*
Berman, Neil Sheldon *retired chemical engineering professor*
Brack, O. M., Jr. *language educator*
Bradford, Steven Paul *film educator, department chairman*

Carlyle, Eric *real estate company executive*
Carpenter, Ray Warren *engineering educator, materials engineer*
Chiriac, Victor Adrian *aerospace engineer, researcher*
Cochran, Mary Leffler *volunteer*
Colgate, Catharine Pamella *secondary school educator*
Cortright, Barbara Jean *public relations executive, writer*
Crellin, Alan W. *air transportation executive*
Crouch, Peter E. *engineering educator*
Crow, Michael M. *academic administrator*
Crown, Eric J. *information systems executive*
Crown, Timothy A. *computer technology company executive*
Culy, Douglas G. *mechanical engineer, consultant*
Curtiss, Roy III *life sciences professor*
Dhillon, Janet L. *lawyer*
Emerson, Charles LeRoy *religious studies educator*
Fennessy, Richard A. *information technology executive*
Ferry, David Keane *electrical engineering educator*
Fulton, Ira *construction executive*
Gordon, Leonard *retired social sciences educator*
Goronkin, Herbert *physicist*
Green, Monica H. *history professor*
Guo, Hongbin *education educator*
Haggerson, Nelson Lionel, Jr. *education educator*
Harris, Warren Lynn *computer engineer*
Hechter, Michael Norman *sociologist*
Herald, Cherry Lou *medical researcher, educator*
Hickson, Robin Julian *mining company executive*
Hölldobler, Berthold Karl *zoologist*
Humphreys, Jere Thomas *music educator, consultant*
Iverson, Peter James *historian, educator*
Jacobs, Mark *biology professor, dean*
Johanson, Donald Carl *physical anthropologist*
Johnson, Shane Richard *research scientist, consultant*
Jungbluth, Kirk E. *real estate appraiser*
Juvet, Richard Spalding, Jr. *chemistry professor*
Kambhampati, Subbarao *computer scientist, educator*
Karády, George György *electrical engineering educator, consultant*
Kaufman, Herbert Mark *finance educator*
Kerr, Derek J. *transportation executive*
Kim, Joochul *urban planner, educator*
Koetter, Dirk *college football coach*
Laybourne, Stanley *computer technology company executive*
Li, Wei *social sciences educator*
Lohr, Dennis E. *research scientist, education educator*
Lombardi, Eugene Patsy *retired conductor, musician, educator*
MacKinnon, Stephen R. *Asian studies administrator, educator*
Mahajan, Subhash *electronic materials educator*
Marchant, Gary Elvin *lawyer*
Marshall, Kimberly *music educator, musician*
Matheson, Alan Adams *law educator*
Maynard, Michael *librarian*
McKelvy, Michael John *chemist, research scientist*
Meehan, Robert Henry *human resources executive, business educator, electronics executive*
Morrison, John Haddow, Jr. *engineering company executive*
Myint, Soe Win *geographer, educator*
Nagrin, Daniel *dancer, educator, choreographer, writer*
Page, Robert Eugene, Jr. *biology professor*
Pany, Kurt Joseph *finance educator, consultant*
Parker, W. Douglas (Doug Parker) *air transportation executive*
Pasqualetti, Martin J. *geography educator*
Peck, Ernest James, Jr. *academic administrator*
Peralta, Pedro *mechanical engineer, educator, consultant*
Pettit, George Robert *chemist, educator, cancer researcher*
Playford, Nancy Jean *medical association administrator*
Poe, Jerry B. *financial educator*
Poste, George Henry *biology professor, former pharmaceutical company executive*
Prescott, Edward C. *economist, educator*
Raby, William Louis *writer, consultant*
Rankin, William Parkman *communications educator, academic administrator*
Reckers, Philip Merle *accountant, educator*
Reyes, Guillermo Augusto *playwright, educator*
Richards, Gale Lee *communications educator*
Roudenko, Svetlana *mathematics professor*
Rowley, Beverley Davies *sociologist*
Ryaby, James Thomas *pharmaceutical executive, cellular biologist*
Sackton, Frank Joseph *public affairs educator*
Schmidt, Sherrie *library director, dean*
Schneller, Eugene Stewart *health administration and policy educator*
Schroder, Dieter Karl *electrical engineering educator*
Seeling, Patrick *research scientist, educator*
Shaw, Milton Clayton *mechanical engineering educator*
Simes, Michael Louis *lawyer*
Simon, Sheldon Weiss *political science professor*
Smith, Branson M. *computer technology company executive*
Smith, David John *physicist, researcher*
Smith, Harvey Alvin *mathematics professor, consultant*
Sol'Sax, *artist, educator*
Spritzer, Ralph Simon *lawyer, educator*
Tabbara, Hadi *director, researcher*
Theodore, David *research scientist*
Thor, Linda M. *college president*
Tsakalis, Konstantinos *electrical engineer, educator*
Uttal, William R(eichenstein) *psychology and engineering educator, research scientist*
Wang, Ning *education educator*
Warner, Kurt (Kurtis Warner) *professional football player*
Weigend, Guido Gustav *geographer, educator*
Wetsel, William David *literature educator*

White, Patricia Denise *dean, law educator*
Wills, J. Robert *academic administrator, theater educator, writer*
Winter Chaser, Vivian Janice *elementary school educator*
Wong, Timothy C. *language and literature educator*
Yau, Stephen Sik-sang *computer scientist, information scientist, educator*
Younger, Jarred Wayne *research scientist*
Zeitlin, Marilyn Audrey *museum director*

**Tonopah**
Pallin, Samuel Lear *ophthalmologist, educator, medical director*

**Tubac**
Chilcote, Samuel Day, Jr. *trade association administrator*
Pardue, A. Michael *retired plastic and reconstructive surgeon*

**Tucson**
Ablin, Richard Joel *immunologist, educator*
Acker, Loren Calvin *medical products executive*
Acker, Robert Flint *retired microbiologist*
Adjarian, Maude Madeleine *literature educator, researcher*
Aguilar, Darla J. *adult education educator*
Allen, John Jeffrey Beck *psychology professor*
Alpert, Joseph Stephen *cardiologist, educator*
Amhowitz, Harris J. *lawyer, educator*
Angel, James Roger Prior *astronomer*
Arcus, Sam George *social worker, educator, writer*
Arenas, Alberto *education educator*
Arnell, Walter James William *engineering educator, consultant*
Ashby, Garmon J.N. *music educator, director*
Aurand, Charles Henry, Jr. *music educator*
Axinn, George Harold *rural sociology educator*
Baker, Robert Kerry *college administrator, author, editor*
Baker, Victor Richard *geologist, hydrologist, researcher, research scientist, educator*
Barrett, Bruce Richard *physics professor*
Bartlett, David Carson *state legislator*
Barton, Stanley Faulkner *retired management consultant*
Bernmúdez, Carmen *trust company executive*
Betteridge, Frances Carpenter *retired lawyer, mediator*
Birkinbine, John, II *philatelist*
Blackman, Jeffrey William *lawyer*
Block, Michael Kent *economics professor, law educator, former government official*
Bloembergen, Nicolaas *physicist, researcher*
Bootman, J. Lyle *pharmacy educator*
Bootzin, Richard R. *psychology professor, researcher*
Boyle, Christopher George *language educator, counseling administrator*
Brammer, J. William, Jr. *judge, lawyer*
Breiger, Ronald Louis *social sciences educator*
Brett, Peter D. *writer*
Broadfoot, Albert Lyle *physicist*
Brunton, Daniel William *mechanical engineer*
Brusca, Richard Charles *biologist, researcher, educator, science administrator*
Butcher, Russell Devereux *writer, photographer*
Cain, Vernon *retired diversified financial services company executive*
Capp, Michael Paul *pediatrician, educator*
Carleton, Willard Tracy *retired finance educator*
Carman, Mary Ann *realtor, writer, retired medical/surgical nurse*
Christie, Nancy Gail *psychology professor*
Clarke, James Weston *political science professor, writer*
Coakley, Stephanie Joy *museum educator*
Coan, Richard Welton *psychologist, educator*
Conant, Howard Somers *artist, educator*
Cooper, Corinne *communications consultant, lawyer*
Corrigan, James John, Jr. *pediatrician, educator, dean*
Cota, Hortensia *social studies educator*
Crawford, David L. *astronomer*
Crooks, Roselyn June *artist, writer*
Cullen, Shawn L. *music educator*
Dalen, James Eugene *cardiologist, educator*
Das, Manabendra *mechanical engineer, researcher*
Daum, Bryan Edwin *lawyer*
Davenport, Sandra *cultural organization administrator*
Davis, Cathy *publishing executive*
Davis, Rendell Ashton *minister, social worker*
Davis, Stanley Nelson *hydrologist, educator*
Deal, Mike Gary *educator*
DeLuca, Dominick *medical educator, researcher*
Dereniak, Eustace L. *engineering educator, researcher*
De Young, David Spencer *astrophysicist, educator*
Díaz, Elena R. *community health nurse*
Dickey, Jerry R. *theater educator*
Dinnerstein, Leonard *historian, educator*
Dobbs, Dan Byron *lawyer, educator*
Dolan, Susan Mae *museum staff member*
Donoghue, John Charles *application developer, consultant*
Duan, Jennifer Guohong *civil engineer, educator*
Dunn, Floyd *biophysics professor, biomedical engineering educator*
Dyer-Raffler, Joy Ann *retired special education diagnostician, educator*
Emerson, Kirk *government agency administrator*
Esposito, Joseph Louis *lawyer*
Ewy, Gordon Allen *cardiologist, researcher, educator*
Fajardo, Sarah Elizabeth Johnson *financial consultant*
Falco, Charles Maurice *physicist, researcher*
Favre, Kelly Ann *surgeon*
Fay, Mary Anne *retail executive*
Feldman, Stanley George *lawyer*
Fredericksen, Dick Hartman *retired computer programmer*
Frieden, B. Roy *mathematical physicist*
Fritts, Harold Clark *botanist, educator*
Froman, Sandra Sue *lawyer*
Gaither, William Samuel *civil engineering executive, consultant*

Gantz, David Alfred *lawyer, academic administrator*
Gelfand, Howard Michael *history professor*
Gerba, Charles Peter *microbiologist, educator*
Giberti, Tina Shereen *principal*
Girardeau, Marvin Denham *physics professor*
Goldman, Gloria A. *lawyer*
Goltz, Pat *artist, web site designer*
Gonzales, Richard Joseph *lawyer*
Graham, Anna Regina *pathologist, educator*
Grand, Marcia *civic worker*
Grand, Richard D. *lawyer*
Green, Richard Frederick *astronomer*
Griffith, Caitlin Ann *science educator*
Gruhl, James *energy scientist, artist*
Gutsche, Carl David *chemistry professor*
Hale, William Bryan, Jr. *newspaper editor*
Hall, Henry Kingston, Jr. *chemistry professor*
Haney, Robert Locke *retired insurance company executive*
Hanson, Thor *retired health agency executive, retired naval officer*
Harrington, Roger Fuller *electrical engineering educator, consultant*
Hasselmo, Ann Hayes Die *executive recruiter, consultant, psychologist, educator, retired academic administrator*
Hattery, Robert Ralph *radiologist, educator*
Hawke, Robert Francis *dentist*
Hay, Richard Le Roy *geology educator*
Haynes, Caleb Vance, Jr. *geology and archaeology educator*
Hays, James Fred *geologist, educator*
Hayt, Therese D. *newspaper executive*
Heller, Frederick *retired mining executive*
Hellon, Michael Thomas *financial analyst, political organization worker*
Herrnstadt, Richard Lawrence *American literature educator*
Hildebrand, John G(rant) *neuroscientist, educator*
Hill, Henry Allen *physicist, researcher*
Hoffert, Paul Washington *surgeon*
Horne, William McHenry *finance educator*
Houser, Harold Byron *epidemiologist*
Hubbard, William Bogel *planetary sciences educator*
Hughes, John Harold *surgeon, educator*
Hughes, Malcolm Kenneth *dendrochronologist, educator, administrator*
Hull, Herbert Mitchell *botanist, researcher*
Hunten, Donald Mount *planetary scientist, educator*
Ingram, Charles Owen *priest, educator*
Jamison, Harrison Clyde *retired oil company executive*
Jefferies, John Trevor *astrophysicist, director*
Jeter, Wayburn Stewart *retired microbiologist, educator*
Johnson, John Gray *retired university chancellor*
Johnson, Paula D. *veterinarian*
Johnstone, Craig S. *elementary school educator*
Jones, Frank Wyman *management consultant, director, mechanical engineer*
Jurkowitz, Daniel S. *lawyer, prosecutor, judge*
Jurkowitz, Lisa Amy *language educator*
Kaltenbach, C(arl) Colin *dean, educator*
Karkoschka, Erich *planetary science researcher, writer*
Katakkar, Suresh Balaji *hematologist, oncologist*
Kearney, Joseph Laurence *retired athletic conference administrator*
Kececioglu, Dimitri Basil *reliability engineering educator, consultant*
Kennicutt, Robert Charles, Jr. *astronomer*
Kerwin, William James *electrical engineering educator, consultant*
Kessler, John Otto *physicist, researcher*
Kimble, William Earle *lawyer*
King, James Edward *retired museum director, consultant*
King, Joseph Willet *child psychiatrist*
Kischer, Clayton Ward *human embryologist, educator*
Kohloss, Frederick Henry *retired engineer*
Kozolchyk, Boris *law educator, consultant*
Kuklin, Susan Beverly *law librarian, lawyer*
Kuykendall, Gregory John *lawyer*
Lacagnina, Michael Anthony *judge*
Lai, LiWen *geneticist, educator*
Lamb, Willis Eugene, Jr. *physicist, researcher*
Lane, Melissa D. *planetary geologist, researcher*
Larwood, Laurie *psychologist*
Lascelles, Susan *artist*
Leonard, Michael A. *retired automotive executive*
Levenson, Alan Ira *psychiatrist, physician, educator*
Lewis, Wilbur H. *educational management consultant*
Lomicka, William Henry *investor*
Longan, George Baker III *real estate company executive*
Lucas, Pierre *materials scientist, educator*
Manning, Laura Shelton *assistant principal*
Marchalonis, John Jacob *immunologist, educator*
Marcialis, Robert Louis *planetary astronomer*
Marcus, Frank Isadore *cardiologist, educator*
Markman, Sherman *investment banker, venture capitalist, financial consultant*
Marquez, Alfredo C. *federal judge*
Martin, June Johnson Caldwell *journalist*
Martin, Loren Winston *allergist*
Martin, Marci *writer, former advertising specialist*
Martinez Sanchez, Mary Ann *academic administrator*
Massaro, Toni Marie *dean, law educator*
Matthew, Neil Edward *artist, educator*
Maxon, Don Carlton *mining executive, construction executive, consultant*
Mc Donald, John Richard *lawyer*
McGrath, Dominic Vincent *chemistry professor*
McNamara, Michael *lighting designer, educator*
McPherson, Guy Randall *ecology educator, researcher*
Meehan, Michael Joseph *lawyer*
Meijer, Arend *geochemist, consultant*
Meislin, Harvey Warren *emergency medicine physician, professional society administrator*
Mense, Allan Tate *research and development engineering executive*
Mercker, Mary Alice *aviation school administrator*
Miller, Michael Douglas *lawyer*

Moran, Nancy A. *ecologist, educator*
Morrison, Roger Barron *geologist*
Morrow, James Franklin *lawyer*
Mould, Jeremy Richard *astronomer*
Mullen, Rod *nonprofit organization executive*
Nachman, Michael William *education educator*
Neff-Encinas, Julie Gay *bilingual education specialist, consultant*
Nelson, Edward Humphrey *architect*
Neugebauer, Marcia *physicist, researcher*
Neuman, Shlomo P. *hydrologist, educator*
Ogilvie, T(homas) Francis *marine engineering educator*
Ostromencki, Nancy Lee *music educator*
Pace, Thomas M. *lawyer*
Pacholczyk, Andrzej Grzegorz *astrophysicist*
Patla, John Thomas *protective services official*
Peeler, Stuart Thorne *gas industry executive, consultant*
Perret, Gary William *priest, educator*
Peters, Charles William *nuclear energy industry executive*
Peterson, Thomas W. *engineering educator*
Piccarreta, Carl Alan *lawyer*
Pintozzi, Chestalene *librarian*
Portney, Paul Rogers *dean*
Prewitt, Charles Thompson *geochemist*
Quan, Stuart Fun *internist, educator*
Raab, Diane *special education educator*
Ramirez, Raul *academic administrator*
Reitan, Ralph Meldahl *clinical neuropsychologist, former educator*
Riggs, Lew *foundation executive*
Riley, Mark Richard *biochemical engineer, educator*
Roemer, Elizabeth *retired astronomer, retired educator*
Rogers, Lee Frank *radiologist*
Roll, John McCarthy *judge*
Rose, Carol Marguerite *law educator*
Rose, Hugh *management consultant*
Ruscher, Charles B. *finance educator, consultant*
Russell, Findlay Ewing *physician*
Ryan, Kenneth J. *immunologist, educator*
Samet, Dee-Dee *lawyer*
Satten, Wayne Richard *psychologist*
Schannep, John Dwight *brokerage house executive*
Schorr, S. L. *lawyer*
Schulz, Renate Adele *German studies and second language acquisition educator*
Seaman, Arlene Anna *retired musician*
Seehausen, Richard Ferdinand *architect*
Serido, Joyce *psychologist, researcher*
Shelton, Robert Neal *academic administrator, physics professor, researcher*
Shropshire, Donald Gray *hospital executive*
Sibley, William Austin *neurologist, educator*
Simmons, Sarah R. *lawyer*
Slack, Donald Carl *agricultural engineer, educator*
Smerdon, Ernest Thomas *engineering educator*
Smith, David Wayne *psychologist, educator*
Smith, Kenneth Rodger *finance educator*
Smith, Verne V. *astronomer*
Snyder, Richard Gerald *research scientist, administrator, educator, consultant*
Soren, David *archaeologist, educator, writer, filmmaker*
Soto, Angela C. *elementary school educator*
Spaeth, Jan Mills *jury consultant*
Sprague, Ann Louise *aerospace scientist*
Staubitz, Arthur Frederick *retired lawyer, retired health products executive*
Stini, William Arthur *anthropologist, educator*
Stitt, Mari Leipper *poet*
Stoffle, Carla Joy *university library dean*
Strittmatter, Peter Albert *astronomer, educator*
Strong, John William *lawyer, educator*
Swalin, Richard Arthur *scientist, company executive*
Tang, Esther Don *real estate developer, consultant, social worker*
Thompson, Kathleen Shambaugh *marriage and family counselor*
Thompson, Raymond Harris *retired anthropologist, educator*
Thomson, Donald Arthur *education educator*
Tifft, William Grant *retired physics professor, scientist*
Tindall, Robert Emmett *lawyer, educator*
Tirrell, John Albert *organization executive, consultant*
Titley, Spencer Rowe *geology educator*
Treadwell-Rubin, Pamela A. *lawyer*
Underwood, Jane Hainline Hammons *anthropologist, educator*
Venkata, Subrahmanyam Saraswati *engineering educator, researcher*
Walker, Franklin Curtis *federal agency administrator*
Walker, Ronald Hugh *retired management consultant*
Walkup, Robert E. *mayor*
Wallach, Leslie Rothaus *architect*
Walsh, Craig T. *composer, educator*
Ward, Robin A. *mathematics professor*
Weil, Andrew Thomas *physician, educator*
Whitaker, Ewen Adair *retired astronomer*
White, Herbert Spencer *library and information scientist, educator, dean*
Wickham, John Adams, Jr. *retired army officer*
Williams, Alan Keiser *management consultant*
Williams, Joy *writer*
Willoughby, Stephen Schuyler *mathematics professor*
Wolfe, William Jerome *librarian, language educator*
Wolff, Sidney Carne *astronomer, science administrator*
Woolfenden, James Manning *nuclear medicine physician, educator*
Woosley, Raymond *pharmacologist, educator*
Wyant, James Clair *engineering company executive, educator*
Wyatt, Roland Gratts *music educator, voice educator, consultant*
Yocum, Harrison Gerald *horticulturist, botanist, educator, researcher*
Yuan, Nicole Patricia *healthcare educator*
Zegura, Stephen Luke *biologist, anthropologist, educator*
Zepeda, Ofelia *linguist, educator*

Ziehler, Tony Joseph *insurance agent*
Zlaket, Thomas Andrew *lawyer, former state supreme court chief justice*
Zou, Changping *research scientist, educator*

### Vail
Cardieri, Alexander M. *music specialist, music educator*
Reichlin, Seymour *endocrinologist, educator*

### Waddell
Turner, Warren Austin *state legislator*

### Wickenburg
Daniel, James Richard *accountant, corporate financial executive*

### Wikieup
Brattstrom, Bayard Holmes *biology professor*

### Williams
Erickson, Edward Grant *electrical engineer*

### Window Rock
Shirley, Joe, Jr. *Native American tribal leader*

### Youngtown
Black, Robert Frederick *retired gas industry executive*

### Yuma
Anderson, John Albert *physician*
Hodson, Roy Goode, Jr. *retired logistician*
Hossler, David Joseph *lawyer, law educator*
Houggard, Santa Carol Hall *family nurse practitioner, consultant*
Hudson, John Irvin *retired career officer*
Hunt, Gerald Wallace *lawyer*
Kiley, Thomas *rehabilitation counselor*
Mendoza, San Juana Jane *school psychologist*
Norton, Dunbar Sutton *economic developer*
Rush, Dorie Mae *nursing educator*
Straley, Forrest Alvin Chip *theater educator, director, actor*

## ARKANSAS

### Arkadelphia
Buscher, Darin G. *mathematics professor*
Dunn, Charles DeWitt *academic administrator*
Elrod, Ben Moody *academic administrator*
Futrell, Alvin *director*
Grant, Daniel Ross *retired academic administrator*
Graves, John William *historian*
Trofimova, Irina (Irene) Alexeevna *literature and language professor*
Webster, Robert Lee *accounting educator, researcher*

### Ashdown
Edmonson, Phyllis Denty *artist*
Finley, John Cyrus III *lawyer, judge*

### Bald Knob
Barber, Leah Adrianne *elementary school educator, literacy educator*

### Batesville
Bennett, Linda Lou *library director*
Carius, Robert Wilhelm *mathematics professor, retired military officer*
Harkey, John Norman *judge*
Meinzer, Beverly Anne *chemist, educator*
Stephens, Anna Jo *finance educator*
Williams, Darrick Shad *mathematician*

### Bella Vista
Johnson, A(lyn) William *chemistry professor, writer, researcher, consultant*
Medin, Alice Louise *librarian*
Medin, Myron James, Jr. *city manager*
Pogue, William Reid *retired astronaut, foundation administrator, aerospace scientist, consultant*
Zehring, Lawrence Edward *music educator*

### Benton
Krueger, Marlo Bush *retired lawyer*

### Bentonville
Castro-Wright, Eduardo *retail executive*
Chambers, Susan (M. Susan Chambers) *retail executive*
Degn, Douglas J. *retail executive*
Dillman, Linda M. *retail executive*
Dobbs, Johnnie *retail executive*
Duke, Michael T. *retail executive*
Fleming, John *retail executive*
Ford, Rollin *retail executive*
Gean, Thomas C. *lawyer, former prosecutor*
Glass, David D. *retail executive, professional sports team executive*
Herkert, Craig R. *retail executive*
Hyde, Thomas D. *lawyer*
Jackson, Lawrence V. *retail executive*
McMillon, Doug *retail executive*
Menzer, John Bruce *retail executive*
Mora, Alberto J. *retail executive, lawyer*
Schoewe, Thomas M. *retail executive*
Scott, H. Lee, Jr. (Harold Lee Scott Jr.) *retail executive*
Simon, William *retail executive*
Walton, Helen *philanthropist*
Walton, Jim Carr *bank executive*
Walton, Rob (Samuel Robson Walton) *discount department store chain executive*
Watts, Claire A. *retail executive*
Zorn, Eric Stuart *retail executive*

### Berryville
Brown, Frances Louise (Grandma Fran) *artist, art gallery director*
Sanders, Larry Dale *funeral director, coroner*

### Blytheville
Baker, Carlene Poff *real estate agent, reporter*
Edmonds, Revis L., Jr. *history educator*
Fulling, Sharon S. *college nursing program director*
Slowik, Richard Andrew *air force officer*

### Camden
Bradshaw, Otabel *retired primary school educator*

### Cherokee Village
Burke, Richard Kitchens *lawyer, educator*
Hollingsworth, John Alexander *retired science and mathematics educator, writer*
Payne, Howard James *retired insurance company executive*

### Clarksville
Stone, George Clifford *education educator, researcher*

### Conway
Cloyd, J. Timothy *academic administrator*
Duan, Qiang *computer scientist, educator*
Hatcher, Joe Branch *management consultant*
Horton, Joseph Julian, Jr. *economics and finance educator*
Johnson, James Douglas (Jim Johnson) *lawyer*
Larroya Runge, Saroj Nilu *biologist, educator*
Leffler, Jean Riise *religious organization administrator*
McNew, Bennie Banks *retired finance educator*
Pearson, Brooks C. *geography educator, consultant*
Peeples, James Thomas *computer engineer, musician*
Reddin, George *religious organization administrator*
Stiritz, Marette McCauley *English language educator, consultant*
Thompson, Winfred Lee *academic administrator, lawyer*
Ziegler, John Alan *historian, political scientist, educator*

### Crossett
Hubbell, Billy James *lawyer*

### Dumas
Schexnayder, Charlotte Tillar *state legislator*

### El Dorado
Barnes, Harry Francis *federal judge*
Cossé, Steven A. *lawyer*
Deming, Claiborne Payne *oil industry executive*
Lee, Vernon Roy *minister*
Nolan, William C., Jr. *energy executive*
Tommey, James Eldon *retired surgeon*
Watkins, Jerry West *retired oil company executive, lawyer*

### Eureka Springs
McCullough, V. Beth *pharmacist, educator*

### Farmington
Schoppmeyer, Martin William, Jr. *school system administrator*

### Fayetteville
Abu-Safe, Husam Hamza *physics professor*
Aiello, Thomas *historian, educator*
Andrew, Horowitz Warren *economics professor*
Andrews, John Frank *retired civil and environmental engineering educator*
Banks, David Russell *former health care executive*
Bassett, Woodson William, Jr. *lawyer*
Bell, Debbie McCulley *science educator*
Brown, Avert Hayden *animal scientist, educator*
Brown, Connell Jean *retired animal science educator*
Burton, Scot *finance educator*
Cantrell, Andrea E. *library administrator*
Chung, Donghun *communications educator*
Costrell, Robert Michael *economist*
Epley, Lewis Everett, Jr. *retired lawyer*
Farley, Roy Carl *counselor educator*
Ferritor, Daniel E. *retired chancellor*
Fink, William James *retired surgeon*
Gaddy, James Leoma *chemical engineer, educator*
Hay, Robert Dean *retired management educator*
Hendren, Jimm Larry *federal judge*
Jackson, Barbara Ann Garvey *music educator*
Jones, Louis, Jr. (Bucky Jones) *academic administrator*
Jones, Phillip John *librarian*
Kellogg, David Wayne *agricultural studies educator, researcher*
Kester, Charles Melvin *lawyer*
King, Jerry Wayne *chemist, researcher, engineer*
Levine, Daniel Blank *classical studies educator*
Mc Gimsey, Charles Robert III *anthropologist*
Mendez, Fabio *economist, researcher*
Morris, Justin Roy *food scientist, consultant*
Mosebach, Michael *education educator*
Musacchia, X(avier) J(oseph) *physiology and biophysics educator*
Musick, Gerald Joe *retired entomology educator*
Nance, Cynthia Eleanor *law educator*
Naumov, Ivan I. *physicist, educator*
Pearson, Charles Thomas, Jr. *lawyer, director*
Roberts, Michael T. *law educator, lawyer*
Rosenberg, Leon Joseph *marketing educator*
Scharlau, Charles Edward III *natural gas company executive*
Schoppmeyer, Martin William *education educator*
Sears, Derek William George *education educator, researcher*
Smith, Lavenski R. (Vence Smith) *federal judge*
Smith, Robert Victor *academic administrator, educator*
Steele, Kenneth Franklin, Jr. *hydrologist*
Sutherland, Daniel Ellyson *historian*
Venkatesh, Viswanath *information systems professional, educator, consultant*
White, John Austin, Jr. *engineering educator, academic administrator*
Wilkins, Charles L. *chemist, educator*
Williams, Miller *retired poet, writer, translator*
Wilson, Charles Banks *artist*

### Fort Smith
Babb, Douglas J. *lawyer*
Balfe, Robert Cramer III *prosecutor*
Churchey, Randy L. *health facility administrator*
Colbert, Alice Taylor *history professor*
Coleman, Michael Dortch *nephrologist*
Cooper, Richard F. *lawyer*

### Daily
Daily, Thomas A. *lawyer*
Davidson, Robert A. *trucking executive*
Flanders, Donald Hargis *manufacturing executive*
Gooden, Benny L. *school system administrator*
Howell, James Tennyson *allergist, immunologist, pediatrician*
Meadors, C. Brian *lawyer*
Momand, Elizabeth Blanton *singer, music educator*
Snider, James Rhodes *radiologist*
Timmons, William Todd *chemical engineer, educator*
Young, Robert A. III *freight systems executive*

### Gravette
Legler, Kristin M. *music educator*

### Greenwood
Walters, Bill *retired state senator*

### Greers Ferry
Martindale, Carla Joy *retired librarian*
Robbins, Etta Jo *music educator*

### Hardy
Jones, Shirley J. *elementary school educator*

### Harrison
Rickman, William Thomas *choral director*
Street, Susan Lee *elementary school educator*

### Heber Springs
Niehaus, Sherry M. *social welfare administrator*
Rawlings, Paul C. *retired government official*

### Helena
Kontos, George John, Jr. *surgeon*
Roscopf, Charles Buford *lawyer*

### Hindsville
Peirce, Carole *elementary school educator*

### Hot Springs
Bailey, Robert E. *behaviorist, biologist, chemist, consultant*
Smart, Catherine Anne *retired administrative assistant*

### Hot Springs National Park
Farris, Jefferson Davis *university administrator*
Selix, Karen Elizabeth *writer, artist, vocalist*

### Hot Springs Village
Henning, Lloyd Craig *retired inventory executive*
Smith, W. Preston *publishing executive, educator, real estate broker*

### Huntsville
Carr, Gerald Paul *retired astronaut, retired engineer, retired marketing professional, retired military officer*
Roach, Lonnie Calvin *social studies educator*

### Jefferson
Binienda, Zbigniew Karol *research scientist, consultant*
Moon, Hojin *statistician*
Schwetz, Bernard Anthony *toxicologist*

### Jonesboro
Bartee, Neale *music educator, musician, conductor*
Deacon, John C. *lawyer*
Elkins, Francis Clark *historian, educator, director*
Frego, Georgia Kaye *elementary school educator*
Groves, Mark *music director*
Jones, Kenneth Bruce *surgeon*
Malinsky, Marci Ann *education educator*
Perkins, George Brant *lawyer*
Schaefer, Kelly Marie *theater educator, costume designer*
Smith, Eugene Wilson *retired academic administrator, education educator*
Tims, Robert Austin *data processing official, pilot*

### Little Rock
Allen, H. William *lawyer*
Alsobrook, David Ernest *library director, archivist, historian*
Anderson, Philip Sidney *lawyer*
Arnold, Morris Sheppard *federal judge*
Baker, Russell Pierce *archivist*
Barr, Frederick Reichert, Jr. *marketing executive*
Bass, Evelyn Elizabeth *elementary school educator*
Beebe, Mike *state attorney general*
Bell, Joseph R. *finance executive*
Bell, Richard Eugene *agricultural products executive, state official*
Bemis, Michael B. *utility company executive*
Bird, Samuel N. *judge*
Boe, Myron Timothy *lawyer*
Boswell, Bill Reeser *religious organization executive*
Braithwaite, Wilfred John *physics professor*
Briscoe, David Lloyd *academic sociologist, educator*
Brown, Larry Douglass *research consultant, writer*
Bruce, Thomas Allen *physician, educator*
Buehling, Cynthia Gwynne *music educator*
Campbell, Gilbert Sadler *surgeon, educator*
Casciano, Daniel Anthony *biologist, educator*
Chappelle, Richard Allen, Sr. *bishop*
Cheek, James Richard *ambassador*
Cherry, Sandra Wilson *lawyer*
Chiang, Chia-Chu *computer scientist, educator*
Chilcote, Lugean Lester *retired architect, researcher*
Clark, Shawn L. *psychologist, educator*
Coffman, Deborah Kay *director*
Corbin, Donald L. *state supreme court justice*
Cothren, Martha Rose *history educator*
Cross, J. Bruce *lawyer*
Cummins, Bud *prosecutor*
Daniels, Charlie *state official*
Darsey, Jerome Anthony (Jerry Darsey) *chemistry professor, consultant*
Davis, Suanna Jeanette *music educator, mezzo-soprano*
Dickey, Betty C. *state supreme court justice*
Dillard, Mike *retail executive*

Dillard, William, II, *department store chain executive*
Elders, Joycelyn (Minnie Jocelyn Elders, Minnie Joycelyn Lee) *public health service officer, endocrinologist, former Surgeon General of the United States*
Fisher, Jimmie Lou *state official*
Fitzhugh, Kathryn Corrothers *law librarian*
Ford, Joe Thomas *telephone company executive, former state senator*
Ford, Scott T. *telecommunications industry executive*
Frantz, Francis X. *telecommunications industry executive, lawyer*
Fribourgh, James Henry *retired university administrator*
Gealt, Michael A. *environmental microbiologist, educator*
Givens, John Kenneth *automotive executive*
Glaze, Thomas A. *state supreme court justice*
Good, Mary Lowe (Mrs. Billy Jewel Good) *investment company executive, educator*
Goodner, Norman Wesley *governmental relations specialist*
Green, Johnnie D. *loan officer*
Greenberg, Paul *editor*
Greene, Tristan Dorian *state agency administrator*
Groesbeck, Rolf Alfred *music history and ethnomusicology educator*
Gulley, Wilbur Paul, Jr. *retired savings and loan association executive*
Gunter, James Houston, Jr. *state supreme court justice*
Gunter, Russell Allen *lawyer*
Hall, John Wesley, Jr. *lawyer*
Hannah, James *state supreme court justice*
Hargis, David Michael *lawyer*
Hart, Ronald Wilson *radiobiologist, educator, toxicologist, business adviser*
Hathaway, Charles E. *academic administrator*
Haught, William Dixon *lawyer, writer*
Hope, Ronald Arthur *lawyer*
Hough, Aubrey Johnston, Jr. *pathologist, physician, educator*
Huckabee, Michael Dale *governor*
Imber, Annabelle Clinton *state supreme court justice*
James, T. Kenneth *school system administrator*
James, William Owen, Jr. *lawyer*
Jansen, G. Thomas *dermatologist*
Jaquiss, Robert Douglas Benjamin *pediatric cardiac surgeon*
Kaza, Greg John *economist, educator*
Lang, Nicholas Paul *surgeon*
Ledbetter, Calvin Reville, Jr., (Cal Ledbetter) *political science professor, legislator*
Lemke, Judith A. *lawyer*
Levy, Eugene Pfeifer *architectural firm executive, architect*
Liem, Pham H. *geriatrician*
Light, Jo Knight *stockbroker*
Lucy, Dennis Durwood, Jr. *neurologist, educator*
Malone, David Roy *educational association administrator, director*
May, Ronald Alan *lawyer*
McCaleb, Annette Watts *executive secretary*
McCoy, Stuart Sherman *manufacturing executive*
McIntyre, Nina M. *counseling administrator*
McSwain, Byrdie Engle *laboratory scientist, immunohematologist*
Metzler, James Robert *musician*
Mrak, Robert Emil *neuropathologist, educator*
Mulkey, Jack Clarendon *retired library director*
Murphey, Arthur Gage, Jr. *law educator*
Nelson, Edward Sheffield *lawyer, retired utilities executive*
Nunn, Patarica Dian *poet*
O'Brien, Mark Stephen *pediatric neurosurgeon*
Olden, Kevin William *medical researcher*
Orsini, Tom *retired telecommunications company executive*
Parkhurst, Ted A. *publishing executive*
Portis, Charles McColl *reporter, writer*
Priest, Sharon Devlin *retired state official, not-for-profit developer*
Raney, Miriam Day *actress*
Raphael, Jay E. *theater educator, director, actor*
Raza, Asim *psychiatrist*
Reece, E. Albert *dean, obstetrician, gynecologist, perinatologist*
Roaf, Andree Layton *judge*
Safirstein, Robert Louis *nephrologist, medical educator, medical researcher*
Schroeder, Paul J., Jr. *lawyer*
Scivally, Bart Murnane *accountant, auditor*
Shell, Robert J. *construction executive*
Sherman, William Farrar *lawyer, former state legislator*
Smith, Griffin *editor*
Smith, Paula Yvette *education educator*
Sotomora-von Ahn, Ricardo Federico *pediatrician, educator*
Stewart, Amy Lee *lawyer*
Stockburger, Jean Dawson *lawyer*
Thomas, Lestene *nurse*
Truemper, John James, Jr. *retired architect*
Truex, Dorothy Adine *retired university administrator*
Ursery, Frederick Stanley *lawyer*
Vinikas, Vincent *historian, educator*
Ward, Harry Pfeffer *hematologist, retired academic administrator*
Weiss, Richard A. *state official*
Whiteside, Charles B. III *investment company executive*
Wight, Patricia Anne *neuroscience educator*
Wilson, I. Dodd *dean*
Wilson, William R., Jr. *federal judge*
Witherspoon, Carolyn Brack *lawyer*
Wright, Susan Webber *federal judge*
Xu, Xiaowei *education educator, researcher*

### Lonoke
Ross, Philip Rowland *retired library director*

### Lowell
Garrison, Wayne *transportation executive*
Hunt, J. B. (Johnnie Bryan Hunt) *retired transportation executive*
Thompson, Kirk *transportation executive*

**Magazine**
Cleveland, Jared Allen *superintendent*

**Magnolia**
Avard, Joseph L. *mathematician, educator*
Harrison, Betty Carolyn Cook *retired education educator, administrator*
Juniker, Anthony Michael *real estate developer, consultant*

**Malvern**
Schultz, Marvin E. *historian, educator*

**Marion**
Hughes, Michael Randolph *evangelist*

**Mena**
Eddleman, Floyd Eugene *retired language educator*
Wiles, Betty Jane *accountant*

**Monticello**
Annulis, John Thomas *mathematics professor*
Babin, Claude Hunter *history professor*
Ball, William Kenneth *lawyer*
Guenter, Helen Marie Giessen *librarian*

**Morrilton**
Lord, Penny *writer*
Lord, Robert *writer*

**Mountain Home**
Baker, Robert Leon *military officer*

**Mountainburg**
Roper, Paul Kirk *elementary school educator*

**Nashville**
Couch, Holly G. *secondary school educator*
Martin, Marie Ann *art association administrator*

**Newport**
Hembrey, Shea *artist*

**North Little Rock**
Clothier, Jeffrey Lane *neuropsychiatrist, educator*
Lierly, John A. *psychologist*
Patty, Claibourne Watkins, Jr. *lawyer*
Welch, Morgan E. *lawyer*

**Omaha**
Shaddox, Michael Scott *social studies educator*

**Osceola**
Young, Marilyn Virginia *elementary school educator*

**Palestine**
Taylor, Barbara Mae Helm *artist, educator*

**Pangburn**
Roe, Sandy C. *gifted and talented educator*

**Pearcy**
Burch, Bobby Joe *secondary school educator*

**Pine Bluff**
Bock, Joe Ann *educational examiner*
Bradford, Jay Turner *insurance company executive, state legislator*
Brown-King, Kimberly Kaye *finance educator*
Davis, Lawrence A., Jr. *academic administrator*
Engle, Carole Ruth *aquaculture economics professor*
Hudspeth, Harvey Gresham *history professor*
Hunt, Kami Mays *psychologist, educator*
Jones, John Harris *retired lawyer*
Lakew, Dejenie Alemayehu *mathematician*
Long, Edward Arlo *management consultant, retired manufacturing executive*
Shannon-Gragg, Tenita Leanette *computer scientist, educator*
Sims, David Lloyd *lawyer*
Strode, Joseph Arlin *lawyer*
Walker, Richard Brian *chemistry professor*

**Powhatan**
Clark, Lloyd Wayne *social studies educator, minister*

**Prairie Grove**
Dunn, Anne Ewald Nefflen *retired elementary school educator*

**Prescott**
Vasser, Albert Glenn *lawyer*

**Rogers**
Cooper, John Alfred, Jr. *community development company executive*
Nunneley, Janelle Annette *education educator*
Spainhower, James Ivan *retired college president*

**Russellville**
Cooper, Robert Michael *consultant, retired nuclear energy industry specialist*
Eidson, Martha Head *elementary school educator*
Finan, Marcel Bassil *mathematics professor, researcher*
Herrick, Nita Marie *music educator*
Morris, Lois Lawson *retired education educator*
Zimmer, Connie Whitlow *librarian*

**Scranton**
Uzman, Betty Ben Geren *retired pathologist*

**Searcy**
Burks, David Basil *academic administrator, educator*

**Sherwood**
George, James Edward *accountant*

**Siloam Springs**
Wubbena, Jan Helmut *music professor*

**Springdale**
Beach, Jean Mrha *food products executive*
Bond, Richard L. *food products executive*

Cordell, Beulah Faye *retired special education educator*
Dunn, Jeri R. *food products executive*
Gonzalez-Pita, J. Alberto *lawyer*
Hudson, R. Read *lawyer, food products executive*
Leatherby, Dennis *food products executive*
Lee, Greg W. *food company executive*
Rosenschein, Guy Raoul *pediatric and visceral surgeon, airline pilot*
Schaffer, Archie III *food products executive*
Tyson, John H. *food products executive*

**Star City**
Scifres, Teresa Ellen *reporter, educator*

**State University**
Barredo, Ronald De Vera *physical therapist, educator*
Bouldin, Jennifer L. *research scientist*
Milner, Clyde A., II, *historian*

**Stuttgart**
Counce, Paul Allen *physiologist, educator*

**Texarkana**
Stroud, John Fred, Jr. *judge*

**Tontitown**
McMennamy, Roger Neal *automotive executive*

**Van Buren**
Peer, Diana Kay *principal*

**Warren**
Claycomb, Hugh Murray *lawyer, writer*

**West Fork**
Higgins, Sarah Jean *literature and language professor*

**West Memphis**
Fogleman, Julian Barton *lawyer*
Howell, Kathy Aileen *advertising executive*
Peoples, Johnny Ray *music educator*

**White Hall**
Scott, Vicki Sue *school system administrator*

**Wickes**
Riley, Faith Lynch *retired historian, writer*

**Winslow**
Burggraf, Frank Bernard, Jr. *landscape architect, retired educator*

## CALIFORNIA

**Agoura Hills**
Curiale, Joseph James *composer, writer*
Currie, Malcolm Roderick *aerospace executive, automotive executive, research scientist*
deCiutiis, Alfred Charles Maria *oncologist, television producer*
Gressak, Anthony Raymond, Jr. *sales executive*
Kuzmanovic, Jane Violet *academic administrator*
Merchant, Roland Samuel, Sr. *health facility administrator, educator*
Teresi, Joseph *publishing executive*

**Alameda**
Bartalini, C. Richard *judge*
Billings, Thomas Neal *computer and publishing executive, management consultant, entrepreneur, journalist, writer*
Boltwood, Russell Lewis *lawyer, telecommunications industry executive*
Brooks, Aaron Lafette *professional football player*
Caldwell, William Mackay, IV, *cloning and stem cell research company executive*
Chen, Arthur *physician, hospital administrator*
Cho, Myeong-Je *plant biologist, researcher*
Davis, Allen *professional football team executive*
Herrera, John *professional football team executive*
Janowitz, Jeffrey Mark *management consultant*
Jordan, LaMont *professional football player*
LaRose, Katherine Stencel *music educator*
Leong, Jonathan R. *insurance company executive*
Lu, Hong Liang *telecommunications industry executive*
Moss, Randy *professional football player*
Ngo, Tung Thanh *writer, photographer*
Potash, Jeremy Warner *public relations executive*
Potash, Stephen Jon *public relations executive*
Rubin, Charles Alexis *writer*
Sapp, Warren Carlos *professional football player*
Schoeler, George Bernard *medical entomologist*
Shell, Art (Arthur Shell Jr.) *professional football coach*
Troll, Lillian Ellman *psychologist, educator*
Verrill, Kathleen Wills *special education educator*
Whorton, M. Donald *physician, epidemiologist*
Williamson, Robert F. *pharmaceutical executive*

**Alamo**
Bouret, Pierre George *brokerage house executive*
Liggett, Lawrence Melvin *vacuum equipment manufacturing company executive*
Madden, Palmer Brown *lawyer*
Shiffer, James David *retired utilities executive*
Whalen, John Sydney *management consultant*

**Albany**
Boris, Ruthanna *dancer, educator, choreographer, dance therapist*
Daniels, Lydia M. *health care administrator*
Marsh, Richard Charles *psychologist, educator, writer*
Schwimmer, Sigmund *food enzymologist*

**Alhambra**
Austin, Elizabeth Ruth *retired elementary school educator*
Duke, Donald Norman *publishing executive*
Huang, Jia-Sheng Jack *optics scientist, researcher*
Im, Jaemo *research scientist*
Ly, Allan Q. *medical technician*
Suzuki, Bob H. *retired academic administrator*

**Aliso Viejo**
Blum, Scott Allen *Internet company executive*
Boeckmann, Alan L. *engineering company executive, construction management company executive*
Carroll, Adeline F. *special education educator*
Cohen, Sasha (Alexandra Pauline Cohen) *ice skater*
Fisher, Lawrence N. *lawyer, engineering company executive*
Grover, Neel *Internet company executive*
Kizer, Kenneth Wayne *emergency physician, medical educator, physician executive*
La Marca, Jeffry Peter *language educator, consultant*

**Alpine**
Greenberg, Byron Stanley *newspaper and business executive, consultant*
Oliverio, Ponzio *protective services official, educator*
Roberts, Dwight Loren *engineering consultant, writer*

**Alta Loma**
Campbell, Ellen Feyk *elementary school educator*
Haskvitz, Alan Paul *elementary school educator, consultant*
Klein, Henry *lawyer*
Maloof, Sam *woodworker*
Straka, Laszlo Richard *retired publishing consultant*

**Altadena**
Burden, Jean Prussing *retired poet, editor*
Coles, Donald Earl *retired engineering educator*
Dobbins, Maggie Sonne *real estate investment company executive*
Dutton, Pauline Mae *fine arts and reference librarian*
Eisen, Glenn Philip *management consultant, educator*
Klages, Karen Louise *music educator, musician*
Willans, Jean Stone *bishop, religious organization administrator*

**Alviso**
Ramsay, Michael *communications company executive*
Rogers, Thomas Sydney *communications company executive*
Sordello, Steve *communications executive*

**Anaheim**
Anderson, Garret *professional baseball player*
Barry, Sandra *school system administrator*
Baumgartner, Anton Edward *automotive sales professional*
Bennett, Genevieve *artist*
Burke, Brian *professional sports team executive*
Carlyle, Randy *professional hockey coach, retired professional hockey player*
Frank, Judith Ann (Jann Frank) *retired entrepreneur, small business owner*
Glazer, Sidney *physician, director*
Gobar, Alfred Julian *retired economic consultant, educator*
Goodspeed, Kathryn Ann *pre-school educator*
Green, Travis *professional hockey player*
Gregg, James R. *optometrist, educator*
Guajardo, Elisa *counselor, educator*
Halligan, Joseph William *snack food industry executive*
Kallay, Michael Frank, II, *medical products executive*
Lano, Charles Jack *retired financial executive*
Lee, Donna Jean *retired nurse*
McNulty, James Francis *engineering executive*
Miller, Mark A. *information technology training executive*
Moreno, Arturo (Arte Moreno) *major league baseball team owner, former advertising executive*
Nelipovich, Sandra Grassi *artist*
Niedermayer, Scott *professional hockey player*
Pringle, Curt *mayor*
Pronger, Chris *professional hockey player*
Schubert, Joseph Edward *music educator*
Selanne, Teemu *professional hockey player*
Unan, George Vincent *adult education educator*
Watson, Oliver Lee III *aerospace engineer, manufacturing executive*

**Angwin**
Maxwell, Donald Malcolm *clergyman, theology studies educator*

**Antelope**
Nenov, Ivo P. *mathematical and software researcher*

**Antioch**
Adams, Liliana Osses *music performer, harpist*
Archuleta, Keith Anthony *entrepreneur, business and management consultant*
Molina, Ron Joseph *music educator*

**Apple Valley**
Yule, Caroll Jane *real estate broker*

**Aptos**
Bohn, Ralph Carl *educational consultant*
Heron, David Winston *librarian*
Hirsch, Bette G(ross) *academic administrator, language educator*
Nicholson, Joseph Bruce *real estate developer*
Trounstine, Philip John *communications consultant, academic administrator*

**Arcadia**
Baltz, Patricia Ann (Pann Baltz) *retired elementary school educator*
Belnap, David F. *journalist*
Chih, Luke *music educator, conductor*
Gamboa, George Charles *retired oral surgeon, educator*
Guo, Xin *music educator, editor*
Ingram, C. Kendal (Ken Ingram) *information technology executive, non-profit organization administrator*

Matsuura, Kenneth Ray *counseling administrator*
Yen, Wen-Hsiung *language and music professional, educator*

**Arcata**
Bailey, Stephen Fairchild *retired museum director, ornithologist*
Bowker, Lee Harrington *sociologist, educator, writer*
Emenhiser, JeDon Allen *political science professor, dean*
Land-Weber, Ellen *photography professor*
McCrone, Alistair William *retired academic administrator*

**Arleta**
Kelley, Frances A. *occupational therapist, consultant*

**Aromas**
Fleischman, Paul *children's author*

**Arroyo Grande**
Grisez, James Louis *physician, plastic surgeon*
Oseguera, Palma Marie *retired career officer*

**Artesia**
Costa, David Lourenco *music educator, conductor*

**Atascadero**
Jones, Kathryn Cherie *pastor*
Locke, Virginia Otis *writer*
Ogier, Walter Thomas *retired physics educator*
Rios, Evelyn Deerwester *columnist, musician, artist, writer*

**Atherton**
Anderson, Harry W. (Hunk) *retired food service executive*
Bales, Royal Eugene *philosophy educator*
Coleman, Robert Griffin *geology educator*
Ferris, Robert Albert *lawyer, venture capitalist*
Fried, John H. *chemist*
Gill, Stephen Paschall *retired physicist, mathematician*
Goodman, Sam Richard *electronics executive*
Hogan, Clarence Lester *retired electronics executive*
Lane, Joan Fletcher *academic administrator*
Lowry, Larry *engineering company executive*
Sollman, George Henry *venture capitalist*
Walsh, William Desmond *investor*

**Atwater**
Ryan, Kelli Lorraine *ballerina, educator*

**Auburn**
Ferber, Robert Rudolf *retired physics researcher, educator, science administrator*
Henrikson, Donald Merle *forensic pathologist*
Hess, Patrick Henry *chemist, researcher*
Jeske, Howard Leigh *retired insurance company executive, lawyer*
Lyon, Bruce Arnold *lawyer, educator*
Miller, Susan L. *social services administrator*
Moore, Billie Jo *minister*
Rothwell, Elaine B. *artist*
Sanborn, Dorothy Chappell *retired librarian*

**Avalon**
Pedersen, Jeannine Lynn *curator*

**Azusa**
Esselstrom, David Dwight *literature educator, writer*
Hoffman, Joy Lynn *educational association administrator*
Liegler, Rosemary Menke *dean*
Miyake, Stephanie Ann *psychology professor, director, marriage and family therapist*
Pacino, Maria Antonieta *education educator, department chairman*
Parham, Thomas David *education educator*

**Bakersfield**
Ashburn, Roy *state senator*
Bacon, Leonard Anthony *accounting educator*
Bernard, Alexander *protective services official*
Chidgey, Guy Clement *real estate company executive*
Davisson, Scott Louis *secondary school educator*
Duquette, Diane Rhea *library director*
Enriquez, Carola Rupert *museum director*
Fiedler, Joseph Robert *mathematician, educator*
Flachmann, Michael Charles *English language educator*
Frazier, Jo Frances *religious organization administrator, writer*
Fuller, Jean *school system administrator*
Hancock, Tapp *elementary school educator*
Huerta, Dolores Fernandez *labor union administrator*
Kegley, Jacquelyn Ann *philosophy educator*
Kempf, Robert Louis *theater educator, theater director*
Kreber, Lisa Ann *neuroscientist, psychologist*
McAlister, Michael H. *architect*
Meyers, Christopher *humanities educator, consultant*
Osterkamp, Dalene May *psychology educator, artist*
Peterson, Pamela Carmelle *language educator*
Provencio, Roberto Enrique *music educator, music minister*
Prunes, Fernando *plastic surgeon, surgeon*
Reed, James Michael *music educator, singer*
Reep, Edward Arnold *artist*
Rump, Marjorie *library director*
Sawyer, Nelson Baldwin, Jr. *credit union executive*
Sio, Jimmy Ong *embryologist*
Thomason, Scott *automobile executive*
Tornstrom, Robert Ernest *lawyer, oil industry executive*
Zarra, Ernest Joseph III *secondary school educator, researcher*

**Baldwin Park**
Feng, Mark I. *urologist, surgeon*

**Banning**
Gladden, Garnett Lee *psychologist, educator*

Wieczorek, John Richard *application developer, systems analyst*
Wiegel, Robert Louis *consulting engineering executive*
Wilensky, Harold L. *political science professor, sociologist, researcher*
Williamson, Oliver Eaton *economics professor, law professor*
Winkelstein, Warren, Jr. *physician, educator*
Wolf, Joseph Albert *mathematician, educator*
Wolfinger, Raymond Edwin *retired political science professor*
Wolfram, Charles William *law educator*
Woodhouse, Thomas Edwin *lawyer, trust company administrator*
Wright, Paul Kenneth *mechanical engineering educator*
Xie, Ganquan *mathematician, computational geophysical scientist, educator*
Yang, Peidong *material science researcher*
Yeung, Ronald Wai-Chun *engineering educator, researcher*
Yoo, John Choon *law educator, former federal agency administrator*
Zaentz, Saul *film producer, former record company executive*
Zelmanowitz, Julius Martin *mathematics professor, academic administrator*
Zimring, Franklin E. *lawyer, educator*
Zwerdling, Alex *language educator*
Zysman, John Adler *political scientist, educator*

## Bermuda Dunes

Eppert, Luana Kyle *retired secondary school educator, sculptor, writer*

## Berry Creek

Miller, Joseph Arthur *manufacturing engineer, consultant, educator*

## Beverly Hills

Abdul, Paula (Paula Julie Abdul) *singer, dancer, choreographer*
Abrams, J.J. (Jeffrey Jacob Abrams) *television producer, scriptwriter*
Alexander, Jason (Jay Scott Greenspan) *actor*
Allen, Debbie *actress, choreographer, dancer, television director*
Allen, Joan *actress*
Allen, Ted *television personality*
Allen, Tim (Timothy Allen Dick) *actor, comedian*
Ambrose, Lauren (Lauren Anne D'Ambruoso) *actress*
Anderson, Kenneth Allen *lawyer, hotel executive*
Anderson, Pamela Denise *actress*
Anderson, Wes (Wesley Wales Anderson) *film director*
Ann-Margret, (Ann-Margret Olsson) *actress, performer*
Apatow, Judd *scriptwriter, television producer, film producer*
Arieff, Allen Ives *physician*
Arnold, Tom *actor, comedian, television producer*
Arquette, Patricia *actress*
Avary, Roger Roberts (Frank Brauner) *film director, producer, writer*
Aykroyd, Daniel Edward *actor, writer*
Bacon, Kevin *actor*
Badham, John MacDonald *motion picture director*
Balash, Jeffrey Linke *investment banker*
Ball, Alan *screenwriter*
Banderas, Antonio *actor*
Bao, Katherine Sung *pediatric cardiologist*
Barclay, Paris *television director, television producer*
Barkin, Ellen *actress*
Barrymore, Drew *actress*
Barton, Mischa *actress*
Basichis, Gordon Allen *writer, scriptwriter, novelist, marketing consultant, media consultant*
Bass, Ronald *screenwriter*
Bateman, Jason *actor*
Bates, Kathy *actress*
Bay, Michael Benjamin *film director*
Beatty, Warren *actor, film director, film producer*
Bello, Maria Elana *actress*
Belushi, James A. *actor*
Bening, Annette *actress*
Berenger, Tom (Thomas Michael Moore) *actor*
Berg, Jeffrey Spencer *talent agency executive*
Bergman, Nancy Palm *real estate investment company executive*
Berkus, James *talent agent*
Berney, Bob *film company executive*
Biel, Jessica *actress, model*
Bisset, Jacqueline *actress*
Black, Jack (Thomas Black) *actor*
Blaine, David *magician*
Blanchett, Cate (Catherine Elise Blanchett) *actress*
Bogdanovich, Peter *film director, writer, producer, actor*
Bollenbach, Stephen Frasier *hotel executive*
Bonham-Carter, Helena *actress*
Bortman, David *lawyer*
Bosworth, Kate *actress*
Bradshaw, Terry (Terry Paxton Bradshaw) *sports announcer, former professional football player*
Bratt, Benjamin *actor*
Braun, Zev *motion picture and television producer*
Brenneman, Amy *actress*
Bridges, Jeff *actor*
Brillstein, Bernie J. *producer, talent manager*
Brockovich-Ellis, Erin *legal researcher*
Broderick, Matthew *actor*
Brokaw, Norman Robert *talent agency executive*
Buckland, Marc *television director*
Burnett, Carol *actress, comedienne, singer*
Burnham, John Ludwig *agent*
Burns, Marvin Gerald *lawyer*
Burstyn, Ellen (Edna Rae Gillooly) *actress*
Busfield, Timothy *actor*
Bush, Sophia *actress*
Bymel, Suzan Yvette *talent manager, film producer*
Byrne, Gabriel *actor*
Campbell, Neve *actress*
Cantor, Alan Bruce *management consultant, application developer*
Capshaw, Kate (Kathy Sue Nail) *actress*
Carpenter, John Howard *director, screenwriter*
Carradine, Keith Ian *actor, singer, composer*

Carrere, Tia (Althea Rae Duhinio Janairo) *actress*
Carrey, Jim *actor*
Carter, Lynda *actress, entertainer*
Caruso, David *actor*
Castellaneta, Dan (Daniel Louis) *actor*
Caster, Andrew Ian *ophthalmologist*
Castle-Hughes, Keisha *actress*
Caton-Jones, Michael *film director, film producer*
Cattrall, Kim *actress*
Catz, Boris *endocrinologist, educator*
Caviezel, James Patrick *actor*
Channing, Carol *actress*
Chappelle, Dave (David Chappelle) *actor, comedian*
Chase, David (David DeCaesare) *scriptwriter, television producer, television director*
Cheadle, Don *actor*
Christensen, Hayden *actor*
Chritton, George A. *theater producer*
Church, Thomas Hayden *actor*
Clooney, George *actor*
Close, Glenn *actress*
Coen, Ethan *film director, writer*
Coen, Joel *film director, writer*
Collette, Toni *actress*
Columbus, Chris *film director, screenwriter*
Condon, Tom *sports agent*
Condon, William (Bill) *film director, writer, producer*
Congdon, Amanda *actress, web video blogger, writer*
Connelly, Jennifer *actress*
Connery, Sir Sean (Thomas Sean Connery) *actor*
Cook, Dane (Dane Jeffrey Cook) *comedian, actor*
Corbett, John *actor*
Corbin, Barry *actor, writer*
Corwin, Stanley Joel *book publisher*
Covitz, Carl D. *investment company executive, federal official, state official*
Cox Arquette, Courteney *actress*
Craig, Daniel *actor*
Cristofer, Michael *actor, writer, playwright, scriptwriter*
Croll, Tony *cinematographer, television director*
Cronenberg, David *film director*
Crowe, Cameron *screenwriter, film director*
Cruz, Penelope *actress*
Culkin, Macaulay *actor*
Curry, Tim *actor*
Curtis, Jamie Lee *actress*
Cusack, Joan *actress*
Cusack, John *actor*
Daly, Tyne *actress*
Daniels, Jeff *actor, playwright*
Davis, Geena (Virginia Davis) *actress*
DeGeneres, Ellen *actress, comedienne, talk show host*
Delaney, Kim *actress*
De Niro, Robert *actor, film producer, film director, restaurant owner*
Dennehy, Brian *actor*
Depp, Johnny *actor*
Dern, Bruce MacLeish *actor*
DeVito, Danny Michael *actor, film director*
Diesel, Vin (Mark Vincent) *actor*
Donaldson, Roger *film director, film producer*
Donner, Richard *film director, producer*
Dooley, Paul *actor, writer*
Dorff, Stephen *actor*
Dotrice, Roy Louis *actor*
Dourdan, Gary *actor*
Drescher, Fran *actress*
Dreyfuss, Richard Stephan *actor*
Duchovny, David *actor*
Duke, Patty (Anna Marie Duke) *actress*
Duncan, Michael Clarke *actor*
Duvall, Robert (Robert Selden Duvall) *actor*
Duvall, Shelley *actress*
Eastwood, Clint (Clinton Eastwood Jr.) *actor, film director, film producer*
Eikenberry, Jill *actress*
Elfman, Jenna (Jennifer Mary Butala) *actress*
Elliott, Sam *actor*
Elwes, Cary *actor*
Emanuel, Ari (Ariel Z. Emanuel) *talent agent*
Emmerich, Roland *film director, producer, writer*
Epps, Omar *actor*
Evans, Louise *investor, retired psychologist*
Eyre, Chris *film director*
Factor, Max III *arbitrator, mediator*
Fagel, Bruce G. *lawyer, former emergency physician*
Falco, Edie *actress*
Fallon, Jimmy *actor*
Farrelly, Bobby (Robert Leo Rarrelly Jr.) *scriptwriter, film director, film producer*
Favreau, Jon *actor, film director, film producer*
Fein, William *ophthalmologist*
Fellowes, Julian *actor*
Ferguson, Craig *actor*
Ferrell, Conchata Galen *actress, performing arts educator*
Ferrell, Will (John William Ferrell) *actor*
Ferretti, Dante *display designer*
Fey, Tina *actress*
Filicia, Thom *television personality, interior designer*
Filosa, Gary Fairmont Randolph V., II, *columnist, theater producer, film producer*
Fine, Richard Isaac *lawyer*
Fisher, Garth (Donald Garth Fisher) *plastic surgeon*
Flaum, Marshall Allen *television producer, writer, director*
Flockhart, Calista *actress*
Foch, Nina *actress, creative consultant, film director, educator*
Fonda, Jane *actress*
Ford, Tom *apparel designer, apparel executive*
Forsythe, William *actor*
Fox, Michael J. *actor*
Fox, Vivica *actress*
Foxworth, Robert Heath *actor, film director*
Foxx, Jamie (Eric Bishop) *actor, comedian*
Franken, Al (Alan Stuart Franken) *comedian, writer, actor*
Fraser, Brendan *actor*
Frears, Stephen *film director*
Friedman, Robert Lee *film company executive*
Gabler, Elizabeth Brand *film company executive*
Gaghan, Stephen *scriptwriter, film director*
Gandolfini, James *actor*

Ganis, Sidney *film company executive, producer*
Garofalo, Janeane *actress, comedienne*
Garr, Teri (Ann) *actress*
Gelbart, Larry *scriptwriter, television producer, theater producer*
Getty, Balthazar *actor*
Gilpin, Peri *actress*
Glazer, Guilford *real estate developer*
Glover, John *actor*
Glover, Savion *actor, dancer*
Goldsmith, Bram *banker*
Golshani, S. Daniel *plastic surgeon*
Gooding, Cuba, Jr. *actor*
Goodman, John *actor*
Gordy, Berry *entrepreneur, film producer, recording industry executive*
Gores, Tom T. *investment company executive*
Gosnell, Raja *film editor, film director*
Graham, Heather *actress*
Graham, Lauren *actress*
Grant, Hugh *actor*
Grant, Michael Ernest *educational administrator, management educator*
Grazer, Brian *film company executive*
Grenier, Adrian *actor*
Griffin, Kathy *comedienne, actress*
Griffin, Merv Edward *former entertainer, television producer, entrepreneur*
Griffith, Andy (Andrew Samuel Griffith) *actor*
Griffith, Clark Dexter *corporate financial executive*
Grodin, Charles *actor, writer, theater director*
Groening, Matthew (Matthew Abram Groening) *writer, cartoonist*
Guest, Christopher *actor, director, screenwriter*
Gugino, Carla *actress*
Gyllenhaal, Jake *actor*
Gyllenhaal, Maggie *actress*
Hackford, Taylor *film director*
Hackman, Gene (Eugene Alden Hackman) *actor*
Hallstrom, Lasse *film director*
Hamilton, Linda *actress*
Hanks, Tom *actor, film producer, film director*
Hannah, Daryl *actress*
Hanson, Curtis *film director, scriptwriter*
Harden, Marcia Gay *actress*
Hardy, Sean *chef*
Harmon, Angie (Angie Sehorn) *actress*
Harrelson, Woody *actor*
Harris, Mel (Mary Ellen Harris) *actress*
Harris, Neil Patrick *actor*
Hart, Matthew J. *hotel and recreation executive*
Hart, Melissa Joan Catherine *actress*
Hartnett, Josh *actor*
Haskell, Peter Abraham *actor, director*
Hathaway, Anne *actress*
Hawke, Ethan Green *actor*
Hawn, Goldie *actress*
Haworth, Randal Digby *plastic surgeon*
Hayek, Salma *actress*
Haysbert, Dennis *actor*
Heasley, Thomas Allen *composer, musician*
Heaton, Patricia *actress*
Heder, Jon *actor*
Hefter, Lee *chef*
Heller, Paul Michael *film company executive, film producer*
Hershey, Barbara (Barbara Herzstein) *actress*
Heston, Charlton (John Charlton Carter) *actor*
Hewitt, Jennifer Love *actress, singer*
Hill, David *broadcast executive*
Hill, Walter *film director, writer, producer*
Hilton, Barron (William Barron Hilton) *hotel executive*
Hofbauer, John D. *ophthalmologist*
Hoffman, Dustin Lee *actor*
Hogan, Steven L. *lawyer*
Holmes, Katie (Katherine Noelle Holmes) *actress*
Hopkins, Sir Anthony (Philip) *actor*
Hopkins, Stephen *film director, producer*
Hopper, Dennis *actor, writer, photographer, film director*
Horwin, Leonard *retired lawyer*
Howard, Ron *film director*
Howard, Terrence Dashon *actor*
Hughes, John W. *film producer, screenwriter, film director*
Hunt, Bonnie *actress*
Hunt, Helen (Helen Elizabeth Hunt) *actress*
Hunt, Linda *actress*
Hurd, Gale Anne *film producer*
Hurley, Elizabeth *actress, model, film producer*
Hurt, William *actor*
Huston, Anjelica *actress*
Hutton, Timothy *actor*
Idle, Eric *actor, scriptwriter, film producer, lyricist*
Imperioli, Michael *actor*
Isaacman, Alan L. *lawyer*
Israel, David *journalist, scriptwriter, film producer*
Israel, Richard Stanley *investment banker*
Jackson, Janet (Janet Damita Jo Jackson) *vocalist, dancer*
Jaffe, F. Filmore *lawyer, retired judge*
Janseen, Famke *actress*
Jenkins, Patty *film director, scriptwriter*
Johansson, Scarlett *actress*
Johnson, Magic (Earvin Johnson Jr.) *professional sports team executive, development company executive, former professional basketball coach and player*
Jolie, Angelina *actress*
Jones, Cherry *actress*
Jonze, Spike *film director*
Jordan, Glenn *film director, television director, theater director*
Jordan, Neil Patrick *film director, writer*
Josephson, Nancy *talent agency executive*
Judd, Ashley *actress*
Karlin, Michael Jonathan Abraham *lawyer*
Karpman, Harold Lew *cardiologist, educator, writer*
Kaufman, Charlie *scriptwriter*
Keaton, Diane *actress*
Keaton, Michael *actor, comedian*
Keener, Catherine *actress*
Keitel, Harvey *actor*
Keith, David Lemuel *actor*
Kelly, Moira *actress*
Kerkorian, Kirk *investor, former motion picture company executive, consultant*
Kerns, Joanna de Varona *actress, writer, director*
Khan, Chaka (Yvette Marie Stevens) *singer*

Kidman, Nicole *actress*
Kilmer, Val *actor*
King, Charles *agent*
Kingston, Alex (Alexandra Kingston) *actress*
Klein, Arnold William *dermatologist*
Kleiner, Madeleine A. *lawyer*
Klum, Heidi *model, actress*
Knoxville, Johnny (Philip John Clapp) *actor*
Kotler, Robert *cosmetic surgeon*
Krause, Peter *actor*
Kravitz, Lenny *singer, guitarist*
Kressley, Carson *television personality*
La Forgia, Robert M. *hotel executive*
Lahti, Christine *actress*
Lake, Ricki (Ricki Pamela Lake) *talk show host, actress*
Lane, Nathan (Joseph Lane) *actor*
Langella, Frank *actor*
Lansbury, Angela Brigid *actress*
LaPaglia, Anthony *actor*
Law, Jude (David Jude Law) *actor*
Lawrence, Martin *actor, comedian*
Lear, Norman Milton *producer, writer, director*
Leder, Mimi *television director, film director, film producer*
Lee, Ang *film director*
Lee, Jason *actor*
Lee, Whitney Fielding *literary agent*
Leguizamó, John *actor, comedian*
Leigh, Jennifer Jason (Jennifer Leigh Morrow) *actress*
Leonard, Robert Sean *actor*
Levant, Brian *film director*
Levinson, Barry L. *film director*
Levy, Eugene *actor, film director, screenwriter*
Lewis, Juliette *actress*
Limato, Edward Frank *agent*
Lindo, Delroy *actor*
Linney, Laura *actress*
Liotta, Ray *actor*
Liu, Lucy *actress*
Lloyd, Christopher *actor*
Lohan, Lindsay *actress*
Lond, Harley Weldon *editor, publishing executive*
Lord, Marjorie *actress*
Lovett, Richard *talent agency executive*
Lowe, Rob *actor*
Lucas, Josh (Josh Maurer) *actor*
Mac, Bernie *actor, comedian*
MacLaine, Shirley *actress*
Macy, William H. *actor*
Madsen, Michael *actor*
Maher, Bill *television personality, comedian, television producer*
Malick, Terrence (David Whitney II) *film director*
Malkovich, John *actor*
Malone, Jena *actress*
Mandel, Babaloo *scriptwriter*
Mandel, Howie *actor, comedian*
Manheim, Camryn *television and film actress*
Mann, Michael Kenneth *film director, film producer*
Mantello, Joseph *theater director*
Margulies, Julianna *actress*
Markman, Ronald Abraham *psychiatrist, lawyer*
Marsden, James (James Paul Marsden) *actor*
Marshak, Harry *plastic surgeon*
Marshall, Penny (C. Marshall, Carole Penny Marshall) *director, actress*
Martin, Steve *actor, comedian*
Martinson, Constance Frye *television personality, television producer*
Masterson, Mary Stuart *actress*
Mastrantonio, Mary Elizabeth *actress*
Mathis, Samantha *actress*
Mazar, Debi *actress*
McAdams, Rachel *actress*
McCarthy, Jenny *actress*
McDermott, Dylan *actor*
McGagh, William Gilbert *financial consultant*
McGovern, Elizabeth *actress*
McKenzie-Swarts, Molly *human resources specialist, hotel executive*
McMorrow, William J. *finance company executive*
Meirelles, Fernando *film director*
Mendes, Eva *actress*
Menkes, John Hans *pediatric neurologist*
Messing, Debra *actress*
Metcalf, Laurie (Lauren Ophelia Metcalfe) *actress*
Meyer, Breckin *actor*
Milius, John Frederick *film writer, director*
Miller, Bennett *film director*
Miller, Sienna *actress*
Moelleken, Brent Roderick Wilfred *surgeon*
Mol, Gretchen *actress*
Molina, Alfred *actor*
Moore, Demi (Demi Guynes, Demetria Gene Guynes) *actress*
Moore, Julianne (Julie Anne Smith) *actress*
Moore, Mandy (Amanda Leigh Moore) *actress, singer*
Moore, Mary Tyler *actress*
Moore, Michael *film director, writer*
Mortensen, Viggo *actor*
Morton, Samantha *actress*
Mullally, Megan *actress*
Mulroney, Dermot *actor*
Muniz, Frankie (Francisco James Muniz IV) *actor*
Murphy, Cillian *actor*
Murray, Bill *actor, writer*
Nackel, John George *medical association administrator*
Najimy, Kathy *actress*
Neill, Sam *actor*
Neville, Aaron *musician*
Nicita, Rick *agent*
Nixon, Cynthia *actress*
O'Donnell, Chris *actor*
Olmos, Edward James *actor*
Olyphant, Timothy *actor*
Owen, Clive *actor*
Pacino, Al (Alfredo James Pacino) *actor, film director, film producer*
Palmer, Francis Roger III *plastic surgeon*
Palminteri, Chazz *actor*
Paltrow, Gwyneth *actress*
Pantoliano, Joe *actor*
Parker, Alan (William) (Sir Alan Parker) *film director, writer*
Parker, Mary-Louise *actress*
Parker, Sarah Jessica *actress*

Patinkin, Mandy *actor, singer*
Patric, Jason *actor*
Paxton, Bill *actor, film director*
Paymer, David *actor*
Peet, Amanda *actress*
Pepper, Barry *actor*
Perlman, Jon Arthur *plastic surgeon*
Perlman, Rhea *actress*
Petersen, Wolfgang *film director*
Pezzullo, Ralph Michael *writer, playwright*
Phillippe, Ryan *actor*
Phillips, Stacy D. *lawyer*
Piscopo, Joseph Charles *actor*
Pitt, Brad *actor*
Piven, Jeremy *actor*
Platt, Oliver *actor*
Plummer, Christopher (Orme) (Arthur Plummer) *actor*
Polanski, Roman *film director, writer, actor*
Pollack, Sydney *film director*
Pompeo, Ellen *actress*
Portman, Natalie *actress*
Posey, Parker *actress*
Pullman, Bill *actor*
Quaid, Dennis *actor*
Quinn, Aidan *actor*
Quinn, Patricia K. *literary agent*
Rai, Aishwarya *actress*
Ramer, Bruce M. *lawyer*
Ramser, Wanda Tene *librarian, educator*
Reese, Della (Deloreese Patricia Early) *singer, actress*
Reeves, Keanu *actor*
Reiner, Carl *director, actor, writer*
Reiner, Rob *film director, actor*
Rey, Robert M. *plastic surgeon*
Reynolds, Kevin *film director, writer*
Rhames, Ving (Irving) *actor*
Rhys-Meyers, Jonathan *actor*
Ricci, Christina *actress*
Richardson, Patricia *actress*
Riess, Gordon Sanderson *management consultant*
Riley, Jack *actor, writer*
Ringwald, Molly *actress*
Rivers, Joan *entertainer*
Roberts, Julia Fiona *actress*
Rodriguez, Robert *filmmaker*
Rogers, Mimi *actress*
Romero, George A. *film director*
Rosenthal, Richard Jay *psychiatrist*
Rosky, Burton Seymour *lawyer*
Rossellini, Isabella *actress, model*
Roth, Eric *screenwriter*
Rowles, Michael G. *lawyer*
Ruffalo, Mark *actor*
Rush, Geoffrey *actor*
Russell, Irwin Emanuel *lawyer*
Russell, Keri *actress*
Russell, Kurt Von Vogel *actor*
Russo, Anthony *film director*
Russo, Joe *film director*
Ryan, Frank Harry *plastic surgeon*
Ryan, Meg (Margaret Mary Emily Ann Hyra) *actress, film producer*
Sagal, Katey *actress*
Saget, Bob *actor, comedian, writer, television director*
Samberg, Andy *actor*
Sambery, Andy *actor*
Sandrich, Jay H. *television director*
Sands, Kevin B. *dentist*
Sarsgaard, Peter *actor*
Sayles, John Thomas *film director, writer, actor*
Scacchi, Greta *actress*
Schaff, Manya *foundation administrator*
Schaffer, Akiva *writer, director*
Schiff, Gunther Hans *lawyer*
Schneider, Charles Ivan *newspaper executive*
Schneider, Rob *actor*
Schroder, Rick *actor*
Schulian, John (Nielsen Schulian) *screenwriter, author*
Scott, Ridley *film director*
Scott-Thomas, Kristin *actress*
Sedgwick, Kyra *actress*
Seidel, Joan Broude *securities dealer, investment advisor*
Seiff, Stephen S. *ophthalmologist*
Seizer, Fern Victor *retired mental health services administrator*
Sellecca, Connie *actress*
Semel, George Herbert *plastic surgeon*
Sevigny, Chloë *actress*
Sewell, Rufus *actor*
Seymour, Jane *actress*
Shadyac, Thomas *film director, producer*
Shalhoub, Tony *actor, television producer*
Shanley, John Patrick *playwright, screenwriter*
Shapell, Nathan *financial and real estate executive*
Shapiro, Isadore *materials scientist, consultant*
Shapiro-Mathes, Angela *broadcast executive*
Shatner, William *actor*
Sherwood, Kehela (Karen Kehela Sherwood) *broadcast executive*
Shlosberg, Stuart R. *prosthodontist*
Short, Martin *actor, comedian, film critic*
Shue, Elisabeth *actress*
Shuler Donner, Lauren *film producer*
Shyamalan, M. Night (Manoj Nelliyattu Shyamalan) *film producer*
Siciliano, Rocco Carmine *cultural institute executive*
Silverman, Jonathan *actor*
Silverman, Sarah *actress, comedian, writer*
Simmons, Gene (Chaim Witz, Gene Klein) *musician*
Simpson, Jessica Ann *vocalist, actress*
Simpson, Mike *talent agent*
Singer, Bryan *film producer, director, writer, actor*
Sinise, Gary *actor*
Skerritt, Tom *actor*
Slater, Christian *actor*
Smith, Jaclyn *actress*
Snowden, David L. *protective services official*
Sobelle, Richard E. *lawyer*
Sommers, Stephen *film director, scriptwriter, film producer*
Sonnenfeld, Barry *director, cinematographer*
Sorkin, Aaron *scriptwriter, television producer, playwright*
Sorvino, Mira *actress*

Sorvino, Paul *actor*
Spacek, Sissy (Mary Elizabeth Spacek) *actress*
Spader, James *actor*
Spelling, Tori (Victoria Davey Spelling) *actress*
Spheeris, Penelope *film director*
Spielberg, Steven (Steven Allan Spielberg) *film director, film producer*
Stahl, Nick *actor*
Stamos, John *actor*
Statham, Jason *actor*
Steenburgen, Mary *actress*
Steinem, Gloria *writer, editor, advocate*
Stern, Sandor *film director, writer*
Stiers, David Ogden *actor, conductor*
Stiles, Julia *actress*
Stoltz, Eric *actor*
Streep, Meryl (Mary Louise Streep) *actress*
Sutherland, Donald *actor*
Sutherland, Kiefer *actor*
Suvari, Mena *actress*
Swank, Hilary Ann *actress*
Swayze, Patrick *actor, dancer*
Swofford, Beth *agent*
Sykes, Wanda *comedienne, actress*
Taccone, Jorma *writer, director*
Tamblyn, Amber Rose *actress*
Tambor, Jeffrey *actor, theater director, educator*
Tamkin, Curtis Sloane *real estate development company executive*
Taylor, Christine *actress*
Taylor, Lili *actress*
Theron, Charlize *actress*
Thompson, Emma *actress*
Thompson, Larry Angelo *film and television producer, lawyer, motivational speaker, writer*
Thompson, Richard Dickson *lawyer*
Thurman, Uma Karuna *actress*
Tierney, Maura *actress*
Tilly, Jennifer *actress*
Tom, Lauren *actress, singer*
Tomei, Marisa *actress*
Travolta, John *actor*
Tripplehorn, Jeanne *actress*
Tucci, Stanley *actor*
Turlington, Christy *model*
Turner, Kathleen *actress*
Turturro, Nicholas *actor*
Tyler, Liv *actress*
Underwood, Blair *actor, television producer*
Underwood, Ronald Brian *director, producer*
Utley, Nancy *film company executive*
Van Dyke, Dick *actor, comedian*
Van Zandt, Steven *actor, musician, radio personality*
Vardalos, Nia *actress, screenwriter*
Vaughn, Vince *actor*
Verhoeven, Paul *film director*
Victor, Robert Eugene *real estate company executive, lawyer*
Visnjic, Goran *actor*
Wachowski, Andy *film director*
Wachowski, Larry *film director*
Wagner, Lindsay Jean *actress*
Walker, William Tidd, Jr. *investment banker*
Ward, David Schad *scriptwriter, film director*
Ward, Sela *actress*
Waters, John *film director, writer, actor*
Watts, Naomi *actress*
Wayans, Marlon *actor, film producer, writer*
Wayans, Shawn *actor, film producer, writer*
Weaver, Sigourney (Susan Alexandra Weaver) *actress*
Weir, Peter Lindsay *film director*
Weisz, Rachel *actress*
Whaley, Frank *actor*
White, Betty *actress, comedienne*
White, Meg (Megan Martha White) *musician, vocalist*
Whitford, Bradley *actor*
Wiatt, James Anthony *theatrical agency executive*
Wilkinson, Tom *actor*
Williams, Michelle *actress*
Willis, Walter Bruce (Bruce Willis) *actor, vocalist*
Willson, James Douglas *aerospace transportation executive*
Wilson, Luke *actor*
Wilson, Owen *actor*
Winger, Debra *actress*
Winkler, Henry Franklin *actor, film producer, director*
Winters, Dean *actor*
Winthrop, John *wines and spirits company executive*
Wirtschafter, David *talent agency executive*
Witherspoon, Reese (Laura Jean Reese Witherspoon) *actress*
Wolper, David Lloyd *motion picture and television executive*
Wood, Elijah *actor*
Woods, James *actor*
Wright, Jeffrey *actor*
Wright Penn, Robin *actress*
Wu, Yusen (John Woo) *film director*
Yedidsion, Meira *computer artist, sculptor*
Zane, Billy *actor*
Zanuck, Lili Fini *film director, producer*
Zanuck, Richard Darryl *motion picture company executive*
Zarem, Abe Mordecai *management consulting executive*
Zellweger, Renee *actress*

## Bishop

Archer, James Orville *retired aeronautical engineer*
Naso, Valerie Joan *automotive dealership executive, travel company executive*

## Bloomington

Lawrence, William, Jr. *retired elementary school educator*

## Bodega Bay

Clegg, James Standish *physiologist, biochemist, educator*
Cohen, Daniel Morris *museum administrator, marine biologist, researcher*
Freeman, Donna Cook *small business owner*
Hand, Cadet Hammond, Jr. *retired marine biologist*
Sorensen, Linda *lawyer*

## Bolinas

Harris, Paul *sculptor*
Okamura, Arthur Shinji *artist, educator*

## Bonita

Kline, Paul Conley *lawyer*
Ling, Jahja Wang-Chieh *conductor*

## Boonville

Hanes, John Ward *civil engineer, sculptor, rancher, director*

## Boron

Fisher, Richard Paul *chemist*

## Borrego Springs

Strong, John Oliver *plastic surgeon, educator*

## Bradbury

Campbell, Robert Charles *minister, theology studies educator*
Clare, Kenneth Guilford *economist, consultant*

## Brawley

Kellogg, Nancy V. *science educator*

## Brea

Brown, Ronald Malcolm *engineering corporation executive*
Curtis, James Richard *writer, editor*
Oh, Tai Keun *business educator, consultant*
Painchaud, Phillip Andre *metrologist*
Tamura, Cary Kaoru *consultant*

## Brentwood

Albers, Lucia Berta *land developer*
Groseclose, Wanda Westman *retired elementary school educator*
Semtner, Emma Margarette *music educator*

## Brisbane

Baadh, Valerie *choreographer, movement educator, theater producer, production designer*
Daniels, Caroline *publishing executive*
Mashouf, Manny *apparel executive*

## Browns Valley

Stevens, Aileen *retired secondary school educator*

## Buellton

Porter, Bruce Jackman *computer engineer, application developer, portfolio manager, civil engineer*

## Buena Park

Carcich, Ronald A. *secondary school educator*
Kristy, James E. *financial consultant, consultant*

## Burbank

Ancier, Garth Richard *television broadcast executive*
Aviv, Oren R. *film company executive*
Baker, Rick *make-up artist*
Barber, Gary *motion picture company executive*
Bender, Jack *television producer, television director, actor*
Berman, Bruce *entertainment company executive, television producer*
Big Boy, (Kurt Alexander) *radio personality, actor*
Bloomberg, Stu *television producer*
Bower, Richard James *minister*
Branch, Michelle *musician*
Brandis, Bernardine *lawyer*
Braverman, Alan N. *lawyer*
Bublé, Michael *singer*
Burk, Bryan *television producer*
Bush, Billy *television personality*
Caouette, David Paul *public relations executive*
Cher, (Cherilyn Sarkisian) *singer, actress*
Clapton, Eric *musician*
Clark, Dick *performer, producer*
Connelly, Mary *television producer*
Cook, Richard W. (Dick Cook) *film company executive*
Crane, David *producer*
de Ravin, Emilie *actress*
DiBonaventura, Lorenzo *film company executive*
Eubanks, Kevin *jazz guitarist*
Feltenstein, George *film producer, entertainment company executive*
Fishburne, Laurence III *actor*
Fleishman, Susan Nahley *entertainment company executive*
Fogerty, John Cameron *musician, composer*
Franco, James *actor*
Garcia, Jorge *actor*
Glavin, Edward P. *television producer*
Gold, Stanley Phillip *diversified investments executive*
Handel, William Wolf *radio personality*
Henley, Don *singer, drummer, songwriter*
Higgins, Jean *television producer*
Hoffman, Mark *broadcast executive*
Horn, Alan F. *film company executive*
Howard, James Newton *composer*
Iger, Robert Allen *entertainment company executive*
Janollari, David *television broadcasting executive, cable producer, television producer*
Joseff, Joan Castle *manufacturing executive*
Jovovich, Milla (Natasha Militza Jovovich) *model, actress*
Kaye, Jhani *radio station executive, television producer, television director*
Kilgariff, Karen *television producer*
Kroll, Sue *broadcast executive*
Kwan-Rubinek, Veronika *broadcast executive*
Lang, K. D. (Katherine Dawn Lang) *country music singer, composer*
Lanois, Daniel *record producer, musician, popular music singer*
Lassner, Andy *television producer*
Lee, Paul *broadcast executive*
Letterie, Kathleen *broadcast executive*
Lindelof, Damon *television producer, scriptwriter*
Madison, Paula *broadcast executive*
Marinelli, Janice *broadcast executive*
McGraw, Tim *country music singer*
McPherson, Stephen *broadcast executive*
Mc Vie, Christine Perfect *musician*
McVie, John *musician*

## Bonita

Meyer, Barry Michael *motion picture executive*
Michel, Donald Charles *editor*
Mitchell, Joni (Roberta Joan Anderson) *singer, songwriter*
Murphy, Michael George *actor*
Navarro, Dave (David Michael Navarro) *musician, recording artist*
Neill, Ve *make-up artist*
Nelson, Diane W. *broadcast executive*
Neumann, Nancy Ruth *private school educator*
O'Dell, Nancy *television personality*
O'Quinn, Terry (Terrance Quinn) *actor*
Pedowitz, Mark *broadcast executive*
Petty, Tom (Thomas Earl Petty) *musician, composer*
Piddock, James Anthony *actor*
Raulinaitis, Pranas Algis *electronics executive, consultant*
Rawlinson, Joseph Eli *foundation administrator, lawyer*
Remini, Leah *actress*
Renfroe, Owen *television director*
Renner, Andrew Ihor *surgeon*
Rhimes, Shonda *producer, director, writer*
Rimes, LeAnn *country music singer*
Rivera, Miluka *actress, journalist, poet*
Robinov, Jeff *film company executive*
Ross, Rich *broadcast executive*
Rzeznik, Johnny *singer, musician*
Schiff, Richard *actor*
Schumacher, Joel *film director, scriptwriter*
Schumacher, Thomas *film company executive*
Shore, Howard Leslie *composer*
Silver, Joel *film producer*
Sklar, Marty (Martin A. Sklar) *entertainment company executive*
Staggs, Thomas O. *entertainment company executive*
Stewart, Rod (Roderick David Stewart) *singer*
Sweeney, Anne M. *cable television company executive*
Taubin, Dawn *film company executive*
Thornton, Cameron Mitchell *financial planner*
Tourapis, Alexandros *signal processing engineer, researcher*
Watros, Cynthia *actress*
Weiskopf, Wanda *mezzo soprano, writer, poet*
Welinsky, Howard Steven *film distribution executive*
Wells, John Marcum *producer, writer*
Wonder, Stevie (Steveland Hardaway Judkins, Stevland Morris) *musician*
Young, Neil *musician, songwriter*
Younger, Laurie *broadcast executive*
Zimmer, Hans Florian *composer*
Zucker, Jeffrey *broadcast executive*

## Burlingame

Azarnoff, Daniel Lester *pharmaceutical executive, consultant*
Cotchett, Joseph Winters *lawyer, writer*
Mendelson, Lee M. *film company executive, film producer, film director, writer*
Schwantes, Robert Sidney *international relations executive*

## Calabasas

Carner, Charles Robert, Jr. *screenwriter, director*
Christensen, Donn Wayne *insurance executive*
Dreier, R. Chad *construction and mortgage company executive*
Geckle, Timothy J. *lawyer*
Goldfield, Emily Dawson *finance company executive, artist*
Grimwade, Richard Llewellyn *lawyer*
Jones, Richard K. *information technology executive*
Levy, Dena Christine *television producer, director*
McLaughlin, Thomas Keith *diversified financial services company executive*
Milne, Gordon A. *construction executive, mortgage company executive*
Mozilo, Angelo R. *diversified financial services company executive*
Phillips, Teddy Steve, Sr. *conductor, saxophone player, production company executive*
Presland-Byrne, Peter *mortgage company executive*
Rubin, Rick (Frederick Jay Rubin) *record producer*
Sambol, David E. *diversified financial services company executive*
Samuels, Sandor Eli *diversified financial services company executive, lawyer*
Sieracki, Eric P. *diversified financial services company executive*
Stark, Martin J. *management consultant*
Walker, Larry A. *secondary school educator*

## California City

Paiva, Clifford Anthony *physicist, consultant*

## Camarillo

Arthington, Carol Ann *elementary school educator*
Bowman, Bruce *art educator*
Bryan, Bob *professional tennis player*
Cleary, Thomas Charles *technology company executive*
Cobb, Shirley Ann Dodson *public relations consultant, journalist*
d'León, Omar *artist*
MacAlister, Robert Stuart *retired oil industry executive*
Rush, Richard R. *academic administrator*
Sullivan, Michael Evan *investment company executive*
Van House, Robert Arthur *small business owner, contractor*
Weiss, Carl *aerospace company executive*

## Cambria

Harden, Marvin *artist, educator*
Morse, Richard Jay *human resources specialist, consultant*
Salaverria, Helena Clara *retired language educator*

## Cameron Park

Vorce-Tish, Helene R. *writer*

## Camino

McCarthy, Brian Nelson *real estate developer*

## Campbell

Ross, Hugh Courtney *electrical engineer*
Vincent, David Ridgely *financial consultant*

## Canoga Park

Alexander, Sue *writer*
Hajela, Gyaneshwar P. *systems engineer, educator*
Lederer, Marion Irvine *cultural administrator*
Meier, Sue A. *marriage and family therapist, director*
Taesch, Richard Edmond *music educator*

## Canyon Lake

Schilling, Frederick Augustus, Jr. *geologist, consultant*
Sparks, Dale Boyd *allergist, health facility administrator*

## Capitola

Jackson, Kingsbury Temple *educational consultant, financial consultant*
Stobbe, Colleen Sue *elementary school educator, consultant*

## Carlsbad

Benjamin, Theresa Mary *retired psychotherapist*
Chopra, Deepak *preventive medicine physician, writer*
Conway, Daniel Edward *management consultant*
Craig, Jenny *human services manager*
Crooke, Stanley Thomas *pharmaceutical executive*
Fikes, Jay Courtney *anthropology educator, art dealer*
Fox, Roger Edwin *retired physician*
Golding, Brage *university president*
Halberg, Charles John August, Jr. *mathematics professor*
Hale, David Fredrick *biotechnology executive*
Hanscom, Eric Alan *lawyer*
Heckmann, Richard J. *sporting goods company executive*
Howard, Robert Staples *newspaper publisher*
Kauderer, Bernard Marvin *retired naval officer, consultant*
Lu, Taijin *physical chemist, researcher*
McCracken, Steven Carl *lawyer*
Misiorowski, Elise Besson *museum director*
Missett, Judi Sheppard *dancer, jazzercise company executive*
Moore, David Robert *lawyer*
Owen, Charles Theodore *journalist, publishing executive*
Rodak, Sharon Lorraine *elementary school educator, researcher*
Smith, Warren James *optical scientist, consultant, lecturer, author*
Sperling, Irene R. *publishing executive*
Wilson, Donald Grey *management consultant*

## Carmel

Alsberg, Dietrich Anselm *electrical engineer, consultant*
Aurner, Robert Ray, II *retail development executive*
Barton, Hugh Perry *bank executive*
Bengert, W. Raymond *chemical engineer*
Chung, Kyung Cho *Korean history specialist, educator, writer*
de Vos, Paula Francesca *finance company executive, investment advisor, consultant*
Dobey, James Kenneth *banker*
Faul, June Patricia *education specialist*
Felch, William Campbell *internist, editor*
Freed, Sharon Lou *retired principal*
Gordon, David Jamieson *tenor*
Hamilton, Beverly Lannquist *investment executive*
Hamilton, Lyman Critchfield, Jr. *telecommunications industry executive*
Hobbs, C. Fredric *artist, filmmaker, writer*
Jacobs, Ralph, Jr. *artist*
Koeppel, Gary Merle *publishing executive, art gallery owner, writer*
Lockton, David Ballard *entrepreneur, information technology executive*
Mollman, John Peter *publishing executive*
Pippi, Mikel Eugene *food service executive*
Reamy, Michaelin *marriage and family therapist, educator, consultant*
Skidmore, Howard Franklyn *public relations counsel*
Smith, Gordon Paul *management consultant*
Vagnini, Livio Lee *chemist, consultant, forensic specialist*
Vardamis, Alex A. *foundation administrator, retired military officer*
Wright, Constance Storey *retired humanities educator*
Youngdahl, Paul Frederick *mechanical engineer*

## Carmel Valley

Chapman, Robert Galbraith *retired hematologist, administrator*
Kasson, James Matthews *electronics executive*
Meckel, Peter Timothy *arts administrator, educator*
Wolfe, Maurice Raymond *retired museum director, educator*

## Carmichael

Hellmuth, William Frederick *economics professor*
O'Leary, Marion Hugh *retired dean, chemist*

## Carpinteria

Adizes, Ichak *management consultant, writer*
Puzder, Andrew F. *food service executive, lawyer*
Schmidhauser, John Richard *political science professor*
Williams, Benjamin, IV, *headmaster, history educator*

## Carson

Anuakan, Robyn Iset *archivist, educator, film producer*
Bensussen, Gale K. *health products company executive*
Berenato, Joseph C. *manufacturing executive*
Brassell, Danny *education educator*
Cienfuegos, Mauricio *professional soccer player*
Delfin, Donna K. *writer, web programmer*
Del Prado, Sergio *professional soccer team executive*

---

Fisher, Farah Lee *education educator*
Han, Jianchao *science educator*
Heiser, James S. *manufacturing executive*
Hirsch, Gilah Yelin *artist, writer*
Lalas, Alexi (Panayotis Alexander Lalas) *professional sports team executive, retired professional soccer player*
Mende, Howard Shigeharu *mechanical engineer*
Mori, Allen Anthony *academic administrator, consultant*
Oropeza, Jenny *state official*
Palmer, Beverly Blazey *psychologist, educator*
Ruiz Gutierrez, Carlos Humberto *professional soccer player*
Schmid, Sigi *professional soccer coach*
Stuart, Nancy Giovinazzo *secondary school educator*
Zimmerer, Kathy Louise *museum director*

## Castaic

Holmes, Dale Arthur *optics scientist*

## Castro Valley

Morrison, Glenn Leslie *minister*
West, Doyle Thomas *retired music educator*
Wycoff, Charles Coleman *writer, retired anesthesiologist*

## Cathedral City

Berry, Ester Lorée *vocational nurse*
Jackman, Robert Alan *retail executive*
Poppe, Eugene Dale *banker*
Sexton, Douglas Robert *education educator*

## Cayucos

Shahan, Sherry Jean *writer, educator*

## Century City

Clark, Shaun C. *lawyer*
Mak, Kitty *lawyer*

## Ceres

Carrico, Kimberly Anne *elementary school educator*
Wedlake, Philip Russell, Jr. *school system administrator*

## Cerritos

Rosenberg, Steve *secondary school educator*
Shavelle, Robert *medical researcher, consultant*
Woodson-Glenn, Yolanda *social worker*

## Chatsworth

Bhartia, Prakash *defense research management executive, researcher, educator*
Cassar, Jon Francis *television director, film director*
Gunn, Stanley Veerin *retired engineer*
Komm, Kermit Matthew *software engineer*
Stephenson, Irene Hamlen *biomedical researcher, consultant, editor, educator*
Strieby, B. Lorraine *artist*
Weisbrod, Ken (Joseph Louis Weisbrod) *marketing professional*

## Chico

Akimoto, Martin Wayne *mental health services professional*
Allen, Charles William *mechanical engineer, educator*
Bernhardt, Victoria L. *director, researcher*
Esteban, Manuel Antonio *academic administrator, language educator*
Hanton, E. Michael *public information officer, consultant*
Hornaday, Richard H. *artist, retired art educator*
Hyde, Geraldine Veola *retired secondary school educator*
Kistner, David Harold *biology professor*
Livingston, Myran Jay *author, film writer, director and producer*
McNall, Scott Grant *sociologist, educator, academic administrator*
Mejia, Barbara Oviedo *retired chemistry professor*
Smith, Valene Lucy *anthropologist, educator*
Van Auken, Stuart *marketing educator*
Zingg, Paul Joseph *academic administrator*

## China Lake

Bennett, Jean Louise McPherson *physicist, research scientist*

## Chino

Determan, John David *lawyer*
Goodman, Lindsey Alan *furniture manufacturing executive, architect*
Lopez, Sonja *education educator*

## Chino Hills

Fisher, Teresa Marie *psychologist, forensic specialist*
Kim, Kenny H. *secondary school educator*
Nash, Sylvia Dotseth *management consultant*

## Chula Vista

Bauman, Noel James *psychologist*
Blankfort, Lowell Arnold *newspaper publisher*
Briggs, Franklin Henry *retired naval officer*
Cohen, Elaine Helena *pediatrician, cardiologist, educator*
Heise, Steven Anthony *surveyor, consultant*
Nelson, Carl Alfred *writer, international business educator*
Ryan, Candace I. *writer, director, editor*
Sullivan, Patrick Allen *strategic management educator*
Weiss-Cornwell, Amy *interior designer*
Worthington, George Rhodes *retired naval officer*

## Citrus Heights

Daves, Sandra Lynn *poet, lyricist*
Leisey, Donald Eugene *educational association administrator*
Osaki, Mark Stephen *foundation administrator, writer*
Walker, Ronald Craig *artist, educator*

## City Of Commerce

Martin, Richard J. *food wholesale executive*

---

Plamann, Alfred A. *wholesale distribution executive*

## City Of Industry

Cavanaugh, Janis Lynn *protective services official, educator*
Contreras-Sweet, Maria *bank executive*
Fernandez, Manuel G. *food products executive*
Perry, William Joseph *food processing company executive*
Roski, Edward P., Jr. *real estate developer, professional sports team executive*

## Claremont

Ackerman, Gerald Martin *art historian, consultant*
Alexander, John David, Jr. *college administrator*
Ansell, Edward Orin *lawyer*
Atlas, Jay David *philosopher, consultant, linguist, educator*
Barron, Hal S. *historian, history professor*
Bekavac, Nancy Yavor *academic administrator, lawyer*
Benjamin, Karl Stanley *artist, art educator*
Blizzard, Alan *artist*
Borcherding, Thomas Earl *economist*
Burdekin, Richard Charles Keighley *economics professor*
Burns, Richard Dean *historian, educator, writer*
Christian, Suzanne Hall *financial planner*
Coleman, Courtney Stafford *mathematician, educator*
Comba, Steve Scott *museum director, artist*
Cramer, Alfred William *musician, educator*
Csikszentmihalyi, Mihaly *psychology professor*
Davis, Nathaniel *humanities educator*
Deese, E(thel) Helen *retired literature and language professor*
Dunye, Cheryl *artist, filmmaker*
Dym, Clive Lionel *engineering educator*
Ferguson, Cleve Robert *lawyer, educator*
Forti, William Bell *manufacturing executive*
Gann, Pamela Brooks *academic administrator*
Genung, Dan Baldwin *minister, writer*
Gonzales-Day, Kenneth Robert *artist, educator*
Grabiner, Judith Victor *mathematics professor*
Grabiner, Sandy *mathematics professor*
Halpern, Diane F. *psychology educator, professional association executive*
Hansch, Corwin Herman *chemistry professor*
Hawkins, Gregory J. *consumer products company executive*
Helliwell, Thomas McCaffree *physicist, researcher*
Henriksen, Melvin *mathematician, educator*
Huang, Hao H. *music educator, department chairman*
Jaffa, Harry Victor *political philosophy educator emeritus*
Johnson, Jerome Linné *cardiologist, educator*
Kates, Gary *academic administrator*
Klawe, Maria Margaret *academic administrator, engineering and computer science educator*
Kucheman, Clark Arthur *philosophy educator, religious studies educator*
Kucij, Timothy Michael *engineer, minister, musician*
Lasswell, Marcia Lee *psychologist, educator*
Leeb, Charles Samuel *psychologist*
Liggett, Thomas Jackson *retired seminary president*
Likens, James Dean *economics professor*
Lipman-Blumen, Jean *public policy and organizational behavior educator*
Lofgren, Charles Augustin *historian, educator*
Maguire, John David *academic administrator, educator, writer*
Martin, Jay Herbert *psychoanalyst, language professor, political science professor*
McKirahan, Richard Duncan *classics and philosophy educator*
Molinder, John Irving *engineering educator, consultant*
Monson, James Edward *electrical engineer, educator*
Morgan, Ann Marie *psychologist*
Moss, Myra Ellen (Myra Moss Rolle) *philosophy educator*
Myhre, Janet *mathematician, educator*
Oxtoby, David William *academic administrator, chemistry professor*
Pedersen, Richard Foote *diplomat, academic administrator*
Phillips, Ian M. *physiologist, educator*
Pinney, Thomas Clive *retired English language educator*
Pippenger, Nicholas John *mathematician, researcher, computer scientist, educator*
Platt, Joseph Beaven *former college president*
Rankaitis, Susan *artist*
Raval, Alpan *computational biologist, mathematics professor*
Riley, Judith Merkle *writer, educator*
Rossum, Ralph Arthur *political science educator*
Sanders, James Alvin *retired minister, retired religious studies educator*
Shimkhada, Deepak *art historian*
Skandera Trombley, Laura Elise *academic administrator, literature educator*
Sontag, Frederick Earl *philosophy educator*
Stanley, Peter William *former academic administrator*
Strauss, Jon Calvert *retired academic administrator*
Tanenbaum, Basil Samuel *engineering educator*
Tilden, Wesley Roderick *writer, retired application developer*
Vallabhajosyula, Ravishankar Rao *application developer*
Van Hecke, Gerald Raymond *chemist, educator*
Wachtel, Albert *writer, educator*
Wheeler, Geraldine Hartshorn *historian, writer*
Woodress, James Leslie, Jr. *language educator*
Zehr, Connie *sculptor, art educator*
Zornes, Milford *artist*

## Clarksburg

Merwin, Gregory King *farmer*

## Clayton

Bower, Fay Louise *academic administrator, nursing educator*

---

## Clovis

Badgley, Clifford W. *music educator*
Brahma, Chandra Sekhar *civil engineering educator*
Kawashima, Hope Nozomi *musician*
Shields, Allan Edwin *writer, photographer*
van der Paardt, Tamara Ann *music educator*
Von Prince, Kilulu Magdalene *retired occupational therapist, sculptor*

## Coachella

Gonzales, Martha *elementary school educator*

## Coalinga

Frame, Ted Ronald *lawyer*
Russell, Beverly Ann *librarian, writer*

## Colton

Allen, Blair Hamilton *writer, poet, artist, editor, photographer*
Brown, Jack H. *supermarket company executive*

## Colusa

Carter, Jane Foster *agricultural industry executive*

## Commerce

Crabtree, James Robert *nursing educator*

## Compton

Drew, Sharon Lee *sociologist*
Dymally, Mervyn Malcolm *retired congressman*
Maradiaga Kieffer-Aanonsen, Nora Ludmila *language educator*
McKnight, Carl Phillip *psychologist*
Shiloh, Allen *writer*

## Concord

Accatino, Steven C. *instrumental music educator, orchestra conductor*
Blair, Virginia Devoto *music educator*
Crandall, Ira Carlton *electrical engineer, consultant*
Orris, Donald C. *freight transporation executive*
Seshadri, Srivatsan *optics scientist*
Travers, Judith Lynnette *human resources executive*
Turnbull, Thomas Leigh *social studies educator, secondary school educator*

## Copperopolis

Whisnand, Rex James *association housing executive*
Wooster, Kelly C. *lawyer*

## Corona

Buchen, David A. *lawyer*
Chao, Allen Y. *pharmaceutical executive*
Everett Nollkamper, Pamela Irene *legal association administrator, educator*
Silva, A. R. *surgeon, educator*
White, Joy Mieko *retired communications executive*
Wood, Brenda Jean *pastor, evangelist*

## Corona Del Mar

Allen, Russell G. *lawyer*
Britten, Roy John *biophysicist*
Delap, Tony *artist*
Freeman, Richard Dean *new business start-up service company executive*
Holley, Colin C. *prosecutor*
Indiek, Victor Henry *finance corporation executive*
Jacobs, Donald Paul *architect*
Morisseau, Nan Kruger *television personality*
O'Brien, John William, Jr. *management consultant*
Tobis, Jerome Sanford *physician*
Yeo, Ron *architect*

## Coronado

Axelson, Joseph Allen *professional sports team executive, publishing executive*
Baumer, Edward Ferdinand *finance company executive*
Butcher, Bobby Gene *retired military officer*
Herring, Charles David *lawyer, educator*
Hostler, Charles Warren *retired ambassador, international affairs consultant*
Mock, David Clinton, Jr. *internist*
Moore, Edward, Jr. *career officer*
Raushenbush, Walter Brandeis *retired law educator*
Sack, Edgar Albert *electronics company executive*
Smith, Albert Cromwell, Jr. *investment company executive, writer*

## Corte Madera

Dalpino, Ida Jane *retired secondary school educator*
Tate, John William *consumer products company executive, former food products executive*

## Costa Mesa

Barbarosh, Craig A. *lawyer*
Berman, Stuart B. *information technology executive*
Brady, John Patrick, Jr. *electronics educator, consultant*
Caldwell, Courtney Lynn *lawyer, real estate consultant*
Chambers-Belida, Candace R. *radio personality, writer, television producer, educator*
Cohen, Stanley *commercial real estate developer*
Daniels, James Walter *lawyer*
DeMille, Dianne Lynne *mathematics professor, academic administrator*
Escobar, Evelyn Ernestine *psychologist*
Fones, Monty Garth *secondary school educator*
Frieden, Clifford E. *lawyer*
Gay, William Tolin *lawyer*
Giannini, Valerio Louis *investment banker*
Gottlieb, Jeffrey Paul *journalist*
Grogan, Virginia S. *lawyer*
Guilford, Andrew John *lawyer*
Hay, Howard Clinton *lawyer*
Jones, H(arold) Gilbert, Jr. *lawyer*
Kiang, Assumpta (Amy Kiang) *brokerage house executive*
Lattanzio, Stephen Paul *astronomy educator*
Marshall, Ellen Ruth *lawyer*

Metzger, Vernon Arthur *management educator, consultant*
Mohajer, Dineh *cosmetics company executive*
Mooradian, George T. *lawyer*
Morrow, Donald L. *lawyer*
Muller, Jerome Kenneth *photographer, art director, editor*
Mumford, Lawrence R. *composer, educator*
Ratcliff, Donald Earl *minister, educator*
Rose, I. Nelson *lawyer, educator*
Ruben, Richard S. *lawyer*
Schaaf, Douglas Allan *lawyer*
Scheuneman, Christine A. *lawyer*
Sharpe, Constantine *engineer, consultant, mathematics professor*
Tennyson, Peter Joseph *lawyer*
Williams, William Corey *theology educator, consultant*

**Cotati**
Hill, Debora Elizabeth *writer, journalist, screenwriter*

**Coto De Caza**
Sheehy, Jerome Joseph *electrical engineer*

**Covina**
Baker, Elenora Frances *retired elementary school educator*
Li, Baoyan *science educator, researcher*
Paulson, Raymond Arnold *engineering executive*
Wilkerson, Andrea Leta *musician, educator*

**Cowan Heights**
Ruttencutter, Brian Boyle *manufacturing company executive*

**Crescent City**
Carter, Neville Louis *geophysicist, educator*

**Crestline**
Douglas, Cindy Holloway *financial consultant*
Merrill, Steven William *research and development company executive*

**Crockett**
Silverman, Mervyn F. *health science association administrator, consultant*

**Cromberg**
Kolb, Ken Lloyd *writer*

**Culver City**
Blake, Jeff *film company executive, lawyer*
Boonshaft, Hope Judith *public relations executive*
Brooks, James L. *film producer, director*
Brooks, Mel *film producer, actor, film director, scriptwriter*
Chaffin, Cean *producer*
Coolidge, Matthew *curator*
Eckel, James Robert, Jr. *financial planner*
Evans, Linda (Linda Evanstad) *actress*
Finkelman Cox, Penney *film producer*
Fisher, Lucy *film producer*
Geiselman, LucyAnn *college president*
Grant, Joan Julien *artist*
Hall, Barbara *television producer*
James, Kevin III *actor*
Kaufman, Richard Stuart *conductor*
Landau, Yair *film company executive*
Leve, Alan Donald *electronics executive*
Lynton, Michael *film company executive*
Maltzman, Irving Myron *psychology professor*
Mann, Michael Martin *engineering executive*
Marshall, Garry K. (Garry Kent Marsciarelli) *film producer, director, writer*
Netzel, Paul Arthur *fundraising management executive, consultant*
Nicholas, Frederick M. *lawyer*
Pascal, Amy Beth *film company executive*
Russell, Robin J. *broadcast executive*
Sakai, Richard *motion picture and television executive, producer*
Shamberg, Michael *film producer*
Simmons, Kimora Lee *apparel designer, television personality, model*
Sussman, Deborah Evelyn *interior designer, small business owner*
Thomas, Marlo (Margaret Julia Thomas) *actress*
Tisch, Steven Elliot *television and movie producer*
Trebek, Alex *television game show host*
Van Galder, Valerie *broadcast executive*
Vollack, Lia *broadcast executive*
Wick, Douglas *producer*
Wigan, Gareth *film company executive*
Ziskin, Laura *television producer, film producer*

**Cupertino**
Bregman, Mark *information technology executive*
Clyde, Robert Allan *computer software engineer*
Courville, Arthur F. *lawyer*
Edson, William Alden *retired electrical engineer, researcher*
Fletcher, Homer Lee *librarian*
Haskell, Barry Geoffry *computer engineer, researcher*
Ive, Jonathan *information technology executive, product designer*
Jobs, Steven Paul *computer company executive*
Johnson, Allison *corporate communications specialist, marketing executive*
Johnson, Ron *information technology executive*
Knapp, George Griff Prather *retired insurance executive*
Krauss, Kirk J. *application developer, writer*
Lyon, Mary Lou *retired secondary school educator*
Mathias, Leslie Michael *electronic manufacturing company executive*
Nielsen, Tod *information technology executive*
Oppenheimer, Peter *computer company executive*
Schiller, Philip W. *information technology executive*
Serlet, Bertrand *information technology executive*
Sobrato, John A. *construction executive*
Svalya, Phillip Gordon *lawyer*
Tamaddon, Sina *information technology executive*
Thompson, John W. *information technology executive*

**Cypress**
Cully, Joseph Andrew *hazard substance scientist*
Edmonds, Ivy Gordon *retired writer*
Garrett, Sharon *health services company executive*
Henrickson, Leslie Ann *educational consultant, researcher*
Konowiecki, Joseph Samuel *lawyer, health facility administrator*
Olschwang, Alan Paul *lawyer, crossword puzzle author*
Romero, Tony *information technology executive*
Scott, Gregory W. *health care company executive*
Turbow, David Joseph *education educator, musician*

**Daly City**
Batlin, Robert Alfred *retired newspaper editor*
Hargrave, Sarah Quesenberry *consulting company executive, public relations executive*
Kennedy, Gwendolyn Debra *artist, scriptwriter, playwright*
Sun, Edward Chih-Yu *surgeon, orthopedist*

**Dana Point**
Walker, Doris Isaak *writer, historian, educator*
Wolf, Karl Everett *aerospace transportation executive, communications executive*

**Danville**
Bergsten, James Robert *computer technology architect*
Candland, D. Stuart *lawyer*
Cross, Christopher T. *educational association administrator, consultant*
Harks, Helene Louise *elementary school educator*
Jones, Orlo Dow *retired lawyer, retired pharmaceutical executive*
Whalen, Thomas Earl *psychology professor*
Wisniewski, Stephen Adam *professional football player*

**Darwin**
Palazzo, Robert Paul *lawyer, accountant*

**Davis**
Al-Asaad, Hussain *electrical engineer, educator*
Altisent, Marta *language educator*
Ardans, Alexander Andrew *veterinarian, educator, lab administrator*
Ball, Barry Allen *veterinarian, researcher*
Barakat, Abdul I. *engineering educator*
Barbour, Michael G(eorge) *botanist, educator, ecologist, consultant*
Bartosic, Florian *lawyer, educator*
Basile, Marie Elisabeth *historian, researcher*
Baskin, Ronald Joseph *biophysicist educator, dean*
Bauer, Herbert *retired physician*
Bauer, Ross *composer, music educator*
Biggart, Nicole Woolsey *dean*
Bombardelli, Fabián Alejandro *hydraulic engineer, researcher*
Bower, John Richard Fenn *archaeologist, educator*
Bruch, Carol Sophie *law educator*
Bryant, Brenda K. *psychologist*
Bunch, Richard Alan *writer, educator, poet, philosopher*
Burri, Betty Jane *research chemist*
Cahill, Thomas Andrew *physicist, researcher*
Cannon, William Bernard *retired academic administrator*
Cardiff, Robert Darrell *pathology educator*
Chancellor, William Joseph *agricultural engineering educator*
Cheney, James Addison *civil engineering educator*
Cohen, Lawrence Edward *sociologist, educator, criminologist*
Colvin, Harry Walter, Jr. *physiology educator*
Conn, Eric Edward *plant biochemist*
Day, Howard Wilman *geology educator*
DePaoli, Geri M. (Joan DePaoli) *artist, art historian*
Druzhnikov, Yuri Ilya *literature educator, writer*
Eastin, Delaine Andree *education educator*
Eerkens, Jelmer W. *archaeologist, educator*
Enders, Allen Coffin *anatomy educator*
Epstein, Emanuel *plant physiologist*
Faller, Roland *education educator*
Fannjiang, Albert *mathematician, educator*
Flowers, Ross A. *psychologist*
Gardner, Murray Briggs *pathologist, educator*
Gates, Bruce Clark *chemical engineer, educator*
Gottlieb, Leslie *geneticist, educator*
Greenwood, M. R. C. *biologist, nutrition educator, former academic administrator*
Groth, Alexander Jacob *political science professor*
Hayden, John Olin *English literature educator, writer*
Hess, Charles Edward *environmental horticulture educator*
Hinshaw, Virginia *academic administrator*
Hoffman, Michael Jerome *humanities educator*
Holyoak, Marcel *ecologist, educator*
Hope, Hakon *research scientist*
Horwitz, Barbara Ann *physiologist, educator, consultant*
Imwinkelried, Edward John *law educator*
Irwin, Robert McKee *Spanish educator*
Jensen, Marie Margrete *pathologist, educator*
Jones, Edward George *neuroscience educator, neurologist*
Jungerman, John Albert *physics professor*
Kaloper, Nemanja *physics professor, researcher*
Knittel, Christopher Roland *economics professor, consultant*
Lauchli, Andre E. *science educator*
Liu, Gang-Yu *chemist, educator*
Liu, Kai *physics professor*
Major, Clarence Lee *writer, educator*
Marino, Miguel Angel *engineering educator*
Mason, William A(lvin) *psychologist, educator, researcher*
Maurer, Frank W, Jr. *land trust administrator*
McHenry, Henry Malcolm *anthropologist, educator*
Meyer, Margaret Eleanor *retired microbiologist*
Moyle, Peter Briggs *marine biologist, educator*
Mukherjee, Amiya K. *metallurgy and materials science educator*
Murphy, Terence Martin *biology professor*
Musolf, Lloyd Daryl *political science professor, educational association administrator*

Nash, Charles Presley *chemistry professor*
Ohara, Noriaki *hydrologist*
Owings, Donald Henry *psychologist, educator*
Palmer, Philip Edward Stephen *radiologist*
Pan, Ning *engineering educator*
Patricelli, Gail Lisa *biology professor*
Perschbacher, Rex Robert *dean, law educator*
Pessah, Isaac Ness *pharmacology and toxicology educator*
Poulos, Joan Graham *lawyer*
Pritchard, William Roy *former university systems administrator*
Qualset, Calvin O. *agronomist, educator*
Quinzii, Martine *economics professor*
Rappaport, Lawrence *plant physiology and horticulture educator*
Rhode, Edward Albert *veterinary medicine educator, veterinary cardiologist*
Richman, David Paul *neurologist, educator, researcher*
Ronald, Pamela C. *plant pathologist, educator*
Rost, Thomas Lowell *retired botany educator*
Roth, John Roger *geneticist, biology educator*
Rothchild, Donald Sylvester *political science professor*
Schneeman, Barbara Olds *nutritionist, educator*
Schoener, Thomas William *zoology educator, researcher*
Shackelford, James Floyd *materials science educator, researcher*
Sharrow, Marilyn Jane *library administrator*
Sillman, Arnold Joel *physiologist, educator*
Simonton, Dean Keith *psychology professor*
Skinner, G(eorge) William *anthropologist, educator*
Smith, Michael Peter *social sciences educator, educator*
Sosnick, Stephen Howard *economics professor*
Spindler, George Dearborn *anthropologist, educator, writer*
Springer, Sally Pearl *university administrator*
Stern, Judith Schneider *nutritionist, researcher, educator*
Stroeve, Pieter *chemical engineering researcher, educator*
Stumpf, Paul Karl *biochemistry professor emeritus*
Su, Zhendong *computer scientist, educator*
Sumner, Daniel Alan *economist, educator*
Tanno, John W. *university librarian*
Temple, John Blake *mathematics professor*
Tracy, Craig Arnold *mathematics educator*
Treguboff, William Jack *psychologist*
Trimmer, Jim *neuroscientist, educator*
Troy, Frederic Arthur, II, *medical biochemistry professor*
Turcotte, Donald Lawson *geophysical sciences educator*
Turnlund, Judith Rae *nutritionist*
Van Alfen, Neal K. *plant pathologist*
Vanderhoef, Larry Neil *academic administrator*
Volman, David Herschel *chemistry professor*
Waddington, Raymond Bruce, Jr. *language educator*
Wang, Shih-Ho *electrical engineer, educator*
Watt, Kenneth Edmund Ferguson *zoology educator*
Wegelin, Jacob Andreas *statistician*
Wegge, Leon Louis François *retired economics educator*
Williamson, Alan Bacher *literature educator, poet, writer*
Willis, Frank Roy *historian, educator*
Wolk, Bruce Alan *law educator*
Wydick, Richard Crews *lawyer, educator*

**Del Mar**
Boynton, Robert Merrill *retired psychology professor*
Farquhar, Marilyn Gist *cell biologist, pathologist, educator*
Fricke, Martin Paul *science company executive*
Kaye, Peter Frederic *columnist*
Morton, Frederic *author*
Quinn, Katherine Sarah *psychologist*
Scherger, Joseph Edward *family physician, educator*
Seitman, John Michael *arbitrator, mediator, lawyer*
Wilkinson, Eugene Parks *nuclear engineer, director*

**Delano**
Salmassi, Sadegh *physician*

**Desert Hot Springs**
Laws, Maurice Wesley *set decorator, museum exhibit designer*
Zarres, Sharon L. *marriage and family therapist, health facility administrator*

**Diablo**
Burnison, Boyd Edward *lawyer*

**Diamond Bar**
Domeño, Eugene Timothy *elementary education educator, principal*
Snoop Dogg, (Calvin Broadus) *vocalist, actor*

**Dinuba**
Leps, Thomas MacMaster *civil engineer, consultant*
Surabian, Carol Anne *language educator, consultant*

**Discovery Bay**
Mikalow, Alfred Alexander, II, *deep sea diver, marine surveyor, marine diving consultant*

**Downey**
Achon, Raquel Andrea *music educator, consultant*
Baumann, Theodore Robert *aerospace engineer, consultant, military officer*
Brooks, Lillian Drilling Ashton (Lillian Hazel Church) *adult education educator*
Gong, Henry, Jr. *internist, researcher, educator*
Perry, Jacquelin *orthopedist, surgeon*
Robles, Darline P. *school system administrator*
Shapiro, Richard Stanley *physician*
Takagi, Carol *educational consultant*
Todd, Margaret Donnellan *librarian, director*
Victoroff, Jeff *neurology professor, psychology professor*

Wayman, Joseph McKelden *editor, researcher*

**Duarte**
Bhatia, Smita *epidemiologist, researcher, pediatric oncologist, educator*
Driskill, James Lawrence *minister*
Mojica, Pablo *surgeon*
Riggs, Arthur D. *health facility administrator, research scientist*
Smith, Steven Sidney *molecular biologist*
Yoshida, Akira *biochemist*

**Dublin**
Chen, John S. *computer company executive*
King, Suzanne Dampier *chemistry educator*
Lloyd, Leonard Edward *marriage and family therapist, consultant*
Whetten, John D. *food products executive*

**East Palo Alto**
Bates, William III *lawyer*
Lesser, Henry *lawyer*
Rinsky, Arthur C. *lawyer*
Vaughan, Winston C. *otolaryngologist, surgeon*

**Edwards**
Brand, Vance Devoe *astronaut, director*
Liu, Chi Tsieh *aerospace scientist, researcher*

**El Cajon**
Anthony, Roy Sanford, Jr. *secondary school educator*
Ostermeyer, Maryann *secondary school educator, writer*
Silverberg, Lewis Henry *lawyer, consultant*
Summers, Stanley Eugene *mechanical engineer*
Thomas, Esther Merlene *elementary and adult education educator*

**El Centro**
Gaede, Robert Matthew *music educator*
Steensgaard, Anthony Harvey *federal agency administrator*

**El Cerrito**
Alldredge, Noreen S. *librarian*
Burger, Edmund Ganes *architect*
Kao, Yasuko Watanabe *retired library director*
Ma, L. Eve Armentrout *television producer, educator*
Tayler, David S. *musician*

**El Dorado Hills**
Bartlett, Robert Watkins *metallurgist, educator, consultant*
Sparks, Robert Dean *medical administrator, gastroenterologist*
Tierney, Kevin Allen *elementary school educator*

**El Granada**
Heere, Karen R. *astrophysicist*

**El Macero**
Stowell, Robert Eugene *pathologist, retired educator*

**El Monte**
Mestas, Luis Herrera *theater educator, dancer*

**El Segundo**
Abbassian-Kashi, Mandana *industrial engineer, systems engineer*
Brekke, John Peters *aerospace engineer*
Bryant, Kobe *professional basketball player*
Buss, Jeanie *professional sports team executive*
Carey, Chase (Charles G. Carey) *broadcast executive*
Daughaday, Douglas Robert *computer engineer*
Divac, Vlade *professional basketball player*
Eckert, Robert A. *consumer products company executive*
Fisk, Hayward Dan *lawyer, computer company executive*
Freeland, Pete *aerospace transportation executive, consultant*
Hamel, Michael A. *career officer*
Harwick, Wayne Thomas *economist*
Honeycutt, Van B. *computer company executive*
Hunter, Larry Dean *lawyer*
Jackson, Philip Douglas *professional basketball coach*
Kay, Kenneth Jeffrey *real estate company executive*
Kilpatrick, Frank Stanton *marketing executive*
Laphen, Michael W. *computer company executive*
Leslie, Lisa DeShaun *professional basketball player*
McCarty, Shirley Carolyn *consumer products company executive*
McQuillin, Richard Ross *management consultant*
Milton-Jones, DeLisha *professional basketball player*
Muhlbach, Robert Arthur *lawyer*
Musk, Elon *aerospace transportation executive*
Odom, Lamar Joseph *professional basketball player*
Oei, Lok S. *digital communications systems and DSP engineer, researcher*
Palkovic, Michael W. *broadcast executive*
Seymour, Scott *science administrator*
Thiry, Kent J. *health products executive*
Toler, Penny *former professional basketball player, sports team executive*
Tucker, Paul Thomas *computer company executive*
Vollrath, Frederick E. *human resources specialist, career officer*
Weatherspoon, Teresa Gaye *professional basketball player*
Webb, Darryl Willard *systems engineer*
Willis, Judy Ann *lawyer*

**Eldridge**
Schain, Richard *neurologist, consultant*

**Elk Grove**
Forbes, Kenneth Albert Faucher *urologist, retired surgeon*
Lichtman, Debbie *writer, secondary school educator*

McDavid, Douglas Warren *executive research consultant*
Moe, Janet Anne *elementary school educator, church organist*
Romano, Sheila June *telecommunications industry professional, writer, artist*

**Elmira**
Montoya, Malaquias *art educator, artist*

**Emerald Hills**
Chao, Kwang-Chu *chemical engineer, educator*

**Emeryville**
Bartels, Ursula Brennan *lawyer*
Bax, Simon Tristan *film company executive*
Bird, Brad *film director, writer, animator*
Catmull, Edwin E. *film company executive, computer graphics engineer*
Chiasson, William B. *electronic games executive*
Choi, Doo-Sup *molecular biologist*
Fields, Howard Lincoln *neurologist, physiologist, educator*
Goldstein, Jack *biopharmaceutical executive, microbiologist*
Gombocz, Erich Alfred *biochemist*
Houghton, Michael *geneticist*
Howe, Drayton Ford, Jr. *lawyer*
Hurst, Deborah *pediatric hematologist*
Kalinske, Thomas J. *education, video game and toy company executive*
Katz, Jeffrey G. *electronic games executive*
Lasseter, John A. *film company executive, computer animator*
Masri, Merle Sid *biochemist, consultant*
Palmer, Craig *digital music and media company executive*
Pien, Howard *pharmaceutical executive*
Renton, Hollings C. *health products executive*
Roberts, Dale (Ty) *digital music and media company executive*
Roth, Joe *motion picture company executive*
Smith, Christopher Allen *information technology executive, financial executive*
Teufel, William Lockwood *emergency physician*
White, Raymond Leslie *geneticist*
Zwoyer, Eugene Milton *retired consulting engineering executive*

**Encinitas**
Ford, William Francis *retired bank holding company executive*
Kim, Kyehee *environmental engineer, consultant*
Litvin, Inessa Elizabeth *piano educator*

**Encino**
Bright, Kevin S. *producer*
Church, Kathy Lynn *education educator, consultant*
Friedman, George Jerry *aerospace engineer, engineering executive*
Genga, John Michael *lawyer*
Glickman, Daniel Robert *motion picture association executive, former congressman*
Greenberg, Allan *advertising and marketing research consultant*
House, Karen Sue *nursing consultant*
Ingels, Marty *agent, broadcast executive*
Irmas, Audrey Menein *not-for-profit developer*
Kempisty, Michael *artist, writer, actor*
Knuth, Eldon Luverne *engineering educator*
Lesavoy, Malcolm Alan *plastic surgeon*
Parrott, Dennis Beecher *retired insurance company executive*
Pisano, A. Robert *former actors guild executive, former film company executive*
Rawitch, Robert Joe *journalist, educator*
Shire, David Lee *composer*
Smith, Selma Moidel *lawyer, composer*
Sungaila, Mary-Christine (M.C. Sungaila) *lawyer*
Taylor, Renee *actress, writer*
Vogel, Susan Carol *nursing administrator*
Westmore, Michael George *make-up artist, writer*
Wilder, Gene *actor, film director, writer*

**Escalon**
Barton, Gerald Lee *food products executive*

**Escondido**
Bakko, Orville Edwin *retired health facility administrator*
Briggs, Edward Samuel *naval officer*
Carey, Catherine Anita *artist, art educator*
Damsbo, Ann Marie *psychologist*
Dannenberg, Otto Doyle *retired optometrist*
Ehrhart, Joseph Edward *retired broadcast technician*
Guinn, Stanley Willis *lawyer*
Kennedy, Robert Philip *civil engineer*
Linzey, Verna May *minister, writer*
McCarberg, Bill Harold *physician*
Moore, Marc Anthony *retired academic administrator, writer, retired military officer*
Newman, Barry Ingalls *retired bank executive*
Newsome, Melinda *anthropologist*
Rockwell, Elizabeth Goode *dance company director, consultant, educator*
Sanders, Adrian Lionel *retired educational consultant*
Sloan, Anne Elizabeth *food scientist, writer*
Tomomatsu, Hideo *chemist*
Walker, Patricia Ann *special education educator*

**Eureka**
Cox, Christopher Mark *music educator*
Hannaford, Peter Dor *public relations executive, writer*
Robinson, Michael Kevin *lawyer*

**Fair Oaks**
Chernev, Melvin *retired beverage company executive*
Hoehn, Robert Guthrie *science educator*
Hutton, Essex Clark, Sr. *adult education educator*
Lemke, Herman Ernest Frederick, Jr. *retired elementary school educator, consultant*
Potter, George Kenneth *artist*

**Fairfax**
Kadoyama, Margaret *anthropology educator, management consultant*

**Fairfield**
Gelpke, Peter Hall *science educator, department chairman*
Haas, Richard *lawyer*
Herring, Lynne D. *secondary school educator*
Schunke, Hildegard Heidel *accountant*
Spake, Reuben Michael *mathematics professor, researcher*

**Fallbrook**
Freeman, Harry Lynwood *retired accountant*
Harsha, Philip Thomas *retired aerospace engineer*
Ragland, Jack Whitney *artist*
Sorbello, Joseph Charles *retired lawyer*

**Felicity**
Istel, Jacques Andre *mayor*

**Felton**
Kulzick, Ken Stafford *retired lawyer, writer*

**Flintridge**
Johnston, Oliver Martin, Jr., (Ollie Johnston) *animator*

**Folsom**
Anderson, Jeffrey Lee *physician, anesthesiologist, consultant*
Bahbah, Amr G. *application developer, consultant*
Ewing, Russell Charles, II, *physician*
Haga, Enoch John *computer educator, writer*
Jefferds, William John *military officer*
Krishnaswamy, Dilip *computer architect*
Regan, William Joseph, Jr. *energy company executive*
Ryu, Woong Hwan *electrical engineer*
Sarraf, Shirley A. *secondary school educator*

**Fontana**
Afagh, Arman *physician*
Ferreri, Michael Victor *optometrist*
Johna, Samir *surgeon*

**Fort Bragg**
Gjerde, Rosalie Carolyn *music educator, conductor*

**Fortuna**
Johnson, Louanna B. *retired small business owner*
Souza, Jonathan Raymond *music educator, conductor*

**Foster City**
Bischofberger, Norbert W. *medical products company executive*
Butcher, C. Preston *real estate company executive*
Coghlan, John Philip *corporate financial executive*
Denny, James M. *pharmaceutical executive, former retail executive*
Hotz, Henry Palmer *retired physicist*
Liu, Leonard *software services company executive*
Lonnquist, George Eric *lawyer*
Lutvak, Mark Allen *computer company executive*
Martin, John C. *pharmaceutical company executive*
Miller, Jon Philip *marketing professional, pharmaceutical executive*
Scheer, Janet Kathy *mathematics professor*
Yan, Martin *celebrity chef*
Zaidi, Iqbal Mehdi *biochemist, research scientist*

**Fountain Valley**
Armstrong, Jeffrey Lee *oceanographer*
Berman, Steven Richard *computer company executive*
Broderick, Daniel P. *lawyer*
Davis, Jeremy Matthew *chemist*
Einstein, Stephen Jan *rabbi*
Hoffman, Richard W. *automotive executive*
Kieu, Quynh Dinh *pediatrician, not-for-profit developer*
Le, Vinh Tu *retired language educator, translator*
Otto, Marie (Bertha Otto) *educational administrator, educational consulting company executive*
Smith, Marie Edmonds *real estate agent, property manager*
Treadway-Dillmon, Linda Lee *actress, stuntwoman, dancer, dispatcher*

**Fowler**
Bowman, Joseph Paul *protective services official, writer, retired military officer*

**Frazier Park**
Edwards, Sarah Anne *social worker, psychologist*

**Fremont**
Bagley, James W. *semiconductor equipment company executive*
Berman Salot, Jeannette Goldberg *retired elementary school educator*
Bray, Richard Daniel *librarian*
Chen, Wai-Kai *electrical engineering and computer science educator, consultant*
Chien-Hale, Elizabeth *lawyer*
Clarke, Christina *epidemiologist, educator*
Duan, Xiaodong *engineer*
Henry, Leo G. *engineer, consultant*
Huang, Robert *electronics executive*
Jensen, Paul Edward Tyson *business executive, consultant*
Korn, Laurence *health products executive*
Lankford, James E. *food service executive*
Le, Thuy Trong *nuclear engineer, educator*
Liang, Christine *import company executive*
Lin, Sharon Shiang Chien *librarian*
Lyons, Irving (Bud) III *corporate financial executive*
Newberry, Stephen G. *semiconductor equipment company executive*
Parikh, Mihir *consumer products company executive*
Pipkin, Robert Donald *quality assurance professional, cardiologist*
Rusch, Thomas William *manufacturing executive*
Smith, Bernald Stephen *retired pilot*
Tang, John *network technician, information scientist, engineer*
Tantra, Muljadi *corporate marketing professional*
Venturini, Judith Anne *education educator*

Wood, Linda May *librarian*
Wu, James Chen-Yuan *aerospace engineering educator*
Yamamoto, Masako *music educator*
Zimmer, George A. *men's apparel executive*

**Fresno**
Anglen, Brandy Lynn *geologist, educator*
Autry, Alan *mayor, actor, former professional football player, film company executive*
Battista, Matthew Antonio *psychologist, neuroscientist*
Bundy-DeSoto, Teresa Mari *language educator, vocalist*
Burnett, Lynn Barkley *health science educator*
Corless, Dorothy Alice *nursing educator*
Cornish, Bonita Clark *retired secondary school educator*
Coyle, Robert Everett *federal judge*
Cunningham, Mark Alan *surgeon*
Dackawich, S. John *sociology educator, academic administrator*
Darden, Edwin Speight, Sr. *architect*
Dauer, Donald Dean *investment company executive*
De La Cruz-Reyes, Pilar L. *nursing administrator*
Edwards, Lynne Marie *information technology consultant*
Epperson, Robert Dale *farmer*
Ewell, A. Ben, Jr. *lawyer, small business owner*
Fortune, Larry M. *real estate broker*
Ganulin, Judy *public relations professional*
Garrison-Finderup, Ivadelle Dalton *writer, educator*
Genini, Ronald Walter *retired history educator, historian*
Gorman, Michael Joseph *library director, educator*
Harris, Breck Anthony *business educator, writer, researcher*
Ishii, Anthony W. *judge*
Jenkins, David Ray *lawyer*
Joseph, James William *political scientist, consultant, educator*
Kauffman, George Bernard *chemistry professor*
Kouymjian, Dickran *art historian, educator*
Kristensen, Allan Erik *music educator*
Lambe, James Patrick *lawyer*
Lanter, Lanore *writer, educator*
Leigh, Hoyle *psychiatrist, educator, writer*
Little, Kevin Gerard *lawyer*
McConnell, Charles Prescott *retired science educator*
Misakian, Jo Ellen Priest *school librarian, dean*
Morales, Hugo *broadcast executive*
O'Connor, Kevin John *psychologist, educator*
Ortiz, John Michael *provost*
Palmer, Samuel Copeland III *lawyer*
Patnaude, William Eugene *architect*
Patton, Jack Thomas *family practice physician*
Pings, Anthony Claude *architect*
Rank, Everett George *federal agency administrator*
Raven, Patricia Elaine (Penny Raven) *real estate broker, developer, columnist, gas industry executive*
Rojeski, Hallie E. *elementary school educator*
Shmavonian, Gerald S. *political organization administrator*
Smith, Richard Howard *banker*
Steinbock, John Thomas *bishop*
Tellier, Richard Davis *management educator*
Tudman, Cathi Graves *elementary school educator*
Wample, Robert Lee *research scientist, director*
Welch, Jack Hamill *retired internist*
Welty, John Donald *academic administrator*
Wilson, James Ross *communications educator, broadcast executive*
Winslow, Norman Eldon *small business owner*
Winter, Robert Frank *biologist, educator*
Xiong, Tousu Saydangnmvang *minister, theology studies educator*

**Fullerton**
Ackerman, Richard Charles *lawyer, state legislator*
Ayala, John L. *retired librarian, dean*
Baugh, William Preston *dermatologist*
Bush, William Merritt *lawyer*
Carrithers, Joseph Edward *English composition and literature educator*
Chaudhry, Maqsood Ahmed *electrical engineer, educator*
Childers, James Gregory *physicist, educator, research scientist*
Dolhinow, Rebecca *geographer, educator*
Donoghue, Mildred Ransdorf *education educator*
Fischer, Robert Blanchard *academic administrator, researcher*
Foote, Paul Sheldon *business educator, administrator, consultant*
Frost, Jacqueline Beth *cinematographer, educator*
Garrett, Scott T. *medical products executive*
Goldstein, Edward David *lawyer, former glass company executive*
Johnson, Carolyn Elizabeth *librarian*
Kaisch, Kenneth Burton *psychologist, priest*
Levesque, Paul Joseph *religious studies educator*
Lewandoski, Robert Henry *editor, publisher*
May, William Hathaway *lawyer*
McNamee, Lawrence Ross, Jr. *manufacturing executive*
Miller, Arnold *electronics executive*
Moerbeek, Stanley Leonard *lawyer*
Montgomery, Thom Mathew *health program administrator, counselor*
Monty, Louis Harold *psychiatrist*
Parman, Susan Morrissett *anthropologist, writer*
Roberts, Mark Scott *lawyer*
Rubin, Arthur Leonard *systems engineer, mathematician*
Sadrudin, Moe *humanitarian organization executive*
Shapiro, Mark Howard *physicist, educator, dean*
Smith, Ephraim Philip *academic administrator*
Sowder, Kathleen Adams *marketing executive*
Steinmeyer, Robert Jay *retired lawyer*
Sugarman, Michael *physician, rheumatologist*
Wareham, John P. *medical products executive*
Wiley, David Cole *television producer*
Woods, Betty *insurance company executive*
Woyski, Margaret Skillman *retired geology educator*
Zettel, Laura A. *psychology professor, researcher*

**Garberville**
Nyokka, Suzette *artist, natural health educator*

**Garden Grove**
Greenslade, Cindy Louise *psychologist*
Lichty, Jolene Jennings *elementary school educator*
Schuller, Robert Harold *minister, writer*
Schwalm, Laura *school system administrator*
Williams, J(ohn) Tilman *insurance company executive, real estate agent, municipal official*

**Garden Valley**
Price, Lew Paxton *writer, engineer*

**Gardena**
Bornino-Glusac, Anna Maria *retired mathematics professor*
Harvey, Cyril Leslie *education educator*
Hite, Janet Sue *elementary school educator*
Hume-Dawson, Rodney Babatune *education educator*

**Gilroy**
Barham, Warren Sandusky *horticulturist*
McCarty, Robert Clarke *mathematician*
Wu, Wayne Wen-Yau *artist*

**Glen Ellen**
Berkland, James Omer *geologist*
Haslag, Karen Christine *art educator, musician*
Hurlbert, Roger William *information technology executive*

**Glendale**
Belk, Jennifer Elizabeth *human resources specialist*
Blackwell, Linda Jane *elementary school educator*
Coleman, Lewis Waldo *film company executive, former bank executive*
Cross, Richard John *bank executive*
Dallas, Saterios (Sam Dallas) *aerospace engineer, researcher, consultant*
Daly, Ann Michelle *broadcast executive*
de Grassi, Leonard *art historian, educator*
DeLuca, Michael *film company executive*
Ebersole, Todd Michael *lawyer*
Ebert, Gerard (Gerry Ebert) *hypnotherapist, freelance/self-employed writer*
Enrico, Roger A. *film company executive, retired soft drink company executive*
Gedjeyan, Hovannes John *real estate broker*
Geffen, David Lawrence *film company executive, former recording company executive*
Gibbons, Leeza *television and radio talk show host, entertainment reporter*
Hadley, Paul Ervin *international relations educator*
Hoffman, Donald M. *lawyer*
Hong, Christian Sang *history educator*
Hughes, Bradley Wayne *storage company executive*
Irwin, Dianne E. *psychology professor*
Katzenberg, Jeffrey *film company executive*
Kay, Alan C. *computer scientist, nonprofit organization executive*
Kazanjian, Phillip Carl *lawyer, educator*
Kendrick, Katherine *lawyer*
Khatchaturian, Hovik Malhami *real estate broker*
King, Keith B.W. *lawyer*
MacDonald, Kirk Stewart *lawyer*
MacDonald, Laurie *film company executive*
Martinetti, Ronald Anthony *lawyer*
Michelson, Lillian *librarian, researcher*
Misa, Kenneth Franklin *management consultant*
O'Day, Anita Belle Colton *entertainer, musician, vocalist*
Parkes, Walter F. *film company executive*
Robinson, Smokey (William Robinson) *singer, composer*
Ross, Bruce Shields *lawyer*
Scott, A. Timothy *lawyer*
Shahshahani, Ahmad *economics professor*
Snider, Stacey *film company executive*
Sotelo, Eduardo (El Piolín) *radio personality*
Spring, Carl Chaffee, Jr. *writer*
Sprosty, Joseph Patrick *film producer, writer, motion picture weapons specialist*
Stack, Kevin J. *lawyer*
Stewart, Julia A. *food service executive*
Thallander, Mark Alan *music educator*
Uhrich, Kevin Patrick *editor*
Whalen, Lucille *retired academic administrator*
Woolls, Esther Blanche *library science educator*

**Glendora**
Haile, Benjamin Carroll, Jr. *retired chemical engineer, retired mechanical engineer*
Lasko, Allen Howard *pharmacist*
Prukesatonkul, Kamol *music educator*
Schiele, Paul Ellsworth, Jr. *retired academic administrator, writer*
Thornburg, Lee Ellis *film executive, director*

**Gold River**
Andrew, John Henry *lawyer, writer*
Shaw, Eleanor Jane *newspaper editor*

**Goleta**
Everhart, Thomas Eugene *retired academic administrator, engineering educator*
Gilbert, Richard Keith *education educator, researcher*
Jerphagnon, Olivier L. *telecommunications industry executive*
Sensiper, Samuel *electrical engineer*
Tighe, Thomas *non-profit organization executive*
Wu, Jingchun *research scientist*
Zuk, Carmen Veiga *psychiatrist*

**Granada Hills**
Aller, Wayne Kendall *psychologist, educator, computer company executive, property manager*
Paton, Jim Glenn *voice educator*
Pulido-Ragus, Elisa S. *secondary school educator, department chairman*
Shoemaker, Harold Lloyd *information scientist*

**Granite Bay**
Hartmann, Frederick Howard *retired political science professor*

**La Habra Heights**
Agajanian, Gilda *pianist*

**La Jolla**
Adams, Marc Anthony *medical statistician, researcher*
Akiskal, Hagop Souren *psychiatric researcher, educator*
Andre, Michael Paul *physicist, educator*
Anthony, Harry Antoniades *retired city planner, architect, educator*
Antin, David *poet, critic*
Arnold, James Richard *chemist, educator*
Asaro, Robert J. *engineering educator*
Asmus, John Fredrich *physicist*
Atai, Manucher *surgeon*
Atkinson, Richard Chatham *academic administrator, cognitive scientist*
Backus, George Edward *theoretical geophysicist*
Baesel, Stuart Oliver *architect*
Bailey, David Nelson *pathology educator, dean, academic administrator*
Bardwick, Judith Marcia *management consultant*
Barrett-Connor, Elizabeth Louise *epidemiologist, educator*
Barshop, Bruce A. *science educator*
Bavasi, Peter Joseph *sports management executive*
Beebe, Mary Livingstone *curator*
Berger, Wolfgang H. *oceanographer, educator, geologist, space director*
Best, Brookie Manning Dugan *pharmacist*
Beutler, Ernest *physician, research scientist*
Blanchard, Daniel G. *cardiologist*
Bloom, Floyd Elliott *internist, neuroscientist*
Boger, Dale L. *chemistry professor*
Bottini, Massimo *medical researcher*
Bower, Christopher James *investment banker*
Bradner, Hugh *retired physics professor*
Branscomb, Lewis McAdory *physicist, researcher*
Brooks, Charles Lee III *computational biophysicist, educator*
Buchholz, Debby *lawyer*
Bucko, Carroll Dennis *plastic surgeon*
Burbidge, E. Margaret *astronomer, educator*
Burbidge, Geoffrey *astrophysicist, educator*
Burgin, George Hans *computer scientist, educator*
Cain, William Stanley *experimental psychologist, educator, researcher*
Carmichael, David Burton *physician*
Cavenee, Webster K. *director*
Chandler, Marsha *academic administrator, educator*
Chang, William Shen Chie *electrical engineering educator*
Chien, Shu *physiology and bioengineering educator*
Chisari, Francis V. *pathologist*
Chrispeels, Maarten Jan *biology professor*
Cleveland, Don W. *biomedical researcher*
Coburn, Marjorie Foster *psychologist, educator*
Continetti, Robert E. *chemistry professor*
Copley, David C. *newspaper publishing company executive*
Counts, Stanley Thomas *retired military officer, retired electronics executive*
Cowhey, Peter Francis *international relations educator, consultant*
Cox, Charles Shipley *oceanography researcher, educator*
Dalessio, Donald John *internist, neurologist, educator*
Dandan, Randa Hilal *pharmacologist, researcher*
Davidow, Jeffrey *former ambassador to Mexico*
Davies, Hugh Marlais *museum director*
Davis, Brian Keith *biophysicist, researcher*
Dennis, Edward Alan *chemistry and biochemistry professor*
Deutsch, Alin Bernard *computer scientist, educator*
Dimsdale, Joel Edward *psychiatry educator*
Dixon, Frank James *pathologist, educator*
Dixon, Jack Edward *biological chemistry professor, consultant*
Drake, Hudson Billings *aerospace executive, electronics executive*
Driscoll, Charles Frederick *physicist, educator*
Edelman, Gerald Maurice *biochemist, neuroscientist, educator*
Edgington, Thomas S. *pathologist, educator, molecular biologist, vascular biologist*
Edwards, Charles Cornell *surgeon, medical association administrator*
Elander, Richard Paul *microbiologist, consultant*
Elman, Jeffrey Locke *cognitive sciences educator*
Emr, Scott David *biology professor, consultant*
Evans, Ronald M. *microbiologist, educator*
Farson, Richard Evans *psychologist*
Feher, George *biophysicist, educator*
Fogler, Michael *physicist*
Foley, L(ewis) Michael *real estate company officer*
Fowler, Raymond Dalton *psychologist, educator*
Foxe, Marye Anne *academic administrator*
Freedman, David Noel *religious studies educator*
Freedman, Jonathan Borwick *journalist, writer, educator*
Friedmann, Theodore *physician*
Fung, Yuan-Cheng Bertram *bioengineering educator, writer*
Gaasterland, Terry *biotechnologist, educator*
Garland, Cedric Frank *epidemiologist, educator*
Geckler, Richard Delph *retired metal products executive*
Gilbert, James Freeman *geophysics educator*
Gill, Gordon N. *medical educator*
Glatt, Stephen Joseph *psychiatry educator*
Granger, Clive William John (Sir Clive Granger) *retired economist*
Guillemin, Roger C.L. *physiologist*
Haddad, Gabriel D. *pediatrician, educator*
Halkin, Hubert *mathematics professor, research mathematician*
Hallin, Daniel Clark *communications educator*
Hamburger, Robert N. *pediatrician, educator, consultant*
Han, Jiahuai *medical researcher*
Harilal, Sivanandan S. *physicist, researcher*
Harris, Philip Robert *management and space psychologist*
Harris, T. George *editor*
Harrison, Larry J. *health facility administrator*
Hawkinson, Tim *sculptor*

Haxo, Francis Theodore *marine biologist*
Heeb, Mary Jo *biochemist, researcher*
Helinski, Donald Raymond *biologist, educator*
Hendrickson, David Norman *chemistry professor*
Henig, Suzanne *retired academic administrator, editor, writer*
Hermann, Thomas C. *chemistry professor*
Hester, Perrietta Burke *artist, educator*
Hofmann, Alan Frederick *biomedical researcher, educator*
Holmes, Edward Warren *dean, medical educator*
Horner, Anthony Adam *pediatrician, educator*
Imana, Jorge Garron *artist*
Itano, Harvey Akio *biochemistry educator*
Jacobson, Gary Charles *political science professor*
Jambon, Martin Rufus *research scientist*
Kaback, Michael *medical educator*
Kabantsev, Andrey *physicist, educator*
Kadonaga, James Takuro *biochemist*
Kaplan, Robert Malcolm *health researcher, educator*
Karbhari, Vistasp M. *engineering educator, researcher*
Karin, Sidney *computer science engineering educator*
Karlen, Peter Hurd *lawyer, writer*
Kassel, Daniel Brian *biotechnologist, researcher*
Katzman, Robert *neurologist, medical educator*
Kearns, David Richard *chemistry professor*
Kehler, Andrew S. *computer scientist, educator*
Kelly, Jeffrey W. *chemist, educator*
Kennel, Charles Frederick *physics professor, academic administrator, government official*
Kent, Paula *public relations, marketing and management consultant, lecturer*
Khan, Imran *education educator*
Kirchheimer, Arthur E(dward) *lawyer, stock exchange executive*
Kitada, Shinichi *biochemist*
Klonoff-Cohen, Hillary Sandra *epidemiologist*
Kolodner, Richard David *biochemist, educator, director*
Lake, David A. *political science professor*
Lal, Devendra *nuclear geophysics educator*
Langacker, Ronald Wayne *linguistics educator*
Lauer, James Lothar *physicist, researcher*
Ledermann, Robert Joseph *social worker, psychotherapist*
Levy, Ralph *engineering executive, consultant*
Lewin, Ralph Arnold *biologist*
Liu, Shumo *molecular biologist*
Low, Mary Louise (Molly Low) *documentary photographer*
Low, Philip Steven *research scientist*
Lydon, Nicholas B. (Nick Lydon) *biochemist, pharmaceutical executive, researcher*
Macagno, Eduardo R. *biology professor, dean*
Machina, Mark Joseph *economist*
Mah, Silvia Armitano *director, educator*
Mandler, George *psychologist, educator*
Mandler, Jean Matter *psychologist, educator*
Maple, M. Brian *physics professor*
Marti, Kurt *chemistry professor*
Martin, James John, Jr. *systems analyst, retired research and development company executive*
Mayer, James Hock *lawyer, mediator*
McCammon, James Andrew *chemistry professor*
McDonald, Marianne *classicist*
Mendoza, Stanley Atran *pediatric nephrologist, educator*
Merrim, Louise Meyerowitz *artist, actress*
Miller, David R. *academic administrator*
Miller, Stanley Lloyd *chemistry and biochemistry professor*
Milstein, Laurence Bennett *electrical engineering educator, researcher*
Miyoshi, Masao *literature educator, writer*
Molina, Mario Jose *physical chemist, educator*
Moossa, A. R. *surgeon, educator*
Nahavandi, Amir Nezameddin *retired engineering firm executive*
Najmabadi, Farrokh *engineering educator*
Nakamura, Robert Motoharu *pathologist*
Nemat-Nasser, Sia *engineering educator, researcher*
Nicolaou, K. C. *chemistry professor*
Nyhan, William Leo *pediatrician, educator*
Olafson, Frederick Arlan *philosophy educator*
O'Neil, Thomas Michael *physicist, researcher*
Oreskes, Naomi *science historian*
Patton, Stuart *biochemist, educator*
Penner, Stanford Sol *director*
Phelps, Jerry Scott *psychologist, educator*
Poole, Keith T. *political science professor*
Rahman, Yueh-Erh *biologist*
Rajasekar, Arcot *computer scientist*
Rauch, James E. *economics professor*
Rearden, Carole Ann *clinical pathologist, educator*
Reed, John C. *physician, researcher*
Reynolds, Roger Lee *composer, educator*
Richman, Douglas Daniel *medical virologist, educator, internist*
Ride, Sally Kristen *physics professor, research scientist, retired astronaut*
Rinaker, Samuel Mayo, Jr. *retired utilities executive*
Rosen, Judah Ben *computer scientist*
Rotenberg, Manuel *physics professor*
Rubin, Lewis J. *physician, researcher*
Rudee, Mervyn Lea *engineering educator, researcher*
Saldivar, Enrique *bioengineer, researcher*
Savoia, Maria Christina *vice dean*
Schimmel, Paul Reinhard *biochemist, biophysicist, educator*
Schmid-Schoenbein, Geert Wilfried *biomedical engineer, educator*
Schneider, Benjamin *psychology professor, consultant*
Schneider, Gerald L. *plastic surgeon*
Schottlaender, Brian E.C. *university librarian*
Schroeder, Julian Ivan *biology professor*
Schuller, John Kohn *physicist*
Scull, Andrew T. *sociologist, educator*
Seagren, Stephen Linner *oncologist*
Seible, Frieder *structural engineer, educator*
Shakespeare, Frank *ambassador*
Sham, Lu Jeu *physics professor, physicist*
Sharpless, K. Barry *chemist, educator*
Sherman, Irwin William *biological sciences educator, academic administrator*

Shor, George G., Jr. *geophysicist, oceanographic administrator, engineer*
Shuler, Kurt Egon *chemist, educator*
Siegel, Jay Steven *chemistry educator*
Silver, Dee Edward *physician, neurologist*
Singer, Robert *plastic surgeon*
Sinha, Sunil Kumar *physicist*
Snyder, Evan *cloning and stem cell company administrator, educator, neuroscientist*
Somerville, Richard Chapin James *atmospheric scientist, educator*
Starr, Ross Marc *economist, educator*
Steinberg, Daniel *preventive medicine physician, educator*
Stone, Donald Diamond *investment and sales executive*
Sullivan, Robert S. *college dean*
Swain, Judith Lea *cardiologist, educator*
Tan, Eng Meng *immunologist, biomedical researcher*
Taupenot, Laurent *medical educator, researcher*
Taylor, Palmer W. *pharmacology educator*
Taylor, Susan Serota *biochemist, researcher*
Telengator, Alexander M. *engineer*
Thiemens, Mark H. *chemistry professor*
Thomas, Charles Allen, Jr. *molecular biologist, educator*
Thompson, Charlotte Ellis *pediatrician, educator, writer*
Thompson, Emily *historian*
Tsien, Roger Yonchien *chemist, cell biologist*
Tsuang, Ming Tso *psychiatrist, educator*
Tsuji, Frederick Ichiro *biochemist, molecular biologist*
Tyrberg, Björn *cell biologist*
Van Lint, Victor Anton Jacobus *physicist*
Waddy, Lawrence Heber *writer*
Walker, Richard Hugh *orthopaedic surgeon*
Wallach, Nolan R. *mathematician, consultant*
Wang, Lei *biochemist*
Wang, Xudong *network architect, researcher*
Watson, Kenneth Marshall *physics professor*
Wesling, Donald Truman *English literature educator*
West, John Burnard *physiologist, educator*
Whaley, Storm Hammond *retired federal agency administrator*
Wilkie, Donald Walter *retired biologist, aquarium administrator*
Wilkins, Floyd, Jr. *lawyer, educator*
Wilson, Bonnie Jean *lawyer, educator, investor*
Wolynes, Peter Guy *chemistry researcher, educator*
Wright, Andrew *English literature educator*
Wulbert, Daniel Eliot *mathematician, educator*
Yen, Samuel S(how)-C(hih) *obstetrician, gynecologist, educator, endocrinologist*
yLang, Lenore Schulman *visual artist*
Zhongren, Cao *chemical engineer, researcher*
Zimmermann, Joerg *biophysicist*

**La Mesa**
Boghairi, Anoushiravan *cardiologist*
Browne, Juanita Maria *academic administrator, social sciences educator*
Charleton, Margaret Ann *child care administrator, consultant*
Hansen, Grant Lewis *retired air transportation executive*
Kinzel, David L. *elementary school educator*
Schmidt, James Craig *retired bank executive, savings and loan association executive*

**La Mirada**
Edwards, John Kent *religious studies educator, minister*

**La Palma**
Knowles, Marie L. *transportation executive*
Levy, Elaine Ann *music educator*
Thelander, Beverly *oil company executive*

**La Puente**
Hitchcock, Frederick E., Jr., (Fritz Hitchcock) *automotive company executive*
Rojo De Santos, Anita *shop owner, writer*
Vetter, Lawrence Anthony *art educator, consultant*

**La Quinta**
Calvin, James Willard *thoracic and vascular surgeon*
Eversole, Barbara Louise *administrative assistant*
Henry, Nancy Louise *hospitality executive, mayor*
Hull, Kathryn Blomquist *music educator, composer, consultant*
Knoblauch, Mary Reilly (Mary Louise Reilly) *retired music educator, writer*
Pitkin, Roy Macbeth *retired obstetrician, educator*
Sylk, Robert F. *casino marketing executive*

**La Verne**
Barrett, Robert Matthew *lawyer, educator*
Fleck, Raymond Anthony, Jr. *retired academic administrator*
Jalbert, Janelle Jennifer *executive recruiter, secondary school educator*
Kent, Steven Kyle *theater director, educator*
Lou, Yiming *chemical engineer*
Morgan, Stephen Charles *academic administrator*
O'Brien, James D. *language educator, communications executive*

**Lafayette**
Davies, Paul Lewis, Jr. *retired lawyer*
Dethero, J. Hambright *banker*
Edwards, Aura C. *political organization worker, volunteer*
Krueger, Robert Edward *mechanical engineer, manufacturing executive*
Lewis, Sheldon Noah *technology consultant*
Shurtleff, Akiko Aoyagi *artist, consultant*

**Laguna Beach**
Anderson, Elizabeth Carmal (Bette Anderson) *librarian, writer*
Arnold, John David *management counselor*
Bent, Alan Edward *political science professor*
Bernstein, Jean Newman *retired public health information officer*
Chevli, Lyn *writer*
Dana, Edward Runkle *retired physician*

Englund, Robert *actor, director, producer*
Foote, Kay Rebber *artist*
Hanauer, Joe Franklin *real estate company officer*
Matzdorff, James Arthur *investment banker, internet marketing professional*
Pelton, Virginia Lue *small business owner*
Taylor, Theodore Langhans *retired author*

**Laguna Hills**
Green, Millie Ann *mathematician, educator*
Hammond, R. Philip *chemical engineer*
Reinglass, Michelle Annette *lawyer*
Rossiter, Bryant William *chemistry consultant*
Widyolar, Sheila Gayle *dermatologist*

**Laguna Niguel**
Axon, Donald Carlton *architect*
Bauer, Barbara A. *financial consultant*
Greenberg, Lenore *public relations professional*
York, James Orison *real estate executive*

**Laguna Woods**
Badgley, John Roy *architect*
Berk, Jack Edward *gastroenterologist, educator*
Hussey, William Bertrand *retired diplomat*
Leonard, Elizabeth Adney *social worker*
McClure, Hal H. *film producer*
Ross, Mathew *medical educator*
Wheatley, Melvin Ernest, Jr. *retired bishop*

**Lagunitas**
Holman, Arthur Stearns *artist*

**Lake Arrowhead**
Fitzgerald, John Charles, Jr. *investment banker*

**Lake Elsinore**
Druskoff, Barbara Therese *elementary school educator*
Young, Patricia Janean *speech pathology/audiology services professional*

**Lake Forest**
Blackley, Daniel John *theater educator, theater director*
Boccia/Stacy, Judy Elaine *home health agency executive, consultant*
Cranmer, Scotty *professional trick bike rider*
Fahim, Amr *electrical engineer*
Goldsmith, David L. *health facility administrator*
Higby, Lawrence M. *medical products executive*
Massengill, Matthew H. *data storage company executive*
McCurley, Thomas W. *manufacturing executive*
Milligan, Steve *retail executive*
Schroeder, John A. *systems engineering consultant, educator*
Shakeel, Arif *retail executive*
Smoot, Skipi Lundquist *psychologist*

**Lakeside**
Seaberg, Eric Dayle *audio engineer*

**Lakewood**
Baptista, Arnaldo D. *secondary school educator*
Bogdan, Carolyn Louetta *financial specialist, retired small business owner*
Carr, Firpo Wycoff *bible scholar, educator, writer*
Marthell, Yvette Jessica *photographer, educator, filmmaker*
Welch, Lynne G. *language and music educator*

**Lancaster**
Bell, Gary Lynn *owner production company, video and audio producer*
Ellsworth, Richard German *psychologist*
Hodges, Vernon Wray *mechanical engineer*
Holley, Susan L. *psychologist*
Wooster, Larry D. *music educator*

**Larkspur**
Aster, Richard (Rick) F., Jr. *diversified financial services company executive*
Dellar, Michael D. *restaurant owner, hospitality industry consultant*
Greenberg, Myron Silver *lawyer*
Ratner, David Louis *retired law educator*
Saxton, Lloyd *psychologist, writer*
Willson, Prentiss, Jr. *retired lawyer*

**Lemoore**
Barnes, Kirsten Aileen *school counselor*
Gerhard, H. John *orthopaedic surgeon, military officer*
Schwerdtfeger, Henry Douglas *military officer, physiologist*

**Lincoln**
Chong, Vernon *retired surgeon, retired military officer*
Dorn, Mary Ann *retired auditor*
Helzer, James Dennis *retired health facility administrator*
Johnson, Ursula Anne *artist*
Rockwell, Don Arthur *retired psychiatrist*

**Live Oak**
Spilman, Janet Lynne *special education educator*

**Livermore**
Alder, Berni Julian *physicist, researcher*
Anastasio, Michael R. *science foundation director*
Banerjee, Souvik *process engineer, researcher*
Cowgill, Donald Franklin *physicist*
Darter, Thomas Eugene, Jr. *composer, musician, writer*
Fong, Nelson S. *secondary school educator*
Glassley, William E. *geochemist, researcher*
Glenzer, Siegfried Heinz *physicist, educator, researcher*
Goodwin, Bruce T. *engineer*
Hiskes, Dolores G. *language educator*
Hooper, Edwin Bickford *physicist*
Johnson, Roy Ragnar *electrical engineer, researcher*
Kidder, Ray Edward *physicist, consultant*
King, Ray John *electrical engineering educator, engineering company executive*
Kirkwood, Robert Keith *applied physicist*
Lassila, David H. *materials scientist, researcher*

Leith, Cecil Eldon, Jr. *retired physicist*
Nuckolls, John Hopkins *physicist, researcher*
Raymond, Jason *geneticist, microbiologist*
Reyes, Susana *nuclear engineer*
Sack, Seymour *nuclear scientist*
Santer, Benjamin David *atmospheric scientist*
Shotts, Wayne J. *nuclear scientist, federal agency administrator*
Spiller, Eberhard Adolf *physicist, researcher*
Tarter, Curtis Bruce *physicist, science administrator*
Tripodes, James G. *nuclear safety and environmental regulatory affairs professional*
Weber, Stephen Vance *physics researcher*
Xie, Shaocheng *atmospheric scientist*

## Livingston
Foster, Ron *agricultural products supplier, agricultural products executive*

## Lodi
Bishop-Graham, Barbara *secondary school educator, journalist*
Reinold, Christy Diane *school counselor, consultant*
Siler, Virginia Carlisle *retired elementary school educator*
Tan, Robert C. *music educator*

## Loma Linda
Bailey, Leonard Lee *surgeon*
Behrens, Berel Lyn *physician, academic administrator, health facility administrator*
Bull, Brian Stanley *pathologist, educator*
Bullock, Weldon Kimball *health facility administrator, pathologist, educator*
Chan, Philip J. *medical educator*
Cimpoeru, Petre *archivist, educator*
Coggin, Charlotte Joan *cardiologist, educator*
Condon, Stanley Charles *gastroenterologist*
Dayes, Lloyd Albert *neurosurgeon, minister*
Goodacre, Charles J. *dean, academic administrator*
Herrmann, Paul C. *physician, chemist*
Kyle, James Lewis *dean, physician*
Llaurado, Josep G. *nuclear medicine physician, researcher*
Llerandi Phipps, Carmen Guillermina *nutritionist and dietitian*
Longo, Lawrence Daniel *physiologist, educator, obstetrician, gynecologist*
Mace, John Weldon *pediatrician*
Molnar, Violet *mental health nurse*
Pendergraft, Janice Gayle *volunteer*
Schwab, Ernest Roe III *physiology educator, researcher*
Slater, James Munro *radiation oncologist*
Strother, Allen *biochemical pharmacologist, researcher*
Taylor, Barry Llewellyn *microbiologist, educator*
Vermeersch, David Adam *psychologist*
Wareham, Ellsworth Edwin *cardiothoracic surgeon, educator*

## Lomita
Balcom, Orville *engineer*

## Lompoc
Belisle-Foreman, Karen *music educator*
Bongiorno, James William *electronics executive*
Lyra, Jon Robert *music educator, artist*
Means, James Andrew *engineer*
Wagner, Geraldine Marie *nursing educator, consultant*

## Long Beach
Adler, Jeffrey D. *media consultant, management consultant*
Alexander, F. King *academic administrator*
Alkana, Linda Kelly *history professor*
Baber, Walter Franklin *political science professor*
Barron, (Mary Lou) Slater *artist, retired art educator*
Bauer, Roger Duane *chemistry professor, consultant*
Beebe, Sandra E. *retired language educator, artist, writer*
Bowen, Fern Chambers *artist, educator*
Braunstein, Terry Malikin *artist*
Brown, Lester B. *social worker, educator*
Brown, Roxanne (Jerene Roxanne Brown) *sales executive*
Burnett, Ella M. Glenn *education educator*
Bursley, Kathleen A. *lawyer*
Calhoun, John R. *lawyer*
Collins, Aristide J., Jr. *academic administrator*
Davlin, Grace Lucille *real estate educator*
Davis, Mark Hezekiah, Jr. *electrical engineer*
de Soto, Simon *mechanical engineer*
Deukmejian, George *lawyer, retired governor*
Dillon, Michael Earl *engineering executive, mechanical engineer, educator*
Duran, Matias Martin *retired adult education educator*
Engle, Robert Irwin *music educator, translator*
Fischler, Sandy Lynn *charitable and informational organization executive*
Fleming, Jane Williams *retired elementary school educator, writer*
Gahungu, Prosper *mathematics educator*
Glenn, Constance White *art museum director, educator, consultant*
Haile, Lawrence Barclay *lawyer*
Halili, Antonio Marquez *facilities maintenance mechanic*
Hancock, John Walker III *banker*
Helwick, Christine *lawyer*
Hershberger, Scott Laurence *psychologist, educator, statistician, researcher*
Higginson, John *retired career officer*
Hu, Chi Yu *retired physicist, educator*
Huyck, Charles Krishna *geographer, consultant*
Jeynes, William Hettich *religious studies educator, religious organization administrator, minister*
Karentte, Betty *state legislator*
Keller, J(ames) Wesley *credit union executive*
Kumar, Rajendra *electrical engineering educator*
Kusaba, Clifford Noboru *historian, educator*
Kwaan, Jack Hau Ming *retired physician*
Lathrop, Irvin Tunis *retired dean*
Lauda, Donald Paul *dean*

Locklin, Gerald *language educator, poet, writer*
Luke, Gregorio *museum director*
Macer, George Armen, Jr. *orthopedic hand surgeon*
Mathieu, Susan Leifer *recreational therapist, educator*
McGaughey, Charles Gilbert *retired biochemist*
Mills, Don Harper *pathology and psychiatry educator, lawyer*
Molina, Joseph Mario (Mario Molina) *medical administrator*
Mullins Berg, Ruth Gladys *nurse*
Myers, John Wescott *air transportation executive*
Nelson, Harold Bernhard *museum director*
Nguyen, Huong Tran *former elementary and secondary language educator, former district office administrator*
O'Neill, Beverly Lewis *mayor, former college president*
Proust, Joycelyn Ann *retired librarian*
Pullman, Alan *architect*
Reed, Charles Bass *chief academic administrator*
Reichard, Gary Warren *academic administrator, historian, educator*
Rutherford, Vicky Lynn *special education educator*
Sato, Eunice Noda *former mayor, consultant*
Schubel, Jerry Robert *marine scientist educator, dean*
Sinclitico, Dennis J. *lawyer*
Singhal, Meena *education educator*
Sosoka, John Richard *consulting firm executive, engineer*
Springer, Wilma Marie *retired elementary school educator*
Stemmer, Edward Alan *surgeon, educator*
Tang, Paul Chi Lung *philosophy educator*
Viola, Bill *artist, writer*
Wagdy, Mahmoud Fawzy *engineering educator*
Welch, Ronnie Scott *health facility administrator*
Wells, James H. *plastic surgeon*
Wise, George Edward *lawyer*
Withers, Aldina *educational consultant*
Wollmer, Richard Dietrich *statistics and operations research educator*
Worcester, Howard Lester *internist*
Wu, Sing-Yung *physician, researcher*
Yousef, Fathi Salaama *communications educator, management consultant*

## Los Alamitos
Aberman, Harold Mark *veterinarian*
Eckelman, Richard Joel *engineering specialist*
Lee, Jhemon Hom *physician*
Weinberger, Frank *information management consultant*

## Los Altos
Beer, Clara Louise Johnson *retired electronics executive*
Carsten, Jack Craig *venture capitalist*
Collins, Gordon Dent *recording industry executive*
Davies, Paul Anthony *composer, music educator*
Fraknoi, Andrew *astronomy educator, astronomical society executive*
Gough, William Cabot *engineer*
Justice-Moore, Kathleen E. *lawyer*
King, Chi-Yu *research scientist*
Larson, Carol S. *foundation administrator, lawyer*
Nivison, David Shepherd *language educator, philosopher*
Orman, Nanette Hector *psychiatrist*
Orr, Susan Packard *small business owner, foundation administrator*
Peterson, Victor Lowell *aerospace engineer, consultant*
Scifres, Donald Ray *finance company executive*
Sharpe, Roland Leonard *structural engineer, consultant*
Spiller, Gene Alan *nutritionist, health facility administrator*
Vickers, Roger Spencer *physicist, researcher, environmental artist*
Wilbur, Colburn Sloan *foundation consultant and trustee, former executive*
Yang, Roxana Hwu *lawyer, investor*
Yu, Oliver Shukiang *corporate executive, educator, technology strategist*
Zebroski, Edwin Leopold *risk management consultant*

## Los Altos Hills
Archibeque, Charlene Paullin *retired music educator*
Fondahl, John Walker *civil engineering educator*
Robbins, Doren Gurstein *poet, educator, artist*

## Los Angeles
Aaron, Benjamin *law educator, arbitrator*
Abell, Nancy L. *lawyer*
Aberbach, Joel David *political science professor, writer*
Aberle, Denise Ru *radiologist, researcher*
Abrams, Norman *academic administrator, law educator*
Adamek, Charles Andrew *lawyer*
Adams, Thomas Merritt *lawyer*
Adell, Hirsch *lawyer*
Adleman, Leonard M. *computer scientist, educator*
Adler, Erwin Ellery *lawyer*
Adler, Fred Peter *retired electronics company executive*
Adler, Michael I. *lawyer*
Adler, Sara *arbitrator, mediator*
Agnew, John A. *science educator*
Ahrens, Mary Elizabeth *lawyer*
Alarcón, Arthur Lawrence *federal judge*
Alden, John W. *lawyer*
Alkalay, Arie L. *pediatrician*
Alkin, Marvin C. *education educator*
Alkon, Ellen Skillen *physician*
Alkon, Paul Kent *language educator*
Allen, David C. *lawyer*
Allen, Michael John Bridgman *language educator*
Allen, Sharon *accounting firm executive*
Allen, Suzanne *financial planning executive, insurance agent, writer, educator*
Allen, Walter Recharde *sociology educator*
Allen, William Richard *retired economist*
Allred, Gloria Rachel *lawyer*
Alpers, Edward Alter *history professor*

Altman, Scott *law educator, dean*
Alvarado, Pablo *day laborer organizer & immigrant rights activist*
Álvarez, Rodolfo *sociology educator, consultant*
Aminian Baghai, Arash *lawyer*
Anawalt, Patricia Rieff *anthropologist, researcher*
Andersen, Ronald Max *health services researcher, educator*
Anderson, Charles David *lawyer*
Anderson, John Edward *diversified holding company executive, lawyer*
Anderson, W. French *biochemist, physician, educator*
Angel, Arthur Ronald *lawyer, consultant*
Angeloff, Dann Valentino *brokerage house executive*
Antin, Michael *lawyer*
Antonovich, Michael Dennis *county official*
Aoki, Masanao *economics professor*
Apfel, Gary *lawyer*
Apple, Jacki (Jacqueline B. Apple) *artist, educator, writer*
Apt, Charles *artist*
Apt, Leonard *physician*
Apuzzo, Michael Lawrence John *neurological surgeon*
Arbisser, Aton *lawyer*
Archer, Anne *actress*
Archerd, Army (Armand A. Archerd) *columnist, retired commentator*
Arenella, Peter Lee *law educator*
Arkin, Adam *actor*
Armstrong, Lloyd, Jr. *academic administrator, physics professor*
Arnett, Will *actor*
Arnold, Dennis B. *lawyer*
Aronoff, Vera *law librarian*
Aronowitz, Joel Alan *plastic and reconstructive surgeon*
Aronson, Seth *lawyer*
Aronzon, Paul S. *lawyer*
Arquette, Rosanna (Rosanna Lauren Arquette) *actress*
Ash, Roy Lawrence *former federal official*
Ashwell, Rachel *entrepreneur, interior designer*
Asperger, James *lawyer*
Austen, Karl Ramsdell *lawyer*
Averbook, Beryl David *retired surgeon*
Azad, Susan Stott *lawyer*
Bacharach, Burt *composer, conductor*
Bahr, Ehrhard *Germanic languages and literature educator*
Bain, Conrad Stafford *actor*
Bakaly, Charles George, Jr. *lawyer, mediator*
Baker, Donald P. *lawyer*
Baker, Robert Frank *molecular biologist, educator*
Ballard, Glen *composer*
Bamattre, William *fire chief*
Banerjee, Utpal *biology professor, research scientist*
Banks, Tyra (Tyra Lynne Banks) *retired model, television personality*
Baquet, Dean Paul *newspaper editor*
Barberie, Jillian *newscaster, meteorologist*
Bardem, Javier *actor*
Barker, Robert William (Bob Barker) *television personality*
Baron, Melvin Farrell *pharmacy educator*
Barrack, Thomas J., Jr. *real estate investor, lawyer*
Barren De Serres, Bruce Willard (H.R.H. The Duke Bruce Willard Barren de Serres) *merchant banker*
Barrett, Jane Hayes *lawyer*
Barron, Stephanie *curator*
Barry, Brent Robert *professional basketball player*
Barsky, Wayne Mitchell *lawyer*
Bart, Peter Benton *editor, film producer, writer*
Barth, Uta *artist, educator*
Barth Menzies, Karen Ann *lawyer*
Barton, Alan Joel *lawyer*
Barza, Harold A. *lawyer*
Bas, Hernan *artist*
Basak, Saroj Kumar *medical researcher*
Basil, Douglas Constantine *writer, educator*
Batamack, Patrice Theodore Desire *chemistry professor, researcher*
Bates, Marcia Jeanne *information scientist educator*
Battista, Richard *entertainment company executive*
Baum, Michael Lin *lawyer*
Bauman, Stephen Adrian *lawyer*
Baumann, Richard Gordon *lawyer*
Baumbach, Noah *screenwriter*
Baumgarten, Ronald Neal *lawyer*
Baylor, Elgin Gay *professional basketball team executive*
Beart, Robert W., Jr. *colon and rectal surgeon, educator*
Beck, (Beck Hansen) *musician, songwriter*
Begley, Ed, Jr. *actor*
Bekey, George Albert *computer scientist, educator*
Belkind, Elizabeth *chef*
Bell, Lee Phillip *television personality, television producer*
Bell, William J., Jr. *television producer*
Beltramo, Michael Norman *management consultant*
Benatar, Pat (Pat Andrzejewski) *rock singer*
Bender, Charles William *lawyer*
Bender, Dean *public relations executive*
Bendix, Helen Irene *lawyer*
Bennett, Brent Jackson *architect*
Bennett, Charles Franklin, Jr. *biogeographer, educator*
Bennett, Joel Herbert *construction executive*
Bennis, Warren Gameliel *business administration educator*
Benson, Sidney William *chemistry researcher*
Bergman, Emily Anne *librarian*
Bergman, Marilyn Keith *lyricist, writer*
Berman, Gail *film company executive*
Berman, Geoffrey Louis *diversified financial services company executive*
Berman, Richard Keith *television producer, film producer*
Bernacchi, Richard Lloyd *lawyer*
Bernstein, Arthur Harold *venture capital executive*
Bernstein, Leslie *academic administrator, biostatistician, epidemiologist*
Bernstein, Sol *cardiologist, educator*
Bertero, Karen E. *lawyer*

Bessman, Samuel Paul *pediatrician, educator, biochemist*
Beyer, Robert D. *corporate financial executive*
Bhaumik, Mani Lal *physicist*
Bhidayasiri, Roongroj *neurologist, researcher*
Bianchi, Carisa *advertising company executive*
Bibicoff, Hillary Sue *lawyer*
Bice, Scott Haas *dean, law educator*
Biggs, Jason *actor*
Biles, John Alexander *pharmacologist, chemist, educator*
Binder, Gordon M. *venture capitalist*
Bindingnavele, Vijay Krishna *plastic surgeon*
Bing, Steve *film producer*
Birren, James Emmett *research and development company executive*
Bitting, William M. *lawyer*
Black, Lewis *comedian, actor*
Blahd, William Henry *physician, nuclear medicine physician, director*
Blake, Rob *professional hockey player*
Blencowe, Paul Sherwood *lawyer, private investor*
Blendell, Elizabeth A. *lawyer*
Bloch, Paul *public relations executive*
Bloom, Claire *actress*
Bloomberg, Coe Arthur *lawyer*
Blumberg, Grace Ganz *lawyer, educator*
Bobbitt, Leroy *lawyer*
Bodey, Bela *immunologist, pathologist, oncologist*
Bodkin, Henry Grattan, Jr. *lawyer*
Boehm, Barry William *computer science educator*
Boehmer, Richard Arthur *lawyer*
Bogen, Andrew E. *lawyer*
Bohle, Sue *public relations executive*
Boime, Albert Isaac *art historian, educator*
Boles, Richard Gregory *clinical geneticist, researcher*
Bologna, Joseph *actor*
Bondareff, William *psychiatrist, educator*
Bonesteel, Michael John *lawyer*
Bonner, Robert Cleve *lawyer*
Boras, Kim *lawyer*
Bordy, Michael Jeffrey *lawyer*
Borenstein, Daniel Bernard *psychiatrist, educator*
Borsting, Jack Raymond *business administration educator*
Borvitz, Mark Jay *rabbi, counselor*
Bosley, Tom *actor*
Boswell, James Douglas *medical research executive*
Bottjer, David John *earth science and biology educator*
Boxer, Lester *lawyer*
Boyce, David S. *lawyer*
Boyd, Malcolm *minister, writer*
Boyer, Paul D. *biochemist, educator*
Boyle, Barbara Dorman *film company executive*
Boyle, Kevin Richard *lawyer*
Brackmann, Derald E. *otolaryngologist*
Bradley, Lawrence D., Jr. *lawyer*
Bradshaw, Murray Charles *musicologist, educator*
Branca, John Gregory *lawyer, consultant*
Brand, Elton *professional basketball player*
Brand, Michael *museum director*
Brandler, Jonathan M. *lawyer*
Bratton, William J. *police chief, former police commissioner*
Braun, David A(dlai) *lawyer*
Braunstein, Glenn David *physician, educator*
Bremond, Duane Benjamin *marketing professional*
Brendel, Bettina *abstract artist*
Breslow, Lester *public health physician, educator*
Bressan, Paul Louis *lawyer*
Breuer, Stephen Ernest *religious organization administrator*
Brian, Brad D. *lawyer*
Brill, Laura W. *lawyer*
Brittenham, Skip *lawyer*
Broad, Eli *finance company executive, art collector*
Brodie, Simon *genetic cloning company executive*
Brodwin, Martin George *counselor, educator*
Brolin, James (James Brunderlin) *actor*
Brown, Carol *make-up artist*
Brown, Jason Robert *composer, arranger*
Brown, John S. *computer scientist*
Brown, Kathleen *diversified financial services company executive*
Brown, Kwame *professional basketball player*
Brown, Michael K. *lawyer*
Brubaker, William Rogers *sociology educator*
Bruce, William A. *airport executive*
Bryan, Greyson *lawyer*
Bryan, Karen Smith *lawyer*
Buffington, Gary Lee Roy *safety engineer, construction executive*
Bufford, Samuel Lawrence *federal judge*
Burch, Robert Dale *lawyer*
Burke, Yvonne Watson Brathwaite (Mrs. William A. Burke) *lawyer*
Burnett, T-Bone (Henry John Burnett) *music producer, musician*
Burrows, James *television and motion picture director, producer*
Burton, Brian Joseph (Danger Mouse) *sound recording engineer, musician*
Burton, Tim (Timothy William Burton) *film director*
Bush, Wes *defense, technology contracting executive*
Butcher, Larry L. *neuroscientist, educator*
Buzzi, Ruth *comedienne*
Byrd, Christine Waterman Swent *lawyer*
Byrnes, James Bernard *museum director, consultant*
Caine, Michael *actor*
Calabrese, Joseph A. *lawyer*
Campbell, Bebe Moore *writer*
Campbell, Glen *singer, entertainer*
Campbell, Martin *film director, producer, writer*
Campion, Robert Thomas *manufacturing executive*
Caram, Eve La Salle *language educator, writer*
Carey, Stevens Anthony *lawyer*
Carlin, George Denis *comedian, actor*
Carlson, Robert Edwin *lawyer*
Carnesale, Albert *former academic administrator*
Caroompas, Carole Jean *artist, educator*
Carothers, A.J. *scriptwriter*
Carr, Willard Zeller, Jr. *retired lawyer*
Carrillo, Elpidia *actress*
Carroll, Pete *college football coach*

Carson, Margaret *human services administrator*
Casamassima, Christopher T. *lawyer*
Cassavetes, Nick *film director, actor*
Cassell, Samuel James *professional basketball player*
Castro, Leonard Edward *lawyer*
Catanzarite, David M. *theater educator, director*
Cate, Jan Harris *lawyer*
Cates, Gilbert *television producer, theater director, film producer*
Catlin, Don H. *molecular pharmacologist, educator*
Cecere, Domenico *homebuilding company executive*
Cechmanek, Roman *professional hockey player*
Cee-Lo, (Thomas DeCarlo Callaway) *singer*
Cermak, John Frank, Jr. *lawyer*
Champagne, Duane Willard *sociology educator*
Champlin, Charles Davenport *television personality, critic, writer*
Chan, David Ronald *tax specialist, lawyer*
Chandor, Stebbins Bryant *pathologist*
Chang, Edward H. *computer company executive*
Chang, Henry C. *library administrator*
Chang, Jane P. *chemical engineering educator*
Chapman, Carolyn *broadcasting director*
Chapman Collins, Janice *school system administrator*
Chapman Holley, Shawn Snider *lawyer*
Charen, Mona *columnist*
Chavez, Victor Edwin *judge*
Chazen, Stephen I. *oil industry executive*
Cheeseboro, Margrit *retired economics educator*
Chen, Francis F. *physics and engineering educator*
Chen, Tony F. *mathematics professor, dean*
Cheng, Hong *library and information scientist*
Cheng, Tsen-Chung *electrical engineering educator*
Chernin, Peter F. *multimedia company executive*
Cherry, James Donald *pediatrician*
Chew, Elaine *engineering educator, musician*
Chiate, Kenneth Reed *lawyer*
Chiklis, Michael *actor*
Chobotov, Vladimir Alexander *aerospace engineer, educator*
Chopra, Inder Jit *endocrinologist*
Chow, Stephen (Sing-Chi Chow) *actor*
Christ, Roxanne E. *lawyer*
Christol, Carl Quimby *lawyer, political science professor*
Christopher, Warren Minor *lawyer, former secretary of state*
Chu, Chi-Cheng *research scientist*
Chu, Morgan *lawyer*
Chung, Tong Soo *lawyer*
Churgin, Amy *publishing executive*
Ciccone, Amy Navratil *art librarian*
Clair, John J., Jr. *lawyer*
Clark, Burton Robert *sociologist, educator*
Clark, R(ufus) Bradbury *lawyer, director*
Clarke, Peter *communications and health educator*
Clarke, Steven Gerard *chemistry professor*
Cleary, William Joseph, Jr. *lawyer*
Clemente, Carmine Domenic *anatomist, educator*
Clow, Lee *advertising agency executive*
Coates, Thomas J. *medical association administrator*
Cochran, Steve *lawyer*
Cohee, Kevin *bank executive*
Cohen, Aryell *music educator*
Cohen, Cynthia Marylyn *lawyer*
Cohen, Marcia Fran Baltimore *writer, psychologist*
Cohen, S(tephen) Marshall *philosophy educator*
Cohn, Gary Dennis *journalist*
Cole, K.C. *journalist, writer*
Cole, William L. *lawyer*
Coleman, Paul Jerome, Jr. *physicist, researcher*
Coleman, Rexford Lee *lawyer, educator*
Colletti, Ned *professional sports team executive*
Collier, Anna *photographer*
Collier, Charles Arthur, Jr. *lawyer*
Collins, Audrey B. *judge*
Combs, Holly Marie *actress*
Compton, William Henry, Jr. *mental health services professional*
Conley, Mark A. *lawyer*
Connor-Dominguez, Billie Marie *science information professional*
Cook, Ian Ainsworth *psychiatrist, researcher, educator*
Cook, Melanie K. *lawyer*
Cooley, Steve *prosecutor*
Cooper, Chris *actor*
Cooper, Robert E. *lawyer*
Copeland, Trent Brehon *lawyer*
Cora, Cat *chef*
Cordova, Richard D. *hospital administrator*
Corman, Roger William *film director*
Cornwall, John Michael *physics professor, consultant*
Coroniti, Ferdinand Vincent *physics professor, astronomy educator*
Cortines, Ramon C. *former school superintendent*
Corwin, Norman *scriptwriter, film producer, film director*
Costello, Kenneth R. *lawyer*
Coston, Suzanne *television producer*
Cote, Richard James *pathologist, researcher*
Cotsen, Lloyd E. *retired consumer products company executive*
Coulter, David A. *investment banker*
Coupe, James Warnick *lawyer*
Court, Michelle Williams *lawyer, director*
Cowan, Marie Jeanette *dean, nurse, medical educator*
Cox, Brian *actor*
Craft, Cheryl Mae *neurobiologist, anatomist, researcher*
Crampon, Jean Elaine *librarian*
Crawford, Marc *professional hockey coach*
Crockett, Donald Harold *composer, music educator*
Crombie, Douglass Darnill *aerospace communications system engineer*
Crosby, Peter Alan *management consultant*
Cuadra, Carlos Albert *library and information scientist, consultant*
Cunneen, Scott Anthony *surgeon*
Curran, Darryl Joseph *photographer, educator*
Curtiss, Thomas, Jr. *lawyer*

Cushman, John C. III *real estate company executive*
Dabrowska, Dorota Maria *statistician, educator*
D'Accone, Frank Anthony *music educator*
Dale, Jim *actor*
Dallmeyer, Robert Frederick *art educator, writer*
Daly, Robert Anthony *international relief organization executive, former professional sports team executive, retired film company executive*
Dana, Lauren Elizabeth *lawyer*
D'Angelo Melby, Donna Marie *lawyer*
Daniels, John Peter *lawyer*
Danoff, Dudley Seth *surgeon, urologist*
Dantzscher, Jamie *gymnast*
Danziger, Bruce Edward *structural engineer*
Darby, G(eorge) Harrison *lawyer*
Darby, Michael Rucker *economist, educator*
Darden, Christopher Allen *lawyer, actor, writer*
Dastin, Barry L. *lawyer*
Daum, John F. *lawyer*
Davidson, Ezra C., Jr. *obstetrician, gynecologist, educator, academic administrator*
Davidson, Gordon *theater producer, theater director*
Davidson, Herbert Alan *Near Eastern languages and cultures educator*
Davidson, Jeffrey S. *lawyer*
Davidson, Robert C., Jr. *manufacturing executive*
Davis, Gray (Joseph Graham Davis) *lawyer, former governor*
Davis, John A. *film producer*
Davis, Michael Rico *county official*
Davis, Susie Francisca *psychologist*
Dawson, Rosario *actress, singer*
Day, Robert Addison, Jr. *investment management company executive*
Dayton, Sky *telecommunications company executive*
De Brier, Donald Paul *lawyer*
de Castro, Hugo Daniel *lawyer*
Decker, Richard Jeffrey *lawyer*
Dee, Ruby (Ruby Dee Davis) *actress, writer, film director*
Dekmejian, Richard Hrair *political science professor*
De La Hoya, Oscar *boxer*
Delaney, Matthew Sylvester *mathematics professor, academic administrator*
De Larios, Dora *artist*
de la Rocha, Castulo *health services executive*
Delgadillo, Rockard J. (Rocky Delgadillo) *lawyer*
Delugach, Albert Lawrence *journalist*
Demeter, Dan A. *executive recruiting company executive*
Demick, Barbara *journalist*
Dempsey, Patrick *actor*
Demsetz, Harold *economist, educator*
Denham, Robert Edwin *lawyer, investment company executive*
dePaolis, Potito Umberto *food company executive*
Detels, Roger *epidemiologist, retired dean*
Dewey, Donald Odell *dean, academic administrator*
Dhir, Vijay K. *mechanical engineering educator*
Diamond, Jared Mason *biologist, writer*
Diamond, Stanley Jay *lawyer*
Didkovsky, Leonid V *engineer*
Diehl, Dolores *performing company executive*
Diehl, Kristin *education educator*
Dignam, William Joseph *obstetrician, gynecologist, educator*
DiMeglio, David J. *lawyer*
Dinel, Richard Henry *lawyer*
Dodd, Jan Eve *lawyer*
Dolan, Mary Anne *journalist, columnist*
Doll, Lynne Marie *public relations agency executive*
Donahue, Ann M. *television producer*
Donovan, John Arthur *lawyer*
Dorfman, William M. *dentist*
Dorman, Albert A. *engineering executive, consultant, architect*
Dorrell, Karl *college football coach*
Dows, David Alan *chemistry professor*
Dragan, Alexandra *mechanical engineer, consultant, environmental engineer, researcher, engineering educator*
Dr. Dre, (Andre Young) *rapper, record producer*
Drew, J.D. *professional baseball player*
Dr. Phil, (Phillip Calvin McGraw) *psychologist, television personality*
Dudziak, Mary Louise *law educator*
Duke, Margaret Joyce *sound recordist, broadcast engineer*
Dumitrescu, Domnita *Spanish language educator, researcher*
Dummett, Clifton Orrin *dentist, educator*
DuMont, James Kelton, Jr. *actor, theater producer*
Dunham, Scott H. *lawyer*
Dunleavy, Mike, Sr. *professional basketball coach*
Dunn, Arnold Samuel *biochemistry educator*
Dunn, Bruce Sidney *materials scientist, educator*
Dunst, Kirsten *actress*
Durant, Sam *artist*
Duritz, Adam *musician*
Dworsky, Daniel Leonard *architect, educator*
Dwyre, William Patrick *journalist*
Easton, Mark *lawyer*
Eatman, Louis Perkins *lawyer*
Eckhart, Aaron *actor*
Edgerton, Bradford Wheatly *plastic surgeon*
Edmonds, Tracey E. *film company executive*
Edwards, Blake *film director*
Eisenstein, Edward Milton *psychologist, physiologist, biophysicist, educator*
Eliel, Ruth Louise *performing company executive*
Ellenberg, Marcia Stamler *retired elementary school educator*
Ellickson, Bryan Carl *economics professor*
Elrod, Lu *retired music educator, actress*
Elswit, Robert *cinematographer*
Emanuel, William Joseph *lawyer*
Emanuele, R.M. *pharmaceutical executive*
Emigh, Rebecca Jean *social sciences educator*
English, Stephen Raymond *lawyer*
Engvall, Bill *comedian, actor*
Enstrom, James Eugene *epidemiologist*
Eo, SuRak *plastic surgeon, educator*

Erdos, Joanna E. *school counselor, secondary school educator*
Erichsen, Peter Christian *foundation administrator*
Eskenazi, Bonnie Elise *lawyer*
Ettenger, Robert Bruce *physician, pediatric nephrologist*
Evans, Gregory Lawrence *lawyer*
Faber, George Donald *retired communications executive*
Fairbank, Robert Harold *lawyer*
Fairchild, Morgan (Patsy McClenny) *actress*
Fanselow, Michael Scott *psychology professor*
Farmer, Robert Lindsay *lawyer*
Farrar, Stanley F. *lawyer*
Farrell, Joseph *film producer, financial analyst, film company executive, sculptor, writer*
Feig, Stephen Arthur *pediatrician, educator, preventive medicine physician, hematologist, oncologist*
Feigen, Brenda S. *lawyer, film producer, writer*
Fein, Irving Ashley *television and motion picture executive*
Fein, Ronald Lawrence *lawyer*
Feinstein, Michael Jay *singer, pianist, musicologist, actor*
Feldman, Lewis G. *lawyer*
Fenning, Lisa Hill *lawyer, mediator, retired judge*
Ferry, Richard Michael *retired executive recruiter*
Fickett, Edward Hale *architect, educator, arbitrator*
Field, Ted (Frederick Field) *film company executive, recording industry executive*
Fielding, Jonathan Evan *city health department administrator, pediatrician*
Fields, Bertram Harris *lawyer*
Fields, Henry Michael *lawyer*
Fields, Robin *reporter*
Fincher, David *film director, film producer*
Findley, John Allen, Jr. *publishing executive*
Finegold, Sydney Martin *microbiology educator*
Finkel, Evan *lawyer*
Finnegan, Michael J. *lawyer*
Firstenberg, Jean Picker *film institute executive*
Fischer, Alfred George *geology educator*
Fisher, Richard N. *lawyer*
Fitz-Carter, Aleane *retired elementary school educator, composer*
Flagel, Mark Alan *lawyer*
Flanagan, Fionnula Manon *actress, writer, theater director*
Flanigan, James J(oseph) *journalist*
Fleer, Keith George *lawyer, retired film company executive*
Fleischmann, Ernest Martin *performing arts executive, consultant*
Fleming, Macklin *retired judge*
Floyd, Tim *men's college basketball coach, former professional basketball coach*
Fodor, Peter Bela *plastic surgeon*
Follick, Edwin Duane *law educator, dean, chiropractor*
Fonkalsrud, Eric Walter *pediatric surgeon, educator*
Forness, Steven Robert *educational psychologist*
Foss, Robert Fletcher *lawyer*
Foster, Sutton *actress*
Frackman, Russell Jay *lawyer*
Fragner, Matthew Charles *lawyer*
Francis, Charles K. *medical educator*
Frank, Peter Solomon *art historian, curator, art critic*
Franz, Dennis *actor*
Freehling, Allen Isaac *rabbi*
Freier, Elliot G. *lawyer*
Friedlander, Sheldon Kay *chemical engineering professor*
Frimmer, Paul Norman *lawyer*
Fuhrman, Jed Alan *biological oceanographer*
Fulco, Armand John *biochemist*
Furcal, Rafael *professional baseball player*
Futami, Norman *lawyer*
Gabriel, Ronald Samuel *child neurologist*
Gadal, Louis Stephen *artist*
Gagne, Eric *professional baseball player*
Gale, Jeffrey *management consultant, business educator*
Gallo, Jon Joseph *lawyer*
Galton, Stephen Harold *lawyer*
Ganas, Perry Spiros *physicist*
Ganz, Julian, Jr. *retail executive*
Garbacz, Gregory A. *lawyer*
Garciaparra, Nomar (Anthony Nomar Garciaparra) *professional baseball player*
Garrett, Elizabeth *law educator, academic administrator*
Garrett, Spencer *actor, writer, director*
Gasich, Welko Elton *retired aerospace transportation executive, management consultant*
Gasparetti, Lorenzo E. *lawyer*
Gasson, Judith C. *research scientist*
Gatti, Richard A. *medical educator, medical geneticist*
Gehry, Frank Owen *architect*
Gelber, Danielle Arna *broadcast executive*
Geller, Debra F. *academic administrator, educator*
Geller, Michael D. *engineering educator*
Geller, Stephen Arthur *pathologist, educator*
Geragos, Mark John *lawyer*
Gest, Howard David *lawyer*
Gewertz, Bruce Labe *surgeon, educator*
Ghez, Andrea Mia *astronomy educator, physics educator*
Ghil, Michael *atmospheric scientist, geophysicist*
Gianopulos, Jim *film company executive*
Giffin, Margaret Ethel (Peggy Giffin) *management consultant*
Gifford, Kathie Lee *television personality, vocalist*
Gilbertson, John T. *lawyer*
Gillespie, Craig *art director*
Gilligan, Thomas W. *dean, finance educator*
Gilman, John Joseph *research scientist*
Girard, Robert David *lawyer*
Girardi, Thomas Vincent *lawyer*
Glazer, Michael *lawyer*
Glover, Stephen I. *lawyer*
Goedde, Alan George *financial company executive*
Goin, Marcia Kraft *physician*
Goldberg, Robert B. *molecular biologist, biology professor*
Golden, Arthur *writer*

Goldman, Allan Bailey *lawyer*
Goldman, Benjamin Edward *lawyer*
Goldman, Donald Aaron *lawyer*
Goldman, Stanley A. *law educator*
Goldschmidt, Walter Rochs *anthropologist*
Goldstein, Michael Saul *sociologist*
Golomb, Solomon Wolf *mathematician, educator, director, electrical engineer*
Gomez, Elizabeth M. *community organization administrator*
Gondry, Michel *film director*
Gonick, Harvey Craig *nephrologist, educator*
Good, Edith Elissa (Pearl Williams) *writer*
Goodman, Max A. *lawyer, educator*
Goodwin, Scott Craig *interventional radiologist*
Gordon, Allen Barry *musician, composer*
Gordon, Basil *retired mathematics professor*
Gordon, David *research scientist*
Gordon, Malcolm Stephen *biology professor*
Gores, Alec E. *venture capitalist*
Gorman, Joseph Gregory, Jr. *lawyer*
Gorney, Roderic *psychiatrist, educator*
Gosling, Ryan (Ryan Thomas Gosling) *actor*
Gothold, Stuart Eugene *school system administrator, education educator*
Gottfried, Ira Sidney *management consulting executive*
Gould, David *lawyer*
Govan, Michael *museum director*
Grady, Mark F. *law educator, former dean*
Grammer, Kelsey *actor*
Grant, Mark Antonio *organization administrator*
Grassian, Esther Stampfer *librarian, educator*
Graves, Anna Marie *lawyer*
Gray, Jan Charles *lawyer, business owner*
Gray, Jeremy J.F. *lawyer*
Green, William Porter *lawyer*
Greenberg, Barry Michael *talent executive*
Greenberg, Gordon Alan *lawyer*
Greenberger, Martin *biotechnologist, information scientist, educator*
Greenfield, Mark Steven *art gallery director, artist*
Grinnan, Katie *artist*
Grinnell, Alan Dale *neuroscientist, educator*
Grobe, Charles Stephen *lawyer, accountant*
Grode, Susan A. *lawyer*
Grody, Wayne William *physician*
Gronnier, Henry Maurice *violinist, educator*
Gross, Allen Jeffrey *lawyer*
Gross, Larry Paul *communications educator*
Gross, Lee *chef*
Grossman, Steven L. *lawyer*
Grotjahn, Mark *painter*
Guo, Wei *research scientist*
Guo, Zhanhu *researcher*
Gupta, Yash *dean*
Gurfein, Peter J. *lawyer*
Hahn, Elliott Julius *lawyer*
Haight, G. Timothy *academic administrator, consultant*
Halberstadter, David *lawyer*
Haley, Roslyn Trezevant *educational program director*
Halkett, Alan Neilson *lawyer*
Hamilton, Patricia Rose *art dealer*
Hancock, Herbert Jeffrey (Herbie Hancock) *composer, pianist, publisher*
Handler, Carole Enid *lawyer, city planner*
Handler, Joel F. *law educator*
Handzlik, Jan Lawrence *lawyer*
Hannah, David H. *metal products executive*
Hansell, Dean *lawyer*
Hansen, Alexander E. *advertising agency executive*
Hansen, B(obby) J. *management consultant, real estate investor and developer*
Hanson, John J. *retired lawyer*
Harberger, Arnold Carl *economist, educator*
Harbert, Ted (Edward W. Harbert III) *broadcast executive*
Harkness, Nancy P. *lawyer*
Harris, D. Alan *lawyer*
Harrison, Blair *information technology executive*
Harrison, Gail G. *public health educator*
Hart, Mary *television talk show host*
Hartigan, John Francis *lawyer*
Hartsough, Gayla Anne Kraetsch *management consultant*
Harvey, James Gerald *educational consultant, researcher*
Harvey, Randy *editor, reporter*
Hashemi, Hossein *engineering educator*
Hatamiya, Lon Shoso *consultant, former state official*
Hateley, J. Michael *human resources executive*
Havel, Richard W. *lawyer*
Haviland, Peter L. *lawyer*
Hawley, Philip Metschan *retired retail executive, management consultant*
Hayes, Reggie *actor*
Hayutin, David Lionel *lawyer*
Haywood, L. Julian *cardiologist, educator*
Hebert, William N. *lawyer*
Hefner, Hugh Marston *editor-in-chief*
Heigl, Katherine Marie *actress*
Heinke, Rex S. *lawyer*
Heller, Philip *lawyer*
Hellwarth, Robert Willis *physicist, researcher*
Helm, Robert Wilbur *federal official*
Helms, Ed *comedian, actor*
Hemminger, Pamela Lynn *lawyer*
Henderson, Brian Edmond *dean, physician, educator*
Henderson, Florence *actress, singer*
Henkel, Kathy *composer*
Henriksen, Eva Hansine *retired anesthesiology educator*
Henry, Carl Nolan *lawyer*
Hernandez, Antonia *foundation administrator, lawyer*
Herron, Vincent H. *lawyer*
Herzog, Doug *broadcast executive*
Hess, Frederick Scott *artist*
Hextall, Ron *professional sports team executive, former professional hockey player*
Heyck, Theodore Daly *lawyer*
Heyler, Grover Ross *retired lawyer*
Hieronymus, Edward Whittlesey *retired lawyer*
Hight, B. Boyd *retired lawyer*
Hill, Bonnie Guiton *consulting company executive*
Hill, Millicent E. *English educator*
Hiltzik, Michael *journalist*

Hines, Thomas Spight *historian, educator, architecture critic*
Hirabayashi, Keith Cooke *actor, martial arts instructor*
Hirai, Denitsu *surgeon*
Hirano, Irene Ann Yasutake *museum director*
Hirsch, Anthony Terry *physician*
Hoang, Duc Van *pathologist, educator*
Hockney, David *artist*
Hoff, Christian *actor*
Hoffman, Philip Seymour *actor*
Hoi, Samuel Chuen-Tsung *academic administrator*
Hollander, Daniel *gastroenterologist, medical educator*
Holliday, Thomas Edgar *lawyer*
Holly, Krisztina J. *entrepreneur, academic administrator*
Holmes, Fontayne *city librarian*
Holscher, Mark Charles *lawyer*
Holtzman, Robert Arthur *lawyer*
Hopkins, Bernard *professional boxer*
Hopkins, Henry Tyler *museum director, art educator*
Horn, Cindy Harrell *environmental advocate*
Horovitz, Adam (King Adrock) *recording artist*
Horowitz, Ben *health facility administrator*
Horowitz, David Charles *consumer advocate, radio and television commentator, newspaper columnist, director*
Horowitz, David Joel *author*
Horwitz, David A. *rheumatologist, educator*
Hostovich, Teena Maria *insurance brokerage executive*
Houk, Kendall Newcomb *chemistry professor*
House, John William *otolaryngologist*
Houston, Ivan James *insurance company executive*
Hovanessian, Shahen Alexander *electrical engineer, educator, consultant*
Howland, Ben *men's college basketball coach*
Hoye, Maria Pilar *lawyer*
Hubbard, John Randolph *retired academic administrator, department chairman, diplomat*
Hudson, Jeffrey Reid *lawyer*
Huebner, David *lawyer*
Huerta, Sergio *physician, researcher*
Hufstedler, Seth Martin *lawyer*
Hufstedler, Shirley Mount (Mrs. Seth M. Hufstedler) *lawyer, former federal judge*
Hundley, Norris Cecil, Jr. *historian, educator*
Hurt, William Holman *investment management company executive*
Hurwitz, Mitchell *television producer, writer*
Husar, Linda S. *lawyer*
Hutchins, Joan Morthland *manufacturing executive, farmer*
Hyde, Manly Richard *thoracic surgeon*
Hyman, Jonathan *lawyer*
Hyman, Milton Bernard *lawyer*
Hyman, Ursula H. *lawyer*
Ibarra, Irene M. *foundation administrator*
Ice-T, (Tracy Marrow) *rap artist, actor*
Ignarro, Louis J. *pharmacology educator*
Im, Hyepin Christine *not-for-profit developer*
Ingram, Theodore Francis *transportation executive*
Inman, James Russell *claims consultant*
Intriligator, Michael David *economist, educator*
Iovine, Jimmy *recording industry executive*
Irani, Ray R. *oil, gas and chemical company executive*
Iredale, Nancy Louise *lawyer*
Ireland, Kathy *actress, apparel designer*
Irving, Paul Howard *lawyer*
Irwin, Philip Donnan *lawyer*
IsHak, Waguih William *psychiatrist*
Islam, Mohammad *chef*
Itabashi, Hideo Henry *medical educator, consultant, coroner, pathologist*
Itoh, Tatsuo *engineering educator*
Ivins, Molly (Mary Tyler Ivins) *columnist, writer*
Jacobson, Marcus J. *retired mechanical engineer*
Jacoby, Neil Herman, Jr. *astronautical scientist, engineer, consultant*
Jadvar, Hossein *nuclear medicine physician, biomedical engineer*
Jagger, Sir Mick (Michael Philip Jagger) *singer, musician*
Jalali, Behnaz *psychiatrist, educator*
Jeffrey, Sheri *lawyer*
Jensen, David Gram *management consultant*
Jin, Yan *adult education educator*
Johnson, Cage Saul *hematologist, educator*
Johnson, Charles Floyd *television executive, producer*
Johnson, E. Eric *insurance company executive*
Johnson, Earl, Jr. *judge, author*
Johnson, Jeffrey M. *publishing executive*
Johnson, Jonathan Edwin, II, *lawyer*
Johnston, Ynez *artist, educator*
Jones, Gerald Paul *information technology educator*
Jones, Quincy *producer, composer, arranger, conductor, trumpeter*
Jones, Sir Tom (Thomas Jones Woodward) *singer*
Jordan, Martha B. *lawyer*
Jordan, Robert Leon *lawyer, educator*
Joseph, George *insurance company executive*
Ju, Jiann-Wen *mechanics educator, researcher*
Judge, Mike *animator*
Kalis, Murray *advertising agency executive, writer*
Kamil, Elaine Scheiner *pediatric nephrologist, educator*
Kamine, Bernard S. *lawyer*
Kanoff, Mary Ellen *lawyer*
Kanter, Sandra May *lawyer*
Kaplan, Isaac Raymond *chemistry professor*
Kaplan, Nadia *writer*
Karatz, Bruce E. *construction executive*
Karst, Kenneth Leslie *law educator*
Kassner, Michael Ernest *materials science educator, researcher*
Katz, Jason Lawrence *lawyer, insurance company executive*
Katz, Ronald Lewis *physician, educator*
Katzenstein, Andrew M. *lawyer*
Kaufman, Francine R. *pediatric endocrinologist*
Kaunitz, Jonathan Davidson *physician*
Kedes, Laurence Herbert *biochemistry professor, physician, researcher*
Keith, David *symphony orchestra conductor*
Kelleher, Robert Joseph *judge*

Kellerman, Sally Claire *actress*
Kelley, David E. *producer, writer*
Kelley, Malcolm David *actor*
Kelley, Robin Davis Gibran *history professor, writer*
Kelly, Arthur Paul *physician*
Kelly, Daniel *neurosurgeon*
Kelly, Henry Ansgar *language educator*
Kelly, Robert Edward *engineer, educator*
Kent, Jeffrey Franklin *professional baseball player*
Keville, Terri Donna *lawyer*
Khawli, Leslie Albert *research scientist, educator*
Kieffer, George David *lawyer*
Kiley, Katie *printmaker, painter*
Kim, Kwang-Jin *medical educator*
Kimmel, Jimmy (James Christian Kimmel) *television personality*
Kindel, James Horace, Jr. *lawyer*
King-Ning, Tu *materials science and engineering educator*
Kirwan, Betty-Jane *lawyer*
Kirwan, R. DeWitt (Kyle) *lawyer*
Kitchens, Dean J. *lawyer*
Kittles, Kerry *professional basketball player*
Kivelson, Margaret Galland *physicist*
Klausen, Raymond *theatre set designer, television production designer, sculptor*
Klauss, Kenneth Karl *composer, music educator*
Kleeman, Charles Richard *medical educator, nephrologist, researcher*
Klein, Benjamin *economics professor, consultant*
Klein, Eric A. *lawyer*
Kleingartner, Archie *dean, educator, academic administrator*
Kleinrock, Leonard *computer scientist*
Kline, Richard Stephen *public relations executive*
Klinger, Marilyn Sydney *lawyer*
Knapp, Cleon Talboys *publishing executive*
Knight, Henry L. *minister*
Koeffler, H. Phillip *health facility administrator*
Koga, Rokutaro (Rocky Koga) *physicist*
Kollar, Linda Randlett *lawyer*
Kolve, V. A. *English literature educator*
Komaroff, Linda *curator*
Kozberg, Joanne Corday *public affairs consultant*
Kraft, Scott Corey *news correspondent*
Kramer, Barry Alan *psychiatrist, educator*
Kranwinkle, Conrad Douglas *lawyer, broadcast executive*
Krieger, Ellie *chef, dietitian, TV personality*
Kristof, Kathy M. *journalist*
Krupka, Robert George *lawyer*
Krupp, Edwin Charles *astronomer*
Kuechle, John Merrill *lawyer*
Kuehl, Hans Henry *electrical engineering educator*
Kunowski, Herbert Peter *lawyer*
Kupietzky, Moshe Joseph *lawyer*
Kupper, Ketti *artist*
Kveton, Kyle *lawyer*
Kwoh, Stewart *lawyer, cultural organization administrator*
Kwon, Ohyun *chemist, educator*
Kyles, Cedric Antonio (Cedric the Entertainer) *comedian, actor*
La Force, James Clayburn, Jr. *economist, educator*
Lagasse, Emeril *chef, restaurant owner, television show host, writer*
Laird, David *humanities educator emeritus*
Lake, James *microbiologist, educator*
Landers, Audrey *actress, singer*
Langan, Kenneth J. *lawyer*
Langberg, Barry Benson *lawyer*
Langguth, Arthur John *journalist, educator, writer*
Lappen, Chester I. *lawyer*
Larkin, Thomas Ernest, Jr. *investment management company executive*
Larrubia, Evelyn *reporter*
Larry the Cable Guy, (Daniel Lawrence Whitney) *comedian, radio personality*
Lasorda, Thomas Charles (Tommy Lasorda) *professional baseball team manager*
Lauchengco, Jose Yujuico, Jr. *lawyer*
Lavin, Laurence Michael *lawyer*
Lavin, Stephen Michael *university basketball coach*
Lawler, Jean Marie *lawyer*
Lawrence, Sanford Hull *physician, immunochemist, author*
Layne, Jonathan K. *lawyer*
Layton, Harry Christopher *art director*
Lazareff, Jorge Antonio *neurosurgeon, researcher*
Lazarus, Mell *cartoonist*
Leach, Anthony Raymond *financial executive*
Leanse, Thomas J. *lawyer*
Lear, Lyn Davis *psychologist*
LeBeau, Mary Delle *dancer, educator, writer*
Lechago, Juan *pathologist, educator*
Ledger, Heath *actor*
Lee, Dorothy Wong *art educator*
Lee, John Joon *research scientist, minister*
Lee, Kwan Min *communications educator, consultant*
Lee, Stan (Stanley Martin Lieber) *cartoon publisher, writer*
Leeves, Jane *actress*
LeFevre, David *chef*
Leff, Daniel V. *venture capitalist*
Leibow, Ronald Louis *lawyer*
LeMay, Harry Adrian *artist, educator*
Lemkin, Jeffrey W. *lawyer*
Lennon, Sean Taro Ono *musician*
Lentz, David *chef*
Leonard, Jack *reporter*
Lesser, Joan L. *lawyer*
Letwin, Leon *law educator*
Leung, Frankie Fook-Lun *lawyer*
Levenson, Laurie L. *law educator*
Levey, Gerald Saul *dean, internist, educator*
Levine, Jerome L. *lawyer*
Levine, Meldon Edises *lawyer, retired congressman*
Levine, Michael *public relations executive, author, television and radio personality*
Levine, Pamela *film company executive*
Levine, Philip *classics educator*
Levine, Raphael David *chemistry professor*
Levine, Robert Arthur *economist, educator, policy writer*
Levine, Thomas Jeffrey Pello *lawyer*
Lewis, Marjorie Ehrich *lawyer*

Lewis, Samella Sanders *artist, educator*
Lhuillier, Monique (Diane Monique Lhuillier) *apparel designer*
Li, Andrew J. *gynecologist, oncologist*
Li, Yong-Gang Frank *research scientist, educator*
Liberman, Robert Paul *psychiatry educator, researcher, writer*
Lieber, David Lee *university vice president*
Lieber, Michael Randall *biochemist, educator*
Lightfoot, Peter *music educator, baritone*
Liguori, Peter *film company executive*
Lindholm, Dwight Henry *lawyer*
Lindley, F. Haynes, Jr. (Francis Haynes Lindley Jr.) *foundation executive, lawyer*
Linkletter, Arthur Gordon *radio and television broadcaster*
Linsk, Michael Stephen *real estate company executive*
Linsman, Joseph F. *retired radiologist*
Lipsig, Ethan *lawyer*
Litewka, Albert Bernard *publishing executive, entertainment executive*
Little, William Grady (Grady Little) *professional baseball coach*
Lizarraga, David C. *non-profit community development corporation administrator*
Ljubimov, Alexander V. *molecular biologist, cell biologist, researcher*
Lloyd-Jones, Dadiva Bocobo *nursing assistant, writer*
Logan, Ben H. III *lawyer*
Lombardi, Dean *professional sports team executive*
London, Andrew Barry *film editor*
Long, Gregory Alan *lawyer*
Looney, Claudia Arlene *health facility administrator*
Lopez, George *actor, comedian*
Lopez, Steve *journalist*
Lopez-Arce Martinez, Paula *geologist, researcher*
Lowenthal, Abraham Frederic *international relations educator*
Lowy, Peter *corporate financial executive*
Lozano, Monica Cecilia *publishing executive*
Lu, John Kuew-Hsiung *physiology educator, endocrinologist*
Lui, Elwood *lawyer*
Lund, James Louis *lawyer*
Lunden, Joan *television personality*
Lunt, Owen Raynal *biologist, educator*
Lynch, Beverly Pfeifer *education and information studies educator*
Lynch, Patrick *lawyer*
Lyons, James Richard *research scientist*
Macavinta-Tenazas, Gemorsita *physician*
MacIntosh, Jay W. *lawyer, realtor, actress*
Mack, James Curtis, II, *cultural organization administrator*
MacLachlan, Kyle *actor*
MacLaughlin, Francis Joseph *lawyer*
Maddux, Gregory (Gregory Alan Maddux) *professional baseball player*
Madni, Asad Mohamed *engineering executive*
Mager, Artur *retired aerospace executive*
Maguire, Tobey (Tobias Vincent Maguire) *actor*
Mahony, Roger Michael *archbishop*
Maki, Kazumi *physicist, researcher*
Malamuth, Neil Moshe *psychology and communication educator*
Malden, Karl (Malden Sekulovich) *actor*
Malkin, Michelle *syndicated columnist*
Mall, William John, Jr. *aerospace transportation executive, retired military officer*
Malone, Carolyn Lucia Marino *education educator*
Malone, Nancy *actress*
Maloney, Kristen *gymnast*
Maloney, Robert Keller *ophthalmologist, medical educator*
Maltin, Leonard *commentator, writer*
Maltzan, Michael Thomas *architect*
Mamer, John William *business educator*
Man, Lawrence Kong *architect, art dealer*
Mancino, Douglas Michael *lawyer*
Mandel, Joseph David *academic administrator, lawyer*
Mandles, Martinn Heroe *facility services company executive*
Manella, Nora Margaret *judge*
Mann, Nancy Louise (Nancy Louise Robbins) *entrepreneur*
Marciano, Maurice *apparel executive*
Marder, John Adam *lawyer*
Margo, Rod David *lawyer*
Marjoram, Paul *medical educator, researcher*
Markland, Francis Swaby, Jr. *biochemist, educator*
Marmarelis, Vasilis Zissis *engineering educator, writer, consultant*
Marmorstein, Victoria E. *lawyer*
Maronde, Robert Francis *internist, pharmacologist*
Marshall, Consuelo Bland *federal judge*
Marshall-Daniels, Meryl *mediator, executive coach*
Martin, Donald A. *mathematics professor*
Martin, J(ohn) Edward *architectural engineer*
Martin, Shane Patrick *education educator, consultant*
Martinez, Maritza Araceli *elementary school educator*
Martinez, Miguel Acevedo *urologist, consultant, lecturer*
Mataric, Maja J. *engineering educator*
Mathias, Alice Irene *business management consultant*
Maxworthy, Tony *mechanical and aerospace engineering educator*
Mayorkas, Alejandro *lawyer, former prosecutor*
Mays, Vickie M. *psychology professor*
McAniff, Edward John *lawyer*
McCabe, Edward R. B. *hospital administrator, educator, physician*
McCarthy, Paul *artist*
McConaughey, Matthew *actor*
McCormick, Carolyn *actress*
McElyea, Jacquelyn Suzanne *accountant, real estate consultant*
McFarlane, Seth *animator, director*
McFarling, Usha Lee *newswriter*
McGarry, Dorothy *librarian*
McGregor, Judith Ann *education educator*
McKenna, Robert Joseph, Jr. *thoracic surgeon*
McKinzie, Carl Wayne *lawyer*
McKnight, Frederick L. *lawyer*

McLane, Frederick Berg *lawyer*
McNevin, Christopher J. *lawyer*
McQueen, Justice Ellis (L. Q. Jones) *actor, television director*
McRaney, Gerald *actor*
Meer, Jon Douglas *lawyer*
Meisinger, Louis M. *lawyer*
Melby, Donna D. *lawyer*
Mellinkoff, Sherman Mussoff *medical educator*
Mellor, Ronald John *history professor*
Melnick, David *geneticist, educator*
Mendel, Jerry Marc *electrical engineering educator*
Mendoza, Ron *chef*
Mersel, Marjorie Kathryn Pedersen *lawyer*
Mesereau, Thomas Arthur, Jr. *lawyer*
Meshki, Hamed *lawyer*
Messerli, Douglas *writer, publisher*
Metzger, Robert Streicher *lawyer*
Meyer, Bruce D. *lawyer*
Meyer, Catherine Dieffenbach *lawyer*
Meyer, Michael Edwin *lawyer*
Michaelson, Jon *lawyer*
Mihan, Richard *retired dermatologist*
Milchan, Arnon *film producer*
Miles, Jack (John Russiano) *journalist, educator*
Millard, Neal Steven *lawyer, educator*
Millauer, Liselotte *journalist*
Miller, Milton Allen *lawyer*
Miller, Timothy Alden *plastic and reconstructive surgeon*
Min, Taegee *aerospace engineer, researcher, mechanical engineer*
Minkova, Donka *language educator*
Mintz, Marshall Gary *lawyer*
Miranda, M. Jeanne *psychiatrist*
Miscavige, David *head of religious order*
Mobley, Cuttino Rashawn *professional basketball player*
Mock, Theodore Jaye *finance educator*
Modabber, Zia F. *lawyer*
Moe, Stanley Allen *architect, consultant*
Mohr, John Luther *biologist, environmental consultant*
Molina, Gloria *municipal official*
Mondino, Bartly J. *ophthalmologist*
Montgomery, Robert K. *lawyer*
Montoya, Velma *economist, consultant*
Moore, Shemar *actor*
More, Philip Harvey Birnbaum *business administration educator*
Moreno, Rita (Rosita Dolores Alverio) *actress*
Morgan, Elizabeth *plastic surgeon*
Morgenthaler-Lever, Alisa *lawyer*
Morgner, Aurelius *economist, educator*
Morin, JoyAnn Hauge *education educator*
Morissette, Alanis Nadine *singer*
Moriuchi, K. Derek *secondary school educator*
Morrison, Donald Graham *business educator, consultant*
Morrison, Sherie Leaver *microbiologist, educator*
Morrissey, J. Richard *lawyer*
Morrow, Winston Vaughan *financial executive*
Mort, Peter J. *lawyer*
Morton, Joe *actor*
Moschovakis, Yiannis Nicholas *mathematics professor*
Mosich, Anelis Nick *accountant, writer, educator, consultant*
Mosk, Richard Mitchell *judge*
Moskowitz, Joel Steven *lawyer*
Moss, Jerome (Jerry) S. *recording industry executive*
Moss, Susan Hecht *artist, writer*
Moxley, John Howard III *internist*
Moy, Ronald Leonard *dermasurgeon*
Mueller, Carl Richard *theater arts educator, author*
Muldaur, Diana Charlton *actress*
Mullan, John H. *science administrator*
Muller, Dave *artist*
Munger, Molly *lawyer*
Munro, JP *artist*
Muntz, Eric Phillip *aerospace and mechanical engineering educator, consultant*
Mureika, Jonas R. *physics professor*
Murphree, A. Linn *ophthalmologist*
Murray, Alice Pearl *data processing company executive*
Murray, Anthony *lawyer*
Myers, Albert F. *aerospace executive*
Nadler, Gerald *management consultant, educator*
Nael, Kambiz *radiologist, educator*
Nakanishi, Don Toshiaki *Asian American studies educator, writer*
Nakell, Martin R. *literature educator, writer*
Natarajan, Sathima *pathologist*
Nathwani, Bharat N. *pathologist, educator*
Needleman, Jack *education educator, researcher*
Neely, Sally Schultz *lawyer*
Neil, Daniel *journalist*
Neiter, Gerald Irving *lawyer*
Nelson, Grant Steel *law educator*
Nelson, Howard Joseph *geographer, educator*
Nelson, Larry Dean *telecommunications and computer systems company executive, consultant*
Nelson, Marvin Dale, Jr. *radiologist, educator*
Nelson, Steven D. *art history professor*
Neufeld, Elizabeth Fondal *biochemist, educator*
Neutra, Dion *architect*
Newhart, Bob (George Robert Newhart) *entertainer*
Newman, Michael Rodney *lawyer*
Newman, Randy *singer, songwriter, musician*
Newman, Richard G. *engineering company executive*
Nicholas, William Richard *lawyer*
Nicholson, Jack *actor*
Nield, Margaret *nursing researcher*
Nikias, Chrysostomos L. (Max Nikias) *engineering educator*
Niles, John Gilbert *lawyer*
Nimni, Marcel Ephraim *biochemistry educator*
Nissenson, Allen Richard *physician, educator*
Nobe, Ken *chemical engineering professor*
Noble, Douglas *architecture educator*
Noble, Ernest Pascal *pharmacologist, biochemist, educator*
Noble, James Wilkes *actor*
Nobumoto, Karen S. *prosecutor*
Nochimson, David *lawyer*

Nogales, Luis Guerrero *investment company executive*
Noguchi, Thomas Tsunetomi *writer, pathologist*
Norris, William Albert *lawyer, mediator, retired judge*
North, Oliver Laurence (Ollie North) *syndicated columnist, retired military officer*
Nuechterlein, Keith H. *psychology professor*
Nugent, Gary W. *lawyer*
Nyman, Michael Lawrence *composer*
Oakes, Jeannine *education educator*
O'Brien, Pat *television personality*
Ochoa, Arthur J. *lawyer, hospital administrator*
O'Connell, Kevin *lawyer*
O'Donnell, Pierce Henry *lawyer*
Ogilvie, Lloyd John *clergyman*
Oh, Angela E. *lawyer*
Ohlgren, Joel R. *lawyer*
Ohlmeyer, Donald Winfred, Jr. *film and television producer*
Okrent, David *engineering educator*
Olah, George Andrew *chemist, educator*
Oldham, Granville Murl, Jr. *conductor, educator*
Oldman, Gary *actor*
O'Leary, Prentice Lee *retired lawyer*
Oliver, Dale Hugh *lawyer*
Olivier, Kathy Ricks *college basketball coach*
Olsen, Ashley Fuller *actress*
Olsen, Frances Elisabeth *law educator, theorist*
Olsen, Mary-Kate *actress*
Olson, Ronald Leroy *lawyer*
O'Neil, Harold Francis *psychologist, educator*
O'Neil, William Scott *publishing executive*
O'Neill, Russell Richard *engineering educator*
Oppenheim, Charles B. *lawyer*
Oppenheimer, Randy (Mark Randall Oppenheimer) *lawyer*
Ordin, Andrea Sheridan *lawyer*
Ordonez, Fernando Ivan *adult education educator*
Orme, Antony Ronald *geography educator*
Ostroff, Dawn T. *broadcast executive*
Ostroff, Peter I. *lawyer*
O'Toole, James Joseph *business educator*
Owen, Michael Lee *lawyer*
Owens, Laura *painter*
Ownbey, Vance Scott *corporate financial executive*
Pachino, Barton P. *lawyer*
Palevsky, Max *industrialist, director*
Palmer, Pamela S. *lawyer*
Palmieri, Victor Henry *lawyer, director, investment advisor*
Pare, Michael *actor, singer*
Parente, Robert Bruce *electrical engineer, consultant*
Park, No-Hee *dean, academic administrator*
Park, Sam-Koo *transportation executive*
Parks, Michael Christopher *journalist, educator*
Parmelee, Arthur Hawley, Jr. *pediatric medical educator*
Parsky, Gerald Lawrence *lawyer*
Pasich, Kirk Alan *lawyer*
Patrick, Robert *playwright*
Patron, Susan Hall *librarian, writer*
Paulson, Donald Robert *chemistry professor*
Pearl, Judea *computer scientist, educator*
Peel, Mark *chef, restaurant owner*
Pellegrini, Claudio *physicist, educator*
Peña, Elizabeth *actress*
Penn, Sean *actor*
Penny, Brad *professional baseball player*
Perenchio, Andrew Jerrold *film and television executive*
Perez, Edith R. *lawyer*
Perkins, William Clinton *manufacturing executive*
Perlis, Michael Fredrick *lawyer*
Perrine, Richard Leroy *environmental engineer, educator*
Perron, Edward Adrian *lawyer*
Perry, Ralph Barton III *lawyer*
Pesta, Ben W., II, *lawyer, writer*
Petak, William John *systems management educator*
Petersen, Robert E. *magazine publishing executive*
Peterson, Kurt C. *lawyer*
Peterson, Linda S. *lawyer*
Petrocelli, Daniel M. *lawyer*
Petroff, Laura R. *lawyer*
Pfeiffer, Norman *architectural firm executive*
Phelps, Barton Chase *architect, educator*
Philbin, Ann *art facility director*
Phillips, Geneva Ficker *academic editor*
Phillips, Keith Wendall *minister*
Phillips, Todd *film director, film producer*
Phoenix, Joaquin Raphael *actor*
Pi, Edmond Hsin-Tung *psychiatry educator*
Picot, Pierre Bernard *artist, educator*
Pierskalla, William Peter *dean, finance educator, engineering educator*
Piller, Charles Leon *journalist*
Pircher, Leo Joseph *lawyer, director*
Piuze, Michael Joseph *lawyer*
Plate, Thomas Gordon *columnist, educator*
Pohost, Gerald Michael *cardiologist, medical educator*
Poindexter, William Mersereau *lawyer*
Poledna, Mathias *video artist*
Pollock, John Phleger *lawyer*
Pondel, Roger S. *public relations executive*
Port, Sidney Charles *mathematician, educator*
Porter, John E. *lawyer*
Powell, James Lawrence *educational association administrator, museum director, geologist*
Power, John Bruce *lawyer*
Prager, Susan Westerberg *academic administrator, law educator*
Preonas, George Elias *lawyer*
Presant, Sanford Calvin *lawyer, educator, writer, tax specialist*
Prewitt, Jean *not-for-profit organization executive*
Price, William Charlie *lawyer*
Priselac, Thomas M. *health facility executive, educator*
Pritzker, Jean *film producer*
Pruetz, Adrian Mary *lawyer*
Pryor, Richard Walter *telecommunications executive, retired air force officer*
Qiao, Jian-Hua *pathologist, researcher*
Quicksilver, William Todd *lawyer*
Quinn, John B. *lawyer*
Quinn, John J. *lawyer*
Rabinovitz, Joel *lawyer, educator*

Rachelefsky, Gary Stuart *medical educator*
Racine, Scott H. *lawyer*
Racklin, Barbara Cohen *fundraising consultant*
Rae, Matthew Sanderson, Jr. *lawyer*
Raeder, Myrna Sharon *lawyer, educator*
Rafeedie, Edward *federal judge*
Rakow, Jay *lawyer, film company executive*
Raksin, Alex *reporter, writer*
Ramer, Lawrence Jerome *corporation executive*
Ramo, Simon *retired engineering executive*
Ramos, Jorge *newscaster*
Rando, John *theater director*
Rappeport, Ira J. *lawyer*
Rasgon, Natalie Luzina *psychiatrist*
Rassman, William R. *plastic surgeon*
Rath, Howard Grant, Jr. *lawyer*
Raven, Bertram H(erbert) *psychology professor*
Ray, Gilbert T. *lawyer*
Reagins-Lilly, Soncia Rae *dean*
Reddick, C.N. (Frank)lin III *lawyer*
Reed, George Ford, Jr. *investment executive*
Reeves, Barbara Ann *lawyer*
Reid, E. Lewis *lawyer*
Reinman, Glenn D. *computer scientist, educator*
Reisman, Ellen Kelly *lawyer*
Reiss, Howard *chemistry professor*
Renwick, Edward S. *lawyer*
Resnick, Lynda *corporate financial executive*
Resnick, Stewart Allen *diversified company executive*
Reuben, Don Harold *lawyer*
Reyes Robbins, Ann Marie *lawyer, researcher, educator, former magistrate judge*
Reynolds, Burt *actor, film director*
Rice, Constance LaMay *lawyer*
Rice, Regina Kelly *marketing executive*
Rice, Thomas Howard *healthcare educator*
Rich, Alan *film critic, writer*
Rich, Andrea Louise *museum administrator*
Richards, Eric Albert Stephan *lawyer*
Richardson, James *chef*
Richardson, John Vinson, Jr. *library and information science professor*
Richland, Kent Lewis *lawyer*
Richmond, Rocsan *television executive producer, small business owner*
Richter, Stuart M. *lawyer*
Rickles, Donald Jay *comedian, actor*
Riff, Lawrence P. *lawyer*
Rimoin, David Lawrence *medical geneticist*
Riordan, George Nickerson *investment banker*
Rishwain, James Michael, Jr. *lawyer*
Rising, Kevin D. *lawyer*
Roberts, Paul Harry *mathematics professor*
Roberts, Robert Winston *social worker, educator, dean*
Roberts, Sidney *biological chemist*
Robinson, James W. *fire captain*
Robitaille, Luc *retired professional hockey player*
Robleto, Dario *artist*
Robson, Glenn R. *engineering and design company executive*
Roby, Thomas Carter *conservator*
Rodriguez, Daniel *tenor, former protective services official*
Roeder, Richard Kenneth *business owner, lawyer*
Rogers, David Booth *lawyer*
Rogers, Wayne M. *actor, investor, investment strategist, consultant*
Rohrer, Susan Earley *film producer, film director, scriptwriter*
Rosen, Kevin S. *lawyer*
Rosenberg, Alan *actors guild executive*
Rosenfeld, John Lang *geology educator*
Rosenstock, Linda *dean, medical educator*
Rosenthal, J. Thomas *hospital administrator, medical educator*
Rosenthal, Sol *lawyer*
Rosenzweig, Richard Stuart *publishing company executive*
Rosett, Arthur Irwin *lawyer, educator*
Rosett, Daniel J. *film company executive*
Ross, Marion *actress*
Ross, Robert K. *foundation administrator, physician*
Ross, Stan *real estate company executive*
Rosser, James Milton *academic administrator*
Rotell, Cynthia A. *lawyer*
Roth, Tim *actor*
Rothenberg, Alan I. *lawyer, professional sports association executive*
Rouse, Richard Hunter *historian, educator*
Rouze, Jeffrey Alan *real estate executive*
Roven, Alfred Nathan *surgeon*
Rowell, Victoria *actress*
Roy-Burman, Pradip *molecular biology and virology educator*
Roychowdhury, Vwani *electrical engineer, educator*
Rubin, Robert Terry *psychiatrist, researcher, educator*
Rubin, Stanley Creamer *television producer, film producer*
Rubinstein, Moshe Fajwel *engineering educator*
Rudkin, George Henry *plastic surgeon*
Ruhl, Mary B. *lawyer*
Rush, Herman E. *television executive*
Ruskin, Joseph Richard *actor, director*
Russell, Joseph Allen *engineer, consultant*
Russo, Rene *actress*
Rust, Neil W. *lawyer*
Rust, Patricia Joan *television executive*
Ruthberg, Miles N. *lawyer*
Rutter, Marshall Anthony *lawyer*
Ryan, Stephen Joseph, Jr. *ophthalmologist, educator*
Saban, Haim *investment company executive, television producer*
Sachs, George *biology professor, physician*
Sacks, Robert A. *lawyer*
Safadi, M. Oussama *engineering educator*
Safonov, Michael George *electrical engineering educator, researcher*
Saltzman, Joseph *journalist, educator, television producer*
Salvaty, Benjamin Benedict *lawyer*
Samaha, Elie *producer, film company executive, business owner*
Samet, Jack I. *lawyer*
Sample, Steven Browning *academic administrator*
Samuels, Mark A. *lawyer*

Sanders, Kathryn A. *lawyer*
Sands, Rick (Richard Sands) *film company executive*
Sanford, James L. *science administrator*
San Giacomo, Laura *actress*
Santaolalla, Gustavo *musician, composer, record producer*
Sargent, Joseph Daniel *motion picture and television director*
Sarma, Radha J. *cardiologist, educator*
Sarnat, Bernard George *plastic surgeon, educator, researcher*
Sarnoff, Thomas Warren *television executive*
Sawyer, Toni *actress*
Saxe, Deborah Crandall *lawyer*
Scates, Allen Edward *coach*
Schaefer, William David *language educator*
Scheibel, Arnold Bernard *psychiatrist, educator, research director*
Schelbert, Heinrich Ruediger *nuclear medicine physician*
Schill, Michael H. *dean, law educator*
Schmidt, Karl A. *lawyer*
Scholtz, Robert Arno *electrical engineering educator*
Schopf, James William *paleobiologist, researcher, educator*
Schott, Robert W. (Bob Schott) *film producer, actor, film director*
Schuchard, Robert L. *lawyer*
Schuetze-Coburn, Marje *university librarian*
Schulberg, Budd *author*
Schulman, Cathy *film producer*
Schwartz, Robert M. *lawyer*
Schwarz, Ernst Ruediger *cardiologist, researcher*
Scott, Michael Dennis *lawyer*
Scott, Robert Lane *chemist, educator*
Scott, Tony *film director*
Scoular, Robert Frank *lawyer*
Sears, David O'Keefe *psychology professor*
Sedaris, Amy *writer, actress*
See, Carolyn *English language educator, writer, book critic*
Sella, Anthony *film company executive*
Selleck, Tom *actor*
Serafin, Thomas Joseph *photographer, writer*
Seto, Theodore Paul *lawyer, educator*
Settles, F. Stan, Jr. *engineering educator, manufacturing executive*
Sewell, William George III *electronics engineer, writer*
Shahinian, Hrayr K. *surgeon*
Shakely, John Bower (Jack Shakely) *foundation executive*
Shank, Russell *librarian, educator*
Shanks, Patricia L. *lawyer*
Shapiro, Jerald Steven *chemist, bank executive*
Shapiro, Mel *playwright, educator, theater director*
Shapiro, Robert *lawyer*
Shay, Anthony Victor *choreographer, dance historian*
Shearer, Derek Nocross *political science professor, diplomat, academic administrator*
Sheedy, Ally (Alexandra Elizabeth Sheedy) *actress*
Sheehan, Lawrence James *lawyer*
Shelby, Carroll Hall *automotive designer*
Sheldon, Sidney *writer, television director, television producer*
Sheller, John Willard *lawyer*
Shen, Wei-Chiang *medical educator*
Sherman, Randolph *plastic and reconstructive surgeon, educator*
Sherrell, John Bradford *lawyer*
Sherwood, Allen Joseph *retired lawyer*
Shideler, Ross Patrick *literature and language educator, writer, translator, poet*
Shields, Patrick M. *lawyer*
Shields, William Donald *physician, educator*
Shneidman, Edwin S. *psychologist, thanatologist*
Shoaf, R. Wayne *librarian*
Shortz, Richard Alan *lawyer*
Shultz, John David *lawyer*
Shuster, Alvin *journalist, reporter*
Shuster, Beth *editor*
Siegel, Michael Elliot *nuclear medicine physician, educator*
Siegel, Robert (Bob) A. *lawyer*
Siegel, Sheldon C. *pediatrician, immunologist, allergist*
Siegel, Stuart Elliott *pediatric oncologist, educator*
Sigband, Norman Bruce *communications educator*
Silbergeld, Arthur F. *lawyer*
Silverstein, Suzanne *art therapist*
Simmons, Donna Marie *neuroscientist, histotechnologist, neuroendocrinologist, researcher*
Simmons, Gary *artist*
Simmons, Richard J. *lawyer*
Sinay, Joseph *retail executive*
Sinenko, Sergey A. *biologist, geneticist, researcher*
Singleton, Joan Vietor *publishing executive, writer, film producer*
Siniawski, Matthew *science educator*
Sinner, Steve *sculptor*
Sivertsen, Linda Joyce *writer, editor, publishing consultant*
Skaggs, David L. *orthopedist, educator*
Sklar, Richard Lawrence *political science professor*
Slamon, Dennis J. *research scientist*
Slavkin, Harold Charles *dean, biologist*
Sloan, Harry Evans *film company executive*
Smiley, Tavis *radio talk show host*
Smith, Bruce R. *language educator*
Smith, Emil L. *biochemist, educator*
Smith, Jean Webb (Mrs. William French Smith) *civic worker*
Smith-Meyer, Linda Helene (Linda Smith) *artist*
Smits, Jimmy *actor*
Snider, Darryl *lawyer*
Sohaili, Hushmand *lawyer*
Solish, Jonathan Craig *lawyer*
Solnik, Meir Jonathon *gynecologist, educator*
Solomon, David Harris *geriatrician, educator*
Song, Yongyi *librarian*
Sonnenschein, Ralph Robert *physiologist*
Sood, Neeraj *economist, researcher*
Speigel, Brennan Mason Ross *internist, gastroenterologist, researcher*

Spindler, Paul *communications executive, consultant*
Splichal, Joachim *chef, restaurant owner*
Stahl, Frieda Axelrod *physicist, researcher, physics professor*
Stamm, Alan *lawyer*
Stamp, Terence Henry *actor*
Stancill, James McNeill *finance educator, consultant*
Stanish, Charles *anthropologist, educator*
Stansfield, Claire *apparel designer*
Stanton, Harry Dean *actor*
Stanton, Robert James, Jr. *geologist, educator*
Stapleton, Jean (Jeanne Murray) *actress*
Starrett, Lucinda *lawyer*
Stein, James Eric *pediatric surgeon*
Stein, Laurence Jay *lawyer*
Stein, Sheryl E. *lawyer*
Stellwagen, Robert Harwood *biochemistry professor*
Stephens, George Edward, Jr. *lawyer*
Stephens, Loren M. *publishing executive, writer*
Sterling, Donald T. *real estate mogul, professional basketball team executive*
Stern, James Coper *sales executive*
Stern, Susan Toy *human resources specialist*
Stevanovic, Milan V. *surgeon*
Stevenson, Robert Murrell *music educator*
Stewart, David Wayne *marketing educator, psychologist, consultant*
Stiehm, E. Richard *pediatrician, educator*
Stier, Byron G. *law educator*
Stinehart, William, Jr. *retired lawyer*
Stockwell, Robert Paul *linguist, educator*
Stoddart, J. Fraser *chemistry professor*
Stone, Gregory Paul *lawyer*
Stone, Lawrence Maurice *lawyer, educator*
Stoughton, W. Vickery *healthcare executive*
Straatsma, Bradley Ralph *ophthalmologist, educator*
Strack, Stephen Naylor *psychologist*
Streisand, Barbra Joan *singer, actress, film director*
Strick, Jeremy *curator*
Strickland, Julia B. *lawyer*
Strong, Gary Eugene *librarian*
Strong, George Gordon, Jr. *lawyer, management consultant*
Sugar, Ronald D. *aerospace executive*
Sullivan, Stuart Francis *anesthesiologist, educator*
Sultan, Wafa *psychiatrist*
Sutterby, Larry Quentin *internist*
Swamikannu, Xavier *environmental engineer, state official*
Swartz, Roslyn Holt *real estate company executive*
Sweeney, Paul W., Jr. *lawyer*
Synolakis, Costas E. *engineering educator*
Szego, Clara Marian *cell biologist, educator*
Tabachnick, Norman Donald *psychiatrist, educator*
Tabatabai, Jay (Magid) *travel company executive*
Taciroglu, Ertugrul *civil engineer, educator*
Takei, George Hosato *actor*
Talley, Vernon Andrew *museum administrator*
Tamkin, S. Jerome *manufacturing executive, consultant*
Tao, Terence Chi-Shen *mathematics professor*
Tardio, Thomas A. *public relations executive*
Tarr, Ralph William *lawyer, former federal government official*
Tassler, Nina *broadcast executive*
Taylor, Charles Ellett *biologist, educator*
Taylor, Daniel J. *film company executive*
Taylor, Leigh Herbert *dean*
Taylor, Minna *lawyer*
Taylor, Peter J. *diversified financial services company executive*
Taylor, Shelley E. *psychology researcher, educator*
Tellem, Nancy Reiss *broadcast executive*
Telles, Cynthia Ann *psychologist*
Tepper, R(obert) Bruce, Jr. *lawyer*
Territo, Mary C. *health facility administrator, hematologist, educator*
Terry, Timothy P. *lawyer*
Terry, W. Burks *lawyer*
Tevrizian, Dickran M., Jr. *judge*
Thomas, Geoffrey L. *lawyer*
Thomas, John David *composer, musician, compact disc artist, photographer, music and arts business owner*
Thompson, Anne Kathleen *entertainment journalist*
Thompson, Earl Albert *economics professor*
Thompson, Elizabeth *bank executive*
Thompson, Judith Kastrup *nursing researcher*
Thompson, Paul Matthew *neuroscientist*
Thompson, Richard Frederick *psychologist, educator, neuroscientist*
Thorne, Richard Mansergh *physicist*
Thorpe, Geogory B. *lawyer*
Timlin, Robert J. *judge*
Title, Gail Migdal *lawyer*
Tobisman, Stuart Paul *lawyer*
Tolo, Vernon Thorpe *orthopedist, educator*
Toluie, Kamran *cardiologist, electrophysiologist*
Toman, Mary Ann *federal official*
Tomlin, Lily *actress*
Tontonoz, Peter *molecular biologist, educator*
Torchetti, John *former professional hockey coach*
Torres, Cynthia Ann *marketing professional*
Torres-Gil, Fernando M. *academic administrator, educator*
Totten, George Oakley III *political science professor*
Toumari, Arman *environmental engineer, chemistry professor*
Treister, George Marvin *lawyer*
Trembly, Cristy *television executive*
Trembly, Dennis Michael *musician*
Trenton, Patricia Jean *art historian*
Tribble, Denise Hall *registrar*
Trimble, Stanley Wayne *hydrologist*
Tritle, Lawrence Alan *history professor*
Trost, Glenn W. *lawyer*
Troy, Nancy J. *art history educator*
Trumbull, Stephen Michael *entrepreneur, musician*
Trygstad, Lawrence Benson *lawyer*
Tsao, Jennie Ching-I *research scientist, educator*
Tsircou, Kyriacos Stavrou *lawyer*
Turner, Craig *editor, journalist*
Turner, Ralph Herbert *sociologist, educator*
Udvar-Hazy, Steven F. *leasing company financial executive*

Moore, George W. *electronics executive*
O'Connor, Kevin *electronics executive*
Ogawa, Joichi Raphael *director, consultant*
Patel, Kiran *manufacturing executive*
Pursel, David G. *lawyer*
Saha, Samar Kanti *electronics engineer, educator*
Stevens, Glenn H. *lawyer*
Talwalkar, Abhi Y. (Abhijit Y. Talwalkar) *computer company executive*
Treichel, Helmuth W.A. *technology executive*
Tufano, Paul J. *computer company executive*
Veremey, Volodimir *electrical engineer, researcher*
Wang, Susan S. *manufacturing executive*

### Mission Hills
Strazzeri, James C. *orthopedist, surgeon, health facility administrator*

### Mission Viejo
Berger, William Ezial *allergist, director*
Faley, Robert Lawrence *retired instruments company executive*
Glasky, Alvin Jerald *retired medical research scientist*
Mc Afee, Margaret Anne *retired art educator*
Ruben, Robert Joseph *lawyer*
Tuohey, Conrad Gravier *lawyer*

### Modesto
Berry, John Charles *psychologist, academic administrator*
Fedorchak, Timothy Hill *facility planning and program consulting executive*
Gallo, Ernest *vintner*
Gallo, Joseph E. *vintner*
Jacisin, John James *psychiatrist*
Jones, Mary Cunningham *music educator*
Khanna, Kanwal *rheumatologist*
Kushar, Kent *information technology executive*
Long, David R. *food products executive*
Mattos, William Harold *trade association administrator, publishing executive*
Moe, Andrew Irving *veterinarian*
Nicholson, Coy Lee *English educator, writer*
Norton, Max C. *writer, educator*
Piccinini, Robert M. (Bob Piccinini) *grocery store chain executive*
Price, Robert William *school superintendent, consultant*
Rogers, Wanda Faye *vocalist*
Smith, Chester *broadcast executive*
Smith, Heather Lynn *psychotherapist, recreational therapist*
Suntra, Charles Ratapol *surgeon, educator*
Truong, D. Hiep *lawyer*
Whiteside, Carol Gordon *foundation executive*

### Moffett Field
Berenji, Hamid Reza *research scientist, educator*
Cohen, Malcolm Martin *psychologist, researcher*
Freund, Friedemann T. *research scientist, educator*
Friedmann, E(merich) Imre *biologist, educator*
Harper, Lynn D. *biologist*
Kittel, Peter *research scientist*
Lissauer, Jack Jonathan *astronomy educator*
Makeev, Maxim A. *physicist*
Malkova, Natalia *physicist, mathematician, researcher*
Mattioda, Andrew Lige *research chemist, scientist*
Morrison, David *science administrator, researcher*
Nemani, Ramakrishna Rao *research scientist*
Sharma, Surendra Prasad *aerospace engineer, scientist*
Srivastava, Ashok Narain *computer scientist, consultant*
Statler, Irving Carl *aerospace engineer*
Straume, Tore *biophysicist, researcher*
Vercoutere, Wenonah Annrea *research scientist*

### Mojave
Binnie, Brian *pilot, transportation executive*
Melvill, Michael W. *aircraft company executive, experimental test pilot*
Rutan, Burt (Elbert Leander Rutan) *aircraft designer, aircraft company executive*

### Monarch Beach
Dougherty, Elmer Lloyd, Jr. *retired chemical engineering professor, consultant*

### Monrovia
Brown, Gwendolyn Williams *music educator*
Comings, David Edward *medical geneticist*
Edwards, Kenneth Neil *chemical engineering executive*
Jemelian, John Nazar *management consultant*
Kimnach, Myron William *botanist, horticulturist*
Mountjoy, Dennis Lee *state official*
Pray, Ralph Emerson *metallurgical engineer*
Stevens, Gary *retired jockey*
Zolodz, Melissa D. *scientist*

### Montclair
Boyd, Mary H. (Mary H. Merrill) *social services administrator*
Duvall, Michele Denise *school psychologist, marriage and family therapist*

### Montebello
Calderon, Ronald *state official*
Lopez, Donald Robert *parochial school educator, writer*

### Montecito
Burford, Jerrad Dalon *corporate financial executive, writer*
Hanley, Kevin Lance *maintenance company executive*
Meghreblian, Robert Vartan *manufacturing executive, physicist*
Purl, O. Thomas *retired electronics company executive*
Wheelon, Albert Dewell *physicist*

### Monterey
Black, Robert Lincoln *pediatrician, educator*
Boger, Dan Calvin *science professor, consultant*
Bomberger, Russell Branson *lawyer, writer*
Browder, John Glen *former congressman, educator*

Butler, Jon Terry *computer engineering educator, researcher*
Denning, Peter James *computer scientist, engineer*
Gaver, Frances Rouse *lawyer*
Goldstein, Kenneth F. *entertainment company executive, publishing executive*
Haddad, Louis Nicholas *paralegal*
Hanlon, James Allison *confectionery company executive*
Hoivik, Thomas Harry *military educator, international consultant*
Jiang, Qingfang *research scientist*
Le, Ly Ngoc (Le Ngoc Ly) *environmental physicist, educator, research scientist*
Lehr, Jeffrey Marvin *immunologist, allergist*
Luqi, *computer science professor*
Marto, Paul James *retired mechanical engineering educator, consultant, researcher, dean*
Matthews, David Fort *career officer*
Nesheim, Robert Olaf *retired food products executive*
Neta, Beny *mathematics educator, researcher*
Packard, Julie *aquarium administrator*
Packard Burnett, Nancy *biologist*
Peet, Phyllis Irene *women's studies educator*
Reese, William Albert III *clinical neuropsychologist*
Reneker, Maxine Hohman *librarian*
Robinson, Marla Holbrook *community care nurse*
Schrady, David Alan *civilian military employee, educator*
Soskin, William H. *lawyer, accountant*
Widmer, Chad L. *marine biologist, researcher*

### Monterey Park
Amezcua, Charlie Anthony *social science counselor*
Sekiguchi, Eugene *dentist*
Smith, Betty Denny *county official, administrator, fashion executive*
Stapleton, Jean *journalism educator*
Tsao, Gus *information technology executive*
Wilson, Linda *librarian*

### Moorpark
Kessner, Dolly Eugenio *music educator, concert pianist*
Young, Victoria E. *occupational health nurse, lawyer*

### Moraga
Allen, Richard Garrett *healthcare educator*
O'Brien, Bea Jae *artist*
Tom, Randolph L. *corporate financial executive*

### Moreno Valley
Calley, Tranquil Hudson *travel consultant, educator*
Guerrero, Donna Marie *sales executive*
Marshall, Debra Lynn *secondary school educator*
Moulthrop, Rebecca Lee Stilphen *retired elementary school educator*
White, Charles R. *former mayor*

### Morgan Hill
Foster, John Robert *lawyer*
Freimark, Robert (Bob Freimark) *artist*
Horning, Barbara Hortense Scheer *retired elementary school educator*
Singh, Loren Chan *writer, educator*

### Morro Bay
LaLanne, Jack (François Henri LaLanne) *physical fitness specialist, entrepreneur*

### Moss Beach
Glauthier, T. J. *management consultant*

### Moss Landing
Brewer, Peter George *ocean geochemist*
Clague, David A. *geologist*
Lange, Lester Henry *mathematics professor*
Robison, Bruce H. *marine biologist*

### Mountain View
Abel, Elizabeth Ann *dermatologist*
Armstrong, Tim *information technology executive*
Baker, Mitchell *computer software development foundation administrator*
Bennett, Stephen M. *computer company executive*
Bills, Robert Howard *political party executive*
Bishop, Robert R. *computer company executive*
Bosworth, Adam *software engineer*
Brilliant, Larry (Lawrence Brilliant) *preventive medicine physician, epidemiologist, technology pioneer, writer, educator, entrepreneur, social venture capitalist*
Brin, Sergey Mihailovich *information technology executive*
Brown, Shona *information technology executive*
Burton, Jeremy *information technology executive*
Cabrol, Nathalie Agnes *research scientist*
Campbell, William V. *computer company executive*
Cassidy, Sukhinder Singh *information technology executive*
Cerf, Vinton Gray *information technology executive*
Cook, Scott David *computer software company executive*
Coughran, William M., Jr. *information technology executive, researcher*
Di Muccio, Mary-Jo *retired librarian*
Drummond, David C. *information technology executive, lawyer*
East, John *computer company executive*
Eustace, Alan *information technology executive*
Gillis, Edwin *information technology executive*
Hagerman, Kristof *information technology executive*
Huber, Jeff *information technology executive*
Hughes, Gregory *information technology executive*
Hwang, Dennis (Dennis Hwang-Jung-moak) *graphic computer artist*
Isaacs, Nicholas Stephen *music educator, director*
Johnson, Conor Deane *mechanical engineer*
Jonaris, George G. *electrical engineer, computer engineer*
Kamangar, Salar *information technology executive*
Kobza, Dennis Jerome *architect*

Kordestani, Omid *information technology executive*
Kwon, Taek *Internet company executive*
Malachowsky, Chris Alan *electrical engineer*
Matin, Arthur *information technology executive*
Mayer, Marissa Ann *information technology executive*
Nash, Horace Lyons *lawyer*
Oulianov, Dmitri A. *laser engineer*
Page, Larry (Lawrence E. Page) *information technology executive*
Pasahow, Lynn Harold *lawyer*
Qureishi, A. Salam *computer company executive*
Reyes, George *information technology executive*
Rivera, Miriam *information technology executive, lawyer*
Rosenberg, Jonathan *information technology executive*
Rosing, Wayne *information technology executive*
Sandberg, Sheryl *information technology executive*
Schmidt, Eric Emerson *information technology executive*
Schneier, Bruce *information technology executive*
Schrage, Elliot *information technology executive*
Sclavos, Stratton *information technology executive*
Shostak, G. Seth *astronomer, writer*
Showalter, Mark Robert *astronomer*
Singh, Sangita *information technology and marketing executive*
Summers, David Patrick *chemist, astrobiologist*
Tarter, Jill Cornell *science foundation director, astronomer, researcher*
Urman, Jeffrey David *physician, educator*
Warren, Richard Wayne *obstetrician, gynecologist*
Yan, Qing *bioinformatics scientist*
Zhou, Peng *mechanical engineer*

### Murrieta
Cloud, Mark F. *film director, film editor, film producer, musician*
deVries-White, Donna Lynn *education educator, consultant*
Geffe, Philip Reinhold *electrical engineer, consultant*
Lake, Bruce Meno *physicist*
Plachno, Ronald John *electrical engineer*

### Napa
Battisti, Paul Oreste *retired municipal official*
Bogdan, Michael Andrew *plastic surgeon*
Chiarella, Peter Ralph *vintner*
Chiarello, Michael *chef*
Eissmann, Walter James *consulting company executive*
Gillespie, Marcia Lou *tax specialist, accountant, musician*
Hennings, Dorothy Ann *financial advisor*
Hess, Donald Marc *diversified financial services company executive*
Jeffords, Tracy H. *real estate company officer*
Loar, Peggy Ann *foundation administrator, museum administrator*
Morgese, Vincent John *neurosurgeon*
Pickett, Justus Cunningham *medical association administrator*
Schmidt, Hollie *secondary school educator*
Shin, Ernest Eun-Ho *physicist, educator, researcher*
Snow, Tower Charles, Jr. *lawyer*

### National City
Beauchamp, Miles Philip *editor, columnist, consultant*
Quigley, Deborah Hewitt *adult education educator*

### Needles
Thomas, Michael J. *secondary school educator*

### Nevada City
Clausen, Jeanne Lorraine *musician*
Hersh, Howard Douglas *composer, conductor, writer*
Whitsel, Richard Harry *retired biologist, entomologist*

### Newark
Dong, Weimin *risk management consultant*
Gupta, Anju *risk management consultant*

### Newbury Park
Bleiberg, Leon William *surgeon, podiatrist*
Ebrahimi, Nercy Bozorg *process engineer*
Lindsey, Joanne M. *flight attendant, poet*
Monteau, Norman Keith *gemologist*
Violano, Stella Marie *artist*

### Newhall
Stein, Karl N. *plastic and reconstructive surgeon*

### Newport Beach
Allison, M(arvin) Lawrence (Larry Allison) *psychologist*
Amyes, Edwin Westby *neurosurgeon*
Baskin, Scott David *lawyer*
Belić Weiss, Zoran *artist, design educator, director*
Bennett, Bruce W. *retired construction executive, civil engineer*
Bissell, George Arthur *architect*
Blankenship, Edward G. *architect*
Bren, Donald L. *real estate company executive*
Bron, Guillermo (Bill Bron) *lending company executive*
Brown, Giles Tyler *history professor, lecturer*
Bruggeman, Terrance John *corporate financial executive*
Bryant, Thomas Lee *magazine editor*
Cai, Weizhong (Will) *electronics engineer, researcher, physicist*
Cano, Kristin Maria *lawyer*
Carmichael, David Richard *lawyer*
Casey, Thomas Clark *retired trust company executive, investment advisor*
Chiu, John Tang *physician*
Clark, Thomas P., Jr. *lawyer*
Connolly, John Earle *surgeon, educator*
Currie, Robert Emil *retired lawyer*
Dean, Paul John *magazine editor*
Di Massa, Ernani Vincenzo, Jr. *communications executive, television producer, writer*
Durand, Robert Matthew *investment company executive*

Fawcett, John Scott *real estate developer*
Fehner, Michael Richard *lawyer*
Goldstein, Michael Gerald *lawyer, director*
Gould, Marilyn A. *writer, educator*
Gross, William H. (Bill Gross) *financial analyst, investment company executive*
Halmos, Jeff *apparel designer*
Herron, J. Jay *lawyer*
Johnson, William Stanley *metal distribution company executive*
Kenney, William John, Jr. *real estate developer*
Klink, Fredric J. *lawyer*
Kolyer, John McNaughton *materials scientist, retired chemist*
Lamberto-Egan, Josia *apparel designer*
Landau, Martin *actor*
Lyon, William, Sr. *construction executive*
Mallory, Frank Linus *lawyer*
Mandel, Maurice, II, *lawyer, educator, mediator*
Marcoux, Carl Henry *insurance company executive, writer, historian*
McCue, Dennis Michael *management consultant*
Mc Culloch, Samuel Clyde *history professor*
Millar, Richard William, Jr. *lawyer*
Morris, James T. *insurance company executive*
Olenicoff, Igor *real estate company executive*
Ortlund, Anne (Elizabeth Anne Ortlund) *writer, musician*
Prince, Thomas E. *bank executive*
Quinlan, Francis E. *lawyer*
Richardson, Walter John *architect*
Rogers, Robert Reed *manufacturing executive*
Schiff, Laurie *lawyer*
Schnapp, Roger Herbert *lawyer, consultant*
Schwarzstein, Richard Joseph *lawyer*
Shamoun, John Milam *plastic surgeon*
Shipley, Sam *apparel designer*
Shonk, Albert Davenport, Jr. *advertising executive*
Singer, Gary James *lawyer*
Solmer, Richard *surgeon*
Spitz, Barbara Salomon *artist*
Steelberg, Chad *broadcast advertising company executive*
Steelberg, Ryan *broadcasting advertising company executive*
Steinberg, Leigh William *sports agent*
Sutton, Thomas C. *insurance company executive*
Thompson, Jennifer Lee *lawyer*
Thorp, Edward Oakley *investment management company executive*
Tracy, James Jared, Jr. *retired legal association administrator*
Tran, Khanh T. *insurance company executive*
Viehe, Richard B. *podiatrist*
Wade, Michael Robert Alexander *marketing specialist*
Weissbard, Samuel Held *lawyer*
Wentworth, Diana von Welanetz *author*
Wentworth, Theodore Sumner *lawyer*
Whitledge, John *apparel designer*
Whittemore, Paul Baxter *psychologist*

### Newport Coast
Evanoff, George C. *retired consumer products company executive*
Pavony, William H. *retail executive, consultant*
Rollans, James O. *service company executive*
Swan, Peer Alden *public utility executive*

### Norco
Hamilton Boone, Jeanmarie *director*
Lu, Guiyang *electrical engineer, engineering executive*
McNeal, Phyllis Paulette *parole agent*
Morrison, James V. *biology professor*
Tuttle, Timothy Joseph *secondary school educator*

### North Hills
Deets, Richard M. *secondary school educator, consultant*
Iacocca, Lee (Lido Anthony Iacocca) *retired automotive manufacturing executive, venture capitalist*

### North Hollywood
Campos, Luis *puzzle writer*
Chang, Wung *academic administrator, investment advisor, educator*
Cottrell, David Milton *sound recording engineer, producer, singer, songwriter*
Davis, Edmond Ray *lawyer*
de la Houssaye, Brette Angelo-Pepe *electrical engineer, researcher, engineering educator*
Fanning, Dakota *actress*
Holmes, Michael *performing company executive, performing arts educator*
McMartin, John *actor*
Meat Loaf, (Marvin Lee Aday) *popular musician, actor*
Miller, Philip Gray *artist*
Newton-John, Olivia *singer, actress*
Reynolds, Debbie (Mary Frances Reynolds) *actress*
Smothers, Tom *actor, singer*
Stone, Sharon *actress*
Thomas, Tony *producer*
Thomson, John Ansel Armstrong *biochemist*
Toplitt, Gloria H. *music educator, actress, vocalist*
Totton, Carl Allen, II, *psychologist*
Toussieng, Yolanda *make-up artist*

### Northridge
Ackerman, Sue Ann *mathematics educator*
Avsharian, Roupen *prosecutor, academic administrator*
Bassler, Robert Covey *artist, educator*
Boberg, Dorothy Kurth *author*
Bradshaw, Richard Rotherwood *engineering executive*
Cartwright, Nancy *actress, television producer*
Curzon, Susan Carol *academic administrator*
Dart, John Seward *journalist, editor*
Duran, Karin Jeanine *librarian*
Jumonville, Felix Joseph, Jr. *physical education educator, real estate company officer*
Kiddoo, Robert James *engineering service company executive*
Koester, Jolene *academic administrator*
Logan, Lee Robert *orthodontist*
Loudon, Craig Michael *video specialist*
Mallard, Benjamin Franklin *engineering educator*

Chang, Carmen *lawyer*
Chen, Stephen Shi-hua *pathologist, biochemist*
Cherno, Melvin *humanities educator*
Chinnis, C. Cabell, Jr. *lawyer*
Christiansen, Susan Putnam *artist, educator, consultant*
Climan, Richard Elliot *lawyer*
Cohen, Karl Paley *nuclear energy consultant*
Coyle, Edward Leo *lawyer, retired banker*
Cullen, James G. *telecommunications industry executive*
Davidson, Gordon Kirby *lawyer*
de Alcuaz, Anthony *lawyer*
del Calvo, Jorge A. *lawyer*
Dement, William Charles *medical researcher, educator*
Denzel, Nora *information technology executive*
Diffie, Whitfield (Whit) *computer and communications engineer*
Dugger, Marguerite J. *retired special education educator*
Dunn, Debra L. *computer company executive*
Ernst, Wallace Gary *geology educator, dean*
Estrin, Judith *computer company executive*
Fairman, Marc P. *lawyer*
Fajardo, Luis Felipe *pathologist, educator, director*
Farmer, David Wayne *mathematician*
Feldman, Boris *lawyer*
Flanagan, Robert Joseph *economics professor*
Flaum, Keith Avery *lawyer*
Flaxman, Jon E. *computer company executive*
Flory, Curt Alan *research physicist*
Forbes, Alfred Dean *religious studies researcher*
Fordis, Jean Burke *lawyer*
Frankle, Diane Holt *lawyer*
Fries, James Franklin *internal medicine educator*
Fromm, Jeffery Bernard *lawyer*
Fruchterman, James Robert, Jr. *computer company executive, not-for-profit executive*
Frye, William Emerson *physicist, engineer*
Gaither, James C. *lawyer*
Galel, Susan Alpert *transfusion medicine physician*
Gerety, Robert John *microbiologist, researcher, pediatrician, pharmaceutical executive*
Greco, Joseph A. *lawyer*
Greene, Diane *information technology executive*
Halloran, Jean M. *human resources specialist*
Halluin, Albert Price *lawyer*
Hamilton, David Mike *publishing executive*
Hammett, Benjamin Cowles *psychologist*
Haque, Promod *venture capitalist*
Hays, Marguerite Thompson *nuclear medicine physician, educator*
Heneveld-Story, Christy Jean *educational researcher*
Herrick, Tracy Grant *fiduciary*
Herring, Conyers (William Conyers Herring) *retired physicist, educator*
Hiscox, Frank S. *lawyer*
Hodge, Philip Gibson, Jr. *mechanical and aerospace engineering educator*
Holman, Halsted Reid *medical educator, physician*
Horngren, Charles Thomas *finance educator*
Huberman, Bernardo A. *physicist*
Hurd, Mark V. *computer company executive*
Ivey, Thomas J. *lawyer*
Jackson, Cynthia L. *lawyer*
Johnson, Noble Marshall *research scientist*
Joshi, Vyomesh I. *computer company executive*
Kapoor, Ashok Kumar *engineer*
Kase, Kenneth R. *radiation physicist, consultant*
Kawasaki, Guy *venture capitalist, investment banker, evangelist, entrepreneur, blog writer, writer*
Kaye, Ronald Lee *physician, educator*
Keeffe, Emmet Britton *medical educator*
Kim, Wan Hee *engineering educator*
King, Kenton J. *lawyer*
Klein, Robert Nicholas, II, *real estate developer*
Knoles, George Harmon *history educator*
Korman, Martin *lawyer*
Lal, Dhananjay *information technology executive, researcher*
Lampman, Richard H. (Dick Lampman) *computer company executive*
Lane, Alfred Thomas *medical educator*
Lee, Virginia Fern *community volunteer*
Lo, Yee On *composer*
Loewenstein, Walter Bernard *nuclear energy industry executive*
Lucente, Sam *industrial designer*
Luh, Howard H. *aerospace engineer*
Lynch, Timothy Jeremiah-Mahoney *lawyer, educator, theologian, realtor, writer*
Lyons, Cathy *computer company executive*
Martin, Robert Bruce *chemistry professor*
Masur, Joshua Michael *lawyer*
Mayo, Robert N. *computer science researcher*
McCall, Jennifer Jordan *lawyer*
McIntyre, Robert Wheeler *retired conservation organization executive*
Michie, Sara H. *pathologist, educator*
Miller, Michael Patiky *lawyer*
Miller, Scott D. *lawyer*
Moll, John Lewis *retired electronics engineer*
Mommsen, Katharina *retired literature and language professor, foundation administrator*
Monroy, Gladys H. *lawyer*
Montgomery, Kevin *information technology executive*
Moon, Ronald Leslie *materials scientist*
Moore, Cassandra Chrones *real estate broker*
Moos, Rudolf H. *psychologist, researcher*
Moss, Richard B. *pediatrician*
Mott, Randall D. (Randy Mott) *computer company executive*
Neal, Stephen Cassidy *lawyer*
Needleman, Philip *cardiologist, pharmacologist*
Nichols, William Ford, Jr. *foundation administrator, educator, health science association administrator*
Nopar, Alan Scott *lawyer*
Nordlund, Donald Craig *lawyer*
Nuchi, Lior O. *lawyer*
Ober, Josiah *history educator*
O'Brien, Raymond Francis *transportation executive*
O'Rourke, C. Larry *lawyer*
Park, Marina H. *lawyer*
Parker, James Wesley *former naval officer, investment company executive*

Patten, Valerie Lynn *lawyer*
Patterson, Robert Edward *lawyer*
Payton, Paul Max *application developer*
Peng, Stanford Lee-Yu *physician*
Penn, Lee *information scientist, consultant, journalist*
Perez de Alonso, Marcela *human resources specialist, information technology executive*
Perl, Martin Lewis *physicist, educator, chemical engineer*
Petkanics, Donna M. *lawyer*
Phair, Joseph Baschon *lawyer*
Pitchford, Mark B. *lawyer*
Pizzo, Philip A. *pediatrician, educator, dean*
Quate, Calvin Forrest *engineering educator*
Radcliffe, Mark Flohn *lawyer*
Raffin, Thomas A. *physician*
Rehman, Saifur *web site design company executive*
Renfro, John M. *human resources specialist*
Richardson, Tom (Edward Thompson Richardson) *artist*
Robinson, Walter J. III *lawyer*
Robison, Shane V. *computer company executive*
Roos, John Victor *lawyer*
Salmon, Denis R. *lawyer*
Salvatierra, Oscar, Jr. *transplant surgeon, urologist, educator*
Sanders, William John *research scientist*
Saper, Jeffrey D. *lawyer*
Saxena, Arjun Nath *physicist*
Schafer, Ronald William *electrical engineering educator*
Schendel, Stephen Alfred *surgeon, educator*
Scher, Erik *physical chemist*
Schnabel, Rockwell Anthony *former ambassador*
Schulz, Michael *physicist*
Schurman, David Jay *orthopedic surgeon, educator*
Scitovsky, Anne Aickelin *economist, researcher*
Seethaler, William Charles *international business executive, consultant*
Shen, Bo *research scientist*
Sherlock, Phyllis Krafft *psychologist*
Shi, Qin *lawyer, technologist*
Shuer, Lawrence Mendel *neurosurgery educator*
Shulman, Ron E. *lawyer*
Silverman, Norman Henry *cardiologist, educator*
Skoll, Jeffrey S. *philanthropist, former internet company executive*
Skoog, Douglas Arvid *retired chemistry educator, writer*
Smith, Gregory C. *lawyer*
Sonsini, Larry W. *lawyer*
Staprans, Armand *electronics executive*
Strober, Samuel *immunologist, educator*
Sullivan, Denis R. *lawyer*
Sullivan, William P. *electronics executive*
Sundheim, George (Duf) *lawyer, political organization worker*
Sunshine, Philip *pediatrician*
Taylor, John Joseph *nuclear engineer, researcher*
Ticknor, Carolyn M. *computer company executive*
Tiffany, Joseph Raymond, II, *lawyer*
Title, Alan M. *astrophysicist*
Tsien, Richard Winyu *biology professor*
Tune, Bruce Malcolm *pediatrics educator, renal toxicologist*
Unkovic, Nicholas C. *lawyer*
Urquhart, John *medical researcher, educator*
Van Atta, David Murray *lawyer*
Van de Walle, Chris Gilbert *physicist*
Vaughn, Issac J. *lawyer*
Voight, Jerry D. *lawyer*
Walker, Ann Yvonne *lawyer*
Waller, Peter William *public relations executive*
Waltzer, Garrett J. *lawyer*
Wayman, Robert Paul *computer company executive*
Weng, Wen-Kai *oncologist, medical researcher*
Wheeler, Raymond Louis *lawyer*
White, Rick *lawyer, former congressman*
Wick, Michael M. *biotechnology executive*
Winkler, Michael *computer company executive*
Wong, Y(ing) Wood *real estate investment company executive, real estate development company executive, venture capital investment company executive*
Wright, Kirby Michael *writer, editor*
Yuan, Nanci *pediatrician, pulmonologist, educator*
Zuckerberg, Mark (Mark Elliot Zuckerberg) *Internet company executive, entrepreneur, programmer*

**Palo Cedro**
Aust, Elizabeth Ann (Betty) *artist*

**Palos Verdes Estates**
Abbott, A. Dwight *retired astronautical engineer*
Blackman, Lee L. *lawyer*
DeLuce, Richard David *lawyer*
DiPaul, Christopher *psychologist*
Hayter, Karyn Leanne *theater educator*
Lazzaro, Anthony Derek *academic administrator*
Mackenbach, Frederick W. *welding products manufacturing company executive*
Mennis, Edmund Addi *investment management consultant*
Paulikas, George Algis *retired physicist*
Raue, Jorg Emil *electrical engineer*
Seide, Paul *civil engineering educator*
Sharp, Jane Shriver *artist*
Smith, Stephen Randolph *aerospace executive*
Yarbrough, Allyson Debra *electrical engineer*

**Palos Verdes Peninsula**
Christie, Hans Frederick *retired utilities executive*
Denke, Paul Herman *retired aircraft engineer*
Grant, Robert Ulysses *retired manufacturing executive*
Julien, Gail Leslie *model, public relations professional*
Leone, William Charles *retired manufacturing executive*
Manning, Christopher Ashley *finance educator, consultant*
Mirels, Harold *aerospace engineer*
Narasimhan, Padma Mandyam *physician*
Slayden, James Bragdon *retired retail executive*
Slusser, Robert Wyman *aerospace transportation executive*

Thomas, Claudewell Sidney *psychiatrist, educator*
Thomas, Hayward *manufacturing executive*
Van Der Meulen, Joseph Pierre *neurologist*
Wilson, Theodore Henry *retired electronics executive, aerospace engineer*

**Panorama City**
Bass, Harold Neal *pediatrician, medical geneticist*
Janis, Elinor Raiden *artist, educator*
Sue, Michael Alvin *allergist*

**Paradise**
Barr, Donald Roy *statistics and operations research educator, statistician*
Bernstein, Elizabeth Ann *retired executive secretary*
Haws, Hale Louis *medical association administrator, consultant*

**Paramount**
Hall, Howard Harry *lawyer*
Williams, Vivian Lewie *retired counseling administrator*

**Parlier**
Stapleton, James Jay *agricultural scientist, consultant*

**Pasadena**
Abelson, John Norman *biology professor*
Albee, Arden Leroy *geologist, educator*
Ali, Ahmed Haider *geophysicist*
Allen, Clarence Roderic *geologist, educator*
Anderson, Don Lynn *geophysicist*
Arnold, Frances Hamilton *chemistry educator*
Arnott, Robert Douglas *investment company executive*
Atkins, David Charles *psychology professor*
Axelson, Charles Frederic *retired accounting educator, food products executive*
Baltimore, David *former academic administrator, microbiologist, educator*
Barish, Barry C. *physics professor, researcher*
Barnes, Charles Andrew *physicist, researcher*
Baroff, Lynn Elliott *engineering executive*
Beauchamp, Jesse Lee (Jack Beauchamp) *chemistry professor*
Beer, Reinhard *atmospheric scientist*
Bishop, Robert Calvin *pharmaceutical company executive*
Boehm, Felix Hans *physicist, researcher*
Bogaard, William Joseph *mayor, lawyer, educator*
Boochever, Robert *judge*
Bosley, Edward Richmond *historical site administrator*
Boulos, Paul Fares *civil and environmental engineer*
Bradley, James Edwin *religious studies educator*
Breckinridge, James Bernard *optical engineer*
Bridges, William Bruce *electrical engineer, researcher, engineering educator*
Brogden-Stirbl, Shona Marie *writer, researcher*
Brotman, Richard Dennis *counselor*
Brown, Michael E. *astronomer, astronomy educator*
Buchwald, Jed Zachary *environmental health researcher, science history educator*
Byun, Sung Hun *research scientist*
Caine, Stephen Howard *data processing executive*
Call, Merlin Wendell *lawyer*
Calleton, Theodore Edward *lawyer, educator*
Candes, Emmanuel Jean *mathematics professor*
Chahine, Moustafa Toufic *atmospheric scientist*
Chameau, Jean-Lou *academic administrator*
Chan, Sunney Ignatius *chemist, educator*
Chen, Sandra Yi-Ting *political organization worker*
Chiang, Wen-Li *hydrologist*
Chu, Benjamin K. *hospital administrator*
Crowley, John Crane *real estate developer*
Culick, Fred Ellsworth Clow *engineering educator, physics professor*
D'Angelo, Robert William *lawyer*
Davidson, Eric Harris *molecular and developmental biologist, educator*
Dervan, Peter Brendan *chemistry professor*
DeSalvo, Riccardo *research scientist*
Dickinson, Michael *physiologist*
Douglas, Kimberly *university librarian*
Dressler, Alan Michael *astronomer*
Duxbury, Thomas Carl *planetary scientist*
Elachi, Charles *aerospace educator*
Fernandez, Ferdinand Francis *federal judge*
Fisher, Raymond Corley *federal judge*
Frautschi, Steven Clark *physicist, researcher*
Fredericks, Ward Arthur *venture capitalist*
Freedman, Wendy Laurel *astronomer, educator*
Fu, Lee-Lueng *oceanographer*
Gilman, Richard Carleton *retired college president*
Glovsky, Myron Michael *medical educator*
Goei, Bernard Thwan-Poo (Bert Goei) *architectural and engineering firm executive*
Goldreich, Peter Martin *astrophysics and planetary physics educator*
Golombek, Matthew Philip *research scientist, planetary geologist*
Goodstein, David Louis *physics professor*
Goodwin, Alfred Theodore *federal judge*
Gould, Roy Walter *engineering educator*
Gray, Harry Barkus *chemistry professor*
Gregory, Timothy Peter *historian, consultant*
Gross, Bill *energy executive*
Grubbs, Robert Howard *chemistry professor*
Gurnis, Michael Christopher *geological sciences educator*
Haight, James Theron *lawyer*
Hall, Cynthia Holcomb *federal judge*
Halsted, Margo *music educator, carillonneur*
Harvey, Joseph Paul, Jr. *orthopedist, educator*
Heindl, Clifford Joseph *physicist, researcher*
Hickman, Rose *lawyer*
Hilbert, Robert S(aul) *optical engineer*
Hitlin, David George *physicist, researcher*
Holmes, Louis Ira *physician assistant, educator, photojournalist*
Holzmann, Gerard Johan *computer science researcher*
Horak, Jan-Christopher *filmmaker, educator, curator*
Horner, Althea Jane *psychologist*
Hornung, Hans Georg *aeronautical engineering educator, science administrator*

Huang, Alice Shih-hou
Hunt, Gordon *lawyer*
Hunt, Hazel Analue Stanfield *retired accountant*
Hunter, Milton *construction company executive, retired career military officer*
Hwang, Li-San *technology executive*
Jennings, Paul Christian *civil engineering educator, academic administrator*
Johnson, Barbara Jean *retired judge, lawyer*
Jones, Lawrence Wager *physician, researcher*
Jun, Insoo *nuclear scientist, researcher*
Kaplan, Gary *executive recruiter*
Karlin, Jan M. *violinist, performing company executive*
Kavanagh, Ralph William *physics professor*
Keller, Herbert Bishop *mathematics professor*
Kennard, Lydia H. *airport terminal executive*
Keviczky, Tamas *electrical engineer, researcher, educator*
Keys, Scott *bank executive*
Kincaid, Hazel Victoria *evangelist*
Knowles, James Kenyon *applied mathematician, educator*
Koelzer, George Joseph *lawyer*
Konishi, Masakazu *neuroscientist, educator*
Koshalek, Richard *academic administrator, former museum director, consultant*
Kousser, J(oseph) Morgan *historian, educator*
Kozinski, Alex *federal judge*
Lake, Kevin Bruce *medical association administrator*
Lange, Andrew E. *astrophysicist*
Ledyard, John Odell *economics professor, consultant*
Leeson, Peter *lawyer*
Lester, Henry Allen *biology professor*
Lingenfelter, Sherwood Galen *academic administrator, retired anthropologist*
List, Ericson John *environmental engineering science educator, consultant*
Litvine, Vladimir A. *research scientist, physicist*
Logan, Francis Dummer *retired lawyer*
Lopes, Rosaly Mutel Crocce *astronomer, planetary geologist*
Lu, Thomas T. *lab administrator, information technology executive*
Luxemburg, Wilhelmus Anthonius Josephus *mathematics professor*
Marcus, Rudolph Arthur *chemist, educator*
Markley, William C. *lawyer*
Marlen, James S. *chemical, plastics and building materials manufacturing company executive*
Martin, Craig Lee *engineering company executive*
Matthews, Mildred Shapley *freelance/self-employed editor*
Mayo, Stephen L. *biochemist*
Mc Carthy, Frank Martin *oral surgeon, educator*
McGill, Thomas Conley *physics educator*
Mc Koy, Basil Vincent Charles *theoretical chemist, educator*
McNulty, James F. *construction company executive*
Menefee, John William III *cinematographer, film producer*
Meyerowitz, Elliot Martin *biologist, educator*
Mosher, Sally Ekenberg *lawyer, musician*
Mueth, Joseph Edward *lawyer*
Munger, Edwin Stanton *political geography educator*
Munich, Mario Enrique *research scientist, electronics executive*
Muñoz Fernández, Michela *electrical engineer, researcher*
Murray, Richard M. *engineering educator*
Myers, R(alph) Chandler *lawyer*
Nelson, Dorothy Wright (Mrs. James F. Nelson) *federal judge*
Newell, Michael Alfred *electrical engineer*
O'Bryant, Daniel R. *manufacturing executive*
Oemler, Augustus, Jr. *astronomer, educator*
Opel, William *medical research administrator*
Paez, Richard A. *federal judge*
Parker, Robert Allan Ridley *federal agency administrator, astronaut*
Parr, James Allan *literature professor*
Pashgian, Margaret Helen *artist*
Patton, Richard Weston *retired mortgage company executive*
Perry, Michael W. *bank executive*
Phillips, Robert *engineering educator, researcher*
Politzer, Hugh David *physicist, educator*
Poon, Peter Tin-Yau *engineer, physicist*
Preskill, John Phillip *physics professor*
Quake, Stephen R. *physics professor, researcher*
Revel, Jean-Paul *biology professor*
Rinaldi, James J. *federal agency administrator*
Roberts, John D. *chemist, educator*
Roshko, Anatol *aeronautical engineer*
Rymer, Pamela Ann *federal judge*
Sabersky, Rolf Heinrich *mechanical engineer*
Sackmann, Inge-Juliana *astrophysicist*
Sandage, Allan Rex *astronomer*
Sargent, Anneila Isabel *astrophysicist*
Sargent, Wallace Leslie William *astronomer, educator*
Scott, David Clinton *research scientist*
Scudder, Thayer *anthropologist, educator*
Seinfeld, John Hersh *chemical engineering professor*
Sekanina, Zdenek *astronomer*
Shaw, Anthony *pediatric surgeon, retired educator*
Shimada, Katsunori *retired electrical engineer*
Short, Elizabeth M. *internist, educator, retired federal agency administrator*
Shuster, Marguerite *minister, educator*
Siemon-Burgeson, Marilyn M. *education administrator*
Smith, Howard Russell *manufacturing executive, director*
Smith, Michael Robert *electro-optical engineer, physicist*
Smith, Milan Dale, Jr. *federal judge*
Smolke, Christina *chemical engineer*
Solis, Carlos *lawyer*
Spector, Phil *record company executive*
Spilker, Linda Joyce *aerospace scientist*
Staehle, Robert L. *foundation executive*
Steidel, Charles C. *astronomy educator*
Stevens, Roy W. *sales and marketing executive*
Stolper, Edward Manin *secondary school educator*
Stone, Edward C. *physicist, researcher*

Tanner, Dee Boshard *retired lawyer*
Tashima, Atsushi Wallace *federal judge*
Thomas, Joseph Fleshman *retired architect*
Thorne, Kip Stephen *physicist, researcher*
Tirrell, David A. *research scientist, educator*
Todd, John *mathematician, educator*
Tollenaere, Lawrence Robert *retired industrial products company executive*
Tombrello, Thomas Anthony, Jr. *physics professor*
van Schoonenberg, Robert G. *lawyer*
Varshavsky, Alexander Jacob *molecular biologist*
Villanueva, Daniel D. *former communications executive, investment company executive*
Villanueva, Daniel L., Jr. *investment company executive*
Vogt, Rochus Eugen *physicist, researcher*
Wadden, Christopher David *food products executive*
Wang, Jia *research scientist*
Wardlaw, Kim A. McLane *federal judge*
Wasserburg, Gerald Joseph *geology and geophysics educator*
Watkins, John Francis *management consultant*
Watson, Noel G. *construction executive*
Webster, Christopher R. *chemist, physicist, research scientist*
White-Thomson, Ian leonard *retired mining executive*
Wilcox, Jaroslava Zitkova *physicist*
Williams, Bradley Bennett *historian*
Wong, Raymond Shiu-Loong *radiologist*
Wood, Lincoln Jackson *aerospace engineer*
Wyatt, Joseph Lucian, Jr. *lawyer, writer*
Yariv, Amnon *electrical engineering educator, research scientist*
Yeager, Caroline Hale *writer, retired radiologist, consultant*
Yeomans, Donald Keith *astronomer*
Yohalem, Harry Morton *lawyer*
Zewail, Ahmed Hassan *chemistry and physics educator, consultant, editor*

**Paso Robles**
Boxer, Jerome Harvey *data processing executive, consultant, accountant, management consultant, vintager*
Brown, Benjamin Andrew *retired journalist*
Webster, David Arthur *retired life insurance company executive*

**Patton**
Ermshar, Annette Lorene *psychologist, educator*

**Pauma Valley**
Lewis, Gerald Jorgensen *judge*

**Pearblossom**
Goldman, Gary Steven *computer scientist, consultant*

**Pebble Beach**
Dallmann, William Charles *speech educator, writer*
Hotelling, Neal Barry *historian, director*
Mauz, Henry Herrward, Jr. *retired naval officer*
Mortensen, Gordon Louis *artist, printmaker*
Neville, Roy Gerald *research scientist, chemical executive, consultant*
Peper, George Frederick *writer, retired publishing executive*

**Penn Valley**
Longan, Suzanne M. *retired elementary school educator*
Sands, Sharon Louise *art director, publishing executive, artist*
Throner, Guy Charles, Jr. *aerospace engineering executive, scientist, inventor, consultant*

**Penngrove**
Haslam, Gerald William *writer, educator*

**Petaluma**
Bailey, Preston Edward *music educator*
DeLaurenti McClure, Tracy *elementary school educator*
Frederickson, Arman Frederick *mining executive, petroleum engineer*
Gervais, Cherie Nadine *small business owner*
Hass, Robert L. *writer, literature educator*
Klemenok, Kevin John *music educator*
McChesney, Robert Pearson *artist*
O'Hare, Sandra Fernandez *education educator*
Pronzini, Bill John (William Pronzini) *writer*
Purcell, Steven Richard *international management consultant, engineer, economist*
Rodriguez, Luis J. *writer*
Sebold, Alice *writer*
Skalagard, Hans Martin *artist*
Spiegelman, Art *writer, cartoonist*
Thomas, Nancy Hinckley *special education educator*

**Petrolia**
Cockburn, Alexander *journalist*
St. Clair, Jeffrey *editor*

**Piedmont**
Montgomery, Theodore Ashton *physician*
Putter, Irving *retired French language educator*
Reich, Stanley Benjamin *radiologist, medical educator*

**Pilot Hill**
Freitas, Robert Archibald, Jr. *research scientist*

**Pinole**
Emmanuel, Jorge Agustin *chemical engineer, environmental consultant*
Naughton, James Lee *internist*

**Pittsburg**
Williams-Thomas, Elizabeth A. *financial planner, consultant*
Williscroft-Barcus, Beverly Ruth *retired lawyer*

**Placentia**
Cash, Jeanie Maritta *educational association administrator*
Zweifel, Donald Edwin *editor, lobbyist, consultant*

**Placerville**
Magelitz, Larry L. *construction company executive*
Nesbitt, Paul Edward *historian, author, educator*
Sundgren, Donald E. *construction executive*
Wessels-McCoy, Denise Wendy *pre-school administrator, consultant*
Wilkinson, Rosemary Regina Challoner *poet, writer*

**Playa Del Rey**
Cairns, Diane Patricia *motion picture executive*
McNeill, Daniel Richard *writer*
Mishelevich, David Jacob *medical products executive*
Weir, Alexander, Jr. *chemical engineer, consultant*

**Playa Vista**
Noh, Jun-yong *computer scientist, researcher*

**Pleasant Hill**
Abraham-Helman, Cheryl Goodrich *small business owner*
Bastrenta, Brigitte Elisabeth *school administrator*
Hollister, Arthur Clair, Jr. *epidemiologist, consultant, retired public health service officer*
Nelson, Bette Sturr *secondary school educator*
Richard, Robert Carter *psychologist*

**Pleasanton**
Askanas, Mark S. *lawyer*
Balmuth, Michael A. *retail executive*
Bergquist, Rick *software company executive*
Burd, Steven A. *food service executive*
Dubois, Guy *software company executive*
Edwards, Robert L. *corporate financial executive*
Fehlberg, Robert Erick *architect*
Ferber, Norman Alan *retail executive*
Gordon, Robert A. *food products executive, lawyer*
Gregoire, Michael P. *software company executive*
Gupta, Ram *software company executive*
Novak, Randi Ruth *systems engineer, computer scientist*
Opperwall, Stephen Gabriel *lawyer*
Peters, James C. *retail executive*
Renda, Larree M. *retail executive*
Roshong, Dee Ann Daniels *dean, educator*
Shaw, Charles Alden *engineering executive*
Stallings, Charles Henry *retired physicist*
Van Dreser, Merton Lawrence *ceramics engineer*
White, James D. *food products executive*
Wu, Jia Hao *transportation executive, researcher, consultant*

**Point Mugu**
Fisk, Charles John *meteorologist, researcher, consultant*

**Point Richmond**
Edginton, John Arthur *lawyer*

**Pollock Pines**
Johnson, Stanford Leland *finance educator*
Rickard, Margaret Lynn *library director, educator*

**Pomona**
Agvanian, Youri *mathematician, educator, physicist*
Ambrose, William Wright, Jr. *dean, educator, academic administrator*
Arriaga, Jesus V. *automotive parts company executive*
Barsugli, Jesse Benjamin *lab administrator*
Bidlack, Wayne Ross *nutritional biochemist, toxicologist, food scientist*
Cranston, John Welch *historian, educator*
Dishman, Rose Marie Rice *academic administrator, researcher*
Fetterly, Barbara Louise *artist*
Gambone, Joseph Charles *medical educator, consultant*
Garrity, Rodman Fox *psychologist, educator*
Jackson, Mary Ellen *librarian, consultant*
Keating, Eugene Kneeland *animal scientist, educator*
Lin, Lianlian *management educator*
Mezey, Robert *poet*
Okamoto, Mark P. *pharmacist, educator, dean*
Patten, Thomas Henry, Jr. *finance educator, personnel director*
Saviola, Beatrice Jeaneane *microbiologist*
Stallones, Jared Reuel *education educator*
Teague, Lavette Cox, Jr. *systems educator, consultant*
Tomiyasu, Kiyo *retired consulting engineer*
Trotter, F(rederick) Thomas *retired academic administrator*
Vo, Huu Dinh *pediatrician, educator*
Wilson, Stanley Charles *artist, educator, curator, art gallery director, consultant*

**Port Hueneme**
Schneider, Arthur Paul *retired videotape and film editor, author*

**Porterville**
Golden, Raymond Lee *retired theology studies educator, retired minister*
Hayes, Shirley Ann *special education educator*
Miller, Gary Lee *secondary school educator*
Syrdahl, Rickelle Lyn *biology professor*

**Portola Valley**
Carnochan, Walter Bliss *retired humanities educator*
Fogarty, Thomas James *surgery educator*
Garsh, Thomas Burton *publisher*
Graham, William James *packaging company executive*
Hafkenschiel, Joseph Henry, Jr. *cardiologist, educator*
Kuo, Franklin F. *computer scientist, electrical engineer*
March, James Gardner *social sciences educator*
Nycum, Susan Hubbell *lawyer*
Olson, Walter Gilbert *lawyer*
Ward, Robert Edward *retired political science professor, academic administrator*

**Potrero**
Reider, Shirley Ann *travel company executive*

**Poway**
Conant, Kim Untiedt *retired elementary school educator*
Mueller, Gerhard Gottlob *retired financial accounting standard setter, retired educator*
Uke, Alan Kurt *finance company executive*

**Prather**
Coren, Lance Scott *automotive executive, consultant*

**Quartz Hill**
McAllister, Bruce Richard *art educator*
Nettelhorst, Robin Paul *academic administrator, writer*

**Ramona**
Hoffman, Wayne Melvin *retired airline official*
Van Zant, Susan Lucille *principal*
Yoldas, Bulent Erturk *materials scientist, educator*

**Rancho Cordova**
Harrell, Gary Paul *lawyer*
Kasch, Mary Courteol *occupational therapist*

**Rancho Cucamonga**
Alvarez, Tirso Reyes, Jr. *engineer*
Buckley, Lawrence G. *dean*
Clarke, Orville Oliver, Jr. *art history educator*
Donaldson, Kelley Lynnae *fire prevention specialist*
Dutton, Robert D. *state official*
Jones, Nancy Langdon *financial planning practitioner*
Okoye, Christian Emeka *professional football player*
Quinn, Dennis Michael *history professor*

**Rancho Dominguez**
Janura, Jan Arol *apparel manufacturing executive*

**Rancho Mirage**
Blixseth, Timothy *real estate developer*
Chuang, Tsu-Yi *dermatologist, epidemiologist, educator*
Cone, Lawrence Arthur *medical educator*
Ford, Gerald Rudolph, Jr. *38th President of the United States*
Fromm, Erwin Frederick *retired insurance company executive*
Kramer, Gordon *mechanical engineer*
Leydorf, Frederick Leroy *lawyer*
Novak, Joe *artist*
Pierno, Anthony Robert *lawyer*
Steele, Charles Glen *retired accountant*
Weil, Max Harry *internist, cardiologist, educator, medical researcher*
Wyatt, Lenore *civic worker*

**Rancho Murieta**
Irelan, Robert Withers *retired metal products executive*

**Rancho Palos Verdes**
Douglass, Craig Bruce *computer technology executive*
Frassinelli, Guido Joseph *retired aerospace engineer*
Hillinger, Charles *journalist, writer*
Kwan, Benjamin Ching Kee *ophthalmologist*
McFadden, Thomas *academic administrator*
Neilan, Aidan Joseph *radiologist*
Smirnov, Alexei Vladimirovich *research scientist, consultant*
Vanderlip, Elin Brekke *professional society administrator, volunteer*
Yassin, Robert Alan *museum director, curator*
Zar, Judith L. (Mickey McBride) *writer*

**Rancho Santa Fe**
Affeldt, John Ellsworth *retired physician*
Best, Jacob Hilmer, Jr. *retired hotel chain executive*
Byrd, Betty Rantze *writer*
Carr, David Turner *physician*
Creutz, Edward Chester *physicist, museum director*
Derbes, Daniel William *manufacturing executive*
Dieffenbach, Otto Weaver III *real estate company executive*
Jordan, Charles Morrell *retired automotive designer*
Kessler, A. D. *investment advisor, consultant, commentator*
Laidlaw, Pamela Nielsen *psychologist*
Legro, Stanley Wayne *environmental lawyer*
Matthews, Leonard Sarver *advertising and marketing executive*
Mezzullo, Louis Albert *lawyer*
Nadler, Henry Louis *pediatrician, educator, geneticist*
O'Driscoll, Margaret Millar (Peggy O'Driscoll) *real estate broker*
Peterson, Nad A. *retired lawyer*
Rockoff, S. David *radiologist, physician, educator*
Ruiz, Ramón Eduardo *history professor*
Schirra, Walter Marty, Jr., (Wally Schirra) *business consultant, retired astronaut*
Step, Eugene Lee *retired pharmaceutical executive*
Woolley, Roger Swire *lawyer*

**Rancho Santa Margarita**
Berta, Melissa Rose *mathematics professor*
Bunkis, Juris *plastic surgeon*
Curtis, John Joseph *lawyer, writer*
Lawson, Thomas Cheney *fraud examiner*
Parth, Frank R. *consulting company executive, educator*
Shusterman, Neal Douglas *writer, scriptwriter*

**Red Bluff**
Kennedy, James William, Jr., (Sarge Kennedy) *special education administrator, consultant*

**Redding**
Emmerson, Archie Aldis (Red Emmerson, A.A. Emmerson) *sawmill owner*
Nicholas, David Robert *minister, college president*
Nwangburuka, Okechukwu Nkem *psychiatrist*
Potter, James Vincent *association executive*

**Redlands**
Bangasser, Ronald Paul *physician, director*
Burgess, Larry Eugene *library director, historian, educator*
Clopine, Gordon Alan *consulting geologist, educator*
Coleman, Arlene Florence *retired pediatrics nurse*
Griesemer, Allan David *retired museum director*
Hanson, Gerald Warner *retired county official*
Heiss, David James *editor*
Huntley, William Barney *religious studies professor*
Pedace, Roberto L. *economics professor*
Pick, James Block *business professor, writer*
Rankin, Alex C. *management executive*
Ristau, Jacob Robert *art educator, graphics designer*
Salmon, Catherine Anne *education educator*
Simnjanovski, Riste *nurse counseling administrator*
Skomal, Edward Nelson *retired aerospace transportation executive, electromagnetic environments consultant*
Wilson, Lois Fair *retired school system administrator*
Zeller, Anchard Frederic *retired psychologist*

**Redondo Beach**
Abernethy, Robert John *real estate developer*
Battles, Roxy Edith *novelist, consultant, educator*
Brodsky, Robert Fox *aerospace engineer, educator, author*
Casey, Michael Scott *mathematician*
Foster, John Stuart, Jr. *physicist, former defense industry executive*
Grzesik, Jan Alexander *electronics engineer, mathematician*
Kagiwada, Reynold Shigeru *electronics executive*
Kich, Rolf *communications scientist, consultant*
Martin, Melissa Carol *radiological physicist*
McWilliams, Margaret Ann *home economist, educator, writer*
Mulvey, Gerald John *meteorologist*
Nella, John *aerospace engineer*
Richards, Denise *actress*
Shellhorn, Ruth Patricia *landscape architect*
Sloan, Michael Dana *information systems specialist, management consultant*

**Redwood City**
Bell, Frank Ouray, Jr. *lawyer*
Burkhardt, Roger *information technology executive*
Catz, Safra *computer software company executive*
Cooperman, Daniel *computer software company executive, lawyer*
Davidson, Mary Ann *information technology executive*
Ellis, Eldon Eugene *surgeon*
Ellison, Larry (Lawrence Joseph Ellison) *computer software company executive*
Fitzpatrick, Will *lawyer*
Hagart-Alexander, Claud *software engineer*
Henley, Jeffrey O. *computer software company executive*
Hoy, Linda Jo *theater educator, actress*
Lee, V. Paul *entertainment software company executive*
Millard, Richard Steven *lawyer*
Nosler, Peter Cole *construction company executive*
Phillips, Charles E., Jr. *computer company executive*
Powers, Matthew Douglas *lawyer*
Probst, Lawrence F. III *game systems company executive*
Rohde, James Vincent *software systems company executive*
Sharpnack, Rayona *management consultant*
Smith, Nancy L. *information technology executive*
Spangler, Nita Reifschneider *volunteer*
Stone, Herbert Allen *management consultant*
Sullivan, Kathleen Marie *lawyer, educator, former dean*
Sweet, Victoria *medical educator, physician*
Wang, Chen Chi *electronics executive, real estate company executive, diversified financial services company executive*
Wilhelm, Robert Oscar *lawyer, civil engineer*
Wookey, John *computer software company executive*

**Redwood Valley**
Speed, Cynthia Agnes *retired mathematics professor*

**Reedley**
Carey, Ernestine Gilbreth (Mrs. Charles E. Carey) *writer, educator*
Dick, Henry Henry *minister*
Walter, Burl Leroy, Jr. *retired music educator*

**Rescue**
Ackerly, Wendy Saunders *construction company executive*

**Reseda**
Wagner, Robert *actor*

**Rialto**
Alav, Faramarz *cardiologist, internist*
Gilbert, Joanne Toone *director, educator*
Hunley, John Dillard *retired historian, ombudsman*

**Richmond**
Arnon, Stephen Soulé *physician, research scientist*
Biddle, Michael *plastics company executive*
Corbin, Rosemary MacGowan *former mayor*
Desmond, Edward *microbiologist, consultant*
Dolberg, David Spencer *lawyer*
Janda, John Michael *microbiologist*
Jenkins, Everett Wilbur, Jr. *lawyer, writer, historian*
Ofteness, Ove (O.V. Michaelsen) *writer, musician*
Paré, Jocelyn Marie *elementary school educator, consultant*
Shladover, Steven Elliot *transportation research professional*

Wessel, Henry *photographer*

## Ridgecrest
Bennett, Harold Earl *physicist, optics researcher*
Finholm, Scott Robert *secondary school educator*
St. Amand, Pierre *geophysicist*

## Riverside
Balandin, Alexander A. *electrical engineer, educator*
Barkin, Kenneth David *history professor*
Bell, Helen Lavin *artist*
Beni, Gerardo *engineering educator, electrical engineer*
Boldt, William Gregory *academic administrator, consultant*
Bosse, Mark Thomas *social services administrator*
Bricker, Neal S. *physician, educator*
Calfee, Robert Chilton *psychologist, educator*
Carney, Jane W. *lawyer*
Carpenter, Mark Warren *social sciences educator*
Chamberlain, Willard Thomas *retired metal products executive*
Chang, Sylvia Tan *health facility administrator, educator*
Chen, Wilfred *education educator*
Clegg, Michael Tran *genetics educator, researcher*
Córdova, France Anne-Dominic *academic administrator, astrophysicist*
Darling, Scott Edward *lawyer*
Day, Renee Noelle *secondary school educator, special education educator*
Deal, Kevin Paul *furniture designer*
Elliott, Emory Bernard *language educator, school system administrator*
Evangelista, Allan *surgeon, medical researcher*
Everett, Carl *professional baseball player*
Fontana, Sandra Ellen Frankel *special education educator*
Geraty, Lawrence Thomas *academic administrator, archaeologist, educator*
Gonzalez-Rivera, Gloria *economics professor*
Green, Harry Western, II, *geology and geophysics professor*
Griffin, Keith Broadwell *retired economics professor*
Hall, Anthony Elmitt *agriculturist, physiologist*
Heiting, James Otto *lawyer*
Holmes, Dallas Scott *judge, educator*
Hyman, Bradley C. *biology professor, geneticist*
Jackson, Marguerite Faye Thurston *rhetoric and intercultural communications and language educator*
James, Etta (Jamesetta Hawkins) *recording artist*
Jung, Timothy Tae Kun *otolaryngologist*
Kordus, Marcella Natasha *psychologist*
Kuzina, Ludmila V. *microbiologist, researcher*
Linaweaver, Walter Ellsworth, Jr. *physician*
Lyubomirsky, Ilya *engineering educator*
Mao, Changxuan *statistician*
Marlatt, Michael James *lawyer*
McGill, Leonard John *lawyer*
McLaughlin, Leighton Bates, II, *journalist, educator, retired reporter*
Millar, Jocelyn G. *entomologist, educator*
Page, Albert Lee *soil science educator, researcher*
Peterson, Arthur Laverne *foundation administrator*
Petrinovich, Lewis Franklin *psychologist, educator*
Plowman, Boyd R. *automotive executive*
Pogorelov, Nikolai *physicist, researcher*
Pratt, John Jackson *property manager, retired utilities worker*
Prosser, Michael Joseph *college librarian*
Rabenstein, Dallas Leroy *chemistry professor*
Rainey, Susan J. *school system administrator*
Ratliff, Louis Jackson, Jr. *mathematics professor*
Rosenthal, Robert *psychology professor*
Russo, Marisa N. *media consultant*
Salzman, Michele Renee *historian, educator*
Shapiro, Victor Lenard *mathematics professor*
Smith, Dorothy Ottinger *apparel designer, volunteer*
Smith, Elden Leroy *recreational vehicle and manufactured housing company executive*
Smith, Richard Charles *not-for-profit administrator, educator, consultant, advocate*
Snyder, Henry Leonard *historian, educator, writer*
Sokolsky, Robert Lawrence *journalist*
Suyenaga, Elsie Sakae *retired elementary school educator*
Turk, Austin Theodore *social studies educator*
Valadez, Rudolph Antonio *security firm executive, consultant, writer, artist*
Van Gundy, Seymour Dean *plant pathologist, educator*
Warren, Katherine Virginia *art gallery director*
White, Clara Jo *small business owner, consultant*
Wudka, Jose *physics professor*
Yacoub, Ignatius I. *dean*
Yount, Gwendolyn Audrey *humanities educator*

## Rocklin
Blank, Lenore Kim *literature and language professor, consultant*
Dwyer, Darrell James *finance company executive*
Tal, Jacob *electronics executive*

## Rohnert Park
Arminana, Ruben *academic administrator, educator*
Babula, William *dean, writer*
Byrne, Noel Thomas *sociologist, educator*
Cominsky, Lynn Ruth *physics and astronomy educator*
Halavais, Mary Hoyt *history professor, researcher*
Johnson, Herman Leonall *retired research nutritionist, researcher*
Nowak, Linda Ilene *education educator*
Poe, William Clay *archaeologist, educator*
Steiner, John Michael *sociologist, educator*

## Rolling Hills
Rumbaugh, Charles Earl *arbitrator, mediator, educator, lawyer*

## Rolling Hills Estates
Bellis, Carroll Joseph *surgeon, educator*
Conrad, Paul Francis *cartoonist*
Diaz-Zubieta, Agustin *nuclear engineer, engineering executive*
McCreight, Louis Ralph *retired materials scientist*

Wong, Sun Yet *engineer, consultant*

## Rosemead
Bryson, John E. *utilities executive*
Collins, Jodi M. *utilities executive*
Danner, Bryant Craig *lawyer*
Fohrer, Alan J. *utilities company executive*
Jin, Jing Yi *photographer, film director*
McDaniel, Thomas R. *utilities executive*
Pizarro, Pedro *electric power industry executive*
Rosenblum, Richard Mark *utilities executive*
Smith, Anthony L. *utilities executive*

## Roseville
Arnold, Barbara Cook *librarian*
Grant, Barbara *venture capitalist*
Larson, Kenneth Leroy, Jr. *psychologist, educator*
Netto, Paul V. *critical care nurse*
Reichmann, Péter Iván *mathematics professor*
Smith, Kaye Train *artist*
Yarrigle, Charlene Sandra Shuey *realtor, investment advisor*

## Ross
Godwin, Sara *writer*
Nicholson, William Joseph *energy and environmental consultant*

## Running Springs
Liddle, Sidney George *retired mechanical engineer, researcher*

## Rutherford
Staglin, Garen Kent *computer company executive, venture capitalist*

## Sacramento
Abdur-Rahim, Shareef (Julius Shareef Abdul-Rahim) *professional basketball player*
Acree, G. Hardy *airport executive*
Ahmed, Ashraf Ibrahim *structural engineer, researcher*
Aldrich, Thomas Albert *former brewing executive, consultant*
Allan, William George *artist, educator*
Amezcua, Esther Hernandez *elementary school educator*
Artest, Ron (Ronald William Artest Jr.) *professional basketball player*
Baccigaluppi, Roger John *agricultural products executive*
Barankin, Joseph Paul *director, consultant*
Bass de Martinez, Bernice *academic administrator, consultant*
Behrman, Bruce Ward *social sciences educator*
Bell, Wayne S. *lawyer, state agency official*
Bersin, Alan Douglas *state agency administrator, lawyer*
Bettenhausen, Matthew Robert *state official, lawyer*
Betts, Bert A. *retired treasurer, accountant*
Bibby, Mike *professional basketball player*
Blake, D. Steven *lawyer*
Block, Alvin Gilbert *academic administrator*
Bogren, Hugo Gunnar *radiology educator*
Bowen, Debra Lynn *lawyer, state legislator*
Bruce, Thomas Edward *thanatologist, psychology professor*
Bustamante, Cruz M. *lieutenant governor*
Callahan, Consuelo Maria *federal judge*
Campbell, Tom *state agency administrator, dean, former congressman*
Carmona, Tamyra Rae *biology professor*
Carr, Gerald Francis *language educator*
Caso, Anthony T. *lawyer*
Chapman, Michael William *orthopedist, educator*
Chason, Robert *health facility administrator*
Chu, Judy May *assemblywoman*
Clover, Haworth Alfred *elementary school educator, historian*
Cole, Glen David *minister*
Covin, David L. *retired political science professor*
Crawford, Robert Lawrence *mathematics professor*
Crimmins, Philip Patrick *retired metallurgical engineer, lawyer*
Cunningham, Mary Elizabeth (Mary Cunningham-Lusby) *physician*
Dager, William Erling *pharmacist, educator*
Day, James McAdam, Jr. *lawyer*
Dong, Michael Hon *toxicologist*
Drachnik, Catherine Meldyn *recreational therapist, artist, counselor*
Drummond, Marshall Edward (Mark Drummon) *academic administrator*
Dunnett, Dennis George *retired state official*
Fait, Glenn A. *lawyer, educator*
Fargo, Heather *mayor*
Faust, Mara Leah *prosecutor*
Forsyth, Raymond Arthur *civil engineer, consultant*
Franz, Jennifer Danton *public opinion and marketing researcher*
Friedman, Morton Lee *lawyer*
Fung, Maxwell Alexander *medical educator*
Gardner, Jerry Lee *financial consultant*
Gebers, Michael A. *research scientist*
Gerringer, Elizabeth (The Marchioness de Roe Devon, Poet Julie de Vontine) *writer, lawyer*
Gerth, Donald Rogers *retired university president, educator*
Gordon, Vahl Scott *computer scientist, educator*
Gosfield, Margaret *secondary school educator, school system administrator, consultant, editor*
Gray, Walter P. III *historian, archivist, consultant*
Greene, Richard *association executive*
Griffith, Yolanda Evette *professional basketball player*
Harvey, Ian *artist, educator*
Heningburg, Keith Rudolph Valenteno *history professor, director*
Henson, Glenda Maria *newswriter*
Heym, Roger H. *literature and language educator*
Houpt, James Edward *lawyer*
Howell, Lydia Pleotis *pathologist, educator*
Hummel, John *information technology executive*
Hunter, Patricia Rae (Tricia Hunter) *state official*
Jackson, Richard Joseph *epidemiologist, educator, pediatrician, preventive medicine physician*
Jelinek, David *education educator, writer*
Jones, Lial A. *museum director*
Karlton, Lawrence K. *federal judge*

Keddy, James *religious organization administrator*
Keiner, Christian Mark *lawyer*
Killian, Richard M. *library director*
Kon, Alexander A. *pediatrician, educator*
Kondos, Gregory *painter, art educator*
Kravitz, Richard L. *medical educator, director*
Kuehl, Sheila James *state legislator*
Lam, Siuwa Monica *education educator, consultant*
Lathi, Bhagawandas Pannalal *retired electrical engineering educator*
Leong, Albin B. *pediatric pulmonologist, educator, pediatric allergist*
Levi, David F. *federal judge*
Lewin, John Calvert *medical association administrator*
Lim, Alan Young *plastic surgeon*
Lionakis, George *architect*
Lippold, Roland Will *retired surgeon*
Liu, Carol *state representative*
Lockyer, Bill (William Lockyer) *state attorney general*
Lukenbill, Gregg *real estate developer, sports promoter*
Lundstrom, Marjie *editor, columnist*
Lynch, Peter John *retired dermatologist*
Majesty, Melvin Sidney *psychologist, consultant*
Malkin, Harold Marshall *retired medical researcher*
Malloy, Michael Patrick *law educator, consultant*
Marin, Rosario *state agency administrator, former federal agency administrator*
Mazzaferro, James Joseph *music educator*
McCann, Kim Lou M. *theater educator, director*
McCarthy, Kevin *state representative*
McFarland, Kevin John *foundation administrator*
McPherson, Bruce A. *state official, former state legislator*
Meindl, Robert James *language educator, poet*
Metzer, Laren Wayne *government agency administrator, archivist*
Morrow, Bill *state legislator*
Moulds, John F. *judge*
Munitz, Barry *former arts and foundation administrator*
Musselman, Eric *professional basketball coach*
Myrrdin, Terry A. *state agency administrator*
Nagy, Stephen Mears, Jr. *physician, allergist*
Newland, Chester Albert *public administration educator*
Nice, Carter *conductor*
Norman, Ben Eric *mathematician, educator*
O'Connell, Jack *school system administrator*
Opperman, Rosanna Resendez *vice principal*
Parker, Dennis Rey *finance educator*
Parker, Elizabeth Rindskopf *dean, law educator*
Patino, Douglas Xavier *government agency administrator, academic administrator*
Pavley, Fran J. *state representative*
Philip, Tom *reporter*
Piper, Jami Kathleen *music educator, composer, musician*
Piskoti, Carol Lee *art educator*
Post, August Alan *retired economist, artist*
Pruitt, Gary B. *publishing company executive*
Purdy, James Aaron *medical physics professor*
Quinn, Francis A. *bishop*
Rab, George T. *pediatric orthopedic surgeon*
Rainwater, Eric *composer, music educator*
Robbins, Stephen J. M. *lawyer*
Roberts, Paul Dale *state agency administrator, writer*
Robinson, Muriel Cox *psychiatrist*
Rosenberg, Dan Yale *retired plant pathologist*
Rosenfeld, Arthur H. *physics professor, researcher*
Ross, Jean M. *think-tank executive*
Sanborn, Kathy *career planning administrator, consultant*
Schwarzenegger, Arnold Alois *governor*
Scott, McGregor W. *prosecutor, lawyer*
Sharma, Arjun Dutta *cardiologist*
Sherwood, Robert Petersen *retired social sciences educator*
Shriver, Maria Owings *news correspondent*
Silva, Joseph, Jr. *dean, medical educator*
Starr, Kevin *librarian, educator*
Stevenson, Thomas Ray *plastic surgeon*
Strickland, Anthony *state representative*
Styne, Dennis Michael *physician, educator*
Swatt, Stephen Benton *communications executive, consultant*
Taylor, Joseph Evans *law educator*
Totton, Gayle *professional sports team executive*
Tract, Larry Scott *construction management consultant*
Tran, Van Thai *state legislator*
Tung, Prabhas *plastic surgeon*
Van Camp, Brian Ralph *judge*
Vixie Sandy, Mary Dolores *educational association administrator*
von Friederichs-Fitzwater, Marlene Marie *researcher*
Walsh, Denny Jay *reporter*
Walters, Daniel Raymond *political columnist*
Wasserman, Barry L(ee) *architect*
Welter, Paula Joy *singer, songwriter*
Wilmer, Robin Louise *music educator*
Winterton, Shaun Leslie *entomologist, educator*
Wolfman, Earl Frank, Jr. *surgeon, educator*
Wolkov, Harvey Brian *oncologist, researcher*
Wyland, Mark *state official*
Yang, Yung Y. *economics professor, consultant*
Yee, Leland Y. *state legislator*
Zaidi, Emily Louise *retired elementary school educator*
Zhang, Du *engineering educator*

## Saint Helena
Sakopoulos, Andreas George *cardiac and vascular surgeon*
Seavey, William Arthur *lawyer, vintner*
Sone, Hiro *chef, restaurant owner, writer*
Wiggins, Rita Cassidy *poet*

## Salinas
Bernhard, Nancy Lynn *secondary school educator*
Chester, Lynne *foundation administrator, artist*
Etienne, Myron E., Jr. *lawyer*
Jeffries, Russell Morden *communications company official*
Newberry, Conrad Floyde *aerospace engineering educator*

Puckett, Richard Edward *artist, consultant, former recreation executive*
Rosen, Jacqueline I. *musician, educator*
Stevens, Wilbur Hunt *accountant*

## San Andreas
Breed, Allen Forbes *social services administrator*
Maris, Anthony, Jr. *environmental services administrator*
Prema, Nitya *marriage and family therapist, artist*

## San Anselmo
Chiaverini, John Edward *construction company executive*
Crawley, Cheryl K. *school system administrator*
Harper Haines, Jan Frances *writer, educator*
Murphy, James *lawyer*
Truett, Harold Joseph, III, (Tim Truett) *lawyer*

## San Bernardino
Andersen, Jennifer Lotte *literature and language professor*
Aylmer, Francoise *academic administrator*
Baek, Eun-Ok *instructional technology educator*
Burgess, Michael *librarian, writer*
De Haas, David Dana *emergency physician*
Del Riego, Rutilio J. *bishop*
Evans, Hiram Kraig *forensic chemist*
Fernandez-Miyakawa, Mariano Enrique *biologist, research scientist*
Harter-Speer, Joan E. *human services educator*
Martinez, Benjamin Ray *security officer, retired military non-commissioned officer*
Roberts, Katharine Adair *retired bookkeeper*

## San Bruno
Bradley, Charles William *podiatrist, educator*
Chandy, John Attupurathu *computer engineer*

## San Carlos
Dafforn, Geoffrey Alan *biochemist*
Eby, Michael John *marketing research and technology consultant*
Gutow, Bernard Sidney *packaging manufacturing company executive*
Lee, John Jin *lawyer*
Love, Ted W. *biotechnology company executive*
Oliver, Nancy Lebkicher *artist, retired elementary school educator*
Rathmann, George Blatz *genetic engineering company executive*
Schumacher, Henry Jerold *museum director, retired military officer*
Symons, Robert Spencer *electronics engineer*
Wolff, Ronald Keith *toxicologist, researcher*

## San Clemente
Butler, Russell *artist*
Clark, Earnest Hubert, Jr. *tool company executive*
Lopez, George A. *medical products executive*
Petruzzi, Christopher Robert *business educator, consultant*
Riem, Michelle Johanna *science educator*
Steinberg, Howard *chemical company executive, consultant*
Wolfram, Thomas *physicist, educator*

## San Diego
Adams, Loretta *marketing executive*
Adler, Christopher Alan *composer, educator*
Allen, P. Blake *lawyer*
Altamar, Hernan Orlando *urologist, military officer*
Altman, Steven R. *telecommunications executive*
Amstadt, Nancy Hollis *retired language educator*
Anderson, Karl Richard *aerospace engineer, consultant*
Anderson, Paul Maurice *electrical engineering educator, researcher, consultant*
Armstong, Robert G. *lawyer*
Astroth, Margo Foltz *mental health nurse, nurse psychotherapist*
Auld, Robert Henry, Jr. *biomedical engineer, educator, consultant, writer*
Ballinger, Charles Edwin *educational association administrator*
Bartus, Raymond Thomas *neuroscientist, writer, pharmaceutical executive*
Bates-Romeo, Delores Alvenia *music educator, consultant*
Baxter, Robert Hampton *insurance company executive*
Bell, Robert Jeffrey *lawyer*
Benirschke, Kurt *retired pathologist, educator*
Bennett, Andrew David *alcohol/drug abuse services professional*
Bernstein, Sanford Irwin *biology professor*
Blanchard, Jennifer Neely *physician, educator*
Blas, Marlene Jambaro *academic administrator, educator*
Bleiler, Charles Arthur *lawyer*
Bliesner, James Douglas *municipal/county official, consultant*
Bochy, Bruce *professional sports team manager, coach*
Bowie, Peter Wentworth *judge, educator*
Brandes, Charles H. *investment company executive*
Brandes, Raymond Stewart *historian, educator, dean*
Breen, Stephen P. *editorial cartoonist*
Brennan-Sparks, Jennifer Anne *writer*
Brewster, Rudi Milton *judge*
Brierton, Cheryl Lynn *lawyer*
Brom, Robert H. *bishop*
Brooks, John White *lawyer*
Brooks, Juanita Rose *lawyer*
Brown, Barbara Sproul *retired librarian, consultant, writer*
Brown, LaMar Bevan *lawyer*
Brownlie, Robert William *lawyer*
Bryan, John Rodney *management consultant*
Buska, Sheila Mary *controller, writer, columnist*
Butterfield, Alexander Porter *government agency administrator, air transportation executive*
Cabrera, Quincy Rodolfo *minister, educator*
Caldwell, Joan Marie *artist, educator*
Campbell, Ian David *opera company director*
Canales, Viola *management consulting executive, writer*
Cantor, Charles Robert *biochemistry professor*
Carretero, Ricardo *science educator*
Cartwright, Derrick *museum director*

Blum, Robert M. *lawyer*
Bocobo-Balunsat, Dalisay *librarian, journalist*
Boles, Roger *otolaryngologist*
Bomse, Stephen V. *lawyer*
Bondoc, Rommel *lawyer*
Bonds, Barry Lamar *professional baseball player*
Bonnie, Shelby W. *computer company executive*
Borowsky, Philip *lawyer*
Bostwick, James Stephen *lawyer*
Botvinick, Elias H. *nuclear medicine physician, researcher, medical educator*
Bourne, Henry R. *medicine, cellular and molecular pharmacology educator*
Boven, Douglas George *lawyer*
Bracken, Thomas Robert James *real estate investment executive*
Bradford, David S. *surgeon*
Brand, Jeffrey S. *dean, law educator*
Brandel, Roland Eric *lawyer*
Bratton, Christopher Alan *academic administrator, videographer, art educator*
Brechka, Frank Tilson *retired librarian, historian*
Broadway, Nancy Ruth *landscape company executive, consultant, model, actress*
Bronstein, Phil *publishing executive*
Brosnahan, James (Jerome) *lawyer*
Brothers, Lynda Lee *lawyer*
Brotman, Martin *gastroenterologist*
Brown, Donald Wesley *lawyer*
Brown, Eric Joel *biomedical researcher*
Brown, Walter Francis, Jr. *lawyer*
Browner, Warren Seth *internist, educator, academic administrator*
Browning, James Robert *federal judge*
Broyles, Deborah J. *lawyer*
Bruen, James A. *lawyer*
Buchanan, John Edward, Jr. *museum director*
Buckmaster, Jim *online community bulletin board company executive*
Buckner, John Knowles *investor*
Bull, Henrik Helkand *architect*
Burden, James Ewers *lawyer*
Burlingame, Alma Lyman *chemist, educator*
Burns, Brian Patrick *lawyer*
Burt, Richard *lawyer*
Bushnell, Roderick Paul *lawyer*
Butenhoff, Susan Grace *public relations executive*
Cabraser, Elizabeth Joan *lawyer*
Callaham, Michael L. *emergency physician, educator*
Callahan, Patricia R. *bank executive*
Camahort, Steve L. *lawyer*
Cameron, Heather Anne *publishing executive*
Campbell, Janet Coral *architect*
Campbell, Jeffrey C. *pharmaceutical executive*
Campbell, Scott Robert *lawyer, former food products executive*
Canady, Richard Warren *lawyer*
Canales, James Earl, Jr. *foundation president*
Caniparoli, Val William *choreographer, dancer*
Capaldini, Lisa Claire *physician, educator*
Carrow, Robert Duane *lawyer, barrister*
Carr-Ruffino, Norma *management educator*
Cartmell, Nathaniel Madison III *lawyer*
Cepeda, Orlando *retired professional baseball player*
Chaet, Vicky Isabel *visual artist*
Chang, Patti *foundation administrator*
Chao, Cedric C. *lawyer*
Chase, Alexandra Nin *psychologist, writer*
Cheng, Wan-Lee *mechanical engineer, educator*
Cherny, Robert Wallace *historian, educator*
Chi, John H. *neurosurgeon*
Chin, Ming W. *state supreme court justice*
Chin, Sue Soone Marian (Suchin Chin) *artist, photojournalist*
Ciccarone, Daniel *medical educator, researcher, physician*
Cirese, Robert Charles *economist, real estate consultant*
Cisneros, Evelyn *dancer*
Clever, Linda Hawes *physician*
Clifford, Geraldine Joncich (Mrs. William F. Clifford) *retired education educator*
Clowes, John Howard *lawyer*
Cluff, Lloyd Sterling *earthquake geologist*
Coan, Eugene Victor *environmental services administrator*
Cobbs, Price Mashaw *social psychiatrist*
Cohn, Roger *editor*
Coleman, Kathryn Anne *lawyer*
Coleman, Thomas Young *lawyer*
Collins, Mary Ann *lawyer*
Colman, Shoshana S. *pharmaceutical executive, researcher*
Colton, Roy Charles *management consultant*
Cominos, Dion Nicholas *lawyer*
Conway, Craig A. *retired computer company executive*
Coombe, George William, Jr. *lawyer, retired bank executive*
Cooper, Allen David *medical researcher, educator*
Corash, Michèle B. *lawyer*
Corrigan, Carol A. *state supreme court justice*
Corrigan, Robert Anthony *academic administrator*
Costa-Zalessow, Natalia *foreign language educator*
Cranston, Mary Bailey *lawyer*
Crawford, J. Brooks *ophthalmologist, educator*
Crawford, Michael Howard *cardiologist, educator, researcher*
Crawford, Roy Edgington III *lawyer*
Cree, Bruce *neurologist*
Croughan, Mary *medical educator*
Cuggino, Michael Joseph *financial executive*
Curran, Mary *lawyer*
Czachor, Bruce *lawyer, consultant*
Dallman, Mary F. *physiologist, science educator*
Danko, Gary J. *chef*
Danoff, Eric Michael *lawyer*
Darbee, Peter A. *electric power company executive*
David, George *psychiatrist, economic theory lecturer*
Davidson, Keay *newswriter*
Davis, Patricia Margaret Alice *psychology educator, religion educator*
Davis, Roger Lewis *lawyer*
Dawson, Chandler Robert *ophthalmologist, educator*
Deicken, Raymond Friedrich *psychiatrist, neuroscientist*
Delaney, Martin *not-for-profit developer*

Del Campo, Martin Bernardelli *architect*
Dell, Robert Michael *lawyer*
Dellas, Robert Dennis *investment banker*
Demarest, David Franklin, Jr. *banker, retired government official*
DeMuro, Paul Robert *lawyer*
Dennehy, Raymond Leo *philosopher, educator*
DeRisi, Joseph L. *science educator, biochemist*
Des Jardins, Traci *chef, restaurant owner*
DeSoto, Lewis Damien *art educator, artist*
Deviren, Vedat *orthopedist, educator*
de Vries, Brian *gerontologist, researcher*
Dickey, Glenn Ernest, Jr. *sportswriter*
Dickinson, Eleanor Creekmore *artist, educator*
Dickinson, Wade *oil industry executive, educator*
Diekmann, Gilmore Frederick, Jr. *lawyer*
Dill, Kenneth Austin *pharmaceutical chemistry educator*
Dodds, Christopher V. *finance company executive*
Dolby, Ray Milton *engineering company executive, electrical engineer*
Dolinko, Robert A. *lawyer*
Donnelly, Thomas M. *lawyer*
Donnelly, Trisha *artist*
Donner, Michael F. *lawyer*
Dracup, Kathleen Anne *dean, nursing educator*
Draper, William Henry III *venture capitalist*
Dryden, Robert Eugene *lawyer*
Dryovage, Mary Margaret *lawyer*
Duffy, Jan *lawyer*
Dugoni, Arthur A. *dean, orthodontics educator*
Duncan, David Ewing *editor, writer*
Dunn, Patricia Cecile *investment company executive*
Dunne, Kevin Joseph *lawyer*
Durham, Ray *professional baseball player*
Duscha, Julius Carl *journalist*
Dwyer, Carrie Elizabeth *lawyer*
Eastham, Thomas *retired foundation administrator*
Eddington, Thomas L. *human resources specialist, consultant*
Edelstein, Michael R. *psychologist, writer*
Edwards, C. Webb *bank executive*
Edwards, Robin Morse *lawyer*
Egan, Patricia Jane *foundation administrator, retired director*
Eigner, Richard Martin *lawyer*
Elder, Muldoon *artist, poet, film producer*
Ellis, John *urban designer*
Emery, Vince *writer, educator*
Enfield, Donald Michael *insurance company executive*
Eng, Catherine *health facility administrator, physician*
Engleman, Ephraim Philip *rheumatologist*
Epsen, Robert A. *lawyer*
Epstein, Charles Joseph *pediatrician, geneticist, biochemist, educator*
Epstein, John Howard *dermatologist*
Ericson, Bruce Alan *lawyer*
Erskine, John Morse *surgeon*
Estes, Carroll Lynn *sociologist, educator*
Eth, Jordan David *lawyer*
Etheridge, Melissa Lou *singer, lyricist*
Eurich, Judith *art appraiser, printmaker*
Fainaru-Wada, Mark *journalist*
Fake, Caterina *Internet company executive*
Falk, Jerome B., Jr. *lawyer*
Falk, Steven B. *newspaper publishing executive*
Falkner, Elizabeth *chef*
Fanning, Shawn *information technology executive*
Felstiner, Mary Lowenthal *history professor*
Fergus, Gary Scott *lawyer*
Ferlinghetti, Lawrence *poet*
Ferriero, Donna M. *pediatric neurologist*
Ferris, Russell James, II, *writer*
Fessel, Walford Jeffrey *rheumatologist*
Field, Carol Hart *writer, news correspondent, journalist*
Field, John Louis *architect*
Finberg, James Michael *lawyer*
Finberg, Laurence *pediatrician, educator, dean*
Finck, Kevin William *lawyer*
Fink, Scott Alan *lawyer*
Fisher, Donald G. *retail executive*
Fisher, Doris *retail executive*
Fisher, Robert J. *retail executive*
Fisher, Robert Morton *foundation administrator, academic administrator*
Fitzgerald, Paul A. *endocrinologist, educator*
Fitzmaurice, Deanne *photojournalist*
Fleishhacker, David *school administrator*
Fletcher, William A. *federal judge, law educator*
Flittie, Clifford Gilliland *retired petroleum company executive*
Fogel, Paul David *lawyer*
Folberg, Harold Jay *lawyer, educator, dean*
Folkman, David H. *retail, wholesale and consumer products consultant*
Folkman, Susan *research psychologist*
Fong, Kevin Murray *lawyer*
Foret, Mickey Phillip *retired air transportation executive*
Foster, David Scott *lawyer*
Fox, Patrick John *sociology educator*
Fox, Steve *editor-in-chief*
Freud, Nicholas S. *lawyer*
Freund, Fredric S. *real estate broker, real estate manager*
Frick, Oscar Lionel *pediatrician, educator*
Friedman, Barbara Lorie *lawyer*
Friedman, K. Bruce *lawyer*
Friedman, Tully Michael *corporate financial executive*
Friedrichs, Edward Charles *architect*
Friese, Robert Charles *lawyer*
Fuller, James William *financial planner*
Furth, Frederick Paul *lawyer*
Gamson, Joshua Paul *sociology educator, writer*
Ganem, Donald E. *immunologist*
Ganong, William F(rancis) *physiologist, educator*
Garchik, Leah Lieberman *journalist*
Garvey, Joanne Marie *lawyer*
Gekelman, Diana *dentist, dental educator, researcher*
Gellin, Gerald Alan *dermatologist*
Gensler, M. Arthur, Jr. *architect*
George, Ronald M. *state supreme court chief justice*
German, William *newspaper editor*

Gerwick, Ben Clifford, Jr. *civil engineer, consultant*
Getto, Ernest John *lawyer*
Gibbs, Patricia Hellman *physician*
Gillette, Frankie Jacobs *retired savings and loan association executive, federal agency administrator, social worker*
Gillette, Patricia K. *lawyer*
Gimon, Juliette *foundation administrator, volunteer*
Giovinco, Joseph *non profit agency administrator, writer*
Glantz, Stanton A. *medical researcher*
Glazer, Jack Henry *lawyer*
Glynn, Robert D., Jr. *electric power and gas industry executive*
Gockley, David (Richard David Gockley) *opera director*
Goldman, Richard N. *foundation administrator*
Goldstein, David Baird *energy executive, physicist*
Goldstein, Sydney Rachel *photographer, writer, radio producer*
Goldstine, Stephen Joseph *art educator*
Gooding, Charles Arthur *radiologist, physician, educator*
Gooding, Gretchen Ann Wagner *physician, educator*
Goodwin, David B. *lawyer*
Gordon, Judith *communications consultant, writer*
Granik, Vladimir *mechanic engineering educator, researcher*
Graw, LeRoy Harry *diversified financial services company executive*
Gray, James N. *computer scientist*
Graysmith, Robert *political cartoonist, author*
Greene, Richard Lawrence *lawyer*
Greene, Warner Craig *medical educator, medical association administrator*
Greenspan, Deborah *dental educator*
Greenspan, Francis S. *physician*
Greenspan, John S. *dental and medical educator, researcher, academic administrator*
Gregoratos, Gabriel *medical educator*
Gregory, Sara Susan (Sudie) *musician, singer, lyricist, poet, recording industry executive, sound recording engineer, archivist*
Gresham, Zane Oliver *lawyer*
Griggs, Lewis Brown *executive producer, speaker, trainer*
Grodsky, Gerold Morton *biochemistry professor*
Grossman, William *medical researcher, educator*
Grumbach, Melvin Malcolm *pediatrician, educator*
Gudmundsson, Dadi *computer company executive*
Guggenhime, Richard Johnson *lawyer*
Guillermo, Tessie *foundation administrator*
Guttentag, Lucas *advocate, lawyer*
Haas, Raymond F. *lawyer*
Haas, Robert Douglas *apparel executive*
Haber, Scott R. *lawyer*
Haerle, Paul Raymond *judge*
Hafner, Katie *reporter*
Hagenbuch, John Jacob *investor*
Hale, Cecil *communications educator, business educator*
Hale, Victoria G. *chemist, pharmaceutical executive*
Halliday, John Meech *investment company executive*
Halloran, Michael James *lawyer*
Halprin, Lawrence *landscape architect, urban planner*
Hamilton, Joan Nice *editor-in-chief*
Hammergren, John H. *pharmaceutical executive*
Hansen, Carol Louise *literature and language professor*
Hara, George *computer company executive*
Haratani, Joan Mei *lawyer*
Harlan, Neil Eugene *retired health facility administrator*
Harris, Kamala D. *prosecutor*
Harriss, Cynthia Therese (Cynthia Therese Clarke) *retail executive*
Harvey, D. Peter *lawyer, educator*
Hasson, Kirke Michael *lawyer*
Hastings, Edward Walton *theater director*
Havel, Richard Joseph *physician, educator*
Hawkins, Trip *electronics executive*
Hecker, Peter S. *lawyer*
Heilbron, David Michael *lawyer, arbitrator, mediator*
Hellman, F(rederick) Warren *investor*
Henderson, Isaac Craig *oncologist, researcher*
Henderson, Thelton Eugene *federal judge*
Hendrick, James T. *lawyer*
Heng, Donald James, Jr. *lawyer*
Henson, Ray David *law educator, consultant*
Hernandez, Gary A. *lawyer*
Herrera, Dennis J. *lawyer*
Herringer, Frank Casper *diversified financial services company executive*
Hewitt, Conrad W. *former comissioner, accountant*
Heyneman, Donald *parasitology and tropical medicine educator*
Higashida, Randall Takeo *radiologist, neurosurgeon, medical educator*
Higgins, Daniel B. *lawyer*
Hills, Austin Edward *vineyard executive*
Hilton, Stanley Goumas *lawyer, educator, writer*
Hinman, Frank, Jr. *urologist, educator*
Hinman, Harvey DeForest *lawyer*
Hirsch, (William) Reece *lawyer*
Hisert, George Arthur *lawyer*
Ho, Doreen Woo *bank executive*
Hoffman, William Yanes *plastic surgeon*
Hofmann, John Richard, Jr. *retired lawyer*
Holden, Frederick Douglass, Jr. *lawyer*
Holland, April Anne *elementary school educator*
Honig, Al *artist*
Hosie, Spencer *lawyer*
Howard, Carl *retired lawyer*
Howard, David E. *artist*
Hoyt, David A. *bank executive*
Hsu, Chi-yuan *nephrologist, researcher*
Hubbell, Robert B. *lawyer*
Hudner, Philip *lawyer, banker*
Hudson, Darril *political scientist, educator*
Hui, Helen Yuen Hing *lawyer*
Hunt, James L. *lawyer*
Hunter, William Dennis *lawyer*

Ikeda, Clyde Junichi *plastic and reconstructive surgeon*
Ikuta, Sandra Segal *federal judge*
Illston, Susan Y. *federal judge*
Im, Subin *marketing educator*
Jaffe, Seth Roth *lawyer, retail executive*
James, David Lee *lawyer, writer, international advisor*
James, George Barker, II, *investment company executive*
James, Thomas Larry *chemistry professor*
Jamison, Dean Tecumseh *economist*
Jarvis, Donald Bertram *judge*
Jenkins, Margaret Ludmilla *choreographer, dancer*
Jewett, George Frederick, Jr. *forest products company executive*
Johns, Christopher P. *corporate financial executive*
Johnson, Michelle L. *lawyer*
Johnson, Stephen Patrick Howard *lawyer*
Jolly, Todd B. *music educator, minister*
Jones, Frances Mary *law librarian*
Jones, J. Gilbert *private investigator*
Jones, Stanton William *management consultant*
Jonsen, Albert R(upert) *retired medical ethics educator*
Joseph, Allan Jay *lawyer*
Judd, Bruce Diven *architect*
Julian, Paul C. *health products executive*
Julius, David *biochemist*
Juster, Kenneth Ian *lawyer*
Kamm, John *non-profit organization administrator, human rights activist*
Kan, Yuet Wai *hematologist, educator*
Kane, Mary Kay *academic administrator, law educator*
Kao, John Sterling *mathematician, educator*
Kapor, Mitchell David *application developer, foundation administrator*
Kasanin, Mark Owen *lawyer*
Katz, Jeff *television personality*
Katz, Mitchell H. *city health department administrator*
Katzung, Bertram George *pharmacologist*
Kee, Terry Michael *lawyer*
Keker, John Watkins *lawyer*
Keller, Edward Lowell *electrical engineer, educator*
Kelley, Michael Garhart Roosevelt *historian, educator, writer*
Kelly, J. Michael *lawyer*
Kelly, James Anthony *priest*
Kennard, Joyce L. *state supreme court justice*
Kennedy, Raoul Dion *lawyer*
Kenyon, Cynthia J. *medical researcher*
Kerlikowske, Karla *research scientist*
Kern, Brad D. *lawyer*
Kern, John McDougall *lawyer*
Kertzman, Mitchell E. *former software company executive, venture capitalist*
Kessler, David Aaron *dean, medical educator*
Khosla, Ved Mitter *oral and maxillofacial surgeon, educator*
Kielarowski, Henry Edward *marketing executive*
Kimmich, Robert André *psychiatrist*
Kimport, David Lloyd *lawyer*
Kirincic, Paul E. *human services administrator*
Klammer, Joseph Francis *retired management consultant*
Klein, Marc S. *editor, publishing executive*
Knapp, Charles Lincoln *law educator*
Knebel, Jack Gillen *lawyer*
Knutzen, Martha Lorraine *lawyer*
Koeppel, John A. *lawyer*
Koffel, Martin M. *engineering company executive*
Kolkey, Daniel Miles *former judge, lawyer*
Koltzova-Rang, Yulia K. *internist*
Koo, John Ying Ming *psychiatrist, dermatologist*
Kovacevich, Richard M. *bank executive*
Kozloff, Lloyd M. *dean, microbiologist, educator*
Kozloff, Theodore J. *lawyer*
Krames, Elliot Stephan *anesthesiologist*
Krane, Hilary K. *lawyer*
Krevans, Rachel *lawyer*
Krippner, Stanley Curtis *psychologist*
Kuhl, Paul Beach *lawyer*
Kunwar, Sandeep *neurosurgeon*
Kunz, Heidi *healthcare company executive*
LaBelle, Thomas Jeffrey *research executive, academic administrator*
Lacovara, Michael *lawyer*
La Farge, Timothy *retired plant geneticist*
Lamberson, John Roger *insurance company executive*
Lane, Mary B. *education educator, writer*
Lane, Nathan III *lawyer*
Laret, Mark R. *health facility executive*
Larrabee, Matthew L. *lawyer*
Larson, John William *lawyer*
Laspa, Jude *engineering company executive*
Lau, Jenny Kwok Wah *theater educator, consultant, film educator, consultant*
Lazarus, David *journalist*
LeBlanc, Tina *dancer*
Lee, Iara *filmmaker*
Lee, Pamela Anne *bank executive, accountant, financial analyst*
Lee, Richard Diebold *lawyer, educator*
LeFurgy, Rich *advertising executive*
Leshy, John David *lawyer, educator, solicitor*
Lester, W. Howard *retail executive*
Levie, Mark Robert *lawyer*
Levin, Barry Steven *lawyer*
Levine, Alison *entrepreneur, leadership development consultant, adventurer*
Leviton, Alan Edward *curator*
Levy, Jay A. *medical educator*
Lieber, Tom Alan *painter*
Lieff, Robert Lawrence *lawyer*
Likova Mineva, Lora T. *research scientist*
Lindstrom, Gregory P. *lawyer*
Liu, Hanmin *foundation administrator*
Livermore, Samuel Morgan *lawyer*
Livsey, Robert Callister *lawyer*
Lo, Bernard *medical educator*
Londen, Jack W. *lawyer*
Lopes, James Louis *lawyer*
Low, Arnold Kinman *systems executive*
Low, Randall *internist, cardiologist*
Lowell, Frederick K. *lawyer*
Lowenthal, Steven R. *lawyer*
Lucia, Marilyn Reed *physician*

Luft, Rene Wilfred *civil engineer*
Lyon, David William *research executive*
Lyons, James Elliott *lawyer*
Maas, Corey *plastic surgeon*
MacNaughton, Angus Athole *finance company executive*
Maffre, Muriel *ballet dancer*
Magowan, Peter Alden *professional sports team executive, retail executive*
Mahley, Robert W. *health facility administrator*
Mahoney, Michael James *investment company executive*
Maier, Peter Klaus *lawyer*
Malkin, Joseph M. *lawyer*
Maly, Michael Kip *lawyer*
Mandra, York T. *geology educator*
Mann, Bruce Alan *lawyer, bank executive, investment banker*
Manning, Jerome Alan *retired lawyer*
Marchant, David Judson *lawyer*
Marduel, Alix *venture capitalist*
Marineau, Philip Albert *apparel executive*
Markoff, John *reporter*
Márquez-Magaña, Leticia Maria *biology professor*
Marshall, Grayson William, Jr. *materials scientist, biomedical engineer, health sciences educator, dentist*
Marshall, Patrick C. *lawyer*
Marshall, Raymond Charles *lawyer*
Marston, Michael *economist, consultant*
Martel, John Sheldon *lawyer, writer*
Martin, Fred *artist, academic administrator*
Martin, John L. *airport executive*
Martinez, Belinda *health insurance company executive*
Martinez Tucker, Sara *educational association administrator*
Masaoka, Jan *not-for-profit executive*
Masio, Richard Frank *sales executive, director*
Mason, Dean Towle *cardiologist*
Mathes, Stephen John *plastic and reconstructive surgeon, educator*
Mattern, Douglas James *think-tank executive*
Mattes, Martin Anthony *lawyer*
McAninch, Jack Weldon *urological surgeon, educator*
McCauley, Matthew K. *apparel executive*
McClintock, Jessica *fashion designer*
McCollam, Sharon L. *retail executive*
McCormick, Frank *research scientist*
McCracken, Harry *journalist*
McCulley, Timothy J. *ophthalmologist, surgeon, educator*
McCune, Joseph Mike *epidemiologist, educator, researcher*
McDiarmid, Bruce W. *lawyer*
McElhinny, Harold John *lawyer*
McGettigan, Charles Carroll, Jr. *investment banker*
McGinnis, James Landon *lawyer*
McGrath, Don John *bank executive*
McGuckin, John Hugh, Jr. *lawyer*
McGuire, Kathleen Alison *conductor*
McGuire, William Albert *humanities educator*
McKeever, Michael Pierce, Sr. *economics and business educator*
McKenzie, John F. *lawyer*
McKeon, Jami Wintz *lawyer*
McNally, Thomas Charles III *lawyer*
Meader, Keith Alan *social services administrator*
Mellor, Robert E. *building materials company executive, lawyer*
Meyerson, Ivan D. *lawyer, corporate financial executive*
Michels, Dirk *lawyer*
Miles, Donald F. *lawyer*
Miller, Ann G. *lawyer*
Miller, Ronald D. *medical educator, researcher*
Miller, Walter Luther *pediatrician, educator*
Miller, William Napier Cripps *lawyer*
Miller, William Napier Cripps *lawyer*
Minar, Paul G. *interior designer, consultant*
Ming, Jenny J. *retail apparel company executive*
Minnick, Malcolm David *lawyer*
Minor, Halsey *multimedia company executive*
Mitchell, Bruce Tyson *lawyer*
Mitchell, Theodore Reed *educational association administrator, former academic administrator*
Moe, Michael *diversified financial services company executive*
Molland, Maria U. *Internet company executive*
Moore, Kenneth G. *foundation administrator, former manufacturing executive*
Moore, Kristen L. *marketing professional*
Moore, Steven E. *foundation administrator*
Moreno, Albert F. *apparel executive, lawyer*
Moreno, Carlos R. *state supreme court justice*
Moris, Lamberto Giuliano *architect*
Morrissey, John Carroll, Sr. *lawyer*
Morris-Tyndall, Lucy *construction executive*
Motto, David M. *music educator, writer*
Munio, David J. *bank executive*
Muranaka, Hideo *artist, educator*
Murdoch, Colin *academic administrator*
Muren, Dennis E. *special effects expert*
Murillo, Juan A. *civil engineer*
Murphy, Kathleen Anne Foley *communications executive*
Murphy, Sheigla Brighid *sociologist, researcher*
Murray, Kathleen Anne *lawyer*
Musfelt, Duane Clark *lawyer*
Mustacchi, Piero *preventive medicine physician, educator*
Nedelman, Adam *entrepreneur*
Needleman, Jacob *philosophy educator, writer*
Newmark, Craig Alexander *communications executive*
Newsom, Gavin *mayor*
Newton, Nell Jessup *dean, law educator*
Noonan, John T., Jr. *federal judge, law educator*
Norris, Philip John *medical educator, researcher*
Oakes, Nancy *chef, restaurant owner*
Oberman, Ida *research and evaluation director, consultant*
O'Connor, G(eorge) Richard *ophthalmologist*
O'Connor, Sheila Anne *freelance writer*
Odgers, Richard William *lawyer*
Offer, Stuart Jay *lawyer*
Okeke, Christian Nwachukwu *law educator*
Olson, Steven Kent *dentist*
Olson, Karl *lawyer*

Olson, Robert Howard *lawyer*
Oman, Mark C. *bank executive*
O'Neal, Stephen V. *lawyer*
O'Neill, Brian *national recreation area administrator*
Ong, Lance Orion *writer*
Osborne, Donald Eugene *performing company executive*
Ostler, Clyde W. *banker*
Ousterhout, Douglas Kenneth *plastic surgeon*
Owen, Marc *health products executive*
Owens, Ronald Stephen (Ronn Owens) *radio talk show host*
Oxarart, Frank *broadcast executive*
Palmer, Venrice Romito *lawyer, educator*
Palmer, William Joseph *accountant*
Pape, Glenn Michael *lawyer, financial planner*
Park, Roger Cook *law educator*
Parker, Derek *architectural firm executive*
Parker, Diana Lynne *restaurant manager, special events director*
Patel, Marilyn Hall *judge*
Paterson, Eva *legal association director, educator*
Paterson, Richard Denis *corporate financial executive*
Paxton, Jay Lee *lawyer*
Pazour, Don *publishing executive*
Penhoet, Edward *foundation administrator, former biochemicals company executive, former dean*
Penskar, Mark Howard *lawyer*
Perisic, Igor *engineer*
Perlman, David *journalist*
Perloff, Carey *performing company executive, theater director, playwright*
Petersen, Roland *artist, printmaker*
Peterson, Linda Lou *special education educator*
Petrakis, Nicholas Louis *epidemiologist, medical researcher, educator*
Petty, George Oliver *lawyer*
Pfaff, Laura King *auction house executive*
Philipps, Kinga (Szpakiewicz) *TV show host*
Phillips, Theodore Locke *radiologist, educator*
Pickett, Donn Philip *lawyer*
Pierson, Jay Arthur *music educator*
Pimentel, Benjamin Impelido *journalist*
Pipes, Sally C. *think-tank executive*
Plaisance, Melissa C. *consumer products company executive*
Platto, Jamie Scott *lawyer*
Plishner, Michael Jon *lawyer*
Pollack, Jeffrey Lee *restaurateur*
Pollitt, Byron H., Jr. *retail executive*
Pope, Carl *environmental organization administrator*
Pope, Marcia L. *lawyer*
Popofsky, Melvin Laurence *lawyer*
Presniakov, Alexander *artist, sculptor, inventor, writer*
Pressler, Paul S. *retail executive*
Preuss, Charles Frederick *lawyer*
Pringle, Paul C. *lawyer*
Pritzker, John A. *leisure services executive*
Privett, Stephen A. *academic administrator, priest*
Pure, Pamela J. *information technology executive*
Quick, William Thomas *writer, scriptwriter*
Quittner, Josh *editor*
Raciti, Cherie *artist*
Radlo, Edward John *lawyer, mathematician*
Raeber, John Arthur *architect, construction consultant*
Ragan, Charles Ransom *lawyer*
Ratum, Cecilia Bangloy *retired psychologist*
Reding, John Anthony, Jr. *lawyer*
Redo, David Lucien *investment company executive*
Reese, John Robert *lawyer*
Reilly, William Kane *former government official, educator, lawyer, conservationist*
Renfrew, Charles Byron *lawyer*
Renne, Paul A. *lawyer*
Renstrom, Lisa *environmental organization administrator*
Rice, Denis Timlin *lawyer*
Rice, Dorothy Pechman (Mrs. John Donald Rice) *medical economist*
Richards, Norman Blanchard *lawyer*
Richey, Ellen *credit card company executive*
Richey, Mary Ellen *lawyer*
Richtel, Matt (Theron Heir) *reporter, cartoonist*
Rinder, Lawrence R. *curator*
Ristow, Brunno *plastic surgeon*
Rivlin, Gary *writer, reporter*
Robertson, Armand James, II, *judge*
Robinson, Ralph W. *lawyer*
Rock, Arthur *venture capitalist*
Roe, Benson Bertheau *surgeon, educator*
Roehrman, Todd Frederick *costume designer, educator*
Roethe, James Norton *lawyer*
Rogan, Richard A. *lawyer*
Roger, Kent M. *lawyer*
Romano, James John *plastic surgeon*
Rosales, Suzanne Marie *hospital coordinator*
Rosedale, Philip *computer software company executive*
Rosen, Joshua Nathan *lawyer*
Rosen, Moishe *religious organization founder*
Rosen, Sanford Jay *lawyer*
Rosenberg, Betsy *radio personality, environmentalist*
Rosenberg, Pamela *opera director, conductor*
Rosenfeld, Robert A. *lawyer*
Rosenheim, Daniel Edward *journalist, television news director*
Rosinski, Edwin Francis *medical educator*
Ross, Ivy *apparel executive, artist*
Ross, Jeffrey S. *lawyer*
Roth, Michael S. *academic administrator, art educator*
Rowen, Harvey Allen *investment company executive*
Royer, Kathleen Rose *pilot*
Rubenstein, Donald P. *lawyer*
Rubenstein, Steven Paul *newspaper columnist*
Rubin, Michael *lawyer*
Rubin, Seth Isaiah *psychologist*
Rudolph, Abraham Morris *pediatrician, educator*
Rugoff, Ralph *curator*
Runnicles, Donald *conductor*
Rusher, William Allen *writer, commentator, columnist*
Russell, Sabin *newswriter*

Russoniello, Joseph Pascal *lawyer, dean*
Rutherford, George Williams III *preventive medicine physician*
Rutter, William J. *biochemist, educator*
Ryan, Kevin V. *prosecutor, lawyer*
Sachs, Marilyn Stickle *writer, educator, editor*
Saeger, Rebecca *advertising executive*
Sage-Gavin, Eva Marie *retail executive*
Sakamoto, Katsuyuki *retired academic administrator, psychologist, educator*
Salmi, Mika *information technology executive*
Samuelson, Kristin Weaver *clinical psychologist, educator*
Sanders, Joel Steven *lawyer*
Sano, Emily Joy *museum director*
Sansweet, Stephen Jay *journalist, writer, marketing executive*
Sasaki, Robert J. *financial services executive*
Satin, Joseph *language educator, retired dean*
Satre, Derek Davies *psychologist, researcher*
Savage, Mark Randall *lawyer*
Sax, Paul J. *lawyer*
Schmidt, Jason *professional baseball player*
Schmidt, Robert Milton *preventive medicine physician, educator, medical association administrator*
Schrock, Theodore R. *surgeon*
Schroeder, Steven Alfred *medical educator*
Schwab, Charles R. *brokerage house executive*
Schwarz, Glenn Vernon *newspaper editor*
Schwarzer, William W. *federal judge*
Seabolt, Richard L. *lawyer*
Seago, Jean Ann *science educator*
Sedway, Lynn Massel *real estate economist*
Seebach, Lydia Marie *physician*
Seegal, John Franklin *lawyer*
Seeger, Laureen E. *health products executive*
Seelenfreund, Alan *retired pharmaceutical company executive*
Seff, James M. *lawyer*
Seneker, Carl James, II, (Kim Seneker) *lawyer*
Shackley, Douglas John *fire alarm company executive*
Shank, J. William *art conservator*
Shansby, John Gary *investor*
Shaw, Richard Eugene *cardiovascular researcher*
Shenk, George H. *lawyer*
Sherr, Elliott Harold *neurologist, researcher*
Sherratt, Holly *art appraiser*
Shiffman, Michael A. *lawyer*
Shinefield, Henry Robert *pediatrician*
Shinohara, Katsuto *medical educator*
Shorenstein, Walter Herbert *commercial real estate development company executive*
Shorenstein Hays, Carole *theater producer*
Shushkewich, Kenneth Wayne *structural engineer*
Sickles, Edward *radiologist*
Siebel, Kenneth *investment advisor*
Silk, Thomas *lawyer*
Sillman, Amy *cell biologist*
Silverman, Victoria Lillian *consultant, fundraiser, cultural organization administrator*
Singer, Allen Morris *lawyer*
Singh, Jai *online news executive*
Siniscalco, Gary Richard *lawyer*
Slipsager, Henrik C. *building services company executive*
Smegal, Thomas Frank, Jr. *lawyer*
Smith, Brian D. *lawyer*
Smith, David Elvin *physician*
Smith, Jennie *artist*
Smith, Kerry Clark *lawyer*
Smith, Lloyd Hollingsworth *physician*
Sneed, Joseph Tyree III *federal judge*
Snyder, Darin W. *lawyer*
Soberon, Presentacion Zablan *state bar administrator*
Soh, Chunghee Sarah *anthropology educator*
Soler, Esta *foundation administrator*
Solomon, Neal Edward *management consultant, executive recruiter, social theorist, entrepreneur, author*
Sommers, Stephen Anthony *lawyer*
Sparks, Thomas E., Jr. *lawyer*
Speidel, John Joseph *public health professional, educator*
Spivey, Bruce E. *ophthalmologist, educator, health facility administrator*
Spratt, Randall N. *health products executive*
Sproul, John Allan *retired utilities executive*
Spustek, Maria S. *lawyer*
Stamper, Robert Lewis *ophthalmologist, educator*
Staring, Graydon Shaw *lawyer*
Stauffer, Thomas Michael *former university president*
Steel, Michael J. *lawyer*
Steele, Shari *think-tank executive*
Steer, Reginald David *lawyer*
Stephens, Elisa *college president*
Stephens, Shand Scott *lawyer*
Steppe, Stephen *management consultant*
Sterkina, Sofiya *writer*
Stermer, Dugald Robert *designer, writer, consultant, illustrator*
Stewart, Richard Edwin *insurance consulting company executive*
Steyer, Thomas Fahr *investment company executive*
Stinnett, Terrance LLoyd *lawyer*
Story, Joan H. *lawyer*
Straw, Lee *music educator, actor*
Street, Paul Shipley *lawyer*
Stromberg, Ross Ernest *lawyer*
Strother, James M. *lawyer*
Studley, Jamienne Shayne *lawyer, educator*
Stump, David James *philosopher, educator*
Stumpf, John G. *bank executive*
Sugarman, Myron George *lawyer*
Sullivan, Robert Edward *lawyer*
Sutton, John Paul *lawyer*
Tantum, James Kent *artist, publisher*
Tarnoff, Peter *federal agency administrator, consultant*
Tasooji, Michael B. *retail executive*
Taylor, William James (Zak Taylor) *lawyer*
Ternar, Mine Y. *artist, art educator*
Thacker-Estrada, Elizabeth Lorelei *librarian, historian*
Thiebaud, Wayne Morton *artist*
Thiel, Peter A. *investment company executive*
Thistlethwaite, David Richard *architect*

Thomas, William Scott *lawyer*
Thompson, Adam Clay *reporter*
Thompson, Patrick S. *lawyer*
Thompson, Robert Charles *lawyer*
Thornton, Charles Victor *lawyer*
Tlsty, Thea Dorothy *research scientist, educator*
Tobin, James Michael *lawyer*
Tolstedt, Carrie L. *bank executive*
Tomasson, Helgi *dancer, choreographer, dance company executive*
Toney, Anita Karen *printmaker*
Traynor, John Michael *lawyer*
Tricaro, Robert Collet *biologist, educator, editor, poet*
Tripp, Alan H. *educational association administrator, consultant*
Trott, Mena *application developer*
Tully, Herbert Bullard *chemical manufacturing executive*
Turner, Ross James *investment company executive*
Tyler, Christopher William *scientist, director*
Uilkema, John K. *lawyer*
Ullman, Myron Edward, III, (Mike Ullman) *retail executive*
Uri, George Wolfsohn *accountant*
Uyehara, Otto Arthur *mechanical engineering educator emeritus, consultant*
Van Buskirk, Ronald E. *lawyer*
van den Daele, Leland Douglas *psychology professor, psychological measurement company executive*
Van Dyck, Wendy *dancer*
Van Dyke, Craig *psychiatrist, director*
Vazquez-Azpiri, A. James *lawyer*
Veaco, Kristina *lawyer*
Vega, Frank J. *newspaper publishing executive*
Venning, Robert Stanley *lawyer*
Vercruysse, Raymond James *director*
Vesely, Jeffrey M. *lawyer*
Vidwans, Smruti Jayant *microbiologist*
Vizcaino, Jose Luis Pimental *professional baseball player*
Vizquel, Omar Enrique *professional baseball player*
Volpe, Peter Anthony *surgeon*
Vuoto, Anthony *corporate financial executive*
Wald, Peter Allen *lawyer*
Walker, Vaughn R. *federal judge*
Walsh, Joan *editor-in-chief*
Walter, Peter *biochemist*
Wang, An-Yi (Anne) Chou *real estate broker*
Wang, Wayne *film director*
Wang, William Kai-Sheng *law educator*
Warnecke, John Carl *architect*
Warner, Harold Clay, Jr. *banker, investment company executive*
Warner, Rollin Miles, Jr. *economics educator, real estate broker*
Way, E(dward) Leong *pharmacologist, toxicologist, educator*
Weber, Arnold I. *lawyer*
Weber, Paula M. *lawyer*
Weihrich, Heinz *management educator*
Weir, Robert H. *lawyer*
Weisel, Thomas W. *investment company executive*
Weitzel, Mark P. *lawyer*
Welborn, Caryl Bartelman *lawyer*
Werb, Zena *cell biologist, educator*
Werdegar, Kathryn Mickle *state supreme court justice*
Wescott, William Burnham *oral maxillofacial pathologist, educator*
Whelan, John William *law educator*
Whitehead, David Barry *lawyer*
Wild, Nelson Hopkins *lawyer*
Williams, Lance *journalist*
Williams, Linda C. *lawyer*
Williamson, Laird *theater director, actor*
Willner, Jay R. *consulting company executive*
Wilson, John D. *lawyer*
Wilson, John Pasley *law educator*
Winblad, Ann *investment company executive*
Wingate, C. Keith *law educator*
Winkler, Agnieszka M. *marketing executive*
Winn, Steven Jay *critic*
Wintroub, Bruce Urich *dermatologist, educator, researcher*
Wirum, Andrea A. *lawyer*
Wolfe, Cameron Withgot, Jr. *lawyer*
Wolff, Sheldon *radiobiology educator*
Wolford, Richard G. *food products executive*
Wong, Stanton D. *lawyer*
Wonner, Paul John *painter*
Wood, Robert Warren *lawyer*
Woods, James Robert *lawyer*
Worthington, Bruce R. *lawyer*
wwGiacomini, Gary T. *lawyer*
Wyle, Frederick S. *lawyer*
Wyse, Roger Earl *physiologist, department chairman*
Yamamoto, Keith Robert *molecular biologist, educator*
Yao, John Sen *physician*
Yellen, Janet Louise *bank executive*
Yost, Nicholas Churchill *lawyer*
Young, Bryant Llewellyn *lawyer*
Young, Douglas Rea *lawyer*
Young, Lowell Sung-yi *health facility administrator, medical educator*
Zeldin, Kim S. *lawyer*
Zellerbach, William Joseph *retired paper company executive*
Ziegler, R. W., Jr. *lawyer, consultant*
Ziering, William Mark *lawyer*
Zilber, Norman Albert *lawyer*
Zimmerman, Bernard *judge*
Zippin, Calvin *epidemiologist, educator*
Zischke, Michael Herman *lawyer*

**San Gabriel**

Chen, John Calvin *psychiatrist, educator*
Shao, Zhenhua *electrical engineer, consultant*
Wong, Ronald W. *communications executive*

**San Jacinto**

Hert, Theresa M. *mathematics educator*
Smith, Diane Jans *librarian, educator*
Stange, Sharon (Sherri) *science educator*
Willis, Ralph Walker *retired firefighter*

## San Jose

Arvizu, Charlene Sutter *elementary school educator*
Ashburn, Thomas *information technology executive*
Avakoff, Joseph Carnegie *medical consultant, law consultant*
Bandic, Zvonimir Z. *physicist, researcher, electrical engineer*
Bannick, Matthew *Internet company executive*
Barnholt, Edward W. *former computer company executive*
Beizer, Lance Kurt *priest, lawyer*
Bell, W. Donald *electronics executive*
Belluzzo, Rick E. (Richard E. Belluzzo) *information technology executive, former computer software company executive*
Berman, Shawn L. *finance educator*
Boac, Thelma Blantucas *principal*
Bodensteiner, Lisa M. *utilities executive, lawyer*
Boston, Brad *information technology executive*
Bostrom, Susan L. *marketing executive*
Braden, Jeffery P. *psychology educator*
Brooks, Allison Ruth *music educator*
Brundage, Adrienne Leane *biologist, educator, entomologist*
Bunn, Charles Nixon *management consultant*
Capellas, Michael D. *telecommunications industry executive*
Carey, Peter Kevin *reporter*
Carle, Matt *professional hockey player*
Carstens, Marilynn *freelance/self-employed music educator*
Cedolini, Anthony John *psychologist*
Ceppos, Jerome Merle (Jerry Ceppos) *newspaper editor*
Chambers, John Thomas *computer systems network executive*
Cheechoo, Jonathan *professional hockey player*
Chen, Deanford Frederick *software engineer*
Chizen, Bruce R. *computer company executive*
Chuang, Alfred S. *information technology executive*
Cobb, William C. *Internet company executive*
Coleman, William T. *information technology executive*
Collins, Alison *opera singer, music educator*
Connors, Mary Jean *communications executive*
Cottle, Karen Olson *lawyer*
Craford, M. George *physicist, research administrator*
Curtis, Ann B. *utilities executive*
Dalis, Irene *mezzo soprano, performing arts association administrator*
D'Arrigo, Stephen, Jr. *agricultural company executive*
Davido, Scott *retail executive*
Davis, Robert *police chief*
Dennison, Ronald Walton *engineer*
Denver, Thomas H.R. *lawyer*
Derr, Kenneth T. *energy executive*
Diamond, Diana Louise *editor, journalist*
DiGiacomo, Richard *social studies educator, writer*
Dowd, Susan Carol *art educator*
Dutta, Rajiv *Internet company executive*
Effren, Gary Ross *financial executive*
Eigler, Donald Mark *physicist*
Ellner, Michael William *art educator*
Es-Haq, Fereidoun *minister, marriage and family therapist*
Estabrook, Reed *artist, educator*
Farnham, Timothy *information technology executive*
Fishback, Dennis *information technology executive*
Fister, Michael J. *computer company executive*
Fleck, Andrew J *education educator*
Fry, John C. *electronics executive*
Furr, Randy W. *electronics manufacturing executive*
Gallo, Joan Rosenberg *lawyer*
Goldberg, Susan *editor*
Goldston, Daniel A. *mathematics professor, researcher*
Gonzales, Ron *mayor, former county supervisor*
Ha, Kiet Tuan *hospital administrator*
Hall, Robert Emmett, Jr. *investment banker, realtor*
Harris, Jay Terrence *communications educator*
Haycock, Kenneth Roy *academic administrator, educator, academic administrator, consultant*
Helleboid, Olivier *information technology executive*
Hernández, Fernando Vargas *lawyer*
Hernandez, Jo Farb *museum director, consultant*
Hill, Richard S. *manufacturing executive*
Ho, Yinhsin *retired mathematician, artist*
Hoang, Loc Bao *electrical engineer*
Hoffman, Charles E. *information technology executive*
Holyer, Erna Maria *adult education educator, writer, artist*
Hooper, Mark Scheller *engineer, educator*
Hung, Donald Lu-Cheng *electrical engineer, computer engineer, educator*
Ill, Charles III *information technology executive*
Jacobson, Michael R. *lawyer, Internet company executive*
Jiang, William Yuying *business educator, consultant, researcher*
Johnson, Allen Halbert *surgeon*
Jordan, Jeff *Internet company executive*
Justice, Richard *computer company executive*
Karandikar, Yogesh Dinkar *software engineer*
Katzman, Richard Alan *lawyer, arbitrator*
Keegan, Daniel T. *museum director*
Kim, Young-Hoon *systems engineer, researcher*
Klein, William M. (Bill Klein) *information technology executive*
Kraw, George Martin *lawyer, writer*
Landis, Kevin *diversified financial services company executive*
Lee, Stanley Tak *dentist*
Light, Jane Ellen *librarian*
Lippe, Philipp Maria *neurosurgeon, educator, academic administrator*
Lobig, Janie Howell *special education educator*
Loiacono, John P. *information technology executive*
Loventhal, Milton *writer, playwright, lyricist*
Macias, E. James *utilities executive*

Madra, Satbir Singh *materials researcher, mechanical engineer*
Maekawa, Koji Ogura *technology company administrator*
Malis, Andrew Gary *telecommunications company executive*
Mason, Thomas R. *utilities executive*
Matusow, Steven S. *mathematics professor*
May, Robert P. *energy executive*
McDonald, Susan *publishing executive*
McDowell, Jennifer *sociologist, composer, playwright*
McKeithen, R.L. Smith (Smith McKeithen) *lawyer*
McManis, James *lawyer*
Meltzer, Cliff *information technology executive*
Mendoza, Martha *reporter*
Migielicz, Geralyn *photojournalist*
Mitchell, David Walker *lawyer*
Morgridge, John P. *computer systems network executive*
Morrison, William Fosdick *business educator, retired electrical company executive*
Nahat, Dennis F. *performing company executive, choreographer*
Narayen, Shantanu *computer software company executive*
Nardi, Glen *publishing executive*
Near, Timothy *theater director*
Nelson, Lionel M. *otolaryngologist*
Ngo, Chiu Y. *electrical engineer*
Nissly, Kenneth L. *lawyer*
Okerlund, Arlene Naylor *academic administrator, writer*
Omidyar, Pierre M. *Internet company executive*
Parkin, Stuart Stephen Papworth *materials scientist*
Patryshev, Vlad *application developer*
Perlegos, George *electronics executive*
Pham, Christopher Hoang *electrical engineer, educator*
Powell, Dennis D. *computer systems network executive*
Prasad, Neil A. *telecommunications industry executive, computer company executive*
Press, Barry Harris Jay *plastic surgeon*
Prestine, Joan Singleton *writer, educator, editor*
Purpura, Grace *artist, retired art educator*
Quadros, Paul D. *health products executive*
Richardson, James *computer company executive*
Ridder, P. Anthony (Paul Anthony Ridder) *newspaper company executive*
Robinson, Archie Stirling *lawyer*
Roelandts, Willem P. *data processing executive*
Rossi, Steven B. *newspaper publishing company executive*
Rothblatt, Donald Noah *urban and regional planner, educator*
Russo, Paul M. *electronics executive*
Sauers, William Dale *lawyer, playwright*
Sauvageau, Yvon *application developer*
Schaller, Anthony Josef *technology management executive*
Scheinman, A. Daniel *computer system networks executive*
Schmidt, Cyril James *librarian*
Schroeder, Kenneth L. *electronics executive*
Scott, Edward William, Jr. *computer company executive*
Selinger, Patricia Griffiths *computer science professional*
Shao, Otis Hung-I *retired political science professor*
Silver, Melvyn David *lawyer, arbitrator*
Smith, David Eugene *business administration educator*
Sola, Jure *electronics executive*
Song, Jessica Chuyunn *pharmacist, educator*
Sraon, Dilber S. *dentist*
Stapleton, Beverly Cooper *aerospace executive*
Stein, John C. *lawyer*
Stevens, David Alec *medical educator*
Stutzman, Thomas Chase, Sr. *lawyer*
Sultanov, Namig, 2d Baronet *musician, music educator*
Swan, Robert H. *information technology executive*
Swope, William Clarence *computer scientist, researcher*
Tabbut, Loreen M. *power industry executive*
Tanaka, Richard Koichi, Jr. *architect, planner*
Taylor, Richard Cordia *mathematics educator*
Thornton, Joe *professional hockey player*
Togasaki, Shinobu *computer scientist*
Towery, James E. *lawyer*
Volpi, Mike *computer company executive*
Voth, Alden H. *political science professor*
Wallace, Richard P. *computer company executive*
Warnock, John Edward *computer company executive*
Wesson, Kenneth Alan *educational consultant*
White, David L. *electronics executive*
Whitman, Margaret C. (Meg Whitman) *Internet company executive*
Whyte, Ronald M. *judge*
Wickramasinghe, Hemantha Kumar *electrical engineer, physicist*
Wilson, Douglas Frederick *professional sports team executive, retired professional hockey player*
Wilson, Ronald Lawrence *professional hockey coach*
Winters, Harold Franklin *physicist*
Wolverton, Edward Lee Allen *writer*
Yiotis, Kristin *librarian, educator*
Yoshizumi, Donald Tetsuro *dentist*
Yu, Paul *academic administrator*
Zafiropoulo, Arthur *electronics executive*
Zaro, Brad A. *research and development company executive, biologist*
Zes, Tikey A. *music minister*
Zwern, Arthur Louis *computer company executive*

## San Juan Bautista

Nutzle, Futzie (Bruce John Kleinsmith) *artist, writer, animator*
Wolfe, Michael Bramson *film producer, writer*

## San Juan Capistrano

Carlson, Lawrence Arvid *retired English language educator, real estate agent*
Ealy, Cynthia Pike *artist, real estate agent*
Fisher, Delbert Arthur *pediatric endocrinologist, educator, health facility administrator*

Gardner, Carol Ann *insurance company executive*
Hawkins, Brandon James *podiatrist, surgeon*
Larwood, Susan Elizabeth *elementary school educator*
Peterson, Fred McCrae *retired librarian*
Suzuki, Yasuhiko *retired law educator*
Warren, Rick Duane *minister, writer*
White, Beverly Jane *cytogeneticist*
Zalta, Edward *otolaryngologist, physician*

## San Leandro

Dolgin, Stephen Mark *secondary school educator, retired social worker*

## San Luis Obispo

Aiello, Michael Benjamin *secondary school educator*
Anderson, Warren Ronald *electrical engineering educator*
Ayral-Clause, Odile *language educator, writer*
Baker, Warren J(oseph) *university president*
Blakeslee, Diane Pusey *financial planner*
Bunge, Russell Kenneth *writer, poet, editor*
Deasy, Cornelius Michael *retired architect*
DuFresne, Armand Frederick *management consultant, engineering consultant*
Ericson, Jon Meyer *academic administrator, language educator*
Fairbanks, William Louis, II, *anthropologist, educator*
Fisher, Eric O'Neill *economist*
Gardebring, Sandra S. *academic administrator*
Grismore, Roger *physics professor, researcher*
Hafemeister, David Walter *physicist*
Haile, Allen Cleveland *academic administrator*
Hosn, Wally *plastic surgeon*
Lynch, Joseph James *philosophy educator*
McCorkle, Robert Ellsworth *agribusiness educator*
Pinkel, Donald Paul *pediatrician*
Shlaudeman, Harry Walter *retired diplomat*
Thatcher, Janet Solverson *financial advisor, writer*
Williams, David Alexander *retired chief pilot*

## San Luis Rey

Melbourne, Robert Ernest *civil engineer*

## San Marcos

Ball, Betty Jewel *retired social worker, consultant*
Barnes, Howard G. *communications executive, film producer*
Fabry, Victoria Joan *biology professor*
Harmon, Harry William *architect, former university administrator*
He, Shaoyi *information systems educator*
Houk, Benjamin Noah *performing company executive, choreographer*
Johnson, Christopher Stephen *history professor*
Jones, William Henry *retired military officer*
Kagan, Stephen Bruce (Sandy Kagan) *corporate financial executive*
Lilly, Martin Stephen *retired university dean*
Purdy, Alan Harris *biomedical engineer*
Sheath, Robert Gordon *botanist, educator*
Snow, Tiffany *writer, healer, composer*
Watts, Jill Marie *history educator*

## San Marino

Benzer, Seymour *neuroscience educator*
Cranston, Howard Stephen *lawyer, management consultant*
Footman, Gordon Elliott *educational administrator*
Galbraith, James Marshall *lawyer, corporate financial executive*
Gouw, Julia Suryapranata *bank executive*
Grantham, Richard Robert *financial consultant*
Lashley, Virginia Stephenson Hughes *retired computer science educator*
Martin, Olivia Jean *social studies educator*
Mortimer, Wendell Reed, Jr. *judge*
Murdoch, John *museum director*
Ng, Dominic *bank executive*
Rolle, Andrew *historian, writer*
Sherwood, Midge *writer*
Terry, Roger *retired pathologist, consultant*
Tomich, Lillian *lawyer*
Travis, Albert Hartman *retired ancient language educator*
Zall, Paul Maxwell *language educator, consultant*

## San Mateo

Anderlini, P. Terry *lawyer*
Baio, James R. *diversified financial services company executive*
Bhatia, Sandeep *financial services company executive*
Burton, Al *television producer, television director, writer*
Chabra, Anand *public health physician, epidemiologist*
Chen, Steve *Internet company executive*
Davis, Troy Edward *music educator*
Farmer, Dan *computer security researcher, computer programmer*
Fletcher, Vernon Jerome *dental association administrator, director*
Ginn, Sam L. *telephone company executive*
Gordon, William Bingham (Bing Gordon) *software marketing executive*
Grill, Lawrence J. *lawyer, accountant, bank executive*
Helfert, Erich Anton *management consultant, writer, educator*
Hurley, Chad M. *Internet company executive*
Huxley, Mary Atsuko *artist*
Johnson, Charles Bartlett *corporate financial executive*
Johnson, Gregory E. *diversified financial services company executive*
Johnson, Leland Henry, Jr. *orthopedic surgeon*
Johnson, Rupert Harris, Jr. *finance company executive*
Kennedy, W(ilbert) Keith, Jr. *retired electronics executive, transportation executive*
Kenney, William Fitzgerald *lawyer*
Krikorian, Blake *entrepreneur, consumer electronics company executive*
Krikorian, Jason *consumer electronics company executive*
Land, Karl-Heinz *corporate communications specialist*
Monaco, Daniel Joseph *lawyer*

Mullin, Gene *state legislator*
O'Reilly, Terence John *lawyer*
Pileggi, Jennifer Wendy *transportation services executive*
Rabbat, Guy *electronics executive, consultant*
Saldinger, Anne Grenn *cultural organization administrator, psychologist*
Shah, Bhupen *consumer electronics company executive*
Shaheen, George T. *software company executive*
Siebel, Thomas M. *software company executive*
Simpson, Murray L. *lawyer*
Slabach, Stephen Hall *lawyer*
Stotlar, Douglas W. *transportation executive*
Strohm, David *venture capitalist*
Sutherland, Vanna Rae *psychiatrist*
Trabitz, Eugene Leonard *aerospace company executive*
Van Kirk, John Ellsworth *retired cardiologist*
Watters, Ann Oliva *psychologist, educator*
Wong, Otto *epidemiologist*

## San Pablo

Woodruff, Kay Herrin *pathologist, educator*

## San Pedro

Bowling, Lance Christopher *recording industry executive*
Ellis, George Edwin, Jr. *chemical engineer*
Gaines, Jerry Lee *retired secondary school educator*
Kline, Frank Menefee *psychiatrist*
McCarty, Frederick Briggs *electrical engineer, consultant*
Parkhurst, Violet Kinney *artist*
Simmons, William *retired aerospace engineer, research and development company executive*

## San Rafael

Adcock, Muriel W. *special education educator*
Amada, Gerald *retired psychotherapist*
Barker, Celeste Arlette *computer scientist*
Bartz, Carol A. *computer software company executive*
Bass, Carl *computer software company executive*
Blakeslee, Helen P. *columnist*
Brubeck, David Warren *musician*
Burks, Rocky Alan *disability access coordinator, consultant*
Chilvers, Robert Merritt *lawyer*
Djordjevich, Miroslav-Michael *bank executive*
Drexler, Kenneth *lawyer*
Fink, Joseph Richard *academic administrator*
Finkelstein, James Arthur *management consultant*
Friesecke, Raymond Francis *health company executive, director*
Greene, John Clifford *dentist, retired dean*
Gryson, Joseph Anthony *orthodontist*
Ingram, Robert Bruce *lawyer*
Keegan, Jane Ann *insurance executive, consultant*
Lesh, Philip Chapman *musician, composer*
Lucas, George Walton, Jr. *film director, film producer, scriptwriter*
Malifrando, Frank *healthcare executive, theater producer, consultant, film producer, international real estate investor, publisher*
Marsh, Marian E. *voice educator*
Morgan, Michael Brewster *publishing executive*
Nelson, James Carmer, Jr. *writer, editor, advertising executive*
Pomerantz, Martin Arthur *astronomer, educator, physicist*
Roth, Hadden Wing *lawyer, mediator, arbitrator*
Roulac, Stephen E. *real estate consultant*
Santana, Carlos *guitarist*
Sterling, Marcia Kemp *lawyer*
Thomas, Mary Ann McCrary *counselor, school system administrator*
Wilson, Ian Holroyde *management consultant, futurist*

## San Ramon

Bethancourt, John E. *oil industry executive*
Cronin, Patricia Romero *computer company executive*
Crowe, Stephen J. *comptroller*
Gass, John D. *oil industry executive*
Harris, Philip III *movie theater executive, lawyer*
James, Charles Albert *lawyer*
Kalicki, Jan H. *economist, political scientist, energy executive*
Laidlaw, William Samuel Hugh *oil company executive*
Litman, Robert Barry *physician, writer, television and radio commentator*
Moore, Justin Edward *information technology executive*
O'Reilly, David J. *oil industry executive*
Robertson, Peter James *oil company executive*
Salazar-Tio, Rafael *physicist, researcher*
Schofield, James Roy *computer programmer*
Vaughn, John Rolland *auditor*
Watson, John S. *oil company executive*
Wirth, Michael K. (Mike Wirth) *oil company executive*
Zygocki, Rhonda I. *oil industry executive*

## San Ysidro

Ortiz, Antonio Ignacio *public relations executive*
Schneider, Christine Lynn *customs inspector*

## Sand City

Coile, Russell Cleven *electrical engineer, consultant*

## Santa Ana

Abramo, Guy P. *information technology executive*
Adams, John M. *library director*
Afifi, Alaa Youssef *cardiothoracic surgeon*
Aitken, Wylie A. *lawyer*
Amoroso, Frank *retired communication system engineer, consultant*
Anderson, N. Christian III *newspaper publisher*
Balzer, Robert Lawrence *journalist*
Barr, James Norman *retired federal judge*
Borges, Fredrick Mario *lawyer*
Brusic, Ken *editor*
Cahill, Richard Frederick *lawyer*
Callahan, Daniel J. *lawyer*
Capizzi, Michael Robert *prosecutor*
Carter, Curtis William *communications executive*

Daly, Tom *county official*
Dean, William Evans *aerospace engineer, engineering company executive, consultant*
DeRoy, Craig I. *title insurance company executive, lawyer*
Digorgio, Kenneth *lawyer*
Dillard, John Martin *lawyer, pilot*
Donchey, Sheryl Diane *theater educator, department chairman*
Ferguson, Warren John *federal judge*
Flastrup, Asger *information technology executive*
Foster, Kent B. *information technology executive*
Harley, Robison Dooling, Jr. *lawyer, educator*
Hueston, John Charles *prosecutor*
Hughes, Chrstopher *real estate company executive*
Humes, William D. *computer company executive*
Katz, Tonnie *newspaper editor*
Kelly, James Patrick, Jr. *retired engineering executive*
Kennedy, Parker S. *finance company executive*
Klemens, Thomas A. *insurance company executive*
Koppen, Hans T. *information technology executive*
Kropp, William Rudolph *physicist*
Lawson, Barbara Slade *elementary school educator, artist*
Martinez, Rueben *entrepreneur*
Mei, Tom Y. K. *lawyer*
Moore, David Gene *academic administrator*
Murai, Kevin *information technology executive*
Myers, Marilyn Gladys *pediatric hematologist, oncologist*
Payne, Steven M. *musician, director*
Re Velle, Jack B(oyer) *statistician, consultant*
Ricketts, James F. *treasurer*
Salem, Karen E. *information technology executive*
Spierkel, Gregory M. *information technology executive*
Sporty, Lawrence Douglas *psychiatrist*
Steinken, William Theodore, Jr. *military officer, secondary school educator*
Storer, Maryruth *law librarian*
Stotler, Alicemarie Huber *federal judge*
Tanaka, Richard I. *computer company executive*
Torrez, Caroline Herminia *human resources specialist, director, actress, musician, singer, dancer*
Veasey, Byron Keith *information systems consultant*
Wagner, John Leo *lawyer, retired judge*
Wellborn, Michael *county official*

## Santa Barbara

Abbinante, Christopher *finance company executive*
Abbott, Horace Porter *English literature educator*
Ackerman, Marshall *publishing executive*
Ahlers, Guenter *physicist, researcher*
Aldisert, Ruggero John *federal judge*
Anderson, Donald Meredith *bank executive*
Aswani, Shankar (Shankar Aswani-Canela) *anthropologist, educator*
Auston, David Henry *former academic administrator, electrical engineer, educator*
Awschalom, David Daniel *physicist*
Aylesworth, Owen Roy *retired firefighter, genealogist, philanthropist*
Badash, Lawrence *science history educator*
Bartlett, James Lowell III *investment company executive*
Behrens, June Adelle *writer*
Ben-Dor, Gisselle *conductor, musician*
Bischel, Margaret DeMeritt *physician, consultant*
Boehm, Eric Hartzell *information technology executive*
Bohn, Henning *economist, educator*
Bowers, Michael Thomas *chemistry professor*
Boyan, Norman J. *retired education educator*
Brilliant, Ashleigh Ellwood *cartoonist, writer*
Brodhead, James E(aston) *actor, writer*
Brown, J'Amy Maroney *journalist, media consultant, investor*
Bruice, Thomas C. *chemist, educator*
Burgee, John Henry *architect*
Caldwell, David Orville *physics professor*
Campbell, William Steen *publishing executive, writer, chaplain*
Canfield, Jack *writer, speaker, trainer*
Cappello, A. Barry *lawyer*
Castro, Joseph Isaac *academic administrator, educator*
Chafe, Wallace LeSeur *linguist, educator*
Christman, Arthur Castner, Jr. *science advisor, consultant*
Cirone, William Joseph *educational administrator*
Coffin, Dwight Clay *retired grain company executive*
Coldren, Larry Allen *electrical engineering educator, consultant*
Collins, Robert Oakley *history professor*
Comanor, William S. *economist, educator*
Conley, Philip James, Jr. *retired air force officer*
Corbani, Candace Bedford *antiques broker, political campaign consultant, researcher*
Cotton, John Whealdon *psychology professor*
Crawford, Donald Wesley *philosophy educator, university official*
Crowell, John C(hambers) *geology educator, researcher*
Cunningham, Julia Woolfolk *author*
Davidson, Roger H(arry) *political science professor*
Del Chiaro, Mario Aldo *art historian, archaeologist, etruscologist, educator*
Dow, Brian Christopher *academic administrator*
Dubroff, Henry Allen *editor, journalist*
Dunne, Thomas *geology educator*
Egan, Susan Chan *securities analyst, writer*
Eguchi, Yasu *artist*
Elliott, Warren G. *lawyer*
Ellis, Eugene Joseph *cardiologist*
Emmeluth, Bruce Palmer *investment company executive, venture capitalist*
Emmons, Robert John *corporate executive, poet*
Erasmus, Charles John *anthropologist, educator*
Evans, Anthony Glyn *materials scientist, educator*
Feigin, Joel *composer, educator*
Fingarette, Herbert *philosopher, educator*
Fisher, Steven Kay *neurobiology educator*
Ford, Peter C. *chemistry professor*
Gartrell, David Christian *archivist*
Göllner, Marie Louise *musicologist, retired educator*
Goodchild, Michael Frank *geographer, educator*

Gossard, Arthur Charles *physicist, researcher*
Gross, David Jonathan *physicist*
Gunn, Giles Buckingham *language educator, religious studies educator, global and international studies educator*
Hayward, Jean *artist, musician, interior designer, performance artist*
Heeger, Alan Jay *physicist, educator*
Helgerson, Richard *English literature educator*
Herman, James Edward *lawyer*
Hong, Dongwoo *electrical engineer*
Horne, Marilyn Berneice *mezzo-soprano*
Hubbard, Arthur Thornton *chemist, educator*
Jackson, Beverley Joy Jacobson *columnist, educator*
Jochim, Michael Allan *archaeologist*
Johnsen, Eugene Carlyle *mathematician, educator*
Jovanovic, Lois *medical researcher*
Karpeles, David *museum director*
Kendler, Howard H(arvard) *psychologist, educator*
Kennedy, John Harvey *chemistry professor*
Kohn, Roger Alan *surgeon*
Kohn, Walter *physicist, retired educator*
Kokotovic, Petar V. *electrical and computer engineering educator*
Kozyrev, Andrei Nikolaevich *research scientist*
Kramer, Edward John *materials engineering educator*
Kroemer, Herbert *electrical engineering educator*
Kruger, Kenneth Charles *architect*
Kryter, Karl David *retired research scientist*
Kuczynski, John-Michael Maxime *writer*
Kuhn, Peter Joseph *economics professor, consultant*
Langer, James Stephen *physicist, researcher*
Larsgaard, Mary Lynette *librarian, writer*
Lawrance, Charles Holway *retired civil and sanitary engineer*
Levine, Joshua H. *medical products executive*
Lick, Wilbert James *mechanical engineering educator*
Liebhaber, Myron I. *allergist*
Lovelace, Jon (Jonathan Bell Lovelace) *investment management company executive*
Lucas, Gene *academic administrator*
Luyendyk, Bruce Peter *geophysicist, educator, academic administrator*
Macdonald, Ken Craig *geophysicist*
Mack, Judith Cole Schrim *retired political scientist*
Mahlendorf, Ursula Renate *literature educator*
Mathews, Barbara Edith *gynecologist*
Maudsley, Ronald R. *finance company executive*
Mayer, Richard Edwin *psychology professor*
McCaw, Wendy Petrak *publishing executive*
McCoy, Lois Clark *retired social services administrator, retired county official, editor*
Mc Duffie, Malcolm *oil industry executive*
McGee, James Sears *historian, educator*
McMeeking, Robert Maxwell *mechanical engineer, educator*
Meinel, Aden Baker *optics scientist*
Mikhailovsky, Alexander *research and development company executive*
Minc, Henryk *mathematics professor*
Mitchell, Shawne Maureen *author*
Mitra, Sanjit Kumar *electrical and computer engineering educator*
Morgan, Alfred Vance *management consulting company executive*
Murdoch, Helen Claire *secondary school educator*
Nakamura, Shuji *engineering educator*
Norris, Virginia Oakley *secondary school educator*
O'Dowd, Donald Davy *retired university president*
Peale, Stanton Jerrold *physics educator*
Pilgeram, Laurence Oscar *biochemist*
Pochini, Judy Hay *interior designer, writer, editor*
Polchinski, Joseph G. *physicist, science educator*
Potter, David Samuel *former automotive company executive*
Prindle, William Roscoe *retired glass company executive*
Ramsay, William Charles *writer, composer*
Ray, Charles Dean *neurosurgeon, spine surgeon, bioengineer, inventor*
Rehm, Susan J. *social services professional*
Riemenschneider, Paul Arthur *retired physician, retired radiologist*
Roddick, Hawley *writer, editor, personal historian*
Rose, Mark Allen *humanities educator*
Rosenthal, Earl Edgar *art history educator*
Russell, Jeffrey Burton *historian, educator*
Salotti, Kathryn E. *marriage and family therapist*
Sanger, Robert Marshall *lawyer*
Scheinfeld, James David *retired travel company executive*
Schneider, Edward Lee *botanist, researcher*
Schultz, Arthur Warren *retired communications executive*
Sebastian, Suzie *television producer*
Shackman, Daniel Robert *psychiatrist*
Shames, Henry Joseph *lawyer*
Sherman, Alan Robert *psychologist, educator*
Simons, Stephen *mathematics professor, researcher*
Sinsheimer, Robert Louis *retired academic administrator, educator*
Smith, Bill *religious organization administrator*
Sneddon, Thomas William, Jr. *prosecutor*
Sudbrack, Eli *(assume vivid astro focus) artist*
Tilton, David Lloyd *savings and loan association executive*
Tirrell, Matthew V. *engineering educator*
Tucker, Shirley Lois Cotter *botanist, educator*
Wade, Glen *electrical engineer, educator*
Weidemann, Celia Jean *social sciences educator, management consultant, financial consultant*
White, Robert Stephen *retired physics professor*
Wilkins, Burleigh Taylor *philosophy educator*
Witherell, Michael S. *physicist, educator*
Yang, Henry T.Y. *chancellor, educator*
Young, Michael Kent *physics professor*

## Santa Clara

Alexander, George Jonathon *lawyer, educator*
Arrillaga, John *real estate company executive*
Atkinson, Darren C. *education educator*
Barrett, Craig R. *electronics company executive*
Barrett, Ronald W. *biopharmaceutical executive*
Bechtolsheim, Andy (Andreas Bechtolsheim) *software executive*
Berg, Carl E. *real estate developer*

Beveridge, Crawford *information technology executive*
Bray, Tim (Timothy William Bray) *computer company executive, software developer*
Bryant, Andy D. *computer company executive*
Burke, Conrad *energy executive*
Cachopo, Patricia Ann *music educator*
Canepa, Mark A. *information technology executive*
Chan, Shu-Park *electrical engineering educator*
Chastain, Brandi Denise *professional soccer player*
Chin, Albert Kae *research physician*
Claflin, Bruce L. *software company executive*
Clark, John M. III *lawyer*
Culbertson, Leslie S. *computer company executive*
Cutler, Leonard Samuel *physicist*
Dai, Guang-ming George *optics scientist*
Dai, Weili *information technology executive*
Dave, Tushar A. *Indo-US venture capital company executive*
DeBartolo-York, Denise *sports team executive*
Der Torossian, Papken *engineering executive*
Dham, Vinod K. *Indo-US venture capitalist company executive*
Dilfer, Trent *professional football player*
Dillon, Michael A. *lawyer*
Dorchak, Glenda *electronics company executive*
Dunlap, F. Thomas, Jr. *lawyer, retired electronics executive*
Elkus, Richard J., Jr. *electronics company executive*
Faggin, Federico *electronics executive*
Field, Alexander James *economics professor, dean*
Foldvary, Fred Emanuel *economist, educator*
Gelsinger, Patrick P. *computer company executive*
Gilbert, Lucia Albino *psychology professor*
Glancy, Dorothy Jean *lawyer, educator*
Gope, Dipanjan *computer engineer*
Gozani, Tsahi *nuclear physicist*
Grove, Andrew Steven *electronics executive*
Gutierrez, Si *electronics executive*
Halla, Brian L. *electronics executive*
Haskell, Timothy O. *academic administrator*
Hopkinson, Shirley Lois *library and information scientist, educator*
Howe, Bill *information technology executive*
Hsieh, Marina Cing *lawyer, educator*
Huang, Jen-Hsun *electronics executive*
Hutcheson, Jerry Dee *manufacturing company executive*
Kamal, Abu Hena M. *electrical engineer, researcher*
Kelley, Robert Suma *network engineer*
Koomen, Cornelis Jan *telecommunications and electronics executive*
Lane, Holly Diana *artist*
Lau, John Hon Shing *electronics scientist*
Lee, Chan-Yun *physicist, process engineer, educator*
Lehman, Michael Evans *information technology executive*
Ling, Nam *dean*
Locatelli, Paul Leo *academic administrator*
Maloney, Sean M. *computer company executive*
McGowan, Stephen T. *corporate financial executive*
McNealy, Scott Glenn *information technology executive*
Medepalli, Kamesh *engineer, researcher, educator*
Moberg, Dennis *director*
Moore, Gordon E. *electronics executive, researcher*
Morgan, James C. *manufacturing executive*
Morris, Sandra K. *computer company executive*
Murray, Patricia *electronics company executive*
Nolan, Mike *professional football player*
Ostwald, Venice Eloise Varner *librarian, educator, minister, writer*
Otellini, Paul S. *electronics company executive*
Papadopoulos, Gregory Michael *computer company executive*
Parden, Robert James *engineering educator, management consultant*
Peterson, Marissa *information technology executive*
Plummer, Ahmed *professional football player*
Polden, Donald *dean, law educator*
Pollace, Pamela L. *public relations executive*
Rivera, George *museum director*
Roknaldin, Farzam *mechanical engineer, educator*
Rong, Haisheng *research scientist*
Roy, Abhra *plasma engineer, researcher*
Rozman, James D. *school system administrator, minister*
Samenuk, George *software security company executive*
Schwartz, Jonathan Ian *information technology executive*
Shannon, David M. *lawyer*
Shavers, Cheryl L. *technology and business consultant*
Simmons, Janet Bryant *writer, publishing executive*
Simon, James Lowell *lawyer*
Smith, Alex *professional football player*
Smith, Stephen Allen *mathematician, educator*
Sodhani, Arvind *computer company executive*
Splinter, Michael R. *manufacturing executive*
Sunwolf, *law educator, writer*
Sutardja, Sehat *information technology executive*
Talbot, Nyna Lucille *psychologist, writer*
Turner, Norv (Norval Eugene Turner) *professional football coach*
Vu, Quat Thuong *electrical engineer*
Wang, Min *electronics engineer*
Weinberg, William Henry *chemical engineer, physicist, educator*
Yee, Keith Philip *finance company executive, accountant*

## Santa Clarita

Ayres, Glenn Alex *scriptwriter, film producer*
Boyer, Carl III *not-for-profit developer, retired mayor, municipal official, secondary school educator*
Feldman Nebenzahl, Bernardo *composer, educator*
Garcia, Andrew B. *chemical engineer*
Kotler, Richard Lee *lawyer*
Lavine, Steven David *academic administrator*
Plew, Paul Timothy *music educator, dean*
Walker, Robert F. *social studies educator*

## Santa Cruz

Berger, Harry *literature and art history professor emeritus*
Blumenthal, George *academic administrator, astronomy and astrophysics professor*
Brown, George Stephen *physics professor*
Bunnett, Joseph Frederick *chemist, educator*
Carson, Benjamin Leeds *composer, educator*
Chemers, Martin M. *psychologist, educator*
Cheung, Yin-Wong *economics professor*
Child, Frank Clayton *economist, educator*
Davis, Angela Yvonne *political activist, educator, writer*
Delaney, Margaret L. *academic administrator*
Dilbeck, Charles Stevens, Jr. *real estate company executive*
Eischen, Donald F. *psychologist, educator, writer*
Epps, Harland Warren *astronomy educator, optical design consultant*
Faber, Sandra Moore *astronomer, educator*
Flatté, Stanley Martin *physicist, researcher*
Garcia-Luna-Aceves, J.J. *education educator*
Griggs, Gary Bruce *science administrator, oceanographer, geologist, educator*
Haussler, David H. *molecular biologist, educator*
Hill, Terrell Leslie *chemist, researcher, biophysicist*
Huskey, Harry Douglas *information and computer science educator*
Kang, Sung-Mo (Steve Kang) *electrical engineering educator*
Klein, Spencer Robert *physicist, researcher*
Kraft, Robert Paul *astronomer, educator*
Langenheim, Jean Harmon *biologist, educator*
Langhout, Regina D. *psychology professor*
Lay, Thorne *geosciences educator*
Martinez, Alma R. *actress, theater director, educator*
Osterbrock, Donald E(dward) *astronomy educator*
Pettigrew, Thomas Fraser *social psychologist, educator*
Pletsch, Marie Eleanor *plastic surgeon*
Pratkanis, Anthony Richard *social psychologist, educator*
Rabus, Dominik Gerhard *electrical engineer, researcher*
Resneck-Sannes, Helen *psychologist*
Ripma, Mary *librarian*
Roby, Pamela Ann *sociologist, educator*
Rothwell, Wendy *biology educator*
Russell, Laura Wimberly *artist*
Sands, Matthew Linzee *physicist, researcher*
Shorenstein, Rosalind Greenberg *internist*
Smith, M(ahlon) Brewster *retired psychologist, educator*
Stevens, Stanley David *historian, researcher, retired librarian, archivist*
Stormes, John Max *systems analyst*
Suckiel, Ellen Kappy *philosophy educator*
Wiberg, Donald Martin *electrical engineering educator, consultant*
Widom, Harold *mathematician, educator*
Winston, George *solo pianist, guitarist, harmonica player*
Wipke, W. Todd *chemistry professor*

## Santa Maria

Armstrong, James D. *school system administrator, musician*
Roadarmel, Stanley Bruce *civilian military employee*

## Santa Monica

Aaron, David L. *diplomat, author*
Adams, Ryan (David Ryan Adams) *musician*
Alexander, Peter Houston *artist*
Almqvist, Pelle *singer*
Alpert, Herb *composer, recording artist, producer, painter*
Angel, Steven *musician*
Anthony, Polly *broadcast executive*
Apple, Fiona (Fiona Apple Maggart) *singer, songwriter*
Archambault, Nicole Marie *speech pathology/audiology services professional, consultant*
Auriana, Angelo *chef*
Bachrach, Charles Lewis *advertising agency executive*
Baer, Walter S. *think-tank executive*
Benjamin, Stuart *film producer*
Bosman, Richard *artist, printmaker*
Brainard, Cecilia Manguerra *writer*
Brook, Robert Henry *public health service officer, internist, educator*
Bruckheimer, Jerry *producer*
Burrell, Orville Richard (Shaggy) *popular musician*
Calacanis, Jason McCabe *internet entrepreneur, blogger*
Cameron, James *film director, screenwriter, producer*
Carr, Ruth Margaret *plastic surgeon*
Carrabba, Christopher Ender *singer*
Casso, Jesse, Jr. *investment company executive, investment advisor*
Cooper, Jay Leslie *lawyer*
Crichton, Michael (John Michael Crichton) *writer, film director*
Cron, Steven Michael *lawyer*
Curran, Leigh *actress, playwright*
Davie, Jill *chef*
Davis, Stephen Edward Folwell *banker*
Dienes, Louis Robert *lawyer*
Ellickson, Phyllis Lynn *political scientist*
Eminem, (Marshall Mathers III) *rap artist*
Eve, (Eve Jihan Jeffers) *rap artist, actress*
Feltheimer, Jon *entertainment company executive*
Feniger, Susan Jan *chef, television personality, writer*
Foley, Jane Deborah *foundation executive*
Friedman, Monroe *psychologist, educator, consultant, editor, writer*
Frot-Coutaz, Cecile *television production producer*
Geiser, Thomas Christopher *lawyer, insurance company executive*
Giannulli, Mossimo *designer, apparel business executive*
Goldman, Charles A. *science administrator*
Grace, Maggie *actress*
Gray, Laura B. *psychology professor, counselor*
Greifinger, David Ross *lawyer*

Griffith, Huw *advertising executive*
Gritton, Eugene Charles *nuclear engineer, director*
Grossman, Marshall Bruce *lawyer*
Grubisich, Tom *screenwriter, editor, writer*
Hannigan, Alyson *actress*
Haroon, Nasreen *artist*
Heimbuch, Babette E. *bank executive*
Henderson, Rosemary C. *elementary school educator*
Hinerfeld, Robert Elliot *lawyer*
Hoefflin, Steven M. *plastic surgeon*
Horowitz, Zachary I. *entertainment company executive*
Hu, Kelly *actress*
Huffington, Arianna (Arianna Stassinopoulos) *writer*
Intriligator, Devrie Shapiro *physicist*
Jewison, Norman Frederick *film producer, director*
Jones, William Allen *lawyer*
Kanin, Josh David *film studies educator*
Katina, Elena Sergejevna *singer*
Katz, Roger *pediatrician, educator, allergist, immunologist*
Kawamoto, Henry K. *plastic surgeon*
Kayton, Myron *engineering company executive*
Kennedy, Kathleen *film producer*
Kinney, James Howard *lawyer, real estate company executive*
Kirkland, John C. *lawyer*
Klowden, Michael Louis *think-tank executive*
Koning, Hendrik *architect*
Kurtzman, Joel Allan *economist*
Lawton, Eric *lawyer, artist, photographer, writer*
Leaf, Paul *film producer, writer*
Lederman, Bruce Randolph *investment company executive, retired lawyer*
Lempert, Philip *advertising executive, writer, news correspondent*
Leonard, Elmore John *writer, scriptwriter*
Levin, Marvin Eugene *lawyer*
Li, Jet (Li Lian Jie, Lei Lin-Git) *actor*
Lincoln, Thomas L. *pathologist, educator*
Littlefield, Warren *television executive*
Lochte, Richard Samuel *writer*
Lohner, Henning *composer, filmmaker*
Louis-Dreyfus, Julia *actress*
Maglione, Margaret A. *public policy analyst, researcher*
Markoff, Steven C. *finance company executive*
Marshall, Frank W. *film producer, director*
Masucci, Michael James *artist*
Mayne, Thom *architect*
McGlynn, Elizabeth A. *health policy analyst*
McGuire, Michael Francis *plastic surgeon*
McGuire, Michael John *environmental engineer*
McMahon, Julian *actor*
McMillan, M. Sean *lawyer*
Milken, Michael R. *think-tank executive, philanthropist*
Milliken, Mary Sue *chef, television personality, writer*
Minghella, Anthony *film director, screenwriter*
Modisett, Jeffrey A. *lawyer, former state attorney general*
Mora, Philippe *screenwriter, producer, director, painter*
Morgan, Kermit Johnson *lawyer*
Morgenstern, Joe *film critic*
Moses, Samuel B. *accountant, consultant*
Moskos, Charles C. *social studies educator*
Orlando, Maria *behavioral scientist*
Ovitz, Michael S. *communications executive*
Park, Edward Cahill, Jr. *retired physicist*
Patel, Chandra Kumar Naranbhai *communications executive, educator, entrepreneur, researcher*
Peña, Michael Anthony *actor*
Postaer, Larry *advertising executive*
Preble, Laurence George *lawyer*
Rand, Robert Wheeler *neurosurgeon, educator*
Redford, Robert (Charles Robert Redford) *actor, film director*
Resnick, Jeffrey I. *plastic surgeon*
Reville, Robert T. *economist*
Reznor, Trent *musician*
Rice, Donald Blessing *biotechnology executive, former federal official*
Rice, Pamela Ann *marriage and family therapist*
Rich, Michael David *think-tank executive, lawyer*
Rifkin, Arnold *film company executive*
Risman, Michael *lawyer, real estate developer, broker*
Roberts, Tony (David Anthony Roberts) *actor*
Roney, Robert Kenneth *retired aerospace transportation executive*
Rubin, Gerrold Robert *advertising executive*
Ryan, Jane Frances *corporate communications executive*
Salveson, Melvin Erwin *management sciences company executive, educator*
Schaeffer, Leonard David *health insurance company executive*
Schultz, Victor M. *physician*
Scott, Jill *poet, musician*
Shamban, Ava T. *dermatologist*
Sherman, Victor *lawyer*
Sherman, Zachary *civil engineer, aerospace engineer, consultant*
Shiffrin, Nancy *writer, educator*
Shim, Elisabeth K. *dermatologist*
Siart, William Eric Baxter *non-profit education organization administrator*
Simpson, India.Arie *musician*
Singer, Frederick Raphael *medical researcher*
Smith, Anna Deavere *actress, educator, playwright*
Smith, James Patrick *economist*
Sohaili, Monira *retired special education educator*
Soloff, Laura J. *academic administrator*
Spataro, Janie Dempsey Watts *freelance/self-employed writer*
Stern, Walter Eugene *neurosurgeon, educator*
Stewart, Patrick *actor*
Stone, Oliver *film director, film producer, scriptwriter*
Straus, Matthew *wine director*
Summer, Donna (La Donna Adrian Gaines) *singer, songwriter, actress*
Sun, Li *statistician*
Suschitzky, Peter *cinematographer*
The Edge, (David Howell Evans) *musician*
Thompson, Dennis Peters *plastic surgeon*
Thomson, James Alan *think-tank executive*

Timmer, Barbara *state agency administrator*
Tito, Dennis Anthony *former aerospace engineer, financial advisor*
Tompkins, Ronald K. *retired surgeon, educator*
Unterman, Thomas *venture capitalist, lawyer*
Vrabeck, Kathy *videogame publishing executive*
Wachs, Martin *urban planning educator, author, consultant*
Wang, Jeffrey C. *surgeon*
Wangard, Gregg *chef*
Watanabe, Ken *actor*
Watson, Doc (Arthel Lane Watson) *vocalist, guitarist, banjoist, recording artist*
Williams, Kenneth Scott *entertainment company executive*
Wilson, Hugh Steven *lawyer*
Wolf, Charles, Jr. *economist, educator*
Zarem, Harvey Alan *plastic surgeon*

**Santa Paula**
Edwards, Samuel Roger *internist*
Lattimore, Steven *classicist, educator*
Tushla, Richard James *physician*

**Santa Rosa**
Aman, Reinhold Albert *philologist, writer*
Ash, John *chef*
Banks, Peter Morgan *physics professor*
Biderman, Charles Israel *diversified financial services company executive*
Borglum, Keith Carsten *health care business consultant*
Bozdech, Marek Jiri *physician, educator*
Callum, Myles *magazine editor, writer*
Clement, Clayton Emerson *lawyer*
Cohn, Joseph David *surgeon*
Courteau, Girard Robert *retired prosecutor*
Flanagan, Michael Brendan *obstetrician, gynecologist*
Gentemann, Chelle Leigh *oceanographer*
Grundy, Richard David *engineer*
Guglielmino, Jude Patch *writer, humanitarian aid worker*
Jackson, Jess S. *vintner*
Jandrey, Becky Lee *psychologist*
Leuty, Gerald Johnston *osteopathic physician, surgeon*
Monk, Diana Charla *small business owner*
Morris, Jack G. *architecture educator, writer*
O'Connor, Paul Daniel *lawyer*
Pearson, Roger Lee *library director*
Person, Evert Bertil *retired newspaper and radio executive*
Rosaschi, Jim *librarian*
Schafer, John Francis *plant pathologist, researcher*
Smith, Thomas Kent *retired radiologist*
Swofford, Robert Lee *editor, journalist*
Trucker, Albert *retired plastic surgeon*
Wagner, Harold A. *retired gas industry executive*
Webb, Charles Richard *retired university president*

**Santee**
Cantor, Thomas *research and development company executive*
Hardy, Ben (Benson B. Hardy) *orchid nursery executive*
Morris, Henry Madison III *minister, writer, speech professional, consultant*
Peters, Raymond Eugene *historian, writer*
Schenk, Susan Kirkpatrick *nursing educator, consultant, small business owner*

**Saratoga**
Barna, Lillian Carattini *school system administrator*
Chisholm, Margaret Elizabeth *retired library director*
Houston, Elizabeth Reece Manasco *correctional education consultant*
Houston, Joseph Brantley, Jr. *optical instrument company executive*
Reagan, Joseph Bernard *retired aerospace executive, management consultant*
Rollo, F. David *healthcare company executive, cardiologist*
Syvertson, Clarence Alfred *management consultant, engineer*

**Sausalito**
Albert, Ronald Peter *lawyer*
Apatoff, Michael John *entrepreneur*
Battelle, John *journalist, educator, writer, entrepreneur*
Berkman, William Roger *lawyer, army reserve officer*
Casals, Rosie *retired professional tennis player*
Gordon, Robert Eugene *lawyer*
Gulland, Frances M. *veterinarian, researcher*
Hansen, Charles Morton *editor, retired military officer*
Hawthorne, Lou *genetic cloning research company executive, researcher*
Hyde, Catherine Ryan *short story writer*
Jampolsky, Gerald G. (Jerry Jampolsky) *psychiatrist*
Orbison, James Archer, Jr. *cardiologist, surgeon*
Ornish, Dean *medical association administrator, medical educator*
Polejaeva, Irina *genetic cloning company executive, researcher*
Wiley, William T. *artist*

**Scotia**
Hise, Mark Allen *dentist*

**Scotts Valley**
Crandell, Kenneth James *management consultant, entrepreneur*
Haisch, Bernard Michael *astronomer, researcher*
Janssen, James Robert *consulting software engineer*
Luczo, Stephen J. *computer equipment company executive*
Park, Chong S. *computer company executive*
Pope, Charles C. *computer hardware company executive*
Watkins, William D. *computer hardware company executive*
Wingert, Michael J. *computer company executive*

**Seal Beach**
Burge, Willard, Jr. *software company executive*

Cunningham, Terence Thomas III *hospital administrator*
Matz, Sean Cormick *electrical engineer*
Pipes, Doris Perry *secondary school educator, consultant*
Reynales, Barbara Wallace *literature educator*

**Seaside**
Anderson, David Louis *academic administrator, history professor*
Gales, Samuel Joel *retired civilian military employee, counselor*
May, James Harvey *communications educator*
Mendoza, Ruben G. *anthropologist, educator, archaeologist*
Paget, Ruth Pennington *academic administrator, educator, writer*
Panetta, Leon Edward *former White House chief of staff, former congressman*

**Sebastopol**
Drever, Richard Alston, Jr. *consulting architect*
Marler, Joan *writer, educator*
McCarthy, Thomas Edward *retired telecommunications executive*
Norman, Arnold McCallum, Jr. *engineer*
O'Reilly, Tim *computer book publishing company executive, open sourcer advocate*
Rappaport, Stuart Ramon *lawyer*
Sabsay, David *library director, consultant*
Worthington, Nancy G. *sculptor, multi-media artist*

**Sepulveda**
Yano, Elizabeth Martin *epidemiologist, researcher*

**Shadow Hills**
Bangs, Cate (Cathryn Margaret Bangs) *film production designer, interior designer*

**Shafter**
Ulloa, Mauricio *geneticist, researcher*

**Shasta Lake**
Innes, Rob *product designer*

**Sherman Oaks**
Ardalan, Pezhman Christopher *lawyer*
Bakula, Scott *actor*
Blair, Linda Denise *actress*
Caren, Robert Poston *aerospace scientist*
Clark, Susan (Nora Goulding) *actress*
Cook, Paul Maxwell *technology company executive*
Crump, Gerald Franklin *retired lawyer*
Dawson, David Smith *television executive*
Drudge, Matt *journalist*
Elfman, Danny *composer*
Feldman, Phillip *lawyer*
Gibbs, Antony (Tony Gibbs) *film editor*
Heffner, Daniel Jason *film producer*
Hein, Todd Jonathan *accountant*
Holden, William Willard *insurance executive*
Howe, Daniel Walker *historian, educator*
Jackson, Chris *real estate broker*
Jordan, Bonita Adele *television producer*
Karras, Alex *actor, retired professional football player*
Krueger, Kenneth John *nutritionist, educator*
Leighton, Carolyn *foundation administrator*
Levin, Evanne Lynn *lawyer, educator*
Medearis, Miller *lawyer*
Milgrim, Darrow A. *insurance company executive*
Norwood, Brandy Rayana (Brandy) *singer, actress*
Reiner, Thomas Karl *manufacturing executive, engineering scientist*
Ross, Jeff *communications executive*
Sabella, Ernie *actor*
Schlessinger, Laura *radio talk show host*
Taylor, Elizabeth (Dame Elizabeth Rosemond Taylor) *actress*
Winkler, Lee B. *business consultant*
Yasnyi, Allan David *communications company executive*

**Sierra Madre**
Browder, William Bayard *lawyer*
Converse, Elizabeth *artist, writer*
Nation, Earl F. *retired urologist, educator*

**Signal Hill**
Vandament, William Eugene *retired academic administrator*

**Silverado**
Mamer, James Michael *secondary school educator*

**Simi Valley**
Blackwood, Duke (R. Duke Blackwood) *library director*
Eberhard-Neveaux, Christine *aviation executive, dispute resolution executive*
Erzinger, Kathy McClam *nursing educator*
Hochheiser, Marilyn *writer, actress*
Lewis, Richard B. *manufacturing and logistics executive*
Ritacco, Patsy Richard *sales executive*

**Solana Beach**
Agnew, Harold Melvin *physicist*
Beck-von-Peccoz, Michele *retired secondary school educator, writer*
Gildred, Theodore E. *former diplomat, real estate developer*

**Soledad**
Casillas, Jesse Diaz *protective services official*

**Solvang**
Roberts, Monty *horse trainer, writer*
Rymer, Ilona Suto *artist, retired art educator*

**Somerset**
Carr, Les *psychologist, educator*

**Somis**
Kehoe, Vincent Jeffré-Roux *photographer, cosmetics executive*
Premack, Ann J. *writer*

**Sonoma**
Beckmann, Jon Michael *publishing company executive*
Emery, John Edward *plastic surgeon, vintner*
Fellows, Alice Combs *artist*
Gelpi, Armand Philippe *internist*
Kizer, Carolyn Ashley *poet, educator*
Markey, William Alan *health facility administrator, consultant*
Muchmore, Robert Boyer *engineering executive, consultant*
Obninsky, Victor Peter *lawyer*
Sasaki, Y(asunaga) Tito *engineering executive*
Woodbridge, John Marshall *architect, urban planner*

**Sonora**
Chandler, Edwin Russell *clergyman, writer*
Clarke, Paula Katherine *anthropologist, researcher, social studies educator*
Tolhurst, Jeffrey Wayne *science educator, information systems educator*
Wheeler, Elton Samuel *financial executive*

**Soquel**
Stephens, Robert *horticulturist*
Tomash, Erwin *retired computer company executive*

**South Lake Tahoe**
Nason, Rochelle *conservation organization administrator*
Williams, Mark Didrik *music educator, composer*

**South Pasadena**
Askin, Walter Miller *artist, educator*
Finnell, Michael Hartman *mining executive*
Fuller, Kathy J. *special education educator, consultant, researcher*
Girvigian, Raymond *architect*
Hsieh, Ming *information technology executive*
Kopp, Eugene Howard *electrical engineer*
Mantell, Suzanne Ruth *editor*
Martin, Richard D. *social studies educator*
Sverdlove, Zolita *artist, painter, printmaker*
Whang, Sukoo Jack *pathologist, microbiologist*
Yett, Sally Pugh *art educator, consultant*

**South San Francisco**
Brewer, Richard B. *biotechnology company executive*
Caro, Ivor *dermatologist*
Cittadini, Pete *reporting applications platform company executive*
Desmond-Hellmann, Susan *medical products manufacturing executive*
Goodman, Corey Scott *neuroscientist, educator, biotechnologist*
Gower, James M. *biotechnology company executive*
Grandsaert, John Leo *judge*
Hull, Cordell William *engineering, construction, and project management executive, investor*
Humphrey, Patrick Paul *pharmacologist*
Lee, Leonard S. *health facility administrator*
Letts, Nathan P. *biotechnology executive, lawyer*
Levinson, Arthur David *biotechnology research company executive*
Lewis, Jason Alvert, Jr. *communications executive*
Lipsky, Ian David *manufacturing executive, science administrator, director*
Nierenberg, Nico *software developer company executive*
Potter, Myrtle S. *research and development company executive*
Ruggles, Sandra Waugh *biophysicist*
Ryan, Tom *reporting applications platform company executive*
Scheller, Richard H. *physiologist, science educator*
Tananbaum, James *medical engineering company executive*
Tessier-Lavigne, Marc Trevor *neurobiologist, researcher*

**Stanford**
Abraham, Spencer (Edward Spencer Abraham) *former Secretary of Energy*
Abrams, Herbert LeRoy *radiologist, educator*
Alexander, Janet Cooper *law educator*
Anderson, Martin Carl *economist*
Anderson, Theodore Wilbur *statistics educator*
Andreopoulos, Spyros George *writer*
Arber, Daniel Alan *hematologist, pathologist*
Arrow, Kenneth Joseph *economist, educator*
Arvin, Ann Margaret *microbiology and immunology educator, researcher*
Aziz, Khalid *petroleum engineering educator*
Baker, Keith Michael *history professor*
Baker, Patricia Ann *publishing executive*
Baldwin, Robert Lesh *biochemist, educator*
Bandura, Albert *psychologist, educator*
Bankman, Joseph *law educator*
Banks, R. Richard *law educator*
Barron, Brigid *education educator*
Batzoglou, Serafim *computer scientist, educator*
Bauer, Eugene Andrew *dermatologist, educator*
Baylor, Denis Aristide *neuroscientist, educator*
Bendor, Jonathan *economics professor, researcher*
Benkard, Charles Lanier *economics professor*
Berg, Paul *biochemist, educator*
Bienenstock, Arthur Irwin *physicist, educator, federal official*
Blandford, Roger David *science educator*
Blau, Helen Margaret *pharmacology educator*
Boaler, Jo *education educator*
Bobo, Lawrence D. *sociologist*
Boudart, Michel *chemical engineer, consultant, chemist, educator*
Bracewell, Ronald Newbold *engineering educator*
Brauman, John I. *chemist, educator*
Bresnan, Joan W. *literature and language professor*
Brinegar, Claude Stout *retired oil industry executive*
Brody, Richard Alan *political science educator, researcher*
Brown, J. Martin *oncologist, educator*
Brown, Patrick O. *molecular biologist, educator*
Bube, Richard Howard *retired materials scientist, educator*
Bulow, Jeremy Israel *economist*

Bunzel, John Harvey *political science professor*
Campbell, Allan McCulloch *bacteriology educator*
Cannon, Robert Hamilton, Jr. *aerospace engineering educator*
Chase, Robert Arthur *surgeon, educator*
Chui, Chi On *electrical engineer, researcher*
Cohen, Albert *musician, educator*
Cohen, Harvey Joel *pediatric hematology and oncology educator*
Cohen, Paul Joseph *mathematician*
Cohen, Stanley Norman *geneticist, educator*
Cohen, William *law educator*
Cole, G. Marcus *law educator*
Collman, James Paddock *chemistry professor*
Conquest, Robert (George Robert Acworth Conquest) *writer, historian, poet*
Cork, Linda Katherine *veterinary pathologist, educator*
Corn, Wanda Marie *art educator*
Cottle, Richard Warren *retired operations research educator*
Cox, Donald Clyde *electrical engineering educator*
Craswell, Richard *law educator*
Cuban, Larry *education educator, researcher*
Dahan, Michael Haim *obstetrician, gynecologist, researcher*
Daily, Gretchen Cara *ecologist, environmental services administrator*
Daines, Robert M. *law educator*
Damon, William Van Buren *developmental psychologist, educator, writer*
Danielson, Elena Schafer *retired archivist*
David, Paul Allan *economist, economic historian*
Davis, Mark M. *microbiologist, educator*
Davis, Ronald Wayne *genetics researcher, biochemistry educator*
Dekker, George Gilbert *literature educator, writer*
Derksen, Charlotte Ruth Meynink *librarian*
Diamond, Larry *political scientist*
Dimopoulos, Savas *physics professor, theoretical physicist*
Dirzo, Rodolfo *science educator, researcher, biologist*
Djerassi, Carl *writer, retired chemistry professor*
Donaldson, Sarah Susan *radiologist*
Duus, Peter *retired historian*
Efron, Bradley *statistician, educator*
Egbert, Peter Roy *ophthalmologist, educator*
Ehrlich, Paul Ralph *biology professor*
Ehrlich, Thomas *law educator*
Eisner, Elliot W. *education educator*
Eitner, Lorenz Edwin Alfred *art historian, educator*
Eliashberg, Yakov *mathematician, educator*
Elliott, David Duncan III *science company executive*
Enthoven, Alain Charles *economist, educator*
Eshleman, Von Russel *electrical engineering educator, aerospace scientist*
Etchemendy, John *academic administrator, educator*
Eustis, Robert Henry *design company executive, mechanical engineer*
Evers, Williamson Moore *education policy analyst, political scientist*
Farquhar, John William *physician, educator*
Fee, Willard Edward, Jr. *otolaryngologist*
Feigenbaum, Edward Albert *retired computer science educator*
Felstiner, John *literature educator, translator*
Fetter, Alexander Lees *theoretical physicist, educator*
Fetterman, David Mark *anthropologist, educator*
Fire, Andrew Z. *pathologist, educator, geneticist*
Fisher, George *law educator*
Flinn, Paul Anthony *materials scientist*
Ford, Richard Thompson *law educator*
Francke, Uta *geneticist, educator*
Frank, Curtis W. *chemical engineer, department chairman*
Franklin, Gene Farthing *engineering educator, consultant*
Franklin, Marc Adam *law educator*
Fredrickson, George Marsh *history professor*
Fried, Barbara H. *law educator*
Friedman, Gary David *epidemiologist*
Friedman, Lawrence M. *law educator*
Friedman, Milton *retired economist*
Fuchs, Victor Robert *economist, educator*
Fuller, Margaret Tatnall *biomedical researcher*
Gage, Nathaniel Lees *retired psychologist, retired educator*
Garber, Alan Michael *internist, educator, economist*
Gelpi, Albert Joseph *language educator, department chairman, critic*
Gilson, Ronald Jay *law educator*
Goldstein, Paul *lawyer, educator*
Goodman, Joseph Wilfred *electrical engineering educator*
Gould, William Benjamin, IV, *lawyer, educator, federal agency administrator*
Greely, Henry T. (Hank Greely) *law educator*
Greif, Avner *economics professor*
Grey, Thomas C. *law educator*
Grundfest, Joseph Alexander *law and business educator*
Hall, Robert Ernest *economics professor*
Hanawalt, Philip Courtland *biology professor, researcher*
Hansen, Peter Reinhard *economics professor*
Harbaugh, John Warvelle *geologist, educator*
Harbury, Pehr A.B. *biochemist, educator*
Harrison, Walter Ashley *physicist, researcher*
Heller, Thomas Charles *law educator*
Henderson, Victor Warren *behavioral and geriatric neurologist, epidemiologist, researcher, educator*
Hennessy, John L. *academic administrator*
Henriksen, Thomas Hollinger *academic administrator*
Hensler, Deborah Rosenfield *law educator*
Hesselink, Lambertus *electrical engineering and physics educator*
Hickman, Bert George, Jr. *economist, educator*
Hilton, Ronald *international relations educator*
Hlatky, Mark Andrew *cardiologist, medical researcher*
Holloway, Charles Arthur *public and private management educator*

Howard, Ronald A. *systems engineer, educator*
Howell, James Edwin *economist, educator*
Huntington, Hillard Griswold *economist*
Inkeles, Alex *sociology educator*
Jacobs, Charlotte De Croes *medical educator, oncologist*
Jardetzky, Oleg *medical educator, researcher*
Joss, Robert L. *dean*
Jurafsky, Daniel *linguist*
Kailath, Thomas *electrical engineer, educator*
Kamil, Michael *education educator*
Karlan, Pamela Susan *law educator*
Karlin, Samuel *mathematics professor, researcher*
Kays, William Morrow *academic administrator, mechanical engineer*
Keller, Joseph Bishop *mathematician, educator*
Keller, Michael Alan *librarian, musicologist*
Kennedy, David Michael *historian, educator*
Kennedy, Donald *environmental scientist, educator, editor*
Keren, Kinneret *biophysicist*
Khosla, Chaitan S. *chemical engineer*
Kino, Gordon Stanley *electrical engineering educator*
Klausner, Michael David *law educator*
Knuth, Donald Ervin *computer sciences educator*
Koller, Daphne *computer scientist*
Kool, Eric T. *chemist, educator*
Kornberg, Arthur *biochemist, educator*
Kornberg, Roger David *biochemist, structural biologist*
Kovach, Robert Louis *geophysics educator*
Koza, John R. *medical educator, writer*
Kraemer, Helena Antoinette Chmura *psychiatry educator*
Kramer, Larry *dean, law educator, lawyer*
Krasner, Stephen David *federal agency administrator, political science educator*
Krawinkler, Helmut *engineering educator, consultant*
Krensky, Alan Michael *pediatrician, educator*
Krumboltz, John Dwight *psychologist, educator*
Kunz, John Clayton *engineering company executive*
Kurz, Mordecai *economics professor*
Lai, Tze Leung *mathematician, educator*
Laitin, David Dennis *political science professor*
Lambers, James Vincent *mathematician, researcher, petroleum engineer*
Laughlin, Robert B. *academic administrator, physics professor*
Law, Kincho H. *engineering educator*
Lee, Peter Poon-Hang *biotechnologist, educator*
Lehman, I(srael) Robert *biochemist, educator*
Leibel, Steven Arnold *radiologist*
Lemley, Mark Alan *law educator*
Lepper, Mark Roger *psychologist, educator*
Lessig, L. Lawrence III *lawyer, law educator, writer*
Levy, Ronald *medical educator, researcher*
Lewis, John Wilson *political science professor*
Linvill, John Grimes *engineering educator*
Little, William Arthur *physicist, researcher*
Loeb, Susanna *education educator*
Loftis, John, Jr., (John Clyde Loftis Jr.) *language educator*
Long, Sharon Rugel *dean, molecular biologist, educator*
Lotan, Rachel *education educator*
Luo, Liqun *medical educator*
Lyman, Richard Wall *foundation administrator, academic administrator, historian*
Maccoby, Eleanor Emmons *psychology professor*
Macovski, Albert *electrical engineer, educator*
Malenka, Robert C. *psychiatrist, educator*
Mann, J. Keith *retired law educator, arbitrator*
Mansour, Tag Eldin *pharmacologist, educator*
Mark, James B. D. *surgeon, educator*
Marmor, Michael Franklin *ophthalmologist, educator*
Marsh, Martha H. *hospital administrator*
Marshall, Lawrence C. *law educator*
Martin, Joanne *social sciences educator*
Martin, Richard Peter *classics educator, consultant*
Martinez, Jenny S. *lawyer*
Matson, Pamela Anne *environmental scientist, science educator*
McCarthy, John *computer scientist, educator*
McCarty, Perry Lee *civil and environmental engineering educator*
McConnell, Susan K. *neuroscientist*
McDevitt, Hugh O'Neill *immunologist, educator*
McDonald, John Gregory *financial investment educator*
McDougall, Iain Ross *nuclear medicine educator*
Mc Lure, Charles E., Jr. *economist, consultant*
Mc Namara, Joseph Donald *researcher, retired protective services official*
Méndez, Miguel Angel *law educator*
Mignot, Emmanuel *medical researcher*
Miller, William Frederick *research and development company executive, educator, financial consultant*
Mitchell, Beverly Shriver *hematologist, oncologist, educator*
Mitchell, Reginald Eugene *mechanical engineering educator*
Monin, Benoit *psychology professor*
Montgomery, David Bruce *marketing educator*
Mooney, Harold Alfred *plant ecologist*
Moore, Thomas Gale *economist, educator*
Moretti, Franco *professor of comparative literature*
Mueller, Holger *physicist*
Muendermann, Annegret *researcher*
Ngo, Khiem Viet *research scientist*
Noll, Roger Gordon *economist, educator*
Oberhelman, Harry Alvin, Jr. *surgeon, educator*
Olcott, Cornelius, IV, *surgeon*
Orr, Franklin Mattes, Jr. *petroleum engineering educator*
Osheroff, Douglas Dean *physics professor, researcher*
Ott, Wayne Robert *environmental engineer*
Owens, Douglas K. *physician, researcher*
Oyer, Paul *economist*
Palm, Charles Gilman *academic administrator*
Parkinson, Bradford Wells *astronautical engineer, educator*
Paté-Cornell, Marie-Elisabeth Lucienne *finance educator, engineering educator*
Pea, Roy *education educator*

Pearson, Scott Roberts *retired economics professor*
Perry, William James *education educator, former secretary of defense*
Pfeffer, Jeffrey *business educator*
Plummer, James D. *electrical engineering educator*
Polan, Mary Lake *obstetrics and gynecology educator*
Polinsky, A. Mitchell *law and economics educator*
Predmore, Michael Pennock *Spanish language and literature educator*
Purevdorj-Gage, Laura Boloroo *research scientist*
Rabin, Robert L. *law educator*
Radin, Margaret Jane *law educator*
Raisian, John *academic administrator, economist*
Reddy, Vadiyala Mohan *cardiothoracic surgeon*
Reitz, Bruce Arnold *cardiac surgeon, educator*
Rhee, Soo-Yon *information scientist*
Rhode, Deborah Lynn *law educator*
Ricardo-Campbell, Rita *economist, educator*
Riggs, Henry Earle *academic administrator, engineering educator*
Robbins, Robert Clayton *surgeon*
Roberts, Donald Frank, Jr. *communications educator*
Roberts, Donald John *economics professor, business professor, consultant*
Robinson, Paul Arnold *historian, educator, writer*
Rosenberg, Saul Allen *oncologist, educator*
Ross, John *physical chemist, educator*
Roughgarden, Joan E. *biology professor*
Rubenstein, Edward *physician, educator*
Rubin, Karl Cooper *mathematics educator*
Schatzberg, Alan Frederic *psychiatrist, researcher*
Schoen, Richard Melvin *mathematics professor, researcher*
Scott, Kenneth Eugene *lawyer, educator*
Scott, W(illiam) Richard *sociology educator*
Segall, Paul *geologist, educator*
Shapiro, Lucy *molecular biology educator*
Shavelson, Richard *education educator*
Sheehan, James John *historian, educator*
Shenker, Stephen *physics educator*
Shooter, Eric Manvers *retired neurobiology professor, consultant*
Shultz, George Pratt *economics professor, former secretary of state*
Siekierski, Maciej M. *curator*
So, Yuen T. *neurologist, educator*
Sofaer, Abraham David *lawyer, educator, judge, consultant*
Solomon, Edward Ira *chemistry professor, researcher*
Somerville, Christopher Roland *botanist, educator*
Sowell, Thomas *economist, syndicated columnist*
Spaulding, Norman W. III *law educator*
Spence, Andrew Michael (A. Michael Spence) *former dean, finance educator*
Springer, George Stephen *mechanical engineering educator*
Spudich, James A. *biology professor*
Stamey, Thomas Alexander *urologist, educator*
Stansky, Peter David Lyman *historian, writer, retired history professor*
Stearns, Timothy P. *biology professor, geneticist*
Steele, Shelby *writer, educator*
Stefanick, Marcia Lynn *medical educator, researcher*
Stipek, Deborah Jane *dean, education educator*
Stone, William Edward *academic administrator, consultant*
Street, Robert Lynnwood *civil, mechanical and environmental engineer*
Strena, Robert Victor *lab administrator, director*
Strnad, Jeff (James Frank Strnad II) *law educator*
Strober, Myra Hoffenberg *education educator, consultant*
Stryer, Lubert *biochemist, educator*
Sturrock, Peter Andrew *space science and astrophysics educator*
Suppes, Christine Johnson *publishing executive*
Susskind, Leonard *physicist, educator*
Swartz, James R. *chemical engineer, educator*
Theriot, Julie *microbiologist, medical educator*
Thompson, Buzz (Barton H. Thompson Jr.) *law educator*
Thompson, George Albert *geophysicist, educator*
Tomlin, Claire J. *aeronautical engineer, educator*
Traugott, Elizabeth Closs *linguist, educator, researcher*
Trost, Barry Martin *chemist, educator*
Ullman, Jeffrey David *computer scientist, educator*
Umetsu, Dale T. *pediatrics educator, physician*
Van Dyke, Milton Denman *aeronautical engineering educator*
Van Horne, James Carter *economist, educator*
Voinott, Arthur Fales, Jr. *university educator*
Vincenti, Walter Guido *aeronautical engineer, emeritus educator*
Wagoner, Robert Vernon *astrophysicist, educator*
Walt, Martin *physicist, educator*
Weiner, Allen S. *law educator*
Weisberg, Robert *law educator*
Weissman, Irving L. *medical researcher*
Wender, Paul Anthony *chemistry professor*
White, Robert Lee *electrical engineer, educator*
Whitney, Rodger Franklin *academic administrator*
Whittemore, Alice *biostatistician*
Williams, Howard Russell *law educator*
Wojcicki, Stanley George *physicist, researcher*
Wolak, Frank Anthony *economics professor*
Wolff, Tobias (Jonathan Ansell Wolff) *writer*
Wotipka, Christine Min *education educator*
Yanofsky, Charles *biology educator*
Zahedi, Sina *electrical engineer, researcher*
Zare, Richard Neil *chemistry professor*
Zarins, Christopher Kristaps *surgeon, educator*
Zimbardo, Philip George *psychologist, educator, writer*
Zitzewitz, Eric *economics professor*

## Stanton

Zabel-Durham, Martha L. *retired secondary school educator*

## Stevenson Ranch

Krainin, Julian Arthur *film director, film producer, cinematographer, writer*

## Stinson Beach

Metz, Mary Seawell *retired foundation administrator, retired academic administrator*

Schwarm, Harold Chambers *artist*

## Stockton

Ballot, Michael Harvey *business administration educator, consultant*
Biddle, Donald Ray *aerospace transportation executive*
Blodgett, Elsie Grace *small business owner, property manager*
Cobb, Judy Lynn *elementary school educator*
DeRicco, Lawrence Albert *retired college president*
Derosa, Donald V. *academic administrator*
Dornbush, Vicky Jean *medical billing systems executive*
Fish, Tom *special education educator, vocational school educator*
Gilbertson, Philip *academic administrator*
Gross, Paul Hans *retired chemistry professor*
Hackley, Carol Ann *public relations educator, consultant*
Haines, Joybelle *retired elementary school educator*
Jackson, Jewel *retired state agency administrator*
Jacobs, Marian *advertising executive*
Kareem, A'isha *educational consultant, counselor*
Knapp, Christian Jakob *lawyer*
Knight, Norman Gladstone *minister*
Limbaugh, Ronald Hadley *retired historian, cultural organization administrator*
Magness, Rhonda Ann *retired microbiologist*
McCarthy, Beverly Fitch *retired civic leader, educator*
Meissner, Katherine Gong *municipal official*
Michailoff, Ian Robert *real estate broker, land use planner*
Murphy, Jeremiah T. *professional sports team executive, construction executive*
Nakanishi, Alan *ophthalmologist, state representative*
Null, Paul Bryan *minister*
Oak, Claire Morisset *artist, educator*
Parish, William Henry *lawyer*
Ren, Jianhua *education educator*
Roll, Renée F. *retired psychologist*
Samoshin, Vyacheslav Vladimirovich *chemistry professor, science educator, researcher*
Singleton, Marvin Ayers *state legislator, otolaryngologist*
Sorby, Donald Lloyd *dean*
Sumida, Gregory Zio *artist, photographer, musician, astronomer*
Taylor, Francis Michael *auditor, municipal official*
Viscovich, Sir Andrew John *educational management consultant*
Weick, Cynthia Wagner *business educator*
Whiteker, Roy Archie *retired chemistry professor*
Wilcox, Helena Marguerita (Rita) *music educator*
Wright, Evelyn Louise *artist*

## Studio City

Basinger, Kim (Kimila Ann Basinger) *actress*
Boyett, Joan Reynolds *performing company executive*
Brommer, Gerald Frederick *artist, writer*
Chambers, Clytia Montllor *retired public relations consultant*
Delnik, Alexander *engineering executive, consultant*
Devane, William *actor*
Easterson, Sam *artist*
Frumkin, Simon *political organization worker, writer*
Gallardo, Sandra Silvana *television producer, actress*
Gold, Arnold Henry *judge*
Grace, Topher *actor*
Kelley, Jan *publishing executive, musician*
Kenney, H. Wesley, Jr., (Harry Wesley Kenney Jr.) *television producer, television director*
King, Carole (Carole Klein) *lyricist, singer*
Laba, Marvin *management consultant*
Manders, Susan Kay *artist*
Mc Donald, Meg *public relations executive*
Meenan, Alan John *clergyman, theology studies educator*
Miller, Charles Maurice *lawyer*
Moseley, Chris Rosser *marketing executive*
Najee, (Jerome Najee Rasheed) *musician*
Parish, James Robert *writer, cinema historian*
Richman, Anthony E. *textile rental industry association executive*
Rogers, Suzanne C. *actress*
Shavelson, Melville *scriptwriter, theater producer, director*
Silverman, Bruce Gary *advertising executive, consultant*
Sinbad, (David Adkins) *actor, comedian*
Steinberg, Roy Bennett *television producer, director, educator*
Werner, Tom *television producer, professional baseball team executive*

## Sugarloaf

Black, Victoria Lynn *writer, artist*

## Summerland

Cannon, Louis Simeon *journalist, writer*

## Sun City

Holl, Walter John *architect, interior designer*

## Sun Valley

Casey, Paul Arnold *writer, producer, photographer, composer, director*
Mayhue, Richard Lee *dean, minister, writer*
Miller, Flemon Marshall *public works manager*
Sweet, Harvey *set designer, lighting designer*

## Sunland

Nepales, Ruben Viado *journalist*

## Sunnyvale

Andreessen, Marc *software company executive, internet innovator*
Bazzi, Samer *application developer, consultant*
Benhamou, Eric A. *information technology company executive*
Brachman, Ron *research and development company executive*
Braun, Lloyd *Internet company executive*

Brigden, John *lawyer*
Burkett, Marvin D. *electronics executive*
Butterfield, Stewart *Internet company executive*
Calderoni, Robert M. *software company executive*
Callahan, Michael John *lawyer*
Cambou, Bertrand *information technology executive*
Castellino, Ronald Augustus Dietrich *radiologist, educator*
Chang, William Zhi-Ming *research scientist*
Chen, Xiao *process engineer*
Coleman, Gregory G. *former magazine publisher*
Daltchev, Ana Ranguel *sculptor*
Decker, Sue (Susan L. Decker) *Internet company executive*
Dunaway, Cammie *marketing executive*
Edwards, William T. (Billy Edwards) *information technology executive*
Filo, David *Internet company executive*
Garner, Shirley Imogene *retired music educator*
Gelman, Bob Mark *retired systems engineer*
Gifford, John F. *computer company executive*
Goo, Jung-Suk *semiconductor company research engineer*
Harari, Eli *computer company executive*
Hawkins, Jeff *information technology company executive*
Holmes, Richard Brooks *mathematical physicist*
Koogle, Timothy K. *communications executive*
Kriens, Scott G. *information technology executive*
Lanaro, Clara Marrama *music educator, writer*
Leong, Chia Ken *mechanical engineer*
Lin, Frank C. *computer company executive*
McCollam, Craig A. *manufacturing executive*
McCoy, Thomas *information technology executive*
McVeigh, Patrick (Pat) *software developer company executive*
Merrill, Wendy Jane *financial services company executive*
Meyer, Derrick R. *information technology executive*
Morris, Iain *information technology executive*
Nagel, David *software developer company executive*
Nazem, Farzad *information technology executive*
Olson, James (Jim Olson) *telecommunications industry executive*
Parnafes, Itzik *Internet company executive*
Perdikou, Kim *information technology executive*
Raghavan, Prabhakar *Internet company executive*
Ratchev, Boris A *management consultant*
Rosensweig, Daniel L. *Internet company executive*
Ruiz, Hector de Jesus *information technology executive*
Sanders, Walter Jeremiah *computer company executive*
Sartain, Libby *human resources specialist*
Schneider, Hilary A. *Internet company executive*
Schwartz, Eleanore Anita *retired elementary school educator, small business owner*
Semel, Terry S. *Internet company executive*
Siddiqee, Muhammad Waheeduddin *electrical engineer*
Sindu, Pradeep *information technology executive*
Tinianov, Brandon Dillan *engineering executive, acoustical engineer*
White, Christine A. *internist, oncologist, pharmaceutical executive*
Wu, Yider *research scientist*
Xie, Ken *software company executive*
Yang, Jerry *Internet company executive*
Yang, Ming-Hsuan *research scientist*

### Sunset Beach
Anderson, William (Bill) Maxwell *artist, educator*
Pridham, Thomas Grenville *retired microbiologist*

### Sutter Creek
Sanders, Elizabeth Anne Weaver (Betsy Sanders) *management consultant, writer*

### Sylmar
Corry, Dalila Boudjellal *internist, educator*
Foster, Dudley Edwards, Jr. *musician, educator*
Froelich, Beverly Lorraine *foundation administrator*
Kamangar, Nader *pulmonologist, educator*
Liu, Paul Ishen *pathologist, educator*
Scheib, Gerald Paul *art educator*
Tully, Susan Balsley *pediatrician, educator*
Valdez, Denise *newscaster*

### Tarzana
Firestone, Morton H. *finance company executive*
Goldberg, Harvey *corporate financial executive*
Handelsman, Yehuda *endocrinologist, preventive medicine physician*
Hansen, Robert Clinton *electrical engineer, consultant*
Lauter, James Donald *retired stockbroker*
Lindley, Charles Alexander *aerospace engineer, consultant*
Neece, Olivia Helene Ernst *investment company executive, consultant*
Richman, Peter Mark *actor, painter, film producer*
Rinsch, Maryann Elizabeth *occupational therapist*
Smith, Mark Lee *architect*
Steinberg, Jeffrey Mark *obstetrician, gynecologist, medical researcher*
Weil, Leonard *banker*

### Tehachapi
Mitchell, Betty Jo *publishing executive, writer*
Smith-Thompson, Patricia Ann *public relations consultant, educator*
Sprinkle, Martha Clare *elementary school educator*

### Temecula
Bathaee, Soussan *engineering technician*
Betz, Martin G. *art association administrator*
Cherrington, Pamela Jo *special education educator*
Chung, Hee M. *retired nuclear engineer*
Minogue, Robert Brophy *retired nuclear engineer*
Ojeda, Nelson A., II, *musician*

### Templeton
Abernathy, Shields B. *allergist, immunologist, internist*
Foster-Wells, Karen Margaret *artist*
Girolo, Nella Sue *retired voice educator*

### The Sea Ranch
Baas, Jacquelynn *museum director, art historian*
Carter, Richard Duane *management educator*
Hayflick, Leonard *microbiology educator, writer*

### Thermal
Wallis, Judith Lynn *science educator*

### Thousand Oaks
Albertson, Marty P. *music company executive*
Benedek, Kálmán Pál *biochemist, consultant*
Brogden, Stephen Richard *library director*
Dahl, Richard J. *food products executive*
Eisenberg, Paul Richard *cardiologist, consultant, educator*
El Fattah, Yousri M. *computer scientist*
Everson, Joseph *theology studies educator*
Ferber, Samuel *publishing executive*
Gentile, Joseph F. *lawyer, educator*
Gregory, Calvin *real estate investor*
Herman, Joan Elizabeth *health insurance company executive*
Heyer, Carol Ann *illustrator*
Hudson, Barbara *writer, actor*
Loren, Sophia *actress*
Malmuth, Norman David *research scientist*
Nanula, Richard *health products executive*
Pakula, Anita Susan *dermatologist*
Reaves, Michaela Crawford *history professor*
Remmele, Richard L., Jr. *research scientist*
Rooney, Mickey (Joe Yule Jr.) *actor*
Scott, David J. *lawyer*
Sharer, Kevin W. *medical products company executive*
Sladek, John R., Jr. *academic administrator, neurobiology and anatomy educator*
Sladek, Lyle Virgil *mathematician, educator*
Sloane, J.P. *television producer, theologian, entertainer, writer*
Smith-Kielland, Ingvald Alain *product designer*
Stephens, Diana L. *counselor, educator*
Valdez, Josh *health insurance company executive*
Venable, Diane Dailey *retired elementary school educator*
Wolff, Stuart *online real estate executive*
Zhang, Zhongqi *chemist*
Zhou, Sophia Huai *biomedical engineering scientist*

### Tiburon
Barron-Druckrey, Eleanor *psychologist*
Cohn, Nathan *retired lawyer*
Widman, Gary Lee *lawyer*

### Toluca Lake
Beal, John Everett *composer, conductor*
Morton, Hugh Wesley *television producer, television director*
Ragan, Ann Talmadge *media and production consultant, actor*

### Torrance
Adelsman, Jean (Harriette Adelsman) *newspaper editor*
Amemiya, Koichi *motor vehicle company executive*
Bell, Scott Andrew *financial consultant*
Bhargave, Ashish *systems engineer, electrical engineer*
Brasel, Jo Anne *pediatrician, educator*
Brass, Eric Paul *internal medicine and pharmacology educator, academic administrator*
Brown, Adriane M. *aerospace transportation executive*
Bryan, Sharon Ann *lawyer*
Budoff, Matthew Jay *cardiologist*
Carlson, Terrance L. *lawyer, aerospace transportation executive*
DeMoss, Juliet Julee *civil engineer, music educator*
Ebeling, Vicki *marriage and family therapist, psychotherapist, writer*
Emmanouilides, George Christos *physician, educator*
Enright, Stephanie Veselich *investment company executive, financial consultant*
Esmond, Donald V. *transportation executive*
Everts, Connor *artist*
Hammer, Terence Michael *physician*
Hansen, James Edward *medical educator, researcher*
Ho, Mat Hoang *gynecologist, researcher, medical educator*
Howell, Irvin Wendell, Jr. *physician, consultant*
Imbarus, Aura *language educator, consultant*
Kerstiens, Gene J. *mathemagenician, consultant*
Kim, Keehoon *cybernetic scientist*
Kohan, Betsy Burns *lawyer*
Kuc, Joseph A. *research scientist*
Lieberman, Robert Arthur *physicist*
Mehringer, Charles Mark *medical educator*
Moore, Christopher M. *lawyer*
Myhre, Byron Arnold *pathologist, educator*
Oudiz, Ronald *cardiologist*
Petillon, Lee Ritchey *lawyer*
Pfund, Edward Theodore, Jr. *electronics company executive*
Rogers, Howard H. *retired chemist*
Shitabata, Paul Kent *pathologist*
Signorovitch, Dennis J. *communications executive*
Sorstokke, Susan Eileen *systems engineer*
Stabile, Bruce Edward *surgeon*
Sun, Nora Chi-Jun *pathologist*
Swerdloff, Ronald S. *medical educator, physician, researcher*
Tanaka, Kouichi Robert *hematologist, educator*
Yamamoto, Akimasa *transportation executive*

### Tracy
Hammer, (Stanley Kirk Burrell) *musician*
Johnson, Ronald Leonard *information technology executive, small business owner*
Kiggins, Mildred L. *marketing professional*
Waziri, Ghaus Ghulam *diplomat*

### Travis Afb
Wible, Julie Lynn *human services administrator, military officer*

### Trinidad
Conant, Ralph Wendell *retired academic administrator, writer, educator*

### Truckee
Todd, Linda Marie *nutrition researcher, circulation manager, financial consultant, pilot*

### Tujunga
Ancu, Edward Florin *veterinarian*
Loehwing, Lord Rudi Charles *publicist, radio broadcasting executive, journalist*

### Tulare
Berge, Anna Catharina Björnsdotter *veterinarian, epidemiologist*
Hefflefinger, Clarice Thorpe *retired real estate broker*

### Turlock
Ahlem, Lloyd Harold *psychologist*
Burns, James W. *academic administrator, researcher, consultant*
Harris, Randall Duane *management consultant, educator*
Shirvani, Sir Hamid *architect, educator, philosopher, writer, university president*
Sutherland, Andrew C. *actor, educator*

### Tustin
Braunstein, Herbert *pathologist, educator*
Herdeg, Howard Brian *retired physician*
Hester, Norman Eric *chemical company technical executive, chemist*
Kim, Dong Wook *information technology executive*
Kim, Han Pyong *researcher*
Kraft, Henry Robert *lawyer*
Mazzucato, Carla Carli *artist*
Prasad, Birendra (Brian) *mechanical engineer*

### Twain Harte
Kinsinger, Robert Earl *property company executive, educational consultant*

### Twentynine Palms
Clemente, Patrocinio Ablola *secondary school educator*
Fultz, Philip Nathaniel *management analyst*

### Ukiah
Lind, Leslie J. *music educator*
McClintock, Richard Polson *dermatologist*
Newell, Barbara Ann *coatings company executive*

### Union City
Feinberg, Richard Alan *psychologist*
Lindsey, Tommie *secondary school educator*
Muñoz, Eduardo Rafael *elementary school educator*

### Universal City
Bismuth, Pierre *artist*
Bowen, Andrea *actress*
Bromstad, Angela *broadcast executive*
Chavira, Ricardo Antonio *actor*
Cross, Marcia *actress*
Denton, James *actor*
Finkelstein, Rick *film company executive*
Golper, John Bruce *lawyer*
Hammer, Bonnie *broadcast executive*
Hatcher, Teri *actress*
Huffman, Felicity (Flicka Huffman) *actress*
Langley, Donna *film company executive*
Lawless, Lucy (Lucille Francis Ryan) *actress*
Linde, David *film company executive*
Longoria, Eva (Eva Jacqueline Longoria, Eva Longoria Christopher) *actress*
McCormack, Eric *actor*
Menendez, Belinda *broadcast executive*
Merkerson, S. Epatha *actress*
Meyer, Ron *film company executive*
Parent, Mary *film company executive*
Press, Terry *marketing executive*
Randall, Karen *film company executive*
Reitman, Ivan *film director, producer*
Rocco, Nikki *film company executive*
Savant, Doug *actor*
Schulz, Diana *film company executive*
Sheridan, Nicolette *actress*
Shmuger, Marc *film company executive*
Strong, Brenda *actress*
Stuber, Scott *film company executive*
Wolf, Dick (Richard A. Wolf) *television producer*
Woodard, Alfre *actress*

### Upland
Barden, Shirley Ramsey *credit union executive*
Cullen, Robert John *financial planner, investment advisor*
Goodman, John M. *construction executive*
Hawks, Wesley Howard *retired director, music educator*
Horton, Michael L. *mortgage company executive, publishing executive*
Jordan, Charles Wesley *retired bishop*
Kennedy, Mark Alan *secondary school educator*
Likens, John David *rehabilitation services professional*
Suh, Jung Sook Ky *personnel consultant*

### Vacaville
Longoria, Steve *security firm executive, consultant*

### Valencia
Anguiano, Lupe *advocate*
Jones, Christopher Charles *psychologist*
Joy, Alexa *small business owner, artist, educator*
King, Wayne T. *lawyer*
Klahr, Lewis *film director*
Levy, Ezra Cesar *aerospace scientist, real estate agent*
Mann, Alfred *pharmaceutical executive*
Millar, Michael William *musician*
Parks, Suzan Lori *playwright*
Pocrass, Richard Dale *management consultant*
Windsor, William Earl *consulting engineer, sales representative*
Wolfson, Jeremy *investment advisor*

### Vallejo
Brown, Earl Kent *historian, minister*
Crosley-Mayers, Diane *social worker*
Davis, William Albert *parks director*
McGowan, Thomas Randolph *retired religious organization administrator*
Toms, Kathleen Moore *nurse*
Towne, Sarah Patton *physician*
Wilson, Carrie Lee Stroud *principal*
Womack, Thomas Houston *manufacturing executive*
Zingale, Donald Paul *academic administrator, educator*

### Valley Center
Arciniega, Tomas Abel *university president*
Camp, Joseph Shelton, Jr. *film producer, director, writer*

### Valley Springs
Vitrac, Jean-Jacques Charles *international business consultant*

### Valley Village
Barkin, Elaine Radoff *composer*
Bench, Johnny Lee
Diller, Phyllis (Phyllis Ada Driver Diller) *actress, writer*

### Van Nuys
Ahern, Sean Christopher *aerospace scientist*
Arabian, Armand *arbitrator, mediator, lawyer*
Becker, Frawley *writer, dialogue director, location manager*
Boone, Deborah Ann (Debby Boone) *singer*
Dea, Fay Suey *counselor, educator*
Ewing, Guin Porter *historian, art collector*
Graham, Roger John *photography professor, journalism professor*
Greenberg, Daniel *electronics rental company executive*
Greene, Albert Lawrence *healthcare executive*
Vasilyeva, Anna *artist, writer*
Walsh, Thomas Francis, Jr. *producer, writer, director*
Wright, Judith Ann *elementary school educator*
Zucker, Alfred John *English and history educator, academic administrator, historian*

### Venice
Adams, Lisa Kay *artist*
Alf, Martha Joanne *artist*
Beery-Polglase, Penelope (Pixie) *education educator*
Bill, Tony *producer, director*
Binns, Tom *jewelry designer*
Chartoff, Robert Irwin *film producer*
Chipman, Jack *artist*
Choo, Kristy *chef*
Eliot, Alexander *writer*
Eversley, Frederick John *sculptor, engineer*
Mankin, Donald Aaron *management consultant, writer*
Padilla, Mario René *literature educator, writer*

### Ventura
Abul-Haj, Suleiman Kahil *pathologist*
Barber, Jerry Randel *medical device company executive*
Bradley, Jerry Alan *psychologist, consultant*
Chouinard, Yvon *sportswear outfitter executive*
Downs, Floella McIntyre *retired ferry pilot, instructor, flight examiner*
Gallagher, Timothy J. *newspaper editor*
Gaynor, Joseph *chemical engineer, management consultant*
Greig, William Taber, II, *publishing company executive*
Hoffman, Kenneth *music educator*
Howry, Joe R. *newspaper editor*
Lawson, Robert Earl *music educator, conductor*
Naurath, David Allison *engineering psychologist, researcher*
Orfalea, Paul *printing, copying company founder, investment company executive*
Shifman, Ruth Miri *dentist*
Turturro, John *actor*
Villaveces, James Walter *allergist, immunologist, consultant*

### Vernon
Gavina, Pedro *coffee company executive*

### Victorville
Scott, Deborah Elizabeth *school system administrator, poet*
Sedeño, Eugene Raymond *electrical engineer, consultant*
Toner, Stephen J. *education educator*

### Villa Park
Britton, Thomas Warren, Jr. *retired management consultant*
Hawe, David Lee *manufacturing consultant, venture capitalist*

### Visalia
Anderson, Maureen Anne *retired librarian*
Burnett-Sousa, Jennifer Carrie *agricultural studies educator*
Carrillo, Melchor Paul *voice educator*
Crowe, John T. *lawyer*
Garcia, William L. *academic administrator*
Gray, Kris Diane *nursing consultant, forensic specialist*
Hsu, Shu-Dean *hematologist, oncologist*
Levine, Suzin Nancy Leah *religious organization administrator*
O'Leary, Deanna Kay *benefits compensation analyst, consultant*
Porterfield-Pyatt, Chaumonde R. *music educator, advocate*
Riegel, Byron William *ophthalmologist*

### Vista
Cavanaugh, Kenneth Clinton *retired real estate consultant*
Dyson, Brian G. *business consulting company executive, former beverage company executive*
Ferguson, Margaret Ann *tax specialist, consultant*

Hawk, Tony *professional skateboarder*
Linhart, Letty Lemon *editor*
Mitchell, Thomas Edward, Jr. *communications cabling executive*
Nolte, Linda Marie *language educator*
Rodriguez-Cruz, Sandra Enid *chemist, researcher*
Way, Danny *professional skateboarder*

**Walnut**
Budzak, Stephen Howard *tax specialist, consultant*
Cheng, Shide *engineer, researcher*
Johnson, Keith Liddell *retired chemicals executive*
Karr, Joanne Fern *theater educator*
McKee, Catherine Lynch *lawyer, educator*
Tan, Colleen Woo *communications educator*

**Walnut Creek**
Bryant, Warren F. *retail executive*
Cannon, Grace Bert *retired immunologist*
Carson, Jay Wilmer *pathologist, educator*
Chu, Valentin Yuan-ling *author*
Costa, Walter Henry *architect*
Curtin, Daniel Joseph, Jr. *lawyer*
Gill, Margaret Gaskins *lawyer*
Ginsburg, Gerald J. *lawyer, management consultant*
Hanschen, Peter Walter *lawyer*
Hanson, Robert Duane *engineering educator*
Hassid, Sami *architect, educator*
Heftmann, Erich *biochemist*
Henshaw, Guy Runals *management consultant*
Keith, Bruce Edgar *political scientist, genealogist*
Laddon, Michael M *retail executive*
Lilly, Luella Jean *retired academic administrator*
Man, Pang Ling *retired psychiatrist*
McCauley, Bruce Gordon *financial consultant*
Nolan, Janiece Simmons *health facility administrator*
Nord, Paul Elliott *lawyer, accountant*
Ostrander, Willis Frederick *retired real estate appraiser*
Pagter, Carl Richard *lawyer*
Rainey, William Joel *lawyer*
Reimann, Arline Lynn *artist*
Rhody, Ronald Edward *bank executive, communications executive*
Saavedra, Charles James *retired banker*
Satz, Louis K. *publishing executive*
Schneider, Gisela Helga *medical technician*
Seaborg, David Michael *evolutionary biologist*
Skaggs, Sanford Merle *lawyer*
Trousdale, Stephen Richard *newspaper editor*
Walston, Roderick Eugene *federal official*
Wu, Tse Cheng *chemist, researcher*

**Watsonville**
Brown, Alan Charlton *retired aeronautical engineer*
Dehner, David Anthony *music educator, voice educator*
Desimone, Richard Louis *principal*
Dorey, William G. *construction executive*
Watts, David H. *construction company executive*
West, Karrie L. *school psychologist*

**Weed**
Schaefer, M. Elaine *music educator, conductor*

**Weimar**
Kerschner, Lee R(onald) *academic administrator, political scientist, educator*

**West Covina**
Ebiner, Robert Maurice *lawyer*
Galen, Albert John *retired lawyer*
McHale, Edward Robertson *retired lawyer*
Musich, Robert Lorin *motivational speaker*
Torres, Esteban Edward *congressman, trade association administrator*

**West Hills**
Duzy, Merrilyn Jeanne *artist, educator*
Monosson, Ira Howard *physician*
Shirk, Jack Andrew *executive recruiter*
Smith, Chad A. *band director*

**West Hollywood**
Annakin, Kenneth Cooper *film director, writer*
Antin, Jonathan *hairstylist, entrepreneur*
Arnaz, Lucie Desiree *actress*
Barker, Clive *artist, film director, film producer, scriptwriter*
Bassett, Angela *actress*
Baxter, Meredith *actress*
Berry, Halle Maria *actress*
Burke, Clem *musician*
Cage, Nicolas (Nicolas Coppola) *actor*
Cole, Natalie Maria *singer*
Currin, John *artist*
Deschanel, Caleb *cinematographer, film director*
Destri, Jimmy *musician*
DeWolfe, Chris T. *Internet company executive*
Einstein, Clifford Jay *advertising executive*
Estevez, Luis de Galvez *designer, manufacturer*
Feidelson, Marc *advertising executive*
Franklyn, Audrey Pozen *talent promoter, television personality*
Goin, Suzanne *chef*
Grey, Brad *film company executive*
Harper, Robert *actor*
Harry, Deborah Ann *singer*
Hayes, Sean (Sean Patrick Hayes) *actor, comedian*
Hodal, Melanie *public relations executive*
Holloway, Josh *actor*
Huntsberry, Frederick D. *film company executive*
Jackson, Randy *music producer, television personality, musician*
Joseph, J. Jonathan *interior designer*
Krabbe, Jeroen Aart *actor*
Lefebvre, Ludovic *chef*
Margolin, Bruce M. *lawyer*
Morris, Brian *advertising executive*
Perry, Troy D. *minister, religious organization administrator*
Peyton, Elizabeth Joy *writer, painter*
Presley, Priscilla (Pricilla Ann Wagner, Priscilla Beaulieu Presley) *actress*
Romijn, Rebecca *actress, model*
Sackett, Barnard (Barney) *actor, film producer, director, scriptwriter*
Shaye, Robert Kenneth *film company executive*

Shearmur, Alli *broadcast executive*
Slade, Bernard *playwright*
Stein, Ben (Benjamin Jeremy Stein) *television personality, writer, lawyer, economist*
Stein, Chris *musician*
Suissa, David *advertising executive*
Tarantino, Quentin Jerome *film director, scriptwriter*
Thornton, Billy Bob *actor, film producer*

**West Los Angeles**
Hirschhorn, Charles *media company executive*

**West Sacramento**
Anderson, William Wallace *financial executive*
Coyne, William J. *retail executive, former member house representatives*
Kalachov, Ellada *realtor*
Teel, Joyce Raley *retail executive*
Wilson, Eric F.G. *information technology executive*

**Westlake Village**
Caligiuri, Joseph Frank *retired engineering executive*
Carter, C. Michael *lawyer*
Colburn, Keith W. *electronics executive*
Detterman, Robert Linwood *financial planner*
Dimitriadis, Andre C. *health care executive*
Erdelyi, Eileen Edith *financial planner, financial advisor*
Feiman, Thomas E. *investment company executive*
Gleim, Frances Hollearn *elementary school educator*
Kodigala, Subba Ramaiah *research scientist*
Long, W. Michael *real estate company executive*
Munson, John Backus *computer scientist, retired data processing executive*
Murdock, David H. *food products executive*
Nichols, Steven *apparel executive*
Power, J.D., III, (James David Power III) *marketing executive*
Seymour, Jeffrey Alan *governmental relations consultant*
Strote, Joel Richard *lawyer*
Troxell, Lucy Davis *management consultant*
Weiss, Barbara G. *artist*

**Westminster**
Allen, Merrill James *marine biologist*
Armstrong, Gene Lee *systems engineer, consultant, retired aerospace transportation executive*
Le, Anh Quang *mathematics professor*
Luong, Khanh Vinh Quoc *nephrologist, researcher*
Nguyen, Duoc Tan *small business owner*
Nguyen, Lan Thi Hoang *physician, educator*
Zeng, Eddy Yongping *chemist*

**Whittier**
Arenowitz, Albert Harold *psychiatrist*
Drake, E. Maylon *academic administrator*
Hearn, Kathleen E. *psychologist*
Korf, Jean Prinz *retired theater educator*
Prickett, David Clinton *physician*
Rahiman, Karla Molina *school counselor*
Reid, Ivonne Figueroa *language educator*
Rinard, Arthur Calvin *secondary school educator*
Weismiller, Eleanor Kovacs *library director*

**Wilmington**
Hamai, James Yutaka *manufacturing executive*
Hatch, Ronald Ray *engineer*
Smith, Samantha Denice Akers *primary school educator*

**Wilton**
Harrison, George Harry, III, (Hank Harrison) *publishing executive, author*

**Windsor**
Fieri, Guy *chef*
Sparks, Bennett Sher *military officer*

**Woodland**
Bauer, Cynthia Renae *nurse*
Gray, Sue *elementary school educator*
Squires, Richard Felt *research scientist*

**Woodland Hills**
Babayans, Emil *financial planner*
Chiodini, John Allen *musician, composer*
Clarey, Patricia T. *health insurance company executive, former state official*
Deters, Thomas C. *publishing executive, educator*
Ennis, Thomas Michael *management consultant*
Even, Randolph M. *lawyer*
Fox, James Michael *orthopedic surgeon*
Fox, Stuart Ira *physiologist*
Gellert, Jay M. *health and medical products executive*
Glick, Earl A. *lawyer*
Greaves, Roger F. *health maintenance organization executive*
Harris, Barbara S. *publishing executive, editor-in-chief*
Helwig, David S. *healthcare insurance company executive*
Hokana, Gregory Howard *engineering executive*
Jacobson, Sidney *editor*
Kaufman, Albert I. *lawyer*
Lehr, Leslie Joyce *writer*
McCluggage, Kerry *film and television executive*
Morishita, Akihiko *manufacturing executive*
Mulligan, David Keith *consulting company executive, securities arbitrator*
Mund, Geraldine *judge*
O'Connor, Brian D. A. *music educator, French horn musician*
Pettit, John W. *health facility administrator*
Piersol, Allan Gerald *mechanical engineer*
Piszel, Anthony S. *corporate financial executive*
Pregerson, Harry *federal judge*
Preston, John Elwood *lawyer*
Putman, John A. *biofeedback practitioner, consultant*
Rafter, Tracy *publishing executive*
Rich, Marvin P. *health association executive*
Russell, Anne M. *editor-in-chief*
Schor, Suzi *lawyer, psychologist*

Sharma, Brahama D. *chemistry professor*
Stahlecker, Barbara Jean *marketing professional, consultant*
Stratton, Gregory Alexander *application developer, director, mayor*
Tuthill, Walter Warren *accountant, management consultant*
Valladares-Barbush, Lisette Marie *mathematics educator*
Westen, Brodie Curtis, Jr., (Curt Westen) *lawyer*
Yates, Gary L. *marriage and family therapist*
Zeitlin, Eugenia Pawlik *librarian, educator, writer*
Zeitlin, Herbert Zakary *college administrator, real estate consultant, writer*

**Woodside**
Arthur, Greer Martin *leasing firm executive*
Blum, Richard Hosmer Adams *foundation administrator, educator*
Fisher, Kenneth Lawrence *investment management firm executive*
Freitas, Antoinette Juni *insurance company executive*
Gates, Milo Sedgwick *retired construction company executive*

**Yorba Linda**
Lunde, Dolores Benitez *retired secondary school educator*
Lynch, Frank Thomas *aeronautical engineer, consultant*
Naftali, Timothy J. *library director, historian, educator, writer*
Porcello, Leonard Joseph *engineering research and development executive*
Stavropoulos, Rose Mary Grant *community activist, volunteer*

**Yosemite National Park**
Forgang, David M. *curator*

**Yountville**
Bedell, Jay Dee *small business owner, writer*
Keller, Thomas A. *chef*
Lee, Corey *chef*

**Yreka**
Smith, Vin *editor, small business owner, writer*

**Yuba City**
Kemmerly, Jack Dale *retired state official*
Price, Ardythe Bernadeane *nurse*

**Yucaipa**
Crise, Robert D., Jr. *mathematics professor*

**Yucca Valley**
Dockendorff, Robert Lawrence *computer graphics designer*

# COLORADO

**Alamosa**
Garcia, Castelar Medardo *lawyer*

**Alma**
Swanson, Erik Christian *museum director*

**Arvada**
Ball, Kenneth (Ken) Weston *landscape architect, sculptor*
Bett, Robert Scott *music educator*
Bindel, Thomas Herbert *chemistry educator*
Ferguson, Lloyd Elbert *retired manufacturing engineer*
Glodava, Mila Garcia *entrepreneur, educator, consultant*
Halley, Diane Esther *artist*
Holden, George Fredric *food products executive, consultant, public information officer, writer*
Krohnfeldt, Gretchen Ann *secondary school educator, genealogist*
Kurth, Suzanne M. *criminalist*
Mullineaux, Donal Ray *geologist*
Robey, Mark Douglas *lawyer*
Weitzel, Ginger M. *entrepreneur, critical care nurse*
Yamamoto, Kaoru *retired psychology professor*

**Aspen**
Berkeley, Edward *performing arts association administrator, music educator*
Bucksbaum, Melva *foundation administrator*
Fischl, Eric *artist*
Hayes, Mary Eshbaugh *editor, writer*
Manosevitz, Martin *psychologist*
Mitchell, Karen Frances *artist, jewelry designer*
Oden, Robert Rudolph *surgeon*
Schendler, Auden *recreational facility executive*
Soldner, Paul Edmund *artist, ceramist, educator*
Thomas, William Daniel *journalist*
Tsontakis, George *composer, conductor*

**Aurora**
Alvero, Ruben J. *medical educator*
Battaglia, Frederick Camillo *physician*
Bunn, Paul A., Jr. *oncologist, educator*
Churchill, Mair Elisa Annabelle *medical educator*
D'Amico, Sandra Hathaway *art educator*
Dooley, J. Gordon *food scientist*
Farmer, Keith Allen *music educator*
Haas, Robert Lance *surgeon, consultant*
Heller, Austin Norman *chemical and environmental engineer*
Holmes, Randall Kent *microbiology educator, academic administrator, internist, epidemiologist*
Horwitz, Kathryn Bloch *molecular biologist, educator, breast cancer researcher*
Hughes, Brad, Jr. *economist*
Katz, Michael Jeffery *lawyer*
Khanna, Kishanlal K. *lawyer, educator*
La Rosa, Francisco Guillermo *pathologist, researcher, educator*
Mellette, Julian Ramsey, Jr. *dermatologist, dermatologic surgeon*
Morrow, Caroline Donovan *retired social worker*
Nelson, Marvin Ray *retired life insurance company executive*

Nichols, Clyde Richard *minister, consumer products company executive*
Nora, Audrey Hart *physician*
Olson, Allison W. *social studies educator*
Onyeuku, Alfred Eme *small business owner, consultant*
Reitan, Harold Theodore *management consultant*
Robertson, James Mueller *civil engineer, educator*
Roberts-Ramsbotham, Hazel Ruth *piano educator*
Rust, Stephen Thomas *geriatrician*
Sheffield, Nancy *city agency administrator*
Shore, James H(enry) *psychiatrist*
Sorenson, Katherine Ann *elementary school educator*
Stauffer, Scott William *lawyer, accountant*
Stifel, Frederick Benton *minister, biochemist, nutritionist*
Taraborelli, Janice Conti *humanities educator, academic administrator*
Ton, Paul *investor, educator*
Tovani, C. Cristine *literature and language educator, writer*
Weedin, James Frank *biology professor, researcher*

**Basalt**
Moya, Sharon Staggs *language educator*
Weill, Hans *medical educator*

**Bayfield**
Collins, William Leroy *retired telecommunications engineer*
Horton, Frank Elba *academic administrator, geographer, educator*

**Berthoud**
Davis, Donald Alan *news correspondent, writer, lecturer*

**Bethune**
Williams, Donna M. *social studies educator*

**Black Hawk**
Jones, Linda May *tour guide, writer*

**Boulder**
Adams, William Walter III *science educator*
Adler, Patricia Ann *sociologist, educator*
Anderson, Ronald Delaine *education educator*
Anseth, Kristi S. *tissue engineer, engineering educator*
Araujo-Pradere, Eduardo A. *geophysicist, researcher*
Armstrong, David Michael *biology professor*
Bangs, F(rank) Kendrick *former business educator*
Barchilon, Jacques *foreign language educator, researcher, writer*
Barnes, Frank Stephenson *electrical engineer, educator*
Bartlett, David Farnham *physics professor*
Beer, Francis Anthony *political science professor*
Bernstein, Giora *artistic director*
Bintliff, Barbara Ann *law educator, library director*
Blacker, Helen Virginia *business manager, aeronautical engineer*
Bolomey, Roger Henry *sculptor*
Borko, Hilda *education educator*
Bourne, Lyle Eugene, Jr. *psychology professor*
Brown, Hank *academic administrator, former senator*
Bruff, Harold Hastings *law educator, former dean*
Buck, Michael Charles *electrical engineer, researcher*
Burns, Daniel Hobart *management consultant*
Byerly, Radford, Jr. *science administrator*
Carlson, Devon McElvin *architect, educator*
Chappell, Charles Franklin *meteorologist, consultant*
Churchill, Ward L. *social sciences educator, advocate*
Clark, Melvin Eugene *chemical company executive*
Clark, Wallace Lee, Jr. *physicist*
Clifford, Steven Francis *science administrator, director*
Clos, Lynne Mobley *magazine publisher, paleontologist*
Collins, Jim *management researcher, author*
Conroy, Daniel Frederick *writer, playwright, poet, painter*
Cornell, Eric Allin *physics professor*
Corotis, Ross Barry *civil engineer, educator, academic administrator*
Davis, Robert Heater *chemical engineering educator*
Deaktor, Darryl Barnett *lawyer*
Denning-Adams, Barbara *science educator*
DePuy, Charles Herbert *chemist, educator*
DiStefano, Philip *academic administrator*
Dryer, Murray *physicist, educator*
Dubin, Mark William *neuroscientist, educator, academic administrator*
Dudhia, Jimy *atmospheric scientist*
Echohawk, John Ernest *lawyer*
Eisele, Fred Louis *atmospheric chemist*
Ellis, Homer Godsey *mathematics professor, physicist, researcher*
El Mallakh, Dorothea Hendry *editor, publishing executive*
Engel, Barbara Alpern *history professor*
Esposito, Larry Wayne *planetary astronomer*
Faller, James Elliot *physicist, researcher*
Fenster, Herbert Lawrence *lawyer*
Fiflis, Ted James *lawyer, educator*
Fink, Robert Russell *music educator, retired dean, music theorist*
Fleming, Rex James *meteorologist*
Flowers, William Harold, Jr. *lawyer*
Floyd, Ted *ornithologist, writer*
Garstang, Roy Henry *astrophysicist, educator*
Glover, Fred William *information scientist, director, educator*
Gonzalez-del-Valle, Luis Tomas *Spanish language educator*
Gosling, John Thomas *space plasma physicist, researcher*
Gray, William R. *lawyer*
Greenberg, Edward Seymour *political science professor*
Hall, John Lewis *physicist, researcher*
Hanna, William Johnson *electrical engineering educator*

Hauser, Ray Louis *engineer, researcher, entrepreneur*
Hawkins, Brian Lee *academic administrator, educator*
Hayes, Richard Johnson *association executive, retired lawyer*
Heath, Josephine Ward *foundation administrator*
Hermann, Allen Max *physics professor*
Hess, John Warren *professional society administrator*
Hibbs, John David *computer company executive, electrical engineer, small business owner*
Hill, David Allan *electrical engineer*
Hill, Melvin James *retired oil industry executive*
Ho, Shu-Peng *research scientist*
Hogg, David Clarence *physicist*
Holdsworth, Janet Nott *women's health nurse*
Horikis, Theodoros *research scientist*
Irvine, Leslie *sociologist, educator*
Jessor, Richard *behavioral science educator, director, psychologist, educator*
Jin, Deborah *physicist, educator*
Jin, Xiaoying *electrical engineer, computer engineer, researcher*
Johnston, Laurance Scott *foundation director*
Johnstone, Sally Mac *educational association administrator, psychology educator*
Joselyn, Jo Ann *space scientist*
Joy, Edward Bennett *electrical engineer, educator, consultant*
Kapteyn, Henry Cornelius *physics professor, engineering educator*
Kellogg, William Welch *meteorologist, researcher*
Kenney, Belinda Jill Forseman *information technology executive*
King, Edward Louis *retired chemistry professor*
Kintsch, Walter *retired psychology professor*
Kirshbaum, Daniel Joseph *researcher*
Knoelker, Michael T.F. *science observatory director*
Koch, Tad Harbison *chemistry professor, researcher*
Kotter, Rita Joan *theatre educator, design consultant*
Kuhn, Timothy R. *finance educator*
Lacy, Mary T. (Mary Keenan) *prosecutor*
Landesman, Howard M. *retired academic administrator*
LeMasurier, Wesley Ernest *geology educator, researcher*
LeMone, Margaret Anne *atmospheric scientist*
Lenzen, Glenn Howard, Jr. *lawyer*
Leuliette, Eric W. *research scientist*
Limerick, Patricia Nelson *history professor*
Linsky, Jeffrey L. *astrophysicist*
Low, Boon Chye *physicist*
Lu, Chungu *meteorologist, researcher, educator*
Mahlman, Jerry David *retired meteorologist*
Malde, Harold Edwin *retired federal government geologist*
Mancino, John Gregory *software company executive*
Matthews, Eugene Edward *artist*
McDonald, Dorcas *psychologist, educator*
McFarland, Robert Bruce *physician*
Mehalchin, John Joseph *entrepreneur, finance company executive*
Meier, Mark Frederick *research scientist, educator, artist, small business owner*
Melicher, Ronald William *finance educator*
Mendez, Celestino Galo *mathematics professor*
Menken, Jane Ava *demographer, educator*
Middleton-Downing, Laura *psychiatric social worker, artist, small business owner*
Mitchell, Joan LaVerne *research scientist*
Mooney, William Piatt *actor*
Mulhern, Martin Robert *engineer*
Murnane, Margaret Mary *engineering and physics educator*
Mycielski, Jan *retired mathematics professor*
Nehls, Richard Charles *lawyer*
Neinas, Charles Merrill *sports association executive, consultant*
Nordgren, Ronald Paul *engineering educator, researcher*
O'Brien, Elmer John *librarian, educator*
Oh, Seongshik *physicist, researcher*
Pace, Norman R. *science educator, microbiologist*
Pankove, Jacques Isaac *retired physicist, researcher*
Peterson, Courtland Harry *law educator*
Peterson, G. P. (Bud Peterson) *academic administrator*
Phelps, Arthur Van Rensselaer *physicist, consultant*
Porzak, Glenn E. *lawyer*
Princeton, Joy Carol *retired nursing educator*
Randa, James Paul *physicist, electrical engineer*
Ravishankara, Akkihebal R. *chemist*
Reitsema, Harold James *aerospace engineer*
Ritzel, Brent Paul *publishing executive, consultant*
Roberts, Pamela Ranger *secondary school educator*
Roble, Raymond Gerald *science administrator*
Rodriguez, Juan Alfonso *information technology executive*
Roellig, Leonard Oscar *physics professor*
Rood, David S. *linguistics educator*
Rundle, John Belting *physicist, researcher*
Sable, Barbara Kinsey *retired music educator*
Salby, Murry L *atmospheric and oceanic sciences professor*
Sani, Robert LeRoy *chemical engineering professor*
Sarson, John Christopher *television producer, director, writer*
Schleiner, Anne-Marie *computer graphics designer*
Schneider, Vivian I. *psychologist, researcher*
Serafin, Robert Joseph *science center administrator, electrical engineer*
Shanahan, Eugene Miles *flow measurement instrumentation company executive*
Smith, Ernest Ketcham *electrical engineer*
Smythe, William Rodman *physicist, educator*
Snow, Theodore Peck *astrophysics educator*
Southwick, Charles Henry *zoologist, educator*
Staehelin, Lucas Andrew *cell biology professor*
Stanton, William John, Jr. *marketing educator, author*
Stepanek, Joseph Edward *real estate developer, consultant*

Stern, Alan (S. Alan Stern, Sol Alan Stern) *astrophysicist, researcher*
Steuben, Norton Leslie *lawyer, educator*
Tatarskii, Valerian Il'Ich *physics researcher*
Timmerhaus, Klaus Dieter *chemical engineering professor*
Tolbert, Bert Mills *biochemist, educator*
Tolbert, Margaret A. *geochemistry educator*
Trenberth, Kevin Edward *atmospheric scientist*
Uberoi, Mahinder Singh *aerospace engineer, researcher*
Underwood, Anthony Paul *lawyer*
Walker, Deward Edgar, Jr. *anthropologist, educator*
Washington, Warren Morton *meteorologist*
Wertheimer, Marilyn Lou *librarian, educator*
Westwater, Edgeworth Rupert *physicist*
White, Gilbert F. (Gilbert Fowler White) *geographer, educator*
Wieman, Carl E. *physics professor*
Williams, James Franklin, II, *dean, librarian*
Wilson, M. Roy *academic administrator, medical educator*
Wittemyer, John *lawyer*
Wolfe, Lynn Robert *art educator*
Wolzien, Charles Frederick *dean, music educator, musician*
Wood, William Barry III *biologist, educator*
Yee, Sienho *law educator*
Zable, Jack Louis *mechanical engineer, educator*

## Breckenridge
Ehrhorn, Richard William *electronics executive*

## Brighton
Bacon, Melvin Leon *secondary school educator*
Rinkenberger, Richard Krug *physical scientist, geologist, consultant*
Wagner, Samuel Albin Mar *recording industry executive, educator*

## Broomfield
Baker, Charles E. *lawyer*
Crowe, James Quell (Jim Crowe) *communications executive*
Drouillard, Thomas F., II, *aerospace engineer*
Flanders, Eleanor Carlson *community volunteer*
Gill, Michael Gerard *music educator*
Hoover, R. David *packaging company executive*
O'Hara, Kevin J. *information technology executive*
Patel, Sunit *telecommunications industry executive*
Potter, James Michael *archaeologist, consultant*
Scott, Gregory Kellam *former state supreme court justice, lawyer*
Seabrook, Raymond J. *corporate financial executive*
Stacks, Karen Beth *music educator*
Stortz, Thomas C. *lawyer, communications executive*
Williams, John James, Jr. *architect*

## Calhan
Henderson, Freda LaVerne *elementary school educator*

## Canon City
Cochran, Susan Mills *research librarian*

## Carbondale
Cowgill, Ursula Moser *biologist, educator, environmental consultant*

## Castle Rock
Corboy, James McNally *investment banker*
Sjostrom, Joan Sevier *retired travel company executive*

## Centennial
Bryan, A(lonzo) J(ay) *retired service club official*
Buxton, Zane Kelly *pastor*
Chandramouli, Srinivasan (Chandra Chandramouli) *management and systems consultant*
Councell, Randall Eugene *protective services official*
Frame, Roger Everett *mental health counselor*
Galaznik, Judith Ann *elementary school educator*
Goughnour, Roy Robert *civil engineer, educator*
Grant, Paul *chemical engineer, real estate broker, lawyer*
Heath, Jayne Marie *music educator*
Miller, Cheryl Lynn *former paralegal, artist, art educator*
Milliken, Douglas Gordon *financial consultant, municipal official*
Milliken, John Gordon *research economist*
Owens, Marvin Franklin, Jr. *oil industry executive, director*
Ulevich, Neal Hirsh *photojournalist*

## Cherry Hills Village
Conroy, Mary Elizabeth *history professor*
Stapleton, Katharine Hall (Katie Stapleton) *commentator, writer*
Van Loucks, Mark Louis *venture capitalist, financial planner*

## Clifton
Konola, Claudette June *finance company executive, consultant*

## Colorado City
Stelle, Robert E. *physician, retired educator*

## Colorado Springs
Adams, Bernard Schroder *retired college president*
Adams, Deborah Rowland *lawyer*
Adnet, Jacques Jim Pierre *astronautical and electrical engineer, consultant*
Anderson, Paul Nathaniel *oncologist, educator*
Ansorge, Iona Marie *musician, educator, real estate agent*
Ashcraft, Vernon Arthur *music educator*
Barber, Michael J. *cardiologist, educator*
Bartalo, Theresa Marie *elementary school educator*
Beard, Amanda *swimmer, Olympic athlete*
Bobek, Nicole *professional figure skater*
Bondurant, David William *marketing professional*

Bowen, Clotilde Marion Dent *retired military officer, psychiatrist*
Bramschreiber, Terry Lee *science educator*
Brooks, Glenn Ellis *political science professor, educational association administrator*
Budington, William Stone *retired librarian*
Burdo, Amy *elementary school educator*
Bybee, Rodger Wayne *science administrator*
Cameron, Paul Drummond *health facility administrator*
Cash, Swin (Swintayla Marie Cash) *professional basketball player*
Celeste, Richard F. *academic administrator, retired ambassador, retired governor*
Cheek, Joey *Olympic athlete*
Christensen, C. Lewis *real estate developer*
Clay, Bryan Ezra *Olympic track and field athlete*
Coker, Carolyn Ann *music educator*
Coppock, Richard Miles *retired not-for-profit administrator*
Corry, Charles Elmo *geophysicist, not-for-profit developer*
Coughlin, Natalie *Olympic athlete*
Cramer, Owen Carver *classics educator, department chairman*
Crocker, Ian *Olympic athlete*
Dassanowsky, Robert von *language educator, film producer, educator, writer*
Driscoll, David Lee *chiropractor*
Driscoll, Lori *neuroscientist, educator*
Elias, John *lab administrator*
Fagin, Barry Steven *computer science educator, writer*
Farrer, Claire Anne Rafferty *anthropologist, educator*
Fielden, C. Franklin III *early childhood education consultant*
Gardner, Rulon E. *Olympic athlete*
Gatlin, Justin *Olympic track and field athlete*
Gibson, John Robert *software engineer*
Gifford, Marilyn Joyce *emergency physician, consultant*
Goehring, Kenneth *artist*
Granato, Catherine (Cammi Granato) *Olympic athlete*
Greene, Edith Leslie *legal consultant, psychology educator*
Haas, Julian L. *researcher, educator*
Hall, Gary, Jr. *Olympic athlete*
Hamilton, Tyler *professional cyclist, Olympic athlete*
Hamm, Morgan *Olympic athlete*
Hawley, Nanci Elizabeth *professional society administrator*
Hayes, Joanna *Olympic track and field athlete*
Heilman, John Edward *engineering consultant*
Herron, Sherry Shelton *biology professor*
Hinkle, Betty Ruth *retired academic administrator*
Hughes, Sarah *figure skater*
Johnson, Daniel Kent Neil *economist, educator*
Johnson, Henry Fred *clergy*
Killian, George Ernest *retired educational association administrator*
Krayzelburg, Lenny *Olympic athlete*
Kubida, William Joseph *lawyer*
Kupets, Courtney *Olympic athlete*
Kwan, Michelle Wing *professional figure skater*
Lamont, Mary *nurse*
LeMieux, Linda Dailey *museum director*
Ligety, Ted *Olympic athlete*
Loux, Gordon Dale *philanthropic consultant*
May, Misty *Olympic athlete*
McCool, Courtney *Olympic athlete*
McCready, Guy Michael *lawyer*
McDonough, Ann Patrice *ice skater*
Miller, Zoya Dickins *civic worker, consultant*
Morris, Steven Lynn *engineering consultant, retired military officer*
Nikodinov, Angela *professional figure skater, Olympic athlete*
Noyes, Richard Hall *bookseller*
Ogrean, David William *sports association executive*
Pappas, Tom *Olympic track and field athlete*
Patterson, Carly *Olympic athlete*
Payne, Billy (William Porter Payne) *real estate lawyer, sports association executive*
Phelps, Michael *Olympic athlete*
Quann, Megan *Olympic athlete*
Randall, Jessy *curator, writer*
Rangaswamy, Kulumani M. *mathematician, educator*
Riley, Ruth Ellen *professional basketball player*
Rivera, Lionel *mayor*
Sargent, Walter Harriman, II, *lawyer*
Saviano, Jeffrey D. *criminologist, consultant*
Schultz, Richard Dale *national athletic organization executive*
Schulzki, Anton G. *history educator*
Scott, Carla Anne *music educator, musician*
Shockley-Zalabak, Pamela Sue *academic administrator*
Siddoway, Christine Helen Smith *geology educator*
Simmons, George Finlay *retired mathematics professor*
Sinclair, William Donald *state legislator, retired church official*
Skora, Wayne Philip *retired air force officer*
Stahl, Philip Anthony *physicist, educator*
Standing Bear, Zug Guelgeres Galafach *criminologist, educator, forensic specialist*
Stavig, Mark Luther *language educator*
Strickland, Sylvia Raye *social worker*
Sturdevant, Katherine Scott *historian, educator*
Swanson, Victoria Clare Heldman *lawyer*
Swihart, James W., Jr. *diplomat*
Teter, Hannah *Olympic athlete*
Torres, Dara *Olympic athlete*
Tucker, Frank Hammond *history professor*
Tueting, Sarah *professional hockey player*
Vandeputte, Dixie Dianne *psychologist, educator*
Van Ness, Lottye Gray *writer, genealogist*
Walsh, Kerri Lee *Olympic athlete*
Wariner, Jeremy *Olympic track and field athlete*
Watts, Oliver Edward *engineering company executive*
West, Ralph Leland *veterinarian*
Yaney, George *retired history professor*
Yanney, Patrick Steven *human resources specialist*
Zapel, Arthur Lewis *book publishing executive*

Zhou, Xiaobo *computer scientist, educator*
Ziemer, Rodger Edmund *electrical engineering educator, consultant*

## Columbine Valley
Gagin, Lawrence Vincent *ceramics engineer, consultant*

## Commerce City
Colon, Alan Brian *protective services official, federal agency administrator*

## Conifer
Boese, Michelle Lynne *accountant, consultant*

## Cortez
Kristin, Karen *artist*
Skinner, Eulalia Ardith *retired secondary school educator*

## Crawford
Cocker, Joe *popular musician*

## Crestone
Thompson, William Irwin *writer, educator*

## Delta
Lowell, Lauretta Jane *craftsman, poet*

## Denver
Abo, Ronald Kent *freelance/self-employed architect*
Adelman, Jonathan Reuben *political science professor*
Adkins, Jeanne M. *state agency administrator*
Adler, Charles Spencer *psychiatrist*
Agostini, Juan C. *surgeon*
Albino, Judith Elaine Newsom *university president*
Alvarado, Linda G. *construction executive*
Anderson, Donald H. *energy executive*
Anderson, John David *architect*
Anderson, Norma V. *retired state legislator*
Anthony, Carmelo F. *professional basketball player*
Apodaca, Bob *professional baseball coach*
Aro, Edwin Packard *lawyer*
Ashton, Rick James *retired librarian*
Atkins, Dale Morrell *retired physician*
Austin, H(arry) Gregory *lawyer*
Avi, (Avi Wortis) *author*
Axelrod, Evan M. *psychologist, educator*
Babayev, Djangir Ali Ikram *physicist, researcher*
Bader, Gerald Louis, Jr. *lawyer*
Baer, Richard N. (Rich Baer) *lawyer*
Bain, Donald Knight *lawyer*
Balboa, Marcelo *professional soccer player*
Banks, Britt D. *lawyer*
Barbour, Alton Bradford *retired human communication studies educator*
Barr, Lois Faye *public relations executive, freelance/self-employed writer*
Barry, Henry Ford *chemicals executive*
Belitz, Paul Edward *lawyer*
Bell, Stephen D. *lawyer*
Bender, Michael Lee *state supreme court justice*
Benson, Robert Eugene *lawyer*
Benton, Auburn Edgar *lawyer*
Berry, Robert Worth *lawyer, retired law educator, retired military officer*
Bess, Charles Wayne *lawyer*
Bialasiewicz, Jan Tadeusz *electrical engineering educator*
Black, Gary D. *investment company executive*
Blair, Andrew Lane, Jr. *lawyer, educator*
Blatter, Frank Edward *travel company executive*
Blitz, Stephen M. *lawyer*
Blum, Gary Bernard *lawyer*
Bogdan, Gregory Michael *toxicologist, researcher*
Bosworth, Bruce Leighton *school administrator, educator, consultant*
Boyer, William Joseph *food products executive*
Bradburn, James Henry *architectural firm executive*
Brantigan, Charles Otto *surgeon*
Breeskin, Michael Wayne *lawyer*
Brega, Charles Franklin *lawyer, director*
Brega, Kerry Elizabeth *physician, researcher*
Bricker Janzen, Donna Lee *music educator*
Briggs, Steve Clement *lawyer*
Brom, Libor *journalist, educator*
Brown, Keith Lapham *retired ambassador*
Brownson, Jacques Calmon *architect*
Buckstein, Caryl Sue *writer*
Bufe, Charles Glenn *geophysicist, researcher*
Burrell, Calvin Archie *minister*
Burrows, Bertha Jean *retired academic administrator*
Burshtan, John Willis *television producer*
Butler, David *lawyer*
Bye, James Edward *lawyer*
Byyny, Richard Lee *academic administrator*
Cain, Douglas Mylchreest *lawyer*
Caine, Jonathan Saul *geologist, researcher*
Camby, Marcus D. *professional basketball player*
Campbell, Leonard M. *lawyer*
Campbell, William J. *lawyer*
Carbone, Rocco William III *elementary school educator*
Carlson, Erik B. *lawyer*
Carrigan, Jim R. *arbitrator, mediator, retired judge*
Case, Paul Watson, Jr. *communications executive*
Case, Steve (Stephen M. Case) *healthcare investment company executive, former media and entertainment company executive*
Cashman, Michael Richard *small business owner*
Ceci, Jesse Arthur *violinist*
Chamberlain, Adrian Ramond *transportation engineer*
Chaput, Charles J. *archbishop*
Charlip, Ralph Blair *military officer, health facility administrator*
Chavez, Jeanette *editor*
Cheris, Elaine Gayle Ingram *business owner*
Cheroutes, Michael Louis *lawyer*
Childears, Linda *foundation administrator*
Chu, Roderick Gong-Wah *academic administrator*
Clark, Gary R. *newspaper editor*
Clark, Suzanne *accountant*
Clinch, Nicholas Bayard III *small business owner*
Coan, Patricia A. *judge*
Coats, Nathan B. *state supreme court justice*

**Eagle**
Lammers, Monica *elementary school educator*

**Edwards**
Chambers, Joan Louise *retired librarian, retired dean*

**Eldorado Springs**
Lovins, L. Hunter *public policy institute executive, consultant, educator*

**Elizabeth**
Brownson, Sue McPherson *music educator*
Travis, Mitchell G. *secondary school educator*

**Englewood**
Ahearn, Joseph August *military officer, civil engineer*
Bailey, Champ *professional football player*
Burnett, George A. *directory publishing executive*
Campbell, Michael L. *recreational facility executive*
Chavez, L.G., Jr., (Lloyd G. Chavez Jr.) *automotive executive*
Chavez, Lloyd G. *automotive executive*
Corson, Jeff Gordon *history educator*
DeMuth, Alan Cornelius *lawyer*
DeMuth, Laurence Wheeler, Jr. *lawyer, utilities executive*
Erickson, William Hurt *retired state supreme court justice*
Fote, Charles T. *information technology company executive*
Fries, Michael T. *communications executive*
Gertz, David Lee *homebuilding company executive*
Gilboy, Margaretta *artist, educator*
Gloss, Lawrence Robert *fundraising executive*
Guggenheim-Boucard, Alan Andre Albert Paul Edouard *international consultant*
Hakim, Joy *writer*
Haliw, Jerome Michael *civil engineer*
Han, Bernard L. *communications executive*
Hardy, Wayne Russell *insurance and investment broker*
Karstaedt, Arthur R. III *lawyer*
Keesling, Ruth Morris *foundation administrator*
Knize, David Maurice *plastic surgeon*
Kubik, Timothy Robert White *director, history educator*
Lessey, Samuel Kenric, Jr. *foundation administrator*
Lidstone, Herrick Kenley, Jr. *lawyer*
Lynch, John Terrence *professional football player*
Macdonald, Patricia Lynn *gifted and talented educator*
Maffei, Gregory B. *media company executive, former computer software company executive*
Malone, James Richard *manufacturing executive*
Malone, John C. *media company executive*
Manley, Richard Walter *insurance company executive*
McCrary, Brian Fountain *physician*
McGraw, Jack Wilson *federal agency administrator*
Miles, Amy E. *recreational facility executive*
Morton, John Douglas *retail executive*
Moskowitz, David K. *lawyer*
Neiser, Brent Allen *foundation executive, public information educator, finance educator*
Olcer, Nuri Yelman *engineering researcher, educator*
Orsini, Rosemary *lawyer*
Peterson, Ralph Randall *engineering executive*
Plummer, Jason Steven (Jake Plummer) *professional football player*
Rheney, Susan O. *paper company executive*
Rosser, Edwin Michael *mortgage company executive*
Schleyer, William T. *cable company executive*
Shanahan, Mike *professional football coach*
Shields, Marlene Sue *elementary school educator*
Smith, Mark Christopher *lawyer*
Smith, Rod *professional football player*
Spencer, Margaret Gilliam *lawyer*
Steinhauser, John William *retired lawyer*
Tanabe, Charles Y. *lawyer*
Touff, Michael *lawyer*
Vogel, Carl E. *communications executive*
Woodward, John Simpson, Jr. *orthopedic surgeon*
Zoeller, Mark L. *lawyer, printing company executive*

**Erie**
Alpers, John Hardesty, Jr. *financial planner, retired military officer*
Nichols, Janet Hildreth *elementary school educator, childbirth and parenting educator*
Plehaty, Phyllis Juliette *retired curator*

**Estes Park**
Calden, Diane Dorothy *reading educator*
Ojalvo, Morris *civil engineer, educator*
Piper, Mark Harry *retired banker*
Webb, Richard C. *engineering company executive*

**Evergreen**
Dobbs, Gregory Allan *journalist*
Evans, David Lynn *management consultant*
Haun, John Daniel *petroleum geologist, educator*
Heyl, Allen Van *geologist*
Jackson, William Richard *entrepreneur*

**Fort Collins**
Abt, Steven R. *civil engineer, educator*
Bai, Ying *research scientist*
Baldwin, Lionel Vernon *retired university president*
Bamburg, James Robert *biochemistry professor*
Barbezat, Eugene LaVar *computer engineer, retired military officer*
Bennett, Thomas LeRoy, Jr. *clinical neuropsychology educator*
Bikos, Daniel Ernest *meteorologist*
Carlson, Alan Douglas *lawyer*
Cermak, Jack Edward *engineer, educator*
Cheng, William Y. Y. *meteorologist, educator*
Chong, Edwin K. P. *engineering educator*
Chorpenning, H. R. III *minister*
Colbert, Debora A. *director*
Eddy, Gladys Louise *educational administrator*

**Ewing**, Jack Robert *accountant*
Fixman, Marshall *chemist, educator*
Follett, Ronald Francis *soil scientist*
Gandy, H. Conway *retired judge, state official*
Grandin, Temple *industrial designer, science educator*
Guo, Yuanqing *research scientist*
Harper, Judson Morse *retired university administrator, consultant, educator*
Hobbs, N. Thompson *science administrator*
Hughes, Harrison G. *horticulture educator*
Jensen, Margaret *real estate broker*
Johnson, Donald Edward, Jr. *lawyer*
Johnson, Robert Britten *geology educator*
Kang, Soo K. *social sciences educator*
Keim, Wayne Franklin *retired agronomist, geneticist*
Kinnison, Robert Wheelock *retired accountant*
Knaff, John Albert *research engineer*
Kogan, Lori R. *psychology professor, consultant*
Konor, Celal Sukru *meteorologist, researcher*
Kraus, David (Dirk) Bruce *musician, educator*
Lokupitiya, Ravindra Shanthakumar *research scientist*
Lumb, William Valjean *veterinarian*
Maher, Thomas George *academic administrator, producer, media educator*
Martin, Denise Ann *safety and environmental health manger*
Matthies, Frederick John *civil and environmental engineer*
Mc Clellan, William Monson *retired library director*
McComb, David Glendinning *history professor*
Meyers, Albert Irving *chemistry professor*
Mielke, Paul William, Jr. *statistician, consultant*
Mortvedt, John Jacob *soil scientist, researcher*
Murphy, Dennis Joseph *lawyer*
Neil, Stuart *management consultant, real estate broker*
Patton, Carl Elliott *physicist, educator*
Peng, Junhua *molecular biologist*
Penley, Larry Edward *academic administrator, finance educator*
Peterson, Gary Andrew *agronomics researcher*
Phemister, Robert David *veterinary medical educator*
Pluth, Joseph, Jr. *music educator*
Rennick, John H. *psychiatrist, director*
Ricard, Virginia Belle *adult education educator*
Richardson, Everett Vern *hydraulic engineer, educator, administrator, consultant*
Roesner, Larry August *civil engineer*
Rogers, Garth Winfield *lawyer*
Rolston, Holmes III *theology studies educator, philosopher*
Sankaran, Mahesh *ecologist*
Savage, Eldon Paul *retired environmental health educator*
Schaffer, Robert (Bob Schaffer) *former congressman*
Schendel, Winfried George *insurance company executive*
Schwartz, Allen R. *lawyer*
Sedei Rodden, Pamela Jean *psychologist, director*
Seidel, George Elias, Jr. *zoology educator*
Seward, Nathan William *biologist, researcher*
She, Chiao-Yao *physics professor, researcher*
Simmons, Mark Pitkin *botanist, educator*
Suinn, Richard Michael *psychologist*
Terauds, Juris *retired science educator, research scientist*
Thiem, Jon Edgar *literature educator*
Thilmany, Dawn Denise *economist, educator*
Tremblay, William Andrew *language educator, writer*

**Fort Garland**
Boyer, Lester Leroy, Jr. *architecture educator, consultant*

**Fort Morgan**
Overton, Larry Dean *music educator, musician*

**Fountain**
Hazlett, David Lawrence *social studies educator*

**Fraser**
Shaw, Roger Walz *physicist, educator*

**Frederick**
Emlen, Warren Metz *retired computer company executive*

**Frisco**
Helmer, David Alan *lawyer*

**Georgetown**
Etcheson, Christopher Carlyle *public health service officer*
Stern, Mort(imer) P(hillip) *communications educator, editor, reporter, consultant*

**Glenwood Springs**
Jaffrey, Ira *educator*
Kelley, Robert Daryl *biology professor, mathematics professor*

**Golden**
Baron, Robert Charles *publishing executive*
Bettinghaus, Erwin Paul *research scientist*
Bickart, Theodore Albert *university president emeritus*
Coors, Jeffrey H. *technology manufacturing executive*
Coors, Peter Hanson *brewery company executive*
DeSanto, John A. *physicist, educator, mathematics educator*
Dickinson, Carol Rittgers *art historian, writer*
Eckley, Wilton Earl, Jr. *humanities educator*
Eiberger, Carl Frederick *lawyer*
Hamilton, Warren Bell *geologist, researcher, geophysicist, educator*
Keyser, Matt *transportation engineer*
Kiely, W. Leo III *brewery company executive*
Kopel, David Benjamin *lawyer*
Krauss, George *metallurgist*
Lee, SeHee *energy scientist*
Lufkin, John L. *geologist, educator, publishing executive*

Matthews, Thomas Michael *former energy company executive*
Metzger, Wyatt K. *physicist*
Myers, Daryl Ronald *engineer*
Olson, Marian Katherine *management consultant*
Pegis, Anton George *retired language educator*
Petrick, Alfred, Jr. *economist, educator*
Phillipson, Donald E. *lawyer*
Pollack, Gerald Leslie *physicist, researcher*
Rodgers, Frederic Barker *judge*
Shea, Dion Warren Joseph *academic administrator, fundraiser*
Sloan, Earle Dendy, Jr. *chemical engineering educator*
Spurck, Richard Francis *materials engineer*
Taylor, P. Craig *physics professor*
Trefny, John Ulric *college president*
Truly, Richard H. *academic administrator, retired pilot, retired federal agency administrator*
von Roedern, Bolko Graf *energy executive, researcher*
Wang, Dong *chemist, researcher*
Weimer, Robert Jay *geology educator, energy consultant, civic leader*
Zhong, Dalong *materials scientist, consultant*

**Granby**
Holzworth, Robert Haviland *retired physician*
Johnson, William Potter *publishing executive, director*

**Grand Junction**
Agapito, J. F. T. *mining engineer, mineralogist*
Armstrong, Alden Arthur *retired elementary school educator, photographer, writer*
Bacon, Phillip *geographer, author, consultant*
Bishop, Tilman Malcolm *retired state legislator*
Bragdon, Lynn Lyon *library administrator*
Burdick, Margaret Seale (Marge Burdick) *interior designer*
Freeman, Neil *accounting executive, computer consulting firm executive*
Hoagland, Christina Gail *occupational therapist, industrial drafter*
Janson, Richard Anthony *plastic surgeon*
Michels, Ruth Yvonne *retired cytologist*
Morton, Louis George *retired social sciences educator*
Phillips, Ruth Amelia *retired music educator, artist*
Rutz, Richard Frederick *physicist, researcher*
Scott, Pamela Sue *middle school educator*
Skogen, Haven Sherman *investment company executive*

**Greeley**
Bond, Richard Randrol *foundation administrator, legislator*
Carrico, Stephen J. *construction company executive*
Copley, R. Evan *music educator*
Cordell, Larry Kenneth (L. Kenny) *agricultural products executive*
Downey, Matthew T. *history professor, writer*
Duff, William Leroy, Jr. *retired dean, finance educator*
Jackson, Patricia Anne *primary school educator, consultant*
James, Philip J. *agricultural products executive*
Jaouen, Richard Matthie *plastic surgeon*
McDaniel, Bruce Alan *economist, educator*
Miccio, Elizabeth Petrick *artist*
Miller, Diane Wilmarth *retired human resources director*
Miller, Nathaniel Gregory *mathematics professor*
Morgensen, Jerry Lynn *construction company executive*
Murray, Robert Patrick *music educator, musician*
Schrenk, Gary Dale *foundation executive*
Smith, Jack Lee *bank executive*
Szczyrba, Igor Nicholas *mathematical physicist, consultant*
van Gorp, Gary Wayne *clergyman*
Willis, Connie (Constance E. Willis) *writer*
Wilson, Sharon Rose *literature educator, researcher*
Womble, Ken *theater educator, film director, writer, actor*
Worley, Lloyd Douglas *language educator*
Yagami, Kazuo *historian*

**Greenwood Village**
Appel, Joel *household cleaner manufacturing executive*
Arvizu, Dan Eliab *mechanical engineer*
Aspinwall, David Charles *lawyer, insurance company executive*
Benson, Robert Craig III *business consultant*
Chico, Beverly Ann *history professor, humanities educator*
Davidson, John Robert (Jay) *bank executive*
Dewald, Bruce Wayne *lawyer*
Duques, Ric (Henry C. Duques) *information technology company executive*
Dymond, Lewis Wandell *lawyer, educator*
Evans, Nola Lea *healthcare specialist*
Gold, Christina A. *data processing company executive*
Grainger, John R. *medical association administrator*
Lesh-Laurie, Georgia Elizabeth *academic administrator, biology professor, medical researcher*
Liniger, Dave *real estate company executive*
Poe, Robert Alan *lawyer*
Ramsey, John Arthur *lawyer*
Rothrock, Lindsey Nichole *lawyer*
Sims, Douglas D. *bank executive*
Walter, Heath Allen *music educator*
Whealy, Michael Thomas *data processing executive, lawyer*
Wittman, Vanessa Ames *communications executive*

**Gunnison**
Gelwicks, James M. *retired communications educator*
Javernick, Amy Sue *special education educator*

**Henderson**
Reibold, Dorothy Ann *accountant, researcher*

**Highlands Ranch**
Brierley, Corale L. *geological and biomining engineer*
Brierley, James Alan *biohydrometallurgy consultant*
Bublitz, Deborah Keirstead *pediatrician*
Eberhard, Jacob John *software engineer*
Fiess, Stephen Charles Edward *musician, music educator*
Harris, Douglas Clay *retired newspaper executive*
Hendrick, Hal Wilmans *human factors educator*
Judson, Philip Livingston *retired lawyer, consultant*
Lampard, Greg Edward *computer scientist, educator*
Snell, Michael Steven *music educator*

**Howard**
Hopkins, Donald J. *retired lawyer*

**Jefferson**
Maatsch, Deborah Joan *manufacturing executive*

**Joes**
Crawford, Dorothy Hill *retired secondary school educator*

**Johnstown**
French, Irene Wagdy *special education educator*

**La Jara**
Portnoy, Darin Arthur *medical association administrator*

**La Veta**
Emsden, Katharine Nicely *retired history educator, writer*
Schneider, Kenny *artist, educator*
Zehring, Peggy Johnson *artist*

**Lafayette**
Mehl, Albert L. *pediatrician, poet, composer*
Short, Ray Everett *minister, sociologist, educator, writer*
Thornbury, John Rousseau *radiologist, physician*

**Lake George**
Norman, John Barstow, Jr. *graphics designer, educator*

**Lakewood**
Axley, Hartman *retired financial planner, underwriter*
Fugate, Ivan Dee *banker*
Guyton, Samuel Percy *retired lawyer*
Hadley, Marlin LeRoy *financial planner, consultant*
Hansen, Richard Olaf *geophysicist, educator, director*
Heath, Gary Brian *manufacturing executive, engineer*
Hickman, Ruth Virginia *Bible educator*
Humphrey, Charles Edward, Jr. *lawyer*
Isely, Henry Philip *association executive, integrative engineer, writer, educator*
Joy, Carla Marie *history educator*
Knott, William Alan *library director*
Kulkarni, Kishore Ganesh *economics professor, consultant*
Martinen, John A. *travel company executive*
McBride, Guy Thornton, Jr. *college president emeritus*
McElwee, Dennis John *lawyer, former pharmaceutical company executive*
Nelson, Deborah Jane *family and consumer science educator*
Nichols, Vicki Anne *financial consultant, librarian*
Peters, Julie Anne *writer*
Quinn, John Michael *physicist, geophysicist*
Reed, Joan-Marie *special education executive*
Samal, Abani Ranjan *geologist*
Stromberg, Patricia Roberts *retired school librarian*
Woodruff, Kathryn Elaine *literature and language professor*

**Lamar**
Banker, Carol Anne *elementary school educator*
Green, Eric Roger *librarian*

**Laporte**
Riba, Shirley *artist*

**Leadville**
Watson, Jack Crozier *retired state supreme court justice*

**Limon**
Richards, Ann Adair *psychologist*

**Littleton**
Alykova, Valentina *musician, music educator*
Battilega, John A. *research and development company executive*
Bennett, Janice Lynn *publisher, educator*
Bush, Stanley Giltner *secondary school educator*
Clark, Julie *consumer products company executive*
Day, Susan Marie *music educator, composer*
Dugan, Michael T. *communications executive*
Ergen, Charles W. *communications professional*
Forstot, Stephan Lance *ophthalmologist*
Fryt, Monte Stanislaus *petroleum company executive, speaker, advisor*
Grant, Newell M. *real estate investment manager*
Greenberg, Elinor Miller *director, consultant*
Groothuis, Douglas Richard *minister, educator*
Grounds, Vernon Carl *seminary administrator*
Hill, Thane Clayton *science educator*
Hopping, William Russell *hospitality industry consultant, appraiser*
Johansson, Alicia Barbara *musician*
Keats, Donald Howard *composer, educator*
Keogh, Heidi Helen Dake *advocate*
Kleinknecht, Kenneth Samuel *retired air transportation executive*
Kullas, Albert John *management consultant, systems engineer*
Lode, Trygve Tennyson *entrepreneur, actor*
Marion, John Martin *instructional technology educator*

McDonnell, Michael R. *communications executive*
Meyer, Milton Edward, Jr. *retired lawyer, artist*
Michaels Hollander, Erica *law educator*
Paull, Richard Allen *geologist, educator*
Reinker, Mary Stefanich *musician, music educator*
Shepherd, Donna Lou *interior designer*
Sutton, Robert Edward *investment company executive*
Tucker, James Raymond *primary school educator*
Udevitz, Norman *publishing executive*
Vail, Charles Daniel *veterinarian, consultant*
Volpe, Richard Gerard *insurance accounts executive, consultant*
Wittbrodt, Edwin Stanley *financial planner, consultant, retired military officer*
Wolfer, Dale *retired music educator*
Zwilling, Mark C. *music director*

**Lone Tree**
Spelts, Richard John *lawyer*
Spisak, John Francis *management consultant executive*
Washington, Reginald Louis *pediatric cardiologist*

**Longmont**
Breuer, Werner Alfred *retired plastics company executive*
Dierks, Richard Ernest *veterinarian, academic administrator*
Doyle, James Thomas *electronics engineer*
Jones, Beverly Ann Miller *nursing administrator, retired patient services administrator*
Newman, Dean Gordon *business consultant*
Sandler, Thomas R. *accountant, director*
Watkins, John Goodrich *psychologist, educator*
Zable, Barbara A. *manufacturing executive*

**Louisville**
Adams, Eula L. *data storage executive*
Brault, James William *physicist*
Kocol, Robert S. *information technology executive*
Maddock, Jerome Torrence *library and information scientist*
Marsh, Donald Pete *chaplain*
Martin, Patrick J. *technology company executive*
Roellig, Mark D. *lawyer*
Schonbrun, Michael K. *senior housing developer and operator*
Shively, Merrick Lee *pharmaceutical scientist, consultant*
Stahler, Joyce Ann *history educator*

**Loveland**
Ahmann, John Stanley *retired psychologist*
Balsiger, David Wayne *television director, writer, television producer, television director, researcher*
Bierbaum, J. Armin *petroleum company executive, consultant*
Bierbaum, Janith Marie *artist*
Clark, Roger Earl *lawyer*
DiFalco, John Patrick *lawyer, arbitrator*
Fleischer, Gerald Albert *industrial engineer, educator*
Kaufman, William George *lawyer*
King, Joan Caluda *medical educator, neuroscientist*
Kreutz, Robert A. *music educator, musician*
Lundeen, George Wayne *artist*
Porfilio, John Carbone *federal judge*
Rodman, Alpine C. *arts and crafts company executive, photographer*
Rodman, Sue A. *wholesale company executive, artist, writer*
Schilling, Arleen Marie *social studies educator*
Walker, Laurie Shannon *psychologist, counselor*
Weresh, Thelma Faye *sculptor*

**Lyons**
Spring, Kathleen *writer*

**Mancos**
Brown, Joy Alice *social services administrator*
Whitehead, Linda Sue *English, American history, and special education educator*

**Manitou Springs**
Hopwood, Brian Keith *music educator, musician*

**Masonville**
Dubrovin, Vivian *writer*

**Meeker**
Omer, Robert Wendell *hospital administrator*

**Monte Vista**
Rausch, Paul Matthew *financial executive*

**Montrose**
Boice, Judith Lynette *physician, writer, educator*
Davis, Christopher Thomas *music educator, musician*
Fritze, Sheila Kay *librarian*
Gates, Viola R. *writer*
Kontny, Vincent L. *rancher, retired engineering executive*
Radovich, Donald *painter, illustrator, retired art educator*

**Monument**
Boggs, Steven Eugene *real estate broker, lawyer*
Breckner, William John, Jr. *retired military officer*
De Francesco, John Blaze, Jr. *public relations consultant, writer*
Hutchison, Jon McKee *music educator*
Karasa, Norman Lukas *home builder, developer, geologist*
McIver, Deborah Kay *tax specialist, entrepreneur, small business owner*

**Morrison**
Bowen, Peter Geoffrey *arbitrator, finance educator*
Myers, Harry J., Jr. *retired publisher*

**Nederland**
Lutz, Frank Wenzel *education administration educator*
Morrison, K. Jaydene *education counseling firm executive*

Thomas, Daniel Foley *retired diversified financial services company executive*

**Niwot**
Buss, Kathleen E. *music educator*
Farrington, Helen Agnes *personnel director*

**Northglenn**
Hemlock, Roberta Leigh *veterinary technician*
Kappler, Karen L. *music educator, musician*

**Norwood**
Brantingham, Andrya J. *special education educator*
Reagan, Harry Edwin III *lawyer*

**Nucla**
Sandefur, Denice Lee *science educator*

**Ordway**
Fosdick, Jacque Janelle *literature and language educator, theater educator*

**Pagosa Springs**
Kelly, Reid Browne *lawyer*

**Palisade**
Barnewall, Marilyn MacGruder *retired banker*
Fay, Abbott Eastman *history professor*

**Paonia**
Noonan, Robert Harry *art and music educator*

**Parker**
Greenberg, Morton Paul *lawyer, consultant, life settlement broker*

**Peterson Afb**
Keating, Timothy J. *career military officer*
Lord, Lance W. *career military officer*

**Peyton**
Dunn, Doris *retired critical care nurse, artist, rancher*

**Pine**
Jones, David Milton *economist, educator*

**Pritchett**
Hall, Carol Ann *music educator*

**Pueblo**
Brown, Courtney Allison *composer, writer, singer*
Deasy, Irene M. *retired protective services official*
Farley, Thomas T. *lawyer*
Genova, Wayne D. *music educator, consultant*
Maio, Heather Allen *environmental services administrator*
Mara, Patrick Scott *mathematics educator*
O'Callaghan, R.J. Patrick *lawyer*
Occhiato, Michael Anthony *municipal official*
Puls, Elaine Allison *retired librarian*
Ramirez, Monica E. *education educator, consultant*
Shomaker, Gordon Alexander, Jr. *poet, writer*
Sisson, Ray L. *retired dean, author*
Werner, Betty Ann *academic administrator*

**Pueblo West**
Kogovsek, Daniel Charles *lawyer*

**Ridgway**
Lathrop, Kaye Don *nuclear scientist, educator*

**Rocky Ford**
Mendenhall, Harry Barton *lawyer*

**Salida**
Strawn, Melvin Nicholas *artist, educator*

**Sedalia**
Cooley, Andrew Lyman *computer company executive*

**Silverthorne**
Riley, Mary Jane *computer scientist*

**Snowmass Village**
DiBiaggio, John A. *university president*
Strand, Curt Robert *hotel executive*

**Springfield**
Wessler, Melvin Dean *farmer, rancher*

**Steamboat Springs**
Hanlon, Dean William *physical therapist*
Potter, William Bartlett *diversified financial services company executive*

**Superior**
Forshee, Gladys Marie *insurance agent, writer*
Middlebrooks, Eddie Joe *environmental engineer*

**Thornton**
Parker, Alice Jeanne *music educator*

**Towner**
Fees, Ruth Anna *secondary school educator*

**Twin Lakes**
Homan, Ralph William *finance company executive*

**U S A F Academy**
Born, Dana H. *dean, career military officer*
DeBerry, Fisher *college football coach*
Galema, Joseph M. *music director*
Mertz, Bryan Paul *science educator*
Musselman, Randall L. *electrical engineer, educator*
Post, Martiqua Leigh *engineering educator*
Regni, John F. *academic administrator, career military officer*
Veverka, Donald Victor *science educator*
Weida, Johnny A. *career military officer*
Westermann, Edward Burton *military officer, analyst, educator*

**Vail**
Bevan, William Arnold, Jr. *emergency physician*

Hoover, Gary Lynn *banker*
Kelton, Arthur Marvin, Jr. *real estate developer*
McGee, Michael Jay *protective services official, educator*
Vosbeck, Robert Randall *architect*

**Walden**
Ary, Bonnita Ellen *registrar, federal official*

**Walsh**
Lancaster, Robert Carl *secondary school educator*

**Wellington**
Grant, Lewis O. *agricultural products executive, meteorology educator*

**Westminster**
Eaves, Stephen Douglas *high school and vocational administrator, educator, consultant*
Kopperud, Marilyn Sue *music educator*
Lingle, JoLynn Fleishman *writer, educator*
Michael, Hart E. *pharmaceutical executive*
Reynolds-Sakowski, Dana Renee *science educator*
White, John David *composer, musician*

**Wheat Ridge**
Fleischaker, Gordon Henry, Jr. *pediatrician*
Gerlick, Helen J. *tax practitioner, accountant*
Morriss, Frank *writer, educator*
Ogsbury, James Stanley III *neurosurgeon, educator*
Scherich, Erwin Thomas *civil engineer, consultant*
Wilcox, Mary Marks *retired Christian education consultant, educator*

**Windsor**
Downey, Arthur Harold, Jr. *lawyer, mediator*
Mayer, Victor James *geologist, educator*
Schumacher, Tara *biology educator*

**Winter Park**
Groswold, Gerald F. *retired resort executive, lawyer*

**Wolcott**
Flacke, Joan Wareham *physician, anesthesiologist, educator*

**Woodland Park**
Cockrille, Stephen *art director, business owner*
Critchlow, Bryan Douglas *music educator*

**Woody Creek**
Jenkins, Robert Berryman *real estate developer*

**Yuma**
Hertneky, Randy Lee *optometrist*

## CONNECTICUT

**Ansonia**
Kerpa, Gary J. *computer science consultant*

**Avon**
Behrend, Donald Fraser *academic administrator, educator*
Freymann, John Gordon *physician, educator*
Griggs, Julie Hinds *foundation administrator, marriage and family therapist*
Hinz, Carl Frederick, Jr. *immunologist, educator*
Kling, Phradie (Phradie Kling Gold) *small business owner, educator*
Mazur, Edward John, Jr. *financial planner*
Odenheimer, Robert W. *health care services company executive*
Shulman, Steven J. *health services company executive*
Weiss, Robert Michael *dentist*
Wu, George Yung-hsing *medical educator, gastroenterologist*

**Beacon Falls**
Feige, Mary S *literature and language educator*
Vignola, Andrew Michael, Sr. *computer company executive*

**Bethany**
Barnes, Richard Barton *mechanical engineer, musician*
Niederman, James Corson *retired internist, educator*

**Bethel**
Kurfehs, Harold Charles *real estate executive*
Shepard, Jean Heck *retired publishing consultant*
Tesar, Jenny Elizabeth *freelance/self-employed writer, freelance/self-employed editor*
Tomasko, Edward A. *financial planner*

**Bloomfield**
Baccus, R. Eileen Turner *retired academic administrator*
Boltes, Carlos *musician, educator*
Coburn, Richard Joseph *electronics executive, electrical engineer*
Cornell, Robert Witherspoon *engineer, consultant*
Cronin, Daniel Anthony *emeritus archbishop*
De Maria, Anthony John *electrical engineer*
Kissa, Karl Martin *electrical engineer*
Mamlok, Walter Joseph *music educator, musician*
Messemer, Glenn Matthew *lawyer*
Santanella, Richard Charles, Jr. *music educator*
Shimelman, Susan Fromm *state agency administrator*
Thorpe, James *retired researcher*
Young, Albert Frederick Antonio *director*

**Bolton**
Banas, Conrad Martin *mechanical engineer, chief scientist*
Reyna, Magdalena Bessy *writer*

**Branford**
Chapman, Roger Stevens, Jr. *construction company executive*
Charlot, Joseph Leonce, Jr. *preventive medicine physician*
Gejdenson, Sam *former congressman*

Johnson, Eva Jo *educational consultant*
Resnick, Idrian Navarre *foundation administrator*
Sipprell, George Sidney *aerospace engineer, consultant*
Smith, Richard Emerson (Dick Smith) *make-up artist*
Tchernev, Velizar Tzvetanov *physician, research scientist*
Wegener, Peter Paul *engineering educator, writer*
Whitaker, Thomas Russell *English literature educator*

**Bridgeport**
Bowen, Patrick Harvey *lawyer, consultant*
Chih, Chung-Ying *physicist, consultant*
Eginton, Warren William *federal judge*
King, Sister Eleace *special education services professional*
Laccavole, Dennis Mark *lawyer*
Lanci, Janet Mead *academic administrator, educator*
Lobdell, David Hill *pathologist*
Lori, William E. *bishop*
Macdonald, Karen Crane *occupational therapist, geriatrics services professional*
Maloney, Maureen Murphy *social sciences educator*
Mcpherson, Craig A. *cardiologist, educator*
Nijensohn, Daniel Edgardo *neurosurgeon*
Pagano, Celeste Ann *social services coordinator*
Richard, Ellen *theater executive*
Semple, Cecil Snowdon *retired manufacturing executive*
Sheehan, Geoffrey *theater educator*
Simoneau, Cynthia Lambert *editor, educator*
Trefry, Robert J. *health facility administrator*
Wasmer, Pedro E. *technology leasing company executive*

**Bridgewater**
Crooke, Robert Andrew *media consultant, writer, educator*

**Bristol**
Barnes, Carlyle Fuller *manufacturing executive*
Barnes, Wallace *manufacturing executive*
Berman, Chris *sportscaster*
Bodenheimer, George *broadcast executive*
Brantley, Jeffrey Hoke *baseball analyst, retired professional baseball player*
Corso, Lee *former football coach, football analyst*
Driessen, Christine F. *broadcast executive*
Flutie, Doug (Douglas Richard Flutie) *retired professional football player*
Gammons, Peter *columnist, commentator*
Greenberg, Mike *sportscaster*
Gwynn, Anthony Keith (Tony Gwynn) *former professional baseball player*
Jaworski, Ron *sports analyst*
Kruk, John Martin *retired professional baseball player, sportscaster*
LaGanga, Donna Brandeis *dean*
Levy, Steve *sports anchor, studio host*
Mayne, Kenny *sports anchor*
Mielcarz, Sharon Marie *assistant principal*
Mortensen, Chris *sports analyst, reporter*
Olney, Robert Stanbury III *sportswriter and baseball analyst*
Paolantonio, Sal *sports correspondent*
Piniella, Louis Victor *professional baseball team manager*
Scott, Stuart *sports anchor*
Simmons, Bill *sportswriter*
Sutcliffe, Rick (Richard Lee Sutcliffe) *professional baseball player*
Theismann, Joseph Robert (Joe Theismann) *former professional football player, announcer*
Tirico, Mike *sportscaster*
Wynalda, Eric *professional soccer player*

**Broad Brook**
Kement, Isabella Viniconis *retired construction company executive*

**Brookfield**
Cohen, Mark Steven *dentist*
Gerstein, Mordicai *illustrator, writer*
Lock, Timothy G. *psychologist*
Stern, Michael Lawrence *psychologist, educator*

**Brooklyn**
McIlvane, Edward James *stained glass artist, educator*

**Canaan**
Thorne, Francis *composer*

**Canterbury**
Yaworski, James John III *elementary school educator*

**Canton**
Jordan, Evora Ruth *writer, researcher, publishing executive*
Richardson, Dana Roland *technology consultant*

**Canton Center**
Humphrey, Samuel Stockwell *town official, physicist*

**Centerbrook**
Grover, William Herbert *architect*
Harper, Robert Leslie *architect, educator*

**Chaplin**
Wood, Wendy Deborah *filmmaker*

**Cheshire**
Condon, Thomas Brian *retired hospital executive*
Keiser, David Wharton *pharmaceutical executive*
Rowland, Ralph Thomas *retired architect*
Tufte, Edward Rolf *statistician, educator*
Walter, Kenneth Gaines *library director*

**Chester**
Frost-Knappman, (Linda) Elizabeth *publishing executive, editor, writer*
Harwood, Eleanor Cash *retired librarian*
Hilsman, Roger *political scientist, educator*
Stark, Evelyn Brill *poet, musician*

## Clinton

Adler, Peggy Ann *writer, illustrator, consultant, protective services official*
Panayotov, Christo Angelov *research scientist, consultant*

## Colchester

Bartkowski, Kathleen Susan *musician*
Huzmezan, Mihai *aerospace engineer*
Latman, Joel *history educator*
Nikirk, Silva Susan *minister, writer, dancer*

## Colebrook

Burrows, John Edward *communications company executive*
McNeill, William Hardy *retired historian, writer*

## Collinsville

Whitney, Carol Marie *securities trader*

## Cos Cob

Halvorsen, Ole Andreas *financier*
Hauptman, Michael *broadcasting company executive*
Kane, Jay Brassler *banker*
Kane, Margaret Brassler *sculptor*
Leamy, Nancy M. *professional athletics coach*
Murphy, Robert Blair *management consulting company executive*

## Coventry

Aho, Sandra Christine *conservator*

## Cromwell

Günther-Stirn, Dagmar Dorothea *retired social sciences educator*
Izzo, Lucille Anne *sales representative*

## Danbury

Anderson, Alan Reinold *real estate company executive, computer security firm executive, consultant*
Angel, Stephen F. *chemicals executive*
Belsky, Joseph L. *endocrinologist*
Burns-DeMelo, Heather Ellsworth *publishing executive*
Collar, Emilio, Jr. *information systems consultant*
Hawkes, Carol Ann *academic administrator*
Hirshfield, Louis Russell *music educator, musician*
Johns, William David *nuclear medicine physician, internist*
Lagardere, Arnaud *publishing executive*
Leebens, Patricia Kay *psychiatrist*
Mann, Richard O. *public relations consulting company executive*
Martens, Juergen A. *pharmaceutical executive*
Meyers, Abbey S. *foundation administrator*
Moskowitz, Stanley Adam *finance company executive*
Nelson, Willie Hugh *musician, lyricist*
Proctor, Richard Jerome, Jr. *business educator, expert witness, accountant*
Reilley, Dennis H. *chemicals executive*
Reynolds, Jean Edwards *publishing executive*
Sawyer, James S. *manufacturing executive*
Tolor, Alexander *psychologist, educator*
Williamson, Brian David *information systems executive, consultant*
Yamin, Robert Joseph *lawyer*

## Danielson

Thibodeau, Joan Marie Serafin *writer, educator*

## Darien

Anderson, Robert Alexander *portrait artist*
Brooke, Avery Rogers *publisher, writer*
Cronk, Leonard *management consultant*
Dordelman, William Forsyth *food company executive*
Forman, J(oseph) Charles *chemical engineer, consultant, writer*
Kobak, James Benedict *management consultant*
Koontz, Carl Lennis, II, *investment counselor*
Lim, Ralph Wei Hsiong *finance educator*
Mapel, William Marlen Raines *retired bank executive*
McKim, Paul Arthur *management consultant, retired gas industry executive*
Morano, Gerard John *marketing executive*
Ossi, James Matthew *artist*
Penrose, Charles, Jr. *professional society administrator*
Prince, Kenneth Stephen *lawyer*
Schell, James Munson *finance company executive*
Smith, Elwin Earl *mining and oil company executive*
Sprole, Frank Arnott *retired pharmaceutical executive, lawyer*
Workman, Sharon Joy *journalist*

## Dayville

Funk, Michael S. *food products executive*
Townsend, Steven H. *food products executive*

## Deep River

Cobb, Hubbard Hanford *magazine editor, writer*

## Derby

Katz, David Lawrence *preventive medicine physician, researcher*
McEvoy, Sharlene Ann *law educator*

## East Glastonbury

Smith, David Clark *research scientist*

## East Granby

Carter, Adrian Lindsey Gould *information technology manager*
Kozlowski, Michael *automotive equipment executive*
Scanlon, Lawrence Eugene *language educator*

## East Haddam

Borton, John Carter, Jr., (Terry Borton) *theatrical producer*
Clarke, Cordelia Kay Knight Mazuy *management consultant, artist*
Clarke, Logan, Jr. *management consultant*
Frost, Susan Beth *theater producer*

## East Hartford

Barredo, Rita M. *auditor*
Cao, Ming *mechanical engineer*
Cassidy, John Francis, Jr. *industrial technology executive*
Chatell, Roger Armand *youth agency executive, camp director*
Dubin, Joseph William *federal mediator*
Jackson, Joseph Essard *religious organization administrator*
Jacobson, Clas A. *engineering educator, director*
Lautzenheiser, Barbara Jean *insurance company executive*
Staroselsky, Alexander *mechanical engineer, materials scientist*
Teller, Adam J. *lawyer*

## East Haven

Vermette, Raymond Edward *retired health facility administrator*

## East Lyme

Mylari, Banavara L. *retired chemist*

## Easton

Enos, Randall *cartoonist, illustrator*
Lorenz, Lee Sharp *cartoonist*
Maloney, John Joseph *writer*
Meyer, Alice Virginia *state official*

## Enfield

Doty, Victoria Skower *elementary school educator*
Oliver, Bruce Lawrence *retired information systems educator*
Squires, William Allen *distribution company executive*

## Essex

Hieatt, Allen Kent *retired language educator*
Hieatt, Constance Bartlett *English language educator*
Miller, Elliott Cairns *retired bank executive, lawyer*
Miller, Walter Neal *insurance company consultant*
Thompson, George Lee *retail executive, consultant*

## Fairfield

Barone, Rose Marie Pace *writer, retired educator*
Beccalli, Ferdinando *manufacturing executive*
Bennedum, Charles L. *computer scientist, educator, band director*
Booth, George Keefer *corporate financial executive*
Brett, Arthur Cushman, Jr. *banker*
Bryan, Barbara Day *retired librarian*
Bullard, Roger Perrin *artist*
Burd, Robert Meyer *hematologist, oncologist, educator*
Carlucci, David R. *information technology executive*
Caruso, Daniel F. *lawyer, judge, former state legislator*
Cassidy, Katherine *energy executive*
Conaty, William J. *electric power industry executive*
Cooper, L.E., Jr. *bank executive, lawyer, writer*
Daley, Pamela *diversified services, technology and manufacturing company executive*
Denniston, Brackett Badger III *lawyer*
Eigel, Edwin George, Jr. *mathematics professor, retired university president*
Fash, Victoria R. *business executive*
Gad, Lance Stewart *investment advisor, lawyer, private investor*
Henson, Daniel S. *manufacturing executive*
Hodgkinson, William James *publishing executive*
Howell, Karen Jane *private school educator*
Immelt, Jeffrey R. *diversified technology and services company executive*
Johnsen, Walter Craig *security firm executive*
Kaff, Albert Ernest *reporter, writer*
Kleine, Herman *economist*
Lakeland, Paul Francis *religious studies educator*
Levitt, Jesse *retired foreign language educator*
Loris, Michelle *psychologist, educator*
Luther, David Byron *management consultant*
Miles, Leland Weber *retired academic administrator*
Miller, Frederick Edwin, Jr. *history professor, government agency administrator*
Morehouse, Sarah McCally *retired political science professor*
Neal, Michael A. *corporate financial executive*
Newton, Lisa Haenlein *philosopher, educator*
Paolini, Claire Jacqueline *dean, educator*
Reiner, Gary M. *diversified technology and services company executive*
Rice, John G. *diversified technology and services executive*
Shelton, Carolyn Johnson *professional society administrator*
Sherin, Keith S. *electrical manufacturing company executive*
Trotter, Lloyd G. *electric power industry executive*
Upton, Barbara M. *music director*
Ury, Frederic Stephen *lawyer*
Wales, Gwynne Huntington *retired lawyer*
Wexler, Herbert Ira *retail company executive*

## Falls Village

Cronin, Robert Lawrence *painter*
Purcell, Mary Louise Gerlinger *retired adult education educator*
Toomey, Jeanne Elizabeth *animal activist*

## Farmington

Bronner, Felix *physiologist and biophysicist, educator, painter*
Centofanti, Joseph *accountant*
Deckers, Peter John *dean*
DiCicco, Tony *soccer coach*
Donaldson, James Oswell III *neurologist, educator*
Ford, Burch Tracy *headmaster*
Goodson, Richard Carle, Jr. *chemist*
Hall, Robert Stevens *dentist*
Ioannidou, Efthimia *periodontist, educator*
Ledgerwood, David M. *psychologist, researcher*
Liebowitz, Neil Robert *psychiatrist*
Melekote, Swathanthra Kumar *education educator*
Osborn, Mary Jane Merten *biochemist, educator*

## Gaylordsville

Dunn, Virginia *artist*

## Georgetown

Julian, Alexander, II, *menswear designer*

## Glastonbury

Bollinger, Lori *economist*
Cassotto, Mary Lou Grace *counselor, educator, lawyer*
Dixon, Robert F. *telecommunications executive*
Googins, Sonya Forbes *state legislator, retired banker*
Singer, Paul Richard *ophthalmologist*

## Greens Farms

Deford, Frank *sportswriter, commentator, writer*

## Greenwich

Alonzo, Martin Vincent *mining and aluminum company executive, investor, financial consultant*
Atkins, Ronald Raymond *lawyer*
Badman, John III *real estate developer, architect*
Ball, John Fleming *advertising executive, film company executive*
Bara, Jean Marc *finance and communications executive, artist*
Bedrosian, Gregory Ronald *investment banker*
Berkley, William Robert *insurance holding company executive*
Bjornson, Edith Cameron *foundation administrator, communications consultant*
Blumberg, Joel Myron *cardiologist*
Brandrup, Douglas Warren *lawyer*
Brant, Peter M. *magazine publishing executive, real estate developer*
Cameron, Dort *electronics executive*
Carmichael, William Daniel *management consultant, educator*
Clements, Robert *insurance executive*
Coleman, Joel Clifford *lawyer*
Davenport, Lee Losee *physicist*
Davidson, Thomas Maxwell *oil industry executive*
DeCrane, Alfred Charles, Jr. *petroleum company executive*
Dettmer, Robert Gerhart *retired beverage company executive*
de Visscher, Francois Marie *investment banker*
Donley, James Walton *management consultant*
Duff, Philip *investment company executive*
Ewald, William Bragg, Jr. *writer, consultant*
Farbish, Alfred B. *waterproofing materials executive*
Fleming, Martin *economist, strategist*
Ford, William E. *investment company executive*
Fuller, Theodore *retired insurance executive*
Ganek, David Kent *investor*
Gelfman, Robert William *retired lawyer*
Ghogawala, Zoher *neurosurgeon*
Gierer, Vincent A., Jr. *tobacco and wine holding company executive*
Goergen, Robert B. *consumer products company executive*
Grant, Ronald Alfred *psychiatrist, pastoral counselor, psychoanalyst*
Griggs, Nina M. *realtor*
Grossman, Sanford Jay *former economics professor, financial consultant*
Hewitt, Dennis Edwin *financial executive*
Hoberman, Mary Ann *author*
Horton, Jared Churchill *retired diversified financial services company executive, metal products executive*
Jacobs, Bradley S. *rental company executive*
Johnson, Herbert Michael *publisher*
Jones, Paul Tudor, II, *investment executive*
Kovner, Kathleen Jane *civic worker, portrait artist*
Krauser, Robert Stanley *health care executive*
Kreiger, Bruce D. *lawyer*
Lampert, Edward *investment company executive*
Landau, Jon *music producer, manager*
Lanning, Christopher Glenn *lawyer*
Long, Thomas Michael *investment banker*
Lynch, William Redington *lawyer*
Macaulay, William Edward *financial executive*
Mandel, Stephen, Jr. *financier*
Mango, Wilfred Gilbert, Jr. *construction executive, real estate company executive*
Marram, Ellen R. *investment company executive*
Moffly, John Wesley, IV, *magazine publishing executive*
Moore, John Plunkett Dennis *publisher*
More, Douglas McLochlan *lawyer*
Nevin, Crocker *investment banker*
Nimetz, Matthew *lawyer, investment company executive*
Pados, Frank John, Jr. *investment company executive*
Pascarella, Henry William *lawyer*
Paul, Roland Arthur *lawyer*
Paulson, Allen Joseph *advertising executive*
Perless, Ellen *advertising executive*
Perless, Robert L. *sculptor*
Reeves, Michael Spencer *investment company executive*
Rudy, Kathleen Vermeulen *small business owner*
Russell, William Edwards, IV, *educational association administrator, researcher*
Schlafly, Hubert Joseph, Jr. *communications executive*
Schneider, John Arnold *investor*
Schoonmaker, Samuel Vail III *lawyer*

Owens, Guy *retired neurosurgeon*
Reeves, John Drummond *retired English language professional, writer*
Robinson, Peter J. *dean, periodontal educator, pathologist*
Rothfield, Lawrence I. *microbiology educator*
Rothfield, Naomi Fox *physician*
Runowicz, Carolyn Dilworth *physician*
Schenkman, John Boris *pharmacologist, educator*
Spencer, Richard Paul *biochemist, educator, physician*
Trani, John M. *former consumer products company executive*
Walker, George W. *bishop*
Walker, James Elliot Cabot *physician*
Wand, Martin *ophthalmologist, educator*
Wiechmann, Eric Watt *lawyer*

## Groton

Daniel, J. Christopher *health facility executive, family medicine physician, military officer*
English, James Fairfield, Jr. *former college president*
Harwood, Harold James, Jr. *biochemist*
Kennedy, Evelyn Siefert *foundation executive, textiles executive*
Stoddard, Patrick Clare *retired military systems consultant, computer engineer*
Swindell, Archie Calhoun, Jr. *research biochemist, statistician*
Umlauf, Jon *physician, director*
Wallach, Morton L. *scientist*

## Guilford

Chatt, Allen Barrett *psychologist, neuroscientist*
Colish, Marcia Lillian *history professor*
Handschumacher, Robert Edmund *biochemistry professor*
Hare, Peter Hewitt *philosophy educator*
Morgan, Leon Alford *retired utilities executive*
Pease, David Gordon *artist, educator*
Peters, William *writer, film producer, film director*
Shelton, Darlene *psychologist, consultant*
Speth, James Gustave *dean, environmental studies educator, lawyer*
Springgate, Clark Franklin *physician, researcher*
Stevens, Lydia Hastings *community volunteer*

## Hamden

Adair, Eleanor Reed *environmental biologist*
Bigland-Ritchie, Brenda Rachel *physiologist, educator, neurophysiology researcher*
Brown, Jay Marshall *retired secondary school educator*
Cole-Schiraldi, Marilyn Bush *occupational therapist, educator*
Forman, Charles William *religious studies educator*
He, Xiaohong *finance educator*
Hines, Haywoodene *elementary and middle school educator*
Kagan, Donald *historian, educator*
Leddy, James Francis *protective services official*
Lucas, Doina C. *librarian*
Malherbe, Abraham Johannes *retired religious studies educator, writer*
Margulies, Martin B. *lawyer, educator*
McClellan, Edwin *literature educator*
Nuland, Sherwin *surgeon, writer*
Peterson, George Emanuel, Jr. *retired lawyer*
Reiser, Morton Francis *psychiatrist, educator*
Robson, Carol Ann Shaffner *retired secondary school educator*
Roche, (Eamonn) Kevin *architect*
Smith, David Martyn *retired forestry educator*
Weinstein, Stanley *Buddhist studies educator*

## Hampton

Roenigk, Martin Allen *insurance company executive*

## Hartford

Alfano, Charles Thomas, Sr. *lawyer*
Amatuli, Robert Alexander *architect*
Ancona, Cara D. *psychologist, educator*
Anthony, Julian Danford, Jr. *lawyer*
Apruzzese, Philip John *educational association administrator, educator*
Ayer, Ramani *insurance company executive*
Bennett, Alan M. *corporate financial executive*
Berall, Frank Stewart *lawyer*
Bergenn, James Walter *lawyer*
Bermel, John J *insurance company executive, corporate financial executive*
Bertolini, Mark T. *insurance company executive*
Bieluch, William Charles *judge*
Blumberg, Phillip Irvin *law educator*
Blumenthal, Richard *state attorney general*
Bolton, Roger *insurance company executive*
Boman, Paul Eric *engineering executive*
Bonee, John Leon III *lawyer*
Borden, David M. *state supreme court justice*
Brennan, Troyen A. *insurance company executive, medical educator, lawyer*
Bronzino, Joseph Daniel *electrical engineer*
Brown, W. Miller *faculty dean*
Buck, Gurdon Hall *lawyer, urban planner, mediator*
Bucknall, William L., Jr. *human resources professional*
Butler, Gregory B. *utilities executive, lawyer*
Bysiewicz, Susan *state official*
Cain, George Harvey *lawyer, legal association administrator*
Campbell, Timothy Reid *financial services company executive*

## Scott — Wyman (column)

Scott, John Constante *marketing company executive*
Scott, Mariette A. *marketing executive*
Selby, Leland Clay *lawyer*
Sexton, David Farrington *lawyer, bank executive*
Shimchick, Marie *music educator*
Smith, Phillips Guy *banker*
Smith, Rodger Field *financial executive*
Srere, Benson M(ortimer) *communications executive, consultant*
Stauffer, Valerie Vilas *civic volunteer*
Stockman, David Alan *investment banker*
Storms, Clifford Beekman *lawyer*
Swarz, Jeffrey Robert *investment banker, biotechnologist, neuroscientist*
Tarantino, Dominic A. *retired professional services firm executive*
Tournillon, Nicholas Brady *investment company executive*
Urstadt, Charles J. *real estate company officer*
Van Dijk, Frits *food products executive*
Verheij, Richard H. *lawyer*
Wallach, Magdalena Falkenberg (Carla Wallach) *writer*
Welling, Kathryn Marie *editor*
Welt, Philip Stanley *lawyer, consultant*
Whitmore, George Merle, Jr. *management consulting company executive*
Wiener, Malcolm Hewitt *historian, writer*
Winkler, Charles Howard *investment company executive*
Wyman, Ralph Mark *security firm executive, healthcare company executive*

Chaet, Bernard Robert *artist, educator*
Chandler, William Knox *physiologist*
Cheng, Yung-Chi Tommy *medical educator*
Chevalier, Judith A. *economics professor, finance professor*
Chilton, William David *architect*
Chua, Amy *law educator*
Chupka, William Andrew *chemical physicist, educator*
Cicchetti, Domenic Vincent *research scientist, educator*
Ciuparu, Dragos Mihael *research scientist, educator*
Clarie, Thomas Cashin, II, *librarian*
Cleary, Paul David *sociomedical educator*
Coe, Michael Douglas *retired anthropologist*
Cohen, Lawrence Sorel *internist, educator*
Coifman, Ronald R. *mathematician, educator*
Cole, Elsa Kircher *lawyer*
Coleman, Jules L. *law educator*
Collins, William F., Jr. *neurosurgery educator*
Comer, James Pierpont *psychiatrist, educator*
Conklin, Harold Colyer *anthropologist, educator*
Cooper, Jack Ross *pharmacology educator, researcher*
Crakes, Gary Michael *economics professor*
Cullen, Mark Richard *medical educator*
Curran, Lisa M. *environmental scientist, educator*
Dalton, Harlon L. *law educator*
Damaska, Mirjan Radovan *law educator*
Danaher, John Anthony III *prosecutor*
Davey, Lycurgus Michael *neurosurgeon*
Days, Drew S. III *lawyer, educator*
Degutis, Linda Christine *adult education educator, epidemiologist, researcher*
De Rose, Sandra Michele *psychotherapist, educator, administrator*
Donohue, John Joseph *law educator*
Dorsey, Peter Collins *federal judge*
DuBois, Arthur Brooks *physiologist, educator*
Duke, Steven Barry *law educator*
Dyson, William R. *state legislator, educator*
Edelson, Richard L. *dermatology educator, director*
Ehrenkranz, Richard Allan *pediatrician*
Ellickson, Robert Chester *law educator*
Ember, Carol R. *anthropology educator, writer*
Ember, Melvin Lawrence *anthropologist, educator*
Engelman, Donald Max *molecular biophysics and biochemistry educator*
Erikson, Kai *sociologist, educator*
Errington, James Joseph *anthropology educator*
Eskridge, William Nichol, Jr. *law educator*
Esty, Daniel Cushing *law educator, lawyer*
Evenson, Robert Eugene *economist, educator*
Fair, Ray Clarence *economics professor*
Fairbanks Harris, Theresa Louise *art educator, restorer*
Feigenbaum, Joan *computer scientist, mathematician*
Feinstein, Rochelle *artist, educator*
Feldman, Grace A. *musician*
Ferholt, J. Deborah Lott *pediatrician*
Fikrig, Erol *rheumatologist, medical educator*
Fischer, Michael John *computer science educator*
Fiss, Owen M. *law educator*
Fleischman, Gary Franklin *acupuncturist*
Followay, Jonathan Scott *history professor*
Foster, Roger Sherman, Jr. *surgeon, educator, health facility administrator*
Frank, Roberta *literature educator*
Freed, Daniel Josef *law educator*
Fuchs, Elinor *film critic, playwright, educator*
Galantucci, Bruno *research scientist*
Galston, Arthur William *biology professor*
Garten, Jeffrey E. *finance educator*
Gastwirth, Donald Edward *lawyer, literary agent*
Geisler, Thomas Milton, Jr. *lawyer*
Genel, Myron *pediatrician, educator*
Gewirtz, Paul D. *lawyer, educator*
Gilbert, Creighton Eddy *art historian*
Gildea, Brian Michael *lawyer*
Girvin, Steven Mark *physicist, researcher*
Goffart, Walter André *history professor*
Gonzalez, Caleb *ophthalmologist, educator*
Goodrich, Isaac *neurosurgeon, educator*
Graedel, Thomas Eldon *industrial ecology educator, researcher*
Graetz, Michael J. *law educator*
Grausman, Philip *sculptor*
Green, Donald Philip *political scientist, educator*
Greene, Liliane *literature and language educator, editor*
Greenfield, James Robert *lawyer*
Grey, Margaret *nursing educator*
Gross, Ian *academic pediatrician, neonatologist*
Gueorguieva, Ralitza *biostatistician*
Hallo, William Wolfgang *literature and language professor, writer*
Hansmann, Henry Baethke *law educator*
Harries, Karsten *philosophy educator, researcher*
Harrison, Henry Starin *real estate appraiser, educator, entrepreneur*
Heninger, George Robert *psychology professor, researcher*
Hennah, Vivian Lisa *school system administrator*
Hersey, George Leonard *retired art historian*
Hickey, Leo Joseph *museum curator, educator*
Hollander, John *humanities educator, poet*
Holquist, James Michael *literature educator, department chairman*
Hong, Baoming *research scientist, engineer*
Horwich, Arthur L. *medical educator*
Horwitz, Sarah McCue *educator*
Hostetter, Margaret K. *pediatrician, medical educator*
Huwiler, Joan P. *public relations executive, consultant*
Hyman, Paula E(llen) *history professor*
Insler, Stanley *philologist, educator*
Jacob, Deirdre Ann Bradbury *manufacturing executive, finance educator, consultant*
Jatlow, Peter I. *pathologist, medical educator, researcher*
Johnson, Lester Fredrick *artist*
Johnstone, Quintin *law educator*
Jones, Katherine R. *nursing educator*
Kahan, Dan M. *law educator*
Kahn, Paul W. *law educator*
Kalyanpur, Arjun *radiologist*
Kashgarian, Michael *pathologist, educator*

Kevles, Daniel Jerome *historian, educator, writer*
King, Robert Alan *psychiatrist, educator*
Klevorick, Alvin K. *law and economics educator*
Koh, Harold Hongju *dean, law educator*
Korchagin, Vladimir *astrophysicist*
Krauss, Judith Belliveau *nursing educator*
Kronman, Anthony Townsend *dean, law educator*
Kushlan, Samuel Daniel *internist, educator, hospital administrator*
Lamar, Howard Roberts *academic administrator, historian*
Langbein, John Harriss *lawyer, educator*
LaPalombara, Joseph *political science educator, industrial management educator*
Leckman, James Frederick *psychiatry and pediatrics educator*
Leeney, Robert Joseph *newspaper editor*
Leffell, David Joel *dermatologist, surgeon, writer, photographer, medical school administrator, educator*
Levin, Rick (Richard Charles Levin) *academic administrator, economist*
Levine, Robert John *internist, educator*
Lewis, Melvin *psychiatrist, pediatrician, psychotherapist*
Lindroth, Linda (Linda Hammer) *artist, writer, curator*
Lopez, Javier *psychiatrist*
Lord, Ruth *retired researcher, philanthropist, writer*
Lorimer, Linda Koch *university educator*
Lytton, Bernard *urology educator*
Mac Dowell, Samuel Wallace *retired physics professor*
Macey, Jonathan R. *law educator*
Malawista, Stephen E. *medical educator*
Marchesi, Vincent Thomas *biochemist, educator*
Marcus, Edward Leonard *lawyer, political organization worker*
Marcus, Ruth Barcan *philosopher, educator, writer, lecturer*
Margulis, Gregory A. *mathematics professor, researcher, science educator*
Marks, Lawrence Edward *psychologist, educator*
Marmor, Theodore Richard *political science professor*
Martignetti, Frank Anthony III *music educator, church music director*
Massey, William S. *mathematician, educator*
Mattina, MaryJane Incorvia *chemist*
Mayhew, David Raymond *political science professor*
Mazzotta, Giuseppe Francesco *literature and language professor*
McClain, Brenda C. *pain management physician*
McClatchy, J. D. *editor, writer, educator*
McCorkle, Ruth *oncological nurse, educator, researcher*
McGuire, William James *psychologist, educator*
McNamara, Julia Mary *academic administrator, foreign language educator*
Meeks, Wayne A. *religious studies educator*
Meyers, Amy *museum director*
Miller, I. George *physician, educator, researcher*
Molaei, Goudarz *research scientist*
Mostaghimi, Mehdi *economist, educator*
Mostow, George Daniel *mathematics professor*
Mukherjee, Sandip Kumar *cardiologist*
Musto, David Franklin *medical researcher, educator, historian, consultant*
Narendra, Kumpati Subrahmanya *electrical engineer, educator*
Newick, Craig David *architect*
Nolan, Victoria *theater director*
Norton, Cheryl J. *academic administrator*
Novick, Peter J. *cell biologist, educator*
O'Connor, Kevin James *prosecutor, lawyer*
Pagani, Mark *education educator, researcher*
Parker, Peter D.M. *physicist, educator, researcher*
Patterson, Peyton R. *bank executive*
Pelli, Cesar *architect*
Persing, John Arthur *surgeon*
Peters, Jean Koh *law educator*
Peterson, Linda H. *English language educator*
Petit, Emmanuel J. *architecture educator*
Phillips, Caryl *writer*
Phillips, Peter Charles Bonest *economist, educator, researcher*
Podolny, Joel M. *dean, management educator*
Pollard, Thomas Dean *cell biologist, educator*
Pollitt, Jerome Jordan *art historian, educator*
Pospisil, Leopold Jaroslav *anthropologist, educator, law educator*
Post, Robert Charles *law educator*
Poutrina, Ekaterina *optics scientist, researcher*
Powsner, Seth *psychiatrist, educator, medical researcher*
Powsner, Seth M. *psychiatrist, educator*
Priest, George L. *law educator*
Prochaska, Alice *historian, librarian*
Proctor, Deborah Denise *gastroenterologist, educator*
Pronin, Anatoly *photographer*
Prown, Jules David *art historian, educator*
Ramirez, Ainissa *materials scientist*
Ranis, Gustav *economist, educator*
Rawson, Claude Julien *literature and language professor*
Redmond, Donald Eugene, Jr. *neuroscientist, educator*
Reed, Robert James, Jr. *painter, art educator*
Reisman, William Michael *lawyer, educator*
Resnik, Judith *law educator*
Reynolds, Jock *artist, curator, art gallery director*
Ritchie, J. Murdoch *pharmacologist, educator*
Robinson, Fred Colson *language educator*
Roemer, John E. *economics educator*
Rose, Aron D. *ophthalmologist, educator*
Rose-Ackerman, Susan *law and political economy educator*
Roth, Harold *architect*
Rubenfeld, Jed *law educator*
Ruchkin, Vladislav *psychiatrist*
Russett, Bruce Martin *political science professor*
Saltzman, W. Mark *engineering educator*
Sandweiss, Jack *physicist, researcher*
Sartorelli, Alan Clayton *pharmacologist, educator*
Sasaki, Clarence Takashi *surgeon, educator*
Saunders, Martin *chemistry educator, researcher*
Scarf, Margaret (Maggie Scarf) *author*
Schepartz, Alanna *biochemist, educator*

Schleifer, Alison Pedicord *educational consultant*
Schlessinger, Joseph *pharmacology educator*
Schloss, Irving Steven *lawyer*
Schneider, David Walter *lawyer*
Schottenfeld, Richard Steven *psychiatrist*
Schowalter, John Erwin *child and adolescent psychiatry educator*
Schuck, Peter Horner *lawyer, educator*
Schultz, T. Paul *economics professor*
Schwartz, Alan *law educator*
Scully, Vincent Joseph, Jr. *architectural historian, educator, writer*
Sease, Catherine *conservator, consultant*
Seashore, Margretta Reed *physician, educator*
Seilacher, Adolf *special education educator*
Shapiro, Eugene David *pediatrician, epidemiologist, educator*
Shaywitz, Bennett Arthur *medical educator*
Shepherd, Gordon Murray *neuroscientist, educator*
Shiller, Robert James *economist, educator*
Shubik, Martin *economics professor*
Shulman, Gerald I. *physician, scientist, endocrinologist, educator*
Shulman, Robert Gerson *biophysics professor*
Sico, Jason Jonathon *neurologist, internist, consultant*
Siegel, Reva *law educator*
Silk, James J. *law educator*
Singer, Jon Douglas *foundation administrator, writer*
Skowronek, Stephen Lee *political scientist, educator*
Smith, Brian Richard *hematologist, oncologist, pathologist*
Smith, Henry E. *law educator*
Smith, John Edwin *philosophy educator*
Snyder, Timothy David *history professor, writer*
Solomon, Robert A. *law educator*
Sommers, Alexis Nigel *academic administrator, engineering educator*
Sorkin, Jenni *curator, critic*
Spence, Jonathan Dermot *historian, educator*
Spencer, Dennis Dee *medical educator, director*
Stahl, Nanette *librarian, biblicist*
Stahl, Richard Sheldon *surgeon*
Stapleton, James Francis *lawyer*
Steitz, Joan Argetsinger *biochemistry professor*
Stern, Robert *psychiatrist*
Stevens, Joseph Charles *psychology professor*
Stewart, Paul James, Jr. *history educator*
Stiber, Julie Anne *social worker*
Stith-Cabranes, Kate *law educator*
Stone, Alfred Douglas *physicist, educator*
Storr, Robert *curator, art educator, painter*
Stuehrenberg, Paul Frederick *librarian*
Sullivan, Shaun Stuart *lawyer*
Summers, William Cofield *science educator*
Swain, James Edward *psychiatrist, researcher*
Sweet, Alec Stone *law educator*
Tirro, Frank Pascale *music educator, composer, writer*
Torgler, Benno *economist, researcher*
Tsai, James C. *ophthalmologist, researcher*
Tully, John Charles *research chemical physicist*
Turner, Frank Miller *historian, educator*
Underdown, David Edward *historian, educator*
Volkmar, Fred Robert *psychiatrist, educator, director*
Waggoner, Paul Edward *agricultural scientist*
Wagner, Allan Ray *psychology professor*
Wagoner, Walter Dray, Jr. *lawyer*
Walbert, Kate *writer, educator*
Walker, John Mercer, Jr. *federal judge*
Wandycz, Piotr Stefan *historian, educator*
Warshaw, Marvin D. *conductor, educator, musician*
Waxman, Stephen George *neurologist, neuroscientist*
Weiss, Robert M. *urologist, educator*
Wessel, Morris Arthur *retired pediatrician*
Wiberg, Kenneth Berle *chemist, educator*
Winroth, Anders *historian, educator*
Winter, Ralph Karl, Jr. *federal judge*
Wolf, Werner Paul *physicist, researcher*
Wolterstorff, Nicholas Paul *philosophical theology educator*
Wynn, Karen *psychologist, educator, researcher*
Yeargan, Michael *scenic designer*
Yeazell, Ruth Bernard *English language educator*
Zaret, Barry Lewis *cardiologist, medical educator*
Zedillo Ponce de León, Ernesto *former president of Mexico*
Zeller, Michael Edward *physicist, researcher*
Zhang, Xiang Yang *psychiatrist, researcher*
Zhang, Yawei *epidemiologist*
Zigler, Edward Frank *psychologist, educator*
Zimmermann, Jeremy Gray *lawyer*

## New London

Asselin-Connolly, John Thomas *lawyer*
Bald, Ronald James *military officer*
Carpenter, Bruce William *information technology manager, director*
Clarke, Florence Dorothy *minister, educator*
Dudden, Alexis *history professor*
Espinosa, Resurreccion *playwright, theater director, writer*
Fainstein, Norman *sociology professor, former academic administrator*
Hammond, Ulysses Bernard *academic administrator*
Higdon, Leo Ignatius, Jr., (Lee Higdon) *academic administrator*
Johnson, Diana Atwood *business owner, innkeeper*
Reardon, Robert Ignatius, Jr. *lawyer*
Schoenberger, Steven Harris *physician, research consultant*
Tassinari, Melissa Sherman *reproductive toxicologist*
Urbanetti, John Sutherland *internist, consultant*
Van Sice, James *career military officer, academic administrator*
Zimmer, Marc *chemistry professor*

## New Milford

Fabricand, Burton Paul *physicist, researcher*

## New Preston

Grizzard, George *actor*

## Newington

Anderson, Kathryn Parks *music educator*

Bell, Kenneth Leman, Jr. *music educator, musician*
Cohen, Fern K. *music educator*
Sumner, David George *association executive*

## Newtown

Coates, John Peter *technical executive*
Cole, Richard John *marketing executive*
Cottingham, Robert *artist*
Forger, Robert Durkin *retired professional association administrator*
Goodwick, David Lee *advertising executive*

## Niantic

Butler, Jonathan Putnam *architect*
Deakyne, William John *library director, musician*
Douglas, Robert Gordon, Jr. *physician*
Hunt, Francis Howard *retired navy laboratory official*
Morrill, Billie Alberta *librarian*

## Noank

Leeds, Robin Leigh *transportation executive*

## Norfolk

Jessup, Philip Caryl, Jr. *retired lawyer*
Mermann, Alan Cameron *retired pediatric educator, chaplain*

## North Branford

Gasparine, Barbara Ellen *elementary school educator*
Houghton, Alan Nourse *educational association administrator, consultant*
Ingram, George *manufacturing executive*
Logan, John Arthur, Jr. *retired foundation executive*
Mead, Lawrence Myers, Jr. *retired manufacturing executive*
Womer, Charles Berry *retired hospital executive, management consultant*

## North Canton

Swibold, Gretchen Ann *librarian, writer*

## North Grosvenordale

Kornbluth, Frances Helen Schachter *artist*

## North Haven

Bennett, Harry Louis *history professor*
Dahl, Robert Alan *political science professor*
Fuggi, Gretchen Miller *education educator*
Glaser, Gilbert Herbert *retired neuroscientist, educator*
Herzenberg, Arvid *physicist, researcher*
Hudson, Richard L. *retired adult education educator, minister*
Katsaros, Thomas *historian, educator*
Mahl, George Franklin *retired psychologist, educator*
Westerfield, Carolyn Elizabeth Hess *urban planner*

## North Stonington

Keane, John Patrick *retired secondary school educator*
Svengalis, Kendall Frayne *law librarian, educator, publishing executive*

## North Windham

Careau, James Thomas *music educator*

## Northford

Gregan, Edmund Robert *landscape architect*
James, William Hall *former state official, educator*

## Norwalk

Babcock, Catherine Evans *artist, educator*
Bays, John Theophanis *consulting engineer*
Bennett, Carl *retired discount department store executive*
Bortolot, Gary *writer, educator*
Brown, William Terrel *psychology professor, educational consultant*
Burton, David K. *lawyer*
Cammaker, Sheldon Ira *lawyer*
Carius, Michael Lee *emergency medicine physician*
Chesser, Leicle E. *corporate financial executive*
Czajkowski-Barrett, Karen Angela *human resources specialist*
DeCesare, Donald E. *broadcast executive*
Dvornek, Linda Smith *chemist*
Eagan, Sherman G. *producer, communications executive*
Falsone, Jack Joseph *physician*
Fischman, Eric D. *psychologist, special education educator*
Gold, Richard N. *management consultant*
Guzzi, Anthony J. *construction executive*
Harris, Holton Edwin *plastics machinery manufacturing executive*
Hathaway, Carl Emil *investment company executive*
Jacobs, Mark Randolph *lawyer*
Johnson, Robert James *psychology educator*
Knopp, Alex *lawyer, mayor*
MacInnis, Frank T. *construction executive, securities trader, holding company executive*
Nelson, Paula Morrison Bronson *reading specialist*
Nightingale, William Joslyn *management consultant*
O'Connell, William Egan *English professor*
Peppet, Russell Frederick *accountant*
Perry, Charles Owen *sculptor*
Piper, Thomas Laurence III *banker*
Raikes, Charles FitzGerald *retired lawyer*
Sawch, William B. *lawyer*
Scheinman, Stanley Bruce *corporate financial executive*
Soper, Jeannine *real estate agent*
Stella, George *chef*
Swift, Richard J. *engineering company executive*
Tropin, Kenneth G. *fund management executive*
White, Tony L. *health and medical products executive*
Wilks, Paul Almy, Jr. *engineering educator*
Yeosock, Michael Michael *funeral director, civil engineer*

## Norwich

Cote, Michael Richard *bishop*

Hart, Daniel Anthony *bishop*
Pudlo, Steven Edward *computer technician*

**Oakville**
Carroll, Constance Marie *piano educator, organist, director*

**Old Greenwich**
Allen, Jefferson F. *oil industry executive*
DeOrchis, Frankie Juanita *forester, writer*
Dixon, John Morris *magazine editor*
Gayda, Michael D. *lawyer*
Lorefice, Laurence Santo *psychiatrist*
Parris, Sally Nye *real estate agent*
Walton, Constance Williams *music educator*

**Old Lyme**
Algiere, Scott G. *health facility administrator*
Chandler, Elisabeth Gordon (Mrs. Laci De Gerenday) *sculptor, musician*
Doersam, Charles Henry, Jr. *engineer, educator, entrepreneur, writer*
Fairfield-Sonn, James Willed *management educator, consultant*
Johnson, James Myron *psychologist, educator*
Osborne, Judith Barbour *artist*
Stula, Nancy *museum director, curator*

**Old Saybrook**
Hoffman, Ellendale McCollam *psychologist, counselor*
Neal, Irene Collins *artist, educator*
Norcia, Stephen William *advertising executive*
Phillips, William E. *advertising agency executive*
Purcell, Bradford Moore *publishing company executive*

**Orange**
Conant, Sally Lorensen *textile conservator, art historian*
Davies, Richard Warren *lawyer*
Davis, David Brion *historian, educator*
Lobay, Ivan *mechanical engineering educator*
Miller, Henry Forster *architect*
Powers, Timothy H. *electric power industry executive*

**Oxford**
Marano, Richard Michael *judge*

**Plainfield**
Barfield, Kem *director, educator*

**Plainville**
Glassman, Gerald Seymour *metal products executive*

**Pleasant Valley**
Decker, Robert Owen *history professor, clergyman*

**Prospect**
Powell, Raymond William *financial planner, school administrator*

**Putnam**
Craig, Robert James *ornithologist, educator*
Day, John Anthony, Jr. *pulmonologist*

**Redding**
Addison, Jason Lawrence *multifamily community development executive*
Begell, William *publisher*
Benyei, Candace Reed *psychotherapist*
Campbell, Joseph John *retired finance company executive*
Gooch, Anthony Cushing *retired lawyer*
Macintyre, Malcolm Scott *retired secondary education educator*
McClure, Grover Benjamin *management consultant*
Quinn, Andrew Peter, Jr. *lawyer, retired insurance company executive*
Welsh, John Francis *retired advertising executive*

**Ridgefield**
Brewster, Carroll Worcester *former academic administrator*
Davie, Malcolm Henderson *minister, retired municipal official*
Egan, Kenneth J. *dermatologist*
Habashy, Tarek *oil industry executive, director*
Kantor, James Graham *music educator, composer*
Levine, Paul Michael *paper company executive, consultant*
Lindsay, Dianna Marie *educational administrator*
Lodewick, Philip Hughes *equipment leasing company executive*
McConnell, John Edward *retired electrical engineering company executive*
Mesznik, Joel R. *investment banker*
Swartout, Torin Sherwin Roberts *logistics executive, transportation consultant*
Taylor, Edwin R. *music director*
Wiegley, Roger Douglas *lawyer*

**Riverside**
Coulson, Robert *retired professional society administrator, arbitrator, writer*
Deering, Allan Brooks *retired soft drink company executive*
Geismar, Richard Lee *communications executive*
McSpadden, Peter Ford *retired advertising agency executive*
Powers, Claudia McKenna *state legislator*
Schur, Jeffrey *advertising executive*

**Rocky Hill**
Burnett, Claire Conklin *music educator*
Chu, Hsien-Kun *chemist, researcher*
Powers, Helen *columnist, writer*

**Roxbury**
Friedman, John Maxwell, Jr. *lawyer*
Gurney, Albert Ramsdell *playwright, educator*
Styron, Rose *human rights activist, poet, journalist*

**Salisbury**
Block, Zenas *retired management consultant, educator*

Kilner, Ursula Blanche *genealogist, educator, writer*

**Sharon**
Gordon, Nicholas *broadcast executive, performing arts executive*
Johns, Jasper *artist*
Learsy, Raymond J. *private investor*
Mesniaeff, Gregory *economist, securities analyst*

**Shelton**
Kantrowitz, Jonathan Daniel *publishing executive, educator, lawyer*
Vine, Leo *lawyer*
Williamson, Keith Harvey *lawyer*

**Sherman**
Cowley, Robert William *editor, writer, consultant, lecturer*

**Simsbury**
Berberich, Patricia Louise *librarian*
Borges, Francisco Lopes *venture capitalist*
Houlihan, Charles Daniel, Jr. *lawyer*
Long, Ann Marie *health facility administrator*
Roberts, Celia Ann *librarian*
Yagudin, Alexei *Olympic athlete, ice skater*

**Somers**
Blake, Stewart Prestley *retired ice cream company executive*

**South Kent**
Baker, John Milnes *architect*
Keehner, Michael Arthur Miller *investment banking executive*
Samartini, James Rogers *retired appliance company executive*

**South Windsor**
Baretta, Marsha Motyl *elementary school physical education educator*
Famiglietti, Nancy Zima *computer company executive*
Hobbs, David Ellis *mechanical engineer*

**Southbury**
Atwood, Edward Charles *economist, educator*
Auerbach, Ernest Sigmund *lawyer, insurance company executive, writer*
Bergen, Polly *actress*
Bowen, Christopher Edward *researcher, director*
Caravatt, Paul Joseph, Jr. *communications executive*
Foxworth, Johnnie Hunter *retired state agency administrator*
Hopf, Frank Rudolph *retired dentist*
Rine, Maureen S. *elementary school educator*
Rorick, William Calvin *librarian, educator, portrait artist*
Russell, Allan David *lawyer*
Welton, Sharon Marie *food service executive*

**Southington**
Byeff, Peter David *hematologist, oncologist*

**Southport**
Ambrosino, Ralph Thomas, Jr. *retired telecommunications executive*
Cappeto, Michael Arnold *university dean*
Damson, Barrie Morton *oil and gas exploration company executive*
Twiname, John Dean *minister, human services administrator*
Walker, Charles Dodsley *conductor, organist*
Wheeler, Wilmot Fitch, Jr. *diversified manufacturing company executive*
Wilbur, E. Packer *investment company executive*

**Stafford Springs**
Zeldes, Benjamin *retired optometrist*

**Stamford**
Azam, Zeshan Raza *diversified financial services company executive*
Babson, Jane Frances *artist, writer*
Bainton, J(ohn) Joseph *lawyer*
Balduino, Michael J. *paper company executive*
Barker, James Rex *water transportation executive, director*
Barreca, Christopher Anthony *lawyer*
Bijur, Peter I. *retired petroleum company executive*
Birenbaum, Jonathan *lawyer*
Bostin, Marvin Jay *hospital and health services consultant*
Britt, Glenn Alan *media company executive*
Burns, Ursula M. *printing company executive*
Burston, Richard Mervin *marketing executive*
Burton, Robert Gene *printing company executive*
Buzzard, James A. *paper, packaging and chemical company executive*
Caldwell, Philip *retired automobile manufacturing company executive, retired finance company executive*
Carter, Jerome N. *human resources specialist, paper company executive*
Cassidy, Denis Andrew *artist, architect*
Chang, Ted T. *chemist*
Chickering, Howard Allen *insurance company executive, lawyer*
Chisholm, Andrea Lynne *trade association administrator, foundation administrator*
Clement, Bill *hockey analyst*
Cohen, Steven A. *investment company executive*
Colthup, Norman Bertram *retired spectroscopist*
Cook, Colin Burford *psychiatrist*
Critelli, Michael J. *lawyer, manufacturing executive*
Dammerman, Dennis Dean *diversified technology and services company executive*
Dell, Warren Frank, II, *management consultant*
Dennies, Sandra Lee *city official*
duPont, Augustus Irénée *lawyer*
Elizondo, Patricia *sales executive*
Erichson, Robert B. *hematologist, oncologist*
Evans, Robert Sheldon *manufacturing executive, director*
Faraci, John Vincent, Jr. *paper company executive*
Farren, J. Michael *former government official, lawyer*

Fast, Eric Carson *manufacturing executive*
Fein, Ronnie *journalist, writer*
Fisher, Richard S. *lawyer*
Frank, Laura Jean *computer scientist*
Freeborn, Philip *information technology executive*
Frenkel, Steven I. *lawyer*
Friedman, Michael *pharmaceutical executive*
Gilman, Kenneth B. *retail executive*
Gladstone, Herbert Jack *manufacturing executive*
Gold, Steven Michael *lawyer*
Goldsmith, Donna *sports association executive*
Gonnelli, Patrick M. *finance company executive*
Goodhue, Peter Ames *obstetrician, gynecologist, educator*
Graf, Rudy J. *communications company executive*
Griffith, Forrest Lee III *lawyer*
Gross, Ronald Martin *consumer products company consultant*
Harper, Arthur H. *manufacturing executive*
Harrington, Richard J. *information business executive*
Hawkins, John Donald, Jr. *lawyer*
Hawley, Frank Jordan, Jr. *venture capital executive*
Hecht, Harvey Leon *radiologist*
Herlands, E. Ward *poet, printmaker*
Hicks, Wayland R. *rental company executive*
Hogan, Frank W. III *lawyer, manufacturing executive*
Hollinger, Morton *small business owner, artist*
Hood, Todd Anthony *computer company executive, director*
Horrigan, D. Gregory *packaging products executive*
Hubschman, Henry A. *lawyer*
Hudson, Harold Jordon, Jr. *retired insurance executive*
Jason, J. Julie *portfolio manager, writer, lawyer*
Johnson, Dwayne Douglas (The Rock) *professional wrestler, actor*
Karp, Steve *agent*
Kisseberth, Paul Barto *retired publishing executive*
Klein, Neil Charles *physician*
Koproski, Alexander Robert *real estate company executive*
Kucic, Joseph *management consultant, industrial engineer, network engineer, information security specialist*
Lane, Hana Umlauf *editor*
La Penta, Robert Vincent *venture capitalist*
Lesko, Newland A. *paper company executive*
Lessin, Andrew Richard *accounting executive*
Levitan, Gutman *research and development company executive, communications engineer*
Loh, Arthur Tsung Yuan *finance company executive*
Luke, John Anderson, Jr. *paper, packaging and chemical company executive*
Mactas, Mark V. *diversified financial services company executive*
Macurdy, John Edward *bass*
Mahony, Edward B. *corporate financial executive*
Malloy, Dannel Patrick *mayor*
Martin, Murray D. *manufacturing executive*
Masino, Frank A. *radiation oncologist*
Mayer, John Anton, Jr. *bank executive*
Mayes, Michele Coleman *lawyer*
McGeeney, John Stephen *lawyer*
McGrath, Richard *lawyer*
Mc Kinley, John Key *retired oil company executive*
McMahon, Linda E. *sports association executive*
McMahon, Vince (Vincent Kennedy McMahon) *sports entertainment company executive*
Merritt, William Alfred, Jr. *retired lawyer, real estate company executive*
Miller, Gregory James *lawyer*
Miller, Wilbur Hobart *retired management consultant*
Mitten, Russ *lawyer, telecommunications industry executive*
Morgan, William J. *accounting company executive*
Motroni, Hector John *manufacturing executive*
Mulcahy, Anne Marie *printing company executive*
Munera, Gerard Emmanuel *manufacturing executive*
Nazemetz, Patricia *human resources specialist*
Neal, A. Michael *utilities executive*
Nevans, Roy Norman *food products executive, producer*
Nichols, Ralph Arthur *lawyer*
Nissen, David R. *utilities executive*
Pansini, Michael Samuel *financial analyst, tax specialist*
Pappas, Alceste Thetis *consulting company executive, educator*
Pardue, Bill *publishing executive*
Parra, Marianno M. *paper and lumber company executive*
Perle, Eugene Gabriel *lawyer*
Peterson, Elizabeth Holly *art association administrator*
Rand, A. Barry *financial services executive*
Reardon, Michael J. *finance company executive*
Robins, Robert Sidwar *political science professor, department chairman*
Rose, Richard Loomis *lawyer*
Rudman, Joan Eleanor *artist, educator*
Sackler, Mortimer D.A. *pharmaceutical executive*
Schiff, Jayne Nemerow *underwriter*
Scott, Gregory Alan *pharmacist, writer*
Shanman, James Alan *lawyer*
Shassian, Donald R. *telecommunications company executive*
Silver, Charles Morton *communications company executive*
Silver, R. Philip *packaging products executive*
Skidd, Thomas Patrick, Jr. *lawyer*
Smith, J. Gordon *automotive executive*
Snediker, David E. *lawyer*
Staab, Diane D. *lawyer*
Steenburgh, Frank D. *consumer products company executive*
Stillings, Irene Ella Grace Cordiner *retired foundation executive*
Teeters, Nancy Hays *economist, director*
Teitell, Conrad Laurence *lawyer, writer*
Thomas, Dennis *retired paper company executive, retired federal official*
Tow, Leonard *television executive*
Tregurtha, Paul Richard *water transportation executive*

Udell, Howard R. *pharmaceutical executive*
Valentine, Bobby (Robert John Valentine) *professional baseball manager*
Vandebroek, Sophie Verdonckt *printing company executive*
Walsh, Thomas Joseph *ophthalmologist*
Weitzel, William Conrad, Jr. *lawyer*
Wilderotter, Maggie (Mary Agnes Wilderotter) *software company executive, former cable television executive*
Wilens, Michael Engber *information technology executive, biologist, microscopist*
Williams, Reba White *corporate financial executive, writer, researcher*
Willkie, Wendell Lewis, II, *lawyer*
Wilson, Mark *corporate financial executive*
Zimmerman, Lawrence A. *printing company executive*

**Stonington**
Brown, Meredith M. *lawyer*
Cole, Richard A. *retired lawyer*
Elliott, Osborn *journalist, educator, retired dean*
Stoddard, Alexandra *interior designer, educator, writer*

**Storrs**
Baxter, Donald Leon Murray *education educator*
Kiene, Susan Maria *psychologist*
Petrovic, Kimberly Ann *nursing researcher, nursing educator*

**Storrs Mansfield**
Auriemma, Geno *women's college basketball coach*
Austin, Philip Edward *academic administrator*
Baldwin, Carlita Rose *minister*
Bartram, Ralph Herbert *physicist*
Bzymek, Zbigniew Marian *engineering educator*
Calhoun, Jim *men's college basketball coach*
Cazel, Fred A., Jr. *history professor*
Charters, Ann *literature educator*
Coons, Ronald Edward *historian, educator*
Crossgrove, Roger Lynn *art educator*
Croteau, Maureen Elizabeth *journalism educator*
Deotte, Michael J. *marketing professional*
Devereux, Owen Francis *retired metallurgy educator*
Farr, William Joseph *secondary school educator*
Franklin, Brinley *library director*
Franklin, Wayne S. *literature and language professor, writer*
Gaxiola, Roberto Adrian *plant biologist, researcher*
Gross, Robert Alan *history professor*
Gui, Changfeng *mathematics professor*
Katz, Leonard *psychology professor, researcher*
Kerr, Kirklyn M. *academic administrator, veterinarian, pathologist*
Klemens, Paul Gustav *physicist, researcher*
Kline, Nancy Mattoon *librarian*
Laufer, Hans *developmental biologist, educator*
MacDonald, John Thomas *school system administrator*
Maier, Romulus *journalist*
Marcus, Harris Leon *materials science educator*
Marcus, Philip Irving *virology educator, researcher*
Nicholls, Peter J. *academic administrator*
Overmyer-Velazquez, Mark *history professor*
Pitkin, Edward Thaddeus *aerospace engineer, consultant*
Price, Glenda Delores *dean, college president*
Reifsnider, Kenneth Leonard *metallurgist, educator*
Rimland, Lisa Phillip *writer, composer, lyricist*
Rose, Dale A.J. *performing arts educator*
Saternow, Tim *set designer, lighting designer, theater educator, painter*
Shaw, Montgomery Throop *chemical engineering professor*
Stephens, Jack Edward *civil engineer, consultant*
Stwalley, William Calvin *physics professor, chemistry professor*
Tucker, Edwin Wallace *law educator*
Wang, Guiling *education educator, researcher*
Woods, David G. *dean*
Zhang, Yuwen *mechanical engineer, researcher*

**Stratford**
Blair, Sylvia H. *aerospace engineer*
Feinberg, Dennis Lowell *dermatologist*
LaDonna, Frank *psychologist*
Mahoney, Maurice Jeremiah *medical educator*
O'Rourke, James Louis *lawyer*
Spodick, Pearl Blegen *counselor, medical psychotherapist*

**Suffield**
Bianchi, Maria *critical care nurse, acute care nurse practitioner*
Hanzalek, Astrid Teicher *public information officer, consultant*
Sullivan, Edmund Bertram *writer*

**Taconic**
Medvecky, Patricia *retired elementary school educator*

**Terryville**
Doughty-Jenkins, Bonnie-Marie *middle school educator*

**Thomaston**
Mühlanger, Erich *ski manufacturing company executive*

**Torrington**
Drobena, Thomas John *minister, educator*
Handelman, William Alan *physician*
Marshall, Kathleen Ann *elementary school educator*

**Trumbull**
Allen, Richard Stanley (Dick Allen) *literature and language professor, writer*
Berg, Charles G. *insurance company executive*
Ewing, Anna M. *stock exchange executive*
Lang, James Richard *education consultant*
Nevins, Lyn (Carolyn A. Nevins) *school disciplinarian*

Norcel, Jacqueline Joyce Casale *educational association administrator*
Watson, Donald Ralph *architect, dean, writer, artist*
Williams, Ronald Doherty *lawyer*

### Uncasville
Lobo, Rebecca *professional basketball player*

### Unionville
Dublac, Robert Revak *artist*

### Vernon Rockville
Marmer, Ellen Lucille *pediatrician, cardiologist*
Purnell, Oliver James III *judge*
Putnam, Richard *dentist, educator*
Roden, Jon-Paul *retired educator, labor union organizer, educational consultant*
Wolff, Gregory Steven *insurance company executive*

### Voluntown
Caddell, Foster *artist*
Thevenet, Patricia Confrey *social studies educator*

### Wallingford
Cline, John Carroll *psychologist*
Cohen, Gordon S. *health products executive*
Hartz, Richard Allen *research scientist*
Jia, Weitao *dental products executive, researcher*
Lauttenbach, Carol *artist*
Lelas, Snjezana *pharmacologist, researcher*
Loeffler, Martin H. *electronics executive*
Neff, John Adam *artist*
Shanahan, Edward J. *headmaster*
Tyczynski, Jerzy Edward *epidemiologist*
Wojtasik, Joseph T. *retired military officer, small business owner*

### Washington
Grimes, Margaret Whitehurst *artist, educator*
Leab, Daniel Joseph *history professor*

### Washington Depot
Pendleton, Moses Robert Andrew *dancer, choreographer*
Tracy, Michael Cameron *choreographer, educator*

### Waterbury
Brown, Lillian Hill *retired academic administrator*
Dost, Mark W. *lawyer*
Dudrick, Stanley John *surgeon, research scientist, educator*
Fischbein, Charles Alan *pediatrician*
Garsten, Joel Jay *gastroenterologist*
Harper, Barbara Clara *educational program administrator, counselor*
Koliani, Leonardi *physician*
Lang, Christine JoAnn *elementary school educator*
Luedke, Frederick Lee *manufacturing executive*
Lum, Johnny *physician assistant, consultant*
Mador, Jonathan Mark *director, education educator*
Martone, Eric Anthony Domenic *history educator*
McDonald, Francis Michael *judge trial referee, retired state supreme court justice*
Pape, William James, II, *newspaper publisher*
Sanders, Richard L. *academic administrator*
Smith, James Copenhaver *bank executive*
Upson, Thomas Fisher *judge, retired state senator, lawyer*
Wolfe, Harriet Munrett *lawyer*
Wood, Robert L. *chemicals executive*

### Waterford
Commire, Anne *playwright, writer, editor*
Hinkle, Janet *psychologist*
Hinkle, Muriel Ruth Nelson *naval warfare analysis company executive*
Johnson, Gary William *environmental scientist, consultant*
London, David Bruce *psychiatrist*
Pierson, Anne Bingham *physician*
Walsh, Peter Joseph *marketing professional*

### Watertown
Watson, Michael Thomas *biology educator*

### West Cornwall
Engel, Jeffrey Mark *musician, music educator*
Simont, Marc *artist*

### West Hartford
Bigler, Harold Edwin, Jr. *retired investment company executive*
Boothe, Power *visual artist, filmmaker, set designer*
Braus, Ira L. *music educator, researcher*
Calip, Roger *writer, educator*
Clear, Albert F., Jr. *retired hardware manufacturing company executive*
Coleman, Winifred Ellen *academic administrator*
Collins, Alma Jones *language educator, writer*
Detmar-Pines, Gina Louise *business strategy and policy educator*
Dubé, Cynthia Christine *physics educator, consultant, video producer*
Faude, Wilson Hinsdale *museum director, consultant*
Gitterman, Alex *social work educator*
Glasser, Joseph *management consultant, educator*
Gould, Laurence Ira *physicist*
Harrison, Walter Lee *university president*
Karotkin, Rose A. *marketing professional*
Keller, Dorothy Bosch *art educator*
Malone, Thomas Francis *academic administrator, meteorologist*
Markham, Claire Agnes (M. Clare Markham) *retired chemistry educator, consultant*
Raffay, Stephen Joseph *manufacturing executive, director*
Silver, Herbert *physician*
Tonkin, Humphrey Richard *academic administrator, educator*
Wessel, Frederick Warner *artist, educator*
Wilder, Michael Stephen *former insurance company executive*

### West Haven
Boronico, Jess Stephen *management science educator, dean*

Ellis, Lynn Webster *retired finance educator, retired telecommunications consultant*
Haley, George Thomas *marketing educator*
Haley, Usha C.V. *international business educator*
Hatch, Annia *gymnast*
Kyriakides, Tassos Constantino *biostatistician*
Lisi, Anthony James *chiropractor, educator*
Onton, Ann Louise Reuther *chemist*

### West Mystic
Liberty, Frank J. *lawyer*

### West Redding
Rhodes, Stanley Williams *retired secondary school educator*

### West Simsbury
Morest, Donald Kent *neuroscientist, educator*

### Westbrook
Fuller, Martha M. *poet*

### Weston
Aibel, Howard James *arbitrator, mediator*
Bleifeld, Stanley *sculptor*
Cohen, Fred Howard *lawyer, investment company executive*
Daniel, James *curator, writer*
Diforio, Robert George *literary agent*
Falber, Harold Julius *marketing professional*
Fredrik, Burry *theater producer, theater director*
Kilty, Jerome Timothy *playwright, theater director, actor*
Murray, Stephen James *lawyer*
Murray, Thomas J. *advertising executive*
Oliver, Sandra *art dealer, painter*
Thompson, N(orman) David *insurance company executive*
Wiseman, Carter Sterling *writer, educator*
Zimmerman, Bernard *investment banker*

### Westport
Aasen, Lawrence Obert *public relations executive*
Baker, Leonard Morton *manufacturing executive*
Barberi, Robert Obed *lawyer*
Blau, Barry *marketing professional, financial consultant*
Breitbarth, S. Robert *manufacturing executive*
Carr, Cynthia *lawyer*
Chernow, Ann Levy *artist, educator*
Clausman, Gilbert Joseph *retired medical librarian*
Cohen, Eric I. *lawyer*
Daw, Harold John *lawyer, director*
Defeo, Ronald M. *machinery manufacturing executive*
Donaldson, James Neill *banker*
Feliciano, José *entertainer*
Ferris, Roger Patrick *architect*
Fisher, Leonard Everett *artist, educator, writer*
Freedman, Judith Greenberg *retired elementary school educator, state legislator*
Frese, Edward Scheer, Jr., (Ted Frese) *information technology executive, consultant*
Goodman, Stanley Erwin *surgeon*
Hedge, Arthur Joseph, Jr. *manufacturing executive*
Heyman, Ronnie Feuerstein *lawyer*
Hotchner, Aaron Edward *author*
Kelly, Paul Knox *investment banker*
Kovatch, Carol Wilhelm *small business owner*
Kramer, Sidney B. *publishing executive, literary agent, lawyer*
Kurz, Mitchell Howard *marketing communications executive*
Levien, Roger Eli *strategy and innovation consultant*
Lewis, Margaret Mary *marketing professional*
MacCormack, Charles Frederick *international relief organization executive*
Manley, John Frederick *political scientist, educator*
Margolis, Emanuel *lawyer, educator*
McCormack, Donald Paul *newspaper consultant*
McKane, David Bennett *business executive*
Newman, Paul *actor, food products executive, race car driver*
O'Keefe, John David *brokerage house executive*
Razzano, Pasquale Angelo *lawyer*
Ready, Robert James *finance company executive*
Reilly, Nancy (Anne Caulfield Reilly) *painter*
Rudd, Nicholas *investor, consultant*
Sacks, Herbert Simeon *psychiatrist, educator, consultant*
Samberg, Arthur J. (Art Samberg) *investment company executive*
Schriever, Fred Martin *management consultant, financial investor*
Sheiman, Ronald Lee *lawyer*
Siff, Marlene Ida *artist, space designer*
Smith, Andrew James Thomas *music educator*
Smith, Peter Wolfgang *physicist, artist*
Solum, John Henry *flutist, educator, author*
Stern, Robert D. *publishing executive*
Stewart, Martha Kostyra *entrepreneur, lecturer, author*
Walton, Alan George *venture capitalist*
Warner, Kerstin Julianna *gifted and talented educator*
Weiss, Harvey *artist, educator*
Widman, Phillip C. *machinery manufacturing executive*

### Wethersfield
Osborne, Louise *publishing executive*

### Willimantic
Barbuto, Leah M. *early childhood and technology educator, consultant*
Brodie, Ellen Faith *theater educator, director*
Carter, David George, Sr. *academic administrator*
Escoto, Carlos Aurelio *psychology professor, researcher*
Free, Rhona Campbell *economics professor*
Singh, Delar K. *education educator*
Wilson, Margaret Sullivan *retired executive dean, consultant*

### Wilton
Adams, Thomas Tilley *lawyer*
Bair, Tom *publishing executive*
Binder, Steven F. *publishing executive*
Bishop, William Wade *advertising executive*

Brown, James Thompson, Jr. *operations research specialist, information scientist*
Davis, Joel *publisher*
Duke, Robert Dominick *lawyer*
Farley, James Parker *retired advertising agency executive*
Frank, Robert Allen *media consultant*
Fricke, Richard John *lawyer*
Grunewald, Donald *former college president, educator*
Healy, James Casey *lawyer*
Hersh, Ira Paul *tax specialist, financial consultant*
Kaskell, Peter Howard *professional society administrator, lawyer*
Mitchell, Richard Boyle *security firm executive*
Nickel, Albert George *advertising agency executive*
Poundstone, Sally Hill *library director*
Reilly, Kathleen C. *director, retired secondary school educator*
Seitz, Nicholas Joseph *editor, journalist*
Slater, Ralph Evan *lawyer*
Tarde, Jerry (Gerard Tarde) *magazine executive*
Weiland, Juliette Marie *public relations executive, freelance photographer, writer*
Wright, Joseph Robert, Jr. *corportate executive*

### Windsor
Auten, Arthur Herbert *history professor*
Ferraro, John Francis *investment banker*
Weigel, Russell H. *headmaster*

### Windsor Locks
Coelho, Sandra Signorelli *secondary school educator, consultant*

### Winsted
Atkins, Adam Preston *music educator, singer*
Stawicki, Joseph John, Jr. *marketing executive*

### Woodbridge
Alvine, Robert *industrialist, entrepreneur, world business leader, philanthropist, business owner*
Cone, Virginia Williams *retired historian*
Conte, Alberta *language educator*
Dupré, Louis *retired philosopher, educator*
Kleiner, Diana Elizabeth Edelman *art historian, educator, academic administrator*
Malloy, Ina Arlene *secondary school educator, photographer*
Menchaca, Frank *editorial director*
Westerberg, Kermit Berndt *librarian*

### Woodbury
Skinner, Brian John *geologist, educator*

### Woodstock Valley
Allaby, Stanley Reynolds *clergyman*

## DELAWARE

### Bear
Hudson, Kelly Marie *music educator*
McCann, Richard Stephen *lawyer*
Stewart, Shirley Anne *elementary school educator*

### Camden Wyoming
Bailey, Kay Wood *management consultant*
Jones, Jay Paul *environmental engineer*
Pfeuffer, Robert John *musician*

### Dagsboro
Hanna, Anne Marie *artist*
Mortenson, Thomas Theodore *health products executive, management consultant*

### Dover
Amick, Steven Hammond *state legislator, lawyer*
Braverman, Ray Howard *secondary school educator*
Britt, Maisha Dorrah *protective services official*
Carney, John C., Jr. *lieutenant governor*
Ennis, Bruce Clifford *retired lawyer*
Fondong, Vincent N. *virologist, educator*
Kim, Dae Ryong *management information systems educator*
Minner, Ruth Ann *governor*
Ridgely, Henry duPont *state supreme court justice*
Sessoms, Allen Lee *academic administrator, physicist, educator, retired diplomat*
Smyth, Joel Douglas *newspaper executive*
Sorenson, Liane Beth McDowell *director, state legislator*
Spence, Terry R. *state legislator*
Taylor, Suzonne Berry Stewart *real estate broker*
Wilson, Samuel Mayhew *surgeon*
Windsor, Harriet Smith *state official*
Woodruff, Valerie *state agency administrator*
Young, Robert Bond *lawyer*

### Georgetown
Holland, Randy James *state supreme court justice*
Orlando, John D. *elementary school educator*

### Greenville
DeWees, Donald Charles *security firm executive*
Long, Linda Ann *lawyer*
Parets, Paul L. *music educator*
Reeder, Charles Benton *retired economic consultant*
Reynolds Cooch, Nancy D. (Mrs. Edward W. Cooch Jr.) *sculptor*
Schroeder, Herman Elbert *scientific consultant*
Walker, Sally Barbara *retired glass company executive*

### Hockessin
Croyle, Barbara Ann *health facility administrative executive*
Sawin, Nancy Churchman *educational consultant*
Valbuena-Briones, Angel Julian *retired language educator, author*

### Laurel
Selby, Cora Norwood *retired elementary school educator*

### Lewes
Beaufait, Frederick W(illiam) *retired engineering educator*

Costigan, Constance Frances *artist, educator*
DeBastiani, Roberta *school psychologist*
Fried, Jeffrey Michael *health care administrator*
Neal, Carole Elkins *music educator*
Poulterer, William Taylor III *river pilot*
Rudmann, Brent L. *museum director, educator*
Saliba, Anis Khalil *surgeon*
Spence, Sandra *retired professional society administrator*
Warden, Richard Dana *government labor union official*

### Middletown
Cataldi-May, Lauren Michelle *head of religious order, music director*
Hall, Peter Michael *physics professor, electronics engineer*
Harney, Edward Gary *music educator*
Roach, Daniel T., Jr., (Tad Roach) *headmaster*

### Milford
Bergmann, William J. *personnel director*

### Millsboro
Lasher, Hiram Nelson *entrepreneur, consultant*

### Millville
Zinman, David Joel *conductor*

### Milton
Carrow, Milton Michael *law educator*
Lindsay, Joyce W. *secondary school educator*
Provost, Thomas Taylor *dermatology educator, researcher*

### New Castle
Almquist, Don *illustrator, artist*
Brownson, Kenneth C. *dean*
Cansler, Leslie Ervin *retired newspaper editor*
Guidry, A. Gail *secondary school educator*
Newell, Katherine Claiborne *librarian*
Rolland, Kathy Ann *elementary school educator*
Sanderson, Devon Lee *elementary school educator*

### Newark
Allen, Herbert Ellis *environmental chemistry educator*
Appelbaum, Ian *research scientist, educator*
Bailey, Daniel Carl *higher education administrator*
Berk, Dawn *mathematics professor*
Bilinsky, Yaroslav *political scientist*
Boncelet, Charles George *engineering educator*
Boylan, Anne Mary *historian*
Brown, Hilton *artist, educator, writer*
Burmeister, John Luther *chemistry professor, consultant*
Butkiewicz, James Leon *economics professor, researcher, consultant*
Byrne, John Michael *energy and environmental educator*
Campbell, Linzy Leon *molecular biology researcher, educator*
Cha, Daniel K. *environmental engineer, educator*
Chapman, H. Perry *art educator*
Colton, David Lem *mathematician, educator*
Dawson, Carl *English literature educator*
Day, Robert Androus *literature and language professor, retired library director, editor, publisher*
DeLorme, Michael *toxicologist, researcher*
DePietropaolo, Daniel L. *physician, educator*
DeVivo, Sal J. *newspaper executive*
DiRenzo, Gordon James *sociologist, psychologist, educator*
Dybowski, Cecil *chemistry educator*
Elson, Charles Myer *law educator*
Esrey, Elizabeth Gove Goodier *chemist, biologist*
Gantzer, Mary Lou *medical products executive*
Gehrlein, William Vincent *business professor*
Gibson, Ann Eden *art historian, educator*
Godwin, Ralph Edward *retired computer operator*
Homer, William Innes *art history educator, art expert, writer*
Jackson, Marvin Dennis *journalism educator, writer*
Kim, Hee June *engineer*
Lathrop, Thomas Albert *language educator*
Le Min, Thomas Francis *law enforcement official, educator*
Lemole, Gerald Michael *surgeon*
Levia, Delphis F., Jr. *geography professor*
Luke, David Russell *mathematician, educator*
Mangone, Gerard J. *maritime law educator*
Matsumoto, Roger Lee Ken *research scientist, artist*
Mitchell, Peter Kenneth *educational consultant*
Murray, Richard Bennett *retired physics professor*
Neal, James Preston *state senator, project engineer*
Pika, Joseph A. *political scientist, educator, educational association administrator*
Polenova, Tatyana *chemistry professor, researcher*
Rayle, Heather Lynnette *chemist*
Ritter, William Frederick *civil and agricultural engineering educator, consultant*
Robinson, Marie Hadley *voice educator*
Roselle, David Paul *academic administrator, mathematician, educator*
Rowe, Charles Alfred *artist, graphics designer, educator*
Russell, Thomas William Fraser *chemical engineer, educator*
Sandler, Stanley Irving *chemical engineering educator*
Sarkar, Kausik *acoustical engineer, educator*
Sawyer, John Edward *management educator*
Schaefer, Paul William *retired entomologist*
Semmel, Stuart *history professor*
Stark, Robert Martin *mathematician, civil engineer, educator*
Steiner, Roger Jacob *linguistics educator, writer, researcher*
Stick, Thomas Howard Fitchett *architect, construction litigation consultant*
Tannian, Francis Xavier *economist, educator*
Vassiliou, Eustathios *chemist, consultant*
Velury, Uma *finance educator, researcher*
Wagner, Norman Joseph III *chemical engineering educator, researcher*
Weintraub, Stanley *arts and humanities educator, writer*
Wilson, Deborrah *physical education educator*

Dimberg, Lennart Axel *medical researcher, physician*
Diner, Bryan C. *lawyer*
Dingell, John David *congressman*
Dinh, Viet D. *law educator*
Dionne, E. J., Jr. *columnist*
DiPerna, Frank Paul *photographer, educator*
Disheroon, Fred Russell *lawyer*
Dixon, Glenn *art critic*
Dixon, Michel L. *educational administrator*
Dixson, Diane Elizabeth *acquisitions librarian, tax preparation business owner*
Doan, Lurita Alexis *federal agency administrator*
Doan, Michael Frederick *editor*
Dobriansky, Paula Jon *federal agency administrator*
Dodd, Christopher John *senator*
Doebbler, Curtis F.J. *lawyer*
Doggett, Lloyd Alton, II, *congressman, retired judge*
Dolan, Edward Charles *lawyer*
Dolan, Michael William *lawyer*
Dole, Bob (Robert Joseph Dole) *lawyer, retired senator*
Dole, Elizabeth Hanford (Liddy Dole) *senator, former federal agency administrator*
Dolin, Mitchell F. *lawyer*
Domenech, Edgar A. *government agency administrator*
Domenici, Pete Vichi (Vichi Domenici) *senator*
Domingo, Placido *tenor*
Dominguez, Cari M. *federal official*
Donahue, Thomas Reilly *trade union official*
Donaldson, Samuel Andrew *journalist*
Donegan, Charles Edward *lawyer, educator*
Donilon, Thomas E. *federal official*
Donlon, Claudette *performing company executive*
Donna, Roberto *restaurateur, chef*
Donnelly, Shaun Edward *government agency administrator*
Donohoe, Cathryn Murray *journalist*
Donohue, Thomas Joseph *business association administrator*
Donovan, George Joseph *transportation executive, consultant*
Dooley, Calvin Millard *former congressman*
Doolittle, Jesse William, Jr. *lawyer*
Doolittle, John Taylor *congressman*
Doran, Charles Francis *political scientist, consultant*
Dorfman, Cynthia Hearn *government agency administrator*
Dorgan, Byron Leslie *senator*
Doria, Marilyn L. *lawyer*
Dorn, Georgette Magassy *library official*
Dorn, James Andrew *editor*
Dorn, Jennifer Lynn *federal official*
Dorr, Thomas C. *federal agency administrator*
Dorsen, David M(ilton) *lawyer*
Dotson, Donald L. *lawyer*
Doty, Shayne Taylor *organist*
Dougherty, Jude Patrick *philosopher, educator, dean*
Douglas, Leslie *investment banker*
Doumato, Lamia *librarian, historian*
Dowd, John Maguire *lawyer*
Dowd, Maureen *columnist*
Downie, Leonard, Jr. *editor, writer*
Downie, Richard Duncan *government agency administrator, retired military officer*
Downs, Anthony *economist, consultant, real estate consultant*
Downs, Thomas Michael (Tom Downs) *transportation executive*
Doyle, A. Patrick *lawyer*
Doyle, Michael F. (Mike Doyle) *congressman*
Drake, Thelma Day *congresswoman*
Dreeben, Michael R. *federal agency administrator*
Dreier, David Timothy *congressman*
Drew, Elizabeth *commentator, journalist, writer*
Drinan, Robert Frederick *law educator*
Droms, William George *finance educator, investment advisor*
Drysdale, Douglas D. *lawyer*
Duberstein, Kenneth Marc *management consultant, former White House chief of staff*
Dublin, Thomas David *retired preventive medicine physician*
DuBois, April L. *not-for-profit developer, director*
DuBois, Raymond Francis, Jr. *civilian military employee, former marketing professional*
Duemling, Robert Werner *diplomat, museum director*
Duff, James C. *lawyer*
Duffey, Joseph Daniel *academic administrator*
Duffy, Brian P. *editor*
Duffy, John Fitzgerald *lawyer, educator*
Duffy, Michael F. *commissioner*
Dugan, John Cunningham *federal agency administrator, lawyer*
Duggan, Juanita D. *trade association administrator*
Dujack, Stephen Raymond *editor*
Dukert, Betty Cole *television producer*
Dunbar, Leslie Wallace *writer, consultant*
Duncan, John J., Jr. *congressman*
Duncan, Robert Michael *lawyer, political organization administrator*
Dunn, David B. *ambassador*
Dunn, H. Stewart, Jr. *lawyer*
Dunn, James Milton *retired religious organization administrator*
Dunn, Michael M. *academic administrator, career military officer*
Dunn, Michael V. *commissioner*
Dunne, Patrick W. *federal agency administrator, retired military officer*
Dunner, Donald Robert *lawyer*
Dunton, James Raynor *publisher*
Durbin, Dick (Richard Joseph Durbin) *senator*
Durney, Michael Cavalier *lawyer*
Dutro, John Thomas, Jr. *geologist, paleontologist*
Dutta, Biprodas *physics professor*
Duvall, Tyler Davis *federal agency administrator*
Dwyer, Maureen Ellen *lawyer*
Dwyer Southern, Kathy *museum administrator*
Dybul, Mark Richard *ambassador*
Dye, Rebecca Feemster *commissioner*
Dye, Stuart Selley *lawyer*
Dyer, Susan Kristine *editor, librarian*
Dyk, Timothy Belcher *federal judge*

Dyke, Charles William *retired army officer*
Eads, George Curtis *economic consultant*
Eagleburger, Lawrence Sidney *former secretary of state*
Earll, Jerry Miller *internist, educator, endocrinologist*
Earp, Naomi Churchill *federal official, lawyer*
Easterbrook, Gregg Edmund *writer*
Eastin, Keith E. *civilian military employee, lawyer*
Eastment, Thomas James *lawyer*
Easton, John Jay, Jr. *lawyer*
Eaton, Sabrina Catherine Elizabeth *journalist*
Eaton, William A. *ambassador, former federal agency administrator*
Eckenhoff, Edward Alvin *health facility administrator, educator*
Eckland, William S *lawyer*
Economon, Paul David *lawyer, management consultant*
Eddy, John Joseph *diplomat*
Edelman, Eric Steven *federal agency administrator, former ambassador*
Edelman, Marian Wright *not-for-profit developer, lawyer*
Edelman, Peter Benjamin *lawyer, educator*
Edge, Joe D. *lawyer*
Edlavitch, Susan T. *lawyer*
Edsall, Thomas Byrne *reporter*
Edson, Charles Louis *lawyer*
Eduardo, Ley *economist*
Edwards, Bob (Robert Alan Edwards) *radio news anchor*
Edwards, Chet (Thomas Chester Edwards) *congressman*
Edwards, Harry Thomas *federal judge*
Effron, Andrew S. *federal judge*
Efros, Ellen Ann *lawyer*
Eftekhari, Abe *computer scientist, department chairman*
Eggenberger, Andrew Jon *federal agency administrator*
Ehlers, Vernon James *congressman*
Ehrenhaft, Peter David *lawyer*
Ehrlich, Alan Marshall *lawyer, educator*
Eichen, Jeffrey L. *lawyer*
Ein, Daniel *allergist*
Eisenberg, Meyer *lawyer*
Eisenberg, Pablo Samuel *non-profit organization executive*
Eisenstat, David H. *lawyer*
Eisenstein, Laurence Jay *lawyer*
Eisner, Howard *engineering educator, engineering executive*
Eizenstat, Stuart Elliot *lawyer, former federal agency administrator*
Elcano, Mary S. *lawyer*
Elfin, Mel *magazine editor*
El-Fishawy, Saad Samuel *lawyer*
Elias, Thomas Sam *botanist, author*
El Khadem, Hassan Saad *chemistry professor, researcher*
Eller, Matthias M. *mathematics professor*
Ellett, Ted (E. Tazewell Ellett) *lawyer*
Ellicott, John LeMoyne *lawyer*
Elliott, Edwin Donald, Jr. *lawyer, educator, federal agency administrator*
Elliott, Emerson John *education consultant, policy analyst*
Elliott, Graham John *music educator, director*
Elliott, Thomas Michael *retired association executive, educator, consultant*
Ellis, Courtenay *lawyer*
Ellis, Joe W. *federal agency administrator*
Elmer, Brian Christian *lawyer*
El-Nakib, Hesham Moussa *diplomat*
Elrod, Eugene Richard *lawyer*
Elsasser, Glen Robert *journalist*
Elwood, Patricia Cowan *district secretary, political consultant, international relations education specialist*
Ely-Raphel, Nancy *diplomat*
Emanuel, Rahm *congressman*
Emden, Craig A. *lawyer*
Emely, Mary Ann *association executive*
Emerson, Jo Ann H. *congresswoman*
Engel, Eliot Lanze *congressman*
Engel, John *lawyer*
Engel, Margaret *journalist*
England, Gordon Richard *federal agency administrator*
Engleman Connors, Ellen G. *federal agency administrator*
Engler, Renata Johanna Martha *allergist, immunologist, internist, educator*
English, Philip Sheridan *congressman*
English, Richard Allyn *sociologist, educator*
Ensenat, Donald Burnham *ambassador, lawyer*
Ensign, John Eric *senator, former congressman*
Entman, Robert Mathew *communications educator, consultant*
Enzi, Michael Bradley *senator, accountant*
Epps, Roselyn Elizabeth Payne *pediatrician, educator*
Epstein, Ellen Chubin *prosecutor*
Epstein, Gary Marvin *lawyer*
Epstein, Gerald Lewis *technology and security policy analyst*
Epstein, Lionel Charles *lawyer*
Epstien, Jay Alan *lawyer*
Erdmann, Charles Edgar *federal judge, former state supreme court justice*
Erdtmann, Frederick J. *physician, retired military officer*
Ericsson, Sally Claire *not-for-profit official*
Ershler, William Baldwin *biogerontologist, educator*
Escobedo Cabral, Anna *federal official*
Escolar, Diana M. *neurologist, researcher*
Esfandiary, Mary S. *physicial scientist, operations consultant*
Eshoo, Anna Georges *congresswoman*
Etheridge, Bob (Bobby Ray Etheridge) *congressman*
Etter, Delores M. *civilian military employee*
Etzioni, Amitai *sociologist, educator*
Evans, David C. *lawyer*
Evans, Donald Louis *think-tank executive, former secretary of commerce*
Evans, Joy *foundation administrator*
Evans, Lane *congressman*
Evans, Robert David *legal association executive*

Everett, Ralph Bernard *lawyer*
Everett, Terry *congressman*
Everson, Mark Whitty *federal agency administrator*
Ewing, Ky Pepper, Jr. *lawyer*
Faden, Alan Ira *neurology educator*
Faherty, Robert Louis *publishing executive*
Fahey, John M., Jr. *book publishing executive*
Fahmy, Nabil *ambassador*
Fahmy Hudome, Randa *lawyer*
Fairbanks, David Nathaniel Fox *otolaryngologist, surgeon, educator*
Fairbanks, Richard Monroe III *lawyer, retired ambassador*
Faith, Thomas Iain *historian, educator*
Faleomavaega, Eni Fa'auaa Hunkin *congressman*
Fales, Lisa Jose *lawyer*
Falk, Diane M. *research information specialist, librarian, writer, editor, director*
Fall, Dorothy *artist, art director, art association administrator*
Farabow, Ford Franklin, Jr. *lawyer*
Farr, Judith Banzer *retired literature educator, writer*
Farr, Michael Keogh *investment company executive*
Farr, Sam *congressman*
Farrell, Michael W. *judge*
Fattah, Chaka *congressman, former state legislator*
Faust, Emanuel, Jr. *lawyer*
Fedders, John Michael *lawyer*
Feder, Judith *dean*
Feeney, Tom *congressman*
Feffer, Gerald Alan *lawyer*
Feil, Michael Bruce *statistician*
Feinberg, Kenneth Roy *lawyer, law educator*
Feingold, Russell Dana *senator, lawyer*
Feinstein, Dianne *senator*
Feld, Karen Irma *columnist, journalist, commentator, speech professional*
Feldbaum, Carl *biotechnologist*
Feldhaus, Stephen Martin *lawyer*
Feldman, Clarice Rochelle *lawyer*
Feldman, Mark B. *lawyer*
Feldman, Roger David *lawyer*
Felix, Larry R. *federal agency administrator*
Fels, Nicholas Wolff *lawyer*
Fendrich, Roger Paul *lawyer*
Fennell, Stephen A. *lawyer*
Ferguson, Michael A. *congressman*
Ferrand, Louis George *lawyer*
Ferrara, Ralph C. *lawyer*
Ferrell, Elizabeth Ann *lawyer*
Ferrell, Michael J. *lawyer*
Ferren, John Maxwell *judge*
Ferretti, Maddalena Funicello *humanities educator*
Ferris, Charles Daniel *lawyer, former government official*
Feshbach, Murray *demographer, educator*
Feuer, Michael J. *educational association administrator, educator*
Feulner, Edwin J., Jr. *research foundation executive*
Fiedler, Marc *lawyer, advocate*
Field, Andrea Bear *lawyer*
Fielding, Fred Fisher *lawyer*
Fields, Stuart Howard *labor relations specialist*
Fields, Suzanne Bregman *syndicated columnist*
Figueroa, Orlando *federal agency executive*
Filner, Bob *congressman*
Fine, Glenn A. *federal agency administrator*
Fineberg, Harvey Vernon *medical institute administrator*
Fineman, Howard David *news correspondent*
Fingar, Thomas *federal official*
Finkel, David *journalist*
Finkel, Eugene Jay *lawyer*
Finkelstein, James David *physician, educator*
Finkle, Jeffrey Alan *professional association executive*
Finley, James I. *federal agency administrator*
Finneran, John Patrick, Jr. *finance company executive, educator*
Firestone, Charles Morton *lawyer, educator*
Fischer, Elizabeth (Betsy) *television producer*
Fishburne, Benjamin Postell III *lawyer*
Fishel, Andrew S. *managing director*
Fisher, Alice S. *federal agency administrator, lawyer*
Fisher, Bart Steven *lawyer, educator, investment banker*
Fisher, John R. *judge*
Fisher, Miles Mark, IV, *education educator, religious studies educator, minister*
Fisher, Robert Dale *stockbroker, retired naval officer*
Fishman, Ira *lawyer*
Fithian, John *trade association administrator, lawyer*
Fitton, Tom J. *lawyer*
Fitzgerald, Helen Teresa *social worker, writer*
Fitzgerald, Kevin C. *lawyer*
Fitzmyer, Joseph Augustine *theology studies educator, priest*
Fitzpatrick, James Franklin *lawyer*
Fitzpatrick, Michael G. *congressman, lawyer*
Flagg, Ronald Simon *lawyer*
Flaherty, Sister Mary Jean *dean*
Flake, Jeff *congressman*
Flake, L. Gordon *think-tank executive*
Flannery, Ellen Joanne *lawyer*
Flavin, Christopher *think-tank executive*
Fleischaker, Marc L. *lawyer*
Fleischman, Aaron I. *lawyer*
Fleisher, Eric Wilfrid *retired foreign service officer*
Fleming, Lee Virginia *art critic, writer, curator*
Flory, Peter Cyril Wyche *federal agency administrator*
Flowe, Carol Connor *lawyer*
Flügelman, Máximo Enrique *financier, composer*
Flyer, Michael R. *lawyer*
Foer, Franklin *editor*
Fogleman, Guy Carroll *physicist, mathematician, educator*
Foley, Mark Adam *congressman*
Foley, Maurice Brian *federal judge*
Foley, Tom (Thomas Stephen Foley) *former ambassador, former congressman*
Fong, Phyllis Kamoi *federal agency administrator, lawyer*

Forbes, James Randy *congressman*
Ford, Ann K. *lawyer*
Ford, Carl W., Jr. *consulting firm executive, former federal agency administrator*
Ford, Cecilia Sparks *federal agency administrator*
Ford, Charles A. *ambassador*
Ford, Harold Eugene, Jr. *congressman, lawyer*
Fore, Henrietta Holsman *federal agency administrator*
Foreman, Carol Lee Tucker *consumer advocate*
Foresman, George W. *federal agency administrator*
Forester, John Gordon, Jr. *lawyer*
Forgey, Benjamin Franklin *architecture and art critic*
Forkan, Patricia Ann *foundation executive*
Forrest, Herbert Emerson *lawyer*
Forrester, Patricia Tobacco *artist*
Forsten, Robert Douglas *military officer, psychiatrist*
Fort, Randall Martin *federal agency administrator*
Fortenberry, Jeffrey Lane *congressman*
Fortuño, Luis *congressman*
Fortuno, Victor M. *lawyer*
Foscarinis, Maria *lawyer*
Foss, Clive Frank Wilson *history professor*
Fossella, Vito John, Jr. *congressman*
Foster, C(harles) Allen *lawyer*
Foster, Hope S. *lawyer*
Foulke, Edwin Gerhart, Jr. *federal agency administrator, lawyer*
Fox, Hamilton Phillips, III, (Phil Fox) *lawyer*
Fox, James Edward, Jr. *federal agency administrator*
Fox, Thomas C. *lawyer*
Fox, William F. *dean, law educator*
Foxx, Virginia Ann *congresswoman, small business owner*
Francke, Rend Rahim *ambassador*
Franco, Omar *government agency administrator*
Francois, Francis Bernard *retired professional society administrator, lawyer, transportation consultant*
Frank, Barney *congressman*
Frank, Richard Asher *lawyer, health products executive*
Frank, Robert J. *lawyer*
Frank, Theodore David *lawyer*
Franklin, Barbara Hackman *former government official*
Franks, Trent *congressman*
Franzen, Byron T. (John Franzen) *media specialist*
Fraser, William M. III *career military officer*
Fratto, Tony (Salvatore Antonio Fratto) *federal agency administrator*
Fraulino, Philip Samuel *telecommunications industry executive*
Frawley Bagley, Elizabeth *government advisor, ambassador*
Frazer, Jendayi Elizabeth *federal agency administrator, former ambassador*
Freed, Joel M. *lawyer*
Freedman, Jay Weil *lawyer*
Freeman, Catherine E. *government policy advisor*
Freeman, Chas W., Jr. *federal agency administrator, writer, ambassador*
Freeman, Sharee M. *federal agency administrator*
Frelinghuysen, Rodney P. *congressman*
French, Roderick Stuart *university chancellor*
French, Valerie *history professor*
Fried, Bruce Merlin *lawyer*
Fried, Daniel *federal agency administrator, former ambassador*
Friedman, Daniel Mortimer *federal judge*
Friedman, Gregory H. *energy administrator*
Friedman, Robert Sidney *political science professor*
Friedman, Thomas Loren *foreign correspondent, writer*
Friend, Patricia A. *trade association administrator*
Fries, Helen Sergeant Haynes *civic leader*
Frisby, Herbert Russell *lawyer*
Frist, Bill (William Harrison Frist) *senator, thoracic surgeon*
Fritsche, Claudia *diplomat, ambassador*
Fritts, Edward O. *broadcasting association executive*
Froman, Veronica Zasadni *career officer*
Fromer, Kevin *federal agency administrator*
Frost, Edmund Bowen *lawyer*
Frost, Martin, III, (Jonas Martin Frost III) *lawyer, former congressman*
Fujimara, Makota *painter*
Fuller, Edwin Daniel *hotel executive*
Fulton, Kenneth Ray *professional association administrator*
Furash, Edward Elliott *investment company executive, banker, educator, writer, theater producer*
Furchtgott-Roth, Harold Wilkes *economist, consultant*
Furey, Roger P. *lawyer*
Furgurson, Ernest Baker, Jr., (Pat Furgurson) *writer*
Fusco, Aurilla Marie *director*
Gable, Edward Brennan, Jr. *lawyer*
Gadson, Sandra L. *nephrologist, medical association administrator*
Gage, John *labor union administrator*
Gajarsa, Arthur J. *judge*
Gajewski, Donald Andrew *orthopedist, surgeon*
Gale, Joseph H. *federal judge*
Gallagher, Michael David *lawyer, former federal agency administrator*
Gallagher, Patricia E. *government agency administrator*
Gallas, Philip S. *lawyer*
Gallegly, Elton William *congressman*
Gallo, Anthony Ernest *playwright, economist*
Galloway, Hoyt Wilson *library director*
Galloway, Joseph Lee, Jr. *writer, journalist*
Galston, William Arthur *political scientist, educator*
Gambatesa, Donald Anthony *federal agency administrator*
Ganter, Susan Lynn *foundation administrator, retired mathematics professor*
Gapen, Michael T. *economist*
Gardiner, Kent A. *lawyer*
Gardner, William Albert, Jr. *pathologist, medical products executive*

Garland, Gloria Jean *lawyer, consultant*
Garland, Merrick Brian *federal judge*
Garman, David Kline *federal agency administrator*
Garnette, Cheryl Petty *government agency administrator*
Garr, Sally D. *lawyer*
Garrels, Anne *news correspondent*
Garrett, Scott (E. Scott Garrett) *congressman, lawyer*
Garrett, Theodore Louis *lawyer*
Garrish, Theodore John *lawyer*
Garrison, Gwen E. *educational researcher, consultant*
Garthoff, Raymond Leonard *retired diplomat, diplomatic historian, researcher*
Garvey, Jane *public relations executive*
Gaskell, Judith Ann *law librarian*
Gati, Toby T. *international advisor*
Gatons, Anna-Marie Kilmade *government official*
Gaynor, Kevin Allen *lawyer*
Gaynor, Suzanne Marie *healthcare executive, researcher*
Gearan, Mark D. *former federal agency administrator*
Gehrig, Leo Joseph *retired surgeon*
Gelernter, David H. *critic, painter, educator*
Geller, Kenneth Steven *lawyer*
Gelmann, Edward Paul *oncologist, educator*
Geltman, Edward Alan *lawyer*
Genetski, Christian S. *lawyer*
Geniesse, Robert John *lawyer*
Gentner, Paul LeFoe *architect, consultant*
George, Warren S. *labor union administrator*
Georgieva, Rennie T. *medical librarian*
Gephardt, Dick (Richard Andrew Gephardt) *lawyer, former congressman*
Gerber, Joel *federal judge*
Gerber, Melanie K. *lawyer*
Geren, Pete (Preston M. Geren III) *civilian military employee, former congressman*
Gerlach, Jim (James William Gerlach) *congressman*
Gerry, Dale Francis *military officer, legislative staff member*
Gersh, Darren *television correspondent*
Gershman, Carl Samuel *foundation administrator*
Gerson, Elliot Francis *foundation administrator*
Gerson, Stuart Michael *lawyer*
Gesner, Lawrence H. *lawyer*
Gessaman, Donald Eugene *retired government executive*
Gest, Kathryn Waters *public relations executive*
Geyer, Georgie Anne *columnist, educator, commentator, writer*
Giallorenzi, Thomas Gaetano *optical engineer*
Giambastiani, Edmund P., Jr. *career military officer*
Gibbons, James Arthur *congressman*
Gibbons, Petch *real estate company executive*
Gibbs, Lawrence Blake *lawyer*
Giblin, Vincent J. *labor union administrator*
Gibson, Cecelia Anne *registrar*
Gibson, Emmitt E. *career officer*
Gibson, Florence Anderson *talking book company executive, narrator*
Gibson, Paul Raymond *international trade and investment development company executive*
Gibson, Reginald Walker *federal judge*
Gideon, Kenneth Wayne *lawyer*
Giffin, Gordon D. *former ambassador, lawyer*
Gilburne, Miles R. *venture capitalist*
Gilchrest, Wayne Thomas *congressman, secondary school educator*
Gilfoyle, Nathalie Floyd Preston *lawyer*
Gill, Clair F. *military career officer*
Gillan, Kayla J. *lawyer*
Gillespie, Edward Walter *former political organization executive*
Gilliam, Sam *artist*
Gillingham, Robert Fenton *economist, consultant*
Gilliom, Judith Carr *federal official*
Gillis, John W. *federal agency administrator*
Gillman, Daniel W. *information scientist*
Gilmor, Paul Eugene *congressman, lawyer*
Gillon, Peter M. *lawyer*
Gilman, Benjamin Arthur *former congressman, lawyer*
Gingrey, Phil (John Phillip Gingrey) *congressman*
Gingrich, Newt (Newton Leroy Gingrich) *former congressman*
Ginsberg, Marc Charles *former diplomat, investment company executive*
Ginsburg, Charles David *lawyer*
Ginsburg, Douglas Howard *federal judge*
Ginsburg, Gilbert J. *lawyer, educator*
Ginsburg, Martin David *lawyer, educator*
Ginsburg, Paul B. *health facility administrator*
Ginsburg, Ruth Bader (Joan Ruth Bader Ginsburg) *United States Supreme Court Justice*
Gioia, Dana (Michael Dana Gioia) *poet, critic, cultural organization administrator*
Girard, James Emery *chemistry professor*
Girod, Bernard A. *electronics executive*
Gittleman, Michael M. *lawyer*
Giuliano, Louis J. *former industrial manufacturing company executive*
Givhan, Robin Deneen *journalist*
Glancz, Ronald Robert *lawyer*
Glantz, Gina *political consultant*
Glasbrenner, Karl Christian *federal agency administrator*
Glasgow, Norman Milton *lawyer*
Glass, Andrew James *newspaper editor*
Glassman, James Kenneth *editor, writer, publishing executive*
Gleklen, Jonathan Ian *lawyer*
Glendening, Parris Nelson *former governor, political science educator*
Glick, Leslie Alan *lawyer*
Glickman, Stephen H. *judge*
Glover, Jere Walton *lawyer*
Glynn, Edward F., Jr. *lawyer*
Gnehm, Edward W., Jr. *ambassador*
Godsey, John Drew *retired minister, theology educator emeritus*
Goelzer, Daniel Lee *lawyer*
Goewey, David W. *lawyer*
Gohmert, Louis Buller, Jr. (Louie Gohmert) *congressman, former judge, lawyer*
Gold, Peter Frederick *lawyer*

Goldberg, Fred T., Jr. *lawyer*
Goldberg, Jolande Elisabeth *law librarian, lawyer*
Goldberg, Jonah Jacob *political columnist*
Goldberg, Seth A. *lawyer*
Goldblatt, Steven Harris *law educator*
Golden, Cornelius Joseph, Jr. *lawyer*
Golden, James Leslie *information technology executive, retired military officer*
Golden, Olivia Ann *human services administrator*
Goldin, Daniel S. *former federal agency administrator*
Goldman, Neil *association administrator*
Goldman, Steven Mark *lawyer*
Goldsmith, Barry Richard *lawyer, former federal agency administrator*
Goldsmith, Stephen *social services administrator, former mayor*
Goldsmith, Willis Jay *lawyer*
Goldstein, Allan Leonard *biochemist, educator*
Goldstein, Frank Robert *lawyer*
Goldstein, Michael B. *lawyer*
Goldstein, Thomas C. *lawyer*
Goldston, David James *state representative*
Goldway, Ruth Y. *federal agency administrator*
Goler, Wendell *political correspondent*
Golkiewicz, Gary J. *federal official*
Gollin, Michael A. *lawyer*
Goldner, Jack *labor association official*
Gonzales, Alberto R. *United States Attorney General, former state supreme court justice*
Gonzalez, Charles A. *congressman*
Gonzalez, Emilio T. *federal agency administrator*
Goode, Virgil H., Jr. *congressman*
Goodlatte, Bob (Robert William Goodlatte) *congressman, lawyer*
Goodman, Valerie Rene *secondary school educator*
Goodwin, Robert Keer *foundation administrator*
Gopnik, Blake *art critic*
Gordon, Barton Jennings (Bart Gordon) *congressman, lawyer*
Gordon, James Samuel *psychiatrist*
Gordon, Lincoln *political economist*
Gorelick, Jamie Shona *lawyer*
Gorham, William *organization executive*
Gorman, Joyce J(ohanna) *lawyer*
Gorman, Patricia Jane *editor*
Gorn, Janet Marie *government official*
Gorrell, J. Warren, Jr. *lawyer*
Goshorn, Richard Henley *lawyer*
Gostin, Lawrence O. *lawyer, educator*
Gottfried, Keith Evan *lawyer*
Gottlieb, Robert Gene *lawyer*
Gradison, Bill (Willis David Gradison Jr.) *former congressman*
Graham, Donald Edward *publishing company executive*
Graham, John H., IV, *association executive*
Graham, Lindsey Olin *senator*
Graham, Thomas, Jr. *lawyer*
Graham, Thomas Richard *lawyer*
Graham, William Pierson *investment banker, entrepreneur*
Grainger, Amanda R. *lawyer*
Grandmaison, J. Joseph *federal agency administrator*
Granger, Kay *congresswoman*
Grant, Carl N. *communications executive, sales executive*
Grapin, Jacqueline G. *economist*
Grassley, Chuck (Charles Ernest Grassley) *senator*
Graves, Samuel B., Jr. *congressman, retired state legislator*
Graves-Roman, Patricia Ann *language educator, writer*
Gray, Bradford Hitch *health service researcher*
Gray, George M. *federal agency administrator*
Gray, Lyons *federal agency administrator*
Gray, Mary Wheat *statistician, lawyer*
Gray, Sheila Hafter *psychiatrist, researcher*
Grealy, Mary R. *medical association administrator*
Greaux, Cheryl Prejean *federal agency administrator*
Green, Al *congressman*
Green, Donald Hugh *lawyer*
Green, Douglas G. *lawyer*
Green, Gene (Raymond Eugene Green) *congressman*
Green, Joyce Hens *federal judge*
Green, Madeleine F. *educational association administrator*
Green, Mark Andrew *congressman, lawyer*
Green, Richard C. *lawyer*
Green, Thomas Charles *lawyer*
Greenberger, I. Michael *lawyer*
Greene, Marcia Slacum *editor*
Greene, Thomas Hardy *architect*
Greene, William P., Jr. *federal judge*
Greenhalgh, Paul *museum director*
Greenhouse, Linda Joyce *journalist*
Greenwald, John Doyle *lawyer*
Greer, Mark Francis *information technology executive*
Gregg, Judd Alan *senator, former governor*
Gregor, Clark R. *public information officer*
Gregorian, Raffi *diplomat*
Grenier, Edward Joseph, Jr. *lawyer*
Griffenhagen, George Bernard *trade association executive*
Griffin, Christine M. *commissioner*
Griffin, Kelly Ann *public relations executive, consultant*
Griffin, Michael D. *federal agency administrator, aerospace scientist*
Griffin, Paul L. *publishing executive, fraternal organization administrator*
Griffin, Richard J. *federal agency administrator*
Griffin, Robert H. *career military officer*
Griffin, Robert Thomas *automotive company executive*
Griffis, Kirby T. *lawyer*
Griffith, Thomas Beall *federal judge*
Grigsby, Sharlyn Ann *human resources specialist*
Grijalva, Raul *congressman*
Grimaldi, James V. *journalist*
Grimes, John Grayson *federal agency administrator*
Griner, G. Christopher *lawyer*
Grob, George Frederick *health science association administrator*
Gross, Kenneth Andrew *lawyer*

Gross, Leon Jay *psychometrician*
Gross, Patrick Walter *information technology executive*
Grossman, Claudio M. *dean, law educator*
Grossman, Marc Issaiah *former federal agency administrator*
Grosvenor, Gilbert Melville *journalist, educator, publishing executive*
Grove, Brandon Hambright, Jr. *diplomat*
Gruenberg, Martin J. *federal agency administrator, lawyer*
Grunberg, Nancy R. *lawyer*
Guard, Patricia J. *federal agency administrator*
Gubser, Peter Anton *political scientist, writer, educator*
Guenther, Jack Donald *banker*
Guhin, Michael A. *ambassador*
Gulland, Eugene D. *lawyer*
Gulliford, James B. *federal agency administrator*
Gumpert, Gunther *artist*
Gunderson, Steven Craig *association executive, former congressman*
Gurdak, Michael P. *lawyer*
Gutierrez, Carlos M. *secretary of commerce, former grocery manufacturing company executive*
Gutierrez, Jay Matthew *lawyer*
Gutierrez, Luis V. *congressman, elementary education educator*
Gutknecht, Gilbert William, Jr. *congressman, former state legislator*
Gutman, Roy William *reporter*
Guttman, Egon *law educator*
Guzda, Henry Peter *industrial relations specialist*
Guzy, Carol *photojournalist*
Gwaltney, Corbin *publishing executive, editor*
Haber, Jonathan H. *lawyer*
Hachana, Mohamed Nejib *ambassador*
Hadley, Stephen John *national security advisor*
Hagee, Michael W. *career military officer*
Hagel, Chuck (Charles Timothy Hagel) *senator*
Hagel, Lawrence B. *federal judge*
Hagen, Wendy W. *public relations executive*
Hager, John Henry *federal agency administrator, former lieutenant governor*
Hager, Mary Hastings *nutritionist, educator, consultant*
Hager, Susan Kulka *public relations executive*
Hagin, Joseph Whitehouse, II, *federal official*
Hagner, John D. *lawyer*
Hahn, Lorna *political organization executive, author*
Hailey, Gary D. *lawyer*
Haines, Harry Allen *federal judge*
Haines, Martha Mahan *lawyer*
Halaska, Terrell *federal agency administrator*
Hale, David M. *ambassador*
Haley, John *risk management consultant*
Haley, Roger Kendall *librarian*
Hall, Dale (H. Dale Hall) *federal agency administrator*
Hall, Jason Piers Wilton *biologist*
Hall, Ralph Moody *congressman*
Hallgren, Richard Edwin *meteorologist*
Halperin, Jerome Arthur *retired pharmaceutical executive*
Halperin, Morton H. *political scientist*
Halperin, Samuel *education and training policy analyst*
Halpern, James S. *federal judge*
Halsey, Ashley III *newspaper editor*
Halstead, Edward Allen (Ted Halstead) *think-tank executive*
Halvorson, Newman Thorbus, Jr. *lawyer*
Hamburg, Margaret Ann (Peggy Hamburg) *public health administrator*
Hamilton, Lee Herbert *educational association administrator*
Hamlisch, Marvin *composer, conductor, musician, entertainer*
Hammond, Allen Lee *editor, consultant, former broadcaster, non-profit policy research center executive*
Hammond, William Michael *historian, educator*
Hampden Thompson, Gillian M.H. *research scientist*
Hampton, Philip G., II, *lawyer*
Hamre, John J. *think-tank executive, former federal agency administrator*
Hand, John Oliver *museum curator*
Hand, Lloyd N. *lawyer*
Hanley, Allison Anne *federal agency administrator*
Hanlon, Glen *professional hockey coach*
Hanlon, Stephen F. *lawyer*
Hanlon, William R. *lawyer*
Hannah, John P. *federal official*
Hansen, Charles Martin III *lobbyist*
Hansen, Joseph T. *labor union administrator*
Hansen, Kenneth *lawyer*
Hanzlik, Rayburn DeMara *lawyer*
Harbour, Pamela Jones *commissioner, lawyer*
Harding, Fann *retired science administrator*
Harkin, Thomas Richard *senator*
Harlem, Susan Lynn *librarian*
Harling, Barbara Jean *social worker*
Harman, Jane *congresswoman*
Harman, Sidney *audio and video company executive*
Harman, William Boys, Jr. *lawyer*
Harpham, Virginia Ruth *violinist*
Harrington, Anthony Stephen *lawyer, diplomat, business executive*
Harrington, Clifford M. *lawyer*
Harrington, Kathleen M. *public relations company executive, former federal agency administrator*
Harris, Don Victor, Jr. *lawyer*
Harris, Jeffrey *lawyer*
Harris, Katherine *congresswoman*
Harris, Scott Blake *lawyer*
Harrison, Earl David *lawyer, real estate company officer*
Harrison, Marion Edwyn *lawyer*
Harrison, Mark B. *lawyer*
Harrison, Patricia de Stacy *broadcast executive, former federal agency administrator*
Harrison, Todd A. *lawyer*
Harrop, William Caldwell *retired ambassador*
Hart, Christopher Alvin *lawyer*
Hart, Melissa Anne *congresswoman*
Hart, Sarah V. *federal agency administrator*

Harter, Donald Harry *neurologist, medical educator*
Harting, Harry Lloyd, Jr. *government agency administrator, retired military officer*
Hartman, Carl (Howard Carl Hartman) *reporter*
Hartman, Gary E. *pediatric surgeon*
Hartman, George Eitel *architect*
Hartmann, Robert Sankey *health facility administrator, not-for-profit fundraiser*
Hartwell, Stephen *investment company executive*
Harvey, Eleanor Jones *museum curator*
Harvey, Francis J. *civilian military employee*
Harvey, John Collins, Jr. *military officer*
Harvey, Sheila McCafferty *lawyer*
Harwit, Martin Otto *astrophysicist, writer, educator, museum director*
Harwood, John H., II, *lawyer*
Hassett, Joseph Mark *lawyer*
Hastert, Dennis (John Dennis Hastert) *congressman*
Hastings, Alcee Lamar *congressman, retired judge*
Hastings, Doc (Richard Norman Hastings) *congressman*
Hastings, Douglas Alfred *lawyer*
Hastings, George L. *federal official*
Hatch, Cary Collins *advertising executive*
Hatch, Orrin Grant *senator*
Hatfield, Fred *federal agency administrator*
Hauptman, Gregory B. *lawyer*
Hauser, Richard Alan *lawyer, foundation administrator*
Hausfeld, Michael D. *lawyer*
Havemann, Joel *editor*
Havlicek, Franklin J. *communications executive*
Hawke, Paul Henry *historian*
Hawkins, Philip Linton *real estate executive*
Hayden, Michael Vincent *CIA Director, career military officer*
Hayes, David John *lawyer*
Hayes, John C., Jr. *lawyer*
Hayes, Paula Freda *federal agency administrator*
Hayes, Robin (Robert Cannon Hayes) *congressman*
Haynes, R. Michael *lawyer*
Haynes, William James, II, *lawyer*
Hays, Dennis K. *former ambassador*
Haythe, Winston McDonald *lawyer, educator, real estate investor*
Hayworth, John David, Jr., (J.D. Hayworth) *congressman, former sportscaster*
Hazen, Robert Miller *research scientist, writer*
Headden, Susan M. *editor*
Hebert, Jay Howell *lawyer*
Hecht, Marjorie Mazel *editor*
Heckman, Jerome Harold *lawyer*
Heddell, Gordon S. *federal agency administrator*
Hedges, Harry George *retired computer scientist*
Hedges, Kamla King *library director*
Heelan, Patrick Aidan *philosophy educator*
Heenan, Michael Terence *lawyer*
Heffernan, James Vincent *lawyer*
Hefferon, Thomas Michael *lawyer*
Hefley, Joel Maurice *congressman*
Hefter, Laurence Roy *lawyer*
Heideman, Richard D. *lawyer*
Height, Dorothy I. *former foundation administrator*
Heimberg, Scott M. *lawyer*
Hein, Jay F. *federal official*
Heintz, John Edward *lawyer*
Heinz Kerry, Teresa F. (Maria Teresa Thierstein Simoes-Ferreira) *foundation administrator*
Heiss, Harry Glen *archivist*
Helgerson, John Leonard *federal agency administrator*
Heller, Jack Isaac *lawyer*
Heller, John Roderick III *lawyer, corporate financial executive*
Heller, Mark A. *lawyer*
Hellmuth, George William *architect*
Helmly, James R. *career military officer*
Helms, Robert Brake *economist, science administrator*
Hemingway, Thomas L. *career military officer, lawyer*
Henderson, Douglas Boyd *lawyer*
Henderson, Frances J. *lawyer*
Henderson, Karen LeCraft *federal judge*
Henderson, Wade J. *civil rights advocate, law educator*
Henke, Michael John *lawyer, educator*
Henke, Robert Joseph *federal agency administrator*
Henke, Tracy Ann *federal agency administrator*
Hennessy, Ellen Anne *lawyer, financial analyst, educator*
Henry, Ed *news correspondent*
Henry, Emil W., Jr. *federal agency administrator*
Henry, John Cooper *journalist*
Henry, Ronald Kenneth *lawyer*
Hensarling, Jeb *congressman*
Hensler, David J. *lawyer*
Herbold, Patricia Louise *ambassador*
Herbst, John Edward *federal agency administrator, former ambassador*
Herger, Walter William *congressman*
Herlihy, Scott C. *lawyer*
Herman, Andrea Maxine *newspaper editor*
Hernandez, Livan Eisler *professional baseball player*
Herrett, Richard Allison *agricultural research institute administrator*
Herridge, Catherine *political correspondent*
Herrling, Christopher J. *lawyer*
Herseth, Stephanie Marie *congresswoman, lawyer*
Hershey, Robert Lewis *mechanical engineer, management consultant*
Hersman, Deborah A. P. *federal agency administrator*
Herzstein, Robert Erwin *lawyer*
Hess, Michael Edward *federal agency administrator*
Hess, Stephen *political scientist, writer*
Hevel, Gary Francis *public information officer, consultant*
Hewitt, Emily Clark *federal judge, minister*
Hewitt, Paul Buck *lawyer*
Heymsfeld, David Alan *lawyer*
Heyward, Peter E. *lawyer*
Hiatt, Fred *journalist*

Hiatt, Jonathan Paul *lawyer, labor union administrator*
Hiebert, Ray Eldon *writer, educator*
Higgins, Bradford R. *federal agency administrator*
Higgins, Brian *congressman*
Higgins, Claudia R. *lawyer*
Higgins, James Henry III *marketing executive*
Higgins, Kathryn O'Leary (Kitty O'Leary Higgins) *federal agency administrator, former consulting firm executive*
Higgins, Paul John *medical director, career military officer*
Higham, Scott *reporter*
Hightower, Dennis Fowler *retired entertainment company executive, educator*
Higuchi, Shirley A. *lawyer*
Hileman, Bette *journalist*
Hill, Christopher R. *federal agency administrator, former ambassador*
Hill, Edwin D. *trade association administrator*
Hill, John H. *federal agency administrator*
Hill, Kent Richmond *federal agency administrator*
Hilleary, (William) Van *former congressman, lawyer*
Hillen, John Francis *federal agency administrator*
Hillman, Jennifer Anne *federal official*
Hills, Carla Anderson *lawyer, former secretary of housing and urban development*
Hills, Roderick M. *lawyer, former government official*
Hills, Stephen P. *publishing executive*
Hillsman, Sally T. *sociologist*
Hinchey, Maurice D. *congressman*
Hinden, Stanley Jay *newspaper editor*
Hinojosa, Rubén *congressman*
Hirji, Rafik F. *water resources expert*
Hirschhorn, Eric Leonard *lawyer*
Hite, William P. *labor union administrator*
Hittner, George J. *lawyer*
Hoagland, Jimmie Lee *newspaper editor*
Hobbins, William T. *career officer*
Hobbs, Ann S. *lawyer*
Hobbs, Caswell O. III *lawyer*
Hobbs, Ira *federal agency administrator*
Hobson, David Lee *congressman, lawyer*
Hodges, Heather M. *ambassador*
Hoekstra, Peter *congressman, manufacturing executive*
Hoffa, James P. *labor union administrator*
Hoffinger, Adam Steven *lawyer*
Hoffman, Alfred, Jr. *ambassador, real estate developer*
Hoffman, E. Leslie *economist*
Hoffman, Joel Elihu *lawyer*
Hoffman, Kenneth R. *lawyer*
Hogan, Felicity *artist*
Holbrooke, Richard Charles Albert *investment banker, former ambassador*
Holden, Tim (Thomas Timothy Holden) *congressman, protective official*
Holder, Eric H. *lawyer, former federal agency administrator*
Holdsclaw, Chamique Shaunta *professional basketball player*
Holladay, Wilhelmina Cole *interior designer, museum director*
Hollingsworth, Joe Gregory *lawyer*
Hollis, Sheila Slocum *lawyer*
Holmes, Mark V. *judge*
Holt, Helen *librarian, consultant, former government official*
Holt, Rush D. *congressman, physics educator, researcher, consultant*
Honda, Michael M. *congressman*
Hong, Mun Kyung *internist*
Hooks, Aubrey *ambassador*
Hooley, Darlene *congresswoman*
Hope, William Duane *retired zoologist, curator*
Hopson, Mark D. *lawyer*
Horahan, Edward Bernard III *lawyer*
Horn, Charles M. *lawyer*
Horn, Donald Herbert *lawyer*
Horn, Marian Blank *federal judge*
Horn, Sharon K. *government agency administrator*
Horn, Wade Frederick *federal agency administrator*
Horne, Michael Stewart *lawyer*
Horner, Constance Joan *federal agency administrator*
Hornyak, Joseph P. *lawyer*
Horowitz, Herbert Eugene *retired diplomat*
Horowitz, Philip Martin *lawyer*
Horton, James Oliver *history educator*
Horton, Philip W. *lawyer*
Hostettler, John N. *congressman*
Hotez, Peter Jay *research scientist, educator*
House, W(illiam) Michael *lawyer*
Howard, Glen Scott *foundation executive, lawyer*
Howard, Jack *industrial relations specialist, consultant*
Howard, Jeffrey Hjalmar *lawyer*
Howard, John *federal agency administrator*
Howard, Roscoe Conklin, Jr. *lawyer, former prosecutor*
Howe, Fisher *management consultant, retired government agency administrator*
Hoyer, Steny Hamilton *congressman*
Hoyt, Clark Freeland *journalist, editor*
Hsia, Judith Ann *physician*
Huband, Frank Louis *educational association executive*
Hubbard, Allan Brooks *federal official, former chemical company executive*
Hubbard, Richard L. *lawyer*
Huberman, Benjamin *technology consultant*
Huberman, Richard Lee *lawyer*
Hudgins, Willie L., Jr. *lawyer*
Hudnut, William Herbert III *political scientist*
Hudson, Michael Craig *political science professor*
Hufbauer, Gary Clyde *economist, lawyer, educator*
Huge, Harry *lawyer*
Huggins, James Bernard *communications executive*
Hughes, Elizabeth R. (Beth) *lawyer*
Hughes, Karen Parfitt *federal agency administrator*
Hughes, Kent Higgon *economist*
Hughes, Marija Matich *law librarian*
Hughes, Sharon Mary *trade association executive*
Hughes, Thomas Lowe *foundation executive*
Huhtala, Marie Therese *federal agency administrator, former ambassador*

Hulkower, Mark J. *lawyer*
Hulse, Carl *newspaper executive*
Hulshof, Kenny Charles *congressman*
Hume, Brit (Alexander Britton Hume) *journalist*
Hume, Cameron R. *ambassador*
Hungar, Thomas G. *federal agency administrator, lawyer*
Hungate, Joseph Irvin III *information technology executive*
Hunnicutt, Charles Alvin *lawyer*
Hunt, Albert R. *editor*
Hunt, Earl Stephen *federal agency administrator*
Hunt, Wayne Robert, Sr. *non-profit organization executive*
Hunter, Duncan Lee *congressman*
Hunter, Michael James *state government official, lawyer, educator*
Huntress, Wesley Theodore, Jr. *research scientist*
Hussain, Syed Taseer *biomedical researcher, educator*
Huston, John Wilson *military officer, historian*
Hut, A. Stephen *lawyer*
Hutchinson, Asa (W. Asa Hutchinson) *lawyer, former federal agency administrator*
Hutchinson, James S. (Jamie) *lawyer*
Hutchison, Claude B., Jr. *federal agency administrator*
Hutchison, Kay Bailey *senator*
Hutt, Peter Barton *lawyer*
Huttler, Stephen B. *lawyer*
Hyatt, Thomas Karl *lawyer*
Hyde, Henry John *congressman*
Hyman, Lester Samuel *lawyer*
Ihrie, John Richard III *art educator*
Ijaz, Mansoor *news correspondent*
Inglis, Bob (Robert Durden Inglis) *congressman*
Inhofe, James M. *senator*
Innis, Pauline *writer, publishing company executive*
Inouye, Daniel Ken *senator*
Inslee, Jay Robert *congressman*
Ireland, Oliver *lawyer*
Irving, Thomas L. *lawyer*
Isaacs, Amy Fay *political organization executive*
Isaacson, Walter Seff *think-tank executive*
Isakson, Johnny (John Hardy Isakson) *senator, former congressman*
Isbell, David Bradford *lawyer, educator*
Ischinger, Wolfgang *ambassador, diplomat*
Ishaq, Ashfaq *foundation administrator, economist, educator*
Ishimaru, Stuart Jon *commissioner, former federal agency administrator*
Iskandar, Harris *attache*
Israel, Steven Jay *congressman*
Issa, Darrell E. *congressman*
Istook, Ernest James, Jr., (Jim Istook) *congressman, lawyer*
Iverson, Kristine Ann *federal agency administrator*
Jackson, Alphonso Roy *secretary of housing and urban development*
Jackson, Beverly Roberson *state agency administrator, former ambassador*
Jackson, Darryl W. *federal agency administrator*
Jackson, Jeanine E. *ambassador*
Jackson, Jesse Louis, Jr. *congressman*
Jackson, John Howard *lawyer, educator*
Jackson, Margaret Elizabeth *science educator*
Jackson, Michael P. *federal agency administrator, former engineering company executive*
Jackson Lee, Sheila *congresswoman*
Jacobs, David Ernest *environmental health scientist*
Jacobs, Julian I. *federal judge*
Jacobs, Madeleine *professional society administrator, writer*
Jacobs, Verne Louis *physicist, researcher*
Jacobsen, Hugh Newell *architect*
Jacobsen, Raymond Alfred, Jr. *lawyer*
Jacobson, Allen Howard *economist*
Jacobson, David Edward *lawyer*
Jacobson, Louis Alan *journalist*
Jacobson, Michael Faraday *consumer advocate, writer*
Jacobson, Richard Lee *lawyer, educator*
Jacobson, Tracey Ann *ambassador*
Jakes, J. Michael *lawyer*
Jamar, Steven Dwight *law educator*
James, Bruce Richard *publishing executive*
Jamison, Antawn *professional basketball player*
Janes, Jackson *research institute executive*
Janes, William Sargent *real estate company executive*
Jankowsky, Joel *lawyer*
Janney, Christopher G. *lawyer*
Jarque, Carlos M. *former federal official*
Jarrett, Jeffrey D. *federal agency administrator*
Jarvis, Charlene Drew *academic administrator, former scientist*
Jaskot, Richard D. *academic administrator, career military officer*
Jasper, John A. *writer, lawyer*
Jaspersen, Frederick Zarr *economist*
Jatras, James George *lawyer*
Jecklin, Lois Underwood *art corporation executive, consultant*
Jefferson, William Jennings (Jeff Jefferson) *congressman*
Jeffery, Reuben III *federal agency administrator*
Jeffords, James Merrill *senator*
Jeffress, William Horace, Jr. *lawyer*
Jehl, Douglas *news correspondent*
Jenkins, Thomas H. *lawyer*
Jenkins, William Lewis (Bill Jenkins) *congressman*
Jennings, Deborah E. *lawyer*
Jensen, Mark A. *lawyer*
Jensen, Thomas C. *lawyer*
Jenson, William G. *federal agency administrator*
Jiechi, Yang *ambassador*
Jindal, Bobby Piyush *congressman*
Jochum, James J. *lawyer, former federal agency administrator*
Johanns, Michael Owen *secretary of agriculture, former governor*
John, Christopher Charles *lobbyist, former congressman*
John, Frank Herbert, Jr. *real estate appraiser, investor, marketing executive*
Johns, Christopher George *photojournalist, editor*

Johnson, Brenda LaGrange *ambassador*
Johnson, Charles E. *federal agency administrator*
Johnson, Clay III *federal official*
Johnson, David Raymond *lawyer*
Johnson, David Timothy *diplomat*
Johnson, Eddie Bernice *congresswoman*
Johnson, Henry Louis *federal agency administrator, former school system administrator*
Johnson, James A. *finance company executive*
Johnson, Jennifer J. *federal official*
Johnson, Kelly A. *federal agency administrator*
Johnson, Nancy Lee *congresswoman*
Johnson, Philip McBride *lawyer*
Johnson, Richard A. *lawyer*
Johnson, Richard Kent *publishing executive*
Johnson, Samuel (Sam Johnson) *congressman*
Johnson, Sheila Crump *entrepreneur*
Johnson, Stephen L. *federal official*
Johnson, Timothy Peter *senator*
Johnson, Timothy Vincent *congressman, lawyer*
Jolly, Bruce O. *lawyer*
Jonas, John Francis *lawyer*
Jonas, Richard Andrew *medical educator*
Jonas, Tina Westby *federal agency administrator*
Jones, A. Elizabeth *corporate communications specialist, former federal agency administrator*
Jones, Aidan Drexel *lawyer*
Jones, Alice Samuels *elementary education educator, reading specialist*
Jones, Boisfeuillet, Jr., (Bo Jones) *publishing executive*
Jones, Coletta L. *senior pastor*
Jones, George Washington, Jr. *lawyer*
Jones, James Robert *ambassador, retired congressman, lawyer*
Jones, Judith Miller *director*
Jones, Kelsey A. *lawyer, educator*
Jones, Michael D. *lawyer*
Jones, Richard Henry *ambassador*
Jones, Stanley Boyd *retired researcher*
Jones, Stephanie Tubbs *congresswoman, lawyer, prosecutor*
Jones, Susan Dorfman *real estate broker, writer*
Jones, Walter Beaman, Jr. *congressman*
Joo, Douglas D.M. *newspaper and video production and aviation executive*
Jordan, Eddie *professional basketball coach*
Jordan, Irving King *university president*
Jordan, Robert Elijah III *lawyer*
Jose, Pedro A. *physician*
Joseph, Robert G. *federal agency administrator*
Journey, Drexel Dahlke *lawyer*
Joyce, Anne Raine *editor*
Joyce, Frederick Mark (Rick) *lawyer*
Joyner, Christopher Clayton *international relations educator*
Justesen, Troy Ralph *federal agency administrator*
Kabel, Robert James *lawyer*
Kafka, Gerald Andrew *lawyer*
Kahan, Jonathan Seth *lawyer*
Kahn, Charles N., III, (Chip Kahn) *medical association administrator*
Kahn, Deborah *artist, educator*
Kahn, Edwin Leonard *lawyer*
Kahn, Michael *stage director*
Kail, Floyd Michael *lawyer*
Kaiser, Michael M. *performing company executive*
Kaiser, Philip Mayer *retired diplomat*
Kalb, Marvin *public policy and government educator*
Kalfatovic, Martin Robert *librarian, writer*
Kaltchev, Ivo *musician, educator*
Kaludis, George *management consultant, publishing executive, educator*
Kamber, Victor Samuel *political consultant*
Kammer, Jerry *reporter*
Kamras, Jason *mathematics educator*
Kanjorski, Paul Edmund *congressman, lawyer*
Kao, Timothy Wu *civil engineering educator*
Kapikian, Catherine Andrews *artist*
Kaplan, Gilbert B. *lawyer*
Kaplan, Joel David *federal official*
Kaplan, Paul A. *lawyer*
Kaplan, Steven *lawyer*
Kaplun, Paul T. *lawyer*
Kapp, Robert Harris *lawyer*
Kappes, Stephen R. *federal agency administrator*
Kappler, Ann M. *lawyer, finance company executive*
Kaptur, Marcia Carolyn (Marcy Kaptur) *congresswoman*
Karl, Jonathan David *television journalist*
Karle, Isabella L. *chemist*
Karle, Jerome *physicist, researcher*
Karpinski, Gene Brien *not-for-profit developer, think-tank executive*
Karsner, Andy (Alexander Armand Karsner) *federal agency administrator*
Kass, Benny Lee *lawyer*
Kass, Leon Richard *humanities educator*
Kassinger, Theodore William (Ted R. Kassinger) *lawyer, former federal agency administrator*
Kasten, Robert W., Jr. *former senator*
Kato, Ryozo *ambassador*
Katyal, Neal K. *law educator*
Katz, Irv *not-for-profit executive*
Katz, John W. *lawyer, state official*
Katz, Sherman E. *lawyer*
Katzen, Sally *lawyer, educator*
Kaufman, Joshua Jacob *lawyer*
Kaufman, Leonard H. *psychologist*
Kaufman, Roger E. *engineering educator*
Kaufman, Thomas Frederick *lawyer, educator*
Kauzlarich, Richard Dale *retired ambassador, political scientist, consultant*
Kavanaugh, Brett Michael *federal judge*
Kaveeshwar, Ashok G. *federal agency administrator*
Kazin, Michael *historian, writer*
Keane, Kevin W. *beverage association administrator*
Keaney, Thomas Addis *academic administrator, management consultant, educator, military officer*
Kearney, Stephen Michael *federal agency administrator*
Keating, Francis Anthony, II, *retired governor, lawyer*
Keegel, C. Thomas *labor union administrator*

Keeley, Robert Vossler *retired academic administrator, ambassador*
Keenan, Nancy A. *pro-choice association executive*
Keeney, John Christopher *lawyer*
Keeney, John B., Jr. *lawyer*
Keeny, Spurgeon Milton, Jr. *professional society administrator*
Keevey, Richard Francis *federal official, state official, educator*
Keiner, R(obert) Bruce, Jr. *lawyer*
Keisler, Peter Douglas *federal agency administrator, lawyer*
Keitelman, Jeffrey Robert *lawyer*
Keller, Craig Lee *social services administrator*
Keller, Ric *congressman, lawyer*
Kelley, Colleen M. *labor union administrator*
Kelley, David Christopher *philosopher*
Kelley, Patrick W. *health science association administrator, preventive medicine physician*
Kelliher, Joseph T. *commissioner*
Kelly, David M. *lawyer*
Kelly, John Joseph, Jr. *federal official*
Kelly, Marguerite Stehli *fashion executive, consultant*
Kelly, Paul Vincent *federal agency administrator*
Kelly, Sue W. *congresswoman*
Kelly, Suedeen G. *commissioner*
Kelly, Thomas J., Jr. *lawyer*
Kelly, William Charles, Jr. *retired lawyer*
Kemp, Geoffrey Thomas Howard *political scientist, consultant*
Kemp, Jack French *former congressman*
Kempthorne, Dirk Arthur *secretary of the interior, former governor*
Kendall, David E. *lawyer*
Kendall, Peter Landis *television news executive*
Kendrick, John Whitfield *economist, educator, consultant*
Kendrick, Kim *federal agency administrator*
Kennard, Mary Elizabeth *lawyer*
Kennedy, Anthony McLeod *United States Supreme Court Justice*
Kennedy, Dane Keith *history professor*
Kennedy, Eugene Richard *microbiologist, university dean*
Kennedy, Mark Raymond *congressman*
Kennedy, Patrick F. *federal agency administrator, former ambassador*
Kennedy, Patrick Joseph *congressman*
Kennedy, Richard Odell *physician*
Kennedy, Robert Emmet, Jr. *historian, educator*
Kennedy, Ted (Edward Moore Kennedy) *senator*
Kennelly, Barbara B. *retired congressman, federal agency administrator*
Kenney, Kristie Anne *ambassador*
Kenney, Robert James, Jr. *lawyer*
Kent, Jill Elspeth *entrepreneur, art appraiser, lawyer*
Kern, Paul John *retired military officer*
Kerr, Stuart H. *lawyer, think-tank executive*
Kerry, John Forbes *senator*
Kerwin, Cornelius Martin *academic administrator, educator*
Kesselman, Marc L. *federal agency administrator*
Kessler, Gladys *federal judge*
Kessler, Judd Lewis *lawyer*
Ketchum, James Roe *curator*
Keyworth, George Albert *physicist, consulting company executive*
Khozeimeh, Issa *electrical engineer, educator*
Kienzl, Gregory Stephen *education researcher*
Kies, Kenneth J. *lawyer*
Kiko, Colleen Duffy *lawyer*
Kiko, Philip George *lawyer*
Kilberg, William Jeffrey *lawyer, director*
Kildee, Dale Edward *congressman*
Kilgore, Edwin Carroll *retired federal agency administrator*
Kilian, Pamela Reeves *journalist, writer*
Killefer, Campbell *lawyer*
Killgore, Andrew Ivy *former ambassador*
Kilpatrick, Carolyn Cheeks *congresswoman*
Kim, Mikyong Minsun *education educator*
Kim, Sukhan *lawyer*
Kim, Wan J. *federal agency administrator, lawyer*
Kimes, Don Mark *artist, educator*
Kimmitt, Robert Michael *federal agency executive, former business executive*
Kinberg, Robert *lawyer*
Kincannon, Louis (Charles Louis Kincannon) *federal agency administrator*
Kind, Ronald James *congressman, lawyer*
King, Colbert Isaiah *editor*
King, Gwendolyn S. *retired utility company executive, retired federal official*
King, James C. *retired military officer*
King, Larry (Larry Zeiger) *broadcaster, radio personality*
King, Llewellyn Willings *publishing executive, educator, commentator, writer*
King, Patricia Ann *law educator*
King, Peter Thomas *congressman, lawyer*
King, Steve *congressman*
King, Warren R. *judge*
Kingham, Richard Frank *lawyer*
Kingsley, Mary Lee *marketing professional*
Kingston, Jack *congressman*
Kinsley, Michael E. *newspaper columnist*
Kiplinger, Knight Austin *journalist, publishing executive*
Kirch, Darrell Gene *medical association administrator, former academic administrator, former dean*
Kirk, Artemis G. *university librarian*
Kirk, Dennis Dean *lawyer*
Kirk, Donald *journalist*
Kirk, Mark Steven *congressman*
Kirkpatrick, David D. *news correspondent*
Kirkpatrick, Jeane Duane Jordan *political scientist, federal official*
Kirsanow, Peter N. *federal agency administrator*
Kirsch, Laurence Stephen *lawyer*
Kiser, Chérie R. *lawyer*
Kissel, Peter Charles *lawyer*
Kitchen, John Howard *economist*
Kittrell, Steven Dan *lawyer*
Kittrie, Nicholas *international lawyer, writer*
Klain, Ronald Alan *lawyer*
Klarfeld, Peter James *lawyer*
Klawiter, Donald Casimir *lawyer*

Matsui, Doris Okada *congresswoman*
Mattsson, Ake *psychiatrist, physician*
Maxey, Randall W. *medical researcher, health science association administrator*
Maxwell, David Ogden *federal agency administrator, mortgage company executive*
May, Stephen *writer, federal official, historian*
May, Timothy James *lawyer*
Mayer, Haldane Robert *federal judge*
Mayers, Daniel Kriegsman *lawyer*
Maynes, Charles William *foundation executive*
Mayo, George Washington, Jr. *lawyer*
Mayo, John W. *finance educator*
Mays, Janice Ann *lawyer*
Mazo, Mark Elliott *lawyer*
McAdams, Melinda Jeanne *copy editor*
Mc Afee, William *government official*
McBee, Susanna Barnes *retired journalist*
McBride, Jonathan Evans *management consultant, director*
McBride, Michael Flynn *lawyer*
McCabe, Edward Aeneas *lawyer*
McCain, John Sidney III *senator*
McCallum, Robert Davis, Jr. *ambassador, former federal agency administrator*
McCann, Clifton Everett *lawyer*
McCarron, Douglas J. *labor union administrator*
McCarthy, Carolyn *congresswoman*
McCarthy, Maura *critic, editor*
McCaul, Elizabeth *investment advisor, former state agency administrator*
McCaul, Michael T. *congressman*
McCaw, Susan Rasinski *ambassador*
McClung, Gwendolyn *soil microbiologist*
McClure, Frederick Donald *lawyer*
McClure, William Pendleton *lawyer*
McCollam, William, Jr. *utilities executive*
McCollum, Betty *congresswoman*
McConnell, Bruce William *information technology executive*
McConnell, Mitchell, Jr., (Addison Mitchell McConnell Jr.) *senator, lawyer*
McConnell, Nicholas Stillwell *lawyer*
McCormack, Douglas P. *lawyer*
McCormack, Sean Ian *federal agency administrator*
McCormally, Kevin Jay *editor*
McCormick, David H. *federal agency administrator*
McCormick, Walter Bernard, Jr. *trade association administrator*
McCormick, William Paul *ambassador*
McCrabb, Donald Raymond *pastoral field educator*
McCrery, James (Jim McCrery) *congressman*
McCutchen, Tammy Dee *federal agency administrator*
McDaniel, James Arthur *educational association administrator*
McDaniels, William E. *lawyer*
McDavid, Janet Louise *lawyer*
McDermott, James A. *congressman, psychiatrist*
McDiarmid, Robert Campbell *lawyer*
McDonald, Frances D. *government official, editor, lawyer*
McDowell, Heather L. *lawyer*
McDowell, Robert M. *commissioner*
McDowell-Craig, Vanessa Dennise *supervisor, consultant*
McEldowney, Nancy *ambassador*
McElroy, Edward J. *labor union administrator*
McElveen, Junius Carlisle, Jr. *lawyer*
McElveen-Hunter, Bonnie *international relief organization executive*
McEntee, Christine W. *architecture association administrator, former medical association administrator*
McEntee, Gerald W. *labor union administrator*
McFeatters, Ann Carey *journalist*
McGee, James M. *federal agency administrator*
McGee, Robert Merrill *oil industry executive*
McGinnis, James Michael *physician*
McGinnis, Patricia Gwaltney *non-profit organization executive*
McGovern, James P. *congressman*
McGovern, Michael *lawyer*
McGrath, Kathryn Bradley *lawyer*
McGreevey, Lisa S. *investment company executive*
McGuan, Kathleen H. *lawyer*
McGuire, John F. *international relief organization executive*
McGuirl, Marlene Dana Callis *law librarian, educator*
McHenry, Patrick Timothy *congressman*
McHugh, James Lenahan, Jr. *lawyer*
McHugh, John Michael *congressman*
McIntosh, David M. *former congressman*
McIntyre, Mike (Douglas Carmichael McIntyre II) *congressman*
McIsaac, Christopher C. *lawyer*
Mc Kay, Emily Gantz *civil rights and nonprofit professional*
McKay, Margo Marquita *federal agency administrator, lawyer*
McKee, Margaret Jean *federal agency administrator*
McKeever, Joseph Francis III *lawyer*
McKenna, Frank Joseph *ambassador, lawyer*
McKeon, Howard Phillip (Buck McKeon) *congressman, former mayor*
McKinney, Cynthia Ann *congresswoman*
McKinney, David Duane *museum director, architectural historian*
McKinnon, John D. *reporter*
McLarty, Thomas F., III, (Mack McLarty) *former governement advisor, business executive*
McLaughlin, David *foundation administrator*
McLaughlin, John J. *broadcast executive, television producer, journalist, political commentator*
McLean, R. Bruce *lawyer*
McLeod, David G. *urologist, educator*
McLucas, William Robert *lawyer, former federal agency administrator*
McMahon, Joseph Einar *lawyer, consultant*
McMillin, Stephen S. *federal agency administrator*
McMillion, Charles Wayne *economist, educator, consultant*
McMorris, Cathy *congresswoman*
McMurray, Claudia Anne *federal agency administrator, lawyer*

McNamara, Michael T. *lawyer*
McNamara, Robert Strange *former President of the World Bank, former Secretary of Defense*
McNulty, Michael Robert *congressman*
McNulty, Paul J. *federal agency administrator, former prosecutor*
McPhee, George *professional sports team executive*
Mc Phee, Henry Roemer *lawyer*
Mc Pherson, Harry Cummings, Jr. *lawyer*
McPherson, James E. *judge*
McPherson, Peter (M. Peter McPherson) *educational association administrator, former academic administrator*
McPherson, Ted R. (Edward Russell McPherson) *federal agency administrator*
McPhie, Neil Anthony Gordon *federal official*
McQueary, Charles E. (Chuck McQueary) *federal agency administrator*
McQuillan, Laurence Joseph *communications consultant, educator*
McSlarrow, Kyle E. *telecommunications association executive, former federal agency administrator*
Mead, Christopher *lawyer*
Mead, Kenneth Minor *lawyer, former federal agency administrator*
Means, Thomas Cornell *lawyer*
Mederos, Carolina Luisa *public policy consultant*
Meece, Roger A. *ambassador*
Meehan, Martin Thomas *congressman, lawyer*
Meehan, Shirley *human services administrator*
Meek, Kendrick B. *congressman*
Meeks, Gregory Weldon *congressman*
Meese, Edwin III *law and public policy educator, former United States attorney general*
Meggers, Betty Jane *anthropologist, researcher*
Megginson, Elizabeth R. *legislative staff member, director, lawyer*
Mehlman, Bruce P. *former federal agency administrator, trade association administrator*
Mehlman, Kenneth B. *poltical organization administrator, former federal official*
Meijer, Paul Herman Ernst *physicist, educator*
Meisburg, Ronald Edward *federal agency administrator, lawyer*
Melamed, Arthur Douglas *lawyer*
Melancon, Charles *congressman*
Melendy, David Russell *newscaster, reporter*
Mellor, John Williams *economist, consultant*
Melnick, Howard A. *hotel executive*
Meloy, Sybil Piskur *retired lawyer*
Melton, Carol A. *communications executive*
Memmott, Scott A. *lawyer*
Menaker, Frank H., Jr. *lawyer*
Mencher, Bruce Stephan *judge*
Mendelsohn, Bruce S. *lawyer*
Mendoza, Julie C. *lawyer*
Menendez, Robert *senator, former congressman*
Menkel-Meadow, Carrie Joan *law educator*
Merow, James F. *federal judge*
Merrell, Jesse Howard *lawyer*
Merrifield, Dudley Bruce *finance educator, federal official*
Merritt, Carolyn *government agency administrator*
Meshulam, Deborah R. *lawyer*
Messiah-Jiles, Sonceria *publishing executive*
Meyer, Dennis Irwin *lawyer*
Meyer, Katherine Anne *lawyer*
Meyer, Lindsay Beardsworth *lawyer*
Meyer, Paul *information technology executive*
Meyerrose, Dale William *federal official, retired military officer*
Meyers, Linda Dee *non-profit administrator, researcher*
Meyers, Wayne Marvin *microbiologist, physician*
Meyerson, Adam *foundation administrator*
Meyerson, Harold *journalist*
Mica, John L. *congressman*
Michaelson, Martin *lawyer*
Michaud, Michael Herman *congressman*
Michel, Paul Redmond *federal judge*
Michelman, Kate *advocate*
Michnich, Marie E. *health policy analyst, consultant, educator*
Mickey, Paul F(ogle), Jr. *lawyer*
Miers, Harriet Ellan *federal official, lawyer*
Migdal, Nelson *lawyer*
Mikulski, Barbara Ann *senator*
Milam, William Bryant *former ambassador, senior policy scholar*
Milch, Thomas H. *lawyer*
Miles, David Michael *lawyer*
Miles, John Jeffries *lawyer*
Millar, James Robert *economist, educator, university official*
Millender-McDonald, Juanita *congresswoman*
Miller, Andrew Pickens *lawyer*
Miller, Brad (Ralph Bradley Miller) *congressman*
Miller, Candice S. *congresswoman*
Miller, Christine Odell Cook *federal judge*
Miller, Ewing Harry *retired architect*
Miller, Gary G. *congressman*
Miller, George *congressman*
Miller, George W. *federal judge, lawyer*
Miller, H. Todd *lawyer*
Miller, James Clifford III *economist*
Miller, James Forrest *lawyer*
Miller, Jeanne-Marie Anderson (Mrs. Nathan J. Miller) *language educator, academic administrator*
Miller, Jeff *congressman*
Miller, John *federal agency administrator, former news correspondent*
Miller, John T., Jr. *lawyer, educator*
Miller, Margery *psychologist, educator, speech pathology/audiology services professional, mental health services professional*
Miller, Marshall Lee *lawyer*
Miller, Mary Jeannette *retired management consultant*
Miller, Nicole *art columnist*
Miller, R. Charles *lawyer*
Miller, Richard N. *former medical association administrator*
Miller, William Green *former ambassador*
Millian, John C. *lawyer*
Mills, Thomas L. *lawyer*
Milman, Natalie *education educator*
Milstein, Elliott Steven *lawyer, educator, academic administrator*

Minardi, Ann Segura *lawyer, musician*
Minarik, Joseph John *economist, researcher*
Mineta, Norman Yoshio *former secretary of transportation, management consultant*
Minkoff, Alice Sydney *interior designer stylist*
Mirengoff, Paul E. *lawyer, political blogger*
Mirkow, Frank J. *lawyer*
Mirvahabi, Farin *lawyer*
Mishel, Lawrence *economics research director*
Mishkin, Barbara Friedman *lawyer*
Mishkin, Frederic Stanley *bank executive, economics educator*
Missar, Charles Donald *retired librarian*
Mistral, Jacques *economist*
Mitchell, Andrea *journalist*
Mitchell, Ruthie Yvette *human services administrator, director*
Moates, G. Paul (Paul Moates) *lawyer*
Moe, Richard Palmer *lawyer*
Moe, Ronald Chesney *public administration researcher*
Moeller, Philip D. *commissioner*
Moffitt, William Benjamin *lawyer*
Mogel, William Allen *lawyer*
Mohrman, Kathryn j. *academic administrator*
Mok, Samuel Tinsing *federal agency administrator*
Moler, Elizabeth Anne *lawyer*
Molinari, Susan *former congresswoman*
Mollohan, Alan Bowlby *congressman*
Mombouli, Serge *ambassador*
Mondello, Lisette McSoud *federal agency administrator*
Monroe, Jane D. *federal agency administrator*
Monroe, Stephanie Johnson *federal agency administrator*
Montanez-Johner, Nancy *federal agency administrator*
Montedonico, Joseph *lawyer*
Montelongo, Michael *federal agency administrator, military officer*
Montgomery, Brian D. *commissioner*
Montgomery, John A. *physicist*
Montoya, Regina T. *association executive, lawyer*
Moody, Sheryl L. *educational association administrator*
Mooney, John Joseph *chemical engineer*
Mooney, Marilyn *lawyer*
Moore, Amy Norwood *lawyer*
Moore, Barbara C. *fraternal organization administrator*
Moore, Bob Stahly *communications executive*
Moore, Dennis *congressman*
Moore, Gwendolynne S. (Gwen Moore) *congresswoman*
Moore, Jacquelyn Cornelia *retired labor union administrator, editor*
Moore, Jerry A. III *lawyer*
Moore, Kimberly Ann *federal judge, law educator*
Moore, Powell Allen *former federal agency administrator*
Moore, Robert Madison *food products executive, lawyer*
Moorehead, Donald V. *lawyer*
Moorman, William A. *federal judge, retired career military officer*
Morales, Hector E., Jr. *bank executive, lawyer*
Moran, Anne E. *lawyer*
Moran, Jerry *congressman*
Moran, Jim (James Patrick Moran Jr.) *congressman, stock broker*
Moran, Terry *news correspondent*
Moreno, Jaime *professional soccer player*
Morgan, Bruce Ray *management consultant*
Morgan, Daniel Louis *lawyer, educator*
Morgan, Linda Joan *former federal agency administrator, lawyer*
Mori, Yoshiko *language educator*
Moring, John Frederick *lawyer*
Morris, Robert Crane *management training executive*
Morrissey, Patricia A. *federal agency administrator*
Morse, John B., Jr. *corporate financial executive*
Morse, Larry Eugene *botanist, conservationist*
Morse, M. Howard *lawyer*
Mosbacher, Robert A. *investment company executive*
Moschella, William Emil *federal agency administrator*
Moseley, T. Michael (Teed Michael Moseley) *career military officer*
Moses, Alfred Henry *lawyer, writer, diplomat*
Moss, Madison Scott *editor*
Mostoff, Allan Samuel *lawyer, consultant*
Mough, Scott Thomas *chemist*
Moy, Edmund C. *federal agency administrator*
Moyer, Homer Edward, Jr. *lawyer*
Muckenfuss, Cantwell Faulkner III *lawyer*
Mudd, Daniel H. *finance company executive*
Mueller, Robert Swan III *FBI Director*
Mueller, Sharon Lee (Sherry Mueller) *educational organization executive*
Muir, J. Dapray *lawyer*
Mujica, Barbara Louise *language educator, writer*
Muleta, John B. *lawyer*
Mullen, Michael G. *career military officer*
Muller, Steven *international studies educator, academic administrator*
Mulloy, Patrick Aloysius *lawyer*
Munson, Richard Jay *government agency administrator*
Murguia, Janet *non-profit organization administrator*
Muris, Timothy Joseph *former federal agency administrator, lawyer, educator*
Murkowski, Lisa Ann *senator*
Murphy, Betty Southard (Mrs. Cornelius F. Murphy) *lawyer*
Murphy, Caryle Marie *foreign correspondent*
Murphy, Frances M. *federal agency administrator*
Murphy, Gerard Norris *trade association executive*
Murphy, J. Andrew *lawyer*
Murphy, Joanne Becker *writer*
Murphy, Joseph Albert, Jr. *lawyer*
Murphy, Timothy F. *congressman*
Murray, Charles Alan *social scientist*
Murray, Christopher Charles III *architect*
Murray, James Joseph III *association executive*
Murray, Patty (Patricia J. Murray) *senator*
Murray, Robert Fulton, Jr. *physician*

Murry, Harold David, Jr. *lawyer*
Murtha, John Patrick, Jr. *congressman*
Musgrave, Marilyn N. *congresswoman*
Mussa, Michael L. *economist, educator*
Mwenda, Kenneth Kaoma *legal association administrator, consultant*
Myaing, U. Linn *ambassador*
Myers, Julie L. *federal agency administrator*
Myrick, Sue Wilkins *congresswoman, former mayor*
Nabholz, Joseph Vincent *biologist, ecologist*
Nace, Barry John *lawyer*
Nader, Ralph *advocate, lawyer, writer*
Nadler, Jerrold Lewis *congressman, lawyer*
Naeve, Clifford Mike *lawyer*
Nagel, Trevor W. *lawyer*
Nager, Glen D. *lawyer*
Nagorski, Zygmunt *political scientist, writer*
Nakayama, Granta Y. *federal agency administrator, lawyer*
Namrow, Eric S. *lawyer*
Napolitano, Grace F. *congresswoman*
Narasaki, Karen Keiko *advocate, lawyer*
Nardi Riddle, Clarine *chief of staff*
Nash, James Lee *poet, security official*
Nash, John Davidson, Jr. *economist*
Nason, Nicole R. *federal agency administrator*
Nastal, David Thomas *secondary school educator*
Natividad, Irene *women's rights advocate*
Natsios, Andrew Stephen *diplomat, former federal agency administrator*
Navarro, Bruce Charles *lawyer*
Nazareth, Annette LaPorte *commissioner, lawyer*
Neal, Darwina Lee *federal agency administrator*
Neal, Richard Edmund *congressman, former mayor*
Negroponte, John Dimitri *Director of National Intelligence, former ambassador*
Neiditch, H. Michael *historian*
Nelsen, Hart Michael *sociologist, educator*
Nelson, Ben (Earl Benjamin Nelson) *senator, former governor, lawyer*
Nelson, Bill (Clarence William Nelson) *senator, former state treasurer*
Nelson, Keith A. *federal agency administrator*
Nemeroff, Michael Alan *lawyer*
Nesbitt, La Fonte *lawyer*
Ness, Andrew David *lawyer*
Nethercutt, George Rector, Jr. *lawyer, consultant, former congressman*
Nethery, John Jay *government official, military officer*
Neufeld, Michael John *curator, historian*
Neugebauer, Randy (Robert R. Neugebauer) *congressman*
Neureiter, Norman P. *science association director*
Neviaser, Robert Jon *orthopaedic surgeon, educator*
Newberry, Edward J. *lawyer*
Newell, Mark E. *lawyer*
Newman, Pauline *federal judge*
Newman, Sherryl Hobbs *former district secretary*
Newstead, Jennifer G. *lawyer*
Ney, Bob (Robert William Ney) *congressman*
Nicely, Olza M. (Tony) *insurance company executive*
Nichols, Rob (Robert Stanley Nichols) *think-tank executive, former federal agency administrator*
Nicholson, Jim (Robert James Nicholson) *secretary of veterans affairs, former ambassador*
Nicholson, Richard Selindh *educational association administrator*
Nickel, Henry V. *lawyer*
Nickles, Don (Donald Lee Nickles) *former senator*
Nicolson, Dan Henry *plant taxonomist*
Niehuss, John Marvin *lawyer*
Niemeier, Charles D. *accountant*
Nightingale, Elena Ottolenghi *pediatric geneticist, academic administrator, educator*
Nightingale, Stuart Lester *public health service officer*
Nirenberg, Darryl D. *lawyer*
Niskanen, William Arthur, Jr. *economist, think-tank executive*
Nitze, William Albert *government official, lawyer, not-for-profit developer, energy executive*
Noe, Adrianne *museum administrator*
Nolan, John Edward *lawyer*
Noland, Marcus *economist, educator*
Nordhaus, Robert Riggs *lawyer*
Nordlinger, Gerson *investor*
Norland, Donald Richard *retired foreign service officer*
Norquist, David L. *federal agency administrator*
Norquist, Grover Glenn *economist*
North, Gary L. *career military officer*
Northup, Anne Meagher *congresswoman*
Norton, Eleanor Holmes *congresswoman, lawyer, educator*
Norton, Floyd Ligon, IV, *lawyer*
Norwood, Charles Whitlow, Jr. *congressman*
Norwood, Deborah Anne *law librarian*
Novak, Robert David Sanders *columnist, commentator*
Novelli, William Dominic *retirement association executive*
Novick, Robert T. *lawyer*
Novitch, Mark *physician, retired pharmaceutical executive*
Nuland, Anthony C. J. *lawyer*
Nunes, Devin *congressman*
Nunn, Sam (Samuel Augustus Nunn) *former senator, lawyer*
Nussle, James Allen *congressman*
Nwagbaraocha, Joel Onukwugha *academic administrator, educator*
Oakley, Robert Louis *law librarian, educator*
Obama, Barack H. *senator, former state legislator*
Oberdorfer, John L. *lawyer*
Obering, Trey (Henry A. Obering) *federal agency administrator, career military officer*
Oberstar, James L. *congressman*
Oberwetter, James C. *ambassador*
Obey, David Ross *congressman*
Obiozor, George Achulike *ambassador*
O'Brien, Edwin Frederick *archbishop*
O'Brien, Patrick Michael *federal agency administrator*
O'Brien, Soledad *news anchor*
O'Brien, Steven D. *lawyer*

O'Brien, Timothy Andrew *journalist, writer, lawyer, educator*
O'Callaghan, Thomas Aloysius *artist, librarian*
O'Connell, David M. *academic administrator, priest*
O'Connor, Eileen J. *federal agency administrator*
O'Connor, Karen *political science professor, researcher, writer*
Odle, Robert Charles, Jr. *lawyer*
Odom, William Eldridge *career military officer*
O'Donnell, Patrick Emmett *lawyer*
O'Donnell, Terrence *lawyer*
O'Donovan, Leo Jeremiah *former academic administrator, priest, theologian*
Oehme, Wolfgang Walter *landscape architect*
Oertel, Yolanda Castillo *pathologist, educator*
Ohanian, Bernard Jay *writer, editor*
Ohl, Joan Eschenbach *federal agency administrator*
Ohle, David H. *military career officer*
Ohlke, Amanda Anne *museum administrator, educator*
Oka, Takashi *journalist, consultant, educator*
O'Kane, Margaret E. *non-profit organization executive*
Okun, Deanna Tanner *federal official*
Olchyk, Samuel *lawyer*
Olender, Jack Harvey *lawyer*
Oliver, LeAnn Michelle *government official*
Olmstead, Cecil Jay *lawyer*
Olsen, Jody (Josephine K. Olsen) *federal agency administrator*
Olson, Lyndon Lowell, Jr. *ambassador*
Olson, Mark Walter *not-for-profit organization administrator, former bank executive*
Olson, Pamela Faith *lawyer, former federal agency administrator*
Olson, Theodore Bevry *lawyer, former federal agency administrator*
Olver, John Walter *congressman*
O'Malley, Susan *professional basketball team executive*
Oman, Ralph *lawyer*
Omass, George A. *federal agency administrator*
Omole, Duncan Wambogo *information scientist, corporate communications specialist*
O'Neil, Thomas Francis III *lawyer*
O'Neill, Brian Dennis *lawyer*
O'Neill, John H., Jr. *lawyer*
O'Neill, William Patrick *lawyer*
Onel, Suzan *lawyer*
Ong, Laureen E. *broadcast executive*
Oosterhuis, Paul William *lawyer*
Opfer, George J. *federal agency administrator*
Oppenheimer, Franz Martin *lawyer*
Orbach, Raymond Lee *federal agency administrator, physicist, researcher*
Orr, Bobette Kay *diplomat*
Orszag, Jonathan Marc *economist, consultant*
Orszag, Peter Richard *economist*
Ortiz, Solomon Porfirio *congressman*
Ortner, Donald J. *biological anthropologist, educator*
Osborne, Tom (Thomas William Osborne) *congressman, former college football coach*
Oshinsky, Jerold *lawyer*
Osicka, Teresa D. *health economist, consultant*
Osnos, David Marvin *lawyer, director*
O'Sullivan, Michael *writer, art critic*
O'Sullivan, Stephanie L. *federal agency administrator*
O'Sullivan, Terence M. *labor union administrator*
O'Toole, Francis J. *lawyer*
Otremba, Geraldine Marie *congressional and international relations executive*
Otter, Clement Leroy (Butch Otter) *congressman*
Otto, Robert L. *information technology executive*
Outlaw, Wanda Cecelia *priest*
Ovechkin, Alexander *professional hockey player*
Overman, Dean Lee *lawyer, investor, writer*
Owen, Henry *former ambassador, consultant*
Owen, Roberts Bishop *lawyer, arbitrator*
Owen, Stephen Lee *lawyer*
Owens, Major Robert Odell *congressman*
Owsley, Douglas W. *forensic osteologist, researcher, anthropologist*
Oxley, Michael Garver *congressman*
Oyler, Gregory Kenneth *lawyer*
Pace, David *journalist*
Pace, Peter *Chairman of the Joint Chiefs of Staff*
Pachter, Marc *museum director*
Padden, Preston *broadcast executive*
Padgett, Nancy Weeks *law librarian, consultant, lawyer*
Page, Clarence E. *columnist*
Page, Rodney Fred *lawyer*
Page, Tim *music critic, writer, producer*
Paige, Kathleen K. *naval officer*
Painter, William Hall *law educator*
Pallone, Frank, Jr. *congressman, lawyer*
Palmer, Christopher E. *lawyer*
Palmer, Stacy Ella *periodical editor*
Palomares, Ronald S. *psychologist*
Palumbo, Benjamin Lewis *public relations executive, consultant*
Pane, Natalia *policy and research analyst, strategic planner*
Panero, Hugh Edward *broadcast executive*
Pantaleo, Peter S. *lawyer*
Panuthos, Peter J. *federal judge*
Pape, Stuart M. *lawyer*
Paper, Lewis J. *lawyer, educator*
Parde, Duane Arthur *association executive*
Parish, Norman *artist, art gallery director*
Park, Alice Mary Crandall *author, genealogist*
Park, Jin-Suk *lawyer*
Parker, Rich *lawyer*
Parr, Carolyn Miller *federal judge*
Parris, Mark Robert *former ambassador, policy advisor*
Parsons, Gary M. *broadcast executive*
Pascrell, William J., Jr. *congressman*
Pascual, Carlos *ambassador*
Passage, David *diplomat*
Passaic, Joseph G. *lawyer*
Pastor, Edward *congressman*
Pasurka, Carl A., Jr. *economist*
Pate, Michael Lynn *lawyer*
Patenaude, Pamela Hughes *federal agency administrator*

Patrick, Richard M. *professional hockey team executive*
Patrick, Susan D. *federal agency administrator*
Patron, June Eileen *former government official*
Patterson, Anne Woods (Anne Brevard Woods Patterson) *federal agency administrator, former ambassador*
Patterson, Sally Jane *communications executive, consultant*
Patton, Sharon F. *museum director*
Patton, Thomas Earl *lawyer*
Paul, Jerald S. *federal agency administrator, former state representative, lawyer*
Paul, John Charles *lawyer*
Paul, William McCann *lawyer*
Paulison, R. David (Robert David Paulison) *federal agency administrator*
Paulson, Hank (Henry Merritt Paulson Jr.) *secretary of the treasury, former diversified financial services company executive*
Paulson, Jerome Avrom *pediatrician*
Pavlick, John J., Jr. *lawyer*
Paxon, L. William *former congressman*
Payne, Donald Milford *congressman*
Payne, Fred J. *epidemiologist, educator*
Payton, John *lawyer*
Payton, Sue C. *civilian military employee*
Peacock, Marcus C. *federal agency administrator*
Pearce, Drue *federal official, former state legislator*
Pearce, Steve (Stevan E. Pearce) *congressman*
Pearlman, Ronald Alan *lawyer, educator*
Pearse, Warren Harland *obstetrician, gynecologist, medical association administrator*
Pearson, Daniel R. *federal official*
Pearson, Rebecca E. *lawyer*
Pearson, Roger *organization executive*
Peck, Louis Moses *editor*
Peck, Robert Stephen *lawyer, educator*
Pedersen, William Francis *lawyer*
Peirce, Neal R. *journalist*
Pelavin, Sol Herbert *research company executive*
Pelham, Ann *publishing executive, department chairman*
Pell, Terence J. *legal association administrator*
Pellegrino, Edmund Daniel *internist, educator, retired academic administrator*
Pelosi, Nancy Patricia *congresswoman*
Pemberton, Alan A. *lawyer*
Pence, Michael Richard *congressman*
Pendleton, Florence Howard *shadow senator*
Pendleton, Miles Stevens, Jr. *diplomat*
Penniman, Nicholas *editor*
Pensabene, Judith K. *lawyer*
Peretz, Martin *publishing executive, educator*
Perino, Dana Marie *federal official*
Perito, Robert Michael *political scientist*
Perkins, Lucian *photographer*
Perkins, Nancy Leeds *lawyer*
Perl, Peter *editor*
Perle, Richard Norman *former federal agency administrator*
Perlman, Matthew Saul *lawyer*
Perlstein, William James *lawyer*
Perry, George Lewis *research economist, consultant*
Perry, James Michael *museum administrator, historian*
Persinger, Del Louis *pharmaceutical company executive*
Peters, Frederick Whitten *lawyer*
Peterson, Charles Hayes *lawyer*
Peterson, Collin C. *congressman*
Peterson, John E. *congressman*
Petito, Margaret L. *foundation administrator*
Petrash, Jeffrey Michael *lawyer*
Petri, Thomas Evert *congressman*
Petruzzelli, Julie A. *lawyer*
Pfeiffer, Margaret Kolodny *lawyer*
Pfeiffer, Steven Bernard *lawyer*
Phalen, Patricia Frances *media specialist, educator*
Phillips, Carter Glasgow *lawyer*
Phillips, James D. *retired diplomat*
Phillips, John R. *lawyer*
Phillips, Karen Borlaug *economist, rail transportation executive*
Phillips, Susan Meredith *academic administrator, economist*
Piccininno, Anthony Ray *government administrative executive*
Pickenpaugh, Thomas Edward *archaeologist, anthropologist*
Pickens, Scott E. *lawyer*
Pickering, Chip (Charles Willis Pickering Jr.) *congressman*
Pickholtz, Raymond Lee *electrical engineering educator, consultant*
Pierce, John Randall *medical inspector, pediatrician*
Pierson, Stuart F. *lawyer*
Pilcher, Carl B. *astrobiologist*
Pincus, Stephanie Hoyer *dermatologist*
Pincus, Walter Haskell *news editor*
Pines, Wayne Lloyd *public relations executive*
Pinkerton, James Pearson *columnist, political analyst*
Pionk, Jerome Lee *federal official, trade association administrator*
Piorkowski, Joseph D., Jr. *lawyer, physician, educator, military officer*
Piromya, Kasit *ambassador*
Pistole, John S. *federal agency administrator*
Pitt, Harvey Lloyd *risk management consultant, former federal agency administrator*
Pittman, Lisa *lawyer*
Pittman, R. Allen *federal agency administrator*
Pitts, James T. *lawyer*
Pitts, Joseph R. (Joe Pitts) *congressman*
Pizzella, Patrick *federal agency administrator*
Placke, James Anthony *retired diplomat*
Plager, S. Jay *federal judge*
Plaine, Daniel J. *lawyer*
Plaine, Lloyd Leva *lawyer*
Plattner, Marc Florea *foundation administrator, editor*
Platts, Howard Gregory *cultural organization administrator, not-for-profit fundraiser, director*
Platts, Todd Russell *congressman, state legislator*
Plave, Lee Jonathan *lawyer*
Player, Thelma B. *librarian*
Plotkin, Mark Elliott *lawyer*

Podberesky, Samuel *lawyer*
Podesta, John David *law educator, former White House chief of staff*
Poe, David Russell *lawyer*
Poe, Ted *congressman, former judge*
Pojeta, John, Jr. *geologist, researcher*
Polito, Robert J. *federal agency administrator*
Pollack, Ronald Frank *healthcare organization executive, lawyer*
Pollock, Alexander John *banker*
Polon, Ira H. *lawyer*
Polt, Michael C. *ambassador*
Pombo, Richard William *congressman, rancher, farmer*
Pomeroy, Earl Ralph *congressman, retired commissioner*
Poneman, Daniel Bruce *lawyer*
Poos, Lawrence Raymond *history educator*
Pope, Andrew *health science association administrator*
Popkin, Joel *economist, consultant*
Popofsky, Mark S. *lawyer*
Porges, Lawrence Michael *editor*
Porter, John Edward *former congressman*
Porter, John Weston *counselor, consultant, educator*
Porter, Jon Christopher, Sr. *congressman*
Portman, Robert Jones *federal official, former ambassador, former congressman*
Portnoy, Elliott Ivan *lawyer*
Postol, Lawrence Philip *lawyer*
Potenza, Joseph Michael *lawyer*
Potter, Caryl A. III *lawyer*
Potter, Jack (John E. Potter) *federal agency administrator*
Potter, John Francis *oncologist, surgeon*
Potter, Lorraine K. *career military officer*
Potts, Stephen Deaderick *lawyer*
Pouillon, Nora Emanuela *food service executive, chef*
Povich, David *lawyer*
Powell, Benjamin Albond *federal agency administrator, lawyer*
Powell, Dina Habib *federal agency administrator*
Powell, Michael Kevin *investment company executive, former federal official*
Powell, Nancy Jo *federal official, former ambassador*
Powers, Mary Ellen *lawyer*
Powers, Richard Edward, Jr. *lawyer*
Pozen, Sharis Arnold *lawyer*
Pratt, Carin *television executive*
Pratt, Dana Joseph *publishing consultant*
Press, Frank *geophysicist*
Preston, Richard McKim *lawyer*
Preston, Stephen W. *lawyer*
Preston, Steven C. *federal agency administrator, former service company executive*
Prestowitz, Clyde Vincent, Jr. *economist, researcher*
Prettyman, Elijah Barrett, Jr. *lawyer*
Prezioso, Giovanni P. *lawyer*
Price, Daniel Martin *lawyer*
Price, David Eugene *congressman, education educator*
Price, Griffith Baley, Jr. *lawyer*
Price, Joseph Hubbard *lawyer*
Price, Thomas E. *congressman*
Priest, Dana *journalist*
Prina, L(ouis) Edgar *journalist*
Principi, Anthony Joseph *pharmaceutical company executive, former secretary of veterans affairs*
Pritchard, Therese D. *lawyer*
Proger, Phillip A. *lawyer*
Prosper, Pierre-Richard *federal agency administrator*
Prost, Sharon *federal judge*
Pryce, Deborah Denine *congresswoman*
Pryor, Mark Lunsford *senator*
Przypyszny, John R. *lawyer*
Puchalski, Christina M. *physician, medical educator*
Pucie, Charles R., Jr. *public affairs executive*
Pupkin, Barry A. *lawyer*
Pusey, William Anderson *lawyer*
Putnam, Adam Hughes *congressman, farmer, rancher*
Putzel, Michael *journalist, editor*
Pyke, Thomas Nicholas, Jr. *science administrator*
Pyle, Robert Noble *public relations executive*
Quainton, Anthony Cecil Eden *diplomat*
Quale, John Carter *lawyer*
Quarles, Randal Keith *federal agency administrator, lawyer*
Quarterman, Cynthia Louise *lawyer*
Quello, James Henry *government official*
Quigley, Michael *lawyer*
Quigley, Thomas J. *lawyer, director*
Quinn, Jack (John Francis Quinn) *former congressman, English language educator*
Quinn, Kenneth Phillip *lawyer*
Quinn, Thomas H. *lawyer*
Quint, Arnold Harris *lawyer*
Quintanilla-Villanueva, Rosalinda *economist*
Rabinovitz, Bruce H. *lawyer*
Raby, Julian *art gallery director*
Racicot, Marc F. *insurance association executive, lawyer, former governor*
Racine, Karl A. *lawyer*
Racine, Richard B. *lawyer*
Radanovich, George P. *congressman*
Rademaker, Stephen Geoffrey *legislative staff member, former federal agency administrator*
Rader, Randall Ray *federal judge*
Radice, Anne-Imelda Marino *museum director, former federal agency administrator*
Radin, Alex *former association executive, consultant*
Radner, Roy *economist, educator, researcher*
Rahall, Nick Joe, II, (Nick Rahall) *congressman*
Raher, Patrick Michael *lawyer*
Railton, W. Scott (William Scott Railton) *commissioner*
Raim, David Matthew *lawyer*
Raimi, Burton Louis *lawyer*
Raimo, Bernard (Bernie Raimo) *lawyer*
Rainey, Jean Osgood *public relations executive*
Raju, Minnie M. *nursing administrator, critical care nurse*
Rales, Mitchell P. *automotive parts company executive*

Rales, Steven M. *automotive parts company executive*
Ralston, Joseph W. *retired military officer*
Ramberg, Walter Dodd *architect*
Ramey, Carl Robert *lawyer*
Ramirez, Ted L. *lawyer*
Ramphele, Mamphela A. *international organization administrator, physician, former academic administrator*
Ramsey, Charles H. *police chief*
Ramstad, James *congressman, lawyer*
Ranck, Edna Runnels *academic administrator, researcher*
Randall, Robert L(ee) *ecological economist*
Randolph, A. Raymond (Arthur Raymond Randolph) *federal judge*
Randt, Clark Thorp, Jr. *ambassador, lawyer*
Rangel, Charles Bernard *congressman*
Rankin, Edward Anthony *orthopedist, surgeon*
Rankin, Robert Arthur *journalist*
Ranneberger, Michael E. *ambassador*
Rao, Mahadev *pharmacologist, researcher, molecular biologist*
Raphael, Louise Arakelian *mathematician, educator*
Rasmus, John Charles *trade association administrator, lawyer*
Raspberry, William James *journalist*
Ratner, Ellen Faith *news analyst, news correspondent, writer*
Rato y Figaredo, Rodrigo *international banking official*
Rauh, Carl Stephen *lawyer*
Raul, Alan Charles *lawyer*
Raut, Lakshmi Kanta *economist, educator*
Ravenal, Earl Cedric *international relations educator, writer*
Rayner, Victoria Leigh *medical educator, consultant*
Reade, Claire Elizabeth *lawyer*
Reaman, Gregory Harold *pediatric hematologist, oncologist*
Redd, Kenneth Eric *statistician, researcher*
Redd, Teresa M. *English language educator*
Reddel, Carl Walter *academic administrator*
Redman, Robert Shelton *pathologist, dentist*
Reed, John Francis (Jack Reed) *senator*
Reed, John Hathaway *former ambassador*
Reed, Travis Dean *public relations executive*
Reeder, Joe Robert *lawyer, former federal official*
Rees, Nina Shokraii *federal agency administrator*
Reger, Lawrence Lee *trade association administrator*
Regula, Ralph Straus *congressman, lawyer*
Rehberg, Dennis R. *congressman*
Rehnquist, Janet *lawyer, former federal agency administrator*
Rehr, David K. *broadcast association executive*
Reich, Bernard *political science professor*
Reich, John M. *federal agency administrator*
Reich, Walter *psychiatrist, museum director, educator*
Reichert, David G. (Dave Reichert) *congressman*
Reichertz, Peter Stuart *lawyer*
Reichs, Kerry E. *lawyer*
Reid, Harry Mason *senator*
Reid, Inez Smith *lawyer, educator, judge*
Rein, Bert Walter *lawyer*
Reinsch, William Alan *association executive, educator*
Reischauer, Robert D. *research organization executive*
Relch, John *banker, federal agency administrator*
Relyea, Harold Clarence *political scientist, writer*
Renick, James Carmichael *educational association administrator, former academic administrator*
Renuart, Victor E., Jr. *career military officer*
Renzi, Rick *congressman*
Ressel, Teresa Mullett *federal agency administrator*
Retz, William Andrew *naval consultant, retired naval officer*
Reyes, Silvestre *congressman*
Reynolds, Jerry (Gerald A. Reynolds) *federal agency administrator*
Reynolds, Nicholas S. *lawyer*
Reynolds, Thomas M. *congressman*
Reznik, Mykhailo B. *ambassador*
Ricciardone, Francis Joseph, Jr. *ambassador*
Riccini, Kenneth A. *government agency administrator*
Rice, Condoleezza *secretary of state, former national security advisor*
Rice, Lois Dickson *retired computer company executive*
Rice, Paul Jackson *lawyer, educator*
Rice, Susan Elizabeth *foreign policy analyst, former federal agency administrator*
Rich, Dorothy Kovitz *educational association administrator, writer*
Rich, John Townsend *lawyer*
Richards, Femi Soyinka *lawyer*
Richards, Suzanne V. *lawyer*
Richardson, Ann Bishop *foundation executive, lawyer*
Richardson, Paul Joseph *economist*
Richardson, Scott *federal official, researcher, writer*
Richeson, James Grady, Jr. *dentist*
Richlen, Scott Lane *federal government program administrator*
Richmond, David Walker *retired lawyer*
Richmond, Marilyn Susan *lawyer*
Rickard, Lisa Ann *lawyer*
Rickert, Anthony H. *lawyer*
Ridenour, Amy Moritz *research center administrator*
Ridgeway, James Fowler *journalist*
Riechmann, Deb *reporter*
Riedel, Bunnie *not-for-profit organization executive*
Riehle, B. Hudson *trade association executive*
Rieser, Joseph A., Jr. *tax specialist*
Rifkin, Ned *museum director*
Riggs, Barbara *federal agency administrator*
Rill, James Franklin *lawyer*
Ring, Carlyle C. *lawyer*
Rios, Elena *health association administrator*
Risen, James E. *journalist*
Rissetto, Harry A. *lawyer*
Rives, Jack L. *judge, career military officer*

Rivlin, Alice Mitchell *economics professor, former federal official*
Rizzi, Robert A. *lawyer*
Robb, James Willis *romance languages educator*
Robb, Lynda Johnson *writer*
Robbins, Robert B. *lawyer*
Roberts, Carter S. *environmental services administrator*
Roberts, Charles Patrick (Pat Roberts) *senator*
Roberts, Cokie (Corinne Boggs Roberts) *newscaster*
Roberts, James Harold III *lawyer*
Roberts, Jeanne Addison *retired literature educator*
Roberts, John *news anchor*
Roberts, John Glover, Jr. *United States Supreme Court Chief Justice*
Roberts, John W. *historian, federal agency official*
Roberts, Markley *economist, educator*
Roberts, Michael G. *lawyer*
Roberts, Michele A. *lawyer*
Roberts, Walter Ronald *retired diplomat*
Robertson, James *federal judge*
Robinson, Frank *professional baseball manager, retired professional baseball player*
Robison, Victor James, Jr. *retired military officer*
Rochon, Mark *lawyer*
Rockefeller, Edwin Shaffer *lawyer*
Rockefeller, John Davison, IV, (Jay Rockefeller) *senator, retired governor*
Rocque, Vincent Joseph *lawyer*
Rodemeyer, Michael Leonard, Jr. *lawyer*
Rodgers, Clifton Eugene, Jr. *trade association administrator, lobbyist*
Rodley, Carol A. *federal agency administrator*
Rodman, Peter Warren *federal agency administrator*
Rodriguez, Rita Maria *economist*
Roemer, Timothy John *think-tank executive, former congressman*
Rogan, Michael P. *lawyer*
Rogers, Harold Dallas (Hal Rogers) *congressman*
Rogers, Judith Ann Wilson *federal judge*
Rogers, Mike (Michael J. Rogers) *congressman*
Rogers, Mike *congressman*
Rogers, Thomasina Venese *federal commissioner*
Rogers, William Dill *lawyer*
Rogovin, John A. *lawyer*
Rogowsky, Robert Arthur *federal official, educator*
Rohner, Ralph John *lawyer, educator, dean*
Rohrabacher, Dana *congressman*
Rohrbach, Peter Alpaugh *lawyer*
Roll, David Lee *lawyer*
Romanow, Josh *lawyer*
Romeo, Peter John *lawyer*
Romig, Thomas J. *judge, career military officer*
Rooney, Francis *ambassador*
Rosch, John Thomas (Tom Rosch) *commissioner, lawyer*
Rose, Deedie Potter *arts patron*
Rose, George Andrew *application developer, information systems specialist*
Rose, Jonathan Chapman *lawyer*
Rose, Mary McNally *federal official*
Rosebush, James Scott *management consulting executive, former government official*
Rosen, Gerald Robert *editor*
Rosen, Jeffrey Adam *lawyer, federal agency administrator*
Rosenau, James Nathan *political scientist, educator, writer*
Rosenberg, Jerome David *physicist*
Rosenberg, Joel Barry *government economist*
Rosenblatt, Jason Philip *literature and language professor*
Rosenblatt, Peter Ronald *lawyer, former ambassador*
Rosenbloom, David Harry *political science and law educator*
Rosenbloom, H(arry) David *lawyer*
Rosenfeld, Arthur F. *federal official, lawyer*
Rosenfeld, Ronald Allen *federal agency administrator*
Rosenhauer, James Joseph (Jim Rosenhauer) *lawyer*
Rosenker, Mark Victor *federal agency chairman*
Rosenkrantz, Steven Jay *lawyer*
Rosenthal, Douglas Eurico *lawyer*
Rosenthal, Steven Siegmund *lawyer*
Roshwald, Aviel Isaiah *history professor*
Ros-Lehtinen, Ileana Carmen *congresswoman*
Rosman, Michael E. *lawyer*
Ross, Dennis B. *former diplomat*
Ross, Donald K. *lobbyist, environmental organization administrator, lawyer*
Ross, Douglas *lawyer*
Ross, Malcolm *minerals consultant*
Ross, Mike *congressman*
Ross, Robinette Davis *publisher*
Ross, Stanford G. *lawyer, government official*
Ross, Terence P. *lawyer*
Rossides, Eugene Telemachus *lawyer, writer*
Rostropovich, Mstislav Leopoldovich *conductor, musician, music director*
Rotberg, Eugene Harvey *investment banker, lawyer*
Rothenberg, Pamela V. *lawyer*
Rother, John *association executive, lawyer*
Rothkopf, Arthur J. *association executive*
Rothman, Steven R. *congressman*
Rothstein, Barbara Jacobs *federal judge*
Rothstein, Paul Frederick *lawyer, educator*
Rottman, Ellis *public information officer*
Rotunda, Donald Theodore *public relations consultant*
Roundtree, Jacqueline Washington *public relations executive, federal agency administrator*
Rouse, Leo E. *dean, dental educator*
Rouvelas, Emanuel Larry *lawyer*
Rove, Karl Christian *federal official*
Rovelstad, Mathilde V(erner) *retired library and information scientist, educator*
Rowden, Marcus Aubrey *lawyer, retired government agency administrator*
Rowe, Richard Holmes *lawyer*
Rowland, Diane *health facility administrator, researcher*
Roybal-Allard, Lucille *congresswoman*
Royce, Ed (Edward Randall Royce) *congressman*
Roycroft, Howard Francis *lawyer*

Royle, David Brian Layton *television producer, journalist*
Rubel, Eric A. *lawyer*
Rubin, Kenneth Allen *lawyer*
Ruckman, Roger Norris *pediatric cardiologist*
Ruddy, Frank *lawyer, retired ambassador*
Ruehle, Charles Joseph *pathologist, military officer*
Ruetter, Gunter H *surgeon*
Ruiz, Vanessa *judge*
Rule, Charles Frederick (Rick Rule) *lawyer*
Rumsfeld, Donald Henry *secretary of defense*
Runge, Jeffrey William *federal agency administrator*
Rupp, Kalman *economist*
Ruppersberger, Charles Albert, III, (Dutch Ruppersberger) *congressman*
Rush, Bobby L. *congressman*
Ruskin, Robert Sterling *educational association administrator*
Russell, Mark *comedian*
Russell, Michael James *lawyer*
Russell, William Joseph *educational association administrator*
Russert, Timothy John *broadcast journalist, broadcast executive*
Russin, Jonathan *lawyer, consultant*
Rust, William David, Jr. *retired structural engineer*
Ruthenberg, Kirk R. *lawyer*
Rutherford, Boyd Kevin *federal agency administrator*
Rutledge, Peter J. *federal agency administrator*
Rutstein, David W. *lawyer, food products executive*
Ruttenberg, Charles Byron *lawyer*
Ruttinger, George David *lawyer*
Ruwe, Robert Paul *federal judge*
Ryan, David Alan *systems analyst*
Ryan, Paul *congressman*
Ryan, Timothy J. *congressman*
Ryerson, Paul Sommer *lawyer*
Ryn, Claes Gösta *political science professor*
Ryun, James Ronald *congressman*
Sabo, Martin Olav *congressman*
Sabshin, Melvin *psychiatrist, educator, health science association administrator*
Sachar, Howard Morley *history educator*
Sacher, Steven Jay *lawyer*
Saffuri, Khaled Ahmad *cultural organization executive*
Safire, William *journalist, foundation administrator*
St. John, Julie *mortgage company executive*
Salamon, Linda Bradley *English literature educator*
Salant, Jonathan D. *reporter*
Salazar, John T. *congressman*
Salazar, Ken Lee (Kenneth Lee Salazar) *senator, former state attorney general*
Salem, George Richard *lawyer*
Salisbury, Dallas L. *researcher, director*
Salsbury, Michael H. *lawyer*
Saltzburg, Stephen Allan *law educator, consultant*
Salyer, Stephen Lee *educational program administrator*
Sampson, David Allan *federal agency administrator*
Sams, Ronald F. *career military officer*
Samsot, Robert Louis *editor, consultant*
Samuelson, Kenneth Lee *lawyer*
Sanchez, Linda T. *congresswoman*
Sanchez, Loretta *congresswoman*
Sanchez Mills, Peggy *women's association executive*
Sanchez-Way, Ruth Dolores *public health administrator*
Sanders, Bernard (Bernie Sanders) *congressman*
Sanders, Jackie Wolcott *ambassador*
Sandkuhler, Kevin M. *military officer*
Sandler, Bernice Resnick *women's rights specialist*
Sandman, James Joseph *lawyer*
Sanford, Bruce William *lawyer*
Sant, Roger W. *retired energy executive*
Sant, Victoria P. *museum administrator*
Santorum, Rick (Richard John Santorum) *senator*
Santos, Leonard Ernest *lawyer*
Saperstein, Marc Eli *religious studies educator, rabbi*
Sarbanes, Paul Spyros *senator*
Sartori, Michael A. *lawyer*
Sasso, John *advertising and public strategies executive*
Satcher, David *public health service officer, former Surgeon General of the United States*
Satloff, Robert B. *think-tank executive*
Satterthwaite, Janet F. *lawyer*
Sauerbrey, Ellen Elaine Richmond *federal agency administrator, former ambassador*
Saunders, Alan Keith *professional football coach*
Saunders, Harold Henry *foundation administrator*
Saunders, Mary Jane *lawyer*
Savage, Nora V. *environmental engineer*
Sawhill, Isabel Van Devanter *economist*
Saworotnow, Parfeny Pavlovich *mathematician, educator*
Saxton, Jim (Hugh James Saxton) *congressman*
Sayler, Robert Nelson *lawyer, educator*
Sayre, Edward Vale *chemist*
Sayre, Robert Marion *ambassador*
Scalia, Antonin *United States Supreme Court Justice*
Scanlon, Kerry Alan *lawyer*
Scanlon, Terrence Maurice *foundation administrator*
Scarlett, Lynn (Patricia Lynn Scarlett) *federal agency administrator*
Schafer, Jacqueline Ellen *federal agency administrator*
Schaitberger, Harold *protective services official, labor union administrator*
Schakowsky, Janice *congresswoman*
Schall, Alvin Anthony *federal judge*
Schapiro, Mary L. *financial regulatory service executive*
Schaumber, Peter Carey *federal agency administrator*
Scheffman, David Theodore *economist, management educator, consultant*
Scheibel, Kenneth Maynard *journalist*
Scheinberg, Phyllis F. *federal agency administrator*

Schieck, Frederick W. *federal agency administrator*
Schieffer, Bob *newscaster*
Schieffer, John Thomas *ambassador, former professional baseball team executive*
Schiff, Adam Bennett *congressman, lawyer*
Schiff, Janis Boyarsky *lawyer*
Schiffer, Lois Jane *lawyer*
Schill, Charles F. *lawyer*
Schiller, Harvey W. *risk management company executive*
Schiller, Jonathan David *lawyer*
Schlesinger, B. Frank *architect, educator*
Schley, Wayne Arthur *political scientist, consultant*
Schlicher, Ronald Lewis *ambassador*
Schlickeisen, Rodger Oscar *non-profit environmental organization executive*
Schmeltzer, Edward *lawyer*
Schmidt, Jean *congresswoman*
Schmidt, Susan *journalist*
Schmidt, William Arthur, Jr. *lawyer*
Schmitt, John K. *army officer*
Schmoke, Kurt L. *dean, former mayor*
Schneider, Ann Imlah *federal agency administrator, education consultant*
Schneider, Carol Geary *educational association administrator*
Schneider, Cynthia Perrin *former ambassador, political science professor*
Schneider, Lawrence Alan *lawyer*
Schneider, Mark *political science professor*
Schneider, Mark Lewis *foreign policy executive, retired government agency administrator*
Schneider, Matthew Roger *lawyer*
Schneller, Marina Velentgas *lawyer*
Schnitzer, Steven C. *lawyer*
Schoelen, Mary Jeanette *federal judge*
Schoettle, Enid C.B. *federal agency administrator*
Schofield, Regina Brown *federal agency administrator*
Schoomaker, Peter J. *career military officer*
Schorr, Lisbeth Bamberger *sociologist, researcher*
Schorsch, Louis L. *metal products executive*
Schram, Martin Jay *journalist*
Schroeder, Patricia Scott *trade association administrator, former congresswoman*
Schuelein, Marianne Ida *neurologist, educator*
Schulte, Gregory L. *ambassador*
Schumer, Chuck (Charles Ellis Schumer) *senator*
Schwaab, Richard Lewis *lawyer*
Schwab, Susan Carroll *ambassador, former academic administrator*
Schwalb, Brian L. *lawyer*
Schwartz, Allyson Y. *congresswoman*
Schwartz, Daniel C. *lawyer*
Schwartz, Norton A. *career military officer*
Schwartz, Victor Elliot *lawyer, educator*
Schwartzman, Andrew Jay *lawyer*
Schwarz, Gerard *conductor, musician, music director*
Schwarz, John J.H. (Joe Schwarz) *congressman, physician*
Schwebel, Stephen Myron *arbitrator, mediator, legal advisor*
Schwelb, Frank Ernest *judge*
Schwinger, David *lawyer*
Scoblic, J. Peter *magazine editor*
Scott, Charneta Claudetta *psychologist, educator*
Scott, David Albert *congressman*
Scott, Gary Thomas *historian*
Scott, Robert Cortez *congressman, lawyer*
Scott, Thomas Jefferson, Jr. *lawyer, electrical engineer*
Scowcroft, Brent *former national security advisor, retired military officer*
Scrivner, Ellen M. *psychologist*
Scully, Thomas A. *lawyer, former federal agency administrator*
Seale, Ronald Armbrust *lawyer*
Sears, John Patrick *lawyer*
Sears, Mary Helen *lawyer*
Seats, Peggy Chisolm *public affairs executive*
Seck, Mamadou Mansour *ambassador, military officer*
Sedgwick, Jeffrey Leigh *federal agency administrator, political science professor*
Sega, A. Christopher *lawyer*
Sega, Ronald Michael *civilian military employee, former dean*
Segal, Theodore D. *lawyer*
Segall, Wynn H. *lawyer*
Seidman, L(ewis) William *television commentator, publisher*
Seifert, Jeffrey W. *political scientist, researcher*
Selin, Ivan *entrepreneur*
Sell, Clay (Jeffrey Clay Sell) *federal agency administrator*
Sellin, Theodore *diplomat, consultant*
Semas, Philip Wayne *editor*
Senger, Jeffrey M. *lawyer*
Sensenbrenner, F. James, Jr., (Frank James Sensenbrenner Jr.) *congressman*
Sentelle, David Bryan *federal judge*
Serrano, José Enrique *congressman*
Sessions, Jeff (Jefferson Beauregard Sessions III) *senator, former state attorney general*
Sessions, Pete *congressman*
Sessions, William Steele *lawyer, former FBI director*
Severino, Roberto *language educator, academic administration executive*
Sewell, John Williamson *research association executive*
Shadegg, John Barden *congressman*
Shadid, Anthony *journalist*
Shaffer, David James *lawyer*
Shales, Thomas William *television and film critic, writer, journalist*
Shambaugh, David Leigh *political scientist, educator, writer*
Shanahan, Sheila Ann *pediatrician, educator*
Shane, Jeffrey Neil *federal agency administrator, lawyer*
Shanks, Hershel *editor, writer*
Shannon, Donald Hawkins *retired editor*
Shannon, Thomas A., Jr. *federal agency administrator*
Shanny, Ramy *physicist*
Shapero, Donald Campbell *physicist, government official*
Shapiro, Howard M *lawyer, former prosecutor*

Shapiro, Walter Elliot *columnist*
Sharma, Tina *lawyer*
Sharp, Walter L. (Gary Sharp) *career military officer*
Shaw, E. Clay, Jr., (Clay Shaw) *congressman*
Shaw, Russell Burnham *writer, journalist*
Shaw, Theresa S. (Terri Shaw) *federal official*
Shaw, William Frederick *statistician*
Shaw, William J. *hotel facility executive*
Shaw-Eagle, Joanna *art critic*
Shay, Albert W. *lawyer*
Shays, Christopher *congressman*
Shear, Natalie Pickus *conference and event management executive*
Shearer, Paul Scott *federal agency administrator, trade association administrator*
Sheehan, Neil *reporter, writer*
Shelby, Richard Craig *senator, former congressman*
Shelley, Herbert Carl *lawyer*
Shenon, Philip *journalist*
Shepherd, Alan J. *construction executive, management consultant*
Sheppard, Scott S. *astronomer*
Sherer, Samuel Ayers *lawyer, urban planner, consultant*
Sherman, Bradley James *congressman*
Sherman, Gerald Howard *lawyer, educator*
Sherman, Jonathan Henry *lawyer*
Sherwood, Donald Lewis *congressman*
Sherzer, Harvey Gerald *lawyer*
Shields, Christopher Andrew *website director*
Shih, J. Chung-wen *Chinese language educator*
Shimkus, John Mondy *congressman*
Shiner, Josette Sheeran *federal agency administrator*
Shinn, David Hamilton *former diplomat, educator, writer*
Shirzad, Faryar *federal official*
Shivakumar, Sujai *political economist, policy advisor*
Shore, Bill *nonprofit organization executive*
Shrier, Adam Louis *investment company executive, consultant*
Shrinsky, Jason Lee *lawyer*
Shriver, Timothy Perry *sports association executive*
Shulenburger, David Edwin *educational association administrator, economics educator, former academic administrator*
Shull, Joe A. *lawyer*
Shulman, Stephen Neal *lawyer*
Shumaker, Gregory M. *lawyer*
Shuster, William (Bill Shuster) *congressman*
Sibolski, John Alfred, Jr. *educational association executive*
Siegel, David B. *lawyer*
Siegel, Frederic Richard *geology educator*
Siegel, Lloyd Harvey *architect, real estate developer, consultant*
Siegel, Richard David *lawyer, former government official*
Siegel, Robert Charles *broadcast journalist*
Siekman, Thomas Clement *lawyer*
Sigal, Jill L. *federal agency administrator*
Sikora, Clifford S. *lawyer*
Silberg, Jay Eliot *lawyer*
Silbert, Earl J. *lawyer*
Silver, Brian Quayle *broadcast journalist, musician, educator*
Silver, Harry R. *lawyer*
Silverman, Leslie E. *commissioner*
Silverman, William A. *lawyer*
Silverstein, Martin J. *lawyer, former ambassador*
Simko, Jan *English, foreign language and literature educator*
Simmons, Anne L. *federal official*
Simmons, Robert Ruhl *congressman*
Simon, Gary Leonard *internist, educator*
Simon, Gregory *lawyer*
Simon, John A. *investment company executive*
Simon, Karla W. *law educator*
Simon, Kenneth Mark *lawyer*
Simon, Raymond Joseph *federal agency administrator, former school system administrator*
Simons, Lawrence Brook *lawyer*
Simonson, Stewart Gerard *retired federal agency administrator*
Simpson, Cam *reporter*
Simpson, James S. *federal agency administrator*
Simpson, John M. *lawyer*
Simpson, Louis A. *insurance company executive*
Simpson, Michael K. *congressman*
Sims, Joe *lawyer*
Sinel, Norman Mark *lawyer*
Singer, Daniel Morris *lawyer*
Singer, Maxine Frank *retired biochemist, science association director*
Singer, Richard M. *lawyer*
Singleton, Harry Michael *lawyer*
Sinick, Marshall S. *lawyer*
Sinn, Jerry L. *army officer*
Sirri, Erik R. *federal agency administrator, economist*
Sizemore, Richard Tom III *government agency administrator*
Sjoblom, Thomas V. *lawyer*
Skall, Gregg P. *lawyer*
Skancke, Nancy J. *lawyer*
Skelton, Ike (Isaac Newton Skelton IV) *congressman*
Skinner, Richard L. *federal agency administrator*
Skinner, Robert Earle, Jr. *civil engineer, engineering executive*
Skinner, Thomas V. *federal agency administrator*
Skol, Michael *counter-money laundering consultant*
Skolfield, Melissa T. *public relations executive, government official*
Skolnik, Merrill I. *electrical engineer*
Slade, John Danton *lobbyist*
Slafka, Kristi Lynne *lawyer*
Slater, Jim *sportswriter, journalist*
Slater, Rodney E. *lawyer, emergency management executive, former secretary of transportation*
Slater, Valerie A. *lawyer*
Slatkin, Leonard Edward *conductor, musician, music director*
Slaughter, Kenneth S. *lawyer*

Villarosa, Shari *ambassador*
Villarreal, June Patricia *retired sales executive*
Vince, Clinton Andrew *lawyer*
Visclosky, Peter John *congressman, lawyer*
Viso, Olga *museum director*
Vita, Michael *economist*
Vitter, David Bruce *senator, former congressman*
Vodra, William Wilson *lawyer*
Vogelsong, Diana Louise *librarian*
Voinovich, George Victor *senator, former governor*
Voll, John Obert *history professor*
Volner, Ian D. *lawyer*
Voorhees, Theodore, Jr. *lawyer*
Vose, Kathryn Kahler *marketing executive, communications executive*
Wagner, Annice McBryde *judge*
Wagner, Curtis Lee, Jr. *judge*
Wagner, Martha Jo *lawyer*
Wainstein, Kenneth L. *federal agency administrator, former prosecutor*
Waite, Barbara L. (Pixie) *lawyer*
Walcott, John L. *communications executive*
Wald, Douglas L. *lawyer*
Wald, Patricia McGowan *retired federal judge*
Wald, Robert Lewis *lawyer*
Walden, Greg *congressman*
Waldman, Amy *journalist*
Waldman, Daniel *lawyer*
Waldron, Gerard J. *lawyer*
Walgren, Doug *lawyer, former congressman*
Walker, Audrey Thayer *social worker, psychotherapist*
Walker, Barbara Dodson *cultural organization administrator, educator*
Walker, Daniel *museum director*
Walker, David Alan (David Alan Walker) *finance educator*
Walker, David Michael *federal official*
Walker, Edward S., Jr. *former ambassador*
Walker, Martin Alan *journalist*
Walker, Mary L. *lawyer*
Walker, Robert Smith *former congressman*
Wall, Christopher Read *lawyer*
Wallace, Don, Jr. *law educator*
Wallace Douglas, Jean *conservationist*
Wallis, Jim *religious speaker, activist, writer*
Walpole, Jim (James R. Walpole) *lawyer*
Walsh, Alexandra M. *lawyer*
Walsh, James Thomas (Jim Walsh) *congressman*
Walsh, John *television show host, missing children and victims' rights advocate*
Walsh, Michael J. *lawyer*
Walter, Sheryl Lynn *lawyer*
Walters, John P. *federal official*
Walton, Reggie Barnett *judge*
Wamp, Zachary Paul *congressman*
Wand, Patricia Ann *librarian*
Wang, John Cheng Hwai *communications engineer, researcher*
Wang, Kim *commissioner, librarian*
Ward, Alan S. *lawyer*
Ward, David *academic administrator, educator*
Ward, Erica Anne *lawyer, educator*
Warder, Lawrence A. *federal agency administrator*
Ware, Marilyn *ambassador, former utilities company executive*
Warin, Roger E. *lawyer*
Warner, John William *senator*
Warren, David Liles *educational association executive*
Warren, Jack Duane *professional society administrator, historian, writer*
Warren Ellison, Tasheaya L. *tax attorney*
Warsh, Kevin Maxwell *bank executive*
Wartman, Steven A. *medical association administrator*
Washington, Eric T. *judge*
Wasko-Flood, Sandra Jean *artist, educator*
Wasserman-Schultz, Debbie *congresswoman*
Wasshausen, Dieter Carl *botanist*
Waters, Jennifer Nash *lawyer*
Waters, Maxine *congresswoman*
Watkin, Virginia Guild *retired lawyer*
Watson, Arthur Dennis *federal official*
Watson, Diane Edith *congresswoman*
Watson, Harlan L(eroy) *federal agency administrator, physicist, economist*
Watson, Peter S. *former federal agency administrator*
Watson, Rebecca Wunder *federal agency administrator, lawyer*
Watt, Melvin Luther *congressman, lawyer*
Wattenmaker, Richard Joel *archivist, director*
Watts, Doris Earlene *retired librarian*
Watts, J. C., Jr. *former congressman, retired professional football player*
Waxman, Henry Arnold *congressman*
Waxman, Seth Paul *lawyer*
Wayne, Earl Anthony *ambassador, former federal agency administrator*
Wayne, Stephen J. *government educator, writer*
Weatherstone, Sir Dennis *retired bank executive*
Weaver, Christopher E. *naval officer*
Weaver, Reg (Reginald Weaver) *educational association administrator*
Webber, Richard John *lawyer*
Webre, Septime *ballet company artistic director, choreographer*
Webster, William Hedgcock *lawyer, former CIA director*
Wedgwood, Ruth *law educator, international affairs expert*
Weems, Kerry N. *federal agency administrator*
Wegener, Mark Douglas *lawyer*
Weicher, John Charles *economist, research director*
Weidenfeld, Edward Lee *lawyer*
Weidenfeld, Sheila Rabb *television producer, writer*
Weigel, George Shillow, Jr. *theologian*
Weigel, Kenneth George *lawyer*
Weimer, Thomas R. (R. Thomas Weimer) *federal agency administrator*
Weiner, Anthony David *congressman*
Weiner, Edward *civil engineer, federal agency administrator*
Weiner, Kenneth Brian *lawyer*
Weiner, Robert Neil *lawyer*
Weiner, Robert Stephen *federal agency administrator*
Weingarten, Reid H. *lawyer*

Weinhold, Linda Lillian *psychologist, researcher*
Weinman, Howard Mark *lawyer*
Weinmann, Eric *retired lawyer*
Weinreich, Gadi *lawyer*
Weinstein, Harris *lawyer*
Weintraub, Sidney *economist, educator*
Weisgall, Jonathan Michael *lawyer*
Weisman, Steven Roger *newspaper editor*
Weiss, Arnold Hans *lawyer*
Weiss, Charles, Jr. *educator*
Weiss, Mark Anschel *lawyer*
Weiss, Rick *reporter*
Weiss, Stephen J. *lawyer*
Weissman, William R. *lawyer*
Welch, C. David *assistant secretary of state, former ambassador*
Weldon, Curt (Wayne Curtis Weldon) *congressman*
Weldon, David Joseph, Jr. *congressman, physician*
Wellen, Robert Howard *lawyer*
Weller, Gerald C. *congressman*
Wellinghoff, Jon *commissioner*
Wells, Linton, II, *federal agency administrator*
Wells, Thomas B. *federal judge*
Wenner, Charles Roderick *lawyer*
Wennergren, David M. *civilian military employee*
Werkman, Sidney Lee *psychiatrist, educator*
Werner, Robert William *federal agency administrator*
Werronen, Betsy Warren *political organization administrator*
Wertheim, Mitzi Mallina *information technology executive*
Wertheimer, Fredric Michael *professional society administrator*
Wertz, Virginia Loryma *retired librarian*
Wesberry, James Pickett, Jr. *anti-corruption specialist, management consultant*
West, Gail Berry *lawyer*
West, Joseph D. *lawyer*
West, Robert MacLellan *science educator, consultant*
West, Togo Dennis, Jr. *lawyer, retired cabinet member*
West, W. Richard *museum director*
Westbrook, Reeves C. *lawyer*
Westmoreland, Lynn A. *congressman*
Wexler, Anne *government relations and public affairs consultant*
Wexler, Robert *congressman*
Weyrich, Paul Michael *think-tank executive*
Wheeler, Douglas Paul *conservationist, state agency administrator, lawyer*
Wheeler, Stephen Anthony *biology educator*
Wheeler, Thomas Craig *federal judge*
Wheeler, Thomas Edgar *private equity executive*
Wherry, Robert Allen, Jr. *federal judge, lawyer*
Whitaker, Scott *former federal agency administrator, lobbyist*
White, John Arnold *physics professor, research scientist*
White, John W. *federal agency administrator, lawyer*
White, Robert Edward *think-tank executive*
White, Robert I. *lawyer*
White, Robert Mayer *meteorologist*
Whitehurst, Grover Jay *psychologist, educator, federal official*
Whitfield, Edward (Wayne Whitfield) *congressman*
Whiting, Richard Albert *lawyer*
Whitney, Benson K. *ambassador*
Whittlesey, Judith Holloway *public relations executive*
Whitworth, Horace Algernon *mechanical engineer*
Whitworth, William A. *magazine editor*
Wholley, Michael Christopher *retired military officer, lawyer*
Wiacek, Raymond J. *lawyer*
Wicker, Roger F. *congressman, lawyer*
Wieder, Bruce Terrill *lawyer, electrical engineer*
Wiesel, Sam W. *medical educator, academic administrator*
Wilchins, Howard Martin *lawyer*
Wilder, Roland Percival, Jr. *lawyer*
Wilensky, Gail Roggin *economist, researcher*
Wiley, Richard Emerson *lawyer*
Wilhelm, John W. *labor union administrator*
Wilkes, Donna Natalie *historian*
Wilkins, David Horton *ambassador, former state legislator*
Wilkins, Robert L. *lawyer*
Wilkison, David *editor*
Will, George Frederick *editor, journalist, commentator*
Willard, Robert F. *career military officer*
Williams, Andrew W. *energy executive*
Williams, Anthony A. *mayor*
Williams, Darlene F. *federal agency administrator*
Williams, E. Faye *lawyer, political organization executive, health products executive*
Williams, Eddie Nathan *retired think-tank executive*
Williams, Ella Marilyn *mathematics educator*
Williams, James A. *labor union administrator*
Williams, Juan *news correspondent*
Williams, Julie Lloyd *federal agency administrator, lawyer*
Williams, Karen Hastie *lawyer*
Williams, Leaford Clemetson *writer, political scientist*
Williams, Mary Ellen Coster *federal judge*
Williams, Stephen Fain *federal judge*
Williamson, Carl Augustus *engineering executive*
Williamson, Edwin Dargan *lawyer, former federal official*
Willis, Kevin *airport administrator*
Willner, Ann Ruth *political scientist, educator*
Willner, Dorothy *anthropologist, educator*
Wilner, Thomas Bernard *lawyer*
Wilson, Carl *information technology executive*
Wilson, D. Edward, Jr. *lawyer*
Wilson, Gary Dean *lawyer*
Wilson, Heather Ann *congresswoman*
Wilson, Joe (Addison Graves Wilson) *congressman, former senator, lawyer*
Wilson, Michael Moureau *lawyer, physician*
Wilson, Ross *ambassador*
Winans, Cece *gospel vocalist*
Wine, L. Mark *lawyer*
Winfrey, Carey Wells *journalist, editor*

Winkenwerder, William, Jr. *federal agency administrator*
Winland, Thomas W. *lawyer*
Winnie, Glenna Barbara *pediatric pulmonologist*
Winston, Judith Ann *lawyer*
Winter, Donald C. *civilian military employee, former science administrator*
Winter, Douglas E. *lawyer, writer*
Winter, Thomas Swanson *publishing executive*
Wintrol, John Patrick *lawyer*
Wise, Bob (Robert Ellsworth Wise Jr.) *former governor, former congressman*
Wise, Joan S. *lawyer*
Wise, Lorraine E. *educational consultant*
Wiseman, David M(itchell) *lawyer*
Wiseman, Laurence Donald *foundation executive*
Wiseman, Thomas G. *lawyer*
Wiss, Marcia A. *lawyer*
Witek, John W. *history professor*
Withuhn, William Lawrence *curator, financial consultant*
Witt, James Lee *management consultant, former federal agency administrator*
Wittmann, Marshall *political organization worker*
Wixon, Henry N. *lawyer*
Wolanin, Barbara Ann Boese *curator, art historian*
Wolanin, Thomas Richard *federal agency administrator, educator*
Wolf, Frank Rudolph *congressman, lawyer*
Wolf, John S. *ambassador, federal agency administrator*
Wolf, William B., Jr. *lawyer*
Wolfe, Leslie R. *think-tank executive*
Wolfe, Sidney Manuel *physician*
Wolff, Alan William *lawyer*
Wolff, Candida (Candi Wolff) *federal official*
Wolff, Elroy Harris *lawyer*
Wolff, Karen Lias *music educator*
Wolff, Otto J. *federal agency administrator*
Wolff, Paul Martin *lawyer, sculptor*
Wolfowitz, Paul Dundes *President of the World Bank, former federal agency administrator*
Wolski, Victor J. *federal judge, lawyer*
Wolters, Curt Cornelis Frederik *foreign service officer*
Wood, Michael M. *ambassador*
Woodall, Samuel Roy, Jr. *lawyer*
Woodley, John Paul, Jr. *civilian military employee, lawyer*
Woodward, Bob (Robert Upshur Woodward) *newspaper reporter, writer*
Woodworth, Ramsey Lloyd *lawyer*
Woofter, Vivien Perrine *interior designer, consultant*
Wooldridge, Sue Ellen *federal agency administrator, lawyer*
Woolsey, Lynn C. *congresswoman*
Wootan, Margo G. *nutritionist, director*
Work, Charles Robert *lawyer*
Worsley, James Randolph, Jr. *lawyer*
Worthy, K(enneth) Martin *retired lawyer*
Worthy, Patricia Morris *lawyer, educator*
Wortley, George Cornelius *congressman, consultant*
Wraase, Dennis Richard *utilities executive, accountant*
Wrathall, James R. *lawyer*
Wray, Christopher Asher *lawyer, former federal agency administrator*
Wray, Robert *lawyer*
Wright, Daniel V. *judge, carrer military officer*
Wright, James Ralph *lawyer*
Wright, Sylvia *government agency administrator*
Wu, Benjamin H. *federal agency administrator, lawyer*
Wu, David *congressman*
Wulf, William Allan *foundation administrator, information scientist, educator*
Wunderlich, Gooloo S. *demographer, statistician, policy analyst*
Wuzor, Geoffrey Onyema *psychotherapist*
Wyatt, Richard L., Jr. *lawyer*
Wyden, Ron (Ronald Lee Wyden) *senator*
Wynn, Albert Russell *congressman*
Wynne, Michael Walter *civilian military employee*
Wyss, John Benedict *lawyer*
Yablon, Jeffery Lee *lawyer*
Yambrusic, Edward Slavko *lawyer, consultant*
Yanai, Shunji *former diplomat*
Yannucci, Thomas David *lawyer*
Yardley, Jonathan *journalist*
Yarwood, Bruce *health science association administrator*
Yerkes, David Norton *architect*
Yochelson, Ellis L(eon) *paleontologist*
Yoches, Edward Robert *lawyer*
Yoder, Ronnie A. *judge*
Yost, Paul Alexander, Jr. *foundation executive, retired military officer*
Young, Bill (Charles William Young) *congressman*
Young, Donald Alan *federal agency administrator*
Young, Donald E. *congressman*
Young, Howard J. *lawyer*
Young, John Jacob, Jr. *federal agency administrator*
Young, William H. *labor union administrator*
Youtcheff, John Sheldon *physicist*
Yulish, Charles Barry *retired public relations executive*
Zacharias, Norbert *astronomer*
Zagaris, Bruce *lawyer*
Zahn, Paula *newscaster*
Zaleski, Gary George *federal agency administrator, accountant*
Zane, Phillip Craig *lawyer*
Zarate, Juan Carlos *federal official*
Zaucha, Jerome J. *lawyer*
Zax, Leonard A. *lawyer*
Zeidman, Philip Fisher *lawyer*
Zelikow, Philip David *federal official, public policy educator*
Zentay, John H. *lawyer*
Ziegler, Janice H. *lawyer*
Zikmund, Barbara Brown *minister, religious organization administrator, educator*
Ziman, Barry Russell *government relations executive*
Zimmer, Richard Alan *lawyer, retired congressman*
Zimmerman, Edwin Morton *lawyer*
Zinmeister, Karl *federal official*

Zinni, Anthony Charles *retired military officer*
Zipp, Joel Frederick *lawyer*
Zoeller, Jack Carl *finance company executive*
Zolandz, Michael E., Jr. *lawyer*
Zotter, Bruce C. *lawyer*
Zuckman, Harvey Lyle *law educator*
Zwillinger, Marc J. *lawyer*

## Washington Navy Yard

Campbell, Regan Helen *engineer*

# FLORIDA

## Alachua

Carlisle, Casey Allen *chemist, educator*
Gaines, Weaver Henderson *lawyer*
Schneider, Richard T. (Richard Theodore Schneider) *optics scientist, researcher, engineer*

## Altamonte Springs

Heindl, Phares Matthews *lawyer*
LeBlanc, Janet M. *addictions and relationship counselor*
Nanton, Nicholas David *lawyer*

## Altoona

Westbrook, Clinton Howard *retired military petty officer, retired protective services official*

## Alva

Darlow, George Anthony Gratton *investor*

## Amelia Island

Adelman, Robert Paul *retired construction executive, lawyer*
Lilly, Wesley Cooper *marine engineer*
Schiebler, Gerold Ludwig *pediatrician, educator*

## Anna Maria

Hoffmann, Carl Konrad *lawyer*
Kaiser, Albert Farr *manufacturing executive*

## Apopka

Reinecke, William T. *conductor, educator*

## Arcadia

White, Will Walter III *public relations consultant, writer*

## Atlantic Beach

Gartland, Alice Johnson *artist*
Preble, Robert Curtis, Jr. *insurance executive*
Walker, Richard Harold *pathologist, educator*

## Aventura

Fishel, Peter Livingston *finance company executive*
Garcia, Marc Anthony *diplomat*
Johnson, Ray R. *artist*
Kliger, Milton Richard *diversified financial services company executive*
McKenna, Peter Dennis *lawyer*
Meltzer, Brad *writer*
Perkel, Robert Simon *photojournalist, educator*
Wolfenson, Azi U. *electrical, mechanical and industrial engineer, consultant*

## Babson Park

Morrison, Kenneth Douglas *writer, columnist*
Reeb, W. Suzanne *retired elementary and middle school educator and nurse*

## Bal Harbour

Spiegel, Siegmund *architect*

## Bartow

Etheredge, Edward Ezekiel *retired surgeon*
Kincart, Robert Owen *technological executive*
Logan, Heidi Christine *elementary school educator*
Meuser, Fredrick William *retired church administrator, historian*

## Bascom

Brooten, Kenneth Edward, Jr. *lawyer, writer, researcher*
Hart, James Whitfield, Jr. *retired public relations executive, lawyer*

## Bay Harbor Islands

Rosenbluth, Morton *periodontist, educator*

## Bay Pines

Law, David Hillis *physician*
Stewart, Jonathan Taylor *psychiatrist, educator*

## Bayonet Point

Errington, Norman *television producer, photographer*

## Belleair

Blackmar, Charles Blakey *state supreme court justice*
Dexter, Helen Louise *dermatologist, consultant*

## Belleair Beach

Ayers, Richard Wayne *electric power industry executive, writer, journalist*
Fuentes, Martha Ayers *playwright*

## Belleair Bluffs

Alexander, Christina Anamaria *translator, performing company executive*
Sexton, Donald Lee *retired business administration educator*

## Belleview

Bellis, Arthur Albert *financial executive, government official*

## Beverly Hills

Larsen, Erik *retired art history educator*

## Big Pine Key

Fleischer, Roland Edward *art history professor*

## Boca Grande

Carlson, Jane Cartwright *painter*

de Saint Phalle, Thibaut *investment banker, financial consultant*
Stolley, Alexander *advertising executive*
Winterer, Victoria Thompson *small business owner*

## Boca Raton

Agler, Richard Dean *rabbi*
Andrews, Holdt *investment banker*
Anise, Nader *lawyer*
Arden, Eugene *retired university provost*
Arent, Albert Ezra *retired lawyer*
Armstrong, Edward Bradford, Jr. *oral and maxillofacial surgeon, educator*
Babbar, Sunil *finance educator*
Barbarosh, Milton Harvey *merchant banking executive*
Batmasian, Marta Tersakian *investment company owner*
Baumgarten, Diana Virginia *gerontological nurse*
Beber, Robert H. *lawyer, diversified financial services company executive*
Bell, Marc H. *investment company executive*
Boykin, Anne Jane *dean*
Breakstone, Robert Albert *information technology executive, consumer products company executive, consultant*
Broadfield, Douglas *biological anthropologist, researcher*
Brogan, Frank T. *academic administrator, former lieutenant governor*
Buckstein, Mark Aaron *lawyer, educator, mediator*
Chestnov, Richard Franklin *private investor*
Collins, Robert Arnold *literature and language professor*
Connor, Frances Partridge *retired education educator*
Cowen, Edward S. *lawyer, consultant*
Dorfman, Allen Bernard *international management consultant*
Dower Gold, Catherine Anne *music history educator*
Dunhill, Robert *advertising executive*
Feinberg, Marc H. *neurologist*
Feld, Joseph *construction executive*
Fier, Elihu *lawyer, educator*
Fineman, Geraldine Gottesman *artist*
Fishenfeld, Grace *artist, educator*
Fowler, Gary Allen *management consultant*
Frank, Andrew K. *history professor*
Frankel, Charles James III *banker*
Friedland, Michael Lawrence *medical educator*
Friend, Harold Charles *neurologist*
Furman, Mark Evan *neuroscientist*
Garelick, Martin *retired transportation executive*
Godofsky, Stanley *lawyer*
Goldberger, Melvin Tobias *bank executive*
Goldman, Stuart Miles *podiatrist*
Goray, Gerald Allen *real estate company executive, lawyer*
Gracin, Hank *lawyer*
Gralla, Eugene *natural gas company executive*
Handel, Morton Emanuel *film company executive, management consultant*
Harris, S. Buddy *architect, interior designer*
Hermann, Philip J. *lawyer*
Hung, Chao-shun *economics professor, researcher*
Hunter, Barry C. *secondary school educator*
Iacobucci, Edward E. *air transportation executive, former software company executive*
Innes-Brown, Georgette Meyer *real estate broker, insurance broker*
Jessup, Jan Amis *arts volunteer, writer*
Johr, Robert Henry *dermatologist*
Kassner, Herbert Seymore *lawyer*
Kaye, Barry *insurance company executive*
Keyes, Daniel *author*
Kitzes, William Fredric *lawyer, advocate, researcher*
Koch, Robert Charles *lawyer, community activist*
Kramer, Cecile Edith *retired medical librarian*
Land, Judith Broten *stockbroker*
Langbort, Polly *retired advertising executive*
Lazar, Charna L. *private investigator, security consultant, retired CIA officer*
Leary, William James *educational association administrator*
Lee, Xiaoyang *scientist*
Lemanski, Larry Fredrick *medical educator, academic administrator*
Levine, Irving R. *commentator, dean, writer, educator*
Lin, Yukweng M. *engineer, educator*
Louda, J. William *chemist, biochemist, educator*
Man, Daniel *plastic surgeon*
Martin, James Russell *lawyer*
McNair, Russell Arthur, Jr. *lawyer*
McQueen, Scott Robert *broadcast executive*
Miles, Jesse Mc Lane *retired accounting company executive*
Miller, Eugene *academic administrator, finance educator*
Miller, Tonya Alicia *training and development specialist*
Monroe, William Lewis *human resources executive*
Mussenden, Georg Antonio *electronics engineer*
Norris, Charles Richard, Jr. *physician, psychiatrist*
O'Connell, Theresa Aurora *title company executive*
Oussani, James John *manufacturing executive*
Pasternack, Stefan Alan *psychiatrist, psychoanalyst*
Perel, David *editor*
Ponzi Kay, Marylou *human resources specialist*
Reinstein, Joel *lawyer*
Ricciardi, Salvatore *wholesale distribution executive*
Richardson, R(oss) Fred(erick) *insurance company executive, consultant*
Richman, Joseph Herbert *retired public health service officer*
Roselli, Richard Joseph *lawyer*
Rosenberg, Lee Evan *financial planner*
Ross, Kevin McAndrew *academic administrator*
Rothberg-Blackman, June Simmonds *retired nursing educator, psychotherapist*
Rubinson, Howard Alan *physician*
Russ, Fenee L. *principal, consultant*
Samuels, William Mason *physiology association executive*
Schechterman, Lawrence *chef, business consultant*
Shalom, Galit *psychologist*
Sigel, Marshall Elliot *financial consultant*

Sperry, Len Thomas *psychiatrist and preventive medicine educator*
Tennies, Robert Hunter *headmaster*
Turner, Lisa Phillips *human resources executive*
Wallach, Steven Ernst *lawyer, pilot*
Warshaw, Carole Klein *education educator, consultant*
Weiner, Howard Marc *physician*
Weissbach, Herbert *biochemist, researcher*
Wyatt, James Luther *drapery hardware company executive*
Yaffa, Andrew Bryan *lawyer*
Yoder, Patricia Doherty *public relations executive*

## Bokeelia

Judd, Jacqueline Vogel *retired middle school educator*

## Bonita Springs

Becker, Richard Charles *retired college president*
Brown, Theodore Lawrence *chemistry professor*
Costley, Gary Edward *food company executive*
Dignan, Thomas Gregory, Jr. *lawyer*
Dougherty, James *retired orthopedist*
Hastings, Vivien N. *lawyer*
Hauserman, Jacquita Knight *management consultant*
Johnson, Franklyn Arthur *academic administrator*
Katzen, Raphael *consulting chemical engineer*
McManigal, Shirley Ann *retired dean*
Nevin, Hugh Williamson, Jr. *lawyer*
Powell, Robert Ellis *mathematics professor, dean*
Starkey, Jerry L. *real estate developer*
Trudnak, Stephen Joseph *landscape architect*

## Boynton Beach

Allison, Dwight Leonard, Jr. *investor*
Bartholomew, Arthur Peck, Jr. *accountant*
Bernstein, Edwin S. *judge*
Bryant, Donald Loyd *insurance company executive*
Frankenberger, Bertram, Jr. *investor, consultant*
Glickman, Franklin Sheldon *dermatologist, educator*
Honeycutt, Kevin *construction executive, consultant*
Jacobs, Wendy *editor, realtor*
Jensen, Reuben Rolland *former automotive company executive*
Klein, Bernard *publishing executive*
Lisan, Philip *medical educator*
Mittel, John J. *diversified financial services company executive, economist*
Osipow, Lloyd I. *chemist, consultant*
Pataky, Paul Eric *ophthalmologist*
Polinsky, Janet Naboicheck *retired state official, retired state legislator*
Solkoff, Scott M. *lawyer*
Sondak, Arthur *retired management consultant*
Warga, Jack *mathematician, educator*
Warshaw, Stanley Irving *federal official, consultant*
Waterman, Daniel *mathematician, educator*
Wick, Mitchell A. *physician*
Winters, Darcy LaFountain *medical association administrator*

## Braden River

Wilkerson, Janet Stafford *publishing executive, educator*

## Bradenton

Bailey, Higgins D. *health products executive*
Beall, Robert Matthews, II, *retail executive*
Blanchard, Leonard Albert *writer, consultant, educator*
Brenner, Frank *lawyer*
Brunk, William Edward *astronomer*
Carnes, James Edward *retired electronics executive*
Castro, Valentino *psychologist, counseling administrator*
Compton, Charles Daniel *chemistry professor*
Crouthamel, Thomas Grover, Sr. *editor, consultant*
Diana, John Nicholas *physiologist*
Dudley, Perry, Jr. *retired electronics executive*
Engelman, Melvin Alkon *retired dentist, dental products executive*
Garvick, Kenneth Ryan *broadcast engineer, announcer, educator*
Green, Raymond Ferguson St. John *marketing and advertising executive*
Haas, Tommy (Thomas Mario Haas) *professional tennis player*
Hashmi, Sajjad Ahmad *finance educator, dean*
Heffernan, John William *retired journalist*
Houston, Stanley Dunsmore *retired public relations executive*
Howe, Carroll Victor *construction equipment company executive*
McFarland, Richard Macklin *retired journalist*
Moore, John Hampton *academic administrator*
Padgett, Gail Blanchard *lawyer*
Pillot, Gene Merrill *retired school system administrator*
Price, Edgar Hilleary, Jr. *manufacturing executive, consultant*
Robinson, Hugh R. *retired marketing executive*
Rutstein, Stanley Harold *apparel retailing company executive*
Smith-Gonzalez, April Renee *music educator*
Stewart, Priscilla Ann Mabie *art historian, educator*
Vereb, Teresa B. *psychiatrist*
Voorhees, Stephanie Robin Faught *retired art educator*
Watkins, William, Jr. *electric power industry executive*
White, Dale Andrew *journalist*
Wolf, John Michael *adult education seminar consultant*
Woodson-Howard, Marlene Erdley *former state legislator*

## Brandon

Curry, Clifton Conrad, Jr. *lawyer*
Mack, Arthur Neal *emergency medicine and family practice physician*
Pantano, Daniele *poet, educator*
Stephens, Robert David *environmental engineering executive*

## Brooksville

Anderson, Richard Edmund *city manager, management consultant*
Brown, James Milton *law educator*
Cario, Jeffrey Peter *lawyer*
Flannery, Michael Sidney *environmental scientist*
Lauer, Harry Curtis *retired civil engineer*
McBride, Tamera Shawn Dew *geologist*

## Cantonment

Coakley, William Travis *music educator*

## Cape Canaveral

Hess, Terry Lee *writer, educator, logistician*

## Cape Coral

(Harrison) Flint, Nancy Elizabeth *retired medical association administrator*
Graham, Dorothy E. *elementary school educator*
Hopkins, Lee Bennett *writer, educator*
Martin, Benjamin Gaufman *ophthalmologist*
Milaski, John Joseph *management consultant*
Nightingale, Suzanne M. *management consultant*
Parrett, Sherman O. *lawyer*
Shuman, Carolyn Rae (Thorburn) *psychologist, columnist, writer, nurse*
Stuart, Robert *container manufacturing executive*
Wendel, Joan Audrey *music educator*

## Carol City

Cabrera, Miguel *professional baseball player*
Girardi, Joseph Elliott (Joe Girardi) *professional baseball manager, former professional baseball player*

## Casselberry

Pantuso, Vincent Joseph *food service consultant*
Renee, Lisabeth Mary *small business owner, art designer*

## Cedar Key

Starnes, Earl Maxwell *retired urban and regional planner, retired architect, retired educator*

## Celebration

Johnson, Derrick M. *information technology executive*
Renard, Meredith Anne *marketing and advertising professional*
Schroeder, James White *retired lawyer*
Whelden, Craig B. *retired army officer*

## Chattahoochee

Carrasco, José Aníbal *recreational therapist*

## Clearwater

Bailey, Robin Keith *medical educator*
Barry, Joyce Alice *dietician, consultant*
Bazzone, Theresa (Terry) A. *sales executive*
Blumencranz, Peter William *surgeon*
Brady, Sheila Ann *manufacturing executive*
Brosious, Matthew James *manufacturing executive*
Campolettano, Thomas Alfred *international contract manager*
Chisholm, William DeWayne *retired contractor*
Coleman, Jeffrey Peters *lawyer*
Coraggio, James Thomas *educational measurement consultant, researcher*
Crites, Richard Ray *financial planner, finance company executive, investment advisor*
Cross, Beverly Jean *music educator*
Dougall-Sides, Leslie K. *lawyer*
Duerst, Andreas *information technology executive*
Dutkowsky, Robert M. *computer company executive*
Feldman, Marvin Herschel *financial consultant*
Glymph, Dianne Tyler *librarian*
Grala, Jane M. *security firm executive*
Greer, George W. *judge*
Halsey, Jean Michele *nursing educator*
Henderson, Janet Lynn *small business owner*
Hogan, Elwood *lawyer*
Howells, Jeffrey P. *computer company executive*
Johnson, Timothy Augustin, Jr. *lawyer*
Kiehl, E. Robert *manufacturing executive, consultant*
Luginbuehl, Marsha L. *psychologist*
Martino, Richard *application developer, mathematician, educator*
Maxwell, Richard Anthony *retail executive*
Peterson, James Robert *engineering psychologist*
Pope, Fred Wallace, Jr. *lawyer*
Raymund, Steven A. *computer company executive*
Sandefer, G(eorge) Larry *lawyer*
Shimel, John *game company executive*
Slade, Roy *artist, college president, museum director*
Smith, Marion Pafford *retired avionics company executive*
Tragos, George Euripedes *lawyer*
Turley, Stewart *retired retail company executive*
VanMeer, Mary Ann *publishing executive, writer, webmaster*
Vasilyadis, Leon *retired social worker*
Vetter, David R. *lawyer*
Zschau, Julius James *lawyer*

## Clearwater Beach

Whedon, George Donald *medical association administrator, researcher*

## Clermont

Cox, Margaret Stewart *photographer*
Kemp, Gretchen Laurel *choral director, music educator*
Richardson, Dot (Dorothy Gay) *former Olympic softball player, physician*
Sides, I. Ruth S. *retired music educator*

## Clewiston

Oeffner, Barbara Dunning *writer, educator, scriptwriter*

## Cocoa

Block, David L. *solar engineering executive*
Gamble, Thomas Ellsworth *academic administrator*
Pound, Frank R., Jr. *lawyer*
Rickling, Iraida Badillo *librarian*

## Cocoa Beach

Adkisson, Hubert Keith *military officer*
Wirtschafter, Irene Nerove *tax specialist, consultant, military officer*

## Coconut Creek

Brenner, Egon *academic administrator, education consultant*

## Coconut Grove

Alarcon, Raul, Jr. *broadcast executive*
Martinez-Carbonell, Karelia *not-for-profit fundraiser*
Softness, John *public relations executive*

## Cooper City

Garrard, Patricia Renick *elementary school educator*
Maugere, Dennis Paul *historian, educator*

## Coral Gables

Anthony, Andrew John *lawyer*
Asmus, Edward Paul *music educator*
Balkany, Thomas Jay *otolaryngologist*
Balzebre, Anthony Francis, Sr. *real estate developer, investor*
Brandt, Frederic Sheldon *dermatologist*
Brownell, Edwin Rowland *banker, civil engineer, land surveyor*
Buchsbaum, Karen Fuson *public relations executive, consultant*
Buell, Rodd Russell *lawyer*
Burini, Sonia Montes de Oca *apparel manufacturing executive, public relations executive*
Cole, Todd Godwin *management consultant transportation*
Dady, Robert Edward *lawyer*
De Sena, Ferdinando *composer, educator*
Einspruch, Norman Gerald *physicist, engineering educator*
Fitzgerald, John Thomas, Jr. *religious studies educator*
Frohock, Fred Manuel *political science professor*
Glaser, Luis *biochemistry educator*
Gould, Taffy *Internet company executive, real estate executive*
Hall, Miles Lewis, Jr. *lawyer*
Harriell, Kysha *athletic trainer, educator*
Hertz, Arthur Herman *communications executive*
Hirschberg, Joseph Gustav *physicist, educator*
Hirschhorn, Joel *lawyer*
Hoffman, Carl H. *lawyer*
Humphries, Joan Ropes *psychologist, educator*
Kohen, Elli *science educator*
Landon, Robert Kirkwood *volunteer*
Leblanc, Roger Maurice *chemistry professor*
Lomonosoff, James Marc *marketing professional*
Lucà-Moretti, Maurizio *research scientist, medical researcher, nutritionist, researcher*
Mangravite, Ronald *education educator, writer*
Matthews, Joseph Michael *lawyer*
McGrane, Miles A. III *lawyer*
Milton, Jose *real estate development company executive*
Milton, Joseph *real estate development company executive*
Moss, Ambler Holmes, Jr. *lawyer, educator, former ambassador*
Musgrave, Franklyn Garfield *obstetrician, gynecologist*
Nijman, Jan *geographer, educator*
Nunez-Portuondo, Ricardo *investment company executive*
Perez, Josephine *psychiatrist, educator*
Prilleltensky, Isaac *dean*
Quillian, Warren Wilson, II, *pediatrician, educator*
Rew, William Edmund *civil engineer*
Roberts, Samuel Smith *television news executive*
Sabat-Rivers, Georgina *Latin American literature educator*
Sacher, Charles Philip *lawyer*
Saffir, Herbert Seymour *structural engineer, consultant*
Shalala, Donna Edna *academic administrator, former secretary of health and human services*
Shyu, Mei-Ling *information scientist, educator*
Steinberg, Alan Wolfe *investment company executive*
Sumanth, David Jonnakoty *industrial engineer, educator*
Touby, Kathleen Anita *lawyer*
Van Vliet, Carolyn Marina *physicist, researcher*
Wiles, David Ernest *academic administrator*
Williams, Lowell E. *theater educator*
Wolf, Aizik Loft *neurosurgeon*
Zvijac, John E. *orthopedist, surgeon*

## Coral Springs

Burg, Ralph *art association executive*
Kristofferson, Kris *singer, lyricist, actor*
Singh, Vijay *professional golfer*
Sommerer, John *accountant, former mayor*
Wechsler, Arnold *obstetrician, gynecologist*

## Crawfordville

Brumby, James Remley, III, (Knox Brumby) *retired priest*
Siamis, Janet Neal *painter*

## Crestview

Scott, George Gallmann *accountant*

## Dade City

Bala, Sam G. *surgeon*
Brennan, Thomas Emmett *lawyer*
Brown-Waite, Virginia (Ginny Brown-Waite) *congresswoman*
Burdick, Glenn Arthur *physicist, engineering educator*

## Dania

Fernander, Karen Geneine *secondary school educator*

## Dania Beach

Satin, Claire Jeanine *sculptor, artist*
Spieler, Richard Earl *oceanographer, educator*

## Davie

Boston, David *professional football player*

**Capers, Dom (Dominic Capers)** *professional football coach*
**Culpepper, Daunte** *professional football player*
**Harrington, Joey** *professional football player*
**Morris, Joseph Raymond** *finance educator*
**Mularkey, Mike** *professional football coach*
**Saban, Nick** *professional football coach*
**Schwab, Judith** *artist, educator, sculptor*
**Taylor, Jason Paul** *professional football player*
**Thomas, Zach Michael** *professional football player*
**Upadhiaya, Umesh Chandra** *engineer, consultant*
**Walkinshaw, Nicole M.** *performing arts educator*

## Daytona Beach

**Adams, John Carter, Jr.** *insurance executive*
**Ahn, Shi Hyun** *professional golfer*
**Alvarez, Marianne** *artist, photographer, educator*
**Amick, William Walker** *golf course architect*
**Andrews, Donna L.** *professional golfer*
**Baena, Marisa** *professional golfer*
**Barrett, Tina** *professional golfer*
**Bennett, Byron Lee** *chemistry professor, researcher*
**Bivens, Carolyn Vesper** *former advertising executive, golf association commissioner-elect*
**Bodine, Geoff** *race car driver*
**Cardwell, Harold Douglas, Sr.** *retired rehabilitation services professional*
**Carmona, José Antonio** *Spanish language educator, English language educator*
**Creamer, Paula** *professional golfer*
**Dalia, Vesta Mayo** *artist*
**David, Valentina S.** *physics professor*
**Davidson, Herbert M., Jr., (Tippen Davidson)** *newspaper owner*
**Davies, Laura** *professional golfer*
**DeLuca, Annette** *professional golfer*
**Dhainaut, Jean-Michel Maurice** *engineering educator*
**Doolan, Wendy** *professional golfer*
**Duma, Richard Joseph** *epidemiologist, microbiologist, educator, pathologist, researcher, physician*
**Dumm, Robert Wayne** *musician, educator, writer*
**Foushee-Higgs, Rosa** *elementary school educator, artist*
**France, Brian Z.** *sports association executive*
**France, James C.** *professional sports executive*
**France, William Clifton, Jr.** *professional sports executive*
**Gordon, Jeff** *race car driver*
**Green, Betty Nielsen** *education educator, consultant*
**Han, Hee-Won** *professional golfer*
**Harris, Christy Franklin** *lawyer*
**Helfrick, Albert Darlington** *electronics engineering educator, consultant, department chairman*
**Hurst, Patricia Ann** *professional golfer*
**Inkster, Juli** *professional golfer*
**Jang, Jeong** *professional golfer*
**Kane, Lorie** *professional golfer*
**Kerr, Cristie** *professional golfer*
**Kim, Christina** *professional golfer*
**Kim, Mi Hyun** *professional golfer*
**King, Betsy** *professional golfer*
**Klein, Emilee** *professional golfer*
**Kruse, Marylin Lynn** *retired language educator*
**Kuiper, Dirk** *performing arts educator, writer*
**Kung, Candie** *professional golfer*
**Libby, Gary Russell** *museum director emeritus, writer*
**Lincicome, Brittany** *professional golfer*
**Mallon, Meg** *professional golfer*
**Mc Collister, John Charles** *writer, minister, educator*
**Mears, Casey** *race car driver*
**Neitzke, Eric Karl** *lawyer*
**Neumann, Liselotte** *professional golfer*
**Ochoa, Lorena** *professional golfer*
**Pagan Ortiz, Alex Omar** *computer systems analyst, educator*
**Pak, Se Ri** *professional golfer*
**Park, Grace** *professional golfer*
**Park, Hee-Jung (Hee Jong Park)** *professional golfer*
**Poitier, Constance Rena** *music specialist, educator*
**Robbins, Kelly** *professional golfer*
**Rosales, Jennifer** *professional golfer*
**Rudd, Ricky** *race car driver*
**Saiki, Kim** *professional golfer*
**Samuelson, Fred Binder** *artist, educator*
**Scott, John Brooks** *retired research and development company executive*
**Seenith, Sivasundaram** *mathematician, educator*
**Sheehan, Patty** *professional golfer*
**Sigerson, Marjorie Lorraine** *librarian*
**Sorenstam, Annika** *professional golfer*
**Steinhauer, Sherri** *professional golfer*
**Stupples, Karen** *professional golfer*
**Teske, Rachel** *professional golfer*
**Votaw, Ty M.** *golf association commissioner*
**Webb, Karrie** *professional golfer*
**Whitworth, Kathrynne Ann** *professional golfer*
**Wie, Michelle Sung** *professional golfer*
**Zenkovsky, Betty Jean** *modern languages educator*

## Debary

**Coble, Alicia Sharon** *retired elementary school educator, retired secondary school educator*
**Pelosi, Haydee** *sculptor*

## Deerfield Beach

**Allaire, Gaston George** *music educator, researcher*
**Brown, Colin** *automotive executive*
**Gambino, S(alvatore) Raymond** *lab administrator, educator*
**King, Don** *boxing promoter*
**Laser, Charles, Jr.** *oil company executive*
**Moran, James M.** *automotive sales executive*
**Moran, Patricia Genevieve** *corporate financial executive*
**Nieto, Mario** *civil engineer*
**Panitz, Daniel R.** *psychologist, consultant*
**Siegel, Steven L.** *finance company executive, consultant*
**Solomon, Barry Jason** *human services administrator, consultant*
**Yerves, Ken** *information technology executive*

## Deland

**Bailey, T. Wayne** *political science professor*
**Blais, Michael Roland** *retired urologist*
**Bradford, Jane Turner** *librarian*
**Caccamise, Genevra Louise Ball (Mrs. Alfred E. Caccamise)** *retired librarian*
**Dascher, Paul Edward** *dean, accounting educator*
**Freeman, Ronald Eugene** *environmental engineer*
**Goldberg, Paul Bernard** *gastroenterologist, clinical researcher*
**Hodges, Brian W.** *consumer products company executive*
**Langston, Paul T.** *dean, composer, music educator*
**Lee, Howard Douglas** *academic administrator*
**Mendez, Elsie Noemi** *elementary school educator*
**Musco, Lynn Ann** *music educator*
**Niemann, Chester S., Jr.** *retired band director, customer service administrator*
**Plane, Donald Ray** *retired management science educator*
**Rattman, William John** *electronics and electro-optic engineer*
**Ryan, Susan Magness** *librarian, educator*
**Wittich, John Jacob** *retired academic administrator, finance company executive*

## Delray Beach

**Beckman, Frank Samuel** *computer science educator, researcher*
**Brown, Charles E.** *retail executive*
**Carter-Miller, Jocelyn** *retail executive*
**Charyk, Joseph Vincent** *retired satellite telecommunications executive*
**Chavin, Walter** *biological sciences educator, researcher*
**Dye, Thomas Roy** *political science professor*
**Ehrlich, Geraldine Elizabeth** *management consultant*
**Ellsweig, Phyllis Leah** *retired psychotherapist*
**Fannin, David Cecil** *lawyer*
**Goldenberg, George** *retired pharmaceutical executive*
**Hardiman, Joseph Raymond** *security firm executive*
**Hegstrom, William Jean** *retired mathematics professor*
**Hofman, Elizabeth Elveretta** *retired mathematics educator, guidance counselor, dean*
**Holifield, Mark** *retail executive*
**Jacobson, Herbert Leonard** *electronics executive*
**Larry, R. Heath** *lawyer, director*
**Leeds, Susanne** *special education educator, writer*
**Levinson, Harry** *psychologist, educator*
**Luechtefeld, Monica** *retail executive*
**Make, Isabel Rose** *multicultural studies educator, adult education educator, small business owner*
**McKay, Patricia A.** *corporate financial executive*
**Mills, Agnes Eunice Karlin** *artist*
**Odland, Steve** *consumer products company executive*
**Rippeteau, Darrel Downing** *retired architect*
**Rosenfeld, Steven Ira** *ophthalmologist*
**Ross, Donald Edward** *former academic administrator*
**St. George, Elaine** *art educator*
**Salsberg, Arthur Philip** *publishing executive*
**Schenkel, Suzanne Chance** *retired natural resource specialist*
**Sherwood, Louis Maier** *endocrinologist, pharmaceutical executive*
**Silberman, Charlotte Schatzberg** *retired lawyer, artist*
**Smith, Charles Oliver** *retired engineer*
**Spyker, Harry A. III** *music educator*
**Stewart, Patricia Carry** *foundation administrator*
**van Kaldekerken, Rolf** *retail executive*
**Wells, Mary Elizabeth Thompson** *deacon, director, chaplain, director*
**Zarwyn, Berthold** *physicist, consultant*

## Deltona

**Bondinell, Stephanie** *counselor, academic administrator*
**Drewry, Marcia Ann** *physician*
**Marrett, Caroline Denise** *special education educator*

## Destin

**Blossman, Alfred Rhody, Jr.** *banker*
**Burden, William R.** *plastic surgeon*
**Burns, Jurate** *library director*
**Deel, Frances Quinn** *retired librarian*
**De Revere, David Wilsen** *retired professional society administrator*
**Robinson, Wilkes Coleman** *retired federal judge*

## Dover

**Pearson, Walter Donald** *editor, columnist*

## Duck Key

**Prout, George Russell, Jr.** *medical educator, urologist*

## Dunedin

**Asefa, Tirusew** *hydrologist*
**Goodale, Arthur Worthington** *civil engineer, researcher*
**Huffman, Thomas David** *church music director, organist*
**Klingbiel, Paul Herman** *retired information scientist*
**Metcalf, Robert John Elmer** *industrial consultant*
**O'Dea, J. David** *psychologist, educator*
**Rosa, Raymond Ulric** *retired banker*
**Ruff, Kenneth** *management consultant, information technology manager*

## Dunnellon

**Dixon, W(illiam) Robert** *retired psychologist*
**Fonseca, Julio** *retired secondary school educator*

## Edgewater

**Michajlow, Eustachy Iom** *artist*
**Schubert, Jeanne** *artist*

## Eglin Afb

**Franzen, Larry William** *aerospace electronics engineer*
**Head, William Christopher** *military officer, health care administrator*

**Richardson, Douglas J.** *career officer*

## Ellenton

**Edson, Herbert Robbins** *retired foundation and hospital executive, retired military officer*

## Englewood

**Clark, Bret Shawn** *lawyer*
**McCall, Gene William** *conservator, sculptor, artist, furniture designer*
**Sanders, W(illiam) Eugene, Jr.** *retired internist*
**Simis, Theodore Luckey** *investment banker, information technology executive*
**Watts, Ronald Lester** *retired military officer*

## Estero

**Brown, William Robert** *trade association administrator, consultant*
**Brush, George W.** *college president*
**Routh, Donald K. (Donald Kent Routh)** *psychologist, educator*
**Steele, Richard J.** *management consultant*

## Eustis

**Chorosinski, Eugene Conrad** *writer, poet, author*
**King, Robert Howard** *marketing professional*

## Fernandina Beach

**Ash, Frederick Melvin** *retired manufacturing executive*
**Barlow, Anne Louise** *pediatrician, medical researcher*
**Kurtz, Myers Richard** *retired hospital administrator*
**Smeeton, Thomas Rooney** *government affairs consultant*

## Fort Lauderdale

**Adams, Nancy R.** *nurse, retired military officer*
**Adams, S. C(hase)** *lawyer, writer, radio and television commentator, financial consultant*
**Alpert, Martin Jeffrey** *chiropractic physician*
**Ambrose, Judith Ann** *wedding planner*
**Arneson, Margaret Susan** *lawyer*
**Atkinson, Christopher Lee** *county official*
**Austin, John Norman** *classics educator*
**Azrin, Nathan Harold** *psychologist, educator*
**Bamberg, Louis Mark** *wealth planning and business insurance specialist*
**Bass, Harold Michael** *plastic surgeon*
**Beach, Cecil Prentice** *librarian*
**Beach, Marcia Ellen** *judge*
**Berrard, Steven R.** *investment company executive, former automotive retail company executive*
**Bogenschutz, J. David** *lawyer*
**Borras, Jaime** *telecommunications industry executive*
**Bowen, Judith Reina** *fundraising executive*
**Brogan, Francis B., Jr.** *lawyer*
**Bronstein, Dina B.** *lawyer*
**Bunnell, George Eli** *lawyer, director*
**Burleigh, A. Peter** *ambassador*
**Bustamante, Nestor** *lawyer*
**Cannon, Robert Eugene** *library director*
**Cantwell, John Walsh** *advertising executive*
**Castillo, Carmen** *staffing company executive*
**Cavendish, Kim L. Maher** *museum administrator*
**Chernow, Bart** *critical care physician*
**Chung, Chia Mou (Charles Chung)** *former Oriental art business owner*
**Cobb, David Keith** *accountant*
**Coleman, Phyllis** *law educator*
**Collins, Ronald William** *psychologist, educator*
**Cordesman, Michael J.** *waste management administrator*
**Cox, Linda Susan** *allergist, immunologist*
**Craib, Kenneth Bryden** *research and development company executive, physicist, economist*
**Donaway, Carl D.** *messenger service executive*
**Dressler, Robert A.** *lawyer*
**Droege, Marcus** *medical educator, researcher*
**Duke, James T** *art educator, consumer products company executive*
**Dwors, Robert F.** *retail executive*
**Edmund, Norman Wilson** *educational researcher*
**Feldman, Les J.** *finance educator*
**Ferrando, Jonathan P.** *retail executive*
**Fine, Howard Alan** *management consultant*
**Fischler, Abraham Saul** *retired academic administrator, educator*
**Fleetwood, Clifford Gene ("The Father of Philosophical Art" Fleetwood)** *recording industry executive, publishing executive*
**Gagnon Blodgett, Michelle Dawn** *psychologist*
**Gerbino, John** *advertising executive*
**Glick, Richard Stephen** *internist, rheumatologist*
**Gonzalez, Jose Alejandro, Jr.** *federal judge*
**Gunzburger, Suzanne Nathan** *municipal official, social worker*
**Haliczer, James Solomon** *lawyer*
**Hanbury, George Lafayette, II,** *academic administrator*
**Hargrove, John Russell** *lawyer*
**Hartz, Deborah Sophia** *editor, writer*
**Haugen, Christine** *plastic surgeon*
**Hershenson, Miriam Hannah Ratner** *librarian*
**Hess, George Franklin, II,** *lawyer*
**Hester, Julia A.** *lawyer*
**Hills, John Merrill** *educational association administrator, consultant, public relations executive, researcher*
**Hirsch, Jeffrey Allan** *lawyer*
**Horvitz, David W.** *investment company executive*
**Huizenga, H. Wayne** *entrepreneur, professional sports team executive*
**Hull, Richard Franklin** *insurance brokerage executive*
**Itkin, Ivan** *nuclear scientist, mathematician*
**Jackson, Michael J.** *automotive retail company executive*
**Jarvis, Robert Mark** *law educator*
**Johnson, Mary Margaret Dickens** *governmental and commercial researcher, consultant*
**Jotcham, Thomas Denis** *marketing communications consultant*
**Kelly, John Patrick** *lawyer*
**Kilgus, Edward Chip** *singer, actor, writer, poet*
**Kjellmark, Eric William, Jr.** *management consultant, performing company executive*
**Knight, Kenneth Vincent** *entrepreneur, venture capitalist*

**Koch, Katherine Rose** *communications executive*
**Kornblau, Barbara L.** *physical therapist, educator*
**Krause, Roy G.** *office staffing firm executive*
**Kubler, Frank Lawrence** *lawyer*
**Lataif, Lawrence P.** *lawyer*
**Leach, Ralph F.** *banker*
**Leighton, James H.** *law educator, department chairman*
**LeRoy, Miss Joy** *model, apparel designer*
**Levy, Michael** *electronic manufacturing company executive*
**Levy, Michael** *philosopher, writer*
**Lilley, Mili Della** *insurance company executive, entertainment management consultant*
**Littman, Marlyn Kemper** *information scientist, educator*
**Lodwick, Gwilym Savage** *radiologist, educator*
**Lyons, Bruce M.** *lawyer*
**Mahan, Mary Hoyle** *retired physical educator*
**Markos, Chris** *retired real estate company executive*
**Markus, Robert Michael** *retired journalist*
**Maroone, Michael E.** *car and truck sales executive*
**Mathis, Donald Raymond** *music educator*
**McCan, James Lawton** *education educator*
**McCluskey, Neil Gerard** *gerontologist, educator, literary agent*
**McIntyre, Jennifer Noel** *academic administrator*
**Meeks, William Herman III** *lawyer*
**Monaghan, Craig Thomas** *automotive executive*
**Morris, Gerald Michael** *lawyer, educator*
**Moss, Stephen Bruce** *lawyer*
**Neimark, Cort Alan** *lawyer*
**Nyce, John Daniel** *lawyer*
**O'Brien, Patrick T.** *lawyer*
**O'Connor, James E.** *waste management executive*
**Oliet, Seymour** *endodontics educator, dean, dentist*
**Oltman, John Harold** *patent lawyer*
**Packer, Billy** *sports announcer (broadcast)*
**Parker, Sasha Smilka** *medical educator, nurse, consultant*
**Parrish, Lori Nance** *property appraiser*
**Peltzer, Douglas Lea** *manufacturing executive*
**Pohlman, Randolph A.** *business administration educator, dean*
**Putnam, Gene Chumley** *music educator*
**Randi, James (Randall James Hamilton Zwinge)** *magician, educator*
**Ray, Raymond B.** *federal judge*
**Rentoumis, Ann Mastroianni** *psychotherapist*
**Revis, Don Ray, Jr.** *plastic surgeon*
**Richmond, Gail Levin** *law educator*
**Riggs, Donald Eugene** *librarian, academic administrator*
**Rodriguez, Carlos Augusto** *lawyer*
**Rojas, Jesus Jon** *health products executive, researcher*
**Ruffner, Frederick G., Jr.** *book publisher*
**Russell, Terrence Joseph** *lawyer*
**Sanders, Dale R.** *lawyer*
**Sanders, Howard** *investment company executive*
**Sanderson, Rita Marye** *history educator*
**Schnoor, Jon Peter** *military officer*
**Schreiber, Alan Hickman** *lawyer*
**Schulte, Frederick James** *newspaper editor*
**Seltzer, Barry S.** *federal judge*
**Seyoum, Belay** *business educator*
**Sherman, Richard Allen, Sr.** *lawyer*
**Shoemaker, William Edward** *corporate financial executive*
**Siegel, Michael Alan** *dental educator*
**Smith, Mark W.** *management consultant*
**Stayton, James Michael** *music educator*
**Sullivan, Edward Delano** *lawyer, investor*
**Sun, Junping** *computer science professor*
**Tacher, Robert Frederick** *lawyer*
**Taylor, Ralph Orien, Jr.** *real estate developer, investor*
**Thayer, Charles James** *investment banker*
**Tristano, Antonio Gino** *medical researcher*
**Trubey, Lillian Priscilla** *retired secondary school educator*
**Turner, Hugh Joseph, Jr.** *lawyer*
**Uchin, Robert Allen** *dean, endodontist*
**Udolf, Bruce Lee** *lawyer*
**Valdes, Arlene H.** *assistant principal*
**Vasquez, William Leroy** *business educator, consultant*
**Velez, Ines** *oral pathologist, educator*
**Vladem, Paul Jay** *investment advisor*
**Webster, Ernest Wesley** *musician, educator*
**Weiss, David I.** *real estate company executive, lawyer, writer*
**Whitmore, Douglas Michael** *physician*
**Wilbur, Colleen Patricia** *elementary school educator, principal*
**Williamson, William Paul, Jr.** *journalist*
**Wojcik, Cass** *decorative supply company executive, retired municipal official*
**Zfaz, Martin** *medical director, treatment professional, consultant*
**Zimmerman, Jordan** *advertising executive, marketing professional*
**Zloch, William J.** *federal judge*

## Fort Mc Coy

**Cromer, Don M.** *secondary school educator, music educator*

## Fort Myers

**Antonic, James Paul** *international marketing consultant*
**Arnall, Robert Esric** *physician, health facility administrator*
**Barbour, William Rinehart, Jr.** *retired book publisher*
**Beever, James William III** *biologist*
**Benbenisty, Keith Mitchell** *dermatologist*
**Canham, Pruella Cromartie Niver** *music educator*
**Colasurd, Richard Michael** *lawyer*
**Colgate, Doris Eleanor** *sailing school owner, administrator*
**Curtin, Constance O'Hara** *language educator, writer*
**Curtin, David Yarrow** *chemist, educator*
**Drushal, Mary Ellen** *parish educator, education educator, former academic administrator*
**Faith, Ruth L.** *retired mathematician*
**Fox, Beverly** *marketing professional*
**Fulker, Edmund Norman** *management consultant*

**Indian River Shores**
Ahrens, William Henry *architect*
Wiegner, Edward Alex *manufacturing executive*

**Inverness**
Cross, Sandra Kay *primary school educator*
Esquibel, Edward V. *psychiatrist, health facility administrator*

**Islamorada**
Gates, Richard Daniel *retired manufacturing executive*
Shelton, Dorothy Aubinoe *interior designer*

**Jacksonville**
Adams, Scott Leslie *accountant*
Aldana, Philipp Roque *neurosurgeon*
Aleschus, Justine Lawrence *retired real estate broker*
Ansbacher, Barry Barnett *lawyer*
Appel, Laurence Bruce *lawyer, retail executive*
Arbogast, Gordon Wade *systems engineer, educator, consultant, retired military officer*
Atteberry, Linda Rose *surgeon, retired military officer*
Barrow, Sally Settle *media specialist, librarian*
Bartley, George B. *ophthalmologist, surgeon*
Beattie, Donald A. *aerospace scientist, consultant*
Bedell, Elizabeth Snyder (Betty Bedell) *editor-in-chief, marketing professional*
Beytagh, Francis X. *law educator*
Blount, Yolanda Denise *social services administrator, psychologist*
Bodkin, Ruby Pate *real estate broker, educator*
Bosworth, William Posey *physician, physical education educator*
Boyer, Tyrie Alvis *lawyer*
Boyer, Tyrie William *judge, law educator*
Boylan, Kevin Bernard *neurologist*
Bradford, Dana Gibson, II, *lawyer*
Bruns, Robert A. *history educator*
Bullock, Bruce Stanley *lawyer*
Cagle, Margaret Broughton *retired parochial school educator*
Callender, John Francis *lawyer*
Campo, Dave *professional football coach*
Cannon, Carl N. *publishing executive*
Cannon, L. Kinder III *lawyer*
Carpenter, JoAnn Deakin *history professor*
Cavendish, Michael Robert *lawyer*
Chambers, Jack Allen *application developer, educator*
Chang, Hernan Robert *infectious disease consultant*
Clarkson, Charles Andrew *real estate investment executive*
Commander, Charles Edward *lawyer, real estate consultant*
Costin, Rea-Silvia *civil engineer*
Crowe, Jeffrey C. *transportation executive*
Cruz, Theresa Lavaina *mental health services professional, educator*
Davis, Fred *journalist, educator*
Davis, Linda Lennon McConnell *critical care nurse*
Delaney, John Adrian *academic administrator*
Delaney, Kevin Francis *retired military officer, consultant*
Del Rio, Jack *professional football coach, former professional football player*
De Soto, Hernando *pediatric anesthesiologist*
Dikici, Engin *research scientist*
Duke, Andrea K. *music educator*
Dundon, Margo Elaine *museum director*
Eden, F. Brown *artist*
Edwards, Marvin Raymond *investment counselor, economical consultant*
Enders, Lawrence John *preventive medicine physician, educator*
Eschen, James L. *historian, educator*
Fahner, Harold Thomas *marketing executive*
Fanniel, Ronald Noel, Sr. *educational consultant*
Farmer, Guy Otto, II, *lawyer*
Fawbush, Andrew Jackson *lawyer*
Ferguson, Thomas Crooks *lawyer*
Fine, Cory R. *education educator, consultant*
Fisher, Michael D. *retail executive*
Fortado, Bruce *management educator*
Francis, James Delbert *oil industry executive*
Gabel, George DeSaussure, Jr. *lawyer*
Gerkens, Henry H. *trucking executive*
Getman, Willard Etheridge *lawyer, arbitrator, mediator*
Godfrey, John Munro *economic consultant*
Goldhagen, Jeffrey Lee *city health department administrator*
Goodwin, Jane Ayers *pediatric anesthesiologist*
Gubbin, Barbara Ashley Brendon *library director*
Halil, Susan Terrell *dental hygienist*
Hardesty, W. Marc *lawyer, educator*
Hartmann, Frederick William *newspaper editor*
Hill, Debra S. *lawyer*
Hill, James Clinkscales *federal judge*
Holliday, Patricia Ruth McKenzie *evangelist*
Homsley, Denise Louise *music educator*
Hovey, Charles William *mortgage company executive*
Huber, Mary Susan *music educator*
Hughes, Carolyn Wright *elementary school educator, director*
Israel, Kimberly Held *lawyer*
Jackson, Julian Ellis *food company executive*
Jamrich, John Xavier *retired university administrator*
Johnson, Douglas William *radiologist*
Jones, Herman Otto, Jr. *agricultural products executive*
Kanders, Warren Beatty *manufacturing executive, investment banker*
Kelso, Linda Yayoi *lawyer*
Kent, John Bradford *lawyer*
Killea, Michael F. *lawyer*
Kinne, Frances Bartlett *academic administrator*
Kneller, Michael *transportation services executive*
Laymon, April Marie *music educator*
Lee, Lewis Swift *lawyer*
Leftwich, Byron Antron *professional football player*
Legler, Mitchell Wooten *lawyer*
Lehmbeck, John Pierce *journalist, writer*
Leonard, Thomas Michael *university program director, educator*

Lestage, Daniel Barfield *retired military officer, physician*
Lynch, Peter L. *retail executive*
Lyon, Wilford Charles, Jr. *insurance executive*
Main, Edna Dewey (June Main) *education educator*
Main, James L. *lawyer*
Mandal, Prabir Kumar *biologist, educator*
Mass, M. F. *allergist, immunologist*
Matta, Mark W. *human resources specialist, manufacturing executive*
Maxwell, W(ilbur) Richard *retired management consultant*
McBurney, Charles Walker, Jr. *lawyer*
McCook, Richard Paul *grocery chain financial executive*
McWilliams, John Lawrence III *lawyer*
Melton, Howell Webster, Sr. *federal judge*
Milton, Joseph Payne *lawyer*
Mizrahi, Edward Alan *allergist*
Monsky, John Bertrand *investment company executive*
Montgomery, Suzanne Howard *psychologist*
Mordecai, Monica Myers *anesthesiologist*
Morgan, William Newton *architect, educator*
Moseley, James Francis *lawyer*
Motsett, Charles Bourke *sales, marketing and leadership executive*
Muehrcke, Derek David *thoracic and cardiovascular surgeon*
Mueller, Cherone *religious organization administrator, writer, minister*
Mueller, Edward Albert *retired transportation engineer*
Nussbaum, Bennett *printing/copying company executive*
O'Connor, R. D. *retired health services administrator*
Olin, Marilyn *secondary school educator*
Osborn, Marvin Griffing, Jr. *educational consultant*
Owen, Dennis P. *lawyer*
Page, Willis *conductor*
Patel, Vinod Motibhai *accountant*
Pavlick, Pamela Kay *nurse, consultant*
Payne, Timothy D. *information technology executive*
Perdikis, Galen *plastic surgeon*
Portell, Keith S *application developer, consultant*
Prussin, Jeffrey A. *management consultant*
Radisky, Derek Charles *biomedical researcher, educator*
Raynor, Eileen Margolies *otolaryngologist, educator*
Rinaman, James Curtis, Jr. *lawyer*
Robinson, Christine Marie *mathematics professor*
Rutherford, John *sheriff*
Sandercox, Robert Allen *academic administrator, minister*
ScarborougH, Marion Nichols *nutritionist, recreational facility executive*
Schlesinger, Harvey Erwin *judge*
Schramm, Bernard Charles, Jr. *retired advertising agency executive*
Schultz, Frederick Henry *investor, former government official*
Schupp, Robert Warren *law educator*
Sederbaum, William *marketing professional*
Sheppard, William J. *lawyer*
Skelton, H. Jay *retail executive, investment company executive*
Skinner, Halcyon E. *lawyer*
Smith, David A. *medical services executive*
Smith, Stephen Mark *music educator*
Stanley, Helen Camille *composer, musician*
Stanton, Robert John, Jr. *language educator*
Stein, Jay *retail executive*
Stewart, Sandra Kay *music educator*
Supanich, Barbara Ann *physician*
Taylor, Fred *professional football player*
Taylor, Gavin Hall *music educator*
Taylor, Robert M. *minister*
Thomas, Archibald Johns III *lawyer*
Thorsteinsson, Gudni *physiatrist*
Tjoflat, Gerald Bard *federal judge*
Tomlinson, William Holmes *management educator, retired military officer*
Tyler Guidry, Carolyn E. *bishop*
Van Cleve, Robert Baldwin *cardiologist*
Vane, Terence G., Jr. *finance company executive, lawyer*
Vasana, Susan (Chun-Ye) *engineering educator*
Vincent, Norman Fuller *broadcast executive*
Ward, Michael J. *rail transportation executive*
Washington, MaliVai *retired professional tennis player, foundation administrator*
Watkins, Julia Anne *healthcare educator, researcher*
Weaver, Dianne Jay *lawyer*
Welch, Philip Burland *electronics and office products company executive*
White, Edward Alfred *lawyer*
Williams, Leola Wilkerson *social worker, writer*
Zenni, Elisa Alter *pediatrician*

**Jacksonville Beach**
Mahorner, James M. *lawyer*
Saltzman, Irene Cameron *consumer products company executive*

**Jasper**
McCormick, John Hoyle *lawyer*

**Jensen Beach**
Aho, Paul Richard *artist, art educator*
Gamble, Raymond Wesley *retired marriage and family therapist, clergyman*
Kraynak, Helen *special education consultant*
Peterson, David Frederick *retired government agency administrator*

**Juno Beach**
Holmes, Melvin Almont *insurance company executive*
Knapp, George M. *lawyer*

**Jupiter**
Baum, Herbert Merrill *consumer products company executive*
Click, David Forrest *lawyer, investment advisor*
De George, Lawrence Joseph *diversified financial services company executive*

Ernst, Calvin Bradley *retired vascular surgery educator*
Feinberg, Herbert *apparel executive, real estate company executive*
Garfinkel, Harmon Mark *retired specialty chemicals company executive*
Gerson, Irwin Conrad *advertising executive*
Jacobson, Jerry Irving *biophysicist, theoretical physicist, medical researcher*
Kobylarski, Rebecca Lee *music educator*
Kulok, William Allan *entrepreneur, venture capitalist*
Migliaro, Marco William *electrical engineer*
Nessmith, H(erbert) Alva *dentist*
Sykes, Robin Alexis *plastic surgeon*
Vanatta, Bob *athletic administrator*
Weissmann, Charles *molecular biologist, educator*
Wolff, Edward Alvin *electronics engineer*
Zelnick, Ronald Stuart *surgeon*

**Kennedy Space Center**
DiBiase, Catherine Priscilla *nurse*
Feldman, Stephen *academic administrator*
Hancock, Randy A. *safety engineer*
Tang, Philip W. *engineer, educator*

**Key Biscayne**
Cardozo, Richard Nunez *marketing professional, educator, entrepreneur*
Clay, Cynthia Joyce *writer, editor-in-chief*
de la Cruz, Carlos *wholesale distribution executive*
de la Cruz, Rosa *art collector*
Evans, Peter Kenneth *advertising executive*
Palmer, Roger Farley *pharmacology educator*
Pope, John Edwin *editor, columnist*
Reynolds, Paul Davidson *social sciences educator*
Ross, Marilyn J. *language educator, communications educator*
Wilson, Robert Gordon *investment banker*

**Key Largo**
Chevins, Anthony Charles *retired advertising agency executive*
Daenzer, Bernard John *insurance company executive, consultant*
Davidson, Thomas Noel *metal products executive*
Frankovich, Thomas Anthony *biologist, researcher*
Kennedy, Mary Sussock *artist*
Mattson, James Stewart *lawyer, environmental scientist, educator*

**Key West**
Buffett, Jimmy (James William Buffett) *vocalist, songwriter, writer*
Congdon, Kirby *writer*
Evans, John Derby *telecommunications industry executive*
Kalb, Chester H. *mathematics professor*
Keenan, Mike (Micheal E. Keenan) *former professional sports team executive*
MacDougall, Peter *retired lawyer*
Mathews, Harry Burchell *poet, writer, educator*
McIntosh, Jon Charles *illustrator, graphics designer, painter*
Pennington, Claudia *museum director*
Taylor, Victoria *real estate rehabilitator, sculptor*
Trammell, Herbert Eugene *retired physicist*
Wisniewski, P. Michelle *retired obstetrician, gynecologist*
Wolz, Robert Joseph *museum director*

**Keystone Heights**
Ohanian, Mihran Jacob *nuclear engineer, educator, dean, researcher*

**Kissimmee**
Goode, Betty Ruth *retired social worker*
Haynes, Ulric St. Clair, Jr. *retired dean*
McCann, Jean Friedrichs *artist, educator*
Norris, Marty Todd *elementary school educator*
Rajyaguru, Vrajlal Laljibhai *anesthesiologist*
Sherwood, Jack Robert *quality engineer, logistics consultant*
Toothe, Karen Lee *elementary and secondary school educator*
Weaver, Russell *music educator*

**Labelle**
Pratt, Donald Dwayne *protective services official*

**Lady Lake**
Akins, Zane Vernon *agricultural products executive*
Di Benedetto, Ann Louise *retired accounting administrator*
Granger, Robert Alan *mechanical and aerospace engineering educator*
Hartzler, Genevieve Lucille *physical education educator*
Langevin, Thomas Harvey *educational association administrator, consultant*
Rosene, Paul Earl *music educator*

**Lake Alfred**
Chung, Kuang-Ren *plant pathologist, educator*
Kender, Walter John *horticulturist, educator*

**Lake Buena Vista**
Cerri, Robert Noel *photographer*
Rasulo, James A. *theme park executive*

**Lake City**
Gay, John Marion *retired federal agency administrator, financial analyst*

**Lake Forest**
Ross, Jimmy Douglas *retired military officer*

**Lake Helen**
Finn, Stephen Martin *film producer, venture capitalist*

**Lake Mary**
Bachmann, Bill *photographer*
Bindley, William Edward *pharmaceutical executive*
Bowden, Helen Frances *psychologist*
Cosler, Steven Douglas *diversified financial services company executive*

Nagda, Durga Shanker *environmental engineer, researcher*
Reagan, Bettye Jean *artist*
Shanahan, Rebecca M. *lawyer*
Swonger, Thomas K. H., Jr. *insurance company executive*

**Lake Placid**
Adams, Herbert Ryan *management consultant, retired minister, mediator*
Roberts, William B. *lawyer*
Viater, John Ronald *investment company executive*

**Lake Suzy**
Ogan, Russell Griffith *real estate broker*

**Lake Wales**
Connor, John Thomas, Jr. *portfolio manager*
Luing, Gary Alan *financial management educator*
Robinson, Richard Allen, II, *security firm executive, director*
Walton, Madalyn Carol *music educator*

**Lake Worth**
Bachrach, Howard L. *biochemist*
Carlisle, Ervin Frederick *university provost, educator*
Copeland, Richard Loyd *electrical engineer*
Feuer, Bradley Scott *lawyer, physician*
Franco, Don Alvado *veterinarian*
Goldstein, Jerome Charles *retired professional society administrator, otolaryngologist, surgeon*
Pecker, David J. *magazine publishing company executive*
Saffir, Leonard *public relations executive*
Taylor, Clifford Otis *retired principal*
Wilson, William J. *language educator*

**Lakeland**
Ashmore, Kathryn Louise *education educator*
Attaway, John A., Jr. *lawyer*
Barnett, Hoyt R. (Barney Barnett) *supermarket company executive*
Boyer, Naomi Rose *education educator, director*
Buckmaster, Matthew Tobe *music educator, musician, small business owner*
Cooper, James Russell *retired law educator*
Dusing, Michael Lee *theology educator*
Hatten, William Seward *manufacturing executive, consultant*
Holland, Leland Norman, Jr. *dean, educator*
Hrabusa, John T. *human resources specialist, food products executive*
Jacobson, Barbara Dinger *music educator*
Jakub, James Ward *physician, surgical oncologist*
Jenkins, Howard M. *supermarket executive*
Kittleson, Henry Marshall *lawyer*
Koren, Edward Franz, Jr. *lawyer*
MacDonald, Susan Priest *media specialist, writer*
Mahr, Aaron Lee *government agency administrator*
Masters, Sharon Kay *sociologist, educator*
Matheny, Pamela Bemko *secondary school educator*
McFarlin, Richard Francis *retired industrial chemist, researcher*
Meads, Walter Frederick *communications executive, consultant, writer*
Morris, Gregory K. *minister, consultant*
Mutz, Oscar Ulysses *manufacturing and distribution executive*
Phillips, David P. *grocery company executive*
Plastow, Edward George *business administration educator*
Pospichal, Marcie W. *neuroscientist, psychologist, educator*
Reich, David Lee *library director*
Rogers, James Gordon, Jr. *art educator*
Roth, William Joseph *dermatologist*
Schultz, David Franklin *psychologist*
Siedle, Robert Douglas *management consultant*
Spencer, Mary Miller *civic worker*
Stark, Bruce Gunsten *artist*
Washington, Gloria Dunn *secondary school educator*
Waugaman, Richard William *sales executive*
Wendel, John Fredric *lawyer, consultant*

**Land O Lakes**
Mallon, Kellie Jane *special education educator*
O'Connell, Carmela Digristina *appraisal executive, consultant*
Quackenbush, Roger E. *retired secondary school educator*

**Lantana**
Balis, Moses Earl *biochemist, educator*
Barrett, Robert James III *investment banker*

**Largo**
Benoit, Christopher Louis *music educator*
Bentz, Laura Marie *supervisor*
Bush, Debra W. *occupational health nurse*
Camara, Vincent Antonin Reginald *mathematician, educator, statistician, researcher*
Dolan, John E. *retired utilities executive, consultant*
Frantzis, Theodosios George *periodontist*
Grove, Jeffrey Scott *family practice physician*
Hamlin, Robert Henry *public health service officer, educator, management consultant*
Krolick, Merrill A. *cardiologist*
MacDonald, Joseph Lester *retired metal products executive*
Osborne, Mary Gagliardi *elementary school educator, director*
Shillinglaw, Gordon *retired finance educator*
Szalkowski, Deborah *music educator*
Wheat, Myron William, Jr. *cardiothoracic surgeon*

**Lauderdale By The Sea**
Wynne, Brian James *retired professional society administrator*
Yonkman, Fredrick Albers *lawyer, management consultant*

**Lauderhill**
Swisher, Charles Francis *electrical engineer, consultant*

## Lecanto

Max, Buddy (Boris Max Pastuch) *musician*
Wheatley, Deborah A. *music educator*

## Leesburg

Bayus, Lenore Weatherly *writer, public relations executive, consultant*
Bolden, Kristin Elizabeth *secondary school educator*
Duffy, John Lewis *retired Latin, English and reading educator*
Fechtel, Vincent John *legal administrator*
Moore, Wistar *cardiovascular surgeon*
Smith, Kathy L. *elementary school educator, cosmetics executive, consultant*

## Lighthouse Point

Autry, Herman Allen, Sr. *lobbyist, writer, music executive*
Gauthier, Doreen Ann *librarian*

## Longboat Key

Frankel, Jack *pediatrician, allergist*
Freeman, Richard Merrell *retired lawyer*
Gollobin, Leonard Paul *chemical engineer*
Hazan, Marcella Maddalena *writer, educator, consultant*
Herzog, Godofredo Max *physician*
McCollough, Newton Clark III *orthopaedic surgeon*
Morse, Marvin Henry *retired judge*
Schneiderman, Julius *retired orthopedic surgeon*
Stapleton, Harvey James *physics professor*
Tata, Robert Joseph *retired geographer, educator*
Workman, George Henry *structural engineering consultant*

## Longwood

Bernabei, Raymond *management consultant*
Calderón, Jaime A. *psychologist, educator*
Cirello, John *utility and engineering company executive*
Faller, Donald E. *marketing and operations executive*
Gasperoni, Ellen Jean Lias *interior designer*
Gasperoni, Emil, Sr. *realtor, real estate developer*
Johnson, Nancy Plattner *secondary school educator*
Palmer, R. Scott *food products executive, educator*
Smyth, Joseph Patrick *retired military officer, physician*
Tomasulo, Virginia Merrills *retired lawyer*
Zahn, Richard Gregory *construction executive*

## Lutz

Anderson, Karl Franklin *systems engineer, researcher*
Cualing, Hernani Del Mundo *physician, researcher*
Currey, Cecil Barr *retired history professor*
Ellis, Leslie Elaine *psychologist*
Hacker, Michelle Wendy *auditor, researcher, finance educator*
Koff, Fred William *retired research chemist*
Kolb, Richard Maurice *sports writer, sportscaster*
Miller, Bonnie Sewell *marketing professional, writer*

## Lynn Haven

Durden, Paul Alan *mathematics educator, mathematics professor*

## Madison

Hiss, Sheila Mary *librarian*
Shaw, Roderick Kirkpatrick III *dentist*
Steen, Morris Grissom, Jr. *academic administrator, retired military officer*

## Maitland

Cicilioni, Orlando Joseph *plastic surgeon*
Vallee, Judith Delaney *environmentalist, writer, not-for-profit fundraiser*
Von Hilsheimer, George Edwin III *neuropsychologist*

## Manalapan

Hyatt, Susan Marie *theater educator, director, actress*

## Marathon

Wiecha, Joseph Augustine *language educator*

## Marco Island

Cooper, Thomas Astley *bank executive*
Foster, Edward John *engineer, physicist*
Guerrant, David Edward *retired food company executive*
Kaner, Harvey Sheldon *lawyer*
Kelly, Robert Donald *management consultant*
Kerstetter, Wayne Arthur *law educator*
Krause, Charles Joseph *otolaryngologist*
Pettersen, Kjell Will *securities trader, consultant*
Zecchino, Vincent *retired surgeon*

## Marianna

Brunner, William F. *surgeon*
Duffee, Betty B. *biology educator*

## Mary Esther

McTyeire, Robert Adams *sound engineer, music company executive, consultant*

## Medley

Leinbach, Tracy A. *transportation executive*
O'Meara, Vicki A. *lawyer*
Quirch, Guillermo, Jr., (Bill Quirch) *food distribution executive*

## Melbourne

Allington, Maynard *writer*
Ballantyne, Richard Lee *lawyer*
Brown, Seymour R. *lawyer*
Buchanan, Richard Kent *electronics company executive*
Cacciatore, S. Sammy *lawyer*
Catanese, Anthony James *academic administrator*
Elder, Stewart Taylor *dentist, retired military officer*
Farmer, Phillip W. *communications executive*
Fox, Thomas George *academic administrator*

Greenblatt, Hellen Chaya *immunologist, microbiologist*
Grenevicki, Lance Francis *surgeon*
Helmstetter, Charles Edward *microbiologist*
Helmstetter, Wendy Lee *librarian*
Hughes, A. N. *psychotherapist*
Jones, Elaine Hancock *humanities educator*
King, Virginia Shattuck *painter, retired school nurse, educator*
Koenig, Harold Paul *management consultant, ecologist, evangelist, writer*
Kreines, Joseph Melvin *conductor*
Lakshmikantham, Vangipuram *mathematics professor*
Lance, Howard L. *communications executive, industrial engineer*
Laposata, Joseph Samuel *army officer*
Magee, Thomas Henry *radiologist, educator*
Maloratsky, Leo G. *electrical engineer*
Menezes, Ronaldo P. *computer scientist, educator*
Mikolajczyk, Mark S. *publishing executive*
Nelson, Gordon Leigh *chemist, educator*
O'Neal, Kathleen Len *communications executive, writer, management speaker, financial consultant*
Pocoski, David John *cardiologist*
Savickis, Rodney Fredrick *theater educator, theater director*
Shaikh, Muzaffar Abid *management sciences educator*
Simokaitis, Frank Joseph *military officer, lawyer*
Storrs, Eleanor Emerett *science administrator, consultant*
Trefry, John H. III *chemical oceanographer, educator*
Weaver, Lynn Edward *academic administrator, consultant, editor*
Winkelmann, Kurt Joseph *science educator*
Wiseman, Floyd Landis *chemist*
Zabel, Dianne Donnelly *retired elementary school educator*

## Melbourne Beach

Cooper, Roger Merlin *information technology executive, school system administrator, federal agency administrator*
Glaubinger, Lawrence David *retired manufacturing company executive*
Harrington, Peter Tyrus *emergency management company executive, public relations executive, consultant, writer, photographer*
Harris, Jack Howard, II, *financial consultant, director*

## Melrose

Burt, Alvin Victor, Jr. *journalist*

## Merritt Island

Johnson, Clarence Traylor, Jr. *state judge*
McClanahan, Leland *university director*
Roub, Bryan R(oger) *electronics executive*
Smith, David Edward *small business owner, aerospace engineer, aerospace scientist*
Yoh, William Harry, Jr. *music educator*
Young, Nancy Mayer *retired secondary school educator, artist*

## Miami

Aberson, Sim David *meteorologist, researcher*
Acosta, Alex (Rene Alexander Acosta) *prosecutor, former federal agency administrator*
Aguirre-Sacasa, Francisco Xavier *international banker, diplomat*
Ajamil, Luis *civil engineer*
Allen, Charles Norman *television, film and video producer*
Alperin, Stanley I. *writer, editor, consultant*
Alschuler, Al *freelance/self-employed writer*
Alvarez, Cesar L. *lawyer*
Amos, Betty Giles *food service executive, accountant*
Anderson, Douglas Richard *ophthalmologist, educator, researcher*
Anderson, Terence James *law educator*
Arango, Jorge Sanin *architect*
Arango, Penelope Corey *psychologist, consultant*
Arison, Marilyn Barbara (Lin Arison) *foundation administrator*
Arison, Micky *cruise line company executive, professional sports team executive*
Arison, Shari *investment company executive*
Armstrong, F. Daniel *psychologist, educator*
Armstrong, Pamela Kay *principal*
Aronovitz, Tod *lawyer*
Arsht, Adrienne *lawyer, broadcast executive, bank executive*
Astigarraga, Jose I(gnacio) *lawyer*
Auerbach, Ethel Louise *healthcare facility administrator*
Ayala, Melvin *electrical engineer, researcher*
Backman, Gerald Stephen *retired lawyer*
Baker, Thomas Eugene *law educator*
Bald, Gary M. *cruise line executive, former federal agency administrator*
Banas, Suzanne *middle school educator*
Bandstra, Emmalee S. *physician, pediatrician, researcher, educator*
Bannard, Walter Darby *artist, art critic*
Barkett, Rosemary *federal judge*
Bass, Hilarie *lawyer*
Batcheller, Joe Ann *entrepreneur*
Baumberger, Charles Henry *lawyer*
Beck, Morris *allergist*
Benestante, Vincenzo *writer*
Benjamin, Latanya T. *dermatologist*
Berg, Martin David *lawyer*
Berman, Bruce *lawyer*
Berman, Mona S. *actress, playwright, theater director, theater producer*
Bird, Vincent G. *urologist, researcher*
Black, Creed Carter *newspaper executive*
Black, Roy *lawyer*
Blechman, Wilbur Jordan *medical educator*
Block, Norman Louis *oncologist, educator*
Bloom, Mark David *lawyer*
Blumberg, Edward Robert *lawyer*
Bogusky, Alex *advertising executive*
Bolooki, Hooshang *cardiac surgeon*
Borkan, William Noah *electronics executive, biomedical engineer, entrepreneur, venture capitalist, real estate developer*

Braman, Norman *automotive executive, former sports team executive*
Bravo, Irene Maria *psychologist, educator*
Brochin, Robert M. *lawyer*
Brooten, Dorothy *retired dean, nursing educator*
Brown, Judith Oropallo *academic administrator, political science professor*
Brown, Lewis Nathan *lawyer*
Brown, Robert Donald *lawyer*
Buchwald, Peter Sandor *science association director*
Buell, Edward Rick, II, *lawyer*
Burgher, Cedric W. *food service executive*
Burke, Redmond Paul *pediatric cardiologist, surgeon*
Burnett, Henry *lawyer*
Burnett, Keitha Denise *social studies educator*
Burr, Scott Allen *lawyer*
Camner, Howard *writing educator, writer, poet*
Campos-Orrego, Nora Patricia *lawyer, consultant*
Candocia, Frank *computer engineer, educator*
Capraro, Franz *accountant*
Cardenas, Rene F. *nuclear medicine physician, oncologist*
Carey-Shuler, Barbara *county commissioner*
Casares, Raul *manufacturing executive*
Casey, Daniel Arthur *lawyer*
Cefaratti, Anthony Joseph *retired diplomat*
Cekauskas, Cynthia Danute *social worker*
Cento, Juan N. *delivery service executive*
Centro, Juan N. *air transportation executive*
Chambers, Elenora Strasel *artist*
Chang-Mota, Roberto *electrical engineer*
Chaplin, Harvey *wine and liquor wholesale executive*
Chapman, Alvah Herman, Jr. *retired newspaper executive*
Chen, Shu-Ching *computer science educator*
Chidsey, John W. *food service executive*
Chwat, Anne *food service executive*
Ciancio, Gaetano *transplant surgeon, urologist*
Clark, James H. *former software company executive, real estate company executive*
Clarke, Peter John *computer scientist, educator, educational consultant*
Clarkson, John G. *academic administrator, ophthalmologist*
Claure, R. Marcelo *telecommunications industry executive*
Clem, Ralph S. *career officer, educator*
Cobb, Hugh Dimmock III *meteorologist*
Codina, Armando M. *real estate developer*
Cohen, Jeffrey Michael *lawyer*
Coker, Larry *college football coach*
Comras, Rema *retired library director*
Connor, Terence Gregory *lawyer*
Cooper, Johnnie Edward, Jr. *advocate*
Cosgrove, John Francis *lawyer, mayor*
Cosner, George Christopher *mathematics professor*
Craddock, Bantz J. *career military officer*
Cristol, A. Jay *federal judge*
Critchlow, Richard H. *lawyer*
Cubas, Jose M(anuel) *advertising agency executive*
Culmer, Leome Frances *consultant*
Dann, Oliver Townsend *psychoanalyst, psychiatrist, educator*
Dasburg, John Harold *restaurant executive*
Davis, Edward Bertrand *retired federal judge, lawyer*
Davis, Janet *physician*
Davis, Richard Edmund *plastic surgeon*
de Cespedes, Carlos M. *pharmaceutical executive*
de Cespedes, Jorge L. *pharmaceutical executive*
Delehanty, Suzanne *museum director*
de Leon, Lidia Maria *magazine editor*
Diaz, Manuel A. *mayor*
Diaz, Tania *psychology professor*
Diaz Oliver, Remedios *manufacturing executive*
Dienstag, Cynthia Jill *lawyer*
Diez, Oliver *music educator*
Di Liddo, Michael *music educator, musician*
Dimitriou, Dolores Ennis *computer consultant*
Donelan, Mark Anthony *physicist*
Dorion, Robert Charles *entrepreneur, investor*
Duchesne, Carlos A. *epidemiologist, military officer*
Dunn, Richard M. *lawyer*
Dye, H. Michael *marketing professional*
Eftekhari, Nasser *physiatrist*
Ehrlich, Morton *marketing executive, management consultant*
Eisdorfer, Carl *psychiatrist, health facility administrator*
Elsas, Louis Jacob, II, *medical educator*
Embden, Dawn Terris *medical/surgical nurse, writer*
England, Arthur Jay, Jr. *lawyer, former state justice*
Epstein, Gary M. *lawyer*
Eshraghi, Adrien A. *head and neck surgeon, medical educator, researcher*
Fain, Richard David *cruise line executive*
Falagan, Margarita Martinez *art educator*
Falco-Leshin, JoAnna M. *literature and language professor*
Fatovic, Robert Dean *lawyer, transportation executive*
Feinberg, Wendie *television producer*
Feito, Jose *architect*
Feldenkreis, George *apparel executive*
Ferrari, Leonardo *small business owner*
Ferré, Maurice Antonio *entrepreneur*
Ferrell, Milton Morgan, Jr. *lawyer*
Fichtner, Margaria *journalist*
Fiedler, Tom *editor-in-chief*
Field, Julia Allen *futurist, strategist, environmentalist*
Fine, Jeffrey Louis *psychologist, educator, writer*
Fine, Rana Arnold *chemical and physical oceanographer*
Fish, Stanley Eugene *dean, language educator*
Fisher, Ann *recording industry executive, lawyer*
Fleit, Martin *lawyer*
Foote, Edward Thaddeus, II, *academic administrator, lawyer*
Forgione, Dana Anthony *accounting educator*
Fornaris, Carl A. *lawyer*
Freire, Jose A. *physicist, writer*
Freshwater, Michael Felix *hand surgeon, educator*
Frigo, James Peter Paul *industrial hardware company executive*

Fromkin, Ava Lynda *management consultant, healthcare risk management services*
Frost, Phillip *pharmaceutical executive, dermatologist*
Furst, Alex Julian *thoracic and cardiovascular surgeon*
Gabor, Frank *insurance company executive*
Galatas, Ruth Ann *musician, publishing executive, educator*
Gang, Robert C. *lawyer*
Garrett, Richard G. *lawyer*
Gelband, Henry *pediatric cardiologist*
Germain, Marie-Line *education educator*
Ginsberg, Myron David *neurologist*
Giusto, Richard J. *lawyer*
Glatzer, Richard L. *orthopedist, surgeon*
Goin-Harding, Cecilia Margaret *poet*
Goldberg, Lee Dresden *endocrinologist, educator*
Golden, John Dennis *lawyer*
Goldstein, Burton Jack *psychiatrist*
Gong, Edmond Joseph *lawyer*
Goodman-Milone, Constance B. (Connie Malone) *writer*
Goodwin, W. Jarrard *otolaryngologist, educator*
Gorson, Matthew B. *lawyer*
Gragg, Karl Lawrence *lawyer*
Graham, Donald Lynn *federal judge*
Greer, Alan Graham *lawyer*
Grewer, Christof Theodor *biophysicist*
Gross, Leslie Jay *lawyer, real estate broker, mortgage company executive*
Grossman, Robert Louis *lawyer*
Gutgsell, Nancy Snowden *medical researcher*
Guzman, Iris Vila *music educator*
Hall, Adam Stuart *lawyer*
Hall, Andrew Clifford *lawyer*
Halsey, Douglas Martin *lawyer*
Hampton, John Lewis *retired newspaper editor*
Hampton, Mark Garrison *architect*
Hansell, Dennis A. *oceanography educator*
Harmon, Monica Renee *music educator*
Harrison, Stanley L. *editor, publisher, writer*
Hartz, Steven Edward Marshall *lawyer, educator*
Hector, Louis Julius *lawyer*
Heggen, Arthur William *insurance company executive*
Henderson, Gene M. *marketing professional*
Hernandez, Marie *nurse*
Heros, Roberto Cosme C. *neurosurgeon*
Herz, Marvin Ira *psychiatrist, researcher*
Heuer, Robert Maynard, II, *opera company executive*
Highsmith, Shelby *federal judge*
Higley, Bruce Wadsworth *orthodontist*
Himburg, Susan Phillips *dietician, educator*
Hoffman, Kenneth Cary *lawyer*
Hoffman, Larry J. *lawyer*
Holifield, Marilyn J. *lawyer*
Horner, Diane L. *dean*
Houlihan, Gerald John *lawyer*
Howell, Ralph Rodney *pediatrician, geneticist, educator*
Hrinak, Donna Jean *lawyer, former ambassador*
Hudson, Robert Franklin, Jr. *lawyer*
Huysman, Arlene Weiss *psychologist, educator, writer*
Ibarguen, Alberto *foundation administrator, former newspaper executive*
Ibler, Gerold *finance company executive, consultant*
Imperato, Joseph John *lawyer, composer*
Iver, Robert Drew *dentist*
Jacobson, Bernard *lawyer*
Jhabvala, Farrokh *lawyer*
Johnston, Philip Connelly *lawyer*
Jones, Janice Cox *elementary school educator, writer*
Kahn, Jack Merrill *television producer*
Kaiser, Gerard A. *hospital administrator*
Kanet, Roger Edward *political science professor*
Kaplan, Betsy Hess *retired school board member*
Kasbar, Michael J. *energy executive*
Katz, Lawrence Sheldon *lawyer*
Katz, Sandra *educational consultant, psychologist, education educator*
Kelley, Michael James *medical services executive, author*
King, James Lawrence *federal judge*
King, John Allan, Jr. *history professor*
Kingman, Barbara *music educator*
Kislak, Jean Hart *art director*
Klock, Joseph Peter, Jr. *lawyer*
Knight Crane, Marjorie *foundation administrator*
Kooima, Linda Kay *neonatal and pediatrics nurse*
Korchin, Judith Miriam *lawyer*
Kragg, Judith Lynn *accountant*
Kreitzer, Michael N. *lawyer*
Krishan, Awtar *educator*
Laje, Zilia L. *writer, publisher, translator*
Lampen, Richard Jay *lawyer, investment banker*
Landy, Burton Aaron *lawyer*
Lasseter, Kenneth Carlyle *pharmacologist*
Lawrence, David, Jr. *journalist*
Lechner, Suzanne Caryn *psychology professor*
Lee, J. Patrick *academic administrator*
Leeder, Ellen Lismore *literature and language professor, literary critic*
Leibowitz, Max Adam *lawyer*
Lemberg, Louis *cardiologist, educator*
Levin, Oscar *lawyer*
Levine, Robert Jeffrey *lawyer*
Levy, Cesar *mechanical engineer, educator*
Lew, Salvador *radio station executive*
Lewis, John Milton *cable television company executive*
Li, Qi *research scientist, consultant*
Liddle, Howard A. *psychologist, researcher*
Llorente, Maria D. *psychiatrist, geriatrician, educator*
Long, Maxine Master *lawyer*
Lopez, Miriam *bank executive, department chairman*
Loria, Jeffrey H. *sports team executive*
Louis, Paul Adolph *lawyer*
Loumiet, Juan P. *lawyer*
Lubs, Herbert Augustus *genetics educator, administrator*
Lynch, Catherine Gores *social services administrator*
Madurga, Gonzalo F. *performing company executive, actor, singer*

Magrath, Kathleen Barry *retired municipal official*
Maidique, Modesto Alex *academic administrator*
Majumdar, Sharanya Jyoti *meteorologist, educator*
Malinin, Theodore *medical educator, researcher*
Manzello, Derek Paul *marine biologist*
Marcus, Stanley *federal judge*
Marley, Damian Robert Nesta (Jr. Gong) *reggae artist*
Martin, Jacques *professional hockey coach, professional sports team executive*
Martinez, Carlos *insurance agent*
Martinez-Fraga, Pedro J. *lawyer*
Mas Santos, Jorge *foundation administrator, telecommunications industry executive*
Mauch, Diane Farrell *music educator*
Mayfield, Max *meteorologist*
McCabe, Robert Howard *college president*
McCain, David B. *lawyer*
McCall, Anthony *filmmaker*
McLaughlin, Margaret Brown *adult education educator, writer*
Mehta, Eileen Rose *lawyer*
Mena, Daniel *lawyer, arbitrator*
Mencio, George, Jr. *lawyer*
Mendez, Luis Eduardo *medical educator, researcher*
Menendez Cambo, Patricia *lawyer*
Miller, James M. *lawyer*
Miller, Stuart A. *real estate executive, lawyer*
Miller Udell, Bronwyn *judge*
Milstein, Richard Craig *lawyer*
Mintz, Daniel Harvey *endocrinologist, educator, academic administrator*
Mooers, Christopher Northrup Kennard *physical oceanographer, educator*
Moran, Kate *sculptor, photographer*
Morgan, Dahlia *museum director, art educator*
Morgan, Marabel *writer*
Morrison, Glenn *neurosurgeon*
Morrison, Richard A. *lawyer*
Muench, Karl Hugo *clinical geneticist*
Murphy, Timothy James *lawyer*
Mustelier, Margarita M. *psychologist, director*
Nachwalter, Michael *lawyer*
Nadeau, Joseph Eugene *health care management consultant, information systems consultant*
Nahmad, Albert H. *manufacturing executive*
Natoli, Joseph T. *financial administrator, former publishing executive*
Navarro, Jose F., Jr. *retail executive*
Nestor Castellano, Brenda Diana *real estate company executive*
Neu, Charles Eric *historian, educator*
Newton, Terry Fernando *health facility specialist, writer*
Noonan, John Gerard *bishop*
Nuernberg, William Richard *lawyer*
Nunez-Lawton, Miguel G. *financial analyst*
Nunez Ojeda, Elpidio *food distribution executive*
O'Bryon, Linda Elizabeth *broadcast executive*
O'Connor, Kathleen Mary *lawyer*
O'Neal, Shaquille Rashaun *professional basketball player*
Osinski, Martin Henry *healthcare consultant*
Osman, Edith Gabriella *lawyer*
Ostlund, H. Gote *marine biologist, educator*
Page, Larry Keith *neurosurgeon, educator*
Pan, Guoquan Victor *mathematics professor, computer science educator*
Panthaki, Zubin Jal *medical educator, plastic surgeon*
Papy, Charles C. III *lawyer*
Parks, Arva Moore *historian*
Payton, Gary Dwayne *professional basketball player*
Pelton, Margaret Marie Miller *retired art educator, academic administrator, artist*
Pena, Guillermo Enrique *lawyer*
Perez, Jorge M. *real estate developer*
Pettigrew, Grady Gil Landers *biology professor*
Pham, Si Mai *cardiothoracic surgeon*
Pietrocarlo, Nick *artist, consultant, information technology manager*
Pilafian, Audrey Kalenian *music educator*
Pinder, Renee Monique *diplomat*
Pitts, Leonard Garvey, Jr. *columnist, writer*
Planas, Carlos *automotive executive*
Pochi, Subbarayan Ramalingam *biomedical researcher*
Pogede, Alexander *consulting company executive*
Pomeranz, Felix *accounting educator*
Porter, Wayne Randolph *dermatologist*
Pratt, John Patrick *lawyer*
Puliafito, Carmen Anthony *ophthalmologist, healthcare executive*
Quentel, Albert Drew *lawyer*
Raffel, Leroy B. *real estate developer*
Rawl, Arthur Julian (Lord of Cursons) *retail executive, consultant, accountant, writer*
Regev, Arie *gastroenterologist, researcher, hepatologist*
Reilly, Kenneth James *lawyer*
Reiter, Luis *lawyer*
Remek, Robert Thomas *music educator, church musician*
Revis-Pyke, Robin Lynn *educator*
Richards-Vital, Claudia *small business owner, recreational facility executive*
Ricordi, Camillo *surgeon, medical researcher*
Riley, Patrick James *professional basketball coach*
Riley, Terence *curator, architect*
Risi, Louis James, Jr. *manufacturing executive*
Rodriguez, Irmina Bestard *science educator*
Rodriguez, Josefa Nieves *special education educator, language educator*
Rodriguez-Walling, Matilde Barcelo *special education educator*
Rose-Singh, Judith Angella *elementary school educator*
Rozek, Thomas M. *health facility administrator*
Rubell, Donald *gynecologist, hotel executive, art collector*
Rubin, Steven D. *lawyer*
Ruiz, Olga *lawyer, educator*
Rusconi, Paolo *pediatric cardiologist*
Russell, Elbert Winslow *neuropsychologist*
Russell, James Webster, Sr. *editor, columnist*
Saland, Deborah *psychotherapist, educator*
Salazar, Luis *management consultant, lawyer*
Salazar-Carrillo, Jorge *economics professor*
Salinas, Baruj *artist, architect*

Salinas, María Elena *newscaster, columnist*
Salvaneschi, Luigi *real estate developer, management consultant, educator*
Samole, Myron Michael *lawyer, management consultant*
Sanchez, Danmary *research scientist*
Santiago, Raymond *library director, educator*
Saralegui, Cristina Maria *Spanish language television personality, journalist*
Sarkar, Malancha *research scientist, educator*
Savage, James Francis *editor*
Schafer, Marie *nurse, educator*
Schally, Andrew Victor *endocrine oncologist, researcher*
Schild, A. Frederick *surgeon*
Schor, Olga Seemann *mental health counselor, real estate broker*
Schuette, Charles A. *lawyer*
Schulman, Clifford A. *lawyer*
Schwartz, Gerald *public relations and fundraising agency executive*
Schwartz, Kessel *modern language educator*
Scully, Sean Patrick *orthopaedic surgeon, educator*
Seitz, Patricia Ann *judge*
Selin, Nina Evvie *museum director, electric power industry executive, volunteer*
Sherman, Beatrice Ettinger *hotel executive*
Shusterman, Nathan *underwriter, financial consultant*
Siegel, Paul *judge*
Simmons, Sherwin Palmer *lawyer*
Sirvén, José E. *lawyer*
Skolnick, Holly R. *lawyer*
Skolnick, S. Harold *lawyer*
Skyler, Jay S. *medical educator, consultant*
Smith, Richard C. (Dick) *lawyer*
Sonberg, Steven *lawyer*
Sparkman, Barry Steven *artist, art educator, museum administrator*
Spear, Laurinda Hope *architect*
Stanley, Sherry A. *lawyer*
Stansell, Leland Edwin, Jr. *lawyer, mediator, educator*
Stebbins, Paul H. *energy executive*
Steinbaum, Bernice *art dealer*
Steinberg, Marty *lawyer*
Stiehm, Judith Hicks *director, political scientist, educator*
Stokes, Paul Mason *lawyer*
Stotts, Dennis Martin *lawyer*
Strafer, G. Richard *lawyer*
Stratos, Kimarie Rose *lawyer, sports association executive*
Sussmane, Jeffrey Brett *pediatrician*
Swaminathan, Sethuraman *pediatrician, cardiologist*
Swienton, Gregory T. *transportation company executive*
Tejada, Francisco *physician, educator*
Thaller, Seth Ray *plastic surgeon*
Thornburg, Frederick Fletcher *lawyer*
Todd, Karyn L. *lawyer*
Traurig, Robert Henry *lawyer*
Treyz, Joseph Henry *librarian*
Troen, Bruce Robert *medical educator*
Tsai, John Jengshyong *publishing executive*
Tzakis, Andreas Gerasimos *surgeon, educator, research scientist*
Ungaro-Benages, Ursula Mancusi *federal judge*
Van Aken, Norman *chef*
Van Wyck, George Richard *insurance company executive*
Vento, M. Thérèse *lawyer*
Veziroglu, Turhan Nejat *mechanical engineering educator, researcher*
Vielot, Alain J. *elementary school educator*
Wade, Dwyane *professional basketball player*
Walkley, Mary L. *voice and music educator*
Walton, Rodney Earl *lawyer*
Walz, Leo R. *conductor*
Warren, Mark Edward *cruise line executive, lawyer*
Wated, Guillermo *psychology educator*
Watson, Doug *information technology executive*
Wax, William Edward *photojournalist*
Weagraff, Patrick James *psychology professor, writer*
Weeks, Marta Joan *retired priest*
Weems, Lori K. *lawyer*
Weiner, Lawrence *lawyer*
Weinger, Steven Murray *lawyer*
Weinstein, Andrew H. *lawyer*
Weiser, Ralph Raphael *oil industry executive*
Weiser, Sherwood Manuel *hotel and corporation executive, lawyer*
Welch, Judy Ann *language educator*
West, Macdonald *real estate executive*
Wheeler, Steve Dereal *neurologist*
Williams, Eric Joseph *transportation executive*
Williams, Jason Chandler *professional basketball player*
Willis, Dontrelle *professional baseball player*
Wilson, Dave *editor*
Wilson, Thomas Strong, Jr., (Tam Wilson) *judge*
Wing, James David *lawyer*
Wiseheart, Malcolm Boyd, Jr. *lawyer*
Wolff, Grace Susan *pediatric cardiologist*
Wolfson, Aaron Howard *radiation oncologist, educator*
Zack, Stephen Neal *lawyer*
Zaleski-Vegazo, Ilene *librarian*
Zayas-Bazan, Eduardo *foreign language educator*
Zaydon, Thomas John, Jr. *plastic surgeon*
Zwerling, Leonard Joseph *physician, educator*

## Miami Beach
Agatston, Arthur Stephen *cardiologist*
Arbuz, Joseph Robert *lawyer*
Camber, Diane Woolfe *museum director*
Carnase, Thomas Paul *graphics designer, consultant*
Cohen, Philip Herman *accountant*
Danzis, Rose Marie *emeritus college president*
Gardiner, Pamela Nan *performing company executive*
Gitlow, Abraham Leo *retired dean*
Howard, Melvin *financial executive*
Kalsner-Silver, Lydia *psychologist*
Lanzkron, Rolf Wolfgang *manufacturing executive*
Lawson, Eve Kennedy *dancer*
Lehr, Mira Tager *artist*

Martz, Willard Harry *physician*
Nash, Seymour Cy *surgeon, urologist*
Rogers, Mark Charles *physician, entrepreneur, anesthesiologist, pediatrician, educator*
Rosenhaus, Drew *professional sports agent*
Rut, Wanda E. *artist, educator, writer*
Sharlach, Jeffrey *public relations executive*
Shula, Don Francis *retired professional football coach, professional sports team executive*

## Miami Gardens
Bell, Taunjah Patrease *research scientist*
Conley, James W. *English language educator, language arts educator*
Ersek, Gregory Joseph Mark *lawyer*
Light, Alfred Robert *law educator*
Vangates, Dess *retired military officer*
Wilson, Isabel Gomez *elementary school educator, consultant*

## Miami Lakes
Perez de la Mesa, Manuel Jose *swimming pool company executive*

## Miami Shores
Diener, Betty Jane *business educator*
Favalora, John Clement *archbishop*
Gonzalez, Pedro Blas *philosopher, educator*
Raphael, Amy Beth *director*

## Milton
Arnold, Margaret Morelock *music educator, soprano*
Collins, Joda Lee *minister*
Losee, Michael Patrick *music director*
McKinney, George Harris, Jr. *training systems analyst*
Seaton, Carolle Carter *writer, educator*

## Miramar
Catalano, Carl Philip *small business owner*
Huang, Guiyou *English studies educator, writer*
Rissmann, William John *medical products executive*
Stewart Simpson, Donnamay Angela *interior designer*

## Montverde
Perry, Douglas Skip Dale *music educator*

## Mount Dora
Crone, Eugene N. *addictions specialist, retired educator*
Kirton, Jennifer Myers *artist*
Langgood, Judith Ann *art educator*
Scharfenberg, Margaret Ellan *retired elementary school educator*
Trundle, W(infield) Scott *publishing executive, newspaper, lawyer*

## Mulberry
Bowman, Hazel Lois *retired English language educator*

## Naples
Alpert, Hollis *writer*
Anderson, John Thomas *lawyer*
Askins, Wallace Boyd *manufacturing executive*
Ayres, John E., Jr. *hotel executive, astronomer*
Baldwin, Ralph Belknap *retired manufacturing executive, educator*
Berman, Robert S. *marketing consultant*
Bileydi, Sumer *advertising agency executive*
Birdsall, Stephanie E. *artist*
Blevins, Charles Russell *publishing executive*
Blumenthal, Ronnie *lawyer*
Brooks, Joae Graham *psychiatrist*
Bruce, Jackson Martin, Jr. *lawyer*
Burdick, Robert W. *newspaper editor*
Butler, Frederick George *retired drug company executive*
Capelle-Frank, Jacqueline Aimee *writer*
Clapp, Roger Howland *retired publishing executive*
Clarke, John Patrick *retired newspaper publisher*
Cobb, Brian Eric *broadcast executive*
Cotrone, Janice Lynne *nursing consultant*
Crandall, Blane Mitchell *obstetrician, gynecologist*
Crehan, Joseph Edward *lawyer*
Cremer, Richard Eldon *marketing professional*
Delano, Victor *retired naval officer*
de Maleissye Melun, Countess Judith *realtor*
Dorio, Martin Matthew, Jr. *real estate company executive, investor*
Doub, William Offutt *lawyer*
Dykstra, David Allen *real estate company executive*
Eldridge, David Carlton *art and antique appraiser*
Ericson, Roger Delwin *lawyer, forest resource company executive*
Faison, William Franklin, II, *lawyer, retired manufacturing corporation executive*
Farnham, Robert E. *health facility administrator*
Fogg, Joseph Graham III *investment company executive*
Frantzen, Henry Arthur *retired investment company executive*
Frazer, John Howard *tennis association executive, retired manufacturing executive*
Gade, Marvin Francis *retired paper company executive*
Gehring, David Austin *cardiologist, physician, health facility administrator*
Gindin, William Howard *retired judge*
Greene, David *surgeon, researcher*
Hall, Beverly Barton *librarian*
Hansen, Claire V. *financial executive*
Hathcock, William Parker III *studio director, publicist, curator*
Hollenbeck, Karen Fern *foundation administrator, consultant*
Jones, Philip Howard *broadcast journalist*
Jones, Richard Wallace *interior designer*
Keller, Theodore G., Jr. *investment property owner and manager*
Kinder, Suzanne Fonay Wemple *retired historian, retired educator*
Kirby, Charles William, Jr. *dancer, choreographer*
Kley, John Arthur *banker*
Kozitka, Richard Eugene *retired consumer products company executive*

Kvetko, Colleen M. *bank executive*
LaRusso, Anthony Carl *company executive, educator*
Leitner, Alfred *retired mathematical physicist, educator, educational film producer*
Lewis, Gordon Gilmer *golf course architect*
Lickhalter, Merlin *architect*
Llewellyn, Leonard Frank *real estate broker, investment company executive*
Lowery, William Herbert *lawyer*
Ludwig, Richard Joseph *small business owner*
Lynn, Larry (Verne Lauriston Lynn) *engineering executive*
Madigan, Joseph Edward *financial executive, director, consultant*
Mahalawich, Anne Mary *retired mathematics educator*
Mancuso, John Henry *retired lawyer, bank executive*
Marcuvitz, Nathan *physicist, educator*
Marino, William Francis *telecommunications industry executive, consultant*
Marshall, Charles *communications company executive*
Martinuzzi, Leo Sergio, Jr. *banker*
McCaffrey, Judith Elizabeth *lawyer*
McMackin, F. Joseph III *lawyer*
McSwiney, Charles Ronald *lawyer*
Mehaffey, John Allen *marketing executive, publishing executive*
Mills, Dorothy Jane (Dorothy Z. Seymour) *editor, consultant*
Monaghan, Thomas Stephen *philanthropist*
Moore, Mechlin Dongan *communications executive, management consultant*
Myers, Robert Jay *retired air transportation executive*
Norton, Elizabeth Wychgel *lawyer*
Ordway, John Danton *retired pension fund administrator, lawyer, accountant*
Parry, Timothy R. *lawyer*
Penniman, Nicholas Griffith, IV, *retired newspaper publisher*
Petersen, David L. *lawyer*
Randall, Neil Warren *gastroenterologist*
Rowe, Herbert Joseph *retired trade association executive*
Salentine, Thomas James *pharmaceutical executive*
Sampson, John Eugene *food products executive, consultant*
Schwartz, Stephen Gregory *ophthalmologist*
Sekowski, Cynthia Jean *health products executive, medical consultant, contact lens specialist*
Slaff, Allan Paul *military officer, academic administrator, educator, entrepreneur*
Smith, Numa Lamar, Jr. *lawyer*
Snyder, Marion Gene *lawyer, retired congressman*
Sowman, Harold Gene *ceramics engineer, researcher*
Stastny, John Anton *real estate executive*
Stevens, William Kenneth *lawyer*
Suziedelis, Vytautas A. *retired engineering corporation executive*
Synnott, William Raymond *retired management consultant*
Temple, Donald *retired allergist, dermatologist*
Thampi, Mohan Varghese *environmental health and civil engineer*
Thomas, Gary Lynn *information technology executive*
Thomas, John Melvin *retired surgeon*
Vanderslice, Thomas Aquinas *electronics executive*
Vickery, Robert Remsen *painter*
Vickrey, Robert Remsen *artist*
von Arx, Dolph William *food products executive*
Vumbacco, Joseph V. *health services executive*
Wedel-Cowgill, Millie Redmond *secondary school educator, performing arts educator, communications educator, education educator*
Weeks, Lee *hotel executive*
Weiss, Daniel Edwin *minister, educator*
Westman, Carl Edward *lawyer*
White, Roy Bernard *performing arts association administrator*
Williams, George Earnest *retired engineer, retired corporate financial executive*
York, Tina *painter*

## Navarre
Bare Grounds, Patricia Kelly *personal trainer, alcohol/drug abuse services professional, medical products executive*

## Neptune Beach
Palmer, Jane G. *music educator*

## New Port Richey
Adams, Jean Marie *biology professor*
Charters, Karen Ann Elliott *critical care nurse, health facility administrator*
Day, Peter Rodney *geneticist, educator*
Deasy, Theresa *finance company executive, accountant*
Focht, Theodore Harold *lawyer, educator*
Hanahan, James Lake *retired insurance executive*
Lake, Victor Hugo *former manufacturing company executive*
Miller, Harvey William *retired military officer*
Mills, Edward Warren *lawyer*
O'Farrell, Mark Theodore *religious organization administrator*
Rhodes, Eric Foster *employee relations consultant, writer*
Vajk, Hugo *manufacturing executive*

## New Smyrna Beach
Dunagan, Walter Benton *lawyer, educator*
Faherty, Sandra Lee *social worker, psychotherapist*

## Newberry
Thornton, J. Ronald *technology consultant*

## Niceville
Clark, Steven Jay *plastic surgeon, consultant*
Crawford, Jackie R. *retired federal agency administrator*
Fitzpatrick, James Thomas *music educator*
Havens, Jason Edward *lawyer*
Hinze, Vicki Kay *writer, educator*
Litke, Donald Paul *acquisition executive, retired military officer*

## Palmetto Bay
Nakashima, Tadayoshi *retired biochemist, researcher*

## Panama City
Caiazzo, Tom A *political scientist, educator*
Cortes, Enric *marine biologist*
D'Arcy, Gerald Paul *engineering executive, consultant*
Fejer, T. William *musician, composer, architect, furniture designer*
McWhorter, Susan Carol *English language educator*
Moore, Derrick Lanier *military officer*
Navon, Robert *real estate investor, retired publisher*
Phelps, Daniel Christopher *information scientist, researcher*
Reedy-Dewey, Madeline Anne *retired occupational therapist*
Roberts, Paul Craig III *economics professor, writer, columnist*
Schafer, John Stephen *poet*

## Panama City Beach
Nelson, Edith Ellen *dietician*
Reading, Anthony John *retired psychiatrist, educator*

## Parrish
Wood, Benton *retired editor, priest*

## Patrick Afb
Kohn, Paul Franklin *mathematician*
McAlwee, Martin Frederick *lawyer*

## Pembroke Pines
Embergher, Mary Louise *elementary school educator*
Schaefer, Bonnie (E. Bonnie Schaefer) *retail executive*
Schaefer, Marla L. *retail executive*

## Penney Farms
Muilenburg, John Powell *minister*

## Pensacola
Apap, Antonio *finance educator, portfolio manager*
Appleyard, Diane Paige *human service administrator*
Arnold, Barry Raynor *philosophy educator, medical ethicist*
Bennett, Wayne A. *marine biologist, educator*
Bookman, Alan B. *lawyer*
Bowden, Jesse Earle *editor, writer, cartoonist, journalist, educator*
Bozeman, Frank Carmack *lawyer*
Bradshaw, Bascom Kyle *surgeon, science educator*
Brown, Susan Louise *philosopher, educator*
Bullock, Ellis Way, Jr. *architect*
Canady, Alexa Irene *pediatric neurosurgeon, educator*
Davis, Wesley D. *psychologist, educator*
Dorman, Jo-Anne *elementary school educator*
Ferguson, Michael Lambert *lawyer, educator*
Ford, Kenneth M. *computer scientist, educator*
Furlong, George Morgan, Jr. *museum program director, retired military officer*
Geeker, Nicholas Peter *lawyer, judge*
Gill, Becky Lorette *retired psychiatrist*
Holloway, Barbara Jean Chambers *retired secondary school educator*
Howell, Everette Irl *physicist, researcher*
Jaffe, Alberto P. *musician, educator*
Jones, Harry Gordon *electronics executive*
Kaplan, Joyce Bridget *zoologist, educator*
Killian, Lewis Martin *sociology educator*
Levin, Fredric Gerson *lawyer*
Maddock, Lawrence Hill *retired language educator, writer*
Maygarden, Jerry Louis *health care foundation executive*
Mazzeo, Daniel Patrick *aerospace engineer, consultant*
Mountcastle, William Wallace, Jr. *philosophy and religion educator*
Müeller, Susan Jones *school system administrator*
Olsen, Richard Galen *biomedical engineer, consultant*
Rashid, Muhammad Harunur *electrical engineering educator*
Redmond, Michael R. *ophthalmologist*
Ricard, John H. *bishop, educator*
Rubardt, Peter Craig *conductor, educator*
Sharma, Venkatanarayanan *surgeon, consultant, medical educator*
Shimmin, Margaret Ann *women's health nurse*
Soloway, Daniel Mark *lawyer*
Steinhoff, Raymond O(akley) *consulting geologist*
Stuart, Walter Bynum III *retired banker*
Vuksta, Michael Joseph *surgeon*
Windham, John Franklin *lawyer, educator*
Woolf, Kenneth Howard *architect*
Wright, Shannon Marie *psychotherapist, counselor*

## Pinellas Park
Benedict, Gail Cleveland *music educator*

## Placida
McClister, Michael *writer*
Prabhudesai, Mukund M. *pathology educator, health facility administrator, researcher, academic administrator*

## Plant City
Buchman, Kenneth William *lawyer*
Golden, Sonya A. *mathematics professor*
Henry, J. Myrle *pharmacist*
Sparkman, Steven Leonard *lawyer*

## Plantation
Alisetti, Edwin Luis *engineer, corporate financial executive*
Cher Killigan, Beatriz M. *art educator*
Costa, Paul Joseph *psychologist*
Fellows, John *delivery service executive*
Gonshak, Isabelle Lee *nurse, volunteer*
Harris, Eleanor Lynne K. (E. Lynn Harris) *religious studies educator, literature educator, minister, writer*

Hsu, Jiun-Jia *engineering educator, transportation engineer*
Jaegerman, Patricia *psychologist*
Schink, Robert Kelly *sales executive*
Smartt, Bill *air courier company executive*
Stein, Alvin *surgeon*
Treible, Kirk *retired academic administrator, foundation administrator*
Waller, Stephen *air transportation executive*
Young, William Benjamin *retired special education educator*

## Poinciana
Spero, Barry Melvin *retired health facility administrator*
Williams, Donald John *physicist, researcher*

## Polk City
Closen, Michael Lee *retired law educator*

## Pompano Beach
Calatchi, Ralph Franklin *investment banker, writer*
Calevas, Harry Powell *management consultant*
Cherla, Gautam V. *physician, nephrologist, researcher*
Dunn, Eston Robert *healthcare educator, director*
Fauss, David H. *legal consultant*
Grossman, Daniel V *investor*
Gude, Nancy Carlson *lawyer*
Hinson, Robert William *advertising executive, consultant*
Johnson, Dorothy Curfman *elementary school educator*
Kester, Stewart Randolph *banker*
Rifenburgh, Richard Philip *investment company executive*
Roen, Sheldon R. *publishing executive, psychologist*
Williams, Cloretta Mae *retired elementary school educator*

## Ponte Vedra Beach
Agassi, Andre Kirk *retired professional tennis player*
Berry, Clare Gebert *real estate broker*
Blake, James Riley *professional tennis player*
Campbell, Chad *professional golfer*
Cink, Stewart *professional golfer*
Coria, Guillermo *professional tennis player*
Curtis, Ben Clifford *professional golfer*
Davis, Wendell, Jr. *lawyer*
de Selding, Edward Bertrand *retired bank executive*
DiMarco, Christian *professional golfer*
Draper, J(osiah) Everett *artist, author, educator*
Ferrero, Juan Carlos *professional tennis player*
Finchem, Tim *sports association executive*
Garcia, Sergio *professional golfer*
Gaudio, Gaston *professional tennis player*
Ginepri, Robby (Robert Louis Ginepri) *professional tennis player*
Gold, Keith Dean *advertising and design executive*
Green, Norman Kenneth *retired oil industry executive, former naval officer*
Grosjean, Sebastien Rene *professional tennis player*
Hamilton, William Berry, Jr. *retired transportation executive*
Kuhn, Bowie K. *lawyer, former professional baseball commissioner, consultant*
Langer, Bernhard *professional golfer*
Leek, Jay Wilbur *management consultant*
Linnen, Thomas Francis *international strategic management consulting executive*
MacKowski, John Joseph *retired insurance company executive*
Moya, Carlos *professional tennis player*
Nalbandian, David *professional tennis player*
Novak, Jiri *professional tennis player*
O'Brien, Raymond Vincent, Jr. *banker*
Patterson, Oscar III *academic administrator*
Pavin, Corey Allen *professional golfer*
ReMine, William Hervey, Jr. *retired surgeon*
Rodriguez, Chi Chi (Juan Rodriguez) *professional golfer*
Slayton, Gus *foundation administrator*
Soderberg, Nancy *former court official, writer*
Tyler, Diane Lazzelle *elementary school educator*
Watson, John Lawrence III *former trade association executive*
Weir, Mike *professional golfer*
Wilson, Dean *professional golfer*
Wood, Quentin Eugene *oil industry executive*
Wu, Hsiu Kwang *economist, educator*

## Port Charlotte
Asperilla, Marianito O. (Mark Asperilla) *epidemiologist*
Donovan, William Alan *retired librarian*
Hill, Richard Earl *academic administrator*
Kidd, A. Paul *health facility administrator, government agency administrator*
Kok, Hans Gebhard *consulting engineer*
Norris, Dolores June *elementary school educator*
Reynolds, Helen Elizabeth *management consultant*
Von Holden, Martin Harvey *psychologist*
Wall, Edward Millard *environmental consulting executive*
Winters, Stanley B. *history professor, consultant, writer*
Wolff, Diane Patricia *writer, film and television producer*

## Port Orange
Chesnut, Nondis Lorine (Angel Love) *education educator, writer, learning specialist, scriptwriter*
Collyer, Robert B. *trade association administrator*
Johnson, Susan F. *elementary school educator*
Millar, Gordon Halstead *mechanical engineer, agricultural products executive*

## Port Richey
Fry, Ronald Sylvan *music educator, director*
Long, Michael Eldon *government and history educator*

## Port Saint Lucie
Augelli, John Pat *geographer, educator, writer, consultant, rancher*
Austin, Philip *research scientist*

Beatrice, Ruth Hadfield *hypnotherapist, retired elementary school educator, financial administrator*
Earley, Deborah Loraine *education educator, researcher*
Guglielmino, Lucy Margaret Madsen *education educator, researcher, consultant*
Guglielmino, Paul Joseph *educator*
Lambert, George Robert *lawyer, realtor*
Rothschild, Mary Ann *music educator*
Sommers, Robert Thomas *editor, writer*
Staub, Carol Anne *artist*

## Punta Gorda
Fullman, Robert Louis *metallurgy consultant*
Haswell, Carleton Radley *banker*
Hollinshead, Ariel Cahill *oncologist, educator, researcher*
Kitson, Don E. *music educator*
Klarik, Bela William James Clark *retired school system administrator*
McDaniel, Norwood Allan *insurance agent*
Miles, Frank Charles *retired newspaper executive*
O'Neal, Lyman Henry *biology educator*
Ott, Walter Richard *information technology executive*
Pollard, Herschel Newton *artist, psychologist*
Presley, Brian *investment company executive*
Smith-Mooney, Marilyn Patricia *city government official, management consultant*
Spaulding, Mar *retired special education educator*
Stratas, Teresa (Anastasia Strataki) *soprano*

## Quincy
Hochmuth, George J. *horticultural educator*

## Reddick
Corwin, Joyce Elizabeth Stedman *construction company executive*

## Redington Beach
Alpert, Barry Mark *insurance company and banking executive*

## Riverview
Ingersoll, Ronald J. *corporate financial executive*

## Riviera Beach
Berliner, Hans Jack *retired computer scientist*

## Rockledge
Means, Michael David *hospital administrator*
Ollie, Pearl Lynn *artist, singer, lyricist*

## Rosemary Beach
Rose, Michael Elvin *oil and gas exploration company executive*

## Rotonda West
Durham, Olga Kalapaca *retired art educator, volunteer*

## Royal Palm Beach
Delgado, Rizal Reyes *psychiatrist, retired internist*
Gardner, Elizabeth Michelle *lawyer*

## Ruskin
Briscoe, Anne M. *retired science educator*
Dickson, Tim *music educator, marine life administrator*

## Safety Harbor
Banks, Allan Richard *artist, art historian, researcher*
Crafton-Masterson, Adrienne *real estate company executive*
Dail, Joseph Garner, Jr. *retired judge*
Olbrick, Valerie Lyn *management consultant, information technologist*

## Saint Augustine
Banton, Theodore Daniel *school system administrator*
Bishop, Claire DeArment *small business owner, retired librarian*
Brady, James Joseph *labor arbitrator*
Couture, Sister Diane Rhea *sister, artist, educator*
Danielson, Reva Annette *pianist, music educator*
DeLaughter, Thomas Glenn *business administration educator, consultant*
Gilmore, H. James *film producer, educator*
Henderson, Hazel *economist, writer*
Johnson, Timothy John *writer, educator*
Jurgens, Julie Graham *mathematics professor*
Kelly, Yvan J. *economics professor, professional basketball scout*
Lund, Frederick Henry *aerospace and electrical engineer*
McCarty, Doran Chester *religious organization administrator*
Nolan, Joseph Thomas *journalism educator, communications consultant*
Okech, Bernard Achero *parasitologist, entomologist*
Oliver, Elizabeth Kimball *historian, writer*
Preysz, Louis Robert Fonss III *management consultant, educator*
Proctor, William Lee *college chancellor*
Sappington, Sharon Anne *retired school librarian*
Wilkes, Delano Angus *architect*
Xue, Rui-De *entomologist*

## Saint Cloud
Everett, Woodrow Wilson *electrical engineer, educator*
Ortiz, Anthony *hotel executive*

## Saint Leo
Hammond, Bruce Ray *academic administrator, consultant*

## Saint Petersburg
Allshouse, Merle Frederick *educational organization administrator*
Armacost, Peter Hayden *academic administrator*
Bairstow, Frances Kanevsky *arbitrator, mediator, educator*
Barnes, Andrew Earl *former newspaper executive*
Battaglia, Anthony Sylvester *lawyer*

Belich, John Patrick, Sr. *journalist, private investigator*
Benham, Emily *fundraiser*
Bercu, Barry Bernard *pediatric endocrinologist*
Betzer, Susan Elizabeth Beers *physician, geriatrician*
Biasotti, Robert E. *lawyer*
Bryant, Timothy Clark *investment brokerage executive*
Buckspan, Randy Jay *plastic surgeon*
Byrd, Isaac Burlin *retired biologist*
Cardenas-Valencia, Andres Manuel *chemical engineer, researcher*
Carnesoltas, Ana-Maria *lawyer*
Carroll, Charles Michael *music educator*
Chenneville, Tiffany Ann *psychologist, educator*
Clijsters, Kim *professional tennis player*
Coetzer, Amanda *professional tennis player*
Collins, Carl Russell, Jr. *industrial engineer*
Collins, Paul Steven *vascular surgeon*
Connelly, David O'Brien *museum administrator, journalist*
Corty, Andrew P. *publishing executive*
Craybas, Jill *professional tennis player*
D'Elia, Christopher Francis *marine biologist, educator, academic administrator*
Dementieva, Elena *professional tennis player*
Dennis, Brady *journalist*
Dimas, Marilyn J. *health products executive*
Dinsdale, Carol Ellen *special education educator*
Emerson, William Allen *retired investment company executive*
Erman, Aila *small business owner*
Escarraz, Enrique III *lawyer*
Fishman, Mark Brian *computer scientist, educator*
Fleming, William Sloan *energy executive, computer company executive*
Fraser, John Wayne *insurance executive, consultant, underwriter*
Frazier, A. D., Jr. *information technology executive, lawyer*
Freeman, Corinne *financial analyst, retired mayor*
Galperin, Boris *mathematician, physicist, oceanographer, educator*
Georges, Richard Martin *lawyer, educator*
Gilbert, Gordon Joel *neurologist, electroencelographer*
Glass, Roy Leonard *lawyer*
Godbold, Francis Stanley *investment banker, security firm executive*
Godwin, Benjamin Braxton *finance company executive*
Granville, Laura *professional tennis player*
Grube, Karl Bertram *judge*
Haiman, Robert James *editor, journalist, educator, media consultant, critic*
Hamilton, John McFarland *plastic surgeon, real estate developer*
Hooker, Robert Wright *journalist*
Hsu, Tsong Han *chemist, researcher*
Hunsicker, Gerry *sports association executive*
Hurley, John Kenneth *real estate company executive, merchant banking executive*
Iyer, Mohan N. *surgeon*
Jacob, Bruce Robert *law educator*
James, Thomas A. *investment company executive*
Janney, Oliver James *lawyer*
Jenkins, Robert Norman *reporter, editor*
Johnson, Edna Ruth *editor*
Jordan, William Reynier, Sr. *retired therapist, poet*
Kanstoroom, David Arnold *real estate developer, entrepreneur*
Keane, Michael J. *lawyer*
Kent, Allen *library and information sciences professor*
Kiefner, John Robert, Jr. *lawyer, educator*
Kubiet, Leo Lawrence *advertising executive, consultant, marketing executive*
Kuznetsova, Svetlana *professional tennis player*
Lang, Joseph Hagedorn *lawyer*
Lanza, Donald Charles *otolaryngologist, rhinologist*
Lemoi, Brian Andr *religious organization administrator, religious studies educator, writer*
Lewis, Chris A. *manufacturing executive*
Linde, Shirley *writer, travel company executive*
Linhart, Joseph Wayland *retired cardiologist, educational administrator*
Lowery, Solomon J. *social studies educator*
Maddon, Joe *professional baseball coach*
Main, Timothy L. *electronics company executive*
Mallory, Jeannine Marek *public relations and marketing professional*
Mann, Sam Henry, Jr. *retired lawyer*
Matecki, Paul L. *lawyer*
Meyer, Robert Allen *finance educator*
Mills, William Harold, Jr. *construction executive*
Mondello, Mark T. *manufacturing executive*
Morean, William D. *manufacturing executive*
Mueller, O. Thomas *molecular geneticist, pediatrics educator*
Myskina, Anastasia *professional tennis player*
Naimoli, Vincent Joseph *diversified financial services company executive*
Naughton, James Martin *journalist*
Nichols, Katie *investment company executive*
Nussbaum, Leo Lester *retired college president, consultant*
Patterson, Eugene Corbett *retired editor, publishing executive*
Paver, Robert L. *lawyer*
Petty, M. S. Marty *publisher*
Pflum, William John *physician*
Pittman, Robert Turner *retired newspaper editor*
Putnam, J. Stephen *corporate financial executive*
Roney, Paul Hitch *federal judge*
Root, Allen William *pediatrician, educator*
Rosenblum, Martin Jerome *ophthalmologist*
Rosenblum, Zina Michelle Zarin *psychology professor, marketing professional, researcher*
Ross, Howard Philip *lawyer*
Sebastien, Anya Celita *academic administrator, consultant*
Sharapova, Maria *professional tennis player*
Shaughnessy, Meghann *professional tennis player*
Short, James F. *investment company executive*
Shuck, Robert F. *financial executive*
Silver, Lawrence Alan *retired marketing professional*
Simpson, Lisa Ann *physician, educator*
Smith, Betty Robinson *elementary school educator*

Southworth, William Dixon *retired education educator*
Stokes, Melvin Kirklin *psychologist*
Tash, Paul Clifford *editor, publishing executive*
Thomas, Patrick Robert Maxwell *oncologist, educator, academic administrator*
Wales, Jimmy Donal (Jimmy Donal "Jimbo" Wales) *Internet company executive*
Wasserman, Susan Valesky *accountant, artist, yoga instructor*
Wedding, Charles Randolph *architect*
White, June Miller *mathematics professor, educational consultant*
Zimmer, Donald William *former professional baseball coach, former professional baseball manager*

**Saint Petersburg Beach**
Bradshaw, John Robert Covington III *Internet company executive*
Garnett, Stanley Iredale, II, *utilities executive, lawyer*
Hurley, Frank Thomas, Jr. *realtor*

**San Antonio**
Beverland, Jack Edwin *retired retail executive, folk artist*

**Sanford**
Capps, James Leigh, II, *lawyer, military officer*
Dickison, Alexander Kane *physical science educator*
Mamele, Richard Louis *lawyer*
Oostwouder, Peter Henry *physician*
Scott, Mellouise Jacqueline *retired media specialist*

**Sanibel**
Allen, Patricia J. *library director*
Ball, Armand Baer *former association executive, consultant*
Brodbeck, William Jan *marketing professional*
Crown, David Allan *criminologist, educator*
Hasselman, Richard B. *retired rail transportation executive*
Ray, Charles Albert *photojournalist*
Rothschild, Donald Phillip *retired lawyer, arbitrator*
Trevor, Alexander Bruen *information technology manager, consultant*

**Santa Rosa Beach**
Rees, Lane Charles *industrial relations consultant*

**Sarasota**
Allen, Charles Franklin *music educator*
Apfelbach, George Leonard, Jr. *urologist*
Arreola, John Bradley *financial planner*
Atwell, Robert Herron *academic administrator*
Aull, Susan *physician*
Bailey, Robert Elliott *financial executive*
Balliett, John William *entrepreneur, real estate company executive*
Beck, Robert Alfred *hotel executive, educator*
Bennett, William F. *orthopedist, surgeon*
Benowitz, June Melby *historian, educator*
Berkoff, Charles Edward *pharmaceutical and biotech consultant*
Boersma, Lawrence Allan (Larry Allan) *animal welfare administrator, photographer*
Bowers, Charles Richard *surgeon*
Brandhorst, Wesley Theodore *retired library and information scientist*
Bushey, Alan Scott *retired insurance holding company executive*
Carr, Patricia Ann *community health nurse*
Carstens, Charlene B. *composer, music educator*
Cavanagh, Denis *gynecologist, obstetrician, educator, gynecological oncologist*
Chase, Jeanne Norman *artist, educator*
Christopher, William Garth *lawyer*
Clark, Eugenie *zoologist, educator*
Cleland, Sherrill *college president*
Cooper, William Ewing, Jr. *retired army officer*
Culkin, Charles Walker, Jr. *retired trade association administrator*
Cummings, Martin Marc *medical educator, physician, academic administrator*
Daoust, Donald Roger *pharmaceutical executive, microbiologist, cosmetics executive*
De Gennaro, Richard *retired library director*
Deutsch, Sid *biomedical engineer, educator*
Dryce, H. David *accountant, consultant*
Dungy, Kathryn R. *humanities educator*
Edwards, Michael Donald *artistic director, drama educator*
Ehrlich, Bernard Herbert *lawyer, trade association administrator*
El Shahawy, Mahfouz *internist, educator, cardiologist*
Faron, Sally Rogers *performing arts association administrator, consultant*
Fendrick, Alan Burton *retired advertising executive*
Fulton Ross, Gale *artist, actor*
Garland, Richard Roger *lawyer*
Gauch, Eugene William, Jr. *retired air force officer*
Geithner, Paul Herman, Jr. *retired banker*
Gittelson, Bernard *public relations consultant, author, lecturer*
Goodacre, Glenna *sculptor*
Gordon, Sanford Daniel *economics professor*
Greenfield, Robert Kauffman *retired lawyer*
Harmon, Foster (Loren Foster Harmon) *arts consultant*
Harris, Judith Ann White *occupational health nurse, educator*
Heiser, Rolland Valentine *former army officer, foundation administrator*
Heitler, George *lawyer*
Hoffman, Oscar Allen *retired forest products company executive*
Holcomb, Constance L. *sales and marketing management executive*
Hughes, Allen *music critic*
Hull, J(ames) Richard *retired lawyer*
Hummel, Dana D. Mallett *librarian*
Iverson, Robert Louis, Jr. *internist, physician*
Jackel, Lawrence *publishing executive*
Jacobson, Melvin Joseph *mathematician, educator*
Jelks, Mary Larson *retired pediatrician*

Jones, Sally Daviess Pickrell *writer*
Jones, Tracey Kirk, Jr. *retired minister, educator*
Kaminsky, Stuart M. *screenwriter, writer*
Keltner, Robert Earl *lawyer, researcher, hotel executive*
Kerr, Donald Craig *retired minister*
Kessler, Leonard *writer, illustrator*
Knickerbocker, Robert Platt, Jr. *retired lawyer*
Landis, Edgar David *business consultant*
Lee, Nancy Ranck *management consultant*
Leidel, Katherine *journalist, newscaster*
Lengyel, Alfonz *art history educator, archeology educator, museology educator*
Levitt, Jaren *real estate company officer*
Levy, Gerhard *pharmacologist*
Long, Robert Radcliffe *fluid mechanics engineer, educator*
Lynch, Martin Francis *psychology professor*
Magenheim, Mark Joseph *physician, epidemiologist, educator*
Mahadevan, Kumar *marine life administrator, researcher*
Marino, Eugene Louis *publishing executive, director*
Markin, Sheila Ruben *community relations executive*
Marks, Charles *surgeon, educator*
Martia, Dominic Francis *academic administrator*
Masters, John Christopher *psychologist, educator, writer*
Mattran, Donald Albert *management consultant, educator*
McCollum, John Morris *tenor*
McFarlin, Diane Hooten *publisher*
McMaster, Gloria (Gloria Bugni Juhn) *mezzo-soprano, educator*
Metzger, Sidney *retired communications engineer*
Meyer, B. Fred *small business executive, home designer and builder, product designer*
Middleton, Norman Graham *social worker, psychotherapist*
Miles, Arthur J. *financial planner, consultant*
Miranda, Carlos Sa *food products company executive*
Mizer, Joyce Taylor *music educator*
Morris, Gordon James *financial company executive, consultant*
Morrow, William Earl *retired government official, retired law educator*
Mullane, John Francis *pharmaceutical executive*
North, Marjorie Mary *columnist*
Oelbaum, Harold *lawyer*
Oldshue, James Y. *chemical engineering consultant*
O'Malley, Thomas Anthony *gastroenterologist, internist*
Phillips, Howard William *investment banker*
Pierce, Richard Harry *oceanographer*
Platt, Franklin Dewitt *retired history professor*
Poppel, Harvey Lee *management consultant, investment banker*
Proffitt, Waldo, Jr. *newspaper editor*
Retzer, Mary Elizabeth Helm *retired librarian*
Ross, Gerald Fred *electrical engineering executive, researcher*
Roth, James Frank *chemicals executive, chemist*
St. John, Terri *secondary school educator*
Sarakatsannis, Leonidas Nicholas *musician, concert pianist, music educator, composer, conductor*
Scanlon, Janice Lynn *retired gifted and talented educator*
Schlegel, John Frederick *management consultant, personal trainer*
Schmalzried, Marvin Eugene *financial consultant*
Schwartz, Francis *music educator, composer*
Shulman, Arthur *communications executive*
Slocum, Donald Hillman *consumer products company executive*
Stevens, Elisabeth Goss (Mrs. Robert Schleussner Jr.) *journalist, writer, graphic artist*
Stewart, Donald George *musician, composer, music industry executive*
Straight, Elsie Hosking *retired librarian, sculptor*
Tachna, Ruth C. *retired lawyer*
Taplin, Winn Lowell *historian, retired federal agency administrator*
Thompson, Annie Figueroa *retired academic administrator*
Torrey, Richard Frank *utilities executive*
Tourkantonis, Arthur Charles *real estate consultant, lawyer*
Tuch, Howard Stanley *long-term care administrator, geriatrics services professional*
Umanoff, Dan F. *medical association administrator*
Vasilaki, Linda Boozer *music educator*
Wadsworth, Dyer Seymour *metal products executive, treasurer, environmental services administrator*
Watson, Joyce Morrissa *forensic and clinical psychologist*
Weeks, Albert Loren *writer, educator, journalist*
Welch, John Dana *retired urologist*
West, Bob *pharmaceutical executive*
Wetenhall, John *museum director*
Wilson, Kenneth Jay *writer*
Zahn, Carl Frederick *museum program director, photographer, graphics designer*
Zavon, Mitchell Ralph *occupational medicine physician*

**Satellite Beach**
Clark, John F. *space systems engineering educator*
Loney, Mary Rose *former airport administrator, aviation industry consultant*
Miller, Susan Laura *real estate company executive, retired special education educator*
Rains, Baxter Smith *sculptor, consultant*
Van Arsdall, Robert Armes *engineer, retired military officer*

**Sebastian**
Lagin, Neil *landscape designer, consultant*
Mauke, Otto Russell *retired college president*
Pieper, Patricia Rita *artist*

**Sebring**
DeWitt, Carol A. *writer*
McCollum, James Fountain *lawyer*
Sherrick, Daniel Noah *real estate broker*

**Seffner**
Jackson, Greg L. *academic administrator*
Seaman, Jeffrey *consumer products company executive*

**Seminole**
Carrere, Charles Scott *law educator, judge*
Evans, Thomas Passmore *management consultant*
Schmitz, Dolores Jean *primary school educator*

**Singer Island**
Dixson, J. B. *communications executive*

**South Daytona**
Fernández, Lianne *elementary school educator, consultant*

**South Florida**
Hoffman, Randy Michael *automotive executive*

**South Miami**
Keedy, Christian David *lawyer*
Villacian, Vanessa Luisa *psychologist*

**Sparr**
Tovi, Murray *futurist, research scientist*

**Spring Hill**
Post, Wendy *elementary school educator*
Rothenberg, Linda Ann *science educator*
Timmins, Allan S. *information technology manager, educator*
Vanderburg, Paul Stacey *insurance executive, consultant*
Whyte, Raymond A. *artist*
Wood, Shelton Eugene *education educator, minister, consultant*

**Stuart**
Ankrom, Charles Franklin *golf course architect, consultant*
Cocoves, Anita Petzold *psychotherapist*
Derrickson, William Borden *manufacturing executive*
Gary, Willie E. *lawyer*
Johnson, Sailee *realtor*
Kooluris, Hortense Dolan *performing arts educator, consultant, dancer*
Moreno, Christine Margaret *lawyer*
Riordan, James Quentin *retired oil industry executive, lawyer*
Robinson, Michael Hill *retired zoological park director, biologist*
Smithson, Charles Wayne *economist, consultant*
Stark, Richard Boies *surgeon, artist*
Stocks, Donna Brandenburg *school system administrator*

**Sugarloaf**
Greenberg, Linda Garrett *education educator, volunteer, singer*

**Summerfield**
Lynne-O'Brien, Vincent *theater director, actor*
McNulty, Carrell Stewart, Jr. *retired manufacturing executive, architect*

**Sun City Center**
Chapman, Lenora Rosamond *day care provider, social service organization director*
Crow, Harold Eugene *physician, educator*
Edwards, Paul Beverly *retired science and engineering educator*
Gummere, Walter Cooper *finance educator, consultant*
Hall, John Fry *retired psychologist*
Hottinger, Joseph Earle *retired government agency administrator*
Jeffries, Robert Joseph *retired engineer, information technology executive, educator*
Kochanski, Lois Whidden *foundation administrator*
Leonard, William Norris *economist, educator*
Malkin, Moses Montefiore *retired employee benefits administration company executive, diversified financial services company executive*

**Sunny Isles Beach**
Edelcup, Norman Scott *management and financial consultant*

**Sunrise**
Bainton, Donald J. *diversified manufacturing company executive*
Belfour, Ed *professional hockey player*
Larionov, Igor *professional hockey player*
Maken, Sonny *real estate company executive, real estate developer*
Odelein, Lyle *professional hockey player*
Offerdahl, John Arnold *former professional football player, food service executive*
Singer, Richard P. *neurologist, researcher, director*
Sorensen, Allan Chresten *service company executive*

**Tallahassee**
AbdelRazig, Yassir A. *engineering educator*
Anstead, Harry Lee *state supreme court justice*
Ashler, Philip Frederic *international trade and development advisor*
Aurell, John Karl *lawyer*
Baggett, Fred W. *lawyer*
Bagley, James Robert *freelance writer*
Bailey, Theresa L. *director, consultant*
Barnett, Martha Walters *lawyer*
Bartlett, Richard Adams *retired history professor*
Bell, Kenneth B. *State Supreme Court Justice*
Bielby, Lorence Jon *lawyer*
Blaber, Michael *education educator*
Blair, Maudine *psychotherapist, communications executive, management consultant*
Blanton, Faye Wester *legislative official*
Bowden, Bobby *college football coach*
Braswell, Jackie Boyd *state agency administrator*
Buck, Thomas Randolph *retired lawyer, retired diversified financial services company executive*
Buford, Barbara Fest *retired state agency administrator*
Burkman, Ernest, Jr. *education educator*
Burnaman, Ross Stafford *lawyer*

Bush, Jeb (John Ellis Bush) *governor*
Butler, Robert Olen *writer, educator*
Bye, Raymond Erwin, Jr. *academic administrator*
Calhoun, Joseph Patrick *economics professor, researcher*
Campbell, Frances Harvell *real estate developer*
Cantero, Raoul G. III *state supreme court justice*
Cherniga, Michael J. *lawyer*
Choppin, Gregory Robert *chemistry professor*
Cobb, Sue McCourt *state official, former ambassador*
Coleman, Robert H. *theater educator*
Coloney, Wayne Herndon *civil engineer*
Corzine, Jennifer Jean *music educator*
Crist, Charles (Charlie Crist) *state attorney general*
Cronin, Jerome Joseph, Jr. *marketing educator, consultant*
Cummings, Frederic Alan *lawyer*
Curtin, Terrence N. *lawyer*
Dadisman, Joseph Carrol *retired newspaper executive*
Dariotis, Terrence Theodore *lawyer*
Das, Himangshu Shekhar *civil engineer*
Davis, Larry Michael *air force officer, healthcare manager, consultant*
Dea, David Young Fong *electrical engineer, consultant*
DeFoor, J. Allison, II, *lawyer*
De Forest, Sherwood Searle *agricultural engineer, agricultural products executive*
Elsner, James Brian *meteorologist, educator*
Ervin, Charles Phifer, Jr. *education educator, retired military officer*
Ervin, Robert Marvin *lawyer*
Fiore, Carole Diane *library consultant*
France, Belinda Takach *lawyer, business owner*
Gilmer, Robert *mathematics professor*
Gleeson, Thomas Alexander *retired meteorologist*
Glover, Erica D. *lawyer*
Glueckauf, Robert Lewis *psychologist, educator*
Golden, Leon *classicist, educator*
Goldstein, Julia Sonia *librarian*
Grant, Sydney R. *education educator, consultant*
Greene, Daniel E. *pastel artist*
Grimes, Stephen Henry *retired state supreme court justice*
Gunnarsson, Roy *government agency administrator, consultant*
Guy, Mary Ellen Johnston *political science professor*
Hall, Houghton Alexander *electrical engineer, municipal official*
Halpern, Paul G. *history professor*
Harding, Major Best *former state supreme court chief justice*
Harper, Robert Augustus *lawyer*
Harrison, Luvada A. *voice educator, singer*
Harsanyi, Janice *retired soprano, educator*
Hernandez, Jose Yolando Balagtas *surgeon*
Hernandez, Minerva Cuadrante *physician, consultant*
Herndon, Roy Clifford *physicist*
Herrick, Nathan *biologist*
Hetrick, Charles Brady *retired county official*
Holcomb, Lyle Donald, Jr. *retired lawyer*
Holcombe, Randall Gregory *economics professor*
Humphrey, Louise Ireland *civic worker, equestrienne*
Humphries, Frederick S. *former university president*
Hunt, Mary Alice *retired humanities educator*
Hunter, Christopher *retired mathematics professor*
Jennings, Toni *lieutenant governor*
Johnson, Benjamin F., VI, *economist, consultant*
Johnson, Kelly Overstreet *lawyer*
Johnson, Margaret Anderson *writer, publishing executive, agricultural products executive*
Kaelin, Eugene Francis *retired philosophy educator*
Kercheval, Alec Norton *mathematician*
Kerns, David Vincent *lawyer*
Khalil, Mohammed K. *research scientist, medical educator*
Kickliter, Raymond Lawton *retired secondary school educator*
Knetsch, Joe *historian*
Kroto, Harold Walter *chemistry researcher, educator*
Ladner, Kysandra Marie *information technology manager*
Laird, Doris Anne Marley *retired humanities educator, musician*
Laird, William Everette, Jr. *economics professor*
Lamont, Bruce Thomas *management educator*
Laughlin, William Page *retired electric power industry executive*
Lee, Peter John *research engineer*
Levine, A. Kenneth *lawyer*
Lewis, R. Fred *state supreme court justice*
Lick, Dale Wesley *educational leadership educator*
Lisenby, Dorrece Edenfield *realtor*
Loper, David Eric *geophysicist, mathematician*
Losh, Susan Carol *education educator, researcher*
Maguire, Charlotte Edwards *retired pediatrician*
Mamatey, Victor Samuel *historian, educator*
Marshall, Alan George *chemistry and biochemistry educator*
McCord, Guyte Pierce, Jr. *retired judge*
Mele, Alfred R. *philosophy educator*
Miller, Gregory R. *prosecutor*
Miller, Morris Henry *lawyer*
Mills, Belen Collantes *early childhood education educator*
Mindlin, Steven Todd *lawyer*
Minnick, Bruce Alexander *lawyer*
Mooney, Krista Michele *academic administrator*
Morgan, Lucy Ware *news correspondent, journalist*
Morgan, Robert Marion *educational research educator*
Morgante, John-Paul *human resources specialist*
Mortham, Sandra Barringer *former state official*
Moulton, Grace Charbonnet *retired physicist*
Nam, Charles Benjamin *demographer, sociologist, educator, writer*
Nasser, Joseph Yousef *public safety administrator, consultant*
Navon, Ionel Michael *mathematics professor*
Nichols, Eugene Douglas *mathematics professor*

Palladino-Craig, Allys *museum director, educator*
Pariente, Barbara J *state supreme court justice*
Pettijohn, Fred Phillips *retired publishing executive*
Pfeffer, Richard Lawrence *meteorology and geophysics educator*
Phipps, Benjamin Kimball, II, *lawyer*
Pugh, Thomas Doering *architecture educator, educator*
Quince, Peggy A. *judge*
Ramsey, Sally Ann Seitz *retired state official*
Reid, Sue Titus *law educator*
Robson, Donald *physics professor*
Rogers, William Warren *historian, educator, publishing executive, writer*
Rushing, John Alan *business educator*
Schrieffer, John Robert *physics professor, science administrator*
Scott, Fran *adult education educator*
Scott, Marcus Lewis Elliot *music educator*
Shaftel, Matthew Robert *music educator, tenor, conductor*
Shamsham, Fadi Michel *cardiologist*
Sliger, Bernard Francis *academic administrator, economist, educator*
Stebleton, Michelle Marie *music educator, musician*
Streem, James Kenneth *musician, educator*
Strickland, Delphene Coverston *judge*
Terry, Anne Curtis *lawyer, writer*
Teson, Fernando Roberto *law educator, consultant*
Thomas, James Bert, Jr. *retired federal agency administrator*
Thompson, Gregory Lee *social sciences educator*
Thompson, Jean Tanner *retired librarian*
Thompson, Omar *art educator, artist*
Tourtet, Christiane Andrée *writer, photojournalist, reporter, advocate*
Turnbull, Marjorie Reitz *foundation executive, retired state legislator*
von Molnár, Stephan *physics professor, director*
Waas, George Lee *lawyer*
Waas, Harriet Issner *elementary school educator*
Walker, Karen D. *lawyer*
Washington, Cecile Fernando *career planning administrator*
Washington, Karen *librarian, educator*
Weale, Mary Jo *artist*
Weaver, Thomas Harold *health facility administrator*
Webster, Peter David *judge*
Weidner, Donald J. *dean, law educator*
Weinberger, Steven *lawyer, educator*
Wells, Charles Talley *state supreme court justice*
Wetherell, Thomas Kent *academic administrator*
Winn, John L. *school system administrator*
Yang, Xiaojun *education educator*
Yecke, Cheri Pierson *educational researcher, administrator, columnist, writer*
Yerg, Beverly Johnson *physical education educator, researcher*
Zachert, Martha Jane *retired librarian*
Zaiser, Kent Ames *lawyer*
Zou, Xiaolei *meteorologist, educator*
Zwilich, Ellen Taaffe *composer*

## Tamarac

Auletta, Joan Miglorisi *construction company executive, mortgage broker, insurance broker*
Baron-Malkin, Phyllis *artist, art educator*
Froehlich, Fritz Edgar *communications educator, telecommunications scientist*
Krause, John L. *retired optometrist*
O'Neil, Thomas *dentist*

## Tampa

Abdelrahman, Talaat Ahmad Mohammad *financial executive*
Abizaid, John Philip *career military officer*
Afield, Walter Edward *psychiatrist, educator, health facility administrator*
Agazzi, Siviero *neurosurgeon*
Albritton, Arthur Dallas *lawyer*
Aldrich, David Alan *accountant, consultant*
Alexander, William Olin *finance company executive*
Alstott, Michael Joseph (Mike Alstott) *professional football player*
Andreychuk, David *professional hockey player*
Anton, John Peter *philosopher, educator*
Barkin, Marvin E. *lawyer*
Barness, Lewis Abraham *physician*
Barnett, Michael L. *strategic management educator*
Barrow, Frederica Harrison *education educator, social worker*
Barrow, Lionel Ceon, Jr. *communications consultant, marketing consultant*
Barton, Bernard Alan, Jr. *lawyer*
Bedgood, Alvin J. *information technology manager*
Berarducci, Adrienne *nursing educator, researcher*
Bishopric, Karl *insurance company executive, retired investment banker, real estate company executive, retired advertising executive*
Black, Caroline Kapusta *lawyer*
Blacklidge, Raymond Mark *lawyer*
Boutros, Linda Nelene Wiley *medical/surgical nurse*
Branch, William Terrell *urologist, educator*
Brooks, Derrick Dewan *professional football player*
Brown, Troy Anderson, Jr. *retired electric power industry executive*
Bruner, Darlene York *education educator, consultant*
Bunker-Soler, Antonio Luis *physician*
Burke, Sean *professional hockey player*
Campbell, Richard Bruce *lawyer*
Campos, Jackie C. *insurance agent*
Cancio, Margarita R. *infectious disease physician*
Cardoso, Anthony Antonio *artist, educator*
Carnahan, Robert Paul *civil engineer, educator, researcher, consultant*
Castellano, Josephine Massaro *medical records specialist*
Christian, Terry Clifton *lawyer*
Clendinen, Craig P. *lawyer*
Coleman, Rodney Albert *political scientist, consultant*
Corcoran, Clement Timothy III *lawyer, retired judge*

Cress, William Douglas *biology professor, researcher*
Cunningham, Anthony Willard *lawyer*
Dalton, William Steven *oncologist, educator*
Davidson, Charles Thomas *lawyer*
Davis, Blondell Gilliam *business manager, evangelist, artist, author, poet*
Davis, Helen Gordon *retired state senator*
Davis, Richard Earl *lawyer*
de Chant, Dell *religious studies educator*
DeFosset, Don *retired manufacturing executive*
de Lama, Alberto *artist*
DeVane, Mindy Klein *financial planner*
Diehr, Beverly Hunt *lawyer*
Doliner, Nathaniel Lee *lawyer*
Dsurney, John *psychologist*
Dupuis, John James *music educator, composer*
Edberg, Judith Florence *music educator*
Eddy, Colette Ann *aerial photography studio owner, photographer*
Eichberg, Rodolfo David *physiatrist, educator*
El-Hadidy, Bahaa *information scientist, educator, consultant*
Ellwanger, Thomas John *lawyer*
Erickson, Linda E. *retired academic administrator*
Farha, Todd S. *health products executive*
Feaster, Jay *professional sports team executive*
Flom, Edward Leonard *retired metal products executive*
Forsythe, Robert Elliott *economics professor*
Freedman, Sandra Warshaw *former mayor*
Friedlander, Edward Jay *journalist, educator*
Frisch, Stefan A. *language educator*
Galloway, Joe *professional football player*
Gaska, Christine *accountant*
Genshaft, Judy Lynn *psychologist, educator*
Genter, John Robert *grocery industry executive*
Germroth, Peter *biologist, educator*
Ghiu, Silvana Melania Stefania *process and development engineer*
Gilbert, Leonard Harold *lawyer*
Gilbert-Barness, Enid F. *pathologist, educator*
Gironda, Ronald James *psychologist*
Glazer, Malcolm *professional sports team executive*
Gonzalez, Joe Manuel *lawyer*
Grammig, Robert (Bob) James *lawyer*
Greenfield, George B. *radiologist*
Gruden, Jon *professional football coach*
Haggis, Arthur George, Jr. *retired military officer, educator, publisher*
Hamilton, William F. *lawyer*
Hanford, Agnes Rutledge *retired investment advisor*
Hanford, Grail Stevenson *writer*
Hankenson, E(dward) Craig, Jr. *performing arts executive*
Hankins, Phillip R. *music educator*
Harkness, Mary Lou *librarian*
Hegarty, Thomas Joseph *academic administrator, history educator*
Henard, Elizabeth Ann *controller*
Hernandez, Gilberto Juan *accountant, auditor, management consultant*
Hickman, Hugh V. *science educator, researcher*
Hlavay, Jay Alan *financial analyst*
Holliday, Ronald Sturgis *lawyer*
Howey, John Richard *architect, writer*
Hudson, Sherrill W. *energy executive*
Huey, Peggy J. *communications educator, performing company executive*
Huneycutt, Alice Ruth *lawyer*
Hunter, Larry Lee *retired electrical engineer*
Hyland, Gregory E. *home building products executive*
Iorio, Pam *county official*
Jacobs, Timothy Andrew *epidemiologist, consultant*
Jacobsen, Paul *psychologist*
Jacobson, Howard Newman *obstetrics and gynecology educator, researcher*
Jacobus, Mary *publishing executive*
Jamieson, Michael Lawrence *lawyer*
Jenkins, Elizabeth Ann *federal judge*
Jennewein, James Joseph *architect*
Johnson, Anthony O'Leary (Andy Johnson) *meteorologist, consultant*
Johnson, Thomas S. *electronics executive*
Jones, Franklin Ross *education educator*
Jones, John Arthur *lawyer*
Jones, Vaughn Paul *construction marketing executive*
Joseph, Babu *chemical educator*
Jurado, Jaime *construction and energy company executive*
Karver, Marc Stuart *psychologist, educator*
Kasum, Michael *humanities educator, writer*
Keller, Shari Ann *small business owner*
Kelly, Thomas Paine, Jr. *retired lawyer*
Kersaint, Gladis *mathematics professor, researcher*
Killinger, Dennis Karl *physicist, educator*
Kimmel, Ellen Bishop *psychologist, educator*
Knox, Michael Dennis *medical educator, research center administrator*
Kovachevich, Elizabeth Anne *judge*
Krone, Norman Bernard *real estate developer, lawyer*
Kruschwitz, Walter Hillis *retired physics educator*
Lallance, Leroy Odom *music minister*
Lane, Robin *lawyer*
LaRussa, Rudy G. *lawyer*
Lashley, Keith Livingstone *architect, educator*
Lebouitz, Martin Frederick *diversified financial services company executive, consultant*
Lecavalier, Vincent *professional hockey player*
Leopold, Blake *music educator*
Leto, Sharon Ann *secondary school educator, consultant*
Levine, Jack Anton *lawyer*
Lim, Daniel Van *microbiology educator*
Lockey, Richard Funk *allergist, immunologist, educator*
Luddington, Betty Walles *school library media specialist*
Lynch, Michael Joseph *criminologist, educator*
MacDonald, Thomas Cook, Jr. *lawyer, mediator*
MacManus, Susan Ann *political science professor, researcher*
Mahan, Charles Samuel *public health educator*
Malone, John I. *pediatrics educator, biomedical researcher*

Mangiapane, Joseph Arthur *information technology executive*
Martin, Gary Wayne *lawyer*
Matheny, Charles Woodburn, Jr. *former army officer, civil engineer, city official*
McAdams, John Pope *lawyer*
McBride, William Howard, Jr. *lawyer*
McCook, Kathleen de la Peña *librarian, educator*
McDevitt, Sheila Marie *lawyer, energy executive*
McIlwain, Harris H. *physician, researcher*
Meisels, Gerhard George *academic administrator, chemist, educator*
Michaels, John Patrick, Jr. *investment banker, media broker*
Milito, Connie Marie *education administrator, government relations administrator*
Miliziano, John C. *social studies educator*
Mitchell, Mozella Gordon *language educator, minister*
Moltzon, Richard Francis *data processing executive*
Moszkowski, Neal *health products executive*
Muroff, Lawrence Ross *nuclear medicine physician, educator*
Murthy, Uday *accountant, educator*
Natarelli, Larissa Ivanovna *language educator, researcher*
Nichols, Nancy Diane *music educator*
Nord, Walter Robert *business administration educator, researcher, consultant*
Norman, Robert Andrew *dermatologist, educator*
O'Brien, Mary Ellen Christina *artist, educator*
Ohrt, William F. *manufacturing executive*
Older, Jay Justin *ophthalmic plastic surgeon*
Olson, Robert Eugene *physician, biochemist, educator*
O'Neill, Albert Clarence, Jr. *lawyer*
Ortinau, David Joseph *marketing specialist, educator*
Palmer, Denise E. *publishing executive*
Pasetti, Louis Oscar *retired dentist*
Pellett, Jon Michael *lawyer*
Perez, Paul Ignatius *prosecutor, lawyer*
Perret, Gerard Anthony, Jr. *orthodontist*
Perry, James Frederic *philosophy educator, writer*
Pfeiffer, Eric Armin *psychiatrist, gerontologist, writer*
Piper, John Richard *political science professor*
Platt, Jan Kaminis *former county official*
Plumeri, Joseph James, II, *financial executive*
Pollara, Bernard *pediatrician, educator, immunologist*
Powers, Pauline Smith *psychiatrist, educator, researcher*
Pribor, Hugo Casimer *physician*
Reed, Donna Marie *editor*
Richards, Brad *professional hockey player*
Rifkin, Stephen *nephrologist*
Roberson, Bruce Heerdt *lawyer*
Roberts, Jill Carolyne *researcher, educator*
Robinson, John William, IV, *lawyer*
Roop, Mitchell A. *information scientist*
Rowlands, David Thomas *pathology educator*
St. Louis, Martin *professional hockey player*
Sanberg, Paul Ronald *medical educator*
Sanchez, Mary Anne *retired secondary school educator*
Sasso, Gary L. *lawyer*
Sbramaniam, Chitra P. *educational consultant*
Schild, Nancy Lois *realtor, music educator*
Schueler, John R. *newspaper executive*
Schultz, Barbara Marie *investment advisor*
Schwenke, Roger Dean *lawyer*
Scialdo, Mary Ann *music educator, musician*
Seyfang, Andreas Georg *biochemist, educator*
Shenefelt, Philip David *dermatologist*
Shephard, Bruce Dennis *obstetrician, educator, medical writer*
Siegel, Richard Lawrence *immunologist, allergist*
Sigety, Charles Birge *investment company executive*
Silbiger, Martin L. *radiologist, educator, dean*
Sinnott, John Thomas *internist, educator*
Smith, David John, Jr. *plastic surgeon*
Smith, William Reece, Jr. *lawyer*
Somers, Clifford Louis *lawyer*
Sopher, Vicki Elaine *appraiser*
Spellacy, William Nelson *obstetrician, gynecologist, educator*
Spielberger, Charles Donald *psychologist, educator*
Stallings, Norman (Charles Norman Stallings) *lawyer*
Stalnaker, Lance Kuebler *lawyer*
Stefanov, Ivanka *music educator*
Stiles, Mary Ann *lawyer, writer, lobbyist*
Studer, William Allen *security consultant, retired military officer*
Sullebarger, John Thompson *internist, educator, cardiologist*
Sullivan, Christopher *restaurant executive*
Sullivan, Joseph Peter *risk and insurance management consultant*
Tebbi, Cameron K *hematologist, oncologist*
Thelen, Gil *publishing executive*
Thomas, Gregg Darrow *lawyer*
Thomas, Wayne Lee *lawyer*
Torres-Roca, Javier Francisco *medical educator*
Tortorella, John *professional hockey coach*
Tully, Darrow *newspaper publisher*
Vogt, Martha Diane *lawyer*
Wagner, Frederick William (Bill Wagner) *lawyer*
Waller, Edward Martin, Jr. *lawyer*
Watkins, Joan Marie *osteopath, physician*
Weaver, Janet S. *editor*
Weiner, Irving Bernard *psychologist*
Wilson, Charles Reginald *federal judge*
Wujcik, Theo Frank *artist*
Yang, Grace H. *lawyer*
Yerrid, C. Steven *lawyer*
Young, Gwynne A. *lawyer*
Young, William Henry *education educator, writer, consultant*
Zayas-Castro, José *engineering educator, researcher*
Zhu, Yiliang *research scientist, educator*
Zhukon, Tatyana Anatoly *biologist, researcher*

## Tarpon Springs

Byrne, Richard Hill *counselor, educator*
Crismond, Linda Fry *public relations executive*
Johnson, Randall Clyde *mortgage company executive*

Leisner, Anthony Baker *publishing company executive*

## Tavares

Gross, Paul Allan *health products executive*
Reynolds, Bruce Grahlmann *physicist*

## Temple Terrace

Barlar, Rebecca Nance *music educator*
Crispell, Brian Lewis *history professor*
Rink, Wesley Winfred *retired bank executive*

## Tequesta

Larson, Edythe K. *science educator*
Swets, John Arthur *psychologist, researcher*
Turrell, Richard Horton, Sr. *banker*

## The Villages

Behrendt, Richard Louis *academic administrator*
Oetjen, David L. (Jon David Douglas) *writer, film producer*
Phillips, Patricia Jeanne *retired school system administrator*

## Thonotosassa

Jordan, Frederick Leroy *trucking executive*

## Tierra Verde

Gaffney, Thomas Francis *private investor*
Stewart, John Murray *retired bank executive*

## Titusville

Arnold, Arthur Joseph *writer, journalist*
Atwood, Freida Garland *small business owner, computer scientist, consultant*
Duffy, John Charles *psychiatrist, educator, consultant*
Morton, Craig Richard *real estate investor*
O'Sullivan, Patricia Ann *principal, writer*
Robinson, Christina Anne *secondary school educator*
Stewart, David Witherington *business consultant*

## Treasure Island

Dunn, Craig Andrew *entertainer, conductor, writer, composer, educator*

## Trenton

Ivey, James Frederick, Jr. *health facility administrator, physician*

## Umatilla

Balandran, Stella Varona *interpreter, lyricist, composer, writer*

## University Park

Compain, Rita *librarian*
Walker, Jane Stewart *small business owner, publishing executive, educator*

## Valparaiso

Merritt, Phyllis June *music educator, director*

## Valrico

Hess, Bonnie B. *physical education educator, volleyball coach*
Jurch, George R., Jr. *retired science educator*
McCrystal, Jennifer Cross *elementary school educator*

## Venice

Asp, William George *librarian*
Barritt, Evelyn Ruth Berryman *nurse, educator, dean*
Bluhm, Barbara Jean *communications agency executive*
Clarke, Edward Owen, Jr. *lawyer*
Cool, Kim Patmore *editor, publishing executive, retail executive*
Corrigan, William Thomas *retired broadcast news executive*
Feldmann, Edward George *pharmaceutical chemist, pharmacologist*
Finlay, Susan Sparling *education educator*
Gabriele, Charles *composer, educator*
Girman, Dee-Marie *artist, singer*
Gooding, Charles Thomas *psychologist, educator, retired academic administrator*
Hrachovina, Frederick Vincent *retired osteopathic physician*
Kleinlein, Kathy Lynn *training and development executive*
Lanford, Luke Dean *retired electronics company executive*
Meyerhoff, Jack Fulton *corporate financial executive*
Miller, Allan John *lawyer*
Nevins, John J. *bishop*
Przemienicki, Janusz Stanislaw *engineering executive, former government senior executive and college dean*
Slate, Floyd Owen *retired engineering educator*
Tausan, Carol A. *music educator*

## Vero Beach

Ahrensfeld, Thomas Frederick *retired lawyer*
Bennett, Jack Franklin *oil industry executive*
Beran, Denis Carl *publisher*
Binney, Jan Jarrell *publishing executive, marketing professional*
Bright, Willard Mead *retired manufacturing executive, retired director*
Case, Douglas Manning *lawyer*
Christopher, Robert Paul *retired physical medicine physician*
Clokey, Rebecca Louise *minister*
Conway, Earl Cranston *business educator, retired manufacturing company executive, educator*
Crosby, John Griffith *investment banker*
Darsie, Richard Floyd, Jr. *medical entomologist*
David, Ivo *artist, poet, real estate broker*
Enhorning, Goran *obstetrician, gynecologist*
Ferrell, Catherine K. *sculptor, painter*
Fisher, Andrew *management consultant*
Fitzgeorge, Harold James *former oil and gas company executive*
Freeman, Donald Wilford *real estate developer, horse breeder*
Gedeon, Lucinda Heyel *museum director*
Grimes, Howard Ray *management consultant*

Hardie, James Carl *academic administrator, consultant*
Harris, Nancy Lee *special education educator, behavior analyst*
Havens, Charles William III *retired lawyer*
Higgs, John H. *lawyer*
Hilker, Robert Reuben John *medical educator, researcher, administrator, consultant*
Ingwersen, Martin Lewis *water transportation executive*
Janicki, Robert Stephen *retired pharmaceutical executive*
Kamman, Alan Bertram *communications consulting company executive*
Koontz, Alfred Joseph, Jr. *financial analyst, consultant*
Leonsis, Ted *media executive, professional sports team executive*
Massey, Howard Clayland *writer*
McNamara, John J(oseph) *advertising executive, writer*
Nichols, Carl Wheeler *retired advertising agency executive*
Proctor, William Gilbert, Jr. *writer*
Reed, Sherman Kennedy *chemicals executive, consultant*
Riefler, Donald Brown *financial consultant*
Satuloff, Barth *accountant, dispute resolution professional, investment strategist, publishing executive, rancher*
Schwarz, Berthold Eric *psychiatrist*
Sheehan, Charles Vincent *investment banker*
Spivak, Alvin A. *retired public relations executive*
Standish, John Spencer *textile manufacturing company executive*
Wilcox, Harry Wilbur, Jr. *retired manufacturing executive*

**Village Of Golf**
Birle, James Robb *investor*
Boer, F. Peter *chemical company executive*
Sutter, William Paul *lawyer*

**Weeki Wachee**
Finney, Roy Pelham, Jr. *urologist, surgeon, inventor*
Luffsey, Walter Stith *air transportation executive, consultant*

**Wellington**
Guillama-Alvarez, Noel Jesus *merchant banker, healthcare executive*

**Wesley Chapel**
Mendelsohn, Louis Benjamin *financial analyst*
Revelle, Donald Gene *manufacturing and health care company executive, consultant*

**West Palm Beach**
Aaron, M. Robert *electrical engineer*
Ackerman, David P. *lawyer*
Addison, Ferguson Lofton Lightbourne *retired bank executive*
Barre, Steven Craig *lawyer*
Beall, Kenneth Sutter, Jr. *lawyer*
Beasley, James W., Jr. *lawyer*
Benavides, Christopher *special education educator*
Bergmann, Arthur M. *writer, retired journalist, retired county official*
Bernhardt, Marcia Brenda *mental health counselor*
Bregman, Howard *lawyer*
Brown, Paul A. *medical services executive*
Brumback, Clarence Landen *physician*
Burgess, R. Brandon (Roy Brandon Burgess) *communications executive*
Chopin, L. Frank *lawyer*
Chopin, Susan Gardiner *lawyer*
Clark, David William *lawyer, councilman*
Clarke, David H. *industrial products executive*
Coloso, Victor Francisco *pediatrician*
Conrad, Bette Anne Kester *lawyer, writer, minister*
Cooper, Margaret Leslie *lawyer*
Coppock, Mark Stephen *not-for-profit executive*
Coyle, Dennis Patrick *lawyer, retired utilities executive*
Damsel, Charles H., Jr. *lawyer*
Darter, Jeffrey Allen *data processing professional*
Davis, Paul B. *retired mechanical engineer, civil engineer*
Doto, Paul Jerome *retired accountant*
Fanjul, Alfie, Jr., (Alfonso Fanjul) *food products executive*
Fanjul, Pepe (José Fanjul) *food products executive*
Floyd, Raymond Loran *professional golfer*
Furlaud, Richard Mortimer *pharmaceutical executive*
Gildan, Phillip Clarke *lawyer*
Giuffrida, Tom A. *publisher*
Gold, Bela *economist, educator*
Gottlieb, Andrew D. *aquatic ecologist*
Gronlund, Robert B. *art collector, fund raising consultant*
Groves, Ann M. *mathematician, educator*
Gu, Binhe *environmental scientist*
Hagerthey, Scot Edward *environmental scientist*
Hale, Marie Stoner *artistic director*
Henry, Rene Arthur *writer, consultant*
Henry, Thornton Montagu *lawyer*
Herrick, John Dennis *financial planner, consultant, retired food products executive*
Hill, Thomas William, Jr. *lawyer, educator*
Jenkins, Ruben Lee *chemicals executive*
Johnson, Martin Allen *publishing executive, artist*
Kamen, Michael Andrew *lawyer*
Kapnick, S. Jason *oncologist*
Kiely, Dan Ray *telecommunications industry executive, bank executive, consultant*
Koch, William I. *energy company executive*
Kramer, Eleanor *retired real estate broker, tax specialist, financial consultant*
Lamb, Kevin Thomas *lawyer*
Levin, Ronald Mitchell *geriatrician*
Link, Scott J. *lawyer*
Livingstone, John Leslie *accountant, economist, management consultant, educator*
Longhofer, Gordan Allen *art educator, performance artist*
Loring, Arthur *lawyer, diversified financial services company executive*
Lozito, Gilda Lelia *artist, painter*
Maktouf, Samir *education company executive*

Marker, Shaun James *lawyer*
Marshall-Beasley, Elizabeth *landscape architect*
Miller, Richard Jackson (Rick Miller) *lawyer*
Montgomery, Robert Morel, Jr. *lawyer*
Moore, George Crawford Jackson *lawyer*
Most-Levin, Carol Lynn *physician, geriatrician*
Mrachek, Lorin Louis *lawyer*
Newmark, Emanuel *ophthalmologist*
Nolan, Richard Thomas *clergyman, educator*
Ogden, John Clifton III *environmental scientist, director*
Orlovsky, Donald Albert *lawyer*
Orr-Cahall, Anona Christina *museum director, art historian*
Paine, James Carriger *federal judge*
Passy, Charles *writer*
Phillips, Kenneth Wayne *music educator*
Pingpank, Robert Charles *retired mathematics educator*
Pinsky, Mark A. *plastic surgeon*
Pottash, A. Carter *psychiatrist, hospital executive*
Raab, Ira Jerry *lawyer, judge*
Rhoads, B. Eric *entrepreneur, artist*
Robinson, Raymond Edwin *conductor, music educator, writer*
Ronan, William John *management consultant*
Rosen, Marvin Shelby *lawyer*
Ross, Edward Joseph *architect*
Royce, Raymond Watson *lawyer, rancher, citrus grower, investor*
Rukeyser, M.S., Jr. *television consultant, writer*
Scott, Adam *professional golfer*
Sears, Edward Milner, Jr. *newspaper editor*
Stauderman, Bruce Ford *advertising executive, writer*
Terry, Karen Elizabeth *lawyer*
Terwillegar, Jane Cusack *librarian, educator*
Thomashow, Steven Roy *military officer, intelligence officer*
Vecellio, Leo Arthur, Jr. *construction company executive*
Vilchez, Victoria Anne *lawyer*
Westman, Steven Ronald *rabbi*
Whitfield, Graham Frank *orthopedic surgeon*
Wisnicki, Jeffrey Leonard *plastic surgeon*
Zeller, Ronald John *lawyer*

**Weston**
Alexander, Cynthia Louise *psychologist, educator*
Barnes, William Douglas *advertising executive*
Faierman, Tamy M. *plastic surgeon*
Gamarra, Alberto Neil *psychologist, educator*
Gordon, Lori Heyman *psychotherapist, author, educator*
Holtzman, Gary Yale *retired diversified financial services company executive*
Kortlander, Susan Elizabeth *psychologist*
Malave, Andres *pharmacologist, educator*
McGovern, Mark Edward *pharmaceutical company executive, researcher*
Messa, Charles Angelo III *plastic surgeon*
Napp, Gudrun F. *artist*
Nogueras, Juan Jose *surgeon*
Samson, Michel Charles *plastic surgeon*

**Wewahitchka**
de Abreu, Sue *elementary school educator*
Stryker, Terence Wayne *secondary school educator*

**Wilton Manors**
Kaufmann, Vicki Marie *social services administrator*

**Wimauma**
Palmer, Louis Thomas *pathologist*
Shober, Amy *education educator*

**Windermere**
Hahn, Dowon *pharmaceutical researcher, educator*
McGuire, Edward David, Jr. *lawyer*

**Winter Garden**
Ellis, Missie Lynne *music educator*
Gillet, Pamela Kipping *special education educator*
Reeher, James Irwin *minister*

**Winter Haven**
Benton, Obie Folsom *publishing executive, writer*
Boully, LaJuan Bonnie *minister, religious studies educator*
Burns, Arthur Lee *architect*
Goodman, Karen Lacerte *financial services executive*
Grierson, William *retired agriculturist*
Johnson, Gordon Selby *consulting electrical engineer*
Schepis, Anthony Joseph *artist, educator*
Susac, John Obren *neurologist, consultant*

**Winter Park**
Alfond, Theodore B. *retired shoe company executive*
Baker, James L., Jr. *plastic surgeon*
Benedict, Dorothy Jones *genealogist, researcher*
Beute, Brian Arthur *music educator*
Bloodworth, Velda Jean *librarian, educator*
Blossey, Erich Carl *chemistry professor*
Carpan, Ann Carolyn *school librarian, educator*
Dempsey, Bernard Hayden, Jr. *lawyer*
Figner, William James *computer engineer*
Granberry, Edwin Phillips, Jr. *safety engineer, consultant*
Gray, Anthony Rollin *retired finance company executive*
Hadley, Ralph Vincent III *lawyer*
Haendiges, Anne R. *marriage and family therapist*
Halladay, Laurie Ann *public relations consultant, food products executive*
Heinle, Richard Alan *lawyer*
Jernigan, Donald *hospital administrator*
Jontz, Jeffry Robert *lawyer*
Kaston, Lisa Marsha *social services administrator*
Kincaid, Rodney Lyle *construction company executive*
Kindlund, Newton Carlton *retail executive*
Koltko-Rivera, Mark Edward *research scientist*
Kraft, Kenneth Houston, Jr. *insurance agency executive*
LaCognata, John Patrick *music educator*
Ladha-Karmali, Shainoor *lawyer*

Mason, Aimee Hunnicutt Romberger *retired philosophy and humanities educator*
McKean, Thomas Wayne *dentist, retired military officer*
Merrill, Harvie Martin *manufacturing executive, director*
Morgan, Mary Ann *lawyer*
Olsson, Nils William *former association executive*
Pineless, Hal Steven *neurologist*
Powers, Ronald George *management consultant*
Rogers, Rutherford David *librarian*
Rooks, Linda *writer*
Seymour, Thaddeus *language educator*
Starr, Martin Kenneth *management educator*
Steward, Sherry Ann *information technology executive, educator*
Therrien, Francois Xavier, Jr. *business and tax consultant*
Troutman, Holmes Russell *lawyer*
Wallace, Curtis Wilbern, Jr. *music director, organist*
Whitworth, Hall Baker *forest products company executive*
Wilson, Robley Conant, Jr. *language educator, editor, writer*
Wrancher, Elizabeth Ann *music educator, opera singer*
Zhang, Wenxian *librarian*
Zivot, Eric *actor, educator*

**Winter Springs**
San Miguel, Manuel *painter, writer*

**Zephyrhills**
Anderson, Lisa D. *graphics designer, educator*
Barron, Ilona Eleanor *secondary school educator, consultant*
Walton, Shirley Dawn *retired medical technician*

## GEORGIA

**Acworth**
Hutchins, Robert William *social studies educator, military officer*
Oloni, Anthony Olushegun *medical association administrator, director*

**Adairsville**
Dobson, Suzanne *science educator*

**Albany**
Carmichael, Ann Louise *elementary school educator*
Forsyth, Rosalyn Moye *middle school educator*
Jenkins, Patricia Ann *early childhood educator*
Johnson, Debra Pope *education educator*
Keith, Carolyn Austin *secondary school counselor*
Marbury, Ritchey McGuire III *engineering executive, surveyor*
Peach, Paul E. *physician, health facility administrator*
Revills, Isaiah *minister*
Robinson, J. Mack *communications executive*
Rodriguez, Sergio Raul *music educator, conductor*
Shields, Portia Holmes *academic administrator*
Stallworth, Charles Derotha, Jr. *psychologist*
Wernick, Joel *health facility administrator*
Wooden, Ontario Sherrod *academic administrator*
Young, Scott Christopher *music educator, musician*

**Alpharetta**
Adams, Kenneth Francis *automotive executive*
Balows, Albert *microbiologist, educator*
Bolton, Robin Jean *artist, painter*
Braxton, Jerry W. *communications executive*
Bridges, Alan Lynn *physicist, researcher, application developer, computer scientist*
Chatlen, Stanley Lee *transportation executive*
Cline, Stewart M. *real estate executive*
Corby, Francis Michael, Jr. *finance company executive*
Deitrich, Wayne H. *manufacturing executive*
Esher, Brian Richard *manufacturing executive*
Filliat, Elizabeth Hartley *retired secondary school educator*
Fowler, Vivian Delores *insurance company executive*
Freeman, Douglas K. *bank executive*
Greene, Melinda Jean *retail maintenance analyst*
Harris, James Herman *pathologist, neuropathologist, consultant, educator*
Hatcher, Barbara A. *lawyer*
Heyman, John H. *energy executive*
Johnston, William David *biotechnologist, director*
Kurtz, Robert Arthur *finance company executive*
Lademacher, Hartmut *computer software and services company executive*
Marsella, Anthony Joseph *psychologist, educator*
McCormick, James K. *application developer*
McCullough, Ross A., Jr. *delivery service executive*
Mock, Melinda Smith *orthopedic nurse specialist, consultant*
Mulhauser, Craig H. *energy executive*
Rettig, Helen B. *construction executive*
Roberts, Paul C. *paper company executive*
Smith, Derek V. *risk management consultant*
Thomas, Robert L. *retired manufacturing company executive*
Thompson, Peter J. *manufacturing executive*
Travers, James M. *application developer*
Walker, Thomas H. *industrial designer*
Weitz, John Jerome, Jr. *city planner*
Whitley, Lena Frances *French educator*
Yeatman, Henry Clay *mechanical engineer*

**Americus**
Capitan, William Harry *university president emeritus*
Hooks, George Bardin *state legislator, insurance and real estate company executive*
Isaacs, Harold *history professor*
Palmer, Edward Kent *charitable organization executive*
Reckford, Jonathan Thomas More *nonprofit organization administrator*
Stanford, Henry King *college president*

**Andersonville**
Boyles, Frederick Holdren *historian*

**Athens**
Abdel-Hadi, Ali Ismail *engineer, educator*
Adams, Michael Fred *academic administrator, political scientist, educator*
Algeo, John Thomas *association executive, retired educator*
Allsbrook, Ogden Olmstead, Jr. *retired economics professor*
Andrews, Grover Jene *adult education educator, administrator*
Annis, Patricia Anne *textile engineer, educator*
Avise, John Charles *geneticist, educator*
Baile, Clifton A. *biologist, researcher*
Bargmann, Rolf Erwin *computer scientist, educator*
Beard, James Ralph *lawyer, educator, dean*
Bennetzen, Jeffrey L. *molecular biologist*
Benson, P. George *dean, finance educator*
Bertsch, Gary Kenneth *political science professor*
Black, Clanton Candler, Jr. *biochemistry professor, researcher*
Black, Marsha C. *environmental scientist*
Bowen, John Metcalf *pharmacologist, toxicologist, educator*
Box, Elgene Owen *ecologist, educator*
Bullock, Charles Spencer III *political science educator, author, consultant*
Carlson, Ronald Lee *law educator*
Castenell, Louis Anthony *academic administrator*
Cederbaum, Sandra Bloomfield *biologist*
Chaffin, Verner Franklin *lawyer, educator*
Chu, Chung Kwang *medicinal chemistry professor*
Clute, Robert Eugene *political science professor*
Crowley, John Francis III *university dean*
Cunningham, Tess *marketing professional*
Darvill, Alan G. *biochemist, botanist, educator*
Delgado, Mark Crawford *chemist, educator*
DeZurko, Edward Robert *art educator*
Donovan, James M. *librarian, anthropologist*
Dunham, Richard E. III *lighting designer, consultant, set designer, educator*
Dunn, Delmer Delano *political science professor*
Ellington, Charles Ronald *lawyer, educator*
Feldman, Edmund Burke *art critic*
Fincher, Cameron Lane *psychology professor*
Fink, Conrad Charles *journalist, educator, communications executive, consultant*
Freer, Coburn *language educator*
Garbin, Albeno Patrick *sociology educator*
Harshman, Melissa Ann *art educator*
Hellerstein, Walter *lawyer*
Herbert, James Arthur *retired art educator, artist, filmmaker*
Houser, Ronald Edward *lawyer, arbitrator, mediator*
Huszagh, Fredrick Wickett *lawyer, educator, information technology executive*
Johnson, Michael Kenneth *chemistry professor*
Kamerschen, David Roy *economist, educator*
Kaufman, Glen Frank *art educator*
Kretzschmar, William Addison, Jr. *language educator*
Kurtz, Paul Michael *law educator*
Law, John Harold *biochemistry educator*
McAlister, Sheila Anne *archivist*
McBee, Mary Louise *retired state legislator, retired academic administrator*
McCutcheon, Steven Clifton *ecological and environmental engineer, hydrologist*
Melton, Wayne Charles *real estate executive*
Miller, Herbert Elmer *accountant*
Miller, Ronald Baxter *language educator, writer*
Nelson, Stuart Owen *agricultural engineer, researcher, educator*
Nichols, William Curtis *psychologist, educator, marriage and family therapist, consultant*
Oh, Yongseok *physicist*
Olsen, Richard James *artist, educator*
Paul, William Dewitt, Jr. *retired art educator, photographer, videographer, museum director*
Pollack, Robert Harvey *psychology professor*
Potter, William Gray, Jr. *library director*
Power, Chandra Lynn *elementary school educator*
Puckett, Elizabeth Ann *law librarian, educator*
Richt, Mark *college football coach*
Schaefer, Henry Frederick III *chemistry professor*
Shipley, David Elliott *lawyer, educator*
Shockley, Floyd Wayne *entomologist*
Shoemaker, Rene Denise *librarian, artist*
Smagorinsky, Peter *education educator*
Smith, Susan Carlton *artist, illustrator*
Soloski, John *journalism and communications educator*
Staub, August William *theater producer, educator*
Stipe, Michael *musician, film producer*
Thomas, Patricia Joanne *journalist, writer*
Tolley, Edward Donald *lawyer*
Toma, J. Douglas *education educator*
Tyler, David Earl *retired veterinary medical educator*
Wessler, Susan R. *biologist, educator*
White, Rebecca Hanner *dean, law educator*
Wraga, William Gerard *education educator*
Yang, Charles Qi-Xiang *chemistry educator, researcher, consultant*
Yen, William Mao-Shung *physicist, consultant*
Ziemke, Earl Frederick *history professor, researcher*
Zinkhan, George Martin III *marketing educator*

**Atlanta**
Aaberg, Thomas Marshall, Sr. *academic administrator*
Aaron, Hank (Henry L. Aaron) *professional baseball team executive*
Abbott, Herschel Lee, Jr. *lawyer*
Abdel-Khalik, Said Ibrahim *nuclear and mechanical engineering educator*
Abdul-Ghaffar, Aswad Jawhar *physiologist, consultant*
Abernathy, Thomas Edwards, IV, *lawyer*
Abrams, Harold Eugene *lawyer*
Adams, David Porterfield III *business appraiser*
Addison, James W. *lawyer*
Affonso, Dyanne D. *dean*
Aiken, Vernoy Fred *government agency administrator*
Albert, Ross Alan *lawyer*

Aldridge, John *lawyer*
Alexander, Alonzo III *music educator, composer*
Alexander, Cecil Abraham *academic administrator, consultant, retired architect*
Alexander, Kent B. *lawyer*
Alexander, Miles Jordan *lawyer*
Allan, Alexander R.C. (Sandy Allan) *food products executive*
Allen, Pinney L. *lawyer*
Allen, Randall L. *lawyer*
Alleyne, Mark Dacosta *communications educator, journalist*
Allison, Stuart Anthony *chemistry professor, researcher*
Altman, Robert *lawyer*
Amanpour, Christiane *news correspondent*
Ames, William Francis *mathematician, educator*
Anderson, Al H., Jr. *communications executive*
Anderson, Barbara Allen *alcohol/drug abuse services professional, archivist*
Anderson, Peter Joseph *lawyer*
Anstrom, Decker *broadcast executive*
Anthony, Barbara Cox *foundation administrator*
Antunes, Joël *chef*
Appeadu, Charles Edward *finance educator, researcher*
Arani, Ardy A. *marketing professional, sports association administrator*
Arroyo, F. Thaddeus *telecommunications industry executive*
Arthur, Thomas Carlton *former dean, law educator*
Asbill, Richard M. *lawyer*
Ashby, Eugene Christopher *chemistry professor*
Attridge, Richard Byron *lawyer*
Austin, Dallas *record company executive, producer*
Austin, Jeannette Holland *genealogist, writer*
Austin, Jesse Hinnant III *lawyer*
Austin, Johnta *musician*
Bahl, Roy Winford *economist, educator, consultant*
Bainbridge, Frederick Freeman III *architect*
Baird, Marianne Saunours *critical care clinical nurse specialist, administrator*
Baker, Thomas William *lawyer*
Baker, Thurbert E. *state attorney general*
Bales, Virginia Shankle *health science association administrator*
Bankoff, Joseph R. *art association administrator*
Banks, Marvin R., Jr. *investment company executive*
Bao, Gang *biomedical engineer, educator*
Barker, William Daniel *hospital administrator*
Barkoff, Rupert Mitchell *lawyer*
Barksdale, Richard Dillon *civil engineer, educator*
Barnard, Patricia A. *human resources specialist*
Barnes, David A. *delivery service executive*
Barnett, Preston B. *lawyer, communications executive*
Barr, Robert Laurence, Jr. *lawyer*
Barron, Patrick Kenneth *bank executive*
Barros, Paulino R. *communications executive*
Barwick, William D. *lawyer*
Bassett, Peter Q. *lawyer*
Bastian, Edward H. *air transportation executive*
Batson, Richard Neal *lawyer*
Bawa, Avantika *artist, educator*
Beazer, Brian C. *construction executive*
Beckham, Walter Hull III *lawyer*
Bekkers, John *food products executive*
Bell, Griffin Boyette *lawyer, former United States attorney general*
Bellamy, Ivory *elementary school educator, consultant*
Bellamy, Walter *professional basketball player*
Bellanca, Joseph Paul *engineering construction executive*
Benario, Herbert William *classicist, educator*
Benham, Robert *state supreme court justice*
Bennett, Jay D. *lawyer*
Benston, George James *accountant, economist*
Benveniste, Lawrence M. *dean*
Bergeson, Donna Pottis *lawyer*
Berkelhamer, Jay Ellis *pediatrician*
Bernardino, Carlo Roberto *ophthalmologist, educator*
Berry, Dennis (G. Dennis Berry) *publishing executive*
Betts, Jennifer Leah *secondary school educator*
Betty, Charles Garry (Garry Betty) *Internet company executive*
Beystehner, John J. *transportation executive*
Bibb, Daniel Roland *art restorer*
Biggins, J. Veronica *bank executive*
Bihary, Joyce *federal judge*
Billington, Barry E. *lawyer*
Birch, Stanley Francis, Jr. *federal judge*
Bird, Francis Marion, Jr. *lawyer*
Bird, Wendell Raleigh *lawyer*
Birdsong, Alta Marie *volunteer*
Bisher, James Furman *journalist, writer*
Black, Kenneth, Jr. *retired insurance company executive*
Blackburn, William Stanley *lawyer*
Blackstock, Jerry B. *lawyer*
Blake, Francis Stanton *retail executive, lawyer*
Blank, A(ndrew) Russell *lawyer*
Bloodworth, Albert William Franklin *lawyer*
Blum, Terry C. *dean*
Boisseau, Richard Robert *lawyer*
Bolch, Carl Edward, Jr. *petroleum company executive, lawyer*
Bonds, John Wilfred, Jr. *lawyer*
Bondurant, Emmet Jopling, II, *lawyer*
Boone, J. William *lawyer*
Boone, John Temple *lawyer*
Booth, Gordon Dean, Jr. *lawyer*
Bostic, James E., Jr. *paper company executive*
Bostwick, John III *plastic surgeon, department chairman, medical educator*
Bowden, Henry Lumpkin, Jr. *lawyer*
Bowling, Daniel S. III *lawyer*
Bradshaw, Rod Eric *personnel consultant*
Braine, David Thomas *university athletic director*
Branch, Thomas Broughton III *lawyer*
Brandenburg, David Saul *gastroenterologist, educator*
Bratton, James Henry, Jr. *lawyer*
Brecher, Armin George *lawyer*
Brelsford, Theodore William, Jr. *theology studies educator*

Bremner, James Douglas *psychiatrist, researcher, education educator*
Brewster, William Howard *lawyer*
Brice Ross, Carla Yvette *school counselor*
Bridges, Shirley Walton *air transportation executive*
Bright, David Forbes *academic administrator, classicist, educator*
Broadnax, Walter D. *university president, educator*
Brock, John F. *beverage company executive*
Brown, Janine *lawyer*
Brown, Lorene B(yron) *retired library educator*
Brown-Olmstead, Amanda *public relations executive*
Bryant, Gregory Alexander *bishop*
Buffenstein, Daryl R. *lawyer*
Bull, Frank James *retired architect*
Buoch, William Thomas *corporate executive*
Burandt, Michael Charles *lumber company executive, paper company executive, chemicals executive, consumer products company executive*
Burdell, George P. *retired mechanical engineer*
Burge, William Lee *retired credit manager*
Burns, Thomas Samuel *history professor*
Burstein, Fernando David *plastic surgeon*
Butler, Gloria Singleton *state legislator*
Butler, Richard J. *federal agency administrator, consultant*
Butterworth, S. Kendall *lawyer*
Byrne, Granville Bland III *lawyer*
Cadenhead, Alfred Paul *lawyer*
Calhoun, David *lawyer*
Cantley, Kevin Rilous *architectural firm executive*
Capper, Natasha Lee *pastry chef*
Carbonell, Joaquin R. III *telecommunications industry executive, lawyer*
Carley, George H. *state supreme court justice*
Carnes, Julie Elizabeth *judge*
Carpenter, David Allan *lawyer*
Carroll, Blayne Earl *mathematics educator*
Carson, Christopher Leonard *lawyer*
Carter, Jimmy (James Earl Carter Jr.) *39th President of the United States*
Carter, Stephen M. *telecommunications manufacturing industry executive*
Cates, Christopher Upton *cardiologist*
Cathy, S. Truett *food products executive*
Cavin, Kristine Smith *lawyer*
Chafee, Ingrid Roberta Hoover Coleman *retired language educator*
Chambers, Anne Cox *publishing executive, former diplomat*
Chambers, Robert William *diversified financial services company executive*
Chandler, Robert Charles *healthcare consultant*
Chapman, Hugh McMaster *banker*
Chartier, Kirk Lee Freund *business services executive*
Chasen, Sylvan Herbert *data processing executive, financial planner*
Chau, Pin Pin *bank executive*
Chiang, Tze I. *economist, researcher, consultant*
Chilivis, Nickolas Peter *retired lawyer*
Chisholm, Tommy *lawyer, utilities executive*
Cilella, Mary Winifred *director*
Circeo, Louis Joseph, Jr. *research scientist, civil engineer*
Clarke, Thomas Hal *lawyer*
Cleage, Pearl Michelle *writer, playwright, journalist*
Clift, W.E. *telecommunications industry executive*
Clough, Gerald Wayne (Wayne Clough) *academic administrator*
Cobb, Charles Kenche, Jr. *lawyer, real estate broker*
Cohen, Ezra Harry *lawyer*
Cohen, George Leon *lawyer*
Cohen, Lori G. *lawyer*
Cohen, N. Jerold *lawyer*
Coleman, Terry Lewis *state legislator*
Collins, Steven M. *lawyer*
Compans, Richard W. *microbiology educator*
Comstock, Robert Donald, Jr. *real estate executive*
Conboy, Kevin *lawyer*
Concha, Mario *chemicals executive*
Connell, Paul J. *lawyer*
Connelly, Terrence John, Sr. *television and cable station executive*
Cook, Don Lloyd *lawyer, consultant, marketing educator*
Cook, John M. *retired finance company executive*
Cook, Philip Carter *lawyer*
Cooper, Gerald Rice *clinical pathologist*
Cooper, Jerome Maurice *architect*
Cooper, Thomas Luther *retired printing company executive*
Cooper-Ruspoli, Annie Nataf *psychiatrist, director*
Copenhaver, John Barns *not-for-profit executive, lawyer*
Corr, James Vanis *furniture manufacturing executive, accountant*
Costello, John H. III *business and marketing executive*
Cowan, Keith O. *telecommunications industry executive*
Cox, Bobby (Robert Joe Cox) *professional baseball manager*
Cox, Cathy *state official*
Cox, Kathy *school system administrator*
Cox, Nancy Jane *microbiologist*
Cramer, Howard Ross *geologist, environmental consultant*
Cressler, John David *electrical engineering educator*
Crews, William Edwin *lawyer*
Croft, Terrence Lee *lawyer, mediator, arbitrator*
Culhane, John Joseph *lawyer*
Cummings, Alexander B., Jr. *food products executive*
Cupp, Robert Erhard *golf course architect, land use planner*
Curran, James W. *epidemiologist, educator, dean*
Curry, Toni Griffin *counseling center executive, consultant*
Curtis, J. Vaughan *lawyer*
Curtis, Philip Kerry *executive recruiter*
Cutshaw, Kenneth Andrew *lawyer*
Cwiak, Carrie Ann *obstetrician, gynecologist*
Dakhli, Mourad *finance educator*
Dalton, John Joseph *lawyer*

Danielson, Gilbert Lawrence *consumer products company executive*
Darden, Calvin *delivery service executive*
Darden, Claibourne Henry, Jr. *marketing research professional*
David, Todd R. *lawyer*
Davis, Benjamin Alando *lawyer*
Davis, D. Scott *corporate financial executive*
Davis, Erroll Brown, Jr. *academic administrator, former utilities executive*
Davis, Frank Tradewell, Jr. *lawyer*
Davis, Lawrence William *radiation oncologist*
Davis, Marvin Arnold *manufacturing executive*
Davis, Michael *medical educator*
Day, Janet S. *academic administrator*
Dayhoff, James Edward *retired state official*
Dean, James Edward *retired state official*
Deane, Richard Hunter, Jr. *former federal judge, lawyer*
DeAngelo, Joe *retail executive*
DeCosta, Benjamin R. *airport executive*
de la Vega, Ralph *wireless telecommunications industry executive*
Deming, N. Karen *lawyer*
Denmark, Darron B. *academic administrator*
Denny, Richard Alden, Jr. *retired lawyer*
DeRodes, Robert P. *manufacturing executive*
De Rosa, Christopher Thomas *biomedical researcher*
DeSimone, Samuel Richard *lawyer*
Despriet, John G. *lawyer*
de Waal, Frans B.M. *biologist, psychology professor*
Dickinson, Robert Earl *atmospheric scientist, educator, retired science administrator*
Diedrich, Richard Joseph *architect*
Dietz, William Harry *pediatrician*
Dobson, Bridget McColl Hursley *television executive, writer*
Domby, Arthur H. *lawyer*
Donald, James Edward *retired career officer, government agency executive*
Donovan, Dennis M. *manufacturing executive*
D'Orsi, Carl Joseph *medical educator, radiologist, researcher*
Dotson, Albert *not-for-profit fundraiser*
Douglas, J. Alexander M. (Sandy Douglas) *beverage company executive*
Douglas, John Lewis *lawyer*
Douglas, Lee (Charles Douglas) *basketball team executive*
Douglas, William W. *corporate financial executive*
Dowling, Roderick Anthony *investment banker*
Dramis, Francis (Fran) A., Jr. *communications executive*
Draper, Stephen Elliot *lawyer, engineer*
Driver, Walter W., Jr. *lawyer*
Duffey, William Simon, Jr. *federal judge, former prosecutor*
Duffie, L. Traywick *lawyer*
Dunlevie, Steven S. *lawyer*
Durrett, James Frazer, Jr. *retired lawyer*
Dutt, Kamla *medical educator*
Dykes, Ronald Mitchell *retired telecommunications industry executive*
Easterly, David Eugene *communications executive*
Eastman, Charles (Chuck) M. *architecture educator*
Eckert, Charles Alan *chemical engineering educator*
Eckl, William Wray *lawyer*
Edmondson, Earnest Eugene *secondary school educator*
Edmondson, J.L. (James Larry Edmondson) *federal judge*
Edson, Margaret *playwright*
Edwards, Stephen Allen *lawyer*
Egan, Michael Joseph *retired lawyer, state legislator*
Elgison, Martin J. *lawyer*
Ellingwood, Bruce Russell *structural engineer, educator*
Elliott, Mark Lee *lawyer*
Ellison, Earl Otto *computer scientist*
Eskew, Michael L. *package distribution company executive*
Esser, Patrick J. *communications executive*
Etheridge, Jack Paul *arbitrator, mediator, retired judge*
Evans, Orinda D. *federal judge*
Falk, Henry *pediatrician, epidemiologist, researcher*
Fancher, Kristen L. *lawyer*
Fanning, Thomas Andrew *corporate financial executive*
Farnham, Clayton Henson *lawyer*
Fayard, Gary P. *beverage company executive*
Feidler, Mark L. *telecommunications industry executive*
Feldman, Joel Martin *magistrate judge*
Felton, Jule Wimberly, Jr. *lawyer*
Fenton, Jeffrey J. *management consultant, wholesale distribution executive*
Fermanis, Ernest George *urological surgeon*
Fernandez, Frank L. *lawyer, retail executive*
Ferris, James Leonard *academic administrator*
Fifty Cent, (Curtis James Jackson) *rap artist*
Finan, Irial *beverage company executive*
Fine, Frederick L. *computer company executive, health products executive*
Finkelstein, David Ritz *physicist, educator, consultant*
Finley, Michael Valton *foundation executive*
Flagg Davis, Vivian Annette *librarian, researcher, public information officer*
Flannery, James William *performing arts educator, theater director, singer*
Fleming, Julian Denver, Jr. *lawyer*
Fletcher, Kathy Jordan *music educator*
Fleury, Marc *application developer*
Flynn, Owen V. *information technology executive*
Foege, William Herbert *public health administrator, educator*
Foley, James David *computer scientist, educator*
Forbes, Theodore McCoy, Jr. *arbitrator, mediator, retired lawyer*
Forney, Larry J. *chemical engineer, educator*
Forry, Robert H. *lawyer*
Fortenberry, James Donald *pediatrician*
Fortin, Judy *cable news anchor*
Fortin, Raymond D. *lawyer*

Fowler, Bruce Andrew *toxicologist, researcher, public health service official*
Fox, John T. *health facility administrator*
Fox, Ronald Forrest *physicist, educator*
Fox-Genovese, Elizabeth Ann Teresa *humanities educator*
Frank, Erica *preventive medicine physician*
Franklin, Shirley Clarke *mayor*
Frederick, Paula J. *lawyer*
Freedman, Louis Martin *dentist*
Frias, Jaime Luis *retired pediatrician, educator*
Fry-Johnson, Yvonne Wilkins *pediatrician*
Fuller, S(heri) Marce *energy executive*
Gailey, Chan, Jr. (Thomas Chandler Gailey) *college football coach*
Galambos, John Thomas *internist, medical educator*
Gallagher, Thomas C. *diversified manufacturing executive*
Gambrell, David Henry *lawyer*
Ganaway, George Kenneth *psychiatrist, psychoanalyst, educator, researcher*
Garland, LaRetta Matthews *psychologist, nursing educator*
Gary, Marc *lawyer*
Gay, Robert Derril *behavioral health consultant*
Gayle, Helene D. *pediatrician, public health service officer*
Gayles, Joseph Nathan, Jr. *medical association administrator, not-for-profit fundraiser, chemist*
Genberg, Ira *lawyer*
Gerakitis, Richard *lawyer*
Gerberding, Julie Louise *federal agency administrator*
Gibson, Michael Allen *music educator*
Giddens, Don Peyton *engineering educator, researcher*
Gignilliat, R. Read *lawyer*
Girth, Marjorie Louisa *lawyer, educator*
Glass, Roger I. *virologist*
Goizueta, Javier C. *beverage company executive*
Goizueta, Olga (Olga Casteleiro de Goizueta) *foundation administrator, philanthropist*
Goizueta Rawls, Olga Maria *lawyer*
Gold, Hazel *Spanish language educator*
Goldman, John Abner *rheumatologist, immunologist, educator*
Goldstein, Elliott *lawyer, director*
Gonzalez, Ruben Rene *biochemist, researcher*
Goodwin, George Evans *public relations executive*
Gordon, Frank Jeffrey *medical educator*
Grady, Kevin E. *lawyer*
Gramlich, Larry E. *lawyer*
Grant, Susan *television executive*
Graves, Judson *lawyer*
Greco, Anthony Joseph *artist, educator, dean*
Green, Holcombe Tucker, Jr. *investment company executive*
Greene, Kevin C. *lawyer*
Greer, Bernard Lewis (Ben), Jr. *lawyer*
Gregory, Henry D., Jr. *real estate company executive*
Gregory, Mel Hyatt, Jr. *retired insurance company executive*
Gregory, Wilton D. *archbishop*
Grice, Richard W. *lawyer*
Grinstein, Gerald *air transportation executive*
Groton, James Purnell *lawyer, arbitrator*
Grout, Robert W. *lawyer*
Grumet, Priscilla Hecht *fashion specialist, consultant, writer*
Guberman, Sidney *painter, writer*
Guest, Rita Carson *interior designer*
Hackett, Stanley Hailey *lawyer*
Hakes, Jay Edward *library director, former federal agency administrator*
Hall, Beverly L. *school system administrator*
Hall, Wilbur Dallas, Jr. *medical educator*
Hallen, Barry *philosopher, educator*
Hanagud, Sathyanaraya V. *aerospace engineer, educator*
Hanna, Frank Joseph, Jr. *credit company executive*
Hanthorn, Dennis Wayne *performing arts association administrator*
Haralson, Michael *real estate agent*
Hardman, John B. *psychiatrist, director*
Harkey, Robert Shelton *retired lawyer*
Harris, Harold Stephen, Jr. *lawyer*
Harrison, George Brooks *engineer, researcher, retired military officer*
Hartle, Robert Wyman *retired literature and language professor*
Hartley, Bob *professional hockey coach*
Harvey, Adia M. *sociology professor*
Harvey, James A. *lawyer*
Hasson, James Keith, Jr. *lawyer, educator*
Hatcher, Charles Ross, Jr. *surgeon, health facility administrator*
Hatcher, James A. *lawyer*
Hawks, Barrett Kingsbury *lawyer*
Hay, Peter Heinrich *law educator*
Hayes, Jimmy W. *media company executive*
Hays, Richard R. *lawyer*
Heberton, George H. *lawyer*
Henry, John Dunklin, Sr. *hospital executive*
Henry, Ronald James Whyte *academic administrator, physicist, educator*
Henry, Thomas Reid *education educator, researcher*
Herman, John C. *lawyer*
Hewitt, Paul Harrington *basketball coach*
Higginbotham, Eve Juliet *ophthalmologist, educator, dean*
Higgins, Shaun Brian *beverage company executive*
Hill, Allen Edward *transportation services executive*
Hilliard, Robert Glenn *insurance company executive, lawyer*
Hinchey, John William *lawyer*
Hines, Preston Harris *state supreme court justice*
Hinson, H. Douglas *lawyer*
Hodges, Dewey Harper *aerospace engineer, educator*
Hoff, Gerhardt Michael *lawyer, insurance company executive*
Hoffman, Fred L. *human resources specialist*
Hogan, John Donald *retired college dean, finance educator*
Hollis, Timothy Martin *bank executive*
Holtzheimer, Paul E. III *medical educator*
Honaman, J. Craig *health facility administrator*

Stokes, James Sewell *environmental services administrator, not-for-profit developer*
Stormont, Richard Mansfield *hotel executive*
Strekowski, Lucjan *chemistry professor*
Su, Kendall Ling-Chiao *engineering educator*
Summerlin, Glenn Wood *retired advertising executive*
Swanagan, Jeffery S. *aquarium administrator*
Sweeney, Neal James *lawyer*
Swift, Frank Meador *lawyer*
Tanenbaum, Allan Jay *lawyer*
Tanner, W(alter) Rhett *lawyer*
Taylor, Andrew T., Jr. *radiologist, educator*
Taylor, George Kimbrough, Jr. *lawyer*
Taylor, Mark *lieutenant governor*
Taylor, Robert N. *medical researcher, department chairman*
Taylor, Tom *marketing executive*
Teepen, Thomas Henry *editor, journalist*
Tennant, Thomas Michael *lawyer*
Tentzeris, Emmanouil Manos *engineering educator, researcher*
Terrel, James E. *controller*
Terwilliger, J. Ronald *real estate company executive*
Thacker, Stephen Brady *medical association administrator, epidemiologist*
Thomas, Able Mable *communications executive, state legislator, councilwoman*
Thomas, Lizanne *lawyer*
Thomas, Peter Charles *psychologist, educator*
Thompson, Herbert Alden *microbiologist, public health scientist*
Thompson, Hugh P. *state supreme court justice*
Thompson, Shirley Williams *mathematics professor*
Thompson, Wallace Reeves III *physical education educator*
Thorpe, Jane Fugate *lawyer*
Thrower, Randolph William *lawyer*
Thuesen, Gerald Jorgen *industrial engineer, educator*
Thursby, Jerry Gilbert *economics professor, consultant, department chairman*
Tilley, Tana Marie *pharmaceutical executive*
Tillman, Mary Norman *urban affairs consultant*
Tincher, Wayne Coleman *engineering educator*
Tomaszewski, Richard Paul *market representation executive*
Tome, Carol B. *corporate financial executive*
Toner, Michael F. *journalist*
Towslee, Janet L. *special education educator*
Travis, Robert M. *lawyer*
Tucker, Cynthia Anne *journalist*
Tuggle, Clyde Cebron *beverage company executive*
Udoff, Eric Joel *diagnostic radiologist*
Vachio, Vincent J. *consumer products company executive*
Vachon, Reginald Irenee *mechanical engineer*
Van Houten, G. David, Jr. *beverage company executive*
Varner, Chilton Davis *lawyer*
Vaughn, Michael S. *law educator*
Verrill, F. Glenn *advertising executive*
Vigtel, Gudmund *retired museum director*
Villwock, Kenneth James *management company executive*
Vito, Raymond P. *engineering educator, researcher*
Vulgamore, Allison *performing arts association administrator*
Waddell, Don *professional sports team executive*
Wade, Nicole Jennings *lawyer*
Wagner, James Warren *academic administrator, engineering educator*
Wakefield, Stephen Alan *lawyer*
Wald, Michael Leonard *economist*
Wallace, Gladys Baldwin *librarian*
Wallace, Julia Diane *newspaper editor*
Wallace, Peter Marsden *radio producer, commentator, writer*
Walsh, W. Terence *lawyer*
Walton, Carole Lorraine *clinical social worker*
Walton, Jim *news network executive*
Wang, Yuhang *science educator*
Ward, Horace Taliaferro *federal judge*
Waring, George Oral III *ophthalmologist, surgeon*
Warren, Stephen Theodore *human geneticist, educator*
Waters, John W. *minister, educator*
Watkins, Tionne (T-Boz) *singer*
Weatherly, Alvis Morrison, Jr. *retired association developer*
Webb, Robert W., Jr. *lawyer*
Weed, Roger Oren *rehabilitation services professional, educator*
Weidman, Sheila *marketing professional*
Wellon, Robert G. *lawyer*
Wells, James M. III *bank executive*
Wenger, Nanette Kass *cardiologist, researcher, educator*
Wesley, Nicole Leigh *dancer, choreographer*
Westney, Gloria Elaine *medical educator*
Weyand, Cornelia M. *medical educator*
Wheeler, Chris D. *investment company executive*
White, Benjamin Taylor *lawyer*
White, Ronald Leon *financial management consultant*
Whitt, Richard Ernest *reporter*
Wieland, John *real estate executive*
Wiesenfeld, Kurt Arn *physicist, researcher*
Wiglesworth, Michael Bland *advertising executive*
Wigmore, Steven P. *lawyer*
Wilding, Diane *computer scientist, consultant*
Williams, David Howard *lawyer*
Williams, James Bryan *banker*
Williams, Neil, Jr. *lawyer*
Williams, Ralph Watson, Jr. *retired security firm executive*
Williams, Robert P., II, *lawyer*
Williams, Sondra Beth *social studies educator, department chairman*
Williamson, R. Mark *lawyer*
Willis, Isaac *dermatologist, educator*
Wilson, Brent Lawrence *lawyer, mediator*
Wilson, Debora J. *broadcast executive*
Wilson, James Hargrove, Jr. *lawyer*
Winchester, Jesse Gregory *commercial real estate company executive*
Winer, Ward Otis *mechanical engineer, educator*

Wineski, Lawrence E. *medical educator, biomedical researcher*
Winograd, Audrey Lesser *retired advertising executive*
Withrow, William N., Jr. *lawyer*
Wofford, Milton Russell, Jr. *lawyer*
Wong, Ching-Ping *chemist, materials engineer*
Wong, Faye Ling *public health service officer*
Wood, L. Lin, Jr. *lawyer*
Woodard, Diane E. *music educator*
Woodson, Mike *professional basketball coach*
Wright, Frederick Lewis, II, *lawyer*
Wright, Peter Meldrim *lawyer*
Wu, De Ting *mathematics professor, researcher, writer*
Wussler, Robert Joseph *broadcast executive, media consultant*
Wylly, Barbara Bentley *performing arts association administrator*
Yancey, Asa Greenwood, Sr. *physician, educator*
Yancey, Carolyn Dunbar *academic administrator*
Yates, Ella Gaines *librarian, consultant*
Yates, Jerome William *medical association administrator*
Yavari, Arash *engineering educator*
Yoganathan, Ajit Prithviraj *biomedical engineer, educator*
Young, James E. *banker*
Young, Joyce L. *chemicals executive*
Zadeh, Javad Hamadani *mathematics professor*
Zeng, Fanxing *chemist*
Zhang, Guoqiang *finance educator*

### Auburn

Hutchinson, Leslie Julian *preventive medicine physician*

### Augusta

Baker, Carleton Harold *physiology educator*
Baker, Philip Steven *dentist, educator*
Bollag, Wendy Bollinger *medical educator*
Bowen, Dudley Hollingsworth, Jr. *federal judge*
Carroll, James Edwin *child neurologist, researcher*
Cheng, Wu C. *retired patent examiner*
Craig, Cynthia Mae *mathematics professor*
Davis, Catherine Lucy *psychologist, diabetes researcher*
Davis, Minnie P. *minister*
Denton, Frank M. *publishing executive*
Dolen, William Kennedy *allergist, immunologist, pediatrician, educator*
Drisko, Connie Lee Hastings *dean, dental educator*
Dyer, James Harold, Jr. *language educator*
Ellison, Lois Taylor *internist, educator, medical association administrator*
Fincher, Ruth Marie Edla *medical educator, dean*
Gambrell, Richard Donald, Jr. *endocrinologist, educator*
Gillespie, Edward Malcolm *hospital administrator*
Given, Kenna Sidney *surgeon, educator*
Glaser, Nancy Jane *museum director*
Hand, Maryanne Kelly *artist, educator*
Hooks, Vendie Hudson III *surgeon*
Horuzsko, Anatolij *medical researcher*
House, Fredrick Crisler *allergist*
Hsu, Stephen De *medical educator*
Inscho, Edward William *physiology educator*
Jackson, Rosa M. *retired elementary school educator*
Johnson, William Michael *physician*
Klacsmann, Karen Towers *art historian, writer*
Knox, Wyckliffe Austin, Jr. *lawyer*
Lee, Gregory Price *neuropsychology educator*
Logan, Betty Mulherin *human services specialist*
Luxenberg, Malcolm Neuwahl *ophthalmologist, educator*
MacLeod, James L. *minister, finance company executive, art gallery owner*
Mansberger, Arlie Roland, Jr. *surgeon*
Miller, Alfred Montague *lawyer*
Mixon, Kenneth Wayne *history professor, department chairman*
Osborne, James B., Sr. *academic administrator*
Owen, Mary Anne *nuclear scientist, educator*
Ownby, Dennis Randall *pediatrician, educator, allergist, researcher*
Parish, Michael J. *controller*
Parrish, Robert Alton *retired pediatric surgeon, educator*
Phillips, Marjorie Shaw *pharmacist, educator*
Puryear, Joan Copeland *academic administrator*
Rogers, Michael Bruce *orthodontist*
Ryan, James Walter *physician, medical researcher*
Schultz, Nancy Jansson *artist*
Sullivan, Jennifer Case *research scientist*
Tedesco, Francis Joseph *retired academic administrator, medical educator*
Woodhurst, Robert Stanford, Jr. *architect*
Wray, Betty Beasley *allergist, immunologist, pediatrician*
Yu, Robert Kuan-jen *biochemistry professor*

### Austell

Orr, Zellie *entrepreneur, educator, writer, researcher*
Pope, Jacqueline Privette *music educator*
Smiley, Jacquelyn *voice educator*

### Avondale Estates

Bastin, Clinton *retired chemical engineer, retired nuclear energy industry executive*
Carroll, Jane Hammond *artist, writer, poet*

### Bainbridge

Dixon, Lugenia *psychology educator*
Miley, Jenna Yvonne *education educator, consultant*

### Ball Ground

Tucker, Robert Dennard *health care products executive*

### Barnesville

Brown, Angelia *poet*
Gahr, Allan Arthur *chemistry professor*
Robbins, Dan S. *theater educator, theater director*

### Baxley

Williams, David Alfred *elementary school educator*

Williams, Sonia Kay *retired secondary school educator*

### Bethlehem

Sass, Joshua Lee *music educator*

### Big Canoe

Bendelius, Arthur George *engineering firm executive*

### Bishop

Bower, Douglas William *counseling administrator, psychotherapist, clergyman*

### Blairsville

Jones, Mary Emma B. *psychologist*
Sterling, Colleen *artist*

### Blue Ridge

Watkins, Nancy Ann *music and art educator*

### Braselton

Copper, James Robert *manufacturing executive*
Greene, William L. *marketing professional, consultant*
Romer, Denise Patrice *lawyer*

### Brooklet

McCormick, Paula Shurling *elementary school educator*

### Brunswick

Douglas, Christopher Thomas *music educator, musician*
Herndon, Alice Patterson Latham *public health nurse*
Iannicelli, Joseph *chemical company executive, consultant*
Mihal, Sandra Powell *research scientist*
Moran, John Bernard *retired government official*
Patrick, Connie L. *federal official*
Perniciaro, Charles Vincent *dermatologist, educator, entrepreneur*
Pittman, Catherine Sylvia *secondary school educator*
Spencer, Shirley Ann *secondary school educator, speech educator, literature educator*

### Buford

Byrd, Larry Donald *behavioral pharmacologist*

### Byron

Bai, Cheng *biochemist, researcher*

### Cairo

Oliver-Warren, Mary Elizabeth *retired library science educator, library and information scientist*

### Calhoun

Lorberbaum, Jeffrey S. *textiles executive*
Milam, Ben William *music educator*
Perillo, Salvatore J. *lawyer*
Thornton, H Monte *textiles executive*

### Camilla

Daniels, Deloria *elementary school educator*

### Canton

Fitzgerald, Gregory Allan *real estate broker, entrepreneur*
Harrison, David E. *secondary school educator*
Horton, Delories Epps *gifted and talented educator*
Wilson, Brian Andrew *computing performance consultant, educator, writer, editor*

### Carrollton

Bleuel, John Stephen *music educator*
Cao, Li *social studies educator*
Clark, Janet Eileen *political science professor*
Cochran, J. Guyton, Jr. *corporate financial executive*
Harris, Randa R. *research scientist, educator*
Holcombe, Brenda Sue *performing arts educator*
Hunter, James Lee (Lee Hunter) *manufacturing executive*
Hynes, Thomas John *academic administrator*
Pope, W. Alan *psychology professor, psychotherapist*
Reber, Jeffrey Stephen *psychology professor*
Sethna, Beheruz Nariman *academic administrator, educator, management consultant*
Steely, Melvin T. *language educator*
Thorn, Stuart Wallace *marketing and financial executive*

### Cartersville

DiMassimo, Thomas *secondary school educator, military officer*
Hopkins, Seth M. *museum director*
Wheeler, Susie Weems *retired school system administrator*

### Cataula

Averill, Ellen Corbett *retired secondary education science educator, administrator*

### Cave Spring

Morrow, Winifred Bryant *artist, educator*

### Cedartown

Burgess, Peggy Biggers *special education educator*
Garner, Robby Glen *software research executive, roboticist*

### Chamblee

Pearson-King, Lynn *music educator, director*

### Chatsworth

Howard, Timothy Ray *elementary school educator, historian*

### Clarkesville

Dowden, Thomas Clark *telecommunication executive*

### Clarkston

Charania, Barkat *real estate consultant*

### Cleveland

Durden, Julie Mariann *music educator*
Edwards, John Carver *retired archivist*
Kendrick, Brenda Cloyd *school counselor*

### Cochran

Agnew, Charlie Martin *art educator, artist*
Ricks, John Addison III *history professor*

### College Park

Bradley, Lynn Hecht *school librarian*
Patterson, P(ickens) Andrew *lawyer*

### Columbus

Amos, Daniel Paul *insurance company executive*
Anthony, Richard E. *bank executive*
Beall, Charles Donald *former special education educator*
Blanchard, James Hubert *finance company executive*
Brinkley, Jack Thomas *lawyer, retired congressman*
Chan, Philip *retired dermatologist, retired military officer*
Cloninger, Kriss III *insurance company executive*
Cockrell, Pearl Hand *writer*
Diaz-Verson, Salvador, Jr. *investment advisor*
Duncan, Frances Murphy *retired special education educator*
Gibbons, Dona Alden Coe *electrical engineer, director*
Golden, Joseph David *music educator*
Haneman, Vincent Siering, Jr. *consulting engineer, educator, dean*
Harbison, Ed *state legislator, broadcast journalist, motivational speaker*
Hiatt, Florence Ellen *musician*
Ingram, Rhea *education educator*
James, Elizabeth R. (Lee Lee James) *bank executive*
Jinright, Noah Franklin *vocational school educator, security firm executive*
Laney, John Thomas III *federal judge*
Lester, James D. III *insurance company executive*
Loudermilk, Joey M. *insurance company executive, lawyer*
Lumbard, Trina Yvette *mathematician, educator*
McFarland, Samuel P., Jr. *psychologist*
McGlamry, Max Reginald *retired lawyer*
Montgomery, Anna Frances *elementary school educator*
Musgrove, Katherine E. *theater educator*
Page, William Marion *lawyer*
Patrick, James Duvall, Jr. *lawyer*
Poydasheff, Robert Stephen *lawyer*
Prescott, Thomas W. *bank executive*
Riggsby, Dutchie Sellers *education educator*
Rumbelow, Robert Wesley *composer, conductor, director*
Simmons, Lynda Teel *nurse, healthcare executive*
Sprouse, James Edward *lawyer*
Sweeney, Robert David *retired communications engineer*
Tipton, James D. *retired military officer, education educator*
Wooten, Joel Orba, Jr. *lawyer*

### Conley

Marcus, James Elbert *manufacturing executive*

### Conyers

Grider, Rhonda Patriece *elementary school educator, writer*
Kelly, John Hubert *diplomat*
Sobh, Lou *automotive executive*
Spearman, Maxie Ann *financial analyst, administrator*
Waters, Roger Allen *music educator*

### Cordele

Bell, Andrew C. *music educator*
Helms, Bobby Gillespie *music educator, consultant*
Mitchell, James Marshall, Jr. *artist, educator*
Partin, Stephen Andrew *music educator*

### Covington

Fallings, Gloria Vondell *special education educator*
Norwood, Brandi Aisha *middle school educator*

### Crawford

Spears, Louise Elizabeth *minister, secondary school educator*

### Cumming

Drew, Paul S. *entrepreneur*
Nelson, Dennis Stephen *protective services official*
Willadsen, Michael Chris *marketing professional, sales executive*

### Dacula

Murphree, Harold T. *retired minister*

### Dahlonega

Newman, Thomas Daniel *archaeologist, school system administrator, minister*
Nourbakhsh, M. Reza *medical educator*
Potter, David L. *academic administrator*

### Dallas

Coley, Linda Marie *retired secondary school educator*
Erwin, Patrick Michael *music educator*

### Dalton

Bouckaert, Carl M. *manufacturing executive*
Ford, Katherine Michelle *special education educator*

### Dawsonville

Carroll, Martha Lynn *music educator, church pianist, editor, writer, illustrator*
Jorgensen, Alfred H. *retired data processing executive, retired telecommunications industry executive*

### Decatur

Bain, James Arthur *pharmacologist, educator*
Barrs, Thomas Jackson III *pharmacist*

Brown, William Virgil *internal medicine educator*
Cavallaro, Joseph John *retired microbiologist*
Clarke, Erskine *religious history professor, writer*
Dillingham, William Byron *literature educator, author*
Duffy, Thomas M. *transportation services executive, lawyer*
Grace, George H. *not-for-profit fundraiser*
Gregory, Sharon E. *neonatal clinical nurse specialist, nurse practitioner*
Hale, Cynthia Lynette *religious organization administrator*
Hamilton, Frank Strawn *musician, composer, educator*
Harris, Maurice Daniel *internist*
Henderson, Ralph Hale *physician*
Hinman, Alan Richard *public health physician, epidemiologist*
Kelly, Karen Deloris *addiction counselor, administrator*
Kiss, Elizabeth *academic administrator, philosophy educator*
Knight, Walker Leigh *publishing executive, minister*
Lucius, Randall H. *psychologist*
Majette, Denise *former congresswoman*
Manley, Frank *language educator, writer*
Mc Intosh, James Eugene, Jr. *interior designer*
Nease, Judith Allgood *marriage and family therapist*
Ray, Amy *vocalist, guitarist*
Rosenberg, Mark L. *health facility administrator*
Saliers, Emily *singer, musician*
Selby, Gail Diana *computer scientist*
Shaw, Jeanne Osborne *editor, poet*
Solomon, Hilda Pearl *wholesale executive*
Strain, Michael L. *music director, performing company executive*
Wheelan, Belle S. *educational association administrator*
Williams, Rita Tucker *lawyer*

**Demorest**
Rogers, Elizabeth (Betty) Carlisle *education educator, consultant*

**Doraville**
Wempner, Gerald Arthur *engineering educator*

**Douglas**
Hayes, Dewey *lawyer*
Seward, Lori A. *speech educator*

**Douglasville**
Adams Johnson, Arnita D. *chemist, educator*
Hébert, Rebecca Lapczynski *archivist*
Yates, Brenda H. Carroll *secondary school educator*

**Dublin**
Giannini, A. James *psychiatrist, educator, researcher, author*
Greene, Jule Blounte *lawyer*
Sapp, Peggy G. *pastor, editor, writer, speech professional*

**Duluth**
Beck, Andrew H. *farm equipment manufacturing executive*
Brody, Aaron Leo *food and packaging consultant*
Colwell, Gene Thomas *engineering educator*
Derro, Robert Arthur *retired physician*
Evans, Paul *osteopath*
Gillcrist, Kathy Ann *theater educator*
Guillory, Barbara Ann *elementary school educator*
Hunter, Douglas Lee *electronics executive*
Jellison, Brian D. *manufacturing executive*
Kimmich, Madeline P. *business operations consultant*
Koch, Linda Marie *elementary school educator*
Kramer, Edward E. *screenwriter, editor*
Laubscher, Robert James *consumer products company executive*
Luger, Donald R. *engineering company executive*
Lupton, Stephen D. *lawyer*
McClung, Samuel Brenton *music educator, consultant*
McCracken, William Henry *retired mining executive*
Reed, Ralph Eugene, Jr. *political consultant, former political organization administrator*
Richenhagen, Martin H. *manufacturing executive*
Sloan, Donnie Robert, Jr. *lawyer*
Stubbs, Thomas Hubert *public relations executive*

**Dunwoody**
Callison, James W. *retired lawyer, air transportation executive*
Duvall, Marjorie L. *English and foreign language educator*
Maddox, Jerry Aven *retail executive*

**East Point**
Bridgewater, Herbert Jeremiah, Jr. *radio personality*
Johnson, Hardwick Smith, Jr. *school psychologist*

**Eatonton**
Thompson, Laura Key *school system administrator*

**Epworth**
Burgess, Lesa L. *language educator*

**Evans**
Feldman, Elaine Bossak *medical nutritionist, educator*
McCorkle, Pamela Loveridge *elementary school educator*
Stout, Elva Carolyn Fraser *elementary school educator*
Zachert, Virginia *retired psychologist*

**Experiment**
Reeves, Alan M. *automotive company executive*

**Fairburn**
Holyfield, Evander *professional boxer*
Johnston, Carolyn Judith *construction engineer*
Milam, Lynne Morgan *special education educator*

**Fayetteville**
Borders, Donna Turner *elementary school educator*
Cokuslu, Lynda Elizabeth McCord *medical assistant*
Hood, Barbara W. *musician, educator*
Neal, Joan Burkes *librarian*
Turnipseed, Barnwell Rhett III *journalist, public relations consultant*

**Fitzgerald**
Newsome, John David, Jr. *music educator*

**Flowery Branch**
Abraham, John *professional football player*
Blank, Arthur M. *professional sports team executive, retired lumber company executive*
Coll, Edward Girard, Jr. *university president*
Congdon, Jon Harvey *music company executive*
Crumpler, Alge *professional football player*
Dunn, Warrick *professional football player*
Hall, DeAngelo *professional football player*
McKay, Richard James *professional sports team executive*
Monroe, Melrose *retired bank executive*
Mora, Jim, Jr. *professional football coach*
Reynolds, George Anthony, Jr. *engineering executive*
Vick, Michael (Michael Dwayne Vick) *professional football player*

**Folkston**
Crumbley, Esther Helen Kendrick *retired real estate agent, retired secondary school educator, councilman*

**Forest Park**
Honoré, Russel L. *career military officer*

**Forsyth**
Coleman, Steven Andrew *surveyor*

**Fort Benning**
Kotwal, Russ Steven *military officer, physician*

**Fort Gordon**
Windhorn, Richard J. *dentist*

**Fort Mcpherson**
Emery, Carolyn Vera *civilian military employee, retired non-commissioned officer*
Piacentini, Nicholas A., Jr. *military officer*
Stultz, Jack C. *career military officer*

**Fort Stewart**
Thompson, Frankie Mazie *school psychologist*
Warner, Christopher Hugh *psychiatrist*
Webster, William G., Jr. *career military officer*

**Fort Valley**
Archer, Lloyd Daniel *communications educator*
Maddox, Richard *manufacturing executive*

**Gainesville**
Battle, Julie Vicknair *psychology professor*
Burd, John Stephen *retired academic administrator, music educator*
Floyd, Hazel McConnell *special education educator*
Frank, Mary Lou Bryant *psychologist, educator*
Jones, William Benjamin, Jr. *retired electrical engineering educator*
Leet, Richard Hale *oil industry executive*
Lowrey, Alex Andre *biology professor*
May, Sterling Randolph *biology professor, department chairman*
Nichols, Dana *language educator*
Schuder, Raymond Francis *lawyer*
Thrasher, Karen Hewell *counseling administrator*

**Georgetown**
Briggs, Niwana Page *editor, writer*

**Glennville**
Craft, Mary Faye *public relations executive, consultant, television producer, poet*

**Griffin**
Doyle, Michael Patrick *microbiologist, educator, director*
Lindsey, James Robert, II *music educator, director, secondary school educator*
Phillips, Audrey Patricia (Pat Phillips) *secondary school educator*
Shockley, Carol Frances *psychologist, psychotherapist*

**Guyton**
Murray, Anthony David *music educator, director*

**Hamilton**
Byrd, Gary Ellis *lawyer*

**Hapeville**
Meshack, Marques D. *social studies educator*

**Hartwell**
Rushing, Tonnie Austin Page *musician, educator*

**Hawkinsville**
Whipple, Woodrow Thomas *artist, educator*

**Hephzibah**
Golphin, Elouise *writer, educator*

**Hiawassee**
Davis, Nighta J. *photographer, artist*

**Hinesville**
Wise, Carl Stamps *accounting educator*

**Hiram**
Crutchfield, Veda Maria Sharp *elementary school educator*
Stevens, Charles Thomas, Sr. *drafting technology educator*

**Hoschton**
Campbell, Leslie Caine (Caine Campbell) *writer, historian*

**Ila**
Greene, Sheree' Jeane *elementary school educator, consultant*

**Jackson**
Beasley, Anita Claire *reading specialist, consultant*

**Jasper**
Ledford, Shirley Louise *practical nurse*
Marger, Edwin *lawyer*
Moss, Anna Lee *construction executive, music educator*
Wiltse, James Cornelius *retired electrical engineer*

**Jeffersonville**
Capece, Michelle René *elementary school educator*
Hawthorne, Sarah Beck *reading educator*

**Jekyll Island**
Bentley, James Luther *former journalist*
McKinley, Douglas Webster (Webb McKinley) *consultant*

**Jonesboro**
Colburn, Donald Eugene *protective services official*
Galvin, John Rogers *retired army officer, law educator*
Harris, Queen Wiggs *mathematician, educator*

**Kennesaw**
Adams, Dean (Lewis Adams) *theater director*
Barnett, Benjamin Lewis, Jr. *retired physician, educator*
Kidonakis, Nikolaos *physicist*
Kinnick, Katherine Neil *communications educator, academic administrator*
Kruger, Harry *retired conductor, retired music educator*
Martinez, Ricardo *emergency medicine company executive*
Petersen, David M. *electrical engineer*
Robinson, Kenneth Charles *management educator*
Roebuck, Deborah Mae Britt *management consultant, educator*
Sherr, Laurence E. *music educator, composer*
Siegel, Betty Lentz *university president*
Stiles, Cheryl *writer, librarian, educator*
Whittingham, Harry Edward, Jr. *retired banker*
Xu, Chong-wei *computer scientist, educator*

**Keysville**
Cartwright, Maggie B. *retired nurse*

**Kingsland**
Huygens, Remmert William *architect*

**Lagrange**
Ault, Ethyl Lorita *special education educator, consultant*
Bledsoe, L. Bernard, Jr. *retired textile engineer*
Copeland, Robert Bodine *internist, cardiologist*
Gittinger, Laurie Ellen *music educator, elementary school educator*
Hudson, Charles Daugherty *insurance executive*
West, John Thomas *retired surgeon*

**Lake Park**
Blanton, Vallye J. *elementary school educator*
Carpenter, Paula Jo *elementary school educator*

**Lawrenceville**
Bannick, Janice Carol *automotive dealerships executive*
Brannon, Ronald Roy *retired minister*
Crain, Mary Ann *elementary school educator*
Fetner, Robert Henry *radiobiologist*
Folds, Frank Elliott *music educator*
Gericke, Paul William *minister, educator*
McDonald, James Francis *electronics company executive*
Schoen, Marc Alan *pension and employee benefits executive*
Swanson, Lynnette Sue *special olympics coordinator, special education educator*
Veysey, Michael Charles *lawyer*
Walker, Donald Murray *minister*

**Leesburg**
Hilley, Mary Kay *music educator*

**Lexington**
Newsome, Christa Anne *elementary school educator*

**Lilburn**
Baranco, Gregory T. *automobile dealership executive*
Bendelius, Bonnie Sue *elementary school educator*
Frapwell, Sharon Ann *mathematics educator*
Hester, Felicia Campbell *science educator*
Jamie, Parker Scott *elementary school educator, music educator, director*
Lynberg, Christopher A. *systems analyst, researcher*
Magnan, Sarah E. *court reporter*
Neumann, Thomas William *archaeologist*

**Lithia Springs**
Boyle, Michael J. *communications company executive*
Longobardo, Guy Alfred *lawyer*
Moore, Lindy A. *librarian*

**Lithonia**
Baxter, Gene Francis *chemical researcher, consultant*
Greene, John Edward, Jr. *network technician*

**Loganville**
McGonigle, Terry L. *theater educator, consultant*
Smelser, Thelma Ann *writer, tax specialist*

**Lookout Mountain**
Brown, Jeanell S. *music educator*

**Louisville**
Abdich, Robert Nicholas *band director, musician*
Hoover, John Elwood *former military officer, consultant, author, United States military history speaker*

**Lovejoy**
Onukwuli, Francis Osita *computer scientist, secondary school educator, mathematician*

**Mableton**
Rowe, Bonnie Gordon *music company executive*

**Macon**
Aldridge, Melvin Dayne *engineering educator*
Anderson, Robert Lanier III *federal judge*
Beaulier, Scott Alex *economics professor*
Brin, Foster Blake *psychiatrist*
Brown, Stephen Phillip *judge*
Cook, Charlotte C. *psychologist*
Davis, Anita Yvonne *small business owner, writer*
Davis, David Scott *academic administrator, chemistry professor*
Dunwody, Eugene Cox *architect*
Ennis, Edgar William, Jr. *lawyer*
Floyd, Daisy Hurst *dean, law educator*
Fontenot, Chester J. *humanities educator, minister*
Franklin, Roosevelt *minister*
Hails, Robert Emmet *retired aerospace engineer, manufacturing executive, retired military officer*
Hershner, Robert Franklin, Jr. *judge*
Huffman, Joan Brewer *history professor*
Huthnance, Edward Dennis, Jr. *mathematics professor*
Jones, Frank Cater *retired lawyer*
Kitchens, William Charlie *accountant*
Knight Olson, Beverly *foundation administrator*
Leonard, Michael Steven *industrial engineering educator*
Lewis, Sandra Combs *research psychologist, writer*
Mayes, Alva Louie *physician, pediatrician*
Owens, Wilbur Dawson, Jr. *federal judge*
Patterson, Kenneth *nurse*
Pilcher, Christie W. *special education educator*
Preuit, Theresa *librarian*
Quiroga, Alicia Espinosa *physiatrist*
Reitnauer, Otto Charles *fine arts director*
Rigsby, Sheila Goree *accounting firm executive*
Robinson, Joe Sam *neurosurgeon, educator*
Robinson, W. Lee *lawyer*
Schnell, Frederick Mark *oncologist, hematologist*
Staton, Cecil Pope, Jr. *writer, educator, broadcast executive*
Steeples, Douglas Wayne *retired university dean, consultant, researcher*
Walton, DeWitt Talmage, Jr. *dentist*
Wiggins, James L. *lawyer*
Wood, Frank Maxwell *prosecutor, lawyer*
Young, Henry E. *tissue engineering medical educator*

**Madison**
Aldridge, John Watson *language educator, writer*
DuBose, Charles Wilson *lawyer*

**Marietta**
Anderson, Vanessa Alferea *educational association administrator*
Aronoff, Craig Ellis *business educator, consultant*
Barksdale, Daryl *historic preservationist*
Bentley, Fred Douglas, Sr. *lawyer*
Blount, Daniel J. *lumber company executive*
Carnes, James Donald *real estate manager*
Clarkson, Lawrence William *air transportation executive*
Clay, Charles Commander (Chuck Clay) *lawyer, former state senator*
Devigne, Karen Cooke *retired amateur athletics executive*
Dudley, Guy Edward *psychologist*
Dunwoody, Kenneth Reed *magazine and book editor*
Edwards, Charles Mundy III *financial consultant*
Eggersman, Denise *computer engineer, educator*
Fitzgerald, John Edmund *retired civil engineering educator*
Fletcher, Carlos Alfredo Torres *video and film production company executive*
Gannon, Tom *paper company executive*
Gibb, Ginari Rene *psychiatrist*
Hagood, Murl Felton *surgeon*
Hays, Robert William *communications educator, consultant, writer*
Hellrung, Stephen Andrew *lawyer*
Henderson, Cynthia *medical librarian*
Houston, Dorothy Middleton *elementary school educator*
Humphrey, Stephen M. *paperboard company executive*
Ingram, Robert D. *lawyer*
Kanter, Donald Richard *pharmaceutical executive*
Kelly, William Watkins *educational association executive*
Kendall, Susan Gardes *librarian*
Kiger, Ronald Lee *retired contract negotiator*
Lahtinen, Silja Liisa *artist*
Lee, Raymond William III *institutional stockbroker*
Levere, Richard David *internist, educator*
McAuley, Thomas H. *real estate executive*
McEntire, Betty *health facility administrator*
Miles, Thomas Caswell *aerospace engineer*
Morisco, Jerid Simon *music educator, conductor*
Moscato, Joseph Louis, Jr. *health facility administrator, military officer*
Nowland, James Ferrell *lawyer*
Opre, Thomas Edward *retired editor, retired film company executive*
Poor, Andrew Ford *music educator*
Ranu, Harcharan Singh *biomedical scientist, administrator, orthopaedic biomechanics educator*
Reed, James Whitfield *internist, educator, endocrinologist*
Rivers, Alma Faye *secondary school educator*
Roach, Carole Hyde *music educator*
Rossbacher, Lisa Ann *academic administrator*
Shaw, Judith Ann *secondary school educator, human resources specialist, consultant*
Short-Mayfield, Patricia Ahlene *business owner*

Smith, Baker Armstrong *management executive, lawyer*
Smith, George Thornewell *retired state supreme court justice*
Spann, George William *management consultant*
Swanson, William Fredin III *manufacturing executive*
Volentine, Richard J., Jr. *lawyer*
Wenk, Michael Scott *regulatory administrator*
Williamsen, Dannye Sue *publishing executive, writer*

**Martinez**
Chaudhary, Shaukat Ali *ecologist, plant taxonomist*
Colborn, Gene Louis *anatomy educator, researcher*
Meyers, Nicholaus *music educator*

**Mc Rae**
Allen, Annette *minister*

**Mcdonough**
Hall, Mark *youth pastor, christian rock artist*
Mauney, Brandi Savage *special education diagnostician*
Wilson, Russell Edward *music educator*

**Metter**
Doremus, Ogden *lawyer*
Farmer, DeWayne Mark *director, photographer*
Guido, Michael Anthony *evangelist*

**Milledgeville**
Barron, Sheree S. *psychology professor, consultant*
Davis, Matthew Scott *curator, history professor*
Engerrand, Doris Dieskow *retired business educator*
Oetter, Doug R. *geography professor*
Ragan, Charlotte Ann *music educator*
Williamson, John Thomas, Sr. *minerals company executive*

**Morrow**
Culver, Dan Louis *federal agency administrator*
Gooden, Randall Scott *historian, archivist*
Totty, Totty Okoro *soccer coach*

**Moultrie**
Collum, Rick Daniel *lawyer*
Newberry, Daniel M. *elementary school educator*
Vereen, William Jerome *uniform manufacturing company executive*

**Mount Berry**
Davis, John Edward *music educator, musician*
Mew, Thomas Joseph, III, (Tommy Mew) *artist, educator*

**Mount Vernon**
Bowdidge, Mark *music educator*
Toll, Larry Allen *history professor*

**Nashville**
Cosson, Mary Gwendolyn *music educator*

**Newnan**
Barron, Thomas Willis *real estate broker*
Drake, W. Homer, Jr. *federal judge*
Franklin, Bruce Walter *lawyer*
Krach, Dale James *science educator, athletic trainer*
McBroom, Thomas William, Sr. *aviation consultant*
Royal, Nancy B. *primary school educator*

**Norcross**
Atkinson, A. Kelley *insurance company executive*
Beck, Joshua James *information technology executive*
Cohen, Barry P. *real estate investment management company executive*
Conway, Hobart McKinley, Jr. *futurist*
Cramer, James Perry *management strategist, architectural author, educator*
Dibb, David Walter *research association administrator*
Galfas, Timothy, II, *wholesale distribution executive*
Granger, Philip Richard *minister*
Harrison, Gordon Ray *engineering executive, consultant, research scientist*
Hellyer, Christine Frances *secondary school educator, art educator*
Koperniak, Matthew Ryan *music educator, director, secondary school educator*
McIntosh, Robert B. *lawyer*
Moreno, Veronica *food products executive*
Penninger, Samuel A., Jr. *consumer products company executive*
Rubright, James Alfred *paperboard and packaging company executive*
Strange, J. Leland *computer company executive*
Tufano, Charles C. *paper company executive*
Wagner, Robert Earl *retired agronomist*
Xie, Jeff Zhengquan *lawyer*

**Oakwood**
Jondahl, Terri Elise *importing and distribution company executive*
Martin, Johnny Benjamin *accountant*
Phillips, Ernie Howard *music educator*

**Oxford**
Cody, William Bermond *political science professor*
Patrick, Heather R. *chemistry professor*
Sitton, Claude Fox *newspaper editor*

**Peachtree City**
Barnes, Marylou Riddleberger *retired academic administrator*
Clark, James Kermit, Jr. *real estate executive*
Day, Annette J. *music educator*
Dillard, George Stewart III *minister*
Ebneter, Stewart Dwight *utility industry management consultant*
Nix, Kemie Richards *educational association administrator, editor*

Roobol, Norman Richard *chemistry professor, consultant*
Turner, Lynda E. *science educator*

**Pembroke**
Woodward, Serena *school psychologist*

**Perry**
Geiger, James Norman *lawyer*
Giles, Lisa Lanette *elementary school educator*

**Pine Mountain**
Bishop, Michael *writer*
Callaway, Howard Hollis *resort executive*

**Powder Springs**
Drawdy, Larry Wayne *elementary school educator*

**Reidsville**
Saad, Fathy Zaki *medical association administrator, physician*

**Richmond Hill**
Budde, Neil Frederick *publishing company executive, editor, publisher*

**Rincon**
Purcell, Ann Rushing *state legislator, human services manager*

**Riverdale**
Lambert, Ethel Gibson Clark *secondary school educator*

**Robins Afb**
Manley, Nancy Jane *environmental engineer*

**Rockmart**
Vinson, Victoria Dean *middle school educator*

**Rome**
Borchardt, Marc *nurse anesthetist*
Davis, Susan Lynn *music educator, musician*
Doyle, James Donald, Jr. *librarian*
Harbin, Frank Rockwell *psychologist*
Hodges, Thomas C. *art educator*
Janowski, Thaddeus Marian *architect*
Johnson, Alberta Clark *psychology professor*
Mosley, Mary Mac *retired librarian*
Murphy, Harold Loyd *federal judge*
Sellers, Jimmie *construction executive*
Slack, Clemontene *education educator*

**Roopville**
Huckeba, Emily Causey *retired elementary school educator*

**Roswell**
Baker, Anita Diane *lawyer*
Birmingham, Richard Gregory *lawyer*
Boley, Dennis Lynn *construction company executive*
Bridges, Chris (Ludacris) *musician, actor*
Bruckner, William J. *lawyer*
Christopher, Lin *artist*
Dolan, Dennis Joseph *pilot, lawyer*
Herron, Harriette A. *retired occupational health nurse*
Hill, Donald Dee *management consultant, educator, writer*
Klein, John Jacob *retired economist*
McCloud, Melody Theresa *obstetrician-gynecologist, surgeon*
McCraw, Earl C., Jr. *textiles executive*
Nilsen, Arthur Christian *lawyer*
Peterson, Donald Robert *editor, vintage automobile consultant*
Polatty, Rose Jackson *civic worker*
Rayburn, Boyd Dale *artist*
Rogers, Richard Hilton *hotel executive*
Roland, Raymond William *lawyer, mediator*
Siepi, Cesare *opera singer*
Welch, Robert Bennett *retired music educator, retired conductor*

**Saint Marys**
Berry, Stephen L. (Steve) *writer, lawyer*
Hall, Lois Bremer *secondary school educator, volunteer*
Keating, Mary Tucker *retired school system administrator*
Smith, Charles Courtland, Jr. *lawyer, state legislator*

**Saint Simons Island**
Bell, Ronald Mack *university foundation administrator, consultant*
Douglas, William Ernest *retired commissioner*
Mathis, Luster Doyle *academic administrator, political scientist, educator*
Schneider, Duane Bernard *English literature educator*
Spivey, Ted Ray *language educator*
Taylor, Philip Raymond *lawyer*
Thau, William Albert *lawyer*
Turbidy, John Berry *investor, management consultant*
Webb, Lamar Thaxter *architect*

**Sandy Springs**
Owen, Robert Hubert *lawyer, real estate broker*

**Savannah**
Aja-Herrera, Marie *fashion designer, educator*
Aquadro, Jeana Lauren *graphic designer, educator*
Berry, Jack K. *lawyer*
Boland, John Kevin *bishop*
Bowman, Catherine McKenzie *lawyer*
Brown, Carlton E. *college president*
Cartledge, Raymond Eugene *retired paper company executive*
Cebula, Richard John *economist, educator*
Chong, Bruce Simon *dean, broadcast executive*
Clemmons, John B. *bank executive, director, retired mathematics educator*
Coffey, Thomas Francis, Jr. *retired writer*
Court, Stacie Lorraine *musician, tax specialist*
Dickey, David Herschel *lawyer, accountant*
DiClaudio, Janet Alberta *health information administrator*

Dirlam, David Kirk *education educator*
Dixon, Harry D., Jr., (Donnie Dixon) *lawyer, former prosecutor*
Dodge, William Douglas *risk management consultant*
Eaves, George Newton *science foundation director, educator*
Edenfield, Berry Avant *federal judge*
Everhard, Martin E. *surgeon*
Felcyn, Diane Marian *museum educator*
Field, Jonathan David *art educator*
Fischer, Thomas Jeffrey *art educator*
Fishburne, John Ingram, Jr. *retired obstetrician/gynecologist, educator*
Foley, Marilyn Lorna *artist*
Forbes, Morton Gerald *lawyer*
Gillespie, Daniel Curtis, Sr. *retired not-for-profit developer*
Granger, Harvey, Jr. *retired manufacturing executive*
Holland, Robert D. *music educator*
Hoskins, William John *obstetrician, educator, gynecologist*
Houngues, Desire Mensanh *dean*
Hsu, Ming-Yu *engineering educator*
Hung, Chin-Cheng *art educator, artist*
Hutchinson, Michael E. *music educator, conductor*
Johnson, Eric B. *state legislator*
Krahl, Enzo *retired surgeon*
Lee, Ernest William, II, *lawyer*
Leighton, Richard Frederick *retired dean*
Lesko, Diane *museum director, curator*
Lindley, James Gunn, Jr. *neurosurgeon*
Lindqvist, Gunnar Jan *management consultant, international trade consultant*
Moore, William Theodore, Jr. *federal judge*
Otter, John Martin III *retired television advertising consultant*
Phillips, Robert L., Jr. *application developer, consultant*
Polite, Evelyn C. *retired elementary school educator, evangelist*
Purnell, Elissa T. *biology professor*
Rowan, Richard G. *academic administrator*
Sanders, James Grady *biogeochemist*
Searcy, William Nelson *lawyer, director*
Shanken, Edward A. *art educator, design educator*
Sheehy, Barry Maurice *management consultant*
Skelton, William Douglas *physician*
Smith, David Lee *retired editor*
Smith, Elizabeth Mackey *retired financial consultant*
Spitz, Seymour James, Jr. *retired fragrance company executive*
Stillwell, Walter Brooks III *lawyer*
Tessema, George *mathematician, educator*
Thomas, Dwight Rembert *writer*
Thompson, Larry James *retired gifted and social studies education educator*
Thompson, Richard S. *lawyer, former prosecutor*
Wallace, Paula S. *academic administrator*
Walter, Paul Hermann Lawrence *chemistry professor*
Windom, Herbert Lynn *oceanographer, environmental scientist*
Wirth, Fremont Philip, Jr. *neurosurgeon, educator*
Wood, Lisa Godbey *prosecutor*
Yang, Dihua *architecture educator, researcher*
Zoller, Michael *otolaryngologist, head and neck surgeon, educator*

**Sea Island**
Mc Swiney, James Wilmer *retired pulp and paper manufacturing company executive*
Revoile, Charles Patrick *lawyer*

**Sky Valley**
Geer, Ronald Lamar *mechanical engineer, consultant, retired oil industry executive*
Wilkinson, Albert Mims, Jr. *lawyer*

**Smyrna**
Atkins, William Austin, Sr., (Bill Atkins) *former state legislator*
Dean, Martha Elizabeth *music educator*
Kell, Michael Jon *physician, researcher*
Lnenicka, Wade Sheridan *purchasing agent, councilman*
Rife, Elizabeth *musician, music educator*
Seigler, Michael Edward *lawyer, librarian*
Tripp, Victor K. *electrical engineer, researcher*

**Snellville**
Dodd, Violet M. *nursing educator, recreational therapist, counselor*

**Social Circle**
Penland, John Thomas *retired import/export and development company executive*

**Statesboro**
Adhikari, Dharma Nanda *journalist, writer, educator*
Barjis, Joseph *computer scientist, educator*
Bartels, Jean Ellen *nursing educator*
Franklin, James Burke *lawyer*
Henry, Nicholas Llewellyn *public administration educator*
Li, Xiezhang *education educator*
Lloyd, Margaret Ann *psychologist, educator*
Murkison, Eugene Cox *finance educator*
Nettles, Saundra R. Murray *psychologist, writer, educator*
Olvey, Pamela Hagan *elementary school educator*
Stewart, Lewis Moore *finance educator*
Whitaker, Mical Rozier *theater director, educator*
Wilson, LeVon Edward *lawyer, educator*
Woods, James M. *history professor*

**Stockbridge**
Collins, Oliver Jack *military officer, secondary school educator*
Friedman, Robert Barry *neurosurgeon*
Grimes, Richard Allen *banker, educator*
Sanders, Curtis Arra *music educator*

**Stone Mountain**
Allen (Irvin M.N.), Georgianne Lydia Christian *writer, poet*
Bacon, Louis Albert *retired consulting civil engineer*

Brown, Rhonda Jean *special education educator*
Dees, Julian Worth *retired academic/research administrator*
Fairweather, Daniel Edward *music educator*
Farngalo, Rosemarie Merritt *school psychologist*
Gotlieb, Jaquelin Smith *pediatrician*
Malone, Embry *property manager, advocate*
Moales, Yvonne Edwards *school psychologist*
Reichert, Leo Edmund, Jr. *biochemist, department chairman, endocrinologist*
Torbush, Deborah Nickels *psychology educator*
Warthan, Helen Patricia *retired secondary school educator*

**Suwanee**
Cox, Albert Harrington, Jr. *economist*
Decker, Richard John *neuroscientist*
Frankel, Andrew Joel *management consultant, information scientist*
Harriman, John *music educator*
Stanley, Gwen G. *elementary school educator*

**Swainsboro**
Stracher, Glenn Blair *geology educator, research scientist*
Watt, Dwight, Jr., (Arthur Dwight Watt Jr.) *computer programming and microcomputer specialist*

**Sylvania**
Harper, Michael Christopher *music educator*

**Sylvester**
Kroll, Francis Scott *music educator*

**Thomasville**
Avera, Stephen R. *food products company executive, lawyer*
Deese, George E. *food products company executive*
Flowers, Langdon Strong *foods company executive*
Stepanek, David Leslie *financial services company executive*
Williams, Gerald Arnett *academic administrator*

**Tifton**
Dorminey, Henry Clayton, Jr. *allergist*
McClusky, Duncan Kemp *librarian*
Reinhardt, George Robert *lawyer*
Roberts, Curtis Creed *minister, writer*
Robinson, John Christopher *music educator*

**Tiger**
Ring, Yvonne Ann *special education educator*

**Toccoa**
Maypole, John Floyd *real estate company executive*

**Toccoa Falls**
Brock, Dorothy Dixon *psychologist, psychology professor*
Council, Thomas Maurice *music educator*
Gardner, Donna Rae (Diehl) *education educator*

**Townsend**
Hicks, Harold Eugene *chemical engineer*

**Tucker**
Hardy, Michael C. *performing arts administrator*
Stewart, Connie Ward *retired academic administrator*
Streeb, Gordon Lee *diplomat, economist*
Taylor, George B., Jr. *lawyer*

**Union City**
Bryant, Curtis *composer, educator*
Drake-Hamilton, Lillie Belle *retired secondary school educator*

**Valdosta**
Bailey, Hugh Coleman *university president*
Beal, John M. *surgeon, medical educator*
Burnette, Ada M. Puryear *program coordinator*
Cronin, Kevin Stewart *historian, educator*
Dodd, Roger J. *lawyer*
Edwards, Edith Martha *lawyer*
Halter, Henry James, Jr., (Diamond Jim Halter) *retail executive*
Lindsay, LeVonne D. *costume designer, educator*
McLendon, Richard Charles *music educator*
Morgan, Joe Leland *physician, psychiatrist*
Wares, Arsalan *mathematics professor*
Warrick, Emory Lawrence *retired education educator*

**Vidalia**
Findley, LaRee *history educator*
Fountain, Edwin Byrd *minister, librarian, poet*
Melton, Thomas Ronald *history professor*

**Villa Rica**
Blevins, Ernest Everett *genealogist, researcher, historian*

**Waleska**
Muzyka, Pola Marie *film producer, artist*

**Warner Robins**
DePriest, C(harles) David *engineering executive, retired military officer*
Gayton, Johnny Lee *ophthalmologist, educator, recreational facility executive*
Merk, P. Evelyn *librarian*
Nugteren, Cornelius *air force officer*

**Watkinsville**
Leathers, Joyce Carol *secondary school educator*
Williams, Vivian (Vinnie) Marie *publishing executive, editor, writer*
Wright, Robert Joseph *lawyer*

**West Point**
Albarado, Rebecca Hill *elementary school educator*
Andrews, Gerald Bruce, Sr. *textiles executive*
Glover, Clifford Clarke *retired construction company executive*
Humphries, M. Clayton, Jr. *lawyer*

**Whitesburg**
Nicholson, Diane M. *special education educator*

**Wildwood**
Dombrowski, Bob *artist, writer*

**Woodbine**
Konetzni, Albert H., Jr. *career officer*

**Woodstock**
Austin, John David *retired financial executive*
Christmas, Bobbie Jaye *freelance/self-employed writer*
Colgan, George Phillips *real estate developer, real estate appraiser*
Collins, David Browning *religious institution administrator*
Moses, Marjorie *elementary school educator*

**Young Harris**
Arnold, Paul T. *biologist, educator*
Richardson, Vernal Edward *retired music educator*
Wolfersteig, Eloise Smith *retired music educator*

# HAWAII

**Aiea**
Manabe, Shari A *education educator*

**Camp H M Smith**
Fallon, William J. *career military officer*

**Ewa Beach**
Lewis, Mary Jane *film producer, film director, scriptwriter*

**Hawaii National Park**
Swanson, Donald Alan *geologist*

**Hilo**
Brown, Daniel Edward *social sciences educator*
Dinges, Richard Allen *entrepreneur*
Dixon, Paul William *psychologist, educator*
Figueroa-Centeno, Ramón *mathematics professor*
Grabar, Andrew *art educator, artist*
Li, Shuguang *mathematics professor, researcher*
Pezzuto, John Michael *dean, pharmacology educator*
Tseng, Rose *academic administrator*

**Holualoa**
Scarr, Sandra Wood *retired psychology educator, researcher*

**Honolulu**
Abbott, Isabella Aiona *retired biology educator*
Abe, Gregg Koyei *music educator*
Acoba, Simeon Rivera, Jr. *state supreme court justice, educator*
Adams, Jo-Ann Marie *lawyer*
Agrusa, Jerome *tourism studies educator*
Ahmed, Iqbal *psychiatrist, consultant*
Aiona, James R., Jr. *lieutenant governor*
Akiba, Lorraine Hiroko *lawyer*
Akinaka, Asa Masayoshi *lawyer*
Akinnuoye-Agbaje, Adewale *actor*
Albano, Andres, Jr. *real estate developer, real estate broker*
Andrews, Naveen William Sidney *actor*
Aucan, Jerome Pierre *oceanographer*
Baker, Rosalyn Hester *state senator*
Bender, Byron Wilbur *linguistics educator*
Bennett, Mark J. *state attorney general*
Betts, Barbara Stoke *artist, educator*
Betts, James William, Jr. *financial analyst, consultant*
Bitterman, Morton Edward *psychologist, educator*
Bloede, Victor Carl *lawyer, consultant, director*
Boas, Frank *retired lawyer*
Botsai, Elmer Eugene *architect, architecture educator, retired dean*
Brady, Stephen R.P.K. *physician*
Brill, Richard C. *physical science educator*
Bronster, Margery S. *retired state attorney general, lawyer*
Cadman, Edwin Clarence *health facility administrator, retired medical educator*
Callies, David Lee *lawyer, educator*
Case, James Hebard *lawyer*
Chapman, Duane Lee (Dog) *bail enforcement agent*
Char, Vernon Fook Leong *lawyer*
Chen, Wai-Fah *civil engineering educator*
Cheung, Edward Leonard *physician*
Ching, Chauncey Tai Kin *agricultural studies educator, economist*
Cho, Lee-Jay *social scientist, demographer*
Chock, Raelene *school system administrator*
Chun, Jacqueline Clibbett *artist, educator*
Chung, Kea Sung *television broadcasting executive*
Chyba, Monique *mathematics professor*
Clifton, Richard Randall *federal judge*
Cooke, Mary Moragne *volunteer*
Cooke, Samuel Alexander *retired brokerage house executive*
Cowan, Stuart Marshall *lawyer*
Cox, Richard Horton *civil engineering executive*
Curb, Jess David *medical educator, researcher*
Dang, Marvin S.C. *lawyer*
Deaver, Phillip Lester *lawyer*
Devaney, Donald Everett *law enforcement official*
Devenot, David Charles *human resources specialist, artist*
Devens, Paul *retired lawyer*
Doane, W. Allen *water transportation executive*
Dousset, Benedicte *research scientist*
Duffy, James Earl, Jr. *state supreme court justice*
Dupont, Ralph Paul *lawyer, educator*
Dyen, Isidore *linguistic scientist, educator*
Edmunds, John Sanford *lawyer*
Edwards, John Wesley, Jr. *urologist*
Englert, Peter *academic administrator, educator*
Fale, Kim Kimball *secondary school educator, director*
Farris, William Wayne *history professor*
Finney, John Edgar III *food products executive*
Finucane, Melissa Lucille *psychologist, researcher*
Fischer, Joel *social work educator*

Flynn, David A. *librarian*
Fok, Agnes Kwan *retired cell biologist, educator*
Fong, Bernard W.D. *physician, educator*
Fujita, James Hiroshi *history educator*
Fukumoto, Leslie Satsuki *lawyer*
Fukushima, Barbara Naomi *financial advisor*
Fullmer, Daniel Warren *former psychologist, educator*
Gay, E(mil) Laurence *lawyer*
Gee, Chuck Yim *dean*
Gelber, Don Jeffrey *lawyer*
Ghasemi Nejhad, Mehrdad N. *mechanical engineering educator*
Gillmor, Helen *federal judge*
Godbey, Robert Carson *lawyer*
Goldstein, Sir Norman *dermatologist*
Gonsalves, Margaret Leboy *elementary school educator*
Goodhue, William Walter, Jr. *pathologist, military officer, educator*
Greeley, Burnham H. *lawyer*
Gubler, Duane J. *research scientist, educator, virologist*
Guerrero, Reuben Castro *oncologist, internist*
Guthrie, Edgar King *artist*
Hack, Randolph C. *advocate, educator, counselor*
Haig, David M. *diversified financial services company executive*
Haight, Warren Gazzam *investor*
Halloran, Richard Colby *writer, reporter, communications executive, editor*
Hamada, Duane Takumi *architect*
Hamamoto, Patricia *school system administrator, educator*
Hammar, Sherrel Leyton *medical educator*
Hannemann, Mufi *mayor*
Harris, Jeremy *former mayor*
Hart, Brook *lawyer*
Hawke, Bernard Ray *planetary scientist, researcher*
Hays, Ronald Jackson *career officer*
Hazlett, Mark A. *lawyer*
Heller, Ronald Ian *lawyer*
Hey, Richard Noble *marine geophysicist*
Higa, D. Puanani *secondary school educator*
Hirai, Craig Kazuo *accountant*
Ho, Don (Donald Tai Loy Ho) *entertainer, singer*
Ho, Reginald Chi Shing *medical educator*
Hook, Ralph Clifford, Jr. *business educator*
Hu, Ching Yuan *academic administrator*
Hue, Nguyen Van *soil scientist, chemist, educator*
Hughes, Robert Harrison *former agricultural products executive*
Hunt, Terry L. *archaeologist, educator*
Ihrig, Judson La Moure *chemist*
Imanaka, Mitchell Akio *lawyer*
Ingersoll, Caroline Yee *director*
Ishikawa-Fullmer, Janet Satomi *psychologist, educator*
Jensen, Barbara Wood *interior design business owner*
Johnson, Katherine Marie *elementary school educator*
Johnson, Lawrence M. *retired bank executive*
Jordan, Amos Azariah, Jr. *foreign affairs educator, retired military officer*
Kadohiro, Jane K. *nurse, educator, consultant*
Kaholokula, Joseph Keaweaimoku *mental health services professional, researcher*
Kamemoto, Fred Isamu *retired zoologist*
Kane, Thomas Jay III *surgeon, educator*
Kanehiro, Kenneth Kenji *insurance educator, risk analyst, consultant*
Katayama, Robert Nobuichi *retired lawyer*
Keil, Klaus *geology educator, consultant*
Keith, Kent Marsteller *academic administrator, writer, lawyer, recreational facility executive*
Kelley, Richard Roy *hotel executive*
Kennedy, Faye *retired social worker, author*
Keogh, Richard John *firearms and explosives consultant*
Keyes, Saundra Elise *newspaper editor*
Khan, Mohammad Asad *geophysics educator, retired minister, former senator of Pakistan*
Kim, S. Peter *psychiatrist, educator, health facility administrator, researcher*
Klobe, Tom *art gallery director*
Koide, Frank Takayuki *electrical engineering educator*
Konan, Denise *academic administrator, economics professor*
Kong, Laura S. L. *geophysicist*
Kudritzki, Rolf-Peter *astronomer, educator*
Lacy, John Robert *lawyer*
Laney, Leroy Olan *economist, banker, educator*
Langham, Edward Allen *drama and theater educator*
Lau, Constance H. (Connnie Lau) *electric power industry executive*
Lau, H. Lorrin *obstetrician, gynecologist*
Lebedev, Konstantin Vladimirovich *oceanographer, researcher*
Lee, Dale W. *lawyer*
Lee, Lorrin L. *internet marketing entrepreneur, architect, writer*
Lee, Sang-Hyop *economist*
Lee, Yeu-Tsu Margaret *surgeon, educator*
Levinson, Steven Henry *state supreme court justice*
Levister, Raymond Lee *psychologist*
Leyden, Michael Joseph, II, (Lei Jie Ming) *entrepreneur, writer*
Lighter, Eric Aaron *real estate developer, law enforcement software developer, consultant*
Lilly, Michael Alexander *lawyer, writer*
Lingle, Linda *governor*
Loo, Wilson M.N. *lawyer, judge*
Louie, David Mark *lawyer*
Lum, Jean Loui Jin *nursing educator*
Ma, Kougen *engineering educator, researcher*
Maddock, Jay E. *medical educator*
Mader, Charles Lavern *chemist*
Magaoay, Michael Y. *state representative*
Mandel, Morton *molecular biologist*
Mark, Shelley Muin *economist, educator*
Marks, Michael J. *lawyer*
Masters, Elaine *religious studies educator, writer*
Mau-Shimizu, Patricia Ann *lawyer*
McClain, David Stanley *academic administrator, business and management professor*
McMurtry, Gary Michael *geochemist, educator*

Merrifield, Donald Paul *ministries coordinator*
Midkiff, Robert Richards *trust company executive, finance company executive, consultant*
Migimoto, Fumiyo Kodani *retired secondary school educator*
Miller, Richard Sherwin *law educator*
Miyasaki, Shuichi *lawyer*
Moon, Ronald T.Y. *state supreme court chief justice*
Moreno-Cabral, Carlos Eduardo *cardiac surgeon*
Morrison, Charles E. *think-tank executive*
Nakata, Gary Kenji *lawyer*
Nakayama, Paula Aiko *state supreme court justice*
Nasky, H. Gregory (Harold Gregory Nasky) *lawyer*
Ng, Wing Chiu *accountant, educator, application developer, lawyer, advocate*
Nishimura, Pete Hideo *oral surgeon*
Noguchi, Hideo *insurance company executive*
Nordyke, Eleanor Cole *demographer, researcher, community health nurse*
O'Brien, Kendra Allen *psychologist, researcher*
Ogburn, Hugh Bell *chemical engineer, consultant*
Ogburn, Nancy Wrenn *civic volunteer*
Okimoto, Glenn Michiaki *state official*
Okinaga, Lawrence Shoji *lawyer*
O'Neill, Charles Kelly *marketing professional, retired advertising executive*
Osborne, Larry Norman *dean, consultant*
O'Shughnessy, Edward Joseph *urologist, retired medical educator*
Overstreet, Maryann Elizabeth *literature and language professor*
Paige, Glenn Durland *political scientist, educator*
Pakvasa, Sandip *physicist*
Palia, Aspy Phiroze *marketing educator, researcher, consultant*
Parsa, Fereydoun Don *plastic surgeon*
Pauka, Kirstin *theater educator, director*
Pearsall, Paul *psychologist, educator*
Pedersen, Paul Bodholdt *psychologist, educator*
Perkins, Frank Overton *academic administrator, marine biologist*
Perushek, Diane *university librarian*
Pickens, Alexander Legrand *retired education educator*
Pickens, Frances Jenkins *artist, educator*
Pinckney, Neal T. *psychologist, retired educator*
Platte, Mark *editor*
Plourde, William E. *secondary school educator*
Portnoy, Jeffrey Steven *lawyer*
Preble, Sarah Hamilton *art librarian, author, writer*
Raleigh, Cecil Baring *geophysicist*
Ramler, Siegfried *foundation administrator*
Reber, David James *lawyer*
Rehg, Kenneth Lee *linguistics educator*
Rexner, Romulus *publishing executive*
Rhee, Mooweon *business educator*
Riggs, Fred Warren *political science professor*
Robinson, Robert Blacque *foundation administrator*
Roley, V. Vance *dean, finance educator*
Sagawa, Yoneo *horticulturist, educator*
Saiki, Patricia (Mrs. Stanley Mitsuo Saiki) *federal agency administrator, congressman*
Sakamoto, Norman Lloyd *state legislator, civil engineer*
Sakamoto, Ronald Rikio *lawyer, construction executive*
Sato, Glenn Kenji *lawyer*
Schatz, Irwin Jacob *cardiologist, educator*
Schindler, Jo Ann *librarian, director*
Schneider, Niklas *educator*
Seff, Karl *chemistry educator*
Seidensticker, Edward George *Japanese language and literature educator*
Silva, Clarence *bishop*
Silva, Jana Kaida *obstetrician, maternal/fetal medicine specialist*
Silva, Mary Barnes *retired elementary school educator*
Simonds, John Edward *retired newspaper editor*
Soifer, Aviam *dean, law educator*
Solidum, James *finance and insurance executive*
Sparks, Robert William *retired publishing executive*
Staats, Arthur W. *psychology professor*
Starshak, James L. *lawyer*
Stephan, John Jason *historian, educator*
Sterrett, James Melville *accountant, consultant*
Stigall, Phyllis Graham *retired librarian*
Stockholm, Charles M. *diversified financial services company executive*
Sugiki, Shigemi *ophthalmologist, educator*
Suh, Dae-Sook *political science professor*
Swanson, Richard William *retired statistician*
Takimi, Roy Mitsuo *state legislator*
Tanner, Jerré E. *composer, retired publishing executive*
Tanoue, Donna A. *bank executive, former federal agency administrator*
Titchenal, Charles Alan *nutrition educator*
Turbin, Richard *lawyer*
Uhl, Philip Edward *artist, photographer, cinematographer*
Usui, Leslie Raymond *apparel executive*
Varley, Herbert Paul *Japanese language and cultural history educator*
Wang, Jaw-Kai *bioengineering educator*
Watanabe, Corinne Kaoru Amemiya *judge, state official*
Wee, Christine Dijos *elementary school educator*
Wellein, Marsha Diane Akau *military educator, director*
Wertheimer, Andrew B. *library and information scientist, educator*
White, Emmet, Jr. *retirement community administrator*
White, Gary Richard *electrical engineer*
Wilson, William James *healthcare executive*
Wolff, Herbert Eric *banker, former army officer*
Wright, Chatt Grandison *academic administrator*
Yeh, Raymond Wei-Hwa *architect, educator*
Zamzow, Jill Patricia *biologist, consultant*

**Kalulului**
Domingo, Cora Maria Corazon Encarnacion *minister*
Tolliver, Dorothy *librarian*

**Kailua**
Bone, Robert William *writer*
Buratynski, Theresa Joan *physician*
Lundquist, Dana Richard *health facility administrator*
Rosendal, Hans Erik *retired meteorologist*
Shank, Charles Vernon *science administrator, educator, physicist*
Stamper, Ewa Szumotalska *psychologist*
Tavares, Samantha *psychologist, educator*
Tubbs, Mary S. *curriculum coordinator*
Wong, Wallace *real estate investor*
Wright, John Cotton *archivist, consultant*
Young, Jacqueline Eurn Hai *former state legislator, consultant*

**Kailua Kona**
Clewett, Kenneth Vaughn *academic administrator*
Diama, Benjamin *retired secondary school educator, artist, composer, writer*
Iolana, Patricia Elvira *foundation administrator, consultant*
Leonardo, Ann Adamson *marketing and sales consultant*
Liepack, Scot Alan *psychologist*
Spitze, Glenys Smith *retired teacher and counselor*

**Kamuela**
Mc Dermott, John Francis *psychiatrist, physician*
Morgan, Andrew Lane *urologist, educator*

**Kaneohe**
Ashley, Elizabeth *dean, educator*
Lagoria, Georgianna Marie *curator, writer, editor, visual art consultant*
LaMarchina, Marilynne May *elementary school educator*
Maeshiro, Mitzi (Mikilani) *literature and language educator*
McGlaughlin, Thomas Howard *publishing executive, retired military officer*
Poliahu, George *retired music educator*
Talbert, Geal Fukumoto *investment representative*
Vincent, Thomas James *retired manufacturing executive*
Young-Pohlman, Colette Lisa *music educator*

**Kapaa**
Klontz, Bradley T. *psychologist, consultant*
Veylanswami, Satguru Bodhinatha *head of religious order*

**Kapaau**
Jankowski, Theodore Andrew *artist*
McFee, Richard *electrical engineer, physicist*
Ralston, Joanne Smoot *public relations executive*

**Kapolei**
Adachi, Athan Ken *civil engineer*
Dudley, Doris S. *music educator, small business owner*
Moriyama, Karen Ito *educational association administrator*

**Kihei**
Borchers, Robert Reece *physicist, science administrator*
Burns, Richard Gordon *retired lawyer, writer, consultant*

**Koloa**
Cobb, Rowena Noelani Blake *real estate broker*
Donohugh, Donald Lee *physician*

**Kula**
Maloney, Michael Patrick *lawyer, mediator, arbitrator*
Richardson, Robert Allen *retired lawyer, educator*
Rohlfing, Frederick William *lawyer, retired judge, political scientist*

**Lahaina**
Percy, Helen Sylvia *physician*

**Laie**
Gorman, Vicki Pfluger *voice educator*
Miller, Ronald Mellado *education educator*
Shumway, Eric *academic administrator*

**Lihue**
Culliney, John James *radiologist, educator*
Stevens, Robert David *librarian, educator*

**Mililani**
Gardner, Sheryl Paige *gynecologist*
Hunkele, Lester Martin III *retired federal agency administrator*
Magee, Donald Edward *retired national park service administrator*
Okita, George Torao *retired pharmacologist*
Olsen, Harris Leland *diplomat, writer, real estate company executive, educator*

**Naalehu**
Carroll, Mary Colvert *not-for-profit developer, consultant*

**Oahu**
Moose, Charles A. *former protective services official*

**Pahoa**
Lewis, Jack (Cecil Paul Lewis) *publishing executive, editor*

**Paia**
Loomis, James Cook *mathematician, cyberneticist, writer, educator, navigator*

**Pearl City**
Sue, Alan Kwai Keong *dentist*

**Princeville**
Forth, Kevin Bernard *beverage distributing industry consultant*
Taylor, James Walter *business and management educator*

**Volcano**
Nicholson, Marilyn Lee *arts administrator*

**Wahiawa**
Camery, John William *computer engineer*

**Waianae**
Holifield, Pearl Kam (Kam Holifield, Momi Kam Holifield) *poet*

**Waikoloa**
Calvert, Delbert William *retired energy executive*
Copman, Louis *radiologist*
Morris, Victor Franklin, Jr. *retired meteorology educator*

**Wailuku**
DeVey, Graham Richard *secondary school educator, retired engineering executive*

**Waipahu**
Chang, Walter Tuck, Sr. *draftsman, real estate agent, religious studies educator*
Look, Pauwilo *media specialist, architectural engineer*

## IDAHO

**Arco**
Jardine, Cindy M. *music educator*

**Blackfoot**
Asmus, Elaine G. *science educator*

**Boise**
Aitken, Paul Arthur *composer, conductor*
Andrus, Cecil Dale *academic administrator*
Ansbach, Thomas M. *academic administrator*
Appleton, Steven R. *electronics executive*
Benham, James H. *state official*
Black, Pete *retired state legislator, educator*
Boyce, Carolyn *political organization administrator*
Brownson, Mary Louise *counselor, educator, artist*
Burdick, Roger S. *state supreme court justice*
Cleary, Edward William *retired diversified forest products company executive*
Close, Timothy *museum director*
Cory, Wallace Newell *retired civil engineer*
Eastland, Larry L. *entertainment and theme park development executive*
Eismann, Daniel T. *state supreme court justice*
Elg, Annette *food products executive*
Geston, Mark Symington *lawyer*
Griffin, Sylvia Gail *reading specialist*
Hanks, Stephen Grant *construction executive, lawyer*
Harad, George Jay *retired manufacturing executive*
Herbert, Kathy J. *retail executive*
Hlobik, Lawrence S. *agricultural products executive*
Hofflund, Mark *theater director*
Holt, Isabel Rae *radio program producer*
Howard, Marilyn *state school system administrator*
Hunsucker, Wayne (Carl Wayne Hunsucker) *architectural firm executive, educator*
Ilett, Frank, Jr. *trucking executive, educator*
Johnston, Lawrence R. *food products executive*
Jones, James Thomas *state supreme court justice, former state attorney general*
Juetten, George H. *company executive*
Kent, E(verett) Allen *performing arts association administrator, theater producer*
Keough, Shawn *state legislator*
Kirklin, Vance Lane *software company executive*
Leroy, David Henry *lawyer*
Lewis, Roderic W. *electronics executive, lawyer*
Lodge, Patti Anne *state senator*
Long, William D. *grocery store executive*
Mahoney, James E. *information technology executive*
Maloof, Giles Wilson *academic administrator, educator, author*
Markuson, Richard K. *former pharmaceutical association executive*
McDevitt, Charles Francis *retired judge, lawyer*
McGown, John, Jr. *lawyer*
McLuskie, Ed *communications educator*
Meyer, Christopher Hawkins *lawyer*
Minnich, Diane Kay *legal association administrator*
Moss, Thomas E. *prosecutor*
Myers, William Gerry III *lawyer*
Neil, J. Meredith *historian*
Nelson, Thomas G. *federal judge*
Overgaard, Willard Michele *retired political scientist*
Park, William Anthony (Tony Park) *lawyer*
Pfouts, Ralph William *economist, consultant*
Punnoose, Alex *physics professor*
Redshaw, James Douglas *neurologist*
Richardson, Betty H. *lawyer, former prosecutor*
Ricks, Mark G. *lieutenant governor, former state senator*
Risch, James E. *governor, former lieutenant governor, former state legislator*
Rubocki, Melanie Goedeker *lawyer*
Schultz, Richard H. *state agency administrator*
Shurtliff, Marvin Karl *lawyer*
Silak, Cathy R. *lawyer, former state supreme court justice*
Simplot, John R. *agribusiness executive*
Sims, John R. *lawyer*
Slaughter, Richard Arthur *political scientist, economist, educator*
Smith, Marsha H. *state agency administrator, lawyer*
Stover, Wilbur G., Jr. *manufacturing executive*
Sullivan, James Kirk *management consultant*
Terteling-Payne, Carolyn Ann *city official*
Thornton, Felicia D. *food service company executive*
Trott, Stephen Spangler *federal judge*
Trout, Linda Copple *state supreme court justice*
Uranga, Jean R. *lawyer*
Van Helden, Pete *food products executive*
VanHole, William Remi *lawyer*
Wasden, Lawrence *state attorney general*

**Bonners Ferry**
McClintock, William Thomas *health care administrator*

**Burley**
Vargas, Teresa Marie Bradley *elementary school educator*

**Caldwell**
Hendren, Robert Lee, Jr. *academic administrator*
Hoover, Robert Allan *university president*
Kerrick, David Ellsworth *lawyer*

**Coeur D' Alene**
Dahlgren, Dorothy *museum director*
Flygare, Richard Andrew *physician assistant*
Gumprecht, Jane Caroline Doering *retired physician*

**Cottonwood**
Wicks, Dwight Earl *elementary school educator*

**Donnelly**
Ferensowicz, Michael Jay *real estate company executive*

**Emmett**
Bennett, Gary Lee *physicist, consultant*

**Gooding**
Larson, Lynn Wood *artist, musician*

**Hagerman**
Roberts, Ronald John *education educator, director*

**Hailey**
Dolas, Evelyn Ann *poet, musician*
Youngblood, Deborah Sue *lawyer, speech pathology/audiology services professional*

**Harrison**
Carlson, George Arthur *artist*

**Heyburn**
Barson, Ross J. *music educator, assistant principal*

**Idaho Falls**
Abbott, Michael Lehman *environmental scientist*
Barbe, Betty Catherine *marketing professional, retired financial analyst*
Finnigan, Bernard Keith *filmmaker, writer*
Harris, Darryl Wayne *publishing executive*
King, Ronald Amos *federal official, retired communications professional*
Lee, Glenn Richard *medical association administrator, educator*
Miller, Gregory Kent *structural engineer*
Planchon, Harry Peter, Jr. *research development manager*
Riemke, Richard Allan *nuclear engineer*
Rydalch, Ann *federal agency administrator*
Shindurling, Jon J. *judge*
Smith, Gregg *brewing industry executive, writer*
Thorsen, James Hugh *retired aviation director, retired airport manager*
Thorsen, Nancy Dain *real estate broker*

**Inkom**
Ambrose, Tommy W. *chemical engineer, engineering executive*
Jackson, Allen Keith *retired museum administrator*

**Jerome**
Akers, Sharron Loella *language educator*
Bell, Maxine Toolson *state legislator, librarian*

**Kamiah**
Mills, Carol Margaret *public relations executive, consultant*
Mills, Lawrence *lawyer, business and transportation consultant*

**Ketchum**
Holland, Robert James *retired lawyer*
McElhinny, Wilson Dunbar *banker*
Ziebarth, Robert Charles *management consultant*

**Kimberly**
Strausbaugh, Carl Alan *plant pathologist*
Tasumi, Masahiro *science educator*

**Lewiston**
Branting, Steven D. *gifted and talented consultant*
Marshall, Josie *secondary school educator*
Tait, John Reid *lawyer*
Thomas, Dene Kay *academic administrator, educator*

**Mccall**
Pace, James T. *Internet company executive*
Romano, Michael *publishing executive, consultant*

**Meridian**
Ascuena, Vikki Pepper *secondary school educator*
Bach, William Kenneth, Jr. *financial consultant, director*
Rehder, Jon *social studies educator*
Thorsted, V. Darleene *neonatal/perinatal nurse, community health nurse*

**Moscow**
Abraham, Terry *school librarian*
Bobisud, Larry Eugene *mathematics professor*
Bohach, Carolyn Hovde *science educator, researcher*
DeShazer, James Arthur *biological engineer, educator, administrator*
Fiske, Janet Morray *volunteer, elementary school educator, researcher*
Force, Ronald Wayne *librarian*
Greene, Timothy Geddes *lawyer*

**Harris**, Robert Dalton *history professor, researcher, writer*
Jankowska, Maria Anna *school librarian, educator*
Miller, Maynard Malcolm *geologist, educator, science administrator, former state legislator*
Renfrew, Malcolm MacKenzie *chemist, educator*
Roberts, Lorin Watson *botanist, educator*
Shafii, Bahman *statistician, educator, researcher*
Shreeve, Jean'ne Marie *chemist, educator*
Vincenti, Sheldon Arnold *law educator, lawyer*
White, Timothy Peter *academic administrator, physical education educator*

**Mountain Home**
Jett, Sandra *elementary school educator*

**Nampa**
Bowers, Curtis Ray, Jr. *chaplain*
Johnson, Daniel D. *music educator*
Rambo, Helen Marie *librarian*

**Ola**
Farr, Reeta Rae *special education administrator*

**Osburn**
Bardelli, Frederick Ketchell *artist, art educator*

**Parma**
Lee, Jungmin *food scientist, researcher*

**Pocatello**
Baergen, Ralph Neil *humanities educator*
Berrey, Eleanor G. *elementary school educator*
Eichman, Charles Melvin *counselor*
Jacobsen, Richard T. *mechanical engineering educator*
Lawson, Jonathan Nevin *academic administrator, educator*
Leung, Solomon W. *engineering company executive, researcher*
Piland, Neill Finnes *health services economist, researcher, educator*
Robinson, Evelyn Etta *principal*
Stucki, Margaret Elizabeth *art gallery director, writer, painter*
Valentine, Ralph Schuyler *chemical engineer, director*

**Post Falls**
Hasalone, Annette Leona *research and development company executive*
Riggs, Jack Timothy *emergency physician, retired lieutenant governor*
Soss, Daniel Lee *social work educator*

**Preston**
Seare, Paul Dearden *music educator*

**Rexburg**
Barrus, Charles LaMar, Jr. *music educator*
Clark, Kim Bryce *academic administrator*
Hartvigsen, M. Kip *literature and language professor*
Ivers, John Joseph *language educator, dean*

**Sandpoint**
Bowne, Martha Hoke *editor, consultant*
Glock, Charles Young *sociologist, writer*
Schultz, Stephen W. *art educator*

**Sun Valley**
Cassell, William Comyn *retired college president*
Stewart, John Todd *economist, consultant*
Tillinghast, Charles Carpenter III *retired marketing company executive*

**Troy**
Hepler, Merlin Judson, Jr. *real estate broker*

**Twin Falls**
Hohnhorst, John Charles *judge*
Mathews, Donna Mae *special education educator*
Startin, W. Lane *insurance agent*
Williams, Ashlee Jean *English educator, psycho-social rehabilitation specialist*

**White Bird**
Lathrop, Lawrence Erwin, Jr. *retired small business owner, retired forester*

**Yellow Pine**
Auth, Robert Ralph *art educator*

## ILLINOIS

**Abbott Park**
Dempsey, William G. *pharmaceutical executive*
Flynn, Gary L. *pharmaceutical executive*
Frazier, Douglas Byron *healthcare manufacturing manager*
Freyman, Thomas C. *pharmaceutical executive*
Gonzalez, Richard A. *pharmaceutical executive*
Kempf, Dale J. *chemist*
Leiden, Jeffrey Marc M. *pharmaceutical executive, molecular biologist, cardiologist*
Nemmers, Joseph M., Jr. *pharmaceutical executive*
White, Miles D. *pharmaceutical executive*

**Addison**
Christopher, Doris K. *consumer products company executive*
Klemens, Thomas Lloyd *editor*
McDonald, David Eugene *transportation operator*

**Albion**
Curtis, Cyril Dean *retired physicist*

**Alexander**
Eck, Gail Ann *elementary school educator*

**Algonquin**
Gnutek, Anthony Edward *music educator*
Wise, Jack Ronald *music educator*

**Alpha**
Hunt, Brenda Sue Davis *missionary outreach executive, secondary school educator*

**Alsip**
Fournier, Maureen Mary *physical education educator*

**Alton**
Boyle, Ann M. *dean, dental educator*
Greenwood, John E. *investment advisor*
Kessler, William Eugene *healthcare executive*

**Argonne**
Abrikosov, Alexei Alexeyevich *physicist*
Ahmad, Irshad *physicist, nuclear scientist*
Ahmed, Shabbir *chemical engineer*
Ban, Stephen Dennis *gas industry executive*
Chang, Yoon Il *nuclear engineer*
Derrick, Malcolm *physicist*
John, Charles J. *public health service officer, educator*
Jorgensen, James Douglas *research physicist*
Kim, Yeon Soo *nuclear engineer, researcher*
Kopasz, John Peter *chemist*
Kukhtin, Alexander V. *chemist*
Kumar, Romesh *chemical engineer*
Lindert, Eric Alton *operations research specialist, small business owner*
Perlow, Gilbert Jerome *retired physicist, retired editor*
Peshkin, Murray *physicist*
Reed, Claude Brinton *systems engineer*
Schriesheim, Alan *science administrator*
Shpyrko, Oleg G. *physicist*
Srinivasan, Shankar Pattamadai *materials scientist, researcher*
Steindler, Martin Joseph *chemist*
Uprety, Krishna K. *physicist, materials scientist*
Vivio, Frank Michael *education educator, researcher*

**Arlington Heights**
Baptist, Allwyn J. *healthcare consultant*
Baumann, Daniel E. *publishing executive*
Church, Herbert Stephen, Jr. *retired construction company executive*
Fields, Sara A. *travel company executive*
Griffin, Jean Latz *political strategist, writer, publisher*
Hudson, Ronald Morgan *aviation planner*
Jensen, Lynn Edward *retired medical association administrator, economist*
Johnson, Margaret H. *welding company executive*
Kopielski, Camille Ann *counseling administrator, volunteer*
Lampinen, John A. *newspaper editor*
Leon, Edward *investor*
Li, Norman N. *chemicals executive*
Ray, Douglas Kent *newspaper executive*
Ruder, John Regan *physician*
Smith, Norman Obed *retired physical chemist, educator*
Telleen, Judy *counselor*
Tongue, William Walter *economics and business consultant, educator*
Tucker, Bowen Hayward *lawyer*

**Athens**
Curry, John Wesley *retired secondary school educator*

**Aurora**
Daugherty, Diane Ruth *music educator*
Daugherty, Patricia Ann *retired elementary school educator*
Easley, Pauline Marie *retired elementary school educator*
Elgar, Sharon Kay *science educator*
Fisher, Thomas Lee *gas industry executive*
Gregson, Timothy Howard, II, *music educator, musician, singer*
Keutzer, Ronald Eugene *mathematics educator*
Koopman, Richard Nelson *engineer, consultant*
Lee, Robert Hugh *management executive*
Lundquist, Robert Science *educator*
McCarthy, Mary Elizabeth (Beth) Constance *conductor, music educator*
Noglows, William P. *electronics executive*
Pappas, Margene *retired music educator*
Porzio, Donald Timmis *mathematics educator*
Stephens, Steve Arnold *real estate broker*
Wear, Jean Ann *accountant*

**Barrington**
Burrows, Brian William *retired research and development company executive, retired manufacturing executive*
Carter, Jeanie *performing company executive*
Chung, Joseph Sang-hoon *economics professor*
Furst, Warren Arthur *retired corporate executive*
Graham, Berta *humanities educator, researcher*
Kunkel, Nancy Angela *psychologist*
Lee, William Marshall *lawyer*
Murphy, Robert *executive search consultant*
Nadig, Gerald George *retired manufacturing executive*
Perry, I. Chet *petroleum company executive*
Ross, Frank Howard III *management consultant*
Schwan, Howard W. *manufacturing executive*
Stephens, Norval Blair, Jr. *marketing consultant*
Vertino, Anthony Dominic *psychologist*
Wood, Andrée Robitaille *archaeologist, researcher*
Worrell, Sharyn Dianne *volunteer, retired flight attendant*
Wyatt, James Frank, Jr. *lawyer*
Wynn, Thomas Joseph *judge, educator*
Young, Michael Phillip *orthopedist, surgeon*

**Batavia**
Balbekov, Valeri I. *physicist, researcher*
Brown, Gerald Curtis *retired military officer, retired engineering executive*
Chen, Mu-Chun *physicist, researcher*
Jonckheere, Alan Mathew *physicist*
Kosek, Wayne Richard *retired secondary school educator*
Lach, Joseph Theodore *physicist*
Lykken, Joseph David *physicist*
Mokhov, Nikolai V. *physicist, researcher*
Morefield, Michael Thomas *financial executive*
Oddone, Piermaria Jorge *experimental particle physicist*
Raja, Rajendran *physicist*

Rakhno, Igor *physicist*
Yeary, Sheridan Todd *pastor, educator*

## Beecher
Dettmer, Janet Kay *retired elementary school educator*
Squier, Victoria (Vicki) J. *mathematics educator*

## Belleville
Andersen, Barbara Jo *technologist, educator*
Baricevic, Sister John LaLande *nun, mathematician, educator*
Bauman, John Duane *lawyer*
Braxton, Edward K. *bishop*
Fietsam, Robert Charles *accountant*
Hedges, Patrick Armand *security firm executive*
Hess, Frederick J. *lawyer*
Hilgenbrink, Robert J. *academic administrator*
Jones, Donald Leigh *retired music educator*
Kappel, Stephen R. *retired orthopedist*
Miller, Jan Paul *lawyer, former prosecutor*
Pounds, Regina Dorothea *writer*
Ripplinger, George Raymond, Jr. *lawyer*
Shim, Sang Koo *mental health services professional*
Stone, William David *secondary school educator, consultant*
Studer, Louis *priest, religious organization administrator*
Thien-Stasko, Vicki Lynn *civil engineer*
Wittenbrink, Boniface Leo *priest*

## Bellwood
Miller, Denyce Karlina *tax specialist*

## Belvidere
Luhman, William Simon *community development administrator*
Mc Nelly, Frederick Wright, Jr. *psychologist*

## Bement
Vezina, Vicky Lynne *middle school educator*

## Bensenville
Lance, Joseph G. *sales executive*

## Benton
Foreman, James Louis *retired judge*
Gilbert, J. Phil *federal judge*

## Berwyn
Forst, Edmund Charles, Jr. *communications educator, administrator, consultant*
Hudik, Martin Francis *hospital administrator, educator, consultant, writer*
Parker, Alan John *veterinary neurologist, educator, researcher*
Wunderlich, Dorothy Anastasia *superintendent*

## Bloomingdale
Flaherty, John Joseph *quality assurance company executive*
Irgang, Lisa Beth *psychologist*
Wolande, Charles Sanford *former computer company executive*

## Bloomington
Blackburn, John D. *insurance company executive*
Bragg, Michael Ellis *lawyer, insurance company executive*
Bridges, Roger Dean *historian*
Brown, Jared *theater director, educator, writer*
Brunner, Kim M. *insurance company executive, lawyer*
Cook, Richard Kent *music educator, musician*
Curry, Alan Chester *insurance company executive*
Dietz, William Ronald *corporate management consultant*
Farmer, Doc *security firm executive, consultant*
Moham, Carren *music educator, singer*
Olson, Rue Eileen *retired librarian*
Pannell, Thierry Edgard *engineer, information technology manager*
Rust, Edward Barry, Jr. *insurance company executive, lawyer*
Skillrud, Harold Clayton *minister, retired bishop*
Stroyan, Susan Elizabeth *librarian, administrator*
Sullivan, Laura Patricia *lawyer, insurance company executive*
Switzer, Jon Rex *architect*
Tipsord, Michael L. *insurance company executive*
Trefzger, Richard Charles *surgeon*
Trosino, Vincent Joseph, Sr. *insurance company executive*
Vayo, David Joseph *composer, music educator*
Wilson, Richard F. *academic administrator*

## Blue Island
Heckenast, Sherri *auto parts executive, sports association executive*
Tisch, Carrie Catherine *elementary school educator*
Yager, Vincent Cook *retired bank executive*

## Bolingbrook
Caddy, Edmund H.H., Jr. *architect*
Day, Mary Ann *medical/surgical nurse*
Malicay, Manuel Alaban *physician*
Price, Theodora Hadzisteliou *individual, child and family therapist*
Sabau, Carmen Sybile *retired chemist*
Sheehan, James Patrick *printing company executive, former media company executive*

## Bourbonnais
Armstrong, Douglas *organic chemist, educator*
Dalton, Martha Gomer *music educator*
Rezba, Patricia Louise *middle school educator*
Wilkey, Elmira Smith *illustrator, artist, writer, educator*

## Braidwood
Zolecki-Browning, Diana M. *middle school educator*

## Bridgeview
Henson, Sheila J. *elementary school educator, assistant principal*

## Broadview
Bland, Pamela June *special education educator*

Lazar, Jill Sue *home healthcare company executive*

## Brookfield
Rabb, George Bernard *zoologist, conservationist*
Rudnick, Jamie *geneticist, research scientist*

## Buffalo Grove
Johnson, Craig Theodore *portfolio manager*
Kosobayashi, Kevan Takashi *music educator*
Kuennen, Thomas Gerard *journalist*
Leonetti, Michael Edward *financial planner*
Rai, Rajat *health facility administrator*
Samors, Neal *publishing executive, writer*
Schrader, Kara Jean *science educator*
Tracy, Allen Wayne *management consultant*
True, Michelle Ailene *editor, writer*

## Burr Ridge
Bottom, Dale Coyle *marketing executive, director, management consultant*
Brennan, James Joseph *lawyer, bank executive*
Decker, Richard Knore *lawyer*
McCormack, Robert Cornelius *investment banker*
Parker, James John *engineer, marketing professional*
Rosenberg, Robert Brinkmann *information technology executive*
Wyatt, Robert Odell *journalism educator*
Zaccone, Suzanne Maria *sales executive*

## Bushnell
Cortelyou, Cynthia Ann *elementary school educator*

## Byron
Love, LeeAnn *elementary school educator*

## Cahokia
Healy, Steven Michael *accountant, city official*

## Calumet City
Kovach, Joseph William *management consultant, psychologist, educator*
Muñoz, Romeo Solano *audio visual curator*
Scullion, Annette Murphy *lawyer, educator*
Swansey, Micah Kassio *psychologist*

## Carbondale
Ammon, Harry *history professor*
Asoh, Derek Ajesam *information scientist, educator*
Baker, Clora Mae *education educator*
Bauner, Ruth Elizabeth *library director*
Bekele, Elias Getahun *research scientist*
Benford, Robert Dee *social studies educator, editor*
Burr, Brooks Milo *zoology educator*
Carlson, David H. *dean*
Clark, M. H. *quantitative psychologist*
Clemons, John Robert *lawyer*
Cole, Brad *mayor*
Dixon, Billy Gene *academic administrator, educator*
Duggan, James Edgar *law librarian*
Gilbert, Glenn Gordon *retired linguistics educator*
Hahn, Robert Alan *philosophy educator*
Headrick, Todd Christopher *mathematical statistician, educator*
Herstein, Gary L. *philosophy professor, researcher*
Kawewe, Saliwe Moyo *social work educator, researcher*
Lanigan, Richard Leo, Jr. *humanities educator, writer, editor*
Lee, Mark Richard *lawyer, educator*
Mathur, Ike *finance educator*
Mohanty, Manoj K. *mineral engineer, educator*
Neuman, Edward George *mathematician, educator*
Oyana, Tonny J. *geoscientist, educator*
Patwardhan, Amit *research scientist*
Pinter, Nicholas *geologist*
Poshard, Glenn (Glendal W. Poshard) *academic administrator, former congressman*
Quisenberry, Nancy Lou *academic administrator, educator*
Scott, Shirley Clay *dean*
Snyder, Carolyn Ann *education educator, librarian, director*
Townsend, Gregory Williams *music educator*
Weeks, Theodore R. *history professor*
Werlich, David Patrick *history professor*
Whitlock, John Joseph *museum director*

## Carlinville
Bellm, Joan *civic worker*
Witham, Craig Ray *biology and chemistry educator*

## Carol Stream
Bemis, Mary Ferguson *magazine editor*
Franzen, Janice Marguerite Gosnell *magazine editor*
Gale, Neil Jan *Internet company executive, computer scientist, consultant*
Mollet, Emily A. *secondary school educator*

## Carrollton
Strickland, Hugh Alfred *lawyer*

## Carterville
Barkley Giffin, Adrienne F. *museum administrator, academic administrator*
Krapf, Keith Alan *science educator*

## Carthage
Glidden, John Redmond *lawyer*

## Cary
Narusis, Regina Gyté Firant *lawyer*

## Centralia
Whitten, Mary Lou *nursing educator*

## Cerro Gordo
Gilpin, Vicky Sue *literature and language educator, former congressman*

## Champaign
Abd-El-Khalick, Fouad Sami *science educator*
Arnould, Richard Julius *economist, educator, consultant, dean*

Baker, Jack Sherman *architect, educator*
Balbach, Harold Edward *environmental scientist*
Batzli, George Oliver *ecology educator*
Becker, Lawrence Paul *educator*
Bernhardt, Mark Daniel *economics educator*
Boubekri, Mohamed *architecture educator*
Brighton, Gerald David *retired finance educator*
Buschbach, Thomas Charles *geologist, consultant*
Cartwright, Keros *hydrogeologist, researcher*
Davis, James Henry *retired psychology educator*
Dmitriev, Dmitry A. *entomologist, researcher*
Douglas, George Halsey *language educator, writer*
Drasgow, Fritz *psychology professor*
Dulany, Donelson Edwin, Jr. *psychology professor*
Dulany, Elizabeth Gjelsness *editor*
Eriksen, Charles Walter *psychologist, educator*
Fredrickson, L(awrence) (L)homas *composer*
Freedman, Philip *internist, educator*
Ghosh, Avijit *dean*
Gold, Paul Ernest *psychology and behavioral neuroscience educator*
Gross, David Lee *geologist*
Guttenberg, Albert Ziskind *planning educator*
Hansen, Kathryn Gertrude *editor, retired state official*
Harroff, Natasha Karena *science educator, consultant*
Herman, Richard H. *academic administrator*
Hopkins, Lewis Dean *architecture educator*
Hurd, Heidi M. *dean, humanities educator, law educator*
Ikenberry, Stanley Oliver *education educator, director, former university president*
Joy, Richard Marks *lawyer*
Kindt, John Warren *lawyer, educator*
Korst, Helmut Hans *mechanical engineer, educator*
Kotoske, Roger Allen *artist, educator*
Krause, Harry Dieter *law educator*
Kroner, Fred L. *journalist*
Krug, Edward Charles *environmental scientist*
Levin, Geoffrey Arthur *botanist*
Loeb, Jane Rupley *academic administrator, educator*
Maggs, Peter Blount *lawyer, educator*
Mamer, Stuart Mies *lawyer*
May, Linda Karen Cardiff *occupational health nurse, safety engineer, consultant*
McConkie, George Wilson *education educator*
Mc Cord, John Harrison *lawyer, educator*
McCulloh, Judith Marie *editor*
McDonough, Jerome Patrick *librarian*
McGlathery, James Melville *retired foreign language educator*
Meyer, August Christopher, Jr. *broadcast executive, lawyer*
Mies, John Charles *Internet company executive*
Miller, Harold Arthur *lawyer*
Moore, Jerry Jay *sales executive, retired archaeologist*
Morrissette, Jason William *theater educator, actor, director*
Mueller, Rodney Alan *music educator*
Nowak, John E. *law educator*
Perry, Kenneth Wilbur *finance educator*
Rayward, Warden Boyd *librarian, educator*
Rebeiz, Constantin Anis *plant biochemist, educator, lab administrator, foundation administrator*
Reedy, Frances Starr *music educator, cellist*
Ridlen, Samuel Franklin *agriculture educator*
Riley, Robert Bartlett *landscape architect*
Roese, Neal J. *psychology professor, consultant*
Rose, Walter Deane *retired engineering educator*
Roussos, Louis Ablen *statistician, psychology professor*
Ruan, Lian Jin *library director*
Schnarre, Thomas Dale *education educator*
Schoenfeld, Hanns-Martin Walter *finance educator*
Scott, Anna Marie Porter Wall *sociology educator*
Semonin, Richard Gerard *retired state official*
Slichter, Charles Pence *physicist, researcher*
Smith, Ralph Alexander *cultural and educational policy educator*
Spice, Dennis Dean *financial consultant*
Spodek, Bernard *early childhood educator*
Stotler, Edith Ann *retired grain company executive*
Summerfield, Gale *director, educator*
Triandis, Harry Charalambos *psychologist, educator*
Turquette, Atwell Rufus *logician*
Turquette, Frances Bond *editor*
Watson, Jessica Lewis *writer*
Watts, Emily Stipes *retired English language educator*
Watts, Robert Allan *publisher, lawyer*
Wolfram, Stephen *physicist, computer company executive*
Young, Paul *graphic designer, edcator*

## Charleston
Ball-Saret, Jayne Adams *small business owner*
Coutant, Mary McElwee *retired editor*
Daum, John LaVern *retired band director, educator*
Dulaney, John Robert *music educator*
Eberly, Charles *counseling and student development educator*
Fine, Elaine Sarah *composer, musician*
McBride, Jonica Helene *mathematics professor*
NeSmith, Richard A. *education educator, consultant*
O'Rourke, Kathleen Ann *education educator*
Rives, Stanley Gene *retired academic administrator*
Surles, Carol D. *academic administrator*
Thornburgh, Daniel Eston *retired university administrator, journalism educator*

## Chatham
Chew, Keith Elvin *health facility administrator*

## Chebanse
McLaughlin, Barbara Lyn *elementary school educator*

## Chester
Welge, Donald Edward *food manufacturing executive*

## Chicago
Abcarian, Herand *surgeon, educator*

Abelson, Herbert Traub *pediatrician, educator*
Abrams, Lee Norman *lawyer*
Acker, Ann E. *lawyer*
Acker, Frederick George *lawyer*
Adams, Austin A. *bank executive*
Adams, John S. *insurance company executive*
Adelman, Pamela Bernice Kozoll *education educator*
Adelman, Stanley Joseph *lawyer*
Adelman, Steven Herbert *lawyer*
Adelson, Lawrence Seth *electronics executive, lawyer*
Adomavicius, Jonas *gastroenterologist, writer*
Ahern, Joseph James, Jr. *television station executive*
Aifantis, Ioannis *medical educator*
Alberts, Barry S. *lawyer*
Albrecht, Ronald Frank *anesthesiologist*
Albrecht-Buehler, Guenter Wilhelm Herbert *biologist*
Albright, Chris *professional soccer player*
Alcantara, Anita Luisa *community arts administrator*
Alexander, Karen *museum staff member*
Allen, Belle *management consulting firm executive, communications executive*
Allen, Henry Sermones, Jr. *lawyer*
Allen, Ronald Jay *law educator*
Allen, Thomas Draper *lawyer*
Almen, Lowell Gordon *church official*
Amberg, Thomas L. *public relations executive*
Amft, Robert Ernest *artist, photographer*
Amstadter, Laurence *retired architect*
Andersen, Burton Robert *immunologist, educator, medical historian*
Anderson, Craig Allen *retired art educator, artist*
Anderson, David Boyd *lawyer, metal products executive*
Anderson, J. Trent *lawyer*
Anderson, Karl Stephen *editor*
Anderson, Kimball Richard *lawyer*
Anderson, William Cornelius III *lawyer*
Andolino, Rosemarie *airport terminal executive*
Andreoli, Kathleen Gainor *nurse, educator, dean*
Angelson, Mark A. *printing company executive*
Angst, Gerald L. *lawyer*
Angulo, David Sigfredo *computer scientist, educator*
Anthony, Michael Francis *lawyer*
Antonio, Douglas John *lawyer*
Anvaripour, M. A. *lawyer*
Apelbaum, Phyllis L. *delivery messenger service executive*
Appel, Nina Schick *law educator, dean, academic administrator*
Archer, James G. *retired lawyer*
Armstrong, Edwin Richard *lawyer*
Arnold, Damon Theodore *physician*
Aronson, Virginia L. *lawyer*
Arpino, Gerald Peter *performing company executive*
Arruda, Jose *nephrologist*
Artner, Alan Gustav *art critic, journalist*
Artz, Andrew *hematologist, researcher*
Aschenbrenner, Matthias Josef *mathematician, educator*
Ash, J. Marshall *mathematician, educator*
Ast, Bruno *architecture educator*
Athas, Gus James *lawyer*
Aubin, Barbara Jean *artist*
Auerbach, Marshall Jay *lawyer*
Avery, Robert Dean *lawyer*
Axley, Frederick William *lawyer*
Babcock, Lyndon Ross, Jr. *environmental engineer, educator*
Baca, Stacey *newscaster*
Bacevicius, John Anthony, V, (John Bace) *research and development company executive*
Badel, Julie *lawyer*
Baer, John Richard Frederick *lawyer*
Bailey, Nettie Whitney *retired elementary school educator, retired assistant principal*
Bailey, Robert, Jr. *advertising executive*
Bailey, Robert Short *lawyer*
Baines, Harold Douglass *retired professional baseball player, baseball bench coach*
Baird, Douglas Gordon *law educator, dean*
Baird, James *lawyer*
Bajich, Milena Tatic *psychologist*
Bakay, Roy Arpad Earle *neurosurgeon, educator*
Baker, Bruce Jay *lawyer*
Baker, Dusty (Johnnie B. Baker Jr.) *professional baseball team manager*
Baker, Pamela *lawyer*
Bakris, George L. *nephrologist, educator, clinical researcher*
Bakwin, Edward Morris *banker*
Balanoff, Clem *county election director*
Balasi, Mark Geoffrey *architect*
Baldwin, DeWitt Clair, Jr. *pediatrician, educator*
Baldwin, Shaun McParland *lawyer*
Baley, Joan Marie *elementary school educator*
Balk, Robert A. *medical educator*
Balsam, Theodore *physician*
Balzekas, Stanley, Jr. *museum director*
Banerjee, Prashant *industrial engineer, educator, computer scientist*
Banoff, Sheldon Irwin *lawyer*
Barbour, Claude Marie *minister, educator*
Barden, Larry A. *lawyer*
Barker, Walter Lee *thoracic surgeon*
Barker, William Thomas *lawyer*
Barnes, Brenda C. *food products executive*
Barnes, James Garland, Jr. *lawyer*
Barney, Carol Ross *architect*
Baron, Joseph Mandel *hematologist*
Barr, Emily L. *broadcast executive*
Barr, John Robert *retired lawyer*
Barr, John W. *investment company executive, foundation administrator*
Barr, Sanford Lee *dentist*
Barré, Laura *finance company executive*
Barron, Harold Sheldon *lawyer*
Barron, Howard Robert *lawyer*
Barron, John *lawyer*
Bart, Susan Therese *lawyer*
Bartholomay, William C. *insurance brokerage company executive, professional baseball team executive*
Bartlit, Fred Holcomb, Jr. *lawyer*

Barton, John Joseph *obstetrician, gynecologist, educator, health facility administrator, researcher*
Bartter, Brit Jeffrey *investment banker*
Basden, Cameron *ballet mistress, dancer*
Bashwiner, Steven Lacelle *lawyer*
Bauer, William Joseph *federal judge*
Baugher, Peter V. *lawyer*
Baum, Bernard Helmut *sociologist, educator*
Baumgardt, Justi Michelle *professional soccer player*
Baumgartner, William Hans, Jr. *lawyer*
Bayles, Deborah Lynn *lawyer*
Bayless, Rick *chef*
Beane, Marjorie Noterman *academic administrator*
Beasley, DaMarcus Lamont *professional soccer player*
Beaudet-Francès, Patricia Suzanne *photography editor*
Beck, Philip S. *lawyer*
Beck, Robert N. *nuclear medicine educator*
Becker, Gary Stanley *economist, educator*
Becker, Heather Shawn *art association administrator, artist*
Becker, Michael Allen *internist, rheumatologist, educator*
Becker, Scott *lawyer*
Beem, Jack Darrel *retired lawyer*
Beemster, Joseph Robert *risk management consultant*
Begel, Thomas M. *manufacturing executive*
Beitler, J. Paul *real estate developer*
Bell, Carl Compton *psychiatrist, researcher*
Bell, James A. *aerospace transportation executive*
Bellows, Laurel Gordon *business lawyer*
Belluschi, Anthony C. *architect*
Bennett, Robert William *law educator*
Bennington, Thomas Francis *lawyer, county official*
Bensinger, Peter Benjamin *consulting firm executive*
Benson, Al Bowen III *oncologist, educator*
Berens, Mark Harry *lawyer*
Berenzweig, Jack Charles *lawyer*
Berger, Miles Lee *land economist*
Berger, Robert Michael *lawyer*
Bergonia, Raymond David *venture capitalist*
Bergstein, Melvyn *information technology executive*
Berhalter, Gregg *professional soccer player*
Berk, Harlan Joseph *numismatist, writer*
Berkoff, Adam T. *lawyer*
Berkowitz, Sean M. *prosecutor*
Berkson, Sadie *volunteer*
Berman, Arthur Leonard *retired state legislator*
Berman, Debbie *lawyer*
Berman, Laura *sex therapist*
Bernard, Robert *company executive*
Bernardin, Thomas L. *advertising executive*
Bernatowicz, Frank Allen *management consultant*
Berner, Robert Lee, Jr. *lawyer*
Bernstein, Charles Bernard *lawyer*
Bernstein, H. Bruce *lawyer*
Bernstein, Lisa E. *law educator*
Berolzheimer, Karl *lawyer*
Bertenthal, Bennett Ira *psychologist, educator*
Be Sant, Craig *marketing executive*
Bess, Ronald W. *advertising executive*
Betz, Hans Dieter *theology studies educator*
Beugen, Joan Beth *communications executive*
Bevington, David Martin *English literature educator*
Bidwell, Charles Edward *sociologist, educator*
Biebel, Paul Philip, Jr. *lawyer*
Bigg, Susan Jeanette *educational consultant*
Biggs, Robert Dale *Near Eastern studies educator*
Bindenagel, James Dale *university executive*
Binion, Celious *retired parochial school educator*
Bitner, John Howard *lawyer*
Bixby, Frank Lyman *retired lawyer*
Black, Henry Richard *physician*
Black, Robert Durward *television producer*
Blair, Edward McCormick *investment banker*
Blake, Aileen *finance company executive*
Bleifuss, Joel *journalist*
Bleiweiss, Shell J. *lawyer*
Block, Neal Jay *lawyer*
Block, Philip Dee III *retired investment company executive*
Blount, Michael Eugene *lawyer*
Bluhm, Neil Gary *real estate company executive*
Blumberg, Avrom Aaron *physical chemistry professor*
Boberg, Wayne D. *lawyer*
Bobins, Norman R. *banker*
Bobrinskoy, Charles Kellogg *investment banker*
Bocanegra, Carlos *professional soccer player*
Bodenstein, Ira *lawyer*
Boehnen, Daniel A. *lawyer*
Bogaard, Jonathan Harvey *lawyer*
Boggs, Catherine J. *lawyer*
Boggs, Joseph Dodridge *pediatric pathologist, educator*
Bogolub, David Louis *physician*
Bohn, Charlotte Galitz *retired real estate executive*
Boies, Wilber H. *lawyer*
Bona, Jerry Lloyd *mathematician, educator*
Bonaparte, William *communications company executive*
Bonow, Robert Ogden *medical educator*
Borenstine, Alvin Jerome *search company executive*
Borisy, Gary G. *molecular biology professor*
Bosselman, Fred Paul *law educator*
Bouma, Robert Edwin *lawyer*
Bourdon, Cathleen Jane *professional society administrator*
Bowe, William J(ohn) *lawyer*
Bowen, Stephen Stewart *lawyer*
Bower, Glen Landis *judge, lawyer*
Bowman, Cynthia Grant *law educator*
Bowman, James Edward *pathologist, educator*
Bowman, Leah *fashion designer, consultant, photographer, educator*
Boyer, John William *history professor, dean*
Boykins, Michael L. *lawyer*
Boyle, John Francis *lawyer*
Bradley, Thomas A. *insurance company executive*
Brake, Cecil Clifford *retired diversified manufacturing executive*

Brakel, Samuel Jan *public safety executive, law educator*
Bramnik, Robert Paul *lawyer*
Bramson, James B. *dentist, dental association administrator*
Brandt, William Arthur, Jr. *consulting executive*
Brasher, Aimee Elizabeth *surgeon*
Brauer, Sasha Gerritson *church musician, music educator*
Breen, Neil Thomas *publishing executive*
Brendler, Charles Burgess *urologist, educator*
Brennan, Michael *real estate company executive*
Brice, Roger Thomas *lawyer*
Bridgman, Thomas Francis *retired lawyer*
Brinkman, John Anthony *historian, educator*
Briones, Teresita Landicho *medical researcher, educator*
Brizzolara, Charles Anthony *lawyer, director*
Bro, Ruth Hill *lawyer*
Broadhead, Glenn J. *communications educator, consultant*
Brock, Kathy *newscaster*
Brodsky, William J. *investment company executive*
Brogan, Lisa S. *lawyer*
Bromley, Richard *lawyer*
Brookens, Carl *psychologist*
Brooker, Thomas Kimball *oil industry executive*
Brotman, Barbara Louise *journalist, writer*
Brown, Alan Crawford *lawyer*
Brown, Donald James, Jr. *lawyer*
Brown, Elizabeth McCarthy *social services administrator*
Brown, Gregory K. *lawyer*
Brown, Jeremy Earle *advertising executive*
Brown, Matthew S. *lawyer*
Brown, Richard Holbrook *library director, historian, researcher*
Brown, Rosellen *writer*
Brumback, Charles Tiedtke *retired newspaper executive*
Brummel, Mark Joseph *religious organization administrator*
Bryan, John Henry *food and consumer products company executive*
Bryant, David J. *lawyer*
Bryant, Fred Boyd *psychology professor*
Buchh, Basharat *pediatrician*
Buckley, Joseph Paul III *computer technician*
Bucklo, Elaine Edwards *United States district court judge*
Bucksbaum, John *real estate company executive*
Bucksbaum, Matthew *real estate investment trust company executive*
Buehrle, Mark *professional baseball player*
Bulger, Brian Wegg *lawyer*
Bulka, Micheal *art critic*
Buniak, Raymond *educational professional*
Burck, Joseph Russell *medical educator, consultant, minister*
Burke, Anne M. *state supreme court justice*
Burke, John Michael *lawyer*
Burke, Thomas Joseph, Jr. *lawyer*
Burkhardt, Edward Arnold *rail transportation executive*
Burnitz, Jeromy *professional baseball player*
Burns, Diann *newscaster*
Burns, Robert Patrick *law educator*
Burns, Terrence Michael *lawyer*
Burroughs, Margaret Taylor Goss *artist*
Burton, Cheryl *newscaster*
Busey, Roxane C. *lawyer*
Buss, Emily *law educator*
Butler, John William, Jr. *lawyer*
Bynoe, Peter Charles Bernard *real estate developer, lawyer*
Cafferty, Pastora San Juan *education educator*
Calabresi, Steven G. *law educator*
Callahan, Michael R. *lawyer*
Callahan, Timothy T. *real estate company executive*
Cameron, Kenzie Alynn *medical researcher, educator*
Campbell, Gavin Elliott *real estate investor and developer*
Campbell, William Henry, Jr. *financial consultant, former federal agency administrator*
Campbell, William J., Jr. *lawyer*
Camper, Fred *freelance writer, educator*
Camper, John Jacob *writer, academic administrator*
Canty, Dawn M. *lawyer*
Cappo, Joseph C. *journalist, writer*
Carey, Charles P. *commodities exchange executive*
Carlin, Dennis J. *lawyer*
Carlson, LeRoy Theodore, Jr. *telecommunications industry executive*
Carlson, Michael *chef*
Carlson, Walter Carl *lawyer*
Caro, William Allan *dermatologist, educator, pathologist*
Carpenter, David William *lawyer*
Carr, Jeffrey W. *lawyer, manufacturing executive*
Carr, Walter Stanley *lawyer*
Carren, Jeffrey P. *lawyer*
Carroll, David *writer, illustrator*
Carroll, James J. *lawyer*
Carroll, William Kenneth *lawyer, educator, psychologist, theologian*
Case, Donni Marie *investment company executive*
Case, Gregory C. *insurance company executive*
Case, Mary Anne *law educator*
Castillo, Mario Enrique *artist, educator*
Castillo, Ruben *federal judge*
Castorino, Sue *communications executive*
Ceko, Theresa C. *law educator, lawyer*
Celesia, Gastone Guglielmo *neurologist*
Cesario, Robert Charles *retail executive, consultant*
Chacko, Samuel *association official*
Chafetz, Barry Richard *lawyer*
Chakrabarty, Ananda Mohan *microbiologist*
Chakrabarty, Dipesh *history professor*
Chaleff, Carl Thomas *investment company executive*
Chambers, Donald Arthur *biochemistry and molecular medicine educator*
Champagne, Ronald Oscar *medical association administrator*
Chan, Lawrence Siu-Yung *dermatologist, educator*
Chandiwal, Amito *research scientist*
Chandler, Kent, Jr. *lawyer*

Chang, Peter M.J. *musicologist, educator*
Chang, Yi-Cheng *insurance agent*
Chang, Yong *research scientist*
Chapman, Alger Baldwin *finance company executive, lawyer*
Chapman, John Stuart *lawyer*
Chapman, Stephen James *columnist*
Charles, Allan G. *obstetrician, educator*
Charrow, Joel *pediatrician, educator, geneticist, director*
Chatterton, Robert Treat, Jr. *reproductive endocrinology educator*
Chauhan, Neelima B. *neuroscientist, researcher*
Cheely, Daniel Joseph *lawyer*
Chemers, Robert Marc *lawyer*
Cherdunulo, Steve *professional soccer player*
Chereska, Steven Edward *counselor, paralegal*
Cherry, Daniel Ronald *lawyer*
Childers, Mary Ann *newscaster*
Chiles, Stephen Michael *lawyer*
Ching, Brian *professional soccer player*
Chiu, Brian Chih-Hung *epidemiologist*
Chmell, Samuel Jay *orthopedic surgeon*
Choldin, Marianna Tax *librarian, educator*
Chorengel, Bernd *international hotel corporation executive*
Christianson, Stanley David *finance company executive*
Christoffel, Katherine Kaufer *pediatrician, epidemiologist, educator*
Chromizky, William Rudolph *accountant*
Chung, Paul Myungha *mechanical engineer, educator*
Chunprapaph, Boonmee *physician, educator*
Ciezadlo, Janina A. *art critic, educator*
Citera, Peter M *mortgage company executive*
Claeys, Jerome Joseph III *investment company executive*
Clark, Frank M. *utilities executive*
Clark, James Allen *lawyer, educator*
Clark, James E. *lawyer*
Clark, Raymond S. *architectural firm executive*
Clayton, Robert Norman *chemist, educator*
Clemens, Richard Glenn *lawyer*
Cline, William Chambers *automotive executive*
Cloonan, James Brian *investment company executive*
Cloutier, Kevin M. *lawyer*
Coase, Ronald Harry *economist, educator*
Coe, Fredric L. *internist, educator, medical researcher*
Coffey, Susanna Jean *art educator, artist*
Cohen, Charles Emil *art historian, educator*
Cohen, Melanie Rovner *lawyer*
Cohen, Melvin R. *physician, educator*
Cohen, Ted *philosopher, educator*
Cohler, Bertram Joseph *social sciences educator, psychologist*
Cole, Thomas Amor *lawyer*
Colker, David A. *stock exchange executive*
Collen, John *lawyer, educator*
Collens, Lewis Morton *academic administrator, law educator*
Colley, Karen J. *medical educator, researcher*
Comella, Phillip L. *lawyer*
Congalton, Christopher William *lawyer*
Conklin, Thomas William *lawyer*
Conlon, Suzanne B. *federal judge*
Conlon, William F. *lawyer*
Conrad, Jimmy *professional soccer player*
Conroe, Henry Gerald *psychiatrist*
Convey, Bobby (Robert Francis Convey) *professional soccer player*
Conway, James Joseph *radiologist, educator*
Conway, Michael Maurice *lawyer*
Cook, Bruce Lawrence *editor*
Cooke, Michael *editor-in-chief, publishing executive*
Cooper, Charles Gilbert *cosmetics executive*
Copeland, Edward Jerome *lawyer*
Corrin, Dean C. *theater educator, playwright*
Costello, John William *lawyer*
Costin, Joseph Laurence, Jr. *information services executive*
Cottone, Dominic Patrick *director*
Covalt, Robert Byron *chemicals executive*
Cox, Allan James *management consultant*
Cox, Charles C. *economist*
Craig, John Bruce *former ambassador, air transportation executive*
Craine, Thomas Knowlton *not-for-profit developer*
Crane, Barbara Bachmann *photographer, educator*
Crane, Charlotte *law educator*
Crane, Mark *lawyer*
Crane, R.H. *poet*
Craven, George W. *lawyer*
Crawford, Dewey Byers *lawyer*
Cressey, Bryan Charles *venture capitalist*
Crisham, Thomas Michael *lawyer*
Crnkovich, Ruth Anne *art appraiser, museum director*
Crocker, Douglas, II, *real estate executive*
Crockett, George Ephriam *secondary school educator*
Crone, Anna Lisa *Russian literature educator*
Cronin, James Watson *physicist, researcher*
Cropsey, Joseph *retired political science professor*
Crosby, John Bartlett *lawyer, health science association administrator*
Cross, Robert Clark *journalist*
Crossan, John Robert *lawyer*
Crown, James Schine *investment company executive*
Crown, Lester *manufacturing executive*
Cruickshank, John Douglas *publishing executive*
Crull, Jan, Jr. *lawyer*
Cruthird, Robert Lee *sociology educator*
Cudahy, Richard D. *federal judge*
Cueto, Rochelle E. *elementary school educator*
Cullen, Charles Thomas *historian, librarian*
Culp, Kristine Ann *dean, theology studies educator*
Cummings, Andrea J. *lawyer*
Cunningham, Robert James *lawyer*
Cuno, James *museum director*
Cupps, Anthony S. *investment company executive*
Currie, David Park *law educator*
Curry, Raymond Howard *physician*
Curwen, Randall William *journalist, editor*
Cusack, John Thomas *lawyer*
Custer, Charles Francis *lawyer*

Dabrowski, Edward John *television technical director*
Daley, Michael Joseph *lawyer*
Daley, Richard Michael *mayor*
Daley, Susan Jean *lawyer*
Daley, Vincent Raymond, Jr. *real estate company executive, consultant*
Daly, Patrick F. *real estate executive, architect*
Dam, Kenneth W. *law educator, former federal agency administrator*
Dan, Bernard W. *commodities exchange executive*
Dancewicz, John Edward *investment banker*
Dandridge, LeNor *paralegal*
Daniel, Elnora D. *academic administrator*
Daniel, T. *mime performer, theater director, choreographer*
Darabi, Houshang *engineering educator*
Darby, Edwin Wheeler *retired columnist*
Darchun, Lino Auksutis *real estate professional*
Dardai, Shahid Moinuddin *computer science educator*
Dasso, James Daniel *lawyer*
Davidson, Michael H. *cardiologist, researcher*
Davidson, Richard Laurence *geneticist, educator*
Davis, Addie L. *mathematics educator*
Davis, Mary Ellen K. *library director*
Davis, Michael W. *lawyer*
Davis, Muller *lawyer*
Davis, Scott Jonathan *lawyer*
Davison, Richard *internist, educator*
Davros, Michael George *education educator*
Dawson, Michael C. *political science professor*
Dayal, Vijay Shanker *medical educator, physician*
De Armas, Frederick Alfred *foreign language educator*
Debus, Allen George *historian, educator*
Dechene, James Charles *lawyer*
Dee, Ivan Richard *book publisher*
Dees, Richard Lee *lawyer*
de Hoyos, Debora M. *lawyer*
Deitrick, William Edgar *lawyer*
de Lasa, José M. *lawyer*
Deli, Anne Tynion *retail executive*
DeLong, Ray *editor*
Delp, Wilbur Charles, Jr. *lawyer*
Dembowski, Peter Florian *foreign language educator*
D'Emilio, John *humanities educator, writer*
DeMoss, Jon W. *insurance company executive, lawyer*
Dempsey, Clinton (Clint) Drew *professional soccer player*
Dempsey, Mary A. *commissioner, lawyer*
Dempster, Ryan Scott *professional baseball player*
Denvir, Robert F. *lawyer*
Desideri, Lawrence R. *lawyer*
Desjardins, Claude *physiologist, dean*
Despa, Florin *research scientist*
D'Esposito, Julian C., Jr. *lawyer*
Despres, Leon Mathis *lawyer, former city official*
Devine, Richard A. (Dick DeVine) *lawyer*
DeVries, James Howard *lawyer*
DeWolfe, John Chauncey, Jr. *lawyer*
DeYoe, David P. *lawyer*
Diamond, Seymour *physician*
Diamond, Shari Seidman *law professor, psychology professor*
Dickman, Martin J. *federal agency administrator*
Diederichs, Janet Wood *public relations executive*
Dienst, Daniel W. *metal products executive*
DiStasio, Richard P. *manufacturing executive*
Dittmer, Frances R. *curator*
Dix, Rollin C(umming) *mechanical engineering educator, consultant*
Dixon, Stewart Strawn *lawyer, consultant*
Dockterman, Michael *lawyer*
Doetsch, Virginia Lamb *former advertising executive, writer*
Doherty, Brian Gerard *alderman*
Dohner, Markos *museum staff member, artist*
Dolan, Michael F. *lawyer*
Dolan, Thomas Christopher *professional society administrator*
Dold, Robert Bruce *journalist*
Dondanville, Patricia *lawyer*
Donlevy, John Dearden *lawyer*
Donnelley, James Russell *printing company executive*
Donohue, Craig S. *mercantile exchange executive*
Donovan, Landon *professional soccer player*
Douglas, Charles W. *lawyer*
Dowlatshahi, Kambiz *surgeon, educator*
Downs, Robert K. *lawyer*
Doyle, John Robert *lawyer*
Dragonette, Rita Hoey *public relations executive*
Drake, Francis LeBaron *law librarian*
Draut, Eric J. *insurance company executive*
Drinfeld, Vladimir Gershonovich *mathematician, educator*
Driskell, Claude Evans *college director, educator, dentist*
Drizin, Steven A. *law educator, lawyer*
Dube, Monte I. *lawyer*
DuCanto, Joseph Nunzio *lawyer, educator*
Dudley, Rick (Richard C. Dudley) *professional sports team executive*
Duffy, Terrence A. *mercantile exchange executive*
Duhl, Michael Foster *lawyer*
Dull, Charles C. *educational association administrator*
Dunaif, Andrea Elizabeth *endocrinologist*
Duncan, Bruce W. *real estate company executive, hotel executive*
Duncan, John Patrick Cavanaugh *lawyer*
Dunea, George *nephrologist, educator*
Dunlop, Karen Owen *lawyer*
Dunn, Edwin Rydell *lawyer*
Dunning, Jean *artist*
Dunning, Jeffrey Patrick *lawyer*
Dunning, Richard L. *health products executive*
Dupont, Todd F. *mathematics professor*
Durburg, Jack E. *real estate company executive*
Durchslag, Stephen P. *lawyer*
Durkin, Kevin P. *lawyer*
Dutta, Mitra *engineer, educator*
Dwyer, Dennis D. *information technology executive*
Dye, Jermaine *professional baseball player*
Dykstra, Paul Hopkins *lawyer*
Easterbrook, Frank Hoover *federal judge*
Eastman, Dean Eric *physicist, researcher*

Iyer, Kishore *transplant surgeon*
Jachino, Daneen L. *legal administrator*
Jackson, Jesse Louis *political organization worker, clergyman*
Jacobs, Caryn Leslie *lawyer, former prosecutor*
Jacobson, Marian Slutz *lawyer*
Jacobson, Richard Joseph *lawyer*
Jacoby, John Patrick *lawyer*
Jacover, Jerold Alan *lawyer*
Jager, Melvin Francis *lawyer*
Jameson, James Larry *medical educator, endocrinologist, internist*
Jamieson, James M. *manufacturing executive*
Janners, Erik Nikolas *music educator, conductor*
Jao, Chiang *information technology educator*
Jarrett, Tukoi Demarco *director*
Jarrett, Valerie Bowman *real estate company executive, stock exchange executive*
Jegen, Sister Carol Frances *religious studies educator*
Jensen, Harold Leroy *medical liability insurance administrator, physician*
Jerome, Jerrold V. *retired insurance company executive*
Jezuit, Leslie James *manufacturing executive*
Jilhewar, Ashok *gastroenterologist*
Joern, Charles Edward, Jr. *lawyer*
John, Peter C. *lawyer*
Johnson, Eddie *professional soccer player*
Johnson, Elmer William *lawyer*
Johnson, Garrett Bruce *lawyer*
Johnson, Gary Thomas *cultural organization administrator*
Johnson, Glenn Thompson *retired judge*
Johnson, Janet Helen *literature educator*
Johnson, Mary Ann *vocational school owner*
Johnson, Richard Fred *lawyer*
Johnson, Timothy Patrick *health and social researcher*
Jones, Cobi *professional soccer player*
Jones, Emil, Jr. *state legislator*
Jones, Linda *communications educator*
Jones, Mary Laura *not-for-profit developer*
Jones, Sandra Yvonne *lawyer*
Jones, Tony *academic administrator*
Jordan, Karen *newscaster*
Joseph, Robert Thomas *lawyer*
Joslin, Rodney Dean *lawyer*
Judge, Bernard Martin *editor, publishing executive*
Julmy, Camille P. *real estate company executive*
Junewicz, James J. *lawyer*
Kadanoff, Leo Philip *physicist, educator*
Kaegi, Walter Emil *history professor*
Kahrilas, Peter James *medical educator, researcher*
Kallick, David A. *lawyer*
Kalt, David *diversified financial services company executive*
Kamerick, Eileen Ann *corporate financial executive, lawyer*
Kaminski, David P. *lawyer*
Kamyszew, Christopher D. *film executive, educator, curator*
Kantrow, Josh Mark *lawyer*
Kaplan, Jared *lawyer*
Kaplan, Joel H. *lawyer*
Kaplan, Morton A. *political science professor*
Kaput, Jim *science administrator, educator*
Karanikas, Alexander *language educator*
Karlin, Edward J. *lawyer*
Karlin, Sy N. *social studies educator*
Karow, Thomas Robert *public relations executive*
Katz, Adrian Izhack *medical educator*
Katz, Avrum Sidney *lawyer*
Katz, Friedrich *history educator*
Katz, Stuart Charles *lawyer, musician*
Kauffman, Peter H. *lawyer, energy executive*
Kaufman, Andrew Michael *lawyer*
Kearney, John Walter *sculptor, painter*
Keenan, James George *classics educator*
Keiderling, Timothy Allen *chemistry educator, researcher*
Keller, Julia *reporter*
Keller, Kasey *professional soccer player*
Kellman, Sandra Y. *lawyer*
Kelly, Arthur Lloyd *investment company executive*
Kelly, Charles Arthur *lawyer*
Kelly, Curtis Hartt *retired publishing executive*
Kelly, Jerry Bob *social services administrator*
Kennedy, Lawrence Allan *mechanical engineering educator*
Kenney, Colleen M. *lawyer*
Kenney, Crane H. *lawyer*
Kenney, Estelle Koval *artist, educator*
Kenney, Frank Deming *lawyer*
Kerbis, Gertrude Lempp *architect*
Khabibulin, Nikolai *professional hockey player*
Khan, M. Wasiullah *academic administrator*
Khodarev, Nikolai Nikolaevich *biologist, researcher*
Kikoler, Stephen Philip *lawyer*
Kilbride, Thomas L. *state supreme court justice*
Kim, Danial *publishing executive*
Kim, Michael Charles *lawyer*
Kincaid, Richard D. *real estate company executive*
King, Andre Richardson *architectural graphic designer*
King, Quintin L. *trade association administrator, lobbyist*
King, Sharon Louise *lawyer*
Kins, Juris *lawyer*
Kirkpatrick, Anne Saunders *systems analyst*
Kirschner, Barbara Starrels *gastroenterologist*
Kirsner, Joseph Barnett *physician, educator*
Kisor, Henry Du Bois *editor, columnist, critic, writer*
Kissel, Richard John *lawyer*
Kistenbroker, David H. *lawyer*
Kitch, Paul R. *lawyer*
Kite, Steven B. *lawyer*
Kittle, Charles Frederick *surgeon*
Klapthor, James *news media relations specialist*
Klatt, Wayne Roy *editor, writer*
Klaviter, Helen Lothrop *editor-in-chief, magazine editor*
Klebba, Raymond Allen *property manager*
Klenk, James Andrew *lawyer*
Klenk, Timothy Carver *lawyer*
Kleppa, Ole J. *chemistry professor*
Kloss, Linda L. *medical association administrator*
Knapp, Paul Raymond *think-tank executive*

Knappenberger, Paul Henry, Jr. *science museum director*
Kneen, John W. *venture capitalist*
Knight, Christopher Nichols *lawyer*
Knight, Cranston S. *history professor*
Knox, James Marshall *lawyer*
Knutson, Kristen Lynn *anthropologist, sleep researcher*
Kobs, James Fred *direct marketing consultant*
Koch, Steven *lawyer, investment banker, finance company executive*
Koellner, Laurette *human resources specialist, aerospace transportation executive*
Koernig, Stephen K. *marketing professional, educator*
Kohn, Shalom L. *lawyer*
Kolek, Robert Edward *lawyer*
Konerko, Paul *professional baseball player*
Kopelman, Ian Stuart *lawyer*
Koppelman, Andrew Martin Mayer *law educator*
Kornick, Michael *chef*
Kouvel, James Spyros *physicist, educator*
Kozak, John W. *lawyer*
Kramer, Andrea S. *lawyer*
Krantz, Claire Wolf *artist, freelance critic, curator*
Krashesky, Alan *newscaster*
Krasny, Paula J. *lawyer*
Kraus, Herbert Myron *public relations executive*
Krause, James R. *stock exchange executive*
Kravitt, Jason Harris Paperno *lawyer*
Krawczyk, Eva *information scientist, educator*
Krawetz, Arthur Altshuler *chemist, science administrator*
Kreis, Jason *professional soccer player*
Krent, Harold J. *dean, law educator*
Kresse, William Joseph *lawyer, educator, accountant*
Kriss, Robert J. *lawyer*
Kritz, Robert *composer*
Krivicich, John Augustine *lawyer*
Krivkovich, Peter George *advertising executive*
Kroll, Barry Lewis *retired lawyer*
Kroot, Jason M. *lawyer*
Krueger, Bonnie Lee *editor, writer*
Kubistal, Patricia Bernice *educational consultant*
Kubo, Gary Michael *advertising executive*
Kuczwara, Thomas Paul *federal agency administrator, lawyer*
Kudish, David J. *financial executive*
Kuiken, Todd Alan *medical researcher, rehabilitation services professional, educator*
Kullberg, Duane Reuben *accounting firm executive*
Kuner, Charles *secondary school educator*
Kurish, James Brian *finance executive*
Kwembe, Tor Anthony *mathematics professor, researcher*
Lach, Alma Elizabeth *food and cooking writer, consultant*
Ladd, Jeffrey Raymond *lawyer*
Laidlaw, Andrew R. *lawyer*
Lal, Anil *health facility administrator*
Landan, Henry Sinclair *financial and business consultant*
Landeck, Carl *corporate financial executive*
Landerholm, Elizabeth Jane *early childhood education educator*
Landes, William M. *law educator*
Landow-Esser, Janine Marise *lawyer*
Landsberg, Lewis *dean, endocrinologist, medical researcher*
Laner, Richard Warren *lawyer*
Lang, Gordon, Jr. *retired lawyer*
Lanznar, Howard S. *lawyer*
Larsen, Erik *retired surgeon*
Larson, Allan Louis *political scientist, educator, lay worker*
Larson, Nancy Celeste *information technology manager*
Larson, Roy *journalist, publishing executive*
Lassar, Scott R. *lawyer, former prosecutor*
Lathon, Sheraine *clergyman*
Latimer, Kenneth Alan *lawyer*
Lau, Lester F. *science educator, researcher*
Laumann, Edward Otto *sociology educator*
Lavani, Romeen M. *physician*
LaVelle, Avis *consulting firm executive*
Lawler, James Ronald *French language educator*
Lazar, Ludmila *concert pianist, music educator*
Lazarus, Steven *technology company exective*
Lee, Bao-Shiang Bob *biochemist, researcher*
Lee, Derrek Leon *professional baseball player*
Lee, Raphael Carl *plastic surgeon, biomedical engineer*
Lee, Yoon Mo *state official*
Lefco, Kathy Nan *law librarian*
Leff, Alan Richard *medical educator, researcher*
Lefkow, Joan Humphrey *federal judge*
Legge Kemp, Diane *architect, landscape architect*
Leighton, George Neves *retired judge*
Leinenweber, Harry D. *federal judge*
Lemein, Gregg D. *lawyer*
Leonard, Sister Anne C. *school system administrator*
Leonard, Laura L. *lawyer*
Lerman, Zafra Margolin *science and public policy professor*
Lerner, Alexander Robert *insurance company executive*
Lerner, Barbara *writer, researcher*
Lerner, Wayne M. *healthcare executive*
LeRoy, Spencer III *lawyer*
Leszinske, William O. *investment company executive*
Letts, Tracy *actor, playwright*
Levandowski, Barbara Sue *education educator*
Levenfeld, Milton Arthur *lawyer*
Leventhal, Bennett Lee *psychiatry and pediatrics educator, academic administrator*
Levi, John G. *lawyer*
Levin, Charles Edward *lawyer*
Levin, Jack S. *lawyer*
Levin, Lawrence Daniel *lawyer*
Levine, Laurence Harvey *lawyer*
Levitt, Steven D. *economics professor*
Levmore, Saul *dean, law educator*
Levy, Deborah *security company executive*
Levy, Peter A. *lawyer*
Lewis, Eddie *professional soccer player*
Leyhane, Francis John III *lawyer*
Li, Wen-Hsiung *geneticist*
Liao, Shutsung *biochemist, molecular oncologist*

Libowsky, Stephen David *lawyer*
Liebenow, Franklin Eastburn, Jr. *English literature educator*
Lien, John Donovan *lawyer*
Lies, Valerie Sharp *foundation administrator*
Liggio, Carl Donald *lawyer*
Lilly, Kristine Marie *professional soccer player*
Lin, James Chih-I *biomedical engineer, electrical engineer, educator*
Linden, Henry Robert *chemical engineer, researcher*
Lindgren, James *law educator*
Lindquist, Lee A. *geriatrician, educator*
Linklater, William Joseph *lawyer*
Lipinski, Ann Marie *publishing executive*
Lipton, Lois Jean *lawyer*
Litwin, Burton Howard *lawyer*
Liu, Ben-chieh *economist*
Livingston, Bradford Lee *lawyer*
Lochbihler, Frederick Vincent *lawyer*
Lockwood, Gary Lee *lawyer*
Loesch, Katharine Taylor *communication and theatre educator*
Logemann, Jerilyn Ann *speech pathologist, educator*
Lona, Marie A. *lawyer*
Longworth, Richard Cole *journalist*
Loo, Nancy *newscaster*
Looman, James R. *lawyer*
Lopes, Demetrius Klee *neurosurgeon*
Lopez, Carolyn Catherine *physician*
Lorch, Kenneth F. *lawyer*
Lorch, Robert K. *corporate financial executive*
Lorenz, Hugo Albert *retired insurance executive, consultant*
Lowe, Sandra Elveta *psychologist*
Lower, Joseph *air transportation executive*
Lowinger, Frederick Charles *lawyer*
Lowry, James Hamilton *management consultant*
Lubet, Steven *law educator*
Lubin, Donald G. *lawyer*
Lucas, Robert Emerson, Jr. *economist, educator*
Luchins, Daniel Jonathan *psychiatrist*
Luning, Thomas P. *lawyer*
Lurain, John Robert III *gynecologist*
Lurie, Ann LaSalle *investment company executive, foundation administrator*
Luscombe, George A., II, *lawyer*
Lusk, Peggy June *retired counseling administrator*
Lutter, Paul Allen *lawyer*
Luttig, J. Michael (John Michael Luttig) *aerospace transportation executive, former federal judge*
Lyerla, Bradford Peter *lawyer*
Lynch, John Peter *lawyer*
Lyon, Charles Herbert Randolph *investment banker*
Lythcott, Marcia A. *newspaper editor*
Macaulay, Susan Jane *lawyer, law educator*
MacCarthy, John L. *lawyer*
MacCarthy, Terence Francis *lawyer*
MacDougal, Gary Edward *corporate board member, foundation trustee*
Mack, Alan Wayne *interior designer*
MacKinnon, Kevin Scott *lawyer*
MacMillan, Shannon Ann *professional soccer player*
Madara, James Lee *dean, pathologist, educator, epitheliologist*
Madigan, Lisa *state attorney general*
Madsen, Dorothy Louise (Meg Madsen) *writer*
Magazine, Todd *food products executive*
Mahaffey, John Christopher *medical association executive*
Makinen, Marvin William *biophysicist, educator*
Malinowski, Arthur Anthony *lawyer, arbitrator*
Malkin, Cary Jay *lawyer*
Malkinson, Frederick David *dermatologist, educator*
Mallory, Robert Mark *controller, finance company executive*
Malovany, Howard *lawyer*
Mancoff, Neal Alan *lawyer*
Mandell, Floyd A. *lawyer*
Manelli, Donald Dean *scriptwriter, film producer*
Manning, Sylvia *language educator*
Mansfield, Karen Lee *lawyer*
Mansueto, Joseph Daniel *publisher*
Manzo, Edward David *lawyer*
Marcovici, Michael *investment company executive*
Marshall, Cody *bishop*
Marshall, Kerry James *artist*
Martin, Arthur Mead *lawyer*
Martin, Gary Joseph *medical educator*
Martin, Laura Keidan *lawyer*
Martinez, David Grey *classicist, educator*
Martinez, Natalie *newscaster*
Marwedel, Warren John *lawyer*
Mason, Gregory Wesley, Jr. *secondary school educator*
Mason, Richard J. *lawyer*
Mason, Terry *city health department administrator, urologist*
Mason, William *opera company director*
Mastroeni, Pablo *professional soccer player*
Matanky, James E. *real estate developer*
Mateles, Richard Isaac *biotechnologist*
Matis, Nina D. *lawyer*
Matsakis, Elias N. *lawyer*
Matthei, Edward Hodge *architect*
Matuano, Tony *chef*
May, Aviva Rabinowitz *music educator, musician, linguist*
Mayer, Raymond Richard *business administration educator*
Mazany, Terry *foundation administrator*
McCaleb, Malcolm, Jr. *lawyer*
McCallister, Richard Anthony *business consulting company executive*
McCann, Renetta *advertising executive*
Mc Carter, John Wilbur, Jr. *museum executive*
McCaskey, Raymond F. *insurance company executive*
McChesney, Fred S. *law educator*
McClain, Shawn *chef*
McClintock, Martha K. *biologist, educator*
McCloskey, Deirdre Nansen *economics and history educator*
McCloskey, Michael *social sciences educator*
McCloy, Elizabeth K. *lawyer*

McClure, James Julius, Jr. *lawyer, former city official*
McConnell, E. Hoy, II, *advertising and public policy executive*
McCormick, Steven D. *lawyer*
McCracken, Thomas James, Jr. *lawyer*
McCrank, Lawrence J. *dean, school librarian*
McCray, Curtis Lee *academic administrator*
McCue, Judith W. *lawyer*
McCullagh, Grant Gibson *retired architect*
McCullough, Richard Lawrence *advertising executive*
McCurry, Margaret Irene *architect, educator, furniture designer, interior designer*
McDaniel, Charles-Gene *journalism educator, writer*
McDermott, John Henry *lawyer*
McDonagh, Steve *chef*
McDonald, Sally J. *lawyer*
McDonald, Theresa Beatrice Pierce (Mrs. Ollie McDonald) *church official, minister*
McDonald, Thomas Alexander *lawyer*
McDonald, William Brice *educational association administrator*
McDonnell, David Croft *diversified financial services company executive*
McDonough, John Michael *lawyer*
McElheny, Josiah G. *sculptor*
McGaan, Andrew Raymond *lawyer*
McGovern, Peter John *law educator*
McGowan, Michael Jeremy *lawyer*
McGrail, Jeane Kathryn *artist*
McGrath, Michael G. *finance company executive*
McGrath, William Joseph *lawyer*
McIntyre, Sarah Elizabeth *vocalist*
McKay, Melinda *hotel executive*
McKee, Keith Earl *manufacturing technology executive*
McKinney, William T. *psychiatrist, educator*
McLaren, Richard Wellington, Jr. *lawyer*
McLaughlin, T. Mark *lawyer*
McLawhon, Ronald William *pathology educator, biochemist*
McMath, Lula Wray *retired elementary school educator, realtor*
McMenamin, John Robert *lawyer*
McNally, Andrew, IV, *publishing executive, director*
McNeill, G. David *psychologist, educator*
McNerney, James, Jr., (W. James McNerney) *aerospace transportation executive, former manufacturing executive*
McPherson, Michael Steven *academic administrator, economist*
McVisk, William Kilburn *lawyer*
Meccia, Francis (Frank) Anthony *physician assistant*
Mecklenburg, Gary Alan *hospital executive*
Mehlman, Mark Franklin *lawyer*
Mehrberg, Randall Eric *lawyer*
Melbinger, Michael S. *lawyer*
Melnick, Jane Fisher *writer, educator, photographer*
Melton, David Reuben *lawyer*
Meltzer, Bernard David *law educator*
Meltzer, David Owen *internist, educator, economist*
Menchik, Daniel Aron *sociologist, researcher*
Menchin, Robert Stanley *marketing executive*
Menendez, Marcelino Eulogio (Marc Menendez) *marketing professional*
Metcalf, James *manufacturing executive*
Metz, Charles Edgar *radiology educator*
Michaels, Richard Edward *lawyer*
Michaels, Robert A. *real estate development company executive*
Michaels, Walter Benn *English professor, writer*
Michalak, Edward Francis *lawyer*
Michod, Susan Alexander *artist, painter*
Migala, Lucyna J. *journalist, broadcast executive, artistic director*
Miglis, Thomas G. *financial services company executive*
Mihelic, Tracey L. *lawyer*
Mikesell, Marvin Wray *geography educator*
Mikva, Abner Joseph *lawyer, retired judge*
Milbrett, Tiffeny Carleen *professional soccer player*
Miletich, Ivo *library and information scientist, bibliographer, educator, linguist, literature research specialist*
Miller, Benjamin K. *retired state supreme court justice*
Miller, Irving Franklin *chemical engineer, educator, biomedical engineer, academic administrator*
Miller, Kenneth W. *lawyer*
Miller, Lee I. *lawyer*
Miller, Paul J. *lawyer*
Miller, Peter C. *lawyer*
Miller, Stephen Ralph *lawyer*
Miller, Verne William *computer engineer, consultant*
Millichap, Joseph Gordon *neurologist, educator*
Millien, Raymond *lawyer*
Mims, Joyce Elaine *lawyer*
Mindes, Gayle Dean *education educator*
Miner, Thomas Hawley *entrepreneur*
Minichello, Dennis *lawyer*
Minkowycz, W. J. *mechanical engineering educator*
Minogue, John P. *academic administrator, educator, priest*
Minow, Josephine Baskin *civic volunteer*
Minow, Newton Norman *lawyer, educator*
Mirkin, Bernard Leo *pharmacologist, pediatrician*
Mirza, Leona Lousin *elementary school educator, director*
Mitchell, J. Barry *corporate financial executive*
Mitchell, Lee Mark *communications executive, investment banker, lawyer*
Moawad, Atef *obstetrician, gynecologist, educator*
Montgomery, Charles Barry *lawyer*
Montgomery, Charles Howard *retired bank executive*
Montgomery, William Adam *lawyer*
Moog, Matthew *Internet company executive*
Moore, Patrick J. *paper company executive*
Moran, James Byron *federal judge*
More, José *photojournalist*
Morency, Paula J. *lawyer*

Shindler, Donald A. *lawyer*
Short, Marion Priscilla *neurogenetics educator*
Shulruff, Stuart P. *lawyer*
Shuman, Ann *investment company executive*
Siegel, Howard Jerome *lawyer*
Siegler, Mark *internist, educator*
Sigmon, Joyce Elizabeth *professional society administrator*
Silberman, Alan Harvey *lawyer*
Silets, Harvey Marvin *lawyer*
Silverman, Gary R. *lawyer*
Silverman, Ross O. *lawyer*
Simmons, Adele Smith *foundation executive, former educator*
Simon, George T. *lawyer*
Simon, John Bern *lawyer*
Simon, Seymour *lawyer, former state supreme court justice*
Simons, Helen *school psychologist, psychotherapist, educator*
Simpson, Dick Weldon *political science educator*
Singer, Emel *staffing industry executive*
Singer, Martin H. *Internet company executive*
Sinha, Raj P. *education educator, researcher*
Sippey, Roger Boyd *corporate executive*
Sivananthan, Sivalingam *science educator*
Sive, Rebecca Anne *public relations executive*
Skiles, Scott Allen *professional basketball coach*
Skilling, Raymond Inwood *lawyer*
Skinner, Mary Jacobs *lawyer*
Sklarsky, Charles B. *lawyer*
Slansky, Jerry William *investment company executive*
Slemmons, Rod *museum director, art educator, curator*
Sljivic-Simsic, Biljana B. *Slavic and Baltic languages educator*
Slyde, Jimmy (James T. Godbolt, King of Slides) *tap dancer*
Smagner, John Patrick *applied behavior analyst, educator*
Smalheiser, Neil Raymond *neurobiologist*
Small, Richard Donald *travel company executive*
Smart, Allen Rich, II, *retired lawyer*
Smedinghoff, Thomas J. *lawyer*
Smith, Adrian Devaun *architect*
Smith, Art *chef*
Smith, Arthur B., Jr. *lawyer*
Smith, Cynthia Janese *science educator*
Smith, Dan *chef*
Smith, David Paul *psychologist, researcher*
Smith, Earl Charles *nephrologist, educator*
Smith, Elizabeth Angele Taft *curator*
Smith, Lewis J. *medical educator, researcher*
Smith, Raymond Thomas *anthropology educator*
Smith, Sam *columnist, writer*
Smith, Scott Clybourn *media company executive*
Smith, Stan Vladimir *economist, finance company executive*
Smith, Todd A. *lawyer*
Smolen, Lee M. *lawyer*
Snyder, Edward Adams *dean, economics professor*
Snyder, Graydon F. *religion educator*
So, Kevin *singer*
Sobrero, Kate (Kathryn Michele Sobrero) *professional soccer player*
Sochen, June *history professor*
Socol, Michael Lee *obstetrician, gynecologist, educator*
Solaro, Ross John *physiologist, biophysicist*
Solow, Michael Barry *lawyer*
Sonderby, Susan Pierson *federal judge*
Song, David *plastic surgeon, medical educator*
Sotelino, Gabino *chef*
Southwell, Donald G. *insurance company executive*
Spain, Richard Colby *lawyer*
Sparberg, Marshall Stuart *gastroenterologist, educator*
Spector, David M. *lawyer*
Spellmire, George W. *lawyer*
Spergel, Irving Abraham *social worker, researcher*
Spindler, George S. *lawyer, retired oil industry executive*
Spring, Bonnie Joan *psychology professor*
Springer, Jerry *television talk show host, radio personality*
Sproger, Charles Edmund *retired lawyer*
Sprowl, Charles Riggs *lawyer*
Srivastava, Anurag K. *research scientist*
Stacey, James Henry *writer, columnist*
Stack, Michael *artist*
Stack, Paul Francis *lawyer*
Stack, Stephen S. *manufacturing executive*
Staller, John Edward *archaeologist, anthropologist, educator*
Stallworth, Stanley B *lawyer*
Standberry, Herman Lee *school system administrator, educational consultant*
Stanhaus, James Steven *lawyer*
Stanley, Amy Dru *history professor*
Starkman, Gary Lee *lawyer*
Stassen, John Henry *lawyer*
Stead, James Joseph, Jr. *security firm executive*
Stearns, Neele Edward, Jr. *investment company executive*
Steele, Eric Henry *sculptor, lawyer*
Steinberg, Morton M. *lawyer*
Steinberg, Rubin *retired art educator, artist*
Steinberg, Salme Elizabeth Harju *academic administrator, historian*
Steiner, Donald Frederick *biochemist, physician, educator*
Steinfeld, Manfred *furniture manufacturing executive*
Steinhorn, Robin H. *neonatologist, educator*
Stern, Carl William, Jr. *management consultant*
Sternstein, Allan J. *lawyer*
Stetler, David J. *lawyer*
Stevens, Mark *banker*
Stevens, Stanley M. *lawyer*
Stevenson, Adlai Ewing III *lawyer, retired senator*
Stiegel, Michael Allen *lawyer*
Stigler, Stephen Mack *statistician, educator*
Stillman, Nina Gidden *lawyer*
Stirling, James Paulman *investment banker*
Stoklosa, Gregory A. *publishing executive*
Stoll, John Robert *lawyer, educator*
Stone, Alan *container company executive*
Stone, Geoffrey Richard *lawyer, educator*

Stone, Howard S. *retired baking industry executive, art collector*
Stone, Susan A. *lawyer*
Storb, Ursula Beate *molecular genetics and cell biology educator*
Stovall-Brooks, Patricia *elementary school educator, writer*
Stover, Leon (Eugene Stover) *retired anthropology professor, critic, writer*
Strassner, Howard Taft, Jr. *obstetrician, educator*
Stratman, Deborah *filmmaker, film and video educator*
Strauss, David A. *law educator*
Strauss, Deborah *foundation administrator*
Streff, William Albert, Jr. *lawyer*
Strobel, Pamela B. *energy executive*
Stroger, John H., Jr. *county official*
Strohm, Bruce C. *lawyer, real estate company executive*
Stroscio, Michael Anthony *physicist, researcher*
Strubel, Ella Doyle *advertising executive, public relations executive*
Strubel, Richard Perry *Internet company executive*
Stulberg, Samuel David *surgeon, physician*
Suchomel, Mark *publishing executive*
Sulkin, Howard Allen *academic administrator*
Sullivan, Barry *lawyer*
Sullivan, Bernard James *accountant*
Sullivan, Marcia Waite *lawyer*
Sullivan, Peggy *librarian, consultant*
Sullivan, Thomas Patrick *lawyer*
Sunstein, Cass Robert *law educator*
Sviokla, John Julius *technology consultant*
Swanson, Don Richard *university dean*
Sweeney, James Raymond *retired lawyer*
Swibel, Howard Jay *lawyer*
Swibel, Steven Warren *lawyer*
Swiecicki, Peter *lawyer*
Swift, Edward Foster III *investment banker*
Swiger, Elinor Porter *lawyer*
Swinand, Andrew *advertising executive*
Szydlowski, Joseph Edward *music librarian*
Tabin, Julius *lawyer, physicist*
Talbot, Pamela *public relations executive*
Tallman, Martin Stuart *hematologist, oncologist*
Tallon, Dale *professional sports team executive*
Tambur, Anat *lab administrator*
Tanabe, Paula *nursing educator, researcher*
Tangora, Martin Charles *mathematician, educator*
Tanna, Angelo Peter *ophthalmologist, educator*
Tarun, Robert Walter *lawyer*
Taub, Richard Paul *social sciences educator*
Taylor, Koko *singer*
Teichner, Lester *general management executive*
Telfer, Margaret Clare *internist, hematologist, oncologist*
Teller, Alan *museum program director, photographer, educator*
Teolis, Michael Francis *music educator, musician, conductor, composer*
Terkel, Studs (Louis Terkel) *writer, journalist*
Terrassa, Jacqueline *museum director*
Tessing, Louise Scire *graphic designer*
Tetzlaff, Theodore R. *lawyer*
Thaden, Edward Carl *history professor*
Thall, Robert *photographer, educator*
Theobald, Edward Robert *lawyer*
Theobald, Thomas Charles *banker*
Thies, Richard Brian *lawyer*
Thisted, Ronald Aaron *statistician, educator, consultant*
Thistlethwaite, Susan Brooks *religious organization administrator*
Thomas, Barbara L. *not-for-profit executive*
Thomas, Cherryl T. *former federal agency administrator*
Thomas, Frederick Bradley *lawyer*
Thomas, Leona Marlene *healthcare educator*
Thomas, Robert R. *state supreme court justice*
Thomas, Stephen Paul *lawyer*
Thomas, Tim *professional basketball player*
Thome, Jim *professional baseball player*
Thompson, James Robert, Jr. *lawyer, former governor*
Thompson, Jayne Carr *public relations and communications executive, lawyer*
Thompson, John H. *research and development company executive*
Thompson, Michael *lawyer*
Thompson, Richard *psychologist*
Thurston, Stephen John *pastor*
Tigerman, Stanley *architect, educator*
Tiller, Emerson H. *law educator*
Tilton, Glenn F. *air transportation executive*
Tipton, Margaret Ann *religious organization administrator, writer*
Toback, Paul A. *recreational facility executive*
Tobin, Craig Daniel *lawyer*
Tomaino, Joseph Carmine *former retail executive, former postal inspector*
Tomar, Russell Herman *pathologist, educator, researcher*
Toohey, James Kevin *lawyer*
Topinka, Judy Baar *state official, political organization worker*
Torgersen, Torwald Harold *architect, consultant*
Toth, Bruce A. *lawyer*
Townsend, Robert Morris *economics professor, researcher*
Tramonto, Rick *chef*
Treston, Sherry S. *lawyer*
Tribbett, Charles *executive recruiter*
Trifilio, Steven Michael *pharmacist, educator*
Trost, Eileen Bannon *lawyer*
Trotter, Carl *lawyer*
Trotter, Cortez *city official, former fire commissioner*
Truran, James Wellington, Jr. *astrophysicist, educator*
Truskowski, John Budd *lawyer*
Truwit, Mitchell *Internet company executive*
Tryban, Esther Elizabeth *lawyer*
Tryloff, Robin S. *food products executive*
Tsai, Jingpha (Jeffrey Tsai) *computer scientist, educator*
Turner, Michael Stanley *astrophysics professor, researcher*
Turow, Scott F. *writer, lawyer*
Tyree, James C. *insurance company executive*
Tyson, Kirk W. M. *management consultant*
Ullrich, Polly *art critic*

Umans, Alvin Robert *manufacturing executive*
Underwood, Robert Leigh *venture capitalist*
Ungaretti, Richard Anthony *lawyer*
Upshaw, Harry Stephan *psychologist, educator*
Urrea, Luis Alberto *writer*
Usiskin, Zalman Philip *mathematics educator*
Valerio, Joseph Mastro *architectural firm executive, educator*
Valukas, Anton Ronald *lawyer, former prosecutor*
Valyi-Nagy, Tibor G. *neuropathologist, virologist*
Van Den Hende, Fred J(oseph) *human resources executive*
VanderBeke, Patricia K. *architect*
Van Patten, Bill *foreign language educator*
Van Pelt, Robert Irving *retired firefighter*
Van Zandt, David E. *dean, law educator*
Venturini, Tisha Lea *professional soccer player*
Veres, Bob *editor*
Vermeule, Adrian *law educator*
Verschoor, Curtis Carl *business educator, consultant*
Vezeau, Timothy J. *lawyer*
Vie, Richard Carl *insurance company executive*
Vincent, Jim *performing company executive*
Vinci, John Nicholas *architect, educator*
Vishneski, John Stanley III *lawyer*
Vishny, Paul Harvey *lawyer*
Vitale, Gerald Lee *finance company executive*
Vojcanin, Sava Alexander *lawyer*
Volgman, Annabelle Santos *cardiologist, educator*
von Rhein, John Richard *music critic, journalist, writer*
Vowell, Sarah *writer, radio personality*
Vrablik, Edward Robert *import/export company executive*
Vree, Roger Allen *lawyer*
Vroman, Kendal *investment company executive*
Wagner, Rose Mary *retired librarian*
Wakschlag, Milton Samuel *lawyer*
Walberg, Herbert John *psychologist, educator, consultant*
Walker, Debra Bess *lawyer*
Walker, Matthew *radiologist*
Walker, Thomas Ray *city aviation commissioner*
Wall, James McKendree *minister, editor*
Wallace, Ben *professional basketball player*
Walsh, Mathew M. *construction executive*
Walsh, Matthew M. *real estate developer*
Walsh, Michael S. *lawyer*
Walter, Mark R. *investment company executive*
Walton, Robert Lee, Jr. *plastic surgeon*
Wambach, Abby (Mary Abigail Wambach) *Olympic athlete*
Wander, Herbert Stanton *lawyer*
Wang, Albert James *violinist, educator*
Wang, Yanbin *physicist, researcher*
Wanke, Ronald Lee *lawyer*
Wasan, Darsh Tilakchand *academic administrator, chemical engineer, educator*
Wasendorf, Russell R., Sr. *brokerage house executive*
Wasson, Jeffrey *music educator*
Waters, Ronald V. III *candy company executive*
Watson, Easter Jean *psychotherapist, financial program consultant*
Waxler, Beverly Jean *anesthesiologist, physician*
Weaver, Timothy Allan *lawyer*
Webb, Dan K. *lawyer*
Weber, Hanno *architect*
Weber, Susan A. *lawyer*
Webster, James Randolph, Jr. *physician*
Weese, Benjamin Horace *architect*
Weil, Roman Lee *finance educator*
Weinberg, David B. *investor*
Weinberg, Lila Shaffer *editor, writer*
Weinberg, Walter S. *lawyer*
Weiner, Gerald Arne *stockbroker*
Weiner, Lynn Yvette *history professor, academic administrator*
Weinfurter, Daniel Joseph *business services executive*
Weinkopf, Friedrich J. *lawyer*
Weinsheimer, William Cyrus *lawyer*
Weintraub, Joseph Barton *publishing executive*
Weisbach, David A *law educator*
Weiss, John Robert *lawyer*
Weissman, Michael Lewis *lawyer*
Welsh, Kelly Raymond *lawyer, investment company executive*
Weselak, Anna Marie Schmidt *educational association administrator, media consultant*
Weston, Roger Lance *banker*
Whalen, Wayne W. *lawyer*
Wham, David Buffington *secondary school educator*
Wharton, Margaret Agnes *artist*
White, C. Vanessa *director*
White, Henry F., Jr. *legal association administrator, retired military officer*
White, Linda Diane *lawyer*
White, Linda Marie *former fraternal organization administrator*
Whitington, Peter Frank *pediatrics educator, pediatric hepatologist*
Whitney, Kent R.E. *securities trader*
Whitney, Patrick Foster *design educator*
Wieczorek, Dennis E. *lawyer*
Wied, George Ludwig *physician*
Wiens, Ann *artist, writer, editor, art critic*
Wier, Patricia Ann *publishing executive, consultant*
Wildman, Max Edward *lawyer, director*
Wilhelm, David C. *investment company executive*
Wilhelm, John L. *health facility administrator*
Wille, Lois Jean *retired editor*
Williams, Ann Claire *federal judge*
Williams, Philip Copelain *obstetrician, gynecologist*
Williams, Richard Lucas III *electronics executive, director, lawyer*
Williamson, Wayne C. *internist, geriatrician*
Willoughby, William Franklin, II, *retired physician, researcher*
Wilmouth, Robert K. *commodities trader*
Wilson, Cleo Francine *foundation administrator*
Wine-Banks, Jill Susan *lawyer*
Winfrey, Oprah *television talk show host, actress, television producer*
Winjum, Stephen J. *medical association administrator*
Winnecke, Joycelyn *editor*
Winslow, Robert A. *real estate company executive*

Winters, Anne *poet, educator*
Wirszup, Izaak *mathematician, educator*
Wirtz, William Wadsworth *real estate company executive, professional sports team executive*
Wise, William Jerrard *lawyer*
Wissler, Robert William *pathologist*
Witcoff, Sheldon William *lawyer*
Wittbrodt, Elizabeth Stratton *education educator*
Wittenberg, Jon Albert *accountant*
Wolf, Charles Benno *lawyer*
Wolfe, David Louis *lawyer*
Wolfe, Sheila A. *journalist*
Wolfert, Frederick E. (Rick Wolfert) *healthcare financial services company executive*
Wolff, Josh *professional soccer player*
Wong, Thomas Tang Yum *engineering educator*
Wood, Diane Pamela *federal judge*
Wood, James Nowell *museum director and executive*
Wood, Kerry *professional baseball player*
Wood, Mark D. *lawyer*
Wood, Patrick Henry III *former federal official*
Woodford, Peter C. *lawyer*
Wooldridge, Patrice Marie *marketing professional, personal trainer*
Wooten, Robert E. *music educator*
Workman, Michael *editor-in-chief, publishing executive, art critic*
Wright, Judith Margaret *law librarian, educator, dean*
Wrigley, William, Jr. *candy company executive*
Yaghmai, Dina *dermatologist, educator*
Yale, Seymour Hershel *dental radiologist, educator, gerontologist, dean*
Yamada, Tohru *biologist, educator, researcher, director*
Yandle, Stephen Thomas *dean*
Yao, Mike *otolaryngologist*
Yao, Tito Go *pediatrician*
Yawney, Trent *professional hockey coach, retired professional hockey player*
Yost, Emery Joseph *music industry producer, educator*
Young, Lauren Sue Jones *education educator*
Young, Scott Thomas *business management educator*
Youngman, Owen Ralph *newspaper executive*
Yu, Anthony C. *religion and literature educator*
Yu, Linda *newswoman, television anchorwoman*
Yudkowsky, Rachel *medical educator*
Yuracko, Kimberly *law educator*
Zabel, Sheldon Alter *lawyer, educator*
Zagel, James Block *federal judge*
Zagel, Margaret Maxwell *lawyer*
Zajicek, Jeronym *retired music educator*
Zee, Phyllis C. *physician, educator, researcher*
Zeine, Rana Ramsey *neuropathologist, research professor*
Zellner, Arnold *economics, econometrics and statistics professor*
Zemm, Sandra Phyllis *lawyer*
Zenner, Sheldon Toby *lawyer*
Zerbe, Darell *metal products executive*
Zhang, John X *medical educator*
Zhao, Jia *lawyer*
Zheng, James *architectural firm executive*
Ziliak, Stephen T. *economics professor*
Zimmer, Robert J. *academic administrator, mathematician, educator*
Zolno, Mark S. *lawyer*
Zoloth, Laurie Susan *bioethicist*
Zonis, Marvin *political scientist, educator*
Zucaro, Aldo Charles *insurance company executive*
Zucker, David F. *information technology executive*
Zwecker, William Rene, Jr., (Bill Zwecker) *newspaper columnist, television reporter*

### Chicago Heights

Buishas, Kristin Maureen *elementary school educator*
Cifelli, John Louis *lawyer*
Croarkin, Donald J. *librarian*
Kavis, George *engineer, photographer*
Nowocin, Debra Terese *gifted and talented secondary education educator*
Reed, Scott C. *music educator, writer*
Stanko, Susan G. *librarian*
Yalavarthi, Ramaraja *physician*

### Chillicothe

Tallon, Edward Joseph *social studies educator*

### Cicero

Paprocki, Thomas John *lawyer, priest*

### Cisne

White, Sharon *elementary school educator*

### Cissna Park

McCullough, Edward L. *artist, educator*

### Clarendon Hills

Choice, Priscilla Kathryn Means (Penny Choice) *retired educational association administrator*
Moritz, Donald Brooks *mechanical engineer, consultant*

### Coal City

DiGiusto, Elaine Bessie *science educator*

### Collinsville

Daugherty, Phyllis Lyn *secondary school educator*

### Country Club Hills

McClelland, Helen *music educator*
Scott, Earline *school system administrator*

### Crestwood

Haggard, Edward (Ned) Roy *writer, consultant*

### Crete

Langer, Steven *personnel director, psychologist*

### Crystal Lake

Althoff, J(ames) L. *construction company executive*
Anderson, Lyle Arthur *retired manufacturing executive*

Chamberlain, Charles James *railroad labor union executive*
Faulds, Marguerite Zita *music educator*
Halperin, Richard George *information technology executive*
Keller, William Francis *publishing consultant*
Kruper, John Gerald (Jack Kruper) *sales and marketing executive*
Pearson, Nels Kenneth *retired manufacturing executive*
Shank, William O. *lawyer*
Wade, Edwin Lee *lawyer, writer*

**Danville**
Anderson, Claudia Smith *lawyer*
Lindemann, Ruth Burridge *librarian*

**Darien**
Bland, Robert S. *insurance company executive*
Friedrich, Charles William *industrial relations specialist*
Gardner, Howard Garry *pediatrician, educator*
Hanson, Martin Philip *mechanical engineer, farmer*
Jordan, Ronald P. *pharmacist, pharmaceutical executive, consultant*
Kulkarni, Bidy *reproductive endocrinologist, biomedical researcher, consultant*

**Davis**
Fulfer, Matrona Penny *retired school librarian, columnist*

**Decatur**
Andreas, G. Allen, Jr., (Glenn Allen Andreas Jr.) *agricultural company executive*
Coryell, Sandra Kay *music educator*
Decker, Charles Richard *investment company executive, educator*
Dunn, John Francis *lawyer, state representative*
Gaffney, Sean *information scientist*
Koucky, John Richard *metallurgical engineer, manufacturing executive*
Mulhollem, Paul B. *agricultural products executive*
Munoz, Joseph Mark *education educator, consultant*
Reising, Richard P. *lawyer*
Schmalz, Douglas J. *agricultural company executive*
Smith, David James *corporate lawyer*
Stafford, John H., II, *composer, music educator*
Staley, Henry Mueller *manufacturing executive*
Woertz, Patricia Ann *agricultural company executive, retired oil company executive*

**Deerfield**
Adams, Jennifer *medical products executive*
Bernauer, David W. *retail executive*
Bialek, Paul Richard *mathematics professor*
Birmingham, William Joseph *retired lawyer*
Boyd, Joseph Don *diversified financial services company executive*
Green, Dana I. *lawyer, human resources specialist*
Heiman, Marvin Stewart *finance company executive*
Howell, George Bedell *investment company executive*
Lezak, Carol Spielman *communications executive, editor, writer, design consultant, medical librarian*
Miller, Michael Thurman *architect*
Nitzki-George, Diane M. *pharmacist, medical writer*
Park, Jeffrey Bryan *controller*
Parkinson, Robert L., Jr. *medical products executive, health facility administrator*
Pearson, Louise S. *lawyer*
Persky, Marla Susan *lawyer*
Prete, Gayle Compton *advertising and marketing executive*
Reid-Anderson, James *diagnostic equipment company executive*
Rein, Jeffrey A. *retail executive*
Rudolphsen, William M. *retail executive*
Sabatino, Thomas Joseph, Jr. *lawyer*
Saida, Toyoyasu *chemical and biochemical engineer*
Sanner, John Harper *retired pharmacologist*
Scott, Theodore R. *retired lawyer*
Shakno, Robert Julian *hospital and social services administrator*
Tashjian, Beatrice Charmian *composer, educator*
Taylor, Trent E. *retail executive*
Vollen, Robert Jay *lawyer*
Wrobbel, Karen *education educator, consultant*
Zywicki, Robert Albert *retired electric power industry executive*

**Dekalb**
Crosser, Carmen Lynn *marriage and family therapist, social worker, consultant*
Dyshkant, Alexander Sergeevich (Alexandre Sergeevich Dychkant) *physicist, researcher*
Ewell, John Albert III *mathematician, educator*
Gelman, Alexander *theater director, educator*
Goldenberg, William Bruce *music educator, musician*
Hamilton, David Arnold *retired librarian*
Hosmane, Narayan Sadashiv *chemistry professor*
Kimball, Clyde William *physicist, researcher*
Kong, Xuan *electrical engineer, educator*
Legg, J. Ivan *academic administrator*
Molnar, Andrea Katalin *anthropology professor*
Monat, William Robert *university official*
Shernoff, David Jordan *psychology professor*
Shi, Lin *marriage and family therapist, educator*
Slotsve, George Aaron *economist, educator, consultant*
Splansky, Sandra J. *director*
Troyer, Alvah Forrest *agricultural products executive, horticulturist*
Valentiner, David Peter *psychologist, educator*

**Des Plaines**
Adatto, Irving Jack *physician*
Banach, Art John *retired graphic artist*
Canfield, Jinhee *mathematics professor*
Clapper, Marie Anne *magazine publisher*
Coburn, James LeRoy *academic administrator*
D'Anca, John Arthur *psychotherapist, educator*

Drake, Ann M. *consumer products company executive*
Frank, James S. *automotive executive*
Gochnauer, Richard Wallis *wholesale distribution executive*
Gold, Deidra D. *lawyer*
Kaczor, Diane L. *marketing professional, researcher*
Lee, Margaret Burke *college president, language educator*
Lyu, Seung Won *metallurgical engineer, environmental scientist*
Miesse, James Everett *librarian*
O'Dwyer, Mary Ann *automotive executive*
Orme, Marianne Linette *librarian*
Pannke-Smith, Peggy *insurance company executive*
Pestova, Ekaterina *scientist*
Quintanilla, Antonio Paulet *retired physician, educator*
Relwani, Nirmal Murlidhar (Nick Relwani) *mechanical engineer*
Santisteban, Joseph Henry *human resources specialist*

**Dixon**
Hertel, William John *music educator*
Huber, Marianne Jeanne *art dealer, art appraiser*
Polascik, Mary Ann *ophthalmologist*

**Dolton**
Hahn, Gerald Eugene *industrial education educator*

**Dow**
Schuler, Dorothy R. *education educator, consultant, retired elementary school educator*

**Downers Grove**
Brekke, Stewart Ernest *retired chemistry and physics educator*
Choudhury, A. N. M. Masum *optical engineer*
Clement, Paul Platts, Jr. *performance technologist, educator*
DuBose, Michael T. *manufacturing executive*
Feeney, Don Joseph, Jr. *psychologist*
Green, David William *chemist, educator*
Hornish, Ronald Frederick *music educator*
Hubbard, Lincoln Beals *medical physicist, consultant*
Jacklin, William Thomas *retired county official, educator*
Kaput, Jim L. *lawyer*
McGarr, Frank James *retired federal judge, consultant*
Mrozek, Ernest J. *customer service administrator*
Piekarz, Frank Jeffrey *music educator*
Punt, Leonard Cornelis *educational services company executive*
Roselieb, Craig Alan *band director*
Schwemm, John Butler *printing company executive, lawyer*
Siedlecki, Nancy Therese *lawyer, funeral director*
Soenen, Michael J. *consumer products company executive*
Spainhour, J. Patrick *outsourcing company executive, former apparel executive*
Tedeschi, Thomas E., Jr. *music educator*
Veluchamy, Pethinaidu *marketing executive*
Wristen, Edward L. *health facility administrator*
Yeager, David P. *transportation executive*

**Du Quoin**
Ibendahl, Jean Ayres *retired elementary and secondary educator*

**Dundee**
Carlini, James *management consultant*
Ulakovich, Ronald Stephen *real estate developer*
Weck Farrag, Kristin W. *bank executive*

**East Alton**
DiPaolo, Marcella Kay *elementary school educator*

**East Dubuque**
Kussmaul, Donald *academic administrator*

**East Dundee**
Simons, Gail S. *artist, educator, librarian*

**East Peoria**
Frison, Rick *agricultural company executive*
May, Janet Sue *playwright, lyricist*
Twitty, Susan Kay *music educator*
Wadsworth Walker, Cherilee *music educator*

**East Saint Louis**
Jones, Laura M. *psychologist, consultant*
Lane-Trent, Patricia Jean *social worker*
Thomas, Mary Lee *property manager*
Wright, Katie Harper *educational administrator, journalist*

**Edwardsville**
Anderson, Mary Jane *music educator*
Anop, Lenora-Marya *violinist, music educator*
Banks, Ronald Dwayne *academic administrator, industrial engineer, educator*
Browne, Dallas *anthropologist, educator*
Brugam, Richard Blair *biology educator*
Claudson, William Dolan *music educator*
DeGarmo, Denise Kay *political scientist, educator*
Douglas, Thomas John *healthcare educator*
Gupchup, Gireesh Vijay *pharmacist, educator*
Hampton, Phillip Jewel *artist, educator*
Johnson, Charlotte Lee *librarian*
Kuba, Joan Carol *special education educator*
Liu, Yuliang *linguist, educator*
Malone, Robert Roy *artist, art educator*
Petry, Alice Hall *scholar, educator, writer*
Rehg, Jennifer *anthropology educator*
Schultz, Norbert J. *retired music educator*

**Effingham**
Franklin, William Price *computer programmer*
Lewis, Linda Sue *retired elementary school educator*
Wallace, Bradford F. *music educator*

**Elburn**
Hansen, H. Jack *management consultant*

**Elgin**
Barnett, Sue *nurse*
Bassoul, Selim A. *food products executive*
Beyer, Karen Haynes *social worker*
Carl, Jeffery *art educator*
Golden, Loren S. *lawyer*
Jakle, Kenneth Richard *broadcast executive*
Mao, Ruixuan (Rick Mao) *dean*
Puotinen, Arthur Edwin *college president, minister*
Rogers, Carleton Carson, Jr. *trade show and convention executive*
Turnquist, Jerry L. *communications educator, journalist*
Yarkony, Gary Michael *physician, researcher*

**Elk Grove Village**
Brace, Frederic F. (Jake Brace) *air transportation executive*
Field, Larry *paper company executive*
Jan, Chwu-Ching Hwang *environmental chemistry consultant*
Lovejoy, Paul Robert *lawyer*

**Elmhurst**
Blain, Charlotte Marie *internist, educator*
Choyke, Phyllis May Ford (Mrs. Arthur Davis Choyke Jr.) *management executive, editor, poet*
Duchossois, Craig J. *manufacturing executive*
Fischer, Bruce Douglas *management consultant, educator*
MacInnes, Sally Ackerman *computer education educator*
Malo, Michele Lee *marketing professional*
Moffitt, Ray *social worker, consultant*
Pollack, Judy Barbara *special education educator*
Pruter, Margaret Franson *editor*
Sample, Steven Dale *secondary school educator*
Scurlock, Jo Ann *history professor, researcher*
Stanger, John Goodman *literature and language professor, archivist*

**Elmwood**
Vaughan, Patricia Ann *elementary school educator*

**Elmwood Park**
Spina, Anthony Ferdinand *lawyer*

**Eureka**
Staudenmeier, William John, Jr. *academic administrator, dean, sociology professor*
Wells, Christopher Lindell *art educator, football coach, baseball coach*

**Evanston**
Allred, Albert Louis *chemistry professor*
Altman, Edith G. *sculptor*
Backman, Vadim *biomedical engineer, educator*
Basolo, Fred *chemistry professor*
Bazant, Zdenek Pavel *engineering educator*
Beatty, Virginia Lewis *librarian, archivist, consultant*
Belting, Hans *art historian, educator, writer*
Belytschko, Ted *engineering educator*
Bethel, Kathleen Evonne *librarian*
Bienen, Henry Samuel *academic administrator, political scientist, educator*
Bishop, David Fulton *library administrator*
Bloomer, William David *radiologist, oncologist, educator*
Bobco, William David, Jr. *consulting engineering company executive*
Borcover, Alfred Seymour *journalist*
Boye, Roger Carl *academic administrator, journalism educator*
Braeutigam, Ronald Ray *economics professor, educational association administrator*
Brown, Eric Ricardo *biology educator*
Brown, Laurie Mark *physicist, researcher*
Canes-Wrone, Brandice *political scientist, educator*
Carr, Stephen Howard *materials engineer, educator*
Cates, Jo Ann *library director*
Chang, R. P. H. *materials science educator*
Christian, Richard Carlton *dean, former advertising agency executive*
Colgate, J. Edward *mechanical engineering educator*
Conger, William Frame *artist, educator*
Corey, Gordon Richard *financial advisor, former utilities executive*
Crawford, Isiaa Wilhlm *psychologist, educator, administrator*
Crawford, Susan *library director, educator, editor, writer*
Creamer, Robert Allan *lawyer*
Dallos, Peter John *neurobiologist, educator*
Dana, Steven B. *academic administrator*
Danilov, Victor Joseph *museum administrator, educator, writer*
Daskin, Mark Stephen *engineering educator*
Davis, Shani *Olympic athlete*
Davis, Stephen Howard *applied mathematics professor*
Deming, Thomas Edward *publishing executive*
Devinatz, Allen *retired mathematician, educator*
Dranove, David Stuart *business educator, consultant, economist*
Dumas, Lawrence B. *academic administrator*
Eberley, Helen-Kay *opera singer, recording industry executive, poet*
Enroth-Cugell, Christina Alma Elisabeth *neurophysiologist, educator*
Felknor, Bruce Lester *publishing executive, consultant, writer*
Fessler, Raymond R. *metallurgical engineering consultant*
Fine, Morris Eugene *materials engineer, educator*
Frey, Donald Nelson *industrial executive, educator, retired manufacturing executive*
Gaiha, Vishnu Das *cardiologist*
Galvin, Kathleen Malone *communications educator*
Gentner, Dedre *psychology professor*
Ghiglione, Loren Frank *journalism professor*
Gibbons, William Reginald, Jr. *poet, writer, translator, editor*

Godwin, Hilary A. *chemistry professor, research scientist*
Goldstick, Thomas Karl *biomedical engineering educator*
Gordon, Julie Peyton *foundation administrator*
Gordon, Robert James *economics professor*
Grunsfeld, Ernest Alton III *architect*
Hacek, Donna Marie *microbiologist, researcher*
Hall, Bruce A. *music educator*
Hemke, Frederick L. *academic administrator*
Hixson, Kathryn *art critic*
Holton, Lisa *writer, editor, researcher*
Hughes, Edward F. X. *healthcare educator, preventive medicine physician*
Hunwick, John Owen *history professor, language educator*
Hurter, Arthur Patrick *economist, educator*
Ibers, James Arthur *chemist, educator*
Irons, William George *anthropology educator*
Jacobs, Donald P. *retired dean, banking and finance educator*
Jacobs, Norman Joseph *publishing executive*
Jacobson, Andrew Darin *geochemist*
Jain, Dipak Chand *dean, marketing educator, consultant*
Jennings, Hamlin Manson *materials scientist, educator*
Jerome, Joseph Walter *mathematics professor*
Jones, Robert Russell *retired magazine editor*
Kalai, Eliud *economist, researcher, educator*
Keer, Leon Morris *engineering educator*
Kertész, Imre *writer*
Khandekar, Janardan Dinkar *oncologist, educator*
Kieckhefer, Richard *religion educator*
Kotler, Philip *marketing educator, writer*
Kraut, Richard *humanities educator*
Krizek, Raymond John *engineering educator, consultant*
Kuenster, John Joseph *editor*
Kujala, Walfrid Eugene *musician, educator*
Lambert, Joseph Buckley *chemistry professor*
Larson, Paul William *public relations executive*
Lewis, Charles A. *foundation administrator*
Lewis, Dan Albert *education educator*
Liang, Chuang *optical engineer, researcher*
Macsai, John *architect*
Malthouse, Edward Carl *finance educator*
Manin, Yuri Ivanovich *mathematician*
Margoliash, Emanuel *biochemist, educator*
Matkowsky, Bernard Judah *mathematician, educator*
McCarron, John Francis *editor*
McDonough, Bridget Ann *music theatre company director*
Menke, Allen Carl *manufacturing executive*
Miller, Stephen Herschel *surgeon, educator*
Mills, Edwin Smith *economics professor*
Mineka, Susan *psychology professor*
Moore, C. Bradley *chemistry professor*
Morrison, John Horton *lawyer*
Murphy, Gordon John *electrical engineer, educator*
Mustoe, Thomas Anthony *physician, plastic surgeon*
Neaman, Mark Robert *hospital administrator*
Nechin, Herbert Benjamin *lawyer*
Nelson, Richard Lawrence, Jr. *surgeon, educator*
Novales, Ronald Richards *zoologist, educator*
Oakes, Robert James *physics professor*
Odom, Teri Wang *chemist*
Olmstead, William Edward *mathematics professor*
Olszewski, Wojciech *economist, mathematician*
Ottino, Julio Mario *engineering educator*
Otwell, Ralph Maurice *retired newspaper editor*
Peck, Abraham *editor, writer, educator, media consultant*
Peters, Gordon Benes *retired musician*
Peterson, Lance Robert *physician*
Peterson, Penelope Loraine *dean, education educator*
Pierrehumbert, Janet Breckenridge *language educator*
Power, Peggy Ann *elementary school educator*
Prince, Thomas Richard *accountant, educator*
Pritchard, Sarah Margaret *library director*
Reiss, Lenore Ann *language educator, retired secondary school educator*
Reiter, Stanley *economist, educator*
Richeson, Jennifer Anne *psychology professor, researcher*
Rielly, John Edward *educational association administrator*
Robbins, Henry Zane *public relations and marketing executive*
Robertson, David Alan *museum director, educator*
Rosengart, Todd Kenneth *cardiothoracic surgeon, researcher, neurosurgeon, educator*
Sachtler, Wolfgang Max Hugo *chemistry professor*
Salafsky, Ira S. *pediatrician, educator*
Salem, Richard Allen *mediator*
Satterthwaite, Mark A. *economics professor*
Sawhney, Mohanbir S. *finance educator*
Schiff, Molly Jeanette *artist, researcher*
Schofer, Joseph Landy *civil engineer, educator*
Scholten, Menno Nico *mortgage banker*
Schulte, Bruce John *lawyer*
Schwartz, Neena Betty *endocrinologist, educator*
Scott, Walter Dill *management educator*
Sedgwick, Timothy Foster *religion educator*
Seidman, David N(athaniel) *materials scientist, engineer, educator*
Sener MD, Stephen Francis *oncologist, surgeon*
Shah, Surendra Poonamchand *engineering educator*
Sheldon, Mark *assistant dean*
Sheridan, James Edward *history professor*
Silverman, Richard Bruce *chemist, educator, biochemist*
Smith, Spencer Bailey *engineering and business educator*
Sobel, Alan *electrical engineer, physicist*
Sprang, Milton LeRoy *obstetrician, gynecologist, educator*
Stern, Louis William *marketing educator, consultant*
Stumpf, David Allen *pediatric neurologist*
Taflove, Allen *electrical engineer, educator, researcher, consultant*
Tanner, Martin Abba *statistician, educator*
Thrash, Patricia Ann *retired educational association administrator*

Tornabene, Russell C. *communications executive*
Traisman, Howard Sevin *retired pediatrician*
Ulmer, Melville Paul *physics and astronomy educator*
Van Duyne, Richard Palmer *analytical chemistry educator, chemical physics educator*
Van Ness, James Edward *electrical engineering educator*
Van Zanten, David Theodore *humanities educator*
Ver Steeg, Clarence Lester *historian, educator*
Vick, Nicholas A. *neurologist*
Walter, Robert Irving *retired chemistry professor*
Weber, Arnold Robert *academic administrator*
Weber, Klaus *finance educator*
Weertman, Johannes *materials science educator*
Weertman, Julia Randall *materials engineering educator*
Weil, Irwin *literature and language professor*
Weisbrod, Burton Allen *economist, educator*
Well, Irwin *language educator*
Wessels, Bruce W. *materials scientist, educator, department chairman*
Widom, Jonathan *biology professor*
Wilhelm, Frank L. *publisher, writer*
Wills, Garry *historian*
Witwer, Samuel Weiler, Jr. *lawyer*
Wright, Ellen *writing educator*
Wright, John *classics educator*
Wu, Tai Te *biological sciences and engineering educator*
Zelinsky, Daniel *mathematics professor*
Zhou, Hai *engineering educator*
Zimmerman, Mary Alice *performing arts educator*
Ziomek, Jonathan S. *journalist, educator*
Zipperer, Lorri Ann *librarian, consultant*

### Fairfield
Thomason, Nola Faye *emergency physician*

### Fairview Heights
Tenpas, Ronald J. *prosecutor, lawyer*

### Flanagan
Keck, Gerald Ray *music educator*

### Flora
Shrum, John *equal rights officer*

### Flossmoor
Cary, William Sterling *retired church executive*
Crum, James Francis *waste recycling company executive*
Day, Gregory Lynn *music educator*
Garrison, Ray Harlan *lawyer*
MacMaster, Daniel Miller *retired museum official*
Pierce, Shelby Crawford *oil industry executive, consultant*

### Forest Park
Poplawska, Anna *artist, educator, art critic*

### Forreston
Braker, William Paul *music educator*
Harn, Amy Helen *music educator, director*

### Forsyth
Graf, Karl Rockwell *nuclear engineer*

### Fox River Grove
Abboud, Alfred Robert *banker, consultant, investor, director*

### Frankfort
Burhoe, Brian Walter *automotive service executive*
Coughlin, Kimberly Ann *music educator*

### Franklin Park
Miller, Bryan Michael *music educator*
Simpson, Michael *retired metals service center executive*

### Freeport
Fiorenza, Samuel Thomas, Jr. *English educator*
Giaimo, Paul Sebastian *English and philosophy educator*
Vogt, Lorna Corrine *retired librarian, small business owner*
Weaver, Michael Glenn *pharmacist*

### Galena
Alexander, Barbara Leah Shapiro *clinical social worker*
Bezkorovainy, Anatoly *medical educator, retired biochemist*
Crandall, John Lynn *retired insurance company executive, consultant*
Narkiewicz-Laine, Christian K. *museum director, painter, poet*
Sipiera, Paul P., Jr. *foundation administrator, retired geology and astronomy professor*

### Galesburg
Fitch, Martha Jean *minister*
Haywood, Bruce *retired academic administrator*
Hellenga, Robert Riner *language educator, writer*
Metz, Robin O. *writer, educator, poet*
Polay, Bruce *music educator, conductor*
Ridlon, Kathleen *dancer, educator*
Schwartzman, Peter David *environmental scientist, educator*
Taylor, Roger Lee *academic administrator, lawyer*
Tourlentes, Thomas Theodore *retired psychiatrist*

### Galva
Everett, Reynolds Melville, Jr. *lawyer*
Massie, Michael Earl *lawyer*
Swatos, William Henry, Jr. *priest, sociologist*

### Geneva
Klenke, Deborah Ann *band and choral director, department chairman*
Montgomery, Joel Robert *communications executive, consultant*
Tyler, Lloyd John *retired lawyer*
Weiler, Rory Thomas *lawyer*
Young, Jack Allison *financial executive*

### Genoa
Cromley, Jon Lowell *lawyer*

### Gilberts
Barilich, Thomas Anthony *risk management consultant*

### Gillespie
Schwab, Sharon Kay *language arts educator, drama educator*

### Gilman
Ireland, Herbert Orin *retired engineering educator*

### Glen Carbon
Jarabak, Phyllis A. *music educator*
Lazerson, Earl Edwin *retired academic administrator*

### Glen Ellyn
Baloun, John Charles *retired wholesale distribution executive*
Bollendorf, Robert Fredrick *retired education educator, psychologist*
Conti, Paul Louis *management consulting company executive*
Cummings, Joan E. *health facility administrator, educator*
Cvengros, Joseph Michael *manufacturing company executive*
Dieter, Raymond Andrew, Jr. *physician, thoracic and vascular surgeon*
Frateschi, Lawrence Jan *economist, statistician, educator*
Grosser, William F. *science educator*
Hudson, Dennis Lee *lawyer, retired arbitrator, federal official*
King, Peggy Marsha *special education educator, researcher*
Lenard, Anthony Edward *mathematics professor*
Maciejewski, Nora Jean *elementary school educator*
Mooring, F. Paul *physics editor*
Neurauter, Elizabeth Strain *secondary school educator*
Nunamaker, Susan Sun *mathematics professor*
O'Connell, Daniel James *lawyer*
Patten, Ronald James *university dean*
Poromanska, Margarita Kirilova *science educator, environmental scientist*
Rothmaler, Peter Antell *mathematician, educator*
Sandrok, Richard William *lawyer*
Ulrich, Werner *patent lawyer*
Whisenhunt, William Benton *history professor*

### Glencoe
Dean, H. Clark *retired civil engineer, genealogist*
Isaacs, Roger David *public relations executive*
Milloy, Frank Joseph, Jr. *surgeon*
Nebenzahl, Kenneth *rare book and map dealer, author*
Perlberg, Jules Martin *lawyer*
Siske, Regina *artist*

### Glendale Heights
Cook, Doris Marie *retired accountant, educator*
Rawal, Darshan Lal *civil engineer, structural engineer, consultant*

### Glenview
Berkman, Michael G. *lawyer*
Blase, Anthony Idomeneus *retired electronics executive, writer, poet*
Bruns, Nicolaus, Jr. *retired agricultural products executive, lawyer, educator*
Casas, Laurie Ann *plastic surgeon*
Corley, Jenny Lynd Wertheim *elementary school educator*
Coulson, Elizabeth Anne *physical therapist, educator, state representative*
Dawson, Suzanne Stockus *lawyer*
Epstein, Barbara Myrna Robbin *retired language educator*
Farber, Isadore E. *psychologist, educator*
Franklin, Lynne *corporate communications specialist, writer*
Geller, William Alan *criminologist, consultant, protective services official*
Gillis, Marvin Bob *retired chemical executive, consultant*
Graff, Jeffrey G. *emergency physician*
Grubbs, Robert W. *computer services company executive*
Haebich, Arthur T. *retired surgeon, retired thoracic surgeon*
Hickey, John Thomas *retired electronics company executive*
Hough, Winston *artist*
King, Billie Jean Moffitt *retired professional tennis player*
Kinigakis, Panagiotis *research scientist, researcher, engineer, writer*
Kinney, Jon C. *metal products executive*
Knox, James Edwin *lawyer*
Levin, Donald Robert *business and finance executive, motion picture producer, professional sports team owner*
Martin, James Frederick *media consultant*
Mc Nitt, Willard Charles *food products executive*
Mukoyama, James Hidefumi, Jr. *security firm executive*
Olson, Roy Arthur *retired government official*
Panarese, William C. *civil engineer*
Rorig, Kurt Joachim *chemist, science association director, educator*
Smith, Harold B. *manufacturing executive*
Speer, David Blakeney *industrial executive*
Turner, Lee *travel company executive*
Van Zelst, Theodore William *civil engineer, engineering company executive*

### Godfrey
King, Ordie Herbert, Jr. *oral pathologist*

### Granite City
Humphrey, Owen Everett *retired education administrator*
Rarick, Philip Joseph *lawyer, retired state supreme court justice*
Roberds, Wyatt Kayne *music educator*

### Grayslake
Barrington, Leonard Barry *chemist, educator, writer*

Cayari, Christopher *music educator*
Lorence, Michael Franklin *social sciences educator*

### Great Lakes
Tiba, Amer *research scientist*

### Greenview
Full, Susan Gayle *librarian, educator*

### Greenville
Filby, Ivan Leonard *management educator*
Flowers, Creole Duane *publishing executive*
Hall, Tracy Lynn *physician*

### Griggsville
Evans, H. Todd *music educator*

### Gurnee
Hall, Terry *accountant*
Halsne-Baarda, Alana Michelle *secondary school educator*
Myren, Allen W(illiam) *retired music educator*
Sommerlad, Robert Edward *environmental research engineer*

### Hanover
Bleveans, John *lawyer*

### Harrisburg
Rushing, Philip Dale *retired social worker*

### Harvey
Heilicser, Bernard Jay *emergency physician*

### Havana
Sass, Gregory George *ecologist, researcher*

### Hazel Crest
Freed, Melvyn Norris *retired educational association administrator, writer*

### Herrin
Gauto, Nelson Fernando *plastic surgeon, consumer products company executive*

### Herscher
Van Meter, LeRoy Ray *music educator*

### Hickory Hills
Lustig, Margaret Gallagher *lawyer*

### Highland Park
Afterman, Allan B. *accountant, educator, financial consultant, researcher*
Bakalar, John Stephen *printing company executive, publishing executive*
Cohen, Burton David *food service executive, lawyer*
Dirsmith, Ronald *architect*
Dubin, Arthur Detmers *retired architect*
Gash, Lauren Beth *lawyer, state legislator*
Greenblatt, Miriam *writer, editor, educator*
Harris, Thomas L. *public relations executive*
Hawkins, Margaret *art critic, writer, educator*
Hershenson, Martha Bradford *history educator*
Hobson, Stephen Gilbert *conductor, music educator*
Hoy, Suellen *historian*
Hulseman, Robert L. *manufacturing executive*
Humay, Priscilla *artist*
Johnson, Curtis Lee *publishing executive, editor, writer*
Karol, Nathaniel H. *lawyer, consultant*
Korzenski, Robert M. *manufacturing executive*
Nelson, Richard David *lawyer*
Pattis, S. William *publishing executive*
Roy, Hemant Kumar *gastroenterologist, researcher*
Rudo, Milton *retired manufacturing executive*
Rutenberg-Rosenberg, Sharon Leslie *retired journalist*
Saltzberg, Eugene Ernest *emergency physician, educator*
Schindel, Donald Marvin *retired lawyer*
Slavick, Ann Lillian *retired art educator*
Stein, Paula Jean Anne Barton *hotel real estate company executive, real estate broker*
Tobin, Calvin Jay *retired architect*
Tribbey, Fern *mathematics educator*
Uhlmann, Frederick Godfrey *securities trader*

### Highwood
Brown, Lawrence Haas *retired banker*

### Hillsboro
Doss, JoAnn Trauernicht *retired elementary school educator*
Mulch, Robert F., Jr. *physician*

### Hillside
Savic, Jelena *technologist, educator*

### Hines
Best, William Robert *internist, educator, dean*

### Hinsdale
Allen, James Edward *preventive medicine physician*
Brueschke, Erich Edward *physician, researcher, educator*
Dederick, Robert Gogan *economist*
Denton, Ray Douglas *insurance company executive*
Dillon, Jane Elizabeth *otolaryngologist*
Gruft, James Harris *physiatrist, educator*
Kaminsky, Manfred Stephan *physicist*
Kim, Micaela *speech pathology/audiology services professional*
Lonchyna, Vassyl A. *thoracic surgeon*
Mehuron, William Otto *retired federal official*
Peckenpaugh, Robert Earl *investment advisor*
Taylor, T(homas) Roger *educational consultant, educator*
Unikel, Eva Taylor *interior designer*
Urbik, Jerome Anthony *financial consultant*
Whitney, William Elliot, Jr. *advertising agency executive*

### Hoffman Estates
Crowley, William C. *retail executive*

Dunn, Christopher Joseph *public affairs consultant*
Good, Mark *retail executive*
Kahn, Elizabeth *language educator, department chairman*
Kelly, Gerald F. Jr. *retail executive*
Larson, John M. *educational consultant*
Lee, Gregory A. *human resources specialist*
Lewis, Aylwin B. *retail executive, former food service company executive*
Meads, Mindy *merchandising and design executive*
Nicholas, Arthur Soterios *manufacturing executive*
O'Leary, Robert J. *retail executive*
Rooney, John Edward *communications company executive*
White, William III *retail executive*
Winckler, Alicia Jean *human resources director*
Zopp, Andrea Lynne *lawyer, retail executive*

### Homewood
Parker, Eugene Newman *retired physicist, retired educator*
Schillings, Denny Lynn *retired history professor, educational and grants consultant*

### Hoopeston
Hicks, Carol Ann *small business owner, educator*

### Hudson
Mills, Frederick VanFleet *art educator, watercolorist*

### Huntley
Balk, Alfred William *journalist*
Saporta, Jack *psychologist, educator*

### Indian Head Park
Bamberger, Mary Ann *archivist, consultant*

### Ingleside
D'Andrea, Dana M. *medical/surgical nurse, lawyer*

### Itasca
Balasa, Mark Edward *investment consultant*
Broad, Matthew *lawyer*
Civgin, Don *corporate financial executive*
Constant, Anita Aurelia *publisher*
Duncan, Sam K. *retail executive*
Fellowes, James *manufacturing executive*
Gallagher, J. Patrick, Jr. *insurance company executive*
Garratt, Reginald George *electronics executive*
Porter, Ethel Mae *publishing executive*
Rosengren, John Charles *lawyer*

### Jacksonville
Anderson, Michael R. *elementary school educator, writer*
Calderhead, Kyle D. *mathematics professor*
Chaffee, James *academic administrator*
Findley, Paul *former congressman, author, educator*
Gallas, Martin Hans *librarian*
Hardin, Susan Jean *social studies educator, department chairman*
Hayter, John Eldon *retired music educator*
Johns, Beverley Anne Holden *special education administrator*
Kuster, Larry Donald *lawyer*
Mathews, Jack Sherman *foundation administrator, retired insurance company executive*
Walters, Christopher Matchette *music director*
Ware, Jon Dean *retail executive*

### Joliet
Anderson, Carol Lee *communications executive*
Easton, Kenneth Glenn *retired utilities executive*
Holmgren, Myron Roger *social sciences educator*
Johnston, James Robert *library director*
Kaffer, Roger Louis *bishop*
Layman, Dale Pierre *medical educator, researcher, writer*
Lenard, George Dean *lawyer*
Ring, Alvin Manuel *pathologist, educator*
Teas, Richard Harper *lawyer*
Tijani, Hakeem Ibikunle *history professor, researcher*

### Kankakee
Deck, Gregory A. *lawyer*
Roy, Sudipta D. *education educator*

### Kenilworth
Bott, Harold Sheldon *accountant, management consultant*
Cook, Stanton R. *media company executive*
Corrigan, John Edward, Jr. *retired banker, lawyer*
Feng, Paul Yen-Hsiung *lawyer, chemist*
Hayes, M. M.M. *publishing executive*
McKittrick, William Wood *lawyer*
Schneider-Criezis, Susan Marie *architect*
Steingraber, Frederick George *management consultant*
Weaver, Clifford Lee *retired lawyer, winery owner*

### La Grange
Kerr, Alexander Duncan, Jr. *lawyer*
Mehlenbacher, Dohn Harlow *civil engineer, consultant*
Reggio, Vito Anthony *retired management consultant*
Zethmayr, Ellen Lolakos *music educator, writer*

### La Grange Park
Butler, Margaret Kampschaefer *retired computer scientist*
Perkins, William H., Jr. *retired finance company executive*

### Lafox
Seils, William George *lawyer*

### Lake Barrington
Morris, Ralph William *chronopharmacologist*

### Lake Bluff
Fryburger, Vernon Ray, Jr. *advertising executive, finance educator*
Griem, John Michael *management consultant*

Kyncl, John Jaroslav *pharmacologist*
Marozsan, John Robert *retired publishing company executive*
Ochsner, Othon Henry, II, *importer, restaurant critic*
Schreiber, George Richard *publishing executive, writer*
Scott, Karen Bondurant *consumer catalog company executive*
Snader, Jack Ross *publishing company executive*

**Lake Forest**
Begley, Christopher B. *pharmaceutical executive*
Benson, Cedric *professional football player*
Bramhall, Robert Richard *management consultant*
Callan, Clair Marie *physician, consultant*
Campbell, Andrew *manufacturing executive*
Carroll, Barry Joseph *manufacturing and real estate executive*
Carter, Donald Patton *retired advertising executive*
Chieger, Kathryn Jean *recreational facility executive*
Clark, Wesley M. *manufacturing executive*
Covington, George Morse *retired lawyer*
Crawford, Robert W., Jr. *furniture rental company executive*
Damico, Joseph F. *medical products executive*
Donovan, Timothy R. *automotive executive, lawyer*
Dreimann, Leonhard *manufacturing executive*
Emerson, William Harry *retired lawyer*
Faulkner, James Vincent, Jr. *lawyer*
Feinberg, Jeffrey Enoch *religious studies educator, writer*
Francois, William Armand *lawyer*
Frederick, Virginia Fiester *state legislator*
Gayle, Carol *history educator, educational association administrator*
Griese, Brian *professional football player*
Hamilton, Peter Bannerman *manufacturing executive, lawyer*
Hammar, Lester Everett *retired manufacturing executive*
Haser, William H. *automotive executive*
Herron, Orley R. *college president*
Howard, John Lawrence *federal agency lawyer*
Johnson, Richard Darrell *management consultant*
Jones, Gordon Kempton *dentist*
Jones, Philip Newton *internist, educator*
Kelly, Daniel John *physician*
Keyser, Richard Lee *distribution company executive*
Krasnewich, Kathryn *water transportation executive*
Lambert, John Boyd *chemical engineer, consultant*
Larson, Peter N. *manufacturing executive*
Leemputte, Peter G. *manufacturing executive*
Levy, Nelson Louis *immunologist, educator, surgeon*
McCaskey, Michael B. *professional football team executive*
McCoy, Dustan Elwood *manufacturing executive, lawyer*
Miller, Arthur Hawks, Jr. *librarian, archivist*
Miller, Mark C. *waste management administrator*
Mohr, Roger John *retired advertising agency executive*
Morell, William Nelson, Jr. *foreign trade association executive, government agency administrator*
Muhammad, Mushin *professional football player*
Orton, Kyle *professional football player*
Palmer, Ann Therese Darin *lawyer*
Park, David William *humanities educator*
Parker, Dean E. *lawyer*
Pawl, Ronald Phillip *neurosurgery educator*
Prochnow, Herbert Victor, Jr. *retired lawyer*
Rand, Kathy Sue *public relations consultant, public relations executive*
Romans, Donald Bishop *manufacturing executive*
Ross, Robert Evan *bank executive*
Salter, Edwin Carroll *retired pediatrician*
Schulze, Franz, Jr. *critic, educator*
Seaman, Irving, Jr. *banker*
Sikorovsky, Eugene Frank *retired lawyer*
Smith, Lovie *professional football coach*
Smith, Marschall Imboden *lawyer*
Stecko, Paul T. *packaging company executive*
Taylor, Barbara Ann Olin *writer, educational consultant*
Trammell, Kenneth R. *automotive executive*
Urlacher, Brian *professional football player*
Weinberg, Milton, Jr. *retired cardiovascular and thoracic surgeon*
Weston, Arthur Walter *chemist, consultant, retired chemicals executive*
Weston, Dawn Thompson *artist, researcher*
Wilbur, Richard Sloan *medical association administrator, physician*
Young, Ronald Faris *commodities trader*
Ysasi-Diaz, Gloria *wholesale distribution executive*

**Lake In The Hills**
Kay, Dennis Matthew *retired publishing company official*

**Lake Villa**
Kastor, Matthew Anton *secondary school educator, music educator*

**Lake Zurich**
Juknelis, Nick *music educator*
Krolopp, Rudolph William *retired industrial designer, consultant*
Schultz, Carl Herbert *real estate developer*
Scott, John Joseph *lawyer*
Thompson, Joshua M. *music educator*

**Lanark**
Abbott, David Henry *manufacturing executive*

**Lebanon**
Jewett, Thomas O. *science educator, writer*

**Lemont**
Hayes, Randy Alan *family therapist*
Inokuti, Mitio *physicist, educator*
Williams, Jack Marvin *research chemist*

**Libertyville**
Grote, Jonathan *chemist, researcher*

Korenev, Sergey Alexandrovich *physicist*
Maczulski, Margaret Louise *event marketing professional, meeting manager*
Schroeder, W(illiam) Widick *religion educator*
Shen, Xiaohui *application developer, researcher*
Szini, Istvan Janos *electronics engineer*
True, Raymond Stephen *editor, writer*
Trzyna, Chris *physical education educator*
Tullman, Glen *management consultant*

**Lincoln**
Wilson, Robert Allen *religion educator*

**Lincolnshire**
Anderson, David J. *manufacturing executive*
Boyton, Rick *theater director, actor*
Carbonari, Bruce A. *metal products executive*
Fradin, Russell P. *human resources company executive, former computer company executive*
Knopik, Robert *retail executive, consultant*
Lemonis, Marcus *automotive executive*
Martin, John Driscoll *school administrator*
Michalik, John James *legal association administrator*
Para, Gerard Albert *lawyer, real estate broker, consultant*
Roche, Mark A. *consumer products company executive, lawyer*
Schauble, John Eugene *physical education educator*
Simes, Stephen Mark *pharmaceutical executive*
Wesley, Norman H. *metal products executive*

**Lincolnwood**
Akos, Francis *retired violinist, conductor*
Beck, Cynthia Marie *archivist, researcher*
Carroll, Howard William *state legislator*
Earnest, Craig Hopkins *psychologist, consultant*
Greenblatt, Deana Charlene *elementary school educator*
Lebedow, Aaron Louis *consulting company executive*
Zaremski, Miles Jay *lawyer*

**Lisle**
Colbert, Marvin Jay *retired internist, educator*
Gaddis, Vincent Ray *history professor*
Harris, Gregory Todd *customer service administrator*
Hayes, Richard J., Jr. *engineering company executive*
Krehbiel, Frederick August, II, *electronics executive*
Krehbiel, John H., Jr. *retired electronics company executive*
Mallak, Augustine Kenneth *monk, music educator*
Meeker, Ralph D. *computer scientist, information scientist, educator*
Ruyle-Hullinger, Elizabeth Smith (Beth Ruyle) *municipal financial advisor, consultant*
Skweres, Thomas W. *entrepreneur, writer, poet, investor, consultant, advertising executive*
Slark, Martin P. *electronics executive*
Smith, Jared Russell William *research executive, research scientist, consultant, poet*
Townsley, Lisa Gail *mathematics professor*
Ware, George Henry *botanist*

**Litchfield**
Deaton, Beverly Jean *nursing administrator, educator*
Floreth, Frederick Dennis *lawyer*
Talley, Hayward Leroy *communications executive*

**Lockport**
Whyte, Kelly Ann *music educator*

**Lombard**
Ahlstrom, Ronald Gustin *artist*
Bachop, William Earl, Jr. *retired anatomist, zoologist*
Barnholt, Brandon K. *retail executive*
Benning, Joseph Raymond *principal*
Garrett, Paul James *financial planner*
Henkin, Robert Elliott *nuclear medicine physician*
Lindsay, Diane Miller *music educator*
McCoy, Jeanie Shearer *analytical chemist, consultant*

**Long Grove**
Ausman, Robert K. *surgeon, research and development company executive*
Conway, John K. *lawyer*
Davis, Britton Anthony *retired lawyer*
Obert, Paul Richard *lawyer, manufacturing executive*
Wilson, Stephen Ray *fertilizer manufacturing company executive*

**Loves Park**
Dixon, John James *music educator*

**Lovington**
Duncan, Linda B. *social sciences educator*

**Machesney Park**
Vaughn, Linda Marie *municipal official*

**Macomb**
Barclay, Martha Jane *science educator, research scientist*
Bauerly, Ronald John *marketing educator*
Bean, Matt *theater educator*
Deng, Yongxin *geography educator, ecology educator*
Dexter, Donald Harvey *surgeon, educator*
Goldfarb, Alvin *academic administrator*
Hayes, Paul Robert *retired field and clinical experiences coordinator*
Hetzel-Riggin, Melanie Dyan *psychology professor*
Hopper, Stephen Rodger *hospital administrator*
Kim, Chung-Ha *music educator*
Kyllonen Rose, Julie Frances *college program administrator*
Solomonson, Glen Terrance *music educator, musician*
Thompson, James Lynn *music educator*
Walker, Tammie Leigh *music educator*
Walzer, Norman Charles *economics professor*
Woods, Jeannie Marlin *theater educator*

**Madison**
Purdes, Alice Marie *retired adult education educator*

**Mahomet**
Thompson, Margaret M. *physical education educator*

**Malta**
Ragan, Dennis M. *mathematics educator*

**Maple Park**
Nickels, John L. *retired state supreme court justice*

**Marengo**
Franks, Herbert Hoover *lawyer*
Meredith, Owen Nichols *public relations executive*
Mrkvicka, Edward Francis, Jr. *writer, finance company executive*

**Marion**
Crane, Hugh Wingate *railroad executive*
Schaede, Richard Edwin *retired family practice physician*

**Markham**
Majeski, Susan Saxer *elementary school educator*
Peacock, Marilyn Claire *primary school educator*

**Marseilles**
Nellett, Gaile H. *adult education educator*

**Marshall**
Freeman, Charles E. *writer, musician*

**Maryville**
Stark, Patricia Ann *psychologist*

**Matteson**
Garrett-Wilson, Shirlyn Maria *social services administrator*
van der Hoek, Sherry A. *counselor*

**Mattoon**
Black, Todd Ronald *music educator*
Horsley, Jack Everett *bank executive, writer, lawyer*
Phipps, John Randolph *retired army officer*

**Maywood**
Albain, Kathy S. *oncologist*
Aranha, Gerard V. *surgeon*
Barbato, Anthony L. *hospital administrator, medical educator*
Bermes, Edward William, Jr. *biochemist, educator*
Biller, Jose *neurologist, educator*
Dado, Diane Valentina *plastic and reconstructive surgeon*
Gamelli, Richard Louis *surgeon, educator*
Gaynor, Ellen Rose *hematologist*
Gianopoulos, John George *obstetrician*
Hanin, Israel *pharmacologist, educator*
Lid, Glenn David *chemistry educator*
Light, Terry Richard *orthopedic hand surgeon*
Miele, Lucio *physician, medical researcher, pharmacologist*
Moran, John Francis *cardiologist*
Nand, Sucha *medical educator*
Newman, Barry Marc *pediatric surgeon*
Picken, Maria M. (Maria M. Mrozowicz-Picken) *pathologist*
Stankiewicz, James A. *otolaryngologist*
Ward, Kathleen Anne *radiologist*
Warpeha, Raymond Leonard *surgeon, educator*
Wheeler, John S., Jr. *urologist*

**Mc Gaw Park**
Bernardo, Angelito Alday *nephrologist, medical products executive*
Kesman, Anthony K. *medical products executive*

**Mchenry**
Carson, Linda Marie *elementary school educator*
Chisu, Ioan *artist*

**Melrose Park**
Bernick, Carol Lavin *consumer products company executive*
Bernick, Howard Barry *manufacturing executive*
Cernugel, William John *consumer products company executive, distributor*
Giancola, James J. *bank executive*
Klein, Lloyd William *cardiologist, researcher*
Kloster, Carol Good *wholesale distribution executive*
Lavin, Bernice E. *cosmetics executive*
Schmidt, Gary P. *lawyer, personal care industry executive*
Wechter, Clari Ann *manufacturing executive*

**Metamora**
Harbers, Rebecca Ann *physical education educator*

**Mokena**
Lighty, Michelle McCowan *secondary school educator*
Sangmeister, George Edward *lawyer, consultant, congressman*
Wright, Chely *country singer*

**Moline**
Arnell, Richard Anthony *radiologist*
Garvin-Hunthey, Lynn M. *psychologist*
Gleich, Carol S. *health professions education executive*
Jenkins, James Robert *lawyer, chemicals executive*
Johnson, Mary Lou *lay worker, educator*
Jones, Nathan Jerome *farm machinery manufacturing company executive*
Lane, Robert W. *farm equipment manufacturing executive*
Middleton, Marc Stephen *corporate insurance risk manager*
Milberg, Joachim *retired automotive executive*
Mitchell, Lucille Anne *retired elementary school educator*
Nowinski, Frank Lawrence *lawyer*
Penn, J. B. *economist*

Schwiebert, Deborah Johnson *marketing executive*
Stodt, F. Chloe *piano educator*
Taylor, Byron Keith *industrial engineer*

**Monmouth**
Bruce, Mary Hanford *academic administrator, educator, writer*

**Monroe Center**
Coulahan, Mike J. *principal*

**Morton**
Corey, Judith Ann *retired elementary school educator*

**Morton Grove**
McKenna, Andrew James *wholesale distribution executive, printing company executive, sports association executive*
Smolyansky, Julie *consumer products company executive*
Vega, Steve *poet*

**Mount Carmel**
Fornoff, Frank J(unior) *retired chemistry educator, consultant*

**Mount Carroll**
Rogers, Ward Junior *retired industrial designer*

**Mount Prospect**
Eliason, Birdell *painter, educator*
Epstein, Stephen Roger *financial executive*
Rueggeberg, Erna M. *nursing consultant, nursing administrator, researcher*
Sayers, Gale *computer company executive, retired professional football player*

**Mount Sterling**
Tracy, Patrick F. *food products executive*

**Mount Vernon**
Hall, Sharon Gay *retired language educator, artist*
Harvey, Morris Lane *lawyer*
Withers, W. Russell, Jr. *broadcast executive*

**Mundelein**
Raviv, Gabriel *medical products executive*

**Muscatine**
Housh, E. William *manufacturing executive*

**Naperville**
Arzoumanidis, Gregory G. *chemist*
Bell, Bradley J. *water treatment company executive*
Benson, Kevin E. *transportation executive*
Birck, Michael John *telecommunications industry executive*
Briseno, Kathleen *education educator*
Bufalino, Vincent John *cardiologist, medical administrator*
Calamos, John Peter, Sr. *brokerage house executive*
Calamos, Nick P. *diversified financial services company executive*
Corvino, Beth Byster *lawyer*
Cowlishaw, Mary Lou *government educator*
Crawford, Raymond Maxwell, Jr. *nuclear engineer*
Desch, Theodore Edward *retired insurance company executive, lawyer*
Dombeck, Harold Arthur *insurance company executive*
Florence, Ernest Estell, Jr. *special education educator*
Folk, Frank Anton *surgeon, educator*
Fritz, Roger Jay *management consultant*
Gracey, Paul C., Jr. *lawyer, utilities executive*
Grimley, Jeffrey Michael *dentist*
Hawley, Richard L. *utilities executive*
Holba Puacz, Jeanne *librarian, educator*
Joyce, William H. *engineering company executive, chemical engineer*
Katai, Andrew Andras *chemical company executive*
Larson, Mark Edward, Jr. *lawyer, educator, financial planner*
McCallum, Gerald Christopher *clinical psychologist*
Miller, Charles E. *gynecologist*
Modery, Richard Gillman *marketing executive, sales executive*
Navin-O'Meara, Cynthia L. *school psychologist*
Penisten, Gary Dean *entrepreneur*
Pollak, Raymond *general and transplant surgeon*
Prabhu, Krish Anant *telecommunications industry executive, educator*
Raccah, Dominique Marcelle *publisher*
Rosenthal, Edward Leonard *secondary school educator*
Sellers, Gregory Jude *physicist*
Smetana, Mark *food products executive*
Spunt, Avery L. *pharmacist*
Stangl, Peter E. *transportation executive*
Strobel, Russ M. *gas industry executive, lawyer*
Tan, Li-Su Lin *accountant, insurance company executive, consultant*
Tibble, Douglas Clair *lawyer*
Vanagas, Rimantas (Ray) Andrius (Ray Vanagas) *entrepreneur, real estate developer, real estate company executive*
Vora, Manu Kishandas *chemical engineer, consultant*
Wake, Richard W. *food products executive*
Wake, Thomas G. *food products executive*
Wilde, Harold Richard *college president*
Xiao, Yanan *physicist, researcher*
Zinger, Michael *reproductive endocrinologist*

**Nashville**
Barber, Donald Gene, Jr. *purchasing agent*
Karmeier, Lloyd A. *state supreme court justice*

**Nauvoo**
Ivie, Evan Leon *computer science educator*

**New Baden**
Gregov, Maria Irma Pott *retired elementary school educator*

**New Lenox**
Hesser, Christa E. *secondary school educator*

**Niles**
Beton, John Allen *communications company executive*
Foster, Martha Mitchell *television director, writer*
Grace, John Joseph *retired priest*
Herb, Marvin J. *food products executive*
Kessell, Charles Arthur *music educator, musician*
Martinez, Euri Anthony *music educator, small business owner*

**Normal**
Alferink, Larry Allen *psychology professor*
Bowman, C. Alvin *academic administrator*
Brehm, Joan M. *training services executive*
Brown, Lauren Evans *zoologist, researcher, educator*
Buller, Chrysalis Chablis *director*
Cooley, William Emory, Jr. *radiologist*
Devinatz, Victor Gary *industrial relations specialist, educator*
Hickrod, George Alan Karnes Wallis *educational administration educator*
Miller, Wilma Hildruth *education educator*
Musick, Marilyn Irene *retired secondary school educator*
Olsen, Patrice Elizabeth *history professor, photographer*
Presley, John Woodrow *academic administrator*
Shields, John Charles *literature educator*
Temple, Mark Allen *adult education educator, consultant*
Trouille, Mary Seidman *foreign language educator*

**Norridge**
Petrakis, Myron Titos *retired mechanical engineer*

**North Aurora**
Sabey, Richard Homer *retired graphics designer*

**North Chicago**
Barsano, Charles Paul *medical educator, dean*
Bush, Eugene Nyle *pharmacologist, researcher*
Chedid, Antonio *pathologist, educator, researcher*
Gall, Eric Papineau *internist, educator*
Hawkins, Richard Albert *medical educator, administrator*
Kim, Yoon Berm *immunologist, educator*
Loga, Sanda *physicist, researcher*
Nair, Velayudhan *pharmacologist, educator, academic administrator*
Olejniczak, Edward Thaddeus *research scientist*
Roberts, Barry Lester *biologist, educator*
Rudy, David Robert *physician, educator*
Sierles, Frederick Stephen *psychiatrist, educator*

**Northbrook**
Abbey, G(eorge) Marshall *lawyer, retired health facility administrator*
Adler, Robert *electronics engineer*
Ben-Arie, Ronit Peleg *elementary school educator*
Boettcher, Robert Walter *civil engineer*
Bohlender, Hugh Darrow *lawyer*
Clarey, John Robert *executive recruiter, consultant*
Colburn, David Dunton *investment advisor*
Crockett, Joan M. *human resources executive*
Cruikshank, John W. III *insurance agent*
Cucco, Ulisse P. *retired obstetrician, gynecologist*
Di Spigno, Guy Joseph *industrial psychologist, international management consultant*
Edelson, Ira J. *venture capitalist*
Feibel, Frederick Arthur *financial consultant*
Gratalo, John, Jr. *banker, small business owner*
Green, David *manufacturing executive*
Gyoerkoe, Kevin L. *psychologist, director*
Hale, Danny Lyman *diversified financial services company executive*
Hindo, Walid Afram *radiology educator, researcher*
Kahn, Sandra S. *psychotherapist*
Keehn, Silas *retired bank executive*
King, Robert Charles *biologist, educator*
Lapin, Harvey I. *lawyer*
Levy, Arnold S(tuart) *real estate company executive*
Liddy, Edward M. *insurance company executive*
Mandel, Karyl Lynn *accountant*
McCabe, Michael J. (Mick) *insurance executive, lawyer*
Metz, Adam S. *real estate company executive*
Mulhall, Kimberly A. *business manager*
Noeth, Carolyn Frances *speech and language pathologist*
Perelman, Jeffrey E. *real estate company executive*
Pesmen, Sandra (Mrs. Harold William Pesmen) *editor, educator*
Pike, Robert William *insurance company executive, lawyer*
Pulsifer, Edgar Darling *retired leasing and sales company executive*
Rosemarin, Carey Stephen *lawyer*
Rosenberg, Auria Eleanor *secondary school educator*
Rosenfeld, Robert Lee *psychiatrist*
Ross, Debra Benita *marketing executive, jewelry designer*
Rotchford, Patricia Kathleen *lawyer, mediator*
Ruter, Allan J. *literature and language educator*
Sernett, Richard Patrick *lawyer*
Siegal, Judy A. *social services administrator*
Slattery, James Joseph (Joe Slattery) *actor*
Sprieser, Judith A. *former software company executive*
Stewart, Charles Leslie *lawyer*
Sudbrink, Jane Marie *sales and marketing executive*
Wajer, Ronald Edward *management consultant*
Wallace, Harry Leland *lawyer*
Wilson, Thomas Joseph *insurance company executive*

**Northfield**
Carlin, Donald Walter *retired food products executive, consultant*
Hadley, Stanton Thomas *manufacturing executive, director, lawyer*
Knight, James Atwood *manufacturing executive*
Lubawski, James Lawrence *healthcare consultant*

Lynch, Kirsten *food products executive*
Mamet, David Alan *playwright, theater producer*
Pratt, Murray Lester *manufacturing executive*
Rosenfeld, Irene B. *food products company executive*
Shabica, Charles Wright *geologist, earth science educator*
Shillestad, John Gardner *diversified financial services company executive*
Smeds, Edward William *retired food company executive*
Sneed, Paula Ann *food products executive*
Stepan, Frank Quinn *chemicals executive*
Stepan, Frank Quinn, Jr., (F. Quinn Stepan Jr.) *chemical company executive*
Vilim, Nancy Catherine *advertising executive*

**Northlake**
Haack, Richard Wilson *retired police officer*

**O Fallon**
Bjerkaas, Carlton Lee *information technology executive*
Fairchild, David Lawrence *music educator*
Lang, Matthew *music educator*
Ritzel, Tracey L. *special education educator*
Voellger, Gary A. *business consulting executive, retired air force officer*

**Oak Brook**
Alvarez, Ralph *food products executive*
Armario, Jose *restaurant executive*
Barnes, Karen Kay *lawyer*
Bennett, Margaret Airola *lawyer*
Biedron, Theodore John *publishing executive, advertising executive*
Bower, Barbara Jean *nurse, consultant*
Christian, Joseph Ralph *physician*
Ciccarone, Richard Anthony *financial executive*
Congalton, Susan Tichenor *lawyer*
Crump-Caine, Lynn *food service executive*
DeLorey, John Alfred *printing company executive*
Ding, Jianchi *embryologist, researcher*
Duerinck, Louis T. *retired rail transportation executive, lawyer*
Fenton, Tim *food service executive*
Fields, Janice L. *food service executive*
Floersch, Richard *human resources specialist*
Glenn, J. Thomas *consumer products company executive*
Hodnik, David F. *retail company executive*
Hoffmann, Joan Carol *retired academic dean*
Hollins, Mitchell Leslie *lawyer*
Iles, Eileen Marie *bank executive, risk management consultant*
John, Richard C. *enterprise development organization executive*
Khoshabe, Steven Y. *mortgage company executive*
Koufis, John Theodore *accountant*
Marinaccio, Lee Anthony *lawyer*
Nelson, Robert Eddinger *retired management consultant*
Onstead, R. Randall, Jr. *food products executive*
Paull, Matthew H. *food service executive*
Quist, Arjan *biotechnologist, director*
Santona, Gloria *lawyer*
Sherman, Jennifer L. *lawyer*
Skinner, James A. (James A. Skinner) *food products executive*
Skogsbergh, James H. *health facility administrator*
Spohr, Earl Clyde *retired investment advisor, retired military officer*
Stoelting, Curtis W. *consumer products company executive*
Thompson, Don *food products executive*
Turner, Fred L. *retired fast food company executive*
Veno, Ronald James, Jr. *travel industry executive*

**Oak Forest**
Aukes, Matthew H. *band educator*
Kogut, Kenneth Joseph *engineer, consultant*

**Oak Lawn**
Jachna, Joseph David *photographer, educator*
Jandes, Kenneth Michael *superintendent of schools*
Martin, Charles E. *music educator*
Sullivan, Michael *writer, retired mathematics professor*
Wiechert, Barbara Theresa *school nurse practitioner*

**Oak Park**
Adelman, William John *retired academic administrator, industrial relations specialist*
Bachand, Cheryl Ann *curator, art history educator*
Cannon, Patrick Francis *public relations executive*
Clark, John Peter III *engineer, consultant*
Devereux, Timothy Edward *advertising executive*
Matsuda, Takayoshi *surgeon, educator, biomedical researcher*
Schubert, Blake H. *lawyer*
Sengpiehl, Paul Marvin *lawyer, retired state official*
Varchmin, Thomas Edward *public health service officer*
Venerable, Shirley Marie *retired gifted and talented educator*
Young, Jessica S.E. *secondary school educator*

**Oakbrook Terrace**
Becker, Robert Jerome *allergist, consultant*
Catalano, Gerald *accountant*
Hegenderfer, Jonita Susan *public relations executive*
Keller, Dennis James *management educator*
Levine, Norman M. *academic administrator*
Overbye, David Lawrence *dean, researcher*
Pauldine, David J. *marketing executive, educator*
Tang, George Chickchee *investment company executive*
Taylor, Ronald Lee *academic administrator*

**Oakland**
Eriksen, Barbara Ann *writer, researcher*

**Olympia Fields**
Nuding, Doris Leona *law librarian, researcher*

**Oregon**
Haynes, Gary Allen *photojournalist, editor*

**Orland Park**
Antia, Kersey H. *industrial and clinical psychologist, consultant*
Burfeind, Betty Ruth *science educator*
Drugas, Theodore George *retired surgeon*
Gittelman, Marc Jeffrey *manufacturing and financial executive*
Osmanski, Adam E. *social studies educator*
Ritchey, Lauretta Marie *secondary school educator*
Saubert, Nicole J. *communications educator, social studies educator*

**Oswego**
May, Frank Brendan, Jr. *lawyer*

**Ottawa**
Ballowe, James *writer, educator*
Thornton, Edmund B. *philanthropist*

**Palatine**
Bokhari, Naila *mathematician, educational consultant*
Butler, John Musgrave *financial consultant*
Hershenhorn, Robert Gene *bank executive*
Keres, Karen Lynne *literature and language professor*
Kieft, Gerald Nelson *mechanical engineer*
Matsushima, Akira Paul *manufacturing executive*
Medin, Lowell Ansgard *management executive*
Pohl, Frederik *freelance/self-employed writer*
Spinner, Lee Louis *accountant*
Victor, Michael Gary *lawyer, physician*
Wilk, Pamela June *elementary school educator*
Zamarin, Ronald George *lawyer*

**Palos Hills**
Crawley, Vernon Obadiah *academic administrator*
Healy, Judith Ann *social worker*
McGarel-Warkocki, Lynn M. *history educator*

**Palos Park**
Nelson, Lawrence Evan *manufacturing executive, consultant*
Peckenpaugh, Donald Hugh *psychologist, consultant, writer*

**Park City**
Aquino, Armando Co *minister, consultant*

**Park Forest**
Billig, Etel Jewel *theater director, actress*
Goodrich, John Bernard *lawyer, consultant*
Orr, Marcia *pre-school administrator, consultant*
Steinmetz, Jon David *health facility administrator, psychologist*
Williams, Jack Raymond *civil engineer*

**Park Ridge**
Albert, Elizabeth Franz (Mrs. Henry B. Albert) *investor, artist, conservationist*
Barnett, Patrick Shawn *music educator*
Bitran, Jacob David *internist*
Campbell, Bruce Crichton *hospital administrator*
Carr, Gilbert Randle *retired railroad executive*
Ewald, Robert Frederick *insurance company executive, consultant*
Hrejsa, Allen Francis *physicist, consultant*
Kenney, John Patrick *dentist*
LaRue, Paul Hubert *retired lawyer*
Matthews, Roy S. *management consultant*
Pielet, Bruce William *obstetrician*
Pippen, Jennifer Lynn *therapist, consultant*
Russell, William Steven *treasurer*
White, John Vincent *surgeon, consultant*
Williams, Sandra Lynn *ethics consultant*

**Pecatonica**
Duncan, Linda M. *elementary school educator*

**Pekin**
Dancey, Charles Lohman *retired newspaper executive*
Rimington, James Earl *music educator, consultant*
White, Richard Lee, Jr. *secondary school educator*

**Peoria**
Allen, Lyle Wallace *lawyer*
Banwart, Sidney C. *human resources specialist*
Bertschy, Timothy L. *lawyer*
Buda, James B. *lawyer, manufacturing executive*
Burritt, David B. *corporate financial executive*
Chamberlain, Joseph Miles *retired astronomer, educator*
Davis, Charisse Maria *doll maker, folk artist*
Estes, Norman C. *surgeon, educator*
Golan, Kim Marie *facility interior designer*
Grebner, Bernice Prill *author, astrological counselor*
Heiple, James Dee *retired state supreme court justice*
Hindi, Riyadh *engineering educator, researcher*
Huffcutt, Allen Ivan *psychology professor*
Kelly, Grace Dentino *secondary school educator*
Kroll, Dennis Edwards *industrial engineering educator*
Kurtzman, Cletus Paul *microbiologist, researcher*
Lanzino, Giuseppe *physician*
McCollum, Jean Hubble *medical technician*
McConnell, John Thomas *publishing executive*
Meriden, Terry *physician*
Mihm, Michael Martin *federal judge*
Murphy, Sharon Margaret *retired communications educator*
Nielsen, Harald Christian *retired chemist, researcher*
Owens, James W. *manufacturing executive*
Parsons, Donald James *retired bishop*
Parsons, Richard Hugo *lawyer*
Sanderson, Kenneth Jerome *school system administrator, consultant*
Sattler, Joan Tilda *education educator, dean*
Saxon, Randall Lee *pastor, author, educator*
Tuggle, Marla L. *science educator*
Vaughan, David John *corporate financial executive*
Walker, Philip Chamberlain, II, *health facility administrator*
Woods, Michael Lee *lawyer*

**Peotone**
Hilsenhoff, Robert Dean *retired pharmacist*

**Pontiac**
Ewing, Thomas William *congressman, lawyer*
Schultz, Heidi Renee *psychologist*

**Princeton**
Collins, N. Dana *art gallery owner, consultant, retired art educator*
Webber, Adam Brooks *science educator*

**Prophetstown**
Bohms, Stephanie A. *music educator, director*

**Prospect Heights**
Aldinger, William F. III *diversified financial services company executive*
Anderson, Hugh George *bishop*
Armishaw, Andrew C. *financial services company executive*
Byrne, Michael Joseph *manufacturing executive*
Derickson, Sandy *bank executive*
Harvey, Kenneth M *corporate financial executive*
Leopold, Mark F. *lawyer*
Lynch, William Thomas, Jr. *advertising executive*
Mooney, Timothy *playwright, actor, theater director*
Robinson, Martin (Marty Robinson) *television and radio broadcaster, media consultant*

**Quincy**
Centanni, Ross J. *engineering executive*
Daniels, James M. *medical educator*
Mallory, Troy L. *accountant*
Points, Roy Wilson *municipal official*
Reynolds, Judith Amy *nutritionist, consultant, animal scientist, educator*
Tomczak, Patricia Ann *dean, archivist*
Tyer, Travis Earl *librarian, consultant*

**Rantoul**
Weber, Rochelle Irene *editor, writer*

**Richton Park**
Nevins, Patrick Fredrick *librarian*
Pierce, Mary E. *retired elementary school educator, public relations consultant*
Piucci, Virginio Louis *academic administrator*

**River Forest**
Batlivala, Robert Bomi D. *oil industry executive, economics professor*
Bogojevich, Natasha *composer, educator*
Carroll, Donna M. *academic administrator*
Coe, Donald Kirk *retired academic administrator*
Douglas, Kenneth Jay *food products executive*
Froehle, Bryan Thomas *sociologist, director*
Heggerty, Michael *school system administrator, consultant, writer*
Moore, Vernon John, Jr. *pediatrician, consultant, lawyer*
O'Meara, Thomas Franklin *priest, educator*
Saffold, Monroe *science educator, consultant*
Tiesenga, Marvin Francis *surgeon*
Valauskas, Edward Justin *librarian, editor, Internet consultant*
Wirsching, Charles Philipp, Jr. *retired brokerage house executive, securities trader*

**River Grove**
Litzsinger, Richard Mark *retail executive*
Stanton, Kathryn *retail executive*
Stein, Thomas Henry *social sciences educator*

**Riverside**
Dengler, Robert Anthony *management consultant*
Marty, Martin Emil *theology studies educator*
Van Cura, Joyce Bennett *librarian*

**Riverwoods**
Douglas, Bruce Lee *oral and maxillofacial surgeon, occupational and geriatric health educator, consultant*
Hochschild, Roger C. *investment company executive*

**Robinson**
Chapman, Roger Eugene *historian, educator*
Wolfe, Ellen Darlene *school librarian, elementary school educator*

**Rochester**
Petterchak, Janice A. *writer*

**Rock Island**
Anderson, Richard Charles *geology educator*
Bahls, Steven Carl *academic administrator, educator*
Clay, Carol Sue *reading specialist*
Hand, Angela Rene *singer*
Hendrickx, Irene S. *elementary school educator*
Horstmann, James Douglas *retired academic administrator*
Kirklin-Darif, Dianna Lynn *small business owner*
Lardner, Henry Petersen (Peter Lardner) *insurance company executive*
Leinicke, Kris Gayman *museum director, educator*

**Peru**
Carus, Milton Blouke *children's periodicals publisher*

**Petersburg**
Wood, Harlington, Jr. *federal judge*

**Pinckneyville**
Cawvey, Clarence Eugene *retired physician*

**Plainfield**
Chakrabarti, Subrata Kumar *marine research engineer*
Reichenbach, Linda Louise *mathematician, educator, language educator*
Schinderle, Robert Frank *retired hospital administrator*
Serna, Phillip Woodrow *music educator, musician*

**Pleasant Plains**
Thomas, Evelyn B. *agricultural products supplier*

**Kanosky**, Albert Leo *history educator, small business owner*

Skahill, Nathan B. *historian, educator*
Symons, Van Jay *humanities educator*

### Rockford

Albert, Janyce Louise *human resources specialist, retired business educator, banker, consultant*
Aniol, Scott Michael *pastor*
Bippus, David Paul *manufacturing executive*
Borling, John Lorin *military officer*
Bradley, Charles MacArthur *retired architect*
Clodius, Robert LeRoy *retired economist*
Doran, Thomas George *bishop*
Eliason, Jon Tate *electrical engineer*
Fleming, Thomas J. *editor, publishing executive*
Hartz, Linda M. *elementary school educator*
Heerens, Robert Edward *physician*
Heflin, Tom Pat *artist*
Hicks, Stephen Ronald Craig *philosopher, educator*
Hoshaw, Lloyd *retired historian, educator*
Howard, John Addison *retired academic administrator*
Jacobi, Fredrick Thomas *newspaper publisher*
Johnson, Thomas Stuart *lawyer*
McClelland, Patricia G. *minister*
O'Donnell, William David *retired construction firm executive*
Reinhard, Philip G. *federal judge*
Reno, Roger *lawyer*
Schlub, Teresa Rae *minister*
Steele, Carl Lavern *academic administrator*
Steely, Allen Merle *secondary school educator*
Tuite, Gerald Francis *lawyer, commercial real estate manager*
Turner, Dallas G., Jr. *physics professor*
Wallem, Paul Sigurd *financial planner*

### Rockton

Pennell, Danny Joe *social worker*
Polaski, Thomas Brian *social studies educator, department chairman*

### Rolling Meadows

Bassi, Suzanne Howard *retired secondary school educator, volunteer*
Bauer, Lorain *art educator*
Breakstone, Donald S. *lawyer*
Cangemi, Michael Paul *accountant, author, consultant*
Eckel, James J. *aerospace engineer*
Roti, Thomas David *judge*
Yerkan, Robert R. *educational consultant*

### Romeoville

Mitchell, Paul *computer graphics designer, educator*
Sprovieri, Bridgette Ann *social worker, school system administrator*

### Rosemont

Good, William Allen *professional society executive*
Le Menager, Lois M. *incentive merchandise and travel company executive*
Meinert, John Raymond *apparel executive, investment banker*
Nichols, Robert Hastings *lawyer*
Reyes, J. Christopher *food products distribution executive*

### Rossville

Tracy, Christina L. *secondary school educator*

### Round Lake

Abdullah, Bashar Y. *pharmacist, researcher*

### Round Lake Beach

Harold, Kathleen T. *elementary school educator*

### Saint Anne

Holtzman, Michael *alcohol abuse professional*

### Saint Charles

LaHood, Julie Ann *small business owner*
Malinowski, Maryellen *photographer, artist*
O'Shea, Lynne Edeen *management consultant, educator*
Stovall, April Leanne *music educator*

### Saint Francisville

Harezi, Ilonka Jo *medical technology research executive*

### Saint Jacob

Carter, Dennis R. *music educator, band director, musician*

### Sandwich

Meier, Carolyn K. *elementary school educator*

### Savoy

Bednar, Susan Gail *social worker, consultant, social sciences educator*
McConnell, William Stewart *application developer*
Sinclair, James Burton *retired plant pathology educator, consultant*

### Schaumburg

Adrianopoli, Barbara Catherine *librarian*
Aryanfar, Farshid *electrical engineer, electronics engineer*
Brown, Gregory Q. *communications executive*
Cabay, Robert John *physician, dentist*
Delaney, Eugene A. *electronics executive*
Desai, Samir T. *electronics executive*
Devonshire, David W. *financial executive*
Dodohara, Jean Noton *music educator*
Fattori, Ruth A. *human resources specialist, electronics executive*
Galvin, Robert W. *electronics executive*
Hanna, Nessim *marketing educator*
Hill, Raymond Joseph *packaging company executive*
Janssen, Carron Joyce *music educator*
Kornowski, Robert Richard *engineer, science educator*
Lawson, A. Peter *lawyer*
Little, Bruce Washington *professional society administrator*
Maluchnik, Rosemary Pellicore *elementary school educator*

Marshall, John David *lawyer*
Morrison, Patricia B. *information technology executive*
Nehs, William Scott (Scott Nehs) *lawyer*
O'Connor, James, Jr., (Jim O'Connor) *telecommunications industry executive*
Otis, James, Jr. *architect*
Richter, Glenn *retail executive*
Riffel, Karen Sheffer *music educator*
Roman, Ray *communications executive*
Soderberg, Leif G. *electronics company executive*
Soon-Shiong, Patrick *pharmaceutical executive*
Spada, Alfred Thomas *publishing executive*
Tompson, Marian Leonard *professional society administrator*
Warrior, Padmasree *communications executive*
Westlund, Maribeth *secondary school educator*
Zander, Edward J. *communications executive*

### Scott Air Force Base

Hendricks, Ian P.B. *military officer, health facility administrator*

### Seymour

Carringer, Robert *language educator*

### Shabbona

Feken, John E. *music educator, director*

### Shorewood

Heaphy, John Merrill *lawyer*

### Silvis

Bobb, Harold Daniel *chiropractor, consultant*

### Skokie

Anthony, Carolyn Additon *librarian*
Brennan, William P. (Bill Brennan) *computer company executive*
Bush, Gail *librarian, educator, director, writer*
Corley, William Gene *engineering research executive*
Gleason, John Patrick, Jr. *trade association executive*
Gregerman, Daniel P. *choral director*
Guillermo, Linda *clinical social worker*
Hoopis, Harry Peter *insurance executive, entrepreneur*
Karp, Gary *marketing and public relations executive*
Langguth, Margaret Witty *health facility administrator*
Levy, Mark Hirsch *internist, researcher, medical educator*
McCarthy, Michael Shawn *health care company executive, lawyer*
Montague, Ann Hood *veterinarian*
Polus Gerstner, Lillian *educational association administrator, director*
Siegal, Burton Lee *product designer, consultant, inventor*
Sperzel, George E., Jr. *former personal care industry executive*
Weidmann, K. Timothy *not-for-profit fundraiser, writer*

### South Barrington

Kissane, Sharon Florence *writer, consultant, educator*

### South Chicago Heights

Misdom, Amanda Michelle *elementary school educator, music educator*

### South Holland

Anderson, Paul Martin *music educator, musician*
Connolly, Carla Marie *librarian*
Doty, Brandon S. *history educator*

### Springfield

Aiello, Elizabeth Blackwell *secondary school educator*
Bandyopadhyay, Sucharita *research scientist*
Beckwith, Peter Hess *bishop*
Bell, John Perry *minister, religious organization administrator*
Blagojevich, Rod R. *governor, former congressman*
Carmichael, Buff *publishing executive*
Collins, Annazette R. *state representative*
Currie, Barbara Flynn *state legislator*
Daniels, Lee Albert *state legislator*
Darby, Karen Sue *legal association administrator*
Davis, George Cullom *historian*
Dodge, Edward John *retired insurance company executive*
Dodge, James William *lawyer, educator*
Dunn, Randy J. *school system administrator*
Elble, Rodger Jacob *neurologist, researcher*
Evans, Charles H. *federal judge*
Frank, Stuart *cardiologist*
Godwin, John E. *hematologist*
Hallmark, Donald Parker *museum director, educator*
Hannig, Gary L. *state representative*
Hicks, David Eric *retired sports association executive*
Holland, John Madison *retired family practice physician*
Jackson, Jacqueline Dougan *literature educator, writer*
Jefferson, Charles E. *state representative*
Johnson, Paul Harold *music director*
Kerr, Gary Enrico *lawyer, educator*
Klingler, Gwendolyn Walbolt *state representative*
Kocis, Janet Kay *elementary school educator*
Kosel, Renée *state representative*
LeBlang, Theodore Raymond *law educator, lawyer*
Londrigan, Thomas Foster *lawyer*
Malany, Le Grand Lynn *lawyer, engineer, bank executive*
Martinez, Iris *state senator*
Masternak, Michal Mateusz *biotechnologist, educator, molecular biologist, researcher*
Mathewson, Mark Stuart *lawyer, editor*
Mc Millan, R(obert) Bruce *retired museum director, anthropologist*
Mikell, Frank Leonard *cardiologist*
Mills, Richard Henry *federal judge*
Mims, Merrill Ted *computer scientist, department chairman*

Morris, Donald *tax specialist*
Munyer, Edward Arnold *zoologist*
Myers, Phillip Ward *otolaryngologist*
Pankau, Carole *state senator*
Parke, Terry Richard *state legislator*
Phelps, David Dwain *state agency administrator, former congressman*
Phillips, John Robert *political scientist, educator*
Poorman, Robert Lewis *retired academic administrator*
Rabinovich, Sergio *physician, educator*
Schroeder, Joyce Katherine *state agency administrator, research analyst*
Schroeder, Raymond Ernest *educational administrator*
Schroeder-Lein, Glenna Ruth *librarian, historian*
Schroyer, Michael Kevin *healthcare consultant, hospital executive*
Simpson, William Arthur *insurance company executive*
Snyder, Darlene Nootens *science educator, mathematics educator*
Stroh, Raymond Eugene *retired personnel executive*
Stuart, Robert Allan, Jr. *lawyer*
Sumner, David Spurgeon *surgeon, educator*
Temple, Wayne Calhoun *historian, writer*
Travis, Lawrence Allan *accountant*
Turner, Sharon Lou Willson *elementary and gifted education educator*
Van Meter, Abram DeBois *lawyer, retired banker*
Wehrle, Leroy Snyder *economist, educator*
White, Jesse *state official*
Woodson, Gayle Ellen *otolaryngologist*
Yaffe, Stuart Allen *physician*
Zaricznyj, Basilius *orthopedic surgeon*

### Sterling

Fitzgerald, Carol J. *foundation administrator, not-for-profit organization administrator*
McCord, Julie Ann *retired conductor*
Pace, Ole Bly III *lawyer*
Tóth, Peter Paul *physician, researcher*

### Stoy

Rhoten, Kenneth Dale *writer*

### Streamwood

Ackert, Lynee L. *social studies educator*

### Sugar Grove

Debartolo, Hansel Marion, Jr. *otolaryngologist, plastic surgeon*
DeLay, Larry Gene *science educator, photographer*
Del Medico, Amy *mathematics professor*
Norris, Blanche Lee *business consultant, educator*

### Summit Argo

Koutchma, Tatiana Nicolaevna *food scientist, educator*

### Sycamore

Ballee', Shawn Alexander *engineering educator*
Burzynski, James Bradley *state legislator*
Johnson, Yvonne Amalia *elementary school educator, consultant*
Stone, Van Courtright *not-for-profit developer*
Tucker, Watson Billopp *lawyer*

### Table Grove

Thomson, Helen Louise *retired artist*

### Taylorville

Austin, Daniel William *lawyer*

### Techny

Vanderstappen, Harrie Albert *art educator*

### Tinley Park

Cox, Carrie Lee *secondary school educator*
Daniels, Kurt R. *speech and language pathologist*
Kenny, Mary Alice *lawyer*
Lobes, Mark Robert *graphic design educator, coach*

### Toledo

Prather, William C. III *lawyer, writer*

### Trenton

Barnett, Thomas Glen *manufacturing executive*

### Troy

Perkins, Sandra Laird *biology educator*

### Tuscola

Henderson, E. Suzanne *elementary school educator*

### Union

Perlick, Richard Allan *steel company executive*

### University Park

Hakala, Reino William *mathematician, educator*
Keys, Paul Ross *academic administrator, educator*
Patton, June Odessa *writer, consultant, educator, researcher*

### Urbana

Althaus, Scott L. *political science professor*
Amir, Eyal *computer scientist, educator*
Antonsen, Elmer Harold *Germanic languages and linguistics educator*
Arnstein, Walter Leonard *retired historian*
Baer, Werner *economist, educator*
Baker, David Hiram *nutritionist, educator*
Balbach, Stanley Byron *lawyer*
Baron, Dennis E. *English language educator*
Basak, Chandramallika *psychologist, researcher*
Beak, Peter Andrew *chemistry professor*
Bennett, Scott Boyce *retired librarian, consultant*
Berenbaum, May Roberta *entomology educator*
Bergeron, Clifton George *engineer, educator*
Bernard, Richard Lawson *retired geneticist, educator*
Blahut, Richard Edward *electrical and computer engineering educator*
Braatz, Richard Dean *chemical engineer*
Brichford, Maynard Jay *archivist*
Brover-Lubovsky, Bella *musicologist*

Buckius, Richard O. *mechanical engineer, educator*
Buetow, Dennis Edward *physiologist, educator*
Burkholder, Donald Lyman *mathematician, educator*
Carmen, Ira Harris *political scientist, educator*
Carroll, Robert Wayne *mathematics professor*
Chao, Bei Tse *mechanical engineering educator*
Charlevoix, Donna J. *meteorologist, educator*
Chato, John Clark *mechanical and bioengineering educator*
Chow, Poo *forester*
Christians, Clifford Glenn *communications educator*
Coleman, James J. *electrical engineer, educator*
Conry, Thomas Francis *mechanical engineering educator*
Crang, Richard Francis Earl *botanist, writer, research scientist*
Crofts, Antony Richard *biochemistry and biophysics educator*
Dash, Leon DeCosta, Jr. *journalist*
Delcomyn, Fred *physiology educator, neurobiology educator*
Do, Minh N. *engineering educator*
Dovring, Karin Elsa Ingeborg *writer, poet, playwright, media specialist*
Eddy-Johnson, Deanna M. *home health care advocate*
Eden, James Gary *electrical engineer, educator, physicist, researcher*
Edgar, Jim *former governor*
Ehrlich, Gert *science educator, researcher*
Endres, Arthur Bryan *law educator*
Erdman, John W. *nutritionist, educator*
Fitz-Gerald, Roger Miller *lawyer*
Foulonneau, Muriel *education educator*
Frazzetta, Thomas Henry *evolutionary biologist, educator*
Frederick, Robert George *lawyer*
Gabriel, Michael *psychology professor*
Garcia, Marcelo Horacio *engineering educator, consultant*
Giles, Eugene *anthropology educator*
Ginsberg, Donald Maurice *physicist, researcher*
Gove, Samuel Kimball *retired political science professor*
Granato, Andrew Vincent *physics professor, researcher*
Gray, John Walker *mathematician, educator*
Greene, Joseph E. *material science researcher*
Greenough, William Tallant *psychobiologist, educator*
Grossman, Margaret Rosso *law educator*
Gruebele, Martin *chemistry professor, biophysicist, educator*
Haile, H. G. *German language and literature educator*
Hall, William Joel *retired civil engineer, educator*
Hannon, Bruce Michael *engineering educator*
Hedlund, Ronald *baritone*
Heichel, Gary Harold *agronomist, educator*
Hendrick, George *retired English language educator*
Henson, C. Ward *mathematician, educator*
Hess, Karl *electrical and computer engineering educator*
Hicks, Darren Scott *music educator*
Hoeft, Robert Gene *agricultural studies educator*
Holonyak, Nick, Jr. *electrical engineering educator*
Holt, Donald A. *agronomist, consultant, researcher, retired academic administrator*
Hou, Xiaoqiang *mineralogist, geochemist, spectroscopist*
Hoxie, Frederick Eugene *history professor*
Huang, Thomas Shi-Tao *electrical engineering educator, researcher*
Iben, Icko, Jr. *astrophysicist, educator*
Jackson, Edwin Atlee *retired physicist, retired educator*
Jacobson, Sheldon Howard *engineering educator*
Jeon, Won J. *research scientist*
Jonas, Jiri *chemist, educator*
Kaufman, Jerome Benzion *retired neurosurgeon*
Kaufman, Paula T. *librarian*
Kaufmann, Urlin Milo *English literature educator*
Keys, Henson *theater educator, actor, theater director*
Kieffer, Susan Werner *geologist, educator, media consultant*
Kim, Chin-Woo *linguist, educator*
Kirkpatrick, R(obert) James *geology educator*
Klein, Miles Vincent *physics professor*
Knight, Frank Bardsley *mathematics professor*
Knobloch, Neil A. *education educator*
Koenker, Diane P. *history professor*
Krock, Curtis Josselyn *pulmonologist*
Kuhlenschmidt, Mark Stuart *microbiologist, researcher*
Kumar, Panganamala Ramana *electrical and computer engineering educator*
Kwasinski, Alexis *research scientist*
Larkin, Denis M. *geneticist, researcher*
Lauterbur, Paul Christian *chemistry professor*
Leggett, Anthony James *physics professor, researcher*
Leuthold, Raymond Martin *agricultural economics professor*
Lieberman, Laurence *poet, educator*
Liebman, Judith Rae Stenzel *retired operations research specialist*
Loui, Michael Conrad *engineering educator*
Love, Joseph LeRoy *history professor, former cultural studies center administrator*
Lu, Yi *chemistry professor*
Lüschen, Günther Rudolf Friedo *social sciences educator*
Martinez, Todd J. *chemistry professor*
Mayes, Paul Eugene *engineering educator, consultant*
McColley, Robert McNair *historian, educator*
Mc Glamery, Marshal Dean *agronomist, educator, weed scientist*
McKay, John Patrick *history professor*
Meyer, Richard Charles *microbiologist, educator*
Middeljans, April Lynn *literature educator*
Miley, George H. *nuclear and electrical engineering educator, plasma engineer, energy conversion scientist*
Misic, Mark M. *exercise physiologist, researcher*

Nanney, David Ledbetter *geneticist, educator*
Nelson, Cary Robert *language educator*
Nelson, Ralph Alfred *physician*
Nettl, Bruno *anthropologist, musicologist, educator*
Newmark, Phillip Allan *biology professor*
Nichols, John Alden *retired history professor*
O'Brien, Nancy Patricia *librarian, educator*
Oliphant, Uretz John *physician, surgeon*
O'Morchoe, Charles Christopher Creagh *anatomist, surgeon, educator*
Ono, Kent Alan *communications educator*
Park, Jae Hyun *mechanical engineer, researcher*
Petrov, Ivan *physicist, materials scientist*
Prussing, Laurel Lunt *mayor, economist*
Ra, Hyungshim Yoo *biologist, researcher*
Rao, Nannapaneni Narayana *electrical engineer*
Resek, Robert William *economist*
Rich, Robert F. *law educator, political science professor*
Ridgway, Marcella Davies *veterinarian*
Robinson, Gene Ezia *biologist, educator*
Rowland, Theodore Justin *physicist, researcher*
Salamon, Myron Ben *physicist, educator, dean*
Sandvig, Christian Edward *communications educator, researcher*
Schleis, Thomas Henry *music educator, organist*
Schmidt, Stephen Christopher *agricultural economist, educator*
Schupp, Paul Eugene *mathematician, educator*
Schweizer, Kenneth Steven *physics professor*
Seigler, David Stanley *botanist, educator, chemist*
Sharif, Behzad *research scientist*
Snoeyink, Vernon L. *civil engineer, educator*
Snyder, Lewis Emil *astrophysicist, educator*
Soffer, Olga *archaeologist, educator*
Solberg, Winton Udell *historian, educator*
Spitze, Robert George Frederick *agricultural studies educator*
Splittstoesser, Walter Emil *botanist, educator*
Sreenivas, Ramavarapu S. *mathematics professor*
Strano, Michael *chemical engineer*
Stukel, James Joseph *academic administrator, mechanical engineer, educator*
Suslick, Kenneth Sanders *chemistry professor*
Switzer, Robert Lee *biochemistry professor*
Talbot, Emile Joseph *French language educator*
Thompson, Robert Lee *agricultural economist, educator*
Tondeur, Philippe Maurice *mathematician, educator*
Visek, Willard James *nutritionist, animal scientist, physician, educator*
Wah, Benjamin Wan-Sang *electrical and computer engineering educator*
Walker, William Hamilton *civil engineer, educator*
Watson, Paula D. *retired librarian*
Watson, William Douglas *astrophysicist*
Webber, Carl Maddra *lawyer*
Whitt, Gregory Sidney *evolution educator*
Williams, Martha Ethelyn *information science educator*
Wirt, Frederick Marshall *retired political scientist, educator*
Woese, Carl R. *biophysicist, microbiology educator*
Yoon, Wonyong *computer scientist, researcher*
Yu, George Tzuchiao *political science professor*
Zimmerman, Steven Charles *chemistry professor*

## Vermont

Datcu, Ioana *artist*

## Vernon Hills

Claassen, W(alter) Marshall *employment company executive*
Edwardson, John Albert *security firm executive*
Kaplan, Edward L. *electronics executive*
Klein, Barbara A. *information technology executive*
Krasny, Michael P. *investment company executive*
Leahy, Christine A. *information technology executive*
Powers, Anthony Richard, Jr. *educational sales professional*
Sundell, Randy *music educator*

## Villa Park

Antonelli, Joseph K. *musician, educator*
Camp, Jeffery Mark *web site designer, military officer*
Gordon, Rachel Singer *editor*
Russo, Cheryl Jean *elementary school educator, special education educator*

## Virginia

Webster, Kim S. *music educator*

## Wadsworth

Ahmad, Moghisuddin *chemist, researcher*

## Walnut

Meisenheimer, Sharon Lee *nurse*

## Warrenville

Boardman, Robert A. *retired lawyer*
Covey, Steven K. *lawyer*
Darukhanavala, Phiroz P. (Daru Darukhanavala) *energy executive*
Data, Art J. *information technology executive*
Horne, John R. *farm equipment company executive*
Johnson, Douglas Wells *lawyer*
Lannert, Robert Cornelius *manufacturing executive*
Ustian, Daniel C. *trucking executive*

## Washington

Schupp, Joyce Elaine *elementary school educator*
Stine, Robert Howard *retired pediatrician, allergist*

## Waterloo

Hoffmann, Mary Jukich *voice educator*

## Wauconda

Gotthardt, Mary Jane *religious studies educator*
Meehan, Jean Marie Ross *human resources, occupational health and safety management consultant*

## Waukegan

Akouris, Dianne Frances *school system administrator*
Drapalik, Betty R. *volunteer, artist, educator*
Henrick, Michael Francis *lawyer*
Houle, Jeanne Larson *retired music educator*
Miller, Helen Elizabeth *art educator, adult education educator, artist*

## Wayne City

Staggs, Teresa Laverne *special education educator*

## West Brooklyn

Mays, K. J. *writer, musician*

## West Chicago

Kramer, Pamela Kostenko *librarian*
Mott, Thomas Charles *science educator*
Noonan, Josette Marie *music educator*
Paulissen, James Peter *retired pediatrician, county official*

## Westchester

Calder, Robert Austin *preventive medicine physician, administrator*
Clarke, Richard Lewis *health science association administrator*
Faison, Ralph E. *communications equipment manufacturing executive*
Faulkner, Robert Lloyd *advertising executive, graphics designer*
Lightford, Kimberly A. *state legislator*
Masterson, John Patrick *retired language educator*
Pavelka, Elaine Blanche *mathematics professor*
Scott, Samuel C. *food products executive*
Tutins, Antons *electrical and audio engineer*
Webb, Emily *retired plant morphologist*

## Western Springs

Hanson, Heidi Elizabeth *lawyer*
Harken, Bruce R. *social studies educator*
Thomas, Paul Augustus, Jr. *retired thoracic surgeon*
Zamora, Marjorie Dixon *retired political science professor*

## Westmont

Ford, Ralph A. *lawyer, moving and relocation company executive*
Harten, Ann M. *relocation services executive*
Kelley, Brian P. *transportation executive*
Schefdore, Ronald L. *dentist*
Tricase, Elizabeth *gymnast*
Warner, H. Ty *entrepreneur, manufacturing executive*

## Wheaton

Ali, Fatima Z. *physician*
Back, Robert Wyatt *investment company executive, pharmaceutical executive, consultant*
Bogdonoff, Maurice Lambert *physician*
Hambley, Douglas Frederick *geological and environmental engineer*
Holman, James Lewis *financial consultant, management consultant*
Kincaid, John Bruce *lawyer*
Leston, Patrick John *judge*
Lim, Cheryl Cheon-Ae *music educator*
Litfin, A. Duane *academic administrator*
Long, Charles Franklin *retired corporate communications executive*
Martin, Marcia Gray *retired architecture educator, artist, designer*
McCartney, Charles Price *retired obstetrician, retired gynecologist*
Noll, Mark A. *historian*
Pape, Patricia Ann *social worker, consultant*
Pappas, Barbara Estelle *biblical studies educator, author*
Riley, Betty Anne *psychologist, educator*
Schwanda, Tom *religious studies educator*
Stein, Lawrence A. *lawyer*
Taylor, Mark Douglas *publishing executive*
Thompson, Bert Allen *retired librarian*
Tucker, Beverly Sowers *library and information scientist*
Warner, William Kent, Jr. *religious organization administrator, consultant*

## Wheeling

Jackson, Carolyn M. *school librarian*
Keats, Glenn Arthur *manufacturing executive*
Kenny, James Casey *ambassador, construction company executive*
Levitin, Yelena *surgeon*
Long, Sarah Ann *librarian*
Meehan, Tamiye Marcia *library director*
Schulman, Alan Michael *small business owner*

## Williamsville

Pruitt, David R. *music educator, musician*

## Willow Springs

Jashel, Larry Steven (L. Steven Rose) *entrepreneur, media consultant*

## Willowbrook

Burrows, Donald Albert *artist, painter, photographer, dean*
Foley, Joseph Lawrence *sales executive*
Walton, Stanley Anthony III *lawyer*

## Wilmette

Albright, Townsend Shaul *brokerage house executive, consultant*
Atkinson, Jeff John Frederick *lawyer, educator, writer*
Baisley, James Mahoney *retired lawyer*
Ballard, Patricia Jo *elementary school educator*
Boyle, Antonia Barnes *writer, editor*
Brindel, June Rachuy *writer*
Brink, Marion Francis *trade association administrator*
Bunge, Jonathan Gunn *lawyer*
Chiaro, A. William *retired management consultant*
Coughlan, Gary Patrick *pharmaceutical executive*
Ellis, Helene Rita *social worker*
Griffiths, Robert Pennell *banker*
Hansen, Andrew Marius *retired library director*
Hier, Daniel Barnet *neurologist*

Hurley, Andrew John *musician*
Jampole, Michael *music educator, composer*
Kenamore, Jane Allen *archivist*
Mandel, Judith Lynn *primary school educator*
Merrier, Helen *actress, writer*
Miripol, Jerilyn Elise *poet, writer, writing therapist*
Monter, E. William *retired history professor*
Muhlenbruch, Carl W. *civil engineer*
Pearlman, Jerry Kent *electronics company executive*
Rocek, Jan *chemist, educator*
Schloss, Nathan *retired economist*
Smutny, Joan Franklin *academic director, educator*
Stump, Patrick Martin *musician*
Trohman, Joseph Mark *editor*
Wadden, Richard Albert *environmental engineer, educator, science administrator, consultant*
Walker, Ronald Edward *psychologist, educator*
Wentz, Peter (Peter Lewis Kingston Wentz III) *musician*
Wishner, Maynard Ira *retired finance company executive, lawyer*

## Winnetka

Bundy, Blakely Fetridge *pre-school administrator*
Burke, John Edward *communications editor*
Cole, Kathleen Ann *advertising executive, social worker*
Crowe, Robert William *lawyer, mediator*
Ellwood, Scott *lawyer*
Greenblatt, Ray Harris *lawyer*
Hales, Daniel B. *lawyer*
Huggins, Charlotte Susan Harrison *retired secondary school educator, writer, travel company executive*
Johnson, Julie West *secondary school educator, writer*
Klapperich, Frank Lawrence, Jr. *investment banker*
Krueger, Deborah A. Blake *school psychologist, consultant*
Ladd, David Scott *music educator*
Markey, Maurice *food products executive*
McKee, Judith Nelson *elementary school educator, educational consultant*
McWhirter, Bruce J. *retired lawyer*
Piper, Robert Johnston *retired architect, urban planner*
Plowden, David *photographer*
Puth, John Wells *manufacturing executive, consultant*
Quaal, Ward Louis *broadcast executive*
Rossi, Ennio C. *internist, educator*
Rubnitz, Myron Ethan *pathologist, educator*
Schlossman, John Isaac *architect*
Sick, William Norman, Jr. *technology company executive*
Thomas, John Thieme *management consultant*
Webster, David Macpherson *lawyer*
Weldon, Theodore Tefft, Jr. *manufacturing executive*

## Wood Dale

Goodwin, James E. *retired air transportation executive*
Storch, David *manufacturing executive*

## Wood River

Shelton, Michael Patrick *principal*

## Woodridge

Farrug, Eugene Joseph, Sr. *retired lawyer*
O'Connor, William Michael *search company executive*
Puthenpurakal, Joseph Mathew *information technology executive*
Rathke, Barbara Joanne Andrews *art educator*
Shen, Sin-Yan *physicist, acoustical engineer, musicologist*
Stall, Alan David *packaging company executive*

## Woodstock

Ackley, Robert O. *lawyer*
Dorn, Diane M. *science educator*
Trausch, Thomas Vincent *art educator, artist*
Wertheimer-Sexton, Willa Renee *clinical psychologist*

## Yorkville

Freese, Carolyn Lee *art educator*

# INDIANA

## Alexandria

Irwin, Gerald Port *physician*

## Anderson

Bracken, Linda Darlene *medical/surgical nurse*
Carrell, Terry Eugene *manufacturing executive*
Clanin, Douglas Edward *editor, researcher*
Conrad, Harold August *retired religious pension board executive*
King, Charles Ross *physician*
Kufeldt, George *biblical educator*
Lambert, Lloyd Laverne *minister*
Nicholson, Robert Arthur *college president*
Rountree, James Paul *retired music educator*

## Batesville

Classon, Rolf Allan *pharmaceutical company executive*
de Maynadier, Patrick D. *lawyer*
Soderberg, Peter H. *health products executive*
Sorenson, Scott K. *manufacturing executive*

## Bedford

Freeman, Beth Ellen *music educator, real estate agent*
Hunter, Harlen Charles *orthopedic surgeon*

## Beech Grove

Byrkett, Gary Lee *information technology manager*
Hughes, Charles E. III *plastic surgeon*

## Bicknell

Ford, Andrea Michelle *mathematics educator*

## Bloomington

Alderson, Arthur Stancliff III *education educator*

Aman, Alfred Charles, Jr. *law educator*
Anderson, Judith Helena *English language educator*
Arnove, Robert Frederick *education educator*
Assensoh, Akwasi Bretuo *historian, educator*
Barnes, A. James *dean*
Basu, Abhijit *geologist, educator*
Baude, Patrick Louis *law educator*
Baye, Michael Roy *economics professor*
Becker, William Edward *economist, consultant*
Belth, Joseph Morton *retired business educator*
Bernhardt-Kabisch, Ernest Karl-Heinz *English and comparative literature educator*
Bishop, Michael D. *emergency physician*
Bonser, Charles Franklin *public administration educator*
Bornholdt, Laura Anna *academic administrator*
Brehm, Sharon Stephens *psychology professor, former academic administrator*
Brinkman, Paul Del(bert) *retired foundation administrator, journalist, educator*
Brown, Keith *musician, educator*
Buente, Wayne Gerald *information scientist, researcher*
Calinescu, Adriana Gabriela *curator, art historian*
Cameron, John M. *nuclear scientist, educator, science administrator*
Chafel, Judith Ann *education educator*
Chaifetz, Marshal Lawrence *educational consultant, educator*
Choksy, Jamsheed Kairshasp *historian, religious scholar, humanities educator, language educator*
Clark, Gracia Courtright *anthropologist*
Clemmer, David E. *chemistry professor, researcher*
Clevenger, Sarah *botanist, consultant*
Connally, Sandra Jane Oppy *retired art educator, artist*
Conrad, Geoffrey Wentworth *archaeologist, educator*
Cook, William Alfred *medical products executive*
Dalton, Dan R. *finance educator, former dean*
DeHayes, Daniel Wesley *business educator*
Dunn, Jon Michael *logician, dean*
Dunning, Jeremy David *application developer, dean, educator*
Easton, Susan Dawn *biochemist, educator*
Edmondson, Frank Kelley *retired astronomer*
Effron, David Louis *conductor, performing company executive*
Engber, Cheryl Ann *retired language educator, linguist*
Estes, William Kaye *psychologist, educator*
Gest, Howard *microbiologist, educator*
Gordon, Paul John *management educator*
Gremillion, Helen Claudia *humanities educator, director*
Gros Louis, Kenneth Richard Russell *humanities educator*
Guth, Sherman Leon (S. Lee Guth) *psychologist, educator*
Hanson, Gail G. *physicist, researcher*
Hanson, Karen *philosopher, educator*
Hattin, Donald Edward *geologist, educator*
Henn, Barbara Jeanne *academic librarian*
Henson, Jane Elizabeth *information management professional, adult education educator*
Herbert, Adam William, Jr. *academic administrator, educator*
Hites, Ronald Atlee *chemist, educator*
Huffman, John Curtis *chemist*
Hustad, Thomas Pegg *marketing educator*
Jacobi, Peter Paul *journalism educator, writer*
Johnson, Owen Verne *historian, educator*
Johnson-D'Alessio, Anna *writer, poet*
Jorgensen, Estelle Ruth *music educator*
Juergens, George Ivar *history professor*
Kauffman, Erle Galen *geologist, paleontologist*
Ketterson, Ellen D. *biologist, educator*
Kiesgen, Paul *music educator*
Kreft, Steven Francis *economics professor*
Kuratko, Donald F. *entrepreneur, educator, consultant*
Lebano, Edoardo Antonio *foreign language educator*
Lee, Don Yoon *publishing executive, academic administrator, writer*
Legler, April Arington *librarian, educator*
Letsinger, Robert Lewis *chemistry professor*
Louis, Kenneth R.R. Gross *academic administrator*
Lucas, Judith Ann *secondary school educator*
Macfarlane, Malcolm Harris *physicist, educator*
Mac Watters, Virginia Elizabeth *singer, music educator, actress*
McRobbie, Michael Alexander *computer scientist, researcher, academic administrator*
Mehlinger, Howard Dean *education educator*
Meho, Lokman I. *library and information scientist, educator*
Mickel, Emanuel John *foreign language educator*
Mobley, Tony Allen *foundation administrator, former dean, recreation educator*
Moore, Ward Wilfred *medical educator*
Murphy, Otis *music educator*
Nolan, Val, Jr. *retired biologist, lawyer*
Nordloh, David Joseph *literature and language professor, dean*
Nunn, Ken *lawyer*
Oh, Sangyoon *research scientist*
O'Hearn, Robert Raymond *stage designer*
O'Loughlin, Valerie Dean *medical educator*
O'Meara, Patrick O. *political science professor*
Ostrom, Elinor *political science professor, researcher*
Ostrom, Vincent A(lfred) *political science professor*
Patrick, John Joseph *social sciences educator*
Pedersen, Paul Mark *sportswriter, educator, columnist*
Peebles, Christopher Spalding *anthropologist, educator, dean, academic administrator*
Perkins, William Clyde *business educator*
Peters, Dennis Gail *chemist*
Peterson, M. Jeanne *historian, educator*
Phillips, Harvey G. *musician, educator, performing arts educator*
Pollock, Robert Elwood *nuclear scientist*
Prosser, Franklin Pierce *computer scientist*
Purdom, Paul Walton, Jr. *computer scientist*
Puri, Madan Lal *mathematics professor*
Ransel, David Lorimer *history professor*

Brenner, Mark Lee *academic administrator, physiologist, educator*
Brickley, Richard Agar *retired surgeon*
Brooks, Susan W. *prosecutor*
Broome, Marion *dean*
Brown, Edwin Wilson, Jr. *preventive medicine physician, educator*
Brown, Randy *human resources specialist*
Broxmeyer, Hal Edward *medical educator*
Buechlein, Daniel Mark *archbishop*
Buhner, Byron Bevis *health science facility administrator*
Buranello, Raymond Terrence *quality assurance executive, chemist*
Burgomaster, Frederick *music director*
Burr, David Bentley *anatomy educator*
Butt, P. Lawrence *lawyer*
Caine, Virginia A. *city health department administrator*
Capello, William Naldo *surgeon*
Cardwell, Sue Webb *psychology professor*
Carey, Edward Marshel, Jr. *accountant*
Carlisle, Rick *professional basketball coach*
Carmichael, Daniel P. *lawyer*
Carney, Joseph Buckingham *lawyer*
Carter, Steve *state attorney general*
Catchings, Tamika Devonne *professional basketball player*
Chen, Jake Yue *computer scientist, bioinformatician*
Cheng, Liang *pathologist*
Choplin, John M., II, *lawyer*
Christen, Arden Gale *dental educator, researcher, consultant*
Clark, Charles M., Jr. *medical school administrator*
Cliff, Johnnie Marie *mathematics professor, chemistry professor*
Coffey, Charles Moore *communication research professional, writer*
Cohen, Alan H. *retail executive*
Cohoat, Matthew A. *real estate company executive*
Colby, David C. *healthcare management company executive*
Coleman, John Joseph III *surgery educator*
Connor, Ulla M. *linguistics educator*
Coomer, Steven Robert *music educator, musician*
Corley, William Edward *hospital administrator*
Cravens, Gary Dean *information scientist, physician*
Crews, Kenneth Donald *law educator, legal consultant, dean*
Croffie, Joseph M. *gastroenterologist, educator*
Crookall, Simon *performing company executive*
Croshere, Austin *professional basketball player*
Crow, Paul Abernathy, Jr. *retired minister*
Dai, Yuan-Shun *education educator*
Dalsing, Michael Cletus *surgeon, educator*
Daly, Walter Joseph *medical educator*
Daniels, Deborah Jean *lawyer, former federal agency administrator*
Daniels, Mitchell Elias, Jr. *governor, former federal official*
Davis, Edgar Glenn *public health service officer, educator*
Davis, Kenneth Wayne *language educator, business communication consultant*
Dawes, Dominique *Olympic athlete*
DeCaro, James L. *band director*
Dickinson, Richard Donald Nye *clergyman, theology studies educator*
Dickson, Brent E. *state supreme court justice*
Divita, James J. *retired social studies educator, writer, researcher*
Dorr, Marjorie W. *healthcare insurance company executive*
Downs, Thomas K. *lawyer*
Drentlicher, David *lawyer, educator, physician*
Dunayevich, Eduardo *pharmaceutical executive*
Dungy, Tony *professional football coach*
Dutton, Stephen James *lawyer*
Dyken, Mark Lewis, Jr. *neurologist, educator*
Eigen, Howard *pediatrician, educator*
Einhorn, Lawrence Henry *oncologist, medical educator*
Elberger, Ronald Edward *lawyer*
Enright, William Gerald *religious institute administrator*
Everly, Jack *conductor*
Ewbank, Thomas Peters *lawyer, retired banker*
Faller, Keith *healthcare insurance company executive*
Fastenau, Philip S. *neuropsychologist, educator*
Featherstonaugh, Henry Gordon *psychologist, health facility administrator*
Fels, James Alexander *lawyer*
Feng, Gen-sheng *medical educator, researcher*
Fife, Wilmer Krafft *retired chemistry professor*
Fine, Pamela B. *newspaper editor*
Finley, Katherine Mandusic *professional society administrator*
Fisher, Gene Lawrence *controller, accountant*
Fisher, James R. *lawyer*
FitzGibbon, Daniel Harvey *lawyer*
Floyd, James M., Jr. *adult education educator*
Foley, Brian Scott *physiatrist, medical educator*
Fortner, Nell *professional athletics coach*
Foster, Kennard P. *magistrate judge*
Freeney, Dwight *professional football player*
French, Tarence Wade, Sr. *minister*
Fruehwald, Kristin Gail *lawyer*
Fuller, A. James *history professor*
Funk, David Albert *retired law educator*
Furlow, Mack Vernon, Jr. *retired chief financial officer, treasurer, financial analyst*
Gardner, Thomas Allen *urologist, researcher*
Garmel, Marion Bess Simon *retired arts journalist*
Gaunce, Michael Paul *insurance company executive*
Gerdes, Ralph Donald *fire safety consultant*
Ghetti, Bernardino Francesco *pathologist, educator, neuroscientist*
Gibbs, David Richard *musician, journalist, photographer, writer*
Gilliland, John Campbell, II, *lawyer*
Gilman, Alan B. *restaurant company executive*
Givan, Richard Martin *retired judge*
Glasscock, Larry Claborn *health insurance company executive*
Gnat, Raymond Earl *librarian*
Goldblatt, Lawrence I. *dean, educator, researcher*

Goodwin, William Maxwell *financial executive*
Gooldy, Patricia Alice *retired elementary school educator*
Green, Morris *pediatrician, educator*
Greene, Maurice *Olympic athlete, track and field athlete*
Gregg, Stephen Thompson *political scientist, consultant*
Gregory, Valiska *writer*
Griffith, Roy Lloyd *design engineer*
Grosfeld, Jay Lazar *surgeon, educator*
Hale, Douglass Stuart *urogynecologist, director*
Hall, Emily Marie *editorial assistant*
Hamilton, David F. *judge*
Hamm, Richard L. *church administrator*
Handel, David Jonathan *health facility administrator*
Hansell, Richard Stanley *obstetrician, gynecologist, educator*
Harden, Anita Joyce *nurse*
Hardin, Boniface *academic administrator*
Harrison, Marvin *professional football player*
Harrold, John Andrew *education educator, consultant*
Hartsfield, James Kennedy, Jr. *orthodontist, geneticist*
Henry, Barbara Ann *publishing executive*
Hitchens, William Randolph (Randy Hitchens) *healthcare executive*
Holden, Robert Watson *radiologist, educator, dean*
Holigrocki, Richard *educator*
Hollingsworth, Martha Schmidt *lawyer*
Houser, Nathan *philosopher, educator*
Hovde, F. Boyd *lawyer*
Hubbard, Jesse Donald *retired pathology educator*
Hunt, Robert G. *construction company executive*
Ilgen, Dorothy L. *arts foundation executive*
Inui, Thomas Spencer *physician, educator*
Irsay, James Steven *professional football team owner*
Irwin, Glenn Ward, Jr. *medical educator, physician, academic administrator*
Jackson, Stephen *professional basketball player*
Jackson, Valerie Pascuzzi *radiologist, educator*
Jegen, Lawrence A. III *law educator*
Johnston, Cyrus Conrad, Jr. *medical educator*
Johnstone, Robert Philip *retired lawyer*
Jones, Marion *track and field athlete*
Kahlenbeck, Howard, Jr. *retired lawyer*
Kamendulis, Lisa M. *medical educator*
Kappes, Philip Spangler *lawyer*
Kashani, Hamid Reza *lawyer, computer consultant*
Kaufman, Barton Lowell *financial services company executive*
Kaye, Gordon Israel *pathologist, anatomist, educator*
Keaton, Margaret-Ann Coleman *education educator*
Keflezighi, Mebrahtom *professional marathon runner*
Kemper, James Dee *lawyer*
Kennedy, Russell Edward *academic administrator*
Kerr, William Andrew *lawyer, educator*
Kessler, Marcia Lynn *school psychologist*
Kirk, Carol *lawyer*
Kirkham, James Alvin *manufacturing executive*
Kirkpatrick, Robert Hugh *communications executive*
Klaper, Martin Jay *lawyer*
Knebel, Donald Earl *lawyer*
Knoebel, Suzanne Buckner *cardiologist, educator*
Koeller, Robert Marion *lawyer, director*
Krasean, Thomas Karl *historian*
Kunkler, Arnold William *retired surgeon, educator*
Kury, Bernard Edward *lawyer*
Lacy, Andre Balz *industrial executive*
Ladd, Alan Preston *pediatrician, pediatric surgeon*
Lamkin, Martha Dampf *lawyer, foundation administrator*
Landis, Larry Seabrook *state agency administrator*
Lau, Pauline Young *chemist*
Lechleiter, John C. *pharmaceutical executive*
Lee, Stephen W. *lawyer*
Lehman, Glen A. *gastroenterologist*
Lemberger, Louis *pharmacologist*
Lewis, Randall J. *healthcare insurance company executive*
Lilly, Ruth E. *philanthropist*
Lisher, Mary Katherine *lawyer*
Livers, Catherine McGhee *writer*
Lobley, Alan Haigh *retired lawyer*
Lofton, Thomas Milton *lawyer*
Long, Clarence William *accountant*
Lorell, Beverly H. *medical products executive*
Lowe, Louis Robert, Jr. *lawyer*
Lowe, Mary Katherine *technology company executive, writer*
Lugar, Thomas R. *manufacturing executive*
Lumeng, Lawrence *physician, educator*
Lytle, L(arry) Ben *insurance company executive, lawyer*
MacDougall, John Duncan *thoracic surgeon*
Madura, James Anthony *surgeon, educator*
Maine, Michael Roland *lawyer*
Malone, Jean Hambidge *educational consultant*
Manders, Karl Lee *neurosurgeon*
Manning, Peyton Williams *professional football player*
Marsh, Don Ermal *supermarket executive*
Mason, Thomas Alexander *historian, educator, author*
Matthews, Dewayne *foundation administrator*
Mays, William G. *chemical company executive*
McCall-Rodriguez, Leonor *healthcare services company executive, entrepreneur*
McCarthy, Harold Charles *retired insurance company executive*
McConnell, William F., Jr. *medical products executive*
McCrory, Michael Keith *lawyer*
Mc Farland, H. Richard *food products executive*
McKeag, Douglas Bruce *physician, educator*
McKeand, Patrick Joseph *newspaper publisher, educator*
McKinney, E. Kirk, Jr. *retired insurance company executive*
McKinney, Larry J. *federal judge*
Mead, Susanah M. *dean*
Mehta, Rakesh Peter *medical educator*
Merrill, William H., Jr. *lawyer, corporate financial executive*

Mikelsons, J. George *air transportation executive*
Miller, David W. *lawyer*
Mills, Jeffrey D. *prosecutor*
Mirola, William Andrew *sociologist, educator*
Mirsky, Arthur *retired geologist, educator*
Miyamoto, Richard Takashi *otolaryngologist*
Moelhman, Amy Jo *social worker*
Molitoris, Bruce Albert *nephrologist, educator*
Montoya, Juan Pablo *professional race car driver*
Moratz, Karen Evans *musician*
Mullen, Thomas Edgar *real estate consultant*
Murphy, Meissa Bleu *music educator, behaviorist*
Mutz, John Massie *foundation administrator, former state official, former energy executive*
Najjar, Diana *elementary school educator*
Neff, Robert Matthew *lawyer, finance company executive*
Newman, Norman Richard *lawyer*
Niederberger, Jane *information technology executive*
Nnaemeka, Obioma Grace *French language and women's studies educator, consultant, researcher*
Noffze, Jennifer Noel *museum administrator*
Nolan, Alan Tucker *lawyer, writer, arbitrator*
Norins, Arthur Leonard *dermatologist, educator*
Nurnberger, John I., Jr. *psychiatrist, educator*
Nussbaum, Samuel *healthcare insurance company executive, medical educator*
Ochs, Sidney *neurophysiology researcher, editor, writer*
Odell, James Calvin *history professor, theology studies educator*
Oklak, Dennis D. *real estate company executive*
Olson, Byron Louis *biochemist, educator*
O'Neal, Jermaine *professional basketball player*
Onochie, Florence N. *accountant*
Organ, Rita C. *museum administrator, consultant*
Osborn, Kathy *lawyer*
Padgett, Gregory Lee *lawyer*
Page, Curtis Matthewson *minister*
Paul, Stephen Howard *lawyer*
Pence, Linda Lee *lawyer*
Pennamped, Bruce Michael *lawyer*
Peribere, Jerome A. *agricultural products executive*
Petersen, James L. *lawyer*
Peterson, Bart *mayor*
Pilgrim, Jill *lawyer, consultant*
Pishchalnikov, Yuri A. *researcher*
Pitt, Henry Anthony *surgeon, researcher, medical educator*
Pitts, Beverley J. *academic administrator*
Plater, William Marmaduke *literature and language professor, educator, academic administrator*
Pockrass, Joseph Craig *music educator*
Poel, Robert Walter *military officer, physician*
Poinsette, Donald Eugene *engineering executive, management consultant*
Polak, Jonathan G. *lawyer*
Polston, Mark Franklin *minister*
Ralston, Ronald Lee *manufacturing tradesman*
Ramos, Jose A. *engineering educator*
Reed, Suellen Kinder *school system administrator*
Rees, Fred Joseph *music educator*
Reid, William Hill *mathematics professor*
Reynolds, Robert Hugh *lawyer*
Rhoad, Richard E. *healthcare executive*
Rhoades, Rodney Allen *physiologist, educator*
Rice, Derica *pharmaceutical company executive*
Richter, Judith Anne *pharmacologist, educator*
Riegsecker, Marvin Dean *pharmacist, state senator*
Robbins, N. Clay *foundation administrator*
Roberts, William Everett *lawyer*
Robinson, Rebecca Lynne *medical researcher*
Roger, Janice Lowenstein *cantor*
Rogers, Robert Ernest *medical educator*
Rokita, Todd *state official*
Rosenblatt, Alice F. *healthcare insurance company executive*
Roth, Lawrence Max *pathologist, educator*
Ruben, Gary A. *marketing and communications consultant*
Rucker, Robert D. *state supreme court justice*
Russell, David Williams *lawyer*
Russell, Frank Eli *retired newspaper publishing executive*
Rusthoven, Peter James *lawyer*
Rutledge, Joanne *artist, consultant*
Ryder, Henry Clay *lawyer*
Sawada, Stephen George *cardiologist, researcher*
Scaletta, Phillip Ralph III *lawyer*
Schenk, William Earl III *senior special agent, criminal investigator*
Schlegel, Fred Eugene *lawyer*
Schmetzer, Alan David *psychiatrist*
Schmid, John A. *musician, voice educator*
Scism, Daniel Reed *lawyer*
Seevers, Robert H. *chemist*
SerVaas, Beurt Richard *manufacturing executive*
SerVaas, Cory *editor-in-chief*
Sheehan, Kevin Edward *venture capitalist*
Shepard, Randall Terry *state supreme court chief justice*
Sherman, Stuart *internist, gastroenterologist*
Shi, Lizheng *health economist*
Shula, Robert Joseph *lawyer*
Siderys, Harry *surgeon, educator*
Simon, David *real estate company officer*
Simon, Herbert *real estate developer, professional basketball team executive*
Simon, Melvin *real estate developer, professional sports team executive*
Simon, Melvon *real estate company officer*
Skillman, Becky Sue *lieutenant governor, former state legislator*
Slocum, Judith Ann *retired elementary school educator*
Smith, Donald Archie *religious business executive, consultant*
Smith, James Warren *pathologist, educator, microbiologist, parasitologist*
Smith, K. Clay *machinery transport company executive*
Smith, Kenneth Dale *civil engineer, consultant*
Snare, Leroy Earl *physicist, physics educator*
Sokolov, Richard Saul *real estate company executive*

Solomon, Marilyn Kay *primary school educator, consultant, small business owner*
Sommer, James Koch *lawyer*
Sorley, Rebecca Ellen *music educator*
Spanogle, Robert William *marketing and advertising company executive, association administrator*
Speth, Gerald Lennus *educational consultant, management consultant*
Stayton, Thomas George *lawyer*
Stehman, Frederick Bates *obstetrician, gynecologist, educator*
Sterrett, Steven E. *real estate company officer*
Stewart, Paul Arthur *pharmaceutical company executive*
Stocker, Michael Aubrey *health insurance company executive*
Stoker, Daniel J. *academic administrator*
Storm, Janet S. *psychiatric social worker*
Strain, James Arthur *lawyer*
Strauss, Diane Jayne *retired elementary and secondary school educator, small business owner*
Sullender, Joy Sharon *retired elementary school educator*
Sullivan, Frank, Jr. *state supreme court justice*
Sutton, Gregory Paul *obstetrician, gynecologist*
Sweezy, John William *political party official*
Swindle, Ralph Wilson, Jr. *research psychologist*
Tabler, Bryan G. *lawyer*
Tabler, Norman Gardner, Jr. *lawyer*
Tabler, Susan Beidler *lawyer*
Tatom, John Anthony *economist*
Taurel, Sidney *pharmaceutical executive*
Taylor, Angelo *Olympic athlete*
Tempel, Eugene Raymond (Gene Tempel) *foundation administrator, speaker, researcher*
Terry, Linda Faye *librarian*
Thomas, Jerry Arthur *soil scientist*
Thuesen, Peter Johannes *religious studies educator, writer*
Towne, Edgar Arthur *theologian, educator*
Townsend, Earl C., Jr. *lawyer, writer*
Venzago, Mario *conductor, music director*
Vereen, Robert Charles *retired trade association administrator*
Vinatieri, Adam Matthew *professional football player*
Ware, J(oe) Anthony *cardiologist*
Warner, Joanne Rains *nursing educator, associate dean*
Watanabe, August Masaru *physician, educator, retired science association director*
Watkins, Harold Robert *minister*
Watts, John S., Jr. *insurance company executive*
Waynick, Catherine Elizabeth Maples *bishop*
Weber, George *oncology and pharmacology educator, researcher*
Weinberger, Myron Hilmar *medical educator*
Wensits, David L. *aerospace transportation executive*
Westra, Mitzi Sue *music educator*
Whale, Arthur Richard *retired lawyer*
Wheeler, Daniel Scott *management executive, editor*
White, James Patrick *law educator*
Wilkinson, Laura *Olympic athlete*
Williams, Bernard *Olympic athlete*
Wilson, Fred M., II, *ophthalmologist, educator*
Wishard, Gordon Davis *lawyer*
Wong, David T. *biochemist, researcher*
Wood, William Jerome *lawyer*
Woodring, DeWayne Stanley *religious organization administrator*
Woody, John Frederick *retired secondary school educator*
Woolling, Kenneth Rau *vascular internist*
Wright, David Burton *retired newspaper publishing company executive*
Wu, Min *cell biologist, researcher, educator*
Yao, Yongxue *immunologist*
Yee, Robert Donald *ophthalmologist*
Young, Philip Howard *library director*
Yovits, Marshall Clinton *information scientist, educator, dean*
Zipes, Douglas Peter *cardiologist, researcher*
Zoeller, David Louis *lawyer*

## Inglefield

James, Marion Ray *retired publishing executive, editor*

## Jasper

Brenner, Raymond Anthony *priest*
Newman, Leonard Jay *retail jewel merchant, gemologist*

## Jeffersonville

Hoehn, Elmer Louis *lawyer, educator, state agency administrator, consultant, federal agency administrator*
Morgan, Roberta Diane *music educator*
Phillips, Arlene Marie *retired secondary school educator*
Reisert, Charles Edward, Jr. *realtor*
Walburn, John Clifford *mental health services professional*

## Kentland

Hiatt, Tony John *biology educator, director*

## Knightstown

Richardson, Shirley Maxine *editor*

## Kokomo

Coppock, Janet Elaine *mental health nurse*
Highlen, Larry Wade *music educator, piano rebuilder, tuner*
Hockney, Dean Wesley *editor, writer*
Maugans, John Conrad *lawyer*
Miller, Robert Frank *retired electronics engineering executive*
Ramos, Jamie *information scientist*
Stein, Eleanor Bankoff *retired judge*
Wysong, Earl Edward *sociologist, educator*

## La Porte

Casey, Keith Allen *accountant*
Johnson, Bruce Ross *elementary school educator*
Kaminski, Leon R. *lawyer*

Morris, Leigh Edward *mayor, retired health facility administrator*

**Lafayette**
Caldwell, Barrett Scott *industrial engineering educator*
Drazin, Michael Peter *mathematician, researcher*
Etzel, James Edward *environmental engineering educator*
Feuer, Henry *retired chemist*
Fox, Robert William *mechanical engineering educator*
Gartenhaus, Solomon *physicist, educator*
Geddes, Leslie Alexander *engineering educator, forensic engineer, physiologist*
Hamdi, Hamid S. *neurologist, neurorehabilitation specialist, consultant, researcher*
Hardin, Lowell Stewart *retired economics professor*
Hart, Russell Holiday *retired lawyer*
Helmuth, Ned D. *financial planner*
Kanne, Michael Stephen *federal judge*
Laszynski, Robert Steven *lawyer*
Liley, Peter Edward *retired engineering educator*
Loeffler, Frank Joseph *physicist, educator*
Maickel, Roger Philip *pharmacologist, educator*
McBride, Angela Barron *nursing educator*
McCully, Thomas Richardson *lawyer*
McKowen, Dorothy Keeton *librarian, educator*
Meyer, Brud Richard *retired pharmaceutical executive*
Minor, Ronald Ray *minister*
Mitchell, Pamela Lee *elementary school educator*
Mobley, Emily Ruth *library director, educator, dean*
Nicholson, Ralph Lester *botanist, educator*
Osborn, John Robert *retired engineering educator*
Pipes, Robert Byron *mechanical engineer, educator*
Porile, Norbert Thomas *chemistry professor*
Renzetti, Phyllis Jean *retired technical editor*
Roush, Nadine Marie *elementary school educator*
Schönemann, Peter Hans *psychologist, educator*
Schweickert, Richard Justus *psychologist, educator*
Troutner, Joanne Johnson *director, consultant, secondary school educator*

**Lagrange**
Brown, George E. *judge, educator*
Roth, Gayle Yvonne *elementary school educator*

**Lake Village**
Emmrich, Mary Kaylene *librarian*

**Lawrenceburg**
Dautel, Charles Shreve *retired mining company executive*
Edwards, Marie D. *social services administrator*

**Lebanon**
Goodwin, John Charles *social studies educator*

**Leopold**
Spence, Rodney Glen *education educator, coach*

**Liberty**
Pringle, Lewis Gordon *marketing professional, educator*
Sowers, Marilyn Rae *librarian*

**Linden**
Eutsler, Therese Anne *physical therapist*

**Lizton**
King, Richard Gene *superintendent*
Rauch, Eric *biology educator*

**Logansport**
Brewer, Robert Allen *physician*
Hetzler, Kathy E. *nursing educator, nursing administrator*
Howland, Bette *writer*
Walter, Patricia L.. *psychotherapist, consultant*

**Lowell**
Stewart, Bradley Mitchell *secondary school educator*

**Madison**
Grahn, Ann Wagoner *retired science administrator*
Tatera, James Frank *chemist*
Williams, Carole Lee *secondary school educator*

**Marion**
Felton, Wanda June *curator*
Fisher, Pierre James, Jr. *physician*
Lawson, Diane Sue *elementary school educator*
Maher, John Gene *music educator, musician*
Miller, Peter Karl *music educator*
Walker, Corean Jones *evangelist*

**Martinsville**
Kendall, Robert Stanton *newspaper editor, journalist, automotive executive*

**Merrillville**
Brenman, Stephen Morris *lawyer*
Compton, Clyde D. *lawyer*
Doumanian, Heratch Ohannes *radiologist*
Gioia, Daniel August *lawyer*
Marchina, Darlene B. *religious coordinator*
Miller, Richard Allen *lawyer*
Neale, Gary Lee *utilities executive*
Skaggs, Robert C., Jr. *utilities executive, lawyer*
Wang, Josephine L. Fen *physician*

**Michigan City**
Manny, Carter Hugh, Jr. *architect, foundation administrator*
Mothkur, Sridhar Rao *radiologist*
Varro, Barbara Joan *retired editor*
Wiegand, Elizabeth *musician, educator*

**Middlebury**
Corson, Thomas Harold *retired manufacturing executive*
Dickey, Lucy Jane *elementary school educator*
Guequierre, John Phillip *manufacturing executive*

**Mishawaka**
Haley, David Alan *healthcare executive*
Kendall, Michael Jay *music educator, musician*
Klopfenstein, Reginald Lee *music educator*
Kummeth, Beth A. *elementary school educator*
Ponko, William Reuben *architect*
Rubenstein, Pamela Silver *manufacturing executive*
Silver, Neil Marvin *manufacturing executive*
Sobol, Zbigniew W. *orthopedist, surgeon*
Troyer, LeRoy Seth *architect*

**Modoc**
Shore, Randy *secondary school educator*

**Monroeville**
Ray, Annette D. *executive secretary*

**Morgantown**
Callon, Margaret Joann *writer, minister*

**Mount Summit**
Bales, James Lavon *music educator*

**Muncie**
Ali, Mir Masoom *statistician, educator*
Amman, E(lizabeth) Jean *academic administrator*
Anderson, Stefan Stolen *retired banker*
Ballard, Jeffrey Dale *music educator, tenor*
Barber, Earl Eugene *management consultant*
Bell, Stephen Scott (Steve Bell) *journalist, educator*
Blume, Peter Frederick *museum director*
Bogg, Richard Allan *sociologist, educator*
Bower, Connie Ilene *bank executive*
Cartwright, Susan Merrick *mathematician, educator*
Cheng, Chu Yuan *economics professor*
Dennis, Ralph Emerson, Jr. *lawyer*
Dickson, Nancy Starr *retired elementary school educator*
Dolak, Fritz *librarian, information administrator*
East, David Harold *mathematics professor*
Elvin, George *architecture educator*
Farr, Barbara F. *minister*
Fillwalk, John Alfred *art educator, artist*
Fisher, John Wesley *manufacturing executive, director*
Glass, James Arthur *historian, educator*
Gora, JoAnn M. *academic administrator*
Greve, Todd Allen *minister*
Harris, Joseph McAllister *retired chemist*
Hayashi, Tetsumaro *retired literature educator, writer, editor*
Hendrix, Jon Richard *biology professor*
Henzlik, Raymond Eugene *zoophysiologist, educator*
Hoffman, Mary Catherine *retired nurse, anesthetist*
Hunter, Miriam Eileen *artist, educator*
Kelly, Eric Damian *lawyer, educator*
Kitchens, Frederick Lynton III *education educator, researcher*
Klotz, Ann Marie *director*
Kroehler, Beth Ann *librarian*
Lawhead, Victor Bernard *education educator*
Lynch, Bill *university football coach*
Maurer, Kathleen Marie *music educator, vocalist*
Mertens, Thomas Robert *biology professor*
Nanko, Raymond S. *physician*
Norris, Tracy Hopkins *retired public relations executive*
Popovich, Karen *health facility administrator*
Roch, Lewis Marshall, II, *ophthalmic surgeon, medical entrepreneur*
Roothaan, John *music educator, jazz pianist*
Schaefer, Patricia *retired librarian*
Seymour, Richard Deming *technology educator*
Shobe, Franklin Dale *mathematician, educator*
Smith, Van P. *diversified financial services company executive*
Stewart, Rita Joan *academic administrator*
Swartz, B(enjamin) K(insell), Jr. *archaeologist, educator*
Thornbro, William Graden *writer*
Turner, Nancy K. *archivist, librarian*
Wise, Charles Davidson *science educator*
Yeamans, George Thomas *librarian, educator*
Zhuk, Sergei Ivanovich *history professor, researcher*

**Munster**
Amber, Douglas George *lawyer*
Corsiglia, Robert Joseph *retired electrical construction company executive*
Neff, Bonita Dostal *communication development facilitator*
Potempa, Philip Matthew *journalist, columnist, communications educator*
Singh, Manmohan *orthopedic surgeon, educator*
Taylor, Gloria A. *minister, educator*

**Nashville**
Wills, Katherine V. Tsiopos *language educator*

**New Albany**
Beeby, James Matthew *history professor*
Bourne, James E. *lawyer*
Chowhan, Naveed Mahfooz *oncologist*
Crump, Claudia *geographer, educator*
Rhodes, Betty Fleming *rehabilitation services professional, nurse*
Riehl, Jane Ellen *education educator*
Thackeray, Frank W. *history professor*

**New Castle**
Chilton, Todd Longstreet *psychologist*
Nipp, Tom *mayor, protective services official, artist*

**New Harmony**
Rice, David Lee *university president emeritus*

**New Haven**
Powelson, Gale Dawn *elementary school educator*

**Newburgh**
Culiver, Elizabeth Ann *elementary school educator*
Tierney, Gordon Paul *real estate broker, genealogist*

**Noblesville**
Monical, Robert Duane *engineering company executive*
Morrison, Joseph Young *transportation executive, consultant*
Wilson, Norman Glenn *church administrator, writer*

**North Manchester**
Mason, Stephen Olin *not-for-profit developer*
Switzer, Jo Young *college president*

**Notre Dame**
Appleby, R(obert) Scott *history educator*
Arnold, Peri Ethan *political scientist*
Bartell, Ernest *economist, educator, priest*
Bennett, David Paul *astrophysicist*
Blakey, G. Robert (George Robert Blakey) *law educator*
Burish, Thomas Gerard *academic administrator, psychology professor*
Burns, Peter C. *science educator, engineering educator*
Crosson, Frederick James *retired dean, humanities educator*
Cummings, Edward Mark *psychology professor, researcher*
Davis, Stacy Nicole *religious studies educator*
Despres, Leo Arthur *sociologist, anthropologist, educator, academic administrator*
Evens, Samuel Robert *mathematics professor*
Goetz, Abraham *retired mathematics professor*
Goulet, Denis André *development ethicist*
Gray, William Guerin *engineering educator*
Green, Catherine Gertrude *retired speech educator, retired secondary school educator*
Gunn, Alan *retired law educator*
Hallinan, Maureen Theresa *sociologist, educator*
Hayes, Stephen Matthew *librarian*
Huber, Paul William *biochemistry professor, researcher*
Incropera, Frank Paul *mechanical engineering educator*
Jemielity, Thomas John *language educator*
Jenkins, John I. *academic administrator*
Jensen, Richard Jorg *biologist, educator*
Kogge, Peter Michael *computer scientist, educator*
Kulpa, Charles F. *microbiology professor, department chairman*
Ladewski, Roman Sebastian *priest, educator*
Lanzinger, Klaus *language educator*
Loving, Charles Roy *museum director, curator*
Malloy, Edward Aloysius *academic administrator*
Marmion, Daniel Keith *school librarian*
Marsden, George M. *history professor, writer*
Matthias, John Edward *English literature educator*
Maurice, Patricia Ann *geochemist, educator*
Maziar, Christine M. *academic administrator*
McInerny, Ralph Matthew *philosopher, educator, writer*
Meisel, Dan *chemist*
Merz, James Logan *electrical and materials engineering educator, researcher*
Michel, Anthony Nikolaus *electrical engineering educator, researcher*
Mirowski, Philip Edward *economics professor*
O'Hara, Patricia Anne *dean, law educator*
O'Meara, Onorato Timothy *academic administrator, mathematician*
O'Rourke, William Andrew *literature and language professor, writer*
Ovaert, Timothy Christopher *mechanical engineering educator*
Pollard, Morris *microbiologist, educator*
Raymer, John David *literature and language professor*
Reilly, Frank Kelly *business educator*
Robinson, John Hayes *law educator*
Sandusky, Billy Ray *art educator, artist*
Scheidt, W. Robert *chemistry educator, researcher*
Schmitz, Roger Anthony *chemical engineer, educator, academic administrator*
Shannon, William Norman III *finance educator, food service executive*
Shrader-Frechette, Kristin *science educator*
Sommese, Andrew John *mathematics professor*
Stadtherr, Mark A. *chemical engineer, educator*
Stamper, John W. *architecture educator, academic administrator*
Swartz, Thomas R. *economist, educator*
Trozzolo, Anthony Marion *chemistry professor*
Vakulenko, Sergei Borisovich *medical researcher, educator*
Valenzuela, Julio Samuel *sociologist, educator*
Vecchio, Robert Peter *business management educator*
Walshe, Aubrey Peter *political science professor*
Weigert, Andrew Joseph *sociology educator*
Weis, Charlie *college football coach*
Welch, Michael R. *sociologist, educator*
Williams, Oliver Franklin *priest, educator*
Woehr, Andreas *physics professor*
Woo, Carolyn Yauyan *dean*
Younger, Jennifer A. *university librarian*
Zuckert, Catherine Heldt *political science educator, writer, editor*

**Pittsboro**
Swango, Colleen Jill *science educator*

**Plainfield**
Fivel, Steven Edward *lawyer*
Laikin, Robert J. *electronics executive*

**Portage**
Popp, Joseph Bruce *manufacturing executive*
Schroeder, Marvis Lynn *accountant, artist*
Williams, Susan Marie *music educator*

**Princeton**
Okamoto, Seizo *transportation executive*

**Richmond**
Bennett, Douglas Carleton *academic administrator*
Cooper, Jamie Lee *writer*
Farber, Evan Ira *librarian*
Kirk, Thomas Garrett, Jr. *librarian*
Routson, Susan Hutchins *secondary school educator, consultant, peer counseling specialist*

**Roanoke**
Cutshall-Hayes, Diane Marion *elementary school educator*
Geyer, Catherine S. *elementary school educator*

**Rockport**
Davis, Karen Sue *hospital nursing supervisor*
Smith, Mary Lee *civil engineer, technician*

**Russiaville**
Berry, Patricia A. *elementary school educator*
Suffield, Judith Kreutz *secondary school educator*

**Salem**
Davis, Duane L. *music educator, vocalist*

**Santa Claus**
Edwards, James Dallas III *management consultant*

**Schererville**
Jarrett, Alexis *insurance agent, lawyer*
Opacich, Milan *protective services official, musician*

**Scottsburg**
Dockery, Linda *writer*
Kho, Eusebio *surgeon*

**Shelbyville**
Lisher, James Richard *lawyer*
McNeely, James Lee *lawyer*

**Shoals**
Boyd, Earl E., Jr. *councilman*

**South Bend**
Agbetsiafa, Douglas Kofi *financial consultant, management consultant*
Anderson, Kenneth Paul *nephrologist, administrator*
Carey, John Leo *lawyer*
Carrington, Michael Davis *criminal justice and security consultant*
Cerny, William *retired education educator, musician*
Cohen, Ronald S. *accountant*
Cook, Pamela Margaret *French educator*
Davis, Glen Anthony *pediatrician*
Davis, Katherine Lyon *former lieutenant governor*
Dowty, Alan Kent *political scientist, educator*
Doyle, Colleen Elizabeth *secondary school educator*
Fitzpatrick, Eileen Theresa *chemistry educator*
Harriman, Gerald Eugene *retired business administrator, retired economics professor*
Hellyer, Timothy Michael *protective services officer*
Horsbrugh, Patrick *architect, educator, environologist*
Jones, Wellington Downing III *banker*
Larkin, Eugene David *artist, educator*
Manion, Daniel Anthony *federal judge*
Muniz, Jorge *composer, music educator*
Reinke, William John *lawyer*
Ripple, Kenneth Francis *federal judge*
Seall, Stephen Albert *lawyer*
Shaffer, Thomas Lindsay *lawyer, educator*
Sharp, Allen *federal judge*
Smith, E. Berry *television and radio consultant*
Smith, Thomas Gordon *architect*
Stankrauff, Alison Harper *archivist*
Storin, Matthew Victor *academic administrator, educator, retired editor*
van Inwagen, Peter Jan *philosophy educator*
Vogel, Nelson J., Jr. *lawyer*

**Spencer**
Young, Frederic Hisgen *information systems executive, data processing consultant*

**Spencerville**
Clark, Donna M. *retired elementary school educator*

**Sullivan**
Chavez, Mary Ann *osteopathic family physician*

**Syracuse**
Metcalf, Philip Leslie *mathematics professor, career planning administrator*

**Tell City**
Arterberry, Patricia *retired elementary school educator*
Thrasher, May Alif Maruroft *educator, social worker*

**Terre Haute**
Aldridge, Sandra *civic volunteer*
Badar, M. Affan *engineering educator*
Bagert, Donald Joseph *computer scientist, educator*
Baker, Ronald Lee *folklore educator*
Betts, Katherine Helen *academic administrator, educator*
Bopp, James, Jr. *lawyer*
Carmony, Marvin Dale *retired linguist, educator*
Chambers, Curtis Allen *clergyman, church administrator*
Dando, William Arthur *academic administrator, geography and geology educator*
De Marr, Mary Jean *English language educator*
Frey, Susan M. *information specialist*
Gennaro, Rocco Joseph *philosopher, educator*
Guthrie, Frank Albert *chemistry professor*
Halpern, Arthur Merrill *chemistry professor*
Hardin, Steve *librarian*
Hunt, Effie Neva *retired dean, literature educator*
Inlow, Jennifer Kay *chemistry professor, researcher*
Lamis, Leroy *artist, retired art educator*
Leach, Ronald George *education educator, librarian*
Leigh, Janis *clinician*
Malooley, David Joseph *electronics and computer technology educator*
Mehrens, Christopher Emile *musicologist, music librarian*
Mellor, J. P. *education educator*
Olsen, Christopher John *education educator*

Roshel, John Albert, Jr. *orthodontist*
Sparks, Dale W. *biologist, research scientist*
Steinbaugh, Robert P. *management and finance educator*
Vincent, Richard C. *communications educator, researcher*
Vollmer, David *museum director*

**Trail Creek**
Nagle, Ronald K. *music educator*

**Upland**
Kesler, Jay Lewis *retired academic administrator*

**Valparaiso**
Blaschke, Lawrence Raymond *electronic security services professional*
Canganelli, Vincent Guglielmo *retired psychiatrist*
Cook, Addison Gilbert *chemistry professor*
Gaffney, Edward McGlynn *law educator, dean*
Hillila, Bernhard Hugo Paul *retired education educator*
Kobak, Alfred Julian, Jr. *obstetrician, gynecologist*
Mosco, Scott Morris *small business owner*
Mundinger, Donald Charles *retired college president*
Olson, Lynn *sculptor, painter, writer*
Peters, Howard Nevin *foreign language educator*
Pritchett, Daniel R. *music educator*
Schlender, William Elmer *management sciences educator*
Schnabel, Robert Victor *retired academic administrator*
Startt, James Dill *history educator*
Taylor, Heather Marie *director*
Zhou, Yiqun *humanities educator*

**Versailles**
Perry, Donna Sue *special education educator*

**Vincennes**
Emison, Ewing Rabb, Jr. *lawyer*

**Wabash**
Scales, Richard Lewis *retired sales representative*

**Walton**
Chu, Johnson Chin Sheng *retired physician*
Krug, Don L. *secondary school educator, director*

**Wanatah**
Moser, Sandra Kay *secondary school educator*

**Warsaw**
Elliott, J. Raymond *medical products executive*
Hann, Daniel P. *medical products executive, lawyer*
Leno, Sam R. *corporate financial executive*
Mroczkowski, Matthew *biomedical engineer*
Noblitt, Niles L. *medical products executive*
Utter, Brenda Lu *adult education educator*

**Washington**
Graham, David Bolden *food products executive*

**Waterloo**
Johnson, George Axil III *television producer*

**West Lafayette**
Abhyankar, Shreeram Shankar *mathematics professor*
Adelman, Steven Allen *chemist, educator*
Ahmed, Shaikh Shahid *physicist, researcher*
Albright, Jack Lawrence *animal science and veterinary educator*
Albright, Lyle Frederick *chemical engineering educator*
Altschaeffl, Adolph George *retired civil engineering educator*
Amstutz, Harold Emerson *veterinarian, educator*
Andres, Ronald Paul *chemical engineer, educator*
Andrews, Theodora Anne *retired librarian, educator*
Asher, J. William *education educator, psychology professor*
Barany, James Walter *industrial engineering educator*
Barnes, Virgil Everett, II, *physics professor*
Baumgardt, Billy Ray *professional society administrator, agriculturist*
Beering, Steven Claus *academic administrator, medical educator*
Belcastro, Patrick Frank *pharmacist, researcher*
Bertolet, Rodney Jay *philosophy educator*
Blickenstaff, Channing Blount *retired language educator*
Borowitz, Joseph Leo *pharmacologist, educator*
Brey, Eric Trent *hospitality and tourism educator*
Broden, Thomas Francis III *French language educator*
Buckmaster, Dennis Rene *agricultural engineer, educator*
Chang, Ching-jer *medicinal chemistry educator*
Christian, John Edward *health science association administrator, educator*
Cicirelli, Victor George *psychologist*
Cohen, Raymond *mechanical engineer, educator*
Connor, John Murray *economics professor*
Contreni, John Joseph, Jr. *humanities educator*
Cooks, R(obert) Graham *chemist, educator*
Cooper, Arnold Cook *management educator, researcher*
Cosier, Richard A. *dean, finance educator*
Cramer, William Anthony *biochemistry and biophysics researcher, educator*
Danielli-Garofalo, Donatella *mathematics professor*
Delleur, Jacques William *retired engineering educator*
Diamond, Sidney *chemist, educator*
Drnevich, Vincent Paul *engineering educator*
Dumas, Jean E. *psychology professor*
Dyrenfurth, Michael John *education educator, academic administrator*
Farris, Paul Leonard *agricultural economist*
Frey, Harley Harrison, Jr. *retired anesthesiologist*
Gennett, Timothy *academic administrator*
Gruen, Gerald Elmer *psychologist, educator*
Horwich, George *economist, educator*
Hoxie, Robert Prynne *retired entomologist*

Hunt, Michael O'Leary *wood science educator, engineering educator*
Ichiyama, Dennis Yoshihide *art educator, educational association administrator*
Irudayaraj, Joseph M. *engineering educator*
Jabbari, Esmaiel *polymer scientist, researcher*
Jackson, Mark James *engineering educator*
Jackson, Scott Allen *biology professor*
Jang, SooCheong (Shawn) *education educator*
Janick, Jules *horticultural scientist, educator*
Jischke, Martin C. *academic administrator*
Judd, William Robert *engineering geologist, educator*
Katehi, Linda P.B. *engineering educator*
Kirchmaier, Ann *biochemist, researcher*
Kirksey, Avanelle *nutrition educator*
Ladisch, Michael R. *engineering educator*
Landgrebe, David Allen *electrical engineer*
Lechtenberg, Victor L. *agricultural studies educator*
Le Master, Dennis Clyde *forester, educator, retired economist*
Lewellen, Wilbur Garrett *management educator, consultant*
Lin, Pen-Min *electrical engineer, educator*
Lipschutz, Michael Elazar *chemistry professor, consultant, researcher*
Markee, Katherine Madigan *librarian, educator*
Marshall, Francis Joseph *aerospace engineer*
Mason, Sally Kay Frost *biology professor, academic administrator*
Mauer, Lisa *education educator*
Mc Bride, William Leon *philosopher, educator*
McMillin, David Robert *chemistry professor*
Mork, Gordon Robert *historian, educator*
Morrison, Harry *chemistry professor*
Moskowitz, Herbert *management educator*
Moyars-Johnson, Mary Annis *retired history professor*
Naik, Sameer Vijaykumar *mechanical engineer, educator*
Negishi, Ei-ichi *chemistry professor*
Nelson, Philip Edwin *food scientist, educator*
Newby, Timothy James *education educator, researcher*
Nixon, Judith May *librarian*
Ohm, Herbert Willis *agronomy educator, agriculturist*
Ong, Chee-Mun *engineering educator*
Orvis, Kathryn S. *science educator*
Overhauser, Albert Warner *physicist*
Peck, Garnet Edward *pharmacist, educator*
Peroulis, Dimitrios *engineering educator, consultant*
Perrucci, Robert *sociologist, educator*
Phillips, Terry LeMoine *investment advisor*
Poulos, James Thomas *endocrinologist, educator*
Preckel, Paul Veitch *agricultural economics educator, researcher*
Ramkrishna, Doraiswami *chemical engineering educator, researcher*
Reckowsky, Michael J. *academic administrator*
Ringel, Robert Lewis *academic administrator*
Rossmann, Michael George *biochemist, educator*
Rud, Anthony Gordon, Jr. *education educator*
Rutledge, Charles Ozwin *pharmacologist, educator*
Salvendy, Gavriel *industrial engineer, educator*
Savaiano, Dennis Alan *education educator, dean*
Schendel, Dan Eldon *management consultant, finance educator*
Scholer, Sue Wyant *retired state legislator*
Schwartz, Richard John *electrical engineering educator, researcher*
Shaw, Stanley Miner *pharmacist, educator*
Sherman, Louis Allen *biology professor, department chairman*
Shertzer, Bruce Eldon *education educator*
Shively, Gerald E. *economist, educator*
Silva, Tony *education educator, editor*
Sims-Curry, Kristy *women's college basketball coach*
Stahly, G. Patrick *chemist*
Stob, Martin *retired physiology educator*
Swensen, Clifford Henrik, Jr. *psychologist, educator*
Taber, Margaret Ruth *retired engineering technology educator*
Tacker, Willis Arnold, Jr. *medical educator, researcher*
Thomas, Marlin Uluess *industrial engineer, educator, academic administrator*
Tyner, Wallace Edward *agricultural economics educator*
VanFossen, Phillip J. *academic administrator*
Varma, Arvind *chemical engineering educator, researcher*
Viskanta, Raymond *mechanical engineering educator*
Wankat, Phillip Charles *chemical engineering educator*
Weidenaar, Dennis Jay *retired economics professor*
Weinstein, Michael Alan *political science professor*
Williams, Theodore Joseph *engineering educator*
Wood, Terry Lee *mathematics professor*
Woodman, Harold David *historian, educator*
Yao, Bin *mechanical engineering educator*

**Westfield**
Bradbury, Betty Marie *history educator, music educator*

**Westville**
Serwatka, Judy Ann *computer and information systems educator*

**Whiting**
Dowen, Madeline Elizabeth *retired hospital librarian*

**Winamac**
Ligocki, Gordon Michael *artist, educator*

**Winona Lake**
Davis, John James *religion educator*
Julien, Thomas Theodore *religious denomination administrator*
Norris, Mark Marston *historian, educator*
Swartzentruber, Don Michael *artist, educator*

**Zionsville**
Garfunkel, Art *singer, actor*

# IOWA

**Akron**
Hultgren, Dennis Eugene *farmer, management consultant*

**Algona**
Aboud, John Anthony *music educator*

**Alton**
LeTendre, Beth Ann *language educator*

**Ames**
Abbott, David L. *agricultural products executive*
Allen, Benjamin J. *academic administrator*
Alumbaugh, JoAnn McCalla *magazine editor*
Anderson, Lloyd Lee *physiologist, educator*
Anderson, Robert Morris, Jr. *electrical engineer*
Armstrong, Daniel Wayne *chemist, educator*
Avalos, Hector Ignacio *language educator*
Barnes, Richard George *physicist, researcher*
Barton, Thomas Jackson J. *chemistry professor, researcher*
Baumann, Edward Robert *environmental engineering educator*
Beran, George Wesley *veterinary microbiology educator*
Black, James Robert *industrial engineer*
Brown, Robert C. *engineering educator*
Bruene, Barbara Jane *artist, educator*
Buchele, Wesley Fisher *retired agricultural engineering educator*
Bugeja, Michael Joseph *director, educator, writer*
Bytautas, Laimutis *chemist, educator*
Chimenti, Dale E. *engineering educator*
Clem, John Richard *physicist, educator*
Courteau, Joanna *foreign language educator*
Crabtree, Beverly June *retired dean*
Dahiya, Rajbir Singh *mathematics professor, researcher*
David, Herbert Aron *retired statistician, educator*
Davis, Wayne Pitman *public relations executive*
Ebbers, Larry Harold *education educator*
Fennelly, William *basketball coach*
Fleming, Jon Lee *gastroenterologist*
Fox, Karl August *economist, educator, eco-behavioral scientist*
Fritz, James Sherwood *chemist, educator*
Fuller, Wayne Arthur *statistics educator*
Geoffroy, Gregory L. *academic administrator, educator*
Greve, John Henry *veterinary parasitologist, educator*
Hallauer, Arnel Roy *geneticist*
Harl, Neil Eugene *economist, educator, lawyer, writer*
Hatfield, Jerry Lee *plant pathologist, meteorologist*
Hendrich, Suzanne *toxicologist*
Hong, Mei *chemistry professor*
Horowitz, Jack *biochemistry educator*
Hunger, J(ohn) David *business educator*
Jackson, George Arthur dean, *educator*
Jacobson, Norman L. *retired agricultural educator, researcher*
Jacobson, Robert Andrew *chemistry professor*
Jenks, Cynthia J. *research scientist*
Johnson, Lawrence Alan *cereal technologist, educator, administrator*
Kang, Dae-Ki *computer scientist*
Karlen, Douglas Lawrence *soil scientist, researcher*
Kaufmann, Jeffrey Baer *finance educator*
Larsen, William Lawrence *engineering educator*
Lee, Seong-Jae *research scientist*
Lewis, Calvin Fred *architect, educator*
Lo, Chester C.H. *research scientist*
Manatt, Richard *retired education educator*
Mattila, Mary Jo Kalsem *elementary and art educator*
Maxwell Dial, Eleanore *foreign language educator*
Mengeling, William Lloyd *retired veterinarian, virologist*
Mertins, James Walter *entomologist*
Moore, Kenneth James *agronomist, educator*
Munkvold, Gary P. *plant pathologist, educator*
Nostwich, Theodore Daniel *literature educator, researcher*
O'Berry, Phillip Aaron *retired veterinarian*
Okiishi, Theodore Hisao *mechanical engineering educator*
Palermo, Gregory Sebastian *architect*
Pohlman, Lynette *museum director, curator*
Retallick, Michael S. *agricultural studies educator, director*
Rodde, James F. *music educator*
Ross, Richard Francis *veterinarian, educator, dean, microbiologist*
Sanders, Wallace Wolfred, Jr. *civil engineer*
Schlagel, Deborah "Devo" Lynn *chemist, materials scientist*
Seaton, Vaughn Allen *retired veterinary pathology educator*
Sebranek, Joseph G. *science educator*
Smith, John Francis *materials science educator*
Solensten, John Martin *retired English and American studies educator, writer*
Tabatabai, M. Ali *chemist, biochemist*
Thompson, Louis Milton *agronomy educator, researcher*
Topel, David Glen *agricultural studies educator*
Tylka, Gregory L. *plant pathologist, educator*
Wilder, David Randolph *retired materials engineer*
Willham, Richard Lewis *zoology educator*
Work, George Paul *cellist*
Yeung, Edward Szeshing *chemist*

**Anita**
Stender, Julia Mae *mathematics educator*

**Ankeny**
Lamb, Ronald M. *convenience stores executive*
Stahr, Curtis Brent *photographer, art association administrator, educator*
Weigel, Ollie J. *dentist, former mayor*
Wirtz, Eli J. *lawyer, retail executive*

**Atlantic**
Johnson, Joan (Jan) Hope Voss *communications executive, photojournalist, public relations executive*

**Belmond**
Martinek, Cynthia L. *principal*

**Bettendorf**
Hengst, Herbert Randall *retired adult education educator*
Heyderman, Arthur Jerome *engineer, civilian military employee*
Rathje, James Lee *broker*
Schulz, Sally Ann *pastoral musician, conductor, educator*

**Burlington**
Hoth, Steven Sergey *lawyer, educator*

**Camanche**
DeLacy, Gary Richard *principal*
Fuglsang, Steven M. *principal*

**Cambridge**
Colvin, Thomas Stuart *agricultural engineer, farmer*

**Cedar Falls**
Blakesley, Kimberly Kay *art educator, consultant*
Broadie, Richard R. *history professor*
Chesnutt, Rod Martin *music educator*
Fanelli, Michael Paul *musician, educator, writer*
Gilgen, Albert Rudolph *retired psychologist, retired educator*
Glockner, Richard Peter *theater educator, actor, theater director*
Golczewski, Artur *art history educator*
Haack, Joel K. *mathematics professor, academic administrator*
Koob, Robert Duane *chemistry professor, academic administrator*
Lettow, Lucille Jane *school librarian, education educator*
Lindberg, Duane R. *bishop, historian*
Olivares-Cuhat, Gabriela Antonia *literature and language professor*
Olsen-Dunbar, Jessica Ida *sign language educator*
Rajendran, Kadiampatti Natarajan *marketing educator*
Schnucker, Robert Victor *historian, educator*
Shimp, Karen Ann *accountant, corporate financial executive*
Skaine, James C. *retired communications educator*
Skaine, Rosemarie Keller *writer, consultant, publisher*
Taylor, Darrell Richard *art gallery director, artist*

**Cedar Rapids**
Arnold-Olson, Helen B. *not-for-profit consultant*
Baermann, Donna Lee Roth *real estate property executive, retired insurance analyst*
Bahadur, Birendra *displays research specialist*
Brighi, Robert J. *principal*
Chadick, Gary Robert *lawyer*
Collins, Kevin Heath *lawyer*
Erickson, Lawrence A. (Larry Erickson) *electronics executive*
Fitzpatrick, John Charles *humanities educator, curator*
Gilmor, Jane Ellen *artist, educator*
Hansen, David Rasmussen *federal judge*
Jones, Clayton M. *computer and electronics company executive*
Keller, Eliot Aaron *broadcast executive*
Knepper, Eugene Arthur *realtor*
Larson, Charles W. *prosecutor*
Maikon, Marc Steven *podiatrist*
Mc Manus, Edward Joseph *federal judge*
Melloy, Michael J. *federal judge*
Nazette, Richard Follett *lawyer*
Norris, Albert Stanley *psychiatrist, educator*
Nyquist, John Davis *retired radio manufacturing company executive*
Pundt, Richard Arthur *lawyer*
Renter, Lois Irene Hutson *retired librarian*
Riley, Tom Joseph *lawyer*
Rohr, Carol Ann *composer, music educator*
Smith, Bruce Vaughn *electrical engineer*
Stephens, Ralph Renne *massage therapy educator*
Stolte, Larry Gene *marketing executive, retired computer and publishing company executive*
Urbanowski, Melena Haskovec *elementary school educator*
Wax, Nadine Virginia *retired bank executive*
Whipple, William Perry *foundation administrator*
Wiese, Daniel Edward *marketing and communications researcher*
Wilson, Robert Foster *lawyer*
Ziese, Nancylee Hanson *social worker*

**Centerville**
Moritz, Dana Dee *language educator*

**Chariton**
Stuart, William Corwin *judge*

**Charles City**
Mc Cartney, Ralph Farnham *lawyer*

**Cherokee**
Gordon, Roma Dianne *music educator*
Henke, Marcia Ann *secondary school educator*
Rice, Christina Lynn Bochtler *literature and language educator*

**Clarinda**
Boysen, Katharine *school system administrator, director*

**Clear Lake**
Broshar, Robert Clare *architect*
Brown, Robert Grover *engineering educator*
Enabnit, Ted *retired lawyer*
Siska, Robert John *software engineer*

**Clinton**
Engelson, Robert Allen *music educator*
Kearney, Michael John *banker*

Smith, Lauren Ashley *lawyer, clergyman, physicist, journalist*
Woodman, Grey Musgrave *psychiatrist*

**Clive**
Miller, Kenneth Edward *sociologist, educator*
Neis, Arthur Veral *healthcare and development company executive*

**Coralville**
Aly, Al S. *plastic surgeon*
Behlke, Mark Aaron *biotechnologist, research scientist*
Coulter, Charles Roy *lawyer*
Dong, Jun *mechanical engineer, researcher*

**Council Bluffs**
Alley, Mary Lou Vande Woude *retired medical/surgical nurse*
Bragg, MaryAnn *technical facilitator*
Davids, Roger Alex *food service executive*
Guttau, Michael K. *state agency administrator, banker*
Kurt, Johnny Thomas *music educator*
Lippoldt, Vaughn Arthur *retired music educator*
Peterson, Richard William *retired judge, retired lawyer*

**Creston**
Dillenburg, Carolyn Eva Lauer *retired secondary school educator*
Nurnberg, Roger C. *county official*

**Davenport**
Achs, Jack Horst *social studies educator*
Beguhn, Sandra E. *poet, writer*
Chowdhury, Ali Asraf *electrical engineer, researcher*
Dcamp, Charles Barton *music educator*
Dettmann, David Allen *lawyer*
Foster, James Franklin *professional sports management executive*
Gehl, Eugene Patrick *aerospace engineer*
Hood, James Michael *lawyer*
Hudson, Celeste Nutting *education educator, consultant, reading clinic administrator*
Juckem, Wilfred Philip *manufacturing executive*
MacNaughton, Neil Scot *nursing educator*
Meyer, Jane Mary *elementary school educator*
Nagle, John E. *accountant*
Pedersen, Karen Sue *electrical engineer*
Runge, Kay Kretschmar *library director*
Shammas, Nicolas Wahib *internist, cardiologist*
Sievert, Mary Elizabeth *small business owner, retired secondary school educator*
Skora, Susan Sundman *lawyer*
Wiese, Glenda Coppersmith *librarian, archivist*

**Decorah**
Farwell, Elwin D. *minister, consultant*
Kath, Ruth Robert *foreign language educator*
Kemp, H. Jane *librarian*
Lord-Dinan, Elizabeth Ann *nursing administrator, director*

**Des Moines**
Abel, Gregory E. *utility company executive*
Anderson, Eric Anthony *city manager*
Archer, Julian Pratt Waterman *history professor*
Bartschat, Klaus Richard Wilhelm *physics professor*
Begleiter, Martin David *law educator, consultant*
Begleiter, Ronni Frankel *lawyer*
Bergman, Bruce E. *municipal official*
Boettger, Nancy J. *state legislator*
Bremer, Celeste F. *judge*
Brickman, Kenneth Alan *state agency administrator*
Brooks, Roger Kay *insurance company executive*
Bukta, Polly *state representative*
Butler, Gayle *editor-in-chief*
Butz, John Newton *theater educator, actor*
Cady, Mark S. *state supreme court justice*
Carroll, Frank James *lawyer, educator*
Carter, James Harvey *state supreme court justice*
Charron, Joseph L. *bishop*
Clark, William Robert, Jr. *lawyer*
Claypool, David L. *lawyer*
Colloton, Steven M. *federal judge*
Conlin, Roxanne Barton *lawyer*
Corning, Joy Cole *retired state official*
Critelli, Nicholas (Nick) *lawyer, barrister*
Crook, Charles Samuel III *lawyer*
Culver, Chester J. (Chet Culver) *state official, educator*
Deluhery, Patrick John *state official*
Demorest, Allan Frederick *retired psychologist*
DeWulf Nickell, Karol *editor-in-chief*
Dukes, Vanessa Johnson *dietician*
Ellis, Mary Louise Helgeson *information technology company executive*
Fagg, George Gardner *federal judge*
Fisher, Thomas George *lawyer, media specialist*
Fisher, Thomas George, Jr. *lawyer*
Foxhoven, Jerry Ray *lawyer*
Gaines, Ruth Ann *secondary school educator*
Gartner, Michael Gay *editor, baseball executive, television executive*
Gersie, Michael H. *insurance company executive*
Godlasky, Thomas C. *insurance company executive*
Graham, Diane E. *newspaper editor*
Griswell, J. Barry *insurance company executive*
Gronstal, Tom *commissioner, bank executive*
Habib, Shahid *medical association administrator*
Haggerty, Joseph K. *lawyer, insurance company executive*
Hansell, Edgar Frank *lawyer*
Harris, Charles Elmer *retired lawyer*
Harris, K. David *senior state supreme court justice*
Hecht, Daryl L. *state supreme court justice*
Heiden, Cara *mortgage company executive*
Hill, Luther Lyons, Jr. *lawyer*
Holland, Brent Andrew *art educator, painter*
Huser, Geri D. *state official*
Jacobs, Libby Swanson *state official*
Jeffrey, Judy *school system administrator*
Jensen, Dick Leroy *lawyer*
Jochum, Pam *state representative*

Kalainov, Sam Charles *insurance company executive*
Kandris, Michael *trucking executive*
Kelley, Bruce Gunn *insurance company executive, lawyer*
Kerr, William T. *publishing executive, broadcasting executive*
Koehn, William James *lawyer*
Kramer, Mary Elizabeth *ambassador, former state legislator*
Lacy, Stephen M. *publishing and broadcasting executive*
Landwehr, Amy Marie *lawyer*
Larson, Jerry Leroy *state supreme court justice*
Leach, Dave Francis *editor, musician*
Malm, Richard Allan *lawyer*
Marsh, Wendy K. *pharmacist, lawyer*
Martens, Harvey Arthur *retired government worker, academic administrator*
Maxwell, David E. *academic executive, educator*
McGivern, Arthur A. *former state supreme court chief justice*
McGuire-Riggs, Sheila *Democratic party chairman*
Miller, Thomas J. *state attorney general*
Mitchell, Stuart *medical entomologist, consulting physician*
Myers, Mary Kathleen *publishing executive*
Nelson, Charlotte Bowers *public administrator*
Nickerson, Don C. *lawyer, retired prosecutor, judge*
Norris, Glenn L. *lawyer*
Olds, John Ward *internist*
Pappajohn, John G. *venture capitalist*
Paterik, Frances Sue *secondary school educator, actress*
Peddicord, Roland Dale *lawyer*
Pederson, Sally *lieutenant governor*
Power, Joseph Edward *lawyer*
Quirmbach, Herman Charles *economics professor*
Ragan, Amanda *state senator*
Reece, Maynard Fred *artist, writer*
Rosen, Matthew Stephen *botanist, consultant*
Scholten, Gary P. *finance company executive*
Shaff, Karen E. *lawyer, insurance company executive*
Shors, John Dennis *lawyer*
Simmons, Suzan *psychologist*
Simpson, Lyle Lee *lawyer*
Smith, Diana Marie *business educator*
Sokol, David L. *energy services provider company executive*
Song, Joseph *pathologist, educator*
Stier, Mary P. *publishing executive*
Streit, Michael J. *state supreme court justice*
Szymoniak, Elaine Eisfelder *retired state senator*
Ternus, Marsha K. *state supreme court chief justice*
Thompson, Jerome Lafayette *curator*
Van Zante, Shirley M(ae) *magazine editor*
Vaughan, Therese Michele *insurance educator*
Vietor, Harold Duane *federal judge*
Vilsack, Thomas *governor*
Wallace, Samuel Taylor *health system administrator*
Walters, Ross A. *federal judge*
Wattleworth, Roberta Ann *physician*
Webb, Mary Christine *reading recovery educator, in-class reading specialist*
Wharton, John Michael *lawyer*
Whitaker, Matthew George *prosecutor*
Wiggins, David Stewart *state supreme court justice*
Williams, Carl Chanson *insurance company executive*
Witke, David Rodney *retired newspaper editor, consultant*
Woehler, Joel Lee *real estate asset manager*
Wolfe, Charles Robert *judge*

**Dubuque**
Barker, Barbara Yvonne *nursing home administrator*
Barland, Charles John *music educator*
Beardsley, Shelley J. *science educator*
Burkhart, John Ernest *minister, theology studies educator*
Crahan, Jack Bertsch *retired manufacturing executive*
Frommelt, Molly Kathleen *nursing educator*
Hammer, David Lindley *lawyer, writer*
Hanus, Jerome George *archbishop*
Haugen, Jane S. *elementary school educator*
Lickteig, Mary Joan *elementary school educator*
Patterson, David *music educator*
Toale, Thomas Edward *school system administrator, minister*
Tully, Thomas Alois *building materials executive, consultant, educator*

**Eagle Grove**
Sundberg, Gordon Neil *retired mathematics and computer sciences instructor*

**Eldridge**
Downing, Paul R. *sports science educator*

**Emmetsburg**
Farnsworth, Steven Robert *safety engineer*

**Epworth**
Boice, Daniel Gene *college librarian*

**Fairfield**
Hagelin, John Samuel *political organization administrator, theoretical physicist*
Rogers, Benjamin Franklin *retired history professor*

**Fayette**
Barker, Richard Alexander *organizational psychologist*

**Forest City**
Biggs, Douglas Lee *historian, educator*
Tillman, Joseph Edward *elementary school educator*

**Fort Dodge**
Cassady, Daniel Bennet *music educator*
Kitterman, Ralph Donald *retired member of clergy*

**Fort Madison**
Moon, Julie Ann *elementary school educator*

**Glenwood**
Campbell, William Edward *mental hospital administrator*

**Grinnell**
Adelberg, Arnold Melvin *mathematics professor, researcher*
Fyffe, Richard Coleman *librarian*
Kaiser, Daniel Hugh *historian, educator*
Kintner, Philip L. *history professor*
McKee, Christopher Fulton *librarian, historian, educator*
Michaels, Jennifer Tonks *foreign language educator*
Mitchell, Orlan E. *clergyman, academic administrator*
Osgood, Russell King *academic administrator*
Swartz, James Edward *chemistry professor, educator, dean*
Walker, Waldo Sylvester *biologist, educator, academic administrator*

**Grundy Center**
Kliebenstein, Don *retired lawyer*

**Harlan**
Salvo, J. C. *lawyer*
Sondag, Mary Jo *elementary school educator, education administrator*

**Holstein**
Soseman, Eleanor Douglass *volunteer*

**Holy Cross**
Ross, Christine Marie *media coordinator, small business owner, disc jockey, educator*

**Hubbard**
Wessel, Gregory James *music educator*

**Humboldt**
Dodgen, John N. *manufacturing executive*

**Ida Grove**
Snell, Bruce M., Jr. *retired judge*

**Indianola**
Croskery, Virginia *music educator, vocalist*
Dyer, Cynthia Myers *school librarian, archivist*
Kazmerzak, Richard Anthony *art educator*
Larsen, Robert LeRoy *artistic director*
Mace, Jerilee Marie *performing arts association administrator*
Poulsen, James Viggo III *music educator, composer*

**Iowa City**
Abboud, Francois Mitry *physician, educator*
Adams, Brian David *orthopaedic surgeon, educator*
Addis, Laird Clark, Jr. *philosopher, educator, musician*
Afifi, Adel Kassim *physician*
Albrecht, William Price *economist, educator, government official*
Anderson, Rachel L. *healthcare educator, researcher*
Andreasen, Nancy Coover *psychiatrist, educator, neuroscientist*
Apicella, Michael Allen *microbiologist, educator*
Aspel, Paulene Violette *retired language educator*
Baker, Nancy L. *university librarian, educator*
Baker, Richard Graves *geologist, educator, palynologist*
Barkan, Joel David *political science professor*
Barrera, Susan Cristina *secondary school educator*
Beaver, Hilary A. *medical educator, ophthalmologist*
Bedell, George Noble *internist, educator*
Bell, Marvin Hartley *poet, language educator*
Bentz, Dale Monroe *retired librarian*
Berg, Mary Jaylene *pharmacy educator, researcher*
Bishara, Samir Edward *orthodontist*
Bognar, Matthew *statistician, educator*
Bonfield, Arthur Earl *lawyer, educator*
Bowlsby, Bob *athletic director*
Boyd, Willard Lee *academic administrator, educator, lawyer, museum director*
Bozeman, Theodore D. *religion educator*
Brennan, Robert Lawrence *educational director, psychometrician*
Broffitt, James Drake *statistician, educator*
Buckwalter, Joseph Addison *orthopedic surgeon, educator*
Buckwalter, Kathleen C. *academic administrator, educator*
Burns, C(harles) Patrick *hematologist, oncologist*
Burton, Donald Joseph *chemistry professor*
Campbell, Kevin Peter *physiology and biophysics educator*
Clifton, James Albert *physician, educator*
Cogan, Nancy Adams *chaplain, poet*
Collins, Daniel W. *accountant, educator*
Conway, Thomas William *biochemist, educator*
Cooper, Reginald Rudyard *orthopedic surgeon, educator*
Craft-Rosenberg, Martha Jane *nursing educator, researcher*
Densen, Paul Maximillian *retired health facility administrator*
Donelson, John Everett *biochemistry professor, molecular biologist*
Dove, Edwin L. *engineering educator*
Downer, Robert Nelson *lawyer*
Dreher, Melanie Creagan *dean, nursing educator*
Duerlinger, James Peter *philosopher, educator*
Duff, Kevin *neuropsychologist, psychiatry professor*
Eckstein, John William *internist, educator, retired dean*
Ertl, Wolfgang *German language and literature educator*
Feldt, Leonard Samuel *academic administrator, educator*
Fellows, Robert Ellis *medical educator, researcher*
Ferentz, Kirk *college football coach*

Fethke, Gary C. *economics professor, academic administrator*
Field, Robert W. *epidemiologist, health physicist, educator*
Folsom, Lowell Edwin *language educator*
Fuller, John Williams *economics professor*
Galask, Rudolph Peter *obstetrician, gynecologist*
Gantz, Bruce Jay *otolaryngologist, educator*
Gelfand, Lawrence Emerson *historian, educator*
Geweke, John Frederick *economics professor*
Gittler, Josephine *law educator*
Gray, George Trumon *test development professional*
Green, Peter Morris *classics educator, writer, translator*
Gronbeck, Bruce Elliot *communications educator*
Grose, Charles Frederick *pediatrician, epidemiologist*
Gurnett, Donald Alfred *physics professor*
Hammond, Harold Logan *oral and maxillofacial pathologist, educator*
Hartz, Arthur J. *medical researcher*
Hausler, William John, Jr. *microbiologist, educator, public health service officer*
Hawley, Ellis Wayne *historian, educator*
Heistad, Donald Dean *cardiologist*
Herman, Ronald Alton *pharmacokineticist, educator*
Hines, Norman William *law educator, retired dean*
Hogan, Michael *academic administrator*
Hogg, Robert Vincent, Jr. *mathematical statistician, educator*
Holland, Charles Joseph *lawyer*
Husted, Russell Forest *research scientist*
Huttner, Sidney Frederick *librarian*
Iannettoni, Mark David *thoracic surgeon, department chairman*
Ingram, Beth F. *academic administrator*
Johnsen, David C. *dean, dental educator*
Johnson, Nicholas *writer, lawyer, educator*
Jones, Carolyn *dean, law educator*
Jorgensen, Palle E.T. *mathematician, educator*
Katen-Bahensky, Donna *health facility administrator*
Kennedy, Colleen M. *medical educator*
Kerber, Linda Kaufman *historian, educator*
Kerber, Richard E. *cardiologist*
Kessel, Richard Glen *zoology educator*
Kim, Chong Lim *political science professor*
Kisker, Carl Thomas *pediatrician, educator*
Konety, Badrinath R. *surgeon, researcher*
Kottick, Edward Leon *musician, educator*
Kurtz, Alice Kaufman *elementary school educator*
Kurtz, Sheldon Francis *lawyer, educator*
Lamping, Kathryn G. *medical educator, medical researcher*
Lasansky, Mauricio *artist*
Lauer, Ronald Martin *pediatric cardiologist, researcher*
Lim, Ramon (Khe-Siong Lim) *neuroscience educator, researcher*
Loening-Baucke, Vera *pediatrician, educator*
Loewenberg, Gerhard *political science professor*
Long, John Paul *pharmacologist, educator*
Marshall, Jeffrey Scott *mechanical engineer, educator*
Mason, Edward Eaton *surgeon*
Mather, Roger Frederick *retired music educator, writer*
Maxson, Linda Ellen *biologist, educator*
McCartney, David Farnham *archivist, educator*
Medh, Jheem D. *medical educator, biochemist, researcher*
Merrill, Christopher Lyall *writer*
Miller, Dwight Merrick *archivist, historian*
Miller, Jordan D. *physiologist*
Mills, Margaret H. *linguist*
Montgomery, Rex *biochemist, educator*
Moore, Brian Edward *mathematics professor*
Morriss, Frank Howard, Jr. *pediatrics educator*
Muir, Ruth Brooks *alcohol/drug abuse services professional, consultant*
Mullan, Brian *medical educator*
Mullins, Robert F. *cell biologist*
Murray, Jeffrey C. *medical educator, pediatrician*
Myers, Virginia Anne *art educator*
Nathan, Peter E. *psychologist, educator*
Nelson, Herbert Leroy *psychiatrist*
Nesbitt, John Arthur *recreational therapist, writer, educator, researcher*
Neumann, Roy Covert *architect*
Niebyl, Jennifer Robinson *obstetrician, gynecologist, educator*
Olin, William Harold *orthodontist, educator*
Olshansky, Brian *internal medicine and cardiology educator, researcher, physician*
Packer, ZZ (Zuwena) *writer, literature educator*
Park, Joon Bu *biomedical engineer, researcher, educator*
Patel, Virendra Chaturbhai *mechanical engineer, educator*
Peloso, Paul Michael *medical educator*
Pessin, Jeffrey E. *physiology educator*
Pierce, Jennifer Burek *library and information scientist*
Plapp, Bryce Vernon *biochemistry educator*
Ponseti, Ignacio Vives *orthopaedic surgery educator*
Porter, Horace Anthony *literature educator, writer*
Preucil, Doris Bogen *music educator*
Prisinzano, Thomas Edward *chemistry professor, researcher*
Raeburn, John Hay *language educator*
Richerson, Hal Bates *internist, allergist, immunologist, educator*
Riesz, Peter Charles *marketing educator, consultant*
Robertson, Timothy Joel *statistician, educator*
Robillard, Jean Eugene *dean, educator*
Roe, Gerald Bruce *director, writer*
Schmidt, Julius *sculptor*
Scott, John Beldon *art history educator, writer*
Sheffield, Val C. *medical geneticist*
Siebert, Calvin D. *economist, educator*
Simon, J. Richard (Jennings Richard Simon) *psychologist, educator*
Skinstad, Anne Helene *psychologist, researcher*
Snyder, Peter M. *medical educator, medical researcher*
Solbrig, Ingeborg Hildegard *literature educator, writer*

Sonka, Milan *electrical and computer engineering educator*
Spriestersbach, Duane Caryl *academic administrator, speech pathology/audiology services professional, educator*
Stay, Barbara *zoologist, educator*
Stein, Robert A. *writer, educator, military officer*
Strauss, John Steinert *dermatologist, educator*
Swensen, Cole *poet, educator*
Titze, Ingo Roland *physics professor*
Tomkovicz, James Joseph *law educator*
Tsalikian, Eva *physician, educator*
Van Gilder, John Corley *neurosurgeon, educator*
Wasserman, Edward Arnold *psychology professor*
Weinberger, Miles M. *pediatrician, educator*
Weintraub, Neal L. *medical educator, cardiologist*
Welsh, Michael James *medical educator, biophysicist, educator*
Williams, Richard Dwayne *physician, educator, urologist*
Wing, Adrien Katherine *law educator*
Wunder, Charles C(ooper) *physiologist, biophysicist, educator*
Wurster, Dale Erwin *pharmacist, educator, retired dean*
Yang, Jingzhou *engineer, educator*
Young, Laura Elizabeth *artist*
Ziegler, Ekhard Erich *pediatrics educator*

**Jefferson**
Pauley, James Leroy, Jr. *retired lawyer*

**Johnston**
Hattel, Carson Matthew *elementary school educator*
Poppe, Pamela J. *accountant*

**Kellogg**
Anderson, Dale C. *state agency professional, travel consultant*

**Keokuk**
Hoffman, James Paul *lawyer*
Wendt, David Allen *literature and language educator*

**Le Grand**
Ryan, Deloris Kay *elementary school educator*

**Le Mars**
Hallberg, Theodore Forest *music educator*
Murphy, Patrick Neil *lawyer*
Niebuhr, Paul David *music educator*
Rebstock, Theodore Lynn *chemist, educator, retired research scientist*

**Leon**
Miller, Eleanora Genevieve *freelance/self-employed poet*

**Madrid**
Handy, Richard Lincoln *civil engineer, educator*

**Mapleton**
Stodola, Steven James *science educator*

**Maquoketa**
Tubbs, Edward Lane *banker*

**Marion**
Pate, Paul Danny *mayor*
Ritchie, Ronald Thomas *history educator*

**Marshalltown**
Bousum, Julie Kaye *art educator*
Brennecke, Allen Eugene *lawyer*
Cassidy, Eugene Patrick *pathologist*
Price, Bernice Irene *retired elementary school educator*
Thomas, David Llewellyn *physician*
Weidenaar, Bradley William *literature and language educator*

**Mason City**
Backlin, William Wayne *music educator, composer*
Collison, Jim *publishing executive*
Rodamaker, Marti Tomson *bank executive*
Slaven, Timothy William *theater educator, set designer*

**Milford**
Fontaine, Sue (Jeane Fontaine) *public relations professional*

**Monticello**
Balster, Barbara Ann *elementary school educator*

**Mount Pleasant**
Brereton, Todd Richard *history professor*
Crane, Frederick Baron *retired music educator*
Edwards, Jason Ray *music educator, musician*
Larsen, Christopher Svend *music educator*

**Mount Vernon**
Will, Frederic *university administrator, writer*

**Moville**
Baker, Kent Alfred *broadcasting executive, publishing company executive*

**Muscatine**
Askren, Stan A. *manufacturing executive*
Johnson, James I. *lawyer*
Mowl, Linda *special education educator*
Nepple, James Anthony *lawyer*
Phillips, Janet K. *music educator*
Stanley, Richard Holt *consulting engineer*
Thomopulos, Gregs G. *consulting engineering company executive*

**Nevada**
Countryman, Dayton Wendell *lawyer*

**New Hampton**
Herman, Claudia Bernice *elementary school educator*

**Newton**
Brostrom, Dennis Alan *music educator*
Moore, George C. *manufacturing executive*

Padilla, Sue Ann *librarian*
Scholten, Roger Keith *lawyer*
Tisdale, Thomas J. *social studies educator*
Ward, Doree Maxine *secondary school educator*

**North Liberty**
Crowner, Dee Kay *library administrator*

**Oelwein**
Flaucher-Falck, Velma Ruth *retired special education educator*
McFarlane, Beth Lucetta Troester *retired mayor*

**Ogden**
Bardole, Richard Allen *music educator*

**Okoboji**
Pearson, Gerald Leon *food products executive*

**Osceola**
Reynoldson, Walter Ward *retired judge, lawyer*

**Oskaloosa**
Burrow, Paul Irving *secondary school educator*
Mangold, Archie Wayne, II, *insurance agent*
Porter, David Lindsey *history and political science professor, writer*

**Ottumwa**
Krafka, Mary Baird *lawyer*
Lang, Janelle J. *accountant*
Lechner, Jane Ann *mathematics educator*
Newquist, Judy Lynne Roos *elementary school educator, education educator*
Stannard, Natalie Marie *secondary school educator*
Vasconez, Dennis Cornelius *secondary school educator, voice educator*
Wormhoudt, Pearl Shinn *voice educator, writer*

**Panora**
Hartman, James Austin *retired geologist*

**Parkersburg**
Schmitz, Marianina Alice *literature and language educator*

**Pella**
Den Adel, Raymond Lee *classics educator*
Dout, Anne Jacqueline *manufacturing and sales company executive*
Eastin, Matthew David *science educator*
Hartman, Mark LeRoy *music educator, musician*
Muether, Charles Alexander *writer, educator*

**Pleasant Valley**
Myatt, William Howard *theater educator, director, actor*

**Red Oak**
Higdon, Hal *sportswriter*
Stoner, Leonard D. *automotive parts company executive*

**Riverside**
Rew, Ken E. *physical education educator, healthcare educator, coach*

**Rock Valley**
Bulthuis, Sidney Aaron *secondary school educator*
Ortman, Don L. *principal*

**Rockwell City**
Erkenbrack, Lori Jean *county official*

**Seymour**
Horton, Laura Kaye *special education educator*

**Sheffield**
VanHorn, Bradley Kent *musician*

**Sheldon**
Gifford, Carla J. *education educator*
St. Clair, Clifford Mark *music educator*

**Sioux Center**
De Boer, Douglas F. *engineering educator*

**Sioux City**
Andersen, Leonard Christian *former state legislator, real estate investor*
Ayi, Bertha Serwa *infectious disease specialist, internist*
Bennett, Michael L. *agricultural products executive*
Doyle, Donald Vincent *retired state legislator, lawyer*
Fredregill, Alan *lawyer*
Hassenger, James Michael *writer, retired small business owner*
Kelly, Mary Elizabeth Wiese *medical educator*
Mack, Thomas Russell *foundation administrator, management consultant*
Mayne, Wiley Edward *lawyer*
Mounts, Nancy *secondary school educator*
O'Brien, Donald Eugene *federal judge*
Peterson, Delaine Charles *lawyer, bank executive*
Rants, Carolyn Jean *academic administrator, educator*
Waller, Ephraim Everett *retired association executive*
Young, Janet Marie *secondary school educator*

**Sioux Rapids**
Jarvis, Steve Lee *religious studies educator, coach*

**Spencer**
Lemke, Alan James *environmental specialist*

**Spirit Lake**
Quaday-Gray, Ailene Diann *retired speech pathology/audiology services professional*

**Springville**
Beals, Karen Marie Downey *pastor*

**Storm Lake**
Lenzmeier, Brian A. *biology professor, researcher*

**Sully**
Fopma, Mary Louise *music educator*

**Tipton**
Farwell, Walter Maurice *vocalist, educator*

**Toddville**
Hazeltine, Gerald Lester *food products executive*

**Urbandale**
Hoyt, Kenneth Boyd *education educator, writer*

**Vinton**
Ramsey, Ardeth Jane *retired elementary school educator*

**Walford**
Brooks, Debra L. *healthcare executive, neuromuscular therapist*

**Washington**
Buchholz, Lee William (Leroy William Buchholz) *retired music educator*

**Waterloo**
Green, Nancy Loughridge *publishing executive*
Kober, Arletta Refshauge (Mrs. Kay L. Kober) *supervisor*
Mathys, Gordon D. *accountant, educator*
Waters, Ronald W. *theology studies educator, church administrator, pastor*

**Waverly**
Brunkhorst, Robert John *computer programmer, analyst*
Rose, Mary Mabel *retired elementary school educator*

**West Bend**
Wuebker, Colleen Marie *retired librarian*

**West Branch**
Mather, Mildred Eunice *retired archivist*
Walch, Timothy George *library director*

**West Burlington**
Sharp, Joan Diane *biology professor*
Trousil, Hans Kurt *mayor*

**West Des Moines**
Alberts, Marion Edward *retired physician*
Bakari, Rosenna *educational psychology professor, consultant*
Conner, William Bruce *facilty engineer*
Cortese, Joseph Samuel, II, *lawyer*
Dooley, Donald John *retired publishing executive*
Henderson, Jason Craig *financial advisor*
Hockenberg, Harlan David *lawyer*
Lynch, David William *physicist, retired educator*
Marshall, Russell Frank *consulting company executive*
Matthews, Alexander *health facility administrator*
McEnroe, Michael Louis *lawyer*
Pearson, Ronald Dale *retail food stores corporation executive*
Pomerantz, Marvin Alvin *manufacturing executive*
Stines, Fred, Jr. *publisher*
Thornton, John Edwin *social studies educator*
Tully, Robert Gerard *lawyer*

**Wever**
Hardy, Julia Irene *elementary school educator*

**Windsor Heights**
Beadel, Stephen Jay *author*

## KANSAS

**Abilene**
Britt, Ronald Leroy *retired manufacturing company executive*
Holt, Dan *library director*

**Andover**
Whiteside, Mel L. *information technology manager, educator, small business owner*

**Arkansas City**
Bruton, Rebecca Ann *mayor, commissioner*

**Atchison**
Jackson, Dan Adrian *language educator*
Lane, Elizabeth Ann *genealogist, researcher*

**Baldwin City**
Baker, Margaret Moore-Fritz *retired school librarian, retired humanities educator*
Long, Patricia N. *academic administrator*
Rosenthal, Dan *retired director*

**Basehor**
Hart, Paul Vincent, Jr. *emergency and acute care physician, inventor*

**Baxter Springs**
Whiteley, Henry Howard *religious studies educator, minister*

**Bern**
Dassel-Stuke, Donna Jane *psychologist, educator*

**Bucyrus**
Hoffman, John Raymond *lawyer*

**Burr Oak**
Underwood, Deanna Kay *librarian*

**Caney**
Wilmoth, Marsha Hope *elementary school educator*

**Chanute**
Dillard, Dean Innes *English language educator, academic administrator*
Smith, David *music educator*

**Chetopa**
Reid, William R. *agricultural studies educator*

**Claflin**
Burmeister, Paul Frederick *farmer*

**Clay Center**
Braden, James Dale *former state legislator*

**Clearwater**
Taverner, Pamela Johnson *secondary school educator*

**Clifton**
Compton, Doris Martha *lay worker*

**Coffeyville**
DeRosa, Michael L. *elementary school educator, artist*
Garner, Jim D. *state official, lawyer*
Hawley, Raymond Glen *pathologist*
Partridge, Sharon Sue *secondary school educator*

**Colby**
Baldwin, Irene S. *hotel executive, real estate developer*
McVay, Micheal Ray *social sciences educator, department chairman*
Morrison, James Frank *optometrist, state legislator*

**Coldwater**
Adams, Elizabeth Herrington *banker*

**Concordia**
Fowler, Wayne Lewis, Sr. *internist*

**Copeland**
Birney, Walter Leroy *religious administrator*

**Cottonwood Falls**
Dodez, Diane M. *principal*

**De Soto**
Strubbe, Thomas R. *insurance industry executive*

**Derby**
Clark, Susan Matthews *psychologist*

**Dighton**
Stanley, Ellen May *historian, consultant*

**Dodge City**
Sewell, Carol Ann *artist*

**El Dorado**
Garber, Ronald Lee *music educator*

**Emporia**
Alshare, Khaled A. *information systems educator*
Bartruff, Jim *theater educator, director*
Emerson, Marion Preston *mathematics professor*
Fowler, Barbara J. *elementary school educator*
Lovett, Christopher C. *history professor, consultant*
Mallein, Darla J. *social studies educator*
Sundberg, Marshall David *biology professor*
Wenger, James L. *education educator*

**Enterprise**
Wickman, John Edward *librarian, historian*

**Eskridge**
Taylor, Russell Benton *mining executive*

**Eudora**
Miller, David Groff *insurance agent*

**Eureka**
Ditko, Pamela Ann *physical education educator, coach*

**Fort Leavenworth**
Anderson, David Allen *military officer, educator*
Berlin, Robert Harry *military studies educator*
Cupp, Orville Shawn *military officer*
King, Curtis Steeble *history professor*
Mullis, Tony Randall *social studies educator*
Petraeus, David Howell *career military officer*
Wilhelm, Gary Bretz *physician*

**Frontenac**
Wilson, Donald Wallin *academic administrator, communications educator*

**Garden City**
Alam, A.N.M. Mahbub Ul *engineer, educator*
Hauschild, Barbara A. *principal*
Loyd, Ward Eugene *lawyer, state legislator*
Thomas, Gregory Hall *psychology professor*
Tidwell, Russell Murray *secondary school educator*
Wright, J. Clayton *music educator*

**Garden Plain**
Stovall, Carla Jo *former state attorney general*

**Gaylord**
Whelchel, Butch E. *agricultural studies educator*

**Gem**
Ziegelmeier, Patricia Kay *music educator, executive secretary*

**Great Bend**
Gaunt, Glenna Sue *voice educator*
Rittenhouse, Nancy Carol *elementary school educator*

**Halstead**
Bender, Jack Sinclair III *retired lawyer*
Orr, Jim (James D. Orr) *editor, writer, publishing executive*

**Hays**
Budig, Jeanette *special education educator*
Bustos, Rudolph R. *health facility administrator*
Caprez, Judith V. *social worker, director*
Coyne, Patrick Ivan *physiological ecologist*
Harbin, Calvin Edward *retired educator*
Kuksi, Kris M. *artist*
Purvis, Karen R. *sanitary engineer*

## Hillsboro

Kyle, Richard Granville *history professor, religion educator*

## Holton

Cripe, Elizabeth Ann (Betty Cripe) *investment company executive*

## Horton

Radford, Virginia Rodriguez *retired secondary school educator, librarian*

## Hoyt

Morris, Sandra N. *elementary school educator*

## Hugoton

Kelling, Sherry Lee *music educator, interior designer, educator*

## Humboldt

Finney, Paul *acupuncturist, Chinese herbologist, entrepreneur*

## Hutchinson

Baumer, Beverly Belle *journalist*
Brewer, William Thomas *theater educator, theater director*
Buchanan, Bruce *publishing executive*
Buzbee, Richard Edgar *retired newspaper editor*
Crater, Timothy Andrews *internist*
Davis, Mary Elizabeth *speech pathologist, educator, counselor*
Dick, Harold Latham *manufacturing executive*
Gamber, Kenneth M. *mathematics professor, farmer*
Hayes, John Francis *lawyer*
Kerr, Dave *state official, marketing professional*
O'Neal, Michael Ralph *state legislator, lawyer*
Swearer, William Brooks *lawyer*
Widener, Charlene *theater director, educator*

## Independence

Wright, Tami LaDonna *pre-school educator*

## Iola

Lynn, Emerson Elwood, Jr. *retired newspaper editor/publisher*
Strickler, Ivan K. *dairy farmer*
Tebbets, Gary Duane *music educator*

## Junction City

Heesch, Marcella B. *art educator*
Werts, Merrill Harmon *retired management consultant*

## Kansas City

Aljitawi, Omar Salah *hematologist, oncologist*
Anderson, Harrison Clarke *pathologist, educator, biomedical researcher*
Arakawa, Kasumi *physician, educator*
Atkinson, Barbara F. *dean, medical educator, executive vice chancellor*
Baska, James Louis *wholesale grocery company executive*
Benien, Ruth Marie *lawyer*
Burke, Thomas Richard *community college administrator*
Clifton, Thomas E. *academic administrator, minister*
Damjanov, Ivan *pathologist, educator*
Drake, Kenneth David *geologist*
Dunn, Marvin Irvin *physician*
Gattone, Vincent Henry, II, *medical researcher, anatomist*
Godwin, Harold Norman *pharmacist, educator*
Grantham, Jared James *nephrologist, educator*
Hudson, Robert Paul *medical educator*
Huet, Raul *psychiatrist*
Jerome, Norge Winifred *nutritionist, anthropologist, educator*
Johnson, Joy Ann *diagnostic radiologist*
Jones, Charles W. *labor union executive*
Keleher, James P. *bishop*
Krantz, Kermit Edward *obstetrician, department chairman*
Kriet, J. David *medical educator*
Lawrence, Walter Thomas *plastic surgeon*
Lee, Kyo Rak *radiologist, educator*
Lungstrum, John W. *federal judge*
McCallum, Richard Warwick *medical researcher, clinician, educator*
Miller, Karen L. *dean, nursing educator*
Mohn, Melvin Paul *anatomist, educator*
Naumann, Joseph F. *archbishop*
Olofson, Tom William *technology company executive*
Penick, Elizabeth C. *psychologist*
Rawitch, Allen Barry *medical educator, academic administrator*
Sanders-Hall, Patricia E. *health facility administrator*
Schloerb, Paul Richard *surgeon, educator*
Sciolaro, Charles Michael *cardiothoracic and vascular surgeon*
Smarr, Tracy Jean *psychologist*
Suzuki, Tsuneo *molecular immunologist*
Swint-Kruse, Liskin *biochemist, educator*
Vacek, James *cardiologist*
Voogt, James Leonard *medical educator*
Vratil, Kathryn Hoefer *federal judge*
Warne, Alan M. *adult education educator, consultant*
Waxse, David John *judge*
Ziegler, Dewey Kiper *neurologist, educator*

## Lansing

Rawlings, Gregory Owen *science educator, consultant*

## Lawrence

Alexander, John Thorndike *historian, educator*
Ammar, Raymond George *physicist, researcher*
Angino, Ernest Edward *retired geology educator, retired engineering educator*
Armitage, Kenneth Barclay *retired biology professor*
Barnett, William Arnold *economics professor*
Beedles, William LeRoy *finance educator, financial consultant*

Benjamin, Bezaleel Solomon *architectural engineer, educator*
Berry, James Lee *retired military educator*
Boyd, Beverly *English literature educator*
Brejcha, Vernon L. *artist, art educator*
Briscoe, Mary Beck *federal judge*
Buck, Henry William, Jr. *obstetrician, gynecologist*
Byers, George William *retired entomology educator*
Casad, Robert Clair *legal educator*
Castle, Joyce *mezzo soprano*
Cienciala, Anna Maria *history professor*
Conard, John Joseph *finance company executive*
Crowe, William Joseph *librarian*
Darwin, David *engineering educator, consultant*
Dickinson, William Boyd, Jr. *media consultant*
Dooley, Patrick John *graphic designer, design educator*
Dreschhoff, Gisela Auguste Marie *physicist, researcher*
Eldredge, Charles Child III *art history educator*
Enos, Paul *geologist, educator*
Frederickson, Horace George *retired academic administrator, humanities educator*
Gaumer Erickson, Amy Sue *special education educator*
Gerhard, Lee Clarence *geologist, educator*
Grabow, Stephen Harris *architecture educator*
Green, Don Wesley *chemical and petroleum engineering educator*
Greenfield, Michael Dennis *biology educator, researcher*
Gunn, James Edwin *language educator*
Hale, Richard Lee *magazine editor*
Hardy, Saralyn Reece *museum director*
Haricombe, Lorraine *library director, dean*
Harmony, Marlin Dale *chemistry professor*
Heller, Francis Howard *retired political science professor, retired law educator*
Hemenway, Robert E. *academic administrator, language educator*
Hilding, Jerel Lee *music and dance educator, retired dancer*
Himmelberg, Charles John III *mathematics professor, researcher*
Hoeflich, Michael Harlan *law educator, department chairman*
Johnson, Wallace Stephen, Jr. *Asian languages educator*
Johnston, Richard Fourness *biologist, educator*
Kaesler, Roger L. *paleontologist, educator*
Karcz, Andrzej *literature educator*
Landgrebe, John Allan *chemistry professor*
Lariviere, Richard Wilfred *academic administrator, educator*
Lerner, David Evan *mathematician*
Li, Chu-Tsing *art historian, educator*
Lichtwardt, Robert William *mycologist*
Locke, Carl Edwin, Jr. *academic administrator, engineer, educator*
McAllister, Stephen Robert *dean, law educator*
Mc Coin, John Mack *social worker*
McDiarmid, Diane *education educator, researcher*
McGowan, Rodger Alan *administrative assistant*
Merriam, Daniel F(rancis) *geologist*
Miller, Don Robert *surgeon, educator*
Mitscher, Lester Allen *chemist, educator*
Moore, Richard Kerr *electrical engineering educator*
Muirhead, Vincent Uriel *retired aerospace engineer*
Pasik-Duncan, Bozenna Janina *mathematics professor, researcher*
Peterson, Nancy *special education educator*
Pozdro, John Walter *retired music educator, composer*
Ralston, John Peter *theoretical physicist, educator*
Roskam, Jan *aerospace engineer*
Rowland, James Richard *electrical engineering educator*
Saul, Norman Eugene *historian, educator*
Schoeck, Richard J. *English and humanities scholar, poet*
Shankel, Delbert Merrill *microbiologist, biologist, educator*
Simons, Dolph Collins, Jr. *publishing executive, editor*
Smith, Henry Heller *music educator, director*
Stella, Valentino John *chemistry professor*
Stull, Donald David *anthropologist, educator*
Tacha, Deanell Reece *federal judge*
Tsubaki, Andrew Takahisa *theater director, educator*
Turnbull, Ann Patterson *special education educator, consultant, research director*
Turnbull, H. Rutherford III *lawyer, educator*
Tuttle, William McCullough, Jr. *history professor*
Wiechert, Allen LeRoy *educational association administrator*
Williams, Sheryl Katheryn *archivist, librarian*
Winter, Winton Allen, Jr. *lawyer, state legislator*
Woelfel, James Warren *philosophy and humanities educator*
Worth, George John *retired English literature educator*

## Leavenworth

Crow, Martha Ellen *lawyer*
Crow, Michael P. *lawyer*

## Leawood

Devlin, James Richard *lawyer*
Dykes, Archie Reece *finance company executive*
Garwood, Julie *writer*
Gray, Thomas Alva, Jr. *writer, minister, retired protective services official*
Hartzler, Geoffrey Oliver *retired cardiologist*
Ivey, Donald James *historian, archivist*
Joslin, Janine Elizabeth *preservationist, consultant*
Karmeier, Delbert Fred *engineer, consultant, realtor*
King, Barbara Sackheim *travel company executive*
Talley, Melvin Gary *academic administrator*
Terry, Robert Brooks *food products executive, lawyer*
White, Shanon Kathleen *accountant, consultant*

## Lenexa

Ascher, James John *pharmaceutical executive*
Capps, Jack Lee *military officer, educator*

Russo, Guy J. *financial services company executive*
Warenskjold, Dorothy *singer, educator*
Williams, Larry R. *music educator*

## Liberal

Hicks, Linda Reona *elementary school educator*
Richard, Loren Dru *bank executive*
Smothermon, Reba Maxine *elementary school educator*

## Lincoln

Crangle, Robert D. *lawyer, management consultant, entrepreneur*

## Lindsborg

Fisk, Irwin Wesley *financial investigator*
Mahraun, Daniel Allen *musician, director*

## Linwood

Coatney, Sharon Ann *librarian, educator, editor*

## Manhattan

Babcock, Michael Ward *economics professor*
Barkley, Andrew Paul *economics professor*
Benton, Stephen LeRoy *psychology professor, researcher*
Bhadriraju, Subramanyam Venkata *entomologist, consultant*
Coffman, James Richard *academic administrator, veterinarian, educator*
Das, Sanjoy *engineering educator, researcher*
Dissanayake, Sunanda *engineering educator*
Durkee, William Robert *retired internist*
Erickson, Howard Hugh *veterinarian, physiology educator*
Eyman, Susanne Kohn *clinical psychologist*
Foerster, Bernd *architecture educator*
Gillispie, Harold Leon *minister*
Hagen, Lawrence Jacob *agricultural engineer*
Hammaker, Robert Michael *chemist, educator*
Higham, Robin *historian, editor, publisher*
Jiang, Hongxing *physics professor, researcher*
Johnson, William Howard *retired agricultural engineer, retired educator*
Kirkham, M. B. *plant physiologist, educator*
Klabunde, Kenneth J. *chemistry professor, researcher*
Kren, Margo *artist, educator*
Krysko, Michael Alexander *history professor*
Le, Anh-Thu *physicist, researcher*
Lee, E(ugene) Stanley *engineering educator*
McKee, Richard Miles *retired agricultural studies educator*
Mortenson, Kristin Oppenheim *musician*
Motipalli, V. V. Satish Kumar *mechanical engineer, researcher*
Muir, William Lloyd III *academic administrator*
Murray, John Patrick *psychologist, educator, researcher*
Myers, Richard Bowman *former Chairman of the Joint Chiefs of Staff*
Oehme, Frederick Wolfgang *medical researcher, research consultant, writer*
Olds, David Andrew *food scientist, educator*
Patterson, Deb *women's college basketball coach*
Phares, E. Jerry *retired psychology professor*
Posler, Gerry Lynn *agronomist, educator*
Prasad, P.V. Vara *agricultural studies educator, researcher*
Seaton, Edward Lee *editor, publishing executive*
Shanklin, Carol W. *dietician, educator*
Sheu, Chwen *finance educator*
Simons, Gale Gene *nuclear and electrical engineer, educator*
Streeter, John Willis *information systems manager*
Swanson, Diane L. *business management and economics educator, researcher*
Thomas, Lloyd Brewster *economics professor*
Wefald, Jon *academic administrator*
White, Warren John *education educator*

## Marion

Beckham, Dwight Russel, Sr. *music educator, composer*
Meyer, Bill *publishing executive, editor*

## Mcpherson

Kilgus, Ocie Arlene *language educator*

## Meade

Brannan, Cleo Estella *retired elementary school educator*

## Mission

Bresky, H. Harry *agricultural products executive*
Bresky, Steven J. *agricultural products executive*
Churchill, James Garton *retired finance company executive*
Merrill, Donna *special education educator*
Trevino, Lee Buck *professional golfer*
Watson, Thomas Sturges *professional golfer*

## Mission Hills

Rose, Stephen F. *columnist*

## Morganville

Clark, Anne Louise *music educator, musician*

## Moundridge

Clark, Rustin *school system administrator*

## Mulvane

Kraft, William Earl *social studies educator*

## Neodesha

James, Charles (Chuck) Edward *small business owner, writer*

## Neosho Falls

Bader, Robert Smith *biology and zoology educator, researcher*

## Newton

Rogers, Rita Doris Luck *family nurse practitioner*

## North Newton

Ediger, Marlow *education educator*
Eitzen, David Stanley *sociologist, educator*
Goering, Jacob D. *retired psychoanalyst*

Snider, Marie Anna *syndicated columnist*
Sprunger, Keith L. *historian, educator*

## Ogden

Armendariz, Jim *principal*

## Olathe

Anderson, Peggy C. *elementary school educator*
Burrell, Gary *retired manufacturing executive*
Dodd, James B. *internet executive*
Goodwin, Becky K. *educational technology resource educator*
Graham, James C. *food service executive*
Harmon, Roger E. *environmentalist*
Hart, Michele *real estate agent*
Kao, Min H. *manufacturing executive*
Mathews, Valinda Gail *theater educator, gifted and talented educator*
Menke, Diana Lynn *elementary school educator*
Monzon, Carlos Manuel *physician*
Morrison, Ray Leon *library director, education educator*
Obenhaus, Steven Lee *secondary school educator*
Roby, Brian L. *bank executive*
Roller, Robert H. *academic administrator, finance educator*
Stevens, Diana Lynn *elementary school educator*

## Onaga

Dillinger, Susan Alice *reading specialist*

## Ottawa

Davidson, Medora Lea *dance educator*
Forrest, Daniel Ernest *composer, music educator*
Howe, William Hugh *artist*

## Overland Park

Amundson, Beverly Carden *artist*
Balloun, Joseph Eugene *lawyer*
Betts, Gene M. *telecommunications industry executive*
Burger, Henry G. *vocabulary scientist, anthropologist, writer*
Callahan, Michael Thomas *arbitrator, consultant, construction executive, writer*
Carpenter, Nancy E. *mathematics professor*
Christian, Shirley Ann *journalist, author*
Cummings, Jan Norman *interior designer, educator*
Damron, Nancy Lynn *secondary school educator*
Daniel, Karen *engineering and design company executive*
Ferrell, James Edwin *nuclear energy industry executive*
Fuller, Michael B. *communications executive*
Gaar, Norman Edward *lawyer, former state senator*
Gerke, Thomas A. *communications executive, lawyer*
Gerson, Steven Marc *technology writing professor, consultant*
Goetz, Kenneth Lee *cardiovascular physiologist, research consultant, writer*
Griswold, Thomas L. *lawyer*
Guckenheimer, Daniel Paul *financial advisor*
Hill, Lloyd Lester *food service executive*
Hodgell, Murlin Ray *university dean*
Horen, Jeffrey Harry *telecommunications executive*
Kempf, Andrea Caron *librarian, educator*
Keplinger, Bruce (Donald Keplinger) *lawyer*
Klamann, John Michael *lawyer*
Kuppuswamy, Carthy *telecommunications industry executive*
Lamb, Gordon Howard *music educator*
Landry, Mark Edward *podiatrist, researcher*
Leonard, Markus Dayle *software systems engineer*
Linville, Randal L. *agricultural company executive*
Lucas, James Raymond *project manager*
McCann, Vonya B. *federal agency administrator, telecommunications industry executive*
Murray, Thomas Veatch *lawyer*
Ostby, Frederick Paul, Jr. *meteorologist, retired government official, science administrator*
Plese, Joseph Marshall *education educator, actor*
Pretzel, Mark William *musician*
Rodman, Leonard C. *engineering and construction executive*
Stanton, Roger D. *lawyer*
Stem, Carl Herbert *business educator*
Strandjord, M. Jeannine *telecommunications industry executive*
Tubbs, David Eugene *mechanical engineer, marketing professional*
Vaughan, Brad *engineering and design company executive*
Voska, Kathryn Caples *consultant, facilitator*
Vratil, John Logan *state legislator, lawyer*
Whelan, Richard J. *retired academic administrator*
Woods, Richard Dale *lawyer*
Wornall, Ilah Ruth (Ruthie) *publishing executive, educator*
Zinke, Michael Duane *finance and accountancy manager*
Zollars, William D. *freight company executive*

## Oxford

Browning, Terri L. *secondary school educator*

## Paola

Krum, Jack Kern *food products executive*

## Parsons

Lomas, Lyle Wayne *agricultural research administrator, educator*
Walker, Robert R. *music educator*

## Pittsburg

Harris, James Dean *computer scientist, educator*
Krug, Harry E. *art educator, artist*
Lee, Earl Wayne *library science educator*
Morgan, Lyle Warner, II, *medical educator*
Nettels, George Edward, Jr. *retired mining executive*
Runyan, Charles Kent *education educator*
Sullivan, William John *osteopath*
Trent, Darrell M. *ambassador, academic administrator*

## Pleasanton

Earnest, Ola May *curator*

**Pomona**
Gentry, Alberta Elizabeth *elementary school educator*

**Prairie Village**
Fairchild, Robert Charles *pediatrician*
Newton, Dean *state representative*
Vogel, Arthur Anton *clergyman*

**Pratt**
Hart, Don Lee *academic administrator, writer*
Loomis, Howard Krey *banker, director*
Shrack, Christopher George *curator, educator*

**Russell**
Branick, Terry Lynn *secondary school educator*

**Saint John**
Robinson, Alexander Jacob *retired psychologist*

**Saint Marys**
Byers, Walter *athletic association executive*

**Salina**
Bell, Mark Gerald *physician, surgeon*
Entriken, Robert Kersey, Jr. *editor, writer*
Horst, Deena Louise *state legislator*
Owens, William Dean *lawyer*

**Shawnee**
Wilson, Eugene Rolland *retired foundation executive*

**Shawnee Mission**
Allen, Janet Lee *special education educator*
Badgerow, John Nicholas *lawyer*
Barger, Donald Gordon, Jr. *automotive products company executive*
Barton, Betty Louise *school system administrator*
Bell, Deloris Wiley *physician*
Black, Lisa Zahn *elementary school educator*
Bond, Richard Lee *lawyer, state senator*
Braude, Michael *commodities trader, researcher*
Breen, Katherine Anne *speech and language pathologist*
Fleming, Michael O. *physician*
Flora, Jairus Dale, Jr. *statistician*
Gamet, Donald Max *appliance company executive*
Green, John Lafayette, Jr. *educational association administrator*
Henley, Douglas E. *medical association administrator*
Ingenthron, Mary Kay *marketing executive, museum consultant*
Johnson, Bradford McClure *financial consultant, investor*
Johntz, John Hoffman, Jr. *lawyer*
Mandl, Herbert Jay *rabbi*
Martin, Donna Lee *retired publishing company executive*
McEachen, Richard Edward *banker, lawyer*
Mealman, Glenn *corporate marketing executive*
Moeller, Laura Lee *retired retail executive, library and information consultant*
Mooney, Justin David *motel executive, consultant*
Nulton, William Clements *retired lawyer*
Pressman, Ronald R. *utilities executive*
Price, James Gordon *physician, educator*
Putman, Dale Cornelius *management consultant, lawyer*
Sader, Carol Hope *former state legislator*
Snyder, Willard Breidenthal *lawyer*
Sparks, Billy Schley *lawyer*
Starrett, Frederick Kent *lawyer*
Sweeney, Leo Joseph *university administrator*
Thomas, Christopher Yancey III *surgeon, educator*
Vandever, William Dirk *lawyer*
Watts, Carl Douglas *music educator*

**Stilwell**
Keith, Dale Martin *management consultant*

**Sublette**
Myers, Connie Lanine *elementary school educator*
Swinney, Carol Joyce *secondary school educator*

**Topeka**
Allegrucci, Donald Lee *state supreme court justice*
Bearman, Alan *historian*
Beier, Carol Ann *state supreme court justice*
Bunten, William Daniel *retired banker*
Cantrell, Duane L. *retail executive*
Carlin, Sydney *state representative*
Chandler, Charles Q., IV *energy executive*
Concannon, James M. *lawyer, educator, dean*
Corkins, Bob *school system administrator*
Crow, Sam Alfred *judge*
Dan, Johnson *state representative*
Davis, Robert Edward *state supreme court justice*
Dunning, John Wilson, II *voice educator, director*
Elrod, Linda Diane Henry *lawyer, educator*
Eubank, Steven Eugene *secondary school educator*
Farley, Jerry B. *academic administrator*
Frahm, Sheila *association executive, academic administrator, former government official*
Fyler, Carl John *dentist*
Gamboa, Norman Armando *conductor, educator*
Goetz, Roger Melvin *minister*
Gordon, Lana G. *state representative*
Griffin, Ronald Charles *law educator*
Haines, James S., Jr. *energy executive*
Hayse, Richard Franklin *lawyer*
Hecht, Robert D. *lawyer*
Hedrick, Lois Jean *investment company executive, state official*
Hejtmanek, Danton Charles *lawyer*
Hollomon, Frederick Shelton *retired minister*
Irick, Larry D. *lawyer, energy executive*
Jenkins, Lynn M. *state official, former state legislator*
Johns, William Howard *psychiatrist, neurologist*
Karst, Gary Gene *architect*
Keefer, J(ames) Michael *lawyer*
Kellim, Kevin D. *music educator*
Kirk, Nancy A. *state legislator, nursing home administrator*
Kline, Phillip D. *state attorney general*
Knecht, Robert Lee *archivist*
Larson, Edward *retired state supreme court justice*

Luckert, Marla Jo *state supreme court justice*
Marquardt, Christel Elisabeth *judge*
McFarland, Kay Eleanor *state supreme court chief justice*
McFarland, William Joseph (Joe McFarland) *academic administrator*
Menninger, William Walter *psychiatrist*
Merrick, Raymond F. *state representative*
Moore, John Eddy *lieutenant governor*
Nason, Barry Mark *systems engineer, mathematician, educator*
Nuss, Lawton R. *state supreme court justice*
Osinski, Kay *nursing educator, medical/surgical nurse*
Perry, Nancy *foundation administrator*
Peters, Barbara Waterman *artist, educator*
Petty, Marge D. *state senator*
Porzig, Ullrich E. *retail executive*
Randall, Anthony Shields *environmental scientist, military officer*
Robinson, Julie Ann *judge*
Rogers, Richard Dean *federal judge*
Rosen, Eric S. *state supreme court justice*
Rubel, Matthew Evan *retail executive*
Saville, Pat *state senate official*
Schmidt, Derek *state legislator*
Schroer, Gene Eldon *lawyer*
Schultz, LeAnne *violinist, performer, music educator*
Sebelius, Kathleen Gilligan *governor*
Sipes, Karen Kay *communications executive*
Slemmons, Robert Sheldon *architect*
Snyder, Brock Robert *lawyer*
Spencer, William Edwin *retired telecommunications industry executive, engineer*
Spohn, Herbert Emil *psychologist*
Storm, Suzanne *state representative*
Thornburgh, Ron E. *state official*
Varner, Charleen LaVerne McClanahan *nutritionist, educator, dietician*
Wilson, Peggy Jo *secondary school educator*

**Westwood**
Brown, Gerald Eugene *minister*

**Wichita**
Andrew, Kenneth L. *physicist, researcher, physics professor*
Arnel, Kevin J. *lawyer*
Ayres, Ted Dean *lawyer*
Badger, Ronald Kay *lawyer*
Bovee, David Steven *historian, educator*
Brown, Wesley Ernest *federal judge*
Burket, George Stuart, Jr. *retired family physician*
Cadman, Wilson Kennedy *retired utilities executive*
Cress, Jerry W. *music educator*
Da'Luz Vieira-Jones, Lorraine Christine C. *acupuncturist, researcher*
Dierks, Melinda Adair *science educator*
Docking, Thomas Robert *lawyer, former state lieutenant governor*
Dorr, Stephanie Tilden *psychotherapist*
Ericson, David Frank *political scientist, educator*
Etter, Gregg Wayne, Sr. *police officer, educator*
Farmer, Steven *psychology professor*
Feilmeier, Steve *energy executive*
Ferris, Bruce G. *plastic surgeon, educator*
Fitch, Diane K. *human services administrator*
Guthrie, Diana Fern *nursing educator*
Guthrie, Richard Alan *physician*
Hatteberg, Larry Merle *photojournalist*
Herr, Peter Helmut Friederich *sales executive*
Jackels, Michael Owen *bishop*
Johnson, C. Nicholas *dance company executive*
Johnson, Ellen Schultz *retired music librarian, researcher*
Johnson, Kevin Blaine *lawyer, educator*
Johnson, Steven M. *food service executive*
Jones, Schuyler *museum director, anthropologist*
Knight, Robert G. *mayor, investment banker*
Koch, Charles de Ganahl *industrial company executive*
Koch, David Hamilton *chemical company executive*
Lerman, Kenneth Barry *marketing professional, consultant*
Liao, Haitao *science educator, researcher*
Manske, Robert C. *physical therapist, educator*
Maust, Ezma Minnie *music educator*
McKee, George Moffitt, Jr. *civil engineer, consultant*
Melgren, Eric Franklin *prosecutor, lawyer*
Menefee, Frederick Lewis *advertising executive*
Meyer, Russell William, Jr. *air transportation executive*
Moore, Leon, Jr. *social studies educator*
Park, Chan Hyung *cell biologist, physician*
Philson, Richard Michael *academic administrator*
Platt, George Milo *university administrator*
Pottorff, Jo Ann *state legislator*
Powell, Shirley Theressa *elementary school educator*
Rieger, James A. *plastic surgeon*
Rogers, Michael E. *exercise physiology educator, researcher*
Rueb, Sheree A. *social services administrator*
Sevart, Daniel Joseph *lawyer*
Steiner, Charles K. *museum director, painter*
Stephenson, Richard Ismert *lawyer*
Sullivan, Mitzi *accountant*
Thompson, Lee (Morris Thompson) *lawyer*
Vaughn, Kerri Lynn *elementary school educator*
Vliet, Marni *foundation administrator*
Waters, Mary A. *literature and language professor*
Weber, W. David *music educator*
Wilhelm, William Jean *civil engineering educator*

**Winfield**
Gray, Ina Turner *fraternal organization administrator*

**Yates Center**
Edwards, Mary Lee *retired secondary school educator, home economist*
Stockebrand, Larry Dean *physical education educator, director*

**KENTUCKY**

**Albany**
Sell, James Douglas *music educator*
Smith, Eugenia Sewell *funeral home executive*

**Ashland**
Hatfield, Bennett K. *mining executive*
Weaver, Carlton Davis *retired oil industry executive*
Yancey, Robert Earl, Jr. *retired oil industry executive*

**Bellevue**
Carpenter, Woodrow Wilson *manufacturing executive, ceramics engineer*

**Benton**
Glass, Mary Jean *management executive*
Pagel, Andrew W. *history educator*

**Berea**
Krug, John Carleton (Tony Krug) *academic administrator, library director, consultant*
Lamb, Irene Hendricks *medical researcher*
Majumdar, Kingshuk *physics professor, researcher*

**Bowling Green**
Ahmed, S. Basheer *research and development company executive, educator*
Atwell, Nedra Wheeler *education educator, consultant*
Berry, Mark Sean *music educator*
Buntzman, Gabriel Franklin *investor, educator*
Burch, Barbara G. *academic administrator*
Butts, Vanessa Oldham *secondary school educator*
Cangemi, Joseph Peter *psychologist, consultant, educator*
Cofoid, Paul Brian *physician*
Garrison, Geneva *retired administrative assistant*
Gipson, Jim *wholesale distribution executive*
Haynes, Robert Vaughn *retired academic administrator, historian*
Holland, John Ben *clothing manufacturing company executive*
Huddleston, Joseph Russell *judge*
Jackson, Carlton L. *history professor, writer*
Marcus, Jeffrey M. *science educator*
Minton, John D., Jr. *state supreme court justice*
Minton, John Dean *historian, educator*
Rabold, Charlene Franklin *librarian*
Rudloff, William Joseph *lawyer*
Sexton, Timothy Curt *music educator*
Slocum, Donald Warren *chemist, researcher*
Smith, Charles Hyde *librarian, historian*
Wells, Jerry *protective services official*
Wilcher, Larry K. *lawyer*
Xing, Guangming *engineering educator*

**Brandenburg**
Bowen, Patricia Lederer *dental educator*

**Bromley**
Sloan, David B. *lawyer*

**Brooksville**
Dorton, Truda Lou *medical/surgical nurse, geriatrics nurse*

**Buckner**
Thompson, Deborah J. *mathematics educator*

**Burkesville**
Burris, Larry Brent *music educator, director*

**Burlington**
Mitchell, Timothy Lynn *music educator*

**Calvert City**
Butler, Sheila Morris *occupational health nurse*
Madison, Vicki DiAnne *retired music educator*

**Campbellsville**
Burch, John Russell, Jr. *library director*
Chowning, John E. *political scientist, educator, minister*
Gaddis, John Robert *music educator*
Martin, J(ames) Kenneth *music educator*
McArthur, Lisa R. *music educator, musician*
Spurling, Teresa Phillips *education educator*

**Campton**
Drake, David Lee *electronics engineer*

**Clarkson**
Day, John Nelson *music educator*

**Cold Spring**
May, Debra Hardyman *librarian*

**Columbia**
Reliford, Judy Lynn Petty *science educator*

**Corbin**
Barton-Collings, Nelda Ann *political organization worker, bank executive*
Doby, John Thomas *social psychologist*

**Covington**
Berg, Lorine McComis *retired guidance counselor*
Gemunder, Joel Frank *healthcare company executive*
Hausrath, David L. *lawyer*
Kerr, Thomas Robert *lawyer*
McQueen, Regenia *writer*
Mehling, Christopher John *lawyer*
O'Brien, James J. *manufacturing executive*
Robinson, William T.(Bill) III *lawyer*
Stepner, Donald Leon *lawyer*
Surber, David Francis *public relations executive, consultant, television producer, journalist*

**Crescent Springs**
Chellgren, Paul Wilbur *energy industry executive*

**Crestwood**
Ray, Ronald Dudley *lawyer*
Roy, Elmon Harold *minister*
Snow, Edwin Fawcett *management consultant*

**Cynthiana**
Bandurski, Bruce Lord *retired ecologist, environmental scientist*

**Danville**
Breeze, William Hancock *academic administrator*
Kennan, Elizabeth Topham *academic administrator, retired historian*
Morris, Alvin Leonard *retired dentist, academic administrator*
Nickens, Harry Carl *medical association administrator*
Pappas, Marjorie L. *library studies educator*
Roush, John A. *academic administrator*

**Elizabethtown**
Phelps, Dennis Lane *minister, educator, author*
Rahman, Rafiq Ur *oncologist, educator*

**Elkton**
Manthey, Frank Anthony *physician, director*

**Erlanger**
Cuneo, Dennis Clifford *automotive company executive*

**Eubank**
Karriker, Danny Allen *small business owner, protective services official*

**Florence**
Gorman, Gayla Marlene Osborne *consumer affairs executive*

**Fort Knox**
Barnes, Larry Glen *journalist, editor, educator*
Olive, Karl William *elementary education educator, secondary educator*
Tucker, Brenda Brunette *elementary school educator*

**Fort Mitchell**
Drees, David G. *construction executive*
Drees, Ralph *construction executive*
Silvers, Gerald Thomas *retired publishing executive*

**Fort Thomas**
Clinkenbeard, Janelle Darlene *retired elementary school educator*
Lutz, Mark *computer graphics designer, art educator*
Wehr, William James *judge*

**Fort Wright**
Sullivan, Connie Castleberry *artist*

**Frankfort**
Al-Hamdani, Wasim A. *computer science educator*
Bowling, Charles Bryan *legal association administrator*
Breeding, Carl Wayne *lawyer*
Carroll, Julian Morton *lawyer, retired governor, state senator*
Collins, Hubert *real estate broker, state representative*
Embry, Michael Dale *writer, editor*
Fleming, Juanita Wilson *nursing educator, academic administrator*
Fletcher, Ernie (Ernest Lee Fletcher) *governor, former congressman*
Fletcher, Winona Lee *theater educator*
Frye, Wilbur Wayne *retired soil science educator, researcher, administrator*
Gibbons, Judith A. *librarian*
Gomelsky, Boris *geneticist, educator*
Grayson, Trey (C.M. Grayson) *state official*
Hatchett, Edward Bryan, Jr. *lawyer*
Huebner, Ruth A. *science educator, researcher*
Lambert, Joseph Earl *state supreme court chief justice*
Marcotte, Paul Henry *state representative*
Palmore, John Stanley, Jr. *retired lawyer*
Palumbo, Ruth Ann *state legislator*
Pence, Stephen Beville *lieutenant governor*
Pullin, Tanya *state representative*
Reid, George Willis *college president*
Richards, Jody *state legislator, communications educator, small business owner*
Scott, Will T. *state supreme court justice*
Shabazz, David Lorenzo *vocational school educator*
Sias, Mary *university president*
Sonego, Ian G. *assistant attorney general*
Stine, Katie Kratz *state legislator*
Stumbo, Gregory D. *state attorney general*
Wintersheimer, Donald Carl *state supreme court justice*
Zourarakis, Demetrio Periferachis *natural resource scientist*

**Franklin**
Baldock, Brian F. *corporate financial executive*
Clark, James Benton *retired rail transportation executive*
Kelley, Brad M. *conservationist, real estate developer*
Law, Jerriann Marcella *artist, poet, writer*

**Georgetown**
Bates, Clyde Thomas *retired economics professor*
Caroland, William Bourne *structural engineer*
Hall, Sara Y. *retired music educator*
Klotter, James C. *historian, educator*

**Glasgow**
Baker, Walter Arnold *lawyer*
Knicely, Carroll Franklin *publishing executive*

**Goshen**
Strode, William Hall III *photojournalist*

**Grayson**
Hunt, Andrea Wheaton *nurse*

**Greenville**
Beaty, Ted Hugh *music educator*
Walters, Sue Fox *broadcast executive, accountant*

## Grethel
Hughes, Cindi Baker *special education educator*

## Guston
Yundt, Betty Brandenburg *elementary school educator*

## Hagerhill
Blevins, Danny Keith *science educator, astronomer*

## Hardin
Morrow, Bruce William *academic administrator, management consultant*

## Harlan
Greene, James S. III *school administrator*

## Harrods Creek
Keeney, Steven Harris *lawyer*

## Harrodsburg
Herman, Alice Gertrude *retired nursing educator*

## Hartford
Taylor, David Michael *elementary school educator*

## Hazard
Cory, Cynthia Strong *mathematics professor*
Stewart, Sharon Rose *mathematics professor*

## Henderson
Gold, Steven Douglas *lawyer*
Logan, John A. III *hospital administrator*
Sullivan, William Litsey *lawyer*

## Hickman
Black, David A. *secondary school educator*

## Highland Heights
Donnelly, Sharlotte K. B. Neely *anthropology educator, writer*
Kennedy, Colleen Jo Ann *librarian, educator*
Kenny, Gregory B. *industrial equipment executive*
Luse, Kimberly Ann *radiologist, educator*
Ramage, James Alfred *history professor*

## Hopkinsville
Neville, Thomas Lee *food service company executive*
Soberal, Isabel M. *minister, music educator, social worker*
Wilkinson, Daniel Melvin *music educator*

## Independence
Hopgood, James F. *anthropologist, educator*

## Jeffersontown
Williams, Petra Schatz *antiquarian, director*

## La Grange
Morgan, Mary Dan *librarian*

## Lancaster
Taylor, Senica Duwayne *music educator*

## Lexington
Allison, Jonathan Mackinnon *university professor, researcher*
Anderson, James Wingo *physician*
Baker, Merl *engineering educator*
Barr, Philip Douglas *lawyer*
Baumann, Robert Jay *child neurology educator*
Beal, Donald Gordon *clinical psychology educator*
Belin, Bruce *surgeon*
Bennett, Victoria Elizabeth *rehabilitation nurse, dialysis technician*
Beshear, Steven Lynn *lawyer*
Birchfield, Martha *librarian*
Bodenbender, Michael Thomas *historian*
Boyd, James Robert *energy executive*
Bricker, John Timothy *pediatric cardiologist*
Brock, Carolyn Pratt *chemist, educator*
Brock, Louis Milton, Jr. *engineering educator, researcher*
Burris, Ashley Paige *director, educator*
Calderhead, William John *special education educator, researcher*
Calvert, C. Emmett *former state agency administrator*
Cameron-Mickens, Vertrelle Diane *singer, conductor, voice educator*
Campbell, Tracy *history professor*
Chance, Kenneth Bernard, Sr. *endodontist educator, academic administrator*
Charnigo, Richard John, Jr. *statistician, educator*
Chen, Zhi *electrical engineering educator*
Chowdhury, Dipak K. *pharmaceutical executive, researcher*
Clawson, David Kay *orthopedic surgeon*
Coffman, Edward McKenzie *retired history professor*
Coffman, Jennifer Burcham *judge*
Cole, Henry Philip *educational psychology educator*
Cole, Vincent J. *lawyer*
Cross, Alvin Miller (Al Cross) *journalist*
Curlander, Paul Joseph *technology executive*
Curtz, Chauncey S.R. *lawyer, real estate company executive*
Davey, Diane Davis *pathologist, educator, medical association administrator*
DeLuca, Patrick Phillip *pharmacist, educator, medical association administrator*
Diedrichs, Carol Pitts *librarian, dean*
Donohew, Robert Lewis, Sr. *communications educator*
Drake, Vaughn Paris, Jr. *electrical engineer*
Ehmann, William Donald *chemistry professor*
Elitzur, Moshe *physicist, researcher*
Ettensohn, Frank Robert *geologist, educator*
Farrar, Donna Beatrice *health facility administrator*
Fedorchuk, Mary Kathrine *social worker*
Fryman, Virgil Thomas, Jr. *lawyer*
Gable, Robert Elledy *real estate investment company executive*
Gallagher, Eugene Bennett *sociologist, medical educator*
Garman, Ray Fillmore *occupational physician, director*

Garmer, William Robert *lawyer*
Gill, Karen V. *secondary school educator, consultant*
Girard, C. Jack *art educator, artist*
Goldman, Alvin Lee *lawyer, educator, arbitrator*
Gornik, Kathy *electronics executive*
Guskey, Thomas Robert *education educator*
Hagen, Michael Dale *family physician educator*
Hamilton-Kemp, Thomas Rogers *organic chemist, educator*
Hayes, Don, Jr. *physician, researcher*
Hiestand, Sheila Patricia *lawyer*
Hochstrasser, Donald Lee *cultural anthropologist, community health and public administrator*
Hojahmat, Marhaba *research scientist*
Holland, Robert, Jr. *food products executive*
Holsapple, Clyde Warren *decision and information systems educator*
Holsinger, James Wilson, Jr. *physician*
Huffman, Gerald P. *science administrator, educator*
Humphries, Asa Alan, Jr. *biologist, educator, dean*
Isaac, Teresa Ann *mayor, lawyer*
Kaplan, Martin P. *allergist, immunologist, pediatrician*
Karpf, Michael *medical administrator*
Kasperbauer, Michael John *plant physiology educator, researcher*
Keeling, Larry Dale *journalist*
Keller, James *retired state supreme court justice*
Kelly, Timothy Michael *newspaper publisher*
Kern, Bernard Donald *retired physicist*
Kibler, William Benjamin *orthopedist, surgeon*
Kissling, Fred Ralph, Jr. *publishing executive, insurance agency executive*
Kwolek, Christopher John *surgeon, educator*
Leaumont, Anne Parlanti *special education educator*
Lewis, Robert Kay, Jr. *fundraising executive*
Male, Alan Thomas *engineering educator, foundation administrator*
Martin, Craig Allen *infectious diseases pharmacist*
Mason, Ellsworth Goodwin *retired librarian*
McRoberts, J. Williams *urologist, surgeon, researcher*
Means, Robert Taylor, Jr. *hematologist, educator*
Millard, James Kemper *marketing executive*
Miller, Daniel Harlan *lawyer*
Miller, Pamela Gundersen *mayor*
Mitchell, George Ernest, Jr. *zoology educator*
Mostert, Paul Stallings *retired mathematician*
Mudd, Angela *social worker*
Mukherjee, Debabrata *cardiologist, researcher*
Norman, Charlene Wilson *secondary school educator*
O'Brien, Stephen Mazyck III *lawyer*
O'Hurley, John *actor*
Okeson, Jeffrey Paul *dental educator, director*
Omar, Mohammed A. *engineering educator, consultant*
Piper, George Chilton *lawyer*
Prado, Edgar *horse racing jockey*
Puffer, James C. *sports medicine physician, educator, medical association administrator*
Reed, Michael Robert *agricultural economist*
Roach, John C. *state supreme court justice*
Robinson, Thomas Christopher *health science educator*
Romanowitz, Byron Foster *architect, engineer*
Rowe, Melinda Grace *public health service officer*
Sandoval, Arturo Alonzo *artist, educator*
Sekulic, Dusan P. *science educator, engineering educator, researcher*
Sexton, Robert Fenimore *educational organization executive*
Sineath, Timothy Wayne *librarian, educator, dean*
Smith, Michael Earl *jockey*
Steensland, Ronald Paul *librarian*
Stempel, John Dallas *international studies educator*
Straus, Robert *behavioral sciences educator*
Sullivan, Patrick Giles *education educator, researcher*
Thapar, Amul R. *prosecutor*
Thelin, John Robert *historian, educator, researcher*
Timoney, Peter Joseph *veterinarian, educator, virologist, consultant*
Todd, Lee Trover, Jr. *academic administrator, electrical engineer*
Tollison, Joseph W. *family practice physician*
Turner, Sharon P. *dean, dentist, educator*
Varellas, Sandra Motte *judge*
Vestal, Allan W. *dean, law educator*
Walsh-Piper, Kathleen A. *museum director*
Walton, William W., Jr. *surgeon*
Warth, Robert Douglas *history professor*
Waltzel, William David *psychiatrist*
Wethington, Charles T., Jr. *academic administrator*
Whayne, Thomas French, Jr. *cardiologist, educator*
Wildasin, David E(arl) *economics professor*
Worell, Judith P. *psychologist, educator*
Young, Paul Ray *medical association administrator, physician*
Young, Sandra Cooper *retired librarian*
Zack, George J. *conductor*
Zito, Nick *horse trainer, breeder*

## London
Felts, Mark A. *voice educator*
Keller, John Warren *lawyer*
McFadden, David Michael *music educator, director*
Siler, Eugene Edward, Jr. *federal judge*

## Louisville
Adams, Robert Waugh *state agency administrator, economist, educator*
Amin, Mohammad *urology educator*
Andrews, Billy Franklin *pediatrician, educator*
Appleberry, James Bruce *educational association administrator*
Ardery, Philip Pendleton *lawyer*
Aronoff, George Rodger *medicine and pharmacology educator*
Atz, Sarah J. *music educator*
Ballew, Laurie K. *psychiatrist*
Barnett, Joyce Lyndel *freelance/self-employed writer*
Barr, James Houston III *lawyer*
Beck, Peter *marketing educator, minister*
Becker, Gail Roselyn *museum director*

Beggan, James K. *sociologist, educator*
Belanger, William Joseph *chemist, consultant*
Bell, Mary Margaret *archivist*
Blandford, Jim, Jr. *social studies educator*
Bloem, James H. *managed health care executive*
Boggs, Danny Julian *federal judge*
Boykin, Gladys *retired religious organization administrator*
Brown, Owsley, II, *diversified consumer products company executive*
Buckaway, William Allen, Jr. *lawyer*
Byerlein, Anne P. *human resources specialist, food products executive*
Callen, Jeffrey Phillip *dermatologist, educator*
Campbell, Christian Larsen L. *lawyer*
Carlisle, Douglas R. *health facility administrator*
Carranza, Jovita *delivery service executive*
Casi, Paul Aldo, II, *lawyer*
Cecil, Bonnie Susan *elementary school educator*
Chaires, Jonathan Bradford *research scientist, educator*
Chien, Sufan *surgeon, educator*
Choi, Namok *education educator*
Conner, Stewart Edmund *lawyer*
Cook, Larry Norman *pediatrician, neonatologist, educator*
Cornelius, Wayne Anderson *electrical and computer engineering consultant*
Cowan, Frederic Joseph *lawyer*
Crutcher, Michael Bayard *lawyer, consumer products company executive*
Dale, Judy Ries *religious organization administrator, consultant*
Danzl, Daniel Frank *emergency physician*
Datta, Somnath *statistician, educator*
Davidson, Gordon Byron *lawyer*
Deering, Ronald Franklin *librarian, minister*
Diaz, Paul J. *health products executive*
Dilger, Craig *lawyer*
Dudley, George Ellsworth *lawyer*
Duffy, Martin Patrick *lawyer*
Early, Jack Jones *foundation executive*
Egilmez, Nejat K. *science educator*
Elin, Ronald John *pathologist, educator*
Ethridge, Larry Clayton *lawyer*
Faller, Rhoda *lawyer*
Farman, Allan George *radiologist, pathologist, educator*
Fenner, Chris *music educator*
Ford, Gordon Buell, Jr. *literature educator, writer*
Foster, William R. *zoological park developer*
Foulks, Gary Neal *ophthalmologist, educator*
French, Michael Bruce *marketing executive*
Fuchs, Olivia Anne Morris *lawyer*
Galandiuk, Susan *colon and rectal surgeon, educator*
Gall, Stanley Adolph *immunologist, researcher*
Garcia, Rafael Jorge *retired chemical engineer*
Garretson, Henry David *neurosurgeon*
Gilman, Sheldon Glenn *lawyer*
Glogower, Michael Howard *real estate company executive, consultant*
Goheen, Nan J. *psychologist*
Goldstein, Irvin L. *elementary school educator*
Goodman, Bruce *health products executive*
Gray, Joan S. *head of religious order*
Greaver, Joanne Hutchins *mathematics educator, writer*
Greer, Ginger Dell *music educator*
Guillaume, Raymond Kendrick *banker*
Hale, Roger W. *utilities company executive*
Hanson, Dennis Michael *retired health facility administrator*
Hathcock, Bonita Catherine (Bonnie Hathcock) *managed health care company executive*
Hawpe, David Vaughn *editor, journalist*
Hayes, William Meredith *pilot, retired military officer*
Haynes, Douglas Martin *obstetrician, gynecologist, educator*
Heiden, Charles Kenneth *metal products executive, consultant, retired military officer*
Hernandez, John E. *musician, music educator*
Heyburn, John Gilpin, II, *federal judge*
Hipwell, Arthur P. *lawyer, managed health care company executive*
Holt, Homer Anthony, Jr. *urologist, educator*
Hopson, Edwin Sharp *lawyer*
Huber, David L. *prosecutor*
Hultgren, John Robert *information systems professional, flight paramedic*
Hunter, William Jay, Jr. *lawyer*
Jenne, Sue Oak *secondary school educator*
Jones, David A., Jr. *insurance company executive*
Juber, David L. *prosecutor*
Kamardzhi, Mehmed M. *engineering educator*
Kaplan, Henry Jerrold *ophthalmologist, educator*
Kaplan, Joel A. *academic administrator*
Karwowski, Waldemar *adult education educator*
Keisling, Bruce Lowell *librarian*
Kelly, Thomas Cajetan *archbishop*
Kirkpatrick, G. Leon *music educator*
Klotter, John Charles *retired law educator*
Kuntz, Edward Lawrence *healthcare executive*
Lay, Norvie Lee *law educator*
Lechleiter, Richard A. *medical products executive*
LeClaire, Brian P. *health benefits company executive*
Lockwood, William Byron *physician*
Lofton, Kevin Eugene *medical facility administrator*
Lord, Jonathan T. (Jack Lord) *medical association administrator*
Luber, Thomas J(ulian) *lawyer*
Lunsford, W. Bruce *health facility administrator, health products executive*
Lyndrup, Peggy B. *lawyer*
Margulis, Heidi *health products executive*
Marks-Morgan, Linda Lee *music educator*
Martin, Boyce Ficklen, Jr. *federal judge*
Martin, David Allen *application developer, computer scientist*
Mather, Elizabeth Vivian *healthcare executive*
McAnulty, William E., Jr. *state supreme court justice*
McCall, John Richard *lawyer*
McCallister, Michael B. *insurance company executive*
McCormick, Steven Thomas *insurance company executive*
McKim, Ruth Ann *financial planner*

McMasters, Kelly Marc *surgeon, educator*
Mellen, Francis Joseph, Jr. *lawyer*
Mohler, Richard Albert, Jr. *academic administrator, theologian*
Morell, Michael John *actuary*
Morrin, Peter Patrick *museum director*
Mountz, Wade *retired healthcare executive*
Mowery, Ward Franklin *retired music educator*
Moya, Steve *health products executive*
Muezzinoglu, Mehmet Kerem *research scientist*
Nasraoui, Olfa *computer scientist, educator, electrical engineer*
Northern, Richard *lawyer*
Novak, David C. *restaurant company executive*
Novick, Aileen Mary *historic site director, educator*
Oates, Thomas R. *university executive*
Oglesby, Joseph Woodson (Mike English) *writer, publishing executive*
Osborn, John Simcoe, Jr. *lawyer*
Palmer, Larry Isaac *lawyer, educator*
Parker, Joseph Corbin, Jr. *pathologist, educator, department chairman*
Parkins, Frederick Milton *dental educator, dean*
Pasic, Resad *medical educator*
Pedley, Lawrence Lindsay *lawyer*
Pelfrey, D. Patton *lawyer*
Pence, Hobert Lee *physician*
Petrino, Bobby *college football coach*
Pitino, Richard *collegiate basketball coach, former professional basketball coach*
Polk, Hiram Carey, Jr. *surgeon, educator*
Portes, Pedro René *psychology professor, department chairman*
Potter, Harold Claude *philosopher*
Power, David M. *advertising executive*
Power, Michael L. *advertising executive*
Rainer, Thomas Spratling *pastor*
Rempala, Grzegorz A. *mathematician, statistician, educator*
Richardson, James David *surgeon*
Riedman, Mary Suzanne *lawyer*
Robinson, David Lowell *biology professor*
Ronald, Peter *utilities executive*
Rose, Charles Alexander *lawyer*
Rosky, Theodore Samuel *insurance company executive*
Rothstein, Laura *dean, law educator*
Runyon, Keith Leslie *lawyer, editor*
Saunders, Robert Samuel *venture capitalist*
Schwab, John Joseph *psychiatrist, educator*
Scott, Ralph Mason *retired radiologist, educator*
Shah, Atique R. *gaming activities executive*
Sherman, Mildred Mozelle *music educator, vocalist, actress, opera director*
Shield, Gene *health products executive*
Shobe, David Soren *librarian, director*
Silverthorn, Robert Sterner, Jr. *lawyer*
Simpson, Charles R. III *judge*
Simpson, David Michael *financial planner, educator*
Singh, Amar V. *research scientist*
Skees, William Leonard, Jr. *lawyer*
Smith, Donald Ray *magazine dealer*
Staffieri, Victor A. *energy executive*
Stanton, M(orris) Duncan *psychologist, researcher, dean*
Street, William May *beverage company executive*
Swain, Donald Christie *retired academic administrator, historian, educator*
Syed, Ibrahim Bijli *medical educator, physicist*
Talbott, Ben Johnson, Jr. *lawyer*
Tanguay, Peter Eugene *child and adolescent psychiatry educator*
Tasman, Allan *psychiatry educator*
Taylor, Kenneth Grant *chemistry professor*
Taylor, Robert Lewis *finance educator*
Thompson, Kathy C. *bank executive*
Thongboonkerd, Visith *nephrologist, researcher*
Towles, Donald Blackburn *retired publishing executive*
Tran, Long Trieu *industrial engineer*
Travis, Nigel *food service executive*
Varga, Paul C. *beverage products executive*
Vish, Donald H. *lawyer, writer, photographer*
Vogel, Werner Paul *retired machine company executive*
Waddell, William Joseph *pharmacologist, toxicologist*
Wagner, James Miller *funeral director*
Wagoner, Ruth R *education coach*
Watson, Gary Alan *management consultant*
Weeter, John Montgomery *plastic surgeon*
Weisskopf, Bernard *pediatrician, child behavior, development and genetics specialist, educator*
Welsh, Mr Alfred John *lawyer, investment advisor*
Westberry, Robert Kent *lawyer*
Wood, Phoebe A. *food products executive*
Wright, Jesse Hartzell *psychiatrist, educator*
Yazdanpanah, Mehdi Mohammad *physicist, researcher*
Zepeda, Susan Ghozeil *foundation administrator*
Zimmerman, Gideon K. *minister*

## Madisonville
Deger, Robert John, Jr. *college dean*
Kington, Barry Clark *investor, consultant*
May, Richard Warren *writer*
Spain, Thomas B. *retired state supreme court justice*

## Marion
Henley, Darl Heathcott *librarian, educator*

## Masonic Home
Coryell, Glynn Heath *financial services executive*

## Mayfield
Murray, Helen *writer*

## Maysville
Trimble, Garnet O'Cull *retired music educator*

## Middlesboro
Daniel, Barbara Ann *realtor, advertising executive*
Owens, Chuck *secondary school educator, broadcast technician*

## Monticello
Sexton, Scotty Eugene *music educator, gifted and talented educator*

## Morehead

Besant, Larry Xon *retired librarian, administrator, consultant*
Detweiler, Greg Jeffrey *music educator*
Klecker, Beverly McCauley *academic administrator*
Miller, Green Russell *economist, educator*
Nutter, Carol Angell *academic librarian*
Pritchard, Elsie Tomlinson *librarian*
Reilley, Sean Patrick *psychology professor, consultant*

## Mount Sterling

Aileen-Donohew, Phyllis Augusta *educational consultant*
Johnston, Jacqueline Anne *school administrator, director*

## Murray

Boston, Betty Lee *investment company executive, financial consultant, financial planner*
Buckingham, David Cowan *judge*
Ferreyra, Rafael Andres *agricultural and biological engineer, consultant, researcher*
Guy, Sallie T. *artist*
Hill, Todd Edwin *band director*
Keller, Randal Joseph *toxicology educator*
Whisenhunt, Donald Wayne *historian, educator, dean*

## Newport

Castellini, Robert H. (Bob Castellini) *food products executive, professional sports team executive*
Clinkenbeard, James Howard *principal*
Giuliani, Michael J. *medical educator*

## Nicholasville

Armstrong, Marcy Lynn *literature and language educator, special education educator*
Burton, Malinda Daugherty *school librarian*
Midkiff, Dinah Lee *retired elementary and middle school educator*

## Owensboro

Adams, Robert Douglas *cardiothoracic surgeon*
Caplan, Geralyn Marie *biology professor*
Cinnamond, Robert E. *education educator, writer*
Humphreys, Daniel James *elementary school educator*
Lee, Anthony Wayne *literature and language professor*
McRaith, John Jeremiah *bishop*
Roberts, Brian Wayne *middle school educator, minister*
Stovall, Beth Roop *music educator*
Webb, Otis D. *retired underwriter*
West, William Robert *history professor*
Whear, J. Kevin *information technology executive*

## Paducah

Fejes, Robert R. *minister*
Graves, John William *state supreme court justice*
Justice, Phillip Howard *marketing professional*
King, W. David *judge*
Stice, Dwayne Lee *broadcasting company executive*

## Paintsville

Hovee, Mark John *psychologist*

## Paris

Steffer, Robert Wesley *clergyman*

## Pewee Valley

Gill, George Norman *newspaper publishing company executive*

## Pikeville

Hunter, Trudy Pearl *surgical nurse*
Smith, Harold Hasken *university administrator*
Van Tatenhove, Gregory F. *federal judge, former prosecutor*

## Pineville

Whittaker, Bill Douglas *minister*

## Princeton

Earnest, Melissa Webb *education educator*
Faughn, Dale *biology educator*

## Prospect

Aberson, Leslie Donald *lawyer*
Kehlbeck, Joseph H. *software developer, consultant*
Willenbrink, Rose Ann *retired lawyer*

## Radcliff

Cole, Jessie Mae *nursing assistant, freelance/self-employed writer*

## Richmond

Ballard, Michael Ray (Mickey Ballard) *minister, music educator*
Blanchard, Paul *academic administrator, educator*
Branson, Branley Allan *biology professor*
Chenault, James Stouffer *judge*
Coleman, David William *history professor*
Gershtenson, Joe *political science professor*
Hall, Kathy *health facility administrator*
Huch, Ronald Kind *historian, educator*
Inman, Larry Joe *basketball coach*
Machado-Echezuria, Marianella Perpetua *composer, writer, educator*
Nguyen, A. Minh Thong *philosopher, educator*
Wright, John Daniel *minister*

## Rineyville

Jackson, Charles Wayne *food products executive, former telecommunications industry executive*

## Russell Springs

Floyd, Christopher Chad *music educator, director*

## Russellville

Harper, Shirley Fay *nutritionist, educator, consultant, lecturer*
Rogers, Gina Insco *medical association administrator*
Sauerbrunn, Mark Aaron *music educator*

## Saint Catharine

Donathan, David Allen *retired military officer*

## Shelbyville

Hedrick, William David *secondary school educator, musician*
Miller, Mary Helen *retired state government administrator*

## Shepherdsville

Austin, Jim E. *secondary school educator*
Pike, Burlyn *retired bank director, lawyer*

## Somerset

Armstrong, Anthony L. *mathematics professor*
Huntsman, Mary Taylor *librarian, history professor*
Pennington, Aubrey El *director*

## Southgate

Glenn, Jerry Hosmer, Jr. *retired language educator*

## Stanford

Underwood, Ray Stuart *music educator*

## Sturgis

Thornsberry, Willis Lee, Jr. *chemist*

## Versailles

Farish, William S. *former ambassador, horse breeder*
Stober, William John, II, *economics professor*
Taylor, Elizabeth *secondary school educator*
Troutt, Kenny *communications executive*

## Villa Hills

Giesbrecht, Martin Gerhard *retired economics professor, musician*

## Waco

Hackman, Vicki Lou *physician*

## Warsaw

Davis, Michael L. *guidance counselor*

## Wickliffe

Frueh, Deborah K.A. (Debi Frueh) *artist, poet*

## Wilmore

Kinlaw, Dennis Franklin *clergyman, religious organization administrator*
Pohl, Gunther Erich *retired library administrator*

## Winchester

Book, John Kenneth (Kenny Book) *retail store owner*
Snowden, Ruth O'Dell Gillespie *artist*
Studebaker, John Milton *utilities engineer, consultant, educator*

# LOUISIANA

## Alexandria

Fletcher, Keith Merril *mathematics educator*
Gist, Howard Battle, Jr. *lawyer*
Hanley, Henry Gorman *cardiologist*
Maples, Mary Lou *elementary school educator*
Norem, Richard Frederick *surgeon*
Robinson, Cathy D. *science educator*
Slipman, Ronald (Samuel Slipman) *hospital administrator*
Smith, Joe Dorsey, Jr. *retired newspaper executive*
Thevenot, Maura Travis *retired home economist*
Webb, Watts Rankin *surgeon*
Wesse, David Joseph *higher education administrator, consultant*

## Baker

Cross, James Edward *electrical engineering educator*

## Bastrop

Bonsall, Vicki J. *art educator*

## Baton Rouge

Alam, Mohammmad Shah *engineering educator, researcher*
Arceneaux, William *historian, educator, educational association administrator*
Ater, Al *state official*
Barfield, Tim *manufacturing executive*
Baron, Stuart *art, art educator, director*
Bedeian, Arthur George *business educator*
Bensman, Stephen J. *school librarian, researcher*
Bernhard, James M. *engineering executive*
Besch, Everett Dickman *veterinarian, dean emeritus, educator*
Blackman, John Calhoun, IV, *lawyer*
Blanco, Kathleen Babineaux *governor*
Boyce, Bert Roy *university dean emeritus, library and information science educator*
Bray, George August *internist, researcher, educator*
Broussard, Malcolm Joseph *pharmacist, consultant*
Buchmann, Molly O'Banion *choreographer, educator*
Burns, Paul Yoder *forester, educator*
Burt, Vickie P. *theater educator, theater director*
Caffey, Horace Rouse *academic administrator, agricultural company executive*
Calabrese, Michael Raphael *lawyer, consultant*
Cargill, Jennifer S. *librarian, dean, educator*
Chapman, Russell Leonard *botany educator*
Chatman, Dana (Pokey Chatman) *women's college basketball coach*
Chen, Peter Pin-Shan *engineering educator, computer science and internet/web educator, data processing executive*
Cherry, William Ashley *surgeon, state health official, educator*
Cole, Luther Francis *former state supreme court associate justice*
Combe, John Clifford, Jr. *lawyer*
Cooper, William James, Jr. *history professor*
Corripio, Armando Benito *chemical engineering professor*
Cramer, Gail Latimer *economist*

Crumbley, Donald Larry *accounting educator, writer*
Culbert, David Holbrook *historian, educator, editor, writer*
Davis, Carol *educational association administrator, researcher*
Deng, Zhi-Qiang *civil and environmental engineering educator, researcher*
DeVille, Donald Charles *accountant*
Doty, Gresdna Ann *theatre historian, educator*
Dugas, David Roy *prosecutor, lawyer*
Dumais, Susan A. *sociology professor*
Finney, Clifton Donald *publishing executive*
Foti, Charles C., Jr. *state attorney general*
Gammon, Malcolm Ernest, Sr. *surveying and engineering executive*
Gettys, Thomas Wigington *medical researcher*
Gill, Richard F. *construction engineering executive*
Gilmore, Clarence Percy *editor-in-chief, writer*
Goodell, Rosemary Wilson *artist, educator*
Graphia, Gary P. *lawyer*
Green, Stuart Paul *law educator*
Greer, Jennifer *records analyst*
Guedry, Leo J. *agricultural economics educator*
Guzik, Theodore Gregory *astrophysicist, researcher*
Hamed, Shadpour *research assistant*
Hansel, William *biology professor*
Hardy, John Edward *language educator, writer*
Harper, Robert D. *state agency administrator*
Harper, Sandra Stecher *academic administrator*
Harrelson, Clyde Lee *retired secondary school educator*
Hartzog, Elizabeth Windham *music educator*
Hayward, Olga Loretta Hines (Mrs. Samuel Ellsworth Hayward) *retired librarian*
Head, Jonathan Frederick *cell biologist*
Hirst, Edwin Timothy *music educator*
Hoffman, Paul Everett *history professor*
Hymel, L(ezin) J(oseph) *lawyer, former prosecutor*
Ishler, Harold LeRoy, Jr. *family medicine physician*
Jenkins, William L. *academic administrator*
Kastin, Abba Jeremiah *endocrinologist, researcher*
Khonsari, Michael M. *mechanical engineering educator*
Kidd, James Marion III *allergist, immunologist, educator*
Kinnison, Phyllis Marie *archivist*
Koehler, Robert Brien *priest*
Laine, Roger A. *biology professor*
Landrieu, Mitchell Joseph *lieutenant governor*
Litvinoff, Saul *law educator, lawyer*
Lopez, Mandi J. *veterinarian, scientist*
Lott, Bret *literature and language professor, writer*
Lusk, Glenna Rae Knight (Mrs. Edwin Bruce Lusk) *librarian*
Madden, David *author*
Mathews, Sharon Walker *performing company executive, secondary school educator*
Mc Call, Jerry Chalmers *retired federal official*
Mc Cameron, Fritz Allen *retired university administrator*
McCoy, Wesley Lawrence *musician, educator, conductor*
Mc Glynn, Sean Patrick *physical chemist, educator*
McKay, Michael Wendell *lawyer*
McKnight, Michelynn *librarian*
Meyinsse, Joseph Appolinaire *mathematics professor, researcher*
Miles, Les *college football coach*
Moody, Gene Byron *engineering executive, small business owner, minister*
Morvant, Barbara L. *nursing administrator*
Mueller, Lisel *writer, poet*
Mugnier, Clifford John *engineering educator, consultant*
Nave, J. L. *performing company executive*
Ngandu, Pius Nkashama *education educator*
Noland, Christine A. *judge*
Norem, Richard Frederick, Sr. *musician, educator*
O'Connell, Robert Francis *physics professor*
O'Keefe, Sean Charles *academic administrator, former federal agency administrator*
Okeil, Ayman M. *educator*
Parker, John Victor *judge*
Parks, James William, II, *public facilities executive, lawyer*
Patterson, Clara Darold *librarian, educator*
Perkins, Huel Davis *retired academic administrator*
Phillabaum, Leslie Ervin *publisher*
Picard, Cecil *school system administrator*
Pike, Ralph Webster *chemical engineer, educator, academic administrator*
Polozola, Frank Joseph *federal judge*
Prestage, James Jordan *university chancellor*
Pugh, George Willard *law educator*
Puyau, Francis Albert *retired radiology educator, physician*
Quartararo, Philip, Jr. *mathematics professor*
Reich, Robert Sigmund *landscape architect*
Ricapito, Joseph Virgil (Giuseppe Ricapito) *literature educator*
Richards, Marta Alison *lawyer*
Riddick, Winston Wade, Sr. *lawyer*
Riedlinger, Stephen C. *federal judge*
Riopelle, Arthur Jean *psychologist*
Risinger, Beth N. *elementary school educator*
Robinson, James William *chemistry professor*
Rubin, Michael Harry *lawyer, educator*
Rutledge, Katherine Burck *artist*
Sanders, Mary Elizabeth *writer, historian*
Sandoz, George Ellis, Jr. *political science educator*
Schechter, Lynn Renee *psychologist*
Sinclair, Glenn Bruce *mechanical engineering educator, researcher*
Skillman, Ernest Edward, Jr. *real estate sales and management executive*
Sluyter, Andrew *geographer, educator*
Smith, Michael *academic administrator*
Smith, James *retired music educator*
Spell, Derrick W. *oncologist, educator*
Stapp, Dan Ernest *retired lawyer, utilities executive*
Superneau, Duane William *geneticist, physician*
Tandberg, Gerilyn Gay *theater educator, costume designer*
Taylor, John McKowen *lawyer*

Thomas, Jeffrey Cone *financial executive, consultant*
Tipton, Kenneth Warren *retired agricultural administrator, researcher*
Torns, David Loren *conductor, director, musician*
Travagli, Renato Alberto *neuroscientist, researcher*
Traynham, James Gibson *chemist, educator*
Tsai, Frank Tsung-Chen *engineering educator, researcher*
Tumay, Mehmet Taner *geotechnical engineering educator, researcher*
Tyagi, Mayank *research scientist*
Unglesby, Lewis O. *lawyer*
Warner, Isiah Manuel *chemistry professor*
Wheeler, Otis Bullard *retired language educator, retired director*
Witcher, Robert Campbell, Sr. *bishop*
Wong, Wai Hing *marine biologist, researcher*
Yarbrough, Martha Cornelia *music educator*
Younathan, Ezzat Saad *retired biochemistry educator*
Young, David P. *physics professor*
Zhou, Liming *environmental scientist*

## Belle Chasse

Arimura, Akira *biomedical researcher, educator*

## Benton

Hudson, Marguerite W. *secondary school educator*

## Bogalusa

Gallaspy, Dixie *interior designer, innkeeper*
Villarrubia, Glenda Boone *reading specialist, reading coordinator, educational consultant, educator*

## Bossier City

Paris, Norma Jean *psychologist, educator*

## Bunkie

Laborde, Terry James *secondary school educator*

## Cecilia

Girouard, Tina *artist, curator*

## Centerville

Mancuso, Monica Laughlin *educational administrator*

## Chauvin

Sammarco, Paul W. *marine science researcher and educator*
Sammarco, Paul William *ecologist, researcher*

## Choudrant

Ford, John Charles *artist*

## Columbia

McGee, Bruce D. *evangelist*

## Coushatta

Wiggins, Mary Ann Wise *small business owner, educator*

## Covington

Doody, Louis Clarence, Jr. *retired accountant*
Files, Mark Willard *business and financial consultant*
Flattmann, Alan Raymond *artist, educator*
Gilman-Anderson, Susan Ellen *real estate company executive, consultant*
Maurin, James E. *real estate executive*
Rice, Winston Edward *lawyer*
Snyder, Charles Aubrey *lawyer*
Stahr, Beth A. *librarian*
Vercellotti, John Raymond *chemist, researcher*

## Crowley

Foreman, Alfred G. *theologian, philosopher*
Privat, Ruby (Ruby Thibodeaux) *elementary school educator*

## Cut Off

Mestayer, Mary Frances *science educator*

## Denham Springs

Grimmer, Cindy C. *social studies educator*
May, Kenneth Nathaniel *retired food industry consultant*

## Deridder

Mallory, Patricia Jody *museum curator*

## Destrehan

Ates, J. Robert *lawyer*
Griffith, Steven Franklin, Sr. *lawyer, insurance agent*

## Donaldsonville

Watson, Stanley Ellis *clergyman, small business owner*

## Doyline

Willis, Gladden Williams *pathologist, scientific photographer, tree farmer*

## Dubach

Straughan, William Thomas *engineering educator, structural engineering consultant*

## Elm Grove

Livingston, John H. *retired engineer, retired military officer*
Turner, Steven Jay *director*

## Eunice

Attole, Mary Bertha *writer*
Joubert, Lorrie B. *mathematics professor*

## Fort Polk

Lubbers, Alice Dianne *operating room nurse*

## Franklin

Fairchild, Phyllis Elaine *school counselor*

## Gilbert

Bell, Wallace Edward *minister, insurance agent*

**Glenmora**
Burns, Linda D. *elementary school educator*

**Gonzales**
Adams, Jason D. *obstetrician, gynecologist*

**Grambling**
Francis, Norman C. *academic administrator*
Judson, Horace Augustus *academic administrator, chemistry educator*
Porter, Wilma Jean *retired educational consultant*
Robinson, Eddie Gay *college football coach*
Seetala, Naidu V. *physics professor, researcher*

**Gretna**
Kennedy, Maydra Jane Penisson (J.P. Kennedy) *poet*
Layman, Kim Florinda Marie *pharmacist, writer*

**Hammond**
Hill, Catherine Parham *school psychologist*
Levi, Danilo *sociologist, educator, director*
Parish, Richard Lee *engineer, consultant*
Parker, Clea Edward *retired university president*
Pittman, Iddo, Jr. *retired lawyer*
Ratliff, Joy *music educator, singer*
Richardson, Thaddeus Maurice *funeral director*
Valverde, Roldan Arturo *education educator, researcher*

**Harahan**
O'Neal, Edgar Carl *psychology professor*

**Harvey**
Simon, Keith R. *safety engineer, petroleum engineer, radio personality*
Weekley, Judy Liddington *special education educator*

**Houma**
Adams, Richard David *music educator*
Dagenhardt, Glynn Anthony *secondary school educator*
Walters, Steven Anthony *small business owner, consultant*

**Iowa**
Kuykendall, Richard G. *music educator*

**Kaplan**
LeMoine, Frank Eugene *lawyer, judge*

**Kenner**
Farber, George Allan *dermatologist, educator*
Hallila, Bruce Allan *welding engineer*
Kuebler, David Wayne *insurance company executive, private investigator*
McShan, Clyde Griffin, II, *diversified financial services company executive*

**La Place**
Cicet, Donald James *lawyer*
Fiffie Proctor, JoAnn *media and technology specialist*
Lodwick, Judith Lynne *nursing educator*

**Lacombe**
Hendricks, Donald Duane *retired school librarian*

**Lafayette**
Angers, Winston Thomas *lawyer, publishing executive*
Authement, Ray Paul *college president*
Brasseaux, Carl Anthony *historian, educator, academic administrator, curator*
Cain, Judith Sharp *mathematics professor, consultant*
Carstens, Jane Ellen *retired library science educator*
Clark, Elsa Myriam *artist*
Colbert-Cormier, Patricia A. *secondary school educator*
Culotta, Frank Jay, Jr. *preventive medicine physician*
Daniel, Margaret Hagen *music and voice educator*
Dasgupta, Subrata *director*
Davidson, James Joseph III *lawyer*
Davis, William Eugene *federal judge*
Domingue, Emery *retired consulting engineering company executive*
Duhe, John Malcolm, Jr. *federal judge*
Fang, Cheng-Shen *chemical engineering professor*
Fekih, Afef *education educator*
Gaines, Ernest James *author*
Goforth, William H. *lawyer*
Hail, Karen L. *bank executive*
Henderson, Mary Stanley *museum director, writer*
Judice, Marc Wayne *lawyer*
Lim, Chan Kiat *music educator*
Marshak, Alan Howard *electrical engineer, educator*
Meza, Luis Alberto *internist, researcher*
Neuner, Frank X., Jr. *lawyer*
Oller, John W., Jr. *educator, writer*
Petry, Ruth Vidrine *retired principal*
Raffel, Burton Nathan *literature educator, poet, translator*
Redding, Evelyn A. *dean*
Rickey, Horace B., Jr. *retired civil engineer, retired architectural engineer*
Rieck, William Albert *education educator, academic administrator*
Saloom, Kaliste Joseph, Jr. *lawyer, retired judge*
Sides, Larry Eugene *advertising executive*
Skinner, Michael David *lawyer, lobbyist, consultant*
Stravinska, Sarah *dance educator*

**Lake Charles**
Beam, James Carroll (Jim Beam) *retired newspaper editor*
Clement, Richard Joseph *retired obstetrician, gynecologist*
Drez, David Jacob, Jr. *orthopedic surgeon, educator*
Fields-Gold, Anita *retired dean*
Gunderson, Clark Alan *orthopedic surgeon*
Hebert, Robert D. *academic administrator*
Lacoste, Alan Daniel *physician, educator, medical company executive*

**Levingston**, Ernest Lee *engineering company executive*
Middleton, George, Jr. *clinical child psychologist*
Mount, Willie Landry *state legislator*
Stacey, Truman *journalist, consultant*
Veron, J. Michael *lawyer, writer*

**Leesville**
Gutman, Lucy Toni *social worker, educator*
Thompson, Darlene Bennett *realtor, musician*

**Madisonville**
Young, Lucy Cleaver *retired physician*

**Mandeville**
Aaron, Shirley Mae *retired tax specialist*
Arrowsmith, Marian Campbell *elementary school educator, supervisor, educator*
Childress, Joel M. *medical educator*
Christian, John Catlett, Jr. *lawyer*
Deano, Edward Joseph, Jr. *lawyer, retired state legislator*
Ewen, Pamela Binnings *retired lawyer*
Genevay, Kelly Elizabeth *music educator*
Lamid, Sofjan *physician, educator*
Landry, Joseph L., Jr. *retired affirmative action specialist*
Treuting, Edna Gannon *retired nursing administrator, educator*

**Many**
Behari, Vishnu N. *physician, health facility administrator*
Dutton, Frank Elroy *data processing executive, writer*

**Marksville**
Riddle, Charles Addison III *district attorney, former state legislator*

**Marrero**
Kushner, Frederick Gary *cardiologist, medical educator*

**Metairie**
Album, Jerald Lewis *lawyer*
Arthur, Jett Clinton *retired chemist*
Blunt, Joyce Omega *special education educator*
Brees, Drew *professional football player*
Bush, Reggie *professional football player*
Casselli, Henry Calvin, Jr. *artist, painter*
Chambers, Thomas Edward *academic administrator, psychologist*
Crosby, Deborah Berry *artist*
Crosby, Marena Lienhard *retired academic administrator*
Dickerson, Lon Richard *library administrator*
Edisen, Clayton Byron *physician*
Evans, Carol Rockwell *nursing administrator*
Falco, Maria Josephine *political scientist*
Fantaci, James Michael *lawyer*
Feran, Russell G. *sales executive*
Gereighty, Andrea Saunders *diversified financial services company executive, poet*
Grau, Shirley Ann (Mrs. James Kern Feibleman) *writer*
Grimm, John Lloyd *marketing professional*
Grotkowski, Edward Michael *music educator, director*
Jacobs, Benjamin Franklin *cardiologist*
Lake, Wesley Wayne, Jr. *internist, allergist, medical educator*
Nehrbass, Seth Martin *lawyer*
Nicoladis, Michael F. *engineering company executive*
Nix, Linda Ann Bean *public relations executive*
Payton, Sean *professional football coach*
Pizzo, Andrew Joseph *music educator*
Rosen, Charles, II, *retired lawyer*
St. John, Bridgette Alayne *secondary school educator*
Villia, Morris Sabastian *music producer, publishing executive, writer*
Wood, Jonathan Stuart *economist, educator*

**Minden**
Kemmerly, James Robert *obstetrician, gynecologist*

**Monroe**
Bulot, James John *gerontologist, educator*
Cofer, James Erwin *academic administrator*
Cooksey, John Charles *ophthalmologist, retired congressman*
Ewing, R. Stewart *telecommunications company executive*
Foreman, Teresa *educational consultant, educator*
Fouts, James Fremont *mining company executive*
Galle, Jeffrey Wayne *literature and language professor, department chairman*
Hawley, Jeffrey Lance *investments executive, accountant*
Huntington, Lisa Lynee *music educator*
Mickel, Ruth Phelps *commentator, librarian*
Post, Glen Fleming III *telecommunications industry executive*
Profit, Loretha Spurs *retired elementary school educator*
Sartor, Daniel Ryan, Jr. *lawyer*
Smith, Donald Raymond *librarian*
Smith, Pamela LaTrice *school psychologist*
Trapp, A.C. *retired music educator*

**Napoleonville**
Blanchard, Donald Pierre, Jr. *petroleum engineer*

**Natchitoches**
Anzaldua, Lori Anne *music educator*
Egan, Shirley Anne *retired nursing educator*
Findley, James Lee *academic administrator, history professor*
Lacina, Lorna J. *education educator*
LeBreton, Marietta M. *history professor*
Moreau, Robert Daniel, Jr. *art educator*
Wells, Carol McConnell *genealogist, retired archivist*
Whitehead, Malcolm T. *research scientist*
Wolfe, George Cropper *retired private school educator, artist, writer*

**New Iberia**
Hamilton, Roger Paul, Jr. *lawyer*
Hockless, Mary Fontenot *educational consultant*

**New Orleans**
Abaunza, Donald Richard *lawyer*
Abbott, Hirschel Theron Jr. *lawyer*
Acomb, Robert Bailey, Jr. *lawyer, educator*
Adkerson, Richard C. *mining executive*
Agrawal, Krishna Chandra *pharmacology educator*
Allen, Gary Curtiss *geology educator*
Allerton, William III *public relations executive*
Alsobrook, Henry Bernis, Jr. *lawyer*
Amoss, Walter James, III, (Jim Amoss) *editor*
Andrews, E. Wyllys *archaeologist, educator*
Bacot, Marie *management consultant, researcher*
Bailey, Barry Stone *sculptor, educator*
Balée, William L. *anthropology educator*
Ball, Millie (Mildred Porteous Ball) *editor, journalist*
Barach, Jeffrey Alvan *management educator*
Barry, Francis Julian, Jr. *lawyer*
Beard, Elizabeth Letitia *physiologist, educator*
Beck, David Edward *surgeon*
Beer, Peter Hill *federal judge*
Benjamin, Adelaide Wisdom *retired lawyer, retired community volunteer and activist*
Benjamin, Edward Bernard, Jr. *lawyer*
Bennett-Johnson, Earnestine Rose *education educator, consultant*
Berenson, Gerald Sanders *physician*
Berrigan, Helen Ginger *federal judge*
Bieck, Robert Barton, Jr. *lawyer*
Birtel, Frank Thomas *mathematician, philosopher, educator*
Blackwell, James E. *retired science educator*
Bookhardt, Fred Barringer, Jr. *architect*
Boudreaux, Kenneth Justin *economist, educator*
Brinkley, Douglas *historian, writer, educator*
Brown, Jerry A. *federal bankruptcy judge*
Brumfield, William Craft *Slavic studies educator, photographer, writer*
Bullard, Edgar John III *museum director*
Calogero, Pascal Frank, Jr. *state supreme court justice*
Canizaro, Joseph *real estate developer*
Cargille, Charles M. *internist, pain management physician, educator*
Carter, James Clarence *pastor, educator*
Casellas, Joachim *art gallery executive*
Chetta, Holly Ann *transportation executive*
Childress, Steven Alan *law educator*
Christovich, Alvin Richard, Jr. *lawyer*
Clark, Joshua Maker *publishing executive*
Claverie, Philip deVilliers *lawyer*
Clement, Edith Brown *federal judge*
Cody, Wilmer St. Clair *educational policy researcher*
Cohn, Isidore, Jr. *surgeon, educator*
Coleman, James Julian *lawyer*
Coleman, James Julian, Jr. *lawyer, industrialist, real estate company executive*
Collins, Harry David *forensic engineer, mechanical engineer, nuclear engineer, claims consultant*
Cook, Victor Joseph, Jr. *finance educator, consultant*
Cospolich, James Donald *electronics executive, consultant*
Cotton, John G. *career military officer*
Cowen, Scott S. *academic administrator*
Creppel, Claire Binet *hotel owner*
Crumley, David Oliver *publishing executive, writer, corporate executive*
Crusto, Mitchell Ferdinand *lawyer, educator*
Culbertson, Richard Allen *healthcare educator, health facility administrator*
Dahlberg, Carl Fredrick, Jr. *entrepreneur*
Dennis, James Leon *federal judge*
Didriksen, Caleb H. III *lawyer*
Doley, Harold Emanuel, Jr. *securities company executive*
Domer, Floyd Ray *pharmacologist, educator*
Duncan, Margaret Caroline *physician*
Duplantier, Adrian Guy *federal judge*
Duval, Stanwood Richardson, Jr. *judge*
Easson, William McAlpine *psychiatrist, educator*
Ernest, Tabi Elise *art educator, photographer*
Espinoza, Luis Rolan *rheumatologist, researcher*
Ewin, Dabney Minor *surgeon*
Fagaly, William Arthur *curator*
Falgoust, Dean Thomas *lawyer, accountant*
Ferguson, Charles Austin *retired newspaper editor*
Fisher, James William *pharmacologist, medical educator*
Fleischer, Barbara Jane *organizational psychologist, consultant, researcher*
Flower, Walter Chew III *investment counselor*
Force, Robert *law educator*
Frantz, Phares Albert *architect*
Friedmann, Patricia Ann *writer*
Frohlich, Edward David *medical educator*
Fuselier, Harold Anthony, Jr. *urologist, director, educator*
Garcia, Patricia A. *lawyer*
Gay, Esmond Phelps *lawyer*
Goins, Richard Anthony *lawyer, educator*
Gordon, Joseph Elwell *university official, educator*
Gould, Harry J. III *neurology educator*
Griffin, Jeffrey Farrow *surgeon*
Hà, Tài Huy *mathematician*
Harvey, John Grover *mathematics professor, information scientist*
Hasselbach, Karlheinz *literature educator, dean*
Healy, George William III *lawyer, mediator*
Herman, Russ Michel *lawyer*
Hoffman, Donald Alfred *lawyer*
Hollier, Larry Harold *vascular surgeon, hospital administrator, dean*
Hovland, Eric Jeffrey *dean, endodontics educator*
Howard, Richard Ralston, II, *medical health advisor, researcher, financial consultant*
Hughes, Alfred Clifton *archbishop*
Hurley, Grady Schell *lawyer*
Hyman, Albert Lewis *cardiologist, educator*
Hyslop, Newton Everett, Jr. *infectious disease specialist*
Incaprera, Frank Philip *internist*
Irons, Paulette Riley *state legislator, lawyer*

Ivens, Mary Sue *microbiologist, medical mycologist*
Johnson, Arnold Ray *public relations executive*
Johnson, Bernette Joshua *state supreme court justice*
Johnson, Peter Forbes *transportation executive, business owner*
Jones, Glenn Earle *property management executive*
Jones, Philip Kirkpatrick, Jr. *lawyer*
Judell, Harold Benn *lawyer*
Kelly, Eamon Michael *university president emeritus*
Kewalramani, Laxman Sunderdas *surgeon, consultant*
Khaton, Sabrina Roslyn *librarian, accountant*
Kimball, Catherine D. *state supreme court justice*
Klingman, John Philip *architect, educator*
Knoll, Jeannette Theriot *state supreme court justice*
Kolinsky, Michael Allen *emergency physician*
Langston, Thomas Samuel *political science professor*
Lannes, William Joseph III *electrical engineer*
Lemann, Thomas Berthelot *lawyer*
Letten, James B. *prosecutor*
Lewy, John Edwin *pediatric nephrologist*
Lind, Thomas Otto *barge transportation company executive*
Lintinger, Gregory John *electrical engineer, educator*
Livaudais, Marcel, Jr. *federal judge*
Locke, William *retired endocrinologist*
Longwell, Kelly (A. Kelton Longwell) *lawyer*
Looney, Joseph W. *lawyer*
Lopez, Manuel *immunology and allergy educator*
Lovett, William Anthony *law and economics educator*
Lowe, Robert Charles *lawyer*
Lundy, Larry *food franchise company executive*
Lupo, Robert Edward Smith *real estate developer and investor*
Luza, Radomir Vaclav *historian, educator*
Marcus, Bernard *lawyer, arbitrator, mediator*
Marks, Charles Dennery *insurance consultant*
Martin, David Hubert *internist, epidemiologist, educator*
Mathes, Edward Conrad *architect*
Matthews, Brenda J. *human resources specialist*
Mbadugha, Loretta Nkeiruka Akosa *social services administrator, consultant*
McCall, John Patrick *college president, educator*
McFadden, P. Michael *physician, surgeon*
McFarland, James W. *finance educator*
McFerren, Martha Dean *writer, librarian*
McGlone, Michael Anthony *lawyer*
McMillan, Lee Richards, II, *lawyer*
McSwain, Norman Ellsworth, Jr. *surgeon, educator*
Mentz, Henry Alvan, Jr. *retired federal judge*
Michney, Todd Michael *history professor*
Miller, Pierre Valcour, II, *lawyer*
Millikan, Larry Edward *dermatologist*
Mintz, Albert *lawyer*
Mitchell, Kenneth David *physiologist, educator*
Moely, Barbara E. *psychologist, educator*
Moffett, James Robert *mining executive*
Molony, Michael Janssens, Jr. *lawyer, arbitrator, mediator*
Nagin, Ray (Clarence Ray Nagin Jr.) *mayor*
Navar, Luis Gabriel *physiology educator, researcher, director*
Nicholl, Jeffrey Scott *neurologist, educator*
Nichols, Ronald Lee *surgeon, educator*
Norwood, Colvin Gamble, Jr. *lawyer*
Novakov, George John, Jr. *gifted and talented educator, consultant, administrative assistant*
Nuzum, Robert Weston *lawyer*
Ochsner, John Lockwood *thoracic-cardiovascular surgeon*
Olson, Richard David *psychology professor*
O'Quinn, April Gale *obstetrician, gynecologist, educator*
Ortique, Revius Oliver, Jr. *retired judge*
Osakwe, Christopher *lawyer, educator*
Pankey, George Atkinson *internist, educator, researcher*
Paolini, Gilberto *literature educator*
Paradise, Louis Vincent *education educator, dean*
Pearce, John Y. *lawyer*
Peoples, Gerald C. *college president*
Perdew, John Paul *physics professor*
Perlis, Sharon A. *lawyer*
Phelps, Ashton, Jr. *newspaper publisher*
Poesch, Jessie Jean *art historian*
Ponoroff, Lawrence *dean, law educator, consultant*
Pope, John Marvin *journalist*
Porteous, G. Thomas, Jr. *judge*
Prockop, Darwin Johnson *biochemist, medical educator*
Puschett, Jules B. *nephrology educator, researcher*
Query, Lance D. *dean, university librarian*
Rajan, Latha *microbiologist, educator*
Reck, Andrew Joseph *philosopher*
Redmann, John William *lawyer, consultant, school system administrator*
Reza, Ali Hajmohammad *cardiologist*
Riddick, Frank Adams, Jr. *physician, healthcare administrator*
Roberts, Gary Raymond *lawyer, educator*
Rock, John Aubrey *gynecologist, obstetrician, educator, healthcare administrator, retired chancellor*
Rodriguez, Antonio Jose *lawyer*
Roesler, Robert Harry *media consultant*
Rosen, William Warren *lawyer*
Rosensteel, George Thomas *physics professor, nuclear physicist*
St. Julien, Thais Mary *soprano, musician*
Scelfo, Chris *university football coach*
Schalow, Frank Hickey *philosopher, educator*
Scherr, Kevin John *art gallery owner*
Schulte, Francis B. *retired archbishop*
Sherman, Edward Francis *dean, law educator*
Simon, H(uey) Paul *lawyer*
Singreen, Shirley Ann Basile (Mrs. Harry Voss Singreen) *lawyer, consultant*
Skinner, Robert Earle *librarian, author*
Smith, Juanita Bérard *lawyer, artist*
Stansbury, Harry Case *state commissioner*
Stewart, Gregory Wallace *physician*
Straumanis, John Janis, Jr. *psychiatrist, educator*

Tahir, Mary Elizabeth (Liz Tahir) *marketing professional, consultant, writer*
Taylor, Phyllis Miller *energy executive*
Teamer, Charles Carl, Sr. *former fraternal organization administrator*
Thomas, Joseph Winand *lawyer*
Thompson, Martyn Philip *political and literary studies educator, translator*
Thornell, Jack Randolph *photographer*
Threefoot, Sam Abraham *physician, educator*
Timmcke, Alan Edward *colon and rectal surgeon*
Tipler, Frank Jennings III *physicist*
Traylor, Chet D. *state supreme court justice*
Ukpolo, Victor *economics educator*
Usdin, Gene Leonard *psychiatrist*
Vance, Robert Patrick *lawyer*
VanLandingham, Mark Jennings *sociologist, educator*
Vaudry, J. William, Jr. *lawyer*
Vella, Christina *history professor*
Victory, Jeffrey Paul *state supreme court justice*
Wang, Ting *mechanical engineering educator*
Waring, William Winburn *pediatric pulmonologist, educator*
Weimer, John L. *state supreme court justice*
Wiener, Jacques Loeb, Jr. *federal judge*
Williams, Anthony Ervin *music educator*
Williams, Ronald David *telecommunications industry executive*
Witherspoon, Lynn Ralph *physician*
Wolfe, Richard Peel *lawyer*
Worley, Robert Bruce, Jr. *lawyer*
Yang, DaGang *mathematician, educator*
Zhang, Jun *finance educator*

### Newllano
Boren, Lynda Sue *gifted education educator*

### Norco
Munch, Christopher Joseph *music educator*

### Opelousas
Lafleur, Kenneth Charles *ophthalmologist*
Pinac, André Louis III *obstetrician, gynecologist*
Underwood, Lorainne Ballard *literature and language educator*

### Pearl River
Cantrell, Joseph Sires *chemistry professor*
Thiel, David Brian *physician assistant*

### Pineville
Conway, Evelyn Atkinson *accountant, financial analyst*
Lott, Johnnye Jo *elementary school educator, writer*
Nanna, Michael Edward *chemist, researcher*
Smith, Mabel Hargis *retired secondary school educator, musician*
Thrasher, Fay C. *clinical psychologist*

### Ponchatoula
Kuechmann, Christopher Robert *library director*
Kuhn, James Edward *judge*
Warden, Waldia Ann *archdiocese official, director*

### Ruston
Barron, Brian Richard *education educator*
Bourgeois, Patricia McLin *women's health and pediatrics nurse, educator*
Bukowski, Marie Diane *artist, educator*
Crook, Paul B. *performing arts educator, director*
Deasy, William John *construction, engineering, and mining company executive*
Dodge Robbins, Dorothy Ellin *language educator*
Freasier, Aileen W. *special education educator*
Halliburton, Lloyd *Romance philology educator*
Hankins, Jeffery Robin *history professor*
Hudnall, Jarrett, Jr. *management consultant, educator, marketing professional*
Kim, B. J. *technologist, educator*
Marbury, Virginia Lomax *insurance and investment executive*
Maxfield, John Edward *retired university dean*
Mesak, Hani Ibrahim *marketing educator*
Nassar, Raja *statistics educator, researcher, consultant*
Phillips, Thomas J., Jr. *accountant, educator*
Sale, Tom S. III *financial economist*
Sterling, Raymond Leslie *civil engineering educator, researcher, consultant*
Taylor, Foster Jay *retired university president*
Zhu, Huiguang *research educator*

### Saint Martinville
Fournet, Patricia Sibley *retired secondary school educator*

### Schriever
Shaffer, Margaret Minor *retired library director*

### Scott
Richardson, Cindy Guidry *voice educator, music educator, religious education administrator*

### Shreveport
Achee, Roland Joseph *lawyer*
Amin, Helen Jewitt *special education educator*
Blondin, Joan *nephrologist educator*
Brandl, Mary-Katherine *mathematics professor*
Brannon, Guy Emilio *psychiatrist*
Brazile, Orella Ramsey *library director*
Bryant, J(ames) Bruce *lawyer*
Burton, George Aubrey, Jr. *accountant*
Carmody, Arthur Roderick, Jr. *lawyer, director*
Chastain, Merritt Banning, Jr. *lawyer*
Conrad, Steven Allen *critical care and emergency physician, biomedical engineer, educator*
Cox, John Thomas, Jr. *lawyer*
Dai, Yong *psychologist, educator*
Feldman, Larry, Jr. *lawyer*
Foreman, John Patrick *electrical engineer*
Fort, Arthur Tomlinson III *obstetrician, educator*
Friend, William Benedict *bishop*
Goodman, Robert Uhle *lawyer*
Goodman, Sylvia Klumok *film center executive*
Griffith, Robert Charles *allergist, educator*
Harbuck, Edwin Charles *insurance agent*
Heacock, Donald Dee *social worker*
Heldmann, Maureen Gail *physician, radiologist*

Hetherwick, Gilbert Lewis *lawyer*
Hughes, Mary Sorrows *artist*
Hummel, Kay Jean *physical therapist*
Jawahar, Ajay *neurosurgeon, educator*
Jenkins, Clifford *music educator*
Joiner, Gary Dillard *cartographer, writer, history professor*
Jones, Kenneth B., Jr. *surgeon*
Jose, Bisquerra *psychiatrist*
Knight, Adina Kay *allergist, immunologist*
Lazarus, Allan Matthew *retired newspaper editor*
London, Steve Norman *obstetrician, gynecologist, educator*
Makishi, Yasuko *securities trader, writer*
McDonald, John Clifton *surgeon*
McLemore, Laura Lyons *archivist, history educator*
Misra, Raghunath Prasad *physician, educator*
Nelson, Ralph Stanley *lawyer*
Payne, Roy Steven *lawyer*
Pelton, James Rodger *librarian*
Perlman, Jerald Lee *lawyer*
Plummer, Marguerite Reynolds *historian, educator*
Ramey, Cecil Edward, Jr. *lawyer*
Rigby, Perry Gardner *medical association administrator, internist, medical educator*
Robinson, Garry Lewin *television news executive*
Ryder, Randall Taylor *nuclear medicine technologist, director*
Sandifer, Kevin Wayne *archival services executive*
Shea, Joseph Lawrence, Jr. *lawyer*
Shelby, James Stanford *surgeon, researcher*
Shemwell, Mary Anne *adapted physical education specialist*
Shemwell, Robert H. *federal judge*
Stagg, Tom *federal judge*
Stewart, Carl E. *federal judge*
Street, Jeanne *psychologist*
Sutton, Hal Evan *professional golfer*
Tandon, Neeraj *cardiologist, educator*
Tinker, Paul David *music educator*
Washington, Donald W. *prosecutor*
Webb, Donald Arthur *minister*
Wolf, Robert Edward *physician, educator*
Wood, Julienne Louise *librarian, historian*

### Slidell
Dabdoub, Paul Oscar *academic administrator*
Dearing, Reinhard Josef *city official*
Fincher, Margaret Ann *retired secondary school educator*
Larson, Sandra Pauline *music educator*
Lovell, Emily Kalled *retired journalist*
Marton, Kathryn Widman *secondary school educator*
McBurney, Elizabeth Innes *dermatologist, physician, educator*
Muller, Robert Joseph *gynecologist*
Singletary, Alvin D. *lawyer*
Stroud, Robert Arlen *medical equipment company executive*
Stuart, Charles Edward *electrical engineer, oceanographer*
Tewell, Joseph Robert, Jr. *retired electrical engineer*

### Sorrento
Welch, Joe Ben *academic administrator*

### Springhill
Morgan, Larry Ronald *minister*
Thomas, Faye Evelyn J. *elementary and secondary school educator*

### Sulphur
Fuller, Betty Stamps *music educator*
Toniette, Sallye Jean *physician*

### Tallulah
Gilbert, Rochelle Wilhelmina *education educator, consultant*

### Thibodaux
Breaux, Annette Lalande *education educator, writer*
Harris, Rose M. *academic administrator*
Hulbert, Stephen Thompson *academic administrator*

### Tioga
Brandow, Stephen Jon *priest*

### Ville Platte
Patsicostas, Susan Joanna *mental health services professional, psychotherapist*

### Walker
Michel, Jacqueline *geochemist*

### West Monroe
Ford, Mary Ann *secondary school educator, educator*
North, Sherri L. *elementary school educator*

### Westlake
Ecker, John J. *music educator*
Grantham, Camille Renee Theriot *high school librarian, media specialist*
Yarbrough, Frances Carole *music educator*

### Westwego
Brehm, Loretta Persohn *retired art educator, librarian, consultant*

### Zachary
Mills, Elizabeth Jennings *art educator*

## MAINE

### Acton
Cunningham, Joyce Wentworth *retired secondary school educator*

### Allagash
Hafford, Faye O'Leary *writer*

### Andover
Kaltsos, Angelo John *electronics executive, educator, photographer*

### Auburn
Clifford, Robert William *state supreme court justice*
Matthews, Margaret Ellen *physician*

### Augusta
Baldacci, John Elias *governor, former congressman*
Bourque, Bruce Joseph *archaeologist, educator*
Clark, Beth *retired minister*
Cragin, Charles Langmaid *lawyer*
Crosby, Nathaniel Howard *elementary school educator*
Dakivich, Brian Alan *hospital administrator, psychologist*
Donahue, Joseph Gerald *lawyer*
Dunlap, Matthew Gordon *state official, former state legislator*
Edmonds, Beth *state legislator, lieutenant governor*
Gendron, Susan Ann *school system administrator*
Gervais, Paul Nelson *foundation administrator, psychotherapist, writer, public relations executive*
Hussey, John Francis *physician, geriatrician*
Jacobson, James Lamma, Jr. *data processing company executive*
Johnson, Phillip Edward *lawyer*
Martin, John Lewis *state legislator*
McCormick, Dale *state official*
Nickerson, John Mitchell *political science professor*
Randall, Richard J. *academic administrator*
Rowe, G. Steven *state attorney general*
Wilkinson, Lester F., Jr. *lawyer*

### Bangor
Ballesteros, Paula Mitchell *nurse*
Bickford, Meris J. *lawyer, bank executive*
Bullock, William Clapp, Jr. *banker*
Coffman, Michael S. *international organization official, ecologist*
Foster, Walter Herbert, Jr. *real estate company executive*
Kelley, Barbara Bannin *physical education educator*
King, Stephen Edwin *writer, scriptwriter*
King, Tabitha *author*
MacTaggart, Terrence Joseph *professor, former university chancellor*
McKinnon, Carolyn Ann *child care center director*
Palmer, Thomas Howard, Jr. *retired surgeon*
Rea, Ann W. *librarian*
Rosen, Clifford James *internist*
Rudman, Paul Lewis *lawyer, former state supreme court justice*
Silver, Warren M. *state supreme court justice*

### Bar Harbor
Carpenter, William Morton *language educator, writer*
Coleman, Douglas *research scientist, educator*
Gould, Douglas Bradley *biomedical researcher*
Krevans, Julius Richard *academic administrator, internist*
Leiter, Edward Henry *cell biologist, researcher*
Nass, Meryl J. *physician, writer, research scientist*
Swazey, Judith Pound *academic administrator, science educator*

### Bath
Galleher, Gay *psychologist*
Stoudt, Howard Webster *biological anthropologist, consultant*

### Belfast
DeSilvey, Dennis Lee *cardiologist, educator, academic administrator*
Griffith, Patricia King *journalist*
Worth, Mary Page *mayor*

### Belgrade Lakes
Kany, Judy C(asperson) *retired state senator*

### Biddeford
Ford, Charles Willard *medical educator*

### Blue Hill
Young, David Michael *biochemist, molecular biologist, internist, educator*

### Bremen
Wilson, Linda Smith *retired academic administrator*

### Brewer
Cote Robbins, Rhea Jeannine *writer, educator*

### Bristol
Sabin, William Albert *writer*

### Brooklin
Schmidt, Klaus Dieter *marketing professional, management consultant, educator*
Schmidt, Lynda Wheelwright *psychotherapist*

### Brunswick
Aranson, Robert *physician, director*
Broene, Richard Dale *chemistry professor*
Fuchs, Alfred Herman *psychologist, educator*
Greason, Arthur LeRoy, Jr. *retired university administrator*
Hodge, James Lee *German language educator*
King, Angus S., Jr. *former governor*
Kline, Katy *museum director*
Levine, Daniel *historian, educator*
McEwen, Craig A. *dean*
Mills, Barry *academic administrator, lawyer*
Owen, H. Martyn *retired lawyer*
Page, David Sanborn *biochemist, educator, environmental scientist, consultant*
Pfeiffer, Sophia Douglass *retired state legislator, lawyer*
Putnam, Samuel Patrick *psychologist*
Schwartz, Elliott Shelling *composer, writer, music educator*
Visser, Richard Edgar *minister*

### Bryant Pond
Conary, David Arlan *investment company executive*

### Bucksport
Ives, Edward Dawson *folklore educator*

### Camden
Dyer, Barbara F. *retired accountant, writer*
Etter, Howard Lee *artist*
Kidder, Rushworth Moulton *journalist*
Moran, Elizabeth Ames *library director*

### Cape Elizabeth
Cotter, Joseph Francis *retired bank executive, hotel executive*
Materson, Edward Arthur *sculptor, artist*
Rich, John Hubbard, Jr. *news correspondent*

### Cape Neddick
Ksypka, Helen *organizational consultant*

### Casco
Brown, Ronald Osborne *telecommunications and computer systems consultant*

### Castine
Berleant, Arnold *philosopher*
Bernstein, Lester *editorial consultant*
Davis, Peter Frank *filmmaker, writer*
Wiswall, Frank Lawrence, Jr. *lawyer, educator*

### Chebeague Island
Traina, Albert Salvatore *publishing executive*

### Corea
Harward, Donald West *retired academic administrator*

### Cumberland Foreside
Martin, Joseph Robert *retired corporate financial executive*

### Cushing
Magee, Alan *artist*

### Damariscotta
Blake, Bud (Julian Watson) *cartoonist*
Fuller, Melvin Stuart *botany educator*

### Deer Isle
Smith, Gardner Watkins *physician*

### Dixmont
Cummings, James William *poet*

### Dresden
Iserbyt, Charlotte Thomson *researcher, consultant, writer, educator*
Turco, Lewis Putnam *language educator*

### East Boothbay
Eldred, Kenneth McKechnie *acoustician, consultant*
Ford, Richard *writer*
Gibson, Barry Joseph *editor*

### Edgecomb
Carlson, Suzanne Olive *architect*

### Ellsworth
Whedon, Ralph Gibbs *manufacturing executive*

### Fairfield
Martin, James *retired education educator*

### Falmouth
Cabot, Lewis Pickering *manufacturing company executive, art consultant*
Hathaway, Lynn McDonald *education advocate, administrator*
Kendrick, Peter Murray *communications executive, investor*
Pierce, Philip Sargent *clinical psychologist*
Rohsenow, Warren Max *retired mechanical engineer, educator*
Winton, Linda *international trainer and consultant*

### Farmington
Kalikow, Theodora June *academic administrator*
Mathews, Linnea Koons *science educator, librarian*
Melcher, James Patrick *political scientist, educator*

### Fort Fairfield
Shapiro, Joan Isabelle *lab administrator, medical/surgical nurse*

### Fort Kent
Cost, Richard Willard *academic administrator, educator*

### Freeport
Cushman, Margaret Jane *herbalist, nurse*
Panish, Morton B. *retired physical chemist*

### Friendship
MacIlvaine, Chalmers Acheson *retired financial executive, former association executive*

### Gardiner
Dunbar, Robert Everett *writer, educator*
Gosline, Norman Abbot *real estate appraiser, consultant*

### Georgetown
Chapin, Maryan Fox *civic worker*
Chapin, Richard *arbitrator, director*

### Gorham
Carey, David R., Jr. *history professor*
Chaulet, (Frédérique) Emmanuelle *performing company executive, actress, educator*
Chen, Ray Gow Hwei *art educator, department chairman, artist*
Lehmann, Robert Alexander *conductor, musician, director*

### Gouldsboro
Thayer, Cynthia A. *farmer, writer*

### Hampden
Scroggins, M. Suzanne Paonessa *budget analyst*

**Hancock**
Blasi, Antonio *music educator*

**Hancock Point**
Silvestro, Clement Mario *museum director, historian*

**Hebron**
Marchetti-Ponte, Karin *lawyer, land conservation consultant*

**Islesboro**
Rogers, William Raymond *retired academic administrator, psychologist, educator*

**Kennebunk**
Betts, Edward *artist*
Damon, Edmund Holcombe *retired plastics company executive*
Escalet, Frank Diaz *small business owner*
Pozdeev-Freeman, Yuri *research scientist*
Rollerson, Marnie Loreen *secondary school educator, art educator*

**Kennebunkport**
Featherman, Bernard *steel company executive*
Featherman, Sandra *academic administrator, political science professor*
Mulvihill, James Edward *periodontist, educator*
Ray, Virginia H. S. *columnist, writer*

**Kingfield**
Silver, Sally *minister*
Wescott, Seth *Olympic athlete*

**Kittery**
McNally, James Henry *physicist, defense consultant*

**Kittery Point**
Green, Edward Crocker *research scientist*

**Lamoine**
Schmidt, Christine Alice *art gallery owner*

**Lewiston**
Bessire, Mark H.C. *museum director*
Hansen, Elaine Tuttle *academic administrator*
Reich, Jill *dean*
Semon, Mark David *physicist, researcher*

**Lincoln**
Kneeland, Douglas Eugene *retired newspaper editor*

**Little Deer Isle**
Mills, David Harlow *psychologist, professional society administrator*

**Lubec**
Hayes, Ernest M. *podiatrist*

**Milbridge**
Enslin, Theodore Vernon *poet*

**Moody**
Wagstaff, Barbara Jane *marketing executive*

**Mount Desert**
Crawford, Richard Bradway *biologist, biochemist, educator*

**New Gloucester**
Jaccaci, August Thayer, Jr. *social architect, educator*
Jasinski, Kenneth M. *energy executive*

**New Harbor**
Carr, James Revell *writer, curator, retired museum director*
Fradley, Frederick Macdonell *retired architect*
Lyford, Cabot *sculptor*

**New Vineyard**
Smith, Frederick Orville, II, *agricultural products executive, retired military officer*

**North Yarmouth**
Fecteau, Rosemary Louise *educational administrator, educator, consultant*

**Ogunquit**
West, Norman Ellsworth *artist*

**Old Orchard Beach**
Day, Marlene E. *elementary school educator*

**Old Town**
Alex, Joanne DeFilipp *elementary school educator*
Nelligan, Annette Frances *social worker*
Priest, Jeffrey Arnold *music educator*
Ritz, George F. *forester, consultant*

**Orono**
Cohn, Steven Frederick *sociology educator, consultant*
Cox, Dennis Keith *music educator, conductor*
Dalton, Timothy John *economics professor*
Dodge, Clayton Willard *mathematics professor*
Estler, Suzanne E. *education educator*
Goldstone, Sanford *psychologist, educator*
He, Zhongqi *chemist, researcher*
Innis, Daniel Eugene *dean, consultant*
Kennedy, Robert Alan *educational administrator*
Rice, Edward Perry *secondary school educator*
Risberg, Erica Lynn *archivist, film producer*
Szymanski, Edna Mora *dean*
Townsend, David W. *director*
Weiss, Robert Jerome *psychiatrist, educator*
Wiersma, G. Bruce *dean, forester, educator*

**Orrs Island**
Nelson, Robert Louis *lawyer*

**Palermo**
Anderson, Alfred Oliver *mathematician, consultant*

**Peaks Island**
Bohan, Thomas Lynch *physicist, lawyer*

**Penobscot**
dePaolo, Ronald Francis *editor-in-chief, writer*

**Portland**
Alexander, Donald G. *state supreme court justice*
Blair, Bonnie Kathleen *former professional speedskater, former Olympic athlete*
Bradford, Carl O. *judge*
Bucci, Thomas Vincent *music educator, pianist, composer*
Buckley, Paul Richard, Sr. *insurance executive*
Calkins, Susan W. *state supreme court justice*
Candage, Howard Everett *insurance management consultant, agent, broker*
Carter, Gene *judge*
Chow, Amy *gymnast, Olympic athlete*
Clark, Gordon Hostetter, Jr. *physician*
Coburn, Andrew F. *research scientist educator*
Coffin, Frank Morey *federal judge*
Dana, Howard H., Jr. *state supreme court justice*
Dill, William Rankin *college president*
Duff, John A. *law educator*
Gainey, Louis F., Jr. *biology educator*
Glassman, Caroline Duby *state supreme court justice*
Graffam, Ward Irving *lawyer*
Haddad, Freddie Duke, Jr. *not-for-profit fundraiser, consultant*
Harvey, Charles Albert, Jr. *lawyer*
Hornby, David Brock *federal judge*
Hunt, David Evans *lawyer*
Ives, Samuel Clifton *minister*
James, Tillian *ergonomist*
Keith, Robert Gordon *data processing executive, historian, researcher*
Khoury, Colleen A. *dean*
Knudsen, Chilton Abbie Richardson *bishop*
Lancaster, Ralph Ivan, Jr. *lawyer*
LeBlanc, Richard Philip *lawyer*
Levy, Jon D. *state supreme court justice*
Lipez, Kermit V. *federal judge, former state supreme court justice*
Lyons, Charles M. *education educator, former academic administrator*
Maher, Christine R. *biologist, educator*
McKusick, Vincent Lee *retired judge, arbitrator, lawyer, mediator*
Miller, Buffy *dancer*
Mitchell, Carol L. *lawyer*
Montegut, Alain J. *physician, consultant*
Neavoll, George Franklin *writer*
Nelson, Michael Allan *lawyer*
O'Brien, Murrough Hall *lawyer*
O'Leary, Dan *museum director*
Opperman, John R. *lawyer*
Pattenaude, Richard Louis *university administrator*
Powers, Ross *Olympic athlete*
Rockefeller, Richard Gilder *medical association administrator*
Rundlett, Ellsworth Turner III *lawyer*
Ryden, Kent C. *social studies educator*
Saufley, Leigh Ingalls *state supreme court chief justice*
Schwanauer, Francis *philosopher, educator*
Sigfridson, Andrew Carl *real estate broker, investor*
Silsby, Paula D. *prosecutor*
Stanley, Eliot Hungerford *small business owner, writer, lawyer*
Stauffer, Eric P. *lawyer*
Thompson, Peter L. *lawyer*
Vincent, Christine *academic administrator*
von Schack, Wesley W. *utilities executive*
Weir, Anne *writer*
White, Jeffrey Munroe *lawyer*
Wipfler, William John *health facility administrator*
Zarr, Melvyn *lawyer, educator*

**Presque Isle**
Burgher, Karl E. *academic administrator*

**Raymond**
Coughlan, Patrick Campbell *lawyer, mediator*
Sinclair, Louis *artist, writer*

**Readfield**
Gower, Shane *social studies educator*

**Rockland**
Collins, Samuel W., Jr. *judge*
Crosman, Christopher Byron *museum director*

**Rockport**
Goodwin, Doris Helen Kearns *historian, writer*

**Saco**
Ames, Ted *environmental scientist*
Mason, Nancy Tolman *retired state agency administrator*
Morgan, Robin Evonne *poet, writer, journalist, editor*
Prescott, Dana E. *lawyer*

**Sanford**
Allan, Jonathan David *autograph dealer, pop culture historian*

**Sangerville**
Harris, Norman Edwin *food scientist, consultant*

**Scarborough**
Raisbeck, Gordon *systems engineer, consultant*
Sadik, Marvin Sherwood *art historian, consultant, retired museum director*
Shire, Donald Thomas *retired chemicals executive, lawyer*

**Seal Harbor**
Forbes, Peter *architect*

**Searsport**
Barnes, Robert Myrrdyn *artist, educator*

**Sedgwick**
Donnell, William Ray *small business owner, communications executive*
Schroth, Thomas Nolan *editor*

**Skowhegan**
Ross, James Owen *education educator, researcher*

**South Bristol**
Lasher, Esther Lu *minister*
Wells, Arthur Stanton *retired manufacturing executive*

**South Paris**
Allen, Daniel Hersey *contractor, music educator, director*

**South Portland**
Delva, Paul D. *lawyer*
Fetteroll, Eugene Carl, Jr. *human resources professional*
Harris, Penny Smith *fundraising consultant*
Huntoon, Abby Elizabeth *artist, educator*
Manuel, Peter Jay *poet, librettist, literature and language professor*
Thompson, Mark S. *electronics executive*
Wheeler, Hewitt Brownell *surgeon, educator*

**South Thomaston**
Buffington, Audrey Virginia *elementary school educator, writer*

**Southport**
Gibson, Edgar Thomas *retired surgeon, educator*

**Southwest Harbor**
Drummond, Carol Cramer *voice educator, lyricist, writer, artist*

**Stockton Springs**
Snyder, Arnold Lee, Jr. *retired military officer, research director*

**Stonington**
Pitts, Edgar Thurlow *writer, retired educator*

**Sullivan**
Davis-Wexler, Ginia *singer, director*

**Sumner**
Rudd, David William *management consultant, chemical engineer, consultant*

**Surry**
Pickett, Betty Horenstein *psychologist*

**Tenants Harbor**
Bates, John Cecil, Jr. *lawyer*

**Topsham**
Arnold, Charles Burle, Jr. *psychiatrist, writer*
Palesky, Carol East *tax accountant*
Rosser, Richard Franklin *educational association administrator, consultant*

**Vinalhaven**
Indiana, Robert (Robert Clark) *artist*

**Waterford**
Stockwell, William F. *not-for-profit fundraiser, consultant*

**Waterville**
Adams, William D. *academic administrator*
Bassett, Charles Walker *literature and language professor*
Benissan, Jordan Messan *music educator*
Chapman, James R. *business and technology educator*
Cook, Susan Farwell *director*
Gemery, Henry Albert *economics professor*
Gilkes, Cheryl Louise Townsend *sociologist, educator, minister*
Laurence, Robert Lionel *chemical engineering professor*
Muehlner, Suanne Wilson *library director*
Simon, David L. *art historian*
Yeterian, Edward Harry *psychologist, educator, administrator*

**Wayne**
Rosenkrantz, Roger Daniel *writer, educator*

**Wells**
Carleton, Joseph George, Jr. *lawyer, state legislator*

**West Baldwin**
Simmonds, Rae Nichols *musician, composer, educator*

**West Bath**
Jorgensen, Jenny *mathematician, educator*

**West Boothbay Harbor**
Goes, Joaquim Ignacio *oceanographer, researcher*
Marshall, Howard Lowen *musicologist, retired music educator*

**Westbrook**
Bride, John W. *communications executive, entrepreneur*
Larochelle, Patricia Anne *technologist*
Lee, Shepard *automobile dealership owner*

**Whitefield**
Marden, Kenneth Allen *advertising executive*

**Wilton**
Emerson, Kathy *writer*

**Wiscasset**
Leslie, Seaver *artist*

**Yarmouth**
Bischoff, David Canby *retired university dean*
Grover, Mark Donald *application developer, computer scientist*
Hart, Loring Edward *academic administrator*
Haynes, Peter Lancaster *utilities executive*
Northrup, Christiane *obstetrician, gynecologist*

**York**
Freeman, Neal Blackwell *communications corporation executive*
Hallam, Beverly (Beverly Linney) *artist*
Lyman, William Welles, Jr. *retired architect*

Minard, Maryann Johnson *elementary school educator, secondary school educator, director*
Roché, Robert Richard *artist*
Smart, Mary-Leigh Call (Mrs. J. Scott Smart) *civic worker*

**York Beach**
MacRury, King *management consultant*

## MARYLAND

**Aberdeen**
Cassady, Shawn Lawrence *psychiatrist*

**Aberdeen Proving Ground**
Carrieri, Arthur Helmut *physicist, researcher*
Clayton, John Daniel *mechanical engineer, researcher*
Cozby, Richard Scott *electronics engineer, military officer*
Craig, Stephen C. *osteopathic physician, army officer*
Davis, Randolph Joseph *museum administrator, consultant*
Halstead, Rebecca S. *career military officer*
Kalinowski, Caroline Marie *environmental scientist*
Mackay, Raymond Arthur *chemist*
Steger, Ralph James *chemist*
Stuebing, Edward Willis *research scientist*
Willens, Scott *pharmacologist, military officer*

**Abingdon**
Wolf, Martin Eugene *lawyer, educator*

**Accident**
Nicklin, Shawn Douglas *history educator*

**Accokeek**
Beddow, Richard Harold *retired judge*
Kutchi, Judith Ann *elementary school educator*

**Adamstown**
Church, Martha Eleanor *retired academic administrator*
Munson, John Christian *acoustician*
Tidball, Charles Stanley *computer scientist, educator*

**Adelphi**
Agwu, Idika Ume *chemist, educator, reading specialist*
Bayne, Stephen B. *electronics engineer, researcher*
Brandt, Howard Edward *physicist*
Gaunaurd, Guillermo C. *physicist, researcher, engineer*
Heeger, Gerald Arthur *university president*
Kirwan, William English, II, *mathematics professor, academic administrator*
Monroe, Bryan *publishing executive, trade association administrator*
Podlesak, Thomas F. *electronics engineer*
Sutherland, Alan Roy *business educator*
Walker, Mamie Odena *retired secondary school educator*
Young, S. Susan *electrical engineer, researcher*

**Ammendale**
Goodpaster, John Vincent *chemist*

**Annapolis**
Ames, Steven Reede *financial planner*
Andrews, Archie Moulton *retired federal official*
Barve, Kumar P. *state legislator*
Battaglia, Lynne Ann *judge*
Berg, Gordon Hercher *banker*
Bontoyan, Warren Roberts *chemist, lab administrator*
Bowen, Linnell R. *director*
Branand, Claire Diane *advertising executive, writer*
Brann, Eva Toni Helene *philosophy educator*
Busch, Michael *state legislator*
Clagett, Virginia Parker *state official*
Clotworthy, John Harris *oceanographic consultant*
Connolly, Janet Elizabeth *retired sociologist, retired criminal justice educator*
Crawford, Carol Gloria *mathematician, educator*
Crosby, Ralph Wolf *communications executive*
Devanny, Louise Bell *public relations executive*
DiPentima, Renato Anthony *corporate financial executive*
Doory, Ann Marie *legislator*
Ehrlich, Robert L., Jr. *governor, former congressman*
Erskine, Janis *educational association administrator*
Finerty, Martin Joseph, Jr. *editor, military officer*
Fry, Virginia Milne *artist, poet*
Galvin, Michael Francis *state agency administrator, arborist*
Gavian, Peter Wood *securities analyst*
Goldwater, Marilyn R(ubin) *medical/surgical nurse, state legislator*
Green, David Charles *retired surgeon*
Greene, Clayton, Jr. *judge*
Grooms, Bruce Estes *career military officer*
Halpern, Joseph Alan *physician*
Hammer, Jacob Myer *physicist, consultant*
Hollinger, Paula Colodny *state legislator*
Jacobs, Linda Joan *secondary school educator*
Jansson, John Phillip *architect, consultant*
Jefferson, Ralph Harvey *international affairs consultant*
Johnson, Bruce *engineering educator*
Kane, Mary Deely *state official*
Kelley, Delores Goodwin *state legislator*
Klejnot, Getha Jean *school nurse practitioner, music educator*
Kolmus, Ryan Francis *music educator*
Kopp, Nancy Kornblith *state official*
Kushner, Jack *retired physician*
Lee, Susan C. *state legislator, lawyer*
Levin, Gilbert Victor *biotechnology company executive*
Levitan, Laurence *lawyer, retired state senator*
Lillard, John Franklin III *lawyer*
Love, Mary Ann E. *state legislator*
Madden, Martin Gerard *former state legislator*

Marienthal, George *telecommunications industry executive*
Markman, Ronald *artist, educator*
Martino, Peter Dominic *financial software company executive, real estate developer, real estate broker, federal agency administrator, consultant, management consultant*
Mason-Chaney, Lisa *curator*
McGuirk, Ronald Charles *retired bank executive, economic advisor*
Miller, John Grider *writer*
Miller, Richards Thorn *naval architect, engineer*
Miller, William Charles *academic administrator, retired naval officer*
Nolan, James P. *lawyer*
Papenfuse, Edward Carl, Jr. *archivist, state official*
Perkins, Roger Allan *lawyer*
Pinkney, Alfred Eli *environmental scientist*
Poe, Luke Harvey, Jr. *lawyer*
Rempt, Rodney P. *career military officer, academic administrator*
Rogers, David Freeman *aerospace engineering educator*
Ruben, Ida Gass *state senator*
Salem, Thomas Eric *electrical engineer, educator*
Schaefer, William Donald *state official, former governor*
Schleicher, Nora Elizabeth *bank executive, treasurer, accountant*
Schneider, Carl Stanley *physics professor, researcher*
Seep, Dorothy M. *music educator*
Sheppard, John Wilbur *computer research scientist*
Steele, Michael *lieutenant governor*
Stern, Margaret Bassett *retired special education educator, author*
Symonds, Craig *historian, writer*
Thoms, Josephine Bowers *artist*
Tosé, Maurice B. *communications executive*
Trescott, Sara Lou *water resources engineer*
Trost, Carlisle Albert Herman *retired naval officer*
Welch, Robert Bond *ophthalmologist, educator*
Werking, Richard Hume *librarian, historian, academic administrator*
Wolf, Alfred A. *physicist, educator*

### Arnold

Constants, Dorothy Marie *manufacturing executive*
Harris, Roger Clark *psychiatrist, consultant*
Marder, Barbara Hermling *theater educator, department chairman*
Smith, Martha A. *academic administrator*
Williams, James Arthur *retired military officer, information technology executive*

### Ashton

Smith, Kent Ashton *information scientist, consultant*
Whelan, Roger Michael *lawyer, educator*

### Baldwin

Kiper, Mel, Jr. *sports commentator*

### Baltimore

Abd-Elmoniem, Khaled Zakarya *biomedical engineer, researcher*
Abrams, Rosalie Silber *retired state agency official*
Achinstein, Peter Jacob *philosopher, educator*
Adams, Harold Lynn *architect*
Allan, Janet D. *dean*
Allen, Norma Ann *librarian, educator*
Allen, Ronald John *astrophysics educator, researcher*
Alves, Donald W. *emergency physician, educator*
Anderson, Gerard Fenton *economist, academic administrator*
Anderson, Jean R. *women's health physician*
Angelos, Peter G. *professional sports team executive, lawyer*
Apsel, Alyssa *electrical engineer, computer engineer*
Arlotta, John J. *pharmaceutical executive*
Arrindell, Nicholas J. *academic administrator, educator*
Asuncion-Miller, Lana Martina *school psychologist*
Aumann, R. Karl *commissioner, former state official*
Aurelian, Laure *medical sciences educator*
Bahrami, Hossein *epidemiologist, physician*
Baines, Henry T., Sr. *supermarkets executive*
Baker, Constance H. *lawyer*
Baker, R. Robinson *surgeon*
Baker, Timothy Danforth *physician, educator*
Baldwin, Henry Furlong *banker*
Baldwin, John Wesley *history professor*
Ball, Gregory Francis *biological psychology educator*
Ball, Marion Jokl *academic administrator*
Barnhart, Jo Anne B. *federal agency administrator*
Barnhill, Gregory Hurd *investment banker*
Barth, John Simmons *writer, educator*
Bartlett, James Wilson III *lawyer*
Batten, Sonja Victoria *psychologist, educator*
Baumgartner, William Anthony *cardiac surgeon*
Bausell, R. Barker, Jr. *research methodology educator*
Bedard, Erik *professional baseball player*
Beer, Michael *biophysicist, educator, environmentalist*
Beilenson, Peter Lowell *former public health official*
Bell, Robert M. *judge*
Bellack, Alan Scott *clinical psychologist*
Belzberg, Allan Joel *neurosurgery educator*
Benson, Kris *professional baseball player*
Berghuis, Brian *investment company executive*
Berlage, Jan Ingham *lawyer*
Berns, Peter Vernon *lawyer*
Bhardwaj, Anish *neuroscientist, medical educator*
Bigelow, George E. *psychology and pharmacology scientist*
Blake, Catherine C. *judge*
Blakemore, Karin Jane *obstetrician, geneticist*
Blanton, Edward Lee, Jr. *lawyer*
Blattner, William Albert *physician, epidemiology researcher*
Boardman, John Michael *mathematician, educator*
Bochner, Bruce Scott *immunologist, educator*
Bolger, Doreen *museum director*
Bowman, Donald Eugene *investment advisor*

Bradford, Peter Durgin *elementary school educator*
Bradley, Wanda Louise *librarian*
Brady, Joseph Vincent *behavioral biologist, educator*
Bredar, James Kelleher *judge*
Brem, Henry *neurosurgeon, educator, researcher*
Bridges, John Francis Patrick *healthcare educator, researcher*
Brieger, Gert Henry *medical educator*
Bright, Margaret *sociologist*
Brock, Roslyn McCallister *association executive*
Brockmeyer, Michael F. *lawyer*
Broda-Hydorn, Susan *entomologist*
Brodie, Angela M. *biomedical researcher, educator*
Brodie, Menasha J. (Jay Brodie) *architect, city planner, government executive*
Brody, Eugene Bloor *psychiatrist, educator, editor*
Brody, William Ralph *academic administrator, radiologist, educator*
Broening, Walter Stephens, Jr. *journalist, history educator*
Brotman, Phyllis Block *advertising executive, public relations executive*
Brown, Donald David *biology professor*
Brown, Eddie C. *investment company executive*
Browne, Lovetie W. *special education educator, small business owner*
Burch, Francis Boucher, Jr. *lawyer*
Busuttil, Steven James *surgeon*
Byron, William James *minister, retired academic administrator, finance educator*
Cain, Marcena Jean Beesley *retail executive*
Calvert, Walter Randolph *lawyer*
Cameron, Duke Edward *cardiac surgeon, educator*
Campbell, Jacquelyn C. *community health nurse*
Cao, Dengfeng *pathologist*
Capute, Courtney G. *lawyer*
Carbine, James Edmond *lawyer*
Carlin, Paul Victor *legal association executive*
Carper, Gertrude Esther *small business owner, real estate developer*
Carrier, France *medical educator*
Carson, Benjamin Solomon *neurosurgeon*
Cason, Alan C. *lawyer*
Catania, A(nthony) Charles *psychologist, educator*
Celenza, Christopher S. *language educator*
Chagnoni, Kathleen *energy executive*
Chalk, David *lawyer*
Chapelle, Suzanne Ellery Greene *history professor*
Chaplin, Peggy Louie *lawyer*
Chen, Yu *acupuncturist, Chinese herbologist*
Chiu, Hungdah *law educator*
Choudhury, Dipa *mathematician, educator*
Ciccolo, Angela *lawyer*
Civiletti, Benjamin Richard *lawyer, former United States attorney general*
Clarizio, Lynda M. *advertising executive, lawyer*
Clements, Mary Lou *epidemiologist, educator*
Cohen, Steven Paul *anesthesiologist, researcher*
Cohen, Warren I. *history professor*
Cole, Emried Dargan, Jr. *lawyer*
Coleman, Carolyn Quilloin *association executive*
Colgan, Richard *medical educator*
Colomer, Veronica *medical educator, researcher*
Constantine, Andrew *conductor*
Conway de Macario, Everly *immunologist, molecular biologist*
Cook, Bryson Leitch *lawyer*
Coons, Thomas Wayne *lawyer*
Cooper, Jerrold Stephen *historian, educator*
Cooper, Joseph *political scientist, educator*
Coppel, Lawrence David *lawyer*
Corley, Rose Ann McAfee *government official*
Cornwell, Edward E. III *surgeon*
Crawford, Fred Lee *public information officer*
Crockett, Bryan Lane *language educator, consultant*
Crowe, Thomas Leonard *lawyer*
Cummings, Charles William *otolaryngologist, educator*
Curley, John Francis, Jr. *mutual fund executive*
Curran, J. Joseph, Jr. *state attorney general*
Curran, Robert Bruce *lawyer*
Dang, Chi Van *hematology and oncology educator*
Dannenberg, Arthur Milton, Jr. *experimental pathologist, immunologist, educator*
Dawson, Valina L. *science educator*
DeAngelis, Catherine D. *pediatrics educator*
Deeley, C. Carey, Jr. *lawyer*
DeLateur, Barbara Jane *medical educator*
Del Rosso, Jeana Marie *literature educator*
DePaulo, J. Raymond, Jr. *psychiatrist, researcher*
Derby, Ernest Stephen *federal judge*
DeTolla, Louis James *research scientist, veterinarian*
Deutsch, Robert William *physicist*
Devan, Deborah Hunt *lawyer*
DeVito, Mathias Joseph *retired real estate company executive*
DeWeese, Theodore L. *radiation oncologist*
Dewey, Joel Allen *lawyer*
Diaz-Montes, Teresa P. *oncologist, obstetrician, gynecologist*
DiBiagio, Thomas Michael *lawyer, former prosecutor*
Dicello, John Francis, Jr. *physicist, researcher*
Dickey, George Edward *economist, educator, water transportation executive*
Dickfeld, Timm-Michael *electrophysiologist, cardiologist, educator*
Dickinson, Jane W. *retired executive secretary, volunteer*
Dietze, Gottfried *political science professor*
Diop, Nafissatou *research scientist*
Ditz, Toby Lee *history professor*
Dobs, Adrian Sandra *endocrinologist, educator*
Dodge, Calvert Renaul *education and training executive, author, educator*
Donkervoet, Richard Cornelius *architect*
Donovan, Dianne Francys *journalist*
Dorsey, John Russell *journalist*
Dougherty, John C. *lawyer*
Drachman, Daniel Bruce *neurologist, educator*
Duncan, Lionel Sebastian *artist, educator*
Dunn, Jeffrey A. *lawyer*
Duquette, Jim *professional sports team executive*
Durbin, Dean D. *marketing executive*
Eichhorn, Gunther Louis *chemist, researcher*
Eisenberg, Howard Michael *neurosurgeon*

Eisner, Jonathan David *lawyer*
Ellin, Marvin *lawyer*
Ellis, Brother Patrick (H. J. Ellis) *academic administrator*
Englar, Nancy Ellen *nurse, consultant, nursing educator*
Epstein, Daniel Mark *poet, dramatist, biographer*
Erozan, Yener Sahir *pathologist, educator*
Evans, Nolly Seymour *lawyer*
Eveleth, Janet Stidman *law association administrator*
Faden, Ruth R. *medical educator, ethicist, researcher*
Farber, Donna Lynn *medical researcher, educator*
Fassel, Jim (James E. Fassel) *professional football coach*
Ferencz, Charlotte *pediatrician, epidemiologist, preventive medicine physician, educator*
Ferentz, Kevin Scott *physician*
Fergenson, Arthur Friend *lawyer*
Fisher, Alan Hall *guidebook writer*
Fisher, Morton Poe, Jr. *lawyer*
Ford, John Gilmore *interior designer*
Foster, Lester Anderson, Jr. *metal products executive*
Fox, Harold Edward *obstetrician, researcher, gynecologist, educator*
Franklin, Timothy A. *editor*
Freeland, Claire Ann Bennett *psychologist*
Freischlag, Julie Ann *surgeon*
Frenkil, Steven David *lawyer*
Frerichs, Herbert Donald, Jr. *lawyer*
Friedman, Louis Frank *lawyer*
Friedman, Maria Andre *public relations executive*
Fuentealba, Victor William *professional society administrator*
Fulton, Thomas *theoretical physicist, educator*
Gabriel, Donald Albert *real estate company executive*
Gaither, John Francis, Jr. *lawyer, health products executive*
Gall, Joseph Grafton *biologist, researcher, educator*
Gallo, Robert Charles *research scientist*
Garbis, Marvin Joseph *judge*
Gartner, John D. *clinical psychologist, educator*
Gately, Mark Donohue *lawyer*
Gauvey, Susan Kathryn *judge*
Gendron, Andrew *lawyer*
Giacconi, Riccardo *astrophysicist, educator*
Gifford, Donald George *dean, law educator*
Gillece, James Patrick, Jr. *lawyer*
Gimenez, Luis Fernando *physician, educator*
Glassman, Jon David *aerospace executive*
Gleichmann, Frances Evangeline *retired elementary school educator*
Godenne, Ghislaine Dudley *physician, psychotherapist, educator*
Goldberg, Alan Marvin *toxicologist, educator*
Goldberg, Morton Falk *ophthalmologist, educator*
Goldman, Brian Arthur *lawyer, accountant*
Goldman, Lynn Rose *medical educator*
Gonya, Jeffrey Keenan *lawyer*
Gooden, Eric *government agency administrator, real estate agent*
Goodman, William Richard *insurance adjusting company executive*
Gordis, Leon *physician*
Gordon, Bruce S. *civil rights organization executive, former telecommunications company executive*
Gracias, David H. *chemical engineer, educator*
Grant, Leslie Edwina *dentist, dental association administrator*
Grasmick, Nancy S. *school system administrator*
Gray, Frank Truan *lawyer*
Gray, Oscar Shalom *lawyer*
Green, Bert Franklin, Jr. *retired psychology professor*
Green, Robert Edward, Jr. *physicist, researcher*
Greene, Jack Phillip *historian, educator*
Greenough, William Bates III *medical educator*
Greider, Carol Widney *molecular biology professor*
Griffin, John W. *neurologist, medical educator*
Griffith, Lawrence Stacey Cameron *cardiologist, educator*
Grossman, Joel B(arry) *political science educator*
Guben, Jan K. *lawyer*
Guler, Osman *education educator, researcher*
Gustafson, Thomas *medical association administrator*
Haan, James Mathew *surgeon, researcher*
Hackerman, Willard J. *construction executive*
Haddaway, Heather Michelle *elementary school educator, music educator*
Hafets, Richard Jay *lawyer*
Haig, Frank Rawle *physics professor, priest*
Hanks, James Judge, Jr. *lawyer*
Hansen, Barbara Caleen *physiologist, science educator*
Harris, James Carol Overton, Jr. *psychiatrist, pediatrician*
Harris, Reginald Mervyn, Jr. *librarian, writer*
Harris, Yael *health policy executive*
Harrison, Michael *opera company director*
Harvey, Alexander, II *retired federal judge*
Hauser, Michael George *astrophysicist*
Hayden, Carla Diane *library director, educator*
Hayes, Dennis Courtland *civil rights association executive, lawyer*
Hecht, Alan Dannenberg *insurance executive*
Hecht, Donald D. *lawyer*
Heller, Barbara R. *former dean, nursing educator*
Hellmann, David Bruce *medical educator*
Helm, Donald Cairney *geologist, engineer, educator*
Henderson, Donald Ainslie *public health service officer*
Henderson, Lenneal Joseph, Jr. *political science professor*
Hicks, Sherman Gregory *pastor*
Himelfarb, Richard Jay *investment company executive*
Hirsh, Allan T. III *book publisher*
Hirsh, Allan Thurman, Jr. *publishing executive*
Hirsh, Theodore William *lawyer*
Hofkin, Gerald Alan *gastroenterologist*
Holder, Lawrence Edward *radiologist, educator*
Honemann, Daniel Henry *lawyer*
Hopkins, Samuel *retired investment banker*

Howard, J. Woodford, Jr. *retired political science professor*
Howard, John Vincent, Jr. *lawyer*
Howell, Harley Thomas *lawyer*
Howes, James Guerdon *communications executive*
Hsueh, Mingkai *researcher*
Hug, Richard Ernest *small business owner*
Huganir, Richard Lewis *neuroscientist, educator, researcher*
Huggins, Amy Branum *music educator*
Hungerford, David Samuel *orthopedic surgeon, educator*
Ihrie, Robert *oil, gas and real estate company executive*
Immelt, Stephen J. *lawyer*
Irwin, John Thomas *humanities educator*
Isable, Alisha *elementary school educator*
Jaar, Bernard Georges *nephrologist, researcher*
Jackson, Stanley Edward *retired special education educator*
Jacobs, Richard James *banker, educator*
Jacobson, Katherine Louise *musician, music educator*
Jelinek, Frederick *electrical engineer, educator*
Johns, Richard James *physician, educator*
Johnson, Harry Sterling *lawyer*
Johnson, Kenneth Peter *neurologist, researcher*
Johnson, Michael Paul *historian, educator*
Johnson, Richard Tidball *microbiology and neuroscience educator, virologist, researcher*
Johnston, Edward Allan *lawyer*
Johnston, George W. *lawyer*
Jones, Hendree Evelyn *research scientist, psychologist*
Jones, John Martin, Jr. *lawyer*
Jones, Nicholas P. *civil engineering educator*
Jones, Raymond Moylan *strategy and public policy educator*
Joyce, David Lyle *surgeon*
Judd, Brian Raymond *physicist*
Judson, Horace Freeland *history professor, writer*
Kandel, Nelson Robert *lawyer*
Kaplan, Abner J. *social worker, public relations executive*
Kaplan, Alexander Efimovich *physics educator, engineering educator*
Karni, Edi *economics professor*
Karpa, Jay Norman *surgeon*
Kastor, John Alfred *cardiologist, educator*
Katarzyna, Macura J. *radiologist, researcher*
Kattel, Bheem Prakash *engineering educator, consultant*
Katz, Joseph Louis *chemical engineer, educator*
Kelen, Gabor David *emergency physician*
Keller, George Charles *higher education consultant, writer*
Kelly, Deanna Lynn *pharmacologist, educator*
Kenney, Brigid E. *lawyer*
Kent, Edgar Robert, Jr. *investment banker*
Kenyatta, David Roger Joseph *director, lawyer*
Kerr, Douglas Anthony *neurologist, researcher*
Kessler, Herbert Leon *art historian, educator, academic administrator*
Kessler, Irving Isar *epidemiologist, consultant*
Kim, Lillian G. Lee *retired administrative assistant*
Kirkhart, Matthew Wayde *psychology professor*
Klitzke, Theodore Elmer *arts consultant, retired college dean*
Knapp, David Allan *pharmaceutical educator, researcher, dean*
Knight, Franklin W. *historian, educator*
Kolkin, Mitchell *lawyer*
Kremen, Richard M. *lawyer*
Krolik, Julian Henry *astrophysicist, educator*
Kues, Irvin William *financial planner*
Kumar, Martha Joynt *political science educator*
Kumin, Libby Barbara *speech language pathologist, educator*
Kurth, Lieselotte *foreign language educator*
Kwon, Chul Soo *psychiatrist*
Langmead, Joseph Michael *accountant, consultant, educator*
Lawrence, Robert Swan *physician, educator*
Lawson, Edward Earle *neonatal/perinatal nurse practitioner*
Lazarus, Fred, IV, *academic administrator*
Lazarus, Gerald Sylvan *dermatologist, educator, dean*
Lederer, William Julius *author*
Lee, Michael Kiwon *neuroscientist*
Lee, Steven Xavier *museum director, artist and environmentalist*
Lee, Yung-Keun *physicist, researcher*
Legg, Benson Everett *federal judge*
Legum, Jeffrey Alfred *holding company executive*
Lemer, Andrew Charles *engineer, economist*
Leonard, Angela Michele *librarian, educator*
Leonard, Joseph Howard *staff specialist*
Levien, David Harold *surgeon*
Levin, Edward Jesse *lawyer*
Levine, Richard E. *lawyer*
Lewis, Edwin Augustus Stevens *physics educator*
Lewis, Jamal *professional football player*
Lewis, Ray *professional football player*
Lewison, Edward Frederick *surgeon*
Liberto, Joseph Salvatore *retired federal bank executive*
Lichtenstein, Lawrence Mark *immunologist, allergist, educator*
Lidtke, Doris Keefe *retired computer science educator*
Lidtke, Vernon LeRoy *history professor*
Liebmann, George W(illiam) *lawyer*
Litrenta, Frances Marie *psychiatrist*
Littlefield, John Walley *geneticist, cell biologist, pediatrician*
Long, Donlin Martin *surgeon, educator*
Longo, Dan Louis *internist, researcher, oncologist*
Lorizzo, Robert P. *science administrator*
Loucks, Allen Frazier *prosecutor, lawyer*
Lucas, Barbara B. *electrical equipment manufacturing executive*
Lundy, Audie Lee, Jr. *lawyer*
Macario, Alberto Juan Lorenzo *physician*
Maccini, Louis John *economist, educator*
Mackowiak, Philp Arthur *medical educator, epidemiologist*
MacWilliams, Michael Broughton *lawyer*
Magnuson, Nancy *librarian*
Manson, Paul Nellis *plastic surgeon*
Margolis, Simeon *physician, educator*

Margon, Bruce Henry *astrophysicist, educator*
Marsh, Bruce David *geologist, educator*
Mason, Raymond Adams *finance company executive*
Massey, Garnetta D. *bank executive*
Massey-Burzio, Virginia *librarian, writer*
Massof, Robert William *neuroscientist, educator*
Matheson, Nina W. *medical researcher*
Mathias, James D. *lawyer*
Mathias, Robert Joseph *lawyer*
Matjasko, M. Jane *anesthesiologist, educator*
Matthews, Rondra J. *publishing executive*
Maw, Nicholas *composer, music educator*
McAdam, Paul Edward *retired library administrator*
McCarthy, Patricia Anne *reading educator*
McClung, A(lexander) Keith, Jr. *retired lawyer*
McDaniel, Wayne Allen *transportation executive, consultant*
McHugh, Paul R. *psychiatrist, neurologist, educator*
McKusick, Victor Almon *geneticist, educator, physician*
McMillan, Julia A. *pediatrician*
McNair, Steve LaTreal *professional football player*
McNatt, Glenn *art critic*
McPartland, James Michael *academic administrator*
McPherson, Donald Paxton III *lawyer*
McWilliams, John Michael *lawyer*
Meagher, Anthony L. *lawyer*
Melick, Clifford Francis *sociologist, researcher*
Meltzer, Arthur Adam *researcher, researcher*
Mendell, Joshua T. *molecular biologist, geneticist, educator*
Mfume, Kweisi *civil rights association executive, former congressman*
Miller, Decatur Howard *lawyer*
Miller, Edward Doring *anesthesiologist, hospital administrator, dean*
Miller, Michael *physician, educator*
Millspaugh, Martin Laurence *real estate developer, consultant*
Mixson, Archibald James *research scientist, internist, endocrinologist*
Mocko, George Paul *minister*
Moloney, Herbert W. III *advertising executive*
Moos, H. Warren *physicist, educator, astronomer, director*
Morford, Thomas *health facility administrator*
Moser, Hugo Wolfgang *physician*
Moser, M(artin) Peter *lawyer*
Motz, Diana Gribbon *federal judge*
Motz, John Frederick *federal judge*
Moulton, Lawrence Hale *statistician, educator*
Mountcastle, Vernon Benjamin *retired neuroscientist*
Murphy, Frances Louise, II, *retired newspaper publisher*
Myslinski, Norbert Raymond *medical educator*
Nasr, Nadia *librarian*
Natarajan, Ananth *medical products executive, biomedical engineer*
Nathanson, Harvey Charles *electrical engineer*
Nelkin, Barry David *oncology researcher and educator*
Nelson, Douglas W. *foundation administrator*
N'guerekata, Gaston Mandata *mathematician, department chairman*
Nichols, David Gregory *anesthesiologist, pediatrician, educator*
Nichols, Stephen George *Romance languages educator*
Niemeyer, Paul Victor *federal judge*
Njie, Veronica P.S. *clinical nurse, educator*
Norman, Colin Arthur *astrophysics educator*
Norman, Philip Sidney *physician*
Nyquist, Paul Alan *neurologist, researcher*
Ogden, Jonathan *professional football player*
Ohly, D. Christopher *lawyer*
Oji, Pauline E. *secondary school educator*
O'Malley, Martin Joseph *mayor, lawyer, retired councilman*
Orman, Leonard Arnold *lawyer*
Otal, Monica D. *music educator*
O'Toole, Tara Jeanne *medical educator, former federal agency administrator*
Owsley, Thomas L. *oil industry executive*
Palmeiro, Rafael Corrales *professional baseball player*
Pan, William Kuang-Yao *research scientist*
Park, Mary Woodfill *information consultant, librarian, writer*
Parvis, Peter P. *lawyer*
Paulson, Ronald Howard *language educator, humanities educator*
Perler, Bruce Alan *surgeon*
Perschetz, Arthur Driban *lawyer*
Peterson, Ronald R. *health service administrator*
Pinkard, Anne Merrick *foundation administrator*
Plank, Kevin A. *apparel executive*
Plant, Albin MacDonough *lawyer*
Pokempner, Joseph Kres *lawyer*
Pollak, Joanne Elizabeth *lawyer*
Pollak, Mark *lawyer*
Posner, Gary Herbert *chemist, educator*
Powe, Neil Richard *physician, educator, epidemiologist, public health service officer*
Provorny, Frederick Alan *lawyer, educator*
Puzia, Thomas H. *astronomer, researcher*
Quinn, Michael Desmond *diversified financial services executive*
Radding, Andrew *lawyer*
Ranum, Orest Allen *historian, educator*
Ravenell, Kenneth W. *lawyer*
Rayson, Glendon Ennes *internist, preventive medicine specialist, writer*
Rea, Evan Andrew *curator*
Redden, Roger Duffey *lawyer*
Redfield, Robert R. *virologist, medical educator*
Reid, Lauretta Glasper *retired principal*
Reinsel, Joseph Thomas *art educator, artist*
Rene, Vidal *electrical engineer, educator*
Reno, Russell Ronald, Jr. *lawyer*
Reynolds, William Leroy *lawyer, educator*
Riepe, James Sellers *investment company executive*
Riess, Adam Guy *astronomer, educator*
Roberts, Rosalinda Cusido *medical researcher, educator*

Robinson, Brooks Calbert, Jr. *former professional baseball player, sports commentator, business consultant*
Robinson, Retiana Cecelia *secondary school educator*
Robinson, Zelig *lawyer*
Roby, Mary Lorraine *special education educator*
Roche, George Augustine *investment management executive*
Rodowsky, Lawrence Francis *retired state judge*
Rodricks, Daniel John *columnist, television commentator*
Rogers, Brian Charles *portfolio manager, investment company executive*
Rose, Noel Richard *immunologist, microbiologist, educator*
Roseman, Saul *biochemist, educator*
Rosenberg, Edwin Harold *systems analyst*
Rosenberg, Frank Blaustein *petroleum company executive*
Rosenberg, Henry A., Jr. *petroleum executive*
Rosenstein, Rod J. *prosecutor*
Rosenthal, William J. *lawyer*
Ross, Richard Starr *retired medical school dean, cardiologist, educator*
Rothenberg, Karen H. *dean, law educator*
Roupe, James Paul *accountant*
Rousuck, J. Wynn *theater critic*
Rubin, Aviel David *computer science educator, writer*
Rumbaugh, Jeffrey Arlin *neurologist, neuroscientist*
Ruppert, Joseph Alphonsus *music educator, language educator*
Rzepkowski, James Edward *state agency administrator*
Saba, Walter Pedro *health products executive*
Sachs, Murray B. *audiologist, educator*
Sack, George Henry, Jr. *molecular geneticist*
Salamon, Lester Milton *political science professor*
Samet, Jonathan Michael *epidemiologist, educator*
Sanders, Deion Luwynn *professional football player*
Sanders, Julius Ray *music company executive*
Saudek, Christopher D. *medical educator*
Savonenko, Alena *neuroscientist, educator*
Scales, Robert H., Jr. *former academic administrator, retired army officer*
Schaefer, Robert Wayne *banker*
Schilling, Franklin Charles, Jr. *retail management professional*
Schlaff, Barbara E. *lawyer*
Schochor, Jonathan Jamyer, educator*
Schoenrich, Edyth Hull *internist, preventive medicine physician*
Schultheis, Patricia Ann *writer, editor*
Schumann, Jill *religious organization administrator*
Schuster, Marvin Meier *retired physician, educator*
Schwartz, Howard S. *lawyer*
Scriggins, Larry Palmer *lawyer, director*
Sentinek, Kelly Marie *social studies educator*
Seurkamp, Mary Pat *college president*
Sfekas, Stephen James *lawyer, educator*
Shamoo, Adil Elias *biochemist, educator*
Shannon, Joe *art critic, painter*
Shapiro, Harry Dean *lawyer*
Sharfstein, Joshua M. *city health department administrator, pediatrician*
Shattuck, Mayo Adams III *utilities executive*
Shea, James L. *lawyer*
Shelton, Robert Arthur *lawyer*
Shepherd, Kevin L. *lawyer*
Shiffman, Bernard *mathematician, educator*
Short, Alexander Campbell *lawyer*
Sidransky, David *molecular biologist*
Silbergeld, Ellen Kovner *epidemiologist, researcher, toxicologist*
Siliciano, Robert F. *immunologist, medical educator*
Silver, Michael Joel *lawyer*
Silverberg, Steven George *pathologist, educator*
Silverstone, Harris J. *chemistry professor*
Simmons, Howard L. *education educator*
Sinha, Neeti *biophysicist, researcher*
Sirota, Wilbert H. *lawyer*
Skirpan, Richard Michael *conductor, music educator*
Smith, David Jeddie *American literature educator*
Smith, E. Follin *corporate financial executive*
Smith, Robert G. *lawyer*
Smith, Robert W., Jr., (Jay Smith) *lawyer*
Smith, Stephen Ross *endocrinologist*
Snead, James Arrington *architect*
Snyder, Solomon Halbert *psychiatrist, pharmacologist*
Somer-Oneil, Penny Lynn *lawyer*
Sommer, Alfred *ophthalmologist, medical educator, researcher*
Song, Danny *radiation oncologist*
Sorkin, Alan Lowell *economist, educator*
Sroka, Karen Jean *clinical director*
Stanley, Steven Mitchell *paleontologist, educator*
Starfield, Barbara Helen *pediatrician, educator*
Steiner, Robert Frank *biochemist*
Stephens, Joseph *psychiatrist, researcher*
Sterne, Joseph Robert Livingston *editor, educator*
Stewart, Doris Mae *biology professor*
Stohler, Christian S. *dean, dental educator*
Strickland, Marshall Hayward *bishop*
Strull, Gene *technology consultant, retired manufacturing executive*
Suggs, Kenneth *lawyer*
Summers, Thomas Carey *lawyer*
Suskind, Sigmund Richard *microbiology educator*
Sykes, Melvin Julius *lawyer*
Tabb, Winston *librarian*
Taguchi, Katsuyuki *science educator*
Talalay, Paul *pharmacologist, educator*
Talbot, Donald Roy *management consultant*
Tejada, Miguel *professional baseball player*
Thakor, Nitish Vyomesh *biomedical engineering educator*
Thompson, Otho M. *lawyer, former solicitor*
Tiburzi, Paul A. *lawyer*
Tiefenwerth, William Philip *university program director*
Tilghman, Richard Carmichael, Jr. *lawyer*
Tillapaugh, Daniel Weston *academic administrator*
Tocco, Elaine Kay *insurance agent*
Townsend, Craig Arthur *chemistry educator*

Townsend, John Cunningham *optometrist*
Trpis, Milan *vector biologist, educator*
Trujillo, J. Roberto *virologist*
Tucker, James L., Jr. *art educator, artist*
Tyler, Anne (Mrs. Taghi M. Modarressi) *writer*
Uhl, Scott Mark *state agency administrator*
Van Riper, Robert Austin *writer, retired public relations executive*
Vikan, Gary Kent *museum director*
Vogelstein, Bert *oncology educator*
Wadsworth, Julie Bell *secondary school educator*
Walker, Irving Edward *lawyer*
Walsh, Patrick Craig *urologist*
Walter, Harold Mark *lawyer*
Wang, Tza-Huei (Jeff Wang) *engineering educator*
Warren, Melissa Allison *lawyer*
Washington, Strother Lee, Jr. *mechanical engineer, design engineer*
Wasserman, Richard Leo *lawyer*
Waterbury, Larry *physician, educator*
Watkins, John B. *lawyer*
Weaver, Kenneth Newcomer *geologist, state agency administrator*
Weisfeldt, Myron Lee *cardiologist, educator*
Weisgal, Jeanne Nancy *writer*
Weiss, James Lloyd *cardiology educator*
Welker, James Anthony *physician*
White, Pamela Janice *lawyer*
Whitman, Marland Hamilton, Jr. *lawyer*
Wierman, John Charles *mathematician, educator*
Williams, Roy L. *public relations executive, advocate*
Willis, John T. *former secretary of state*
Wilson, Donald Edward *internist, educator, dean*
Wilson, Thomas Matthew III *lawyer*
Winn, James Julius, Jr. *lawyer*
Wolman, M. Gordon *geography educator*
Woodson, Leon C. *mathematics professor*
Wright, James Dorsey *lawyer*
Wu, Albert W. *medical educator*
Yang, Stephen C. *thoracic surgeon*
Yantis, Steven George *psychology educator*
Yates, Sharon *artist*
Yoskowitz, Irving Benjamin *lawyer, merchant banker*
Young, Barbara *psychiatrist, psychotherapist, educator, photographer*
Yue, Wusi *computer engineer, researcher*
Zaveri, Dimple Jigish *microbiologist, medical technician*
Zaveri, Jigish Shirish *chemical engineer, educator*
Ziff, Larzer *literature and language professor*
Zinkham, W. Robert *lawyer*

## Bel Air

Helfrich, Cornelius David *lawyer*
Lu, David John *historian, writer*
O'Bryon, James Fredrick *defense conusltant*
Thursfield, Fred Falconer, II, *foundation administrator*

## Belcamp

Tapp, Mamie Pearl *educational association administrator*

## Beltsville

Bae, Hanhong *molecular biologist, researcher*
Bruckner, Daniel Raymond *history educator*
Collins, Anita Marguerite *research geneticist*
Klun, Jerome Anthony *entomologist, researcher*
Luo, Yaguang *food scientist, researcher*
Miller, Ted Robert *management consultant*
Nemes, Attila *soil scientist, researcher*
Palm, Mary Egdahl *mycologist*
Quirk, Frank Joseph *management consulting company executive*
Ritz, David M. *photographic retail company executive*
Schneider, Edwin Kahn *research scientist*
Stolwijk, Jan Adrianus Jozef *physiologist, biophysicist*
Tso, Tien Chioh *federal agency administrator, researcher, agronomist*

## Berlin

Brodsky, Allen *retired biophysicist*
Passwater, Barbara Gayhart *real estate broker*
Passwater, Richard Albert *biochemist, author*

## Bethesda

Abdoo, Elizabeth A. *lawyer*
Abrams, David B. *federal agency administrator*
Achin, Milos Kosta *historian, writer*
Aisenberg, Irwin Morton *retired lawyer*
Akhondi, Hossein *internist, researcher*
Alexander, Duane Frederick *federal agency administrator, pediatrician, researcher*
Allmon, Charles W. *investment advisor*
Allnutt, Robert Frederick *management consultant, lawyer*
Alter, Harvey J. *hematologist, educator*
Alving, Barbara *federal agency administrator, hematologist*
Anderson, George Kenneth *physician, retired military officer, foundation administrator*
Apud, Jose Antonio *psychiatrist, researcher*
Arons, Bernard S. *psychiatrist, educator, health services administrator*
Ashkin, Ronald Evan *international executive*
Ashwell, Jonathan D. *medical researcher*
Baird, Bruce Allen *lawyer*
Banik, Sambhu Nath *psychologist*
Barros, Colleen *federal agency administrator*
Barton, Jean Marie *psychologist, educator*
Basavappa, Ravi *biophysical science educator*
Battey, James F., Jr. *federal agency administrator, neurologist*
Bauersfeld, Carl Frederick *lawyer*
Beall, Robert Joseph *foundation executive*
Becker, Edwin Demuth *chemist, director*
Bennink, Jack Richard *immunologist, researcher*
Benson, Elizabeth Polk *art specialist*
Berg, Jeremy Mark *federal agency administrator, biochemist, researcher*
Berger, Robert Lewis *retired biophysicist*
Berman, Marshall Fox *lawyer*
Berzofsky, Jay A. *medical researcher*
Biddle, Albert George Wilkinson, III, (Jack Biddle) *venture capitalist*
Bowsher, Charles Arthur *retired government official, financial executive*

Brady, Roscoe Owen *neurogeneticist, educator*
Brinton, Louise A. *cancer epidemiologist*
Brown, Dudley Earl, Jr. *psychiatrist, educator, health science association administrator, federal agency administrator, retired military officer*
Brown, Elizabeth E. *epidemiologist*
Buetow, Kenneth H. *federal agency administrator*
Bukh, Jens *medical researcher*
Bulas Kurzrok, Dorothy Isabella *pediatrician*
Bulger, Roger James *academic administrator*
Burbage, Tom *aeronautical engineer*
Burdeshaw, William Brooksbank *engineering executive*
Burkhalter, Susan Shively *music educator, organist*
Burns, Drusilla Lorene *microbiologist*
Cai, Tao *biomedical researcher*
Cairo, Armon Anthony *physician*
Camardo, Michael F. *engineering company executive*
Camerini-Otero, Rafael Daniel *biochemist, geneticist, molecular biologist, physician, researcher*
Candotti, Fabio *pediatrician*
Cao, Jie Jane *cardiologist, researcher*
Castelli, Alexander Gerard *accountant*
Catherino, William Henry *endocrinologist*
Chanock, Robert Merritt *pediatrician*
Chapman, Gerald Frederick *lawyer, banker*
Chebaane, Mohamed *water management specialist, consultant*
Chen, Kevin Gang *oncologist, researcher, molecular pharmacologist*
Child-Olmsted, Gisèle Alexandra *retired language educator*
Choyke, Peter L. *radiologist, researcher*
Christopher, Austin *neurologist, researcher*
Chronister, Gregory Michael *newspaper editor*
Clark, A. James *real estate company executive*
Cleary, Timothy Finbar *professional society administrator*
Coates, Paul M. *government agency administrator*
Cody, Thomas Gerald *management consultant, writer*
Cohen, Robert Abraham *retired physician*
Cohen, Sheldon Gilbert *physician, historian, immunologist*
Collins, Francis S. *federal agency administrator, geneticist, physician*
Comey, James B., Jr. *lawyer, aerospace company executive, former federal agency administrator*
Compton, Wilson Martindale *psychiatrist, researcher*
Cope, Laurence Brian *utilities executive, economist, consultant*
Corn, Milton *dean, physician, consultant*
Cornish, Edward Seymour *magazine editor*
Coutts, Robert B. *electronics corporation executive*
Crout, J(ohn) Richard *pharmacologist, researcher*
Cutting, Mary Dorothea *audio and audio-visual communications company executive*
Danforth, David Newton, Jr. *surgeon, oncologist*
Daniel, Charles Dwelle, Jr. *retired military officer*
Daniels, Michael Paul *lawyer*
Day, Robert Dwain, Jr. *foundation administrator, lawyer*
De Cherney, Alan Hersh *obstetrics and gynecology educator*
Deckelbaum, Nelson *lawyer*
Dennin, Joseph Francis *former government official, lawyer*
Dietrich, Robert Anthony *pathologist, consultant, medical association administrator*
Dignac, Geny (Eugenia M. Bermudez) *sculptor*
Di Paolo, Joseph Amedeo *geneticist*
DiPietro, Ralph John *lawyer*
Doroshow, James Halpern *federal agency administrator, oncologist*
Dorr, Ann Pierce *science educator*
Downey, Arthur Thomas III *lawyer*
Dulin, Maurine Stuart *volunteer*
Duncan, Constance Catharine *psychologist, educator, researcher*
Durek, Thomas Andrew *computer company executive*
Dyda, Fred P. *biochemist, researcher*
Ehrenfeld, Ellie (Elvera Ehrenfeld) *biologist, researcher*
Elliott, George Armstrong III *artist, journalist*
Emanuel, Ezekiel J. *oncologist, bioethicist*
English, Michela *entertainment company executive*
English, William deShay *lawyer, director*
Eule, Norman Louis *lawyer*
Fales, Henry Marshall III *chemist*
Fauci, Anthony Stephen *federal agency administrator, allergist, immunologist*
Fee, Elizabeth *medical historian, administrator*
Fefferman, Hilbert *government official, lawyer*
Feuerstein, Donald Martin *lawyer*
Fine, Howard A. *medical researcher*
Fleisher, Thomas Arthur *physician*
Fleming, Patricia Stubbs (Patsy Fleming) *artist*
Forster, Peter C. *construction executive*
Francomano, Clair Ann *geneticist*
Frank, Martin *physiologist, educator, medical association administrator*
Frank, Richard Sanford *retired magazine editor*
Fraser, Catriona Trafford *art gallery director, photographer*
Fraumeni, Joseph Francis, Jr. *federal agency administrator, epidemiologist*
Freedman, Joseph *retired sanitary and public health engineering consultant*
Frosh, Brian Esten *lawyer, state senator*
Gaarder, Mary *speech pathologist*
Gabelnick, Henry Lewis *medical research administrator*
Gallin, John I. *medical researcher*
Gastwirth, Glenn Barry *medical association administrator*
Germain, Gale Inoff *research psychologist*
Gershengorn, Marvin Carl *internist, researcher, educator*
Giedd, Jay Norman *psychiatrist*
Goldstein, Murray *medical research administrator*
Gonzalez, Frank J. *medical researcher*
Goodwin, Frederick King *psychiatrist*
Gottesman, Michael Marc *biomedical researcher*
Gould, W. Scott *financial administrator*
Govern, Frank Stanley *health facility and research administrator, healthcare educator, writer*

Grady, Patricia A. *federal agency administrator*
Graeff, Alan S. *health association executive*
Grau, John Michael *trade association executive*
Greenberg, Judith Horovitz *geneticist*
Greenwald, Peter *epidemiologist, researcher*
Gress, Ronald E. *oncologist*
Grisham, Joe Wheeler *cell biologist, educator*
Gruber, Jack *virologist, medical researcher*
Gude, Gilbert *former federal official, former state official, nurseryman, writer*
Guttman, Helene Nathan *biomedical researcher, consultant, transpersonal counselor*
Hager, Gordon Lee *molecular biologist*
Hallett, Mark *neurologist, educator, medical researcher, director*
Hamilton, J-Mauri *academic administrator*
Hanson, Glen R. *pharmacologist, educator*
Harford, Joe B. *federal agency administrator*
Harlan, Linda Carol *epidemiologist*
Harris, Curtis Craig *medical researcher*
Harris, Stanley S. *retired judge, arbitrator, mediator*
Haseltine, Florence Pat *obstetrician, gynecologist, medical association administrator*
Hausman, Steven Jack *health science association administrator*
Helman, Lee J. *medical researcher*
Hemming, Val G. *retired dean, educator*
Hempstone, Smith, Jr. *diplomat, journalist*
Heravi, Mehdi *economist*
Herman, Edith Carol *journalist*
Herman, Mary Margaret *neuropathologist*
Hewes, Laurence Ilsley III *lawyer, management consultant*
Highfill, Philip Henry, Jr. *retired language educator*
Hingson, Ralph W. *medical educator*
Hodes, Richard J. *federal agency administrator, immunologist, researcher*
Hoffman, Dax *neuroscientist, researcher*
Holland, Robert Carl *economist*
Horwitz, Barry *neuroscientist, researcher*
Hrynkow, Sharon Hemond *federal agency administrator, neuroscientist, researcher*
Hsu, S. Dana *technologist*
Huebner, John Stephen *geologist*
Humphreys, Betsy L. *librarian*
Hutton, John Evans, Jr. *surgeon, educator, retired military officer*
Insel, Thomas R. *federal agency administrator, psychiatrist*
Ito, Yoichiro *pathologist, researcher*
Jaffe, Elaine Sarkin *pathologist*
Jamieson, Graham A. *biochemist, researcher, retired organization official*
Javitt, Jonathan C. *ophthalmologist*
Jeong, Soo-Jin *cell biologist*
Johann, Donald Joseph *biomedical researcher*
Johnson, Eugene Clare *data processing company executive*
Johnson, Robert Louis *broadcast executive, professional sports team executive*
Jonas, Gary Fred *healthcare executive*
Jones, John Franklin, Jr., (Jack F. Jones) *federal agency administrator*
Joo, Jungnam *statistician*
Joy, Robert John Thomas *medical educator*
Joyce, Bernita Anne *retired federal agency administrator*
Kapikian, Albert Zaven *physician, epidemiologist*
Kaplan, Marjorie *broadcast executive*
Katz, Stephen Ira *federal agency administrator*
Kavanaugh, Everett Edward, Jr. *trade association executive*
Kawazoe, Robin Inada *federal official*
Keiser, Harry Robert *retired physician*
Kelly, Kathleen *medical researcher*
Kem, Richard Samuel *retired army officer*
Kemelhor, Robert E(lias) *mechanical engineer*
Kempster, Norman Roy *journalist*
Kennevan, Walter James *computer science educator*
Khil, Pavel *physicist, researcher*
Kinsey, John Allen *systems engineer, technical director*
Kirby, Harmon Elwood *retired ambassador*
Kirschstein, Ruth Lillian *physician*
Klee, Claude Blenc *medical researcher*
Knable, Michael *medical researcher*
Knachel, Philip Atherton *librarian*
Koonce, Calvin Scott *brokerage firm executive, physicist*
Korn, Edward David *biochemist*
Koslow, Stephen Hugh *health science association administrator, pharmacologist*
Kramer, Barnett Sheldon *oncologist*
Krantz, David S. *psychology educator, researcher*
Krause, Richard Michael *medical scientist, government official, educator, senior researcher*
Kruger, Gustav Otto, Jr. *retired oral surgeon, educator, department chairman*
Kubasik, Christopher E. *aerospace transportation executive*
Kuehl, W. Michael *medical researcher*
Kunos, George *pharmacologist*
Kutemeyer, Peter Martin *industrial engineering executive*
Lai, Zhennan *research scientist*
Laingen, Lowell Bruce *diplomat*
Landis, Story Cleland *federal agency administrator, neurobiologist*
Lane, H. Clifford *internist*
Lannan, Maura Anne Kelly *reporter*
Larionov, Vladimir L. *medical researcher*
Larrabee, Barbara Princelau *retired intelligence officer*
Larrabee, Donald Richard *publishing executive*
Less, Anthony Albert *retired naval officer*
Levy, Richard C. *television production executive, author, producer, inventor*
Li, Qingdi Quentin *physician, research scientist, medical educator*
Lichten, Michael J. *microbiologist, researcher*
Lindberg, Donald Allan Bror *library director, pathologist, educator*
Linehan, William Marston Marston *urologic surgeon, cancer researcher*
Lo, Cecilia Wen-Ya *biomedical researcher*
Longfellow, David *administrator*
Lorber, Mortimer *retired physiology educator*
Lowy, Douglas Ronald *oncologist, researcher*

Lystad, Mary Hanemann (Mrs. Robert Lystad) *sociologist, writer*
Mackall, Crystal L. *medical researcher*
MacKay, Charles Robert *federal official, consultant*
Manasse, Henri Richard, Jr. *pharmaceutical executive*
Marini, Ann Marie *medical researcher, educator*
Marks, Jonathan Bowles *mediator, arbitrator*
Marriott, Richard Edwin *hotel and contract services executive*
Mattison, Donald Roger *gynecologist, toxicologist, educator, medical association administrator, public health service officer*
McClure, Brooks *management consultant*
McCray, Alexa T. *health science association administrator, director*
McCurdy, Harry Ward *otolaryngologist*
McDonough, Thomas P. *health facility administrator*
Mc Gurn, Barrett *communications executive, writer*
McHale, Judith A. (Judith Ottalloran) *broadcast executive, lawyer*
McMurphy, Michael Allen *energy company executive, lawyer*
Meakem, Carolyn Soliday *investment executive, financial planner, money manager, consultant*
Melenhorst, Jan Joseph *immunologist*
Mellor, James Robb *electronics executive*
Merlino, Glenn T. *medical researcher*
Metcalfe, Dean Darrel *medical research physician*
Metzger, Henry *federal research institution administrator*
Millstein, Richard Allen *federal agency administrator*
Mishkin, Mortimer *neuropsychologist*
Mitchell, James B. *medical researcher*
Mock, Beverly A. *geneticist, researcher*
Monjan, Andrew Arthur *health facility administrator*
Morgan, John Davis *government agency administrator, consultant*
Moriyama, Iwao Milton *statistician, consultant*
Morrison, Bruce Andrew *federal official, public information officer*
Morrison, Nancy Anne *public affairs consultant*
Moshman, Jack *statistical consultant*
Moss, Bernard *virologist, researcher*
Mullan, Fitzhugh *public health physician*
Muraro, Paolo A. *immunologist, neurologist*
Murayama, Makio *biochemist*
Murrett, Robert B. *federal agency administrator, career military officer*
Musil, Robert Kirkland *educator*
Nabel, Elizabeth G. *cardiologist, researcher*
Nakamura, Richard *mental health services professional*
Nash, Howard Allen *geneticist, researcher*
Nassetta, Christopher J. *hotel facility executive*
Naylor, Phyllis Reynolds *writer*
Neill, Denis Michael *management consultant*
Nejelski, Paul Arthur *retired judge, freelance writer*
Nelson, John Howard (Jack Howard Nelson) *journalist*
Nelson, William Eugene *lawyer*
Neumann, Ronald Daniel *nuclear medicine physician, educator*
Niederhuber, John Edward *federal agency administrator, oncologist, surgeon, immunologist*
North, A. Frederick *physician*
North, William Haven *foreign service officer*
Nyirjesy, Istvan *obstetrician, gynecologist*
Obrams, Gunta Iris *clinical research administrator*
O'Callaghan, Jerry Alexander *federal agency administrator*
Ochej, Helen Wanda *biologist, researcher, information scientist*
Oddis, Joseph Anthony *health associations executive*
Ognibene, Frederick Peter *internist*
Oldfield, Edward Hudson *neurosurgeon, researcher*
Oldham, Roger Jay *plastic surgeon*
Olmsted, Jerauld Lockwood *telephone company executive*
Olson, Lynn *editor*
Ommaya, Ayub Khan *neurosurgeon, educator*
Orr, Larry L. *economist*
Ostrander, Elaine A. *federal agency administrator, geneticist*
Palumbo, James Fredrick *finance company executive*
Park, Yonil *mathematician*
Pastan, Ira Harry *medical researcher*
Pasternak, N. Alfred *lawyer, accountant*
Paul, William Erwin *immunologist, researcher*
Peck, Edward Lionel *retired foreign service officer, corporate executive*
Penn, Audrey S. *federal agency administrator*
Perlin, Seymour *psychiatrist, educator*
Peterson, Charles Marquis *medical educator*
Petralia, Ronald Sebastian *entomologist, neurobiologist*
Pettigrew, Roderic I. *federal agency administrator, radiologist, researcher*
Pickerell, James Howard *photojournalist*
Pinn, Vivian W. *federal agency administrator, pathologist*
Pipkin, James Harold, Jr. *lawyer*
Poggi, Matthew Michael *radiation oncologist, researcher*
Pollard, Harvey B. *medical educator, neuroscientist*
Polsby, Gail K. *psychotherapist*
Pommier, Yves Georges *pharmacologist*
Popescu, Daniel *interior designer*
Pospisil, George Curtis *health science administrator*
Purcell, Robert Harry *virologist, researcher*
Quinnan, Gerald Vincent, Jr. *medical educator*
Quon, Michael James *medical researcher, internist*
Rabson, Alan Saul *federal agency administrator, pathologist, educator*
Rall, Joseph Edward *physician*
Rapoport, Judith *psychiatrist*
Raullerson, Calvin Henry *political scientist, consultant*

Reed, Berenice Anne *cultural organization administrator, educator, artist*
Reed, Miriam Bell *legislative staff member*
Rennert, Owen Murray *pediatrician, geneticist, educator*
Revesz, Akos George *physicist*
Reynolds, Herbert Young *internist*
Reynolds, Robert Joel *economist, consultant*
Rhim, Johng Sik *physician, medical researcher*
Ricciardi, Richard *military officer*
Rice, Charles Lane *surgeon, educator*
Rice, Jerry Mercer *biochemist, consultant, pathologist*
Rice, Kenner Cralle *medicinal chemist*
Richardson, John *retired international relations executive*
Rider, Lisa G *pediatric rheumatologist, researcher*
Robbins, John Bennett *medical researcher*
Robinson, Sharon Beth *health science association administrator*
Rosenbaum, Greg Alan *merchant banker, consultant*
Rosenberg, Mark Louis *lawyer*
Rosenberg, Steven A. *surgeon, researcher*
Ross, William Warfield *lawyer*
Rossouw, Jacques E. *preventive medicine physician, researcher*
Rowell, Edward Morgan *retired foreign service officer, educator*
Ruffin, John *federal agency administrator, researcher*
Ruiz-Bravo, Norka *federal agency administrator*
Rumbaugh, John R. *health facility administrator, military officer*
Ryan, Joseph *lawyer*
Saffiotti, Umberto *pathologist*
Salisbury, Tamara Paula *foundation executive*
Salmoiraghi, Gian Carlo *physiologist, educator*
Samelson, Lawrence Elliot *medical researcher*
Sanoff, Alvin Paul *writer, educational consultant*
Sarnoff, Lili-Charlotte (Lolo Sarnoff) *artist*
Saul, B. Francis, II, *bank executive, director*
Saunders, Charles Baskerville, Jr. *retired association executive*
Saville, Thorndike, Jr. *coastal engineer*
Scarpa, Antonio *medical educator, researcher, director, physiologist*
Schaeffer, Charles Perry *writer, editor*
Schifter, Richard *lawyer*
Schlom, Jeffrey Bert *research scientist*
Schmidt, Raymond Paul *military officer, historian, government agency administrator*
Schoettler, James Anthony, Jr. *lawyer*
Schrump, David Stuart *medical association administrator, researcher*
Schwarz, Louis Jay *financial advisor*
Sewell, Rodney milton *biologist*
Shamburek, Robert Dean *gastroenterologist*
Shapeero, Lorraine G. *physician, researcher, educator*
Shulman, Lawrence Edward *biomedical researcher, rheumatologist*
Sieving, Paul A. *federal agency administrator, ophthalmologist, educator*
Silver, David *lawyer*
Silver, David Martin *chemist*
Singer, Alfred *immunologist, researcher*
Singer, Dinah S. *federal agency administrator, immunologist, researcher*
Smith, Albert E. *areonautics company professional*
Smoller, Bruce Melvyn *psychiatrist*
Sokoloff, Louis *physiologist, neuroscientist*
Solomon, Henry *university dean*
Solomon, Robert *economist*
Spector, Eleanor Ruth *manufacturing executive*
Springfield, Sanya A. *federal agency administrator*
Sprott, Richard Lawrence *foundation administrator, researcher*
Stadtman, Earl Reece *biochemist, researcher*
Stanfield, Brent B. *federal agency administrator*
Starkey, Russell Bruce, Jr. *energy executive*
Stetler-Stevenson, William George *pathologist*
Stoddard, Philip Hendrick *foreign affairs analyst, consultant, writer*
Stone, Jeremy Judah *professional society administrator*
Stover, Ellen L. *health scientist, psychologist*
Straus, Stephen Ezra *federal agency administrator, biomedical researcher*
Sturtz, Donald Lee *surgeon, educator, military officer*
Tabak, Lawrence A. *federal agency administrator, dentist*
Taylor, Lindsay David, Jr. *healthcare executive, bank executive, federal agency administrator*
Taylor, William Jesse, Jr. *international security studies educator, research institute senior advisor*
Terragno, Paul James *information industry executive*
Thorgeirsson, Snorri Sveinn *medical researcher*
Tilley, Carolyn Bittner *information scientist*
Tourino, Ralph Gene *aerospace transportation executive*
Tracy, Thomas Miles *international health organization official*
Trus, Benes Louis *structural chemist*
Udey, Mark C. *dermatologist, researcher*
Ursano, Robert Joseph *psychiatrist*
Vaitukaitis, Judith Louise *medical researcher*
van der Linden, Frank Morris *historian*
Vanderryn, Jack *environmental services administrator*
Vaughan, Martha *biochemist, educator*
Vest, George Southall *retired diplomat*
Volkow, Nora Dolores *medical researcher, director*
Vonderhaar, Barbara K. *medical researcher*
Wagner, Cynthia Gail *editor, writer*
Waldmann, Thomas Alexander *medical researcher, physician*
Walter, W. Edward *hotel executive, corporate financial executive*
Webster, Henry de Forest *neuroscientist*
Webster, Thomas Glenn *psychiatrist, educator*
Weinberger, Alan David *lawyer, business executive*
Weinberger, Daniel R. *psychiatrist, neurologist*
Weiss, George Herbert *mathematician, consultant*
Welch, John Kirtland *nuclear energy industry executive*
Western, Karl August *physician, epidemiologist*
White, Jeffrey D. *federal agency administrator*

Wickner, Sue Hengren *biochemist*
Wiese, Wolfgang Lothar *physicist, researcher*
Wise, Allen F. *health care administrator*
Witkop, Bernhard *chemist*
Wolf, Dale B. *health facility administrator, corporate financial executive*
Wolpert-DeFilippes, Mary K. *science administrator*
Woodall, Jerry M. *research scientist, educator*
Woodard, Geoffrey Esty *molecular physiologist*
Work, Henry Harcus *psychiatrist, educator*
Wright, Pamela Ann *surgeon*
Wu, Carl *medical researcher*
Yamada, Kenneth Manao *cell biologist*
Yang, Key Paik *librarian, archivist*
Yuspa, Stuart Howard *oncologist*
Zerhouni, Elias Adam *federal agency administrator*
Zheng, Gang *mathematician, statistician, researcher*
Zielinski, Thomas C. *lawyer*
Zierdt, Charles Henry *retired microbiologist*
Zoon, Kathryn Christine *biochemist*
Zwanzig, Robert Walter *chemist, physical science educator*

### Betterton
Kohl, Benjamin Gibbs *historian, educator*

### Boonsboro
Butler, Naomi Witmer *librarian, educator*

### Bowie
Bushnell, David Sherman *social psychologist, consultant*
Caire, Kaleem (Michael) Steven *not-for-profit fundraiser*
Dawodu, Segun Toyin *sports medicine physician, physiatrist*
Fox, Kenneth *physicist, educator, lawyer*
Gourdine-Tyson, Natachia *investment company executive, writer*
Hillsman, Joan Rucker *music educator*
LeCounte, Lola Houston *literature and language professor, educational consultant*
Littlefield, Roy Everett III *association executive, law educator*
Lowe, Calvin W. *university president*
Mondale, S. Janiece *librarian*
Speller-Brown, Barbara Jean *pediatric nurse practitioner*
Sterling, Richard Leroy *English and foreign language educator*
Stone, Edward Harris, II, *landscape architect*
Wardrip, Elizabeth Jane *retired librarian*
Yager, Joseph Arthur, Jr. *economist, consultant*

### Boyds
Bu, Rulei *artist, educator*

### Bozman
Wyatt, Wilson Watkins, Jr. *communications executive, public affairs executive, writer*

### Brandywine
Briggs, John Harold, Sr. *music educator*
Jaffe, Morris Edward *insurance executive*
Johnson, Madge Richards *business owner, fundraiser, consultant*

### Brentwood
Kaskey, Raymond John *sculptor*

### Burtonsville
Hudson, McKinley *retired military officer, retired zoological park administrator*
Kettell, II, Ralph Wallis *mining executive, mining engineer*

### Cabin John
Ingraham, Edward Clarke, Jr. *retired foreign service officer*
Shropshire, Walter, Jr. *biophysicist, pastor*
Townsend, John William, Jr. *physicist, retired federal agency administrator*

### California
Powell, Melchior Daniel *educational administrator, lawyer*

### Cambridge
Rihanna, (Robyn Rihanna Fenty) *singer*
Spahr, Elizabeth *environmental research administrator*
Tenanty, Jane Elizabeth *secondary school educator*

### Camp Springs
Barnet, Christopher Dwight *physicist*
Pryor, Kenneth *meteorologist*
Tallapragada, Vijay Kumar *research scientist*

### Catonsville
Clelland, Nelda Diane *mathematics professor*
Hubbard, Herbert Hendrix *lawyer*
Toomey, Sister Stephana *small business owner*
Wynn, John Charles *clergyman, retired theology studies educator*
Zumbrun, Alvin John Thomas *law and criminology educator*

### Centreville
Griffith, Alan Richard *retired banker*

### Chester
Dabich, Eli, Jr. *insurance company executive*

### Chestertown
Amos, James Lysle *photographer*
Bish, Richard Hayes *missionary, educator*
Clarke, Garry Evans *composer, educator, academic administrator, musician*
Docksteader, Karen Kemp *marketing professional*
Littlefield, Lauren Montenegro *psychologist, educator*
Rather, Lucia Porcher Johnson *library administrator*
Tipson, (Lynn) Baird *academic administrator, religious studies educator*
Wendel, Richard Frederick *economist, educator, consultant*

## Cheverly

Miller, Mark Karl *journalist, editor*

## Chevy Chase

Adler, James Barron *publishing executive*
Albright, Raymond Jacob *federal official*
Alexander, Arthur Jacob *economist*
Alpert, Seymour *anesthesiologist, educator*
Atkin, Flora Blumenthal *playwright, theater director*
Auerbach, Seymour *architect*
Bacon, Donald Conrad *writer, editor*
Baruch, Jordan Jay *retired management consultant*
Basa, Enikö Molnár *retired librarian*
Bissinger, Frederick Lewis *retired manufacturing executive*
Broide, Mace Irwin *public information officer*
Bruder, George Frederick *lawyer*
Bruno, Harold Robinson, Jr. *retired journalist, writer*
Cech, Thomas Robert *chemistry professor*
Cheng, David Keun *engineering educator*
Choppin, Purnell Whittington *science administrator*
Cline, Ruth Eleanor Harwood *translator*
Coerper, Milo George *lawyer, priest*
Cowen, Eugene Sherman *broadcast executive*
Curzan, Myron Paul *lawyer*
Ewing, Frank Marion *paper company executive, real estate developer*
Feldman, Bruce Allen *otolaryngologist*
Fern, Alan Maxwell *art historian, retired museum director*
Gavin, James Raphael III *biochemist*
Gildenhorn, Joseph Bernard *lawyer, real estate company executive, retired diplomat*
Glaser, Vera Romans *journalist*
Groner, Beverly Anne *retired lawyer*
Harlan, William Robert, Jr. *internist, educator, researcher*
Hickman, R(obert) Harrison *political pollster, strategist*
Hunt, Frederick Talley Drum, Jr. *association executive*
Kandel, Eric Richard *neuroscience educator*
Khairalla, Eric William *plastic surgeon*
Kilborn, Peter Thurston *journalist*
Kranking, Margaret Graham *retired artist, educator*
Kriegsman, Alan M. *arts critic*
Krupnick, Janice Lee *psychologist, psychotherapist, educator*
Lebow, Irwin Leon *communications engineering consultant*
Lee, Brenda Baker *real estate company executive*
Linowes, David Francis *finance educator, corporate financial executive*
Lukens, Alan Wood *retired ambassador, retired federal official*
Lynn, D. Joanne *physician, researcher*
Mackall, Laidler Bowie *retired lawyer*
Michaelis, Michael *management and technical consultant*
Mielke, James Edward *geochemist*
Murphy, John Condron, Jr. *lawyer*
Nelson, John Marshall *medical information services company executive*
Nichols, Henry Eliot *lawyer, director, savings and loan association executive*
Noonan, Patrick Francis *conservation executive*
Norwood, Bernard *economist*
Norwood, Janet Lippe *economist*
Opper, Barbara Negri *financial economist*
Pedersen, Wesley Niels M. *public relations and public affairs counselor*
Pilkerton, Arthur Raymond, Jr. *surgeon, educator*
Pitofsky, Robert *federal agency administrator, law educator*
Pogue, John Marshall *physician*
Pollard, Michael Ross *lawyer, health science association administrator*
Rayburn, Wendell Gilbert, Sr. *educational consultant*
Reilly, Edward Francis, Jr. *federal agency administrator, former state senator*
Resnik, Harvey Lewis Paul *psychiatrist*
Rockwell, Theodore *nuclear engineer*
Rose, John Charles *internist, educator*
Shannon, Stephen Curtis *medical association administrator, occupational health physician*
Shipler, David Karr *journalist, writer*
Shogan, Robert *news correspondent*
Sinclair, Rolf Malcolm *retired physicist*
Smith, Hedrick Laurence *journalist, television producer*
Sperling, Godfrey, Jr. *retired journalist*
10th, Robert James *retired journalist*
Towsner, Cynthia Merle *academic administrator, educator*
Toy, Charles David *lawyer*
Williams, Charles Laval, Jr. *retired preventive medicine physician*

## Clarksville

Hung, Mei-Jong Chow *social worker*

## Clinton

Cruz, Wilhelmina Mangahas *critical care physician, educator*
Davis, Mark Cameron *radiologist*
Whittington, Ralph Edward *curator, librarian*

## Cockeysville

Barnes, Peter *federal official*

## Cockeysville Hunt Valley

Whitehurst, William Wilfred, Jr. *management consultant*

## College Park

Abd-Almageed, Wael *research scientist*
Anderson, John David, Jr. *aerospace engineer*
Antman, Stuart Sheldon *mathematician, educator*
Aruoba, S. Boragan *economics professor*
Ayyub, Bilal M. *engineer, educator, engineering executive, researcher*
Barbe, David Franklin *electrical engineer, educator*
Basili, Victor Robert *computer science educator*
Beasley, Maurine Hoffman *journalism educator, historian*

Benedick, Richard Elliot *diplomat*
Berlin, Ira *historian, educator*
Bernstein, Melvin *provost*
Boehmler, Debra *chemist, educator*
Brazile, Donna *advocate*
Brodsky, Marc Herbert *physicist, research and publishing executive*
Brush, Stephen George *historian, educator*
Carver, Sean Goodwin *research scientist*
Coffey, Timothy *physicist*
Collins, Merle *English and comparative literature educator*
DeSilva, Alan W. *physics professor, researcher*
Destler, I. M(ac) *political scientist, foreign policy writer*
Destler, William W. *academic administrator*
Diener, Theodor Otto *plant pathologist, researcher*
Dieter, George Elwood, Jr. *academic administrator*
Dill, Bonnie Thornton *sociology educator*
Dragt, Alexander James *physicist, educator*
Dusold, Laurence Richard *chemist, computer specialist*
Epstein, Norman B. *psychologist, marriage and family therapist, educator*
Esh, Christian Rusell *history professor*
Fanning, Delvin Seymour *soil science educator*
Faria, Jose Alberto *engineering educator, consultant*
Farquhar, James *geochemist, researcher*
Farvardin, Nariman *engineering educator*
Fenselau, Catherine Clarke *chemistry professor*
Fisher, Michael Ellis *physicist, educator, chemist*
Frank, Howard *dean, information technology executive*
Frese, Brenda *women's college basketball coach*
Fu, Michael C. *management science educator*
Gansler, Jacques Singleton *public policy educator*
Gaylin, Ned L. *psychologist, educator*
Gomery, Douglas *communications educator, writer*
Granatstein, Victor Lawrence *electrical engineer, educator*
Greenberg, Oscar Wallace *physicist, researcher*
Griem, Hans Rudolf *physicist, researcher*
Grunig, James Elmer *communications educator, researcher, public relations consultant*
Gupta, Ashwani Kumar *mechanical engineering educator*
Haggh-Huglo, Barbara Helen *musicologist, educator*
Hall, William Sterling *psychology educator*
Hallett, Judith Peller *classical studies educator*
Hehn, Jack Gordon *physicist, educator*
Helz, George Rudolph *chemistry professor*
Hendler, James Alexander *computer science educator, consultant*
Hey, Nancy Henson *educational administrator*
Hill, Clara Edith *psychologist, educator*
Howe, Ann Clark *science educator*
Huglo, Michel Victor *musicologist*
Ingold, Catherine White *academic administrator*
Izaurralde, Roberto César *science educator, researcher*
Jabaji, Ramsey George *academic educator*
Jeffery, William Richard *developmental biology educator, researcher*
Johnson, Haynes Bonner *journalist, writer, commentator*
Just, Richard Eugene *economist, consultant, agriculturist, educator*
Kang, Kyeongpyo *transportation engineer, researcher*
Katz, Ronald Alan *dermatologist*
Khoury, Bernard V. *educational administrator*
Kleidon, Axel *geographer, educator*
Kundu, Mukul Ranjan *physics professor, astronomy professor*
Kurtz, Michael Joseph *archivist, educator*
Langenberg, Donald Newton *retired academic administrator, physicist*
Lathan, Corinna Elisabeth *aerospace engineer*
Lee-Kim, Jennie *research scientist*
Lent, Robert William *psychologist*
Leventhal, Marvin *physicist*
Levine, William Silver *electrical engineer, educator*
Li, Zhanqing *meteorologist, educator*
Loiselle, Andrea Pugsley *archivist*
Lowell, Howard Parsons *archivist, federal agency administrator*
Lowry, Charles Bryan *librarian, dean*
Lubkin, Gloria Becker *physicist*
Lucas, Henry Cameron, Jr. *information scientist, educator, writer*
Marcus, Steven Irl *electrical engineering educator*
Meagher, Joseph Patrick *law educator, consultant*
Miller, Raymond Edward *computer science educator*
Miller, Raymond Jarvis *agronomy educator*
Minker, Jack *computer scientist, educator*
Misner, Charles William *physics professor*
Mote, Clayton Daniel, Jr. *academic administrator, mechanical engineer, educator*
Murdoch, Amelia Clara *educational association administrator*
Nerlove, Marc Leon *economics professor*
Newcomb, Robert Wayne *electrical engineer*
O'Connor, John Dennis *biology professor*
Olson, Charles Eric *economist*
Olson, Keith Waldemar *historian, educator*
Orloff, Jonathan Harris *engineering educator*
Oster, Rose Marie Gunhild *foreign language professional, educator*
Paik, Ho Jung *physics professor*
Panichas, George Andrew *language educator, critic, editor*
Pasch, Alan *philosopher, educator*
Presser, Harriet Betty *social studies educator*
Presser, Stanley *social sciences educator, researcher*
Qi, Jianwei *mechanical engineer, researcher*
Quester, George Herman *political science professor*
Quick, Edward Raymond *museum director, educator, curator*
Rabin, Herbert *physicist, educator, dean*
Radhakrishnan, Anand *aerospace engineer, researcher*
Redish, Edward Frederick *physicist, researcher*
Richardson, W.C. *painter*

Rosenberg, Norman Jack *agricultural meteorologist, educator*
Rust, John Philip *economist, educator*
Sacks, Charles Bernard *psychiatrist, educator*
Schelling, Thomas Crombie *economist*
Shen, Weixing *meteorologist*
Sigall, Harold Fred *psychology professor*
Silverman, Joseph *chemistry professor*
Sims, Henry P., Jr. *management educator*
Skibniewski, Miroslaw Jan *engineering educator*
Smidts, Carol *mechanical engineer, educator*
Sorenson, Georgia Lynn Jones *political science professor*
Souza, Gilvan Castro *operations and management educator*
Stover, Carl Frederick *foundation executive*
Strickland, Lee Stephen *educator, consultant*
Tabatabaee, Vahid *architectural engineer, researcher*
Taylor, Leonard Stuart *engineering educator, consultant*
Toll, John Sampson *retired academic administrator, physics professor*
Walters, William Ben *chemistry professor*
Warner, C(harles) Robert *mathematics professor*
Wasserman, Paul *library and information science professor*
Weart, Spencer Richard *historian*
Weinstein, Allen *archivist*
White, Marilyn Domas *information science educator*
Whittemore, Edward Reed, II, *poet, retired educator*
Wong, Yanyi Liu *physicist, researcher*
Yorke, James Alan *mathematician, educator*
Zen, E-an *research geologist, educator*

## Columbia

Bennett, P. Tyson *lawyer*
Campbell-Alston, Deirdre Adina *anatomist, physiologist, researcher*
Canahuati, Judy *lactation consultant*
Cheng, Jian-Yu *mechanical engineer, researcher, application developer*
Closson, Walter Franklin *child support prosecutor*
Davis, Benjamin George *theologian, educator*
Davis, Guy Donald *research scientist*
Deering, Anthony Wayne Marion *real estate developer*
DeRosa, Thomas J. *investment banker, investment company executive*
Duncan, Mary Ellen *academic administrator*
Festa, Fred E. (Alfred E. Festa) *chemicals executive*
Fishbune, Robert *food products executive*
Fisher, Dale John *retired chemist, medical investigator*
Fritz, Steven L. *physicist*
Gillespie, Charles Kevin *priest, educator*
Gray, Kirk Lamond *social investment firm executive, anthropologist*
Gregorie, Corazon Arzalem *operations research specialist*
Greyson D'Otazzo, Meaghan Regina *literary critic*
Gruhl, Andrea Morris *librarian*
Hyman, Lawrence Robert *psychiatrist*
Jones-Wilson, Faustine Clarisse *retired education educator*
Kearns, Ronald Edwin *music educator*
Khare, Mohan *chemist, researcher*
Klein, Sami Weiner *librarian*
Kurlander, Neale *accountant, law educator*
Lok, Joan Mei-Lok *community affairs specialist, artist*
Maseritz, Guy B. *lawyer*
McCuan, William Patrick *real estate company executive*
McGregor, Douglas A. *real estate company executive*
Moore, Darla D. *investment company executive*
Norris, Paul J. *chemicals executive*
Pacifico, Joseph Carl *counselor*
Piou-Brewer, Magalie *psychotherapist, educator, small business owner*
Privitera, Joseph F. *retired foreign service official, writer, researcher*
Purcell, James Nelson, Jr. *cultural organization administrator*
Rogers, Thomas Francis *foundation administrator*
Rovelstad, Gordon H. *dentist, researcher*
Saini, Simarjeet Singh *electronics engineer*
Scates, Alice Yeomans *retired federal official*
Shaw, Donald Hardy *lawyer*
Strahlman, Richard Scott *pediatrician*
Straja, Sorin Radu *chemical engineer, mathematician, computer programmer*
Weems, Helen Rachel *music educator, musician*
Whiting, Albert Nathaniel *former university chancellor*
Zhu, Jian Zhong *research scientist*
Ziegler, Gwendolyn Woods *minister, consultant*

## Crofton

Freeman, Ernest Robert *engineering executive*
Jamieson, Perry David *historian*
Laurenson, Robert Mark *mechanical engineer*
Mahaffey, Redge Allan *movie producer, director, writer, actor, scientist, business executive*
Ross, E(dwin) Clarke *association executive, educator*
Williams, J. Linda *librarian*

## Crownsville

Irish, Leon Eugene *lawyer, educator, non-profit organization executive*

## Cumberland

Heckert, Paul Charles *sociologist, educator*
Keller, Karen Lee *science educator*

## Damascus

Nelligan, William David III *professional association executive*
Splete, Marilyn Detweiler *retired secondary school educator*
Styer, Joanne Louise *retired dietician*

## Darnestown

Cohen, Sanford Irwin *physician, educator*
Gottlieb, Julius Judah *podiatrist*
Lightner, Gene Cleek *investment banker*

## Davidsonville

Montague, Brian John *consulting company executive*

## Dayton

Ferrera, Arthur Rocco *food distribution company executive*
Fischell, Robert Ellentuch *physicist*

## Denton

Doster, Rose Eleanor Wilhelm *artist*

## Derwood

Crawford, Stephen *think tank executive*
Mylonakis, Stamatios Gregory *lawyer, consultant*
Stadtman, Thressa Campbell *biochemist*

## Easton

Behm, Mark Edward *academic administrator, consultant*
Colton, Elizabeth Wishart *government agency administrator*
Ikenberry, Henry Cephas, Jr. *lawyer*
Kerr, James Wilson *engineer*
Maffitt, James Strawbridge *lawyer*
Peterson, James Kenneth *manufacturing executive*
Rever, George Wright *psychiatrist, health facility administrator*
U'Ren, Marie Rita *retired travel company executive, pre-school educator*
Wilson, Laura Ann *newspaper editor*

## Elkridge

Byrd, Alicia D. *minister, sociologist*

## Elkton

Jasinski-Caldwell, Mary L. *insurance company executive*
Moon, William Neal *music educator*
Xu, Ping *chemist*

## Ellicott City

Bruley, Duane Frederick *academic administrator, consultant, engineer*
Freeman, Lisa Marie Yacono *psychologist*
Galinsky, Deborah Jean *county official*
Loerke, William Carl *art historian, educator*
McNaughton, Kenneth John *former publisher*
Wann, Michael Stephen *music educator*
Webster, Sharon B. *economist*
Wheltle, Margaret Maie *retired secondary school educator*

## Emmitsburg

Fields, Victor Lee *music educator*
Houston, George R., Jr. *college president*
O'Toole, William Edward, 3rd, *mathematics professor, computer science professor*

## Essex

Bunn, Wm. Jeffrey *secondary school educator, director*

## Federalsburg

Kennedy-Milligan, Diana Lynne *secondary school educator*

## Forest Hill

Klein, Shirley Snyderman *retail executive*
McIntosh, L(orne) William *research and development company executive*

## Fort George G Meade

Alexander, Keith B. *federal agency administrator, career military officer*
Black, William B., Jr. *federal agency administrator*
Kera, Tiiu *career officer*
Schmitt, Robert Lee *computer scientist*

## Fort Washington

Alexander, Gary R. *lawyer, state legislator, lobbyist*
Bull, Sharon Kay *elementary school educator*
Cameron, Rita Giovannetti *writer, publishing executive*
Canlas, Luzano Pancho, Sr. *writer, researcher*
Satterthwaite, George, II, *security firm executive*
Smoot, Burgess Howard *federal official*
Vaughan, James Joseph Michael *lawyer*
Wooten, Ralph G. *career officer*

## Frederick

Albright, Joseph William *civilian military employee*
Anderson, Arthur Osmund *pathologist, immunologist, military officer*
Baker, Joanne Evelyn *retired government agency administrator*
Blumenthal, Robert P. *medical researcher*
Brauer, Ethel May *secondary school educator*
Burkhard, Fred (Bud) *academic administrator*
Byrd, R. Andrew *medical researcher*
Byron, Beverly Butcher *retired congresswoman*
Carlson, David Emil *physicist, researcher*
Colburn, Nancy Hall *medical researcher*
Copeland, Neal G. *medical researcher*
Deveneni, Mohan *pharmacist*
Garver, Robert Vernon *retired research physicist*
Gustchina, Alla *molecular biologist, researcher*
Hanna, Michael George, Jr. *immunologist, pharmaceutical executive*
Henderson, Madeline Mary (Berry Henderson) *chemist, engineer, consultant*
Hughes, Stephen H. *virologist, researcher*
Iverson, Warren Philip *retired microbiologist, research scientist, consultant*
Keefer, Larry Kay *medical researcher*
Kelsey, Ronald Grant *retired military officer, environmental engineer*
Knisely, John Franklin *retired microbiologist*
Le Grice, Stuart F.J. *medical researcher*
Lin, George *research and development company executive, biomedical researcher*
Malin, Howard Gerald *podiatrist*
Marquez, Victor E. *medical researcher*
Marx, Patricia Anne *education educator*
McDowell, Eugene Charles *systems analyst, bioethicist*
McMahon, James Brislin *medical researcher*

McNeil, Scott *research scientist*
Merrill, Daniel A. *program manager*
O'Brien, Stephen James *geneticist*
Oppenheim, Joost J. *allergist, immunologist, researcher*
Ortaldo, John R. *immunologist, researcher*
Pastoor, Robertus Antonius *academic administrator*
Randall, Frances *technical writer*
Reynolds, Craig W. *research scientist*
Sharifi, Nima *oncologist, researcher*
Stewart, Colin L. *biologist, researcher*
Strathern, Jeffrey N. *medical researcher*
Weissman, Allan M. *medical researcher*
Whelihan, Alan Stuart *real estate developer, automotive executive*
Wiltrout, Robert H. *federal agency administrator*
Wlodawer, Alexander *medical researcher*

**Friendship**
Clagett, Diana Wharton Sinkler *museum docent*

**Friendsville**
Biser-Rinard, Kendra May *music educator*

**Frostburg**
Bauman, Jon Ward *retired music educator*
Gibralter, Jonathan C. *academic administrator*
Gira, Catherine Russell *retired academic administrator*
Horner, Ronald George *music educator, musician*
Root, Edward Lakin *education educator, academic administrator*
Teker, Kasif *engineering educator*

**Fulton**
Hamlin, George L. *writer*

**Funkstown**
Mallery, Mary Silcox *librarian, director*

**Gaithersburg**
Adams, James Michael *nuclear physicist*
Aiuto, Russell *science education consultant*
Bremenstuhl, David P. *elementary school educator*
Brodine, Charles Edward *physician*
Burnett, John Huszagh *physicist*
Cahn, John Werner *metallurgist, educator*
Caplin, Jerrold Leon *health physicist*
Carasso, Alfred Sam *mathematician*
Carey, John Edward *communications executive*
Caswell, Randall Smith *physicist*
Celotta, Robert James *physicist*
Clark, Charles Winthrop *physicist*
Cookson, Alan Howard *electrical engineer, researcher*
Delgado, Dwighd D(ubied) *electric power industry executive*
Dermody, William Christian *biomedical consultant*
Dizdaroglu, Miral *chemist*
Dowd, Carolyn Lay *social worker*
Ferrell, Charles Madison *nuclear engineer, physicist*
Fratantoni, Joseph Charles *medical researcher, biotechnologist, hematologist*
French, Judson Cull *federal official*
Glass, Lawrence *research scientist*
Gloyd, Rita A. *retired social worker*
Hall, Arthur Raymond, Jr. *retired minister*
Harman, George Gibson *physicist, consultant*
Hertz, Harry Steven *government official*
Hsu, Stephen Ming *materials scientist, chemical engineer*
Hubbell, John Howard *radiation physicist*
Jacox, Marilyn Esther *chemist*
Jahanmir, Said *materials scientist, mechanical engineer*
Jeffrey, William Alan *federal agency administrator, physicist*
Jestrab, Frank F. *retired lawyer*
Johnson, George H. *finance company executive*
Kibira, Deogragias *electronics engineer, educator*
Killgore, William Dale (Scott), Jr. *neuropsychologist*
Kulvatunyou, Boonserm *research scientist*
Landel, Michel *food service and management company executive*
Lenfant, Claude Jean-Marie *physician, director*
Levine, Robert Sidney *chemical engineer, consultant*
Li, Zhigang *physicist*
Long, Gabrielle Gibbs *physicist*
Lynn, Jeffrey Whidden *research physicist, educator*
Madhavan, Raj *electrical engineer, electronics engineer*
Martinez, Richard Isaac *research scientist, science administrator, music composer and producer, education and health policy consultant*
McDowell, Donna Schultz *lawyer, educator*
Outola, Iisa Emma Janika *research scientist*
Owen, Thomas Barron *aerospace transportation executive, retired military officer*
Phillips, William Daniel *physicist*
Pierce, Daniel Thornton *physicist*
Quraishi, Mohammed Sayeed *retired health facility administrator, research scientist*
Reader, Joseph *physicist*
Reddy, Thikkavarapu Ramachandra *electrical engineer*
Rosenblatt, Joan Raup *mathematical statistician*
Rupert, Hoover (Lynn Hoover Rupert) *minister, writer*
Ruth, James Perry *financial planner*
Saunders, George Wendell *management consultant, retired government official*
Schlenoff, Craig *mechanical engineer*
Schwartzberg, Allan Zelig *psychiatrist, educator*
Semerjian, Hratch Gregory *federal agency administrator*
Sengers, Johanna M. H. Levelt *physicist*
Shin, Myung-Ki *computer scientist, researcher*
Taylor, Barry Norman *physicist*
Tesk, John Aloysius *materials scientist*
Tirumala, Vijaya Raghavan *materials scientist*
Wang, Chung Shan *physicist*
Weber, Alfons *physicist*
Werner, Samuel Alfred *physicist, educator*
Wright, Richard Newport III *retired engineering executive, engineering educator*
Young, Russell Dawson *physicist, consultant*

**Galena**
Hunsperger, Elizabeth Jane *art and design consultant, educator*

**Galesville**
Whaley, Garwood *music company executive*

**Gambrills**
Messner, Howard Myron *professional association executive*

**Garrett Park**
Baldwin, Calvin Benham, Jr. *retired science administrator*
Kornberg, Warren Stanley *journalist*

**Germantown**
Chawla, Tejpal Singh *lawyer*
Foulke, Judith Diane *health physicist*
Iqbal, Zafar *neuroscientist, biochemist, educator*
Lewis, Robert John Cornelius Koons *retired library director*
Norcross, Marvin Augustus *veterinarian, researcher, retired federal official*
Patrinos, Aristides *environmental scientist, federal agency administrator*
Sorensen, John Noble *retired mechanical and nuclear engineer*
Taylor, Douglas Howard *translator*
Weiner, Claire Muriel *freelance writer*

**Gibson Island**
Forster, William Hull *management consultant*

**Glen Arm**
Lotz, George Michael *retired computer company executive, graphics designer, photographer*

**Glen Burnie**
Mc Cabe, Gerard Benedict *retired library administrator*
Sanchez-Barnett, Susan Lynn *historian, educator*

**Glen Echo**
Stevenson, A. Brockie *retired artist*

**Glenelg**
Niese, Henry Ernst *artist, educator*

**Glyndon**
Colhoun, Howard Post *financial executive*
Renbaum, Barry Jeffrey *lawyer*

**Grasonville**
Timony, Peter Edward *chemist, researcher*

**Great Mills**
Bufis, Matthew Peter *music educator*

**Greenbelt**
Al-Bassyiouni, Moustafa *engineering company executive, engineering educator*
Amato, Deborah Douglass *aerospace engineer*
Bernstein, Kenneth J. *secondary school educator*
Billingsley, Lance W. *lawyer*
Bryant, Paul T. *electronics engineer*
Cede, Alexander *physicist*
Chasanow, Howard Stuart *retired judge, mediator*
Comiso, Josefino Cacas *research scientist*
Danchi, William C. *astrophysicist*
Fax, Charles Samuel *lawyer*
Fontaine, Kathleen Sturey *policy analyst*
Greenwald, Andrew Eric *lawyer*
Heirtzler, James Ransom *geophysicist*
Hlavka, Dennis Lee *meteorologist*
Hogensen, Margaret Hiner *retired librarian, consultant*
Jenkins, Norman *accountant*
Jeong, Seong-Il *aerospace engineer, researcher*
Kniffen, Donald Avery *astrophysicist, educator, researcher*
Kuchner, Marc Jason *astrophysicist*
Mather, John Cromwell *astrophysicist*
Matthews, Darryl R., Sr. *not-for-profit fundraiser*
Messitte, Peter Jo *judge*
Middleton, Elizabeth McPhee *research scientist*
Miller, Alwin Vermar *educational association administrator, consultant*
Moore, Virginia Bradley *librarian*
Morris, Joseph Anthony *retired health science association administrator*
Mumma, Michael Jon *research scientist*
Obamogie, Mercy A. *physician*
Pulkkinen, Antti Aleksi *research scientist*
Simpson, Joanne Malkus *meteorologist*
Stubbs, Timothy John *physicist*
Titus, Roger Warren *judge*
Vranish, John Michael *electrical engineer, researcher*
Weiler, Edward J. *federal agency administrator*
Weltz, Martin David *hematologist*
Wood, H(oward) John III *astrophysicist, astronomer*

**Gwynn Oak**
Hughes, Catherine L. (Cathy Hughes) *radio personality, broadcast executive*

**Hagerstown**
Baer, John Metz *entrepreneur*
Berkson, Jacob Benjamin *lawyer, writer*
Cooper, G. David *psychologist*
Harrison, Lois Smith *hospital executive, educator*
Higgins, M. Eileen *management consultant, educator*
Ksienski, Aharon Arthur *retired electrical engineer*
Lasky, William M. *manufacturing executive*
Nickerson, Rosemary Grzesik *humanities educator*
Poole, D. Bruce *lawyer*
Potash, Martin H. *English educator*
Shaper, Christopher Thorne *sales executive*
Ward, Spring Tina *history and political science educator*
Warner, Charles David III *academic administrator*

**Hampstead**
Dotterweich, Patrick Timothy *social studies educator*

**Hanover**
Bisciotti, Stephen J. *staffing company executive, professional sports team executive*

**Harwood**
Dudley, William Sheldon *historian*

**Havre De Grace**
Alegi, Marc Patrick *middle school educator*
Wetter, Virginia Forwood Pate *broadcast executive*

**Hollywood**
Freeman, Michael Anthony *academic administrator, educational consultant*
Newhouse, Alan Russell *retired federal official*

**Hunt Valley**
Carmean, C. William *lawyer*
Carney, Stephen Patrick *lawyer, retired insurance company executive*
Igusa, Jun-Ichi *mathematician, educator*
Kinstlinger, Jack *engineering executive, consultant*

**Hyattsville**
Arias, Elizabeth *research scientist, educator*
Asongu, Januarius Jingwa *information technology executive*
Chang, Jim C. I. *air force executive*
Embody, Daniel Robert *biometrician*
Golden, Marita *English language educator, foundation executive*
Gonzalez, Joe Fred, Jr. *mathematical statistician, educator*
Levy, David Lawrence *retired lawyer, legal association administrator*
Lovick, Norman *accountant*
O'Connor, Kevin Thomas *religious organization administrator*
Rodgers, Mary Columbro *literature educator, writer, academic administrator*
Shestack, Alan *museum administrator*
Shinolt, Eileen Thelma *artist*
Wuerl, Donald William *archbishop*

**Indian Head**
Latimer, Paul Jerry *industrial engineer*
Price, Teresa Annette *elementary school educator*

**Jarrettsville**
Brennan, Molly B. *music educator*

**Jefferson**
Beall, James Robert *toxicologist, consultant*

**Joppa**
Bates, Martha Copenhaver *elementary school educator*

**Kensington**
Chiazze, Leonard, Jr. *biostatistician, epidemiologist, educator*
Dauster, William Gary *lawyer, economist*
Ellwanger, Albert Thompson III *secondary school educator*
Fasusi, Jimmy Adebayo *small business owner*
Forrest, Sidney *clarinetist, music educator*
Holloway, William Jimmerson *retired education educator*
Hum, Vance York *technology consulting executive*
Jackson, William David *research and development company executive*
Mintz, Suzanne *association executive*
Mirkin, Gabe Baron *physician, medical educator, writer, radio personality*
Rosenthal, Alan Sayre *government official, lawyer*
Suraci, Charles Xavier, Jr. *retired federal agency administrator, air transportation executive, consultant*
Szára, Stephen István *pharmacologist, consultant*

**Keymar**
Meakin, Matthew *director*

**Kingsville**
Standiford, Ronald Dawson *minister, educator*

**La Plata**
Herdman-Fisher, Carolyn A. *music educator*
Mariya, Deborah Luethje *minister*
Zinn, Michael Wallace *aerospace engineer*

**Landover**
Grasselli, Margaret Morgan *curator*
Maduka, Chikezie *journalist*
Powell, Earl Alexander III *art museum director*

**Lanham**
Criscimagna, Ned Henry *engineer*
Degnan, John James III *physicist*
Godwin, Mary Jo *editor, librarian, consultant*
Ingraham, Cynthia Louise Johnson *educational consultant*
Lyons, James Edward (Jed) *publishing executive*
Reupke, William Albert *engineer*

**Lanham Seabrook**
Liggins, Alfred C. III *broadcasting company executive*

**Lanham-Seabrook**
Hogie, Keith *systems engineer, computer engineer*

**Largo**
Martin, Flora Y. *music educator*
Ryan, Carol J. *educational administrator*
Seon, Yvonne *cultural educator, minister*

**Laurel**
Babin, Steven Michael *atmospheric scientist, researcher*
Cebula, Thomas Adam *geneticist, researcher*
Chrismer, Ronald Michael *federal agency administrator*
Damarla, Thyagaraju *electronics engineer*
Dorsey, John Wesley, Jr. *retired academic administrator, economist*
Eaton, Alvin Ralph *aeronautical engineer, electronics executive, systems engineer*
Heaton, Harold Irving, Jr. *research scientist, consultant*

**Hunter**, Edwina Earle *elementary school educator*
Krimigis, Stamatios Mike *physicist, researcher, engineering executive, consultant*
Land, H. Bruce III *electronics engineer, aerospace engineer*
Land, Henry Bruce III *electronics engineer, researcher*
Landis, Donna Marie *nursing administrator, women's health nurse*
Levitt, Gerald Steven *engineering executive*
Lui, Anthony Tat Yin *physicist*
Maurer, Richard Hornsby *physicist*
McMenamin, Terence Michael *economist*
Mitchell, Donald G. *physicist*
Pikas, Christina Kirk *librarian, researcher*
Rorie, Conrad Jonathan *research scientist, retired military officer*
Sommerer, John Curtis *physicist, educator*
Stumpff, Robert Thomas *retired academic administrator*
Weerackody, Vijitha *electrical engineer, researcher*
Williams, Barbara Ivory *educational researcher*

**Lexington Park**
Donely, George Anthony Thomas III *retired economist*
Jackameit, Kevin Charles *statistician*

**Linthicum**
Billig, Donal Michael *surgeon*

**Linthicum Heights**
Skillman, William Alfred *consulting engineering executive*
Stein, David Eric *physicist, defense analyst, futurist, retired military officer*

**Lothian**
Messenger, Barbara Beall *artist*

**Lusby**
Eshelman, Ralph Ellsworth *historian, consultant, paleontologist*
Ladd, Culver Sprogle *secondary school educator*
Sprague, Edward Auchincloss *retired professional society administrator, economist*

**Lutherville**
Baramki, Theodore Atallah *gynecologist, reproductive endocrinologist*
Goodman, Valerie Dawson *psychiatric social worker*
Panuska, Carolyn Marie *science educator*
Parekh, Dhirajlal Gokaldas *electrical engineer*
Smith, Michelle Sun *psychologist*

**Lutherville Timonium**
Bevis, Robert E. *retired oil industry executive*
Brown, Ellyn L. *lawyer, consultant*
Brustein, Abram Isaac *sales executive, insurance company executive*
Cappiello, Frank Anthony, Jr. *investment advisor*
Cedrone, Louis Robert, Jr. *retired critic*
Meyer, Jon Keith *psychiatrist, psychoanalyst, educator*
Muuss, Rolf Eduard *retired psychologist, author*
Park, Lee Crandall *psychiatrist*
Sternberger, Ludwig Amadeus *neurologist, educator*

**Madison**
Hoffman, Alicia Coro *retired federal executive*
Hoffman, Kenneth Myron *mathematician, educator*

**Marion Station**
Handy, Mary Thomas *retired elementary school educator*

**Marriottsville**
Strange, Donald Ernest *healthcare company executive*

**Marydel**
LaBarge, Christopher W. *priest*

**Mc Henry**
Kelly, Robert William *economist*

**Millersville**
DiAiso, Robert Joseph *civil engineer*
Hicks, Robert *park ranger*
Sipple, William Stanton *ecologist, educator*

**Mitchellville**
Ball, Robert M. *social security and health insurance specialist*
Ball, Robert M(yers) *retired social security, welfare and health policy specialist, writer, lecturer*
Blasier, Cole *political scientist*
Brubaker, Lauren Edgar *minister*
Embree, Ainslie Thomas *history professor*
Heald, Morrell *humanities educator*
Henle, Peter *retired economist, arbitrator*
Kendall, Katherine Anne *social worker*
Marsh, Caryl Amsterdam *retired curator, retired psychologist*

**Monkton**
Parker, Robert M., Jr., (Bob Parker) *wine critic, writer*

**Montgomery Village**
Durning, Steven James *internist, educator*
Kushner, Lawrence Maurice *physical chemist, consultant*
Murray, Peter *retired metallurgist, manufacturing executive*
O'Connell, James Sheridan *physicist, researcher*
Robinson, Henry Ward *meteorologist*
Zabrek, Albert Samuel *architect*

**Mount Airy**
Spohn, William Gideon, Jr. *mathematician, retired musician*

**New Market**
Schuettinger, Bruce Michael *conservator*

**North Bethesda**

Flax, Herman Jacob *physiatrist*
Lerner, Theodore *real estate company executive*
Richards, Mark E. *plastic surgeon, educator*
Sherman, Deane Murray *culture organization administrator*
Szabo, Daniel *federal official*

**North East**

Goldbach, Jennifer DeBerdine *bank executive*
Perry, Josie Lynn *social studies educator*

**North Potomac**

Busche, Leon Frank *secondary school educator*
Lehman, Leonard *retired lawyer, consultant*
Lide, David Reynolds *editor-in-chief*

**Oakland**

Harman, Yolanda Michelle *science educator*
Zakaluzny, Ihor Andrew *surgeon*

**Ocean City**

Corun, Ronald Lewis *asphalt refining executive*

**Ocean Pines**

Crawford, Norman Crane, Jr. *academic administrator, consultant*
Fullerton, Jean Leah *retired language educator, researcher, census researcher*

**Odenton**

Lambert, Vickie Ann *retired dean, nursing consultant*

**Olney**

Baker, Carl Gwin *retired science administrator, educator*
Delmar, Eugene Anthony *architect*
Hails, Barbara Geldermann *artist*
Uscinski, Ronald Henry *medical educator*

**Owings**

Oring, Stuart August *audio-visual specialist, writer, photographer, researcher*
Redmond, John Andrew *elementary school educator*

**Owings Mills**

Billick, Brian *professional football coach*
Colussy, Dan Alfred *aviation executive*
Earnhardt, David Lu *retired literature and language educator, writer, musician*
Heck, Albert Frank *retired neurologist*
Holdridge, Barbara *book editor, writer, consultant*
McNiesh, Celeste Angela *sales executive*
Newsome, Ozzie *professional sports team executive*
Ryan, Judith W. *geriatrics nurse, educator*
Sanner, George Bradley *bank executive*
Swartz, Eugene Robert, Jr. *music educator, minister*

**Oxford**

Bellinger, Edgar Thomson *lawyer*
Shepard, William Seth *diplomat, writer*

**Oxon Hill**

Demby, Byron Gerard *military officer*

**Parkton**

Cummins, Paul Zach, II, *insurance company executive*
Fitzgerald, Edwin Roger *physicist, researcher*

**Parkville**

Jensen, Arthur Seigfried *retired engineering executive, physicist, consultant*

**Pasadena**

De Pauw, Linda Grant *historian, educator, writer*

**Patuxent River**

Fitzhugh, David Michael *lawyer*
Hebert, Matthew Wayne *aerospace physiologist*
Stroup, Darryl Ray *systems engineer*
Vitatoe, Lee Anne *aerospace medicine executive, aerospace physiologist*

**Perryville**

Quesenbery, Erika Lynn *media specialist, curator*

**Phoenix**

Meyerhoff, Robert E. *real estate developer, philanthropist, art collector, horse breeder*

**Pikesville**

Putzel, Constance Kellner *lawyer*
Stein, Bernard Alvin *retail executive, consultant*

**Pittsville**

Richards, Samuel J. *secondary school educator*

**Poolesville**

Kapsch, Robert James *engineering and architectural historian*

**Potomac**

Brewer, Nathan Ronald *veterinarian, consultant*
Broderick, John Caruthers *retired librarian*
Carper, Fern Gayle *small business owner, writer*
Casella, Russell Carl *physicist*
Christian, John Kenton *publishing executive, marketing professional, consultant*
Cotton, William Robert *retired dentist*
Crowson, Henry Lawrence *mathematician, educator*
Dickerman, Serafina Poerio *real estate broker, consultant*
Eaves, Maria Perry *realtor*
Epstein, Mark Robert *electronics executive*
Feldman, Myer *lawyer*
Foley, Joseph Patrick *public relations executive*
Fox, Arthur Joseph, Jr. *editor*
Frieder, Gideon *computer scientist, educator*
Fthenakis, Emanuel John *air transportation executive*
Gaston, Marilyn Hughes *health facility administrator*
Hall, William Darlington *lawyer*
Harvey, John Collins *internist, educator*

Ingram, Richard Thomas *retired educational association executive, consultant*
Johnson, Anne Hale *educational association administrator, director*
Johnson, Sue O'Neill *retired library and information scientist*
Jones, Sidney Lewis *economist, researcher, educator*
Karnow, Stanley *journalist, writer*
Keefe, Arthur Thomas III *non-profit fund raising executive*
Kessler, Ronald *author*
Korengold, George Matthew *physician*
Kuykendall, Crystal Arlene *educational consultant, lawyer*
Medin, A. Louis *computer company executive*
Medin, Julia Adele *mathematics professor, researcher*
Meyer, Lawrence George *lawyer*
Navarro, Joseph Anthony *retired statistician, consultant*
Oertel, Goetz Kuno Heinrich *physicist, professional society administrator*
Oh, John Kie-Chiang *political science professor, academic administrator*
Pastan, Linda Olenik *poet*
Peter, Phillips Smith *lawyer*
Pietzsch, Jan Benjamin *engineering company executive*
Reback, Richard Neal *lawyer*
Redding, Robert Ellsworth *lawyer*
Reichley, A. James *political scientist*
Rhode, Alfred Shimon *finance educator*
Roesser, Jean Wolberg *state official*
Rosenberg, Sarah Zacher *retired cultural organization administrator*
Rotberg, Iris Comens *social scientist*
Sammons, Morgan Taylor *psychologist*
Shapiro, Richard Gerald *retail executive, consultant*
Sherwood, Arthur Lawrence *lawyer*
Shirvinski, Adam John *management consultant*
Sirotin, Peter *musician, educator*
Sundick, Sherry Small *journalist, writer, poet*
Tai, Tsze Cheng *aerodynamicist, researcher*
Troffkin, Howard Julian *lawyer*
Vadus, Gloria A. *scientific document examiner*
Walker, Charls Edward *economist, consultant*
Waugaman, Richard Merle *psychiatrist, educator*
Wolman, Eric *health care consultant*
Wonnacott, Paul *retired economics professor*

**Princess Anne**

Acquah, Sarah Nipah *agricultural educator*
Chigbu, Paulinus *fisheries biologist, educator, research scientist*
Parveen, Salina *microbiologist, educator*
Sharma, Dinesh Kumar *management science educator*
Thompson, Thelma Barnaby *university president, classical languages educator*

**Pylesville**

Roth, George Stanley *biochemist, researcher, physiologist*

**Queenstown**

Corn, Morton *environmental engineer, educator*

**Randallstown**

Holt, John J. *mediator, retired human resources specialist, arbitrator*

**Reisterstown**

Frank, Robert Louis *lawyer*
Gloth, F. Michael III *geriatrician*
Stefano, Toni Amanda *voice educator*
Tannenbaum, Harvey *defense technology consultant*
Tirone, Barbara Jean *retired health insurance administrator*

**Riverdale**

Bernard, Cathy S. *management corporation executive*

**Rock Hall**

Mariner, Linda Ketterman *minister*

**Rockville**

Abron, Lilia A. *chemical engineer*
Ashar, Hansraj G. *structural engineer, nuclear regulator*
Barbera, Thomas P. *health care company executive*
Bardack, Paul Roitman *cultural organization administrator*
Barkley, Brian Evan *lawyer, political organization worker, consultant*
Barr, Solomon Efrem *allergist, educator*
Berryman, Richard Byron *lawyer*
Birns, Mark Theodore *physician*
Boettcher, Helene *retired lawyer*
Buchanan, John Donald *retired nuclear scientist*
Burdick, William MacDonald *biomedical engineer*
Burt, Marvin Roger *financial advisor, investment manager*
Cantelon, Philip Louis *historian*
Carter, Kenneth Charles *geneticist*
Cheston, Sheila Carol *lawyer*
Chiogioji, Melvin Hiroaki *retired federal official, entrepreneur*
Chohayeb, Aida A. *dentist, educator*
Chretien, Paul Bernard *oncologist, medical researcher*
Clancy, Carolyn M. *internist, federal agency administrator*
Clancy, Patrick L. *lawyer*
Clark, Harry Westley *federal agency administrator*
Clarke, Nina Honemond *historian, writer, retired principal*
Conroy, J. Michael *lawyer, judge*
Croyle, Robert T. *federal agency administrator, psychologist, educator*
Curie, Charles G. *federal agency administrator*
Dal Pan, Gerald J. *federal agency administrator*
Davies-Venn, Christian *environmental engineer*
Davis, Beverly Watts *federal agency administrator*
Davis, James H. *lawyer*
De Jong, David Samuel *lawyer, educator*
Dodgen, Daniel W. *health policy advisor, psychologist*

Donnally, Robert Andrew *lawyer*
Drum, Bruce Alan *physicist*
Duke, Elizabeth M. *federal agency administrator*
DuPont, Robert Louis *psychiatrist, physician*
Edinger, Stanley Evan *clinical chemist*
Edwards, Bert Tvedt *accountant*
Epstein, Jay Stuart *federal agency administrator*
Ermolaeva, Maria D. *biophysicist, researcher*
Etter, Paul Courtney *oceanographer*
Frazier, Walter Ronald *real estate investment company executive*
Frye, Roland Mushat, Jr. *lawyer*
Futrovsky, Cheryl Jean *foundation administrator, performing company executive*
Gail, Mitchell H. *science foundation executive*
Geem, Zong Woo *engineer*
Gibson, William M. *technology company executive*
Gluckstein, Fritz Paul *veterinarian, biomedical information specialist*
Gonzalez-Licea, Augustin *pathologist, public health service officer*
Goodman, Jesse *physician, director, public health facility administrator, research scientist*
Graham, Robert *medical association executive*
Grandy, Fred *foundation administrator, former congressman, former actor*
Gray, Paulette Styles *federal agency administrator, biologist*
Greenberg, Jerrold Selig *health education educator*
Griffith, Jerry Dice *energy executive, management consultant*
Grim, Charles W. *federal agency administrator*
Groban, Mark D. *health care company executive*
Grozbean, Stuart Harvey *lawyer*
Haber, Margaret Wilson *informatics specialist, director*
Hamilton, Parker *library director*
Hawk, Ernest T. *federal agency administrator*
Herrera, Hector H. *urologist*
Hewlett, Richard Greening *historian*
Hisada, Michie *physician, epidemiologist*
Hoffman, Jeffrey David *school psychologist*
Howard, Lee Milton *international health consultant*
Jacques, Joseph William *investment advisor*
Jaczko, Gregory Bela *commissioner, physicist*
Kadish, Richard L. *lawyer*
Kamerow, Martin Laurence *accountant*
Karp, Ronald Alvin *lawyer*
Karson, Emile *lawyer*
Kerxton, Alan Smith *lawyer*
Klein, Dale Edward *federal agency administrator, engineering educator*
Kline, Raymond Adam *professional organization executive*
Klosson, Michael *foreign service officer*
Knight, Edward S. *lawyer, federal official*
Kogan, Felix Naum *environmental scientist, researcher*
Kohlmeier, Louis Martin, Jr. *newspaper reporter*
Kowalchick, Edward M. *headmaster*
Kowarski, Allen Avinoam *endocrinologist, educator*
Kruger, Jerome *materials science educator, consultant*
Landon, John Campbell *research and development company executive*
Lavoie, Daniel Joseph, II, *archivist, historian*
Leach, Berton Joe *medical educator*
Leef, James Lewis *biology professor, immunology research executive, immunologist, director*
Leventhal, Carl M. *neurologist, consultant, retired government agency administrator*
Lide, James H. *historian*
Lloyd, Douglas Seward *physician, public health administrator*
Long, Cedric William *health facility administrator*
Loyevsky, Mark Michael *biochemist, parasitologist, researcher*
Lumpkin, Murray M. *federal agency administrator*
Lyons, Peter B. *commissioner*
MacArthur, Diana Taylor *advanced technology executive*
Madle, Robert Albert *writer*
Malik, Waheed Ahmad *cardiologist*
Manderscheid, Ronald William *program administrator*
Marcuccio, Phyllis Rose *retired educational association administrator, editor*
Massie, Tammy Jeanne Parliment *statistician*
McCormick, Kathleen Ann Krym *geriatrics nurse, computer information specialist, federal agency administrator*
McDonald, Capers Walter *biomedical engineer, manufacturing executive, entrepreneur, educator*
McGaffigan, Edward, Jr. *commissioner*
McMurry, James Finley, Jr. *endocrinologist, researcher*
Mealy, J. Burke *clinical psychologist*
Megan, Thomas Ignatius *retired judge*
Mehan, Ashok *information technology executive*
Merrifield, Jeffrey S. *commissioner*
Meyer, F. Weller *bank executive*
Miller, Claire Ellen *editor, educator, writer*
Miller, Kenneth Michael *electronics executive, director*
Morgan, William Bruce *naval architect*
Moritsugu, Kenneth Paul *internist, federal official*
Mummaneni, Padmaja *research scientist, educator*
Niewiaroski, Trudi Osmers (Gertrude Niewiaroski) *social studies educator*
O'Donnell, James Francis *retired health scientist administrator*
Parham-Hopson, Deborah *health programs administrator*
Paulhus, Norman Gerard, Jr. *aerospace engineer*
Peele, Roger *hospital administrator*
Pehrson, Gordon Oscar, Jr. *lawyer, venture capitalist*
Pennello, Gene Anthony *statistician*
Petzold, Carol Stoker *state legislator*
Power, A. Kathryn *federal agency administrator*
Proffitt, John Richard *information technology executive, educator, public official*
Raker, Irma S. *judge*
Rao, Potarazu Krishna *environmental consultant*
Rashid, Mushfiqur M *statistician*
Renninger, Mary Karen *retired librarian*
Reyes, Luis A. *federal agency administrator*
Rosen, Saul Woolf *research scientist, health facility administrator*

Rothenberg, Alan David *lawyer*
Ryan, Kevin William *virologist, clinical research administrator*
Sansalone, William Robert *biochemist, educator, biomedical researcher*
Scherf, Uwe *research scientist*
Schindler, Albert Isadore *physicist, researcher*
Scully, Martha Seebach *speech and language pathologist*
Seagle, Edgar Franklin *environmental engineer, consultant*
Shapiro, Maurice Mandel *nuclear astrophysicist*
Shekar, Sam S. *federal agency administrator*
Sparks, David Stanley *academic administrator*
Stansfield, Charles W. *educational administrator*
Stefano, Kenneth *psychologist, psychotherapist*
Steinberg, William Mark *physician*
Strausberg, Robert L. *federal agency administrator*
Sundlof, Stephen Frederick *veterinary administrator*
Tandon, Narendra Nath *research scientist, director*
Tarrio, Charles *physicist*
Taubenberger, Jeffery Karl *pathologist, molecular biologist*
Telesetsky, Walter *federal agency administrator*
Temple, Robert *physician, federal agency administrator*
Thompson, James Lee *lawyer*
Tomar, Richard Thomas *lawyer*
Uhl, Kathleen *federal agency administrator*
Um, Ki Sung *research scientist*
Umbreit, Wayne William *bacteriologist, educator*
Valenti, Elizabeth Jeanne *environmental services administrator*
van Dyck, Peter Cuyler *federal agency administrator*
Van Grack, Steven *lawyer*
Venter, J. Craig (John Craig Venter, Craig Venter) *science foundation director, geneticist*
von Eschenbach, Andrew C. *federal agency administrator, oncologist, urologic surgeon*
Vorosmarti, James *physician*
Ware, Theresa *reading specialist, educator*
Watkins, H. Thomas *biopharmaceutical company executive*
Whitescarver, Jack Edward *federal agency administrator*
Woodcock, Janet *federal official*
Zhao, Xiaoliang *mechanical engineer, researcher*

**Rosedale**

Gretz, Ronald John *music educator, conductor*

**Saint Leonard**

Seifert, Betty L. *conservator, consultant*

**Saint Marys City**

Clifton, Lucille Thelma *author*
Froom, David *composer, music educator*
O'Brien, Jane Margaret *academic administrator*

**Saint Michaels**

Brown, Omer Forrest, II, *lawyer*
Feisel, Lyle Dean *retired dean, electrical engineer, educator*
Jones, Raymond Edward, Jr. *brewing executive*
Peck, Charles Edward *retired construction and mortgage executive*

**Salisbury**

Booker, Betty Mae *poet*
Bowden, Derek Thomas *orchestra director, educator*
Cathell, Dale Roberts *judge*
Clarke, William A. Lee III *lawyer*
Gorrow, Teena Ruark *education educator*
Heller, R. Andrew *communications educator, theater educator, director*
Jones, Elizabeth Carol *language educator*
Kleiman, Gary Howard *broadcast, advertising and cellular communications consultant*
Losonczy-Marshall, Marta Elizabeth *psychologist, educator*
Moultrie, Fred *geneticist, researcher*
Nutter, David George *city planner*
Perdue, James A. (Jim Perdue) *food products executive*
Romanowski, Autumn Dawn *health facility administrator*
Schoyen, Jeffrey Gerald *music educator, conductor*
Wilmer, Ann *public relations executive*
Wolter, John Amadeus *librarian, federal official*

**Severna Park**

Allison, John Langsdale *naval architect, marine engineer*
Daly, Charles Arthur *health facility administrator*
Davis, John Adams, Jr. *electrical engineer, research and development company executive*
Hall, Marcia Joy *non-profit organization administrator*
Humphreys Troy, Patricia *communications executive*
Lively, Carter Cunningham *museum director*
Meima, Ralph Chester, Jr. *retired diplomat, real estate company executive*
Rheinstein, Peter Howard *healthcare company executive, physician, lawyer*
Schick, Edgar Brehob *language educator*
Windsor, Patricia (Katonah Summertree, Perrin Winters, Anna Seeling) *author, educator, lecturer*

**Shady Side**

Devine, Donald J. *political science professor, consultant*

**Silver Spring**

Adams, Diane Loretta *physician*
Ahmad, Mirza Muzaffar *economic advisor*
Alexander, Herbert E. *political scientist*
Altschul, B. J. *public relations counselor*
Aranya, Gwendalin Qi *painter, sculptor, educator*
Baskerville, Lezli *educational association administrator*
Bassett, William, Jr. *regional analyst*
Beach, Bert Beverly *clergyman*
Beard, Lillian B. McLean *pediatrician, consultant*
Bennett, Carol(ine) Elise *retired reporter, actress*
Berger, Allan Sidney *psychiatrist, educator*

Bergmann-Leitner, Elke S. *immunologist, researcher*
Bernard, Hugh Yancey, Jr. *law educator, retired law librarian*
Biberman, Lucien Morton *retired physicist*
Blakeney, Barbara A. *public health service officer*
Borkovec, Vera Z. *literature and language professor*
Brandt, Carl David *research virologist*
Brandt, Elsa Lund Erickson *music educator*
Brog, David *former air force officer, consultant*
Brush, Julianna R. *marine biologist*
Burgos-Sasscer, Ruth *chancellor emeritus*
Burke, Margaret Ann *computer company executive, communications executive*
Calinger, Ronald Steve *historian*
Calvert, Gordon Lee *retired legal association executive*
Camphor, James Winky, Jr. *educational administrator*
Carson, Steven Lee *newspaper publisher*
Carter-Johnson, Jean Evelyn *management consultant*
Chacko, George Kuttickal *management science educator, consultant*
Chery, Reginald *minister*
Ciment, Melvyn *mathematician*
Coates, Robert Jay *retired electronics executive*
Cole, Wayne Stanley *historian, educator*
Coles, Anna Louise Bailey *retired dean, nurse*
Cooper, Nannie Coles *education educator, consultant*
Corwin, Jeff *biologist, anthropologist, television host*
Craig, Paul Max, Jr. *retired lawyer*
Cunningham, Keith Allen *nuclear energy industry executive, accountant, lawyer, engineer*
Dalton, J. Joseph *psychologist, consultant*
Doherty, William Thomas, Jr. *historian, retired educator*
Doolan, Denise Louise *molecular biologist*
Dunnigan, John H. *federal agency administrator*
Ehrlich, Charles David *physicist*
Eiserer, Leonard Albert Carl *publishing executive*
Ewing, Blair Gordon *federal official*
Fitzgerald, Joseph Patrick *artist*
Fockler, Herbert Hill *foundation executive*
Frassrand, Pete *art educator*
Fustero, Robert Raymond *retired political organization worker*
Gandy, Kim Allison *feminist organization executive, lawyer*
Gaydos, Joel Carl *physician*
Gilbert, Charles Richard Alsop *obstetrician, gynecologist, surgeon, educator*
Hayman, Harry *professional society administrator, electrical engineer*
Haynes, Leonard L. III *director*
Heppner, Donald Gray, Jr. *immunology research physician, army officer*
Herbers, Tod Arthur *publisher*
Hong Duc, Duong *economic development company executive*
Hsueh, Chun-tu *political scientist, educator, foundation administrator, historian*
Hubbell, Katherine Jean *retired marketing professional*
Hudson, Ralph P. *physicist*
Jacobs, George *broadcast engineering consulting company executive*
Johnson, David L. *federal agency administrator, retired military officer*
Johnson, Richard August *literature and language professor*
Kant, Gloria Jean *retired neuroscientist*
Kellner, Mark Allen *writer*
Kline, Jerry Robert *retired administrative judge, ecologist*
Koltnow, Peter Gregory *engineer, consultant*
Koppel, Ted *newscaster*
Kurata, Phillip Cedomir *journalist*
Lathrop, Daniel Perry *physics professor, director*
Latson, Richard Charles *retired audio-visual specialist*
Ledsinger, Charles A. *hotel executive*
Lipstein, Robert A. *lawyer*
Maas, Joe (Melvin Joseph Maas) *retired federal agency administrator*
Mahoney, James R. *federal agency administrator*
McCray, Lora *real estate developer*
Miller, Karla Patricia *elementary school educator*
Miller, Kendra Danette *art services business owner, consultant*
Misbin, Robert *medical executive*
Mitchum, Cassandra *poet, writer*
Mohr, Christina *retired economist*
Mok, Carson Kwok-Chi *structural engineer*
Moon, Marilyn Lee *economist*
Moreno, Donna Marie *communications executive*
Mosholder, Andrew Donald *psychiatrist*
Neuhauser, Frank Louis *retired lawyer*
Null, Elisabeth Higgins *librarian, editor*
Okigbo, Franklin C. *engineering company executive*
Oliver, Kimberly *Teacher of the Year*
O'Meara, Noel P. *priest, religious organization administrator*
Oswald, Rudolph A. *economist*
Pacuska, Alison Brandi *paralegal*
Papas, Irene Kalandros *English language educator, poet, writer*
Peiperl, Adam *sculptor, photographer*
Rachanow, Gerald Marvin *lawyer, pharmacist*
Rayburn, Carole Ann (Mary Aida) *psychologist, researcher, writer, consultant*
Rice, Rick Blackburn *application developer, systems analyst*
Rodgers, Johnathan *broadcast executive*
Rothberg, Morey David *historian, editor*
Sammet, Jean E. *computer scientist*
Scipio, L. Albert, II, (Louis Albert Scipio II) *retired aerospace science engineering educator, historian*
Secular, Sidney *actor, writer, fundraiser, consultant*
Shalowitz, Erwin Emmanuel *civil engineer*
Shih-Carducci, Joan Chia-mo *food service executive, educator, medical technologist, writer, biochemist*
Sibley, Lynn M. *anthropologist, educator*
Sirken, Monroe Gilbert *statistician*

Smedley, Lawrence Thomas *retired organization executive*
Soderberg, Susan Cooke *historian, writer*
Striner, Herbert Edward *economics professor*
Sucher, Dorothy *writer, psychotherapist*
Taubman, Claudia *gynecologist*
Truitt, Gordon Edward *editor, writer*
Vernon, Weston, III, (Wes Vernon) *broadcaster, writer, actor*
Waldrop, Francis Neil *physician*
Walsh, Douglas Shawn *medical association administrator, dermatologist, director, military officer*
Ware, Thaddeus Van *retired government official*
Weiss, Leonard *mathematician, consultant*
Whalen, John Philip *retired academic administrator, priest, lawyer*
Whitaker, Joel *publishing executive, public official*
White, Edmund William *chemical engineer*
Whitmore, Frank Clifford, Jr. *retired geologist*
Whitten, Leslie Hunter, Jr. *writer, poet, reporter*
Williams, Paul *retired federal agency administrator*
Wilson, William Stanley *oceanographer*
Winston, Michael Russell *foundation executive, historian*
Woolard, Connie Ward *retired art gallery manager, art director*
Yasher, Michael *retired accountant*
Young, Jay Alfred *chemical safety and health consultant, editor, writer*

### Simpsonville
Altschuler, Bruce Robert *research dentist*
Bluher, Gregory *computer scientist, mathematician*

### Solomons
Dorsey, James Francis, Jr. *naval officer*
Harrington, John Vincent *retired communications executive, engineer, educator*

### Sparks
Lawless, Robert J. *food products executive*
Rallo, James Gilbert *management company executive*
Suarez-Murias, Marguerite C. *retired language educator, retired literature educator*

### Sparks Glencoe
Contino, Francis A. *food products executive*

### Springdale
Keith, Patricia *multi-media specialist*

### Stevenson
Hendler, Nelson Howard *physician, health facility administrator, director*
Hilgenberg, John Christian *corporate financial executive, consultant*
Manning, Kevin James *academic administrator*
Middendorf, Alice Carter *volunteer*

### Stevensville
Barrett, John Anthony *publishing and printing company financial executive*
Engel, Bradford Charles *educational association administrator, secondary school educator*
Lain, David Cornelius *health scientist, researcher*

### Street
Spangler, Ronald Leroy *retired television executive, aircraft executive, automobile consultant*

### Suitland
Basinger, William Daniel *computer programmer*
Brooks, Richard C. *electrical engineer, federal official*
Johnson, Jessica Susan *conservator*
McClain, Edward Fifer, Jr. *retired physicist*
Rueda, Leopoldo M. *entomologist, research scientist*

### Sunderland
Franklin, Jon Daniel *writer, journalist, educator*

### Swanton
Cummins, Delmer Duane *academic administrator, historian*

### Takoma Park
DeVaris, Panayotis Eric *architect*
Fatiadi, Alexander John *retired chemist*
Leitma, Grant *psychologist, educator*
Stephenson, Patricia Ann *public health researcher, educator*
Urciolo, John Raphael, II, *real estate developer, real estate educator, finance educator*
von Hake, Margaret Joan *librarian*

### Temple Hills
Ourisman, Mandell J. *automotive executive*
Smith, Irving *gerontologist*
Strauss, Simon Wolf *chemist, materials scientist*

### Timonium
Forrester, Alfred Whitfield *psychiatrist, educator*
Sagerholm, James Alvin *retired naval officer*

### Towson
Adams, Joseph Andrew *internist, health facility administrator, educator*
Ali, Omar H. *history professor*
Ayres, Jeffrey Peabody *lawyer*
Baker, Jean Harvey *history professor*
Bowen, Lowell Reed *lawyer*
Brennan, Michael J. *lawyer*
Brooks, Gavin *artist*
Caret, Robert Laurent *academic administrator*
Carney, Bradford George Yost *lawyer, educator*
Chase, Jacquelyn Veronica *marketing professional*
China, Daniel William *lawyer*
Coughlin, James Patrick *mathematician, educator*
Crawford, Leneida Marie *singer, educator*
Decker, Michael John *music educator, musician*
Dzbinski, Alex J. *music educator*
Forrest, Juliet *dancer, educator, choreographer*
Hoch, David Allen *athletic director*
Jothen, Michael Jon *music educator, composer, conductor*

Kissel, William Thorn, Jr. *sculptor*
Lazar, Jonathan Kumin *computer scientist, educator*
Lutz, Randall Matthew *lawyer*
McManus, Walter Leonard *brokerage house executive*
Meny, Robert George *former medical research administrator, physician*
Nelson, H. Wayne *gerontologist, advocate*
Passano, E. Magruder, Jr. *management consultant*
Proctor, Kenneth Donald *lawyer*
Propst, M. Teresa Carson *historian*
Saylor, Charlotte Vernelle *biology professor*
Sell, Jeffrey Edward *heart surgeon*
Shah, Shirish Kalyanbhai *computer science, chemistry and environmental science educator*
Spodak, Michael Kenneth *forensic psychiatrist*
Tull, Willis Clayton, Jr. *retired librarian*
Vettori, Paul Marion *lawyer*
Wilkinson, Charles P. *ophthalmologist*
Wilner, Alan M. *judge*
Yao, Dong-Qing *research scientist, educator*
Zink, John H. III *lawyer*
Zweback, Stanley *psychologist, educator*

### Trappe
Blades, G(ene) Granville *accountant*
Burns-Bowie, Maureen Elizabeth *sculptor*
Paul, James Caverly Newlin *law educator, retired dean*

### Union Bridge
Hannah, Judy Challenger *private education tutor*

### University Park
Beckenstein, Myron *journalist*

### Upper Marlboro
Brown, Mary Louvinia *literature and language professor, lawyer*
Buffenbarger, Thomas (R. Thomas Buffenbarger, Robert Thomas Buffenbarger) *labor union administrator*
Harrell, Glenn T., Jr. *judge*
Jones-Lukács, Elizabeth Lucille *physician*
Morrison, Anne Deinlein *law librarian*
Symlar, Jesse Lee *finance executive*
Wesley, Ruby LaVerne *nursing educator, administrator, researcher*

### Waldorf
Raiman, Rosemary A. *advocate*
Wiggins, Stephen Edward *physician*

### West Bethesda
Scully, Roger Tehan, II, *lawyer*
Sevik, Maurice *acoustical engineer, researcher*
Vogelgesang, Sandra Louise *former ambassador, writer, consultant*

### Westminster
Dulany, William Bevard *lawyer*
Erb, Betty Jane *retired real estate agent*
Gribben, Michele Ann *humanities educator*
McKay, Gretchen Kreahling *dean, educator, director*
Pearson, Steven Robert *artist, art educator*
Preston, Charles Michael *lawyer*
Rogers, Jeffery Paul *music educator*
Rosenthal, Michael Ross *academic administrator, consultant*
Saxton, Celeste Dawn *social studies educator, consultant*
Spencer, Kimberly Ann *psychologist*
Wheatley, Charles Henry III *information technology executive*

### Wheaton
White, Martha Vetter *allergist, immunologist*

### White Hall
Radigan, Frank Xavier *retired pharmaceutical executive*

### Woodbine
Mc Indoe, Darrell Winfred *retired nuclear medicine physician*
Nuss, Barbara Gough *artist*

### Wye Mills
Schnaitman, William Kenneth *retired finance company executive*

## MASSACHUSETTS

### Acton
Benz, Edward John, Sr. *clinical pathologist*
Boghani, Ashok Balvantrai *entrepreneur, management consultant*
Buck-Moore, Joanne Rose *nursing administrator, educator*
Conoby, Joseph Francis *chemist*
Evans, Robert, Jr. *economics professor*
Hicks, Walter Joseph *electrical engineer*

### Agawam
Kantor, Simon William *chemistry professor*
Sylvester, John Andrew *social studies educator*

### Allston
Becton, Henry Prentiss, Jr. *broadcast executive*
Kneece, Richard C. *information technology executive*
Mills, Daniel Quinn *business educator, consultant, author*
Spencer, Lara *television personality, journalist*

### Amesbury
Heyman, Joseph Martin *obstetrician, gynecologist*

### Amherst
Adrion, William Richards *academic administrator, computer and information sciences educator, writer*
Anderson, Ronald Trent *artist, educator*
Archer, Ronald Dean *chemist, educator*
Averill, James Reed *psychology professor*
Avrunin, George Sam'l *mathematician, computer scientist, educator*

Baker, Lynne Rudder *philosophy educator*
Benson, Lucy Wilson *historian, consultant*
Bentley, Richard Norcross *regional planner, writer, educator*
Berger, Seymour Maurice *social psychologist*
Bradley, Raymond Stuart *education educator, researcher*
Bridegam, Willis Edward, Jr. *retired librarian*
Broadbridge, Anne Falby *history professor*
Brooks, A. Taeko *historian*
Calabrese, Edward J. *toxicologist*
Call, Gregory S. *academic administrator, mathematics professor*
Cornish, Geoffrey St. John *golf course architect*
Cox, David Archibald *mathematics professor*
Dabrowski, Thaddeus E. *art educator, art consultant, painter*
Daehler, Marvin William *psychology professor*
Donohue, Therese Brady *artistic director, choreographer, costume and set designer*
Fink, Richard David *chemist, educator*
Fleischman, Paul Robert *psychiatrist, writer*
Folbre, Nancy *economics professor*
Foulis, David James *retired mathematics professor*
Franks, Lewis E. *electrical and computer engineering educator, researcher*
Gibson, Walker *retired language educator, poet, writer*
Goldstein, Joseph Irwin *materials scientist, educator*
Hallock, Robert Bruce *physics professor*
Hartwell, Alfred Stedman *international relations educator, consultant*
Howland, Richard Moulton *retired lawyer*
Immerman, Neil *academic administrator, computer science educator*
Keen, Rachel *psychology professor*
Kinney, Arthur Frederick *humanities educator, writer*
Klare, Michael Thomas *social sciences educator, director*
Larson, Joseph Stanley *environmentalist, educator*
Lasch, Pat *artist, educator*
Levin, Robert Eugene *science educator*
Liebling, Jerome *photographer, educator*
Lombardi, John V. *academic administrator, historian*
MacKnight, Carol Bernier *educational association administrator*
MacKnight, William John *chemist, educator*
Manz, Charles Craig *management educator*
Margulis, Lynn (Lynn Alexander) *evolutionist, educator*
Marx, Anthony W. *academic administrator*
May, Ernest Dewey *academic administrator, musician*
Minear, Richard Hoffman *history professor*
Morse, Stearns Anthony *science educator*
Mullin, William Jesse *physics professor*
Muriel, Ana *education educator*
Nash, William Arthur *civil engineer, educator*
Oates, Stephen Baery *retired historian*
Palmer, John Derry *physiology educator*
Peterson, Gerald Alvin *physics professor*
Prince, Gregory Smith, Jr. *retired college president*
Pritchard, William H. *literature educator, writer*
Rabin, Monroe Stephen Zane *physicist*
Rayner, Keith *psychology professor, researcher*
Reed, Daphne Stevenson *artist*
Roberts, Chris *strategy and finance educator, researcher*
Roeper, Thomas Walter *linguist, educator*
Rosbottom, Ronald Carlisle *language educator, humanities educator*
Rubin, Emanuel Leo *musicologist, composer*
Sandweiss, Martha Ann *writer, history professor*
Schafer, Gerald Lewis (Jay Schafer) *library director*
Seymour, Charlena *academic administrator*
Spratlan, Lewis *composer, educator*
Strickland, Bonnie Ruth *psychologist, educator*
Swift, Calvin Thomas *electrical and computer engineering educator*
Tate, James Vincent *poet, English educator*
Taubman, Jane Andelman *literature and language professor*
Taubman, William Chase *political science professor, writer*
Vogl, Otto *polymer science and engineering educator*
Webley, Wilmore Christopher *microbiologist, researcher*
Wills, David Wood *minister, educator*
Winter, Horst Henning *chemical engineer, educator*
Wolff, Robert Paul *philosophy educator*
Woodbury, Richard Benjamin *anthropologist, educator*
Wyman, David Sword *retired historian, educator*
Yarde, Richard Foster *art educator*

### Andover
Agassounon, William B. G. *engineer, researcher*
Dalton, Kathleen *history professor*
Darling, Beverly Jones *retired real estate agent, artist*
Hatcher, Rebecca E. *field services representative, library archives consultant*
Jakes, William Chester *electrical engineer*
Keleher, David *electronics executive*
Loschi, Richard Paul *middle school educator*
Simone, Joseph *clergyman, educator*
Yannalfo, Brett Conlon *bank executive*

### Arlington
Dahill, Thomas Henry *artist, educator*
Fulmer, Vincent Anthony *retired college president*
Halperin, Helena Stacy *writer, educator*
Junger, Miguel Chapero *retired acoustics researcher*
Simpson, Russell Avington *retired lawyer*
Tollen, Cynthia Joyce *photographer, writer*
Zimmer, Anna Held *social worker*

### Ashfield
Bannister, Geoffrey *academic administrator, geographer*
Gabriel, Peter Paul *business educator*

### Ashland
Pettinella, Nicholas Anthony *corporate financial executive*

Eddleston, Kimberly Ann *management educator*
Edelin, Kenneth Carlton *physician*
Edmonds, Dean Stockett, Jr. *physicist, educator, director*
Egbert, Richard Michael *lawyer*
Egdahl, Richard Harrison *surgeon, educator, health science association administrator*
Ehrlich, M. Gordon *lawyer*
Eichler, Jeremy *music critic*
Eisenberg, Leon *psychiatrist, educator*
Elasmar, Michael *director, educator*
El-Baz, Farouk *science administrator, educator*
Elefante, Michael Barrett *lawyer*
El-Erian, Mohamed A. *investment manager*
Elfner, Albert Henry III *retired portfolio manager*
Ellis, Franklin Henry, Jr. *surgeon, educator*
Ellis, Randall Poor *economist, educator*
Elrifi, Ivor R. *lawyer*
Elshamy, Wael M. *medical educator*
Emerson, Anne Devereux *museum administrator*
Enfanto, Frank W. III *health insurance company executive*
Engel, David Lewis *lawyer*
Englander, John C. *lawyer*
Epler, Gary Robert *physician, author, educator*
Epstein, Arnold M. *medical educator*
Epstein, Franklin Harold *internist, educator*
Epstein, Theo N. *professional sports team executive*
Eskandarian, Edward *advertising executive*
Essex, Myron Elmer *microbiology and virology educator*
Estin, Hans Howard *retired brokerage house executive*
Eurich, Richard Rex *lawyer*
Falb, Peter Lawrence *mathematician, educator, investment company executive*
Farmer, Paul Edward *medical anthropologist*
Farrar, Constance Mosher *marketing executive*
Fay, Michael Leo *lawyer*
Federman, Daniel David *medical educator, academic administrator, endocrinologist*
Feeherry, Anthony M. *lawyer*
Feelisch, Martin *research scientist, consultant*
Feeney, Joan N. *judge*
Feeney, Mark *journalist*
Fein, Rashi *health sciences educator*
Felter, John Kenneth *lawyer*
Fertitta, Angela *dean*
Fesko, Colleene *art appraiser*
Fetter, Thomas *portfolio manager*
Fifer, Michael A. *cardiologist, educator*
Fine, David A. *lawyer*
Finegold, Maurice Nathan *architect*
Finn, Terrence M. *lawyer*
Finnegan, Neal Francis *retired banker*
Finucane, Anne M. *communications executive, marketing executive*
Firth, Everett Joseph *timpanist*
Fischer, Eric Robert *lawyer, educator*
Fischer, Mark Alan *lawyer*
Fishman, Len *state commissioner*
FitzGerald, Maura *public relations executive*
Fitzgerald, Warren Franklin *lawyer*
Flaherty, Lois Talbot *editor, psychiatrist, educator*
Flansburgh, Earl Robert *architect*
Fletcher, Stephen L. *art appraiser*
Flier, Jeffrey S. *endocrinologist*
Flockhart, Barbara Townsley *publishing executive*
Floor, Richard Earl *lawyer*
Foer, Jonathan Safran *writer*
Folkman, Moses Judah *surgeon, educator*
Fong, Cynthia Ann *language educator*
Foote, Warren Edgar *neuroscientist, psychologist, educator*
Foreman, Judy *journalist*
Forse, Robert Armour *surgeon*
Fortier, Albert Mark, Jr. *lawyer*
Fortunato, D'Anna E. *voice educator, mezzo soprano*
Foulke, Keith Charles *professional baseball player*
Fowler, Floyd Jackson, Jr. *researcher*
Fox, Edward A. *retired finance company executive*
Fox, Francis Haney *lawyer*
France, Joseph David *financial analyst*
Francona, Terry Jon *professional baseball manager*
Frank, Richard G. *healthcare educator*
Frank, Samuel Arthur *neurologist*
Frank-Kamenetskii, Maxim D. *biomedical engineer*
Frankl, Spencer Nelson *dean, dentist*
Franzen, Wolfgang *physicist, researcher*
Fraser, Donald C. *engineering executive, educator*
Fraser, Robert Burchmore *lawyer*
Freedberg, A. Stone *physician*
Freedman, Joel F. *lawyer*
Freeman, Joseph *automotive historian*
Frei, Emil III *physician, educator, researcher*
Freishtat, Harvey W. *lawyer*
Friedman, Paula Konowitch *dentist, academic administrator*
Frigoletto, Fredric David, Jr. *physician*
Gaff, Brian Michael *lawyer*
Galvani, Paul B. *lawyer*
Galvin, William Francis *state official*
Gamst, Frederick Charles *social anthropologist*
Garber, Carol Ewing *physiology educator*
Garber, Jeffrey Richard *endocrinologist*
Gardner, Geoff *chef*
Gardner, Timothy S. *biomedical engineer, educator*
Garvin, Michele M. *lawyer*
Gaudreau, Russell A., Jr. *lawyer, educator*
Gault, Robert Mellor *lawyer*
Gauron, Paul R. *lawyer*
Gawande, Atul A. *surgeon, writer*
Gelb, Richard Mark *lawyer*
Gelfand, Jeffrey Alan *physician, educator*
Gelman, Simon *anesthesiologist, educator*
German, Katherine L. *international consultant*
Gertsen, John *bar chef*
Ghabbour, Elham A. *research scientist, educator*
Gibson, Nigel C. *education educator*
Gifford, Charles K. *banker*
Gifford, Nelson Sage *finance company executive*
Gilbert, David A. *lawyer*
Gilchrest, Barbara Ann *dermatologist*
Giles, Roscoe C. *engineering educator*
Gill, Robert Tucker *lawyer*
Gilmore, Maurice Eugene *mathematics professor*

Gimbrone, Michael Anthony, Jr. *research scientist, pathologist, educator*
Giner, A. Silvana *lawyer*
Gipson, Ilene Kay *ophthalmologist, educator*
Giso, Frank III *lawyer*
Glassroth, Jeffrey *internist, educator*
Gleason, Daniel J. *lawyer*
Gleason, Jean Berko *psychology professor*
Glimcher, Melvin Jacob *orthopedic surgeon*
Glosband, Daniel Martin *lawyer*
Godine, David Richard *publishing executive*
Goldberg, Irving Hyman *molecular pharmacology and biochemistry educator*
Golden, Daniel *journalist*
Goldie, Sue J. *health service researcher*
Goldstein, Jane D. *lawyer*
Goldstein, Nathan *artist, writer*
Goldstein, Sara *music educator*
Golub, Todd R. *research scientist*
Gomes, Ryan *professional basketball player*
Gonson, S. Donald *lawyer*
Gonzalez, Juan (Alberto Vazquez) *professional baseball player*
Goodman, Louis Allan *lawyer*
Goody, Joan Edelman *architect*
Gormley, Pamela D. *controller*
Gorton, Nathaniel M. *federal judge*
Gossels, Claus Peter Rolf *lawyer*
Gottlieb, Alice B. *dermatologist*
Gottlieb, Leonard Solomon *pathology educator*
Gozonsky, Edwin O. O. *investment broker*
Grammer, Jeffrey *wireless semiconductor company executive*
Grant, Barbara Hurwitz *history educator*
Greaney, John M. *state supreme court justice*
Greco, Michael S. *lawyer*
Green, Karen F. *lawyer*
Greenblatt, David J. *pharmacologist*
Greenes, Robert A. *medical educator*
Greer, Allen Curtis, II, *lawyer, investment management executive*
Gregory, Shawn Alen *physician, researcher*
Grillo, Hermes Conrad *surgeon*
Grillone, Gregory Angelo *otolaryngologist*
Grogan, Paul Stanley *foundation administrator*
Groopman, Jerome *medical educator*
Grossman, Frances Kaplan *psychologist*
Grousbeck, Wyc *professional sports team executive*
Grundfast, Kenneth Martin *otolaryngologist*
Guertin, Robert Powell *physics professor, dean*
Gura, Kathleen Marie *pediatric pharmacist, educator*
Habener, Joel Francis *medical educator, researcher*
Haddad, Ernest Mudarri *lawyer*
Haddad, Mark E. *lawyer*
Hadlock, Theresa Anne *surgeon, otolaryngologist*
Halamka, John D. *emergency physician, information technology executive*
Haldeman, Ed (Charles Edgar Haldeman Jr.) *investment company executive*
Haley, Paul Richard *lawyer, state legislator*
Hall, David *law educator, dean, department chairman*
Hall, Henry Lyon, Jr. *lawyer*
Halston, Daniel William *lawyer*
Halström, Frederic Norman *lawyer*
Hammond, Norman David Curle *archaeology educator, researcher*
Hamrah, Pedram *ophthalmologist, researcher*
Handly, Kevin John *lawyer, educator*
Hanlon, Francis X. *lawyer*
Hardy, Victoria Elizabeth *finance educator*
Harkness, John Cheesman *retired architect*
Harper, Marvin Bruce *pediatrics educator, hospital administrator*
Harrington, John Michael, Jr. *lawyer*
Harris, Andrew Michael *director*
Harris, Barbara Clementine *bishop*
Harris, Gayle Elizabeth *bishop*
Harvey, Christopher P. *lawyer*
Harvey, Mark Sumner *composer, educator, retired minister, musician*
Haseltine, William Alan *virology educator, former biopharmaceutical company executive*
Hawkey, G. Michael *lawyer, real estate developer*
Hawley, Anne *museum director*
Hayes, Andrew Wallace, II, *consumer products company executive*
Hayes, Robert Francis *lawyer*
Hayes, Robert Herrick *technology management educator*
Hayes, Samuel Linton III *business educator*
Hayter, Robert Glenn *physician*
Healey, Kerry Murphy *lieutenant governor*
Healy, Gerald Burke *otolaryngologist*
Healy, Martin Russell *lawyer*
Hebard, Barbara Adams *conservator*
Hedges, Inez Kathleen *comparative literature educator*
Hedley-Whyte, John *anesthesiologist, educator*
Hedlund, Ronald David *academic administrator, researcher, educator*
Hehir, J. Bryan *priest, educator, social services administrator*
Henry, DeWitt Pawling, II, *literature educator, art association administrator, writer*
Henry, John W. *professional sports team executive*
Herndon, James Henry *orthopedic surgeon, educator*
Hershey, Nona *artist, printmaker, educator*
Herzlinger, Regina *economist, educator, writer*
Herzog, David Brandeis *psychiatrist*
Hettmer, Simone *hematologist, oncologist*
Hiatt, Howard H. *internist, educator*
Hickey, Paul Robert *anesthesiologist, educator*
Hieken, Charles *lawyer*
Hilgenberg, Alan D. *surgeon, educator*
Hill, Nicholas S. *physician, researcher*
Hill, Richard Devereux *retired banker*
Hillery, Thomas Hungiville *journalist, financial consultant*
Hills, Patricia Gorton Schulze *curator, art historian*
Hintikka, Jaakko *philosopher, educator*
Hirsch, Erwin F. *surgeon, educator*
Hoffman, Stanley Marc *composer, editor*
Holland, James R. *real estate company officer*
Hoort, Steven Thomas *lawyer*
Horrigan, Brian Richard *economist*

Hoskins, William Keller *pharmaceutical executive, lawyer, mediator, arbitrator*
Hostetter, Amos Barr, Jr. *cable television executive*
Howe, Janice W. *lawyer*
Howley, Peter Maxwell *pathology educator*
Hoyer, Jed *professional sports team executive*
Hoyt, Herbert Austin Aikins *television producer*
Hrones, Stephen Baylis *lawyer, educator*
Hu, Chengcheng *statistician, medical researcher*
Hubel, David Hunter *physiologist, science educator*
Hung, Kuo-Ting *operations research specialist, educator*
Hunter, Durant Adams *executive search company executive*
Hurd, J. Nicholas *executive recruiting consultant, former banker*
Hurwitz, Mark David *oncologist*
Hurwitz, Sidney *printmaker*
husbands, andy *chef*
Huston, Julia *lawyer*
Ingwall, Joanne S. *medical educator, department chairman*
Ireland, Roderick L. *state supreme court justice*
Irimia, Daniel *biomedical researcher*
Ives, J. Atwood *financial executive*
Jacoby, Jeff *journalist, commentator*
Jaff, Michael Ritt *osteopath, internist*
Jain, Rakesh K. *chemical engineering educator, tumor biology educator*
James, Bill *baseball writer, statistician*
Janos, Ellen L. *lawyer*
Järbe, Torbjörn Ulf Christian *psychologist, educator*
Jehlen, Patricia D. *state legislator*
Jin, Xuefei (Ha Jin) *literature educator, writer*
Jochum, Veronica *pianist*
Johansen, Erling *retired dental educator, dean*
Johnson, Abigail Pierrepont *investment company executive*
Johnson, Edward Crosby, III, (Ned Johnson) *investment company executive*
Johnston, Richard Alan *lawyer*
Johnston, Susan A. *lawyer*
Jonas, Stephen P. *investment company executive*
Jones, Daniel Bougere *surgeon*
Jones, Jeffrey Foster *lawyer*
Jones, Sheldon Atwell *retired lawyer*
Jordan, Alexander Joseph, Jr. *lawyer*
Joyce-Brady, Martin Francis *medical educator*
Kahn, Barbara B. *endocrinologist*
Kahn, C. Ronald *research laboratory administrator*
Kalkstein, Joshua Adam *lawyer*
Kandror, Konstantin *biochemist, educator*
Kane, Daniel E. *nurse*
Kang, Jing X. *medical researcher, educator*
Kanin, Dennis Roy *lawyer*
Kantoff, Philip W. *oncologist*
Kaplan, Marshall Myles *medical educator, researcher, gastroenterologist*
Kaplan, Robert S. *business educator, former investment banker*
Karnovsky, Morris John *pathologist, biologist*
Karpovsky, Mark Girsh *computer engineering educator, research laboratory director*
Kassirer, Jerome Paul *medical educator*
Katsoulomitis, Georgia *foundation administrator, lawyer*
Katz, Paul *musician, music educator*
Katzmann, Gary Stephen *judge*
Kaufmann, Patrick J. *business educator*
Kazemi, Homayoun *internist, educator*
Kearns, Ellen Cecelia *lawyer*
Keating, Mark Taylor *physician, medical educator*
Keating, Michael Burns *lawyer, educator*
Keeton, Robert Ernest *federal judge*
Kehoe, William Francis *lawyer*
Keller, Stanley *lawyer*
Kelly, Edmund Francis *insurance company executive*
Kelly, Francis J. III *global marketing company president and COO*
Kempuraj, Duraisamy *research scientist*
Kennedy, Joseph Patrick, II, *utilities executive, former congressman*
Kennedy, Louise Avery *theater critic, newspaper editor, writer*
Kerry, Cameron F. *lawyer*
Kesari, Santosh *neurologist, oncologist, neuroscientist*
Kessler, Diane Cooksey *religious organization administrator, minister*
Keusch, Gerald Tilden *academic administrator*
Khalsa, Sat Bir Singh *biomedical researcher*
Kiang, Nelson Yuan-sheng *medical educator*
Kidder, George Howell *lawyer*
Kieff, Elliott Dan *medical educator*
Kilbourne, Jean *media analyst, educator*
Kim, Ducksoo *radiologist, inventor, educator*
Kimball, George Edward III *sports columnist*
King, Nick *newspaper editor*
Kircher, Moritz Florian *radiologist, researcher*
Kirchick, William Dean *lawyer*
Kirkpatrick, Edward Thomson *retired academic administrator, retired mechanical engineer*
Kirsch, Robert L. *lawyer*
Kitz, Richard John *anesthesiologist, educator*
Klarfeld, Jonathan Michael *journalism educator*
Kleiner, Fred Scott *art historian, archaeologist, educator, editor*
Kleinman, Ronald Ellis *pediatrician*
Klem, Christopher A. *lawyer*
Klema, Donald David *architect*
Klieman, Rikki Jo *lawyer, legal analyst*
Klotz, Charles Rodger *water transportation executive, investment company executive*
Knag, Paul Everett *lawyer*
Knight, Norman *volunteer, retired broadcast executive*
Knott, Bill *poet, literature educator*
Kocher, Mininder Singh *pediatric orthopaedic surgeon, epidemiologist*
Kociubes, Joseph Leib *lawyer*
Koh, Howard Kyongju *academic administrator, educator, former public health commissioner*
Kojic, Milos *research scientist, educator*
Komaroff, Anthony Leader *physician*
Kopans, Daniel B. *radiologist, educator*
Kopelman, Leonard *lawyer*
Kornberg, Sir Hans Leo *biochemist, educator*

Kotting, Joey *artist*
Kotz, Nathan Kallison (Nick Kotz) *news correspondent, author*
Krakoff, Robert Leonard *publishing executive*
Krane, Stephen Martin *rheumatologist, educator*
Kressel, Herbert Yehude *medical educator*
Kumar, Vikram Sheel *information technology executive*
Kuo, Winston Patrick *biomedical researcher*
Kuttner, Robert Louis *editor, writer, columnist*
Lahiri, Jhumpa (Nilanjana Sudeshna) *writer*
Lamont, John Thomas *gastroenterologist, educator*
Lampert, James B. *lawyer*
Landsmark, Ted *academic administrator*
Lane, Kathy S. *information technology executive, consumer products company executive*
Lange, Harry W. *investment company executive*
Langer, Robert Martin *retired chemical engineering company executive, consultant*
Langwell, Dennis J. *corporate financial executive*
Larkin, Michael John *editor, journalist*
Lasker, Morris E. *judge*
Last, Michael P. *lawyer*
Lataif, Louis Edward *dean*
Laufer, Marc R. *obstetrician*
Lawner, Ron *advertising executive*
Lawrence, Merloyd Ludington *editor*
Lawrence, Paul Roger *retired psychology professor*
Lazar, Harold Lee *cardiothoracic surgeon*
Lazarow, Robin S. *lawyer*
Leahy, John L. *software development company executive*
Leaman, J. Richard, Jr. *paper company executive*
LeBlanc, Marianne Camille *lawyer*
Lee, Charles *cytologist*
Lee, David Stoddart *retired investment company executive*
Lee, Donald Young (Don Lee) *publishing executive*
Lee, Thomas Henry *internist, cardiologist, healthcare executive*
Lee, William F. *lawyer*
Leetch, Brian Joseph *professional hockey player*
Leff, Deborah *library director*
Leibowitz, Hal J. *lawyer*
Leland, Timothy *retired newspaper executive*
Lepore, Ralph Thomas III *lawyer*
Le Quesne, Philip William *chemistry educator, researcher*
Lesser, Laurence *musician, educator*
Lettieri, Richard J. (Richard Joseph Lettieri) *lawyer*
Levine, William Michael *lawyer*
Levitin, Lev Berovich *research scientist, educator*
Levy, Paul Finanque *health facility administrator*
Levy, Stephen Raymond *retired data processing executive*
Levy, Stuart B. *molecular biologist, educator, science administrator, researcher*
Lewis, Dave *professional hockey coach, former professional hockey player*
Licata, Arthur Frank *lawyer*
Lieberman, Michael J. *lawyer*
Linde, Edward H. *real estate manager*
Lindsay, Reginald Carl *judge*
Ling, Pei-Ra *medical educator*
Liotta, Jeanne *film director, film instructor*
Little, John Bertram *radiologist, educator, researcher*
Litwin, Paul Jeffrey *lawyer*
Liu, Ta-Chiang *research scientist, physician, consultant*
Livingston, David Morse *internist, biomedical researcher*
Lockhart, Keith Alan *conductor, music director*
Loder, John Mark *lawyer*
Lodge, George C(abot) *business administration educator*
Loeser, Hans Ferdinand *lawyer*
Lo Gerfo, Frank William *surgeon*
Logue, Ronald E. *finance company executive*
Looney, William Francis, Jr. *lawyer*
Loretta, Mark *professional baseball player*
Loria, Martin A. *lawyer*
Loscalzo, Joseph *cardiologist, biochemist*
Loth, Renée *editor*
Lovejoy, George Montgomery, Jr. *real estate company executive*
Lowell, Mike *professional baseball player*
Lowell, Richard Lee *music educator, musician*
Lowenstein, Arlene Jane *nursing educator, health facility administrator*
Lowry, Lois (Lois Hammersberg) *writer*
Lublin, Robert Ian *theater educator*
Ludwig, David S. *endocrinologist*
Lundgren, Lena Margareta *social sciences educator, researcher*
Lundgren, Richard John *real estate executive, preservationist, city planner*
Luongo, C. Paul *public relations executive*
Lynch, Barbara *chef, restaurant owner*
Lynch, Sandra Lea *federal judge*
Lyons, David Barry *philosophy and law educator*
Lyons, Paul Vincent *lawyer*
MacCombie, Bruce Franklin *composer, college administrator*
Macdonald, Peter J. *lawyer*
MacLeish, Roderick, Jr. *lawyer*
Maffeo, Pino *chef*
Magazini, Brother John Bernard *academic administrator*
Malenka, Bertram Julian *physicist, researcher*
Malt, Ronald Bradford *lawyer*
Mandell, James *health facility executive, urologist, educator*
Mankin, Henry Jay *orthopedist, educator, health facility administrator*
Mannick, John Anthony *surgeon*
Manning, Peter Kirby *criminal justice educator*
Mansfield, Christopher Charles *lawyer*
Manson, JoAnn Elisabeth *endocrinologist*
Margolis, Bernard Allen *library administrator*
Markey, John K. *lawyer*
Markham, Jesse William *economist, educator*
Marsh, Milton R.W. *composer*
Marshall, Margaret Hilary *state supreme court chief justice*
Marshall, Martin Vivan *business administration educator, consultant*

Walker, Antoine Devon *professional basketball player*
Walrath, Patricia A. *state legislator*
Walz, Thomas *biology professor*
Wang, Zhi *biomedical researcher*
Ware, Paul F., Jr. *lawyer*
Warner, John J.P. *orthopedist, surgeon*
Warshaw, Andrew Louis *surgeon, researcher*
Watanabe, Mark David *pharmacist, educator*
Wedge, Carole C. *architectural firm executive*
Weiner, Stephen Mark *lawyer*
Weiss, Earle Burton *physician*
Weitzel, John Patterson *lawyer*
Wellington, Carol Strong *law librarian*
Weltman, David Lee *lawyer*
Wendorf, Richard Harold *library director, educator*
Werchniak, Andrew Eugene *dermatologist, educator*
Wermuth, Paul Charles *retired language educator*
Westcott, John McMahon, Jr. *lawyer*
Westra, James R. *lawyer*
Wheeler, W(illiam) Scott *composer, conductor, music educator*
White, Barry Bennett *lawyer*
White, Deborah O. *forensic psychologist*
Whitley, L. Tracee *lawyer*
Whitlock, John L. *lawyer*
Whittemore, Anthony Dunster *vascular surgeon, chief medical officer*
Whitters, James Payton III *lawyer, educator*
Wiesel, Elie *writer, educator*
Wiesner, David *illustrator, children's writer*
Wigglesworth, Margaret *property manager*
Wilcox, Steven Alan *lawyer*
Willett, Walter Churchill *epidemiologist, educator*
Williams, John Taylor *lawyer*
Williams, John Towner *composer, conductor*
Willock, Marcelle Monica *retired medical educator*
Winn, Joseph Lampher *retired electronics executive*
Wizwer, Phillip *pharmacist, consultant*
Wolf, Alice Koerner *state legislator, former mayor*
Woodard, Fredrick James, Jr. *music educator, musician*
Woodburn, Ralph Robert, Jr. *lawyer*
Wu, Guofa Felix *computer company executive*
Wu, Tung *curator, artist, art historian, educator*
Wyszynski, Diego Federico *epidemiologist, educator*
Xu, Xiping *adult education educator, director*
Yaroslavsky, Anna *biophysicist, educator*
Yeager, Peter Cleary *sociologist, educator*
Yoon, Young-sup *medical educator*
Yoshida, Hiroyuki *mathematician, computer scientist, educator, medical science educator*
Young, Anne B. *neurologist, educator*
Young, David William *management educator*
Young, Laura *dance educator, choreographer*
Young, Raymond Henry *lawyer*
Young, William Glover *federal judge*
Yuan, Junying *medical educator, researcher*
Zack, Arnold Marshall *lawyer, mediator, arbitrator, judge*
Zaleznik, Abraham *psychoanalyst, management specialist, educator*
Zannieri, Nina *museum director*
Zawaideh, Samer K. *orthodontist*
Zelnick, Carl Robert *writer, educator*
Zervas, Nicholas Themistocles *neurosurgeon*
Zinner, Michael Jeffrey *surgeon, educator*
Zobel, Rya Weickert *federal judge*
Zon, Leonard I. *pediatrics educator, researcher*
Zungolo, Eileen H. *dean*

**Bourne**
Fantozzi, Peggy Ryone *geologist, environmental planner*

**Boxboro**
Parmese, Gabriel J. *corporate financial executive*

**Boxford**
Siegert, Barbara (Barbara Marie Siegert) *health care administrator*

**Boylston**
Hanshaw, James Barry *pediatrician, educator*
Larson, Roland Elmer *health facility administrator*
Schofield, Edmund Acton, Jr. *botanist, academic administrator*

**Braintree**
Hallenbeck, Rachel Kirsten *music educator, director*
Robertson, Michael Swing *minister*

**Brewster**
Johnson, Jill Ann *lyricist, actress*
Stoltenberg, Donald Hugo *artist, writer*

**Bridgewater**
Heffernan, Peter John *state official*
Holton, Susan A. *communications educator*
Karavites, Peter *retired historian*
Tinsley, Adrian *former college president*

**Brighton**
Garber, Paul William *lawyer*
Holley, Michael *sportswriter, sportscaster*
Leistyna, Pepi *linguistics educator*
O'Malley, Sean Patrick Cardinal *Archbishop of Boston, cardinal*
Valianti, Deborah L. *playwright*

**Brockton**
Carlson, Desiree Anice *pathologist*
Lightford, Melvin *minister*
Moore, Mary Johnson *nurse*
Rothschild, William Baron *psychiatrist, educator*
Sullivan, Brendan Paul *state official, consultant, communications educator*

**Brookfield**
Anderson, Theodore Robert *physicist, small business owner*
Couture, Ronald David *art association administrator, web site designer, consultant*

**Brookline**
Alarcon, Rogelio Alfonso *retired internist, retired researcher*
Barron, Ros *artist*
Bourne, Katherine Day *journalist, educator*
Burns, Ikuko Kawai *artist*
Burns, Padraic *physician, psychiatrist, psychoanalyst, educator*
Cromwell, Adelaide M. *sociology educator*
Dow, Elias Charles *endocrinologist*
Frankel, Ernst Gabriel *shipping and aviation business executive, educator*
Goldsmith, Gary Norman *psychiatrist, psychoanalyst*
Jakab, Irene *psychiatrist*
Michopoulos, Aristotle V. *humanities educator, researcher*
Moon, John Ellis van Courtland *retired historian*
Moses, Harry Elecks *physicist, mathematician*
Nash, Leonard Kollender *retired chemistry professor*
Reedy, Harry Lee *financial services executive*
Rubin-Katz, Barbara *sculptor, human services manager*
Schwartz, Bernard *physician*
Skeete, Helen Watkins *minister, counselor*
Swirnoff, Lois *artist, educator*
Tyler, H. Richard *physician*

**Brookline Village**
Frankenthaler, Stan *food service executive*

**Burlington**
Angle, Colin *electrical engineer, robotic company executive*
Berkoben, John Perri *physician*
Cerveny, David John *lawyer*
Choi, In-Sup *radiologist*
Clerkin, Eugene Patrick *physician, educator*
Cosgrove, Garth Rees *neurosurgeon*
Dyer, Joseph Wendell *retired naval officer*
Flanigan, Thomas Christopher *research scientist*
Freidberg, Stephen Roy *neurosurgeon*
Gawoski, John Michael *physician*
Greiner, Helen *mechanical engineer*
Hurd, Joseph Kindall, Jr. *obstetrician, gynecologist*
Moschella, Samuel L. *dermatology educator*
Oberfield, Richard Alan *oncologist*
Rhee, Sokwoo *mechanical engineer*
Schoetz, David John, Jr. *colon and rectal surgeon, educator*
Sproull, Robert Fletcher *research and development company executive*

**Buzzards Bay**
Cirillo, Jeannine L. *pharmacist*

**Byfield**
deGrasse, Olga I. *language educator*
Doggett, John Martin, Jr. (Marty Doggett) *headmaster*
Kozol, Jonathan *writer*
Yesair, David Wayne *biochemist*

**Cambridge**
Abernathy, Frederick Henry *mechanical engineering educator*
Acemoglu, Daron (K. Daron Acemoglu) *economics professor*
Ackerman, James *fine arts educator*
Adams, Jody *chef, restaurant owner*
Alberty, Robert Arnold *chemistry professor*
Alcalay, Albert S. *artist, design educator*
Alcock, Charles Roger *science educator*
Alesina, Alberto *economist, educator*
Alexander, Seth *investment company executive*
Alford, William P. *law educator*
Allen, Thomas John *finance educator*
Alt, James Edward *political science professor*
Anderson, James Gilbert *chemistry professor*
Anderson, Stanford Owen *architect, architectural historian, educator*
Anderson, William Henry *psychobiology educator*
Andrews, William Dorey *law educator*
Angrist, Joshua D. *economics educator*
Anquetil, Patrick Armond *investment company executive, researcher*
Apostolakis, George E. *engineering educator, researcher*
Aronson, Michael Andrew *editor*
Asani, Ali S. *foreign language and religious studies educator*
Bailyn, Bernard *historian, educator*
Bailyn, Lotte *psychologist, educator*
Bakanowsky, Louis Joseph *artist, educator, architect*
Baker, Tania Ann *biology professor, researcher*
Bane, Mary Jo *dean, political science professor*
Banerjee, Abhijit Vinayak *economics professor*
Barger, James Edwin *physicist*
Barlow, David S. *pharmaceutical executive*
Barnett, David Philip *horticulturist*
Barnhart, Cynthia *engineering educator, researcher*
Barrett, J. Carl *medical researcher, molecular biologist, researcher*
Barron, David Jeremiah *law educator*
Bartee, Thomas Creson *computer scientist, educator*
Bartel, David *biology professor, researcher*
Bartholet, Elizabeth *law educator*
Bator, Francis Michel *economist, educator*
Battin, Richard Horace *aeronautical engineer*
Bawendi, Moungi G. *chemist, educator*
Bear, Mark Firman *neuroscientist, educator*
Bebchuk, Lucian Arye *law educator, finance educator*
Beér, János Miklós *engineering educator*
Belcher, Angela *engineering educator*
Ben-Akiva, Moshe Emanuel *civil engineering educator*
Benedict, Manson *retired chemical engineer, educator*
Beranek, Leo Leroy *acoustical engineer, educator*
Berger, Harvey James *pharmaceutical executive, physician, educator*
Berlowitz, Leslie *cultural organization administrator*
Berndt, Ernst Rudolf *economist, educator*
Berwick, Donald Mark *medical institute administrator*

Bhabha, Homi K. *humanities educator, writer*
Bianchi, Claudine *marketing executive*
Binzel, Richard P. *astrophysicist, educator*
Bishop, Robert Lyle *economist, educator*
Bizzi, Emilio *neurophysiologist, educator*
Blackmer, Donald Laurence Morton *political scientist*
Blair, Ann *historian*
Blout, Elkan Rogers *retired biological chemistry professor, retired dean*
Bok, Derek Curtis *law educator, former university president*
Bolster, Arthur Stanley, Jr. *history professor*
Borjas, George J(esus) *economics professor*
Botkin, James W. *leadership and executive coach*
Brackett, Prilla Smith *artist, educator*
Bradt, Hale Van Dorn *physicist, x-ray astronomer, educator*
Bras, Rafael Luis *engineering educator*
Bremer, Gabriel *chef*
Brenner, Howard *chemical engineering educator*
Brewer, Scott *law educator*
Brooks, Rodney Allen *information technology executive, educator*
Brusch, John Lynch *physician, educator, hospital administrator*
Brustein, Robert Sanford *literature and language professor, theater director, writer*
Buell, Lawrence Ingalls *language educator*
Bulovic, Vladimir *engineering educator*
Burke, Bernard Flood *physicist, researcher*
Burns, Virginia *social worker*
Burr, Winthrop Ames *psychiatrist*
Bush, Michael *architectural firm executive*
Calabrese, Joseph D. *psychologist, educator*
Campbell, Robert *architect, writer*
Canizares, Claude Roger *astrophysicist, educator*
Cao, Junwei *research scientist*
Caplice, Christopher *engineering educator*
Capozzola, Christopher *historian*
Caramazza, Alfonso *psychology professor*
Carter, Ashton Baldwin *former federal agency administrator*
Cestnick, Laurie L. *neuropsychologist, educator, scientist*
Ceyer, Sylvia T. *chemistry professor, department chairman*
Champion, Hale (Charles Hale Champion) *academic administrator, lecturer, government official, consultant*
Chandler, Fay Martin *artist*
Chatterjee, Sharmila *marketing educator*
Chen, Lincoln Chin-ho *medical educator*
Chen, Sow-Hsin *nuclear engineering educator, researcher*
Cheng, Susan *medical researcher*
Chisholm, Sallie Watson *biological oceanography educator, researcher*
Chodorow, Nancy Julia *psychotherapist, educator*
Chomsky, (Avram) Noam *linguistics and philosophy educator*
Chung, Soon-Jo *engineer, researcher*
Clark, Maynard Stephen *vegetarian resource center administrator*
Clark, Robert Charles *law educator, former dean*
Clausen, Wendell Vernon *retired classics educator*
Clay, Phillip L. *academic administrator*
Cleary, David Michael *composer, critic, library assistant*
Clifford, Gari David *engineering educator, biomedical engineer*
Coates, John C., IV, *law educator*
Cohen, Joshua *political science professor*
Cohen, Preston Scott *architecture educator*
Cohen, Robert Edward *chemical engineering professor, consultant*
Cole, Heather Ellen *librarian*
Colton, Clark Kenneth *chemical engineering professor*
Conley, Tom Clark *literature educator*
Connick, Harry, Jr. *musician, actor, vocalist, composer, lyricist*
Conway, Jill Kathryn Ker *former academic administrator, writer*
Cooper, Richard Newell *economist, educator*
Copenhagen, Edward Blake *archivist, librarian*
Corey, Elias James *chemistry professor*
Covert, Eugene Edzards *aerospace engineer, aeronautics professor*
Craig, Albert M. *history professor, researcher*
Crandall, Stephen Harry *engineering educator*
Crawley, Edward Francis *aerospace engineering educator*
Cummins, Christopher C. *chemistry professor*
d'Arbeloff, Alexander V. *electronics executive*
Davis-Millis, Nina *librarian*
de Marneffe, Barbara Rowe *historic preservationist*
de Monteiro, Nadsa *chef*
de Neufville, Richard Lawrence *engineering educator*
Dennis, Jack Bonnell *computer scientist, educator*
Dershowitz, Alan Morton *law educator*
Desan, Christine *law educator*
Deutch, John Mark *chemistry professor, former CIA Director*
de Varon, Lorna Cooke *choral conductor*
de Weck, Oliver *engineering educator, researcher*
Dewey, Clarence Forbes, Jr. *engineering educator*
DiCamillo, Kate *writer*
Dilday, Judith Nelson *judge*
Dobson, Parrish *photographer, educator*
Dominguez, Jorge Ignacio *political scientist, educator*
Donahue, Charles, Jr. *law educator*
Donahue, John David *federal agency administrator, educator*
Doty, Paul Mead *biochemist, educator, arms control specialist*
Dowling, John Elliott *biology professor*
Downey, Richard Ralph *lawyer, consultant, accountant, management consultant*
Drake, Elisabeth Mertz *chemical engineer, consultant*
Dresselhaus, Mildred Spiewak *physics professor, engineering educator*
Dudley, Richard Mansfield *mathematician, educator*
Duffy, Robert Aloysius *aeronautical engineer*
Dugundji, John *aeronautical engineer*
Dulac, Catherine *biology professor, researcher*

Dunsire, Deborah *pharmaceutical executive*
Dyck, Martin *literary theorist, mathematics historian*
Eagar, Thomas Waddy *metallurgist, educator*
Eagleson, Peter Sturges *civil engineer, environmental engineer, educator*
Eckaus, Richard Samuel *economist, educator*
Edgerly, William Skelton *banker*
Eggan, Kevin C. *molecular and cellular biology professor, researcher*
Ehrenreich, Henry *physicist, researcher*
Eisen, Herman Nathaniel *immunology researcher, medical educator*
Eisenberg, Carola *psychiatrist, educator*
Elhauge, Einer Richard *law educator*
Elkies, Noam D. *mathematics professor*
Elkins, Caroline M. *history professor, writer*
Ellison, Peter Thorpe *anthropology professor*
Ellwood, David Tabor *dean, public policy educator*
Elmore, Richard F. *education educator*
Emanuel, Kerry Andrew *academic administrator, meteorologist, oceanographer, educator*
Engell, James Theodore *language educator, department chairman*
Erikson, Raymond Leo *biology professor*
Essigmann, John M. *chemistry professor*
Ette, Ene Ikpong *clinical pharmacologist*
Eurich, Nell P. *education educator*
Ewing, Scott Edwin *physiatrist, educator*
Fallon, Richard H., Jr. *law educator*
Fanger, Donald Lee *Slavic language and literature educator*
Farver, Jane *museum director*
Faust, Drew Gilpin *historian, educator*
Fay, James Alan *mechanical engineering educator*
Feininger, Theodore Lux *artist*
Feld, Michael Stephen *physics professor*
Feldman, Gary Jay *physicist, researcher*
Feldstein, Martin Stuart *economist, educator*
Ferguson, Niall Campbell *history professor, writer*
Ferrari, Raffaele *oceanographer, educator*
Ferrell, Allen F. *law educator*
Field, Martha Amanda *law educator*
Field, Robert Warren *chemistry professor*
Fink, Yoel *science educator, researcher*
Fiorenza, Francis P. *religion educator*
Fischer, Kurt Walter *education educator*
Fisher, Philip J. *English language educator, literature educator*
Fisher, Roger Dummer *negotiation expert, law educator*
Fisher, William W. III *law educator*
Fishman, Mark Charles *biomedical researcher*
Flad, Rowan Kimon *social sciences educator*
Flannery, Susan Marie *library administrator*
Fleming, Ronald Lee *urban planner, consultant*
Flemings, Merton Corson *engineering educator, materials scientist*
Flier, Michael Stephen *Slavic languages educator*
Forbes, Kristin J. *economics professor, former federal official*
Ford, Patrick Kildea *Celtic studies educator*
Forney, G(eorge) David, Jr. *retired electronics executive*
Fox, John Bayley, Jr. *university dean*
Fox, Maurice Sanford *retired molecular biologist, educator*
French, Anthony Philip *physicist, educator*
Frey, Daniel D. *engineering educator, researcher*
Frey, Frederick August *geochemist, researcher, educator*
Friedman, Benjamin Morton *economics professor*
Friedman, Jeffrey Robert *psychiatrist, educator*
Friedman, Jerome Isaac *physics professor, researcher*
Frisch, Rose Epstein *population sciences researcher*
Frosch, Robert Alan *retired automobile manufacturing executive, physicist*
Frug, Gerald E. *law educator*
Fujimoto, James G. *electrical engineering educator*
Gabrielse, Gerald *physics professor*
Gaensler, Bryan Malcolm *astronomer, educator*
Gagliardi, Ugo Oscar *systems software architect, educator*
Gallager, Robert Gray *electrical engineering educator*
Gardner, Howard Earl *psychologist, educator, writer*
Garland, Carl Wesley *chemist, educator*
Gaskell, Ivan George Alexander De Wend *art museum curator*
Gates, Henry Louis, Jr. *literature and language professor, historian*
Geller, Margaret Joan *astrophysicist, educator*
Georgi, Howard *physics professor*
Gergen, David Richmond *federal official, magazine editor*
Gibbons, Joe *filmmaker*
Gilbert, Daniel *psychology professor*
Gilbert, Walter *molecular biologist, educator*
Giles, Robert Hartmann *journalist, educator*
Gingerich, Owen Jay *astronomer, educator*
Glaeser, Edward Ludwig *research economist, educator*
Glauber, Roy Jay *physics professor*
Glendon, Mary Ann *law educator*
Goldberg, Marc Evan *biotechnology venture capitalist*
Goldberg, Ray Allan *agriculturist, educator*
Goldstone, Jeffrey *physicist, educator*
Goldwasser, Shafrira *computer scientist*
Gomes, Peter John *clergyman, educator*
Goodman, Ellen Holtz *journalist*
Graham, Jorie *writer, educator*
Graham, Loren Raymond *historian, educator*
Graham, Patricia Albjerg *education educator*
Graham, William Albert *religious studies educator, history educator*
Gray, Paul Edward *academic administrator*
Greenberg, Jerry A. *information technology executive*
Greenblatt, Stephen Jay *literature and language professor, writer*
Greene, Frederick Davis, II, *chemistry professor*
Greenspan, Harvey Philip *applied mathematician, educator*
Greenstone, Michael *economics professor, researcher*

Griffith, Linda G. (Linda Griffith-Cima) *biomedical engineer, chemical engineer, educator*
Grindlay, Jonathan Ellis *astrophysics educator*
Gross, Benedict H. *mathematician*
Grosz, Barbara Jean *computer science educator*
Grove, Timothy Lynn *geology educator*
Gund, Graham *architectural firm executive*
Guthke, Karl Siegfried *language educator*
Gyftopoulos, Elias Panayiotis *mechanical and nuclear engineering educator*
Halley, Janet E. *law educator*
Halperin, Bertrand Israel *physics professor*
Halperin, Daniel I. *law educator*
Hamner, Suzanne Leath *retired history educator*
Hamner, W. Easley *architect*
Hanan, Patrick Dewes *foreign language professional, educator*
Hansen, Kent Forrest *nuclear engineering educator*
Hanson, Jon D. *law educator*
Hao, Tian *physical chemist, materials scientist*
Harbison, John *composer*
Harris, Wesley L. *aeronautical engineer, educator*
Hart, Oliver D'Arcy *economics professor*
Hastings, Daniel *aeronautical engineer, educator*
Hastings, John Woodland *biologist, educator*
Hauser, John Richard *marketing and management science educator*
Hausman, Jerry Allen *economics professor, consultant*
Hausmann, Ricardo *economics professor, director*
Havens, Leston Laycock *psychiatrist, educator*
Hay, Bruce L. *law educator*
Heineman, Benjamin Walter, Jr. *lawyer*
Helgason, Sigurdur *mathematician, educator*
Heller, Eric Johnson *physicist, educator, digital abstract artist*
Herschbach, Dudley Robert *chemistry professor*
Hewitt, Jacqueline N. *astronomy educator*
Heywood, John Benjamin *mechanical engineering educator*
Himmelstein, David U. *medical educator*
Hirsch, Martin Stanley *internist, epidemiologist, researcher*
Hockfield, Susan *academic administrator, medical educator*
Hoffman, Paul Felix *geologist, educator*
Hoffmann, Inge Schneier *psychologist, educator*
Hofmann, Hans A. *neuroscientist*
Holdren, John Paul *physicist, educator, writer*
Holmberg, Arthur Carl *performing arts educator, director, theater critic*
Holmstrom, Bengt R. *philosopher, educator*
Holton, Gerald *physicist, educator, science historian*
Hopkins, Nancy H. *biology professor*
Horn, Henry Eyster *retired minister*
Horvitz, Howard Robert *biology professor, researcher*
Horwitz, Morton J. *law educator*
How, Hoton *electrical engineer*
Howitt, Arnold Martin *academic administrator, educator*
Hubbard, Ruth *retired biology professor*
Huchra, John Peter *astronomer, educator*
Hunt, Swanee G. *public policy educator, former ambassador*
Hunter, Ian W. *engineering educator, researcher*
Huntington, Samuel Phillips *political science educator*
Huth, John E. *physicist, educator*
Hyman, Steven Edward *academic administrator, physiatrist, educator*
Hynes, Richard Olding *biology researcher, educator*
Iagnemma, Karl *robotics scientist, researcher, writer*
Ippen, Erich Peter *electrical engineer, educator, physicist*
Iriye, Akira *historian, educator*
Jackiw, Roman *physicist, researcher*
Jackson, Howell E. *law educator*
Jacob, Wendy *artist, art educator*
Jacobs, Vicki Ann *education educator*
Jacobsen, Eric N. *chemistry professor*
Jacoby, Henry Donnan *economist, educator*
Jaffe, Arthur Michael *mathematician, physicist, educator*
Jencks, Christopher Sandys *sociologist, educator*
John, Richard Rodda *transportation executive*
Johnson, Howard Wesley *retired academic administrator, finance company executive*
Johnson, Willard Raymond *political science professor*
Jolls, Christine Margaret *law educator*
Jonas, Joan (Joan Amerman Edwards) *artist*
Jones, Alex S. *reporter, writer*
Jones, Christopher Prestige *classicist, educator, historian, consultant*
Jones, Mary M. *landscape architect*
Jorgenson, Dale Weldeau *economist, educator*
Joskow, Paul Lewis *economist, educator*
Joss, Paul Christopher *astrophysicist, atmospheric physicist, educator*
Kac, Victor G. *mathematician, educator*
Kagan, Elena *dean, law educator*
Kagan, Jerome *psychologist, educator*
Kalb, Johannes Andreas *research scientist*
Kamentsky, Louis Aaron *biophysicist*
Kaplan, Benjamin *judge*
Kaplan, Justin *author*
Kaplow, Louis *law educator*
Kaufman, Andrew Lee *law educator*
Kaufman, Gordon Dester *theology studies educator*
Kaysen, Carl *economics professor*
Kazhdan, David *mathematician, educator*
Kazimi, Mujid Suliman *nuclear engineer, educator*
Kellogg, Peter Newman *biotechnology company executive*
Kelly, Sean Dorrance *philosophy educator*
Kelman, Steven Jay *education educator*
Kelsey, Robin E. *art history educator*
Keniston, Kenneth *psychologist, educator*
Kennedy, David William *law educator*
Kennedy, Duncan McLean *law educator*
Kennedy, Roger George *museum program director, parks director*
Kennedy, Stephen Dandridge *economist, researcher*

Kerman, Arthur Kent *physicist, researcher*
Kerwin, Justin E. *naval engineer, educator*
Ketterle, Wolfgang *physics professor*
Keyfitz, Nathan *sociologist, educator, demographer*
Keyser, Samuel Jay *linguist, educator*
Khorana, Har Gobind *chemist, educator*
Khoury, Philip S. *academic administrator*
King, William Bruce *retired lawyer*
Kirby, William C. *dean, history professor*
Kleinman, Arthur Michael *medical anthropology and psychiatry educator*
Klemperer, Willian *chemistry professor*
Kleppner, Daniel *physicist, researcher*
Knickrehm, Glenn Allen *management executive*
Knoll, Andrew Herbert *biology professor*
Knowles, Jeremy Randall *chemist, educator*
Kobus, Richard Lawrence *architect*
Koepp, Donna Pauline Petersen *librarian*
Koester, Helmut Heinrich *history professor*
Kraakman, Reinier Herman *law educator*
Kraus, Rozann B. *performing company executive*
Kremer, Michael *economist, educator*
Kruger, Kenneth *architect*
Kujawa-Holbrook, Sheryl *theology studies educator, academic administrator*
Ladd, Charles Cushing III *civil engineer, educator*
Ladd, Florence Cawthorne *writer*
Lagace, Paul Alfred *aeronautical engineering educator*
Lagemann, Ellen Condliffe *history and education educator, former dean*
Laiou, Angeliki Evangelos *history professor*
Lamberg-Karlovsky, Clifford Charles *anthropologist, archaeologist*
Lander, Eric Steven *geneticist, molecular biologist, mathematician*
Langer, Ellen Jane *psychologist, educator, writer, artist*
Langer, Robert Samuel, Jr. *chemical, biomedical engineering educator*
Langermann, John W. R. *financial services company executive*
Lau, Vincent W. *lawyer*
Lauder, George V. *marine biologist*
Lawrence-Lightfoot, Sara *education educator, sociologist*
Lee, Barbara *political activist, foundation administrator*
Lee, Patrick A. *physics educator*
Lee, Se-Hee *electrical engineer, researcher*
Lenger, John Richard *journalism educator*
Lentz, Thomas W. *museum director, curator*
Leonard, Herman Beukema (Dutch Leonard) *public finance, management, and leadership educator*
Leveson, Nancy G. *aeronautical engineer*
Levi, Herbert Walter *biologist, educator*
Lewis, Henry Rafalsky *manufacturing executive*
Liau, Gene *medical educator*
Lieber, Charles *chemistry professor, researcher, materials scientist*
Lieberson, Stanley *sociologist, educator*
Light, Richard Jay *statistician, educator*
Lindquist, Susan Lee *biology and microbiology professor*
Lindzen, Richard Siegmund *meteorologist, educator*
Linsky, Marty *public policy educator, consultant*
Lipscomb, William Nunn, Jr. *retired chemistry professor*
Lipson, Pamela *information scientist*
Little, John Dutton Conant *management scientist, educator*
Liu, David Ruchien *biochemist*
Liu, Xiong *physicist*
Livingston, James Duane *physicist, researcher*
Lloyd, Seth *physicist*
Lomon, Earle Leonard *physicist, educator, consultant*
London, Irving Myer *physician, educator*
Long, Alan K. *research administrator*
Losick, Richard M. *biology professor*
Lydon, Amanda *chef*
Lynch, Nancy Ann *computer scientist, educator*
MacKinnon, Rebecca *media consultant, researcher*
MacMaster, Robert Ellsworth *historian, educator*
Maeda, John *graphics designer, artist, computer scientist*
Magee, Christopher L. *systems engineer*
Magnanti, Thomas L. *management educator, engineering educator*
Maher, Brendan Arnold *retired psychology educator, editor*
Maier, Charles Steven *history professor*
Maier, Pauline *historian, educator*
Malmstad, John Earl *literature and language professor*
Malone, Thomas W. *business educator, researcher*
Mancusi-Ungaro, Carol *conservator, educator*
Mandelbrot, Benoit B. *mathematician, research scientist, educator*
Mandl, Robert *application developer*
Mankiw, Gregory (Nicholas Gregory Mankiw) *economics professor, former federal official*
Manning, John F. *law educator*
Mansbridge, Jane Jebb *political scientist, educator*
Mansfield, John H. *law educator*
Marcus, Richard Sargon *research scientist*
Marini, Robert Charles *environmental engineering executive*
Markey, Winston Roscoe *aeronautical engineering educator*
Marks, David Hunter *civil engineering educator*
Marsden, Brian Geoffrey *astronomer*
Martin, Harry Stratton III *law educator, law librarian*
Martin, Paul Cecil *physicist, researcher*
Mathews, Joan Helene *pediatrician*
Matsui, Connie L. *pharmaceutical executive*
Maws, Tony *chef*
Mazlish, Bruce *historian, educator*
Mazur, Barry Charles *mathematician, educator*
Mazur, Michael *artist*
McBride, Robert Albert *training services executive*
McCartney, Kathleen *dean, education educator*
McCunney, Robert Joseph *physician*
McDonald, Christie Anne *literature and language professor, writer*
McGurk, Michael R. *lawyer*
McKenna, Margaret Anne *academic administrator*

Mc Kie, Todd Stoddard *artist*
McMullen, Curtis T. *mathematics professor*
McNally, Richard James *clinical psychologist, educator*
Mei, Chiang Chung *civil engineer, educator*
Melton, Douglas A. *molecular and cell biology educator*
Meltzer, Daniel J. *law educator*
Menand, Louis *literature educator, writer*
Meng, Xiao-Li *statistician*
Meselson, Matthew Stanley *biochemist, educator*
Meyer, John Robert *economist, educator*
Michelman, Frank I. *law educator*
Mikaelian, Tsoline *aerospace engineer*
Milgram, Jerome H. *marine and ocean engineer, educator*
Miller, Arthur Raphael *law educator*
Miller, Steven E. *professor of international affairs*
Milner, Richard Gerard *physicist*
Mindell, David A. *engineering educator*
Minow, Martha Louise *law educator*
Mitchell, William J. *academic administrator, architecture educator*
Mitten, David Gordon *classical archaeologist*
Mnookin, Robert Harris *law educator*
Moavenzadeh, Fred *engineering educator*
Mohamed, Mustafa A. *management educator*
Moncton, David *physicist*
Moniz, Ernest Jeffrey *physics professor*
Moore, J. Stuart *information technology executive*
Moore, Mark Harrison *criminal justice and public policy educator*
Moore, Sally Falk *anthropology educator*
Mootha, Vamsi Krishna *biomedical researcher, educator*
Moran, James Michael, Jr. *astronomer, educator*
Mori, Toshiko *architecture educator*
Moses, Joel *computer scientist, educator*
Motl, Lubos *physics professor, researcher*
Mullen, James C. *biotechnology company executive*
Munguia Tapia, Emmanuel *electrical engineer, researcher, computer scientist*
Murray, Andrew W. *biology professor, researcher*
Narayan, Ramesh *astronomy educator*
Narayanamurti, Venkatesh *health science association administrator*
Nathanson, Larry *medical educator*
Negele, John William *physics professor, consultant*
Negroponte, Nicholas *media specialist, educator*
Nesson, Charles R. *law educator*
Newman, Dava Jean *aerospace engineering educator, director*
Nightingale, Deborah Seifert *systems engineer, consultant*
Nordell, Hans Roderick *journalist, retired editor*
Nye, Joseph Samuel, Jr. *political science professor, former dean*
Nykrog, Per *French literature educator*
Oettinger, Anthony Gervin *mathematician, educator*
Ogletree, Charles J., Jr. *law educator*
O'Neil, Wayne *linguist, educator*
Oppenheim, Irwin *chemical physicist, educator*
Orchard, Robert John *theater producer, educator*
Orfield, Antonia Marie *optometrist, researcher*
O'Shea, Erin K. *biomedical researcher*
Owen, Edward Roger John (E. Roger Owen) *Middle Eastern studies professor, writer*
Pardue, Mary-Lou *biology professor*
Parker, Richard Davies *law educator*
Patton, Bruce M. *law educator, management consultant*
Paul, William *physicist, researcher*
Payack, Peter *poet, writer, artist, educator*
Penfield, Paul Livingstone, Jr. *electrical engineering educator*
Perkins, Dwight Heald *economics professor*
Petersen, Ulrich *geology educator*
Pettengill, Gordon H(emenway) *physicist, researcher*
Pfister, Donald Henry *biology professor*
Pian, Theodore Hsueh-Huang *engineering educator, consultant*
Pierce, Naomi Ellen *biology professor, researcher*
Pinker, Steven A. *psychologist, educator*
Pinkham, Daniel *composer*
Poggio, Tomaso Armando *physicist, educator, computer scientist, researcher*
Porter, Roger Blaine *federal official, educator*
Porter, William Lyman *architect, educator*
Poterba, James Michael *economist, educator*
Pounds, William Frank *management educator*
Powell, Adam Clayton *engineering educator, consultant*
Power, Samantha J. *public policy educator, writer*
Prinn, Ronald G. *atmospheric science educator*
Pritchard, David Edward *physics professor*
Probstein, Ronald Filmore *mechanical engineering educator*
Putnam, Robert D. *education educator*
Pye, Lucian Wilmot *political science professor*
Quinn, William (Chip) Gorman *biology professor, researcher*
Ramcharan, Bertrand *former international organization official*
Ramsey, Norman F. *physicist, researcher*
Ramseyer, J. Mark *law educator*
Randall, Lisa *physics professor*
Raskar, Ramesh *computer scientist*
Ratti, Carlo Filippo *architect, researcher*
Redwine, Robert Page *physicist, researcher*
Reif, L. Rafael *academic administrator, engineering educator*
Rensberger, Boyce *science journalism fellowship program administrator*
Reyes-Cubides, William *language educator, researcher, writer, actor*
Rhoda, Janice Tucker *writer, educator, musician*
Rightmire, George Philip *anthropology educator*
Riley, Lynne F. *lawyer*
Ritvo, Harriet *historian*
Rivest, Ronald L. *engineer*
Roberts, Edward Baer *technology management educator*
Roberts, Nancy *computer scientist, educator*
Rodrik, Dani *economics and international affairs educator*
Rogers, Peter Phillips *environmental engineer, educator, urban planner*
Rogoff, Kenneth Saul *economics professor*

Roos, Daniel *engineering educator*
Rose, Robert Michael *materials engineering educator*
Rosenberg, Charles Ernest *historian, educator*
Rosenblum, Nancy Lipton *political science professor*
Rosenkrantz, Barbara Gutmann *science and medicine historian*
Rosovsky, Henry *economist, educator*
Rotberg, Robert Irwin *historian, political scientist, educator, academic administrator*
Rowe, Mary P. *organizational ombudsman, management educator*
Rowe, Peter Grimmond *architecture educator, researcher*
Rowley, Geoffrey Herbert *management consultant*
Rubin, Donald Bruce *statistician, educator, research and development company executive*
Rubin, Lawrence Gilbert *physicist, science administrator*
Ruina, Jack Philip *electrical engineer, educator*
Russell, Kenneth Calvin *metallurgical engineering educator*
Sabeti, Pardis Christine *researcher*
Sadoway, Donald Robert *materials science educator*
Sampson, Robert J. *sociologist, educator*
Samson, Leona D. *biological engineering educator, research center director*
Samuelson, Paul Anthony *economist, educator*
Sander, Frank Ernest Arnold *law educator*
Santos, Adèle Naudé *architect, educator*
Sapers, Carl Martin *lawyer, educator*
Sapienza, Tony *public relations executive*
Sapolsky, Harvey Morton *political scientist, educator*
Sargentich, Lewis D. *law educator*
Sarma, Sanjay E. *electronics engineer, researcher*
Saywell, Edward *curator*
Schattenburg, Mark L. *physicist, educator*
Schaub, Robert George *pharmaceutical executive*
Schauer, Frederick Franklin *law educator*
Scherer, Frederic Michael *economics professor*
Schmalensee, Richard Lee *dean*
Schmid, Wilfried *mathematician, educator*
Schrag, Daniel P. *geochemist, educator*
Schrock, Richard Royce *chemistry professor*
Schuessler Fiorenza, Elisabeth *theology studies educator*
Scott, Hal S. *law educator*
Sen, Amartya Kumar *economist, educator*
Sevcenko, Ihor *history professor, literature professor*
Seyferth, Dietmar *chemist, educator*
Shaheen, C. Jeanne *political organization administrator, former governor*
Shapiro, David Louis *law educator*
Shapiro, Irwin Ira *physicist, researcher*
Sharp, Phillip Allen *biologist, educator*
Shavell, Steven M. *law educator*
Shaw, Anthony Raymond, Jr. *research executive*
Sheffi, Yossi *engineering educator, researcher*
Shinagel, Michael *dean, English literature educator*
Siegel, Abraham J. *economics professor, academic administrator*
Sigel, Anthony B. *art conservator*
Silbey, Robert James *chemistry professor, researcher, consultant*
Simmons, Kenneth Joseph *lawyer*
Simon, Eckehard (Peter) *foreign language educator*
Sims, Ezra *composer*
Singer, Isadore Manuel *mathematician, educator*
Singer, Joseph William *law educator*
Skolnikoff, Eugene B. *political science professor*
Slive, Seymour *museum director, art educator*
Slosburg-Ackerman, Jill Rose *artist, educator*
Smail, Daniel Lord *history professor*
Smith, Amy B. *mechanical engineer, engineering educator*
Smith, David Julian *educational consultant*
Smith, Kenneth Alan *chemical engineer, educator*
Smith, Merritt Roe *history professor*
Soljacic, Marin *physicist, educator*
Sollors, Werner *literature and language educator*
Solow, Robert Merton *economist, educator*
Soon, Willie Wei-Hock *environmental scientist*
Sortun, Ana *food service executive*
Spaepen, Frans August *physicist, educator*
Spunt, Shepard Armin *real estate company executive, management and financial consultant*
Staelin, David Hudson *electrical engineering educator, consultant*
Stager, Lawrence E. *archaeologist, educator*
Stanley, Richard P. *mathematics professor*
Stauffer, John William *cultural historian*
Steadman, Stephen Geoffrey *physicist*
Steel, Robert K. *former diversified financial services company executive*
Steiker, Carol S. *law educator*
Steiner, Henry Jacob *law and human rights educator*
Steinfeld, Jeffrey Irwin *chemistry professor, educator, writer*
Stevens, Kenneth Noble *electrical engineer, educator*
Stevenson, Howard Higginbotham *business educator*
Stock, James H. *economics professor*
Stoddard, Roger Eliot *scholar*
Strandberg, Malcom Woodrow Pershing *physicist*
Strang, William Gilbert *mathematician, educator*
Stroock, Daniel Wyler *mathematician, educator*
Stubbe, JoAnne *chemistry professor*
Stuntz, William John *law educator*
Subramanian, Guhan *law educator*
Suh, Nam Pyo *mechanical engineering educator*
Summers, Lawrence Henry *former academic administrator, former secretary of the treasury*
Suresh, Subra *materials engineer, educator*
Susskind, Lawrence Elliott *urban planner, educator, mediator*
Sussman, Joseph *engineering educator, researcher*
Swager, Timothy Manning *chemistry educator*
Szolovits, Peter *computer scientist*
Tannenbaum, Steven Robert *toxicologist, chemist*
Tarokh, Vahid *engineering educator*
Tarrant, Richard J(ohn) *classicist, educator*
Taymor, Betty *political science professor*
Teevan, Jaime *application developer, researcher*

Termeer, Henricus Adrianus *pharmaceutical executive*
Thaddeus, Patrick *physicist, researcher*
Thernstrom, Stephan *historian, educator*
Thiemann, Ronald Frank *dean, religious studies educator*
Thomas, Edward LaBelle *company executive*
Thomason, Moriah Elizabeth *neuroscientist*
Thompson, Dennis Frank *political science professor, consultant*
Thompson, Robert L., Jr. *pharmaceutical executive, lawyer*
Thorburn, David *literature educator*
Tian, Gang *mathematics professor*
Ting, Samuel Chao Chung *physicist, researcher*
Tinkham, Michael *physicist, researcher*
Tirman, John *academic research director*
Todreas, Neil Emmanuel *nuclear engineering educator*
Tonegawa, Susumu *biology professor*
Toomre, Alar *applied mathematician, theoretical astronomer*
Triantafyllou, Michael Stefanos *engineering educator*
Tribe, Laurence Henry *law educator*
Trilling, Leon *aeronautical engineering educator*
Troccoli, Mariano *astrophysicist, researcher*
Trumpbour, John *historian, researcher, director*
Tsoi, Edward Tze Ming *architect, urban planner, interior designer*
Tucker, Louis Leonard *retired historical society administrator*
Tuller, Harry Louis *materials scientist*
Ulrich, Laurel Thatcher *historian, educator*
Ungar, Eric Edward *mechanical engineer*
Vagts, Detlev Frederick *law educator*
Valenstein, Arthur F. *psychiatrist, educator*
Valiant, Leslie Gabriel *computer scientist, educator*
Vander Velde, Wallace Earl *aeronautical and astronautical engineering educator*
Vanger, Milton Isadore *historian, educator*
Vendler, Helen Hennessy *literature educator, poetry critic*
Verba, Sidney *political science professor, academic administrator*
Vessot, Robert Frederick Charles *physicist, researcher*
Vigier, François Claude Denis *city planning educator*
Vogel, Ezra F. *sociology educator*
von Hippel, Eric Arthur *innovation educator*
Wacker, Warren Ernest Clyde *internist, educator*
Walker, Graham Charles *biology professor*
Ward, David Wayne *physicist, researcher*
Ware, Susan W. *historian*
Warren, Alvin Clifford, Jr. *law educator*
Warren, Elizabeth A. *law educator*
Waters, Mary Catherine *sociology educator*
Watson, Rubie S. *museum director*
Watts, Ross Leslie *finance educator*
Waugh, John Stewart *chemist, educator*
Weinberg, Robert Allan *biochemist, educator*
Weinreb, Lloyd Lobell *law educator*
Weitzman, Arthur Joshua *language educator*
Welsch, Roy Elmer *statistician, educator*
Westfall, David *lawyer, educator*
Westheimer, Frank Henry *chemist, educator*
White, David Calvin *electrical engineer, educator, energy executive, consultant*
White, Lucie E. *law educator*
White, Shelby *art association administrator*
Whitesides, George McClelland *chemistry professor*
Whitlock, Charles Preston *former university dean*
Whitman, Robert Van Duyne *civil engineer, educator*
Widnall, Sheila Evans *aeronautical educator, former secretary of the airforce, former university official*
Wilcox, Maud *editor*
Wilczek, Frank Anthony *physics professor*
Wilkins, David Brian *law educator*
Williams, James Henry, Jr. *mechanical engineer, educator, consultant*
Willie, Charles Vert *social sciences educator*
Wilson, Edward Osborne *biologist, educator, writer*
Wilson, William Julius *sociology educator*
Win, Moe Z. *information scientist, educator*
Wirasinha, Hemamali Anushka *computer scientist, researcher*
Wirth, Peter *lawyer*
Wittrup, Karl Dane *chemical engineer, educator*
Wodiczko, Krzysztof *artist, architect, educator*
Wojciech, Matusik *computer scientist*
Wolfman, Bernard *lawyer, educator*
Wolpert, Ann J. *library director*
Wood, John Armstead *planetary scientist, geological sciences educator, artist*
Wood, Pamela Sharon *music educator, soprano*
Wood, Richard Robinson *real estate company executive*
Wu, Tai Tsun *physicist, researcher*
Wuensch, Bernhardt John *ceramic engineering educator*
Wurtman, Richard Jay *neuroscientist, educator*
Xie, Xiaoliang Sunney *chemist, educator*
Yannas, Ioannis Vassilios *polymer science educator*
Yau, Shing-Tung *mathematics professor*
Yergin, Daniel Howard *writer, consultant*
Yi, Wei *physicist*
Yip, Winnie *health economics educator*
Young, Laurence R. *biomedical researcher, biomedical engineer, aeronautical engineer, aerospace engineer*
Young, Laurence Retman *biomedical engineer, educator*
Young, Rick (Richard Allen Young) *molecular biologist, educator*
Zaldarriaga, Matias *cosmologist, physics professor*
Zeidenstein, George *population educator*
Zhang, Cynthia Hongbing *lawyer*
Zhang, Ji-Hu *biochemist, researcher*
Zhang, Shuguang *biomedical engineer*
Zinberg, Dorothy Shore *educator, educator*
Ziolkowski, Jan Michael *medievalist educator*
Zittrain, Jonathan L. *law educator*
Zollar, Alfred *computer company executive*
Zuber, Maria T. *geophysicist, educator*

## Canton

Bentas, Lily Haseotes *retail executive*
Bihldorff, John Pearson *hospital director*
Brenner, Harry J. *retail executive*
Daley, Charles Mike *consumer products company executive*
Fireman, Paul Barry *footwear and apparel company executive*
Fuchs, Lawrence Howard *federal official, educator*
Harrington, Paul *apparel executive*
Hayes, Michelle Christine *artist, educator*
Judson, Arnold Sidney *management consultant*
Kelley, Irene W. *retired librarian, musician, artist*
Luther, Jon *food service executive*
Pace, David A. *lawyer*
Parker, Virginia Marie *language educator*
Reichman, Joel H. *retail executive*
Sawtelle, Carl S. *psychiatric social worker*

## Carlisle

Drew, Philip Garfield *retired engineering company executive, consultant*
Fohl, Timothy *investment company executive*

## Carver

Neubauer, Richard A. *library science educator, consultant*

## Centerville

Anderson, Gerald Edwin *retired utilities executive*
Condon, Ann Blunt *psychotherapist*
Scherer, Harold Nicholas, Jr. *electric power industry executive*
Shapiro, Harvey *sales executive, journalist, writer, lyricist*

## Charlestown

Abdelwahid, Eltyeb *research scientist*
Ackerman, Jerome Leonard *biomedical researcher*
Bhide, Pradeep G. *neuroscientist, researcher*
Faustman, Denise L. *immunologist*
Hadjikhani, Nouchine *neuroscientist, researcher*
Isselbacher, Kurt Julius *internist, educator*
Kiihne, Robert Spencer *exhibit director*
Leaf, Alexander *preventive medicine physician, epidemiologist*
Moskowitz, Michael Arthur *neuroscientist*
Ntziachristos, Vasilis *bioengineer*
Potts, John Thomas, Jr. *physician, educator*
Wetherell, David S. *communications executive*
Zamecnik, Paul Charles *oncologist, medical researcher*

## Chatham

Bohman, Raynard Frederick, Jr. *transportation executive, consultant, professional society administrator*
Escalante, Judson Robert *business consultant*
O'Connell, Brian *public health service officer, educator, writer*
Popkin, Alice Brandeis *lawyer*

## Chelmsford

DiPillo, Patricia Anne *language educator, researcher*
Fulks, Robert Grady *computer company executive*
Menitoff, Paul Alan *psychiatrist*

## Chelsea

Jenkins, Alexander III *consumer products company executive, consultant*
Kaneb, John A. *oil industry executive*
Petrowski, Joe *oil industry executive*

## Cheshire

Vincent, D. Christopher *history educator*

## Chestnut Hill

Altbach, Philip *director, educator*
Bando, Patricia Alice *academic administrator*
Bartunek, Jean Marie *management educator*
Beaton, Albert Eugene *education educator*
Bedell, Kevin Shawn *physicist, researcher*
Blanchette, Oliva *philosophy educator*
Burgess, Ann Wolbert *nursing educator*
Carfora, John Michael *economics professor, academic administrator*
Cohen, David Joel *medical educator*
Deese, David Allen *education educator, researcher*
Flax, Martin Howard *pathologist, retired educator*
Gaiser, Ted Joseph *academic administrator, minister*
Goizueta, Roberto Segundo *theology studies educator*
Gottlieb, Marise Suss *epidemiologist*
Gow, Peter *secondary school educator, writer*
Hachey, Thomas Eugene *British and Irish history educator*
Helmick, Raymond Glen *priest, educator*
Keating, Patrick J. *academic administrator*
Kelley, Shana O. *biochemist*
Kosasky, Harold Jack *fertility researcher*
Leahy, William Patrick *academic administrator, historian, educator*
Mc Innes, William Charles *priest, academic administrator*
Munro, Barbara Hazard *nursing educator, dean, researcher*
Nemerowicz, Gloria *academic administrator*
Netzer, Nancy *museum director, art historian, educator*
O'Block, Robert Paul *management consultant*
O'Brien, Tom *college football coach*
O'Toole, James Michael *history educator*
Reed, James Eldin *historian, consultant, educator*
Rosensaft, Lester Jay *management consultant, lawyer*
Safizadeh, M. Hossein *finance educator*
Salib, Philip I. *orthopedic surgeon*
Shen, Tsung Ying *medicinal chemistry educator*
Smith, Richard Alan *publishing and specialty retailing executive*
Stanbury, John Bruton *retired pharmacologist, educator*
Thier, Samuel Osiah *physician, educator*
Valette, Jean Paul *writer*
Valette, Rebecca Marianne *Romance languages educator*
Van Flandern, Geoffrey James *orthopedist, surgeon*

Yavarkovsky, Jerome Harold *library director*

## Chicopee

Dame, Catherine Elaine *acupuncturist*

## Chilmark

Lazarus, David *physicist, researcher*

## Clinton

Lanza, Robert Paul *medical scientist*

## Cohasset

Dickstein, Harvey Leonard *pharmaceutical executive, educator*
Rabstejnek, George John *manufacturing executive*
Replogle, David Robert *publishing executive*

## Concord

Andrews, Joseph Lyon, Jr. *internist, pulmonologist, medical educator, writer*
Bander, Edward Julius *law librarian emeritus, lawyer*
Bethell, Charlyn *music educator*
Brooker, Richard I. *architect*
Coles, Robert *child psychiatrist, educator, writer*
Davidson, Frank Paul *retired macroengineer, retired lawyer*
Davies, Michael A. M. *management consultant*
Delehant, Joseph Henry *lawyer*
Dresden, Jacob A. *headmaster*
Eberle, William Denman *international management consultant*
Emerson, Richard B. *marketing company executive*
Giles, Kathleen C. *headmaster*
Gomberg, Sydelle *dancer educator*
Gorny, Marina Dubinsky *music educator*
Heinle, Beverly Diane *publishing executive*
Horwitz, Paul *physicist*
Ihara, Michio *sculptor*
MacNeill, Frederick Douglas *artist*
Plummer, William Torsch *optical physicist*
Schiller, Pieter Jon *retired venture capital executive*
Smith, Eric Parkman *retired railroad executive*
Villers, Philippe *mechanical engineer*
Weiss, James Michael *financial analyst, portfolio manager*
Wickfield, Eric Nelson *investment company executive*
Woll, Harry J. *electrical engineer*

## Cotuit

Ballou, Kenneth Walter *retired business executive, retired dean*
Housewright, David W. *writer*
Miller, Robert Charles *retired physicist*

## Cummington

Smith, William Jay *author*
Wilbur, Richard Purdy *writer, educator*

## Danvers

Beauregard, John *college librarian, consultant*
Clark, Sharon Jackson *private school administrator*
Dolan, John Ralph *retired electronics executive*
Fox, John Joseph, Jr. *historian, educator*
Haber, Frederic *lawyer*
Southwick, Paul *retired public relations executive*
Waite, Charles Morrison *food products executive*

## Dartmouth

Connors, Robert Leo *city official*
Kahrl, Benjamin Richards *social studies educator, department chairman*
Nieviedgal, Carol Belmarce *elementary school educator*
Notaros, Branislav M. *electrical engineer, educator*
Washburn, Stewart Putnam *management consultant*

## Dedham

Frazier, Ronald F. *non-profit association administrator*
Magner, Jerome Allen *performing company executive*
Redstone, Shari E. *amusement company executive*
Redstone, Sumner Murray *broadcast executive, lawyer*

## Deerfield

Widmer, Eric *headmaster*

## Dennis

Cetto, Teresa *art educator*

## Dennis Port

Singer, Myer R(ichard) *lawyer*

## Devens

Sizer, Theodore R. *education educator*

## Dighton

Buote, Rosemarie Boschen *retired special education educator*

## Dorchester

Jackson, Jimmie L. *retired music educator, retired organist*
James, Elaine McLean *retired librarian*
Medeiros, Jennifer Lynn *school psychologist, consultant*
Smith, Survilla Marie *social services administrator, artist, poet*

## Douglas

Bachelder, Beverly Brandt *secondary school educator, assistant principal, director*

## Dover

Aldrich, Frank Nathan *banker*
Bonis, Laszlo Joseph *marketing executive, mechanical engineer, chemist*
Buyse, Marylou *pediatrician, geneticist, medical association administrator*
Craver, James Bernard *lawyer*
Edwards, Carl Norman *lawyer*
Mehta, Narinder Kumar *marketing executive*

## Dudley

Bickford, Crystal *literature and language professor, director*

## Duxbury

Erickson, Phyllis Traver *marketing executive*
Keleher, Chantal Stone *marketing professional*
Swanson, Richard Oscar *history educator, department chairman*
Thrasher, Dianne Elizabeth *mathematics educator, computer scientist, consultant*
Van der Veen, Steven Roger *manufacturing executive*
Wangler, William Clarence *retired insurance company executive*
Zachmann, William Francis *computer and communications industry market research company executive*

## East Boston

Coy, Craig P. *airport terminal executive*
Crawford, Linda Sibery *lawyer, educator*
Patinkin, Terry Allan *physician*

## East Longmeadow

Skutnik, Bolesh J. *optics scientist, lay worker, lawyer*

## East Orleans

Burkert, Robert Randall *artist*
Natale, Barbara Gustafson *retired librarian*
Romey, William Dowden *geologist, educator*

## Easthampton

Lake, Shelley *artist*
Perkins, Homer Guy *manufacturing executive*

## Easton

Barrett, Mary Kathleen *secondary school educator*

## Edgartown

Gatting, Carlene J. *lawyer*
MacDonald, Duncan *broadcaster, writer, communications consultant*
Rosenfeld, Walter David, Jr. *architect, writer*

## Everett

Blake, Margaret Mary *director*

## Fairhaven

Hotchkiss, Henry Washington *real estate broker, financial consultant*

## Fall River

Alam, Akm A. *ceramics engineer*
Andrade, Manuela Pestana *art educator*
Brenner, Rylan *theater educator, director*
Brion, Norma M. *real estate broker*
Tinberg, Howard *language educator*
Wilner, Marion Leonard *art educator*

## Falmouth

Adelman, William J., Jr. *biophysicist*
Brock, Nancy Jeanne *composer, writer, music educator*
Goody, Richard Mead *geophysicist*
Lamont, Rosette Clementine *language educator, journalist, translator*
Litschgi, Richard John *computer manufacturing company executive*
McInnes, Donald Gordon *rail transportation executive*
Milkman, Marianne Friedenthal *retired city planner*
Milkman, Roger Dawson *genetics educator, molecular biologist, researcher*
Sato, Kazuyoshi *pathologist*

## Fiskdale

Costello, Christine Ann *fine arts director, church organist*

## Fitchburg

Bartsch, Noel R. *lawyer*
Jareckie, Stephen Barlow *museum curator*
Wellman, Robert Jonathan *medical educator*

## Florence

Platt, Rutherford Hayes *law educator, geographer, consultant*

## Foxboro

Belichick, Bill (William Stephen Belichick) *professional football coach*
Brady, Tom (Thomas Edward Patrick Brady Jr.) *professional football player*
Bruschi, Tedy *professional football player*
Bush, Raymond T. *accountant, architectural firm executive*
Dillon, Corey *professional football player*
Karelitz, Richard Alan *treasurer, lawyer*
Kennedy, Susan Marie *music educator*
Kraft, Robert K. *professional sports team executive*
Martin, Peter Gerard *computer technician, consultant, secondary school educator*
Pierce, Francis Casimir *civil engineer*
Surgenor, Timothy R. *neurotechnology company executive*

## Framingham

Antal, John J. *retired physicist, consultant*
Aronson, Benjamin *artist*
Austin, Sandra Ikenberry *nursing educator, consultant*
Bogard, Carole Christine *soprano*
Bose, Amar Gopal *electronics executive, electrical engineering educator*
Cammarata, Ben (Bernard Cammarata) *retail executive*
Casper, Leonard Ralph *American literature educator*
Crossley, Frank Alphonso *retired metallurgical engineer*
DeWerth, Gordon Henry *management consultant*
Feldberg, Sumner Lee *retired retail executive*
Feldman, Nan Hass *artist, educator*
Feldman, Susan Eleanor *technology analyst*
Flanagan, Timothy James *academic administrator, criminal justice educator*

Harrington, Joseph Francis *educational company executive, history educator*
Heineman, Helen L. *retired academic administrator*
Hodgins, Beatrice Davis *retired elementary school educator, primary school educator*
Kendall, Julius *consulting engineer*
Klapholz, Henry *obstetrician, gynecologist, educator*
Komola, Christine T. *corporate financial executive*
Lavin, Philip Todd *medical researcher*
Lesser, Richard G. *retired apparel executive*
Levy, Joseph Louis *publishing company executive*
Lindsay, Leslie *packaging engineer*
Lucci, Dorothy Ann *educational consultant, psychologist*
Mahoney, John J. *office supply company executive*
Margolis, Bruce Lewis *human resources executive*
Meador, Charles Lawrence *management and systems consultant, educator*
Meyrowitz, Carol *retail executive*
Miles, Michael A., Jr. *retail executive*
Naylor, Jeffrey Gordon *retail executive*
Ramachandran, Vasan Srini *medical educator*
Sargent, Ronald L. *retail office and business products executive*
Struyk, Pieter M. *music educator*
Twombly, Stephen Doane *magazine publisher*
VanWoerkom, Jack A. *lawyer, retail executive*
Vassalluzzo, Joseph S. *retail company executive*
Vrabel, Joseph P. *lawyer*
Zamvil, Linda Susan *psychiatrist, educator*

**Franklin**
Benjamin, Bernard Edward *school system administrator, director*
Maril, David C. *editor*

**Gardner**
Du Buske, Lawrence Michael *immunologist, rheumatologist*
Hawke, Robert Douglas *retired state legislator*
Herrnkind, Hilda Marie *writer, military volunteer*

**Georgetown**
Ramseur, T. Michael *social worker*

**Gloucester**
Birchfield, John Kermit, Jr. *lawyer*
Hausman, William Ray *fund raising and management consultant*
Junger, Sebastian *writer*
Littlefield, Paul Damon *retired management consultant*
McCarl, Henry Newton *economist, geologist, consultant, venture capitalist*
Nicholls, Bruce Gilbert *lawyer*
Oder, Frederic Carl Emil *retired aerospace transportation executive*
Sallah, Majeed (Jim Sallah) *retired real estate developer*
Socolow, Arthur Abraham *geologist*
Steele-Goetemann, Judith Ann *artist, educator, art gallery owner*
White, Harold Jack *pathologist*
White, Lucette Darby *painter, sculptor*

**Granby**
Ingham, Norman William *literature educator, genealogist*
Mucha, Sister Marlene M. *secondary school educator*

**Granville**
Brown, Stephen Pat *artist*

**Great Barrington**
Curtin, Phyllis *music educator, dean, vocalist*
Frye-Moquin, Marsha Marie *social worker*
Rodgers, Bernard Francis, Jr. *literature and language professor*

**Greenfield**
Curtiss, Carol Perry *health facility administrator, consultant, nurse*
Hutcheson, Thomas Worthington *trade association administrator*

**Groton**
Anthony, Sylvia *social welfare organization executive*
Commons, Richard B. *headmaster*
Wiggins, D. Scott *headmaster*

**Hampden**
Joubert, Raymond Ernest *retired electrical engineer*

**Hanover**
Barreira, Brian Ernest *lawyer*
Lonborg, James Reynold *dentist, former professional baseball player*

**Hanscom Afb**
Carney, David John *computer scientist, music theorist*
Harper, David Taylor *civilian military employee*
Johnson, Charles L., II, *military officer*
Mailloux, Robert Joseph *physicist*
Mittleman, Steven David *physicist, researcher*

**Hanson**
Norris, John Anthony *health products executive, lawyer, educator*

**Harvard**
Monath, Thomas Patrick *physician*

**Harwich**
Steward, Aleta Joanna *fine artist, digital artist*
Worrell, Francis Toussaint *retired physics professor*

**Harwich Port**
Smith, Ralph Wesley, Jr. *retired federal judge*
Staszesky, Francis Myron *electric power industry executive, consultant*

**Hatfield**
Yolen, Jane *writer*

**Haverhill**
Bigelow, Peter *electronics executive*
DeSchuytner, Edward Alphonse *biochemist, educator*
Newman, Rochelle Joyce *artist, educator, writer*

**Haydenville**
Shallcross, Doris Jane *education educator*

**Hingham**
Llewellyn, John Schofield, Jr. *former food company executive*
Macchia, David Alan *management consultant*
Menzies, Ian Stuart *newspaper editor*
Noel, Barbara Hughes McMurtry *retired music educator*
Pallai, David Francis *publishing executive*
Richie, Margaret Bye *architectural historian*

**Holbrook**
Crandlemere, Robert Wayne *engineering executive*

**Holden**
O'Neil, William Francis *academic administrator*

**Holyoke**
Resnic, Burton S. *lawyer*

**Hopkinton**
Dacier, Paul T. *electronics company executive, lawyer*
Moran, Wendy Jacqueline *music educator, musician*
Newbrander, William Carl *health economist, management consultant*
Ruettgers, Michael Cadet *electronics executive*
Teuber, William J, Jr. *corporate financial executive*
Tucci, Joseph M. *computer software and services executive*

**Hubbardston**
Marceau, Judith Marie *retired elementary school educator, small business owner*

**Hudson**
Osoff, Jeffrey Arlin *media company executive*

**Hull**
Anderson, Timothy Christopher *educational association administrator*

**Hyannis**
Capparella (Muller), Nancy Lisa *music educator*
Nicholson, Ellen Ellis *clinical social worker*
O'Brien, Kathleen L. *special education educator*
Segersten, Robert Hagy *lawyer, investment banker*

**Hyde Park**
Harris, Emily Louise *special education educator*

**Indian Orchard**
Daley, Veta Adassa *educational administrator*

**Ipswich**
Dion Faust, Debra *secondary school educator*
Getchell, Charles Willard, Jr. *lawyer, publisher, foundation executive*
Herrmann, Robert Lawrence *biochemist, educator*
Jennings, Frederic Beach, Jr. *economist, saltwater flyfishing guide*
Lombardo, Ann Marie *special education educator, writer, artist*
Munro, Donald William, Jr. *non-profit organization executive*
Roberts, Richard John *molecular biologist, consultant, scientific officer*
Wilson, Doris H. *volunteer*

**Jamaica Plain**
Pierce, Chester Middlebrook *retired psychiatrist, educator*
White-Hammond, Gloria E. *pastor, pediatrician, human rights advocate*

**Jefferson**
Parham, Valerie deForest Byron *artist*

**Lakeville**
Kolva, Matthew *marketing professional*
Ledwith, Edward J *elementary school educator*

**Lawrence**
Barbagallo, Joseph C. *small business owner*
Weaver, Peter David *bishop, religious organization administrator*

**Leeds**
Deane, James Garner *editor, conservationist*

**Lenox**
Biron, Margaret M. *historian, educator*

**Leominster**
Ford, John Stephen *treasurer*
Kerns, Christian Randolph *chemist*
Zephir, Jeanne Yvonne *artist*

**Leverett**
Margolis, Nadia *language educator, translator, medievalist*

**Lexington**
Aldrich, Nancy Cook *engineer*
Aronin, Lewis Richard *metallurgical engineer*
Bailey, Fred Coolidge *retired engineering consulting company executive*
Baron, Sheldon *research and development company executive*
Bazzaz, Fakhri A. *plant biology educator, administrator*
Benitz, Gerald Robert *electrical engineer*
Beusch, John Ulrich *engineer, researcher*
Bombardieri, Merle Ann *psychotherapist*
Buchanan, John Machlin *biochemistry professor*
Bussgang, Julian Jakub *electronics engineer, consultant*
Cohen, Judah Levi *environmental services administrator*
Coleman, Loring W. *artist*

Collins, Allan Meakin *education educator*
Davis, Robert J. *internet company executive*
Dinneen, Gerald Paul *electrical engineer, retired federal official*
Dionne, Gerald Francis *research physicist, educator, consultant*
Dougherty, Richard Hamlen *management consultant, healthcare consultant*
Drouilhet, Paul Raymond, Jr. *retired science administrator, electrical engineer*
Ehrenfeld, John Roos *environmental policy educator*
Fillios, Louis Charles *retired science educator*
Freed, Charles *engineering consultant, researcher*
Freitag, Wolfgang Martin *retired librarian, educator*
Frey, John Ward *landscape architect*
Garing, Ione Davis *civic worker*
Garrelick, Joel Marc *acoustical scientist, consultant*
Gelb, Arthur *electrical and systems engineering executive*
Gibbs, Martin *biologist, educator*
Goell, James Emanuel *electronics executive*
Hines, Edward Francis, Jr. *lawyer*
Huang, Robin K. *research scientist*
Jordan, Judith Victoria *clinical psychologist, educator*
Kaledin, Eugenia Oster *American studies educator*
Keicher, William Eugene *electrical engineer*
Kennedy, X.J. (Joseph Kennedy) *writer*
Kent, Robert Brydon *law educator*
Klein, Lawrence Allen *finance educator*
Li, Tongchuan *pharmacologist, researcher*
Linkov, Igor *conservationist, consultant*
McFarland, Philip James *secondary school educator, writer*
McGirr, David William John *pharmaceutical executive*
Morrow, Walter Edwin, Jr. *electrical engineer, lab administrator*
Nichols, Albert L. *economic consultant*
Oliner, Arthur Aaron *physicist, researcher*
Ott, John Harlow *museum administrator*
Papanek, Gustav Fritz *economist, educator*
Paul, Norman Leo *psychiatrist, educator*
Schafer, Alice Turner *retired mathematics professor*
Silverman, Sam Mendel *physicist, lawyer*
Smith, Robert Louis *construction company executive*
Steiner, John William *retired biophysicist*
Thernstrom, Abigail *federal agency administrator, writer*
Waksman, Byron Halsted *immunologist, educator, medical association administrator*
Wang, Chi Hua *chemist, education educator*
Williamson, Richard Cardinal *physicist*
Zayhowski, John J. *electrical engineer, researcher*

**Lincoln**
Bracken, (Myra) Jeanne Munn *librarian, writer*
Brandt, John Henry *physician*
Donald, David Herbert *writer, history professor*
Giles, Allen *pianist, composer, music educator*
Gnichtel, William Van Orden *lawyer*
Hawkins, Malcolm *music educator, composer*
Kerrebrock, Jack Leo *aeronautics and astronautics engineering educator, department chairman*
LeGates, John Crews Boulton *information scientist*
Nenneman, Richard Arthur *retired publishing executive*
Payne, Roger Searle *zoologist, researcher, science administrator, conservationist*

**Littleton**
Ramakrishnan, Kadangode Krishnamoorthy *computer science researcher*

**Longmeadow**
Ezrin, Myer *retired director*
Gallup, John Gardiner *retired paper company executive*
Katz, Barbara Stein *special education educator*
Keady, George Cregan, Jr. *judge*
Leary, Carol Ann *academic administrator*
Lemnios, Andrew Zachery *aerospace engineer, educator, researcher*
Lo Bello, Joseph David *bank executive*

**Lowell**
Aste, Mario Andrea *foreign language educator*
Carlsmith, Christopher *history professor*
Collins, Sean Michael *physical therapist, educator*
Curtis, James Theodore *lawyer*
Dinh, Khanh Thi *psychology professor, consultant*
Dubner, Daniel William *pediatrician*
Gonzalez-Velasco, Enrique Alberto *mathematics professor*
Hill, Duane Paul *biologist, researcher, entrepreneur*
Kannenberg, Lloyd Chambers *physicist, researcher*
Karakashian, Aram Simon *physics professor*
Karr, Ronald Dale *librarian, historian*
Martin, William Francis, Jr. *lawyer*
McAfee, Noelle Claire *philosopher, educator*
McAloon, Noreen Marie *elementary school educator*
O'Donnell, Kathleen Marie *lawyer*
Pullen, David John *physicist, researcher*
Teague, Bernice Rita *accountant*
Ting, John M. *dean, engineering educator*
Zhang, Xiaoqi *education educator*

**Ludlow**
Budnick, Thomas Peter *social worker*

**Lynn**
Astuccio, Sheila Margaret *educational administrator*
Chow, Humphrey Wai *mechanical engineer*
D'Entremont, Edward Joseph *application developer, educator*
Farris, Robert Harold, Jr. *artist, educator*
Petchkis, Anthony James *artist*
Ryder, Edward Francis *secondary school educator*

**Lynnfield**
Hodgkins, Douglas Wendell *music educator*
Kerrigan, Nancy *professional figure skater, retired Olympic athlete*

McGivney, John Joseph *lawyer*
Meyer, Piotr Jan *electronics engineer*

**Malden**
Driscoll, David P. *school system administrator*
Guild, Richard Samuel *trade association management company executive*
Jonker, Jean Elizabeth *educational consultant*
Madhappan-Kempuraj, Bhuvaneshwari *medical researcher*

**Manchester**
Porter, Henry Homes, Jr. *investor*

**Marblehead**
Green, Richard John *architect*
Heins, Esther *artist, illustrator*
Kennedy, Elizabeth Mae *musician*
Page, George Alfred, Jr. *lawyer*
Peterson, Pam M. *museum director*
Quigley, Stephen Howard *executive editor*
Snow, George Bartlett *accountant, city manager*
Speller, Kerstin G. Rinta *psychologist*
Tamaren, Michele Carol *spiritual director, writer, retired special education educator, personal coach, presenter*

**Marion**
Latham, Christopher Robert *alumni and development director*
McPartland, Patricia Ann *educational association administrator, health educator*
Worley, Robert William, Jr. *retired lawyer*

**Marlborough**
Bennett, C. Leonard *electrical engineer*
Murray, R. Scott *computer software company executive*

**Marstons Mills**
Martin, David Standish *education educator*
Martin, Susan Katherine *librarian*

**Mashpee**
Jamison, John L. *music educator, musician*
Kilmartin, Joseph Francis, Jr. *information technology executive*

**Mattapoisett**
Ellis, Stanley Weston *musician, educator*
Mazer, Mike *cardiologist, retired nephrologist, artist*

**Maynard**
Pastore, William M. *insurance company executive*
Taylor, Jeff *Internet company executive*

**Medfield**
McQuillen, Jeremiah Joseph *distribution executive*
Phillips, Marion Grumman *civic volunteer, writer*

**Medford**
Abriola, Linda Marie *civil engineer, environmental engineer*
Almedom, Astier M. *healthcare educator, researcher*
Ambady, Nalini *social psychologist, educator, researcher*
Antonelli, Pattie Ellen *public relations executive*
Bacow, Lawrence Seldon *academic administrator, environmental scientist, educator*
Bedau, Hugo Adam *philosophy educator*
Belovari, Susanne *archivist, historian*
Berman, David *lawyer, poet*
Bharucha, Jamshed *academic administrator*
Bishop, Richard Woodrow *lawyer, writer*
Bosworth, Stephen Warren *dean, former ambassador*
Cavallaro, Mary Caroline *retired physics professor*
Chaturvedi, Pravin R. *pharmaceutical executive*
Conklin, John Evan *sociology educator*
DeBold, Joseph Francis *psychologist, educator*
Elkind, David *psychology professor*
Fyler, John Morgan *language educator*
Glaser, James M. *dean, political science professor*
Goldberg, Pamela Winer *entrepreneur, educator*
Greif, Robert *mechanical engineering educator*
Gunther, Leon *physicist, educator*
Jackendoff, Ray Saul *linguistics educator*
Kerr, Barbara E. *librarian, writer*
Kouguell, Susan *film educator*
Kumar, Krishna *chemistry professor*
McKay, Ryan Thomas *psychologist*
Michalak, Jo-Ann *library director*
Miczek, Klaus Alexander *psychology professor*
Mujat, Mircea *optics scientist*
O'Leary, David *priest, theologian, educator*
Penick, Ann Clarisse *minister, counselor*
Ruskai, Mary Beth *mathematics professor*
Salacuse, Jeswald William *lawyer, educator*
Schneps, Jack *physics professor, department chairman*
Sherwin, Martin J. *history professor*
Shultz, Mary Jane *chemist, educator*
Simpson, Theodore Brian *set designer, educator*
Sommers, Samuel R *psychologist*
Spolaore, Enrico *economist*
Sternberg, Robert Jeffrey *dean, psychology professor, researcher*
Ueda, Reed Takashi *historian, educator*
Uhlir, Arthur, Jr. *electrical engineer, academic administrator*
Walker, Peter John Charles *science foundation director*

**Medway**
Burnett, Calvin *artist, educator*
Hoag, David Garratt *retired aerospace engineer*

**Melrose**
Burnim, Kalman Aaron *retired theater educator*
Desforges, Jane Fay *retired internist, hematologist, educator*
Henken, Bernard Samuel *clinical psychologist, speech pathologist*

**Merrimac**
Ketchen, Deborah Ann *food scientist*

**Methuen**
Lattini, James Tufic *music educator*

McNaughton, William John *retired bishop*

**Middleton**
Stanley, (Malchan) Craig *school system administrator, consultant, psychologist, researcher*

**Milford**
Kashyap, Nitu *internist*
Lopez, Alvaro Benito *psychiatrist, director*

**Mill River**
Dunsay, Charles William *elementary school educator*
Jaffe, Katharine Weisman *retired librarian*

**Millbury**
Yonda, Alfred William *mathematician*

**Milton**
Daggett, David Marshall *mathematics professor*
Frazier, Marie Dunn *speech professional, public relations executive, personnel director*
Randall, Lilian Maria Charlotte *museum curator*
Robertson, Robin Alayne *headmaster, anthropologist*
Wengler, Marguerite Marie *counseling administrator*

**Nantucket**
Frasca, Gabriel *chef*
Kales, Paul Albert *engineering educator, cartoonist*
Philbrick, Nathaniel *writer*
Rorem, Ned *composer, writer*
Sangree, Walter Hinchman *social anthropologist, educator*

**Natick**
Abele, John E. *medical products executive*
Berglund, Larry Glenn *mechanical engineer, educator*
Best, Lawrence C. *medical products executive, manufacturing executive*
Blaha, Michael Douglas *research biologist*
Dareshshori, Nader Farhang *publishing sales executive*
Geller, Esther (Bailey Geller) *artist*
Gottlieb, Michael Norman *internist, educator, health facility administrator*
Grassia, Thomas Charles *lawyer, writer*
Latanision, Ronald Michael *materials science and engineering consultant*
LaViolette, Paul A. *medical products executive*
Miller, George David *retired military officer, not-for-profit executive*
Nicholas, Peter M. *medical products executive*
Oulton, Donald Paul *lawyer*
Pokorny, Joseph Wenceslaus III *engineer*
Rendell, Kenneth William *rare and historical documents dealer, consultant*
Russell, Mary E. *medical products executive, cardiologist*
Sandman, Paul William *lawyer*
Sedo, Manuel Arturo *neuropsychologist, researcher*
Strauss, Harlee Sue *environmentalist, consultant*
Sullivan, Brianne May *history educator, educational program director*
Tobin, James Robert *biomedical device manufacturing company executive*
Walker, Kellye L. *lawyer*
Wedge, Michael T. *wholesale distribution executive*
Zarkin, Herbert J. *retail executive*

**Needham**
Boulding, Elise Marie *sociologist, educator*
Branfman, Steven Jay *artist, educator*
Bronner, Michael *advertising executive, education assistance company executive*
Celli, Paul *art educator*
Cogswell, John Heyland *retired telecommunications industry executive, financial consultant*
Di Domenica, Robert Anthony *musician, composer*
Grasso, James Anthony *public relations executive, educator*
Greenway, Hugh Davids Scott *journalist*
Holt, Stephen S. *astrophysicist*
Kenslea, Timothy Joseph *historian, educator*
Kolb, Gloria Ro *medical products executive*
Kossuth, Joanne M. *academic administrator*
Lyons, Maureen P. *social studies educator*
Miller, Richard Keith *academic administrator, engineering educator*
Osser, David Neal *psychiatrist, educator*
Rafferty, James Paul *telecommunications executive*
Rodman, Sumner *insurance company executive*
Ryan, Una Scully *health science association administrator, medical educator*
Stein, Martin Matthew *management consultant*
Zambone, Alana Maria *special education educator, consultant*

**Needham Heights**
Salhany, Lucille S. (Lucy Salhany) *broadcast executive*

**New Bedford**
Benoit, Richard Armand *lawyer, retired police chief*
Bullard, John Kilburn *educational association administrator*
LaPorte, Adrienne Aroxie *nursing administrator*
Matsumoto, Carolee Setsuko *researcher, education developer and administrator*
Rothschild, Brian James *marine biologist, educator*
Spongberg, Andrew K. *otolaryngologist, law educator*

**Newbury**
Vilma, Jonathan Polynice *professional football player*

**Newburyport**
Connolly, James Thomas *lawyer*
Robinson, Enders Anthony *geophysicist, educator, writer*

Robinson, Joyce McPeake *academic administrator*

**Newton**
Aronow, Saul *radiological physicist, consultant*
Bagalay, John Earl *information technology executive, consultant*
Baron, Charles Hillel *lawyer, educator*
Bassuk, Ellen Linda *psychiatrist*
Benner, Mary Wright *freelance/self-employed conference director*
Bernier, George Matthew, Jr. *oncologist, educator, dean*
Chubb, Stephen Darrow *health products executive*
Coquillette, Daniel Robert *lawyer, educator*
Dunlap, William Crawford *physicist*
Frankenheim, Samuel *retired lawyer*
Glazer, Donald Wayne *lawyer, corporate financial executive, educator*
Glick-Weil, Kathy *library director*
Holbik, Karel *economics professor*
Huber, Richard Gregory *lawyer, educator*
Hume, Ellen Hunsberger *media analyst, educator, journalist*
Jeanloz, Roger William *biochemist, educator*
Jellinek, Michael Steven *psychiatrist, pediatrician*
Jencks, Penelope *sculptor*
Karp, Stephen R. *real estate developer*
Knez, Brian J. *publishing executive*
Lev-Ari, Hanoch *electrical engineering educator*
Li, Fan *pianist, music educator*
Lichtin, Norman Nahum *chemistry professor*
Marrone, Philip A. *chemical engineer*
Marshall, Robert Lewis *musicologist, educator*
Matteson, Carol J. *academic administrator*
May, Harold Louis *retired surgeon, not-for-profit developer*
Metzer, Patricia Ann *lawyer*
Mullen, Maureen Ann *social worker*
Nahigian, Robert John *real estate company executive, consultant*
O'Connell, Sister Virginia M. *school librarian*
Osborne, Charles David *singer, composer, conductor*
Peterson, Lloyd, Jr. *academic administrator, consultant*
Rivlin, Rachel *lawyer*
Saffran, Kalman *entrepreneur, venture capitalist*
Sasahara, Arthur Asao *cardiologist, educator, researcher*
Sheridan, Thomas Brown *mechanical engineering and applied psychology educator, researcher, consultant*
Teig, Marlowe Gilman *investment banker*
Wahlberg, Mark *actor*
White, Burton Leonard *retired educational psychologist, writer, consultant*

**Newton Center**
Adams, F. Gerard *economist, educator*
Copithorne, David A. *public relations executive*
Eichler, Marc *neurosurgeon*
Garvey, John Hugh *dean, law educator*
Philippe, Paul *chemist*
Schuller, Gunther Alexander *composer*
Snyder, John Gorvers *lawyer*
Williamson, Susan *mathematician, educator*

**Newton Highlands**
Bricklin, Daniel *software designer, consultant*
Hummel, Margaret P. *state representative*

**Newtonville**
Polonsky, Arthur *artist, educator*
Porter, Jack Nusan *writer, sociologist, educator, political organization worker*

**North Adams**
McConnell, Matthew Stephen *composer*
Newby, Kelli *education educator*
Sloan, Julie L. *stained glass artist, consultant*
Thurston, Donald Allen *broadcast executive*

**North Andover**
Becker, Lawrence Wilfred *headmaster*
Bradley, Michael John *mathematics professor*
Goldstein, Charles Henry *architect, consultant*
Grady, Kenneth Alan *lawyer*
Jannini, Ralph Humbert III *electronics executive*
Kurzweil, Raymond C. *computer scientist, entrepreneur*
Norris, Rebecca Sachs *religious studies educator*
Swallow, Kathleen Clinedinst *chemistry professor*
Wenzel, James Andrew *religious studies educator*

**North Attleboro**
Koussa, Harold Alan *insurance account executive*

**North Billerica**
Chu, Jeffrey Chuan *manufacturing executive, consultant*
Mellon, Timothy *transportation executive*

**North Brookfield**
McNeaney, Lee Anne *physical education educator*

**North Chatham**
O'Brien, Robert Emmet *insurance company executive*
Rhinesmith, Stephen Headley *management consultant*
Wilson, E. B. *manufacturing executive, consultant, writer*

**North Chelmsford**
Erkkila-Ricker, Barbara Howell *writer, photographer*
Kotelly, George Vincent *editor, writer, electrical engineer*

**North Dartmouth**
Barrow, Clyde Wayne *social sciences educator*
Hsu, Jong-Ping *physicist, educator*
Peters, Morgan James *language educator, social studies educator, actor, writer, film director*
Yoken, Mel B(arton) *language educator, writer, radio personality*

**North Dighton**
Cserr, Robert *psychiatrist, physician, hospital administrator*

Silvia, David Alan *insurance broker*

**North Easton**
Bundy, Annalee Marshall *library director*
Churchill, Jean Frances *secondary school educator, finance educator*
Varella, Hazel L. *historian, educator*

**North Grafton**
Schwartz, Anthony *veterinary surgeon, educator*

**North Oxford**
Carney, Roger Francis Xavier *retired military officer*

**North Reading**
Eracar, Yonet *information technology manager*

**Northampton**
Birdsall, Jeanne *writer, photographer*
Christ, Carol Tecla *academic administrator*
Derr, Thomas Sieger *religion educator*
Donfried, Karl Paul *theology studies educator, minister*
Doss-Quinby, Eglal *language professional, educator*
Elkins, Stanley Maurice *historian, educator*
Ellis, Frank Hale *retired English literature educator*
Fabing, Suzannah *museum director*
Hastings, Wilmot Reed *lawyer, writer*
Holbert, Kelly McKay *exhibition coordinator, art historian*
Jakuc, Monica *music educator, pianist, fortepianist*
Levy, Ralph Jacob, Jr. *retired theater educator*
Mahoney, Maureen A. *academic administrator*
Miles, Harry Lehman *lawyer, educator*
Naegele, Philipp Otto *musician, educator*
Nehring, Fletcher Aldrich *pharmacist*
Newman, Lesléa *writer*
Palser, Barbara F. *retired botanist*
Piccinino, Rocco Michael *librarian*
Robinson, John Alan *information scientist, educator*
Rose, Peter Isaac *sociologist, writer*
Rupp, Sheron Adeline *photographer, educator*
Schneider, Katy *painter, educator*
Schuleit, Anna *artist*
Smith, Malcolm Barry Estes *philosopher, educator, lawyer*
Swyers, Donald G. *information scientist*
von Klemperer, Klemens *historian, educator*

**Northborough**
Fulmer, Hugh Scott *physician, educator*

**Northfield**
Stevens, Donald John *secondary school educator*

**Norton**
Crutcher, Ronald Andrew *music educator, academic administrator*
Holden, William *food service executive*
Marshall, Dale Rogers *academic administrator, political scientist, educator*
Taylor, Robert Sundling *language educator, critic*
Worthley, Harold Field *retired minister, educator*

**Norwell**
Brett, Jan Churchill *illustrator, author*
Case, David Knowlton *management consultant*

**Norwood**
Berliner, Allen Irwin *dermatologist*
Bermani, Eric J. *musician, conductor*
Fishman, Jerald G. *semiconductor executive*
Pence, Robert Dudley *biomedical researcher, consultant, hospital administrator*
Reilley, Margaret Randall *secondary school educator*
Sheingold, Daniel H. *electrical engineer*

**Oak Bluffs**
Ball, Diane Altman *librarian*

**Orange**
Rivers, Robert Alfred *microwave company executive*

**Orleans**
Baird, Julian Thompson, Jr. *art dealer*
Day, Emerson *physician*

**Osterville**
Schwarztrauber, Sayre Archie *former naval officer, maritime consultant*
Sommers, William Paul *management consultant, research and development company executive*

**Oxford**
Schur, Walter Robert *physician*

**Palmer**
Dupuis, Robert Simeon *sales executive*

**Paxton**
Clarke, Edward Nielsen *engineering science educator*

**Peabody**
Bierman, George William *retired food scientist*
Finch, Rogers Burton *association management consultant*
Generazzo, Arlene Diamond *retired elementary school educator*
Gordon, Bernard M. *computer company executive*
Lipman, Richard Paul *pediatrician*
McDonald, Michael Perry *retired transportation engineer, musician*
Peters, Leo Francis *environmental engineer*

**Pelham**
Fetler, Andrew *author, educator*

**Pepperell**
Holmes, Jean Louise *real estate investor, humanities educator*

**Petersham**
Chivian, Eric Seth *psychiatrist, environmental scientist, educator*

**Pittsfield**
Begley, Charlene *electronics executive*
Fawcett, Gayle P. *bank executive*
Feigenbaum, Armand Vallin *systems engineer, information technology executive*
Hochfelder, Scott Z. *toy company executive, lawyer*
Malkani, Prakash *neuroradiology educator*
Norris, Jeannie *headmaster*
Page, Daniel Bennett *dean, musician*
Rich, Philip Dewey *publishing executive*
Shammas, Nazih Kheirallah *environmental engineer, consultant, engineering educator*
Staley, Greg *retail executive*
Wenner, Gene Charles *arts management executive*
Wood, Elizabeth Ann *special education educator*
Zelka, Sandra Lynn *finance company executive*

**Plainville**
Zani, Frederick Caesar *retired financial consultant*

**Plymouth**
Della-Giustina, Jo-Ann Subotin *lawyer*
Flood, H. Gay (Hulda Gay Flood) *editor, consultant*
Goldman, Ralph Frederick *research physiologist, educator*
Gregory, Dick *comedian, volunteer*
Woodburn, Norma Denman *biology educator*

**Plympton**
Smith, Robert Rutherford *dean, communications educator*

**Prides Crossing**
Crate, Darrell W. *investment company executive, political organization administrator*
Garcia, Adolfo Ramon *lawyer*

**Provincetown**
Collins, Larry Richard *artist, educator, art gallery director*
Hutchinson, Peter Arthur *artist*
Oliver, Mary *poet*
Sturner, Lynda *performing company executive*

**Quincy**
Adams, Ronald G. *elementary school educator*
Britt, Margaret Mary *finance educator*
Chisholm, Maureen *academic administrator*
Colgan, Sumner *manufacturing engineer, chemical engineer*
Conley, Olga L. *retail executive*
Hall, John Raymond, Jr. *fire protection executive*
Hayes, Mary Dianne Wixted *lawyer*
Holway, David J. *labor union administrator*
Levin, Robert Joseph *food products executive*
Lippincott, Joseph P. *photojournalist, educator*
Moran, James Joseph, Jr. *insurance company executive*
Spangler, Arthur Stephenson, Jr. *psychologist*
Wilson, Blenda Jacqueline *foundation administrator*
Young, Richard William *chemicals executive*

**Randolph**
Huntington, Robert Howard *business management executive*
Johnson, Laurence Michael *lawyer*
Morrissey, Edmond Joseph *philologist*

**Raynham**
Brown, Jeff *pharmaceutical executive*

**Reading**
Burbank, Nelson Stone *investment banker*
Frey, Joanne Alice Tupper *art educator*
Hambartsoumian, Edouard *obstetrician, researcher, embryologist*
Nordstrand, Nathalie Elizabeth Johnson *artist*

**Revere**
Paananen, Victor Niles *language educator*
Recupero-Faiella, Anna Antonietta *poet*

**Rockland**
Blethen, Sandra Lee *pediatric endocrinologist*
Dunne, Myra Schley *nurse, consultant*

**Rockport**
Bissell, Phil (Charles P. Bissell) *cartoonist*
Mosher, Donald Allen *artist*
Nicholas, Thomas Andrew *artist*
Whitcomb, Kay *artist*
Wiberg, Lars-Erik *occupational compatibility consultant*

**Roslindale**
Sullivan, Dorothy Rona *state official*

**Roxbury**
Peters, Alan *anatomy educator*
Simons, Elizabeth R(eiman) *biochemist, educator*

**Salem**
Doran, Kathleen Brewer *dean, consultant*
Goss, Laurence Edward, Jr. *geographer, educator*
Higgins, Gina O'Connell *psychologist, writer*
McKenzie, Walter L. *information technology executive, consultant*
Melby, John B. *composer, educator*
Moran, Philip David *lawyer*
Rabchenuk, Paul Thomas *lawyer*

**Sandisfield**
Burtis, Herbert *musician*

**Sandwich**
Troy, Robert Sweeney, Sr. *lawyer*

**Scituate**
Spangler, Stanley Eugene *international relations educator*

**Sharon**
Edmonds, Nick *sculptor*

### West Chatham
Rowley, Glenn Harry *lawyer*

### West Falmouth
Bass, Norman Herbert *neurologist, educator, research scientist, hospital administrator, academic administrator*
Carlson, David Bret *retired lawyer*
King, Richard Hood *retired newspaper executive*

### West Hyannisport
Gingold, George Norman *insurance company executive, lawyer*

### West Newbury
Dooley, Ann Elizabeth *freelance writers cooperative executive, editor*

### West Roxbury
Ellenbogen, George *poet, educator*
Frisbie, James Howard *retired internist*
Lovell, Francis Joseph *retired investment company executive*
Roach, Maureen S. *primary school educator*
Seltzer, Richard Warren, Jr. *writer, editor, consultant*

### West Springfield
Desai, Veena Balvantrai *obstetrician, gynecologist, educator*

### West Tisbury
Méras, Phyllis Leslie *journalist*
Schwartz, Edward Arthur *lawyer*

### West Wareham
Worrell, Cynthia Lee *bank executive*

### Westborough
Antalek, Eileen Elizabeth *educational psychologist, consultant*
Bok, Joan Toland *utilities executive*
Horwitz, Eleanor Catherine *public information officer*
Nichols, Guy Warren *retired institute executive, retired utilities executive*
Schrager, Mindy Rae *software company professional*
Staffier, Pamela Moorman *psychologist*
Stillitano, Joseph Michael *music educator*

### Westfield
Buckmore, Alvah Clarence, Jr. *computer scientist, ballistician*
Conant, Patricia Carol *printmaker, educator*
Niles, DeBorah Olive *benefits compensation analyst*
Zayac, Linda Mary *sociologist, educator*

### Westford
Antón-Oldenburg, Mary Felice *principal*
Paine, Robert J. *environmental scientist, consultant*

### Weston
Alcock, George Lewis, Jr., (Peter Alcock) *investor, business strategist*
Barry, William Anthony *priest, writer*
Daly, Charles Ulick *foundation executive*
Goldstein, Arthur Louis *retired utilities executive*
Higgins, Sister Therese *literature educator, former college president*
Jarzavek, John Brian *English and art history educator*
Jayasankar, Subramanyan *orthopaedic surgeon*
Katz, William Emanuel *retired chemical engineer*
Kraft, Gerald *economist*
Lashman, L. Edward *arbitrator, mediator, consultant*
Lin, Alice Lee Lan *physicist, researcher, educator*
Oates, Mary Josephine *historian, educator*
Sanzone, Donna S. *publishing executive*
Tenney, Sarah G. *music educator*
Thomas, Roger Meriwether *lawyer*
Valente, Louis Patrick (Dan Valente) *financial planner, director*
Wang, Chia Ping *physicist, researcher*
Wood, Jeremy Scott *architect, urban designer*

### Westport
Gormley, Robert John *retired publishing executive*
Nichols, C. Walter III *retired trust company executive*
Norcross, Alvin Watt *retired personnel administrator, consultant*

### Westport Point
Fanning, William Henry, Jr. *computer specialist*

### Westwood
Bier, Louis Henry Gustav *minister*
Bloomingdale, Lewis Morgan *retired psychiatrist*
Borgman, George Allan *journalist*
Gillette, Hyde *retired brokerage house executive*
Kushner, Jeffrey L. *manufacturing executive*
Liberman, Judith *artist*
Plimpton, Calvin Hastings *retired internist, university president*
Riley, Henry Charles *banker*

### Weymouth
Gillespie, Barbara Joan *language educator*
Lamothe, Joanne Lewis *library director, consultant*

### Whitinsville
Plaud, Joseph Julian *psychology educator*

### Whitman
Daley, James L. *coach, director*

### Wilbraham
Dailey, Franklyn Edward, Jr. *electronic image technology company executive, analyst, consultant*

### Williamstown
Bell, Robert *literature educator*
Blair, Phyllis E. *artist*
Bolton, Roger Edwin *economist, educator*
Chandler, John Wesley *educational consultant*

Conforti, Michael Peter *museum director, art historian*
Corrin, Lisa G. *museum director*
Cramer, Phebe *psychologist*
Crampton, Stuart Jessup Bigelow *physicist, researcher*
Dalzell, Robert Fenton, Jr. *historian, educator*
Dew, Charles Burgess *historian, educator*
Eusden, John Dykstra *theology studies educator, minister*
Fuller, Renee Nuni *psychologist, educational publisher*
Fuqua, Charles John *classicist, educator*
Graver, Lawrence Stanley *language educator*
Graver, Suzanne Levy *English literature educator*
Hill, Victor Ernst, IV, *retired mathematics professor, musician*
Jaffe, Andrew William *music educator, composer*
Kassin, Saul *psychology professor*
Markgraf, J(ohn) Hodge *chemist, educator*
Morgan, Frank *mathematics professor*
Niemeyer, Peter Eduard *history educator*
Norton, Glyn Peter *literature educator*
Nowicki, George Lucian *retired chemical company executive*
Oakley, Francis Christopher *historian, educator*
Park, David Allen *physicist, researcher*
Pasachoff, Jay Myron *astronomer, educator*
Pasachoff, Naomi *writer*
Pistorius, George *language educator, educator*
Robinson, Hobart Krum *management consulting company executive*
Rudolph, Frederick *history professor*
Schapiro, Morton Owen *academic administrator*
Sheahan, John Bernard *economist, educator*
Solomon, Paul Robert *neuropsychologist, educator*
Sprague, John Louis *management consultant*
Stamelman, Richard Howard *French and humanities educator*
Stuebner, Erwin August, Jr. *internist*
Weiner, Bruce Barnet *psychologist*
Wilkins, Earle Wayne, Jr. *retired surgery educator*
Wobus, Reinhard Arthur *geologist, educator*

### Wilmington
Vakhshoori, Daryoosh *chemicals executive*

### Winchester
Bigelow, Robert P. *lawyer, arbitrator, mediator, journalist*
Blackham, Ann Rosemary (Mrs. J. W. Blackham) *realtor*
Brennan, Francis Patrick *banker*
Ferrara, Lee *graphics designer, artist, educator*
Fitch, Blake *museum director, photographer, curator*
Hansen, Robert Joseph *civil engineer*
Irving, Gitte Nielsen *secondary school educator*
Jackson, Francis Joseph *research and development company executive*
Koppel, Lowell B. *chemical engineer*
Milburn, Richard Henry *physics professor*
Neuman, Robert Sterling *art educator, artist*
Ockerbloom, Richard C. *newspaper executive*
Rahmeier, Lynne Jillson *primary school educator, secondary school educator*
Reno, John F. *foundation administrator*
Taggart, Ganson Powers *management consultant*
von Stackelberg, Katherine Ellen *environmental scientist, consultant*

### Windsor
Leaf, Martin Norman *lawyer*

### Winthrop
Brown, Patricia Irene *retired law librarian, lawyer*

### Woburn
DeCrosta, Susan Elyse *graphic designer*
Doyle, Thomas R. *archivist, consultant*
Guo, Ling *musician, consultant*
Li, Chiang J. *pharmaceutical executive, physician scientist*
Lundquist, Eric *editor-in-chief*
Mehra, Raman Kumar *aerospace and defense technology executive, automotion and control engineering researcher*
Popov, Oleg *physicist*
Preve, Roberta Jean *librarian, researcher*
Tramonte, Michael Robert *education educator*
Winson, Ellen-Marie (Macone) *school system administrator, reading specialist*

### Woods Hole
Behn, Mark Dietrich *marine geophysicist, educator*
Berggren, William Alfred *geologist, research micropaleontologist, educator*
Cohen, Seymour Stanley *biochemist, educator*
Evans, Rob L. *geophysicist, researcher*
Farrington, John William *academic administrator, dean, research scientist*
Felzer, Benjamin Seth *ecologist, researcher*
Gagosian, Robert B. *chemist, educator*
Gifford, Prosser *retired library administrator*
Hart, Stanley Robert *geochemist, educator*
Laster, Leonard *internist, gastroenterologist, academic administrator, educator, writer, biomedical researcher*
Nepstad, Daniel C. *ecologist, educator*
Newman, John Nicholas *naval architect educator*
Sogin, Mitchell L. *biologist, educator*
Speck, William T. *former physician, health facility administrator*
Steele, John Hyslop *marine scientist, oceanographic institute administrator*
Stephen, Ralph Archibald *geophysicist, researcher*
Uchupi, Elazar *geologist, researcher*
Woodwell, George Masters *ecologist, conservationist*

### Worcester
Angelescu, Amanda Goseco *pediatrician, endocrinologist*
Angelini, Michael P. *insurance company executive*
Bagshaw, Joseph Charles *molecular biologist, educator*
Baldiga, Joseph Hilding *lawyer*
Barr, Dorothy *librarian*
Bassett, John E. *academic administrator, language educator*

Bennett, Bruce S. *publishing executive*
Berkey, Dennis Dale *university president*
Bernhard, Jeffrey David *dermatologist, educator, editor*
Billias, George Athan *historian, educator*
Boroff, Henry Jack *federal judge, educator*
Brooks, John Edward *college president*
Candib, Murray A. *retail executive, consultant*
Chandok, Dinesh *cardiologist, consultant*
Chaudhury, Sujoy Krishna *research scientist*
Chen, Chun-Jen *immunologist, researcher*
Chernin, Russell Scott *lawyer*
Corbin, Frank Wayne *music educator*
Cowan, Fairman Chaffee *lawyer*
Curran, Louis Jerome, Jr. *choral master*
Delorey, John Francis *music educator*
Dolgon, Corey *sociology educator, political activist*
Donnelly, James Corcoran, Jr. *lawyer*
Drachman, David Alexander *neurologist*
Dunlap, Ellen S. *library administrator*
Eppinger, Frederick H., Jr. *insurance company executive*
Falco, Richard Gerard *music educator*
Gaudette, Glenn R. *biomedical engineer, educator*
Geller, Jeffrey L. *psychiatrist, educator*
Gnanaraj, Joseph Sathiya *research scientist*
Greenberg, Nathan *accountant*
Hagar, Richard Joseph *music educator, musician*
Harding, Beth Ann *middle school educator*
Harper, Doreen C. *nursing educator*
Hatfield, Renee S.J. *music educator*
Hovsepian, Leon *artist, designer*
Huber, J. Kendall *lawyer*
Hunt, John David *retired bank executive*
Hunter, Richard Edward *retired physician*
Indic, Premananda *education educator, researcher*
Katz, Robert Nathan *ceramics engineer, educator*
Kaufman, Paul D. *biomedical researcher, researcher*
Kennedy, Linda Mann *neuroscience educator, researcher*
Kuklinski, Joan Lindsey *librarian*
Lazare, Aaron *dean, psychiatrist*
Lou, Wenjing *engineering educator*
Lougee, David Louis *lawyer*
Madison, John Mark *pulmonologist, educator*
Malone, Joseph James *mathematics professor, researcher*
Mardilovich, Ivan P. *education educator, researcher*
Marik, Paul Ellis *physician*
Mathisen, Howard *psychologist, educator, minister*
McCorison, Marcus Allen *librarian, cultural organization administrator*
McFarland, Michael C. *academic administrator*
Mello, Craig C. *molecular medicine educator, researcher*
Menon, Mani *urological surgeon, educator*
Mirick, John O. *lawyer*
Morse, Abraham Nicholas *obstetrician, gynecologist, educator*
Morse, Leonard J. *epidemiologist, public health service officer*
Murray, Timothy P. *mayor*
Novarro, Neva K. *economics professor*
Ott, Attiat Farag *economist, educator*
Palmer, John Anthony III *secondary school educator, music educator, language educator*
Parrish, Edward Alton, Jr. *electrical and computer engineering educator, academic administrator*
Parsons, Edwin Spencer *clergyman, educator*
Pockwinse, Shirwin M. *research scientist, educator*
Reilly, Daniel Patrick *retired bishop*
Richard, Stella Marie Schwarz *veterinary science professor*
Roorbach, Bill Forsyth *English language educator, writer*
Selin, Lisa K. *physician*
Smith, H. Kerner *manufacturing executive, heavy*
Thompson, Michael David *physician*
Tonkonogy, Joseph Moses *physician, neuropsychiatrist, researcher*
Townes, Philip Leonard *pediatrician, educator*
Van Nostrand, Richard Charles *lawyer*
Varpahovsky, Andrey *computer scientist, educator*
Vaughan, Alden True *history professor*
Vellaccio, Frank *academic administrator*
Vick, Susan *playwright, educator, director, actress*
Vickstrom, Kristina Rose *medical researcher*
Welu, James A. *art museum director*
West, Michael D. *cloning and stem cell research company executive*
Woolhouse, Maureen Ann *mathematics professor*
Young, Stephen Bernard *urogynecologist, surgeon*
Zeugner, John Finn *historian, educator, writer*
Zurier, Robert Burton *rheumatology educator*

### Wrentham
Bittenbender, Brad James *environmental engineer*

### Yarmouth Port
Gordon, Benjamin Dichter *pediatrician, educator, health facility administrator*
Hall, James Frederick *retired college president*
Nichols, Robert Lyman *retired foreign service officer, lecturer*
Phelps, Judson Hewett *health facility administrator, marketing professional*
Weiner, Charles *historian, educator*

## MICHIGAN

### Ada
DeVos, Richard Marvin, Sr. *former network marketing company executive*
Lyall, Lynn *consumer products company executive*
McCallum, Charles Edward *lawyer*
Van Andel, Steve Alan *consumer products company executive*
Weiss, Joseph Joel *consulting company executive*

### Adrian
Caine, Stanley Paul *college administrator*
Dodson, John Thomas *orchestra conductor*
Fosbender, Jule Joann *retired librarian*
Geyer, Richard Douglas *librarian, poet*
Lamprecht, Elizabeth Ann *mathematics professor*
Warner, Joanne Marie *theater educator*

Weathers, Milledge Wright *retired economics professor*
Yehuda, Simone Naomi *education educator*

### Akron
Wright, Michelle Denise *elementary school principal*

### Albion
Raj, Selva J. *religious studies educator*

### Algonac
Paquet, Gary Lee *elementary school educator*

### Allen Park
Kirby, Dorothy Manville *social worker*
Kitna, Jon *professional football player*
Marinelli, Rod *professional football coach*
Millen, Matt *professional sports team executive*
Pollard, Marcus *professional football player*
Williams, Roy *professional football player*

### Allendale
Ambrose, Bradley Scott *physics professor, researcher*
Bazany, Ted Bruce *music educator*
Campbell, Arthur J. *music educator*
El-Said, Mostafa M. *computer science educator, information systems educator*
Haas, Thomas Joseph *academic administrator, chemistry educator*
Murray, Diane Elizabeth *librarian*
Nikitin, Alexey G. *biology professor, researcher*

### Alma
Swanson, Robert Draper *college president*
Tracy, Saundra J. *academic administrator*

### Alpena
Sumerix, Kendall J. *science educator*

### Ann Arbor
Abrams, Gerald David *pathologist, educator*
Adriaens, Peter *environmental engineer, consultant*
Agno, John G. *management consultant*
Agranoff, Bernard William *biochemist, educator*
Akerlof, Carl William *physics professor*
Akil, Huda *neuroscientist, educator, researcher*
Allen, Layman Edward *law educator, research scientist*
Allen-Meares, Paula G. *social work educator, dean*
Annesley, Thomas Michael *clinical chemist, pathology educator*
Ansbacher, Rudi *physician*
Apperson, Jean *psychologist*
Arlinghaus, Sandra Judith Lach *mathematical geographer, educator*
Ash, Major McKinley, Jr. *dentist, educator*
Ashe, Arthur James III *chemistry professor*
Atreya, Sushil Kumar *planetary-space science educator, astrophysicist*
Bacon, George Edgar *pediatrician*
Bagian, James Philip *former astronaut, public health service officer, medical educator*
Bailey, Reeve Maclaren *museum curator*
Ball, Deborah Loewenberg *dean, education educator*
Barsan, William George *emergency physician*
Bartell, Lawrence Sims *chemist, educator*
Bartlett, Robert Hawes *surgeon*
Bashshur, Rashid L. *health facility administrator, educator*
Beaubien, Anne Kathleen *librarian*
Beaver, Frank Eugene *critic, historian*
Becher, William Don *retired electrical engineer, engineering educator, writer*
Beckley, Robert Mark *architect, educator*
Bedard, Patrick Joseph *editor, writer, consultant*
Beeton, Alfred Merle *lab administrator, director, biologist, educator, environmentalist*
Behling, Charles Frederick *psychologist, educator*
Belcher, Louis David *marketing professional, retired mayor*
Benford, Harry Bell *naval architect*
Ben-Shahar, Omri *law and economics educator*
Beutler, Frederick Joseph *information scientist*
Beutler, Suzanne A. *retired secondary school educator, artist*
Bigelow, Wilbur Charles *retired education educator*
Bilello, John Charles *engineering educator, director*
Bishop, Elizabeth Shreve *psychologist*
Blair, David Clark *information scientist, educator*
Blinder, Seymour Michael *chemistry professor, physics professor, educator*
Bloom, Jane Maginnis *emergency physician*
Blouin, Francis Xavier, Jr. *history professor*
Bornstein, George Jay *literary educator*
Bornstein, Morris *economist, educator*
Bowdler, Anthony John *internist, educator*
Boxer, Laurence Alan *physician, research educator*
Brandon, David A. *food service executive*
Brown, Donald Robert *psychology professor*
Brown, William Ernest *dentist*
Bryant, Barbara Everitt *academic administrator, researcher, retired marketing professional, retired federal agency administrator*
Buesser, Anthony Carpenter *lawyer*
Burdi, Alphonse Rocco *anatomist*
Burke, Robert Harry *surgeon, educator*
Cadman, Charles *mathematician*
Cai, Hongliang *medical researcher*
Cain, Albert Clifford *psychologist, educator*
Caminker, Evan H. *dean, law educator*
Carlson, Bruce Martin *anatomist*
Carney, Thomas Daly *lawyer*
Carr, Lloyd *college football coach*
Casey, Kenneth Lyman *neurologist*
Caslini, Corrado *molecular biologist*
Cerny, Joseph Charles *urologist, educator*
Chaffin, Don Brian *industrial engineering educator, research director*
Chang, Chun-Shu *historian, educator, writer*
Chang, Hsueh-lun Shelley *historian, researcher, writer*
Chey, William D *physician, researcher*
Chin, Chen Ooi *dean*
Choe, Seungho *physicist, researcher*

Davis, Laura Arlene *retired foundation administrator*
Jenness, James M. *grocery manufacturing company executive*
Lincoln, Margaret *library media specialist*
Mackay, A. D. David *food products executive*
Markey, James Kevin *lawyer*
Matthews, Wyhomme S. *retired music educator, academic administrator*
Pilnick, Gary H. *food products executive, lawyer*
Risukhin, Vladimir Nikolayevich *aeronautical engineer, educator*
Speirn, Sterling K. *foundation administrator*
Stewart, Joseph Melvin *manufacturing executive, former food products executive*

**Bay City**
Greve, Guy Robert *lawyer*
Hiner, John Patrick *newspaper editor*
Van Dyke, Clifford Craig *retired bank executive*

**Bay Harbor**
Sargent, Charles Lee *manufacturing executive*

**Belleville**
Ibrahim, Faroog Abdel-Kareem *information technology executive*
Palmer, James F. *corporate financial executive*
Stebbins, Donald J. *car parts manufacturing company executive*
Van Tassel, Michael L. *music educator*
Wilson, David James *chemistry researcher, educator*

**Belmont**
Powers, Linda S. *art association administrator*

**Benton Harbor**
Binkley, David A. *human resources specialist*
Brown, Mark E. *manufacturing executive*
Fettig, Jeff M. *manufacturing executive*
Hopp, Daniel Frederick *manufacturing company executive, lawyer*
Lundgren, Colleen Bowling *elementary school educator, consultant*
Periquito, Paulo F.M.O. *manufacturing executive*
Templin, Roy *corporate financial executive*
Tennant-Snyder, Nancy *appliance company executive*
Thieneman, Michael D. *manufacturing executive*
Todman, Michael A. *manufacturing executive*
Watkins, M(artha) Anne *family practice nurse practitioner*
Yoder, Dale Roy *history educator*

**Berrien Springs**
Homan, Michele Annette *language educator*
Lesher, William Richard *retired academic administrator*
Lundgren, Dennis David *elementary school educator, secondary school educator*
Maguad, Ben Abrico *management educator*
Ritzenthaler, Beatriz Augusta *musician, educator*
Wiltse, Richard Arthur *music educator*

**Beulah**
Auch, Walter Edward *security firm executive*
Edwards, Wallace Winfield *retired automotive executive*
Tanner, Helen Hornbeck *historian, consultant*

**Beverly Hills**
Castle, Maurice Emmett *orthopedist, surgeon*
Hertzberg, David Gordon *retired lawyer*

**Big Rapids**
Ryan, Ray Darl, Jr. *academic administrator*
Tymes, Nathaniel, Jr. *statistician, educator*
Westman, Craig Ellery *academic administrator*

**Bingham Farms**
Baumkel, Mark S. *lawyer*
Giles, Conrad Leslie *ophthalmic surgeon*
Goren, Steven Eliot *lawyer*
Gratch, Serge *retired mechanical engineering educator*
Krevsky, Margery Brown *talent agency executive*
Silverman, Gilbert B. *retired real estate developer, art collector*

**Birch Run**
Thompson-Christie, Heather Marie *adult education educator*

**Birmingham**
Carter, Marsha Jean *public relations executive, poet*
Edwards, Michael Gerard *physician*
Elsman, James Leonard, Jr. *lawyer*
Filter, Terrance Anderson *clinical psychologist*
Foxen, Richard William *manufacturing executive*
Kienbaum, Thomas Gerd *lawyer*
Kozlow, Richard *artist*
Lerner, Martin A. *infectious disease physician*
Maxwell, Jack Erwin *manufacturing executive*
McCuen, John *finance and tooling company executive, columnist, educator*
Smith, George Wolfram *physicist, researcher*
Sweeney, Thomas Frederick *lawyer*
Wagner, Bruce Stanley *marketing professional*
Wells, Steven Wayne *lawyer*

**Bloomfield**
Gabriel, Martin George *engineering consultant*

**Bloomfield Hills**
Adams, Charles Francis *advertising executive, real estate company executive*
Ball, Patricia Ann *physician*
Banas, C(hristine) Leslie *lawyer*
Berline, James H. *advertising executive, public relations executive*
Bokhari, Raza Ali Babar *former marketing strategist*
Brent, Robert Lewis *urologist*
Burstein, Richard Joel *lawyer*
Charla, Leonard Francis *lawyer, publishing executive*
Clippert, Charles Frederick *lawyer*
Coburn, Ronald Murray *ophthalmologist, surgeon*

Cregg, Roger A. *construction executive*
Cuffe, Stafford Sigesmund *business, technology, manufacturing and management consultant*
Dawson, Stephen Everette *lawyer*
Devaney, Dennis Martin *lawyer, educator*
DiFeo, Samuel X. *automotive executive*
Dugas, Richard J., Jr. *construction executive*
Gagliardi, Raymond Alfred *physician*
Gold, Edward David *lawyer*
Googasian, George Ara *lawyer*
Greenwood, Frank *information scientist, educator*
Guarascio, Philip *advertising executive*
Haidostian, Alice Berberian *concert pianist, volunteer, not-for-profit fundraiser*
Kasischke, Louis Walter *lawyer*
Kirk, John MacGregor *lawyer*
Larson, Robert Craig *real estate company officer*
Ledwidge, Patrick Joseph *lawyer*
LoPrete, James Hugh *lawyer*
Martin, J(oseph) Patrick *lawyer, judge*
Mathog, Robert Henry *otolaryngologist, educator*
McCuen, John Francis, Jr. *lawyer*
McDonald, Patrick Allen *lawyer, educator, arbitrator*
Mc Gehee, H(arry) Coleman, Jr. *retired bishop*
Meyer, George Herbert *lawyer*
Nern, Christopher Carl *lawyer*
Norris, John Hart *lawyer, director*
Papai, Beverly Daffern *retired library director*
Pickard, William Frank *plastics company executive*
Poth, Stefan Michael *retired diversified financial services company executive*
Prasad, Niru *physician, television personality*
Pulte, William J. *construction executive*
Rader, Ralph Terrance *lawyer*
Robinson, Jack Albert *retail executive*
Rumbell, Mary Beth *secondary school educator*
Sandy, William Haskell *training and communication systems executive*
Simon, Evelyn *lawyer*
Smith, H(arold) Lawrence *lawyer*
Snyder, George Edward *lawyer*
Solomon, Mark Raymond *lawyer, educator*
Sommerfeld, David William *lawyer, educator*
Stewart, Michael B. *lawyer, mechanical and aerospace engineer*
Stivender, Donald Lewis *mechanical engineering consultant*
Stoller, John R. *lawyer*
Stunz, John Henry, Jr. *retired physician, consultant*
Sugrue, Dennis Patrick *psychologist*
Swift, Jonathan *television personality, educator*
Syme, Daniel Bailey *rabbi, institution executive*
Taubman, Robert S. *real estate developer*
Tolia, Vasundhara K. *pediatric gastroenterologist, educator*
Weil, John William *technology management consultant*
Williams, J. Bryan *lawyer*
Williams, Walter Joseph *lawyer*
Wise, John Augustus *lawyer, director*

**Bloomfield Township**
Brown, Lynette Ralya *journalist, publicist*

**Brighton**
Schroeder, Stephanie Lynn *human resources specialist, director*
Wolf, Robert John *music educator*

**Brimley**
Elder, Richard Wayne *history professor*

**Brooklyn**
Vischer, Harold Harry *manufacturing executive*

**Brownstown**
Slingerland, Mary Jo *writing educator*

**Burt**
Wolverton, Thomas Frank *automotive company supervisor*

**Burton**
Farmer, Philip José *writer*
Johnson, Jolene Carole *music educator*

**Byron Center**
VanderJagt, Kathleen Sue *parochial school educator*

**Cadillac**
DeVito, Karen Smith *French educator*
Walker, Dale Maxwell *city official*

**Calumet**
Smith, Thomas Hugh (T. Kilgore Splake) *poet, writer, photographer*

**Camden**
Falls, Kathleene Joyce *photographer*

**Canton**
Wickus, James D. *food service executive*
Wiloch, Thomas *poet, editor*

**Capac**
Wagner, Dorothy Marie *retired senior creative designer, artist*

**Carleton**
Ely, Deborah D. *elementary school educator*

**Caro**
Hile, Michele Vera *middle school educator*

**Cass City**
Althaver, Lambert Ewing *manufacturing executive*

**Cedar Lake**
Berlin, Gregory Alan *library director*

**Charlevoix**
Miles, David Loren *museum director*

**Chassell**
Spain, James Dorris, Jr. *biochemist, educator*

**Chelsea**
Crane, Horace Richard *physicist, researcher*

Kendall, Kay Lynn *interior designer, consultant*
Paulsen, Serenus Glen *architect, educator*
Weinreich, Gabriel *physicist, minister, educator*
Yarows, Steven Allen *internist*

**Clarkston**
Keough, James Gillman, Jr. *minister*
Kruzan, James Brendan *financial planner*
Wydra, Frank Thomas *healthcare executive*

**Commerce Township**
Smith, Barbara Kathryn *retired elementary school educator*

**Dearborn**
Bannister, Michael E. *corporate financial executive*
Barton, Robert H. III *automotive executive*
Beauford, Sandra *nurse, data processing executive*
Beyer, Roberta *dean, education educator, writer, researcher*
Bovich, Edward Hugh *manufacturing executive*
Brown, James Ward *mathematician, educator, author*
Buckingham, Lance *automotive executive*
Cairns, James Robert *mechanical engineering educator*
Cape, James Odies E. *fashion designer*
Chatterjee, Anjan *automotive executive*
Chou, Clifford Chi Fong *research engineering executive*
Fields, Mark *automotive executive*
Ford, Bill (William Clay Ford Jr.) *automotive company executive*
Ford, William Clay *automotive executive, professional sports team executive*
Fordyce, James George *physician*
Fox, Stacy L. *lawyer*
Gandhi, Haren S. *chemical engineer*
Hamp, Steven K. *automotive executive*
Henderson, Stanley Elwood *academic administrator, consultant*
Hogan, Brian Joseph *editor*
Jie, Min *mechanical engineering educator, researcher*
Johnston, Michael Francis *auto parts company executive*
Kahn, Mark Leo *arbitrator, educator*
Kiska, Timothy Olin *communications educator, radio producer*
Krygier, Roman J. *automotive executive*
Laymon, Joe W. *human resources specialist, automotive executive*
Leclair, Don (Donat R. Leclair Jr.) *automotive executive*
Lee, Hei Wai *finance educator, researcher*
Leet, Kenneth H.M. *automotive executive*
Little, Daniel Eastman *philosopher, educator, director*
Little, Robert Eugene *engineering educator*
Lundy, J(oseph) Edward *retired automobile company executive*
Marcin, Robert H. *automotive executive*
Mays, J. C. *automotive executive*
McKeage, Alice Jane *computer programmer*
Mi, Chunting Chris *engineering educator*
Mohan Iyengar, Raj *automotive executive, researcher*
Mulally, Alan R. *automotive company executive, former aerospace company executive*
Musson, Warren R. *investment banker*
Papazian, Dennis Richard *historian, educator, commentator*
Parker, Gordon Arthur *chemistry professor*
Parry-Jones, Richard *automotive executive*
Pestillo, Peter John *auto parts company executive, lawyer*
Popovich, George Lee *theater educator*
Ross, Dennis E. *retired automotive executive, retired lawyer*
Scheele, Nicholas V. *automotive executive*
Shim, Taehyun *mechanical engineer*
Smither, Nick *automotive executive*
Taub, Robert Allan *lawyer*
Thai-Tang, Hau *automotive engineer*
Thursfield, David W. *automotive executive*
Yang, Guangbin *engineer*
Zhu, Qiang *education educator*
Zimmerman, Martin B. *automotive executive*

**Dearborn Heights**
Abramson, Marc A. *dentist*
Carter, Julia Marie *secondary school educator*
Johns, Diana *secondary school educator*

**Delton**
Collier-Horn, Mary Eliza *literature and language educator*
Waring, Walter Weyler *literature and language professor*

**Detroit**
Abramson, Hanley Norman *pharmacy educator*
Abt, Jeffrey *art educator, art historian, artist, writer*
Afonso, Luis C. *cardiologist*
Albom, Mitch David *sports columnist*
Ali, Murad Cajetan *transportation executive, writer*
Alpert, Daniel *broadcast executive*
Amsden, Ted Thomas *lawyer*
Anderson, Gerard M. *energy executive*
Anderson, Thomas Caryl *dean*
Andrews, Caesar *editor*
Anger, Paul *newspaper editor*
Ansari, Mohammed Rafiullah *surgeon*
Archer, Dennis Wayne *lawyer, former mayor*
Babb, Ralph W., Jr. *bank executive*
Babcock, Mike *professional hockey coach*
Barclay, Kathleen S. *automotive executive*
Barnhart, Mary C. *health facility administrator*
Barrett, Nancy Smith *academic administrator*
Bassett, Tina *communications executive*
Beal, Graham William John *museum director*
Beierwaltes, William Howard *physiologist, educator*
Bell Wilson, Carlotta A. *state official, consultant*
Bennett, Grace *publishing executive*
Beran, John R. *banker*
Bilstrom, Jon Wayne *lawyer*
Bing, David *retired professional basketball player, metal products executive*

Blomquist, David Wels *journalist*
Bock, Brooks Frederick *emergency physician*
Boocock, Stephen William *lawyer*
Booth, Betty Jean *retired daycare administrator, poet*
Bowen, David R. *science and technology educator, consultant*
Bowman, William Scott (Scotty Bowman) *professional hockey coach*
Boykin, Peter Jeffrey *humanities educator*
Braid, Ralph M. *economics professor*
Brake, Willie Edward *computer company executive, educator*
Brand, George Edward, Jr. *retired lawyer*
Bridge, Patrick David *education educator*
Brill, Lesley *literature and film studies educator*
Brunk, Thomas Walter *art historian*
Brustad, Orin Daniel *lawyer*
Bryant, Marchelle Dionne *performing arts educator*
Bully-Cummings, Ella M. *police chief*
Burns, Lawrence D. *automotive executive*
Burnside, Wanda Jacqueline *elementary school educator*
Burzynski, Susan Marie *newspaper editor*
Butler, David J. *newspaper editor*
Butler, Timothy W. *business educator*
Buttigieg, Joseph J. *bank executive*
Calkins, Stephen *lawyer, educator*
Callahan, J(ohn) William (Bill Callahan) *judge*
Candler, James Nall, Jr. *lawyer*
Cantoni, Louis Joseph *retired psychologist, sculptor, poet*
Charfoos, Lawrence Selig *lawyer*
Chelios, Christos K. *professional hockey player*
Clarke, Troy A. *automotive executive*
Cohan, Leon Sumner *lawyer, retired electric company executive*
Cohen, Norton Jacob *lawyer*
Cohen, Sanford Ned *pediatrician, educator, academic administrator*
Colby, Joy Hakanson *critic*
Collier, James Warren *retired lawyer*
Collins, Jeffrey G. *lawyer, former prosecutor*
Connor, Laurence Davis *lawyer, director*
Cooke, William Nelson *labor management professor, consultant*
Corbitt, Eumiller Mattie *special education educator*
Corrigan, Maura Denise *state supreme court justice*
Cothorn, John Arthur *lawyer*
Covensky, Edith *language educator, poet*
Cranmer, Thomas William *lawyer*
Dale, Shirley Marie *protective services official*
Dane, Jefic *internist, cardiologist*
Darr, Alan Phipps *curator, historian*
Datsyuk, Pavel *professional hockey player*
Datta, Sudip *finance educator*
Dauch, Richard E. *automotive executive*
Deason, Herold McClure *lawyer*
Demos, Dave *marketing executive*
DeRamus, Betty Jean *columnist*
Devellano, James Charles *professional hockey manager, baseball executive*
Di Chiera, David *opera company director*
Diehl, Nancy J. *lawyer*
Dombrowski, Mitchell Paul *obstetrician, researcher*
Dore-Duffy, Paula *neuroscientist, educator*
Drescher, Dennis George *biochemist, researcher*
Drutchas, Gregory G. *lawyer*
Dudley, John Henry, Jr. *lawyer*
Duensing, Dorothy Jean *music educator, vocalist*
Duggan, Michael E. *health facility administrator*
DuMouchelle, Ernest J. *art appraiser*
DuMouchelle, Lawrence F. *art appraiser*
Dunn, William Bradley *lawyer*
Dworkin, Aaron *violinist, educator*
Dwyer, John M. *mathematician, statistician, computer scientist*
Earley, Anthony Francis, Jr. *utilities company executive, lawyer*
Edelstein, Tilden Gerald *academic administrator, historian, educator*
Edmunds, Nancy Garlock *federal judge*
Elias, Arturo *automotive executive*
Ellyn, Lynne *energy executive*
Ewing, Stephen E. *natural gas company executive*
Fay, Sister Maureen A. *university president*
Feikens, John *federal judge*
Field, Judith Judy *librarian*
Fladung, Thom *managing editor*
Fleming, George Robert *psychologist*
Forster, Carl-Peter *automotive executive*
Frade, Peter Daniel *chemist, educator, administrator*
Francis, Edward D. *architect*
Frank, Richard Calhoun *architect*
Friedman, Bernard Alvin *federal judge*
Gamache, Kathleen Anne *law librarian*
Gardin, Julius Markus *cardiologist, educator*
Gee, Ramondo Reginald *internal revenue service territory manager*
Gerosa, Peter R. *automotive executive*
Gershel, Alan M. *prosecutor*
Gettelfinger, Ron *labor union administrator*
Gillum, Roderick D. *automotive executive*
Godzak, Roman Paul *archivist*
Goodman, Allen Charles *economist, educator*
Gottschalk, Thomas A. *automotive executive, lawyer*
Green, Charles Adam *retired education educator, psychologist*
Greene, Harold H. *psychology professor*
Gross, James George *lawyer*
Gupta, Suraj Narayan *physicist, researcher*
Gushee, Richard Bordley *lawyer*
Hall, Elliott Sawyer *lawyer*
Hampton, Verne Churchill, II, *lawyer*
Hasek, Dominik *professional hockey player*
Hashimoto, Ken *dermatologist, educator*
Henderson, Frederick A. (Fritz Henderson) *automotive executive*
Herstein, Carl William *lawyer*
Higby, Mary A. *marketing executive, educator*
Hill, Elizabeth Marie *research scientist*
Holland, Ken *professional sports team executive*
Hunke, David L. *publisher*
Ilitch, Marian *professional hockey team executive, food service executive*

Ilitch, Michael *professional hockey team executive, food products executive*
Jeffs, Thomas Hamilton, II, *retired bank executive*
Jefic, Dijana *nephrologist*
Jendrzejewski, Roxanne Marie *social studies educator, language educator*
Jenkins-Anderson, Barbara Jeanne *pathologist, educator*
Johnson, Lester Larue, Jr. *artist, educator*
Kahalas, Harvey *business educator*
Kahkonen, Dorothy M. *endocrinologist*
Kalman, Andrew *manufacturing executive, director*
Kaltenbach, James Albert *neurobiologist, educator*
Kamins, John Mark *lawyer*
Kantrowitz, Jean *health products executive*
Kaplan, Joseph *pediatrician*
Keith, Damon Jerome *federal judge*
Kelley, Mark Albert *physician, educator, health products executive*
Kelly, Marilyn *state supreme court justice*
Kennedy, Cornelia Groefsema *federal judge*
Kessler, Philip Joel *lawyer*
Kilpatrick, Kwame Malik *mayor*
Kim, Do Gyoon *biomedical researcher*
Kirschner, Stanley *chemist*
Krawetz, Stephen Andrew *molecular medicine and genetics scientist, educator*
Krouse, Helene June *nursing educator*
Krsul, John Aloysius, Jr. *lawyer*
Kummler, Ralph H. *chemical engineer, educator, dean*
Lamborn, LeRoy Leslie *law educator*
LaNeve, Mark R. *automotive executive*
Lawrence, John Kidder *lawyer*
Lee, Joon Sang *engineering educator*
Lerner, Stephen Alexander *microbiologist, physician, educator*
Levin, Charles Leonard *state supreme court justice*
Lewis, David Baker *lawyer*
Lidstrom, Nicklas *professional hockey player*
Lim, Henry Wan-Peng *dermatologist*
Lisak, Robert Philip *neurologist, researcher, educator*
Lockman, Stuart M. *lawyer*
Lupulescu, Aurel Peter *medical educator, researcher, physician*
Lusher, Jeanne Marie *pediatric hematologist, educator*
Lutz, Robert Anthony *automotive company executive*
Madgett, Naomi Long *poet, editor, publisher, educator*
Maida, Adam Joseph Cardinal *cardinal*
Maiese, Kenneth *neurologist, neuroscientist*
Mallett, Conrad LeRoy, Jr. *former state supreme court chief justice, hospital administrator*
Mamat, Frank Trustick *lawyer*
Mani, Nandita S. *medical librarian*
Mari, Giancarlo *obstetrician, gynecologist, educator*
Martin, John E *psychologist, educator*
Martz, Mike *former professional football coach*
Marunick, Mark Timothy *medical educator, dental educator*
Maseru, Noble A.W. *city health department administrator*
Maurer, David Leo *lawyer*
McCrae, Jocelyn Diane *psychologist*
McIntyre, Michael John *lawyer, educator*
McKim, Samuel John III *lawyer*
Mclorie, Gordon Arthur *urologist, educator*
McTyre, Robert Earl *publishing executive*
McWhorter, Sharon Louise *engineering executive, inventor, consultant*
Middlebrook, John G. *marketing executive, advertising executive*
Mika, Joseph John *library director, educator*
Miller, George DeWitt, Jr. *lawyer*
Miller, Orlando Jack *obstetrician, gynecologist, educator, geneticist*
Mitchell, Connie *director*
Mitseff, Carl *lawyer*
Moldenhauer, Judith A. *graphic design educator*
Monroe, Craig *professional baseball player*
Morford, Craig S. *prosecutor*
Morgan, Virginia Mattison *judge*
Moses, Gregory H., Jr. *health services administrator*
Moss, Leslie Otha *homeland security specialist*
Mubarak, Kamal K. *pulmonologist*
Murphy, Stephen Joseph III *prosecutor*
Myers, Rodman Nathaniel *lawyer*
Nathanson, Saul David *oncologist, surgeon, educator*
Neithercut, Mark Edward *foundation consultant*
Newton, Kenneth Kurt *physician, educator, administrator*
Noland, Mariam Charl *foundation executive*
Novak, Raymond Francis *environmental services administrator, pharmacology educator*
Nunn, Andre' Ronald *surgeon, health facility administrator*
O'Connell, John Bernard, Jr. *medical educator, department chairman*
Oliver, John Preston *chemistry professor*
Ordonez, Magglio *professional baseball player*
Osgood, Chris *professional hockey player*
Parrish, Maurice Drue *museum executive*
Parry, Dale D. *newspaper editor*
Parsons, Anne *performing company executive*
Peck, William Henry *curator, archaeologist, educator, art historian, writer*
Peres, Edward M. *preventive medicine physician, educator*
Peters, John Douglas *lawyer, artist*
Peterson, Bruce D. *lawyer*
Pietrofesa, John Joseph *psychologist, educator*
Piper, William Howard *bank executive*
Powell, Ronald Rowe *library science educator*
Prasad, Ananda Shiva *medical educator*
Rassel, Richard Edward *lawyer*
Rathod, Mulchand *mechanical engineering educator*
Raymond, Richard Gerard, Jr. *lawyer*
Reddy, Daniel Joseph *vascular surgeon*
Redman, Barbara Klug *nursing educator*
Reece, Terry Allen *travel company executive, Internet company executive*
Reilly, David N. (Nick Reilly) *automotive executive*

Risner, Doug S. *performing arts educator, researcher*
Rivers, Emanuel P. *emergency physician, medical educator*
Rivin, Evgeny Izrailevich *mechanical engineer, consultant*
Robinson, Joel D. *manufacturing executive*
Rodriguez, Ivan Torres *professional baseball player*
Rogers, Hon Paulletto *researcher, writer*
Rosen, Gerald Ellis *federal judge*
Rosman, Howard S. *cardiologist, educator*
Rozof, Phyllis Claire *lawyer*
Ryan, James Leo *federal judge*
Saxton, William Marvin *lawyer*
Schlichting, Nancy Margaret *hospital administrator*
Schreiber, Bertram Manuel *mathematics professor*
Schwartz, Alan E. *lawyer, director*
Schwartz, Matthew Barahal *historian*
Schwartz, Michael Robinson *insurance company executive*
Schweitzer, Peter *advertising agency executive*
Scott, John Edward Smith *lawyer*
Scott, Nina Elizabeth Ray *music educator*
Sedler, Robert Allen *law educator*
Shannon, Margaret Anne *lawyer*
Shields, Anthony Frank *oncologist, hematologist*
Silverman, Norman Alan *cardiac surgeon*
Sims, Howard F. *architectural firm executive*
Skowronski, Nancy *library director*
Small, Melvin *historian, educator*
Smith, Gary Richard *technology educator*
Smith, James Albert *lawyer*
Smith, Wilbur Lazar *radiologist, educator*
Smyntek, John Eugene, Jr. *editor*
Soave, Anthony *manufacturing executive*
Sokol, Robert James *obstetrician, gynecologist, educator*
Soltanian-Zadeh, Hamid *research scientist, educator*
Sparrow, Herbert George III *lawyer, educator*
Speegle, Laura Ann *elementary school educator*
Spoutz, Eric I. *art dealer, conservator, curator, investor, consultant*
Spyers-Duran, Peter *librarian, educator*
Steiman, H. Robert *dean, dental educator*
Stewart, Melbourne George, Jr. *physicist, researcher*
Svoboda, Mary Beth *health physicist, environmental science educator*
Szygenda, Ralph J. *automotive executive*
Taraza, Dinu *engineering educator, researcher*
Tarnacki, Duane L. *lawyer*
Taylor, Anna Diggs *federal judge*
Taylor, Jeff *reporter, editor*
Thelen, Bruce Cyril *lawyer*
Thurber, Peter Palms *lawyer*
Timm, Roger K. *lawyer*
Turner, Reginald Maurice, Jr. *lawyer*
Tyburski, James Gerard *surgeon*
Valade, Alan Michael *lawyer*
Vanzura, Liz (Elizabeth K. Vanzura) *automotive executive*
Venegas, Frank, Jr. *construction executive*
Vigneron, Allen Henry *theology studies educator, rector, auxiliary bishop*
Volz, William Harry *lawyer, educator*
Wagoner, Rick (G. Richard Wagoner Jr.) *automotive executive*
Warden, Gail Lee *healthcare executive*
White, Katherine E. *law educator*
Whitehouse, Fred Waite *endocrinologist, researcher*
Whiteman, Richard Mark *lawyer*
Whitmer, Richard E. *insurance company executive*
Whittum-Hudson, Judith Anne *education educator, researcher*
Wiener, Joseph *pathologist, educator*
Wittlinger, Timothy David *lawyer*
Wolf, Barry *geneticist, pediatric educator*
Wu, Frank H. *law educator, journalist*
Wyrick, Jermaine Albert *lawyer*
Yee, Sandra Gayle Brown *librarian*
Yoo, George H. *otolaryngologist, medical educator*
Yzerman, Steve (Stephen Gregory Yzerman) *professional sports team executive, retired professional hockey player*
Zak, Imad *radiologist, educator*
Zemlicka, Jiri *medical educator, researcher*

### Dexter
Hanamey, Rosemary T. *nursing educator*

### Dowagiac
Murphy, Lllis *association management executive*
Ott, C(larence) H(enry) *ambassador, accounting professor*

### East Lansing
Abeles, Norman *psychologist, educator*
Abolins, Maris Arvids *physicist, educator*
Abramson, Paul Robert *political scientist, educator*
Aggarwal, Vaneet *research scientist*
Andersland, Orlando Baldwin *engineering educator*
Anderson, David Daniel *retired humanities educator, writer, editor*
Anderton, James Franklin, IV, *real estate company executive*
Austin, Sam M. *physicist, educator*
Baillie, Richard Thomas *economist, educator*
Ballbach, Philip Thornton *political consultant, investor*
Bandes, Susan Jane *museum director, educator*
Beckmeyer, Henry Ernest *anesthesiologist, pain management specialist, medical educator*
Blosser, Henry Gabriel *physicist*
Bresnahan, Roger Jiang *humanities educator, researcher*
Brody, Theodore Meyer *pharmacologist, educator*
Brophy, Jere Edward *education educator, researcher*
Brown, Boyd Alex *physicist, researcher*
Bruno, Maria Frances *writing and cultural educator*
Bukovac, Martin John *horticulturist, educator*
Byerrum, Richard Uglow *college dean*
Case, Eldon Darrel *materials science educator*

Chapin, Richard Earl *retired librarian*
Chen, Kun-Mu *electrical engineering educator*
Cheng, Betty Hsiao-Chih *education educator, researcher*
Crewe, Nancy Moe *retired psychologist*
Cross, Aureal Theophilus *geology and botany educator*
Cutts, Charles Eugene *retired engineering educator*
Dennis, Frank George, Jr. *retired horticulture educator*
Dewhurst, Charles Kurt *museum director, curator, language educator*
D'Itri, Frank Michael *environmental research chemist*
Dow, Steven Benjamin *social studies educator*
Dye, James Louis *chemistry professor*
Essa, Daniel F. *lawyer*
Fisher, Alan Washburn *historian, educator*
Foss, John Frank *mechanical engineering educator*
Freedman, Eric *journalist, educator, writer*
Gass, Gertrude Zemon *psychologist, researcher*
Gelbke, Claus-Konrad *nuclear physics educator*
Goodman, Erik David *engineering educator*
Gottschalk, Alexander *radiologist, educator*
Greenberg, Bradley Sander *communications educator*
Hackel, Emanuel *science educator*
Haider, Steven John *economics professor*
Haka, Clifford Roby *library director*
Harrison, Ann Tukey *foreign language educator*
Harrison, James Francis *chemistry professor, researcher*
Harrison, Jeremy Thomas *dean, law educator*
Harrison, Michael Jay *physicist, researcher*
Hine, Darlene Clark *history educator, administrator*
Honhart, Frederick Lewis III *academic director*
Iglesias, Emma Maria *economics professor*
Izzo, Thomas *college basketball coach*
Johnson, Clark Cumings *lawyer, educator, dean*
Kanatzidis, Mercouri G. *chemist, educator*
Kang, Jun-Koo *finance educator*
Kaplan, Thomas Abraham *physicist, educator*
Kirk, Edgar Lee *retired musician, educator*
Koo, Anthony Ying Chang *economist, educator*
Kravchenko, Alexandra N. *agricultural studies educator*
Kreinin, Mordecha Eliahu *economics professor*
Ladenson, Mark Lawrence *economist, educator*
La Ferle, Carrie *advertising executive, educator*
Lashbrooke, Elvin Carroll, Jr. *law educator, consultant*
Lloyd, John Raymond *mechanical engineering educator*
Luccock, Thomas Nelson *auditor, director*
Magen, Jed Gary *child psychiatrist*
Manderscheid, Lester Vincent *agricultural economics educator*
Mansour, George P. *Spanish language and literature educator*
McMeekin, Dorothy *botanist, plant pathologist, educator*
Menchik, Paul Leonard *economist, educator*
Miracle, Gordon Eldon *advertising educator*
Natoli, Joseph *language educator*
Ngouajio, Mathieu *horticulturist, researcher*
Noel, Mary Margaret *nutritionist, educator*
Pathak, Dorothy Rybaczyk *epidemiologist, researcher*
Perrin, Robert *writer, consultant*
Petrides, George Athan *ecologist, educator*
Petropoulos, Evangelos *former health institute director, educator, researcher*
Pierre, Percy Anthony *engineering educator*
Preiss, Jack *biochemistry professor*
Press, Charles *retired political science professor*
Pysh, Joseph John *neurologist*
Ralph, David Clinton *communications educator*
Revelos, Constantine Nicholas *law educator, writer*
Ristow, George Edward *neurologist, educator*
Robinson, Mitchell *music educator*
Root-Bernstein, Robert Scott *biologist, educator*
Rosenman, Kenneth D. *medical educator*
Rothert, Marilyn L. *dean, nursing educator*
Saint Arnault, Denise Marie *education educator, researcher*
Saul, William Edward *engineering educator*
Schemske, Douglas William *science educator*
Schmitt, Neal *psychology professor, department chairman*
Schoenl, William James *history professor*
Seaton, James *humanities educator*
Simon, Lou Anna Kimsey *academic administrator*
Sisk, Cheryl *neuroscientist, educator*
Smoody, James Ernest *education educator*
Sparks, Harvey Vise, Jr. *physiologist*
Stapleton, James Hall *statistician, educator*
Strampel, William Derkey *dean, medical educator*
Tiedje, James Michael *microbiologist, educator, ecologist*
Tzitsikas, Helene *retired literature educator*
Uludag, Umut *electrical engineer, researcher*
Unsworth, Michael Edward *university librarian*
Velicer, Janet Schafbuch *retired elementary school educator*
von Bernuth, Robert Dean *agricultural engineering educator, consultant*
Von Tersch, Lawrence Wayne *engineering educator, dean*
Wakoski, Diane *poet, educator*
Watson, Ralph Edward *internist, educator*
Wilkinson, William Sherwood *lawyer*
Wilson, R. Dale *marketing educator*
Winder, Clarence Leland *psychologist, educator*
Yang, Lijian *educator*
Young, Raymond James *retired education educator*

### Eastport
Tomlinson, James Lawrence *mechanical engineer*

### Edwardsburg
Floyd, Alton David *cell biologist, consultant*

### Elk Rapids
Thompson, Richard Thomas *academic administrator*

### Escanaba
Wood, D. Ann *language and music educator*

### Essexville
Gabil, Diane Rapson *retired special education educator*

### Farmington
Bryfonski, Dedria Anne *publishing executive*
Ellens, J(ay) Harold *philosopher, educator, psychotherapist, minister*
Ginsberg, Myron *computer scientist*
Itin, Thomas William *merchant, investment banker, consultant*
Neyer, Jerome Charles *consulting civil engineer*
Penberthy, Stanley Josiah, Jr. *publisher*
Werba, Gabriel *public relations consultant*

### Farmington Hills
Barry, Essie Marilyn *elementary school educator, writer*
Brodhead, William McNulty *lawyer, retired congressman*
Chapman, Gilbert Bryant *physicist*
Ellmann, Sheila Frenkel *investment company executive*
Faxon, Jack *headmaster*
Fenton, Robert Leonard *lawyer, writer, film producer*
Gordon, Craig Jeffrey *oncologist, educator*
Goslin, Gerald Hugh *concert pianist, educator*
Hagerty, Robert E. *academic administrator*
Hurd, Mary K. *civil engineer, writer*
Luby, Elliot Donald *psychiatrist, educator*
Meyer, Philip Gilbert *lawyer*
Plaut, Jonathan Victor *rabbi*
Robinson, Amorie Alexia *psychologist, educator*
Seifman, Barry A. *lawyer*
Shaevsky, Mark *lawyer*
Smith, Isabel Francis *financial planner*
Tedrick, Deborah Lynne *singer, actress, educator*
Theodore, Ares Nicholas *chemist, researcher*
Toth, Brian M. *social studies educator*
Yagahashi, Takashi *chef*

### Fennville
Kamman, Curtis Warren *retired ambassador*

### Ferndale
Pennock, Peggy Ann *secondary school educator*
Purtan, Dick (Paul Purtan) *radio personality*

### Fife Lake
Knecht, Richard Arden *family practitioner*

### Flat Rock
Cerasuolo, Jennifer Lyn *preservationist*

### Flint
Acuff, A. Marshall, Jr. *retired investment company executive*
Belcher, Max *social services administrator, dean*
Bonner, Darlene E. *minister, writer*
Chaney, Carol A. *multimedia artist*
Conyers, Jean Louise *chamber of commerce executive*
Davidek, Stefan *artist*
Echempati, Raghu *mechanical engineering educator, consultant*
Henry, John Bailey *museum director*
Marcinkoski, Annette Marie *retired elementary school educator*
Maynard, Olivia P. *foundation administrator*
Munerlyn, Lorraine *foundation administrator*
Simmons, Robert Randolph *principal*
Smith, Catherine Jean *artist, educator*
Stone, Pamela Ann *accountant*
Tomblinson, James Edmond *architect*
White, William Samuel *foundation executive*
Wigston, David Lawrence *biologist, dean*
Williams, Veronica Myres *psychotherapist, social worker*

### Flushing
Bain, William David *electronics engineer, writer*

### Frankenmuth
Shetlar, James Francis *physician*

### Frankfort
Foster, Robert Carmichael *banker*
Gerberding, Miles Carston *lawyer*
Schmidt, Robert Charles, Jr. *finance company executive*
Storrer, William Allin *theater educator, consultant*

### Franklin
Pappas, Edward Harvey *lawyer*
Reinhart, Anne Christine *special education educator, consultant*
Sax, Mary Randolph *speech and language pathologist*

### Fraser
Winget, Larry J., Sr. *automotive industry executive*

### Fremont
Edwards, Loren Allan *secondary school educator*

### Garden City
Elmouchi, Joan Leslie *library director*

### Gaylord
Cooney, Patrick Ronald *bishop*

### Grand Blanc
Byerly, Carl Wesley *music educator, academic administrator*
Riley, Ronald Jim *industrial engineer, consultant*

### Grand Haven
Disbrow, Sidney Arden, Jr. *chiropractor*
Johnson, Dorothy A. *foundation administrator*

### Grand Ledge
Evert, Sandra Florence (Sandra Wheeler) *medical/surgical nurse, consultant*

### Grand Rapids
Auwers, Stanley John *motor carrier executive*
Baker, Hollis MacLure *furniture manufacturing company executive*
Barnes, Thomas John *lawyer*

Beals, Paul Archer *religious studies educator*
Becker, Robert Joseph *database consultant, application developer, educator, computer science specialist*
Beeke, Joel Robert *minister, educator, writer*
Bell, Robert Holmes *federal bank*
Biser, Larry *music educator, director*
Bolinder, Scott W. *publishing company executive*
Bolt, Eunice Mildred DeVries *artist*
Botsford, Jon Douglas *lawyer*
Bradshaw, Conrad Allan *retired lawyer*
Brenneman, Hugh Warren, Jr. *judge*
Brinkmeyer, Scott S. *lawyer*
Bursch, John Joseph *lawyer*
Bytwerk, Randall Lee *communication educator*
Carlotti, Ronald John *food scientist*
Carpenter, Joel Allan *historian*
Carpenter, John R. *finance educator*
Chiara, Margaret M. *prosecutor, lawyer*
Currie, William G. *forest products executive*
Curtin, Timothy John *lawyer*
Daniels, Joseph *neuropsychiatrist*
Davis, Henry Barnard, Jr. *lawyer*
DeLapa, Judith Anne *business owner*
DeVries, Robert K. *retired publisher, consultant*
Diekema, Anthony J. *college president, consultant*
Dykstra, William Dwight *management executive, consultant*
Garver, Frederick Merrill *industrial engineering executive*
Giambernardi, Troy A. *research scientist*
Glenn, Michael B. *forest products executive*
Gordon, Dan A. *food service executive*
Hackett, James P. *manufacturing executive*
Harris, Richard W. *law educator, lawyer, accountant*
Horn, Joyce Elaine *music educator*
Hurley, Walter Allison *bishop*
Jackoboice, Sandra Kay *artist*
Jones, Ora McConner *retired foundation administrator*
Kaczmarczyk, Jeffrey Allen *journalist, music critic, dance critic*
Keane, James P. *manufacturing executive*
Keller, Fred P. *engineering company executive*
Kelly, Ruth Ellen *elementary school educator*
Lake, Veronica *director*
Logie, John Hoult *former mayor, lawyer*
Lubbers, Arend Donselaar *retired academic administrator*
Luttikhuizen, Henry M. *art historian, curator*
Maupin, Karin Louise *secondary school educator*
Mavima, Paul *finance educator*
Mayo, David Wayne *sportswriter*
McGarry, John Everett *lawyer*
Mears, Patrick Edward *lawyer*
Meijer, Hank *retail company executive*
Menninga, Clarence *retired geologist*
Messner, James W. *advertising executive*
Miles, Wendell A. *federal judge*
Murray, Mark Andrew *food products executive, former academic administrator, economist*
Paterson, Hattie P *philanthropist*
Pisacreta, Richard *psychology professor*
Posthumus, Richard Earl *former lieutenant governor, farmer*
Purchase-Owens, Francena *marketing professional, consultant, educator*
Quist, Gordon Jay *federal judge*
Sadler, David G(ary) *manufacturing executive*
Schmidt, Gary David *language educator*
Schwanda, Grace Elaine *music educator*
Secchia, Peter F. *forest products executive, former United States ambassador to Italy*
Sherman, Gregory Albert *psychologist*
Shoemaker, Allen L. *psychology professor, consultant*
Sieger, Diana R. *foundation administrator*
Spaulding, Dan *public relations executive*
Staples, David M. *corporate financial executive*
Sturken, Craig C. *retail executive*
Sytsma, Fredric A. *lawyer*
Taylor, Mark Lyman *music educator*
Tiemstra, John Peter *economics professor*
Vande Woude, George Franklin *molecular biologist, cancer researcher*
Van Dyke, Michelle *bank executive*
VanHarn, Gordon Lee *academic administrator*
Verdier, David D'Ooge *ophthalmologist, educator*
Walters, George O. *lawyer*
Watkins, James Kelley *retired urologist*
Webb, Mark Russell *music educator*
Wendt, Vernon Earl *internist, cardiologist*
Williams, Janice H. *business executive*
Wilt, Jeffrey Lynn *pulmonary and critical care physician, educator*
Woodrick, Robert *food products executive*
Zigerelli, Lawrence *retail products company executive*

**Grayling**
Lasby, Terri Darlene *adult education educator*

**Greenbush**
Paulson, James Marvin *retired engineering educator*

**Grosse Ile**
Smith, Veronica Latta *real estate company officer*
Stump, M. Pamela *sculptor*

**Grosse Pointe**
Beltz, Charles Robert *retired engineering executive*
Caldwell, John Thomas, Jr. *communications executive*
Casey, Genevieve M(ary) *librarian, educator*
Goss, James William *lawyer*
Hill, Draper *editorial cartoonist*
Manetta, Richard L. *chemicals executive, lawyer*
Marshall, Douglas William *health research administrator, consultant*
Mengden, Joseph Michael *retired investment banker*
Sphire, Raymond Daniel *anesthesiologist, educator*
Whittaker, Jeanne Evans *retired journalist*
Wilkinson, Warren Scripps *manufacturing executive*

**Grosse Pointe Farms**
Christian, Edward Kieren *broadcasting station executive*

Fromm, Joseph L. *financial consultant*
Krentzin, Earl *sculptor, silversmith*
Obolensky, Marilyn Wall (Mrs. Serge Obolensky) *metals company executive*
Surdam, Robert McClellan *retired banker*
Weingart, Robert Paul *financial consultant*

**Grosse Pointe Park**
Centner, Charles William *lawyer, educator*
Elsila, David August *editor*
Knapp, Mildred Florence *retired social worker*
Krebs, William Hoyt *industrial hygienist, health science association administrator*
Mogk, John Edward *law educator, association executive, consultant*
Orton, Colin George *medical physicist*

**Grosse Pointe Shores**
Holness, Gordon Victor Rix *engineering executive, mechanical engineer*
LaHood, Mary Anne *real estate investor*

**Grosse Pointe Woods**
McWhirter, Glenna Suzanne (Nickie McWhirter) *retired columnist*
Sul, Yi Chul *neurologist*

**Gwinn**
Lasich, Vivian Esther Layne *secondary school educator*

**Hale**
Lixey, Elizabeth Voulgarakis *secondary school educator*

**Harbor Beach**
Falkenberg, Mary Elaine *small business owner*

**Harbor Springs**
Cappel, Constance *educational consultant, writer*
Smith, Wayne Richard *lawyer*

**Harper Woods**
Barba, Lance Elliott *financial consultant, investment advisor*

**Harsens Island**
Woodford, Arthur MacKinnon *retired library director, historian*

**Haslett**
Hotaling, Robert Bachman *urban planner, educator*
Warrington, Willard Glade *retired university official*

**Hastings**
Adrounie, V. Harry *retired military medical service officer, science educator, environmentalist*
Jones, Kensinger *advertising executive, educator*
Yarger, James Richard *protective services official, director*

**Hickory Corners**
Bristol, Norman *lawyer, arbitrator, retired food products executive*
Lauff, George Howard *biologist*

**Highland**
Brown, Ray Kent *biochemist, physician, educator*
Bullard, Willis Clare, Jr. *lawyer*

**Hillsdale**
Frudakis, Anthony Parker *sculptor, educator*
Knecht, Melissa *music educator, musician*
Stewart, David *history professor, researcher*

**Holland**
Cook, James Ivan *clergyman, educator*
De Jong, James Edward *conductor*
Franken, Darrell *counselor, writer, publishing executive*
Garlough, William Glenn *marketing executive*
Haworth, Gerrard Wendell *office furniture manufacturing company executive*
Haworth, Richard G. (Dick Haworth) *office furniture manufacturer*
Holmes, Jack Edward *political science professor*
Nieuwsma, Milton John *writer, journalist*
Nyenhuis, Jacob Eugene *academic administrator*
Schieringa, Paul Kenneth *special education educator, entertainer*
Stynes, Stanley Kenneth *retired chemical engineer, educator*
Van Noord, Diane C. *artist, educator*
Van Voorst, Robert E. *theology educator, minister*
Van Wylen, Gordon John *former college president*
Zuidema, George Dale *surgeon, educator*

**Holly**
Evans Snowden, Audra Lynn *counselor*
Stolpin, William Roger *printmaker*

**Holt**
Smith, Betty W. *librarian*
Wood, Mary Elizabeth *retired secondary school educator, church musician*

**Houghton**
Brown, Richard Edwin *chemistry professor, researcher*
Crittenden, John Charles *engineering educator*
Fink, William Orman *retired federal agency administrator, management consultant*
Heckel, Richard Wayne *metallurgical engineering educator*
Huang, Eugene Yuching *civil engineer, educator*
Hungwe, Kedmon Nyasha *education educator, researcher*
Mishra, Piyush *computer engineer, researcher, educator*
Narain, Amitabh *aerospace and mechanical engineering educator*
Utt, Glenn S., Jr. *retired medical products executive*
Welch, Eric D. *electrical engineer, consultant*
Wray, Kent *academic administrator*
You, Zhanping *civil engineer, educator*

**Houghton Lake**
Manley, Janet Zeegers *retired small business owner*

**Howell**
Rohrabacher, Janet Hammond *genealogist, archivist*
Tupper, Leon F. *manufacturing executive*
Watkins, Curtis WinthroP *artist*

**Idlewild**
Wooley, Geraldine Hamilton *poet, writer*

**Inkster**
Bullock, Steven Carl *lawyer*

**Interlochen**
Kimpton, Jeffrey S. *academic administrator*
Nadji, Taoufik *physics professor, mathematician*

**Ionia**
Ulmer, Evonne Gail *health science association administrator*

**Ironwood**
Rondeau, Clement Robert *petroleum geologist*

**Jackson**
Carrera, Jose *psychiatrist, child psychiatrist, psychoanalyst*
Copeland, Eric *protective services official*
Graham, Donald James *food technologist, hygienic design consultant*
Joos, David W. *energy executive*
Kelly, Robert Vincent, Jr. *metal products executive*
Marcoux, William Joseph *lawyer*
Nugent, Ted (Theodore Anthony Nugent) *musician*
Popp, Nathaniel *archbishop*
Smith, S. Kinnie, Jr. *lawyer*
Smith, Stanton Kinnie, Jr. *lawyer*
Webb, Thomas J. *utilities executive*
Whipple, Kenneth *utilities executive*
Wingblade, Loren Charles *education educator*

**Jenison**
Frye, Della Mae *portrait artist*

**Jerome**
Dillon, Merton Lynn *historian, educator*

**Kalamazoo**
Askew, Thomas Rendall *physics educator, researcher, consultant*
Badra, Robert George *theology studies educator, humanities educator*
Bailey, Judith Irene *academic administrator, consultant*
Bennett, Arlie Joyce *clinical social worker*
Bergy, Dean H. *health products executive*
Breisach, Ernst A. *historian, educator*
Bricker, Luan Alan *medical educator*
Burns, James W. *education educator*
Bus, Roger Jay *lawyer*
Carver, Norman Francis, Jr. *architect, photographer*
Coss, Barbara Sue *humanities educator*
Curry, John Patrick *insurance company executive, management consultant*
Dahlinger, Martha Louise *elementary school educator*
Dybek, Stuart *language educator, writer*
Enslen, Pamela Chapman *lawyer*
Enslen, Richard Alan *federal judge*
Evans, Oliver H. *college administrator*
Gordon, Edgar George *retired lawyer*
Greenfield, John Charles *biochemist*
Grotzinger, Laurel Ann *librarian, educator*
Haenicke, Diether Hans *academic administrator emeritus, educator*
Hall, Curtis E. *lawyer*
Hudson, Roy Davage *retired pharmaceutical executive*
Hueng, Chiayang James *educator*
Huffman, David Lee *chemistry professor, researcher*
Julien, Catherine *history professor*
Kasdorf, Thomas Roger *music educator*
Kim, Moonkoo *marine environmental chemist*
Kujawski, Daniel *science educator*
Lander, Joyce Ann *retired nursing educator, retired medical/surgical nurse*
Lawrence, William Joseph, Jr. *retired corporate executive*
Light, Christopher Upjohn *freelance/self-employed writer, photographer*
Light, John Richard *sculptor*
Litynski, Daniel Mitchell *engineering educator, retired military officer*
MacMillan, Stephen P. *health products executive*
Marshall, Vincent de Paul *industrial microbiologist, researcher*
Mc Allister, Lester Belden *economics professor*
Ortiz-Button, Olga *social worker*
Palchick, Bernard S. *academic administrator, art educator*
Petersen, Anne C. (Cheryl Petersen) *foundation administrator, educator*
Ratner, Carl Joseph *opera stage director, baritone*
Saber, Alan A. *surgeon*
Showalter, Shirley H. *academic administrator*
Toledo-Pereyra, Luis Horacio *transplant surgeon, researcher, historian educator*
Truesdell, Timothy L. *private investor*
Vander Weg, Phillip Dale *art educator, academic administrator, sculptor*
Webber, John Charles *composer, music educator*
Yang, Li *computer scientist, educator*

**Keego Harbor**
Gee, Sharon Lynn *funeral director, educator*

**Kentwood**
Yovich, Daniel John *chemist, educator*

**Laingsburg**
Collins, Mary Alice *psychotherapist, social worker*

**Lake Angelus**
Kresge, Bruce Anderson *retired physician*

**Lake Orion**
Bernia, John Charles, Jr. *secondary school educator*
Leonard, Jacquelyn Ann *retired elementary school educator*
Robinson, Marietta S. *lawyer*

**Lakeview**
Clingan, Nancy Beth *secondary school educator*

**Lanse**
Augustine, Henry Joseph *secondary school educator*

**Lansing**
Arends, Herman Joseph *former insurance company executive*
Baker, Frederick Milton, Jr. *lawyer*
Brewer, Mark Courtland *lawyer*
Brown, Nancy Field *editor*
Cavanagh, Michael Francis *state supreme court justice*
Cawthorne, Dennis Otto *lawyer*
Cherry, John D., Jr. *lieutenant governor*
Christian, Sandra Svec *retired state official*
Couto, C. Douglass *state agency administrator*
Cox, Mike *state attorney general*
Demlow, Daniel J. *lawyer*
Ewert, Quentin Albert *lawyer, consultant*
Feight, Theodore J. *financial planner*
Fink, Joseph Allen *lawyer*
Fisher, John W. *insurance company executive*
Flanagan, Michael P. *school system administrator*
Foster, Joe C., Jr. *lawyer, lawyer*
Granholm, Jennifer Mulhern *governor*
Hetrick, Esther *music educator*
Hoffman, Philip Edward *legislative consultant*
Hopgood, Hoon-Yung *state representative*
Howard, David L. *conductor, baritone*
Johnson, Veronica Ann Wilkerson *library director*
Kelley, Frank Joseph *lawyer, former state attorney general*
Kepros, John Paul *trauma surgeon*
Kleine, Robert J. *state official*
Kulick, Peter J. *lawyer*
Land, Terri Lynn *state official*
Looyenga, Roger L. *insurance company executive*
Markman, Stephen J. *state supreme court justice*
Marvin, David Edward Shreve *lawyer*
McKeague, David William *judge*
Nicholas, Caroline Jean *retired nurse, consultant*
Nsofor, Leslie Monagolum *food scientist, researcher*
Reason, Elizabeth M. *health facility administrator*
Shirtum, Earl Edward *retired civil engineer*
Stockmeyer, Norman Otto *law educator, consultant*
Stowers, Mark David *chemicals executive*
Straus, Kathleen Nagler *academic administrator, educator*
Suhrheinrich, Richard Fred *federal judge*
Sweet, Margaret Ann *psychologist, educator*
Taylor, Clifford Woodworth *state supreme court justice*
Vincent, Frederick Michael, Sr. *neurologist, educator*
Weiner, William P. *law educator*
Young, Robert P., Jr. *state supreme court justice*

**Lawrence**
Applewhaite, Carlisle S. *special education educator, consultant*
Bourg, Louise Janette *retired secondary school educator*

**Leland**
Small, Hamish *chemist*
Soutas-Little, Robert William *mechanical engineer, educator*

**Lincoln**
Martinico, Jennifer Marie *music educator*

**Livonia**
Baskin, Victoria *child and adolescent psychiatrist*
Cantie, Joseph S. *automotive executive*
Chowdhury, Subir *management consultant*
Drouin, Joe *automotive executive*
Gepford, Barbara Beebe *retired nutrition educator*
Gilbert, Daniel *mortgage company executive*
Haggard, Joan Claire *church musician, piano instructor, accompanist, adjudicator*
Hoffman, Barry Paul *lawyer*
Holtzman, Roberta Lee *French and Spanish language educator*
Kujawa, Sister Rose Marie *academic administrator*
Maibach, Ben C., Jr. *consumer products company executive*
McCotter, Thaddeus George *congressman*
McDowell, Richard William *academic administrator*
McHard, James Lorin *corporate financial executive, freelance/self-employed composer, writer*
Plant, John Charles *automotive equipment company executive*
Uicker, Joseph Bernard *retired engineering company executive*
Valerio, Michael Anthony *diversified financial services company executive*

**Ludington**
Puffer, Richard Judson *retired college chancellor*

**Macomb**
Farmakis, George Leonard *retired education educator*

**Madison Heights**
Janke, Kenneth *investment consultant*
Kafarski, Mitchell I. *chemical processing company executive*

**Mancelona**
Whelan, Joseph L. *neurologist*

**Manistee**
Trussell, Charles Tait *columnist*

**Manistique**
Jeffcott, Janet Bruhn *statistician, consultant*

**Maple City**
Duff, James George *retired finance company executive, automotive executive*

**Marine City**
Brown, Ronald Delano *endocrinologist*
Robinson, Michelle A. *elementary school educator*

**Marquette**
Camerius, James Walter *marketing educator, corporate researcher*
Clumpner, Krista Ellis *library science educator*
Lincke, Eric Theodore *retired surgeon*
Mahmood, Tallat *oncologist, hematologist*
Manning, Robert Hendrick *retired audio-visual services executive*
Nicholson, Howard Lee *history professor*
Pesola, William Ernest *restaurant management executive*

**Marshall**
Hammond, Jane Pamela *adult education educator*

**Mason**
Dart, Kenneth B. *food container manufacturing executive*
Yoakam, Lynn Kelly *harpist, educator*

**Mattawan**
Greene, Timothy James *industrial engineering educator*

**Mesick**
Johnson, David Allen *history and English educator*

**Midland**
Adams, Thomas Walton *corrections official*
Allemang, Arnold A. *chemicals executive*
Barker, Nancy Lepard *university official*
Belton, Betty Kepka *retired art educator, artist*
Burns, Stephanie A. *chemicals executive*
Bus, James Stanley *toxicologist*
Carbone, Anthony J. *chemicals executive*
Chao, Marshall *chemist*
Cook, Phillip H. *chemicals executive*
Davidson, John Hunter *agriculturist*
Dorman, Linneaus Cuthbert *retired chemist*
Dreyfuss, M(ax) Peter *research chemist, educator*
Duncan, Christopher *information technology executive*
Gambrell, Michael R. *chemicals executive*
Gross, Richard M. *chemicals executive*
Grzesiak, Katherine Ann *primary school educator*
Hampton, Leroy *retired chemical company executive*
Hoerneman, Calvin A., Jr. *economics professor*
Holder, Julie Fasone *chemicals executive*
Kalil, Charles James *lawyer, chemicals executive*
Kepler, David E., II, *chemicals executive*
Klosin, Jerzy *research chemist*
Kreinberg, Romeo *chemicals executive*
Liveris, Andrew N. *chemical company executive*
Meister, Bernard John *retired chemical engineer*
Merrington, Adrian *researcher, educator, rheologist*
Merszei, Geoffrey E. *corporate financial executive*
Nowak, Robert Michael *chemist*
Potts, Sandra *library director*
Reinhard, Joao Pedro *chemicals company executive*
Schmidt, William C. *retired chemicals executive*
Veurink, Gary R. *chemicals executive*
Walthie, Theo H. *chemicals executive*

**Milford**
Bennur, Mallikarjuna *automotive executive*
Oliveri, Eugene Alfred *gastroenterologist*

**Millersburg**
Bergstedt, Roger Allen *biologist, researcher*

**Monroe**
Cohn, Morton Ray *lawyer*
Darrow, Kurt L. *manufacturing executive*
DeVries, James E. *historian, educator*
Graham, W. Thomas *lawyer*
Lipford, Rocque Edward *lawyer*
Nuechterlain, James Howard *music educator*
Pixley, Sylvia Kay *artist*

**Montague**
Davis, Robert Leach *retired federal official*

**Mount Clemens**
Gielniak, Michael Gerard *non-profit executive, education consultant*
Robinson, Earl, Jr. *marketing executive, transportation executive, educator, retired air force officer*

**Mount Pleasant**
Beehr, Terry A. *psychology professor*
Dietrich, Richard Vincent *geologist, educator*
Garver, Michael Scott *finance educator*
Jeon, Yongil *economics professor*
Lee, Carl *statistician, educator*
Lynch, John Joseph *lawyer*
Messick, Frederic Morton *librarian*
Orlik, Christina Bear *music educator*
Petrick, Michael Joseph *journalism educator*
Peyrefitte, Ashton George, Jr. *meteorologist, educator*
Primeau, Ronald *literature educator, writer*
Scott, Renay Marie *academic administrator, educator*
Smallwood, Carol *writer*
Traines, Rose Wunderbaum *sculptor, educator*

**Munising**
Hughes, Patti L. *social sciences educator*

**Muskegon**
Akker, Arlene F. *social sciences educator*
Chu, Xuefeng *science educator*
Crummett, Allan Warren *psychologist*

**Naubinway**
Beaudoin, Robert Lawrence *small business owner*

**New Era**
Grubb, Daniel Studd *literature and language professor, priest*

**New Haven**
Shaw, Charles Rusanda *retired government investigator*

**Niles**
Gibbs, Denis Laurel *radiologist*
Marshall, Gerald Francis *optical engineer, consultant, physicist*
Tenney, Jane Morris *real estate developer*

**North Branch**
Stevenson, James Laraway *engineering company executive, electronics engineer, computer engineer, communications engineer, engineering educator*

**Northport**
Schultz, Richard Carlton *plastic surgeon*
Scripps, Douglas Jerry *music educator, conductor*
Thomas, Philip Stanley *economist, educator*

**Northville**
Bohm, Henry Victor *physicist*
Cauley, Patrick C. *lawyer*
Clawson, Curtis J. *manufacturing executive*
Clemens, Michael Terrence *furniture manufacturing representative*
Green, Jody *real estate company executive, real estate broker*
Sawyer, Harriet Behner *retired secondary school educator*
Yost, James A. *manufacturing executive*

**Novi**
Chow, Chi-Ming *retired mathematics professor*
Jeffe, Sidney David *automotive executive, engineer*
Johnson, Anthony *automotive executive*
Kinsey, Charles John *industrial auctioneer, consultant, farmer, cattle breeder*
Ligocki, Kathleen A. *auto parts company executive*
Mallak, James A. *auto parts company executive*
Maniscalco, Joseph *artist, educator*
Nanian, Marjorie Kay *lawyer, photographer, educator*

**Okemos**
Burnett, Jean B. (Mrs. James R. Burnett) *biochemist, educator*
Edwards, Caryn Louise *educational consultant, special education educator*
Klunzinger, Thomas Edward *writer, actor, film director*
Monson, Carol Lynn *osteopath, psychotherapist*
Solo, Robert Alexander *economist, educator*

**Onaway**
Wregglesworth, Kymberli April *social studies educator*

**Onsted**
Freeman, Fred Wesley *forester, educator*

**Orchard Lake**
Majewski, Karen Marie *curator*

**Ossineke**
Larson, Ilene Kay *elementary school educator*

**Owosso**
Acton, David L(awrence) *automobile company executive*
Uptigrove, Kenneth R. *library administrator*

**Oxford**
Smith, Jay Lawrence *financial planning company executive*

**Pentwater**
Noffke, Frank Edward *educational planner, writer, educator*

**Perry**
Suehr, Cindy L. *social studies educator, language educator*

**Petoskey**
Meengs, William Lloyd *cardiologist*
Nicholson, William Noel *clinical neuropsychologist*
Switzer, Carolyn Joan *artist, educator*

**Pigeon**
Maust, Joseph J. *agricultural products supplier*

**Pinckney**
Britton, Clarold Lawrence *lawyer, consultant*

**Plainwell**
Mundo, Paul L. *music educator*

**Plymouth**
Bain, Elaine Rugienius *secondary school educator*
Berry, Charlene Helen *librarian, musician*
deBear, Richard Stephen *library director, consultant*
Haynes, Richard Terry *lawyer*
Leuliette, Timothy D. *automotive executive*
Longhofer, Ronald Stephen *lawyer*
Lou, Zheng (David) *technical specialist*
Martina, Carlo Jack *lawyer*
Moore-Viculin, Charlotte Anne *artist, musician*
Robinson, Logan Gilmore *lawyer*
Vlcek, Donald Joseph, Jr. *food products executive, wholesale distribution executive, writer*

**Pontiac**
Beemer, Dawn Marie *public health service officer*
Hampton, Philip Michael *consulting engineering company executive*
Hatten, Angela *secondary school educator*
Love, Sharon Irene *elementary school educator*
Wang, Yucong *engineering executive*

**Port Huron**
Moss, Carl Arthur *psychologist*
Rowark, Maureen *fine arts photographer*
Wu, Harry Pao-Tung *retired librarian*

**Portage**
Brown, John Wilford *health products executive*
Seely, Robert Eugene *management consultant*
Taylor, Karen Lynn *biology educator*
Zhang, Charles C. *financial planner*

**Quinnesec**
Opolka, Jayme Lyn *medical writer, researcher*

**Rapid City**
Ring, Ronald Herman *lawyer*

**Redford**
Behen, Daniel James *elementary school educator*
Hoeft, Stacy *principal*
Hoge, Ann Cancilla *music educator*
Karpinski, Huberta *library trustee*
Schnuell-Ruth, Karen D. *elementary school educator*

**Reed City**
Rautiola, Norman A. *small business owner, manufacturing executive*

**Republic**
Wixtrom, Donald Joseph *translator*

**Richland**
Atkinson, Arthur John, Jr. *pharmacologist, educator, consultant*

**Riverdale**
Kirby, Kent Bruce *artist, educator*

**Riverview**
Wilczynski, Christie Louise *secondary school educator, counselor*

**Rochester**
Clark, Jon Brian *psychologist*
Elder, Ken R. *physicist, educator*
Estes, Todd A. *historian*
Fazzalari, Frank *cardiothoracic surgeon*
Haskell, Richard Edmund *engineering educator*
Kleimola, Sharon Leigh *retired elementary school educator*
Loh, Robert N. K. *engineering educator*
Packard, Sandra Podolin *education educator, consultant*
Polis, Michael Philip *engineering educator*
Russi, Gary D. *academic administrator*
Yang, Lianxiang *optical engineer, educator*

**Rochester Hills**
Badalament, Robert Anthony *urologist, oncologist*
Denton, Lawrence A. *automotive executive*
Eisenhower, Laurie *performing company executive*
Fritzsche, Hellmut *physics professor*
Parker, Catherine L. *theater educator*
Romero, Josefino Tabernilla *nurse anesthetist*
Unakar, Nalin Jayantilal *biological sciences educator*

**Rockford**
Loux, Jonathan Dale *business development consultant, director*

**Rogers City**
Lamp, Brenda S. *elementary school educator*

**Romeo**
Stryker, James William *retired automotive executive, former military officer*
Tsukamoto, Daniel *piano instructor, church organist*

**Roscommon**
Mainprize, Donald Charles *minister, writer*
Thiel, John Robert *history professor*

**Roseville**
Diez, Gerald F. *manufacturing executive, advertising executive*
Lane, Debra Lillian *secondary school educator*
Pires, Luis A. *cardiologist, researcher*

**Royal Oak**
Britt, Stephen Thomas *medical educator*
Cook, Noel Robert *manufacturing executive*
Dworkin, Howard Jerry *nuclear medicine physician, educator*
Ernstoff, Raina Marcia *neurologist*
Fragomeni, James Mark *mechanical engineer, educator*
LaBan, Myron Miles *physician, hospital administrator*
O'Neill, William Walter *physician, educator*
Pike, Charlene Helen *retired secondary school educator*
Pricer, Wayne Francis *counseling consultant*
Proctor, Conrad Arnold *physician*
Stanalajczo, Greg Charles *computer company executive*

**Saginaw**
Carlson, Robert James *bishop*
Chaffee, Paul Charles *newspaper editor, publisher*
Cline, Thomas William *real estate leasing company executive, management consultant*
Coughlin, Jeannine Marie *music educator*
Eschmann, Paul David *music educator, mathematics educator*
Evans, Harold Edward *banker*
Ferlinz, Jack *cardiologist, educator*
Hammel, Iriana Simona *geriatrician*
Houshiar, Bobbie Kay *language arts educator*

**Pontiac** → continued

**Saint Clair Shores**
Manning, John Warren III *retired surgeon, medical educator*
Marsh, Doris Elaine *retired ballet school owner*
Moyer, Genevieve J. *counselor*
Scharffe, William Granville *academic administrator, educator*
Shinaver, Alan L. *educator*
Zanot, Craig Allen *lawyer*

**Saint Clair Shores**
Hausner, John Herman *retired judge*
Kaminski, Margaret *retired librarian*
Rodriguez, Daniela M. *plastic surgeon*
Ryan, Harold Martin *judge*
Skoney, Sophie Essa *educational administrator*
Smith, Frank Earl *retired trade association administrator*

**Saint Joseph**
King, George Raleigh *retired manufacturing executive*
Rommel, James Joseph *elementary school educator*
Wood, Dirk Gregory *surgeon, physician, forensic consultant*

**Saline**
Anderson, Austin Gothard *lawyer, consultant, academic administrator*
Cruden, Robert William *botany educator*

**Saugatuck**
Genetski, Robert James *economist*

**Sault Sainte Marie**
Balfantz, Gary Leonard *communications and drama educator*
Miller, Jennifer Jean *lawyer, law educator*
Morello, Steven John *lawyer*
Youngblood, Betty J. *academic administrator*

**Scottville**
Pollock, Kevin Alexander *academic administrator*

**Shelby Township**
Aukland, Neil Ralph *electronics engineer, researcher*
Chalil, Joseph Mathew *sales executive, consultant*
Fillbrook, Thomas George *telephone company executive*
Luz, Kyle Stuart *physics educator*
Nagy, Louis Leonard *engineering executive, researcher*

**Skandia**
Johnson, Judy M. *artist, writer*

**Sodus**
Handy, Virginia Mae *writer*

**South Haven**
LaRocque, Linda Lou *interior designer, educator, playwright*
Llorens, Merna Gee *elementary school educator, retired music educator*

**South Lyon**
Palmer, Kimberly Anne *director*

**Southfield**
Alapont, José Maria *automotive executive*
Andreoff, Christopher Andon *lawyer*
Barnett, Marilyn *advertising executive*
Bassey, Ronald D. *tax attorney*
Battah, Hammam Jamil *civil engineer, utilities executive*
Bindschadler, David E. *mathematician, department chairman, application developer*
Boyce, Daniel Hobbs *finance company executive*
Brooks, Ernie L. *lawyer*
Caponigro, Jeffrey Ralph *public relations counselor*
Catallo, Heather *newscaster*
Chambers, Charles MacKay *academic administrator, lawyer, consultant*
Darling, Robert Howard *lawyer*
Dawson, Dennis Ray *lawyer, manufacturing executive*
Dean, Kelly A. *principal*
DelGrosso, Douglas G. *manufacturing executive*
Fieger, Geoffrey Nels *lawyer*
Gayle, Monica *broadcast journalist*
Gleichman, John Alan *protective services official*
Goulday, Glenn Charles *manufacturing executive*
Graves, Ray Reynolds *retired judge*
Gregory, Karl Dwight *economics professor, consultant*
Hotelling, Harold *law and economics educator*
Ibrahim, Ibrahim N. *bishop*
Jackson, Roger A. *human resources specialist, automotive executive*
Kalter, Alan *advertising agency executive*
Lee, James Edward, Jr. *educational consultant*
Leuchtman, Stephen Nathan *lawyer*
Lynch, George Michael *auto parts manufacturing executive*
Maibach, Ben C. III *construction company executive*
Makupson, Amyre Porter *broadcast executive*
Margolis, Sherry *newscaster*
Martin, Marcella Edric *retired community health nurse*
McKeen, Alexander C. *retired engineering executive, foundation executive*
Miller, Nancy Ellen *computer scientist, consultant*
Morganroth, Mayer *lawyer*
Naber, Faith *retired librarian, educator*
Ninivaggi, Daniel A. *lawyer*
O'Hara, John Paul III *orthopedic surgeon*
Perez-Cruet, Mick (Miguelangelo) Jorge *neurosurgeon, educator*
Ponitz, John Allan *lawyer*
Porter, Thomas W.B. *lawyer*
Primo, Joan Erwina *retail and real estate consulting business owner*
Rawden, David *financial services company executive*
Ritchie, Alexander Buchan *lawyer*
Rochkind, Louis Philipp *lawyer*

Rossiter, Robert E. *interior auto parts manufacturing executive*
Saidi, Reza F *researcher*
Sedler, Rozanne Friedlander *social worker, educator*
Sherbin, David M. *lawyer*
Shields, Robert Emmet *merchant banker, lawyer*
Sobel, Robert A. *retired orthopedic surgeon*
Song, Xubin *mechanical engineer, researcher*
Stinger, Fanchon *newscaster*
Sullivan, Robert Emmet, Jr. *lawyer*
Thimotheose, Kadakampallil George *psychologist*
Thomas, Judy Janet *reporter, public health service officer*
Timmons, Robbie *news anchor*
Toll, Sheldon Samuel *lawyer*
Tuttle, Edward X. *architect, lawyer*
Vandenberghe, James H. *financial executive*
Weiner, Karen Colby (Karen Lynn Colby) *psychologist, lawyer*
Willingham, Edward Bacon, Jr. *ecumenical minister, administrator*
Winzenreid, James Ernest *lawyer, entrepreneur*
Zubroff, Leonard Saul *surgeon*

### Spring Arbor
Thompson, Stanley B. *church administrator*

### Spring Lake
Bussard, Janice Wingeier *retired secondary school educator*

### Sterling Heights
Bohy, Ric *writer, commentator*
Fleming, Mac Arthur *retired labor union administrator*
Lane, Wendall Chenney, Jr. *automotive engineer*
Novak, Joseph Anthony *law librarian*
Stephens, Karen Lorene *librarian*

### Sturgis
Hair, Robert Eugene *editor, writer, historian*

### Suttons Bay
Periard, Douglas Dee *social studies educator*

### Swartz Creek
Russell, Charles Harry *music educator, restaurant manager*

### Sylvan Lake
Derdarian, Christine Anne *lawyer*

### Taylor
Barry, Alan H. *consumer products company executive*
Coleman, Fay *literature and language educator, director*
Gusky, Stacy L *private school educator*
Hirsch, David L. *lawyer*
Hunt, Brian Keith *special education educator*
Lavery, Ian C. *colon and rectal surgeon, medical association administrator*
Leekley, John Robert *lawyer*
Manoogian, Richard Alexander *manufacturing executive*
Rosowski, Robert Bernard *manufacturing executive*
Wadhams, Timothy *consumer products company executive*

### Tecumseh
Herrick, Todd W. *manufacturing executive*

### Three Rivers
Boyer, Nicodemus Elijah *chemist, consultant*

### Traverse City
Alzuny, Thomas *secondary school educator*
Bullis, Jo Louise *social services administrator, educator*
Burton, Betty June *retired pastor*
Clous, James M. *electrical equipment company executive, engineer*
Czarny, Thomas Gerard *secondary school educator*
Faulmann, Roger Ray *retired music educator*
Frick, James Carlton *physician assistant, director*
Parsons, John Thoren *manufacturing executive*
Quandt, Joseph Edward *lawyer, educator*
VanderKolk, Mary DeDecker *nursing educator*
Weaver, Elizabeth A. *state supreme court justice*
Zimmerman, Paul Albert *retired academic administrator, minister*

### Trenton
Cicotte, Melony *elementary school educator*
Go, Benedict Anthony *internist*
Tang, Cyrus *investment company executive*
Wukovits, John Francis *secondary school educator, writer*

### Troy
Adderley, Terence Edward *human resources executive*
Alterman, Irwin Michael *lawyer*
Arbuckle, Brad B. *lawyer*
Arking, Lucille Musser *nurse, epidemiologist*
Austin, Karen *retail executive*
Baker, Vernon G., II, *lawyer*
Barton, Stanley L. *ophthalmologist, consultant*
Battenberg, J. T. III *automotive company executive*
Blahnik, John G. *electronics executive*
Buschmann, Siegfried *retired manufacturing executive*
Butler, Kevin M. *electronics executive*
Camden, Carl T. *human resources company executive*
Cunningham, Gary H. *lawyer*
Dellinger, Robert J. *corporate financial executive*
DeSantis, Mike G. *social studies educator*
Elder, Irma *retail executive*
Gelder, John William *lawyer*
Golusin, Millard R. *obstetrician, gynecologist*
Haron, David Lawrence *lawyer*
Healy, Karen *automotive executive*
Hillegonds, Paul *former state legislator*
Hilton, Michael E. *lawyer*
Kruse, John Alphonse *lawyer*
Lobo, Carlos *automotive executive*

---

Lueken, Harold W. *retail executive*
Macher, Frank E. *automotive executive*
Mahone, Barbara Jean *automotive executive*
Marshall, John Elbert III *foundation executive*
May, Alan Alfred *lawyer*
McClure, Charles G. *automotive executive*
Meerschaert, Joseph Richard *physician*
Meyers, Christine Laine *marketing and media executive, consultant*
Miller, Robert Stevens, Jr. *automotive executive*
Moore, Daniel Michael *lawyer*
Nefske, Donald Joseph *engineer*
O'Neal, Rodney *automotive company executive*
Opie, John D. *retired electric power industry executive*
Pasricha, Atul *automotive executive*
Pearce, Harry Jonathan *lawyer, manufacturing executive*
Potts, Anthony Vincent *optometrist, orthokeratologist*
Rapson, Richard (Rip Rapson) *foundation administrator*
Sastry, Shivashankar Kudur *retired entomologist*
Schafer, Sharon Marie *anesthesiologist*
Sharf, Stephan *automotive executive*
Sloan, Hugh Walter, Jr. *automotive executive*
Strome, Stephen *distribution company executive*
Thoms, David Moore *lawyer*
Walker, Bette *automotive executive*
Walker, Bette M. *information technology executive*
Webster, Robert Byron *lawyer*
White, James, Jr. *psychiatric, mental health nurse, consultant*
Zhenyu, Kong *industrial engineer*

### University Center
Boyse, Peter Dent *academic administrator*
Clarey, Timothy Lee *geologist, educator*
Gilbertson, Eric Raymond *academic administrator, lawyer*
Hall, David McKenzie *business and management educator*
Hill, Alan Gordon *sociologist, educator*

### Utica
Egan, Ron *corporate financial executive*

### Walled Lake
Gillespie, J. Martin *sales and distribution company executive*
Remer, Deborah Jane *elementary school educator*

### Warren
Bell, Julie Marie *health facility administrator, consultant*
Cutter, Jeffrey S. *music educator*
Herbst, Jan Francis *physicist, researcher*
Hopp, Anthony James *advertising agency executive*
Kolakowski, Diana Jean *county commissioner*
Zoubareff, Kathy Olga *administrative assistant*

### Waterford
Anderson, Francile Mary *secondary school educator*
Gulda, Edward James *diversified financial services company executive*
Hall, Terrence Lyon *lawyer*
Houston, E(rnest) James, Jr. *banker, consultant*
James, William Ramsay *broadcast executive*
Laing, James Thomas *retired not-for-profit developer*
Randall, Karl W. *air transportation executive, lawyer*

### Watersmeet
Freund, William Frederick *retired art educator, artist*

### West Bloomfield
Barr, Martin *science educator, academic administrator*
Brin, David *writer, astronomer*
Cox, Clifford Ernest *information systems consulting executive, former academic administrator*
Harwood, Julius J. *metallurgist, educator*
Jones, Lewis Arnold, Jr. *physician, radiologist, consultant*
Mamut, Mary Catherine *retired entrepreneur*
Marx, Thomas George *economist*
Rauwerdink, William Jay *accountant*
Sarwer-Foner, Gerald Jacob *psychiatrist, educator*
Sawyer, Howard Jerome *physician*
Simpson, Robert Lee *academic administrator, department chairman, biologist, educator*
Smith, Nancy Hohendorf *sales executive, marketing professional*
Williamson, Marilyn Lammert *literature educator, academic administrator*

### West Branch
Krzyminski, MaryAnn Marie *literature and language educator*

### White Lake
Clyburn, Luther Linn *real estate broker, real estate appraiser*

### Whitehall
Squier, David Louis *manufacturing executive*

### Williamston
Johnson, Tom Milroy *dean, physician, educator*

### Wixom
Sugiyama, Toru Tom *automotive executive*

### Wyandotte
Kaurin, Douglas Edward *protective services official*
Pentiuk, Randall Alan *lawyer*

### Wyoming
Couch, Katrina Denise *elementary school educator*
Nelson, Tami Sue *music educator*

### Yale
Hedge, Janice Faye *secondary school educator*

---

### Ypsilanti
Barnes, James Milton *physics professor, astronomy professor*
Bengtsson, Erling Blöndal *musician, retired music educator*
Boone, Morell Douglas *information technology educator*
Cere, Ronald Carl *languages educator, consultant, researcher*
Eggertsen, John Hale *lawyer*
Evans, Gary Lee *communications educator, consultant*
Fairfield, Richard Thomas *art educator*
Farah, Badie Naiem *computer information systems educator, consultant*
Fox, Diane Porretta *nursing educator*
Harris, Michael *academic affairs administrator, public policy and administration educator*
Kramer, Catherine Ann *elementary school educator*
Lewis-White, Linda Beth *elementary school educator*
Lottie, Adrian Jerome *writer, educator, consultant*
Okafor, Victor O. *journalist, educator*
Peoples, Alice Leigh *not-for-profit executive*
Reifel Werner, Melody Ann *academic administrator*
Robbins, Jerry Hal *educational administration educator*
Stuppard-Byars, Doris J. *minister*
Weinstein, Jay A. *social sciences educator, researcher*
Willis, Craig Dean *academic administrator*

### Zeeland
Volkema, Michael A. *office furniture manufacturer*
Walker, Brian C. *manufacturing executive*

## MINNESOTA

### Ada
Sillerud, Arlen Roger *retired secondary school educator*

### Aitkin
Lane, Chuck J. *real estate developer*

### Alexandria
Weigel, Dennis Philip *orthopedic surgeon*

### Anoka
Chamberlain, Sonja Kay *music educator*
Lindbergh, Reeve *writer, poet*

### Austin
Alcorn, Wallace Arthur *minister, writer*
Budd, Jim *communications manager*
Cavanaugh, James W. *lawyer*
Ettinger, Jeffrey M. *food products executive, lawyer*
Holman, Ralph Theodore *retired biochemistry professor, nutritionist*
Johnson, Joel W. *food products executive*
Rioux, Pierre August *psychiatrist*
Schmid, Harald Heinrich Otto *biochemistry educator, academic administrator*

### Bayport
Garofalo, Donald R. *window manufacturing executive*
Humphrey, James E. *manufacturing executive*

### Bemidji
Bridston, Paul Joseph *strategic management consultant*
Kief, Paul Allan *lawyer*
Martinson, Ida Marie *medical/surgical nurse, educator, physiologist*
Skinner, Jauneth *art educator, graphic artist*
Sterbenk-Lund, Jacquelyn Marie *chemistry educator, biology educator*
Weaver, Will(iam Weller) *language educator, writer*
Wold, Kenneth Jon *music educator*

### Benson
Duncan, J. Brock *music educator*

### Big Lake
Fillafer, Richard *music educator*

### Blaine
Olson, Bruce Van *music educator*

### Bloomington
Bekrenev, Anatoliy *physicist*
Broeker, John Milton *lawyer*
Grinnell, Joseph Fox *lawyer*
Knotek, Robert Frank *retired management consultant, educator*
Kuntz, Lila Elaine *business educator*
Larson, Michael Len *newspaper editor, hospital administrator, publishing executive*
Mooty, John William *lawyer*
Nichols, Donna Mardell *nurse anesthetist*
Ohnsorg, Brian Gregory *music educator, singer*
Ouyang, Jun *electrical engineer, researcher*
Smith, Henry Charles III *symphony orchestra conductor*
Tsu, I-Fei *materials engineer*

### Blue Earth
Siem, Pauline M. *library director*

### Brainerd
Peterson, Donn Neal *forensic engineer, engineering company executive*
Samuelson, Donald B. *former state legislator*

### Brooklyn Park
DeBusk, Charles Richard *engineer, consultant*
Kiland, Lance Edward *art educator*

### Burnsville
Fischer, Michael W. *minister, musician*
Foss, Emma Thoren *retired social worker*
Lakin, James Dennis *allergist, immunologist, director*

---

O'Brien, Gerald James *utilities executive*

### Caledonia
Kranz, Eliott Gregory *music educator*
Kranz, Kimberly Renee *elementary music educator*

### Canby
Larson, Gary Arthur *farmer, financial consultant*

### Chanhassen
Prince, (Prince Rogers Nelson) *musician, actor*
Severson, Roger Allan *bank executive*

### Chaska
Braun, Mary Edna *museum director*
Olin, Peter Joel *landscape architect, educator*

### Chatfield
Opat, Matthew John *lawyer*

### Chisago City
Miller, Robert Carl *retired library director*

### Chisholm
Fleming, Jennifer Renee *history educator, coach*
Peterson, Marjorie *former mayor*

### Circle Pines
Davis, Richard Carlton *rehabilitation services administrator*
Lahann, Jon Clifford *music educator*

### Coleraine
Jones, Gail *elementary school educator*

### Collegeville
Hassler, Jon Francis *novelist*
Reinhart, Dietrich Thomas *academic administrator, social studies educator*
Sayles, Letory Bruno *retired priest, monk*

### Coon Rapids
Bordner, Patricia Anne *insurance agent, writer*
Vogel, Scott Charles *music educator*
Wilson, Sylvia Alyce *musician, educator*

### Cottage Grove
Hudnut, Robert Kilborne *clergyman, writer*
Russell, Christopher John *secondary school educator, music educator*

### Crookston
Balke, Victor H. *bishop*

### Detroit Lakes
Stowman, David L. *lawyer*

### Duluth
Amberg, Deborah Ann *lawyer*
Aufderheide, Arthur Carl *pathologist*
Bowman, Roger Manwaring *real estate company officer*
Burns, Richard Ramsey *lawyer*
Gallian, Joseph Anthony *mathematics professor*
Johnson, Arthur Gilbert *microbiology educator*
Latto, Lewis M. *broadcast executive*
McKee, David Charles *neurologist*
Morath, Max Edward *entertainer, composer, writer*
Nelson, Dennis Lee *finance educator*
Pearce, Donald Joslin *retired librarian*
Rapp, George Robert (Rip Rapp) *geology and archeology educator*
Salmela, David Daniel *architect*
Schroeder, Fred Erich Harald *humanities educator*
Stauber-Johnson, Elizabeth Jane *retired elementary school educator*
Tezla, Albert *language educator*
Trachte, George Joseph *pharmacology educator*
Whiteman, Richard Frank *architect*
Ziegler, Richard J. *dean, educator*

### Eagan
Clemens, T. Pat *manufacturing executive*
Gouin, Warner Peter *information technology consultant*
Johnson, Jaren Lee *lawyer*
Sievwright, Julia Ann *elementary school educator*
Simon, Barry Philip *lawyer, air transportation executive*
Steenland, Douglas M. *air transportation executive*
Todd, John Joseph *lawyer*

### Eden Prairie
Arthur, Lindsay Grier *retired judge, editor, writer*
Borlik, Robert W. *information technology executive*
Carver, Gloria Jean *documentation specialist*
Cervilla, Constance Marlene *marketing consultant*
Childress, Brad *professional football coach*
Feuss, Linda Anne Upsall *lawyer*
Gilbert, James H. *lawyer, former state supreme court justice*
Hanson, Dale S. *retired bank executive*
Hardman, Harold Francis *pharmacology educator*
Henningsen, Peter, Jr. *manufacturing executive*
Higgins, Robert Arthur *electrical engineer, educator, consultant*
Jackson, Darren Richard *retail executive*
Jackson, Michael L. *wholesale distribution executive*
Johnson, Brad *professional football player*
Johnson, Howard Arthur, Jr. *corporate executive, operations analyst, financial officer*
Knickerbocker, Vicky Ann *academic administrator*
Knous, Pamela K. *wholesale distribution executive*
Lindbloom, Chad M. *transportation executive*
Luther, William P. *former congressman*
McCombs, Billy Joe (Red McCombs) *professional football team executive*
Nilles, John Michael *lawyer*
Noddle, Jeffrey *retail and food distribution executive*
Radunz, Paul A. *transportation executive*
Smoot, Fred *professional football player*
Switz, Robert E. *telecommunications executive*
Thompson, Sally Ann *editor*
Verdoorn, D.R. (Sid) *food service executive*
Wiehoff, John P. *trucking executive*

Woods, Gary V. *professional football team executive, former professional basketball team executive, automotive executive*

**Edina**
Anderson, Gregory Shane *insurance executive*
Bakken, Eric Allen *lawyer*
Bean, Glen Atherton *entrepreneur*
Bisping, Bruce Henry *photojournalist*
Brown, Charles Eugene *retired electronics company executive*
Brown, Laurence David *retired bishop*
Burk, Robert S. *lawyer*
Campbell, James Robert *retired bank executive*
Fenwick, Sheridan Mellon *psychologist, director*
Finkelstein, Phil *retail executive*
Froemming, Herbert Dean *retired retail executive*
Gottesman, Irving I. *psychologist, educator*
Kunin, Myron *hair care company executive*
Markgraf, Cheryl Lee *church musician, conductor*
Neff, Fred Leonard *lawyer*
Pauley, Marlene Joan *musician, conductor*
Putnam, Frederick Warren, Jr. *bishop*
Rucker, Richard Douglas, Jr. *emergency physician*
Sandy, Lewis Gordon *physician, healthcare executive*
Schwarzrock, Shirley Pratt *author, educator*
Tagatz, George Elmo *retired obstetrician, gynecologist, educator*
Van Beek, Allen Lester *plastic surgeon*
Worthing, Carol Marie *retired minister*

**Elk River**
Richardson, Mark P. *protective services official, educator*

**Ellsworth**
Shurr, George W. *geologist, consultant*

**Elmore**
Kortgard, Karen Marie *special education educator, counselor*

**Ely**
Sagen, Harry Bradley *education educator*

**Elysian**
Thayer, Edna Louise *health facility administrator*

**Excelsior**
Bilka, Paul Joseph *retired physician*
Fenske, Jerald Allan *minister*
Martinson, Elmer James *retired surgeon*
Parker, Robert Chauncey Humphrey *clergyman, publishing executive*

**Faribault**
Collins, Ruth Ann *principal*

**Farmington**
Wurdeman, Lew Edward *Internet company executive, consultant*

**Forest Lake**
Marchese, Ronald Thomas *ancient history and archaeology educator*

**Frontenac**
Hedin, Robert Alexander *writer*

**Glenwood**
Tessman, Wes *secondary school educator*

**Golden Valley**
Ainsworth, Louis Lynde *lawyer, manufacturing executive*
Allen, Martin *chemistry educator, consultant*
Harrison, David D. *corporate financial executive*
Hogan, Randall J. *manufacturing executive, electronics executive*
Leppik, Margaret White *municipal official*
Savitt, Steven Lee *computer scientist*
Schlichting, William Henry *lawyer, writer*
Spake, Mary Barbara *music educator*

**Goodridge**
Hanson, Norma Lee *farmer*

**Grand Marais**
Dupre, Lonnie *arctic explorer, writer, photographer*
Hattery, Robert Wilber *political science educator*
Hennessy, William Joseph *prosecutor*
Napadensky, Hyla Sarane *engineering consultant*

**Grand Rapids**
Hall, Frieda Atlas *history educator*
King, Sheryl Jayne *secondary school educator, counselor*
Merrill, Arthur Lewis *retired theologian*

**Hallock**
Malm, Roger Charles *lawyer*

**Hamel**
Tiller, Thomas C. *manufacturing executive*

**Harmony**
Webster, Jeffrey Leon *graphic designer*

**Hastings**
Avent, Sharon L. Hoffman *manufacturing company executive*
Orr, Jennie Marie (Jennie Thomas) *family physician*

**Hibbing**
Calligan, William Dennis *retired life insurance company executive*

**Hopkins**
Dunlap, William DeWayne, Jr. *advertising agency executive*

**Inver Grove Heights**
Howarth, Mark Evans *secondary school educator*
Johnson, John D. *grain company executive*
Kastelic, David Allen *lawyer*
Koenig, Robert August *minister, educator*
Schmitz, John *grain company executive*

**La Crescent**
Gelatt, Charles Daniel *manufacturing executive*

**Lake Crystal**
Pawlitschek, Donald Paul *management consultant*

**Lake Elmo**
Schultz, Clarence John *minister*
Tomljanovich, Esther M. *retired judge*

**Lake Lillian**
Marquardt, Steve Robert *advocate*

**Lakeville**
Setterholm, Jeffrey Miles *systems engineer*

**Lauderdale**
Resch, Joseph Anthony *neurologist*

**Lindstrom**
Messin, Marlene Ann *plastics company executive*

**Lino Lakes**
Jezierski, Scott *wireless monitoring, security, and surveillance company executive*

**Little Falls**
Morgan, Mary Jo *school system administrator*
Perfetti, Robert Nickolas *educational consultant*

**Madison**
Husby, Donald Evans *engineering company executive*
Omland, Kim Marie *music educator, department chairman*

**Mahtomedi**
Brainerd, Richard Charles *human resources executive, consultant, educator*
Holmen, Reynold Algott Emanuel *chemist*

**Mankato**
Benner, Autumn Rae *science educator*
Dumke, Melvin Philip *dentist*
Friend, Donald Agar *geographer, educator*
Janc, John J. *language educator*
Lopez, Jose Javier *geographer, educator*
McCarl, David *costume designer, educator*
Nickerson, James Findley *retired education educator*
Orvick, George Myron *religious organization administrator, minister*
Preska, Margaret Louise Robinson *historian, educational association administrator*
Purscell, Keith William *minister*
Schreier, Bradley *management executive*
Taylor, Glen A. *direct mail and technology executive, professional sports team executive*

**Maple Grove**
Boyd, Kelly A. *lawyer, law educator*
Kirpes, Anne Irene *elementary school educator*
Ones, Deniz S. *psychologist, educator*

**Maple Plain**
Erdmann, John Baird *environmental engineer*

**Mapleton**
John, Hugo Herman *natural resources educator*

**Maplewood**
St. Germain, Sharon Marie *writer*

**Marcell**
Aldrich, Richard John *agronomist, educator*

**Marine On Saint Croix**
Gavin, Robert Michael, Jr. *educational consultant*

**Marshall**
Beadle, John M. *food products executive*
Bonnstetter, Rhonda S. *education educator*
Burr, Tracy L. *food products executive*
Danahar, David C. *academic administrator, historian, educator*
Meffert, Robert Lee *music educator*
Paskach, David M. *lawyer, food products executive*
Pichaske, David Richard *language educator*
Pippin, M. Lenny *food products executive*
Schwan, Alfred *food products executive*
Van Overbeke, Debbie Ann *education educator*

**Medford**
Paschke, Jerry Bryan *lawyer*

**Medina**
McConnell, Mary Patricia *lawyer*

**Mendota Heights**
Frechette, Peter Loren *dental products executive*

**Milaca**
Wig, Robert Curtis *retired music educator, conductor*

**Minneapolis**
Aamoth, Gordon M. *medical association administrator*
Abi-Ghanem, Georges Victor *civil engineer, environmental engineer*
Ackerman, Eugene *biophysics professor*
Adams, John Stephen *geography educator*
Agyenkwah, Kennedy Seth *communications executive*
Ahern, Michael James *lawyer*
Ahlers, Linda L. *retail executive*
Alton, Ann Leslie *judge, lawyer, educator*
Anderson, Eric Scott *lawyer*
Anderson, John Edward *mechanical engineering educator*
Anderson, Leslie J. *lawyer*
Anderson, Richard H. *health insurance company executive, former air transportation executive*
Arbisi, Paul Anthony *psychologist, educator*
Arendt, Elizabeth Ann *orthopedist, educator*
Ariyur, Kartik Balasubramanian *control systems engineer, researcher*
Atwood, John Brian *dean*
Augustus, Seimone *professional basketball player*

Avella, Joseph Ralph *business professor*
Bache, Robert James *physician, medical educator*
Bader, Kathleen M. *chemicals executive*
Bagan, Mark G. *grain exchange executive*
Baillie, James Leonard *lawyer*
Baker, John Stevenson (Michael Dyregrov) *writer*
Bales, Kent Roslyn *language educator*
Bancroft, Ann E. *polar explorer*
Banerjee, Subir Kumar *science educator*
Beilman, Greg J. *medical educator, researcher*
Berens, William Joseph *lawyer*
Berg, Thomas Kenneth *lawyer*
Bergerson, David Raymond *lawyer*
Berry, David J. *former financial services company executive*
Berryman, Robert Glen *finance educator, consultant*
Berscheid, Ellen S. *psychology professor, writer, researcher*
Binger, Erika L. *foundation administrator*
Bingham, Christopher *statistics educator*
Birk, Peggy J. *foundation administrator*
Blackburn, Henry Webster, Jr. *retired epidemiologist*
Blackwell, Todd V. *human resources specialist*
Blaes, Anne Hudson *internist*
Boelter, Philip Floyd *real estate company officer, construction executive*
Bonneville, Katherine Ann *human resources specialist, consultant*
Boone, Bret Robert *professional baseball player*
Borger, John Philip *lawyer*
Bouchard, Thomas Joseph, Jr. *psychology professor, researcher*
Bowie, Norman Ernest *university official, educator*
Brand, Steve Aaron *lawyer*
Branson, Timothy E. *lawyer*
Brasket, Curt Justin *systems analyst*
Breimayer, Joseph Frederick *patent lawyer*
Bress, Michael E. *retired lawyer*
Brink, David Ryrie *lawyer*
Brown, Robert John *social sciences educator, consultant*
Bruininks, Robert H. *academic administrator, psychologist, educator*
Bruner, Philip Lane *lawyer*
Buchwald, Henry *surgeon, educator, researcher*
Buckingham, Elizabeth C. *lawyer*
Buhrmaster, Robert C. *manufacturing executive*
Buratti, Dennis P. *lawyer*
Burchell, Howard Bertram *retired internist*
Burns, Matthew Kevin *psychology professor*
Busdicker, Gordon Gene *retired lawyer*
Campbell, Jon R. *diversified financial services company executive*
Caplan, Allan Hart *lawyer*
Carlson, Arne Helge *former governor*
Carlson, Jennie Peaslack *bank executive*
Carr, Peter William *chemistry professor*
Casey, Dwane *professional basketball player*
Cattanach, Robert Edward, Jr. *lawyer*
Chakraborty, Sombuddha *research scientist*
Champlin, Steven Kirk *lawyer*
Chapman, David Wilfred *education educator*
Chavers, Blanche Marie *pediatrician, educator, researcher*
Chemberlin, Peg *minister, religious organization administrator*
Chipman, John Somerset *economist, educator*
Christiansen, Jay David *lawyer*
Christopherson, Howard M. *artist*
Ciresi, Michael Vincent *lawyer*
Clary, Bradley G. *lawyer, educator*
Clemence, Roger Davidson *landscape architect, educator*
Cohen, Andrew David *language educator, applied linguist*
Cole, Phillip Allen *lawyer*
Collins, Arthur D., Jr. *medical products executive*
Conn, Gordon Brainard, Jr. *lawyer*
Constantine, Katherine A. *lawyer*
Cook, William M. *manufacturing executive*
Cooper, William Allen *bank executive*
Cope, Lewis *journalist*
Corrigan, Frederic W. *agricultural products executive*
Cowles, John, Jr. *publishing executive, women's sports promoter, philanthropist*
Cowles, John Jay III *investment company executive, entrepreneur*
Crabtree, Vicki Gail *musician*
Cracchiolo, James M. *diversified financial services company executive*
Craig, James Lynn *physician, health services administrator*
Croll, Jillian Kathleen *dietician, researcher*
Crosby, Jacqueline Garton *newspaper editor, journalist*
Cunningham, Bruce Langdon *plastic and reconstructive surgeon, educator*
Curler, Jeffrey H. *packaging manufacturing executive*
Cussler, Edward Lansing, Jr. *chemical engineer, educator*
Dale, John Sorensen *investment company executive, portfolio manager*
Dallas, H. James *medical products executive*
Dalluge, Joseph James *chemist*
Danielson, James Walter *retired research microbiologist*
Davis, Howard Ted *engineering educator*
Davis, Michael J. *judge*
Davis, Richard K. *bank executive*
deBruin Sample, Anne *human resources specialist*
DeNavaez, Denny *health facility administrator*
Diemand, Kim Eugene *human resources executive*
DiGangi, Frank Edward *academic administrator*
Dimond, Robert B. *food products executive*
Diviney, Craig David *lawyer*
Domino, Constance Mae *genetics researcher*
Dorenkamp, Theodore III *lawyer*
Doroschak, John Z. *dentist, consultant*
Doty, David Singleton *federal judge*
Drake, Dallas Sumner *researcher*
Dunn, Brian J. *retail executive*
Durkin, G. Michael *food products executive*
Durocher, Vernie C. (Skip), Jr. *lawyer*
Dworkin, Martin *microbiologist, educator*
Dykstra, Dennis Dale *physiatrist*
Eck, George Gregory *lawyer*
Edwardson, Sandra *dean, nursing educator*

Elm, Dawn Rae *management educator*
Eng, Holly S.A. *lawyer*
Engh, N. Rolf *lawyer*
Erdrich, Louise (Karen Erdrich) *writer, poet*
Erickson, Gerald Meyer *classical studies educator*
Erickson, W(alter) Bruce *business and economics educator, entrepreneur*
Erstad, Leon Robert *lawyer*
Fallon, Patrick R. *advertising executive*
Farah, Caesar Elie *language educator*
Faricy, John Hartnett, Jr. *lawyer*
Fauth, John J. *venture capitalist*
Feldman, Nancy Jane *insurance company executive*
Fergus, Patricia Marguerita *language educator, writer, editor*
Ferrari, Giannantonio *electronics executive*
Fetler, Paul *retired composer*
Finkelstein, Paul D. *personal care industry executive*
Firchow, Evelyn Scherabon *German language and literature educator, writer*
Firchow, Peter Edgerly *language professional, educator, writer*
Fisch, Robert Otto *medical educator*
Flanagan, Barbara *journalist*
Flom, Gerald Trossen *lawyer*
Foreman, Edward Vaught *voice educator, book publisher, writer, translator, composer, singer*
Forncris, Jeanne M. *lawyer*
Forsyth, Ann *urban planner, educator*
Forsythe, Thomas M. *communications executive*
Fowke, Benjamin G.S. III *energy executive*
Francis, Michael R. *retail executive*
Frase, Richard Stockwell *law educator*
Freese, Andrew *neurosurgeon, educator*
French, John Dwyer *retired lawyer*
Fulop, Laszlo G. *architect*
Gage, Edwin C., III, (Skip Gage) *travel and marketing services executive*
Gagnon, Craig William *lawyer*
Galambos, Theodore Victor *civil engineer, educator*
Gardenhire, Ronald Clyde *professional athletics manager*
Garner, Shirley Nelson *language educator*
Garnett, Kevin *professional basketball player*
Garon, Philip Stephen *lawyer*
Garton, Thomas William *lawyer*
Genereux, L. Joseph *lawyer*
George, William Wallace *former manufacturing executive*
Georgopoulos, Apostolos P. *neuroscientist, neurologist, educator*
Gerberich, Susan Goodwin *epidemiologist, educator, medical researcher*
Gerdner, Linda Ann *nursing researcher, educator*
Gill, Richard Lawrence *lawyer*
Gockel, John Raymond *construction executive*
Gogel, Raymond E. *energy executive*
Goldberg, Luella Gross *diversified financial services company executive*
Goldman, Allen Marshall *physics professor*
Gordon, Corey Lee *lawyer*
Gorham, Eville *retired ecologist*
Gottschalk, Stephen Elmer *lawyer*
Graham, Allister P. *food products executive*
Gralnek, Minda *retail executive*
Greener, Ralph Bertram *lawyer*
Greenfield, Lee *state legislator*
Griffith, Sima Lynn *investment banker, consultant*
Griswold, William M. *museum director, curator*
Grundhofer, Jerry A. *bank executive*
Grundhofer, John F. *bank executive*
Grussing, Bruce Douglass *lawyer*
Gulliver, John Stephen *civil engineering educator*
Gyllenhaal, Anders *publishing executive, editor*
Haase, Ashley Thomson *microbiology professor, researcher*
Hagedorn, Hildi *psychologist, researcher*
Hagglund, Clarance Edward *lawyer, publishing executive*
Haines, Stephen John *neurosurgeon*
Halbreich, Kathy *museum director*
Hale, James Thomas *retail executive, lawyer*
Hale, Roger Loucks *manufacturing executive, director*
Halley, James Woods *physics professor*
Hallman, Gary L. *photographer, educator*
Hamel, Mark Edwin *lawyer*
Hamel, William John *church administrator, minister*
Hansen, Jo-Ida Charlotte *psychology professor, researcher*
Hansen, Robyn L. *lawyer*
Hanson, Arthur Stuart *physician, consultant*
Hanson, Daniel R. *psychiatrist, educator*
Hanson, Kent Bryan *lawyer*
Harper, Donald Victor *retired transportation and logistics educator, consultant*
Harris, Michael Lawrence *psychologist, consultant*
Hart, Buster Clarence *lawyer*
Hawkins, William A. *medical products executive*
Hayes, Caroline Clark *engineering educator*
Haynsworth, Harry Jay, IV, *law educator*
Hays, Thomas S. *medical educator, medical researcher*
Hayward, Edward Joseph *lawyer*
Heiberg, Robert Alan *lawyer*
Hemsley, Stephen J. *healthcare company executive*
Hendrixson, Peter S. *lawyer*
Henson, Robert Frank *lawyer*
Herbison, Priscilla Joan *social services administrator, law educator*
Herr, David Fulton *lawyer, educator*
Hillstrom, Thomas Peter *engineering executive*
Hinderaker, John Hadley *lawyer, political blogger*
Hippee, William H., Jr. *lawyer*
Hobbins, Robert Leo *lawyer*
Hoffman, Michael J. *manufacturing executive*
Hoffmann, Thomas Russell *business management educator*
Holden, Susan M. *lawyer*
Holen, Norman Dean *art educator, artist*
Hollencamp, Greg *architectural firm executive*
Holt, Robert Theodore *political science professor, educator, dean*
Hom, David Brian *surgeon*
Howland, Joan Sidney *law librarian, educator*
Hudson, Troy *professional basketball player*
Hunt, Kay Nord *lawyer*

Hurwicz, Leonid *economist, educator*
Hyslop, David Johnson *retired arts administrator*
Ingbar, David H. *physician, researcher*
Jackson, J. David *lawyer*
Jacob, Bernard Michel *architect*
Jacobs, Benjamin M *education educator*
Jacobs, Irwin Lawrence *diversified corporate executive*
Jarboe, Mark Alan *lawyer*
Jemmerson, Ronald *science educator, researcher*
Johannsen, Marc Alan *lawyer*
Johnson, Alex Moore *dean, law educator*
Johnson, David Chester *academic administrator, sociologist, educator*
Johnson, Donald Clay *librarian, curator*
Johnson, Gary L. *publishing executive*
Johnson, Gary M. *lawyer*
Johnson, John Warren *retired professional society administrator*
Johnson, Kenneth Harvey *veterinary pathologist*
Johnson, Larry Walter *lawyer*
Johnson, Lola Norine *retired advertising and public relations executive, educator*
Johnson, Margaret Ann (Peggy) *library administrator*
Johnson, Walter Kline *civil engineer*
Jonason, William A. *lawyer*
Joseph, Daniel Donald *aeronautical engineer, educator*
Joseph, Marilyn Susan *gynecologist*
Joyce, Joseph M. *lawyer*
Judson, Patricia Lynn *obstetrician, gynecologist, oncologist*
Kaess, John Philip *music educator, director*
Kane, Robert Lewis *public health service officer, educator*
Kaplan, Sheldon *lawyer, director*
Karras, Ruth Mazo *history professor*
Keane, William Francis *nephrology educator, research foundation executive*
Keets, John David, Jr. *insurance company executive*
Keiser, Kenneth E. *food products executive*
Keller, Kenneth Harrison *engineering educator*
Kelly, A. David *lawyer*
Kelly, Charles Harold *advertising executive*
Kelly, Richard C. *energy executive*
Kelly, Tom (Jay Thomas Kelly) *retired professional sports team manager*
Keppel, William James *lawyer, educator, writer*
Keyes, Jeffrey J. *lawyer*
Kilbourne, Barbara Jean *health and housing executive*
Kim, Suck-Won *psychiatrist, educator*
King, Lyndel Irene Saunders *museum director*
Kinney, Earl Robert *mutual funds company executive*
Kirtley, Jane Elizabeth *law educator*
Klaas, Paul Barry *lawyer*
Knatterud, Mary E. *editor, educator, writer*
Knoke, David Harmon *sociology educator*
Knopf, Matthew J. *lawyer*
Kohlstedt, David Lee *geophysicist, educator*
Kohlstedt, Sally Gregory *historian, educator*
Koneck, John Michael *lawyer*
Korotkin, Fred *writer, philatelist*
Koscheyev, Victor S. *emergency physician, researcher*
Koutsky, Dean Roger *advertising executive*
Koyano-Nakagawa, Naoko *biologist, researcher*
Krause, Timothy Gilbert *academic administrator, web strategist*
Kreiser, Frank David *real estate executive*
Kudrle, Robert Thomas *economist, educator*
Kuhi, Leonard Vello *astronomer, academic administrator*
Kukla, Edward Richard *rare books & special collections librarian*
Kvalseth, Tarald Oddvar *mechanical engineer, educator*
Laing, Karel Ann *magazine publishing executive*
Lambert, Robert Frank *electrical engineer, educator, consultant*
Lancaster, Peter McCreery *lawyer*
Landry, Paul Leonard *lawyer*
Larson, Sheryl Ann *social worker, researcher*
Lavik, Bricker L. *lawyer*
Lawrence, James A. *food products executive*
Lazar, Raymond Michael *lawyer, educator*
Lebedoff, David Miller *lawyer, writer*
Lebedoff, Jonathan Galanter *retired judge, mediator*
Lehman, Tom (Thomas Edward Lehman) *professional golfer*
Leon, Arthur Sol *research cardiologist, exercise physiologist*
Leppik, Ilo E. *neurologist, educator*
Lerner, Harry Jonas *publishing executive*
Leuchovius, Deborah *advocate, special education services professional, consultant*
Levinson, David Matthew *engineering educator, civil engineer*
Lewis, Stephen Richmond, Jr. *economist, educator*
Lillehaug, David Lee *lawyer*
Lin, Jizhen *otolaryngologist, researcher*
Lindau, Philip *commodities trader*
Lindell, Edward Albert *academic administrator, religious organization administrator*
Lindsay, Michael Anthony *lawyer*
Lipovetsky, Stan (Stanislav Lipovetsky) *statistician, mathematician*
Lloyd, Patrick M. *dean, dental educator*
Loh, Horace H. *pharmacology educator*
Loken, James Burton *federal judge*
Lougee, Wendy Pradt *library director, educator*
Lucke, Stephen P. *lawyer*
Lueck, Martin R. *lawyer*
Luepker, Russell Vincent *epidemiology educator*
Lumpkins, Robert L. *food products executive*
Magid, Creighton (Chip) Reid *lawyer*
Magnuson, Roger James *lawyer*
Malmquist, Carl Phillip *psychiatrist*
Mandel, Sheldon Lloyd *dermatologist, educator*
Mansfield, William L. *manufacturing executive*
Manthey, Thomas Richard *lawyer*
Markus, Lawrence *retired mathematics professor*
Marling, Karal Ann *art history educator, social sciences educator, curator*
Marshak, Marvin Lloyd *physicist, researcher*
Marshall, Ron *retail executive*
Marshall, Siri Swenson *lawyer*

Martin, Judith Moran *lawyer*
Martin, Phillip Hammond *lawyer*
Martin, Roger Bond *landscape architect*
Martinson, Bradley James *lawyer*
Maruyama, Geoffrey *academic administrator, educator*
Mason, Barbara Fountain *minister*
Matthews, James Shadley *lawyer*
Mauer, J *professional baseball player*
McClanahan, Harry Allen III *management consultant*
McConnell Serio, Suzie Theresa *former professional basketball player, professional basketball coach*
McDermott, Kathleen E. *lawyer*
McDonald, John J., Jr. *lawyer*
McGuire, Tim *editor*
McGuire, William W. *health insurance company executive*
McGunnigle, George Francis *lawyer, judge*
McHale, Kevin Edward *professional sports team executive, retired professional basketball player*
McIntyre, John Lawrence *lawyer*
McLaughlin, Patrick J. *lawyer*
McQuarrie, Donald Gray *surgeon, educator*
McSorley, Stephen J. *medical educator*
Meador, Ron *newspaper editor, writer*
Mellum, Gale Robert *lawyer*
Melrose, Kendrick Bascom *manufacturing executive*
Mengler, Thomas M. *dean*
Meshbesher, Ronald I. *lawyer*
Meyers, Miriam Watkins *retired language educator*
Mickelson, Stacey *state legislator*
Miles, Steven Haverstock *geriatric medicine educator*
Miller, Alan M. *editor, writer, educator, television host*
Miller, William Alvin *clergyman, author, lecturer*
Miner, James Ross *emergency physician, educator*
Moffett, David McKenzie *bank executive*
Mohanty, Sunil K. *finance educator, researcher*
Molina, J. Ernesto *thoracic surgeon, educator*
Moller, James Herman *pediatrician, educator*
Mondale, Joan Adams *wife of former Vice President of United States*
Mondale, Walter Frederick *former Vice President of United States, lawyer, diplomat*
Monson, Cindy Lou *music educator*
Monson, Dan *college basketball coach*
Montgomery, Ann D. *federal judge, educator*
Montgomery, Henry Irving *financial planner*
Montgomery, Lynn Marie *educational consultant*
Moore, Cornell Leverette *financial services executive, lawyer*
Moran, Lewis Terrill *architect*
Morrison, Fred LaMont *law educator, dean*
Morrison, John M. *bank executive*
Mouser, Les (Lyman Mouser) *advertising executive*
Moyer, J. Keith *publishing executive*
Munsell, William A. *healthcare insurance company executive*
Murphy, Daniel J., Jr. *aerospace and defense manufacturing company executive, military officer*
Murphy, Diana E. *federal judge*
Murphy, Joseph Edward, Jr. *broadcast executive*
Najarian, John Sarkis *surgeon, educator*
Nanne, Louis Vincent *professional hockey team executive*
Nelson, Gary Michael *lawyer*
Nelson, Richard Arthur *lawyer*
Nevin, Phillip *professional baseball player*
Newman, Eric A. *neuroscientist*
Nicholson, Bruce J. *insurance company executive*
Nightingale, Edmund Joseph *clinical psychologist, educator, consultant*
Noel, Franklin Linwood *judge*
Novak, Leslie Howard *lawyer*
Nyrop, Donald William *air transportation executive*
Oesterle, Stephen N. *medical products executive, cardiologist, medical educator*
Oh, Allen James *lawyer*
O'Keefe, Michael *academic administrator, physicist*
O'Keefe, Thomas Michael *academic administrator*
Oliver, Edward Carl *retired state legislator, retired insurance company executive, small business owner*
Olowokandi, Michael *professional basketball player*
Olson, James Richard *retired transportation executive*
O'Neill, Brian Boru *lawyer*
Oriani, Richard Anthony *metallurgical engineer, educator*
Osander, John *secondary school educator*
Ostrem, Walter Martin *librarian, educator, consultant*
Ostrom, Don *political science professor*
O'Toole, Stephen Joseph *special education educator*
Overmier, J. Bruce *psychology professor*
Palmer, Brian Eugene *lawyer*
Parhi, Keshab Kumar *electrical and computer engineering educator*
Paulose, Rachel *prosecutor*
Paulu, Frances Brown *retired international center administrator*
Pazandak, Carol Hendrickson *liberal arts educator*
Perlman, Lawrence *retired information technology executive*
Persson, Erland Karl *electrical engineer, engineering educator*
Peterson, Neal N. *lawyer*
Peterson, William George *lawyer*
Pfau, James Michael *lawyer*
Pfender, Emil *mechanical engineering educator*
Phibbs, Clifford Matthew *surgeon, educator*
Pick, Anne Danielson *psychology professor*
Piper, Addison Lewis *securities executive*
Platt, Nina *law librarian*
Pletcher, Carol H. *chemicals executive*
Pohlad, Carl R. *bank executive, professional sports team executive*
Pohlad, Robert C. *consumer products company executive*
Porter, Philip Wayland *geography educator*

Portoghese, Philip Salvatore *medicinal chemist, educator*
Powell, Deborah Elizabeth *pathologist, dean*
Powell, Kendall J. *consumer products company executive*
Pratte, Robert John *lawyer*
Preuss, Roger Emil *artist*
Price, Joseph Michael *lawyer*
Pyles, Lee Allan *cardiologist, biomedical researcher*
Quie, Paul Gerhardt *pediatrician, educator*
Radmer, Michael John *lawyer, educator*
Ramalho-Ahrndt, Maria Gabriela *art educator*
Randall, Roger David *publishing executive*
Raskind, Leo Joseph *law educator*
Rasmussen, Teresa J. *lawyer, insurance company executive*
Ratchye, Boyd Havens *lawyer*
Redhead, Ruth Willard *foreign language educator*
Reha, Rose Krivisky *retired finance educator*
Reichgott Junge, Ember Darlene *retired senator, lawyer, writer, broadcast commentator, radio personality*
Reinhart, Robert Rountree, Jr. *lawyer*
Reiss, Ira Leonard *retired sociology educator, writer*
Reister, Raymond Alex *retired lawyer*
Remele, Lewis Albert, Jr. *lawyer*
Reyelts, Paul C. *chemical company executive*
Rockenstein, Walter Harrison, II, *lawyer*
Rockwell, Winthrop Adams *lawyer*
Roe, John H. *manufacturing executive*
Roe, Roger Rolland, Jr. *lawyer*
Rompala, Richard M. *chemical company executive*
Rose, Thomas Albert *artist, educator*
Rosenbaum, James Michael *federal judge*
Ross, Donald, Jr. *language educator, academic administrator*
Roth, Thomas *marketing executive*
Rothenberg, Elliot Calvin *lawyer, writer*
Rowan, Herman T. *art educator, artist*
Rudelius, William *marketing educator*
Rybak, R. T. *mayor*
Sadraie, Hamid Reza *civil engineer, researcher*
Saeks, Allen Irving *lawyer*
Safley, James Robert *lawyer*
Sanger, Stephen W. *consumer products company executive*
Santana, Johan Alexander *professional baseball player*
Sawicki, Zbigniew Peter *lawyer*
Sawyer, Charles F. *lawyer*
Scallen, Thomas Kaine *broadcast executive*
Schneider, Elaine Carol *lawyer, researcher, writer*
Schnell, Robert Lee, Jr. *lawyer*
Schnobrich, Roger William *lawyer*
Schreiner, John Christian *economics consultant, software publisher*
Schuh, G(eorge) Edward *dean, agricultural economist*
Schulze, Richard M. *retail executive*
Schuman, Leonard M. *medical educator, academic administrator*
Schwartz, Howard Wyn *business and marketing educator, consultant*
Scovanner, Douglas *retail executive*
Scoville, James Griffin *industrial relations professor*
Scriven, L. E(dward) *engineering educator*
Seidel, Robert Wayne *science historian, educator*
Selander, Lucy Mae *librarian*
Serrin, James Burton *mathematics professor*
Serstock, Doris Shay *retired microbiologist, civic worker, educator*
Severinsen, Doc (Carl H. Severinsen) *conductor, musician*
Shaheen, Christopher T. *lawyer*
Shapiro, Burton Leonard *dentist, geneticist, educator*
Shaughnessy, Thomas William *retired librarian*
Shemchuk, Mary Elizabeth *occupational therapist*
Shifman, Mikhail *physicist*
Shively, William Phillips *political scientist, educator*
Shnider, Bruce Jay *lawyer*
Short, Marianne Dolores *lawyer*
Silver, Alan Irving *lawyer*
Simonson, James S. *lawyer*
Sinha, Akhouri A. *cell and development biologist, researcher*
Sipkins, Peter W. *lawyer*
Sippel, William Leroy *lawyer*
Sisk, Gregory Charles *lawyer, educator*
Skare, Robert Martin *lawyer, director*
Slade, George Gilbert *art historian*
Slettehaugh, Thomas Chester *retired art educator*
Slocum, Rosemarie *physician services consultant, recruiter*
Smetanka, Mary Jane *reporter*
Smith, Justin P. *technology analyst, lab consultant*
Smith, Katie (Katherine May Smith) *professional basketball player*
Soland, Norman R. *corporate lawyer*
Sortland, Paul Allan *lawyer*
Spear, Allan Henry *state legislator, historian, educator*
Spoor, William Howard *food products executive*
Sprenger, Gordon M. *hospital administrator*
Sprewell, Latrell Fontaine *professional basketball player*
Srirangarajan, Seshan *electrical engineer, researcher*
Stageberg, Roger V. *lawyer*
Steen-Hinderlie, Diane Evelyn *social worker, musician*
Steinberg, Michael *music critic, educator*
Steinhafel, Gregg W *retail executive*
Stenwick, Michael William *retired internist, geriatrician, consultant*
Stephenson, Vivian M. *former retail executive*
Stern, Gary Hilton *bank executive*
Stern, Leo G. *lawyer*
Stoeri, William R. *lawyer*
Stone, Harold B. *artist, educator*
Struthers, Margo S. *lawyer*
Struyk, Robert John *lawyer*
Stuebner, James Cloyd *real estate developer, contractor*
Sullivan, Alfred Dewitt *academic administrator*
Sullivan, E. Thomas *law educator*

Suryanarayanan, Raj Gopalan *pharmacist, researcher, consultant, educator*
Svendsbye, Lloyd August *academic administrator, theologian, educator*
Swanson, David P. *lawyer*
Swenson, Mark Gregory *architect*
Tandon, Rajiv *training company executive*
Taylor, Frederick R. *health facility administrator*
Thompson, Roby Calvin, Jr. *orthopedic surgeon, educator, department chairman*
Thompson, Theodore Robert *pediatric educator*
Thorson, Steven Greg *lawyer*
Tinkham, Thomas W. *lawyer*
Tollefson, Lee *architect*
Tomlinson, Patricia Short *nursing scientist, educator*
Toscano, James Vincent *medical foundation administrator*
Tracy, James Donald *historian, educator*
Trestman, Frank D. *distribution company executive, director*
Troup, Elliott V., Jr. *psychologist*
Trucano, Michael *lawyer*
Truhlar, Donald Gene *chemist, educator*
Tuckson, Reed V. *academic administrator*
Turner, John Gosney *insurance company executive, director*
Turner, Ronald L. *information services executive*
Ulrich, Robert J. *retail executive*
Ulstrom, Robert A. *retired pediatrician*
Vander Molen, Thomas Dale *lawyer*
Van Dyke, William Grant *manufacturing executive*
Van Ryn, Michelle *healthcare educator*
Vanska, Osmo *music director*
Veblen, Thomas Clayton *management consultant*
Veldey, Bonnie *special education educator*
Verby, John Edward, Jr. *physician, educator*
Viault, Raymond G. *food company executive*
Wahoske, Michael James *lawyer*
Walden, John *retail executive*
Wang, Yang *cardiologist, educator, medical researcher*
Ward, David Allen *sociology educator*
Warman, Eduardo Norberto *research scientist*
Warner, William Hamer *mathematician*
Warring, Douglas Franklin *education educator, psychologist, director*
Watson, Dennis Wallace *microbiologist, educator*
Wegerson, Edward J. *lawyer*
Weinberg, Richard Alan *psychologist, educator*
Weiss, Gerhard Hans *German language educator*
Wejcman, Linda *retired state legislator*
Werner, Lawrence H. *editor*
Whelpley, Dennis Porter *lawyer*
White, Robert James *retired columnist*
Wickesberg, Albert Klumb *retired management consultant*
Wicks, John R. *lawyer*
Wikman, Michael Raymond *advertising executive*
Wild, John Julian *surgeon, researcher, medical educator*
Wilhelm, Gretchen *retired secondary school educator, volunteer*
Williams, Yolanda Yvette *music educator*
Windhorst, John William, Jr. *lawyer*
Wollan, Curtis Noel *theater producer, theater director*
Woodman, Stewart *chef*
Wright, Herbert E(dgar), Jr. *geologist*
Wu, Baolin *statistician*
Wurtele, Christopher Angus *paint and coatings company executive*
Yost, Gerald B. *lawyer*
Younger, Judith Tess *law educator*
Yourzak, Robert Joseph *management consultant, educator, engineer*
Ysseldyke, James Edward *psychology professor*
Zahler, Noel Barry *composer, music educator*
Zaleske, David Joseph *surgeon, research scientist, health facility administrator*
Zalk, Robert H. *retired lawyer*
Zimmermann, Robert Laurence *marketing professional*

**Minnetonka**

Anderson, Tad Stephen *landscape architect, consultant, photographer*
Bahl, Tracy L. *healthcare executive*
Bell, William Robert *music educator*
Bissell, Brent John *advertising and direct marketing executive*
Dapper, L. Robert *healthcare insurance company executive*
Erlandson, Patrick J. *health products executive*
Freeman, Gerald Russell *lawyer*
Gillies, Donald Richard *marketing and advertising consultant, educator*
Heckt, Melvin Dean *lawyer*
Johnson, Lennart Ingemar *materials engineering consultant*
Los, Cornelis Albertus *risk analyst, economist, finance educator*
Lubben, David J. *lawyer*
Moon, James Russell *technology education educator*
Nelson, Marilyn Carlson *hotel executive, travel company executive*
Pearson, Kevin *health facility administrator*
Penshorn, John S. *health facility administrator*
Pillsbury, George Sturgis *retired investment advisor*
Porter, Jim *human resources specialist*
Quam, Lois *healthcare company executive*
Rivet, Jeannine M. *insurance company executive*
Robbins, Orem Olford *insurance company executive*
Rogers, James Devitt *judge*
Schmidt, Russel Alan, II, *sales executive*
Sheehy, Robert J. *insurance company executive*
Van Brunt, William A. *lawyer*
Weisman, Eric *music company executive*
Wigfield, Rita L. *elementary school educator*

**Monticello**

Krohn, Brett Duane *music educator*

**Moorhead**

Buckley, Joan N. *retired literature and language professor*
Dille, Roland Paul *college president*
Eyler, David Paul *music educator*

Halmrast, Lynn James *psychologist*
Heuer, Gerald Arthur *mathematician, educator*
Noblitt, Harding Coolidge *political scientist, educator*
Rothlisberger, Rodney John *music educator*
Shoptaugh, Terry Lee *historian, archivist*
Stafford, Bonnie *social studies educator*
Strong, Judith Ann *chemist, educator*
Trainor, John Felix *retired economics professor*
Treumann, William Borgen *university dean*

**Moose Lake**
DeVillion, Kevin John *information scientist, consultant*

**Morris**
Kim, Jong-Min *education educator*
Kleinwolterink, John Evan *music educator*
Ordway, Ellen *biologist, educator, entomologist, researcher*

**Mound**
Whaley, Roger Glenn *music educator*

**Mounds View**
Wang, Aixue *translator, writer*

**Nevis**
Stibbe, Austin Jule *retired accountant*

**New Brighton**
Appel, William Frank *pharmacist*
Carlson, Kaye Lilien *retired music educator*
Hankes, Margaret Ellen *parochial school educator, consultant*

**New Hope**
Johnson, David Paul *writer, poet, publishing executive*

**New Ulm**
Moldenhauer, Kermit Gene *music educator*
Schubkegel, Joyce Catherine *music educator, composer*
Sprung, William *school system administrator*

**Newport**
Yelland, Mary Virginia *artist*

**Nisswa**
Meier, Christian Beach *pastor*

**North Branch**
Zumwalde, Barry *music educator*

**North Oaks**
Engle, Donald Edward *retired rail transportation executive, lawyer*
Woods, Robert Edward *lawyer*

**North Saint Paul**
O'Brien, Daniel William *lawyer, lumber company executive*

**Northfield**
Appleyard, David Frank *mathematics professor*
Benkowski, Ann Marie *writer*
Boardman, Shelby J. *academic administrator*
Cederberg, James *retired physics professor*
Clark, Clifford Edward, Jr. *history professor*
Clark, William Hartley *political science professor*
Iseminger, Gary Hudson *philosophy educator*
Levin, Burton *diplomat*
Lundergan, Barbara Keough *lawyer*
Nau, Richard William *mathematics professor, consultant, computer scientist, educator*
Noer, Richard J. *physics professor, researcher*
Oden, Robert A., Jr. *academic administrator*
Paas, John Roger *language educator*
Schuster, Seymour *mathematician, educator*
Soule, George Alan *literature educator*
Sovik, Edward Anders *architect, consultant*
Steen, Lynn Arthur *mathematician, educator*
Swanson, Stephen Olney *minister, retired English educator*
Yandell, Cathy Marleen *language educator*

**Oakdale**
Nagdimon, Ellen Tara *artist, educator*
Tran, Nang Tri *research scientist, electrical engineer*

**Olivia**
Cosgriff, James Arthur *physician*

**Osseo**
Anya, Adamma Chukwudi *special education educator*

**Ottertail**
Anderson, Bob *state legislator, retired small business owner*
Blaha, Verle Dennis *consumer products company executive, electrical engineer*

**Owatonna**
Annexstad, Albert T. *insurance company executive*
Birk, Peg J. *lawyer*

**Park Rapids**
Novak, Larry Ray *secondary school educator, music educator, director*

**Pequot Lakes**
Gray, Allen (Ernest Bungaard) *communications executive*
Lane, Kathleen Margaret *refrigeration company official*

**Pipestone**
Scott, William Paul *lawyer*

**Plymouth**
Friswold, Fred Ravndal *manufacturing executive*
Gauger, Beth Lynn *literature and language educator*
Kahler, Herbert Frederick *manufacturing executive*
Saville, Derric James *lawyer*
Shadley, Robert D. *retired army officer*
Trump, Stephanie *music educator, director*

Vieth, William Chapman *secondary school educator*

**Richfield**
Amdahl, Douglas Kenneth *retired state supreme court justice*
Anderson, Bradbury H. *retail executive*
Devlin, Barbara Jo *school district administrator*
Reilly, Jill Marlene *school system administrator*
Thompson, Steve Allan *writer*

**Robbinsdale**
Anderson, Scott Robbins *hospital administrator*

**Rochester**
Aksamit, Allen J. *neurologist*
Archibald, Reginald Mac Gregor *pediatrician, endocrinologist, chemist, educator*
Bartholomew, Lloyd Gibson *physician*
Boeve, Bradley F. *neurologist*
Bowie, E(dward) J(ohn) Walter *hematologist, researcher*
Brown, Arnold Lanehart, Jr. *pathologist, educator, dean*
Cofield, Robert Hahn *orthopedic surgeon, educator*
Cooper, Leslie Trumbull *cardiologist, educator*
Cortese, Denis A. *healthcare executive, medical educator*
Cross, Shelley Ann *neurologist, neuro-ophthalmologist*
Currier, Bradford Leonard *spine and orthopedic surgeon*
Danielson, Gordon Kenneth, Jr. *cardiovascular surgeon, educator*
DeBoer, Stephen W. *dietician*
DeRemee, Richard Arthur *internist, educator, researcher*
Dilger, John Anthony *anesthesiologist, consultant*
Dittrich, Steven Michael *lawyer*
Douglass, Bruce E. *physician*
Elkin, Peter Lewis *medical educator*
Engel, Andrew George *neurologist*
Fervenza, Fernando C. *nephrologist, educator*
Forstrom, Lee Arthur *physician*
Fye, W. Bruce III *cardiologist*
Geda, Yonas Endale *psychiatrist, researcher*
Gervais, Sister Generose *hospital consultant*
Gorman, Colum Alphonsus *retired endocrinologist*
Gracey, Douglas Robert *internist, educator, physiologist*
Greenleaf, James Fowler *biophysics educator*
Haddy, Francis John *internist, educator*
Hauri, Peter J. *psychology professor, researcher*
Hiniker, LuAnn *management consultant, educator, researcher, grants consultant*
Hodgson, Harriet W. *health and wellness writer*
Hodgson, Jane Elizabeth *obstetrician, gynecologist, consultant*
Hunder, Gene Gerald *rheumatologist, educator*
Kantarci, Kejal *radiologist, researcher*
Kao, Pai Chih *clinical chemist*
Key, Jack Dayton *librarian*
Knopman, David S. *neurologist*
Kyle, Robert Arthur *medical educator, oncologist*
Lange, Elizabeth Ann *retired librarian*
LaRusso, Nicholas F. *gastroenterologist, educator, scientist*
Lee, Hon-Chi *medical educator*
Lee, Kendall Han *neurosurgeon*
Lindor, Keith D. *gastroenterologist, researcher, hepatologist, dean*
Lucas, Alexander Ralph *child psychiatrist, educator, writer*
Mackenzie, Ronald Alexander *anesthesiologist*
Maher, L. James III *molecular biologist*
Malkasian, George Durand, Jr. *obstetrician, educator*
McAlpine, Donald Eugene *physician*
Moir, Christopher Robert *surgeon*
Mrazek, David Allen *psychiatrist*
Neel, Harry Bryan III *surgeon, scientist, educator*
Nelson, Audrey May *physician*
Nienow, Beth Marie *librarian*
Ordog, Tamas *research scientist, educator*
Pairolero, Peter Charles *surgeon, educator*
Perry, Harold Otto *dermatologist*
Phillips, Sidney Frederick *gastroenterologist, educator*
Piepgras, David G. *neurosurgeon, educator*
Pittelkow, Mark Robert *physician, dermatologist, educator, medical researcher*
Platt, Jeffrey Louis *surgeon, director, immunologist, educator, pediatric nephrologist*
Prendergast, Franklyn G. *health facility administrator medical educator*
Pulido, Jose S. *physician*
Raffel, Corey *neurosurgeon, pediatrician*
Reitemeier, Richard Joseph *physician*
Riggs, Jeanette Templeton *civic worker*
Rinden, David Lee *clergyman*
Robbins, Thomas Landau *researcher, editor*
Rogers, Roy Steele III *dermatologist, educator, dean*
Rosenow, Edward Carl III *medical educator*
Sanchez-Sotelo, Joaquin *surgery consultant*
Schnelldorfer, Thomas *surgeon*
Shampo, Marc Anthony *retired editor*
Shepard, Laura Ann *microbiologist, researcher*
Siekert, Robert George *retired neurologist, retired educator*
Sim, Franklin H. *orthopedic surgery educator*
Smith, Hugh Cadham *cardiovascular diseases physician*
Solbrig, Harold Ralph *systems analyst*
Steckelberg, James *epidemiologist, educator*
Stegall, Mark D. *surgeon, medical educator*
Stickler, Gunnar Brynolf *pediatrician*
Stockwell, Linda M. *principal*
Talley, Nicholas Joseph *medical educator, research scientist, physician*
Van Dyke, Daniel L. *geneticist*
Ward, Louis Emmerson *retired physician*
Weinshilboum, Richard M. *pharmacologist, educator, biomedical researcher*
Wells, Lloyd Allen *psychiatrist, educator*
Whisnant, Jack Page *neurologist*
Wiebers, David Owen *physician*
Wood, Douglas Lynn *medical educator*
Wood, Michael B. *medical products executive*
Woods, John Elmer *plastic surgeon*

**Rosemount**
Aadland, Thomas Vernon *minister*

**Roseville**
Marten, Gordon Cornelius *agronomist, educator, federal agency administrator*
McMillan, Mary Bigelow *retired minister, volunteer*
Miller, Suzanne Marie *library director, educator*
Seagren, Alice *school system administrator, former state legislator*

**Round Lake**
Holger, Jon C. *social studies educator*

**Rushford**
Stras, Penny Lynn *director*

**Saint Bonifacius**
Ingolfsland, Dennis Eldon *school librarian, religious studies educator*

**Saint Cloud**
Frank, Stephen Ira *political science professor, department chairman*
Gangopadhyay, Partha *management consultant*
Hofsommer, Donovan Lowell *history professor*
Inkster, Christine Davis *librarian, educator*
Krystyniak, Rebecca Ann *chemistry professor*
Martinson, Jody Marie *voice educator*
Olagunju, Amos Omotayo *computer science educator, consultant*
Olson, Barbara Ford *physician*
Prout, Robert Stephen *higher education consultant, law enforcement consultant*
Specht-Jarvis, Roland Hubert *fine arts educator, humanities educator, dean*
Supanvanij, Janikan *finance educator*
Wertz, John Alan *retired secondary school educator*

**Saint James**
Ferdig, Jerald Jim *music educator*

**Saint Joseph**
Kirick, Daniel John *agronomist*
Rowland, Howard Ray *mass communications educator*

**Saint Louis Park**
Beecher, Lee Hewitt *psychiatrist*
Carpel, Emmett Franklin *ophthalmologist, consultant*
Frestedt, Joy Louise *research scientist, science administrator*
Kalman, Marc *radio station executive*

**Saint Paul**
Allison, John Robert *lawyer*
Alsop, Donald Douglas *federal judge*
Amidon, Paul Charles *publishing executive*
Anderson, G. Barry *state supreme court justice*
Anderson, Paul Holden *state supreme court justice*
Anderson, Russell A. *state supreme court chief justice*
Archabal, Nina M(archetti) *historic site director*
Arora, Puneet Singh *endocrinologist, consultant, educator*
Axelrod, Leonard *management consultant*
Baker, Douglas M., Jr. *service industry executive*
Barker, Frederick Keith *biologist*
Barnwell, Franklin Hershel *zoology educator*
Barry, Anne M. *public health officer*
Bauer, Jean Warner *educator*
Bell, Lawrence T. *lawyer*
Benet, Jay S. *insurance company executive*
Bessette, Andy F. *diversified financial services company executive*
Boudreau, Lynda L. *state agency administrator*
Braun, Richard J. *lab administrator*
Bree, Marlin Duane *publisher, author*
Broccard, Alain F. *pulmonologist*
Brooks, Phillip *advertising executive*
Bruhn, JoAnn Marie *radiologic technologist, writer, speaker*
Brushaber, George Karl *academic administrator, minister*
Buckley, George W. *manufacturing executive*
Burke, Mary Griggs (Mrs. Jackson Burke) *art collector*
Burton, Charles Victor *neurosurgeon*
Busch, Robert Henry *geneticist, researcher*
Campbell, Patrick D. *manufacturing executive*
Cavert, Henry Mead *retired physician, retired medical educator*
Chaudhary, Satveer *state senator*
Cheng, Hwei H(sien) *soil scientist, agronomic and environmental science educator*
Cohen, Neal S. *former air transportation executive*
Coppock, Bruce *orchestra executive*
Courtney, Eugene Whitmal *computer company executive*
Dahlberg, Eric Ross *music educator*
Daly, Joseph Leo *law educator*
Davis, Margaret Bryan *paleoecology researcher, educator*
Deretich, George *lawyer*
Diesch, Stanley La Verne *veterinarian, educator*
Doermann, Humphrey *writer, consultant*
Domnisoru, Cristian *science educator*
Donaghy, James Edison *retired manufacturing executive, engineering educator*
Dybvig, Mary McIlvaine *educational consultant, psychologist*
Dykstra, Robert *retired education educator*
Edwards, Jesse Efrem *pathologist, educator*
Eibensteiner, Ron *political organization administrator, venture capitalist*
Ek, Alan Ryan *forester, educator*
Farrell, W. James *metal products manufacturing company executive*
Feinberg, David Erwin *publishing executive*
Ferrey, Mark Laurence *environmental scientist, researcher*
Fishman, Jay Steven *financial services executive*
Fitzgerald, Janice S. *public relations executive, academic administrator*
Fitzharris, Joseph Charles *history educator*
Flynn, Harry Joseph *archbishop*
Fritze, Steven L. *service industry executive*

Fulton, Robert Lester *sociology educator*
Galvin, Michael John, Jr. *lawyer*
Gehan, Mark William *lawyer*
Geis, Jerome Arthur *lawyer, law educator*
Gorski, Paul Cameron *education educator, consultant*
Goyal, Sagar M. *virologist, educator*
Granger, Steven Tandvig *archivist, consultant*
Habiger, James David *religious studies educator*
Haertl, Kristine Lynn *occupational therapist, educator*
Hanna, Kathryn Lura *university administrator*
Hanson, Samuel Lee *state supreme court justice*
Harvey, Patricia A. *school system administrator*
Hatch, Mike *state attorney general*
Havelin, Kate *writer, editor*
Heyman, William Herbert *financial services executive*
Hobbie, Russell Klyver *physics professor*
Holter, Arlen Rolf *cardiothoracic surgeon*
Hopper, David Henry *theologian, educator*
Hornbach, Daniel J. *academic administrator, biologist, educator*
Hubbard, Stanley Stub *broadcast executive*
Huber, Sister Alberta *academic administrator*
Huzar, Eleanor Goltz *historian, educator*
Janzen, Peter S. *lawyer*
Jessup, Paul Frederick *financial economist, educator*
Johnson, Badri Nahvi *social studies educator, real estate company officer*
Johnson, James Erling *insurance executive*
Johnson, Paul Oren *lawyer*
Jones, C. Paul *lawyer, educator*
Jones, Patricia L. *lawyer*
Kalliainen, Loree K. *surgeon, educator*
Keillor, Garrison Edward *writer, radio personality*
Kiffmeyer, Mary *state official*
King, Jack Burge *academic librarian*
Kirsch, Steven Jay *lawyer*
Kirwin, Kenneth Francis *law educator*
Kling, William Hugh *broadcast executive*
Knudson, Mark Bradley *health products executive, venture capitalist*
Kommedahl, Thor *plant pathology educator*
Kurtz, Harold Paul *foundation executive*
Kurzer, Mindy Susan *adult education educator*
Kyle, Richard House *federal judge*
Lancaster, Joan Ericksen *judge*
Larson, David Allen *law educator*
Lasansky, Leonardo *artist, educator*
Lay, Donald Pomeroy *federal judge*
Lebedoff, Randy Miller *lawyer*
Lee, Andrea Jane *academic administrator, nun*
Leighton, Robert Joseph *lawyer*
Lemaire, Jacques *professional hockey coach*
Leonard, Kurt John *retired plant pathologist, director*
Lipp, Robert I. *insurance company executive*
Lofquist, Vicki L. *journalist*
Mather, Richard Burroughs *retired Chinese language and literature educator*
Matteson, Clarice Chris *artist, educator*
May, Georgiana *biologist, educator*
McCormick, James Harold *academic administrator*
McGegan, Nicholas *music director*
McKinnell, Robert Gilmore *retired zoologist, biology professor, geneticist*
McNamee, Sister Catherine *theology studies educator*
Meyer, Helen M. *state supreme court justice*
Michael, Alfred Frederick, Jr. *physician, medical educator*
Minge, David *former congressman, lawyer, law educator*
Mlinar, John R. *mechanical engineer*
Molnau, Carol *lieutenant governor*
Monson, Dianne Lynn *literacy educator*
Nash, Nicholas David *retail executive*
Newmark, Richard Alan *chemist*
Ollmann, Brad Eric *music educator*
Ouderkirk, Andrew J. *corporate scientist*
Owens, B. Mitchell *lab administrator*
Page, Alan C. *state supreme court justice*
Pampusch, Anita Marie *foundation administrator*
Pappas, Sandra Lee *state senator*
Pawlenty, Timothy J. *governor*
Perry, James Alfred *environmental scientist, consultant, science educator, academic administrator*
Phillips, Ronald Lewis *plant geneticist, educator*
Policinski, Chris *food products executive*
Prager, Stephen *chemistry professor*
Pratt, Jon *not-for-profit executive*
Risebrough, Doug *professional sports team executive*
Roberts, William O. *sports medicine physician*
Rogness, Michael *religious studies educator, minister*
Rosenberg, Brian C *academic administrator*
Rossmann, Jack Eugene *psychologist, educator*
Rothmeier, Steven George *merchant banker, investment company executive*
Roy, Robert Russell *toxicologist*
Rubens, Sidney Michel *physicist, consultant*
Ruttan, Vernon Wesley *agricultural economist, educator*
Sadowsky, Michael J. *microbiologist, educator*
Schoonover, James A. *lab administrator*
Schram, Lee J. *manufacturing executive*
Schuman, Allan L. *chemicals executive*
Senkler, Robert L. *insurance company executive*
Seymour, McNeil Vernam *lawyer*
Shepherd, Terry L. *health facility administrator*
Skillingstad, Constance Yvonne *social services administrator, educator*
Spence, Kenneth F. III *lawyer*
Stadelmann, Eduard Joseph *retired plant physiologist, educator, researcher*
Starks, Daniel J. *medical technology and services executive*
Stauber, Karl Neill *foundation administrator*
Stroucken, Albert P. L. *chemical company executive*
Swaiman, Kenneth Fred *pediatric neurologist, educator*
Tylevich, Alexander V. *sculptor, architect*
Van Pilsum, John Franklin *biochemist, educator*
Vecoli, Rudolph John *retired history educator, director*

Wagner, Mary Margaret *library and information scientist, educator*
Wehrwein, Austin Carl *freelance/self-employed reporter*
Weiner, Carl Dorian *historian*
Weisberg, David Steven *healthcare consultant*
Weschcke, Carl Llewellyn *publishing executive*
Westermeyer, Joseph John *psychiatrist*
Wheelock, Pam *financial executive*
Wiersma, Kevin *lab administrator*
Willis, Bruce Donald *judge*
Wilson, Gary Lee *airline company executive*
Wilson, Leonard Gilchrist *medical educator*
Wiltz, James W. *medical products executive*
Wohlman, Matthew Jerry *legislative staff member*
Yessman, Timothy *insurance company executive*
You, Yali *music educator*
Zibell, Donald Fredrick *lawyer*
Ziegler, Richard Ferdinand *lawyer*
Zuraitis, Marita *insurance company executive*

**Saint Peter**
Costello, Patricia Anne *neuroscientist, educator*
Haeuser, Michael John *library administrator*
Hilbert, Richard Andrew *sociologist, educator*
Jodock, Darrell Harland *minister, educator*
Mc Rostie, Clair Neil *economics professor*
Myers, Donald James *museum director, art historian, educator*

**Sauk Centre**
Ross, Jeffrey Alan *social studies educator*

**Savage**
Soderquist, Ronald Bruce *minister, consultant, religious organization administrator*

**Shakopee**
Gertis, Neill Allan *writer*
McCloud, Samuel Alfred *lawyer*
Qiu, Peihua *statistician, researcher, educator*

**Sleepy Eye**
Jirak, Sarah Reed *secondary school educator*

**South Saint Paul**
Atkins, Joseph Eugene *lawyer, state representative*
Metzen, James P. *state legislator, bank executive*
Pugh, Thomas Wilfred *lawyer*

**Stillwater**
Asch, Susan McClellan *pediatrician*
Horsch, Lawrence Leonard *venture capitalist, corporate financial executive*
Lane, Stephen S. *ophthalmologist*

**Tracy**
Myhr, Gayle E. *consumer science educator*

**Vadnais Heights**
Martinez, Kathryn Marie *music educator*
Polakiewicz, Leonard Anthony *foreign language and literature educator*

**Virginia**
Knabe, George William, Jr. *pathologist, educator*

**Walker**
Collins, Thomas William *caterer, consultant*

**Warba**
Currie, Earl James *transportation executive*

**Waseca**
Deike, Keith Lawrence *lawyer*
Frederick, Edward Charles *university official*
Strand, Melvin LeRoy *English educator*

**Waubun**
Christensen, Marvin Nelson *venture capitalist*

**Wayzata**
Alton, Howard Robert, Jr. *lawyer, food company executive, real estate executive*
Blodgett, Frank Caleb *retired food company executive*
Brown, Neil W. *bank executive*
Johnson, Sankey Anton *manufacturing executive*
Luthringshauser, Daniel Rene *manufacturing executive*
Muschenheim, Frederick *retired pathologist*
Nagorske, Lynn A. *bank executive*
Reutiman, Robert William, Jr. *lawyer*
Rich, Willis Frank, Jr. *banker*
Schoen, Charles Judd *service executive*
Skrowaczewski, Stanislaw *conductor, composer*
Staley, Warren R. *agricultural products and diversified services company executive*
Sullivan, Austin Padraic, Jr. *retired diversified food company executive*
Swanson, Donald Frederick *retired food company executive*
Waldera, Wayne Eugene *crisis management executive*
Wyard, Vicki Shaw *investment and insurance company executive*

**West Saint Paul**
Cento, William Francis *retired newspaper editor*

**White Earth**
Vizenor, Erma J. *Native American tribal leader*

**Winona**
Beyer, Mary Edel *primary education educator*
Brosnahan, Roger Paul *retired lawyer*
Bures, Ruth Ellen *music educator, composer*
Franz, Craig Joseph *academic administrator, biology professor*
Holm, Joy Alice *goldsmith, psychology professor, artist, art educator*
Krueger, Darrell William *academic administrator*
Nasstrom, Roy Richard *educational consultant*
Oberton, Willard D. *industrial supply company executive*

**Woodbury**
Beck, Warren Randall *retired glass technologist*
Sandberg, Steve Jason *music educator*
Woodruff, Ellen Louise *chaplain*

**Young America**
Luecke, Robert Kenneth *social studies educator, department chairman*

**Zumbrota**
Post, Diana Constance *retired librarian*

## MISSISSIPPI

**Aberdeen**
Davidson, Glen Harris *federal judge*

**Ackerman**
Coleman, Frances McLean *secondary school educator*
Miller, Birthalene *writer*

**Alcorn State**
Dodgen, Anthony Bruce *mathematics professor*
Hawkins, Sidney Taylor *mathematician, educator*
Hunt, Clinton, Jr. *chemistry professor*
Wyatt, Helen J. *special education educator*
Yu, May Huang *librarian, educator*

**Amory**
Bending, Martha King *music educator*
Llewellyn, Charles Ray *secondary school educator*

**Batesville**
Carlson, George Clarence, Jr. *state supreme court justice*

**Bay Saint Louis**
Bernstein, Joseph *lawyer*
Corbin, James H. *engineering executive, meteorologist, oceanographer*
Hurlburt, Harley Ernest *ocean modeling and prediction scientist*
Lewando, Alfred Gerard, Jr. *oceanographer*

**Biloxi**
Brinsmade, Akbar Fairchild *chemical engineering consultant*
Brown, Sheba Ann *elementary school educator*
Dornan, Donald C., Jr. *lawyer*
Farrior, James L. III *lawyer*
Love, James Sanford III *communications executive*
Manners, Pamela Jeanne *secondary school educator*
Zocchi, Louis Joseph *product designer, game company executive*

**Brandon**
Cooper, Cynthia F. *accountant, consultant*
Schoolar, Laurel Ann *artist, educator*

**Carthage**
Moran, Mitch *lawyer*

**Clarksdale**
Lucy, William (Bill Lucy) *labor union administrator*
Schmidt, John Frederick III *government agency administrator, consultant*

**Cleveland**
Boschert, Thomas Neville *historian, educator*
Lane, Randy James *education educator, consultant*
Wojcik, John Casimir *music educator, director*

**Clinton**
Bigelow, Martha Mitchell *retired historian*
Cook, Stephen Day *art educator*
Gore, Samuel Marshall *art educator, sculptor*
Hensley, John Clark *religious organization administrator, minister*
Hutson, Martha Gillon *social studies educator, consultant*
Montgomery, Keith Norris, Sr. *insurance agent, military officer*

**Columbus**
Gingerich, Samuel Beryl *chemistry professor, academic administrator*
Holt, Robert Ezel *data processing executive*
Kaye, Samuel Harvey *architect, educator*
Labensky, Sarah Ross *culinary educator*
Summer, Emily Eugenia *artist, art educator*
Tousley, Rebecca Perkins *retired librarian*
Wheeley, Nancy Janine *librarian*

**Crystal Springs**
Bates, Lura Wheeler *retired trade association executive*

**Decatur**
Gordon, Marcus *judge*

**Ecru**
Mounce, Carolyn P. *retired school librarian*

**Ellisville**
McNair, Emma Louise *minister*

**Enterprise**
McCarty, Margaret Jane *retired elementary school educator*

**Ethel**
Glaskox, Anna C *secondary school educator*

**Eupora**
Meek, Walter Buchanan *retired lawyer, director*

**Fayette**
La Salle, Arthur Edward *historic foundation executive*

**Flora**
Das, Suman Kumar *plastic surgeon, researcher*

**Flowood**
Barnes, Harris H., III, (Trip Barnes) *tax lawyer*
Byrd, Joyce Marie *dentist*
Wilson, William Roberts, Jr., (Bob Wilson) *lawyer, apparel executive*

**Fulton**
Mastin, Lynn P. *biology professor*

**Gautier**
Egerton, Charles Pickford *anatomy and physiology educator*

**Goodman**
King, Kathy Cooper *music educator*

**Greenville**
Martin, Andrew Ayers *lawyer, physician, educator*
Orlansky, Julian David *judge*

**Greenwood**
Horn, Lawrence Charles *retired music educator*
Swayze, Charles J., Jr. *lawyer*

**Gulfport**
Biffle, Tony *editor*
Conrad, Harold Theodore *psychiatrist*
LaBorde, Oriel *civil engineer*
Opel, Pamela Lynn *elementary school educator*
Owen, Joe Sam *lawyer*
Phillips, Joy Lambert *lawyer, banker*
Senter, Lyonel Thomas, Jr. *federal judge*
Swetman, Glenn Robert *literature and language professor, poet*
Thatcher, George Robert *banker, writer, journalist, columnist*

**Hattiesburg**
Adelman, Michael Schwartz *lawyer*
Barthelme, Frederick (Rick) *writer, literature educator*
Bedenbaugh, Angela Lea Owen *chemistry educator, researcher*
Bower, Janie Pittman *mathematics educator*
Chain, Bobby Lee *electrical contractor, former mayor*
Chambers, Douglas Brent *history professor*
Davis, Charles Raymond *political scientist, educator*
De Chiaro, John Paul *music educator*
Doty, Duane Harold *business educator*
Griffith, Jerry A. *environmental science educator*
Gunther, William David *academic administrator, economics professor*
Henry, Myron *academic administrator*
Hickman, Ronald Lee *media broker, broadcast executive*
King, Ernest Wade *law educator*
Lucas, Aubrey Keith *retired university president*
Malone, Mark Hugh *music educator*
McRaney, Joan Katherine *artist*
Miao, Wujian *chemistry professor*
Nanda, Ajaya Kumar *chemist, educator*
Noonkester, James Ralph *retired college president*
St. John, Robert *chef, writer*
Scarborough, William Kauffman *historian, educator*
Shin, Jae-Hwa *educator*
Sulbaran, Tulio *education educator, researcher*
Sutton, Robert James *social studies educator, special education educator*
Zeigler-Hill, Virgil *psychology professor*

**Hernando**
Brown, William A. *lawyer, mediator, arbitrator*

**Holly Springs**
Beckley, David Lenard *academic administrator*

**Indianola**
Matthews, David *clergyman*

**Itta Bena**
Ahanonu, Chukwuma Smart *education educator*
Wax, Benjamin *physical education educator, consultant*

**Iuka**
Segars, Kelly Scott, Sr. *physician, banker*

**Jackson**
Adams, Charles P., Jr. *lawyer*
Anglin, Linda McCluney *retired elementary school educator*
Banks, Fred Lee, Jr. *former state supreme court presiding justice, lawyer*
Barbour, Haley Reeves *governor*
Barksdale, Rhesa Hawkins *federal judge*
Barrett, Gene Richard *orthopedist*
Bloom, Sherman *retired pathology educator, photographer*
Bounds, Hank M. *school system administrator*
Bradley, Betsy *museum director*
Broome, Kathryn *secondary school educator*
Burch, Donald Victor *lawyer*
Burns, Robert, Jr. *retired architect, painter*
Chatham, Lloyd Reeve *lawyer*
Cho, Hyun Jung *biology professor*
Chung, Sung *pathologist*
Clark, David Wright *lawyer*
Clark, Eric C. *state official*
Cobb, Kay Beevers *state supreme court justice, retired state senator*
Coleman, Mary H. *state legislator*
Collins, Deloris Williams *secondary school educator*
Corlew, John Gordon *lawyer*
Cowan, Bryan D. *medical educator, department chairman*
Cruse, Julius Major, Jr. *pathologist, educator*
Dale, T.D. *architectural firm executive*
de-Shazo, Richard Denson *medical educator, academic administrator*
Diaz, Oliver E., Jr. *state supreme court justice*
Dickinson, Jess H. *state supreme court justice*
Easley, Charles D., Jr. *state supreme court justice*
Eldek, Abdelnasser A. *engineering educator, researcher*
Ellingburg, C. Michael *lawyer*
England, John F. *lawyer*
Franks, James R. (Jamie), Jr. *lawyer, state legislator*
Freeland, Alan Edward *orthopedic surgery educator, physician*
Fuselier, Louis Alfred *lawyer*
Girtman, Paxton M *music educator*

Gordon, Granville Hollis *church official*
Graves, James E. *state supreme court justice, educator*
Guise, Linda Jackson *music educator*
Hafter, Jerome Charles *lawyer*
Hall, John E. *medical educator*
Hendrix, Albert Randel *social services administrator*
Henegar, John C(lark) *lawyer*
Herndon, Robert McCulloch *neurologist, researcher*
Hood, Jim *state attorney general*
Hosemann, C. Delbert, Jr. *lawyer*
Houston, Gerry Ann *oncologist*
Howell, Joel Walter III *lawyer*
Hughes, Byron William *oil industry executive*
Hughson, Michael Donald *pathologist, researcher, medical educator*
Hupp, James R. *dean, dental educator*
Hutchison, Mark Stevenson *lawyer*
Islam, Saleem *pediatric surgeon, researcher*
Izevbigie, Ernest B. *biomedical researcher*
Jolly, E. Grady *federal judge*
Julian, Michael *grocery company executive*
Krause, Denise D. *information technology manager, educator*
Kyle, Patrick B. *biomedical researcher, educator*
Lampton, Dunn O. *prosecutor*
Lampton, Leslie B., Sr. *oil industry executive*
Lee, Tom Stewart *judge*
Lewis, Robert Edwin, Jr. *pathology and immunology educator, researcher*
Lindsay, Arnold Arness *reporter*
Luse, Lender *biology educator*
Marshall, Gailen Daugherty, Jr. *allergist, educator*
Mayeaux, Anne Russell *education educator*
McDavid, John Sanford *lawyer*
McElvaine, Robert Stuart *writer, educator*
McIntyre, James G. *lawyer*
Minocha, Anil *physician, educator, researcher*
Mitchell, Jerry *reporter*
Moize, Jerry Dee *lawyer, federal official*
Moll, George William *pediatrician, educator*
Moore, Mike *former state attorney general*
Munera, Pedro Antonio *child and adolescent psychiatrist*
Olendski, Oleg *physicist*
O'Mara, James Wright *lawyer*
Phillips, Joshua Phillips *pediatrician*
Purdy, William Richard *lawyer*
Randolph, Michael K. *state supreme court justice*
Rawson, John Elton *neonatologist, medical educator*
Risley, Rod Alan *educational association administrator*
Roberts, Richard Charlton III *lawyer*
Roy, Sitesh Ranen *pediatrician, allergist, immunologist, educator*
Scanlon, Pat H. *lawyer*
Smith, Carnice *music educator, director*
Smith, Edgar Eugene *biochemist, educator, academic administrator*
Smith, James W., Jr. *state supreme court justice*
Smith, Sharman Bridges *state librarian*
Stanton, Sylvia Doucet *artist, art gallery owner*
Suess, James Francis *retired psychiatry educator*
Sugg, Robert Perkins *retired judge*
Sullivan, Bettye Yarborough *foundation administrator*
Sweet, Dennis C. III *lawyer*
Tchounwou, Paul Bernard *environmental health specialist, toxicologist, educator*
Thames, Lee Davis *lawyer*
Thigpen, James Tate *oncologist, educator*
Tuck, Amy *lieutenant governor*
Waites, Robert Guinn *utilities executive*
Waller, William Lowe, Jr. *state supreme court justice*
Welch, W(alter) Scott III *lawyer*
Winter, William Forrest *retired governor, lawyer*

**Keesler Afb**
Van Goor, Anthony Jay *military officer*

**Kiln**
Mathur, Abhinav *research engineer*

**Kosciusko**
Shoemaker, William C. *journalist*

**Laurel**
Lacey, Peeler Grayson *diagnostic radiologist*
Lindstrom, Eric Everett *ophthalmologist*

**Leakesville**
Hollinghead, Juanita Green *elementary school educator*

**Lumberton**
Wisznia, Walter *architectural firm executive*

**Madison**
Watts, Thomas Parrish *history educator, consultant*

**Magnolia**
Coney, Elaine Marie *language educator*

**Mayhew**
Marsh, Patricia Guyton *humanities educator*

**Mc Cool**
Miller, Charlotte Faye *speech pathology/audiology services professional*

**Mccomb**
Chamberlin, Mary Ellen *music educator*

**Meridian**
Church, George Millord *retired real estate company executive*
Havard, Jeanne S. *finance educator*
Leewer, William George, Jr. *education educator*

**Minter City**
Mitchell, Patsy Malier *religious school founder, administrator*

**Mississippi State**
Acar, Erdem *aerospace scientist, researcher*

Babski-Reeves, Kari *industrial and systems engineering educator*
Chrisman, James Joseph *management educator*
Clynch, Edward John *political science professor, public information officer*
Croom, Sylvester *football coach*
Delgado, Marica LaDonne *librarian, educator*
Eksioglu, Burak *engineering educator*
Foglesong, Robert H. *academic administrator, career military officer*
Hosie, Thomas Walsh *counselor, educator*
Janus, Jonathan Mark *aerospace engineer, educator*
Lowery, Charles Douglas *historian, educator, dean*
Martin, Edward Curtis, Jr. *landscape architect, educator*
Potirniche, Gabriel Petru *mechanical engineer, researcher*
Rabideau, Peter Wayne *dean, chemistry professor, educator*
Reddy, Kambham Raja *botanist, educator*
Shah, Vijay Pravin *electrical engineer, researcher*
Thompson, Joe Floyd *aerospace engineer, researcher*
Topsakal, Erdem *science educator*
Truax, Dennis Dale *civil engineer, educator, consultant*
Vance, David A. *information systems educator*

**Moorhead**
Tabb, Vicki Clark *mathematics professor*

**Morton**
Cox, Marlina R. *social studies educator*

**Moss Point**
Bolton, Betty J. *medical/surgical nurse, poet*

**Mound Bayou**
Kamphefner, Pius *minister*

**Natchez**
Bramlette, David C. III *federal judge*
Kirk, Susanne Smith *editor*
McLemore, Joan Meadows *librarian, consultant*
Wynn, Bobbye Faye *music educator*

**Nettleton**
Cherry, Jeffrey Lynn *history educator*

**Ocean Springs**
Austin, Claude Lidell *retired surgeon*
Biber, Patrick D. *oceanographer*
Brown-Peterson, Nancy J. *biologist*
Culberson, Gary Michael *hotel manager*
Lee, Kathleen Mary *health facility administrator, nursing educator*
Luckey, Alwyn Hall *lawyer*
Parrott, Linda Susan *chemistry educator*

**Olive Branch**
Leary, Frances Elizabeth Cooper *secondary school educator*
McRae, Carol Reeves *secondary school educator, theater director*

**Oxford**
Carter, Gail Marie *special education educator*
Greenlee, Jim Ming *prosecutor*
Hoffheimer, Michael Harry *law educator*
Howorth, David Bishop *lawyer*
Keiser, Edmund Davis, Jr. *biologist, educator*
Landon, Michael de Laval *retired history professor*
Mills, Michael Paul *judge*
Moorhead, Sylvester Andrew *retired education educator*
Rego, Cesar *science educator, researcher*
Walton, Gerald Wayne *retired university official*

**Pascagoula**
Rideout, Jan G. *ship manufacturing company executive*

**Pass Christian**
Clark, John Walter, Jr. *water transportation executive*
Henrion, Rosemary Provenza *psychotherapist, educator*
McCardell, James Elton *retired naval officer*

**Pearl**
Latham, Robert Richard, Jr. *retired state agency administrator*

**Philadelphia**
Duncan, Mark *district attorney*
Montgomery, Kathryn Suzainne *elementary school educator*

**Poplarville**
Hague, Ronn *museum director*

**Raymond**
Walker, Carol McRaney *mathematics professor, consultant*

**Ridgeland**
Ghirmai, Tadesse *engineering educator, researcher*
Harmon, George Marion *academic administrator*
Lewis, Larry Lisle *human resources specialist company executive*
Long, Roger Leonard *artist*
Pemberton, William Bertram, II, *lawyer*

**Saltillo**
Newell, Joyce R. *social studies educator*

**Saucier**
Finley, Emma Rosemary *science educator*

**Senatobia**
Banham, Sandra Rodgers *language educator*
Latham, Amy Moore *academic administrator*

**Shaw**
Garner, Mable Tecola *health facility administrator*

**Southaven**
Dale, Randy Neil *music educator*

Taylor, Ronald Louis *lawyer*

**Starkville**
Ford, Robert MacDonald III *architect, educator*
Gregg, Billy Ray *seed industry executive, consultant*
Huang, Junmin *chemist, researcher*
Jacob, Paul Bernard, Jr. *electrical engineering educator*
Liu, Qingyun *thermal and mechanical research engineer*
Mabry, Donald Joseph *retired academic administrator, history professor*
Martin, Theodore Krinn *former university administrator*
Oppenheimer, Bonnie Lou *mathematics professor*
Thomas, Garnett Jett *accountant*

**Stennis Space Center**
Chin-Bing, Stanley Arthur *physicist, educator*
Lever, John A. *civilian military employee*

**Stoneville**
Morales-Ramos, Juan Alfredo *entomologist, researcher*
Ranney, Carleton David *retired plant pathologist*

**Sumrall**
Downey, James Cecil *retired music educator, retired humanities educator*

**Tougaloo**
Whittington, Felicia Trenise *social services administrator, educator*

**Tupelo**
Clayton, Claude F., Jr. *lawyer*
Cleveland, Mary Heloise *elementary school educator*
Hawkins, Bridgett Burnett *elementary school educator*
Miles, Sharon Kathleen *microbiologist, educator*
Nash, Henry Warren *marketing educator*
Parker, Jennifer Merri *writer, editor, educator*
Ramage, Martis Donald, Jr. *banker*

**Tutwiler**
Brooks, Sister Anne *osteopath*

**University**
Aranchuk, Vyacheslav *research scientist*
Breazeale, Mack Alfred *research scientist, educator*
Cheng, Alexander Hung-Darh *engineering educator, consultant*
Davis, Samuel Marion *dean, law educator, researcher*
Dor, George W. K *music educator*
Duke, Stephen Oscar *physiologist, research scientist, educator*
Jordan, Winthrop Donaldson *historian, educator*
Kiger, Joseph Charles *history professor*
Matalgah, Mustafa Muhammad *engineering educator, researcher*
O'Sullivan, Daniel E. *language educator*
Pulliam, Rene E. *performing arts educator*
Shughart, William Franklin, II, *economics professor, consultant*
Smith, Allie Maitland *engineering educator*
Stephens, Earnest B. *academic administrator*
Wei, Bing *mathematics professor*
Wicker, Nancy Lynn *art history educator*
Willson, David E. *music educator*
Yakovlev, Alexander B. *electrical engineer, educator*

**Vancleave**
Anthony, Geneva Jo *poet, writer*

**Vicksburg**
Faith, Jonathan Mark *retired military officer*
Houston, James R. *government agency administrator*
Keulegan, Emma Pauline *special education educator*
Nichols, William Owen *conservationist*

**Walls**
Tharnish, Rose Maries Lehman *veterinarian*

**Washington**
Branyan, Cheryl Munyer *museum administrator*

**West Point**
Cliett, Charles Baron *retired aeronautical engineer, retired educator, retired academic administrator*

**Whitfield**
Montgomery, John Harold *psychiatrist*

## MISSOURI

**Advance**
Lanpher, Ben Evert *psychologist, researcher*

**Alton**
Scott, Lori Denise *music educator, musician*

**Anderson**
Coble, Mary Gloria *protective services official, rancher*

**Arcadia**
Davis, Jo *nurse, writer, professional speaker, small business owner, photographer*

**Arnold**
Kasey, Arthur R. III *secondary school educator*
Miller, Pamela Sue *elementary school educator*

**Ash Grove**
Johnson, Iver Christian *retired real estate appraiser*

**Aurora**
Lyon, Lucy *school system administrator*

**Bakersfield**
Barnes, Sandra Lynn *special education educator*

**Ballwin**
Ackerson, Charles Stanley *minister, educator, social worker*
Bond, Dennis Earl *auditor*
Cornell, William Daniel *mechanical engineer*
Geis, Milton Arthur *painter, writer*
Pallozola, Christine *not-for-profit executive*

**Belton**
Blim, Richard Don *retired pediatrician, health facility administrator*
Hoye, Linda Lee *special education educator*
Short, Joel Barton *secondary school educator, department chairman*

**Bethel**
Coonrod, Delberta Hollaway (Debbie Coonrod) *retired elementary school educator, consultant*

**Bloomfield**
Ferrell, Paul Cleveland *writer*

**Blue Springs**
Baker, Jean Morrison *writer*
Hiles, Barbara Lynn *retired elementary school educator*
Hochgrebe, Nolan Robards *secondary school educator*
Page, Leslie Andrew *retired consumer products company executive*
Washburn, Gladys Haase *retired church musician, educator, director*

**Bolivar**
Brown, Autry *psychology professor, clergyman*
Gott, Wesley Atlas *art educator*
Harris, Beverly Howard *retired mathematics professor, genealogist*
Huser, Carl Frank *retired biology professor*
Tarrant, James Richard III *music educator*

**Bowling Green**
Bruce, Judith Esther *retired music educator, elementary school educator*

**Branson**
Lanning, James Wilford *sales executive, retired music educator*
Ownby, Jerry Steve *landscape architect, educator*

**Bridgeton**
Asma, Lawrence Francis *priest*
Brunngraber, Eric Henry *banker*
Faulk, Marshall William *professional football player*
Hylla, Linda Kay *sister, social worker*
Kenison, Raymond Robert *fraternal organization administrator, director*

**Butler**
Turner, Vicky Jo *music educator*

**Canton**
Cochell, Gary G. *mathematician, educator*
Galloway, Robert Edward *literature and language professor, retired municipal official*

**Cape Girardeau**
Blanton, Lewis M. *federal judge*
Grand, Stanley I. *museum director, educator*
King, Cynthia Rose *literature and language educator, theater arts director*
Langenfeld, Mark E. *healthcare educator*
Limbaugh, David *lawyer*
McManaman, Kenneth Charles *lawyer*
Smallwood, Glenn Walter, Jr. *utility marketing management executive*

**Carl Junction**
Pulliam, Frederick Cameron *educational administrator*
Wostal, Holly Ann *music educator*

**Carthage**
Flanigan, Matthew C. *manufacturing executive*
Haffner, David S. *manufacturing executive*
Jett, Ernest Carroll, Jr. *paper company executive, lawyer*
McAfee, Diana Mae *media specialist, music educator*
Skaggs, Ronald Lee *controller, history professor, religious studies educator*
Wright, Felix E. *manufacturing executive*

**Centralia**
Everhart, James Gray *retired manufacturing executive*

**Charleston**
Cassell, Lucille Richardson *small business owner*

**Chesterfield**
Ashworth, Ronald Broughton *health facility executive, accountant*
Bunch, Bob *manufacturing executive*
Bunch, C. Robert *oil industry executive, lawyer*
Carpenter, Will Dockery *chemicals executive*
Denneen, John Paul *lawyer*
Diamandis, Peter H. *foundation administrator*
Gerard, Jules Bernard *law educator*
Gietschier, Steven Philip *journalist, historian*
Hier, Marshall David *lawyer*
Kleffner, Gregory William *retail executive, accountant*
Landram, Christina Louella *librarian*
Mirza, Azam A. *insurance company executive*
Morley, Harry Thomas, Jr. *real estate executive*
Pollihan, Thomas Henry *lawyer*
Qazi, Mujtaba A. *ophthalmologist*
Ross, E. Earl *small business owner*
Salem, Bakr Ibramim *cardiologist*
Selfridge, George Dever *retired dentist, retired military officer*
Stork, Donald Arthur *advertising executive*
Welshans, Merle Talmadge *management consultant*
Williams, Luther Steward *research scientist*

**Chillicothe**
Kapono, Francie Napuaonalani Josie *music educator*
Logan, Janet Louise *retired elementary school educator*
Stull, Kenneth Lee *social studies educator*

**Clayton**
Costas, Bob (Robert Quinlan Costas) *sportscaster*
Davenport, Dennis Lynn *protective services official*
Kemper, David Woods, II, *banker*
Lamoureux, Gerard William *container manufacturing company executive*
Mohrman, Henry Joe, Jr. *lawyer, investment manager*
Novelly, Paul Anthony *petrochemical and refining company executive*
Pain, George H. *lawyer*
Post, Stephen Lightner *retired psychoanalyst, educator*
Rogers-Beard, Donna Jane *history educator*
Rupp, Joseph D. *metal products executive*
Tremayne, Eric Flory *lawyer*
Vecchiotti, Robert Anthony *management and organizational consultant*

**Clinton**
Kelsay, David Roland *chemist*

**Columbia**
Almony, Robert Allen, Jr. *librarian*
Anderson, Ralph Robert *endocrinologist, educator*
Arunpachalam, V. *accountant, educator*
Bank, Barbara J. *sociology educator*
Bauman, John E., Jr. *chemistry professor*
Beem, John Kelly *retired mathematician, educator*
Benoit, William Lyon *communication educator*
Biddle, Bruce Jesse *social psychologist, educator*
Bien, Joseph Julius *philosophy educator*
Blevins, Dale Glenn *agronomy educator*
Brekhus, Wayne Herbert *sociologist, educator*
Brushwood, Mack Lewis *labor union administrator*
Bunn, Ronald Freeze *lawyer, academic administrator*
Burgoyne, Suzanne *theater educator, writer*
Chambers, Glenn Darrell *film company executive, art director*
Cogswell, Jim *library director*
Colwill, Jack Marshall *physician, educator*
Creighton, Donald Louis *mechanical engineer, consultant*
Crist, William Miles *dean, pediatrician, educator*
Cunningham, Billie M. *accounting educator*
Cunningham, Milamari Antoinella *retired anesthesiologist*
Day, Cecil LeRoy *agricultural engineering educator*
Deaton, Brady J. *academic administrator*
Decker, Wayne Leroy *meteorologist, educator*
Dessem, R. Lawrence *dean, law educator*
Dolbashian, Edward John *conductor*
Dreier, Keith Lynn *not-for-profit fundraiser*
Easton, Stephen Douglas *law educator, lawyer*
Edgington, Bobbie George *communications engineer, consultant*
Eggers, George William Nordholtz, Jr. *anesthesiologist, educator*
Finkelstein, Richard Alan *retired microbiology educator, consultant*
Fisch, William Bales *law educator*
Flinn, Mark van Doren *education educator*
Flournoy, Nancy *statistician, educator*
Frisby, James Curtis *retired agricultural engineering educator*
Fulweiler, Howard Wells *language professional*
Gehrke, Charles William *biochemistry professor*
George, Melvin Douglas *retired university president*
Goodrich, James William *retired historian executive*
Govindarajan, Gurushankar *cardiologist, researcher*
Gu, Zhimang *engineer*
Gysbers, Norman Charles *counselor, educator*
Hanrahan, Timothy Ryan *elementary school educator*
Hardin, Christopher Demarest *medical educator*
Harter, Philip J. *lawyer, educator*
Hawthorne, Marion Frederick *chemistry professor*
Helvey, William Charles, Jr. *communications specialist*
Hensley, Elizabeth Catherine *nutritionist, educator*
Horner, Winifred Bryan *humanities educator, researcher, consultant, writer*
James, Elizabeth Joan Plogsted *pediatrician, educator*
Janda, Mark William *history educator*
Katti, Kattesh V. *biochemist, educator, research scientist*
Kausler, Donald Harvey *retired psychology professor*
Keyvan, Shahla *nuclear engineer, educator*
Kirawanich, Phumin *electrical engineer*
König, Peter *pediatrician, educator*
Kramer, Michael W. *communications educator*
Kvanvig, Jonathan Lee *philosophy educator*
LaCrue, Alexis Nichole *parasitologist*
Lansford, Raymond William *retired finance educator*
LeMaster, Joseph William *physician, epidemiologist*
Lewis, Michael Robert *medical researcher, educator*
Libby, Wendy B. *academic administrator*
Loory, Stuart Hugh *journalist*
Looser, Devoney Kay *English literature educator*
LoPiccolo, Joseph *psychologist, educator, author*
Mashhoon, Bahram *physicist, researcher*
Maxcy, Brendan David *education educator*
Mays, William Gay, II, *lawyer, real estate developer*
McDermott, Dennis Michael *trade association executive*
McKinley, Lori *education educator*
Men, Hongsheng *biologist, researcher*
Micheas, Athanasios Christou *finance educator*

Miller, Paul Ausborn *adult education educator*
Mitchell, Roger Lowry *retired agronomy educator*
Morehouse, Lawrence Glen *veterinarian, educator, academic administrator*
Mullen, Edward John, Jr. *Spanish language educator*
Mustapha, Azlin *food scientist, educator*
Nikolai, Loren Alfred *accounting educator*
O'Connor, John Thomas *civil engineering educator*
Overby, Osmund Rudolf *art historian, educator*
Perry, Michael Clinton *internist, educator, academic administrator*
Phillips, Walter Ray *law educator*
Pinkerton, Marjorie Jean *librarian, educator*
Pittman, Von Veron *education educator*
Poehlmann, Carl John *agronomist, researcher*
Potts, Jeffrey Thomas *biomedical researcher*
Pringle, Oran Allan *mechanical and aerospace engineering educator*
Puckett, Charles Linwood *plastic surgeon, educator*
Puttler, Benjamin *entomologist*
Randall, Douglas D. *biochemist, educator*
Randall, Linda Lea *biochemist, educator*
Retzloff, David George *engineering educator*
Roberts, R. Michael *animal scientist, biochemist, educator*
Rowlett, Ralph Morgan *archaeologist, educator*
Sanders, Keith Page *journalism educator*
Schaeffer, Mary L. *geneticist*
Schwartz, Richard Brenton *English language educator, dean, writer*
Shende, Rajesh V. *chemical engineer, materials scientist, researcher*
Smith, Charles Jeffrey *radiologist, educator, research scientist*
Speakman, Robert J. *archaeologist, chemist, researcher*
Stack, Frank Huntington *painter, retired art educator*
Stephenson, Hugh Edward, Jr. *retired surgeon*
Strickland, Arvarh Eunice *history professor*
Sun, Albert Yung-Kwang *pharmacologist, educator*
Tarnove, Lorraine *medical association executive*
Timberlake, Charles Edward *historian, educator*
Tobias, Joseph Drew *pediatric anesthesiologist*
Triplett, Gregory Edward *educator, researcher*
Van Sambeek, Jerome William *physiologist, educator*
Vogt, Albert Ralph *forester, educator, program director*
Weisman, Gary Andrew *biochemist*
Welliver, Warren Dee *lawyer, retired judge*
Westbrook, James Edwin *law educator*
Whitman, Dale Alan *lawyer, educator*
Witten, David Melvin *retired radiology educator*
Yanders, Armon Frederick *biological sciences educator, science administrator*
Zylstra, Alexandria *lawyer*

**Conway**
Day, Sandy J. *gifted and talented educator, tax specialist*
Maxwell, Quentin D. *art educator*

**Creve Coeur**
Bockserman, Robert Julian *chemist*
Faust, John Joseph, Jr. *performing arts educator, theater director*
Randle, Bernadette *musician, composer, graphics designer*

**Cuba**
Work, Bruce Van Syoc *small business owner, consultant*

**De Soto**
Jackson, Candine Lee *performing arts educator, English and speech educator*

**Dearborn**
McInnis, Robin Lynn *voice educator*

**Des Peres**
Sadlo, Kenneth Louis *poet, writer*

**Dover**
Jobe, Angela Francine *postmaster, writer*

**Earth City**
Anderhalter, Oliver Frank *educational organization executive*
Bulger, Marc *professional football player*
Chandler, Christopher Mark (Chris Chandler) *professional football player*
Coakley, Dexter *professional football player*
Holt, Torry *professional football player*
Kroenke, E. Stanley *real estate developer, professional sports team executive*
Wallace, Bob (Robert Eugene Wallace Jr.) *lawyer*

**Edwards**
Findley, Kathryn E.C. *psychologist*

**Eldon**
Hannah, Melody Lorraine *music educator, elementary school educator*

**Ellisville**
Henry, Roy Monroe *financial planner*

**Eureka**
Baker, Donna Kay *music educator, director*
Lindsey, Susan Lyndaker *zoologist*

**Ewing**
Lueckenhoff, Mark Albert *elementary school educator*

**Excelsior Springs**
Mitchell, Earl Wesley *clergyman*

**Fayette**
Inman, Marianne Elizabeth *academic administrator*
Keeling, Joe Keith *theology studies educator, retired dean*
Vandelicht, Roy Dean *music educator*

Woodward, Ralph Lee, Jr. *historian, educator*

**Fenton**
Hoffman, Gilbert L. *information technology executive*
Huber, Scott *transportation services executive*
Kienker, James W. *marketing executive*
Lipovsky, Robert P. *marketing executive*
Maritz, W. Stephen *marketing professional, service executive*
McClure, Richard H. *transportation executive*
Powers, James G. *corporate financial executive*
Stadler, Gerald P. *transportation executive*

**Ferguson**
Chubb, Charles Ray *physicist, researcher*

**Festus**
Auchly, Christopher M *music educator*
Baker, Marycarol Germaine *physical therapist, educator*

**Florissant**
Ashhurst, Anna Wayne *foreign language educator*
James, Dorothy Louise King *special education educator*
Jones, Brian Keith *speech educator*
Kralemann, William Joseph *retired chemistry educator*
Linn, Dale E. *secondary school educator*
Reese, Alferd George *retired army civilian logistics specialist*
Stevens, Robert Edward *engineering company executive*
Stormer, John Anthony *retired minister, writer, publisher*
Tanphaichitr, Kongsak *rheumatologist, allergist, immunologist, internist*

**Forsyth**
Klinefelter, Sarah Stephens *retired dean, broadcast executive*

**Fortuna**
Ramer, James LeRoy *civil engineer*

**Four Seasons**
Bivins, Susan Steinbach *systems engineer*

**Fredericktown**
Sudmeyer, Alice Jean *art gallery owner*

**Fulton**
Backer, William Earnest *food products executive*
Forsythe, George Barnett *academic administrator, dean*
Garcia, Alfred Gerard *emergency physician, director*
Lamkin, Fletcher M., Jr. *academic administrator*
McClain, Cindy Dunstan *music educator*
Pierson, Katricia Guyn *language educator*

**Gainesville**
Sayles, Wayne Gerald *numismatist, writer*

**Graham**
Svoboda, Robert Ray *music educator*

**Grain Valley**
Olsson, Björn Eskil *railroad supply company executive*

**Granby**
Sparkman, Lyle Bruce *academic administrator, education educator*

**Grandview**
Ferguson, Cathy Lynne *elementary school educator*

**Gray Summit**
Desloge, Christopher Davis, Sr. *real estate company executive, merchant banking and consulting executive*

**Green City**
Bender, Patricia Ann *secondary school educator*

**Greenwood**
Zeller, Marilynn Kay *retired librarian*

**Hannibal**
Corkern, David E. *music educator*
Katsion, John Roy *communications educator*

**Harrisonville**
Mathew, Kip *music educator*

**Hazelwood**
Burleski, Joseph Anthony, Jr. *information technology executive*
O'Reilly, Mary Catherine *elementary school educator*

**Herculaneum**
Smelser, Douglas Martin *music educator*

**Hermann**
Mahoney, Catherine Ann *artist, educator*
Wilson, C. Daniel, Jr. *library director*

**High Ridge**
Karll, Jo Ann *retired judge, lawyer*

**Hillsboro**
Howald, John William *lawyer*
Stinson, Stanley Thomas *project manager*

**Holden**
Martin, Laurabelle *property manager*

**Hollister**
Canfield, Cindy Sue *art educator*
Herron, Gayle Ann *health facility administrator, forensic psychotherapist, consultant*
Hopper, Ruby Lou *clergy member*
Lowther, Gerald Halbert *lawyer*

**House Springs**
Grassino, Sandra Smith *theater educator, language educator*

**Independence**
Albano, Michael Santo John *lawyer*
Barker, Keith Rene *investment banker*
Burnett, Crystal Blythe *marketing professional*
Cady, Elwyn Loomis, Jr. *medicolegal consultant*
Devine, Michael J. *library director, educator*
Evans, Margaret Ann *human resources administrator, business owner*
Francis, Mary Frances Van Dyke *small business owner, real estate company executive, retired editor*
Franklin, J. Richard *principal*
Jackson, James Bruce *lawyer*
Lemon, Leslie Roy *radar meteorologist*
Pinick, Sariah Kay *music educator*
Pointer, Rosanne Elise *music educator*
Potts, Barbara Joyce *retired historic site director*
Rees, Elaine *chemistry educator*
Starks, Carol Elizabeth *retired principal*
Terry, Jack Chatterson *lawyer*
Tyree, Alan Dean *clergyman*
Wilding, Richard *library director*
Willett, Teri Kay *art educator*

**Ironton**
Sebastian, Phylis Sue (Ingram) *real estate broker, antique appraiser, real estate appraiser*

**Jefferson City**
Baker, Wade Franklin *retired state bar executive*
Bardwell, Rosemary Ann *elementary school educator*
Barrett, David F. *lawyer*
Bartlett, Alex *lawyer*
Blunt, Matt (Matthew Roy Blunt) *governor, former state official*
Brown, Vicki Knasel *newswriter*
Bussabarger, Mary Louise *retired mental health services professional*
Carnahan, Robin *state official*
Craver, Charles Henry *illustrator*
Deutsch, James Bernard *lawyer*
Farmer, Nancy *state official*
Kinder, Peter D. *lieutenant governor, former state legislator*
King, D. Kent *school system administrator*
Knox, William Arthur *judge*
Limbaugh, Stephen Nathaniel, Jr. *state supreme court judge*
Mahoney, Carolyn Ray *academic administrator*
McCaskill, Claire *auditor*
McDaniel, Sue Powell *writer*
Nixon, Jeremiah W. (Jay Nixon) *state attorney general*
Novotney, Donald Francis *superintendent of schools*
Parker, Sara Ann *librarian, consultant*
Price, William Ray, Jr. *state supreme court justice*
Russell, Mary Rhodes *state supreme court justice*
Stith, Laura Denvir *state supreme court justice*
Teitelman, Richard B. *state supreme court judge*
Tettlebaum, Harvey M. *lawyer*
White, Ronnie L. *state supreme court justice*
Wolff, Michael A. *state supreme court judge*

**Jennings**
Jansen, Michele R. *curriculum and instruction specialist*

**Joplin**
Habermann, James Herbert *retired pathologist*
Hand, Linda Marie *mathematics professor*
Massa, Richard Wayne *retired communications educator*
Scott, Robert Haywood, Jr. *lawyer*

**Kansas City**
Abuissa, Hussam *cardiologist*
Acheson, Allen Morrow *retired engineering executive*
Allen, John L., Jr. *journalist, writer*
Allen, Marcus *retired professional football player*
Amigoni, Michael *information technology executive*
Amoury, Raymond Anthony *retired surgeon, educator*
Anderson, Christopher James *lawyer*
Angoff, Gerald Harvey *cardiologist*
Atkinson, David Neal *law educator*
Ayers, Jeffrey David *lawyer*
Baisden, Eleanor Marguerite *retired airline compensation executive, consultant*
Baker, John Russell *utilities executive*
Baker, Ronald Phillip *service company executive*
Baker, Sharlynn Ruth *livery and limousine service owner*
Barnes, Kay *mayor*
Bass, Lee Marshall *food products company executive*
Bates, William Hubert *lawyer*
Batiuk, Thomas Martin *cartoonist*
Beck, William G. *lawyer*
Beckett, Theodore Charles *lawyer*
Beihl, Frederick *retired lawyer*
Belzer, Irvin V. *lawyer*
Benner, Richard Edward, Jr. *marketing consultant, volunteer, investor*
Benton, William Duane *federal judge*
Berkley, Eugene Bertram (Bert Berkley) *envelope company executive*
Berkowitz, Lawrence M. *lawyer*
Bevan, Robert Lewis *lawyer*
Blanton, W. C. *lawyer*
Bloch, Henry Wollman *diversified financial services company executive*
Bowman, Pasco Middleton, II, *judge*
Boysen, Melicent Pearl *finance company executive*
Bradshaw, Jean Paul, II, *lawyer*
Brake, Timothy L. *lawyer*
Brandmaier, Jeff *diversified financial services company executive*
Brandt, William Perry *lawyer*
Brett, George Howard *baseball executive, former professional baseball player*
Brisbane, Arthur Seward *newspaper publisher*
Brous, Thomas Richard *lawyer*
Brown, Peter C. *movie theater company executive*

Bugher, Robert Dean *professional society administrator*
Burger, Delores Theresa *historian, writer*
Busby, Marjean (Marjorie Jean Busby) *retired journalist*
Butler, Merlin Gene *physician, medical geneticist, educator*
Byers-Pevitts, Beverley *college administrator, educator*
Cao, Qing *information scientist, educator*
Caulfield, Joan *director, educator*
Chambers, Gina *school system administrator, education educator*
Cheng, Kuang Lu *chemist, educator*
Chesser, Michael J. *gas and electric power industry executive*
Churchman, Michael Steele Bright *educational consultant, educator*
Clarke, Milton Charles *lawyer*
Clegg, Karen Kohler *lawyer*
Collins, Kathleen *academic administrator, art educator*
Connor, Kevin M. *lawyer*
Courson, Marna B.P. *public relations executive*
Cozad, Rachael Blackburn *museum director*
Cross, William Dennis *lawyer*
Cunningham, Gunther *professional football coach*
Cunningham, Paul George *minister*
Danner, Kathleen Frances Steele *federal official*
Davis, James Robert *cartoonist*
Davis, John Charles *lawyer*
Davis, (Francis) Keith *civil engineer*
Davis, Richard Francis *city government official*
Deacy, Thomas Edward, Jr. *lawyer*
Dees, Stephen Phillip *agricultural products executive, lawyer*
Delaware, Richard Raymond *mathematician, educator*
Dias, Jerry Ray *chemistry professor, researcher*
Dicus, Stephen Howard *lawyer*
Diehl, James Harvey *church administrator*
Dietrich, William Gale *lawyer, real estate developer, consultant*
Dillingham, John Allen *marketing professional*
Dimond, Edmunds Grey *medical educator*
Dinakar, Chitra *immunologist, allergist*
Dobson, Rick *energy executive*
Dunn, Terrence P. *manufacturing executive*
Dwyer, William Michael *health care company marketing executive*
Eddy, Charles Alan *chiropractor*
Edmiston, Kelly Dane *economist, researcher*
Edwards, Herman *professional football coach*
Egan, Charles Joseph, Jr. *lawyer, consumer products company executive*
Eldridge, Truman Kermit, Jr. *lawyer*
Ernst, Mark A. *diversified financial services company executive*
Eubanks, Eugene Emerson *education educator, consultant*
Fetsch, Susan Hackler *nursing administrator, educator*
Finn, Robert W. *bishop*
Fiorella, Russell Michael *pathologist*
Foster, Mark Stephen *lawyer*
Frantze, David Wayne *lawyer*
Freeman, Frederick Roe *lawyer*
Friedlander, Edward Robert *pathologist*
Gallagher, Maggie *columnist*
Gansler, Robert *professional soccer coach*
Gardner, Brian E. *lawyer*
Geroe, Michael R. *lawyer*
Gibson, John Robert *federal judge*
Glaros, Alan G. *psychologist, researcher*
Gonzalez, Tony *professional football player*
Gorman, Gerald Warner *lawyer*
Gray, Helen Theresa Gott *editor*
Green, Frank Earl *civil engineer*
Green, Jerry Howard *investment banker*
Green, Trent Jason *professional football player*
Guilliland, Martha W. *academic administrator*
Gusewelle, Charles Wesley *journalist, writer*
Hagan, John Charles III *ophthalmologist*
Hall, Donald Joyce, Sr. *greeting card company executive*
Hall, Donald Joyce, Jr. *consumer products company executive*
Hamilton, Richard Alfred *academic administrator, marketing executive*
Hawley, R. Scott *research scientist*
Hebenstreit, James Bryant *agricultural products executive, venture capitalist*
Hebenstreit, Jean Estill Stark *religion educator, practitioner*
Heeter, James A. *lawyer*
Heymach, George John III *physician, educator, health facility administrator, consultant*
Hindman, Larrie C. *lawyer*
Hodges Morgan, Anne *historian*
Hoenig, Thomas M. *bank executive*
Hoffman, Gloria Levy *communications executive*
Hoffmann, Donald *architectural historian*
Holmes, Priest *professional football player*
Hunt, Lamar *professional football team executive*
Ibsen, Van *theater director*
Ingraham, James H. *diversified financial services company executive*
Johnson, Larry, Jr. *professional football player*
Johnson, Mark Eugene *lawyer*
Johnson, Mark P. *lawyer*
Johnson, Richard Dean *pharmaceutical consultant, educator*
Johnston, John Steven *lawyer*
Johnston, Lynn Beverley *animator*
Jonas, Harry S. *medical education consultant*
Judd, Barbara Anne *history educator, counselor*
Kaplan, Harvey L. *lawyer*
Kemper, Rufus Crosby, Jr. *retired bank executive*
Kilroy, John Muir *lawyer*
Kilroy, William Terrence *lawyer*
King, Richard Allen *lawyer*
Kirch, Donald Allen *writer, composer*
Knight, John Allan *clergyman, theology studies educator*
Krieg, Nancy Kay *social worker, poet, musician*
Krumlauf, Robert Eugene *neuroscientist, educator*
Kuenn, Marjorie Asp *music educator*
Langworthy, Robert Burton *lawyer*
Lashley, Curtis Dale *lawyer*
Laughrey, Nanette Kay *federal judge*
Lee, Margaret Norma *artist*

Armstrong, Theodore Morelock *corporate financial executive*
Arnold, Fred English *lawyer*
Arnold, John Fox *lawyer*
Atwood, Hollye Stolz *lawyer*
Aylward, Ronald Lee *lawyer*
Babler, Wayne E. *lawyer, retired utilities executive*
Bach, Richard Gordon *internist, cardiologist, educator*
Bachmann, John William *security firm executive*
Bacon, Bruce Raymond *physician*
Baernstein, Albert, II, *mathematician, educator*
Bagby, Robert L. *investment company executive*
Baker, Shirley Kistler *academic administrator*
Baker, W. Randolph *brewery executive*
Baldwin, Edwin Steedman *lawyer*
Balint, David Lee *engineering company executive*
Ball, Dan H. *lawyer*
Ballinger, Walter Francis *surgeon, educator*
Banks, Eric Kendall *lawyer*
Barksdale, Clarence Caulfield *retired banker*
Barmann, Lawrence Francis *historian, educator*
Barnickol, Karl R. *lawyer*
Bascom, C. Perry *retired foundation administrator*
Baum, Gordon Lee *lawyer, non-profit organization administrator*
Baum, M(ary) Carolyn *occupational therapist*
Baumer, Martha Ann *minister*
Baxter, Warner L. *energy executive*
Bealke, Linn Hemingway *banker*
Beck, Lois Grant *anthropologist, educator, author*
Becker, David Mandel *law educator, author, consultant*
Bellville, Margaret (Maggie Bellville) *communications executive*
Bender, Carl Martin *physics professor, consultant*
Berg, Leonard *retired neurologist, educator, researcher*
Berger, Wayne C. *retail executive*
Berland, David I. *psychiatrist, educator*
Bernstein, Donald Chester *brokerage house executive, lawyer*
Bextermiller, Theresa Marie *architect, computer engineer*
Bhatia, Sanjiv K. *math and computer science professor*
Bickel, Floyd Gilbert III *investment counselor*
Biondi, Lawrence *academic administrator, priest*
Bjerregaard, Preben *cardiologist, educator*
Blake, Allen H. *bank executive*
Blanton-Kuhl, Wendy Renee *social studies educator*
Blasingame, David Thomas *academic administrator*
Blumenthal, Herman Theodore *retired pathologist*
Bobak, Mark T. *lawyer*
Boddie, Don O'Mar *recording industry executive*
Bonacorsi, Mary Catherine *lawyer*
Boothby, William Munger *retired mathematics professor*
Borders, John Gillespie *psychotherapist, retired corporate financial executive*
Boyce, Gregory H. *energy executive*
Bradley, Marilynne Gail *advertising executive, educator*
Brauer, Camilla Thompson (Kimmy Thompson Brauer) *civic leader*
Brauer, Stephen Franklin *diplomat, manufacturing company executive*
Breece, Robert William, Jr. *lawyer*
Brickey, Kathleen Fitzgerald *law educator*
Brickler, John Weise *lawyer*
Brickson, Richard Alan *lawyer*
Bridgewater, Bernard Adolphus, Jr. *retired retail executive*
Briggs, William Benajah *retired aerospace engineer*
Brighton, Louis Andrew *religious studies educator*
Brockhaus, Joyce Patrica Dees *counselor, family therapist, consultant, family business consultant*
Brockhaus, Robert Herold, Sr. *business educator, consultant*
Brody, Lawrence *lawyer, educator*
Browde, Anatole *electronics company executive, consultant*
Browman, David L(udvig) *archaeologist*
Brown, Bobby R. *retired coal company executive*
Brown, JoBeth Goode *food products executive, lawyer*
Brownlee, Robert Hammel *lawyer*
Bryan, Henry C(lark), Jr. *retired lawyer*
Bryant, Donald L., Jr. *insurance and benefits company executive*
Bryant, Ruth Alyne *banker*
Buckley, Kevin William *lawyer*
Buggs, Dwayne Andre *fine arts coordinator, music educator*
Burgess, James Harland *physics professor, researcher*
Burgess, Robert Ronald *human resources executive*
Burgin, Richard Weston *writer, educator, editor*
Burke, Raymond Leo *archbishop*
Burke, William *neurologist*
Burkhart, Mark *real estate company executive*
Burroughs, Harold R. *lawyer*
Busch, August A., IV, *food products executive*
Busch, August Adolphus III *brewery executive*
Byrnes, Christopher Ian *engineering educator*
Cahill, Richard Anderson *medical educator*
Cain, James Nelson *arts school and concert administrator*
Capps, W. Lee III *retail executive*
Carlson, Arthur Eugene *accounting educator*
Carp, Larry *lawyer*
Carpenter, Chris *professional baseball player*
Carr, Gary Thomas *lawyer*
Case-Schmidt, Mary E. *pathologist, educator*
Chaitman, Bernard Raymond *internist*
Chaplin, David Dunbar *medical research specialist, educator*
Chaplin, Hugh, Jr. *preventive medicine physician, educator*
Charlson, Alan Edward *lawyer, retail executive*
Chole, Richard Arthur *otolaryngologist, department chairman*
Clark, John Walter *physics professor*
Clausen, Robert A. *chemicals executive*
Clear, John Michael *lawyer*
Cloninger, Claude Robert *psychiatrist, researcher, epidemiologist, educator*

Colletti, Ronald F. *chemist, researcher*
Concibido, Vergel C. *research and development company executive, writer, inventor*
Conner, Patrick T. *lawyer*
Conran, Joseph Palmer *lawyer*
Constantino, John Nicholas *medical educator, researcher*
Copeland, Douglas Allen *lawyer*
Corich, Evelyn Frances *mathematician, educator*
Cornfeld, Dave Louis *lawyer*
Cornfeld, Richard Steven *lawyer*
Correa-Perez, Juan Ramon *embryologist, science educator, director, lab administrator*
Corrigan, William M. *lawyer*
Costigan, Edward John *retired investment banker*
Cotton, W(illiam) Philip, Jr. *architect*
Cousins, Steven *lawyer*
Covington, Ann K. *lawyer, former state supreme court justice*
Cowsik, Ramanath *physics professor*
Crider, Robert Augustine *international financier, protective services official*
Cross, Anne Haney *neurologist, medical researcher*
Cryer, Philip Eugene *endocrinologist*
Cullen, James D. *lawyer*
Cupples, Stephen Elliot *lawyer*
Curran, Michael Walter *management consultant*
DaCorte, Allan Francis *financial consultant*
Danforth, John Claggett *lawyer, former ambassador, former senator*
Danforth, William Henry *retired academic administrator, physician*
Davidson, John *professional sports team executive, former hockey analyst*
Davis, Irvin *advertising executive, public relations executive, broadcast executive*
de Chasca, Edmund *editor, writer*
Demitra, Pavol *professional hockey player*
Devers, Gail *track and field athlete*
Dewald, Paul Adolph *psychiatrist, educator*
Di Bisceglie, Laureen Gail *pianist, accompanist, educator*
Dierberg, James F. *bank executive*
Ding, Cody *science educator*
Dodge, Paul Cecil *academic administrator*
Dodge, Philip Rogers *neurologist, educator*
Doggett, John Nelson, Jr. *clergyman*
Donati, Robert Mario *physician, educational administrator*
Dorsett, Dale *medical educator*
Dorwart, Donald Bruce *lawyer*
Dougherty, Charles Hamilton *pediatrician*
Dowd, Edward L., Jr. *lawyer, former prosecutor*
Dowd, Thomas F. *lawyer*
Downey, Michael Patrick *lawyer*
Dreifke, Gerald Edmond *electrical engineering educator*
Drey, Leo *environmentalist*
Drury, Charles Louis, Jr. *hotel executive*
Dudukovic, Milorad P. *chemical engineering educator, consultant*
Duesenberg, Richard William *lawyer*
Dugan, Jean Brodshaug *public relations executive*
Duhme, Carol McCarthy *civic worker*
Duncan-Hewitt, Wendy Carolyn *dean, medical educator*
Dykewicz, Mark Steven *physician*
Eagleton, Thomas Francis *lawyer, former senator*
Ebert, Robert T. *lawyer*
Eckstein, David *professional baseball player*
Edison, Bernard Alan *retired apparel executive*
Edmonds, James Patrick (Jim Edmonds) *professional baseball player*
Ehrlich, Ava *broadcast executive*
Elgin, Sarah Carlisle Roberts *biology professor, researcher*
Elkins, Ken Joe *retired broadcast executive*
Elliott, Howard, Jr. *lawyer, gas industry executive*
Elliott, Susan Spoehrer *information technology executive*
Ellis, Dorsey Daniel, Jr. *lawyer, educator*
Engelhardt, Irl F. *coal company executive*
Engelhardt, Thomas Alexander *editorial cartoonist*
Entessar, Tahmineh *political scientist, educator*
Epner, Steven Arthur *computer consultant*
Epstein, Robert Harry *lawyer*
Evans, Lawrence E. *lawyer, educator*
Evens, Ronald Gene *radiologist, educator, health facility administrator*
Evers, Alex Steven *anesthesiologist, internist, educator*
Eyerman, Charlotte *curator, art historian*
Ezenwa, Josephine Nwabuoku *social worker*
Fahrenkrog, Eugene Henry, Jr. *lawyer*
Falk, William James *lawyer*
Fanetti, Mary-June *writer, editor*
Farr, David N. *electronics executive*
Farria, Dione Marie *radiologist, educator*
Ferguson, Gary Warren *retired public relations executive*
Fessenden, Ann T. *law librarian*
Filippine, Edward Louis *federal judge*
Fingleton, Thomas D. *retail executive*
Fitch, Coy Dean *internist, educator*
Fitch, Rachel Farr *health policy analyst*
Fitzpatrick, Susan *biochemist, neurologist, foundation administrator*
Fleshman, James W. *medical association administrator*
Fletcher, Bill, Jr. *political organization executive, activist*
Flye, M. Wayne *surgeon, immunologist, educator, writer*
Folz, Carol Ann *benefits compensation analyst*
Fondaw, Ronald Edward *artist, educator*
Fontana, Luigi *internist, researcher*
Fournie, Raymond Richard *lawyer*
Foy, Betsy D. *health facility administrator, educator*
Fraley, Robert T. *biotechnologist*
Freiling, Marianne *principal*
Frieden, Carl *biochemist, educator*
Friedlander, Michael Wulf *physicist, researcher*
Fritz, Tarren Denise *elementary school educator*
Fritz, Gayle Peycke *music educator*
Fromm, Ronald A. *apparel executive*
Galvin, Walter J. *electrical equipment manufacturing executive*
Gass, William H. *writer, educator*
Gauen, Patrick Emil *news correspondent*

Gay, William Arthur, Jr. *thoracic surgeon*
Gelberman, Richard H. *orthopedist, surgeon*
George, Thomas Frederick *academic administrator*
Gibbons, Patrick Chandler *physicist, researcher*
Gilligan, Sandra Kaye *private school director*
Gillis, John Lamb, Jr. *lawyer*
Godiner, Donald Leonard *lawyer*
Goebel, John J. *lawyer*
Gokel, George William *organic chemist, educator*
Goldberg, Anne Carol *physician, educator*
Goldberg, Norman Albert *music publisher, writer*
Goldman, Scott Barry *psychologist*
Goldstein, Julius Lester *biomedical engineer, consultant*
Goldstein, Steven *lawyer*
Goran, Mark H. *lawyer*
Gordon, J. Eric *orthopedist, surgeon*
Gordon, Jeffrey Ivan *gastroenterologist, educator, molecular biologist, researcher*
Gould, Phillip Louis *engineering educator, department chairman*
Graff, George Stephen *aerospace transportation executive*
Grant, Hugh *biotechnology company executive*
Gray, Charles Elmer *lawyer, rancher, investor*
Greaney, Thomas L. *law educator, lawyer*
Green, Dennis Joseph *lawyer*
Green, Joyce *book publishing company executive*
Green, Maurice *molecular biologist, educator, virologist*
Greenbaum, Stuart I. *economist, educator*
Greenley, Beverly Jane *lawyer, educator*
Griffith, Thea R. L. *psychologist, researcher*
Griggs, Leonard LeRoy, Jr. *air transportation executive, consultant*
Gross, Michael Lawrence *chemistry professor*
Grossberg, George Thomas *psychiatrist, educator*
Grubb, Robert L., Jr. *neurosurgeon*
Grudzielanek, Mark James *professional baseball player*
Gruender, Raymond W. *federal judge, former prosecutor*
Guarigila, Dale A. *lawyer*
Guenther, Charles John *librarian, writer*
Guerin, Bill *professional hockey player*
Guerri, William Grant *lawyer*
Gupta, Surendra Kumar *chemicals executive*
Gustafson, David I *environmental scientist, researcher*
Hackmann, Frank H. *lawyer*
Haley, Johnetta Randolph *music educator*
Hamilton, Jean Constance *judge*
Hammerman, Marc Randall *nephrologist, educator*
Hanaway, Catherine Lucille *prosecutor*
Hancock, Camilla Ann *pharmacist*
Handel, Peter H. *physics professor*
Hanley, Thomas Patrick *obstetrician, gynecologist*
Hansen, Charles *lawyer*
Hansman, Robert G. *art educator, artist*
Harris, Whitney Robson *lawyer, educator, military officer, volunteer*
Harvey, David R. *chemical company executive*
Haslett, Jim *professional football coach*
Hassell, Stephen C. *information technology executive*
Hawkins, Pamela Leigh Huffman *biochemist*
Hayman, Randy E. *lawyer*
Hays, Howard H. (Tim Hays) *editor, publisher*
Heaney, Gerald William *federal judge*
Heiken, Jay Paul *physician*
Hellmuth, Theodore Henning *lawyer*
Herbert, Kevin Barry John *classics educator*
Hicks, Shirley E. *director*
Hiles, Bradley Stephen *lawyer*
Hirsch, Raymond Robert *chemicals executive, lawyer*
Hmiel, Stanley Paul *pediatrician, nephrologist, educator*
Hoessle, Charles Herman *zoological park administrator, director*
Holden, Robert (Bob Holden) *former governor*
Holliman, W. G. (Mickey), Jr. *furniture manufacturing executive*
Holmes, Nancy Elizabeth *pediatrician*
Holt, Glen Edward *editor*
Holtzman, David Michael *neurologist*
Howard, Michael Joseph *neuroscientist, researcher*
Hsueh, Eddy C. *surgeon, oncologist*
Huang, Yan (Christine) *informatics analyst*
Hungerford, Thomas William *mathematician, educator*
Hunt, Kevin J. *food products executive*
Hunt, Norma Jean *retired elementary school educator*
Hunter, Earle Leslie III *retired professional association executive*
Hunter, John C. III *chemicals executive*
Husar, Rudolf Bertalan *mechanical engineering educator*
Hyers, Thomas Morgan *internist, biomedical researcher*
Inkley, John James, Jr. *lawyer*
Israel, Martin Henry *astrophysicist, educator, academic administrator*
Izuchukwu, John Ifeanyichukwu *industrial engineer, mechanical engineer*
Jackson, Carol E. *federal judge*
Jacobsohn MD, Eric *anesthesiologist*
Jaudes, Richard Edward *lawyer*
Jayne, Thomas R. *lawyer*
Johnson, E. Perry *lawyer*
Johnson, Robert Graham *surgeon, educator, researcher*
Johnson, Sandra Hanneken *law educator*
Joley, Lisa Annette *lawyer*
Jones, Robert Gerard *lawyer*
Joyner, Dee Ann *bank executive*
Joyner Kersee, Jackie (Jacqueline Joyner Kersee) *retired track and field athlete*
Kalyanaraman, Ramki *education educator, researcher*
Kamel, Hosam Kamal *medical educator, researcher, geriatrician*
Kaminski, Donald Leon *surgeon, gastroenterologist, educator*
Kass, Michael Alan *ophthalmologist, educator*
Kaul, Siddharth *neuroscientist, researcher*
Keffler, Karl Joseph *investment company executive, lawyer*
Keller, Juan Dane *retired lawyer*
Kennedy, Craig *rental company executive*

Kennelly, Sister Karen Margaret *retired academic administrator, church administrator, nun*
Keyes, Marion Alvah, IV, *manufacturing executive*
Khoury, George Gilbert *printing company executive, sports association executive*
Kieschnick, Gerald B. *religious organization administrator*
Killenberg, George Andrew *publishing executive, consultant, retired editor*
Kimmey, James Richard, Jr. *foundation administrator*
King, Joseph, Jr. *federal agency administrator*
Kipnis, David Morris *physician, educator*
Kitchen, Mike *professional hockey coach, retired professional hockey player*
Klein, Ward M. *consumer products company executive*
Kling, Merle *political scientist, university official*
Klobasa, John Anthony *lawyer*
Knutsen, Alan Paul *pediatrician, immunologist, allergist*
Koehler, Harry George *real estate executive*
Koff, Robert Hess *academic administrator, adult education educator*
Kolker, Allan Erwin *ophthalmologist*
Kornblet, Donald Ross *retired communications company executive*
Kornfeld, Stuart A. *hematology educator*
Korotev, Randall L. *research scientist, editor*
Kouchoukos, Nicholas Thomas *surgeon*
Krasney, Rina Susan *school librarian*
Krem, Maxwell Masters *internist*
Kroll, Kristen L. *medical educator*
Kuhlmann, Fred Mark *lawyer*
Kusky, Timothy M. *geologist, educator*
Lackey, Kayle Diann *elementary school educator*
Ladd, Debbie K. *theater educator, director*
Lalime, Patrick *professional hockey player*
Lambright, Stephen Kirk *brewing company executive, lawyer*
Lane, Frank Joseph, Jr. *lawyer*
La Russa, Tony, Jr., (Anthony La Russa Jr.) *professional baseball manager*
Lauenstein, Ann Gail *librarian*
Lause, Michael Francis *lawyer*
Leavitt, Lynda *school system administrator, educator*
Lebowitz, Albert *lawyer, writer*
Lederle, Kenneth Joseph *director, secondary school educator*
Leer, Steven F. *mining executive*
Leguey-Feilleux, Jean-Robert *political scientist, educator*
Lents, Don Glaude *lawyer*
Lents, Peggy Iglauer *marketing professional*
Lenzen, Dana Diane *social studies educator*
Leonard, Judith Price *educational advisor*
Leven, Charles Louis *economics professor*
Le Vine, Victor Theodore *retired political science professor*
Lewis, Jeffrey E. *dean, law educator*
Lewis, Jodi A. *secondary school educator, theater educator*
Lewis, Robert David *ophthalmologist, educator*
Lieberman, Edward Jay *lawyer*
Liggett, Hiram Shaw, Jr. *retired diversified financial services company executive*
Limbaugh, Stephen Nathaniel *federal judge*
Lin, Tien-Sung Tom *chemistry professor*
Linehan, Scott *professional football coach*
Lock, Albert Larry, Jr. *finance company executive*
Loevinger, Jane *psychologist, educator*
Lohman, Janette Massie *lawyer, educator*
Lonsberg, John V. *lawyer*
Lovelace, Eldridge Hirst *retired landscape architect, city planner*
Lowenhaupt, Charles Abraham *lawyer*
Lowther, Thomas Edward *lawyer*
Lubbock, James Edward *retired writer, photographer, media consultant*
Ludmerer, Kenneth Marc *medical educator*
Ludwig, Fredrick J. *lawyer*
Lutz, John Thomas *author*
Lynch, Robert Martin *lawyer, consultant*
Macias, Edward S. *chemistry professor, dean, academic administrator*
Mahan, David James *retired academic administrator*
Mahsman, David Lawrence *writer*
Majerus, Philip Warren *physician*
Malone, Rich L. *financial services company executive*
Mandelstamm, Jerome Robert *lawyer*
Mantovani, John F. *pediatric neurologist*
Marti, Paul Edgar, Jr. *architect, educator*
Martin, Kevin John *nephrologist, educator*
Martin, Lisa Demet *lawyer*
Martínez-Solís, Luis Fernando *journalist, writer, historian*
Massey, Raymond Lee *lawyer*
Maurer, Frederic George III *bank executive*
McCarter, Charles Chase *lawyer*
McDaniel, James Edwin *lawyer*
McDonnell, Sanford Noyes *air transportation executive*
McGinnis, W. Patrick *diversified company executive*
McGuire, Walter F. *library director*
McKelvey, James Morgan *chemical engineering educator, retired dean*
McKinnis, Michael B. *lawyer*
McMahon, Robert M. *physician, lawyer*
McNamara, William P. *retail executive*
Medler, Mary Ann L. *federal judge*
Meisel, George Vincent *lawyer*
Merrell, James Lee *writer, minister*
Merrill, Charles Eugene *lawyer*
Metcalfe, Elizabeth Brokaw *art educator*
Metcalfe, Walter Lee, Jr. *lawyer*
Michaelides, Constantine Evangelos *architect, educator*
Michenfelder, Albert A. *lawyer*
Middelkamp, John Neal *pediatrician, educator*
Miller, Gary J. *political economist*
Miller, James Gegan *research scientist*
Miller, Judith Braffman *writer*
Mitchell, Louise Tyndall *special education educator*

**Wheeling**
Roe, Mary Ann *postmaster*

**Willow Springs**
Hinds, C. Robert (Bob) *retired writer*

**Windyville**
Condron, Barbara O'Guinn *philosopher, educator, academic administrator, writer*
Condron, Daniel Ralph *academic administrator, metaphysics educator*

**Wright City**
Schaffer, William D. *music educator, alderman*

## MONTANA

**Baker**
Whiteman, Jill Karen *music educator*

**Big Sky**
Ryan, Raymond D. *retired steel company executive, insurance company executive*
Strickler, Jeffrey Harold *pediatrician*

**Big Timber**
Bratvold, James *music educator*

**Bigfork**
Wetzel, Betty Preat *writer*

**Billings**
Barnea, Uri N. *conductor, musician*
Carter, Gary Wayne *environmental health specialist*
Cochran, William Michael *librarian*
Corey, Scott D. *music educator*
Cromley, Brent Reed *lawyer, state senator*
Fagg, Russell *judge, lawyer*
Glenn, Guy Charles *pathologist*
Habein, Harold Clinton *retired surgeon*
Haughey, James McCrea *lawyer, artist*
Jones, Doris Logan *artist, art educator*
Larsen, Kimbert E. *journalist*
Larsen, Richard Lee *city manager, consultant, retired mayor, arbitrator*
Mace, Michael R. *academic administrator, real estate development consultant, mortgage executive*
Mercer, William W. *prosecutor*
Nance, Robert Lewis *oil industry executive*
Paul, Bessie Margrette *retired weaher forecaster*
Peterson, Robyn Gayle *museum director*
Sample, Joseph Scanlon *foundation executive*
Stapleton, Corey *financial planner*
Thomas, Sidney R. *federal judge*
Thompson, James William *lawyer*
Towe, Thomas Edward *lawyer*
Zulkowski, Karen *nursing educator, researcher*

**Bonner**
Smith, Annick *writer*

**Bozeman**
Buonamici, April Graham *elementary school educator, music educator*
Cokelet, Giles Roy *biomedical engineering educator*
Davis, Nicholas Homans Clark *finance company executive*
DeHaas, John Neff, Jr. *retired architecture educator*
Duffié, Mary Katharine *anthropologist, educator*
Gamble, Geoffrey *academic administrator*
Gray, Philip Howard *former psychologist, writer, educator*
Grieco, Paul Anthony *chemistry professor*
Han, Jiaping *research scientist*
Horner, John Robert *paleontologist, researcher, curator*
Hufstetler, Mark Allan *historian*
Jacobsen, Jeffrey Scott *environmental scientist*
Langford, Chad *music educator, composer*
Mandell, John F. *chemical engineer, educator*
Mian, Ahsan *engineering educator, mechanical engineer*
Nehrir, M. Hashem *electrical engineer, educator*
Nelson, Steven Dwayne *lawyer*
Patten, Duncan Theunissen *ecologist educator*
Sanks, Robert Leland *environmental engineer, retired educator*
Stanislao, Joseph *engineering educator, consultant*
Stohr, Kate (Katherine A. Stohr) *freelance journalist*
Stroup, Richard Lyndell *economist, educator, writer*
Vick, Jeffrey Harrison *music educator, musician*
Warrick, Kimberley Kaye *language educator, social studies educator*
Welder, Rachael Mae *mathematician, educator*
Wylie, Paul Richter, Jr. *lawyer*

**Browning**
Thomas, Patrick *Native American tribal leader*

**Butte**
Clark, Gloria A. *music educator*
Gilmore, W. Franklin (Frank Gilmore) *academic administrator*
Harrington, Dan William *state senator*
Haugen, Margaret Ellen *daycare administrator*
L'heureux, Richard Allen *academic administrator, consultant*
Spear, Terry M *education educator, consultant*

**Clancy**
Ekanger, Laurie *retired state official, consultant*

**Colstrip**
Birk Shy, Dawn Marie *psychologist*

**Columbia Falls**
Chisholm, Dean D. *lawyer*
Spade-Shenker, George Lawrence (George Shenker) *research scientist*

**Cut Bank**
Roush, Glenn A. *state senator*

**Dayton**
Catalfomo, Philip *retired university dean*
von Volborth, Alexis *geochemist, geological engineering educator*

**Dillon**
Suenram, Andy *lawyer*
Tash, Bill *state senator*

**Emigrant**
Logan, Jesse A. *ecologist, researcher*

**Eureka**
Atherton, Michael Ward *music educator*
Kessler-Hodgson, Lee Gwendolyn *actress, performing company executive*

**Forsyth**
Heser, Cheryl J. *library director*

**Glendive**
McDonough, Russell Charles *retired state supreme court justice*

**Great Falls**
Anderson, Norman F. *social studies educator*
Davidson, David Scott *retired architect*
Doherty, Steve *lawyer, state legislator*
Hartelius, Channing Julius *lawyer*
Johnson, Gordon James *performing company executive, conductor*
Knudson, Ruthann *environmental consultant, anthropologist, archaeologist*
Kumar, Rajeev *research scientist*
Manning, John Willard *lawyer*
Santin, Antonio *plastic surgeon*
Stevens, George Alexander *real estate broker*
Voss, Lisa Marie *music educator*
Walker, Leland Jasper *civil engineer*

**Hamilton**
Henley, Jack Carson *retired military officer*

**Harlem**
Brekke, Alan Lee *industrial engineer*

**Havre**
Maristuen, Keith A. *lawyer*

**Helena**
Benyus, Janine M. *writer*
Bohlinger, John C. *lieutenant governor, former state legislator*
Cooney, Mike *former secretary of state*
Cotter, Patricia O'Brien *state supreme court justice*
Craig, Mary Lauri *accountant*
Fitzpatrick, Lois Ann *library administrator*
Franz, Holly Jo *lawyer*
Gray, Karla Marie *state supreme court justice*
Harrison, John Conway *retired state supreme court justice*
Hill, Richard (Rick) Allan *former congressman*
Johnson, Brad *state official*
Johnson, John Philip *geneticist, researcher*
Jones, Charles Irving *bishop*
Leaphart, W. William *state supreme court justice*
Lindgren, Robert Kemper *securities investor, auditor*
Mahlum, Dale Duane *state legislator, small business owner*
Mazurek, Joseph P. *lawyer, former state legislator*
McCulloch, Linda *school system administrator*
McGrath, Mike *state attorney general*
Meadows, Judith Adams *law librarian, educator*
Morris, Brian *state supreme court justice*
Nelson, James C *state supreme court justice*
Rabenberg, John *farmer, political organization worker*
Regnier, James *retired state supreme court justice*
Rice, Jim *state supreme court justice*
Scheet, Ethel Louise *rental company executive, consultant*
Schweitzer, Brian *governor*
Stearns, Sheila MacDonald *academic administrator*
Toole, Joan Trimble *financial consultant*
Trebon, Thomas *academic administrator*
Warner, John Arnan *state supreme court justice*

**Kalispell**
Freiberg, Robert Jerry *engineering executive*
Slater, Allen J. *music educator*
Vickers, Lee Louise *minister*

**Lodge Grass**
Rockabove, Magdalene M. *special education educator*

**Lolo**
Stewart, JoAnne *retired director*

**Manhattan**
Sanddal, Nels Dodge *foundation executive, consultant*

**Medicine Lake**
Nelson, Linda J. *state legislator*

**Missoula**
Borrie, William Thomas *communications educator*
Bowman, Jean Louise *lawyer, civic worker*
Brown, Bob (Robert Joseph Brown) *former state official*
Brown, Perry Joe *dean*
Brown, Robert Munro *museum director*
Brumit, Lawrence Edward III *oil industry executive*
Dennison, George Marshel *academic administrator*
Fawcett, Don Wayne *retired anatomist*
George, Alexander Andrew *lawyer*
Gillespie, Donald N. *immunologist, pediatrician*
Grieves, Forest Leslie *political science professor, department chairman*
Haines, John Meade *poet, translator, writer*
Jakobson, Mark John *retired physics professor*
Kittredge, William Alfred *humanities educator*
Latino, Chad Gregory *history educator*
Lopach, James Joseph *political science professor*

**McKeown, Ashley** *biological anthropologist, educator*
Millin, Laura Jeanne *museum director*
Molloy, Donald William *federal judge, lawyer*
Pavilack, Joann Clements *history professor*
Sullivan, Robert John *lawyer*
Tonev, Thomas (Toma) V. *mathematics professor*
Vogelsberg, Ross Timm *education educator, researcher*
Willey, Charles Wayne *lawyer*
Willstein, Gary Jay *orthopedist, surgeon*
Wollersheim, Janet Puccinelli *psychology professor*
Yee, Albert Hoy *writer, retired psychologist, educator*

**Moccasin**
Chen, Chengci *science educator, research scientist*

**Monarch**
Baker, David Warren *earth scientist*

**Polson**
Turnage, Jean Allen *retired state supreme court chief justice*

**Pony**
Anderson, Richard Ernest *agricultural engineer, consultant, rancher*

**Rollins**
Greer, Willis Roswell, Jr. *finance educator*

**Troy**
Sherman, Signe Lidfeldt *portfolio manager, former research chemist*

**Victor**
Davenport, Anne Marilyn *dietitian*

**Whitefish**
DeFranco, Boniface Ferdinand Leonard (Buddy DeFranco) *clarinetist, bandleader*
Miller, Ronald Alfred *family physician*

**Whitehall**
Bernard, Donald Ray *retired law educator*

**Winifred**
Butcher, Edward Bernie *state senator*

**Wolf Point**
Ulrickson, Virginia Gayle *elementary school educator, librarian*

## NEBRASKA

**Alliance**
Haefele, Edwin Theodore *political theorist, consultant*

**Arlington**
Moskus, Jerry Ray *retired academic administrator*

**Atkinson**
Sutherland, John Campbell *pathologist, educator*

**Aurora**
Lockmon, Nancy *mathematics educator*

**Beatrice**
Clawson, Rita Louise *curator*
Riedesel, Laureen Falk *library director*

**Bellevue**
Dorsey, Jacquelyn A. *secondary school educator*
Kayne, Jon Barry *academic administrator, psychologist*
Muller, John Bartlett *university president*
Stohlman, Bruce Richard *secondary school educator*

**Bellwood**
Lunde, Keith A. *music educator, animal breeder*

**Bennington**
Burgher, Louis William *physician, educator, academic administrator*

**Boys Town**
DiBacco, T. Jay *financial services executive, retired military officer*
Lynch, Thomas Joseph *museum director*

**Broken Bow**
Bigbee, Darlene Mae *retired medical/surgical nurse*
Sennett, John O. *lawyer*

**Cairo**
Wiebe-Brown, Beverly *music educator*

**Cedar Bluffs**
Fleischman, Brian William *mathematics educator*

**Chadron**
Carnot, Mary Jo *psychologist, educator*
Stack, Robert Vernon *dean, mathematics professor*
Younglove, Georgia A. *agricultural studies educator*

**Clay Center**
Hahn, George LeRoy *agricultural engineer, biometeorologist*

**Columbus**
Antholz, Marty *music educator*
Cunningham, Paris Lynn *systems administrator, consultant*
Schumacher, Paul Maynard *lawyer*
Thoms, Christopher Michael *elementary school educator*

**Crete**
Fahrlander, Eric *music educator*
Holmes, Andrea *chemistry professor, researcher*

**Elkhorn**
Walk, Louis Bernard *physician*

**Fort Calhoun**
Ware, Frederick *internist, educator, nephrologist*

**Fremont**
Dunklau, Rupert Louis *financial planner, consultant*
Roesch, Robert Eugene *dentist*

**Friend**
De Bevoise, Lee Raymond *editor, writer*

**Gering**
Peters, Gretchen J. *artist, educator*
Raines, Robert Randle *music educator*

**Grand Island**
Weseman, Vicki Lynne *elementary school educator*

**Gretna**
Druliner, Marcia Marie *education educator*

**Harrison**
Coffee, Virginia Claire *civic worker, former mayor*

**Hastings**
Dungan, John Russell, Jr., (12th Viscount Dungan of Clane, Hereditary Prince of Fermoy and Arra) *anesthesiologist, health facility administrator*
Katen, Troy William *basketball coach, academic administrator*

**Hebron**
Dunback, M. Kathleen Meyer *literature and language educator*

**Holdrege**
Cooper, Angela Dawn *historic site director*
Hendrickson, Bruce Carl *life insurance company executive*

**Hooper**
Poessnecker, Myron *music educator*

**Kearney**
Buckner, Nathan Andrew *music educator, musician*
Gonzalez, Eduardo *language educator, interpreter, translator*
Hardesty, Larry Lynn *librarian*
Johnston, Gladys Styles *university official*
Rohrer, James Russell *history professor*
Schnoor, Neal Henry *music educator*
Squires, Allison P. *nursing educator*

**Kimball**
Walker, Judy Lou *special education educator, director*

**Leigh**
Welsch, Kevin Eugene *music educator*

**Lincoln**
Beam, Clarence Arlen *federal judge*
Beermann, Allen J. *former state official*
Bicknell- Holmes, Tracy *librarian*
Bilder, Christopher R. *statistician, educator*
Binning, John Harlan *lawyer*
Blanke, Henry H., Jr. *retired theater educator*
Bradley, Richard Edwin *retired academic administrator*
Bruning, Jon Cumberland *state attorney general*
Bruskewitz, Fabian W. *bishop*
Burnham, Stephen Jenn *civil engineer*
Byrd, Lorelee *state treasurer*
Callahan, Bill *college football coach*
Christensen, Douglas D. *school system administrator*
Collier, Nathan Morris *musician, educator*
Connolly, William M. *state supreme court justice*
Deegan, Mary Jo *sociology educator*
Digman, Lester Aloysius *management educator*
Dixon, Wheeler Winston *film and video studies educator, writer*
Drullinger, Leona Pearl Blair *obstetrics nurse*
Dyer, William Earl, Jr. *retired newspaper editor*
Dyrland, Jonathan David Ellis *music educator, tenor*
Eckhardt, Craig Jon *chemistry professor*
Edison, Allen Ray *electrical engineer, educator*
Edwards, Donald Mervin *systems engineer, educator, dean*
Falcone, Anthony M. *music educator*
Fisher, Calvin David *food products executive*
Fleharty, Mary Sue *government agency administrator*
Francis, Charles Andrew *agronomy educator, consultant*
Gale, John A. *state official*
Gaskell, C. Martin *astronomer, educator, composer*
Genoways, Hugh Howard *systematic biologist, educator*
Gerrard, John M. *state supreme court justice*
Geske, Norman Albert *museum director*
Giesecke, Joan Ruth *librarian, dean*
Grady, Marilyn L. *education educator*
Grew, Priscilla Croswell *academic administrator, geologist, educator*
Guthery, John M. *lawyer*
Hanrahan, Kevin *music educator*
Hanway, Donald Grant *retired agronomist, educator*
Hardin, Martha Love Wood *civic leader*
Harris, Bernard *statistician, mathematician, educator*
Harwood, David M. *geologist, educator*
Hastings, William Charles *retired state supreme court chief justice*
Hawley, Kimra *computer company executive*
Heineman, David Eugene *governor*
Hendry, John V. *state supreme court justice*
Hewitt, James Watt *retired lawyer*
Hoffmann, Richard John *biology professor, dean*
Howard, Dan F. *retired art educator, artist*
Jones, Lee Bennett *chemistry professor, academic administrator*

Baloglu, Seyhmus *hospitality and tourism educator*
Bandt, Paul Douglas *radiologist*
Becker, Nancy Anne *state supreme court justice*
Bernstein, Maureen Ann *theater educator, director*
Bersi, Ann *lawyer*
Bishop, Leo Kenneth *clergyman, educator*
Bogden, Daniel G. *prosecutor*
Borovicka, Marsha Lorraine *music educator*
Boyd, William S. *hotel and entertainment facility executive*
Brammell, Stephen Harrison *lawyer*
Bridges, B. Ried *lawyer*
Broca, Laurent Antoine *aerospace scientist*
Brock, Holly Melinda *marketing professional*
Brown, Joseph Wentling *lawyer*
Bryan, Richard H. *lawyer, educator, former senator*
Buzard, Kurt Andre *ophthalmologist*
Bybee, Jay Scott *federal judge, former federal agency administrator*
Capanna, Albert Howard *neuroscientist, neurosurgeon, lawyer, banker*
Carnes, Zandy *trade association administrator*
Cho, Hokwon Anthony *mathematics professor*
Christensen, John William *lawyer*
Cole, Ann Harriet *psychologist, consultant*
Collins, Frank Edwin *lawyer*
Consul, Vincent A. *lawyer*
Culp, Gordon Louis *consulting engineer, management consultant*
DeBusk, Lorraine *elementary school educator*
DeLury, Bernard Edward, Jr. *lawyer*
Donaghy, Henry James *literature educator, academic administrator*
Donohue, Bradley Christopher *psychology professor*
Douglas, Michael Lawrence *state supreme court justice*
Dragone, Franco *performing company executive*
Duncombe, Patricia Warburton *retired social worker*
Duva-Mikhail, Donna Marie *financial executive*
Egidio, Martha L. *real estate broker and salesman*
Ensign, Michael S. *resort company executive*
Ernst, Suzanne *academic administrator, educator*
Faiss, Robert Dean *lawyer*
Ferrillo, Patrick J., Jr. *dean, endodontist*
Fleischer, Eric Matthew *music educator*
Frances, Marie Cecilia *theater producer, television producer*
Francis, Timothy Duane *chiropractor*
Freeman, J. P. Ladyhawk *vicar, underwater exploration, security and transportation executive, educator, model*
Frigard, Monique Denise *journalist*
Gafford, Mary May Grimes *retired humanities educator*
Gardner, Grace Joely *writer, consultant, psychologist*
Gaspar, Anna Louise *retired elementary school educator, consultant*
Gentile, Dominic P. *lawyer*
Gilchrist, Ann Roundey *medical/surgical nurse*
Goldblatt, Hal Michael *photographer, accountant*
Goodall, Leonard Edwin *public administration educator*
Goodenberger, Daniel Marvin *medical educator*
Goodman, Oscar Baylin *mayor, lawyer*
Goodwin, Nancy Lee *computer company executive*
Gostin, Irwin *retired lawyer*
Goulet, Robert Gerard *entertainer*
Gremse, David Albert *pediatrician, educator*
Griesche, Robert Price *hospital purchasing executive*
Haas, Robert John *aerospace engineer*
Hall, Gene E. *education educator*
Hamby, Jennifer Lynne *elementary school educator*
Hardie, George Graham *casino executive*
Hashem, Zouheir Anwar *engineering company executive, educator*
Herridge, Elizabeth *museum director*
Herzlich, Harold J. *chemical engineer*
Hilbrecht, Norman Ty *lawyer*
Hobbs, Guy Stephen *financial executive*
Hoepfner, Mark Thomas *surgeon*
Honsa, Vlasta *retired librarian*
Hua, Fred Huizhong *materials scientist*
Huston, Joyce A. *web site design company executive*
Jabara, Michael Dean *real estate developer, former technology entrepreneur*
Jackson, Charles Anthony *music educator, radio personality*
Jacobs, Gary N. *hotel executive, lawyer*
Jakopec, Carl Thomas *pharmaceutical executive*
James, Mark A. *lawyer, former state legislator*
Jelen, Ted G. *political scientist*
Jones, Fletcher, Jr. *automotive company executive*
Kasama, Hideto Peter *international business and investment advisor*
Kendell, Ken *music educator*
Knight, Gladys (Gladys Maria Knight) *singer*
Kurlinski, John Parker *physician*
Lally, Norma Ross *retired federal agency administrator*
Landau, Ellis *hotel executive*
Lanni, Terry (Joseph Terrence Lanni) *hotel corporation executive*
Laub, William Murray, Sr. *retired utilities executive*
Le Blanc, Suzanne *museum director*
Lee, Theodore Bo *real estate developer*
Leleu, Jonathan Paul *lawyer*
Lewis, Jerry (Joseph Levitch) *comedian*
Lima, Donald Roger *retired computer programmer*
Liu, Qunli *engineering educator, researcher*
Lovell, Carl Erwin, Jr. *lawyer*
Loveman, Gary W. *gaming company executive*
Luckett, Byron Edward, Jr. *chaplain, retired military officer*
Lukens, John Patrick *lawyer*
MacPherson, Grant *chef*
Mahan, James Cameron *judge*
Manley, Edward Harry, Jr. *professional association administrator, food products executive, retired military officer*
Marcella, Joseph *information scientist*
Marlon, Anthony M. *healthcare company executive, cardiologist*

Marnell, Anthony Austin, II, *architect*
Martinez, Adriana *political organization worker, photographer*
Massier, Paul Ferdinand *mechanical engineer*
Mataseje, Veronica Julia *sales executive*
Mc Elroy, John Harley *electrical and industrial engineering educator*
McNeal, Betty Jean *librarian, writer*
McNulty, James Francis, Jr. *lawyer, consultant*
Meiner, Sue Ellen Thompson *adult nurse practitioner, consultant, gerontologist*
Merkin, Albert Charles *pediatrician, allergist*
Messenger, George Clement *engineering executive, consultant*
Michel, Mary Ann Kedzuf *nursing educator*
Miller, Valerie Carol *journalist*
Mon, Kevin G. *research scientist*
Moore, Michael James *information technology executive*
Morgan, Richard J. *dean, law educator*
Moritz, Timothy Bovie *psychiatrist*
Moss, Gary Curtis *lawyer*
Muhlenbruck-Fleischer, Deborah Lynn *music educator*
Murren, James Joseph *recreational facility executive, hotel executive*
Neilsen, Craig H. *hotel executive*
Neumann, Edward Schreiber *transportation engineering educator*
Nicholson, R. Stephen *former cultural organization administrator*
Noback, Richardson Kilbourne *medical educator*
Norville, Craig Hubert *lawyer*
Palmer, Lynne *writer, astrologer*
Phillips, Karen *secondary school educator*
Pierce, Thresia Korte (Tish Pierce) *primary school educator*
Pro, Philip Martin *judge*
Ramos, Albert A. *electrical engineer*
Ramsey, Inez Linn *librarian, educator*
Rawlinson, Johnnie Blakeney *federal judge*
Reed, Ellen Beth *librarian*
Rieckenberg, Desiree *academic administrator*
Roberts, Lia *investor, political organization worker*
Robins, David *chef*
Rodgers, Steven Edward *tax practitioner, educator*
Root, Alan Charles *diversified manufacturing company executive*
Rosen, Leon *lawyer*
Sadineni, Suresh Babu *research scientist*
Safford, Florence Viray Sunga *travel agent, consultant*
Sakugawa, June Elizabeth *music educator*
Satre, Philip Glen *casino entertainment executive, lawyer*
Schaeffer, Glenn William *casino corporate financial executive*
Scherf, Dietmar *publishing executive, artist, minister*
Schneiter, George Malan *professional golfer, real estate developer*
Shannon, Samuel A. *chemist*
Shaw, Jeffrey William *gas industry executive*
Sheets, Thomas R. *lawyer, gas industry executive*
Shelton, Samantha *psychologist*
Sherry, Krystal A. *real estate broker*
Shires, George Thomas *surgeon, educator*
Shively, Judith Carolyn (Judy Shively) *administrative assistant*
Shuman, R. Baird *academic administrator, consultant, language educator, writer*
Shuster, Carl *food products executive*
Sillerman, Robert F. X. *communications executive, banker*
Silver, N. Clayton *psychology professor, consultant*
Singer, Clifford *mathematics educator, artist*
Sklar, Alan Curtis *lawyer*
Smith, Jimmy Wayne, Sr. *forensic specialist*
Snyder, John Henry *computer science educator, consultant*
Solomon, Jack Avrum, Jr. *lawyer, automotive executive, art dealer*
Sorrell, Michael E. *consulting company executive, hospitality executive*
Speck, Eugene Lewis *internist*
Spencer, Carol Brown *retired educational association administrator*
Stanley, Tim *information technology executive*
Stark, S. Daniel, Jr. *diversified financial services company executive*
Sturman, Glorida J. *lawyer*
Sulich, Vassili *artistic director*
Sullivan, Christopher David *real estate broker, real estate attorney*
Tash, Martin Elias *publishing company executive*
Teng, Francis W. *surgeon*
Tollman, Aaron Paul *military officer*
Trigiano, Lewis Ilวนศ *physician*
Trivelpiece, Craig Evan *computer electronics executive*
Walker, Randall H. *air transportation executive*
Wall, Clarence Vinson *state legislator*
Weeks, Gerald *psychologist, educator*
Welter, William Michael *marketing and advertising executive*
Wiemer, Robert Ernest *film and television producer, writer, educator*
Wiener, Valerie *state senator, writer, communications executive*
Williams, Mary Irene *business education educator*
Wilmott, Timothy J. *recreational facility executive*
Wilson, Joseph Morris III *lawyer*
Wooten, Glen Donovan *media consultant*
Wynn, Stephen A. *hotel and entertainment facility executive*

### Logandale
Smiley, Robert William, Jr. *investment banker*

### Minden
Bently, Donald Emery *electrical engineer*

### Nellis Afb
Malachowski, Nicole *pilot*

### North Las Vegas
Benson, Allen B. *chemist, educator, consultant*
Davis, Jennifer Ann *elementary school educator*
Folden, Norman C. (Skip Folden) *information systems executive, consultant*

Kelly, Christopher Pat *dean, educator*
Miller, Eleanor *English language and literature educator*
Talley, Brenda S. *performing arts center director, theatrical light designer*

### Pahrump
Evans, Charles Wayne, II, *biologist, researcher*

### Reno
Adams, Kenneth Robert *gaming analyst, writer, consultant, historian*
Aldrich, Gary O. *singer, educator*
Apassa, Cyril Omo-Osagie *clergyman, educator*
Bell, Robert Cecil *lawyer*
Binns, James Edward *retired banker*
Brennan, Susan Mallick *utilities executive*
Brunetti, Melvin T. *federal judge*
Burnett, John A. *director*
Carr, James Russell *engineering educator*
Cathey-Gibson, Sharon Sue Rinn *principal, academic administrator*
Chapman, Samuel Greeley *political science professor, criminologist*
Chrystal, William George *minister*
Clontz, Donna *lawyer, writer, consultant*
Cornell, Annie Aiko *nurse, administrator, retired military officer*
Crognale, Michael Anthony *medical educator, neuroscientist, consultant*
Crowley, Joseph Neil *political science professor, former academic administrator*
Cummings, Nicholas Andrew *psychologist*
Daniels, Ronald Dale *conductor*
Danko, George *engineering educator*
Dietrich, Dean Forbes *academic administrator*
East, Ernest Earl *lawyer, electric power industry executive*
Fletcher, Douglas Charles *lawyer*
Ford, Victoria *retired public relations executive, writer, oral historian*
Frank, Lillian Gorman *human resources executive, management consultant*
Fuerstenau, M(aurice) C(lark) *metallurgical engineer*
Gifford, Gerald Frederic *retired science educator*
Glick, Milton Don *academic administrator, chemist*
Goin, Peter Jackson *art educator*
Gundersen, Wayne Campbell *energy executive, consultant*
Guneyi, Umit Ahmet *physician, consultant*
Hafter, Jacob Louis *lawyer, paramedic*
Harder, Kelsie T. *artist, educator*
Harsh, Antoinette Mollett *investor*
Hayes, Steven Charles *psychologist, educator*
Haynes, Gary Anthony *archaeologist*
Hengstler, Gary Ardell *publisher, editor, lawyer*
Herzog, Serge *academic administrator, researcher*
Hibbs, Loyal Robert *lawyer*
Higgins, Walter M. III *electric power industry executive*
Howard, Christopher Philip *management consultant, investor*
Hug, Procter Ralph, Jr. *federal judge*
Jacobson, Raymond Earl *electronics executive*
Je, Chung-Hwan *engineering educator, researcher*
Johnson, David D. *lawyer, game company executive*
Kemmelmeier, Markus *sociologist, psychologist, educator*
Kleinfeld, Erwin *mathematician, educator*
Kleppe, John Arthur *electrical engineer, educator, engineering executive*
Klinefelter, Gary V. *lawyer*
Lee, H. Helen *music educator*
Leland, Joy Hanson *retired anthropologist, researcher*
MacKintosh, Frederick Roy *oncologist*
Mandl, William John *electronics engineer, researcher*
Mashour, Steve *pulmonologist*
Matthews, Thomas J. *game company executive*
McKibben, Howard D. *federal judge*
McLeod, Carolyn Louise *artist*
Middlebrooks, Deloris Jeanette *retired nursing educator*
Mitchell, David Lancaster *research educator*
Pagni, Albert Frank *lawyer*
Perry, Jean Louise *retired dean, academic administrator*
Pinson, Larry Lee *pharmacist, state agency administrator*
Price, Jonathan G. *geologist*
Ragavan, Anpalaki Jeyabalasinkham *software developer, researcher*
Raggio, William John *state legislator*
Reed, Edward Cornelius, Jr. *federal judge*
Robison, Kent Richard *lawyer*
Ross, Robert Donald *library director*
Sandoval, Brian Edward *federal judge, former state attorney general*
Santos, Herbert Joseph, Jr. *lawyer*
Savoy, Douglas Eugene *bishop, writer, religious studies educator*
Shoen, Edward Joseph *transportation and insurance companies executive*
Sladek, Ronald John *physics professor*
Small, Elisabeth Chan *psychiatrist, educator*
Smith, Catherine Parsons *music educator*
Svahn, John Alfred *federal agency administrator*
Taranik, James Vladimir *geologist, educator*
Vasquez, Victor R. *chemical engineering educator*
Veropoulos, Konstantinos *computer scientist, researcher*
Walrath, Harry Rienzi *retired minister*
Weinberg, Leonard Burton *political scientist*
Weniger-Phelps, Nancy Ann *media specialist, photographer*
White, John, Jr. *lawyer*
Zager, Bernard Solomon *physician, consultant*
Zaliapin, Ilya *geophysical statistician*

### Sandy Valley
Visculgia, Jenny Lou *music educator*

### Silver Springs
O'Malia, Mary Frances *special education educator*

### Sparks
Bonham, Harold Florian *research geologist, consultant*

Boyer, Patricia W. *publishing executive, editor*
Holder, Harold Douglas, Sr. *investor, hotel executive*
Lagasse, Bruce Kenneth *retired structural engineer*

### Stateline
Sprague, Billy Michael *aerospace transportation executive*

### Winnemucca
Hesse, Martha O. *gas industry executive*

### Yerington
Burrowes, Robert Arthur *transportation consultant, travel-tour operator*
Price, Judith Holm *educational psychologist*
Scatena, Lorraine Borba *retired rancher, women's rights advocate, researcher*

## NEW HAMPSHIRE

### Alstead
Holloway, Robert Charles *musician, composer*
Moore, Michele Claire *physician*

### Alton
Stevens, Thomas D., Jr. *secondary school educator, music educator*

### Amherst
Atwater, Verne Stafford *finance educator*
Buff, Margaret Anne *psychiatric nurse practitioner*
Johnson, Daryl Diane *painter*

### Auburn
Herman, William George *municipal official*

### Bedford
Cronin, Timothy Cornelius III *computer manufacturing executive*
Hall, Pamela S. *environmental services administrator*
Pasquerreli, Shawna *forensic specialist*
Steadman, David Rosslyn Ayton *corporate financial executive, director*

### Bennington
Verney, Richard Greville *paper company executive*

### Berlin
Doherty, Katherine Mann *librarian, writer*

### Bow
Emery, Paul Emile *psychiatrist*

### Brentwood
Bunker, Dusty (Sandra Coby) *writer*

### Campton
Benton, Geraldine Ann *preschool owner, director*
Scrimshaw, Nevin Stewart *physician, nutritionist, educator*

### Center Harbor
Shaw, Robert William, Jr. *management consultant, venture capitalist*

### Center Sandwich
Booty, John Everitt *retired theology studies educator*

### Colebrook
Bernard, Susan Shattuck *retired secondary school educator*

### Concord
Ayotte, Kelly A. *state attorney general*
Bagan, Merwyn *neurological surgeon*
Baldwin, Carolyn Whitmore *lawyer*
Barbadoro, Paul James *federal judge*
Blankenstein, Elizabeth M. *director, educator*
Broderick, John T., Jr. *state supreme court chief justice*
Brown, Tom Christian *newspaper publishing executive*
Chaney, Michael Parker *not-for-profit developer, writer*
Clemons, Jane Andrea *state legislator*
Colantuono, Thomas Paul *prosecutor, former state legislator*
Cote, David Edward *state legislator*
Dalianis, Linda Stewart *state supreme court justice*
DiClerico, Joseph Anthony, Jr. *federal judge*
Duggan, James E., Jr. *state supreme court justice*
Eaton, Thomas R. *state legislator*
Ferland, Brenda L. *state representative*
Flora, Kathleen M. *retired state representative*
Foster, Linda Timberlake *state legislator*
Francoeur, Sheila T. *state representative*
Galway, Richard E., Jr. *state supreme court justice*
Gardner, William Michael *state official*
Gartrell, Donald Everett *lawyer*
Gatsas, Ted (Theodore L. Gatsas) *state legislator*
Ginsburg, Ruth *state representative*
Hager, Elizabeth Sears *state legislator, social services administrator*
Heard, Charles Wolfe *lawyer, consultant*
Hesse, Richard A. *law educator*
Hicks, Gary Ellis *state supreme court justice*
Hill, Donald S. *state commissioner*
Hilliard, Russell F. *lawyer*
Howard, Jeffrey R. *federal judge*
Jillette, Arthur George, Jr. *school system administrator, educator*
Kaen, Naida *state representative*
Larsen, Sylvia B. *state legislator*
Laughlin, Larry *communications media executive*
Lynch, John H. *governor*
Matthews, William R., Jr., (Bill Matthews) *headmaster*
McAuliffe, Steven James *federal judge*
McCall, Junietta Baker *psychotherapist, minister*
Mevers, Frank Clement *state agency administrator, archivist*
Muirhead, James Russell *federal judge*
Norelli, Terie Thompson *state legislator*
Nowe, Ronald John *state legislator, small business owner*

Pilliod, James P. *state legislator, physician*
Potter, Fred Leon *lawyer, retired insurance company executive*
Rath, Thomas David *lawyer, retired prosecutor*
Resnick, Kenneth *photography director*
Richardson, Barbara Hull *state legislator, social worker*
Roberts, George Bernard, Jr. *management and government relations consultant, former state legislator*
Robinson, V. Gene (The Right Reverend V. Gene Robinson) *bishop*
Stickney, Nancy Carver *state legislator*
Thompson, Rob Roy *legislator, writer*
Tracy, Lyonel B. *school system administrator*
Uchida, Richard Y. *lawyer*
Vidaver, Robert Maxwell *medical educator*
White, Jeffrey George *healthcare consultant*
Young, Sherilyn Burnett *lawyer*

**Cornish**
Atkinson, James Blakely *writer, editor*

**Deering**
Spitzer, Morton Edward *management consultant*

**Derry**
Holmes, Richard Dale *history consultant*
Katsakiores, George Nicholas *state legislator, retired food service executive*
Sanborn, George Freeman, Jr. *genealogist*
Sapareto, Frank Vincent, II, *investment advisor, state legislator*

**Dover**
Catalfo, Alfred, Jr., (Alfio Catalfo) *lawyer*
Denaco, Parker Alden *state official, lawyer, arbitrator*
Nelson, Michael Underhill *educational association administrator*
Parks, Joe Benjamin *entrepreneur, retired state legislator*
Pelletier, Arthur Joseph *state legislator, data processing executive, educator*
Pelletier, Marsha Lynn *secondary school educator, poet*

**Dublin**
Hale, Judson Drake, Sr. *publishing executive, editor, writer*

**Durham**
Aitkenhead-Peterson, Jacqueline Ann *soil scientist, educator*
Allen, Michael Austin *language educator*
Appel, Kenneth I. *mathematician, educator*
Croce, Ronald Victor *neuroscientist, educator*
DeMitchell, Todd Allan *education educator*
Farrell, William Joseph *university chancellor*
Ford, Daniel (Daniel Francis Ford) *writer*
Gold, Janet Nowakowski *Spanish language educator*
Hapgood, Robert Derry *language educator*
Harris, John William *historian, educator*
Kaye, David Julian *theater educator*
Mallory, Bruce *academic administrator*
McCann, Francis (Frank) Daniel (Frank McCann) *historian, educator*
McConnell, Michael *art educator*
Newman, J. Bonnie *academic administrator, former government official*
Palmer, Stuart Hunter *sociology educator*
Pistole, Thomas Gordon *microbiology professor, researcher, department chairman*
Romoser, George Kenneth *political and social science educator*
Shea, Christine M. *education educator*
Simic, Charles *language educator, poet*
Wheeler, Katherine Wells *retired state legislator*
White, Ralph Paul *automotive executive, consultant*
Young, Arthur Price *librarian, educator*

**East Andover**
Gould, Donald Everett *retired chemical company executive, consultant*

**Enfield**
Gamache, Richard Donald *retired business development executive*

**Etna**
Picoult, Jodi *writer*

**Exeter**
Harmon, Richard Wingate *management consultant*
Thomas, Jacquelyn May *librarian*
Tingley, Tyler C. *headmaster*
Wicklein, John Frederick *journalist, educator*

**Farmington**
Panek, William Dominick *systems engineer executive*

**Fitzwilliam**
Schott, John Robert *international consultant, educator*

**Francestown**
Foster, Margery Somers *economics professor*
Milton, Peter Winslow *artist*

**Franconia**
Schaffer, David Edwin *retired systems administrator*

**Franklin**
Galloway, Jeanne Marie *public health service officer, consultant*

**Gilford**
Wood Parrish, Victoria Ann *minister*
Wool, Alan D. *mathematics educator*

**Glen**
Zager, Ronald I. *chemist, consultant*

**Goffstown**
Day, Russell Clover *state agency administrator*
Holden, Carol Helen *county official*

Martel, Eva Leona *accountant*
Wajenberg, Arnold Sherman *retired librarian, educator*

**Grantham**
Figley, Melvin Morgan *radiologist, physician, educator*
Grimley, Robert Thomas *chemistry professor*
Hansen, Herbert W. *management consultant*

**Hampstead**
Hargreaves, David William *retired communications company executive*

**Hampton**
Clark, Kevin P. *medical products executive*
Della Penta, David T. *medical products executive*
DuChene, Todd Michael *lawyer*
Meister, Paul M. *medical products executive*
Montrone, Paul Michael *scientific instruments company executive*

**Hancock**
Pollaro, Paul Philip *artist*

**Hanover**
Anthony, Robert Newton *retired management educator*
Bien, Peter Adolph *language educator, writer*
Boghosian, Varujan Yegan *sculptor, educator*
Bower, Richard Stuart *retired economist*
Brooks, H. Allen *architectural educator, author, lecturer*
Burnham, Patricia White *consultant, advocate, writer, business executive*
Chapman, Robert James *psychiatrist, educator*
Cook, William Wilbert *literature and language professor, department chairman*
Copenhaver, Marion Lamson *retired state legislator*
Crory, Elizabeth Lupien *retired state legislator*
Curphey, Thomas John *chemist, researcher*
Daniell, Jere Rogers, II, *retired historian*
Danos, Paul *dean, accounting educator*
Demko, George Joseph *geographer*
Dmitrovsky, Ethan *oncologist, medical educator, researcher*
Dong, Kui *music educator, composer*
Doyle, William Thomas *physicist, retired educator*
Ehrlich, David Gordon *film director, educator*
Fesen, Robert A. *astronomer, educator*
Fischel, William Alan *economics professor*
French, Kenneth Ronald *finance educator*
Fuechtner, Veronika *language educator*
Gardner, Peter Jaglom *lawyer, publishing executive*
Garthwaite, Gene Ralph *historian, educator*
Gazzaniga, Michael S. *neuroscientist, psychologist*
Gert, Bernard *philosopher, educator*
Govindarajan, Vijay *finance educator*
Green, Ronald Michael *bioethics educator*
Guerinot, Mary Lou *biology professor*
Hall, Raymond *social studies educator*
Heffernan, James Anthony Walsh *language and literature educator*
Hennessey, John William, Jr. *academic administrator, educator*
Horrell, Jeffrey Lanier *library administrator*
Hughes, Russell Profit *chemistry professor*
Kantrowitz, Arthur *physicist, researcher, educator*
Kemp, Karl Thomas *insurance company executive*
Kleck, Robert Eldon *psychology professor*
Koop, C. Everett (Charles Everett Koop) *former Surgeon General of the United States, educator*
Kritzman, Lawrence David *humanities educator*
Kurtz, Thomas Eugene *retired mathematics professor*
Lamperti, John Williams *mathematician, educator*
Langford, George Malcolm *cell biology educator*
Logue, Dennis Emhardt *finance educator, consultant, dean, writer, banker*
Lotko, William *engineering educator*
Lundquist, Weyman Ivan *lawyer*
Luxon, Thomas Hyatt *language educator, director*
Lyons, Gene Martin *political scientist, educator*
Mansell, Darrel Lee, Jr. *language educator*
Masters, Roger Davis *political scientist, educator, toxicologist*
Montgomery, David Campbell *retired physics professor*
Moss, Ben Frank III *art educator, painter*
Murdza, Peter John, Jr. *actuary*
Oxenhandler, Neal *literature educator, writer*
Peteraf, Margaret Ann *strategic management and organization educator*
Petitto, Laura-Ann *cognitive neuroscience educator*
Queneau, Paul Etienne *metallurgical engineering educator*
Riggs, Lorrin Andrews *psychologist, educator*
Rockmore, Daniel Nahum *mathematician*
Rolett, Ellis Lawrence *cardiologist, educator*
Russell, Robert Hilton *Romance languages and literature educator*
Rutter, Jeremy Bentham *archaeologist, educator*
Scher, Steven Paul *literature educator*
Scherr, Barry Paul *foreign language educator*
Shewmaker, Kenneth Earl *history professor*
Spielberg, Stephen Paul *dean, educator*
Starzinger, Vincent Evans *political scientist, educator*
Walp, Susan Jane *illustrator, educator*
Wegner, Gary Alan *astronomer*
Welsch, Robert Louis *anthropologist, curator*
Wright, James Edward *academic administrator, historian, educator*
Zubkoff, Michael *medical educator*

**Henniker**
Braiterman, Thea Gilda *economics professor, state legislator*
Gleason, James D. *lawyer*
Nitschke-Shaw, Debra Ann *education educator, dean*

**Holderness**
Butler, George Tyssen *film director, producer, photographer, writer*

**Hudson**
Ainley, David James *systems engineer, electrical engineer*

**Jaffrey**
Press, Fred *artist*
Walling, Cheves Thomson *chemistry professor*

**Keene**
Baldwin, Peter Arthur *psychologist, educator, author, minister*
Bell, Ernest Lorne III *retired lawyer*
Cohen, Richard B. *grocery company executive*
Crocker, Matthew Hallowell *historian, educator, writer, researcher*
Gooding, Judson *writer*
Gross, Mark *lawyer, food products executive*
Hackett, John Thomas *retired economist*
Harris, Reuben *wholesale distribution executive*
Higgins, Roland Louis *history professor*
Lichtenstein, Sally (Ali) Tucker *small business owner, writer, English and women's studies educator*
Miller, Rita *die-casting company executive, personnel consultant*
Pelletier, John B., Jr. *mathematics professor, consultant*
Salcetti, Marianne *newswriter, educator*
Scioli, Anthony *psychologist, educator*

**Kingston**
Walen, Harry Leonard *historian, lecturer, author*

**Laconia**
Brody, Spencer John *pediatrician*
Dhillon, Samjot Singh *pulmonologist*
Parthasarathy, Vinod *manufacturing engineer, consultant*

**Lancaster**
Pratt, Leighton Calvin *retired state legislator*

**Lebanon**
Bernat, James Lawrence *neurologist, educator*
Cohen, Jeffrey Allen *neurologist, educator*
Collins, E. Dale *surgeon, educator*
Cronenwett, Jack LeMoyne *vascular surgeon educator*
Darnall, Robert Allen *pediatrician, physiologist, educator*
Dillon Rydman, Linda Gay *nurse, consultant*
Emery, Virginia Olga Beattie *psychologist, researcher*
Fanger, Michael W. *medical educator*
Ferrell, Richard Bradley *neuropsychiatrist*
Fillinger, Mark F. *vascular surgeon, researcher*
Glass, Donald David *anesthesiologist*
Gosselin, Benoit Jean *otolaryngologist, facial plastic surgeon, head and neck reconstructive surgeon*
Kelley, Maurice Leslie, Jr. *gastroenterologist, educator*
Linnell, Robert Hartley *editor-in-chief*
McCollum, Robert Wayne *epidemiologist, educator*
McDonald, Brenna Cathleen *psychologist*
Munck, Allan Ulf *physiologist, educator*
Oxman, Thomas Elliot *psychiatrist*
Rosenberg, Stanley David *psychologist, educator*
Silberfarb, Peter Michael *psychiatrist, educator*
Waugh, Theodore Rogers *orthopedic surgeon*
Whitley, Rob *medical educator, sociologist, researcher*

**Lee**
Young, James Morningstar *internist, military officer*

**Litchfield**
Darlington, David William *management consultant*
Miller, Dawn Marie *retired meteorologist*

**Littleton**
Gallagher, James C. *lawyer*
Kelly, Dorothy Helen *pediatrician, educator*
Merritt, Thomas Butler *lawyer*

**Londonderry**
Osen, Gregory Alan *water conditioning company executive*
Parten, Priscilla M. *medical and psychiatric social worker, educator*

**Loudon**
Moore, Beatrice *religious organization administrator*

**Lyme**
Carmichael, Donald Scott *retired lawyer, retired corporate financial executive*
Cornwell, Gibbons Gray III *retired internist, educator*
Dwight, Donald Rathbun *publishing executive, corporate communications specialist*
McIntyre, Oswald Ross *physician*

**Manchester**
Arnold, Barbara Eileen *state legislator*
Bolduc, Diane Eileen Mary Buchholz *psychotherapist*
Carrier, Celine A. *psychologist*
Christian, Francis Joseph *bishop*
Danby, F. William *dermatologist, educator*
Ehrlich, Charles Gordon *insurance company executive, lawyer*
Haffer, Edward Anthony *lawyer*
Holmes, Ralph F. *lawyer*
Hower, Philip Leland *semiconductor device engineer*
Hutchins, Peter Edward *lawyer*
Joshuah, Richard Totten-Greenwood *elementary school educator*
Kamen, Dean *biomedical engineer*
Maloney, Simone *accountant*
Marchesseault, Anita *music educator*
Merideth, Susan Carol *business administration educator*
Middleton, Jack Baer *lawyer*
Monson, John Rudolph *lawyer*
Perkins, Charles III *newspaper and website editor*
Pochampally, Kishore K. *engineering educator*
Sklar, Daniel William *lawyer*
Wells, Robert Alfred *lawyer*
Wright, Mark A. *lawyer*

**Meredith**
Fahey, Mary Crane *elementary school educator*
Hatch, Frederick Tasker *research scientist, consultant*
Heald, Bruce Day *English educator, historian, music educator*
Lovett, Miller Currier *retired management educator, minister, educator*
Nyhan, Mary E. *literature and language educator*

**Meriden**
Brent, Patricia Lee *health facility administrator, writer*

**Merrimack**
Gallup, Patricia *computer company executive*

**Middleton**
Feyler, Carrie A. *elementary school educator*

**Milford**
Queeney, Deborah Ann *special education educator*

**Milton**
Edelman, Hendrik *library and information science professor*
Shean, Timothy Joseph *manufacturing executive*

**Mirror Lake**
Culleton, James Frederick *neurologist*

**Moultonborough**
Patten, Betsey Leland *state legislator*

**Nashua**
Arthur, Rose Ann Horman *dean*
Egan, John Frederick *retired electronics executive*
Grasso, Kristina Marie *lawyer*
Hanson, Arnold Philip *retired lawyer*
Hemming, Walter William *financial consultant*
Hermansen, Marcus C. *pediatrics professor, director*
Knights, Edwin Munroe *pathologist*
Lerch, Carol M. *mathematics professor*
Lumbard, Eliot Howland *lawyer, educator*
Mitsakos, Charles Leonidas *education educator, consultant*
Phelps, Bonnie Noreen *language educator, secondary school educator*
Pignatelli, Debora Becker *state official*
Provencher, Jeanne Stansfield *secondary school educator*
Seidel, Carl William *pharmaceutical executive, consultant*
Siroty, William Charles *physician*
Smith, Thomas Raymond III *software engineer*
Twedell, Terri Danni *writer, educator, artist*
Woodruff, Thomas Ellis *electronics consulting executive*
Wright, Elizabethada Amanda *communications educator*
Yannone, Ronald Matthew *systems engineer, researcher*

**New Castle**
Baker, Robert I. *manufacturing executive*
Friese, George Ralph *retail executive*

**New London**
Condict, Edgar Rhodes *manufacturing executive, minister*
Crane, Robert Kendall *engineering educator, researcher, consultant*
Ponder, Anne *academic administrator*

**Newmarket**
Ellis, David Wertz *retired museum director*
Getchell, Sylvia Fitts *librarian*
Jernigan, David Bruce *men's college basketball coach*

**Newport**
Gayvoronsky, Ludmila *artist, educator*
Stamatakis, Carol Marie *lawyer, former state legislator*

**North Hampton**
Taylor, Donald *retired manufacturing executive*

**Orford**
Karol, John J., Jr. *producer, filmmaker*
Martin, Allen *retired lawyer*

**Peterborough**
Bass, Perkins *retired lawyer, congressman*
Day, John Sidney *management sciences educator*
Eppes, William David *arts and humanities advocate*
Thomas, Elizabeth Marshall *writer*

**Pike**
Teschner, Douglass Paul *project administrator*

**Plainfield**
Brown, Judith Olans *retired lawyer, educator*

**Plaistow**
Goddu, Kevin Albert *secondary school educator*
Wilder, Dwight Safford *academic administrator*

**Plymouth**
Berona, David A. *library director, educator*
D'Aleo, Judith Anne *biotechnologist, consultant*
Gorin, Stephen H. *social worker, educator*
McGuire, Keven James *hydrologist, educator*
Roberts, William J. *mathematics professor*

**Portsmouth**
Baumann, Hans D. *engineering executive*
Bourgeault, Ronald *art appraiser*
Breen, Edward Deveaux *manufacturing executive*
Cunningham, Valerie S. *historic preservationist, researcher*
Doleac, Charles Bartholomew *lawyer*
Dumont, Mary *chef*
Harter, Hugh Anthony *foreign language educator*
Hopkins, Jeannette Ethel *book publisher, editor*
Lauter, M. David *physician*
Lytton, William Bryan *lawyer*
McCann, Margaret Hazel *artist, educator*

Nylander, Jane Louise *museum director, educator, writer*
Powers, Henry Martin, Jr. *oil industry executive*
Tober, Stephen Lloyd *lawyer*
Volk, Kenneth Hohne *lawyer*
Wener, Brian D. *psychologist*

**Randolph**
Bradley, Paula E. *former state legislator*

**Raymond**
Benz, Marilyn Christine *elementary school educator*

**Richmond**
Rogers, Barbara Radcliffe *writer*

**Rindge**
Burns, Gerald Thomas *literature and language professor*
Martin, Frederick Nichols *school system administrator*

**Rochester**
Coviello, Robert Frank *retail executive*
Dworkin, Gary Steven *insurance company executive*

**Rye**
Wilson, Ralph Sloan *retinal surgeon*

**Salem**
Courtois, Michael G. *biology educator*
Simmons, Marvin Gene *retired geophysics educator*
Smith, Laurence Roger *journal editor*
Stone, Patricia A. *special education services professional, consultant*

**Sanbornton**
Weiant, Elizabeth Abbott *retired biology professor*

**Sanbornville**
Berg, Warren Stanley *retired bank executive*

**Silver Lake**
Tregenza, Norman Hughson *investment banker*

**Somersworth**
Dahms, Bruce John *secondary school educator*
Gow, Linda Yvonne Carignan Cherwin *travel executive*

**Stoddard**
Cahill, George Francis, Jr. *physician, educator*

**Stratham**
Green, Catherine Cooper *artist*
Swartz, Jeffrey B. *apparel executive*
Terry, Elizabeth Hays *artist, small business owner*

**Tilton**
Found, Sandra Thrall *mathematics educator, mathematics professor*

**Walpole**
Burns, Kenneth Lauren *filmmaker, historian*

**Warner**
Coolidge, Daniel Scott *lawyer*
Hunt, Everett Clair *engineering educator, researcher, consultant*

**Waterville Valley**
Saenger, Bruce Walter *consulting firm executive*

**Weare**
White, Karen Ruth Jones *information systems executive*

**West Chesterfield**
Garinger, Louis Daniel *religion educator*

**West Lebanon**
Halperin, George Bennett *education educator, retired military officer*
Lawton, Jacqueline Agnes *retired communications executive, management consultant*

**West Swanzey**
Faulkner, Mary E. *treasurer*

**Wilmot**
Zuehlke, Richard William *communications executive, consultant, writer*

**Winchester**
MacKay, Neil Duncan *plastics company executive, consultant*

**Windham**
Arndt, Janet S. *former state legislator, educator*
Levin, Murray Newman *retired surgeon*

**Wolfeboro**
Bonin, Suzanne Jean *artist*

## NEW JERSEY

**Absecon**
Cartlidge, Edward Sutterley *mechanical engineer*

**Adelphia**
Carter, Harry Robert *fire protection consultant*

**Allendale**
Bisanzo, Mark Thomas *sales executive*
DeFeo, Neil P. *consumer products company executive*
DiBlasi, Dianne Clark *editor*
Petersen, Martin Ross *public affairs executive*
Ruth, Rodney *musician, music consultant, contractor, educator*

**Allentown**
Sulyok, Paul David *music educator, composer*

**Allenwood**
Carbone, Diane M. *psychologist, consultant*

**Asbury**
Hannay, Janneka Evans *artist*

**Asbury Park**
Avella, John Thomas *educational administrator*
Rosenbloom, Norma Frisch *lawyer*

**Atlantic City**
Jamieson, John Edward, Jr. *social services administrator, minister*
Knight, Edward R. *judge, psychologist, law educator*
Perry, James Benn *casino and hotel executive*
Pullman, Jennifer King *art educator, artist*

**Atlantic Highlands**
Hawley, Joseph B. *property management executive, educator*
Levine, George Lewis *literature and language professor, literary critic*
Tice, George A(ndrew) *photographer*

**Avenel**
Berg, Louis Leslie *investment executive*

**Avon By The Sea**
Bruno, Grace Angelia *accountant, retired educator*
Potter, Emma Josephine Hill *language educator*

**Barnegat**
Bronkowski, Mark John *textiles executive, real estate agent*

**Barnegat Light**
Gibbs, Frederick Winfield *lawyer, communications executive*

**Basking Ridge**
Besch, Lorraine W. *special education educator*
Buist, Richardson *retired corporate executive, retired banker*
Collis, Sidney Robert *retired telephone company executive*
Conklin, Donald Ransford *retired pharmaceutical executive*
Craven, Pamela F. *lawyer*
D'Ambrosio, Louis J. *telecommunications industry executive*
Drewry, Don Neal *fire protection engineer*
Evdukimow, David Z. *plastic surgeon*
Matthews, Craig Gerard *retired energy executive*
McGuire, Garry K., Sr. *communications executive*
McNamee, James M. *lab administrator*
Moden, Joleen *communications executive*
Morgan, Samuel P(ope) *physicist, applied mathematician*
Panzarino, Saverio Joseph *physician*
Peterson, Donald Kent *telecommunications industry executive*
Probert, Edward Whitford *foundation executive, volunteer*
Riesenberger, John Richard *science administrator*
Tamarelli, Alan Wayne *venture capitalist*

**Bay Head**
O'Brien, Robert Brownell, Jr. *banker, consultant, yacht broker, opera company executive*

**Bayville**
Worth, Katherine Marie *retired vocalist*

**Beach Haven**
Van Buren, William Benjamin III *retired pharmaceutical executive*

**Bedminster**
David, Edward Emil, Jr. *electrical engineer, engineering executive, management consultant*
Delehanty, Martha *human services administrator*
Eslambolchi, Hossein *communications executive*
Flaherty, Kathleen Ruth *telecommunications industry executive*
Gardner, David John *communications executive, sound recording engineer*
Graddick-Weir, Mirian *human resources specialist*
Hannigan, William J. *telecommunications industry executive*
Hart, Terry Jonathan *communications executive*
Hudacsko, Dennis Wayne *urban planner*
Laroia, Rajiv *communications executive*
Ripp, Joseph Allen *information technology executive*
Strigl, Dennis F. *telecommunications industry executive*
Weaver, Constance *communications executive*

**Belle Mead**
Brown, Elizabeth Schmeck *fashion historian*
Goodnick, Paul Joel *psychiatrist*
Sarle, Charles Richard *health facility executive*
Shiv, Kumar *bioscientist*

**Belleville**
Resciniti, John William *music educator, protective services official*
Salvini, Emil Robert *publishing executive, writer, historian*
Shuhan, Janice-Lynn Nazziola *secondary school educator*

**Belmar**
Downes, Laurence M. *gas industry executive*
Swett, Stephen Frederick, Jr. *artist, educator*

**Belvidere**
Walsh, John Alfred *retired social worker*

**Bergenfield**
Clark, Fred *writer, editor*
Davidson, Marilyn Copeland *writer, music educator, musician*
Dello Russo, Joseph *ophthalmologist*
Glazer, Gilda F. *musician, educator*
Marciano, Lisa Oggioni *musician, music educator*

**Berkeley Heights**
Geusic, Joseph Edward *physicist*

Mac Rae, Alfred Urquhart *physicist, electrical engineer*
Momeni, Reza *plastic surgeon*
Shaffer, Gail Dorothy *secondary school educator*

**Bernardsville**
Coheleach, Guy Joseph *artist*
Cooperman, Saul *retired educational association administrator*
Dixon, Richard Wayne *retired communications company executive*
Dixon, Rosina Berry *physician, pharmaceutical executive, consultant*
Robinson, Maureen Loretta *retired secondary school educator*
Spofford, Sally (Sally Hyslop) *artist*
Teiger, David *management consultant*

**Blairstown**
Bean, Bennett *artist*
Fechisin, Wendy Leigh *mathematics educator*

**Bloomfield**
Conta, Richard Vincent *actuary*
Glasser, Lynn Schreiber *publisher*
Glasser, Stephen Andrew *publishing executive, lawyer*
Lordi, Katherine Mary *lawyer*
Marcus, Phillip Ronald *management consultant*
Weisert, Kent Albert Frederick *lawyer*

**Bogota**
Condon, Francis Edward *retired chemistry professor*
McCann, Barry John *music educator*
Oakland, Ron *violinist*

**Boonton**
Bona, Frederick Emil *public relations executive*
Lunt, Alan Nicholas *rehabilitation services professional*
Ward, Solveig Maria *marketing professional*

**Bordentown**
Barker, Al C. (Albert Charles Barker) *artist*

**Bound Brook**
Shive, Richard Byron *architect*

**Bradley Beach**
Unger, Irwin *historian, educator*

**Branchburg**
Hulse, Robert Douglas *biotechnologist*

**Branchville**
MacMurren, Harold Henry, Jr. *psychologist, lawyer*
Murphy, Gregory E. *insurance company executive*
Pasvolsky, Richard Lloyd *retired parks, recreation, and environment educator*
Thomas, William H. *anthropologist, director*

**Brick**
Roache, Patrick Michael, Jr. *management consultant*
Shortess, Edwin Steevin *marketing consultant*
Tozer, Jean Frame *gifted and talented educator*

**Bridgeton**
Howell, James Burt III *retired agricultural products company sales consultant*

**Bridgewater**
Albrethsen, Adrian Edysel *metallurgist, consultant*
Bernson, Marcella S. *psychiatrist*
Dahling, Gerald Vernon *lawyer*
Faruqi, Abdul Rab *physician, consultant, researcher*
Glesmann, Sylvia-Maria *artist*
Hart, Karen Jean *special education educator*
Hirsch, Paul J. *orthopedist, surgeon, health facility administrator, medical educator*
Kennedy, James Andrew *chemical company executive*
Lowman, Tyrone David *entrepreneur*
Maynard, Kenneth Irwin *pharmaceutical executive, medical educator, researcher*
Patton, Diana Lee Wilkoc *artist, educator, illustrator*
Scully, John Thomas *obstetrician, gynecologist, educator*
Sethi, Shyam Sunder *management consultant*
Skidmore, James Albert, Jr. *management, computer technology and engineering services company executive*
Steinhart, Jessica *lawyer*
Taylor, Duncan Paul *pharmacologist, researcher*

**Brigantine**
Kickish, Margaret Elizabeth *elementary school educator*

**Brookside**
Fairchild, Samuel Wilson *investor, retired federal agency administrator, financial services executive*

**Browns Mills**
Cha, Se Do *internist*
Moore, Roger Addison *pediatrician, anesthesiologist*
Rakes, Randi Lee *elementary school educator, test developer*

**Budd Lake**
Webb, John Gibbon III *lawyer*

**Burlington**
Britt, Donna Marie *school nurse*
Haws, Elizabeth Anne *psychologist, director*
Rowlette, Henry Allen, Jr. *social worker, counseling psychologist*
Tang, Paul C. *lawyer*

**Butler**
Abdelsalam, Sylvia Claire *secondary school educator*
Ward, Robert Allen, Jr. *advertising executive*

**Caldwell**
Castano, Gregory Joseph *lawyer*
Lukabu Khabouji N'Zaji, *diplomat*
Mann, Robert Christopher *communications educator, television producer, television personality*
Palombo, Lisa *artist*
Savage, Joseph George *academic administrator*
Werner, Patrice (Patricia Ann Werner) *academic administrator*

**Califon**
Rosen, Carol Mendes *artist*

**Camden**
Ances, I. G. (I. George Ances) *obstetrician, gynecologist*
Beck, Susan J. *academic librarian*
Blyn, George *economics professor*
Brooks, Gail Denise *school system administrator, consultant*
Brotman, Stanley Seymour *federal judge*
Conant, Douglas R. *food products executive*
Daniels, Albertina Diana *secondary school educator*
Galante, Joseph A. *bishop*
Golub, Harvey *food products executive, former financial services company executive*
Gordon, Walter Kelly *retired academic administrator, retired language educator*
Harrison, Russell Sage *political science professor, consultant, social studies educator*
Hollenberg, Steven Michael *physician, researcher*
Irenas, Joseph Eron *judge*
Kaden, Ellen Oran *lawyer, consumer products company executive*
Laskin, Lee B. *judge, state senator*
Madan, Deepak S. *engineering executive*
Parra, Raul O. *urologist, educator*
Parrillo, Joseph Edison, Jr. *allergist, immunologist, cardiologist*
Pomorski, Stanislaw *lawyer, educator*
Rajaram, Sri-Sujanthy *internist, medical educator*
Reardon, Nancy Anne *food products executive*
Simandle, Jerome B. *federal judge*
Solomon, Rayman Louis *dean, law educator*
Uhler, Walter Charles *government official, writer*
Venegas, Arturo, Jr. *protective services official*
Whalen, Thomas Vincent *pediatric surgeon*
Worrall, John Dennis *economics professor, consultant, writer*
Yamada, Tetsuji *health economist, educator*

**Cape May**
Fox, Matthew Ignatius *publishing executive*
Savage, Maureen Walls *retired history professor*
Turner, Almon Richard *retired art historian, educator*

**Cape May Court House**
Altman, Brian David *pediatric ophthalmologist*
Cohen, Daniel Edward *writer*
Cohen, Susan Lois *writer*
Pierson, Jeffrey Lynn *protective services officer*

**Cape May Point**
Chandler, Marguerite Nella *real estate company executive*
Fraser, Malcolm Cavanagh *mayor*
Jordan, Joe J. *architect*

**Carteret**
Neff, Richard B. (Richie Neff) *consumer products company executive*
Standley, John T. *food market executive*
Strassler, Marc A. *corporate lawyer*
Vitrano, Frank G. *supermarket executive*
Volla, Steven L. *food products executive*

**Cedar Grove**
Carlozzi, Catherine L. *corporate communications consultant, writer*

**Chatham**
Earle, Jean Buist *finance company executive, computer company executive*
Finestein, Russell Mark *lawyer*
Hurley, Allyson Kingsley *dentist*
Jacobs, Andrew Robert *lawyer*
Kane, Cynthia M. *editor, writer*
Leonett, Anthony Arthur *banker*
Meagher, James Proctor *editor*
Murphy, Joseph James *chiropractic physician*
Sundberg, Carl-Erik Wilhelm *telecommunications executive, researcher*
Tepper, David A. *hedge fund manager*
Zegas, Alan Lee *lawyer*

**Cherry Hill**
Batterman, Steven Charles *engineering mechanics and bioengineering professor, consultant*
Berman, Steven Eric *audiologist*
Blakney, Juanita Mosley *psychotherapist*
Bryan, Henry Collier *clergyman, retired secondary school educator*
Clauser, Donald Roberdeau *musician*
Collins, Erica Harriet *communications executive, media consultant*
Copsetta, Norman George *real estate executive*
Erving, Julius (Julius Winfield Erving II) *retired professional basketball player, business executive*
Gardner, Joel Robert *writer, historian*
Garrigle, William Aloysius *lawyer*
Goldberg, Jack *hematologist*
Grado-Wolynies, Evelyn (Evelyn Wolynies) *nursing educator*
Hill, Vernon W., II, *bank executive*
Kahn, Marc Leslie *orthopedic surgeon*
Kole, Janet Stephanie *lawyer, writer*
Levin, Joshua Zev *computer scientist, consultant, transportation engineer*
Margolis, Gerald Joseph *psychiatrist, psychoanalyst*
Marrella-Davis, Christy Elizabeth *history educator*
Myers, Daniel William, II, *lawyer*
Olearchyk, Andrew *cardiothoracic surgeon, educator*
Rabic, James William *music educator, personal trainer*

Resor, Randolph Richardson *transportation consultant*
Rose, Joel Alan *legal consultant*
Rudman, Solomon Kal *magazine publisher*
Schelm, Roger Leonard *information systems specialist*
Swibinski, Edward Thomas *internist, endocrinologist, educator*
Trotter, Jeremiah *professional football player*
Van Syoc, Clifford Lee *lawyer*
Weinstein, Steven D. *lawyer*
Werbitt, Warren *gastroenterologist, educator*

**Chester**
Lynch, Beverly Love *language educator*

**Cinnaminson**
Edwin, Robert *voice educator*
Hanejko, Francis Gary *metallurgical engineer, metallurgist*
Lorenz, Betsy M. *elementary school educator*

**Clayton**
Bertenshaw, William Howard III *radio and television producer*

**Clementon**
Albee, Gloria *playwright*

**Cliffside Park**
Chelariu, Ana Radu *library director*
Goldstein, Howard Bernard *investment banker*
Perhacs, Marylouise Helen *musician, educator*

**Cliffwood**
Jaros, Robert James *information technology executive*

**Clifton**
Bronkesh, Annette Cylia *public relations executive*
DiNicola, Robert J. *consumer products company executive*
Feinstein, Miles Roger *lawyer*
Giles, William (Bill) T. *retail executive*
Klein-Von Reiche, Samuelle *psychologist*
Minkoff, John *mathematician, educator*

**Clinton**
Bosch, Robert John, Jr. *mechanical engineer*

**Closter**
Ribary, Urs *neuroscientist, educator*

**Colonia**
Wiesenfeld, Bess G. *interior designer*

**Colts Neck**
Borisov, George P. *music educator*
Crowder-Pagano, Linda Louise *special education educator*
Mauro, Anthony Peter *small business owner*
Schmalz, Elizabeth Moody *cosmetics company executive*

**Columbia**
Timcenko, Lydia Teodora *secondary school educator, biochemist*

**Columbus**
Litman, Bernard *electrical engineer, consultant*

**Cranbury**
Hawver, Dennis A. *psychologist, consultant*
Jaharis, Michael *pharmaceutical executive*
Kemmerer, Peter Ream *financial executive*
Yoseloff, Julien David *publishing company executive*

**Cranford**
Bergen, Bruce Harry *lawyer*
Bodian, Nat G. *publishing and marketing consultant, author, lecturer, lexicographer, historian*
Halleck, George Thomas *marketing professional*
Jenssen, Warren Donald *microbiologist, consultant*
Mack, William L. *real estate investment company executive*
Mazur, Leonard L. *pharmaceutical company executive*
McCreedy, Edwin James *lawyer*
Mendelson, Joel Stuart *allergist, immunologist*
Petryshyn, Wolodymyr V. *retired mathematician*
Russell, John Joseph *English educator*

**Cream Ridge**
Tomson, Jon Scott *management consultant*

**Cresskill**
Jurasek, John Paul *mathematics professor, counselor*
Marion, Winifred Zenorini *retired elementary school educator*
Smyth, Craig Hugh *fine arts educator*
Uehling, Gordon Alexander, Jr. *investment company executive*

**Deal**
Becker, Richard Stanley *music publisher*

**Delanco**
Lane, Carrie Belle (Hairston) *retired music educator*

**Demarest**
Dornfest, Burton Saul *anatomy educator*
Ruderman, Warren *chemist*

**Denville**
Doane, Eileen Maloney *learning disabilities teacher consultant*
Husar, Walter Gene *neurologist, neuroscientist, educator*
Minter, Jerry Burnett *electronics executive*
Tartaglia, Richard V. *priest*
Veech, Lynda Anne *musician, educator*

**Deptford**
Johns, Michael Douglas *healthcare executive, medical device executive, former federal government official*

**Dover**
Kassell, Paula Sally *editor, publisher*
Seadler, Stephen Edward *philosopher, writer*

**Dumont**
Sadock, Geoffrey J. *English professor*

**East Brunswick**
Applebaum, Charles *lawyer*
Daniel, Charles Timothy *transportation engineer, consultant*
Dombrowski, Anne Wesseling *retired microbiologist*
Hurst, Gregory Squire *investment company executive, theater director, theater producer*
Johnson, Edward Elemuel *psychologist, educator*
Kish, John R. *secondary school educator, music educator*
McDowell, Wilbur Benedict *retired chemist consultant*
Meningall, Evelyn L. *retired educational media specialist*
Savio, Frances Margaret Cammarotta *music educator*

**East Hanover**
Bess, Alan L. *pharmaceutical executive, physician*
Dodsworth, Roy W. *pharmaceutical company executive*
Harshman, Richard R. *manufacturing executive*
Iovel, Alla *music educator, writer*
Nelson, Barbara Kasztan *marketing professional*
Nemecek, Georgina Marie *molecular pharmacologist*
Purkayastha, Das D. *biostatistics director*
Tamburro, Peter James, Jr. *secondary school educator*

**East Orange**
Brundage, Gertrude Barnes *pediatrician*
Fielo, Muriel Bryant *interior designer*
Hudson-Zonn, Eliza *nurse, psychologist*
Ilogienboh, Caroline O. *protective services official, publishing executive*
Jones-Gregory, Patricia *art educator*
Tarver, Antonio *professional boxer*
Wolff, Derish Michael *economist, department chairman*

**East Rutherford**
Accorsi, Ernest William, Jr. *professional football team executive*
Arrington, LaVar *professional football player*
Brodeur, Martin *professional hockey player*
Burress, Plaxico *professional football player*
Carter, Vince *professional basketball player*
Cartwright, James William (Bill Cartwright) *professional basketball coach, retired professional basketball player*
Cathey, Gertrude Brown *retired medical/surgical nurse*
Coughlin, Tom *professional football coach*
Elias, Patrik *professional hockey player*
Frank, Lawrence *professional basketball coach*
Gionta, Brian *professional hockey player*
Gomez, Scott *professional hockey player*
Guevara, Amado *professional soccer player*
Jefferson, Richard *professional basketball player*
Julien, Claude *professional hockey coach*
Kempner, Michael W. *public relations executive*
Kidd, Jason *professional basketball player*
Kluge, John Werner *broadcasting and advertising executive*
Kutzer, Jamie *construction materials company executive*
Lamoriello, Louis Anthony *professional sports team executive*
Langenbrunner, Jamie *professional hockey player*
MacLean, John *professional hockey coach, former professional hockey player*
Manning, Eli (Elisha Nelson Manning) *professional football player*
Mashburn, Jamal *professional basketball player*
Mogilny, Alexander *professional hockey player*
Robinson, Clifford *professional basketball player*
Shockey, Jeremy Charles *professional football player*
Stevens, Scott *retired professional hockey player*
Strahan, Michael Anthony *professional football player*
Toomer, Amani *professional football player*
Umenyiora, Osi *professional football player*
Vanderbeek, Jeffrey *professional sports team executive*

**East Windsor**
Park, Hyosang *music educator*
Shoemaker, Frank Crawford *retired physicist*

**Eatontown**
Priesand, Sally Jane *rabbi*
Sullivan, Timothy Patrick *telecommunications company executive*

**Edgewater**
Berliner, Barbara *retired librarian, consultant*
Paci, Ruth A. *freelance/self-employed writer*

**Edgewater Park**
Mednick, Sheldon Ira *pharmacist*

**Edison**
Alexander, John Charles *pharmaceutical executive, preventive medicine physician*
Barnes, Peter J., Jr. *assemblyman*
Behr, Omri M. *lawyer*
Brisman, Jonathan *neurosurgeon*
Chen-Maxham, Li-Chan *soprano*
Currie, Robert *communications executive*
Fan, Shirley Tsui-Yu *music educator*
Gilmore, Adam Matthew *biophysicist*
Gizzi, Martin Sherman *neurologist, neurophysiologist*
Grewal, Raji Paul *neurologist, educator, medical researcher*
Hecht, William David *accountant*
Hunter, Michael *publishing executive*
Islam, Naushad S. *pharmacist, government agency administrator*
Miniere, Michael Anthony *mathematician, educator*

**Egg Harbor City**
Earl, Donald W. *treasurer, executive secretary*
Farris, Vera King *former college president*

**Egg Harbor Township**
Lashman, Shelley Bortin *retired judge*
Nelson, Edward R. *pianist, composer, educator, consultant*
Polillo, Ronald R. *federal official*
Schreiber, Eileen Sher *artist*

**Elizabeth**
Berger, Harold Richard *physician*
Bollwage, J. Christian *mayor*
Bomrind, Mitchel J. *rabbi*
de la Viña-Sierra, Diana Maria *music educator*
Gellert, George Geza *food importing company executive*
Lucco, James Perry *writer*
Pompey-Plummer, Danielle Nicole *counselor*
Rauh, Linda Ann *rehabilitation services professional, counselor*
Rosenstein, Neil *surgeon, genealogist, researcher*
Sananman, Michael Lawrence *neurologist*

**Elmwood Park**
Grodman, Marc D. *lab administrator, physician, medical educator*
Mangano, Louis *lawyer*

**Englewood**
Anuszkiewicz, Richard Joseph *artist*
Bloomenstein, Richard B. *plastic surgeon*
Chiorazzi, Mary Lorraine *psychiatrist*
Cohen, Wendy E. *neurologist*
Dallas, Dorothy Benz *painter, printmaker*
Dardik, Herbert *vascular surgeon, general surgeon*
DeJarnett, Rodney *headmaster*
Deresiewicz, Herbert *retired mechanical engineering educator, retired academic administrator*
Elias, Steven *surgeon*
Fay, Toni Georgette *communications executive*
Frieden, Faith Joy *obstetrician*
Goldweit, Richard Scott *cardiologist*
Gulko, Edward *healthcare executive, consultant*
Harish, Ziv *allergist, immunologist*
Kramer, Orin Stuart *investment services company executive*
Saliba, Philip E. *archbishop*
Schlossman, Howard Harvey *psychoanalysis educator*
Schmidt, Ronald Hans *architect*
Svezia, Vera Tisheff *concert pianist*
Tobias, Geoffrey *otolaryngologist, plastic surgeon*
Wuhl, Charles Michael *psychiatrist*

**Englewood Cliffs**
Books, Roberta Paula *real estate finance executive*
Dobrzynski, Judith Helen *journalist, commentator*
Farrell, Patricia Ann *psychologist, educator, writer*
Haltiwanger, Robert Sidney, Jr. *book publishing executive*
Insana, Ronald Gerard *newscaster*
Kim, Jae Taik *adult education educator*
Neis, Arnold Hayward *pharmaceutical company executive*
Saible, Stephanie Irene *magazine editor*
Yu, Fei *internist*

**Erial**
Browna, Jo McIntyre *nurse*

**Ewing**
Brunda, Daniel Donald *retired aerospace engineer, consultant, inventor, writer*
Gitenstein, Donna M. *academic administrator*
Liu, Xinru *history professor, researcher*
McCarty, John Albert *management educator*

**Fair Haven**
Di Turi, Christopher *dentist, educator*
McKissock, David Lee *retired manufacturing company executive*
Wyndrum, Ralph William, Jr. *communications consultant*

**Fair Lawn**
Carrera, Jaganath *acupuncturist, yoga educator*
Hurewitz, Florence *painter, educator*
Namerow, David Mark *pediatrician*

**Fairfield**
Byer, Theodore Scott *accountant*
Connell, William Terrence *lawyer, judge*
Sangiuliano, Barbara Ann *tax consultant*
Stein, Robert Alan *electronics executive*

**Far Hills**
Alexandre, Kristin Kuhns *public relations executive, writer*
Burns, Amy Margaret *music educator*

**Farmingdale**
Schluter, Peter Mueller *electronics executive*

**Flanders**
Hilbert, Rita L. *librarian*
Kuzma, Deborah J. *vice principal, music educator*

**Flemington**
Buchsbaum, Peter A. *judge*
Jacobsen, Betty *artist, art educator*
Kettler, Carl Frederick *airline executive*
Lance, Leonard *state legislator*
Miller, Louis H. *lawyer*

Pedescleaux-Muckle, Gail *retired business analyst, writer, artist*
Riley, Barbara Polk *retired librarian*
Roskoski, John *religious studies educator, coach*
Samek, Edward Lasker *medical transcription executive*
Traub, Richard Kenneth *lawyer*
Vellucci, Margaret Mary *librarian*
Vercammen, Kenneth Albert *lawyer, prosecutor*
Walters, Arthur Scott *neurologist, educator, clinical research scientist*
Winter, Robin Okner *health facility administrator*

Rubin, Arkady *biostatistics and data management researcher, executive*
Rushton, Alan R. *physician, medical researcher, historian*
Salamon, Renay *real estate broker*
Thomas, Anne Moreau *former newspaper owner*
Van Ost, Lynn *physical therapist, Olympic team official*
Wolfson, Barbara Libensperger *guidance counselor*
Zulker, Charles Bates *broadcasting company executive*

**Florham Park**
Altieri, James M. *lawyer*
Bossen, Wendell John *retired financial planner*
Brodkin, Adele Ruth Meyer *psychologist*
Chase, Eric Lewis *lawyer*
Fischer, Pamela Shadel *public relations executive*
Gale, Stan *real estate company executive*
Hardin, William Downer *retired lawyer*
Hull, Gerald W., Jr. *lawyer*
Kandravy, John *lawyer*
Laulicht, Murray Jack *lawyer*
Lavey, Stewart Evan *lawyer*
Long, Stephen R. *lawyer*
Malone, Robert K. *lawyer*
Naimark, George Modell *marketing and management consultant*
Negi, Devendra S. *communications services company administrator*
Nittoly, Paul Gerard *lawyer*
O'Connell, Daniel Francis *lawyer*
Pantel, Glenn Steven *lawyer*
Reid, Charles Adams III *lawyer*
Rexford, Jennifer *communications engineer*
Ridley, John A. *lawyer*
Rosenthal, Jeffrey M. *lawyer*
Smith, Theodore S. *lawyer*
Stryker, David Michael *lawyer*
Weisberg, Lynne Willing *psychiatrist, consultant*
Yeager, Mark *real estate company executive*

**Fords**
Ayers, Christopher James *special education educator*
Blond, Stuart Richard *magazine editor*
Brown, James *singer, broadcasting executive*

**Forked River**
Novak, Dennis E. *physician*

**Fort Dix**
Adams, Keith Robert *military officer*

**Fort Lee**
Altomara, Rita Ecke *library director, writer*
Amara, Lucine *vocalist*
Armellino, Michael Ralph *retired portfolio manager*
Baiul, Oksana *former figure skater, clothing designer*
Chessler, Richard Kenneth *gastroenterologist, endocrinologist*
Goldberg, Harry Finck *lawyer, consultant*
Goldfarb, Joel Peter *internist, gastroenterologist*
Kofman, Mikhail *economist, engineering executive*
Li, Tien-Shun *obstetrician, gynecologist, educator*
Lippman, William Jennings *investment company executive*
Morozova, Irina *musician, music educator*
Orman, Suze *news correspondent, writer*
Seitel, Fraser Paul *public relations executive*
Soejima, Daisuke *diversified financial services company executive, economist*
Stuart, Carole *publishing executive*
Sugarman, Alan William *educational consultant*
Thomopoulos, Michael *music educator*
Treskov, Yakov Maks *engineer*
Weinstock, George David *financial services company executive*

**Fort Monmouth**
Perlman, Barry Stuart *electrical engineer, researcher*
Schwering, Felix Karl *electronics executive, researcher*
Thornton, Clarence Gould *electronics executive, civilian military employee*

**Franklin Lakes**
Baker, Cornelia Draves *artist*
Considine, John *pharmaceutical company executive*
Friedman, Martin Burton *retired chemicals executive*
Ginsberg, Barry Howard *endocrinologist, educator*
Healy, Bridget M. *lawyer*
Ludwig, Edward J. *medical technology executive*
Machlowitz, David Steven *lawyer*
McGill, Kenneth, Jr. *mental health services professional*
Reed, JoAnn A. *corporate financial executive*
Snow, David B. *pharmaceutical executive*
Williams, Edward David *information technology management consultant*

**Freehold**
Anderson, James Francis *lawyer*
Cheng, Grace Zheng-Ying *music educator*
Christ, Duane Marland *retired computer systems engineer*
Foster, Eric Harold, Jr. *retail executive*
Greenstein, Gary *periodontist, dental educator*
Jawidzik, Edward Mark *priest*

**Galloway**
Carson, Keith Elmer *history professor*
Newell, Eric James *financial planner, retired insurance company executive*

**Garfield**
Herpst, Robert Dix *lawyer, optical materials company executive*
Yakimovich, Vladimir *chemist, director*

**Garwood**
Jannotti, Gene Patrick *business consultant, telecommunications professional*

**Gillette**
Knorr, Michael Jeffrey *architect*
Nathanson, Linda Sue *publishing executive, writer*

**Gladstone**
Close, Donald Pembroke *management consultant*
Kenny, Jane M. *management consulting executive*
Ocello, Claudia Barbara *museum program director*

**Glassboro**
Dahm, Kevin *chemical engineer, educator*
D'Augustine, Robert *academic administrator, lawyer*
Gephardt, Donald Louis *academic administrator*
Murashima, Kumiko *artist, educator*
Ramanujachary, Kandalam V. *chemistry professor, researcher*
Slater, C. Stewart *chemical engineering educator*
Wasserman, Burton *artist, educator*
Wright, William Cook *archivist, director*

**Glen Gardner**
Orfe, N. Michael *secondary school educator*

**Glen Ridge**
Addison, Herbert John *consulting editor, writer*
Agnew, Peter Tomlin *employee benefit consultant*
Pendley, Donald Lee *association executive*
Rubin, Roberta Gail *retired pathologist*
Zbar, Lloyd Irwin Stanley *otolaryngologist, educator*

**Glen Rock**
D'Angelo, Thomas J. *not-for-profit developer, financial consultant*
Mc Elrath, Richard Elsworth *retired insurance company executive*
Savoie, Brietta Dolores *retired librarian*

**Green Brook**
Balsamello, Melissa (Marley) *elementary school educator*
Bohanan, David John *management consultant*
Hertzberg, Henry *retired radiologist*
Spoeri, Randall Keith *healthcare company executive*

**Green Village**
Swift, John Francis *retired health care advertising company executive*

**Greenwich**
Lane, Mark *lawyer, educator, writer*

**Guttenberg**
Wright, Jane Cooke *oncologist, educator, consultant*

**Hackensack**
Abut, Charles C. *lawyer*
Agress, Harry, Jr. *radiologist, nuclear medicine physician*
Ahearn, James *columnist*
Basile, Anthony Stephen *pharmacologist, researcher*
Borg, Malcolm Austin *publishing executive*
Burt, Gwynne Elayne *minister, theology studies educator*
Caminiti, Donald Angelo *lawyer*
Corcoran, Robert Thomas *lawyer*
De Groote, Robert David *general and vascular surgeon*
Ferguson, John Patrick *health facility administrator*
Greenberg, Steven Morey *lawyer*
Gross, Peter Alan *epidemiologist, researcher*
Haines, Kathleen Ann *pediatrician, educator*
Heilborn, George Heinz *investor*
Horowitz, Donald *lawyer*
Kestin, Howard H. *judge*
Latimer, Stephen Mark *lawyer*
Margulies, James Howard *editorial cartoonist*
Masullo, Alfredo Salvatore *dermatologist*
Mavrovic, Paul J. *information technology executive*
Mullin, Patrick Allen *lawyer*
Parisi, Cheryl Lynn *art educator*
Pecora, Andrew Louis *hematologist, oncologist*
Pollinger, William Joshua *lawyer*
Rich, Tara Schillari *lawyer*
Smith, Daniel *oncologist, gynecologist*
Stein, Gary S. *retired judge, lawyer*
Vort, Robert A. *lawyer*
Williamson, (Eulah) Elaine *elementary school educator*

**Hackettstown**
Berrie, Marily Monteith *music educator*
Lamour, Kenol *artist, educator*
Mulligan, Elinor Patterson *lawyer*
Quade, Robert Thomas *finance educator*
Scalza, Margaret T. *publishing executive*
Singh, Harjit *medical educator, artist*
Van Campen, Stephen Bernard *executive recruiter, consultant*
Wiedemann, Charles Louis *dentist*

**Haddon Heights**
Westfield, Margaret Ann Hoyert *architect*

**Haddonfield**
Baltake, Susan *marketing professional*
Bauer, Raymond Gale *sales professional*
Capelli, John Placido *nephrologist, educator*
Chu, Horn Dean *chemical engineer*
Ewan, David E. *lawyer*
Fisher, George Ross III *physician, educator*
Gatti, Eugene Anthony *immunologist, pediatrician*
Iavicoli, Mario Anthony *lawyer*
Jensh, Ronald Paul *retired anatomist*

**Hainesport**
Sylk, Leonard Allen *manufacturing executive, real estate developer*

**Haledon**
Dougherty, June Eileen *librarian*

**Hamilton**
Blohm, Robert *investment banker, economist, statistician*

Cosentino, Andrew J. *retired art historian, curator*
Ebert, Lawrence Burton *lawyer*
Gideon, Richard Walter *broadcasting management consultant*
Paul, William Gerald *educational psychologist*
Sipski, Mary Leonide *physiatrist, health facility administrator*
Sporn, Aaron Adolph *physician, educator*

**Hamilton Square**
Ridolfi, Dorothy Porter Boulden *nurse, real estate broker*

**Hammonton**
Henshaw, Louise Ann *school psychologist*

**Hampton**
Yates, Michael Francis *management consultant*

**Harrison**
Srinivasan, Purushothaman *electrical engineer, researcher*
Winkleblech, Eileen *computer technology educator, career planning administrator*

**Hasbrouck Heights**
Colon, José Mariano *obstetrician, gynecologist, endocrinologist, educator*
Orchard, Robert A. *system science educator*
Perham, Roy Gates III *industrial psychologist*
Reutty, Michele Marie *library director*

**Haworth**
Strum, Brian J. *real estate company officer*

**Hazlet**
Marcus, Abir A. *psychiatrist*
Shea, James Bryan *writer*
Wilson, Elizabeth Sawin *psychiatrist*

**Helmetta**
Gabay, Eleonora V. *mechanical engineer, educator*

**Hewitt**
Mollenkott, Virginia Ramey *English literature and language educator, writer, guest lecturer*
Selwyn, Donald *engineering administrator, researcher, inventor, educator*

**Highland Park**
Blum, Lisa Carrie *social worker, researcher*
Brudner, Harvey Jerome *physicist*
Cheiten, Marvin Harold *playwright, manufacturing executive*
Feuerwerker, Elie *biologist, educator*
Fogiel, Max *publishing executive*
Grady, Joyce (Marian Joyce Grady) *psychotherapist, consultant*
Kolodzei, Natalia A. *art association administrator, art historian, curator*
McGoldrik, Monica *marriage and family therapist, researcher*
Spencer, Herbert Harry *structural engineer, researcher, computer analyst*
Youm, Gunwoong *food scientist*

**Highlands**
Hansen, Christian Andreas, Jr. *plastics and chemical company executive*
Psuty, Norbert Phillip *marine sciences educator*
Saunders Furda, Denise Elizabeth *music educator*
Skidmore, Nancy Lynne *music educator, pre-school educator*

**Hightstown**
Darr, Walter Robert *financial analyst*
Drotch, Eric Jay *artist, educator, researcher*
Elliott, Frank Nelson *retired college president*
Finn, Gerald C. *real estate company executive*
Finn, Jeffrey M. *real estate company executive*
Green, John F. *headmaster*
Hull, Gretchen Gaebelein *lay worker, writer, lecturer*
Miller, Mary Kathleen *secondary school educator*
Schorske, Carl Emil *historian, educator*
Szarawarski, Carollee *special education educator*

**Hillsborough**
Herman, David J. *infectious diseases physician*
Kenyhercz, Thomas Michael *pharmaceutical company executive*
Sun, Wei *electrical engineer*
Yuster-Freeman, Leigh Carol *broadcast executive*

**Hillsdale**
Copeland, Lois Jacqueline *physician*

**Hillside**
Dickerson, Martin Lee *principal*
Franks, Robert D. (Bob Franks) *former congressman*

**Ho Ho Kus**
Bryan, Thomas Lynn *lawyer, educator*
Deupree, Marvin Mattox *financial consultant*
Van Slooten, Ronald Henry Joseph *dentist*

**Hoboken**
Abel, Robert Berger *science administrator*
Boesch, Francis Theodore *electrical engineer, educator*
Bose, Ajay Kumar *chemistry professor*
Bostwick, Randell Armour *retired food service executive*
Chapman, Natalie Prichard *publishing executive*
Chassapis, Constantin *mechanical engineer, educator*
Eide, Hans A. *physicist, educator*
Erbe, Gary Thomas *artist*
Fassoulis, Satiris Galahad *communications company executive*
Griskey, Richard George *chemical engineering professor*
Hakki, Ayesha *editor-in-chief*
Lawrence, Victor B. *computer engineer, systems engineer*
Malek, Manu *information scientist, educator*
Moon, Deok Hyun *research scientist*
Raveché, Harold Joseph *academic administrator*

Savitsky, Daniel *retired structural engineer, retired educator*
Schmidt, George *physicist, educator*
Schultz, Kenneth Carl *antiques dealer*
Sisto, Fernando *mechanical engineering educator*
Sommers, George R. *lawyer*
Spring, Michael *editor, writer*
Tabora, Carolos Alberto *mathematician, educator*
Tardiff, Jill Alexandria *publishing executive, photographer*
Ubell, Robert Neil *editor, educator, publishing executive, consultant*
Upchurch, Leslie Purcell *music educator*
Voloshin, Yury *chemical engineer*
Widdicombe, Richard Palmer *librarian*
Xing, Yiping *electrical engineer, researcher*
Yao, Yu-Dong *electrical engineer, educator, electrical engineer, researcher*
zur Muehlen, Max *information systems educator, researcher*

**Holmdel**
Kogelnik, Herwig Werner *electronics company executive*
Lang, Howard Lawrence *electrical engineer*
Meyer, Robert Alan *management consultant*
Papadias, Constantinos Basil *electrical engineer*
Slovik, Sandra Lee *retired art educator*
Smith, Sibley Judson, Jr. *historic site administrator, educator*
Snyder, Michael F. *telecommunications industry executive*

**Hopatcong**
Ferderber-Hersonski, Boris Constantin *process engineer*
Oken, Robert *retired neuroscientist, consultant*
Reese, Harry Edwin, Jr. *electronics executive*

**Hope**
McDonald, John Joseph *electronics executive*

**Hopewell**
Baeckler, Virginia Van Wynen *librarian*
Lester, Pamela Robin *lawyer*
Woodward, Daniel Holt *librarian, researcher*

**Indian Mills**
Schroeder, James Edward *minister, consultant*

**Irvington**
Paden, Harry *municipal official*

**Iselin**
Accardi, Joseph Ronald *accountant*
Dornbusch, Arthur A., II, *lawyer*
Ilinich, Oleg *chemist, researcher*
Liu, Xinsheng *chemist*
Perry, Barry W. *manufacturing executive*
Smith, Orin Robert *chemical company executive*
Sperduto, Michael A. *corporate financial executive*

**Jackson**
Arminas, Scott Arnold *chemist, poet, writer*
Cohen, Walter Stanley *financial consultant*
Hagberg, Carl Thomas *financial executive*
Heck, Roberta M. *poet, writer*
Leveson, Irving Frederick *economist*
McCormick, Harold J. *music educator*
Ranone, John Louis *school board executive*
Tague, Charles Francis *retired engineering company executive, real estate company executive, construction executive*
Woodman, G. Roger *management consultant*

**Jersey City**
Al-Bashir, Mohamed Fahmi *surgeon*
Altamura, Mauro A. *artist, educator*
Balter, Leslie Marvin *business communications educator*
Bulaong, Grace F. *library director*
Coreil, Raymond Clyde *language educator*
Coyne, Frank J. *insurance industry executive*
Demos, Nicholas John *physician, surgeon, researcher*
Ezrati, Milton Joseph *investment manager, economist, writer*
Farrior, Evan Bell *special education educator, writer*
Goldberg, Arthur *merchant banker, financial consultant, educator*
Gurevich, Grigory *visual artist, educator, mime*
Hayes, Isaac *rhythm and blues singer, composer*
Healy, Jerramiah *mayor*
Hitchcock, John C. *communications media executive*
Ingrassia, Paul Joseph *publishing executive*
Jeng, Judy Horng *librarian*
Jennings, Sister Vivien *literature and language professor*
Katz, Colleen *publisher*
Klyatis, Lev Matusovich *test and reliability scientist*
Koster, Emlyn Howard *geologist, educator*
Kramer, Helene *banking executive*
Laski, John N. *finance educator*
Lipschutz, Neal S. *editor*
Mastro, Victor John *mathematician, educator*
Metallo, Frances Rosebell *mathematics professor*
Morales, Carlos *director, educator*
O'Dea, William Patrick *research and development company executive*
Ohiwerei, Godwin Oiseozoje *sociologist, educator*
Ott, Gilbert Russell, Jr. *lawyer*
Perhach, James Lawrence *pharmaceutical executive*
Pietrini, Andrew Gabriel *automotive aftermarket executive*
Queen Latifah, (Dana Owens) *recording artist, actress*
Shamburg, Christopher *education educator*
Singer, Howard Jack *biology professor, researcher*
Soo Hoo, Tsung (Bill) Yao *security studies educator, consultant*
Stine, Rick D. *editor*
Tang, C. Mark *investment banker, venture capitalist*
Thor, Ira P. *sports director*
Urso, Ida *psychologist*
Vasmatzidis, Ioannis *systems engineer*
Warren, Maredia Delois *music educator*

Yaworsky, Bohdan *law educator*

**Kearny**
John, Ricky *state official*

**Keasbey**
Hari, Kenneth Stephen *painter, sculptor, writer*

**Kendall Park**
DeLollis-Fitzgerald, Heather A. *special education educator*
Hershenov, Bernard Zion *research and development company executive*
Kesarwala, Hemant *pediatrician, educator*

**Kenilworth**
Bertolini, Robert J. *pharmaceutical executive*
Connors, Joseph Conlin *lawyer, pharmaceutical executive*
Cox, Carrie *pharmaceutical executive*
Gen, Martin *protective services executive*
Hassan, Fred *pharmaceutical executive*
Hoffman, John Fletcher *lawyer*
Jia, Yanlin *research scientist*
Johnson Velazco, Nancy Ruth *marketing professional*
Korfmacher, Walter Averill *chemist, researcher*
Pickett, Cecil B. *pharmaceutical executive*
Pickett, Cecil Bruce *cell biologist*
Yang, Tsong-Toh (T.T.) *pharmacist, researcher*

**Keyport**
Colmant, Andrew Robert *lawyer*

**Kinnelon**
Haller, Charles Edward *engineer, consultant*
Klaas, Nicholas Paul *management consultant*
Preston, Andrew Joseph *pharmacist, drug company executive*

**Kirkwood Voorhees**
Barr, J. James *company executive*

**Lafayette**
Muscalo, David *geologist, environmental consultant*

**Lakewood**
Bielory, Abraham Melvin *lawyer, finance company executive*
Conklin, Jack L. *education educator*
Fanuele, Michael Anthony *retired electronics engineer, research engineer*
Forbes, Gordon Maxwell *sportswriter, commentator*
Houle, Joseph E. *mathematics professor*
Karol, Frederick John *retired industrial chemist*
Levine, Stephen M. *psychologist, educator*
Levovitz, Pesach Zechariah *rabbi*
Pilgram, Suzanne *artist, art educator*
Williams, Barbara Anne *retired academic administrator*

**Lambertville**
Cusworth, Christyl J. *conservator, artist*
Thorstensen, Shelley M. *artist, educator*

**Landing**
Taylor, Alexander A. *information technology analyst, freelance/self-employed musician*

**Lanoka Harbor**
Lake, William Robert *school district administrator*

**Laurel Springs**
Cleveland, Susan Elizabeth *library administrator, researcher*
Roma, Aida Clara *artist*
Wood, Leonard James *lawyer*

**Lawrenceville**
Adams, Christine Hanson *advertising executive*
Ben-Asher, Daniel Lawrence *photojournalist, retired legislative staff member*
Coleman, Wade Hampton III *management consultant, mechanical engineer, retired banker*
Cox, Teri Polack *public relations executive*
Jordan, Mildred Rice Loretta *education educator*
Lackie, Robert Jonathan *university librarian, educator, consultant*
Oglesby, Jennifer Marie *clinical psychologist, neuropsychologist*
Pouleur, Hubert Gustave *cardiologist, consultant*
Rosenthal, Albert Lester *dermatologist, educator*
Rozanski, Mordechai *academic administrator*
Stehle, Edward Raymond *secondary education educator, school system administrator*
Stein, Sandra Lou *educational psychology professor*
Tharney, Leonard John *education educator, consultant*
Weaver, Charles Lyndell, Jr. *marketing executive, educational consultant*
Witte, Arnold Stewart *neurologist*

**Layton**
Seely, Maribeth Walsh *elementary school educator*

**Lebanon**
Barto, Susan Carol *writer*

**Leonardo**
Bianchi, Hollis Dolce *writer, poet, artist*

**Leonia**
Deutsch, Nina *pianist, vocalist*
Dondysh, Victoria *pianist*
Greenwald, Martin *publishing company executive*
Kurtz, Anthony David *physicist*

**Liberty Corner**
Apruzzese, Vincent John *lawyer*
Ganz, Felix *marketing professional*

**Lincoln Park**
Sichuk, George *entrepreneur, quantum biochemist, educator*

**Lincroft**
Benham, Helen *music educator*

Ruiz Madas, Yesenia *educational counselor*
Zigo, Paul Edward *historian, educator*

**Linden**
Bedrick, Bernice *retired principal, science educator*
Bukosky, Richard J. *allergist*
Covino, Charles Peter *chemicals executive*
Purves, Dennis Patrick *library director*
Suliga, Joseph *small business owner*

**Lindenwold**
Jackson, Yocontalie Ann *entertainment company executive*

**Linwood**
Chernoff, Deborah Shelley *art educator*
Sutman, Francis Xavier *university dean*

**Little Falls**
Berra, Yogi (Lawrence Peter Berra) *former professional baseball player, coach and manager*
Birnberg, Jack *financial executive*
Birnberg, Jeffrey *small business owner*
Casey, Karen Anne *banker*
Oliver, Raymond A. *lawyer*
Shern, Stephanie Marie *investment company executive, accountant*
Viil, Heino *retired engineer*

**Little Ferry**
Briggs, Alice *clinical child psychologist*
Hayes, Lynda Margaret *elementary school educator*

**Little Silver**
Brennan, William Joseph *manufacturing executive*
Schmidt, Daniel Edward, IV, *lawyer, arbitrator*

**Livingston**
Adelsberg, Harvey *hospital administrator*
Beerman, Herbert *art educator*
Brody, Martin *hotel executive*
Candido, A. Michael *contracting company executive, real estate manager*
Daman, Ernest Ludwig *mechanical engineer*
Friedman, Merton Hirsch *retired psychologist, educator*
Hallman, Thomas B. *finance company executive*
Ingato, Robert Joseph *lawyer*
Klein, Peter Martin *lawyer, retired transportation executive*
Leone, Joseph M. *finance company executive*
Peek, Jeffrey M. *corporate financial executive*
Rickert, Robert Richard *pathologist, educator*
Rinsky, Joel Charles *lawyer*
Samojlik, Eugeniusz *medical educator, health facility administrator*
Sikora, Barbara Jean *library director*
Stevens, William Dollard *mechanical engineer, consultant*

**Lodi**
Guillory, Ann Verrett *psychologist, educator*
Karetzky, Joanne Louise *librarian*
Karetzky, Stephen *library director, educator, researcher*
McParland, Robert Patrick *literature educator, writer*

**Long Branch**
Lagowski, Barbara Jean *writer, editor*
Luria, Martin Jay *endocrinologist*
Pachman, Frederic Charles *library director*
Stewart, Georgiana Liccione *writer*
Tesser, Dorothy *artist*
Woolwich, Madlyn-Ann Crawford *artist, educator*

**Lumberton**
Campagnolo, Mary Frances *physician*

**Lyndhurst**
Bunda, Stephen Myron *political advisor, counselor, lawyer, classical philosopher*

**Madison**
Armstrong, Richard William *bank executive, management consultant*
Beland, Matthew Robert *library assistant*
Bull, Vivian Ann *retired academic administrator, educator*
Byrd, Stephen Fred *human resource consultant*
Chang, Darwin Ray *civil engineer*
Demain, Arnold Lester *microbiologist, educator*
Ellenbogen, Leon *nutritionist, biochemist, retired pharmaceutical executive*
Essner, Robert Alan *pharmaceutical executive*
Goodman, Michael B(arry) *communications educator*
Jennings, George Harold *psychology professor*
Kaboub, Fadhel *economics professor, consultant*
Mahady, Joseph M. *former pharmacy products company executive*
Martin, Kenneth J. *pharmaceutical executive*
Mertz, Francis James *university president*
Monte, Bonnie J. *performing arts company executive, director, educator*
O'Brien, Mary Devon *communications executive, consultant*
O'Connor, Charles P. *lawyer*
Parker, Henry Griffith III *insurance executive*
Poussot, Bernard Jean *pharmaceutical executive*
Rosales Herrera, Raúl Joaquin *language educator*
Rubinstein, Ernest *librarian, educator*
Shelby, Bryan Rohrer *information systems management consultant*
Skaggs, Merrill Maguire *humanities educator*
Stein, Lawrence V. *lawyer*
Weisbuch, Robert Alan *academic administrator*
Wojtaszek, Kevin Joseph *director, video editor*

**Mahwah**
Bear, Larry Alan *retired lawyer, educator*
Davis, Henry Vance *education educator*
Gerstein, David Brown *manufacturing executive, professional sports team executive*
Gibbons, Robert Philip *management consultant, director*
Hailparn, Diana Finnegan *psychotherapist, writer*

Hilpert, Dale W. *retail shoe company executive*
Morneweck-Fuld, Lynn E. *music educator*
Padovano, Anthony Thomas *theologian, educator, literature educator*
Perez-Strumolo, Lysandra Marie *psychologist, educator*
Potocka, Katarzyna *mathematics professor*
Rakotobe-Joel, Thierry *engineering educator, researcher, department chairman*

**Manahawkin**
Barton, Noreen Duffy *secondary school educator*
Turkot, Dorothy Regester Felton *writer, illustrator*

**Manalapan**
Altruda, Paul F. *lawyer*
Chatterjee, Subhajit *information technology executive*
Mamoun, John Sami *dentist*
Stone, Fred Michael *lawyer*

**Manasquan**
Abate, John E. *electrical engineer, consultant*
Barr, Ted Walker *music educator*
Boodey, Cecil Webster, Jr. *retired political science professor*
Kelman, Marybeth *retired health care consultant, health policy analyst*
Nardone, Vincent Joseph *artist, educator*

**Maple Shade**
Abidi, S. Manzoor *neurologist*
Gordon, Paul *retired dentist, artist*

**Maplewood**
Ennis, Boyce *art facilitator, music director*
Haggerty, Mary Ann *medical educator*
Joel, Amos Edward, Jr. *telecommunications consultant*
Johnson, Dewey, Jr. *retired biochemist*
Joseph, Susan B. *lawyer*
Lally, Michael David *writer, actor*
Rabadeau, Mary Frances *protective services official*
Safian, Gail Robyn *public relations executive*
Shuttleworth, Anne Margaret *psychiatrist*
Tatyrek, Alfred Frank *retired chemist, environmental engineer*
Woods, Krystyna Janina *artist, pharmacist*

**Margate City**
Videll, Jared Steven *cardiologist*

**Marlboro**
Bass, David Steven *law educator, arbitrator, mediator*
Miller, Duane King *health and beauty care company executive*

**Marlton**
Cheney, Eleanora Louise *retired secondary school educator*
Clemens, David Allen *minister*
Farwell, Nancy Larraine *public relations executive*
Gorenberg, Charles Lloyd *finance company executive*
Kahn, Sigmund Benham *retired internist, dean*
Klein, Gerhart Leopold *public relations executive*
Laubach, Roger Alvin *accountant*

**Marmora**
Johnson, Joyce Ann *elementary school educator*

**Martinsville**
Raby, John Cornelius *secondary school educator*
Weiss, Allan Joseph *transport company executive, lawyer*

**Matawan**
Amato, Vincent Vito *marketing and business consultant*
Campbell, Earl Duncan *computer consultant*
Fennessy, James Gerard *retired engineer*
Liggett, Twila C. *academic administrator, broadcast executive, educator*
Nolan, Sharon Theresa *nurse, educator*
Rivera-Dominguez, Alberto *mathematician, educator, mechanical engineer*
Thompson, Samuel Donald *assemblyman*
Updegraff, Steven Phillip *music educator*

**Mays Landing**
May, John T. *college president*

**Medford**
Henderson, Rita Elizabeth *literary agent, journalist*
Kondracki, Edward Anthony *lawyer*
Lawson-Ndu, Ovunda A. *emergency physician, surgeon*
Mayer, Joyce Harris *artist*
Micko, Alexander S. *corporate financial executive, educator, treasurer*
Sheffer, James Thomas *music educator, elementary school educator*
Springer, Douglas Hyde *retired food products executive, lawyer*

**Mendham**
Allen-Scerbo, Susan Lynn *secondary education educator, counselor*
Bennett, Nancy Evans *secondary school educator*
Hambleton, George Blow Elliott *retired management consultant*
Kirby, Allan Price, Jr. *investment company executive*
Pierson, Robert David *investor*
Posunko, Barbara *retired elementary school educator*
Sagurton, Wilma *retired secondary school educator, musician, historian*

**Metuchen**
Arbeiter, Joan *artist, educator*
Demkovitz, Russell Bernard *deacon, cemetary director*
Kushinsky, Jeanne Alice *humanities educator*
Lasz, Anais *school librarian*
Macarin-Mara, Lynn *psychotherapist, consultant*

Massey, Eleanor Nelson *school librarian, media specialist*
Rhodes, Linda *pharmaceutical executive*
Smyth, David *writer, editor*
Stummer, Helen M. *photographer*
Zatz, Arline *writer, photographer*

**Middlesex**
Hilliard, Robert Allan *secondary school educator*

**Middletown**
Lundgren, Carl William, Jr. *physicist*
Rosenberg, Eric *mathematician*
Vitalo, Sandra Lynn Liddy *music educator, singer*

**Millburn**
Diamond, Richard S. *lawyer*
Kuttner, Bernard A. *retired judge, lawyer*
Tinning, Herbert Peter *association executive*
Wagenheim, Kal *journalist, editor*

**Milltown**
Haws, Robert John *lawyer*

**Monmouth Beach**
Danikas, Dimitrios *plastic surgeon*
Herbert, LeRoy James *retired accounting firm executive*

**Monmouth Junction**
Brolin, Robert Edward *physician, surgeon*
Lancaster, Barbara Mae *management consulting company executive*
Lawton, Deborah Simmons *librarian*
Lien, Ting-Ting *music educator*
Prestbo, John Andrew *editor, writer, journalist*

**Monroe Township**
Cushman, Helen Merle Baker *retired management consultant*
Meshowski, Frank Robert *business consultant*
Reichek, Morton Arthur *retired magazine editor, writer*
Spierer, Robert *family practice physician*
Zelin, Jerome *retired retail executive*

**Montclair**
Adarkar, Aditya *humanities educator*
Campbell, Stewart Fred *foundation administrator, consultant*
Chinard, Francis Pierre *physiologist, educator, consultant physician*
Cioffi, Patrizia *soprano, voice educator, arts consultant*
Cole, Susan A. *academic administrator, language educator*
Delbourgo, Joëlle Lily *publishing executive*
Delgado, Ramon Louis *theater educator, author, director, playwright, lyricist*
Du, Chunguang Charles *biologist, educator*
Eager, George Sidney, Jr. *electrical engineer, engineering executive*
Gill, Nia H. *state legislator*
Goldring, Nancy Deborah *artist, educator*
Gollob, Herman Cohen *retired publishing executive*
Green, Amy *psychiatrist*
Greenwald, Robert *public relations executive*
Holmes, Nathaniel J. *surgeon*
Lang, Gerhard *psychology professor*
Luftglass, Murray Arnold *corporate financial executive*
McConnell, Lorelei Catherine *retired library director*
Nielsen, Wendy Christine *literature educator*
Passchier, Sandra *geologist, educator*
Robila, Stefan Alexandru *education educator*
Rosen, Allen David *plastic surgeon*
Sims, Patterson *curator*
Stertz, Stephen Allen *historian, educator*
Walker, George Theophilus, Jr. *composer, music educator, pianist*
Williamson, Philemona *artist*

**Montvale**
Henkel, Herbert Ludwig *manufacturing executive*
Nachtigal, Patricia *lawyer*
Politi, Beth Kukkonen *publishing services company executive*
Scullion, Tony *pharmaceutical executive*
Unterbeck, Axel Joachim *pharmaceutical executive, director*

**Montville**
Birkett, Norman Myles *private school educator, writer*
Klapper, Byron D. *finance company executive*
Leeson, Lewis Joseph *pharmacist, researcher*
Lucibello, Alan Joseph *history professor*
Teubner, Ferdinand Cary, Jr. *retired publishing executive*

**Moonachie**
Ueltschi, Albert Lee *air transportation executive*

**Moorestown**
Bennington, William Jay *management consultant*
Buckman, William H. *lawyer*
Carson, William Charles *sales and marketing executive*
Clark, Maryliz M. *retired minister*
McDaniel, Joanava B. *nurse*
Missel, Esther Barbara *artist*
Schwerin, Horace S. *marketing research consultant*

**Morganville**
Sternfeld, Marc Howard *finance educator*

**Morris Plains**
Bennett, John Charles *former engineering and construction executive*
Fielding, Stuart *psychopharmacologist*
Goldenberg, David Milton *experimental pathologist, oncologist*
Spong, John Shelby *retired bishop, writer, columnist*

**Morristown**
Adler, Kenneth R. *oncologist*

Anderson, David J. *corporate financial executive*
Aspero, Benedict Vincent *lawyer*
Bromberg, Myron James *lawyer*
Cameron, Nicholas Allen *manufacturing executive*
Coleman, James H., Jr. *lawyer, former state supreme court justice*
Cote, David M. *diversified technology and manufacturing company executive*
Detrizio, Charles Santo *lawyer*
Fiel, Stanley Bruce *internist, pulmonologist, educator, researcher*
Finkel, Marion Judith *internist, pharmaceutical administrator*
Flynn, Marie Cosgrove *portfolio manager, corporate financial executive*
Fredericks, Robert Joseph *language company executive*
Gillen, James Robert *lawyer, insurance company executive*
Gilligan, Kevin *manufacturing executive*
Hafer, Frederick Douglass *utilities executive*
Haselmann, John Philip *management consultant*
Hastings, Mary Jane *minister*
Healey, Thomas J. *former government official, brokerage house executive*
Herzberg, Peter Jay *lawyer*
Humick, Thomas Charles Campbell *lawyer*
Hyland, William Francis *lawyer*
Kearns, William Michael, Jr. *investment banker*
Kirby, Fred Morgan, II, *manufacturing executive*
Kirby, Jefferson W. *investment company executive*
Kittelberger, Larry E. *engineering executive*
Korf, Gene Robert *lawyer*
Kreindler, Peter Michael *lawyer*
Lieberman, Lester Zane *engineering company executive*
Lieblich, Frederich *real estate consultant*
Martine, Cathy *telecommunications industry executive*
McConnell, John Howard *personnel management consultant, writer*
Miller, Steven H. *museum director*
Moore, Milo Anderson *banker*
Musa, John Davis *information technology executive, writer*
Nadaskay, Raymond *architect*
Nagle, Ronald T. *lawyer*
Newman, John Merle *lawyer*
Nolan, J. Michael, Jr. *retired lawyer*
O'Grady, Dennis Joseph *lawyer*
Olcott, John Whiting *air transportation executive*
Parker, Mary Lou *lawyer*
Parr, Grant Van Siclen *surgeon*
Pollock, Stewart Glasson *lawyer, state supreme court justice*
Prince, Leah Fanchon *lab administrator, executive secretary*
Prisco, Dorothy DeSteno *academic administrator*
Rainal, Attilio Joseph *retired electronics engineer*
Rose, Robert Gordon *lawyer*
Scott, Richard Thomas, Jr. *reproductive endocrinologist*
Sherman, Sandra Brown *lawyer*
Stanton, Patrick Michael *lawyer*
Stiskal, Joseph Alexander *neonatologist*
Venezia, William Thomas *school system administrator, counseling consultant*
Weidenkopf, Thomas W. *human resources specialist*
Williams, Joseph Dalton *pharmaceutical executive*
Wong, James Robert *oncologist, educator*
Zaubler, Thomas Scot *psychiatrist, educator*

**Mount Holly**
Hersh, David William *director*
Wille, John Jacob, Jr. *medical products executive, biologist*

**Mount Laurel**
Batory, Ronald Louis *rail transportation executive*
Giampetro, Kathleen A. *school psychologist*
Huttner, Louise Ann *mathematician, educator*
Mann, Louis Eugene *financial planner*
Rabbe, David Ellsworth *oil industry executive*

**Mountain Lakes**
Daniel, Royal Thomas III *lawyer, mechanical engineer, accountant*
Loomis, Rebecca C. *psychologist*

**Mountainside**
Bertsch, Patricia Ann *nature center director*
Helander, Robert Charles *lawyer, arbitrator*
Holton, Carlotta *editor-in-chief, writer*
Horner, Shirley Jaye *columnist, writing and publishing consultant*
Lipton, Bronna Jane *marketing communications executive*
Nielsen, Gwyn English *writer, illustrator, publishing executive, language educator*
Slabe, James F. *publishing executive*
Vice, Susan F. *medicinal chemist*
Weigele, Richard Sayre *police officer*

**Mullica Hill**
Rose, Carol Ann *retired air transportation executive*

**Murray Hill**
Brewington, James *telecommunications industry executive*
Bruch, Ruth E. *information technology executive*
Christy, Cindy *telecommunications industry executive*
Davidson, Janet G. *telecommunications industry executive*

**Neptune**
Aguiar, Adam Martin *chemist, educator*
Hanna, Niveen *surgeon*
Hersh, Steven Lance *hypnotherapist, writer*
Laraya-Cuasay, Lourdes Redublo *pediatrician, pulmonologist, educator*
Manuel, Sandra Lorraine *minister*
Rice, Stephen Gary *medical educator, pediatrician, sports medicine physician*
Zurick, Jack *electrical engineer, consultant*

**Neptune City**
Axelrod, Glen Scott *publishing executive, pet product company executive*

DeValue, John M. *retired computer science educator*

## Neshanic Station
Muckenhoupt, Benjamin *retired mathematics professor*

## New Brunswick
Alexander, Robert Jackson *economist, educator*
August, David Allen *surgeon*
Bachmann, Gloria Ann *obstetrician, gynecologist, educator*
Bertino, Joseph Rocco *physician, educator*
Biribauer, Richard Frank *lawyer*
Borah, Gregory *surgeon, educator*
Bowden, Henry Warner *religion educator*
Boyarsky, Andrew Harold *surgeon, educator*
Bradley, Dondeena G. *consumer products company executive*
Bunch, Charlotte *advocate*
Carson, Jeffrey L. *internist*
Chandler, James John *surgeon, educator*
Chatterjee, Indrani *history educator, researcher*
Clauss-Ehlers, Caroline S. *psychologist, educator, journalist*
Corbett, Siobhan Aiden *surgeon*
Coscia, Anthony R. *state agency administrator, lawyer*
Darretta, Robert J. *pharmaceutical executive*
Day-Salvatore, Debra Lynn *medical geneticist*
Deyo, Russell C. *health products executive*
Dormer, Michael J. *health products executive*
Dougherty, Neil Joseph *physical education educator, consultant*
Drachman, Richard Allan *pediatrician, educator*
Durnin, Richard Gerry *education educator*
Ehrenfeld, David William *biology professor, writer*
Elias, Maurice Jesse *psychology educator*
Ettinger, Lawrence Jay *pediatric hematologist, oncologist, educator*
Feigenson, Mark Daniel *geologist, educator*
Findley, Patricia Ann *social worker, health services researcher, educator*
Fine, Roger Seth *pharmaceutical executive, lawyer*
Foley, Eugene Arthur *accountant, consultant*
Foster-Cheek, Kaye I. *health products executive*
Funk, Cyril Reed, Jr. *agronomist, educator*
Gambino, Anthony Thomas *music educator, musician*
Gaunt, Marianne I. *university librarian*
Gillette, William *historian, educator*
Glasser, Paul Harold *sociologist, educator, social worker, university administrator*
Glickman, Norman Jay *economist, urban policy analyst*
Goggins, Colleen A. *health products executive*
Golbe, Lawrence Ingram *neurologist*
Goldberg, Michael Ira *obstetrician, gynecologist*
Greenberg, Michael Richard *urban studies and community health educator*
Greenwald, Alfred Emanuel *retired cosmetic surgeon*
Griffin, Gary Arthur *technological products executive*
Grob, Gerald N. *historian, educator*
Haines, William Joseph *retired pharmaceutical executive*
Hartman, Mary Susan *historian, educator*
Horowitz, Irving Louis *publisher, educator*
Huhmann, Maureen Brigitte *dietitian, researcher*
Jaluria, Yogesh *mechanical engineering educator, department chairman*
Jenkins, Alyce Mitchem *writer, educator*
Jenkins, Reese V. *historian, educator*
Kahn, Jeffry *mathematics professor*
Kamen, Barton A. *pediatrician, educator*
Katz, James E. *communications educator*
Kaufman, Kenneth Roland *psychiatrist, educator*
Kelley, Donald Reed *historian*
Khachadurian, Avedis *physician*
Kostis, John Basil *cardiologist*
Kruskal, Martin David *mathematical physicist, astrophysicist, educator*
Kubik, Jan *political science professor*
Kulikowski, Casimir Alexander *computer scientist, engineer, educator*
Lachance, Paul Albert *food science educator, clergyman*
Lacy, Clifton R. *internist, commissioner*
Lambert, George H. *physician, director*
Larsen, Ralph S(tanley) *retired pharmaceutical executive*
Lenehan, James T. *pharmaceutical executive*
Lepore, Frederick Everett *neurologist, educator*
Leventhal, Elaine A. *internist*
Leventhal, Howard *health psychology educator, researcher*
Liao, Mei-June *pharmaceutical executive, researcher*
Ma, Jun *researcher*
Mann, Richard Alan *physician, educator*
Maramorosch, Karl *virologist, educator*
Martínez, Tomás Eloy *writer, journalist*
McCormick, Richard Levis *academic administrator*
Mechanic, David *social sciences educator*
Miller, Lynn Fieldman *lawyer*
Mills, Dorothy Allen *investor*
Mills, George Marshall *financial consultant*
Moreyra, Abel E. *medical educator*
Nelson, Jack Lee *education educator*
Nissenblatt, Michael Jeffrey *medical oncologist*
Notterman, Daniel A. *pediatrician, educator*
Olson, Robert Martin *plastic surgeon*
O'Neill, William Lawrence *retired history professor*
Onwuchekwa, Michael O. *accountant, educator*
Pandey, Ramesh Chandra *chemist, chemicals executive*
Perry, Gregory J. *museum director*
Peterson, Per A. *health products executive*
Pitchumoni, Capecomorin Sankar *gastroenterologist, educator*
Polanco, Katiusca *lawyer*
Poon, Christine A. *pharmaceutical company executive*
Previdi, Michael *meteorologist, research scientist*
Price, Mitchell R. *pediatric surgeon*
Prince, Jonathan D. *social worker, educator*
Puniello, Françoise Sara *librarian*
Raska, Karel Frantisek Julian, Jr. *pathologist, virologist, educator*

Reed, James Wesley *social historian, educator*
Reock, Ernest C., Jr. *retired social studies educator, director*
Robock, Alan *meteorology professor*
Rockoff, Hugh Touff *economist, educator*
Rosenberg, Seymour *psychologist, educator*
Saidi, Parvin *hematologist, medical educator*
Salas, Max *pediatrician, educator*
Saracevic, Tefko *information science educator*
Scanlon, Jane Cronin *mathematics professor*
Schneider, Stephen Harley *medical educator*
Scholz, Peter M. *surgeon, director*
Scodari, Joseph C. *health products executive*
Sewell, Robert George *librarian*
Smouse, Peter E. *ecologist, educator*
Snyder, Barbara K. *pediatrician, educator*
Sosa, Joseph F. *pharmaceutical executive*
Spotnitz, Alan Jeffrey *cardiothoracic surgeon*
Stanley, Jason *education educator*
Stauffer, George B. *dean, music historian, musician, consultant*
Stich, Stephen Peter *philosophy educator*
Strauss, Ulrich Paul *chemist, educator*
Strawderman, William E. *statistics educator*
Strickland, Dorothy *education educator*
Sullivan, Margaret Wolan *research psychologist, educator*
Tanner, Daniel *education educator*
Tedrow, John Charles Fremont *soils educator*
Tiger, Lionel *social scientist, anthropology consultant*
Toby, Jackson *sociologist, educator*
Todd, Mary Beth *oncologist, researcher*
Townsend, Carmilla D. *history professor, researcher*
Trautman, Mark Allen *conductor*
Trooskin, Stanley Z. *surgeon*
Tu, Ching-I *humanities educator, researcher*
Turock, Betty Jane *library and information science professor*
Valeriani, Nicholas J. *health products executive*
Vintzileos, Anthony Mark *obstetrician, gynecologist*
Weiss, Lynne S. *pediatrician, educator*
Weiss, Robert Edward *urologist, educator*
Weldon, William C. *pharmaceutical executive*
Weng, George Jueng-Cious *engineering educator*
Yorke, Marianne *lawyer, real estate executive*
Yu, Jurong *chemist*
Zachariah, Emmanuel Selvanayagam *science educator, researcher*

## New Milford
Walsh, Joseph Michael *magazine distribution executive*

## New Monmouth
Santos, Sharon Lee *parochial school educator*

## New Providence
Barnes, Sandra Henley *retired publishing company executive*
Blessing, Leonard C. *secondary school educator*
Carapezzi, William R., Jr. *telecommunications industry executive, lawyer*
Chandross, Edwin Arthur *chemist*
Chatterji, Debajyoti *retired manufacturing executive*
D'Amelio, Frank Anthony *communications executive*
Del Tiempo, Sandra Kay *sales executive*
Doescher, William Frederick *communications executive*
Fleming, James William *ceramics engineer*
Gasparyan, Arman *physicist*
Gupta, Piyush *research scientist*
Helfand, Eugene *chemist*
Hirsch, Maxine K. *special education educator, councilman*
Kritzmacher, John A. *telecommunications industry executive*
McCaffrey, Robert Henry, Jr. *retired manufacturing company executive*
McCarthy, G. Daniel *lawyer*
Mejia, Jose A. *telecommunications industry executive*
Netravali, Arun N. *communications executive*
O'Shea, William (Bill) T. *telecommunications industry executive*
Reinsdorf, Judith A. *lawyer*
Ring, Timothy Michael *human services administrator, pharmaceutical executive*
Roth, Robert Howard *psychologist*
Russo, Patricia F. *telecommunications company executive*
SanGiovanni, Mary Elizabeth *writer, freelance manager*
Sivco, Deborah Lee *materials scientist, researcher*

## New Vernon
Bross, Albert Louis, Jr. *artist*
Dugan, John Leslie, Jr. *foundation executive*
Kushen, Allan Stanford *retired lawyer*
McCormack, John Joseph, Jr. *insurance company executive*

## Newark
Adler, Freda Schaffer (Mrs. G. O. W. Mueller) *criminologist, educator*
Altenkirch, Robert A. *academic administrator*
Amalfe, Christine A. *lawyer*
Arabie, Phipps *marketing educator, researcher*
Arbuckle, Peggy Trawick *educational consultant, special education educator*
Aregood, Richard Lloyd *editor*
Arwady, George E. *publishing executive*
Asatryan, Rubik *chemistry professor, researcher*
Askin, Frank *law educator*
Baer, Susan M. *airport executive*
Baker, Herman *medical educator, writer*
Baker, Stephen R. *physician*
Banta, Vivian L. *insurance company executive*
Bar-Ness, Yeheskel *electrical engineer, educator*
Barry, Maryanne Trump *federal judge*
Bergen, Stanley Silvers, Jr. *retired academic administrator*
Berry, Andrew T. *lawyer*
Bethel, Colin Anthony Ivan *pediatric surgeon, educator*
Bielory, Leonard *allergist, immunologist, medical school administrator*

Bikofsky, Veronica M. *dentist*
Bizub, Johanna Catherine *law librarian*
Bloom, Joel S. *academic administrator*
Blount, Susan L. *insurance company executive, lawyer*
Blumrosen, Alfred William *law educator*
Bolden, Marion A. *superintendent*
Booker, Cory Anthony *mayor, lawyer*
Brescher, John B., Jr. *lawyer*
Cahn, Jeffrey Barton *lawyer*
Camacho, Margarita Ticzon *cardiothoracic surgeon, educator*
Carbone, Richard J. *insurance executive*
Carmel, Peter W. *neurosurgeon*
Carroll, John Douglas *mathematical and statistical psychologist, educator*
Cave, Damien *journalist*
Chavis, Janet Daugett *school system administrator*
Cheng, Mei-Fang *psychobiology educator, neuroscientist*
Cherniack, Neil Stanley *pulmonologist, educator*
Christie, Christopher James *prosecutor, lawyer*
Christie, Scott S. *lawyer*
Clymer, Brian William *diversified financial services company executive, retired state official*
Cohen, Stanley *pathologist, educator*
Contractor, Farok *business and management educator*
Cook, Stuart Donald *neurologist, educator*
Corbin Walker, Karol *lawyer*
Correia, Joaquim Jose *physician*
Courter, James A. (Jim Courter) *communications executive, retired congressman*
Cummis, Clive Sanford *lawyer*
Cunningham, LeeAnn *assistant prosecutor*
Czumaj, Artur *education educator*
Darmento, Ralph Joseph *religious organization administrator, school system administrator*
Datiashvili, Ramazi O. *plastic surgeon*
Dauth, Frances Kutcher *journalist, editor*
Day, Edward Francis, Jr. *lawyer*
Debevoise, Dickinson Richards *federal judge*
Dee, Francis X. *lawyer*
Defeis, Elizabeth Frances *law educator, lawyer*
Depre, Christophe *medical educator*
Dhawan, Atam Prakash *engineering educator, dean*
Dickson, Jim *writer, theater producer*
Docarmo, Jerry Soares *academic administrator*
Edwards, Samuel Lawrence, II, *information technology executive, writer*
Eittreim, Richard MacNutt *lawyer*
Ellner, Jerrold Jay *infectious diseases specialist*
Emery, Charles Christian, Jr. *health care and information systems executive*
English, Nicholas Conover *lawyer*
Evans, Hugh E. *pediatrician, educator*
Farmer, John Joseph *lawyer, former state attorney general*
Feldman, Cecile Arlene *dean, dental educator*
Fenster, Saul K. *retired academic administrator*
Ferguson, Yale Hicks *political scientist, educator*
Ferland, E. James *electric power industry executive*
Frenkel, Gerald *biochemist, educator*
Friedland, Bernard *engineer, educator*
Fuentes, Julio M. *federal judge*
Garde, John Charles *lawyer*
Garth, Leonard I. *judge*
Gaussin, Vinciane *science educator*
Gauster, Stephen Wilhelm *lawyer, corporate financial executive*
Gettleman, Jeffrey *journalist*
Gibbons, John Joseph *lawyer, retired federal judge*
Goldman, Glenn *architect, educator*
Goldstein, Bruce I. *lawyer*
Goldstein, Marvin Mark *lawyer*
Granick, Mark S. *medical educator*
Greenaway, Joseph Anthony, Jr. *judge*
Griffith, Hurdis M. *dean*
Hanesian, Deran *chemical engineer, educator, environmental scientist, consultant*
Harber, Kent D. *psychology professor*
Haring, Eugene Miller *lawyer*
Haycock, Christine Elizabeth *retired medical educator*
Heller, William J. *lawyer*
Hiltz, Starr Roxanne *sociologist, educator, writer, consultant, computer scientist*
Hobbs, Patrick Esmond *dean, law educator*
Hochberg, Faith S. *US district court judge*
Holzer, Marc *public administrator educator*
Howard, M(oses) William, Jr. *minister*
Hrycak, Peter *retired engineering educator*
Iffy, Leslie *medical educator*
Izenberg, Jerry *sportswriter, columnist, author*
Joffe, Russell T. *former dean*
Jonas, Howard *communications executive*
Karp, Donald Mathew *lawyer, banker*
Kelley, Tina *journalist*
Kennedy, Leslie W. *dean*
Kott, David Russell *lawyer*
Krovatin, Gerald *lawyer*
Lanzerotti, Louis John *physicist*
La Rocco, Anthony P. *lawyer*
Ledeen, Robert Wagner *neuroscientist, educator*
Levin, Simon *lawyer*
Levine, Benjamin *lawyer*
Little, Alan Brian *gynecologist, educator*
Lorell, Jeffrey W. *lawyer*
Louria, Donald Bruce *medical educator*
Lurie, Jonathan *history professor*
Macal, Zdenek *conductor, music director*
Maran, David *lawyer*
Marino, William J. *insurance executive*
McGuire, William B(enedict) *lawyer*
McGurk, Christopher J. *former film company executive*
McLean, David J. *lawyer*
Mercado, Lillian Amensina *counselor*
Milita, Martin Joseph *lawyer*
Mital, Dinesh Prakash *healthcare educator, consultant*
Miura, Robert Mitsuru *mathematician, researcher, educator*
Muratov, Cyrill B. *mathematician, educator*
Myers, John Joseph *archbishop*
Nash, Alicia *application developer, physicist*
Neuer, Philip David *lawyer, real estate consultant*
Newhouse, Mark William *publishing executive*

Nutt, Amy Ellis *journalist*
O'Flynn, Thomas M. *investment company executive*
Pagán, Gilberto, Jr. *psychologist*
Passantino, Benjamin Arthur *marketing executive*
Petillo, John J. *former academic administrator, former priest*
Pfeffer, Robert *chemical engineer, academic administrator, educator*
Price, Mary Sue Sweeney *museum director*
Pryor, Stefan I. *city manager, real estate developer*
Reichman, Lee Brodersohn *physician*
Reilly, William Thomas *lawyer*
Reynolds, Valrae *museum curator*
Robertson, William Withers *lawyer*
Rosato, Anthony Dominick *mechanical engineer, educator*
Rothschild, Gita F. *lawyer*
Ryan, Arthur Frederick *insurance company executive*
Ryan, Lisa Kathleen *environmental and medical science educator*
Schillinger, Randi *lawyer*
Schleifer, Steven J. *psychiatrist, educator*
Schweizer, Karl Wolfgang *historian, educator, author*
Selover, R. Edwin *lawyer*
Shiffrar, Margaret Mary *education educator*
Siegal, Joel Davis *lawyer*
Simmons, Peter *lawyer, urban planner, educator*
Slaton, Gwendolyn Childs *academic administrator*
Smothers, Ronald *journalist*
Spillers, William Russell *civil engineering educator*
Steinbaum, Robert S. *publishing executive, lawyer*
Stephens, B. Consuela *minister, consultant*
Stewart, Michael T. *lawyer*
Thompson, Hugh Walter *chemistry professor*
Timoni, Stephen Anthony *lawyer, accountant*
Tischman, Michael Bernard *lawyer*
Vaidya, Jaideep Shrikant *engineering educator*
Van Buskirk, William Charles *engineering educator*
Van Deusen, Lois M. *lawyer*
Varzegar, Minoo *literature educator, reading specialist*
Vatner, Stephen F. *physiologist, researcher, research scientist*
Verkhovsky, Boris *computer scientist, educator*
Vincenti, Gene A. *director, consultant*
Vladeck, Bruce Charney *academic administrator, healthcare educator*
Ward, Roger Coursen *lawyer*
Warrington, George D. *rail transportation executive*
Weis, Judith Shulman *biology professor*
Weiss, Gerson *endocrinologist, educator*
Willse, James Patrick *newspaper editor*
Winters, Robert Cushing *insurance company executive*
Yamner, Morris *lawyer*
Zaborszky, Laszlo *neuroscientist*
Zuckerman, Herbert Lawrence *lawyer*

## Newfield
Dreher, Frank H., Jr. *retired optician*

## Newfoundland
Van Winkle, Edgar Walling *retired electrical engineer*

## Newton
Boulware, Bobbie L. *music educator*
Case, Tammy *bank executive*
Colizza, Wayne Anthony *orthopaedic surgeon*
Cox, William Martin *lawyer, educator*
Hollander, Roslyn *artist, educator*
MacMurren, Margaret Patricia *secondary school educator, consultant*
Scales, James Leonard, Jr. *orthopedic surgeon*

## North Bergen
Pohan, Armand *transportation executive, professional hockey club executive, lawyer*
Slatner, Thomas Allen *bookseller*

## North Brunswick
Bern, Ronald Lawrence *management consultant, writer*
Burge, Micah Benjamin *school psychologist*
Frenkiel, Richard Henry *retired systems engineer, consultant*
Ghosh, Alok *pharmaceutical executive*
Jones, Frank A., Jr. *psychiatrist, educator*
Shaw, Roslyn Lee *small business owner, retired elementary school educator*

## North Caldwell
Boronow, John David *music educator*
Imhof, David Charles *music educator*

## North Plainfield
Delger, Leslie Amelia *artist*
Dunbar, Holly Jean *communications executive, public relations executive*
Parrcott, Dorian Lee, II, *music educator*

## Northfield
Margolis, Thomas Ira *vitreoretinal ophthalmologist*
McNeal, Jane Erskine *music educator, musician*

## Northvale
Di Mino, André Anthony *manufacturing executive, consultant*

## Norwood
Murburg, Thelma D. *retired elementary school educator*

## Nutley
Bridge, Thomas Peter *psychiatrist, researcher*
English, Robert Joseph *electronics executive*
Kong, Norman *chemist*
Mallard, Stephen Anthony *retired utilities executive*
Mostillo, Ralph *medical association administrator*
Tò, Stephen Edward *editor, writer*

## Oak Ridge
Kieren, Thomas Henry *management consultant*

**Oakland**

DeFreest, Kevin Albert *music educator*
Dressel, Margaret Jane *artist, art educator*
Guller, Irving Bernard *forensic, clinical psychologist, consultant, writer*
Maccario, Maurice Malcolm *oral and maxillofacial surgeon, consultant*
Manheimer, Heidi *cosmetics company executive*

**Ocean**

Reich, Bernard *communications engineer*

**Ocean City**

Hughes, Robert G. *minister, religious organization administrator*
Hughes, William John *former congressman, diplomat*
Juliana, James Nicholas *manufacturing executive*
Kyriazis, Arthur John (Athanasios Ioannis Kyriazis) *lawyer, biotechnologist*

**Ocean Grove**

Davis, John Mihran *surgeon, educator*
Perwo, George Edward *music educator*

**Oldwick**

Haymaker, Douglas James *psychologist, researcher*
Sinfelt, John Henry *chemist*
Snyder, Arthur *publishing executive*

**Oradell**

Blakeslee, Edward Eaton *lawyer, insurance company executive*
Mavroudis, John M. *lawyer*
Parish, J. Michael *lawyer, mutual fund executive, writer*
Roe, W. Barton *engineering executive*
Rosen, Jay Samuel *urologist, surgeon*
Struck, Norma Johansen *artist*
Tong, Hing *mathematician, educator*

**Orange**

Agarwal, Shashi Kant *cardiologist*
Maynard, Estelle L. *pre-school educator, director*
Thomas, Lois Baskerville *retired language educator*

**Palisades Park**

Schmarge, Agapi Georgiou *social studies educator*

**Paramus**

Agresta, Anthony John *academic administrator, educational consultant, language educator*
Crow, Lynne Campbell Smith *insurance company representative*
Fader, Shirley Sloan *writer*
Forman, Beth Rosalyne *specialty food trade executive*
Gordon, Scott (Harry Scott Buehlmeier) *entertainer, actor*
Grinberg, Efraim *watch manufacturing company executive*
Grinberg, Gedalio *watch manufacturing company executive*
Hadaller, David Lawrence *academic administrator*
Hochberg, Lois J. *school psychologist*
Jacobs, Helen Nichols *artist*
LaMothe, Catherine A. *elementary school educator*
Levy, Joseph *lawyer*
Lieberman, Charles *economist*
Liva, Edward Louis *eye surgeon*
Maclin, Ernest *medical products executive*
Mahoney, Joseph Francis *historian, educator*
Marcel-Calderon, Linda *music educator*
Noguere, Suzanne *trade association administrator, poet*
Perkins-Munn, Tiffany Sabrena *psychologist, researcher*
Saltzman, Jared *performing arts educator, lighting designer*
Wasmer, Carmenia Ann *language educator*

**Park Ridge**

Ciannella, Joeen Moore *small business owner*
Frissora, Mark P. *automobile rental and leasing company executive*
Giovannoli, Joseph Louis *entrepreneur, lawyer*
Kennedy, Brian James *marketing executive*
Koch, Craig R. *automobile rental and leasing company executive*
Popolizio, Rick *music educator*

**Parlin**

Mogensen, Charles Ray, Jr. *retired food service executive*

**Parsippany**

Bablin, Mark Edward *security administrator, mortgage consultant*
Bandi, Nagesh *research scientist*
Belmonte, Steven Joseph *hotel chain executive*
Cox, Melvin Monroe *lawyer*
Ferguson, Thomas George *retired healthcare advertising agency executive*
François, Andre J. *psychologist, educational association administrator*
Iapicca, Michael Alfonso *music educator*
Jones, Charles Hill, Jr. *banker*
Moch, Kenneth Ian *entrepreneur*
Ray, Robert William *lawyer*
Reed, Howie *music educator, minister*
Smay, Connie R. *educational media specialist, educator*
Theiss, Richard Edward *electrical engineer, applications engineer*
Wechter, Ira Martin *tax specialist, financial planner*
Weller, Robert N(orman) *hotel executive*

**Passaic**

Johnson, Myrtle Alice Harris *elementary and secondary school educator*
Sebek, Miklós László *sculptor, educator*

**Paterson**

Daniels, Cheryl Lynn *pediatrics nurse*
Deffaa, Chip *jazz critic*
Fields, Marvin Leon *secondary school educator*

---

Fink, David Leonard *surgeon*
Gaydos, Tim J. *artist*
Mussano, Theodore Anthony *retired court services supervisor*
Papageorgis, Jack *small business owner*
Paulhus, Thomas A. *social studies educator*
Radke, Stephen Lewis *social services administrator*
Salcedo, Jose Rodolfo *nephrologist*

**Peapack**

Eddey, Gary Erwin *physician, administrator, educator*
Rost, Peter *pharmaceutical company executive*
Walsh, Philip Cornelius *retired mining executive*

**Pennington**

Calvo, Roque John *professional society administrator*
Donnelly, Gerard Kevin *marketing and retail executive*
Gundeck, Caroline Nyklewicz *investment company executive*
Kelly, Quentin Thorn *water and power company executive, writer*
Rigg, Lyle D. *headmaster*
Zhang, Hong (Rick) *design engineer, researcher*

**Penns Grove**

Reilley, James Clark *artist, cartoonist, small business owner*

**Pennsauken**

Alday, Paul Stackhouse, Jr. *retired mechanical engineer*
Honickman, Harold *food manufacturing company executive*

**Pennsville**

Ludlam, James Brian *music educator*

**Perth Amboy**

Cruz, Nelson Xavier *healthcare executive*
Richardson-Melech, Joyce Suzanne *music educator, singer*
Washington, Marcel Maurice *statistician, researcher*

**Phillipsburg**

Drago, Joseph Rosario *urologist, educator*
Richards, Jay Claude *photographer, publishing executive, historian*

**Picatinny Arsenal**

Owens, Frank James *physicist*
Zulauf, Madeline Ruth *photographer, artist*

**Pilesgrove**

Mohrfeld, Richard Gentel *marketing professional*

**Pine Brook**

Marlow, Ian Michael *real estate company executive*

**Piscataway**

Agrawal, Shruti *researcher*
Al-Sharab, Jafar Farhan *materials scientist, researcher*
Arnold, Edward (Eddy Arnold) *research scientist, educator*
Balaguru, Perumalsamy *civil engineering educator*
Chaovalitwongse, Wanpracha *mathematician, researcher*
Chu, Brian Christopher *psychology professor*
Cohen, Morrel Herman *physicist, biologist, educator*
Colaizzi, John Louis *dean*
Colcord, Herbert Nathaniel, III, (Skip Colcord) *corporate communications executive*
Demissie, Kitaw *epidemiologist, educator*
Denhardt, David Tilton *molecular and cell biology educator*
Dill, Ellis Harold *university dean*
Escobar, Javier Ignacio *psychiatrist*
Essien, Francine B. *biologist, educator*
Etter, Zana Claire *library director*
Ferstandig Arnold, Gail *research scientist, educator*
Flanagan, James Loton *electrical engineer, researcher, engineering educator*
Goss, Mary E. Weber *sociology educator*
Gustafsson, Mary Beth *lawyer*
Hammer, Peter L. *mathematics professor, researcher*
Idol, James Daniel, Jr. *chemist, educator, inventor, consultant*
Iwaniec, Henryk *mathematics professor*
Jones, Roger Alan *chemistry professor, researcher, consultant*
Kenney, Mary R. *software engineer*
Kormann, Russell Jay *psychologist, consultant*
Kotliar, B. Gabriel *physics professor*
Leath, Paul Larry *physicist, educator, former university official*
Lebowitz, Joel Louis *mathematical physicist, educator*
Lee, Barbara Anne *law educator, dean*
Li, Mei-Ling *medical educator*
Li, Yanyan *mathematician, educator*
Lindenfeld, Peter *physics professor*
Linke, Richard A. *optical engineer*
Manowitz, Paul *biochemist, researcher, educator*
McCrady, Barbara Sachs *psychologist, educator*
McGhee, George Rufus *palebiologist, educator*
Menza, Matthew A. *psychiatrist*
Mizrahi, Isaac *fashion designer*
Monheit, Alan Craig *economist, educator*
Peterson, Donald Robert *psychologist, educator, academic administrator*
Polefka, Thomas Gregory *biochemist*
Poses, Frederic M. *engineering company executive*
Ranzan, David Aldrich *archivist*
Reiley, T(homas) Phillip *systems analyst, consultant*
Rhoads, George Grant *medical epidemiologist*
Robbins, Allen Bishop *physics professor*
Rokhlenko, Alexander *research scientist, educator*
Rosalsky, Barbara Ellen *artist, community health nurse*

---

Sahota, Amrik *medical researcher, educator, lab administrator*
Salkind, Alvin J. *engineering educator, dean, consultant*
Schuler, Randall Steve *education educator, writer*
Schwebel, Milton *psychologist, educator*
Shanefield, Daniel Jay *ceramic engineering educator*
Sincoskie, W. David *computer engineer*
Smith, Bob *lawyer, educator, state senator*
Swee, David Ethan *physician*
Talpade, Rajesh *telecommunications industry executive*
Toby, Sidney *retired chemistry professor*
Trelstad, Robert Laurence *pathology educator, cell biologist*
Trontell, Marie Celestine *dean*
Upton, Arthur Canfield *experimental pathologist, educator*
Welkowitz, Walter *biomedical engineer, educator*
West, Mark Otto *psychology professor*
Yacowitz, Harold *biochemist, nutritionist*
Zerubavel, Eviatar *sociologist, educator*
Zhang, Dajun *biomedical engineering educator*
Zimmermann, Frank Martin *physicist, educator, research scientist*

**Pitman**

Cloues, Edward Blanchard, II, *lawyer*
Reinfeld, George *retired communications educator*

**Plainfield**

Allen, Stuart (Stuart Allen Sup) *film and television company executive*
Ellington II, Michael L. *lawyer*
Frost, David *retired biology professor, medical editor, consultant*
Green, Gerald B. *state legislator*
Holdorf, Harry Hulbert *health facility administrator*
Johnson, Lonnie L., Jr. *information specialist*
Krump, Paul J. *insurance company executive*
Limpert, John H., Jr. *fund raising executive*
Reeder, Hubert *elementary school educator*
Ruiz, Pedro Javier *education educator*

**Plainsboro**

Devine, Hugh James, Jr. *marketing executive*
Dezii, Christopher Michael *medical/surgical nurse, medical researcher*
Khan, Sajid A. *management consultant, entrepreneur*
Lansing, Martha Hempel *physician*
Schreyer, William Allen *retired finance company executive*
Spiegel, Phyllis *public relations consultant, journalist*

**Pleasantville**

Applewhite, Kim *music company executive, educator*
London, Charlotte Isabella *secondary school educator*

**Point Pleasant**

Greene, Ellin *library service educator*
Marjanczyk, Joseph Anicetus *priest*

**Pomona**

Constantelos, Demetrios John *priest, educator*
Sharon, Yitzhak Yaakov *physicist, researcher*

**Pompton Plains**

Guida, Pat *information broker, literature chemist*
Gummel, Hermann Karl *retired physicist, lab administrator*
Kettlewood, Bea Card *artist, retired educator*
Pischl, Adolph John *school administrator*
Shrem, Charles Joseph *metals corporation executive*

**Port Murray**

Kunzler, John Eugene *physicist*

**Port Norris**

Canzonier, Walter Jude *shellfish aquaculturist*

**Princeton**

Aarsleff, Hans *linguistics educator*
Ackourey, Peter Paul *lawyer*
Adler, Stephen Louis *physicist*
Ait-Sahalia, Yacine *finance educator*
Aizenman, Michael *mathematics professor, physics professor, researcher*
Allen, Stanley T. *architect, dean, educator*
Altmann, James Daniel, Jr. *zoologist, educator*
Altmann, Jeanne *zoologist, educator*
Altmann, Stuart Allen *biologist, educator*
Anderson, Ellis Bernard *retired lawyer, pharmaceutical executive*
Anderson, Philip W. *physicist*
Armstrong, Richard Stoll *minister, educator, poet*
Balch, Stephen Howard *professional society administrator*
Ballou, Janice Donelon *research director*
Bartolini, Robert Alfred *electrical engineer, researcher*
Basáñez, Miguel Ebergenyi *political scientist, educator*
Bassler, Bonnie L. *molecular biologist*
Beidler, Marsha Wolf *lawyer*
Belshaw, George Phelps Mellick *bishop*
Benabou, Roland Jean-Marc *economist, educator*
Bergman, Edward Jonathan *lawyer, educator*
Bergman, Richard Isaac *health information executive*
Bergman, Victoria Besterman *small business owner, consultant*
Bhargava, Manjul *mathematics professor, researcher*
Billington, David Perkins *civil engineering educator*
Bishop, James Francis *personnel director, consultant*
Blackman, Sue Anne Batey *economics researcher*
Bland, Calvin *foundation administrator*
Blinder, Alan Stuart *economist, educator*
Bogan, Elizabeth Chapin *economist, educator*
Bois, Yve-Alain *art educator, curator*
Bombieri, Enrico *mathematician, educator*
Boretz, Naomi Messinger *artist, educator*

---

Botstein, David *geneticist, educator*
Bourgain, Jean *mathematician*
Bowersock, Glen Warren *retired historian, educator*
Branker, Anthony Daniel John *music educator, researcher, composer*
Brinkman, William Frank *physicist, research and development company executive*
Brombert, Victor Henri *literature educator, author*
Brown, Leon Carl *historian, educator*
Bryan, Kirk, Jr. *meteorologist, oceanographer, researcher*
Bunnell, Peter Curtis *retired art educator, curator*
Burgess, Robert Kyle *lawyer*
Campbell, Mildred Corum *business owner, nurse*
Campbell, Robert Emmett *retired health products executive*
Carr, Marcus Eugene, Jr. *internist*
Carter, Emily Ann *physical chemist, researcher, educator*
Carver, David Harold *retired pediatrician*
Cava, Robert J. *chemistry professor*
Cavanaugh, James Henry *health products executive, retired federal official*
Chaikin, Paul M. *physicist*
Chamberlin, John Stephen *investor, consumer products company executive*
Chang, Sun-Yung Alice *mathematics professor*
Chazelle, Bernard *computer science educator*
Chen, Thomas *mathematical physicist, researcher, educator*
Choueiri, Edgar Y. *research scientist, physics and engineering educator, director*
Chow, Gregory Chi-Chong *economist, educator*
Christman, Edward Arthur *physicist*
Coffey, Joseph Irving *political scientist, educator*
Connor, Geoffrey Michael *lawyer*
Cook, Michael Allan *social sciences educator*
Cooper, Joel *psychologist, educator*
Cooper, John Madison *philosophy educator*
Cooper, Michael R. *dean*
Corngold, Stanley Alan *language educator, writer*
Cox, Douglas Lynn *management consultant, researcher*
Craigie, James R. *consumer products company executive, former sports equipment apparel company executive*
Crane, David W. *energy executive*
Crawford, Franklin David *publishing executive*
Darnton, Robert Choate *historian, educator*
Das, Jagabandhu *chemist, researcher*
Davidson, Ronald Crosby *physicist, researcher*
Davies, Robert Abel III *consumer products company executive*
Dayanik, Savas *science educator*
Debenedetti, Pablo Gaston *chemical engineering professor*
Deligne, Pierre René *mathematician*
De Lung, Jane Solberger *independent sector executive*
Diller, Elizabeth E. *architect, educator, artist*
Doig, Jameson Wallace *political science professor*
Doll, Robert C. *investment company executive*
Donohue, Andrew John *lawyer, securities executive*
Dougherty, Peter Joseph *publisher*
Drakeman, Donald Lee *biotechnologist, pharmaceutical executive*
Drakeman, Lisa N. *biotechnologist*
Dubrovsky, Gertrude Wishnick *journalist, researcher*
Durst, Robert Joseph, II, *lawyer*
Dyson, Freeman John *retired physics professor*
Enquist, Lynn William *molecular biologist*
Ermolaev, Herman Sergei *Slavic languages educator*
Evslin, Tom *internet telephone service executive*
Fefferman, Charles Louis *mathematics professor*
Felton, Edward William *computer scientist, educator*
Fernholz, Erhard Robert *investment executive*
Fisch, Nathaniel Joseph *physicist*
Fitch, Val Logsdon *physics professor*
Florey, Klaus Georg *chemist, pharmaceutical consultant*
Ford, Jeremiah III *architect*
Fox, Mary Ann Williams *librarian*
Frankfurt, Harry Gordon *philosophy professor*
Frantz, Robert Wesley *lawyer*
Frenier, Diane M. *lawyer*
Frey, Julia Bloch *language educator, art historian, educator*
Friedberg, Aaron Louis *political science professor*
Ganoe, Charles Stratford *banker, consultant*
Geertz, Clifford James *anthropology educator*
George, Thomas *artist*
German, Elaine *physician*
Ghasemi, Seifi *chemicals executive*
Gillham, John Kinsey *chemical engineering professor*
Giordmaine, Joseph Anthony *physicist*
Girgis, Suzette *clinical pharmacologist, researcher*
Girgus, Joan Stern *psychologist, educator, director*
Gmachl, Claire *electrical engineer, educator*
Goddard, Peter *academic administrator, mathematical physicist*
Goheen, Robert Francis *classicist, educator, former ambassador*
Goldblatt, Barry Lance *manufacturing executive*
Goldfarb, Irene Dale *retired financial planner*
Goldston, Robert J. *research scientist*
Gordenker, Leon *political science professor*
Gould, Elizabeth *neuroscientist, educator*
Gould, James L. *biology professor*
Grabar, Oleg *retired art educator*
Grafton, Anthony Thomas *history professor*
Grant, Peter Raymond *biologist, researcher, educator*
Graves, Michael *architect, educator*
Green, Claude *information company executive*
Greenman, Jane Friedlieb *lawyer, human resources executive*
Greenstein, Fred Irwin *political science professor*
Grisham, Larry Richard *physicist*
Gross, Charles Gordon *psychology professor*
Groves, John Taylor III *chemist, educator*
Gu, Henry Hongsheng *pharmacist, researcher*
Gund, Gordon *venture capitalist, investment company executive*
Gunning, Robert Clifford *mathematician, educator*
Haberman, Shelby Joel *statistician, educator*

Habicht, Christian Herbert *history professor*
Haldane, F. Duncan M. (Frederick Duncan Michael Haldane, Duncan Haldane) *physics educator*
Hall, Robert Turnbull III *lawyer*
Hanks, Richard *information company executive*
Happer, William, Jr. *physicist, researcher*
Harford, James *writer*
Harman, Gilbert Helms *philosophy educator*
Hartog, Hendrik *historian*
Harvey, Norman Ronald *retired finance company executive*
Hill, James Scott *lawyer*
Hillier, James *retired technology management executive, researcher*
Hillier, J(ames) Robert *architect*
Hitz, Frederick Porter *public and international affairs educator*
Hochschwender, Karl Albert *international trade and government relations consultant*
Hoebel, Bartley Gore *psychologist, educator*
Hoke, Molly Elizabeth *chemist, research scientist*
Hollander, Robert B., Jr. *romance languages educator*
Hollander, Toby Edward *education educator*
Howarth, William (Louis Howarth) *literature and language professor, writer*
Howell, David Luke *history professor*
Hughes, Robert G. *foundation administrator*
Hulse, Russell Alan *physicist*
Hut, Piet *astrophysics educator*
Hynes, Samuel *language educator, writer*
Jacobs, William Paul *botanist, educator*
Jeffers, Beverly Maynard *volunteer*
Jenkins, Edward Beynon *research astronomer*
Johnson, Barbara Piasecka *volunteer, art historian, investor*
Johnson, Margaret Kennard *artist, educator*
Johnston, Robert Fowler *venture capitalist*
Jordan, William Chester *historian, educator*
Kahneman, Daniel *psychology professor*
Kammen, Daniel Merson *environmental physicist, researcher*
Kaplowitz, Karen (Jill) *lawyer, consultant*
Kassof, Allen H. *foundation administrator*
Kateb, George Anthony *political science professor*
Katz, Nicholas M. *mathematician*
Katz, Stanley Nider *law history educator*
Kauzmann, Walter Joseph *chemistry professor*
Kawarsky, Jay A. *music educator, conductor, composer*
Keeley, Edmund LeRoy *literature educator, writer, translator*
Kehrt, Allan William *architect*
Keller, Suzanne *sociologist, psychotherapist*
Kelly, Paul J. *lab administrator, physician, researcher*
Kenen, Peter Bain *economist, educator*
Kenny, Robert *lawyer*
Kenyon, Regan Clair *educational research executive*
Keohane, Robert Owen *political scientist, educator*
Khutoryansky, Naum M. *mathematician, educator*
Knoepflmacher, Ulrich Camillus *literature educator*
Kobayashi, Hisashi *computer scientist, dean*
Kollár, János *mathematics professor*
Krugman, Paul Robin *economics professor*
Kuebler, Christopher Allen *pharmaceutical executive*
Kurtzer, Daniel Charles *former ambassador*
Landgraf, Kurt M. *educational association administrator*
Langlands, Robert Phelan *mathematician, educator*
Lavizzo-Mourey, Risa Juanita *medical foundation administrator, academic administrator*
Law, Stuart A., Jr. *lawyer*
Lazarus, Arnold Allan *psychologist, educator*
Leader, Solomon *retired mathematics professor*
Lechner, Bernard Joseph *consulting electrical engineer*
Leonard, Naomi Ehrich *aerospace engineer, engineering educator*
Levin, Simon Asher *mathematician, ecologist, educator*
Levine, Richard James *publishing executive*
Levy, Kenneth *music educator*
Lewis, Bernard *retired social studies educator*
Lewis, John Prior *economist, educator*
Lieb, Elliott Hershel *physicist, educator, mathematician, educator*
Lin, Hai *physicist*
Lincoln, Anna *publishing executive, language educator*
Lippincott, Walter Heulings, Jr. *retired publishing executive*
Liu, Bede *electrical engineering educator*
Livstone, Michael S. *database curator*
Logue, Judith Felton *psychoanalyst, educator*
Long, Frank Wesley, Jr. *chemist*
Lu, Xiaoguang *computer scientist*
Luchak, Frank Alexander *lawyer*
Lustig, Graham *artistic director*
MacPherson, Robert Duncan *mathematician, educator*
Makadok, Stanley *management consultant*
Maldacena, Juan *physicist, researcher*
Malkiel, Burton Gordon *economist, educator*
Malkiel, Nancy Weiss *dean, historian, educator*
Manabe, Syukuro *meteorologist*
Manyak, Michael John *urologist, educator, researcher*
Marks, James S. *public health service administrator*
Maskin, Eric Stark *economics professor*
Matlock, Jack Foust, Jr. *diplomat*
McClure, Donald Stuart *physical chemist, educator*
McCullough, John Price *retired oil company executive*
Mc Pherson, James Munro *history professor*
Mc Vicker, Charles Taggart *artist, educator*
Meade, Dale Michael *experimental physicist*
Mehlman, Myron A. *medical educator, toxicologist*
Metzger, Bruce Manning *clergyman, educator*
Miles, Richard Bryant *mechanical and aerospace engineering educator*
Miller, George Armitage *psychologist, educator*
Miller, Patrick Dwight, Jr. *religious studies educator, minister*

Mills, Bradford *merchant banker*
Mollica, Joseph A. *pharmaceutical executive*
Moote, A. Lloyd *history professor*
Morgan, William Jason *geophysics educator*
Morris, Mac Glenn *advertising executive*
Moynahan, Julian Lane *retired literature educator, writer*
Mueller, Peter Sterling *psychiatrist, educator*
Muldoon, Paul *poet, educator*
Nash, John Forbes, Jr. *mathematician, researcher*
Nehamas, Alexander *philosophy educator*
Nied, Thomas Herman *retired media specialist*
Nolet, Guust *geophysicist*
O'Donnell, Laurence Gerard *retired managing editor*
Okounkov, Andrei *mathematics professor*
Olsen, Gregory H. *fiber optic manufacturing executive, researcher*
Ong, Nai-Phuan *physicist, researcher*
Oppenheimer, Michael *physicist*
Orphanides, Nora Charlotte *ballet educator*
Ostriker, Jeremiah Paul *astrophysicist, educator*
Page, Lyman Alexander, Jr. *physicist*
Palomar, Daniel Perez *electrical engineer*
Paret, Peter *historian*
Parry, Scott Brink *psychologist*
Pechura, Constance Mary *foundation administrator*
Pfister, Marc *consumer products company executive, medical researcher*
Picco, Steven Joseph *lawyer*
Pimley, Kim Jensen *financial training consultant*
Plaks, Livia Basch *foundation executive*
Poor, Harold Vincent *electrical engineering educator*
Quandt, Richard Emeric *economics professor*
Rabb, Theodore K. *historian, educator*
Ramaprasad, Kackadasam Raghavachar *physical chemist*
Rodgers, Daniel Tracy *historian, educator*
Rosen, Harvey Sheldon *economics professor, former federal official*
Rothschild, Michael *economics professor*
Royce, Barrie Saunders Hart *physicist, researcher*
Rozman, Gilbert Friedell *sociologist, educator*
Rubin, Dorothy Molly *language educator, writer*
Russel, William Bailey *engineering educator*
Rutherford, Earl Harding *physicist*
Sandman, Peter M. *risk management consultant*
Saville, Dudley Albert *chemical engineering educator*
Schofield, Robert E(dwin) *historian, educator, academic administrator*
Scott, Joan Wallach *historian, educator*
Seawright, James L., Jr. *sculptor, educator*
Seiberg, Nathan *physics professor*
Selberg, Atle *retired mathematician*
Shaohua Kevin, Zhou *research scientist*
Shapiro, Harold Tafler *economics professor, former academic administrator*
Shear, Theodore Leslie, Jr. *archaeologist, educator*
Sheffield, Justin *hydrologist, researcher*
Shenk, Thomas Eugene *molecular biology educator, academic administrator*
Shimizu, Yoshiaki *art historian, department chairman*
Showalter, Elaine *humanities educator*
Shrivastava, Ajay *biologist, researcher*
Siegel, Laurie *human resources specialist*
Sierocki, John Stanley *oncologist*
Sigal, Leonard H. *physician*
Sigmund, Paul Eugene *political science professor*
Silverman, Jane Aresty *not-for-profit organizational consultant*
Sinai, Yakov G. *theoretical mathematician, educator*
Singer, Burton Herbert *statistics educator*
Slabaugh, Gregory Gibran *application developer*
Slaughter, Anne-Marie *dean*
Small, Mario L. *sociologist, educator*
Smith, Arthur John Stewart *physicist, researcher*
Socolow, Robert Harry *engineering educator*
Song, Zhen *electrical engineer, researcher*
Spicer, Michael E. *lab administrator*
Stackhouse, Max Lynn *religious studies educator*
Starr, Paul Elliot *sociologist, educator, editor, writer*
Stein, Elias M. *mathematician, educator*
Stengel, Robert Frank *engineering and applied science educator*
Sterzer, Fred *research physicist*
Stier, Roger Edwin *chemist, researcher*
Sugerman, Abraham Arthur *psychiatrist, educator*
Sullivan, Diane P. *lawyer*
Szwalbenest, Benedykt Jan *lawyer*
Taylor, Edward Curtis *chemistry professor*
Taylor, Joseph Hooton, Jr. *radio astronomer, physicist*
Taylor, Susan M. *museum director*
Theroux, William Gerard *lawyer*
Tienda, Marta *demographer, educator*
Tilghman, Shirley Marie *academic administrator, biology professor*
Torquato, Salvatore *materials scientist, chemistry professor*
Trainer, Karin A. *librarian*
Tremaine, Scott Duncan *astrophysicist*
Treu, Jesse Isaiah *venture capitalist*
Troyanskaya, Olga *biomedical researcher, computer scientist*
Trussell, James *economist, educator, dean*
Tsui, Daniel C. *electrical engineer, physicist*
Ufford, Charles Wilbur, Jr. *lawyer*
Unruh, Howard K., Jr. *military officer, university administrator*
Van Houten, Franklyn Bosworth *geologist, educator*
VanMarcke, Erik Hector *civil engineer, educator*
Vecchi, Gabriel Andrés *geophysicist*
Verdu, Sergio *engineering educator*
Vinicombe, Charles James *lawyer*
Voevodsky, Vladimir *mathematician*
von der Schmidt, Edward III *neurosurgeon, veterinarian*
Walter, Hugo Günther *humanities educator, poet*
Walzer, Michael *political science professor*
Ward, Bess B. *oceanographer, educator*
Warren, William L. *lawyer*
Wei, James *chemical engineering professor, academic dean*

Weiss, Renée Karol *editor, musician*
West, Charles Converse *retired theologian*
West, Cornel Ronald *humanities educator, writer*
Westoff, Charles Francis *demographer, educator*
Wheeler, John Archibald *physicist, educator*
Whipple, William, Jr. *government policy consultant, writer*
White, Morton Gabriel *philosopher, writer, historian, retired educator*
Wieschaus, Eric F. *molecular biologist, educator*
Wightman, Arthur Strong *physicist, researcher*
Wildnauer, Richard Harry *pharmaceutical executive*
Wilentz, Sean *historian, educator, writer*
Wiles, Andrew J. *mathematician, educator*
Williams, C(harles) K(enneth) *poet, educator, literature educator*
Willig, Robert Daniel *economics professor*
Willingham, Warren Wilcox *psychologist*
Wilmerding, John *art historian, educator, curator*
Winn, Paul T. *electronics executive*
Witkin, Evelyn Maisel *retired geneticist*
Witten, Edward *mathematical physicist*
Zhao, Wenyi *systems analyst*
Ziolkowski, Theodore Joseph *literature educator*

## Princeton Junction

Amenta, Peter Sebastian *pathologist*
Bair, William Alois *engineer*
Butorac, Frank George *librarian, educator*
Cohen, Florence Emery *retired financial services executive*
Denlinger, Edgar Jacob *electronics engineering executive, researcher*
Haddad, James Henry *chemical engineer, consultant*
Hirschman, Barry H. *human resources specialist*
Lull, William Paul *engineering consultant*
Norback, Craig Thomas *writer*
Vahaviolos, Sotirios John *electrical engineer, researcher, engineering executive*
Wu, Huan-ter *statistician*

## Rahway

Dolinich-Matuska, Christine *artist*
Freedman, Stanley Lewis *assistant principal*
Garcia, Maria Luisa *biochemist, researcher*
Kaczorowski, Gregory John *biochemist, researcher, science administrator*

## Ramsey

Gipple, Douglas John *theater educator, literature and language educator*
Libin, Laurence Elliot *retired curator*
Underwood, Steven Clark *publishing executive*

## Rancocas

Rowan, Henry M. *electrical engineer*

## Randolph

Chen, Kevin S. *management executive, consultant, educator*
Ghosh, Ajit Kumar *daycare administrator*
Sarmiento-Fernandez, Jorge *mathematics professor, consultant*
Zelante, Thomas Andrew *lawyer*

## Raritan

Bower, David Norman *music educator, director*

## Red Bank

Braddom, Randall Lee *physiatrist, educator*
Brown, Valerie Anne *psychotherapist, social worker, educator*
Carmody, Margaret Jean *retired social worker*
Clever, Marcia Sue *psychiatrist*
Daidone, Lewis Eugene *finance company executive*
Dale, John Denny *economist, business executive*
Fred, Rogers Murray III *veterinary oncologist*
Gutentag, Patricia Richmand *social worker, family counselor, occupational therapist*
Hearth, Blair Anthony *fundraiser, clergyman*
Hertz, Daniel Leroy, Jr. *entrepreneur*
Hovnanian, Ara K. *real estate developer*
Hovnanian, Kevork S. *real estate developer*
McWhinney, Madeline H. (Mrs. John Denny Dale) *economist, director*
Oberst, Robert John *financial analyst*
Reinhart, Peter Sargent *lawyer*
Rose, Arthur Royal *financial planner, tax consultant*
Sorsby, James Larry *home building company executive*
Terris, Albert *metal sculptor*
Watson, Charles M. *financial consultant*

## Ridgefield

Riggs, Rory B. *pharmaceutical executive*
Tracey, Matthew Sean *music educator, musician*

## Ridgefield Park

D'Avella, Bernard Johnson, Jr. *publishing executive, lawyer*
Denning, Karen Craft *finance educator*
Litwinowicz, Anthony *information scientist, researcher*
Magdosko, Paula *school psychologist*

## Ridgewood

Baddoura, Rashid Joseph *emergency physician*
Blakely, Jane McCarthy *secondary school educator*
Bronstein, Eric H. *surgeon*
Clements, Lynne Fleming *marriage and family therapist, application developer*
Farrell, Gregory Alan *biomedical engineer*
Harris, Micalyn Shafer *lawyer, educator, arbitrator, consultant, mediator*
Hayes, Michael Joseph *investment banker, entrepreneur, retail executive*
Healey, Frank Henry *retired chemicals executive*
Kiernan, Richard Francis *publisher*
O'Leary, Paul Gerard *retired insurance company executive*
Ostling, Richard Neil *journalist*
Warner, John Edward *advertising executive*

## Ringoes

Tema-Lyn, Laurie *management consultant*

## Ringwood

Barbour, Arthur J. *artist*

## River Edge

Gass, Manus M. *accountant, construction executive*
Mueller, Richard L.P. *physician*

## Riverton

O'Brien, James Jerome *construction management consultant*

## Rivervale

Becker, Murray Leonard *corporate financial consultant, actuary*
Falcon, Raymond Jesus, Jr. *lawyer*
Moderacki, Edmund Anthony *music educator, conductor*
Posamentier, Alfred Steven *mathematics professor, dean*

## Robbinsville

Biondi, Linda Ann *elementary school educator*

## Rochelle Park

Gaer, Michael Ira *financial planner*
Schapiro, Jerome Bentley *chemicals executive*

## Rockaway

Allen, Dorothea *secondary school educator*
Kelsey, Ann Lee *library administrator*

## Roosevelt

Mallach, Alan *writer, consultant, city planner*
Zuckerman, Mark Alan *composer, consultant*

## Roseland

Benson, James Bracken *lawyer*
Butler, Gary C. *computer company executive*
Clemente, Celestino *physician, surgeon*
Eakeley, Douglas Scott *lawyer*
Golden, Robert Charles *finance company executive*
Graham, Patricia *information technology executive*
Hayden, Joseph A., Jr. *lawyer*
Kohl, Benedict M. *lawyer*
Leit, David Edward *lawyer*
Lowenstein, Alan Victor *lawyer*
Lubit, Beverly Weiss *lawyer, science educator*
Malafronte, Donald *health facility administrator*
McMahon, Edward Richard *lawyer*
Panagides, John *pharmacologist*
Positan, Wayne John *lawyer*
Stern, Herbert Jay *lawyer*
Sugahara, Byron Masahiko *transportation executive*
Tarino, Gary Edward *lawyer*
Vanderbilt, Arthur T., II, *lawyer*
Weinbach, Arthur Frederic *computer company executive*
Wovsaniker, Alan *lawyer, educator*
Zhu, Junhong *biostatistician*

## Roselle

Di Marco, Barbaranne Yanus *principal*

## Roselle Park

Scarpelli, Vito *retired adult education educator, small business owner*

## Rosemont

Torricelli, Robert G. *former senator*

## Rumson

Brenner, Theodore Engelbert *retired trade association administrator*
Mardinly, George John *lawyer*
Rowe, Harrison Edward *electrical engineer*
Strong, George Hotham *private investor, consultant*
Swartz, Renee Becker *civic volunteer*

## Rutherford

Gerety, Peter Leo *archbishop*
Petrie, Ferdinand Ralph *illustrator, artist*
Suarez, Sally Ann Tevis *health facility administrator, nurse, consultant*

## Saddle Brook

Clifton, Nelida *social worker*
Cohn, Albert Linn *lawyer*
Hickey, William V. *manufacturing executive*
Kelsey, David *manufacturing executive*
Pearlman, Peter Steven *lawyer*
White, H. Katherine *lawyer*

## Saddle River

Goodman, Jerome David *psychiatrist*
Lasser, Gail Maria *psychologist, educator*
Noyes, Robert Edwin *publisher, writer*
Roes, Nicholas A. *communications consultant, writer*
Weissmann, Heidi Seitelblum *radiologist, educator*

## Salem

Brauer, Shaun Michael *music educator*

## Scotch Plains

Hallard, Wayne Bruce *retired economist*
Johnsen, Karen Kennedy *marketing professional*
Klock, John Henry *lawyer*
Kraemer, Ira B. *symphony conductor*
Margiotta, Joseph M. *printing company executive*
Shaw, Alan *lawyer*

## Sea Bright

Plummer, Dirk Arnold *chemical, electrical, and electronics engineer*

## Sea Isle City

Tull, Theresa Anne *retired diplomat*

## Seabrook

Damiano, Beth Carole *special education educator*

## Secaucus

Abrams, Dan *broadcast executive, news correspondent*
Arena, Bruce *professional soccer coach*
Bradley, Bob *professional soccer coach*

Carlson, Tucker *political analyst, writer, television host*
Crowley, Monica *political commentator*
Dabah, Ezra *apparel executive*
Diggs, Taye (Scott Diggs) *actor*
Liao, Paul Foo-Hung *electronics executive*
Lynch, Joseph Michael *engineer, consultant*
Marcus, Alan C. *public relations consultant*
Meola, Tony *professional soccer player, actor*
Olbermann, Keith *news analyst, former sportscaster*
Sakiewicz, Nick *professional sports team executive*
Sanders, Summer *Olympic athlete, news correspondent, newscaster*
Silver, Adam *sports association executive*
Unanue, Robert I. *food products executive*

**Sewell**
Crouse, Farrell R. *lawyer*
Gonnella, Renee *school psychologist*
Mandracchia, Vincent Joseph *podiatrist*

**Shiloh**
Garrison, John Raymond *organization executive*

**Ship Bottom**
Shackleton, Richard James *lawyer, director*

**Short Hills**
Alesio, Steven W. *financial services company executive*
Austin, Danforth Whitley *newspaper executive*
Bartels, Stanley Leonard *investment banker*
Chaiken, Bernard Henry *internist, gastroenterologist*
Cooper, Russell John III *lawyer*
Duberstein, Joel Lawrence *internist, pulmonologist, educator*
Fast, Kenneth H. *lawyer*
Gibson, William Lee *financial consultant*
Harwood, Jerry *market research executive*
Hazlehurst, Robert Purviance, Jr. *lawyer*
Howe, James Everett *investment company executive*
Loren, Allan Z. *business information company executive*
MacKinnon, Malcolm D(avid) *retired insurance company executive*
Marshall, John Patrick *lawyer*
Mebane, William Black *controller, financial consultant*
Novack, Robert *lawyer*
Ogden, Maureen Black *retired state legislator*
Price, Michael F. *money management executive*
Robbins-Wilf, Marcia *educational consultant*
Schaefer, Charles James III *advertising executive, consultant*
Schaefer, Eleanor Montville *retired publishing executive*
Schirmeister, Charles F. *retired lawyer*
Siegfried, David Charles *retired lawyer*
Soderlind, Sterling Eugene *newspaper industry consultant*
Wharton, Lennard *engineering company executive*
Winter, Ruth Grosman (Mrs. Arthur Winter) *journalist*

**Shrewsbury**
Baker, Gerald David *marketing executive, consultant*
Feeney, John Robert *banker*
Michaelson, Peter Lee *lawyer*
Westerman, Liane Marie *research scientist executive*

**Sicklerville**
Miller, Audrey Thornton *retired vice principal*
Simpson, Eugene Thamon *music educator, singer*

**Skillman**
Brill, Yvonne Claeys *engineer, consultant*
Cummings, Peggy Ann *counseling administrator*
Diaz, Teresita Perez *chemist*
Eiger, Richard William *retired publisher*
Hackel, Adam William *music educator*
Liro, Joseph R. *diversified financial services company executive*
Rhett, Haskell Emery Smith *educational association administrator*
Sharma, Om Prakash *clinical research and development executive*
Tenenbaum, Bernard Hirsh *entrepreneur, educator*
Wheelock, Keith Ward *retired investment company executive, educator*

**Somerset**
Aronson, Louis Vincent, II, *manufacturing executive*
Becker, Phyllis *systems analyst*
Brophy, Joseph Thomas *computer company executive*
DeMonic, Betty Lee *music educator*
De Salva, Salvatore Joseph *retired pharmacologist, toxicologist*
Jones, Andrew William *pharmaceutical executive*
Karas, James *public relations executive, engineering executive*
King, David T. *communications company financial executive*
Lichtig, Leo Kenneth *health economist*
Mittleberg, Eric Michael *pharmaceutical executive*
Soaries, DeForest B., Jr. *former state official*
Sofia, R. D. *pharmacologist*
Tsou, Yu-Min *science administrator, chemistry researcher*
Wallfesh, Henry Maurice *communications executive, writer*

**Somerville**
Albin, Barry Todd *state supreme court justice*
Biondi, Peter J. *assemblyman*
Dobrinsky, Susan Elizabeth *human resources director*
Fleischman, Joseph Jacob *lawyer*
Gorton-Horan, Ann Hilbert *vice principal*
Grey, Ruthann E. *corporate communications specialist, director*
Hutcheon, Peter David *lawyer*
Robinson, William Richard *lawyer*
Sponzilli, Edward George *lawyer*

Weisblatt, Barbara Ann *secondary school educator*

**South Amboy**
Moskal, Anthony John *retired dean, management consultant, educator*

**South Bound Brook**
Weir, Sonja Ann *artist*

**South Hackensack**
Cohen, Brett I. *health products executive*
Jacobs, George Braun *neurosurgeon*
Wille, Rosanne Louise *educational consultant*

**South Orange**
Amar, A. D. *business educator, management consultant*
Bao, Xue-Ming *librarian, educator*
Budin, Wendy C. *nursing educator, researcher*
Collins, John W., Jr. *retired military officer, technologist, educator*
Delo, Ellen Sanderson *retired lawyer*
Hackett, Mims, Jr. *state legislator*
Hanbury, Kevin M. *dean, priest*
Hanifin, Christopher James *physician assistant, educator*
Hansell, Phyllis Shanley *nursing educator, administrator, researcher, consultant*
Hecht, Marion B. *counselor*
Hoffert, Eric Michael *application developer, information technology executive*
Leshnoff, Susan Kriegel *art educator, artist*
Nowik, John David *music educator, musician*
Riordan, Rick *writer*
Sahiner, Mehmet Alper *physics professor, researcher*
Schectman, Stephen Barry *pharmaceutical executive*
Stringile, Marie Elizabeth *educational administrator*
Toy, Tasha Chantey *academic administrator, educator*

**South Plainfield**
Kennedy, John William *engineering company executive*
Kwon, Ik Hyun *internist*
Lewandowski, Andrew Anthony *utilities executive, consultant*
Santoro, Frank Anthony *lawyer*

**South River**
Jackiewicz, Frederick Waclaw *priest*
Kirshner, Jacob *physician*

**Southampton**
Callaway, Ben Anderson *journalist*

**Sparta**
Bhattacharyya, Dev *information technology executive, consultant*
Jacobs-Quam, Vivien Marie *retired music educator*
McMeen, Elmer Ellsworth III *musician, retired lawyer*
McMeen, Sheila Taenzler *retired lawyer*
Rosser, Alvin Raymon *artist*
Spence, Robert Leroy *publishing executive*
Stickney, Carol Jean *special education educator, consultant*
Truran, William Richard *electrical engineer*

**Spring Lake**
Bonhag, Thomas Edward *insurance company executive, financial planner, financial consultant*
D'Luhy, John James *investment banker*
Harrigan, John Thomas, Jr. *physician, obstetrician, gynecologist*
Krein, Catherine Cecilia *broadcast and journalism educator*
McGreal, Joseph A., Jr. *publishing executive*
O'Connor, Francis X. *financial executive*

**Springfield**
Burford, Peter T. *publishing executive*
Goldsmith, Jeffrey H. *lawyer*
Kerner, Michael Bernard *gastroenterologist*
Kraemer, Waldron *lawyer*
Kwartler, Jed Aryeh *otolaryngologist*
Marino, Natalie Marie *artist*
Mytelka, Arnold Krieger *lawyer*
Shilling, A. Gary *economist, consultant*
Wosnitzer, Morey *urologist*

**Stewartsville**
Busch, Beverly Gull *English language educator, literature educator, instructional resource center administrator*
Eckert, John Andrew *chemist, technical consultant*

**Stirling**
Walsh, Peter Joseph *physics professor*

**Stockton**
Mahon, Robert *photographer*
Schoenherr, John (Carl) *artist, illustrator*

**Stone Harbor**
Koss, Rosabel Steinhauer *retired health and physical education educator*

**Stratford**
Daguisan, Janel *biomedical engineer, electronics and computer educator, music producer*
Levitas, Andrew Stephen *child psychiatrist, educator*

**Succasunna**
Romance, Mary C. *library director*

**Summit**
Baker, Alden *artist*
Barer, Sol Joseph *biotechnology company executive*
Carniol, Paul J. *plastic and reconstructive surgeon, otolaryngologist*
Chynoweth, Alan Gerald *retired telecommunications industry executive*
D'Alessandro, Mari Angelina *art association administrator*

Deming, Frederick Wilson *retired economist, banker*
English, Jerry Fitzgerald *lawyer, educator*
Falletta, Jo Ann *conductor*
Fuess, Billings Sibley, Jr. *advertising executive*
Fukui, Hatsuaki *retired electrical engineer, art historian*
Gaudino, Mario *physician, pharmaceutical company executive, scientist*
Greenberg, Rosalie *child psychiatrist*
Halperin, John Jacob *neurology educator, researcher*
Hodosh, Richard M. *neurosurgeon*
Hyans, Peter *plastic surgeon*
Jackson, John Wyant *biotechnology company executive*
Kahmann, Chesley *composer, music educator, pianist*
Kenyon, Edward Tipton *lawyer*
Lewis, Donald Emerson *banker*
Lindars, Laurence Edward *retired health care products executive*
Longfield, William Herman *health products executive*
Malin, Robert Abernethy *investment company executive*
Mehner, Roger *lawyer*
Mueller, Paul Henry *retired bank executive*
Pace, Leonard *retired management consultant*
Pfaltz, Hugo Menzel, Jr. *lawyer*
Phillips, James Charles *physicist, researcher*
Rosensweig, Ronald Ellis *chemical engineer, consultant*
Rousseau, Irene Victoria *artist*
Sachs, Richard Gregory *cardiologist*
Singleterry, Gary Lee *investment banker*
Starks, Florence Elizabeth *retired special education educator*
Vandenberg, Joka Maria *physicist, researcher*
Weinstein, Stephen Brant *communications executive, researcher, writer*
Woller, James Alan *lawyer*
Zachary, Louis George *chemical company consultant*

**Sussex**
Hoyt, Earl Edward, Jr. *industrial designer*

**Swedesboro**
Lovell, Theodore *electrical engineer, consultant*

**Tabernacle**
DiBella, Russell Thomas *federal investigator*

**Teaneck**
Alperin, Richard Martin *social worker, psychoanalyst*
Brudner, Helen Gross *social sciences educator*
Bullough, John Frank *musician, educator*
Carter, Regina *jazz violinist*
Cassimatis, Peter John *economics professor*
Chandrashekaran, Rajesh *marketing educator*
Chen, Zong *computer scientist, educator*
Connola, Donald Pascal, Jr. *management consultant*
Daddario, Richard *chief financial officer, accountant*
Dewey, Ralph Jay *school system administrator*
Ehrlich, Ira Robert *mechanical engineering consultant*
Feinberg, Robert S. *plastics company executive, marketing professional*
Fjordbotten, Alf Lee *language educator*
Gordon, Lois G. *language educator*
Graham, Janet Lorraine *music educator*
Haas, Gerhard Julius *chemistry professor*
Halper, June *medical center director*
Holmes, Miriam H. *publisher*
Ladenheim, Jules Calvin *neurosurgeon*
Lafer, Fred Seymour *data processing executive*
Meno, John Peter *chorepiscopus*
Reinish, Gloria Brooks *electrical engineer, educator*
Rundback, John H. *radiologist, interventional radiology director*
Smith, Susan Elizabeth *guidance director*
Solá, Victoria M. *announcer, writer*
Walker, Lucy Doris *secondary school educator, writer*
Wallmann, Jeffrey Miner *author*
Weinberg, Loretta *state legislator*
Weiss, Mitchell Joseph *librarian*
Wiener, Joel Howard *historian, educator*
Zwass, Vladimir *computer science and information systems educator*

**Tenafly**
Bernstein, William Robert *banker*
Blank, Marion Sue *psychologist, educator*
Gerst, Paul Howard *physician*
Golomb, Frederick Martin *surgeon, educator*
Koons, Irvin Louis *graphics designer, consultant, marketing professional*
Tall, Susan Porter *music educator*

**Teterboro**
Freeman, Kenneth W. *laboratory executive*
Hagemann, Robert A. *health facility administrator*
Mohapatra, Surya N. *laboratory executive*
Prevoznik, Michael E. *health facility administrator, lawyer*

**Thorofare**
Andrews, Raymond Douglas *financial executive*

**Three Bridges**
Lawrence, Gerald Graham *management consultant*

**Tinton Falls**
Hoelzler, Michael Gebhard *veterinarian, surgeon*
Macdonald, Donald Arthur, Jr. *physician, surgeon*
Ostar, Allan William *educational consultant*

**Titusville**
Bhattacharjya, Ashoke Sanjoy *economist, researcher*
Cooper, Paul *retired mechanical engineer, science association director, researcher*

**Toms River**
Bosley, Karen Lee *language educator, communications educator*
Chopyk, Dan Bohdan *language educator, poet*
D'Alessandro-Fernandez-Phillips, Gina *elementary school educator*
Donaldson, Marcia Jean *lay worker*
Fiore, Carmen Anthony *writer*
Kanarkowski, Edward Joseph *data processing company executive*
Marchese, Michael James, Jr. *radiation oncologist*
Matteo, Christine E. *librarian*
Moran, Jeffrey W., Jr. *county surrogate*
Unger, Howard Albert *artist, photographer, educator*

**Totowa**
Tuthill, Jay Dean, II, *investment executive*

**Trenton**
Abelow, Bradley *state official*
Barclay, Warren M. *human resources specialist, researcher*
Baron, Lisa Ann *environmental scientist*
Bauer, Virginia S. *state agency administrator*
Bigham, William J. *lawyer*
Binder, Elaine Kotell *associations consultant*
Brown, Peggy Lee *academic administrator, consultant, singer*
Caldwell, Wesley Stuart III *lawyer, lobbyist*
Caspersen, Sidney J. *state agency administrator*
Chen, David *reporter*
Christopherson, Elizabeth Good *broadcast executive*
Codey, Richard James *state senator, former governor*
Cole, Richie Thomas *musician, composer, educator*
Cooper, Mary Little *judge*
Corzine, Jon Stevens *governor, former senator*
Cowen, Robert E. *federal judge*
Davy, Lucille E. *school system administrator*
Deltuvia, John Joseph, Jr. *systems and procedural analyst*
Demitry, Elpis Hope *music educator*
Depuglio, Joseph *physics educator*
George, Emery Edward *foreign language and studies educator, writer*
Gervasoni, James E., Jr. *medical researcher, oncologist*
Gomez, William *orthopedist*
Greenberg, Morton Ira *federal judge*
Grossman, David Michael *academic administrator, educator*
Gupta, Rajendra Prasad *physician*
Holt, Jonathan Turner *public relations executive*
Hubbs, Julie Christine *lawyer*
Kocieniewski, David *journalist*
Lattanzi, Gregory Denis *archaeologist*
LaVecchia, Jaynee *state supreme court justice*
Leipzig, Melvin *art educator*
Long, Virginia *state supreme court justice*
Mansnerus, Laura *news correspondent*
Martin, James Hanley *state attorney general*
Miller, Ruane *artist, educator*
Miller, Velvet G. *health science association administrator*
Mojer-Torres, Lisa Nan *lawyer*
Obed, Leonora Rita Villegas *writer*
Old, Hughes Oliphant *theologian, minister*
Palmer, Douglas Harold *mayor*
Poritz, Deborah T. *state supreme court justice, retired state attorney general*
Pruitt, George Albert *college president*
Rabner, Stuart Jeff *state attorney general, lawyer*
Riccards, Michael Patrick *academic administrator*
Rivera-Soto, Roberto A. *state supreme court justice*
Russell, Joyce Anne Rogers *retired librarian*
Scheiring, Michael James *college official*
Smallwood, Robert Albian, Jr. *retired secondary education educator*
Socolow, David Jacob *state agency administrator*
Sterns, Joel Henry *lawyer*
Sullivan, John *news correspondent*
Thatsneyakul, Yaovares *pediatrician, consultant*
Ulsh, Gordon A. *battery manufacturing company executive*
Viscomi, Frank Joseph *pharmaceutical executive*
Wallace, John E. *state supreme court justice*
Wells, Nina Mitchell *state official*
Zanna, Martin Thomas *physician*
Zazzali, James R. *state supreme court justice*

**Turnersville**
DeIrace, Nicholas Louis *physician*
Rabil, Mitchell Joseph *lawyer*

**Union**
Applbaum, Ronald Lee *academic administrator*
Bottitta, Joseph Anthony *lawyer*
Darden, Barbara S. *library director*
Darden, Joseph Samuel, Jr. *health educator*
Eisenberg, Warren *retail executive*
Feinstein, Leonard *retail executive*
Kim, Youn-Suk Ernest *economist, educator*
Lederman, Susan Sturc *public administration professor*
Newman, Stephen Alexander *chemical engineer*
Temares, Steven H. *retail executive*
White, Robert Leslie Gordon, Jr. *aerospace transportation executive*
Zois, Constantine Nicholas Athanasios *meteorologist, educator*

**Union Beach**
Gilmartin, Clara T. *volunteer*

**Union City**
Bozoyan, Sylvia *elementary school educator*
Englese, Damon Joseph *director*
Portes, Fernando A. *project manager*
Sullivan, Kathleen Ann *secondary school educator*

**Upper Montclair**
Tintle, Carmel Joseph *public relations executive*

**Upper Saddle River**
Cappitella, Mauro John *architect*
Oolie, Sam *manufacturing and investment company executive*

Wallace, William III *engineering executive*

## Ventnor City
Bolton, Kenneth Albert *management consultant*
Campbell, Thomas Douglas *legal association administrator*
Robbins, Hulda Dornblatt *artist, printmaker*

## Vernon
Ryan, John Michael *secondary school educator*

## Verona
Aronow, Edward *psychologist, educator*
Ayaso, Manuel *artist*
Malanga, Gerard Anthony *sports medicine physician, director*
Poor, Suzanne Donaldson *advertising and public relations executive*

## Vincentown
Foster, David Ramsey *soap company executive*

## Vineland
Clinton, Lawrence Paul *psychiatrist*
Schmid, Patti A. *library director*
Vaden, Sandra Drake *academic administrator*

## Voorhees
Brahms, William Bernard *librarian, writer*
Correll, Donald L. *water services company executive*
Glasofer, Eric David *allergist, immunologist, pediatrician, educator*
Lampert, S. Henry *retired dentist*
Piermatti, Jack *dentist*
Siskin, Edward Joseph *engineering company executive, construction company executive*
Suflas, Steven William *lawyer*

## Waldwick
Lynch, Carol *special services director, psychologist*

## Wall
De Santo, Donald James *psychologist, educational association administrator*
Gaona, Arlene *secondary school educator*
Monaco, Robert Anthony *radiologist*
Motley, John Paul *psychiatrist, consultant*
Mudd, Mary Cordelia *historian*
Nucciarone, A. Patrick *lawyer*
O'Neill, James Paul *psychiatrist*
Petrovich, Dorothy *elementary school educator*

## Wanamassa
McTague-Dougherty, Amy Elizabeth *speech pathology/audiology services professional*

## Warren
Baxter, Nancy *medical writer*
Blass, Walter Paul *management consultant, educator*
DiFrancesco, Donald T. *lawyer*
DiPietro, Ralph Anthony *management consultant, educator, marketing consultant*
Finnegan, John D. *insurance company executive*
Hartman, David G. *actuary*
Hennings, Dorothy Grant (Mrs. George Hennings) *education educator*
Jacobson, Gary Steven *lawyer*
Kozberg, Donna Walters *rehabilitation services professional*
Kozberg, Ronald Paul *health and human services administrator*
Maull, George Marriner *conductor, educator*
O'Neill, Michael J., Jr. *lawyer, insurance company executive*
O'Reilly, Michael *corporate financial executive*
Wildrick, Kenyon Jones *minister*

## Washington
Castner, Bret A. *social studies educator*

## Watchung
Cohen, Melvin Irwin *retired communications systems and technology executive*
Cox, Archibald, Jr. *investment company executive*
Michaelis, Paul Charles *engineering physicist executive*
Miller, John Ronald *minister*
Tornqvist, Erik Gustav Markus *chemical engineer, research scientist, consultant*

## Wayne
Arthur, Ray *retail executive*
Arthur, Raymond L. *retail toy and game company executive*
Barbour, John *retail executive*
Brockett, Francesca L. *retail executive*
Cetrulo, Jerry *artist, sculptor*
Connell, Joseph F. *academic administrator*
Derby, Deborah *retail executive*
DeRosa, Richard Jerome *composer, musician, educator*
Garcia, Ofelia *art educator, department chairman*
Geiger, David E *engineer*
Gelman, Jon Leonard *lawyer*
Gollance, Robert Barnett *ophthalmologist*
Heyman, Samuel J. *chemical manufacturing company executive*
Jacobs-Carey, Sheila L. *retired immunologist*
Jeffrey, Robert George, Jr. *manufacturing executive*
Kay, Christopher K. *retail executive, lawyer*
Li, Fuan *marketing educator, researcher*
Liu, Timothy *poet, educator*
Markee, Richard L. *retail executive*
Oriji, Gibson K. *medical educator, medical researcher*
Pardo, Janette M. *archivist, librarian*
Rogoff, Paula Drimmer *English and foreign language educator*
Salny, Abbie Feinstein *psychologist*
Schmidt, Barnet Michael *communications and electronic engineer*
Schwartz, David Jay *lawyer*
Speert, Arnold *academic administrator, chemistry educator*
Storch, Gerald L. *retail executive*
Sullivan, Glenn D. *music educator*

---

Tumolo, Michael L. *corporate lawyer*

## Weehawken
Hobson, Burton Harold *publishing executive*
Kelleher, Kathleen *marketing professional*

## West Caldwell
Dixon, Jo-Ann Conte *management consultant*
Giblin, Thomas Patrick *labor union administrator, political organization administrator*
Page, Frederick West *business consultant*
Piel, Emil J. *retired engineering educator*
Schiff, Robert *healthcare consulting company executive*
Surmatis, Joseph D. *retired chemist*

## West Long Branch
Ensor, Linda Lineberger *literature and language educator*
Gaffney, Paul Golden, II, *academic administrator, retired military officer*
Lutz, Francis Charles *dean, civil engineering educator*
Pearson, Thomas Spencer *academic administrator*

## West Milford
Goerig, Marianne *elementary school educator*
Hannon, Patricia Ann *library director*
Stelpstra, William John *minister*

## West New York
Gruenberg, Elliot Lewis *electronics engineer and company executive*
Knopf, Claire *editor, writer*
Schmidt, Nancy Anne *psychotherapist*

## West Orange
Atkins, Richard Bart *film, television producer*
Bojsza, Joan E. *elementary school educator*
Bornstein, Lester Milton *retired health facility administrator*
Brodkin, Roger Harrison *dermatologist, educator*
Casella, Anthony John *cardiologist*
Connolly, Mark A. *biology educator*
De Lisa, Joel Alan *rehabilitation physician, research executive*
Dispaltro, Franklin L. *plastic surgeon*
Eisenberg, R. Neal *restoration company executive*
Filippone, Dennis R. *surgeon, consultant*
Gans, Bruce Merrill *physiatrist, educator, health facility administrator*
Gehl, Raymond Harold *psychiatrist, educator*
Ghali, Anwar Youssef *psychiatrist, educator*
Hill, George James *physician, educator*
Hwang, Karen *research scientist*
Ko, Chia-Wen *biostatistician, researcher*
Kyle, Corinne Silverman *management consultant*
Langsner, Alan Michael *pediatric cardiologist*
Linsenmeyer, Todd Alan *medical educator, physician*
Martin, Boston Faust *neurosurgeon*
Mazur, Thomas A. *music educator*
McKinney, John Adams, Jr. *lawyer*
Pollara, Joanne *learning disabilities educator consultant*
Rinsky, Judith Sue Lynn *foundation administrator, educator consultant*
Rogal, Gary Jeffrey *cardiologist*
Samson, David *lawyer*
Shapiro, Jared *freelance/self-employed emergency medical technician*
Sweeney, Gerald Bingham *lawyer*
Thomas, Gary L. *retired academic administrator*
Zimmerman, David Carl *controller, corporate financial executive*

## West Paterson
Lilley, David *chemicals executive*
Pataki, Andrew *bishop*
Smith, Roy *lawyer*

## West Windsor
Yoseloff, Thomas *publisher*

## Westfield
Balsamello, Jason Reed *principal, educator*
Bhagat, Phiroz Maneck *mechanical engineer*
Bobis, Daniel Harold *lawyer*
Davoren, Steven Michael *marketing professional, psychologist*
McLean, Vincent Ronald *former manufacturing company financial executive*
Schlosberg, Theodore K. *music educator*
Simon, Martin Stanley *economist, consultant*
Vijayakumar, Asha *ophthalmologist*

## Westwood
Fabrikant, Craig Steven *psychologist*
Landzberg, Joel Serge *cardiologist*
Radakovich, Daniel I. *communications executive, consultant*

## Wharton
Krosser, Howard S. *aerospace transportation executive*

## Whippany
Alexander, Mark A. *energy executive*
Lemmo, Peter S. *writer, educational consultant*

## Whitehouse
Shelton, Craig *food service executive*

## Whitehouse Station
Anstice, David W. *pharmaceutical executive*
Avedon, Marcia J. *pharmaceutical executive*
Bossidy, Larry (Lawrence Arthur Bossidy) *pharmaceutical company executive, former industrial manufacturing executive*
Clark, Richard T. *pharmaceutical company executive*
Deese, Willie A. *pharmaceutical executive*
Fiscus, Philip Wayne *underwriter*
Frazier, Kenneth C. *pharmaceutical executive, lawyer*
Gilmartin, Raymond V. *pharmaceutical company executive*
Hunsche, Elke Greta Irma *economist*
Lewent, Judy Carol *pharmaceutical executive*
Loescher, Peter Hans *pharmaceutical executive*

---

Mahmoud, Adel A. *medical educator, pharmaceutical executive*
Martelet, Francois R. *pharmaceutical executive*
McGlynn, Margaret G. *pharmaceutical executive*
McGuire, John Lawrence *pharmaceutical executive*
Scalet, J. Chris (James Christopher Scalet) *pharmaceutical executive*
Wold-Olsen, Per *pharmaceutical executive*
Yarno, Wendy *pharmaceutical executive*

## Whiting
Randall, Lynn Ellen *librarian*
Willis, Ben *writer, artist*

## Wildwood
DiMedio, Michael Joseph *secondary school educator*

## Wildwood Crest
Carey, Steven Everett *music educator*

## Wilkesboro
Jennings, Perry G. *retail executive*

## Williamstown
Ash, Donna Joan-Stillwell *art educator*
Heidemark, George John *elementary school educator*

## Willingboro
Bass, Joseph Oscar *retired minister*
Bevels, Esther Marie *medical technician, director*
Denslow, Deborah Pierson *primary school educator*
Ingerman, Peter Zilahy *systems analyst, consultant*
Jenerette, Joyce Williams *elementary school educator, educational consultant*

## Woodbridge
Ayub, Yacub *financial consultant*
Barcan, Stephen Emanuel *lawyer*
Brown, Morris *lawyer*
Galkin, Samuel Bernard *orthodontist*
Hurley, John *library director*
Qiu, Li-Hui *music educator, actress*
Santulli, Richard T. *air transportation executive*
Warren, Arthur Lee *secondary school educator, school system administrator*
Wood, J. Warren, III, (Joshua Warren Wood III) *lawyer*

## Woodbury
Doughty, A. Glenn *minister*
Stambaugh, John Edgar *oncologist, hematologist, educator, pharmacologist*
Zimmer, Janie Louise *mathematics professor, academic administrator*

## Woodcliff Lake
Jacobs, Charles Nathan *editor, writer*

## Wyckoff
Brown, James Joseph *manufacturing executive*
Gartner, Joseph John, II, *obstetrician, gynecologist*
Lavery, Daniel P. *management consultant*
Marcus, Linda Susan *dermatologist*
Metrey, George David *social work educator, retired academic administrator*
Munson, William Leslie *insurance company executive*
Oberndorf, Mark Robert *artist*
Stahl, Alice Slater *retired psychiatrist*

## Yardville
Lauricella, Margaret Pierce *school system administrator*
Zweig, Steven Frederick *statistician*

# NEW MEXICO

## Abiquiu
Botts, Gregory *artist*
Hamburger, Sydney K. *sculptor*
Howlett, Phyllis Lou *retired athletics conference administrator*

## Alamogordo
Ashdown, Franklin Donald *physician, composer*
Ernst, James Allan *safety engineer, consultant*
McFadin, Helen Lozetta *retired elementary school educator*
Patch, Lisa E. *health services director, nurse*
VanAlstine, Rick G. *secondary school educator*

## Albuquerque
Alexis, Tracy L. *project manager, project specialist, information technology manager, small business owner*
Anaya, Rudolfo *writer, educator*
Anderson, Lawrence Keith *electrical engineer, consultant*
Antreasian, Garo Zareh *artist, lithographer, art educator*
Ardelean, Emil Valentin *mechanical engineer, researcher*
Baker, Laura Kay *art gallery owner, writer*
Bankhurst, Arthur Dale *medical educator, researcher*
Bardacke, Paul Gregory *lawyer, retired federal official*
Barker, Lynn M. *manufacturing executive*
Barry, Steve *sculptor, educator*
Baum, Carl Edward *electrical engineer, researcher*
Beach, Arthur O'Neal *lawyer*
Beiler, Holly Anne *education educator*
Bell, Stoughton *computer scientist, mathematician, educator*
Berman, Stanley Zissman *allergist, immunologist, educator, internist, department chairman*
Black, Bruce D. *judge*
Bova, Vincent Arthur, Jr. *lawyer, consultant, photographer*
Brinker, Charles Jeffrey *chemistry and chemical engineering educator*
Brown, Lee Kelvin *pulmonary, critical care and sleep medicine physician, researcher*
Cadavid, Luis Fernando *biologist*

---

Caldera, Louis Edward *academic administrator, former federal official*
Calkins, Ralph Nelson *retired economics professor*
Caplan, Edwin Harvey *retired dean, retired finance educator*
Cardimona, David Anthony *physicist, researcher*
Cargo, David Francis *lawyer, former governor*
Chang, Barbara Karen *medical educator*
Chavez, Martin Joseph *lawyer, mayor*
Cobb, John Candler *medical educator*
Coleman, Barbara McReynolds *artist*
Condie, Carol Joy *anthropologist, science administrator*
Conway, John E. *federal judge*
Cornelius, Chris James *chemical engineer, researcher*
Cramer, James Dale *physicist, scientific company executive*
Davidge, K. Genevieve *clinical social worker*
Davies, Thomas Mockett, Jr. *history professor*
Davis, Betty Bourbonia *real estate company executive*
Davis, Jon L. *logistics consultant*
DeCandia, Donald Alan *lawyer*
de Gouvea, Raul *educator, consultant*
DelCampo, Robert Gregory *education educator*
Dorato, Peter *electrical and computer engineering educator*
Eaves, John M. *lawyer*
Eichenberg, Peter Thompson *retired criminal investigator*
Eldredge, Jonathan DeForest *medical librarian, educator, social informaticist*
Ellis, James W. *law educator*
Emin, David *physicist*
Enke, Christie George *chemistry professor, consultant*
Erickson, Sue Alice *health educator, consultant, nurse*
Espat, Robert Eduardo, Sr. *industrialist*
Everitt, Elizabeth M. *school system administrator*
Farmer, Terry D(wayne) *lawyer*
Figueroa, Francisco Armando *aerospace transportation executive, accountant*
Finch, Robert Jonathan *communications engineer, consultant*
Fletcher, Marilyn Pendleton *retired librarian*
Flournoy, John Charles, Sr. *retired civilian military employee, retired military officer*
Foster, Judi *interior designer, artist*
Franse, R. Nelson *lawyer*
Freeman, Patricia Elizabeth *multi-media specialist, educational consultant*
Frias, Shirlee N. *elementary school educator*
Friberg, George Joseph *electronics company executive, entrepreneur*
Fry, Donald Edmund *surgeon*
Fuller, Anne Elizabeth Havens *English language and literature educator, consultant*
Gahala, Estella Marie *writer, consultant*
Gander, John Edward *biochemistry educator*
Garcia, F. Chris *academic administrator, political scientist, educator*
Gardner, Lenann McGookey *management consultant*
Giller, Edward Bonfoy *retired government official, retired military officer*
Goldberg, Catherine T. *lawyer*
Gordon, Larry Jean *environmental health educator*
Graff, Pat Stuever *secondary school educator*
Greene, Linda Kay *retired secondary school educator*
Guenther, Arthur Henry *research scientist, educator*
Gurney, Burke *physical therapist, educator*
Gutierrez, Joni Marie *landscape architect, political organization worker*
Gutierrez, Sidney M. *federal agency administrator*
Hadas, Elizabeth Chamberlayne *editor*
Hager, Gordon Douglas *scientist, engineering educator*
Hahn, Betty *artist, photographer, educator*
Hall, Jerome William *research engineering educator*
Hansen, Curtis LeRoy *federal judge*
Hansen, Harold B., Jr. *elementary school educator, assistant principal*
Harris, Fred R. *political scientist, educator, retired senator*
Hart, Frederick Michael *law educator*
Hartz, Harris L *federal judge*
Heffron, Warren A. *physician, educator*
Henderson, Rogene Faulkner *toxicologist, researcher*
Herrera, Gilbert Victor *engineering executive*
Hester, Reid Kevin *psychologist, researcher*
Hopfinger, Anton Joseph *education educator, consultant*
Horner, Harry Charles, Jr. *sales executive*
Hovel, Esther Harrison *art educator*
Hsi, David Ching Heng *plant pathologist, geneticist, educator*
Hutton, Paul Andrew *historian, educator, writer*
Iglesias, David Claudio *prosecutor*
Jaramillo, Mari-Luci *retired federal agency administrator*
Jewell, Donna Louise *choreographer, educator*
Johnson, Robert Hersel *journalist*
Jung, Rex Eugene *psychologist, researcher*
Kaehele, Bettie Louise *accountant*
Keep, Marcus Floyd *neurosurgeon*
Keleher, Michael Lawrence *lawyer*
Kierst, Debra B. *theater educator, theater director*
King, Brian Jeffrey *publishing executive, artist, writer*
King, Lowell Restell *pediatric urologist*
Knospe, William Herbert *medical educator*
Korman, Nathaniel Irving *research and development company executive*
Lambert, Jeffrey Scott *secondary school educator*
Lang, Thompson Hughes *publishing executive*
Lange, Dale Lowell *language educator, researcher*
Lasater, W(illiam) Robert, Jr. *lawyer*
Lattman, Laurence Harold *retired academic administrator*
Leach, Richard Maxwell, Jr., (Max Leach Jr.) *corporate professional, consultant*
Lee, Sang-Joon *statistical professor*
Leeper, Ramon Joe *physicist*
Lewis, Linda Kathryn *librarian*
Liotta, William A. *theater educator*

Enyeart, James L. *museum director*
Evans, Dick *artist*
Ferguson, Glenn Walker *writer, educator, retired ambassador*
Fisher, Robert Alan *laser physicist*
Franzen, Ulrich J. *architect*
Gaddes, Richard *opera company director*
Gallegor, Mary Ellen *mathematics professor*
Gallegos, Mary Ellen *education educator, department chairman*
Garcia, Veronica *school system administrator*
Gell-Mann, Murray *theoretical physicist, educator*
Gilbert, Alan *conductor*
Giovanielli, Damon Vincent *physicist, consultant*
Goorley, John Timothy *nuclear engineer*
Groseclose, Everett Harrison *retired editor*
Hammer, Charles F. *chemistry professor*
Harcourt, Robert Neff *educational administrator, genealogist, journalist*
Harding, Marie *ecological executive, artist*
Harmon, Judith S *anthropologist*
Harroun, Dorothy Sumner *artist*
Hoffmann, Louis Gerhard *immunologist, educator*
Horndeski, Gregory Walter *artist, mathematics educator*
Johnson, Eric B. *police chief*
Johnson, Reverdy *lawyer*
Justice, Jack Burton *retired lawyer, writer*
Kaman, Helen S. *retired aerospace engineer, artist*
Karp, Diane R. *art educator*
Kellner, Richard George *mathematician, computer scientist*
Kelly, Paul Joseph, Jr. *federal judge*
King, George G. *museum director*
Kingsmore, Stephen Francis *physician, research scientist*
Knight, Kenneth Hugh *conductor*
Kotin, Paul *pathologist*
Kronberg, Philipp Paul *physicist, educator*
Kropschot, Richard Henry *retired physicist, lab administrator*
Lee, David Mallin *physicist*
Lehmberg, Stanford Eugene *historian, educator*
Leibowitz, Jack Richard *physicist, educator*
Leon, Bruno *architect, educator*
Lichtenberg, Maggie Klee *publishing executive*
Lynn, John Eric *nuclear physicist, researcher, consultant*
Madrid, Patricia A. *state attorney general*
Maehl, William Henry *historian, academic administrator, consultant*
Maes, Petra Jimenez *state supreme court justice*
McDermott, Sandra *national park administrator*
Melnick, Alice Jean (AJ Melnick) *counselor*
Mercer, James Lee *management consultant*
Merrin, Seymour *computer company executive*
Miller, Dwight Richard *professional hair care industry executive, cosmetologist, consultant*
Miller-Engel, Marjorie *foundation administrator, commissioner, small business owner*
Minzner, Pamela Burgy *state supreme court justice*
Moll, Deborah Adelaide *lawyer*
Morrison, Malcolm Cameron *engineering management professional*
Morrissey, Michael Joseph *investment banker*
Myers, R. David *library director, dean*
Ovitsky, Steven Alan *musician, symphony orchestra executive*
Peat, Randall Dean *military analyst, retired military officer*
Peña, Amado Maurilio, Jr. *artist, curator, educator*
Perry, Nancy Estelle *psychologist*
Pound, John Bennett *lawyer*
Primozic, Daniel Thomas *dean*
Richardson, Bill (William Blaine Richardson) *governor*
Rubenstein, Bernard *orchestra conductor*
Sandoval, Isabelle Medina *education educator*
Schiller, William Richard *surgeon*
Schwartz, George R. *physician, researcher*
Schwarz, Michael *lawyer*
Serna, Patricio *state supreme court justice*
Sloan, Jeanette Pasin *artist*
Sloane, Phyllis Lester *artist*
Smith, Philip Meek *science administrator, consultant*
Snider, Richard Douglas *music educator, director*
Stalker, James Raghi *meteorologist, environmental services administrator*
Stevens, Ron A. *lawyer, advocate, surveyor*
Stieber, Tamar *journalist*
Stolley, Richard Brockway *journalist*
Sumner, Gordon, Jr. *retired military officer*
Tarn, Nathaniel *poet, educator, translator*
Thornburg, Garrett, Jr. *finance company executive*
Vaughn, Gloria C. *state representative*
Vázquez, Martha Alicia *federal judge*
Vigil-Giron, Rebecca *state official*
Watkins, Stephen Edward *accountant, publishing executive*
Welch, Jasper Arthur, Jr. *security company executive, consultant*
White, David Hywel *physics professor, researcher*
Williams, Ralph Chester, Jr. *physician, educator*
Williams, Stephen *anthropologist, educator*
Yalman, Ann *judge, lawyer*
Zlatoff-Mirsky, Everett Igor *violinist*

## Santa Rosa

Alcott, Colin C. *prosecutor*

## Seneca

Monroe, Kendyl Kurth *retired lawyer*

## Shiprock

Atcitty, Fannie L. *elementary school educator, education educator*
Austin-Garrison, Martha A. *education educator, researcher*
Heusinkveld, John Michael *obstetrician, gynecologist*

## Silver City

Bettison, Cynthia Ann *museum director, archaeologist*
Charland, William A., Jr. *writer, educator, consultant*
Fryxell, David Allen *publishing executive*
Gilbert, Kathie Simon *economist, educator*
Hodges, Norman *retired district judge*

Lopez, Linda Carol *social sciences educator*
Snedeker, John Haggner *university president*

## Socorro

Boston, Penelope J. *science educator, researcher*
Schery, Stephen Dale *physicist*
Wang, Bixiang *mathematician*

## Taos

Beck, Ursula *art educator, artist*
Bell, Larry Stuart *artist*
Boles, David LaVelle *lawyer*
Bolls, Imogene Lamb *English language educator, poet*
Brown, David Warfield *management educator, lawyer, academic administrator*
Harmon, Barbara Sayre *artist*
Smith, Dinah Maxwell *painter, photographer*
Vickers, Robert Edwin *retired military officer, historian, writer*
Witt, David L. *curator, writer*

## Tesuque

MacGraw, Ali *actress*

## Truth Or Consequences

Rush, Domenica Marie *health facilities administrator*

## Tucumcari

Barry, Phillip Owen *college president*

# NEW YORK

## Adams Center

Hood, Thomas Gregory *minister*

## Addison

Vona, John David *music educator*

## Akron

Hoover, Eddie Lee *cardiothoracic surgeon, educator*

## Akwesasne

Ransom, James W. *Native American tribal leader*

## Albany

Aceto, Vincent John *librarian, educator*
Alberski, Tadeusz Czeslaw *civil engineer, researcher*
Applebee, Arthur Noble *English education researcher*
Arseneau, James Charles *physician*
Bagyi, John Martin *lawyer*
Barron, Kevin Delgado *physician, educator*
Beverley, Barbara Sally *librarian, educator*
Blount, Stanley Freeman *marketing educator*
Bonventre, Vincent Martin *lawyer, educator*
Bowen, Mary Lu *ecumenical administrator*
Brademas, John *retired academic administrator, former congressman*
Bradley, Edward James *state official, computer programmer and analyst*
Bruno, Joseph L. *state legislator*
Capaldi, Elizabeth Ann Deutsch *psychological sciences professor*
Carl, Allen Laurence *surgery educator*
Carson, JoAnne *art educator, artist*
Catalano, Robert Anthony *ophthalmologist, hospital administrator, writer*
Cavaliere, Rossella *neurologist*
Cellery McCall, Patti *librarian*
Clarey, Donald Alexander *government affairs consultant*
Cogen, Richard M. *lawyer*
Cole, John Adam *insurance executive*
Corelli, John Charles *physicist, researcher*
Covington, Sim Jonathan, Jr. *counseling administrator, director*
Cross, Robert Francis *commissioner*
D'Ambra, Thomas E. *pharmaceutical executive*
Davis, Paul Joseph *endocrinologist*
DeNuzzo, Rinaldo Vincent *pharmacy educator*
Donohue, Mary *lieutenant governor*
Donovan, Robert Alan *language educator*
Ebert, Loretta Caren *university librarian*
Eristoff, Andrew S. *state agency administrator*
Everett, James W., Jr. *lawyer*
Fanuele, Frank John *engineering executive, electrical engineer*
FitzAlan-Howard, Bennett-Thomas Henry Robert *news analyst, consultant, political scientist, theologian*
Fogelman, Martin Lee *information technology manager, educator*
Frank, Joachim *molecular biologist, educator, biophysicist*
Frisch, Harry Lloyd *chemist, educator*
Gellis, Zvi Dan *healthcare educator*
Graffeo, Victoria A. *state appeals court judge*
Greene, Jerry George *physician*
Happ, Harvey Heinz *electrical engineer, educator*
Hartman, Brett Thomas *psychologist, writer*
Hawley, Ilissa Kotzin *social studies educator*
Heshmat, Hooshang *manufacturing executive*
Hevesi, Alan G. *state official, former city manager*
Higgins, Robert J. *retail entertainment executive*
Hoffmeister, Jana Marie *cardiologist*
Howard, Lyn Jennifer *medical educator*
Hubbard, Howard James *bishop*
Huxley, Carole Frances Corcoran *educational association administrator*
Jacobs, Christopher L. *state official*
Jacobs, Rhoda S. *state legislator*
Jennings, Gerald D. (Jerry Jennings) *mayor*
Joyce, William George, Jr. *transportation executive*
Kaye, Judith Smith *state appeals court judge*
Kelly, Raymond Aloysius, Jr. *lawyer, educator*
Kennedy, William Joseph *novelist, educator*
Keyser, Daniel *atmospheric scientist, educator*
Kim, Jai Soo *retired physicist*
Klopott, Zvi Simcha *psychiatrist*
Knee, Michael J. *science librarian, consultant*
Koff, Howard Michael *lawyer*
Kruegler, Catherine A. *sister, parochial school educator*
Kuhla, Donald E. *chemicals executive*

Langer, Judith Ann *language educator*
Lawton, Nancy *artist*
Leichman, Kenneth William *investment executive*
Lepow, Martha Lipson *pediatric educator, consultant*
Levine, Howard Arnold *judge*
Ley, Ronald *psychologist, educator*
Mannella, Carmen A. *research scientist*
Marschilok, Edward *music educator, musician*
Meader, John Daniel *judge*
Menges, Susan Debra Favreau *management consultant, retired protective services official*
Merbler, Candace Anne *librarian*
Miles, Christine Marie *museum director*
Mills, Richard Paul *school system administrator*
Miner, Roger Jeffrey *federal judge*
Molho, Eric Steven *neurologist, researcher*
Morga Bellizzi, Celeste *editor*
Mulholland, Nancy W. *state agency administrator*
Mumpower, Jeryl L. *academic administrator*
Nathan, Richard P(erle) *political science professor*
Novello, Antonia Coello *state health commissioner, pediatric nephrologist, former Surgeon General of the United States*
Ortloff, George Christian, Sr., (Chris Ortloff) *journalist, state legislator*
Pataki, George E. *governor*
Paterson, David Alexander *state legislator*
Paulson, Peter John *librarian, publishing executive*
Pezzulo, Jacqueline *psychologist, researcher*
Polimeni, John Matthew *economics professor*
Powers, John Kieran *lawyer*
Read, Susan Phillips *state appeals court judge*
Reese, William Lewis *philosophy educator*
Reinhold, Karin *mathematics professor*
Rej, Robert *biochemist*
Robbins, Cornelius (Cornelius Van Vorse) *educational administration educator*
Rosenfeld, Harry Morris *editor*
Rosenkrantz, Daniel J. *computer science educator*
Rostow, Charles Nicholas *lawyer, educator*
Roy, Rob J. *biomedical engineer, anesthesiologist, educator*
Ryan, John R. *academic administrator, career military officer*
Salins, Peter D. *academic administrator*
Sandhaas, Jill T. *lawyer*
Schalit, Robert Edward *advertising executive*
Schalk, Gerwin *research scientist, software engineer*
Schneider, Allan Stanford *biophysics, neuroscience and pharmacology educator, biomedical research scientist*
Schulman, Ruth Meryl Aronson *research and development company executive*
Scott, William Proctor III *lawyer*
Sheehan, Deborah Hardick *lawyer*
Shubert, Joseph Francis *librarian*
Smith, Ada LaVerne *state legislator*
Smith, Rex William *journalist*
Smith, Terry Jay *endocrinology educator*
Snitkoff, Gail Goodman *immunologist, educator*
Spitzer, Eliot Laurence *state attorney general*
Stavisky, Toby Ann *state legislator*
Stewart, Margaret McBride *biology professor, researcher*
Swartz, Donald Percy *physician*
Teevan, Richard Collier *retired psychology professor*
Tepper, Clifford *allergist, immunologist, educator*
Thompson, Frank Joseph *political science professor*
Toren, Mark *state official, statistician*
Veille, Jean-Claude *obstetrician, educator*
Verdile, Vincent Paul *dean, emergency physician*
Volker, Dale Martin *state legislator, lawyer*
Ward, Russell Avery *sociologist, educator*
West, Thomas S. *lawyer*
Wilber, Roger Alan *library supervisor, writer*
Wildemann, Gregory Nylund *writer*
Yanas, John Joseph *lawyer, director*
Zimmerman, Earl Abram *neurologist, educator*
Zimmerman, Joseph Francis *political scientist, educator*

## Albertson

Berlin, Mark A. *lawyer*

## Albion

Allamon, Karen Henn *minister*
Minier, Lee N. *funeral director*

## Alfred

Boehlert, Carl Joseph *materials scientist, educator*
Fei, Jun *art educator, graphics designer*
Higby, Wayne (Donald Higby) *artist, educator*
Hunter, John Orr *college president*
Johnson, Carla Conrad *library dean*
Pye, Lenwood David *materials science educator, researcher, consultant*
Scheer, Joseph H. *artist, education educator*
Smith, Mark Arthur *information scientist, educator*

## Alfred Station

Knowlton, Sylvia Kelley *physician*

## Amagansett

Seelbach, Anne Elizabeth *artist*
Zychick, Joel David *lawyer*

## Amenia

Hale, Nathan Cabot *sculptor, artist, poet*

## Amherst

Abbas, June M. *science educator*
Biddle, Paul Daniel *music educator*
Bobinski, Mary Form *library director*
Brogan, Michael Spencer *physical therapist, educator*
Brown, Murray *economist, educator*
Clark, Donald Malin *professional association executive*
Govindaraju, Venu *computer engineer, educator*
Ismail, Abu Zafar Mohamed *physics professor, researcher*
Jen, Frank Chifeng *finance and management educator*
Kurtz, Paul *philosopher, educator, writer, publisher*
Kutsin, Leonid *engineering educator, researcher*
Marone, James Matthew *music educator*
Nickell, Joe *paranormal expert*

Pajak, David Joseph *lawyer, consultant*
Roehmholdt, John Michael *urologist, educator*
Shook, John Robert *philosopher*

## Amityville

Fischer, Stacey Kim *principal*
Imbert, Richard Conrad *insurance company executive, real estate developer*
Palumbo, Anthony *education educator*
Soloway, Richard Lewis *electronics executive*
Upadhyay, Yogendra Nath *physician, educator*
Walker, Lois Virginia *multimedia designer, educator, poet, editor*
Wright, Nannie Bell *retired secondary school educator*

## Ancram

Blechman, R. O. *artist, filmmaker*

## Ancramdale

Weinstein, Joyce *artist*

## Angola

Green, Gerard Leo *priest, educator*
Ross, Sue Hoisington *elementary school educator, music educator*

## Annandale On Hudson

Achebe, Chinua *writer, humanities educator*
Ashbery, John Lawrence *language educator, poet, playwright, art critic*
Botstein, Leon *academic administrator, conductor, historian*
Darrow, Emily M. *public relations executive, writer*
LÊ, An-My *photographer, educator*
Manea, Norman *writer, educator*
Miyagawa, Chiori *theater educator, playwright*
Papadimitriou, Dimitri Basil *economist, educator, academic administrator*
Pfaff, Judy *artist*
Sourian, Peter *writer, language educator, educator*
Tower, Joan Peabody *composer, educator*
Zacharias, Ajit *economist*

## Appleton

Singer, Thomas Kenyon *international business consultant, fruit grower*

## Ardsley

Grad, Arthur *mathematician, educator*
Swift, Michael Ronald *internist, educator*

## Ardsley On Hudson

Guise, David Earl *architect, educator*
Lisle, Laurie *author*
Seaman, Alfred Barrett *journalist, writer*
Stein, Milton Michael *retired lawyer*

## Armonk

Boies, David *lawyer*
Bolduc, Ernest Joseph *management consultant, not-for-profit developer*
Brown, Joseph W., Jr., (Jay Brown) *insurance company executive*
Donofrio, Nicholas M. *information technology executive*
Dunton, Gary C. *insurance company executive*
Ferguson, Roger Walter, Jr. *reinsurance company executive, former bank executive*
Gerstner, Louis Vincent, Jr. *retired information technology executive*
Harreld, James Bruce *information technology executive*
Horn, Paul M. *information technology executive, crystallographer*
Kelly, John E. III *information technology executive*
Kohnstamm, Abby E. *marketing executive*
Lineen, Edward M. *lawyer, information technology executive*
Loughridge, Mark *computer company executive*
Mellors, Robert Charles *physician, scientist, educator*
Quinn, James W. *lawyer*
Rosenberg, Michael *lawyer*
Sanchez, Adalio T. *data processing executive*
Sharpe, Myron Emanuel *publishing executive, writer*
Wago, Mildred Hogan *retired municipal official*
Wertheim, Ram D. *lawyer*

## Astoria

Dutikow, Irene Vladimirovna *librarian*
Francesca, Mike *radio personality*
Griffin, Daniel Bernard, Jr. *writer, scriptwriter, lyricist*
Kaufman, George S. *real estate company executive*
Matheson, Linda *retired social worker*
Russo, Chris *radio personality*
Salzberg, Russ *sportscaster*
Sirignano, Monica Ann *performing company executive, playwright*
Unsal-Tunay, Nuran *geological engineer, researcher*

## Attica

Rogers, Donald L. *music educator, department chairman, animal breeder*

## Auburn

Dello Stritto, Ellen M. *retired social studies educator*
Pelkey, Lawrence Michael *school psychologist*

## Aurora

Purdy, Laura *philosopher, educator*
Ryerson, Lisa M. *academic administrator*
Sievers, Sally Riedel *mathematics professor*

## Averill Park

Haines, Walter Wells *retired economics professor*
Messia, Robert A. III *social studies educator*
Nevai, Lucia *writer*

## Babylon

Brackett, Ronald E. *investment company executive, lawyer*
Collis, Charles *air transportation executive*
Kroll, Brian Walter Thomas *music educator*

Mastrandrea, Patricia *elementary school educator, consultant*
Meirowitz, Claire Cecile *publishing executive*
Schwartz, Benjamin Michael *gynecologist, oncologist*
Schwarz, Barbara Ruth Ballou *elementary school educator*
Vaswani, Sheila Ann *secondary school educator*

**Baldwin**
Chopra, Parveen Chander *management consultant, educator, researcher, community activist*
Onyido, John Chike *lawyer*

**Baldwin Place**
Kurian, George Thomas *publisher*

**Baldwinsville**
Bowen, Jonathan L. *music educator, consultant*
Wilson, Harold Batting *treasurer*

**Ballston Spa**
Barba, Harry *writer, publisher, educator*
Brown, Ifigenia Theodore *lawyer*
Popham, Todd Gordon *insurance company executive*
Wages, Robert Coleman *equity investor*
Westbrook, Jack Hall *metallurgist, consultant*

**Batavia**
Rigerman, Ruth Underhill *mathematics professor*
Steiner, Stuart *college president*

**Bay Shore**
Baradzi, Amelia *stained glass artist, restorationist*
Kirsch, Scott Douglas *family practice physician*
Lindner, Deborah *writer, illustrator, photographer*
Williams, Tonda *entrepreneur, consultant*

**Bayside**
Ausubel, Hillel *librarian*
Chugh, Om Parkash *mathematics professor, researcher, forensics specialist*
Fabricant, Mona *mathematics and computer science educator*
Kennedy, Mary Theresa *mental health services professional*
Li, Rowena Liu-ping *media specialist*
Madden, Joseph Daniel *trade association executive*
Ohrenstein, Roman Abraham *economist, educator, rabbi*
Tovar-Mengibar, Salvador *retired government agency administrator*
Zinn, William *musician, composer*

**Beacon**
Mc Keown, William Taylor *magazine editor, author*
Metz, Ferdinand *chef, educator, academic administrator*
Siejka, George John *artist*

**Bearsville**
Hera, *sculptor*

**Bedford**
Bowman, James Kinsey *publishing executive, rare book dealer*
Chase, Chevy (Cornelius Crane Chase) *comedian, actor, writer*
Husted, William Armstrong *sales executive*
Philip, Peter Van Ness *former trust company executive*
Tischler, Gary Lowell *psychiatrist, educator*

**Bedford Corners**
Greene, Jesse J., Jr. *former computer company executive*
Singer, Craig *entrepreneur, inventor, investor, consultant*

**Bedford Hills**
Fierstein, Harvey Forbes *playwright, actor*
Lustbader, Eric Van *writer*

**Beechhurst**
Wingate, Constance Blandy *retired librarian*

**Bellerose**
Dornagon, Mandy M. *lawyer*
Miller, Paul J. *orthopedist, surgeon*
Stecher, Pauline *painter, educator*

**Bellmore**
Andrews, Charles Rolland *library administrator*
Dacek, Joanne Carole *psychologist*
Feldman, Harriet Ruth *dean*
Lederman, Gary *dentist*

**Bellport**
Regalmuto, Nancy Marie *small business owner, consultant*
Schultheis, Edwin Milford *dean, business educator*
Townsend, Terry *publishing executive*

**Belmont**
Lasher, Sandra Lee *minister, artist*

**Bemus Point**
Erickson, Susan Phillians *secondary school educator*
Ross, Roderic Henry *retired insurance company executive*

**Berlin**
Pelz, Caroline Duncombe *retired educational administrator*

**Bethpage**
Baglio, Vincent Paul *aerospace transportation executive*
Conti, James Joseph *retired chemical engineer, educator*
Dolan, Charles Francis (Charles "Chuck" Dolan) *media and entertainment company executive*
Dolan, James L *communications executive*
Janczak, Andrew Anthony *marketing professional*
Mahony, Sheila Anne *retired communications executive*

McEnroe, Kate *broadcast executive*
Ratner, Hank J. *broadcast executive*
Schwartz, Jonathan D. *lawyer*

**Big Flats**
Keck, Donald Bruce *physicist*
Orsillo, James Edward *computer engineer, information technology executive*

**Binghamton**
Anderson, Warren Mattice *lawyer*
Arcones, Miguel A. *mathematics professor*
Bearsch, Lee Palmer *architect, urban planner*
Best, Robert Mulvane *insurance company executive*
Bix, Herbert Philip *historian, educator*
Brinker-Gabler, Gisela *literature educator*
Coates, Donald Robert *geologist, educator*
DeFleur, Lois B. *academic administrator*
Gaddis Rose, Marilyn *literature educator, translator*
Gates, Gregory Ansel *lawyer*
Gerhart, Eugene Clifton *lawyer*
Gouldin, David Millen *lawyer*
Hilton, Peter John *mathematician, educator*
Isaacson, Robert Lee *psychologist, educator*
James, Gary Douglas *biological anthropologist, educator, researcher*
Jenkins, David Mark *educator*
Kim, Yong Jin *finance educator*
Klir, George Jiri *systems science educator*
Levis, Donald James *psychologist, educator*
Marella, Philip Daniel *broadcasting company executive*
Mazrui, Ali Al'Amin *political science professor, researcher*
Meador, John Milward, Jr. *dean*
Naslund, Howard Richard *geological science educator*
Pavlovskis-Petit, Zoja *literature and language professor*
Peckham, Eugene Eliot *judge, lawyer*
Powell, Barbara Ann *music educator, voice educator*
Silverberg, Carol Eve *theater educator*
Sklar, Kathryn Kish *historian, educator*
Sokolowski, Linda Robinson *artist, educator*
Stahl, Peter William *archaeologist, educator*
Stein, George Henry *historian, educator, administrator*
Swain, Mary Ann Price *university official*
Whittingham, M(ichael) Stanley *chemist*
Wildoner, Nancy Schamu *music educator, fine arts department chairman*
Yu, Ming *engineering educator, researcher*
Zacks, Shelemyahu *mathematical sciences educator*
Zhou, Nan *finance educator*
Zhu, Weixing *ecologist, educator*

**Blasdell**
Smith, Robin E. *music educator*

**Bloomington**
Culver, Michael Patrick *music educator, composer*

**Blue Mountain Lake**
Welsh, Caroline Mastin *curator, art historian*

**Blue Point**
Owen, Thomas Llewellyn *investment company executive*

**Bohemia**
Fisher, Irene B. *lawyer*
Rudolph, Scott *pharmaceutical executive*
Schwartz, Laurie *special education educator*

**Boiceville**
Boms, Michael *secondary school educator*
Thomas, David Clifton *music educator*

**Brainard**
Isaksen, Robert L. *retired bishop*

**Brentwood**
Auguste, Gabriel Joseph *retired mathematics educator*
Burgess, John Thomas *physical education educator, consultant*
Liebert, Lynn Langenbach *psychologist, educator*

**Brewster**
Bates, Barbara J. Neuner *retired municipal official*
Nadel, Norman Allen *civil engineer*
Shepard, Lance Hastings *marketing professional, consultant, newscaster*

**Briarcliff Manor**
Bernstein, Nadia Jacqueline *lawyer*
Bhargava, Rameshwar Nath *physicist*
Bingham, J. Peter *electronics research executive*
Bower, Thomas Michael *lawyer*
Chou, Chun-Ting *engineer, researcher*
Erkamp, Ramon Quido *medical researcher, consultant*
Kennell, Richard Wayne *recording industry executive, consultant*
Kepcher, Carolyn *real estate company executive*
Lew, Leslie *artist*
Oakley, Richard Putney *investment banker*
Pousada, Lidia *physician*
Read, John Conyers *non-profit company executive*
Wheeler, Margaret Jane *actress, soprano, voice educator*
Windham, Revish *poet*

**Bridgehampton**
Phillips, Warren Henry *publishing executive*
Rattiner, Daniel Steven *communications executive*

**Brightwaters**
Kavanagh, Eileen J. *librarian*
North, E(dward) Lee *retired writer, former aerospace company professional*
Zayas, Elinor Abrams *music educator*

**Brockport**
Blake, Robert William *retired literature and language professor, writer*

Dabbagh, Mahmoud *language educator, researcher*
Gemmett, Robert J. *dean, English language educator*
Keiser, John Dougherty *business educator*
Leslie, William Bruce *history professor*
McGhee, Diane Baumann *dance instructor, consultant*
Smith, Daniel Elon *physical education educator*
White, Christopher Todd *language educator, anthropologist*

**Bronx**
Abreu, Bobby *professional baseball player*
Adams, Alice *sculptor*
Adinolfi, Marion Darlyne *research scientist*
Afterman, Jean *professional sports team executive*
Ahmose, Nefertari A. *journalism educator*
Alderman, Elizabeth *pediatrician, educator*
Antwi, Ebenezer Yaw *education educator*
Ask-Nanko, Lorraine Charlotte *music educator*
Bacarella, Flavia *artist, educator*
Balka, Sigmund Ronell *lawyer*
Baranin, Rosemarie *elementary school educator*
Bark, Nigel Martyn *psychiatrist*
Basile, Philip John Anthony *multimedia designer*
Behnken, William Joseph *art educator, artist*
Bella, Jonathan N. *cardiologist*
Bennett, Michael Vander Laan *neuroscience educator*
Bigal, Marcelo E *physician, researcher*
Bingham, June *playwright*
Blaufox, Morton Donald *hypertension specialist, educator, nuclear medicine physician*
Block, Holly *museum director*
Bowers, Francis Robert *educational consultant, literature educator*
Brandt, Lawrence Jay *internist, gastroenterologist, educator*
Bullaro, Grace Russo *literature, film and foreign language educator, critic*
Burgio, Michael *medical researcher*
Cabart, Pavel *molecular biologist*
Carrion, Adolfo, Jr. *city manager*
Carter, Majora *urban planner*
Cashman, Brian *professional sports team executive*
Chimsky-Lustig, Mark Evan *editor, consultant*
Cimino, Christopher *medical educator, dean*
Cohen, Herbert Jesse *pediatrician, educator*
Conlon, Edward *police officer, writer*
Cornfield, Melvin *lawyer, director*
Correa, Nereida *women's health physician*
Coupey, Susan McGuire *pediatrician, educator*
Coyote, Peter (Peter Cohon) *actor*
Damon, Johnny *professional baseball player*
Das, Ashoke Kumar *internist, consultant*
Dean, Nancy *literature educator, retired playwright*
De Luca, Eva *vocalist, writer, composer, entrepreneur, inventor*
Demb, Howard Bertram *psychiatrist, educator, pediatrician, educator*
Doyle, Brian Leahy *theater educator, director*
Drepaul, Loris Omesh *internist, infectious diseases physician*
Dulles, Avery *cardinal, theologian*
Durglishvili, Nana Z. *psychologist, language educator*
Dutcher, Janice Jean Phillips *oncologist*
Elkins, Alfred David *insurance company executive*
Fleischer, Norman Samuel *endocrinology administrator, medical physician*
Fletcher, Judith Ellen *music educator*
Foreman, Spencer *pulmonologist, hospital administrator, director*
Frater, Robert William Mayo *surgeon, educator*
Freeman, John Wheelock *retired editor, writer*
Freeman, Leonard Murray *radiologist, nuclear medicine physician, educator*
Fremman, Leonard Murray *medical educator*
Gallagher, Robert E. *medical educator, researcher*
Gaveras, Harry *architect*
Giambi, Jason Gilbert *professional baseball player*
Gibbs, Karen E. *physician, surgeon*
Gonzalez, Rose A-Navarro *artist*
Goodrich, James Tait *neuroscientist, neurosurgeon*
Grassano, Thomas David *minister*
Greenstein, Stuart Mark *surgical educator*
Hait, Gershon *pediatric cardiologist*
Hallett, Charles Arthur, Jr. *language educator, humanities educator*
Hartil, Kirsten *research scientist*
Hauser, Bernice Worman *director*
Heagarty, Margaret Caroline *retired pediatrician*
Hennessy, Thomas Christopher *priest, educator, retired dean*
Hilaris, Basil S. *radiation oncologist, educator*
Hilliard, Carol *nurse, educator, consultant, researcher*
Himmelberg, Robert Franklin *historian, educator*
Hirano, Asao *neuropathologist, educator*
Hodgson, W(alter) John (Barry Hodgson) *surgeon*
Horwitz, Susan Band *pharmacologist*
Hudson, Frederick Bernard *management consultant*
Hunt, George William *priest, magazine editor*
Iezza, Anita Kay *physician assistant*
Jaffé, Ernst Richard *medical educator, dean*
Jeter, Derek Sanderson *professional baseball player*
Johnson, Randy (Randall David Johnson) *professional baseball player*
Juszczyk, James Joseph *artist*
Kahn, Thomas *medical educator*
Kalnicki, Shalom *radiologist, educator*
Karkanias, George B. *neurologist, educator*
Kassoy, Hortense (Honey Kassoy) *artist, sculptor, painter*
Keating, Tedd Michael *adult education educator*
Kelley, Aloysius Paul *academic administrator, priest*
Kelly, Thomas M. *headmaster*
Kitt, Olga *artist*
Klein, Robert S. *medical educator*
Koranyi, Adam *mathematics professor*
Korman, Barbara *sculptor*
Kornfeld, Robert Jonathan *playwright, photographer*
Koss, Leopold G. *pathologist, educator*
Lee, Dong Hwan *business administration educator*
Lemos, Arthur *retired music educator*
Lieber, Charles Saul *internist, educator*

Lienert, Christoph *physical education educator*
Lyons, Damian M. *computer scientist, director*
Lyons, Maxine Evadney *small business owner, poet*
Macklin, Ruth *bioethics educator*
Maitra, Umadas *biomedical researcher, educator*
Margolin, Leon *physician*
Martinez, Tino *professional baseball player*
Matsui, Hideki *professional baseball player*
Mazzilli, Lee *professional baseball manager*
McKeown, William B. *lawyer*
McShane, Joseph Michael *academic administrator, priest*
Megalli, Maguid Ramzi *health facility administrator*
Mendez, Hermann Armando *pediatrician, educator*
Mendez, Ruben Policarpio *diplomat, educator, economist*
Menthena, Anuradha *research scientist*
Meyer, Edward Henry *business and economics educator, lawyer*
Mittler, Diana (Diana Mittler-Battipaglia) *music educator, pianist*
Moore, Donald Emerson III *zoological park administrator, curator, wildlife biologist*
Muller, Katherine Lynn *clinical psychologist*
Mussina, Michael Cole *professional baseball player*
Nathanson, Melvyn Bernard *academic administrator, mathematician, educator*
Nitowsky, Harold Martin *physician, educator*
Oertel, Michael *researcher, medical educator*
Olerud, John Garrett *professional baseball player*
Olson, Todd Rowland *anatomist, medical educator, consultant*
Ortiz Ruiz, Aida M. *university administrator, educator*
Osborne, Claudina Rosetta *financial analyst*
Parker, Everett Carlton *clergyman*
Pena, Antonio Francisco (Tony Pena) *professional athletics coach*
Posada, Jorge Rafael *professional baseball player*
Powers, Kenneth *urogynecologist*
Purpura, Dominick P. *dean, neuroscientist*
Putterman, Chaim *rheumatologist, researcher*
Radel, Eva *pediatrician, hematologist*
Rajapaksa, Trikante N. *medical educator*
Ramsey, Doris Theresa *elementary school educator*
Rapin, Isabelle *physician*
Rappaport, Lisa N. *psychologist*
Rego, Simon Alexander *psychologist*
Reichgott, Michael Joel *medical educator, dean, physician*
Richman, Murray *lawyer*
Rivera, Mariano *professional baseball player*
Rodriguez, Alex (Alexander Emmanuel Rodriguez) *professional baseball player*
Romney, Seymour Leonard *obstetrician, educator*
Rose, Israel Harold *mathematics professor*
Rosenstreich, David Leon *medical educator, immunologist, allergist*
Rothstein, Anne Louise *academic administrator, educator*
Ruben, Robert Joel *pediatric otorhinolaryngologist, educator*
Rubensky, Mitchell *band director*
Sable, Robert Allen *gastroenterologist*
Safyer, Steven Michael *medical association administrator, educator*
Samuels, Leslie Eugene *marketing consultant, management consultant*
Satir, Birgit H. *medical educator, researcher*
Scanlan, Thomas Joseph *college president, educator*
Schaller, George Beals *zoologist*
Scharff, Matthew Daniel *immunologist, cell biologist, educator*
Schaumburg, Herbert Howard *neurology educator*
Seltzer, William *statistician, social science administrator*
Shafritz, David Andrew *physician, research scientist*
Shapiro, Nella Irene *surgeon, educator*
Sheffield, Gary Antonian *professional baseball player*
Sherman, Judith Dorothy *theater producer, engineer, recording industry executive*
Socol, Sheldon Eleazer *university official*
Solomon, Seymour *neurologist, consultant*
Sonnenblick, Edmund Hiram *medical educator, cardiologist*
Spatt, Hartley Steven *humanities educator*
Spiegel, Allen Michael *dean, internist*
Spitzer, Adrian *pediatrician, educator*
Stanley, F. Richard *biomedical researcher*
Stein, Bernard L. *journalist*
Stein, Ruth Elizabeth Klein *physician*
Steinbrenner, George Michael III *professional baseball team executive, shipbuilding company executive*
Sullivan, Daniel Joseph *biology professor, priest*
Torre, Joe (Joseph Paul Torre) *professional baseball team manager*
Ultan, Lloyd *historian, educator*
Valgemae, Mardi *language educator*
Veith, Frank J. *vascular surgeon, researcher, educator*
Waelsch, Salome Gluecksohn *geneticist, educator*
Walsh, Christine Ann *cardiologist*
Wertheim, Mary Danielle *educational coordinator*
Wertz, Frederick *psychologist, educator*
Widger, Chris *professional baseball player*
Wiernik, Peter Harris *oncologist, educator*
Williams, Bernie (Bernabe Figueroa Williams) *professional baseball player*
Wolkoff, Allan Wayne *gastroenterologist, medical educator*
Yalow, Rosalyn Sussman *biophysicist*
Zalaznick, Sheldon *retired editor, journalist*

**Bronxville**
Bertles, John Francis *physician, educator*
Biscardi, Chester *composer, educator*
Brunale, Vito John *aerospace engineer*
Civiello, Mary *correspondent*
Cutler, Kenneth Burnett *lawyer, investment company executive*
DeMartino, Anthony Gabriel *cardiologist, internist*
Ellinghaus, William Maurice *communications executive*
Falvey, Patrick Joseph *lawyer*

Frost, A. Corwin *architect, consultant*
Fuller, David Otis, Jr. *lawyer*
Garber, Robert Edward *lawyer, insurance company executive*
Gelfand, Neal *oil industry executive*
Hagendorn, William Hull *lawyer*
Lombardo, Philip Joseph *broadcasting company executive*
Morton, Brian *writer, editor*
Myers, Michele Tolela *academic administrator*
Parsons, Andrew John *management consultant*
Peters, Sarah Whitaker *art historian, writer*
Pollin, Burton Ralph *language educator*
Rosenthal, Lucy Gabrielle *writer, editor, educator*

## Brookhaven
Desiderio, Joseph Gerard *music educator*
Grucci Butler, Donna *fireworks company executive*
Kouts, Herbert John Cecil *retired physicist*

## Brooklyn
Abraham, Teena *pharmacist, educator*
Ackerman, Jacob Lewis *ophthalmologist*
Aizin, Gregory *physicist, educator, researcher*
Alfonso, Antonio Escolar *surgeon*
Al-Hafeez, Humza *minister, editor*
Alleva, Paula Savino *principal, elementary school educator*
Allison, Mary Ann *consulting company executive, writer, speaker*
Altura, Bella T. *physiologist, educator*
Altura, Burton Myron *physiologist, educator*
Amendola, Sal John *artist, educator, writer*
Amon, Carol Bagley *federal judge*
Amrhein, Joe *artist*
Anderson, Lennart *artist*
Andrews, Benny *artist*
Anziska, Brian Jeffrey *neurologist, educator*
Arcuri, Leonard Philip *elementary school educator*
Armenakas, Anthony Emmanuel *aerospace engineering educator*
Armstrong, L. C. *artist*
Arseneau, Joseph Arseneau *financial consultant*
Asarian, Armand Paul *surgeon*
Avram, Morrell M. *nephrologist, educator, consultant*
Bandler, Martin *physician*
Barabash, Claire *lawyer, special education services professional, psychologist*
Barran, Thomas Paul *language educator*
Barriere, Isabelle Huguette *science educator, researcher*
Bates, Leo James *artist*
Bernstein, Larry Howard *clinical pathologist*
Bhattacharya, Bhaswati *preventive medicine physician*
Bianco, Anthony Joseph III *newswriter*
Birenbaum, Leo *retired engineering educator*
Birenbaum, William M. *former university president*
Biro, Laszlo *dermatologist*
Bishar, John Joseph, Jr. *utilities executive, lawyer*
Blasi, Alberto *Romance languages educator, writer*
Bloomfield, David Charles *lawyer, educator, not-for-profit public executive*
Bolton, Saul *chef, food service executive*
Bossert, Jill Audrey *author*
Bottiglia, Frank Robert *bank executive*
Bramwell, Henry *federal judge*
Bugliarello, George *academic administrator, educator*
Bui, Phong *painter*
Butler, Alice Gloria *mathematician, educator*
Buttaro, Lucia *language educator, consultant*
Carlile, Janet Louise *artist, educator*
Carswell, Lois Malakoff *botanical garden executive, consultant*
Castleman, Louis Samuel *retired metallurgist, educator*
Catell, Robert Barry *gas industry executive*
Chambers, William Edmond *writer*
Chandan, Jit S. *management consultant, educator*
Charton, Marvin *chemist, educator*
Chernow, Ron *writer, journalist*
Chung, Ping Tsai *education educator*
Clark, Luther Theopolis *physician, educator, researcher*
Cohen, Alan *investment banker*
Collins, Ronald Leslie Leopold *neurosurgeon*
Costello, Jeffrey *apparel designer*
Cottrell, James E. *anesthesiologist, medical educator*
Crânganu, Constantin *engineer*
Cummings, Josephine Anna *writer, consultant, advertising executive*
Curtis-Tweed, Phyllis Marie *humanities educator*
Das, Nirod K. *engineering educator*
Dealy, Michael Thomas *psychology educator*
Dearie, Raymond Joseph *federal judge*
D'Elia, Nicholas *secondary school educator*
Desmarais, Charles Joseph *museum director, writer*
Diamond, Jessica *artist*
DiMarzio, Nicholas Anthony *bishop*
Dinnerstein, Harvey *artist*
Dinnerstein, Simon Abraham *artist, educator*
Doucette, David Robert *information technology executive*
Douglas, Jerry *bluegrass musician, dobro player*
Douglass, Melvin Isadore *school system administrator, humanities educator, composer*
Dubnau, Jenny *artist*
Eliasi, Jennifer Rebecca *dietician, consultant*
Elliot, Cameron Robert *lawyer*
Enseki, Carol *museum director*
Erber, William Franklin *gastroenterologist*
Estern, Neil Carl *sculptor*
Evans, John T. *finance educator, consultant, social sciences educator, researcher*
Evans-Tranumn, Shelia *commissioner, former literature and language educator*
Fairstein, Linda A. *prosecutor, writer*
Faison, Seth Shepard *retired insurance broker*
Fani, Robert J. *gas industry executive*
Feigelson, Eugene B. *dean*
Fischer, R. M. *sculptor*
Fischman, Myrna Leah *accountant, educator*
Flam, Jack Donald *art historian, educator*
Fleyshman, Bentsion *physicist, researcher, retired mathematician*
Forsberg, Suzanne *humanities educator*
Fox, Cynthia F. *journalist, writer*

Franco, Victor *theoretical physics educator*
Freilich, Gerald *mathematics professor*
Friedman, Eli A. *nephrologist, educator*
Frisch, Ivan Thomas *academic administrator, educator, computer and communications company executive*
Furchgott, Robert Francis *pharmacologist, educator*
Gabriel, Mordecai Lionel *biologist, educator*
Galatianos, Gus A. *computer company executive, consultant, real estate developer, educator*
Garaufis, Nicholas G. *district court judge*
Garrett, Nancy Fales *playwright, educator*
Gatten, David *filmmaker*
Gershon, Nina *federal judge*
Gheewala, Anup Rameshchandra *plastic surgeon, consultant*
Gianlorenzi, Nona Elena *art dealer, painter*
Gilmore, Jennifer A.W. *computer specialist, educator*
Gioseffi, Daniela (Dorothy Daniela Gioseffi) *poet, writer, playwright, critic*
Gisolfi, Diana (Diana Gisolfi Pechukas) *art history educator*
Glasser, Israel Leo *federal judge*
Gleeson, John *judge, educator*
Golanski, Alani *lawyer*
Gonsalves, Patricia E. *surgical nurse*
Gotta, Alexander Walter *anesthesiologist, educator*
Grado, Angelo John *artist*
Greene, Gladstone Fitzpatrick *education educator, consultant*
Greenwood, Monique *innkeeper, writer, restaurant owner*
Gross, Stephen Mark *pharmacist, dean*
Gustin, Mark Douglas *healthcare executive*
Haber, Ira Joel *artist, art educator*
Hamarman, Stephanie *psychiatrist, educator*
Haralick, Robert Martin *electrical engineering educator*
Haratz, Natan *obstetrician, gynecologist*
Hawkins, Vivian Agatha *mental health nurse, educator*
Hechtman, Howard *financial analyst*
Helly, Walter Sigmund *engineering educator*
Hero, George A. *history educator*
Hersman, Alicia Claire *editor, artist*
Hill, Elizabeth Anne *academic administrator, lawyer*
Hill, Victoria Ruth *librarian*
Hollander, Gerald Martin *physician*
Holmes, Robert Eugene *legislative staff member, journalist*
Hood, Ernest Alva, Sr. *pharmaceutical company executive*
Hopkins, Karen Brooks *performing arts executive*
Horowitz, Sara *labor organizer*
Horvath, Annette *home care administrator*
Hussein, Osama *computer engineer, educator*
Ierardi, Eric Joseph *school system administrator*
Inwood, David Gerald *psychiatrist*
Irizarry, Dora L. *federal judge*
Isaac-Emmons, Merlyn Hulda *academic administrator, educator*
Iskander, Magued *engineering educator, consultant*
Jacobowitz, Israel Jacob *cardiothoracic surgeon*
Jaffe, Louise *literature and language professor, writer*
Jemisin, Noah *artist, educator*
Johnson, Sterling, Jr. *federal judge*
Jones, Rudolph *minister*
Jones, Susan Emily *fashion educator, administrator, educator emeritus*
Josephson, William Howard *retired lawyer*
Kamins, Barry Michael *lawyer*
Karmel, Roberta Segal *lawyer, educator*
Katavolos, William *architecture educator, furniture designer*
Kawatra, Mahendra P. *physics professor, mathematics professor*
Kemp, James William *graphic artist*
Kimmich, Christoph Martin *academic administrator, educator*
King, Margaret Leah *history professor*
Kirshenbaum, Richard Irving *retired public health physician*
Kjok, Sol *artist, art educator*
Knizhnik, Leonid *engineering educator*
Korman, Edward R. *federal judge*
Kumar, Swati *epidemiologist, researcher*
Kutlin, Andrei *microbiologist, immunologist, researcher*
Landau, Joel *health services administrator*
Lazar, Paul Alan *actor*
Lee, Spike (Shelton Jackson Lee) *film director, film producer*
Lehman, Arnold Lester *museum official, art historian*
Lentini, Francine *physical education educator*
Levy, Norman B. *psychiatrist, educator*
Li, John K.H. *pathologist, department chairman*
Lichstein, Edgar *cardiologist*
Lichter, Stephen Marc *oncologist*
Lieberman, Zachary *artist*
Lipson, Steven Mark *virologist, microbiologist, environmental scientist, educator*
Lish, Bruce Jared *dentist*
Lobron, Barbara L. *speech educator, editor, photographer, writer*
Lockey, James Peter *public health service officer*
Logan, Paula M. *entertainment company executive, accountant*
Lopate, Phillip *language educator, writer*
Lowery, Robert Chesley *thoracic surgeon, educator*
Lutwak, Erwin *mathematician, educator*
Mack-Harvin, Dionne *library director*
Mann, Roanne L. *federal judge*
Mark, Richard Kushakow *internist*
Markowitz, Marty (Martin Markowitz) *city manager*
Maslow, Aaron D. *lawyer*
Mauskopf, Roslynn R. *prosecutor*
Mayer, Ira Edward *gastroenterologist*
McCabe, Paul Christopher *psychologist, educator*
McClaughlin, (Patricia) Tricia Marie *education educator, artist*
Mc Clenney, Byron Nelson *community college administrator*
McLean, William Ronald *retired electrical engineer, consultant*

McQuiggan, John A. *theater producer, writer*
Medbury, Scot Daniel *botanical garden executive*
Menil, Violeta Cruz *mathematician, educator, consultant*
Merlin, Lisa Ruth *neurologist, researcher*
Miller, Daniel Weiss *psychologist*
Mirra, Suzanne Samuels *pathologist*
Mitcheltree, Dennis *musician, educator*
Moehring, Fred Adolf *wholesale distribution executive*
Mook, Sarah *retired chemist*
Moosazadeh, Kioomars *orthopedist, educator, physiatrist, researcher*
Morales, Jose *psychotherapist, writer*
Morgan, Mary Louise Fitzsimmons *fund raising executive, lobbyist*
Morris, Mark William *choreographer*
Mourokh, Lev Grigorievich *physicist, researcher*
Murillo-Rohde, Ildaura Maria *marriage and family therapist, consultant, educator, retired dean*
Murphy, Kathleen Mary *former law firm executive, alternative healing professional*
Nadel, Monroe Stanley *retired architect, landscape architect*
Nash, Richard Edin *publishing executive*
Niesen, James Louis *theater director*
Nii, Yuko *artist*
Norstrand, Iris Fletcher *psychiatrist, neurologist, educator*
Nye, William Roger *psychologist*
O'Connor, Sister George Aquin (Margaret M. O'Connor) *academic administrator, educator*
O'Doherty, Susan Ann *psychologist, writer*
Orenstein, James *federal judge*
Ortner, Everett Howard *magazine editor, writer*
Orugunta, Raveendra Babu *pediatrician*
Otterness, Tom *artist*
Padovano, Anthony John *fine arts educator, artist*
Panwar, Shivendra Singh *education educator, researcher*
Parlamis, Michael Frank *civil engineer, construction executive*
Pearlstein, Seymour *artist*
Pearsall, Otis Pratt *retired lawyer*
Peker, Elya Abel *artist*
Pennisten, John William *computer scientist, actuary, linguist*
Pertschuk, Louis Philip *pathologist, consultant*
Peters, Mercedes *psychotherapist*
Phillips, Gretchen *social worker*
Pickens, Schanica Lynn *homefinding supervisor, online educator*
Piene, Chloe *artist, filmmaker*
Pine, Bessie Miriam *social worker, columnist*
Pitynski, Andrzej Piotr *sculptor*
Plotz, Charles Mindell *physician, educator*
Pollak, Cheryl L. *federal judge*
Ponnambalam, Ananthasekar *pediatrician, gastroenterologist*
Poser, Norman Stanley *law educator*
Price, Ely *dermatologist*
Pucci, Gabrielle Jennine *historian, educator*
Purvin, Jack Mitchell *physician*
Raggi, Reena *federal judge*
Ranck, James Byrne, Jr. *neuroscience researcher, educator*
Ratner, Bruce C. *professional sports team executive, real estate developer*
Rauschenbusch, Stephanie *artist, educator, poet*
Reichbach, Gustin Lewis *state supreme court justice*
Reichel, Walter Emil *advertising executive*
Reinisch, June Machover *psychologist, educator*
Reisler, Helen Barbara *public relations executive*
Remsen, James F., Jr. *biology educator*
Reynolds, Nancy Remick *writer, researcher, editor*
Rezkalla, Laurence *internist*
Rice, John Thomas *architecture educator*
Richmond, Eero *composer, music librarian*
Rocco, Ron *artist*
Rogers, Michael Alan *writer*
Roker, Christopher A. *microbiologist, photographer*
Rosario-Olmedo, Carmen Gloria *principal*
Rose, Arthur Louis *neurologist, educator*
Ross, Allyne R. *federal judge*
Ross, Randolph Ernest *investor*
Roth, Robert *lawyer, journalist*
Ruane, Krista *TV food stylist*
Ryan, Leonard Eames *judge*
Sacchi, Terrence J. *cardiologist*
Sahlene, *singer*
Sakhnovich, Lev Aronovich *mathematics educator, researcher*
Samuel, Carren C. *hospital administrator*
Sanchez Korrol, Virginia *historian, educator*
Sanford, David Boyer *journalist, editor*
Savits, Barry Sorrel *surgeon*
Scalia, Frank R. *neuroscientist*
Schaefer, Marilyn Louise *artist, writer, educator*
Schiffman, Gerald *microbiologist, educator*
Schneider, Adele Goldberg *librarian, educator*
Schwarz, Richard Howard *obstetrician, gynecologist, educator*
Schweikert, Edgar Oskar *dentist*
Sesin, Maria Carmen *psychologist, researcher*
Shalita, Alan Remi *dermatologist*
Sharify, Nasser *librarian, educator, writer*
Shaw, Kendall (George Shaw) *artist, educator*
Shaw, Leonard Glazer *retired electrical engineering educator, consultant*
Shcherbakova, Estella *chemist, mathematician, educator*
Shelov, Steven Patrick *pediatrician, educator*
Sheverev, Valery A. *physics professor, consultant*
Shivcharran, Jaigobin *secondary school educator, consultant*
Shulman, Abraham *otolaryngology educator, hospital administrator*
Sifton, Charles Proctor *federal judge*
Simons, Barbara *retired elementary school educator*
Singer, Eric T. *investment banker*
Slonczewski, Craig (Craig Slon) *composer*
Smith, Bernadine M. *radio personality, filmmaker, writer, film producer, film director*
Smith, John W(esley), Jr. *data processing executive, consultant, educator*
Spector, Robert Donald *language educator*
Streb, Elizabeth A. *choreographer, dancer*
Stuckey, James P. *real estate developer*

Suarez, Maria C. *health care plan company executive*
Tagliapietra, Robert *apparel designer*
Tamir, Theodor *electrophysics researcher, educator*
Taylor, Ian Logan *dean*
Taylor, Shannon *lawyer, not-for-profit developer*
Thomas, Lucille Cole *librarian*
Toranzo, Nilsa Caridad *special education services professional*
Townes, Sandra L. *federal judge*
Trager, David G. *federal judge*
Tunuguntla, Hari Siva Gurunadha Rao *urologist*
Umpaichitra, Vatcharapan *pediatrician, endocrinologist*
Vassalle, Mario *physiologist*
Vidal, Maureen Eris *theater educator, actress*
Viswanathan, Ramaswamy *physician, educator*
Wei, Xinzhou *engineering educator*
Weill, Georges Gustave *mathematics professor*
Weinstein, Jack Bertrand *federal judge*
Werner, Judith *not-for-profit developer, literature educator*
Whitman, Fargo Deborah *artist*
Wiener, Hesh (Harold Frederic Wiener) *publishing executive, consultant*
Williams, Edward Frank *poet, entertainment company executive*
Wilson, Robert Warne *philanthropist*
Witherspoon, Maria Bernarda Pena *principal*
Wolf, Edward Lincoln *physicist, educator*
Wolfe, Ethyle Renee (Mrs. Coleman Hamilton Benedict) *academic administrator*
Wolintz, Arthur Harry *neurologist, ophthalmologist*
Wrotten, Marylean *medical coordinator, counselor*
Yogeswaran, Pararajasingam *physician*
Zakanitch, Robert Rahway *artist*
Zamdborg, Yury *internist*
Zavitsas, Andreas Athanasios *chemistry professor, researcher*
Zisser, Martin Shepherd *fur apparel manufacturer, investor, securities trader*
Zweig, Janet *artist*

## Brookville
Ceraso, Steven *art educator*
Goubeaud, Karleen R. *education educator*
Rhee, Jeong-eun *education educator*
Sugar, Joseph Robert *music educator, conductor, musician*
Swaner, Lynn E *education educator*

## Buffalo
Ahmed, Jamil *rehabilitation service physician*
Amborski, Leonard Edward *retired chemist*
Ambrus, Clara Maria *physician*
Ambrus, Julian L. *physician, medical educator*
Anbar, Michael *biophysics professor*
Anker, Beverly Elaine *retired elementary school educator*
Baier, Robert Edward *chemist, educator*
Ballow, Mark *immunologist, educator*
Barber, Janice Ann *lawyer*
Barrios, George G. *colon and rectal surgeon*
Batt, Ronald Elmer *gynecologist, historian, biomedical research scientist*
Bayles, Jennifer Lucene *museum program director, educator*
Bean, Edwin Temple, Jr. *lawyer*
Bennett, Shirley Ann *business technology educator*
Biondini, Gino *mathematics professor*
Blane, Howard Thomas *alcohol/drug abuse services professional, researcher*
Bobinski, George Sylvan *librarian, educator*
Boyar, Benjamin *music educator*
Bright, Frank Vernon *chemistry professor*
Brody, Harold *neuroanatomist, educator, gerontologist*
Brown, Byron W., Jr. *mayor, former state legislator*
Brydges, Thomas Eugene *lawyer*
Buchanan, Richard N. *dean, dental educator*
Bucki, Carl Leo *judge*
Camhi, Rebecca Ann *librarian, writer*
Carlson, Bruce William *diversified holding company executive*
Cartwright, Alexander N. *electrical engineer, educator*
Cathey, Patrice Antoinette *secondary school educator, director*
Chang, Ching Ming (Carl Chang) *engineering executive, mechanical engineer, educator, writer*
Chu, Tsann Ming *immunochemist, educator*
Churchill, Melvyn Rowen *chemistry professor*
Clarkson, Elisabeth Ann Hudnut *volunteer*
Coburn, Lewis Alan *mathematics professor*
Coles, Robert Traynham *architect*
Creaven, Patrick Joseph *pharmacologist*
Daley, Ruth Margaret *advertising agency administrator*
Day, Donald Sheldon *lawyer*
DiFranco, Ani *music executive, musician*
Dolnick, Bruce Jeffrey *research scientist, consultant*
Drury, Chris *professional hockey player*
Duax, William Leo *biologist, researcher*
Dubber, Markus Dirk *law educator*
Elfvin, John Thomas *federal judge*
Ezzo, David Alber *not-for-profit developer, anthropologist*
Feldman, Irving *poet*
Fine, Edward Jay *neurologist, educator*
Finnegan, Marchand Marie (Shonnie Finnegan) *archivist, consultant*
Flynn, Terrance Patrick *prosecutor, lawyer*
Frerichs, Valerie *chemistry professor, researcher*
Frone, Michael R. *psychologist, researcher*
Fryer, Appleton *sales executive, diplomat*
Gardner, Arnold Burton *lawyer*
Genco, Robert Joseph *immunologist, periodontist, educator, scientist*
Ghadersohi, Ali *veterinarian, researcher*
Giambra, Joel Anthony *municipal official*
Gielow, Kathleen Louise *career planning administrator, consultant, special education educator*
Glanville, Robert Edward *lawyer*
Goldberg, Neil Alan *lawyer*
Goldblatt, Samuel *lawyer*
Goralski, Donald John *public relations executive, counselor*
Gort, Michael *economics professor*

Grant, Nathan L. *literary and cultural studies educator*
Grant, S. G. *education educator*
Grasser, George Robert *lawyer, real estate developer, consultant*
Greene, Robert Michael *lawyer*
Gruen, David Henry *financial analyst*
Halbreich, Uriel Morav *psychiatrist, educator*
Halpern, Ralph Lawrence *lawyer*
Harvey, Steven John *not-for-profit developer*
Hauptman, Herbert Aaron *mathematician, educator, researcher*
Hayes, J. Michael *lawyer*
Headrick, Thomas Edward *lawyer, educator*
Heilman, Pamela Davis *lawyer*
Hoffman, Faith Louise *social worker*
Hohn, David *physician*
Holm, Bruce Allen *academic administrator, researcher*
Houseknecht, Stephen *artist, educator*
Hunt, Jane Helfrich *volunteer*
Iggers, Georg Gerson *history professor*
Irwin, Robert James Armstrong *investment company executive*
Jacobs, Jeremy Maurice, Sr. *diversified financial services company executive, professional sports team executive*
Jain, Piyare Lal *physics professor*
Janiga, Mary Ann *art educator*
Jasen, Matthew Joseph *lawyer, retired judge*
Karwan, Mark Henry *engineering educator*
Kelemen, Arpad *computer scientist, information scientist*
Kelly, Jim (James Edward Kelly) *former professional football player*
Kmiec, Edward Urban *bishop*
Kristoff, Karl W. *lawyer*
Kurlan, Marvin Zeft *retired surgeon*
Lamb, Charles Moody *political scientist, educator*
Lee, Jaekyung *education educator, researcher*
Lele, Amol Shashikant *obstetrician, gynecologist*
Leo, Raphael Jerome *psychiatrist, director, education educator, consultant*
Levy, Kenneth Jay *psychology professor, academic administrator*
Li, Guofang *social sciences educator*
Lippes, Gerald Sanford *lawyer*
Littlewood, Douglas Burden *brokerage house executive*
Lombardo Appleby, Linda Rose *music educator*
Ma, Yingyu *research scientist*
Macomber, Debbie *writer*
Mahaney, Michael C. *library director*
Mahl, Thomas Christopher *physician, educator*
Manes, Stephen Gabriel *concert pianist, educator*
Manning, Kenneth Alan *lawyer*
Mather, Lynn *law educator, political science professor*
McClary, Glen David *education educator*
McKenzie, Denise *religious organization administrator, academic administrator*
McKibbin, William Alex *artist*
Meredith, Dale Dean *civil engineering educator*
Merini, Rafika *humanities educator, writer, language educator*
Merriman, Kevin Thomas *lawyer*
Meshlovitz, Mary E. *educational consultant, special education educator*
Milazzo, David Anthony *mathematics educator*
Milgrom, Felix *immunologist, educator*
Milligan, John Drane *historian, educator*
Mindell, Eugene Robert *surgeon, educator*
Monahan, John Michael *lawyer*
Moran, Charles, Jr. *consumer products company executive*
Mucci, Gary Louis *lawyer*
Mutton, Holly Beth *psychiatrist*
Naughton, Bruce James *geriatrician, consultant*
Naughton, John Patrick *cardiologist, educator*
Neelamegham, Sriram *chemical engineer, educator, researcher*
Nielsen, Nancy H. *health organization executive*
O'Donnell, Denise Ellen *lawyer, former prosecutor*
Odza, Randall M. *lawyer*
Oliver, Dominick Michael *business educator*
O'Loughlin, Sandra S. *lawyer*
Olsen, R. Nils *dean, law educator*
Owens, Cecelie Ann *elementary school educator*
Pados, Dimitris A. *electrical engineer, educator*
Patel, Mulchand Shambhubhai *biochemist, researcher*
Payne, Frances Anne *literature educator, researcher*
Pearson, Paul David *lawyer, arbitrator, mediator*
Pegels, C. Carl *management consultant, educator*
Penniman, W. David *information scientist, educator, management consultant*
Peradotto, John Joseph *retired classics educator, editor*
Piazza, Kris A. *writer, editor*
Piver, M. Steven *gynecologic oncologist*
Rachlin, Lauren David *lawyer*
Reed, Janet *dance educator, choreographer*
Regier, Darcy John *professional sports team executive*
Reinhold, Sandra Lynne *psychologist*
Reismann, Herbert *engineer, educator*
Reitan, Paul Hartman *geologist, educator*
Rich, Robert E., Jr. *frozen foods company executive*
Ridgley, Frank Nelson *veterinarian*
Roberts, Stephen M. *library director*
Ross, Gary Earl *writing educator*
Ruckenstein, Eli *chemical engineering professor*
Ruff, Lindy *professional hockey coach*
Ruppar, Peter Geoffrey *lawyer*
Saab, Maureen Wilson *social worker, consultant*
Sadler, Robert E., Jr. *bank executive*
Sahlem, James Robert *law librarian*
Salisbury, Eugene W. *lawyer, judge*
Sarjeant, Walter James *electrical and computer engineering educator*
Schentag, Jerome John *pharmacy educator*
Schmidli, Keith William *vocational education administrator, educator, researcher*
Segalla, Thomas Francis *lawyer*
Seitz, Mary Lee *mathematics professor*
Seller, Robert Herman *cardiologist, physician*
Shapiro, Stuart Charles *computer scientist, educator*

Shaw, David Tai-Ko *electrical and computer engineering educator, academic administrator*
Shedd, Donald Pomroy *surgeon*
Sherris, David Allan *surgeon, researcher, educator*
Shick, Richard Arlon *finance educator*
Siedlecki, Peter Anthony *English language and literature educator*
Silverman, Robert Mark *education educator, researcher*
Simms, Leonard Jay *psychology professor*
Simpson, John Barclay *academic administrator*
Skretny, William Marion *federal judge*
Spengler, Paul Albert *grants and foundation administrator*
Starks, Fred William *chemicals executive*
Stoll, Howard Lester, Jr. *dermatologist*
Stoss, Frederick Warren *librarian, educator*
Sullivan, Margaret M. *editor*
Tedlock, Barbara Helen *anthropologist, educator, academic administrator*
Treanor, Charles Edward *physicist, researcher*
Trevisan, Maurizio *epidemiologist*
Triggle, David John *dean, pharmacist, consultant*
Trotter, Herman Eager, Jr. (Herman Trotter) *retired music critic*
Tsai, Christina W. *civil engineer, educator*
Tucker, Melvin Jay *education educator, researcher*
Twagilimana, Aimable *language educator, writer*
Urban, Henry Zeller *publishing executive*
Veronica, Debra Clarisse *principal*
Viney, Christopher Robert *health lawyer*
Vishwanath, Arun *information scientist, educator*
Vladutiu, Adrian O. *physician, educator*
Wagle, A. Tina *education educator, researcher*
Wagner, Barbara Lee *musician*
Wang, Jui Hsin *biochemistry educator*
Weber, Thomas William *chemical engineering professor*
Weller, Sol William *chemical engineering professor*
Wiesenberg, Russel John *statistician*
Williams, Lillian Serece *historian, social studies educator*
Wilmers, Robert George *bank executive*
Wisbaum, Wayne David *lawyer*
Wright, John Robert *pathologist, educator*
Yonkman, Mark William *lawyer*
Zaffram, Robert *finance educator*
Zawicki, Joseph Leo *science educator*
Zirnheld, Jennifer L. *engineering educator, researcher*

**Burnt Hills**
DeVries, Robert Charles *research scientist*

**Buskirk**
Johanson, Patricia Maureen *artist, architect*

**Cairo**
Ludwig, Laura Lonshein *poet*

**Caledonia**
Walker, Todd A. *music educator, football coach*

**Cambridge**
Kriss, Gary W(ayne) *priest*

**Camillus**
Albino, Joseph Xavier *writer, educator, photographer*
Armani, Frank Henry *retired lawyer*
Caryl, William R., Jr. *orthodontist*
Deegan, Robert *secondary school educator*

**Campbell Hall**
Greenly, Colin *artist*
Ottaway, James Haller, Jr. *newspaper publisher*

**Canaan**
Belknap, Michael H. P. *real estate developer*
Hooper, Ian (John Derek Glass) *retired marketing communications executive*
Lewis, Marjorie *librarian*
Pennell, William Brooke *lawyer*
Rothenberg, Albert *psychiatrist, educator*
Walker, William Bond *painter, retired librarian*

**Canandaigua**
Barden, George V. *county official, watershed specialist*
Beal, Myron Clarence *osteopath*
Howard, Jeffrey M. *computer science professor*
Love, Robert Lyman *retired education educator, consultant*
Lowther, Frank Eugene *research physicist*
Schwartz, Adam J. *elementary school educator*
Wormer, Thomas Andrew *surgeon*

**Canton**
Auster, Nancy Eileen Ross *economics professor*
Goldberg, Rita Maria *foreign language educator*
Halstead, Ann Marie G. *performing arts educator*
Pollard, Fred Don *finance company executive, director*
Sullivan, Daniel F. *academic administrator, sociologist, educator*
Young, Jeffrey Thomas *economics professor*

**Carle Place**
Collins, Richard David *lawyer, writer*

**Carmel**
Laporte, Cloyd, Jr. *retired lawyer, retired manufacturing executive*
Shen, Chia Theng *retired water transportation executive, religious organization administrator*

**Carthage**
Desrosiers, Michele L. *curator*
Ebbels, Bruce Jeffery *retired physician, health facility administrator*
Mosher, Daniel Lee *music educator*

**Castile**
Krolikowski, Gary E. *social sciences educator*

**Cato**
Labeille, Claudine *elementary school educator*
Sheckler, Ross David *engineering executive*

**Cazenovia**
Carlson, William Clifford *defense industry executive, director, retired military officer*
Shattuck, David Allan *surgeon, researcher, educator*
Wyckoff, Sylvia Spencer *art educator, artist*

**Cedarhurst**
Cohen, Harris L. *diagnostic radiologist, consultant*
Taubenfeld, Harry S. *lawyer*

**Centereach**
Chassman, Karen Moss *educational association administrator*

**Centerport**
McQueeney, Henry Martin, Sr. *publisher*
Stevens, Martin Brian *publisher*
Trotta, Ric Charles *aerospace transportation executive, consultant*

**Central Islip**
Bernstein, Stan *federal bankruptcy judge*
Boyle, E. Thomas *federal magistrate judge*
Cyganowski, Melanie L. *bankruptcy judge*
Eisenberg, Dorothy *federal judge*
Feuerstein, Sandra Jeanne *judge*
Hurley, Denis R. *federal judge*
McCrain, Michael William *accountant, financial planner*
Platt, Thomas Collier, Jr. *federal judge*
Seybert, Joanna *federal judge*
Spatt, Arthur Donald *federal judge*
Voigt, Philip Kenneth *music educator*
Wall, William D. *federal judge*

**Central Valley**
Regan, Richard Felix *secondary school educator, musician, conductor*

**Chappaqua**
Boal, Lyndall Elizabeth *social worker*
George, Jean Craighead *author, illustrator*
Goldberg, Lee Brian *journalist, writer*
Laun, Louis Frederick *government official*
O'Neill, Robert Charles *inventor, consultant*
Pomerene, James Herbert *retired computer engineer*
Romney, Richard Bruce *lawyer*
Schwarz, Wolfgang *psychologist*

**Charlton**
Kekes, John *philosopher, educator*

**Chatham**
Kherdian, David *writer*

**Chautauqua**
Schmidt, Edward Craig *lawyer*

**Chazy**
Ratner, Gayle *special education educator*

**Cheektowaga**
Mruk, Eugene Robert *retired marketing professional, urban planner*
Wozniak, Richard Anthony *computer engineer*

**Cherry Valley**
Sapinsky, Joseph Charles *publishing executive, photographer*

**Chester**
Amelar, Richard Daniel *urologist*
Mackerodt, Fred *public relations specialist*
Munsch, Martin John III *sound recording engineer, music producer*

**Chestnut Ridge**
Day, Stacey Biswas *physician, medical educator*

**Chittenango**
Cassell, William Walter *retired accounting operations consultant*

**Churchville**
Balch, Glenn McClain, Jr. *academic administrator, minister, writer*
Clarke, Stephan Paul *retired language educator, writer*

**Cicero**
Crabtree, Robert Allen *elementary school educator*
DeVault, Travis L *wildlife biologist, researcher*
Pink, (Alecia B. Moore) *singer*

**Clarence**
Greatbatch, Wilson *biomedical engineer*
Johnston, Joan Lawler *director, consultant*
Stringer, Gretchen Engstrom *consulting volunteer administrator*

**Claverack**
Barrett, William Gary *advertising and marketing executive*

**Clifton Park**
St. Clair, Helaine Denise *language educator*
Scher, Robert Sander *instrument design company executive*
Sun, Zuo *mechanical engineer, researcher*

**Clifton Springs**
Spoto, Carl Alexander, Jr. *history educator*

**Clinton**
Bailey, Mark W. *computer scientist, educator*
Behrens, John (Jack) *editor, writer, columnist, educator*
Kay, Lois Jeanne *writer, educator*
Pagani, Albert Louis *aerospace system engineer*
Paris, David C. *academic administrator, political scientist, educator*
Ring, James Walter *physics professor*
Stewart, Joan Hinde *academic administrator*

**Cobleskill**
Ingels, Jack Edward *horticulture educator*
Rivera, Salvador, Jr. *history and sociology educator, researcher*

Wilson, Lewis Lansing *insurance executive*

**Cohocton**
Sarfaty, Wayne Allen *insurance agent, financial planner*

**Cohoes**
Davey, Mark Christopher *assistant principal*

**Cold Spring**
Hodes, Barney *artist*
Posniack, Lee Joseph *secondary school educator*
Pugh, Emerson William *electrical engineer*

**Cold Spring Harbor**
Stillman, Bruce *molecular biologist*
Wallin, James Peter *lawyer*
Watson, James Dewey *molecular biologist, educator*

**College Point**
Mullany, Kevin Fergus *music educator, director*

**Commack**
Kurtz, Joel Barry *finance executive*
Ohman, Franklin Eric *ballet educator, choreographer*
Price, Amelia Ruth *not-for-profit foundation president, artist, small business owner*
Steindler, Walter G. *retired lawyer*

**Conesus**
Dadrian, Vahakn Norair *retired sociology educator*

**Conklin**
Blouch, Timothy Craig *food company executive*

**Cooperstown**
Bordley, James, IV, *surgeon*
Butts, William Lester *entomologist, researcher*
Franck, Walter Alfred *rheumatologist, medical educator, health facility administrator*
Harman, Willard Nelson *malacologist, educator*
Jones, Clyde Ray *historian, consultant*
Kirkpatrick, Megan Leigh *museum administrator*
Mays, Willie Howard, Jr. (Say Hey Kid) *former professional baseball player*
Rich, Walter George *railroad transportation executive*
Sutter, Bruce (Howard Sutter) *retired professional baseball player*
Tilton, Webster, Jr. *contractor*
Veenema, Ralph James *retired urologist*

**Copake**
Johnson, Paul Edward *poet, writer*

**Coram**
Mohanty, Christine Ann *retired language educator, actress*

**Corfu**
Cavanaugh, Michael John *history educator*
Walker, Barbara Hills *secondary school educator*

**Corinth**
Bein, Edward C. *chiropractor, educator*

**Corning**
Beall, George Halsey *ceramics engineer*
Behm, Forrest Edwin *glass manufacturing company executive*
Buechner, Thomas Scharman *artist, museum director, retired glass manufacturing company executive*
Cicerchi, Eleanor Ann Tomb *not-for-profit fundraiser*
Eggers, William D. *manufacturing executive, lawyer*
Fehlner, Francis Paul *chemist, consultant*
Flaws, James B. *technology executive*
Hatton, Vincent Paul *lawyer*
Houghton, James Richardson *manufacturing executive*
Miller, Joseph A. *chemicals executive*
Miller, Roger Allen *physicist*
Peters, Linda S. *musician, educator*
Spillman, Jane Shadel *curator, writer, researcher*
Ughetta, William Casper *lawyer, manufacturing executive, director*
Whitehouse, David Bryn *museum director*
Wilson, Cecilia Ann *special education educator*

**Cornwall On Hudson**
Peirce, Karen Patricia *education educator*

**Corona**
Finkelpearl, Tom *museum director*
Jackson, Andrew Preston *library director*
Smith, Valerie *curator*

**Cortland**
Anderson, Donna Kay *musicologist, educator*
Brush, Florence Clapham *kinesiologist, exercise physiologist, physical education educator*
Taylor, Leland Baridon *lawyer*

**Cortlandt Manor**
Lupiani, Jennifer Lynne *school psychologist*
Rosenberg, Marilyn Rosenthal *artist, poet*
Traille, Joy Myra *microbiologist, eldercare service provider*

**Coxsackie**
Moyna, John Lawrence *priest*

**Cranberry Lake**
Glavin, James Edward *landscape architect*

**Cropseyville**
Makowiec, Judith A. Neilson *family nurse practitioner*

**Cross River**
Gilarde-Green, Michela M. *secondary school educator*
Lang, Robert Mays, Jr. *manufacturing executive*
Thorn, Susan Howe *interior designer*

## Croton On Hudson
Hoffman, Paul Shafer *lawyer*
Johann, Anne Dorothy *visual artist, painter, graphic artist*
Lewins, Steven *financial analyst, investment company executive, legislative staff member, retired military officer*
Plotch, Walter *management consultant, fund raising counselor*
Reinhard, Kenneth Edward *psychologist*
Turner, David Reuben *publisher, author*
Wandel, Sharon Lee *sculptor*

## Crugers
Norman, Jessye *soprano*

## Cutchogue
Dank, Leonard Dewey *medical illustrator, audio-visual consultant*
Reiley, Jorge Alberto *neurologist*

## Dansville
Dearing, Teresa Allison *librarian*

## De Witt
Belden, Sanford Adams *banker*

## Deer Park
Amend, Stephen J. *musician*
Chapman, Ronald Thomas *musician, educator*

## Delhi
Hartmann, James M. *lawyer*
Van Brunt, Arthur Hoffman (Peter) *economist, educator*

## Delmar
Beck, David Christopher *music educator, conductor*
Button, Rena Pritsker *public relations executive*
Houghton, Raymond Carl, Jr. *education educator*
Matuszek, John Michael, Jr. *environmental scientist, educator, consultant*

## Derby
Cuomo, Rivers *singer, songwriter*
Goodell, Joseph Edward *manufacturing executive*
McKeating, Thomas Francis *secondary school educator*
Pordum, Francis J. *former state legislator, educator, marketing professional*

## Dix Hills
Braun, Ludwig *retired engineering educator*
Fouladvand, Hengameh *artist*
Mymit, Chuck W. *music educator, musician*

## Dobbs Ferry
Anbinder, Paul *publishing executive*
Andreadis, Constantine *art educator, art therapist*
Briskin, Efrem *music educator*
Culhane, Hind Rassam *psychologist, educator, historian*
Fritz, Jean Guttery *writer*
Guggenheimer, Tobias Immanuel Simon *architect*
Juettner, Diana D'Amico *lawyer, educator*
Kalvin-Stiefel, Judy *public relations executive*
Kraetzer, Mary C. *sociologist, educator, consultant*
Kravath, Richard Elliot *retired pediatrician, educator*
Poian, Edward Licio *historian*
Postman, Robert Derek *dean, mathematics educator*
Sherin, Edwin *theater director, film director, television director, actor*
Simon, Lothar *publishing executive*
Sutton, Francis Xavier *social services administrator, consultant*

## Douglaston
Balbi, Kenneth Emilio *environmental specialist, researcher*
Levine, Jeffrey E. *real estate developer*
Palatnick, Frank Sidney *educational consultant*
Valero, René Arnold *clergyman*

## Dryden
Alsdorf-Sprout, Elizabeth Ruth *art educator*
Baxter, Robert Banning *insurance company executive*
Powell, Marsha *director, educator, pathologist*
Slocum, Robert Bigney *retired librarian*

## Dundee
Miller, Ronald K. *real estate broker, educator*
Tette, Sharan Flynn *writer*

## Dunkirk
Burlett, Helen Marie *elementary school educator*
Woodbury, Robert Charles *lawyer*

## East Amherst
Fleming, Renee Rizzo *pharmacist*
Watson, Stewart Charles *construction executive*

## East Aurora
Carfagna, Vincent O. *physician*
Keem, Michael Dennis *veterinarian*
Sand, Seaward Alwyn *geneticist, researcher*
Woodard, Carol Jane *educational consultant*

## East Elmhurst
Scott, Lionel Franklin *psychologist, educator*

## East Greenbush
McConville, Edward Patrick *lawyer*
Mucci, Patrick John *financial consultant, realtor, commercial loan broker*
Quenelle, Susannah Sherman *music educator*
Thornton, Thomas E. *literature and language educator*

## East Hampton
Brady, James Winston *commentator, writer, editor*
Bromley, Bruce Ditmas *language educator, writer*
Damaz, Paul F. *architect*
Dello Joio, Norman *composer*
Delson, Sidney Leon *architect*
Ehren, Charles Alexander, Jr. *lawyer, educator*

---

Garrett, Charles Geoffrey Blythe *physicist, consultant*
Garten, Ina *chef*
Good, Allen Hovey *investment banker, real estate broker*
Jaudon, Valerie *artist*
Karp, Harvey Lawrence *metal products executive*
Mencher, Stuart Alan *sales and marketing executive*
Metz, Robert Roy *publishing executive, media consultant*
Nelson, Mark D. *music educator, arts education administrator*
Osterweil, Adam Matthew *elementary school educator, writer*
Riley, Cheryl *artist, educator*
Schetlin, Eleanor M. *retired associate dean*
Scott, Rosa Mae *art educator, artist*
Swerdlow, Amy *historian, educator, writer*
Twomey, Thomas A., Jr. *lawyer, educator*

## East Hills
Cervia, Joseph Steven *medical educator*

## East Islip
Donohue, Claire P. *retired school librarian*

## East Meadow
Adler, Ira Jay *lawyer*
Albert, Gerald *clinical psychologist*
Cymbler, Murray Joel *corporate financial executive*
Fuchs, Jerome Herbert *management consultant*
Harrison, Robert L. *photographer, writer, retired transportation executive, poet, playwright*
Jeziorski, Michael A. *social studies educator*

## East Northport
Juliano, John Louis *lawyer*
Kehoe, Thomas J. *food products executive*
Rose, Richard *secondary school educator*

## East Norwich
Busner, Philip H. *retired lawyer, judge*
Rosen, Meyer Robert *chemical engineer*

## East Patchogue
McAleese, Alice S. *music educator*

## East Rochester
Murray, James Doyle *accountant, educator*

## East Setauket
Badalamenti, Fred Leopoldo *artist, educator*
Maffia, Christina *elementary school educator, consultant*
Malbon, Craig Curtis *pharmacology educator, dean*
Simons, James Harris *technology company executive*
Tuttle, Anne Palmer *artist, education educator*

## East Syracuse
Atlas, Craig Mitchell *lawyer*
Duffy, Nancy Keogh *newscaster, broadcast executive*
McGlynn, Sean *secondary school educator*
Nivarthi, Raju Naga *anesthesiology educator*

## Eastchester
Cherry, Theresa Cotrone *principal*
Giuliano, Robert Paul *pharmacist*
Gottschall, Edward Maurice *editor, writer*
Kravath, Alan Wolfe *education evaluator*
Stern, Louise *artist*

## Eden
Thomas, Jimmy Lynn *retired treasurer*

## Edmeston
Blackman, Dorothy J. *library director*

## Elba
Kauffman, William Joseph *editor, writer*

## Elma
Wirth, Sandra Lee *real estate company owner*

## Elmhurst
Cush, John Patrick *priest, theology studies educator*
Masci, Joseph Richard *medical educator*

## Elmira
Graham, David Richard *orthopedic surgeon*
Leveen, Pauline *retired history professor, government professor*
Meier, Thomas Keith *academic administrator, language educator*
Miran, Barbara Marie *art educator*
Nast, Edward Paul *cardiac surgeon*
Pucci, Anthony J. *English language educator*
Reddick, Bryan DeWitt *language educator, academic administrator*
Winner, George Henry *lawyer*

## Elmont
Butera, Ann Michele *consulting company executive*
Cusack, Thomas Joseph *retired banker*
Kolb, Lisa Marie *music educator*

## Elmsford
Demopoulos, Harry Byron *retired pathologist, pharmaceutical researcher*
Miranda, Robert Nicholas *publishing executive, director*
Panitz, Lawrence *physician*
Price, Richard Galen *sound recording engineer, music producer, conductor*
Raymond, George Marc *city planner, educator*

## Endicott
Dunscombe, Edward Andrew *library director*
Gleason, James Perley *music educator*
Goodwin, Charles Hugh *technology education educator*
Markovich, Voya R. *information technology executive*

---

## Fairport
Bartlett, Cody Blake *retired lawyer*
DeMay, Michael F. *secondary school educator, director*
Englert, John F. *secondary school educator, coach*
Graham, Susette Ryan *retired English educator*
Marshall, Julie Arnitz *biology educator*
Mierswa, Ruth Mildred *counselor, writer*
Sands, Richard E. *food products executive*
Sands, Robert *food products executive*
Summer, Thomas S. *food products executive*

## Far Rockaway
Epstein, Samuel Abraham *sales executive*
Helfgott, Samson *lawyer*
Sussman, Laureen Glicklin *elementary school educator*

## Farmingdale
Bandyopadhyay, Amitabha *engineering educator*
Facchiano, Patricia A. *music educator*
Goodstone, Michael S. *psychology professor, consultant*
Purandare, Yeshwant K. *chemistry educator, consultant*
Winn, John Arthur, Jr. *mathematics educator*

## Fayetteville
Cady, Robert Brown *pediatric orthopedic surgeon*
Chevli, Renate Naren *gynecologist, obstetrician*
Hadyk-Wepf, Sonia Margaret *artist, real estate manager*
Larson, Lori Geralyn *music educator, singer*
Meigs, Montgomery Cunningham, Jr. *retired military officer, educator*
Pachter, Irwin Jacob *pharmaceutical consultant*
Pirodsky, Donald Max *psychiatrist, educator*
Stewart, William A. *medical educator, neurosurgeon*

## Findley Lake
Gundersen, Allison Maureen *management consultant*

## Fishers Island
Baue, Arthur Edward *surgeon, educator, retired health facility administrator*

## Fishkill
Brocks, Eric *ophthalmologist, surgeon*

## Floral Park
Chatoff, Michael Alan *lawyer*
Corbett, William John *lawyer, public relations executive, consultant*
Dudek, Henry Thomas *management consultant*
Isenberg, Henry David *microbiology educator*

## Flushing
Anderson, Michelle J. *dean, law educator*
Baik-Han, Won H. *pediatrician, educator, consultant*
Beltran, Carlos *professional baseball player*
Beveridge, Andrew Alan *sociologist, educator, consultant*
Bird, Thomas Edward *foreign language and literature educator*
Birnstiel, Charles *consulting engineer*
Carlson, Cynthia Joanne *artist, educator*
Cesarano, Michael Ferdinand *theater educator, actor*
Commoner, Barry *biologist, educator*
Delgado, Carlos Juan *professional baseball player*
Engel, Robert Ralph *chemist, educator, dean*
Evans, Cherice M. *chemistry professor*
Evens, Lucie Ann *music educator*
Fichtel, Rudolph Robert *retired association executive*
Glavine, Tom (Thomas Michael Glavine) *professional baseball player*
Goldenshteyn, Vladimir Lev *civil engineer*
Goldman, Norman Lewis *chemistry professor*
Goldsmith, Howard *writer, consultant*
Haller, Hermann W. *romance language educator*
Henshel, Harry Bulova *watch manufacturer*
Hon, John Wingsun *physician*
Hsu, Charles Jui-cheng *manufacturing company executive, advertising agent*
Hu, Huping *biophysicist, lawyer*
Kim, Sun-Hae *retired medical/surgical nurse, writer, retired nurse midwife, retired physical therapist*
Kopp, Ilya Zinovij *engineering educator*
Kroeppel, Warren *airport terminal executive*
Li, Hongzhi *foundation administrator, writer*
Martinez, Pedro Jaime *professional baseball player*
Mendelson, Elliott *mathematician, educator*
Minaya, Omar *professional sports team executive*
Mirkin, Michael V. *chemistry professor*
Nussbaum, Michel Ernest *physician*
Pellitteri, John Steven *psychologist, psychotherapist, educator*
Person, Philip *biomedical consultant, biochemist, dentist*
Rabassa, Gregory *language educator, translator, poet*
Ranald, Margaret Loftus *English literature educator, author*
Randolph, Willie Larry *professional baseball manager*
Reyes, Jose *professional baseball player*
Rosenberg, Deborah A. *special education educator*
Sanborn, Anna Lucille *pension fund administrator, consultant*
Schwartz, Estar Alma *lawyer*
Smaldone, Edward Michael *composer*
Smith, Charles William *social sciences educator*
Stahl, Frank Ludwig *civil engineer*
Totakura, Satyanarayana Raju *secondary school educator*
Trachuk, Arina George *artist, educator*
Tytell, John *literature educator, writer*
Wagner, Billy *professional baseball player*
Wright, David *professional baseball player*
Yeo, Kim Eng *artist*
Zinnes, Harriet Fich *poet, retired English educator, literary and art critic*

## Fly Creek
Dusenbery, Walter Condit *sculptor*

---

## Forest Hills
Addabbo, Dominic Lucian *lawyer*
Brooks, Martin *electronic media company executive*
Buhks, Ephraim *college administrator, technology educator*
D'Addario, Alice Marie *retired school system administrator*
Eden, Alvin Noam *pediatrician, writer*
Henley, Arthur *writer, editor*
Kilgannon, Corey *journalist*
Kourides, Peter Theologos *lawyer*
Kra, Pauline Skornicki *French language educator*
Mathieu Byers, Deborah Anne *performing company executive*
Morgan, Jacqui *illustrator, painter, art educator, writer*
Neeleman, David *air transportation executive*
Polakoff, Abe *baritone*
Reis, Don *publishing executive*
Sanchez, Victor Hugo *retired military non-commissioned officer*
Seldes, Richard M. *orthopedist, consultant*
Spiegel, Andrea *marketing executive*
Tvildiani, Dimitry *cardiologist*

## Forestville
Adams, Lee Towne *lawyer*

## Fort Drum
Youngs, Michael Theron, Jr. *non-commissioned officer*

## Fort Montgomery
Butler, Patricia Claire *retired history educator*

## Franklin Square
Cantilli, Edmund Joseph *safety engineer, educator, translator, writer, consultant*
Indiviglia, Salvatore Joseph *artist, retired military officer*
Vanora, Jerome Patrick *lawyer*

## Fredonia
Aghazadeh, Seyed-Mahmoud *finance educator*
Benton, Allen Haydon *biology professor*
Croxton, Jack Sanders *director, consultant*
Goetz, Thomas Henry Paul *literature educator*
Hewitt, Holly E. *workforce development professional, reporter*
Horvath, Virginia Schaefer *academic administrator*
Sullivan, Michael Joseph *lawyer*

## Freeport
Berg, Alan *lawyer, arbitrator*
Ferentino, Sheila Connolly *psychologist, consultant*
Golici, Nicolae *sculptor*
Martorana, Barbara Joan *secondary school educator*
Pullman, Maynard Edward *biochemist*
Walker, Lula Noriega *educational association administrator*
Zurcher, Zean William *retired music educator, musician*

## Fresh Meadows
Duckett, Lila Wheeler *retired language educator, writer*
Godfrey, Philip M. *plastic surgeon*
Greenberg, Robert Jay *law educator*
Kaplan, Barry Hubert *physician*
Westrich, Geoffrey Howard *orthopaedic surgery*

## Fulton
Jennings, Meghan Young *music educator*
Long, Robert Emmet *author*
Ludington, Janice Fay *speech pathology/audiology services professional*

## Garden City
Amsler, Georgeann Lucille *publishing executive*
Berka, Marianne Guthrie *health and physical education educator*
Boquiren, Sidney Marquez *composer, educator*
Bouchard, Wendy Ann Borstel *language educator*
Brewer, Bruce William *plastic surgeon*
Calamari, Joseph August *law librarian*
Campbell, James R. *transportation executive*
Conlon, Thomas James *marketing executive*
Cook, George Valentine *lawyer, consultant*
DaSilva, Willard H. *lawyer, educator*
Deane, Leland Marc *plastic surgeon, director*
DiMascio, John Philip *lawyer*
Dods, Stuart C. *mathematics educator*
Doucette, Mary-Alyce *computer company executive*
Douglas, Barry K. *plastic surgeon*
Einenkel, Robert Herbert *theater educator, actor, director*
Findlay, Lorraine Anne *medical educator*
Fishberg, Gerard *lawyer*
Freedman, Monroe Henry *law educator*
Good, Larry Irwin *gastroenterologist, educator*
Gray, Phil R. *band director, musician*
Hamblet, Wendy C. *philosopher, educator*
Harwood, Stanley *retired judge, lawyer, arbitrator, mediator*
Hecht, Jennifer Michael *poet, historian*
High, Robert V. *statistician, educator*
Ingber, Larry H. *lawyer*
Jenkins, Kenneth Vincent *literature educator, writer*
Jones, Lawrence Tunnicliffe *lawyer*
Kaplan, Joel Stuart *lawyer*
Klein, Arnold Spencer *lawyer*
Laureano, Mari *government agency administrator, writer*
Mastaglio, Peter James *lawyer*
Meng, M. Kathryn *lawyer*
Minicucci, Richard Francis *lawyer, former hospital administrator*
Moravec, Paul *composer*
Pereira, John William Miller *theater educator*
Persons, John Wade *lawyer*
Podwall, Kathryn Stanley *biology professor*
Prabhakar, Kumkum *biology professor*
Prattis, Susan Marie *veterinarian, educator*
Rhein, John Hancock Willing III *publishing executive*

Schwarz, Carl A., Jr. *lawyer*
Scollard, Patrick John *hospital executive*
Scott, Robert Allyn *academic administrator*
Shuart, James Martin *retired academic administrator*
Tamigi, Peter F. *lawyer*
Toy, Vivian *journalist*
Wetherill-Smith, Linda Marie *music educator, musician, performing arts association administrator*
Wickiewicz, Jessica-Lauren Charlotte *academic administrator*

**Gardiner**
Mabee, Carleton *historian, educator*

**Garnerville**
Evers, Gene *writer*
Zugibe, Frederick Thomas *retired pathologist, forensic specialist*

**Garrison**
Callahan, Daniel John *biomedical researcher*
Goggin, Dan Charles *playwright, composer, theater director*
Murray, Thomas Henry *bioethics educator, writer*

**Geneseo**
Gouvernet, Gerard Raoul *language educator*
Lim, Seong Bae *business educator*
Olczak, Paul Vincent *psychologist, educator*

**Geneva**
Brind, David Hutchison *lawyer, judge*
Lieberg, Olaf U. *orthopaedic surgeon*
Roelofs, Wendell Lee *biochemistry professor, consultant*
Siebert, Karl Joseph *food science educator, consultant*

**Germantown**
Farberman, Harold *conductor, composer*
Rollins, Sonny (Theodore Rollins) *composer, musician*

**Getzville**
Saveth, Edward Norman *historian, educator*

**Glen Cove**
Burnham, Harold Arthur *pharmaceutical executive, physician*
Mills, Charles Gardner *lawyer*
Olsen, Robert C., Jr. *academic administrator, military officer*
Pettersen, Kevin Will *investment company executive*
Woodman, Edward *dentist*
Woodman, Ryan *dentist*

**Glen Head**
Conway, David Antony *marketing professional*
Huber, Don Lawrence *publisher*
Martin, David S. *retired secondary school educator, administrator*
Stack, Edward William *diversified financial services company executive*

**Glen Oaks**
Lencz, Todd *psychologist, researcher*

**Glen Wild**
Kaszas, William Joseph *technology educator*

**Glenmont**
Bellizzi, John J. *law enforcement association administrator, pharmacist, educator*
Haizlip, Viola *medical/surgical nurse*

**Glens Falls**
Bartlett, Richard James *lawyer*
McMillen, Robert Stewart *lawyer*
Pearsall, Glenn Lincoln *brokerage house executive*
Pontiff, Paul E. *lawyer*
Suffolk, Randall *museum director, curator*
Vitvitsky, Jack *physician assistant*

**Glenville**
Anderson, Roy Everett *retired electrical engineer*

**Goshen**
DeMueller, Lucia *investment consultant*
Ward, William Francis, Jr. *real estate investment broker*
Watson, Georgianna *retired librarian*

**Gouverneur**
Leader, Robert John *lawyer*

**Grahamsville**
Pilc, Jean-Michel *composer, musician*

**Grand Island**
Hennigar, William Grant, Jr. *dentist*

**Great Neck**
Appel, Gerald *investment advisor*
Arams, Frank Robert *electronics executive*
Breidbart, Rory Steven *endocrinologist*
Christie, George Nicholas *economist, consultant*
Dines, David Michael *surgeon, educator*
Elkowitz, Lloyd Kent *dental anesthesiologist, dentist, pharmacist*
Feldman, Gary Marc *nutritionist, consultant*
Fiel, Maxine Lucille *journalist, behavior analyst, educator*
Fried, Belle Warshavsky *education educator*
Gold, Alan H. *plastic surgeon*
Goldberg, Melvin Arthur *communications executive*
Goldman, Ira Steven *gastroenterologist*
Hampton, Benjamin Bertram *brokerage house executive*
Hurwitz, Johanna (Johanna Frank) *writer*
Joskow, Jules *economic research company executive*
Kahn, David *editor, author*
Katz, Edward Morris *banker*
Kechijian, Paul *dermatologist, educator*
Lieber, Constance E. *medical association administrator*

Marcus, Philip *dean*
Minkoff, Jack *retired economics professor*
Panes, Jack Samuel *publishing executive*
Puttlitz, Donald Herbert *microbiologist*
Rosenberg, Richard F. *physician, radiologist*
Samuel, Paul *retired cardiologist*
Scherr, Lawrence *internist, educator*
Schlesinger, Irwin D. *neurologist*
Schwartz, Michael Robert *music educator, department chairman*
Seidler, Doris *artist*
Shons, Alan Rance *plastic surgeon, surgical oncologist, educator*
Wolff, Edward *physician*

**Great River**
Hayman, Martin Arthur *psychiatrist, educator*

**Greenlawn**
Bachman, Henry Lee *electrical engineer, engineering company executive*
Lelyveld, Gail Annick *actress*
Popren, Valerie *artist*

**Greenport**
Jackson, Richard Montgomery *air transportation executive*
Monsell, Thomas Oliver *secondary school educator, writer*
Velleman, Ruth Ann *retired librarian, educator*
Watts, Harold Wesley *economist, educator*

**Greenvale**
Cordaro, Matthew Charles *energy and utility executive, educator*
Dinan, Susan Eileen *history educator*
Halper, Emanuel B(arry) *lawyer, real estate developer, consultant, writer*
Krasnoff, Eric *health products executive*
Kusukawa, Akira *demographer, educator*
Manzari, Laura Lynn *law educator*
Rao, Srikumar Srinivas *marketing educator*
Regazzi, John James III *dean, publishing executive*
Schor, Adam Matthew *history professor*
Senft, Mason George *musician*
Shenker, Joseph *academic administrator*
Steinberg, David Joel *academic administrator, historian, educator*
Watt, Stephanie Denise *musician, educator, department chairman*

**Greenwich**
Edsforth, Maureen McGill *instructional technology specialist*
Fung, Paul, Jr. *cartoonist, illustrator*
Smethurst, E(dward) William, Jr. *investment banker*

**Groveland**
Battersby, Harold Ronald *retired anthropologist, archaeologist, linguist*

**Guilderland**
Escobar, Deborah Ann *gifted and talented educator*

**Hamburg**
Calkins, Evan *physician, educator*
Gorline, Lynda Ruth *elementary school educator*
Markulis, Henryk Jon *career military officer*
Meissner, Anita Cohoon *retired elementary school educator*

**Hamilton**
Berlind, Bruce Peter *poet, educator*
Chopp, Rebecca S. *academic administrator*
Edmonston, William Edward, Jr. *retired publishing executive, writer, retired psychology professor*
Frey, Frank Michael *biology professor*
Haines, Michael Robert *economist, educator*
Johnston, Michael (William Johnston) *political science educator, university administrator*
Moynihan, William J. *museum executive*
Pagano, Jo Anne *education educator*
Pinchin, Jane *literature educator*
Rotter, Andrew Jon *history educator*
Simpson, Nicole B. *economics professor*
Soderberg, Dale LeRoy *language educator, drama director, producer*
Staley, Lynn *literature educator*
Tucker, Thomas William *mathematics professor*

**Hancock**
DeLuca, Ronald *former advertising agency executive, consultant*
Geci, Paul DeWitt *music educator*
Senia, Grace Melanie *language and music educator*

**Hannacroix**
Schwebler, Stephen *retired chemist*

**Harpursville**
Cline, Nicole Elizabeth *music educator*

**Harrison**
Kramer, Alan Sharfsin *lawyer*
Northcutt, Marie Rose *elementary school educator, special education educator*
Strone, Michael Jonathan *real estate consultant, lawyer*
Wadsworth, Frank Whittemore *foundation administrator, literature educator*
Wilson, William James *marketing professional*

**Harrisville**
Seelman, Jannet Genevieve *secondary school educator*

**Hartsdale**
Aker, Susan K. *elementary school educator, assistant principal*
Butler, Kevin J. *social studies educator*
Chait, Maxwell Mani *physician*
Greenawalt, Peggy Freed Tomarkin *advertising executive*
Katz, John *investment banker*
Kroll, Arthur Herbert *lawyer, educator, writer*
Lightburn, Anita Louise *dean, social work educator*

Martin, Daniel Richard *pharmaceutical executive*
McMann, Edith Brozak (Edith Brozak) *performing and visual artist*
Pell, Arthur Robert *human resources specialist, consultant, writer*
Schweitzer, Caren S. *social worker*
Sundel, Alfred *retired medical writer*

**Hastings On Hudson**
Cassella, William Nathan, Jr. *retired not-for-profit organization executive*
D'Antoni, Philip *television producer*
Del Colle, Paul Lawrence *communications administrator, educator*
Edelman, Paul Sterling *lawyer*
Landau, Peter Edward *editor*
Reich, Herb *editor*
Rosch, Paul John *internist, educator*
Sharpe, Robert Kent *writer, director, producer, photographer*
Stillman, Jeanne Betsock *public health administrator, consultant*
Weinstein, Edward Michael *architect, consultant*
Wolfe, Stanley *composer, educator*

**Hauppauge**
Bender, Bruce F. *book publishing executive*
Buckley, Robert Matthew *electrical engineer*
Hausman, Howard *electronics executive*
Reid, Margaret Elizabeth *elementary school educator, secondary school educator*

**Haverstraw**
Alpert, Revell Judith *retired data processing executive*
Eidelman, Sharon (Sherry) R. *marriage and family therapist*

**Hawthorne**
Batstone, Joanna Louise *physicist*
Dan, Asit *computer scientist, research scientist*
Gong, Leiguang *computer scientist, researcher*
Lavenberg, Stephen S. *electrical engineer, researcher*
Mihaila, George Andrei *computer scientist, researcher*
Nandedkar, Sanjeev Dattatraya *medical researcher, educator*
Ward, Christopher *computer scientist, researcher*
Wen, Sheree *computer company executive*
Yoffa, Ellen J. *information technology executive*

**Hemlock**
Hodgeman, Michelle A. *technology educator*

**Hempstead**
Aaron, Merik Roy *financial executive, educator, lawyer*
Barak, Benny *marketing and business educator, department chairman*
Berliner, Herman Albert *academic administrator, economist, educator, dean*
Bose, Meena *political science professor*
Bradway, Terry *professional sports team executive*
Coleman, Benjamin Joseph *music educator*
Coles, Laveranues *professional football player*
Connolly, Melissa Kane *public relations executive*
Dyson, Andre *professional football player*
Ferguson, D'Brickashaw *professional football player*
Fiedler, Jay *professional football player*
Glassman, Paul *library administrator, architecture educator*
Goldstein, Stanley Philip *engineering educator*
Graffeo, Mary Thérèse *music educator, performer*
Heuermann-Nowik, Patricia Calhoun *theater director*
Jarvis, Scott E. *language educator*
Lee, Keun Sok *business educator, consultant*
Mahon, Malachy Thomas, Sr. *lawyer, educator*
Mangini, Eric *professional football coach*
Martin, Curtis *professional football player*
Masheck, Joseph Daniel *art critic, educator*
Roble, Carole Marcia *accountant*
Salten, David George *academic administrator*
Schechtman, Saul *conductor*
Shafritz, Keith Michael *psychology professor*
Sodano, Salvatore F. *former stock exchange executive*
Tannenbaum, Mike (Michael Tannenbaum) *professional sports team executive*
Udolf, Roy *psychology professor, lawyer*
Watford, Dolores *elementary school educator*
Wattel, Harold Louis *economics professor*
Zagano, Phyllis *religious studies educator*

**Henrietta**
Byfield, Bert A. *conservative humanitarian novelist*
Wolcott, Kyle B, *secondary school educator*

**Herkimer**
Durham, Jeanette Randall *artist, educator*
Lowery, Kathleen Ann *elementary school educator*

**Hewlett**
Cohen, David Leon *physician*
Mahoney, Eileen Heron *secondary school educator*
Steinfeld, Philip Sheldon *pediatrician*

**Hicksville**
Garner, Beth L. *music educator*
Giuffré, John Joseph *lawyer*
Horowitz, Barry Allan *music company executive*
Kronowitz, Pamela Renee *music educator*
Lieberman, Douglas Mark *lawyer*
Mund, Lorraine G. *English studies educator, writer*
Noll, Amy *secondary educator*
Notaro, Anthony *application developer*
Stein, Melvin A. *accountant*
Tucci, Gerald Frank *manufacturing executive*
Yen, Henry Chin-Yuan *computer systems programmer, software engineer, consulting company executive*

**Highland**
Kells, Albert John *mergers and acquisitions consultant*

Ratcliff, Carter Goodrich *writer, critic, poet*
Ratick, Randie H. *music educator, elementary school educator*

**Highland Mills**
Gross, Mary Anne *author, educator*

**Hillsdale**
Lunde, Asbjorn Rudolph *lawyer*
Parmet, Herbert Samuel *historian, writer*

**Holland**
Loockerman, William Delmer *retired educational administrator*

**Holley**
Ruck, Rosemarie Ulissa *retired social worker, freelance/self-employed writer*

**Hollis**
Jairam, Khelanand Vishvaykanand *lawyer*

**Holtsville**
Iannuzzi, Salvatore *information technology executive*
Lieb, Peter *lawyer*

**Homer**
Bull, Beverly Jane *piano and voice educator*
Gustafson, John Alfred *biology professor*

**Honeoye Falls**
Hillabrandt, Larry Lee *service industry executive*

**Hoosick Falls**
Dodge, Cleveland Earl, Jr. *retired manufacturing executive, director*

**Hopewell Junction**
Donovan, Andrew Joseph *financial consultant*
Lemy, Marie Edith *psychologist, educator*
Nayfeh, Hasan Munir *research scientist*
Novak, Robert Dennis *contractor, real estate developer*

**Hornell**
Piper, W. Stephen *healthcare educator*

**Horseheads**
Andrake, Nancy Carolyn *retired secondary school educator*
Clark, Judy Ann *elementary school educator*

**Houghton**
Chamberlain, Daniel Robert *college president*
Howard, David Allyn *history professor*
Luckey, Robert Reuel Raphael *retired academic administrator*

**Howard Beach**
Leiter, Samuel L. *theater educator*

**Hudson**
Agata, Burton C. *lawyer, educator*
Bothma, Stef-Albert *artist*
Loder, Randolph James *music educator*
Miner, Jacqueline *political consultant*

**Hunter**
Khanzadian, Vahan *tenor*

**Huntington**
Alsop, Reese Fell *medical educator*
Benny, Sandra Marie *artist*
Brettschneider, Rita Roberta Fischman *lawyer*
Christiansen, Donald David *electrical engineer, editor, publishing executive, consultant*
Connor, Joseph Robert *editor*
Engstrand, Beatrice C. *neurologist, educator*
German, June Resnick *lawyer*
Hochberg, Ronald Mark *lawyer*
Kirwin, Barbara Rosa *forensic specialist*
Klein, Richard Daniel *law educator*
LaTourrette, James Thomas *retired electrophysics, electrical engineering and computer science educator*
Masear, Claude *music educator, musician*
Morris, Jeffrey Brandon *law educator*
Munson, Nancy K. *lawyer*
Oler, Kim *voice educator*
Roberts, Elizabeth Anne Stephens *educational consultant*
Selkirk, Alexander MacDonald, Jr. *lawyer*
Sforza, Alfred Vincent *dentist, educator, writer*
Slutsky, Leonard Alan *finance executive, educator*
Tar, Laszlo *artist*
Tucker, William P. *lawyer, writer*

**Huntington Station**
Agosta, Vito *mechanical and aerospace engineering educator*
Cannistraci, Diane Frances *sales executive*
Nagin, Mary Deborah *artist*
Stevens, Susan Seltenreich Cirillo *special education educator*
Williams, Una Joyce *psychiatric social worker*

**Hurley**
Opdahl, Viola Elizabeth *secondary school educator*
Petruski, Jennifer Andrea *speech and language pathologist*
Smith, Lewis Motter, Jr. *retired advertising and direct marketing executive*

**Hyde Park**
Beckmann, Kathleen Ann *music educator*
Hunt, Mark Alan *museum director*
Koch, Cynthia M. *library director*
Rider, Kathleen Mary *dietician*
Ryan, L. Timothy *chef, educator, academic administrator*

**Ilion**
Gay, Douglas MacKenzie *pharmacologist*
Nemyier, Margaret Gertrude *sales executive*

**Interlaken**
Bleiler, Everett Franklin *writer, publishing company executive*

**Irving**
Snyder, Barry E., Sr. *Native American tribal leader*

**Irvington**
Carey, Edward John *utilities executive*
Jackson, Thomas Gene *lawyer*
Lippmann, Janet Gurian *artist, art gallery owner*
Yablon, Leonard Harold *publishing executive*

**Islandia**
Artzt, Russell M. *electronics executive*
Cooper, Nancy E. *computer software company executive*
Cron, Kenneth D. *information technology executive*
Gupta, Yogesh *software company executive*
Handal, Kenneth V. *lawyer*
Pruzansky, Joshua Murdock *lawyer*
Robinson, Douglas *computer company executive*
Swainson, John *software company executive*

**Islip**
Ramsden, Virginia Ann *retired music educator*

**Ithaca**
Abrams, Meyer Howard *language educator*
Alexander, Gregory Stewart *law educator*
Alexander, Martin *microbiologist, educator*
Arquit, Nora Harris *retired music educator, writer*
Ascher, Robert *anthropologist, educator, archaeologist, film producer*
Ashcroft, Neil William *physics professor, researcher*
Barcelo, John James III *law educator*
Bassett, William Akers *retired geologist, educator*
Basu, Kaushik *economics professor*
Bauman, Dale Elton *nutritional biochemistry professor*
Beneria, Lourdes *economist, educator*
Berkelman, Karl *retired physics professor*
Bilderback, Donald Heywood *physicist, researcher*
Billera, Louis J(oseph) *mathematics professor*
Bourne, Russell *publisher, author*
Bramble, James Henry *mathematician, educator*
Brazell, Karen Woodard *literature educator*
Buhrman, Robert A. *physics professor, researcher*
Burns, Joseph Arthur *planetary science educator*
Carlin, Herbert J. *electrical engineering educator, researcher*
Chapman, Lewis Duane *economist*
Cisne, John Luther *mineralogist, educator*
Clermont, Kevin Michael *law educator*
Clune, JoAnn Guardalibene *retired nurse*
Colby-Hall, Alice Mary *language educator*
Cottrell, G. Walton *manufacturing executive*
Craighead, Harold G. *physicist, educator*
Cramton, Roger Conant *lawyer, educator*
Csaki, Csaba *physicist*
Culler, Jonathan Dwight *English language educator*
Daouk, Hazem *finance educator*
Darlington, Richard Benjamin *retired psychologist, retired educator, researcher*
Davies, Peter John *plant physiology educator, researcher*
De Boer, Pieter Cornelis Tobias *mechanical and aerospace engineering educator*
Dev, Chekitan *science educator*
Dick, Richard Irwin *environmental engineer, educator*
Dietert, Rodney Reynolds *immunology and toxicology educator*
Dyckman, Thomas Richard *accountant, educator*
Dynkin, Eugene B. *mathematics professor*
Earle, Clifford John, Jr. *mathematician*
Easley, David *economics professor*
Eastman, Lester Fuess *electrical engineer, educator*
Eddy, Donald Davis *language educator*
Eells, Gregory Todd *psychologist, director*
Eisenberg, Theodore *law educator*
Eisner, Thomas *biologist, educator*
Elber, Ron *computer science educator*
Erickson, David *educator*
Fick, Gary Warren *agronomist, educator*
Firebaugh, Francille Maloch *academic administrator*
Fireside, Harvey Francis *political scientist, educator*
Fitchen, Douglas Beach *physicist, researcher*
Fitzpatrick, John Weaver *ornithologist, researcher*
Fontaine, Michael Till (Michael Scott) *humanities educator*
Foote, Robert Hutchinson *medical educator*
Freed, Jack Herschel *chemist, educator*
Fuchs, W. Kent *engineering educator*
Garrison, Elizabeth Jane *artist*
Germain, Claire Madeleine *law librarian, educator, lawyer*
Gillett, James Warren *ecotoxicology educator*
Ginsparg, Paul *physicist*
Gold, Michael Evan *law educator*
Goldsmith, Paul Felix *physics professor, astronomy professor*
Gottfried, Kurt *physicist, researcher*
Green, Edward Thomas, Jr. *education educator*
Greene, Harry W. *biology professor*
Greisen, Kenneth Ingvard *physicist, emeritus educator*
Grippi, Salvatore William *artist*
Groos, Arthur Bernhard, Jr. *German studies educator, music educator*
Gross, Leonard *mathematics professor*
Hairston, Nelson George, Jr. *ecologist, educator*
Haith, Douglas A. *engineering educator, researcher*
Halpern, Bruce Peter *academic administrator, researcher, educator*
Hartmanis, Juris *computer scientist, educator*
Hay, George Alan *law and economics educator*
Heckathorn, Douglas D. *sociologist, educator, epidemiologist*
Henry, Susan Armstrong *biology professor, dean*
Hess, George Paul *biochemist, educator*
Hillman, Robert Andrew *lawyer, educator, retired dean*

Hoffmann, Roald *chemist, educator*
Hohendahl, Peter Uwe *German language and literature educator*
Hojnowski, Jules Austin *entrepreneur*
Holcomb, Donald Frank *physicist, academic administrator*
Hopcroft, John Edward *computer scientist, educator*
Hoy, Ronald Raymond *neurobiology educator*
Husa, Karel *composer, conductor, educator*
Isakovic, Abdel *physicist, researcher*
Jagendorf, André Tridon *physiologist*
Jarrow, Robert Alan *economist, educator*
Kahn, Alfred Edward *economist, educator, government official*
Kallfelz, Francis A. *veterinary medicine educator*
Kenkel, Donald Scott *economist*
Kennedy, Kenneth Adrian Raine *biological anthropologist, forensic anthropologist*
Kennedy, Wilbert Keith, Sr. *agronomy educator, retired university official*
Kimes, Sheryl Elaine *business educator*
Kingsbury, John Merriam *botanist, educator*
Kinoshita, Toichiro *physicist*
Kleinberg, Jon M. *computer scientist, educator*
Korf, Richard Paul *mycology educator*
Koschmann, J. Victor *history professor, academic program director*
LaCapra, Dominick Charles *historian, educator*
LaFeber, Walter Frederick *historian, educator, writer*
Lee, David Morris *physics professor*
Leibovich, Sidney *engineering educator*
Lengemann, Frederick William *retired physiology educator*
Leopold, A. Carl *plant physiologist*
Lesser, William Henri *marketing educator*
Lifton, Barbara *state legislator, secondary school educator*
Loucks, Daniel Peter *environmental systems engineer*
Lovelace, Richard Van Evera *education educator, research scientist*
Lowi, Theodore Jay *political science professor*
Lumley, John Leask *physicist, researcher*
Lyons, Thomas Patrick *economics professor*
Mackin, Jeanne Ann *journalist, educator*
Mai, William Frederick *plant nematologist, educator*
Majumdar, Mukul Kumar *economist, educator*
Martin, Peter William *lawyer, educator*
Maxwell, William Laughlin *retired industrial engineering educator*
McConkey, James Rodney *literature and language educator, writer*
McCue, Arthur Harry *artist, educator*
McDougal, Stuart Yeatman *comparative literature educator, author*
McGuire, William *civil engineer, educator*
McLafferty, Fred Warren *chemist, educator*
McMurry, John Edward *chemistry professor*
McQuade, Tyler *chemist*
Merle, H. Etienne *restaurateur*
Meyburg, Arnim Hans *transportation engineer, educator, consultant*
Mikhailichenko, Alexander A. *physicist, researcher*
Mikus, Eleanore Ann *artist*
Mooney, Kailen Andrews *ecologist, educator*
Morgan, Robert *writer, poet, educator*
Morgenstern, Matthew *computer scientist*
Mortlock, Robert Paul *microbiologist, educator*
Mueller, Betty Jeanne *social work educator*
Neisser, Ulric *psychology professor*
Nerode, Anil *mathematician, educator*
Nicholson, Sean *science educator*
Nikitin, Alexander Yu. *pathologist*
Norton, Mary Beth *history educator, writer*
Novak, Cheryl Donald *science educator*
Oh, HyungSeon *power systems researcher*
Oliver, Jack Ertle *geophysicist, educator*
Olpadwala, Porus *architecture educator, dean*
Orlov, Yuri F. *nuclear physicist, human rights activist*
O'Rourke, Thomas Denis *civil engineer, educator*
Park, Roy Hampton, Jr. *advertising executive*
Pelto, Gretel H. *nutritional anthropologist, educator*
Perry, Margaret *librarian, writer*
Phelan, Richard Magruder *mechanical engineer*
Pimentel, David *entomologist, educator*
Pinstrup-Andersen, Per *economist, educator*
Pohl, Robert Otto *physics professor*
Poleskie, Stephen Francis *retired art educator, artist, writer, publisher*
Poppensiek, George Charles *retired veterinary scientist, retired educator*
Porte, Joel Miles *language educator*
Provine, William B. *biology professor*
Rader, Nancy Louise de Villiers *psychology professor, consultant*
Radzinowicz, Mary Ann *language educator*
Rawlings, Hunter Ripley III *classicist, former academic administrator*
Regenstein, Joe M. *food scientist, educator*
Reppy, John David, Jr. *physicist, educator*
Rhodes, Frank Harold Trevor *academic administrator, geologist*
Richardson, Robert Coleman *physics professor, researcher*
Rinaldo, Peter Merritt *publishing executive*
Rivas, Ariel L. *biomedical researcher, educator*
Roberts, E. F. *law educator*
Rodríguez, Ferdinand *chemical engineer, educator*
Sakai, Naoki *literature and language professor*
Salpeter, Edwin Ernest *physical sciences educator*
Scheraga, Harold Abraham *physical chemistry professor*
Schlafer, Donald Hughes *veterinary pathologist*
Schneiderman, Anne Mercedes *lawyer, neurobiologist*
Schuler, Mary Callaghan *artist, educational association administrator*
Schwab, Stewart Jon *dean, law educator*
Schwartz, Donald Franklin *communication scientist*
Scott, Norman Roy *academic administrator, agricultural engineer, educator*
Shore, Richard Arnold *mathematics professor*
Silbey, Joel Henry *history professor*
Skorton, David Jan *academic administrator*
Smidt, Seymour *economics professor*

Smith, Julian Cleveland, Jr. *chemical engineering professor*
Smith, Robert John *anthropology educator*
Sosna, Morton Philip *historian, academic administrator*
Squier, Jack Leslie *sculptor, educator*
Squyres, Steven Weldon *astronomy educator, planetary geology researcher*
Steinberg, Michael Philip *history professor*
Stycos, Maria Nowakowska *adult education educator*
Summers, Robert Samuel *lawyer, author, educator*
Swieringa, Robert Jay *dean, accounting educator*
Temple, Elise *neuroscientist*
Thomas, J. Earl *retired physicist*
Thomas, Sarah E. *librarian*
Thorbecke, Erik *economics professor*
Thoron, Gray *lawyer, educator*
Tomek, William Goodrich *agricultural economist*
Trautmann, Nancy Morton *science educator, writer*
Trotter, Leslie Earl *operations research specialist, educator*
Vanek, Jaroslav *economist, educator*
Viands, Donald Rex *plant breeder, educator*
Walcott, Charles *neurobiology and behavior educator*
Waldman, Michael *economist, educator*
Wasserman, Robert Harold *biology professor*
Welch, Ross Maynard *plant physiologist, educator*
Whitaker, Susanne Kanis *veterinary medical librarian*
Widom, Benjamin *chemistry professor*
Williams, Peggy Ryan *academic administrator*
Wills, Michael Stephen *nutritionist, quality assurance professional*
Wootton, John Francis *physiology educator*
York, James Wesley, Jr. *theoretical physicist, educator*

**Jackson Heights**
Chang, Lydia Liang-Hwa *social worker, educator*
Dacey, Paul *artist*
Morrow, Nana Kwasi Scott Douglas *choreographer, director, writer, filmmaker, educator*
Sohmer, Bernard *mathematics professor, administrator*
Stevenson, Amanda (Sandy Stevens) *librettist, composer, songwriter*

**Jamaica**
Angione, Howard Francis *lawyer, retired editor*
Bartilucci, Andrew Joseph *university administrator*
Benson, James Allen *library science educator, academic administrator*
Brown, Kenneth Lloyd *lawyer*
Bunshaft, Charles Edward *elementary school educator, consultant*
Cade, Walter III *artist, actor, musician, vocalist*
Carey, Elaine *education educator, historian*
Castro-Blanco, James *law educator*
Chirico, Donna M. *psychologist, educator, researcher*
Chropufka, Mark A. *information technology executive, poet*
Cline, Janice Claire *education educator*
Coppa, Frank John *historian, educator*
Daly, Mary C. *dean, law educator*
Davis-Jerome, Eileen George *educational consultant, principal*
Faust, Naomi Flowe *education educator*
Flake, Floyd Harold *former congressman*
Galante, Thomas W. *library director*
Garner, Steven C. *radiologist, emergency physician*
Gati, William Eugene *architect, educator*
Geffner, Donna Sue *speech pathology/audiology services professional, audiologist, educator*
Greenberg, Jacob *biochemist, educator, consultant*
Harmond, Richard Peter *historian, educator*
Harrington, Donald James *university president*
Jawin, Ann Juliano *human resource specialist*
Kaplan, Carolyn Sue *elementary school educator*
Keizs, Marcia V. *academic administrator*
Kemeny, M. Margaret *oncologist, surgeon, educator, hospital administrator*
Lee, Joseph *musician, educator*
Lees, Francis *economics professor*
Parmet, Robert David *historian, educator*
Pratt-Johnson, Yvonne Karen *education professor*
Sciame, Joseph *university administrator*
Skirde, Edward George *academic administrator, consultant*

**Jamestown**
Bogey, Brian Allen *secondary school educator, music educator, director*
DJang, Arthur H.K. *pathologist, preventive medicine physician*
Idzik, Martin Francis *lawyer*
Langworthy, Traci I. *history professor*
Walker, Timothy Craig *transportation executive*
Wellman, Barclay Ormes *furniture company executive*

**Jamesville**
DeCrow, Karen *lawyer, educator, writer*

**Jefferson**
Sullivan, Jim *artist*

**Jeffersonville**
Craft, Douglas Durwood *artist*
Harms, Elizabeth Louise *artist*

**Jericho**
Astuto, Philip Louis *retired language educator*
Blau, Harvey Ronald *lawyer*
Dore, Kathleen A. *broadcast executive*
Edson, Andrew Stephen *public relations executive*
Rosen, Robert Arnold *management consultant, real estate owner, manager, developer, investor, farmer*
Schell, Norman Barnett *preventive medicine physician, consultant*
Shinners, Stanley Marvin *electrical engineer*
Spatafore, Anthony R. *financial executive*

**Johnson City**
De Angelo, Jan Joseph *music educator*

Goddard, Bryan Lance *physician, director*
McMillen, Marieta Louise *art educator*

**Johnstown**
DiNitto, Andrew Joseph *political scientist, educator*
Gibson, Jahnn Hansen Swanker *mental health nurse*

**Katonah**
Bashkow, Theodore Robert *electrical engineering consultant, former educator*
Bauman, Jonathan Hugh *psychiatrist*
Brownlee, Delphine *actress, musician*
Carlson, Karen Beth *elementary school educator*
Fry, John *magazine editor*
Giobbi, Edward Giacchino *artist*
Levine, Pamela Gail *business owner*
McCauley, Gerard Francis *literary agent*
Simpson, William Kelly *curator, Egyptologist, educator*
Wenglowski, Gary Martin *economist*

**Kendall**
Rak, Linda Marie *elementary school educator, consultant*

**Kenmore**
Elibol, Tarik *gastroenterologist, educator*
Kenny, John Edward *computer analyst*
Kuhn, William Andrew *music educator*

**Kenoza Lake**
Baumgardner, Matthew Clay *artist*

**Keuka Park**
Armstrong, James Francis III *language educator, writer*

**Kew Gardens**
Adler, David Neil *lawyer*
Aldea, Patricia *architect*
Chen, Yuanlin *composer*
Chipkin, Frederick *textile designer, consultant, artist, writer*
Marshall, Helen M. *city manager*

**Kinderhook**
McCreight, JoAnn Oakley *retired librarian*

**Kings Park**
Fay, Thomas A. *philosopher, educator*
Greene, Robert William *communications educator, media consultant*

**Kings Point**
Mazek, Warren F(elix) *dean, economics professor*
Stewart, Joseph D. *career military officer, academic administrator*

**Kingston**
Johnson, Marie-Louise Tully *dermatologist, educator*
McGuire, Thomas Peter *water transportation executive, secondary school educator*
Tsirpanlis, Constantine N. *theology, philosophy, classics and history educator*

**Kirkwood**
Skinner, Christopher G. *protective services official, farmer*

**La Fayette**
Amidon, David R. *science educator, coach*
Cady, Duane Maynard *surgeon*

**Lake Luzerne**
Goldstein, Manfred *retired management consultant*

**Lake Peekskill**
Bloom, Janet K *audio-visual specialist, poet*
Cutrone, Ronnie Blaise *artist*

**Lake Placid**
Grimmette, Mark *Olympic athlete*
Martin, Brian *Olympic athlete*
Pappalardo, Rosa Gloria *secondary school educator*
Reiss, Paul J. *academic administrator*
Rossi, Ronald Aldo *sports association administrator, Olympic athlete*

**Lake Success**
Lee, Brian Edward *lawyer*
Uchida, Kinya *consumer products company executive*

**Lakewood**
Anderson, Raymond Quintus *diversified company executive*
Deppas, Louis Anthony *financial adviser*

**Lancaster**
Meides, Holly Sue *music educator*
Neumaier, Gerhard John *environmental services administrator, consultant*
Walsh, Edward F. *social studies educator*

**Lansing**
Emelett, Stephen John *electrical engineer, researcher*

**Larchmont**
Berridge, George Bradford *retired lawyer*
Bloom, Lee Hurley *lawyer, consultant, retired consumer products company executive*
Burkett, Bradford Charles *lawyer*
Cavanna, Dino Francesco *chemicals executive*
Folter, Roland *historian, rare book dealer, writer*
Greenwald, Carol Schiro *professional services marketing research executive*
Hinerfeld, Norman Martin *manufacturing executive*
Hinerfeld, Ruth G. *civic organization executive*
Kaufmann, Henry Mark *mortgage banker*
Levi, James Harry *real estate executive, investment banker*
McSherry, William John, Jr. *lawyer, consultant*
Pelton, Russell Gilbert *retired lawyer*

Plumez, Jean Paul *advertising executive, consultant*
Quigley, Martin Schofield *writer, educator*
Rainier, Robert Paul *publisher, consultant*
Rockland, Lawrence Howard *psychiatrist, educator*
Siegel, Nathaniel Harold *sociology educator*
Sklarew, Robert Jay *biomedical research educator, consultant*
Stahl, William Martin *retired surgeon*
White, Thomas Edward *lawyer*
Wit, David Edmund *software company executive*

**Latham**
Catalano, Jane Donna *lawyer*
Conway, Robert George, Jr. *lawyer*
Irwin, Heather May *writer, interior designer*
Schwartz, Robert William *management consultant*
Stallman, Donald Lee *environmental executive*
Wilkes, Brent Ames *management consultant*

**Lawrence**
Berman, Carol *retired commissioner*
Henriquez, Allen *artist*

**Levittown**
Lambert, Bruce *journalist*
Massie, Clifford Michael *music company executive*
Vitello, Paul *journalist*

**Lewiston**
Dexter, Theodore Henry *chemist*
Henry, Leo R. *Native American tribal leader*
LoTempio, Julia Matild *retired accountant*
Moraca-Sawicki, Anne Marie *oncology nurse*
Sheeran, Maureen Flynn *retired secondary school educator*

**Lindenhurst**
Hungerford, Gary A. *insurance executive, columnist, writer, editor*
Kaufman, Susan Shiffman *psychologist*
Snider, Dee (David Daniel Snider) *rock singer, composer, radio personality*

**Little Falls**
Veeder, Donna Clark *artist*

**Little Neck**
Overton, Rosilyn Gay Hoffman *finance company executive*
Weinblatt, Alan S. *psychologist*

**Liverpool**
De Long, Jacob Edward *real estate broker*
Hamlett, James Gordon *electronics engineer, management consultant, educator*
Wightman, Sharon Leilani *librarian*

**Livingston Manor**
Root, Stuart Dowling *lawyer, retired government agency administrator, retired banker*

**Lloyd Harbor**
Sheard, Charles III *dermatologist*

**Lockport**
Carr, Edward Albert, Jr. *pharmacologist, educator, physician*
Leader, Bruce Robert *secondary school educator*
Ludwig, Patricia Marie *pastor*
Penney, Charles Rand *lawyer, civic worker*
Schultz, Gerald Alfred (Jerry Schultz) *retired chemicals executive*
Steinagle, Martin Gene *contractor, paralegal, poet, writer*

**Locust Valley**
Bentel, Carol Rusche *architect*
Bentel, Frederick Richard *architect, educator*
Bentel, Paul Louis *architect, educator*
Comfort, William Twyman, Jr. *banker*
Fairman, Joel Martin *retired broadcast executive*
Fletcher, Mary Lee *retired marketing professional*
Schor, Joseph Martin *pharmaceutical executive, biochemist*
Zulch, Joan Carolyn *retired medical publishing company executive*

**Long Beach**
Cahill, Joan *nun, educator*
Gach, Jay Anthony *composer*
Robbins, Jeffrey Howard *media consultant, research writer, educator*
Shahda Geraci, Carole Anne *elementary school educator*

**Long Eddy**
Hoiby, Lee *composer, concert pianist*

**Long Island City**
Convery, Robert *composer, educator*
Coogan, Timothy Christopher, II, *history professor, researcher*
DiGiovanni, Eleanor Elma *scaffold installation company executive*
Dromm, Daniel Patrick *elementary school educator*
Giaimo, Kathryn Ann *performing arts company executive*
Goodwin, Guy *retired art educator*
Henrikson, C. Robert *insurance company executive*
Lieberman, Janet Elaine *academic administrator*
Lucca, Louis Anthony *academic administrator*
Markus, Maura *bank executive*
McCoy, Ann *artist*
Rein, Catherine Amelia *insurance company executive, lawyer*
Roberts, Kathleen Joy Doty *secondary school educator*
Russo, Lorraine *humanities educator*
Sadao, Shoji *architect*
Young, Aaron *conceptual artist*

**Loudonville**
Booker, James *economics professor, consultant*
Burstein, Sharon Ann *corporate communications specialist, apparel designer*
Toal, James Francis *academic administrator*

**Mahopac**
Gonzalez-Tornero, Sergio *artist*
McCluskey, Frank Bryce *director*

**Malverne**
Benigno, Thomas Daniel *lawyer*
Pollio, Ralph Thomas *editor, consultant*

**Mamaroneck**
Coleman, Marshall Donald *psychiatrist, psychoanalyst*
Halpern, Abraham Leon *psychiatrist*
Martin, Roger Harry *retired college president*
McEnroe, Patrick *former professional tennis player, sports commentator*
McLarnon, Mary Frances *neurologist*
Mizrahi, Abraham Mordechay *retired health products executive, pediatrician*
Pritts, Gloria Piccia *historian*

**Manhasset**
Black, Robert *lawyer*
Bosworth, Jay L. *radiation oncologist*
Brand, Oscar *folk singer, writer, educator*
Budman, Cathy Linda *psychiatrist, physician*
Burke, Alexander James, Jr. *publishing executive*
Calvin, Donald Lee *stock exchange official*
Dabideen, Darrin *research scientist*
D'Olimpio, James Thomas *oncologist*
Esposito, Rick Anthony *physician, thoracic surgeon*
Evans, Bob (Robert Evans) *publishing executive*
Foerst, John George, Jr. *retired fundraising executive*
Gardner, Robert *financial services executive*
Kaminsky, Arthur Charles *lawyer*
Milhorat, Thomas Herrick *neurosurgeon*
Pitti, Donald Robert *financial consultant*
Pogo, Gustave Javier *cardiothoracic surgeon*
Rochelson, Burton L. *obstetrician*
Savage, Clare Leavy *school psychologist*
Schiller, Arthur A. *architect, educator*
Sirooni, Anahid Alice *composer*
Stevens, Thelma Kaplan *artist, educator*
Tippy, Margaret O'Shea *psychologist*
Vizard, Michael *periodical editor*
Wachtler, Sol *lawyer, educator*
Wallace, Richard *editor, writer*
Weitzner, Steve *publishing executive*

**Manlius**
Booth, Patricia Vogt (Trish Booth) *educational consultant*
Cotter, William Donald *retired commissioner, retired editor*
Harriff, Suzanna Elizabeth Bahner *media consultant*
Martonosi, Anthony Nicholas *biochemistry professor, researcher*
O'Reilly, Mary *environmental scientist, educator*
Prior, John Thompson *pathology educator*
Zlomek, Elizabeth A. *customer service/business processes specialist*

**Marcellus**
Baker, Bruce Roy *artist, illustrator*
Pirozzi, Mildred Jean *retired nursing administrator*
Taylor, Robert Wilson *military officer, publishing executive*

**Marlboro**
Parker, Marion Hawkins *retired librarian*

**Maspeth**
Blitz, Nelson, Jr. *entrepreneur*
Heppa, Douglas Van *computer specialist*
Khashu, Bushan *urologist*

**Massapequa**
Turk, Elizabeth Ann *music educator*
Van Gorder, John Frederic *lawyer*
Zwanger, Jerome *physician*

**Massapequa Park**
Blake, Diane Patricia *elementary school educator*

**Mechanicville**
Rhodes, Alan Charles *minister*

**Mecklenburg**
Baptist, Edward E. *history professor*

**Medford**
Brower, Robert Charles *rehabilitation counselor, small business owner*
Kealey, Edward J. *priest, historian*
Lieberman, Carol *healthcare marketing communications consultant*
Saunders, Audrey J. *tax specialist, writer*
Snyder, Mark Jeffrey *financial planner, actuary*

**Medusa**
Groom, Winston Francis, Jr. *writer*

**Melville**
Bergman, Stanley M. *health products executive*
Bongiorno, Joseph John, Jr. *electrical engineering educator*
Breslawski, James P. *health products executive*
Bultan, Aykut *communications systems engineer*
Campofranco, Salvatore *real estate company executive*
Copperman, Stuart Morton *pediatrician, educator*
Damadian, Raymond Vahan *biophysicist*
Davidson, Justin *music critic*
Dooley, James C. *newspaper editor, director of photography*
Ettinger, Michael Saul *lawyer*
Grayson, Gerald Herbert *economist, educator, arbitrator, writer*
Henley, Deborah S. *newspaper editor*
Hildebrand, John Frederick *columnist, educator*
Kanas, John Adam *bank executive*
Kissinger, Walter Bernhard *retired automotive executive*
Klurfeld, James Michael *journalist*
Knight, Timothy P. *publishing executive*
Komaroff, Stanley *lawyer*
Kornberg, Fred *electronics executive*

Krenek, Debby *newspaper editor*
Lane, Arthur Alan *lawyer*
Mancini, John *editor, publishing executive*
McKeon, John C. *publishing executive*
Minicozzi, Rob *electronics executive*
Mitchell, William Edmund *electronics executive*
Moran, Paul James *journalist, columnist*
Olesen, Robert Lind Ole *electrical engineer*
Pinto, Janet Sue *music educator*
Richards, Carol Ann Rubright *retired editor, retired journalist*
Schmid, Charles Ernest *acoustical engineer, academic administrator*
Settle, Mark *information technology executive*
Sobol, Elise Schwarcz *music educator*
Taub, Jesse J. *electrical engineering researcher*
Waddell, John Comer *electronics distribution company executive*
Webber, Pamela D. *information technology executive*

**Merrick**
Cariola, Robert Joseph *artist*
Cherry, Harold *insurance company executive*
Fleischman, Francine D. *secondary school educator*
Garfinkel, Lawrence Saul *academic administrator, educator, television producer*
Gutnik, Zhanna *gastroenterologist, consultant*
Harrison, Marjorie Freeman *secondary education educator, librarian*
Howard, Joyce Anne *elementary school educator*
Poppel, Seth Raphael *entrepreneur*
Sardo, Sanford *music educator*

**Mexico**
Halse, Frank Adams, Jr. *retired minister*
Sade, Donald Stone *anthropology educator*

**Middle Island**
Andrews, Gaylen *public relations executive*
Linick, Andrew S. *direct marketing expert*

**Middle Village**
Katz, Harvey I. *secondary school educator*
Kolatch, Alfred Jacob *publisher*
Walter, John Frederick *historical researcher, genealogist*

**Middletown**
Bedell, Barbara Lee *journalist*
Chevalier, Stefan Gary *plastic surgeon*
Fucci, Joseph Leonard *editor, college librarian*
Henderson, Thomas Emmett *retired language educator, rare book dealer*
Kossar, Ronald Steven *lawyer*
Ojeda, Joseph A. *psychotherapist*
Radeboldt-Daly, Karen Elaine *retired medical/surgical nurse*

**Millbrook**
Burbank, Kershaw *writer*
Della-Volpe, Ralph Eugene *artist*
Duesberry, Joellyn Toler *artist*
Flexner, Josephine Moncure *musician, educator*
Flexner, Kurt Fisher *economist, educator*
Grant, Stephen Allen *lawyer*
Hall, Penelope Coker *editor, writer*
Likens, Gene Elden *biology and ecology educator*

**Millerton**
Hastings, Donald Francis *actor, writer*

**Mineola**
Bartlett, Clifford Adams, Jr. *lawyer*
Christiansen, Colleen M. *physician assistant*
Greenberg, Abby J. *physician*
Halloran, Daniel James *lawyer*
Hammer, Deborah Marie *librarian, paralegal*
Kokotos, William J. *cardiothoracic surgeon*
Lynn, Robert Patrick, Jr. *lawyer*
McGonigle, James Gregory *financial consultant*
Miller, Loring Erik *insurance agent, broker*
Niederman, Michael Steven *physician, educator*
O'Connell, Maureen C. *county official, former state legislator*
Paterson, Basil Alexander *lawyer*
Schaffer, David Irving *lawyer*
Tankoos, Sandra Maxine *court reporting services executive*

**Mohegan Lake**
Paik, John Kee *structural engineer*

**Monroe**
Dierna, Joseph Biagio *construction company executive, land development consultant*
Fontana, John Arthur *employee benefits specialist*
Furman-Markowitz, Joanna Florence *dance educator*
Martin, Stanley Donald *publishing executive, editor*
Winslow, DeLana Lynn *business educator*

**Monsey**
Erickson, Barbara Martha *historian, writer*

**Montauk**
Butler, Thomas William *retired health and social services administrator*
Kahn, Richard Dreyfus *lawyer*
Lavenas, Suzanne *writer, editor, consultant*

**Montgomery**
Moore, Virginia Lee Smith *elementary school educator*
Teutul, Paul, Sr. *television personality, mechanic*

**Montrose**
Matthias, George Frank *retired secondary school educator*

**Morrisonville**
Fuller, Katherine T. *science educator, department chairman*

**Morrisville**
Shayya, Walid H. *natural resources engineer*

**Mount Kisco**
Dore, Anita Wilkes *language educator*
Eastburn, John S., Jr. *venture capitalist*
Frieder, Samuel P. *venture capitalist*
Green, Paul Eliot, Jr. *retired optical engineer*
Hayworth, Scott David *physician*
Hodara, Susan Mina *writer*
Kilbourn, Joseph A. *lawyer*
Kohlberg, James A. *venture capitalist*
Kohlberg, Jerome, Jr., (Jerry Kohlberg) *venture capitalist, lawyer*
Kutty, Malik Anisjervan *plastic surgeon*
Lacovara, Christopher *venture capitalist*
Laster, Richard *biotechnologist, consultant*
Novak, Gregory *marketing professional*
Perez, Louis Anthony *radiologist*
Powell, Jeffrey Scott *endocrinologist*
Romeyn, Prescott C. *venture capitalist*
Schneider, Robert Jay *oncologist*
Wildstein, Evan *venture capitalist*

**Mount Morris**
Leyerle, William Dean *music educator, publishing executive*
Mistretta, Theresa Mary *retired elementary school educator*

**Mount Sinai**
Feinberg, Sheldon Norman *pediatrician, educator*
Kopp, Richard Edgar *electrical engineer*

**Mount Vernon**
Chagula, Paul Machiya *information technology executive, consultant*
Elkind, Arthur H. *physician*
NelsonWilliams, Cecelia Elaine *dietician, nutritionist*
Rossini, Joseph *contracting and development corporate executive*
Sherrill, Milton Lewis *sculptor, painter*
Weisman, Richard Scott *lawyer*
Young, Paula Eva *animal shelter director*

**Munnsville**
Carruth, Hayden *poet*

**Nanuet**
Hurd, David Gary *music educator, actor, musician*

**Narrowsburg**
Krause, Gloria Rose *music educator*

**Nassau**
Benamati, Dennis Charles *librarian, editor, consultant*
Moldoff, William Morris *retired lawyer*

**Nedrow**
Lyons, Oren *Native American chieftain, conservationist*

**Neponsit**
Nicastri, Ann Gilbert *science educator*
Re, Edward Domenic *law educator, retired judge*

**New Berlin**
Tyler, Jean M. *special education services professional*

**New City**
Borelli, Francis J(oseph) (Frank Borelli) *diversified financial services company executive*
Esser, Aristide Henri *psychiatrist*
McCullagh, James Charles *publishing executive*
O'Dowd, Charles Edwyn *physician*

**New Hampton**
Sinnard, Elaine Janice *painter, sculptor*

**New Hartford**
Anthony, Donald Charles *librarian, educator*
Boyle, William Leo, Jr. *educational consultant, retired academic administrator*
Chapin, Mary Q. *arbitrator, director, mediator, writer*
Weiss, Holly Anne *music educator, singer*

**New Hyde Park**
Agin, Herbert *real estate company executive*
Badlani, Gopal *medical educator*
Bonagura, Vincent R. *pediatrician, educator, researcher*
Esiason, Boomer (Norman Julius Esiason) *professional football player*
Flynn, Michael J. *real estate executive*
Gecelter, Gary Raymond *gastrointestinal surgeon, researcher*
Goldberg, Itzhak D. *radiation oncologist*
Henry, David B. *real estate company executive*
Hyman, Abraham *electrical engineer*
Jacobson, Marc Stephen *pediatrician, educator*
Jaffe, Richard S. *lawyer*
Klein, George *manufacturing company executive, systems analyst, consultant*
Lanzkowsky, Philip *physician*
Lehrer, Stanley *magazine publisher, editorial director, museum exhibitor*
Love, Charito *nuclear medicine physician, researcher*
Low, Frederick Emerson *language educator*
Mealie, Carl A. *emergency physician, educator*
Medarov, Boris I. *pulmonologist, researcher, critical care physician*
Myssiorek, David *surgeon*
Neal, Elaine Zirli *health products executive*
Offner, Eric Delmonte *lawyer*
Palestro, Christopher J. *physician*
Pappagallo, Michael V. *realty company executive*
Pegalis, Steven E. *lawyer*
Richards, Bernard *investment company executive*
Rini, Josephine Nancy *nuclear medicine physician*
Seltzer, Vicki Lynn *obstetrician, gynecologist*
Shenker, Ira Ronald *physician*
Smith, Robin Errol *pediatrician, neurologist, educator*
Vultaggio, Don J. (Dominick Vultaggio) *beverage company executive*

**New Paltz**
Azank, Roberto *artist*

Brown, Peter David Gilson *German language educator*
Chikwendu, Sunday C. *engineering educator, mathematician*
Emanuel-Smith, Robin Lesley *special education educator*
Flanagan Kelly, Anne Marie *academic administrator*
Lavallee, David Kenneth *chemistry professor, academic administrator*
Nyquist, Corinne Elaine *librarian*
Poskanzer, Steven Gary *academic administrator, lawyer*
Robinson, Anthony Christopher *novelist, educator*
Schnell, George Adam *geographer, educator*
Smith, Kathleen Tener *bank executive*

**New Rochelle**
Berlage, Gai Ingham *sociologist, researcher*
Black, Page Morton *civic worker, vocalist, musician*
Blotner, Norman David *lawyer, real estate broker, corporate financial executive*
Branch, William Blackwell *playwright, producer*
Cohen, Saul Bernard *retired academic administrator, geographer*
Fauci, Peter Anthony, Jr. *surgeon*
Ferencz, Benjamin Berell *lawyer*
Fitch, Nancy Elizabeth *historian, educator*
Frankl, Evan Stewart *secondary school educator*
Gallagher, John Francis *education educator*
Gitler, Bernard *cardiologist, critical care specialist*
Gunning, Francis Patrick *lawyer, insurance company executive*
Hasson, Adam Isaac *lawyer*
Leaf, Robert Jay *dental insurance consultant*
Lin, Joseph Pen-Tze *retired radiologist*
Margolin, Harold *metallurgical educator*
Menzies, Henry Hardinge *architect*
Perry-Böttinger, Lynne Valencia *interventional cardiologist*
Reddington, Mary Jane *retired secondary school educator*
Rovinsky, Joseph Judah *obstetrician, gynecologist*
Rutstein, Eleanor H. *psychologist*
Saperstein, David *writer, film director, television personality*
Schaffner, Adam David *plastic surgeon*
Slotnick, Mortimer H. *artist*
Sweeny, Stephen Jude *academic administrator*
Tassone, Gelsomina (Gessie Tassone) *metal products executive*

**New Windsor**
MacLeod, Mary Frances *mathematics educator*
Mandel, Joel Emanuel *orthopedist*

**New York**
Aaron, Roger S. *lawyer*
Aaron, Stewart D. *lawyer*
Abate, Catherine M. *retired state legislator*
Abatemarco, Tracy J. *lawyer*
Abbott, Geoffrey Winston *physiologist, researcher*
Abboud, Joseph M. *fashion designer*
Abdel Dayem, Hussein Mahmoud *nuclear medicine physician, radiology educator*
Abe, Nobuyasu *ambassador, international organization administrator*
Abelson, Alan *columnist*
Abelson, Reed *reporter*
Abernathy, James Logan *public relations executive*
Abish, Cecile *artist*
Abraham, Nader G. *biomedical scientist*
Abrahams, Robert M. *lawyer*
Abramovic, Marina *artist*
Abramowitz, Elkan *lawyer*
Abrams, Floyd *lawyer, educator*
Abrams, Robert *lawyer, state attorney general*
Abramson, Jill *newspaper publishing executive*
Abuhoff, Daniel Mark *lawyer*
Acevedo Marte, Matin *political organization worker*
Achenbaum, Alvin Allen *marketing and management consultant*
Ackerman, Lisa Marilyn *foundation administrator, consultant*
Acra, Reem *apparel designer*
Acrivos, Andreas *chemical engineering professor*
Adair, Wendell Hinton, Jr. *lawyer*
Adams, Bryan *vocalist, composer, photographer*
Adams, Daniel Nelson *lawyer*
Adams, Dennis Paul *artist*
Adams, George Bell *lawyer*
Adams, John Brett *investment banker, pharmaceutical executive*
Adams, John Coolidge *composer, conductor*
Adams, John Hamilton *lawyer*
Adams, Robert Brereton *lawyer*
Adams, Scott *cartoonist*
Adcroft, Patti (Patrice Gabriella Adcroft) *editor*
Adjemian, Vart K. *agricultural products executive*
Adler, Amy M. *law educator*
Adler, Barry E. *law educator, academic administrator*
Adler, Edward I. *media and entertainment company executive*
Adler, Jerry *journalist, writer*
Adler, Margot Susanna *journalist, radio producer, radio correspondent, writer*
Adler, Norman Tenner *psychology educator, dean*
Adler, Richard *composer, lyricist*
Adler, Stephen J. *editor-in-chief*
Adler, Tracy L. *curator*
Adlersberg, Jay Ben *internist*
Adri, (Adri Steckling Coen) *fashion designer*
Adrian, Barbara (Mrs. Franklin C. Tramutola) *artist*
Adrian, Tobias *economist*
Adubato, Richard Adam (Richie Adubato) *professional basketball coach*
Agisim, Philip *advertising executive, marketing executive*
Agostinelli, Robert Francesco *investment banker*
Aguiar, Yuri B. *advertising company executive*
Aguilera, Christina *vocalist*
Agwu, Nkechi Madonna *mathematics professor*
Ahmad, Jameel *civil engineer, researcher, educator*
Ahrens, Lynn *lyricist*
Ahrens, Thomas H. *communications executive*
Aidinoff, M(erton) Bernard *retired lawyer*
Aiello, Stephen *public relations executive*

Aigen, Betsy Paula *psychotherapist*
Ailes, Roger Eugene *broadcast executive*
Ainbinder, Bruce *lawyer*
Aitken, Doug *artist*
Akerele, Evaristo Olanrewaju *psychiatrist, educator*
Albano, David Warren *financial executive, business analyst*
Albee, Edward Franklin *playwright, writer*
Albert, Garett J. *lawyer*
Albert, William Joseph *lawyer*
Albertson, Christiern Gunnar (Chris Albertson) *commentator, music critic, writer*
Albrecht, Chris *broadcast executive*
Alcott, Mark Howard *lawyer*
Alda, Alan *actor, film director, scriptwriter*
Alden, Steven Michael *lawyer*
Alderson, Philip Otis *radiologist, educator*
Alemany, Ellen R. *bank executive*
Alessandroni, Venan Joseph *lawyer*
Alex, Paula Ann *foundation administrator*
Alexander, Jane (Jane Quigley) *actress, theater educator, writer*
Alexander, Roy *public relations executive, writer*
Alfano, Michael Charles *academic administrator*
Alfieri, Vincent *lawyer*
Alford, Katherine *food products executive*
Ali, Laylah *artist*
Alikhani, Zoubin *internist, molecular biologist, researcher*
Alizadeh, Kaveh *plastic surgeon, educator*
Allan, Col *editor-in-chief*
Allard, Linda Marie *fashion designer*
Allen, Alice *communications and marketing executive*
Allen, Betty (Mrs. Ritten Edward Lee III) *mezzo-soprano*
Allen, Claxton Edmonds III *investment banker*
Allen, Herbert Anthony, Jr. *investment company executive*
Allen, Leon Arthur, Jr. *lawyer*
Allen, Oliver E. *writer*
Allen, William Thomas *law educator*
Allerhand, Joseph S. *lawyer*
Allison, Herbert Monroe, Jr. *investment company executive*
Allison, Michael David *space scientist, educator*
Alliton, Vaughn *brokerage executive*
Almon, Lorie *lawyer*
Alperin, Stuart N. *lawyer*
Alpert, Warren *oil industry executive, foundation administrator*
Alpert, William Harold (Bill Alpert) *artist, painter*
Alpi, Kristine Markovich *librarian, educator*
Als, Hilton *journalist*
Alschuler, Steven *public relations executive, writer, consultant*
Alt, Carol A. *actress, model, entrepreneur, writer*
Alter, Eleanor Breitel *lawyer*
Alter, Jonathan Hammerman *journalist*
Alter, Paul R. *lawyer*
Altfest, Lewis Jay *financial planner*
Altman, Lawrence Kimball *physician, journalist*
Altman, Robert (Robert Bernard Altman) *film director, writer, producer*
Altman, Roy Peter *pediatric surgeon*
Altman, Steven Lawrence *lawyer*
Altmejd, David *artist*
Alvarez, Julia *writer*
Alves, Flavio P. *researcher, director*
Amdur, Martin Bennett *lawyer*
Amelan, Bjorn G. *sculptor, set designer*
Amen, Robert M. *manufacturing executive, retired paper company executive*
Amenoff, Gregory *artist, educator*
Ames, Richard Pollard *physician, educator, lecturer*
Amihud, Yakov *economics professor*
Amos, Tori *musician, singer*
Amster, Linda Evelyn *newspaper executive, consultant*
Amsterdam, Anthony Guy *law educator*
Amsterdam, Mark Lemle *lawyer*
Anagnost, Dino *artistic director*
Anania, Vincent Jay *film director, educator*
Ananiashvili, Nina *ballerina*
Anastasi, William Joseph *artist*
Andelbradt, Mark *chef*
Anders, David Brian *prosecutor*
Andersen, K(ent) Tucker *investment executive*
Andersen, Mark *musician*
Anderson, Arthur Allan *management consultant*
Anderson, David Poole *sportswriter*
Anderson, Gloria Brown *publishing executive*
Anderson, Richard Theodore *trade association administrator, urban planner*
Anderson, Ross S. *architectural firm executive*
Anderson, Theodore Wellington *portfolio strategist*
Anderson, Walter Herman *editor, educator*
Andjaba, Martin *ambassador*
Andolsen, Alan Anthony *management consultant*
Andrade, Andres *vocalist, educator*
Andre, Michael (Kenneth Andre) *editor-in-chief*
Andreassi, John Lawrence *psychologist, educator*
Andree, Tim *advertising executive*
Andreotti, Lamberto *pharmaceutical executive*
Andresen, Malcolm *lawyer*
Andrews, Gordon Clark *lawyer*
Andrias, Richard T. *judge*
Andriola, Rocco F. *lawyer, diversified financial services company executive*
Andrus, Roger Douglas *lawyer*
Anesh, Mark K. *lawyer*
Angell, Roger *writer, magazine editor*
Angland, Joseph *lawyer*
Angle, Jim *political correspondent*
Angus, Patricia Marie *lawyer*
Annan, Kofi A. *Secretary General of the United Nations*
Antell, Darrick Eugene *plastic surgeon, educator*
Antezzo, Matthew J. *artist*
Anthoine, Robert *lawyer, educator*
Anthony, William Graham *artist*
Antonakos, Stephen *sculptor*
Antonuccio, Joseph Albert *management consultant*
Antunes, Xana *business journalist*
Apcar, Leonard M. *online editor*
Apostolakis, James John *shipping company executive, pharmaceutical executive*
Appel, Albert M. *lawyer*
Appel, Marsha Ceil *advertising executive*
Appelbaum, Ann Harriet *lawyer*

Appelbaum, Paul Stuart *psychiatrist, medical educator, department chairman*
Applebaum, Stuart S. *public relations executive*
Aptekar, Ken *painter*
Apter, Emily *language educator*
Aquila, Francis Joseph *lawyer*
Aquilino, Thomas Joseph, Jr. *federal judge, law educator*
Arabatzis, Constance Elaine *lawyer*
Arcangel, Cory *artist, computer technician*
Archbold, Michael G. *retail executive*
Arditi, Ralph *lawyer*
Arenson, Gregory K. *lawyer*
Arenson, Karen Wattel *reporter*
Arkin, Stanley S. *lawyer*
Arlen, Jennifer Hall *law educator*
Armani, Giorgio *fashion designer*
Armbrust, Joseph W., Jr. *lawyer*
Armen, Garo H. *research and development company executive*
Armenakas, Noel Anthony *medical educator*
Armitage, Karole *dancer*
Arms, Anneli (Anna Elizabeth Arms) *artist, educator*
Armstrong, Neil A. *former astronaut*
Arndt, Cynthia *educational administrator*
Arnold, Ann *artist, illustrator*
Arnold, Martin *editor, journalist*
Aron, Alan Milford *pediatric neurology educator*
Aronson, Clifford Hank *lawyer*
Aronson, Donald Eric *management consultant, tax consultant*
Aronson, Edgar David *venture capitalist*
Arouh, Jeffrey Alan *lawyer*
Arquit, Kevin James *lawyer*
Arrow, Allen H. *lawyer*
Arroyo, Martina *soprano*
Arther, Richard Oberlin *polygraphist, educator*
Arvystas, Michael Geciauskas *orthodontist, educator*
Asakawa, Takako *dancer, educator, choreographer, director*
Ascherman, Jeffrey Alan *plastic and reconstructive surgeon*
Aschoff, Lawrence Michael (Mick Aschoff) *computer information scientist*
Ash, Karen Artz *lawyer*
Ashanti, (Ashanti Shequoiya Douglas) *vocalist*
Ashdown, Marie Matranga (Mrs. Cecil Spanton Ashdown Jr.) *writer, educator, cultural organization administrator*
Asher, Aaron *retired editor, publisher*
Ashley, Dwayne *not-for-profit fundraiser*
Ashley, Willard Walden C., Sr. *minister*
Ashman, Teresa Anne *neuropsychologist*
Ashton, Dore *writer, educator*
Asimov, Eric *wine critic*
Asimov, Janet Jeppson *writer, psychiatrist*
Asner, Edward *actor*
Assael, Henry *marketing educator*
Astley, Amy *editor-in-chief*
Aston, Sherrell Jerone *plastic surgeon, educator*
Astor, David Warren *journalist*
Ataeva, Aksoltan *diplomat*
Atkins, John *concert pianist, voice educator, model*
Atkins, Peter Allan *lawyer*
Atkins, Veronica *philanthropist*
Atlas, James Robert *editor, writer*
Attwood, James Albert, Jr. *investment company executive*
Atwood, Margaret Eleanor *writer*
Audet, Paul L. *diversified financial services company executive*
Aufses, Arthur Harold, Jr. *surgeon, medical educator*
Auletta, Ken *columnist*
Auslander, Mitchell J. *lawyer*
Auster, Paul *writer*
Austin, John H.M. *radiologist*
Axel, Richard *pathology and biochemistry educator*
Axelrod, Charles Paul *lawyer*
Axelrod, Norman N. (Norman Nathan Axelrod) *optical technical planning and application consultant*
Axinn, Stephen Mark *lawyer*
Axthelm, Nancy *advertising executive*
Ayafor, Martin Chungong *ambassador*
Ayoub, Elsa *lawyer*
Azara, Nancy Jean *sculptor, book designer, educator*
Azzoli, Val *music company executive*
Babbio, Lawrence T. *telecommunications industry executive*
Bacall, Lauren (Betty Joan Perske) *actress*
Bach, Thomas Handford *lawyer, investor*
Bachelder, Joseph Elmer III *lawyer*
Bachrach, Nancy *retired advertising executive*
Baden, Michael M. *pathologist, educator*
Bader, Ian *architectural firm executive*
Badertscher, David Glen *law librarian, consultant*
Badgley, Mark *fashion designer*
Baechler, Donald *painter*
Bagatelle, Warren Denis *investment banker*
Bagger, Richard Hartvig *pharmaceutical executive*
Baglivo, Mary L. *advertising executive*
Bagnall, Roger Shaler *history professor*
Baha, Christian J. *investment company executive*
Bahash, Robert J. *publishing executive*
Bahlke, Conrad George *lawyer*
Bahr, Lauren S. *publishing executive*
Baier, Bret *news correspondent*
Bailey, Colin Barry *curator*
Bailey, Darlyne *social worker, educator*
Bailey, Jerome H. (Jerry Bailey) *mercantile exchange executive*
Bains, Leslie Elizabeth *banker*
Baio, Joseph T. *lawyer*
Baird, Lisa P. *marketing executive*
Baird, Penny Drue *interior designer*
Baird, Richard *human resources specialist*
Baird, Zoë *foundation administrator, lawyer*
Baity, John Cooley *lawyer*
Baitz, Jon Robin *playwright*
Baja, Lauro Liboon, Jr. *diplomat*
Baker, Al *journalist*
Baker, Deborah *editor, writer*
Baker, Elizabeth Calhoun *magazine editor*
Baker, Mark M. *lawyer, law educator*
Baker, Paul Raymond *historian, educator*

Baker, Russell Wayne *columnist, writer*
Baker, Stuart David *lawyer*
Baker, William Franklin *public broadcasting company executive*
Balamaceda, Casilda *neurologist, oncologist*
Baldacci, David *writer*
Baldessari, John Anthony *artist*
Baldwin, David Shepard *physician*
Baldwin, Deborah *editor*
Baldwin, William *editor*
Ball, John Paul *publishing company executive*
Ballard, Charles Alan *investment banker*
Balmori, Diana *landscape designer*
Balogh, Mary *writer*
Balter, Bernice *religious organization administrator*
Bamberger, Michael Albert *lawyer*
Bana, Eric *actor*
Bancroft, Margaret Armstrong *lawyer*
Banerjee, Neela *reporter*
Banerjee, (Bimal Banerjee) *artist, educator*
Banga, Ajay *diversified financial services company executive*
Bank, Melissa S. *writer*
Banker, Amy Beth Cohen *artist, writer, educator, curator, actress, poet*
Banks, Michael C. *lawyer*
Bankston, Archie Moore *lawyer*
Bannigan, Eugene F. *lawyer*
Bansal, Preeta D. *lawyer*
Baragwanath, Albert Kingsmill *curator, writer*
Barakat, Richard *oncologist, gynecological surgeon*
Barandes, Robert *lawyer*
Barasch, Clarence Sylvan *lawyer*
Barasch, Mal Livingston *lawyer*
Barber, Lionel *journalist*
Barber, Russell Brooks Butler *television producer*
Barbour, Catherine Jean *actress, set designer, director, mime*
Barbour, Celia *editor*
Barbur, Peter T. *lawyer*
Barchas, Jack D. *psychiatrist, medical researcher, educator, behavioral molecular neurobiologist*
Barckhaus, Rachel *paralegal*
Bardach, Joan Lucile *clinical psychologist*
Bardin, Mary Beth *telecommunications company executive*
Barenberg, Mark *law educator*
Barist, Jeffrey *lawyer*
Barker, Barbara Ann *ophthalmologist*
Barksdale, James Love *communications executive*
Barlow, Anne Julia *curator*
Barlow, Barbara Ann *surgeon*
Barlow, Lou *painter*
Barnard, Kevin Francis *lawyer*
Barnard, Robert N. *lawyer*
Barnes, Clive Alexander *drama and dance critic*
Barnes, Gregg *costume designer*
Barnes, Jhane Elizabeth *fashion design company executive, designer*
Barnet, Peter *curator*
Barnet, Will *artist, educator*
Barnett, Amy DuBois *editor-in-chief*
Barnett, Vivian Endicott *curator*
Barnett, Will *painter*
Barnum, Barbara Stevens *retired nursing educator, writer*
Barolini, Teodolinda *literary critic*
Baron, Andrew Michael *blog website producer, educator, composer*
Baron, Mitchell Neal *lawyer*
Baron, Robert Howard *lawyer*
Baron, Susan *publishing executive*
Barondess, Jeremiah Abraham *physician*
Barquero, Pedro B. *mathematician, researcher*
Barr, Thomas D. *lawyer*
Barr, William Pelham *lawyer, former United States attorney general*
Barrett, David A. *lawyer*
Barrett, Elizabeth Ann Manhart *psychotherapist, consultant, nursing educator*
Barrett, Herbert *performing company executive, management consultant*
Barron, James Turman *journalist*
Barry, Dan *columnist*
Barry, Desmond Thomas, Jr. *lawyer*
Barry, Nancy Marie *bank executive*
Barry, Thomas Corcoran *investment advisor*
Barry, William Garrett III *publishing company executive*
Barse, David M. *financial services executive*
Barshay, Scott A. *lawyer*
Barstow, David *journalist*
Bart, Roger *actor*
Bartfeld, Daniel D. *lawyer*
Bartholomew, Lincoln Edwin *physician*
Bartlett, Elizabeth Easton *interior designer*
Bartlett, Jennifer Losch *artist*
Bartlett, John *fashion designer*
Bartlett, Joseph Warren *lawyer*
Bartlett, Richard Allan *finance company executive*
Bartlett, Thomas A. *telecommunications industry executive*
Bartley, Matthew B. *insurance company executive*
Barton, Lewis *food products executive, consultant*
Barton, Richard N. *computer company executive*
Barton, Thomas Heisler *management consultant*
Bartow, Diane Grace *marketing professional, sales executive*
Baruch, Ralph M. *communications executive*
Bashir, Martin *news correspondent*
Bashkow, Jack Simon *musician*
Baslaw-Finger, Annette *education educator, consultant*
Bason, George R., Jr. *lawyer*
Basquin, Mary Smyth (Kit Basquin) *museum administrator*
Bass, Franklin F. *lawyer*
Bassen, Ned Henry *lawyer*
Bastianich, Lidia Matticchio *chef, food service executive*
Batali, Mario Francis *chef*
Batavia, Mitchell *physical therapist, educator*
Bateman, Maureen Scannell *lawyer*
Bateman, Paul *diversified financial services company executive*
Batts, Deborah A. *federal judge*
Bauer, Douglas F. *retired lawyer*
Bauer, Joel J. *surgeon, educator*
Bauer, Marion Dane *writer*

Bauer, Peter F. *publishing executive*
Baumgardner, John Ellwood, Jr. *lawyer*
Baumgarten, Barbara *human resources specialist*
Baumgarten, Sidney *lawyer*
Baumrin, Bernard Stefan Herbert *lawyer, educator*
Bawden, Nina (Mary Bawden) *author*
Baxter, Violet Diane *artist*
Bazell, Robert Joseph *science correspondent*
Beal, Jack *artist*
Bear, Stephen E. *pharmaceutical executive*
Bearak, Barry *journalist*
Beardsley, Theodore S(terling), Jr. *professional society administrator*
Beattie, Ann *writer, educator*
Beattie, Richard Irwin *lawyer*
Beauford, Carter *musician*
Beausoleil, Doris Mae *retired federal agency housing specialist*
Beck, Andrew James *lawyer*
Beck, Martha Ann *curator, director*
Beck, Nathaniel L. *political science professor*
Becker, Franklin *chef*
Becker, Jonathan *photographer*
Becker, Steven H. *lawyer*
Becker, Susan Kaplan *management and marketing communication consultant, educator*
Beckman, Ericka *artist, filmmaker*
Beckman, Michael *lawyer*
Beckman, Richard David *publishing executive, advertising executive*
Bederson, Benjamin *physicist, researcher*
Bednar, Rudy *television producer, director*
Bedol, Brian *broadcast executive*
Bee, Samantha *comedian, actress*
Beecher, William Manuel *management consultant*
Beeken, Timothy K. *lawyer*
Beekman, William Bedloe *lawyer*
Been, Vicki Lynn *law educator*
Beeney, Garrard Russ *lawyer*
Beerbower, Cynthia Gibson *lawyer*
Beerbower, John Edwin *lawyer*
Beeson, Ann *lawyer*
Beeson, Jack Hamilton *composer, educator, writer*
Begley, Louis *writer, lawyer*
Begley, Sharon Lynn *journalist*
Behar, Joy *television personality*
Behrendt, Greg *comedian*
Beim, David Odell *investment banker, educator*
Beim, Norman *playwright, actor, theater director, writer*
Beinecke, Candace Krugman *lawyer*
Beinecke, Frances G. *environmentalist*
Beinecke, Frederick William *investment company executive*
Beinecke, William Sperry *retired consumer products company executive*
Belag, Andrea Susan *artist*
Beldock, Donald Travis *investor*
Belgorod, Barry Miles *surgeon, educator*
Belknap, Norton *foundation administrator*
Belknap, Robert Lamont *literature educator*
Bell, David Arthur *advertising agency executive*
Bell, Jonathan Robert *lawyer*
Bell, Martin Allen *investment company executive*
Bell, Theodore Augustus, III, (Ted Bell) *writer, former advertising executive*
Bellando, John W. *publishing executive, accountant*
Bellanger, Serge René *bank executive*
Bellas, Albert Constantine *investment executive*
Beller, Gary A. *lawyer, finance company executive, insurance company executive*
Belliveau, Gerard Joseph, Jr. *librarian*
Bellovin, Steven M. *computer science educator*
Bellows, Carl D. *lawyer*
Belson, Ken *reporter*
Belzer, Richard *actor, comedian*
Ben-Ami, Leora *lawyer*
Ben-Avi, Simon Stephen *biomedical researcher, educator*
Bender, John Charles *lawyer*
Bender, Judith *journalist, editor*
Bender, Thomas *historian, educator*
Bendor, Susan Julia *social worker, educator*
Benedek, Melinda *television executive*
Benenson, Mark Keith *lawyer*
Benhabib, Jess *adult education educator*
Ben-Haim, Zigi *artist*
Benjamin, Andre Lauren (Dre, André 3000) *vocalist, actor*
Benjamin, Jeff *lawyer, pharmaceutical executive*
Benkard, James W. B. *lawyer*
Benn, Theodore Alexander (Alec Benn) *writer*
Bennett, Paul B. *stock exchange executive*
Bennett, Robert Scott *lawyer*
Bennett, Scott Lawrence *lawyer*
Benno, Jonathan *chef*
Bensinger, Steven J. *insurance company executive*
Bentley, Eric *writer, playwright, literature educator*
Benton, Daniel C. *investment company executive*
Beraka, George Joseph *plastic surgeon*
Berardi, Loretta A. *human services manager*
Berendt, John Lawrence *writer, editor*
Berenson, Alex *reporter*
Berg, A. Scott (Andrew Scott Berg) *writer*
Berg, Madelaine R. *lawyer*
Bergan, Edmund Paul, Jr. *lawyer*
Bergdoll, Barry G. *architectural historian, educator*
Berger, Frank Milan *biomedical researcher, research scientist, retired pharmaceutical executive*
Berger, George *lawyer*
Berger, Marvin *medical educator*
Berger, Max W. *lawyer*
Berger, Pearl *library director*
Berger, Stephen *finance company executive*
Berger, Thomas Louis *author*
Berghahn, Volker Rolf *history professor*
Bergman, Arlene *lawyer*
Bergman, Charles Cabe *foundation executive*
Bergman, Donald Arthur *endocrinologist, educator*
Bergman, Lowell *television news producer*
Bergmann, Peter George *lawyer*
Bergtraum, Howard Michael *lawyer*
Berk, Paul David *internist, research scientist, educator*
Berke, Richard L. *editor*
Berkery, Rosemary T. *lawyer, investment company executive*

Berkley, Peter Lee *lawyer*
Berkow, Ira Harvey *writer, journalist*
Berkowitz, Brad Alan *financial analyst*
Berkowitz, Richard Lee *obstetrician, gynecologist, director*
Berlin, Andrew Mark *advertising agency executive*
Berlin, Heather Ayn *philosopher, educator*
Berlind, Robert Elliot *artist, educator*
Berman, Ariane R. *artist*
Berman, Carol Wendy *psychiatrist*
Berman, Greg *think-tank executive*
Berman, Keith *solicitor, lawyer*
Berman, Michael Allen *hospital administrator, pediatric cardiologist*
Berman, Richard Miles *judge*
Berman, Russell Scott *oncologist, educator*
Berman, Walter S. *treasurer*
Bermann, George Alan *law educator*
Bermudez, Jorge Alberto *bank executive*
Bern, Marc Jay *lawyer*
Bernard, André Philippe *publishing executive, writer*
Bernard, David George *retired management consultant*
Bernard, Lewis W. *foundation executive, former finance company executive*
Bernard, Richard Phillip *lawyer*
Bernbach, John Lincoln *marketing professional*
Berne, Bruce J. *chemistry professor*
Berner, Andrew Jay *library director, writer*
Bernhard, Lisa *news correspondent*
Bernheimer, G. Max *art appraiser*
Bernick, David M. *lawyer*
Bernstein, Daniel Lewis *lawyer*
Bernstein, David William *lawyer*
Bernstein, Donald Scott *lawyer*
Bernstein, Phyllis J. *financial consultant*
Bernstein, Richard Allen *food products executive*
Bernstein, Robert Jay *lawyer*
Bernstein, Robert M. *dermatologic surgeon*
Bernstein, Warren J. *lawyer*
Berresford, Susan Vail *not-for-profit developer*
Berruga-Filloy, Enrique *ambassador*
Berry, Dean C. *lawyer*
Berry, Gail W. *psychiatrist, educator*
Berry, John Nichols III *publishing executive, editor*
Berson, Anthony M. *oncologist*
Berthot, Jake *artist, educator*
Beshar, Christine *lawyer*
Beshar, Peter Justus *lawyer, insurance company executive*
Beshar, Robert Peter *lawyer*
Beshers, Daniel Newson *retired materials scientist*
Beslow, William S. *lawyer*
Bess, James Lawrence *academic administration educator*
Bessey, Palmer Quintard *surgeon*
Besterman, Douglas *composer, orchestrator*
Bethel, Denise *art appraiser*
Bettis, Jerome Abram *sports commentator, retired professional football player*
Bettman, Gary Bruce *National Hockey League Commissioner*
Betts, Richard Kevin *political science professor*
Beverley, Cordia Luvonne *gastroenterologist*
Bevilacqua, Louis J. *lawyer*
Bewkes, Eugene Garrett, Jr. *investment company executive, consultant*
Bewkes, Jeffrey L. *television broadcasting company executive*
Beyer, Lisa *journalist*
Bezanson, Thomas Edward *lawyer*
Bezozo, Kenneth K. *lawyer*
Bhargava, Peeyush *nuclear medicine physician*
Bhavsar, Natvar Prahladji *artist*
Bholat, Omar *surgeon*
Bialkin, Kenneth Jules *lawyer, director*
Bialler, Nancy *art appraiser*
Bialo, Kenneth Marc *lawyer*
Bibliowicz, Jessica M. *financial analyst*
Bickers, David Rinsey *dermatologist, educator, department chairman, health facility administrator*
Bicks, Peter Andrews *lawyer*
Biddle, Flora Miller *art patron, museum administrator*
Biederman, Barron Zachary (Barry Biederman) *advertising agency executive*
Biel, Leonard, Jr. *urologist*
Bienenstock, Martin J. *lawyer*
Biggs, John Herron *retired insurance company executive*
Biglari, Hamid *investment banker*
Bikel, Theodore *actor, singer*
Billig, Robert Emanuel *psychiatric social worker*
Billington, Ken *lighting designer*
Bilsky, Mark Harvey *neurologist*
Birch, Ian *editor-in-chief*
Bird, Hector Ramón *child psychiatrist, psychoanalyst, educator*
Bird, Paul S. *lawyer*
Birkelund, John Peter *investment company executive*
Birkenhead, Thomas Bruce *theater producer, educator*
Birman, Joseph Leon *physics professor*
Birmelin, Robert *artist*
Birnbaum, Edward Lester *lawyer*
Birnbaum, Sheila L. *lawyer, educator*
Birns, Nicholas Boe *literature educator, editor*
Birstein, Ann *writer, educator*
Bischoff, Theresa Ann *not-for-profit association executive*
Bisignano, Frank *diversified financial services company executive*
Björk, (Björk Guðmundsdóttir) *singer, composer*
Black, Barbara Aronstein *legal history educator*
Black, Carole *broadcast executive*
Black, Cathleen Prunty *publishing executive*
Black, James Isaac (Jib) III *lawyer*
Black, Jerry Bernard *lawyer*
Black, Louis Engleman *lawyer*
Black, Steven D. *diversified financial services company executive*
Blackford, John *magazine editor*
Blackman, Kenneth Robert *lawyer*
Blair, Dike *sculptor, painter*
Blair, Michael Walter *lawyer*
Blair, William Granger *retired reporter*
Blair, William McCormick, Jr. *lawyer*

Blake, Jeremy *artist*
Blalock, Sherrill *investment advisor*
Blamer, Steven W. *advertising executive*
Blanc, Roger David *lawyer*
Blanchard, Kimberly Staggers *lawyer, educator*
Bland, Frederick Aves *architect*
Blank, Matthew C. *broadcast company executive*
Blankfein, Lloyd C. *diversified financial services company executive*
Blaser, Martin Jack *medical educator, researcher*
Blasi, Vincent A. *law educator*
Blassberg, Franci J. *lawyer*
Blatt, Gregory R. *lawyer*
Blattmachr, Jonathan George *lawyer*
Blavatnik, Leonard *investment company executive*
Blazejowski, Carol A. *professional sports team executive, retired professional basketball player*
Blechner, Mark Jacob *psychologist, educator*
Bledel, Alexis (Kimberly Alexis Bledel) *actress*
Bleich, J. David *law educator, rabbi*
Bleifer, Robert *chef*
Bleser, Philip F. *diversified financial services company executive*
Blevins, Jennifer Lynn *insurance company executive*
Blinder, Albert Allan *judge*
Blinken, Donald *ambassador, investment banker*
Blitzer, Andrew *otolaryngologist, educator, research scientist, writer*
Blivaiss, David Harvey *lawyer, accountant*
Bliwise, Lester Martin *lawyer*
Blobel, Günter *cell biologist, educator*
Block, Dennis Jeffrey *lawyer*
Block, Francesca Lia *writer*
Block, Ned *philosopher, educator*
Block, William Kenneth *lawyer*
Bloom, Lisa Read *lawyer*
Bloomberg, Michael Rubens *mayor*
Bloomgarden, Karenne Jo *elementary school educator, small business owner*
Bloomgarden, Kathy Finn *public relations executive*
Blount, Roy Alton, Jr. *freelance/self-employed writer*
Bluh, Bonnie *scriptwriter, actress, novelist, playwright*
Blum, David *editor-in-chief*
Blum, Paul *retail executive*
Blumberg, Barbara Marilyn *history professor, writer*
Blume, Judy *author*
Blume, Lawrence Dayton *lawyer*
Blumkin, Linda Ruth *lawyer*
Boardman, D. Dixon (Dennie Dixon Boardman) *investment banker*
Boardman, Seymour *artist*
Boast, Molly Shryer *lawyer*
Bobrow, Richard S. *lawyer, former diversified financial services executive*
Bochner, Bernard H. *urologic surgical oncologist*
Bochner, Mel *artist*
Bock, Walter Joseph *zoology educator*
Bockstein, Herbert *lawyer*
Bodley, Harley Ryan, Jr. *sportswriter, announcer*
Bodnar, Andrew G. *pharmaceutical executive*
Boffey, Philip M. *journalist*
Bogatin, Marc *lawyer*
Bogdanich, Walt *journalist*
Bogdanos, Matthew F. *lawyer, reserve military officer*
Bogdonoff, Morton David *internist, educator*
Bogert, Jeremiah *journalist*
Bohm, Richard D. *lawyer*
Boice, Craig Kendall *management consultant*
Bolen, Alex *retail executive*
Boley, Bruno Adrian *engineering educator*
Bollinger, Lee Carroll *academic administrator, law educator*
Bolton, John Robert *international organization official, former federal agency administrator*
Bolton, Michael *singer, songwriter*
Bond, Alma Halbert *psychoanalyst, author*
Bond, James Max, Jr. *architect, academic administrator*
Bonfante, Larissa *classics educator*
Bonfield, Andrew R.J. *pharmaceutical executive*
Bonino, Fernanda *art dealer*
Bonnell, Bruno *information technology executive*
Bookspan, Martin *broadcaster, writer*
Booth, Mitchell B. *lawyer*
Booth Corwin, Tami *publishing executive*
Borchard, William Marshall *lawyer*
Borders, William Alexander *journalist*
Borer, Jeffrey Stephen *cardiologist*
Borisoff, Richard Stuart *lawyer*
Bornstein, Gary A. *lawyer*
Borowitz, Sidney *retired physics professor*
Bosl, George Joseph *physician, oncologist*
Bossert, Rex Thomas *editor-in-chief*
Bosses, Stevan J. *mediator, arbitrator*
Boston, Gretha *actress, vocalist*
Bothmer, Dietrich Felix von *curator, archaeologist*
Botkin, Daniel Benjamin *biologist, environmental scientist, writer*
Bottari, Paul J. *lawyer*
Boufford, Jo Ivey *health administrator, educator*
Bouley, David *chef*
Boulhosa, Michael L. *lawyer*
Boulud, Daniel *chef, restaurant owner*
Bourgeois, Louise *sculptor*
Boutis, Tom *artist, painter, printmaker*
Bove, John Louis *chemistry and environmental engineering educator, researcher*
Bovin, Denis Alan *finance company executive*
Bowden, Linda *diversified financial services company executive*
Bowden, William P., Jr. *lawyer, bank executive*
Bowen, Tim *recording industry executive*
Bowen, William Gordon *foundation administrator, economist*
Bowers, Brent *editor*
Bowers, Patricia Eleanor Fritz *economist*
Bowers, William Charles *lawyer*
Bowman, Robert A. *Internet company executive*
Boxer, Leonard *lawyer*
Boxer, Sarah *critic, reporter, writer*
Boxill, Edith Hillman *music therapist, educator, writer*
Boykin, Keith O. *former government official, writer*
Boykin, Richard A. *tax specialist*

Boylan, Elizabeth Shippee *academic administrator, biologist, educator*
Boyle, Edward J. *lawyer*
Boziwick, George E. *music librarian, composer, curator*
Brabeck, Mary Margaret *dean, psychology professor*
Bracco, Lorraine *actress*
Brach, Richard S. *lawyer*
Bradbury, Ray Douglas *writer*
Bradford, Barbara Taylor *writer, journalist*
Bradley, E. Michael *lawyer*
Bradley, Edward R. *news correspondent*
Bradley, John Francis *financial services company executive*
Bradley, Richard (Richard Blow) *writer*
Bradshaw, Dove *artist*
Bradstock, John *advertising executive*
Brady, Adelaide Burks *public relations agency executive, giftware catalog executive*
Brady, Bruce Morgan *lawyer*
Brafman, Benjamin *lawyer*
Braham, Randolph Lewis *political science professor*
Braid, Frederick Donald *lawyer*
Brainin, Gregory *chef*
Brams, Steven John *political science professor*
Branch, Taylor *writer*
Brand, Jason *diversified financial services company executive*
Brandeis, Barry *apparel executive*
Brant, Henry *composer*
Brant, Sandra J. *magazine publisher*
Brantley, Benjamin David *theater critic*
Brashares, Ann *writer*
Brathwaite, Edward Kamau (Kamau Brathwaite, Lawson Edward Brathwaite) *poet, educator*
Bratten, Millie Martini *editor-in-chief*
Braudy, Susan Orr *writer*
Braun, Jeffrey Louis *lawyer*
Brauner, Gary Jules *dermatologist, cosmetic laser surgeon*
Braunstein, Douglas *bank executive*
Braunstein, Lancelot Michael (Lance Braunstein) *financial services company executive*
Braverman, Robert Jay *management consultant, educator*
Bravo, Luis Fernando *investment banker*
Brazinsky, Irv(ing) *chemical engineering educator, department chairman*
Breakstone, Joshua Scott *musician, educator, composer*
Brecher, John *newspaper editor*
Breglio, John F. *lawyer*
Breinin, Goodwin M. *physician*
Brennan, Henry Higginson *architect*
Brennan, Murray Frederick *surgeon, oncologist*
Brennan, Patrick J. *lawyer*
Brennan, Terrance *chef*
Brenner, Beth Fuchs *publishing executive*
Brenner, Douglas *editor*
Bresani, Federico Fernando *manufacturing executive*
Breslin, Jimmy *columnist, writer*
Breslow, Esther May Greenberg *biochemistry professor, researcher*
Breslow, Jan Leslie *scientist, educator, physician*
Breslow, Ronald Charles *chemist, educator*
Breslow, Stephanie R. *lawyer*
Brett, Barry J. *lawyer*
Brett, Harry P. *lawyer*
Brett, Nancy Heléne *artist*
Brewer, Karen *librarian*
Brick, Michael *journalist*
Bricklin, Malcolm *automotive entreprenuer*
Briffault, Richard *law educator*
Brilliant, Richard *art historian, educator*
Brine, Kevin R. *investment company executive*
Bring, Murray H. *retired lawyer*
Brinkley, Alan David *provost, historian*
Brinkley, Christie *model, spokesperson, designer*
Briskman, Robert David *engineering executive*
Brisman, Jennifer *event planning executive*
Britz, Robert G. *stock exchange executive*
Britz Lotti, Diane Edward *investment company executive*
Broad, William J. *science writer*
Broadwater, Douglas Dwight *lawyer*
Brock, Charles Lawrence *lawyer, diversified financial services company executive, investment banker*
Broder, Douglas Fisher *lawyer*
Brodie-Baldwin, Helen Sylvia *retired college and human services administrator*
Brodman, Michael Lewis *gynecologist, educator*
Brodsky, David Michael *lawyer*
Brodsky, Samuel *lawyer*
Brody, Alan Jeffrey *investment company executive*
Brody, Jane Ellen *journalist, researcher*
Brody, Kenneth David *investment banker*
Brody-Lederman, Stephanie *artist*
Brohn, William David *conductor, orchestrator, arranger*
Bromberger, Allen Richard *lawyer*
Brome, Thomas Reed *lawyer*
Bronfman, Edgar Miles, Jr. *recording industry executive*
Bronner, Ethan Samuel *editor*
Brook, David William *psychiatrist, researcher*
Brooke, Linda Hundley *human resources specialist*
Brooks, Daniel Townley *lawyer*
Brooks, David B. *editor, columnist*
Brooks, Jerome Bernard *English and Afro-American literature educator*
Brooks, Mark J. *academic administrator*
Brooks, Roger G. *lawyer*
Brooks, Timothy H. *broadcast executive*
Brothers, Joyce Diane *television personality, psychologist*
Brotman, Steven *venture capitalist*
Broude, Richard Frederick *lawyer, educator*
Browar, Lisa Muriel *librarian*
Browdy, Joseph Eugene *lawyer*
Brown, Andreas Le *retail executive, art gallery owner*
Brown, Arthur Edward *physician*
Brown, Carroll *retired diplomat, association executive, consultant*
Brown, Cecily *artist*
Brown, Chris (Christopher Maurice Brown) *singer*
Brown, Clifford Bryant *financial consultant*

Brown, Dan *writer*
Brown, Darrell James *publishing executive*
Brown, David *motion picture producer, writer*
Brown, Edward James, Sr. *utilities executive*
Brown, Helen Gurley *editor-in-chief*
Brown, James Kevin (Kevin Brown) *professional baseball player*
Brown, Jason Walter *neurologist, educator, researcher*
Brown, Jonathan *art historian, art educator*
Brown, Joyce F. *academic administrator*
Brown, Katie *columnist*
Brown, Lyn *newscaster*
Brown, Mark Malloch *international organization official*
Brown, Paul M. *lawyer*
Brown, Ralph Sawyer, Jr. *retired lawyer*
Brown, Renee *sports association executive*
Brown, Rita Mae *writer*
Brown, Ronald *retired stockbroker*
Brown, Terrence Charles *art association executive, researcher, lecturer*
Brown, Tina *journalist, television personality*
Brown, Trisha *dancer*
Browne, Arthur *newspaper editor*
Browne, Joy *psychologist, radio personality*
Browne, Malcolm Wilde *journalist*
Browne, Thom *apparel designer*
Brownell, Patricia Jane *social worker, educator*
Browning, Candace *corporate financial executive*
Brownstein, Alan P. *health foundation executive, consultant*
Brownstein, Andrew Richard *lawyer*
Brownwood, David Owen *lawyer*
Bruce, Duncan Archibald *investor, writer*
Bruder, Harold Jacob *artist, educator*
Brumley, Tom *museum director, artist*
Brumm, James Earl *lawyer, import/export company executive*
Brun, Henry *publishing executive*
Brundige, Robert William, Jr. *lawyer*
Bruner, Jerome S. *law educator*
Bruni, Frank *restaurant critic*
Brunie, Charles Henry *investment manager*
Brus, Louis Eugene *physical chemist*
Brust, John Calvin Morrison *neurologist, educator*
Brustein, Lawrence *finance company executive*
Bryan, Barry Richard *lawyer*
Bryan, Robert E. *editor*
Bryan, Scott *business owner, chef*
Brychtova, Jaroslava *sculptor*
Brymer, Charles Edward (Chuck Brymer) *advertising executive*
Bryson, Louise Henry *broadcast executive*
Buatta, Mario *interior designer*
Bucchino, John *composer*
Buchanan, Edna *writer, retired journalist*
Buchbinder, Ellen Maud *allergist*
Buchman, M. Abraham *lawyer*
Buck, Joe (Joseph Francis Buck) *sportscaster*
Buck, Louise Zierdt *psychologist*
Buckholz, Robert E., Jr. *lawyer*
Buckles, Robert Howard *retired investment company executive*
Buckley, Christopher Taylor *editor, author*
Buckley, Robert John *academic administrator, researcher*
Buckley, Susan *lawyer*
Buckley, Virginia Laura *editor*
Buckley, William Frank, Jr. *magazine editor, writer*
Buckman, James Edward *lawyer*
Buckman, Thomas Richard *foundation executive, educator*
Buehler, Thomas *psychotherapist, expressive therapist, artist*
Buissonnière, Marine *international organization administrator; physician*
Bujold, Lois McMaster *writer*
Bull, David *fine art conservator*
Buller, Steven E. *diversified financial services company executive*
Bulliet, Richard Williams *historian, educator, writer*
Bundchen, Giselle *model*
Bunts, Frank Emory *artist*
Burak, H(oward) Paul *lawyer*
Burbank, Jane Richardson *historian, educator*
Burch, Stephen A. *telecommunications industry executive*
Burckhardt, Tom *artist*
Burdette, Brooks R. *lawyer*
Burgess, Clara Skipwith *retired principal*
Burgess, Lynne A *lawyer*
Burgheim, Richard *magazine editor*
Burgman, Dierdre Ann *lawyer*
Burgweger, Francis Joseph Dewes, Jr. *lawyer*
Burke, David *corporate and executive chef*
Burke, Delta *actress*
Burke, James Joseph, Jr. *investment banker*
Burke, Kevin *utilities executive*
Burnett, David Alan *photojournalist*
Burnett, Len *publishing executive*
Burnham, Christopher Bancroft *international organization official, former federal agency administrator*
Burns, Arnold Irwin *lawyer*
Burns, John F. *reporter*
Burns, Kevin J. *computer software services executive*
Burns, M. Michele *human resources company executive*
Burns, Red *academic administrator*
Burns, Sarah Ellen *law educator*
Burns, Stephen L. *lawyer*
Burros, Marian Fox *writer*
Burrows, Kenneth David *lawyer*
Burrows, Michael Donald *lawyer*
Bursky, Herman Aaron *lawyer*
Burson, Harold *public relations executive, director*
Burstein, Judd *lawyer*
Burstell, Ed *personal care industry executive*
Burton, John Campbell *accounting educator, former dean*
Burton, Peggy *advertising and marketing executive*
Burton, Thomas M. *journalist*
Burtson, James E. *multimedia company executive*
Buschke, Herman *neurologist*
Bush, Lauren *model*
Bushnell, Candace *columnist, writer*

Bushnell, George Edward III *lawyer*
Busquet, Anne M. *Internet company executive*
Butler, Kerry *actress*
Butler, Samuel Coles *lawyer*
Butler, Vincent Paul, Jr. *internist, educator*
Butler, William Joseph *lawyer, educator*
Butte, Amy S. *brokerage house executive*
Buttenwieser, Lawrence Benjamin *lawyer*
Butterly, Kathy *sculptor*
Butterman, Jay Ronald *lawyer*
Buttner, Jean Bernhard *diversified financial services company executive*
Buttrick, Harold *architect*
Butts, Hugh Florenz *physician, psychiatrist, psychoanalyst*
Buxton, Douglas Francisco *ophthalmologist, educator*
Byer, Diana *performing company executive*
Bylinsky, Gene Michael *magazine editor*
Bynum, Sarah Shun-lien *writer, educator*
Byrd, Eva Wilson *communications executive*
Byrne, Gerard Anthony (Gerry) *publishing executive, consultant*
Byrne, Mary Woods Woods *pediatric nurse practitioner*
Byron, Eric Howard *sculptor, museum researcher and administrator*
Bystryn, Jean-Claude *dermatologist, educator*
Cabalquinto, Luis Carrazcal *freelance writer*
Cabiallavetta, Mathis *insurance company executive*
Caesar, Godfrey Wrensford *biologist, educator*
Cafferty, Jack *news anchor*
Caffrey, Patricia *diversified financial services company executive*
Caginalp, Aydin S. *lawyer*
Cagney, Lawrence K. *lawyer*
Cahan, Cora *not-for-profit developer*
Cahn, Steven Mark *philosopher, educator*
Caiazzo, Nicholas R. *lawyer*
Caine, Edward Peter *religious organization administrator*
Caine, Paul Jason *publishing executive*
Caivano, Ernesto *artist*
Cajori, Charles Florian *artist, educator*
Calabrese, Rosalie Sue *management consultant, writer*
Calame, Byron Edward *journalist*
Calame, Kathryn Lee *microbiologist, educator*
Calder, James J. *lawyer*
Caldwell, Dale Gilbert *publishing executive*
Caldwell, Ian *writer*
Caldwell, L. Scott *actress*
Caldwell, Leslie Ragon *lawyer, former prosecutor*
Calello, Paul *banker*
Calhoun, Craig Jackson *social scientist, educator*
Calio, Nicholas E. *diversified financial services company executive*
Call, Neil Judson *manufacturing executive*
Callagy, John M. *lawyer*
Callahan, Dennis S. *insurance company executive*
Calleja, Jean *media specialist, director*
Callo, Joseph Francis *writer*
Calvano, Phyllis *publishing executive*
Cambria, Christopher C. *lawyer*
Camera, Nicholas J. *lawyer*
Cameron, Timothy G. *lawyer*
Cameron, W. Bruce *writer*
Cami, Russell *lawyer*
Camilleri, Louis C. *consumer goods company executive*
Cammarata, Angelo *surgical oncologist*
Cammisa, Frank P., Jr. *surgeon, educator*
Camp, Sharon L. *reproductive health organization administrator*
Campano, Fred *economics professor, statistician, consultant*
Campbell, Alan *actor*
Campbell, George, Jr. *physicist, university administrator*
Campbell, Judith E. *retired insurance company executive*
Campbell, Mary Schmidt *dean*
Campbell, Robert David *manufacturing executive, metal products executive*
Campbell, Ronald Neil *retired graphics designer*
Campos, Fernando *editor-in-chief*
Canada, Geoffrey *social welfare administrator, writer*
Cancro, Robert *psychiatrist, educator*
Cane, Jeffrey *editor*
Canedy, Dana *editor*
Canellos, Peter Constantine *lawyer*
Canes, Brian Dennis *benefits compensation analyst*
Cannell, John Redferne *lawyer*
Cannell, Michael *editor*
Canonero, Milena *costume designer*
Canoni, John David *lawyer*
Canseco, Jose *retired professional baseball player*
Cantor, Melvyn Leon *retired lawyer*
Cantor, Richard Ira *physician, corporate health executive*
Cantrell, Lana *actress, lawyer, singer*
Capalbo, Carmen *theater director, producer*
Caples, Richard James *performing company executive, lawyer*
Caploe, Roberta *magazine editor*
Capolarello, Joe R. *photojournalist*
Caponnetto, Marianne *information technology executive*
Capozzi, Lou *public relations executive*
Cappellazzo, Amy *art appraiser, writer*
Cappuccio, Paul T. *lawyer, communications executive*
Capriati, Jennifer Maria *professional tennis player*
Capus, Steve *broadcast executive*
Caputo, David Armand *academic administrator, political scientist, educator*
Caputo, Lisa M. *finance company executive*
Caputo, Lucio *trade company executive*
Caputo, Philip Joseph *writer, journalist*
Caraley, Demetrios James *political science professor, writer, editor*
Carboni, Stefano *curator*
Card, Orson Scott (Byron Walley) *writer*
Cardile, Paul Julius *fine arts dealer*
Cardinale, Kathleen Carmel *retired health facility administrator*
Cardozo, Benjamin Mordecai *lawyer*
Cardozo, Michael A. *lawyer*
Cardwell, Diane *journalist*
Carell, Steve *comedian, actor*

Carey, David *publishing executive*
Carey, Kim *veterinarian*
Carey, Peter Philip *writer*
Carey, William Polk *investment banker*
Carlin, David H. *lawyer*
Carlson, Donna *art association administrator, director*
Carlson, Marian Bille *geneticist, researcher, educator*
Carlson, Marvin Albert *theater educator*
Carlson, P(atricia) M(cElroy) *writer*
Carlson, Richard A. *interior designer*
Carlucci, Robert Leonard *curator, anthropologist*
Carman, Gregory Wright *federal judge*
Carmellini, Andrew *chef*
Carmichael, Jesse Royal *musician*
Carmon, Haggai *lawyer*
Carmona, Wayne *television producer*
Carnabuci, Frank J. III *headmaster*
Carneiro, Robert Leonard *curator, anthropologist*
Carnell, Richard Scott *law educator*
Carney, Michael *orchestra leader*
Caro, Robert Allan *historian, writer*
Carpenter, James *glass innovator*
Carr, Arthur Charles *psychologist, educator*
Carr, Gladys Justin *publishing executive, consultant, editor, writer*
Carr, Ronald Edward *ophthalmologist, educator*
Carter, Elliott Cook, Jr. *composer*
Carter, Graydon (Edward Graydon Carter) *editor*
Carter, James Hal, Jr. *lawyer*
Carter, Marshall Nichols *stock exchange executive*
Carter, Peyton Franklin III *accountant*
Carter, Zachary W. *lawyer*
Carucci, John A. *physician*
Carvette, Anthony M. *construction executive*
Case, David Bartlett *internist, educator*
Case, Robert Brown *physician*
Casella, Jim *publishing executive*
Casey, Gerard William *retired food products executive, lawyer*
Casey, Richard Conway *federal judge*
Casey, Thomas Jefferson *clean energy executive and entrepreneur, environmental activist*
Cash, Rosanne *singer, songwriter*
Cashin, Richard M., Jr. *diversified financial services company executive*
Cashman, Gideon *lawyer*
Cassullo, Joanne Leonhardt *foundation administrator*
Castagna, Vanessa J. *retail executive*
Castel, Nico *tenor, educator*
Castel, P. Kevin *federal judge*
Castellano, Michael John *investment company executive*
Castle, John Krob *merchant banker*
Castoro, Rosemarie *sculptor*
Castro, Jan Garden *writer, art educator, consultant*
Catanzaro, Daniel Frank *molecular biologist, educator*
Catley-Carlson, Margaret *not-for-profit executive*
Catsimatidis, John Andreas *retail executive*
Cattelan, Maurizio *artist*
Caulfield, Jerome Joseph *lawyer*
Cavallo, Jo Ann *language educator*
Cavallo, Rob *recording industry executive*
Cavanagh, Michael J. *bank executive*
Cavanagh, Richard Edward *non-profit executive*
Cavanagh, William Q. *lawyer*
Cavior, Warren Joseph *communications executive*
Cavuto, Neil *newscaster, business journalist, television host*
Caws, Mary Ann *literature and language professor*
Cayne, James L. (Jimmy Cayne) *securities trader, diversified financial services company executive*
Caytas, Ivo George *lawyer*
Cazeaux, Isabelle Anne Marie *retired music educator*
Cecil, Donald *retired investment company executive*
Cedarbaum, Miriam Goldman *federal judge*
Cembalest, Robin *arts editor, critic*
Cendali, Dale Margaret *lawyer*
Centrello, Gina *publishing executive*
Cephas, Derrick D. *bank executive, lawyer*
Cesar, Kamala *dancer, educator*
Cesare, Christine B. *lawyer*
Chabon, Michael *writer*
Chaganti, Raju S. *geneticist, educator, researcher*
Chahinian, A(ram) Philippe *oncologist*
Chai, Nelson J. *stock exchange executive*
Chaitman, Helen Davis *lawyer*
Chajet, Clive *brand and corporate image consultant*
Chakravarty, Suvobrata *research scientist, biophysicist*
Chalfie, Martin *biology professor*
Chalsty, John Steele *investment banker*
Chamberlain, John Angus *sculptor*
Chamberlain, Neil Cornelius Wolverton *economist, emeritus educator*
Chambers, William McWillie *artist, art dealer*
Chammah, Walid A. *investment banker*
Champion, Sara Stewart *lawyer*
Chan, Anthony *economist*
Chan, Janet *editorial director*
Chan, Lo-Yi Cheung Yuen *architect*
Chan, Siu-Wai *materials science educator*
Chandler, Michael Jonathan *allergist, physician*
Chandrasekhar, Sujana S. *otologist, educator, neurotologist*
Chaney, Gerald M. *retail executive*
Chang, David *chef*
Chang, Jeannette *publishing executive*
Chang, Joyce *corporate financial executive*
Chang, Laura *editor*
Chang, Marian S. *filmmaker, composer*
Chang, Mona Mei-Hsuan *computer programmer, analyst*
Chang, Stanley *ophthalmologist*
Channing, Stockard (Susan Antonia Williams Stockard) *actress*
Chao, James Si-Cheng *maritime executive*
Chapin, Samuel R. *investment company executive*
Chapin, Schuyler Garrison *retired cultural organization administrator, retired dean*
Chapman, Craig E. *lawyer*
Chapman, Max C., Jr. *investment company executive*
Chapman, Paul B. *oncologist*

Chapnick, David B. *lawyer*
Chappell, John Charles *lawyer*
Chappell, Wallace *performing company executive*
Charash, Bruce D. *cardiologist, educator*
Charles, Michael Harrison *architectural interior designer*
Charney, Marc D. *editor*
Charon, Rita *medical educator*
Charron, Paul Richard *apparel executive*
Chase, Oscar Gottfried *law educator*
Chase, Will *actor*
Chatzinoff, Howard *lawyer*
Chaves, Jose Maria *diplomat, lawyer, foundation administrator, educator*
Chavkin, Jeffrey S. *lawyer*
Chazen, Hartley James *lawyer*
Chazen, Leonard *lawyer*
Cheh, Huk Yuk *electrochemist*
Chell, Beverly C. *lawyer*
Chelstrom, Marilyn Ann *political science educator, consultant*
Chen, Elizabeth Shan Shan *research scientist*
Chen, Gang *research scientist, educator*
Chen, Lucia *foundation administrator*
Chen, Philip Minkang *brokerage house executive*
Chen, Tak-Ming *retired civil engineer, consultant*
Chen, Wesley *lawyer*
Chen, Xi *research scientist*
Chenault, Kenneth Irvine *finance company executive*
Cheney, Richard Eugene *public relations executive, psychoanalyst*
Cheng, Chuen Yan *biochemist, educator*
Cheng-Kingdon, Anla *venture capitalist*
Chenoweth, Kristin *actress*
Chepiga, Michael Joseph *lawyer*
Cherkasky, Michael G. *insurance company executive*
Chermayeff, Ivan *graphics designer*
Chernoff, Allan *correspondent*
Cherry, Sabrina *psychiatrist*
Cherryh, C. J. *writer*
Chesler, Evan Robert *lawyer*
Chesnutt, Jane *publishing executive*
Chess, William *public relations executive*
Chestnut, Colette *broadcast executive*
Chevigny, Paul Graves *law educator*
Chevray, Rene *engineering educator*
Chiang, Yung Frank *law educator*
Chiarchiaro, Frank John *lawyer*
Chicco, Gianfranco *healthcare communications executive*
Chichilnisky, Graciela *mathematician, educator, economist, writer*
Chida, Junaid Hasan *lawyer*
Childs, David M. *architectural firm executive*
Childs, John Farnsworth *retired bank executive*
Chilstrom, Robert Meade *lawyer*
Chin, Denny *federal judge*
Chin, Mel *sculptor*
Chin, Sylvia Fung *lawyer*
Chinn, Adam *lawyer*
Chinn, Yuen Yuey *art educator, painter*
Chira, Susan *editor*
Chirico, Anthony (Tony) *publishing executive*
Chirico, Emanuel *apparel executive*
Chirls, Richard *lawyer*
Chiu, David Tak Wai *surgeon*
Choldenko, Gennifer *writer*
Chopey, Nicholas P. *editor*
Chou, Ting-Chao *inventor, educator*
Chowdhury, Md. Shoaib *engineer*
Christ, Lily Esther Shih *mathematics professor*
Christensen, Anna *art director*
Christensen, Dieter *ethnomusicologist*
Christensen, Henry III *lawyer*
Christensen, Kathleen Elizabeth *foundation administrator*
Christiansen, Keith *curator*
Christodoulou, Marilena *investment banker, finance company executive*
Christoffers, Lynn Beryl *curator, artist*
Christopher, Nicholas *poet, writer*
Christy, Arthur Hill *lawyer*
Chromow, Sheri P. *lawyer*
Chu, C. K. *applied mathematician, educator*
Chun, Eunu *lawyer*
Chunilal, Damian *investment company executive*
Church, Frank Forrester *minister, columnist*
Church, Pamela T. *lawyer*
Chusid, Martin *musicologist, educator*
Chutorian, Abe M. *pediatrician, educator*
Chwast, Seymour *graphic artist*
Ciara, (Ciara Princess Harris) *R&B performer*
Cieply, Michael *editor, writer*
Cioppa, Robert *architectural firm executive*
Ciparick, Carmen Beauchamp *state appeals court judge*
Cipolla, Mark *lawyer*
Cisneros, Sandra *poet, short story writer, essayist*
Clagett, Leslie Plummer *editor, writer*
Claire, Thomas Andrew *financial executive, consultant, educator, writer*
Clamar, Aphrodite J. *psychologist*
Clapp, Stephen Henry *dean, violinist*
Clark, Bruce E. *lawyer*
Clark, Carolyn Cochran *lawyer*
Clark, Howard Longstreth, Jr. *finance company executive, director*
Clark, James Joseph *lawyer*
Clark, Joan Hardy *retired journalist*
Clark, Jonathan Montgomery *lawyer*
Clark, Mayree Carroll *investment banking executive*
Clark, Merrell Edward, Jr. *lawyer*
Clark, Michael K. *diversified financial services company executive*
Clark, Ramsey *lawyer, former United States attorney general*
Clark, Ric *real estate company executive*
Clark, Robert Henry, Jr. *finance company executive*
Clark, Sheryl Diane *physician*
Clark, Victoria *actress*
Clarke, Frank William *communications executive*
Clarke, Kenneth Kingsley *retired electronics executive*
Clarke, Richard Alan *former federal official*
Clarkson, Kelly Brianne *singer*
Clary, Richard Wayland *lawyer*

DeVard, Jerri *marketing professional*
Deveraux, Jude (Jude Gilliam White) *writer*
De Vido, Alfredo Eduardo *architect*
Devine, Donald F. (Don) *lawyer*
DeVita, M. Christine *foundation administrator*
Devitre, Dinyar S. *consumer products company executive, corporate financial executive*
De Vivo, Darryl Claude *pediatrician, neurologist*
Devlin, Robert Manning *diversified financial services company executive*
DeVoe, David, Sr. *publishing executive*
de Vries, Madeline *public relations executive*
Devulder, Arnaud *sommelier*
DeWoody, Beth Rudin *film producer*
Dhondt, Steven Thomas *development officer*
Diamond, Bernard Robin *lawyer*
Diamond, Brian *lawyer*
Diamond, David Howard *lawyer*
Diamond, Heidi Janice *marketing professional*
Diamonstein-Spielvogel, Barbaralee *writer*
Di Angelo, Christopher J. *lawyer*
Dias Griffin, Anne *investment advisor*
Diaz, Angela *pediatrician, educator*
Diaz-Cruz, Mario III *lawyer*
DiBiasio, Adolf R. *entertainment company executive*
DiBlasi, Gandolfo Vincent *lawyer*
Dichter, Barry Joel *lawyer*
Dickey, Eric Jerome *writer*
Didion, Joan *writer*
Diercksen, John W. *telecommunications industry executive*
Dierdorf, Daniel Lee (Dan Dierdorf) *sports commentator, football analyst, former professional football player*
Diggins, Peter Sheehan *arts administrator*
Diker, Charles M. *investment advisor*
Dikkers, Scott *editor*
Dillard, Annie *writer*
Diller, Barry *broadcast executive*
DiMaggio, Frank Louis *civil engineering educator*
Di Meo, Dominick *artist, sculptor, painter*
Di Mitri, Piero *fashion designer*
Dimling, John Arthur *marketing executive*
Dimon, James L. (Jamie Dimon) *diversified financial services company executive*
Dine, Jeffrey Malcolm *lawyer*
Dine, Jim *artist*
Dinerman, Miriam *social work educator*
Di Palma, Joseph Alphonse *investment company executive, lawyer*
DiPiazza, Samuel A., Jr. *finance company executive*
DiResta, Gene Robert *biomedical researcher, director*
DiSalvatore, William P. *lawyer*
DiSciullo, Alan Michael *lawyer*
Diskant, Gregory L. *lawyer*
Disney, Anthea *publishing executive*
Di Vittorio, Salvatore *composer, conductor*
Divon, Michael Y. *obstetrician and gynecologist*
Djeddah, Richard Nissim *investment banker*
Djerejian, Robert Asbed *architect*
Dlugoff, Marc Alan *lawyer*
Dobbins, David Foster *lawyer*
Dobbs, John Barnes *artist, educator*
Dobell, Byron Maxwell *magazine consultant*
Dobrof, Rose Wiesman *gerontology educator*
Doctoroff, Daniel L. *municipal official*
Doctorow, E.L. (Edgar Lawrence Doctorow) *writer, English educator*
Dodd, Lois *artist, art educator*
Dodge, Geoffrey A. *magazine publisher*
Doe, Willo *critic, writer, editor*
Doerfler, Ronald John *communications company executive*
Doherty, Thomas *publisher*
Dohrenwend, Bruce Philip *epidemiologist, social sciences educator*
Dolan, Michael *entertainment company executive, former advertising agency executive*
Dolan, Michael J. *broadcast executive*
Dolan, Raymond Bernard *insurance company executive, director*
Dolan, Regina A. *security firm executive*
Dole-Recio, Lecia *artist*
Dolman, Edward James *auction house executive*
Dolnick, Edward *writer*
Domino, Fats (Antoine Domino) *pianist, singer, songwriter*
Domowitz, Ian *finance company executive*
Donaghy, James K. *construction executive, contractor*
Donald, Arnold W. *health science association administrator, former food products executive*
Donald, Norman Henderson III *lawyer*
Donaldson, John Cecil, Jr. *consumer products company executive*
Donaldson, Stephen Reeder *author*
Donnelly, Patrick L. *broadcast executive, lawyer*
Donneson, Seena Sand *artist*
Donoghue, Denis *language professional, educator*
Donovan, Richard Edward *lawyer*
Doody, John *lawyer*
Dooley, Douglas John *bank executive*
Dooley, Thomas E. *broadcast executive*
Doonan, Simon *window dresser, creative director*
Dooner, John Joseph, Jr. *advertising executive*
Dopf, Glenn William *lawyer*
Dorf, Michael C. *law educator*
Dorfman, Howard David *pathologist, educator*
Dorkey, Charles E. III *lawyer*
Dormann, Henry O. *magazine publisher*
Dorn, Sue Bricker *retired hospital administrator*
Dorsen, Norman *lawyer, educator*
Dorsett, Burt *investment company executive*
Dotson, Robert Charles (Bob Dotson) *news correspondent*
Dougan, Brady W. *diversified financial services company executive*
Douglas, James McCrystal *lawyer*
Douglas, Kyan *television personality*
Douglass, Robert Royal *bank executive, lawyer*
Dowell, James Thomas *artist, filmmaker*
Dowling, Danielle *writer*
Dowling, Edward Thomas *economics professor*
Downes, Lawrence *editor*
Downey, John Alexander *physician, educator*
Downs, Hugh Malcolm *retired radio and television broadcaster*

Doyle, Eugenie Fleri *pediatrician, cardiologist, educator*
Doyle, John *artistic director, designer*
Doyle, Joseph Anthony *retired lawyer*
Doyle, Michael W. *international official, educator*
Doyle, Paul Francis *lawyer*
Dozier, Kimberly *news correspondent*
Draper, James David *art museum curator*
Drasner, Fred *newspaper publishing executive*
Dratch, Rachel *comedienne, actress*
Dray, Philip *history professor, writer*
Drayer, Burton Paul *hospital administrator, neuroradiologist*
Drebsky, Dennis Jay *lawyer*
Drechsler, Beatrice Krain *lawyer*
Dreiling, Richard *retail executive*
Drew, Ina R. *bank executive*
Drexler, Millard S. (Mickey Drexler) *retail executive*
Dreyfuss, Rochelle Cooper *law educator*
Driver, Martha Westcott *literature educator, researcher, writer*
Driver, Tom Faw *theologian, writer, advocate*
Dru, Jean-Marie Paul *advertising executive*
Drucker, Mort *commercial artist*
Drucker, Richard Allen *lawyer*
Drukman, Steven Charles *theater educator, playwright*
Drum, Sydney Maria *artist*
D'Souza, Rohit *investment company executive*
Dubin, James Michael *lawyer*
Dubin, Morton Donald, II, *lawyer*
Dubois, Michel *anesthesiologist*
Dubrow, John *artist*
Ducasse, Alain *chef*
Duch, Stephen *corporate financial executive*
Duchin, Peter Oelrichs *musician*
Duff, Gill *advertising executive*
Duff, Hilary Ann *actress, singer*
Duff, John Ewing *sculptor*
Duffy, Edmund Charles *lawyer*
Duffy, James Henry *writer, retired lawyer*
Duffy, Kevin Thomas *federal judge*
Duffy, W. Leslie *lawyer*
Duffy-King, Jan (John Mitchell Maver Wallace) *journalist, media consultant*
Dufresne, Wylie *chef, food service executive*
Dukakis, Olympia *actress*
Duke, Anthony Drexel *retired sociologist, educator, philanthropist*
Dukmejian, Michael *publishing executive*
Dulaine, Pierre *ballroom dancer*
Dumler, Richard J. *venture capitalist*
Du Mont, Nicolas *psychiatrist, educator*
Dunbar, Leila *antiques appraiser, auction house executive*
Duncan, Patricia *lawyer, broadcast executive*
Duncan, Pearl Rose *writer*
Dunham, Christopher Cooper *lawyer*
Dunham, Wolcott Balestier, Jr. *lawyer*
Dunkelman, Loretta *artist*
Dunn, Martin *editor-in-chief*
Dunn, M(orris) Douglas *lawyer*
Dunn, Thomas E. *lawyer*
Dunn, Vincent *lawyer*
Dunne, Diane C. *marketing professional*
Dunne, Dominick *writer*
Dunning, Jennifer *dance critic, reporter*
Dunst, Laurence David *advertising executive*
Dupont, Jakob *oncologist, researcher*
Du Prez, John *composer*
DuPuy, Bob (Robert A. DuPuy) *major league baseball executive*
Duran, George *chef*
Durang, Christopher *actor, playwright*
Durkin, Dorothy Angela *university official*
Durrant, M. Patricia *diplomat*
Dusick, Ryan Michael *musician*
Dwek, Cyril S. *bank executive*
Dworetzky, Murray *retired physician, educator*
Dworkin, Ronald Myles *law educator*
Dwyer, Gary Joseph *lawyer*
Dwyer, Jim *reporter, columnist*
Dykstra, Gretchen *foundation administrator*
Dylan, Bob (Robert Allen Zimmerman) *singer, composer*
Dyyon, Mario (LeRoy Frazier) *artist*
Eaker, Sherry Ellen *editor*
Eakins, William Shannon *lawyer*
Earl, Christopher D. *health products executive*
Earle, Eugenia *music educator*
Earle, Victor Montagne III *lawyer*
Eastman, Elrich Allan *retired judge*
Easum, Donald Boyd *consultant, educator, former institute executive, diplomat*
Eaton, Richard Kenyon *federal judge*
Ebersol, Dick (Duncan Dickie Ebersol) *television broadcasting executive*
Ebersole, Christine *actress*
Ebony, David *editor, arts critic*
Eckert, Allan Wesley *writer*
Eckhardt, Laurel Ann *biologist, researcher, educator*
Eckman, Fern Marja *journalist*
Edelman, Jack Robert *science educator*
Edelman, Judith H. *architect*
Edelman, Scott A. *lawyer*
Edelson, Gilbert Seymour *lawyer*
Edelson, Mary Beth *artist, educator*
Edelstein, Barbara A. *radiologist*
Edelstein, Mark S. *lawyer*
Edgar, Harold Simmons Hull *legal educator*
Edgerley, Susan *editor*
Edgerton, Malcom James *retired lawyer*
Edidin, Peter *editor*
Edlin, Richard A. *lawyer*
Edling, Lynn M. *knowledge management analyst*
Edlow, Kenneth Lewis *security firm executive*
Edmiston, Mark Morton *publishing company executive*
Edsparr, Patrik L. *diversified financial services company executive*
Edward, Jeffrey N. *diversified financial services company executive*
Edwards, Franklin R. *economist, educator, consultant*
Edwards, Harold Mortimer *mathematics professor*
Edwards, Jeffrey N. *diversified financial services company executive*
Edwards, Steven Mark *lawyer*
Egeland, Jan *international organization official*

Egen, Maureen Mahon *publishing executive*
Egielski, Richard *illustrator*
Ehrenbard, Robert *lawyer*
Ehrenkranz, Joel S. *lawyer*
Eichenwald, Kurt *writer*
Einhorn, David Allen *lawyer*
Einiger, Carol Blum *investment company executive*
Eins, Stefan *artist, curator, science researcher, writer*
Einstein, Steven Henry *lawyer, investment banker*
Eisen, Arnold M. *theologian*
Eisen, LizabethAnn R. *lawyer*
Eisen, Robert L. *lawyer*
Eisenberg, Barbara Anne K. *lawyer*
Eisenberg, Lee B. *writer*
Eisenberg, Marc S. *artist, sculptor*
Eisenberg, Sonja Miriam *artist*
Eisenman, Peter David *architect, educator*
Eisenstadt, G. Michael *diplomat, writer, educator, researcher*
Eisert, Edward Gaver *lawyer*
Eisler, Edith *music educator*
Eisler, Susan Krawetz *advertising executive*
Elder, Janet *editor*
Elderfield, John *art historian, museum curator*
Elgert, Paul A. *cytotechnologist*
Elinson, Jack *social sciences educator*
Elkes, Terrence Allen *communications executive*
Elkin, Judith *lawyer*
Elkin, Michael S. *lawyer*
Ellerbee, Linda (Linda Jane Smith) *reporter*
Elliman, Christopher J. (Kim Elliman) *investment company executive*
Ellin, Doug *film producer, television producer, television director, writer*
Ellingwood, Susan *editor*
Elliott, Eleanor Thomas *foundation executive, volunteer*
Elliott, Missy (Melissa Arnette Elliot) *musician*
Ellis, Albert *clinical psychologist, educator, author*
Ellis, Bret Easton *writer*
Ellis, Rosemary *editor-in-chief*
Ellis, Ross *non-profit organization executive*
Ellis, Scott *theatrical director*
Ellis, Terry *vocalist*
Ellison, Nicholas Howell *literary agent*
Ellroy, James *writer*
Elmer, Russell S. *diversified financial services company executive, lawyer*
Elmore, Leonard Joseph *lawyer*
Elsen, Jon *editor*
Elsen, Sheldon Howard *lawyer*
Elvey, Malcolm *venture capitalist*
Emanuel, Myron *corporate communications specialist, consultant*
Emerson, Andi (Mrs. Andi Emerson Weeks) *sales and advertising executive*
Emerson, Ken *writer*
Emme, (Emme Aronson) *model, apparel designer*
Emmerich, Adam Oliver *lawyer*
Emmerich, Toby *film company executive*
Emmrich, Stuart J. *editor*
Enberg, Dick *sportscaster*
Enders, Anthony Talcott *banker*
Enders, Elizabeth McGuire *artist*
Engel, Amy J. *corporate financial executive*
Engel, David *historian*
Engel, Ralph Manuel *lawyer*
Engelberg, Gail May *fine arts patron*
Englander, Israel A. *financier*
Engle, Robert F. *finance educator*
Engler, Robert *political science professor*
English, Thomas Francis *lawyer*
Engstrom, Erik *publishing executive*
Ensler, Eve *playwright, actress*
Entwistle, Andrew John *lawyer, consultant*
Epling, Richard Louis *lawyer*
Epstein, Cynthia Fuchs *sociology educator, writer*
Epstein, Jeremy G. *lawyer*
Epstein, Matthew *opera company director*
Epstein, Melvin *lawyer*
Epstein, Michael Alan *lawyer*
Ercklentz, Alexander Tonio *investment company executive*
Ercklentz, Enno Wilhelm, Jr. *lawyer*
Erdoes, Mary Callahan *investment banker*
Erickson, Mitchell Drake *chemist, environmental scientist*
Ericson, Robert Walter *lawyer*
Erlanger, Bernard Ferdinand *biochemist, educator*
Erlenmeyer-Kimling, L. *psychiatrist, researcher*
Ernst, John Louis *management consultant*
Eschenbach, Christoph *conductor, musician, music director*
Eshleman, Diane Varrin *bank executive*
Esnault, Tony *chef*
Esposito, Louis *real estate developer*
Esposito, Richard Joseph *journalist, executive*
Essandoh, Hilda Brathwaite *primary school educator*
Estabrook, Alison *surgeon, educator*
Esterow, Milton *publishing executive*
Estes, Richard *artist*
Estes, Simon Lamont *opera singer, bass-baritone*
Estlund, Cynthia *law educator*
Estreicher, Samuel *lawyer, educator*
Ethan, Carol Baehr *psychotherapist, psychoanalyst*
Ettinger, John Riche *lawyer*
Eustis, Oskar (Paul Jefferson Eustis) *performing company executive*
Evanovich, Janet *writer*
Evans, Alfred Lee, Jr. *advertising executive*
Evans, Faith *singer*
Evans, Sir Harold Matthew *editor, publisher, writer*
Evans, James Hurlburt *retired transportation and natural resources executive*
Evans, John Thomas *lawyer*
Evans, Linda Kay *publishing executive*
Evans, Mark Ira *obstetrician, geneticist*
Evans, Martin Frederic *lawyer*
Evans, Mary Johnston *corporate director*
Evarts, Helen Coleman *secondary school educator*
Evarts, William Maxwell, Jr. *lawyer*
Evnin, Anthony Basil *venture capital investor*
Eyre, Paul P. *lawyer*
Faber, Peter Lewis *lawyer*
Fabian, Larry Louis *academic administrator*
Fabricant, Robert Edmund *lawyer*
Fabrikant, Geraldine *journalist*
Fader, Bruce E. *lawyer*

Faedda, Gianni L. *psychiatrist, researcher*
Fagan, Jeffrey A. *law educator*
Fagen, Leslie Gordon *lawyer*
Fager, Jeffrey *broadcast executive*
Fagin, Allen Ian *lawyer*
Fagin, Claire Mintzer *nursing educator, nursing administrator*
Fagin, Dan *science and environmental writer, reporter*
Fahey, James Edward *brokerage house executive*
Fahim, Kareem *journalist*
Fahn, Stanley *neurologist, educator*
Fahour, Ahmed *investment company executive*
Fajors, Nique *marketing executive*
Fakahany, Ahmass L. *finance company executive*
Falai, Tacopo *chef*
Falco, Randy *broadcast executive*
Fales, Haliburton, II, *lawyer*
Falk, Charles H. (Harry Falk) *stock exchange executive*
Falk, Edgar Alan *public relations consulting executive, writer*
Falkenrath, Richard A. *protective services official*
Fallows, James Mackenzie *journalist*
Fantasia, (Fantasia Monique Barrino) *singer*
Farber, David *editor*
Farber, John J. *chemical company executive*
Farber, Saul Joseph *physician, educator*
Farber, Seth C. *lawyer*
Fargis, Alison K. *book developer, literary agent, consultant*
Fargis, Paul McKenna *publisher, publishing executive, consultant, book developer*
Farinelli, Jean L. *management consultant*
Farino, Julian *television director, film director, television producer*
Faris, George N. *management consultant*
Farley, Carole *soprano*
Farley, Katherine G. *real estate company executive*
Farley, Terrence Michael *lawyer*
Farrell, Patrick *editor*
Farris, Robert Linsy *ophthalmologist, director*
Fasman, Zachary Dean *lawyer*
Fasnacht, Heide Ann *artist, educator*
Fass, Peter Michael *lawyer, educator*
Fast, Julius *writer, editor*
Faulkner, Walter Thomas *lawyer, director*
Fausel, Alan *art appraiser*
Fawcett, Christopher Babcock *civil engineer, construction and water resources company executive*
Fazio, Vic (Victor Herbert Fazio Jr.) *lawyer, former congressman*
Fears, Linda *editor-in-chief*
Feczko, Joe *pharmaceutical executive*
Feder, Arthur A. *lawyer, legal association administrator*
Feder, Barnaby *reporter*
Feder, Harry Simon *bank executive*
Feder, Saul E. *lawyer*
Federle, Michael *publishing executive*
Fedunok, Suzanne *retired librarian*
Fehr, Donald M. *baseball union executive*
Feigen, Richard L. *art dealer, collector, writer*
Feiler, William S. *lawyer*
Feiman, Ronald Mark *lawyer*
Feinberg, Wilfred *federal judge*
Feinstein, John *writer, journalist*
Feintuch, Henry Philip *public relations executive*
Feit, Barberi Paull *composer, lyricist, psychotherapist, writer*
Feit, Glenn Martin *lawyer*
Feld, Eliot *dancer, choreographer, performing company executive*
Feldberg, Meyer *investment advisor, university dean emeritus*
Feldberg, Michael Svetkey *lawyer*
Felder, Raoul Lionel *lawyer*
Feldman, Allan Roy *corporate development and marketing executive*
Feldman, Bernard Robert *physician*
Feldman, Franklin retired *lawyer, printmaker*
Feldman, Helaine *editor, public relations associate*
Feldman, Robert C. *public relations executive*
Feldman, Ronald Arthur *sociologist, educator*
Feldman, Samuel Mitchell *neuroscientist, educator*
Fell, M. Ann *publishing executive*
Feltus, Alan Evan *artist*
Fenchel, Gerd Hermann *psychoanalyst*
Feniger, Jerome Roland, Jr. *broadcast executive*
Fenn, Patrick B. *lawyer*
Fenster, Albert M. *lawyer*
Fensterstock, Blair Courtney *lawyer*
Ferber, Linda S. *museum director*
Ferguson, Milton Carr, Jr. *lawyer*
Ferguson, Robert A. *law educator*
Ferguson, Sarah *The Duchess of York*
Ferguson, Tim Wayne *editor, journalist*
Fernandez, James *retail products executive*
Fernandez, Jose Walfredo *lawyer, department chairman*
Fernández, Teresita *sculptor*
Ferrante, Joan Marguerite *language educator, literature educator, writer*
Fertig, Howard *publishing executive*
Fertitta, George A. *marketing executive*
Feskoe, Gaffney Jon *management consultant*
Fessel, Robin D. *lawyer*
Feuerman, Carole A. *sculptor, artist*
Fey, Albert Eugene *lawyer*
Feyer, Thomas *editor*
Field, David Anthony *lawyer*
Field, Patricia *apparel designer*
Field, Steven Philip *medical educator*
Fielding, Helen *writer*
Fields, C. Virginia *city manager*
Fields, Felicia P. *actress*
Filardi, Christopher Edward *biologist, researcher*
Filarski Hasselbeck, Elizabeth *television host/personality*
Fili-Krushel, Patricia *media company executive*
Filkins, Dexter Price *newspaper reporter*
Filler, Ronald Howard *lawyer*
Finch, Edward Ridley, Jr. *lawyer, educator, retired diplomat, ambassador*
Finch, Spencer *artist*
Findakly, Hani K. *investment company executive*
Finder, Alan *reporter*
Finder, Lisa *librarian, researcher*
Findlay, Michael Alistair *art dealer, poet*

Fine, Deborah *Internet company executive, former apparel executive*
Fine, Drew S. *lawyer*
Fine, Jo Renée *management consultant*
Fine, Kit *philosophy educator*
Fine, Michael Joseph *publishing executive, communications executive*
Finegold, Amy Beth *elementary school educator, consultant*
Fineman, Steven E. *lawyer*
Fink, Laurence D. *diversified financial services company executive*
Fink, Matthew E. *health facility executive, educator*
Fink, Robert Steven *lawyer, writer, educator*
Finkelson, Allen *lawyer*
Finkelstein, Allen Lewis *lawyer*
Finkelstein, Bernard *lawyer*
Finkelstein, David S. *lawyer*
Finkelstein, Henry *artist*
Finkelstein, James A. *media executive*
Finkelstein, Stuart M. *lawyer*
Finley, John G. *lawyer*
Finley, Skip *communications executive*
Finley, Steven R. *lawyer*
Finn, Brian D. *financial services executive*
Finn, Edwin Anthony, Jr. *publishing executive*
Finn, Peter *public relations executive*
Finn, Peter Michael *broadcast executive*
Finnerty, Joseph Gregory, Jr. *lawyer*
Finnerty, Joseph Gregory III *lawyer*
Fins, Joseph Jack *internist*
Fiori, Pamela *publishing executive, writer*
Fiorilla di Santa Croce, John Leopoldo *investment company executive, lawyer*
Fireman, Kenneth Howard *journalist*
Firestone, David E. *editor*
First, Harry *law educator*
First, Michael Bruce *psychiatrist, educator*
Fischbach, Gerald D. *dean, neurobiology educator*
Fischer, Carl *photographer, graphic designer, actor*
Fischer, Herbert James *social studies educator*
Fischer, Joseph L. *pharmaceutical executive*
Fischer, Mark David *lawyer*
Fischer, Rob *sculptor*
Fiser, Andras *science educator*
Fishbein, Peter Melvin *lawyer*
Fishbein, William *psychologist, neuroscientist*
Fisher, Ann Bailen *lawyer*
Fisher, Arthur *magazine editor*
Fisher, Joely *actress*
Fisher, Laura Lani *physician, medical educator*
Fisher, Peter R. *investment company executive, former federal agency administrator*
Fisher, Robert I. *lawyer*
Fisher, Vernon *artist, educator*
Fishman, Ellen Beth *lawyer*
Fishman, Fred Norman *lawyer*
Fishman, Steven T. *psychologist*
Fisk, Eliot H. *musician*
Fiske, Robert Bishop, Jr. *lawyer*
Fitch, Janet *writer*
Fitts, Nelson Orus *lawyer*
FitzPatrick, Daniel M. *trust company executive, lawyer*
FitzPatrick, James A., Jr. *lawyer*
Flach, Frederic Francis *psychiatrist*
Flack, Roberta *singer*
Flaherty, Pamela Potter *bank executive*
Flaherty, Tina Santi *corporate communications specialist, writer*
Flanagan, Sean Patrick *publishing executive*
Flaum, Sander Allen *advertising and marketing executive*
Flax, Herschel *surgeon*
Flay, Bobby *chef, restaurateur*
Fleder, Robert Charles *lawyer*
Fleischer, Arthur, Jr. *lawyer*
Fleischman, Albert Sidney (Sid Fleischman) *writer*
Fleischman, Barbara Greenberg *public relations consultant*
Fleischman, Edward Hirsh *lawyer, consultant*
Fleischmann, Dennis C. *lawyer*
Fleming, Gregory J. *finance company executive*
Fleming, Peter Emmet, Jr. *lawyer*
Fleming, Renée L. *opera singer*
Fleming, Ronald A. *lawyer*
Flesher, Gail A. *lawyer*
Fletcher, Anthony Lee *lawyer*
Fletcher, George P. *law educator*
Fletcher, Harry George III *library director*
Flicker, John *foundation executive*
Flinn, Michael de Vluming *investment company executive*
Flint, George Squire *lawyer*
Flom, Jason *music company executive*
Flom, Joseph Harold *lawyer*
Flood, Richard Sidney *curator*
Florence, Tyler *chef*
Florescue, Leonard George *lawyer*
Florin, Sharon *artist*
Florio, Steven T. *magazine executive*
Florio, Thomas A. *magazine publisher*
Flowers, Brandon Richard *singer*
Flowers, J. Christopher *investment banker*
Fluhr, Howard *consulting firm executive*
Flumenbaum, Martin *lawyer*
Flynn, John J. *museum curator*
Flynn, Laurie M. *social worker*
Flynn, Timothy P. *finance company executive*
Flynn, William Joseph *insurance company executive*
Fodor, Susanna Serena *lawyer*
Fogel, Henry *orchestra administrator*
Fogel, Irving Martin *consulting engineer*
Fogelnest, Robert *lawyer*
Fogg, Blaine Viles *lawyer*
Fogg, William V. *lawyer*
Fogler, Dan *actor*
Foley, Ann *broadcast executive*
Folta, Carl D. *communications executive*
Fontaine, John C. *foundation administrator, lawyer, former newspaper company executive*
Fontana, Thomas Michael *television producer, scriptwriter*
Forbes, Christopher (Kip Forbes) *publisher*
Forbes, Sally *researcher, editor, curator*

Forbes, Steve (Malcolm Stevenson Forbes Jr.) *publishing executive*
Forbes, Timothy Carter *publishing executive*
Ford, Mark Patrick *publishing executive*
Ford, Paul B. *lawyer*
Forden, Diane Claire *magazine editor*
Foreman, Richard *theater director, playwright*
Forese, Laura Lee *hospital administrator, orthopedist*
Forman, Leonard P. *media company executive*
Formenti, Silvia C. *radiation oncologist*
Formento, Daniel *radio company executive, writer*
Forrest, David Vickers *psychiatrist, educator*
Forrest, Katherine B. *lawyer*
Forrest, Kenneth B. *lawyer*
Forsberg, Myra *editor*
Forst, Edward C. *investment company executive*
Forstadt, Joseph Lawrence *lawyer*
Forster, Arnold *lawyer, author*
Forstmann, Theodore J. *investment firm executive*
Fortner, Joseph Gerald *surgeon, educator*
Fosler, Gail D. *economist*
Foster, Carter *curator*
Foster, Craig Allen *plastic surgeon*
Foster, Gary *publishing executive, information technology executive*
Foulkes, Llyn *artist, educator*
Fowle, Bruce S. *architect*
Fowler, Beth *actress*
Fowler, John M. *finance company executive*
Fowler, Karen Joy *writer*
Fox, Arthur Charles *cardiologist, educator*
Fox, Daniel Michael *foundation executive, writer*
Fox, Donald Thomas *lawyer*
Fox, Margalit (Eve) *journalist, editor, writer*
Fox, Matthew *actor*
Fox, Mitchell B. *magazine publisher*
Fox, Paula (Mrs. Martin Greenberg) *writer*
Fox, Richard Gabriel *anthropologist, educator*
Fox, Sylvan *journalist, educator*
Fox-Freund, Barbara Susan *real estate company executive*
Fraenkel, George Kessler *chemistry professor*
Fraguela, James *publishing executive*
Fraidin, Stephen *lawyer*
Frances, Richard Joseph *psychiatrist*
Franciosa, Joseph Anthony *healthcare consultant*
Francis, James Clark, IV, *federal judge*
Francis, Steve *professional basketball player*
Franck, Thomas Martin *law educator*
Frank, Elizabeth *writer, educator*
Frank, Frederick *investment banker*
Frank, Lloyd *lawyer, director, retired chemicals executive*
Frank, William Fielding *computer company executive, consultant*
Frank, William P. *lawyer*
Franke, Katherine M. *law educator*
Frankel, Martin Richard *statistician, educator, consultant*
Frankel, Max *retired journalist*
Frankenthaler, Helen *artist*
Frankfort, Lew *consumer products company executive*
Franklin, Blake Timothy *lawyer*
Franklin, Julian Harold *political science professor*
Franks, Martin Davis *broadcast executive*
Frantz, Andrew Gibson *endocrinologist, educator, dean*
Franzen, Jonathan *writer*
Frasch, Ron L. *retail executive*
Frazier, Charles Robinson *writer*
Frazza, George S. *lawyer*
Frear, David J. *broadcast executive*
Fredericks, Ivy Lindstrom *investment banker*
Fredericks, Wesley Charles, Jr. *lawyer*
Fredericks, William Curtis *lawyer*
Freed, Stanley Arthur *retired museum curator*
Freedberg, David Adrian *art educator, art historian*
Freedman, Aaron David *medicine and biochemistry educator, retired dean*
Freedman, Alfred Mordecai *psychiatrist, educator*
Freedman, Gerald M. *lawyer*
Freedman, Helen E. *judge*
Freedman, Michael Leonard *geriatrician, educator*
Freeland, Chrystia *editor, director*
Freeman, David John *lawyer*
Freeman, Scott M. *lawyer*
Frehm, Lynne *painter*
Freiberg, Steven J. *diversified financial services company executive*
Freilich, Joan Sherman *utilities executive*
Freilicher, Morton *lawyer, educator*
French, John III *lawyer*
Frenkel, Jacob Aharon *insurance company executive*
Freudenheim, Milton B. *journalist*
Freund, Fred A. *retired lawyer*
Frey, Andrew Lewis *lawyer*
Frey, James *writer*
Freyer, Dana Hartman *lawyer*
Freyre, Angela Mariana *lawyer*
Freyre, Fabio *publishing executive*
Fribourg, Paul J. *grain company executive*
Fricklas, Michael David *lawyer, broadcast executive*
Fridson, Martin Steven *finance company executive*
Fried, Burton Theodore *lawyer*
Fried, Donald David *lawyer*
Fried, Richard L. *lawyer*
Friedberg, Barry Sewell *investment banker*
Frieden, Thomas R. *city health department administrator, epidemiologist*
Friedenberg, Daniel Meyer *investor, writer*
Friedman, Alan Herbert *ophthalmologist*
Friedman, Alan Roy *lawyer*
Friedman, Barry *law educator*
Friedman, Bart *lawyer*
Friedman, B(ernard) H(arper) *writer*
Friedman, Debbie *singer, songwriter, religious studies educator*
Friedman, Dennis J. *lawyer*
Friedman, George *lawyer*
Friedman, Herbert A. *rabbi, educator, not-for-profit fundraiser*
Friedman, Ira Hugh *surgeon*
Friedman, J. Roger *publisher*
Friedman, Jane *publishing executive*
Friedman, Jeffrey J. *lawyer*
Friedman, Jeffrey M. *medical researcher, educator*

Friedman, Max *lawyer*
Friedman, Rachelle *music retail executive*
Friedman, Robert Laurence *investment company executive*
Friedman, Sam *editor*
Friedman, Samuel Selig *lawyer*
Friedman, Stephen *former federal official, former diversified financial services executive*
Friedman, Wilbur Harvey *lawyer*
Frischling, Carl *lawyer*
Frommer, William S. *lawyer*
Frost, William Lee *foundation executive*
Fruitman, Frederick Howard *investment banker*
Frumkin, Joseph B. *lawyer*
Fry, Elizabeth H. W. *lawyer*
Fry, Morton Harrison, II, *lawyer*
Frye, Channing *professional basketball player*
Frye, Clayton Wesley, Jr. *finance company executive*
Fuchs, Elaine V. *molecular biologist, educator*
Fuchs, Nancy E. *lawyer*
Fudge, Ann Marie *advertising executive*
Fuentez, Tania Michele *journalist*
Fuerth, Glenn J. *lawyer*
Fugazy, William Denis *transportation company executive*
Fuhrman, Susan H. *academic administrator, education educator*
Fujimura, Makoto *artist*
Fuld, Richard Severin, Jr., (Dick Fuld) *investment banking executive*
Fuller, Bonnie *editor-in-chief*
Furman, Anthony Michael *public relations executive*
Furman, Roy Lance *investment banker, theater producer*
Furnas, Barnaby *painter*
Fusaro, Peter C. *environmental scientist, consultant*
Fuster, Valentin *cardiologist, educator*
Futter, Ellen Victoria *museum administrator*
Fuzesi, Stephen, Jr. *lawyer, communications executive*
Gabay, Donald *lawyer*
Gabriel, Trip (Bertram Gabriel III) *editor*
Gabrielson, Charles *publishing executive*
Gabrilove, Jacques Lester *physician*
Gaddipati, Sreedhar *obstetrician*
Gaffney, Elizabeth Mallory *editor, writer, literature educator, translator*
Gaffney, John T. *lawyer*
Gage, Beau *artist*
Gage, Robert Clifford *minister*
Gagosian, Larry *art dealer*
Gaifman, Haim *mathematician, philosopher, educator*
Gaines, Steven S. *writer*
Gainsburg, Roy Ellis *publishing executive*
Galan, Leonidez Vindollo *architect*
Galanter, Eugene *psychologist, educator*
Galanter, Marc *psychiatrist, educator*
Galil, Zvi *engineering educator*
Gallagher, Brian John *lawyer*
Gallagher, Cornelius *chef*
Gallagher, Edward Peter *foundation executive*
Gallagher, Ellen *artist*
Gallagher, Maureen J. *psychologist*
Gallo, David *scenic designer*
Gallo, Martha J. *diversified financial services company executive*
Gallo, William Victor *cartoonist*
Galluzzo, Jay A. *lawyer*
Gamble, Theodore Robert, Jr. *investment banker*
Gambro, Michael S. *lawyer*
Gangwisch, James Edward *social worker, researcher*
Gans, Herbert J. *sociologist, educator*
Gant, Donald Ross *investment banker*
Ganz, Axel *publishing executive*
Ganz, David L. *lawyer*
Ganz, Howard Laurence *lawyer*
Ganzi, Victor Frederick *publishing executive*
Garabedian, Paul Roesel *mathematics professor*
Garber, Donald *Major League Soccer commissioner*
Garbus, Martin Solomon *lawyer*
Garcia, Andy *actor*
Garcia, Angela G. *lawyer*
Garcia, Michael J. *prosecutor, former federal agency administrator*
García, Mildred *academic administrator*
Gardino, Vincent Anthony *broadcast executive*
Gardner, Esther P. *neuroscientist, physiologist, educator*
Gardner, Gary A. *lawyer*
Gardner, H. McIntyre (Mac Gardner) *diversified financial services company executive*
Gardner, Janet Paxton *journalist, film producer*
Gardner, Richard Newton *diplomat, lawyer, educator*
Garfield, Leslie Jerome *real estate executive*
Garfinkel, Barry Herbert *lawyer*
Garfinkel, Lee *advertising agency executive*
Garland, David William *law educator, sociology educator*
Garland, Sylvia Dillof *lawyer*
Garment, Leonard *lawyer, author*
Garner, Albert Headden *investment banker*
Garner, Melvin C. *lawyer*
Garrett, Laurie *journalist, global health scholar*
Garrett, Robert *investment banker, director*
Garrett, Wendell *antiques appraiser, historian, editor*
Garron, Miriam *chef*
Garson, Gary Wayne *lawyer*
Gartner, Murray *lawyer*
Gartner, Steven J. *lawyer*
Garvey, Richard Anthony *retired lawyer*
Garvin, Andrew Paul *computer company executive, writer*
Gasman, Daniel E. *retired history professor, writer*
Gaspar-Martins, Ismael *Angolian diplomat, former government minister, business executive*
Gastwirth, Seth Allen *lawyer*
Gatfield, Stephen J. *advertising executive*
Gath, Jean Marie *architectural firm executive*
Gatje, Robert Frederick *architect, writer*
Gatto, John Taylor *educational consultant, educator*
Gaughan, Eugene Francis *lawyer, retired accountant*

Gavin, Paula Lance *investment company executive*
Gay, Darrell S. *lawyer*
Gay, Peter *historian, educator, writer*
Gazzara, Ben *actor*
Geary, Hilary R. *society editor*
Gebbie, Kristine Moore *medical educator*
Geckle, Robert Alan *manufacturing executive*
Geddes, John M. *editor*
Geelan, John *lawyer*
Gehringer, Richard George *publishing executive*
Geier, Philip Henry, Jr. *advertising executive*
Geiser, Elizabeth Able *publishing company executive*
Geissbuhler, Stephan *graphics designer*
Geistfeld, Mark *law educator*
Geithner, Timothy F. *bank executive*
Gelb, Bruce Stuart *city commissioner, consultant*
Gelb, Judith Anne *lawyer*
Gelb, Leslie Howard *writer, lecturer, consultant*
Gelb, Peter *performing company executive*
Gelband, Michael *investment company executive*
Gelfand, David R. *lawyer*
Geller, Robert James *advertising executive*
Gellert, Michael Erwin *investment banker*
Gellhorn, Alfred *physician, educator*
Gelston, Philip A. *lawyer*
Geltzer, Robert Lawrence *lawyer, arbitrator, mediator, retired retail executive*
Genachowski, Julius *communications executive*
Genader, Robert J. *investment company executive*
Gendler, Ellen *dermatologist*
Genova, Diane Melisano *lawyer*
Genova, Joseph Steven *lawyer*
Genty, Philip *law educator*
Geoghegan, Patricia *lawyer*
George, Elizabeth (Susan Elizabeth George) *writer*
George, Nelson *writer, film producer*
Geraghty, Patrick D. *lawyer*
Gerard, Barbara *visual artist, educator*
Gerard, Whitney Ian *lawyer*
Gerard-Sharp, Monica Fleur *communications executive*
Gerber, Robert Evan *judge*
Gerberg, Judith Levine *management consultant*
Gerdts, William Henry *art history educator*
Gerety, Tom *academic administrator, lawyer, educator, philosopher*
Germano, William Paul *dean, former publishing executive*
Gero, Anthony George *securities and commodities trader*
Gersony, Welton Mark *pediatrician, cardiologist, educator*
Gerspach, Thomas Joseph *lawyer*
Gerth, Jeff *journalist*
Gertjejansen, Doyle *artist, educator*
Gertler, Menard M. *physician, educator*
Gethers, Peter (Russell Andrews) *writer, publishing executive*
Getnick, Neil Victor *lawyer*
Gewirtz, Elliot *lawyer*
Gewirtz-Friedman, Gerry *editor*
Geyer, Thomas Powick *newspaper publisher*
Ghaffari, Avideh Behrouz *interior designer*
Ghani, Cyrus *lawyer*
Gharib, Susie *newscaster*
Giaccio, Anthony *lawyer*
Giancotti, Filippo Giusto *molecular biologist, educator*
Gianinno, Susan McManama *advertising executive*
Giannetti, Stephen P. *publishing executive*
Giannetti, Thomas Leonard *lawyer*
Giardina, Elsa Grace Vonna *cardiologist, educator*
Gibbons, Robert John *lawyer*
Giblin, James Cross *writer, publishing executive*
Giblin, Jennifer *chef*
Gibney, Alex *producer, director, writer*
Gibney, James S. *editor*
Gibson, Arlene Joy *headmaster*
Gibson, Charles DeWolf *newscaster*
Gibson, John *news anchor, correspondent*
Gibson, Ralph H(olmes) *photographer*
Gibson, Sandra *painter, filmmaker*
Giddens-Jones, Emily Jane *architectural and interior designer, consultant*
Giegerich, Thomas William *lawyer*
Gifford, William C. *lawyer, educator*
Gigot, Paul Anthony *editor*
Gilbert, Jack *poet*
Gilbert, Rose Bennett *journalist*
Gill, E. Ann *lawyer*
Gill, Linda A. *advertising executive*
Gillers, Stephen *lawyer, educator, academic administrator*
Gillespie, George Joseph III *lawyer*
Gillespie, John Thomas *retired university administrator*
Gillespie, Michael J. *lawyer*
Gillette, Clayton T. *law educator, academic administrator*
Gilligan, Carol *psychologist, writer*
Gilligan, Edward P. *diversified financial services company executive*
Gillinson, Sir Clive Daniel *performing company executive, former musician*
Gillispie, Robert J. *lawyer*
Gilman, Susan Jane *writer*
Gimblett, Maxwell Harold *artist, art educator*
Giniger, Kenneth Seeman *publisher*
Ginsberg, David Lawrence *architect*
Ginsberg, Elizabeth *artist, educator*
Ginsberg, Henry *medical educator, researcher*
Ginsberg, Hersh Meier *rabbi, religious organization administrator*
Ginsburg, Sigmund G. *management and executive search consultant*
Ginter, Valerian Alexius *urban historian, educator*
Ginzel, Andrew H. *artist*
Giordano, Bill A. *psychotherapist*
Giordano, Mary Ann *editor*
Giraldi, Robert Nicholas *film director*
Girard, Anouck *engineering educator*
Girard, Judy *broadcast executive*
Girardi, Federico Pablo *surgeon, educator*
Girden, Eugene Lawrence *lawyer*
Gissler, Sigvard Gunnar, Jr. *journalist, educator, retired editor*
Gitter, Max *lawyer*
Gittes, Franklin M. *lawyer*
Giuliani, Judith *not-for-profit executive*

Giuliani, Rudy (Rudolph William Louis Giuliani III) *consultant, lawyer, former mayor*
Giurgola, Romaldo *architect, educator*
Gladstone, Bernard *columnist*
Gladstone, Rick *editor*
Gladwell, Malcolm *writer*
Glanze, Walter D. *editor, writer, lexicographer, publishing consultant*
Glanzer, Murray *psychology professor*
Glasberg, H(erbert) Mark *psychiatrist, educator*
Glasberg, Scot Bradley *plastic surgeon*
Glaser, Milton *graphics designer, illustrator*
Glass, David Carter *psychologist, educator*
Glass, Philip *composer, musician*
Glasser, Stephen C. *lawyer*
Glassman, Alexander Howard *psychiatrist, researcher*
Glassman, Debra *dentist*
Glassman, Steven *dentist*
Glassman, Steven J. *lawyer*
Glater, Jonathan D. *reporter*
Glatt, Mitchell Steven *consumer products company executive*
Glekel, Jeffrey Ives *lawyer*
Glesby, Marshall Jay *physician, educator*
Gliatta, Stephen *lawyer*
Glickman, Michael Richard *social studies educator*
Glickman, Robert Morris *health facility administrator, dean*
Glickstein, Steven *lawyer*
Gliklich, Jerry *physician, educator*
Glimcher, Arnold B. *art gallery executive*
Gluck, Carol *history professor*
Glusman, John Alan *editor, writer*
Gochberg, Thomas *real estate investor, investment banker*
Goddard, Donald Letcher *writer, editor*
Godridge, Leslie V. *bank executive*
Godson, Godfrey Nigel *molecular geneticist, educator*
Goelet, Robert G. *investment company executive*
Goetz, Maurice Harold *lawyer*
Goff, Robert Edward *healthcare executive, insurance company executive*
Goines, Leonard *music educator, consultant*
Gold, Arnold P. *neurologist*
Gold, Jeffrey Mark *investment banker*
Gold, Mari S. *public relations executive*
Gold, Martin Elliot *lawyer, educator*
Gold, Richard L. *lawyer*
Gold, Sharon Cecile *artist, educator*
Gold, Simeon *lawyer*
Gold, Stuart Walter *lawyer*
Gold, William Elliott *health care management consultant, educator*
Goldbard, Laura E. *lawyer*
Goldberg, Danny *recording industry executive*
Goldberg, Jay *lawyer*
Goldberg, Nieca *cardiologist, educator*
Goldberg, Victor Paul *law educator*
Goldberger, Paul Jesse *dean, architecture critic, writer*
Golden, Arthur F. *lawyer*
Golden, Daniel H. *lawyer*
Golden, Michael *publishing executive*
Golden, Thelma *curator*
Golden, William Theodore *trustee, corporate director*
Goldfarb, David *investment banking executive*
Goldfarb, David S. *nephrologist, researcher*
Goldfarb, Will *chef*
Goldfein, Shepard *lawyer*
Goldfrank, Lewis Robert *physician*
Goldman, Charles Norton *retired corporate lawyer*
Goldman, George David *psychologist*
Goldman, Lawrence Saul *lawyer*
Goldman, Louis B. *lawyer*
Goldman, Michael S. *lawyer*
Goldman, Peter Louis *writer*
Goldmark, Peter Francis *banker*
Goldschmid, Harvey Jerome *law educator, commissioner*
Goldschmidt, Charles *advertising agency executive*
Goldsmith, Clifford Henry *graphic design company executive*
Goldsmith, Lee Selig *lawyer, physician*
Goldsmith, Merwin *actor, theater director*
Goldsmith, Michael Allen *oncologist, educator*
Goldsmith, Stanley Joseph *nuclear medicine physician, educator*
Goldstein, Alvin *lawyer*
Goldstein, Avraham *mathematician, computer scientist*
Goldstein, Charles Arthur *lawyer*
Goldstein, Gary Sanford *executive recruiter*
Goldstein, Howard Warren *lawyer*
Goldstein, Jeffrey Alan *corporate financial executive*
Goldstein, Jonathan *lawyer*
Goldstein, Marc *surgeon, urologist, educator, health facility administrator*
Goldstein, Marcia Landweber *lawyer*
Goldstein, Martin S. *obstetrician, gynecologist, educator*
Goldstein, Matthew *academic administrator*
Goldstein, Sandra Cara *lawyer*
Goldstein, Steve *corporate financial executive*
Goldston, James *television producer*
Goldstone, Steven F. *former consumer products company executive*
Golici, Ana *artist*
Golick, Toby *law educator, legal services administrator*
Golin, Mark *editor*
Gollub, Marc Jeffrey *radiologist*
Golomb, Susan L. *literary agent*
Golove, David M. *law educator*
Gomez, Francis Dean *consumer products company executive, former foreign service official*
Gomory, Ralph Edward *mathematician, foundation administrator*
Gondolesi, Gabriel Eduardo *transplant surgeon*
Gonnerman, Jennifer *writer, journalist*
Gonzalez, Eugene Robert *investment banker*
Gonzalez-Falla, Sondra Gilman *art collector*
González-Rodríguez, Salvador *dermatologist, educator*
Goodale, James Campbell *lawyer, educator, television producer, media columnist*

Goodale, Toni Krissel *research and development company executive*
Goodell, Roger *national football league commissioner*
Goodfriend, Herbert Jay *lawyer*
Goodhartz, Gerald *law librarian*
Goodman, Edwin A. *venture capitalist*
Goodman, Gary A. *lawyer*
Goodman, George Jerome Waldo (Adam Smith) *writer, television journalist, consultant*
Goodman, Roy Matz *corporate financial executive, former state senator*
Goodnough, Robert Arthur *artist*
Goodridge, Allan D. *lawyer*
Goodstein, Laurie Beth *journalist*
Goodstein, Les *newspaper publishing executive*
Goodwin, Beatrice *nursing educator, consultant*
Goodwin, Michael *labor union administrator*
Goott, Alan F(ranklin) *lawyer*
Gordon, Alan Lee *psychiatrist*
Gordon, David *playwright, theater director, choreographer*
Gordon, David A. *lawyer*
Gordon, Jeffrey Neil *law educator*
Gordon, Leo Maury *federal judge*
Gordon, Linda *history educator*
Gordon, Marsha L. *dermatologist*
Gordon, Mary Catherine *writer*
Gordon, Michael Mackin *lawyer*
Gordon, Robert Jay *lawyer, educator*
Gordon, Stephen Louis *lawyer*
Gordon, Stuart A. *lawyer*
Gorenstein, Ethan Ezra *psychologist, educator*
Gorman, James P. *finance company executive*
Gormley, Kenneth *lawyer*
Goshen, Zohar *law educator*
Gosin, Barry M. *real estate company executive*
Goss, Jared *curator*
Gossett, Robert Francis, Jr. *merchant banker*
Gotbaum, Betsy *municipal official*
Goto, Midori *classical violinist*
Gotschlich, Emil Claus *physician*
Gottesman, David Sanford *investment company executive*
Gotthoffer, Lance *lawyer*
Gotti, Victoria *columnist, writer, actress*
Gottlieb, Beatrice *historian*
Gottlieb, Jerrold Howard *advertising executive*
Gottlieb, Robert *publishing executive*
Gottlieb, Robert W. *lawyer*
Gotto, Antonio Marion, Jr. *internist, educator*
Gotts, Ilene Knable *lawyer*
Gottschalk, Alfred *retired academic administrator, museum administrator*
Gould, Andrew *oil industry executive*
Gould, Harry Edward, Jr. *paper company executive*
Goulden, Joseph Chesley *author*
Goulianos, Konstantin *physicist, educator*
Gourevitch, Philip *writer, editor*
Gourevitch, Jacqueline *artist*
Gourevitch, Philip *editor*
Grace, Nancy A. *news correspondent, former prosecutor*
Grad, Frank Paul *lawyer, educator*
Graf, John A. *finance company executive*
Graf, Peter Gustav *accountant, lawyer*
Graff, George Leonard *lawyer*
Graff, Randy *actress*
Grafstein, Bernice *physiology and neuroscience educator, researcher*
Grafton, Sue *novelist*
Graham, Alma Eleanor *editor, writer, educational consultant*
Graham, Fred Patterson *news correspondent, journalist*
Graham, Philip Lamar *epidemiologist, physician*
Graham, Robert *sculptor*
Granath, Herbert A. *television industry executive*
GrandPré, Mary *illustrator, pastel artist*
Granik, Russ (Russell T. Granik) *sports association executive*
Granito, Frank H. III *lawyer*
Grannan, Katy *photographer*
Grano, Joseph J., Jr. *securities industry executive*
Granoff, Gary Charles *lawyer, investment company executive*
Grant, Cynthia D. *writer*
Grant, Sonia Vivienne *secondary school educator*
Grassi, Joseph F. *lawyer, mediator, arbitrator*
Grau, Marcy Beinish *real estate broker, former investment banker*
Graustark, Barbara *editor*
Graves, Earl G., Jr., (Butch Graves) *publishing executive*
Graves, Earl Gilbert *publishing executive*
Gray, Farrah *entrepreneur, writer*
Gray, James L. *investment company executive*
Gray, Jerry *editor*
Gray, Stacey M. *lawyer*
Grayer, Elizabeth L. *lawyer*
Grayer, Jonathan *education company executive*
Greaney, Michael E. *lawyer*
Grebow, Edward *finance company executive*
Grecich, Daryl George *marketing communications executive, editor-in-chief*
Greeff, Douglas Haven *cosmetics executive*
Greely, Hannah *artist*
Green, Alvin *lawyer, consultant*
Green, Barbara Strawn *psychotherapist*
Green, Dan *publishing executive*
Green, George Edward *retired surgeon*
Green, George Joseph *publishing executive*
Green, Jack Peter *pharmacologist, educator*
Green, Lauren *news anchor and correspondent, concert pianist*
Green, Maurice Richard *neuropsychiatrist*
Green, Micah S. *trade association administrator*
Green, Wayne Hugo *psychiatrist, psychoanalyst*
Green, William D. *management consulting firm executive*
Greenawalt, Robert Kent *lawyer, educator*
Greenbaum, Maurice Coleman *lawyer*
Greenberg, Daniel Lawrence *lawyer*
Greenberg, David I. *consumer products company executive*
Greenberg, Gary Howard *lawyer*
Greenberg, Ira George *lawyer*
Greenberg, Jack *lawyer, educator*
Greenberg, Joel I. *lawyer*
Greenberg, Mark *television producer*

Greenberg, Stephen D. *broadcast executive*
Greenberger, Bette Jo *retired art educator*
Greenberger, Howard Leroy *lawyer, educator*
Greenblatt, Joel *investment company executive, finance educator, writer*
Greene, Bernard Harold *lawyer*
Greene, Douglas A. *internist, educator*
Greene, Ira S. *lawyer*
Greene, Mark I. *lawyer*
Greene, Norman L. *lawyer*
Greene, Richard H. *journalist, writer, policy analyst*
Greenfield, Jeff (Henry Jeff Greenfield) *news analyst*
Greengard, Paul *neuroscientist, educator*
Greenhill, Robert Foster *investment banker*
Greenland, Leo *advertising executive*
Greenman, Frederick F., Jr. *lawyer*
Greenman, Josh *editor*
Greenman, Paula S. *lawyer*
Greenspon, Robert Alan *lawyer*
Greenspun, David Todd *plastic and reconstructive surgeon*
Greenstein, Abraham Jacob *mortgage company executive, accountant*
Greenstein, Scott *broadcast executive*
Greenthal, Jill A. *investment banker*
Greenwald, David *lawyer*
Greenwald, Julie *recording industry executive*
Greenwald, Sheila Ellen *writer, illustrator*
Greenzang, Katherine *lawyer, insurance company executive*
Gregorian, Vartan *foundation administrator*
Gregory, Joseph M. *investment company executive*
Gregory, Robin N. *lawyer*
Grehan, Kevin J. *lawyer*
Greifeld, Robert A. *stock exchange executive*
Greilsheimer, James Gans *lawyer*
Greiner, Stephen W. *lawyer*
Grenquist, Peter Carl *publishing executive, consultant*
Grenrock-Woods, Stacey *comedian, actress*
Greyson, Ann S. *choreographer, theater producer*
Griefen, John Adams *artist, educator*
Griesa, Thomas Poole *federal judge*
Griffel, L. Michael *music educator, researcher*
Griffin, Anne *political scientist, educator*
Griffin, Michael F. *lawyer*
Griffith, William Henry (Bill Griffith) *cartoonist*
Griffith, William R. *lawyer*
Griffiths, Jem *singer*
Griffiths, Richard *actor*
Griffiths, Sylvia Preston *physician, educator*
Griffy, Timothy T. *human resources specialist, finance company executive*
Grimaldi, Nicholas Lawrence *fundraising executive*
Grimes, Martha *author*
Grimes, Suzanne *publishing executive*
Grimes, William *critic*
Grimm, David *playwright*
Grisham, John *writer*
Griswold, Frank Tracy III *bishop*
Groban, Josh *vocalist*
Groberg, James Jay *information technology executive*
Grody, Deborah *psychologist, director*
Grogan, John *writer*
Grohl, David Eric *musician*
Gromada, Thaddeus V. *historian, academic administrator*
Gromek, Joseph R. *apparel executive*
Grooms, Red (Charles Rogers Grooms) *artist*
Gropper, Allan Louis *bankruptcy judge*
Grose, William Rush *publishing executive*
Gross, Amy *editor-in-chief*
Gross, Feliks *sociologist, educator, writer*
Gross, John H. *lawyer*
Gross, Jonathan Light *computer scientist, mathematician, educator*
Gross, Judy E. *publishing executive*
Gross, Karen Charal *lawyer*
Gross, Steven Ross *lawyer*
Grossman, Barbara *artist, educator*
Grossman, Dan Steven *lawyer*
Grossman, Lawrence Kugelmass *former communications executive, advertising executive*
Grossman, Melanie *dermatologist*
Grossman, Michael *economics professor*
Grossman, Nancy *artist*
Grossmann, Edward A. *lawyer*
Groves, Ray John *accountant*
Grubin, Sharon Ellen *lawyer, former federal judge*
Grubman, Allen J. *lawyer*
Gruenberger, Peter *lawyer*
Grune, Steven Bryan *publishing executive*
Grunes, Robert Lewis *engineering executive, consultant*
Grushkin, Jay D. *lawyer*
Gruss, Martin David *investor*
Gubert, Walter Alexander *investment company executive*
Guedry, James Walter *lawyer, retired manufacturing executive*
Guehenno, Jean Marie *international organization official*
Guggenheim, Martin Franklin *lawyer, educator*
Guida, Robert Anthony *otolaryngologist, plastic surgeon*
Guiher, James Morford, Jr. *publisher, writer*
Guillaume, Juanita Connor *financial analyst, minister*
Gulati, Sunil *sports administrator*
Gullo, Stephen Bryan *psychologist, corporate executive*
Gumbinner, Paul S. *advertising and executive recruitment agency executive*
Gumpert, Lynn *gallery director*
Gund, Agnes *retired museum administrator*
Gundle, Sarah Shoshana *psychologist*
Gunn, Nathan *baritone*
Guo, Linfeng *communications engineer, researcher*
Gupta, Paul R. *lawyer*
Gural, Jeffrey R. *real estate company executive*
Gursky, Andreas *artist*
Guskov, Sergey *security firm executive*
Gustafson, Albert Katsuaki *lawyer, engineer*
Gutenbrunner, Kurt *chef, food service executive*
Gutfreund, John Halle *investment company executive, consultant*

Guthrie, Randolph Hobson, Jr. *plastic surgeon, consultant*
Gutman, Robert William *retired art educator*
Gutzwiller, Martin Charles *theoretical physicist, research scientist*
Guyton, Wade *artist*
Guzman, Kathleen McFadden *antiques appraiser, auctioneer*
Gwathmey, Charles *architect*
Gwathmey, Gaines *lawyer*
Gyles, Robert *mathematics professor*
Haacke, Hans Christoph Carl *artist, educator*
Haas, Richard John *artist*
Haase, Leif Wellington *foundation administrator*
Haass, Richard Nathan *federal official*
Habachy, Suzan Salwa Saba *economist, not-for-profit developer*
Haber, Pierre-Claude *psychologist*
Haberman, Clyde *columnist*
Habib, Ibrahim Wahby *computer engineer, educator*
Hackbarth, Steven Lyle *writer, educator*
Hackett, George *editor*
Hackett, Kevin R. *real estate company executive, lawyer*
Hadas, Rachel *poet, educator*
Haddad, Heskel Marshall *ophthalmologist, educator*
Haddad, Jamil Raouf *retired physician*
Hadden, John Winthrop *immunopharmacology educator*
Haddock, Robert Lynn *information services entrepreneur, writer*
Haddon, James Francis *banker*
Haegele, Patricia *publishing executive*
Haessle, Jean-Marie Georges *artist*
Haffner, Alden Norman *academic administrator*
Haffner, F. Kinsey *lawyer*
Hagerty, Patrick K. *publishing executive*
Haggerty, Luane Ruth Davis *theater director, educator, actress*
Hagin, Nancy *printmaker, painter*
Hague, William Edward *writer*
Hahn, Arlene Ann *lawyer*
Haig, Robert Leighton *lawyer*
Haigh, Jennifer *writer*
Haight, Charles Sherman, Jr. *federal judge*
Haight, David Hulen *ophthalmologist*
Haiman, Zoltan *astronomer, educator*
Haimes, Burton Kenneth *lawyer*
Haimes, Todd *artistic director*
Haims, Bruce David *lawyer*
Haines, Thomas Henry *biochemist, educator, researcher*
Hakala, Thomas John *private banker, financial planner, accountant*
Halaby, Samia Asaad *painter, educator, writer*
Halberstam, Malvina *law educator, lawyer*
Haley, James F., Jr. *lawyer*
Hall, Joan *artist*
Hall, John Herbert *lawyer*
Hall, Lisa Gersh *broadcast executive, lawyer*
Hall, Michael C. *actor*
Hall, Peter W. *federal judge, former prosecutor*
Hall, Richard *lawyer*
Hall, Thomas J. *lawyer*
Hall, Trish *editor*
Hallake, Marcello *lawyer*
Halliday, Joseph William *lawyer*
Halmi, Robert, Sr. *film producer, television producer*
Halper, Thomas *political science professor*
Halperin, Jonathan L. *medical school administrator*
Halperin, Richard E. *lawyer, finance company executive*
Halpern, Merril Mark *investment banker*
Halsband, Frances *architect*
Hambrick, George Walter, Jr. *dermatologist, educator*
Hamburg, Charles Bruce *lawyer*
Hamburg, David A. *psychiatrist, foundation administrator*
Hamdan, Lawrence Anise *investment banker, lawyer*
Hamilton, Jane *writer*
Hamilton, Laurell K. *writer*
Hamm, David Bernard *lawyer*
Hammer, Scott M. *medical researcher, educator*
Hammett, Kirk Lee *musician*
Hammond, Darrell *actor*
Hammond, Lou Rena Charlotte *public relations executive*
Hamoy, Carol *artist*
Handelsman, Lawrence Marc *lawyer*
Handforth, Mark *artist*
Handler, Arthur M. *lawyer*
Handler, Daniel (Lemony Snicket) *writer*
Handler, Richard B. *investment company executive*
Handley, Siobhan A. *lawyer*
Hann, Lucy E. *radiologist, educator*
Hansell, Saul Henry *reporter*
Hansen, James E. *physicist, meteorologist, federal agency administrator*
Hansen, Kristopher M. *lawyer*
Hansen, William D. *educational consultant, former federal agency administrator*
Hansmann, Ralph Emil *investment executive, director*
Hanson, Jane *newscaster*
Hanson, Jean Elizabeth *lawyer*
Hanson, Stephen *food service executive*
Haracz, Stephen M. *lawyer*
Harbison, James Wesley, Jr. *lawyer*
Hardwick, Charles Leighton *pharmaceutical executive, former state legislator*
Hardwick, Elizabeth *writer*
Hardy, Hugh *architect*
Hargitay, Mariska Magdolina *actress*
Hariri, Gisue *architect, educator*
Harkavy-Friedman, Jill Martine *psychologist*
Harkrider, John David *lawyer*
Harlan, Leonard Morton *merchant banker*
Harmon, Jane *theater producer*
Harms, David B. *lawyer*
Harper, Emery Walter *lawyer*
Harper, Gerard Edward *lawyer*
Harper, Karen *writer*
Harrell, Ray Evans *performing company executive, conductor, educator*
Harris, Adam C. *lawyer*

Harris, Arlene *lawyer*
Harris, Carla Ann *investment company executive*
Harris, Charles E. *venture capital investment executive*
Harris, Cyril Manton *physicist, educator, acoustical engineer, engineering and architecture educator*
Harris, David Alan *not-for-profit organization executive*
Harris, David Henry *retired life insurance company executive*
Harris, Ethan S. *diversified financial services company executive*
Harris, Frederick John *foreign language and literature educator*
Harris, Henry William *physician*
Harris, Joel B. (Joel Bruce Harris) *lawyer*
Harris, Julie (Julie Ann Harris) *actress*
Harris, Katherine Safford *speech and hearing educator*
Harris, Theresa *lawyer*
Harris, William Vernon *history professor*
Harrison, Gilbert Warner *investment banker*
Harrison, Rachel *artist*
Harrison, S. David *lawyer*
Harrow, Nancy (Mrs. Jan Krukowski) *editor-in-chief, composer, singer*
Hart, Arnold Zackery *lawyer*
Hart, Clare *information company executive*
Hart, Gurnee Fellows *investment counselor*
Hart, Joseph Thomas Campbell *lawyer*
Hart, Mary T. *lawyer*
Hart, Robert M. *lawyer*
Härtl, Roger *physician, researcher*
Hartley, Hal *film director*
Hartman, Bruce L. *apparel executive*
Hartman, Joan Edna *retired literature educator, provost*
Hartnett, William M. *lawyer*
Hartnick, Alan Jay *lawyer, educator*
Hartwick, Gary Glenn *entertainment company executive*
Hartwig, Robert Paul *insurance institute executive, economist*
Harty, Thomas H. *publishing executive*
Hartzell, Andrew Cornelius, Jr. *retired lawyer*
Harvey, La Verne Deborah *writer, theater producer, educator*
Harvey, Peter C. *lawyer, former state attorney general*
Hasday, Robert Joel *lawyer*
Haskell, Barbara *curator*
Haskell, John Henry Farrell, Jr. *investment company executive*
Hass, Lawrence Joel *lawyer*
Hassebo, Yasser Youssef *education educator, researcher*
Hastings, Deborah *bass guitarist*
Hathaway, Gerald Thomas *lawyer*
Hatheway, John Harris *advertising agency executive*
Haubegger, Christy *media consultant, publishing executive*
Hauser, Gustave M. *broadcast executive*
Hauser, Rita Eleanore Abrams *lawyer*
Hawke, Roger Jewett *lawyer*
Hawkins, Katherine Ann *hematologist, educator, lawyer*
Hawkins, Oliver Taylor (Taylor Hawkins) *musician*
Hawkins, Robert Drake *science educator*
Hay, Alex *painter, sculptor*
Hayden, Donald J., Jr. *pharmaceutical executive*
Hayden, Raymond Paul *lawyer*
Hayden, Richard Seth *architectural firm executive*
Hayes, Eddie (Edward W. Hayes) *lawyer*
Hayes, Gerald Joseph *lawyer*
Hayes, John D. *diversified financial services company executive*
Hayes, Joseph G. *cardiologist, educator*
Hazan, Scott L. *lawyer*
Hazzard, Shirley *author*
Headlam, Bruce *editor*
Headley, Mark J. *lawyer*
Heald, Anthony *actor*
Healy, Harold Harris, Jr. *lawyer*
Healy, J. Kevin *lawyer*
Healy, Nicholas Joseph *retired lawyer*
Hearn, George Henry *lawyer, water transportation executive*
Hearst, George Randolph, Jr. *publishing executive, real estate company executive*
Heartney, Eleanor *art critic*
Hebert, Bliss Edmund *opera director*
Hedden, Andrew S. *lawyer*
Hedgpeth, Kim Roberta *trade association administrator*
Heeger, David J. *psychology professor*
Heekin, James Robson III *advertising executive*
Heekin-Canedy, Scott H. *publishing executive*
Heffernan, Virginia *television critic*
Heffner, Richard Douglas *historian, educator, communications consultant, television producer*
Hefter, Michael C *lawyer*
Heftler, Thomas E. *lawyer*
Heicklen, Alice *biologist*
Heilbrun, James *economist, educator*
Heimann, John Gaines *investment banker*
Heinemann, Larry C. *writer*
Heinemann, Peter *artist, educator*
Heintz, Florent M. *art appraiser*
Heinzelman, Kris F. *lawyer*
Heinzerling, Larry Edward *communications executive*
Heisler, Stanley Dean *lawyer*
Heitner, Kenneth Howard *lawyer*
Held, Ivan *publishing executive*
Heleniak, David William *diversified financial services company executive, lawyer*
Hellenbrand, Samuel Henry *lawyer*
Heller, Robert Martin *lawyer*
Hellerer, Mark R. *lawyer*
Helliker, Kevin *journalist*
Helm, Lenora Zenzalai *musician, music educator*
Helmsley, Leona Mindy *hotel executive*
Helsby, Keith R. *stock exchange executive*
Hemmerdinger, H. Dale *real estate executive*
Henderson, Donald Bernard, Jr. *lawyer*
Henderson, Kenneth Lee *lawyer*
Hendin, Josephine Gattuso *language educator, writer*

Hendrickson, Wayne A(rthur) *biochemist, educator*
Henican, Ellis *columnist, political correspondent*
Henkes, Kevin *illustrator, writer*
Hennessy, John Francis III *engineering executive, mechanical engineer*
Henriques, Diana Blackmon *journalist*
Henry, Frederick B. *foundation administrator*
Henry, Robert S. *art educator*
Henry, Sarah M. *museum staff member, historian*
Henryson, Herbert, II, *lawyer*
Henschke, Claudia Ingrid *physician, radiologist*
Hensel, Katherine Ruth *portfolio manager, investment advisor*
Henselmann, Caspar Gustav Fidelis *sculptor*
Henze, William F., II, *lawyer*
Herbert, Bob *columnist*
Herbert, Marilynne *public relations executive, freelance photographer*
Herbst, Todd L. *lawyer*
Herlihy, Edward D. *lawyer*
Herman, Dorothy *real estate broker*
Herman, Kenneth Beaumont *lawyer*
Herman, Mindy *broadcast executive*
Herman, Peter Windley *lawyer*
Herman, Stan *fashion designer*
Hernandez, Keith *retired professional baseball player*
Hernandez, Lazaro *apparel designer*
Hernández, Victor René Christian *medical researcher, consultant*
Hernstadt, Judith Filenbaum *city planner, real estate executive, broadcast executive*
Herr, Harry Wallace *medical researcher, educator, surgeon, urologist*
Herregat, Guy-Georges Jacques *retired banker*
Herrera, Arturo *artist*
Herrera, Carolina *fashion designer*
Herrera, Paloma *dancer*
Herring, Hubert B. *editor*
Herring, Oliver *artist*
Herrmann, Lacy Bunnell *investment company executive, entrepreneur, venture capitalist*
Herron, Cindy *actress, vocalist*
Hersch, Dennis Steven *bank executive, lawyer*
Herschlein, James D. *lawyer*
Hersh, Seymour Myron *journalist, writer*
Hershcopf, Gerald Thea *retired lawyer*
Hershkoff, Helen *law educator*
Hershkop, Shlomo *computer scientist, educator*
Herszenhorn, David *journalist*
Hertog, Roger *investment company executive*
Hertz, Leon *publishing executive*
Hertz, Michael K. *lawyer*
Hertz, Suki *chef*
Hertzig, Margaret E. *psychiatrist*
Herz, Andrew Lee *lawyer*
Herzeca, Lois Friedman *lawyer*
Herzog, John E. *numismatist*
Herzog, Werner (Werner Stipetic) *film director*
Hess, John B. *oil industry executive*
Hess, Michael David *lawyer*
Hesse, Karen (Karen Sue Hesse) *writer, educator*
Hesselbein, Frances Richards *foundation administrator, writer, editor*
Hesser, Amanda Lea *journalist, chef*
Hetfield, James *singer*
Hewitt, John R. *lawyer*
Hewitt, Vivian Ann Davidson (Mrs. John Hamilton Hewitt Jr.) *retired librarian*
Heyde, Martha Bennett *psychologist*
Heymann, C(lemens) David *author*
Heyzer, Noeleen *international organization official*
Hiaasen, Carl *writer, reporter*
Hicklin, Aaron *editor-in-chief*
Hicks, Jonathan P. *journalist*
Hicks, Tyler Gregory *publishing company executive, writer*
Hicks, Weston Milliken *security firm executive, securities analyst*
Hidalgo, David Arthur *plastic surgeon*
Hiden, Robert Battaile, Jr. *lawyer*
Hielscher, Andreas Helmut *biomedical engineer*
Higgins, Edward Tory *psychology professor, research scientist*
Highstein, Jene Abel *sculptor*
Hilchey, Tim *editor*
Hildebrand, Phillip J. *insurance company executive*
Hilderley, Jeriann Gertrude *novelist, educator*
Hill, Alfred *law educator*
Hill, Brian Eugene *music publishing executive, musician, educator*
Hill, J(ames) Tomilson *investment banker*
Hill, Janine *think-tank associate*
Hill, Marjorie Jean *psychologist, association executive*
Hillenbrand, Laura *writer*
Hillman, Peter N. *lawyer*
Hilton, Andrew Carson *investment company executive, retired manufacturing executive, management consultant*
Hines, Walter James *stock exchange executive*
Hinz, Theodore Vincent *architect*
Hippeau, Eric *book publishing executive*
Hirsch, Barry *lawyer*
Hirsch, Charles S. *city health department administrator*
Hirsch, Edward Mark *language educator, poet*
Hirsch, Faye *editor, art critic*
Hirsch, Harvey Stuart *psychiatrist*
Hirsch, Irving B. *lawyer*
Hirsch, Jerome S. *lawyer*
Hirsch, Jules *physician, researcher*
Hirsch, Roseann Conte *publisher*
Hirschfeld, Michael *lawyer*
Hirschhorn, Bernard *educator, historian, researcher, writer*
Hirschhorn, Kurt *pediatrics educator*
Hirschhorn, Rochelle *genetics educator*
Hirschman, David S. *editor*
Hirshfield, Stuart *lawyer*
Hirshon, Sheldon Ira *lawyer*
Hirshowitz, Melvin Stephen *lawyer*
Hjortsberg, William Reinhold *writer*
Ho, Betty Juenyü Yülin *retired music educator, physiologist, educator*
Ho, David D. (Da-i Ho) *research physician, virologist, scientific organization director*
Hoag, Tami *writer*
Hoblin, Philip J., Jr. *securities lawyer*
Hoch, Benjamin *lawyer*

Hochfield, Sylvia *arts editor*
Hochhauser, Richard Michael *marketing professional*
Hochlerin, Diane *pediatrician, educator*
Hodes, Robert Bernard *lawyer*
Hodge, Roger D. *editor*
Hodges, Deborah *investment company executive*
Hodges, Jim *artist*
Hoeflin, Ronald Kent *philosopher, writer*
Hoff, Jonathan M. (Jonathan Morind Hoff) *lawyer*
Hoffert, Martin Irving *aerospace scientist, educator*
Hoffman, Alice *writer*
Hoffman, Jared *music company executive*
Hoffman, Linda M. *chemist, educator*
Hoffman, Linda R. *social services administrator*
Hoffman, Lloyd Alan *plastic surgeon*
Hoffman, Mathew *lawyer*
Hoffman, Nancy *art gallery director*
Hoffman, Ronald L. *manufacturing executive*
Hoffner, Marilyn *university administrator*
Hoge, Warren M. *editor*
Hohn, Harry George *retired insurance company executive, lawyer*
Holden, Stephen *film critic*
Holder, Donald *lighting designer*
Holl, Steven Myron *architect, educator*
Holland, Bernard Peabody *music critic*
Holland, Jimmie C. *psychiatrist, educator*
Holland, Michael Francis *investment company executive*
Holland, Rebecca Lloyd *publishing executive*
Hollander, Joel L. *broadcast executive*
Holley, Steven Lyon *lawyer*
Holliday, Guy D. "Doc" *publishing executive*
Holloway, Ralph Leslie *anthropology educator*
Holman, Bud George *lawyer*
Holmbo, Todd A. *lawyer*
Holmes, Anna-Marie *ballerina*
Holmes, Stephen T. *law educator*
Holodny, Andrei Igor *radiologist*
Holsenbeck, George Penn *lawyer*
Holstad, Christian *artist*
Holt, Peter Rolf *gastroenterologist, educator*
Holt, Sidney Clark *journalist*
Holton, Lisa *publishing executive*
Holton, William *artist*
Holtzman, Elizabeth *lawyer*
Holtzmann, Howard Marshall *lawyer, judge*
Holub, Martin *architect*
Holwell, Richard J. *federal judge*
Holzer, Harold *museum and marketing executive, historian, writer*
Holzman, Robert Stephen *physician*
Hondros, Chris *photojournalist*
Honig, Jonathan David *lawyer*
Hood, Donald Charles *academic administrator, psychologist, educator*
Hooker, Wade Stuart *lawyer*
Hopkins, Deborah C. *diversified financial services company executive*
Horan, Anthony J. *diversified financial services company executive*
Hormats, Robert David *economist, investment banker*
Horn, Karen Nicholson *investment company executive, former bank executive*
Horn, Roni *artist*
Hornstein, Mark *financial executive*
Horowitz, Frances Degen *academic administrator, psychology educator*
Horowitz, Gedale Bob *investment banker*
Horowitz, Joseph Irving *writer, educator*
Horowitz, Steven Gary *lawyer*
Horsfield, Craigie *artist*
Hort, Michael *art collector*
Hort, Susan *art collector*
Horvat, Olga *artist*
Horyn, Cathy *newspaper editor*
Hoskins, Donald W. *retired medical association administrator*
Hosseini, Khaled *internist, writer*
Hotchner, Holly *museum director, curator, conservator*
Hotz, Robert Lee *writer, editor*
Houck, Rudolph S.(Rob) *lawyer*
Houghtelling, Ayres *artist, architectural engineer*
Houghton, James *performing company executive*
Hourigan, Jacqueline (Jack Hourigan) *television personality*
House, David C. *diversified financial services company executive*
Houston, Allan Wade *professional basketball player*
Hovde, Carl Frederick *language professional, educator*
Hoving, Thomas *museum director, consultant, writer*
Howard, David *retired educational association administrator, writer*
Howard, Mildred *sculptor*
Howard, Nathan Southard *brokerage house executive, lawyer*
Howard, Richard (Joseph Howard) *poet, literary translator*
Howat, John Keith *retired museum executive*
Howe, Florence *literature educator, writer, publisher*
Howe, Richard Rives *lawyer*
Howitt, John P. *lawyer*
Howson, Tamar D. *pharmaceutical executive*
Hoxter, Curtis Joseph *international economic advisor, public relations executive*
Hricik, Lorraine E. *bank executive*
Hritz, George F. *lawyer*
Hruska, Alan J. *lawyer*
Hsu, Daphne T. *pediatrician, educator*
Hu, Danian *history professor*
Hu, Winnie *journalist*
Huang, Limin *chemist, researcher*
Hubbard, R. Glenn (Robert Glenn Hubbard, Glenn Hubbard) *academic administrator, former federal official*
Huck, L. Francis *lawyer*
Huckshorn, Kristin *journalist*
Hudes, Nana Brenda *marketing professional*
Hudlin, Reginald Alan *broadcast executive, film director, writer*
Hudson, Christopher John *publisher*
Hudspeth, Stephen Mason *lawyer*
Huey, John Wesley, Jr. *editor*

Hughes, Brigid *former editor*
Hughes, Doug *theater director*
Hugo, Norman Eliot *retired plastic surgeon, retired educator*
Huhs, John I. *lawyer*
Hulbert, Richard Woodward *lawyer*
Hull, Cathy *artist, illustrator*
Hull, Philip Glasgow *lawyer*
Hulsebosch, Daniel Joseph *historian, educator*
Hultquist, Timothy Allen *investment banker*
Hummel, Keith R. *lawyer*
Humphreys, Josephine *writer*
Hunsinger, Peter *publishing executive*
Hunt, Franklin Griggs *lawyer*
Hupper, John Roscoe *retired lawyer*
Hurley, Cheryl Joyce *book publishing executive*
Hurley, Dean C. *bank executive, lawyer*
Hurlin, Dan *theater director*
Hurlock, James Bickford *retired lawyer*
Hurst, Robert Jay *security firm executive*
Hurwitz, Adam *painter*
Hutchings, Peter Lounsbery *retired insurance company executive, director*
Hutchins, Traver *publishing executive*
Hutchinson, Lynda Ronette (Billie Holiday Jr., Princess of Jazz, Munchie) *vocalist, musician, comedian, actress*
Huttner, Constance S. *lawyer*
Huxtable, Ada Louise *architecture critic*
Hyde, David Rowley *lawyer*
Hyman, Alan Barry *lawyer*
Hyman, Bruce Malcolm *ophthalmologist*
Hyman, Earle *actor, educator*
Hyman, Jerome Elliot *lawyer*
Hyman, Morton Peter *private equity investment company executive*
Hynes, Aedhmar *public relations executive*
Hynes, Patricia Mary *lawyer*
Hytner, Nicholas *theatrical director*
Ichel, David W. *lawyer*
Ilacqua, Rosario Salvatore *securities analyst*
Ilchman, Warren Frederick *academic administrator, foundation administrator, educator*
Iles, Greg *writer*
Ilkin, Baki *diplomat, Turkish government official*
Ilse-Neuman, Ursula *curator*
Ilson, Bernard *public relations executive*
Imber, Gerald *plastic surgeon*
Immergut, Mel M. *lawyer*
Imperato, Anthony Peter *publishing executive*
Imperato, Joseph Edward *otolaryngologist*
Impoco, Jim *editor*
Imus, Don (John Donald Imus Jr.) *radio personality*
Incandela, Gerald Jean-Marie *artist*
Ingram, Samuel William, Jr. *lawyer*
Ingrassia, Lawrence *editor*
Innis, Roy Emile Alfredo *foundation executive*
Insel, Michael S. *lawyer*
Intriligator, Marc Steven *lawyer*
Iqbal, Syma U. *information technology executive*
Ireland, Jay *broadcast executive*
Ireland, Patrick *artist*
IRIA, (Irja Leino) *model, artist, painter*
Irish, George Butler *media company executive*
Isaacs, Jeremy M. *finance company executive*
Isaacson, Allen Ira *lawyer*
Isaacson, Steven Robert *surgeon*
Iselin, John Jay *foundation president*
Isenberg, Steven Lawrence *retired publishing executive*
Isherwood, Charles *theater critic*
Ishiguro, Kazuo *writer, scriptwriter*
Isogai, Masaharu *international corporate strategist, retired apparel executive*
Isquith, Fred Taylor *lawyer*
Issacharoff, Samuel *law educator*
Issler, Harry *lawyer*
Istomin, Marta Casals *retired school president, performing company executive*
Iturbide, Graciela *photographer*
Iuzzini, Johnny *chef*
Ivanhoe, Robert J. *lawyer*
Ivanick, Carol W. Trencher *lawyer*
Ivanov, Kalin Hristov *music educator, musician*
Ivanovitch, Michael S. *economist*
Ivory, James Francis *film director*
Ivy, Robert Adams, Jr. *architect, editor-in-chief*
Jack, Bradley H. *investment banker*
Jacker, Corinne Litvin *playwright, writer*
Jackson, Ann Williams *private equity investment executive*
Jackson, Anne (Anne Jackson Wallach) *actress*
Jackson, Henry Nathaniel *clothing designer*
Jackson, Jack P. *lawyer*
Jackson, Keith MacKenzie *retired sports commentator*
Jackson, Kenneth Terry *historian, academic administrator*
Jackson, Reggie (Reginald Martinez Jackson, Mr. October) *former professional baseball player*
Jackson, Yvonne *pharmaceutical executive*
Jackson McCabe, Jewell *not-for-profit developer*
Jacob, Edwin J. *lawyer*
Jacob, Marvin Eugene *lawyer*
Jacobs, Albert Lionel, Jr. *lawyer*
Jacobs, Arnold Stephen *lawyer*
Jacobs, Arnold Stephen *writer, commentator*
Jacobs, Dennis *federal judge*
Jacobs, Jim *actor, composer, librettist, playwright*
Jacobs, Lawrence A. *media company executive, lawyer*
Jacobs, Marc *fashion designer*
Jacobs, Paul *lawyer*
Jacobs, Paul A. *music educator*
Jacobs, Robert Alan *lawyer*
Jacobsen, Theodore H. (Ted H. Jacobsen) *labor union administrator, secondary school educator*
Jacobson, Gilbert H. *lawyer, director*
Jacobson, Jerold Dennis *lawyer*
Jacobson, Julius H., II, *vascular surgeon, writer*
Jacoby, Coleman *scriptwriter*
Jacoby, Jacob *consumer psychology educator*
Jacoby, Robert Harold *management consulting executive*
Jacquette, Yvonne Helene *artist*
Jaffe, Helene D. *lawyer*
Jaffe, Mark M. *lawyer*
Jaffe, Susan *ballerina*

Jagr, Jaromir *professional hockey player*
Jakes, John *author*
James, Christopher Lewis *composer*
James, Hamilton Evans (Tony James) *private equity executive*
James, Marc Stephen *brokerage house executive*
James, Robert Leo *advertising executive, director*
Jamieson, Wendell *editor*
Jamison, Douglas W. *venture capitalist*
Jamison, Jayne *publishing executive*
Jamison, Judith *dancer*
Jan, Dominique Michel *surgeon, educator*
Janiak, Anthony Richard, Jr. *investment banker*
Janklow, Morton Lloyd *lawyer, literary agent*
Janney, Stuart Symington III *investment company executive*
Jannot, Mark Allen *magazine publishing executive*
Jannuzzi, Luigi *playwright, educator*
Janowitz, James Arnold *lawyer*
Jansky, Jeannette Jefferson *learning disabilities specialist*
Janulis, Theodore P. *investment company executive*
Januzzi, James Louis *physician, internist, gastroenterologist*
Jarecki, Henry George *physician, financial planner*
Jaroff, Leon Morton *magazine editor*
Jarrell, Tim *travel guide publishing executive*
Jarvik, Robert Koffler *biomedical research scientist*
Jarvis, Jeff *journalist, former critic, news blogger*
Jason, Kyle *radio personality, musician*
Jasso, Guillermina *sociologist, educator*
Jassy, Everett Lewis *lawyer*
Javitt, Norman B. *medical educator, researcher*
Jay-Z, (Shawn Corey Carter) *rap artist, music company executive*
Jean, Wyclef *musician, recording industry executive*
Jean-Baptiste, Tricia *public relations executive*
Jebara, Tony *science educator*
Jebejian, Sarkis *lawyer*
Jefferson, Denise *dance school director*
Jefferson, Margo L. *journalist*
Jeffrey, Robert *advertising executive*
Jelinek, Vera *dean*
Jelks, Glenn William *plastic surgeon*
Jellinek, George *broadcast executive, music educator, writer*
Jenkins, Paul *artist*
Jenrette, Richard Hampton *investment and insurance company executive*
Jensen, Bill *artist*
Jepson, Hans Godfrey *investment company executive, director*
Jerolmack, Colin *sociologist*
Jerome, John James *lawyer*
Jervis, Robert *political science professor*
Jessell, Thomas M. *medical educator*
Jesselli, Steve *journalist*
Jett, Joan (Joan Larkin) *musician*
Jeydel, Richard K. *lawyer*
Jeynes, Mary Kay *college dean*
Jhabvala, Ruth Prawer *writer*
Jock, Paul F., II, *lawyer*
Joel, Richard Marc *academic administrator, law educator, dean*
Joffe, Robert David *lawyer*
Johansen, Iris *writer*
Johansson, Jerker Mats *investment banker*
Johnnes, Daniel *chef*
Johnson, Betsey Lee *fashion designer*
Johnson, Brooke Bailey *broadcast executive*
Johnson, Clarke Courtney *financial consultant, educator*
Johnson, David J., Jr. *lawyer*
Johnson, Harmer Frederik *art appraiser*
Johnson, Harold Earl *human resources specialist*
Johnson, Horton Anton *pathologist*
Johnson, J. Chester *corporate financial executive, consultant, writer*
Johnson, J. Stewart *curator, art consultant*
Johnson, James D. *lawyer*
Johnson, Jeh Charles *lawyer*
Johnson, John William, Jr. *executive recruiter*
Johnson, Peter James, Jr. *lawyer, legal analyst*
Johnson, Richard *editor*
Johnson, Scott Stuart *merchant banker*
Johnson, Suzanne M. Nora *diversified financial services company executive, lawyer*
Johnson, Thomas Stephen *banker*
Johnson, Verdia E. *marketing professional*
Johnson, Vickie *professional basketball player*
Johnson, W. Clayton *lawyer*
Johnson, Warren Douglas *infectious diseases physician, researcher*
Johnston, David Cay Boyle *journalist*
Jolly, Thomas Alan *journalist*
Jonas, Gilbert *public relations and fund raising executive*
Jonas, Saran *neurologist, educator*
Jones, Abbott C. *investment company executive*
Jones, Barbara S. *federal judge*
Jones, Bill T. *dancer, choreographer*
Jones, David *advertising executive*
Jones, David R. *not-for-profit executive*
Jones, Diana Wynne *writer*
Jones, James A. III *lawyer*
Jones, Laurie Lynn *magazine editor*
Jones, Thomas Wade *financial services executive*
Jones Reynolds, Star (Starlet Marie Jones) *television host, lawyer, former prosecutor*
Jong, Erica Mann *writer*
Joo, Michael *artist, educator*
Jordan, Nora Margaret *lawyer*
Jordan, Vernon Eulion, Jr. *lawyer*
Jordon, John W., II, *investment company executive*
Josell, Jessica (Jessica Wechsler) *public relations executive*
Joseph, Gregory Paul *lawyer*
Joseph, Leonard *lawyer*
Joseph, Michael Sarkies *accountant*
Josephson, Jordan Stuart *otolaryngologist*
Josephson, Marvin *literary agent*
Joynt, Stephen W. *financial services company executive*
Juceam, Robert E. *lawyer*
Judge, Mary Frances *artist*
Juliber, Lois D. *manufacturing executive*
Jung, Andrea *cosmetics company executive*
Jung, Doris *soprano*
Jurinko, Andy Floyd *artist*

Jurka, Edith Mila *psychiatrist, researcher*
Jurkevich, Gayana *Spanish language educator, consultant*
Just, Gemma Rivoli *retired advertising executive*
Kadar, Avraham *immunologist*
Kadden, Jack *editor*
Kaden, Lewis B. *lawyer, educator*
Kadohata, Cynthia *writer*
Kafin, Robert Joseph *lawyer*
Kagan, Ilse Echt *librarian, researcher, historian*
Kagan, Julia Lee *magazine editor*
Kaggen, Lois Sheila *non-profit organization executive, advocate*
Kahan, Marcel *law educator*
Kahane, Jeffrey *conductor, pianist*
Kahn, Alan Edwin *lawyer*
Kahn, Anthony F. *lawyer*
Kahn, Joseph F. *journalist*
Kahn, Norman *dental educator, pharmacologist*
Kahn, Wolf *artist*
Kailas, Leo George *lawyer*
Kaiser, Walter *language educator*
Kaish, Luise Clayborn *sculptor, painter, educator*
Kaish, Morton *artist, educator*
Kaku, Michio *theoretical nuclear physicist, educator*
Kakutani, Michiko *critic*
Kalajian-Lagani, Donna *publishing executive*
Kalech, Marc *newspaper editor*
Kalich, Richard Barry *writer*
Kalik, Mildred *lawyer*
Kalikow, Peter Stephen *real estate developer, former publishing executive*
Kalish, Arthur *lawyer*
Kalish, Myron *lawyer*
Kallir, Jane Katherine *art gallery director, author*
Kalsner, Stanley *pharmacologist, physiologist, educator*
Kamali, Norma *fashion designer*
Kambour, Annaliese Spofford *lawyer, media company executive*
Kamen, D. Jonathan *film producer*
Kamerman, Sheila Brody *social work educator*
Kamin, Sherwin *lawyer*
Kaminer, Ariel *editor*
Kaminsky, Alan *lawyer*
Kamlot, Robert *performing arts executive*
Kamm, Linda Heller *lawyer*
Kampmann, Martin *cell biologist*
Kan, Diana Artemis Mann Shu *painter, art educator, writer*
Kanakaredes, Melina *actress*
Kandarian, Steven A. *insurance company executive*
Kandel, Denise Bystryn *sociologist*
Kandel, Myron *newscaster, columnist*
Kandel, William Lloyd *lawyer, arbitrator, educator, mediator, writer*
Kane, Richard Joseph *lawyer*
Kanick, Virginia *retired radiologist*
Kann, Peter Robert *publishing executive, journalist*
Kanner, Bernice *columnist*
Kanner, Frederick W. *lawyer*
Kanof, Norman B. *dermatologist*
Kanter, Carl Irwin *retired lawyer*
Kanter, Stacy J. *lawyer*
Kanzer, Alan *lawyer*
Kapelman, Barbara Ann *internist, hepatologist, gastroenterologist, educator*
Kapito, Robert S. *diversified financial services company executive*
Kaplan, Carl Eliot *lawyer*
Kaplan, Cathy M. *lawyer*
Kaplan, Jill Rebecca *publishing executive*
Kaplan, Joseph Solte *retired lawyer*
Kaplan, Keith Eugene *insurance company executive, lawyer*
Kaplan, Lawrence Jay *economist, educator*
Kaplan, Lewis A. *federal judge*
Kaplan, Mark Norman *lawyer*
Kaplan, Paul Michael *lawyer, educator*
Kaplan, Peter W. *editor-in-chief*
Kaplan, Robert David *journalist*
Kaplan, Susan *lawyer*
Kaplan, Theodore Norman *insurance company executive*
Kaplan, Todd P. *diversified financial services company executive*
Kaplow, Julie B. *psychologist, educator*
Kapoor, Neera *optometrist, research scientist*
Kappas, Attallah *physician*
Karalekas, George Steven *advertising agency executive, political consultant*
Karan, Donna (Donna Faske) *fashion designer*
Karas, Kenneth M. *federal judge*
Karasu, T(oksoz) Byram *psychiatrist, educator, writer*
Karatz, William Warren *lawyer*
Karchin, Louis Samuel *composer, educator*
Kardon, Janet *museum director*
Karl, Kurt Erskine *economist*
Karlgaard, Rich *publishing executive*
Karlin, Susan *design company executive*
Karls, John Spencer *lawyer, accountant*
Karmazin, Mel *broadcast executive*
Karon, Jan (Janice Meredith Wilson) *writer*
Karp, Brad S. *lawyer*
Karp, David C. *lawyer*
Karp, Martin Everett *management consultant*
Karp, Nolan S. *plastic surgeon*
Karp, Roberta Schuhalter *retail executive, lawyer*
Karpel, Craig S. *journalist, editor*
Karpen, Marian Joan *financial executive*
Karr, Jane *editor*
Karr, Kathleen *writer*
Karr, Robert A. *financier*
Karsen, Sonja Petra *retired literature educator*
Kartiganer, Joseph *retired lawyer*
Kase, Nathan Ginden *dean*
Kasirer, Suri *lobbyist*
Kaslick, Ralph Sidney *dentist, educator*
Kasowitz, Marc Elliot *lawyer*
Kassan, Lee D. *psychotherapist, writer*
Kassebaum, John Philip *lawyer*
Kassel, Catherine M. *community, maternal, and women's health nurse, consultant*
Kassel, Terry *human resources specialist*
Kassel, Virginia Weltmer *television producer, scriptwriter*
Kassimir, Joel Jack *dermatologist*
Kastan, David Scott *literature educator, writer*

Katcher, Richard David *lawyer*
Katsh, Salem Michael *lawyer*
Katz, Abraham *retired foreign service officer*
Katz, Avery W. *law educator*
Katz, Avi *lawyer*
Katz, Bruce Elliot *dermatologist*
Katz, David A. *lawyer*
Katz, Esther *historian, educator*
Katz, Jerome Charles *lawyer*
Katz, Jose *cardiologist, theoretical physicist, educator*
Katz, Lois Anne *internist, nephrologist*
Katz, Robert James *lawyer*
Katz, Ronald Scott *lawyer*
Katz, Stuart Z. *lawyer*
Katzberg, Robert F. *lawyer*
Katzmann, Robert Allen *federal judge*
Katzowitz Shenfield, Lauren *philanthropy consultant*
Kauffmann, Stanley Jules *author*
Kaufman, Bel *author, educator*
Kaufman, David Marc *pediatric neurologist*
Kaufman, Henry *diversified financial services company executive*
Kaufman, Jason Edward *art critic, reporter, editor*
Kaufman, Robert Max *lawyer, director*
Kaufman, Stephen Edward *lawyer*
Kaufman, Victor A. *broadcast executive, retired film company executive*
Kaufmann, Mark Steiner *banker, director*
Kaur, Harminder *language educator*
Kavaler, Thomas J. *lawyer*
Kavalerchik, Boris Yakovlevich *application developer, researcher*
Kavesh, Robert A. *economist, educator*
Kavner, Robert M. *communications executive*
Kavoukjian, Michael Edward *lawyer*
Kaye, Stephen Rackow *lawyer*
Kaye, Walter *corporate financial executive*
Kayle, Bruce E. *lawyer*
Kayse, Kathleen *publishing executive*
Kayser, Leo III *lawyer*
Kazanjian, John Harold *lawyer*
Kazemi, Farhad *political scientist, educator*
Keagy, Dorothy (Dotti Keagy) *copy director*
Kean, Hamilton Fish *lawyer*
Keane, Bil *cartoonist*
Keany, Sutton *lawyer*
Kearney, Lynn *Culinary Manager*
Kearse, Amalya Lyle *federal judge*
Keating, Isabel *actress*
Keegan, Peter W. *diversified financial services company executive*
Keenan, John Fontaine *federal judge*
Keenan, Michael Edgar *marketing professional*
Keenan, Terry *anchor, correspondent*
Keene, Donald *writer, translator, language educator*
Keene, Lonnie *lawyer*
Kehoe, John P. *investor relations executive*
Kehret, Peg *writer*
Keiser, Lauren Keith *publishing executive, composer*
Keithley, Carter *trade association administrator*
Kekst, Gershon *public relations consultant*
Kellar, Charlotte Avrutis *writer*
Keller, Bill *editor*
Keller, Bruce P. *lawyer*
Keller, Marthe *artist, painter*
Kellerman, Jonathan Seth *writer, pediatric psychologist, educator*
Kelley, Darcy B. *biology professor*
Kelley, David N. *lawyer, former prosecutor*
Kelley, Kitty *writer*
Kelley, Mike *artist*
Kellner, George *financial analyst*
Kellogg, Paul *opera company director*
Kelly, Alfred F., Jr. *diversified financial services company executive*
Kelly, Anastasia D. (Stasia Kelly) *telecommunications industry executive, lawyer*
Kelly, Christopher M. *lawyer*
Kelly, Ellsworth *painter, sculptor*
Kelly, James *editor*
Kelly, Mary *sculptor*
Kelly, Patrick Joseph *neurosurgeon, educator*
Kelly, Peter *communications executive*
Kelly, R. (Robert Sylvester Kelly) *musician, recording industry executive*
Kelly, Raymond Walter *police commissioner*
Kelly, Thomas Jesse, Jr. *molecular biologist*
Kelly, Thomas Michael *lawyer*
Kelly, William Michael *investment company executive*
Kelman, Edward Michael *lawyer*
Kelmenson, Leo-Arthur *advertising executive*
Kelson, Richard B. *metal products executive*
Keltner, Thomas Nethery, Jr. *lawyer*
Kemper, Randy *fashion designer*
Kende, Christopher Burgess *lawyer, educator*
Keneally, Kathryn Marie *lawyer*
Kenneally, Michael E. *diversified financial services company executive*
Kennedy, Adrienne Lita *playwright*
Kennedy, David L. *cosmetics company executive*
Kennedy, James M. *editor*
Kennedy, John B. *lawyer*
Kennedy, John Joseph *bank financial officer*
Kennedy, Kevin W. *finance company executive*
Kennedy, Michael John *lawyer*
Kennedy, Robert Francis, Jr. *lawyer, environmentalist*
Kennedy, Thomas Patrick *financial executive*
Kenney, John Joseph *lawyer*
Kenny, Tom *actor*
Keno, Leigh R. *antiques dealer, appraiser*
Keno, Leslie B. *antiques dealer, appraiser*
Kensington, Costa Nicholas *lawyer*
Kent, Deborah Warren *hypnotherapist, consultant, lecturer*
Kent, Julie *dancer, actress, model*
Kent, Linda Gail *dancer*
Kent, Steven *lawyer*
Kent, Susan *library director, consultant*
Kenwright, Bill *theatrical producer*
Keogh, Kevin *lawyer*
Kepets, Hugh Michael *artist*
Kepke, Matthew Aaron *lawyer*
Keppler, Herbert *publishing executive*
Kern, George Calvin, Jr. *lawyer*
Kern, William Bliem, Jr. *minister*

Kernochan, John Marshall *lawyer, educator*
Kerrey, Bob (J. Robert Kerrey) *academic administrator, former senator*
Kerz, Louise *historian*
Kessel, Mark *lawyer*
Kessinger, Kevin M. *diversified financial services company executive*
Kessler, Jeffrey L. *lawyer*
Kessler, Stuart *accountant, financial planner*
Ketchum, Richard G. *stock exchange executive, lawyer*
Keteyian, Armen *news correspondent*
Keys, Alicia (Alicia Augello Cook) *vocalist, musician, songwriter*
Kezsbom, Allen *lawyer*
Khalil, Mohammad Omer *artist, educator*
Khalil, Mounir A. *librarian, educator*
Khan, Shahnawaz *pharmacist, director*
Khan, Sura *film company executive*
Khedoori, Toba *artist*
Kheel, Robert J. *lawyer*
Kheradpir, Shaygan *information technology executive*
Khuri, Nicola Najib *physicist, researcher*
Kidd, Chip *book designer, writer*
Kid Rock, (Robert James Ritchie) *singer*
Kiechel, Walter III *editor*
Kiekhofer, William Henry *lawyer*
Kiernan, John S. *lawyer*
Kies, David M. *lawyer*
Kiessling, B. Robbins *lawyer*
Kilik, Jon *film producer*
Killian, John F. *telecommunications industry executive*
Killip, Thomas *cardiologist*
Kilpatrick, Donald G. *lawyer*
Kim, Atta *photographer*
Kim, Dow *investment company executive*
Kim, Se Jung *civil engineer*
Kimball, Chad *actor*
Kimball, John Devereux *lawyer*
Kimball, Roger *editor, writer, publishing executive*
Kimmelman, Michael Simon *art critic*
Kinberg, Judy *television producer, television director*
Kind, Phyllis *art gallery owner*
Kindler, Jeffrey B. *pharmaceutical company executive, lawyer*
Kindler, Robert Alan *investment banker*
King, B.B. (Riley B. King) *singer, guitarist*
King, Edward Joseph *clinical chemist, laboratory administrator*
King, George A. *technology executive, lawyer*
King, Henry Lawrence *lawyer*
King, Stephen C. *lawyer, commissioner, educator*
Kingsbury, Benedict *law educator*
Kinne, David Weir *retired surgeon*
Kinney, Catherine R. *stock exchange executive*
Kinney, Gilbert Hart *investor*
Kinney, Stephen Hoyt, Jr. *lawyer*
Kinsolving, Charles McIlvaine, Jr. *marketing executive*
Kinstler, Everett Raymond *artist*
Kinzler, Thomas Benjamin *lawyer*
Kipshidze, Nickolas N. *medical association administrator, researcher*
Kirby, John Joseph, Jr. *lawyer*
Kirdar, Nemir Amin *banker*
Kirkham, D. Collier *lawyer*
Kirle, Bruce *theater educator*
Kirsch, Donald *financial consultant*
Kirschbaum, Laurence J. *publishing executive*
Kirschbaum, Myron *lawyer*
Kirsh, Michael Alan *financial estate planner*
Kislik, Richard William *publishing executive*
Kissel, Howard William *drama critic*
Kisselgoff, Anna *dance critic*
Kitahata-Sporn, Amy *movement educator*
Kitashirakawa, Michihisa *head of religious order*
Kizer, Jorge Ruben *cardiologist, epidemiologist*
Klapper, Molly *lawyer, educator*
Klapper, Richard H. *lawyer*
Klass, Sheila Solomon *English language educator, writer*
Kleber, Herbert David *psychiatrist, educator*
Kleckner, Robert George, Jr. *retired lawyer*
Kleeblatt, Norman L. *museum curator*
Klein, Calvin Richard *fashion designer*
Klein, Cynthia *art appraiser*
Klein, Eleazer *lawyer*
Klein, Harvey *medical educator*
Klein, Jason Evan *publishing executive*
Klein, Jeffrey Peter *inventor*
Klein, Joel Irwin *school system administrator*
Klein, Laura Colin *publishing executive*
Klein, Martin I. *lawyer*
Klein, Naomi *journalist*
Klein, Richard S. *lawyer*
Klein, Robert *comedian, actor*
Klein, T(heodore) E(ibon) D(onald) *writer*
Kleinbard, Edward D. *lawyer*
Kleinberg, Norman Charles *lawyer*
Kleinfeld, Klaus *electronics executive*
Klemann, Gilbert Lacy, II, *lawyer*
Kliment, Robert Michael *architect*
Kliment, Stephen Alexander *architect, editor, journalist*
Klimstra, David S. *pathologist*
Kline, Eugene Monroe *lawyer*
Kline, Kevin Delaney *actor*
Klingensmith, Michael *publishing executive*
Klinger, Alan Mark *lawyer*
Klingsberg, David *lawyer*
Klinkenborg, Verlyn *writer, educator*
Klipper, Mitchell S. *book publishing executive*
Klipstein, Robert Alan *lawyer*
Klotz, Florence *costume designer*
Klotz, Martin B. *lawyer*
Kluger, Jeffrey *reporter, author*
Knapp, Albert Bruce *gastroenterologist*
Knapp, Amy K. *insurance company executive*
Knapp, Ellen M. *financial company executive*
Knapp, Robert Charles *retired obstetrics and gynecology educator*
Kneale, Dennis Randall *publishing executive*
Knerr, Anthony David *financial consultant*
Knerr, Theodore *artist, photographer*
Knight, Robert Huntington *lawyer, bank executive*
Knopf, Alfred, Jr. *retired publisher*
Kobak, James Benedict, Jr. *lawyer, educator*
Kobrin, Lawrence Alan *lawyer*

Koch, Edward Irving *lawyer, former mayor*
Koch, Stephen Bayard *writer, language educator*
Koegel, William Fisher *lawyer*
Koeltl, John George *federal judge*
Koen, Robert G. *lawyer*
Koepff, Paul R. *lawyer*
Koepp, Stephen *editor*
Koeppel, Noel Immanuel *financial planner, securities and real estate broker*
Koerner, Brendan I. *columnist*
Kogod, Robert P. *philanthropist, former real estate company executive*
Kohl, Robert L. *lawyer*
Kohlmann, Susan J. *lawyer*
Kohn, A. Eugene *architect*
Kohn, Brenda *pediatrician, endocrinologist, consultant*
Kohn, Immanuel *lawyer*
Koke, Richard Joseph *writer, curator*
Kolata, Gina *journalist*
Kolatch, Myron *magazine editor*
Kolbe, Karl William, Jr. *lawyer*
Kolker, Adam Ross *plastic surgeon, educator*
Kolker, Lawrence Paul *lawyer*
Kolodny, Edwin Hillel *neurologist, geneticist, director*
Kolson, Ann J. *editor*
Komisar, Arnold *otolaryngologist, educator*
Kondo, Reena *science educator, artist*
Konney, Paul Edward *consumer products company executive, lawyer*
Koob, Charles Edward *lawyer*
Koons, Jeff *artist*
Koopersmith, Kim *lawyer*
Koopman, Barbara Goldenberg *psychiatrist*
Kopelman, Richard Eric *management educator*
Kopenhaver, Patricia Ellsworth *podiatrist*
Koplewicz, Harold Samuel *child and adolescent psychiatrist*
Koplik, Michael R. *durable goods company executive*
Koplos, Janet *editor, art critic*
Kopp, Wendy *educational association administrator*
Koppelman, Chaim *artist, educator*
Koppelman, Charles A. *record company executive*
Koppelman, Dorothy Myers *artist, consultant*
Koral, Alan Max *lawyer*
Korda, Michael Vincent *retired publishing company executive, writer*
Kornberg, Alan William *lawyer*
Kornfeld, Neil S. *lawyer*
Kornhauser, Lewis *law educator*
Kornreich, Edward Scott *lawyer*
Korot, Beryl *artist*
Korotkin, Michael Paul *lawyer*
Korvin, Catherine Madeleine *editor*
Koslow, Jonathan L. *lawyer*
Koslow, Sally *editor-in-chief*
Kostelanetz, Richard *writer, artist*
Koster, Elaine *publishing executive*
Koteff, Ellen *periodical editor*
Koten, John F. *editor-in-chief*
Kotlowitz, Robert *writer, editor*
Kotuk, Andrea Mikotajuk *public relations executive, writer*
Kotzwinkle, William *writer*
Kourides, Ione Anne *endocrinologist, researcher, educator*
Kovner, Bruce *investment company executive*
Kowalski, Michael J. *retail products executive*
Kozak, Harley Jane *actress, writer*
Kozik, Susan S. *information technology executive*
Kozinn, Allan *music critic, reporter*
Kozloff, Joyce *artist*
Kozlowski, Cheryl M. *fixed income analyst*
Kraemer, Harry M. Jansen, Jr. *investment company executive, former medical products executive*
Kraemer, Lillian Elizabeth *lawyer*
Kraft, Robert *computer network engineer, publishing executive*
Kraines, Merrill M. *lawyer*
Kram, Shirley Wohl *federal judge*
Kramarsky, Werner H. *art collector*
Kramer, George P. *lawyer*
Kramer, Harry *artist*
Kramer, Linda Konheim *curator, art historian*
Kramer, Marc Z. *publishing executive*
Kramon, Glenn *newspaper business editor*
Krane, Steven Charles *lawyer*
Krantz, Judith Tarcher *novelist*
Krasna, Alvin Isaac *biochemist, educator*
Krasner, Daniel Walter *lawyer*
Krasnow, Kenneth *real estate company executive*
Krasnow, Richard P. *lawyer*
Kraus, Douglas M *lawyer*
Kraus, Norma Jean *human resources executive*
Kraus, Peter Steven *diversified financial services company executive*
Kraushar, Jonathan Pollack *communications and media consultant*
Krauss, Herbert Harris *psychologist*
Kravis, Henry R. *venture capitalist*
Kravitz, Lee *editor*
Krawcheck, Sallie L. *bank executive*
Krebs, Carl F. *architectural firm executive*
Kreek, Mary Jeanne *physician*
Kreidman, Perry L. *lawyer*
Kreisberg, Neil Ivan *advertising executive*
Kreitman, James E. *securities trader*
Kreitzman, Ralph J. *lawyer*
Krementz, Jill *photographer, author*
Kressel, Henry *venture capitalist*
Kreston, Martin Howard *advertising, marketing, public relations, and publishing executive*
Kreuther, Gabriel *chef*
Kriegel, Jay L. *Olympic organizing committee executive, public relations executive*
Krieger, Sanford *lawyer*
Krill, Kay (Katherine Lawther Krill) *apparel executive*
Krimendahl, Herbert Frederick, II, *investment banker*
Krinsky, Carol Herselle *art historian, educator*
Krinsky, Robert Daniel *consulting firm executive*
Kristof, Nicholas Donabet *journalist*
Kroeber, Karl *language educator*
Kroell, Devi *accessories designer*
Kroft, Steve *news correspondent, editor*
Krominga, Lynn *cosmetics executive, lawyer*
Kropf, Susan J. *cosmetics company executive*

Krouse, George Raymond, Jr. *lawyer*
Kruger, Barbara *artist, art critic*
Kruger, Steven F. *literature educator*
Krukowski, Jan *communications executive*
Krupman, William Allan *lawyer*
Krupp, Fred D. *lawyer, environmental services administrator*
Kubek, Gary W. *lawyer*
Kuby, Ronald Lawrence *lawyer*
Kuchta, Ronald Andrew *museum director, editor, curator*
Kuck, Lea Haber *lawyer*
Kudisch, Marc *actor*
Kuh, Richard Henry *lawyer*
Kuhbach, Robert Gerdes *lawyer*
Kuhn, James D. *real estate company executive*
Kujawski, Elizabeth Szancer *art curator, consultant*
Kulish, Nicholas *reporter*
Kunes, Richard W. *cosmetics executive*
Kuntz, Lee Allan *lawyer*
Kuntz, William Francis, II, *lawyer, educator*
Kuo, John Tsungfen *geophysicist, educator, researcher*
Kuperman, Robert Ian *retired advertising agency executive*
Kupper, William P., Jr. *publishing executive*
Kurahara, Ted Naomi *artist, educator*
Kurli, Madhavi *ophthalmologist*
Kurman, Juta *music educator*
Kurnow, Ernest *statistician, educator*
Kurtz, Jerome *retired lawyer, educator*
Kurz, William Charles Frederick *lawyer*
Kurzweil, Edith *social sciences educator, editor*
Kurzweil, Harvey *lawyer*
Kushner, Jared C. *publishing executive, real estate developer*
Kusmierski, Janet Louise *painter, graphics designer, illustrator*
Kutosh, Sue *artist*
Kuttler, Judith Esther *retired psychotherapist*
Kuyper, Joan Carolyn *foundation administrator*
Kyriakou, Linda Grace *communications executive*
La Barbara, Joan Linda *composer, musician, singer*
LaBarre, Dennis W. *lawyer*
LaBelle, Patti (Patricia Louise Holte) *singer, entertainer*
Labovitz, Daniel Lockett *neurologist*
LaBranche, Michael (George M.L. LaBranche IV) *securities trader*
Labunski, Stephen Bronislaw *professional society administrator*
Lachmann, Elisabeth Amanda *physician*
Lack, Andrew R. *music company executive*
Lack, Robert Joel *lawyer*
Lackritz, Marc E. *securities industry association executive*
Lacovara, Philip Allen *lawyer*
Lacy, Robinson Burrell *lawyer*
Laderman, Ezra *composer, educator, college dean*
Ladjevardi, Hamid *portfolio manager*
Lagani, Daniel *publishing executive*
Lagani, Joseph A. *publishing executive*
Lai, W(ei) Michael *mechanical engineer, educator*
Laibman, David *economist, educator*
Laiskonis, Michael *chef*
Lalwani, Anil Kumar *otolaryngologist*
Lam, Derek *apparel designer*
Lamagna, Carlo M. *art educator*
LaMattina, John L. *pharmaceutical executive*
Lamb, Robert Boyden *finance and management educator*
Lamb, Wally *writer*
Lamia, Thomas Roger *lawyer*
Lamle, Hugh Roy *investment advisor, consultant*
Lamm, Donald Stephen *literary agent*
Lamm, Norman *academic administrator, rabbi*
Lammie, James Louis *engineering executive, retired military officer*
Lamont, Lansing *journalist, writer, foundation administrator*
Lamport, Anthony Matthew *venture capitalist*
Lamster, Ira Barry *dean, academic administrator*
Lanchner, Bertrand Martin *lawyer, advertising executive*
Landau, David H. *lawyer*
Landau, Sidney Ivan *lexicographer*
Landman, Jonathan *editor*
Landrigan, Philip John *epidemiologist*
Landry, Donald William *physician scientist*
Lane, Kenneth Jay *jewelry designer*
Lane, Kenneth Robert *producer, distributor*
Lane, Louis *musician, conductor*
Lang, Everett Francis, Jr. *brokerage house executive*
Lang, George *restaurateur*
Lang, Pearl *dancer, choreographer*
Lang, Stephen *actor*
Langan, Marie-Noelle Suzanne *cardiologist, educator*
Langan, Richard F., Jr. *lawyer*
Lange, Jessica Phyllis *actress*
Lange, Liz *apparel designer and executive*
Lange, Phil C. *retired education educator*
Langford, Laura Sue *corporate financial executive*
Langhammer, Fred H. *cosmetics company executive*
Langone, Kenneth G. *investment company executive*
Langton, Cleve Swanson *advertising executive*
Lannamann, Richard Stuart *executive search consultant*
Lanpher, Katherine *radio personality, columnist*
Lansbury, Edgar George *theatrical producer*
Lansner, Gabrielle *choreographer, dancer, performing company executive, actress*
Lansner, Ruth L. *lawyer*
Lanyon, Ellen (Mrs. Roland Ginzel) *artist, educator*
Lapham, Lewis Henry *editor, television personality, writer*
Lapierre, Dominique *writer, historian, philanthropist*
LaQuaglia, Michael Patrick *pediatric surgeon, neuroblastoma researcher*
Laragh, John Henry *cardiologist, surgeon, educator*
Larberg, John Frederick *retired social welfare executive, wine consultant, educator*
Larose, Lawrence Alfred *lawyer*

Larrick, Pamela Maphis *marketing executive*
Larsen, Jonathan Zerbe *journalist*
Larson, Steven Mark *physician*
Lascher, Alan Alfred *lawyer*
Lash, Stephen Sycle *auction company executive*
Lashner, William Mark *writer*
Lasker, Jonathan Lewis *artist*
Lasker, Joseph L. *artist, illustrator*
Laskin, Richard Sheldon *orthopedic surgeon*
Lasser, Joseph Robert *investment company executive*
Lassiter, Phillip B. *insurance company executive*
Lataille, Ronald H. *telecommunications industry executive*
Lattimer, John Kingsley *physician, educator*
Latza, William D. *lawyer*
Lauder, Aerin *cosmetics executive*
Lauder, Evelyn H. *cosmetics executive*
Lauder, Jo Carole *art association administrator*
Lauder, Leonard Alan *cosmetic and fragrance company executive*
Lauder, Ronald Stephen *investor*
Lauder, William P. *cosmetics executive*
Laue, Bruce Antonio *financial consultant, writer*
Lauer, Eliot *lawyer*
Lauer, Matt *television personality*
Laufer, Mark Vladimir *retired engineering educator*
Laufman, Harold *surgeon, consultant*
Laumont, Philippe Emile *communications executive*
Launer, Leland C., Jr. *insurance company executive*
Lauren, Ralph *fashion designer*
Laurence, Jeffrey Conrad *immunologist, educator*
Laurence, Michael Marshall *foundation administrator*
Laurents, Arthur *playwright*
Laurie, Craig *real estate company executive*
Laurie, Nancy Walton *retail executive*
Lavin, Howard S. *lawyer*
Law, Sylvia A. *law educator*
Lawhon, Charla *editor*
Lawrence, Bryan Hunt *investment company executive*
Lawrence, Christopher Rueckert *investment banker*
Lawrence, Lauren *psychotherapist, writer*
Lawrence, Nina *publishing executive*
Lawson, Nigella *cookbook writer, celebrity chef*
Lawson, William *otolaryngologist, educator*
Lawson-Johnston, Peter, II, *investment company executive*
Lawson-Johnston, Peter Orman *foundation executive*
Lax, Peter David *mathematician, educator*
Laybourne, Geraldine B. *broadcast executive*
Layton, Donald Harvey *retired banker*
Lazarcik, Gregor *economist, educator, financial research company executive*
Lazarus, Adrienne *retail executive*
Lazarus, Shelly (Rochelle Braff Lazarus) *advertising executive*
Lazio, Rick Anthony (Enrico Anthony Lazio) *bank executive, former congressman*
Leach, Bryan *music company executive*
Leach, Robin *producer, writer, television host*
Leahey, Lynn *editor-in-chief*
Leahey, Miles Cary *economist*
Leahy, Michael Joseph *retired newspaper editor*
Leahy, Robert Louis *psychologist*
Leaman, Leonard S., Jr. *science educator*
Leandre, Juan (Joan Leandre) *computer graphics designer, artist*
Lebenthal, Alexandra *investment firm executive*
LeBlond, Richard Knight, II, *banker*
Lebow, Mark Denis *lawyer*
LeClerc, Paul *library director*
Lederberg, Joshua *geneticist, educator*
Lederman, Lawrence *lawyer, writer, educator*
Ledger, William Joe *obstetrician, educator*
LeDoux, Joseph E. *neuroscientist, educator*
Lee, Amy *singer*
Lee, Bruce *editor, writer*
Lee, Catherine *sculptor, painter*
Lee, David Hee-Don *trade association administrator, educator*
Lee, Frances Helen *editor*
Lee, Helie *writer*
Lee, In-Young *lawyer*
Lee, Jennifer B. *journalist*
Lee, Jerome G. *lawyer*
Lee, Lillian Vanessa *microbiologist*
Lee, Nancy *radiologist, oncologist*
Lee, Paul Lawrence *lawyer*
Lee, Sally A. *editor-in-chief*
Lee, Sandra *food service executive, product designer*
Lee, Thomas F. *art association administrator*
Lee, Tsung-Dao *physicist, researcher*
Leeds, Norman E. *medical educator, radiologist*
Leepson, Marc *freelance/self-employed writer*
Lees, Alfred William *former magazine editor, writer*
Leet, Mildred Robbins *social welfare administrator, consultant*
Lefcourt, Gerald B. *lawyer*
LeFevre, David E. *lawyer, professional sports team executive*
Lefferts, Gillet, Jr. *architect*
Leffler, Marvin *foundation administrator, writer*
Lefkovits, Albert Meyer *dermatologist*
Lefkowitz, David S. *lawyer*
Lefkowitz, Howard N. *lawyer*
Legato, Marianne *internist, medical educator*
Legend, John (John Stephens) *musician*
LeGrady, George *photographer, educator*
Legrand, Michel Jean *composer*
Legvold, Robert *political science professor*
Lehane, Dennis *writer*
Lehman, Edward William *social studies educator, researcher*
Lehman, Mark E. *lawyer*
Lehmann-Haupt, Christopher Charles Herbert *book reviewer*
Leiber, Gerson August *artist*
Leibert, Burton M. *lawyer*
Leibovitz, Annie *photographer*
Leibovitz, Herbert Akiba *literature and language professor, writer*
Leibowitz, Martin L. *financial services company executive*

Leichtling, Michael Alfred *lawyer*
Leifer, Edgar *physician, retired medical educator*
Leighton, Lawrence Ward *investment banker*
Leighty, Keith *editor*
Leisure, Peter Keeton *federal judge*
Leiter, Al (Alois Terry Leiter) *retired professional baseball player*
Leitman, I. Michael *health facility administrator*
Leive, Cynthia *editor-in-chief*
Lekberg, Barbara *sculptor*
Leland, Richard G(uy) *lawyer*
L'Engle, Madeleine (Mrs. Hugh Franklin) *writer*
Lenobel, Jeffrey A. *lawyer*
Lenox, Adriane *actress*
Leonard, Edwin Deane *lawyer*
Lepore, Nanette *apparel designer*
Leppard, Raymond John *conductor, musician*
Leritz, Lawrence R. *choreographer, singer, dancer*
Lerner, Eric M. *lawyer*
Lerner, Jonathan J. *lawyer*
Lerner, Martin *museum curator*
Lerner, Richard E. *lawyer*
Lerner, Sandra *artist*
Lesch, Michael Oscar *lawyer*
Lesk, Ann Berger *lawyer*
Leslie, Seymour Marvin *communications executive, director*
Lessard, Stefan *musician*
Lessing, Brian Reid *actuary*
Lessing, Stephen M. *finance company executive*
Lessnau, Klaus-Dieter Karl *pulmonologist, director, medical educator*
Letterman, David *talk show host, producer, comedian, writer*
Leubert, Alfred Otto Paul *management consultant*
Leung, Firman *investment bank executive*
Levai, Pierre Alexandre *art gallery executive*
Leval, Pierre Nelson *federal judge*
Levander, Andrew Joshua *lawyer*
Leven, Ann Ruth *financial consultant*
Levie, Joseph Henry *lawyer, banker*
Levin, Alan G. *pharmaceutical company executive*
Levin, Alan M. *television journalist*
Levin, Frances R. *psychiatrist, educator*
Levin, Gail *writer, educator, photographer*
Levin, Henry Mordechai *economist, educator*
Levin, Herbert *retired diplomat, foundation administrator*
Levin, Ira *writer, playwright*
Levin, Janna *physicist, educator*
Levin, Martin P. *publishing executive, lawyer*
Levin, Michael Joseph *lawyer*
Levin, Peter S.W. *lawyer*
Levine, Adam Noah *singer*
Levine, David *artist*
Levine, Ellen R. *editor-in-chief*
Levine, Gail Carson *writer*
Levine, James *conductor, music director, pianist*
Levine, Judy Kendall *real estate broker, interior designer, writer*
Levine, Louis D. *museum director, archaeologist*
Levine, Naomi Bronheim *academic administrator*
Levine, Robert Jay *lawyer*
Levine, Ronald Jay *lawyer*
Levins, Ilyssa *public relations executive*
Levinson, Daryl J. *law educator*
Levinson, Rascha *psychotherapist*
Levinson, Robert Alan *textiles executive*
Levinson, Stephen *television producer*
Levinson, Warren Mitchell *broadcast journalist*
Levitan, David M(aurice) *lawyer, educator*
Levitt, Arthur, Jr. *investment company executive, former federal agency administrator*
Levitz, Paul Elliot *publishing executive*
Levounis, Petros *psychiatrist*
Levoy, Myron *author*
Levy, Albert *physician*
Levy, Clifford J. *reporter*
Levy, Shawn Anthony *writer*
Levy, Stanley Herbert *lawyer*
Lew, Jacob *public administration educator*
Lewin, Betsy R. *illustrator*
Lewin, Robert *lawyer*
Lewis, Edward T. *publishing executive*
Lewis, Jerry Lee *country-rock singer, musician*
Lewis, Jonathan Joseph *surgical oncologist, molecular biologist, educator, entrepreneur*
Lewis, Leland M. *hotel executive*
Lewis, Loida Nicolas *food products holding company executive*
Lewis, Paul *architecture educator*
Lewis, Stephen H. *diplomat*
LeWitt, Sol *artist*
Lewy, Robert Max *physician*
Lewyn, Ann Salfeld *retired English as a second language educator*
Lewyn, Thomas Mark *lawyer*
Li, Tze-chung *lawyer, educator*
Libby, Daniel M. *pulmonologist*
Liberman, Enrique Eduardo *lawyer*
Liberman, Megan Rose *editor*
Libeskind, Daniel *architect*
Libin, Paul *theater producer, theater director*
LiBretto, John Charles *television director*
Lichtblau, John H. *economist*
Liddle, Jeffrey L. *lawyer*
Liden, Hanna *photographer*
Liebenson, Jeffrey M. *lawyer*
Lieberman, Dave *chef*
Lieberman, James Sanford *physiatrist, neurologist*
Lieberman, Nancy Ann *lawyer*
Liebman, Lance Malcolm *law educator*
Liebman, Theodore *architect*
Liebmann, Jeff S. *lawyer*
Liff, Zanvel A. *psychologist*
Liftin, Joan R. *photojournalist, educator*
Liftin, John M. *lawyer*
Lifton, Robert Kenneth *manufacturing executive*
Liles, Kevin *music company executive*
Lilien, Robert Jarrett *diversified financial services company executive*
Lilly, Evangeline *actress*
Lima, Adriana Francesca *model*
Liman, Lewis Jeffrey *lawyer*
Limbaugh, Rush Hudson III *radio talk show host*
Lin, Fang-Hua *mathematics professor*
Lincoln, Edmond Lynch *investment banker*
Lindauer, Erik D. *lawyer*
Lindblom, Marjorie Press *lawyer*
Lindenmayer, Jean-Pierre *psychiatrist*
Lindo, Stephen T. *lawyer*

Lindsay, George Peter *lawyer*
Linen, Jonathan S. *diversified financial services company executive*
Lingeman, Richard Roberts *editor-in-chief, writer*
Link, Robert O., Jr. *lawyer*
Linker, Arthur S. *lawyer*
Linsenmeyer, John Michael *lawyer*
Linton, Donna Joan *foreign language educator, dean*
Linz, Werner Mark *international publishing executive*
Lipkin, Martin *medical educator, researcher*
Lipman, Ira Ackerman *security service company executive*
Lipper, Kenneth *investment banker, film producer, writer*
Lippert, Nels T. *lawyer*
Lippman, Laura *writer*
Lippman, Sharon Rochelle *art historian, filmmaker, art therapist*
Lipscomb, James Louis *lawyer, insurance company executive*
Lipscomb, Thomas Heber III *media company executive*
Lipsey, Robert Edward *economist, educator*
Lipsky, Burton G. *lawyer*
Lipsky, Pat *artist*
Lipson, Allen S. *entertainment company executive, lawyer*
Liptak, Adam *lawyer, reporter*
Lipton, Charles *public relations executive*
Lipton, James *television personality*
Lipton, Joan Elaine *advertising executive*
Lipton, Lester *ophthalmologist, entrepreneur*
Lipton, Martin *lawyer*
Liss, Norman *lawyer*
Littenberg, Michael Richard *lawyer*
Little, Robert David *library science professor*
Littman, Dan R. *microbiologist*
Lituchy, Gregg *dentist*
Litvack, Sanford Martin *lawyer*
Litwin, Ethan *lawyer*
Litwin, Leonard *real estate company executive*
Liu, Kai-Lih *epidemiologist*
Liu, Si-kwang *veterinary pathologist*
Liu, Tony *chef*
Llinás, Rodolfo Riascos *neuroscientist, researcher*
Lloyd, Jean *retired early childhood educator*
Lloyd, Kenneth L. *columnist*
Lloyd, William Frederick *lawyer*
Lo, Anita *chef*
Loacker, Lynn J. *lawyer*
Lobenfeld, Eric Jay *lawyer*
Lobl, Herbert Max *lawyer, writer*
Lobo, Rogerio Arnaldo *obstetrician, gynecologist*
Lockshin, Michael Dan *rheumatologist*
Lodge, Henry Sears *physician*
Loeb, John Langeloth, Jr. *investment counselor, consultant*
Loeb, John Nichols *physician, educator*
Loeb, Larry Morris *communications company executive*
Loeb, Lisa *singer, lyricist*
Loeb, Marshall Robert *journalist*
Loengard, John Borg *photographer, editor*
Loengard, Richard Otto, Jr. *lawyer*
Logan, Don *publishing executive*
Logan, Kenneth Richard *lawyer*
Lohr, Steve *reporter*
Løj, Ellen Margrethe *ambassador*
Lombardi, Joseph J. *retail executive*
London, Herbert Ira *humanities educator, academic administrator*
London, Martin *lawyer*
Loney, Glenn Meredith *theater educator*
Longley, Marjorie Watters *newspaper executive*
Longobardi, David *editor-in-chief*
Longstreth, Bevis *lawyer*
Loo, Marcus Hsieu-Hong *urologist, physician, educator*
Loo, Santos *chef*
Loomis, Carol J. *journalist*
Lopez, Gerald P. *law educator*
Lopez, Pedro Felipe *social worker, educator, playwright, writer*
Lopez, Ralph Ivan *pediatrics educator*
Lopez, Robert *composer, lyricist*
Lorber, Barbara Heyman *communications executive, event producer*
Lorch, Maristella De Panizza *writer, educator*
Lord, M. G. *writer*
Lord, Marvin *apparel executive*
Lorenc, Z. Paul (Paul Lorenc) *plastic surgeon*
Loring, John Robbins *artist, writer*
LoSchiavo, Linda Bosco *library director*
Losier, Marie *film director*
Loss, Margaret Ruth *lawyer*
Lothian, James Robert *economist, educator*
Lotwin, Stanford Gerald *lawyer*
Lou, Liza *artist*
Louderback, Jim *editor-in-chief*
Louganis, Greg E. (Gregory Efthimios Louganis) *retired Olympic athlete, actor*
Loughlin, John P. *publishing executive*
Loughran, Peter J. *lawyer*
Louis, Sean *broadcast executive*
Louizos, Anna Alexandra *set designer*
Love, Shirley *mezzo-soprano*
Lovell, Whitfield *artist*
Low, Anthony *language educator*
Lowe, Ida Brandwayn *information technology manager*
Lowenberg, Marc Gregory *dentist*
Lowenfeld, Andreas Frank *law educator*
Lowenfels, Fred M. *lawyer*
Lowenfels, Lewis David *lawyer*
Lowengrub, Morton *academic administrator*
Lowenstein, Louis *law educator*
Lowry, George S. *art appraiser*
Lowry, Glenn David *art museum director*
Lowry, Nicholas D. *art appraiser*
Lowry, Rich *editor*
Lowy, George Theodore *lawyer*
Lubars, David *advertising executive*
Lubell, Michael Stephen *physicist, educator*
Lubetski, Edith Esther *librarian*
Lubin, Daniel C. *venture capitalist*
Lubovitch, Lar *dancer, choreographer*
Lucander, Henry *investment banker*
Lucas, James E(van) *operatic director*
Lucci, Susan *actress*

Luce, Charles Franklin *retired utilities executive, lawyer*
Lucht, John Charles *management consultant, writer*
Luckman, Sharon Gersten *arts administrator*
Luke, Douglas Sigler *investment company executive*
Luks, Allan Barry *executive director*
Lum, Larry *lawyer*
Lunardini, Christine Anne *writer, historian, school administrator*
Lund, Daniel Peter *lawyer*
Lundberg, George David, II, *medical editor-in-chief, pathologist*
Lundgren, Terry J. *retail company executive*
Lunding, Christopher Hanna *lawyer*
Lundquist, John Milton *librarian, Egyptologist, author, travel writer, photographer*
Lundqvist, Henrik *professional hockey player*
Lunn, Kitty Elizabeth *actress*
Luo, Michael *journalist*
Lupert, Leslie Allan *lawyer*
LuPone, Patti *actress*
Luria, Mary Mercer *lawyer*
Lurie, Alison *writer*
Lurie, Ranan Raymond *political cartoonist, artist, journalist*
Lutnick, Howard William *brokerage house executive*
Lutz, Tina *apparel designer*
Lutzker, Joel E. *lawyer*
Luxenberg, Arthur Martin *lawyer*
Lyden, David Charles *oncologist, cell biologist*
Lyman, Peggy *artistic director, dancer, choreographer, educator*
Lynch, Florence *art gallery director*
Lynch, Gary G. *investment company executive, lawyer*
Lynch, Gerard E. *federal judge*
Lynch, Loretta E. *lawyer, former prosecutor*
Lynch, Luke Daniel, Jr. *lawyer*
Lynn, Theodore Stanley *lawyer*
Lynne, Michael *film company executive*
Lyon, Carl Francis, Jr. *lawyer*
Lyons, Bridget Gellert *language educator*
Lyons, John Matthew *telecommunications industry executive, broadcast executive*
Lyons, Nick *publishing executive*
Ma, Yo-Yo *cellist*
Maack, Thomas *physiology professor*
Maas, Werner Karl *microbiology educator*
Maazel, Lorin *conductor, composer, violinist, music director*
MacAllaster, Archie *investment company executive*
Macan, William Alexander, IV, *lawyer*
MacArthur, John Roderick C. G. (Rick MacArthur) *magazine publisher, journalist*
MacBain, Louise T. Blouin *publishing executive*
Macchiarola, Frank Joseph *academic administrator, educator*
MacCrate, Robert *lawyer*
MacDonald, Alan S. *diversified financial services company executive*
Macdonald, John Stephen *oncologist, educator*
MacDonald, Ronald Francis *diversified financial services company executive*
Macer-Story, Eugenia Ann *writer*
MacGowan, Sandra Firelli *publishing executive, consultant*
Mack, Dennis Wayne *lawyer*
Mack, John J. *diversified financial services company executive*
Mack, Stan *cartoonist*
Macken, Daniel Loos *cardiologist, educator*
Mackey, Patricia Elaine *university librarian*
MacKinnon, Roderick *neuroscientist, educator*
MacKinnon, Roger Alan *psychiatrist, educator*
MacLachlan, Patricia *author*
MacLellan, Steve *diversified financial services company executive*
MacLeod, William Bentley *economics professor, law professor*
Maclin, Amy *editor*
Maclin, Samuel Todd *diversified financial services company executive*
Mac Low, Mordecai-Mark *astrophysicist*
MacRae, Cameron Farquhar III *lawyer*
Macri, Theodore William *book publisher*
Macris, Michael *lawyer*
Madden, John *sportscaster, retired professional football coach*
Madden, John J. *lawyer*
Madden, Michael Daniel *finance company executive*
Madden, Mickey *musician*
Madden-Lunsford, Kerry Elizabeth *writer*
Maddow, Rachel *radio personality, political activist*
Madison, George W. *lawyer*
Mager, Ezra Pascal *investment company executive*
Magro, Cynthia Maria *pathologist*
Maguire, Gregory *writer*
Maher, Jonathan Bannon *finance executive*
Mahon, Arthur Joseph *lawyer*
Mahoney, Margaret Ellerbe *foundation executive*
Maidman, Richard Harvey Mortimer *lawyer*
Maidment, Paul *publishing executive*
Maione, Donna *fashion designer*
Maitland, Guy Edison Clay *lawyer*
Maki, Robert G. *physician, oncologist*
Makovsky, Kenneth Dale *public relations executive*
Malakhov, Vladimir *dancer*
Malamud, Deborah C. *law educator*
Maldonado-Bear, Rita Marinita *economist, educator*
Malefakis, Edward E. *history professor*
Malernee, James Kent, Jr. *financial consultant*
Malfa, Frances *lawyer*
Malgieri, Nick *food service executive, educator, chef, writer*
Malin, Irving *language educator, critic*
Malina, Michael *lawyer*
Malkin, Barry *film editor, consultant*
Malkin, Peter Laurence *lawyer, investor*
Malkin, Stanley Lee *neurologist*
Mallin, Joel *lawyer*
Mallow, Matthew J. *lawyer*
Malloy, Michael Dennis *radio personality*
Mallozzi, Cos M. *public relations executive*
Malman, Laurie L. *law educator*

Maloney, Sean Patrick *lawyer, former federal official*
Malouf, Waldy *food service executive*
Mamlok, Ursula *composer, educator*
Manassah, Jamal Tewfek *electrical engineer, educator, management consultant*
Mandel, Carol *librarian*
Mandel, Irwin Daniel *dentist*
Mandelbaum, Harold Neil *accountant*
Mandelbaum, Jay *diversified financial services company executive*
Mandelstam, Charles Lawrence *lawyer*
Maneker, Morton M. *lawyer*
Maney, Michael Mason *lawyer*
Manger, William Muir *internist, educator, writer, research scientist*
Manges, James Horace *investment banker*
Mangla, Sundeep *radiologist, research scientist*
Manglano-Ovalle, Inigo *sculptor*
Mangold, Robert Peter *artist*
Manilow, Barry (Barry Alan Pincus) *singer, composer*
Manley, James L. *molecular biologist, educator*
Mann, Aimee *singer, songwriter*
Mann, Frank Bert *artist, educator*
Mann, Katinka *artist*
Manning, Dennis J. *insurance company executive*
Manning, Martha Mary *writer, psychologist*
Manoff, Richard Kalman *advertising executive, writer, public health service officer, consultant*
Mansi, Joseph Anneillo *public relations company executive*
Mansouri, Lotfollah (Lotfi Mansouri) *retired performing company executive*
Mantegna, Joe Anthony *actor, playwright*
Mantle, Raymond Allan *lawyer*
Mapes, Glynn Dempsey *newspaper editor*
Marable, Manning *social science educator, writer*
Maraynes, Allan Lawrence *filmmaker, television producer*
Marbury, Stephon *professional basketball player*
Marco, Mitchell *artist*
Marcosson, Thomas I. *management consultant, advertising executive*
Marcus, Eric Peter *lawyer*
Marcus, Eric Robert *psychiatrist*
Marcus, Gwen Ellen *sculptor*
Marcus, Maria Lenhoff *lawyer, educator*
Marcusa, Fred Haye *lawyer*
Marcuse, Adrian Gregory *academic administrator*
Marden, Brice *artist*
Marder, Michael Zachary *dental educator, researcher*
Mardirosian, Tom *actor, playwright*
Margalith, Helen Margaret *retired librarian*
Margolick, David *journalist, writer*
Margolin, Jean Spielberg *artist*
Margolis, Mark Neal *actor*
Margulis, Alexander Rafailo *physician, educator*
Margulis, Howard Lee *lawyer*
Mariani, Michael Matthew *lawyer*
Marin, Deborah B. *psychiatrist, educator*
Marin, Michael L. *vascular surgeon*
Mariner, Jonathan D. *major league baseball executive*
Marino, Dan *sports broadcaster, retired professional football player*
Mark, Jonathan I. *lawyer*
Mark, Reuben *consumer products company executive*
Markard, Marlene Maria *lawyer*
Markel, Gregory Arthur *lawyer*
Markiewicz, Leszek *research biochemist*
Markowitz, Gerald E. *historian, educator*
Markowitz, Martin H. *biomedical researcher*
Marks, Ed *editor*
Marks, Lillian Shapiro *secretarial studies educator, retired, writer, editor*
Marks, Paul Alan *oncologist, cell biologist, educator*
Marks, Ramon Paul *lawyer*
Marlas, James Constantine *diversified financial services company executive*
Marlette, Douglas Nigel *editorial cartoonist, comic strip creator*
Marmor, Michael *epidemiologist, educator*
Maron, Marc *radio personality, comedian, actor, writer*
Maroney, Thomas Joseph *lawyer*
Marooney, Richard T. *lawyer*
Marrero, Victor *federal judge, lawyer*
Marriott, David R. *lawyer*
Marriott, Michel *reporter*
Marron, Donald Baird *venture capitalist*
Marsh, Michele *former newscaster*
Marshall, Alton Garwood *real estate agent, consultant*
Marshall, Kathleen *choreographer, theater director*
Marshall, Robert *film director, television director, theater director, choreographer*
Marshall, Sheila Hermes *lawyer*
Marshall, Thomas Carlisle *applied physics professor*
Marshall, Tom *publishing executive*
Martens, Erwin W. *risk management consultant*
Martin, Cameron *artist*
Martin, George J., Jr. *lawyer*
Martin, John F. *management consultant*
Martin, Judith Sylvia *journalist*
Martin, Malcolm Elliot *lawyer*
Martin, Mary-Anne *art gallery owner*
Martin, Michael Townsend *sports association executive, marketing professional, consultant*
Martin, Paul Ross *editor*
Martin, Renwick D. *lawyer*
Martin, Ricky (Enrique Martin Morales IV) *vocalist, actor*
Martinez, Arthur C. *consumer products company executive, former retail company executive*
Martínez-López, Carmen Leonor *management consultant, educator*
Martini, Richard K. *theatrical producer*
Martins, Peter *ballet master, choreographer, dancer*
Martone, Patricia Ann *lawyer*
Marx, Jeff *composer, lyricist, lawyer, writer*
Marx, Owen Cox *lawyer*
Maryles, Daisy *editor*
Marzorati, Gerald *editor*
Marzulli, John Anthony, Jr. *lawyer*
Masey, Jack *exhibition designer*

Masi, Jane Virginia *marketing and sales consultant*
Masin, Michael Terry *lawyer*
Maslin, Janet *critic*
Maslow, Will *lawyer, legal association administrator*
Masnyj, Yuri *painter, sculptor*
Mason, Bobbie Ann *writer*
Mason, Christopher May *lawyer*
Mason, Frank Herbert *artist, educator*
Mason, Linda *broadcast executive*
Mason, Marshall W. *theater director, educator, author*
Mason, Paul *broadcast executive*
Mason, Susan E. *social sciences educator, consultant*
Masri, Safwan Malek *industrial engineer, educator*
Massad, Timothy G. *lawyer*
Masters, Jon Joseph *corporate governance specialist, management consultant*
Masterson, Ellen Hornberger *accountant*
Masterson, James Francis *psychiatrist*
Matarasso, Alan *plastic and reconstructive surgeon*
Materna, Joseph Anthony *lawyer*
Mathers, William Harris *lawyer*
Mathews, Jack Wayne *journalist, film critic*
Mathis, Catherine J. *publishing executive*
Mattei, Ivan E. *lawyer*
Matteson, William Bleecker *lawyer*
Matthews, Christopher John *political commentator, writer*
Matthews, Dave *singer, musician*
Matthews, Edward E. *retired insurance company executive*
Matthews, Edwin Spencer, Jr. *lawyer*
Mattson, Francis Oscar *retired librarian, rare book dealer, curator*
Mattson, Marlin Roy Albin *health facility administrator, psychiatry educator*
Matus, Wayne Charles *lawyer*
Maupin, Armistead Jones, Jr. *writer*
Maurer, Gilbert Charles *media specialist*
Maurer, Jeffrey Stuart *trust company executive*
Maury, Richard *painter*
Mavroidis, Petros *law educator*
Maxfield, Guy Budd *lawyer, educator*
Maxwell, Anders John *investment banker*
Maxwell, Carla Lena *dancer, choreographer, educator*
May, Gita *literature educator*
May, Peter William *business executive*
May, William Frederick *manufacturing executive*
Mayer, Carl Joseph *prosecutor, lawyer*
Mayer, Christopher *lawyer*
Mayer, John *musician*
Mayer, Rosemary *artist*
Mayer, Theodore V.H. *lawyer*
Mayer, William Emilio *investor*
Mayerson, Philip *classics educator*
Mayerson, Sandra Elaine *lawyer*
Mayeux, Richard *hospital administrator, neurologist*
Mayle, Jane *apparel designer*
Maynard, John Rogers *language educator*
Maynard, Micheline Ann *journalist, writer*
Maynard, Virginia Madden *foundation administrator*
Mayo-Johnston, Julia A. *psychiatry professor, psychotherapist*
Mays, Linda *performing arts association administrator*
Maysilles, Elizabeth *speech communication professional, educator*
Maysles, Albert H. *filmmaker*
Mazzo, Kay *ballet dancer, educator*
Mazzola, Anthony Thomas *editor, graphics designer, consultant*
Mazzola, John William *retired performing company executive, consultant*
Mbanefo, Arthur Christopher Izuegbunan *diplomat*
McAniff, Nora P. *publishing executive*
McAtee, Darin P. *lawyer*
McAveney, Mary Susan *marketing executive*
McCabe, David J. *lawyer*
McCabe, Jim *publishing executive*
McCabe, John Cordell *surgeon*
McCabe, Mary F. *marketing professional*
McCaffrey, Carlyn Sundberg *lawyer*
McCall, Brendan *dancer, educator*
McCall, H. Carl *financial services executive, former state comptroller*
McCann, Robert J. *investment company executive*
McCarrick, Edward R. *magazine publisher*
McCarthy, Cormac (Charles Joseph McCarthy) *writer*
McCarthy, Gloria M *insurance company executive*
McCarthy, Pamela Maffei *magazine editor*
McCarthy, Patrick *publishing executive*
McCarty, V. K. *publishing executive, chaplain, librarian*
McCaslin, Teresa Eve *human resources specialist*
McCaw, Robert Bruce *lawyer*
McClelland, Shearwood Junior *orthopaedic surgeon*
McClelland, W. Carter *bank executive*
McClimon, Timothy John *lawyer*
McClure, Lee *musician, composer, educator*
McCollough, Jack *apparel designer*
McCormack, Richard Thomas Fox *diversified financial services company executive, former ambassador*
McCormack, Thomas Joseph *retired publishing executive, playwright*
McCormack, William F. *lawyer*
McCourt, Frank (Francis McCourt) *writer*
McCoy, Jennifer *artistic collaborator, educator*
McCoy, Kevin *artistic collaborator, educator*
McCrary, Eugenia Lester (Mrs. Dennis Daughtry McCrary) *civic worker, writer*
McCredie, James Robert *fine arts educator*
McCree, Donald Hanna III *diversified financial services company executive*
McCrie, Robert Delbert *editor, educator*
Mc Crory, Wallace Willard *pediatrician, educator*
McCulloch, Kenneth John *lawyer*
McCullough, David *writer, educator*
Mc Cullough, J. Lee *industrial psychologist*
McCutchen, William Walter, Jr. *management educator*
McDade, Herbert H. III *investment company executive*

McDaniel, Raymond W., Jr. *financial information company executive*
McDarrah, Fred William *photographer, editor, writer*
McDavid, William Henry *lawyer*
McDermott, Alice *writer*
McDermott, Ann Elizabeth *chemistry professor*
McDonald, Audra Ann *actress, vocalist*
Mcdonald, Gregory Christopher *author*
McDonald, James S. *investment company executive*
McDonald, Stephen Douglas *banker*
McDonell, Robert Terry *magazine editor, novelist*
McDonell, Terry *publishing executive, writer, editor*
McDowell, David Michael *psychiatrist, educator, researcher*
McElhinney, James Lancel *artist, educator*
McElroy, Kathleen O. *dining editor*
McEwen, Adam *artist*
McEwen, Bruce Sherman *neuroscientist, educator*
McFadden, Cynthia Graham *news correspondent, journalist*
McFadden, Mary Josephine *fashion industry executive*
McFadden, Robert Dennis *reporter*
McFarland, Alan Roberts *investment banker*
McFarland, Kathleen Troia (KT McFarland) *government defense consultant*
McFeely, William Drake *publishing company executive*
McGanney, Thomas *lawyer*
McGarry, Robert Alan *university administrator*
McGeady, Paul Joseph *lawyer*
McGee, Hugh E. III *investment company executive*
McGill, Jay *magazine publisher*
Mc Gillicuddy, John Francis *retired banker*
McGinn, Timothy J. *lawyer*
McGlamery, Barbara Ellen *librarian*
McGlynn, William Charles *brokerage house executive*
McGoldrick, John Lewis *lawyer*
McGonagle, Duncan Francis *mental health nurse, substance abuse counselor*
McGowen, Lorraine S. *lawyer*
Mc Gowin, William Edward *artist*
McGrady, Phyllis *television producer*
McGrath, Eleanor Burns *editor, writer*
McGrath, Eugene R. *utility company executive*
McGrath, Judy (Judith Ann McGrath) *broadcast executive*
McGrath, Thomas John *retired lawyer, writer, film producer*
McGraw, Harold W., III, (Terry McGraw) *information company executive*
McGraw, Harold Whittlesey, Jr. *publishing executive*
McGuire, Raymond J. *investment banker*
McHenry, Barnabas *lawyer*
McHugh, Caril Eisenstein Dreyfuss *art dealer, art gallery director, consultant*
McInerney, Jay *writer*
McIntire, Mike *journalist*
McKagan, Duff (Michael Andrew McKagan) *bassist*
McKay, Geoff *private equity investor*
McKay, Kenneth Gardiner *retired physicist, retired electronics company executive*
McKeever, Kent *library director, law librarian*
McKelvey, Andrew J. *advertising executive*
McKenna, Kevin Patrick *newspaper editor*
McKenna, William Michael *advertising executive*
McKenzie, Kevin Patrick *artistic director*
McKenzie, Mary Beth *artist*
McKeown, Allan John *television producer, theater producer*
McKinley-Haas, Mary *artist*
McKinnell, Hank (Henry A. McKinnell Jr.) *pharmaceutical executive*
McKinnon, Floyd Wingfield *textile executive*
McLaughlin, David *academic administrator, mathematics professor, neural science educator*
McLaughlin, Joseph Michael *federal judge, law educator*
McLaughlin, Joseph Thomas *lawyer*
Mc Lean, Don *singer, instrumentalist, composer*
McLennan, Hamish *advertising executive*
McMullan, Michael Patrick III *investment banker*
McMurtry, Larry Jeff *author*
McNally, Terrence *playwright*
McNamara, J. Donald (John Donald McNamara) *retired lawyer, business executive*
McNamara, Mary Ellen *not-for-profit executive*
Mc Namara, Robert A. *construction company executive*
McNeil, Wendy Lawson Johnston *foundation administrator*
McNulty, James J. *former mercantile exchange executive*
McQuown, Judith Hershkowitz *writer, consultant, financial planner*
Meacham, Jon E. *editor*
Meachin, David James Percy *investment banker*
Meadow, Lynne (Carolyn Meadow) *theater producer*
Meckseper, Josephine *sculptor*
Meehan, Sandra Gotham *corporate financial executive, consultant, venture capitalist*
Meeker, Mary G. *brokerage house executive*
Mehiel, Dennis *investment company executive*
Mehler, Gordon *lawyer*
Mehlman, Lon Douglas *information technology specialist, investment banker, venture capitalist*
Mehta, Linn Cary *literature educator*
Mehta, Sonny (Ajay Singh Mehta) *publishing executive*
Mehta, Zarin *performing company executive*
Meier, Barry *reporter*
Meier, Richard Alan *architect*
Meigher, S. Christopher III *communications and media executive, publisher*
Meigs, James B. *editor-in-chief*
Meili, Barbara *lawyer*
Mekas, Jonas *filmmaker, poet*
Mellencamp, John (John Cougar) *singer, lyricist*
Mellins, Robert B. *pediatrician, educator*
Mello, Dawn *retail executive*
Melloan, George Richard *editor*
Melone, Joseph James *retired insurance company executive*
Melton, Howell W., Jr. *lawyer*

Meltzer, Milton *author*
Meltzer, Roger *lawyer*
Menaker, Daniel *publishing executive*
Mencher, Melvin *journalist, educator*
Mendel, Nate (Nathan Gregor Mendel) *musician*
Mendelson, Edward James *English literature educator*
Mendini, Douglas A. *publishing company executive, writer*
Mendoza, Roberto G., Jr. *banker*
Menicheschi, Edward John *publishing executive*
Menschel, Robert Benjamin *investment banker*
Mentz, Lawrence *lawyer*
Menza, Claudia Marcella *literary agent*
Mercado, David *lawyer*
Merchant, Natalie Anne *musician, singer*
Meriam, Thomas C. *lawyer*
Merin, Mitchell M *corporate financial executive*
Merino, Junior *mixologist*
Meron, Theodor *judge, law educator, researcher*
Merow, John *lawyer*
Merrill, George Vanderneth *lawyer, investment executive*
Merrill, Susan L. *lawyer*
Merrill, Thomas Wendell *lawyer, educator*
Merriss, Philip Ramsay, Jr. *banker*
Merritt, Jean *consulting firm executive, psychotherapist*
Mertens, Joan R. *museum curator, art historian*
Mesnikoff, Alvin Murray *psychiatrist, educator*
Messner, Thomas G. *advertising executive, copywriter*
Mestres, Ricardo Angelo, Jr. *lawyer*
Metz, Emmanuel Michael *investment company executive, lawyer*
Metzger, Evelyn Borchard *artist*
Meunier, Monique *dancer*
Meyer, Edward Henry *advertising agency executive*
Meyer, Fred Josef *finance company executive*
Meyer, James E. *broadcast executive*
Meyer, Janis M. *lawyer*
Meyer, Karl Ernest *journalist*
Meyer, Pearl *compensation executive consultant*
Meyer, Scott *communications executive*
Meyer, Tobias *auction house executive*
Meyer-Bahlburg, Heino F.L. *psychology professor*
Meyerhoff, Erich *librarian, director*
Meyerhoff, Karen *museum director*
Meyers, Dale (Mrs. Mario Cooper) *artist*
Meyerson, Lee A. *lawyer*
Miano, Louis Stephen *arts advisor*
Michaels, Al (Alan Richard Michaels) *sports commentator*
Michaels, Lorne *television writer, producer*
Michaelson, Arthur M. *lawyer*
Michalski, Paul Peter *lawyer*
Michel, Nicolas *international organization administrator*
Michelis, Michael Frank *nephrologist*
Michels, Robert *psychiatrist, educator*
Michelsen, Christopher Bruce Hermann *surgeon*
Michelson, Gertrude Geraldine *retired retail executive*
Middendorf, John Harlan *English literature educator*
Middlebrook, Diane Wood *English language educator, writer*
Middleton, David *physicist, applied mathematician, educator*
Midlarsky, Elizabeth Ruth *psychology professor*
Mikita, Joseph Karl *broadcast executive*
Mikumo, Akiko *lawyer*
Milazzo, Richard T. *writer*
Milbank, Jeremiah *foundation executive*
Milder, Jay *artist*
Mildvan, Donna *infectious diseases physician*
Miles, John R. *real estate development company executive*
Milgrim, Roger Michael *lawyer*
Milhaupt, Curtis J. *law educator*
Millard, Robert B. *investment company executive*
Miller, Arthur Madden *lawyer, investment banker, brokerage house executive*
Miller, Barbara Kenton *retired librarian*
Miller, Beth McCarthy *television director*
Miller, Charles Hampton *lawyer*
Miller, Corbin Russell *investment company executive*
Miller, Dennis *comedian*
Miller, Ernest Charles *management consultant*
Miller, Garfield Lankard III *investment banker*
Miller, George H. *architectural firm executive*
Miller, Harvey S. Shipley *foundation trustee, philanthropist*
Miller, Heidi G. *diversified financial company executive*
Miller, J. Allen *lawyer*
Miller, Michael Jeffrey *editor, columnist*
Miller, Nancy K. *literature educator*
Miller, Neil Stuart *advertising executive*
Miller, Nicole Jacqueline *fashion designer*
Miller, Paul Samuel *lawyer*
Miller, Peter A. *lawyer*
Miller, Peter N. *historian, educator*
Miller, Philip Efrem *librarian*
Miller, Richard Kidwell *artist, actor, educator*
Miller, Richard Steven *lawyer*
Miller, Robert *advertising executive*
Miller, Robert J. *lawyer*
Miller, Ruby Sills *retired gerontologist*
Miller, Sam Scott *lawyer*
Miller, Stuart A. *lawyer*
Miller, Sue *writer*
Miller, Theodore Norman *lawyer*
Miller, Theodore T. *radiologist*
Millman, John Bruce Russell *lawyer*
Millson, Rory Oliver *lawyer*
Millstein, Ira M. *lawyer, educator*
Millstein, Julian Stuart *lawyer*
Millstein, Lincoln *media company executive*
Milman, Doris Hope *retired pediatrician, psychiatrist, educator*
Milmoe, J. Gregory *lawyer*
Milonas, E. Leo *lawyer, former state judge*
Milonas, Minos *artist*
Milstein, Howard P. *bank executive*
Milstein, Paul *real estate development*
Min, Janice Byung *editor-in-chief*
Mina, Richard T. *apparel executive*

Mindich, Eric *investment company executive*
Mingwei, Lee *artist*
Minick, Michael *publishing executive*
Minicucci, Robert A. *investment company executive*
Minkel, Herbert Philip, Jr. *lawyer*
Minkowitz, Martin *lawyer, former state government official*
Minskoff, Edward *architectural firm executive*
Mintz, Norman Nelson *investment banker, educator, retired academic administrator*
Mintz, Samuel Isaiah *language educator, writer*
Mintz, Shlomo *conductor, violist*
Mir, Aleksandra *artist*
Mirabile, Russell Michael *lawyer*
Mironer, Merril A. *lawyer*
Mischel, Walter *psychology professor*
Mischka, James *fashion designer*
Mitchell, Alison N. *newspaper reporter, editor*
Mitchell, Arthur *dancer, choreographer, performing company executive, educator*
Mitchell, Dennis Anthony *dentist, educator*
Mitchell, George John *entertainment company executive, lawyer, former senator*
Mitchell, Patricia Edenfield *broadcast museum administrator*
Mitgang, Herbert *writer, journalist*
Mitterand, Henri C. *literature educator, writer*
Mittman, Lawrence *lawyer*
Miyake, Issey *fashion designer*
Mnuchin, Steven T. *investment company executive*
Moby, (Richard Melville Hall) *musician*
Modlin, Howard S. *lawyer*
Moehringer, J. R. *writer*
Moerdler, Charles Gerard *lawyer*
Moglen, Eben *law educator*
Mohler, Mary Gail *magazine editor*
Mohn, Louis *publishing executive*
Mohr, Jay Preston *neurologist, educator*
Moldow, Susan *publishing executive*
Moleko, Lebohang Kenneth *ambassador*
Molho, Emanuel *publisher*
Molinaro, Samuel L. *investment company executive*
Molnar, Lawrence *lawyer*
Moloney, Thomas Joseph *lawyer*
Monaghan, Dominic *actor*
Monahan, Matthew *artist*
Mondlin, Marvin *retail executive, rare book dealer*
Monk, Debra *actress*
Monk, Meredith Jane *artistic director, composer, choreographer, filmmaker*
Monk Kidd, Sue *writer*
Montero, Sylvia *pharmaceutical executive*
Moody, Rick (Hiram Frederick Moody III) *writer*
Mooney, Richard Emerson *writer*
Mooney, Ted (Edward Comstock Mooney) *editor, art critic, writer*
Moonves, Leslie *broadcast executive*
Moore, Ann S. *publishing executive*
Moore, Anne *physician*
Moore, Charles Hewes, Jr. *manufacturing executive*
Moore, David J. *media company executive*
Moore, Donald Francis *lawyer*
Moore, Leroi *musician*
Moore, Michael Watson *musician, educator*
Moore, Rachel Suzanne *performing company executive, dancer*
Moore, Thomas Ronald (Lord Bridestowe) *lawyer*
Morales, Myron Russell *lawyer*
Moran, Juliette M. *retired chemicals executive*
Moran, Martin Joseph *fundraising company executive*
Moran, Patricia *lawyer*
Moran, Thomas J. *insurance company executive*
Morano, Frank *radio producer, talk show host*
Morawetz, Cathleen Synge *mathematician*
Morehouse, Ward III *theater critic, writer, playwright*
Moreno, Barry *historian, writer*
Morgan, Frank Edward, II, *corporate financial executive*
Morgan, Mary E. *publishing executive*
Morgan, Ted (Le Comte Sanche Armand Gabriel de Gramont) *writer*
Morgenson, Gretchen C. *reporter*
Morgenthau, Robert Morris *prosecutor*
Morhouse, Sanford W. *lawyer*
Morial, Marc Haydel *association executive, former mayor*
Morley, Malcolm A. *artist*
Moroz, Pavel Emanuel *retired research scientist*
Morreale, Joseph Constantino *academic administrator, educator, economist, consultant*
Morris, David S. *publishing executive*
Morris, Dick *columnist, political consultant*
Morris, Douglas Peter *recording company executive*
Morris, Stephen Burritt *marketing information company executive*
Morris, William Charles *investor*
Morrison, John Henry *neuroscientist, educator, lab administrator*
Morrison, Stacy Lynne *magazine editor*
Morrissey, Thomas A. *publishing executive*
Morrow, Lance *journalist, educator, writer*
Morse, Edward Lewis *petroleum industry executive*
Morse, Robert Parker *investment company executive*
Morse, Stephen Scott *virologist, epidemiologist, immunologist, educator*
Morvillo, Robert Guy *lawyer*
Mosbacher, Georgette Paulsin *cosmetics executive*
Moscowitz, Todd *music company executive*
Moses, Jeffrey Warren *cardiologist, educator*
Moskin, John Robert *editor, writer*
Moskin, Morton *lawyer, director*
Moskowitz, Harold J. *lawyer*
Moskowitz, Randi Zucker *nurse*
Moskowitz, Ross F. *lawyer*
Mosler, Bruce E. *real estate company executive*
Mosley, Daniel Lynn *lawyer*
Mosley, Walter *writer*
Moss, Adam Wender *editor*
Moss, Douglas *architectural firm executive*
Moss, Sara E. *delivery service executive, lawyer*
Mossavar-Rahmani, Bijan *oil and gas company executive*
Mossberg, Walter *columnist*

Mosse, Peter John Charles *financial services executive*
Moss-Salentijn, Letty (Aleida Moss-Salentijn) *anatomist, educator*
Motoc, Mihnea Ioan *international organization official*
Mouawad, Jad *reporter*
Moulton, Sara *chef, magazine editor*
Mourning, Paul W. *lawyer*
Moutari, Ousmane *permanent representative to UN Niger*
Mowshowitz, Abbe *computer scientist*
Moy, Richard L. *virologist*
Moyer, David S. *executive search consultant*
Moyers, Bill D. *journalist, writer*
Moyers, Judith Davidson *television producer*
Moyles, Philip Vincent, Jr. *financial services company executive*
Moyne, John Abel *computer scientist, linguist, educator*
Mozenter, Cyrilla *artist*
Mroz, John Edwin *political scientist*
Muccia, Joseph William *lawyer*
Muchnick, Richard Stuart *ophthalmologist, educator*
Mueller, Alfred H. *physics professor, researcher*
Mueller, Shirley Anne *lawyer, real estate broker*
Mukasey, Michael B. *lawyer, former federal judge*
Mullany, Gerry *editor*
Mullen, Peter P. *lawyer*
Muller, Jennifer *choreographer, dancer*
Mulligan, Brian C. *film company executive*
Mulligan, Jeremiah T. *lawyer*
Mulligan, John J. *corporate financial executive*
Mulvihill, William J. *former health science association administrator*
Mundell, Robert Alexander *economist, educator*
Mundheim, Robert Harry *law educator*
Mundinger, Mary O'Neil *nursing educator*
Muñoz, Heraldo (Heraldo Muñoz Valenzuela) *diplomat*
Munro, Alice *writer*
Munro, Eleanor *writer, lecturer*
Munroe, George Barber *retired mining and manufacturing company executive*
Muradian, Vazgen *violist, composer*
Murase, Jiro *lawyer*
Murdoch, Rupert (Keith Rupert Murdoch) *multimedia company executive*
Murdock, Robert Mead *curator*
Murphy, Arthur William *lawyer, educator*
Murphy, Austin de la Salle *economist, educator, banker*
Murphy, Carolyn *model*
Murphy, Catherine *painter*
Murphy, Cullen *writer, editor*
Murphy, Donna *actress*
Murphy, Helen *recording industry executive*
Murphy, James Edward *public relations and marketing executive*
Murphy, John B. *portfolio manager*
Murphy, Kenneth F. *human resources specialist*
Murphy, Liam B. *law educator*
Murphy, Mark Joseph *enterprise sales executive*
Murphy, Ramon Jeremiah Castroviejo *physician, pediatrician*
Murphy, Richard William *retired diplomat*
Murphy, Rosemary *actress*
Murphy, Stacia *health service association executive*
Murray, Brian *publishing executive*
Murray, Eileen N. *investment company executive*
Murray, Elizabeth *artist*
Murray, Richard Maximilian *insurance company executive*
Muscari, Joseph Charles *manufacturing executive*
Muscato, Andrew *lawyer*
Muse, Martha Twitchell *foundation executive*
Musgrave, R. Kenton *federal judge*
Musham, Bettye Martin *consumer products executive*
Myerberg, Marcia *investment banker*
Myers, Gerald E. *humanities educator*
Myers, Roberta *editor-in-chief*
Myerson, Toby Salter *lawyer*
Mynbaev, Djafar K. *engineering physics educator*
Nabi, Stanley Andrew *brokerage house executive*
Nabokov, Peter Francis *writer*
Nadiri, M. Ishaq *economics professor, researcher, consultant*
Nadler-Hurvich, Hedda Carol *public relations executive*
Nafisi, Azar *humanities educator*
Naftalis, Gary Philip *lawyer, educator*
Naftolin, Frederick *gynecologist, educator*
Nagournev, Horbort *publishing company executive*
Naidich, Thomas Paul *neuroradiologist, educator*
Nair, Mira *film director, film producer*
Naka, Yoshifumi *surgeon, researcher*
Nally, Dennis Mathew *finance company executive*
Nam, Heekyung Biya *rehabilitation therapist*
Nama, George *artist*
Nance, Allan Taylor *retired lawyer*
Nantz, James William (Jim Nantz) *television sports announcer*
Napack, Brian *publishing executive*
Napolitano, Andrew P. *legal analyst, lawyer, judge*
Nash, Edward L. *advertising executive*
Nash, Paul LeNoir *lawyer*
Nass, Ruth *pediatric neurologist*
Nassau, Michael Jay *lawyer*
Nasser, Jacques *banker, former automotive company executive*
Nathan, Andrew James *political science educator*
Nathan, Frederic Solis *lawyer*
Nathan, Paul S. *retired editor, writer*
Natori, Josie Cruz (Josefina Almeda Cruz Natori) *apparel executive*
Nauman, Bruce *artist*
Navarra, Tova *writer*
Nazem, Fereydoun F. *venture capitalist, entrepreneur*
Neal, James G. *librarian*
Nearing, Vivienne W. *lawyer*
Nederlander, James Morton *theater executive*
Nederlander, Robert E. *entertainment and television executive, lawyer*
Needell, Benjamin F. *lawyer*
Needham, George Austin *investment banker*
Neff, Daniel A. *lawyer*
Neff, Thomas Joseph *search firm executive*

Neger, Peter C. *lawyer*
Nehal, Kishwer Sultana *dermatologist*
Neidell, Martin H. *lawyer*
Neidich, Brooke Garber *foundation administrator, art patron*
Neiman, LeRoy *artist*
Nelly, (Cornell Haynes Jr.) *rap artist*
Nelson, Anne *playwright, former reporter*
Nelson, Carl *journalist*
Nelson, Dean B. *media company executive*
Nelson, Kathy *broadcast executive*
Nelson, Merlin Edward *retired management consultant, lawyer*
Nelson, Ronald L. *travel services company executive, former film company executive*
Nelson, Sara *editor*
Nelson, William Edward *law educator*
Nemser, Earl Harold *lawyer*
Neria, Yuval Y. *psychologist, educator*
Neshat, Shirin *artist*
Ness, Pamela Miller *elementary school educator*
Netzer, Dick *economics professor*
Neubauer, Peter Bela *psychoanalyst*
Neuberg, Hans W. *internist, educator*
Neuborne, Burt *law educator*
Neufeld, Peter *lawyer*
Neugebauer, Cynthia A. *lawyer*
Neuman, Gerald L. *law educator*
Neumann, Andrew *artist*
Neuwirth, Alan James *lawyer*
Neuwirth, Robert Samuel *obstetrician, gynecologist, educator*
Neveloff, Jay A. *lawyer*
New, Maria Iandolo *pediatrician, educator*
Newberg, Esther *literary agent*
Newbold, John Lowe *retired banker, financial consultant*
Newhouse, Jeffrey H. *radiologist, educator*
Newman, Andy *journalist*
Newman, Charles Michael *mathematician, physicist, educator*
Newman, Eileen *not-for-profit organization executive*
Newman, Fredric Samuel *lawyer, communications executive*
Newman, Geraldine Anne *advertising executive*
Newman, Kenneth E. *lawyer*
Newman, Lawrence *lawyer, educator*
Newman, Lawrence Walker *lawyer*
Newman, Robert Gabriel *physician*
Newman, William Arthur *lawyer*
Newsome, Frederick V. *medical educator*
Newsome, James E. *mercantile exchange executive*
Ney, Alexander *artist, sculptor*
Ney, Edward N. *ambassador, advertising executive, public relations executive*
Nibley, Andrew Mathews *media specialist*
Nicholas, Stephen J. *orthopedic surgeon, sports medicine physician*
Nichols, Edie Diane *real estate broker*
Nick, George *painter*
Nickell, Frank (Nick) T. *diversified financial services company executive*
Nickoloff, Edward Lee *radiology physicist*
Nickson, Graham *artist*
Nicol, Dominik *writer, photographer*
Nicolau, Siobhan *cultural organization administrator*
Nicyper, Dean R. *lawyer*
Nides, Thomas Richard *diversified financial services company executive*
Niemeth, Charles Frederick *lawyer*
Niemiec, David Wallace *investment company executive*
Nieporent, Drew *restaurant group executive*
Nigam, Hemanshu *lawyer, Internet company executive*
Nigo, *fashion designer*
Nimkarn, Saroj *endocrinologist, researcher*
Niño, Deanna Hollye *lawyer*
Nirenberg, Louis *mathematician, educator*
Nisenholtz, Martin Abram *telecommunications executive, educator*
Nish, Wayne Paul *chef, restaurant owner*
Nissim, Shai *special education educator, consultant*
Niven, James Graham *auctioneer, art appreciator, philanthropist*
Noam, Eli Michael *telecommunications industry executive, educator*
Noble, Ronald Kenneth *Secretary General of Interpol*
Noce, Donna *retail executive*
Nocera, Joseph *editor, writer*
Nochlin, Linda *art history educator*
Nogina, Elena Y. *mathematics professor, researcher*
Nolan, William Joseph III *banker*
Nonna, John Michael *lawyer*
Noonan, Peggy *writer*
Norell, Mark Allen *paleontologist, curator*
Norman, Christina *broadcast executive*
Norman, Stephen Peckham *finance company executive*
Norris, Floyd Hamilton *financial journalist*
Norris, Michael Byron *museum staff member*
Norsten, Todd *artist*
North, Julie A. *lawyer*
Norton, David K. *publishing executive, human resources specialist*
Norville, Deborah Anne *news correspondent*
Norwitz, Trevor S. *lawyer*
Noski, Charles H. *telecommunications executive*
Novacek, Michael John *curator, museum director*
Novick, Nelson Lee *dermatologist, internist, consultant, surgeon, writer*
Novick, Stephen Alan *cardiologist*
Novitz, Charles Richard *broadcast executive, reporter*
Novogrod, Nancy Gerstein *editor*
Nozkowski, Thomas *painter*
Nugent, Nelle *theater, film and television producer*
Nurnberg, Charles Gordon *publishing executive*
Nurse, Sir Paul M. *academic administrator*
Nusbacher, Gloria Weinberg *lawyer*
Nusbaum, Jack Henry *lawyer*
Nussbaum, Bernard W. *federal official, lawyer*
Nussbaum, Martin *prosecutor*
Nusum, John Barry *professional soccer player*

Nye, Bill S. *research scientist, engineer, comedian, writer, inventor*
Nyren, Neil Sebastian *publishing executive, editor*
O, Cao K. *cultural organization administrator*
Oates, Joyce Carol *writer*
Oberfield, Sharon Elefant *pediatric endocrinologist*
Oberly, Kathryn Anne *lawyer, diversified financial services company executive*
Oberman, Michael Stewart *lawyer*
Obernauer, Marne, Jr. *technology industry executive*
Obogeanu, Madalina Maria *reporter*
Obolensky, Ivan *investment banker, foundation administrator, writer*
O'Brien, Catherine Louise *museum administrator*
O'Brien, Clare *lawyer*
O'Brien, Conan *talk show host, writer, performer*
O'Brien, Dermot J. *human resources specialist*
O'Brien, Geoffrey Paul *editor, writer*
O'Brien, Kevin J. *lawyer*
O'Brien, Michael J. *lawyer*
O'Bryan, C. Jill *visual artist, writer*
Ocampo, Manuel *artist*
Ochoa, Manuel, Jr. *oncologist*
Ochs, Carol Rebecca *theologian, writer, theology studies educator, philosopher*
O'Connor, Anahad S. *journalist*
O'Connor, Chuck (Charles O'Connor) *painter*
O'Connor, Kevin *computer programing executive*
Odenweller, Robert Paul *philatelist, trade association administrator, retired pilot*
O'Doherty, Brian *writer*
Odoner, Ellen J. *lawyer*
O'Donnell, John Logan *retired lawyer*
Oechler, Henry John, Jr. *lawyer*
Oelsner, Richard S. *lawyer*
Oestreich, James R. *editor*
Oettgen, Herbert Friedrich *physician*
Offit, Morris Wolf *investment company executive*
Offit, Sidney *writer, educator*
Ofri, Danielle *internist*
Ogden, Peggy A. *retired personnel director*
O'Grady, Beverly Troxler *investment executive, counselor*
O'Grady, John Joseph III *lawyer*
Ogunlesi, Adebayo O. *investment banker*
Oh, Joong-Hwan *sociologist*
O'Hara, Robert Sydney, Jr. *lawyer*
Ohlson, Douglas Dean *artist, educator*
O'Keefe, Vincent Thomas *clergyman, educational association administrator*
O'Kelley, Winnie *editor*
Okrent, Daniel *writer*
Oktem, Ozgur *medical researcher*
Okuhara, Tetsu *artist, photographer*
Okun, Herbert Stuart *diplomat, educator*
Okura-Marszycki, Mindy Emi *editor*
Okuwa, Makoto *chef*
Olafsson, Olaf *communications executive*
Olafsson, Olafur Johann *writer, media company executive*
Oldenburg, Richard Erik *auction company executive*
Oldfield, Barney *entertainment executive*
Oldham, Todd *fashion designer*
Oler, Wesley M., IV *portfolio manager*
Olick, Philip Stewart *lawyer*
Olinger, Carla D(ragan) *medical advertising executive*
Olinger, Chauncey Greene, Jr. *investment company executive, editorial consultant*
Oliva, Lawrence Jay *retired academic administrator, history professor*
Olmstead, Clarence Walter, Jr. *lawyer*
Olshan, Bernard *artist*
Olshan, Regina *lawyer*
Olson, Peter *publishing executive*
Olsson, Carl Alfred *urologist, department chairman*
O'Meara, Christopher M. *investment company executive*
O'Nan, Stewart Smith *writer*
O'Neal, E. Stanley (Stanley O'Neal) *diversified financial services company executive*
O'Neal, Hank *theater producer, small business owner*
O'Neil, John Joseph *lawyer*
O'Neil, Robyn *artist*
O'Neill, Charles K. *lawyer*
O'Neill, Joan *editor*
O'Neill, Judith D. *lawyer*
O'Neill, June Ellenoff *economist*
O'Neill, Thomas J. (Tom O' Neill) *engineering company executive*
Openshaw, Jennifer *finance company executive*
Opie, Catherine *photographer*
Oppenheim, Robert *beauty industry executive*
Oppenheimer, Martin J. *lawyer*
Oppenheimer, Paul *literature educator, poet*
Orce, Kenneth W. *lawyer*
Ordorica, Steven Anthony *obstetrician, gynecologist, educator*
O'Reilly, Bill (William O'Reilly Jr.) *commentator, writer*
O'Reilly, Richard John *pediatrician*
Oremus, Stephen *composer*
Orender, Donna *sports association executive*
Oreskes, Irwin *biochemistry educator*
Oricchio, Michael *editor*
Orkin, Louis Richard *physician, educator*
O'Rorke, James Francis, Jr. *lawyer*
Orozco, Gabriel *artist*
Orr, Dennis Patrick *lawyer*
Orr, James F. III *foundation administrator*
Ortman, George Earl *artist*
Osborn, Donald Robert *lawyer*
Osborn, Frederick Henry III *foundation executive*
Osborn, John W. *lawyer*
Osborn, June Elaine *pediatrician, microbiologist, educator, foundation administrator*
Osborne, Mary Pope *writer*
Osborne, Richard de Jongh *mining and metals company executive*
Osgood, Charles *news broadcaster, journalist*
Osgood, Richard Magee, Jr. *electrical engineering professor, researcher*
Osgood, Robert Mansfield *lawyer*
Osnos, Peter Lionel Winston *publishing executive*
Osorio, Pepon *artist*
Ossenberg, Hella Svetlana *psychoanalyst*

Ostermann, Curt *lighting designer, educator*
Ostling, Paul James *corporate financial executive*
Ostrager, Barry Robert *lawyer*
Ostrander, Thomas William *investment banker*
O'Sullivan, Eugene Henry *retired advertising executive, management consultant*
O'Sullivan, Thomas J. *lawyer*
O'Toole, Patricia Ellen *writer, educator*
Otunnu, Olara A. *childrens organization official*
Ouroussoff, Nicolai *architecture critic*
Owen, Richard *federal judge*
Oxnam, Robert Bromley *trust company advisor*
Oz, Frank (Frank Richard Oznowicz) *entertainer, film director*
Oz, Mehmet Cengiz *cardiac surgeon, writer*
Ozolinsh, Sandis *professional hockey player*
Paaswell, Robert Emil *civil engineer, educator*
Pace, Antonietta *chemistry professor*
Pace, Eric Dwight *retired journalist*
Pace, Stephen Shell *artist, educator*
Pace, Wayne H. *communications executive*
Pacheco-Fowler, Victor *medical educator*
Packer, George *writer*
Packer, Linda S. *psychotherapist*
Paddock, Anthony Conaway *financial consultant*
Padmanabhan, Anand *information technology executive*
Page, Kenneth R. *lawyer*
Pagnani, Keith A. *lawyer*
Paige, Roderick Raynor *educational consultant, former secretary of education*
Paik, Myunghee Cho *statistician, educator*
Paik, Younhee *artist*
Pakter, Jean *maternal and child health consultant*
Paley, Alan H. *lawyer*
Palion, Peter Thaddeus *financial planner*
Pall, Ellen Jane *writer*
Palm, Gregory K. *lawyer, investment company executive*
Palmer, Catherine E. *lawyer*
Palmer, Charlie *chef, restaurant manager*
Palmer, Deryck A. *lawyer*
Palmer, Jason Michael *research and development company executive*
Palmer, Jessica *diversified financial services company executive*
Palmer, Michael *poet*
Palmer, Robert Baylis *librarian*
Palsho, Dorothea Coccoli *information services executive*
Palumbo, Anthony John *lawyer*
Panagos, Steven Gregory *food products executive*
Pandolfi, Frances *health facility administrator*
Paneth, Donald Joseph *editor, writer*
Panicek, David *radiologist*
Panken, Peter Michael *lawyer*
Panzera, Anthony *artist*
Papalia, Diane Ellen *humanities educator*
Papell, Helen Gertrude *poet, retired librarian*
Papernik, Joel Ira *lawyer*
Pappagallo, Marco *neurologist, pain medicine specialist*
Pappas, Milton J. *venture capitalist*
Papps, Bruce William *financial analyst, investment company executive*
Pardes, Herbert *health facility executive, psychiatrist, educator*
Pareles, Jon *music critic*
Paretsky, Sara N. *writer*
Parisotto, Gloria *publishing executive, poet, writer*
Park, Barbara *writer*
Park, Cynthia *sociology educator, consultant*
Park, Yong Jin *lawyer*
Parker, Alice *composer*
Parker, C. Allen *lawyer*
Parker, Robert Brown *writer*
Parker, Trey *animator*
Parkhurst, Carolyn *writer*
Parkin, Gerard Francis Ralph *chemistry educator, researcher*
Parkinson, John S. *information technology executive*
Paro, Jeff *publisher*
Parrett, William G. *accounting company executive*
Parrish, Steven C. *consumer products company executive*
Parsons, Estelle *actress, director, theater producer*
Parsons, Richard Dean *communications executive*
Pasierb, Stephen John *advertising executive, marketing professional*
Pask, Scott *set designer*
Paskin, Michael A. *lawyer*
Passano, William M. III *publishing executive*
Passlof, Pat *artist, educator*
Paster, Howard G. *public relations and public affairs company executive*
Pasternack, David *chef*
Pastores, Gregory McCarthy *pediatrician, medical geneticist, researcher*
Pastores, Stephen M. *internist*
Patchett, Ann *writer*
Paterson, Katherine Womeldorf *writer*
Patmos, Marcia *apparel designer*
Patrick, Hugh Talbot *economist, educator*
Patrick, Stephen C. *consumer products company executive*
Patrikis, Ernest T. *lawyer*
Patterson, James Brendan, Jr. *writer, former advertising executive*
Patterson, Robert Porter, Jr. *federal judge*
Patton, Antwan Andre (Big Boi) *vocalist*
Paul, Andrew Mitchell *investment advisor*
Paul, Herbert Morton *lawyer, accountant, educator*
Paul, James William *lawyer*
Paul, Les *entertainer*
Paul, Robert Carey *lawyer*
Paulson, Loretta Nancy *psychoanalyst*
Pavarotti, Luciano *lyric tenor*
Pawliczko, George Ihor *academic administrator*
Paxton, Robert Owen *historian, educator*
Payard, Francois *food service executive*
Payton-Wright, Pamela *actress*
Pearce, Alan S. *lawyer*
Pearl, Mary Corliss *wildlife conservationist*
Pearlman, Steven Jay *otolaryngologist, educator, surgeon*
Pearlstine, Norman *communications consultant, former editor*
Peaslee, James M. *lawyer*
Pechukas, Philip *chemistry professor*

Peck, Andrew Jay *federal judge*
Peck, Fred Neil *economist, educator*
Peckolick, Alan *painter, graphics designer, photographer*
Pedley, Timothy Asbury, IV *neurologist, educator, researcher*
Peerce, Marjorie J. *lawyer*
Peet, Charles D, Jr. *lawyer*
Peetz, Karen B. *bank executive*
Pegram, John Braxton *lawyer*
Pelaccio, Zakary *chef*
Pellegrini, John B. *lawyer*
Peloso, John Francis Xavier *lawyer*
Pelster, William Charles *lawyer*
Peltz, Nelson *manufacturing executive*
Peluso, John *lawyer*
Pelz, Robert Leon *lawyer*
Pendleton, Austin *actor, theater director*
Penn, Stanley William *journalist*
Pennington, William Mark *sportswriter*
Pennisi, Liz *women's health nurse*
Pennoyer, Robert M. *lawyer*
Pepper, Allan Michael *lawyer*
Peppers, Jerry P. *lawyer*
Percus, Jerome Kenneth *physicist, researcher*
Perella, Joseph Robert *investment banker*
Perelman, Ronald Owen *consumer products company executive*
Peresman, Joel *foundation administrator*
Peretsman, Nancy B. *investment banker*
Perez-Firmat, Gustavo Francisco *writer, language educator*
Pérez-Rivera, Francisco (Frank Rivera) *writer*
Perin, Noel I. *neurosurgeon*
Perkins, Lawrence Bradford, Jr. *architect*
Perkins, Roswell Burchard *lawyer*
Perlgut, Mark Ralph *public relations executive*
Perlis, Donald M. *artist*
Perlis, Michael Steven *magazine publisher*
Perlman, Itzhak *violinist*
Perlmuth, William Alan *lawyer*
Perlmutter, Alvin Howard *television and film producer*
Perlmutter, Louis *investment banker, lawyer*
Perna, Michael Lewis *language educator*
Perrin, Charles R. *light manufacturing executive*
Perrineau, Harold *actor*
Perry, Douglas *opera singer*
Perry, Robert Francis *lawyer*
Perry, Stephen R. *law educator*
Perschetz, Martin L. *lawyer*
Persell, Caroline Hodges *sociologist, educator, author, researcher, consultant*
Pershan, Richard Henry *lawyer*
Pesin, Ella Michele *journalist, public relations executive*
Pesner, Carole Manishin *art gallery owner*
Pesner, Steven M. *lawyer*
Petchesky, Rosalind Pollack *political scientist, educator, social sciences educator*
Peters, Bernadette (Bernadette Lazzara) *actress*
Peters, Elizabeth *media organization director*
Peters, Roberta *soprano*
Peterson, Peter George *investment company executive*
Petrie, Donald Joseph *banker*
Petronella, Michael A. *publishing executive*
Petrow, George J. *lawyer*
Pettibone, Peter John *lawyer*
Petz, Edwin V. *real estate company executive, lawyer*
Petzal, David Elias *editor, writer*
Pfeffer, David H. *lawyer*
Pfeifer, Tracy M. *plastic surgeon*
Pfeiffer, Jane Cahill *former broadcasting company executive, consultant*
Phair, Liz *vocalist*
Phelan, John C. *lawyer*
Phelps, Edmund Strother *economics professor*
Philbin, Regis (Regis Francis Xavier Philbin) *television personality*
Philips, Jeremy *media company executive*
Phillips, Anthony Francis *lawyer*
Phillips, Barnet, IV *lawyer*
Phillips, David L. *diplomat, mediator, foundation executive*
Phillips, Gerald Baer *internal medicine scientist, educator*
Phillips, Graham Holmes *retired advertising executive*
Phillips, Karen A. *urban planner*
Phillips, Renée *writer*
Phillips, Stone *television journalist*
Phillips, Tari *professional basketball player*
Philp, Richard Nilson *writer, editor, journalist*
Picard, Leslie *publishing executive*
Picasso, Paloma *fashion designer*
Pidot, Whitney Dean *lawyer*
Pierce, Charles Eliot, Jr. *library director, educator*
Pierce, David *information technology executive*
Pierce, Morton Allen *lawyer*
Pierre, Dwight Anthony *mathematician, educator*
Pierson, Jack *artist*
Pierson, Richard Norris, Jr. *medical educator*
Pietri, Todd T. *venture capitalist*
Pietruski, John Michael, Jr. *pharmaceutical executive*
Pikitch, Ellen Karen *science educator*
Pilati, Stefano *apparel designer*
Pildes, Richard H. *law educator*
Piligian, Georgette A. *insurance company executive*
Piliguian, Tro *advertising executive*
Pincus, Lionel I. *financial executive, entrepreneur*
Pinczuk, Aron *physicist*
Pineda, Patricia Salas *lawyer*
Pines, Burton Yale *media executive*
Pinkwater, Julie *publishing executive*
Pinover, Eugene Alfred *lawyer*
Piombino, Nicholas *psychotherapist*
Pionk, Richard Cletus *artist, educator*
Pistor, Katharina *law educator*
Pitman, Gerald H. *plastic surgeon*
Pitt, Jane *medical educator*
Pittman, Robert Warren *investor*
Pittoni, Luke M. *lawyer*
Pitts, Andrew J. *lawyer*
Piven, Frances Fox *political scientist, educator*
Planitzer, Russell E. *computer company executive*
Plant, Robert Anthony *singer, composer*
Platnick, Norman I. *curator, entomologist*

Platt, Nicholas *retired ambassador*
Plavinskaya, Anna Dmitrievna *artist*
Pleuger, Guenter *diplomat*
Plevan, Bettina B. *lawyer*
Plotkin, Loren H. *lawyer*
Plottel, Jeanine Parisier *foreign language educator*
Plum, Fred *neurologist*
Plummer, William B. *publishing executive*
Pnueli, Amir *computer science educator*
Podesta, Roger E. *lawyer*
Podhoretz, John *editor, writer*
Podrug, Dinko *psychiatrist, educator*
Poe, Randall Ellsworth *public relations executive, author*
Poehler, Amy *comedienne, actress*
Pogrebin, Letty Cottin *writer, educator*
Pogue, David *journalist*
Pogue, Donald Carl *federal judge*
Pogue, Velvie Anne *nephrologist, educator*
Pokorny, Jan Hird *architect, educator*
Polacco, Patricia *writer, illustrator*
Polansky, Andy *public relations executive*
Polenz, Joanna Magda *psychiatrist*
Polevoy, Nancy Tally *lawyer, social worker, genealogist*
Poleway, Christopher J. *publishing executive*
Polin, Jane L. *foundation official*
Poliner, Jason M. *lawyer*
Polisar, Leonard Myers *lawyer*
Polisi, Joseph William *academic administrator*
Politan, Nicholas H. *lawyer*
Polk, Samuel S. *lawyer*
Poll, Robert Eugene, Jr. *bank executive*
Pollack, Barbara Grace *writer*
Pollack, Martin D. *lawyer*
Pollack, Robert Elliot *biologist, educator, writer*
Pollack, Stanley P. *lawyer*
Pollack, Stephen J. *stockbroker*
Pollak, William L. *newspaper publishing executive*
Pollan, Stephen Michael *lawyer, writer, finance expert*
Pollard, Veronica *automotive executive*
Pollock, Paul James *lawyer*
Pollock, Robert B. *insurance company executive*
Pollock-O'Brien, Louise Mary *public relations executive*
Polshek, James Stewart *architect*
Polsky, Cynthia Hazen *artist, art collector, philanthropist*
Poltrack, David F. *broadcast executive, marketing educator*
Polvani, Lorenzo M. *physics professor*
Polydorides, Alexandros Demetrios *pathologist*
Pomerantz, Charlotte *writer*
Pomerantz, Frederick J. *lawyer*
Pomeroy, Lee Harris *architect*
Pomp, Alfons *surgeon*
Pompadur, I. Martin *communications executive*
Pool, Mary Jane *writer, editor*
Poole, William Daniel *writer, editor*
Pooley, Eric *editor-in-chief*
Poons, Larry *artist*
Poor, Peter Varnum *television producer, television director*
Pope, Liston, Jr. *writer, journalist*
Pope, Martin *chemist, educator*
Portale, Alfred *chef, restaurant owner*
Porter, Liliana Alicia *artist, photographer, painter, printmaker, filmmaker*
Porter, Marc Bennett *auction house executive*
Porterfield, Christopher *magazine editor, writer*
Portnow, Marjorie *painter*
Posen, Richard L. *lawyer*
Posen, Susan Orzack *lawyer*
Posin, Kathryn Olive *choreographer*
Posner, Jerome Beebe *neurologist, educator*
Posner, Louis Joseph *lawyer, accountant*
Posner, Michael Hoffman *lawyer*
Post, David Alan *broadcast executive*
Postelnek, Stephen A. *lawyer*
Pote, Harold William *banker*
Potter, Hollis Gromisch *radiologist*
Potter, Nicholas F. *lawyer*
Poulet, Anne Litle *museum director, art historian*
Poulson, Richard Jasper Metcalfe *lawyer*
Pouschine, John Laurence *private equity investment executive*
Powell, Richard Gordon *retired lawyer*
Powell, Scott *diversified financial services company executive*
Powell, Thomas Arthur *publisher*
Powers, Edward Alton *minister, educator*
Powers, Scott *television producer, actor*
Pozzi, Lucio *artist, educator*
Pratt, William *lawyer*
Prendergast, Gil Kieran *former international organization official*
Presby, J. Thomas *financial advisor, director, arbitrator*
Prescott, Darrell *lawyer*
Preska, Loretta A. *federal judge*
Press, James E. *automotive executive*
Preston, Frances Williams *music company executive*
Preston, Julia *journalist*
Previn, André (Andre Ludwig Prewin) *composer, conductor, pianist*
Price, Leontyne (Mary Violet Leontyne Price) *retired concert and opera singer, soprano*
Price, Reynolds *writer, educator*
Price, Robert *media and communications executive, investment banker, lawyer*
Prieto, Monique N. *artist*
Primi, Don Alexis *advertising executive, public relations executive, rail transportation executive*
Primps, William Guthrie *lawyer*
Prince, Alice Sara *pediatrician, educator*
Prince, Charles O., III, (Chuck Prince) *diversified financial services company executive*
Prince, Harold *theatrical director, producer*
Prince-Ramus, Joshua *architect*
Prins, Richard T. *lawyer*
Priore, Christopher Anselmo *artist*
Pritchard, John F. *lawyer*
Prives, Carol *biologist, educator*
Prizzi, Jack Anthony *investment banking executive*
Procope, Ernesta Gertrude *insurance company executive*
Proctor, Georganne C. *investment company executive*
Profusek, Robert Alan *lawyer*

Prounis, Othon A. *lawyer*
Prozes, Andrew *publishing executive*
Prueher, Joseph W. *retired military officer, former ambassador*
Psomiades, Harry John *political science professor*
Ptashne, Mark Steven *molecular biology professor*
Pucknat, John Godfrey *chemist, researcher*
Pujol, Ernesto *artist*
Pulanco, Tonya Beth *special education educator*
Puleo, Frank Charles *lawyer*
Pulos, Virginia Kate *actress, consultant*
Purcell, Karen Barlar *naturopathic physician, nutritionist, opera singer, writer*
Puris, Martin Ford *media company executive*
Purse, Charles Roe *investment banker*
Purtell, Lawrence Robert *lawyer*
Puschel, Philip P. *textiles executive*
Puth, David W. *diversified financial services company executive*
Putnam, Jerry (Gerald D. Putnam) *stock exchange executive*
Putnam, Keri *film company executive*
Putney, Mary Lynn *bank administrator, educator*
Pye, Gordon Bruce *economist*
Qazi, Ashraf Jehangir *ambassador*
Quackenbush, Margery Clouser *psychoanalyst, researcher*
Quackenbush, Robert Mead *artist, writer, psychoanalyst*
Queally, Paul B. *venture capitalist*
Queler, Eve *conductor*
Quennell, Nicholas *landscape architect, educator*
Quick, Peter *stock exchange executive*
Quigley, James B. *diversified financial services company executive*
Quigley, James H. *finance company executive*
Quimby, Fred William *pathology educator, veterinarian*
Quindlen, Anna *journalist, writer*
Quin-Harkin, Janet Elizabeth (Rhys Bowen) *writer*
Quinlan, Guy Christian *lawyer*
Quinlan, Mary Lou *former advertising executive, consultant*
Quinlan, Robert Conrad *real estate developer*
Quinn, Christine Callaghan *councilwoman*
Quinn, Francis Flaherty *lawyer*
Quinn, James E. *retail executive*
Quinn, Jane Bryant *journalist, writer*
Quinn, Yvonne Susan *lawyer*
Quiñones Keber, Eloise *art historian, educator*
Quinson, Bruno Andre *painter, retired publishing executive*
Quint, Ira *retail executive*
Quintero, Ronald Gary *management consultant*
Quirk, John James *investment company executive*
Quisgard, Liz Whitney *artist, sculptor*
Quivers, Robin *radio personality*
Raab, Gail Barbara *painter, educator*
Raab, Jennifer J. *city commissioner*
Raab, Sheldon *lawyer*
Rabb, Bruce *lawyer*
Rabb, Harriet Schaffer *academic administrator, lawyer*
Rabin, Jack *lawyer*
Rabinowitz, Dorothy *television critic*
Rabinowitz, Jack Grant *radiologist, educator*
Rabinowitz, Stephen L. *lawyer*
Rabiu, Badru I.O. *federal official*
Race, Tim *editor*
Rachow, Louis A(ugust) *librarian*
Rackow, Eric C. *hospital administrator*
Radice, Frank J. *communications executive*
Radin, Amy Janine *financial services company executive*
Radin, Sam *lawyer, land use planner*
Radke, Kirk A. *lawyer*
Rado, Peter Thomas *lawyer*
Radon, Jenik Richard *lawyer*
Radwin, Jerome J. *public health service officer*
Rafferty, Emily Kernan *museum administrator*
Rafferty, Thomas G. *lawyer*
Raghavan, Sudheer *hotel executive*
Rahm, Susan Berkman *lawyer*
Rainess, Alan Edward *psychiatrist, neurologist, educator*
Rainis, Eugene Charles *bank executive*
Raisler, Kenneth Mark *lawyer*
Rakoff, Jed Saul *federal judge, author*
Ralli, Constantine Pandia *lawyer*
Ramachandra, Goutham K. *software architect, software developer*
Ramirez, Maria Fiorini *financial consultant*
Ramirez, Sara *actress*
Ramirez, Tina *artistic director*
Rampe, David *editor*
Ramps, Kevin M. *real estate developer*
Ramsay, David Leslie *physician, dermatologist, medical educator*
Ranald, Ralph Arthur *former government official, educator*
Rand, Lawrence Anthony *investor, finance company executive*
Rand, William *lawyer, retired judge*
Randall, Francis Ballard *retired historian, educator, writer*
Randel, Don Michael *foundation administrator, former academic administrator, musicologist*
Randich, Steven J. *financial services company executive*
Randolph, David *conductor*
Rankin, Clyde Evan III *lawyer*
Rapaczynski, Andrzej *law educator*
Rapoport, Bernard Robert *lawyer*
Rapoport, Miles S. *former state offical*
Rapoport, Sandra E. *lawyer, consultant*
Rapp, Adam *writer, playwright*
Rappaport, Charles Owen *lawyer*
Rappaport, Linda Ellen *lawyer*
Rashbaum, William K. *journalist*
Rath, Joseph F. *psychologist, researcher, educator*
Rathbone, Peter B. *art appraiser*
Rather, Dan *news correspondent, former network news anchor*
Rathmann, Peggy *writer, illustrator*
Ratliff, Ben *music critic*
Rattner, Steven Lawrence *investment banker*
Rauch, Arthur Irving *management consultant*
Rauschenberg, Robert *artist*
Rausen, Aaron Reuben *pediatric hematologist, oncologist*
Raven, Abbe *broadcast executive*

Ravetch, Jeffrey Victor *molecular biologist, immunologist, educator*
Ravitch, Diane Silvers *historian, educator, writer, government official*
Rawlinson, Nora *publishing executive*
Rawski, Frederick *lawyer*
Rayfield, Elliot James *medical educator*
Raylesberg, Alan Ira *lawyer*
Raymond, Dorothy Sarnoff *communications consultant, former actress, former singer*
Raymond, Jack *journalist, public relations executive, foundation administrator*
Raynor, Bruce S. *labor union administrator*
Raynor, Richard Benjamin *neurosurgeon, educator*
Raz, Amir *neuroscientist, educator*
Read, Ian C. *pharmaceutical executive*
Read, William Tim *musician*
Reals Ellig, Janice *marketing professional, human resources specialist*
Reboul, John W. *lawyer*
Record, William John *librarian*
Reda, James Francis *business consultant*
Redburn, Tom *newspaper editor*
Reddcliffe, Steven *television critic*
Reddy, Krishna Narayana *artist, educator*
Redgrave, Lynn *actress*
Redlener, Irwin Elliot *health facility administrator, educator*
Redlich, Norman *lawyer, educator*
Redo, S(averio) Frank *retired surgeon*
Redpath, John Sloneker, Jr. *lawyer, publishing executive*
Reece, Thomas L. *manufacturing executive*
Reed, Marc C. *human resources specialist, communications executive*
Reed, W. Allen *automotive executive*
Reese, Tracy *fashion designer*
Reeves, Dianne *singer*
Reeves, Jennifer Todd *filmmaker*
Regan, Judith Terrance *publishing executive*
Reger, Robert J., Jr. *lawyer*
Reges, Marianna Alice *marketing executive*
Reich, Steve *composer*
Reichl, Ruth Molly *editor-in-chief*
Reid, Antonio (L.A. Reid) *music company executive*
Reid, Edward Snover III *lawyer*
Reid, John Phillip *law educator*
Reidenberg, Marcus Milton *physician, educator*
Reidy, Carolyn Kroll *publisher*
Reif Cohen, Jessica *broadcast executive*
Reifler, Stewart *lawyer*
Reig, June Wilson *scriptwriter, television director, television producer*
Reilly, Edward Arthur *lawyer*
Reilly, Edward T., Jr. *advertising executive*
Reilly, John J. *lawyer*
Reilly, Richard R. *lawyer*
Reinhard, Keith Leon *advertising executive*
Reinhart, Charles Lawrence *performing company executive*
Reinhold, Richard Lawrence *lawyer*
Reininghaus, Ruth *retired artist*
Reinking, Ann H. *dancer, actress*
Reinthaler, Richard Walter *lawyer*
Reisberg, Barry *geriatric psychiatrist, neuropsychopharmacologist*
Reisler, Marc S. *lawyer*
Reisman, Sharyl A. *lawyer*
Reisner, Lorin L. *lawyer*
Reiss, Dale Anne *corporate financial executive*
Reiss, Steven Alan *lawyer, educator*
Reitzas, Joshua T. *lawyer, venture capitalist*
Reitzfeld, Alan D. *lawyer, department chairman*
Remington, Deborah Williams *artist*
Remnick, David J. *journalist, editor-in-chief*
Remshard, John W. *insurance company executive*
Renauld, Cyril *chef*
Renehan, Edward John *writer*
Renfro, Charles *architect, educator*
Renick, Kyle *artistic director*
Renna, Cathy *communications executive, activist*
Rennert, Ira Leon *manufacturing executive*
Renney, Tom *professional hockey coach*
Rennie, John *editor-in-chief*
Rescigno, Richard Joseph *editor*
Resika, Paul *artist*
Resnick, Rhoda Brodowsky *psychotherapist*
Resnick, Scott N. *real estate company executive*
Resnicow, Norman Jakob *lawyer*
Ressa, Gregory John *lawyer*
Ressler, Peter D. *executive recruiter*
Restani, Jane A. *federal judge*
Reuben, Gloria *actress, singer*
Reutter, Eberhard Edmund, Jr. *education and law*
Revenkova, Ekaterina *biologist, researcher*
Reverdin, Bernard J. *lawyer*
Revesz, Richard Luis *dean, law educator*
Revkin, Andrew C. *writer, reporter*
Reynolds, David Spencer *humanities educator, writer*
Reynolds, James *management consultant*
Reynolds, John R. *hospital executive*
Rheins, Carl Jeffrey *historian, director*
Rhoads, Geraldine Emeline *editor, consultant*
Rhodes, David *academic administrator*
Rhodes, Randi *radio personality*
Rhodes, Richard (Lee) *writer*
Rhodes, Rosamond *medical educator, philosophy educator*
Rhodes, Samuel *violist, educator*
Rhodes, William Reginald *banker*
Rhone, Sylvia Marie Miller *recording industry executive*
Ricco, Donna *fashion designer*
Rice, Donald Sands *lawyer*
Rice, Joseph Lee III *lawyer*
Rice, Luanne *writer*
Rice, Thomas Charles *lawyer*
Rich, Adrienne *poet*
Rich, Frank Hart *journalist, writer*
Rich, Frederic Carl *lawyer*
Rich, Laura *columnist*
Rich, R(obert) Bruce *lawyer*
Richard, Virginia Rynne *lawyer*
Richards, Bill Arthur *artist, educator*
Richards, Cecile *healthcare network executive*
Richards, David A.J. *law educator*
Richards, David Alan *lawyer*
Richards, Martin *theatrical producer*

Richardson, Alfonso Austin *accountant, financial services executive*
Richardson, Grace Elizabeth *consumer products company executive*
Richert, John Rolin *neuroimmunologist, educator*
Riches, Wendy *magazine publishing executive*
Richieri, Kenneth A. *publishing executive, lawyer*
Richman, Martin Franklin *lawyer*
Richman, Sophia *psychologist*
Richtman, Jack *French language educator*
Ridgway, Delissa Anne *federal judge*
Rieder, Eric *lawyer*
Rieff, David Sontag *editor, critic*
Rielly, John P. (J.P. Rielly) *corporate financial executive*
Rifka, Judy *artist, educator*
Rifkin, Ron *actor*
Rifkind, Arleen B. *pharmacologist, researcher, educator*
Rifkind, Robert S. *lawyer*
Rigg, Dame Diana *actress*
Riggio, Leonard *book store company executive*
Riggio, Stephen *book store company executive*
Rigney, James Oliver, Jr., (Robert Jordan, Chang Lung, Reagan O'Neal, Jackson O'Reilly) *writer*
Rigolosi, Elaine La Monica *lawyer, educator*
Rikon, Michael *lawyer*
Riley, Mark *radio personality, political scientist*
Riley, Thomas Edward *lawyer*
Riley, William *wholesale distribution executive, writer, conservationist*
Rindskopf, David *statistician, educator*
Ringel, Dean *lawyer*
Ringgold, Faith *artist*
Ringler, Kenneth J., Jr. *state agency administrator*
Ripa, Kelly Maria *television personality, actress*
Riss, Eric *psychologist*
Ristich, Miodrag *psychiatrist*
Ritch, Kathleen *diversified financial services company executive*
Ritch, Robert Harry *ophthalmologist, educator*
Ritchie, Richard Lee *media company executive*
Ritter, Ann L. *lawyer*
Ritter, Jodi Gottesfeld *lawyer*
Rivera, Chita (Conchita del Rivero) *actress, singer, dancer*
Rivera, Geraldo *television personality, journalist*
Rivkin, David Wolfe *lawyer*
Rivlin, Benjamin *political science professor*
Rivlin, Richard Saul *internist*
Rizer, Maggie *model*
Rizkin, Iosif *systems, circuits, and computer scientist, writer*
Rizowy, Carlos Guillermo *lawyer, educator, political analyst*
Rizzuto, Richard Peter *entrepreneur*
Roach, John Hendee, Jr. *bank executive, investment banker, financial services executive*
Roach, Margaret *editor-in-chief*
Robb, Kathy McCleskey *lawyer*
Robbins, John Clapp *management consultant*
Robbins, Tim (Timothy Francis Robbins) *actor, film director*
Roberts, Burton Bennett *lawyer, retired judge*
Roberts, Denise (Denise Roberts Hurlin) *dancer*
Roberts, Donald Munier *retired banker, trust company executive*
Roberts, Fletcher *editor*
Roberts, Francis Stone *advertising executive*
Roberts, Jim *editor*
Roberts, Katy *editor*
Roberts, Kevin *advertising executive*
Roberts, Madelyn Alpert *publishing executive*
Roberts, Nora *writer*
Roberts, Thomas Alba *lawyer*
Robertson, Andrew *advertising executive*
Robertson, Edwin David *lawyer*
Robertson, Hugh (Elihu F. Robertson) *lawyer*
Robinson, Barbara Paul *lawyer*
Robinson, Irwin Jay *lawyer*
Robinson, James D. III *venture capitalist*
Robinson, Janet L. *publishing executive*
Robinson, Kim Stanley *science fiction author*
Robinson, Marilynne *writer*
Robinson, Peter M. *business association executive*
Robinson, Richard *publishing executive*
Robinson, Roxana Barry *writer, art historian*
Robison, Paula Judith *flutist*
Robock, Stefan Hyman *retired economics professor*
Roche, Gerard Raymond *management consultant*
Roche, John Edward *college administrator, human resources specialist, educator*
Roche, Joyce M. *marketing executive*
Rock, Allan Michael *ambassador, former Canadian government official*
Rockas, Anastasia T. *lawyer*
Rockefeller, David *banker*
Rocklen, Kathy Hellenbrand *lawyer*
Rockwell, David *architectural firm executive*
Rockwell, John Sargent *dance critic, writer, former arts administrator*
Rodin, Judith Seitz *foundation administrator, former academic administrator, psychologist, educator*
Rodin, Rita Angela *lawyer*
Rodman, Leroy Eli *lawyer*
Rodriguez, Carlos A. *lawyer*
Rodriguez, Freddy *actor*
Rodriguez, Narciso *fashion designer*
Rodriguez, Vincent Angel *lawyer, director*
Roeder, Robert Gayle *biochemist, molecular biologist, educator*
Roehrs, Christopher Scott *lawyer*
Roer, Ricki E. *lawyer*
Roethenmund, Otto Emil *finance company executive, bank executive*
Roff, Sandra *library and information scientist, educator, archivist*
Rogers, James Beeland, Jr., (Jim Rogers) *retired investment company executive*
Rogers, Jenny *artist, interior designer, consultant*
Rogers, Theodore Courtney *investment company executive*
Rogin, Gilbert Leslie *editor, author*
Rohatyn, Felix George *diversified financial services company executive, former ambassador*
Roi, Alice (Alice Roy Blumenthal) *apparel designer*
Roker, Al *newscaster*
Rolfe, Ronald Stuart *lawyer*

Rollin, Betty *writer, television journalist*
Rollins, James (Jim Czajkowski, James Clemens) *writer, veterinarian*
Romano, Clare *artist*
Romano, John Francis *dermatologist*
Romanos, John, Jr., (Jack Romanos) *publisher*
Romans, John Niebrugge *lawyer*
Romas, Nicholas Achilles *urologist, educator*
Romero, Anthony D. *legal association administrator*
Romita, Mauro Charles *plastic surgeon*
Ronde, John Herman *writer, translator*
Roney, Carley *wedding company executive, writer*
Ronstadt, Linda Marie *singer*
Rooney, Paul C., Jr. *retired lawyer*
Roosevelt, Theodore, IV, *investment banker*
Root, Nina J. *librarian, writer*
Root, William Pitt *poet, educator*
Roppel, Mark *lawyer*
Rosaldo, Renato Ignacio, Jr. *cultural anthropology educator*
Rosand, David *art historian, educator*
Rose, Charlie (Charles Peete Rose Jr.) *television journalist*
Rose, Daniel *real estate company executive, consultant*
Rose, Donald Joseph *orthopedist, surgeon*
Rose, Elihu *real estate executive*
Rose, Herman *artist*
Rose, Jalen *professional basketball player*
Rose, Joanna Semel *volunteer*
Rose, Joanne W. *rating service executive*
Rose, Robert Neal *investment banker*
Rose, Victoria Lasdon *publishing executive*
Rosell, Kurt F. *lawyer*
Rosen, Aby J. *real estate developer*
Rosen, Adam B. *lawyer*
Rosen, Jeffrey J. *lawyer*
Rosen, J(oshua) Philip *lawyer*
Rosen, Matthew A. *lawyer*
Rosen, Michael N. *lawyer*
Rosen, Nathaniel Kent *cellist*
Rosenbaum, Joan Hannah *museum director*
Rosenbaum, Richard A. *lawyer*
Rosenberg, Alan David *accountant*
Rosenberg, Alan Stewart *lawyer*
Rosenberg, Alex Jacob *art appraiser, art dealer*
Rosenberg, Harold Nmi *preventive medicine physician, consultant*
Rosenberg, Jerome Ira *lawyer*
Rosenberg, John David *language educator, critic*
Rosenberg, Lawrence *lawyer*
Rosenberg, Mark Fletcher *lawyer*
Rosenberg, Robert Charles *housing corporation executive*
Rosenberg, Terry *artist*
Rosenberg, Tina *reporter*
Rosenbloom, Daniel *investment advisor, lawyer*
Rosenblum, Constance *newspaper editor*
Rosenblum, Jay Alan *neurologist*
Rosenblum, Robert H. *art historian, educator*
Rosenblum, William F., Jr. *lawyer*
Rosenfeld, Gerald *investment company executive, financial analyst*
Rosenfeld, Isadore *cardiologist, educator*
Rosenfeld, Nachman *plastic surgeon*
Rosenfeld, Steven B. *lawyer*
Rosenfield, Allan *medical educator, dean, obstetrician, gynecologist*
Rosengarten, Frank *retired language educator, retired literature educator, writer*
Rosensaft, Menachem Zwi *lawyer, writer, foundation administrator*
Rosenshine, Allen Gilbert *advertising agency executive*
Rosenthal, Andrew *newspaper editor*
Rosenthal, Howard Lewis *political science professor*
Rosenthal, Jane *film company executive*
Rosenthal, Joel Howard *think-tank executive*
Rosenthal, Larry *cosmetic dentist*
Rosenthal, Shirley Lord *cosmetics magazine executive, novelist*
Rosenwasser, Mike *lawyer*
Rosenzweig, Charles Leonard *lawyer*
Rosevear, Cora *curator*
Rosha, Uzi *lawyer*
Roshan, Daniel *obstetrician, gynecologist*
Roskam, Catherine S. *bishop*
Roskin, William A. *communications executive*
Rosow, Stuart L. *lawyer*
Ross, Barry C. *lawyer*
Ross, Brian Elliott *news correspondent*
Ross, Diana (Diana Ernestine Earle Ross) *singer, actress, entertainer, fashion designer*
Ross, George H. *real estate company executive, lawyer*
Ross, Jo Ann *media buyer*
Ross, John T. *artist, educator*
Ross, Mathew P. *lawyer*
Ross, Matthew *lawyer*
Ross, Norman Alan *publisher*
Ross, Stephen M. *real estate company executive*
Ross, Wilbur Louis, Jr. *investment banker*
Rossen, Jordan *lawyer*
Rosset, Barnet Lee, Jr. *publishing executive*
Rossettos, Nicholas J. *research and development company executive*
Rossow, William Brigance *physics professor*
Roth, Daryl *theater producer*
Roth, Eric M. *lawyer*
Roth, Kenneth *human rights advocate*
Roth, Michael I. *communications executive, lawyer*
Roth, Paul Norman *lawyer*
Roth, Sol *rabbi*
Roth, Steven *real estate company executive*
Rothberg, Gerald *editor, publishing executive*
Rothberg, Glenda Fay Morris *lawyer*
Rothenberg, Eleanore *psychotherapist*
Rothenberg, Jerome *writer, literature educator*
Rothenberg, Laraine S. *lawyer*
Rothenberg, Peter Jay *lawyer*
Rothenberg, Robert Philip *public relations counselor*
Rothfeld, Michael B. *theatrical producer, investor*
Rothman, Barbara Katz *sociology educator*
Rothman, David J. *historian, educator*
Rothman, Henry Isaac *lawyer*
Rothman, James Edward *cell biologist, educator*

Rothschild, Amalie Randolph *filmmaker, film producer, film director, photographer*
Rotolo, Susan (Suze) *artist*
Roumani-Denn, Vivienne Rachel *library and information scientist, consultant*
Rouse, Christopher Chapman III *composer, educator*
Rover, Edward Frank *foundation administrator, lawyer*
Rovine, Arthur William *international arbitrator*
Rovit, Richard Lee *neurosurgeon*
Rovner, Michal *video artist, photographer*
Rowe, David Lee *financial advisor*
Rowen, Andrew S. *lawyer*
Rowen, Ruth Halle *musicologist, educator*
Rowland, Esther E(delman) *retired dean*
Rowland, Lewis Phillip *neurology educator, editor, clinical investigator*
Rowley, Cynthia *apparel designer*
Rozbruch, S. Robert *orthopedist, researcher*
Rozen, Jerome George, Jr. *entomologist, researcher, curator*
Rozenberg, Lana *cosmetic dentist*
Ruben, Lawrence *real estate developer, real estate company executive, lawyer*
Rubenstein, Atoosa Behnegar *editor-in-chief*
Rubenstein, Howard Joseph *public relations executive*
Rubenstein, Joshua Seth *lawyer*
Rubenstein, Leonard *engineering company executive*
Rubenstein, William S. *lawyer*
Rubin, Albert Louis *internist, nephrologist, educator*
Rubin, Gabriel Kevi *psychiatrist*
Rubin, Harry Meyer *software industry executive*
Rubin, Herbert *lawyer*
Rubin, Jeffrey Wayne *lawyer*
Rubin, Joel Edward *manufacturing executive*
Rubin, Robert Edward *diversified financial services company executive, former secretary of the treasury*
Rubin, Robert Samuel *investment banker*
Rubin, Stephen Edward *publishing executive, editor, journalist*
Rubin, Theodore Isaac *psychiatrist, writer*
Rubinfien, Leo H. *photographer, filmmaker*
Rubini, Gail *education director*
Rubino, Victor Joseph *academic administrator, lawyer*
Rubinstein, Aaron *lawyer*
Rubinstein, Frederic Armand *lawyer*
Rubin-Vega, Daphne *actress*
Ruda, Howard *lawyer, finance company executive*
Rudel, Julius *conductor*
Rudenstine, Neil Leon *former academic administrator, educator*
Ruder, William *public relations executive*
Rudin, Scott *film and theatre producer*
Rudloff, Udo *surgeon, researcher*
Rudoff, Sheldon *lawyer*
Ruegger, Philip T. III *lawyer*
Ruesterholz, Virginia P. *telecommunications industry executive*
Rufrano, Glenn *real estate company executive*
Ruhl, Sarah *playwright*
Rule, Sheila *editor*
Rumaker, Michael *writer, language educator*
Rumschitzki, David Sheldon *chemical engineering educator*
RuPaul, (Andre Charles) *model, singer*
Rupp, George Erik *international relief organization executive*
Rusch, Valerie Williams *thoracic surgeon*
Rusch, William Graham *religious organization administrator*
Ruscha, Edward *artist*
Rusmisel, Stephen Raymond *lawyer*
Russell, Charlotte Sananes *biochemistry professor, researcher*
Russell, David O. *film director, film producer, scriptwriter*
Russell, Maryanne *photographer*
Russo, Anthony Joseph *public relations professional*
Russo, Thomas Anthony *lawyer*
Russotto, Paul *artist, educator*
Ruta, Thomas V. *professional sports team executive, accounting executive*
Rutenberg, Jim *journalist*
Rutherfurd, John *financial information company executive*
Ryan, Antony L. *lawyer*
Ryan, J. Brendan *advertising executive*
Ryan, Regina Claire (Mrs. Paul Deutschman) *editor, literary agent*
Ryan, Richard *ambassador*
Rylant, Cynthia *writer*
Ryman, Robert Tracy *artist*
Sabat, Robert Hartman *magazine editor*
Sabbatini, Paul *gynecologist, obstetrician*
Sabel, Bradley Kent *lawyer*
Sabel, Charles Frederick *law educator*
Sachar, David Bernard *gastroenterologist, educator*
Sachar, Louis *writer*
Sachs, Jeffrey David *economist, educator*
Sachs, Samuel, II, *museum director*
Sack, Robert David *federal judge, law educator*
Sacks, Ira Stephen *lawyer*
Sacks, Oliver Wolf *neurologist, writer*
Sacripanti, Peter John *lawyer*
Saddler, Donald Edward *choreographer, dancer*
Sadegh, Ali M. *mechanical engineering educator, researcher, consultant*
Sadik, Neil Scott *dermatologist*
Sadik, Nafis *United Nations administrator*
Sadler Edepli, Kirsten *biologist, educator*
Sadock, Benjamin James *psychiatrist, educator*
Sadove, Stephen Irving *retail executive*
Saeed, Faiza J. *lawyer*
Saffar, Jean-Marc *healthcare consultant*
Safian, Robert L. *executive editor*
Safra, Joseph *bank executive*
Safro, Millicent *small business owner, decorative arts scholar, writer*
Saft, Stuart Mark *lawyer*
Sahid, Joseph Robert *lawyer*
Saint-Donat, Bernard Jacques *finance company executive*

St. Martin, Charlotte *trade association administrator*
Salans, Lester Barry *physician, research scientist, educator*
Salembier, Valerie Birnbaum *publishing executive*
Salerno, F. Robert *car rental company executive*
Salerno-Sonnenberg, Nadja *violinist*
Salgo, Peter Lloyd *internist, writer, anesthesiologist, journalist, commentator*
Salinger, J(erome) D(avid) *author*
Salky, Barry A. *surgeon*
Salom, Roberto *financial executive*
Salomon, Richard E. *investment company executive*
Salonen, Esa-Pekka *conductor, music director*
Salonga, Lea *actress, singer*
Salter, James *writer*
Salter, Kevin Thornton *lawyer*
Salter, Mary Jo *poet*
Saltzstein, Susan L. *lawyer*
Salvesen, Magda Abercromby *art and garden historian*
Salzberg, Barry *finance company executive*
Salzman, Robert Jay *accountant*
Samaras, Lucas *artist, photographer*
Sampras, Pete *retired professional tennis player*
Sampson, Hugh Albert, Jr. *medical educator*
Samstein, Benjamin *transplant surgeon*
Samuels, Dorothy J. *journalist, writer*
Samuels, Leslie B. *lawyer*
Samuelsson, Marcus (Kasshun Tsegie) *food service executive*
Sanchez, Manuel *retired social services administrator, writer*
Sand, Leonard B. *federal judge*
Sandelman, Jonathan E. (Jon) *investment banker*
Sanders, Gina Susan *publishing executive*
Sanders, Rhea *artist*
Sandhu, Harvinder Singh *spinal surgeon, educator*
Sandler, Irving Harry *art critic, art historian*
Sandler, Lucy Freeman *art history educator*
Sandler, Richard Jay *lawyer*
Sandler, Robert Michael *insurance company executive*
Sandler, Ross *law educator*
Sands, Harry *psychologist, health administrator, researcher*
Sandstedt, J. Erik *lawyer*
Sandy, Sandra V. *psychologist*
Sanford, John (John Camp) *writer, journalist*
Sanger, Carol *law educator*
Sanseverino, Raymond Anthony *lawyer*
Santiago-Hudson, Ruben *actor*
Santo, Fred M. *lawyer*
Santore, Joseph *painter*
Saperstein, Ivan A. *lawyer*
Saphir, Richard Louis *pediatrician*
Sapir, Tamir *entrepreneur*
Sarachik, Myriam Paula Morgenstein *physics professor, condensed matter physicist*
Sarafpour, Behnaz *apparel designer*
Sarandon, Susan Abigail *actress*
Sarbin, Hershel Benjamin *management consultant, lawyer, publishing executive*
Sard, Susannah Ellen *non-profit executive*
Sareyan, Andy *publishing executive*
Sargent, Pamela *writer*
Sarnelle, Joseph R. *publishing executive*
Sarnoff, Ann M. *publishing executive, former sports association executive*
Sarnoff, Richard *digital publishing executive*
Sasaki, Jun *steel company researcher*
Sasman, Irene Deak Handberg *publishing executive*
Sassoon, Andre Gabriel *lawyer*
Sather, Glen Cameron *professional hockey team executive, coach*
Satine, Barry Roy *lawyer*
Saul, Andrew M. *investment company executive*
Saul, John Woodruff III *writer*
Saunders, Paul Christopher *lawyer*
Saunders, Sylvia Christie *biologist, educator*
Saunders, Thomas A. III *investment banker*
Savage, Frank *insurance executive*
Savas, Emanuel S. *finance educator, public official*
Savrin, Louis *lawyer*
Sawyer, Diane (L. Diane Sawyer) *newscaster, journalist*
Sawyer, Linda *advertising executive*
Sawyers, Al Baker *lawyer*
Saxena, Brij B. *endocrinologist, biochemist, educator*
Saxon, Wolfgang Erik Georg *journalist*
Saxton, Catherine Patricia *public relations executive*
Saxton, Martha *history educator, writer*
Sayre, Linda Damaris *human resources professional*
Sayre, Phil *editor*
Sayres, Edwin J., Jr. *animal welfare organization administrator*
Scaffidi, Judith Ann *academic administrator*
Scanlon, Rosemary *economist*
Scarborough, Charles Bishop III *broadcast journalist, writer*
Scarborough, Chuck *newscaster, writer*
Scarola, John Michael *dentist, educator*
Scarpa, A. Michael *apparel executive, corporate financial executive*
Scarpelli, Bob *advertising executive*
Scaturro, Philip David *investment banker, academic administrator*
Scelsa, Joseph Vincent *sociologist, educator, dean*
Sceusa, Nicholas A. *pharmacologist*
Schaab, Arnold J. *lawyer*
Schachter, James Robert *editor*
Schaefer, John H. *finance company executive, security firm executive*
Schaeffer, Richard *mercantile exchange executive*
Schafer, Milton *composer, pianist, educator*
Schafer, Oscar S. *investment company executive*
Schaffer, Kenneth B. *communications executive, mechanical engineer, consultant*
Schaffer, Scott R. *lawyer*
Schaffer, Seth Andrew *lawyer*
Schaffner, Bertram Henry *psychiatrist*
Schaffzin, Jonathan A. *lawyer*
Schair, Robin A. *lawyer*
Schaller-Demers, Debra Susan *education coordinator*
Schallert, Edwin Glenn *lawyer*

Schama, Simon *historian, educator, author*
Schamus, James Allan *film company executive, film producer, screenwriter*
Schapiro, Donald *lawyer*
Schapiro, Miriam *artist*
Scharf, Y. David *lawyer*
Schatz, Barbara A. *law educator*
Schatz, Gary Stewart *marketing professional*
Schechner, Richard *theater director, educator*
Schechter, Daniel Scott *child and adolescent psychiatrist, researcher*
Scheck, Barry C. *legal association administrator, educator*
Scheeder, Louis *theater producer, director, educator*
Scheiman, Eugene R. *lawyer*
Scheindlin, Raymond Paul *literature educator, religious organization administrator*
Scheler, Brad Eric *lawyer*
Schenk, Deborah Huffman *law educator*
Scher, Howard S. *oncologist*
Schiano, Charles *transportation executive*
Schick, Harry Leon *investment company executive*
Schick, Thomas *diversified financial services company executive*
Schiesel, Seth *reporter*
Schiff, David Tevele *investment banker*
Schiff, Frank *investment company executive*
Schiff, Howard Irwin *urologist*
Schiff, Marlene Sandler *entrepreneur*
Schiffman, Daniel *lawyer, arts advocate*
Schiller, Justin Galland *antiquarian bookseller, researcher, editor*
Schisgal, Murray *playwright*
Schizer, David Michael *dean, law educator*
Schizer, Zevie Baruch *lawyer*
Schjeldahl, Peter *poet, critic*
Schlain, Barbara Ellen *lawyer*
Schlegel, Peter Niles *urologist, educator*
Schlein, Michael Edward *diversified financial services company executive*
Schlesinger, Arthur, Jr., (Arthur Meier Schlesinger) *writer, educator, historian*
Schlesinger, Sanford Joel *lawyer*
Schlesinger, Stephen Cannon *think-tank executive*
Schley, William Shain *otolaryngologist*
Schlosser, Herbert S. *broadcasting company executive*
Schlosstein, Ralph L. *diversified financial services company executive*
Schmemann, Serge *journalist*
Schmertz, Eric Joseph *lawyer, educator, commissioner*
Schmertz, Mildred Floyd *editor-in-chief, writer*
Schmidt, Benno Charles, Jr. *lawyer*
Schmidt, Joseph W. *lawyer*
Schmidt, Stanley Albert *editor, writer*
Schmidt, William E. *editor*
Schmidtberger, Michael J. *lawyer*
Schmidt-Holtz, Rolf *music company executive*
Schmolka, Leo Louis *law educator*
Schmults, Edward *retail executive*
Schnabel, Julian *artist*
Schneck, Jerome M. *psychiatrist, historian, medical educator*
Schneider, Daniel B. *reporter*
Schneider, Howard *lawyer*
Schneider, JoAnne *artist*
Schneider, Martin Aaron *photojournalist, educator, ecologist, engineer, writer, artist, television director, filmmaker, public advocate, medical researcher*
Schneider, Willys Hope *lawyer*
Schneiderman, Irwin *lawyer*
Schneirov, Allison R. *lawyer*
Schoenfeld, Gerald *performing company executive*
Schoenfeld, Robert Louis *biomedical engineer*
Schoenhut, Frederick W. *stock exchange executive*
Schofield, Lorna Gail *lawyer*
Schorer, Suki *ballet teacher*
Schori, Katharine Jefferts *bishop*
Schorr, Brian Lewis *lawyer, writer*
Schorsch, Ismar *theology studies educator, rabbi*
Schotter, Andrew Roye *economics professor, consultant*
Schrader, Michael Eugene *columnist, editor*
Schrager, Ian *hotel executive*
Schreiber, Jay *journalist*
Schreiber, Paul Solomon *lawyer*
Schreyer, Leslie John *lawyer*
Schroeder, Edmund R. *lawyer*
Schubert, Scott E. *corporate financial executive*
Schueneman, Diane L. *diversified financial services company executive*
Schulhof, Michael Peter *electronics company executive*
Schulhofer, Stephen Joseph *law educator*
Schulte, Stephen John *lawyer, educator*
Schulzrinne, Henning G. *computer science educator*
Schumacher, Harry Richard *lawyer*
Schumacher, Robert Denison *banker*
Schuman, Patricia Glass *publishing company executive, educator*
Schumer, Robert B. *lawyer*
Schupak, Donald *merchant banker, lawyer, strategic planner*
Schupak, Leslie Allen *public relations company executive*
Schuselka, Elfi *artist*
Schuster, Carlotta Lief *psychiatrist*
Schuster, Reid S. *advertising executive*
Schwab, Frank, Jr. *management consultant*
Schwab, George David *social sciences educator, writer*
Schwab, Harold Lee *lawyer*
Schwalb, Susan Amelia *artist, educator*
Schwantner, Joseph *composer, educator*
Schwartz, Alan Victor *advertising executive*
Schwartz, Anna Jacobson *economist*
Schwartz, Barry Fredric *lawyer, diversified holding company executive*
Schwartz, Bart *diversified financial services company executive*
Schwartz, Gil (Stanley Bing) *broadcast executive, writer*
Schwartz, Herbert Frederick *lawyer*
Schwartz, Irving Leon *internist, educator, research scientist*
Schwartz, Jordan M. *lawyer*
Schwartz, Marvin *lawyer*

Schwartz, Max J. *lawyer*
Schwartz, Mischa *electrical engineering educator*
Schwartz, Renee Gerstler *lawyer*
Schwartz, Robert *finance educator*
Schwartz, Robert George *retired insurance company executive*
Schwartz, Theodore H. *neurosurgeon*
Schwartz, Wallace L. *lawyer*
Schwartz, William *lawyer, educator*
Schwartzstein, Adam *lawyer*
Schwarz, Frederick A.O., Jr. *lawyer*
Schwarz, Thomas J. *lawyer*
Schwarzman, Stephen Allen *investment banker*
Schwind, Michael Angelo *law educator*
Sclafani, Anthony Paul *plastic surgeon, educator, biomedical researcher*
Sclafani, Joseph L. *diversified financial services company executive*
Sclafani, Susan K. *educational consultant, former federal agency administrator*
Scofidio, Ricardo *artist, educator, architect*
Scott, Bertram *insurance company executive*
Scott, Campbell *actor*
Scott, Dale Allan *major league umpire*
Scott, Helen S. *law educator*
Scott, Margaret Simon *retired mortgage broker*
Scott, Mimi Koblenz *psychotherapist, actress, journalist, playwright*
Scott, Stanley DeForest *real estate company executive*
Scott, Susan Craig *plastic surgeon*
Scott, William Clement III *investor*
Scotto, Rosanna *newscaster*
Scribner, Charles III *art historian, writer*
Sculco, Thomas Peter *surgeon*
Scully, Robert William (Bob Scully) *diversified financial services company executive*
Seal, *musician*
Seaman, Alfred Jarvis *retired advertising agency executive*
Seaman, Barbara (Ann Rosner) *author*
Sean Paul, (Sean Paul Henriques) *singer*
Seary, Lawrence Anthony *cinematographer, editor*
Seborovski, Carole *artist*
Secunda, Eugene *marketing professional, educator*
Sederbaum, Arthur David *lawyer*
Sedlin, Elias David *orthopedist, educator*
See, SawTeen *structural engineer*
Seele, Pernessa C. *immunologist, health science association administrator*
Seelig, Jill *publishing executive*
Seely, Robert Daniel *cardiologist, medical association administrator*
Segal, Jonathan Bruce *editor*
Segal, Lore *writer*
Segal, Martin Eli *retired actuarial and consulting company executive*
Segal, Sheldon Jerome *biologist, educator, foundation administrator*
Seidel, Selvyn *lawyer, educator*
Seiden, Henry (Hank Seiden) *advertising executive*
Seiden, Steven Arnold *executive search consultant*
Seidenberg, Ivan G. *telecommunications industry executive*
Seidler, Alan Richard *composer, musician, music company executive*
Seidler, B(ernard) Alan *lawyer*
Seife, Howard *lawyer*
Seifert, Thomas Lloyd *lawyer*
Seigel, Jerrold Edward *historian, writer*
Seinuk, Ysrael A. *architectural engineer*
Seitz, Frederick *former university administrator*
Selby, Cecily Cannan *dean, science educator*
Selby, Ronald M. *orthopedic surgeon*
Seldes, Marian *actress*
Selig, Bud (Alan H. Selig) *major league baseball commissioner*
Selig, Karl-Ludwig *literature and language professor*
Seliger, Charles *artist*
Seligman, Daniel *editor*
Sellers, Peter Hoadley *mathematician, educator*
Seltzer, Leo *cinematographer, educator*
Selver, Paul Darryl *lawyer*
Semlies, Lori R. *lawyer*
Semple, Robert Baylor, Jr. *editor, journalist*
Sendak, Maurice Bernard *writer, illustrator*
Sendax, Victor Irven *dentist, educator, dental implant researcher*
Sender, Adam D. *investment company executive, art collector*
Senese, Daniel *professional society administrator*
Sengupta, Somini *reporter*
Senior, Enrique Francisco *investment banker*
Senzel, Martin Lee *lawyer*
Serbaroli, Francis J. *lawyer, educator, writer*
Serchuk, Ivan *lawyer*
Serebrier, José *musician, composer, conductor*
Serio, Robert Francis *lawyer*
Serota, James Ian *lawyer*
Serota, Susan Perlstadt *lawyer, educator*
Serra, Matthew D. *consumer products company executive*
Serra, Richard *sculptor*
Servodidio, Pat Anthony *broadcast executive*
Sessions, Roy Brumby *otolaryngologist, educator*
Setrakian, Berge *lawyer*
Severs, William Floyd *actor*
Sevilla-Sacasa, Frances Aldrich *bank executive*
Seward, George Chester *lawyer*
Sexton, Joe *editor*
Sexton, John Edward *academic administrator, law educator*
Sexton, Joseph A. *editor*
Seyedi, Nahid *physiologist, researcher*
Seymour, Everett Hedden, Jr. *lawyer*
Seymour, Karen Patton *lawyer, former prosecutor*
Seymour, Samuel Whitney *lawyer*
Seymour, Sloan *media specialist*
Sguerra, Jaime *insurance company executive*
Shachar, Avishai *lawyer*
Shaffer, Paul *musician, bandleader*
Shaffer, Peter (Sir Peter Shaffer) *playwright*
Shah, Jatin Premanand *head and neck surgeon, educator*
Shahn, Jonathan *sculptor*
Shainwald, Sybil *lawyer*
Shakira, (Shakira Isabel Mebarak Ripoll) *musician*
Shakow, David Joseph *lawyer, educator*
Shallcross, Deanne J. *finance company executive*

Shalom, Liliane Winn *investment company executive, consultant*
Shamask, Ronaldus *fashion designer*
Shambroom, Paul *artist, photographer*
Shanahan, Brendan Frederick *professional hockey player*
Shanahan, William Stephen *consumer products company executive*
Shane, Penny *lawyer*
Shanks, David *publishing executive*
Shanks, Eugene Baylis, Jr. *banker*
Shanor, Donald Read *journalism educator, writer*
Shao, Wei *writer, educator*
Shapiro, E. Donald *lawyer, educator*
Shapiro, Gary Evan *newspaper journalist*
Shapiro, Isaac *lawyer*
Shapiro, James Stephen *English professor*
Shapiro, Joel Elias *artist*
Shapiro, Judith R. *academic administrator, anthropology educator*
Shapiro, Marvin Lincoln *communications company executive*
Shapiro, Meryl *lawyer*
Shapiro, Neal *broadcast executive, television producer*
Shapiro, Robert Frank *investment company executive*
Shapiro, Steven R. *legal association administrator*
Shapiro, Theodore *psychiatrist, educator*
Sharbel, Jean M. *editor*
Shargel, Gerald L. *lawyer*
Sharkey, Catherine Moira *law educator*
Sharoff, Leighsa *nursing educator, researcher*
Sharp, Anne Catherine *artist, educator*
Sharp, J(ames) Franklin *finance educator, portfolio manager*
Sharp, Rob *investment company executive*
Sharpe, Shannon *commentator, retired professional football player*
Shatter, Susan Louise *artist*
Shavin, Helene B. *venture capital company executive*
Shaw, David Elliot *financial executive*
Shaw, Jim *painter*
Shaw, Lacy *academic consultant*
Shaw, Steven A. *information technology executive*
Shaw, Theodore Michael *legal association administrator*
Shawn, Wallace *playwright, actor*
Shea, Edward Emmett *lawyer, educator, writer*
Shea, James William *lawyer*
Shea, Martin M. *communications executive*
Shechet, Arlene J. *artist*
Shecter, Howard L. *lawyer*
Shedlarz, David L. *pharmaceutical executive*
Sheehan, Michael Andrew *former protective services official, former federal agency administrator*
Sheehan, Mike *advertising executive*
Sheehan, Robert C. *lawyer*
Sheehan, Susan *writer*
Sheffery, Michael B. *investment company executive*
Sheik, Duncan *singer, songwriter*
Sheinman, Mort *editor, consultant, writer, photographer*
Shelanski, Michael L. *cell biologist, educator*
Sheldon, Eleanor Harriet Bernert *sociologist, writer*
Shelley, Carole *actress*
Shen, Michael *lawyer*
Shenker, Joseph C. *lawyer*
Shenkman, Mark Ronald *investment and finance executive*
Shepard, Robert M. *lawyer, investment banker, engineer*
Shepard, Stephen Benjamin *journalist, educator, former magazine editor*
Shepard, Thomas Rockwell III *advertising executive*
Shepherd, Gillian Mary *physician*
Sheridan LaBarge, Joan Ruth *publishing executive*
Sherman, Arthur *theater educator, writer, actor, composer, sculptor*
Sherman, Eugene Jay *retired marketing professional, retired economist*
Sherman, Jeffrey Barry *retail executive*
Sherman, John Eric *plastic surgeon*
Sherman, Norman Mark *advertising agency executive*
Sherman, Sarai *sculptor, painter*
Sherman, Spencer E. *ophthalmologist*
Sherrod, Philip Lawrence *artist, composer, painter, poet*
Shields, James Joseph *academic administrator, education, writer*
Shientag, Florence Perlow *lawyer*
Shier, Shelley M. *production company executive*
Shiflett, Chris *musician*
Shineman, Edward William, Jr. *retired pharmaceutical executive*
Shinkle, John Thomas *lawyer*
Shinnar, Reuel *engineering educator, consultant*
Shipley, David *editor*
Shipley, Walter Vincent *retired bank executive*
Shnayerson, Robert Beahan *editor, consultant*
Shneidman, J. Lee *historian, educator*
shoemate, Steven R. *lawyer*
Shorter, James Russell, Jr. *lawyer*
Shortliffe, Edward Hance *internist, medical educator, computer scientist*
Shortz, Will *puzzle editor*
Shoss, Cynthia Renée *lawyer*
Showalter, David Scott *accounting executive*
Shriver, Donald Woods, Jr. *theologian, educator*
Shriver, Lionel (Margaret Ann Shriver) *writer*
Shrut, Arlene R. *entrepreneur, director*
Shulevitz, Uri *writer, illustrator*
Shulman, Max Rees *lawyer*
Shuman, Earl Stanley *songwriter, music publisher*
Shutran, Richard *lawyer*
Shyer, John D. *lawyer*
Sibley, David Allen *illustrator, writer, ornithologist*
Sibony, Gedi *sculptor*
Siconolfi, Michael *editor*
Sidamon-Eristoff, Anne Phipps *not-for-profit developer*
Sidamon-Eristoff, Constantine *lawyer*
Siderow, Neil *real estate company executive*
Sidran, Miriam *retired physicist*

Sidwell, David H. *bank executive*
Siebert, Muriel (Mickie) *brokerage house executive, retired bank executive*
Siegel, Arthur Herbert *finance company executive*
Siegel, Edward M. *lawyer*
Siegel, Herbert Jay *communications executive, director*
Siegel, Jeffrey Norton *lawyer*
Siegel, Lucy Boswell *public relations executive*
Siegel, Marc Monroe *television producer, scriptwriter, director*
Siegel, Marvin *newspaper editor*
Siegel, Randy *publishing executive*
Siegel, Stanley *lawyer, educator*
Siegel, Stephen *real estate company executive*
Siegfried, Jonathan D. *lawyer*
Sievert, Frederick J. *insurance company executive*
Siffert, John Sand *lawyer, educator, writer*
Sifton, Sam *editor*
Sigal-Ibsen, Rose *artist*
Sigmond, Carol Ann *lawyer*
Siguler, George William *diversified financial services company executive*
Sikander, Shahzia *artist*
Siklos, Richard *reporter*
Silber, Steven A. *lab administrator, physician*
Silberberg, Richard Howard *lawyer*
Silberman, John Alan *lawyer*
Silberman, Linda Joy *law educator*
Silbersack, John Walter *literary agent*
Silkenat, James Robert *lawyer*
Silkov, Antonina *research scientist*
Sills, Beverly (Mrs. Peter B. Greenough) *performing company executive, singer*
Silva, Daniel Joseph *writer*
Silver, Joan Micklin *film director, screenwriter*
Silver, Morris *economist, educator*
Silver, Richard Tobias *oncologist, educator*
Silver, Sheldon *state legislator, lawyer*
Silverberg, Michael Joel *lawyer*
Silverman, Arthur Charles *lawyer*
Silverman, Dan *chef*
Silverman, Eric F. *lawyer*
Silverman, Henry Richard *travel services company executive*
Silverman, Leon *lawyer*
Silverman, Martin Morris Bernard *secondary school educator*
Silverman, Moses *lawyer*
Silvers, Robert B. *editor*
Silvers, Sally *choreographer, performing company executive*
Silverstein, Ken *journalist*
Silverstein, Larry A. *real estate developer*
Silverstein, Paul N. *lawyer*
Silverstein, Samuel Charles *cellular biology and physiology professor, researcher*
Simkin, Steven *lawyer*
Simkin, Toby James *theater producer, consultant*
Simmons, Danny, Jr. *artist, poet, art gallery director, foundation administrator*
Simmons, John Derek *retired financial consultant*
Simmons, Joseph (Run Simmons, Reverend Run) *musician*
Simmons, Peter Lawrence *lawyer*
Simmons, Richard Milton Teagle *physical fitness specialist, television personality*
Simmons, Robert J. *treasurer*
Simmons, Sue *newscaster*
Simms, Marsha E. *lawyer*
Simms, Phil *sports commentator, retired professional football player*
Simon, Bruce Harvey *lawyer*
Simon, Eric Jacob *neuroscientist, educator*
Simon, Jacqueline Albert *political scientist, writer*
Simon, Ronald Charles *curator*
Simon, William H. *law educator*
Simonds, Charles Frederick *artist*
Simone, Joseph R. *lawyer*
Simons, Albert III *lawyer*
Simpkins, Neil P. *investment company executive, automotive executive*
Simpson, Mary Michael *priest, psychotherapist*
Sims, Lowery Stokes *museum curator, museum administrator, writer, educator*
Sims, William Jack *secondary school educator*
Sinagra, Jack G. *air transportation executive*
Sinclair, Daisy *communications executive*
Singer, Barbara Helen *photographer*
Singer, Joy Daniels *journalist, consultant*
Singer, Niki *media consultant*
Singleton, Donald Edward *journalist*
Sinsheimer, Warren Jack *lawyer*
Sirena, Antonia M. Fanara *artist*
Sirgado, Jo Anne E. *lawyer*
Sirico, Genaro *actor*
Sirkin, Michael S. *lawyer*
Sis, Peter *illustrator, children's book writer, filmmaker, artist*
Sischy, Ingrid Barbara *editor, art critic*
Siskind, Arthur Michael *lawyer*
Siskind, Donald Henry *lawyer*
Sisto, Elena *artist, educator*
Sitarz, Anneliese Lotte *pediatrician, educator, physician*
Sitomer, Sheila Marie *television producer, television director*
Skaistis, Rachel G. *lawyer*
Skinner, Peter Graeme *retired lawyer*
Skirnick, Robert Andrew *lawyer*
Skolnik, Richard Alan *plastic surgeon*
Skule, John L. *pharmaceutical company executive*
Sladkus, Harvey Ira *lawyer*
Slash, (Saul Hudson) *guitarist*
Slavin, Arlene *artist*
Slawsky, Donna Susan *librarian, singer*
Slazberg, Barry *corporate financial executive*
Sleed, Joel *columnist*
Sleigh, Sylvia *artist, educator*
Slifkin, Daniel *lawyer*
Slitkin, Barbara Ann *artist*
Sliwa, Curtis *radio personality, volunteer*
Sloan, Allan Herbert *journalist*
Sloane, Howard G. *lawyer*
Sloat, Richard Joel *artist*
Slomanson, Lloyd Howard *architect, musician, photographer*
Slone, Sandi *artist*
Slonem, Hunt *artist*
Sloss, John *lawyer*

Slotkin, Todd *diversified financial services company executive*
Sloujitel, Jacob Ben *mathematics professor, researcher*
Slusser, William Peter *investment banker*
Slutsky, Lorie A(nn) *foundation executive*
Small, George LeRoy *geographer, educator*
Small, Jonathan Andrew *lawyer, consultant*
Smart, Thomas A. *lawyer*
Smeall, Christopher *lawyer*
Smigel, Irwin *dentist*
Smit, Hans *law educator*
Smith, Andrew Alfred, Jr. *urban planner*
Smith, Barbara *food service executive, model*
Smith, Barry Hamilton *foundation administrator, physician*
Smith, Betty *writer, not-for-profit developer*
Smith, Brad *journalist*
Smith, Bradley Youle *lawyer*
Smith, Clare *art appraiser*
Smith, Craig Richey *thoracic surgeon*
Smith, Dennis (Edward Smith) *publishing executive, writer*
Smith, Edward Paul, Jr. *lawyer*
Smith, George Bundy *state appeals court judge*
Smith, Gordon H. *civil engineer, consultant, forensic engineer consultant*
Smith, Hilary Cranwell Bowen *investment banker*
Smith, James Walker *lawyer*
Smith, Jason A. B. *lawyer*
Smith, Jeffrey Austen *lawyer*
Smith, Jeffrey G. *lawyer*
Smith, Karen A. *lawyer*
Smith, Kiki *artist*
Smith, Liz (Mary Elizabeth Smith) *columnist, newscaster*
Smith, Malcolm Bernard *investment company executive*
Smith, Malcolm Sommerville *bass*
Smith, Martin Jay *advertising executive, marketing executive*
Smith, Raymond W. *investment banking executive*
Smith, Richard Mills *editor-in-chief*
Smith, Robert Everett *lawyer*
Smith, Robert Sherlock *state appeals court judge*
Smith, Roberta *art critic*
Smith, Shirley *artist*
Smith, Stuart A. *lawyer*
Smith, Thomas A. *lawyer, investment company executive*
Smith, Thomas Ramsaur, Jr. *lawyer*
Smith, Timothy K. *editor*
Smith, W. Keith *bank executive*
Smith, Warren Allen *writer, director, columnist*
Smith, Zak *artist*
Smith-Miller, Henry Houck *architect*
Smoak, Evan L. *lawyer*
Smotrich, David Isadore *architect*
Snider, Jerome Guy *lawyer*
Snow, Dash *photographer*
Snow, Tony *White House press secretary, political commentator, analyst*
Snyder, Jon David *dean*
Snyder, Todd *retail executive*
Snyderman, Nancy *surgeon, medical journalist*
Soave, Rosemary *internist*
Sobel, Gerald *lawyer*
Sobel, Howard D. *dermatologist*
Sobol, Thomas *education educator*
Sochet, Mary Allen *psychotherapist, educator, writer*
Softness, Donald Gabriel *marketing professional, manufacturing executive*
Sokoloff, Audrey L. *lawyer*
Solarz, Alan H. *lawyer*
Solecki, R. Stefan *anthropologist, educator*
Solender, Michael S. *lawyer*
Soley, David Benjamin *composer*
Solnit, Rebecca *writer, critic*
Solomon, Andrew P. *lawyer*
Solomon, Gail Ellen *physician*
Solomon, Howard *pharmaceutical executive*
Solomon, Libertina *pharmacist, educator*
Solomon, Maynard Elliott *musicologist, retired recording industry executive*
Solomon, Richard Hugh *art dealer, publishing executive*
Solomons, Gus, Jr. (Gustave Martinez) *choreographer, dancer, writer*
Som, Peter *apparel designer*
Somerhalder, Ian Joseph *actor*
Somers, John Arthur *insurance company executive*
Sommer, Jeff *journalist*
Sone, Yutaka *artist*
Sonett, Joshua Robert *medical educator, surgeon*
Sonneman, Eve *artist*
Sono, Masayuki *architect, artist*
Sopanen, Jeri Rainer *photography director*
Sorell, Kitty Julia *public relations executive*
Sorell Stehr, Deborah K. *lawyer*
Sorensen, Gillian Martin *United Nations official*
Sorgi, Leonard *lawyer*
Soriano, Nancy Mernit *editor-in-chief*
Sorkin, Andrew Ross *reporter, columnist*
Sorkin, David James *lawyer*
Sorkin, Ira Lee *lawyer*
Sorkin, Laurence Truman *lawyer*
Soros, George *pension fund administrator*
Sorte, John Follett *investment firm executive*
Sorter, George Hans *accounting and law educator, consultant*
Sorum, Matt *drummer*
Soter, George Nicholas *advertising executive*
Soth, Alec *photographer*
Sotomayor, Sonia *federal judge*
Sott, Janny *journalist*
Sourian, Eve Pocquet *French educator*
Soussloff, Andrew D. *lawyer*
Southworth, Robert Alexander, Jr. *education researcher, educator*
Sovern, Michael Ira *law educator*
Soyer, David *cellist, music educator*
Soyster, Margaret Blair *lawyer*
Spade, Kate (Katherine Noel Spade) *apparel designer*
Spanbock, Maurice Samuel *lawyer*
Spanfeller, James John, Jr. *publishing executive*
Spangler, Arnold Eugene *investment banker*
Spatt, Robert Edward *lawyer*
Spatz, Andre *international organization executive*
Spear, Harvey M. *lawyer*

Spears, Britney *singer*
Spector, Anita Frohmann *buyer*
Spector, Johanna Lichtenberg *ethnomusicologist, former educator*
Spector, Warren J. *investment company executive*
Spelfogel, Evan J. *lawyer, educator*
Speller, Robert Ernest Blakefield, Jr. *choreographer*
Spelling, Ian *columnist*
Spellman Sweet, Julia T. *lawyer*
Spence, Sique (Mary Stewart Spence) *art dealer*
Spencer, Charles S. *anthropologist*
Spencer, Frank Cole *medical educator*
Spencer-Fleming, Julia *writer*
Sperakis, Nicholas George *artist*
Spero, Joan Edelman *foundation administrator*
Speros, James Demitrios *advertising executive*
Speyer, James L. *oncologist*
Speyer, Jerry I. *real estate company executive*
Speziale, Richard Salvatore *financial executive*
Spiegel, Elwyn *advertising executive, art director*
Spiegel, Herbert *psychiatrist, educator*
Spielvogel, Sidney Meyer *investment banker*
Spikol, Eileen *artist*
Spillane, Dennis Kevin *lawyer*
Spinak, Jane M. *law educator*
Spindler, James Andrew *not-for-profit executive*
Spinetta, Jean-Cyril *airline executive*
Spinney, Caroll *entertainer, educator*
Spivak, Leonard A. *lawyer*
Sporn, Michael V. *producer, director*
Spoto, Donald *writer, educator*
Sprague, Peter Julian *software company executive, lecturer*
Sprayregen, James H.M. *diversified financial services company executive, lawyer*
Sprizzo, John Emilio *federal judge*
Sproule, Michael E. *insurance company executive*
Squire, Walter Charles *lawyer*
Squires, John *publishing executive*
Srednicki, Richard J. *diversified financial services company executive*
Srulowitz, Marvin *lawyer*
Stade, George Gustav *humanities educator*
Stainrook, Harry Richard *photographer, retired bank executive*
Staley, James E. *diversified financial services company executive*
Stanceu, Timothy Charles *federal judge*
Standard, Kenneth G. *lawyer*
Stang, Arnold *actor, writer, film director*
Stang, Rolf Kristian *vocalist, educator, actor, advertising executive, writer*
Stanger, Ila *editor-in-chief*
Stanley, Alessandra *critic*
Stanton, Amy *marketing executive*
Stanton, Ronald P. *export company executive*
Staples, Brent *writer, reporter*
Stapleton, Benjamin F. III *lawyer*
Starer, Brian Douglas *lawyer*
Starr, Steven Dawson *photographer*
Starren, Justin Bruce *medical educator*
Stasio, Marilyn Louise *columnist*
Stathis, Nicholas John *lawyer*
Stautberg, Susan Schiffer *communications executive*
Steber, John H. *information technology executive*
Steedman, Doria Lynne Silberberg *foundation administrator*
Steel, Danielle Fernande *author*
Steele, Howard L. *psychology professor*
Steere, William Campbell, Jr. *pharmaceutical executive*
Stefanelli, Joseph James (Joe Stefanelli) *artist*
Steffe, Cynthia *fashion designer*
Steiger, Paul Ernest *editor, journalist*
Steiger, Randi Janine *English educator*
Stein, David Fred *investment company executive*
Stein, Ellen Gail *information technology manager*
Stein, Elliot, Jr. *business executive*
Stein, Howard S. *retired banker, investment advisor, consultant*
Stein, Jane Wallison *lawyer*
Stein, Marvin *psychiatrist, historian*
Stein, Ronald J. *lawyer*
Stein, Stephen William *lawyer*
Stein, Zena A. *retired epidemiologist, retired educator*
Steinberg, Arthur Jay *lawyer*
Steinberg, Howard Eli *lawyer, diversified financial services company executive*
Steinberg, Jonathan S. *cardiologist, educator*
Steinberg, Leo *art historian, educator*
Steiner, David M. *dean*
Steiner, Jeffrey Josef *manufacturing executive*
Steinert-Threlkeld, Thomas Miller *editor, journalist*
Steines, John P., Jr. *law educator*
Steinfeld, Allan *sports association administrator*
Steinhardt, Michael H. *diversified financial services company executive*
Stelzer, Paul *cardiac surgeon, educator*
Stengel, Richard *editor*
Stephenson, Alan Clements *lawyer*
Sterling, Robert Lee, Jr. *investment company executive*
Stern, David Joel *National Basketball Association Commissioner*
Stern, Donald Allan *lawyer*
Stern, Fritz Richard *historian, educator*
Stern, Howard Allan *radio personality, television show host*
Stern, James Andrew *investment banker*
Stern, Leonard Norman *real estate developer, former pet supply manufacturing company executive*
Stern, Madeleine Bettina *rare book dealer, writer*
Stern, Mitchell *broadcast executive*
Stern, Robert Arthur Morton *architect, educator, writer*
Stern, Roslyne Paige *magazine publisher*
Stern, Walter Phillips *investment company executive*
Sternberg, Seymour *insurance company executive*
Sternman, Joel W. *lawyer*
Steuer, Richard Marc *lawyer*
Stevens, Mark Whitney *art critic*
Stevens, Michael N. *lawyer*
Stevens, Risë *performing arts association administrator*

Stevens, Rosemary A. *medicine and public health historian, artist*
Stevenson, William Henri *author*
Stever, Donald Winfred *lawyer*
Steves, Gale C. *marketing professional, writer, editor-in-chief, publishing executive*
Stewart, E(dward) Nicholson *investment management executive*
Stewart, Ellen D. *theater producer*
Stewart, Jack *artist, educator, writer*
Stewart, James B. *journalist, writer*
Stewart, Jon (Jonathan Stewart Leibowitz) *comedian, actor*
Stewart, Michael Glenn *otolaryngologist, educator*
Stewart, Richard Burleson *law educator*
Stewart, Ruth Ann *public policy educator*
Stickney, John *editor*
Stiefel, Ethan *dancer, performing company executive*
Stiglitz, Joseph Eugene *economics professor, former federal official*
Stillman, Charles Allen *lawyer*
Stimmel, Barry *cardiologist, educator, internist, dean*
Stimpson, Catharine Rosalind *literature educator, writer*
Stimpson, Scott David *lawyer*
Sting, (Gordon Matthew Sumner) *musician, songwriter, actor*
Stockton, Susan *food products executive*
Stoll, Neal Richard *lawyer*
Stoloff, Carolyn *artist, educator, poet*
Stolper, Pinchas Aryeh *religious organization executive, rabbi*
Stoltzman, Richard Leslie *clarinetist*
Stone, Caroline Fleming *artist*
Stone, David Philip *lawyer*
Stone, Merrill Brent *lawyer*
Stone, Michael Howard *psychiatry educator*
Stoopler, Mark Benjamin *physician*
Stopnik, Scott H. *lawyer*
Storch, Arthur *theater director*
Stork, Gilbert *chemistry professor*
Störmer, Horst Ludwig *physicist*
Storper, David H. *bank executive*
Stossel, John *news analyst*
Stotzky, Guenther *microbiologist, educator*
Stover, Diane Elizabeth *internist*
Strasfogel, Ian *stage director, playwright*
Strasser, Robert *architectural firm executive*
Stratigos, William Narge *computer company executive*
Straton, John Charles, Jr. *investment banker*
Stratton, Walter Love *lawyer*
Straub, Chester John *federal judge*
Straub, Gregory S. *priest*
Straus, Oscar S., II, *foundation executive*
Strauss, Carolyn *broadcast executive*
Strauss, Peter L(ester) *law educator*
Strear, Joseph D. *public relations executive*
Streator, Edward *retired diplomat, management consultant*
Strianese, Michael T. *corporate financial executive*
Strickland, Sidney *neurobiologist; educator*
Strickon, Harvey Alan *lawyer*
Stringer, Sir Howard *electronics company executive, retired media executive*
Stringer, Scott M. *city manager, former state legislator*
Strock, Marcus *lawyer*
Stroke, Hinko Henry *physicist, researcher*
Strom, Milton Gary *lawyer*
Stroman, Susan *choreographer, theater director*
Stroock, Mark Edwin, II, *public relations company executive*
Stross, Randall E. *business history professor, columnist*
Strossen, Nadine *legal association administrator, law educator*
Strum, Jay Gerson *lawyer*
Struve, Guy Miller *lawyer*
Stuart, Alice Melissa *lawyer*
Stuart, Jill *apparel designer*
Stuart, Lori Ames *public relations executive*
Stuart, Michelle Rae *artist*
Stuart, Walter Bynum, IV, *lawyer*
Stübgen, Joerg-Patrick *neurologist*
Stucky, Steven (Edward) *composer, conductor*
Studdard, Ruben (Christopher Ruben Studdard) *singer*
Studer, Patricia S. *psychologist*
Studin, Jan *publishing executive*
Sturm, Susan P. *law educator*
Sturman, Deborah Muscha *lawyer, columnist*
Sturtevant, Peter Mann, Jr. *television news executive*
Suarez-Orozco, Carola Elisabeth *psychology professor*
Subak-Sharpe, Gerald Emil *electrical engineer, educator*
Subkoff, Tara *actress, apparel designer*
Subotnick, Ali *curator, writer*
Sugarman, George *artist*
Sugarman, Irwin J. *lawyer*
Sugihara, Kenzi *publishing executive*
Sugiyama, Kazunori *music producer*
Suh, Mary *editor*
Suhler, John Stuart *investor*
Sui, Anna *fashion designer*
Sulds, Jonathan L. *lawyer*
Sulimirski, Witold Stanislaw *banker*
Sullivan, Alison Elizabeth *pediatrician, child psychiatrist*
Sullivan, Dennis P. *mathematics professor*
Sullivan, John W. *lawyer*
Sullivan, Kenneth Wayne *engineer*
Sullivan, Martin J. *insurance company executive*
Sullivan, Mary Brosnahan *advocate, social services administrator*
Sullivan, Trudy F. *apparel executive*
Sultan, Altoon *artist*
Sultan, Mark R. *plastic surgeon*
Sulzberger, Arthur Ochs *newspaper executive*
Sulzberger, Arthur Ochs, Jr. *newspaper publisher*
Summerfield, Judith Pearl *dean, English language educator*
Summit, Stuart A. *lawyer*
Sundararajan, Arun *economist, educator*
Supino, Phyllis Gail *medical researcher, educator*
Suskind, Dennis A. *investment banker*
Suskind, Ronald Steven *journalist, writer*

Sussman, Alexander Ralph *lawyer*
Sussman, Gerald *publishing company executive*
Sussman, Jeffrey Bruce *public relations and marketing executive*
Sussman, Leonard Richard *foundation executive*
Sutin, Alan N. *lawyer*
Sutton, Karen E. *museum director*
Sutton, Mark B. *diversified financial services company executive*
Suydam, John J. *lawyer*
Svenson, Charles Oscar *investment banker*
Swain, Laura Taylor *federal judge*
Swain, Robert *artist*
Swan, Philip George *librarian, educator, director, artist*
Swan, William *actor*
Swann, Brian *writer, humanities educator*
Sweed, Phyllis *publishing executive*
Sweeney, John Francis *lawyer*
Sweeney, Spencer *artist*
Sweeney, Thomas Joseph, Jr. *lawyer*
Sweet, Robert Workman *federal judge*
Sweetman, Kimberly Burke *librarian, consultant*
Swenson, Erick *painter, artist*
Swid, Stephen Claar *communications executive, director*
Swift, Ronnie Gorman *psychiatrist, educator*
Swing, William Lacy *ambassador*
Swistel, Daniel George *surgeon*
Sykes, John *communications company executive*
Sykes, Plum *writer*
Symonette, Lys *foundation executive, musician, writer*
Synnott, Aidan John *lawyer*
Szarkowski, T(haddeus) John *museum administrator*
Szeto, Yvonne *architectural firm executive*
Szymanczyk, Michael E. *tobacco products executive*
Tabbal, Nicolas G. *plastic surgeon*
Taber, Kenneth W. *lawyer*
Tagliaferri, Lee Gene *investment banker*
Taha, Assad M. *surgeon*
Tahbaz, Christopher K. *lawyer*
Takamura, Jeanette Chiyoko *dean*
Talbot, Phillips *retired Asian affairs specialist*
Talese, Gay *writer*
Talley, Truman Macdonald *publisher*
Tallmer, Margot Sallop *psychologist, gerontologist, psychoanalyst*
Talmi, Yoav *conductor, composer*
Tamaro, George John *consulting engineer*
Tamke, George William *venture capitalist*
Tan, Amy Ruth *writer*
Tanaka, Patrice Aiko *public relations executive*
Tananbaum, Steven Andrew *investment consultant*
Tancredi, Laurence Richard *law educator, psychologist*
Tanenbaum, Edward *lawyer*
Tanenbaum, Jeffrey L. *lawyer*
Tanenbaum, William Alan *lawyer*
Tanenhaus, Sam *editor*
Tang, Terry *editor, writer*
Tannenbaum, Bernice Salpeter *national religious organization executive*
Tanner, Douglas Alan *lawyer*
Tanner, Estelle Newman *oral historian*
Tanner, Harold *investment banker*
Tanselle, George Thomas *language educator, foundation administrator*
Tansey, Mark *painter*
Tapella, Gary Louis *manufacturing executive*
Taran, Leonardo *classicist, educator*
Targoff, Michael Bart *space and communications company executive*
Tarnoff, Jerome *lawyer*
Tarnofsky-Ostroff, Dawn *broadcast executive*
Tarr, Robert Joseph, Jr. *publishing executive, retail executive*
Tarter, Fred Barry *advertising executive*
Tauke, Thomas Joseph *telecommunications company executive, former congressman*
Tavel, Mark Kivey *finance company executive, economist*
Tavernise, Sabrina *journalist*
Taylor, Barbara Alden *public relations executive*
Taylor, Diana Lancaster *state official*
Taylor, Edward A. *lawyer*
Taylor, Errol Bancroft *lawyer*
Taylor, Felicia *newscaster*
Taylor, Humphrey John Fausitt *information technology executive*
Taylor, Jean Ellen *mathematics professor, researcher*
Taylor, John Chestnut III *lawyer*
Taylor, Lance Jerome *economics professor*
Taylor, Marilyn Jordan *architectural firm executive*
Taylor, Mildred D. *author*
Taylor, Paul B. *choreographer*
Taylor, Regina *actress*
Taylor, Richard William *investment banker, portfolio manager*
Taylor, Sherril Wightman *broadcast executive*
Taylor, Susan L. *magazine editor*
Taylor, Terry R. *editor, educator*
Taylor, Willard B. *lawyer*
Tchoumak, Adelina *corporate financial executive*
Teachout, Terry *writer, critic*
Teich, Howard Bernard *lawyer, volunteer, public information officer*
Teiman, Richard Barry *lawyer*
Teleanu, Florin I. *risk management consultant, financial analyst*
Temple, Donald Edward *medical association administrator*
Templeton, Fiona *poet, playwright, director, performance artist*
Tendler, David *investment company executive*
Tenenbaum, Ann G. *art association administrator*
Tenenbaum, Joseph *cardiologist*
Tenney, Dudley Bradstreet *retired lawyer*
Tepper, Lynn Marsha *gerontologist, educator*
Tepper Madover, Arielle *theater producer*
Terrell, J. Anthony *lawyer*
Terris, Lillian Dick *psychologist, health facility administrator*
Terry, Frederick Arthur, Jr. *lawyer*
Terry, James Joseph, Jr. *lawyer*
Tesori, Jeanine *composer*
Testa, Michael Harold *lawyer*

Tester, Leonard Wayne *psychology professor*
Tetzeli, Rick *editor*
Thackeray, Jonathan E. *lawyer*
Thain, John A. *stock exchange executive*
Thal, Steven Henry *lawyer, consultant*
Thalacker, Arbie Robert *lawyer, director*
Thaler, Linda Kaplan *advertising executive*
Tharoor, Shashi *international organization official*
Thattassery, Emil George *internist*
Thayer, Russell III *air transportation executive*
Theis, Martin *neuroscientist, researcher*
Thoman, G. Richard *corporate financial executive*
Thomas, Brooks *publishing executive, director*
Thomas, Cal *syndicated columnist*
Thomas, Dorothy *indexing consultant, writer*
Thomas, Helen Amelia (Mrs. Douglas B. Cornell) *editor-in-chief, former White House correspondent*
Thomas, Isiah Lord III *professional basketball coach, professional sports team executive, retired professional basketball player*
Thomas, Jeremiah Lindsay III *lawyer*
Thomas, Mory *chef*
Thomas, Richard *actor*
Thomas, Roger Warren *lawyer*
Thomas, Stephen Jay *anesthesiologist*
Thomason, Dustin *writer*
Thomasos, Denyse *artist*
Thompson, Donald Raymond *film producer, playwright*
Thompson, Jewel Taylor *music educator*
Thompson, William C., Jr. *school system administrator*
Thomson, Gerald Edmund *physician, educator*
Thomson, Todd Stuart *investment company executive*
Thornburgh, Richard Edward *bank executive*
Thoyer, Judith Reinhardt *lawyer*
Thurm, David Aaron *lawyer, publishing executive*
Thurman, Robert A.F. *theology studies educator, philosopher*
Thurston, Sally A. *lawyer*
Thurston, Thom Buster *economics professor, consultant*
Tiano, Linda V. *lawyer*
Tierney, James Edward *law educator, former state attorney general*
Tiesi, Joseph A. *corporate financial executive*
Tighe, Mary Ann *real estate company executive*
Tilewick, Robert *lawyer*
Tillinghast, David Rollhaus *lawyer*
Tillinghast, Edward Hudson III *lawyer*
Tillman, Vickie A. *financial information company executive*
Tilson, Dorothy Ruth *word processing executive*
Tilson, M(artin) David III *surgeon, scientist, educator*
Tilson Thomas, Michael *conductor, music director*
Timberlake, Justin *vocalist*
Tinsley, Boyd Calvin *musician*
Tirana, Bardyl Rifat *lawyer*
Tisch, Andrew Herbert *corporate executive*
Tisch, James Solomon *diversified holding company executive*
Tisch, Jonathan Mark *hotel company executive*
Tischler, Judith Blanche *retired publishing executive*
Tisch Sussman, Laurie *art gallery director*
Tishman, John L. *realty and construction company executive*
Tizzio, Thomas Ralph *brokerage house executive*
Tobach, Ethel *retired curator*
Toben, Doreen A. *telecommunications industry executive*
Tober, Barbara D. (Mrs. Donald Gibbs Tober) *editor*
Tobin, Eugene Marc *foundation administrator, retired academic administrator*
Tobin, Steve Robert *artist*
Todaro, Michael Paul *economics professor, consultant*
Todd, Ronald Gary *lawyer*
Toepfer, Susan Jill *editor-in-chief, editor*
Tofel, Richard Jeffrey *foundation administrator*
Toi, Zang *apparel designer*
Tolchin, Joan Gubin *psychiatrist, educator*
Toledo, Isabel *apparel designer*
Toll, Barbara Elizabeth *art gallery director*
Tolley, B. Cary III *lawyer*
Tomaselli, Fred *artist*
Tomasulo, Patricia A. *medical librarian, plant pathologist, researcher*
Tomkins, Calvin *writer*
Tommasini, Anthony *music critic, writer, musician*
Tonchi, Stefano *editor*
Tong, Kaity *anchor*
Tooker, George *artist*
Toppeta, William John *insurance company executive, lawyer*
Torrenzano, Richard *public relations executive*
Torres, Dalys E. *music educator, consultant*
Tortolani, Anthony John *surgeon, educator*
Tortorello, Nicholas John *public opinion and market research company executive*
Toulantis, Marie J. *retail executive*
Toumey, Donald Joseph *lawyer*
Tourlitsas, John Constantine *radiologist*
Tourondel, Laurent *chef*
Toussaint, Roger *labor union administrator*
Towbin, A(braham) Robert *investment banker*
Townsend, Alair Ane *publishing executive*
Townsend, Charles H. *publishing executive*
Townsend, Robert I. III *lawyer*
Toy, Stephen J. *corporate financial executive*
Tozer, W. James, Jr. *investment company executive*
Tracey, Dennis Henry III *lawyer*
Trachtenberg, Matthew J. *trust company executive*
Tract, Marc Mitchell *lawyer*
Train, John *investment advisor, federal official*
Traub, J(oseph) F(rederick) *computer scientist, educator*
Traverse, Lyn D. *not-for-profit fundraiser, communications executive*
Travis, Jeremy *academic administrator*
Travis, Sarah *orchestrator*
Treadway, James Crispin Curran Corbett *lawyer, brokerage house executive, investor, federal official*
Treaster, Joseph B. (Joseph Bland Treaster) *journalist*
Trecartin, Ryan *filmmaker*

Tree, Michael *violinist, violist, educator*
Treitel, David Henry *aviation executive*
Trent, Charles H., Jr. *social work educator*
Trepper, Myron *lawyer*
Tribe, Lee *sculptor, educator*
Trillin, Calvin *writer, journalist*
Trinkaus, John William *management educator*
Tritch, Teresa *editor, writer*
Troy, Carol Marie *neuroscientist*
Trujillo, Robert *musician*
Trump, Blaine (Martha Lindley Blaine Beard Trump) *philanthropist*
Trump, Ivanka (Ivana Marie Trump) *model, real estate company executive*
Trupp, Michael Saron *psychiatrist*
Tsao, Vivian J. *artist, educator*
Tscherny, George *graphics designer*
Tschumi, Bernard *architect*
Tse, Charles Yung Chang *pharmaceutical executive, lawyer*
Tsividis, Yannis P. *electrical engineering educator*
Tsoucalas, Nicholas *federal judge*
Tu, Jiufeng J. *physics professor*
Tuchman, Phyllis *critic*
Tuchmann, Eric P. *lawyer*
Tuck, Lily *writer*
Tucker, Alan David *publisher*
Tuft, Thomas E. *diversified financial services company executive*
Tulchin, David Bruce *lawyer*
Tung, Ko-Yung *lawyer*
Turino, Gerard Michael *internist, educator*
Turitzin, John N. *lawyer*
Turley, James S. *corporate financial executive*
Turner, Alice Kennedy *editor*
Turner, E. Deane *lawyer*
Turner, Patrick Noel Waddington *portfolio manager*
Turner, Roger D. *lawyer*
Turro, Nicholas John *chemistry professor*
Turso, Vito Anthony *government agency administrator, public information officer*
Turtil, Lawrence Charles *psychiatrist*
Tusiani, Joseph *foreign language educator, author*
Tuttle, Richard *artist*
Tween, Douglas M. *lawyer, former prosecutor*
Tyler, Dana *anchor*
Tyrangiel, Josh *editor*
Tyson, Neil DeGrasse *astrophysicist, museum director*
Tzimas, Nicholas Achilles *orthopedic surgeon, educator*
Uchitelle, Louis *journalist*
Udell, Richard *lawyer*
Uggams, Leslie *entertainer*
Ule, Guy Maxwell, Jr. *stockbroker*
Ulin, Richard Irwin *pediatric orthopedist, educator*
Ulrich, Lars *drummer*
Umansky, Diane *editor-in-chief*
Underberg, Mark Alan *lawyer*
Underwood, Carrie Marie *singer*
Ungaro, Susan Kelliher *foundation administrator, former magazine editor*
Unger, David C. *journalist*
Unger, Peter Kenneth *philosophy educator*
Unger, Sydney Elliott *lawyer*
Ungvarski, Peter J. *nursing administrator*
Updike, Helen Hill *financial advisor*
Upham, Frank K. *law educator*
Upmacis, Rita Karina *chemist*
Upright, Diane Warner *art dealer*
Upson, Stuart Barnard *advertising agency executive*
Uram, Gerald Robert *lawyer*
Urban, Amanda (Binky Urban) *literary agent*
Ureña, Alex *chef*
Urowsky, Richard J. *lawyer*
Urroz-Rapold, Patricia Julia S. *retired diplomat, writer*
Vaidhyanathan, Siva *journalist, educator*
Valbuena, Vivian *brokerage house executive*
Valdes-Rodriguez, Alisa *writer*
Valente, Peter Charles *lawyer*
Valentine, James Burgon *musician*
Valletta, Amber *actress, model*
Van Bosse, Harold J.P. *orthopedic surgeon*
Van de Bovenkamp, Sue Erpf *foundation administrator*
Vanden Heuvel, Katrina *publishing executive*
Van Dine, Vance *investment banker*
Van Halen, Eddie (Edward Lodewijk Van Halen) *musician*
van Hengel, Maarten *banker*
Van Gelder, Greta Conway *newscaster, lawyer*
Van Tran, Tam *painter*
Vardell, James C. III *lawyer*
Varet, Michael A. *lawyer*
Vargas, Elizabeth *newscaster*
Varmus, Harold Eliot *health science administrator, educator, science researcher*
Varney, Carleton Bates, Jr. *interior designer, columnist, playwright*
Varone, Douglas Joseph *choreographer*
Vassallo, Edward E. *lawyer*
Vassil, John Charles *lawyer*
Vaughan, Edwin Darracott, Jr. *urologist, surgeon*
Vaughn, Dona D. *performing company executive*
Veale, Scott *editor, columnist*
Vecsey, George Spencer *sports columnist*
Vega, Matias Alfonso *lawyer*
Vega, Suzanne *singer, songwriter*
Veneman, Ann Margaret *international organization executive, former secretary of agriculture*
Verde, Michael I. *lawyer*
Vermeer, Maureen Dorothy *sales executive*
Vermeulen, Kevin J. *publishing executive*
Vernon, Darryl Mitchell *lawyer*
Verongos, Helen *editor*
Veronneau-Troutman, Suzanne *retired ophthalmologist*
Versfelt, David Scott *lawyer*
Vetrocq, Marcia E. *editor*
Vick, Edward Hoge, Jr. *advertising executive*
Vick, James Albert *publishing executive, consultant*
Victor, A. Paul *lawyer*
Vidal, David Jonathan *insurance company executive, journalist*
Vidal, Gore *writer*
Vieira, Meredith *television personality*

Viener, John D. *lawyer*
Vig, Vernon Edward *lawyer*
Viladas, Pilar *editor*
Vilcek, Jan Tomas *immunologist, medical educator*
Vilchez, Ricardo S. *library director*
Vine, David *lawyer*
Vine, Stephen M. *lawyer*
Vinegrad, Alan *prosecutor*
Vingoe, D. Grant *lawyer*
Viniar, David *investment banker*
Vining, Barbara *lawyer*
Viñoly, Rafael *architectural firm executive*
Violette, Banks *painter, sculptor*
Virtue, Ted *investment company executive*
Visser, Lesley *sports correspondent*
Vitale, Alberto Aldo *retired publishing company executive*
Vitale, Thomas M. *lawyer*
Vitkalov, Sergey A. *physicist, educator*
Vittor, Kenneth Mark *lawyer*
Vladeck, Judith Pomarlen *lawyer*
Vlahov, David *epidemiologist*
Vlamis, Susan (Suzanne) Anne *editor, photographer*
Vogelman, Joseph Herbert *scientific engineering company executive*
Vogt, Douglas *news cameraman, journalist*
Volk, Kristin *advertising agency executive*
Volk, Norman Ilans *financial executive*
Volk, Stephen Richard *diversified financial services company executive, investment banker, lawyer*
Vollbracht, Michael *apparel designer, illustrator*
Vollmann, William T. *writer*
Vollweiler, Cheryl P. *lawyer*
von Baillou, Astrid *executive search consultant*
von der Heyden, Karl Mueller *retired manufacturing executive*
von Fraunhofer-Kosinski, Katherina *bank executive, advertising executive*
Vongerichten, Jean-Georges *food service executive*
von Mehren, Robert Brandt *retired lawyer*
Vonnegut, Kurt, Jr. *writer*
Voorsanger, Bartholomew *architect*
Vora, Ashok *financial economist*
Voss, Linda I. *finance company executive*
Vourvoulias-Bush, Alberto *arts editor*
Vyskocil, Mary Kay *lawyer*
Wachs, Joel *former city councilman, foundation administrator*
Wachsberger, Chaim *lawyer*
Wachtel, Norman Jay *lawyer*
Wachtell, Herbert M. *lawyer*
Wackermann, William *publishing executive*
Waddell, Mark E. *lawyer*
Wade, Estelle B. *psychologist, psychoanalyst*
Wadsworth, John (Jack) Spencer, Jr. *investment banker*
Wagner, Alan Cyril *television and film producer, consultant, performing arts educator*
Wagner, Robin Samuel Anton *stage and set designer*
Wailand, George *lawyer*
Waks, Jay Warren *lawyer*
Wald, Bernard Joseph *lawyer*
Wald, Richard Charles *media consultant, educator*
Wald, Sylvia *artist*
Wald, Wayne A. *lawyer*
Walden, Jennifer Lee *plastic surgeon*
Walden, Shelton Harrison *radio personality, educator*
Waldenberg, Alan S. *lawyer*
Waldman, Seymour Morton *lawyer*
Waldron, Jeremy James *law educator*
Walgren, Frances J. *art appraiser*
Walker, Alice *writer*
Walker, Jeffrey Clemens *venture capitalist*
Walker, Jennie Louise *not-for-profit fundraiser, consultant*
Walker, John Lockwood *lawyer*
Walker, Kara *artist*
Walker, Kim A. *lawyer*
Walker, Mort *cartoonist*
Walker, Robert Harris *historian, writer, editor*
Wall, Charles R. *lawyer*
Wallace, Christopher *broadcast television correspondent*
Wallace, Daniel *writer*
Wallace, Edward Corbett *lawyer*
Wallace, Nora Ann *lawyer*
Wallace, Thomas C. *editor, publishing executive*
Wallace, Thomas J. *editorial director*
Wallace, Walter C. *lawyer, government official*
Wallach, Eli *actor*
Wallach, Erik Jean *lawyer*
Walleck, Joel Jeffrey *psychiatrist*
Waller, Robert James *writer*
Walpin, Gerald *lawyer*
Walter, Ingo *economics professor*
Walter, Jess *writer*
Walters, Barbara Jill *broadcast journalist*
Walters, Milton James *investment banker*
Walton, Anthony John (Tony Walton) *set designer, illustrator, writer*
Waltuck, David *chef, restaurant owner*
Wanek, William Charles *public relations executive*
Wang, Albert Huai-En *lawyer*
Wang, Frederick Mark *pediatrician, ophthalmologist, educator*
Wang, Guangya *ambassador, international organization official*
Wang, John *not-for-profit company executive*
Wang, Lu-Hai *medical educator, biochemist*
Wang, Vera *fashion designer*
Wang, Xinshing *lawyer*
Wank, Gerald Sidney *periodontist, educator*
Wanner, Eric *foundation executive*
Ward, Aaron *professional hockey player*
Ward, Geoffrey Champion *writer, editor*
Warden, John Lehman *lawyer*
Wardropper, Ian Bruce *museum curator, educator*
Wareham, Raymond Noble *brokerage house executive*
Waren, Stanley Arnold *academic administrator, performing company administrator*
Warner, Miner Hill *investment banker*
Warner, Peter David *publishing executive*
Warnke, Gordon E. *lawyer*
Warren, Arete Bernice *art historian*
Warren, David P. *stock exchange executive*
Warren, Irwin Howard *lawyer*

Warren, James I. *lawyer*
Warren, Russell Frederick *orthopedist*
Warren, William Bradford *lawyer*
Washburn, David Thacher *lawyer*
Washburn, Joan Thomas *small business owner*
Washburn, Phoebe *artist*
Washington, Clarence Edward, Jr. *insurance company executive*
Wasow, Omar *Internet company executive*
Wasser, Henry *retired American literature and sociology educator*
Wasserman, Steve *literary agent*
Wasserstein, Bruce *investment banker*
Waters, Donald Joseph *data processing executive*
Watkins, Charles Booker, Jr. *mechanical engineering educator*
Watson, Anthony L. *health facility executive*
Watson, Robert Jose *professional sports team executive*
Watson, Solomon Brown, IV, *lawyer, publishing executive*
Watt, Douglas (Benjamin Watt) *writer, drama critic*
Wattleton, Faye (Alyce Faye Wattleton) *educational association administrator, advocate*
Waxenberg, Jay David *lawyer*
Waxman, Allen *pharmaceutical executive*
Waxman, Anita *theater producer*
Waxman, Wendy *set designer*
Wayne, Leslie *reporter*
Weber, Lisa M. *insurance company executive*
Weber, Robert Maxwell *cartoonist*
Webster, Catherine T. *telecommunications industry executive*
Webster, Lesley Daniels *bank executive*
Webster, Susan *lawyer*
Wechsler, Gil *lighting designer*
Wedgeworth, Ann *actress*
Weeks, David Frank *foundation administrator*
Weems, Carrie Mae *photographer*
Ween, Martin M. *lawyer*
Weiksner, Sandra S. *lawyer*
Weil, Frank A. *investment banker, lawyer*
Weil, Rex *artist, art critic*
Weiland, Andrew J. *orthopaedic surgeon*
Weiland, Scott Richard *singer*
Weil-Garris Brandt, Kathleen (Kathleen Brandt) *art historian*
Weill, Sanford I. (Sandy Weill) *former diversified financial services company executive*
Weinberg, Adam D. *museum director*
Weinberg, H. Barbara *art historian, educator, curator*
Weinberg, Herschel Mayer *lawyer*
Weinberg, Jeffrey J. *lawyer*
Weinberg, John Sidney *investment banker*
Weinberg, Max *musician*
Weinberg, Peter Amory *investment banker*
Weinberger, Eliot *literary essayist, poet, translator*
Weinberger, Harold Paul *lawyer*
Weinberger, Mark Alan *corporate financial executive, former federal agency administrator*
Weiner, Andrew Jay *lawyer*
Weiner, Earl David *lawyer*
Weiner, Lawrence Charles *artist*
Weiner, Stephen Arthur *lawyer*
Weiner, Timothy Emlyn *newspaper journalist*
Weiner, Walter Herman *bank executive, lawyer*
Weingarten, Marc *lawyer*
Weingarten, Rhonda (Randi Weingarten) *labor union administrator, lawyer*
Weingrow, Howard Louis *finance company executive*
Weinrauch, Harry *physician*
Weinreb, Tzvi Hersh *religious organization administrator, rabbi*
Weinroth, Lois L. *lawyer*
Weinschel, Alan Jay *lawyer*
Weinstein, Herbert *chemical engineer, educator*
Weinstein, I. Bernard *oncologist, director, geneticist, educator*
Weinstein, Martin *aerospace transportation executive, manufacturing executive, materials scientist*
Weinstein, Sidney *retired university program director*
Weinstock, Leonard *lawyer*
Weinstock, Rose *artist*
Weintz, Jacob Frederick, Jr. *retired investment banker*
Weisberg-Samuels, Janet S. *psychologist*
Weisbrod, Carl *lawyer, public official*
Weiss, Carol Juliet *psychiatrist*
Weiss, Donald S. *real estate developer*
Weiss, Jonathan Arthur *lawyer*
Weiss, Lawrence N. *lawyer*
Weiss, Lisa Ann *lawyer*
Weiss, Melvyn I. *lawyer*
Weiss, Myrna Grace *management consultant*
Weiss, Paul Richard *plastic surgeon*
Weiss, Samuel Abraham *psychologist, psychoanalyst*
Weissman, David L. *lawyer*
Weissman, Myrna M. *epidemiologist, researcher, medical educator*
Weissman, Walter *artist, photographer*
Weissmann, Andrew *lawyer, former prosecutor*
Weissmann, Gerald *internist, researcher, educator, editor, writer*
Weithorn, Stanley Stephen *lawyer*
Weitzner, Harold *mathematics professor*
Welch, Martha Grace *physician, researcher*
Weld, Jonathan Minot *lawyer*
Wellin, Keith Sears *investment banker*
Wellington, Harry Hillel *lawyer, educator*
Wells, Christopher M. *lawyer*
Wells, Peter Scoville *retired marketing professional*
Wells, Rebecca *writer*
Wells, Theodore V., Jr. *lawyer*
Welsh, Donald Emory *publisher*
Welshimer, Mark J. *lawyer*
Weltman, Edward S. *lawyer*
Wemple, Erik C. *editor-in-chief*
Wen, George Walter Sun *editor*
Wender, Ira Tensard *lawyer*
Wender, Phyllis Bellows *literary agent*
Wendlandt, Gary E. *insurance company executive*
Wenegrat, Saul S. *art association administrator*
Wenig, Cindy L. *lawyer*
Wenig, Devin Norse *communications executive*

Wenner, Jann Simon *editor, publisher*
Werder, Richard I., Jr. *lawyer*
Werfelman, William Herman, Jr. *public relations executive*
Werman, David Sanford *psychiatrist, psychoanalyst*
Werner, Robert L. *lawyer, consultant*
Werthamer, Nathan Richard *physicist*
Wesely, Edwin Joseph *lawyer*
Wesely, Marissa Celeste *lawyer*
Wesley, Eric *sculptor, artist*
Wesley, John Mercer *artist*
Wesley, Richard C. *federal judge*
West, Kanye *rap artist*
West, Paul Noden *writer, playwright*
West, Stephen Kingsbury *lawyer, director*
Westin, David Lawrence *broadcast executive, lawyer*
Westman, Barbara *artist*
Westphalen, Olav *artist, sculptor*
Westreich, Neil P. *lawyer*
Wetmore, Keith Chidester *lawyer*
Wexelbaum, Michael *lawyer*
Wexler, Allan *architect, educator*
Wexler, Leonard Howard *pediatric oncologist*
Wexler, Patricia Susan *dermatologist, surgeon*
Wexler, Peter John *artist, photographer, theater designer*
Weyman, Todd D. *art appraiser*
Whaley, Charles Henry, IV, *communications company executive*
Wharton, Danny Carroll *zoo biologist*
Wharton, Ralph Nathaniel *psychiatrist, educator*
Wheeldon, Christopher *dancer, choreographer*
Wheeler, Ward Christopher *curator*
Wheeler, William J. *insurance company executive*
Whelan, William J. III *lawyer*
Whitaker, G(eorge) Warren *lawyer*
White, Edmund Valentine *writer*
White, Fred B. III *lawyer*
White, George Cooke *theater director, foundation administrator*
White, Harry Edward, Jr. *lawyer*
White, Jack (John Anthony Gillis) *musician, producer*
White, John Patrick *lawyer*
White, Kate *editor-in-chief*
White, Lawrence J. *economics professor*
White, Lillias *actress*
White, Mary Jo *lawyer, former prosecutor*
White, W. Christopher *lawyer*
Whited, Mary Elizabeth *marketing professional*
Whitehead, Edgar Douglas *urology educator*
Whiteman, Douglas E. *publisher*
Whiting, Anthony *executive search consultant*
Whiting, Gordon James *investment banker*
Whiting, Susan Dickinson *media research company executive*
Whitman, Martin J. *portfolio manager*
Whitmer, Frederick Lee *lawyer*
Whitney, Craig Richard *journalist*
Whitney, Jonathan B. *lawyer*
Whitney, Phyllis Ayame *author*
Whitson, Jerry E. *lawyer*
Whitt, Ward *science educator*
Whittemore, Laurence Frederick *bank executive*
Whittingham, Charles Arthur *library director, publishing executive*
Whitty, Jeff *playwright, actor*
Whoriskey, Robert Donald *lawyer*
Whyatt, Robin M. *healthcare educator*
Wibisono, Makarim *diplomat*
Wickens, Drew C. *finance director*
Widing, Eric P. *auction specialist*
Widlund, Olof Bertil *computer science educator, mathematician*
Wiener, Marvin S. *rabbi, editor, executive*
Wiesel, Torsten Nils *neurobiologist, educator*
Wigley, Mark Antony *architecture educator*
Wigmore, Barrie Atherton *investment banker*
Wijnberg, Sandra S. *professional services company executive*
Wilcox, John Caven *lawyer, financial executive*
Wilcox, T.J. *filmmaker*
Wildermuth, Bruce R. *lawyer*
Wilds, Bonnie *writer, volunteer*
Wile, Joan *composer, lyricist, singer*
Wiles, Michael E. *lawyer*
Wiley-Hart, Debra *musician, educator*
Wilford, John Noble, Jr. *science news correspondent*
Wilkins, Amy P. *publishing executive*
Wilkinson, John Hart *lawyer*
Willams, Michael *editor*
Willen, Liz *reporter*
Willett, John A. *lawyer*
Willett, Roslyn Leonore *public relations executive, food service consultant, writer, editor*
Williams, Anthony *lawyer*
Williams, Brian *network news anchor*
Williams, Christopher *investment company executive*
Williams, Christopher *photographer*
Williams, Dave Harrell *investment company executive*
Williams, Frederick Boyd *priest*
Williams, Ian George *writer*
Williams, Lena *sportswriter*
Williams, Marsha E. *broadcast executive*
Williams, Michael G. *publishing executive*
Williams, Montel *television talk show host*
Williams, Patricia J. *law educator*
Williams, Sue *artist*
Williams, Vanessa (Vanessa Lynn Williams) *recording artist, actress*
Williams, Vaughn Charles *lawyer*
Williams, William John, Jr. *lawyer*
Williamson, Douglas Franklin, Jr. *lawyer*
Williamson, Richard Salisbury *ambassador*
Willig, Kenneth C. H. *lawyer*
Willis, Carol *museum director*
Willis, William Ervin *lawyer*
Willner, Barry A. *lawyer*
Willner, Judith P. *clinical geneticist, pediatrician, educator*
Willumstad, Robert B. *insurance company executive, retired bank executive*
Wils, Madelyn *film company executive*
Wilson, Cassandra *singer*
Wilson, Daniel H. *robotics engineer, writer*

Wilson, Don Matthew III *corporate banking executive*
Wilson, Edwin *theater director*
Wilson, Marie C. *foundation administrator*
Wilson, Mike *journalist*
Wilson, Paul Holliday, Jr. *lawyer*
Wilson, Peter Scott *lawyer*
Wilson, Robert Frank *retired real estate broker, artist*
Wilson, Rowan D. *lawyer*
Winawer, Sidney J. *physician, educator*
Windels, James H.R. *lawyer*
Windels, Paul, Jr. *lawyer*
Windhager, Erich Ernst *physiologist, educator*
Winerip, Michael *reporter*
Winfield, Richard Neill *lawyer*
Wing, John Russell *lawyer*
Winick, Myron *nutrition professor, physician*
Winkelried, Jon A. *investment banker*
Winkler, Matthew Adam *editor-in-chief, reporter, editor*
Winn, H. Richard *surgeon*
Winship, Frederick Moery *journalist*
Winston, Arnold *psychiatrist, educator*
Winston, Mary A. *publishing executive*
Winterer, Philip Steele *lawyer*
Winters, William Thomas *bank executive*
Wintner, Mark S. *lawyer*
Wintour, Anna *editor-in-chief*
Wintrob, Jay S. *insurance company executive*
Wise, Aaron Noah *lawyer*
Wiseman, Michael Martin *lawyer*
Wisner, Frank George *insurance company executive, former ambassador*
Wit, Harold Maurice *retired investment banker, lawyer*
Witherell, Mary *editor*
Witkin, Eric Douglas *lawyer*
Witmeyer, John Jacob III *lawyer*
Witten, Roger Michael *lawyer*
Wittes, Robert E. *physician, science foundation director*
Wittstein, Edwin Frank *theater director, set designer*
Witzel, Steven M. *lawyer*
Wixom, William David *art historian, museum administrator, educator*
Woetzel, Kurt D. *banking executive*
Wohl, Frank Harold *lawyer*
Wohrle, Marta *publishing executive*
Wolden, Suzanne Leesa *pediatric radiation oncologist*
Woletz, Robert G. *editor*
Wolf, Barry M. *lawyer*
Wolf, Naomi *writer*
Wolf, Peter *singer, composer*
Wolf, Peter Michael *investment manager, consultant, writer*
Wolfe, George C. *theater director, producer, playwright*
Wolfe, James Ronald *retired lawyer*
Wolfe, Scott W. *orthopedic hand surgeon*
Wolfe, Tom (Thomas Kennerly Wolfe Jr.) *writer, journalist*
Wolff, Alejandro Daniel *ambassador*
Wolff, Edward Nathan *economist, educator*
Wolff, Jesse David *lawyer*
Wolff, Larry *history professor*
Wolff, Richard Joseph *public relations executive, consultant, historian*
Wolff, Virginia Euwer *writer*
Wolff, William F. III *investment banker*
Wolff, William I. *surgeon, educator*
Wolfson, Jordan *artist*
Wolitzer, Steven Barry *investment banker*
Wolkoff, Eugene Arnold *lawyer*
Wolkoff, Neal L. *stock exchange executive*
Wollman, Eric *lawyer*
Wolman, William *economist, journalist, broadcaster*
Wolnek, Stephen S. *religious organization administrator*
Wong, Andrea *broadcast executive*
Woo, Alex *jewelry designer*
Wood, Jerry *investment company executive*
Wood, Kimba M. *federal judge*
Wood, Ronald *musician*
Woodruff, Bob *newscaster*
Woodruff, Jay Noel *editor, writer*
Woodruff, Mark Reed *magazine editor*
Woods, Dan *information technology manager, consultant*
Woods, Emily *apparel executive*
Woods, Joycelyn Sue *alcohol/drug abuse services professional*
Woods, Stuart *writer*
Woodward, Joanne Gignilliat *actress*
Woodward, Kirk *theater director*
Woolard, Edgar S., Jr. *retired chemical company executive*
Woolery, James C. *lawyer*
Worman, Howard Jay *internist, educator*
Worsham, Hal Glenn *marketing professional*
Wortman, Marlene Stein *historian*
Wortman, Richard S. *historian, educator*
Wray, Cecil, Jr. *lawyer*
Wren, Gayden *playwright, theater director*
Wren, John D. *advertising executive*
Wright, Bob (Robert C. Wright) *broadcast executive*
Wright, Deborah C. *bank executive*
Wright, Douglas *playwright*
Wright, Faith-dorian *artist*
Wright, Gwendolyn *writer, architecture educator, historian*
Wright, Jason Howard Sebastian *communications executive*
Wright, Sarah Elizabeth *writer, poet*
Wright, Tony *advertising executive*
Wrobel, Bruce J. *energy and utilities company executive*
Wucker, Michele *educational association administrator, writer*
WuDunn, Sheryl *journalist, correspondent*
Wunderman, Jan Darcourt *artist*
Wuorinen, Charles Peter *composer*
Wurmfeld, Sanford *artist, educator*
Wyeth, James Browning *artist*
Wylde, Kathryn S. *business organization executive*
Wylie, James Malcolm *adult education educator*
Wynne, William Francis *lawyer*

Wyschogrod, Edith *philosophy educator*
Wyss, David Alen *diversified financial services company executive*
Wyzner, Eugeniusz *diplomat*
Yablon, Heather D. *lawyer*
Yadeka, Theophilus Adeniyi *hospital administrator*
Yaffe, James *writer*
Yalen, Gary N. *retired insurance company executive*
Yamaguchi, Masaya *musician, educator*
Yamin, Michael Geoffrey *lawyer*
Yancey, Richard Charles *investment banker*
Yankwitt, George B(ruce) *lawyer*
Yao, David Da-Wei *engineering educator*
Yardley, Jim *journalist*
Yastine, Barbara A. *diversified financial services company executive*
Yee, Kenton K. *educator*
Yegulalp, Tuncel M. *mining engineer, educator*
Yelenick, Mary Therese *lawyer*
Yerman, Fredric Warren *lawyer*
Yerushalmi, Yosef Hayim *historian, educator*
Yetman, Gary *investment company executive*
Yeung, Bernard Yin *finance educator*
Yglesias, Helen Bassine *author, educator*
Yishan, Zhang *ambassador*
Yodowitz, Edward Jay *lawyer*
Yoffie, Erich H. *religious organization administrator*
Yohay, Steven Jacob *healthcare company executive, consultant*
Yoshiuchi, Ellen Haven *healthcare educator, clinical counselor*
Youm, Thomas *orthopedist, surgeon*
Young, Alice *lawyer*
Young, Bruce Kenneth *obstetrician, gynecologist, educator*
Young, David *publishing executive*
Young, Estelle Irene *dermatologist, educator*
Young, Genevieve Leman *publishing executive, editor*
Young, George Haywood III *investment banker*
Young, John Edward *lawyer*
Young, John Lloyd *actor*
Young, John Sacret *writer, film director, film producer*
Young, Jonathan *lawyer*
Young, Michael Warren *geneticist, educator*
Young, Nancy *lawyer*
Young, Robert Craig *banker*
Younger, Kirsten Jeanne *painting restoration specialist*
Youngwood, Alfred Donald *lawyer*
Yu, Andrew *writer*
Yu, Jean *apparel designer*
Yu, Pauline Ruth *former dean, educational association administrator*
Yu, Yi-Hao *endocrinologist, educator, physician, research scientist*
Yuferov, Vadim *research scientist*
Yurchenco, Henrietta Weiss *musicologist, writer*
Yurt, Roger William *surgeon, educator*
Zabel, William David *lawyer*
Zacharias, Athos *artist*
Zachem, Tyler *investment company executive*
Zackheim, Michele *artist*
Zackheos, H.E. Sotirios *ambassador*
Zagat, Nina *publishing executive*
Zagat, Tim *publishing executive*
Zagorin, Janet Susan *legal firm administrator, marketing professional*
Zahnd, Richard H. *sports association executive, lawyer*
Zaitzeff, Roger Michael *lawyer*
Zalaznick, Lauren *broadcast executive*
Zamarra, Galen *chef*
Zammit, Joseph Paul *lawyer*
Zand, Dale Ezra *business management educator*
Zannino, Richard F. *publishing executive*
Zarghami, Cyma *broadcast executive*
Zauderer, Mark Carl *lawyer*
Zawistowski, Stephen Louis *psychologist, educator*
Zedrosser, Joseph John *lawyer*
Zeichner, Harvey *psychologist*
Zeitlin, Jide James *investor*
Zeldin, Richard Packer *publisher*
Zelinsky, Edward Alan *law educator*
Zeller, Tom, Jr. *journalist*
Zerin, Steven David *lawyer*
Zeuschner, Erwin Arnold *brokerage house executive*
Zhang, Xian *conductor*
Zhang, Xudong *literature and language professor, department chairman*
Ziegler, Henry Steinway *lawyer*
Ziegler, John Augustus, Jr. *lawyer*
Zifchak, William C. *lawyer*
Zimand, Harvey Folks *lawyer*
Zimbalist, Michael *publishing executive*
Zimmer, William *art critic*
Zimmerman, Diane Leenheer *law educator*
Zimmerman, Elyn *artist*
Zimmerman, Sol Shea *pediatrician*
Zimmerman, William Edwin *editor, writer*
Zimmett, Mark Paul *lawyer, educator*
Zinczenko, David *publishing executive*
Zinn, Keith Marshall *ophthalmologist, educator*
Zinoman, Jason *theater critic*
Zirinsky, Bruce R. *lawyer*
Zirinsky, Susan *television producer*
Zito, Robert John Amadeus *lawyer*
Zitrin, Arthur *physician*
Zittel, Andrea *painter, sculptor*
Zivin, Norman H. *lawyer*
Zochowski, T. Robert, Jr. *lawyer*
Zoellick, Robert Bruce *diversified financial services company executive, former federal agency administrator*
Zombie, Rob (Robert Cummings) *musician, filmmaker*
Zoogman, Nicholas Jay *lawyer*
Zorn, John *composer, musician*
Zornow, David Merrill *lawyer*
Zosike, Joanie Fritz *theater director, actress*
Zotos, Frederic P. *research and development company executive*
Zubkoff, Daniel J. *lawyer*
Zucker, Stefan *tenor, writer, editor, commentator*
Zucker-Franklin, Dorothea *internist, educator*

Zuckerman, Mortimer Benjamin *editor, real estate developer*
Zuckerman, Paul Herbert *lawyer*
Zugazagoitia, Julian *museum director*
Zukerman, Michael *lawyer*
Zukerman, Pinchas *concert violinist, violist, conductor*
Zulack, Mary Marsh *law educator*
Zweibel, Joel Burton *retired lawyer*
Zwickler, Allen *investment advisor, educator*

**Newark**
Biddle, Jane Lammert *retired English educator*
Hemmings, Madeleine Blanchet *management consultant, not-for-profit administrator, media consultant*
Reid, James Edward *lawyer*

**Newburgh**
Adams, Barbara *language educator, poet, writer*
Fothergill, Lee James *mathematics professor*
Sakac, Sister Ann *academic administrator*

**Newcomb**
Chatzky, Herbert *music educator*

**Newport**
West, Susan R. *elementary school educator, consultant*
Wilson, Eldon Ray *minister*

**Niagara Falls**
Askins, Arthur James *accountant, auditor*
Bharadwaj, Prem Datta *physics professor*
DeFelice, Eugene Anthony *internist, educator, magician*
DiVita-Frommert, Angela Marie *music educator*
Hawkins De Golier, Danielle *political activist*
Knowles, Richard Norris *chemist*
Schifano, Kath M. *artist, educator*

**Niagara University**
Denig, Stephen Joseph *education educator*
Osberg, Timothy Michael *psychologist, educator, researcher*

**Niakayuna**
Lu, Hai *electrical engineer, physicist*

**Niskayuna**
Eberhard, Jeffrey W. *physicist, researcher*
Edelheit, Lewis S. *research physicist*
Fatić, Vuk Marko *electrical engineer, educator, researcher*
Feitelberg, Alan S. *chemical engineer*
Hu, Qingying *optical engineer*
Huening, Walter Carl, Jr. *retired consulting application engineer*
Kambour, Roger Peabody *retired polymer physical chemist, researcher*
Kapur, Ajay *systems engineer*
Mangan, John Leo *retired electric power industry executive, international trade specialist*
Nichols, Albert Myron *retired minister*
Qu, Ronghai *electrical engineer*
Rawson, James Rulon Young *chemist*
Sanborn, Stephen D. *systems engineer*
Varanasi, Kripa Kiran *research scientist*
Wan, Julin *materials scientist*
White, Frederick Andrew *retired physics professor, retired physicist*
Wright, Theodore Paul, Jr. *political science professor*

**North Babylon**
Zitt, Myron J. *allergist, immunologist*

**North Bellmore**
Trigoboff, Sybelle *artist, educator*

**North Blenheim**
Rotterdam, Paul Zwietnig *artist, retired art educator*

**North Collins**
Bowman, Georgianne *historian, reporter*
Cataldo, John *principal*

**North Salem**
Mittelstadt, Beverly Anne *elementary school educator*

**North Tonawanda**
Greenberg, Michael Jay *accountant*
Megahed, Mohamed Salah *neurologist, educator*
Powers, Bruce Raymond *writer, language educator, consultant*
Zimmerman, Bonnie Elizabeth *physical education educator*

**North White Plains**
Erla, Karen *artist, painter, collagist, printmaker*

**Northport**
De Carolis, Philip Joseph *space designer, educator*
Donenfeld, Kenneth Jay *management consultant*
Graber, Mark L. *internist*
Hohenberger, Patricia Julie *fine arts and antique appraiser, consultant*
Miller, Philip John *insurance agent, consultant*
Reinertsen, Norman *retired air transportation executive*
Weber, Ray Everett *engineering executive, consultant*
Yeh, Shing-shing *geriatrician, researcher, internist*

**Norwich**
Koon, Thomas Robert *engineering educator, consultant*
Mayo, Mary E. *music educator, conductor*

**Norwood**
Church, Richard Dwight *electrical engineer, scientist*

**Nyack**
Chien, Jennie *sculptor*
Cozart, Helen Ray *church administrator, educator*
Degenshein, Jan *architect, planner*

Hendin, David Bruce *literary agent, writer, numismatist, educator*
Karp, Peter Simon *marketing executive*
Keil, John Mullan *advertising executive, artist*
Mann, Kenneth Walker *retired minister, psychologist*
Meriwether, Heath J. *newspaper consultant, retired newspaper publisher*
Oursler, Fulton, Jr. *editor, writer*

**Oakland Gardens**
Polak, Emil Joseph *history professor, researcher*

**Oceanside**
Bider, Bruce Evan *music educator, director*
Kyler, Arlene *advertising executive*

**Ogdensburg**
Cunningham, Robert Joseph *bishop*
Smith, Carol Ann *academic administrator*

**Old Chatham**
Severs, Charles A. III *lawyer*

**Old Westbury**
Adams, Mac *art educator, sculptor*
Altabet, Meryl Joyce *mathematics professor*
Christofides, Fotine *parochial school educator*
Gordon, Florence Shanfield *mathematics professor*
O'Brien, Adrienne Gratia *communications educator*
Ozelli, Tunch *economics professor*
van Wie, Paul David *secondary school educator, historian*

**Olivebridge**
Osborne, Seward Russell *writer*

**Oneida**
Halbritter, Ray (Arthur Raymond Halbritter) *Native American tribal leader*
Matthews, William Doty *lawyer, director, consumer products company executive*

**Oneonta**
Beitzel, Brian *educational psychologist*
Freckelton, Sondra *artist*
Hickey, Francis Roger *physicist, researcher*
Hill, Donald Raymond *anthropologist, educator*
Horner, Carl Matthew *chemistry professor*
Insinga, Richard Charles *manufacturing company executive, marketing educator*
Johnson, Richard David *retired librarian*
Malhotra, Ashok Kumar *philosophy educator*
Pignato, Joseph Michael *composer, music educator, musician*
vom Saal, Walter *psychology professor*
Wyshock, Michael Thomas *artist, educator*

**Ontario**
Blackman, Lani Modica *copy editor*

**Orangeburg**
Filippelli, James Anthony *literature and language educator*
Filoramo, Dorothy Christine *academic administrator*
Greenberg, William Michael *psychiatrist*
Lajtha, Abel *biochemist*
Levine, Jerome *psychiatrist, educator*
Nixon, Ralph Angus *psychiatrist, educator, research neuroscientist*
Yaragudri, Vinod K. *neuroscientist, researcher*

**Orchard Park**
Carducci, Donald Joseph *music educator*
Gloss, Wendy *principal*
Jauron, Dick (Richard M. Jauron) *professional football coach*
Keenan, John Paul *leadership and management educator, consultant, director, psychologist*
Lee, Richard Vaille *internist, educator*
Levy, Marv (Marvin Daniel Levy) *professional sports team executive, former professional football coach*
Mayo, Cynthia Gould *music educator*
McGahee, Willis *professional football player*
Spikes, Takeo Gerard *professional football player*
Sullivan, Mortimer Allen, Jr. *lawyer*
Urbanski, Jane F. *retired microbiologist*

**Orient**
McNaught, William P. *museum director*

**Oriskany**
Jacobson, Karen *retired elementary school educator*

**Ossining**
Dolmatch, Theodore Bieley *management consultant*
Galef, Sandra Risk *state legislator, educator*
Maloney, William James *dentist, educator*
Robinson, Karen Vajda *dietician*
Sadan, Mark *photographer, film producer, artist*
Scheffler, Eckart Arthur *publisher*

**Oswego**
Delaney, Tim *sociologist, educator*
Fox, Michael David *retired art educator*
Garruto, John *counseling educator*
Gordon, Norman Botnick *psychologist, educator*
Greene, Stephen Craig *lawyer*
Malgieri, Lewis Joshua *psychologist, consultant*
Rial, Joseph J. *theater educator, set designer*
Smiley, Marilynn Jean *musicologist*
White, Kevin J. *education educator, consultant*

**Owego**
Kemp, Eugene Thomas *retired veterinarian*
Zendle, Howard Mark *systems engineer, researcher*

**Oxford**
Ryan, Kenneth Eugene *engineer*

**Oyster Bay**
Coates, Winslow Shelby, Jr. *lawyer*
Joel, Billy (William Martin Joel) *musician*
Kuehhas, Thomas Alan *museum director*

Landrón, Ana *school psychologist*
Mooney, James David, Jr. *aerial photographer*
Prey, Barbara Ernst *artist*
Schwab, Hermann Caspar *banker*
Wachsman, Harvey Frederick *lawyer, neurosurgeon*
Walsh, Charles Richard *retired banker*

**Ozone Park**
Bellamy, Renee Adele *secondary school educator*
Catalfo, Betty Marie *public health service officer, nutritionist, educator*
Joanidhi, Zhani *mathematician, educator*
Peeples, Thelma J. *elementary school educator*
Singh, Seopaul *security firm executive*

**Painted Post**
Kirk, Connie Ann *writer*

**Palisades**
Balstad, Roberta *social scientist*
Broecker, Wallace S. *geophysics educator*
Davis, Dorothy Salisbury *writer*
Kellogg, Herbert Humphrey *metallurgist, educator*
Kent, Dennis V. *paleomagnetist, educator, researcher*
Knowlton, Grace Farrar *sculptor, photographer*
Lenton, Roberto Leonardo *environmental services administrator*
Porta, Siena Gillann *sculptor, educator*
Richards, Paul Granston *geophysics educator, seismologist*
Schmetterer, Robert Allen *advertising executive*

**Palmyra**
Rose, Donna Marie *secondary school educator, farmer*

**Patchogue**
Esteve, Edward V. *lawyer*
Lamberta, Gail Carol *recreational therapist, physical education educator*
Marr, Robert Bruce *physicist, researcher*
McPherson, Sherry Lynn *social worker*

**Paul Smiths**
Mills, John W. *academic administrator*

**Pawling**
Berlandi, Brian Lawrence *lawyer*
Caplan, Ronald Mervyn *obstetrician, gynecologist*
Jones, James Earl *actor*
Lester, Helen Doughty *writer*
Peale, Ruth Stafford (Mrs. Norman Vincent Peale) *not-for-profit executive*
Utter, Donald L. *music educator*
Wood, Christopher L.J. *real estate executive*

**Pearl River**
Barringer, William Charles *retired chemist*
Boghaert, Erwin R. *oncology researcher*
Bryant, Karen Worstell *financial advisor, investment company executive*
Hamann, Philip Ross *chemist, researcher*
Matsuka, Yury V. *biochemist, research scientist*
Meyer, Irwin Stephan *lawyer, accountant*
Wang, John Xiaowu *computer company executive*
Yuan, Yonghui *chemist, researcher*
Zagursky, Robert *microbiologist, researcher*

**Peekskill**
Black, Carolyn Rebecca *music educator*
Harte, Andrew Dennis *transportation company executive, travel agent*

**Pelham**
Gaffney, Mark William *lawyer*
Hearle, Douglas Geoffrey *public relations consultant*
Hembury, Todd *science educator*

**Penfield**
Kraft, Donald Eugene *architecture and engineering company executive*
Weerasinghe, Renu M. *quality assurance professional*

**Penn Yan**
Stempien, Joseph Jeffrey *music educator*

**Peru**
Dawson, James Clifford *environmental science educator, geologist*

**Phoenix**
Ackerman, Roger G. *ceramics engineer*

**Piermont**
Berkon, Martin *artist*
Brechtel, Unda Jurka *library director*

**Pine Bush**
Prokopchak, Peter A. *music educator*

**Pine Island**
Rogowski, Cheryl *farmer*

**Pine Plains**
Shafer, Michael Gales *priest*
Trapp, Peter Jarl Rudolf *portfolio manager, farmer*

**Pittsford**
Barker, Julie A. *school system administrator*
Bernstein, Paul *retired academic dean*
Braunsdorf, Paul Raymond *lawyer*
Coleman, Paul David *neurobiology educator, researcher*
Dobbs, Herbert Hotaling *automotive executive, consultant, research scientist, retired military officer*
Faloon, William Wassell *physician, educator*
French, Henry Pierson, Jr. *retired historian, educator*
Goldstein, David Arthur *biophysicist, educator*
Green, Martin Lincoln *retired academic administrator*
Hampson, Thomas Meredith *singer*
Hartman, James Matthew *lawyer*
Herge, Henry Curtis, Jr. *information technology executive, consultant*

Hollingsworth, Jack Waring *mathematics professor*
Snyder, Donald Edward *finance company executive*
Sproull, Robert Lamb *retired academic administrator, physicist, director*
Steamer, Robert Julius *political science professor*
Sterns, Samantha *gerontologist, researcher*
Stonehill, Eric *lawyer*
Thompson, Brian John *academic administrator, optics scientist, educator*
Turri, Joseph A. *lawyer*
Willett, Thomas Edward *lawyer*

**Plainview**
Feller, Benjamin E. *actuary*
Maune, James J. *lawyer*
Newman, Edwin Harold *news commentator*
Nichter, Rhoda Samuels *writer, educator*
Wenderoff, Alan J. *psychologist, educator*
Zhitnik, Alexei *professional hockey player*

**Plandome**
Sherwood, James Webster III *writer*

**Plattsburgh**
Davis, Harley Cleo *retired military officer, manufacturing executive*
Fowler, Alyce Milton *health facility administrator*
Mihuc, Timothy Brian *science foundation director*
Tracy, Ann Blaisdell *retired language educator*
Treacy, William Joseph *electrical and environmental engineer*
Withrow, Gregory B. *director, accountant*

**Pleasant Valley**
Becofsky, Arthur Luke *arts administrator, writer*
Marshall, Natalie Junemann *economics professor*
Odescalchi, Edmond Péry *international financial consultant, author*

**Pleasantville**
Annese, Domenico *retired landscape architect*
Brizel, Michael Alan *lawyer*
Eschweiler, Peter Quintus *planning consultant*
Geltzeiler, Michael S. *publishing executive*
Leo, Jacqueline M. *editor-in-chief*
Loase, John *education educator*
McEwen, Laura *publishing executive*
Meisel, Martin *English and comparative literature educator*
Pia, Pamela Carmel *editor, director*
Pike, John Nazarian *optical engineering consultant*
Rockwood, Maria *magazine editor*
Schrier, Eric Woodside W. *publishing executive*
Tao, Lixin *computer science educator*
Urban, Joseph Jaroslav *engineer, consultant*

**Pomona**
Downey, Bruce L. *medical company executive, lawyer*
Frelow, Robert Dean *retired school system administrator, writer*
Landau, Lauri Beth *accountant, consultant*

**Port Chester**
Ailloni-Charas, Dan *marketing executive*
Brescia, Alicia *science educator, vice principal*
Oppenheimer, Suzi *state legislator*
Sotelo-Dynega, Marlene *psychologist*

**Port Jefferson**
Acker, Kathleen Alice Rusin *writer, editor, poet*
Ahmad, Arif *surgeon*
Dranitzke, Richard J. *surgeon*

**Port Jefferson Station**
Shockley, Alonzo Hilton, Jr. *school system administrator*
Spahr, Clinton S., Jr. *retired elementary school educator*

**Port Jervis**
DeCastro, Alfredo P. *physician, consultant*

**Port Washington**
Bartell, Susan Silver *psychologist, writer*
Candido, Arthur Aldo *publishing and distribution company executive*
Feuss, Judith Farrar *music educator, musician*
Gordon-Tennant, Jennifer Jay *secondary school educator*
Hackett, John Byron *advertising executive, lawyer*
Jay, Frank Peter *retired writer, lexicographer, educator*
Johnson, Ted Stuart *market research company executive*
Kwak, Seung-Keon *research scientist*
Leeds, Richard *computer marketing executive*
Lingelbach, Albert Lane *lawyer*
Ragan, David *publishing company executive*
Roy, Ranja *mathematician, educator*
Rush, Curt Stefan *lawyer*
Starr, Ringo (Richard Starkey) *musician, actor*
Ullman, Leo Solomon *lawyer*
van Schenkhof, Carol Dougherty (Carol Dovan) *soprano, music educator*
Williams, George Leo *historian, retired secondary school educator, landmark director*

**Portville**
Welty, Inga Ann *mathematics educator*

**Potsdam**
Baymak, Melek Sirin *science educator, researcher*
ben-Avraham, Daniel *physics professor*
Chin, Der-Tau *chemical engineer, educator*
Collins, Anthony G. *academic administrator*
Fendler, Janos Hugo *chemistry professor*
Ha, Andrew Kwangho *education educator*
Harder, Kelsie Brown *retired language educator*
Islam, Muhammad Azadul *physicist, educator, researcher*
Kim, Eugene *education educator*
Lanz, Christopher Charles *conductor*
Lunt, Lora G. *language educator, director*
Matijevic, Egon *chemist, educator*
Rengaswamy, Raghunathan *chemical engineering researcher, educator*
Rudiger, Lance Wade *secondary school educator*

Schwaller, John Frederick *academic administrator, historian, educator*
Scott, Jean A. *university president*
Stillwell, Arlene M. *psychologist, educator*
Wickman, Peter M. *sociologist, educator*
Zamankhan, Parsa *mechanical engineer*

**Poughkeepsie**
Bari, Paola *application developer*
Bartlett, Lynn Conant *English literature educator*
Brakas, Nora Jachym *education educator*
Buti, Taqi N. *electrical engineer*
Carino, Aurora Lao *psychiatrist, health facility administrator*
Chu, Richard Chao-Fan *mechanical engineer*
Conklin, Donald David *academic administrator*
Daniels, Elizabeth Adams *English language educator*
Deiters, Sister Joan Adele *psychoanalyst, nun, chemistry professor*
Dolan, Thomas Joseph *judge*
Ellsworth, Michael Joseph, Jr. *mechanical engineer*
Glasse, John Howell *retired philosophy and theology educator*
Griffen, Clyde Chesterman *retired historian*
Hansen, Karen Thornley *accountant*
Hansraj, Kenneth Karamchand *surgeon, research scientist*
Harmelink, Herman III *minister, writer, religious studies educator*
Hathaway, Richard Dean *retired language educator*
Heller, Mary Bernita *psychotherapist*
Hill, Catharine Bond (Cappy Hill) *academic administrator, economics professor*
Hytier, Adrienne Doris *French language educator*
Jackson, Judy Faye *academic administrator*
Johnson, M. Glen (Maurice Glen Johnson) *political science professor*
Kim, David Sang Chul *publishing executive, evangelist, retired academic administrator*
Klingenberg, Beate *management educator, director*
Lang, William Warner *physicist*
Logue, Joseph Carl *electronics engineer, consultant*
Opdycke, Leonard Emerson *retired elementary school educator, publishing executive, writer*
Ostertag, Robert Louis *lawyer*
Padegs, Andris *electrical engineer, engineering company executive*
Parker, Raymon Philip *dean*
Peck, H. Daniel *literature educator*
Phipps, Peter A. *psychology professor*
Rosenblatt, Albert Martin *state appeals court judge*
Scileppi, John A. *psychologist, educator*
Sharp, Ronald Alan *language educator, writer, dean*
Sherman, Ethan *contractor, publisher*
Simons, Robert Edward *mechanical engineer, consultant*
Slade, Bernard Newton *electronics executive*
Steinhorn, Charles Ira *mathematician, educator*
Taphorn, Joseph Bernard *lawyer*
Taylor, Patricia *director*
Teal, Arabella W. *lawyer, former state attorney general*
VanBuren, Denise Doring *corporate communications executive*
Van Zanten, Frank Veldhuyzen *library director*
Willard, Nancy Margaret *writer, educator*
Wilson, Richard Edward *composer, music educator, pianist*
Wolfersteig, Jean Lois *medical association administrator, educator*

**Pound Ridge**
Bennett, Edward Henry *reinsurance executive*
Darcy, Keith Thomas *finance company executive, educator*
Rubino, John Anthony *management and human resources consultant*
Schwebel, Renata Manasse *sculptor*

**Purchase**
Amelio, Bill (William J. Amelio) *computer company executive*
Black, Leon David *private investment company executive*
Bridgman, Peter Alwyn *beverage company executive*
Bryant, Daniel James *food and beverage company executive, former federal agency administrator*
Dostart, Thomas J. *lawyer*
Ehrman, Lee *geneticist, educator*
Finnerty, Louise Hoppe *food products executive*
Frost, Elizabeth Ann McArthur *physician*
Hanft, Noah Jonathan *lawyer*
Hudson, Dawn Emily *food service company executive*
Kelly, Edmund Joseph *lawyer, bank executive, investment banker*
Lacy, Bill *academic administrator, architect*
Lucio, Antonio J. *food products executive*
Magaziner, Elliot Albert *musician, conductor, educator*
McElwaine, James William *music educator*
Moore, Margaret D. *human resources specialist*
Newton, Esther Mary *anthropologist, educator*
Nicholson, Cie (Cynthia Nicholson) *marketing executive, beverage company executive*
Nooyi, Indra K. *food products executive*
Nowell, Lionel L. *food products executive*
O'Sullivan, Frances K. *computer company executive*
Phillips, Carly *writer*
Putman, Jeffrey Scott *academic administrator*
Reinemund, Steven S. *food products executive*
Ryan, Edward W. *economics professor*
Schmitz, Robert Allen *publishing executive, investor*
Selander, Robert W. *finance company executive*
Thompson, Larry Dean *lawyer, former federal agency administrator*
Thompson, Peter M. *retired food products executive*
Vardin, Patricia Anne *education educator*
Wachenheim, Edgar III *investment company executive*
Wallach, Ira David *lawyer, corporate financial executive*

Wallach, Kenneth L. *paper company executive*
Waller, Gary Fredric *language educator, poet*
Ward, Stephen M., Jr. *computer company executive*
White, Michael Dennis *food products executive*
Xiao, Shuyi *finance company executive*
Zimiles, Murray *artist, educator*

**Queens**
Beliavsky, Ninah *linguistics professor*

**Queensbury**
Bower, Rose Janet *psychologist, educator*
Cirillo, James John *music educator*

**Quogue**
Burkhardt, Ronald Robert *advertising executive, writer, artist, filmmaker*
Hines, William Eugene *banker*

**Raquette Lake**
Bridger, Beverly Maria *historic site director*

**Ravena**
Muth, Sharon A. *language educator*

**Red Hook**
Fitzpatrick, John *poet*
Gudenzi-Ruess, Ida Carmen V. *music educator, artist*
Pastrana, Ronald Ray *Biblical theology professor, psychotherapist, retired public school system administrator*

**Rego Park**
Cheng, Iris Yi-Chen *music educator*
Feldman, Rachel Beth *psychologist*
Nakanishi, Yuko June *engineering educator, consultant*
Thomas, James Edward *accountant*
Winter, Darius Gerjon *internist*

**Remsenburg**
Billman, Irwin Edward *publishing executive*

**Rensselaer**
Hull, Raymond Whitford *public relations executive*
Willis, John Patrick *chemist*

**Rensselaerville**
Fletcher, Raymond Russwald, Jr. *lawyer*

**Rexford**
Nitecki, Joseph Zbigniew *librarian*
Schmitt, Roland Walter *retired academic administrator*

**Rhinebeck**
Crum, Albert Byrd *psychiatrist, consultant*
Ewald, Wendy Taylor *photographer, writer, educator*
Scherr, Allan Lee *computer scientist, software executive*
Sloane, Beverly LeBov *writer, consultant, writing instructor*

**Rhinecliff**
Conklin, John Roger *retired electronics company executive*

**Richfield Springs**
Walters, Marjorie Anne *interior designer, consultant*

**Richmond Hill**
Gintautas, Jonas *physician, scientist, administrator*

**Richmondville**
Bartholomew, Debra Lee *publishing executive*

**Ridge**
Adams, Peter David *physicist, writer, editor*
Blume, Martin *physicist*
Carter, Sylvia *journalist*

**Ridgewood**
Jones, Harold Antony *banker*
Monroe, Leonora *surgeon*

**Riverdale**
Yale (Yeleyenide-Yale), Serina *philanthropist, apparel designer*

**Riverhead**
Banfelder, Robert Joseph *writer, literature educator*
Carpenter, Angie M. *small business owner, editor, county legislator*
Gilhooley, Dan *artist, psychoanalyst*
Maggipinto, V. Anthony *lawyer*
Orben, Jack Richard *investment company executive, director*
Roland, David Leonard *retired broadcast production educator*

**Rochester**
Adair, Donald Robert *lawyer*
Adams, Carol H. *dean*
Akiyama, Toshio *cardiologist, educator, researcher*
Alder, Donna Bordelon *biologist, educator*
Anderson, Porter Warren, Jr. *retired pediatrics educator*
Anthamatten, Mitchell Lewis *chemical engineer, educator*
Ashley, Stephen B. *finance company executive*
Aslin, Richard N. *psychology professor, researcher*
Aydelotte, Myrtle Kitchell *retired nursing administrator*
Bannon, Anthony Leo *museum director*
Baum, John *physician*
Berg, Robert Lewis *physician, educator*
Berman, Robert L. *human resources specialist*
Bidlack, Jean Marie *pharmacologist, educator, medical researcher*
Bigelow, Nicholas Pierre *physicist, researcher*
Blanda-Holtzberg, Marianne Lourdes *education educator, consultant*
Blanton, Thomas N. *chemist, researcher*

Bluhm, William Theodore *political scientist, educator*
Blumberg, Neil *hematologist, educator*
Blyth, John E. *lawyer, educator*
Boeckman, Robert Kenneth, Jr. *chemistry professor, organic chemistry researcher*
Bohrer, Brian E. *music educator*
Bonfiglio, Thomas Albert *pathologist, educator*
Bouyoucos, John Vinton *research and development company executive*
Braley, Oleta Pearl *community health nurse, writer*
Brody, Bernard B. *internist, educator*
Brooks, Walter S. *dermatologist*
Brust, Robert H. *film processing company executive*
Buckley, Michael Francis *lawyer*
Buff, Frank Paul *chemist, educator*
Buff, Iva Moore *librarian, musicologist*
Burton, Richard Irving *orthopedist, educator*
Buzard, A. Vincent *lawyer*
Cain, Burton Edward *retired chemistry professor*
Cameros, Alan Lee *finance company executive*
Carstensen, Edwin Lorenz *retired biomedical engineer, retired biophysicist*
Chen, Di *bone biologist*
Chess, Patricia R. *pediatrician, medical educator, researcher*
Chey, William Yoon *physician*
Chiarenza, Carl *art historian, critic, artist, educator*
Chiverton, Patricia Ann *dean, nursing educator*
Christensen, Sonya Marie *school librarian*
Clark, Matthew Harvey *bishop*
Clarkson, Thomas William *toxicologist, educator*
Clifford, Eugene Thomas *lawyer*
Cohen, Ann Ellen *librarian*
Cohen, Jules *former dean, internist, educator*
Cohen, Nicholas *immunologist, educator*
Collins, Christopher Carl *manufacturing executive*
Conwell, Esther Marly *physicist, researcher*
Coumou, David J. *electrical engineer, consultant*
Cunningham, Robert Del *librarian*
Dam, Lee Addison *vice principal*
Davies, Mark G *vascular surgeon, vascular biologist*
Deci, Edward Lewis *psychologist, educator*
DeWeese, James Arville *surgeon, educator*
Dolin, Lonny H. *lawyer*
Doty, Robert William *neuroscientist, physiologist, educator*
Dow, Ronald F. *librarian*
Doyle, Justin P. *lawyer*
Dreyfuss, Eric Martin *allergist*
Duarte, Francisco Javier *physicist, researcher*
DuBrin, Andrew John *management educator, writer, behavioral sciences educator, writer*
Eaves, Morris Emery *English language educator*
Eisenberg, Richard S. *chemistry professor*
Elliott, Ralph H. *minister, educator*
Ertsgaard, Edwin Paul *physicist*
Everett, Claudia Kellam *retired special education educator*
Fallesen, Gary David *journalist, lay worker*
Farmer, Richard Gilbert *academic physician, foundation administrator*
Fausold, Martin Luther *history professor*
Fenno, Richard Francis, Jr. *political scientist, educator*
Ferbel, Thomas *physicist, educator*
Figer, Donald F. *astronomer, educator*
Fitzgerald, John T., Jr. *lawyer*
Freeman, Leslie Jean *neuropsychologist, researcher*
Frisina, Robert Dana *neuroscientist, educator*
Galaria, Noreen Ahmad *physician, medical researcher, consultant*
Garwood, Naomi Fuji *education educator*
Gauldin, Robert L. *music educator, composer*
Geiger, Alexander *lawyer*
Giglio, Mary Ann *executive*
Goldberg-Schaible, Jocelyn Hope Schnier *market research professional*
Golden, Reynold Stephen *geriatrician, educator*
Goldman, Joel J. *retired lawyer*
Goldstein, Marvin Norman *physician*
Golisano, B. Thomas *financial services company executive, professional sports team executive*
Gong, Nancy Y. *artist, small business owner*
Goodell, Gary Lloyd *minister, educator*
Gootnick, Margery Fischbein *lawyer*
Gordon, Dane Rex *philosophy educator, minister*
Goyer, Virginia L. *accountant*
Griggs, Robert Charles *physician*
Gripe, Alan Gordon *minister*
Griswold, Kathy Ann King *academic administrator*
Guillet, Ronnie *pediatrician, educator*
Günter-McCoy, Jane Hutton *singer*
Gustin, Carl E., Jr. *manufacturing executive*
Guzick, David S. *dean, educator*
Hanson, Karen Noble *financial holding company executive*
Harris, Diane Carol *merger and acquisition consulting firm executive*
Harris, J. Wayne Manley *lawyer*
Harter, Ralph Millard Peter *lawyer, educator*
Harvey, Douglass Coate *retired photographic company executive*
Hauser, William Barry *historian, educator*
Herminghouse, Patricia Anne *foreign language educator*
Hoch, Edward Dentinger *writer*
Hollis, Susan Tower *history professor*
Hopkins, Thomas Duvall *economics professor*
Houde-Walter, Susan *optics scientist, educator*
Hurlbut, Robert Harold *health care services executive*
Huston, Samuel Richard *health facility executive*
Huxlin, Krystel Raluka *neuroscientist, educator*
Jackson, Thomas Humphrey *former academic administrator*
Jagannathan, Ramesh *research scientist*
John, Susan V. *state representative*
Johnson, Bruce Marvin *language educator*
Joos, Felipe Miguel *mechanical engineer, researcher*
Joynt, Robert James *academic administrator, physician*
Judge, Jonathan J. *financial services company executive*

Kaidy, Mitchell *retired journalist, legislative staff member*
Kampmeier, Jack August Carlos *chemist, educator*
Kaupa, Mike *music educator, musician*
Keeler, William Conrad III *curator, librarian, archivist*
Kehoe, L. Paul *state judge*
Kelley, Lucille Knight *minister, retired neurology and special duty nurse*
Kelley, Stephen Michael *lawyer*
Kende, Andrew Steven *chemist, educator*
Khorana, Alok Anand *oncologist, medical researcher*
Kirschenbaum, Howard *education educator*
Kissel, Lynn Anne *music educator*
Klinke, Louise Hoyt *volunteer*
Knauer, James Philip *physicist*
Knox, Robert Seiple *physicist, researcher*
Kunkel, Barbara J. *law firm executive*
Kurdziel, Michael Thomas *engineering executive*
Kurlan, Roger *neurologist, educator*
Kurland, Harold Arthur *lawyer*
Kwok, Wingchi Edmund *physicist*
LaBarge, Jeffrey Howard *lawyer*
Lacey, Dorothy Ellen *theology studies educator, religious organization administrator*
Lank, Edith Handleman *journalist, educator*
Lansky, Lewis *history professor*
Larson, Joanne Caroline *educator*
Laties, Victor Gregory *psychologist, educator*
Lavine, James Philip *physicist*
Law, Michael R. *lawyer*
Lebman, Robert Richard *social services administrator*
Lever, O. William, Jr. *chemist*
Levy, Harold David *psycholinguist*
Li, James Chen Min *materials science educator*
Lichtman, Marshall Albert *hematologist, educator, researcher*
Long, John Broaddus, Jr. *economist, educator*
Lundback, Staffan Bengt Gunnar *lawyer*
Lyman, Gary Herbert *epidemiologist, cancer researcher, educator*
Lyness, Jeffrey Marc *psychiatrist, educator*
Macpherson, Daniel Craig *music educator*
Magnuson, Karen M. *editor*
Makous, Walter Leon *visual scientist, educator*
Maples, Philip G. *museum director*
Maquat, Lynne E. *biomedical researcher*
Marriott, Marcia Ann *business and economics educator, health facility administrator*
McAnarney, Elizabeth R. *pediatrician, educator*
McCrory, John Brooks *retired lawyer*
McDonald, Joseph Valentine *neurosurgeon*
McDowell, David J. *psychology professor*
McKenty, Patrick *research scientist*
Mc Kenzie, Lionel Wilfred *economist, educator*
McMeekin, Thomas Owen *dermatologist*
Meconi, Honey *musicologist, writer*
Melissinos, Adrian Constantin *physicist, researcher*
Merritt, Howard Sutermeister *retired art educator*
Meyerhofer, David D. *physicist, educator*
Middleton, J. Richard *religious studies educator*
Mink, Jonathan W. *medical educator, researcher*
Moore, Duncan Thomas *optics scientist, educator*
Moore, James Conklin *lawyer*
Moore, Matthew Scott *publishing executive, advocate, writer*
Morphy, John *manufacturing executive*
Morris, James E. *lawyer, judge, educator*
Morrison, Patrice Burgert *lawyer*
Moss, Arthur Jay *physician*
Munson, Harold Lewis *education educator*
Nace, Morton Oliver, Jr. *human services manager*
Nazarian, Lawrence Fred *pediatrician*
Newport, Elissa L. *psychology professor*
Niemi, Richard Gene *political science educator*
Niznik, Carol Ann *electrical engineer, educator, consultant*
Nusbaum, Beryl *lawyer*
Pacala, Leon *retired professional society administrator*
Palermo, Anthony Robert *lawyer*
Paley, Gerald Larry *lawyer*
Parker, Kevin James *electrical engineer, educator*
Patrick, Paul *emergency physician*
Payment, Kenneth Arnold *lawyer*
Pearson, Thomas Arthur *epidemiologist, educator*
Peloquin, Lori Jeanne *clinical psychologist*
Perez, Antonio M. *imaging company executive*
Pettinella, Edward *real estate company executive*
Phelps, Charles Elliott *economics professor, director*
Phillips, Harold John III *protective services official, consultant*
Pitoniak, Scott Michael *sportswriter*
Polevoda, Bogdan V. *research scientist*
Powers, James Matthew *neuropathologist*
Price, Richard Edward *lawyer*
Primo, David Martin *political science professor*
Ramirez, Stevan G. *consumer products company executive*
Ravina, Bernard Mayer *neurologist*
Regenstreif, S(amuel) Peter *political scientist, educator*
Robbins, Nancy Slinker *volunteer*
Robfogel, Susan Salitan *lawyer*
Rodgers, Suzanne Hooker *physiologist, consultant*
Rose, Robert Charles *virologist, researcher*
Rosenhouse, Michael Allan *lawyer, editor, consultant, columnist*
Rothberg, Abraham *writer*
Rowley, Peter Templeton *pediatrician, educator*
Rulison, Joseph Richard *investment advisor*
Saunders, William Hundley, Jr. *retired chemist, educator*
Schumacher, Jon Lee *lawyer*
Schwert, G(eorge) William III *finance educator*
Scotto, Ciro Gerard *composer, educator*
Seligman, Joel *academic administrator*
Sexstone, Brian Thomas *protective services official*
Sharma, Gaurav *imaging scientist, electrical engineer*
Sherman, Fred *biochemist, educator*
Shirley, Bonnie J. *retired elementary school educator*
Sieg, Albert Louis *photographic company executive*
Simon, Albert *retired physicist, retired engineer, retired educator*

Singer, Alan Daniel *artist*
Siragusa, Charles J. *judge*
Smith, David Harry Watrous *retired secondary school educator*
Smith, Julia Ladd *oncologist, physician*
Smoral, Vincent J. *electrical engineer*
Sottile, Joseph James *elementary school educator, poet*
Sparks, Charles Edward *pathologist, educator*
Sparks, Janet Lindsay Dehoff *pathologist, educator*
Stewart, Sue S. *lawyer*
Stratton, John Alfred *electrical engineer, educator*
Surace, Theresa *special education educator*
Swanton, Susan Irene *retired library director*
Tavli, Bulent *communications engineer, researcher*
Thorndike, Edward Harmon *physicist*
Thym, Jürgen *musicologist*
Tobin, Barbara Kay *minister*
Trueheart, Harry Parker III *lawyer*
Tucker, Jeffrey Allen *education educator*
Turner, Scott MacNeely *lawyer*
VanderLinden, Camilla Denice Dunn *telecommunications industry executive*
Velletri, Thomas Joseph *elementary school educator, artist*
Vernarelli, Michael Joseph *economics professor, consultant, academic administrator*
Vigdor, Justin Leonard *lawyer*
Vojt, Christine M. *quality assurance professional, microbiologist*
Wagner, Aureen Pinto *psychologist, educator*
Waite, Stephen Holden *lawyer*
Wayland-Smith, Robert Dean *retired banker*
Webster, Gordon Visscher, Jr. *minister*
Wegman, Colleen *food service executive*
Wegman, Daniel R. *food service executive*
White, Ann Marie *medical educator*
Wild, Robert Warren *lawyer*
Wiley, Jason LaRue, Jr. *neurosurgeon*
Williams, Thomas Franklin *physician, educator*
Witmer, G. Robert *retired state supreme court justice*
Witmer, George Robert, Jr. *lawyer*
Wygant, Patricia Bryans *artist*
Wynne, Lyman Carroll *psychiatrist*
Xia, Tongsheng *electrical engineer*
Yip, Kwok Leung *physicist, researcher*
Young, Mary Elizabeth *history professor*
Yuan, Bo *computer scientist, educator*
Zagorin, Perez *historian, educator*
Zarrella, Ronald L. *pharmaceutical executive*
Zax, Melvin *psychologist, educator*
Zupan, Mark A. *dean, business professor*

## Rockville Centre

Beyer, Suzanne *advertising agency executive*
Fitzgerald, Janet Anne *philosophy educator, academic administrator*
Lewittes, Don Jordan *psychologist*
Mazzucelli, Colette Grace Celia *author, educator*
Pompan, Jack Maurice *management consultant*
Salvato, Scott Vincent *minister*
Schwartz, Arthur *playwright, poet*
Teyan, Frederick Gene *pediatrician*

## Rocky Point

Falcone, David J. *elementary school educator*
Knapp, Craig Brian *music educator, musician*

## Rome

Bello, Paul F. *computer scientist*
Ferens, Daniel Vincent *civilian military employee*
Min, Balshik *pathologist*
Simonin, Howard A. *biologist*
Simons, Richard Duncan *lawyer, retired judge*

## Romulus

Ostrander, Robert Edwin *retired United Nations interregional advisor, petroleum company executive*

## Ronkonkoma

Saladino, Frank S. *music educator*

## Roosevelt

Adams, Mary A. *retired assistant principal*

## Rosendale

Goldpaugh Brown, Bethany J. (Beverly) *theater educator, writer, costume designer*

## Roslyn

Druz, Regina Shmukler *cardiologist, researcher*
Finke, Leonda Froehlich *sculptor, educator*
Greenberg, Steven M. *physician*
Gulotta, Stephen J. *cardiologist*
Mazlen, Roger Geoffrey *ophthalmologist, pharmacologist*
Rosegarten, Rory *personal manager, television producer, theater producer, film producer*
Siahpoosh, Farideh Tamaddon *librarian*
Stracher, Dorothy Altman *education educator, consultant*
Ulanoff, Stanley M. *communications executive*
Weinberg-Aptekar, Doris Mae *psychotherapist, school psychologist, hypnotherapist*

## Roslyn Heights

Guthart, Leo A. *electronics executive*
Newmark, Marilyn *sculptor*
Rogatz, Peter *retired physician*

## Rouses Point

Weierstall, Richard Paul *retired pharmaceutical chemist*

## Ruby

Cole, Max *artist*

## Rye

Barker, Harold Grant *surgeon, educator*
Crawford, R. George *investment company executive, educator, filmmaker*
Curtin, Brian Joseph *retired ophthalmologist*
Davis, Samuel *hospital administrator, educator, consultant*
Feinberg, Norman Maurice *real estate company executive*

Franklin, Martin E. *consumer products company executive*
Gabelli, Mario J. *diversified financial services company executive*
Gambee, Robert Rankin *investment banker*
Goldstein, Peter Dobkin *lawyer*
Harrington, Diane *librarian, writer*
Hurwitz, Sol *writer, consultant*
Kaulakis, Arnold Francis *management consultant*
Ketchum, William Clarence *author, educator*
Lawi, David Steven *utilities executive, merchant banker*
Lehman, Lawrence Herbert *consulting engineering executive*
Nelson, Vita Joy *editor, publisher*
Newburger, Howard Martin *psychoanalyst*
Pearson, Nathan Williams *communications executive, investment executive*
Rolland, Peter George *landscape architect*
Waltz, Joseph McKendree *neurosurgeon, educator*
Wilmot, Irvin Gorsage *former hospital administrator, educator, consultant*

## Rye Brook

Aquino, Joseph Mario *clinical psychologist*
Berk, Alan S. *accountant*
Kuntzman, Ronald *research and development company executive*
Lo Russo, Diane *radiologist*
Mariam, Thomas Fred *public relations executive, radio producer*
Masson, Robert Henry *paper company executive*

## Sag Harbor

Brody, Eugene David *investment company executive*
Brody, Jacqueline *editor*
Epstein, Jason *publishing company executive*
Immerso, John Joseph *music educator*
Pierce, Lawrence Warren *retired federal judge*
Rizzle, Dan *artist*

## Sagaponack

Cedering, Siv *poet, writer*
Graham, Howard Barrett *publishing company executive*
Van de Bovenkamp, Hans *artist*

## Saint Albans

Norfleet, Leontine Sandra *retired biologist*

## Saint Bonaventure

Dembele, Gaston *adult education educator*
Mazon, Margaret Fausold *language educator*
Pierce, Constance Laundon *artist, educator*

## Saint James

Batule, Robert John *priest, writer*
Kalabza-Balsamo, Debra Alyce *music educator*
Kelly, Michael Joseph *academic administrator, consultant*

## Saint Regis Falls

Johnson, Karleen A. *retired primary school educator*
O'Bryan, Margaret Sundberg *music educator*

## Salisbury Mills

Tersine, Brenda L. *funeral director*

## Sanborn

Godell, Lori B. *elementary school educator*
Michalak, Janet Carol *childhood education educator, coordinator*
Nowak (Jarosz), Linda Therese *special education educator, consultant*
Pogel, Alan Fred *history educator*

## Sands Point

Cullinan, Bernice Ellinger *education educator*
Hoynes, Louis LeNoir, Jr. *lawyer*
Lear, Erwin *anesthesiologist, educator*
Olian, JoAnne Constance *curator, art historian*
Wurzel, Leonard *retired candy manufacturing company executive*

## Saranac

Smith, J. Kellum, Jr. *foundation administrator, lawyer*

## Saranac Lake

Caguiat, Carlos Jose *health facility administrator, priest*

## Saratoga Springs

Anderson, Pauline Harriet *library consultant*
Boyers, Robert *literature and language professor*
Carovano, John Martin *not-for-profit developer*
Caruso, Adrienne Iorio *retired language educator*
Coreno, Mary Elizabeth *lawyer*
Dickinson, Richard Henry *accountant*
Ford, Dexter *retired insurance company executive*
Glotzbach, Philip A. *academic administrator, philosopher, educator*
Greco, Joseph Angelo *supervisor*
Masie, Elliott *training executive*
Miller, Anita Diane *psychologist*
Millhauser, Steven *writer*
Porter, David Hugh *musician, classicist, academic administrator, music educator*
Powell, Louie J. *editor-in-chief, engineer, consultant*
Sainer, Arthur *writer, theater educator*
Stake, Peter *art educator, artist*
Upton, Richard Thomas *artist*
Wait, Charles Valentine *banker*

## Saugerties

Levine, Phillip Paul *application developer, poet, actor*

## Sayville

Grizzaffi, Kimberly Anne *music educator, secondary school educator*
Vigliotta, Margaret D. *secondary school educator, art educator, artist*

## Scarborough

Mohl, Allan S. *social worker*

Parks, Robert Henry *consulting economist, educator*
Wittcoff, Harold Aaron *chemist*

## Scarsdale
Abbe, Colman *investment banker*
Angel, Dennis *lawyer*
Belasco, Steven Ronald *lawyer*
Benedict, James Nelson *lawyer*
Beuchert, Edward William *lawyer*
Blitman, Howard Norton *construction executive*
Borg, Robert Frederic *civil engineer*
Bruck Lieb Port, Lilly *retired advocate, columnist, commentator*
Byers, John Raoul III *food products executive, conservationist*
Clapman, Peter Carlyle *lawyer, finance company and corporate governance consultant*
Clark, Merrell Mays *management consultant*
Cohen, Irwin *economist*
Decaminada, Joseph Pio *retired insurance company executive*
Dulit, Everett Paul *psychiatrist, educator*
Edis, Gloria Toby *pediatrician*
Erbsen, Claude Ernest *retired journalist*
Gelb, Harold Seymour *manufacturing executive, consultant, entrepreneur*
Gerber, Roger Alan *lawyer, consultant*
Gladstone, William Louis *accountant*
Gollin, Stuart Allen *accountant*
Goodman, Jordan Elliot *journalist*
Graff, Henry Franklin *historian, educator*
Heese, William John *retired music publishing company executive*
Hoffman, Richard M. *lawyer*
Holmes, Rupert *playwright, singer, writer*
Huff, Mona L. *information technology executive*
Johnson, Boine Theodore *manufacturing executive, mayor*
Johnson, William Alexander *clergyman, philosophy educator, theology educator*
Kaufman, Robert Jules *communications consultant, lawyer*
Laufer, Leonard Justin *management consultant*
Lipman, Marvin Matthew *medical educator*
Mercando, Anthony Dominic *cardiologist*
Moser, Marvin *physician, educator, author*
Newman, Stacey Clarfield *artist, curator*
O'Brien, Edward Ignatius *corporate financial executive, director, investor, lawyer*
O'Neill, Michael James *editor, author*
Pope, Leavitt Joseph *broadcast company executive*
Porosoff, Harold *chemist, science administrator, research and development company executive*
Ries, Martin *artist, educator*
Rubenstein, Jacob Samuel *rabbi*
Schultz, Harley *consulting company executive*
Soley, Robert Lawrence *plastic surgeon*
Topping, Audrey Ronning *photojournalist*
Topping, Seymour *writer*
Van Gundy, Gregory Frank *retired lawyer*

## Schaghticoke
O'Connor, Abigail Elizabeth *mathematician, educator, science educator*

## Schenectady
Ainlay, Stephen Charles *academic administrator, educator*
Andreen, Aviva Louise *dentist, researcher, academic administrator, educator*
Andresen, Peter Louis *materials engineer*
Board, Joseph Breckinridge, Jr. *political scientist, educator*
Chen, Tao-Seng *medical physicist, consultant*
DeLuke, Dean M. *oral surgeon*
Depan, Harry John *cardiothoracic surgeon*
Fell, Samuel Kennedy (Ken Fell) *infosystems executive*
Finks, Robert Melvin *paleontologist, educator*
Fleischer, Robert Louis *geology professor*
Frost, Robert Edwin *chemistry professor*
Golub, Lewis *supermarket, educator*
Golub, Neil M. *supermarket chain executive*
Hartkern, Danielle Anne *elementary school educator*
Hermance, Myron E., Jr. *conductor, educator*
Hull, Roger Harold *foundation administrator, former academic administrator*
Huszar, Andrew Louis *school psychologist*
Huth, Geoffrey Anthony *archivist, artist*
Katz, Samuel *retired geophysics educator*
Larsen, Einar V. *electrical and systems engineer, consultant*
Mikata, Yozo *mechanical engineer, application developer*
Morris, John Telwyn *philosopher, educator, retired academic administrator*
Murray, Edward Rock *insurance broker*
Oliker, David William *healthcare management administrator*
Otto, Peter *information scientist, educator*
Rice, Ruth Elaine *music educator*
Ringlee, Robert James *consulting engineering executive*
Schenck, John Frederic *physician*
Sternlicht, Beno *research and development company executive*
Stevens, Roy W. *microbiologist, researcher, photographer*
Sutherland, Peter Edward *electrical engineer*
Szokody, Aniko *pianist, educator*
Turin, Lars *secondary school educator, artist*

## Schoharie
Duncombe, Raynor Bailey *lawyer*

## Schroon Lake
Pendell, Zhanna I. *music educator*
Williams, Wayne M. *music educator*

## Scotia
de la Rocha, Carlos A. *retired physician*
Webster, Harold Frank *physicist*

## Scottsville
Williams, Henry Ward, Jr. *lawyer, writer*

## Sea Cliff
Anders, Gerald Randolph *music educator*
Knudson, Rozanne Ruth *writer*

---

Popova, Nina *dancer, choreographer, director*

## Seaford
Setzler, William Edward *retired chemicals executive*
Spencer, Jean *retired business executive*

## Selden
Connors, William Francis, Jr. *academic administrator*
Cook, Lisa Marie *mathematics professor, mathematics learning center coordinator*
Howard, Douglas L. *literature and language professor*

## Selkirk
Christoph, Peter Richard *historical editor, archivist*

## Seneca Falls
Luisi-Potts, Billie *not-for-profit executive*
Norman, Mary Marshall *academic administrator, alcohol/drug abuse services professional, educator*

## Setauket
Levine, Sumner Norton *industrial engineer, educator, editor, writer, financial consultant*
Robinson, Richard M. *communications executive*

## Shady
Malkine-Falvey, Fern Sylvie *writer, journalist, painter*

## Shelter Island
Dowd, David Joseph *banker, construction executive*
Mayer, Martin Prager *writer*
Nicklin, George Leslie, Jr. *psychoanalyst, educator, physician, writer*
Shaw, Alan Roger *retired finance company executive, finance educator*

## Shelter Island Heights
Culbertson, Janet Lynn *artist*

## Sherburne
Dodd, Jack Gordon, Jr. *physicist, researcher*

## Shirley
Harper, Catherine B. *primary school educator*

## Shoreham
Li, Zizhong *research scientist*

## Shrub Oak
Wald, Catherine *writer*

## Sidney
Werner, David A. *paper company executive*

## Silver Creek
Kurzawa, Marilyn Taylor *educational consultant*

## Skaneateles
Huxford, J. David *retired sales executive*
Torrey, Linda A. *art educator*

## Slate Hill
Izzo, I. Victor III *music educator*

## Sleepy Hollow
Chia, David Thien-Shing *internist, gastroenterologist*
Flynn-Connors, Elizabeth Kathryn *reporter, editor*
Marshall, Michael Borden *marketing executive*
Melvin, Russell Johnston (Jay Melvin) *magazine publishing consultant*
Neill, Richard Robert *retired publishing executive*
Schmidt, Klaus Franz *advertising executive*

## Slingerlands
Ipsen, Carol Anne *psychiatrist, educator*
Zacek, Joseph Frederick *historian, educator*

## Smallwood
Golden, Elliott *judge*

## Smithtown
Ariosto-Oill, Lynn Carol *music educator*
Dowis, Lenore *lawyer*
Felice, Lisa M. *special education educator*
Goodman, Richard Shalem *lawyer, orthopedic surgeon*
Haskins, Debra May *academic administrator, educator*
Rockensies, John William *mechanical engineer*

## Snyder
Breverman, Harvey *artist*
Levine, George Richard *language educator*

## Somers
Anderson, John Erling *chemical engineer*
Berisford, John L. *human resources specialist*
Cahill, John T. *consumer products company executive*
Cohn, Howard *retired magazine editor*
Drewes, Alfred H. *consumer products company executive*
Foss, Eric J. *consumer products company executive*
Hehenberger, Michael *chemist, researcher*
Reznick, Steven Michael *orthopedic surgeon, educator*
Rothman, Bernard *lawyer*
Rubin, Samuel Harold *internist, consultant*
Sanford, Linda S. *information technology executive*
Sora, Sebastian Antony *business machines manufacturing executive, educator*
Trzasko, Joseph Anthony *psychologist, educator*
Wladawsky-Berger, Irving *communications executive*

## South New Berlin
Brennan, Brian William *industrial physicist*

## South Richmond Hill
Scheich, John F. *lawyer*
Singh, Ronald *social sciences educator, researcher*

---

## South Salem
Cowles, Frederick Oliver *lawyer*
Schindler, Teri *sports association executive*

## South Setauket
Friedlander, Gerhart *nuclear chemist*
Poli, Kenneth Joseph *editor, writer, photographer*

## Southampton
Brokaw, Clifford Vail III *investment banker*
Brophy, James David, Jr. *humanities educator*
Culp, Michael Bronston *investor, writer, publisher*
Kanovitz, Howard *artist, educator*
Lerner, Abram *museum director, artist*
Lopez, David *lawyer*
Martine, David Bunn *curator, artist*
Platt, Jonathan James *lawyer*
Sheehy, Betty Jo *real estate company executive, investment advisor*
Swift, Mary Lou *art dealer, financial consultant*
Thomas, Violeta de los Angeles *real estate broker*
Tuma, Mym *sculptor, painter, educator*

## Southold
Cowley, Joseph Gilbert *writer*
Small, Bertrice W. *writer*

## Sparkill
Dahl, Arlene *actress, writer, designer, cosmetics executive*
Solomon, Pearl Gold *education educator, consultant*

## Sparrow Bush
Murray, William Bruce *opera singer*

## Spencerport
Broussard, Allison M. *secondary school educator, artist*
Wolsky, Jack *retired art educator*

## Spring Valley
Johnson, Judith A. *educational administrator*
Stedge-Fowler, Joyce *retired clergywoman*

## Staatsburg
Wentworth, Dennis Ladd *historic sites and parks administrator*

## Stamford
Bergleitner, George Charles, Jr. *investment banker*

## Stanfordville
Tetor, David R. *agriculturist, consultant*

## Staten Island
Adler, Barbara Arlene *artist*
Arievitch, Igor *psychology professor*
Auh, Yang John *librarian, educational administrator*
Aurelia, Alan C. *performing company executive, music director*
Black, Lawrence *librarian*
Brady, Christine Ellen *education coordinator*
Bruckstein, Alex Harry *internist, gastroenterologist, geriatrician*
Clark, Sylvia Dolores *business educator*
Dennery, Linda *newspaper publishing executive*
Fafian, Joseph, Jr. *management consultant*
Ferzli, George Salem *surgeon*
Foster, Paul *playwright*
Franzone, Eric Scott *psychologist*
Fusco, Jo Ellen *music educator*
Gavrity, John Decker *retired insurance company executive*
Gelbein, Jay Joel *accountant*
Holder, Calvin Beresford *history professor*
Humphries, Edward Francis *lawyer*
Ionescu, Adrian *information scientist, educator*
Kahn, Jim *former magazine publisher*
Khan, Tariq *marketing professional*
Kuppersmith, Judith Carolyn *psychology professor*
Lazzara, Margo Valentine *counselor, writer*
Lutkenhouse, Anne *non-profit executive*
Maiman, Mitchell *oncologist, gynecologist*
Martin, Frances Lee *nursing educator*
Molinaro, James P. *city manager*
Nadler, Nona Jean *social worker*
Newhouse, Donald E. *newspaper publishing executive*
Newhouse, Samuel Irving, Jr., (Si Newhouse Jr.) *publishing executive*
Nicholaou, Mary C(onstantine) *literature and language professor, publishing executive*
Omogu, Donald *history professor*
Pasciuto, Joseph Doria *priest*
Piedilato, Janet *psychologist*
Piegari, James A. *psychologist*
Popler, Kenneth *behavioral health services administrator, psychologist*
Porter, Darwin Fred *writer*
Prince, Danforth *publishing executive, journalist*
Spada, Dominick *pharmacist*
Springer, Marlene *university administrator, educator*
Stathopoulos, Peter *internist*
Stolz, Theodora *psychologist*
Taranto, Deborah Jean *literature and language professor, writer*
Trogan, Roland Bernard *composer, educator*
Wilson, Alice McAteer *secondary school educator*
Yang, Song-Yu *biochemist*

## Sterling
Anderson, Nancy Marie Greenwood *special education educator*

## Stony Brook
Alexander, John Macmillan, Jr. *chemistry professor*
Anderson, Michael Thomas *mathematics professor, researcher, director*
Andriola, Mary Repole *neurologist, pediatrician*
Baker, David A. *obstetrician, gynecologist, educator*
Barnett, Jeffrey Adam *academic administrator*
Benitez-Silva, Hugo A. *economics professor*
Bennett, Tyrone LaMont *engineer, director*
Bokuniewicz, Henry Joseph *oceanography educator*

---

Bonner, Francis Truesdale *chemist, educator, dean*
Brandwein, Ruth Ann *social welfare educator, social services administrator, writer*
Brown, Gerald Edward *physicist, researcher*
Carr, Edward Gary *psychology professor*
Chen, JiuHua *physics, geophysicist, educator*
Chiang, Fu-Pen *mechanical engineering educator, researcher*
Cochran, James Kirk *dean, oceanographer, educator, geochemist*
Cook, Jeannine Salvo *librarian, consultant*
Corman, Marvin Leonard *surgeon, educator*
Dosik, Michael *breast cancer physician, hospital administrator, consultant*
Dugam, Alexander B. *plastic surgeon*
Fine, Richard Nisan *pediatrician, educator, dean*
Fritts, Harry Washington, Jr. *internist, educator*
Gambino, Richard Joseph *materials engineer, educator*
Gavrilov, Dmitri N. *research scientist*
Geller, Marvin Alan *meteorology educator, researcher*
Glimm, James Gilbert *mathematician, educator*
Goldberg, Homer Beryl *language educator*
Grim, Patrick Neal *philosopher, logician*
Harris, Alice *linguist, educator*
Harvey, Christine Lynn *publishing executive*
Hurst, Lawrence *orthopedic surgeon*
Ihde, Don *philosopher, educator, dean*
Jonas, Steven *preventive medicine physician, author*
Kahn, Peter B. *physics professor*
Kenny, Shirley Strum *academic administrator*
Koppelman, Lee Edward *regional planner, educator*
Kramer, Karen Leslie *anthropologist, educator*
Kuchner, Eugene Frederick *neurosurgeon, educator, neuroscientist*
Kuspit, Donald Burton *art historian, critic, educator*
Lane, Dorothy Spiegel *preventive medicine physician*
Larson, Susan G. *anatomist, educator*
Laspina, Peter Joseph *computer resource educator*
Lawson, H(erbert) Blaine, Jr. *mathematician, educator*
Lennarz, William Joseph *research biologist, educator*
Leske, M. Cristina *medical researcher, educator*
Levin, Richard Louis *retired language educator*
Levine, Martin *printmaker, art educator*
Liang, Jerome Zhengrong *radiology educator*
Meyers, Morton Allen *radiologist, educator*
Mignone, Mario B. *language educator*
Milnor, John Willard *mathematician*
Mirza, Humair *cardiologist, educator*
Monheit, Alan Goodman *obstetrician, gynecologist*
Moore, William Henry *radiologist*
Ohannessian, Harry Haroutune *travel agency executive*
Ojima, Iwao *chemistry professor*
Pekarsky, Melvin Hirsch *artist*
Pindell, Howardena Doreen *artist*
Priebe, Cedric Joseph, Jr. *pediatric surgeon*
Rifkin, Barry R. *dean, dental educator, researcher*
Rohlf, F. James *biologist, educator*
Seifert, Frank C. *thoracic surgeon*
Semmel, Bernard *historian, educator*
Shamash, Yacov *dean, electrical engineering educator*
Simpson, Louis Aston Marantz *language educator, writer*
Sreebny, Leo M. *oral biology and pathology professor*
Steigbigel, Roy Theodore *epidemiologist, educator, research scientist*
Stolzberg, Mark Elliott *psychologist*
Stone, Elizabeth Cecilia *anthropology educator*
Swanson, Robert Lawrence *oceanographer, academic program administrator*
Tanur, Judith Mark *sociologist, educator*
Tewarson, Reginald Prabhakar *retired mathematics educator, consultant*
Travis, Martin Bice *retired political scientist, educator*
Tucker, Alan Curtiss *mathematics professor*
Vencl, Fredric Vincent *biologist, researcher*
Vlay, Stephen Charles *cardiologist, electrophysiologist*
Weisbrot, Deborah Marcia *psychiatrist*
White, Henry J. *engineering educator, consultant*
Zemanian, Armen Humpartsoum *electrical engineer, mathematician*

## Stony Creek
La Grasso, Carol Winter *property rights activist, retired civil engineer*

## Stuyvesant
Tripp, Susan Gerwe *museum director*

## Suffern
Codispoti, Andre John *allergist, immunologist*
Coronel, Victor Felipe *engineering educator*
Garbarini, William Nicholas *pharmaceutical executive*
Ralph, Stanley Lee *performing arts educator, musician*
Raven, Luisa Antonia *psychotherapist, nurse*

## Sugar Loaf
Endico, Mary Antoinette *artist*

## Sunnyside
Gil Orrios, Angel *theater director, lighting designer, translator*

## Syosset
Bermas, Stephen *lawyer*
Cordaro, Joanne *human resources specialist, director*
Greene, Christine Elizabeth *artist*
Kniffin, Paula Sichel *insurance sales executive*
Rehm, Carolyn Agnes *pediatrician, educator*
Theodosius, *retired leader of the Orthodox Church in America*

## Syracuse
Allis, Damian Gregory *technologist, chemist, consultant*
Alston, William Payne *philosophy educator*

Arterian, Hannah R. *dean, law educator*
Baker, Bruce Edward *orthopedic surgeon, consultant*
Baldwin, John Edwin *chemistry professor*
Baldwin, Robert Frederick, Jr. *lawyer*
Barclay, H(ugh) Douglas *ambassador, lawyer*
Becker, Lorne Arthur *family physician*
Belfort-Chalat, Jacqueline *art educator, sculptor*
Birkhead, Guthrie Sweeney, Jr. *political scientist, dean*
Blakely, Caroline Miller *retired editor*
Bodow, Wayne R. *defender*
Boeheim, Jim *college basketball coach*
Braungart, Richard Gottfried *social sciences educator, political scientist*
Bunn, Timothy David *newspaper editor*
Caldicott, Catherine V. *medical educator, researcher*
Call, David Andrew *meteorologist*
Callahan, James Michael *physician, educator*
Cantor, Nancy *academic administrator*
Castro, Alfonso Peter *education educator, consultant*
Cherundolo, John Charles *lawyer*
Chickadonz, Grace Harlow *dean*
Cooper, John Ambrose *management consultant, marketing professional*
Coskun, Erman *information systems educator*
Costello, Thomas Joseph *retired bishop*
Crane, David Michael *prosecutor, former judge advocate, educator*
DeFrancisco, John Anthony *state legislator, lawyer*
Driscoll, Matthew J. *mayor, real estate developer, small business owner*
Elms, Ben *actor, theater director*
Emery, Robert Allan *minister*
Engel, Richard Lee *lawyer, educator*
Fawcett, James Walter *computer engineer, educator*
Fiske, Jordan Jay *lawyer, retired prosecutor*
Fitzgerald, Harold Kenneth *social work educator, consultant*
Fitzpatrick, James David *lawyer*
Flaver, John Anthony *retired music educator*
Forbes, Peter Edwin *sculptor*
Ford, Steven J. *lawyer, manufacturing executive*
Fortune, John B. *medical educator*
Fredrickson, Bruce E. *orthopedist*
Freund, Deborah A. *academic administrator*
Furze, Edward William *fundraising consultant*
Gaal, John *lawyer*
Gartner, Joseph Charles *business systems administrator*
Givas, Thomas Peter *lawyer*
Gold, Joseph *medical researcher*
Grant, William Davis *family medicine educator, dean*
Graver, Jack Edward *mathematics professor*
Gray, Charles Augustus *banker*
Hansen, Per Brinch *computer scientist, researcher*
Hayes, David Michael *lawyer*
Herzog, Peter Emilius *retired legal educator*
Hole, Richard Douglas *lawyer*
Honig, Arnold *physics professor, researcher*
Horst, Pamela Sue *medical educator, physician*
Hsu, Lifang *statistician, department chairman*
Irwin, Peter C. *not-for-profit fundraiser*
Jerge, Marie Charlotte *minister*
Kaplan, Eugene Alken *psychiatry professor, department chairman*
Kerr, Darlene Dixon *electric power company executive*
Kim, Yong-Woo *engineer, educator, consultant*
Krathwohl, David Reading *retired education educator*
Kriesberg, Louis *sociologist, educator*
Lang, James Patrick *priest*
Lawler, Mark Clyde *geology professor*
Lazarow, Victor *theater educator*
Lee, David Ames *lawyer, banker, editor, writer*
Leontieva, Luba *psychologist, researcher, psychiatrist*
Levitsky, Melvyn *former ambassador*
Liu, Lizhong *physicist*
Luchsinger, John Francis, Jr. *lawyer*
Malhotra, Yogesh *computer scientist, educator, computer engineer*
Marcoccia, Louis Gary *accountant, academic administrator*
Masters, Kevin S. *psychology professor*
McCurn, Neal Peters *federal judge*
McIntyre, Laura Lee *psychology professor, consultant*
Meinig, Donald William *geography educator*
Milač, Metod M. *retired school librarian*
Miles, Kenneth Ontario *academic program director*
Monmonier, Mark *geographer, writer*
Mooney, Edward Fiske *religious studies educator*
Moynihan, James M. *bishop*
Mukerji, Indranil *lawyer*
Munson, Howard G. *federal judge*
Murphy, Cornelius B., Jr., (Neil Murphy) *academic administrator*
Nicholson, Scott Richard *library scientist, researcher, educator*
Numann, Patricia Joy *surgeon, educator*
Obbie, Mark Joseph *communications educator*
O'Connor, Michael E. *lawyer*
Orentlicher, John *video research educator, artist*
Ortiz, Fernando, Jr. *commissioner*
Pardee, Otway O'Meara *computer scientist, educator*
Pascucci, Marisa Jonell *curator, art historian*
Peng, Feng *environmentalist*
Phillips, Larry Arthur *artist*
Pooler, Rosemary S. *federal judge*
Powell, James Matthew *history professor*
Prucha, John James *geologist, educator*
Rabuzzi, Daniel D. *medical association administrator*
Richardson, M. Catherine *lawyer*
Rivette, Francis Robert *lawyer*
Rogers, Sherry Anne *physician*
Sargent, Robert George *engineering educator*
Scheinman, Steven Jay *dean, medical educator*
Schiff, Eric Allan *physics professor*
Scullin, Frederick James, Jr. *federal judge*
Shroyer-Keno, Joan Elane *information analyst*
Skoler, Louis *architect, educator*
Smith, Kenneth Judson, Jr. *chemistry professor*

Stam, David Harry *librarian*
Steigerwald, Louis John III *corporate executive*
Sternlicht, Sanford *literature educator, writer*
Stork, Christine Mary *toxicologist, pharmacist*
Streeten, Barbara Wiard *ophthalmologist, medical educator*
Suddaby, Glenn T. *prosecutor, lawyer*
Swartz, Michael Frederick *physician assistant*
Szasz, Thomas Stephen *psychiatrist, educator, writer*
Tatham, David Frederic *art historian, educator*
Taylor, Robert Saxton *retired dean*
Thomas, Sidney *fine arts educator, researcher*
Thorin, Suzanne E. *dean, university librarian*
Traylor, Robert Arthur *lawyer*
Trop, Sandra *museum director*
Verheyen, Peter David *librarian, conservator*
Verrillo, Ronald Thomas *neuroscience educator, researcher*
Vook, Richard Werner *retired physics professor*
Waddy, Patricia A. *historian, architecture educator*
Wallerstein, Mitchel Bruce *dean, educator*
Ware, Bennie *academic administrator*
Wilkinson, Louise Cherry *psychology professor, dean*
Williams, William Joseph *hematologist, educator*
Wolff, Catherine Elizabeth *opera company executive*
Wolff, L. Thomas *physician, educator*
Wrigley, Brenda Jean *communications educator*
Yanjun, Yan *electrical engineer, statistician*

## Tappan
Cardenas, Raul Rodolfo, Jr. *engineering executive, educator, consultant*
Dell, Robert Christopher *sculptor, art educator*
Fox, Muriel *retired public relations executive*
Golbert, Sandra *artist*

## Tarrytown
Bergson, Henry Paul *professional society administrator*
Cocchiarella, Antonio *physician, educator*
Ferrari, Robert Joseph *finance educator, retired bank executive*
Field, Barry Elliot *internist, gastroenterologist*
Hyman, Leonard Stephen *financial consultant, economist, writer*
Kenney, Dion Patrick *information technology executive, entrepreneur*
Ladau, Robert Francis *architect, land use planner*
Marcus, Sheldon *school policy and administration educator*
Maun, Mary Ellen *computer consultant*
Mc Murtry, James Gilmer III *neurosurgeon*
Pontrelli, Laura Alison *psychologist*
Safian, Keith Franklin *hospital administrator*
Stein, Sol *publishing executive, writer*
Weiner, Max *psychology professor*
Yancopoulos, George D. *pharmaceutical executive*

## Thiells
Ziotis, Josephine *elementary school educator, restaurant owner*

## Thornwood
Bassett, Lawrence C *management consultant*

## Tivoli
Keesing, Felicia *biology professor*
Sethi, Gautam *environmental professor*

## Tonawanda
Brett, Jay Elliot *lawyer*
Brunger, Eric Geoffrey *social studies educator, coach*
Drozdziel, Marion John *aeronautical engineer*
Glickman, Marlene *non-profit organization administrator*
Haller, Calvin John *banker*
Loos, William H(enry) *librarian, consultant*
Vacanti, Mary Parisi *director, consultant*

## Treadwell
Norris, Linda Beth *museum administrator*

## Troy
Acar, Evrim *computer scientist*
Ahlers, Rolf Willi *philosopher, theologian*
Berg, Daniel *science and technology educator*
Bergles, Arthur Edward *mechanical engineering educator*
Biyik, Emrah *research scientist*
Block, Robert Charles *nuclear engineering educator*
Brazil, Harold Edmund *political science professor*
Demertzoglou, Pindaro Epaminonda *systems administrator, education educator*
Dobry, Ricardo *engineering educator*
Drew, Donald Allen *mathematical sciences educator*
Dvorak, George J. *mechanics and materials engineering educator*
Ehrlich, Henry Lutz *biology professor*
Ferris, James Peter *chemist, educator*
Finkel, Sanford Norman *lawyer*
Freyssinier Nova, Jean Paul *electrical engineer, educator*
Friedman, Gerald Manfred *geologist, educator*
Friedman, Sue Tyler *technical publications executive*
Frost, Jerome Kenneth *lawyer*
Fusfeld, Herbert Irving *research management and public policy executive*
Geddis, Carol J. *educational association administrator*
Gerhardt, Lester A. *engineering educator, dean*
Giaever, Ivar *physicist*
Gill, William Nelson *chemical engineering professor*
Glicksman, Martin Eden *materials engineering educator*
Haddock, Jorge *industrial engineering educator, consultant*
Haviland, David Sands *retired architectural educator, researcher, administrator*
Hsu, Cheng *decision sciences and engineering systems educator*
Jackson, Shirley Ann *academic administrator, physicist*
Jones, E. Stewart, Jr. *lawyer*

Kahl, William Frederick *retired academic administrator*
Kane, Ravi *biomedical engineer*
Krause, Sonja *chemistry professor*
Lahey, Richard Thomas, Jr. *nuclear engineer, fluid mechanics engineer*
Levinger, Joseph Solomon *physicist, researcher*
Linhardt, Robert John *chemistry professor*
Littman, Howard *chemical engineer, educator*
Luraas, Sandra *elementary school educator, secondary school educator*
Magdon-Ismail, Malik *computer science professor*
Mayo, Robert Raymond *university librarian*
McDermott, Robert J. *commissioner*
McDonald, John Francis Patrick *electrical engineering educator*
Medicus, Heinrich Adolf *physicist, researcher*
Medicus, Hildegard Julie *retired dentist, orthodontist, educator*
Mehta, Shreefal *pharmaceutical executive, educator*
Messac, Achille *mechanical engineer, aerospace engineer*
Neff, Jeanne Henry *academic administrator*
Nelson, John Keith *electrical engineer, educator*
Persans, Peter David *physics educator, researcher*
Phan, Phillip Hin Choi *business educator, consultant*
Phelan, Thomas *clergyman, academic administrator, educator*
Potts, Kevin T. *retired chemistry professor*
Sanderson, Arthur Clark *engineering educator*
Shan, Yufeng *research scientist*
Shephard, Mark Scott *civil and mechanical engineering educator*
Shuey, Richard Lyman *engineering educator, consultant*
Sperber, Daniel *physicist*
Szymanski, Boleslaw Karol *computer scientist, educator, entrepreneur*
Wait, Samuel Charles, Jr. *academic administrator, educator*
Watson, E Bruce *science educator*
Woods, John William *electrical, computer and systems engineering educator, consultant*
Zimmie, Thomas Frank *civil engineer, educator*
Zurbenko, Igor Georg *science educator*

## Tuckahoe
Brecher, Bernd *management consultant*
Mariani, John F. *writer*

## Tupper Lake
Welsh, Peter Corbett *museum director, historian*

## Turin
Klossner, Windy *food products executive*

## Tuxedo Park
Davis, Shelby Moore Cullom *investment company executive, consultant*
Regan, Ellen Frances (Mrs. Walston Shepard Brown) *ophthalmologist, educator*

## Uniondale
Berzow, Harold Steven *lawyer*
DiPietro, Rick *professional hockey player*
Duffy, James Raymond *lawyer*
Guerrera, Lisa E. *financial planner*
Impagliazzo, Jenette Celeste *elementary school educator*
Kotula, Michael Anthony *lawyer*
Kozlov, Viktor *professional hockey player*
Lemle, Robert Spencer *lawyer*
Levy, Robert S. *lawyer*
Milbury, Mike *professional sports team executive, former professional hockey coach*
Nolan, Ted (Theodore John Nolan) *professional hockey coach*
Pratt, George Cheney *law educator, retired judge*
Redder, Thomas *consumer products company executive*
Reddy, Gerard Anthony *consumer banker*
Sanchez, Laura Ann *music educator*
Snow, Garth *professional sports team executive, former professional hockey player*
Stewart, Cynthia Willis *minister*
Trottier, Bryan John *professional sports team executive, former professional hockey player and coach*
Wang, Charles B. *professional sports team executive, former computer company executive*

## Unionville
Kemnitz, Thomas Milton *publisher*

## Upton
Alamgir, Faisal M. *materials scientist*
Baltz, Anthony John *physicist*
Bond, Peter Danford *physicist*
Carsten, Arland Leon *radiobiologist, researcher, educator, consultant*
Chaudhari, Praveen *science administrator, materials physicist*
Foerster, Conrad Louis *project engineer*
Fowler, Joanna S. *chemist*
Goldhaber, Maurice *physicist, researcher*
Hamilton, Leonard Derwent *physician, molecular biologist*
Hendrie, Joseph Mallam *physicist, nuclear engineer*
Lindenbaum, S(eymour) J(oseph) *physicist*
Lowenstein, Derek Irving *physicist*
Mahajan, Devinder *chemical engineer, chemistry professor*
Meinhold, Charles Boyd *health physicist*
Paul, Peter *science administrator*
Rau, Ralph Ronald *retired physicist*
Samios, Nicholas Peter *physicist*
Setlow, Jane Kellock *biophysicist*
Setlow, Richard Burton *biophysicist, researcher*
Steinberg, Meyer *chemical engineer*
Sutherland, Betsy Middleton *biologist*
Sutin, Norman *chemist, researcher*
Tannenbaum, Michael J(ay) *physicist*
Wei, Xiangdong *physicist, researcher*

## Utica
Antzelevitch, Charles *research and development company executive*
Baber, Bob *dean*

Cardamone, Richard J. *federal judge*
Fiori-Blanchfield, Joan *artist, art historian*
Hockey, Christopher Lawrence *academic administrator*
Schweizer, Paul Douglas *museum director*
Wagner, Frederick Reese *retired language educator*

## Valatie
Dorsey, Richard J. *lawyer*
Smith, Albert Aloysius, Jr. *electrical engineer, consultant*

## Valhalla
Aronow, Wilbert Solomon *physician, educator*
Brand, Donald Albert *medical researcher, educator*
Christesen, John D. *business educator*
Cimino, Joseph Anthony *preventive medicine physician, educator*
Cohen, Martin Bruce *physician*
Czarnecki, Anthony J. *correction administrator, educator*
Darzynkiewicz, Zbigniew D. *research scientist*
Del Guercio, Louis Richard Maurice *surgeon, educator*
De Nicola, Peter Francis *photographic distributor*
Fachnie, H(ugh) Douglas *film manufacturing company official*
Frishman, William Howard *cardiologist, educator, department chairman, cardiovascular pharmacologist, gerontologist*
Goldowsky, Michael Philip *mechanical engineer*
Goodman, Alvin Irwin *internist, nephrologist, educator*
Hankin, Joseph Nathan *college president*
Iatropoulos, Michael John *health research executive, pathology educator*
Inchiosa, Mario Anthony, Jr. *pharmacologist*
Kline, Susan Anderson *medical educator, internist*
Leone, Stephen Joseph *language educator, computer technician, consultant*
Madden, Robert Edward *surgeon, educator*
Marks, Stephen J. *neurologist, educator*
Niguidula, Faustino Nazario *surgeon, educator*
O'Connell, Ralph Anthony *dean, psychiatrist, educator*
Peterson, Stephen Joseph *internist*
Sclafani, Charles Carlo *language educator, department chairman*
Slim, Michel S. *surgeon, educator, health facility administrator*
Spielvogel, David *thoracic surgeon*
Stringel, Gustavo *pediatric surgeon*
Stuhlmiller, David Fe *emergency physician*
Urban, Diane *psychologist, educator*
Weinberg, Hubert *plastic surgeon*
Williams, Gary Murray *pathologist, educator*

## Valley Stream
Ellis, Bernice *financial planner, investment advisor*
Gonzalez, Jennifer *school psychologist*
Rachlin, Harvey Brant *writer*
Rodgers, John Joseph III *educational administration consultant, educator*
Wood, Catherine T. *special education educator*

## Vestal
Adour, Colleen McNulty *artist, educator*
Cohen, Marvin A. *writer*
Grinberg, Raul *internist*
Quataert, Donald *historian, educator*

## Victor
Morris, G. Michael *science educator*

## Waccabuc
Krefting, Robert J(ohn) *publishing company executive*
Tognino, John Nicholas *diversified financial services company executive*

## Wainscott
Henderson, William Charles *editor*
Herzog, Arthur III *author*
Russo, Alexander Peter *artist, educator*

## Walden
Murphy, Pamela Ann *music educator, actress, musician*

## Wallkill
Koch, Edwin Ernest *artist, interior designer*
Strauser, Susan Parkyn *performing arts educator, singer*

## Walton
Bolton, Theresa M. *music educator*

## Wantagh
Berk, Adele L. *composer, music educator*
Blum, Melvin *chemical company executive, researcher*
Forman, Anne *artist*
Galvan, Max *humanities educator*
Glaser, David *painter, sculptor*
Smits, Edward John *historian, consultant*
Zinder, Newton Donald *investment advisor, consultant*

## Wappingers Falls
Hogan, Edward Robert *financial services executive*
Johnson, Jeh Vincent *architect*
Maissel, Leon Israel *physicist, engineer*
Maissel, Raina Eve *lawyer*
Nolan, John Thomas, Jr. *retired oil industry administrator*

## Warwick
English, Dennis *music educator*
Kaminsky, Anatol *political science professor, writer*
Linnéa, Sharon *writer, playwright*
McManus, Robert Francis *lawyer*
Simon, Dolores Daly *copy editor*

## Washingtonville
Marcialis, Angelo Vincent *music educator, musician*

**Water Mill**
Chalif, Ronnie *medical association administrator, artist*
Hagstrom, Jack Walter Carl Kling *retired pathology educator*
Kreimer, Michael Walter *financial planner, investment company executive*

**Waterford**
Glavin, James Henry III *lawyer*
Gold, James Paul *museum director*

**Waterloo**
Schreck, Richard Thomas *accountant*

**Watertown**
Coe, Benjamin Plaisted *retired state official*
Francis, Danny Marvin *retired military officer*
Henderson, Gladys Edith *retired social welfare examiner*

**Watervliet**
Bishop, Aisha Suzette *materials engineer*
Elrahman, O. Abd *environmental and transportation engineer, educator*

**Watkins Glen**
Spencer, Dawn Joyce *animal advocate*

**Webster**
Curtis, Deana A. *electronics executive, small business owner*
Cusick, Patricia A. *information technology executive*
Duke, Charles Bryan *electronics executive, physicist, educator*
McCormack, Stanley Eugene *financial consultant*
McWilliams, C. Paul, Jr. *engineering executive*
Nicholson, Douglas Robert *accountant*
Powers, Richard Gerard *history educator*
Zhang, Shengliang *materials scientist, physicist*

**Wellsville**
Van Tyne, Arthur Morris *geologist*

**West Babylon**
Ford, Clara S. *retired secondary school educator*

**West Chazy**
Slosson, Constance Sweet *retired music educator*

**West Harrison**
Verano, Anthony Frank *retired banker*

**West Hempstead**
Guggenheimer, Heinrich Walter *mathematician, educator*

**West Hurley**
Martucci, Vincent James *composer, pianist*

**West Islip**
Cokinos, Stephan George *cardiologist*
Henesch, Stephen *pediatrician, radiologist*
Rifkin, Matthew D. *radiologist*

**West Kill**
Dwon, Larry *retired electrical engineer, educator, consultant*

**West Nyack**
Pringle, Laurence Patrick *writer*

**West Point**
Boettner, Daisie Dawson *military officer, mechanical engineering educator*
Bozeman, Laura Beth *military officer, educator*
Finnegan, Patrick *dean, military officer, lawyer*
Hagenbeck, Franklin Lee *career military officer*
Keith, Bruce Edward *sociologist*
Ross, Robert Joseph (Bobby Ross) *college football coach*
Scaparrotti, Curtis M. *career military officer*
Williams, Craig Stewart *organist, music educator, director*

**West Seneca**
Beehler, Mark *director*
Bidlack, Jerald Dean *manufacturing executive*
Siegel, Carolyn Augusta *judge, lawyer, social worker*
Tanski, Sarah Piatko *mathematics educator*

**Westbury**
Brooks, David H. *manufacturing executive*
Cohen, Abraham Ezekiel *retired health care company executive*
Greenberger, Roni Susan *elementary school educator*
Lorber, Howard Mark *investments executive*
Marks, Debra Jane *special education educator*
McCann, Jim (James F. McCann) *consumer products company executive*
Mondello, John Paul *financial consultant*
Ross-Lee, Barbara *dean, educator*
Sandler, Gerald Howard *computer scientist, educator, information technology executive*

**Westhampton Beach**
Flood, Angela *interior designer, artist*
Maas, Jane Brown *advertising executive*
Perez, Dawn Marie *elementary school educator*

**White Plains**
Abrams, Leigh Jeffrey *manufacturing executive*
Adams, Robert T. *lawyer*
Adkins, Rodney *computer company executive*
Alin, Robert David *lawyer*
Allen, Ralph Dean *diversified company corporate executive*
Arimilli, Ravi K. *computer engineer*
Berlin, Alan Daniel *lawyer, consultant, real estate company officer*
Bernard, Robert William *plastic surgeon*
Biers, Martin Henry *physician*
Blass, John Paul *physician, biochemist*
Bober, Lawrence Harold *retired banker*
Bodnar, Peter O. *lawyer*
Brieant, Charles La Monte *federal judge*
Brown, Ronald C. *hotel executive*

**Bushkin**, Merle Jerome *investment banker*
Carey, John *judge*
Carlisle, Jay Charles, II, *lawyer, educator*
Carlucci, Joseph P. *lawyer*
Colwell, Howard Otis *advertising executive*
Conner, William Curtis *federal judge*
Cotter, Robert F. *hotel executive*
Davenport, Lindsay *professional tennis player*
David, Miles *marketing executive*
Davies, Matt *cartoonist*
Doyle, Dennis T. *lawyer*
Feder, Robert *lawyer*
Fisher, Jerome *apparel executive*
Foderaro, Lisa *reporter*
Foster, John Horace *consulting environmental engineer*
Fowler, James D., Jr. *leadership executive*
Fowlkes, Nancy Lanetta Pinkard *social worker*
Frazier, Amy *professional tennis player*
Freed, Arthur *civil engineer*
Friedman, Stephen J. *lawyer*
Gambardella, Thomas M. *lawyer*
Garrison-Jackson, Zina *retired professional tennis player*
Gilbert, Bradley *professional tennis coach, former professional tennis player, former Olympic athlete*
Gimelstob, Justin *professional tennis player*
Gjertsen, O. Gerard *lawyer*
Gottlieb, Lester M. *entrepreneur*
Greenawalt, William Sloan *lawyer*
Greene, Leonard Michael *manufacturing executive, aerospace transportation executive*
Greenspan, Leon *lawyer*
Haines, Daniel Webster *engineering consultant, engineering educator*
Halpern, Philip Morgan *lawyer*
Handelman, Walter Joseph *lawyer*
Hardin, Adlai Stevenson, Jr. *judge*
Hariton, Jo Rosenberg *psychotherapist, educator*
Heyer, Steven J. *hotel executive, former beverage company executive*
Howse, Jennifer Louise *foundation administrator*
Huang, Han *systems engineer*
Jacobson, Sandra W. *lawyer*
Katz, Michael *pediatrician, educator*
Kaushik, Surendra Kumar *economist*
Kroner, Arnold Friedrich *financial consultant, economist*
Kutscher, Martin L. *pediatrician, neurologist*
Landa, Howard Martin *lawyer, management consultant*
Leish, Kenneth William *retired publishing company executive*
Leung, Betty Brigid *nursing administrator*
Levasseur, Guy J. *lawyer*
Levine, Steven Jon *lawyer*
Liebert, Peter Selig *pediatric surgeon, consultant*
Loranger, Steven R. *industrial manufacturing company executive*
Lukaszewski, James Edmund *communications executive*
MacDonald, J. Randall *information technology executive, human resources specialist*
Machover, Carl *computer graphics designer, consultant, computer engineer*
Madden, M. Stuart *lawyer*
Maffeo, Vincent Anthony *lawyer, director*
Manville, Stewart Roebling *archivist*
Marano, Anthony Joseph *cardiologist*
Mills, Steven A. *information technology executive*
Mitchell, Robert Dale *engineer, consultant*
Morariu, Corina *professional tennis player*
Nastasi, Aldo A. *judge*
Newman, Marie Stefanini *law librarian, educator*
Null, William Seth *lawyer*
O'Brien, H. Michael *lawyer*
O'Brien, James F. *lawyer*
Ottinger, Richard Lawrence *dean emeritus*
Palmisano, Samuel J. *information technology executive*
Parker, Barrington D., Jr. *federal judge, lawyer*
Payson, Martin F. *lawyer*
Pfeffer, Cynthia Roberta *psychiatrist, educator*
Pirro, Jeanine Ferris *prosecutor*
Prabhu, Vasant *corporate financial executive*
Quaranta, Philip *lawyer*
Ramos, Paul-John *composer, writer*
Raymond, Lisa *professional tennis player*
Robinson, Nicholas Adams *law educator*
Rometty, Ginny (Virginia M. Rometty) *information technology executive*
Rubin, Chanda *professional tennis player*
Sacco, John Michael *accountant*
Scott-Williams, Wendy Lee *library and information scientist*
Sedelmaier, J. J. *filmmaker*
Sheehan, Timothy J. *lawyer*
Siegel, Kenneth S. *lawyer, director*
Sloan, F(rank) Blaine *law educator*
Smith, Gerard Peter *neuroscientist*
Steccato, Carl L. *lawyer*
Sternlicht, Barry Stuart *hotel executive*
Straus, Marc Joshua *internist, poet*
Surpris, Joseph W. *research scientist*
Sussberg, Milton Joel *marketing professional*
Szolnoki, John Frank *special education educator, administrator*
Tumbarello, Phillip A. *lawyer*
Ughetta, James C. *lawyer*
Underweiser, Irwin Philip *mining executive, lawyer*
Vernon, Lillian *mail order company executive*
Vignali, Rosario M. *lawyer*
Volpe, Bruce Thomas *neurologist*
Wedge, Chris *animation director, studio executive*
Weisburger, John Hans *medical researcher*
Williams, Edward W. *information technology executive*
Williams, Serena *professional tennis player, apparel designer*
Williams, Ted Vaughnell *physical education educator*
Williams, Venus *professional tennis player*
Young, Steven L. *lawyer*
Zuckerman, Marc Abraham *finance educator*

**Whitesboro**
O'Hara, Cynthia O'Connor *writer, columnist*

**Whitestone**
Bikoff, J. Darius *beverage company executive*

**Rahr**, Stewart *health medical products executive*

**Williamsville**
Ackerman, Philip Charles *utilities executive, lawyer*
Ashton, Adam Keller *psychiatrist, educator*
Berner, Robert Frank *managerial statistics educator, administrator*
Brown, Stephen Ira *philosophy professor*
Canfield, Cheryl Lucas *epidemiologist*
Cloudsley, Donald Hugh *retired library administrator*
Danni, F. Robert *town official*
Drew, Fraser Bragg Robert *language educator*
Huff, Kenneth L. *elementary school educator*
Jones, Robert Alfred *retired clergyman*
Kennedy, Bernard Joseph *retired utilities executive*
Kim, Jung Taek *electrochemical engineer*
Levite, Laurence A. *publishing executive*
Mack, Gregory John *financial executive and consultant*
Metzger, Ernest Hugh *aerospace engineer, research scientist*
Neiman, Joseph Bruce *dermatologist, educator*
Ogra, Pearay L. *pediatrician, educator*
Perry, J. Warren *health facility administrator, educator*
Reisman, Robert E. *allergist, educator*
Whitcomb, James Stuart *videographer, photographer, production company executive*

**Williston Park**
Lynch, Kyle Thomas *lawyer*

**Willow**
Bley, Carla Borg *composer*

**Willsboro**
Gillilland, Thomas *art gallery director*
Reuther, David Louis *retired children's book publisher, writer*

**Wilmington**
Leary, Daniel *artist*

**Windsor**
Warner, Roberta Arlene *retired accountant, financial services executive*

**Wolcott**
Searle, Robert Ferguson *minister*

**Woodbury**
Agresti, Miriam Monell *psychologist*
Barnett, Rochelle *accountant*
Guttenplan, Harold Esau *retired food company executive*

**Woodhaven**
Bolster, Jacqueline Neben (Mrs. John A. Bolster) *communications consultant*

**Woodmere**
Faber, Nan Geist *lawyer*
Ginsburg, Estelle *artist*
Seyfert, Wayne George *secondary education educator, anatomy educator*
Winick, Bernyce Alpert *artist, photographer*

**Woodside**
Hofmann, Herbert C. *diversified financial services company executive*
Sfiroudis, Gloria Tides *library and information scientist, educator*

**Woodstock**
Banks, Rela *sculptor*
Currie, Bruce *artist*
Godwin, Gail Kathleen *writer*
Jordan, John Lester (Gaudeamus) *artist*
Lieberman, Josefa Nina *psychologist, educator, writer*
Ober, Stuart Alan *investment advisor, writer*

**Wyandanch**
Newman, Samuel *retired trust company executive*
Weber, Carl *publishing executive, retail bookstore executive, writer*

**Yaphank**
Narain, Ralph B. *biologist*

**Yonkers**
Baumel, Herbert *violinist, conductor*
Baumel, Joan Patricia French *writer, educator*
Boveroux, Lorie Ann Hansen *secondary school educator, graphics designer*
Capodilupo, Elizabeth Jeanne Hatton *public relations executive*
Chumaceiro, Rolando Jose Mendez *family practice physician*
Colabella, George Michael *management consultant, not-for-profit fundraiser*
Daman, Harlan Richard *allergist, educator*
Fyle, Clifford Nelson *publishing executive, educator*
Gunner, Murray *retired religious organization administrator*
Herman, Martin H. *retired accountant*
Holtz, Gilbert Joseph *steel company executive*
Johansen, Robert Joseph *consulting actuary*
Lee, Claudia S. *retired elementary school educator*
Liggio, Jean Vincenza *adult education educator, artist*
Lukach, Arthur S., Jr. *manufacturing executive*
Lupiani, Donald Anthony *psychologist*
McCarthy, William Joseph *retired lawyer, finance company executive*
McKean, Kevin S. *publishing executive, writer*
Monegro, Francisco *alternative medicine consultant, psychology professor*
Neal, Leora Louise Haskett *social services administrator*
Ortega, Maria A. *security firm executive, educator*
Philipps, Edward William *former banker, real estate appraiser*
Roberson, Doris Jean Herold *retired social worker*
Senator, Ronald Paul *composer, writer, retired music educator*

**Singer**, Cecile Doris *bank executive, former state legislator*
Slade, Margot S. *editor*
Smith, Aldo Ralston, Jr. *brokerage house executive*
Spagnuolo, Mario *physician*
Speirs, Greg *artist*
Torrese, Dante Michael *prosthodontist, educator*
Weston, Francine Evans *secondary school educator*
Westphal, Carol Jean *media specialist*
Wolfson, Irwin M. *insurance company executive*

**York**
Coleman, David Cecil *financial executive*

**Yorktown Heights**
Avouris, Phaedon *chemical physicist*
Berk, George Ellis *cardiologist*
Chen, Jia *science and technology researcher*
Choi, Changhwan *operations research specialist*
Dennard, Robert Heath *engineering executive, scientist*
d'Heurle, François Max *research scientist, engineering educator*
Hoffman, Alan Jerome *mathematician, educator*
Iyengar, Arun K. *computer scientist*
Joshi, Rajiv V. *information technology manager, researcher*
Keyes, Robert W. *physicist, researcher*
Kim, Keunwoo *electrical engineer, researcher*
Koester, Steven John *research scientist*
Kosonocky, Stephen V. *electrical engineer, computer graphics designer, researcher*
Lang, Norton David *physicist*
Lanzerotti, Mary Yvonne *physicist, researcher*
Lei, Hui *computer scientist*
Mayer, Gerard J. *physician*
Ning, Tak Hung *physicist, microelectronic technologist*
Rosenblatt, Stephen Paul *marketing and sales promotion company executive*
Saon, George A. *computer scientist, researcher*
Schiller, Barbara *retired special education educator*
Terman, Lewis Madison *retired electrical engineer, researcher, director*
Tersoff, Jerry David *physicist*
Tutuc, Emanuel *research scientist*
Wade, James O'Shea *editor, writer*
Winograd, Shmuel *mathematician*
Winterton, Joseph Henry *computer software executive*
Wu, Chai Wah *research scientist*
Wynne, James J. *research scientist*

**Youngstown**
Alpert, Norman *chemical company executive*
Askins, Nancy Ellen Paulsen *training services executive*
Gordon, Wilfred Edward Lawrence *retired obstetrician-gynecologist*
Lamb, Charles F. *retired minister, retired educator*

## NORTH CAROLINA

**Advance**
Cochrane, Betsy Lane *former state senator*
Guth, Caryl Joy *retired anesthesiologist*

**Andrews**
Fonda, Ronald Alan *epistemologist*

**Ararat**
Marsh, Joseph Virgil *real estate broker, retired investment advisor*

**Archdale**
O'Hara, Karen Ann *mathematician, educator*

**Arden**
Baker, Kerry Allen *management consultant*

**Asheboro**
Clark, Lawrence James *minister*
Jones, David M. *zoological park administrator*
Mac Kenzie, James Donald *clergyman*

**Asheville**
Bissette, Winston Louis, Jr. *lawyer, mayor*
Brown, David G. *academic administrator*
Burgard, Jesse F. *psychologist*
Childress, Patrick Nicholas *retired lawyer*
Coli, Guido John *chemical company executive*
Dickens, Charles Henderson *retired social sciences educator*
Eglinton, Daniel Thomas *orthopedist*
Gray, Robert Ward *art association administrator*
Haggard, William Henry *meteorologist*
Haynes, John Mabin *retired utilities executive*
Hazlehurst, John Livingston *surgeon*
Horwitz, Bertrand Nathan *finance educator*
Hyde, Herbert Lee *lawyer*
Kessler, Donald Joe *research scientist, physicist, consultant*
King, Joseph Bertram *architect*
Lavelle, Brian Francis David *lawyer*
Letzig, Betty Jean *financial consultant*
Merrill, Deane Whitney, Jr. *secondary school educator, consultant*
Meyerson, Seymour *retired chemist*
Mundt, Barry Maynard *management consultant*
Parresol, Bernard Ross *research scientist, statistician*
Pfeiffer, William Sanborn *education educator, writer*
Puckett, Derek Lee *biologist, researcher*
Sun, Bomin *environmental scientist*
Thompson, Charles Spurgeon *retired music educator, retired conductor*
Thornburg, Lacy Herman *federal judge*
Turcot, Marguerite Hogan *medical researcher*
Tynes, Robert Dick *artist, educator*
Voigt, Ellen *literature educator*
White, Terry Edward *physician*
Wilson, Thomas Douglas, Jr. *lawyer*
Zarnoch, Stanley Joseph *research scientist, statistician*

## Bakersville
Buchanan, Robin Byington *school system administrator*

## Banner Elk
Hutcheson, James Sterling *retired physician, allergist*

## Beaufort
Bonaventura, Celia Jean *biochemist, researcher*
Cox, Tara M. *marine biologist, researcher*
Cullman, Hugh *retired tobacco company executive*
Ramus, Joseph S. *marine biologist*

## Belmont
Ratchford, Melinda Eudy *education educator*
Stowe, Robert Lee III *textile company executive*

## Biltmore Forest
Sgro, Joseph Anthony *retired psychologist, educator*

## Biltmore Lake
Steele, Russell Loren *football coach*

## Black Mountain
Belue, Janie A. *music educator*
Ingle, Robert P. *retail executive*
Lanning, James W. *retail executive*

## Blowing Rock
Barnebey, Kenneth Alan *food products executive*

## Boiling Springs
Lahaie, L. Scot *theater educator*
Vanderburg, Timothy Warren *history professor*

## Boone
Austin, Roberta Jones *elementary school educator*
Conrad, David Paul *business broker, real estate developer, retired food service executive*
Duke, Charles Richard *dean*
Durham, Harvey Ralph *academic administrator*
Harbinson, William Grady *dean, composer*
Kitunda, Jeremiah Mutio *history professor, researcher*
Lugo, Emil J. *retired secondary school educator*
Martin, Vicki Joan *biology professor*
McGaha, Cindy *education educator*
Oelberg, Robert Nathan *landscape architect*
Schneberger, Scott L. *information systems educator*
Warren, Robert Lee *dentist, educator*

## Brevard
Dillon, Doris (Doris Dillon Kenofer) *artist, art historian, educator, interior designer*
Finnerty, Frances Martin *medical administrator*
Flory, Margaret Martha *retired religious organization administrator*
Phillips, Euan Hywel *publishing executive*

## Buies Creek
Guzman, Karen *science educator*
Johnson, George Lloyd *education educator, consultant, writer*
Stanke, Jaclyn *history professor*
Whichard, Willis Padgett *lawyer, educator, retired judge*
Wiggins, Norman Adrian *academic administrator, law educator*
Wright, Mary P. *counselor*

## Burlington
Blevins, James Ray *lawyer, insurance company claims executive*
Elingburg, Wesley R. *health products executive*
Flagg, Raymond Osbourn *retired medical products executive*
Holt, Bertha Merrill *state legislator*
King, David Paul *health services executive, lawyer*
MacMahon, Thomas P. *healthcare company executive*
Malinda, Paul F. *emergency physician*
Phillips, Ruth Ann *retired secondary school educator*
Powell, James Bobbitt *health facility administrator, pathologist*
Wilson, William Preston *psychiatrist, educator*

## Burnsville
Bernstein, William Joseph *glass artist, educator*
Doyle, John Lawrence *artist*

## Camden
Hammond, Roy Joseph *reinsurance company executive*

## Canton
Dixon, Shirley Juanita *retired restaurant owner*
Roberts, Bill Glen *retired protective services official*

## Cape Carteret
Mullikin, Thomas Wilson *mathematics professor*

## Carolina Beach
Mansbery, Sarah Huntsman *music educator*

## Carrboro
Barbarin, Oscar Anthony *psychologist*
Baumhover, Alfred Henry *entomologist, researcher*
Generous, William Thomas, Jr., (Tom Generous) *coach, educator*

## Carthage
Gebhardt, Robert Charles *lawyer*

## Cary
Ashley, James MacGregor *management consultant*
Bogdanovich, Alexander *manufacturing executive*
Bryant, Mynora Joyce *not-for-profit fundraiser*
Buckler, Sheldon A. *technology company executive*
Conrad, Hans *materials science and engineering executive, systems analyst*
Craig, Harold Kent *mechanical contracting executive, systems analyst*
Duan, Jiwen *chemical engineer*
Fan, Wei *operations research specialist*

Goodnight, James H. *software company executive*
Hauser, John Reid *electrical engineering educator*
Kung, Pang-Jen *materials scientist, electrical engineer*
Martin, William Royall, Jr. *retired professional society administrator*
Mata, Elizabeth Adams *language educator, land investor*
Montgomery, Charles Harvey *lawyer*
O'Meallie, Kitty *artist*
Rahmani, Carol Hipp *school system administrator, psychologist*
Sall, John *information technology executive*
Summers, Suzanne Frances Hemenway *elementary school educator*
Taylor, David Wyatt Aiken *retired clergyman*
Thayer, Paul William *psychology educator, consultant*
Vick, Columbus Edwin, Jr. *retired civil engineering design firm executive*
Wait, George William *sales executive*

## Cashiers
O'Connell, Edward James, Jr. *psychologist, educator, systems administrator, consultant*

## Chapel Hill
Adkins, Willis G. *medical association administrator, consultant*
Andreoni, Kenneth A. *surgeon*
Andrews, Richard Nigel Lyon *public information officer, educator, environmental services administrator*
Arnold, Roland R. *dental educator, researcher*
Azar, Henry Amin *retired medical educator*
Bailey, Herbert Smith, Jr. *retired publisher*
Baker, Edward L., Jr. *public health physician*
Baroff, George Stanley *psychologist, educator*
Baron, Samuel Haskell *historian*
Berkowitz, Max *physical chemist, researcher*
Bernard, Stephen Alan *oncologist*
Bolas, Gerald Douglas *museum director, art historian, educator*
Bondurant, Stuart *physician, educational association administrator*
Boucher, David C. *medical educator, researcher*
Bowers, Thomas Arnold *journalism educator, dean*
Bowman, Frederick Oscar, Jr. *retired cardiothoracic surgeon*
Broad, Margaret Corbett (Molly Broad) *academic administrator*
Brookhart, Maurice S. *chemist*
Brooks, Frederick Phillips, Jr. *computer scientist, educator*
Brown, Frank *social sciences educator*
Browning, Christopher R. *historian, educator*
Bursey, Maurice M. *retired chemistry professor*
Callahan, Leigh Fleming *medical educator, researcher*
Carroll, Roy *retired academic administrator*
Carson, Culley Clyde III *urologist, educator*
Cefalo, Robert Charles *obstetrician, gynecologist*
Chang, Kuk Won *theology educator, researcher, pastor*
Clark, Arthur Watts *insurance company executive*
Clemmons, David Robert *internist, educator*
Coeytaux, Remy Rene *physician, researcher*
Cole, Richard Ray *communications educator, former dean*
Coles, William Henry *ophthalmologist, educator*
Collier, Albert M. *pediatrician, educator, director*
Crews, Fulton Timm *pharmacology educator*
Crohn, Max Henry, Jr. *lawyer*
Cromartie, William James *medical educator, researcher*
Cronenwett, Linda Houk *dean, nursing educator*
Cummings, Sandra Eileen *medical products executive*
Davis, Sarah Irwin *retired language educator*
Debreczeny, Paul *retired language educator, writer*
De Friese, Gordon H. *health services researcher*
De Rosa, Guy Paul *orthopedic surgery educator*
Desimone, Joseph M. *chemist, educator*
Dirschl, Douglas Ray *surgeon, educator*
Dixon, Frederick Dail *architect*
Dolan, Louise Ann *physicist*
Edmunds, Douglas B. *information technology executive, educator*
Edwards, John Reid *former senator, lawyer*
Edwards, Richard LeRoy *dean, social sciences educator, management consultant*
Eliel, Ernest Ludwig *chemist, educator*
Erdem, Nurum Filiz *geriatrician*
Feduccia, J. Alan *biologist, educator*
Feinberg, Lawrence Edward *language educator, researcher*
Ferrell, Joseph Stevens *law educator*
Ferris, William Reynolds *humanities organization administrator, folklore educator*
Fieleke, Norman Siegfried *economist, educator*
Filene, Peter Gabriel *history professor*
Fine, J(ames) Allen *insurance company executive*
Finkel, Alan Glen *neurologist, educator*
Fletcher, Suzanne Wright *epidemiologist, medical educator, editor*
Flora, Joseph M(artin) *language educator*
Folkerts, Jean *dean, journalism educator*
Fordham, Christopher Columbus III *dean, academic administrator, medical educator*
Forman, Donald T. *biochemist, educator*
Fowler, Wesley Caswell, Jr. *obstetrician, gynecologist*
Fox, Ronald Ernest *psychologist*
Frampton, Paul Howard *physics researcher, educator*
Freund, Cynthia M. *dean*
Ganley, Oswald Harold *retired director*
Gervais-Gruen, Elizabeth *lawyer*
Gilman, Andrew Lee *pediatrician*
Girdler, Susan Scott *psychologist, educator, researcher*
Godschalk, David Robinson *architect, urban development planner, educator*
Goldsmith, Lowell Alan *medical educator*
Gordon-Larsen, Penny *nutritionist, educator, researcher*
Gottlieb, Gilbert *psychobiologist, educator*
Goyer, Robert Andrew *pathology educator*
Gray, Virginia Hickman *political science professor*
Greganti, Mac Andrew *physician, medical educator*
Grendler, Paul Frederick *historian, educator*

Gressman, Eugene *lawyer*
Gura, Philip Francis *English and American literature educator*
Hammond, David Alan *stage director, educator*
Hartlyn, Jonathan *political scientist, educator*
Haskell, Paul Gershon *retired law educator*
Hawkins, David Rollo, Sr. *psychiatrist, educator*
Heninger, Simeon Kahn, Jr. *language educator*
Henson, O'Dell Williams, Jr. *retired anatomy educator*
Houpt, Jeffrey Lyle *psychiatrist, educator, former dean*
Hughes-Hassell, Sandra *education educator*
Hulka, Jaroslav Fabian *obstetrician, gynecologist*
Illiano, Antonio *language educator, researcher*
James, Alton Everette, Jr. *radiologist*
Jones, Houston Gwynne *archivist, history professor*
Jones, Lyle Vincent *psychologist, educator*
Jones, W. S. (Steve Jones) *dean*
Jordan, Janine *interior designer, consultant, small business owner*
Judd, Burke Haycock *geneticist*
Kenan, Thomas Stephen III *philanthropist*
Kim, Chong Soong *aerosol science and inhalation dosimetry researcher*
Kinnaird, Eleanor Gates *state legislator, lawyer*
Klein, Martin Jesse *physicist, educator, science historian*
Kohn, Richard H. *historian, educator*
Krasno, Richard Michael *foundation executive, educator*
Lachiewicz, Paul Francis *orthopedist, surgeon, educator*
Latané, Bibb *social psychologist*
Lauder, Valarie Anne *editor, educator*
Lavelle, John Paul *urologist*
Lawrence, David Michael *lawyer, educator*
Lee, Kuo-Hsiung *medicinal chemistry professor*
Levine, Madeline Geltman *literature and language educator, translator*
Ligett, Waldo Buford *chemist*
Lilley, Albert Frederick *retired lawyer*
Lochridge, Julie Deane *retired communications executive*
Loeb, Ben Fohl, Jr. *retired law educator*
Lohr, Jacob Andrew *pediatrician, educator*
Lowman, Robert Paul *psychology professor, academic administrator*
Ludington, Townsend *English and American studies educator*
Macdonald, James Ross *physicist, researcher*
Magill, Samuel Hays *academic administrator, consultant*
Marchionini, Gary Joseph *information science educator*
Martikainen, A(une) Helen *retired health specialist educator*
Mc Kean, John Rosseel Overton *university dean*
McKinney, Ross Erwin, Sr. *civil engineering educator*
McMillan, Campbell White *pediatrician, educator, hematologist*
Mersini - Houghton, Laura *physicist, educator*
Merzbacher, Eugen *retired physics professor*
Meyer, Philip Edward *journalism educator*
Michalak, Sarah C. *university librarian*
Miller, C. Arden *physician, educator*
Mitchell, Earl Nelson *physicist, researcher*
Moellering, John Henry *aviation maintenance company executive*
Moeser, James Charles *academic administrator*
Moore, Albert Cunningham *lawyer, insurance company executive*
Moran, Barbara Burns *librarian, educator*
Mueller, Nancy Schneider *retired biology professor*
Murray, Michael Dennis *pharmacist*
Neff, Severine *music educator*
Nelson, Philip Francis *musicologist, consultant, conductor*
Norton, Edward C. *economist, educator*
Okun, Daniel Alexander *environmental engineering educator*
Pagano, Joseph Stephen *internist, researcher, educator*
Palmer, Jeffrss Gary *hematologist, educator*
Parr, Robert Ghormley *chemistry professor*
Peacock, Erle Ewart, Jr. *surgeon, lawyer, educator*
Pease, William Henry *history professor*
Pedersen, Lee G. *chemistry professor*
Perreault, William Daniel, Jr. *business administration educator*
Pillsbury, Harold Crockett III *otolaryngologist*
Powell, Carolyn Wilkerson *retired music educator*
Prange, Arthur Jergen, Jr. *psychology professor, neuroscientist*
Prather, Donna Lynn *psychiatrist*
Proffit, William Robert *orthodontics educator*
Pruett, James Worrell *librarian, educator, musicologist*
Rabil, Albert, Jr. *humanities educator*
Ravenel, Shannon *book publishing professional*
Rial, José Antonio *geophysicist, educator*
Richardson, Stephen Giles *biotechnologist, director*
Riggs, Timothy Allan *museum curator*
Rimer, Barbara K. *health facility administrator, educator, dean*
Rindfuss, Ronald Richard *social studies educator*
Rogers, John James William *geology educator*
Roper, William Lee *dean, preventive medicine physician, health facility administrator*
Rosen, Benson *business administration educator*
Ross, Coleman DeVane *accountant, insurance company executive*
Salgado, Maria Antonia *education educator*
Salmon, Edward Dickinson *cell biologist, educator*
Sancar, Aziz *research biochemist*
Sanders, John Lassiter *retired academic administrator*
Schier, Donald Stephen *language educator*
Schoonover, Brenda B. *ambassador*
Schoultz, Lars *political scientist, educator*
Sheldon, George Frank *medical educator*
Sices, David *language educator, translator*
Simmons, Michael Anthony *pediatrician*
Smith, Dean Edwards *retired men's college basketball coach*
Smith, James Finley *economist, educator*
Smith, Sidney Rufus, Jr. *linguist, educator*

Smithies, Oliver *geneticist, educator*
Soltys, Florence Gray *social worker*
Southern, Robert Allen *lawyer*
Spencer, Elizabeth *writer*
Spencer, Roger Felix *psychiatrist, educator*
Stamm, John William Randolph *dentist, educator*
Stearns, Sally Clark *education educator*
Stenberg, Carl W. III *public administration educator, dean*
Stephens, Laurence David, Jr. *linguist, investor, oil industry executive*
Steponaitis, Vincas Petras *archaeologist, anthropologist, educator*
Stevens, Phyllis A. *conceptual artist*
Stipe, Robert Edwin *retired design educator*
Stockman, James Anthony III *pediatrician*
Strauss, Albrecht Benno *retired language educator, editor*
Strauss, Diane Carol Wheeler *librarian, educator, writer*
Stumpf, Walter Erich *cell biology and pharmacology professor, researcher*
Szejniuk, Nathan M. *disaster preparedness coordinator, health care preparedness consultant*
Taft, Timothy Ned *orthopedist, surgeon, sports medicine physician*
Tindall, George Brown *retired historian, educator*
Tolley, Aubrey Granville *psychiatrist, health facility administrator*
Trejo, JoAnn *medical researcher*
Treml, Vladimir Guy *economist, educator*
Umminger, Bruce Lynn *government agency administrator, research scientist, consultant*
Ware, William Brettel *education educator*
Wasik, Barbara Hanna *psychologist, educator*
Wegner, Judith Welch *lawyer, educator, dean*
Weinstein, Sidney *neuropsychologist*
Weiss, Shirley F. *retired urban and regional planner, economist, educator*
Wescott, Joseph Warren, II, *academic administrator, education educator*
White, Raymond Petrie, Jr. *dentist, educator, dean*
Whybark, David Clay *business educator, researcher*
Wilcox, Benson Reid *cardiothoracic surgeon, educator*
Wilfert, Catherine M. *medical association administrator, pediatrician, epidemiologist, educator*
Williams, John N. *dean, dental educator*
Williams, Roy *college basketball coach*
Williamson, Joel Rudolph *humanities educator, writer*
Wilson, Glenn *economist, educator*
Winfield, John Buckner *rheumatologist, educator*
Wolfenden, Richard Vance *biochemistry educator*
Wright, Deil Spencer *political science professor*
Zeisel, Steven H. *nutritionist, scientist, educator*
Zeng, Ming *molecular biologist, researcher*

## Charlotte
Alexander, R. David *retail executive*
Alphin, J. Steele *bank executive*
Anderson, Gerald Leslie *finance company executive*
Anderson, Paul Milton *energy executive*
Armstrong, James David *editor, educator, minister*
Ayscue, Edwin Osborne, Jr. *lawyer*
Barber, Martha Gayle *lawyer*
Barber, Timothy G. *lawyer*
Barnhill, G. Michael *lawyer*
Barrows, Frank Clemence *journalist*
Bass-Hollis, Cynthia Gibson *environmental services administrator*
Bauroth, Nancy Ann *journalist, former marketing executive*
Belflowers, Timothy Dion *organist, choir director*
Belk, John Montgomery *retired retail executive, former mayor*
Belk, John R. *retail executive*
Belk, Thomas Milburn, Jr., (Tim Belk) *apparel executive*
Bessant, Cathy (Catherine Pombier Bessant) *bank executive, marketing professional*
Bhatnagar, Abha *school system administrator, department chairman*
Bickerstaff, Bernie *professional basketball player*
Blanchfield, Francis J., Jr. *lawyer*
Bonnefoux, Jean-Pierre *art director, choreographer, dancer*
Bowles, Erskine B. *academic administrator, former White House chief of staff*
Brackett, Martin Luther, Jr. *lawyer*
Bragg, Ellis Meredith, Jr. *lawyer*
Brinkley, Amy Woods *bank executive*
Britt, Julia Moody *secondary school educator*
Brown, Edward J III *bank executive*
Brown, Harold Ogden Joseph *religious studies educator*
Browning, Peter Crane *packaging company executive*
Browning, Roy Wilson III *former mortgage banking executive*
Brynn, Edward Paul *former ambassador*
Buchan, Jonathan Edward, Jr. *lawyer*
Burke, Peggy Hudgins (Margaret Hudgins Burke) *auditor*
Calloway, Mark T. *lawyer, former prosecutor*
Campbell, J(ohn) Jette *corporate finance executive*
Carroll, David M. *communications professional*
Carroll, James P. *lawyer*
Casey, John T. *hospital administrator*
Castro, Mary McDermott *language educator*
Chambers, Julius LeVonne *lawyer*
Clark, Ranjana B. *bank executive*
Clayton, William Mimms *lawyer*
Clodfelter, Daniel Gray *state legislator, lawyer*
Cochrane, Eugene W., Jr. *foundation administrator*
Cocklin, Kim Roland *lawyer*
Connor, Michael S. *lawyer*
Conrad, Robert J., Jr. *prosecutor, federal judge*
Cooke, Steven John *chemical engineer, consultant, scientist*
Cooper, Jason P. *lawyer*
Coss, Stephen K. *lawyer*
Cottingham, Tracy Thomas III *lawyer*
Cox, Linda Smoak *real estate broker*
Cramer, Robert W. *lawyer*
Croker, Brent Allen *counseling administrator*

Cummings, Stephen Emery *investment banking executive*
Dagenhart, Larry Jones *lawyer*
D'Amato, Frances Louise *art educator, psychology professor*
Davis, Jean E. *bank executive*
Davis, Stephen *professional football player*
Delhomme, Jake Christopher *professional football player*
de Molina, Alvaro G. *bank executive*
Desoer, Barbara J. *bank executive*
Dickson, Thomas Walter *textile company executive*
DiMicco, Daniel R. *manufacturing executive*
Dubois, Philip Leon *academic administrator, political scientist, educator*
Dunn, Jackson Thomas, Jr. *lawyer, educator*
Elanayar, Sunil K. *research and development engineer*
Eppes, Thomas Evans *advertising executive, public relations executive*
Eppley, Frances Fielden *secondary school educator, writer*
Erdman, David Williams *lawyer*
Ethridge, Mark Foster III *writer, publishing executive, consultant*
Fang, Hongbing *engineering educator, researcher*
Fennebresque, John C. *lawyer*
Ferebee, Stephen Scott, Jr. *architect*
Finley, Glenna *writer*
Fitzpatrick, James Ward, Jr. *engineering educator*
Fowler, Fred J. *energy executive*
Fox, John *professional football coach*
Fox, William J. *bank executive, former federal official*
Freeman, Sidney Lee *minister*
Fretwell, Elbert K., Jr. *retired university chancellor, consultant*
Gage, Gaston Hemphill *lawyer*
Gambrell, Sarah Belk *retail executive*
Goldstein, Stuart N. *lawyer*
Goodwin, William H., Jr. *diversified financial services company executive*
Goolkasian, Paula A. *psychologist, educator*
Gosnell, Guy N. *lawyer*
Gotta, Joseph D. *music company executive*
Graham, Billy (William Franklin Graham) *evangelist*
Graham, Franklin (William Franklin Graham III) *evangelist, missionary*
Gregory, Jeannette T. *publisher, writer*
Grigg, Eddie Garman *minister, educator*
Grimaldi, James Thomas *investment fund executive*
Gunson, Douglas R. *lawyer*
Hahn, Robert J. *lawyer*
Haines, Kenneth H. *sports television broadcasting and marketing executive*
Halas, Paul Anthony, Jr. *business appraisal and valuation specialist, consultant*
Hall, James Bryan *gynecologist, oncologist*
Hammonds, Bruce L. *bank executive*
Hance, James Henry, Jr. *bank executive*
Handy, John W. *shipping company executive, retired military officer*
Hankins, Irvin W. III *lawyer*
Hanley, Edward Nathaniel *surgeon*
Hanna, George Verner III *lawyer*
Harris, John W. *real estate company executive*
Hauser, David L. *electric power industry executive*
Hawker, James Francis *priest, school system administrator*
Herring, Rebecca Royce *music educator, consultant*
Hicks-Ray, Denyse *psychologist, commentator*
Hinson, Bobby D. *lawyer*
Hord, Joy M. *lawyer*
Horn, Carl III *federal judge*
Horoschak, Mark J. *lawyer*
Horowitz, Carol Y. *science educator*
Hough, Michael Brady *music educator*
Huberman, Jeffrey Allen *architect*
Hufanda, Joseph *dentist*
Hutchings-Hoffman, Cathy Jo *early childhood educator*
Huynh, Toan T. *surgeon, researcher*
Ignozzi, Bryan K. *management consultant*
Iley, Martha Strawn *music educator*
Ives, H. Bryan III *lawyer*
Jacobs, Gordon Waldemar *surgeon, educator*
Johnson, Charles E., II, *technology company executive*
Johnson, Jimmie *race car driver*
Jones, Milton H., Jr. *bank executive*
Jordan, Robert Sands *electrical engineer*
Kawczak, Janusz *mathematician, educator*
Kearney, Christopher J. *manufacturing executive, lawyer*
Kelley, Janet Oodsey *lawyer*
Kelly, R. James *retail executive*
Klibanov, Michael Victor *mathematics professor*
Kneisl, Jeffrey S. *oncologist, orthopedist*
Lacey, Trudi *professional athletics coach*
Lapp, Charles Warren *internist, pediatrician*
Larsen, Marshall O. *manufacturing executive*
Lea, Scott Carter *retired packaging company executive*
Levine, Howard R. *retail executive*
Lewis, Kenneth D. *bank executive*
Lilly, James Edward *lawyer*
Linnert, Terrence Gregory *lawyer*
Lisenby, Terry S. *waste management executive*
Locke, Elizabeth Hughes *retired foundation administrator*
Loughridge, John Halsted, Jr. *lawyer*
Lucas, Charles Craft III *executive recruiter*
Lyerly, Elaine Myrick *advertising executive*
Mancuso, Michael John *retired corporate financial executive*
Mayopoulos, Timothy J. *lawyer*
McAfee, Larry W. *chemistry educator*
McBryde, Neill Gregory *lawyer*
McClelland, Richard Lee *dentist*
McClure, Howard Jean, Jr. *advocate*
McCoy, Michael D. *lawyer*
McCrory, Patrick *mayor*
McFayden, Shannon W. *bank holding company executive*
McGee, Liam E. *bank executive*
McKay-Wilkinson, Julie Ann *minister, marriage and family therapist*
McKinnish, Richmond D. *manufacturing executive*
McMillan, William P. *lawyer*

Mehta, Kiran H. *lawyer*
Mercer, Evelyn Lois *retired counseling administrator*
Metz, Catherine Taylor *performing arts educator*
Michalski, Stanley Franklin *music educator, conductor*
Migoya, Carlos *bank executive*
Mills, Stacey Webster *music educator, musician*
Mogg, Jimmy W. *gas industry executive*
Monge, Jay Parry *lawyer*
Montague, Edgar Burwell, III, (Monty Montague) *industrial designer*
Moore, James L., Jr. *beverage company executive*
Moynihan, Brian T. *finance company executive*
Mullen, Thomas C. *manufacturing executive*
Munn, Stephen P. *manufacturing executive*
Myers, Robert Manson *language educator, writer*
Nedzbala, Michael *lawyer*
Neel, Richard Eugene *economist, educator*
Nelson, Thomas C. *manufacturing executive*
Nichols, Debra *bank executive*
Norris, William Robert *engineer, researcher*
Oberkfell, Keith *lawyer*
Okafor, Emeka *professional basketball player*
Oken, Marc D. *retired bank executive*
O'Leary, Patrick J. *manufacturing executive*
Oliver, John William Posegate *minister*
Osteen, Louis *chef*
Parmelee, William Douglas *financial executive, accountant*
Paviet-Hartmann, Patricia *chemist, researcher*
Peacock, A(lvin) Ward *textile company executive*
Pedigo, Paul F. *lawyer*
Peppers, Julius *professional football player*
Perkins, Jim C. *automotive executive*
Peterson, Evonne Stewart *elementary school educator*
Phillips, Harry Robert *language educator*
Pollard, John Oliver *lawyer*
Proehl, Ricky *professional football player*
Pruden, James Norfleet III *lawyer*
Pyle, Gerald Fredric *geographer, educator*
Rachor, Jeffrey C. *automotive executive*
Ragan, Robert Allison *private investment executive, financial consultant*
Reese, Annette Evelyn *music educator*
Rikard, William L., Jr. *lawyer*
Rodite, Robert R.R. *research scientist, finance and computer consultant, educator*
Rogers, James Eugene *electric and gas utility executive*
Ruiz, Macedonio *entomologist*
Schafermeyer, Robert William *emergency physician, educator, health policy consultant*
Schulz, Walter Kurt *accountant, information technology consultant*
Seidel, James P. *manufacturing executive*
Shappert, Gretchen C. F. (Gretchen Cecilia Frances Shappert) *prosecutor, lawyer*
Shaw, Ruth G. *energy company executive*
Siegel, Samuel *metals company executive*
Simmons, Charles B., Jr. *lawyer*
Sink, Robert C. *lawyer*
Sintz, Edward Francis *librarian*
Skains, Thomas E. *gas industry executive*
Slaton, Charles R. *hospital administrator*
Smith, B. Scott *automotive executive*
Smith, O. Bruton *automotive company executive*
Smith, Samantha June *literature and language educator*
Smith, Steve *professional football player*
Spangler, Clemmie Dixon, Jr. *construction company executive*
Spiro, Robert Harry, Jr. *foundation and business executive, educator*
Squires, James Ralph *development company executive*
Staley, Dawn Michelle *professional basketball player*
Stepp, James Michael *finance company executive*
Stinson, Andrea Maria *professional basketball player*
Sulg, Madis *manufacturing executive, entrepreneur*
Sutton, Cecilia (Cece Sutton) *bank executive*
Swecker, Chris (Christophe E. Swecker) *protective services official, former federal agency administrator*
Taylor, Gene *bank executive*
Taylor, R. Eugene *bank executive*
Thames, Rick *publishing executive, editor*
Thigpen, Richard Elton, Jr. *retired lawyer*
Thompson, Jocelyn Pharr *organist, director, music educator*
Thompson, John Albert, Jr. *dermatologist*
Thompson, Ken (G. Kennedy Thompson) *bank executive*
Thompson, Sydnor, Jr., (Charles William Sydnor Thompson Jr.) *lawyer, mediator, arbitrator*
Treanor, Mark C. *lawyer, diversified financial services company executive*
Twisdale, Harold Winfred *dentist*
Tyson, Cynthia Haldenby *academic administrator*
Valasquez, Joseph Louis *industrial engineer*
Van Allen, William Kent *lawyer*
Van Alstyne, Vance Brownell *management consultant*
Van Hoy, Philip Marshall *lawyer*
Vazquez Rivera, Ornela Amliv *psychologist*
Vinroot, Richard Allen *lawyer, mayor*
Voorhees, Richard Lesley *federal judge*
Walker, Billy J. *bank executive*
Walker, Clarence Wesley *lawyer*
Walker, Jewett Lynius *clergyman, church official*
Walker, John Seibels *artist*
Walls, George Rodney *lawyer*
Webster, Murray Alexander, Jr. *sociologist, educator*
Weinke, Chris *professional football player*
Whitfield, Fred, Jr. *professional sports team executive*
Whitney, Frank DeArmon *federal judge, former prosecutor*
Wiggins, Nancy Bowen *real estate broker, market research consultant*
Williams, Edwin Neel *newspaper editor*
Wilson, Paul Lowell *mortgage company executive, lawyer*
Wolson, Craig Alan *lawyer*
Wood, Donald Craig *retired marketing professional*
Wood, William McBrayer *lawyer*

Woodward, James Hoyt *retired academic administrator, retired engineering educator*
Wright, Bonnie H. *elementary school educator*
Wright, Wayne Kenneth *federal agency statistician*
Wyche, James Ramage *lawyer*
Yancy, Dorothy Cowser *college president*
Yaste, Christian *dentist*
Yorke, John Bundy *lawyer*

**Cherokee**
Martin, Harry Corpening *lawyer, retired state supreme court justice*

**Cherryville**
Huffstetler, Palmer Eugene *lawyer*
Mayhew, Kenneth Edwin, Jr. *retired transportation executive*

**Chocowinity**
Castle, William Eugene *retired academic administrator*

**Clayton**
Silberman, H. Lee *public relations executive, consultant*

**Clemmons**
Maloney, Sean Robert *physician, biomedical engineer*
Suber, Robert L., Sr. *toxicologist, researcher*
Taquey, Antony *accountant*

**Clinton**
Davis, William Maxie, Jr. *lawyer*
Griffin, Betty Lou *not-for-profit developer, educator*

**Columbus**
Brooks, Jerry Claude *safety engineer, educator*
Wetherby, Ivor Lois *librarian*

**Concord**
Busch, Kurt *race car driver*
Sheppard, Douglas G. *manufacturing project engineer*
Smith, Ollen Bruton *sports association executive*

**Conover**
Jarrett, Dale *race car driver*

**Cornelius**
Connor, Michael Donnell *art educator, writer, artist*

**Cove City**
Hawkins, Elinor Dixon (Mrs. Carroll Woodard Hawkins) *retired librarian*

**Creedmoor**
Husketh, Alma Ormond *retired language educator*

**Cullowhee**
Bardo, John William *academic administrator*
Beam, Richard Squires *theater educator*
Carlisle, James Steven, Jr. *dean, actor*
Coulter, Myron Lee *retired academic administrator*
Kauffman, N. Leroy *academic administrator*
Lormand, Paul Edward *performing company executive*
Mulligan, Robert Francis, Jr. *economist, civil engineer*
Reed, Alfred Douglas *retired academic administrator*
Willis, Ralph Houston *mathematics professor*

**Dallas**
Brown, Pearlie Murray *school librarian*

**Davidson**
Cole, Richard Cargill *language educator*
Grosch, Laura Dudley *artist, educator*
Jackson, Herb *artist, educator*
Kamp, Barbara Ann *designer, poet, photographer, educator, artist*
Klein, Benjamin Garrett *mathematics professor, consultant*
Palmer, Edward L. *psychologist, educator, writer*
Park, Leland Madison *librarian*
Ross, Clark Grant *economics professor*
Sprague, Raymond *music educator*
Vagt, Robert F. *academic administrator*

**Denver**
Detter, Carla Renee *media specialist*
McIntosh, Anita Jane *retired administrative assistant*

**Dunn**
Hill, Susan Beasley *recreational therapist*
Wilson, Douglas Leonard *minister, educator*

**Durham**
Agre, Peter Courtland *medical educator*
Albala, David Mois *urologist, educator*
Aldrich, John Herbert *political science professor*
Anderson, Jean Bradley *writer*
Anderson, William Banks, Jr. *ophthalmology educator*
Anlyan, William George *surgeon, educator, academic administrator*
Armstrong, Brenda Estelle *pediatrician, cardiologist*
Barker, Karen *restaurant owner, chef*
Bartlett, Katharine Tiffany *dean, law educator*
Bejan, Adrian *mechanical engineering educator*
Bennett, Peter Brian *medical researcher, educator*
Berger, Jeffrey S. *cardiologist*
Bernard, Pamela Jenks *lawyer*
Bettman, James Ross *management educator*
Bevan, William *retired foundation executive*
Beyer, John Leslie *psychiatrist*
Blackburn, John Oliver *economist, consultant*
Blazer, Dan German, II, *psychiatrist, epidemiologist*
Blazing, Michael August *internist*
Blum, Jacob Joseph *physiologist, educator*
Bollinger, Ralph Randal *surgeon, researcher*
Borges-Neto, Salvador *radiologist, cardiologist, educator*

Bradford, William Dalton *pathologist, educator*
Brantley, Jeffrey Garland *health science association administrator*
Breeden, Douglas Tower *dean, financial consultant*
Brodhead, Richard H. *academic administrator*
Brodie, Harlow Keith Hammond *psychiatrist, educator*
Buckley, Rebecca Hatcher *allergist, immunologist, pediatrician, educator*
Budd, Louis John *language educator*
Bunch, Michael Brannen *psychologist, educator*
Burks, A. Wesley *pediatrics educator*
Butters, Ronald Richard *language educator*
Cai, Xinjiang *cardiologist, researcher*
Canada, Mary Whitfield *retired librarian*
Cannon, Herbert Seth *investment banker*
Carrington, Bessie Meek *librarian*
Carrington, Paul DeWitt *lawyer, educator*
Carroll, Kenneth G. *lawyer*
Carson, James Wood *psychologist*
Carter, Calvin H., Jr. *materials engineer*
Carter, James Harvey *psychiatrist, educator*
Case, Richard W. *sports association executive*
Casey, H(orace) Craig, Jr. *electrical engineering educator*
Cayne, Bernard Stanley *editor*
Chafe, William Henry *history professor*
Chapman, Robert Lee III *real estate developer*
Chemerinsky, Erwin *law educator*
Chicquor, Isabel *art educator, artist*
Christie, George Custis *lawyer, educator, writer*
Clotfelter, Charles T. *economics professor*
Cohen, Harvey Jay *geriatrician, hematologist, oncologist, educator*
Cohen, Seth Morris *otolaryngologist, educator*
Cohn, Stephen Andrew *publishing executive*
Colton, Joel *historian, educator*
Colvin, O. Michael *medical association administrator, medical educator*
Conklin, George Henry *sociologist, educator*
Cook, Philip Jackson *economist, educator*
Cook-Deegan, Robert Mullan *physician, educator*
Coppridge, Alton James *urological surgeon*
Cox, James D. *law educator*
Crawford, Jeffrey *oncologist, educator*
D'Amato, Victor Arthur *environmental engineer, consultant*
Davis, Calvin De Armond *historian, educator*
Daw, Amy W. *music educator*
Dellinger, Walter Estes III *lawyer, law educator*
Demott, Deborah Ann *law educator*
Denlinger, Ann T. *school system administrator*
Dennis, Helen Oldham *elementary school educator*
Dorfman, Ariel *writer, educator*
Dorn, Louis Otto *retired minister*
Dowell, Earl Hugh *dean, aerospace and mechanical engineering educator*
Dzau, Victor Joseph *cardiologist, director, researcher*
Edelsbrunner, Herbert *computer scientist, educator, mathematician*
Edwards, Christopher Levon *medical association administrator*
Elliot, Jeffrey M. *political science professor, department chairman*
Falletta, John Matthew *pediatrician, educator*
Faris, Marc R *composer, education educator*
Fisk, Catherine Laura *law educator, lawyer*
Fiske, Edward B. *editor, educator, journalist, consultant*
Foreman, John William *pediatrician, educator*
Frank, Michael M. *physician*
Freemark, Michael Scott *pediatric endocrinologist, educator*
Fridovich, Irwin *biochemistry professor*
Frothingham, Thomas Eliot *pediatrician*
Fulkerson, William *hospital administrator, pulmonologist*
Gainetdinov, Raul Radikovich *pharmacologist, researcher*
Giannopoulos, Athina *physician, surgeon*
Gilbert, John Ray *geneticist, researcher*
Gillham, Nicholas Wright *geneticist, educator*
Gillings, Dennis B. *medical products executive*
Gilliss, Catherine Lynch *nursing educator*
Goestenkors, Gail *basketball coach*
Goforth, Harold W. *physician, psychiatrist*
Goodwin, Frank Erik *materials engineer*
Greenfield, Joseph Cholmondeley, Jr. *physician, educator*
Gunter, Emily Diane *communications executive, marketing professional, educator, real estate developer, writer*
Hammes, Gordon G. *chemistry professor*
Hammond, Charles Bessellieu *obstetrician, gynecologist, educator*
Han, Moo-Young *physicist, educator*
Harrell, Carlton (Benjamin Carlton Harrell) *retired editor, writer*
Havighurst, Clark Canfield *law educator*
Hawkins, William E. N. *newspaper editor*
Hellinga, Homme Wytzes *biochemist, educator, researcher*
Hensen, Steven Lee *archivist, librarian*
Hobbs, Marcus Edwin *retired chemistry professor*
Hodgdon, Timothy John *historian, educator*
Hogan, Brigid L.M. *molecular biologist*
Holder, Angela Roddey *law educator*
Holsti, Ole Rudolf *political scientist, educator*
Holzworth, Donald A. *lab administrator*
Horowitz, Donald Leonard *lawyer, educator, political scientist, arbitrator*
Huestis, Charles Benjamin *former academic administrator*
Jakubs, Deborah *university librarian*
James, Sherman Athonia *epidemiologist, educator*
Jarvis, Erich David *neurobiologist, educator*
Jaszczak, Ronald Jack *physicist, researcher, consultant*
Jeffreys, Arcelia Taylor *education educator*
Jenkins, Richard Erik *patent lawyer*
Jennings, Robert Burgess *experimental pathologist, medical educator*
Jirtle, Randy *medical educator, geneticist*
Joklik, Wolfgang Karl *biochemist, virologist, educator*
Jordan, Kerry Elizabeth *psychologist, researcher*
Katz, Samuel Lawrence *pediatrician, researcher*

Keene, Jack Donald *molecular genetics and microbiology educator*
Kelley, Allen Charles *economist, educator*
Kimmick, Gretchen *oncologist*
Kishnani, Priya Sunil *medical geneticist*
Klitzman, Bruce *physiologist, plastic surgery educator, researcher*
Koepke, John Arthur *hematologist, clinical pathologist*
Krakowski, Jane *actress*
Krzyzewski, Mike *university athletic coach*
Kulminski, Aliaksandr M. *research scientist*
Kuniholm, Bruce Robellet *academic administrator, educator*
Kurtzberg, Joanne *pediatrician, educator*
Kuwahara, Kuldip Kaur *literature and language professor*
Lack, Leon *pharmacology and biochemistry educator*
Ladd, Marcia Lee *medical products executive*
Land, Kenneth Carl *sociologist, educator, demographer*
Lange, Peter *academic administrator*
Lefkowitz, Robert Joseph *physician, educator*
LeGrand, Chris *lab administrator*
Leppert, Phyllis Carolyn *obstetrician, gynecologist*
Lerner, Warren *historian, educator*
Levin, Lawrence Scott *plastic surgeon*
Lieberman, Rochelle Phyllis *small business owner*
Liles, Joseph Marshall III *artist, educator*
Lockhead, Gregory Roger *psychology professor*
Maar, Rosina *medical products executive*
Mackensen, Georg Burkhard *anesthesiologist, educator*
Mark, Daniel Benjamin *cardiologist*
Markert, Mary Louise *pediatrics educator*
Masand, Prakash S. *psychiatrist, researcher*
Matchar, David B. *physician, researcher*
Maxwell, Richard Callender *retired lawyer, educator*
McClain, Paula Denice *political scientist, educator*
McMahon, John Alexander *law educator*
McNamara, James O. *physician, scientist*
Means, Anthony Ross *pharmacology educator*
Mehta, Rajendra H. *cardiologist, researcher*
Meyer, Horst *physics professor*
Meyers, Eric Mark *religion educator*
Michener, James Lloyd *medical educator*
Mikhailov, Stepan Fedorovich *physicist, researcher*
Miller, David Edmond *physician*
Modrich, Paul L. *biochemistry professor*
Moss, Marcia Lynn *retired biochemist*
Mushak, Paul *toxicologist, consultant*
Nakarai, Charles Frederick Toyozo *music educator*
Nevins, Joseph Roy *geneticist, educator*
Nifong, Michael B. *prosecutor*
Ohman, E. Magnus *cardiologist, educator*
Olsen, Elise *dermatologist, researcher*
Olufolabi, Adeyemi John *anesthesiologist*
Ostbye, Truls *medical researcher, educator*
Otterbourg, Robert Kenneth *public relations consultant, writer*
Parker, William *education educator*
Patel, Keyur *medical educator*
Pearsall, George Wilbur *materials scientist, educator, mechanical engineer, consultant*
Pearsall, Samuel Haff III *ecologist, geographer, foundation administrator*
Pericak-Vance, Margaret A. *health facility administrator*
Petroski, Henry *engineering educator, writer*
Pieper, Carl F. *statistician, educator*
Pimm, Stuart L. *ecology educator*
Pinnell, Sheldon Richard *dermatologist, researcher, retired educator*
Pirrung, Michael Craig *chemistry professor, consultant*
Pizzo, Salvatore Vincent *pathologist*
Plonsey, Robert *electrical and biomedical engineer*
Preston, Richard Arthur *historian*
Quinn, Jarus William *physicist, former association executive*
Rabinovich, Egla Consuelo *pediatrician, rheumatologist*
Reckhow, Kenneth Howland *conservationist, educator*
Rennie, John *soccer coach*
Robboy, Stanley J. *pathologist, educator*
Robertson, Horace Bascomb, Jr. *retired law educator*
Roger, Edwin Mclendon *education educator*
Rondinelli, Dennis A(ugust) *business administration educator, researcher*
Rorschach, Kimberly *museum director*
Rossi, Barbara *economics professor*
Rossiter, Alexander, Jr. *publishing executive, editor*
Rouse, Doris Jane *physiologist, research scientist*
Rowe, Thomas Dudley, Jr. *law educator*
Ruch, David S. *orthopedist, surgeon*
Sabiston, David Coston, Jr. *surgeon, educator*
Sanders, Donald Benjamin *neurologist, educator*
Schmalbeck, Richard Louis *dean, lawyer*
Schmidt-Nielsen, Knut *physiologist, educator*
Schwarcz, Steven Lance *lawyer, educator*
Seewaldt, Victoria L. *medical educator, researcher*
Semans, Mary Duke Biddle Trent *foundation administrator*
Sharma, Anand *manufacturing executive*
Shelburne, John Daniel *pathologist*
Shimm, Melvin Gerald *law educator*
Simons, Elwyn LaVerne *physical anthropologist, primatologist, paleontologist, educator*
Sloan, Frank Allen *economist, educator*
Sloan, Maceo Kennedy *lawyer, investment company executive*
Smith, Grover C(leveland) *language educator*
Smith, Harmon Lee, Jr. *clergyman, theology studies educator*
Sowa, Artur *mathematician, researcher*
Staddon, John Eric Rayner *psychology professor, neurobiology professor, zoology professor*
Stafford, Mark Smith *anesthesiologist, researcher, education educator*
Steinmetz, David Curtis *religious studies educator*
Stiff-Roberts, Adrienne D. *electrical engineer, educator*
Surwit, Richard Samuel *psychology professor*
Talley, Joseph Eugene *psychologist*

Taylor, James Francis *marketing professional*
Tedder, Thomas Fletcher *immunology educator, researcher*
Thompson, James Howard *historian, librarian*
Thompson, William Moreau *radiologist, educator*
Tselev, Alexander *physicist, researcher*
Utku, Senol *civil engineer, computer science educator*
Vatavuk, William Michael *chemical engineer, writer*
Ward, Robert *composer, educator, conductor*
Weiner, Richard David *psychiatrist, researcher*
Wells, Samuel Alonzo, Jr. *surgeon, educator*
Westbrook, Don Arlen *minister*
Whitlow, Stacey Mataxis *language educator*
Wilcox, Allen James *epidemiologist*
Wilkins, Robert Henry *neurosurgeon, educator, editor*
Williams, George Walton *language educator*
Williams, Redford Brown *medical educator*
Williams, Robert Sanders (Sandy Williams) *dean, academic administrator, educator, researcher*
Wu, Li-Tzy *alcohol/drug abuse services professional, researcher*
Young, Christopher C. *anesthesiologist*
Young, Terri L. *ophthalmologist*
Yu, Bing *researcher*

## Efland
Weinberg, Gerhard Ludwig *history professor*

## Elizabeth City
Banerjee, Hirendra Nath *educator*
Boyle, Terrence W. *federal judge*
Brown, Flora Bryant *history professor*
Griffin, Gladys Bogues *critical care nurse, educator*
Lee, Jennifer Jarman *social studies educator*
Luton, John Willis *education educator*
Rawat, Kuldeep S. *engineering educator*
Storie, Eric Duane *science administrator*
Weaver, Michael Alan *music educator*

## Elkin
Gillespie, James Davis *lawyer*

## Elon
Artley, Malvin Newton *music educator, composer*
Powell, William Council, Sr. *service company executive*
Tolley, Jerry Russell *academic administrator*
Touchette, Brant William *biologist, researcher*

## Fairmont
Byrne, James Frederick *banker*
Spencer, Melissa Johanna *psychotherapist, special education educator*

## Fairview
Brown, Gregory Neil *academic administrator, forester, educator*
Godard, Jerry Holton Caris *retired dean, psychology and literature professor*

## Fayetteville
Barnicle, Mary Anne *music educator, piano accompanist*
Curtis, Marvin Vernell *music educator*
Dembosky, John A., Jr. *science educator*
Fakhouri, Fouad Kifah *composer, conductor*
Fietsam, Robert, Jr. *physician*
Hagans, Valerie Mae Gee *special education educator*
Jackson, Johnny Loretta *music educator*
Jansen, Michael John *health facility administrator*
Jones, Villie *music educator*
Jordan, Karla Salge *retired primary school educator*
Kendrick, Mark Cleveland *real estate executive*
Lowe, James Edward, Jr. *plastic and reconstructive surgeon*
MacRae, Elizabeth (Elizabeth MacRae Halsey) *counselor, actor*
McKnight, Kelly Marie *psychologist*
Redding, Bobbie Newman *lawyer*
Richardson, Emilie White *manufacturing executive, investment company executive, educator*
Richardson, James Bernard *music educator*
Ruppe, Arthur Maxwell *retired lawyer*
Shaffer, Denny Richard *small business owner*
Truong, Dothang *information scientist, educator*

## Fearrington Village
Cell, Gillian Townsend *retired historian, educator*

## Flat Rock
Bar-Sadeh, Madeleine Kay *writer*
Childress, Richard Thomas *international business consultant*
Daubert, Madeline J. *finance educator*
Oliver, Ann Breeding *secondary school educator, art dealer*

## Fletcher
Seagle, J. Harold *lawyer*

## Fort Bragg
Anderson, Curtis Thorwald, II, *military officer*
Fishback, Ian *military officer*
Stafford, C. Stewart *educational consultant, educator*

## Four Oaks
Jordan, Lyndon Kirkman *physician*

## Franklin
Earhart, Eileen Magie *retired elementary school educator, retired child and family life educator*
Johnson, Herbert Alan *historian, lawyer*
Kinard, Cynthia Cochran *artist, writer*
Maki, Joan Owen *gifted and talented educator*

## Franklinton
Elmore, Cenieth Catherine *music educator*

## Gastonia
Burns, Judith O'Dell *library assistant, educator*
Crissman, Katherine Kolb *counseling administrator*

Duran, Carrie *museum staff member*
Easter, Willie, Jr. *artist, educator*
Fayssoux, Patricia Ann Paysour *music educator*
Kimbrell, Willard Duke *textiles executive*
Lawson, William David III *retired cotton company executive*
Patterson, Elaine Wilcox *art educator*
Stott, Grady Bernell *lawyer*
Teem, Paul Lloyd, Jr. *bank executive*

## Goldsboro
Cannon, Alice Grace *counselor*
Turlington, Patricia Renfrew *artist, educator*

## Graham
Stanberry, D(osi) Elaine *English literature educator, writer*

## Granite Falls
Humphreys, Kenneth King *engineer, educator, professional society administrator*

## Greensboro
Acheampong, Joseph Kofi *pharmacist, researcher*
Allen, Jesse Owen III *organizational behavior specialist*
Blackwell, William Ernest *broadcast executive*
Bynum, Magnolia Virginia Wright *retired secondary school educator*
Chandler, Austin Grace *psychologist*
Clark, Clifton Bob *physicist*
Cole, Johnnetta Betsch *academic administrator, educator*
Cornelius, Polly Butler *voice educator, soprano*
Cross, Dawn Rose *paralegal*
Cushman, Keith *English professor*
Davis, Ferd Leary, Jr. *law educator, consultant*
Davis, Herbert Owen *lawyer*
Deere, James Dickson *voice and music educator, writer*
Drye, Jonathan Reed *voice educator*
Dziordz, Walter Michael *priest*
Englar, John David *finance educator, textiles executive, lawyer*
Evans, Jonathan Christopher *social worker*
Floyd, Jack William *lawyer*
Flynt, Candace Lambeth *writer*
Formo, Brenda Terrell *travel company executive*
French, Lenny Sue *elementary school educator*
Frye, Henry E. *retired state supreme court chief justice*
Fujino, Michimasa *aeronautical engineer*
Gill, Evalyn Pierpoint *editor, writer, publisher*
Goktepe, Ipek *food scientist, educator*
Goldman, Bert Arthur *psychologist, educator*
Goulder, Gerald Polster *retail executive, management consultant, lawyer*
Graham, Anthony *language educator*
Haas, Christopher Eric *theater educator*
Hajek, Ellen *elementary school educator*
Hanson, Randall A. *lawyer*
Harris-Offutt, Rosalyn Marie *counselor, consultant, mental health nurse, writer*
Helms-VanStone, Mary Wallace *anthropology educator*
Horton, Gregory Jerome *theater educator, costume designer*
Houston, Frank Matt *dermatologist*
Hunter, Bynum Merritt *retired lawyer*
Jellicorse, John Lee *communications and theatre educator*
Johnson, Marshall Hardy *investment company executive*
Jones, Thomas Owen, Jr. *finance educator, military officer*
Knesel, Ernest Arthur, Jr. *health facility administrator, chemicals executive*
Koonce, Neil Wright *lawyer*
Kornegay, Horace Robinson *trade association administrator, congressman, lawyer*
Linster, Michelle Lynn *education educator, consultant*
Lloyd, Lila G. *business educator*
Lloyd, Robert Blackwell, Jr. *lawyer*
Locke, John R. *music educator, director*
Lowe, Kevin Brian *finance company executive*
McDaniel, James Mark, Jr. *health care executive*
McDonald, Mackey J. *apparel executive*
Melvin, Charles Edward, Jr. *lawyer*
Middleton, Herman David, Sr. *retired theater educator*
Miller, Robert Louis *dean, chemistry professor*
Mozell, Herbert Lee *mental health services professional*
Noble, Ralph C. *animal scientist, department chairman*
Nolker, David Brett *music educator*
Oliver, Donna H. *academic administrator, secondary school educator*
Oliver, Terry James *electronics engineer, educator, communications engineer*
Orlowsky, Martin L. *executive manager*
Osteen, William L. *federal judge*
Owen, Lindsay Alexander *music director*
Penley, Virginia Long *social worker*
Penninger, Frieda Elaine *retired literature educator*
Perkins, Mark L. *university chancellor*
Proffer, Andrew *psychologist*
Revell, Henry, Jr. *social services administrator, retired education educator*
Russell, Anne Wrenn *property manager*
Russell, Peggy Taylor *soprano, educator*
Sanders, William Eugene *marketing executive*
Saul, Connie Cline *secondary school educator*
Schell, Braxton *lawyer*
Schunk, Dale Hansen *dean*
Schwenn, Lee William *retired health facility administrator*
Semmler, Carl D. *lawyer*
Shaw, Robert Gilbert *retired state legislator, food service executive*
Shelton, David Howard *economics professor*
Simmons, Michelle Holschuh *school librarian, educator*
Slaughter, James H. *lawyer*
Smith, Lanty L(loyd) *lawyer, corporate financial executive*
Staab, Thomas Robert *consumer product company financial executive*
Stevens, Elliott Walker, Jr. *allergist, cardiologist, pulmonologist*

Stocks, William L. *federal judge*
Stone, Theresa M. *communications executive*
Stratton, Jack *artist, art educator, curator, conservator*
Sullivan, Patricia A. *academic administrator*
Swan, George Steven *law educator*
Tilley, Norwood Carlton, Jr. *federal judge*
Vulpi, Frank Joseph *music educator*
Wagoner, Anna Mills S. *prosecutor*
Ward, Charles A. *federal agency administrator*
Waters, Robert Francis, Jr. *music educator, writer*
Watson, Betty *artist*
Watson, Robert Winthrop *poet*
Williams, Ereka Rochelle *education educator*
Wiseman, Eric C. *apparel executive*
Xu, Jinsheng *computer scientist, educator*
Zhong, Haizhen *research scientist, educator*
Zopf, Evelyn LaNoel Montgomery *retired guidance counselor*

## Greenville
Allison, Ron *oncologist, researcher*
Anderson, Patricia Jean *elementary school educator*
Aziz, Shahnaz *psychology professor*
Babb, Joseph Dolby *physician*
Ballard, Steven C. *academic administrator*
Bath, Joanne McMath *music educator*
Bearden, James Hudson *university official*
Beers, Burton Floyd *historian, educator*
Bjorkman, Sylvia Johnson *psychologist*
Colombo, Michael Allen *lawyer*
Cummings, James *pediatrician, educator*
Drought, Michael Hall *academic administrator*
Eakin, Richard Ronald *academic administrator, mathematics educator*
Gilham, Hanna Kaltenbrunner *writer*
Jackson, Bobby Rand *minister*
James, James Franklin *psychiatrist, educator, academic administrator*
Johnson, Cynda Ann *physician, educator*
Lee, Kenneth Stuart *neurosurgeon, educator*
Meggs, William Joel *toxicologist, allergist, emergency physician, educator*
Morehead, Andrew Turner, Jr. *chemistry professor*
Pawlak, Roman Maciej *education educator*
Pories, Walter Julius *surgeon, educator*
Riley, Rhonda Wingate *music educator*
Rouse, William Arthur, Jr. *education educator*
Schenarts, Paul Joseph *surgeon, educator*
Shiber, Joseph R. *emergency physician*
Tingelstad, Jon Bunde *retired pediatrician, educator*
Toburen, Larry Howard *physicist, researcher*
Wallin, Leland Dean *artist, educator*
Waugh, William Howard *physician, research scientist*
Wiley, John Edwin *cytogeneticist*
Wilkerson, William Holton *banker*

## Hamlet
Ewing, Viola P. *elementary school educator*

## Hampstead
Walters, Sherwood George *management consultant, educator*

## Harrisburg
Economaki, Chris Constantine (Christopher Economaki) *publishing executive*
Patchen, Kelly A. *elementary school educator*

## Hayesville
Galloway, David Craig *chemist*

## Henderson
Serafin, Donald *plastic surgeon, educator*

## Hendersonville
Brittain, James Edward *science and technology educator, researcher*
Dalton, Robert Edgar *retired mathematician, computer scientist*
Deskin, William C. *healthcare educator*
Franks, Stephen Field *retired judge*
Harris, James Braxton *retired humanities educator, freelance/self-employed writer*
Heil, Mary Ruth *retired counselor*
Kingsbury, Carolyn Ann *aerospace engineer, craftsman, writer*
Reinhart, John Belvin *retired child and adolescent psychiatrist, educator*
Roberts, James Allen *retired urologist, educator*
Saby, John Sanford *physicist, consultant*
Tatreau, (Dolores) Maxine *artist*
Tatsch, Jacki Lynn *music educator, diversified financial services company executive*
Trexler, Edgar Ray *minister, editor*
Ward, Beverly Allen *church administrator, music educator*

## Hertford
Johnson, Donald Lee *retired agricultural materials processing company executive*
McClung, Kenneth Austin, Jr. *training executive, performance consultant*

## Hickory
Ballenger, Cass (Thomas Cass Ballenger) *former congressman, retired plastics company executive*
Eller, Richard E. *history professor, writer*
George, Boyd Lee *consumer products company executive*
Lefler, Wade Hampton, Jr. *ophthalmologist*
Schlagenhauf, Sherry Denise *music educator*
Smith, Young Merritt, Jr. *lawyer*

## High Point
Baker, Walter Wray, Jr. *lawyer*
Bardelas, Jose Antonio *allergist*
Burton, Ward *professional race car driver*
Corey, James William *political scientist, educator*
Draelos, Zoe Diana *dermatologist, consultant*
Fenn, Ormon William, Jr. *furniture company executive*
Fox, Gerald Trent *social sciences educator, consultant*
Gripper, James Kaiser *mental health services professional, consultant*
Kandt, Raymond S. *neurologist*

McAllister, Kenneth Wayne *lawyer*
Pate, William Patrick *city manager*
Phillips, Earl Norfleet, Jr. *diplomat, financial services executive*
Scearse, Patricia Dotson *nursing educator, dean*
Sheahan, Robert Emmett *lawyer, consultant*
Wood, Stephen Wray *minister, educator, legislator, singer, songwriter*

**Highlands**
Shaffner, Randolph Preston *shop owner, educator, writer, publisher*

**Hillsborough**
Adams, Rex *dean*
Goodwin, Craufurd David *economics professor*
Johnston, William Webb *pathologist, educator*
Piper, Don Courtney *political scientist, educator*
Wallace, Andrew Grover *internist, educator, dean*

**Holly Springs**
Booth, Penelope Partridge *secondary school educator, writer, principal*

**Hope Mills**
McBryde, Cecilia Collins *secondary school educator*

**Horse Shoe**
Roskoski, Robert, Jr. *biochemist, educator, author*

**Huntersville**
Atrak, Taisser M. *pediatrician, director*
Nowlin, Connie Blackwell *artist*
Stewart, Tony *professional race car driver*

**Indian Trail**
Brewer, James Timothy *music educator, director*
Hinson, Robert Wayne *education educator*
Johnson, Frank William *marketing professional*

**Iron Station**
Wise, Kimberly Anne (Schillaci) *music educator, musician*

**Jackson**
Brown, Gary *economic development agency executive*

**Jacksonville**
Brooks, Joli *music educator*
Fischer, Violeta Pèrez Cubillas *Spanish literature and linguistics educator*
Guyer, Charles Grayson, II, *psychologist*
Kimball, Lynn Jerome *historian*

**Jamestown**
Kinard, Jeff Sowers *historian, educator*
Schmitt, William Allen *lawyer*

**Jefferson**
Franklin, Robert McFarland *book publisher*

**Kannapolis**
Griggs, Farrar O'Neal, Jr. *lawyer*
Thigpen, Alton Hill *transportation executive*

**Kernersville**
Miller, Helen *history educator*

**Kings Mountain**
Randall, Susan *education educator*

**Kinston**
Baker-Gardner, Jewelle *interior designer, consultant*
Petteway, Samuel Bruce *college president*

**Kitty Hawk**
Sjoerdsma, Albert *research and development company executive*
Tucker, Don Eugene *retired lawyer*

**Lake Junaluska**
Markey, James Ian *music educator, tenor*
Martinson, Jacob Christian, Jr. *academic administrator*
Stanton, Donald Sheldon *academic administrator*
Tullis, Edward Lewis *retired bishop*

**Lake Waccamaw**
Spaulding, Lila Bernice *marriage and family counselor*

**Landis**
Lynch, Samuel Curlee, Jr., (Sir Saml Lynch) *painter*

**Laurinburg**
Deegan, John, Jr. *academic administrator, educator, researcher*
Gilbert, Marie Rogers *poet*

**Leicester**
Entzi, Karen Russell *orchestra educator*

**Leland**
Barnhardt, Zeb Elonzo, Jr. *lawyer, mediator, arbitrator*
Karch, Jacqueline *artist*

**Lenoir**
Wilson, Hugh Mal *lawyer*

**Lexington**
Brinkley, Walter F. *lawyer*
Cuthrell, Carl Edward *retired clergyman, lawyer, educator*
Frontz, Leslie Kay *art educator*
Mabe, Walter Lee *music educator*
Rector, Phillip Alan *minister, musician*

**Lillington**
Cole, Raymond Eugene *public information officer*
Evans, Warden Lee *social studies educator*

**Louisburg**
Foth, Rodney Stephen *academic administrator, science educator*

Miller, Brian Daniel *music educator, organist*

**Lumberton**
Carter, Angela Barnhill *music educator*
Johnson, Judy Van *minister, educator*
Tolar, Anne Melton *minister, music educator*

**Madison**
Millner, Thomas *manufacturing and holding company executive*

**Maggie Valley**
Pickard, John Benedict *language educator*

**Marion**
Burgin, Charles Edward *lawyer*

**Mars Hill**
Greene, Tena Lorraine *singer, educator, actor*
Newton, Paul George *musician, retired librarian*

**Matthews**
Fox, Beth A. *music educator*
Judge, Joseph Donald *music educator*
Mahoney, George R., Jr. *lawyer*
Rawlins, Donald Ray *lawyer*

**Maxton**
Ellis, Hubert Lee *retired secondary school educator*

**Mebane**
Langley, Ricky Lee *occupational medicine physician*

**Merritt**
de Vos, Peter Jon *ambassador*

**Midland**
Voncannon, Brian Everett *writer, scriptwriter, radio personality, naturopath*

**Mill Spring**
Saunders, Barry Wayne *state official*

**Monroe**
Casstevens, Charles Franklin, Jr. *music educator, minister*
Griffin, Cathy McWhorter *elementary school educator*
Kyle, John Emery *retired religious organization administrator*
Reynolds, Jeffrey Michael *music educator*
Taylor, Jimmy Lynn *retired family practice physician, administrator*

**Montreat**
Struble, Dan *academic administrator*

**Mooresville**
Atlas, Marilyn S. *social worker*
Black, Kenneth W., Jr. *retail executive*
Earnhardt, Dale, Jr. *race car driver*
Edwards, Carl *race car driver*
Elder, Christian *race car driver*
Faires, Ian Matthew *music educator*
Johnston, James Wesley *retired consumer products company executive*
Martin, Mark *race car driver*
McCanless, Ross William *lawyer, retail executive*
Münter, Leilani Maaja *race car driver*
Newman, Ryan *race car driver*
Niblock, Robert A. *consumer home products company executive*
Waltrip, Michael *professional race car driver*

**Morganton**
Dickison, Julie Anne *psychologist, researcher*
Dorman, Lewis Robert, IV, *librarian, archivist*
Hartley, Helen Rosanna *business educator*

**Morrisville**
Bolognesi, Dani Paul *virologist, educator*
Harker, Brian *tobacco company executive*
Roy, Biswadev *scientist*

**Morven**
Lowe, David Wayne *elementary school educator, education educator*

**Mount Airy**
Vaughn, Frances Austin *art educator*
Woltz, Howard Osler, Jr. *retired metal products executive*

**Mount Holly**
Dickson, Alan T. *mill and holding company executive*

**Mount Olive**
Beck, Julie Renee *academic administrator*
Maqbool, Muhammad *physics professor*
Marbais, Peter Christian *language educator*
Raper, William Burkette *retired college president*

**Murfreesboro**
Muller, William Albert III *retired library director*
White, Martin Christopher *academic administrator*

**Murphy**
Bata, Rudolph Andrew, Jr. *lawyer*
Deslauriers, Suzanne Dawsey *secondary school educator, artist*
Kerr, Walter Belnap *retired electrical engineer, language researcher, consultant*
Pezzella, Jerry James, Jr. *investment company executive, real estate company executive*

**Nashville**
Penick, Angela Lucas *elementary school educator*

**New Bern**
Danjczek, Michael Harvey *social services administrator*
Davis, James Lee *lawyer*
Jones, Victor Thomas, Jr. *librarian*
Linkonis, Suzanne Newbold *retired probation officer, retired counselor*
Moeller, Dade William *environmental engineer, educator*

Naumann, William Carl *consumer products company executive*
Overholt, Hugh Robert *lawyer, retired military officer*
Painter, Jack Timberlake *civil engineer*
Phipps, Patsy Duncan *retired auditor*
White, James Edward III *historian, educator*
White, Rhea Amelia *library and information scientist*
Whitehurst, Brooks Morris *chemical engineer*

**Newland**
Lustig, Susan Gardner *occupational therapist*

**Newport**
Rettie, Dwight Fay *retired political science educator, writer*

**North Wilkesboro**
Parsons, Irene Adelaide *management consultant*
Shumaker, Tara L. *performing arts educator*
Whiddon, Thomas E. *retail executive*

**Pembroke**
Curtis, Anthony R. *communications educator*
Curtis, Judith Genevicz *communications educator*
Goins, Jimmy (James Ernest Goins) *Native American tribal leader*
Meadors, Allen Coats *health facility administrator, educator, academic administrator*
Stevens, Robyn Anne *music educator*
Vela, Richard Raul *literature educator*

**Pikeville**
Sauls, Don *clergyman*

**Pilot Mountain**
Smith, Richard Jackson *elementary school educator*

**Pine Knoll Shores**
Benson, Kenneth Victor *manufacturing executive, lawyer*
Graham, Gloria Flippin *dermatologist*

**Pinehurst**
Broadhurst, Judith Buck *art gallery owner*
Carroll, Kent Jean *retired naval officer*
Huizenga, John Robert *nuclear chemist, educator*
Linville, Ray Pate *educational association administrator, retired military officer, editor, writer*
O'Neill, John Joseph, Jr. *retired chemicals executive*
Rees, Clifford Harcourt, Jr., (Ted Rees) *consulting company executive, retired trade association administrator, retired military officer*
Swanson, Richard Everett *physics professor, dean*

**Pisgah Forest**
Albyn, Richard Keith *retired architect*
Kempe, Ludwig George *neurosurgeon*

**Pittsboro**
Boyce, Emily Stewart *retired library and information science educator, retired library and information scientist*
Brownlee, Robert Calvin *pediatrician, educator*
Cotter, Michael William *finance educator, retired ambassador*
Cottrell, Eugene Paul *band director*
Doenges, Byron Frederick *former government official, finance educator*
Griffith, Katherine Scott *retired communications executive, retired librarian*
Kachergis, Joyce W. *book designer*
Richardson, Richard Judson *retired political science professor*
Rubin, Louis Decimus, Jr. *retired language educator, writer, publishing executive*
Squire, Alexander *management consultant*

**Raleigh**
Agamloh, Emmanuel B. *systems engineer, consultant*
Aiken, Clay (Clayton Holmes Aiken) *singer*
Aldridge, Adrienne Yingling *accountant, financial analyst, writer*
Allen, Steven Glen *economics professor, business professor*
Annetta, Len *science educator*
Aronson, Arthur Lawrence *retired veterinarian, toxicologist, educator, pharmacologist*
Aspnes, David Erik *physicist, researcher*
Atkinson, June *school system administrator*
Bailey, Mary Beatrice *retired health science association administrator*
Bakalov, Bojko Nentchev *mathematician*
Baker, Stanley Beckwith *education educator*
Bar, Roselyn R. *legal association administrator, lawyer, executive secretary*
Barefoot, Aldos Cortez, Jr. *forester, educator*
Barish, Charles Franklin *internist, gastroenterologist, researcher*
Barnhardt, Robert Alexander *dean*
Barrett, Rolin Farrar, Jr. *mechanical engineer, consultant*
Bateman, Angela Anderson *anesthetist*
Batson, Jonathon Kingsley *composer, singer*
Beatty, Kenneth Orion, Jr. *chemical engineer, educator*
Benson, D(avid) Michael *plant pathologist*
Bernholc, Jerzy *physicist, educator*
Bitzer, Donald Lester *electrical engineer, educator, retired lab administrator*
Blackburn, James B. III *lawyer*
Brady, Edward Thomas *state supreme court justice*
Brind'Amour, Rod *professional hockey player*
Brown, Robert Dale *wildlife science educator, dean*
Brown, William Harris *editor*
Bruck, Robert Ian *education educator*
Burkholder, Joann M. *botany educator*
Burris, Craven Allen *retired college administrator, educator*
Carlton, Alfred Pershing, Jr. *lawyer*
Carter, Jean Gordon *lawyer*
Case, Charles Dixon *lawyer*
Chou, Wushow *retired computer scientist*

Chukwu, Ethelbert Nwakuche *mathematics professor*
Clapp, Allen Linville *electric supply and communications utility consultant, mediator/arbitrator*
Clarke, Lewis James *landscape architect*
Coffey, John William *museum curator*
Cole, Erik *professional hockey player*
Cook, Maurice Gayle *soil science educator, consultant*
Cooper, Arthur Wells *ecologist, educator*
Cooper, Roy Asberry III *state attorney general*
Crisp, Fred *retired publishing executive*
Daubert, Erik Joseph *organization administrator, consultant*
Davey, Charles Bingham *soil scientist, educator*
Davis, Egbert Lawrence III *lawyer*
Davis, Janice *school system administrator*
Deihl, Susan Galyen *preservationist*
Deitz, Lewis Levering *entomologist, educator, researcher*
Doherty, Robert Cunningham *retired advertising executive*
Dolce, Carl John *education administration educator*
Donadio, Donald A. *lawyer*
Doorn, Michiel Roelof Jan *environmental engineer, consultant*
Dornan, John Neill *public policy center professional*
Dorsett, James K. III *lawyer*
Drew, Nancy McLaurin Shannon *counselor, consultant*
Duncan, Allyson K. *federal judge*
Dunphy, Edward James *science educator, crop science extension specialist*
Eagles, Sidney Smith, Jr. *judge*
Easley, Michael F. *governor*
Eberly, Harry Landis *retired communications company executive*
Edens, Frank Wesley *physiologist*
Edmunds, Robert Holt, Jr. *state supreme court justice*
Edwards, Charles Archibald *lawyer*
Effron, Seth Alan *editor, journalist*
Ellis, Lester Neal, Jr. *lawyer*
Ellis, Richard W. *lawyer*
Evans, Janet *publishing executive*
Evans, Margaret Griffin *music educator*
Fantz, Janet Nelsen *school psychologist*
Fedewa, Michael Joseph *school system administrator*
Flournoy, William Louis, Jr. *landscape architect*
Freeman, Franklin Edward, Jr. *government agency executive*
Fritsch, Edward *real estate company executive*
Gale, James L. *lawyer*
Gardner, Robin Pierce *engineering educator*
Garriss, Phyllis Weyer *music educator, performer*
Geller, Janice Grace *nurse*
Gibson, Ronald P. *finance company executive*
Gillette, Dale Alan *research scientist*
Goodman, Major Merlin *botanical sciences educator*
Gordon, Morris Aaron *medical mycologist*
Gorga, Russell E *polymer engineer*
Graham, William Edgar, Jr. *lawyer, utilities executive*
Hall, John Thomas *lawyer, educator*
Hardin, Eugene Brooks, Jr. *bank executive*
Hardin, James W. *botanist, educator, herbarium curator*
Hargrove, Wade Hampton *lawyer*
Harrison, Cecil W., Jr. *lawyer*
Harrison-Jervay, Evelyn Yvonne *publishing executive*
Hartford, Maureen A. *academic administrator*
Havlin, John Leroy *soil scientist, educator*
Hedican, Bret *professional hockey player*
Henderson, Shirley Elizabeth *minister*
Hergeth, Helmut H. *finance educator, educator*
Herrmann, John C. *music educator, church musician*
Hoch, Paul Frederick, Jr. *history professor*
Hodgson, Ernest *toxicologist, educator*
Holton, William Coffeen *electrical engineering executive*
Hritz, Pamela Lynne *accountant*
Hubbe, Martin A. *chemistry professor, consultant*
Huff, Ann Linnea *music educator*
Hughes, Francis P. *medical association administrator*
Hunt, James Baxter, Jr. *lawyer, former governor*
Hynus, Anita Eileen *music educator*
Imade, Lucky Osagie *political scientist, educator*
Isla, Arturs *professional hockey player*
Jarrett, Polly Hawkins *retired secondary school educator*
Jessen, David Wayne *accountant*
Johnson, Mary Pauline (Polly Johnson) *nursing administrator*
Johnson, William Dean *power company executive*
Joyner, Lorinzo Little *commissioner*
Joyner, Walton Kitchin *lawyer*
Jung, Kang *research scientist*
Kapp, Michael Keith *lawyer*
Karmanos, Peter, Jr. *computer company executive, professional sports team executive*
Kirk-Duggan, Michael Allan *retired law, economics and computer sciences educator*
Kolbas, Robert Michael *electrical engineering educator*
Krallinger, Joseph Charles *entrepreneur, consultant, writer*
Kuhler, Renaldo Gillet *retired museum director, medical illustrator*
Lancaster, H(arold) Martin *congressman, academic administrator*
Larsen, Ralph Irving *environmental research engineer*
Laviolette, Peter *professional hockey coach*
Leak, Robert Edwards *economic development consultant*
Lee, Howard N. *educational association administrator*
Lenard, Mary Jane *finance educator*
Li, Bailian *academic administrator*
Lilliston, Andrew Wilson, Jr. *lawyer*
Littleton, Isaac Thomas III *retired library director*
Loboa, Elizabeth Grace *biomedical engineer, educator*

Lolley, William Randall *minister*
Long, David W. *lawyer*
Loper, Johnny M. *lawyer*
Lowe, Sidney *professional basketball coach*
Lynch, John Christopher *lawyer*
Lyons, Kevin M. *engineering educator*
Mac Cormac, Earl Ronald *retired education educator*
Mackay, Trudy Frances Charlene *genetics professor*
Maidon, Carolyn Howser *director*
Malecha, Marvin John *architect, academic administrator*
Marshall, Elaine Folk *state official*
Martin, Mark D. *State Supreme Court Justice*
Masnari, Nino Antonio *electrical engineer, educator*
McArthur, John R. *utilities executive, lawyer*
McGee, Linda Mace *judge, lawyer*
McGehee, Robert B. *energy executive*
McKinney, Carolyn *educational association administrator, educator*
McKinney, Donald Lee *magazine editor*
McNish, Susan Kirk *retired lawyer*
Memory, Jasper Durham *academic administrator, physics professor*
Millberg, John C. *lawyer*
Mitchell, Burley Bayard, Jr. *lawyer*
Mitchell, Gary Earl *physicist, researcher*
Mitchell, Memory Farmer *retired communications executive*
Moore, Jeannette Aileen *animal nutrition educator*
Moreland, Donald Edwin *physiologist*
Neely, Charles B., Jr. *lawyer*
Neenan, Peter Anthony *state agency administrator*
Nelson, Larry A. *statistics educator, consultant*
Newby, Paul Martin *state supreme court justice*
Newman, Slater Edmund *psychologist, educator*
Nguyen, Hoan Kim Huynh *mathematician*
Nutter, Susan K. *librarian, academic administrator*
Oblinger, James L. *academic administrator*
Odum, Jeffery Neal *mechanical engineer*
Orr, Robert F. *not-for-profit administrator, retired state supreme court justice*
Osteryoung, Janet Gretchen *chemistry professor*
Ozturk, Mehmet Cevdet *engineering educator*
Pao, Chia-Ven *mathematics professor*
Parker, Joseph Mayon *retired publishing executive*
Parker, Sarah Elizabeth *state supreme court chief justice*
Parramore, Barbara Mitchell *education educator*
Parsons, William Jonathan *cardiologist*
Patterson, William S. *lawyer*
Paulson, David Freeman, Jr. *lawyer*
Peele, Katherine N. *architect*
Penick, John E. *education educator*
Perdue, Beverly Eaves *lieutenant governor, geriatric consultant*
Petters, Robert M. *education educator*
Pittman, James Morris (Jack Pittman) *cartoonist, illustrator, character designer, consultant*
Poe, Terry Lynn *music educator*
Powell, Durwood Royce *lawyer*
Prior, William Allen *electronics company executive*
Qu, Rongda *biologist, educator*
Ranjan, Vivek *physicist, researcher*
Reeves, Ralph Bernard III *publishing executive*
Reynolds, C. Lewis, Jr. *materials scientist, educator*
Rhodes, Donald Robert *musicologist, educator, retired electrical engineer*
Risher, James A. *electronics executive*
Riviere, Jim Edmond, Jr. *pharmacologist, educator, toxicologist*
Roach, Wesley Linville *lawyer, insurance executive*
Robinson, Charlotte Hill *artist*
Robinson, Prezell Russell *academic administrator*
Rusher, Mary Nash Kelly *lawyer*
Rutherford, Jim *professional sports team executive*
Sanders, Douglas Charles *horticulturist, researcher, educator*
Sanford, Jo Anne *state agency administrator*
Sangkil, Moon *finance educator*
Schroeder, Michelle Shawn *agricultural studies educator*
Scoggin, Blainard Elmo *religious educator*
Scott, Stephen Carlos *academic administrator*
See, Miles Todd *animal scientist, educator*
Sheng, Quan *chemist*
Simpson, Steven Drexell *lawyer*
Sloan, O. Temple, Jr. *automotive equipment executive*
Smith, Sherwood Hubbard, Jr. *retired electric utilities executive*
Sneed, Ronald Ernest *retired project engineer, engineering educator*
Spearman, Robert Worthington *lawyer*
Speer, Kevin Paul *surgeon*
Spruill, W. Murray *lawyer*
Staal, Eric *professional hockey player*
Stevens, Richard Yates *state senator*
Stevenson, Denise L. *diversified financial services company executive, consultant, realtor*
Stillman, Cory *professional hockey player*
Stuber, Charles William *retired genetics educator, researcher*
Suhr, Paul Augustine *lawyer*
Surh, Gerald *history professor*
Sutton, Ronnie Neal *state legislator, lawyer*
Swaisgood, Harold Everett *biochemist, educator*
Szulik, Matthew J. *information technology executive*
Taddesse, Samuel *economist, consultant*
Teague, Charles Woodrow *lawyer*
Thompson Cornwall, Lonieta Aurora *music educator, consultant*
Timmons, Sean Abbott *lawyer*
Timmons-Goodson, Patricia *state supreme court justice*
Timothy, David Harry *retired biology professor*
Tucker, Helen Welch *writer*
Turinsky, Paul Josef *nuclear engineer, educator*
Tverdovsky, Oleg *professional hockey player*
Valois, Robert Arthur *lawyer*
Wadhwa, Vivek *information technology executive*
Wainwright, George L., Jr. *state supreme court justice*
Ward, Cam *professional hockey player*

Wehring, Bernard William *nuclear engineering educator*
Weisel, Michael Lloyd *lawyer, educator*
Wesley, Glen *professional hockey player*
Wetsch, John Robert *information scientist*
Wetsch, Laura Johnson *lawyer*
Whetzel, Julie Anne *special education educator*
Whitaker, Bruce Ezell *college president*
Whitaker, Thomas Burton *agricultural engineer, educator*
Whitney, Ray *professional hockey player*
Whitten, Jerry Lynn *chemistry professor*
Willer, Edward Herman *real estate broker*
Williams, Hugh Alexander, Jr. *retired mechanical engineer, consultant*
Wilson, Donald Hurst III *mediator, biopharmaceutical industry executive*
Wilson, Sue *newspaper editor*
Windham, Donald Eric *bioinformatics analyst*
Winstead, Nash Nicks *academic administrator, plant pathologist*
Wynne, Johnny Calvin *dean, plant pathologist, researcher*
Zelnak, Stephen P., Jr. *construction materials company executive*
Zorowski, Carl Frank *engineering educator, academic administrator*

## Ramseur
Coward, Pamela Kinney *elementary school educator*

## Randleman
Jordan, Lillian B. *judge*
Petty, Richard *retired race car driver*

## Red Springs
Jacobs, Kimberly Ann *elementary school educator*

## Reidsville
Covington, Bennie Mell, Jr. *music educator*

## Research Triangle Park
Advani, Deepak *computer company executive*
Atkins, John L. III *architect*
Bandrowczak, Steven J. *computer company executive*
Baumann, Karsten *engineer, researcher*
Biemer, Paul Philip *statistician, educator*
Bierman, James L. *contract research organization executive*
Bolen, M. Christopher *lawyer*
Bond, Enriqueta Carter *science administrator*
Bronstein, Lois Helene *marketing professional*
Call, Douglas William *university official, naval officer*
Everett, LaTonya Michelle *computer engineer*
Fisher, Robert Perry *environmental scientist, researcher*
Fought, Lorianne *plant pathologist*
Framil, Armando Ramon *pharmaceutical executive*
Gentzsch, Wolfgang *grid computing and networking service company executive*
Greenwell, Arnold *editor, photographer*
Haynes, Victoria F. *science administrator*
Ingram, Robert A. *pharmaceutical executive*
Isler, Raymond Earl *engineer*
Johnson-Payton, Lori Renee *systems engineer*
Lemieux, Paul *chemical engineer, researcher*
Mumford, Stephen Douglas *research scientist*
Roses, Allen David *neurologist, educator*
Russell, John S. *contract research organization executive*
Schwartz, David A. *federal agency administrator*
Sculley, Patrick David *retired army officer, science honor society director*
Selkirk, James Kirkwood *biochemist, researcher*
Tong, Quansong *environmental scientist*
Wani, Mansukhlal Chhaganlal *chemist*
Welborn, Reich Lee *lawyer*

## Rich Square
Baugham, Samuel McCoy *actor, painter*

## Roanoke Rapids
Adiga, Giridhar U. *geriatrician, pharmacologist, researcher, internist*

## Robbins
Smith, Janet Brewer *secondary school educator*

## Robbinsville
Ginn, Ronn *architect, urban planner, general contractor*

## Rockingham
Evans, Patricia McCormick *psychotherapist*
Perkins, Susan Lammonds *art educator*
Robertson, Ralph S. *secondary school principal*

## Rocky Mount
Ellis, J(ames) Nicholas *lawyer*
Killoran, Thomas M. *mathematics professor, department chairman*
Nelsen, William Cameron *educational consultant*
Stubbs, Will, Jr. *pharmaceutical company manager*
Wordsworth, Jerry L. *wholesale distribution executive*
Zipf, Robert Eugene, Jr. *legal medicine consultant, pathologist*

## Ronda
Somers, Shelley Allen *elementary school educator*

## Roseboro
Cobb, Katherine Simon *theater educator*

## Rougemont
Holeman, Betty Jean *counseling administrator*

## Roxboro
Hollingsworth, Brenda Jackson *employment consultant*

## Rutherfordton
Crummie, Ann Vaughn *mental health services professional*

## Salisbury
Bamberg-Revis, Ethel M. *minister, educator*
Candler, Faxon David *small business owner*
Freeman, Algeania Warren *academic administrator*
Higbee, Dale (Strohe) *musician, retired psychologist*
Jenkins, Jimmy Raymond *academic administrator*
Kishev, Stephen Vasilev *urologist*
Troxler, Willie Thomasene *retired elementary school educator*
Tseng, Howard Shih Chang *business educator, investment company executive, economics professor*
Ward, Brenda Robinson *social worker*

## Saluda
Cutright, Phillips *sociologist, educator*
McCutcheon, John Tinney, Jr. *retired journalist*

## Sanford
Higgins, George Edward *sculptor*
Kelly, Daniel J. *retail executive*
Raisig, Paul Jones, Jr. *lawyer*
Sodini, Peter J. *food service executive*

## Seven Lakes
Reilly, David Henry *retired university dean*

## Shelby
Blanton, Madge Brantley *family practice nurse practitioner*
Edgar, Ruth R. *retired elementary school educator*

## Smithfield
Madern, Laurene Patricia *secondary school educator*
McClain, Gregory David *chaplain*

## Southern Pines
Funderburk, David Britton *retired congressman, ambassador, consultant*
Kaufman, Bernhard Barken *writer, educator*
Owings, Malcolm William *retired management consultant*
Toon, Malcolm *former ambassador*
Ward, Susan Sprinkle *organist*
Warren, Donald William *medical and dental educator*

## Southern Shores
Kegel, William George *mining company executive*
Turnage, Fred Douglas *retired lawyer*

## Southport
Pepper, Jeffrey Mackenzie *publishing executive*
Spain, Sheryl Scarbrough *school counselor, educator*

## Spencer
Barnes, Melver Raymond *retired chemist*
Kiser, Glenn Augustus *retired pediatrician, entrepreneur*

## Spindale
Howard, Elizabeth Ann Blanton *transportation executive*

## Spring Hope
Hildreth, James Robert *retired air force officer*

## Statesville
Allred, Susan G. *school system administrator*
Grogan, David R. *work saver company executive*
Kahne, Kasey *race car driver*
Mayfield, Jeremy *race car driver*
Redman, William Walter, Jr. *realtor*
Stelzner, Paul Burke *textile company executive*

## Stella
Quin, Louis DuBose *chemist, educator*

## Sunset Beach
Mattson, Clarence Russell *safety engineer*

## Swannanoa
Stuck, Roger Dean *electrical engineering educator*
Whittington, Lorin Dale *music educator*

## Tarboro
Hopkins, Grover Prevatte *lawyer*

## Taylorsville
Payne, Ronald Dean, II, *music educator, director*
Ross, David Edmond *church official*

## Thomasville
Mintz, Donna Pierce *elementary school educator*
Sprinkle, Robert Lee, Jr. *podiatrist*

## Todd
Cole, Susan Stockbridge *retired theater educator*

## Trenton
Brown, Clifton *agricultural products supplier, director*
Dillahunty, George Robert *minister*

## Trinity
McIlquham, David J. *consumer products company executive*
Walker, Kenneth Lynn *lawyer*

## Tryon
Flynn, Kirtland, Jr. *accountant*
Mellberg, James Richard *retired dental research chemist*

## Vass
Glassman, Edward *public relations executive, educator, journalist*

## Vilas
Stolberg, Mary Margaret *historian*

## Wadesboro
Hamby, Kristie Lynne *director*

## Wake Forest
Buchanan, Edward A. *education educator*

Gamble, Michael F. *human resources generalist*
Thompson, Christina Elizabeth *music educator, musician*

## Walstonburg
Beaman, Joyce Proctor *retired secondary and elementary school educator, writer*

## Warrenton
Kearney, Irene Spruill *elementary school educator*

## Washington
Blackwell, F. Oris *environmental scientist, educator*
Hackney, James Acra III *industrial engineer, consultant, retired manufacturing executive*
Rader, Steven Palmer *lawyer*

## Waxhaw
Ahern, John James *software company executive*
Edwards, Irene Elizabeth (Libby Edwards) *dermatologist, educator, medical researcher*
Lubs, Lori Deanne *elementary school educator*

## Waynesville
Cole, James Yeager *foundation administrator*
Hale, Joe (Joseph Rice) *church organization executive*
McKinney, Alexander Stuart *retired neurologist*
Stokes, Mack Boyd (Marion Boyd Stokes) *bishop*

## Weaverville
Hall, Linda *secondary school educator*
Parsons, Vinson Adair *retired computer company executive*

## Welcome
Sauter, Johnny *race car driver*

## Weldon
Barringer, Paul Brandon, II, *lumber company executive*
Dhasmana, Bindu *paper company executive, chemist, researcher*

## West Jefferson
Merrion, Arthur Benjamin *mathematics professor, tree farmer*

## Whispering Pines
Kuhn, Matthew *retired engineering company executive*

## Whiteville
Harrelson, Bob Fitzgerald *engineering company executive*
McClary, Gracie Branch *bank executive*

## Wilkesboro
Hull, Robert F., Jr., (Bob Hull) *retail executive*
Thomas, David Lloyd *accountant, consultant*

## Willow Spring
Valvo, Barbara-Ann *lawyer, surgeon*

## Wilmington
Ao, Qi *nuclear scientist, educator*
Boyle, Joseph Hugh *psychiatrist*
Buckland, Wendy *medical products executive*
Cameron, Kay *conductor, composer*
De Maria, Alfred Anthony *neurologist*
Dixon, Daniel Roberts, Jr. *retired lawyer*
Duarte, Hugo *composer*
Fox, James Carroll *federal judge*
Hancock, Robert Douglas *educator*
Herman, Russell Leland *mathematics professor, physics professor*
Kelley, Patricia Hagelin *geology educator*
Leutze, James Richard *television producer, former academic administrator*
Maness, Eleanor Palmer *researcher*
Medlock, Donald Larson *lawyer*
Mintzes, Joel J. *biology professor, researcher*
Moallem, Mahnaz *educational researcher*
Nelson, Tannis Flynn *parliamentarian, retired music educator*
Schuhmann, Peter W. *economist, educator*
Seapker, Janet Kay *museum administrator, historic site director, consultant*
Toplin, Robert Brent *history professor, television producer*

## Wilson
Atkinson, Ann Lennette *funeral director*
Kushner, Michael James *neurologist, consultant, educator*
Ladwig, Harold Allen *neurologist*
McCain, Betty Landon Ray (Mrs. John Lewis McCain) *political party official, state official*
McKinnon, Karl Luther *museum director*
Stewart, Burton Gloyden, Jr. *retired banker*
Wyatt, Edward Avery, V, *city manager*

## Windsor
Mizelle, Alan Keith *minister*

## Wingate
Dirks, Amie Jeanette *physiologist, educator*
Dodd, John Robert *non-profit organization administrator*

## Winston Salem
Adams, Alfred Gray *lawyer*
Adams, Reid C., Jr. *lawyer*
Allison, John Andrew, IV, *bank executive*
Applegate, William Brown *dean, researcher, medical educator, department chairman*
Atala, Anthony John *surgeon*
Barnett, Richard Chambers *historian, educator*
Barnhill, Henry Grady, Jr. *lawyer*
Beardsley, Charles Mitchell *retired insurance company executive*
Beaty, James Arthur, Jr. *federal judge*
Blixt, Charles A. *lawyer, food products executive*
Blynn, Guy Marc *lawyer*
Borwick, Susan Harden *musicologist, educator*
Bourne, Henry Clark, Jr. *electrical engineer, educator, retired academic administrator*
Brewster, Daryl G. *food products executive*
Bulluck, Matthew Heyer *performing arts educator*

Cahill, Eileen Mary *secondary school educator*
Capps, Richard Henry *retired minister*
Chaden, Lee A. *apparel executive, former food products executive*
Chen, Frederick H. *economist*
Chilson, John A. *lawyer, military officer*
Clinard, Keith A. *lawyer*
Constantinidis, Christos *education educator*
Copenhaver, W. Andrew *lawyer*
DeMaio Caprilli, Barbara Jean *music educator*
Donofrio, Peter Daniel *neurology educator*
Dyer, Raymond B. *diagnostic radiology physician*
Ehle, John Marsden, Jr. *writer*
Eldridge, J. Charles *endocrinologist, researcher, medical educator*
Eliason, Russell Allen *judge*
Faccinto, Victor Paul *artist, gallery administrator*
Fleischer, Alan Bernard, Jr. *dermatologist, educator*
Gitter, Allan Reinhold *lawyer*
Gordon, William Charles *academic administrator*
Graham, William Thomas *lawyer*
Graybeal, Barbara *editor, writer*
Greason, Murray Crossley, Jr. *lawyer*
Gregg, Ellen M. *lawyer*
Greven, Kathryn McConnell *radiologist, oncologist*
Grillo, Henry R. *theater educator, technical director*
Griswold, George *marketing, advertising and public relations executive*
Gunter, Michael Donwell *lawyer*
Gunzenhauser, Gerard Ralph, Jr. *management consultant, investor*
Hammon, John William, Jr. *medical educator, thoracic surgeon*
Hanes, Frank Borden *writer, former business executive, farmer*
Hanes, Ralph Philip, Jr. *retired textiles executive, horse breeder*
Harle, Thomas Stanley *radiologist*
Harrelson, Walter Joseph *minister, educator*
Hatch, Nathan Orr *academic administrator*
Hearn, Thomas K., Jr. *academic administrator*
Heckelman, Jac C *economics professor*
Hegde, Ashok *research scientist, educator*
Hendricks, J(ames) Edwin *historian, educator, consultant, author*
Henrichs, W(alter) Dean *dermatologist*
Hite, Robert Duncan *medical educator*
Holton, Walter Clinton, Jr. *lawyer*
Howell, Charles Maitland *dermatologist*
Humphrey, Dudley *lawyer*
Hunt, Ellen *minister, evangelist*
Hwang, Wenke *public health researcher*
Ibdah, Jamal A. *medical educator*
Ivey, Susan M. *tobacco company executive*
James, Francis Marshall III *anesthesiologist*
Jones, F(rancis) Whitney *fund raising executive, consultant*
Karnes, Lucia Rooney *psychologist*
Kaur, Mandeep *dermatologist, educator*
Kerr, William C. *physics professor*
King, Arthur Thomas *economics professor, retired air force officer*
King, Wayne Edgar *journalist, educator*
Kohut, Robert Irwin *otolaryngologist, educator*
Lambeth, Judy (E. Julia Lambeth) *lawyer*
Laxminarayana, Dama *geneticist, researcher, educator*
Leonard, R. Michael *lawyer*
Little, George L. *lawyer*
Locklair, Paula Welshimer *museum administrator, curator*
Ludolf, Marilyn Marie Keaton *lay worker*
Mallett, T. Conn *biochemist, educator*
Margitić, Milorad R. *language educator, researcher*
Marino, Nancy A. *marketing professional*
Maselli, John Anthony *food products executive*
Maynard, Charles Douglas *radiologist*
McKnight, Gregory Richard *research and development director*
Mecimore, Charles Douglas *retired accounting educator*
Medlin, John Grimes, Jr. *banker, director*
Meis, Paul Jean *obstetrics and gynecology educator*
Mendez, John *minister*
Mitchener, John Edward *music educator, musician*
Mohammed, Abdul K. *chemist, educator*
Mokrasch, Lewis Carl *neurochemist, educator*
Moody, Dixon McGuire *radiologist*
Moser, Kenneth Allen *lawyer*
Mueller, John S. *music educator*
Mueller, Margaret S. *musician, educator*
Noll, Richard A. *apparel executive*
O'Donovan, Cormac A. *neurologist, educator*
Oldaker, Guy Brooklyn III *lawyer*
Oliver, Patricia *lawyer*
Osborn, Malcolm Everett *lawyer*
O'Steen, Wendall Keith *anatomist, neurologist, educator*
Patel, Ajay *dean*
Podgorny, George *emergency physician*
Poovey, Mark Nixon *lawyer*
Porter-Kelley, Johanna Marie *microbiology educator, researcher*
Preslar, Len Broughton, Jr. *hospital administrator*
Price, Henry Escoe *broadcast executive*
Quick, Elizabeth L. *lawyer*
Ragland, George A. *lawyer*
Rauschenberg, Bradford Lee *museum program director*
Rights, Graham Henry *retired minister*
Rodgman, Alan *chemist, consultant*
Roth, Marjory Joan Jarboe *special education educator*
Salsbury, Freddie R., Jr. *physics professor, educator*
Sandridge, William Pendleton, Jr. *lawyer*
Sawyer, John Wesley *retired mathematics and computer science educator, consultant*
Schabacker, Elizabeth M. *literature educator*
Schollander, Wendell III *lawyer*
Schollander, Wendell Leslie, Jr. *lawyer*
Schroeder, Thomas D. *lawyer*
Shapere, Dudley *philosophy educator*
Sharpe, Keith Yount *retired lawyer, writer*
Shipko, Renee *marketing executive*
Simon, Jimmy Louis *pediatrician, educator*

Sink, Kaycee M. *geriatrician, medical educator*
Smith, David Coventry *lawyer*
Spach, Jule Christian *church executive*
Steele, Thomas McKnight *law educator*
Stein, Barry Edward *medical educator*
Strickland, Robert Louis *retired retail executive*
Sullivan, William Beaumont *lawyer*
Sutton, Lynn Sorensen *librarian*
Swords, William Edward *microbiologist, educator*
Taylor, Daniel Russell *lawyer*
Toole, James Francis *medical educator*
Torti, Frank Michael *internist, health facility administrator*
Trautwein, George William *conductor, violinist, educator*
Twiggs, Dennis Glenn *psychologist, writer*
Vaughan, Keith W. *lawyer*
Vaughn, Robert Candler, Jr. *lawyer*
Walker, George Kontz *law educator*
Walsh, Robert K. *dean*
Wanders, Hans Walter *banker*
Weller, Robert Stephen *anesthesiologist*
Wells, Dewey Wallace *lawyer*
Whittington, Stephen Lunn *museum director*
Wiley, C. Mark *lawyer*
Wilson, G(rover) Gray *lawyer*
Wilson, Van Cedric *academic administrator*
Winn, Albert Curry *clergyman*
Womble, William Fletcher *lawyer*
Zagoria, Sam D(avid) *reporter, educator, federal agency administrator*
Zubov, Lynn *special education educator, researcher*

**Winton**
Williams, Sue Darden *library director*

**Woodland**
Wilson, Lloyd Lee *registrar, educator*

**Woodleaf**
Nelson, Jennifer *elementary school educator*

**Wrightsville Beach**
Mc Ilwain, William Franklin *newspaper editor, writer*

**Zebulon**
Ruffing, Anne Elizabeth *artist*

# NORTH DAKOTA

**Amidon**
Bergquist, Gene Alfred *farmer, rancher, retired commissioner*

**Ashley**
Kretschmar, William Edward *state legislator, lawyer*

**Bisbee**
Keller, Michelle R. *science educator*

**Bismarck**
Clairmont, William Edward *real estate developer*
Crothers, Daniel J. *State Supreme Court Justice*
Dalrymple, Jack *lieutenant governor*
Evanson, Barbara Jean *middle school education educator*
Gilbertson, Joel Warren *lawyer*
Gray, Arlene *music educator, musician*
Hildestad, Terry D. *energy executive*
Hoeven, John *governor*
Jaeger, Alvin A. (Al Jaeger) *state official*
Joersz, Fran Woodmansee *secondary school educator*
Kapsner, Carol Ronning *state supreme court justice*
Kaushik, Prashant *rheumatologist, educator*
Klemin, Lawrence R. *lawyer*
Loble, Lester Henry, II, *lawyer*
Lundberg, Susan Ona *musical organization administrator*
Maring, Mary Muehlen *state supreme court justice*
McDowell, Jefferey Thomas *information technology educator*
Moore, Sherry Mills *lawyer*
Murry, Charles Emerson *lawyer, federal official*
Nelson, Carolyn *state legislator*
Neumann, William Allen *retired state supreme court justice*
Newborg, Gerald Gordon *state archives administrator*
Nordlie, Margaret A. *biology professor, director*
Ott, Doris Ann *librarian*
Potts, Robert Leslie *academic administrator*
Rettig, Pam *literature educator*
Robinson, Warren Lowe *utilities executive*
Sandstrom, Dale Vernon *state supreme court justice*
Sanstead, Wayne Godfrey *school system administrator*
Schwartz, Judy Ellen *thoracic surgeon*
Seil, Michael James *music educator*
Stenehjem, Wayne Kevin *state attorney general, lawyer*
Stoller, Rose *think-tank executive*
Strutz, William A. *lawyer*
Tornow, L. William *musician*
VandeWalle, Gerald Wayne *state supreme court chief justice*

**Bottineau**
Hagen, Mavis Arlo *elementary school educator*

**Cooperstown**
Surerus, Dorothea Kae *elementary school educator*

**Crystal**
Bradshaw, Glorianne Marie *elementary school educator*

**Devils Lake**
Schiele, James Leo *museum director*

**Dickinson**
Greenwood, Dann Edward *lawyer*
Mattheis, Theresa Judith *webmaster, educator*

**Dunseith**
Ferris, Kade Michael *historian, anthropologist*

**Edgeley**
Jolin, Diane Louise *elementary school educator*
Schimke, Dennis J. *former state legislator*

**Elgin**
Hintz, Pam K. *secondary school educator, science educator*

**Ellendale**
Schlieve, Hy C. J. *school administrator*

**Fargo**
Bright, Myron H. *federal judge*
Bye, Kermit Edward *federal judge, lawyer*
Foss, Richard John *bishop*
Hektner, Joel Martin *psychology professor*
Herman, Sarah Andrews *lawyer*
Holman, Maureen *lawyer*
Ihle, Thomas *physicist, education educator*
Jaseja, Mahesh *chemistry professor, researcher*
Littlefield, Robert Stephen *communications educator, training consultant*
Magill, Frank John *federal judge*
Marcil, William Christ, Sr. *publisher, broadcast executive*
McWilliams, Carey Scott *small business owner, writer*
Meester, Holly *elementary school educator, music educator, sales executive*
Mitchell, James Edward *physician, educator*
Morey, Charlotte Ann *elementary school educator, music educator*
Pauley, Edward E. *museum administrator*
Reitan, Daniel Kinseth *electric and computer engineering educator*
Rice, Jon Richard *health facility administrator, physician*
Riley, Thomas Joseph *anthropologist, educational association administrator*
Schmidt, Claude Henri *retired science administrator*
Tallman, Dennis Earl *chemistry professor, research scientist*
Tallman, Robert Hall *investment company executive*
Tharaldson, Gary Dean *hotel developer, owner*
Thompson, Vern *political organization executive*
Unhjem, Michael Bruce *lawyer*
Wagner, Alexander Johannes *physicist, educator*
Williams, Michael James *lawyer*
Wrigley, Drew H. *prosecutor, lawyer*
Yadav, Om Prakash *reliability engineer, educator*

**Gackle**
Wittmier, Denise Donelle *elementary school educator*

**Grand Forks**
Aune, Adonica Schultz *education educator, consultant*
Bradley, April Rain *psychology professor*
Burgess, Gaye Margaret *theater educator*
Carlson, Edward C. *anatomy educator, cell biologist, department chairman*
Carlson, Steven J. *finance educator*
Crow, Judson Lewis *plastic surgeon*
Gallo, Sergio Roberto *music educator, researcher*
Gjovig, Bruce Quentin *entrepreneur, consultant*
Glassheim, Eliot Alan *editor, state legislator*
Haskins, James P. *finance educator, consultant*
Hoffmann, Mark R. *physical chemist, educator*
Jackson, Jon *medical educator, consultant*
Jones, Arthur Frederick *art university administrator, educator*
Kupchella, Charles Edward *academic administrator, author*
Lerma, Edgar Villanueva *nephrologist*
Milavetz, Barry *academic administrator, molecular biologist*
Mondry, Diane *secondary school educator*
Nielsen, Forrest Harold *research nutritionist*
Nordlie, Robert Conrad *biochemistry educator*
Olson, Myrna Raye *education educator*
Page, Sally Jacquelyn *university official, management educator*
Patton, Gregory Kenneth *management educator*
Penland, James Granville *psychologist*
Ransom, Michael T. *counselor*
Russell, Sue Ann *clinical psychologist*
Seelan, Santhosh Kumar *science educator, department chairman*
Sharma, Sushil K. *medical educator*
Sobus, Kerstin MaryLouise *physician, physical therapist*
Thomasson, Kathryn Ambler *chemistry educator, researcher*
Towne, Gary Spaulding *music educator*
Tyler, John Duke *psychologist, educator*
Wogaman, George Elsworth *insurance company executive, financial consultant*

**Hunter**
Nyberg, Anne Marie *secondary school educator*

**Mandan**
Bair, Bruce Blythe *lawyer*
Hodge, Ann Linton *artist*

**Mayville**
Brunsdale, Mitzi Louisa, (Mallarian) *language educator, critic*
Champion, Kathleen Ann *mathematics professor*
Karaim, Betty June *retired librarian*
McMahon, Dalton Edward *history professor, social sciences educator, department chairman*
Pederson, John Martin *education educator*
Skean, Mark Edgar *finance educator, consultant*

**Minot**
Armstrong, Phillip Dale *lawyer*
Ellis, Lee *social sciences educator*
Jermiason, John Lynn *elementary school educator, farmer, rancher*
Kerian, Jon Robert *retired judge*
Lee, Gary *lawyer*
Moe, Vida Delores *civic worker*
Tollefson, Ben C. *state legislator, retired utilities executive*

Watne, Darlene Claire *county official*

**Oakes**
German, Susan Lee *secondary school educator*

**Rolla**
Seehafer, Brenda Ann *elementary school educator*

**Valley City**
Rogers, Patricia Louise *education educator, consultant*
Stillings, Dennis Otto *research association administrator, consultant*

**Wahpeton**
Dohman, Gloria Ann *librarian*
Reubish, Gary Richard *English language educator*

**Williston**
Adducci, Joseph Edward *obstetrician, gynecologist*
Yockim, James Craig *foundation administrator*

# OHIO

**Ada**
Baker, Kendall L. *academic administrator*
Cooper, Ken Errol *retired management educator*
Durkin, Keith Francis *sociologist, researcher*
Fenton, Howard Nathan III *lawyer, educator*
Henkels, Scott *theater director, educator*
Srinivasa, Vemuru R. *engineering educator, researcher*

**Akron**
Alexander, Anthony J. *electric power industry executive*
Allen, Marc Kevin *emergency physician, educator*
Barker, Harold Kenneth *former university dean*
Barlowe Bodman, Amy *violinist, composer*
Bartek, Dennis J. *lawyer*
Bartlo, Sam D. *lawyer*
Bell, Samuel H. *federal judge, educator*
Bonsky, Jack Alan *lawyer*
Borowiec, Andrew *art educator, photographer*
Briggs, Robert W. *lawyer*
Brown, David Rupert *engineering executive*
Burbach, Mike *editor*
Buzzelli, Charlotte Grace *special education educator*
Castronovo, Thomas Paul *architect, consultant*
Cherpas, Christopher Theodore *lawyer*
Chrisant, Rosemarie Kathryn *law library administrator*
Clinefelter, Ruth Elizabeth Wright *historian, educator*
Collier, Alice Elizabeth Becker *retired social services administrator*
Crawford, Robert John *credit company executive*
Czarnecki, Rita Marie *music educator, pianist*
Duan, Zhong-Hui *education educator, researcher*
Emmett, John Colin *retired inventor, consultant*
Evans, Douglas McCullough *surgeon, educator*
Fisher, James Lee *lawyer*
Frank, John V. *foundation administrator*
Friedman, Richard Everett *curator, art appraiser*
Geier, Kathleen T. *human resources specialist*
Gent, Alan Neville *physicist, researcher*
Haines, Terry L. *plastics company executive*
Harvie, Crawford Thomas *lawyer*
Holloway, Donald Phillip *lawyer*
Ichilov, Nehemia *principal, consultant*
Isayev, Avraam Isayevich *polymer engineer, educator*
Jana, Sadhan C. *engineering educator, researcher*
Kahan, Mitchell Douglas *museum director*
Kaufman, Donald Leroy *building products executive*
Keegan, Robert J. *manufacturing executive*
Kennedy, Joseph Paul *chemist, researcher*
Knepper, George W. *historian, educator*
Komorny, Kenneth Michael *pharmacist*
Korow, Elinore Maria *artist, educator*
Kramer, Richard J. *corporate financial executive*
Kubick, Robert J., Jr. *school psychologist*
LaNasa, Patricia Jeanne *music educator*
Lee, Brant Thomas *lawyer, educator, federal official*
Linberger, Peter *school librarian*
Litman, George Irving *physician, educator*
Lombardi, Frederick McKean *lawyer*
Loud, Keith John *pediatrician*
Marsh, Richard H. *utilities company executive*
Migid, Adel A. *theater educator, set designer, consultant*
Milsted, Amy *biomedical educator*
Moriarty, John Timothy *transportation consultant, writer*
Plummer, Karen Anne *librarian, educator*
Rebenack, John Henry *retired librarian*
Richert, Paul *law educator*
Rouvas, Sakas *singer, gymnast*
Seiberling, John Frederick *retired congressman, lawyer, educator*
Shane, Sandra Kuli *postal service administrator*
Shea-Stonum, Marilyn *federal bankruptcy judge*
Simmons, Debra Adams *editor*
Smart, George M. *energy executive, former packaging company executive*
Snider, George Runyon, Jr. *franchising company executive*
Sonnecken, Edwin Herbert *management consultant*
Spencer, Jeff *biologist, educator*
Taylor, E. Jane *lawyer*
Trotter, Thomas Robert *lawyer*
Vespoli, Leila L. *energy executive, lawyer*
von Spiegel, Janice Krieger *mathematics educator*
Wells, Norman, Jr. *metal products executive*
West, Michael Alan *retired hospital administrator*
Williams, William Proctor *literature educator*
Wolfe, John Leslie *lawyer*
Wortham, James Calvin *retired mathematics educator*
Wright, Bradley Abbott *lawyer*
York, Jeffrey Michael *school psychologist*

**Alliance**
Clem, Harriet Frances *library director*

**Alpha**
James, Francis Edward, Jr. *investment advisor*

**Amelia**
Campbell, John G. *insurance company executive*
Hayden, Joseph Page, Jr. *finance company executive*
Hill, Diane L. *music educator*
Kahles, Cheryl Mary *elementary school educator*

**Archbold**
Henry, Dinah D. *science educator*

**Ashland**
Ford, Lucille Garber *economist, educator*
Gearhart, Randall F. *healthcare educator*
Watson, JoAnn Ford *theology studies educator*

**Ashtabula**
Morisue, Glenn T. *graphics designer*

**Athens**
Ahrens, Kent *museum director, art historian*
Borchert, Donald Marvin *philosopher, educator*
Bruning, James Leon *academic administrator, educator*
Crist, Richard Le Roy *voice educator*
Crowl, Samuel Renninger *retired dean, language educator*
Cuddington, Kim Michelle *ecologist, educator*
Hogan, Terrence James *academic administrator, consultant*
Huang, Wayne Wei *information scientist, educator*
Irwin, Richard Dennis *electrical engineering educator*
Kortlander, William Clark *painter*
Krendl, Kathy *dean*
Lazuka, Robert *artist, art educator*
Matolak, David William *engineering educator*
Matthews, Jack (John Harold Matthews) *language educator, writer*
McDavis, Roderick J. *academic administrator*
McNamara, John Regis *psychology educator*
Metters, Thomas Waddell *sportswriter*
Nance, Richard Damian *geologist, consultant*
Robe, Thurlow Richard *engineering educator, dean*
Scott, Charles Lewis *retired photojournalist*
Stempel, Guido Hermann III *journalism educator*
Stump, Earl Spencer *psychologist*
Torres, Daniel *literature educator*
Tymas-Jones, Raymond *dean*
Ungar, Irwin Allan *botany educator*
Vedder, Richard Kent *economics professor*
Wen, Shih-Liang *mathematics professor*
Whealey, Lois Deimel *humanities scholar*

**Aurora**
Berry, Dean Lester *lawyer*
Eakin, Thomas Capper *sports promotion executive*
Kirchner, James William *retired electrical engineer*
Lawton, Florian Kenneth *artist, educator*
Ross, Violet Bica *retired elementary school educator, retired psychologist*
Su, Sunyu *physicist*

**Austintown**
Kope, Joseph B. *retired humanities educator*

**Avon Lake**
Morton, David Ray *sales and marketing executive*
Newlin, Stephen Dore *chemicals executive*
Parke, M(argaret) Jean *retired business owner, editor*
Pascarella, Perry James *editor, writer*
Patient, William F. *chemicals executive*
Wilson, W. David *corporate financial executive*

**Barberton**
Kitto, John Buck, Jr. *mechanical engineer*

**Bath**
Coyne, Thomas Joseph *economics professor, finance professor*

**Bay Village**
Berry, Edgar Allen *music educator*
Gorman, Elias John *history educator*
Hook, John Burney *investment company executive*
Kapp, C. Terrence *lawyer*

**Beachwood**
Demetriou, Steven J. *metal products executive*
Garber, Joseph Max *meteorologist*
Jacobstein, David M. *real estate company executive*
Krieger, Irvin Mitchell *retired chemistry professor*
Mardell, Carol Dolores *psychology professor*
Moskowitz, Roland Wallace *internist*
Robertson, Edward Neil *dentist*
Varner, Arthur E. *allergist, researcher*

**Beavercreek**
Chachula, Bernard M. *lawyer, consultant*
Gupta, Vijay Kumar *retired chemistry professor*

**Bellaire**
Kniesner, John Thomas *librarian*

**Bellbrook**
Maier, Donna Marie *psychologist*

**Bellevue**
Aigler, William Frank *lawyer*

**Bellville**
Hooker, James Todd *manufacturing executive*

**Beloit**
Barnett, Robert James *music educator, musician*

**Berea**
Atchinson, Kenneth *engineering educator*
Barth, Daniel M. *music educator*
Crennel, Romeo *professional football coach*
Davis, Butch (Paul Hilton Davis) *former professional football coach*
Durst, Richard Wayne *academic administrator*
Fralick, J. R. *music educator*
Kennelly, Laura Ballard *literature educator, writer*
Kevin, Braaten S. *social studies educator*

**Little**, Richard Allen *mathematics professor, computer science educator*
Peart, Sandra Joan *economics professor, researcher*
Sanders, Phyllis May *musician*
Tadych, Christopher Allen *architectural firm executive, architectural engineer*
Tomlin-Houston, Lisa *higher education administrator, director*
Uniatowski, Joanne M. *singer, educator*
Zeitlin, Louise R. *music educator*

**Berlin Center**
Haynali, Carolyn Ann *social services administrator*

**Bexley**
Verde, Brian James *secondary school educator*
Yashon, David *neurosurgeon, educator*

**Blanchester**
Coates, Pamela Marie *principal*

**Bluffton**
Dudley, Durand Stowell *retired librarian*
Liu, Kejing *education educator*
Rich, Ronald Lee *chemistry professor*

**Boardman**
Pavalko, Robert A., II, *music educator*

**Bowling Green**
Baird, James Abington *retired judge*
Berger, Bonnie G. *sport psychologist, educator*
Browne, Ray Broadus *popular culture educator*
Buffington, Robert Marshall *history professor*
Clark, Eloise Elizabeth *biologist, educator*
Darrow, Arthur Lloyd *management consultant, educator*
Gilbert, Erin Leigh *social studies educator*
Guion, Robert Morgan *psychologist, educator*
Hakel, Milton Daniel, Jr. *psychologist, educator, writer, consultant*
Holmes, Robert Allen *former lawyer, law educator, consultant, educator*
Lunde, Harold Irving *retired management educator*
McCaghy, Charles Henry *retired social sciences educator*
Midden, William Robert *chemist, educator*
Mueller, Greg Lester *artist, educator*
Nagi, Lillian S. *biology professor*
Nicolaou, Andreas I. *finance educator, consultant*
Ocvirk, Otto George *artist*
Pelletier, Andrew John *music educator*
Singer, Carol Ann *librarian, researcher*
Thayer, Robert Wilcox *music educator*
Versteeg, Robert John *minister, actor, writer*
Wolcott, Vernon *music educator, musician*

**Bratenahl**
Dunn, Horton, Jr. *organic chemist*
Jones, Trevor Owen *biomedical industry executive, management consultant*

**Brecksville**
Pappas, Effie Vamis *language educator, finance educator, writer, poet, artist*
Ventenilla, Aurora Curamen *psychiatrist*

**Brunswick**
Kuchynski, Marie *physician*
Reed, Jane Garson *entrepreneur*

**Bryan**
Carrico, Virgil Norman *physician*
Oberlin, Earl Clifford III *securities brokerage company executive*

**Bucyrus**
Cooper, April Helen *family practice nurse practitioner*

**Cadiz**
Thompson, Sandra Lee *library administrator*

**Cambridge**
Beldyk, Richard Michael *mechanical engineer*
Marks, Robert Gale *music educator*
Reisner, Andrew Douglas *psychologist*

**Campbell**
Peltz, Ruby *elementary school educator*

**Canal Winchester**
Aho, Eric Ward *music educator, conductor*

**Canfield**
Hill, Thomas Allen *lawyer*
Le Brun, John Leo *education educator, tax specialist*
Scurich, Kelly Lemos *music director*

**Canton**
Bartlette, Donald Lloyd *social worker, consultant, counselor, educator*
Bennington, Ronald Kent *lawyer*
Bridges, Cynthia Lynn *music educator*
Broniak, Lynn Marguerite *gifted and talented educator, technology educator*
Burkhart, William R. *lawyer*
Carson, Harry *retired professional football player*
de Oliveira, Ebenézer Aguiar *psychology professor, researcher*
Ewing, David Charles *automobile dealership executive*
Fernandez, Kathleen M. *cultural organization administrator*
Griffith, James W. *manufacturing executive*
Howland, Willard J. *radiologist, educator*
Mack, Tom *professional football player*
Mann, John Martin *minister*
McIlwain-Massey, Nadine *retired foundation administrator*
Moon, Warren *professional football player*
Nadas, John Adalbert *psychiatrist, educator*
Peck, Douglas Caton *dean, educator*
Perry, Stephen A. *museum administrator, former federal agency administrator*
Schauer, Thomas Alfred *insurance company executive*

Shaw, Billy *retired professional football player*
Swidarski, Thomas W. *manufacturing executive*
Timken, Ward J., Jr. *manufacturing executive*
Tullys, Marilyn Steen *retired elementary school educator*
Wright, Rayfield *professional football player*

**Cedarville**
Firmin, Michael Wayne *psychology professor*
Spencer, Mark William *music educator, minister, announcer*

**Celina**
Fanning, Ronald Heath *architect, engineer*

**Centerville**
Giffen, Daniel Harris *lawyer, educator*
Kauffold, Ruth Elizabeth *psychologist*

**Chagrin Falls**
Brophy, Jere Hall *manufacturing executive*
Brown, Jeanette Grasselli *retired director*
Deihl, Charles L. *former college president*
Heckman, Henry Trevennen Shick *retired metal products executive*
Indriolo, Johna Marie *elementary school educator*
Lingl, Friedrich Albert *psychiatrist*
Miller, John Robert *oil industry executive*
Ostendorf, Joan Donahue *fund raiser, volunteer*
Pierson, Marilyn Ehle *financial planner*
Robertson, Linda F. *educational administrator*
Shakley, Elaine M. *organist, department chairman*
Smith, Barbara Jean *lawyer*
Vail, Iris Jennings *civic worker*

**Chardon**
Dobyns, Brown McIlvaine *retired surgeon, educator*
Horvath, Madelon Toft *secondary school educator*
Orcino, Leonard Anthony *composer, conductor*

**Chesterland**
Aster, Ruth Marie Rhydderch *business owner*
Durn, Raymond Joseph *lawyer*
Korosec, Kenneth David *lawyer, director*
Ruble, Bernard Roy *minister, educator, personnel director, labor relations consultant*
Wood, Kenneth Anderson *small business owner, display designer*

**Chillicothe**
Copley, Cynthia Sue Love *insurance adjuster*
Cunningham, Susan Kathryn *retired secondary school educator*

**Chippewa Lake**
Javorek, Richard Alan *history educator, consultant*

**Cincinnati**
Abate, Anne Katherine *librarian, consultant, educator*
Adams, Edmund John *lawyer*
Adams, Mendle Eugene *minister*
Agrawal, Dharma Prakash *engineering educator*
Aguirre, Fernando *food products executive*
Albainy-Jenei, Stephen R. *lawyer*
Alexander, James Wesley *surgeon, educator*
Alexander, John Kurt *history professor*
Algeo, Thomas John *geologist, educator*
Anderson, James Milton *lawyer, hospital administrator*
Anderson, Jerry William, Jr. *diversified financial services company executive, educator*
Anderson, Joan Balyeat *theology studies educator, minister*
Anderson, William Hopple *lawyer*
Andritzky, Frank William *political science educator*
Anning, Robert Doan Hopkins *brokerage company executive*
Anthony, Thomas Dale *lawyer*
Antoine, Richard L. *human resources specialist, consumer products company executive*
Arnold, Susan E. *consumer products company executive*
Ashley, Kevin Edward *research chemist*
Ashley, Lynn *social sciences educator, consultant*
Ates, Delories *retired counseling administrator*
Bacher, Susan Lorraine *nursing educator*
Bahlman, William Thorne, Jr. *retired lawyer*
Bahr, Donald Walter *retired chemical engineer*
Balistreri, William Francis *pediatric gastroenterologist*
Barrett, John F. *insurance company executive*
Bateman, Sharon Louise *public relations executive*
Beckwith, Barbara Jean *journalist*
Beckwith, Sandra Shank *federal judge*
Bell, Sandra Elizabeth *corporate financial executive*
Bellet, Paul Sanders *pediatrician, educator*
Bellingham, Roger Gerry *librarian, researcher, consultant*
Besier, James Louis *pharmacist, educator*
Bestehorn, Jim Wiltrud *retired librarian*
Betsky, Aaron *art museum director*
Bezerra, Jorge Abdon *pediatrics educator, health facility administrator*
Biagini, Raymond E. *toxicologist, immunochemist*
Bieliauskas, Vytautas Joseph *psychologist, educator*
Birmingham, Stephen *writer*
Biro, Frank M. *pediatrics educator*
Bishop, George Franklin *political scientist, educator*
Black, Robert L., Jr. *retired judge*
Bleznick, Donald William *Romance languages educator*
Bluestein, Venus Weller *retired psychologist, educator*
Boat, Thomas Frederick *pediatrician, researcher, pulmonologist, educator*
Bollen, Sharon Kesterson *artist, educator*
Brady, Darlene Ann *artist, designer, architect*
Briggs, Henry Payson, Jr. *headmaster*
Briskin, Madeleine *oceanographer, paleontologist*
Brod, Stanford *graphics designer, educator*
Broderick, Dennis John *lawyer, retail executive*
Bromberg, Robert Sheldon *lawyer*
Brown, Dale Patrick *retired advertising executive*
Brown, Daniel *curator, executive secretary*
Browning, Robert David *music educator*

Bryant, John *utilities executive*
Buncher, Charles Ralph *epidemiologist, educator, biostatistician*
Burdette, Robert Bruce *retired lawyer*
Burke, Timothy Michael *lawyer, educator*
Burkhead, Phillip Lee *musician, educator*
Burleigh, William Robert *newspaper executive*
Burroughs, Thomas, Jr. *media consultant*
Byrnes, Bruce L. *manufacturing executive*
Cabezas, Heriberto *chemical engineer, researcher*
Cain, Linda Joanne *retired academic administrator*
Callinan, Tom *editor*
Campbell, Audrey Leigh *communications professional*
Campbell, Dell *publishing executive*
Chambliss, Carroll Christopher *professional baseball coach*
Chatterjee, Jayanta *architecture and planning educator*
Chesley, Stanley Morris *lawyer*
Chester, Thomas Lee *chemist*
Ching, Ho *surgeon*
Chistyakov, Dmitry Alexandrovich *research scientist*
Christensen, Paul Walter, Jr. *retired gear manufacturing company executive*
Christenson, Gordon A. *law educator*
Church, Robert Arthur *retired publishing executive*
Ciani, Alfred Joseph *dean*
Cioffi, Michael Lawrence *lawyer*
Cissell, James Charles *lawyer*
Clay, Eric L. *federal judge*
Clifford, Joel Patrick *secondary school educator*
Cloyd, G. Gil *information technology executive*
Cobey, John Geoffrey *lawyer, consultant*
Cody, Thomas Gerald *lawyer*
Conaton, Michael Joseph *diversified financial services company executive*
Cook, Deborah L. *federal judge, former state supreme court justice*
Costigan-Kerns, Louise E. *musician*
Craig, L. Clifford *lawyer*
Crew, Spencer *museum administrator*
Cunningham, Pierce Edward *lawyer, city planner*
Daley, Clayton Carl, Jr. *consumer products company executive*
Davis, Robin *publishing executive*
deCavel, Jean-Robert *chef*
De Courten-Myers, Gabrielle Marguerite *neuropathologist*
Dehner, Joseph Julnes *lawyer*
deKool, L.M. (Theo DeKool) *food products executive*
Dember, William Norton *retired psychologist, educator*
Derstadt, Ronald Theodore *health facility administrator*
DeWitt, Katharine Cramer *museum administrator*
Diller, Edward Dietrich *lawyer*
Dillon, David Brian *retail grocery executive*
Dionysiou, Dionysios Demetriou *adult education educator, researcher*
Diwan, Abhinav *medical educator, researcher*
Dlott, Susan Judy *judge, lawyer*
Dornette, W(illiam) Stuart *lawyer, educator*
Dougherty, Charlotte Anne *financial planner, insurance and securities representative*
Dougherty, David Francis *business process outsourcing executive*
Duffy, Virginia *minister*
Dugan, Timothy P. *director, philosopher, educator*
Dunigan, Dennis Wayne *real estate executive*
Dunn, Adam *professional baseball player*
Dunsker, Stewart B. *neurosurgeon*
Ehrnschwender, Arthur Robert *former utility company executive*
Elluru, Ravindra G. *pediatric otolaryngologist*
Esamann, Douglas F. *utilities executive*
Etges, Frank Joseph *parasitology educator*
Evans, James E. *lawyer*
Everson, Jean Watkins Dolores *librarian, media consultant, educator*
Faller, Susan Grogan *lawyer*
Farage, Miranda A. *research scientist*
Farmer, Richard T. *uniform rental and sales executive*
Farmer, Scott D. *apparel executive*
Federle, Thomas W. *environmental scientist, microbiologist*
Fender, Kimber L. *library director*
Ficke, Gregory C. *utilities executive*
Fink, Jerold Albert *lawyer*
Flanagan, Martha Lang *publishing executive*
Flick, Thomas Michael *mathematician, educator, educational association administrator*
Florez, Mary A. *artist*
Foley, Cheryl M. *electric power industry executive*
Fox, Joan Friedlander *restaurant critic*
Francis, Marion David *consulting chemist*
Friedman, Penny *lawyer*
Frooman, Thomas E. *lawyer*
Fulmer, Michael Clifford *food company administrator*
Gaines, Bennett L. *utilities executive*
Gardner, Adam Daniel *music educator*
Garfinkel, Jane E. *lawyer*
Geis, Stephen Anthony *music educator*
Gettler, Benjamin *lawyer, manufacturing company executive*
Gilbert, Jay *radio personality*
Glendening, Everett Austin *architect*
Goetzman, Bruce Edgar *architecture educator*
Goldstein, Sidney *pharmacist*
Goodman, Bernard *physics professor*
Goodman, Phyllis L. *public relations executive*
Goodman, Stanley *lawyer*
Gottlieb, Kenneth Allen *music educator*
Greenberg, David Bernard *chemical engineering educator*
Greengus, Samuel *academic administrator, theology studies educator*
Griffey, Ken, Jr., (George Kenneth Griffey Jr.) *professional baseball player*
Griffin, David Alan *federal judge*
Griffiths, Kenneth Ross *music educator, voice educator*
Guard, Roger *information technology executive*
Gyuro, Paula Candice *financial planner*
Hale, Nathan Kelly *music educator, artist*
Hardy, William Robinson *lawyer*

Elston, Robert C. *medical educator*
Emrick, Charles Robert, Jr. *lawyer*
Erb, Donald *composer*
Eustis, Joanne D. *university librarian*
Fabens, Andrew Lawrie III *lawyer*
Falcone, Tommaso *reproductive endocrinologist*
FallCreek, Stephanie Jean *non-profit organization executive*
Fallon, Pat *artist, educator*
Falsgraf, William Wendell *retired lawyer*
Fay, Regan Joseph *lawyer*
Fazio, Victor Warren *physician, colon and rectal surgeon*
Feinberg, Paul H. *lawyer*
Finn, Robert *writer, educator*
Fischer, Michelle K. *lawyer*
Fletcher, Robert *retired lawyer*
Fountain, Ronald Glenn *management consultant, corporate financial executive, entrepreneur, educator*
Friedman, Barton Robert *language educator*
Friedman, Harold Edward *lawyer*
Friedman, James Moss *lawyer*
Fung, John Julian *transplant surgeon, immunologist*
Gallagher, Patrick Francis Xavier *public relations executive*
Gambetti, Perluigi *pathologist*
Ganske, Lyle G. *lawyer*
Garcia, Mario Jorge *cardiologist*
Gardner, Richard Kent *retired librarian, educator, editor*
Giannetti, Louis Daniel *film critic, educator*
Gibans, James David *architect*
Gillespie, Robert Wayne *banker*
Gladden, Dean Robert *arts administrator, educator, consultant*
Glaser, Robert Edward *lawyer*
Glickman, Carl David *banker*
Goffman, William *mathematician, educator*
Goins, Frances Floriano *lawyer*
Gold, Gerald Seymour *lawyer*
Goldberg, Jerold S. *dean*
Goldfarb, Bernard Sanford *lawyer*
Goler, Michael David *lawyer*
Gooden, Drew *professional basketball player*
Goodman, David S. *lawyer*
Gould, Bonnie M. *realtor*
Gould, Eric David *musician, educator*
Greppin, John Aird Coutts *philologist, editor, educator*
Grossman, Theodore Martin *lawyer*
Haeck, James F. *manufacturing executive*
Hagen, Daniel C. *lawyer*
Haiman, Irwin Sanford *lawyer*
Hajj-Ali, Rula Adel *rheumatologist, researcher*
Hamilton Brown, Terri *bank executive*
Hardy, Richard Allen *mechanical engineer, engineering executive*
Harris, Paul N *lawyer*
Hartley, Duncan *fundraising executive*
Hastings, Susan C. *lawyer*
Heiman, David Gilbert *lawyer*
Henes, Samuel Ernst *lawyer*
Henman, Tim *professional tennis player*
Hennessy, Sean P. *retail executive*
Henry, Edward Frank *data processing executive*
Hermann, Robert Ewald *retired surgeon*
Hochman, Kenneth George *lawyer*
Hoerner, Robert Jack *lawyer*
Hogg, James Stuart *lawyer*
Hokenstad, Merl Clifford, Jr. *social work educator*
Holland, Brian Joseph *corporate financial executive*
Hollington, Richard Rings, Jr. *lawyer*
Holmes, Arthur S. *manufacturing executive*
Holzbach, Raymond Thomas *gastroenterologist, educator, writer*
Horst, J. Robert *lawyer*
Horvitz, Michael John *lawyer*
Horwitz, Ralph Irving *internist, epidemiologist, educator, dean*
Hundert, Edward M. *former academic administrator, educator*
Iannotti, Joseph Patrick *orthopedic surgeon*
Ilgauskas, Zydrunas *professional basketball player*
Ingram, Lori Ruth *performing arts association administrator*
Ivy, Conway Gayle *paint company executive*
Jackson, Frank G. *mayor*
Jacobs, Leslie William *lawyer*
Jacobs, Michael Roy *microbiologist, researcher*
Jacobs, Richard E. *real estate company executive, sports team owner*
James, LeBron *professional basketball player*
Janke, Ronald Robert *lawyer*
Jenkins, Thomas Llewellyn *physics professor*
Jenks, Carl M. *lawyer*
Jensen, Kathryn Patricia (Kit) *broadcast executive*
Jenson, Jon Eberdt *metal products executive*
Jindra, Christine *editor*
Johnson, John Frank *professional recruitment executive*
Johnson, Victoria Houston *elementary school educator, poet*
Jones, Damon *professional basketball player*
Jorgenson, Mary Ann *lawyer*
Kahrl, Robert Conley *lawyer*
Kalina, Eunice Goldstein *human services director*
Kalmadi, Sujith Rao *oncologist, hematologist*
Kanzeg, David George *radio station executive*
Kaouk, Jihad *urologist*
Karp, Marvin Louis *lawyer*
Kass, Lawrence *hematologist, oncologist, educator*
Katcher, Richard *lawyer*
Katz, Lewis Robert *law educator*
Keithley, Joseph Faber *electronic engineering manufacturing company executive*
Kelly, Dennis Michael *lawyer*
Kelly, John Terence *architect*
Kestner, Robert Steven *lawyer*
Key, Helen Elaine *accountant, educator, consulting company executive*
Kilbane, Catherine M. *lawyer*
Kilbane, Thomas Stanton *lawyer*
King, Joseph Thomas, Jr. *neurosurgeon*
Kinsella, Timothy J. *radiation oncologist*
Klopman, Gilles *chemistry professor*
Knerly, Stephen John, Jr. *lawyer*
Ko, Wen-Hsiung *electrical engineering educator*
Koch, Charles John *credit agency executive*

Kohn, William Irwin *lawyer*
Kolb, David Allen *psychologist, educator*
Kolda, Thomas Joseph *non-profit organization executive*
Korngold, Gerald *law educator, former dean*
Kovel, Ralph Mallory *writer, antique expert*
Kovel, Terry Horvitz *writer, antiques authority*
Kowalski, Kenneth Lawrence *physicist, researcher*
Kraay, Matthew Joseph *orthopedist, educator*
Kramer, Edward George *lawyer*
Kramer, Eugene Leo *lawyer*
Krauss, Lawrence Maxwell *physicist, astronomy educator, researcher, author*
Kuehn, Richard Arthur *telecommunications consultant*
Kurit, Neil *lawyer*
Lamm, Michael Emanuel *pathologist, immunologist, educator*
Landau, Bernard Robert *biochemist, educator, internist*
Lando, Jerome Burton *macromolecular science educator*
Lawniczak, James Michael *lawyer*
Lease, Robert K. *lawyer*
Leavitt, Jeffrey Stuart *lawyer*
Leddy, Patrick John *lawyer*
Lefferts, William Geoffrey *internist, educator*
Leiken, Earl Murray *lawyer*
Lenkoski, Leo Douglas *retired psychiatrist, educator*
Lenn, Stephen Andrew *investment banker*
Lennox, Heather *lawyer*
Lerner, Randolph D. *finance company executive*
Lewis, John Bruce *lawyer*
Lewis, John Francis *lawyer*
Lewis, Peter Benjamin *insurance company executive*
Lopez, Nancy *retired professional golfer*
Lowe, James Allison *lawyer, educator*
Lowe, John Burton *medical association administrator, molecular biologist, educator, pathologist*
Lowenkamp, Cynthia Dellis *lawyer*
Luke, Randall Dan *retired manufacturing executive, lawyer*
Ma, Patrick C. *oncologist, researcher*
Machaskee, Alex *newspaper publishing company executive*
Macklis, Roger Milton *physician, educator, researcher*
Madden, James D. *forensic engineer*
Madison, Robert Prince *architect*
Malangoni, Mark Alan *surgeon, educator*
Maloney, Mary D. *lawyer*
Mandel, Jack N. *manufacturing executive*
Manson, Marilyn (Brian Hugh Warner) *musician*
Markus, Richard M. *judge, arbitrator*
Marting, Michael G. *lawyer*
Mason, Thomas Albert *retired lawyer*
Mast, Bernadette Mihalic *lawyer*
Matia, Paul Ramon *retired judge*
Matthews, Eric Joddy *film director*
Mayland, Kenneth Theodore *economist*
Mayne, Lucille Stringer *finance educator*
Mazzone, Peter *physician*
McArdle, Richard Joseph *retired academic administrator*
Mc Cartan, Patrick Francis *lawyer*
McCarthy, Mark Francis *lawyer*
McCrae, Keith R. *medical educator, researcher*
McCullough, Joseph *retired academic administrator*
McHale, Vincent Edward *political science professor*
McHenry, Martin Christopher *physician, educator*
McKee, Thomas Frederick *lawyer*
McLaughlin, Patrick Michael *lawyer*
McQuarrie, Irvine Gray *neurosurgeon, educator*
Mehlman, Maxwell Jonathan *law educator*
Messinger, Donald Hathaway *lawyer*
Meyer, G. Christopher *lawyer*
Mhanna, Maroun Jean *pediatrician*
Miller, Genevieve *retired medical historian*
Miller, Holly Dara *physician, director, healthcare educator, researcher*
Millisor, Kenneth Ray *lawyer*
Millstone, David Jeffrey *lawyer*
Minai, Omar Ahmad *physician*
Moceanu, Dominique *retired Olympic athlete*
Molyneaux, David Glenn *newspaper travel editor*
Montague, Drogo K. *urologist*
Mooney, Beth *bank executive*
Moore, Karen Nelson *judge*
Moore, Kenneth Cameron *lawyer*
Morgenthaler, David Turner *venture capitalist*
Morris, Thomas William *symphony orchestra administrator*
Myers, Eddie Earl *psychologist*
Nelson, Sue Grodsky *humanities educator, consultant*
Neu, Richard W. *credit agency executive*
Neuhauser, Duncan vonBriesen *medical educator*
Newman, John M., Jr. *lawyer*
Nickerson, Gary Lee *educational consultant*
Nicols, Howard J.C. *lawyer*
Novick, Andrew Carl *urologist*
Oakar, Mary Rose *congresswoman*
O'Hara, Thomas Patrick *managing editor*
O'Keefe, Francis Ronald *lawyer*
Oliver, Solomon, Jr. *judge*
Ollinger, W. James *lawyer*
Olness, Karen Norma *medical educator*
O'Malley, Kathleen M. *federal judge*
Ornt, Daniel B. *physician*
Owendoff, Stephen Peter *lawyer*
Pace, Stanley Dan *lawyer*
Pallam, John James *lawyer*
Parobek, Drew Thomas *lawyer*
Pearlman, Samuel Segel *lawyer, educator*
Perkovic, Robert Branko *retired international management consultant*
Perris, Terrence George *lawyer*
Perry, George Williamson *lawyer*
Pianalto, Sandra *bank executive*
Pidert, Sandy Kristin *finance educator*
Pierce, Mary *professional tennis player*
Pike, Kermit Jerome *cultural organization administrator*
Pilla, Anthony Michael *bishop*
Piraino, Thomas Anthony, Jr. *lawyer*
Plachta, David W. *aerospace engineer*

Podboy, Alvin Michael, Jr. *law librarian, director*
Pogue, Richard Welch *lawyer*
Pollock, R. Jeffrey *lawyer*
Potter, Susan Kuniholm *bank executive*
Powell, Carl R. *academic administrator*
Previts, Gary John *finance educator, consultant*
Pugh, David L. *manufacturing executive*
Pujana, Maria Jose *neurologist*
Putka, Andrew Charles *lawyer*
Queen, Joyce *elementary school educator*
Quigney, Theresa Ann *special education educator*
Quinlan, Mark *credit agency executive*
Raaf, John Hart *surgeon, educator, health facility administrator*
Raghavan, Derek *oncologist, medical researcher and educator*
Rains, M. Neal *lawyer*
Rakita, Louis *retired cardiologist*
Ransohoff, Richard Milton *neurologist, researcher*
Rapp, Robert Neil *lawyer*
Ratner, James *real estate developer*
Rawson, Rachel L. *lawyer*
Rawson, Robert H., Jr. *lawyer*
Rehm, Susan *physician*
Reminger, Richard Thomas *lawyer, artist*
Renwick, Glenn M. *insurance company executive*
Reppert, Richard Levi *lawyer*
Resnick, Martin I. *urologist, educator*
Rhew, Perry James *federal judge*
Rickert, Jeanne Martin M. *lawyer*
Roberts-Mamone, Lisa A. *lawyer*
Rogers, Charles Edwin *physical chemistry professor*
Rome, Ellen S. *physician*
Roop, James John *public relations executive*
Rosenbaum, Jacob I. *retired lawyer*
Rothstein, Fred C. *health facility administrator*
Rub, Timothy F. *museum director*
Ruben, Alan Miles *law educator*
Ruff, Robert Louis *neurologist, physiologist, researcher*
Saada, Adel Selim *civil engineer, educator*
Salem, Dorothy Carlson *social sciences educator, history professor*
Salomon, Roger Blaine *retired language educator*
Sande, Theodore Anton *architect, educator, foundation executive*
Savinell, Robert Francis *engineering educator*
Sawyer, Raymond Terry *lawyer, consultant, theater producer*
Schaefer, David Arnold *lawyer*
Schuele, Donald Edward *retired physics professor, dean*
Schultz, Connie *reporter*
Seaton, Robert Finlayson *retired finance company executive*
Segota, Ena *hematologist*
Seifert, Shelley Jane *bank executive, human resources specialist*
Seles, Monica *professional tennis player*
Shapiro, Fred David *lawyer*
Shashkin, Pavel Nikolayevich *biochemist*
Shatila, Ahmad Hussain *surgeon, oncologist*
Sherry, Paul Henry *minister, religious organization administrator*
Shuck, Jerry Mark *surgeon, educator*
Sibley, Willis Elbridge *anthropology educator, consultant*
Sicherman, Marvin Allen *lawyer*
Siefers, Robert George *banker*
Simmons, Clinton Craig *human resources executive*
Simson, Gary Joseph *dean, law educator*
Slinger, Michael Jeffery *law librarian, director*
Smith, Jerome *not-for-profit developer, film producer, writer*
Smith, Mark Anthony *biochemist, educator*
Sogg, Wilton Sherman *lawyer*
Sola, Srikanth *cardiologist*
Solomon, Randall Lee *lawyer*
Stanley, Hugh Monroe, Jr. *lawyer*
Stanton, R. Thomas *lawyer*
Stanton-Hicks, Michael D'Arcy *anesthesiologist, pain medicine specialist*
Stanziano, Stephen *music educator*
Stavitsky, Abram Benjamin *immunologist, educator*
Steindler, Howard Allen *lawyer*
Stellato, Louis Eugene *lawyer*
Stern, Robert C. *pediatrician, medical educator*
Stevens, Thomas Charles *lawyer*
Stojkovic, Dejan B. *physicist, educator*
Stokes, Louis *lawyer, former congressman*
Storey, Robert Davis *lawyer*
Stratton-Crooke, Thomas Edward *financial consultant*
Strauch, John L. *lawyer*
Striefsky, Linda A(nn) *lawyer*
Strimbu, Victor, Jr. *lawyer*
Stropki, John M., Jr. *electric power industry executive*
Stuhan, Richard George *lawyer*
Summers, William B., Jr. *brokerage house executive*
Summers, William Lawrence *lawyer*
Suri, Jasjit S. *research scientist*
Swartzbaugh, Marc L. *lawyer*
Swetland, David Wightman *real estate company executive, investment company executive*
Szaller, James Francis *lawyer*
Szarek, Stanislaw Jerzy *mathematics professor*
Tary-Lehmann, Magdalena *education educator*
Taw, Dudley Joseph *sales executive, director*
Taylor, Harris C. *endocrinologist, consultant*
Taylor, Margaret Wischmeyer *retired language educator*
Taylor, Nellie Ruby *artist, poet*
Taylor, Steve Henry *zoologist*
Terburg, Bart Paul *physicist, industrial engineer*
Tetzlaff, John Edwin *physician*
Thimmig, Diana M. *lawyer*
Thomas, David Manning *secondary school educator*
Thomas, Dynda A. *lawyer*
Thomas, Richard Stephen *construction executive*
Thomas, Troy D. *banking executive*
Thompson, Paul C. *labor union administrator*
Thornton, Glenda Ann *librarian*
Thurmer, Robert *art gallery director*
Toohey, Brian Frederick *lawyer*
Toomajian, William Martin *lawyer*

Topol, Eric Jeffrey *academic administrator, cardiologist, educator*
Tubbs, Raymond Roy *pathologist*
Tyson, Daniel S. *chemist, researcher*
Ubogu, Eroboghene Ekamereno *physician*
Vande Steeg, Nickolas W. *manufacturing executive*
Venable, Andrew A., Jr. *library director*
von Mehren, George M. *lawyer*
Waldeck, John Walter, Jr. *lawyer*
Wallach, Mark Irwin *lawyer*
Walters, Mark Douglas *obstetrician, gynecologist*
Warner, Carolyn G. *musician, music educator*
Warren, Russell James *investment banker, consultant*
Washkewicz, Donald E. *manufacturing executive*
Watson, Richard Thomas *lawyer*
Weaver, John Carl *chemist, educator*
Weaver, Robin Geoffrey *lawyer, educator*
Weber, Robert Carl *lawyer*
Webster, Leslie Tillotson, Jr. *pharmacologist, educator*
Wedge, Eric *archbishop*
Weidenthal, Maurice David (Bud Weidenthal) *academic administrator, journalist*
Weiler, Jeffry Louis *lawyer*
Weir, Dame Gillian Constance *musician*
Weiss, Morry *greeting card company executive*
Weiss, Zev *corporate financial executive*
Wells, Lesley *federal judge*
Welser-Möst, Franz *conductor, music director*
Wertheim, Sally Harris *director, academic administrator, dean, education educator, consultant*
White, Gregory A. *prosecutor*
Whitney, Richard Buckner *lawyer*
Wilson, Jack *aeronautical engineer*
Wish, Jay Barry *nephrologist, specialist*
Withers, Carl Raymond *lawyer*
Wolfman, Alan *medical educator, researcher*
Wolinsky, Emanuel *internist, educator*
Womack, John W. *pharmacist*
Wong, Margaret Wai *lawyer*
Wood, Paul F. *national health agency executive*
Woods, Jacqueline F. *public relations executive*
Woyczynski, Wojbor Andrzej *mathematician, educator*
Wykle, May L. *dean, educator, researcher*
Yetman, Randall John *plastic surgeon*
Young, James Edward *lawyer*
Young, Jess Ray *retired internist*
Zambie, Allan John *lawyer*
Zhang, Nengli *research scientist*
Zhu, Dongming *materials scientist*
Zung, Thomas Tse-Kwai *architect*

## Cleveland Heights

Baker, Brett E. *music educator*
Chilcote, Lee A. *lawyer*
Close, Carole Lynne *education educator, consultant*
Netzer, Nikolaus C. *physician, medical researcher, publishing executive*
Pease, Robin A. *performing company executive, actress*
Sandburg, Helga *author*

## Columbia Station

Goll, Paulette Susan *education educator*
Yearley, Barbara Ellen *music educator*

## Columbus

Adams, John Marshall *lawyer*
Adeli, Hojjat *engineer, educator, computer scientist*
Adelson, Edward *physicist, educator, musician*
Akers, Saundra Ruth *retired disability rights advocate*
Alban, Roger Charles *small business consultant*
Alexander, Carl Albert *ceramics engineer, educator*
Alger, Chadwick Fairfax *political scientist, educator*
Allen, Lois Arlene Height (Mrs. James Pierpont Allen) *musician*
Altan, Taylan *engineering educator, director*
Alutto, Joseph Anthony *dean, management educator*
Anand, Jaideep *management educator, consultant*
Anderson, Carole Ann *nursing educator, academic administrator*
Anderson, Donald Kennedy, Jr. *language educator*
Anderson, Jon Mac *lawyer, educator*
Armes, Walter Scott *retired vocational school administrator*
Arvia, Anne L. *bank executive*
Ash, Thomas Phillip *school system administrator*
Ausich, William Irl *geology educator*
Babcock, Charles Luther *classics educator*
Bailey, Daniel Allen *lawyer*
Baird, Leonard Lynn *social scientist, educator, researcher, editor*
Balcerzak, Stanley Paul *hematologist, oncologist, director, retired medical educator*
Baliga, Ragavendra Ramakrishna *cardiologist, researcher*
Balkrishnan, Rajesh *education educator*
Banasik, Robert Casmer *health facility administrator, educator*
Barlow-Ware, Jacqueline Sue *music educator*
Barnes, Wallace Ray *retired lawyer*
Barry, James P(otvin) *editor, writer*
Bartels, Robert Louis *retired physical education educator, coach*
Barth, Rolf Frederick *pathologist, educator*
Barthelmas, Ned Kelton *brokerage house executive*
Battersby, James Lyons, Jr. *language educator*
Bechtel, Stephen E. *mechanical engineer, educator*
Beck, Paul Allen *dean, political science professor*
Behrman, Edward Joseph *biochemistry educator*
Beja, Morris *English literature educator*
Bell, Karen A. *dean*
Bennett, Robert Thomas *lawyer, professional athletics manager*
Berndt, Ellen German *lawyer*
Berntson, Gary Glen *psychiatry, psychology and pediatrics educator*
Berry, William Lee *business administration educator*
Beversdorf, David Quentin *neurologist, researcher*
Bhushan, Bharat *mechanical engineer*

Willke, Thomas Aloys *academic administrator, statistician, educator*
Winkler, John Frederick *lawyer, educator*
Wojcicki, Andrew Adalbert *chemist, educator*
Wood, Jackie Dale *physiologist, educator, researcher*
Woodley, Frederick William *molecular biologist, geneticist, educator*
Yancey-Jones, Floristine Darlene *artist, educator*
Yenkin, Bernard Kalman *coatings and resins company executive*
Yu, Chack Yung *pediatrics educator, molecular biologist*
Zakin, Jacques Louis *chemical engineering educator*
Zartman, David Lester *retired zoology educator, researcher*
Zelman, Susan Tave *school system administrator*
Zex, Damon *artist*
Zhao, Fang Li *medical researcher*
Zhu, Xiankui *mechanical engineer, researcher*
Zweben, Stuart Harvey *information scientist, educator, dean*

**Concord**
Ulsenheimer, Dean *language educator*

**Copley**
Weil, Edward David *chemist, researcher, consultant, educator*

**Coshocton**
Boyce, Stanley Edman *retired secondary school educator*
Freund, Carol Louise *social services consultant*

**Cuyahoga Falls**
Barsan, Robert Blake *dentist*
Butcher, Jack Robert (Jack Risin) *manufacturing executive, film producer, actor, artist*
Haag, Everett Keith *architect*
Jones, John Frank *retired lawyer*
Moses, Abe Joseph *financial planner, consultant*
Paulis, Brian E. *conductor, composer*
Roth, Gregory Edward *social studies educator*
Walker, Suzannah Wolf *language educator*

**Dayton**
Ambalavanan, Siva *nephrologist, educator*
Ballal, Dilip Ramchandra *mechanical engineering educator*
Battino, Rubin *retired chemistry professor*
Bednarek, Janet Rose *history professor*
Bocian, Pete *corporate financial executive*
Burick, Lawrence T. *lawyer*
Carbone, Carrie Elizabeth *lawyer*
Carrier, Rachel Esther *music educator, director*
Carson, Dora A. *secondary school educator*
Chernesky, Richard John *lawyer*
Chin, Hong Woo *oncologist, educator, researcher*
Clark, William Alfred *federal judge*
Curran, Daniel J. *academic administrator, sociologist, educator*
Daley, Robert Emmett *retired foundation executive*
Daoud, George Jamil *hotel and motel consultant*
Dermody, Diana Dorothy *elementary school educator*
Duangthip, Thammarat *research scientist*
Duval, Daniel Webster *manufacturing executive*
Farquhar, Robert Nichols *lawyer*
Faruki, Charles Joseph *lawyer*
Freeland, Charles Harrell *literature educator*
Gabbert, Janice Jean *history, literature and language educator*
Geswein, Gregory T. *software company executive*
Gillig, Paulette Marie *psychiatry educator, researcher*
Gladden, Robert Wiley *healthcare executive*
Goldenberg, Kim *academic administrator, internist*
Gomez-Cambronero, Julian *cell biologist, biochemist, educator*
Guan, Shan *materials scientist*
Hadley, Robert James *lawyer*
Hanna, Marsha L. *artistic director*
Harden, Oleta Elizabeth *literature educator, academic administrator*
Harlan, Norman Ralph *construction executive*
Heath, Mariwyn Dwyer *writer, legislative staff member*
Heil, Michael Lloyd *military officer, academic administrator*
Heyman, Ralph Edmond *lawyer*
Hoak, Jonathan S., Sr. *lawyer*
Hofmann, Marie-Claude *cell biologist, educator, research scientist*
Hoge, Franz Joseph *accounting firm executive*
Hopkins, David R. *academic administrator, educator*
Houpis, Constantine Harry *retired electrical engineering educator*
Isaacson, Milton Stanley (Jim Isaacson) *research and development company executive, engineer*
Jenefsky, Jack *wholesale company executive*
Jenks, Thomas Edward *lawyer*
Johnson, C. Terry *lawyer*
Jones, Peter Hayward *design strategist, researcher*
Kinlin, Donald James *lawyer*
Klinck, Cynthia Anne *library director*
Knapp, James Ian Keith *judge*
Lair, Vickie Sue *mathematics professor*
Lashley, William Bartholomew *county official*
Lasley, Thomas J., II, *education educator*
Leigh, Gloria Lorraine *retired religious studies educator*
Leland, Nita Ellen Shannon *artist, writer*
Lockhart, Gregory Gordon *prosecutor*
Look, David Charles *physicist, researcher*
Macklin, Crofford Johnson, Jr. *lawyer*
Matheny, Ruth Ann *editor*
Mathile, Clayton Lee *pet food company executive*
McCloskey, Kathy Ann *psychologist*
McIlroy, Alan F. *manufacturing executive*
McLin, Rhine Lana *mayor, former state legislator*
McWhorter, Stanley Bruce *retired language educator*
Meister, Mark Jay *museum director, professional society administrator*
Michels, Joseph B. *military officer, dean*
Mitakides, Louella Jane *entrepreneur*
Mohler, Stanley Ross *preventive medicine physician, educator*

Monk, Susan Marie *pediatrician, educator*
Mosier, William Arthur *psychiatrist, psychotherapist, director, medical educator, researcher*
Mukhopadhyay, Sharmila Mitra *materials engineer, educator*
Nanagas, Maria Teresita Cruz *pediatrician, educator*
Nielsen, Philip Edward *physicist, research manager*
Nixon, Charles William *acoustician*
Nuti, William R. *computer services company executive*
Part, Howard Mitchell *dean*
Pasupuleti, Venumadhav *information technology executive*
Pestello, Fred P. *academic administrator*
Petrick, Joseph Anthony *small business owner, management consultant, educator*
Phillips, Chandler Allen *biomedical engineer*
Pincetic, Jose E. *information technology executive*
Potter, Dan R. *history educator*
Reiling, Walter Anthony, Jr. *surgeon*
Richmond, Allen *conductor, educator*
Riley, David Richard *management consultant, retired military officer*
Ringler, James M. (James M. Ringler) *computer services company executive*
Rion, John Hayes *lawyer*
Rogers, Richard Hunter *lawyer*
Ruegsegger, Donald Ray, Jr. *radiological physicist, educator*
Saul, Irving Isaac *lawyer*
Schmitt, George Frederick, Jr. *materials engineer*
Simman, Richard *plastic surgeon, researcher*
Singhvi, Surendra Singh *financial consultant*
Stout, Donald Everett *real estate developer, environmental services administrator*
Stutzman, L. Lee *pastor*
Tatar, Jerome F. *business products executive*
Thomas, Marianna *volunteer community activist, writer, speaker*
Vaughn, Noel Wyandt *lawyer*
Vice, Roy Lee *history professor*
Walters, Jefferson Brooks *musician, retired real estate broker*
Wasson, Barbara Hickam *music educator*
Wasson, Steven *music educator, piano technician*
Wasylyna, Victor J. *lawyer*
Weinberg, Sylvan Lee *cardiologist, educator, editor, writer*
Wertz, Kenneth Dean *real estate company officer*
White, Lawrence Edward *treasurer, financial executive*
Wikstrom, Loretta Wermerskirchen *artist*
Wilberding, Merle Francis *lawyer*
Williams, Walker Richard, Jr. *social services administrator*
Wilson, William Campbell McFarland *gastroenterologist*
Winkler, Jonathan Reed *historian, educator*
Wyllie, Stanley Clarke *retired librarian*
Zahner, Mary Anne *art educator*

**De Graff**
Fleming, Lucinda Marie *secondary school educator*

**Defiance**
Yeager, Bobbi Ann *visual arts educator, artist*

**Delaware**
Bahrick, Harry Phillip *science educator, researcher*
Ciochetty, John Bryan *protective services official*
Eells, William Hastings *retired automobile company executive*
Gardner, Bonnie Milne *theater educator, playwright*
Huml, Donald Scott *manufacturing executive*
Jamison, Roger W. *pianist, educator*
Pettigrew, Carolyn Landers *academic administrator, minister*
Schlichting, Catherine Fletcher Nicholson *librarian, educator*
Sparks, William B., Jr. *consumer products company executive*

**Delta**
Miller, Beverly White *former college president, educational consultant*

**Dover**
Haggis, Mary Ripley *nurse, genealogist*

**Doylestown**
Morton, Sallie W. *music educator*

**Dublin**
Anderson, Kerrii B. *food service executive*
Bird, Shelley *communications executive*
Bordelon, Carolyn Thew *elementary school educator*
Borror, Douglas G. *construction company executive*
Clark, R. Kerry (Kerry Clark) *health products executive*
Clement, Henry Joseph, Jr. *diversified building products executive*
D'Antoni, David J. *chemicals executive*
Davids, Jody R. *information technology executive*
Dolch, Gary D. *pharmaceutical executive*
Fong, Ivan Kenneth *lawyer*
Ford, Brendan A. *health facility administrator*
Hammond, David *pharmaceutical executive*
Henderson, Jeffrey W. *corporate financial executive*
Kinman, Gary W. *landscape company executive*
Labrum, Ronald K. *health facility administrator*
Lamp, Benson J. *tractor company executive*
Lynch, Mike *health products executive*
Maloon, Jerry L. *lawyer, director*
McCorkle, Leon Marshall, Jr. *lawyer, educator*
Meek, Violet Imhof *retired dean*
Meyer, Betty Jane *former librarian*
Needham, George Michael *association executive*
Papa, Joseph C. *pharmaceutical executive*
Parrish, Mark *health products executive*
Pickett, James V. *food service executive*
Rishel, James Burton *manufacturing executive, director*

Sanner, Myrna Joyce *elementary school educator*
Santanello, Patricia Jane *theater educator*
Schlotterbeck, David L. *medical products executive*
Singh, Rajendra *mechanical engineering educator*
Slagle, Tom *medical products executive*
Smith, K(ermit) Wayne *computer company executive*
Souch, Mary Pauline *gifted and talented educator*
Tenuta, Luigia *lawyer*
Thomas, Stephen S. *health facility administrator*
Troup, Gordon A. *health facility administrator*
Walsh, Daniel J. *medical products executive*
Walter, Robert D. *health products executive*
Watkins, Carole S. *human resources specialist, medical products executive*
Wilkins, Jeffrey M. *computer company executive*
Williams, Paul Stratton *lawyer*
Winstead, Dwight *medical products executive*

**East Cleveland**
Linderman, Eric Graham *librarian*

**East Liverpool**
Baumgardner, Edward *financial company executive*
Gailey, Joan Dale *retired finance educator*

**East Palestine**
Rohrbaugh, Lisa Anne *librarian*

**Eaton**
Thomas, James William *lawyer*

**Edgerton**
Wu, Lawrence Mg Hla Myin *physician*

**Edon**
Hruska, Bradley J. *elementary school educator*

**Elida**
Dicke, Candice Edwards *librarian, educator*
Roach, Bradley Charles *music educator*

**Elyria**
Foote, Nathan Maxted *retired physical science educator*
Mixon, Aaron Malachi III *medical products executive*
Myers, John T. *physical therapist, educator*
Patton, Thomas James *marketing executive, sales executive*

**Euclid**
Adrine-Robinson, Kenyette *art educator, poet, artist, photographer*
Howson, James G. *photographer*
Obloy, Leonard Gerard *priest*

**Fairfield**
Carmichael, Dan R. *insurance company executive*
Chin, Nee Oo Wong *reproductive endocrinologist*
Crane, Debra K. *lawyer*
Glass, Linda L. *elementary school educator*
Hubbard, Michele Masanek *secondary school educator, soccer coach*
Robertson, Oscar Palmer (Big O Robertson) *chemical company executive, former professional basketball player*
Sheehan, Samantha *gymnast*
Stecher, Kenneth W. *financial corporation executive*
Wilson, James Miller, IV, *cardiovascular surgeon, educator*

**Fairview Park**
Flynn, Patricia M. *director, special education educator, gifted and talented educator*
Fordyce, James Stuart *non-profit organization executive*

**Farmdale**
Grove, Rebecca Irene *mechanical engineer*

**Findlay**
Freed, DeBow *academic administrator*
Fry, Charles George *theologian, educator*
Hanson, David Alan *music educator*
Kline, James Edward *lawyer*
Legg, Harolyn Lee *librarian*
Mattis, Tim *music educator*
Nissley, M. John *dean, educator*
Peters, Milton Eugene *educational psychologist*
Pond, Byron O., Jr. *manufacturing executive*
Stephani, Nancy Jean *social worker, journalist*
Stephens, D. Richard *manufacturing executive*
Thomas, Zachary Adam *music director, educator*
Weaver, Philip G. *tire company executive*
Yammine, Riad Nassif *retired oil industry executive*
Young, Brian A. *academic administrator*

**Fredericktown**
Ackerman, Loretta Ann *retired secondary school educator*

**Fremont**
Johnson, Laurence F. *college executive*
Magoon, Maggie E. *law educator, director*
Ruble, Amanda L. *elementary school educator*
Smart, Judith Ann *mathematics professor*

**Gahanna**
Majtenyi, Steven Istvan *retired civil engineer, consultant*

**Galena**
Berggren, Ronald Bernard *surgeon, retired educator*

**Galion**
Cobey, Ralph *industrialist*

**Gambier**
Holdener, Judy Ann *mathematics professor, researcher*
Leech, Charles Russell, Jr. *lawyer*
Nugent, S. Georgia *academic administrator*
Rutkoff, Peter M. *humanities educator*
Spaid, Gregory P. *academic administrator, art educator*

**Garfield Heights**
Shafer, John Eric *art educator*

**Garrettsville**
Diskin, Michael Edward *plastics company executive, food service executive*

**Gates Mills**
Abbott, James Samuel III *marketing executive*
Enyedy, Gustav, Jr. *chemical engineer*
Reitman, Robert Stanley *management consultant, not-for-profit advisor*
Veale, Tinkham, II, *retired chemicals executive, engineer*

**Geneva**
Carrel, Marianne Eileen *music educator*
Clement, Daniel Roy, IV, *accountant*

**Georgetown**
Fite, Tom W. *retired mathematics educator, farmer*
Ruthven, John A. *wildlife artist*

**Glendale**
Strom, Kristina Chase *writer, consultant*

**Gnadenhutten**
Wolf, Joan Mangon *nursing educator*

**Granville**
Gander, Robert D *theater director, education educator*
Haubrich, Robert Rice *biology professor*
Knobel, Dale Thomas *historian, educator, university president*
Lisska, Anthony Joseph *humanities educator, philosopher*
Santoni, Ronald Ernest *philosophy educator*

**Green**
Davidson, Dale Alan *secondary school educator, director*
Long, Kathy Jean *special education educator*

**Greenville**
Alexander, Paul Richard *illustrator*
Buchy, Jim *food products executive*
Darmer, Ellen Suzanne *school system administrator*
Foureman, Nancy Lee *artist*

**Grove City**
Kilman, James William *surgeon, educator*
Kimethu, Susan Wanja *computer specialist, database manager*
Rudy, Monica Elaine *small business owner, music educator*

**Groveport**
Motts, Warren Earl *museum director*

**Hamilton**
Epp, Mary Elizabeth *retired technologies consultant*
Glass, Robert Edward *retired music educator*
Gruenwald, James Howard *association executive, consultant*
Kerestan, Kitty Wilde *music educator*
Luther, Elissa Meredith *art educator*
Moore, Michael Robert *music educator, band director*
Munson, Richard Howard *horticulturist*
Speckert, Robert E. *engineering educator*
Zahner-Krach, Anne Colette *preschool educator*

**Harrison**
Kocher, Juanita Fay *retired auditor*

**Hebron**
Slater, Wanda Marie Worth *property manager*

**Hemlock**
Johnson, George Warner *gifted and talented educator, consultant*

**Hilliard**
Cupp, David Foster *photographer, journalist*
Pyles, Selma Broadway *music educator*
Riggle, Blair Andrew *educational association administrator, consultant, psychologist, educator*

**Hiram**
Bane, James Wallace *music educator*
Chema, Thomas V. *government official, consultant, academic administrator, lawyer*

**Holland**
Batt, Nick *property and investment executive*
Conlin, Thomas *conductor*
D'Anniballe, Priscilla Lucille *contracting company executive*
Matthews, Christian William, Jr. *minister*
Sacksteder, Thomas Michael *corporate financial executive, entrepreneur, writer*

**Howard**
Lee, William Johnson *lawyer*

**Hubbard**
Trucksis, Theresa A. *retired library director*

**Hudson**
Carducci, Judith Weeks Barker *artist, retired social worker*
Gentile Sachs, Valerie Ann *lawyer*
Goheen, Janet Moore *counseling administrator, sales executive*
Hallenbeck, Linda S. *elementary school educator*
Lambacher, Kathleen Hartwell *education educator*
Merwin, John David *lawyer, former governor*
Roemer, James Paul *data processing executive, writer*
Schneider, Rudolph F. *education educator*
Sorgi, Mercedes Prieto *psychologist*
Stec, John Zygmunt *retired real estate company officer*
Webb, Darrell *retail executive*

**Huron**
Ruble, Ronald Merlin *humanities and theater communications educator*

**Independence**
Dial, David Emory *librarian*
Kola, Arthur Anthony *lawyer*
Lanigan, John *radio personality*
Malone, Jimmy *radio personality*
Van Kirk, Robert John *nursing case manager, educator*

**Ironton**
Allen, Craig Adams *lawyer, director*
Curry, Estella Roberta *education educator, school psychologist, consultant*

**Jackson**
Benson, Steven Clark *management and engineering executive*
Dallura, Sal Anthony *physician*
Lewis, Richard M. *lawyer*

**Jackson Center**
Thompson, Wade Francis Bruce *manufacturing executive*

**Kent**
Allouba, Hassan *mathematics professor*
Baeseman, Jenny L. *environmental scientist, educator*
Bansal, Arvind Kumar *computer scientist, educator*
Beer, Barrett Lynn *historian*
Bianchi, Alison Jean *sociologist, educator*
Bissler, Richard Thomas *mortician*
Buttlar, Rudolph Otto *retired college dean*
Cartwright, Carol Ann *retired academic administrator*
Dahl, Peter Steffen *geologist, educator*
Feinberg, Richard *anthropologist, educator*
Gaston, Paul Lee *academic administrator, language educator*
Gosnell, Davina J. *dean, nursing educator*
Hassler, Donald Mackey, II, *English language educator, writer*
House-Soremekun, Bessie *political science professor*
Lefton, Lester Alan *academic administrator, psychology professor*
Marovitz, Sanford Earl *English language and literature educator*
Maurer, Margaret Beecher *librarian, educator*
McKee, David Lannen *economics professor*
Ozanich, Ruth Shultz *artist, poet, retired elementary school educator*
Phillips, Matthew Todd *history educator*
Reid, S.W. *language educator*
Ryans, John Kelley, Jr. *marketing educator*
Varga, Richard Steven *retired mathematics professor*
Weber, Mark W. *librarian, dean*
Williams, Donald R. *social sciences educator*
Williams, Harold Roger *economist, educator*

**Kettering**
Cline, Allen Lee *endocrinologist, medical educator*
Eubank, David Lynn *lawyer, consultant*
Kankey, Roland Doyle *finance educator*
Meckstroth, Wilma Jean *piano educator, accompanist, music company executive*
Peres, Frank J. *healthcare administrator*
Porter, Walter Arthur *retired judge*
Reynolds, Joan Lorelle *music educator*

**Kirtland**
Armstrong, Mary Ogden *artist, graphics designer*
Asnien, Phyllis Arline *humanities educator, writer*
Basich, Richard B. *mathematics professor*
Johnston, Stanley Howard, Jr. *curator, rare book dealer*
Petrone, John R. *retired music educator, composer*

**Lake Milton**
Glomski, Edward Earl *sales executive*

**Lakeside Marblehead**
Haering, Edwin Raymond *chemical engineering educator, consultant*

**Lakewood**
Condon, George Edward *journalist*
McAndrews, James Patrick *lawyer*

**Lancaster**
Burns, Glenn Richard *dentist*
Katlic, John Edward *management consultant*
Libert, Donald Joseph *lawyer*
Phillips, Edward John *consulting firm executive*
Varney, Richard Alan *health facility administrator*

**Lewis Center**
Heinlen, Daniel Lee *alumni organization administrator*
Lutz, Michael Edward *music educator*
Thomason, Sandra Lee *elementary school educator*

**Lima**
MacBenn, Joseph Vernon *director*
Pranses, Anthony Louis *retired electric power industry executive*
Robenalt, John Alton *lawyer*
Shaw, Sue Ann *church organist*

**Lisbon**
Yonchak, Michael Stephen *music educator*

**Little Hocking**
Corbin, David P. *counselor*

**London**
Harris, Lionel *writer, educator*
Hughes, Clyde Matthew *religious denomination executive*

**Lorain**
Murrell, Jill Pongracz *music educator, director*
Wittlinger, Cheryl A. *elementary school educator*

**Louisville**
Faigley, Joseph Raymond *social studies educator*
Hostetler, Andrew Leon *social studies educator*

**Loveland**
Peters, Thomas J *management consultant, writer*

**Lucasville**
Reno, Ottie Wayne *former judge*

**Macedonia**
Battle, Hilary Howard *minister, educator*

**Madison**
Stafford, Arthur Charles *medical association administrator*

**Mansfield**
Fulginiti, John III *surgeon*
Gorman, James Carvill *manufacturing executive*
Gregory, Deirdre Dianne *secondary school educator*
Gregory, Thomas Bradford *mathematics professor*
Houston, William Robert Montgomery *ophthalmologist, surgeon*
Hussain, Nayyer *economics professor*
Joyce, Steven James *German and comparative studies educator*
Olinger, Angela Marie *adult education educator*
Pesec, David John *data systems executive*
Phelps, Christopher *history professor*
Riedl, John Orth *retired university dean*
Shah, James M. *actuary*
Sheridan, Mark William *mechanical engineer, financial planner*
Sturts, Donna Jean *music educator*

**Marietta**
Fields, William Albert *lawyer*
Francis, Lynne Ann *elementary school educator, music educator*
Fredericks, Margaret Matterson *elementary school educator*
Jache, Albert William *retired chemistry professor, academic administrator, research scientist*
Kessler, Mark (Mickey) Milo *humanities educator, department chairman, playwright*
McCreery, Jean Terrell *retired draftsman, editor*
Neu, Irene Dorothy *historian, educator*
Putnam, Robert Ervin *chemist, consultant*
Schultheis, Rita Virginia *artist*
Wilbanks, Jan Joseph *retired philosopher*

**Marion**
Barker, Tamara Elizabeth *music educator*
Iams, Denise Zucker *retired mathematics educator*
Schwartz, Lance *music educator*

**Martins Ferry**
Douglas, Leslie A. *municipal official*

**Marysville**
Aronowitz, David M. *lawyer, chemicals executive*
Hagedorn, James *landscape company executive*

**Mason**
Beary, John Francis III *rheumatologist, pharmaceutical executive, medical researcher*
Clements, Michael Craig *health services consulting executive, retired renal dialysis technician*
Kohlhepp, Robert J. *apparel executive*
Smith, C. LeMoyne *retired publishing executive*
Wilson, Frederic Sandford *pharmaceutical company executive*

**Massillon**
Eckhart, Marylouise Christine Santilli *pre-school educator*
Netzly, Dwight H. *lawyer*
Steele, Kathryn Ann *social studies educator, gifted and talented educator*

**Maumee**
Burchinow, Naran U. *lawyer*
Fallat, Dale William *lawyer*
Konopinski, Virgil James *industrial hygienist, consultant*
Marsh, Benjamin Franklin *lawyer*
Risley, David Milo *controller*
Tuschman, James Marshall *lawyer*
Witherell, Dennis Patrick *lawyer*

**Mayfield**
Forrester, W Thomas II *insurance company executive*
Jarrett, Charles Elwood *insurance company executive, lawyer*

**Mayfield Heights**
Billick, Steven M. *emergency medical technician*
Chaffee, Mark Anthony *engineer*
Grants, Valdis *engineering manager*
Newman, Joseph Herzl *advertising executive, consultant*
Rankin, Alfred Marshall, Jr. *manufacturing executive*
Rhein, Arthur *computer company executive*

**Mc Donald**
Daigle, Barbara Dianne *elementary school educator*

**Medina**
Ballard, John Stuart *retired mayor, lawyer, educator*
Feola, David Craig *secondary school administrator*
Holliday, Keith Alan *music educator, musician*
Matejka, Robert *chemicals executive*
Rog, Joseph W. *engineering company executive*
Smith, Richey *manufacturing executive*
Sullivan, Frank C. *manufacturing executive*
Sullivan, Thomas Christopher *coatings company executive*
Timco, Joseph Justin *elementary school educator*

**Mentor**
Callsen, Christian Edward *health products executive*

**Combs**, Steven Paul *orthopedic surgeon*
Hale, Jeffrey L. *economics educator*
Herschman, Terry DiFranco *music educator*
Michaels, Edward G. *music educator, musician*

**Miamisburg**
Byrd, James Everett *lawyer*
McLaughlin, Allan D. *information technology executive*
Michaelis, Betty Jane *sculptor, retired small business owner*

**Miamiville**
Franz, Iris Vivian (Vivian Franz) *dean, director*

**Middleburg Heights**
Kosar, James Joseph *secondary school educator*
Maciuszko, Kathleen Lynn *librarian, educator*

**Middletown**
Barrord, John Francis *otolaryngologist*
Gilmore, June Ellen *psychologist*
Gordon, Sandy Gale Combs *medical/surgical nurse*
Horn, David C. *lawyer*
Marine, Susan Sonchik *analytical chemist, educator*
McClain, Michael H. *writer*
Newby, John Robert *metallurgical engineer*
Rathman, William Ernest *retired lawyer, minister*
Schaefer, Patricia Ann *retired librarian*
Wainscott, James Lawrence *steel industry executive*

**Milan**
Henry, Joseph Patrick *chemicals executive*

**Milford**
Creath, Curtis Janssen *pediatric dentist*
Kelley, Donald Frank *retired minister, elementary school educator*

**Millersburg**
Trubee, R. Eldon *minister, writer*

**Millersport**
Harkabus, Noelle Marie *music educator*

**Monroe**
Homer, Gregory C. *protective services official*

**Montpelier**
Deckrosh, Hazen Douglas *retired state agency educator and administrator*

**Moreland Hills**
Groetzinger, Jon, Jr. *lawyer, pharmaceutical executive*
Tolchinsky, Paul Dean *organization design psychologist*

**Morristown**
Tucker, Betty J. *literature and language educator*

**Mount Healthy**
Scheffel, Kenneth Paul *retired archivist*

**Mount Vernon**
Miller, Joyce Catherine *chemistry professor, research scientist*
Ressing, Thomas Garrett *lawyer*
Shriver, William Russell *secondary school educator*
Strouse, Debra J. *director*

**Napoleon**
Bevelhymer, Darlene Pearl *secondary school educator, lawyer*
Meekison, MaryFran *writer*

**Nelsonville**
DiLiberto, Sam Michael *business educator*

**New Albany**
Duggan, Thomas Patrick *management consultant*
Jeffries, Michael S. (Mike Jeffries) *apparel executive*
Page, Linda Kay *bank executive*
Williams, James Case *metallurgist*

**New Bremen**
Dicke, James Frederick, II, *manufacturing executive*

**New Concord**
Boggs, Bennett Gibson *academic administrator*

**New Holland**
Reeves, Nancy Rapp *elementary school educator*

**New Lexington**
Harper, Toni Jane *secondary school educator*

**New Philadelphia**
Doughten, Mary Katherine (Molly Doughten) *retired secondary school educator*

**New Straitsville**
Eaton, Michael Christopher *contractor*

**Newark**
Barner, Bruce Monroe *retired state agency administrator, not-for-profit developer*
Billy, Gerry Dee *protective services official*
Black, Boyd Carson *small business owner*
Kaiser, Judith Arlene *retired elementary school educator*
Mantonya, John Butcher *lawyer*
McConnell, William Thompson *bank executive*
Mencer, Jetta *lawyer*
Meyer, Christopher Richard *lawyer*
Sharrock (Wrentmore), Anita Kay *information technology specialist*

**North Canton**
Dettinger, Warren Walter *lawyer*
Di Simone, Robert Nicholas *radiologist, educator*
Heaphy, Leslie Anne *history professor*
Kairis, Rob *school librarian, consultant*

**Lynham**, C(harles) Richard *manufacturing executive*
Vazzano, Frank Paul *historian, educator*

**North Olmsted**
Bluford, Guion Stewart, Jr. *engineering company executive*
Janson, Patrick *vocalist, educator, actor*

**North Ridgeville**
Cobbledick, Susie Diane *librarian*
Stewart, Arden Ruth *retired automotive executive*

**North Royalton**
Fast, Henryk *mathematician, educator*

**Northfield**
Stavole, Janet M. *librarian, library director*

**Norwalk**
Germann, Richard P(aul) *pharmaceutical company chemist, chemicals executive*
Gutowicz, Matthew Francis, Jr. *radiologist*

**Norwood**
Jones, Hobert W. *health physics and radiochemistry consultant*
Wright, Creighton Bolter *cardiovascular surgeon, educator*

**Oak Harbor**
Randels, David George *retired secondary school educator*
Sievert, Vicki Lee *retired music educator*
Whitaker, Mary Jane *retired elementary school educator*

**Oberlin**
Benzing, David Hill *biologist, educator*
Brown, John Lott *former university president, retired educator*
Carlton, Terry Scott *retired chemist, educator*
Cartier, Brian Evans *consumer products company executive*
Collins, Martha *English language educator, writer*
Crawford, Henry Gerald *music educator*
Dye, Nancy Schrom *academic administrator, historian, educator*
English, Ray *library administrator*
Ganzel, Dewey Alvin *English language educator*
Greenberg, Eva Mueller *retired librarian*
Hoffmann, Richard *composer, educator*
Koppes, Clayton R. *academic administrator*
Luck, Dennis Noel *biologist, educator, researcher*
Moore, Jane Ross *librarian, educator*
Mumford, Jeffrey *composer, educator*
Reinoehl, Richard Louis *social services administrator, scholar*
Rutstein, Sedmara Zakarian *piano educator, concert pianist*
Sepkoski, Dara Henning *museum educator*
Soucy, Robert Joseph *historian, educator*
Taylor, Richard Wirth *retired political science professor*
Taylor, Robert Larry *freelance/self-employed writer*
Weinstock, Robert *physics professor*

**Olmsted Falls**
Faller, Dorothy Anderson *training services executive, consultant*
Semple, Jane Frances *health facility director*

**Oregon**
Bryce, Robert W. *lawyer*
Chablani, Lachman V. *pathologist*
Poad, Flora Virginia *retired librarian, retired elementary school educator*

**Orrville**
Beyeler, Julia *academic administrator*
Harlan, M. Ann *lawyer*
Hennell, Robert William III *secondary school educator*
Smucker, Richard K. *food products executive*
Smucker, Timothy P. *food products executive*
Warner, Patricia Ann *secondary school educator*

**Orwell**
Carlson, Timothy A. *music educator*

**Owensville**
Seifert, Caroline Hamilton *community health nurse*

**Oxford**
Bergen, Doris *psychologist, educator*
Berry, Stephen D. *psychology educator, researcher*
Bolger, Edw. M. *retired mathematics professor*
Brown Manrique, Gerardo *architect, educator*
Cox, James Allan *chemistry professor*
Cronley, Maria Lynn *marketing educator*
Danielson, Neil David *chemistry educator*
Dawisha, Adeed *political science professor*
Eshbaugh, W(illiam) Hardy *botanist, educator*
Ewing, Susan R. *art educator, artist*
Goodell, George Sidney *retired finance educator*
Gordon, Gilbert *chemist, educator*
Hodge, David Charles *academic administrator, geography professor*
Koo, Jeong-Hoi *engineering educator*
Macklin, Philip Alan *retired physics professor*
Miller, Norman Calvin *economist*
Miller, Robert James *educational association administrator*
Pont, John *football coach, educator*
Pratt, William Crouch, Jr. *literature and language professor, writer*
Rauckhorst, William Herman *physics professor, academic administrator*
Rejai, Mostafa *political science professor*
Robinson, Michael Lee *biologist*
Sanders, Gerald Hollie *communications educator*
Sheehan, James Joseph *social studies educator*
Shriver, Phillip Raymond *academic administrator*
Thomas, Robert Jay *music educator, musician*
Thompson, Bertha Boya *retired education educator*
Ward, Roscoe Fredrick *engineering educator*

**Painesville**
Davis, Barbara Snell *education educator*

Filson, Ronald Coulter *architect, educator, dean*
Malchesky, Paul S. *medical association administrator*
McQuaid, Kim *historian, educator, writer*
Orosz, Richard Thomas *lawyer*

**Pandora**
Williams, Mark Ellis *artist, educator*

**Parma**
Brennan, Sean Patrick *secondary school educator, municipal official*
Feldman, Sari *library director*
Indovina, Cynthie Lynn *music educator*
McCarthy, Carrie Ann *secondary school educator, director*
Musat, Katherine Gadus *retired music educator*
Scheffel, Donna Jean *elementary school educator*
Tener, Carol Joan *retired secondary school educator, consultant*

**Pataskala**
Ripley, Randall Butler *political scientist, educator*
Thrasher, Rose Marie *critical care nurse, community health nurse*

**Patriot**
Riggle, Patricia Carol *special education educator*

**Pemberville**
King, Laura Jane *librarian, genealogist*

**Peninsula**
Sigler, Theresa Jane *school system administrator*

**Pepper Pike**
Alexander-Haynes, Sandra *psychologist, educator*
Goodman, Donald Joseph *dentist*
Mc Call, Julien Lachicotte *banker*
Schnell, Carlton Bryce *lawyer*
Stano, Sister Diana *academic administrator*
Vail, Thomas Van Husen *retired publishing executive*

**Perry**
Godfrey, W. Robert *music educator, singer, actor*

**Perrysburg**
Autry, Carolyn *artist, art history educator*
Bohleke, Henry Charles *academic administrator, educator*
Catalano, Dominic *art educator, illustrator*
Cranny, Theresa M. *veterinarian*
King, John Joseph *manufacturing executive*
Kovacik, Neal Stephen *hotel and restaurant executive*
Weaver, Richard L., II, *writer, educator*
Williamson, John Pritchard *retired utilities executive*

**Pettisville**
Poulson, John Franklin *agricultural studies educator, consultant*

**Pickerington**
Callander, Kay Eileen Paisley *business owner, retired education educator, writer*
Collins, Arlene *secondary school educator*
Lang, Lisa Ann *music educator*

**Plymouth**
Hartman, Ruth Campbell *director, educator*

**Poland**
Murphy, Thomas Michael *civil engineer*

**Pomeroy**
Brockert, Joseph Paul *government executive, writer, editor, designer*

**Port Clinton**
Ewersen, Mary Virginia *retired school system administrator, poet*
Peitz, Todd Adam *music educator*
Woodson, Riley Donald *thoracic and cardiovascular surgeon, lawyer*

**Portsmouth**
Akhtar, Muhammad I. *neurologist, researcher*
Baker, Donna L. *history educator*
Brehm, Shawn Lamar *band director*
Hamilton, Virginia Mae *mathematics professor, consultant*

**Pottersburg**
Bilderback, George Garrison III *transportation and logistics professional*

**Powell**
Emanuelson, James Robert *retired insurance company executive*
Lee, Robert J. Y. *marketing professional*
Mitchell, Cathy (C.C.) Christine *art educator*
O'Neal, R. Douglas *music educator, musician*

**Randolph**
Pecano, Donald Carl *automotive manufacturing executive*

**Ravenna**
Turcotte, Margaret Jane *retired nurse*

**Reynoldsburg**
Fiske, Neil S. *retail executive*
Serraglio, Mario *architect*

**Richfield**
Anthony, Leonard Morris *steel company administrator, consultant*
Lewis, Sylvia Davidson *foundation executive*

**Rio Grande**
Hatfield, Barbara Scott *academic administrator*

**Ripley**
Curtis, Russell Glenn *social studies educator*

**Rocky River**
Cronquist, Robert Lee *conductor*

Hosek, John Jude *planning organization executive*
O'Brien, John Feighan *investment banker*
Shively, Daniel Jerome *retired transportation executive*

**Rootstown**
Chiang, John Young Ling *biochemistry professor, researcher*
Nora, Lois Margaret *neurologist, educator, academic administrator, dean*

**Saint Clairsville**
Butler, Andrew Kimmins, Jr. *physiologist, educator*
Morris, Diane L. *mathematics professor*

**Saint Marys**
Anderson, Tracy *literature and language educator*
Kemp, Barrett George *lawyer*
VanderHorst, Monica S. *physical education educator*

**Salem**
Barcey, Harold Edward Dean (Hal Barcey) *real estate consultant*
Fehr, Kenneth Manbeck *retired computer company executive*
Goll, Geoffrey Steven *lawyer*

**Sandusky**
Coffey, Deborah S. Findley *elementary school educator*
Fuller, Jonathan *retired geologist*

**Sardinia**
Evans, C(aroline) Sue *education educator*

**Seaman**
Cartaino, Carol Ann *editor*
Young, Vernon Lewis *retired lawyer*

**Sebring**
Doty, James Edward *minister, psychologist*
Kelley-Hall, Maryon Hoyle *retired social worker*

**Seven Hills**
Stanczak, Julian *artist, educator*

**Shaker Heights**
Bates, Walter Alan *retired lawyer*
Brachna, Gabor (Samuel) *elementary school educator*
Donnem, Sarah Lund *financial analyst, non-profit consultant, political organization consultant*
Ekelman, Daniel Louis *lawyer*
Killeen, Michael F. *retail executive*
Krulitz, Leo Morrion *financial planner, publishing executive, director*
Ludwig, L(owell) Mark *social studies educator*
Siegel, Robert *heat transfer engineer*
Smith, Jonathan David *medical educator*
Solganik, Marvin *real estate executive*
Trefts, Joan Landenberger *retired principal*

**Shandon**
Wilson, James Ray *international business educator*

**Shelby**
Phelan, Martha Armstrong *realtor*

**Sidney**
Leffler, Carole Elizabeth *retired mental health nurse, women's health nurse*
Seitz, James Eugene *retired college president, freelance writer*
Stevens, Robert Jay *magazine editor*

**Silver Lake**
Cantor, Arnold *labor relations official*

**Solon**
Benhoff, Edward Spreng *marketing professional*
Dutile, Robert Arthur *executive management consultant*
Gallo, Donald Robert *retired literature educator*
Rosica, Gabriel Adam *retired manufacturing executive, electrical engineer*
Williams, Jeffery Lynn *secondary school educator, consultant*

**South Charleston**
Weatherby, Donald Alan *telecommunications industry executive, writer*

**South Euclid**
Hall-Chambers, Kymberly Renee *elementary school educator*
Zoller, Karen Ann *library director, art gallery director*

**South Point**
Parikh, Jeannine Lubold *physician*

**Springboro**
Saxer, Richard Karl *metallurgical engineer, retired military officer*
Walden, James William *accountant, educator*

**Springfield**
Dominick, Charles Alva *college official*
Faber, Trudy *music educator*
Harkins, Daniel Conger *lawyer*
Humphries, Jimmy *set designer, educator*
Kinnison, William Andrew *retired university president*
Lagos, James Harry *lawyer*
Little, Stephanie Ann *psychology professor, researcher*
Lowe-Hoover, Steven C. *history educator*
Pitzer, Betty Braun *retired social services administrator*
Ryu, Kyoo-Hai Lee *physiologist*
Todd, Carol *music educator*

**Steubenville**
McGrath, Dennis Michael *secondary school educator*
Scanlan, Michael *priest, academic administrator*
Sheldon, Gilbert Ignatius *clergyman*

**Stockport**
Winebrenner, William Patrick *writer*

**Stow**
Castillo, Katherine Lynn *writer, translator, business owner*
Mangrum, Richard Lee *flight educator*

**Streetsboro**
Cielec, Greg J. *literature and language educator*
Cravcenco, Ludmila *academic administrator*

**Strongsville**
Blumer, Frederick Elwin *retired philosophy educator*
Cameron, David Ronald *entrepreneur, historian, researcher*
Myers, Jack Fredrick *artist, educator, writer*
Pinkerton, Richard LaDoyt *retired management educator*

**Sugar Grove**
Dombrowski, Karen S. *social studies educator, education educator*

**Swanton**
Perry, Nadine Margaret *retired art educator, artist*

**Sylvania**
Bond, Suzanne Mary *gifted and talented educator*
Burkhart, Craig Garrett *dermatologist, researcher*
Garrison, Linda *retired foundation administrator*
Helmer, Robert C. *academic administrator*
Kastner, Michael James *dentist*
Masten, Barbara Jean *education educator, department chairman*
Ring, Herbert Everett *management executive*
Sampson, Earldine Robison *education educator*
Weinblatt, Charles Samuel *retired academic administrator*

**Tallmadge**
Kaul, Mohan Lal *social worker, educator*

**Terrace Park**
Naylor, Paul Donald *retired lawyer*

**Tiffin**
Donaldson, Leonard W. *political science professor*
Einsel, David William, Jr. *retired army officer, educator*
Galipeau, Peter Armand *councilman*
Gridley, Mark Charles *psychologist*
Hillmer, Margaret Patricia *library director*

**Tipp City**
Hartland, James Robert *retired minister*
Tighe-Moore, Barbara Jeanne *electronics executive*

**Toledo**
Anspach, Robert Michael *lawyer*
Averill, Bruce Alan *chemistry professor*
Bacigalupi, Don *museum director*
Baehren, James W. *lawyer*
Bahhur, Nael Osama *physician*
Baker, Richard Southworth *lawyer*
Barrett, Michael John *anesthesiologist*
Berhan, Lesley Michelle *mechanical engineering educator*
Block, Allan James *communications executive*
Block, John Robinson *newspaper publisher*
Block, William K., Jr. *media executive*
Borovicka, Mary Catherine *pharmacist, educator*
Brower, James Calvin *graphic artist, painter*
Brown, David T. *manufacturing executive*
Burns, Michael J. *automotive executive*
Campbell, James *philosopher, educator*
Cardwell, Michael Steven *obstetrician, educator*
Carr, James Gray *federal judge*
Carroll, William J. *municipal official*
Carson, Samuel Goodman *retired bank executive*
Cavanaugh, Steven M. *healthcare company executive*
Chakraborty, Joana *physiologist, educator, science administrator*
Chambers, Virginia Anne *music educator*
Closius, Phillip J. *dean, law educator*
Comerota, Anthony James *vascular surgeon, biomedical researcher*
Cosentino, Mary Jane *retired science educator*
Cousino, Joe Ann *sculptor*
Dalrymple, Thomas Lawrence *retired lawyer*
Davis, David Howard *political science professor*
DeBacker, Michael L. *automotive executive, lawyer*
Elahinia, Mohammad H. *engineering educator, researcher*
El Bialy, Mohamed Sami *mathematician*
Elmer, Lawrence William *neurologist, researcher*
Finkbeiner, Carlton S. (Carty Finkbeiner) *radio personality, former mayor*
Francis, Barbara Joan *nurse, paralegal*
Funk, Jeanne B. *psychology professor*
Geisler, Nathan David *financial consultant*
Gibara, Samir G. *tire manufacturing executive*
Girgis-Hanna, Mary Fahim *music educator*
Glaab, Charles Nelson *historian, educator*
Grundish, Lee Anne *small business owner, writer*
Gutteridge, Thomas G. *academic administrator, consultant, arbitrator*
Harter, James Lester *academic administrator, consultant*
Hasan, Bassam *education educator*
Heintz, Carolinea Cabaniss *retired home economist, retired educator*
Hiltz, Kenneth A. *corporate financial executive*
Jackson, Reginald Sherman, Jr. *lawyer, educator*
Jacobs, Lloyd A. *vascular surgeon*
Knuth, Marya Danielle *special education educator*
Konwinski, Jacqueline Marie Koralewski *secondary school educator*
Koo, Benjamin Hai Chang *structural engineer, educator*
Koppus, Betty Jane *retired savings and loan association executive*
Krull, Stephen Keith *lawyer*
Kunze, Ralph Carl *retired savings and loan association executive*
La Rue, Carl Forman *lawyer*
Lee, Soon Jin *geneticist, educator*

Lessick, Mira Lee *nursing educator*
Mahr, Joe *journalist*
Martin, John Thomas *physician, author, educator*
Martin, Robert Edward *architect*
McCracken, Steven R. *textiles executive*
McGlauchlin, Tom *artist*
McGrady, Angele Vial *psychophysiologist*
McVicker, Michael C. *dentist*
Mulrow, Patrick Joseph *medical educator*
Noormets, Asko *ecologist*
O'Connell, Maurice Daniel *lawyer*
Ormond, David Lan *healthcare company executive*
Paquette, Jack Kenneth *management consultant, writer, historian*
Perz, Sally *academic administrator, former state legislator*
Pham, David Lan *secondary school educator, writer*
Pletz, Thomas Gregory *lawyer*
Rabideau, Margaret Catherine *retired media center director*
Reichert, Christine Edwards *academic administrator*
Rejent, Marian Magdalen *retired pediatrician*
Rokicki, Lori Ann *psychologist*
Romanoff, Marjorie Reinwald *retired education educator*
Romanoff, Milford Martin *retired building contractor*
Royhab, Ronald *journalist, editor*
St. Clair, Donald David *lawyer*
Sallah, Michael D. *journalist*
Scoles, Clyde Sheldon *library director*
Seubert, Lori A. *elementary school educator*
Shaikh, Bahu Sultan *physician, educator*
Shelley, Walter Brown *dermatologist, educator*
Skaff, Anita L. *secondary school educator*
Skiver, Stephen Allen *lawyer, physician*
Smith, Robert Freeman *history professor*
Spitzer, John Brumback *lawyer*
Talmage, Lance Allen *obstetrician, gynecologist, military officer*
Thaman, Michael H. *building material systems executive*
Webb, Thomas Irwin, Jr. *lawyer, director*
Weikel, Malcolm Keith *healthcare company executive*
Weiss, Mitch *journalist*
White, Kathy Jean *educator*
Wicklund, David Wayne *lawyer*
Wolff, Edwin Ray *retired construction engineer, consultant*

**Troy**
DeHart, Karen Trautmann *artist, educator*
Platfoot, Christopher W. *systems administrator, information technology executive*

**Twinsburg**
Bensie, Lori Anne *music educator*

**Uniontown**
Krabill, Robert Elmer *osteopathic physician*

**University Heights**
Carrington, Gary *psychologist*
Cook, Alexander Burns *curator, artist, educator*
Eslinger, Kenneth Nelson *social sciences educator*
Murphy, Paul Regis, Jr. *business educator*
Seaton, Shirley Smith *academic administrator, consultant*
Whelan, John Joseph *education educator*

**Upper Arlington**
Conley, Diana Jean Montenaro *elementary school educator*
Relle, Ferenc Matyas *chemist*

**Upper Sandusky**
Baker, Harrison Scott *application developer, consultant*

**Urbana**
Pencil, Faith Ann *music educator*
Phillips, Julieanne Appleson *history professor*

**Valley View**
Miller, Susan Ann *retired school system administrator*

**Vincent**
Foster, Christopher Robert *music educator*

**Wadsworth**
Furry, Benjamin K. *chemist*
Neumann, Jeffrey Jay *photographer, minister*
Wozniak, Judith T. *pastor*

**Walton Hills**
Elliott, Stanley B. *chemist, researcher*

**Wapakoneta**
Wirth, Tamara L. *music educator*

**Warren**
Dinh, Hai Quang *mathematics professor, researcher*
He, Min *mathematics professor*
Nader, Robert Alexander *judge, lawyer*
Robbins, Robert Marvin *accountant*
Rollo, Richard James *music educator*
Rossi, Anthony Gerald *lawyer*

**Washington Court House**
Dunlap, Jeffrey Lee *minister, educator*

**Wauseon**
Stutzman, Donna J. *minister*

**West Carrollton**
Rabold, Barbara Ann *artist, writer, systems analyst*

**West Chester**
Arasakesari, Subramaniam *chemical engineer, research scientist, consultant*
End, William Thomas *marketing executive*
Mack, Mark Philip *chemical company executive*
Tanov, Romil R. *mechanical engineer, researcher*

**West Farmington**
Smith, Agnes Monroe *history professor*

**West Milton**
Mahaney, Kellie Rose *elementary school educator, consultant*

**West Unity**
Miller, Nancy Celesta *music educator, director*

**Westerville**
Bainbridge, William L. *research firm executive, consultant*
Barr, John Michael *investor, management consultant*
Chaney, Norman Richard *English studies educator*
Dawdy, W. David *pediatrician*
DeVassie, Terry Lee *publishing executive*
DeVore, C. Brent *college president, educator*
Helvey, Edward Douglas *lawyer*
Husarik, Ernest Alfred *educational administrator*
Kerr, Thomas Jefferson, IV, *academic administrator*
Reeves, Roy Franklin *mathematician, engineer, educator*
St. Pierre, Ronald Leslie *public health and medical educator, academic administrator*
Schultz, Arthur LeRoy *clergyman, educator*
Young, Bette Ann *writer*
Young, Sheldon Mike *lawyer, author*

**Westlake**
Doane, Tim *travel company executive*
Donahue, Charles Bertrand, II, *lawyer*
Kuhn, Edwin P. *travel company executive*
Loehr, Marla *chaplain*
Ohno, Apolo Anton *Olympic athlete*
Parra, Derek *Olympic athlete*
Schroth, Joyce Able *social worker*
Skulina, Thomas Raymond *lawyer*
Whitehouse, John Harlan, Jr. *systems software consultant, diagnostician*

**Whitehouse**
Boyle, Daniel Robert *musician, delivery service executive*

**Wickliffe**
Barnes, Lili Darnelle *music educator, director*
Cooley, Charles P. *chemicals executive*
Fisher, Nancy DeButts *library director*
Graves, Pamela Kay *music educator*
Hambrick, James L. *chemicals executive*
Kidder, Fred Dockstater *retired lawyer*
Krause, Marjorie N. *biochemist*
Pevec, Anthony Edward *bishop*
Wainio, Melody F. *registrar*

**Wilberforce**
Anyalewechi, Patrick Okechukwu *psychology professor*
Hargraves, William Frederick, II, *mathematics professor, computer science educator*
Omolewu, Gabriel Adebayo *business educator, researcher*
Onwudiwe, Ebere *humanities educator, writer*
Williamson, Vikki Lyn *university official, financial executive*

**Willoughby**
Abelt, Ralph William *bank executive*
Baker, Charles Stephen *music educator*
Carter, John Robert *retired physician*
Driggs, Charles Mulford *lawyer*
Grossman, Mary Margaret *elementary school educator*
Linsenmeier, Carol Vincent *music educator*
Pennington, John Robert *biology educator, department chairman*
Vokic, Heather Maureen *artist, educator*

**Wilmington**
Evans, Elizabeth Ann West *retired real estate agent*
Hete, Joseph C. *air transportation executive*
Moore, Timothy Isaac *photographer, protective services official*

**Winchester**
Koford, Stuart Keith *electronics executive*

**Wooster**
August, Robert Olin *retired journalist*
Fries, Thomas Anthony *music educator*
Geiser, Robert Neil *computer scientist*
Hales, Raleigh Stanton, Jr. *mathematics professor, academic administrator*
Hickey, Damon Douglas *library director*
Hodgson, David B. *safety engineer, science educator*
Kennedy, Charles Allen *lawyer*
Saif, Linda J. *veterinary scientist, virologist, immunologist*
Schmitt, Wolf Rudolf *consumer products executive*
Schreiber, Clare Adel *journalist*
Velleman, Sandra Gayle *molecular biology educator, researcher*

**Worthington**
Albert, Robert Hamilton *lawyer*
Bernhagen, Lillian Flickinger *retired school health consultant*
Brinkman, Dale Thomas *lawyer*
Compton, Ralph Theodore, Jr. *electrical engineering educator*
Lentz, Edward Allen *consultant, retired health administrator*
Luck, James I. *foundation executive*
Proctor, Allen Joseph *management consultant, economist*
Vladem, Steven Allen *writer, film producer, motivational speaker*
Winter, Chester Caldwell *surgeon, educator, historian, writer*

**Wright Patterson Afb**
Amend, Joseph H. III *military officer*
Boff, Kenneth Richard *engineering research psychologist*
Burggraf, Larry W. *chemist*

Cranston, Stewart E. *career officer*
Fernelius, Nils Conard *physicist*
Garscadden, Alan *physicist*
Palazotto, Anthony N. *aerospace engineering educator*
Pinkus, Alan R. *engineering research psychologist*
Reston, Rocky Russell *anesthesiologist, engineer, educator*
Rodrigues, Stanley John *materials engineer, researcher*

**Wyoming**
Cooley, William Edward *research scientist, consultant*
Jablonsky, Atarah *retired music educator*

**Xenia**
Bigelow, Daniel James *aerospace executive*
Chappars, Timothy Stephen *lawyer*
Drangsholt, James K. *brother, music educator*
Nutter, Zoe Dell Lantis *retired public relations executive*
Vaughan, Doris Celestine Walker *retired librarian, educator*

**Yellow Springs**
Caldwell, John Alvis, Jr. *experimental psychologist*
Cawood, Albert McLaurin (Hap Cawood) *retired newspaper editor*
Fogarty, Robert Stephen *historian, educator, editor*
Graham, Jewel Freeman *social worker, lawyer, educator*
Spokane, Robert Bruce *biophysical chemist*
Trolander, Hardy Wilcox *engineering executive, consultant*
Von Gierke, Henning Edgar *biomedical science educator, former government official, researcher*
Webb, Paul *physiologist, educator, researcher, consultant*

**Youngstown**
Amin, Isam Eldin *science educator, researcher*
Binning, William Charles *political science professor*
Bowers, Bege Kaye *literature educator, communications educator, academic administrator*
Camacci, Michael A. *real estate broker, real estate developer, consultant*
Catoline-Ackerman, Pauline Dessie *small business owner*
Cernica, John N. *engineering educator, civil engineer, consultant*
DeBartolo, Edward John, Jr. *real estate developer, former professional football team owner*
Edirisooriya, Gunapala *finance educator*
Estrin, Melvyn J. *computer products company executive*
Fok, Thomas Dso Yun *civil engineer*
Kessler, Ronald N. *plastics company executive*
Mehra, Jagdish *economics professor*
Miller, Kenneth Lee *counselor, educator*
Pernotto, James Angelo *artist*
Roth, Daniel Benjamin *lawyer, engineering company executive*
Rupeka, Robert W. *court administrator*
Sturgill, James Aaron *museum administrator*
Summers, Michael Edward *music educator*
Theall, Michael *education educator, director*
Usip, Ebenge Etefia *economics professor*
Zorn, Robert Lynn *education educator*

**Zanesville**
Bogard, John Leslie *retired metrologist*
Brown, Karen Rima *orchestra manager, Spanish language educator*
Istok, Christine Markward *retired executive director social service agency, consultant*
Kish, Steven Gene *science educator*
Kopf, George Michael *retired ophthalmologist*
McLaughlin, James Lee *musician, director*
Micheli, Frank James *lawyer*
Ray, John Walker *otolaryngologist, educator, broadcast commentator*

## OKLAHOMA

**Achille**
Gorman, Randall Howard *social sciences educator, real estate appraiser*

**Ada**
Anoatubby, Bill *governor of Chickasaw Nation*
Baggech, Melody A. *music educator*
Baker, Judith Ann *retired computer technician*
Daniel, Arlie V. *speech education educator*
Davenport, Ann Adele Mayfield *retired home care agency administrator*
Greenstreet, Jennifer Kennis *librarian*
Jones, Bret Austin *communications educator, writer*
Stafford, Donald Gene *chemistry professor*
Wang, Mingyu *hydrologist, environmental scientist*
West, Mildred Marie *art educator*
Wilson, John Thomas *microbiologist*

**Allen**
Deaton, Janice Ann *media specialist, elementary school educator*

**Altus**
Carson, Kirk *music educator*
Oden, Waldo Talmage, Jr. *lawyer*

**Alva**
Batalha da Conceicao, Jose Joao *chemistry professor, researcher*
Knedler, Mike *academic administrator*

**Ardmore**
Cawley, Michael A. *foundation administrator, lawyer*

**Bartlesville**
Baker-Morris, Kay *special education educator*
Connor, James William *lawyer*
Doty, Donald D. *retired bank executive*
Hogan, John Paul *chemistry researcher, consultant*
Jackson, Brian Kelly *economics professor*

Mulva, James Joseph *oil industry executive*
Price, Joe D. *pipeline developer*
Silas, Cecil Jesse *retired petroleum company executive*
Sweem, Billy Don *archbishop*

**Bethany**
Alexander, Patrick Byron *hospital administrator, consultant*
Arbuckle, Averil Dorothy (Cookie Arbuckle) *healthcare facility administrator*
Crabtree, John Michael *academic administrator, consultant*
Leggett, James Daniel *bishop*
McGowan, Bernard Wayne (Bernie McGowan) *venture capitalist, writer*
Whitsett, Eleanor Watkins *musician, educator, composer*

**Bixby**
Hawthorne, Karen Lee *school librarian, educator*
Walker, Jerald Carter *academic administrator, minister*

**Bristow**
Primeaux, Henry III *automotive executive, author, speaker*

**Broken Arrow**
Loper, Jana Sue *secondary school educator*
Muller, Patricia Ann *nursing administrator, consultant*
Smith, Jeffrey Andrews *musician, educator, sound recording engineer*
Stewart, Murray Baker *retired lawyer*

**Chandler**
Swanson, Robert Lee *lawyer*

**Cherokee**
Stein, Sam Lee *lawyer*

**Chickasha**
Willoughby-Smith, Dolores Anne *elementary school educator, consultant*

**Choctaw**
Hampton, Brian Wade *information scientist*
Uselton, Bill W. *secondary school educator*

**Chouteau**
Sasser, Charles Wayne *journalist, educator, writer*

**Claremore**
Sneed, Guy Wayne *surgeon*
Steidley, Juan Dwayne *lawyer, judge*
Whinery, Michael Albert *physician*
Winters, Kevin L. *dentist*
Wittenberg, Henry Taylor, Jr. *physician, surgeon*
Woller, Kevin Marc Peter *psychology professor, researcher*

**Cleveland**
Anderson, Patricia Sue *writer*
Henry, Kathleen Marie *marketing executive*

**Davenport**
Walker, Sandra Kay *theater educator*

**Davis**
Patterson, Lyn *director*

**Depew**
Cooper, Wayne *conceptual artist*

**Disney**
Hamilton, Carl Hulet *retired academic administrator*

**Durant**
Daniels-Ayers, Dana Sue *musical theater educator, singer, actress*
Hendricks, John Allen *communications educator*
Kennedy, Elizabeth Carol *psychologist, educator*
Pyle, Gregory E. *Native American tribal leader*

**Edmond**
Harryman, Rhonda L. *special education educator*
Hopwood, Howard Hoppy Perry *military officer*
Lester, Andrew William *lawyer*
Loman, Mary LaVerne *retired mathematics professor*
Loving, Susan Brimer *lawyer, former state official*
Myster, Randall Walton *education educator, researcher*
Necco, Edna Joanne *school psychologist*
Rice, Earl Clifton *retired mathematics educator*
Sibley, William Arthur *academic administrator, physics professor, consultant*
Smock, Donald Joe *information technology manager, political scientist*
Stone, Paul Alan *biologist, educator*

**El Reno**
Hawkins, Anita Lynne *primary school educator*

**Enid**
Camp, Robinson Eugene *chemistry educator*
Jones, Stephen *lawyer*
McCobb, Allan Paul *not-for-profit organization executive*
Moore, Linda Lea LaCroix *literature educator, art educator*
Taveggia, Thomas Charles *management consultant*
Ward, Llewellyn Orcutt III *oil industry executive*

**Fort Towson**
Pike, Thomas Harrison *plant chemist*

**Frederick**
Evans, Michael D. *lawyer*

**Gage**
Fiel, Irene Kay *secondary school educator*

**Goodwell**
Duren, Brad L. *social studies educator*

**Grove**
Trippensee, Gary Alan *retired aerospace executive*

**Guthrie**
Davis, Frank Wayne *lawyer*

**Guymon**
Lim, Jeffrey James *internist*
Wood, Donald Euriah *retired lawyer*

**Hodgen**
Brower, Janice Kathleen *library and information scientist*

**Idabel**
Moy, Henry *museum director*

**Inola**
Paul, Gary Wayne *music educator*

**Jenks**
Abshire, George Edwin *mathematician, educator*

**Jennings**
Nixon, Arlie James *gas and oil company executive*

**Kingfisher**
Allen, Vicky L. *secondary school educator*
Buswell, Arthur Wilcox *physician, surgeon*

**Langley**
Rogers, Chris Ellen *judge*

**Langston**
Haysbert, JoAnn Wright *academic administrator*
Mallik, Muhammad Abdul-Bari *soil microbiologist*

**Lawton**
Baldwin, Larry Todd *voice educator*
Bonnell-Mihalis, Pamela Gay Scoggins *library director*
Carraher, Shawn Michael *investment company executive, management educator*
Davis, Ellen Marie *business educator*
Detweiler, Stanley Bruce *music educator*
Ellenbrook, Carolyn Kay *religious organization administrator*
Hodgson, John *literature educator, editor*
Hooper, Roy B. *lobbyist*
Krishnaiyer, Krishnan *industrial engineer*
Kroll, Connie Rae *librarian, information services consultant*
Leveron, Bud *psychologist, educator*
Mays, Quincy *art educator*
Moore, Roy Dean *retired judge*
Pazoureck, Rebecca Kieffer *food sciences professor*
Smiley, Frederick Melvin *education educator, consultant*
Smith, Michelle *education educator*
Underwood, Kirsten Fedje *musician, educator*
Webb, Orville Lynn *retired physician, pharmacologist, educator*

**Mcalester**
Cornish, Richard Pool *lawyer*

**Miami**
George, Barbara M. *theater educator, department chairman, actor, director*

**Midwest City**
Cook, James Junior *academic administrator*
Gonzalez, Richard Theodore *photographer*
Harrell, Beverly Ellen *mathematics professor*
Smith, Stephen K. *minister*
Thomas, Suzanne Charise *artist, educator*

**Monkey Island**
Vanatta, Chester B. *management consultant, educator*

**Moore**
Chiles, Mary Jane *secondary school educator*
Lee, Myung Woo *accountant, financial secretary*

**Mounds**
Fellows, Esther Elizabeth *musician, music educator*
Halsey, James Albert *entertainer, theater producer*

**Muskogee**
Ehlers, Deborah Layne *theater director*
Fulbright, Denise Nichole *education educator*
Heck, Jennifer Leigh *neonatal/perinatal nurse practitioner, educator*
Henry, Rickey Roy *electrical contractor, educator*
Kang, Heesam *investment analyst, educator*
Kent, Bartis Milton *retired physician*
Sperling, Sheldon J. *prosecutor*
Swanson, Jacqueline V. *academic administrator, educator, women's health nurse practitioner*

**Mustang**
Laurent, Jerry Suzanna *communications executive*
Olson, Jon Philip *music educator, director, voice educator, actor*

**Nichols Hills**
Trost, Louis Frederick, Jr. *banker, financial planner*

**Noble**
Caddell, Lyndal R. *social studies educator*
Winchell, Michael George *lawyer*

**Norma**
Hartel, Austin Stewart *performing arts educator, choreographer*

**Norman**
Affleck, Marilyn *retired sociology educator*
Ambrosini, Armand Anthony *music educator*
Apanasov, Boris N. *mathematics professor, researcher*
Beasley, William H. *meteorology professor*
Bert, Charles Wesley *mechanical and aerospace engineer, educator*
Bluestein, Howard Bruce *meteorology educator*
Boren, David Lyle *academic administrator, former senator*

Brown, Harley Procter, Jr. *zoology educator, entomologist, researcher*
Caldwell, Susan Havens *art educator*
Campbell, John Morgan *retired chemical engineer*
Cochran, Gloria Grimes *retired pediatrician*
Corr, Edwin Gharst *ambassador*
Croft, Janet Brennan *academic librarian*
Dille, John Robert *retired physician*
Doswell, Charles Arthur III *meteorologist*
Drayton, John N. *publishing executive*
Droegemeier, Kelvin K. *meteorologist, educator*
Dryhurst, Glenn *chemistry educator*
Fairbanks, Robert Alvin *lawyer*
Fears, Jesse Rufus *historian, educator, academic dean*
Fillpot, Bob G. *architecture educator*
Gollahalli, Subramanyam Ramappa *engineering educator*
Henderson, Arnold Glenn *architect, educator*
Henderson, George *educational sociologist, educator*
Herstand, Jo Ellen *librarian*
Herstand, Theodore *retired theatre artist, retired educator*
Hoang, Trung Q. *researcher*
Hutchison, Victor Hobbs *biologist, educator*
Ibrahim, Tamer Selim *engineering educator*
Kessler, Edwin *meteorology educator, consultant*
Kudrna, James *architecture educator*
Landers, Thomas Lee *dean, educator*
Lee, Eric McCauley *museum director, art historian*
Lee, Sul Hi *library administrator, dean*
Lester, June *library and information scientist, educator*
Lowitt, Richard *history professor*
MacFarland, Miriam Katherine (Mimi MacFarland) *computer engineer, consultant, writer, educator*
Mergler, Nancy L. *academic administrator*
Morris, Richard Ides *retired petroleum engineer, science educator*
Nelson, Donna Jean *chemistry educator, researcher*
Pappas, James Pete *university administrator*
Pedersen, Jon Erle *education educator, dean*
Petersen, Catherine Holland *lawyer*
Provine, Lorraine *retired mathematics educator*
Savage, William Woodrow, Jr. *historian, consultant, social sciences educator*
Sharp, Paul Frederick *retired academic administrator, educational consultant*
Sherman, Mary Angus *public library administrator*
Sonleitner, Frank Joseph *zoology educator*
Sorey, Thomas Lester, Jr. *architect, educator*
Stoops, Bob *college football coach*
Taylor, Kenneth Lapham *science educator*
Trimble, Preston Albert *retired judge*
Trytten, Deborah Anne *computer scientist, educator*
Van Horn, Richard Linley *academic administrator*
Wallace, Danny P. *library and information scientist, educator*
Wood, Betty Jean *conceptual artist, art educator*
Wren, Jonathan Daniel *research scientist*
Yi, Myongho *library and information scientist*
Zapffe, Nina Byrom *retired elementary school educator*
Zelby, Leon Wolf *electrical engineer, educator, consultant*
Zhai, Yan *education educator, researcher*

## Oklahoma City

Ackerman, Raymond Basil *advertising executive*
Adams, Russell Lee *neuropsychologist*
Alaupovic, Alexandra Vrbanic *artist, educator*
Alaupovic, Petar *biochemist, educator*
Andrews, Mitchell Dewayne *internist, educator, dean*
Arn, Susan Kyle *mathematician, educator*
Askins, Jari *lawyer, department chairman, state representative*
Bahr, Carman Bloedow *internist*
Bailey, Burck *lawyer*
Bailey, David Michael *physician, internist*
Balkman, Thad *lawyer, state representative*
Beltran, Eusebius Joseph *archbishop*
Binning, Bette Finese (Mrs. Gene Hedgcock Binning) *athletic association official*
Blackwell, John Adrian, Jr. *computer company executive*
Boaz, Stephen Scott *lawyer*
Bogardus, Carl Robert, Jr. *radiologist, educator*
Boston, Billie *costume designer, costume history educator*
Bozalis, John Russell *physician*
Bradford, Dennis Doyle *real estate broker, real estate developer*
Branch, John Curtis *biology professor, lawyer*
Brandt, Edward Newman, Jr. *physician, educator*
Bronson, William Cavolt, Jr. *retired counselor*
Brooks, Gene (Leslie Gene Brooks) *cultural organization administrator*
Brophy, Alfred Laurence III *law educator*
Bush, William Arden *federal agency administrator*
Butnev, Viktor Yurievich *research scientist*
Calvey, Kevin *lawyer, state representative*
Campbell, David Gwynne *petroleum executive, geologist*
Carballo, Bernard A. *computer company executive*
Cargill, Lance *lawyer, state representative*
Case, Bill *insurance agent, state representative*
Cauthron, Robin J. *federal judge*
Church, Chelsea O. *pharmacist, educator*
Claflin, James Robert *pediatrician, allergist*
Coats, Andrew Montgomery *dean, lawyer, former mayor*
Colbert, Thomas *state supreme court justice*
Coll, Mario M *engineering company executive*
Collins, William Edward *aeromedical administrator, researcher, psychologist*
Comp, Philip Cinnamon *medical researcher*
Cornett, Mick *mayor*
Cotton, Anita L. *secondary school educator*
Court, Leonard *lawyer, educator*
Craig, George Dennis *economics professor, consultant*
Crawford, James Leroy *minister, retired theology studies educator*
Crawford, Steven Alan *physician, department chairman*

Crites, Carl D. *auditor*
Culkin, Daniel Joseph *urologist, educator, department chairman*
Cunningham, Stanley Lloyd *lawyer*
Davis, Emery Stephen *wholesale food company executive*
Derrick, Gary Wayne *lawyer*
Dubowski, Kurt Max *toxicologist, educator, consultant*
Dunham, Dennis Paul *dean, educator*
Edmondson, Drew (William Andrew Edmondson) *state attorney general*
Edmondson, James E. *state supreme court justice*
Everett, Mark Allen *dermatologist, educator*
Fallin, Mary Copeland *lieutenant governor*
Farag, Noha Hassan *medical researcher*
Feng, Chengde *mathematician, educator*
Fenton, Elliott Clayton *lawyer*
Fernandez, Lisa *softball player*
Filley, Warren Vernon *allergist*
Foerster, David William *plastic surgeon*
Ford, Charles Reed *state legislator*
Forni, Patricia Rose *nursing educator*
Garbrecht, Robert L. *lawyer*
Garrett, Sandy Langley *school system administrator*
Gathright, Julie L. *primary school educator*
Gourley, James Leland *editor, publishing executive*
Gourley, Vicki Clark *publishing executive*
Graves, Virginia Beth *elementary school educator*
Greiner, Kenneth Donald, Jr. *retired management consultant, health facility administrator*
Grupe, Robert Charles *corporate communications specialist*
Gumerson, Jean Gilderhus *health foundation executive*
Hageman, Dale *alternative staffing company executive*
Hale, Sue A. *editor*
Halpin, Anna Marie *retired architect*
Halverstadt, Donald Bruce *urologist, educator*
Hampton, Carol McDonald *priest, educator, historian*
Hampton, James Wilburn *hematologist, oncologist*
Hanna, Terry Ross *lawyer, small business owner*
Hargrave, Rudolph *state supreme court justice*
Harlan, Ross Edgar *retired utility company executive, writer, lecturer, consultant*
Harolds, Jay Alan *radiologist, nuclear medicine physician*
Hefner, William Johnson, Jr., (W. John Hefner Jr.) *oil and gas industry executive*
Henry, Brad (C. Brad Henry) *governor*
Henry, Robert Harlan *federal judge, former attorney general*
Holeman, Lora White *music educator*
Holloway, William Judson, Jr. *federal judge*
Holt, Karen Anita Young *language educator*
Hood, Henry J. *lawyer, energy executive*
Houpt, Jeff *Internet company executive, executive secretary*
Howland, Ellenmarie Myers *retired elementary school educator*
Hutson, Lindel G. *newspaper editor*
Ille, Bernard Glenn *insurance company executive, director*
Jackson, Michael Wayne *academic administrator, researcher*
Jemison, Major Lewis *pastor, religious organization administrator*
Jenkins, Sherry L. *state insurance program administrator*
Johnson, Robert Max *lawyer*
Jones, Renee Kauerauf *health facility administrator*
Jones, Tad *state representative*
Kauger, Yvonne *state supreme court justice*
Kenney, John Arthur *lawyer*
Kerr, Lou C. *foundation administrator*
Kirkpatrick, John Elson *retired oil industry executive, retired naval reserve officer*
Kline, David Adam *lawyer, educator, writer*
Kombe, Ismail *mathematics professor, researcher*
Kraker, Deborah Schovanec *special education educator*
Krempl, Greg *otolaryngologist*
Kriesel, Deanna Jean *education educator*
LaMotte, Janet Allison *retired management consultant*
Lavender, Maxine Knight *special education educator*
Lavender, Robert Eugene *state supreme court justice*
Legg, William Jefferson *lawyer*
Leonard, Timothy Dwight *judge*
Lewis, Russell *toxicologist, researcher*
Ligon, Duke R. *lawyer*
Lopez, John C. *meat processing company executive*
MacDougall, Vicki Lawrence *law educator, writer*
Manchester, Susan Jean *lawyer, artist*
Mass, Michael Don *state legislator*
Mather, Stephanie June *lawyer*
Matlock, Gina Rae *music educator*
McCampbell, Robert Garner *lawyer, former prosecutor*
McClellan, Mary Ann *pediatric nurse practitioner*
McClendon, Aubrey K. *energy executive*
Metcalf, Jordan Patrick *medical educator*
Mildren, Jack *bank executive, retired state official*
Miller, Herbert Dell *petroleum engineer*
Moler, Edward Harold *retired lawyer*
Moore, Billy Don *scriptwriter, film producer*
Moore, Steven E. *energy executive*
Morgan, Catherine Marie *psychologist, writer*
Morgan, Fred *lawyer, state representative*
Murray, James William III *manufacturing executive, lawyer*
Musselman, Lloyd K. *history professor*
Mustion, Alan Lee *pharmacist*
Nelon, Robert Dale *lawyer*
Nesbitt, Charles Rudolph *lawyer, energy executive, consultant*
Neville, Jack L. (Drew), Jr. *lawyer*
Nichols, J. Larry *energy executive, lawyer*
Ogle, James David (David Ogle) *lawyer*
O'Neal, Mike *secondary school educator, state representative*
Opala, Marian Peter *state supreme court justice*
Pain, Betsy M. *lawyer*

Parke, David Wilkin, II, *ophthalmologist, educator, health facility administrator*
Parmley, Jay *political organization administrator*
Paul, Chris *professional basketball player*
Paul, William George *lawyer*
Payne, Gareld Gene *vocal music educator, medical transcriptionist*
Peace, H. W., II, *small business owner, retired oil industry executive*
Perez-Cruet, Jorge *psychiatrist*
Pilcher, Gregory F. *manufacturing executive, lawyer*
Poole, Richard William *economist*
Price Boday, Mary Kathryn *choreographer, small business owner, educator*
Ragsdale, Frank Wayne *voice educator, singer*
Rahhal, Donald K. *obstetrician, gynecologist*
Raj, Tilak D. *anesthesiologist, educator*
Reich, Richard Allen *bank executive*
Reimer, Dennis J. *retired career military officer*
Reneau, Brenda *trade association executive*
Richels, John *energy executive, lawyer*
Richter, John Charles *prosecutor*
Ridley, Betty Ann *theology studies educator*
Riggs, William Gerald *military officer, small business owner*
Riley, Nancy C. *state legislator*
Risser, Paul Gillan *academic administrator, botanist*
Rockett, D. Joe *lawyer, director*
Ross, Elliott Daniel *neurologist, researcher*
Ross, William Jarboe *lawyer*
Rossavik, Ivar Kristian *obstetrician, gynecologist*
Rundell, Orvis Herman, Jr. *psychologist, educator*
Russell, David L. *federal judge*
Ryan, Patrick M. *lawyer*
Savage, Susan M. *state official, former mayor*
Schille, John R. *insurance company executive*
Schimek, John Bradley *music educator, musician*
Schroeder, David J. Dean *psychologist*
Schwartz, Jonathan Royal Lee *medical educator, researcher*
Scott, Byron Alton *professional basketball coach, retired professional basketball player*
Seljeseth, Carol H. *physics educator*
Shelite, Leslie Michelle *vocational school educator*
Shillingburg, Herbert Thompson, Jr. *dental educator*
Shinn, Ronald Theodore *lawyer*
Spencer, Melvin Joe *retired health facility administrator, retired lawyer, retired consultant*
Staggs, Barbara Annette *state representative*
Steinhorn, Irwin Harry *lawyer, educator, corporate financial executive*
Stong, Roger Alan *lawyer*
Stringer, L. E. (Dean Stringer) *retired lawyer*
Sudbury, John Dean *religious organization administrator*
Taylor, Steven W. *state supreme court justice*
Taylor-White-Grigsby, Queen Delores *minister, consultant*
Thadani, Udho *physician, cardiologist*
Thompson, Ralph Gordon *federal judge*
Todd, Joe Lee *historian*
Tompkins, Raymond Edgar *lawyer*
Towery, Curtis Kent *lawyer*
Triplett, E. Eugene *editor*
Trotter, Timothy Howard *thoracic and cardiovascular surgeon, medical educator*
Tuepker, Max C. *lawyer*
Turner, Eugene Andrew *manufacturing executive*
Turpen, Michael Craig *lawyer*
Vaughn, William T *corporate financial executive*
Venters, Harley Eugene *lawyer*
Voth, Douglas W. *dean, educator*
Walsh, Lawrence Edward *lawyer*
Ward, Tom L. *energy executive*
Watt, Joseph Michael *state supreme court justice*
Weigel, Paul Henry *biochemistry educator educator, researcher, consultant*
West, Lee Roy *federal judge*
Wheeler, Jane Frances *protective services official*
Whitener, Carolyn Raye *artist*
Williamson, Marvel *dean, nursing administrator, sexologist, educator, writer*
Winchester, James R. *state supreme court justice*
Wisdom, Peggy Jean *neurologist*
Wohleber, Robert Michael *oil industry executive*
Wolraich, Mark Lee *pediatrician, educator*
Woods, Harry Arthur, Jr. *lawyer*
Woods, Pendleton *college director, author*
Young, Stephen K. *dean, academic administrator*
Yuill, Barbara Krebs *lawyer*
Zhu, Hua *biochemist, researcher*
Zuhdi, Nazih *retired surgeon, hospital administrator*

## Okmulgee

Ellis, A.D. *Native American tribal leader*
Mitcham, Julius Jerome *accountant*

## Owasso

Murray, Todd Anthony *performing company executive*
Reed, Walter George, Jr. *retired osteopath*

## Park Hill

Mankiller, Wilma Pearl *retired tribal leader*
Yeager, Debra Lyn *science educator*

## Pawhuska

Strahm, Samuel Edward *veterinarian*

## Piedmont

DeLozier, Joshua Mark *history educator*

## Ponca City

Gallagher, Gary W(ayne) *educational services executive*
Gong, Xiaoyi *engineer*
Northcutt, Clarence Dewey *lawyer*
Raley, John Wesley, Jr. *lawyer*
Rice, Sue Ann *retired dean, psychologist*
Wann, Laymond Doyle *retired petroleum research scientist*

## Poteau

Sanders, Douglas Warner, Jr. *lawyer, judge*
Spears, Burl Junior *computer technology educator*

## Pryor

Stinson, Marion Dennis *lawyer, land use planner, judge*
Titsworth, Tobie Richard III *academic administrator*

## Ripley

Chlouber, Dale Edward *curator*

## Sand Springs

Quinn, Al Jay *retired veterinarian, educator*
Sedlack, Kashannia Lynn *history educator*

## Sapulpa

Claussen, Alex *music educator*
Gardner, Dale Ray *lawyer*

## Sayre

Brooks, David Eugene *lawyer*

## Seminole

Laule, Gerhard Helmut *chemistry professor, researcher*
Stewart, Jacquelin Maria Connelly *psychology professor, consultant*

## Shawnee

Clark, Don Eugene *voice educator, vocalist*
Farrand, James Clinton *minister, consultant*
Sharp, Ron *secondary school educator*
Stoddard, Allan Lee *writer, musician*
Watson, Kimberly *music educator, pianist*
Way, Helen Sue *science educator*
Wilks, Thomas Milton *religious studies educator, minister*
Wilson, Robert Godfrey *radiologist*

## Skiatook

Harwell, Kenneth E. *chemist, researcher, consultant*

## Stillwater

Anderson, Cookie Gaston *finance educator, computer educator, humanities educator*
Case, Kenneth Eugene *industrial engineering educator*
Chakraborty, Goutam *marketing educator*
Chung, Jong-Moon *education educator*
Clark, Gary Carl *lawyer*
Confer, Anthony Wayne *veterinary pathologist, educator*
Cooper, Donald Lee *physician*
Darcy, Robert Emmett *political science and statistics professor*
DeLacerda, Melissa Griner *lawyer*
Ewing, Sidney Alton *veterinary medical educator, parasitologist*
Fischer, LeRoy Henry *historian, educator*
Fischer, Richard Samuel *lawyer*
Grischkowsky, Daniel Richard *research scientist, educator*
Halligan, James Edmund *academic administrator, chemical engineer*
Jaco, William H. *mathematics professor, researcher*
Jadlow, Janice Wickstead *finance educator*
Kotov, Nicholas Alexander *chemist, educator*
Luebke, Neil Robert *philosophy educator*
Maddox, Robert Nott *chemical engineer, educator*
Madihally, Sundararajan V. *engineering educator*
Max, Elizabeth *retired language educator*
Mize, Joe Henry *industrial engineer, educator*
Mowen, John C. *business educator*
Oliveira, Carlos *engineering educator*
Payton, Mark Edward *statistician, educator*
Rajamani, Vignesh *electrical engineer*
Ramakumar, Ramachandra Gupta *electrical engineering educator*
Royer, Tom A. *entomologist, educator*
Steindl, Frank George *economist, educator*
Thompson, David Russell *engineering educator, dean*
Zhang, Guolong *immunologist, educator*

## Tahlequah

Carment, Thomas Maxwell *accounting educator, consultant, researcher*
Edwards, Terri Lyn Wilmoth *education educator*
Smith, Chad Corntassel *Native American tribal leader*

## Terlton

Bender, John Henry, Jr., (Jack Bender) *editor, cartoonist*

## Tinker Afb

Goodman, Ernest Monroe *military officer*
Livingston, Douglas Mark *lawyer*
Penn, Vernita Lynn *government agency administrator*

## Tulsa

Abbott, William Thomas *private investigator*
Affeldt, Thomas Michael *lawyer*
Angelini, Marcello *artistic director*
Arrington, John Leslie, Jr. *lawyer*
Azar, J. J. *engineering educator*
Ball, Rex Martin *urban planner, architect*
Balman, Steven K. *lawyer*
Barker, John Roy *lawyer*
Belsky, Martin Henry *law educator, dean*
Bender, James J. *oil industry executive, lawyer*
Berlin, Steven Ritt *oil industry executive*
Biolchini, Robert Fredrick *lawyer*
Blais, Roger Nathaniel *physics professor, academic administrator*
Boudreau, Daniel J. *law educator, retired state supreme court justice*
Braumiller, Allen Spooner *gas industry executive, geologist*
Bregman, Martin Louis *geologist, geophysicist, educator*
Briggs, Robert LeRoy *geographer, educator, lawyer*
Brooker, Timothy Douglas *social studies educator*
Bryant, Hubert Hale *lawyer*
Buckley, Thomas Hugh *historian, educator*
Buker, William James *psychotherapist, educator*
Busch, Daniel Adolph *geologist, educator*
Buthod, Mary Clare *school administrator*

**John Day**

Tuttle, Kenneth Lewis *retired engineering educator, consultant, researcher*

**Joseph**

Gilbert, David Erwin *academic administrator, physicist*

**Klamath Falls**

Dow, Martha Anne *academic administrator, biology professor*
Griffin-Smith, Bridgitte M. *bank executive*
Koch, Margaret Rau *writer, artist, historian*
Krowen, Duane E. *elementary school educator*
Wendt, Richard L. *manufacturing executive*
Woodall, David Monroe *engineer, researcher, dean*

**La Grande**

Espinosa, Leandro *composer, conductor, educator*
Thompson, Joan (Jo) *anthropologist*
Woodward, Ralph Frederick, Jr. *elementary school educator, consultant, education educator*

**Lake Oswego**

Bruce, John Allen *retired foundation executive, educator*
Campbell, Colin Herald *former mayor*
Gehrig, Edward Harry *electrical engineer, consultant*
Hill, Gary D. *lawyer*
Hutchens, Tyra Thornton *pathologist, educator*
Julien, Robert Michael *anesthesiologist, writer*
Kuntz, Joel Dubois *lawyer*
Marietta, Elizabeth Ann *real estate broker*
McPeak, Merrill Anthony *retired military officer*
Mylnechuk, Larry Herbert *financial executive*
Parrick, Gerald Hathaway *communications and marketing executive*
Rhinewine, Joseph P. *psychologist*
Zorkin, Melissa Waggener *public relations executive*

**Lebanon**

Griswold, Elaine C. *nurse, consultant*

**Lincoln City**

Arant, Eugene Wesley *lawyer*
Morrow, James Thomas *energy executive*

**Lowell**

Boyle, John Howard *history educator*

**Madras**

Ramsey, Jarold William *literature and language professor, writer*

**Marylhurst**

Hatfield, Mark Odom *former senator*

**Mcminnville**

Nelson, Donna Gayle *state representative*
Thompson, Robert Samuel *retired lawyer*
Walker, Charles Urmston *retired university president*
Yates, Willard Ross *retired humanities educator*

**Medford**

Carter, William G. *lawyer*
Deatherage, William Vernon *lawyer*
De Boer, Sidney B. *automotive executive*
Dixon, Andrew Derart *retired academic administrator*
Entorf, Richard Carl *retired management consultant*
Frost, Orcutt William *historian, educator*
Heimann, M.L. (Dick Heimann) *auto dealership executive*
Hellemose, Aage *minister*
Hennion, Carolyn Laird (Lyn Hennion) *investment executive*
Rogers, Gardner Spencer *railroad company executive*
Schubert, Ruth Carol Hickok *artist, educator*
Shekhar, Stephen S. *obstetrician, gynecologist*
Skelton, Douglas H. *architect*
Straus, David A. *architectural firm executive*

**Milton Freewater**

Agidius, Michael Gregory *music educator*
Gipson, Stephen Richard *journalist, construction executive*
Piefer, Thomas R. *history educator*

**Milwaukie**

Averill, Corey Douglas *music educator*
Eichenger, Marilynne Katzen *museum administrator*
Orloff, Barbara-Lee Marguerite Hewitt *social worker*
Sklovsky, Robert Joel *naturopathic physician, pharmacist, educator*
Walker, Scott Allen *theater and language arts educator, theater director*

**Monmouth**

Balke, Frank H. *language educator, director*
Dantas-Whitney, Maria E. *education educator*
Dunn, Doris Marjory *retired secondary school educator, volunteer*
Oberst, Sharon Stokes *dancer, educator, choreographer*

**Mount Angel**

Petrik, F. A. *music educator*

**Myrtle Point**

Walsh, Don *engineer, consultant*

**Newberg**

Adams, Wayne Verdun *pediatric psychologist, educator*
Johnson, Thomas Floyd *former academic administrator, educator*
Keith, Pauline Mary *artist, illustrator, writer*
Warford, Patricia *psychologist*

**Newport**

Gilhooly, David James III *artist*
Kennedy, Richard Jerome *writer*
Quarles, Jeanne C. *psychology professor*

**North Plains**

Wood, James Anderson *cardiac surgeon*

**Oceanside**

Wadlow, Joan Krueger *retired academic administrator, retired construction executive*

**Ontario**

Gaskill, John William *secondary school educator*

**Oregon City**

Burke, William Romney *urologist*
Lounsbury, Steven Richard *lawyer*

**Pendleton**

Klepper, Elizabeth Lee *retired physiologist*
Muller, Steven John *music educator*
Smiley, Richard Wayne *researcher*

**Port Orford**

Drinnon, Richard *retired historian*

**Portland**

Abravanel, Allan Ray *lawyer*
Ahuja, Jagdish Chand *mathematics professor*
Allen, Rex Whitaker *retired architect*
Al-Rabadi, Anas Naser Essa *electrical engineer, computer engineer*
Anastasiou, Harry *international peace and conflict studies professor*
Arthur, Michael Albert *lawyer, investment advisor*
Attig, Rick *editor*
Backlar, Byron *lawyer*
Bacon, Vicky Lee *lighting services executive*
Bailey, Robert C. *opera company executive*
Baker, Diane R.H. *dermatologist*
Balkowiec, Agnieszka Zofia *science educator, researcher*
Barbeau, Monique Andrée *chef*
Barry, John Maynard *urologist*
Bartlett, Thomas Alva *retired educational administrator*
Bartley, Murray Hill *retired dental educator*
Bates, Doug *editor*
Bauman, Frank Anthony *retired lawyer*
Beatty, John Cabeen, Jr. *judge*
Beauchamp, E(dward) William *priest, lawyer, university administrator, management educator*
Bennett, William Michael *internist, educator, nephrologist*
Berentsen, Kurtis George *music educator, conductor*
Bernstine, Daniel O'Neal *law educator, academic administrator*
Bhatia, Peter K. *editor, journalist*
Blank, Eugene *pediatrician, radiologist, educator*
Bloom, Joseph D. *psychiatrist, medical educator*
Bodin, Kate *dean*
Bosch, Samuel Henry *diversified financial services company executive*
Boulot, Philippe *chef*
Boutwell, Anne Dielschneider *retired artist*
Boyle, Gertrude *sportswear company executive*
Bragdon, Paul Errol *retired academic administrator, educator*
Braun, Stephen Baker *academic administrator*
Brenneman, Delbert Jay *lawyer*
Browne, Joseph Peter *retired librarian*
Buckstein, Steve *think-tank executive*
Bunza, Linda Hathaway *editor, writer, composer, director*
Burke, Bernard Vincent *retired history professor*
Butler, John Lowe, IV, *psychiatrist, educator*
Cable, John Franklin *lawyer*
Cady, Sherry L. *astrobiologist, educator*
Campbell, John Richard *pediatric surgeon*
Canaday, Richard A. *lawyer*
Casey, Daniel E. *psychiatrist, educator*
Chevis, Cheryl Ann *lawyer*
Clark, Jennie L. *lawyer, webmaster*
Claycomb, Cecil Keith *biochemist, educator*
Clinton, Jack W. *dean*
Cohen, Norm *chemist*
Collins, Maribeth Wilson *retired foundation administrator*
Conkling, Roger Linton *management consultant, business administration educator, retired utilities executive*
Cook, Nena *lawyer*
Corbett, Alice Catherine *investor*
Crawshaw, Ralph *psychiatrist*
Crowell, John B., Jr. *lawyer, former government official*
Cunningham, Ward (Howard G. Cunningham) *open source technology executive*
Dailey, Dianne K. *lawyer*
Darnall, Beth Denise *medical educator*
Davis, James Allan *gerontologist, educator*
Davis, Raymond P. *bank executive*
Diver, Colin S. *academic administrator, educator*
Dolan, William J. *media company executive*
Donegan, Mark *metal products executive*
Dow, Mary Alexis *auditor*
Drinkward, Cecil *construction company executive*
Druker, Brian Jay *medical educator, researcher*
Dubanevich, Keith Scott *lawyer*
Dunn, Randall Lawson *judge*
Eakin, Margaretta Morgan *lawyer*
Eifler, Mark Anthony *historian, educator*
Englert, Walter George *classics and humanities educator*
English, Stephen Francis *lawyer*
Epperson, Eric Robert *finance executive, film producer*
Epstein, Edward Louis *lawyer*
Ernst, David A. *lawyer*
Fell, James Frederick *lawyer*
Feuerstein, Howard M. *lawyer*
Finley, Lewis Merren *financial consultant*
Foley, Ridgway Knight, Jr. *lawyer, writer*
Francis, Peter James *physician, ophthalmologist*
Franzke, Richard Albert *lawyer*
Fraunfelder, Frederick Theodore *ophthalmologist, educator*
Furse, Elizabeth *retired congressman, small business owner*
Galbraith, John Robert *insurance company executive*
Glasgow, William Jacob *lawyer, venture capitalist, business executive*
Goodman, Richard H. *biomedical researcher*

Gordly, Avel Louise *state legislator, political organization worker*
Graber, Susan P. *federal judge*
Graves, Earl William, Jr. *journalist*
Greene, Herbert Bruce *lawyer, investor, entrepreneur*
Greer, Monte Arnold *endocrinologist, educator*
Grossmann, Ronald Stanyer *lawyer*
Guillen, Jerome *trucking executive*
Hagenstein, William David *forester, consultant*
Hall, Howard Pickering *engineering and mathematics educator*
Hanlon, Michael Gregory *lawyer*
Harnden, Edwin A. *lawyer*
Harris, Cynthia Viola *principal*
Haug-Chin, Christine Anna *secondary school educator*
Hedges, Jerris *medical educator, health services researcher*
Helmer, M(artha) Christie *lawyer*
Hinckley, Gregory Keith *software industry executive*
Hinkle, Charles Frederick *lawyer, educator*
Hirshon, Robert Edward *lawyer*
Hochstettler, Thomas John *academic administrator, historian*
Horowitz, David A. *history professor, writer*
Houser, Douglas Guy *lawyer*
Hudson, Jerry E. *foundation administrator*
Huggett, Monica *performing company executive, musician*
Immergut, Karin J. *prosecutor*
Jackson, Roberta Q. *music educator*
Jacob, Stanley Wallace *surgeon, educator*
Jaquiss, Nigel *reporter*
Jarvis, Peter R. *lawyer*
Jiang, Bin *mathematician, educator*
Johnson, Mark Andrew *lawyer*
Johnston, Virginia Evelyn *retired editor*
Jolles, Bernard *lawyer*
Jones, Robert Edward *federal judge*
Josephson, Richard Carl *lawyer*
Kanter, Stephen *lawyer, educator, dean*
Katz, Vera *former mayor, former college administrator, state legislator*
Kendall, John Walker, Jr. *internist, researcher, dean*
Kennedy, Jack Leland *lawyer*
Kennedy, R(obert) Evan *engineering executive, consultant, retired structural engineer*
Kester, Randall Blair *lawyer*
Khalil, Mohammad Aslam Khan *environmental science educator, engineering educator, physics professor*
Kirk, Jill *management consultant*
Kitzhaber, John Albert *former governor, emergency physician, former state senator*
Knapp, Robert Stanley *English language educator*
Knoll, James Lewis *lawyer*
Koblik, Steven S. *academic administrator*
Kocaoglu, Dundar F. *engineering management educator, industrial engineer, civil engineer*
Kohler, Peter Ogden *academic administrator, internist, educator*
Kohne, Heidi Ann *church musician*
Korb, Christine Ann *music therapist, researcher, educator*
Kristof, Ladis Kris Donabed *political scientist, writer*
Lang, Philip David *retired state legislator, insurance company executive*
Larpenteur, James Albert, Jr. *retired lawyer*
Larson, Wanda Z. *writer, poet*
Larsson, William Dean *manufacturing executive*
Leavy, Edward *federal judge*
Leupp, Edythe Peterson *retired education educator*
Linstone, Harold Adrian *management consultant, educator*
Livingston, Louis Bayer *lawyer*
Lorenz, Nancy *artist*
Love, Edith Holmes *theater producer*
Love, William Edward *lawyer*
Lowry, David Burton *lawyer*
Maloney, Robert E., Jr. *lawyer*
Margolin, Phillip Michael *lawyer*
Marker, Carl W. *diversified financial services company executive*
Matarazzo, Harris Starr *lawyer*
Matarazzo, Joseph Dominic *psychologist, educator*
Matarazzo, Ruth Gadbois *psychologist, educator*
Mazur, Dennis John *internal medicine physician, educator, features editor*
Mazzola, Michael *lighting designer*
McClave, Donald Silsbee *academic administrator*
McKelvey, Connie Elkins *lawyer*
McMahon, Paul Francis *finance company executive*
McNeil, Mona Margaret *clinical psychologist*
Miller, William Richey, Jr. *lawyer*
Milton, Catherine Higgs *entrepreneur*
Mittelstaedt, Janet Rugen *music educator, composer*
Morgan, James Earl *librarian, administrator*
Mosman, Michael W. *federal judge, former prosecutor*
Mowe, Gregory Robert *lawyer*
Ng, John Daniel *ophthalmologist, educator*
Njoku, Scholastica Ibari *retired college librarian, writer*
Noonan, William Donald *lawyer, physician*
Nunn, Robert Warne *lawyer*
Orloff, Chet *historian*
O'Scannlain, Diarmuid Fionntain *federal judge*
Packard, Robert Goodale III *urban planner*
Paley, Vitaly *chef, food service executive*
Pamplin, Robert Boisseau, Sr. *retired textile manufacturing executive*
Pamplin, Robert Boisseau, Jr. *manufacturing company executive, minister, writer*
Panner, Owen M. *federal judge*
Parsons, Eric E. *financial company executive*
Patterson, Beverly Ann Gross *not-for-profit fundraiser, consultant, social services administrator, writer*
Patterson, James Randolph *physician*
Patterson, Steve *professional basketball team executive*
Pham, Kinh Dinh *electrical engineer, educator, engineering executive*
Phillips, Vicki L. *school system administrator*
Pierson, Wayne George *trust company executive*

Pine, William Charles *foundation executive*
Porter, Elsa Allgood *writer, educator*
Potter, Tom *mayor*
Prendergast, William John *ophthalmologist*
Proctor, James David *environmental scientist, educator*
Purcell, John F. *lawyer*
Raitt, Merritt *cardiologist*
Ramsby, Mark Delivan *lighting designer, consultant*
Ravichandran, Pasala Sankaran *cardiologist, thoracic surgeon, educator*
Rayhill, Stephen Corrigan *surgeon*
Redden, James Anthony *federal judge*
Richardson, Campbell *retired lawyer*
Richter, Peter Christian *lawyer*
Robertson, Joseph E., Jr. *ophthalmologist, educator, dean*
Rooks, Charles S. *foundation administrator*
Rosen, Steven O. *lawyer*
Rowe, Sandra Mims *editor*
Russell, Marjorie Rose *manufacturing executive*
Rutherford, William Drake *investment executive*
Ryan, John Duncan *lawyer*
Ryberg, William A. *orchestra executive*
Sand, Thomas Charles *lawyer*
Schmidt, Stanley Eugene *retired speech educator*
Schmidt, Waldemar Adrian *pathologist, educator*
Schuster, Philip Frederick, II, *lawyer, writer, educator*
Scott, John D. *pharmacologist*
Shangraw, Robert Edward *medical educator, researcher*
Shireman, Joan Foster *social work educator*
Showalter, Marilyn Grace *trade association administrator, director*
Sikora, Darryn Marie *pediatric psychologist*
Silverstein, Paul Adam *education educator, researcher*
Simpson, Robert Glenn *lawyer*
Skopil, Otto Richard, Jr. *federal judge*
Smith, Dennis B. *neurologist, educator*
Snyder, Joan Paula *lawyer*
Standring, James Douglas *real estate developer*
Stanton, John W. *communications executive*
Steinman, Lisa Malinowski *English literature educator, writer*
Stevens, Curtis *consumer products company executive*
Stewart, Marlene Metzger *financial planning practitioner, insurance agent*
Stewart, Milton Roy *lawyer*
Stickel, Frederick A. *publishing executive*
Stone, Richard James *lawyer*
Stott, Peter Walter *investment company executive*
Stowell, Christopher R. *artistic director, choreographer, retired dancer*
Street, Terri M. *artist, educator*
Sullivan, Edward Joseph *lawyer*
Sutherland, Donald Wood *cardiologist*
Suwyn, Mark A. *building products executive*
Swan, Kenneth Carl *surgeon*
Sylvester, Robert *dean, musician*
Taylor, J. Mary (Jocelyn Mary Taylor) *museum director, educator, zoologist*
Taylor, Robert Brown *physician, educator, writer*
Thoen, Doris Rae *retired small business owner*
Tolon, Michael Oded *music educator, director*
Tongue, Thomas Healy *lawyer*
Tucker, Roy W. *lawyer*
Tuska, Jon *writer, publishing executive*
Unger, Karen Virginia *director*
Urbanowski, John Richard *lighting systems company official*
Vanderslice, Ellen *information technology manager, composer*
Van Exel, Nickey Maxwell *professional basketball player*
Van Hoomissen, George Albert *state supreme court justice*
Van Valkenburg, Edgar Walter *lawyer*
Vaughan, Thomas James Gregory *historian, writer*
Voglar, Inés Ana *musician, educator*
Waggoner, James Clyde *lawyer*
Watne, Donald Arthur *retired accountant, educator*
Weber, George Richard *financial and internet marketing executive, writer*
Weeks, Wilford Frank *retired geophysics educator, glaciologist*
Weleber, Richard Gordon *ophthalmologist, geneticist, medical educator, researcher*
Westwood, James Nicholson *lawyer*
Wetzel, Karl Joseph *physics professor, dean*
Whinston, Arthur Lewis *lawyer*
White, Douglas James, Jr. *lawyer*
White, Roberta Lee *financial analyst*
Whitlow, Lillian *retired elementary school educator, poet*
Wieden, Dan G. *advertising executive*
Wiens, Arthur Nicholai *psychology professor*
Williamson, Charles Ready III *lawyer*
Wilson, Owen Meredith, Jr. *lawyer, mediator, arbitrator*
Wilson, Thomas Dale *not-for-profit fundraiser*
Wilson, William Harwell *psychiatrist, educator*
Wood, Marcus Andrew *lawyer*
Workman, Norman Allan *accountant, management consultant*
Wright, Adam *information technology executive*
York, David Pierce *music educator, composer, performing company executive*
Zalutsky, Morton Herman *lawyer*
Zerbe, Kathryn Jane *psychiatrist*

**Redmond**

Blue, Frederick Judd *retired history professor, writer*
Dey, Charlotte Jane *retired community health nurse*

**Roseburg**

Oliphant, Charles Romig *retired physician*
Tilson, Daniel *elementary school educator*

**Salem**

Abrams, Marc *lawyer, political organization worker*
Anderson, Laurie Monnes *state senator*
Balmer, Thomas Ancil *state supreme court justice*
Benson, Steven Donald *marketing professional, mechanical engineer, writer*

Bradbury, William Chapman, III, (Bill Bradbury) *state official*
Breen, Richard F., Jr. *law librarian, lawyer, educator*
Burdick, Ginny Marie *state senator*
Butts, Edward Perry *civil engineer, environmental consultant*
Carson, Wallace Preston, Jr. *state supreme court justice*
Castillo, Susan *school system administrator*
De Muniz, Paul J. *state supreme court chief justice*
Dettwyler, William Karl *medical technologist*
Dmytryshyn, Basil *historian, educator*
Durham, Robert Donald, Jr. *state supreme court justice*
Edge, James Edward *health care administrator*
Erickson, Ray Charles *retired wildlife biologist*
Frank, Gerald Wendel *advocate, journalist*
Gillette, P. Roger *physicist, systems engineer*
Gillette, W. Michael *state supreme court justice*
Haselton, Rick Thomas *lawyer*
Hoff, Reno R. *academic administrator*
Kistler, Rives *state supreme court justice*
Kuhn, Gary D. *speech educator*
Kulongoski, Ted (Theodore Ralph Kulongoski) *governor, former state supreme court justice*
Linde, Hans Arthur *state supreme court justice*
Mainwaring, William Lewis *publishing company executive, author*
Mannix, Kevin Leese *lawyer, political organization executive*
Minnis, Karen *state representative*
Myers, Hardy *state attorney general*
Nafziger, James Albert Richmond *law educator*
Page, Cheryl Miller *elementary school educator*
Pelton, M. Lee *academic administrator*
Peterson, Edwin J. *retired judge, mediator, law educator*
Qutub, Eileen *state legislator, real estate appraiser*
Riggs, R. William *state supreme court justice*
Swaim, Michael E. *lawyer, former mayor*
Tamura, Linda Gayle *education educator*
Tomei, Carolyn *state representative*
Warnath, Maxine Ammer *psychologist, arbitrator*
Winters, Jackie F. *small business owner, foundation administrator*
Wirth, Kelley K. *state representative*
Yih, Mae Dunn *state legislator*
Yoder, Jonathan Paul *secondary school educator*
Zumwalt, Roger Carl *hospital administrator*

**Sandy**
Jensen, Judy Dianne *psychotherapist, consultant*
Rieke, Forrest Neill *lawyer*

**Shedd**
Ruurs, Margriet *writer*

**Spray**
Fussner, F. Smith *history professor, retired rancher*

**Springfield**
Davis, George Donald *executive land use policy consultant*
Lutes, Donald Henry *architect*

**Summerville**
Hopkins, Gerald Frank *trade association administrator*

**Sunriver**
Clough, Ray William, Jr. *civil engineering educator*

**Sutherlin**
Gugel, Merilynn Sue *artist*
Rose, Sarah Elizabeth *genealogist, writer, counselor, web site designer*

**Talent**
Farrimond, George Francis, Jr. *management educator*
MacMillen, Richard Edward *biological sciences educator, researcher*

**The Dalles**
Hayden, I. Jill *secondary school educator*

**Tigard**
Yesilada, Birol Ali *political science professor*

**Troutdale**
Unis, Richard L. *judge*

**Tualatin**
Alley, Allen H. *semiconductor company executive*
Bouchard, Jeffrey B. *semiconductor company executive*
Brown, Robert Wallace *mathematics professor, educator*
Fleischmann, Marc W. *semiconductor company executive*
Greenberg, Robert Y. *semiconductor company executive*
Hick, Kenneth William *marketing executive*
Olsen, Hans H. *semiconductor company executive*
Peters, Robert Wayne *small business owner*
West, Michael G. *electric power industry executive*
Yavorsky, William D. *semiconductor company executive*

**Turner**
Ratzlaff, Ruben Menno *theology studies educator, minister*

**Wallowa**
Wizard, Brian *publisher, author*

**Welches**
Merrill, William Dean *retired architect, medical association administrator*

**West Linn**
Luchterhand, Ralph Edward *financial advisor*
Richards, Herbert East *retired minister, commentator*

**Wilsonville**
Ekman, Donald J. *lawyer, retail executive*
Giesbrecht, F. Bruce *entertainment company executive*
Gordon, John Charles *forestry educator*
Harker, Ron *information technology executive*
Humphrey, Lois Ellen *librarian*
Johnson, Martin Clifton *physician*
Langrock, Karl Frederick *writer, retired academic administrator*
Press, Ron *marketing professional*

**Woodburn**
Oliver, Madison E. *retired engineering executive, mechanical engineer*
Preece, Scott *food products executive*

**Yachats**
Gerdemann, James Wessel *plant pathologist, educator*
Robeck, Mildred Coen *education educator, writer*

# PENNSYLVANIA

**Abington**
Bildersee, Robert Alan *lawyer*
Goldfine, Beatrice *artist*
Halnon, Karen Bettez *sociologist, educator*
Redmond, John *oncologist*
Schuster, Ingeborg Ida *chemistry professor*

**Acme**
Babcock, Marguerite Lockwood *addictions treatment therapist, educator, writer*

**Akron**
Dickinson, Margery Elsie *missionary, clinical psychologist*
Leithmann, David Edward *music educator*

**Alcoa Center**
Ray, Siba Prasad *materials scientist, ceramics scientist*

**Aliquippa**
Drobac, Nikola (Nick Drobac) *education educator, consultant*
Forringer, Letitia Marie *music educator*

**Allentown**
Altemose, Mark Kenneth *lawyer*
Baker, Dexter Farrington *manufacturing executive, director*
Barraco, Robert Don *surgeon*
Beck, Glenn E. *information technology executive*
Beltzner, Gail Ann *music educator*
Biggar, John R. *utilities energy executive*
Brinson, Jennifer L. *social studies educator*
Brown, Robert Wayne *lawyer*
Brown, W(illiam) Douglas *lawyer*
Canfield, Cindy Kay Raup *elementary school educator*
Chang, Chris C.N. *pediatric surgeon*
Clemmer, Richard L. *electronics executive*
Cullen, Edward Peter *bishop*
Dickson, John T. *information technology executive*
Doughty, George Franklin *airport administrator*
Flautz, Nancy A. *librarian*
Foster, Edward Paul (Ted Foster) *process industries executive*
Gaylor, Donald Hughes *surgeon, educator*
Gewartowski, James Walter *retired electrical engineer*
Grey, Robert J. *energy executive, lawyer*
Haddon, Eva W. *principal*
Hansel, James Gordon *engineer, educator*
Hecht, William F. *electric power industry executive*
Heitmann, George Joseph *business educator, consultant*
Hess, Leonard Wayne *obstetrician gynecologist, perinatologist*
Holt, Leon Conrad, Jr. *lawyer, chemicals executive*
Jebitsch, Jenna Lynn *clinician*
Jones, John P. III *chemicals executive*
Kocsis, James Paul *artist*
Lovett, John Robert *retired chemical company executive*
Maffeo, Alphonse A. *anesthesiologist*
McGinley, Thomas Anthony, Jr. *lawyer*
Mealey, Grace Eleanor *music educator*
Miller, James H. *electric power industry executive*
Noonan, Charles Thomas *lawyer*
Orphanides, Otis George *licensing executive*
Palumbo, Robert Craig *sports medicine physician, director, not-for-profit developer*
Pavelich, Judith *secondary school educator*
Platt, William Henry *judge*
Revak, Francis Charles *priest, educator*
Saab, Deanne Keltum *real estate broker, appraiser*
Sacks, Patricia Ann *librarian, consultant*
Sadr, Ann *psychotherapist, educator*
Talsania, Jay S. *orthopedist, surgeon*
Tamboli, Dnyanesh Chandrakant *research scientist*
Weir, Bonnie E. *reliability engineer*

**Allison Park**
Backus, John King *former chemical company research administrator*
Dodani, Sunita *physician, educator*
Ewalt, Henry Ward *lawyer*
Herrington, John David III *retired lawyer, director*
Hollerman, Charles Edward *retired pediatrician*
LaDow, C. Stuart *financial consultant*
Lagnese, Joseph F. *environmental engineer*
Ries, William Campbell *lawyer*
Rulis, Christopher C. *lawyer*
Sullivan, Neil Maxwell *oil and gas company executive*

**Altoona**
Anthony, Bertha M. *minister*
Kinney, Janis Marie *librarian, consultant*
Moffitt, Charles William *art gallery director*
Reed, Carey S. *chemistry professor*
Sheetz, Stanton R. *grocery retail executive*
Weiss, Brock Landon *physics professor*

**Ambler**
Carey, Francis James *investment banker*

**Annville**
Condran, Cynthia Marie *gospel musician*
Foley, Brian Joseph *philosophy educator*
George, Katherine Elizabeth *artist, educator*
Kline, Donald E. *science educator*
McGill, William James, Jr. *academic administrator, writer*
Paustian, Paul Robert *library director*
Tezanos-Pinto, Rosa *Hispanic American literature educator*
Verhoek, Susan Elizabeth *botany educator*

**Ardmore**
Heinzen, Bernard George *lawyer*
Levy, Rochelle Feldman *artist*
Waetzman, Larry Samuel *diversified financial services company executive*

**Arendtsville**
Cope, Jamie H. *music educator*

**Armagh**
Gongaware, Acey M. *music educator*

**Ashland**
Fey, Tammey Lynn *elementary school educator*
Polyakov, Yuriy Sergeyevich *engineer, researcher*

**Aston**
DiMarco, David *mathematician, educator*

**Audubon**
Tanis, James Robert *library director, history professor, clergyman*

**Avondale**
Friel, Daniel Denwood, Sr. *manufacturing executive*

**Avonmore**
Smith, Luella Margaret *special education educator*

**Bakerstown**
Beachley, Michael Charles *radiologist*

**Bala Cynwyd**
Cohen, Rachel Rutstein *financial planner*
Corliss, John Ozro *zoology educator*
Dorwart, Bonnie Brice *historian, retired rheumatologist*
Garrity, Vincent Francis, Jr. *lawyer*
Gleklen, Donald Morse *investment company executive*
Kirschner, Ronald Allen *osteopathic plastic surgeon, ophthalmologist, educator*
Lundy, Joseph E. *lawyer*
Masket, Samuel *medical association administrator*
McGill, Dan Mays *insurance business educator*
Miller, L. Martin *accountant, financial planner*
Murphey, Murray Griffin *history professor*
Oswald, James Marlin *education educator, researcher*
Schwartz, Jeffrey Byron *lawyer*
Shepard, Geoffrey Carroll *insurance company executive*
Shiekman, Philip Miner *lawyer*
Shore, Eric Eugene *internist, consultant, lawyer*
Staley, Kenneth Bernard *civil engineer*
Wiener, Thomas Eli *lawyer*

**Bangor**
Long, Joshua Eric *music educator, small business owner*
Paine, Marlin Craig *band director*
Schiavone, John *state agency administrator*

**Beach Lake**
Chatlos, William Edward *management consultant*

**Beaver**
Strock, Robert S. *retired education educator*

**Beaver Falls**
Copeland, Robert Marshall *music educator, department chairman*
Miller, Albert Jay *retired library director*

**Belle Vernon**
Wapiennik, Carl Francis *manufacturing executive, planetarium and science institute administrator*

**Bellwood**
Broadwater, Robert Paul *publishing executive, writer*

**Bensalem**
Bern, Dorrit J. *apparel executive*
Kang, Benjamin Toyeong *journalist, minister*
Long, Robert C. *retired military officer, management consultant*
O'Toole, Michael Anthony *academic administrator*
Stern, Colin D. *lawyer, retail executive*

**Bentleyville**
Blasko, Barbara Ann *secondary school educator*

**Berwick**
Pasukinis, Cheryl Renee *elementary school educator*
Spencer, Allison Ann *biology educator*

**Berwyn**
Burch, John Walter *mining equipment company executive*
Devlin, Thomas McKeown *biochemist, educator*
Fry, Clarence Herbert *retired retail executive*
Hambrecht, William R. *investment banking firm executive*
McIntyre, James Owen *insurance executive*
Seidel, Arthur Harris *lawyer*
Watters, Edward McLain III *lawyer*
Wood, Thomas E. *lawyer*

**Clemmer**, Leon *architect, space designer*
Hilty, James Walter *historian, educator, media consultant*
Quinn, Colleen M. *reading specialist*

**Bessemer**
Bonnar, Jason *music educator*

**Bethel Park**
Korchynsky, Michael *metallurgical engineer*
Willard, John Gerard *communications executive, consultant, writer, educator*

**Bethlehem**
Anderson, David Martin *environmental health consultant*
Aronson, Jay Richard *economics professor, researcher, academic administrator*
Barnette, Curtis Handley *steel company executive, lawyer*
Barsness, Richard Webster *management educator, academic administrator*
Beidler, Peter Grant *language educator*
Bolash, Robert Benjamin *biomedical researcher*
Caskie, Grace I. L. *statistics professor*
Cole, Jack Eli *physician*
Diggs, David B. *music educator*
Durkee, Jackson Leland *civil engineer*
El-Aasser, Mohamed S. *engineering educator, academic administrator*
Fisher, John William *civil engineering educator*
Gast, Alice Petry *academic administrator, chemical engineering educator*
Ghosh, Bhaskar Kumar *statistics educator, researcher*
Hartmann, Robert Elliott *retired manufacturing executive*
Heindel, Ned Duane *chemistry professor*
Herman, Richard Gerald *research chemist, consultant, educator*
Hobbs, James Beverly *business administration educator, writer, academic administrator*
Humphry, James III *retired librarian, publishing executive, educator*
King, Jane Connell *mathematics professor*
Kodama, Kenneth Philip *science educator, academic administrator*
Leeson, Joseph Francis, Jr. *lawyer*
Lyman, Charles Edson *materials scientist, educator*
Marsh, Robert Harry *chemicals executive*
Mformbele, Akongnwi Clement *mathematician, educator*
Parmet, Harriet Abbey L. *literature educator*
Pense, Alan Wiggins *metallurgical engineer, academic administrator*
Rokke, Ervin Jerome *military officer, academic administrator*
Saeger, James Schofield *history professor, writer*
St. John, Anthony Paul *retired manufacturing executive*
Schattschneider, Doris Jean *retired mathematics professor*
Scheirer, William Kenneth *economist, consultant*
Schumacher, Stanley E. *composer, musician*
Schwartz, Eli *retired economics professor, writer*
Simons, Audrey Kay *music educator*
Smolansky, Bettie Moretz *sociology educator*
Smolansky, Oles M. *retired humanities educator*
Smyth, Donald Morgan *chemistry professor, researcher*
Spillman, Robert Arnold *architect*
Spry, Donald Francis, II, *lawyer*
Steffen, Lloyd Howard *minister, religious studies educator*
Stehney, Ann Kathryn *academic administrator, mathematician, educator*
Stella, John Anthony *financial executive*
Story, Bernard J *academic administrator*
Taggart, Bruce M. *library administrator*
Travers, Jason Eric *art educator, artist*
Tuzla, Kemal *mechanical engineer, researcher*
Warfield, William Leonard *musician, composer, educator*
Wittreich, Warren James *psychologist, consultant*

**Beyer**
Cornell, William Harvey *clergyman*

**Blakeslee**
Albano, Patrick Marino *historian, educator, archivist*
Negri, Rocco Antonio *artist, illustrator*

**Bloomsburg**
Guschel, Timothy James *pharmacist*
Holloway, Sybil Lymorise *psychologist, writer*
Hower, Eileen M. *music educator*
Kozloff, Jessica S. *academic administrator*
Leitzel, Jeffrey Dale *psychology professor*

**Blue Bell**
Brendlinger, LeRoy R. *academic administrator*
Brew, Wayne William *geography educator*
Carrow, John C. *computer company executive*
Deschaine, Barbara Ralph *retired real estate broker*
Elliott, John Michael *lawyer*
Giordano, Nicholas Anthony *brokerage house executive*
Gorby-Schmidt, Martha Louise *pharmacologist, researcher*
Halas, Cynthia Ann *business information specialist*
Haugen, Janet B. *corporate financial executive*
Martino, Babette *artist*
McAdam, Will *electronics executive, consultant*
McGrath, Joseph W. *computer services company executive*
Rounick, Jack A. *lawyer, clothing retail executive*
Sundheim, Nancy Straus *lawyer*
Swansen, Samuel Theodore *lawyer*

**Boalsburg**
Gettig, Martin Winthrop *retired mechanical engineer*

**Boswell**
Croft, Daniel Thomas *music educator*

**Boyertown**
Fortes, Brenda Joyce *language educator*
Jilk, Lawrence T., Jr. *banker*
Kulakowsky, Barry L. *elementary school educator*
Mauger, Cynthia Carroll *secondary school educator*

**Braddock**
Slack, Edward Dorsey III *financial systems professional, consultant*

**Bradford**
Cox, J. Arthur *minister*
Ewert, Kevin *theater educator*
Rice, Lester *electronics company executive*

**Bridgeport**
Lee, Robert *engineer*

**Bridgeville**
Irvine, Peter Bennington *clergyman*

**Bristol**
Boneparth, Peter *apparel executive*
Kimmel, Sidney *apparel company executive*
Lanham, Paul C. *information technology executive*
Shenefelt, Arthur B. *transportation executive, consultant*

**Brodheadsville**
Snyder, Nadine Eldora *music educator*
West, Dana Eric *mathematician, educator*

**Brookville**
Achille, John G. *lawyer*

**Broomall**
DiRosa, Steven Joseph *primary school educator, secondary school educator*
Saunders, Sally Love *poet, educator*

**Brownsville**
Martin, Richard H. *principal*

**Bryn Mawr**
Ackoff, Russell Lincoln *social systems designer, educator*
Anderson, Eric Edward *psychologist, consultant, health facility administrator, educator*
Baird, John Absalom, Jr. *retired academic administrator*
Bedrick, Anthony Edward *oral surgeon, educator*
Braha, Thomas I. *oil industry executive*
Brunt, Manly Yates, Jr. *psychiatrist*
Carbine, Sharon *lawyer*
Cooney, Patricia Ruth *civic worker*
Crawford, Maria Luisa Buse *geology educator*
Dudden, Arthur Power *historian, educator*
Fletcher, Marjorie Amos *librarian*
Frank, Edward David, II, *history educator*
Frick, Benjamin Charles *lawyer*
Gaisser, Julia Haig *classics educator*
Giese, William Herbert *tax accountant*
Goutman, Lois Clair *retired drama educator*
Hackman, Nadine Brokaw *veterinarian*
Hegedus, L. Louis *chemical engineer, retired research and development company executive*
Huth, Edward Janavel *internist, educator, editor*
Kinney, Dale *dean, art history educator*
Krausz, Michael *philosopher, educator*
Kuncl, Ralph *provost*
Lane, Barbara Miller (Barbara Miller-Lane) *humanities educator*
Lang, Mabel Louise *classics educator*
Levitt, Robert E. *gastroenterologist*
Liu, Hans Hamilton *infectious disease physician, educator*
McCabe, Louise Beachboard *language educator*
Mezvinsky, Edward M. *lawyer*
Moyer, F. Stanton *financial executive, pharmaceutical executive*
Narin, Stephen B. *lawyer*
Noone, R. Barrett *plastic surgeon*
Opendak, Irene *academic administrator*
Peters, Douglas Scott *health care executive*
Pew, Robert Anderson *retired real estate and equipment leasing corporation officer*
Porter, Judith Deborah Revitch *sociologist*
Price, Trevor Robert Pryce *psychiatrist, educator*
Trout, Charles Hathaway *historian, educator*
Vickers, Nancy J. *academic administrator*
Wheeler, Grace R. *retired market researcher*

**Buckingham**
Hover, John Calvin, II, *banker*

**Bushkill**
Garretto, Leonard Anthony, Jr. *insurance company executive*

**Butler**
Crytzer, Lynn Carol *music educator*
Hawk, Kathleen Patricia *broadcast consultant*
Miller, Patrick M. *social studies educator*

**California**
Cramer Roh, Joni Lee *physical education educator*
Williams, Paul David *mathematics professor*

**Callery**
Frydryk, Karl Allen *financial executive*

**Camp Hill**
Brandow, Theo *architect*
Burry, Peter Ross *finance company executive*
Crider, Rudyard Lee *psychotherapist*
Crist, Christine Myers *consulting executive*
Custer, John Charles *portfolio manager*
Fazzolari, Salvatore D. *mining products executive*
Hall, Christopher S. *retail executive*
Hathaway, Derek C. *mining products executive*
Johnston, Thomas McElree, Jr. *retired church administrator*
Lovett, Keith W. *retail executive*
Mackin, Charles Philip, Jr. *lawyer*
Markley, Kenneth Alan *psychologist*
Mead, James Matthew *insurance company executive*
Miller, Robert G. *drug store chain company executive*
Rowe, Michael Duane *artist*
Sammons, Mary F. *retail executive*
Sari, Robert B. *lawyer, retail executive*
Shirtliff, Bryan *retail executive*
Swamidoss, Stephenson *pathologist, health facility administrator*

Tokuhata, George K. *retired medical educator, epidemiologist, consultant*
Twomey, Kevin *pharmaceutical executive*
Yates, James Arthur *plastic surgeon*

**Campbelltown**
Jurell, William D. *protective services official*

**Canonsburg**
Coury, Robert J. *pharmaceutical executive*
Mascetta, Joseph Anthony *principal*
Piatt, Jack Boyd *manufacturing executive*
Prado, Gerald M. *investment banker*
Prost, Mary Jane *school nurse*
Puskar, Milan *pharmaceuticals executive*
Southern, David *history professor*
Williams, Stuart Alan *lawyer, educator*

**Canton**
Sutton, Carl *finance educator*

**Carlisle**
Anderson, Howard Wayne, Jr. *training company executive*
Asimakakis, Panagiota *mathematics educator*
Burgett, Gordon P., Jr. *physics educator*
Butler, William Elliott *lawyer, educator*
Durden, William G. *academic administrator*
Fish, Chester Boardman, Jr. *retired editor*
Fox, Arturo Angel *Spanish language educator*
Jones, Oliver Hastings *consulting economist*
Laws, Kenneth L. *physics professor*
Long, Howard Charles *retired physics professor*
McConnaughay, Philip J. *dean, law educator*
Robinson, Ronald Michael *financial executive, financial consultant*
Shrader, Charles Reginald *historian*
Wyn-Jones, Alun (William Wyn-Jones) *software developer, mathematician*

**Center Valley**
Gambet, Daniel G(eorge) *academic administrator, minister*
Risher, William Henry *cardiothoracic surgeon, educator*
Wehr, Matthew *music educator*

**Chadds Ford**
Cohen, Felix Asher *lawyer*
Duff, James Henry *museum director, environmental services administrator*
Gordon, William Edmund, Jr. *lawyer*
Isakoff, Sheldon Erwin *chemical engineer*
O'Hara, Virginia Anne *curator*
Swensson, Evelyn Dickenson *conductor, composer, librettist*
Webster, Owen Wright *chemist*
Whitney, Douglas Edgar, Sr. *retired lawyer*

**Chalfont**
Ashley, Kathleen Labonis *music educator*
Wilson, Jean Louise *retired state legislator*

**Chambersburg**
Furr, Quint Eugene *marketing executive*
Malmont, Andrea G. *education educator*
Neilson, Winthrop Cunningham III *communications executive, financial consultant, photographer*
O'Connor, John Morris III *retired humanities educator*
Rumler, Robert Hoke *agricultural products executive, consultant, retired trade association administrator*
Scarlata, Paul Anthony *oral surgeon*
Yeun, Paul Lorenzo *clergy member*

**Cheltenham**
Weinstock, Walter Wolfe *systems engineer*

**Chester**
Buck, Lawrence Paul *history professor, former academic administrator*
Harris, James Thomas III *college administrator, educator*
Kul, Ismail *chemistry professor*
Saad, Germaine H. *business management educator, researcher*

**Chesterbrook**
Hilzinger, Kurt John *health products executive*

**Cheswick**
Nair, Bala Radhakrishnan *engineer*

**Cheyney**
Wenyi, Bi *science educator*

**Clarion**
Canaday, Doris Charlene *retired traffic representative*
Foreman, Thomas Alexander *dentist*
Grejda, Gail Fulton *dean*
Pope, Kent Smith *lawyer*
Vega, Anthony Jude *meteorologist, researcher*

**Clarks Green**
Kubic, Charles Richard *retired civil engineer*

**Clarks Summit**
Beemer, John Barry *lawyer*
Cagley, Susan A. *history professor*
Janoski, Henry Valentine *investment advisor, former banker*
Maxwell, Brian T. *theatre and communications professor*

**Clearfield**
Singh, Shiwendra Prasad *civil engineer*

**Clifton Heights**
Pagano, Richard Donald *physical education educator, researcher*

**Clinton**
Talbot, Mary Lee *minister*

**Coatesville**
Ainslie, George William *psychiatrist*
Bell, Robert Lloyd *retired neurosurgeon*

Burton, Mary Louise Himes *information technology executive*
Krug, Lee Allen *chemistry educator, coach*
Makous, Norman *retired internist, cardiologist, educator*
Sauer, James Leslie *librarian, educator*
Stenz, Lisa Ann *reading specialist*
Zarychta, William Alex *physician assistant*

**Cochranville**
Sazegar, Morteza *artist*

**Collegeville**
Billiard, Julia *cell biologist, researcher*
Dunstan, Russ Frank *psychological services professional*
Ruffolo, Robert R. *research and development company executive*
Sharifi, Azalea A. *orthodontist and general dentist*
Shen, Hua-Qiong (Joan) *clinical research director*
Stein, Steven H. *pharmaceutical research scientist*
Stiles, Gary Lester *cardiologist, molecular pharmacologist, educator*
Strassburger, John Robert *academic administrator*

**Columbia**
Smith, Thomas Clair *retired manufacturing company executive*
Stuckert, Caroline Morris *retired non-profit executive, anthropologist*

**Connellsville**
Brady, Marsha McCandless *secondary school educator*
Humbert, Kimberly Ramsay *secondary school educator*

**Conshohocken**
Bramson, Robert Sherman *lawyer*
Lotman, Herbert *food processing executive*
Naples, Ronald James *manufacturing executive*
Sigafoos, Thomas W., Jr. *principal*
Spaeth, Karl Henry *retired chemicals executive, lawyer*
Thompson, Pamela Padwick *public relations executive*

**Coopersburg**
Bednar, Charles Sokol *political science professor*
Bolle, Donald Martin *retired engineering educator*
Peserik, James E. *electrical engineer, consultant, safety engineer, computer engineer*
Siess, Alfred Albert, Jr. *engineering executive, management consultant*

**Cooperstown**
Hogg, James Henry, Jr. *retired education educator*

**Coplay**
Norbeck, Jack Carl *library exhibitor*

**Coraopolis**
Beaver, William R. *sociology professor*
Kay, George Paul *environmental engineer*
Koepfinger, Joseph Leo *retired utilities executive*

**Corsica**
Elza, Betty Ann *retired librarian*

**Coudersport**
Kuratomi, Ernie Kazuo *principal*
Kysor, Daniel Francis *psychologist*

**Cranberry Township**
Hogberg, Carl Gustav *retired metal products executive*
Lorenz, John George *librarian, consultant*
Patten, Charles Anthony *management consultant, retired manufacturing company executive, writer, publisher*
Pfeiffer, Gary R. *information technology manager*
Tiller, Olive Marie *retired church worker*

**Cresson**
Rosensteel Way, Nancy Ann *music educator*

**Dallas**
Broskoske, Stephen L. *information technology educator*
Goss, Sheryl E. *director*

**Danville**
Bakri, Younes Noaman *surgeon, oncologist, gynecologist*
Blankenship, James Colegrove *cardiologist*
Chan, Yiumo *biochemist*
Currid, Michael *finance educator, consultant, real estate developer*
Enman, John Aubrey *science educator*
Gubbiotti, Christine M. *lawyer*
Pierce, James Clarence *surgeon, educator*
Ramdas, Jagadeesh *physician*

**Darby**
Eiser, Arnold Robert *physician executive, bioethicist, nephrologist, internist*

**Davidsville**
Pepoy, Marya Alexandra *healthcare educator, coach*

**Delta**
Withrow, James A *music educator*

**Denver**
Milner, Charles Fremont, Jr. *manufacturing executive*

**Derry**
Baltzer, Cynthia Louise *music educator*
Goodman, Frederick Denis *environmental scientist, educator*

**Devon**
Boehne, Edward George *banker*
Earley, Laurence Elliott *retired medical educator*
Porter, Roger John *research and development company executive, neurologist, pharmacologist*
Wilson, Malcolm Campbell *investment trust management executive*

**Dillsburg**
Bowers, Glenn Lee *retired professional society administrator*
Jackson, George Lyman *retired nuclear medicine physician*
Riley, R. Douglas *music educator*
Smith, William Raymond *farmer, horse breeder*

**Dimock**
Rezykowski, Catherine R. *secondary school educator*

**Donora**
Todd, Norma Ross *retired government official*

**Douglassville**
Schwarz, Kathryn J. *gifted and talented educator*

**Dover**
Apgar, Andrew R. *music educator*
Moul, Brian E. *music educator*

**Downingtown**
Romanosky, LuAnn *elementary school educator*
Sweeney, Sarina Marie *psychologist, consultant*
Valentin, Joan Marie *secondary school educator*
Wusinich, Joseph F. III *lawyer, educator*

**Doylestown**
Bowers, Nell S. *psychologist*
Brink, Frank, Jr. *biophysicist, former educator*
Donnelly, Michael William *language educator*
Elliott, Richard Howard *lawyer*
Ginsberg, Barry Gavrille *psychologist, marriage and family therapist*
Maxwell, Clair D. *musician, director, educator*
McCafferty, Barbara Jean (BJ McCafferty) *sales executive*
Meyer, Diane Christine *social worker*
Mishler, John Milton (Yochanan Menashsheh ben Shaul) *science educator, artist*
Solly, Richard Peter *music educator*
Thomas, Ellen Louise *school system administrator*

**Drexel Hill**
Alexander, Lloyd Chudley *author*
Martino, Michael Charles *entertainer, musician, actor*
Schiazza, Guido Domenic (Guy Schiazza) *educational association administrator*
Thompson, William David *minister, educator*
Turnbull, Mary Regina *secondary school educator*

**Du Bois**
Emmer, Barbara Louise *retired librarian*
Forsythe-Adamson, Velma Brown *accountant, consultant, literature educator*
Forthun, Larry F. *science educator, consultant*

**Duncansville**
Smith, D. Brooks *federal judge*

**Dunmore**
Bochicchio, Kim *literature and language educator*
Parmar, Parminder *education educator*
Sebastianelli, Mario Joseph *internist, nephrologist, health facility administrator*
Timlin, James Clifford *bishop*

**East Berlin**
Bamberger, Lauren R. *writer, photojournalist*

**East Petersburg**
Pedrow, Brenda M. *language educator*
Walker, Sue Albertson *retired school system administrator, educational consultant*

**East Stroudsburg**
Amirian, Susan *adult education educator*
Bergo, Conrad Hunter *chemistry professor*
Braithwaite, Barbara Jo *retired secondary school educator*
Henley, Richard James *health facility administrator*
Kansfield, Norman J. *former seminary president*
Miller, Robert W. *music educator, musician*

**Easton**
Bellissimo, Mary E. *art educator*
Brown, Robert Carroll, Jr. *lawyer*
DeGrandis, Ronald Wayne *music educator*
Grunberg, Robert Leon Willy *nephrologist, educator*
Holmes, Larry, Sr. *retired boxer*
Kincaid, John *political science professor, editor*
Lamb-Faffelberger, Margarete Barbara *foreign language educator*
Murphy, Bruce Allen *government educator, law educator, writer*
Pysher, Zane Kermit *retired counselor*
Radisavljevic-Gajic, Verica *mechanical engineer, educator*
Reese, Evan Charles, Jr. *orthopedist*
Scheer, Joel Martin *lawyer*
Schlueter, June Mayer *literature educator, writer*
Stitt, Dorothy Jewett *journalist*
Sun, Robert Zu Jei *manufacturing company executive, inventor, educator*
Teboh-Ewungkem, Miranda Ijang *education educator*
Traldi, Lorenzo *mathematician, educator*
Van Antwerpen, Franklin Stuart *federal judge*
Weiss, Daniel H. *academic administrator, former dean*

**Eddystone**
Fredrick, Susan Walker *tax company manager*

**Edgemont**
Davis, Scott Charles *music educator, political activist*

**Edinboro**
Howell, Allen C. *music educator, choir director*
Miller, G(erson) H(arry) *science administrator, mathematician, computer scientist, chemist*
Obringer, David C. *archivist, educator*
Travis, Grant Carner *lawyer*

**Edwardsville**
Lukas, Edward Michael *retired secondary school educator*

**Eighty Four**
Hardy, Joseph A., Sr. *wholesale distribution executive*
Magerko, Margaret Hardy (Maggie Magerko) *lumber company executive*

**Elizabeth**
Cornelius, David Frederick *band director*
Maurer, Mark Carey *music educator*

**Elizabethtown**
Bartoli, Jill Sunday *reading and language arts educator*
Brown, Dale Weaver *clergyman, theology studies educator*
Garber, Margaret Mary *elementary school educator*
Gordon, Laurie Anne *academic director*
Kenley, David Lynn *history professor*
Kitchen, Otis Dorsey *music educator*
Ritsch, Frederick Field *academic administrator, historian*
Sample, Frederick Palmer *former college president*

**Elizabethville**
McCartney, Chad Edward *music educator*

**Elkins Park**
Davidson, Abraham Aba *art historian, educator, photographer*
Erlebacher, Martha Mayer *artist, educator*
Hart, William C. *underwriter, educator, writer*
Hutapea, Parsaoran *science educator, researcher*
Myers, Kenneth Raymond *lawyer*
Pak, Hyung Woong *community advocate*
Stinnett, Hester Ann *artist, educator, art school administrator*
Verma, Satya Bhushan *optometrist, educator*
Yun, Daniel Duwhan *physician, foundation administrator*

**Elverson**
Sakoian, Lorraine J. *secondary school educator*

**Emlenton**
Berg, Janice Carol *elementary school educator*

**Emmaus**
Bowers, Klaus D(ieter) *electronics executive, researcher*
Bricklin, Mark Harris *magazine editor, publisher*
Denmead, Bruce Palmer *music educator*
Favorule, Denise *publishing executive*
Rodale, Ardath Harter *publishing executive*
Vaccariello, Liz *editor-in-chief*

**Emporium**
Sensenig, Daniel Scot *music educator*

**Enola**
Trout, Gwenn Louise *minister*

**Ephrata**
Reed, Galen K. *music educator*

**Erie**
Ayrault, Evelyn West *psychologist, writer*
Bennett, Charles Andrew *economics professor, department chairman*
Breckenridge, James G. *dean, consultant*
Brown, Gordon Earl *surgeon, consultant*
Collura, Frank Charles *conductor*
Dockstader, Emmett Stanley *civil engineer, construction executive*
Garcia, Philip A. *insurance company executive*
Gottschalk, Frank Klaus *real estate company executive*
Hagen, Thomas Bailey *business owner, former state official, retired insurance company executive*
Henry, Martin Daniel *university president*
Hirt, F. William *insurance company executive*
Ludrof, Jeffrey A. *insurance company executive*
Mason, Gregg Claude *orthopedic surgeon, researcher*
Mencer, Glenn Everell *federal judge*
Michaelides, Doros Nikita *internist, medical educator*
Parihar, Pradeep Singh *sports medicine physician*
Renkis, Alan Ilmars *plastics formulating company executive*
Santillano, Mark Ramon *dancer, educator*
Sensor, Mary Delores *health facility administrator, consultant*
Silverthorn, Ann *writer*
Thelin, Stephen Russell *lawyer*
Trautman, Donald W. *bishop*
Vanco, John L. *art museum director*
Van Gorder, Jan Reid *lawyer, insurance company executive*
Wilson, Shirley Willink *music educator, musician*
Wu, Yi *mechanical engineer*
Yochim, Joseph Adolph *lawyer*
Zelazny, Catherine *elementary school educator*

**Etters**
Garloff, Samuel John *psychiatrist*
Steps, Barbara Jill *lawyer*

**Evans City**
Pagonis, William Gus *retired army general*

**Everett**
Whetstone, Joni Lee *music educator*

**Exeter**
Flickinger, Donald E. *elementary school educator, mathematics educator*
Stocker, Joyce Arlene *retired secondary school educator*

**Exton**
Dorsey, Jeremiah Edmund *pharmaceutical company executive*
Hedges, Donald Walton *lawyer*
Hidalgo, Ismael J. *pharmaceutical scientist*

Roth, William McKinley *psychologist*

**Fairfield**
Freund, John Richard *former English educator*
Westfall, Terri Lee *kindergarten educator*

**Fairless Hills**
Hess, Frances Elizabeth *retired secondary school educator, retired director*
Rosella, John Daniel *clinical psychologist, educator*
Scrocca, Anthony Charles *bank executive*
Steckroat, Patricia A. *special education educator*
Swope, Megan Elizabeth *social studies educator*
Vodicka, Jason Douglas *music educator*

**Fairview**
Krider, Margaret Young *art educator*
Stern, Marilyn Jean *special education educator*

**Farrell**
Patton-Newell, Janet Lavelle *minister*

**Fayetteville**
Daywalt, Lee Eric *minister, museum administrator*
Etchison, Bruce *retired museum director, conservator*
Molitor, Graham Thomas Tate *lawyer*

**Feasterville Trevose**
Dickstein, Jack *chemist*

**Felton**
Shoemaker, Eleanor Boggs *television production company executive*

**Flourtown**
Christy, John Gilray *diversified financial services company executive*
Cooke, Sara Mullin Graff *daycare provider, kindergarten educator, medical assistant*
Dressler, Mark Christopher *writer*
Lee, Adrian Iselin, Jr. *journalist*

**Fogelsville**
Flores, Robin Ann *geriatric program and service consultant*
Hauck, Jeffrey Peter Artorius Martel *lawyer, protective services official*

**Ford City**
Cramer, Dennis F. *music educator, freelance/self-employed musician*

**Fort Washington**
Pezick, Patricia *music educator*
Trombley, Edward Francis III *registrar*

**Fountainville**
Brown, Madeline Morgan *internist*

**Franklin**
Johnston, Steven Roy *music educator*
Sauer, Mary Julia *special education educator*

**Frazer**
Osborn, John Edward *lawyer, pharmaceutical industry executive, former government official*

**Fredericksburg**
Daubert, Harlan Aaron *music educator, director*

**Freeport**
Smits, Ronald Francis *language educator, poet*

**Frenchville**
Hicks, James Thomas *lawyer, physician*

**Friendsville**
Babb, Harold *psychologist, educator*

**Gaines**
Beller, Martin Leonard *retired orthopaedic surgeon*

**Galeton**
Bull, Inez Stewart *retired music educator, curator, director, singer, writer, musician*

**Gettysburg**
Benfield, Ann Kolb *lawyer*
Boritt, Gabor Szappanos *history educator*
Bowman, Christopher Todd *music educator, football coach*
Coughenour, Kavin Luther *career officer, military historian*
Gritsch, Ruth Christine Lisa *editor*
Hallberg, Budd Jaye *management consulting firm executive*
Hansen, Mark R. *music educator*
Hendrix, Sherman Samuel *biology professor, researcher*
Roach, James Clark *federal agency administrator*
Schein, Virginia Ellen *psychologist, editor*
Will, Katherine Haley *academic administrator*

**Gibsonia**
Haas, Eileen Marie *homecare advocate*
Krause, Helen Fox *retired otolaryngologist*

**Gladwyne**
Acton, David *lawyer*
Booth, Harold Waverly *lawyer, finance company executive*
Castetter, William Benjamin *retired education educator, educational director*
Katz, Julian *gastroenterologist, educator*
Kaye, Donald *internist, educator*
Morrison, Gail *internist, nephrologist, educator*
Patten, Lanny Ray *gas industry executive*
Pendergrass, Henry Pancoast *radiologist, nuclear medicine physician*
Webber, John Bentley *orthopedic surgeon*

**Glassport**
Lippard, Thomas Eugene *lawyer*

**Glen Mills**
Churchill, Stuart Winston *chemical engineering educator*
Dunion, Celeste Mogab *municipal official, consultant, foundation administrator*
Turner, Janet Sullivan *painter, sculptor*

**Glenshaw**
Dombrovski, Alexandre Y. *psychiatrist, researcher*
Guentner, James Francis, Jr. *art educator, artist*
Wilkes, John Michael *military officer, auditor*

**Glenside**
Block, Isaac Edward *professional society administrator*
Jones, Elaine F. *psychologist, educator*
Kim, Kathryn Spitzer *geneticist, consultant, science educator*
Medel, Rebecca Rosalie *artist*
Ralston, Steven Philip *portfolio manager, financial analyst*
Rawlins, W. Scott *art educator*
Reiss, George Russell, Jr. *physician*

**Glenwillard**
Milne, Christopher McQuiston Wilmoth *photographer, journalist, educator*

**Grantham**
Kreamer, Carolyn Lee *nursing educator, community health nurse*
Mark, Kenneth Dean *museum director, educator*

**Greencastle**
Horst, Carolyn Diane *accountant*
Wertime, Timothy Ray *music educator*

**Greensburg**
Amari, Suprasad V. *mechanical engineer*
Duck, Patricia Mary *librarian*
Evanson, Paul John *utilities executive*
Fajt, Karen Elaine *art educator*
Ference, Edward W. *engineering executive, structural engineer*
Foreman, John Daniel *financial executive*
Goulding, Philip L. *energy executive*
Langer, Alois *biomedical engineer*
Neff, Mary Ellen Andre *retired elementary school educator*
Ramm, Douglas Robert *psychologist*

**Greentown**
Forcheskie, Carl S. *former apparel company executive*

**Greenville**
Cooper, Brandon Pearce *director*
Root, Brian K. *journalist*

**Grove City**
Lyle, Donald L. *physical education educator, department chairman*
McBride, Milford Lawrence, Jr. *lawyer*
Ranker, Dennis W. *social studies educator*
Schaefer, Paul Robert *religious studies educator*

**Gwynedd**
LeFevre, Perry Deyo *minister, theologian, educator*

**Gwynedd Valley**
McGarry, Lisa Coughlin *language educator*
Owens, Kathleen C. *academic administrator*

**Hamburg**
Pietsch, Douglas K. *music educator*
Schappell, Abigail Susan *retired speech, language and hearing specialist, massage therapist, Reiki master*

**Hanover**
Clark, Sandra Marie *school administrator*
Conway, Samuel Anthony *retired chiropractor*
Kline, Donald *food company executive*
Mayer, Jody Lynn (Jody Lynn Noel) *exercise physiologist*
Shue, Robert A. *social studies educator*

**Hanover Township**
Ginyard, Caleb Nathaniel III *government agency administrator*

**Harleysville**
Browne, Michael L. *insurance company executive*
Browne, Michael Leon *lawyer*
Hauber, Dorothy Marie *elementary school educator*
Kauffman, Robert A. *lawyer*
Smagalski, Carolyn M. *publishing executive, webmaster, director*

**Harmony**
O'Shea, Patrick Alan *elementary school educator*

**Harrisburg**
Adams, Barbara *lawyer*
Angino, Richard Carmen *lawyer*
Antoun, Annette Agnes *editor, publisher*
Bailey, Diandrea Michelle *rehabilitation services professional*
Baker Knoll, Catherine *lieutenant governor*
Barasch, David M. *lawyer, former prosecutor*
Batts, Barbara Jean *academic administrator, director*
Brenner, Thomas Edward *lawyer*
Breslin, Michael Joseph III *social services administrator, educator*
Brown, John Walter *vocational education supervisor*
Burns, Rebecca Ann *elementary school educator, librarian*
Cadieux, Roger Joseph *geriatrics services professional*
Campbell, Carl Lester *banker*
Cline, Andrew Haley *lawyer*
Corbett, Thomas Wingett, Jr. *state attorney general, lawyer*
Cortés, Pedro *state official*
Crahalla, Jacqueline R. *state representative*

Dejoie, Louis Armand *lawyer, management consultant*
DeKok, David *writer, reporter*
Diehm, James Warren *lawyer, educator*
Dinniman, Andrew Eric *international studies and history professor, state senator*
Fine, David R. *lawyer*
Golden, Thomas M. *lawyer*
Gover, Raymond Lewis *retired newspaper executive*
Hafer, Barbara *state official*
Hample, Judy G. *academic administrator*
Hanson, Robert DeLolle *retired lawyer*
Herman, Lynn Briggs *state legislator*
Kane, Yvette *lawyer, judge*
Kelly, Robert Edward, Jr. *lawyer*
Khanzhina, Helen P. *language and literature educator, translator*
Kilbride, Susan A. Richie *physiologist, researcher*
Klein, Michael D. *lawyer*
Knackstedt, Mary V. *interior designer*
Koken, M. Diane *state commissioner*
Kope, Shane Brien *lawyer*
Kraus, David Robert *lawyer*
Lappas, Spero Thomas *lawyer*
Logue, James Nicholas *epidemiologist*
Mahey, John Andrew *retired museum director*
Meilton, Sandra L. *lawyer*
Miller, Leslie Anne *lawyer*
Miller, Sheila *state legislator*
Moritz, Milton Edward *security consultant*
Pizzingrilli, Kim *state official*
Popnik, Marlene Alita *retired school librarian*
Rambo, Sylvia H. *federal judge*
Rendell, Edward Gene *governor, retired mayor, lawyer*
Renner, William Scott *retired military officer*
Rooke, Ben G. *finance company executive, lawyer*
Rudy, Frank R. *pathologist*
Saylor, Thomas G. *state supreme court justice*
Scaringi, Melanie Walz *lawyer*
Sheldon, J. Michael *lawyer, educator*
Smith, Eric Ledell *historian*
Stanley, Edward Alexander *geologist, researcher, retired director, forensic specialist*
Strouss, Carleton O. *lawyer*
Sullivan, John Cornelius, Jr. *lawyer*
Vance, Patricia H. *state senator*
Warshaw, Allen Charles *lawyer*
Wentzel, Paul H., Jr. *state agency administrator*
West, James Joseph *lawyer*
Williams, Constance *state senator*
Wolfe, Gary Donald *retired commissioner, librarian*
Zahorchak, Gerald Lee *school system administrator, executive secretary*
Zavacky, Susan Kline *law librarian*
Zwifka, David Alan *not for profit executive, consultant*

**Harrison City**
McWilliams, Samuel Robert *secondary school educator*

**Hatboro**
Carroll, Lucy Ellen *theater director, educator*
Quigley, Robert Charles *insurance industry consultant*

**Hatfield**
Jesberg, Robert Ottis, Jr. *educational consultant, science educator*

**Haverford**
Aronson, Carl Edward *pharmacology and toxicology educator*
Bean, Philip Albert *dean, historian*
Brand, Charles Macy *history professor*
Dawson, John David *academic administrator, religious studies educator*
DiBerardino, Marie Antoinette *developmental biologist, educator*
Goppelt, John Walter *physician, psychiatrist*
Gutwirth, Marcel Marc *literature educator*
Jorden, Eleanor Harz *linguist, educator*
Kee, Howard Clark *religion educator*
Laird, Shirley Eder *small business owner, communications executive*
Mathews, Timothy Newlyn *lawyer*
Northrup, Herbert Roof *economist*
Palmer, Richard Ware *retired lawyer*
Roelofs, Lyle Dean *physicist, researcher*
Stiller, Jennifer Anne *lawyer*
Stroud, James Stanley *retired lawyer*
Tritton, Thomas Richard *academic administrator, biologist, educator*
Williams, William Earle *artist, educator, curator*

**Havertown**
Bala, Gary Ganesh *lawyer, financial planner*
Brinker, Thomas Michael *finance company executive*
Garrahan-Masters, Mary Patricia *retired social worker, writer*
Hendrickson, Paul Joseph *journalist, writer, educator*
Koenig, Norma Evans *retired religious studies educator*
Koenig, Robert Emil *clergyman*
Siegel, Daniel Joel *lawyer*
Wing, Kennard Thompson *educational organization official*

**Hawley**
Genello, Denise M. *special education educator*

**Hazleton**
DeMelfi, (Ronald) Daniel *music educator, director*
Kemmerer, Kathleen Mary *language educator*
Kraynak, Marcelle Georgeann *not-for-profit developer*
Vice, Daniel Hoy *geologist, educator*

**Hermitage**
Gurgovits, Stephen J. *financial executive*

**Hershey**
Butterfield, Andrea Christine *psychology educator, educational association administrator*
Caputo, Gregory Michael *internist, educator*
Cerminara, Frank *food products executive*

Cherry, Robert A. *surgeon*
Chinoy, Mala R. *biologist, educator*
Christensen, Dawn Michelle *family practice nurse practitioner, consultant*
Cook, Christine *elementary school educator*
Davis, Dwight *cardiologist, educator*
Davis, George F. *food products executive*
Dellasega, Cheryl *humanities educator*
Eyster, Mary Elaine *hematologist, educator*
Gingrich, Shawn M. *music educator, church administrator*
Hopper, Anita Klein *molecular genetics educator*
Jones, Marshall Bush *education educator, researcher*
Kauffman, Gordon Lee, Jr. *surgeon, educator*
Leaman, David Martin *cardiologist, educator*
Lenny, Richard Herbert *food products executive, marketing professional*
Lim, Jung Yul *biomedical engineer*
Mackay, Donald Roy *plastic surgeon, educator*
Marks, James Garfield, Jr. *dermatologist*
Moskowitz, Jay *health science association administrator, educator, dean*
Naeye, Richard L. *pathologist, educator*
Paz, Harold Louis *hospital administrator, internist, educator*
Pierce, William Schuler *cardiac surgeon*
Severs, Walter Bruce *pharmacology educator, researcher*
Snyder, Burton Harold *lawyer*
Tan, Tjiauw-Ling *psychiatrist, educator*
Thomas, Andrea B. *food products executive*
Uhde, Thomas Whitley *medical educator*
Undar, Akif *research scientist, biomedical engineer, educator*
Vesell, Elliot Saul *pharmacologist, educator, dean*
Waldhausen, John Anton *retired surgeon, retired editor*
Wassner, Steven Joel *pediatric nephrologist, educator*
Zagon, Ian Stuart *neuroscience and anatomy educator, researcher, inventor*
Zelis, Robert Felix *cardiologist, educator*

**Hollidaysburg**
Bloom, Lawrence Stephen *retired clothing company executive*
Cottle, Harold Ranson *pathologist, laboratory executive*
Mariano, Ana Virginia *retired pathologist*

**Homestead**
King, Richard Wayne *principal*
Mandel, Herbert Maurice *civil engineer*

**Honesdale**
Barbe, Walter Burke *education educator*
Clark, Christine May *editor, author*

**Hopwood**
Syphers, James Edgar *retired social worker*

**Horsham**
Ahmed, Elias *microbiologist*
Barzilay, Zvi *real estate developer*
Best, Franklin Luther, Jr. *lawyer*
Christian, Mildred Stoehr *health products executive*
Harrison, Deborah Lynn *accountant, consultant*
Nanda, Vivek (Vic Nanda) *software quality executive*
Sachs, Keith L. *manufacturing executive*
Schopp, David L. *music educator*
Toll, Bruce Elliot *real estate developer*
Toll, Robert Irwin *home construction company executive*

**Hughesville**
Boyer, Mark A. *music educator*

**Hulmeville**
Jackson, Mary L. *health services executive*

**Hummelstown**
Clouse, Jerry Allan *architectural historian*

**Hunker**
Springer, Robert Wade *music educator*

**Huntingdon**
Kepple, Thomas Ray, Jr. *college administrator*
Stiffler, Stuart Alden *retired library director*

**Huntingdon Valley**
Cohen, Michael R. *health facility administrator, pharmacist*
Godfrey, John Carl *medicinal chemist*
Isard, Phillip Isaac *medical nutritionist, consultant*
Krzyzanowski, Richard L. *lawyer*
Leibholz, Stephen Wolfgang *physicist, information technology executive, entrepreneur*
Sadoff, Joan Handleman *film producer, social worker*
Vollum, Robert Boone *management consultant*
West, A(rnold) Sumner *chemical engineer*

**Immaculata**
Fadden, Sister R. Patricia *academic administrator, nun*

**Imperial**
Peters, Raymond Andrew *music educator*

**Indiana**
Atwater, Tony *university president*
Barbor, Gretchen Kunst *secondary school educator, theater educator, director*
Bencloski, Joseph W. *geography educator*
Black, Lynanne *psychologist, educator*
Cogar, Theodore Monroe *director*
Falcone, Thomas William *finance educator*
Garvin, C(larence) Alexander, Jr. *economics professor*
Janicak, Christopher A. *academic administrator, educator*
LaRoche, Lynda *artist, educator*
Masilela, Calvin Onias *land use planner, educator*
Mc Cauley, R. Paul *criminologist, educator*
Pettit, Lawrence Kay *university president*
Pidgeon, John Anderson *headmaster*

Reynolds, Virginia Edith *sociologist, anthropologist, educator, artist*
Salser, Scott A. *music educator*
Shim, Leem Seop *computer scientist, educator, researcher*
Stern, T. Noel *political science professor*
Thibadeau, Eugene Francis *education educator, consultant*

**Irwin**
Kuhn, Howard Arthur *engineering executive, educator*
Perich, Terry Miller *retired secondary school educator*

**Ivyland**
Thorne, John Watson III *advertising and marketing executive*

**Jacobus**
Secula, Jennifer Michele *psychologist*

**James Creek**
Durnbaugh, Donald Floyd *church history educator, researcher*

**Jamison**
Touhill, C. Joseph *environmental engineer*

**Jefferson Hills**
Smith, Leslie Edgar *vocational school administrator*

**Jenkintown**
Bales, John Foster III *retired lawyer*
Black, Thomas Donald *retired religious organization administrator*
Booker, Alvin Eugene *publishing executive, consultant*
Dickstein, Joan Borteck *arbitrator, consultant*
Greenspan-Margolis, June E. *psychiatrist*
Haythornthwaite, Robert Morphet *civil engineer, educator*
Johnson, Victor Lawrence *banker, director*
Kaiser, Tracy Misson *paralegal, educator*
Oh, Soojin Susan *elementary school educator*
Sadoff, Robert Leslie *psychiatrist, educator*

**Jim Thorpe**
Meneeley, Edward Sterling *artist*

**Johnstown**
Borkow, Mary P. *small business owner*
Brice, Heather Weidenhofer *consulting librarian*
Depra, Alan Jay *mechanical engineer*
McCleester, Frank Raymond *music educator*
Miloro, Protopresbyter Frank *religious organization administrator, theology studies educator*
Nicholas, (Richard G. Smisko) *bishop*
Samples, Jerry Wayne *military officer, educator*
Sheehan, Edward James *retired night vision and electro-optics specialist*
Smisko, Nicholas Richard *bishop, educator*

**Jones Mills**
Fish, Paul Waring *lawyer*

**Kelton**
Gulick, Walter Lawrence *psychologist, educator, retired academic administrator*

**Kennett Square**
Bell, Philip Wilkes *accountant, economist, educator*
Conard, Alfred Fletcher *legal educator*
Curtin, Philip De Armond *history educator*
Hager, George V., Jr. *health services executive*
Hennes, Robert Taft *former management consultant, investment executive*
Landstrom, Elsie Hayes *retired editor*
Litzenberg, G. Scott *music educator, director*
Martin, George (George Whitney Martin) *writer*
Partnoy, Ronald Allen *lawyer*
Richardson, Dean Wheeler *equine surgeon, veterinary educator*
Wilson, Armin *retired chemist*

**Kimberton**
Williams, Lawrence Soper, Jr. *photographer*

**King Of Prussia**
Bissell, Eugene V.N. *gas industry executive*
Broido, Arnold Peace *music publishing company executive*
Clauson, Sharyn Ferne *consulting company executive, educator*
Filton, Steve G. *corporate financial executive*
Gallis, John Nicholas *retired military officer, executive leadership training consultant*
Gilbert, Bruce Rits *lawyer*
Greenberg, Lon Richard *energy executive, lawyer*
Helmetag, Diana *music educator*
Katz, Arnold Martin *insurance brokerage firm executive*
Liebermann, Lowell *composer, conductor, pianist*
Martini, Perry James *educational consultant*
Mendicino, Anthony J. *gas company executive*
Miller, Alan B. *hospital management executive*
Perlstein, Itay *research scientist*
Rockhold, Frank W. *statistician, pharmaceutical executive*
Rubin, Michael G. *sports internet company executive*
Schneider, Pam Horvitz *lawyer*
Schumann, Paula M. L. *writer*
Volpe, Ralph Pasquale *retired insurance company executive*
Walsh, John L. *energy executive*
Webb, Richard Stephen *manufacturing executive*
Yan, Ying *statistician, researcher*

**Kingsley**
McNabb, Corrine Radtke *librarian*

**Kingston**
Friedman, Pauline Poplin *civic worker, consultant*
Meyer, Martin Jay *lawyer*
Weisberger, Barbara *artistic director, advisor, educator*

**Kintnersville**
Barnes, Francis V. *school system administrator*

**Knox**
Rupert, Elizabeth Anastasia *retired dean*

**Kutztown**
Gupta, Venu Gopal *psychology professor*
Ogden, James Russell *marketing educator, consultant, lecturer, writer*
Pirnot, Thomas Leonard *mathematics professor*
Przydzial, Celine J. *mathematics professor*
Summer, Evan D. *artist, art educator*
Vasko, Francis Joseph *mathematics professor*

**La Plume**
Boehm, Edward Gordon, Jr. *college administrator, educator*
Elliott, David Lindsey *literature educator*

**Lafayette Hill**
Delacato, Carl Henry *education educator*
Delacato, Janice Elaine *special education educator, consultant*
Edwards, JoAnn Louise *human resources executive*
King, Leon *investment advisor*
Miller, Nancy Lois *senior pastor*

**Lake Harmony**
Polansky, Larry Paul *legal association administrator*

**Lancaster**
Ashby, Richard James, Jr. *bank executive, lawyer*
Babic, Michael Walter *lawyer*
Benoit, Philip Grosvenor *communications executive, educator, writer*
Binkley, Luther John *philosophy educator*
Brod, Roy David *ophthalmologist, educator*
Brunner, Lillian Sholtis *nurse, writer*
Burkholder, Michele Stawinski *lawyer*
Burlingame, Mark Wayne *cardiothoracic surgeon*
Carlisle, James Patton *entrepreneur*
Ebersole, J. Glenn, Jr. *engineering, marketing, management, public relations and strategic planning executive*
Ebersole, Mark Chester *emeritus college president*
Freeman, Clarence Calvin *retired diversified financial services company executive*
Fry, John Anderson *academic administrator*
Glick, Garland Wayne *retired theological seminary president*
Graffis, Leister F. *retired engineering executive*
Grube, Rebecca Sue *elementary school educator, consultant*
Heil, Paul Samuel *radio producer*
High, S. Dale *construction executive*
Kelly, Robert Lynn *advertising executive*
Kendall, Leigh Wakefield *retired surgeon*
Kermes, Constantine John *artist, industrial designer*
Kneedler, Alvin Richard (Richard Kneedler) *former academic administrator*
Liddell, W. Kirk *specialty contracting company executive*
Lockhart, Michael D. *manufacturing executive*
Nast, Dianne Martha *lawyer*
Poser, Joan Rapps *artist, writer*
Rigas, John Nicholas *lawyer*
Shaw, Charles Raymond *journalist*
Shenk, Lois Elaine Landis *writer*
Steiner, Robert Lisle *retired language educator*
Taylor, Ann *human resources specialist, educator*
Veitch, Boyer Lewis *printing company executive*
Zeager, Lloyd *librarian*
Zimmerman, Donald Patrick *lawyer*

**Landenberg**
Ness, Norman Frederick *astrophysicist, educator, academic administrator*

**Langhorne**
Cohen, Fredric J. *pharmaceutical executive, consultant*
Heuer, Frederick August III *social studies educator*
Isensee, Paul Ralph *music educator, minister*
Neff, Amy Hancock *elementary school educator*

**Lansdale**
Bierman, Arnold *optometrist*
Fawley, John Jones *retired banker*
Hargens, Charles William III *electrical engineer, consultant*
Nolan, Joan Parmeter *librarian*
Strohecker, Leon Harry, Jr. *orthodontist*

**Lansdowne**
Geist, Lorraine Pinnelli *music educator, director*
Purcell, Mary Hamilton *speech educator*

**Laporte**
DiRado, Linda Marie *mathematician, educator*

**Latrobe**
Botsko, Michael Wayne *mathematics professor*
Cardoso, Carlos M. *metal products executive*
Greenfield, David W. *lawyer*
Maize, Mohamed Anis *physics professor*
Porembka, Michael Richard *assistant principal, supervisor*
Rhodes, Michael E. *biologist, educator*
Tambakeras, Markos I. *machine tool manufacturer*
Tourre, Marc Louis *music educator*
Towey, Jim (H. James Towey) *academic administrator, former federal official*
Will, James Fredrick *academic administrator, former steel company executive*

**Lawrenceville**
Castagnera, James Ottavio *lawyer, journalist*
Chua, Frank *researcher, educator*

**Lebanon**
Balthaser, Gerda Haas *elementary school educator*
Deysher, Paul Evans *retired management consultant*
Fox, Wayne Charles *music educator*

McMindes, Roy James *aggregate company executive*
Moss, Richard Spencer *communications executive*
Seyfert, Paul *social studies educator*

**Leesport**
Jackson, Eric Allen *philatelist*
Schmeck, Deborah M. *literature and language educator*

**Lehman**
Novrocki, Michael W. *secondary school educator*
Williams, Thomas Alan *elementary school educator, small business owner*

**Lemoyne**
Klein, Michael Elihu *physician*

**Levittown**
Henshaw, Jonathan Cook *retired manufacturing executive*
Lombardi, Michael *application developer*
Marable, Simeon-David *artist*
Walker, Patricia Ann Dixon *retired elementary school educator, real estate rehabilitator*
Zhu, Aiming *application developer*

**Lewisberry**
Smith, Bruce I. *state legislator*

**Lewisburg**
Aldrich, Robert Adams *agricultural engineer, consultant*
Candland, Douglas Keith *psychology professor*
Fernsler, John Paul *lawyer*
Huffines, Marion Lois *academic administrator, language and linguistics educator*
Jump, Chester Jackson, Jr. *clergyman, church official*
Kinnaman, Thomas Christopher *economics professor, researcher*
Laszewski, Ronald Thomas *college official*
Mitchell, Brian Christopher *academic administrator*
Muller, Riana Ricci *musician, educator*
Neuman, Nancy Adams Mosshammer *civic leader*
Payne, Michael David *English language educator*
Raymond, Timothy Michael *engineering educator*
Rote, Nelle Fairchild Hefty *management consultant*
Seybold, David James *artist*
Shapiro, Arthur Gilman *science educator*
Sojka, Gary Allan *biologist, educator, academic administrator*

**Lewistown**
Porpotage-Sigler, Marylou M. *academic administrator*
Varner, Vance Sieber *principal*

**Liberty**
Nelson, Thomas John *music educator, musician*

**Ligonier**
Mellon, Seward Prosser *brokerage house executive*
Pilz, Alfred Norman *manufacturing executive*

**Limerick**
Sickler, John J. *manufacturing executive*

**Lincoln University**
Benson, Heidi Lam *art educator*
Nelson, Ivory Vance *academic administrator*
Norris, Jo Anne Wareham *intervention specialist, consultant*
Nwachuku, Levi Akalazu *social sciences and behavioral studies educator*
Van Dover, James Kenneth *education educator*
Venerable, Grant Delbert, II, *chemist, educator, systems scientist*
Williams, Willie, Jr. *physicist, researcher*

**Line Lexington**
Kuehne, Tracy Elizabeth *music educator*

**Lititz**
Buccilla, Brenda Klugh *art educator*
Fulginiti, Todd E. *music educator*
Hartz, Brian David *physical therapist, educator, small business owner*
Hudelson, Judith Giantomass *elementary school educator*
McGlynn, James Francis *chemistry educator, chemical engineer*
Wilczak, Paul Francis *psychologist*

**Little Meadows**
Staby, Dorothy Louise *elementary school educator*

**Lock Haven**
Almes, June *retired education educator, librarian*
Dondong, Jia *nanoscience educator, physics professor*
Forbes, Edward John III *retired developmental psychologist, educator*
Story, Julie Ann *language educator*

**Loretto**
Jareb, Jerome *history professor, researcher*
Shipman, Donald George *academic administrator*

**Lower Gwynedd**
Pendleton, Robert Grubb *pharmacologist*

**Loysburg**
Stuckey, Ellen Mae *music educator*

**Lumberville**
Katsiff, Bruce *artist*

**Lykens**
Sultzbaugh, John Stephan *historian, educator*

**Lyon Station**
Breidegam, DeLight Edgar, Jr. *battery company executive*

**Macungie**
Moore, Joyce Kristina *financial planner, director*
Nenstiel, Susan Kisthart *fundraising professional*

Rubin, Arthur Herman *retired academic administrator*

**Malvern**
Bash, Tamela Sue *educational consultant*
Brighton, Ruth Louise *lay worker, educator*
Cameron, John Clifford *lawyer, health science association administrator*
Espe, Matthew J. *manufacturing executive*
Forese, James John *business machine company executive*
Liang, Jianming *computer scientist, researcher*
Liu, Don H. *lawyer*
Paul, Gerald D. *electronics executive*
Rice, David H. *medical products executive*
Rucker, Donald W. *emergency physician, educator, consultant*
Stetson, John Batterson, IV, *construction executive*
Zandman, Felix *electronics executive*

**Manheim**
Saylor, Carol Hannah *school system administrator, educator*

**Manns Choice**
Braendel, Douglas Arthur *hotel executive*

**Mansfield**
Benjamin, Woan-Jue Jane *education educator, researcher*
Davis, Scott Alan *chemistry professor*
Donahue, Martha *retired librarian*
Haner, Matthew S. *mathematics professor, statistician*
Loeschke, Maravene S. *academic administrator, theater educator*
Sternick, John Lewis *biology professor*

**Maple Glen**
Weaver-Stroh, Joanne Mateer *education educator, consultant*

**Marion Center**
Purdy, David Lawrence *medical products executive*

**Marshalls Creek**
Svoboda, Joanne Dzitko *artist, educator*

**Martinsburg**
Neff, Robert Wilbur *academic administrator, educator, minister*

**Mc Alisterville**
Milliken, Kevin David *music educator*

**Mc Donald**
Chambon, Mary Virginia *social studies educator*

**Mc Elhattan**
Garner, Charles William *retired educational administration educator, consultant*

**Mc Keesport**
Lodor, Marci Ann *dietitian*
Preuss, Mary Herge *Spanish educator*

**Mc Murray**
Brzustowicz, John Cinq-Mars *lawyer*
Celento, Florence M. *librarian*
Langenberg, Frederick Charles *manufacturing executive*
Sherry, John Sebastian *lawyer*

**Meadville**
Adams, Earl William, Jr. *retired economics professor*
Cable, Charles Allen *mathematician*
Dixon, Armendia Pierce *school program administrator*
Fait, Cinda Ruth McGill *elementary school educator*
Gilles, Bruce Carlson *civil engineer*
Steen, John *health policy company executive, consultant*

**Mechanicsburg**
Derr, William James *retired non-commissioned officer*
Eakin, J. Michael *state supreme court justice*
Feaser, Deborah Ellen *mathematics educator*
Gibbons, Miles Joseph, Jr. *foundation administrator*
Hoffman, Diane Mae *special education educator*
Juditz, Lillian Mickley *retired communications educator*
Ortenzio, Robert A. *health and medical products executive*
Ortenzio, Rocco Anthony *health facility administrator*
Owen, Tony Quinn *investment company executive, horse trainer*
Stouffer, Nancy Kathleen *publishing company executive*

**Media**
Barnett, Samuel Treutlen *consultant*
Blake, David Gordon *lawyer*
Brobeck, John Raymond *physiology educator*
Durham, James W. *lawyer*
Emerson, Sterling Jonathan *lawyer*
Ewing, Robert Clark *lawyer*
Garrison, Susan Kay *lawyer*
Garvin, Florence Ward *management consultant*
Heller, Richard Martin *lawyer, educator*
Hemphill, James S. *investment management executive, financial advisor*
Jackson, Katherine Church *retired elementary school educator, literature educator*
Kessler, Carol Farley *English language educator*
Li, Weiye *ophthalmologist, educator, biochemist*
Turner, Letitia Rhodes *artist*
Voltz, Sterling Ernest *physical chemist, researcher*

**Mendenhall**
Reinert, Norbert Frederick *lawyer, retired chemicals executive*
Stone, F. L. Peter *lawyer*

**Mercer**
DaCosta, Caroline Lee *small business owner*
Zellers, Robert Charles *materials engineer, consultant, speaker*

**Mercersburg**
Tompkins, Christopher Robin *director, educator*

**Merion Station**
Gillman, Derek A. *museum director, academic administrator*
Littell, Marcia Sachs *Holocaust and genocide studies professor*

**Middletown**
Walters, Marian R. *research administrator*

**Mifflinburg**
Miller, Mary Lynn *nurse*

**Mifflinville**
Farber, Phillip Andrew *retired biological and allied health sciences educator*

**Milford**
Le Guin, Ursula Kroeber *writer*
Reynolds, Edwin Wilfred, Jr. *retired secondary education educator*

**Milford Square**
Sewell, Gloriana *music educator*

**Mill Hall**
Klacik, Lora Anne *school psychologist*

**Millersville**
Hay, Teri B. *artist, educator*
Miller, Steven Max *humanities educator*

**Millerton**
Kipferl, Christiana A. *special education educator*

**Milton**
Kurtz, Dborah L. *science educator, department chairman*

**Monaca**
Chapin, John R. *communications educator*
Pinchot, Daniel J. *director*

**Monongahela**
Yovanof, Silvana *physician*

**Monroeville**
Furman, L. Robert *principal, music educator*
Read, Robert Allen *music educator*
Skolnick, Marilyn *civic worker*

**Montgomeryville**
Detwiler, Christine Wendler *special education educator*
Schmidt, William Max *management consultant, marketing executive*

**Montoursville**
Carpenter, Dennis Eugene *music educator*
Hunter, Corey Ryan *secondary school educator*

**Moon Township**
Alstadt, Lynn Jeffery *lawyer*
Lawson, John DuVal *communications educator*
Rabosky, Joseph George *engineering consulting company executive*

**Moosic**
Joyce, Patrick Francis *secondary school educator*

**Morgantown**
Dierwechter, David C. *retired elementary school educator, theater director*

**Morrisdale**
Yontosh, Sharlene Mary *principal*

**Mount Gretna**
Okamoto, Jeffrey Akira *psychiatrist*

**Mount Joy**
Lodde, Gordon Maynard *health physics consultant*

**Mount Pleasant**
Collins, Frederick George *music educator, secondary school educator*
Dangelo, Eugene Michael *elementary school educator*

**Mountainhome**
Buttz, Charles William *outdoor advertising executive*

**Muncy**
Temons, Mark Joseph *science educator*

**Murrysville**
Ferri, Karen Lynn *lawyer*
Maurer, Richard Michael *investment company executive*
Yang, Wen-Ching *chemical engineer*

**Nanticoke**
Donohue, Patricia Carol *academic administrator*

**Narberth**
Nathanson, Neal *virologist, epidemiologist, educator*
Strom, Brian Leslie *internist, educator*

**Natrona Heights**
Koharchik, Thomas David *music educator*

**Nazareth**
Bast, Kimberly Ann *social studies educator*
Haynes, Thomas Morris *philosophy educator*

**Nelson**
Kyofski, Bonelyn Lugg *retired education educator*

**Nescopeck**
Shultz, Jack Ellsworth *education educator*

**New Buffalo**
Cramer, John McNaight *lawyer*

**New Castle**
Blaskewicz, Nancy Jane *elementary school educator*
Sands, Christine Louise *retired English educator*
Zumpella, Thomas Joseph *music educator*

**New Cumberland**
Peters, Ralph Edgar *architectural firm executive, engineering executive*

**New Freedom**
Sedlak, Valerie Frances *retired English language educator, retired academic administrator*
Spicer, Barbara Jean Wentz *elementary school educator*

**New Holland**
Fanus, Pauline Rife *librarian*
Papadakis, Emmanuel Philippos *physicist, consultant*
West, Daniel Charles *dentist*

**New Hope**
Ecker, Sidney Wolf *urologist, consultant*
Raabe, Gerhard Karl *epidemiologist*
Sergey, John Michael, Jr. *investment company executive, consultant*

**New Kensington**
Jarrett, Noel *chemical engineer, researcher*
Kalavar, Jyotsna Mirle *education educator*
Wallace, Henry Jared, Jr. *lawyer*

**New Milford**
Burkett, Jeffrey O'Hara *music educator*

**New Oxford**
Martin, Sandra Ann *special education educator, writer*
Rohrbaugh, Nova R. *retired music educator*

**New Paris**
Stoner, Lois Carole *biology educator*

**New Tripoli**
Hess, Darla Bakersmith *cardiologist, educator*

**New Wilmington**
Bolger, Dorita Yvonne Ferguson *librarian*
Long, Kenneth Maynard *chemistry professor*
Moser, Jonathan R. *music educator*

**Newtown**
Booraem, Hendrik, V, *education educator, historian*
Brennan, Thomas John *city and state official, consultant, educator*
Duncan, Stephen Robert *elementary school educator*
Hoffman, Michael Bruce *music educator, composer*
Kardos, Mel D. *lawyer, educator*
Maholic, Julie Lynn *music educator, elementary school educator*
Nowak, Jerry (Gerald C. Nowak) *music educator, musician, writer*
Paghdiwala, Abid F *dentist*
Rao, Sudhakar *aerospace engineer, researcher*
Ross, Edwin William *rubber company executive*
Sheridan, John J. *musician, music educator*
Somers, Anne Ramsay *retired medical educator*
Zicherman, David L. *lawyer, educator, financial consultant*

**Newtown Square**
Benenson, James, Jr. *manufacturer*
Cooper, Charles Fisher *chemist, researcher*
Cordes, Eugene Harold *retired pharmacy and chemistry educator*
de Rivas, Carmela Foderaro *retired psychiatrist, retired health facility administrator*
Garthwaite, Thomas Leonard *medical officer*
Grey, Roger Allen *chemist, researcher*
Grubb, Gary S. *pharmaceutical executive*
Kendall, Robert Louis, Jr. *lawyer*
Lewis, James Earl *investor*
Mestre, Oscar Luis *financial consultant*
Murphy, Arthur Thomas *systems engineer, consultant*
Perrone, Nicholas *engineering company executive*
Staats, Dean Roy *retired reinsurance executive*

**Norristown**
Aman, George Matthias III *lawyer*
Biondi, Anthony *municipal official*
Britt, Earl Thomas *lawyer*
Devine, James I. *lawyer*
Rees, Thomas Dynevor *lawyer*
Steinberg, Arthur Irwin *periodontist, educator*

**North Versailles**
Winkleblech, Jerry A. *band director*

**North Wales**
Kim, Peter Sungbai *pharmaceutical research executive, educator, research and development company executive*

**Nottingham**
White, Richard Edmund *marketing executive*

**Oakmont**
Billings, David Arthur *music educator*

**Oaks**
Marland, Alkis Joseph *leasing company executive, computer scientist, educator, financial planner*
West, Alfred Paul, Jr. *financial services executive*

**Oil City**
Sabousky, Richard Anthony *adult education educator*

**Orefield**
Armor, John N. *chemical company scientist, consultant, research manager*

**Orwigsburg**
Mason, Joan Ellen *nurse*

**Oxford**
Hostert, Leona Teressa *librarian, researcher*

**Palmyra**
Moseley, Marc Robards *sales executive*

**Paoli**
Boehlke, Frederick John *history professor*
Burget, Dean Edwin, Jr. *plastic surgeon*
Denny, William Murdoch, Jr. *investment management executive*
Hermance, Frank S. *electronics executive*

**Pen Argyl**
Cortez, Rita *music educator*
Kovaleski, Diane Marie *secondary school educator*
Martocci, Lewis Nicholas III *writer*

**Penn Valley**
Newhall, John Harrison *retired business executive, management consultant*

**Pennsburg**
Shuhler, Phyllis Marie *physician*

**Perkasie**
Dillingham, Lee *social studies educator*
Ferry, Joan Evans *school counselor*

**Philadelphia**
Aaron, Kenneth Ellyot *lawyer*
Abramowitz, Robert Leslie *lawyer*
Adamany, David Walter *law and political science educator, former academic administrator*
Adawi, Nadia Sharon *energy executive*
Adetunji, Babatunde Abayomi *forensic psychiatrist*
Adler, Matthew *law educator*
Ajzenberg-Selove, Fay *physicist, researcher*
Akers, David *professional football player*
Albertini, William Oliver *retired telecommunications industry executive*
Alchin, John Reginald *cable company executive*
Alexander, Elmore Rosebur III *business educator, dean*
Alexander, William Herbert *business educator, former construction executive*
Alford, Larry P. *university librarian*
Allen-Castellitto, Anita LaFrance *law educator*
Allevi, Angela *pediatrician*
Altschuler, Steven M. *health facility executive, pediatrician, gastroenterologist*
Ammon, Gary D. *lawyer*
Ances, Beau M. *neurologist*
Anders, Jerrold P. *lawyer*
Anderson, Rolph Ely *finance educator*
Angel, Marina *law educator*
Angell, Mary Faith *federal magistrate judge*
Arce, A. Anthony *psychiatrist, educator*
Arem, Lawrence Jay *lawyer*
Armstrong, C. Michael *retired communications executive*
Armstrong, Clay *physiology educator*
Arnold, Lee *library director, archivist*
Asbury, Arthur Knight *neurologist, educator*
Austin, Regina *law educator*
Austrian, Robert *internist, medical educator, department chairman*
Auten, David Charles *lawyer*
Auten, Donald R. *lawyer*
Aversa, Dolores Sejda *educational administrator*
Avery, William Joseph *packaging manufacturing company executive*
Awad, George John *lawyer*
Azzolina, David Sean *librarian*
Babbel, David Frederick *finance and insurance educator*
Bachman, Arthur *lawyer*
Backstrom, C. Stephen *communications executive*
Badler, Norman Ira *computer and information science educator*
Bailin, Michael A. *foundation administrator*
Baker, Stephen C. *lawyer*
Baldwin, Cynthia Ackron *state supreme court justice*
Baltuch, Gordon Hirsh *neurosurgeon*
Banerji, Ranan Bihari *mathematics professor*
Bantel, Linda Mae *former museum curator, consultant*
Barchi, Robert Lawrence *clinical neurologist, neuroscientist, educator*
Barker, Clyde Frederick *surgeon, educator*
Barnett, Bonnie Allyn *lawyer*
Barnett, Jonathan *urban planner, educator, architect*
Barrett, John J., Jr., (John James Barrett Jr.) *lawyer*
Bartlett, Allen Lyman, Jr. *retired bishop*
Barton, Thomas J. *lawyer*
Baserga, Renato Luigi *pathology educator*
Bass, Aaron *school system administrator*
Bates, James Earl *academic administrator*
Battipaglia, Joseph Anthony *lawyer*
Baum, Stanley *radiologist, educator*
Baxt, William Gordon *medical educator*
Beachem, Michael T., IV, *academic administrator, counseling administrator*
Beck, Aaron Temkin *psychiatrist, educator*
Beck, John Robert *pathologist, information scientist*
Beck, Phyllis Whitman *lawyer, retired judge*
Beeman, Richard Roy *historian, educator*
Behrman, Jere Richard *economics professor*
Bell, Michael W. *insurance company executive*
Bennett, Amanda *editor*
Berger, David *lawyer*
Berger, Harold *lawyer, electrical engineer*
Berger, Lawrence Howard *lawyer*
Berkley, Emily Carolan *lawyer*
Berkman, Richard Lyle *lawyer*
Bernard, John Marley *lawyer, educator*
Bernheim, Daniel S. *lawyer*
Bernstein, Charles *poet, writer, educator*
Berry, Mary Frances *history professor, former federal agency administrator*

Bershad, Jack R. *retired lawyer*
Beyer, Aaron Jay *lawyer*
Bibbo, Marluce *physician, educator*
Bilaniuk, Larissa Tetiana *neuroradiologist, educator*
Bilgutay, Nihat Mustafa *engineering educator, associate dean*
Binder, David Franklin *lawyer, writer*
Black, Allen Decatur *lawyer*
Black, Creed C., Jr. *lawyer*
Black, Perry *neurological surgeon, educator*
Blank, Michael Bernard *psychologist*
Blavat, Jerry (Gerald Joseph Blavat) *television personality, actor*
Blaze, Matthew *computer science educator, researcher*
Block, Arthur R. *communications executive, lawyer*
Blumberg, Baruch Samuel *medical researcher, educator*
Blume, Fred *lawyer*
Blume, Marshall Edward *finance educator*
Boden, Guenther *endocrinologist*
Boggia, Eugene Stephen *lawyer*
Bogutz, Jerome Edwin *lawyer, educator*
Bonovitz, Sheldon M. *lawyer*
Booth, Anna Belle *accountant*
Bordogna, Joseph *engineering educator, former science foundation executive*
Borer, Edward Turner *investment banker*
Bortnick, Newman Mayer *research chemist*
Boss, Amelia Helen *lawyer, educator*
Bovaird, Brendan Peter *lawyer*
Bove, Alfred Anthony *medical educator*
Bower, John Arnold, Jr. *architect*
Bowman, Marjorie Ann *physician, educator*
Brady, Luther W., Jr. *radiologist, educator*
Brandt, Jennifer Anne *lawyer*
Breslow, Tina *public relations executive*
Bressler, Barry E. *lawyer*
Brier, Bonnie Susan *lawyer*
Brinster, Ralph Lawrence *biologist, educator*
Briscoe, Jack Clayton *lawyer*
Brookman, Marc D. *lawyer*
Brooman, David J. *lawyer*
Brown, Dave *professional sports team executive*
Brown, Denise Scott *architect, urban planner*
Brown, Lawrence David *statistics professor*
Brown, Stephen D. *lawyer*
Brown, William Hill III *lawyer*
Browne, Stanhope Stryker *lawyer*
Broytman, Vladislav I. *hygenist*
Brucker, Paul C. *academic administrator, physician*
Brunk, Samuel Frederick *oncologist*
Bryans, Henry S. *lawyer*
Buchholz, Carl M. *lawyer*
Buckwalter, Ronald Lawrence *federal judge*
Burbank, Stephen Bradner *law educator*
Burch, Francis Floyd *clergyman*
Burde, Howard Alan *lawyer*
Burdumy, Stephen T. *lawyer*
Burke, Brother Daniel *museum director, educator*
Burke, Stephen B. (Steve Burke) *communications company executive*
Burlingame, Gary Alfred *environmental scientist*
Burstein, Elias *physicist, researcher*
Butler, Marie Gladys *nursing educator*
Cades, Stewart Russell *lawyer, communications executive*
Calabi, Eugenio *mathematician, educator*
Calman, Robert Frederick *mining executive*
Calvert, Jay H., Jr. *lawyer*
Camp, Donald Eugene *experimental photographer, educator*
Canning, Douglas Arthur *pediatrician, urologist*
Cannon, John III *lawyer*
Capers, Gregg *secondary school educator, musician*
Caplan, Arthur Leonard *university program director, educator*
Carey, Arthur Bernard, Jr. *editor, columnist*
Carroll, Mark Thomas *lawyer*
Carven, John Winslow *priest*
Cashman, Wayne *professional athletics coach*
Casper, Charles B. *lawyer*
Cass, David *economist, educator*
Cassel, Christine Karen *physician*
Castille, Ronald D. *state supreme court justice*
Cawley, Michael J. *medical educator, pharmacist*
Cerundolo, Rosario *veterinarian, educator*
Chagares, Michael Arthur *federal judge*
Chang, Howard Fenghau *law educator, consultant*
Chanin, Bernard *lawyer*
Charney, Natalie J. *mental health services professional, educator, researcher*
Cheeks, Maurice Edward *professional basketball coach, retired professional basketball player*
Chen, Lan X. *physician, educator*
Cherken, Harry Sarkis, Jr. *lawyer*
Child, John Sowden, Jr. *lawyer*
Childress, Scott Julius *medicinal chemist*
Chimples, George *lawyer*
Chisum, Melvin J. *retired internist*
Christenbury, T. Daniel *lawyer*
Chrysikou, Evangelia G. *psychology professor*
Clark, John J. *economist, finance educator*
Clark, Peter S., II, *lawyer*
Clark, William H., Jr. *lawyer*
Clarke, Robert Earle (Bobby Clarke) *professional sports team executive*
Clarkin, John Francis *health care management executive*
Clauss, Peter Otto *lawyer*
Clearfield, Harris Reynold *physician*
Cline, Celeste Ann *primary school educator*
Clothier, Robert Clarkson *lawyer*
Coché, Judith *psychologist, educator*
Cohen, David Walter *academic administrator, educator, periodontist*
Cohen, Ira Myron *retired aeronautical and mechanical engineering educator*
Cohen, Johnathan Z. *mortgage company executive*
Cohn, Mildred *retired biochemist, retired educator*
Coleman, Gerald Charles *judge, law educator*
Coleman, Robert J. *lawyer*
Colli, Bart Joseph *lawyer*
Collings, Robert L. *lawyer*
Colman, Robert Wolf *hematologist, educator*
Colson, Rosemary *music educator*
Comisky, Hope A. *lawyer*

Congdon, Charles B. *lawyer*
Conn, Rex Boland, Jr. *pathologist, educator*
Connor, Bernadette Yvonne *retired writer*
Connor, Joseph Patrick III *lawyer*
Conway, John W. *manufacturing executive*
Cooney, J(ohn) Gordon, Jr. *lawyer*
Cooper, Edward Sawyer *cardiologist, internist, educator*
Cooper, Frank G. *lawyer*
Cooper, Richard Alan *hematologist*
Cooper, Richard Lee *newspaper editor, journalist*
Cooperman, Barry S. *academic administrator, chemist, educator*
Corzo, Miguel Angel *academic administrator*
Cotsarelis, George *dermatologist, educator*
Coutifaris, Christos *gynecologist, research scientist*
Cowles, Roger E. *computer consultant*
Cox, Roger Frazier *lawyer*
Coyne, Charles Cole *lawyer*
Cozen, Stephen Allen *lawyer*
Cramer, Harold *lawyer*
Crawford, James Douglas *lawyer*
Creedon, Dennis William *arts education administrator, consultant*
Criner, Gerard Joseph *pulmonologist, director*
Croisetiere, Jacques M. *chemicals executive*
Crumb, George Henry *composer, educator*
Cunningham, Jacqueline Lemmé *psychologist, educator, researcher*
Cunningham, Jessie Jerome *real estate investor, import/export company executive, entrepreneur, small business owner*
Daemmrich, Horst Sigmund *German language and literature educator*
Dagit, Charles Edward, Jr. *architect, educator*
Dalinka, Murray Kenneth *radiologist, educator*
Dalton, David Robert *chemistry professor*
Daly, John M. *surgeon, educator*
d'Amato, Thomas Andrew *thoracic surgeon*
Damsgaard, Kell Marsh *lawyer*
D'Angelo, Christopher Scott *lawyer*
D'Angio, Giulio John *radiologist, educator*
Danien, Elin C. *archaeologist, researcher*
Daryoush, Afshin Samimi *electrical engineer, educator*
Dasgupta, Indranil *physician, educator*
Daugherty, F(rancis) Mark *music educator, conductor, theater director*
Davey, Adam *gerontologist, researcher*
Davis, Alan Jay *lawyer*
Davis, Allen Freeman *history professor, writer*
Davis, Glenn Craig *psychiatrist*
Davis, Paige (Mindy Paige Davis) *television personality and host*
Days, Michael *editor*
de Cani, John Stapley *statistician, educator*
Delacato, Carl Henry *lawyer*
Delaney, Terence (Terry) P. *gas industry executive*
deLisle, Jacques *law educator*
DeLong, David G. *architect, urban planner, educator*
Del Raso, Joseph Vincent *lawyer*
Dennis, Andre L. *lawyer*
de Paulo, Craig J. N. *philosopher, educator*
Desjardins, Eric *retired professional hockey player*
Devlin, John Gerard *lawyer, writer*
Dewan, Vikram H. *zoological park administrator*
d'Harnoncourt, Anne *museum director, museum administrator*
Diamond, Paul Steven *federal judge, lawyer, educator*
Diaz, Magna M. *librarian*
Diaz, Nelson A. *lawyer*
Dichter, Marc Allen *physician*
Dichter, Mark S. *lawyer*
Diebold, Francis X. *economist, educator*
Di Falco, Gerard A. *artist*
Dinoso, Vicente Pescador, Jr. *physician, educator*
DiPalma, Joseph Rupert *pharmacology educator, dean*
Director, Stephen William *electrical and computer engineering educator, academic administrator*
DiTrolio, Joseph *controller*
Djerassi, Isaac *medical researcher*
Dobbs, Stanley *military officer, information quality engineer*
Donaldson, Thomas *finance educator*
Donnelly, Gloria Ferraro *university dean*
Donohue, James J. *lawyer*
Donohue, John Patrick *lawyer*
Dorfman, John Charles *lawyer*
Dougherty Buchholz, Karen *communications executive*
Douglas, Steven Daniel *immunologist, educator, director*
Drake, William Frank, Jr. *lawyer*
Driver, Robert Baylor, Jr. *opera company administrator*
Drosdick, John Girard *oil company executive*
Dubin, Leonard *lawyer*
Duffy, Seamus C. *lawyer*
Dunn, Linda Kay *physician*
Dunn, Mary Maples *academic administrator*
Dunphy, Fran *men's college basketball coach*
Dworetzky, Joseph Anthony *lawyer, city manager*
Dyson, Michael Eric *religious studies educator, writer*
Efstratiades, Anastasius *lawyer*
Ehrlich, George Edward *rheumatologist, consultant*
Eiberson, Jeffrey Lawrence *psychologist, consultant*
Eisen, Howard Joel *internist, researcher*
Eisenstein, Toby K. *microbiology professor*
Eiswerth, Barry Neil *architect, educator*
El-Sherif, Mahmoud A. *electrical engineering educator, engineering executive*
Englander, Sol Walter *biochemistry and biophysics educator, medical educator*
Erdmann, James Bernard *educational psychologist*
Esser, Carl Eric *lawyer*
Evan, William Martin *sociologist, educator*
Ewald, William Bragg III *law educator, philosopher*
Ey, Robert M. *law librarian*
Faberman, Austin S. *lawyer*
Fader, Henry Conrad *lawyer*
Fala, Herman C. *lawyer*
Falkie, Thomas Victor *mining engineer, mining executive*

Fegley, Kenneth Allen *systems engineering educator*
Feirson, Steven B. *lawyer*
Feldman, Arthur M. *cardiologist*
Feldman, Eric Adam *law educator, academic administrator*
Feninger, Claude *food service executive*
Fernandez, Happy Craven (Gladys Fernandez) *academic administrator*
Fickler, Arlene *lawyer*
Fiebach, H. Robert *lawyer*
Fielding, Allen Fred *oral and maxillofacial surgeon, educator*
Finkelstein, Claire *law educator*
Finkelstein, Joseph Simon *educator*
Finney, Graham Stanley *management consultant*
Fischer, Bruce G. *gas industry executive*
Fisher, Aron Baer *physiology educator*
Fisher, Robert *gastroenterologist, health facility administrator*
Fishman, Alfred Paul *physician*
Fitts, Donald Dennis *chemist, educator*
Fitts, Michael Andrew *dean, law educator*
FitzGerald, Garret Adare *medical educator*
Fitzpatrick, J. Michael *chemicals executive*
Flanagan, Joseph Patrick, Jr. *retired lawyer*
Floyd, Michael O'S. *lawyer*
Fodera, Leonard V. *lawyer*
Foo, Susanna *chef*
Forsberg, Peter *professional hockey player*
Fox, Renée Claire *sociology educator*
Frank, Barbara Balis *gastroenterologist, educator*
Frank, George Andrew *lawyer*
Frank, Harvey *lawyer, writer*
Frankel, Francine Ruth *political science professor*
Frankel, Sherman *physicist, educator*
Freeman, Ellen Wood *research professor*
Fretz, Deborah McDermott *oil industry executive*
Friedman, Harvey Michael *infectious diseases educator*
Fritton, Karl Andrew *lawyer*
Frucher, Meyer S. (Sandy Frucher) *stock exchange executive*
Fullam, John P. *federal judge*
Furth, John Jacob *molecular biologist, educator, pathologist*
Fusco, Richard *English literature educator*
Fussell, Paul *writer, literature educator*
Gadon, Steven Franklin *lawyer*
Gagné, Simon *professional hockey player, Olympic athlete*
Gaillard, Theodore Lee, Jr. *information technology manager, English educator*
Gaiser, Robert Raymond *obstetric anesthesiologist, educator*
Gandy, Sam *neurologist, neuroscientist, educator*
Gans, Samuel Myer *temporary employment service executive*
Garcia, Rudolph *lawyer*
Gardner, Timothy Joseph *surgeon, educator*
Garnier, Jean-Pierre *pharmaceutical executive*
Garonzik, Sara Ellen *stage producer*
Gartland, John Joseph *physician, writer*
Gatti, Leonard J. *communications executive*
Gavrin, Jonathan Robert *medical educator, internist*
Gelles, Richard James *sociology professor, psychology professor, academic administrator*
Genkin, Barry Howard *lawyer*
Gerner, Edward William *medical educator*
Giegengack, Robert *university administrator*
Gilbert, Charles *performing arts educator, writer*
Gillick, Patrick
Girard-diCarlo, David Franklin *lawyer*
Givens, Janet Eaton *writer*
Glandt, Eduardo Daniel *chemical engineering educator*
Glass, Dennis Robert *insurance company executive*
Glick, Jane Mills *biomedical researcher, educator*
Glick, John H. *oncologist, medical educator*
Glusker, Jenny Pickworth *chemist*
Godley, Joanne *city health department administrator*
Gogotsi, Yury *materials scientist, educator*
Goldberg, Joseph *lawyer*
Goldhamer, David J. *medical educator, researcher*
Goldstein, William Marks *lawyer*
Gonzalez-Scarano, Francisco Antonio *neurologist, virologist*
Goodenough, Ward Hunt *anthropologist, educator*
Goodman, Sidney *artist*
Goodman, Stephen Murry *lawyer*
Goodrich, Herbert Funk, Jr. *lawyer*
Goon, Arthur David *academic administrator, educator*
Gorberg, David J. *lawyer*
Gordon, Anne Kathleen *editor*
Gordon, Sarah Barringer *law educator*
Gould, Claudia *museum director*
Gowa, Andrew *investor, lawyer*
Goyette, Kimberly Ann *sociology professor*
Graffman, Gary *academic administrator, pianist, music educator*
Granger, Randy William *art educator, consultant*
Grant, M. Duncan *lawyer*
Grant, Richard W. *lawyer*
Grassie, William John *academic administrator*
Greenbaum, Matthew Jonathan *composer*
Greene, Hans *warehouse manager*
Greenstein, Jeffrey Ian *neurologist*
Gregory, Joseph F. *art gallery director, art educator*
Grove, David Lavan *lawyer*
Gueson, Emerita Torres *obstetrician, gynecologist*
Guillen, Mauro Federico *sociology and management educator*
Gupta, Rajiv Lochan *chemicals executive*
Gutmann, Amy *academic administrator, political science and philosophy educator*
Hack, Gary Arthur *dean*
Hackney, Sheldon *former federal agency administrator, history educator*
Hadjiliadis, Denis *physician*
Hahn, Steven *history professor, writer*
Haimm, Neil Keith *lawyer*
Haines, Clifford E. *lawyer*
Hairston, Harold B. *protective services official*
Haley, Vincent Peter *retired lawyer*
Halpern, Eric Franklin *university publishing director*

Hameka, Hendrik Frederik *chemist, educator*
Hamilton, Samuel C. *not-for-profit fundraiser*
Hamilton, Stephen David Derwent *lawyer*
Hammond, Benjamin Franklin *microbiologist, educator*
Han, Yilong *physicist, researcher*
Hangley, William Thomas *lawyer*
Hansen-Flaschen, John Hyman *medical educator, researcher*
Hanway, H. Edward *insurance company executive*
Harbater, David *mathematician*
Harkins, John Graham, Jr. *lawyer*
Harris, Judith E. *lawyer*
Harris, Raymond Jesse *retired federal official*
Harris, Rennie *choreographer*
Hart, Ann Weaver *academic administrator*
Harvey, Gregory Merrill *lawyer*
Harvey, John Adrianne *psychologist, educator, pharmacologist, researcher*
Hatch, Denny (Alden Denison) *publishing executive, writer*
Haviland, Bancroft Dawley *lawyer*
Hayden, Yvonne Meddling *retired accountant, small business owner*
Hayes, John Freeman *architect*
Hemphill, John Lindsay III *administrative assistant*
Henisz, Witold Jerzy *social sciences educator*
Henrich, William Joseph, Jr. *lawyer*
Hickok, D. Alicia *lawyer*
Hindelang, Thomas Joseph *finance educator, dean*
Hine, Thomas *writer*
Hirschmann, Ralph Franz *chemist*
Hitchcock, Ken *professional hockey coach*
Hoelscher, Robert James *lawyer*
Hoffman, Alan Jay *lawyer*
Hofmann, Thomas W. *petroleum company executive*
Hogan, James D. *bank executive*
Holman, Larry Dean *retired healthcare administrator*
Horton, Van H. *military officer, priest, writer*
Horwitz, Eric M. *radiation oncologist*
Hosalkar, Harish Sadanand *pediatrician, orthopedist, surgeon, consultant*
Houshmand, Ali A. *academic administrator*
Houstoun, Feather O'Connor *state official*
Howard, David Miles *lawyer*
Howard, Ryan *professional baseball player*
Hua, Xianxin *cell and cancer biology educator*
Hunter, James Austen, Jr. *lawyer*
Iglewicz, Boris *statistician, educator*
Ingolfsson-Fassbind, Ursula G. *music educator*
Intemann, Robert Louis *physics professor, researcher*
Ischiropoulos, Harry *medical researcher, educator*
Iverson, Allen Ezail *professional basketball player*
Jackson, Harold *journalist*
Jackson, Laird Gray *geneticist, internist, educator*
Jacobs, Jonathan Mark *parliamentary consultant*
Jaffe, Richard Louis *psychiatrist*
Jaron, Dov *biomedical engineer, educator*
Jeffcoat, Marjorie K. *dean, dental educator*
Jenkins, Marc Delano *music educator*
Jessup, Mariell *physician, director*
Jiang, Hao *pharmacologist*
Jimenez, Sergio A. *internist, educator, rheumatologist*
Johnson, Joseph Eggleston III *physician, educator*
Johnson, Shari *elementary school educator*
Johnston, Jason Scott *law educator*
Jones, Robert Jeffries *lawyer*
Jordan, V. Craig *endocrine pharmacologist, educator*
Jordan, Will James *sociologist, educator*
Josephs, Babette *legislator*
Joyner, J(ames) Curtis *judge*
Kadison, Richard Vincent *mathematician, educator*
Kahn, James Robert *lawyer*
Kaier, Edward John *lawyer*
Kaiser, Larry Robert *thoracic surgeon*
Kaiser, Roy *artistic director*
Kaji, Akira *microbiology scientist, educator*
Kang, Ju-Seop *medical educator, consultant, medical researcher*
Kaplan, Barbara Jane *retired city planner*
Kaplinsky, Alan S. *lawyer*
Kassner, Andrew Charles *lawyer*
Katherine, Robert Andrew *chemicals executive*
Katz, Leo *law educator*
Kauffman, Leon A. *internist, educator*
Kaufman, Russel Eugene *hematologist, oncologist*
Kaye, Edward Michael *physician, neurogeneticist*
Kazazian, Haig Hagop, Jr. *pediatrician, researcher, educator*
Kearse, Jevon *professional football player*
Kefalides, Nicholas Alexander *physician, educator*
Kelley, William Nimmons *physician, educator, science administrator, dean*
Kelly, Robert F. *federal judge*
Kennedy, David William *otolaryngologist, medical educator, medical administrator*
Kessler, Alan Craig *lawyer*
Kiefer, J. Richard, Jr. *retired corporate executive*
Kiernan, Edward Philip *lawyer*
Kim, John Y. *insurance company executive*
Kimberly, John Robert *management educator, consultant*
King, Barry M. *museum program director, artist*
Kiniry, William F., Jr. *lawyer*
Kinsella, Thomas *poet*
Klasko, Herbert Ronald *lawyer, educator, writer*
Klausner, Samuel Zundel *sociologist, educator*
Klein, Howard Bruce *lawyer, law educator*
Klein, Julia Meredith *freelance journalist*
Klein, Lawrence Robert *economist, educator*
Klein, Michael Lawrence *research chemist, educator*
Kline, Thomas Richard *lawyer*
Knauer, Georg Nicolaus *philologist*
Knoll, Michael Steven *law educator*
Knopp, Marvin Isadore *mathematics professor*
Knudson, Alfred George, Jr. *medical geneticist*
Koc, Lorraine K(iessling) *lawyer*
Kopp, Charles Gilbert *lawyer*
Koprowski, Hilary *microbiologist, educator*
Kotabe, Masaaki *finance educator*
Kraeutler, Eric *lawyer*
Kraft, Amber Dawn *education program developer*
Kreimer, Seth F. *law educator, lawyer*
Krekstein, Michael Harry *lawyer*

Sugrue, Thomas J. *history professor, social sciences educator*
Suh, Byungse *medical educator*
Sulyk, Stephen *retired archbishop*
Summers, Anita Arrow *finance educator*
Summers, Clyde Wilson *law educator*
Summers, Robert *economics professor*
Suplee, Dennis Raymond *lawyer*
Sutherland, L(ewis) Frederick *food products executive*
Suzuki, Jon Byron *medical educator, periodontist, microbiologist*
Swain, Clifford H. *lawyer*
Sweet, James M. *lawyer*
Szautner, Christian Andreas *lawyer*
Taney, Francis Xavier, Jr. *lawyer*
Tannen, Richard Laurence *nephrology educator*
Tansy, Martin F. *dean*
Tasman, William Samuel *ophthalmologist, educator*
Tegtmeyer, Jordan Michael *financial analyst*
Temin, Michael Lehman *lawyer*
Tepper, H. Marc *lawyer*
Terry, John Joseph *transportation investor*
Testa, Joseph R. *cytogeneticist*
Thomas, Janet Y. *political science professor, researcher*
Thompson, Craig B. *physician*
Tiger, Ira Paul *retired lawyer*
Tileston, Jackie *artist, educator*
Tooker, John Phillip *internist, educator, medical association administrator*
Torg, Joseph Steven *orthopaedic surgeon, educator*
Tourtellotte, Charles Dee *internist, rheumatologist, educator*
Trainer, Nancy Rogo *architect, planner*
Trojanowski, John Q. *medical educator, health facility administrator*
Trulear, Harold Dean *minister, theological educator, social researcher*
Tuan, Kailin *management consultant, educator*
Tucho, Admasu Etafa *education educator*
Tucker, Anita Lynn *science educator*
Turetken, Ozgur *information scientist, educator*
Tüzün, Erdem *neurologist, consultant*
Utley, Chase *professional baseball player*
Vaira, Peter Francis *lawyer*
Van Arsdalen, Keith Norman *urologist*
Vanarsdall, Robert Lee, Jr. *orthodontist, educator*
vanBemmelen, Paul S. *surgeon, educator*
van Rhyn, Jacqueline J. *curator*
Velazquez, Omaida Caridad *vascular surgeon, research scientist*
Venturi, Robert *architect*
Vetri, Marc *chef*
Vetter, Victoria L. *pediatric cardiologist, educator*
Vitek, Vaclav *materials scientist*
Vitez, Michael *reporter*
Voet, Donald Herman *biochemist, educator, writer*
Volgin, Denys V. *medical researcher*
Vredenburgh, Judy *youth organization executive*
Wachman, Marvin *retired academic administrator*
Wachter, Michael L. *law and finance educator*
Wachter, Susan Melinda *finance educator, educator*
Wadden, Thomas Anthony *psychologist, educator*
Wajert, Sean Peter *lawyer*
Wales, Walter D. *physicist, researcher*
Walker, Allen Lyon *engineer*
Walker, Douglas C. *banker*
Wallace, Anthony Francis Clarke *anthropologist, educator*
Wallace, Emily Mitchell *writer, editor, educator*
Walter, William G. *consumer products company executive*
Walters, Christopher Kent *lawyer*
Wang, Jiongjiong *neuroscientist, educator*
Warner, Deborah Courtney *artist, educator*
Warren, Christopher Collins *professional football player*
Wax, Amy Laura *law educator*
Webb, William Yerick *lawyer*
Webber, Chris, III, (Mayce Edward Christopher Webber) *professional basketball player*
Webber, Ross Arkell *management educator*
Weil, Jeffrey George *lawyer*
Wein, Alan Jerome *urologist, educator, researcher*
Weiner, Mark Gordon *medical educator*
Weinstein, David *lawyer, educator*
Weisberg, Morris L. *retired lawyer*
Weitz, Howard Hy *cardiologist, educator*
Welch, Charles Edgar, Jr. *retired English language educator, writer*
Weller, Elizabeth Boghossian *child and adolescent psychiatrist*
Wellington, Ralph Glenn *lawyer*
Welsh, Diane M. *federal judge*
Westbrook, Brian *professional football player*
Whitaker, Linton Andin *plastic surgeon*
White, Howard D. *information science educator*
White, Nicholas John *musician, director, composer*
Whiteside, William Anthony, Jr. *retired lawyer*
Wickstrom, Eric *biophysical chemist, educator*
Wiener, Ronald Martin *lawyer*
Wild, Richard P. *lawyer*
Wiley, James Dee *retired history and biology educator, national park service ranger*
Wilkinson, Signe *cartoonist*
Willet, E. Crosby (Everett Crosby Willet) *artist*
Willi, Steven Matthew *physician, educator, researcher*
Williams, Sankey Vaughan *health services researcher, internist*
Winkler, Gail Caskey *historian, writer*
Winkler, Jeffrey D. *chemist*
Winston, Flaura K. *engineering researcher*
Wint, Dennis Michael *museum director*
Wittels, Barnaby Caesar *lawyer, writer*
Wivel, Nelson Auburn *physician, medical researcher, educator*
Wolfe, John Hall *medical researcher, educator, consultant*
Wolff, Deborah H(orowitz) *lawyer*
Woods, Deirdre *information technology executive*
Woodside, Lisa Nicole *humanities educator*
Woosnam, Richard Edward *venture capitalist, lawyer*
Wright, Barbara Clare *business librarian*
Wright, Minturn Tatum III *retired lawyer*
Wrobleski, Jeanne Pauline *lawyer*

Wu, Hong *pathologist*
Yang, Shu *materials scientist*
Yanoff, Myron *ophthalmologist*
Yaros, Constance Greenberg *painter, sculptor*
Yaruss, Howard Seth *lawyer*
Yohn, William H(endricks), Jr. *federal judge*
Young, Donald Stirling *clinical pathology educator*
Young, Robert Crabill *medical researcher, science administrator, internist*
Zderic, Stephen Anthony *urologist, surgeon*
Zhang, Ruifeng *engineering educator*
Ziegler, Donald Robert *accountant*
Zuberi, Tukufu *sociologist, educator*
Zuckerman, Brian David *lawyer*
Zuckerman, Marvin *retired psychologist*
Zurakowski, Tamara Lee *gerontological nurse practitioner, nursing educator*
Zweiman, Burton *allergist, immunologist, educator*

### Phoenixville

Brundage, Russell Archibald *retired data processing executive*
Hanlon, Barbara Jean *family and consumer sciences educator*
Lukacs, John Adalbert *historian, retired educator*
McClure, A. Glenn *education educator, department chairman*

### Pipersville

Block, Caryn S. *composer*
Erickson, Edward Leonard *biotechnologist, consultant*
McNutt, Richard Hunt *manufacturing executive*
Sigety, Cornelius Edward *small business owner*

### Pitcairn

Rose, Robert Didier *neurophysiologist*

### Pittsburgh

Abbott, Kevin Charles *lawyer*
Ahn, Luis von *computer science educator, computer scientist*
Allen, Rachel Lorey *lawyer*
Allen, Thomas E. *obstetrician, gynecologist*
Amara, Susan *neuroscientist*
Ambrose, Donetta W. *federal judge*
Amemiya, Shigeru *science educator*
Anderson, Scott Richard *geologist, consultant*
Anthony, Edward Mason *linguistics educator*
Apone, Carl Anthony *journalist*
Armstrong, Richard *museum director, curator*
Aronson, Mark Berne *retired lawyer, advocate*
Artz, John Curtis *lawyer*
Asher, Sanford Abraham *chemist, educator*
Atwood, Charles W., Jr. *pulmonologist, researcher*
Baer, Max *state supreme court justice*
Balas, Edith *art historian, educator*
Balas, Egon *mathematician, educator*
Balazs, Kevin *conservator*
Ban, Janet F. *music educator*
Bardyguine, Patricia Wilde *dancer, performing company executive*
Barkus, Bruce E. *health products executive*
Barry, Herbert III *psychologist, educator*
Bartley, Burnett Graham, Jr. *oil industry executive*
Basinski, Anthony Joseph *lawyer*
Becherer, Richard John *architecture educator*
Beck, Paul A. *lawyer*
Belda, Alain J. P. *metal products executive*
Bender, Charles Christian *retail home center executive*
Berenato, Agnus McGlade *women's college basketball coach*
Berkman, Louis *steel company executive*
Bernt, Benno Anthony *entrepreneur, investor*
Berry, Guy Curtis *polymer science educator, researcher*
Bhatt, Bankim Ashok *endocrinologist, educator*
Biegler, Lorenz Theodor *chemical engineering educator*
Biondi, Manfred Anthony *physicist*
Bissoon, Cathy *lawyer*
Black, Samuel Wade *curator*
Bleier, Michael E. *lawyer, director*
Blenko, Walter John, Jr. *lawyer*
Bloom, William Millard *furnace design engineer*
Blum, Eva Tansky *lawyer*
Blumstein, Alfred *urban and public affairs educator*
Bodine, William Beekman, Jr. *museum director*
Booker, Daniel I. *lawyer*
Boswell, William Paret *lawyer*
Bothner-By, Aksel Arnold *chemist*
Boyce, Doreen Elizabeth *foundation administrator, educator*
Branstetter, Lee Gilbert *economics professor*
Braun, Thomas W. *dean, academic administrator*
Brauner, Ronald Allan *theology studies educator*
Brendel, John S. *lawyer*
Brent, David A. *psychiatrist, medical educator*
Brosky, John G. *retired judge*
Brown, David Ronald *lawyer*
Brownlee, David A. *lawyer*
Brustein, William Irving *sociology educator*
Buchanan, Bruce G. *computer scientist, educator*
Buchanan, Mary Beth *prosecutor*
Bunch, Charles E. *manufacturing executive*
Burger, Herbert Francis *retired advertising agency executive*
Burgess, David Lowry *artist*
Burkoff, John Michael *law educator*
Busquets, Miguel Antonio *ophthalmologist*
Caginalp, Gunduz *mathematician, educator, researcher*
Cagney, William Robert *psychologist*
Cahouet, Ann P. *lawyer*
Calabrisi, Robert R. *health facility administrator, educator*
Cameron, Douglas E. *lawyer*
Candris, Aris C. *lawyer*
Cappy, Ralph Joseph *state supreme court chief justice*
Carbo, Toni (Toni Carbo Bearman) *information scientist, educator*
Cardenes, Andres Jorge *musician, educator*
Carlson, Brent *information technology executive*
Caroselli, William R. *lawyer*
Carr, Walter James, Jr. *research physicist, consultant*
Carr, Winifred Walker *artist, historian*

Casasent, David Paul *electrical engineer, educator, data processing executive*
Cassidy, William Arthur *geology and planetary science educator*
Chang, Thomas S. *radiologist*
Charap, Stanley Harvey *electrical engineering educator*
Cheever, George Martin *lawyer*
Cho, Sung K. *education educator*
Choset, Howie *engineering educator, researcher*
Choyke, Wolfgang Justus *physicist*
Clack, Jerry *classics educator*
Cohen, Bernard Leonard *physicist, researcher*
Cohill, Maurice Blanchard, Jr. *federal judge*
Cohon, Jared L. *academic administrator*
Colen, Frederick Haas *lawyer*
Collins, Bobby McManus, II, *dental educator*
Coltman, John Wesley *physicist*
Coney, Aims C., Jr. *lawyer, labor-management negotiator*
Connors, Eugene Kenneth *lawyer, educator*
Constant, Louay *policy analyst*
Conti, Joy Flowers *judge*
Cooley, Cynthia Furber *artist*
Cooper, Thomas Louis *lawyer*
Cotchen, J. Kevin *metallurgical engineer, writer*
Cowan, Barton Zalman *lawyer*
Cowher, Bill (William Laird Cowher) *professional football coach*
Crosby, Sidney *professional hockey player*
Cruz, Robyn Flaum *research scientist*
Curry, Nancy Ellen *psychologist, psychoanalyst, educator*
Dabrishus, Michael John *librarian*
Damianos, Sylvester *architect, sculptor*
Damico, David A. *lawyer*
Daniel, Robert Michael *lawyer*
Das, Phani Bhushan *thoracic surgeon*
Davis, Larry E. *academic administrator*
Davis, Lewis U., Jr. *lawyer*
Davis, Otto Anderson *economics professor*
Dawes, Robyn Mason *psychology professor*
Dawson, Mary Ruth *curator, educator*
Debski, Richard E. *medical educator*
DeForest, Walter Pattison III *lawyer*
DeGroat, William Chesney *pharmacology educator*
DeKosky, Steven Trent *neurologist*
Delano, Jonathan William *lawyer, journalist*
Demchak, William S. *corporate financial executive*
Demmler, John Henry *retired lawyer*
Dempsey, Jerry Edward *retired service company executive*
DeNinno, David L. *lawyer*
Desai, Niranjan A. *chemical engineer*
Desiree, Laura *dancer*
Detre, Thomas *psychiatrist, educator*
DeWalt, Bill *museum director*
Diamond, Gustave *federal judge*
DiMatteo, Tizana *physics professor*
Dixit, Balwant Narayan *pharmacology and toxicology educator*
Doft, Bernard Harvey *ophthalmologist*
Donahue, John Francis *investment company executive*
Donnelly, Thomas Joseph *lawyer, director*
Doty, Robert Walter *lawyer*
Dougherty, Charles John *academic administrator*
Drawbaugh, Daniel *information technology executive, biomedical engineer*
Drescher, Seymour *historian, educator, writer*
Druckenmiller, Stanley F. *investment company executive*
Druzdzel, Marek Jozef *information systems educator, researcher*
Dugan, John F. *lawyer*
Dunlop, Scott Graham *lawyer*
Dunn, Kenneth B. *dean*
Duquesnoy, Rene J. *medical educator, consultant*
Dzombak, David Adam *environmental engineering educator*
Eaton, Joseph W. *sociology educator*
Eckert, Jean Patricia *elementary school educator*
Ehrenwerth, David Harry *lawyer*
Ehrlich, Garth David *molecular biologist*
Einhorn, Jerzy *internist, endocrinologist, consultant*
Ellsworth, Laura E. *lawyer*
Emmerich, Werner Sigmund *physicist, educator*
Evans, Bruce Dwight *lawyer*
Faneca, Alan *professional football player*
Fararo, Thomas John *sociologist, educator*
Fawcett, David B. III *lawyer*
Feingold, David Sidney *microbiology and biochemistry educator, researcher*
Feller, Robert Livingston *chemist, art conservation scientist*
Fernstrom, John Dickson *psychiatry educator, researcher*
Fine, Milton *hotel company executive, lawyer*
Fireman, Philip *pediatrician, allergist, immunologist*
Fischhoff, Baruch *psychologist, educator*
Fisher, Bernard *surgeon, educator*
Fisher, D. Michael *federal judge*
Fisher, Edwin R. *pathologist*
Fitzgerald, Judith Klaswick *federal judge*
Flaherty, John Paul, Jr. *chief justice emeritus*
Flechtner, Harry Marshal *law educator*
Flinn, Michael James *lawyer*
Fontes, Paulo A. *surgeon, educator*
Fox, Debra L. *educational association administrator, business owner*
Frank, Alan I W *manufacturing executive*
Frank, Ronald William *lawyer*
Franklin, Kenneth Ronald *diversified financial services company executive, consultant*
Friday, Gilbert Anthony, Jr. *pediatrician*
Frolik, Lawrence Anton *law educator, lawyer, consultant*
Gale, Robert Lee *retired literature educator, critic*
Geeseman, Robert George *lawyer*
Geibel, Sister Grace Ann *university president*
Gennaula, Charles Paul *family practice physician*
George, John Anthony *health corporation executive*
Gerard, Leo W. *labor union executive*
Gerber, Murry S. *gas, oil and utilities executive*
Gerjuoy, Edward *physicist*
Getz, Jan Mason *announcer, educator*

Gibson, Samuel Norris *educational association administrator, retired clergyman*
Giel, James Arthur, Jr. *employee benefits consultant*
Glaser, Robert *psychology professor*
Goldberg, Mark Joel *lawyer*
Goldstein, Bernard David *public health service officer, educator*
Goldstein, Donald Maurice *historian, educator*
Gollin, Susanne Merle *cell biologist, researcher*
Gomez, Roberto Onofre *physicist, consultant*
Greciano, Sandra Eames *voice educator*
Gu, Zhaoyang *finance educator*
Guadagnino, Frank T. *lawyer*
Gulley, Joan Long *banker*
Gupta, Anil K. *philosophy professor*
Gurtin, Morton Edward *mathematics professor*
Guyaux, Joseph C. *corporate financial executive*
Hackett, Mary J. *lawyer*
Haggerty, Gretchen R. *accounting and finance executive*
Haley, Roy W. *finance company executive*
Halpern, Richard I. *lawyer*
Hansen, Stephen Christian *banker*
Hardesty, Robert Lynch *surgeon, educator*
Harrell, Edward Harding *wine festival executive*
Harris, Ann Birgitta Sutherland *art historian*
Harrison, Eric Jay *construction executive, consultant, artist*
Harrold, Ronald Thomas *research scientist*
Harshman, Richard J. *metal products executive*
Harth, Sidney *musician, educator*
Hartman, Ronald G. *lawyer*
Hartner, John George *language educator*
Harty, James Quinn *lawyer*
Harvey, J. Brett *energy executive*
Hassey, L. Patrick *metal products executive*
Hatfull, Graham F. *microbiologist, educator*
Hearn, Fil *architectural history professor emeritus*
Heath, David Clay *mathematics professor, consultant*
Heckler, Frederick Roger *plastic surgeon*
Heilman, Marlin Stephen *medical products executive*
Heitzenroder, Wendy Roberta *elementary school educator*
Hellman, Arthur David *law educator, consultant*
Hendrickson, Chris Thompson *civil and environmental engineering educator, researcher*
Herberman, Ronald Bruce *medical association administrator, immunologist*
Herring, David John *law educator*
Herrington, Howard Ray *artist*
Hershey, Dale *lawyer, educator*
Hershey, Nathan *lawyer, educator*
Hewitt, Thomas Francis *hotel executive*
Hicks, Wendell *history professor, political scientist, publishing executive*
Hill, John Howard *retired lawyer*
Hillenbrand, David M. *museum administrator*
Hillman, Henry Lea *investment company executive*
Hitt, Leo N. *lawyer, educator*
Hoburg, James Frederick *electrical engineering educator*
Hoglund, J. David *architectural firm executive*
Hollingsworth, Samuel Hawkins, Jr. *bassist*
Hollinshead, Earl Darnell, Jr. *lawyer*
Hollis, Ralph L. *engineering educator*
Holsinger, Candice Doreen *lawyer, accountant*
Holzner, Burkart *retired sociologist, educator*
Horowitz, Carole Spiegel *landscape contractor*
Hull, John Daniel, IV, *lawyer*
Humphrey, Watts Sherman *information technology executive, writer*
Hunker, Jeffrey *dean*
Huntington, James Cantine, Jr. *retired equipment manufacturing company executive*
Hurnyak, Christina Kaiser *lawyer*
Ijiri, Yuji *finance educator*
Ismail, Yahia Hassan *dentist, educator*
Janis, Allen Ira *retired physicist, educator*
Jannetta, Peter Joseph *neurosurgeon, educator*
Jefferson, Joseph Murray *banker*
Jenkins, Georgann Klaus *librarian*
Jeyabalan, Arundhathi *obstetrician, gynecologist*
Jimenez, Joseph *management executive*
Johnson, Robert Alan *lawyer*
Johnson, William R. *food products executive*
Johson, Michael Pennington *finance educator, educator*
Jones, Craig Ward *retired lawyer*
Jones, Elizabeth Winifred *biology professor*
Jones, James M. *lawyer*
Jordan, Angel Goni *electrical and computer engineering educator*
Jordan, Gregory B. *lawyer*
Josey, E(lonnie) J(Unius) *librarian, retired state agency administrator*
Joyner, Claude Reuben, Jr. *cardiologist, educator*
Kalis, Peter John *lawyer*
Kamlet, Mark *provost*
Kanade, Takeo *science educator, director*
Kane-Gill, Sandra Lucille *medical educator*
Keeling, Kenneth Augustus, Sr. *music educator*
Kelly, Robert P. *bank executive*
Kenrick, Charles William *lawyer*
Kerber, Frank John *retired diplomat*
Ketter, David Lee *lawyer*
Khosla, Pradeep Kumar *engineering educator*
Kiger, Robert William *botanist, researcher, science historian, educator*
Kilkeary, Kevin P. *hospitality executive*
Kim, Yongbok *physicist*
King, Elaine A. *curator, art historian, critic*
King, Maxwell E. P. *foundation administrator*
King, Robert Alan *lawyer*
King, William Richard *business educator, consultant*
Klatzky, Roberta Lou *psychologist, educator*
Klett, Edwin L. *lawyer*
Knox, Charles Graham *lawyer*
Kochanek, Patrick Michael *pediatrician, educator*
Koedel, Robert Craig *minister, historian, educator*
Kriebel, Charles Hosey *management sciences educator*
Krishann, Ramayya *information scientist, educator*
Kuehm, Julie K. *nurse, educator*
Kupfer, David J. *psychiatry professor*
Kydland, Finn E. *economics professor*
LaJohn, Lawrence Anthony *research scientist*

Krell-Morris, Cheri Lee *psychologist*
Rhoads, Michael Dennis *sales executive*

**Rydal**
Boreen, Henry Isaac *computer company executive*
Fernberger, Marilyn Friedman *not-for-profit developer, consultant, volunteer*
Heebner, Albert Gilbert *retired economist, retired educator, retired bank executive*
Johnson, Waine Cecil *dermatologist, educator*
Reese, Francis Edward *retired chemical company executive, consultant*

**Sadsburyville**
Gellman, Gloria Gae Seeburger Schick *marketing professional*

**Saegertown**
Ralph, NancyJo *retired music educator*

**Saint Davids**
Bertsch, Frederick Charles III *finance company executive*
Denenberg, Herbert Sidney *journalist, lawyer, educator, retired state official*
Sheftel, Roger Terry *merchant banker*
Smalley, Christopher Joseph *pharmaceutical company professional*

**Saint Marys**
Johnson, J. M. Hamlin *manufacturing executive*

**Saint Peters**
Detterline, Milton E., Jr. *minister*

**Sandy Lake**
Lengauer, Mary Irene *elementary school educator*

**Sayre**
Bentley, Dianne H. Glover *minister, consultant*
Moody, Robert Adams *neurosurgeon*

**Schnecksville**
Labbiento, Julianne Marie *mathematics professor*
Schillow, Ned William *mathematics professor*

**Schuylkill Haven**
Couch, Stephen Robert *sociologist, educator*
Evans, Christopher Jay *music educator*
Sarno, Patricia Ann *biology educator*

**Schwenksville**
Zucker, Barbara J. *artist, educator*

**Scottdale**
Lee, John Lawrence, Jr. *educational administrator*

**Scranton**
Blewitt, Thomas Michael *chief federal magistrate judge*
Brandreth, Elizabeth Anne *library director*
Burke, Henry Patrick *lawyer*
Conaboy, Richard Paul *federal judge*
De Celles, Charles Edouard *theologian, educator*
Eckersley, Richard Laurence *accountant*
Haggerty, James Joseph *lawyer*
Kosik, Edwin Michael *federal judge*
Lawhon, Patricia Patton *literature and language professor, writer educator*
Lynett, William Ruddy *publishing executive, broadcast executive*
Marino, Thomas A. *prosecutor, lawyer*
Marx, David Earl *chemistry professor, consultant*
McKenna, Ann K. *nutritionist, educator*
Nealon, William Joseph, Jr. *federal judge*
O'Malley, Carlon Martin *judge*
Panuska, Joseph Allan *retired academic administrator*
Parente, William Joseph *political science professor*
Passon, Richard Henry *retired academic administrator, language educator*
Shaffern, Robert William *history professor*
Vanaskie, Thomas Ignatius *federal judge*
West, Daniel Jones, Jr. *health care consultant, educator*
Yamanouchi, Midori *social sciences educator*
Zaydon, Jemille Ann *language educator, communications educator*

**Selinsgrove**
Lemons, L. Jay *academic administrator*
Rousu, Matthew C. *economics professor*
Thomforde, Christopher Meredith *minister*
Viker, Erik *theater educator*

**Sewickley**
Bly, James Charles, Jr. *finance company executive*
Bouchard, James Paul *metal products executive*
Fells, Charles Dayton *civil engineer, educator*
Jehle, Michael Edward *financial advisor, lawyer*
Swann, Lynn Curtis *sportscaster, former professional football player*
Thorbecke, Willem Henry *manufacturing executive, consultant*

**Shamokin Dam**
Connolly, Elma Troutman *artist, muralist, art gallery owner*

**Sharon**
Kovac, Shirley Ann *retired elementary school educator*

**Shippensburg**
Basler, Linda Gerber *retired elementary school educator*
Bej, Emil *retired dean*
Cart, Jon Robert *music educator, musician*
Ceddia, Anthony Francis *university administrator*
Collier, Duaine Alden *manufacturing and distribution company executive*
France, Olin Kenneth, Jr. *psychologist*
Hale, Robert L. *psychologist, educator*
Kalist, David E. *economics professor*
Reber, Vera Blinn *history professor*

**Shiremanstown**
Nesbit, William Terry *small business owner, consultant*

**Shohola**
Hess, Judith A. *secondary school educator*

**Sidman**
Coco, Samuel Louis *music educator, musician, composer*

**Sinking Spring**
Bausher, Verne C(harles) *retired bank executive*

**Slippery Rock**
Dailey, David P. *computer scientist, educator*
Mraz, Mark *education educator, researcher*
Mukherjee, Pracheta *management educator, researcher, consultant*
Smiley, Laura Cicely *theater educator, performing company executive*

**Solebury**
Anthonisen, George Rioch *sculptor, artist*
Cross, Robert William *lawyer, venture capitalist*
Valentine, H. Jeffrey *legal association executive*

**Somerset**
Kline, Eva Jane *library services administrator, educator*
Nair, Velupillai Krishnan *cardiologist*

**Souderton**
Hoeflich, Charles Hitschler *banker*
Rosenberger, Janet Thuma *retired elementary school educator*

**South Canaan**
Herman, *archbishop, head of Orthodox Church in America*

**South Park**
Lotze, Barbara *retired physicist*

**South Williamsport**
Ogurcak, Janice L. *museum director, educator*

**Southampton**
Bendiner, Robert *writer, editor*
Gniewek, Debra Lyman *school librarian, consultant*
Goldstein, Scott M. *ophthalmologist, surgeon*

**Southeastern**
Rassbach, Herbert David *marketing executive*
Zlotolow-Stambler, Ernest *real estate executive, architectural executive*

**Spring City**
Britcher, Michael *music educator*
Mayerson, Hy *lawyer*

**Spring House**
Payn, Clyde Francis *technology company executive*
Reitz, Allen Bernard *organic chemist*
Rosoff, William A. *lawyer*
van Steenwyk, John Joseph *healthcare plan consultant*

**Spring Mills**
Songer, Susan Kay *secondary school educator*

**Springfield**
Heath, Michael R. *physical education educator*
Maclay, Donald Merle *retired lawyer*
Mirman, Merrill Jay *physician, surgeon*

**State College**
Albright, Gifford Harry *retired architectural engineering educator, consultant*
Barnoff, Robert Mark *civil engineering educator*
Book, Edward Raymond *retired trade association administrator*
Boone, Tracy Marie *mathematics professor*
Brault, Gerard Joseph *French language educator*
Brown, John Lawrence, Jr. *eletrical engineering educator*
Byrom, Fletcher Lauman *chemical manufacturing company executive*
Coppersmith Fredman, Marian Ungar *magazine publisher*
Dupuis, Victor Lionel *retired curriculum and instruction educator*
Foderaro, Anthony Harolde *nuclear engineering educator*
Garrett, Steven Lurie *physicist*
Ginoza, William *former biophysics educator*
Goldschmidt, Arthur Eduard, Jr. *historian, educator, writer*
Grimes, Dale Mills *physics and electrical engineering educator*
Haas, John C. *architect*
Hettche, L. Raymond *engineering educator, retired research scientist*
Huck, John Lloyd *pharmaceutical executive*
Isenberg, Ann Marie *psychologist*
Katok, Anatole *mathematics professor*
Lamb, Robert Edward *retired diplomat, retired professional society administrator*
Lane, Jill Lyza *instructional systems educator, researcher*
Link, Phoebe Forrest *education educator, writer, social worker, poet*
Madjid, A. Hamid *retired science educator*
McKibbin, William Jeffrey *management consultant*
Olson, Donald Richard *mechanical engineering educator*
Phillips, Janet Colleen *retired educational association administrator, editor*
Redford, Donald Bruce *historian, archaeologist*
Remick, Forrest Jerome, Jr. *former university official*
Robinett, Betty Wallace *linguist, educator*
Schaie, K. Warner (Klaus Warner Schaie) *human development and psychology educator*
Schmalstieg, William Riegel *retired Slavic languages educator*
Shaikh, Nazrul Islam *industrial engineer, researcher*
Sinha, Sunil K. *engineer, educator*
Subler, Edward Pierre *advertising executive*
Swanson, David Carl *engineering educator, researcher*

**Wilson, Keith B.** *rehabilitation educator*
Xu, Jinchao *mathematics professor*

**Steelton**
Zimmerman, Connie Ann *public administrator*

**Strasburg**
Bell, Kurt Robert *archivist*
Lindsay, George Carroll *former museum director*
Morton, D. Holmes *physician*

**Strattanville**
Taylor, Kristie Leigh *performing arts educator, actor*

**Stroudsburg**
Abbruzzese, John A., Jr. *psychologist, retired administrator, educator*

**Sugarloaf**
Goldman-Price, Irene Carolyn *language educator*
Waldron, Theodore Charles *physician*

**Sunbury**
Ely, Donald J(ean) *retired clergyman, secondary school educator*
Mills, William R. *food products executive*
Rich, Norman S. *food service executive*
Weis, Robert Freeman *supermarket company executive*

**Susquehanna**
Purkayastha, Arindam *surgeon*

**Swarthmore**
Bilaniuk, Oleksa Myron *physicist, researcher*
Bloom, Alfred Howard *academic administrator, educator*
Carey, William Bacon *pediatrician, educator*
Devin, Lee (Philip Lee Devin) *dramaturg, author*
Elman, Gerry Jay *lawyer*
Field, Dorothy Maslin *minister*
Frost, Jerry William *religious studies educator, history professor, retired library director, researcher*
Gilbert, Scott Frederick *biologist, educator, author*
Hungerford, Constance Cain *art educator*
Kaufman, Antoinette Dolores *information technology manager*
Keith, Jennie *anthropology educator, academic administrator, writer*
Kelemen, Charles F. *computer science educator*
Krendel, Ezra Simon *systems and human factors engineering consultant*
Krizek, Edwin John *marketing professional*
Marecek, Jeanne *psychologist, educator*
Moreland, Robert Lyle *minister*
Morgan, Kathryn Lawson *retired historian, educator*
North, Helen Florence *classicist, educator*
O'Connell, Virginia Adams *science educator*
Ostwald, Martin *retired classicist*
Pasternack, Robert Francis *chemistry professor*
Redden, Taylor Tilghman *musician*

**Swiftwater**
Brooks, Joyce Maria *music educator*
Kpamegan, Eloi P. *statistician, researcher*

**Tamaqua**
Featro, Susan Mary *language educator, music educator*

**Temple**
Denaro, Anthony Thomas *psychiatrist*
Stump, Richard Carl *environmental services administrator, consultant*

**Thorndale**
Hodess, Arthur Bart *cardiologist*
Ryan, Francis William *history educator, coach, dean*

**Throop**
Moran, Leslie Mason *music educator*

**Tioga**
Sullins, Ken *mathematics, science and computer science educator*

**Titusville**
Altomare, Erica Von Scheven *psychologist*
Campasino, Ellen Marie *elementary school educator*
Tress, Nancy Barsic *biologist, educator*

**Tobyhanna**
Lapidus, Arnold *mathematician, educator*

**Trevose**
Quinn, Holli Jo Bardo *social worker, educator, librarian*
Totaro, Samuel C., Jr. *lawyer*

**Tunkhannock**
Zellner, Ryan Matthew *music educator*

**Tylersport**
Raub, Donald Wilmer *minister, author*

**Union City**
Thomas, Paul Milton *retired science educator*

**Uniontown**
Coldren, Ira Burdette, Jr. *lawyer*

**Unionville**
De Marino, Donald Nicholson *federal agency administrator, diversified financial services company executive*

**University Park**
Alexander, Stephon Haigh-Solomon *physics professor, musician*
Allcock, Harry R. *chemistry professor*
Andrews, George Eyre *mathematics professor*
Antle, Charles Edward *statistics professor*
Askov, Eunice May *adult education educator*
Ayala, Luis F. *engineering educator*
Azmy, Yousry Youssef *computational scientist*

Badding, John Victor *chemistry professor*
Barlow, Jesse Louis *computer scientist, educator*
Barnes, Hubert Lloyd *geochemistry educator*
Blackadar, Alfred Kimball *meteorologist, educator*
Bose, Nirmal Kumar *electrical engineer, mathematics educator*
Brenchley, Jean Elnora *microbiologist, researcher, science administrator*
Brockman, William S. *librarian*
Buskirk, Elsworth Robert *physiologist, educator*
Cahir, John Joseph *meteorologist, educator, educational administrator*
Castleman, Albert Welford, Jr. *physical chemist, educator*
Chan, Moses Hung Wai *physicist, researcher*
Chehab, Ghassan R. *civil engineer, educator*
Coleman, Michael Murray *polymer science educator*
Cross, Leslie Eric *electrical engineering educator*
Davids, Norman *engineering educator, researcher*
De Jong, Gordon Frederick *demography professor, director*
Duda, John Larry *chemical engineering educator*
Dugda, Mulugeta Tuji *education educator*
Dutton, John Altnow *meteorologist, educator*
Eaton, Nancy Ruth Linton *librarian, dean*
Ebitz, David MacKinnon *art historian, educator, museum director*
Eckhardt, Robert Barry *biological anthropologist, geneticist, geneticist, educator*
Elliott, Herschel *agricultural engineer, educator*
Enis, Charles Richard *accountant, educator*
Fedoroff, Nina Vsevolod *research scientist, consultant, educator*
Ford, Donald Herbert *psychologist, educator*
Fowler, H(oratio) Seymour *retired science educator*
Garoian, Charles Richard *artist, educator*
Garrison, Barbara Jane *chemistry professor*
Geiger, Roger Lewis *historian, educator*
Grenfell, Bryan Thomas *biology professor*
Grewal, Rajdeep *marketing professional, educator*
Gurgevich, Elise *academic administrator*
Guthrie, Helen A. *nutritionist, educator, dietician*
Halsey, Martha Taliaferro *Spanish language educator*
Hamburger, Susan *librarian*
Hammond, J. D. *retired academic administrator*
Hedges, Stephen Blair *biology professor, researcher*
Hogan, J. Michael *humanities educator*
Hogg, Richard *process engineer*
Holl, John William *engineering educator*
Hosler, Charles Luther, Jr. *meteorologist, educator*
Howell, Benjamin Franklin, Jr. *geophysicist, educator*
Humphrey, Craig Reed *social studies educator*
Irwin, Mary Jane *engineering educator*
Jackman, Lloyd Miles *chemistry professor*
Jeong, Jae-Weon *architectural engineer, educator*
Joyce, William Leonard *librarian*
Kabel, Robert Lynn *chemical engineering professor*
Kadir, Djelal *literature educator*
Klein, Philip Alexander *economist*
Knott, Kenneth *industrial engineering educator, consultant*
Lai, Chieh-Ping *engineer, researcher*
Lima, Robert *language educator*
Lindberg, Darla V. *architect, educator*
Liu, Peng *information scientist, educator*
Liu, Yongjun *researcher*
Liu, Zi-Kui *materials engineer, educator*
Ma, Xiaoliang *research scientist*
Mahan, Gerald Dennis *physicist, researcher*
Manbeck, Harvey B. *agricultural and biological engineer, educator*
Mann, Michael E. *physicist, educator, climatologist*
Mayers, Stanley Penrose, Jr. *public health service officer, educator*
McCormick, Barnes Warnock *aerospace engineering educator*
McKeown, James Charles *finance educator, consultant*
Mentzer, John Raymond *electrical engineer, educator*
Moore, H. Louis *agricultural economics education*
Mor, Gopal Kumar *materials scientist, researcher*
Muhlert, Jan Keene *art museum director*
Naydan, Michael M. *foreign language educator*
Newsome, Lee Ann *anthropologist, educator*
Olian, Judy D. *dean*
Paterno, Joe (Joseph Vincent Paterno) *college football coach*
Peck, Andrew *psychologist, educator*
Preston, Stephanie Danette *science educator, researcher*
Price, Mitch *biology professor*
Ramani, Raja Venkat *engineering educator*
Ray, William Jackson *psychologist*
Roy, Della Martin *materials science educator, researcher*
Roy, Rustum *citizen scientist*
Scanlon, Andrew *structural engineering educator*
Semali, Ladislaus *education educator*
Snavely, Loanne *library director*
Spanier, Graham Basil *academic administrator*
Stern, Robert Morris *gastroenterologist, psychologist, researcher*
Stinson, Richard Floyd *retired horticulturist, educator*
Stout, Leon James *archivist, librarian*
Thompson, William, Jr. *engineering educator*
Tittmann, Bernhard Rainer *engineering science and mechanics educator*
Todd Copley, Judith A. *engineering educator*
Vannice, M. Albert *chemical engineering professor, researcher*
Varghese, Oomman Kulathinthekkethil *materials scientist, researcher*
Vrentas, James Spiro *chemical engineering professor*
White, William Blaine *geochemist, researcher*
Winograd, Nicholas *chemist*
Witzig, Warren Frank *nuclear engineer, educator*
Wysk, Richard A. *engineering educator, researcher*
Yoder, Edgar Paul *education educator*
Zabel, Diane Marion *school librarian*

Zatsiorsky, Vladimir Moiseevich (Michailovich) *biomechanics educator, researcher*
Zhang, Qiming *engineering educator, researcher*

**Upper Black Eddy**
Sherr, Ronald Norman *artist*

**Upper Darby**
Crouse, Carol K. Mavromatis *elementary school educator*
Fearnley, C. J. *computer company executive*
Hudiak, David Michael *academic administrator, lawyer*
Kahler, Nancy J. *music educator, director*
Leiby, Bruce Richard *secondary school educator, writer*
Samten, Losang *spiritual leader, artist*

**Upper Saint Clair**
Raymond, Bruce Allen *medical association administrator*

**Valley Forge**
Bogle, John Clifton *investment company executive*
Brennan, John Joseph *mutual fund company executive*
Dachowski, Peter Richard *manufacturing executive*
Erb, Robert Allan *physical scientist*
Hilyard, James Emerson *manufacturing executive*
LaBoon, Lawrence Joseph *human resources specialist, consultant*
Medley, Alex Roy *executive minister*
Mesher, John R. *lawyer*
Miller, Betty Brown *freelance writer*
Phelizon, Jean Francois *finance company executive*
Sprague, William Douglas *lawyer*
Wright-Riggins, Aidsand F. III *religious organization executive*

**Vandergrift**
Lizik, Andrea Noreen *elementary school educator*

**Verona**
Bruno, Louis Vincent *principal*

**Villanova**
Beck, Robert Edward *computer scientist, educator*
Bergquist, James Manning *history professor*
Bersoff, Donald Neil *lawyer, educator, psychologist*
Dobbin, Edmund J. *academic administrator*
Donohue, Peter M. *priest, theater educator, director*
Edwards, John Ralph *retired chemist, educator*
Fitzpatrick, M. Louise *dean, nursing educator*
Foight, Michael Patrick *librarian, archivist*
Friend, Theodore Wood III *foundation executive, historian, writer*
Haynor, Patricia Manzi *nursing educator, consultant*
Heitzmann, Ray *education educator, athletic coach*
Helmetag, Charles Hugh *foreign language educator*
Hunt, John Mortimer, Jr. *classical studies educator*
Johannes, John Roland *political science professor, dean*
Langran, Robert Williams *political scientist, educator*
Ludwig, Oliver George *chemistry professor*
Malik, Hafeez *political science professor*
Maule, James Edward *law educator*
McLaughlin, Philip VanDoren, Jr. *mechanical engineering educator, researcher, consultant*
Monck, Mary C. *science educator*
Murphy, John Francis *law educator, consultant*
Nawrocki, David Norman *finance educator*
Norton, Douglas Evatt *mathematician, educator*
Papaefthymiou, Georgia C. *physicist, educator*
Phares, Alain Joseph *physicist, researcher*
Sargent, Mark A. *dean, law educator*
Scheffler, Stuart Jay *lawyer*
Tomlinson, J. Richard *retired engineering services company executive*
Way, Thomas Paul *computer scientist, educator, magician*
Wright, Jay *men's college basketball coach*
Zearfoss, Herbert Keyser *retired lawyer*

**Wallingford**
Adamiec, Jean Kraus *retired advertising executive*
Cook, Harvey Carlisle *law enforcement official*
Morrison, Donald Franklin *statistician, educator*
Severdia, Anthony George *chemistry researcher*

**Warminster**
Ciabarra, Louise *secondary school educator, medical/surgical nurse*
Ciao, Frederick J. *school system administrator, educator*
Gamarnik, Moisey Yankelevich *solid state physicist*
Hull, Lewis Woodruff *manufacturing executive*
Vietri, Linda Smith *gifted and talented educator*

**Warrendale**
O'Donnell, James V. *apparel executive*
Rumbaugh, Max Elden, Jr. *professional society administrator*

**Warrington**
Ward, Hiley Henry *journalist, educator*

**Washington**
Erdner, Jon W. *small business owner, securities trader*
Haring-Smith, Tori *academic administrator*
Kastelic, Robert Frank *aerospace transportation executive*
Klitz, Timothy S. *psychologist, educator*
Lerner, William C. *lawyer*
Mc Cune, Barron Patterson *retired federal judge*
Posner, David S. *lawyer*
Richman, Stephen I. *lawyer*

**Washington Boro**
Snyder, John Jacob *researcher*

**Washington Crossing**
Clevenger, Roy Edward *credit and collections manager*

Roche, Gail Connor *editor*
Wells, Charles *sculptor, printmaker*

**Wayne**
Annenberg, Leonore A. *foundation administrator*
Burton, Betty Jane (B.J. Burton) *playwright*
Burton, Noelle M. *clinical psychologist, psychoanalyst*
Carroll, Robert W. *retired management consultant*
Conde, Cristobal I. *computer company executive*
DePiano, Richard John *medical products executive*
Emmens, Matthew *research and development company executive*
Etris, Samuel Franklin *trade association research consultant*
Fabbri, Anne R. *critic, curator*
Garrison, Guy Grady *librarian, educator*
Gross, Lawrence Alan *lawyer*
Krutsick, Robert Stanley *retired science administrator*
Lefevre, Thomas Vernon *retired utilities executive*
Lief, Harold Isaiah *psychiatrist*
Mann, James L. *computer company executive*
Rubley, Carole A. *state legislator*
Rush, James Edward *retired information scientist*
Salinas, Eliseo *research and development company executive, researcher, psychiatrist*
Sims, Robert John *financial planner*
Stayton, William Ralph *psychologist, educator*
Thelen, Edmund *research executive*
Wilson, Bruce Brighton *lawyer, retired transportation executive*
Wilson, James Lawrence *retired chemical company executive*
Yoskin, Jon William, II, *insurance company executive*
Yost, R. David (David Yost) *pharmaceutical executive*

**Waynesboro**
Coles, Robert Nelson, Sr. *religious organization administrator*
Cryer, Theodore Hudson *ophthalmologist, educator*
Martin, Harold G. *engineering consultant*

**Waynesburg**
Maguire, Mildred May *chemistry professor, researcher*

**Weatherly**
Sipler, Barbara Marie *secondary school educator*

**Wellsboro**
Driskell, Lucile G. *artist*

**West Chester**
Albert, Kristen Ann *music educator*
Babcock, Charles Witten, Jr. *lawyer*
Baxter, Joan Anna Patten *technical writer*
Blasiotti, Robert Vincent *accountant, consultant*
Bove, Patrice Magee *elementary school educator*
Brasfield, Andrew McCollum *artist*
Burton, John Bryan *music educator*
Cinelli, Bethann *school health educator*
Cox-Klaczak, Karen Michelle *finance educator, computer company executive*
Czako, Alan H. *human resources specialist, benefits compensation analyst*
Dunlop, Edward Arthur *computer company executive*
Ewing, Joseph Neff, Jr. *retired lawyer*
Gadsby, Robin Edward *chemicals executive*
Gallagher, Terrence Vincent *editor*
Gingery, Philip Alvah *music educator*
Gougher, Ronald Lee *language educator*
Griffith, Edward *judge*
Griffiths, Jeffrey W. *electronics executive*
Handzel, Steven Jeffrey *accountant*
Hanna, Colin Arthur *management consultant, political organization worker, consultant*
Heaps, Marvin Dale *retired food services company executive*
Heston, Thomas J. *historian, educator*
Hipple, Walter John *language educator*
Kaufman, Daniel J. *lawyer*
Kletzien, Sharon Benge *language educator, department chairman*
Lamb, William H. *lawyer, former state supreme court justice*
Mahoney, William Francis *editor, writer*
Meystel, Michael A. *Internet company executive*
Murray, Lawrence *management consultant*
Pennington, Robert Edgar *music educator*
Tetl, Louis Nicholas *lawyer*
Zlotowski, Martin *psychologist*

**West Conshohocken**
Boenning, Henry Dorr, Jr. *investment banker*
Lenfest, Harold FitzGerald *former cable television executive, lawyer*
Mullen, Eileen Anne *human resources executive*
Newman, Sandra Schultz *state supreme court justice*
Odell, Herbert *lawyer*
Teillon, Louis Pierre, Jr. *lawyer*
Templeton, John Marks, Jr. *retired pediatric surgeon, foundation administrator*
Worley, Richard B. *financial consultant*

**West Grove**
Allman, Margo Hutz *sculptor, painter*
Olson, Leroy Calvin *retired educational administration educator*
Snow, James Byron, Jr. *otolaryngologist, research administrator, educator*

**West Lawn**
Kovary, Loraine Theresa *language educator*

**West Mifflin**
Ardash, Garin *mechanical engineer*
Migliorato, Lynne Gyurisin *elementary school educator*
Skonsky, Caroline Treschow *marriage and family therapist*

**West Point**
Buckland, Barry Christopher *chemical engineer*

Choi, Dennis W. *pharmaceutical executive, neurologist, educator*
Farber, Leonid *materials scientist*
Fleming, Norman Patrick *information scientist*
Schaffner, Carolyn Marie *research administrator, biologist*
Trepakova, Elena S. *research scientist*
Yang, Zhi-Qiang *chemist*

**Westfield**
Walker, Bonnie Lou *social studies educator*

**Wexford**
Bossart, Paul Nathaniel, Jr. *geologist, geophysicist, consultant*
Stefan, Todd Robert *music educator*
Stover, Richard L. *investor*

**Whitehall**
Anonia, Francis *music educator*
O'Connor, M. Carol *private school educator*

**Wilkes Barre**
Baranoski, Joseph Thomas *music educator*
Casale, Alfred Stanley *thoracic and cardiovascular surgeon*
Daniel, Longyhore S. *pharmacist, educator*
Hayes, Wilbur Frank *retired biology professor*
Hepp, John Henry, IV, *historian, lawyer*
Holtzman, Marc Lawrence *catalog chain executive*
Horoszy, Albert John *mathematics educator*
Legg, Timothy James *nursing educator*
Lindemann, George L. *gas industry executive*
McHale, Maureen Bernadette Kenny *controller*
Mech, Terrence Francis *library director*
O'Donnell, Catherine Rose *lawyer*
O'Hara, Thomas J. *priest, academic administrator, educator*

**Williamsburg**
Lewis, David P. *music educator*

**Williamsport**
Albert, Eric *engineering educator*
Carlucci, William Philip *lawyer*
Garner, Ronald A. *automotive technology educator*
Jones, John E. III *judge*
Largen, Joseph *retail executive, purchasing agent*
Loyer, Milton Wayne *statistician, archivist*
Martin, Thomas John *pediatrician, sports medicine physician*
McClure, James Focht, Jr. *federal judge*
McDonald, Peyton Dean *brokerage house executive*
Muir, Malcolm *federal judge*
Rosebrough, Carol Belville *cable television company executive*
Saka, Tuna *technology educator*
Trometter, Mary Gionta *chef, educator*
Weaver, Lucille Mae *retired elementary school educator, radiological technician*
Wittman, Brittany Lyn *design educator*

**Willow Grove**
Asplundh, Christopher B. *tree service company executive*
Burtt, Anne Dampman *special education educator*
Ohama, Gary Louis *dental ceramist*
Schiffman, Louis F. *management consultant*
Suer, Marvin David *architectural consultant*

**Willow Hill**
Dorand, Freda J. *music educator*

**Willow Street**
Blevins, William Edward *management consultant*
Jones, Joseph Louis *retired manufacturing executive*
Keiser, Paul Harold *retired hospital administrator*
Wesbury, Stuart Arnold, Jr. *health science association administrator, educator*
Yrigoyen, Charles, Jr. *retired church denomination executive*

**Windber**
Lee, James Alan *writer, editor*

**Worcester**
Curtis, Alton Kenneth *film company executive, clergyman*

**Wormleysburg**
Grass, Alexander *retail executive*

**Wyulusing**
Kusmierz, Ann Marie Dorothy *elementary school educator*

**Wyncote**
Koppel, Ross *private investigator, sociology professor*

**Wyndmoor**
Brown, Gary Christian *ophthalmologist, director*
Pfeffer, Philip Elliot *biophysicist*

**Wynnewood**
Alter, Milton *retired neurologist*
Anyanwu, Chukwuma Uchenna *clinical pharmacist, biomedical researcher*
Belinger, Harry Robert *retired food service executive*
Bernfeld, Gerald E. *editor, writer, retired nursing educator*
Camp, Kimberly N. *museum administrator, artist*
Cohen, Gordon M. *chemist, executive*
Dunton, Charles Joseph *gynecologist, oncologist*
Frankl, William Stewart *cardiologist, educator*
Kenton, Edgar Jackson III *neurologist*
Kowey, Peter R. *medical educator*
Marks, Gerald *surgeon, educator*
Meyers, Mary Ann *foundation administrator, consultant, writer*
Prendergast, George C. *cancer biologist, researcher*
Robinson, Robert L. *retired diversified financial services company executive, lawyer*
Rosefsky, Jonathan Benensohn *pediatrician*
Rosen, Gerald Harris *physicist, consultant, educator*

Rubin, Leonard Sidney *physiologist, educator, researcher*
Samuels, Louis Edward *cardiothoracic surgeon*
Sider, Ronald J. *theology educator, author*
Wachs, Saul Philip *religious studies educator*

**Wyomissing**
Doherty, Edmond John *retired librarian*
Hildreth, Eugene A. *physician, educator*

**Yardley**
Breitenfeld, Frederick, Jr. *retired educational consultant, broadcast executive*
Fraser, David William *epidemiologist*
Gilmour, D(avid) James *financial analyst, systems analyst*
Hochreiter, Joseph Christian, Jr. *engineering company executive*
Huret, Barry S. *marketing professional, consultant*
Minter, Philip Clayton *retired communications company executive*
Newsom, Carolyn Cardall *management consultant*
Newsom, John Harlan *physician*
Soultoukis, Donna Zoccola *library director*
Stanley, Gerard Francis *language educator*
Weaver, William Clair, Jr., (Mike Weaver) *human resources development executive*

**Yatesville**
Roberts, Anne Marie Gabrielle *chemistry educator*

**York**
Addison, Brian Michael *lawyer*
Alcon, Sonja L. *retired medical social worker*
Andrews, Jennifer Lee *secondary school educator*
Bartels, Bruce Michael *health facility administrator*
Buckel, Mark Andrew *biologist, educator*
Caffrey, Lynn Regina *education educator*
Chervil, Rudy *mechanical engineer*
Davis, Jane G. *lawyer*
Day, Ronald Richard *retired financial executive*
Foster, Timothy Edward *educational association administrator*
Grossman, Robert Allen *transportation executive*
Grumbacher, Tim *retail executive*
Hoffmeyer, William Frederick *lawyer, educator*
Horn, Russell Eugene *engineering executive, consultant*
Horn, Russell Eugene, Jr. *engineering executive*
Kennedy, Christopher Robin *ceramics engineer, director*
Kornblatt, David *corporate financial executive*
Kunkle, Gary K., Jr., (Gerald K. Kunkle) *dental products company executive*
Livingston, Pamela A. *corporate image and marketing management consultant*
Lloyd, June Burk *retired librarian, archivist*
Musone, Amy Lynn *elementary school educator*
Rebert, Jephrey Lee *urban planner, musician*
Rhoads, Jonathan Evans, Jr. *surgeon, medical educator*
Rosen, Raymond *health facility executive*
Sier, Ruth Elaine *music educator*
Thomas, Tracey Williams *researcher*
White, Timothy Paul *brokerage house executive*
Wiles, Lessley Decker *foundation administrator, preservationist*
Wiles, William Wharton *retired federal government official*
Wise, Bret W. *chemical company executive*
Wise, Charles William III *financial advisor*
Worley, Richard Alan *music educator*
Yourist, Sheldon Eric *product designer*

**Youngstown**
Palmer, Arnold Daniel *professional golfer*

**Youngsville**
Montgomery, Christina Lynn *music educator*

**Youngwood**
Duvall, Hollie Jean *music educator*
Henry, Candy A. *education educator, writer*

**Zelienople**
Efaw, Cary Ross *manufacturing executive*

**RHODE ISLAND**

**Barrington**
Carpenter, Charles Colcock Jones *internist, educator*
Deakin, James *writer*
Mihaly, Eugene Bramer *diversified financial services company executive, consultant*
Soutter, Thomas Douglas *retired lawyer*

**Bristol**
Bosco, Susan M. *management professor*
Braver, Adam *writer, educator*
Connell, James Burke *museum director*
Danzberger, Alexander Harris *retired chemical engineer, consultant*
Flanders, Robert G., Jr. *lawyer, educator, legal association administrator*
Hendrix, John Shannon *architecture educator*
McMullen, Susan Taylor *librarian*

**Charlestown**
Rohm, Robert Hermann *sculptor, educator*
Ungaro, Joseph Michael *newspaper publishing executive, consultant*

**Chepachet**
Jubinska, Patricia Ann *ballet instructor, choreographer, artist, anthropologist, archaeologist*

**Coventry**
Chait, Andrea Melinda *psychologist, behavior analyst*
Schweinsburg, Jane Duberg *librarian*

**Cranston**
Alston, Jametta O. *lawyer*
Burge, David Russell *concert pianist, composer, music educator*
Lachance, Philip Roland *music educator*

Langlois, Michael A. *financial consultant*
Parravano, Amelia Elizabeth (Amy Beth Parravano) *recording industry executive*
Perna, Marie Immaculate *retired physical education educator*
Tammelleo, A. David *lawyer, editor, publisher*
Vavala, Domenic Anthony *research scientist, educator, retired military officer*
Wilson, Valerie Petit *health science association director*

### Cumberland
Rossi, Joseph Anthony *film and television make-up artist, educator*

### East Greenwich
Carlson, Shawn Eric *physicist, educator*
Dence, Edward William, Jr. *lawyer, bank executive*
Hunter, Garrett Bell *investment banker*

### East Providence
Spina, Douglas John *priest, educator*
Tripp, Michael Windsor *accountant*

### Foster
Sawyer, Mildred Clementina *retired real estate agent*

### Hope
Stadtmueller, Claire Louise *soprano, performing arts educator*

### Hope Valley
Walker, Howard Ernest *lawyer*

### Jamestown
DiStefano, Gregory John *marketing professional*
Tinker, Thomas Eaton *retired headmaster*
Ullrich, Robert Albert *academic administrator*
Worden, Katharine Cole *sculptor*
Wright, Harrison Morris *historian, educator*

### Johnston
Hurley, Brian J. *insurance company executive*
Merolla, Carol Ann *writer, consultant*
Subramaniam, Shivan Sivaswamy *insurance company executive*
Torelli, Anthony-Alexander *music educator, conductor, musician*

### Kingston
Boving, Thomas B. *hydrologist, educator*
Caldwell, Naomi Rachel *library and information scientist, educator, writer*
Carothers, Robert Lee *academic administrator*
Fastovsky, David E. *geoscientist, educator*
Hufnagel, Linda Ann *biology professor, researcher*
Keefe, Margaret Johnson *librarian*
Kim, Yong Choon *philosopher, theologian, educator*
Markin, Karen Mary *research scientist, journalist*
Mazze, Edward Mark *marketing educator, consultant*
Molloy, David Scott, Jr. *labor relations educator*
Newman, Barbara Miller *psychologist, educator*
Seitsinger, Anne M. *education educator*
Sundlun, Bruce *former governor*
Tolnick Champa, Judith Ellen *art gallery director, curator*
Turnbaugh, William Arthur *archaeologist, educator*

### Lincoln
Barlow, August Ralph, Jr. *minister*
DiMuccio, Robert A. *insurance company executive*
Marsden, Herci Ivana *classical ballet artistic director*

### Little Compton
Middendorf, J. William, II, *investment banker*
Small, Wilfred Thomas *surgeon, educator*

### Middletown
Carroll, Rosemary Frances *historian, educator, lawyer*
Demy, Timothy James *military chaplain*
Ellison, William Theodore *marine engineer*
Jackson, John Edward *adult education educator, retired military officer*
Leighton, Charles Milton *retired specialty consumer products executive*
Peterson, Eric F. *headmaster*

### Narragansett
Goos, Roger Delmon *retired mycologist*
Nixon, Scott West *oceanography science educator*
Pilson, Michael Edward Quinton *oceanography educator*
Pockalny, Robert *geophysicist, researcher*
Stark, Dennis Edwin *private investigator, retired bank executive*

### Newport
Brown, David William *economist, educator, consultant*
Burgin, William Lyle *architect*
Carpenter, Stanley Dean MacDonald *military officer, educator*
Chace, Jameson Fales *ecologist, educator*
Cicilline, J. Clement *mental health services professional, state legislator*
Ellsworth, James Byron *national security educator*
Englander, Roger *television producer, director*
Haas, William Paul *humanities educator, retired academic administrator*
Higgins, Harriet Pratt *investment advisor*
Jae, (Jae French) *sculptor*
Koch, Robert Michael *research scientist, consultant, educator*
Malkovich, Mark Paul III *musician, performing company executive*
McConnell, David Kelso *lawyer*
Mooshagian, Mark Nishan *education educator*
Raum, Mary Beth *performing arts educator*
Roos, Casper *actor*
Rous, Stephen Norman *urologist, educator*
Ruffa, Anthony Armand *mechanical engineer*
Sands, Harold Winthrop *banker, financial planner*
Scheck, Frank Foetisch *retired lawyer*

Shuford, Jacob L. *academic administrator, career military officer*
Stone, Edward Luke *investor, realtor*
Tinney, Harle Hope Hanson *museum administrator*
Wood, Berenice Howland *retired secondary school educator*
Woods, Donald E. *healthcare executive*

### North Kingstown
Jarvis, William David *pharmacologist, researcher*
Kullberg, Gary Walter *advertising agency executive*
Mellor, Kathy *National Teacher of the Year 2004, ESL educator*
Novich, Bruce Eric *chemicals executive*

### Pawtucket
Belliveau, Kathrin Pagonis *lawyer*
Bertini, Richard G. *orthopedist*
Bifulco, Frank *toy company executive*
Charness, Wayne Samuel *public relations executive*
Chopra, Pradeep *physician, educator*
Daya, Jackie *publishing company executive*
Glicksman, Arvin S(igmund) *radiation oncologist*
Goldner, Brian *toy company executive*
Hargreaves, David R. *toy company executive*
Hassenfeld, Alan Geoffrey *consumer products company executive*
Holt, Richard B. *toy company executive*
Huebner, Charles J. *toy manufacturing executive*
Lepore, Lisa *principal*
Nagler, Barry *lawyer*
Orson, Barbara Tuschner *actress*
Romanzi, Kenneth *toy manufacturing executive*
Trueb, Martin R. *toy company executive*
Verrecchia, Alfred Joseph *toy company executive*
Wilson, E. David *toy company executive*

### Portsmouth
Becken, Bradford Albert *engineering executive*
Bergstrom, Albion Andrew *retired military officer, educator*
Levie, Howard S. (Howard Sidney Levie) *lawyer, educator*
Needham, Richard Lee *magazine editor*
Parker, Nancy Knowles (Mrs. Cortlandt Parker) *publishing executive*
Willis, Christopher Scott *school psychologist, writer*

### Providence
Ackerman, Felicia Nimue *philosophy educator, writer*
Ajello, Edith H. *state legislator*
Alfonso, Mariana *education educator, researcher*
Algiere, Dennis Lee *state legislator*
Allio, Robert John *management consultant, educator*
Amaral, Joseph Ferreira *surgeon*
Anderson, James Alfred *cognitive science professor*
Aronson, Stanley Maynard *physician, educator*
Authelet, Keith A. *information technology executive*
Avery, Donald Hills *metallurgist, educator*
Barnhill, James Orris *theater educator*
Barnum, William Milo *architect*
Bensmaia, Reda *French studies educator, researcher*
Berkelhammer, Robert Bruce *lawyer*
Besdine, Richard William *medical educator, researcher*
Biron, Christine Anne *medical science educator, researcher*
Blasing, Mutlu Konuk *English language educator*
Blazar, Andrew S. *reproductive endocrinologist*
Block, Bartley Cavanough *biologist, educator*
Block, Stanley Hoyt *pediatrician, allergist*
Borts, George Herbert *economist, educator*
Bowlby, Raynna R. *school librarian*
Bready, Richard Lawrence *manufacturing executive*
Briant, Clyde Leonard *metallurgist, educator*
Brown, Matthew A. *state official*
Bulman, John *lawyer*
Campbell, Bolaji Victor *art history educator, artist, critic*
Campbell, Lewis B. *aerospace technology executive*
Carcieri, Donald L. *governor*
Carlotti, Stephen Jon *lawyer*
Carpenter, Gene Blakely *crystallography and chemistry educator*
Choquette, Paul Joseph, Jr. *construction company executive*
Conley, Patrick T. *lawyer, writer, historian, educator, real estate developer*
Cooper, Leon N *physicist, researcher*
Coover, Robert *writer, scriptwriter, educator*
Corkery, Timothy James *painter, educator*
Corrente, Robert Clark *prosecutor*
Curran, Joseph Patrick *lawyer*
Dafermos, Constantine Michael *applied mathematics professor*
Dahlberg, Albert Edward *biochemistry professor*
D'Andrea, Vincent Charles *postal clerk*
Davis, Philip J. *mathematician*
Deal, Joseph Maurice *academic administrator, art educator, photographer*
Degroot, Leslie Jacob *medical educator*
Dempsey, Raymond Leo, Jr. *radio and television producer, moderator, writer*
Dill, Sara Worthing *dermatologist*
Donahue, John Edward *physician*
Donnelly, Kevin William *lawyer*
Donoghue, John Phillip *neuroscience educator, neurotechnology company executive*
Donovan, Bruce Elliot *literature educator, dean*
Dowben, Robert Morris *physiologist, researcher*
Dujardin, Richard Charles *journalist*
Easton, J(ohn) Donald *neurologist, educator*
Edwards, James King *retired lawyer*
Elbaum, Charles *physicist, educator, researcher*
Eltringham, Dana Kristin *writer*
Enteman, Willard Finley *retired philosopher*
Erikson, G(eorge) E(mil) (Erik Erikson) *information specialist, anatomist, archivist, science historian*
Estrup, Faiza Fawaz *physician, educator*
Estrup, Peder Jan *physics and chemistry professor*

Ewing, John Harwood *mathematics professor, department chairman, professional society administrator*
Faraone, Philip *organist, director, consumer products company executive*
Farmer, Susan Lawson *retired broadcast executive, former secretary of state*
Farrell, Margaret Dawson *lawyer*
Feldman, Allan Maurice *economist*
Feldman, Walter Sidney *artist, educator*
Ferruolo, Stephen Carl *lawyer, historian*
Fish, Lawrence Kingsbaker *banker*
Fishman, Bernard Philip *museum director*
Flaherty, Francis Xavier *state supreme court justice*
Fleming, Wendell Helms *mathematician, educator*
Fogarty, Charles Joseph *lieutenant governor*
Fogarty, Edward Michael *lawyer*
Fornara, Charles William *historian, classicist, educator*
Francis, Warren William *retired surgeon, educator*
Freiberger, Walter Frederick *mathematics professor, actuarial science consultant*
Frerichs, Ernest Sunley *religious studies educator*
Freund, Lambert Ben *engineering educator, researcher, consultant*
Gamboli, Michael A. *lawyer*
Gasbarro, Pasco, Jr. *lawyer*
Gerritsen, Hendrik Jurjen *physics professor, researcher*
Gibbs, June Nesbitt *state senator*
Gilbane, Thomas F., Jr. *building company executive*
Gilchrist, James Manning *neurologist, researcher, educator*
Gilmore, Judith Marie *physician*
Gleason, Abbott *history professor*
Glicksman, Maurice *engineering educator, retired dean, retired provost*
Goldberg, Maureen McKenna *state supreme court justice*
Golden, Hal *artist, consultant*
Goldscheider, Frances K. *sociologist, educator*
Goldstein, Sidney *sociologist, educator, demographer*
Green, Angel Yvonne *literature educator*
Greer, David Steven *dean, educator, physician*
Guggenheim, Frederick Gibson *psychiatrist, educator*
Hall, Almon C. III *investment company executive*
Hamerly, Michael T. *librarian, historian*
Harleman, Ann *literature educator, writer*
Hazeltine, Barrett *electrical engineer, educator*
Head, James William III *geological sciences educator*
Heath, Dwight Braley *anthropologist, educator*
Hedlund, Ellen Louise *state agency administrator, educator*
Hemmasi, Harriette Ann *university librarian*
Heyman, Lawrence Murray *printmaker, painter*
Hopmann, Philip Terrence *political science educator*
Houston, Stephen D. *anthropologist, educator*
Howes, Lorraine de Wet *fashion designer, educator*
Istrail, Sorin C. *computer scientist, educator*
Jenny, Carole *physician, researcher*
Johnson, Vahe Duncan *lawyer*
Jones, Lauren Evans *lawyer*
Joukowsky, Artemis A. W. *private investor*
Kagan, Marilyn D. *retired architect*
Kane, Agnes Brezak *pathologist, educator*
Kean, John Vaughan *retired lawyer*
Kenna, George Anthony *pharmacist, researcher*
Kertzer, David Israel *academic administrator, anthropology educator, writer*
Kestin, Randi William *educational analyst*
Kim, Jaegwon *philosophy educator*
Knopf, Paul Mark *immunologist*
Konstan, David *classics and comparative literature professor, researcher*
Kraemer, Michael Frederick *lawyer*
Kramer, Ilse Elisabeth *rare book bibliographer, consultant*
Kramer, Peter David *psychiatrist, psychology professor*
Kushner, Harold Joseph *mathematics professor*
LaFrance, William Curt Phillip, Jr. *neuropsychiatrist, educator, medical researcher*
Lagueux, Ronald Rene *federal judge*
Lanou, Robert Eugene, Jr. *physicist, researcher*
Lee, Eugene *theatrical set designer*
Lesko, Leonard Henry *historian, educator, writer*
Levin, Frank S. *physicist, educator*
Lewis, David Carleton *medical educator, academic administrator*
Licht, Richard A. *lawyer*
Lipsey, Howard Irwin *lawyer, educator*
Lisi, Mary M. *federal judge*
López-Morillas, Frances (Mapes) *translator*
Lubar, Steven David *history professor, curator*
Lynch, Patrick C. *state attorney general*
Lynch, William Joseph *lawyer*
Mancebo, Maria Celmira *psychologist*
Mandle, Earl Roger *academic administrator, former museum director*
Marcus, Bess H. *psychologist, medical educator, health facility administrator*
Marsh, Robert Mortimer *sociologist, educator*
McAndrew, Thomas Joseph *lawyer*
McCann, Gail Elizabeth *lawyer*
McCleary, Benjamin Ward *investment banker*
Mc Donald, Charles J. *dermatologist, educator*
McElroy, Michael Robert *lawyer*
McIntyre, Jerry L. *lawyer*
McNeil, Paul Joseph, Jr. *financial analyst*
McSheehy, Cornelia Marie *artist, educator*
McWalters, Peter *school system administrator*
Mittleman, Richard Samuel *lawyer*
Monteiro, George *language educator, writer*
Monteiro, Lois Ann *nursing educator*
Mumford, David Bryant *mathematics professor*
Nails, Kenneth H. *lawyer*
Needleman, Alan *mechanical engineering educator*
Oh, William *physician*
Paolino, Ronald Mario *clinical psychologist, consultant, psychopharmacologist, pharmacist*
Papitto, Ralph Raymond *manufacturing executive*
Pine, Jeffrey Barry *lawyer, former state attorney general*

Pueschel, Siegfried M. *pediatrician, educator*
Putnam, Michael Courtney Jenkins *classics educator*
Putterman, Louis G. *economics professor*
Raaflaub, Kurt Arnold *classics educator*
Recupero, Patricia Ryan *hospital president, psychiatrist, lawyer, health facility executive*
Rhodes, Ramona Lagiers *medical educator, researcher*
Ribbans, Geoffrey Wilfrid *language educator*
Richman, Marc Herbert *engineer, forensic specialist, educator*
Robbins, Mark Walter *historian*
Robert, Stephen *academic administrator*
Robinson, William Philip III *state supreme court justice*
Rohr, Donald Gerard *history professor*
Roney, John M. *lawyer*
Rosenberg, Alan Gene *editor*
Russell, Bill *former professional basketball team executive, former professional basketball player*
Ruth, Sebastian A. *performing company executive*
Ryder, Harl Edgar *economist, educator*
Saint-Amand, Pierre Nemours *humanities educator*
St. Florian, Friedrich Gartler *architect, educator*
Salter, Lester Herbert *lawyer*
Savage, John Edmund *computer science educator, researcher*
Schevill, James Erwin *poet, playwright*
Schmitt, Johanna Marie *plant population biologist, educator*
Schulz, Juergen *art historian, educator*
Schwartz, Richard Evan *mathematician, educator*
Selya, Bruce Marshall *federal judge*
Sgouros, Thomas *artist*
Shapiro, Ronald Gary *psychologist*
Sherman, Deming Eliot *lawyer*
Shu, Chi-Wang *mathematics professor, researcher*
Silverman, Joseph Hillel *mathematics professor*
Simmons, Ruth J. *academic administrator*
Siqueland, Einar *psychologist, educator*
Skasanna, Rey *industrial engineer, department chairman*
Sosa, Ernest *philosopher, educator*
Spoolstra, Linda Carol *minister, educator, religious organization administrator*
Staples, Richard Farnsworth *lawyer*
Stein, Jerome Leon *economist, educator*
Steinbach, Meredith Lynn *writer, educator*
Stout, John Wilson *academic administrator*
Stratt, Richard Mark *chemistry researcher, educator*
Stultz, Newell Maynard *retired political science professor*
Suttell, Paul Allyn *state supreme court justice*
Tagliabue, John Anthony *retired literature educator, poet*
Takao, Motoharu *physiologist*
Tauc, Jan *retired physics professor*
Terras, Victor *literature and language professor*
Tobin, Thomas J. *bishop*
Toro, Stephen Ralph *music educator*
Torres, Ernest C. *federal judge*
Townley, Hugh *sculptor, educator*
Tucci, Joseph Ralph *endocrinologist, educator*
Upfal, Eliezer (Eli Upfal) *computer scientist, educator*
Valles, James M., Jr. *physics professor*
Vezeridis, Michael Panagiotis *surgeon, educator*
Vogel, Paula Anne *playwright*
Waldrop, Rosmarie *writer*
Wanebo, Harold J. *surgeon, educator*
Weiner, Jerome Harris *mechanical engineering educator*
Weinstein, Philip Merrill *lawyer*
Weisberger, Joseph Robert *retired state supreme court justice*
Weitberg, Alan Barry *physician, researcher*
Wells, Alan Hilary *biomedical researcher*
Wetle, Terrie Fox *gerontologist, educator, dean*
Whiting, Brian Christopher *hospitality consultant*
Wideman, John Edgar *English literature educator, novelist*
Williams, Frank J. *state supreme court chief justice, historian, writer*
Withey, Gary David *biomedical researcher*
Wolf, Geralyn *bishop*
Wood, Gordon Stewart *historian, educator, writer*
Wright, Carolyn D. (C.D. Wright) *language educator, poet*

### Riverside
Lekas, Mary Despina *retired otolaryngologist*

### Saunderstown
Donovan, Gerald Alton *retired academic administrator, retired dean*
Knauss, John Atkinson *retired federal agency administrator, oceanographer, educator, retired dean*
Leavitt, Thomas Whittlesey *retired museum director, educator*
Waters, Chris Harold *literature and language professor, poet*

### Scituate
Gorham, Bradford *lawyer*

### Smithfield
Joseph, Antoine L. *sociologist, educator*
Litoff, Judy Barrett *history professor*
Morahan-Martin, Janet May *psychologist, educator*
Seabra, James Joseph *music educator, musician*

### Wakefield
Alexander, Jacqueline Peterson *retired librarian*
Boothroyd, Geoffrey *industrial and manufacturing engineering educator*
Doody, Agnes G. *communications educator, management and communication consultant*
Leete, William White *retired artist*
Mason, Scott MacGregor *entrepreneur, inventor, consultant*
Moore, George Emerson, Jr. *geologist, educator*
Newman, Philip Robert *psychologist*
Wyman, James Vernon *retired publishing executive*

### Warren
Mehlman, Edwin Stephen *endodontist*

### Warwick
Charette, Sharon Juliette *library administrator*

Mood, Francis P., Jr. *lawyer, utilities executive*
Moore, James E. *state supreme court justice*
Morgan, Constance Louise *real estate company executive*
Morrison, Stephen George *lawyer*
Nagpal, Madan Lal *biochemist, educator, researcher*
Newton, Rhonwen Leonard *writer, data processing executive, consultant*
Nexsen, Julian Jacobs *lawyer*
Odom, Jerome D. *academic administrator*
Olenchak, Frank Richard *music educator, musician*
Outin, Mary Louise *business, multi-cultural history and geneology educator*
Page, Randall *state official*
Palms, John Michael *academic administrator, physicist*
Pleicones, Costa M. *state supreme court justice*
Powell, Donald Ashmore *clinical research psychologist*
Preedom, Barry Mason *physicist, researcher*
Pritchett, Samuel Travis *finance and insurance educator, researcher, consultant*
Rawlinson, Helen Ann *librarian*
Raychoudhury, Samir *biology professor, researcher*
Rekers, George Alan *education educator, clinical psychologist*
Robbins, Emmalee Elizabeth *theater director, speech professional*
Rucker, Darius *musician*
Ruffin, Julian Edward *marriage and family therapist, educator*
Samuel, May Linda *environmental scientist*
Sanford, Marshall (Mark Sanford) *governor, former congressman*
Schoen-Giddings, Linda N. *science assessment specialist, science education consultant*
Seigler, Ruth Queen *college nursing administrator, educator, consultant, nurse*
Shafer, John Milton *hydrologist, consultant, data processing executive*
Shedd, Dennis W. *federal judge*
Sheppe, Joseph Andrew *surgeon*
Shmunes, Edward *dermatologist*
Silver, Rick *marketing professional*
Sinclair, Linda Drumwright *educational consultant*
Sorensen, Andrew Aaron *academic administrator*
Sowell, Thornwell F. (Biff) *lawyer*
Sproat, John Gerald *historian, educator*
Sproat, Ruth C. *retired director, consultant*
Spurrier, Steve (Steven Orr Spurrier) *college football coach*
Stamps, Laura Anne *writer, poet*
Starrett, William *dancer, artistic director*
Still, Charles Neal *retired neurologist, medical educator, consultant*
Stroup, Rodger Emerson *historian*
Swerling, Jack Bruce *lawyer*
Synnott, Marcia Graham *history professor*
Tate, Harold Simmons, Jr. *lawyer*
Tenenbaum, Inez Moore *school system administrator*
Timmerman, William B. *utilities executive, accountant*
Toal, Jean Hoefer *state supreme court chief justice*
Toombs, Kenneth Eldridge *librarian*
Tripathi, Ramesh Chandra *ophthalmologist, researcher, educator*
Turk, John Cobb *architect, educator*
Vazsonyi, Nicholas *foreign languages educator*
Waller, John Henry, Jr. *state supreme court justice*
Warren, Charles David *library administrator*
Watabe, Norimitsu *biologist, marine biologist, educator*
Wideman, Ida Devlin *science educator*
Wilder, Ronald Parker *economics professor*
Willis, Paul Allen *librarian, dean*
Wright, Harry Hercules *psychiatrist*
Yarborough, Clinton Joseph *lawyer*
Zimmerman, Nancy Picciano *library and information scientist, educator*

**Conway**
Dame, Richard Franklin *marine biology educator*
Delia, Claude William *retired physician, pathologist*
Martin, Gregory Keith *lawyer, mayor*
McMillan, Michael Reid *retired orthopedic surgeon*

**Cordova**
Hallman, Catherine Owens *art educator*
Hill, Elizabeth Lee *science educator*
Sellers, LaBron E. *art educator, minister*

**Daniel Island**
McConnell, III, Bright *orthopaedic surgeon*

**Denmark**
Bendidi, Rachid *dean, educator*
Dawson, Leonard E. *college president*
Lebby, Gloria C. *history professor*

**Due West**
Carlock, John Bruce, Jr. *language educator*
Haselden, Gregory W. *accountant, educator*

**Easley**
Failing, George Edgar *editor, clergyman, educator*
Howe, Linda Arlene *nursing educator, writer*
Legins, Sarah Otis *information scientist, librarian*
Sustar, T. David *religious organization administrator*

**Edisto Island**
Cannon, David C. *mechanical engineer, consultant*
Van Metre, Margaret Cheryl *performing company executive, dancer, educator*

**Florence**
Agnew, Samuel Gerard *orthopaedic traumatologist*
Baroody, Albert Joseph, Jr. *pastoral counselor*
Carter, Luther Fredrick *university president*
DeMichele, Domenic John *neurologist, neuroradiologist*
Foster, Jackie Green *voice educator*
Imbeau, Stephen Alan *allergist*
Rae, John Gibson III *biology professor*
Waddill, Cynthia Kay *nurse*
West, Jesse Michael *pediatric neuropsychologist*

Wurster, Abigail Michelle *theater educator, costume designer*

**Fort Jackson**
Brinsfield, John Wesley *military officer, educator*

**Fort Mill**
Bowles, Crandall Close *textiles executive*
Cooper, Marvin D. *paper company executive*
Dickey, Martin *music educator*
Honeycutt, Brenda *secondary school educator*
Kutcher, Kenneth E. *manufacturing executive*
Park, John *financial consultant*

**Gaffney**
Griffin, Penni Oncken *social worker, educator*
Griffin, Walter Roland *academic administrator, historian, educator*
Hill, Harry Hoffman, Jr. *musician, educator*
Wilde, Edwin Frederick *retired mathematics professor*

**Georgetown**
Bazemore, Trudy McConnell *librarian*
Schumaker, William Thomas *retired insurance company executive*

**Gilbert**
Padget, Barbara Johnson *elementary school educator*

**Goose Creek**
Vogt, Kathleen Cunningham *musician, music educator*

**Graniteville**
Bell, Robert Morrall *lawyer*
Learnard, James Michael *retired collections and bad debt manager, secondary school educator*

**Green Pond**
Ittleson, H(enry) Anthony *foundation executive*

**Greenville**
Ballou, Kathryn Jeanne *performing arts educator*
Bauknight, Clarence Brock *construction executive, consultant, retail executive*
Baur, Michael L. *information technology executive*
Belk, F. Norman *librarian*
Bonner, Jack Wilbur III *psychiatrist, educator, administrator*
Crawford, William David *real estate broker, consultant*
Cureton, Claudette Hazel Chapman *biology professor*
Davis, Joan Carroll *retired museum director*
DeMint, Jim (James Warren DeMint) *senator, former congressman*
Dobson, Karen Coogler *elementary school educator*
Dreskin, Jeanet Steckler *painter, medical artist, educator*
Edwards, Harry LaFoy *lawyer*
Estridge, Larry D. *lawyer*
Ferguson, Donald Littlefield *retired lawyer*
Fitzgerald, Eugene Francis *management consultant*
Grubbs, R(obert) Howard *lawyer*
Herlong, Henry Michael, Jr. *federal judge*
Hipp, William Hayne *broadcast executive*
Horton, James Wright *retired lawyer*
Hultstrand, Charles John *architect*
Hutson, Melvin Robert *lawyer*
Jones, Bob III *academic administrator*
Jones, Robert Thaddues *principal*
Kilgore, Donald Gibson, Jr. *pathologist*
Maffucci, David G. *paper company executive*
Manly, Sarah Letitia *retired state legislator, ophthalmic photographer, angiographer*
Mann, James Robert *former congressman*
Massey, Raymond David *lawyer*
Mauldin, John Inglis *public defender*
McKinney, Ronald W. *lawyer*
Nemirow, Arnold Myles *paper company executive*
Newman, R. Donald *paper company executive*
Oxner, George Dewey, Jr. *lawyer*
Oxner, Glenn Ruckman *financial executive*
Parker, David G. *music educator, music publisher*
Paterson, David J. *paper company executive*
Payne, George Frederick *academic administrator*
Phillips, Joseph Brantley, Jr. *lawyer*
Porter, Charles Michael (Mike Porter) *business consultant, executive*
Rice, Michael V. *voice educator*
Riley, Richard Wilson *lawyer, former federal official*
Ringenberg, Donna Lou *music educator, conductor*
Schoonmaker, Gail Graham *voice educator, director*
Shi, David E. *academic administrator, historian*
Simmons, Charles Bedford, Jr. *judge*
Sleeman, Anita Marie *education educator, academic administrator, director*
Smith, Philip Daniel *academic administrator, education educator*
Smoak, Lewis Tyson *lawyer*
Todd, John Dickerson, Jr. *retired lawyer*
Townes, Bobby Joe *travel agency executive*
Traxler, William Byrd, Jr. *federal judge*
Trevillian, Wallace Dabney *retired economics professor, retired dean*
Varin, Roger Robert *textile executive*
Walters, Johnnie McKeiver *lawyer*
Westrope, Martha Randolph *psychologist, consultant*
Wilkins, William Walter *federal judge*
Wyche, Cyril Thomas *lawyer*
Wyche, Madison Baker III *lawyer*

**Greenwood**
Cushing, Sara Elizabeth *language educator, writer*
Epps, Susie Rebecca Smith *secondary school educator*
Hughes, Christopher Adam *conductor, educator*
Jackson, Larry Artope *retired college president*
Marino, Louis J(ohn) *mathematics educator*
Marino, Sheila Burris *education educator*
Nexsen, Julian Jacobs, Jr. *lawyer*

**Greer**
Hu, Yiping *metallurgical engineer*

Jackson, J. Garrett (Gary Jackson) *airport terminal executive*
McAbee, Thomas Allen *psychologist*
Sundstrom, Harold Walter *public relations executive*

**Hartsville**
Cecil, Allan *corporate communications executive*
DeLoach, Harris E(ugene), Jr. *manufacturing executive, lawyer*
Hupfer, Charles J. *manufacturing executive*
Menius, Espie Flynn, Jr. *electrical engineer*
Rubinstein, Joseph Harris *education educator*

**Hemingway**
Sumlin, Peggy McDonald *elementary school educator*

**Hilton Head Island**
Adams, William Hensley *ecologist, educator*
Balkin, Alfred *music educator, composer*
Becker, Karl Martin *lawyer*
Birk, Robert Eugene *retired internist*
Brennan, John Thomas *surgeon*
Brock, Karena Diane *dancer, educator*
Brown, Arthur Edmon, Jr. *retired army officer*
Bruun, Per Moller *civil engineer, consultant*
Conn, Margaret Elbow *human resources specialist*
Cunningham, William Henry *retired food products executive*
Davis, Mary Martha (Marty Davis) *small business owner, consultant*
Duvall, Charles Patton *internist, retired oncologist*
Engelman, Karl *physician*
Esposito, John Vincent *lawyer*
Field, James Bernard *internist, educator*
Gruchacz, Robert S. *real estate company officer*
Hagoort, Thomas Henry *lawyer*
Harty, James D. *former manufacturing company executive*
Hewes, Robert Charles *radiologist*
Hoppin, Thomas Edward *retired transportation executive*
Huckins, Harold Aaron *chemical engineer*
Jarvis, William Robert *epidemiologist, educator*
Lattimer, Gary Lee *physician*
Lefer, Allan Mark *physiologist*
Lewis, Gene Evans *retired medical equipment company executive*
Love, Richard Emerson *retired equipment manufacturing company executive*
McKeldin, William Evans *management consultant*
Mersereau, Hiram Stipe *wood products company consultant*
Ostergard, Paul Michael *philanthropy consultant*
Patton, Joseph Donald, Jr. *management consultant*
Pritchard, Dalton Harold *retired electronics executive*
Reed, Frances Boogher *writer, actress*
Roehrig, C(harles) Burns *internist, consultant*
Rulis, Raymond Joseph *manufacturing executive, consultant*
Russell, Allen Stevenson *retired metal products executive*
Selvy, Barbara *dance instructor*
Shepard, Steve *graphic artist, painter*
Simpson, John Wistar *utilities executive, consultant*
Wesselmann, Glenn Allen *retired health facility administrator*
Windman, Arnold Lewis *retired mechanical engineer*
Woodrum, Robert Lee *executive search consultant*
Wright, Marshall *manufacturing executive, diplomat*

**Holly Hill**
Anderson, LaShawn Ecleasha *rehabilitation technician*
Shuler, Karen Bull *elementary school educator*

**Hopkins**
Garrett, Robin Scott *health facility administrator*

**Inman**
D'Ambrosio, Jody (Gigi) Lynn *art educator*
Fogarty, Charles Michael *pulmonologist, researcher*

**Irmo**
Branham, Jennie Jones *artist*
Branham, Mack Carison, Jr. *retired religious organization administrator, minister*
Brown, Leonard Ashleigh (Smokey), Jr. *lawyer*
Parks, Garry Lee *military officer*

**Isle Of Palms**
Elliott, Larry Paul *radiologist, educator*
Wohltmann, Hulda Justine *pediatrician, endocrinologist*

**Johns Island**
Cameron, Thomas William Lane *investment company executive*
Carter, Mary Andrews *paralegal*
Norton, Norman James *retired exploration geologist, educator*

**Johnston**
Jackson, Tracey L *music educator*

**Kershaw**
Wall, Kathy Elliott *secondary school educator*

**Kiawah Island**
Harrigan, Anthony Hart *author*
Korb, William Brown, Jr. *retired manufacturing executive*
Warren, Russell Glen *educational consultant*

**Ladson**
Jackson, Jonathan Michael *computer company executive, writer*

**Lake Wylie**
Buggie, Frederick Denman *management consultant*
Sanford, James Kenneth *public relations executive*

**Lancaster**
Bundy, Charles Alan *retired foundation executive*

**Landrum**
Smith, Constance *retired elementary school educator*

**Leesville**
Crumley, James Robert, Jr. *retired bishop*

**Lexington**
Calloway, Gary R. *choral director, music director*
Kennedy, Sandra Elaine *small business owner*
Lide, Vinton DeVane *lawyer*
Morris, Earle Elias, Jr. *retired state official*
Morrison, Sherrie Crawford *secondary school educator*
Wilkins, Robert Pearce *writer, lawyer*

**Little River**
Maloney, Terry *horticulturist, educator*

**Loris**
Whisnant, Stephen Labron *music educator*

**Lyman**
Morgan, Leon Terrell *environmental health services specialist*

**Marion**
Inabinet, Lawrence Elliott *retired pharmacist*
Kirkpatrick, Donald Robert *secondary school educator*

**Mauldin**
Looper-Wilson, Leah Marie *human resources specialist, controller, interior designer*
Wood, Myra Linden Frank *consultant*

**Moore**
King, Tamara Powers *music educator, musician*

**Mount Pleasant**
Allen, Louise Anderson *education educator*
Bilas, Richard A. *economist*
Friedrich, Lawrence Vincent *research scientist*
Gilbert, James Eastham *academic administrator*
Glenn, Edward Vernon Ferrell *lawyer, consultant*
Gregory, Yvonne Elizabeth Heyning *interior designer*
Hill, Larkin Payne *jewelry designer, manufacturer*
Macdonald, Robert Rigg, Jr. *retired museum director*
Maize, John Christopher *dermatologist, educator*
Royall, Mary-Julia C. *church organist, historian*
Scott, Jeffrey Ryan *music educator*
Thordarson, William *retired hydrogeologist*

**Murrells Inlet**
Justice, Franklin Pierce, Jr. *oil industry executive*
Kelly, Gerald Wayne *chemical coatings company executive*

**Myrtle Beach**
Atkinson, Harold Witherspoon *utilities executive, consultant, real estate broker*
Berry, James W. *athletic trainer, secondary school educator*
Breen, David Hart *lawyer*
Harwell, David Walker *retired judge*
Parker, Donna Tully *elementary school educator, department chairman*
Schwartz, Steve Wendelin *physician*

**Nesmith**
Pressley, Deloris N. *literacy educator*

**New Zion**
Gibbons, Robert Butler, Jr. *retired military officer*

**Newberry**
Lander, James Albert *retired military officer, controller*
McGinnis, Barry Eugene *music educator, musician*
Partridge, William Franklin, Jr. *lawyer*
Partridge, III, W. F. *lawyer, defender*

**North Augusta**
Rowland, Arthur Ray *librarian*

**North Charleston**
Fiedorczyk, Daniel Paul *science educator*
Jarrett, Stephen McAllister *information technology executive*
Mardikian, Paul *conservator*
Zucker, Jerry *chemical manufacturing executive*

**North Myrtle Beach**
Damerst, William *language educator, humanities educator*

**Okatie**
Edwards, Nancy Jo *gifted and talented educator, consultant*

**Orangeburg**
Basher, Hasanul A. *electrical engineer*
Bozinovski, Stevo *computer science educator, researcher*
Byers, Keith Thomas *librarian, educator*
Dalton, Cheryl Renee *entrepreneur*
Hong, Jae-Dong *industrial engineering educator*
Hunter, Terry Keith *artist, educator, art association administrator, consultant*
James, Rodney Arthur *systems administrator, application developer, minister*
Kozachek, Janet Lynne *artist, educator*
Lee, Donald Ray, Jr. *music educator*
McIver, Barbara Basore *language educator*
Sims, Edward Howell *editor, writer*
Smoak, Randolph Duncan, Jr. *surgeon*
Staley, Alvin *artist, educator*
Staley, Bretta *artist, educator*

**Pawleys Island**
Bischoff, Frederick Christopher III *retired accountant*
Grubb, William Francis Xavier *consumer products company executive, marketing professional*
Kay, Thomas Oliver *agricultural consultant*
Matelic, Candace Tangora *museum director, educator*
Noble, Joseph Veach *retired museum director*

Grant, Amy *singer, songwriter*
Heiser, Arnold Melvin *astronomer*
Lee, Robert Erich *information technology consultant*
Mc Creary, James Franklin *lawyer, mediator*
Oonk, Marian Bernice *elementary school educator*
Provine, John Calhoun *retired lawyer*
Scarlett, Joseph H., Jr. *agricultural products executive*
Smith, Wayne Thomas *healthcare company executive*
Stephens, Shirley Lynne *writer, editor*
Taylor, Nicole Renée (Niki Taylor) *model, shop owner*
Tucker, Tanya Denise *singer*
Walker Bonner, Linda Carol *music educator*
Wright, James F. *agricultural products executive*

**Bristol**
Bellamy, John A.A. *lawyer*
Johnson, Opal Burton *retired elementary school educator*
Markison, Brian A. *pharmaceutical executive*

**Brownsville**
Banks, Webb Follin *mayor*
Kalin, Robert *retired mathematics professor*

**Chattanooga**
Bahner, Thomas Maxfield *lawyer*
Barker, William M. *state supreme court justice*
Campbell, Paul III *lawyer*
Campbell, William O'Neal *retired physician*
Copeland, Floyd Dean *insurance company executive, lawyer*
Derthick, Alan Wendell *architect, architectural firm executive*
Edgar, R(obert) Allan *federal judge*
Enriquez, Manuel Hipolito *physician*
Fleury, David Reed *mathematician, educator*
Foy, John N. *real estate company executive*
Franks, Herschel Pickens *judge*
Gartman, Max Dillon *language educator*
Greving, Robert C. *insurance company executive*
Haden, Benjamin *minister, retired publishing executive, broadcast executive*
Harlin, Ray M. *trucking executive*
Hensley, Marble John, Sr. *civil engineer, consultant*
Hodge, Raymond Douglas *minister*
Johnson, Joseph Erle *mathematician*
Lebovitz, Stephen D. *property manager*
Lutgen, Robert Raymond *newspaper editor*
Marshall, Willis Henry *psychiatrist*
Martin, Chester Y. *sculptor, painter*
Mattice, Harry Sandlin, Jr. *federal judge, former prosecutor*
Mills, Olan, II *photography company executive*
Obear, Frederick Woods *academic administrator*
Parks, Susan Jane *artist*
Pate, Lisa M. *transportation services executive, lawyer*
Peck, Douglas Edward *lawyer*
Pollard, C. William *environmental services executive*
Quinn, Patrick *transportation executive*
Rabin, Alan A. *economics professor*
Ragon, Robert Ronald *clergyman*
Resnick, Irven Michael *philosophy educator*
Russe, Conrad Thomas Campbell *accountant*
Schow, Thomas Albert *music educator, educator, military officer*
Shuck, Edwin Haywood III *surgeon*
Stacy, Bill Wayne *academic administrator*
Summers, Gerald Howard (Jerry Summers) *lawyer*
Watjen, Thomas Ros *insurance company executive*
Wilson, Richard Lee *political science professor*

**Chuckey**
Brown, Anne Million *retired elementary school educator*

**Clarksville**
Deitrich, Margaret Alice *education educator*
Hoppe, Sherry Lee *academic administrator*
Lee, Bob D. *music educator, consultant*
Maynard, Terrell Dennis *minister*
Newby, Earl Fernando *education educator*
Puhl, Jennifer Joyce *physiologist*
Staivisky, Jeanne Louise *counselor, alcohol/drug abuse services professional*
Stoddard, Peter Hawkins *education educator, consultant*
Uffelman, Minoa D. *history professor*

**Cleveland**
Breuer, William Bentley *author*
Harper, James Edward, Jr. *academic administrator*
Hughes, Ray Harrison *minister, religious organization administrator*
Miles, Doris Cooper *bank executive*
Preston, Forrest L. *healthcare executive*
Rhodes, Arthur Delano *benefits administrator*
Suits, Janice Crye *elementary school educator*
Taylor, William Al *church administrator*
Thomas, Phillip *music educator, department chairman, musician*
Wittenburg, Michael Shane *concert pianist, music educator*

**Clinton**
Hutchens, Gail R. *chemist*
Seib, Billie McGhee Rushing *nursing administrator, consultant*

**College Grove**
Battle, William Robert (Bob Battle) *retired publishing executive*

**Collegedale**
McKee, Ellsworth R. *food products executive*
Pettibone, Dennis Lynn *history professor*

**Collierville**
Boswell, Rupert Dean, Jr. *retired academic administrator, mathematician, educator*
Culley, J.P. *education educator*
Smith, Vickie M. *chemicals executive*
Springfield, James Francis *retired lawyer, banker*

**Columbia**
Cantrell, Sharron Caulk *principal*
Scheusner, Ronald L. *music educator*
Storey, Pamela T. *elementary school educator*

**Cookeville**
Airhart, Douglas L. *horticulturist, educator*
Chang, Wei Tsun *music educator*
Chowdhuri, Pritindra *electrical engineer, educator*
Dugle, Jon Richard *music educator*
Greeson, James Emerson *educational consultant, educator*
Reynolds, Barbara C. *retired mental health educator, dean*
Sissom, Leighton Esten *engineering educator, dean, consultant*
Smolenski, Lisabeth Ann *physician*
Velu, Yogeshwar Karunakaran *industrial engineer, researcher*
Volpe, Angelo Anthony *retired academic administrator, chemist, educator*
Wang, Chunsheng *chemical engineer, educator*
Wells, John Calhoun *physics professor*

**Cordova**
Cheatham, Wanda M. *music educator*
Haslam, Edward T. *finance company executive*
Isaacson, Bond R. *finance company executive*
Johnson, Lori D. *voice educator, director*
Kiphart, Richard P. *finance company executive*
Labry, Edward A. III *finance company executive*
Nunnikhoven, Thomas Spence *statistician, consultant*
Palmer, Dan M. *finance company executive*
Pugh, Dorothy Gunther *artistic director*
Vaughn, Cary Edward *minister, director*

**Covington**
Gordon, J. Houston *lawyer, political organization worker*
Wright, Bonnie Shankle *assistant principal, choir director*

**Crossville**
Bell, Charles Eugene, Jr. *retired industrial engineer*
Elam, Leslie Albert *retired museum director*
Lansford, Edwin Gaines *accountant*
Sower, Milene A. *nursing educator*

**Dayton**
Cornelius, Richard Meredith *literature and language professor*
Ketchersid, William Lester *history professor*
Luther, Sigrid *music educator*

**Dickson**
Surji, Kemal M. *health facility administrator, consultant*

**Dresden**
Maddox, Mark Lee *academic administrator*

**Dyersburg**
Revell, Bill *mayor*
Robertson, Wanda Sue *secondary school educator*

**Englewood**
Brown, Helen Dodson *retired librarian*

**Farragut**
Riley, Ray Allan *biology educator*

**Fayetteville**
Dickey, John Harwell *lawyer*
Ralston, Joseph Frederick, Jr. *internist*
Wolfhard, Hans Georg *retired research scientist*

**Franklin**
Andrews, William Frederick *manufacturing executive*
Haseltine, Dan *christian rock musician*
Hill, Jon Matthew *science educator, secondary school educator*
Hitt, Leo Richard *mathematician, educator*
Jowdy, Jeffrey William *research and development company executive*
Miller, Dennis Edward *health medical executive*
Moessner, Harold Frederick *allergist*
Morton, James Carnes, Jr. *automotive executive*
Sutter, Lawrence A. *lawyer, educator*
Thornsberry, Clyde *microbiologist*
White, David R. *healthcare company executive*

**Friendsville**
Dees, Linda Jo *nurse, educator*

**Gallatin**
Bradley, Nolen Eugene, Jr. *retired personnel executive, engineer*
Durham, Walter Thomas *historian, researcher*
Ellis, Joseph Newlin *retired wholesale distribution executive*
Ritter, Renee O. *theater educator*

**Gatlinburg**
Cave, Kent R. *parks director*

**Germantown**
Allison, Beverly Gray *retired religious organization administrator, theology studies educator*
Arendall, Charles Steven *management consultant, educator*
Depperschmidt, Thomas Orlando *economist, consultant*
Legett, Benjamin J. III *choral director, composer*
Lieberman, Phillip Louis *allergist, educator*
Loper, Linda Sue *library director*
Mowry, Robert Wilbur *pathologist, educator*
Nolly, Robert J. *pharmacist, health facility administrator, educator*

**Goodlettsville**
Harper, Jewel Benton *pharmacist*
Lanigan, Susan S. *lawyer*
Vatandoost, Nossi Malek *art school administrator*

**Gray**
Combs, Stephen Paul *pediatrician, health facility administrator*

**Greenbrier**
Ault, Andrew Jared *music educator, disc jockey*
Newell, Paul Haynes, Jr. *engineering educator*

**Greeneville**
Corey, Mark *historic site director*
Hull, Thomas Gray *federal judge*
Parsons, Marcia Phillips *judge*
Smith, Myron John, Jr. *librarian, author*

**Harriman**
Vann, Lillie Mae *retired nurse*

**Henderson**
Gardner, Elmer Claude *academic administrator*

**Hendersonville**
Burt, Alvin Miller III *anatomist, educator, cell biologist, writer*
Davis, Robert Norman *hospital administrator*
Kinney, Betty Caudill *elementary school educator*
Spain, Mary Ann *realtor, educator, historian, writer*

**Hermitage**
Lyle, Virginia Reavis *retired archivist, genealogist*
Reid, Donna Joyce *small business owner*
Rosdeutscher, John David *plastic surgeon*
Thompson, Fred Dalton *actor, former senator*

**Hickory Valley**
Weaver, Peggy (Marguerite McKinnie Weaver) *plantation owner*

**Hixson**
Kemp, Robert Bowers, Jr. *investment manager*
Segler, Christopher Paige *surgeon, researcher*

**Humboldt**
Boyte, George Griffin *lawyer*

**Huntland**
Burton, Janet Ruth Wisner *music educator*

**Jackson**
Agee, Bob R. *academic administrator, educator, minister*
Boswell, G(eorge) Harvey *federal judge*
Cole, John Frankland *electrical engineer, educator*
Dale, Karen McCall *music educator*
Evans, Sean *political science professor*
Harper, Ernest Lee, Jr. *sales executive*
Hoyle, Shetina Yevette *librarian*
Kamso-Pratt, Jimmy Michael *physician, administrator*
McRoberts, Terry Allan *music educator*
Nance, William R., Jr. *finance educator*
Swaim, Mark Wendell *physician, molecular biologist, gastroenterologist, photographer*
Todd, James Dale *federal judge*
Weaver, Terry L. *special education educator, writer*

**Jamestown**
Holt, Lesley Lea *music educator*

**Jefferson City**
Baumgardner, James Lewis *history professor*
Muncy, Estle Pershing *physician*
Robertson, Everett B. *performing arts educator, consultant*

**Jellico**
Hausman, Keith Lynn *health facility administrator, physical therapist*

**Johnson City**
Alfonso, Robert John *university administrator*
Beeler, Marsha Colleen *education educator*
Coogan, Philip Shields *pathologist*
Daly, Conrad C. *editor*
Epps, James Haws III *lawyer*
Franks, Ronald Dwyer *dean, psychiatrist, educator*
Giorgadze, Tamar Alfred *pathologist, physician*
Hamdy, Ronald Charles *geriatrician*
Jenrette, Thomas Shepard, Jr. *music educator, choral director*
Kao, Race Li-Chan *medical educator*
Lyle, Valarie Gay *art educator, artist*
Norris, Carol Brooks *retired librarian*
Olsen, Martin E. *obstetrician, educator*
Stewart, Frank Graham *composer, clarinetist*
Tollefson, Terrence Alfred *education educator, consultant*
Zimmern-Reed, Annette Wacks *psychologist*

**Jonesborough**
Gerhardt, E. Alvin, Jr. *retired museum director*
Jenkins, Ronald Wayne *lawyer, engineer, mediator*

**Kenton**
Jenkins-Brady, Terri Lynn *publishing executive, journalist*

**Kingsport**
Brown, Richard E. *music educator*
Coover, Harry Wesley *manufacturing executive*
Crockett, Frank McClung *arts educator, retired music educator*
Deavenport, Earnest W., Jr. *chemical executive*
Ferguson, J. Brian *chemicals executive*
Findley, Don Aaron *manufacturing executive*
Groseclose, Clara Rita *retired secondary school educator*
Hale, Jerry B. *information technology executive*
Head, William Iverson, Sr. *retired chemical company executive*
Lee, Theresa K. *chemicals executive*
Lorraine, Richard *chemicals executive*
McDavid, Jo Collins *library manager*
McKee, Denise Michelle *history educator*
Ogbonnaya, Chuks Alfred *entomologist, agronomist, environmentalist*
Siirola, Jeffrey John *chemical engineer*
Smith, JoAnn Carroll *library and information scientist*
Tant, Martin Ray *chemical engineer, biomedical engineer*
Wolfe, Margaret Ripley *historian, educator, consultant*

**Kingston**
Lannom, Julie Conway Hudson *secondary school educator*

**Knoxville**
Aguilar, Julia Shell *publishing executive*
Alexeff, Igor *retired electrical engineering educator*
Anderson, Edward Riley *state supreme court justice*
Anderson, Ilse Janell *clinical geneticist*
Bass, William Marvin III *anthropology educator*
Beeler, Sandra Gillespie *realtor*
Behrend, Linda *librarian, writer*
Bell, Linda R. *writer, photographer*
Bentley, Michael Lee *science educator*
Blake, Gerald Rutherford *retired banker*
Boling, Edward Joseph *retired academic administrator*
Boling, Mark Edward *music educator*
Bose, Bimal Kumar *electrical engineering educator*
Brady, Patrick *language educator, writer*
Chen, James Pai-fun *biology professor, researcher*
Childers, Michael *science educator*
Cliff, Steven Burris *engineering executive*
Coleman, Shannon DeShae *lawyer, educator*
Congleton, Joseph Patrick *lawyer, preservationist*
Contescu, Cristian Ion *chemist, researcher*
Cottrell, Jeannette Elizabeth *retired librarian*
Creasia, Joan Catherine *dean, nursing educator*
Cutler, Everette Wayne *history professor*
Davis, John Kerr *philosopher, educator, lawyer*
Davis, Marleen Kay *architect, educator*
Dedrick, James R. *prosecutor*
Dewey, Barbara I. *librarian, dean*
Dillard, W. Thomas *lawyer*
Drennen, Jean Cobble *retired public relations executive, linguist*
Drinnon, Janis Bolton *artist, poet, volunteer*
Du, Hongtao *systems engineer*
Dudrick, Paul Stanley *oncologist, surgeon, educator*
Edwards, Brian J. *chemical engineer, educator*
Eleazer, Alan Garrett *church musician, music educator*
Faires, Ross Norbert *manufacturing executive*
Felder-Hoehne, Felicia Harris *librarian, researcher*
Filston, Howard Church *pediatric surgeon*
Fisher, John Hurt *retired English language educator*
Froula, James DeWayne *honor society administrator*
Fulmer, Phillip *university football coach*
Galligan, Thomas C., Jr. *law educator*
Garrison, Arlene Allen *academic administrator, engineering educator*
Gavrilets, Sergey Yurievich *biologist, educator*
Gentry, Robert Vance *physicist, researcher, writer*
Graber, Glenn C. *medical educator, educational consultant*
Harris, Diana Koffman *sociologist, educator*
Harris, Skila *government agency administrator*
Hatcher, Robert Dean, Jr. *geologist, educator*
Hatton, Barbara R. *academic administrator*
Hebbeler, Regis J. *lawyer*
Heppding, Fred, Jr. *history educator, department chairman*
Howard, Herbert Hoover *broadcasting and communications educator*
Infante, Isa Maria *political scientist, educator, lawyer, writer*
Irick, David Kim *engineering educator, consultant*
Jarvis, James Howard, II, *judge*
Jeong, Myong-Kee *information scientist, educator*
Jones, Robert Emmet *sociologist, educator*
Jones, Sherman J. *academic administrator, investment company executive, educator*
Jordan, Robert Leon *judge*
Joy, David Charles *research scientist, educator*
Kahn, Kenneth B. *finance educator, consultant*
Kliefoth, A. Bernhard III *neurosurgeon*
Koschan, Andreas F. *computer engineer, educator*
Lammers, Laura Bea *writer, communications executive*
Lawson, Fred Raulston *banker*
Levy, Robert A. *academic administrator*
Lindeman, Barry James *internal auditor, nurse, minister*
Liu, Yang *geologist, researcher*
Lowe, Alan Conner *library director*
Lucas, John Allen *lawyer*
MacLean, Calvin A. *theater educator, department chairman, theater director*
Mankel, Francis Xavier *retired principal, priest*
Markert, Cynthia Allin *artist*
Martin, James Robert *identification company executive*
Matteson, Karla J. *health science association administrator*
Mayfield, T. Brient, IV, *media and computer executive*
Mazur, Peter *physiologist, cryobiologist*
McCullough, Glenn L., Jr. *electric power industry executive*
Mc Dow, John Jett *biosystems engineering educator*
McGuire, John Albert *dentist*
McGuire, Sandra Lynn *nursing educator*
Mc Hargue, Carl Jack *lab administrator*
McMahon, Susan Henderson *biology professor*
McRae, John Malcolm *dean, educator, architect*
Minkel, Clarence Wilbert *university official*
Mise, Jesse Sherden *structural engineer, consultant*
Moore, Marvelene C. *music educator*
Moore, Richard Wayne *electric power industry executive, former prosecutor*
Moore, Wendy Leigh *anthropology professor*
Murrian, Robert Phillip *retired federal judge, educator*
Naoumov, Viatcheslav I. *mechanical engineer, educator*
Naoumova, Irina Yevgenievna *business educator, consultant*
Nayak, Subhadarshi *research scientist*
Petersen, John D. *academic administrator*
Phillips, Thomas Wade *judge, lawyer*
Plummer, E. Ward *physics professor*
Prados, John William *engineering educator*
Purcell, Aaron D. *archivist, historian*

Collins, Joe Lena *retired secondary school educator*
Collins, Kerry *professional football player*
Compton, John Joseph *philosophy educator*
Conkin, Paul Keith *history professor*
Conley, Richard Scott *orthodontist, educator*
Cook, Ann Jennalie *literature educator, cultural organization administrator*
Cook, E. Gary *manufacturing executive*
Cornfield, Daniel Benjamin *sociology educator*
Covington, Robert Newman *law educator*
Cowart, Richard G. *lawyer*
Creasy, Charles L. *creative director*
Crooke, Philip Schuyler *mathematics professor*
Cui, Yi *computer scientist, educator*
Cyrus, Cynthia J. *dean, music educator*
Daane, James Dewey *banker*
Dachowski, Elizabeth Eileen *history professor*
Dalton, James Edgar, Jr. *health facility administrator*
Darnell, Riley Carlisle *state official, lawyer*
Daughtrey, Martha Craig *federal judge*
Davis, Stephen N. *endocrinologist*
Day, John Arthur *lawyer*
DeHart, Roy Lynch *physician, educator*
Demarcus, Jay (Stanley Demarcus) *country musician, songwriter*
Dennen, Keith Cameron *lawyer*
Dettbarn, Wolf-Dietrich *neurochemist, pharmacologist, educator*
Dickerson, Dennis Clark, Sr. *historian, educator*
Dimitri, Elia Charles *retired medical educator*
Dmochowski, Roger *urologist, educator*
Doyle, William Robert *finance educator*
Draper, James Thomas, Jr., (Jimmy Draper) *clergyman*
Drowota, Frank F. III *retired state supreme court justice*
DuBois, Raymond N. *medical educator, researcher*
Dunn, Ronnie Gene *musician*
Dupont, William Dudley *biostatistician, educator*
Echols, Robert L. *federal judge*
Edge, Kathryn Reed *lawyer*
Edwards, Mark E. *lawyer*
Egli, Martin *crystallographer, educator*
Epps, Anna Cherrie *immunologist, educator, dean*
Estrin, Kari (Karen Ruth Estrin) *theater producer, agent, consultant*
Etherington, Carol A. *medical association administrator*
Evans, Franklin Bachelder *finance educator, consultant*
Evans, Sara *country singer, songwriter*
Fanning, Ellen *biology professor, research scientist*
Farran, Dale Clark *education educator*
Fazio, Sergio *medical educator, researcher*
Feldman, Leonard Cecil *physicist*
Fields, James Perry *dermatologist, dermatopathologist, allergist, pharmacologist, pharmacist*
Fisher, Jeff *professional football coach*
Fitzgerald, Edmund Bacon *electronics executive*
Fleck, Bela *country musician*
Fleischer, Arthur C. *medical educator, radiologist*
Ford, Gerald J. (Jerry) *finance company executive*
Forlines, Franklin Leroy *minister, educator*
Fort, Tomlinson *chemist, chemical engineering educator*
Freudenthal, Ernest Guenter *technology and business educator*
Frist, Thomas Fearn, Jr. *hospital management company executive*
Frost, Richard W. *manufacturing executive*
Frost, Rick *manufacturing executive*
Frusciante, John Anthony *musician*
Gabbe, Steven Glenn *dean, educator, obstetrician, gynecologist*
Gallagher, Martin Joseph *neurologist, neuroscientist*
Galloway, Kenneth Franklin *engineering educator*
Gannon, John Sexton *lawyer, management consultant, arbitrator, mediator*
Gee, Elwood Gordon *academic administrator*
Gentry, Teddy Wayne *country musician*
George, Eddie (Edward Nathan George) *former professional football player*
Gherman, Paul M. *university librarian*
Giles, Joe W. *music educator*
Gillmor, John Edward *lawyer*
Girgus, Sam B. *English literature educator*
Gobbell, Ronald Vance *architect*
Goldberg, Larry M *hospital administrator*
Gorden, David Lee *surgeon, educator*
Gore, Steven Lowell *accountant*
Gore, Tipper (Mary Elizabeth Gore) *wife of the former vice president of the United States*
Granner, Daryl Kitley *physiology and medicine educator*
Green, Lisa Cannon *online editor*
Griffin, Patti Elaine *medical educator, consultant*
Griffith, James Leigh *lawyer*
Griffith, Nanci *singer, songwriter*
Grimes, R. Dale *lawyer*
Guha, Sujata *education educator*
Guinsburg, Philip Fried *alcohol and substance abuse counselor*
Gwin, Dorothy Jean Bird *retired psychology professor, dean*
Hahn, George Thomas *materials engineering educator, researcher*
Hall, Richard Clyde, Jr. *retired religious educational administrator*
Halperin, John William *English literature educator*
Hamilton, Joseph Hants, Jr. *physicist, researcher*
Hanselman, Richard Wilson *entrepreneur*
Hardin, Edward Lester, Jr. *lawyer*
Hargrove, Erwin Charles, Jr. *political science professor*
Harris, Emmylou *singer*
Harris, J(acob) George *health products executive*
Harris, Thomas Raymond *biomedical engineer, educator*
Harrison, Clifford Joy, Jr. *banker*
Hart, Richard Banner *lawyer*
Hartley, Michael J. *travel company executive*
Hassel, Rudolph Christopher *language educator*
Havens, Murray Clark *political scientist, educator*
Hays, Stephen Robert *pediatrician*
Hazelip, Herbert Harold *academic administrator*
Hazen, Samuel N *corporate financial executive*
Heard, Edwin Anthony *banker*

Hefner, James A. *academic administrator*
Henderson, Milton Arnold *professional society administrator*
Hercules, David Michael *chemistry professor, consultant*
Hess, B. Andes, Jr. *chemistry professor*
Hill, Faith *musician*
Hillenmeyer, Henry Reiling, Jr. *restaurant company executive*
Hinshaw, Carroll Elton *economics professor*
Hofstead, James Warner *laundry machinery company executive, lawyer*
Hollon, Steven Dennis *psychology professor, psychologist*
Howell, John Floyd *insurance company executive*
Hwang, Jae-Kwang *physicist, researcher*
Ikizler, Talat Alp *medical educator*
Inagami, Tadashi *biochemistry professor*
Ingram, Orrin Henry, II, *transportation executive*
Jackson, Alan *musician, lyricist*
Jacobs, Sharon O. *lawyer*
Jarman, Mark Foster *language educator*
Jarquin Valdivia, Adrian Alberto *neurologist, researcher*
Jennings, Henry Smith III *cardiologist*
Johnson, David *medical association administrator*
Johnson, Melvin N. *academic administrator, economist*
Johnson, R. Milton *healthcare executive*
Johnston, William P. *health facility administrator*
Juszkiewicz, Henry Edward *musical instrument company executive*
Kaiser, Allen Bernard *health facility administrator*
Kallianpur, Asha R. *epidemiologist*
Kariya, Paul *professional hockey player*
Kasper, Jocelyn A. Alaimo *music educator, musician*
Kiedis, Anthony *vocalist, recording artist, actor*
King, David A. *lawyer*
King, Ed *musician*
Kizilisik, Aydin Tarik *surgeon, researcher*
Krauss, Alison *country musician*
Kuhn, Paul Hubert, Jr. *investment advisor*
Lancaster, John Stevens *historian, museum administrator*
Land, Richard Dale *minister, religious organization administrator*
Lawrence, Tracey *country singer, songwriter*
Lawton, Alexander Robert *immunologist, educator*
Lazar, Irving *psychologist*
Ledyard, Robins Heard *lawyer*
Lee, Donald Han *surgeon, orthopedist*
Lee, Douglas A. *musicologist*
Leipold, Craig L. *professional sports team executive*
LeQuire, Alan Russell *sculptor, educator*
LeVan, Martin Douglas *chemical engineering professor*
Levox, Gary (Gary Wayne Vernon Jr.) *country/rock singer*
Lodge, J. Richard *lawyer*
Longhurst, Robert Russell *retired secondary school educator*
Lukehart, Charles Martin *chemistry professor*
Lynch, John Brown *plastic surgeon, educator*
Lyon, Phillip Kirkland *lawyer*
Madu, Leonard Ekwugha *lawyer, human rights advocate, columnist*
Maguire, Martie (Martha Elenor Erwin Maguire) *musician*
Maier, Harold Geistweit *lawyer, educator*
Maines, Natalie Louise *musician*
Mandrell, Barbara Ann *singer, entertainer, actress, producer, writer*
Manning, Charles W. *university chancellor*
Marney, Samuel Rowe, Jr. *allergist, immunologist, educator*
Martin, Charles Neil, Jr. *health care management company executive*
Martin, Henry Alan *public defender*
Martin, James Larence *dentist, educator*
Martin, Peter Robert *psychiatrist, pharmacologist*
Masulis, Ronald *finance educator*
Masys, Daniel Richard *medical educator, department chairman*
Maupin, John E., Jr. *college president*
Mawn, Louise Ann *ophthalmologist, educator*
May, James M. *medical educator, researcher*
May, Joseph Leserman (Jack May) *retired lawyer*
Mayden, Barbara Mendel *lawyer*
Mayhew, Aubrey *music industry executive*
McBride, Martina *vocalist*
McCabe, Clare *chemical engineer, educator*
McCarty, Richard Charles *psychology professor, dean*
McDonald, Reginald Adrian *musician, educator*
McIntyre, Edward Patrick, Jr. *not-for-profit executive*
McKenzie, Ralph Nelson *mathematician, educator*
McKerley, Annette Elizabeth *school system administrator*
McMurry, Idanelle Sam *educational consultant*
McNally, James Rand (Randy McNally) *pharmacist, state legislator*
Medina, Jose *philosopher, educator*
Merritt, Gilbert Stroud *federal judge*
Mitchell, Angela Carol *elementary school educator*
Montgomery, Dillard Brewster *musician, educator*
Moon, Fletcher Froe *college librarian, multi-media artist, minister*
Moore, William Grover, Jr. *management consultant, retired military officer*
Morrow, Jason Drew *pharmacologist, educator*
Morton, Linda June *academic administrator*
Moses, Harold L. *oncologist*
Neilson, Eric Grant *physician, educator, health facility administrator*
Nelson, Edward Gage *brokerage house executive, bank executive, consultant*
Nichols, Tim *song writer, publisher*
Norris, Thomas Bryant *lawyer*
Norwood, E(dward) Andrew *lawyer*
Oates, John Alexander III *medical educator*
O'Leary, Hazel R. *academic administrator, retired federal official, lawyer*
O'Neill, James Anthony, Jr. *pediatric surgeon, educator*
Orgebin-Crist, Marie-Claire *retired biology professor, department chairman*
Ossoff, Robert Henry *otolaryngologist, surgeon*

Owen, Randy Yeuell *country musician, cattle rancher*
Page, Frank S. *head of religious order*
Paisley, Brad *musician*
Partain, Clarence Leon *radiologist, nuclear medicine physician, educator, health facility administrator*
Pearson, Sela *poet, speaker*
Perlin, Jonathan Brian *health services company executive, former federal agency administrator*
Person, Curtis S., Jr. *state legislator, lawyer*
Petrie, William Marshall *psychiatrist*
Phillips, John A(tlas) III *geneticist, educator*
Pierce, Patricia Ann *university administrator*
Pinkley, Thomas Harold *lawyer*
Pinson, Charles Wright *surgeon, educator, academic administrator*
Pitz, Robert Wendell *professor mechanical engineering*
Poile, David Robert *professional sports team executive*
Policinski, Eugene Francis *foundation administrator, editor, radio personality, television personality, television producer*
Polk, David Brent *pediatrician, educator*
Porter, Andrew Calvin *academic administrator, psychologist, educator*
Powell, Billy *musician*
Quinlan, J(oseph) Michael *lawyer*
Radcliff, Joyce B. *librarian*
Ramer, Hal Reed *academic administrator*
Ramsaur, Allan Fields *legal association administrator, lobbyist*
Ramsey, Lloyd Hamilton *medical educator*
Reschly, Daniel J. *education educator, psychologist*
Reynolds, Doris Elizabeth *management consultant, poet*
Richey, Kimberly Kay *singer, actress, composer*
Ridley, Carolyn Fludd *retired social studies educator*
Risko, Victoria J. *language educator*
Rivera, Maximiano Marquez *academic administrator, educator, researcher, writer*
Roberts, Kenneth Lewis *investor, lawyer, foundation administrator*
Robertson, David *neurologist, educator*
Robison, Emily Burns *musician*
Rooney, Joe Don *country musician*
Roos, Charles Edwin *physicist*
Ross, Joseph Comer *pulmonologist, educator, academic administrator*
Rossington, Gary *musician*
Rothman, Russell L. *medical educator*
Rowan, William Hamilton, Jr. *computer science educator*
Royal, Brenda Campbell *biology educator*
Rubin, Edward *law educator, dean*
Rutherford, William B. *corporate financial executive*
Saff, Edward Barry *mathematics professor, dean*
Sartor, David P. *composer*
Schirg, Brandon Michael *lawyer*
Schnelle, Karl Benjamin, Jr. *chemical engineering professor, consultant, researcher*
Schoggen, Phil H(oward) *psychologist, educator*
Schreiber, Kurt Gilbert *lawyer*
Seivers, Lana C. *school system administrator*
Seligson, Mitchell Allan *political science educator*
Sen, Anjan Ananda *physicist, researcher*
Sergent, John Stanley *hospital administrator, medical educator*
Sevin, Dieter Hermann *literature and language professor*
Shack, R. Bruce *plastic surgeon*
Shallcross, Richard *corporate financial executive*
Shaw, Carole *editor, publisher*
Shell, Owen G., Jr. *retired bank executive*
Sherborne, Robert *editor*
Silberman, Enrique *physicist, director*
Sims, Wilson *lawyer*
Singh, Surendra P. *agricultural economics professor, consultant*
Sisk, Eileen Victoria *writer, journalist*
Smith, Agnes Eyvonda *writer*
Smith, Bradley E. *anesthesiologist*
Smith, Chad Gaylord *musician, recording artist*
Snoddy, Chris Haymond *athletic trainer*
Snyder, Barbara Lou *retired educational association administrator*
Speece, Richard Eugene *civil engineer, educator*
Spengler, Dan Michael *orthopedic surgery educator, surgeon*
Stahlman, Mildred Thornton *pediatrician, pathologist, educator, medical researcher*
Stead, William Wallace *medical educator, researcher, department chairman*
Steele, John M. *human resources specialist*
Sternberg, Paul *ophthalmologist, researcher*
Stewart, David Marshall *librarian*
Stone, Lawrence Mynatt *publishing executive*
Strupp, Hans Hermann *psychologist, educator*
Stuart, Donald Bruce *lawyer*
Summers, Paul G. *state attorney general*
Surowiec, Andrew Julius *biophysicist, researcher*
Swensson, Earl Simcox *architect*
Tarpley, John R. *lawyer*
TeSelle, Eugene Arthur, Jr. *religion educator*
Thomas, Hazel Beatrice *state official*
Thomas, Randall Stuart *lawyer, educator*
Thomas, Robert Paige *lawyer*
Thompson, Dean Allan *cattleman*
Thompson, Jennifer Lynn *lawyer*
Thornton, Spencer P. *ophthalmologist, educator*
Torquati, Alfonso *surgeon, educator*
Trauger, Aleta Arthur *judge*
Trotz, Barry *professional hockey coach*
Tuke, Robert Dudley *lawyer, educator*
Tulsiani, Daulatram P. *biologist, researcher*
Turk, Thomas Liebig *cultural organization administrator*
Twain, Shania (Eilleen Regina Edwards) *musician*
Ullestad, Merwin Allan *tax specialist, director*
Urban, Keith *country singer, songwriter*
Urmy, Norman B. *hospital administrator*
Valentine, Alan Darrell *performing company executive, conductor*
Van Mol, Louis John, Jr. *public relations executive*
Vines, James K. *prosecutor, lawyer*
Viscusi, W(illiam) G. Kip *law and economics educator*

Voegeli, Victor Jacque *historian, educator, dean*
Wadley, Fredia Stovall *state commissioner*
Wasserman, David H. *medical educator, researcher*
Waterman, Robert A. *lawyer*
Waters, Karen Rigsby *music educator*
Watkins, Sara *musician*
Weingartner, H(ans) Martin *finance educator*
Wen, Quan *economics professor, researcher*
Westfield, Fred Meinhard *economics professor*
Wilder, John Shelton *lieutenant governor*
Williams, Hank, Jr., (Randall Hank Williams) *country music singer, songwriter*
Williams, Marsha Rhea *computer scientist, educator, researcher, consultant*
Williams, Noel Brown *information technology executive*
Wilson, Gretchen *vocalist*
Wire, William Shidaker, II, *retired apparel and footwear manufacturing company executive*
Wiseman, Craig *song writer, publisher*
Wiseman, Thomas Anderton, Jr. *federal judge*
Wonders, Pamela Kim *music educator*
Woodruff, Linda Gyjuan *mathematics educator*
Wright, Randy S. *management consultant*
Yang, Edmund Yi-Bin *biomedical researcher, pediatric surgeon*
Morton-Young, Tommie *psychology professor, writer*
Young, Vince Paul, Jr. *professional football player*
Yu, Guoliang *mathematician, educator*
Yuspeh, Alan Ralph *lawyer, health company executive*
Zavalin, Andrey I. *optics scientist, educator*
Zepos, Nicholas S. *academic administrator*
Zhou, Suping *biologist, research scientist, educator*
Zibart, Michael Alan *wholesale book company executive*

### Newport

Ball, Travis, Jr. *school administrator, editor*
Dykeman, Wilma *writer, educator*
Porter, James Kenneth *retired judge*

### Oak Ridge

Ally, Moonis R. *chemical engineer*
Aytug, Tolga *science educator*
Ball, Jacqueline Snyder *librarian, educator*
Bhuiyan, Md Shafiqur Rahman *materials scientist*
Boatner, Lynn Allen *research physicist*
Borie, Bernard Simon, Jr. *retired physicist, educator*
Carlsmith, Roger Snedden *chemistry and energy conservation researcher*
Colston, Freddie Charles *political science professor*
Crawford, Arlene Joanne *music educator, director*
Culiat, Cymbeline Tancongco *geneticist*
David, Stanislaus Antony *metallurgical engineer*
Fogle, Michael Roy, Jr. *physicist*
Goyal, Amit *research scientist*
Hartman, Frederick Cooper *retired biochemist*
Harvey, John Arthur *nuclear physicist*
Holloway, Jacqueline *county commissioner*
Hu, Zhiyu *research scientist, educator*
Jones, Virginia McClurkin *retired social worker*
Katoh, Yutai *materials scientist*
Krause, Manfred Otto *physicist*
Kronenberg, Andreas *nuclear chemist, radiochemist, nuclear technology consultant*
Larson, Bennett Charles *solid state physicist, researcher*
Lynch, Vickie Evette *research scientist*
Maienschein, Fred *retired physicist*
McNeilly, Kathy Eden *librarian, library director*
Messman, Jamie M. *polymer chemist*
Nephew, Edmund A. *physicist, retired mayor*
Pannala, Sreekanth *aerospace engineer*
Pinnaduwage, Lal Ariyaratna *physicist, researcher*
Plasil, Franz *physicist*
Poling, Sheila R. *management consultant*
Pouchard, Line Catherine *research scientist, educator*
Poutsma, Marvin L. *retired chemical research administrator*
Raridon, Richard Jay *retired computer scientist*
Regan-Stanton, Christa Maria *artist*
Rucker, Thomas Lee *physicist*
Runtsch, Clarence Frederick *sculptor*
Schwenterly, Stanley William *physicist, researcher*
Slusher, Kimberly Goode *management consultant*
Spray, Paul Ellsworth *retired surgeon*
Strickler, Dennis Johnson *research scientist*
Wang, Hong *engineer, researcher*
Watson, Evelyn Egner *radiation scientist*
Zucker, Alexander *physicist, researcher*

### Oakland

Terry, Theo B. III *technology executive*

### Ooltewah

Birch, Lorna May *geriatrician*

### Paris

McFarlin, Shannon Dianne *writer, researcher*

### Pigeon Forge

Catron, Stephen Barnard *lawyer, real estate developer, director*
Parton, Dolly Rebecca *singer, composer, actress*

### Pleasant Hill

Hull, Charles William *retired special education educator*

### Pleasant View

Hampton, Margaret Ann Barnes *elementary school educator*

### Powell

Hyman, Roger David *lawyer*
Roach, Janet Ann *music educator*

### Pulaski

Murrell, James Thomas *academic administrator, botanist*

### Ripley

Ammons, H. Ray *band director*

Garner, Harvey Louis *computer scientist, consultant, engineering educator*
Garwood, William Lockhart *federal judge*
Gary, James M. *lawyer*
Gates, Charles Woodley, Sr. *city official*
Gau, George W. *dean*
Gavenda, J(ohn) David *physicist*
Gentle, Kenneth William *physicist*
George, Timothy Merrill *neurosurgeon, educator*
George, Walter Eugene, Jr. *architect*
Gibbins, Bob *lawyer*
Giblin, Pamela M. *lawyer*
Gibson, Jerry Leigh *oil industry executive*
Giddings, Helen *state representative, personnel management director*
Gillman, Leonard *mathematician, educator*
Girling, Robert George William III *business owner*
Glade, William Patton, Jr. *economics professor*
Glenn, Norval Dwight *sociologist, educator*
Goldstein, E. Ernest *lawyer, consultant*
Golemon, Ronald Kinnan *lawyer*
Gonzalez-Gerth, Miguel *literature and language educator, writer*
Goodenough, John Bannister *engineering educator, physicist, researcher*
Gould, Lewis Ludlow *historian, educator*
Gracy, David Bergen, II, *archivist, information science educator, writer*
Graglia, Lino Anthony *lawyer, educator*
Graham, Don Ballew *literature educator, writer*
Graham, Seldon Bain, Jr. *lawyer, engineer*
Granof, Michael H. *finance educator, department chairman*
Grant, Verne Edwin *biology professor*
Green, Paul Warren *state supreme court justice*
Green, Shirley Moore *retired communications executive, public information officer*
Greene, John Joseph *lawyer*
Greenhill, Joe Robert *retired judge, lawyer*
Greig, Brian Strother *lawyer*
Griffy, Thomas Alan *physics professor*
Groat, Charles George *geologist, former federal agency administrator*
Groten, Barnet *energy executive*
Guerin, John William *artist*
Guli, Laura Ann *psychologist, educator*
Gustafsson, Lars Erik Einar *writer, educator*
Haas, Joseph Marshall *retired petroleum consultant*
Hackert, Marvin LeRoy *chemistry professor, biophysical researcher*
Hale, Louis Dewitt *lawyer*
Hamermesh, Daniel Selim *economics professor*
Hamilton, Dagmar Strandberg *lawyer, educator*
Hamilton, Robert Woodruff *retired legal association administrator, retired law educator*
Hancock, Gerre Edward *musician, educator*
Hankins, Michael James-Edwin *broadcast executive*
Hardin, Dale Wayne *political science professor*
Harms, Robert Thomas *linguist, educator*
Harris, Ben M. *education educator*
Harris, Catherine Kirk *law librarian*
Harris, Richard Lee *engineering executive, retired military officer*
Harrison, Richard Wayne *lawyer*
Hatgil, Paul Peter *artist, sculptor, educator*
Hayes, Patricia Ann *health facility administrator*
Haznedar, Haldun *electronics engineer*
Heath, Fred Milton *library director, educator*
Hecht, Nathan Lincoln *state supreme court justice*
Helman, Stephen Jody *lawyer*
Henderson, George Ervin *lawyer*
Henley, Paul Thomas *music educator, researcher*
Hester, Thomas Roy *anthropologist, educator*
Higginbotham, Patrick Errol *federal judge*
High, Timothy Griffin *artist, educator, curator, writer*
Himmelblau, David Mautner *chemical engineer*
Hinojosa, Tish (Leticia Hinojosa) *vocalist*
Hinojosa-Smith, Roland *language educator, writer*
Hitchcock, Joanna *publisher*
Hixson, Elmer L. *retired engineering educator*
Holtzman, Wayne Harold *psychologist, educator*
Holz, Robert Kenneth *retired geography educator*
Houston, Ron *professional society administrator*
Howell, John Reid *mechanical engineering educator, director*
Hubbs, Clark *zoologist, researcher*
Hudec, Michael Robert *geologist, researcher*
Hudspeth, Harry Lee *federal judge*
Hughes, Thomas J.R. *mechanical engineering educator, consultant*
Hull, David George *aerospace engineering educator, researcher*
Hussain, Muhammad Mustafa *research scientist*
Ikard, Frank Neville, Jr. *lawyer*
Inman, Bobby Ray *retired electronics executive*
Ivy, John L. *medical educator, researcher*
Jackson, William Vernon *Latin American studies and library science educator*
Jacobson, Antone Gardner *retired zoology educator*
James, Randall S. *state banking department commissioner*
Janes, Brandon Chaison *lawyer*
Jastrow, Kenneth M. *financial executive*
Jefferson, Wallace B. *state supreme court chief justice*
Jensen, Paul Allen *mechanical engineer*
Jentz, Gaylord Adair *law educator*
Johnson, Lady Bird (Mrs. Claudia Alta Taylor Johnson) *former First Lady of the United States*
Johnson, Philip Wayne *judge*
Johnson, Sandra K. *electrical engineer*
Jones, Matthew Carl *researcher, lawyer*
Jordan, Bryce *retired university president*
Kelley, Henry Paul *academic administrator, psychology educator*
Kendrick, David Andrew *economist, educator*
Kibler, William Westcott *French language and literature educator*
Killough, David E. *lawyer*
Kimberlin, Sam Owen, Jr. *financial consultant*
Kirk, Lynda Pounds *biofeedback therapist, neurotherapist, counselor*
Kirk, Terrence *lawyer*
Knapp, Mark Lane *communications educator, consultant*
Knepp, Christopher A. *lawyer*

Koen, Billy Vaughn *mechanical engineering educator*
Kolar, Mary Jane *trade and professional association executive*
Kuchar Glynn, Tiffany Elizabeth *psychologist*
Lagow, Richard James *chemistry professor*
Lam, Simon Shin-Sing *computer science educator*
Lamb, Jamie Parker, Jr. *retired mechanical engineer*
Lang, Roberta Lynn *food products company executive, lawyer*
Lansford, James Lowell *technologist*
Larkam, Beverley McCosham *social worker, marriage and family therapist*
Larson, Jeanette Carolyn *librarian*
Larson, Kermit Dean *finance educator*
Lary, Banning Kent *film producer, writer*
Leare, Bobbie Jean *musician, educator*
Lemens, William Vernon, Jr. *banker, finance company executive, lawyer*
Lenoir, Gloria Cisneros *secondary school educator, consultant*
Lincoln, Timothy Dwight *library director*
Lindstrom, Naomi Eva *language educator*
Livingston, William Samuel *academic administrator, political scientist, educator*
Lochridge, Lloyd Pampell, Jr. *lawyer*
Lochridge, Patton G. *lawyer*
Lockett, Landon Johnson *retired linguist*
Loehlin, John Clinton *psychologist, educator*
Long, Teresa Lozano *foundation administrator, educator*
Loo, Lynn (Yueh-Lin) *chemical engineer*
Louis, William Roger *historian*
MacKay, Carol Hanbery *literature educator*
Mackey, John P. *food products executive*
Magee, Stephen Pat *economics professor, finance professor*
Mano, Nicolas P. *research scientist*
Mark, Hans Michael *physicist, former federal agency administrator*
Markman, Arthur Brian *psychology professor*
Marshall, Richard Paul, Jr. *lawyer*
Martin, Frederick Noel *audiology educator*
Martin, Stephen F. *chemist, educator, researcher*
Marya, Manuel Paul Claude *metallurgical and materials engineer*
Mathias, Reuben Victor (Vic Mathias) *organization executive, real estate investor*
Mathis, Marsha Debra *customer service administrator*
Matthews, Charles R. *academic administrator*
May, Robert George *dean, accounting educator*
Mayer, Michel *computer company executive*
Mayes, Wendell Wise, Jr. *former broadcasting company executive*
Mazzetti, Robert F. *real estate manager, retired orthopedic surgeon*
McBride, Earle F. *geologist, educator*
McClintic, James A. *lab administrator*
McCullough, Frank Witcher III *lawyer*
McDaniel, Myra Atwell *lawyer, former state official*
McFadden, Dennis *psychologist, educator*
McKeown-Moak, Mary Park *educational consultant*
Mc Ketta, John J., Jr. *chemical engineering professor*
McKetta, John J. III *lawyer*
Mc Kinney, Michael Whitney *trade association executive*
Mear, Charles Eugene *geologist, consultant*
Medina, David *state supreme court judge*
Mersky, Roy Martin *law educator, legal association administrator*
Meston, Cindy M(ay) *psychologist, educator*
Meyers, Lauren Ancel *biologist*
Meyers, Lawrence Edward *state judge*
Middleton, Christopher *Germanic languages and literature educator*
Middleton, Harry Joseph *foundation administrator*
Miller, Charles E. (Chuck Miller) *judge*
Milliken, Kitty Lou *research scientist*
Mills, Stephen *artistic director*
Moag, Rodney Frank *language educator, country and bluegrass singer, musician, record producer*
Mooney, John Bradford, Jr. *oceanographer, consultant, engineer*
Moragné e Silva, Michèle Lowe *language educator*
Morris, Quinton Ilando *music educator, director*
Morrow, Sandra Kay *librarian*
Morton, R. Steven *lawyer*
Moss, Bill Ralph *lawyer*
Moss, Logan Vansen *lawyer*
Mueller, Peggy Jean *dance educator, choreographer, rancher*
Mulconrey, Brian George *management consultant, futurist*
Mullen, Ron *insurance company executive*
Mullenix, Linda Susan *law educator*
Neavel, Celia Beth *medical association administrator*
Neeley, Shirley *school system administrator*
Nichols, Steven Parks *mechanical engineer, educator, lawyer, academic administrator*
Novak, Gordon S., Jr. *computer scientist, educator*
Nowlin, James Robertson *federal judge*
Oden, John Tinsley *engineering educator, mathematician, consultant*
Olasky, Marvin *journalist, educator, editor*
O'Neill, Harriet *state supreme court justice*
Oram, Robert W. *library administrator*
Osborne, Duncan Elliott *lawyer*
Oshinsky, David M *history professor, writer*
Otto, Byron Leonard *lawyer, state agency administrator*
Owen, Priscilla Richman *federal judge, former state supreme court justice*
Painter, Theophilus Shickel, Jr. *internist, allergist*
Parrino, Robert *finance educator*
Parrish, William M. *lawyer*
Patterson, Donald Eugene *research scientist*
Payne, John Ross *archivist, educator, library and information scientist, educator*
Payne, Tyson Elliott, Jr. *retired insurance executive*
Pearson, Jim Berry, Jr. *human resources specialist*
Pena, Richard *lawyer*
Peppas, Nicholas Athanassiou *chemical and biomedical engineering educator, consultant*

Perry, Rick *governor*
Peterson, Robert Allen *marketing educator*
Phillips, Joseph Daniel *geophysicist, oceanographer*
Phillips, Thomas Royal *lawyer, former state supreme court chief justice*
Pickett, Sandra *information scientist*
Pirkey, Louis Thomas *lawyer*
Pope, Andrew Jackson, Jr., (Jack Pope) *retired judge*
Porter, Jenny Lind *writer*
Powers, William Charles, Jr. *academic administrator, law educator*
Prather, Laura Lee *lawyer, educator*
Probus, Michael Maurice, Jr. *lawyer*
Qiu, Lili *science educator*
Rascoe, Paul Stephen *librarian, researcher*
Ray, Cread L., Jr. *retired judge*
Reese, Lymon Clifton *civil engineering educator*
Rich, John Martin *humanities educator, researcher*
Richards-Kortum, Rebecca Rae *biomedical engineering educator*
Richmond, Marvin Elliot *astronomer, educator*
Ritchey, Brent Dylan *lawyer*
Roach, James Robert *retired political science professor*
Roan, Forrest Calvin, Jr. *lawyer*
Romero, Jesse Charles *political consultant*
Rossky, Peter Jacob *chemistry professor, researcher*
Rostow, Elspeth Davies *political science professor*
Roueche, John Edward, II, *education educator, director*
Royal, Darrell K. *university official, retired football coach*
Ruiz, Cookie *performing company executive*
Rylander, Henry Grady, Jr. *mechanical engineering educator*
Salinas, Celena Iris *reading specialist*
Sampson, John J. *law educator*
Sanchez, Isaac Cornelius *chemical engineer, educator*
Sandberg, Irwin Walter *retired electrical and computer engineering educator*
Sands, Dolores S. *dean*
Sawyer, Margo Lucy *artist, educator*
Sawyer, William Dale *internist, educator, dean, foundation administrator*
Schechter, Robert Samuel *chemical engineer, educator*
Schleuse, William *retired psychiatrist, psychoanalyst*
Schmitt, Karl Michael *retired political scientist*
Schoenemann, David Leroy *real estate broker, small business owner*
Schuurman, Willem Gerhard *lawyer*
Schwartz, Aaron Robert *lawyer, former state legislator*
Schwitters, Roy Frederick *physicist, researcher*
Sciance, Carroll Thomas *chemical engineer, educator*
Scott, David Winfield *artist, museum administrator*
Serafine, Mary Louise *psychologist, educator, lawyer*
Sessler, Jonathan Lawrence *chemistry professor*
Seung, Thomas Kaehao *philosophy educator*
Shapiro, Florence *state legislator, advertising executive, public relations executive*
Shea, Andrew Brendan *film director, film producer*
Sherman, Max Ray *lawyer, dean, former state senator*
Shilling, Roy Bryant, Jr. *academic administrator*
Simpson, Beryl Brintnall *botany educator*
Smith, Jeffrey Chipps *art educator*
Sparks, Sam *federal judge*
Spence, Roy Milam, Jr. *advertising executive*
Springer, David William *dean, social sciences educator*
Staley, Thomas Fabian *language professional, academic administrator*
Stapleton, Bill *sports and entertainment agent*
Steinfink, Hugo *chemical engineering professor*
Stewart, Kent Kallam *analytical biochemistry educator*
Stokoe, Kenneth H., II, *civil engineer, educator*
Stoll, William Hermann *real estate company executive*
Stoner, James Lloyd *retired foundation administrator, clergyman*
Stout, Patricia A. *communications educator*
Strauser, Robert Wayne *lawyer*
Streetman, Ben Garland *electrical engineering educator*
Sturley, Michael F. *law educator*
Sullivan, Jerry Stephen *electronics executive*
Sutherland, William Owen Sheppard *retired language educator, consultant*
Sutton, Beverly Jewell *psychiatrist*
Sutton, Harry Eldon *geneticist, educator*
Sutton, John F., Jr. *lawyer, educator, dean*
Swartzlander, Earl Eugene, Jr. *engineering educator, former electronics company executive*
Swinney, Harry Leonard *physics professor*
Tapley, Byron Dean *aerospace engineer, educator*
Tate, John Torrence *mathematics professor, researcher*
Temple, Larry Eugene *lawyer*
Theriot, Edward C. *museum director*
Thornton, Joseph Scott *research and development company executive, materials scientist*
Thurston, George Butte *mechanical and biomedical engineering educator*
Titman, Sheridan *finance educator*
Tottenham, Terry Oliver *lawyer*
Tucker, Richard Lee *civil engineer, educator*
Vande Hey, James Michael *retired air force officer*
Vita-More, Natasha *information technology executive*
Volk, William R. *lawyer*
Voyles, Robb Lawrence *lawyer*
Vykukal, Eugene Lawrence *pharmaceutical executive, director*
Wahlberg, Philip Lawrence *former bishop*
Wainwright, Dale V. *state supreme court justice*
Walter, Virginia Lee *psychologist, educator*
Walton, Charles Michael *civil engineering educator*
Watkins, Joe Bill *lawyer*
Watson, Brenda Bennett *insurance company executive*

Weddington, Sarah Ragle *lawyer, educator*
Weinberg, Louise *law educator, writer*
Weinman, Daryl Gail *lawyer*
Weintraub, Russell Jay *lawyer, educator*
Weismann, Donald Leroy *artist, educator, filmmaker, writer*
Welch, Ashley James *engineering educator*
Wentworth, Earl Jeffrey *lawyer, realtor, state legislator*
West, Royce *lawyer, state legislator*
Westbrook, Jay Lawrence *law educator*
Wheeler, John Craig *astrophysicist, writer*
Whitbread, Thomas Bacon *language educator, writer*
White, John Michael *chemistry professor*
Willett, Don R. *state supreme court justice*
Williams, Mary Pearl *judge*
Williams, Roger *state official*
Williams III, Roberton Capell *economics professor*
Williamson, Barry Scott *conductor, performing arts educator*
Williamson, Thomas Arnold *publishing executive*
Willson, C. Grant *chemical engineering and chemistry professor*
Wilson, Clark R. *geophysicist, educator*
Wilson, Margaret Scarbrough *retail executive*
Wilson, Michael Joseph *newspaper executive*
Winegar, Albert Lee *computer company executive*
Winters, Sam *lawyer*
Wong, Martha Jee *state representative*
Wood, Donald F. *lawyer*
Wurzbach, Linda *educational consultant*
Wynn, Will *mayor*
Xin, Jack *mathematician, educator*
Yacktman, Stephen *investment company executive*
York, Candace A. *marketing professional, writer*
Young, Phyllis Casselman *music educator*
Yudof, Mark George *academic administrator, law educator, federal agency administrator*
Zeng, Hongliu Henry *geophysicist, geologist*
Zlateva, Maria *music educator*

**Bacliff**

Kahn, Kathleen Pica *photojournalist, arbitrator, mediator*

**Baird**

Rodenberger, Charles Alvard *aerospace engineer, consultant*

**Bandera**

Bartley, Dee Gray *information technology executive*
Bartley, William Call *science administrator*

**Bastrop**

Carpenter, Delbert Stanley *educational administration educator*
Reaves, Melvin Junior *retired small business owner*

**Baytown**

Casey, Carole Lynn *elementary school educator, music educator*
Harrison, Paula Jean *church musician*
Leiper, Robert Duncan *local government official*
Williams, Drew Davis *surgeon*

**Beaumont**

Alter, Nelson Tobias *retail executive, wholesale distribution executive*
Aung, Kendrick Than *mechanical engineer, educator*
Bahrim, Cristian *physicist, educator*
Baker, Mary Alice *communications educator, consultant*
Black, Robert Allen *lawyer*
Bradley, Jerry Wayne *language educator, department chairman*
Brailsford, June Evelyn *musician, educator*
Brentlinger, William Brock *college dean*
Brooks, Jack Bascom *former congressman*
Chiou, Paul C.J. *statistician, educator*
Comick, Terrence Christopher *principal*
Davis, Gloria Whittie *educational association administrator*
Denham, Michael Thomas *minister*
Dowell, James Dale *lawyer*
Dryden, Woodson E. *lawyer*
Gagne, Mary *academic administrator*
Hopper, Jack Rudd *chemical engineering professor*
Horton, Henry Hollis III *judge*
Johnson, Leanne *lawyer*
Kemble, Joe David *mathematics professor*
Koehn, Enno *engineering educator, researcher*
Lampson, Nicholas V. *former congressman*
Lord, Evelyn Marlin *mayor*
Lozano, Jose *nephrologist*
Martin, Quincy III *career planning administrator*
Maxey, Debra S. *secondary school educator*
Morales, Emmitt *mechanical engineer, consultant*
Needham, Keith Alan *language educator*
Nelson, Chris B. *physics professor*
Orwig, Matthew Dane *prosecutor, lawyer*
Payne, Elton Curtis, Jr. *adult education educator*
Payne, James Erick *lawyer*
Reay-Jones, Francis Peter Fortnum *entomologist, researcher*
Richardson, Sandra Lynn *mathematics professor*
Roth, Lane *communications educator*
Scofield, Louis M., Jr. *lawyer*
Sooudi, Matthew M. *retired surgeon*
Ward, Debra Yvette *elementary school educator*
Wheatley, Randall *theater educator, theater director, playwright*

**Bedford**

Dawes, Robert Leo *mathematician, consultant*
Horvat, Vashti *online marketing consultant*

**Beeville**

Littlejohn, John Joseph *petroleum engineer*

**Bellaire**

Chavez, Brenda G. *construction executive, real estate agent*
Crayton, Arnell *secondary school educator*
Haywood, Theodore Joseph *physician, educator*
Jacobus, Charles Joseph *lawyer, title company executive, writer*
Kramer, Adam Miles *lawyer*

Anderson, Barbara McComas *lawyer*
Anderson, E. Karl *lawyer*
Anderson, Ron Joe *health facility administrator, internist, educator*
Anglin, Michael Williams *lawyer*
Antioco, John F. *entertainment company executive*
Arbique, Debbie Anita *emergency nurse practitioner*
Arpey, Gerard J. *air transportation executive*
Attanasio, John Baptist *dean, law educator*
Augur, Marilyn Hussman *distribution executive*
Azam, Anwar *cardiologist*
Babcock, Charles Lynde, IV, *lawyer*
Baggett, W. Mike *lawyer*
Bailon, Gilbert *newspaper executive*
Ballesteros, Victor Hugo *dean*
Bangs, Nelson A. (Tony Bangs) *lawyer*
Banzhof, Carl E. *information technology executive*
Barbour, David A. *lawyer*
Barnes, Robert Vertreese, Jr. *construction executive*
Baron, Frederick M. *lawyer*
Barrett, Colleen Crotty *air transportation executive*
Bartlett, Richard Chalkley *writer, conservationist*
Basden, John William *artist*
Baxter, Richard Henry *research scientist*
Bayne, James Elwood *investor*
Beard, Bruce H. *retired psychiatrist*
Becker, Jeffrey M. *lawyer*
Beer, James A. *information technology executive, former air transportation executive*
Bergstresser, Paul Richard *dermatologist, educator*
Berry, Phil Hunter, Jr. *orthopedic surgeon*
Best, Robert Wayne *gas transmission company executive, lawyer*
Betts, Dianne Connally *economist, educator*
Beuttenmuller, Rudolf William *lawyer*
Bick, Rodger Lee *hematologist, researcher, oncologist, educator*
Bickel, John W., II, *lawyer*
Biegler, David W. *energy executive*
Birkeland, Bryan Collier *lawyer*
Bishop, Gene Herbert *corporate financial executive*
Blankenbaker, Zarina *adult education educator, consultant*
Blessen, Karen Alyce *freelance/self-employed journalist, artist*
Blessing, Edward Warfield *petroleum company executive*
Bliss, Robert Harms *lawyer*
Bloom, John (Joe Bob Briggs) *comedian, writer*
Blue, John Ronald (J. Ronald Blue) *evangelical mission executive*
Blumenthal, Karen *newspaper executive*
Bockstruck, Lloyd DeWitt *librarian*
Bondy, Joanne *chef*
Bonte, Frederick James *radiologist, educator, physician*
Boone, Michael Mauldin *lawyer*
Borynack, Zachary A. *psychologist*
Bosch, Joseph A. *human resources specialist*
Boswell, George Marion, Jr. *orthopedist, health facility administrator*
Bowers, Daniel Charles *oncologist*
Boyle, Jane J. *federal judge, lawyer*
Bracken, Frank D. *retail executive*
Bradford, William Edward *oil field equipment manufacturing company executive*
Bradley, John Andrew *health facility administrator*
Brainin, Stacy L. *lawyer*
Bramblett, George, Jr. *lawyer*
Brandt, Carole *theater educator, department chairman*
Braun, Susan J. *foundation administrator*
Brekhus, Melvin G. *construction executive*
Brilakis, Emmanouil S. *cardiologist, educator*
Brin, Royal Henry, Jr. *lawyer*
Brinker, Nancy Goodman *social services administrator, former ambassador*
Brinker, Norman E. *restaurant company executive*
Bromberg, Alan Robert *law educator, lawyer*
Brooks, Ben A. *lawyer*
Brooks, Douglas H. *food service executive*
Brooks, James Elwood *geologist, educator*
Brown, Benjamin A. *investment advisor*
Brown, Colleen *broadcast executive*
Brown, Michael Stuart *geneticist, educator, science administrator*
Brown, Stephen F. *health facility administrator*
Bryant, L. Gerald *management consultant*
Bucker, Robert *educational fundraiser*
Bumpas, Stuart Maryman *lawyer*
Burke, William Temple, Jr. *lawyer*
Burns, Alton Jay *plastic surgeon*
Burns, Scott *columnist*
Byrd, Henry Stephenson (Steve) *plastic surgeon, educator*
Byrne, Susan M. *investment company executive*
Caetano, Raul *psychiatrist, educator*
Cain, David H. *lawyer, former state legislator*
Callahan, Jack F., Jr. *food products executive*
Campbell, Kevin P. *oil industry executive*
Campbell, Raymond III *publication director*
Cantrell, Scott *newspaper music critic*
Cantrill, Thomas H. *lawyer*
Carl, Robert E. *retired marketing company executive*
Carnes, Joseph Sydney *clergyman*
Carpenter, Gordon Russell *retired lawyer, banker*
Case, Thomas Louis *lawyer*
Cavanagh, Harrison Dwight *ophthalmologist, educator*
Cave, Ellis *information technology executive*
Charriere, Suzanne *architectural firm executive*
Chase, J. Scott *lawyer*
Chavez, John Richard *historian, educator*
Chawner, Lucia Martha *language educator*
Cherry, William Speakman *real estate broker, consultant*
Cho, Ho Soon Michelle L. *adult education educator*
Choy, Hak *oncologist*
Cirilo, Amelia Medina *educational consultant*
Clark, Robert Murel, Jr. *lawyer*
Clifton, Matthew P. *petroleum refining company executive*
Cline, Bobby James *insurance company executive*
Cloud, Robert Royce *surgeon*
Cloutman, Edward Bradbury III *lawyer*

Cochran, George Calloway III *retired bank executive, lawyer*
Cochran, Mona Sheinfeld *retired economics professor*
Cockerham, Sidney Joe *professional society administrator*
Coggins, Paul Edward, Jr. *lawyer*
Coldwell, Philip Edward *financial consultant*
Cole, James S. *dean, dental educator*
Coleman, James Edwin, Jr. *lawyer*
Coleman, Robert Winston *lawyer*
Collins, Bruce W. *lawyer*
Collins, Philip A. *management consultant*
Colson, Randall Elwin *lawyer*
Comini, Alessandra *art historian, educator*
Conner, Terry W. *lawyer*
Cook, Gary Raymond *academic administrator, minister*
Copley, Edward Alvin *lawyer*
Corway, Charles Edward *computer draftsman*
Countryman, Edward Francis *historian, educator*
Cowart, T(homas) David *lawyer*
Cowles, Jim E. *lawyer*
Cox, John Michael *lawyer*
Cox, Rody P(owell) *internist, educator*
Crain, John Walter *historian, educator*
Crain, Russell Jon *lawyer*
Creel, Luther Edward III *lawyer*
Crichton, Thomas, IV, *lawyer*
Crockett, Dodee Frost *brokerage house executive*
Croskell, Madelon Byrd *music educator, classical vocalist*
Crotty, Robert Bell *lawyer*
Crow, Trammell *real estate company executive*
Crowley, James Worthington *retired lawyer, investor, financial consultant*
Cruseman, F. Ross (Frederick Ross Cruseman) *advertising agency official*
Cuban, Mark *professional sports team executive, Internet company executive*
Curran, Charles Edward *theology studies educator, priest*
Dalton, Harry Jirou, Jr., (Jerry Dalton) *public relations executive*
Daly, Gail M. *law librarian, educator*
Daves, Don Michael *minister*
Davis, Barry E. *energy executive*
Davis, Clarice McDonald *lawyer*
Davis, Joe A. *lawyer*
Davis, Ray C. *energy executive*
Dawson, Edward Joseph *merger and acquisition executive*
Dawson, William B. *lawyer*
Dealey, Lynn Townsend *artist*
Deason, Darwin *information technology executive*
Dechert, Robert William *newspaper and broadcasting executive*
Deckelman, William L., Jr. *lawyer*
Dederich-Pejovich, Susan Russell *harpist*
Dee, Ronda *poet, photographer, small business owner, journalist*
Deisenhofer, Johann *biochemistry professor, researcher*
Delfassy, Gilles *semiconductor company executive*
Dell, Susan *foundation administrator, apparel designer*
Demarest, Sylvia M. *lawyer*
Diaz Meyer, Cheryl *photojournalist*
Dieste, Tony *marketing professional*
Dillon, David Anthony *editor, educator*
Dinkins, Jane Poling *management consultant, application developer*
Dir, Dave *professional soccer coach*
Doke, Marshall J., Jr. *lawyer*
Doran, Mark Richard *real estate financial executive*
Doty, Elmer *aeronautical engineer*
Dozier, David Charles, Jr. *advertising executive, public relations executive*
Drapkin, Dennis B. *lawyer*
Dufner, Edward Joseph *editor*
Dumerer, Lorraine JoAnne Lori *secondary school educator, consultant*
Durham, Michael Jonathan *investment professional*
Dutton, Diana Cheryl *lawyer*
Duvall, William (Bill) C. *real estate company executive*
Dyess, Bobby Dale *lawyer*
Eads, John A. *accountant*
Eaton, Michael William *lawyer, educator*
Eberhart, Robert Clyde *biomedical engineering educator, researcher*
Edwards, Barry L. *leasing company executive*
Edwards, Warren D. *computer company executive*
Egan, Byron F. *lawyer*
Eichenwald, Heinz Felix *physician*
Eichman, John C. *lawyer*
Einspruch, Burton Cyril *psychiatrist*
Eller, Timothy R. (Tim Eller) *real estate company executive, construction executive*
Elliott, Dorothy Gail *music educator, writer*
Ellis, Alfred Wright (Al Ellis) *lawyer*
Emery, Herschel Gene *lawyer*
Engibous, Thomas (Tom) James *electronics company executive*
England, Julie Spicer *computer company executive*
Engles, Gregg L. *food products executive*
Estep, Robert Lloyd *lawyer*
Etgen, Ann *performing arts educator, choreographer*
Ethridge, Joseph Alfred *manufacturing executive*
Evans, Laurie *library director*
Everbach, Otto George *lawyer*
Fabre, Raul *management consultant*
Fagin, Stephen Andrew *historian*
Fairbairn, Ursula Farrell *human resources executive*
Fanning, Barry Hedges *lawyer*
Farber, Stephen D. *health facility administrator*
Farell, Dan *utilities executive*
Farquhar, Robert Michael *lawyer*
Fegan, Jeffrey P. *airport executive*
Feld, Alan David *lawyer*
Fenner, Suzan Ellen *lawyer*
Fetter, Trevor *healthcare industry executive*
Fielder, Charles Robert *retired oil industry executive*
Fifield, William O. *lawyer*
Figari, Ernest Emil, Jr. *lawyer, educator*
Fijolek, Richard M. *lawyer*
Fillmore, Robert M. *lawyer*

Finkelstein, William Berndt *lawyer*
Flanagan, Christie Stephen *lawyer*
Flatt, Adrian Ede *surgeon*
Flegle, Jim L. *lawyer*
Fontana, Robert Edward *electrical engineer, educator, retired military officer*
Fordtran, John Satterfield *physician*
Forshey, Michael S. *lawyer*
Fortado, Michael George *lawyer*
Foster, Daniel Willett *medical educator*
France, Newell Edwin *retired health facility administrator*
Francisco, Glen Leif *engineer, engineering executive*
Franklin, Janice L. *music educator*
Franklin, Kirk *singer*
Franze, Laura Marie *lawyer*
Free, Mary Moore *biological and medical anthropologist*
Freidel, David Alan *archaeologist, anthropologist, educator*
Freling, Richard Alan *lawyer*
French, Joseph Jordan, Jr. *lawyer*
Frenkel, Eugene Phillip *physician*
Freytag, Sharon Nelson *lawyer*
Friedheim, Jan V. *educational association administrator*
Friedheim, Stephen Bailey *educational consultant*
Frisbie, Curtis Lynn, Jr. *lawyer*
Fritz, Terrence Lee *investment banker, strategic consultant*
Fyfe, Alistair Ian *cardiologist, scientist, educator*
Gafford, Ronald J. *construction executive*
Galvin, Charles O'Neill *law educator*
Gant, Norman Ferrell, Jr. *obstetrician, gynecologist, educator*
Gardner, Stephen Henry *lawyer*
Garner, Bryan Andrew *law educator, consultant, writer*
Garner, Daniel C. *lawyer*
Garreans, Leonard Lansford *protective services official, criminal justice professional*
Gibbs, James Alanson *geologist, consultant*
Gibby, Diane Louise *physician, plastic surgeon*
Gibby, Mabel Enid Kunce *psychologist*
Giggleman, Gene Felton *academic administrator, veterinarian*
Gilchrist, Henry *lawyer*
Gillett, Grover *author*
Gilman, Alfred Goodman *pharmacologist, educator*
Gilmore, Marshall *bishop*
Glancy, Walter John *lawyer*
Glendenning, Don Mark *lawyer*
Glick, Gina Phillips Moran *retired physician*
Glines, Carroll Vane, Jr. *magazine editor*
Godwin, Donald Everett *lawyer*
Goldmann, James Allen *healthcare consultant*
Goldstein, Joseph Leonard *molecular biologist, educator*
Gompf, Henry L. (Hank) *lawyer*
Goodman, John C. *think-tank executive*
Goodstein, Barnett Maurice *lawyer*
Goolsby, Michelle *lawyer, food products executive*
Gores, Christopher Merrel *lawyer*
Grahmann, Charles V. *bishop*
Grammer, John Colquitte *cardiologist*
Granowsky, Alvin *writer, educator*
Grant, Joseph Moorman *finance company executive*
Gratton, Patrick John Francis *oil industry executive*
Gray, James Larry *international business executive*
Greef, Charles E. (Stormy Greef) *lawyer*
Griffeth, Landis King *nuclear medicine physician*
Grimes, David Lynn *communications executive*
Grissom, Mary Anne *speech educator*
Gross, Gary Neil *allergist, physician*
Grzych, Kari Shelton *lawyer*
Guerin, Dean Patrick *metal products executive*
Gupta, Sachin *medical educator, physician*
Guthrie, M. Philip *corporate financial executive*
Haayen, Richard Jan *academic administrator, insurance company executive*
Haggar, J. M. III *retail executive*
Hamas, Robert Steven *plastic surgeon*
Hames, Michael J. *semiconductor company executive*
Hamilton, David Lee *sports association administrator, retired environmental company executive*
Hammond, Herbert J. *lawyer, arbitrator, mediator*
Hankinson, Deborah G. *former state supreme court justice*
Harless, Katherine J. *telecommunications industry executive*
Harmel, Warren *marketing professional*
Harris, Hazel Lynn *medical/surgical nurse*
Harrison, Frank *former university president*
Hartnett, Will Ford *lawyer*
Hartt, Grover III *lawyer*
Hatchell, Steven James *collegiate sports association executive*
Hay, Jess Thomas *retired finance company executive*
Hedrick, Chad *Olympic athlete*
Hegi, Frederick B., Jr. *wholesale distribution executive*
Hennessy, Daniel Kraft *lawyer*
Henry, Vic Houston *lawyer*
Hensley, Noel M. B. *lawyer*
Hernandez, Frank Patrick *lawyer, judge*
Hester, Linda Hunt *retired dean, counseling administrator, sociology educator, health and physical education educator*
Hicks, Marion Lawrence, Jr., (Larry Hicks) *lawyer*
Hinshaw, Chester John *lawyer*
Hirsch, Laurence Eliot *construction executive, investment banker*
Hirschman, Karen L. *lawyer*
Hitt, David Hamilton, Sr. *retired health facility administrator*
Hobbs, Helen Haskell *medical geneticist*
Hoffman, Marguerite Steed *former art gallery director*
Hollingsworth, John Mark *lawyer*
Holman, James *allergist*
Holmes, Bert Otis E., Jr. *retired editor*
Holmes, James Hill III *lawyer*
Hopson, Mary Louise Carstens *marketing consultant*

Horchow, S(amuel) Roger *marketing consultant*
Howland, Grafton Dulany *financial counselor*
Huang, Yen Ti *civil engineer*
Hubach, Francis P. (Frank), Jr. *lawyer*
Hubach, Joseph F. *electronics executive, lawyer*
Hudel, Chestella Alvis *athletics educator*
Huffman, Gregory Scott Combest *lawyer*
Hughes, Vester Thomas, Jr. *lawyer*
Humble, Monty Garfield *lawyer*
Hunt, Ray L. *petroleum company executive*
Hunter, Robert Grams *retired language educator*
Hurd, Eric Ray *rheumatologist, internist, educator*
Hurwitz, Ann *lawyer*
Hutchison, Ray Ray (E. Ray Hutchison) *lawyer*
Ibach, Robert Daniel, Jr. *library director*
Israeloff, Sim *lawyer, mayor*
Jakes, T.D. *bishop*
Jayson, Melinda Gayle *lawyer*
Jennings, James Burnett *oil industry executive*
Jessup, Clifton R., Jr. *lawyer*
Jimenez, Mercy *corporate financial executive*
Jobe, Larry Alton *finance company executive*
Johnson, Avery *professional basketball coach, retired professional basketball player*
Johnson, Benjamin H. *history professor*
Johnson, Mary Elizabeth *music educator, musician*
Johnson, Murray H. *optometrist, researcher, consultant, lecturer*
Johnson, Robert Lee, Jr. *physician, educator, researcher*
Jones, Everett Riley, Jr. *oil industry executive*
Jordan, William Davis *lawyer*
Joyner, Tom *radio personality*
Kaiser, Fran Elizabeth *endocrinologist, gerontologist*
Kangas, Edward A. *healthcare company executive, former diversified financial services company executive*
Karns, Phyllis J. Spear *dean*
Keithley, Bradford Gene *lawyer*
Kelleher, Herbert David *air transportation executive, lawyer*
Kelly, Gary C. *air transportation executive*
Kemper, Robert Van *anthropologist, educator, minister*
Kennedy, Marc J. *lawyer*
Kent, David Charles *lawyer*
Keown, Michael H. *food products executive*
Kerr, Guy Hardie *lawyer*
King, Mark A. *computer company executive*
Kinnebrew, Jackson Metcalfe *lawyer*
Kinzie, Jack L. *lawyer*
Kitner, David N. *lawyer*
Kneipper, Richard Keith *lawyer*
Kobdish, George Charles *lawyer*
Kober, John A. *lawyer*
Koeppel, Peter Stafford *advertising executive*
Kovacevic, Radovan *mechanical engineering educator*
Kroney, Robert Harper *lawyer*
Kruse, Ann Gray *computer programmer*
Kuhn, Willis Evan, II, *lawyer, mediator*
Kunkle, David M. *police chief*
Kutner, Janet *art critic, book reviewer*
Lacy, John Ford *retired lawyer*
Ladik, Steven M. *lawyer*
Laettner, Christian Donald *professional basketball player*
Lake, Joseph Edward *ambassador*
Lan, Donald Paul, Jr. *lawyer*
Landry, Jane Lorenz *architect*
Lane, Alvin Huey, Jr. *management consultant*
Lane, John Rodger *museum director*
Laney, David M. *railroad industry executive, lawyer*
Lang, Douglas Stewart *judge*
Lastelick, Jerry *lawyer*
Lawrence, Annette *artist*
Leatherbury, Thomas Shawn *lawyer*
Lee, Carl B. *lawyer*
Lee, C.S. (Chun-Shing Lee) *semiconductor company executive*
Lee, George Terry, Jr. *lawyer*
Leedom, John Nesbett *manufacturing executive, state legislator*
Lesson, David *photojournalist*
Leven, Stephen H. *human resources professional*
Levenson, Stanley Richard *public relations and advertising executive*
Lewis, Jerry M. *psychiatrist, educator*
Lichliter, Warren Eugene *surgeon, educator*
Lilyhorn, Gregory Dean *security firm executive*
Lindley, Hamilton P. *lawyer*
Liskow, Frederic Cullen (Ric) *printing company executive*
Lister, George *pediatrician*
Litton, Andrew *conductor, music director*
Lovett, Melendy *semiconductor company executive*
Lowe, Gregg A. *semiconductor company executive*
Lowe, John Stanley *law educator*
Lowenberg, Michael *lawyer*
Lowery, David J. *lawyer*
Lumpkin, John O. *news organization executive*
Lynch, William Wright, Jr. *investment company executive, engineer*
Lyne, Kevin Peter *technologist*
Madden, Teresa Darleen *insurance agency owner*
Maddrey, Willis Crocker *medical educator, internist, academic administrator, consultant, researcher*
Madzik, Elizabeth May *hospital administrator*
Makel, Larry A. *lawyer*
Mankoff, Ronald Morton *retired lawyer*
Manteuffel, Robert Lee *lawyer*
March, Kevin P. *electronics executive*
Mareiniss, Darren Peter *lawyer, physician*
Margolin, Solomon Begelfor *pharmacologist, consultant*
Maris, Stephen S. *lawyer, educator*
Marks, James Frederic *pediatric endocrinologist, educator*
Marlow, Patricia Bair Bond *realtor*
Marshall, John Harris, Jr. *geologist, oil industry executive*
Martin, Boe Willis *lawyer*
Martin, Jack *physician*
Massman, Richard Allan *lawyer*
Mathis-Thorton, Dianna Dawn *protective services official, writer, publishing executive, not-for-profit developer*

Feuille, Richard Harlan *lawyer, director*
Flores, Yolanda *speech pathology/audiology services professional, consultant*
Foged, Leslie Owen *mathematician, educator*
Foster, Paul L. *oil industry executive*
Fullerton, Thomas Mankin, Jr. *economist*
Gardner, Kerry Ann *librarian*
Gibson, Sidney Kay *retired lawyer*
Gill, Thomas Edward *science educator*
Goodman, Gertrude Amelia *civic worker*
Hagedorn, Eric A. *physics professor*
Hanbali, Fadi *neurosurgeon, educator*
Harlass, Frederick E. *obstetrician, gynecologist*
Hedrick, Wyatt Smith *pharmacist*
Heide, John Wesley *engineering executive*
Hernandez, Roberto Reyes *secondary school educator*
Howell, Norman Glen *elementary school educator*
Jarvis, Richard S. *academic administrator*
Juarez, Antonio *psychotherapist, consultant, counselor, educator*
Kelley, Sylvia Johnson *financial services firm executive*
Kilbourne, Bruce Deane *history educator*
Korth, Charlotte Williams *retail executive*
Leyva, Yolanda Chavez *historian, educator, writer*
Lujan, Rosa Emma *bilingual specialist, trainer, consultant, assistant principal*
Lyle, James Arthur *real estate broker*
Magana, Jorge Carlos *pediatrician*
Marshall, Richard Treeger *lawyer*
Miller, Deane Guynes *salon and cosmetic studio owner*
Mitchelll, Paula Rae *nursing educator, dean*
Morton, Richard Albert Dunlap *physician*
Moschopoulos, Panagis *science educator*
Moya, Eva M. *health services executive*
Müller, Gene Alan *historian, consultant*
Natalicio, Diana Siedhoff *academic administrator*
Olisa, Nzedegwu Robert III *information technology executive, manufacturing executive*
Oliva, Maricela *education educator*
Pan, Rong *engineering educator*
Penley, Julie Anne *psychologist, educator*
Peralta-Videa, Jose R. *environmental scientist, researcher*
Prendergast, Thomas A. *investments consultant, management consultant*
Reznik, Leonid Carlovich *engineering and information technology educator, researcher*
Riter, Stephen *academic administrator, electrical engineer*
Roberts, Ernst Edward *marketing consultant*
Salas, Guillermo *biologist, educator, medical technician*
Sha, Naijun *statistician*
Silva, Michael Anthony *biologist, educator*
Sipiora, Leonard Paul *retired museum director, art appraiser*
Small, Ray *university administrator*
Smith, Tad Randolph *lawyer*
Stanley, Duffy B. *architect, planner*
Taber, David O. *urological surgeon*
Torres, Richard *literature and language educator*
Vojta-Oswald, Clarice Gertrude *educational diagnostician*
Wardy, Joe *former mayor*
Williams, Darryl Marlowe *medical educator*
Yanar, Maria Luisa (Tita) *director*
Zaloznik, Arlene Joyce *retired oncologist, retired military officer*

**Elgin**
Jordan, Charlene Hanson *writer*
Shelby, Nina Claire *special education educator*

**Ennis**
Swanson, Wallace Martin *lawyer*

**Euless**
Leding, Anne Dixon *artist, educator*
Paran, Mark Lloyd *retired lawyer*
Steffen, Tina Marie *journalist, home economist, elementary school educator*

**Falfurrias**
Cantu, Imelda M. *theater educator*

**Farmers Branch**
Blachly, Jack Lee *lawyer*
Reyes, Czarina Suzanne *mathematics educator*

**Flower Mound**
Flake, Wayne *information technology executive*
Hunt, David Ford *lawyer*
Kolodny, Stanley Charles *oral surgeon, retired military officer*
Kumar, Surinder *food products executive*
Morrish, Thomas Jay *golf course architect*
Ross, Lesa Moore *quality assurance professional*
Salick, Anne *sales executive*

**Fort Bliss**
Dorritie, Mary *military officer, psychologist*

**Fort Hood**
Metz, Thomas Frederic *career military officer*
Moore, Bret A. *psychologist, military officer*
Odierno, Raymond T. *career military officer*
Scott, Karen Lou *systems analyst*

**Fort Sam Houston**
Adams, Bruce Douglas *physician, researcher*
Coppola, Martin Nicholas *military officer, educator*
Gordon, Ella Dean *nursing educator, women's health nurse*
Hewitson, William Craig *physician, career officer*
Kragh, John Frederick, Jr. *orthopedist, educator*
Manguso, John A. *museum director*
Nelson, James Harold *health sciences administrator*
Wojcik, Barbara Elzbieta *statistician, researcher*

**Fort Worth**
Adams, Lavonne Marilyn Beck *critical care nurse, educator*
Alford, Michele T. *theater educator*
Allen, William Marion III *retired graphics designer, artist*
Appel, Bernard Sidney *marketing professional, consultant, retired electronics executive*

Ard, Harold Jacob *library administrator*
Astrup, Jens Leo *retired civil engineer*
Auping, Michael G. *curator*
Bailey, James Stephen *scientist*
Bailey, Susan Rudd *physician*
Bass, Robert Muse *financier*
Bass, Sid Richardson *investment company executive*
Berce, Daniel Eugene *financial services company executive, accountant*
Bernard, Robert William *language educator, theology studies educator, humanities educator*
Black, Timothy Lee *physician*
Blackburn, Wyatt Douglas *insurance executive*
Blanck, Ronald Ray *academic administrator, internist, military officer*
Bonderman, David *investment company executive, lawyer*
Boschetti, Philip J. *oil industry executive*
Boschini, Victor John, Jr. *academic administrator*
Bowler, Peter M. *air transportation executive*
Bradshaw, James Edward (Jim Bradshaw) *consultant*
Brennan, Edward A. *air transportation executive, former retail executive*
Breuer, Bradford R. *former museum director*
Brockman, Leslie Richard *social worker*
Broiles, David *lawyer*
Brown, C. Harold *lawyer*
Brown, George Edward, Jr. *visual arts educator, soccer coach*
Brown, Richard Lee *lawyer*
Brumley, Jon *gas industry executive*
Brumley, Jon S. *oil industry executive*
Brundage, Jeffrey J. *human resources specialist, air transportation executive*
Caldwell, Billy Ray *geologist*
Castro-Balbi, Jesús *musician, educator*
Chalk, John Allen, Sr. *lawyer*
Chambers, Ima Louise *secretarial skills educator, executive secretary*
Clark, Emory Eugene *diversified financial services company executive*
Cliburn, Van (Harvey Lavan Cliburn Jr.) *concert pianist*
Colaluca, Beth *pediatric neurpsychologist*
Corbusier, Drue *apparel and home furnishings executive*
Cottner, Donald *pathologist*
Cox, James Sidney *physician*
Cunningham, Atlee Marion, Jr. *aeronautical engineer*
Currier, Mike *elementary school educator, writer*
Curts, Harold Layne *construction executive*
Day, Julian C. *retail executive*
Dean, Beale *lawyer*
Dees, Sandra Kay Martin *psychologist, research scientist*
DeLotto, Jeffrey Daniel *language educator, writer*
Dent, Edward Dwain *lawyer*
de Tonnancour, Paul Roger Godefroy *library administrator*
Dominiak, Geraldine Florence *retired accounting educator*
Donovan, Nowell *academic administrator*
Doran, Robert Stuart *mathematician, educator*
Dressler, Oscar H. *music educator*
Dunleavy, Willa Gill *music educator, director*
Elliott, Frank Wallace *lawyer, educator*
Endres, Arthur P. (Skip Endres) *rail transportation executive*
Faherty, David Miles *musical instrument repairman*
Fan, Peng *mathematician*
Flynn, Patrick M. *research scientist, educator*
Fortson, Ben J. *oil industry executive*
Fortson, Kay Kimbell Carter *museum administrator*
Friedman, Walker C. *lawyer*
Gilbert, James Cayce *minister*
Gilderhus, Mark Theodore *historian, educator*
Gillette, Paul Crawford *pediatric cardiologist*
Girouard, Marvin J. *retail executive*
Gorman, Rhonda Renee *costume designer, educator*
Gracy, Robert *science educator*
Hahn, Marc B. *physician, dean*
Hall, Randy Jarvis *lawyer*
Harbour, Ted Ira *lawyer*
Harcrow, E. Earl *lawyer*
Hart, John Clifton *lawyer*
Harth-Bedoya, Miguel *conductor*
Hayes, Larry B. *lawyer*
Hernandez, Angel W. *pediatric neurologist, epileptologist*
Hixon, Karen J. *art and environmental patron*
Hoferer, Paul R. *rail transportation executive, lawyer*
Horton, Donald R. *construction executive*
Horton, Thomas W. *air transportation executive, former telecommunications company executive*
Hudson, Edward Randall, Jr. *gas and oil industry executive*
Hund, Thomas N. *rail transportation executive*
Hunt, Dianna *editor*
Hyde, George Lawrence, II *oil industry executive*
Ingram, Denny Ouzts, Jr. *lawyer, law educator*
Jackson, Donald Wilson *political science professor, lawyer*
Jackson, Stephen Eric *public speaker, life strategist*
Johnson, J. Mitchell *communications executive*
Johnson, Melody *school system administrator*
Kankel, Courteneye Ayn *history educator*
Karnes, Keith Dale *portfolio manager*
Kelly, Dee J. *lawyer*
Kelly, Janet *science educator*
Kelly, Raymond Boone III *lawyer*
Kennedy, Gary F. *air transportation executive, lawyer*
King, Steve Mason *judge, lawyer*
Krebs, Robert Duncan *rail transportation company executive*
Lale, Cissy Stewart (Lloyd Lale) *freelance writer*
Lamensdorf, Hugh *urologist, educator*
Law, Thomas Hart *lawyer*
Lawrence, J. Rodney *retired lawyer*
Lawson, Carole Jean *religious educator, author, poet*
Li, Richard T. *retired library director, secondary school educator*

Lichtman, David Michael *retired military officer, orthopedist, educator, health facility administrator*
Lipkin, Seymour *musician, conductor, educator*
Lott, R(obert) Allen *musicologist*
McBryde, John Henry *federal judge*
McConnell, Michael Arthur *lawyer*
Means, Terry Robert *federal judge*
Michero, William Henderson *retired retail executive*
Miller, Kleber C. *lawyer*
Minton, Jerry Davis *lawyer, consultant, retired banker*
Mitchell, Robert Joseph *insurance executive*
Moncrief, Michael Joseph *mayor, former state legislator*
Moncrief, Richard W. *oil industry executive*
Moncrief, William Alvin, Jr. *oil and gas producer*
Mullendore, Walter Edward *retired economist*
Munday, Stephen Dale *writer, artist*
Munn, Cecil Edwin *lawyer*
Nicholas, Nicholas Constantine *retired military officer*
Nichols, James Richard *civil engineer, consultant*
Oropeza, Peter P. *psychologist, consultant*
Palmer, Jeffery Dean *systems engineering manager, consultant*
Pappas-Speairs, Nina *financial planner, educator*
Patoski, Margaret Nancy *historian, educator*
Patterson, Gary *college football coach*
Patterson, Paige *church administrator, former seminary president*
Peipert, James Raymond *journalist*
Piedt, David Lawrence *musician*
Potts, Timothy F. *museum director*
Price, Marla *museum director, curator*
Price, Michael Howard *journalist, critic, composer*
Quarles, Carroll Adair, Jr. *physicist, researcher*
Quinn, Francis Xavier *arbitrator, consultant, mediator, writer, law educator*
Raessler, Kenneth Ray *music educator, university administrator, writer*
Rainwater, Richard Edward *financial consultant, investor*
Record, Phillip Julius *journalist*
Reinecke, Manfred G. *chemistry professor*
Reuter, Frank Theodore *historian, educator*
Roach, John Vinson, II, *retail company executive*
Robin, Clara Nell (Claire Robin) *English language educator*
Rogers, Charles Ray *minister, religious organization administrator*
Roland, Billy Ray *electronics company executive*
Rose, Matthew K. *rail transportation executive*
Saenz, Michael *college president*
Schussler, Irwin *psychiatrist, educator*
Sharpe, James Shelby *lawyer*
Shehan, Geraldean Harrison *ESL educator*
Simmons, Jean Byers *academic administrator, director*
Simpson, Bob R. *energy executive*
Simpson, Dennis Dwayne *psychologist, educator*
Slater, Carmen Rochelle *elementary school educator*
Stevenson, Ben *artistic director*
Stevenson, Ruth Carter *art patron*
Sullenberger, Ara Broocks *mathematics professor*
Teichgraeber, Richard D. *electrical engineer researcher*
Thornton, Charles Victor *metals executive*
Tillman, Karen Sue *lawyer*
Tillman, Massie Monroe *mediator, arbitrator, art gallery owner, retired judge*
Tobey, Martin Alan *cardiologist*
Tomnitz, Donald J. *construction executive*
Tucker, William Edward *academic administrator, minister*
Turner, Wesley R. *publishing executive*
Tyler, Ronnie Curtis *museum director, art historian*
Wallace, R. H., Jr. *lawyer*
Waller, Gary Wilton *administration educator, minister*
Watson, Robert Francis *lawyer*
Webb, Theodore Stratton, Jr. *aerospace scientist, consultant*
Weekley, Frederick Clay, Jr. *lawyer*
West, Robert Grady *lawyer*
West, Sylvia Wandell *small business owner, director, educator, researcher*
Willard, Ralph Lawrence *surgeon, educator, physician, retired academic administrator*
Wilson-Webb, Nancy Lou *educational association administrator*
Witt, Jim *editor*
Woodworth, Steven Edward *history professor, writer*
Yacante, Maria Lucy *music educator, researcher*
Yanni, John Michael *pharmacologist*

**Franklin**
Perry, Anne Marie Litchfield *secondary school educator*

**Fredericksburg**
Arnold, George Lawrence *retired advertising company executive*
Chase, John David *retired dean, retired internist*
Manhart, Marcia Y(ockey) *art museum director*
Scannell, William Edward *aerospace transportation executive, consultant, psychologist*

**Freeport**
Baskin, William Gresham *counselor, vocalist, music educator*
Stevens, James C. *chemist*

**Friendswood**
Moore, Alicia Jane *art educator*

**Frisco**
Armstrong, Doug *professional sports team executive*
Bloskas, John D. *retired finance company executive*
Gajraj, Noor *anesthesiologist, educator*
Hawk, Phillip Michael *service corporation executive*
Hicks, Thomas O. *professional sports team executive, real estate developer*

Kern, Ronald Paul *computer company executive, dean, consultant*
Lim, Jae Doeg *systems engineer, researcher*
Lindros, Eric *professional hockey player*
Lites, James R. *professional hockey team executive*
Mackenzie, John *retired oil industry executive*
Migdol, Marvin Jacob *public relations and marketing executive, consultant*
Mihm, John Clifford *chemical engineer*
Modano, Mike (Michael Modano) *professional hockey player*
Tippett, Dave *professional hockey coach*

**Fulton**
Lamb, Richard *cultural organization administrator*

**Gainesville**
Brooks, Jerry Robert *small business owner*
McCormack, Lowell Ray *oil industry executive, corporate financial executive, consultant*

**Galena Park**
Fierro, Robert, Jr. *librarian*

**Galveston**
Amador, Luis F. *medical educator*
Auslander, Beth Ann *psychologist*
Baker, Robert Ernest, Jr. *retired foundation executive*
Balaban, Alexandru T. *chemistry professor, researcher*
Bloomfield, Maxwell Herron III *retired history professor, retired law professor*
Brown, Paul Sherman, Jr. *surgeon*
Burns, Chester Ray *retired medical educator*
Caldwell, Garnett Ernest *lawyer*
Camacho, Maria E. *geriatrician, educator*
Crown, Eric Daniel *research scientist*
Dawson, Earl Bliss *medical educator*
Ernst, Randy *radiologist*
Esenaliev, Rinat O. *science educator, lab administrator*
Essex, Francis Xavier *physician, educator*
Ferrando, Arny Anthony *medical researcher*
Foster, William Edwin (Bill Foster) *nonprofessional basketball coach*
Frederickson, Christopher John *neuroscientist*
Gold, Daniel Howard *ophthalmologist, educator*
Goodwin, Jean McClung *psychiatrist*
Gorenstein, David G. *chemistry and biochemistry professor*
Gwak, Young Seob *biomedical researcher*
Hargraves, Martha Ann *health services administrator, researcher*
Hawkins, Hal K(enneth) *pathologist*
James, Thomas Naum *cardiologist, educator*
Keeney, Susan E. *pediatrician, educator*
Klein, Gordon Leslie *pediatrician, educator*
Langston, Sue H. *secondary school educator, director*
Lin, Qing *medical educator*
Makino, Shinji *virologist, educator*
Markides, Kyriakos Socrates *gerontology educator*
McLeod, E. Douglas *real estate developer, lawyer*
Moody, Robert Lee *insurance company executive*
Munsell, Debra S. *physician assistant, educator*
Murphy, Frederick Augustus *virologist, researcher*
Neugebauer, Volker Egdar *biomedical scientist, neuroscientist*
Neves, Kerry Lane *lawyer*
Nguyen-Oghalai, Tracy Uyentrang *medical educator, researcher*
Otis, John James *civil engineer*
O'Toole, Austin Martin *lawyer, mediator*
Parisi, Valerie Marie *dean, medical educator*
Rogers, Helen Lynch *physical therapist, educator*
Salch, Steven Charles *lawyer, mediator, arbitrator*
Sandstead, Harold Hilton *physician, researcher, educator, director*
Selig, Oury Levy *port financial consultant*
Shelton, Kenneth R., Jr. *real estate company executive, artist*
Smith, David English *pathologist, educator*
Stobo, John David *dean, educator, physician*
Tesh, Robert Bradfield *epidemiologist, educator*
Townsend, Courtney M. *surgeon*
Tyson, Kenneth Robert Thomas *surgeon, educator*
Vedernikov, Yuri P. *pharmacologist, educator*
White, Robert Brown *medical educator*
Willis, William Darrell, Jr. *neuroscientist, educator*
Yngve, David A. *orthopedist, surgeon*
Zimmerman, Roger Joseph *fishery biologist*

**Garland**
Driver, Joe Luther *state legislator, consultant, insurance agent*
Fain, Thomas Alton, Jr. *music educator*
Haynsworth, Robert Francis, Jr. *anesthesiologist*
Lord, Jacqueline Ward *accountant, photographer, artist*
McGill, Maurice Leon *corporate financial executive*
McGrath, James Thomas *real estate investment company executive*
Quinn, Peggy Armstrong *elementary school educator, writer*
Zimmerman, S(amuel) Morton (Mort Zimmerman) *engineering executive*

**Georgetown**
Aguillon, Charles Christopher *art director*
Brody, Gerald David *academic administrator*
Bryce, William Delf *lawyer*
Busfield, Roger Melvil, Jr. *retired trade association executive, educator*
Deviney, Marvin Lee, Jr. *science administrator, director*
Gerding, Thomas Graham *medical products executive*
Lopreato, Joseph *evolutionary sociologist, writer*
Lovin, Keith Harold *retired academic administrator, philosopher, educator*
Manning, Robert Thomas *internist, educator*
Moore, Pat Howard *engineering and construction executive*
Muir-Broaddus, Jacqueline Elizabeth *psychology educator*
Schofield, James Roy *medical consultant, educator*
Schrum, Jake Bennett *academic administrator*
Sellers, Fred Evans *accounting educator*

Engelhardt, Hugo Tristram, Jr. *physician, educator*
Engerrand, Kenneth G. *lawyer, educator*
Englesmith, Tejas *actor, television producer, curator*
Erikson, Sheldon R. *oil industry executive*
Ertan, Atilla *medical educator, physician, researcher, health facility administrator*
Espree, Mildred Michelle *language educator, writer*
Essmyer, Michael Martin *lawyer*
Estes, Mary K. *virologist*
Estey, Elihu Harris *medical educator*
Eubank, J. Thomas *lawyer*
Evans, Harry Launius *pathology educator*
Evans, Kenya *artist*
Ewing, Patrick Aloysius *professional basketball coach*
Fabugais, Trisha *law librarian*
Farenthold, Frances Tarlton *lawyer*
Farnsworth, T. Brooke *lawyer*
Farrell, John Marshall *architect*
Farris, G. Steven *oil and gas production company executive*
Faulkner, Larry Ray *foundation administrator, former academic administrator*
Feigon, Judith Tova *ophthalmologist, educator, surgeon*
Felleman, Daniel Jay *healthcare educator, science educator*
Ferguson, Christopher J. *astronaut*
Fincke, Edward Michael (Mike) *astronaut*
Fiorenza, Joseph A. *retired archbishop*
Fischer, Craig Leland *physician*
Fishman, Marvin Allen *pediatric neurologist, educator*
Flaitz, Catherine M. *dean, dental educator*
Flato, William Roeder, Jr. *software development company executive*
Florian-Lacy, Dorothy *social worker, educator*
Focht, John Arnold, Jr. *engineer*
Foger, Frances Murchison *minister*
Ford, Thomas W., Jr. *lawyer*
Foreman, Michael J. *astronaut*
Fornage, Bruno Denis *radiologist, educator*
Forney, Jan Lynette *geophysicist*
Foshee, Douglas *gas company executive*
Foss, Michelle Michot *think-tank executive, economist*
Fossati, Humberto Mario *electrical engineer, researcher*
Fossum, Michael E. *astronaut*
Foster, Charles Crawford *lawyer, educator*
Foster, Dale Warren *political scientist, educator, real estate agent, accountant, management consultant*
Francis, James Stephen, Jr. *psychology professor, psychologist*
Frank, Karen Denise *aerospace engineer*
Frederickson, Philip L. *oil industry executive*
Freireich, Emil J. *hematologist, educator*
Freud, Anthony Peter *opera director*
Friedkin, Thomas H. *automotive executive*
Friedman, Paul M. *dermatologist*
Frost, John Elliott *minerals company executive*
Frumovitz, Michael *oncologist*
Fu, Siqing *medical educator*
Fullenweider, Donn Charles *lawyer*
Fulwiler, Robert Neal *oil industry executive*
Furbacher, Stephen A. *energy executive*
Gabbard, Glen Owens *psychiatrist, psychotherapist*
Gaelens, Albert Robert *director, educational administrator, priest*
Gagnon, Stewart Walter *lawyer*
Gallogly, James Lawrence *oil industry executive, lawyer*
Galvin, Kerry A. *lawyer*
Gardezi, Syed A. *medical researcher*
Gardner, Everette Shaw, Jr. *information sciences educator, consultant, author*
Garner, Phil *professional athletics coach*
Garza, Erik David *lawyer*
Gates, Stephen Frye *lawyer, oil industry executive*
Gaucher, Jane Montgomery *retail executive*
Gaut, C. Christopher *gas industry executive*
George, Deveral D. *editor, journalist, advertising consultant*
Gerachis, George Matthew *lawyer*
Getz, Lowell Vernon *financial advisor*
Gibbs, James R. *oil industry executive*
Gibson, Everett Kay, Jr. *aerospace scientist, geochemist*
Gibson, Rex Hilton *lawyer*
Gigli, Irma *dermatologist, educator, academic administrator*
Gilbert, Jill Barson *management consultant*
Gilbert, Mark R. *medical educator*
Giles, Francis J. *medical educator*
Gilpin, Patrick J. *lawyer, educator*
Girouard, Peggy Jo Fulcher *ballet educator*
Gissel, L. Henry, Jr. *lawyer*
Glowinski, Roland *mathematics professor*
Godine, Marion Cecilia *adult education educator*
Goff, Robert Burnside *retired food company executive*
Goldman, Robert W. *retired gas and oil industry executive*
Goldman, Stanford Milton *medical educator*
Goldsmith, Billy Joe *real estate broker, rancher*
Golinkin, Webster Fowler *healthcare executive, media consultant*
Goloby, George William, Jr. *environmental scientist, editor*
Golubitsky, Martin Aaron *mathematician, educator*
Gonzalez, Antonio *academic administrator, educator, title company executive*
Goode, Coralyn *lawyer*
Goodman, Barry Michael *lawyer*
Goodman, Herbert Irwin *petroleum company executive*
Goodman, Joe Read *utilities executive*
Goodman, John B. *heating/air conditioning manufacturing executive*
Goodwin, Heather Marie *educational consultant*
Gordon, Lawrence *geologist, consultant*
Gorman, Sean *lawyer*
Gorry, G. Anthony *medical educator*
Gould, Kenneth Lance *cardiologist, researcher, educator*
Gover, Alan Shore *lawyer*
Graebner, Carol F. *lawyer*

Graf, Hans *conductor, music director*
Graham, David Yates *gastroenterologist*
Graves, Daniel Edward *medical association administrator, researcher*
Gray, Robert F., Jr. *lawyer*
Gray, Robert Steele *publishing executive, editor, writer*
Gregory, William Roger *real estate company executive*
Grigore, Alina M. *anesthesiologist*
Grossberg, Marc Elias *lawyer*
Grossman, Herbert Barton *urologist, researcher*
Grossman, Robert George *neurosurgeon, department chairman*
Guest, Floyd Emory, Jr. *lawyer*
Gunn, Albert Edward, Jr. *internist, educator, health facility administrator, lawyer*
Gunn, Joan Marie *health facility administrator*
Gunter, Joseph Clifford III *lawyer*
Gupta, Monesha *pediatrician, educator*
Gutheinz, James O'Leary *military officer, law clerk*
Gutheinz, Joseph Richard, Jr. *lawyer, writer, retired military officer*
Gutheinz, Michael John *military officer, law clerk*
Guynn, Robert William *psychiatrist, educator*
Hackerman, Norman *chemist, academic administrator*
Hafner, Joseph A., Jr. *food products executive*
Halas, Naomi J. *nanoscale science and engineering educator*
Hall, Anthony W., Jr. *lawyer*
Hall, Charles Washington *lawyer*
Hall, Robert Joseph *internist, educator*
Hamel, Douglas E. *lawyer*
Hamill, Marshall Bowes *medical educator*
Hamilton, Carlos Robert, Jr. *endocrinologist, consultant, academic administrator*
Hamilton, D. Kirk *architectural firm executive*
Hamilton, Jacqueline *arts consultant*
Handlin, Danita L. *lawyer*
Hanks, George Carol, Jr. *state judge*
Hanower, Lee David *lawyer*
Hanrahan, Lawrence Martin *healthcare consultant*
Harding, Steve *real estate company executive*
Harper, A(lfred) J(ohn), II, *lawyer*
Harrington, Bruce Michael *lawyer, investor*
Harris, Venita Van Caspel *retired financial planner*
Harris, Warren Wayne *lawyer*
Hartrick, Janice Kay *lawyer*
Harvin, David Tarleton *lawyer*
Hasen, Michael *engineering company executive, civil engineer*
Hawes, Clay Erik *lawyer*
Hawes, William Kenneth *communication educator, author*
Hawkins, Barbara Reed *mental health nurse*
Hayes, Elvin Ernest *retired basketball player*
Haynes, Richard *lawyer*
Haynie, Thomas Powell III *physician*
Hazelip, Linda Ann *musician, small business owner, executive assistant*
He, Hui *energy executive*
Heard, Larry *real estate company executive*
Heeg, Peggy A. *lawyer, former gas industry executive*
Heinrich, Randall Wayne *lawyer*
Heinsen, Lindsay *newspaper editor*
Helfenstein, Josef *museum director*
Helland, George Archibald, Jr. *manufacturing executive, federal official*
Hemminghaus, Roger Roy *energy company executive, chemical engineer*
Hempel, John P. *mathematics professor*
Hempfling, Linda Lee *nurse*
Henington, David Mead *retired library director*
Henley, Ernest Justus *chemical engineering professor*
Henry, Charles Jay *library director*
Hescht, Billy Wade *theater educator*
Hesterberg, Earl J. *automotive executive*
Hewitt, Lester L. *lawyer*
Higginbotham, Joan E. *astronaut*
Higgins, Pauline Edwards *lawyer*
Hildebrand, Jeffrey D. *oil industry executive*
Hines, Gerald D. *architectural firm executive*
Hinton, Paula Weems *lawyer*
Hirasaki, George Jiro *chemical engineer, educator*
Hittner, David *federal judge*
Hlavinka, Paul Thomas *lawyer*
Hobby, William Pettus *retired broadcast executive*
Hodgess, Erin Marie *statistics educator*
Hoeg, Matthew *lawyer*
Hoffman, Philip Guthrie *former university president*
Hoffman, Ronald Bruce *biophysicist, consultant, life scientist*
Holloway, Gordon Arthur *lawyer*
Hollyfield, John Scoggins *lawyer*
Holmes, Ann Hitchcock *journalist*
Holmes, Harry Dadisman *health care consultant*
Holstead, John Burnham *retired lawyer*
Honeycutt, George Leonard *retired photographer*
Hong, Waun Ki *oncologist, researcher*
Hook, Harold Swanson *former management consulting executive*
Horton, Donald J. *lawyer*
Horton, Thomas Edward, Jr. *mechanical engineering educator*
Horvitz, Paul Michael *finance educator*
Howard, Juwan *professional basketball player*
Howell, Jefferson Davis, Jr. *aerospace transportation executive, retired military officer*
Hoyt, Mont Powell *lawyer*
Hsu, Sylvia *dermatologist, educator*
Hsu, Thomas Tseng-Chuang *civil engineer, educator*
Huang, Hsien-Lu *electrical engineer*
Hubert, Jean-Luc *chemicals executive*
Hudson, Franklin *lawyer, real estate developer*
Hudspeth, Chalmers Mac *lawyer, educator*
Huffington, Roy Michael *business executive, former ambassador*
Hughes, Eloise Stapp *education educator*
Hughes, Lynn Nettleton *federal judge*
Hulet, Randall Gardner *physics professor*
Hull, Robert Joe *lawyer*
Hunsaker, Barry, Jr. *lawyer*
Hunter, Robert Paul *pharmacologist*
Hurley, R. Bruce *lawyer*

Hussain, Moinuddin Syed *geologist, engineer, consultant*
Huston, John Dennis *language educator*
Hutchens, Harry Price, Jr. *engineer*
Hutchison, Brady Lee *editor, history professor*
Hynes, Thomas N. (Toby Hynes) *automotive company executive*
Ifft, Lewis George III *company administrator*
Innes, Debbie *bank executive*
Irvin, Michael P. *lawyer*
Irwin, John Robert *oil and gas industry executive*
Issa, Mariam *volunteer, cultural organization administrator*
Ivanov, Lyuben Dimitrov *naval architecture researcher, educator*
Ivey, Jack Todd *lawyer*
Jackson, Donna Ann *musician, piano teacher*
Jackson, Wanda Britton *secondary school educator*
Jacobs, Mark M. *energy executive, corporate financial executive*
Jamail, Joseph Dahr, Jr. *lawyer*
James, Dean *librarian, author*
Jankovic, Joseph *neurologist, educator*
Jansen, Donald Orville *retired lawyer*
Janssens, Joe Lee *controller*
Jean, Raymond A. *manufacturing executive*
Jemison, Mae Carol *physician, engineer, entrepreneur, philanthropist, educator, former astronaut*
Jenkins, Sheila Alnita *psychologist*
Jett, Brent W., Jr. *astronaut, military officer*
Jetton, Steve *newspaper editor*
Jewell, Robert V. *lawyer*
Jhingran, Anuja *oncologist, educator*
Jines, Michael L. *utilities executive*
Johnson, Alisa B. *lawyer, energy company executive*
Johnson, Marilyn *retired obstetrician, retired gynecologist*
Johnson, Ronald *academic administrator*
Johnson, Wayne D. *gas industry executive*
Jones, Edith Hollan *federal judge*
Jones, Edith Irby *internist*
Jones, Eli III *marketing and sales educator*
Jones, Florence M. *music educator*
Jones, Frank Griffith *lawyer*
Jordan, Paul Howard, Jr. *surgeon, educator*
Jordan, W. Carl *lawyer*
Jordon, Robert Earl *physician*
Joyce, James Daniel *clergyman*
Jurtshuk, Peter, Jr. *microbiologist, educator*
Kagle, Joseph Louis, Jr. *artist, arts administrator, art historian, educator*
Kahan, Barry Donald *surgeon, educator*
Kakadiaris, Ioannis *computer science educator*
Kanellos, Nicolás *language educator, liberal studies educator*
Kaplan, Lee Landa *lawyer*
Karba, Gerhard W. *real estate company executive*
Karff, Samuel Egal *rabbi*
Karner, Stephen Leslie *geophysicist*
Karnes, John Herbert, Jr. *corporate financial executive, lawyer*
Katopodis, Louis *supermarket chain executive*
Kaufman, Raymond Henry *retired physician, retired educator*
Kavandi, Janet Lynn *aerospace power engineer, chemist*
Kavraki, Lydia *computer scientist, educator*
Kay, Joel Phillip *lawyer*
Kearns, Richard J. *surgeon, educator*
Keating, Tim *chef*
Keiser, Robert Lee *retired gas and oil industry executive*
Keith, Susan S. *lawyer*
Kelly, Hugh Rice *lawyer, retired energy executive*
Kelly, James M. *astronaut, military officer*
Kelly, Mark E. *astronaut*
Kelly, T. Mark *lawyer*
Kelly, William Franklin, Jr. *lawyer*
Kennedy, John Edward *lawyer*
Kennedy, Ken *computer science educator*
Kerr, Baine Perkins *oil industry executive*
Ketchand, Robert Lee *lawyer*
Kevan, Larry *chemistry professor*
Key, James Everett *ophthalmologist*
Kiat-amnuay, Sudarat *prosthodontist, educator*
Kientz, Renee *newspaper editor*
Kilrain, Susan *astronaut*
Kimyai-Asadi, Arash *surgeon*
Kinder, Richard Dan *natural gas pipeline, oil and gas company executive*
King, Carolyn Dineen *federal judge*
Kinsey, James Lloyd *chemist, educator*
Kirkland, John David *oil and gas company executive, lawyer*
Kit, Saul *retired biochemist, educator*
Klausmeyer, David Michael *scientific instruments manufacturing company executive*
Klein, Nora J. *pediatrician*
Kline, Mark Wendel *pediatric medicine educator*
Knapp, David Hebard *retired banker*
Kneese, Carolyn Calvin *retired education educator*
Knickel, Carin S. *oil industry executive*
Knobloch, Charles Saron *lawyer, geophysicist*
Kobayashi, Riki *retired chemical engineer, educator*
Kochi, Jay Kazuo *chemist, educator*
Koenig, Rodney Curtis *lawyer, rancher*
Kollaer, Jim C. *real estate executive, architect*
Komaki Cox, Ritsuko U. *medical educator*
Koo, Jaseok Peter *science educator*
Kornbleet, Lynda Mae *insulation, fireproofing and acoustical contractor*
Kors, R. Paul *search company executive*
Kosten, Thomas R. *psychiatrist, educator*
Kouri, Donald Jack *chemist, educator*
Kraft, Irvin Alan *psychiatrist*
Krajewski, Michael *conductor*
Kramer, Phillip D. *oil industry executive*
Kramm, Deborah Ann *information technology executive*
Kratochvil, L(ouis) Glen *lawyer*
Krebs, Arno William, Jr. *lawyer*
Kregel, Kevin R. *astronaut*
Krishen, Kumar *research technologist*
krohn, Tracy W. *oil industry executive, gas industry executive*
Kruse, Layne E. *lawyer*
Kubiak, Gary *professional football coach*

Kuehn, Ronald L., Jr. *natural resources company executive*
Kuntz, Hal Goggan *petroleum exploration company executive, rancher*
LaBoon, Robert Bruce *lawyer*
Lachar, Barbara Leeser *psychologist, educator*
Lacy, Terri *lawyer*
LaFuze, William L. *lawyer*
Lake, Kathleen Cooper *lawyer*
Lake, Sim *federal judge*
Lamb, Sydney MacDonald *language educator*
Lamont, Gene *professional baseball coach, former professional baseball team manager*
Lane, Neal Francis *physics professor, retired federal agency administrator*
Lanier, Mark (W. Mark Lanier) *lawyer*
Lanier, Robert C. (Bob Lanier) *real estate owner, real estate developer, former mayor*
Lannie, Paul Anthony *lawyer*
Lanza, Frank Leo *gastroenterologist, researcher*
Larkin, Lee Roy *retired lawyer*
Larkin, William Vincent, Jr. *corporate financial executive*
Lassetter, Scott D. *lawyer*
Latimer, Roy Truett *museum executive*
Lawrence, Wendy B. *astronaut*
Lawson, Rhea Brown *library director*
Lee, Janie C. *curator*
Leebron, David Wayne *academic administrator, law educator*
Leguillon, Rolande Lucienne *French educator*
Lehrer, Kenneth Eugene *economic consulting company executive*
Lemmer, William C. *lawyer*
Leonard, Charles H. (Chuck Leonard) *air transportation executive*
Lesar, David J. *oil industry executive*
Levin, Bernard *physician*
Levin, Victor A. *neurologist, oncologist, educator*
Levit, Max *wholesale distribution executive, food service executive*
Levy, Eugene Howard *planetary sciences educator, researcher*
Lewis, Chip *lawyer*
Lewis, Edward Clark *lawyer*
Lewis, Kevin Paul *lawyer*
Lewis, Lisa *psychologist, administrator*
Liang, Edison Parktak *astrophysicist, plasma physicist, educator, researcher*
Liberato, Lynne *lawyer*
Lidge, Brad *professional baseball player*
Lienhard, John Henry, IV, *mechanical engineer, educator*
Liles, Clifton Roy *application developer*
Limbacher, Randy L. *energy executive*
Lin, Hong *science and technology educator*
Lin, Peter H. *surgeon, researcher*
Lin, Shiaw-Yih (Phoebus Lin) *cell biologist, researcher, medical educator*
Lindsey, John H. *insurance agency executive*
Lindsey, Steven W. *astronaut, military officer*
Listengart, Joseph *lawyer*
Litvinov, Dmitri *engineering educator*
Liu, Jing *pathologist, educator*
Liu, Jinsong *pathologist*
Liu, Yuhong *geologist*
Locke, Gene L. *lawyer*
Looser, William Gregory *lawyer*
Lopez, David Tiburcio *lawyer, educator, arbitrator, mediator*
Lott, Marley *lawyer*
Lowe, John E. *oil industry executive, accountant*
Lowry, Montecue Judson *military historian*
Lu, Edward Tsang *astronaut*
Lucid, Shannon W. *biochemist, astronaut*
Lukens, Max L. *manufacturing executive*
Luss, Dan *chemical engineering professor*
Lynch, John F. *lawyer*
Lyons, Phillip Michael, Sr. *insurance accounting and real estate executive*
Mackwell, Stephen Joseph *geophysicist, educator*
MacLean, Steve(n) G. *astronaut*
Madrid, Michael John *director*
Mahadeva, Manoranjan *financial executive, accountant*
Malki, Heidar A. *dean*
Mallia, Marianne *medical writer*
Mampre, Virginia Elizabeth *communications executive*
Manrique, Justo Rafael *economist, educator*
Mansell, Joyce Marilyn *retired special education educator*
Mao, Li *molecular biologist, educator*
Marcotte, Michael Steven *municipal official*
Marek, Joycelyn *publishing executive*
Mariotto, Marco Jerome *dean, psychology educator, researcher*
Marks, Lester *automotive dealership owner*
Marshall, Gregory K. *food service executive*
Marston, Edgar Jean III *lawyer*
Martin, J. Clark *lawyer*
Martin, James Kirby *historian, educator*
Martin, Jay Griffith *lawyer*
Martin, Paul Edward *lawyer*
Martin, William C. *social studies educator, writer*
Marzio, Peter Cort *museum director*
Mashburn, Joseph L. *architecture educator*
Mason, Dwayne L. *lawyer*
Massad, Stephen Albert *lawyer*
Matheny, Kenneth L. *oil industry executive*
Mathis, James Forrest *retired petroleum company executive*
Matthews, Charles Sedwick *petroleum engineer, consultant*
Matthews, Kathleen Shive *biochemistry educator*
Mattox, Sharon M. *lawyer*
Max, Ernest *surgeon*
Mayo, Marti *museum director, curator*
Mayor, Heather Donald *molecular biology educator*
Mays, Randall T. *communications company executive*
McArthur, William Surles, Jr. *astronaut, retired military officer*
McCarter, Louis Eugene *lawyer*
McClanahan, David M. *energy executive*
McClure, Daniel M. *lawyer*
McClure, Jeffrey B. *lawyer*
McCollam, Marion Andrus *consulting firm executive, educator*
McCreary, Frank E. III *lawyer*

Wenk, Bridget Kelly *music educator, musician*
Westby, Timothy Scott *lawyer, researcher*
Wheelan, R(ichelieu) E(dward) *lawyer*
Wheelock, Douglas H. *astronaut, military officer*
Whilden, Robert Harral, Jr. *lawyer*
Whitaker, Gilbert Riley, Jr. *economics professor, academic administrator, business economist*
White, Ronald Joseph *biomedical researcher, physiologist, educator*
White, William H. *mayor*
Whiting, Hugh Richard *lawyer*
Whiting, Martha Countee *retired secondary school educator*
Whittenburg, Justin M. *lawyer*
Wilburn, John *editor*
Wilde, Carlton D. *lawyer, director*
Wiley, Michael E. *oil industry executive*
Wiley, Shirley Winona Walters *adult education educator, artist*
Wilkinson, Miles Frome *healthcare educator, researcher*
Willerson, James Thornton *internist, educator*
Williames, Lee John *academic administrator, history professor*
Williams, Edward Earl, Jr. *entrepreneur, educator*
Williams, Lowell Craig *lawyer, employee relations executive*
Williams, Mario *professional football player*
Williams, Michelle (Tenetria Michelle Williams) *singer*
Williams, O'Banion III *lawyer*
Williams, Robert Henry *oil industry executive*
Williams, Sunita L. *astronaut*
Williamson, Bruce A. *gas industry executive*
Williamson, Peter David *lawyer*
Wilson, Carl Weldon, Jr. *construction company executive, civil engineer*
Wilson, Edward Converse, Jr. *oil and natural gas production company executive*
Wilson, Floyd C. *oil industry executive*
Wilson, Gerald Everette *funeral services company executive*
Wilson, Stephanie D. *astronaut*
Wilson, Thomas Leon *physicist, researcher*
Wissel-Littmann, Jeffrey G. *health facility executive*
Witmer, John Richard *librarian*
Wittenbraker, Rick L. *lawyer*
Wood, Michael W *lawyer*
Woodhouse, John Frederick *food distribution company executive*
Woods, Ronald G. *lawyer, former prosecutor*
Worthing, Louie Fabian III *plastic surgeon*
Worthington, William Albert III *lawyer*
Wray, Thomas Jefferson *lawyer*
Wren, Robert James *aerospace engineering manager*
Wriggers, Willy Rudolf *science educator*
Wright, Clark Phillips *computer systems specialist*
Wuensche, Vernon Edgar *construction company executive*
Wyatt, Oscar Sherman, Jr. *energy company executive*
Wynne, John Carlton *lawyer*
Wyrsch, Martha B. *lawyer, energy executive*
Xue, Dong Cynthia *research scientist, consultant*
Yamaoka, Yoshio *gastroenterologist, researcher*
Yatsenko, Yuri Petrovich *economics professor, mathematician*
Yeates, Marie R. *lawyer*
Yelich, Louis James *engineering executive*
Yeoman, Lynn Chalmers *medical educator*
Yetter, R Paul *lawyer*
Yokubaitis, Roger T. *lawyer*
Young, David *anesthesiologist, educator*
Yuen, Benson Bolden *air transportation executive, consultant, software executive*
Yung, Wai Kwan Alfred *neurology and neuro-oncology educator*
Zacharias, Nikolaos Marios *obstetrician, gynecologist*
Zamka, George D. *astronaut*
Zhang, Chunlong *environmental scientist, engineer*
Zhong, Miao *pharmacologist, researcher*
Zhou, Wei *surgeon*
Zhu, Jiang *materials scientist*
Zoghbi, Huda Y. *neurologist, geneticist, educator*
Zubarev, Eugene *chemistry professor*

**Humble**
Hatch, Richard Clawson *small business owner, magician*
Pickle, George Edward *lawyer*
Trowbridge, John Parks *physician*

**Hunt**
Gambrell, James Bruton III *lawyer, educator*

**Huntsville**
Conwell, Halford Roger *physician*
Garner, Randall *medical educator*
Hanssen, Kristina Schirm *costume designer, educator*
Hoffmann, Frank William *library science educator, writer*
Lea, Stanley E. *artist, educator*
Marks, Bobby Kees *academic administrator*
Miller, Rowland Spence *psychologist, writer*
Payne, David Emer *university administrator*
Raymond, Kay E. (Kay Engelmann Raymond) *Spanish language educator, consultant*
Russell, George Haw *video production company executive*
Sower, Victor Edmund *management educator*
Stowe, Charles Robinson Beecher *management consultant, educator, lawyer*
Ward, Richard Hurley *director, dean, writer*

**Hurst**
Bishara, Amin Tawadros *management and consulting firm executive*
Mabry, Philip T. *political scientist, consultant*
Moore, Herff Leo, Jr. *management educator*
Shapley, Gregory Paul *head of religious order, music director*

**Hutto**
Hamilton, Elizabeth Ann *elementary school educator*

**Industry**
Huitt, Jimmie L. *rancher, oil and gas industry executive, real estate developer*

**Ingram**
Riedel, Holly *theater director*

**Iola**
Nelson, John Harrison *mathematics educator*

**Irving**
Abu-Suleiman, Amr *industrial engineer, researcher*
Ali, Ashraf *psychiatrist*
Allen, Larry Christopher *professional football player*
Ashby, Elizabeth Sybil *marketing analyst*
Beach, Charles Addison *lawyer*
Beasley, Mark V. *lawyer*
Birch, Glynn R. *non-profit organization administrator*
Bledsoe, Drew *professional football player*
Brown, Linda Harper *bookkeeping company executive*
Burton, Betsey (Mary Elizabeth Burton) *retail executive*
Buthman, Mark A. *retail executive*
Cavanaugh, Lucille J. *oil industry executive*
Cohen, Kenneth P. *oil industry executive, lawyer*
Conger, Sue Ann *computer information systems educator*
Dahan, Rene *oil industry executive*
Decker, Tristan Quinn *technical director, lighting designer, set designer*
Dingle, Philip *oil industry executive*
D'Spain, Michael Fraser *music educator*
Duffy, Dan *computer company executive*
Eaker, Charles William *chemistry professor*
Falk, Thomas J. *paper company executive*
Gabriel, Eberhard John *lawyer, bank executive*
Glenn, Terry *professional football player*
Halter, Jon Charles *magazine editor, writer*
Hicks, Allen Morley *retired hospital administrator*
Humphreys, Donald D. *oil industry executive*
Jones, Jerry (Jerral Wayne Jones) *professional football team executive*
Jones, Julius *professional football player*
Jorden, Yon Yoon *health services company executive*
Kling, Lewis *multi-industry executive*
Longwell, Harry J. *retired oil industry executive*
Martin, Thomas Lyle, Jr. *academic administrator*
Massah, Cherilyn *auditor*
Matthews, Charles W., Jr. *oil industry executive*
McClean, Murray R. *metal products executive*
McCormack, Grace Lynette *civil engineering technician*
McCray, Ronald David *lawyer*
Means, Richard Nathaniel Griffith *historian*
Molay, Hilary S. *lawyer*
Mulva, Patrick T. *oil industry executive*
Nugent, John Hilliard *communications executive*
Olson, Gary Robert *banker*
Olson, Herbert Theodore *trade association executive*
Owens, Terrell Eldorad *professional football player*
Parcells, Bill (Duane Charles Parcells) *professional football coach*
Pascal, Tracey Michele *software engineer, director*
Plaskett, Thomas George *transportation executive, director*
Potter, Robert Joseph *technical and business executive*
Rabin, Stanley Arthur *metal products manufacturer*
Rees, Frank William, Jr. *architect*
Robinson, Lawrence Dewitt *lawyer*
Rouleau, R. Michael *retail executive*
Sheffield, Scott D. *oil industry executive*
Shuff, Ronald F. *lawyer*
Sigurdson, Mike James *visual art educator*
Sommerfeldt, John Robert *historian, educator*
Strunck, Juergen *printmaker*
Sudbury, David Marshall *lawyer*
Sullivan, Paul E. *lawyer, oil industry executive*
Tillerson, Rex W. *oil company executive*
Vanderjagt, Mike *professional football player*
Walley, James Marvin, Jr. *engineering executive, management consultant, real estate company executive*
Whisennand, Cynthia Simmons *librarian*
Wicks, William Withington *retired public relations executive*
Wilkerson, H. Dean, Jr. *association and organization executive*
Williams, Roy L. *fraternal organization administrator*
Witten, Jason (Christopher Jas Witten) *professional football player*
Wyly, Samuel E. *retail executive*
Young, J. Warren *magazine publisher*

**Jacksboro**
Patterson, Ronald R(oy) *management consultant*

**Jacksonville**
Blaylock, James Carl *clergyman, librarian*
Thrall, Gordon Fish *publishing executive*

**Joaquin**
Gill, Madeline Kay *school and youth counselor*

**Johnson City**
Pollock, Margaret Landau Peggy *elementary school educator*

**Junction**
Evans, Jo Burt *communications executive, rancher*

**Karnes City**
Davis, Troy Arnol *reflexologist, hypnotherapist*

**Katy**
Chavez, Victor Manuel *petroleum engineer, utilities executive*

**Kaufman**
Hausler, Rudolf Heinrich *research chemist*
Tygrett, Howard Volney, Jr. *judge, lawyer*

**Keene**
Doroftei, Mugur Gideon *music educator, conductor, composer, musician*
Miller, Rebecca Lynn *software engineer*

**Keller**
King, Chi-Chi Wong *choir director*
Meixner, Cliff Dale *social studies educator, literature and language professor*
Smith, Eleanor Jane *retired university chancellor, consultant*

**Kerrville**
Burt, Allen Daniel *artist*
Chance, F. Earlayne *artist*
Denke, Margo A. *nutritionist, researcher, endocrinologist*
Dozier, William Everett, Jr. *publishing executive, editor-in-chief*
Freeny, Katherine H. *adult education educator, chemist, researcher*
Frudakis, Evangelos William *sculptor*
Jordan, Sam Latron *minister, mediator*
Shaw, Alan Bosworth *geologist, retired paleontologist*
Sparks, Don Bertrand *retired geophysicist*
Zuber, Randolph Clark *retired urologist*

**Kilgore**
Gosalia, Keyoor Chetan *electrical engineer*
Rorschach, Richard Gordon *lawyer*
Turpin, Michael Hunter *academic administrator*

**Killeen**
Bryan, Arthur Lee *music educator*
Day, Charles R. *plastic surgeon*
Evans, Carl M. *business executive*
Khwaja, Shamsuddin *neurologist, consultant*

**Kingsland**
Watson, Elizabeth Marion *protective services official*

**Kingsville**
Bashir, Sajid *chemist, educator, research scientist*
Bleidt, Barry Anthony *pharmacy educator*
Cecil, David Rolf *mathematician, educator*
Grassman, Lon Irvin, Jr. *research scientist*
Henke, Scott E. *wildlife educator*
Hunter, Leslie Gene *history educator*
Sethi, Rajat *cardiologist, educator, research scientist*
Stanford, (Frances) Jane Herring *management consultant, educator, writer*

**Kingwood**
Hagen, Barbara C. *music educator*
Ribeiro, Frank Henry *bank executive, financial consultant*
van Beem, Janny *geneticist, researcher*

**Kirbyville**
Gaspard, James M. *music educator, musician*

**Kyle**
Atkinson, Valerie J. *writer, webmaster*
Saunders, Patricia Gene Knight *freelance writer, editor*

**La Feria**
Philip, Sunny Koipurathu *municipal official*
Zamarripa, Victor Manuel *sound recording engineer, purchasing agent*

**La Marque**
Bernard, Lora Marie *journalist, public relations and development specialist*
Disher, David Alan *lawyer, consultant*

**La Porte**
Fotsch, George Bernard III *chemical addiction counselor*
Svambera, Beatrice Alice *secondary school educator*

**La Ward**
Lin, Ming T. *plant pathologist*

**Lackland Afb**
Beck, William Joseph *health facility administrator, geophysicist*
Dunn, William Jackson *dental educator, researcher*
Fadare, Oluwole *pathologist, researcher, director*
Perry, William Brian *colorectal surgeon*

**Lake Jackson**
Elbert, James Peak *independent insurance agent, minister*

**Lakehills**
Spears, Diane Shields *art director, elementary school educator*

**Lamesa**
Saleh, John *lawyer*

**Laredo**
Black, Clifford Merwyn *academic administrator, sociologist, educator*
Bruni, Louis H. *judge, oil industry executive*
Cai, Gangshu *computer science professor*
Goonatilake, Rohitha *mathematician, educator*
Greybeck, Barbara Jean *education educator*
Heimes, Charmaine Marie *elementary school educator, poet, writer*
Lakshmana, Viswanath *information technology executive*
Ortiz, Jaime *business educator*
Reuthinger, Georgeanne *special education educator*
Riggs, William W. *social sciences educator*
Shepherd, Terry Lynn *special education educator*
Sosa, Francisco Javier *music educator, consultant*
Soto, Gilberto D. *music educator*
Weber, Janice Ann *library director, grant writer*
Wu, Fuming *computer science educator*
Zaffirini, Judith *state legislator, small business owner*

**League City**
Cherry, Jeffrey Allen *secondary school educator*
Kanuth, James Gordan *chemical engineer*

**Leander**
Erickson, Ralph D. *retired physical education educator, small business owner, consultant*

**Levelland**
Skinner, Peggy June *psychology professor, consultant*

**Lewisville**
Ferguson, R. Neil *computer scientist, consultant*

**Liberty**
Davis, Freida J. *music educator*

**Lindale**
Carter, Thomas Smith, Jr. *retired rail transportation executive*

**Littlefield**
Massengill, Ellen Webb *librarian*

**Livingston**
Davidson, John Robert *retired dentist*
Hayes, Gordon Glenn *civil engineer*
Stovall, Jerry (Coleman Stovall) *insurance company executive*

**Llano**
Wilson, Dena Suzette *elementary school educator*

**Longview**
Gentry, Vernessa Diana *principal, consultant*
Harrison, Guy Newell *lawyer*
Mann, Jack Matthewson *bottling company executive*
Mann, True Sandlin *psychologist, consultant*
McKinley, Jimmie Joe *small business owner*
Statman, Jan B. *artist*
Udy, Rae *columnist, writer*
Welge, Jack Herman, Jr. *lawyer*
Williams, Willie Alvin *retired literature educator*
Winsted, Donald Eugene III *psychologist*

**Lubbock**
Adamcik, Joe Alfred *retired chemistry professor, lawyer*
Aker, Suzanne Deverse *physical movement educator*
Allcorn, Seth Ford *dean, academic administrator*
Aoyama, Katsura *psycholinguist*
Archer, James Elson *engineering educator*
Arnold, Sue *music educator*
Beck, George Preston *anesthesiologist, educator*
Beyer, Gerry Wayne *lawyer, educator*
Blevins, Stanley Nance *minister, educator*
Bullock, James Jefferson, II, *literature and language professor, director*
Chatterjee, Sankar *geology educator*
Chung, Ya-Li *music educator*
Conover, William Jay *statistics educator*
Craighead, Owen Lindsay *writer*
Dennison, Daniel Thomas *environmental compliance administrator, lab administrator*
Doyle, Laurie Ellen *art educator*
Dudek, Richard Albert *engineering educator*
Edwards, Martin S. *political scientist, educator*
Eng, Sothy *research scientist*
Everse, Johannes *biochemist, researcher*
Feola, Mario *researcher*
Fontenot, Andrea Dean *communications executive*
Frezza, Eldo E. *surgeon, educator*
Gilbert, John Haspel *music educator*
Gill, Brian *orthopedist, surgeon*
Gill, Gurdev S. *orthopaedic surgeon*
Haragan, Donald Robert *academic administrator, geologist, educator*
Hart, Melanie A. *secondary school educator*
Hartwell, William Gersham III *retired music educator*
Hentges, David John *microbiology educator*
Huffman, Walter B. *retired army officer, dean, law educator*
Illner-Canizaro, Hana *physician, researcher, oral surgeon*
Jackson, Raymond Carl *cytogeneticist*
Jugenheimer, Donald Wayne *advertising executive, communications educator, academic administrator*
Karp, Tanja Nicolette *electrical engineer, educator*
Kelley, John Timothy *lawyer, animal breeder*
Ketner, Kenneth Laine *philosopher, educator*
Kiesling, Ernst Willie *civil engineering educator, dean*
Knight, Bobby (Robert Montgomery Knight) *college basketball coach*
Kristiansen, Magne *electrical engineer, educator*
Leach, Mike *college football coach*
May, Donald Robert Lee *ophthalmologist, educator, academic administrator, farmer*
Parks, Katie Mae *human services manager*
Phelan, Marilyn Elizabeth *law educator*
Punyanunt-Carter, Narissra *communications educator*
Purdom, Thomas James *lawyer*
Quinn Trank, Christine *education educator*
Rejesus, Roderick Morallo *agricultural and applied economist*
Repman, Judith Lavine *educator*
Sabatini, Sandra *physician*
Seshaiyer, Padmanabhan *mathematician, educator*
Skoog, Gerald Duane *science educator*
Stuart, Frank Adell *county official*
Warren, Donald John *retired surgeon, educator*
Webb, Carl B. *banker*
Wendt, Charles William *soil scientist, educator*
White, Alice Virginia *academic administrator*
White, John Poston *architect, educator*
Wolfe, Verda Nell *pension consultant, financial planner*
Wood, Richard Courtney *library director, educator*
Woolam, Gerald Lynn *surgeon*
Wray, Robert Theodore *music educator*
Yoder-Wise, Patricia Snyder *nursing educator*

**Magnolia**
Bryant, Kimberly Dawn *theater educator, actor*

Girard, Louis Joseph *retired ophthalmologist, educator*

**Mansfield**
Parnell, Charles L. *speechwriter*
Rewoldt, Christian Walter *school psychologist, military officer*

**Marfa**
Chambers Tucker, Johnnie L. *elementary school educator, rancher*

**Marshall**
Branscome, Eric Eugene *music educator, writer*
Capehart, Steven Russell *mathematics professor*
Farmer, T. Brent *music educator*
Magrill, Rose Mary *library director*
O'Day, Patrick Michael *sociologist, educator, criminologist, researcher*
Sudhivoraseth, Niphon *pediatrician, immunologist, allergist*

**Maxwell**
Peters, Carol Ann *secondary school educator*

**Mc Kinney**
Albano, Christine Grace *lawyer*
Dickinson, Richard Raymond *retired oil company executive*
Frank, Steven Neil *chemist*
Gill, David bRIAN *electrical engineer, educator*
Kessler, John Paul, Jr. *financial planner*
McAndrew, Mark S. *insurance company executive*
Wright, Thomas Parker *artist*

**Mcallen**
Casso, Ramiro Raul *physician, academic administrator*
Connors, Joseph Aloysius III *lawyer*
Galdeano, Daniel Rodriguez *social studies educator*
Gonzalez, Rolando Noel *secondary school educator, theology studies educator, photographer*
Hinojosa, Ricardo H. *federal judge*
Huber, Melba Stewart *dance educator, dance studio owner, historian, retailer*
Kadhim, Estelle Beverly *librarian, educator*
McGee, William Howard John *library director*
Millan, Brett Jorge *education educator*
Ramirez, Leo Armando, Sr. *mathematics educator*
Ramirez, Mario Efrain *physician*
Rebuelta, Avelino Luis *public administration educator*
Roney, Glen E. *finance company executive*
Spyker, Leola Edith *missionary*
Sutton, William Blaylock *pastor*
Trainor, Debora Jean *school psychologist, consultant*
Truitt, Rodgers Paul *educator*

**Mclean**
Riley, Jacqulyn (Jacque) Diane *English educator, theater educator*

**Meadowlakes**
Nussbaum, Paul Stowell *retired urologist*

**Megargel**
Robertson, John *principal*

**Mesquite**
Byrd, Kathryn Susan *psychologist, educator*
Dean, Sherry Lynn *language educator, speech professional*
Gant, Linda Gayle *elementary school educator*
Holt, Mildred Frances *special education educator*
Marin, Jackie Willis *music educator, pianist*
Nye, Randall Wayne *music educator*
Sepulvado, Joseph Michael *computer information scientist*
Vaughan, Joseph Lee, Jr. *education educator, consultant*
Wenrich, John William *college president*

**Mico**
McDonald, Mary Helen *special education educator*

**Midland**
Berner, Leo De Witte, Jr. *retired oceanographer*
Bridges, Judy Cantrell *gifted and talented education educator*
Celia, George *composer, writer*
Dawkins, Diantha Dee *librarian*
Dempsey, Christina Marie *reading educator*
Estes, Andrew Harper *lawyer*
Eustace, Natalie Bencowitz *elementary school educator*
Groce, James Freelan *financial consultant*
Grover, Rosalind Redfern *oil and gas company executive*
MacDonald, Leland Lloyd *lawyer*
Martin, C. D. *lawyer*
Morrow, William Clarence *judge, lawyer, arbitrator*
Pysh, Gregory M. *music educator*
Sherpa, Fran Magruder *geography educator*
Syed, Elizabeth Chance *health facility administrator, critical care nurse*
Taylor, Nicholas C. *lawyer, state agency administrator, energy executive*

**Midlothian**
Alderman, Amy Joy Spigel *elementary school educator*
Patty, Patricia Kae *music educator*
Rogers, Robert D. *steel company executive*

**Mineola**
McCann, Evelyn Louise Johnson *retired minister, retired counselor*
Stevenson, David Wayne *municipal official*

**Mineral Wells**
Braun, Gustav Milan *otolaryngologist, surgeon*
Mei, Anhua *mechanical engineer, researcher*
Warfield, Gerald Alexander *composer, writer*

**Mission**
Eyre, Pamela Catherine *retired career officer*

Holkup, Linda Patricia *music educator*
Nichols, Edward Edson *artist*

**Missouri City**
Chang, Jeffrey Chai *dentist, educator, researcher*
de Kanter, Ellen Ann *retired English and foreign language educator*
Hodges, Jot Holiver, Jr. *retired lawyer, corporate financial executive*
Rathnau, Heather Hearn *music educator, writer*
Tchamengo, Mathias Ngoufi *energy executive, mathematician*

**Monahans**
Jones, Evelyn Rojean *theater educator, theater director*

**Montgomery**
Kelsey, Clyde Eastman, Jr. *philosophy educator, psychology professor*
Smith, John Brewster *library administrator*

**Morton**
Black, Rebecca J. *secondary school educator*

**Mount Pleasant**
Giddens, Martha Lynn *health science association administrator, medical educator*
Kirkpatrick, Jim C. *secondary school educator*
McCauley, Dan Paul *dentist*
Vaughn, William Preston *retired historian, retired educator*

**Murchison**
Taweel, Janice M. *artist, art educator*

**Nacogdoches**
Bowen, Donald Edgar *physics professor, former academic administrator*
Jacobsen, Jeffrey Richard *music educator*
Stetz, Phil E. *management educator, entrepreneur*

**New Braunfels**
Barragán, Celia Silguero *elementary school educator*
Benfield, Marion Wilson, Jr. *law educator*
Krueger, Robert Charles *former ambassador, former congressman, former senator*
Oestreich, Charles Henry *retired university president*
Wilson, James Lee *retired geology educator, consultant*

**New Caney**
Hayes, Ann Carson *computer company executive*

**Nocona**
Frailey, S. Clark *minister*

**Normangee**
Cox, Jack Ronald, Jr. *finance educator*
Rector, M. Eugene *community pharmacist*

**North Richland Hills**
Dvorak, Mark Anthony *music educator*
Gedwed, William J. *insurance company executive*
Reed, Glenn W. *lawyer*
Shier, Elizabeth M. *music educator*
Wallace, William Edward *thoracic surgeon*

**Odessa**
Bouquin, Samantha Erin *mathematics professor*
Braswell, Jody Lynn *gifted and talented educator*
Gutierrez, Kristopher James *physicist, researcher*
Moseley, Clifford Wayne *writer, poet*
Robinson, J. Michael *chemistry professor, researcher*
Toruño-Haensly, Rhina M. *literature educator, researcher, writer*
Worley, Robert Michael *criminologist, educator*

**Olney**
Timmons, Gordon David *economics professor, farmer*

**Orange**
Odom, Sarah Bernice *elementary school educator*

**Ovalo**
Mooney, Allan W. *management consultant, foundation administrator*

**Paige**
Trevino, Jerry Rosalez *retired secondary school principal*

**Palestine**
Akin, Charles S. *academic administrator*
Sellers, Wayne Chadick *retired publisher, retired editor*
Williams, Franklin Cadmus, Jr. *bibliographer*

**Pampa**
Cain, Donald Ezell *retired judge*
Crow, Donna Gayle *business educator*
Willingham, Jeanne Maggart *performing arts educator, performing company executive*

**Panhandle**
Sherrod, Lloyd Bruce *retired nutritionist*

**Paris**
McCuen, Maureen E. *history educator*
Proctor, June *retired religious organization administrator, writer*
Proctor, Richard Owen *historian, health facility administrator, military officer*

**Pasadena**
Austin-Goza, Pamela Kay *voice educator*
Blue, Monte Lynn *college president*
Gilley, Mickey Leroy *musician*
Gross, Cynthia Sue *petrochemicals manufacturing executive*
Kenagy, Cheri Lynn *nurse*
Martinez, Fernando V. *civil engineer*
Moon, John Henry, Sr. *banker*
Mullins, Jack Allen *cardiologist, educator*
Rocha, Brenda Duvall *theater educator*
Scott, William Floyd *accountant*

Shapiro, Edward Muray *dermatologist*
Thompson, Marian Nell *poetry, historical, non-fiction and fiction writer, educator, poet*

**Pearland**
Johnson, Hugh James *retired music educator*
McFarlin, Brian Keith *medical educator, researcher*
Shurtleff, Malcolm C. *plant pathologist, consultant*
Visnegarwala, Fehmida *internist, educator*
Würsig, Bernd Gerhard *marine biology educator*
Zhou, Juhua *molecular biologist*

**Pharr**
Liu, David T. *retired librarian*

**Pittsburg**
Goolsby, O. B., Jr. *food products executive*
Pilgrim, Lonnie (Bo Pilgrim) *food products executive*

**Plano**
Altabef, Peter Anthony *lawyer*
Ansari, Amir *digital home and multimedia management technology company executive*
Ansari, Anousheh *digital home and multimedia management technology company executive, first female civilian space traveler*
Ansari, Hamid *digital home and multimedia management technology company executive*
Bain, Travis Whitsett, II, *manufacturing and retail executive*
Bober, Joanne L. *lawyer*
Bonet, Frank Joseph *retired lawyer*
Bravard, Jean-Louis *diversified financial services company executive*
Bru, Abelardo E. *food products executive*
Carver, Rita *not-for-profit fundraiser, consultant*
Cavanaugh, Robert B. *department store executive*
Chopra, Anil *oil industry executive*
Davis, Robert D. *rental company executive*
Day, Kevin Thomas *retired business executive, retired investment banker, retired foundation administrator*
Dillon, Donald Ward *management consultant*
Dougherty, F(rancis) Kelly *data processing executive*
Evans, Pat *mayor*
Fadel, Mitchell E. *rental company executive*
Fahle, William August, Jr. *application developer*
Fay, Donald P. *lawyer*
Feld, Charles S. *information technology executive*
Ford, H. Ross III *real estate company executive*
Friedman, Ronald M. *plastic surgeon*
Fuller, Tony F. *rental company executive*
Glenn, Marshall Andrew *psychologist*
Godbold, Christopher Bourke *curator*
Gordon, Storrow Moss *information technology executive, lawyer*
Harris, Wayne *retail executive*
Heller, Jeffrey M. *data processing executive*
Hemingway, Richard William *law educator*
Hightower, David R. *environmental health specialist, educator*
Hilton, Steven J. *real estate executive*
James, Michael Thames *information technology executive, consultant*
Jensen, Ronald L. *insurance company executive*
Korst, Christopher A. *lawyer, rental company executive*
Landon, John R. *real estate developer*
Levine, Harold *lawyer*
Little, Joseph Hugh *plastic surgeon*
Lombardo, Elizabeth Roessler *psychologist, physical therapist*
MacAlpine, Michelle Lewis *neuroscientist*
Marmol, Guillermo G. (Gil Marmol) *information technology executive*
McClaskey, Michael Keith *information technology executive*
Mick, James Paul *music educator*
Mondul, Donald David *patent lawyer*
Montiel, Alfonso *data processing executive*
Naor, Daniel *food products executive*
Neppl, Walter Joseph *retired retail executive*
Papalia, Rocco Dominic *food products executive*
Parsons, Michael J. *health facility administrator*
Perot, Ross (H. Ross Perot, Henry Ross Perot) *real estate company executive, investment company executive, data processing executive*
Perot, Ross, Jr., (Henry Ross Perot Jr.) *real estate developer, professional sports team executive*
Questrom, Allen I. *retail executive*
Raish, Stephen E *retail executive*
Rhodes, Doris Chaney *freelance/self-employed secondary school educator*
Rodolph, Grant *lawyer*
Ryu, Manho *application developer*
Satz, Jeffrey S. *telecommunications industry executive, consultant*
Schuckenbrock, Stephen *information technology executive*
Schuh, Frank Joseph *oil industry executive, consultant*
Scott, Terry Lee *communications executive*
Shelton, James D. (Denny Shelton) *hospital management company executive*
Sivinski, Tina M. *human resources specialist*
Speese, Mark E. *rental company executive*
Taylor, Paul Peak *pediatric dentist, educator*
Theilmann, Michael T. *human resources specialist*
Vargo, Ronald Paul *information technology applications executive*
Warburton, Ralph Joseph *architect, educator, engineer*
West, Catherine G. *retail executive*
Wyman, Richard Thomas *information technology manager, researcher*

**Port Aransas**
Lehmann, William Leonardo *electrical engineer, educator*
Schake, Lowell Martin *zoology educator, writer*
Turner, Elizabeth Adams Noble (Betty Turner) *real estate company executive*
Van Baalen, Donna Gale *artist, retired pharmacist*

**Port Arthur**
Goza, Jim *chemistry educator*
Munoz, Andrea Lee *human resources specialist*
Vinecour, Oneida Agnes *nurse*

**Post**
Earl, Lewis Harold *economist, consultant, lawyer*
Killian, Lawrence Harding, II, (Larry H. Killian) *sculptor*
Neff, Marie Taylor *museum director, artist*

**Pottsboro**
Hanning, Gary William *utilities executive, consultant, water transportation executive*
Thomas, Ann Van Wynen *retired law educator*

**Powell**
Emerson, Harriett Anne *small business owner*

**Prairie View**
Ciftja, Orion *physicist, researcher*
De Luna-Gonzalez, Elma *accountant, academic administrator*
Qian, Lijun *electrical engineer, educator*

**Quitaque**
Herrington, Patsy Jean Stark *music educator*

**Randolph Afb**
Brennan-Bergmann, Bridget Catherine *special education educator*
Ellis, Edward R. *career officer*
Looney, William R. III *career military officer*

**Red Oak**
Dulworth, Rhonda Rencé *secondary school educator*
Jones, Genia Kay *critical care nurse, consultant*

**Richardson**
Andrews, Melinda Wilson *human development researcher*
Atkins, Howard Gray, Jr. *social services administrator*
Atzori, Marco *neuroscientist, educator*
Berry, Brian Joe Lobley *geographer, educator, urban planner, political economist*
Conkel, Robert Dale *lawyer, consultant*
Cox, David Leon *telecommunications industry executive*
Daniel, David Edwin *academic administrator, civil engineer*
Dian, Jianwei *application developer*
Easttom, Chuck *computer scientist, educator*
Goodspeed, Linda A. *manufacturing executive*
Gray, Donald Melvin *molecular and cell biology educator*
Griffith, Daniel Alva *geography educator*
Heath, Mary Ann *elementary school educator*
Holmes, Jennifer Smith *political scientist, educator*
Krauss, Henry Frederick, Jr. *optometrist*
Long, Allen Floyd *music educator, minister*
Lowe, J. Allen *minister*
Manton, William Inwood *geologist, educator*
Martin, Richard Kelley *lawyer*
McMechan, George *science educator*
Olson, Dennis Oliver *lawyer*
Redman, Timothy Paul *language educator, writer*
Rutford, Robert Hoxie *geologist, educator*
Safka, Jim *information technology executive*
Sall, Larry David *library director*
Sandler, Todd Michael *economist, political scientist, educator*
Schjerven, Robert E. *manufacturing executive*
Senderling, Jon Townsend *journalist, public relations executive, consultant*
Smith, Mark P. *foundation administrator*
Smith, Richard A. *manufacturing executive*
Sowers, Wesley Hoyt *lawyer, management consultant*
Sperrin, Graham Frederick *marketing professional*
Sprague, Charles Warren *geologist*
Stoll, William Frederick, Jr. *lawyer*
Tate, William Fleming, IV, *mathematics educator*
Udeshi, Tushar Jairaj *application developer, consultant*
Williams, James Francis, Jr. *religious organization administrator*
Wiorkowski, John James *mathematics professor*
Wood, Joseph George *neuroscientist, educator*

**Richland Hills**
Haynes, Ruth Elaine *accountant*

**Richmond**
Dholakia, Utpal M. *management educator, consultant*

**Rio Grande City**
Lung, Auristela R. *music educator*

**Robert Lee**
Myers, Sterling *choir director*

**Rockport**
Berkebile, Charles Alan *geology educator, hydrogeology researcher*
Minor, Joseph Edward *civil engineer, educator*

**Rockwall**
Cates, Sue Sadler *educational diagnostician*
Fisher, Gene Jordan *retired chemical company executive*
Johnston, Nicklett Rose *research nurse, clinical perfusionist*
Kotas, Robert Vincent *pediatrician, educator*
Tucker, Kimberly Joan *music educator*
Villarino, Mario Alberto *veterinarian, researcher*
White, Todd William *lawyer, educator*

**Rosenberg**
Haygood, Eithel Marinella *artist, educator*
Lefler, Sherry LynettE *elementary school educator*
Smith, October *elementary school educator*
White, Gretchen Nance *education educator, writer*

**Rosharon**
Jenkins, Judith Alexander *bank consultant*

**Round Rock**
Dell, Michael S. *computer company executive*
Goodman, Kim *marketing professional, computer company executive*
Hudson, Michel Colette *management consultant*

Khalid, Humayun *computer scientist, consultant*
Mountain, Janet *foundation administrator, former computer company executive*
Parra, Rosendo G. *computer company executive*
Puri, Rajendra Kumar *business and tax specialist, consultant*
Ricklefs, Dale Lynne *library director*
Rollins, Kevin B. *computer company executive*
Ryan, Nolan *former professional baseball player*
Schneider, Dennis Ray *microbiology educator and executive*
Schneider, James M. *computer company executive*
Sheskey, Susan E. *computer company executive*
Wahl, William Bryan *marketing professional, real estate company officer*

### Round Top
Killion, Vida Frazier *minister, writer*
Lentz, Edwin Lamar *art historian*

### Rowlett
Bell, Ronald *secondary school educator*

### Rusk
McMinn, J. B. *retired philosophy educator, composer*

### Sachse
Eichelberger, Charles Bell *retired career officer*

### Salado
Parks, Lloyd Lee *oil industry executive*

### San Angelo
Charlesworth, Ernest Neal *allergist, immunologist, dermatologist, educator*
Chatfield, Mary Van Abshoven *librarian*
Davison, Elizabeth Jane Linton *educator*
Fischer, Duncan Kinnear *neurosurgeon*
Lara, Cynthia Lynn *science educator*
Richardson, Shirley R. *librarian*
Smith, Karen B. *educational consultant*
Sutton, John Ewing *lawyer*

### San Antonio
Abramson, Hyman Norman *engineering and science research executive*
Accountius, Patricia L. *dietician, consultant*
Aguirre, Javier Ramos *historian, educator*
Akella, Umasundari Srivenkata *research scientist*
Akopian, David *engineering educator*
Allegrini, Frédéric *research scientist, educator*
Ammann, Lillian Ann Nicholson *writer, editor, small business owner*
Ancira, Ernesto, Jr. *automotive executive*
Anderson, Anita L. *psychology professor*
Arce, Arturo Galvan *military programs instructor*
Arciniega, Armando *mathematics professor*
Artemov, Vladimir Nikolaevich *gymnastics coach*
Arthur, Gary L., Jr. *energy executive*
Atchley, Curtis Leon *mechanical engineer*
Aust, Joe Bradley *surgeon, educator*
Austin, Lola Houston *psychologist*
Avant, Patricia Kay *nursing educator*
Azzi, Jennifer L. *professional basketball player*
Bai, Yidong *molecular biologist, educator*
Baker, Floyd Wilmer *surgeon, retired military officer*
Barnes, Helen Joyce *elementary school educator*
Baron, Robert M. *architecture educator*
Becker, Quinn Henderson *orthopedic surgeon, military officer*
Beckmann, Charles Henry *cardiologist, educator*
Bell, Joy Ann *librarian*
Bellows, Thomas John *political scientist, educator*
Bennett, Sister Elsa Mary *retired secondary school educator*
Bennett, Steven Alan *lawyer*
Bettac, Robert Edward *lawyer*
Blank, Steven A. *energy executive*
Booke, Keith D. *energy executive*
Bowen, Bruce *professional basketball player*
Bowers, Kim *lawyer, energy executive*
(Foote) Boyd, Barbara Jo Ann *quality assurance professional*
Breit, William *economist, educator, writer*
Brewster, Olive Nesbitt *retired librarian*
Brooks, Franklin Ramon *psychologist, military officer*
Brown, Devin *professional basketball player*
Brown, Mary Rose *energy executive*
Browning, Jay D. *energy executive*
Budalur, Thyagarajan Subbanarayan *chemistry professor*
Burch, James Leo *science research institute executive*
Burke, Betty Jane *retired real estate manager*
Butt, Charles Clarence *food service executive*
Callaway, James W. *telecommunications industry executive*
Campbell, Robert Murray, Jr. *surgeon, researcher*
Carr, Cassandra Colvin *communications company executive*
Case, Elizabeth Joy *psychology and educational assessment director*
Catto, Henry Edward *former government official, retired ambassador*
Champion, Michael Edward *physician assistant, clinical perfusionist*
Chasnoff, Barry A. *lawyer*
Chiego, William J. *museum director*
Cicconi, James William *lawyer, telecommunications industry executive*
Ciskowski, Michael S. *energy executive*
Cisneros, Henry G. *homebuilding executive, broadcast executive, retired federal official*
Clark, Robert Phillips *editor, consultant*
Cochran, David L. *periodontist, dental educator, department chairman*
Collins, Kevin Lloyd *lawyer*
Colyer, Kirk Klein *insurance executive, real estate investment executive*
Condos, Barbara Seale *real estate broker, real estate developer, investor*
Condos, J. Alexander *mortgage company executive*
Cordova, Ruben Charles *art historian, educator, curator, photographer*
Corrigan, Helen González *retired cytologist*
Cotae, Paul *communications educator*

Crabtree, Ben C. *neuromuscular therapy clinic director*
Cragnolino, Gustavo Adolfo *research scientist*
Crawford, Edwin Mac (Mac Crawford) *pharmaceutical company executive*
Crichton, Flora Cameron *volunteer, foundation administrator*
Croft, Harry Allen *psychiatrist*
Crownover, Mike *energy executive*
Crutchfield, Sharon Louise *retired librarian*
Cura, Marco Antonio *interventional radiologist, educator*
Dacbert-Friese, Sharyn Varhely *social worker, evangelist*
Daley, William M. *former federal government official*
Danney, Mark Maxwell *pediatrician*
Datta, Rupali *geochemist, educator*
Davis, George Edward *industrial designer*
Davis, Jolene Bryant *magazine publishing executive consultant*
Davis, Marlon Quinn *assistant principal*
Davis, Robert G. *insurance company executive*
Davis, Sarah Jane *health facility administrator*
de la Garza, Luis Adolfo *automotive executive, lawyer*
DeNice, Marcella Louise *counselor*
Dodd, Gerald D. III *radiologist*
Dorman, David W. *telecommunications industry executive*
Dumitru, Daniel *physiatrist*
Duncan, A. Baker *investment banker*
Duncan, Tim *professional basketball player*
Dunlap, Kathryn Sharp *educational association administrator*
Dunn, James David *language educator*
Dyas, Anna Marie *gifted and talented educator*
Edwards, Gene *energy executive*
Ejikeme, Anene *social sciences educator*
Ellis, James D. *telecommunications industry executive, lawyer*
Emery, Nancy Beth *lawyer*
Escobar, Irma *secondary school educator*
Estep, Myrna Lynne *systems analyst, philosophy educator*
Evans, Betty Vaughn *minister*
Eyer, Julia Arlene *speech pathology/audiology services professional, educator*
Fariabi, Said *mathematics professor*
Faules, Barbara Ruth *retired elementary school educator*
Fehrenbach, T.R. (Theodore Reed Fehrenbach) *writer*
Finley, Michael *professional basketball player*
Flores, Belinda Bustos *bilingual educator, administrator*
Fonseca, Joseph Mojica, Jr. *political science professor*
Foster, Nancy Haston *columnist, writer*
Franke, Ernest A. *electrical engineer, educator*
Frazer, Robert Lee *retired landscape architect*
Fuhrmann, Charles J., II, *financial consultant*
Furgeson, William Royal *federal judge*
Furino, Antonio *economist, educator*
Gambitta, Richard Anthony *political science professor*
Garcia, Henry Frank *supply management and project management consultant*
Gardner, Raymond Alan *webmaster, writer*
Garza, Ed *former mayor*
Garza, Emilio Miller *federal judge*
Gates, Mahlon Eugene *retired research and development company executive, retired military officer*
Gibbons, Robert Ebbert *university official*
Ginobili, Manu *professional basketball player*
Glawe, Dawn *engineering educator*
Golden, Stephen L. *lawyer*
Gomez, José H. *archbishop*
Gonzalez, Antonio *voter registration project executive*
Gonzalez, Hector Hugo *nursing educator*
Gorder, Joe *energy executive*
Göring, Harald Heinz Herbert *geneticist, researcher*
Grabinski, Jodi *pharmacist, researcher*
Graf, Dorothy Jo *elementary school educator*
Gray, Suzy *recreation director, educator*
Greehey, William Eugene (Bill Greehey) *energy company executive*
Gribou, Julius M. *architecture educator*
Gruber, John Balsbaugh *physics professor*
Guenther, Jack Egon *lawyer*
Guerra, Fernando A. *pediatrician, health facility administrator*
Guntharp, Elizabeth Anne *librarian*
Gwathmey, Joe Neil, Jr. *broadcast executive*
Hale, Nancy Annette Bills *kindergarten educator*
Hannon, Brenda Ann Marie *psychology professor, researcher*
Hardberger, Phillip Duane *mayor, judge, lawyer, journalist*
Hardy, Harvey Louchard *retired lawyer*
Hare, Henry Phillip, Jr. *psychiatrist*
Heloise, *columnist, writer*
Henderson, Connie Chorlton *retired city planner, artist, writer*
Henderson, Dwight Franklin *dean, educator*
Henry, Peter York *lawyer, mediator*
Hilley, Van Galen *lawyer*
Hogan, John *broadcast executive*
Holt, Peter M. *professional sports team executive, agricultural products executive*
Hood, Sandra Dale *librarian*
Horn, Joe *professional football player*
Hornsby, David McMillan *musician, music educator*
Hudspeth, Almeta Kavanaugh *retired elementary school educator*
Irving, George Washington III *veterinarian, researcher, small business executive*
Jennings, Karen *human resources specialist, telecommunications industry executive*
Jimenez, David Fernando *medical educator, department chairman*
Johnson, Shannon *professional basketball player*
Jones, Daniel Hare *librarian, consultant*
Jones, James Richard *business administration educator*
Kahan, James S. *telecommunications industry executive*

Kalkwarf, Kenneth Lee *dean, dental educator*
Kamada-Cole, Mika M. *allergist, immunologist, medical educator*
Kasinath, Balakuntalam S. *medical researcher*
Katerndahl, David Arthur *medical educator*
Kaye, Celia Ilene *pediatrics educator*
Killinger, Clayton *energy executive*
King, Gregory C. *petroleum company executive*
King, Ronald Baker *federal judge*
Klaerner, Curtis Maurice *gas industry executive*
Klesse, William R. (Bill Klesse) *energy executive*
Kline, John William *retired military officer, management consultant*
Koneru, Suresh *plastic surgeon*
Kotecki, Kevin *beer company executive*
Kovalchuk, Brian *beverage company executive*
Koziol, John Craig (Craig Koziol) *career military officer*
Kreisberg, Jeffrey I. *medical educator, researcher*
Labenz-Hough, Marlene *mediator*
Lalwani, Ashok K. *marketing educator*
Lancaster, Malcolm Clayton *retired hospital administrator*
Langland, Olaf Elmer *retired dental educator*
Lebras, Paul J. *retired career military officer*
Lefeber, Edward James, Jr. *internist, educator*
Leighton, Albert Chester *history professor*
LeMaistre, Charles Aubrey *retired internist, epidemiologist, educator*
Lenke, Joanne Marie *publishing executive*
Leon, Robert Leonard *psychiatrist, educator*
Lin, Ai-Ling *researcher*
Lindner, Richard G. *telecommunications industry executive*
Loeffler, Tom (Thomas Gilbert Loeffler) *lobbyist, former congressman*
Losiewicz, Michael David *biochemist, educator*
Ludzik, Steve *professional hockey coach*
Lyle, Robert Edward *chemist*
Lyons, Kelly Guadalupe *science educator, researcher*
Madrid, Olga Hilda Gonzalez *retired elementary school educator, school system administrator*
Maloney, Marynell *lawyer*
Mamtani, Manju Rameshlal *geneticist, researcher*
Marbut, Robert Gordon *communications executive, electronic security and broadcast executive, investor*
Marcogliese, Richard J. *energy executive*
Markwell, Dick R(obert) *retired chemist*
Martin, James Charles *physician*
Massenburg, Tony *professional basketball player*
Masters, Bettie Sue Siler *biochemist, educator*
Maxwell, Diana Kathleen *education educator, primary school educator*
Mays, L(ester) Lowry *broadcast executive*
Mays, Mark Pitman *communication company executive*
Mc Allister, Gerald Nicholas *retired bishop, minister*
McClane, Robert Sanford *entrepreneur, bank executive*
McComas, David John *science administrator, space physicist*
McFee, Arthur Storer *physician*
McGill, Henry Coleman, Jr. *pathologist, educator, researcher*
McGuire, William Dennis *healthcare consultant*
McIntosh, Dennis Keith *veterinarian, consultant*
McManus, William Paul *police chief*
McSorley, Rita Elizabeth *adult education educator*
Menchaca, Robert *elementary school educator*
Mendoza, Louis G. *literature educator, researcher*
Messina, Paul Francis *finance educator*
Michaels, Willard A. (Bill Michaels) *retired broadcasting executive*
Miller, Forrest E. *telecommunications industry executive*
Mohammed, Nazr *professional basketball player*
Mott, Peggy Laverne *sociologist, educator*
Moya, Francisco Saez *consumer products company executive*
Moynihan, John Bignell *retired lawyer*
Mummidi, Srinivas *veterinarian, research scientist, educator*
Murphy, Sharon B. *health facility administrator*
Myers, Ellen Howell *historian, educator*
Nava, Carmen P. *communications executive*
Navarro, Max *supply chain management company executive*
Nedal, Arar Hamdi *research scientist*
Negrete, George Raymond *chemistry professor, researcher*
Nesterovic, Rasho *professional basketball player*
Newton, Virginia *archivist, historian, librarian*
Nichols, Sharon Louise *educator, researcher*
Nigro, R. Lisa *artist, foundation administrator, director*
Noriega, Elizabeth Govea *elementary school educator*
Odom, Marjorie Mildred Morgan *retired librarian*
Ognibene, Andre John *internist, educator, retired military officer*
Oppenheim, Martha Kunkel *pianist, educator*
Orange, Carolyn *education professor*
O'Rourke, Robert A. *cardiologist, educator*
Palacios, Lisa May *academic administrator*
Palmaz, Julio C. *radiologist*
Paque, Ronald Edward *molecular immunologist*
Parker, Tony *professional basketball player*
Parrish, Charles *lawyer*
Patterson, Jan Evans *epidemiologist, educator*
Paul, Debajyoti *geologist, educator*
Pavuk, Marian *epidemiologist, researcher*
Peak, Howard W. *former mayor*
Pearl, James Hildred *lawyer*
Pensado, Osvaldo *research scientist*
Perry, George *neuroscientist, educator*
Perry, Robert Michael *lawyer, consultant, rancher*
Persellin, Robert Harold *physician*
Pestana, Carlos *surgeon, retired dean, educator*
Peters, Richard Spencer *musician*
Petty, Scott, Jr. *rancher*
Pfeiffer, Philip John *lawyer*
Pietz, Clint A. *pediatrician, educator*
Popovich, Gregg *professional basketball coach*
Pruitt, Basil Arthur, Jr. *surgeon, retired military officer*
Pysher, Alan Guy *retired nurse anesthetist*
Reams, Bernard Dinsmore, Jr. *law educator*

Recker, Patricia Bullion *secondary school educator*
Redfield, Carol Ann Luckhardt *computer scientist, educator*
Renfro, Norm *energy executive*
Restrepo, Ruben Dario *physician, educator*
Reuter, Stewart Ralston *retired radiologist*
Ribble, Ronald George *psychologist, educator, writer, behavioral consultant*
Ridder, Linda Gayle *librarian*
Robertson, Samuel Luther, Jr. *psychotherapist, educator*
Robertson, Sterling Clifton *music educator, musician*
Robinson, David Maurice *professional basketball player*
Robinson, Glenn *professional basketball player*
Robles, Josue, Jr. *insurance company executive*
Rollin, Michael Fredrick *history professor*
Route, Candace *elementary school educator*
Rush, W. Marvin *trucking executive*
Ruttenberg, Frank Z. *lawyer*
Sablik, Martin John *research physicist*
Salvucci, Linda *history professor*
Sanchez, Susie Riojas *elementary school educator*
Schenker, Cecil *lawyer*
Schenker, Steven *internist, educator*
Schlueter, David Arnold *law educator*
Schmitz, John Phillip *maxillofacial surgeon, researcher*
Schmutz, John Francis *lawyer*
Schnitzler, Robert Neil *cardiologist*
Schoenbaum, Alan *lawyer*
Schoenfeld, Lawrence Steven *psychology educator*
Shanklin, Kenneth Dale *plastic surgeon*
Sharpley, Robert Louis *performing arts educator, language educator*
Silantien, John Joseph *music educator*
Sinkin, Fay Marie *environmentalist*
Smith, Bruce Alfred *oil industry executive*
Smith, Rebecca Lynn *language educator*
Smith, Reginald Brian Furness *retired anesthesiologist, educator*
Somlo, Valeska Barbara *medical/surgical nurse*
Spears, Sally *lawyer*
Spiro, Herbert John *political scientist, ambassador*
Spraggins, Johnnie David *sociology and cultural studies educator*
Stallworth, Teresa Louise *psychiatrist, educator*
Steen, John Thomas, Jr. *lawyer*
Stephenson, Randall L. *telecommunications industry executive*
Stevens, Dennis Max *auditor*
Strojuy, Joan E. *writer*
Sutton, Johnny Keane *prosecutor, lawyer*
Swansburg, Russell Chester *nursing educator, consultant, health facility administrator*
Swiggett, Harold E. (Hal Swiggett) *writer, photographer*
Synek, Miroslav *physicist, chemist, world affairs consultant*
Terracina, Roy David *entrepreneur*
Trent, Joyce Miller *librarian*
Triplitt, Curtis Lee *pharmacist, medical educator, researcher*
Upton, Wade *energy executive*
Urbach, Adam Robert *chemistry professor*
Van de Putte, Leticia *pharmacist, state senator*
Vazquez, Gilbert Falcon *lawyer*
Verghese, Abraham Cheeran *internist, educator, writer*
Voigt, Joan (Joan McGuire Voigt) *retired literature and language professor*
von Raffler-Engel, Walburga (Walburga Engel) *retired language educator*
Wahl, Rosemarie *biologist, educator*
Wallis, Ben Alton, Jr. *lawyer*
Walmsley, Judith Abrams *chemistry professor*
Walsh, Nicolas Eugene *rehabilitation services professional, educator*
Wang, Yufeng *science educator*
Watson, Ronald Lynn *theater educator*
Weber, William Wesley *accountant*
Wei, Ronghua *research scientist*
Weinbrenner, George Ryan *aeronautical engineer*
Weir, W. Thomas *lawyer*
Wellberg, Edward Louis, Jr. *insurance company executive*
Wells, Ross M. *secondary school educator, writer*
Wells, Tullos *lawyer*
Wheatley, Seagal V. *lawyer, legal association administrator*
Whitacre, Edward E., Jr. *telecommunications company executive*
Whitesell, Stephen Ernest *parks director*
Wilkins, Christopher Putnam *conductor*
Wilkins, Rayford, Jr. *telecommunications industry executive*
Williams, Docia Schultz *small business owner*
Williamson, Fletcher Phillips *real estate broker*
Winik, Joanne *broadcast executive*
Wiskocil, Angiolina *telecommunications industry executive*
Wood, Thomas Willard *health industry executive, retired military officer*
Wright, Gregory A. *energy executive*
Wright, Wayne E. *education educator*
Wyker, Kenneth E. *lawyer*
Yates, Norris William, Jr. *lawyer*
Young, James Julius *academic administrator, retired military officer*
Zesch, Hal *energy executive*
Zilveti, Carlos Benjamin *preventive medicine physician, pediatrician*

### San Diego
Sankar, Hari *communications engineer*

### San Juan
Guzmán, Belinda F. *elementary school educator*

### San Marcos
Asiabanpour, Bahram *engineering educator*
Chavkin, Nancy Feyl *social worker, educator*
Darling, John Rothburn *business educator*
Dharmasiri, Nihal *molecular biologist, educator*
Erwin, Warner Scott, Sr. *academic administrator, consultant*
Fischer, Joyce Faye *engineering educator*
Hofer, Martha K. *political science professor*
Keeley, Maureen Patricia *communications educator, writer*

Lee, Kathryn S. *education educator, counseling administrator*
McLean, Robert James Cameron *microbiologist, educator*
Moore, Patsy Sites *food service consultant*
Palmer, Roger Raymond *finance educator*
Ronan, Clifford John *literature and language professor*
Schmidt, John Charles *music educator*
Shaw, Donald Keith *physical therapist, educator*
Stovall, Frances Middagh *journalist, preservationist*
Taylor, Ruth Arleen Lesher *marketing educator*
Trepagnier, Barbara A. *sociology educator*
Wilson, Vicki Lynn *executive secretary, administrative assistant*

**Santa Fe**
Lambert, Willie Lee Bell *mobile equipment company owner, educator*

**Schulenburg**
Clark, I. E. *publisher*

**Seabrook**
Patten, Bernard Michael *neurologist, writer, educator*
Spears, James Grady *small business owner*

**Seguin**
Robinson, Ronald Alan *manufacturing executive*

**Seminole**
Summer, Robert E. *automotive executive, educator*

**Sheppard Afb**
Cook, Sharla J. *career officer*

**Sherman**
Brown, Paul Neeley *federal judge*
Cutler, Timothy Spence *music educator, composer*
Joshi, Madhukar *statistician, consultant*
Page, Oscar C. *academic administrator*
Schell, Richard A. *federal judge*

**Shiner**
Burnett, Vida C. *music educator*

**Smithville**
Clark, LaVerne Harrell *writer*
Scofield, Virginia Lee *research scientist*

**Snyder**
Castellano, Dawnmarie *oil industry executive, consultant*
Gray, Donna Lea *small business owner*
Siegel, Mark S. *energy executive*

**Southlake**
Brunig, Robert Arthur *lawyer*
Gilliland, Michael S. (Sam Gilliland) *travel company executive*
Herrmann, Debra McGuire *chemist, educator*
Jackson, Jeffery M. *information technology executive*
Peluso, Michelle *Internet company executive*
Schwarte, David A. *lawyer, travel company executive*
Sorge, Karen Lee *printing company executive, consultant*
Wuetig, Joyce Linda *realtor*

**Spring**
Ciancimino, Joseph Andrew *data processing executive*
Corbett, Luke R. *former energy company executive*
Englert, David John *music educator*
Farley, Andrew Newell *lawyer, consultant*
Griffin, Kelly Ann *science educator*
Hendricks, Randal Arlan *lawyer*
Hunt, T. W. (Thomas Webb Hunt) *retired religion educator*
Jackson, Guida Myrl *writer, editor, literature educator*
Kehoe, John Kimball *finance educator, consultant*
Lewis, Amy Marie *secondary school educator, music educator*
Randazzo, Gary Wayne *newspaper executive*
Rex, Lonnie Royce *religious organization administrator*
Schweiger, Peggy *physics educator*
Szymczak, Edward Joseph *mechanical engineer*
Woodward, Clifford Edward *chemical engineer*

**Spring Branch**
Barban, Arnold Melvin *advertising executive, educator, writer*
Fasano, Anthony John *marketing consultant*

**Springtown**
Marrs, James F., Jr. (Jim Marrs) *writer, journalist, educator*

**Spur**
Warren, Jennifer Elizabeth *family nurse practitioner*

**Stafford**
Krenek, Mary Louise *political scientist, researcher*
Pate, John Gillis, Jr. *financial consultant, educator*

**Stephenville**
Albrecht, Annette C. *education educator, consultant*
Baker, Thomas Lindsay *history professor, museum director, consultant*
Butler, Luther Dale *writer*
Collier, Boyd Dean *finance educator, management consultant*
Dougherty, Thomas Michael *education educator*
Schmelzer, Janet L. *history professor, researcher*
Zelman, Patricia Grace *history educator*

**Sugar Land**
Chatterjee, Nilesh *researcher*
Downs, Hartley H. III *chemist*
Effendi, Wajih Tariq *petroleum engineer*
Goodwin, Anthony Robert Holmes *chemist, editor*
Harribance, Sean Lalsingh *parapsychologist*

Heitzenrater, James F *hospital administrator*
Hitchcock, Bion Earl *lawyer*
Hosley, Marguerite Cyril *civic worker*
Huston, Daniel Cliff *geophysicist*
Kajander, Judy Elaine *social worker*
Keefe, Carolyn Joan *tax accountant*
Le, Chi-Dinh *law educator, writer*
Lester, Jason *singer, music educator*
Martinez, Antonio *choir director, art director*
Matney, Judy McCaleb *secondary school educator*
Victor, Ann Michele *musician, educator*
Wagner, Donald Bert *health facility administrator*

**Sulphur Springs**
Gibson, Jannette Poe *educational consultant*

**Sweetwater**
Taylor, Martha Sue *librarian*

**Tahoka**
Bennett, Hazel Connolly *music educator, small business owner*

**Taylor Lake Village**
Jenicek, Alicia Joanne *nursing consultant*

**Temple**
Asea, Alexzander *research scientist*
Beyer, Richard J. *priest, writer*
Clawson, James F., Jr. *judge, arbitrator, mediator*
Dehmer, Gregory Joseph *cardiologist*
Dostal, David Eugene *education educator, researcher*
Fairlie, Thomas Andrew *director*
Frost, Juanita Corbitt *retired hospital foundation coordinator*
Hayward, Ronald Hamilton *surgeon*
Hoffer, John Lee *health facility administrator, medical educator*
Holleman, Vernon Daughty *internist, educator*
Kuo, Lih *medical educator*
Lynch, Dennis James *plastic surgeon*
McLane, Robert Drayton, Jr. *food products company executive*
Meshack, Geneva Tucker *retired elementary school educator*
Pickle, Jerry Richard *lawyer*
Pinno, John Walter *musician, educator*
Sulak, Patricia Jane *gynecologist, educator*
Wang, Xiuying *agricultural engineer, researcher*
Weber, Robert A. *surgeon*

**Texarkana**
Austin, Sandra Jenelle *school librarian, language educator*
Bertrand, Betty Harleen *nurse*
Malcolm, Molly Beth *political organization worker, counselor*
Presley, James Wright *writer, environmentalist*
Tate, Nancy Jane *secondary school educator*

**Texas City**
Adams, Mark *theater director*
Fuchs, Owen George *chemist*
Hodges, Richard Dean *instrument and electrical technician*
Robertson, Paul Francis *mathematician, educator*

**The Colony**
Mitchell, Melvin Clifford *music educator*

**The Woodlands**
Allison, Robert James, Jr. *retired oil and gas company executive*
Bohannon, Paul M. *lawyer*
Brenneman, Gregory D. *former food service executive*
Cagle, Melinda Reeves *editor*
Desjardins, Raoul *medical association administrator, financial consultant*
Evans, Walter Reed *retired engineering executive, consultant*
Glenn, Gerald Marvin *marketing executive, engineering executive, construction executive*
Griffith, James William *systems engineer, consultant*
Hackett, James T. *oil industry executive*
Hagerman, John David *lawyer, investment advisor*
Holter, Mark E. *musician, educator*
Jones, Lincoln III *military officer*
Larson, James R. *retired oil industry executive*
Logan, Mathew Kuykendall *journalist*
Machle, Edward Johnstone *religious studies educator, philosopher*
Manson, Lewis Aubhal *energy executive*
Mitchell, George Phydias *gas and petroleum company executive*
Morrison, Scott David *management consultant, small business owner*
Ripley, Charlene A. *lawyer*
Schlacks, Stephen Mark *lawyer*
Shannon, Thomas O. *plastic surgeon*
Sharman, Richard Lee *telecommunications executive, consultant*
Stahl, Craig L. *lawyer*
Wilcox, Raymond I. *oil industry executive*

**Trenton**
Yeager, Evan Todd *academic administrator, small business owner*

**Trinidad**
Conant, Allah B., Jr. *lawyer*

**Trophy Club**
Caffee, Virginia Maureen *executive assistant*
Floyd, Judy Louise Casburn *anesthesiologist, political scientist*
Holley, Cyrus Helmer *management consulting service executive*

**Tyler**
Albertson, Christopher Adam *librarian*
Bailey, Nan Hutchins *mathematician, educator*
Baker, Rebecca Louise *musician, music educator, consultant*
Brock, Dee Sala *television executive, educator, writer, consultant*
Brookshire, Bruce G. *retail grocery store executive*
Davidson, Jack Leroy *academic administrator*

Edwards, D. M. *retail executive, wholesale distribution executive, real estate company executive*
Ellis, Donald Lee *lawyer*
Green, Douglas Alvin *retired library director*
Guin, Don Lester *insurance company executive*
Guthrie, Judith K. *federal judge*
Hughes, Arthur Hyde *accountant, energy industry executive, accountant*
Kronenberg, Richard Samuel *physician, educator*
Neuenschwander, Pierre Fernand *medical educator*
Peters, Robert K. *dean, newscaster, newswriter, journalist*
Prater, Emma Lou *retired academic administrator*
Rogers, Cheryl Lynn *music and dance educator*
Rumbley, Philip Lee *music educator, musician, photographer*
Sanchez, Heliodoro Torres, Jr. *education educator*
Sathyamoorthy, Muthukrishnan *engineering educator, dean*
Smith, Howard Thompson *manufacturing executive*
Waller, Wilma Ruth *retired secondary school educator, retired librarian*
Wrenn, Christopher Jay *physician*
Wright, Mary Ellen *theater educator*

**Uvalde**
Graham, Robert Albert *physicist, researcher, curator*
Ramsey, Frank Allen *veterinarian, retired army officer*
Vela, Joel E. *academic administrator*

**Valley Mills**
Odell, Patrick Lowry *mathematics professor*

**Valley Spring**
Bonner, Herbert Dwight *construction management educator*

**Valley View**
Wallace, Donald John III *rancher*

**Van**
Lockwood, Kelly *music educator*

**Vernon**
Malinowski, Dariusz Piotr *horticulturist, educator*
Mikkelsen, Barbara Berry *retired retail executive, rancher*

**Victoria**
Fellhauer, David E. *bishop*
Harrington, Rick *psychology professor*

**Waco**
Albrecht, Karen Elizabeth *voice educator, theater director*
Askins, Sally Lynn *costume designer, educator*
Belew, John Seymour *academic administrator, chemist*
Bennighof, James Malcolm *academic administrator*
Bradley, Walter Lee *mechanical engineer, educator, researcher, consultant*
Brooks, Roger Leon *retired academic administrator*
Chatmas, John Thomas *art educator, artist*
Edgington, Theresa *information technology executive, educator*
Elkins, Gary R. *psychologist, educator*
Emanuel, Gloria Page *retired secondary school educator*
Farison, James Blair *electrical biomedical engineer, educator*
Hillis, William Daniel *biology professor*
Hunt, Maurice Arthur *language educator, researcher*
Iglehart, Patricia Ann *business development and communications executive*
Jeffrey, David Lyle *literature and language professor, writer*
Lilley, John Mark *academic administrator*
Lind, Owen Thomas *biology professor*
Lindsey, Jonathan Asmel *academic administrator, school librarian, educator*
Lowe, John David *information technology educator, educational consultant*
Matlock-Hetzel, Susan *psychologist, educator*
McKinney, Timothy Richmond *music educator*
Mc Swain, Angus Stewart, Jr. *retired law educator*
Morrison, Michael Dean *lawyer, law educator*
Murray, Kathleen Sarah-Jane *literature and language professor*
Pedrotti, Leno Stephano *physics professor*
Reynolds, Herbert Hal *university administrator*
Richie, Rodney Charles *critical care and pulmonary medicine physician*
Rose, John Thomas *finance educator*
Rusling, Barbara N(eubert) *real estate broker*
Scott, Richard Elton *health facility administrator*
Sharp, Ronald Arvell *sociology educator*
Sheng, Qin *mathematics professor*
Sloan, Robert Bryan, Jr. *academic administrator*
Smith, Cullen *lawyer*
Stratton, Margaret Anne *minister*
Talbert, Charles Harold *theologian, educator*
Toben, Bradley J. B. *dean, law educator*
Vander Woude, Richard John *lawyer*
Voight, Carolyn Jean *administrative assistant*
Yang, Michael Vincent *literature and language professor, researcher*

**Warda**
Kunze, George William *retired soil scientist*
Kunze, Otto Robert *retired agricultural engineering educator*

**Waxahachie**
Johnson, Ronald Kay *retail company executive*

**Weatherford**
Banks, Michael Pat *music educator, director*
Bradle, Sue E. *music educator, editor*
Colton, James Patrick *academic administrator*
King, Douglas Michael *lawyer, accountant*
Scott, Geneva Lee Smith *nursing educator*

**Webster**
Farnam, Jafar *allergist, immunologist, pediatrician*

Hartsfield, Henry Warren, Jr. *electronics executive, retired astronaut*
Kobayashi, Herbert Shin *electrical engineer*

**Wellington**
Sims, Lennie Coleman *part-time public relations consultant*

**Weslaco**
Fogarty, Elizabeth Rummans *retired librarian, researcher*

**Wharton**
George, Lila Gene Plowe Kennedy *music educator*
Jackson, Larry C. *publishing executive*

**Whitehouse**
Cavanaugh, Charles Davis *computer scientist, educator*

**Whitewright**
Burg, John Parker *electric power industry executive*
Summers, Bertie Jean *secondary school educator*

**Wichita Falls**
Bourland, D(elphus) David, Jr. *linguist, educator*
Hamlin, Don Auer *financial executive*
Hancock, Carole Patricia *academic administrator*
Lowrance, Muriel Edwards *retired educational specialist*
Parker, Eva Annette *librarian*
Scherler, Kathy Louise *music educator, researcher*
Stringfellow, Catherine Veronique *computer scientist, educator*

**Willis**
Rappaport, Martin Paul *internist, nephrologist, educator*
Snider, Robert Larry *management consultant*

**Wimberley**
Brinsmade, Lyon Louis *retired lawyer*
Ellis, John *small business owner*
Jennett, Joseph Charles *retired academic administrator, engineering educator*
McCoy, John Denny *artist*
Skaggs, Wayne Gerard *retired diversified financial services company executive*

**Windcrest**
Froiland-Baker, Mary Lou *assistant principal*

**Winters**
Reagan, Brilla Jane *principal*

**Wylie**
Flores, Noe Cortez *protective services official*

**Yoakum**
Kvinta, Charles J. *lawyer*
Williams, Walter Waylon *lawyer, agricultural products supplier*

**Zavalla**
Devlin, Cynthia M. *air transportation executive, consultant*

**Zephyr**
Lancaster, Carroll Townes, Jr. *health services executive*

**UTAH**

**Bluffdale**
Bliss, Rick Wayne *engineer*
Harr, Joshua *information technology executive*

**Boulder**
Gove, Walter R. *sociology educator*

**Bountiful**
Burningham, Kim Richard *educational association administrator, former state legislator*
Mangum, Garth Leroy *retired economist*
Ross, Gerald Harvey *family practice and environmental medicine physician*

**Brigham City**
Hepworth, John Leonard *chemist, researcher*

**Brookside**
McMahon, James Patrick *ecologist, consultant*

**Castle Valley**
Zavada, Barbara Johanna *artist, educator*

**Cedar City**
Mayron, Lewis Walter *clinical ecology consultant*
Mills, James *language educator*
Modesitt, Carol Ann *vocalist, music educator, opera director*
Modesitt, Leland Exton, Jr., (L.E. Modesitt Jr.) *writer, poet, consultant*
White, Lynn H. *psychology professor, researcher*

**Cedar Hills**
Ashton, Dawne Belinda *retired secondary school educator*

**Centerfield**
Parkin, Fern Agnes Marvel *medical/surgical nurse, nursing educator*

**Clearfield**
Satterthwaite, Shawn Briscoe *musician, educator*

**Coalville**
Thomas, David Lindsey *lawyer, state senator*

**Corinne**
Ferry, Miles Yeoman *state legislator*

**Draper**
Jacobsen, Laren *retired programmer*
Walz, Angela *retired secondary school educator*
Wright, Stuart I. *materials scientist, materials engineer*

**Dugway**

Benson, Morgan *energy engineer, retired military officer*
Davis, Vernon Thomas *military officer, researcher*
Phan, Richard Man *chemist*

**Hill AFB**

Bergren, Scott C. *career officer*
Embry, Glenn Robert *military officer*
Hill, Mary Frances *curator, researcher*

**Holladay**

McKell, Cyrus M. *retired dean, plant physiologist, consultant*
O'Halloran, Thomas Alphonsus, Jr. *retired physicist, retired researcher*
Silver, Barnard Joseph Stewart *mechanical and chemical engineer, consultant, inventor*

**Ivins**

Theurer, Byron W. *aerospace engineer, business owner*

**Kaysville**

Eads, Penni Daun *music educator*
Houtz, Randy L. *music educator*

**Lindon**

McBride, Darl *information technology executive*
Osmond, Donald Clark (Donny Osmond) *singer*

**Logan**

Albrecht, Stan LeRoy *academic administrator, sociologist, educator*
Aust, Steven Douglas *biochemistry, biotechnology and toxicology educator*
Bowles, David Stanley *engineering educator, consultant*
Culver, Milton Lawrence *historian, educator*
Daines, N. George *lawyer*
Edwards, William Farrell *physics professor, researcher*
Hargreaves, George Henry *civil and agricultural engineer, researcher*
Hruby, George Geoffrey *writer, educator*
Kannan, Vijay R. *business educator*
Keller, Jack *agricultural engineering educator, consultant*
McNeal, Lyle Glen *science educator, rancher, consultant*
Rasmuson, Brent J. *photographer, small business owner*
Rasmussen, Harry Paul *horticulture and landscape educator*
Ren, Wei *control systems educator*
Roberts, Donald Wilson *pathologist, consultant*
Schunk, Robert Walter *space physics research administrator*
Shaver, James Porter *retired education educator, dean*
Subprasom, Kitti *civil engineer*
Symanzik, Juergen *statistician, educator*
West, Stephen Allan *lawyer*

**Manti**

Funk, William Henry *retired environmental engineering educator*
Petersen, Benton Lauritz *paralegal*

**Mapleton**

Hillyard, Ira William *retired pharmacologist, retired educator*

**Midvale**

Dahl, Everett E. *lawyer*
Teerlink, J(oseph) Leland *real estate developer*

**Midway**

Zenger, John Hancock *training company executive*

**Murray**

Volberg, Herman William *electronics engineer, consultant*

**North Logan**

Boyer, Albert Bruce *optometrist, educator*
Edmondson, Richard Shawn *psychologist*
Powers, Linda Sue *biophysicist, educator, biomedical engineer*

**North Salt Lake**

Barden, Robert Christopher *lawyer, writer, psychologist, educator*
Bouley, Joseph Richard *pilot*
Johnson, Frank *educator, retired state official*

**Ogden**

Adams, J. Phillip *oil industry executive*
Ayer, Carol Anne *librarian*
Bedford, Daniel Peter *educator*
Buckner, Elmer La Mar *retired insurance company executive*
Coleman, Robert D. *music critic, educator*
Davidson, Thomas Ferguson *retired chemical engineer*
Harrington, Mary Evelina Paulson (Polly Harrington) *writer, educator*
Jones, Galen Ray *physician assistant*
Mecham, Glenn Jefferson *lawyer, mayor*
Thornburg, Ron *editor*

**Orem**

Benson, Alvin K. *physicist, geophysicist, consultant, educator*
Clark, Bruce Budge *humanities educator*
Hall, Blaine Hill *retired librarian*
Hunt, H(arold) Keith *retired business management educator, marketing consultant*
Jackman, Roderick Victor *distance learning educator*
Michell, Auriel Ibn *lawyer, writer*
Moore, Hal G. *mathematician, educator*
Morey, Robert Hardy *communications executive*
Sawyer, Thomas Edgar *management consultant*
Sederburg, William Albert *academic administrator, former state senator*
Segelman, Alvin Burton *pharmaceutical executive, educator, research scientist*
Snow, Marlon O. *trucking executive, state agency administrator*

Stevens, Lori Ann LaBeau *school librarian, educator*

**Park City**

Baumgardner, Barbara Borke *publishing consultant*
Becker, William Watters *theater producer*
Edwards, Howard Lee *retired oil and gas industry executive, lawyer*
Gallivan, John William *retired publishing executive*
Mancuso, Julia *skier, Olympic athlete*
Miller, Bode *skier*
Milner, Harold William *hotel executive*
Montgomery, James Fischer *savings and loan association executive*
Rude, Lara Peirce *special education educator*
Shea, Jim *Olympic athlete*
White, Shaun Roger *Olympic athlete, professional snowboarder, professional skateboarder*
Young, Steven *retired professional football player*

**Providence**

Montgomery, Michael Davis *research and development company executive, real estate investor*
Vest, Hyrum Grant, Jr. *retired horticultural sciences educator*

**Provo**

Abbott, Charles Favour *lawyer*
Averett, Steven Elmo *law educator*
Bartlett, Leonard Lee *retired communications educator, advertising executive*
Baum, Kerry Robert *retired military officer, director*
Blake, George Rowland *soil scientist, educator, environmental scientist, researcher*
Bott, Jay Cordell *oncologist, hematologist*
Boyter, Scott M. *academic administrator*
Bradshaw, Jerald Sherwin *chemistry educator, researcher*
Brown, Joseph William *retired lawyer*
Brown, Ralph Browning *sociologist, educator*
Bullough, Robert Vernon, Jr. *educational studies professor*
Cheney, Brigham Vernon *physical chemist, consultant*
Comer, David John *engineering educator*
Creer, Thomas Laselle *psychologist, educator, writer*
Crookston, R. Kent *agronomy educator*
Deng, Shenglou *chemistry professor*
Densley, Colleen T. *principal*
Fielding, Eric *set designer, educator*
Fleming, Joseph Clifton, Jr. *dean, law educator*
Forster, Merlin Henry *foreign languages educator, writer, researcher*
Gray, Campbell *museum director*
Gray, Howard Richard *science educator*
Hansen, H. Reese *law educator, former dean*
Harreld, Donald James *history professor*
Hart, Edward LeRoy *poet, educator*
Hastriter, Michael Wayne *medical entomologist*
Henderson, Douglas James *physicist, educator, chemist, researcher*
Hill, Edward Jeffrey *family life educator*
Hill, Ned Cromar *dean, finance educator, consultant*
Hill, Richard Lee *lawyer*
Holbrook, Jay Mack *publishing company executive*
Izatt, Reed M. *chemistry researcher*
Jensen, Michael Allen *engineering educator*
Jensen, Richard Dennis *librarian*
Kunz, Phillip Ray *sociologist, educator*
Lyon, James Karl *German language educator*
McArthur, Eldon Durant *geneticist, researcher*
Mendenhall, Cory J. *music educator, conductor*
Moon, David C. *information technology executive*
Murphy, John Joseph *literature educator, critic, editor*
Nokes, Jeffery D. *history professor*
Olsen, Randy J. *university librarian*
Pedersen, Darhl Max *psychology professor*
Peer, Larry Howard *literature educator*
Peterson, Samuel Ray *dermatologist, department chairman*
Porter, Blaine Robert Milton *sociology professor, psychology professor*
Prater, Mary Anne *special education educator, researcher*
Samuelson, Cecil O., Jr. *academic administrator*
Sawyer, Melvin Wayne *psychologist*
Schofield, Anthony Wayne *judge*
Smoot, Leon Douglas *chemical engineer, educator, retired dean*
Thomas, David Albert *law educator, director*
Valentine, John Lester *state legislator, lawyer*
Vanfleet, Howard Bay *physicist, educator*
Willes, Mark Hinckley *media specialist*
Williams, Gerald R. *law educator*
Woodbury, Dixon John *physiologist, educator, research scientist*
Worthen, Kevin *dean, law educator*
Worthen, Vaughn Eugene *psychologist, educator*
Young, Bruce Wilson *language educator*
Zhang, Libing *botanist*

**Riverton**

Littell, Lon Andrews *elementary school educator*

**Rush Valley**

Pierce, Diane Jean *artist*

**Saint George**

Atkin, Jerry C. *air transportation executive*
Chilow, Barbara Gail *social worker*
Pearce, Carole Ann *poet*
Riley, James Clifford *military career officer*
Strobell, Dan F. *bank executive, writer*
Terry, Gary A. *lawyer, director, former trade association executive*
Wiltsey, Susan A. *secondary school educator, priest*

**Salt Lake City**

Adams, John A. *lawyer*
Adams, Joseph Keith *lawyer*
Allen, Ronald Carl *commissioner, former state senator, former computer company executive, consultant, artist*

Alter, Edward T. *treasurer*
Anderson, Charles Ross *civil engineer*
Anderson, Joseph Andrew, Jr. *retired apparel executive*
Anderson, Ross Carl *mayor, lawyer*
Anderson, Stephen Hale *federal judge*
Anselmi, John Michael *military officer, educator*
Baldwin, John *legal association administrator, lawyer*
Bamberg, Eberhard *engineering educator*
Barney, Kline Porter, Jr. *engineering company executive, consultant*
Barusch, Lawrence Roos *lawyer*
Bassis, Michael Steven *academic administrator*
Baucom, Sidney George *lawyer*
Bauer, A. Robert, Jr., (August Robert Bauer Jr.) *surgeon*
Beall, Burtch W., Jr. *architect*
Bendinger, Gary Frederick *lawyer*
Benjamin, Lorna Smith *psychologist*
Bennion, John Warren *urban education educator*
Berman, Daniel Lewis *lawyer*
Betz, A. Lorris *pediatrician, educator*
Bilginsoy, Cihan *economics professor*
Bird, David R. *lawyer*
Black, Wilford Rex, Jr. *retired state legislator*
Blackburn, Michael Dale *lawyer, educator*
Boozer, Carlos Austin, Jr. *professional basketball player*
Brady, Rodney Howard *diversified financial services company executive, broadcast executive, director, retired academic administrator, retired federal official*
Brems, David Paul *architect*
Brennan, Gerald D. (Jerry Brennan) *biotechnology company executive*
Burke, John Patrick *internist, educator*
Call, Charles H., Jr. *civil engineer*
Capecchi, Mario Renato *genetics educator*
Carey, John Clayton *pediatrician, educator, medical geneticist*
Carlquist, John Frederick *microbiologist, immunologist*
Carnahan, Orville Darrell *retired state legislator, retired academic administrator*
Cash, Roy Don *retired gas and petroleum company executive*
Chaara, Mohammed *statistician, consultant*
Cherkaev, Andrej Vsevolodovich *mathematician, educator*
Chillingworth, Lori *bank executive*
Chong, Richard David *architect*
Christensen, Ray Richards *lawyer*
Christopher, James Walker *architect, educator*
Clark, Deanna Dee *volunteer*
Clark, Glen Edward *judge*
Clayton, Richard D. *lawyer*
Cofield, Philip Thomas *educational association administrator*
Coley, Phyllis Dewing *biology professor*
Conard, Jane Reister *lawyer*
Conway, Nancy Ann *newspaper editor*
Cornaby, Kay Sterling *lawyer, retired state senator*
Courtney-Wilds, Noreen *air transportation executive*
Covey, Stephen Merrill Richards *business consultant, speaker, author*
Curry, Robert A. *music educator*
Davis, Gene *public relations executive, state legislator*
Davis, Loyd Evan *defense industry marketing professional*
DeVries, Kenneth Lawrence *mechanical engineer, educator*
Dewsnup, Ralph L. *lawyer*
Dick, Bertram Gale, Jr. *physics professor*
Dietlein, John R. *physician, health facility administrator*
Drew, Clifford James *dean, psychologist, educator*
Durham, Christine Meaders *state supreme court chief justice*
Durrant, Matthew B. *state supreme court justice*
Dynak, David Michael *theater educator*
Elkins, Glen Ray *retired diversified management services company executive*
Emerson, Norene Rogers *music educator*
Ewers, Anne *opera company director*
Eyring, Henry Bennion *bishop*
Fehr, John William *newspaper editor*
Fields, Debbi (Debra Fields Rose) *cookie franchise executive*
Fogle, Sheryl Kay *voice educator, music educator*
Foltz, Rodger Lowell *chemistry professor*
Frank, Thomas *construction executive, management and design executive*
Fujinami, Robert Shin *neurology educator*
Fukuta, Norihiko *professor emeritus in meteorology, researcher*
Gandhi, Om Parkash *electrical engineer*
Gardiner, Lester Raymond, Jr. *retired lawyer*
George, Sarah B. *museum director*
Ghosh, Sambhunath (Sam Ghosh) *civil engineering educator, environmental engineer*
Gortatowski, Melvin Jerome *retired chemist*
Gray, Douglas D. *child and adolescent psychiatrist*
Greene, John Thomas *judge*
Greenwood, David A. *lawyer*
Gregersen, R(oald) George *newspaper publishing executive*
Grosser, Bernard Irving *psychiatrist, educator*
Hanni, Glenn Charles *lawyer*
Harrington, Patti *school system administrator*
Hatch, George Clinton *television executive*
Hembree, James D. *retired chemical company executive*
Herbert, Gary Richard *lieutenant governor*
Heuman, Joshua I. *curator*
Hickingbotham, Frank D. *food product executive*
Hinckley, Gordon B. *religious organization administrator*
Hofmann, Aaron A. *orthopedist, surgeon, researcher*
Holding, R. Earl (Robert Earl Holding) *oil company executive*
Holland, Jeffrey R. *religious organization administrator*
Holtkamp, James Arnold *lawyer, educator*
Howell, Scott Newell *computer company executive, state legislator*
Hughes, (Robert) John *journalist, educator*
Huntsman, Jon Meade *chemicals executive*

Huntsman, Jon Meade, Jr. *governor, former federal agency administrator*
Huntsman, Peter R. *chemicals executive*
Irish, Carolyn Tanner *bishop*
Jaskowski, Troy D. *immunologist, researcher*
Jenkins, Bruce Sterling *federal judge*
Jensen, Dallin W. *lawyer*
Johnson, Auston Gilbert III *auditor*
Johnson, Jon L. *advertising executive*
Johnson, Xan Stuart *performing arts educator*
Julander, Paula Foil *foundation administrator*
Kåge, Jonas *performing company executive*
Kanner, Richard Elliot *physician, medical educator, consultant*
Kearns, Becky *bank executive*
Keefe, Maureen Ruth *dean*
Kim, Sung Wan *chemistry professor*
Kirkham, John Spencer *lawyer, director*
Kjeldsberg, Karl R. *lab administrator, physician, educator*
Kraus, Peter Leo *librarian, educator*
Kumpfer, Karol Linda *research psychologist*
Layfield, Lester James *pathologist, educator*
Leary, G. Edward *state financial commisioner*
Lee, Blaine Nelson *personnel director*
Liu, Gang *education educator, researcher*
Livne, Nava Levia *psychologist, researcher*
Livne, Oren Eliezer *mathematician, educator*
Lloyd, Ray Dix *health physicist*
Madsen, Brigham Dwaine *history professor*
Markham, Reed B. *education educator, consultant*
Matsumori, Douglas *lawyer*
Mattis, Daniel Charles *physicist, researcher*
McCleary, Lloyd E(verand) *education educator*
Mc Connell, Michael W. *federal judge, law educator*
McGann, Christopher John *cardiologist, educator*
McKay, Monroe Gunn *federal judge*
McLeskey, Charles Hamilton *anesthesiologist, educator, pharmaceutical executive*
Meldrum, Peter Durkee *venture capitalist, biotechnology company executive*
Melton, Arthur Richard *public health administrator*
Mendenhall, Robert W. *information technology executive*
Meyers, Rebecka Louise *pediatric general surgeon*
Middleton, Anthony Wayne, Jr. *urologist, educator*
Miller, Jan Dean *metallurgy educator*
Miller, Joel Steven *inorganic and organic materials chemist*
Miller, Larry H. *professional sports team executive, auto dealer, broadcast executive*
Miller, William Charles *architect, educator*
Mogren, Paul Andrew *librarian*
Monson, Thomas Spencer *religious organization administrator, retired publishing executive*
Moore, Debra *lawyer*
Moore, James R. *lawyer*
Moser, Royce, Jr. *preventive medicine physician, educator*
Motter, Thomas Franklin *medical products executive*
Murphy, Michael R. *federal judge*
Nehring, Ronald E. *state supreme court justice*
Nelson, John C. *obstetrician, gynecologist*
Nelson, Roger Hugh *finance educator, corporate financial executive, consultant*
Nelson, Russell Marion *surgeon, educator*
Newmark, William D. *conservation biologist*
Nicolatus, Stephen Jon *financial consultant*
Niederauer, George H. *bishop*
Nydegger, Rick D. *lawyer*
Ockey, Ronald J. *lawyer*
O'Connell, James F. *anthropologist, educator*
Ogburn, Joyce *library director*
Olson, Ferron Allred *metallurgist, educator*
Osherow, Jacqueline Sue *poet, English language educator*
Owen, Amy *library director*
Parkin, James Lamar *retired otolaryngologist, educator*
Parrish, Jill Niederhauser *state supreme court justice*
Parry, Robert Walter *chemistry professor*
Paulsen, Vivian *editor*
Post, Gina *mathematics professor, researcher*
Poulter, Charles Dale *chemist, educator, consultant*
Prince, William B. *lawyer*
Quinn, Eugene Frederick *diplomat, minister*
Rasmussen, Thomas Val, Jr. *lawyer, small business owner*
Rattie, Keith O. *gas industry executive*
Reeder, F. Robert *lawyer*
Rider, Richard Francis *psychologist*
Roens, Steven Thomas *music educator, associate dean*
Romney-Manookin, Elaine Clive *retired music educator, composer*
Salisbury, Frank Boyer *botanist, educator, writer*
Salomonson, Vincent Victor *meteorologist, educator*
Sam, David *federal judge*
Sandquist, Gary Marlin *engineering educator, researcher, consultant, writer, military officer*
Scofield, David Willson *lawyer*
Shepherd, Karen *retired congresswoman*
Shurtleff, Mark L. *state attorney general*
Sillars, Malcolm Osgood *communications educator*
Silverman, Randy H. *conservator, consultant*
Simmons, Harris H. *banker*
Sloan, Jerry (Gerald Eugene Sloan) *professional basketball coach*
Smith, Donald E. *broadcast engineer*
Smith, Eldred Gee *church leader*
Smith, Janet Hugie *lawyer*
Sohn, Hong Yong *chemical engineer, metallurgical engineer, educator*
Sorensen, John B. *surgeon*
Sorenson, James LeVoy *research and development company executive*
Sorenson, Stephen Jay *prosecutor*
Sparks, Mildred Thomas *state agency administrator, educator*
Spurgeon, Edward Dutcher *lawyer, educator, foundation administrator*
Stang, Peter John *organic chemist*
Stitley, James Walter, Jr. *food manufacturing executive*

Straight, Richard Coleman *photobiologist, natural philosopher*
Stringfellow, Gerald B. *engineering educator*
Tani, Lloyd Yasuo *pediatrician, educator*
Thomas, David Snow *plastic surgeon*
Thompson, Neil Daniel *retired lawyer*
Threedy, Debora Lynn *law educator*
Tolman, Brett L. *prosecutor*
Urie, Alan T *bank executive*
Velick, Sidney Frederick *research biochemist, educator*
Verhaaren, Harold Carl *lawyer*
Walker, Carlene Martin *state senator*
Walker Neve, Diana *singer, voice educator*
Wangsgard, Chris Prince *lawyer*
Warner, Paul Michael *federal judge, former prosecutor*
Wassmer, Theodore Milton *artist*
Weiss, Ronald L. *lab administrator*
West, Jason Brossard *education educator, consultant*
Wilberg, Mack J. *conductor, composer*
Wilkins, Michael Jon *state supreme court justice*
Witty, Christine (Chris Witty) *speed skater*
Wolf, Harold Herbert *pharmacy educator*
Wolfinger, Nicholas H. *educator*
Young, Michael Kent *academic administrator, law educator*
Zhdanov, Michael Semenovich *geophysicist, educator*
Zimmer, Markus Bernhard *legal association administrator*
Zimmerman, Michael David *lawyer*
Zipser, Edward J. *meteorologist, educator*

## Sandy
Durham, Lynn Ellen *school psychologist*
Park, William Laird *agricultural studies educator, dean*
Smith, Willard Grant *psychologist*

## Santa Clara
Tolbert, Beth Willden *real estate company executive, real estate broker*

## South Jordan
Larson, Bryan Alan *lawyer*
Rowley, Maxine Lewis *retired home economics and consumer educator, retired department chairman*
Wirthlin, Richard Bitner *researcher*

## Spanish Fork
Lunt, Rick A. *music educator*

## Springville
Ashworth, Brent Ferrin *lawyer*

## Tremonton
Eakle, Arlene Haslam *genealogist*

## Vernal
Judd, Dennis L. *lawyer*

## Washington
De Vany, Arthur Stacy *economics professor*

## West Jordan
Betenson, Gaye Brinton *secondary school educator*
Huang, Ming-Huang *engineer, materials scientist*

## West Valley City
Peterson, Millie M. *state senator*

## Woods Cross
Blackley, Cheryl Ann *freelance/self-employed music educator, musician*
Hendriksen, Neil Evan *music educator*

# VERMONT

## Arlington
Pond, Thomas Alexander *physics professor, academic administrator*

## Barnard
Larson, John Hyde *retired utilities executive*

## Barre
Black, Percy *psychology professor*
Koch, Thomas Frederick *lawyer*

## Bennington
Bernard, April *poet, literature educator*
Coleman, Elizabeth *college president*
Godwin, Rebecca Thompson *writer, educator, editor*
Graham, Jamie L. *psychologist*
Lum, Mary *artist, art educator*
Wang, Shunzhu *humanities educator, researcher, translator*
Williams, Robert Joseph *retired museum director, educator*

## Brandon
Dwyer, Michael Francis *secondary school educator*
Farnsworth, Frank Albert *retired economics professor*
Konwin, Thor Warner *financial executive*

## Brattleboro
Abrams, Jackie *artist, educator*
Agallianos, Dennis Dionysios *psychiatrist*
Ames, Adelbert III *neuroscientist, educator*
Bellamy, Carol *international organization administrator*
Bussino, Melinda Holden *human services administrator*
Gorman, Robert Saul *architect*
Kotkov, Benjamin *retired clinical psychologist*
Oakes, James L. *federal judge*
Reid, David G. *lawyer*

## Brownsville
Olderman, Gerald *retired medical device company executive*

## Burlington
Allard, Judith Louise *secondary school educator*
Anderson, Thomas D. *prosecutor*
Angell, Kenneth Anthony *bishop*
Burton, Jake (Jake Burton Carpenter) *sports apparel executive*
Cooper, Sheldon Mark *medical educator, immunologist, researcher, rheumatologist*
Cutler, Stephen Joel *sociologist, educator*
Daniels, Robert Vincent *history professor, former state senator*
Davis, John Herschel *retired surgeon, educator*
Delay, Eugene Raymond *psychologist, educator, researcher*
Dinse, John Merrell *lawyer*
Durfee, Herbert Ashley, Jr. *medical educator*
Fogel, Daniel Mark (Daniel Mark Kahn-Fogel) *academic administrator, literature educator, writer*
Gennari, F(rank) John *medical educator*
Gouli, Vladimir Vasilievich *entomologist*
Grunberg, Steven Marc *medical educator*
Hall, Robert William *philosophy educator, religious studies educator*
Hearon, Shelby *writer, educator*
Heinrich, Bernd *biologist, educator*
Keeton, William Scott *ecologist, educator*
Kelly, Sister Marie *school system administrator*
Kindstedt, Paul Stephen *food science educator*
Kirby, David V. *prosecutor*
Kunin, Madeleine May *former ambassador to Switzerland, former governor*
Lawson, Robert Bernard *psychology professor*
Lucey, Jerold Francis *pediatrician*
Montroll, Andrew H. *lawyer, councilman*
Murthy, Sanjeeva N. *education educator, materials scientist*
Naylor, Magdalena Raczkowska *psychiatrist, educator*
Nyborg, Wesley Lemars *physics professor*
Outwater, John Ogden *mechanical engineering educator*
Pinder, George Francis *engineering educator, research scientist*
Post, Peter L. *marketing executive, writer*
Rendall, Donald James, Jr. *lawyer*
Riddick, Daniel Howison *obstetrician, gynecologist, priest*
Sampson, Samuel Franklin *sociology educator*
Sessions, William K. III *federal judge*
Sobel, Burton Elias *internist, educator*
Tamarkin, Kate *conductor*
Tampas, John P. *radiologist*
Thompson, Ellen Ann *elementary school educator*
Vane, Dennis *physician*
Zhao, Feng-Qi *endocrinologist, educator*

## Castleton
Meloy, Judith Marie *humanities educator*
Roper, Scott Christopher *geographer, researcher, research scientist*
Stafford, Robert Theodore *lawyer, retired senator*

## Charlotte
Hamilton, Lawrence Stanley *forest consultant*
Melby, Edward Carlos, Jr. *veterinarian*
Naylor, Thomas Herbert *economist, educator, consultant*
Robinson, Sally Winston *artist*
Sim, Craig Stephen *retired investment banker*

## Chester
Coleman, John Royston *writer*

## Colchester
Blacketor, Paul Garber *minister*
Butenas, Saulius *research scientist*
Jackson, Voleen *perfumer*
Lawton, Lorilee Ann *small business owner, accountant*
Peters, Troy Clark *conductor, composer*

## Corinth
Bellamy, John Stark, II, *librarian*

## Danby
Peel, Harris *retired small business owner*

## Dorset
Bamford, Joseph Charles, Jr. *gynecologist, obstetrician, educator, medical missionary, author*
Hittle, Richard Howard *gas industry executive, oil industry executive, consultant*
Marron, Pamela Anne *artist*

## East Dummerston
Bertone, Thomas Lee *management consultant*

## East Montpelier
Christiansen, Andrew P. *website designer, historic archives digitizer*
Gannon, Robin Bickford *elementary school educator*

## East Thetford
Cummings Rockwell, Patricia Guilbault *psychiatric nurse*

## Enosburg Falls
Svendsen, Alf *artist, art educator*

## Essex Junction
Bisson, Roger *middle school educator*
Jin, Zhenrong *electrical engineer, researcher*
Sweetser, Susan W. *lawyer, advocate, retired state legislator*

## Fairfield
Lazarnick, Sylvia *retired secondary school educator*

## Greensboro
Gilpin, Robert George, Jr. *political science professor*
Hill, Lewis Reuben *horticulturist, nursery owner, writer*

## Hartland Four Corners
Brady, Upton Birnie *editor, literary agent*

## Hinesburg
Carlson, Stephen *publishing executive*
Fay, Glenn Mills, Jr. *science educator*

## Hyde Park
Roberts, Carolyn C. *former hospital administrator*

## Jacksonville
Dell, Ralph Bishop *retired pediatrician, researcher*
Hein, Karen Kramer *pediatrician, epidemiologist*

## Jericho
Bolin, Henry Robert *retired engineer*

## Johnson
Rice, Rebecca Kynoch *writer, consultant, language educator*
Whitehill, Angela Elizabeth *artistic director*

## Lincoln
Kompass, Edward John *consulting editor*

## Lyndon Center
Dame, William Page III *bank executive, educational administrator*

## Lyndonville
Moore, Carol A. *academic administrator*

## Manchester
Carey, James Henry *banker*
Kouwenhoven, Gerrit Wolphertsen *retired museum director*

## Marlboro
Brelsford, Edmund Munger III *musician, educator*
Stevenson, Laura Caroline *writer, educator*

## Middlebury
Albers, Jan Maria *historian, museum director*
Bergesen, Robert Nelson *transportation consultant*
Bumbeck, David *artist, retired educator*
Colander, David Charles *economist, educator*
Ferm, Robert Livingston *religion educator*
Geier, Philip Otto III *foundation executive, consultant, director, academic administrator*
Jacobs, Travis Beal *historian, educator*
Katz, Michael Ray *Slavic languages educator*
Lamberti, Marjorie *retired social studies educator*
Liebowitz, Ronald D. *academic administrator*
MacDonald, Kenneth R., Jr. *author, artist*
Nuovo, Betty A. *state representative*
O'Brien, George Dennis *retired academic administrator*
Pardee, Scott Edward *securities dealer*
Saunders, Richard Henry III *museum director*
Vail, Van Horn *German language educator*
Winkler, Paul Frank, Jr. *astrophysicist, educator*

## Milton
Rivero, Marilyn Elaine Keith *state legislator*

## Montgomery Center
Oktavec, Eileen M. *anthropologist, artist*

## Montpelier
Barbieri, Christopher George *professional society administrator*
Burgess, Brian Louis *state supreme court justice*
Cate, Richard H. *school system administrator*
Diamond, M. Jerome *lawyer, retired state attorney general*
Dobbs, David *writer*
Dooley, John Augustine III *state supreme court justice*
Douglas, Jim (James Holley Douglas) *governor*
Dubie, Brian E. *lieutenant governor*
Dumville, John P. *historic site director*
Errecart, Joyce *lawyer*
Gibson, Ernest Willard III *retired state supreme court justice*
Guild, Alden *retired lawyer*
Johnson, Denise Reinka *state supreme court justice*
Markowitz, Deborah Lynn *state official*
Muncy, Tina Gray *educator, educational coordinator*
Paquin, Edward H., Jr. *retired state legislator, not-for-profit developer*
Pelham, Tom *commissioner*
Reiber, Paul L. *state supreme court chief justice*
Saxman, Anna Esther *lawyer*
Skoglund, Marilyn *state supreme court justice*
Sorrell, William H. *state attorney general*
Valerio, Matthew P. *lawyer*

## Morrisville
Besser, Gretchen Rous *writer, educator*
Lamphere, Leigh Ann *elementary school educator, music educator*
Lechevalier, Hubert Arthur *microbiology educator*
Lechevalier, Mary Pfeil *retired microbiologist, educator*
Simonds, Marshall *retired lawyer*

## Newbury
McGarrell, James *artist, educator*

## Newport
Pepyne, Edward Walter *lawyer, educator, psychologist*

## North Bennington
Adler, Irving *mathematician*

## North Clarendon
Freed, Walter Everett *petroleum company executive, state representative*

## North Pomfret
Crowl, John Allen *retired publishing company executive*
Shepherd, Gaal *artist*

## Northfield
Pondiack, Robert D. *mathematics professor*
Wick, William Shinn *clergyman, chaplain, pastor*

## Norwich
Foster, Michael Kirk *anthropologist, linguist*

## Katz, Arnold Martin *medical educator*
Paine, Walter Cabot *journalist, consultant*
Snapper, Ernst *mathematics professor*
Stetson, Eugene William III *film producer, environmentalist, consultant*
Stevenson, Josiah, IV, *management consultant*

## Pawlet
Buechner, Carl Frederick *minister, author*

## Peacham
Barnes, Harry G., Jr. *advocate, consultant*
Engle, James Bruce *ambassador*

## Pittsfield
Wacker, Susan Regina *graphics designer, consultant*

## Plainfield
Jervis, Jane Lise *academic administrator, historian*

## Poultney
Fingon, Joan Carroll *education educator*
Pentkowski, Raymond J. *principal*

## Quechee
DeRouchey, Beverly Jean *investment company executive*
Vitty, Roderic Bemis *retired financial planner, publishing executive*
Wood, R. Stewart, Jr. *retired bishop*

## Randolph
French, Patsy *property manager, state representative*

## Randolph Center
Sax, Daniel Saul *neurologist, educator*

## Reading
Dike, Rad (Edward Conrad Dike) *artist*

## Rutland
Crowley, Arthur Edward, Jr. *lawyer*
Ferraro, Betty Ann *retired state senator*
Haley, John Charles *retired bank executive*
Norris, Richard Anthony *accountant, waste management administrator*

## Saint Albans
Keenan, Kathleen *state legislator*

## Saint Johnsbury
Marshall, John Henry *lawyer*

## Shelburne
Anderson, Richard Louis *electrical engineer*
Canfield, Andrew Trotter *lawyer, writer*
Mead, Philip Bartlett *healthcare administrator, educator, retired obstetrician*
Myers, David Alan *middle school music educator*
Ryerson, William Newton *non profit organization executive*
Weiger, John George *foreign language educator*
White, William North *retired chemistry professor*

## South Burlington
Pizzagalli, James *construction executive*
Shinozaki, Tamotsu *retired physician, retired anesthesiologist*

## South Londonderry
Spiers, Ronald Ian *diplomat*

## South Royalton
Doria, Anthony Notarnicola *college dean, educator*
Dycus, Stephen *law educator*
Powers, Thomas Moore *writer*
Wroth, L(awrence) Kinvin *law educator*

## Springfield
Lawrence, Wesley M. *lawyer*
Putnam, Paul Adin *federal agency administrator*

## Stamford
Stevens, Lauren Rogers *writer, environmentalist*

## Stowe
Siegel, David Burton *lawyer*
Whiteman, Joseph David *retired lawyer, manufacturing company executive*

## Strafford
Williams, William Magavern *headmaster*

## Swanton
Suitor, Dorcas P. *elementary school educator*

## Thetford
Hoagland, Mahlon *biochemist, educator*
Paley, Grace *author, educator*

## Underhill
Danforth, Elliot, Jr. *medical educator*

## Vergennes
Grant, Edwin Randolph *retail executive, manufacturing executive*
Hiscock, Richard Carson *marine safety investigator*
Lewis, Elizabeth R. *director*

## Waitsfield
Esty, David Cameron *marketing and communications executive*
Parrish, Thomas Kirkpatrick III *marketing consultant*

## Wallingford
Gutmann, David Leo *psychology professor*

## Warren
Raphael, Albert Ash, Jr. *retired lawyer*

## Waterbury
Travis, Randall Howard *retired physiologist, retired endocrinologist*

## VERMONT

### Weathersville
Harris, Christopher *editor, writer*

### West Burke
Van Vliet, Claire *artist*

### West Danville
Pollack, Irwin William *psychiatrist, educator*

### West Glover
Weaver, John Borland *musician, department chairman, composer*

### Weston
Kasnowski, Chester Nelson *artist, educator*
Stettler, Stephen F. *performing company executive*

### White River Junction
Berman, Stephen Alan *neurologist*
Kainen, Michael Roland *lawyer, state representative*
Kobe, Alexander *biology educator, department chairman*
Kutter, Catherine Jane *psychologist*
Madden, Edward Harry *philosopher, retired educator*
Myers, Warren Powers Laird *internist, educator*
Rutter, Frances Tompson *retired publisher*

### Whiting
Jacobson, Edward *retired elementary school educator, retired principal*

### Williston
Essman, Robert Norvel *artist, graphics designer*
Laskarzewski, Debra Sue *language educator*

### Wilmington
Little, Thomas M. *public relations executive*

### Winooski
Higgins, Margaret Ann *medical/surgical nurse*
Racz, Irene *public relations executive*

### Wolcott
Fisher, Neal Floyd *religious organization administrator*
Houston, Nioka Heath *elementary school educator*

### Woodstock
Billings, Franklin Swift, Jr. *federal judge*
Goulazian, Peter Robert *retired broadcasting executive*
Hoyt, Coleman Williams *postal consultant*
Killian, Edward James *retired pediatrician*
Matlins, Stuart M. *management consultant, publisher*
Zonay, Thomas A. *lawyer*

## VIRGINIA

### Abingdon
Jones, James Parker *federal judge*
Jones, Mary Trent *endowment fund trustee*
Moore, Suzan E. *lawyer*
Quillen, Michael J. *energy executive*
Ramos-Cano, Hazel Balatero *caterer, chef, innkeeper, restaurateur, entrepreneur*
Widener, Hiram Emory, Jr. *judge*

### Afton
Stefanovic, Victor R *electrical engineer, consultant*

### Alexandria
Adams, Ranald Trevor, Jr. *retired air force officer*
Ahrari, Ehsan M. *political science professor, dean*
Anderson, Maynard Carlyle *security firm executive*
Armstrong, Cathal *chef*
Artemel, Agnes Palmer *land use planner, director*
Arundel, John Howard *journalist, publisher*
Baker, Brent Harold *foundation executive*
Balch, Charles M. *surgeon, educator*
Baroody, Michael Elias *trade association executive*
Barry, Lance Leonard *judge*
Bartlett, Elizabeth Susan *audio-visual specialist*
Bellon, Venetia Rochelle *financial consultant, educator*
Berger, Patricia Wilson *retired librarian*
Bezold, Clement *futurist*
Birely, William Cramer *investment banker*
Blair, Bryce *real estate company executive*
Blair, Dennis Cutler *career officer*
Blanchette, Theresa Marie *elementary school educator*
Blue, Catherine Anne *lawyer*
Boisi, Geoffrey T. *investment company executive*
Bolger, Robert Joseph *retired trade association administrator*
Borum, Olin Henry *retired government scientist*
Bostetter, Martin V. B., Jr. *bankruptcy court judge*
Bowman, Richard Carl *defense consultant, retired air force officer*
Bozell, Brent (L. Brent Bozell III) *communications executive*
Brinkema, Leonie Milhomme *federal judge*
Brown, Frederic Joseph *military officer*
Bryant, Anne Lincoln *educational association executive*
Burch, John Thomas, Jr. *lawyer*
Burke, Kelly Howard *retired military officer, entrepreneur, philanthropist*
Byrne, John Edward (JEB Byrne) *retired federal official*
Cabral, Sam A. *protective services official, labor union administrator*
Callaghan, John William, Jr. *information technology manager, retired military officer*
Carter, Gene Raymond *professional association executive*
Carter, William Harold, Sr. *physicist, researcher, electrical engineer*
Carville, James, Jr., (Chester James Carville) *political scientist, consultant*
Chen, Fen *mathematician, educator, researcher*
Collins, Cardiss *retired congresswoman*
Connell, Mary Ellen *diplomat*
Cook, Charles William *aerospace engineer, consultant, educator*

Coons, Barbara Lynn *public relations executive, librarian*
Cooper, David Earl Kaleoikaika *foundation executive*
Copulos, Milton Russell *energy executive*
Costagliola, Francesco *retired government official*
Crane, Stephen Charles *professional society administrator*
Cross, Dorothy Abigail *retired librarian*
Cross, Eason, Jr. *architect*
Crundwell, Duncan James *electronics executive*
Curtin, Gary Lee *air force officer*
Davis, Ruth Margaret (Mrs. Benjamin Franklin Lohr) *information technology executive*
Dennison, Donald Lee *lawyer*
Devantier, Paul W. *communications executive, broadcast executive*
DiMuro, Bernard Joseph *lawyer*
Dowling, Dean Edward *information scientist, educator*
Drennan, Joseph Peter *lawyer*
Dubin, Martin Steven *principal*
Dunn, Bernard Daniel *former naval officer, consultant*
Edmonds, Albert J. *career officer*
Eilers, Marlene Anna Louise *librarian, genealogist*
Eluhow, Ljiljana Skoric *musician, educator*
Engler, Brian David *professional society administrator*
Eskew, Henry Lawrence, Jr. *economist, consultant*
Fainberg, Anthony *physicist*
Fedorochko, William, Jr. *retired military officer, military analyst*
Fisher, Donald Wayne *medical association administrator*
Fitton, Harvey Nelson, Jr. *former government official*
Flater, Morris Eugene *lawyer*
Fleming, Douglas Riley *journalist, publishing executive, consultant*
Fosdick, Cora Prifold (Cora Prifold Beebe) *management consultant*
Foster, Robert Francis *communications executive*
Foster, Serrin Marie *non-profit organization executive*
Frommer, Lawrence Julian *retired travel company executive*
Gallagher, Anne Porter *communications executive*
Geary, Patrick Joseph *security and emergency planning administrator, writer*
Georges, Peter John *lawyer*
Gernand, Bradley Elton *archivist, librarian*
Glynn, Ernest B. *civil engineer, environmental engineer*
Goldfarb, Ronald Lawrence *lawyer, writer, literary agent*
Gormley, Dennis Michael *research scholar*
Gould, Charles W. *foundation administrator, lawyer*
Gould, Phillip *engineer*
Grachek, Marianna Kern *healthcare administrator*
Gray, Dorothy Louise Allman Pollet *librarian*
Greenstein, Ruth Louise *think-tank executive, lawyer*
Gutsch, William Anthony, Jr. *astronomer*
Gwadosky, Dan A. *former state official, federal agency administrator*
Hale, Robert Fargo *federal association executive*
Hallman, Linda D. *medical association administrator*
Hark, William Henry *retired federal agency administrator, aerospace physician*
Harris, David Ford *management consultant, retired federal official*
Havens, Harry Stewart *retired federal official, management consultant*
Heil, Alan Lewis, Jr. *retired radio broadcast executive, writer*
Helman, Gerald Bernard *diplomat*
Hesterberg, Larry Allen *aerospace engineer*
Higgins, Mary Celeste *lawyer, researcher*
Hilferty, Bryan Carey *public relations specialist*
Hinkle, Wade P. *political scientist*
Hirsch, Robert Louis *energy analyst, consultant*
Hobbs, Michael Edwin *broadcast executive*
Hobson, James Richmond *lawyer*
Holcomb, Richard Dennis *lawyer*
Huckabee, Harlow Maxwell *lawyer, writer*
Hudgins, David Drake *lawyer*
Hughes, Grace-Flores *federal agency administrator*
Hurtado, Rodrigo Claudio *allergist*
Inman, Stephen Eugene *finance officer*
Ivers, Donald Louis *retired judge*
Jackson, Gary Lee *security consultant*
Jenkins, John Smith *retired dean, lawyer*
Johnson, Edgar McCarthy *psychologist*
Johnson, JoAnn Mardelle *federal agency administrator*
Kelly, Nancy Frieda Wolicki *lawyer*
Kerger, Paula Ann *broadcast executive*
Kim, Sook Cha *artist*
Knowlton, William Allen *federal agency administrator, educator*
Kopp, Eugene Paul *lawyer*
Kotlarchuk, Ihor O. E. *lawyer*
Kratovil, Jane Lindley *think tank associate, not-for-profit developer*
Kroesen, Frederick James *retired army officer, consultant*
Krueger, Gerald Peter *psychologist*
Lachance, Janice Rachel *professional association administrator, retired federal agency administrator, lawyer*
Lantz, Phillip Edward *security firm executive, consultant*
Lapidus, Kevin S. *lawyer*
Larson, Charles Robert *naval officer*
Lasser, Howard Gilbert *chemical engineer, consultant*
Laurent, Lawrence Bell *communications executive, retired journalist*
Leestma, Robert *retired federal agency administrator, educational association administrator*
Lendsey, Jacquelyn L. *foundation administrator*
Lenz, Edward Arnold *trade association administrator, lawyer*
Leonhart, Michele Marie *federal agency administrator*

Lightner, Candy (Candace Lynne Lightner) *non-profit management consultant, advocate*
Lindsey, Sara Ann *sociologist, educator*
Lipnick, Robert Louis *chemist, toxicologist*
Lopatin, Carol Keesler *artist*
Loren, Donald Patrick *retired military officer*
Lundeberg, Philip Karl Boraas *curator, historian*
Lusk, Cody *auto association executive*
MacLaren, William George, Jr. *engineering executive*
Maehara, Paulette V. *fundraising executive*
Mallon, Francis J. *health science association administrator*
Malott, John Raymond *writer, consultant, not-for-profit executive*
Mandil, I. Harry *nuclear engineer*
Mann, Seymour Zalmon *retired political science professor, labor union administrator*
Masterson, Kleber Sanlin, Jr. *physicist*
Matalin, Mary *political consultant*
McConville, Judy Allen *social studies educator*
McDowell, Charles Eager *lawyer, retired military officer*
McMillan, Charles William *consulting company executive*
McNicol, David Leon *retired federal official*
Meisinger, Susan *human resources specialist*
Michael, Ann Dozier Marino *real estate broker*
Milling, Marcus Eugene, Sr. *geologist*
Moshier, David Irwin *church administrator*
Mossinghoff, Gerald Joseph *lawyer, educator*
Muir, Warren Roger *chemist, educator*
Murray, Russell, II, *aeronautical engineer, security consultant*
Nelson, David Leonard *data processing executive*
Nesbitt, Wanda L. *ambassador*
Newton, Hugh C. *public relations executive*
Nicholas, Lynn B. *medical association administrator*
Nodeen, Janey Price *information technology executive*
O'Brien, Patrick Michael *library administrator*
O'Hara, John Patrick *lawyer, consultant*
Palmer, Adam P. *lawyer*
Pastin, Mark Joseph *health science association administrator, educator*
Patel, Manu V. *physics educator*
Paturis, E(mmanuel) Michael *lawyer*
Paulson, Gwen O. Gampel *government relations consultant, life and leadership coach*
Penrose, Cynthia C. *retired health care consultant*
Pitzer, Jack Todd *purchasing agent, consultant, educator*
Poehlein, Gary Wayne *retired chemical engineering professor*
Powell, Colin Luther *former secretary of state, former Chairman of the Joint Chiefs of Staff*
Pringle, Robert Maxwell *diplomat*
Pyle, Howard *lawyer, consultant*
Rabun, John Brewton, Jr. *criminal justice agency administrator*
Rae, Jeneanne *new product development and innovation development consultant, educator*
Rahming, John Christopher *investment company executive, consultant*
Rayman, Russell Barry *physician*
Rector, John Michael *pharmaceutical association executive, lawyer*
Redway, Jonathan *lawyer*
Reinl, Harry Charles *economist, researcher*
Reiss, Richard *environmental consultant*
Rogers, Paul A'Court *management consulting executive*
Romney, Carl F. *seismologist*
Rosenberg, Chuck (Charles P. Rosenberg) *prosecutor*
Salinas, Rodney Jay C. *media company executive*
Schiff, Charlene *adult education educator*
Schubert, Richard Francis *social services administrator, consultant*
Schultz, Franklin H. *retired law educator*
Sepp, Peter John *communications executive, writer*
Sheffield, Greg *liberal media blogger*
Sheffield, Matthew *liberal media blogger*
Shosky, John Edwin *media consultant, speechwriter*
Shrier, Stefan *mathematician, lawyer*
Simmons, Edwin Howard *military officer, historian*
Simmons, Richard De Lacey *mass media executive*
Singletary, Michael *retired professional football player, motivational speaker*
Smith, Jeffrey Greenwood *gas industry executive, retired military officer*
Snyder, Larry *priest, social services administrator*
Stempler, Jack Leon *aerospace executive*
Stone, Ann Elizabeth *marketing agency executive, consultant, entrepreneur, volunteer*
Straub, Peter Thornton *lawyer*
Sturtevant, Brereton *retired lawyer, retired federal official*
Swift, Stephen Christopher *lawyer*
Tandy, Karen P. *federal agency administrator*
Toulmin, Priestley *retired geologist*
Tucker, Alvin Leroy *retired government official*
Tucker, Howard McKeldin *investment banker, consultant*
Verburg, Edwin Arnold *management consultant*
Von Drehle, Ramon Arnold *lawyer*
Vosbeck, Elizabeth Just *retired geneticist*
Vosbeck, William Frederick, Jr. *architect*
Walker, Edward Keith, Jr. *retired management consultant, retired military officer*
Weisberg, Leonard R. *retired engineering executive, researcher*
Whitson, Elizabeth Temple *graphics designer*
Widner, Ralph Randolph *retired public administrator*
Wilcox, David Eric *electrical engineering educator, consultant*
Wilhide, Stephen D. *medical association administrator*
Williams, John Edward *lawyer*
Wilson, Charles H. (Charles Harrison Wilson) *retired air force officer, financial planner, human resource development professional*
Wilson, Tyler J. *medical association administrator*
Wolfe, Thad Allison *air force officer*
Woolley, Mary Elizabeth *science administrator, advocate*

Wynn, Robert E. *electronics executive, retired military officer*
Yoder, Edwin Milton, Jr. *columnist, educator, editor, writer*

### Amherst
Campbell, Catherine Lynn *elementary school educator*

### Amissville
Hunter, Beverly Claire *research scientist, educator*

### Annandale
Abdellah, Faye Glenn *retired public health service executive*
Armstrong, Henry Jere *retired judge*
Bayou, Jean D. *administrative assistant*
Bragg, Cheryl Fuller *psychologist*
Brotton, Joyce Dupras *English language educator*
Carvalho, Julie Ann *psychologist*
Christianson, Geryld B. *government agency administrator, consultant*
Connair, Stephen Michael *financial analyst*
Freeman, Baba Foster *editor*
Gioconda, Thomas F. *government program administrator, retired military flag officer*
Gorsen, Robert Marc *neurosurgeon*
Greinke, Everett Donald *management consultant*
Hulbert, Mark J. *financial analyst, columnist*
Hutcheon, Wallace Schoonmaker *historian, educator*
Jarvis, Elbert, II, (Jay Jarvis) *employee benefits specialist*
Jollie, Susan Barbara *lawyer*
Jones, David Charles *international financial and management consultant*
Jung, Esther *real estate broker, realtor, real estate consultant, small business owner*
Khim, Jay Wook *information technology executive*
Luftglass, Maribeth *information technology manager*
Matuszko, Anthony Joseph *research chemist, administrator, educator*
Ochs, Walter J. *civil engineer, consultant*
Raab, Harry Frederick, Jr. *retired physicist*
Rogers, Stephen Hitchcock *retired ambassador*
Samuelson, Douglas Alan *information technology executive*
Shamburek, Roland Howard *physician*

### Appomattox
Beatson, LeGrande Guerry *environmental health specialist*

### Arlington
Ablard, Charles David *administrative judge*
Abler, Ronald Francis *geography educator*
Adams, Hunter (Patch Adams) *internist, health facility administrator*
Aggrey, Orison Rudolph *former ambassador, consultant, academic administrator*
Alcalde, Hector *public relations executive*
Allard, Dean Conrad *historian, retired historical center director*
Allen, David *systems engineer*
Anthony, Robert Armstrong *lawyer, educator*
Arnold, Gary Howard *film critic*
Askey, Thelma J. *federal agency administrator*
Bakke, Dennis W. *energy company executive*
Baldanza, B. Ben *air transportation executive*
Bass, Judy Marsha *artist, educator*
Beier, Anita P. *air transportation executive*
Bement, Arden Lee, Jr. *science foundation director*
Bennett, Christopher Lawrence *hotel executive, lawyer*
Berg, John Richard *chemist, former federal government executive*
Berkowitz, Edward C. *lawyer*
Bigeleisen, Jacob *chemist, educator*
Blum, Steven (H. Steven Blum) *career military officer*
Boesz, Christine C. *science foundation administrator*
Bolster, Archie Milburn *retired foreign service officer*
Bond, Phillip J. *technology association executive, former advertising executive*
Boorstein, Laurence *economist, educator*
Bradburn, Norman M. *behavioral science educator*
Brenner, Edgar H. *legal association administrator*
Brighton, John A. *mechanical engineer, academic administrator*
Brown, Sandra *forest ecologist, researcher*
Buchanan, Louise *political organization worker, consultant*
Buckley, Francis H. *economist, law educator, lawyer*
Bune, Karen Louise *state agency administrator*
Burgess, David *lawyer*
Cadby, Carol *theater educator, theater director*
Callier, Maria Cecile *writer, journalist, radio producer, voice-over artist, actress*
Caplan, Mitchell H. *diversified financial services company executive*
Cehelsky, Marta *scientific organization executive*
Chafuen, Alejandro Antonio *think-tank executive*
Chattman, Raymond Christopher *association executive*
Chiames, Christopher L. *air transportation executive*
Choksi, Mary *investment company executive*
Chubb, Talbot Albert *physicist, consultant*
Clark, John F. *federal agency administrator*
Claussen, Eileen Barbara *environmental services administrator, former federal agency administrator*
Clayton, James Edwin *journalist*
Clump, Michael Aden *psychologist, educator*
Coady, Philip James, Jr. *retired naval officer*
Coats, Warren L., Jr. *economist*
Cofoni, Paul M. *computer company executive*
Cohen, Sheldon Irwin *lawyer*
Contis, George *medical products executive*
Covington, James Edwin *government agency administrator, psychologist*
Cox, Henry *engineer, researcher*
Crosby, Michael P. *science administrator*
Crouch, Richard Edelin *lawyer*
Davis, David M. *air transportation executive*
Davis, Lynn Etheridge *political scientist, educator*
DeFeo, Charles Joesph *Internet company executive*

Young, M. Dendy *finance company executive*

## Charlottesville

Abbot, William Wright *history professor*
Abraham, Henry Julian *political science professor*
Abraham, Kenneth Samuel *law educator*
Arlet, Vincent *orthopedist, surgeon*
Arnold, Albert James *foreign language educator*
Ayers, Edward *dean*
Aylor, James Hiram *engineering educator*
Balnave, Richard D. *law educator*
Balogun, Rasheed Abiodun *medical educator*
Barrett, Eugene Joseph *physician, educator, researcher*
Battestin, Martin Carey *retired language educator*
Bednar, Michael John *architecture educator*
Belanger, Terry *historian, educator*
Beller, George A. *cardiologist, educator*
Berger, Toby *electrical engineer, educator*
Biltonen, Rodney Lincoln *biochemistry educator, pharmacology educator*
Bloomfield, Louis Aub *physicist, researcher*
Bonnie, Richard Jeffrey *law educator, lawyer, consultant*
Braiman, Mark Stephen *biomedical educator, researcher*
Brewer, Philip Warren *retired civil engineer*
Brodrick, Sheri Mary-Ann *secondary school educator*
Brooks, Peter (Preston) *literature educator, department chairman, writer*
Brown, Holmes *public relations executive*
Buck, D. Ruth *legal research and writing educator*
Bull, George Albert *retired banker*
Cannon, Jonathan Z. *lawyer, educator*
Cano-Ballesta, Juan *Spanish language educator*
Cantrell, Robert Wendell *otolaryngologist, head and neck surgeon, educator*
Carey, Robert Munson *medical educator, physician*
Carter, William Walton *physicist, researcher*
Casey, John Dudley *writer, language educator*
Casteen, John Thomas III *academic administrator*
Chandler, Lawrence Bradford, Jr. *lawyer*
Chapel, Robert Clyde *theater director, educator*
Chase, Karen Susan *English literature educator*
Chevalier, Roger Alan *astronomy educator, consultant*
Chordia, Mahendra Devichand *chemist, researcher*
Click, Patricia C. *historian, educator*
Cohen, George Meredith *law educator*
Cornell, Dewey Gene *psychologist*
Coughlin, Anne M. *law educator*
Crackel, Theodore Joseph *historian*
Crosby, Ivan Keith *cardiac surgeon, educator*
Crutchfield, William Gayle, Jr. *retail executive*
Cushman, Barry *law educator*
Davidson, Hugh MacCullough *French language and literature educator*
Davis, Edward Wilson *business administration educator*
DeMong, Richard Francis *finance and investments educator*
Dooley, Michael P. *law educator*
Dove, Rita Frances *poet, language educator*
Dudley, Earl C., Jr. *law educator*
Elzinga, Kenneth Gerald *economics professor*
Epstein, Robert Marvin *anesthesiologist, educator*
Eubank, Weaver Keith *history professor, writer*
Finley, Robert Van Eaton *minister*
Fitchett, Taylor *law librarian*
Flickinger, Charles John *anatomist, educator*
Forbes, John Douglas *architectural and economic historian*
Forde-Mazrui, Kim Abubakar Ali *law educator*
Forrest, Patricia Anne *publishing executive, editor*
Fox, Charles Dunsmore, IV, *lawyer*
Fraser, Cassandra Lynne *chemist, educator*
Fredrick, Laurence William *astronomer, educator*
Gaden, Elmer Lewis *retired engineering educator*
Garber, Nicholas Jack *civil engineer, educator*
Garrett, George Palmer, Jr. *language educator, writer*
Garrett, Reginald Hooker *biology professor, researcher*
Garson, Arthur, Jr. *dean, medical educator*
Gaskin, Felicia *biochemist, educator*
Gilliam, George Harrison *lawyer*
Goetz, Charles John *law and economics educator*
Good, Richard Standish *geologist*
Graebner, Norman Arthur *historian, educator*
Grimes, Russell Newell *inorganic chemist, educator*
Groiss, Fred George *lawyer*
Guerrant, Richard Littleton *medical educator*
Gunter, Bradley Hunt *capital management executive*
Handler, Jerome Sidney *anthropology educator*
Hanft, Ruth S. Samuels *economist, consultant*
Hanssen, Shirley Mae *retired librarian*
Harris, Robert Shields *finance executive*
Harrison, John Collier *law educator*
Hecht, Sidney Michael *chemistry professor*
Henderson, Stanley Dale *lawyer, educator, arbitrator*
Henry, Laurin Luther *public affairs educator*
Hess, Frederick *social sciences educator, writer*
Hetherington, Eileen Mavis *psychologist, educator*
Hirsch, Eric Donald, Jr. *language educator*
Hobbs, Charles Roderick Bruce, Jr. *retired geologist*
Hochberg, Bayard Zabdial *retired lawyer*
Hodous, Robert Power *lawyer*
Hoel, Lester A. *civil engineering educator, department chairman*
Horgan, Cornelius Oliver *mathematics professor, engineering educator*
Hornberger, George Milton *environmental science educator*
Howard, Arthur Ellsworth Dick *law educator*
Howell, Robert Edward *hospital administrator*
Hudson, John Lester *chemical engineering professor*
Humphreys, Paul William *philosophy educator, consultant*
Hunt, Donald Frederick *chemistry professor*
Hunt, William B. *pulmonologist*
Hurwitz, Deena R. *law educator*
Hymes, Dell Hathaway *anthropologist, educator*
Inigo, Rafael Madrigal *retired electrical engineering educator*
Jeffries, John Calvin, Jr. *dean, law educator*

Jevtovic-Todorovic, Vesna *physician, researcher*
Johnson, Richard Marc *civics educator*
Johnston, Margaret Schuster *volunteer, retired language educator*
Jolly, Bruce Dwight *manufacturing executive*
Jones, Rayford Scott *surgeon, educator*
Jordan, Daniel Porter, Jr. *foundation administrator, historian, educator*
Kaiserlian, Penelope Jane *publishing executive*
Kassell, Neal Frederic *neurosurgery educator*
Kattwinkel, John *pediatrician, educator*
Keats, Theodore Eliot *radiologist, educator*
Kelly, Thaddeus Elliott *medical geneticist*
Kennedy, Cornelius Bryant *retired lawyer*
Kensington, Andrew Justus *litigation specialist*
Kent, Richard W. *mechanical engineer*
Kiewra, Gustave Paul *psychologist, educator*
Kitch, Edmund Wells *law educator*
Kordana, Kevin A. *law educator*
Kraus, Jody S. *law educator*
Krzysztofowicz, Roman *systems engineering and statistical science educator, consultant*
Landess, Fred Stone *retired lawyer*
Lane, Ann Judith *history and women's studies educator*
Langbaum, Robert Woodrow *language educator*
Lee, Jen-shih *biomedical engineering educator*
Leffler, Melvyn P. *history professor*
Leslie, Douglas L. *law educator*
Levenson, Jacob Clavner *language educator*
Lilly, Graham C. *law educator*
Lin, Kant *plastic surgeon, educator*
Linden, Peppy G. *museum director*
Little, W(illia)m A(lfred) *language educator, researcher, musicologist*
Lo, Kwok-Yung *astronomer, educator, researcher*
Louis, Garrick E. *systems engineer, educator*
MacAskill, Lloyd Edwin *systems analyst, consultant*
MacDonald, Timothy Lee *chemistry professor*
Magill, M(ary) Elizabeth *law educator*
Mahoney, Julia Delong *law educator*
Mahoney, Paul G. *law educator*
Mandell, Gerald Lee *internist, educator*
Marshall, John Crook *internal medicine educator, researcher*
Martin, David Alan *law educator*
McCrimmon, Barbara Smith *writer, librarian*
McDonough, William Andrews *architect, former dean*
McGann, Jerome John *language educator*
Meador, Daniel John *law educator*
Megill, Allan D. *historian*
Meiburg, Charles Owen *economist, educator*
Menaker, Michael *biology professor*
Menefee, Samuel Pyeatt *lawyer, researcher*
Middleditch, Leigh Benjamin, Jr. *lawyer, educator*
Midelfort, Hans Christian Erik *history professor*
Mikalson, Jon Dennis *classics educator*
Minehart, Jean Besse *tax accountant*
Mirmira, Raghavendra G. *endocrinologist, researcher, educator*
Molhoek, Kerrington Ramsey *research scientist*
Monahan, John T. *law educator, psychologist*
Moore, John Norton *lawyer, educator, diplomat*
Moreno, Jonathan *bioethicist*
Morgan, Raymond F. *plastic surgeon*
Muller, William Henry, Jr. *surgeon, educator*
Nelson, Caleb Edward *law educator*
Nelson, Raymond John *language educator, dean*
Newsom, David Dunlop *ambassador, educator*
Nohrnberg, James Carson *language educator*
Nolan, Stanton Peelle *surgeon, educator*
O'Brien, David Michael *law educator*
O'Bryant, John Frederick *librarian, educator*
O'Connell, Jeffrey *law educator*
Olsen, Edgar Oliver *economics professor*
Owen, John Atkinson, Jr. *internist, educator*
Parshall, Karen Virginia Hunger *mathematician*
Pate, Robert Hewitt, Jr. *counselor educator*
Perkowski, Jan Louis *language, literature and folklore educator*
Peterson, Kent Wright *physician*
Peterson, Merrill Daniel *historian, educator*
Phillips, Lawrence H., II, *neurologist, educator*
Pierce, Marcia *biomedical engineer, educator*
Platts-Mills, Thomas Alexander E. *immunologist, educator, researcher*
Powers, Robert David *physician*
Quandt, William Bauer *political scientist*
Rehm, Patrice Koch *radiologist, educator*
Reppucci, Nicholas Dickon *psychologist, educator*
Reynolds, Albert Barnett *nuclear engineer, educator*
Reynolds, Robert Edgar *academic administrator*
Rhoads, Steven Eric *political science professor*
Riley, Margaret Foster (Mimi Riley) *law educator*
Rini, Joel *language educator, linguist*
Robinson, Mildred Wigfall *law educator*
Root, James Benjamin *landscape architect*
Roseberry, Edwin Southall *retired state agency administrator*
Ross, Walter Beghtol *music educator, composer*
Rowlingson, John Clyde *anesthesiologist, physician, educator*
Rubin, David Lee *humanities educator, critic, editor*
Rutherglen, George A. *law educator*
Sabato, Larry Joseph *political science professor, director*
Sahr, Morris Gallup *financial planner*
Sarazin, Craig Leigh *astronomer*
Sarembock, Ian Joseph *internist, cardiologist*
Scheld, William Michael *internist, educator*
Schneider, Edward Martin *retired internist, medical educator*
Schuker, Stephen Alan *historian, educator*
Scott, Elizabeth S. *law educator*
Scott, Nathan Alexander, Jr. *minister, educator, critic*
Scott, Robert Edwin *law educator*
Sedgwick, Alexander *retired historian, educator*
Seidelmann, Paul Kenneth *astronomer, educator*
Setear, John K. *law educator*
Shaw, Donald Leslie *Spanish language educator*
Shenkir, William Gary *business educator*
Sibert, Polly Lou *conductor, music educator*
Sihler, William Wooding *finance educator*
Sinclair, Kent *law educator*
Skinner, Jonathan Snowden *economics educator*
Slaughter, Edward Ratliff, Jr. *lawyer*

Smith, Clyde Ray *dean*
Spearing, Anthony Colin *English literature educator*
Stephan, Paul Brooke III *law educator*
Stevenson, Ian *psychiatrist, educator*
Stocker, Arthur Frederick *classics educator*
Sundberg, Richard Jay *chemistry professor*
Sykes, Gresham M'Cready *sociologist, educator, artist*
Templeton, Dennis J. *research scientist, pathologist*
Theodoridis, George Constantin *biomedical engineering educator, researcher*
Thomas, Lawrence Eldon *mathematics professor*
Thompson, Augustine Craig *priest, historian*
Thompson, Kenneth W(infred) *educational association administrator, writer, editor, social sciences educator*
Thorner, Michael Oliver *medical educator*
Thornhill, Arthur H., Jr. *retired publishing executive*
Tillack, Thomas Warner *pathologist, educator*
Tornello, Vincent Joseph *music educator*
Townsend, Miles Averill *aerospace and mechanical engineering educator*
Turner, Robert Foster *law educator, writer*
Tuttle, Jeremy Ballou *neuroscientist*
Vanden Bout, Paul Adrian *astronomer, physicist, educator*
Verkerke, J. Hoult *law educator*
Wadlington, Walter James *law educator*
Wagner, Roy *anthropology educator, researcher*
Wagoner, Jennings Lee, Jr. *historian, educator*
Walker, W. Laurens *law educator*
Walt, Steven David *law educator*
Warren, Russ C. *artist, educator*
Weary, Peyton Edwin *retired medical educator*
Weber, Hans Jürgen *physics professor*
Weinberger, Adrienne *artist, art appraiser*
Wenger, Larry Bruce *law librarian, educator*
Whitaker, John King *retired economics professor*
White, George Edward *law educator, lawyer*
Whitehead, John Wayne *lawyer, educator, writer*
Wiggins, Barbara Sue *pharmacist, educator*
Wilkinson, J. Harvie, III, (James Harvie Wilkinsin III) *federal judge*
Wittenborg, Karin *university librarian*
Wolcott, John Winthrop III *retired manufacturing executive*
Wood, James Arthur *cartoonist*
Woolhandler, Ann *law educator*
Wright, Charles Penzel, Jr. *language educator*
Zunz, Olivier Jean *history professor*

## Charlottesvle

Goodrich, George Herbert *retired judge*
Haigh, Robert William *business professor*
Kraehe, Enno Edward *history professor*
Walker, Beverly Ann *minister, health facility administrator*

## Chatham

Ruef, John Samuel *clergyman*

## Chesapeake

Barnes, Stacy Ray *finance educator, researcher*
Brock, Macon F., Sr. *retail company executive*
Brock, Macon F., Jr. *retail company executive*
Coble, Frederick Charles *retail executive*
Cox, Mark Stanley *public relations professional*
Dixon, Timothy Kaine *music educator*
Hayslett-Wallace, Jeanette *music educator*
Hill, Deborah Nixon *elementary school educator, minister*
Jackson, Cynthia Ann *medical association administrator, health consultant*
Kohns, Jonathan Wesley *secondary school educator*
Kovalcik, Paul Jerome *surgeon*
Lewter, Helen Clark *retired elementary school educator*
Locke, L. Muriel *mathematician, educator*
Myrick, Bismarck *diplomat*
Notti, Donna Betts *special education educator*
Powers, Robert Lawrence *retired civilian military employee*
Raymond, Patricia *gastroenterologist, medical educator*
Sasser, Bob *retail company executive*
Sasser, Robert *retail executive*
Taylor-Hines, Regina Anita *civilian military employee*
Webb, Julia Jones *elementary school educator, minister*

## Chester

Gray, Charles Robert *lawyer*
Gray, Frederick Thomas, Jr., (Rick Gray) *journalist, actor, educator*
Law, Thomas Melvin *academic administrator*
Roane, David James, Jr. *information technology auditor*
Walton, G. Clifford *physician*
White, Jessica Bailey *biology professor*

## Chesterfield

Congdon, John Rhodes *transportation executive*
Davis, Bonnie Christell *judge*
Jacobson, Thomas Elton *urban planner, county official*
Love, Dana Francis Ignatius *telecommunications industry executive*
Shaffer, Earl E., Jr. *music educator*
Tate, Wendy K. *risk management specialist*
Weldon, Thérèse Hemler *secondary school educator, art educator*
Young, Kenneth Wayne *environmental health specialist*

## Christiansburg

Fu, I-Ping Phyllis *language educator, researcher*
Hawley, Rollin James *neurologist*

## Clifton

Brooks, Matthew Wayne *agrichemical regulatory chemist, consultant*
Cavileer, Sharon E. *writer, public relations executive, consultant*
Hennesy, Gerald Craft *artist*
Hoffman, Karla Leigh *mathematician, educator*
Latt, Pamela Yvonne *school system administrator*

## Cobbs Creek

Crum, John Kistler *management consultant*

## Colonial Beach

Miller, Justin Allen *artist, art educator*

## Colonial Heights

Grizzard-Barham, Barbara Lee *artist*
Morgan, Barbara M. *psychotherapist, educator*

## Courtland

Minor, Edward Colquitt *paper company executive, lawyer*

## Covesville

Williams, Patricia Anne *philosopher, writer*

## Covington

Stephenson, Roscoe Bolar, Jr. *state supreme court justice*

## Crozet

Detmer, Don Eugene *health informatics, management and policy researcher*
Reswick, James Bigelow *former government official, biomedical engineer*

## Culpeper

Bahl-Moore, Elizabeth Ann *art educator, artist*
Goddard, Frances Byrd *clinical social worker*
Rector, Donna Lynn *writer, photographer, vocalist*

## Dahlgren

Bressler, Barry Lee *physicist, systems analyst*
Rayms-Keller, Alfredo *molecular biologist*

## Dale City

Baxter, Ruth Howell *educational administrator, psychologist*

## Danville

Aaron, Larry Gene *secondary school educator, writer, minister*
Abreu, Luis Alberto *lawyer*
Hayes, Jack Irby *historian, educator*
Kiser, Jackson L. *federal judge*
Lea, Robert Lee III *social sciences educator*
Pfau, Richard Anthony *university president*
Reaves, Joseph Shane *protective services official*
Regan, Michael Patrick *lawyer*
Talbott, Frank III *lawyer*
Tucker, Gary Allan *information scientist, educator, minister*

## Deltaville

Koedel, John Gilbert, Jr. *retired metal products executive*

## Dinwiddie

McCray, Doris Raines *minister*

## Draper

Whitehurst, Mary Tarr *artist, poet, writer*

## Dublin

Billaud, Louise Ann *musician, educator*
Clark, Shelia Roxanne *sports association executive, legislative analyst*
Wall, Jennifer Grey *assistant principal*

## Dulles

Cheney, Mary Claire *Internet company executive*
Desmond, Ned *editor, writer*
Elias, Antonio L. *aerospace transportation executive*
Glacel, Robert Allan *retired military career officer*
Jacobs, Janice Lee *ambassador*
Mathieu, Gail Dennise *ambassador*
McGraw, Gary *computer scientist, writer*
McKinley, John *information technology executive*
Miller, Jonathan F. *Internet company executive*
Mulford, David Campbell *ambassador, former finance company executive*
Payne, Jeffery E. *software quality management company executive*
Skodon, Emil Mark *ambassador*

## Dumfries

Avrit, Richard Calvin *defense consultant, career officer*
Locigno, Paul Robert *public relations executive*

## Dutton

Washburn, John Rosser *entrepreneur*

## Earlysville

Bartoes, Richard Alan *agricultural products executive*
Brownell, Blaine Allison *educational association administrator, former academic administrator, history professor*
Rotherham, Andrew J. *not-for-profit administrator, consultant*

## Eastville

Williams, Ida Jones *consumer and home economics educator, writer*

## Edinburg

Rhodes, Stephen Michael *poultry company executive*
Trindal, Wesley Steele *mechanical engineer*

## Emory

Jones, Jerry Lee *computer educator*
Morris, Thomas Robbins *political scientist, educator, academic administrator*

## Fairfax

Anderson, David Lawrence *lawyer*
Arntson, Peter Andrew *lawyer*
Baghi, Heibatollah *medical educator*
Bailey, Helen McShane *historian, consultant*
Baird, Charles Bruce *lawyer, consultant*
Baker, Daniel Richard *computer company executive*
Barth, Michael Carl *economist*
Bennett, James Thomas *economics professor*
Bobzien, David P. *lawyer*

Boneau, C. Alan *psychology professor, researcher*
Boone, James Virgil *retired engineering executive, researcher*
Buchanan, James McGill *economist, educator*
Burnett, Michael Bruce *benefits compensation analyst*
Carty, Rita Mary *dean, nurse*
Chen, Chun-Hung *engineering educator*
Clay, Edwin S. III *library director*
Codding, Frederick Hayden *lawyer*
Cook, Gerald *electrical engineering educator*
Cosing, Arthur Paul, Jr. *writer, artist*
Cramer, H. R. (Hal Cramer) *oil industry executive*
Crissey, Rebecca Lynn *special education educator*
Dennis, Rutledge M. *sociologist, educator*
Downey, Richard Lawrence *lawyer*
Drenkard, Karen Neil *nursing administrator*
Fagan, John Ernest *lawyer*
Felsburg, David F. *engineering executive, educator*
Folk, Thomas Robert *lawyer*
Fox, Donna M. *dean, biology professor*
Ganesan, Rajesh *industrial engineer, researcher*
Gardner, Christopher *history professor*
Gertler, Janos John *electrical engineer, educator*
Gillespie, Samuel H. III *lawyer, oil industry executive*
Golden, John Joseph, Jr. *information technology executive*
Hale, Thomas Morgan *professional services executive*
Harrison, Robert Allen *systems analyst*
Haskett, Dianne Louise *retired mayor, lawyer, consultant*
Hollans, Irby Noah, Jr. *retired trade association administrator*
Hopson, Everett George *retired lawyer*
Horton, Lois Elaine *history professor*
Houck, Mark Hedrich *engineering educator*
Johnson, Wallace *retired army officer*
Jones, George Fleming *international consultant*
Kash, Don Eldon *political science professor*
Keith, John A(ugustine) C(hilton) *lawyer*
Kendall Hull, Margarida *art educator, painter*
Kieffer, Jarold Alan *publishing executive, writer*
King, James Cecil *retired literature educator*
Knee, Ruth Irelan (Mrs. Junior K. Knee) *social worker, health care consultant*
Ko, Jang Wan *research scientist, educator*
LaPierre, Wayne R., Jr. *lobbyist*
Larranaga, Jim *men's college basketball coach*
Lavine, Thelma Zeno *philosophy educator*
Lomax, Michael Lucius *non-profit association administrator*
Longin, Thomas Charles *retired academic administrator*
Mackall, Henry Clinton *lawyer*
Mann, Laura Ann *soprano*
Mattson, Joy Louise *oncological nurse*
McAllister, William Howard III *newspaper reporter, columnist, public affairs consultant*
Meamber, Laurie Ann *marketing educator*
Meyer, David Lavon *health administration executive*
Miller, Emilie F. *former state senator, consultant*
Miller, Patricia A. *music educator, opera and concert artist*
Morowitz, Harold Joseph *biophysicist, educator*
Mulvaney, Mary Frederica *systems analyst*
Nicogossian, Anrauld E.T. *education educator*
Palmer, James Daniel *information technology educator*
Pfiffner, James Price *political science professor*
Pisani, Joseph *artist, conservator*
Pruitt, Dean Garner *psychologist, educator*
Pugh, Arthur James (Jay Pugh) *retired retail executive*
Pyatt, Everett Arno *federal official*
Rendine, Maria Farese *retired secondary school educator*
Ricouart, Janine *language educator*
Rieger, Michael Ira *lawyer*
Roberts, Cecil Edward, Jr. *labor union administrator*
Robinson, Kayne B. *lobbyist, former political organization official*
Rosenkranz, Robert Bernard *military officer*
Rust, John Howson, Jr. *lawyer, state legislator*
Sage, Andrew Patrick, Jr. *systems engineering and management educator*
Sanderson, Douglas Jay *lawyer*
Schulman, Joseph Daniel *physician, health facility administrator, medical geneticist, educator*
Siddons, Joy Garbee *music educator*
Silcox, Gordon Bruce *executive coach*
Simon, J. Stephen *oil industry executive*
Simpson, Carter D. *lawyer*
Smith, Vernon Lomax *economist, researcher*
Snyder, Roger Alan *physician, neurologist*
Soyfer, Valery Nikolayevich *geneticist, biophysicist*
Stage, Thomas Benton *psychiatrist*
Stearns, Peter Nathaniel *history professor*
Steele, Howard Loucks *economic development consultant, author*
Steger, Edward Herman *retired chemist*
Stitt, David Tillman *judge*
Suh, Yongsook Victoria *plastic surgeon*
Sun, Donglian *meteorologist*
Tolchin, Susan Jane *political science professor, writer*
Travis, Toni-Michelle C. *political scientist, educator*
Villarreal, Carlos Castañeda *engineering executive*
Wagner, Richard E. *economist, educator*
Ward, George Truman *architect*
Wenner, Debby Linn *mezzo soprano, educator*
Williams, Thomas Rhys *anthropologist, educator*
Williams, Walter E. *economics professor*
Witek, James Eugene *retired public relations executive*
Xing, Guang-Qian *aerospace scientist*
Zhang, Xinwen *computer scientist, researcher*

### Fairfax Station

Barringer, Joan Marie *counselor, educator, artist, writer*
Cantu, Jennifer St. John *gifted and talented educator*
Carver, George Allen, Jr. *retired lawyer*
Duff, William Grierson *electrical engineer, educator*
Randell, Cortes W. *news service executive*

### Falls Church

Akkara, Joseph Augustine *chemist, educator*
Aukofer, Frank Alexander *journalist*
Aziz, Afzal *biology educator*
Bankson, Marjory Zoet *former religious association administrator*
Barkley, Paul Haley, Jr. *architect*
Benton, Nicholas Frederick *publisher*
Beyer, Donald Sternoff, II, *former state offical*
Bingman, Charles Franklin *government executive, educator*
Bruck, Bill *finance company executive*
Brunsvold, Mary Helen Susan (Chica Brunsvold) *artist*
Bryan, Billie Marie (Mrs. James A. Mackey) *retired biologist*
Burroughs, Benton, Jr. *mergers and acquisitions lawyer*
Calkins, Susannah Eby *retired economist*
Cazan, Sylvia Marie Buday (Mrs. Matthew John Cazan) *retired real estate executive*
Chaffin, Jeffrey G. *dentist*
Christman, Bruce Lee *lawyer*
Clizbe, John Anthony *psychologist, social services administrator*
Cooper, Jean Saralee *judge*
Courtney, William Harrison *marketing professional*
Cromley, Allan Wray *retired journalist*
Dao, Thuy Dinh *personal care industry executive*
Dewey-Balzhiser, Anne Elizabeth Marie *lawyer*
Diamond, Robert Michael *lawyer*
Elliott, Virginia F. Harrison *retired anatomist, publisher, educator, investment advisor, kinesiologist, philanthropist*
Fink, Charles Augustin *behavioral systems scientist*
Golden, Wilson *lawyer*
Gosnell, Nanci Little *information technology executive, nurse*
Gray, D'Wayne *retired marine corps officer*
Green, James Wyche *sociologist, anthropologist, consultant, psychotherapist*
Hart, C(harles) W(illard), Jr. *zoologist, curator*
Hibbs, Ernest G. *engineering executive*
Hill, Mack C. *career officer*
Honigberg, Carol Crossman *lawyer*
Isaac, William Michael *brokerage house executive, retired government agency administrator*
Johnson, William David *retired academic administrator*
Jones, Linda R. Wolf *consulting company executive*
Jones, Russel Cameron *civil engineer, educator*
Kaplow, Herbert Elias *journalist*
Klingman, Charles David *health facility administrator*
Klopfenstein, Rex Carter *electrical engineer*
Kurtzke, John Francis, Sr. *neurologist, epidemiologist*
Lefrak, Edward Arthur *cardiovascular and thoracic surgeon*
Leighton, Frances Spatz *writer, journalist*
Lorenzo, Michael *engineer, real estate broker, government official*
Lotz, Denton *minister, church official*
Luchini, Joseph S. *lawyer*
Malek, M. Mike *medical association administrator*
Martin, Lisa Marie *sociologist*
McCue, David J. *information systems specialist, entrepreneur*
McGinly, William C. *healthcare association executive*
Meserve, Richard Andrew *lawyer*
Nason, Charles Tuckey *retired diversified financial services company executive*
Oliver, Walter M. *human resources specialist*
Orben, Robert *scriptwriter, writer*
Perkins, Jack Edwin *lawyer*
Pischke, Vail W. *lawyer, judge*
Poza, Hugo Bernardo *aerospace company executive*
Purvis, Ronald Scott *financial planner, real estate company officer*
Rooney, Kevin Davitt *lawyer*
Rostker, Bernard *civilian military employee*
Roussel, Lee Dennison *economist*
Savner, David A. *lawyer*
Schoonover, Stanley R. *music educator, consultant*
Scott, Hugh Patrick *former surgeon, military officer, medical advisor*
Shipko, Janet M. *human resources manager*
Tether, Anthony John *aerospace executive*
Thomas, William Griffith *lawyer*
Todd, Shirley Ann *school system administrator*
Underwood, Paula Kay *military officer*
Van Cleve, Ruth Gill *retired lawyer*
Walker, William Woodard, Jr. *management consultant, telecommunications technology executive*
Ward, George Frank, Jr. *international programs executive, ambassador*
Ward, Joe Henry, Jr. *retired lawyer*
Waxman, Bruce I. *lawyer*
Waylonis, Jean Lynnette *elementary school educator*
Weiss, Armand Berl *economist, association management executive*
Whitehead, Kenneth Dean *writer, translator, retired federal agency administrator*
Wood, John Martin *lawyer*
Yoshimura, Yoshiko *librarian*

### Farmville

Cormier, Patricia Picard *academic executive*
Dorrill, William Franklin *political scientist, educator*
Kitchie, Matthew Anthony *director*
Palombella, Anthony Lewis *biology professor*
Stein, David Bernard *psychology professor*
Terry, Wayne Gilbert *healthcare educator, hospital administrator*

### Ferrum

Hardt, John Stephen *English language and literature educator*

### Flint Hill

Dietel, William Moore *former foundation executive*
Williamson, Richard Hall *federal agency administrator*

### Floyd

Bosniak, Murray Eli *educational consultant*

### Fort Belvoir

Anderson, Frank J., Jr. *retired career officer*
Clark, Trudy H. *career officer*
Clema, Joe Kotouc *computer scientist*
Crenshaw, Horace, Jr. *military officer*
Harms, John Kevin *lawyer*
Keeney, Leah M. *government agency administrator*
Kiechel, Walter, Jr. *lawyer*
Miglio, Sheryl Ann *computer scientist*
O'Kane, Barbara Lynn *research psychologist*
Parrish-St. John, Florence Tucker *writer, retired federal agency administrator*
St. John, Adrian, II, *retired army officer*
Tegnelia, James A. *federal agency administrator*
Thompson, Carlynn Jean *information scientist*

### Fort Lee

Corona, Joseph Anthony *operations research analyst, mathematician, educator*
Simmonds, Robert Maurer *education educator*
Sterling, Keir Brooks *historian, educator*
Wicker, Christopher Eugene *public health service officer*

### Fort Myer

Hart, Herbert Michael *military officer*

### Franklin

Cobb, G. Elliott, Jr. *lawyer*

### Franktown

Kellam, Caramine *volunteer*

### Fredericksburg

Brown, Harold Eugene *retired magistrate*
Crippen, Timothy Alan *sociology educator*
Dahnk, Jean Patricia *lawyer*
Dorman, John Frederick *genealogist*
Edmunds, Jeffrey Garth *librarian*
Eslinger-Brown, Vanessa Pauline *humanities educator*
Hajek, Otomar *mathematician, educator*
Harrod, Audrey Hunter *retired executive secretary*
Hasenfus, Harold Joseph *retired mechanical engineer, naval technical director*
Jones, Harry Edward *diplomat, writer*
Kusserow, Richard Phillip *federal agency administrator, corporate financial executive*
Medding, Walter Sherman *retired environmental engineer*
Rampersad, Peggy A. Snellings *sociologist, consultant*
Schlegelmilch, Margaret Ann *elementary school educator*
Schmutzhart, Berthold Josef *sculptor, educator*
Sisk, Fred Dean *retired cartographer*
Somma, Thomas P. *art historian, museum director*

### Front Royal

Andes, Larry Dale *minister*
Bonzagni, Vincent Francis *lawyer*
Douglas, J(ocelyn) Fielding *toxicologist, consultant*
Stevens, Loretta Marie *special education educator*

### Gainesville

Bendig, Judith Joan *information systems specialist, computer company executive*
Lee, Won Jay *radiologist*
Levell, Edward, Jr. *retired airport director, aviation consultant*
Lukowsky, Gerhard Hans *internist*
Tuck, Russell R., Jr. *college president emeritus*

### Galax

Dunson, William Albert *biology professor, ecological consultant*

### Garrisonville

Emely, Charles Harry *trade association executive, consultant*

### Glasgow

Riegel, Kurt Wetherhold *environmental protection executive*

### Glen Allen

Anderson, James Frederick *clergyman*
Batzli, Terrence Raymond *lawyer*
Cornwell, Patricia Daniels *writer*
den Hartog, Grace Robinson *lawyer*
Fife, William Franklin *retired drug company executive*
Harter, John J. *economic analyst*
Higday, Paul T. *medical products distribution company executive*
Kirshner, Alan I. *insurance company executive*
Levit, Jay J(oseph) *lawyer*
McCullough, James *composer, writer, retired art association administrator, writer*
Minor, George Gilmer III *drug and hospital supply company executive*
Rogal, Andrew L. *insurance company executive*
Shelby, Ronald Van Dorn *information technology executive, consultant*
Smith, Craig R. *health products executive*
Weaver, Mollie Little *lawyer*

### Gloucester

Hicks, C. Flippo *lawyer*

### Gloucester Point

Bush, Elizabeth Olney *marine lab technician*
Sandridge, Donald Otis *music educator*

### Great Falls

Andrews, Betty Bauserman *retired secondary school educator, real estate manager*
Bachner, John Philip *business consultant*
Cass, Ronald Andrew *lawyer, former dean*
Castro-Klaren, Sara *Latin American literature professor*
Cowhill, William Joseph *retired naval officer, consultant*
DiBona, Charles Joseph *retired trade association administrator*

### Drummond, Alexander R. *priest, church administrator*

Garrett, Wilbur (Bill Garrett) *magazine editor*
Mitchell, Roy Shaw *lawyer*
Neidich, George Arthur *lawyer*
Turner, Stansfield *former CIA director, retired military officer*

### Greenville

Todd, John Edward *retired farmer*

### Grundy

Davis, W. Jeremy *lawyer, dean*
McGlothlin, Michael Gordon *lawyer*
Shinn, Clinton Wesley *lawyer*

### Gum Spring

Dilworth, Robert Lexow *career military officer, educator*

### Hampden Sydney

Arieti, James Alexander *classics educator, writer*
Porterfield, William Wendell *chemist, educator*
Wilson, Samuel V. *academic administrator*

### Hampton

Abner, Harold Loyd *military officer, consultant*
Bartels, Robert Edwin *aerospace engineer*
Bradley, Arthur Thomas *electrical engineer*
Brauer, Harrol Andrew, Jr. *broadcast executive*
Buchanan, Alvin Douglas *music educator*
Choi, Yonghoon *environmental scientist*
Crawford, Tommy F. *career officer*
DeCuir, Bryan Jude *automotive technician, computer engineer*
Dunn, Keith A. *government agency administrator, consultant*
Fadika, Gibril Owereh *research scientist, educator*
Fox, Margaret Louise *retired secondary school educator*
Goode, Constance Loper *elementary school principal*
Harris, Carl G. *music educator*
Harvey, William Robert *university president*
Holmes, Leonard George *psychologist*
Jin, Zhonghai *physicist*
Johnson, Leona Melissa *psychology professor, researcher*
Joshi, Suresh Meghashyam *engineer, researcher*
McAdaragh, Raymon Michael *aerospace engineer, researcher*
Nazaryan, Hovakim *mathematician, researcher*
Nelson, Wallace Jay *lawyer*
Pruitt, Hollis Earl *language educator*
Refaat, Tamer F. *electrical engineer, researcher*
Remsberg, Ellis Edward *meteorologist, researcher*
Roe, Lesa B. *federal agency administrator*
Sobieski, Jaroslaw *aerospace engineer*
Sun, Rensheng *electrical engineer, educator*
Tomassetti, Benjamin *music educator*
Tripathi, Ram Kishore *physicist, researcher*
Verma, Arun K. *mathematician, educator*
Yamakov, Vesselin Ivanov *aerospace scientist, researcher*
Zhu, Weiying *engineering educator*

### Hardyville

White, Gordon Eliot *historian*

### Harrisonburg

Baker, George Harold III *physicist, educator*
Carrier, Ronald Edwin *academic administrator, director*
Choi, In Dal *music educator*
Choi, Yong-Seok *communications engineer, researcher*
Gill, Gerald Lawson *librarian*
Pappas, Eric Charles *director*
Ramsey, Jackson Eugene *management educator*
Rosser, John Barkley, Jr. *economics professor*
Wingard, Christine *music educator*

### Hartfield

Johnson, Carl Randolph *chemist, educator*

### Hayes

Casson, Richard Frederick *lawyer, hotel executive*
Phillips, Elizabeth Jason *lawyer, state agency administrator*

### Haymarket

Doolittle, Warren T. *retired federal official*
Frank, Jacob *lawyer*
Kinz, Alan Charles *musicologist*
Seely, James Michael *retired military officer, defense consultant, small business owner*

### Heathsville

McKerns, Charles Joseph *lawyer*
Stubbs, Susan Conklin *retired statistician*
Winkel, Raymond Norman *aerospace scientist, consultant, retired military officer*

### Herndon

Berry, Fred Clifton, Jr. *editor, writer*
Bridges, Roy Dubard, Jr. *former federal agency administrator*
Burns, Patrick Owen *venture capital company executive*
Douglass, Robert Joseph, Jr. *computer scientist*
Draper, William David *systems administrator*
Gilbert, Douglas Brainerd *telecommunications industry executive*
Hermansen, John Christian *application developer, linguist, consultant*
Hollis, Katherine Mary *information scientist, consultant*
Huntoon, Nancy *security manager*
Jones, Reba (Becki) Pestun *elementary school educator, music educator*
Miller, Donald Lane *publishing executive*
Parker, Kevin T. *computer software company executive*
Walker, Lawrence Howard, Jr. *music educator, department chairman*
Woerth, Duane E. *labor union administrator*

### Hot Springs

Deeds, Robert Creigh *lawyer, state legislator*

**Independence**
Craig, James Hicklin *fine arts consultant*

**Isle Of Wight**
Huber, Janet Barlow *librarian*

**Ivy**
Lord, Richard Dennis *photographer*
Wilcox, Harvey John *lawyer*

**Jamestown**
Kelso, William M. *archaeologist*

**Jeffersonton**
Armor, David J. *sociologist*

**Jonesville**
Geyer, Matthew Douglas *psychologist, educator*

**Keswick**
Nosanow, Barbara Shissler *museum program director, curator*
Pochick, Francis Edward *financial consultant*
Rafajko, Robert Richard *science administrator*
Rowe, William Joseph *internist*
Woods, Reginald Foster *management consulting executive*

**Kilmarnock**
Blake, Robin Bell *middle school educator*
Ibañez, Alvaro *patent design company executive*

**King George**
Agnew, Christopher Mack *minister, historian*
Newhall, David III *retired federal official*

**Lake Ridge**
Ingrassia, Anthony Frank *human resource specialist*

**Langley Afb**
Blalock, Thomas Sullivan, Jr. *military officer*
Keys, Ronald E. *career military officer*
Smail, Leslie Anne *librarian*
Vista, Jeff Peter *emergency medicine physician*

**Lansdowne**
Miller, Dorothy Anne Smith *retired cytogenetics educator*

**Lawrenceville**
Frye, Gary E. *elementary school educator*
Hardy, Sandra Vanessa *elementary school educator*
Williams, Harold Lee *religious studies educator, minister, coach, director*

**Lebanon**
Fuller, Wrenda Sue *music and secondary school educator*

**Leesburg**
Brown, James Robert *retired air force officer*
Budiansky, Stephen Philip *writer*
De Barbieri, Mary Ann *not-for-profit developer, management consultant*
Gunberg, Edwin Woodrow, Jr. *counseling psychologist, consultant, researcher*
Hamman, William Lesley *music educator*
Herrmann, Herbet George, IV, *music educator*
Hetzel, Alice M. *statistician, researcher*
Ink, Dwight A. *government agency administrator*
Johnson, Julia A. *writer*
Levin, Mark Reed *legal foundation administrator, lawyer*
Lobanov-Rostovsky, Oleg *management consultant*
Mahood, Ken *music educator*
Mims, William Cleveland *state legislator, lawyer*
Mitchell, Russell Harry *dermatologist*
Petranek, Stephen Lynn *editor*

**Lexington**
Barrett, John Gilchrist *retired historian*
Beckley, Harlan R. *religious studies educator*
Chambers, Jay Lee *clinical psychologist*
Cline, Philip Lee *business and economics educator*
DeVogt, John Frederick *management science and business ethics educator, consultant*
Duncan, Floyd Harold *social studies educator, department chairman, retired military officer*
Elmes, David Gordon *psychologist, educator*
Gaines, James Edwin, Jr. *retired librarian*
Hamilton, E. William *biology professor*
Jarrard, Leonard Everett *psychologist, educator*
Kirgis, Frederic Lee *law educator*
Koeniger, Alfred Cash *history professor*
Koons, Kenneth Edward *historian, educator, historian, consultant*
Krantz, Linda Law *librarian*
Leach, Maurice Derby, Jr. *librarian, educator*
Luecke, Pamela *editor, educator*
Partlett, David F. *dean, law educator*
Peay, J.H. Binford III *retired army officer*
Ruscio, Kenneth Patrick *academic administrator, political science professor*
Ryan, Halford Ross *speech educator*
Spencer, Edgar Winston *geology educator*
Stuart, Dabney *poet, language educator*
Taylor, Wesley Bayard, Jr. *retired army officer*
Tierney, Michael John *mathematics professor*
Wiant, Sarah Kirsten *law librarian, educator, director*
Williams, H. Thomas (Tom Williams) *academic administrator, physicist, educator*
Winfrey, John Crawford *economist, educator*
Young, Bruce Kenneth *film director*

**Locust Grove**
Gulya, Aina Julianna *retired medical association administrator*
Huntsman, Lawrence Darrow *lawyer, director*
Stein, Richard Louis *chemist, educator*
Walsh, Geraldine Frances *nursing administrator*

**Lorton**
Celentano, Suzanne *movement educator*

**Louisa**
Small, William Edwin, Jr. *association and recreation executive*

**Lovettsville**
Flannery, John Philip *lawyer*
Foard, Douglas W. *historian*
Ryan-Griffith, Mary Kate *special education educator*

**Luray**
Bell, Michael Joseph *business and information technology educator*
Burzynski, Norman Stephen *editor*

**Lynch Station**
Skeen, David Ray *systems engineer, consultant, engineering executive, educator*

**Lynchburg**
Alcindor, Esther *education educator*
Armstrong, Barry K. *education educator*
Bowman, Kathleen Gill *academic administrator*
Burnette, Ralph Edwin, Jr. *judge*
Cornett, Robert Arnold *philosophy educator*
Craddock, Mary Spencer Jack *volunteer*
Curtis, Carl Clifford III *literature and language professor*
Duff, Ernest Arthur *political scientist, educator*
Elson, James Martin *retired landmark director*
Falwell, Jerry Lamon *minister*
Healy, Joseph Francis, Jr. *lawyer, retired air transportation executive*
Henderson, Horace Edward *World War II historian, peace advocate*
Herndon, Merle Puckette *school system administrator*
Howell, Peggy Haas *musician*
Hudson, Walter Tiree *artist*
Johnson, Robert Bruce *historic preservationist, director, small business owner*
Mabry, Cynthia Callands *secondary school educator*
McClenon, John Raymond *retired chemistry professor*
McRorie, William Edward *retired insurance company executive*
Moon, Norman K. *judge*
Morgan, Evan *retired chemist*
Packert, G(ayla) Beth *retired lawyer*
Partie, David John *language educator*
Proffitt, John Daniel, Jr. *education educator*
Pursley, Frank James *retired personal development specialist*
Ross, Jeffrey C. *mathematics educator, department chairman*
Seay, Marlaina Joan *theater educator, set designer*
Smith, Samuel Clayton *history professor*
Snead, George Murrell, Jr. *military officer, research scientist, consultant*
Stephens, Bart Nelson *former foreign service officer*
Terzic, Petar *mathematician, educator*
Wang, Kaihong *mechanical engineer, researcher*
Womack, Edgar Allen, Jr. *energy executive, consultant, nuclear technology consultant*

**Lyndhurst**
Dieter, Melvin Easterday *retired minister, educator*

**Manakin Sabot**
Bright, Craig Bartley *lawyer*
Thompson, Walter David, Jr. *systems analyst*

**Manassas**
Bahner, Sue (Florence Suzanna Bahner) *broadcast executive*
Bruno, Irene Evelyn *mathematician, educator*
Ferguson, Whitworth III *pastor*
Finley, Lucy Layne *artist*
Foley, Michael Patrick *marketing professional educator*
Haddad, Nadim Fawzi *engineer, researcher*
Isbister, Jenefir Diane Wilkinson *microbiologist, researcher, educator, consultant*
Jong, Shung-Chang *mycologist*
Livingston, Jo Ellen Brooks *music educator*
Marshall, Joseph Roman, Jr. *electrical engineer*
Martin, Anna Marie *music educator*
Parrish, Frank Jennings *retired food products executive*
Schlechte, Deborah Whitley *music educator*
Storing, Paul Edward *retired foreign service officer*

**Manassas Park**
Wolle, William Down *foreign service officer*

**Manquin**
Osgood, Nancy Jean *medical educator, writer*

**Marion**
Armbrister, Douglas Kenley *surgeon*
Elledge, Glenna Ellen Tuell *journalist*
Groseclose, Joanne Stowers *special education educator*
Johnson, Douglas Blaikie *lawyer*

**Martinsville**
Plonk, William McGuire *retired minister*

**Mason Neck**
Mc Curdy, Patrick Pierre *editor*

**Mathews**
Busby, Morris D. *former ambassador*

**Mc Dowell**
Harkleroad, Jo-Ann Decker *special education educator*

**Mc Gaheysville**
Kemper, Diana Mede *history educator*

**Mc Lean**
Alexander, Fred Calvin, Jr. *lawyer*
Appler, Thomas L. *lawyer*
Aucutt, Ronald David *lawyer*
Auerbach, Anita L. *psychologist*
Bailar, Gregor S. *finance company executive*
Balakrishnan, Kashyap *information technology manager, consultant*
Barker, Joshua *information technology executive*
Bitsberger, Timothy S. *finance company executive, former federal agency administrator*

Black, David Wayne *lawyer*
Blazer, Randolph C. *diversified financial services company executive*
Boyd, Ralph F., Jr. *finance company executive, former federal agency administrator*
Boydstun, J. Herbert *bank executive*
Brady, Phillip Donley *lawyer*
Brown, Margaret Ann *lawyer*
Brown, Thomas Cartmel, Jr. *lawyer*
Burke, Sheila P. *federal agency administrator*
Byrnes, William Joseph *lawyer*
Cahill, Harry Amory *diplomat, educator*
Calhoun, John Alfred *social services administrator*
Callahan, Vincent Francis, Jr. *state legislator, publishing executive*
Cannon, Mark Wilcox *retired government official*
Carnicero, Jorge Emilio *aeronautical engineer, transportation executive*
Cawley, Thomas J. *lawyer*
Chang, Michael *professional tennis player*
Chapple, Thomas Leslie *lawyer*
Checchi, Alfred A. *air transportation executive, financial consultant*
Church, Randolph Warner, Jr. *lawyer*
Clark-Johnson, Susan *publishing executive*
Corson, J. Jay, IV, *lawyer*
DeGiovanni-Donnelly, Rosalie Frances *biologist, educator*
Dempsey, James Raymon *manufacturing executive*
Dobson, Donald Alfred *retired electrical engineer*
Dong, Hanmin *forest products executive*
Donovan, David P. *lawyer*
Doyle, Frederick Joseph *retired government research scientist*
Dubow, Craig A. *publishing executive*
Duvall, Richard Osgood *lawyer*
Estren, Mark James *communications executive, television producer, writer*
Fairbank, Richard D. *diversified financial services company executive*
Feller, Mimi A. (Millicent Feller) *newspaper publishing executive*
Filerman, Gary Lewis *medical educator*
Finneran, John G., Jr. *lawyer*
Forman, Lee Lavinthal *museum administrator*
Fritz, Thomas Vincent *business executive*
Frostic, Frederick Lee *strategic planning and defense policy consultant*
Gallagher, Brian *editor-in-chief*
Gammon, James Alan *lawyer*
Giallombardo, Leslie *publishing executive*
Gibbons, Sam Melville *retired congressman, government agency administrator*
Gifford, Franklin Andrew, Jr. *meteorologist, consultant*
Giragosian, C. Christopher *lawyer*
Glassman, M. Melissa *lawyer*
Gniewek, Raymond Louis *newspaper editor*
Goktepe, Janet Rose *retired financial analyst*
Gotts, Lawrence J. *lawyer*
Healy, Theresa Ann *retired ambassador*
Herge, J. Curtis *lawyer*
Hess, Adam R. *lawyer*
Hewitt, Lleyton *professional tennis player*
Hjort, Howard Warren *economist, consultant*
Hoffmann, Martin Richard *lawyer*
Horan, Richard T., Jr. *legal association administrator, lawyer*
Hudson, William L. *conductor*
Ingersoll, William Boley *lawyer, real estate developer*
Jackson, Juanita Wallace *educational consultant*
Jackson, William Paul, Jr. *lawyer*
Jayne, Edward Randolph, II, *executive search consultant*
Johnson, Omotunde Evan George *economist*
Kappaz, Michael H. *engineering and energy executive*
Kautt, Glenn Gregory *financial planner, consultant*
Kimberly, William Essick *investment banker*
Klaassen, Paul J. *personal care industry executive*
Knebel, John Albert *lawyer, retired government agency administrator*
Koehler, Robert H. *lawyer*
Kohli, Harinder S. *economist, corporate executive*
Laning, Robert Comegys *retired physician, retired military officer*
Layman, Lawrence *naval officer*
LeSourd, Nancy Susan Oliver *lawyer, writer*
Lewis, James (Jim) M. *lawyer*
Lillard, Mark Hill III *computer scientist, consultant, military officer*
Lion, Linda N. *retired federal agency administrator*
Mahan, Clarence *federal agency administrator, writer*
Main, David C. *lawyer*
Malley, Raymond Charles *retired foreign service official, industrial executive*
Mandl, Alex J(ohann) *telecommunications company executive*
Marino, Michael Frank III *lawyer*
Mars, Forrest E., Jr. *candy company executive*
Mars, Jacqueline Badger *food products executive*
Mars, John Franklyn *candy company executive*
Martore, Gracia *publishing company executive*
Mathews, Linda McVeigh *newspaper editor*
Mazzarella, David *editor*
McCambridge, John James *civil engineer*
McCorkindale, Douglas Hamilton *publishing executive*
McInerney, James Eugene, Jr. *trade association executive*
McQuade, Eugene M. *finance company executive, former bank executive*
Meltzer, Steven Lee *lawyer*
Miller, David L. *lawyer*
Miller, Donald Eugene *lawyer*
Molineaux, Charles Borromeo *lawyer, arbitrator, columnist, poet*
Moon, Craig A. *publishing executive*
Moore, Dennis *news correspondent*
Morlan, Merwyn Eugene *retired music educator*
Morris, James Malachy *lawyer*
Mortensen, Robert Henry *landscape architect, golf course architect*
Murphy, Mary *retired librarian*
Murphy, Thomas Patrick *lawyer*
Nobil, James Howard, Jr. *real estate investor, developer, broker, consultant*

Norman, William Stanley *travel and tourism executive*
Nothaft, Frank Emile *economist*
O'Brien, Morgan Edward *communications executive, lawyer*
Olson, Walter Justus, Jr. *management consultant*
Orkand, Donald Saul *management consultant*
Parshall, Gerald *journalist*
Paschall, Lee McQuerter *retired communications executive*
Paul, Andrew Robert *defense and legislative consultant*
Paulson, Kenneth Alan *editor*
Percival, Meghan Jeanne *secondary school educator*
Persavich, Warren Dale *diversified manufacturing company executive*
Porter, Philip Drew *lawyer*
Price, Ilene Rosenberg *lawyer*
Prichard, Peter S. *newspaper editor*
Reiff, Laura Foote *lawyer*
Ritter, Hal *newspaper editor*
Rose, Susan Porter *management and governmental affairs consultant*
Rosenbaum, David Mark *engineering executive, consultant, educator*
Russell, Theodore Emery *diplomat*
Safer, John *artist*
Schauer, Franz Peter *civil and nuclear engineer, educator*
Schneider, Peter Raymond *political scientist*
Schools, Charles Hughlette *banker, lawyer*
Shrader, Ralph W. *management consultant*
Singh, K. Paul *telecommunications industry executive*
Sirilla, George M. *lawyer*
Sitilides, John *government relations executive*
Smith, Esther Thomas *communications executive*
Smith, Russell Jack *diplomat, consultant*
Sparks, Robert Ronold, Jr. *lawyer*
Spaulding, Wallace Holmes *retired federal agency professional*
Stackpole, Kerry Clifford *association executive*
Stine, John Andrew *communications engineer, researcher*
Stowe, Alexis Mariani *accountant, consultant*
Stump, John Sutton *retired lawyer*
Syron, Dick (Richard Francis Syron) *finance company executive, economist*
Talbot, Lee Merriam *ecologist, educator, director*
Talbot, Martha Hayne *conservationist, biologist*
Tansill, Frederick Joseph *lawyer*
Theon, John Speridon *meteorologist, researcher*
Townsend, Christopher Gordon *lawyer*
Trout, Maurice Elmore *diplomat*
Ullmann, Owen *journalist*
Vandemark, Robert Goodyear *retired retail executive*
Van Lare, Wendell John *lawyer, director*
Verhalen, Robert Donald *consumer safety executive*
Wall, Barbara Wartelle *lawyer*
Wallace, Barbara Brooks *writer*
Wallace, Robert Bruce *retired surgeon*
Walsh, Marie Leclerc *nurse*
Watson, Jerry Carroll *advertising executive*
Webber, Diana L. *management consultant executive, engineering educator*
Weiss, Susan *newspaper editor*
Williams, John A. (Jack Williams) *newspaper publishing executive*
Wilton, Elisabeth Starr *management consultant*
Woolsey, R. James (Robert James Woolsey) *lawyer, former CIA director*
Wright, William Evan *physician, consultant*
Yancik, Joseph John *retired government official*
Yarborough, William Glenn, Jr. *military officer, forester*
You, Harry L. *consulting company executive, former computer software company executive*
Youngs, William Ellis *photographer, electronics engineer*
Zakheim, Dov Solomon *economist, government official*
Zirkle, Warren E. *lawyer*

**Meadowview**
Kingsolver, Barbara Ellen *writer*

**Mechanicsville**
Gerrish, Brian Albert *theologian, educator, retired minister*
Hinkle, Barton Leslie *retired electronics company executive*
Tromblay, Erik John *social studies educator*
Watkins, Carol A. *special education educator*
Wells, Mary Julia *psychologist*

**Melfa**
Harmon, Patricia Marie *retired special education educator*

**Merrifield**
Earner, William Anthony, Jr. *naval officer*

**Middlebrook**
Bernstein, Arthur D(onald) *lawyer, consultant*

**Middleburg**
Beddall, Thomas Henry *lawyer*
Boardman, Harold Frederick, Jr. *lawyer, retired corporate financial executive*
Langley, Rolland Ament, Jr. *engineering and management consultant*
McNichols, Gerald Robert *consulting company executive*
Parkinson, James Thomas III *investment consultant*
Sodolski, John *retired professional society administrator*
vom Baur, Daphne de Blois *artist*

**Middletown**
Morgan, Curtis Franklin *history professor*

**Midlothian**
Chapman, Gilbert Whipple, Jr. *publishing executive*
Crutchfield, George Thomas *journalism educator*
Friedel, Robert Oliver *physician*

Hall, Franklin Perkins *lawyer, bank executive, state official*
Hanes-Stevens, LaVerne E. *minister, social services administrator*
Lamont-Gordon, Melissa Lynne *orchestra director, music educator*
MacAvery, Tristan Alexander (Tristan Black Wolf) *small business owner, writer, actor*
Nuckols, Otis Wills *lawyer, educator*
O'Shanick, Gregory John *physician, medical association administrator*
Stringham, Luther Winters *retired economist, retired health facility administrator*
Wadsworth, Robert David *advertising executive*

**Millboro**
Minetree, James Lawrence III *retired military officer, educator*

**Mineral**
Donald, James Robert *federal agency administrator, writer, economist*
Mayo, Louis Allen *diversified financial services company executive*
Speer, Jack Atkeson *publisher*

**Monterey**
Akaike, Hiroko *music educator, conductor*
Tabatznik, Bernard *retired cardiologist*

**Montross**
Fountain, Robert Roy, Jr. *retired engineering company executive, farmer, military officer*

**Mount Vernon**
Belden, David Leigh *professional society administrator, engineering educator*
Rees, James Conway, IV, *historic site administrator*

**Newington**
Clark-Bourne, Kathryn Orpha *consul*

**Newport News**
Abbott, Beverly Stubblefield *artist*
Alexick, David Francis *art educator*
Anglin, Betty Lockhart *artist, educator*
Banks, Charles Augustus III *manufacturing executive*
Behlmar, Cindy Lee *medical association administrator, management consultant*
Cardman, Lawrence Santo *physics professor, researcher*
Donaldson, Coleman duPont *retired aeronautical engineer, aerospace engineer, consultant*
Eastman, John Robert *education educator*
Epelbaum, Evgeny *physicist*
Goldberg, Stanley Irwin *real estate company executive*
Harris, Charles George *research scientist, consultant*
Heuvel, Sean Michael *humanities educator*
Hightower, John Brantley *arts administrator, educator*
Hubbard, Harvey Hart *aeroacoustician, noise control engineer, consultant*
Kyte, Shannan Dyan *multimedia designer*
Le Mons, Kathleen Ann *securities company executive, portfolio manager, investment officer*
Lenwell, John D. *music educator*
Mazur, Rhoda Himmel *community volunteer*
McDonald, Karis Jeanine *elementary school educator, adult education educator*
Rossettini, Timothy James *music educator, director*
Santoro, Anthony Richard *history professor*
Schievelbein, Thomas Clayton *shipyard executive, sales executive*
Sheaks, Barclay *artist*
Snider, Diane Meier *organist, choir director, music educator*
Summerville, Richard M. *mathematician, academic administrator*
Trible, Paul Seward, Jr. *former United States senator*
Wargo, Lovetta Lynn *medical educator, physical therapist, writer*
Warren, Daniel Churchman *health facility administrator*
Whitesides, John Lindsey, Jr. *aerospace engineering educator, researcher*

**Norfolk**
Aluhamal, Alfred Z. *obstetrician, gynecologist, educator*
Adams, David Huntington *judge*
Addis, Kay Tucker *newspaper editor*
Albert, Alan Dale *lawyer*
Andrews, Mason Cooke *mayor, obstetrician, gynecologist, educator*
Baird, Edward Rouzie, Jr. *retired lawyer*
Barry, Richard Francis III *publishing executive*
Batten, Frank *newspaper publisher, cable broadcaster*
Bishop, Bruce Taylor *lawyer*
Blount, Robert Haddock *management consultant, retired military officer*
Bonney, Hal James, Jr. *federal judge*
Bourie, Elizabeth Conley *gifted resource specialist*
Bucher, Katherine Toth *educational association administrator, librarian*
Byrne, William Andrew *historian, educator*
Combs, Charles Donald *academic administrator*
Corcoran, Andrew Patrick, Jr. *lawyer*
Cranford, Page Deronde *lawyer*
Davis, Russell Haden *psychotherapist, consultant*
Davis, Terry Hunter, Jr. *lawyer*
Dennison, Stanley Scott *retired forest products company executive, consultant*
Dhali, Shirshak Kumar *engineering educator*
Dimino, Joseph C. *lawyer*
Drescher, John Webb *lawyer*
Dungan, William Joseph, Jr. *insurance agent, educator, economist*
Earl, Archie William, Sr. *mathematician, educator*
Fabrizio, Michael Dean *urologist*
Fang, Ming *mathematics professor*
Farmer, Evan R. *dermatologist, researcher*
Faulconer, Robert Jamieson *pathologist, educator*
Gallagher, Carol Joy *bishop*

Goode, David Ronald *transportation company executive*
Grierson, Kevin William *lawyer*
Griffith, Charles Dee, Jr. *state official*
Haoudi, Abdelali *science educator*
Harper, William Thomas III *psychologist, educator*
Hartman, Deanna Mears *retired family counselor, addiction counselor*
Heck, Henry D'Arcy *retired toxicologist, consultant*
Hilliard-Bradley, Yvonne *library administrator*
Hirrel, Leo P. *historian, retired military officer*
Holloway, John Early *lawyer*
Hood, Antoinette Foote *dermatologist*
Hu, Fang Q. *adult education educator*
Jackson, Raymond A. *federal judge*
James, Gus John, II, *lawyer*
Jeng, Hueiwang Cook *environmental science professor*
Karim, Mohammad Ataul *electrical engineering educator, researcher*
Kernan, William Frank *career officer*
Klein, Nancy Kirkland *choral music educator*
Koch, James Verch *academic administrator, economist*
Kreger, David Lawrence *gastroenterologist*
Lester, Richard Garrison *radiologist, educator*
Magee, Kathleen S. *foundation executive*
Magee, William Preston, Jr. *plastic surgeon*
Maly, Kurt John *computer science educator*
Mark, Peter *performing company executive, conductor*
McCune, Thomas Robert *nephrologist, medical educator*
McDemmond, Marie Valentine *academic administrator, consultant*
McKee, Timothy Carlton *taxation educator*
McKinney, Sueanne E. *education educator*
McKinnon, Arnold Borden *retired transportation company executive*
Meyers, Carolyn Winstead *academic administrator, mechanical engineer, educator*
Miller, Khadijah Olivia *education educator*
Moorman, Charles W. *transportation executive*
Morgan, Henry Coke, Jr. *judge*
Musgrave, Thea *composer, conductor*
Nathman, John B. *career military officer*
Neumann, Serina Ann Louise *psychologist, researcher*
Nixon, Patricia Saunders *music educator, actress*
Noginov, Mikhail A. *physicist, researcher, educator*
Oehninger, Sergio C. *endocrinologist, obstetrician, gynecologist*
Oelberg, David George *neonatologist educator, researcher*
Padgett, John David *lawyer*
Panneton, Jean M. *vascular surgeon*
Parker, Richard Wilson *lawyer, retired rail transportation executive*
Pearson, John Yeardley, Jr. *lawyer*
Poston, Anita Owings *lawyer*
Quinlan, Kenneth J., Jr. *military officer*
Rabadi, Ghaith *engineering educator, consultant*
Reason, J. Paul *naval officer*
Rephan, Jack *lawyer*
Richards, Jeffrey Hamilton *English language educator*
Rohn, Reuben David *medical educator, director*
Runte, Roseann *academic administrator*
Russell, C. Edward, Jr. *lawyer*
Ryan, John Morgan *lawyer*
Samuels, John M., Jr. *industrial engineer*
Seow, Ming-Jung *computer engineer, researcher*
Shannon, John Sanford *lawyer, retired rail transportation executive*
Sharpe, Martha Anne Smith *academic administrator, consultant*
Sims, Hunter W., Jr. *lawyer*
Sinacori, John Todd *surgeon, educator*
Sirjani, Mojtaba B. *education educator*
Sizemore, William Howard, Jr. *journalist*
Smith, Lance L. *career military officer*
Stallings, Valerie A. *physician, state agency administrator*
Steele, James Eugene *retired school system administrator*
Stillman, Gregory N. *lawyer*
Thompson, VeRita Jean *music educator*
Tobias, Stephen C. *rail transportation executive*
Train, Harry Depue, II, *retired naval officer*
Wadsworth, J. Trad *otolaryngologist, medical researcher*
Wei, Benjamin Min *engineering educator*
White, Edith Reynolds *librarian*
Wilson, Harold Stacy *history professor, writer*
Wiltse, James Clark *civil engineer*
Wolcott, Hugh Dixon *obstetrics and gynecology educator*
Young, Joy W. *gifted and talented educator*

**North**
Fang, Joong *philosopher, mathematician, educator*

**North Garden**
May, Eleanor Goddard *retired business administration educator*
Moses, Hamilton III *hospital administrator, neurologist*

**Oak Hill**
Okay, John Louis *management consultant*
Ritter, Elza K. *music educator*

**Oakton**
Condit, Robert B. *counselor*
Duesenberg, Robert H. *retired lawyer*
Entzminger, John Nelson, Jr. *federal agency administrator, electrical engineer*
Frost, S. David *retired naval officer*
MacCracken, Thomas Gregg *musicologist*
Mosemann, Lloyd Kenneth, II, *research and development company executive*
Terzian, Grace Paine *communications executive*
Travis, Tracy Leigh *emergency physician*

**Occoquan**
Nemecek, Albert Duncan, Jr. *retail executive, investment banker, management consultant*
Vercauteren, Richard Frank *career officer*

**Onancock**
Verrill, John Howard *museum director*

**Orange**
Thomas, Franklin A. III *lawyer*
Thompson, Louis Milton, Jr. *investment company executive, consultant*

**Paeonian Springs**
Sloyan, Patrick Joseph *journalist*

**Penhook**
Coar, Richard John *mechanical engineer, aerospace transportation executive, consultant*
Hahn, John William *retired insurance company executive*

**Petersburg**
Abbott-Ryan, Pat *painter, writer*
Benn, Candace Marilea *elementary school educator*
Brown, Jack D(elbert) *chemist, researcher*
Burns, Cassandra Stroud *prosecutor*
Everitt, Alice Lubin *labor arbitrator*
Garrott, Carl Lee *foreign language educator*
Spero, Morton Bertram *retired lawyer*
Stronach, Carey Elliott *physicist, researcher*
Watson, Samuel Ray *academic administrator*

**Philomont**
Kok, Frans Johan *investment banker*

**Poquoson**
Holloway, Paul Fayette *retired aerospace transportation executive*
Tai, Elizabeth Shi-Jue Lee *library director*

**Portsmouth**
Hammond, Robie Lee *health science association administrator*
Mapp, Alf Johnson, Jr. *writer, historian, educator*
Moody, Barbara Keller *systems administrator*
Nolen, Crystal Me'Kelle *poet, educator*
Paquette, William Arthur *historian, educator*
Porter, J. Ridgely III *lawyer*
Rampersaud Lundy, Sheryll *special education educator*
Wolf, Jeffrey Stephen *physician*

**Potomac Falls**
Trainor, Bernard Edmund *retired military officer*

**Powhatan**
Robertson, Penetha Browning *secondary school educator*

**Prince George**
Brown, Del M. Mauhrine *lawyer, educator*

**Prince William**
Foote, John Holland *lawyer*

**Prospect**
Shield, Julie Marie Karst *artist, educator*

**Pulaski**
McCarthy, Thomas James, Jr. *lawyer*

**Purcellville**
Grow, Robert Theodore *economist, trade association executive*
Sharples, Winston Singleton *automobile importer and distributor*

**Quantico**
Dotto, Peter Attilius *retired marine corps officer, defense consultant*
Mangan, Terence Joseph *retired federal agency administrator*
Stout, Mary Webb *dean*

**Quinton**
Hinkle, Douglas Paddock *retired languages educator*

**Radford**
James, Clarity (Carolyne Faye James) *mezzo soprano*
Kyle, Penelope Ward *academic administrator*
McNeil, Ramsey English *religious studies educator*
Turk, James Clinton, Jr. *lawyer*
Zweifel, Paul Frederick *retired physics professor*

**Rapidan**
Grimm, Ben Emmet *library director, consultant*

**Reston**
Ancell, Robert Manning *leadership organization executive*
Blakely, William D. *lawyer*
Blum, Edward Howard *investment banker*
Bornmann, Robert Clare *physician, medical consultant*
Bradley, Murray L(ee) *librarian*
Bredehoft, Elaine Charlson *lawyer*
Brennan, Norma Jean *professional society administrator, director*
Burgujian, Richard V. *lawyer*
Carey, Jack H. *publishing executive*
Choi, Michael Kamwah *aerospace engineer, mechanical engineer, researcher*
Conway, William E., Jr. *telecommunications industry executive, venture capitalist*
Dickman, Robert S. *aerospace institute administrator, retired military officer*
Di Trapani, Marcia A. *health facility administrator, community health nurse, educator*
Donahue, Timothy M. *telecommunications industry executive*
Easton, Glenn Hanson, Jr. *management consultant, federal official, military officer*
Eldridge, Gloria Nicole *health care policy expert, researcher, financial consultant*
Esh, Laura Rae *music educator*
Ewell, Dena Lynette *administrative management executive*
Fernandez, Raul J. *data processing executive*
Fitzpatrick, Thomas J. (Thomas J. Fitzpatrick) *finance company executive*

Foley, Christopher P. *lawyer*
Forsee, Gary D. *telecommunications industry executive*
Fowler, David Lucas *corporate lawyer*
Frankel, Kenneth M. *lawyer*
Gates, James David *retired professional society administrator*
Gearheart, Galen Grant *pharmacist, educator*
Grivner, Carl J. *telecommunications industry executive*
Harris, Paul Lynwood *retired aerospace transportation executive*
Harrison, William Henry *retired medical educator*
Higgs, Joey L. *music educator*
Hill, David Warren *lawyer*
Hirsch, Robert Maurice *hydrologist*
Hope, Samuel Howard *accreditation organization executive*
Icahn, Carl Celian *investor*
Jumper, John Phillip *retired military officer*
Kahn, Robert E. *electrical engineer*
Kasten, Stanley Harvey *professional sports team executive*
Keefe, James Washburn *educational writer, researcher, consultant*
Keler, Marianne Martha *lawyer*
Kelly, Thomas N., Jr. *telecommunications industry executive*
Kennedy, Leonard Jervey *telecommunications industry executive, lawyer*
Kirkland, Rodney F. *information technology executive, consultant*
Kirsch, Mark A. *lawyer*
Kramer, Kevin M. *human resources specialist, consultant*
Kramish, Arnold *physicist, historian, writer*
Kreyling, Edward George, Jr. *retired railroad executive*
Lee, Jong Rim *strategic sourcing executive*
Lipsey, Charles E. *lawyer*
Lister, Harry Joseph *financial company consultant*
Lord, Albert L. *finance company executive*
Lynch, Monique Christine *mathematics educator*
Madry-Taylor, Jacquelyn Yvonne *educational association administrator*
Maher, David Willard *Internet company executive*
McJunkin, John G. *lawyer*
Mendis, Patrick *economist, geographer, educator*
Miller, John Edward *military officer, educational association administrator, information technology executive*
Miller, Lynne Marie *environmental services administrator*
Minton, Joseph Paul *retired safety organization executive*
Mitchell, Ellen Clabaugh *investment executive*
Mogge, Harriet Morgan *educational association executive*
Montoni, Richard A. *management consultant*
Myers, Mark D. *federal agency administrator, geologist*
Naeser, Nancy Dearien *geologist, researcher*
Natale, Patrick J *professional society administrator*
Naylon, Michael Edward *retired army officer*
Pasternack, Robert Harry *former federal agency administrator*
Payne, Roger Lee *geographer*
Platt, Leslie A. *lawyer*
Pocalyko, Michael Nicholas *investment banker, venture capitalist*
Polemitou, Olga Andrea *accountant*
Posey, Ada Louise *human resources specialist*
Powell, Anne Elizabeth *editor-in-chief*
Rastogi, Anil Kumar *health products executive*
Rau, Lee Arthur *lawyer*
Ringo, Jerome *conservationist*
Rosendhal, Jeffrey David *federal agency administrator, educator, astronomer*
Ruxin, Robert H. *lawyer*
Saleh, Paul N. *telecommunications industry executive*
Salisbury, Alan Blanchard *information technology officer*
Sarreals, Sonia *data processing executive, consultant*
Saville, Paul C. *construction executive*
Schar, Dwight C. *construction executive*
Scharff, Joseph Laurent *lawyer*
Scheeler, James Arthur *architect*
Schick, Michael William *public relations executive*
Shank, Fred Ross *food scientist*
Shelton, Hugh (Henry Hugh Shelton) *former Chairman of the Joint Chiefs of Staff*
Shindler, Steven *telecommunications industry executive*
Smith, Ralph Lee *writer, musician*
Spander, Deborah L. *lawyer*
Stone, Lawrence D. *software company executive*
Studeman, Bill (William Oliver Studeman) *aerospace transportation executive, former federal agency administrator, retired naval officer*
Tifford, John Mark *lawyer*
Toole, John Harper *lawyer*
Wang, Jin *research scientist*
West, Barry J. *telecommunications industry executive*
Westermeier, John Thomas, Jr. *lawyer, educator*

**Richlands**
Thornhill, M. Jerry *mathematics professor*

**Richmond**
Agee, G. Steven *state supreme court justice*
Aiken, Peter Haynes *systems engineer, educator, architect, consultant, data engineer*
Alewine, Betty *retired telecommunications executive*
Amado, Joseph S. *information technology executive*
Aristides, Sismanis *education educator, department chairman*
Atkinson, Richard Lee, Jr. *internal medicine educator*
Austin, John D. *corporate financial executive*
Ayres, Stephen McClintock *physician, educator*
Bagley, Philip Joseph III *lawyer*
Bagley, Terrence M. *lawyer*
Balster, Robert Louis *alcohol/drug abuse services professional*
Bankos, Jean *educational association administrator, educator*

Barker, Thomas Carl *retired health facility administrator*
Bates, John Wythe III *lawyer*
Beales, Randolph A. *lawyer, former state attorney general*
Belcher, Dennis Irl *lawyer*
Benesek, John Patrick *psychologist*
Betts, James Edward *lawyer*
Black, Robert Perry *bank executive*
Blake, Peter *state agency administrator*
Blankenship, Don L. *energy executive*
Blumberg, Michael Zangwill *allergist*
Boadle-Biber, Margaret Clare *physiologist, educator*
Bohannon, Sarah Virginia *personnel professional*
Bolling, Bill (William T. Bolling) *lieutenant governor, former state senator*
Booker, Lewis Thomas *lawyer*
Bovender, Jack Oliver, Jr. *hospital management company executive*
Brackenridge, N. Lynn *not-for-profit developer*
Brasfield, Evans Booker *lawyer*
Brissette, Martha Blevins *lawyer*
Brockenbrough, Henry Watkins *lawyer*
Brown, Marilyn Branch *retired educational administrator*
Bryan, John Stewart III *newspaper publisher*
Bryson, William Hamilton *law educator*
Budd, Richard Wade *academic administrator, dean, priest*
Bunzl, Rudolph Hans *retired manufacturing executive*
Burke, John K(irkland), Jr. *lawyer*
Burner, Clara Miller *librarian*
Burrus, Robert Lewis, Jr. *lawyer*
Cafritz, Diane L. *lawyer*
Capps, Thomas Edward *utilities company executive, lawyer*
Capps, Thos E. *energy executive*
Carlton, Buzz (Clyde Gordon Carlton Jr.) *singer, songwriter, entertainer, recording artist*
Carrell, Daniel Allan *lawyer*
Carrico, Harry Lee *retired judge*
Casini, Jane Sloan *wholesale distribution executive*
Catlett, Richard H., Jr. *retired lawyer*
Chandler, Theodore Lindy, Jr. *title insurance company executive, lawyer*
Charlesworth, Arthur Thomas *mathematics professor*
Chewning, Thomas N. *energy executive*
Choi, Hongsik *computer science professor*
Clinard, Robert Noel *lawyer*
Coalter, Milton J., Jr. *library director, educator*
Cogbill, John Valentine III *lawyer*
Compton, Olin Randall *consulting electrical engineer, researcher*
Cooper, William Edwin *academic administrator, psychologist, linguist, educator*
Corona, Rosalie *psychology educator*
Cutchins, Clifford Armstrong, IV, *lawyer*
Dan, Michael T. *security firm executive*
Daniel, Wilbon Harrison *history professor*
Davenport, Bradfute Warwick, Jr. *lawyer*
DeMary, Jo Lynne *school system administrator, elementary school educator*
Denny, Collins III *lawyer*
Derry, William R., Jr. *lawyer*
Devolites, Jeannemarie Aragona *state legislator*
Dias, Fiona P. *retail executive*
DiLorenzo, Francis X. *bishop*
Doss, Marilyn Ruth *music educator*
Drain, Cecil B. *dean, nursing educator, retired military officer*
Dray, Mark Stanley *lawyer*
Dunn, Leo James *obstetrician, gynecologist, educator*
Dutz-Kohout, Elfriede *physician, educator*
Eckstein, Maya M. *lawyer*
Edmonds, Thomas Andrew *legal association administrator*
Ellis, Andrew Jackson, Jr. *lawyer*
Erb, James Bryan *music educator, conductor, musicologist*
Face, E. Joseph, Jr. *state agency administrator*
Farrell, Thomas Francis *energy executive*
Fauls, Ted (Thomas E. duB. Fauls) *lawyer*
Fenn, John Bennett *chemist, educator*
Fierro, Marcella Farinelli *forensic pathologist, educator*
Fitzsimmons, Ellen Marie *lawyer*
Fleisher, Paul *retired elementary school educator*
Folliard, Thomas J. *automotive executive*
Foster, Charles H. *title insurance company executive*
Fowler, Alpha Alsbury III *physician, researcher*
Fox, Sandra Gail *insurance marketing executive*
Fraizer, Michael D. *insurance company executive*
Framme, Lawrence Henry III *political organization administrator, lawyer*
Freed, David Clark *artist*
Freeman, Edward Carl, Jr. *music minister*
Freeman, George Clemon, Jr. *lawyer*
Freund, Emma Frances *technologist*
Fuller, Reginald Horace *clergyman, biblical studies educator*
Gandy, Gerald Larmon *rehabilitation counseling educator, psychologist, writer*
Gary, Richard David *lawyer*
Geary, David Patrick *criminal justice educator, consultant, writer*
Geerdes, James D(ivine) *retired chemicals executive*
Gehr, Lynne Connolly *anesthesiologist*
Ginder, Gordon Dean *internist, educator*
Gluck, Michelle H. *lawyer*
Goodpasture, Philip Henry *lawyer*
Goodwin, Mark B. *transportation services executive, lawyer*
Goolsby, Allen Cunningham III *lawyer*
Gottwald, Floyd Dewey, Jr. *chemicals executive, director*
Greenberg, Martin Alan *criminologist, educator*
Gregory, Roger Lee *federal judge*
Grey, Robert J., Jr. *lawyer*
Guzmàn, David R. *information technology executive*
Hackney, Virginia Howitz *lawyer*
Hagan, Michael Philip *radiation oncologist*
Hall, James Curtis *business professor*
Hall, James H(errick), Jr. *philosophy educator, writer*

Hall, Stephen Charles *lawyer*
Hamel, Dana Bertrand *academic administrator*
Hanley, Katherine Keith *state official*
Hardy, Richard Earl *rehabilitation counseling educator*
Harris, Barbara McDaniel-Wolfe *retired elementary school educator*
Hassell, Leroy Rountree, Sr. *state supreme court chief justice*
Heaton, Stuart Alan *lawyer*
Helwig, Arthur Woods *retired chemical company executive*
Henderson, Harriet *librarian, director*
Henry, Robert Randolph Ran *newswriter, educator*
Hettema, John Michael *psychiatrist, researcher*
Hettrick, George Harrison *lawyer*
Hughes, Mike *advertising executive*
Hulsey, Timothy Lee *psychology professor, director, dean*
Hunt, Ronald J. *dean, dental educator*
Ingram, Thomas Bryan *religious development consultant*
Irwin, Donald Paulding *lawyer*
Jacobs, Harry Milburn, Jr. *advertising executive*
Jamgochian, Victoria *interior designer*
Janis, William R. *lawyer, state legislator*
Jewell-Sherman, Deborah *school system administrator*
Joel, William Lee, II, *interior and lighting designer*
Johnson, Patricia Lee *mathematics educator*
Johnston, Francis Claiborne, Jr. *lawyer*
Jones, Jeanne Pitts *pre-school administrator*
Joynes, Barbara Cole *marketing executive*
Kaczka, Jeff *trucking and relocation services executive*
Kaine, Timothy Michael *governor*
Kalmanson, Daniel Patrick *academic administrator*
Karahaliloglu, Koray *electrical engineer, educator*
Kearfott, Joseph Conrad *lawyer*
Keenan, Barbara Milano *state supreme court justice*
Kendler, Kenneth S. *medical educator*
Kennedy, Patricia Berry *retired music educator*
Kevorkian, Richard *artist*
Kilgore, Jerry W. *lawyer, former state attorney general*
King, Allen B. *tobacco company executive*
King, Robert Leroy *business administration educator*
King, William H., Jr. *lawyer*
Kinser, Cynthia D. *state supreme court justice*
Konvicka, Jason Wade *lawyer*
Koontz, Lawrence L., Jr. *state supreme court justice*
Kozlowski, Ronald Stephan *retired librarian*
Krug, Jeffrey Alan *international business educator*
Lacker, Jeffrey Malcolm *bank executive, economist*
Lacy, Elizabeth Bermingham *state supreme court justice*
Landin, David Craig *lawyer*
Langston, Nancy Sue Friedrich *dean*
Laskin, Daniel M. *oral and maxillofacial surgeon, educator*
Lawrence, Walter, Jr. *surgeon, educator*
Leary, David Edward *psychologist, educator*
LeBlanc, Daniel G. *state official*
Ledbetter, David Oscar *lawyer*
Lee, Peter James *bishop*
Leggett, Gloria Jean *minister*
Lemons, Donald W. *state supreme court justice*
Levit, Héloïse B. (Ginger Levit) *art historian, journalist, art dealer, consultant*
Lingerfelt, Alan Thomas *civil engineer, real estate company executive*
Lutz, Jacob A. (Jake) III *lawyer*
Lyons, Curtis A. *archivist*
Mahoney, George LeFevre *lawyer*
Manjili, Masoud H. *immunologist, educator*
Mann, Stephen Ashby *financial consultant*
Marshall, Gary S. *lawyer*
Massenburg, Johnnye Smith *speech pathology/audiology services professional, minister*
Mattauch, Robert Joseph *retired electrical engineering educator, retired dean*
McClard, Jack Edward *lawyer*
McClenahan, John Lorimer *retired radiologist*
McDaid, Jennifer Davis *archivist*
McDermid, Margaret E. *information technology executive, engineer*
McDonnell, Bob (Robert Francis McDonnell) *state attorney general, former state legislator*
McElligott, James Patrick, Jr. *lawyer*
McFarlane, Walter Alexander *lawyer, educator*
McGee, Henry Alexander, Jr. *academic administrator*
McQuigg, Michele Berger *state legislator*
Meath, James V. *lawyer*
Melcher, Elizabeth *musician*
Merrell, Ronald Clifton *surgeon, educator*
Minardi, Richard A. (Rick), Jr. *lawyer*
Mollen, Edward Leigh *pediatrician, allergist, clinical immunologist*
Moore, Andrew Taylor, Jr. *banker*
Moore, T. Justin III *lawyer*
Moore, Thurston Roach *lawyer*
Morgan, Elizabeth Seydel *writer, educator, retired writer*
Morkoç, Hadis *electrical engineer, educator*
Morris, James Carl *architect*
Morris, James Watson III *lawyer*
Mullinax, Perry Franklin *rheumatologist, immunologist, allergist*
Murphey, Robert Stafford *pharmaceutical executive*
Neal, Gail Fallon *physical therapist, educator*
Neal, Stu M. *finance educator, writer*
Nestler, John Edwin *endocrinology educator*
Newsome, Heber H., Jr. *retired academic administrator*
Northrop, Mary Ruth *retired mental health nurse*
Nyerges, Alexander Lee *museum director*
Oliver, Amie *artist, educator*
O'Toole, Deborah Shea *lawyer*
Owen, Duncan Shaw, Jr. *internist, retired educator*
Palen, J(oseph) John *social sciences educator*
Palmer, Robert J. *corporate financial executive*
Pauley, Stanley Frank *manufacturing executive*
Petera, Anne Pappas *state official*

Phillips, Thomas Edworth, Jr. *investment company executive, consultant*
Pinckney, Charles Cotesworth *lawyer*
Pollard, Overton Price *retired lawyer*
Pope, Robert Dean *lawyer*
Powell, Lewis Franklin III *lawyer*
Pulley, J. Waverly, III, (Waverly Pulley) *lawyer*
Rainey, Gordon Fryer, Jr. *lawyer*
Ravenal, John B. *curator*
Redmond, David Dudley *lawyer*
Reed, Austin F. *lawyer*
Reshchikov, Michael A. *physics professor, researcher*
Reynolds, Sheri *writer*
Rhoads, Mark B. *lawyer*
Richardson, David L. *lawyer*
Richardson, David Walthall *cardiologist, educator, consultant*
Rick, Roseleen P. *lawyer*
Rigsby, Linda Flory *lawyer*
Rilling, John Robert *history professor*
Rinaca, James M. *lawyer*
Ritter, Robert T. *diversified financial services company executive*
Robertson, Gregory B. *lawyer*
Robertson, LaVerne *minister*
Robinson, Susan Estes *pharmacology educator*
Rohman, Thomas P. *lawyer*
Rohr, Mark C. *chemicals executive*
Rolfe, Robert Martin *lawyer*
Rowe, William L. S. *lawyer*
Ryland, Walter H. *lawyer*
Salley, John Jones *retired academic administrator, oral pathologist*
Savedge, Anne Creery *artist, educator*
Schieken, Richard Merrill *physician*
Schoonover, Philip J. *retail executive*
Schwarzschild, Jane L. *lawyer*
Scott, Sidney Buford *finance company executive*
Seabolt, Robert D. *lawyer*
Seals, Margaret Louise Crumrine *managing editor*
Selden, Jane Tibbs *biology educator*
Sharer, John Daniel *lawyer*
Sharp, Richard L. *retail company executive*
Shiembob, Mark S. *lawyer*
Shipman, Jean Pugh *medical librarian*
Simmons, Martha R. *mortgage company executive*
Sirica, Alphonse Eugene *pathology educator*
Slater, Thomas Glascock, Jr. *lawyer*
Slaughter, Alexander Hoke *lawyer*
Sledd, Robert C. *food products executive*
Slotnick, Robert D *food products executive*
Smith, Julious Perry, Jr. *lawyer*
Smith, R. Gordon *lawyer*
Smolla, Rodney Alan *dean, law educator*
Somerville, George Arnold *lawyer*
Spahn, Gary Joseph *lawyer*
Spindler, Judith Tarleton *elementary school educator*
Spinner, Steven L. *food products executive*
Sprinkle, William Melvin *acoustical engineer, engineering executive*
Starke, Harold Eugene, Jr. *lawyer*
Starr, Edward H., Jr. *lawyer*
Stone, Jacquelyn Elois *lawyer*
Strauss, Jerome Frank III *reproductive endocrinologist, educator*
Strickland, William Jesse *lawyer*
Stutts, James F. *lawyer*
Suggs, Leo H. *transportation executive*
Sun, Qiang *scientist, educator*
Swartz, Charles Robert *lawyer*
Talley, Charles Richmond *retired bank executive*
Terry, Robert Meredith *foreign language educator*
Thomas, John Charles *lawyer*
Thompson, Paul Michael *lawyer*
Thro, William Eugene *lawyer*
Tice, Douglas Oscar, Jr. *federal bankruptcy judge*
Torres Filho, Ivo *medical educator*
Toscan, Richard Eric *dean, theater educator*
Totten, Randolph Fowler *lawyer*
Trani, Eugene Paul *university president, educator*
Treadway, Sandra Gioia *library director*
Trott, Sabert Scott, II, *marketing professional, consultant*
Troy, Anthony Francis *lawyer*
Tuck, Grayson Edwin *real estate agent, gas industry executive*
Turner, Elaine S. *allergist, immunologist*
Vann, John Daniel III *library consultant, historian*
Van Neste, Karen Lane *librarian, editor*
Vaughan, C. Porter III *lawyer*
Vijayaraman, Pugazhendhi *medical educator*
Waddell, William Robert *lawyer*
Wagner, Jody M. *treasurer*
Walsh, Scott Wesley *reproductive physiologist, researcher*
Walsh, William Arthur, Jr. *lawyer*
Ward, Harry Merrill *history professor*
Warthen, Harry Justice III *lawyer*
Watkins, Hays Thomas *retired railroad executive*
Watts, Robert Glenn *retired pharmaceutical executive*
Watts, Stephen Hurt, II, *lawyer*
Wellford, Hill B., Jr. *lawyer*
Whitehurst, Lucinda Snyder *school librarian*
Wilder, L(awrence) Douglas *mayor, former governor*
Wilkinson, David Stanley *pathologist, consultant, researcher, educator*
Williams, Amy McDaniel *lawyer*
Williams, Karen Johnson *federal judge*
Williams, Richard Leroy *federal judge*
Winslett, Stoner *artistic director*
Witt, Walter Francis, Jr. *lawyer*
Wright, Wiley Reed, Jr. *lawyer, retired judge, mediator*
Xi, Lei *medical educator*
Yeudall, William Andrew *biochemist, molecular oncologist*

**Ridgeway**
Keen, Joe Louis *biology professor*

**Roanoke**
Allen, Mike *writer*
Al-Zubaidi, Amer Aziz *physicist, researcher*
Anderson, Phillip V. *lawyer*
Bates, Harold Martin *lawyer*
Bradshaw, James R. *music educator*
Brownlee, John L. *prosecutor*
Butler, Manley Caldwell *retired lawyer*

Castellani, Lawrence P. *automotive executive*
Coppola, Michael N. *automotive parts executive*
Effel, Laura *lawyer*
Fishwick, John Palmer *retired lawyer, railroad executive*
Fitzgerald, Mary Eileen *museum program director*
Glenn, Robert Eastwood *lawyer*
Gray, Jeffrey T. *automotive executive*
Hutcheson, Jack Robert *hematologist, medical oncologist*
Kennedy, Byron S. *medical researcher*
Kinzie, Brenda Asburry *counselor*
Klein, Deborah Rae *nurse*
Landis, John William *retired engineering executive, consultant, government advisor*
Lemon, William Jacob *lawyer*
Magee, A. Carter *lawyer, educator*
Manns, Essie Jeanette Delaney *advocate*
Margolin, Eric Mitchell *lawyer*
Marshall, Heman Alexander III *lawyer*
Schumm, Darla Yzonne *religious studies educator*
Smith, Nora Nunnery *information scientist, educator*
Steele, Anita Martin (Margaret Anne Martin) *law librarian, law educator*
Thomson, Paul Rice, Jr. *lawyer*
Turk, James Clinton *federal judge*
Waldron, Karen *development, construction, and management company executive*
Wallace, Linda Kay *mathematics professor*
Wickstead, Laura Stuart *librarian, archivist*
Woodrum, Clifton A. III *lawyer, retired state legislator*

**Rockbridge Baths**
Glidden, Robert Burr *academic administrator, consultant, music educator*

**Rose Hill**
Lane, Mary Winston *secondary school educator*

**Roseland**
Stemmler, Edward Joseph *physician, retired health facility administrator, dean*

**Rosslyn**
Seidel, Charles Kenneth *military officer*

**Round Hill**
Tice, Raphael Dean *military officer*

**Ruther Glen**
Unison-Pace, Wendy Jane *nursing professor*

**Salem**
Brand, Edward Cabell *retail executive*
Cirasunda, Esther Bond *librarian*
Day, John T. *academic administrator, dean*
Fisher, Charles Harold *chemistry educator, researcher*
Griffith, H(oward) Morgan *lawyer*
Pearson, Henry Clyde *retired judge*
Sailer, Rachel Ann *secondary school educator*
Selby, John Gregory *history professor*
Shaffner, Patrick Noel *retired architectural engineering executive*
Young, James Marion *lawyer*
Zopf, Eric Paul *mortgage lending company executive*

**Sandston**
Manson, Zynora Davis *music educator, minister*

**Seaford**
Jenkins, Margaret Bunting *human resources executive*

**Shenandoah**
Atkins, Denise Beth *elementary school educator*

**Smithfield**
Hoovestol, Teresa V. *reading specialist*
Luter, Joseph Williamson III *meat packing and processing company executive*
Pope, C. Larry *food products executive*

**South Riding**
Murray, Michael Patrick *lawyer*

**Spotsylvania**
Clower, William Dewey *retired trade association executive*
Hardy, Dorcas Ruth *business and government relations executive*
Hill, Jimmie Dale *retired federal agency administrator*
Manthei, Richard Dale *retired lawyer, health products executive*
Peters, Joanna Eilene *music educator*
Singleton, Tanya *nursing educator*

**Spring Grove**
Davis, Shirley Stancil *retired elementary education educator*

**Springfield**
Bartlow, Gene Steven *professional society administrator, retired military officer*
Benson, William Edward (Barnes) *geologist*
Brown, Margaret Catherine *artist*
Bruen, John Dermot *management consultant*
Campbell, Francis James *retired chemist*
Casazza, John Andrew *electrical engineer, energy executive*
Chappell, Milton Leroy *lawyer*
Chatelier, Paul Richard *aviation psychologist*
Dake, Marcia Allene *retired nursing educator, dean*
de Haan, Henry John *research psychologist*
Doran, Doris Jeanne *librarian*
Edwards-LeBoeuf, Renee Camille *public relations executive, protective services official*
Englert, Roy Theodore *lawyer*
Ginn, Richard Van Ness *retired military officer, health products executive*
Kalkwarf, Leonard V. *minister*
Khalid, Humayun *neurosurgeon, educator*
Kimball, Steven Paul *music educator*
Kurth, Ronald James *retired academic administrator, retired military officer*

Larson, Reed Eugene *foundation administrator*
Meikle, Philip G. *engineer, retired government agency executive*
Myers, Elissa Matulis *publishing executive, professional society administrator*
Price, Arnold Hereward *historian*
Quick, Danny Richard *computer systems engineer*
Sonnemann, Harry *electrical engineer, consultant*
Stottlemyer, David Lee *federal official*
Williams, Cecilia Lee Pursel *optometrist*

**Stafford**
Garrison, Anne-Marie Dickinson *middle school educator*
Williams, Carlisle M., Jr. *municipal official, insurance company executive*

**Stanardsville**
Anns, Arlene Eiserman *publishing company executive*
Anns, Philip Harold *brokerage house executive, pharmaceutical executive*
Gladstone, Arthur M. *artist, writer, aerospace engineer*
Keel, Alton Gold, Jr. *ambassador*

**Staunton**
Balsley, Philip Elwood *entertainer*
Cochran, George Moffett *retired judge*
Jolloff, Nilda Elizabeth *art educator, artist*
Lossing, Wallace William *inventor, minister*
Sorrells, Nancy Taylor *publishing executive, writer, historian*
Thompson, George Fletcher *editor, publishing executive*

**Stephenson**
Johnson, Eva Maria *retired translator*

**Sterling**
Basham, Michael Eric *music educator, director*
Bernal-Labrada, Emilio *writer, poet, interpreter, translator*
Blum, John Curtis *agricultural economist*
Chavez, Linda *civil rights organization executive*
Clegg, Roger Burton *lawyer*
Cleveland, Harlan *political scientist, public affairs executive*
Friedheim, Jerry Warden *museum consultant*
Hadden, Robert Lee *librarian*
Hough, Lawrence A. *former financial organization executive*
Jefferson, Sandra Traylor *choreographer*
Lacey, Aaron Michael *actor, director, film producer, scriptwriter*
Martin, Roger John *computer scientist*
Oller, William Maxwell *retired energy executive, retired military officer*
Schrader, William L. *communications executive*
Steffens, Brian Douglas *elementary school educator, director*
Thompson, David Walker *astronautics company executive*
Wellisch, David *Internet company executive*

**Stuart**
Clark, Martin F(illmore), Jr. *judge*

**Stuarts Draft**
Taylor, James A. *music educator*

**Suffolk**
Birdsong, George Yancy *manufacturing executive*
Bollinger, Michael *artistic director*
Bowman, Dorothy Marie *retired librarian*
Brown, Alvenice Hortense Bryan *educator*
Burd, Joyce Ann *librarian*
Carroll, George Joseph *pathologist, educator*
Hall, Wayne Michael *management consultant*
Holloway, Christopher Matthew *brokerage house executive*
Langston, Suzanne Jordan *social studies educator, department chairman*
Noblitt, Nancy Anne *aerospace engineer*
Phipps, Patrick Michael *plant pathology educator*
Picotte, Leonard Francis *naval officer*
Sorensen, Carl Edward *manufacturing executive*
Williams, Nikkia Sekeena *science educator*

**Sumerduck**
McCamy, Sharon Grove *English educator*

**Susan**
Ambach, Dwight Russell *retired foreign service officer*

**Sweet Briar**
Miller, Reuben George *retired economics professor*
Muhlenfeld, Elisabeth S. *academic administrator, literature educator, writer*
Piepho, Lee (Edward Lee Piepho) *humanities educator*
Wassell, Stephen Robert *mathematics professor, researcher*

**Swoope**
Avery, Robert Newell *sculptor*

**Tappahannock**
McGuire, Lillian Hill (Lillian Elizabeth Hill McGuire) *historian, researcher, retired education educator, writer*

**Tazewell**
Claytor, Katherine W. Moss *secondary school educator*
Weeks, Ross Leonard, Jr. *museum executive*

**The Plains**
Gibbons, John Howard (Jack Gibbons) *federal official, physicist*

**Triangle**
Thomas, Lindsey Kay, Jr. *research ecology biologist, educator, consultant*

**Upperville**
Johnson, Manuel Holman, Jr. *government official, economics educator, business executive*

Powell Gebhard, Joy Lee (Bok Sin Lee) *small business owner*
Ross, John Emerson *public relations executive, writer*

**Victoria**
McLaughlin, Sally Crump *elementary school educator*

**Vienna**
Allen, Jane Folger *psychologist*
Anderson, Eric C. *aerospace transportation executive*
Beyer, Barbara Lynn *transportation executive, consultant*
Bhide, Manohar Gopal *nuclear scientist, educator*
Burr, Ronald Edwin *publisher*
Chandler, Hubert Thomas *former army officer*
Cook, Jane Hampton *communications consultant*
DeWitt, Charles Barbour *federal official*
Dolan, William D. III *lawyer*
Edwards, Phillip Milton *retired import/export company executive*
Gardenier, John Stark *statistician, philosopher, researcher, writer*
Gardenier, Turkan Kumbaraci *statistician, researcher*
Gary, Stuart Hunter *lawyer*
Gavin, Donald Glenn *lawyer, educator*
Higginbotham, Wendy Jacobson *legislative staff member, writer*
Hock, Randolph Edward *adult education educator, writer*
Jenkins, Robert Gordon *retired military officer, federal official*
Jones, Terrence Dale *foundation executive, consultant*
Kader, Nancy Stowe *nursing consultant, bioethicist, philosopher*
Keiser, Bernhard Edward *engineering executive, communications engineer, consultant*
Kinsolving, Sylvia Crockett *musician, educator*
Kropp, Edward H. *education educator, consultant*
Kumar, Verinder *accountant, financial executive*
Liu, Cejun *science educator, researcher, program analyst*
Mackesey, Daniel R. *lawyer*
Maguire, Margaret Louise *lawyer*
Maiwurm, James John *lawyer*
Marx, Gary Dean *educational consultant, futurist, think-tank executive*
Mc Arthur, George *journalist*
McElveen, Joseph James, Jr. *journalist, writer, newscaster, educator*
Monroe, Robert Rawson *national security consultant*
Olshaker, Mark Bruce *scriptwriter, filmmaker*
Peters, Geoffrey Wright *lawyer, fundraising executive*
Razzano, Frank Charles *lawyer*
Rogers, Raymond Jesse *retired federal railroad associate administrator*
Salah, Sagid *retired nuclear engineer*
Schwartz, Philip *lawyer*
Schwartz, Richard Harvey *pediatrician*
Sheinbaum, Gilbert Harold *international management consultant*
Titus, Bruce Earl *lawyer*
Townsend, Irene Fogleman *accountant, tax specialist*
Tyler, Robert R. *psychologist, consultant*
Walsh, William L., Jr. *lawyer*
Webb, William Loyd, Jr. *retired military officer*
Welters, Anthony *health services executive*
Whitaker, Thomas Patrick *lawyer*
Wiesnet, Donald Richard *retired hydrologist*
Woodward, Kenneth Emerson *retired mechanical engineer*
Yamaguchi, Yuriko Fujita *artist*
Yurow, Michael Jay *lawyer*

**Virginia Beach**
Adams, David Franklyn *music educator*
Alexander, William Powell *business advisor*
Antol, Joseph J. *artist*
Apperson, Jack Alfonso *retired army officer, management executive*
Baldwin, Stanley F. *lawyer*
Barney, Michael E. *lawyer*
Bradshaw, Denis James *engineer, graphic designer*
Carlston, John A. *allergist*
Christiansen, Margaret Louise *law librarian, lawyer*
Christy, Larry Todd *publisher*
Denzler, James Wyatt *pharmacist*
Dixon, John Spencer *performing arts association administrator*
Fink, Eloise Bradley *art director*
Forbes, Cynthia Ann *music educator*
Friedman, Andrew Mitchell *director housing and neighborhood preservation*
Garcia, Franc C. *music educator, director*
Gardner, Karen High *special education educator*
Goffigan, Christopher Wayne *research associate*
Gregory, Roger Thorpe *surgeon, consultant*
Harrell, Charles Lydon, Jr. *lawyer*
Hilgers, John Jack William *management and transportation consultant*
Jones, Robert Clair *middle school educator*
Jones, Robert Griffith *law educator, mayor*
Kennedy, David W. *marketing professional*
Lewis, Donald Sykes, Jr. *artist*
Lowe, Cameron Anderson *dentist, endodontist, educator*
Lutsyshyn, Oksana *concert pianist, organist*
McDaniel, David Henry *physician*
McDonald, Linda L. *massage therapist*
McWaters, Jeffrey L. *healthcare executive*
Melsheimer, Mel P(owell) *venture capitalist*
Melvin, Carole Ramey *educational consultant*
Morgan, Raymond Franklin *education educator*
Oberndorf, Meyera E. *mayor*
Panoff, Stephen Edward *music educator*
Pickett, Owen Bradford *lawyer, former congressman*
Poe, Kenneth Donovan *secondary school educator*
Prescott, David I. C., Jr. *music educator*
Pugsley, Richard Dallas *mathematics professor*
Robertson, Pat (Marion Gordon Robertson) *religious broadcasting executive, university president and chancellor*

Schreiber, Mark Traudt *psychiatrist*
Sekulow, Jay Alan *lawyer*
Selig, William George *academic administrator*
Seward, William W(ard), Jr. *writer, educator*
Snead, David N. *music educator*
Spitzli, Donald Hawkes, Jr. *lawyer*
Spivak, Maurice Sidney *civil engineer, consultant*
Stansberry, James Wesley *air force officer*
Stanton, Pamela Freeman *interior designer, writer*
Taylor, Lewis Jerome, Jr. *retired priest*
Tuskey, Laura Jeanne *music educator, pharmacologist*
Ventura, Roland P. *music educator*
Von Mosch, Wanda Gail *middle school educator*
Watkins, Brenda L. *music educator*
Weber, Alban *professional society administrator, lawyer*
Wick, Robert Thomas *retired food service executive*
Williams, John Rodman *theologian, educator, clergyman*
Ziegler, Rochelle Elizabeth *special education educator*

**Wallops Island**
Krause, David John *aerospace engineer, director*

**Ware Neck**
McVey, Henry Hanna III *retired lawyer*
Tabb, Waller Crockett *retired allergist, retired immunologist*

**Warrenton**
Brimelow, Peter *journalist*
Gullace, Marlene Frances *systems engineer, consultant*
Malmgren, Harald Bernard *economist*
Otallah, John August *school psychologist*
Pribram, Karl Harry *neuroscience and psychology educator, brain researcher*
Uygur, Mustafa Eti *engineering educator*

**Washington**
Arbelbide, C(indy) L(ea) *librarian, historian, author*

**Waynesboro**
Dillon, William Henry *retired secondary school educator*
Lane, Lawrence Jubin *retired electrical engineer, consultant*
Wade, Dianne Elizabeth *secondary school educator*

**Weems**
Martin, William Raymond *retired financial manager*

**Weyers Cave**
Wright, James Nash *healthcare educator, psychologist*

**White Stone**
Duer, Ellen Ann Dagon *anesthesiologist, general practitioner*
Sparks, Kenneth R. *association executive*
Wroth, James Melvin *retired military officer*

**Williamsburg**
Aaron, Bertram Donald *engineering executive, management consultant*
Ackerman, Lennis Campbell *retired management consultant*
Ainscough, Thomas Lee, Jr. *business educator, internet marketing consultant*
Aldrow-Liput, Priscilla Reese *retired elementary school educator*
Axtell, James Lewis *history professor*
Ball, Donald L. *retired language educator*
Barausky, Kenneth P. *aerospace company executive*
Blakey, Michael Louis *anthropologist, educator*
Brooks, Philip Coolidge, Jr. *archivist, curator, historian*
Calver, Richard Allen *retired dean*
Campbell, Colin Goetze *foundation president*
Cauthen, Charles Edward, Jr. *retired retail executive, management consultant*
Chandler, Kimberley Lynn *educational association administrator*
Chappell, Miles Linwood, Jr. *art historian, educator*
Christison, Muriel Branham *retired museum director, education educator*
Church, Dale Walker *lawyer*
Clark, Morton Hutchinson *lawyer*
Cohen, Lewis Carroll *sculptor, educator*
Coleman, Henry Edwin *art educator*
Connell, Alastair McCrae *physician*
Crapol, Edward P. *history professor*
Davis, Richard Bradley *pathologist, educator, internist*
Eliason, Nancy Carol *education consultant*
Farrar, John Thruston *health facility administrator*
Fedorov, Andriy Yuri *computer scientist, researcher*
Flanders, Raymond Alan *dentist, governmental health agency administrator*
Gavaler, Joan Susan *dance educator*
Gentry, James William *retired state agency administrator*
Gordon, Baron Jack *stockbroker*
Gottfried, Mark Ellis *accountant, consultant*
Gough, Carolyn Harley *library director*
Graham, David Browning *lawyer*
Griffith, Melvin Eugene *entomologist, public health service officer*
Guastaferro, Angelo *space science administrator, consultant*
Hargrove, Roy Belmont III *stockbroker*
Herbert, Albert Edward, Jr. *interior and industrial designer*
Herrmann, Benjamin Edward *former insurance executive*
Hight, Orian Langley *retired education educator*
Hoffman, Ronald *historian, educator*
Holmes, David Lynn *religion educator*
Holstein, William Kurt *business administration educator*
Hoving, John Hannes Forester *consulting firm executive*

Jacoby, William Jerome, Jr. *internist, retired military officer*
Kottas, John Frederick *business administration educator*
Krakauer, Sarah Yael *psychologist*
Landen, Robert Geran *retired historian, academic administrator*
Lange, Carl James *retired psychology professor*
Lorenz, Hans Ernest *photographer*
Maloney, Milford Charles *retired internal medicine educator*
Marcus, Paul *law educator*
Margolin, Robert Jeremy *lawyer*
McCarthy, Connie Kearns *university librarian*
McGiffert, Michael *retired historian*
McLennan, Barbara Nancy *tax specialist*
Merritt, James Edward *lawyer*
Messmer, Donald Joseph *business management educator, marketing consultant*
Moorman, John A. *librarian*
Morris, Robert Louis *management consultant*
Nettels, Elsa *English language educator*
Nichol, Eugene R. *academic administrator*
Nichol, Gene Ray, Jr. *academic administrator, law educator*
Novikova, Irina *science educator*
O'Connell, William Edward, Jr. *retired finance educator*
Paige, Hilliard Wegner *corporate financial executive, consultant*
Pearson, Roy Laing *business administration educator*
Reveley, Walter Taylor III *dean, law educator*
Ringlesbach, Dorothy Louise *retired nurse, writer*
Roberson, Robert S. *investment company executive*
Robinson, Jay (Jay Thurston Robinson) *artist*
Rodman, Leiba *mathematician*
Sherman, Richard Beatty *historian, educator*
Smith, Roger Winston *retired political theory educator*
Smith, William Henry Preston *freelance/self-employed writer, editor, former telecommunications industry executive*
Spencer, Donald Spurgeon *historian, academic administrator*
Spitzer, Cary Redford *avionics consultant, electrical engineer*
Starnes, William Herbert, Jr. *chemist, educator*
Starry, Donn Albert *retired aerospace corporate executive, retired military officer*
Steinsmith, William *internist, research scientist*
Sullivan, Timothy Jackson *lawyer, educator, retired academic administrator*
Wallach, Alan *art historian, educator*

**Winchester**
Aiosa, Charlotte Nelson *music educator*
Bechamps, Gerald Joseph *surgeon*
Behr, Ken *religious organization administrator*
Bonometti, Robert John *technology management and strategy executive*
Byrd, Harry Flood, Jr. *publishing executive, retired senator*
Engelage, James Roland *management consultant*
Gaither, George Manney *marketing consultant*
Havrda, Dawn E. *pharmacist, educator*
Helentjaris, Diane *physician*
Holland, James Tulley *retired plastics company executive*
Holman, Karen Marie Anderson *purchasing agent*
Hughes, Donna Jean *librarian*
Kidd, Robert Scott *pharmacist, educator*
Lin, Susan Hamady *occupational therapist, educator*
Ludwig, George Harry *retired physicist, electrical engineer*
Meschutt, David Randolph *historian*
Nelson, Paul D. *retired religious organization administrator*
Ojeda Eiseley, Jaime de *former Spanish ambassador, educator*
Pulliam Plummer, Joyce *medical technician*
Tisinger, Catherine Anne *retired history professor*
Zimmermann, Laura *psychology professor, researcher*

**Wise**
Benke, Robin Paul *librarian*
Michael, George Joseph *political science professor*
Seay, Joseph Daniel *music educator*
Smiddy, Joseph Charles *retired academic administrator*

**Woodberry Forest**
Campbell, Dennis Marion *academic administrator, educator, theologian*

**Woodbridge**
Andrews, Michael William *library and information scientist*
Binder, L. James *retired magazine editor, journalist*
Brittain, Lara Michelle *music educator*
Denison, Cynthia Lee *accountant, tax specialist*
Erickson, Robert W. *military officer, educator, consultant*
Flori, Anna Marie DiBlasi *health facility administrator, nurse, anesthesiologist*
Garon, Richard Joseph, Jr. *political organization worker*
Grassilli, Leo Joseph *retired military officer, fuel consultant*
Hollingsworth, Bobby G. *career officer*
Hood, Ronald Chalmers III *historian, writer*
Kreipke, Merrill Vincent *civil engineer, consultant*
McMahon, Janet Mankiewich *critical care nurse*
Messerschmidt, William Harclerode *non-commissioned officer, musician*
Monaco, Anthony John *retired health facility administrator, writer*
Noorbakhsh, Masood *county official*
Phillips-LeSane, Fay M. *mental health professional*

**Woodford**
Orrock, Robert Dickson *agricultural educator, state legislator*

**Woodstock**
Mrosko, Matthew L. *music educator*
Walton, Morgan Lauck III *lawyer*

## Yorktown

Douthat, Rebecca Arlene *retired secondary school educator*
Elmahboub, Widad Ibrahim *science educator*
Goetz, Kevin Edward *instructional specialist*
Gross, Leroy *retired sugar company executive*
Kirsch, Darren Matthew *music educator*
Lee, Veverlyn A. *history educator*
Romjue, John Lawson *historian, writer*
Wood, James Edward, Jr. *religion educator, author*

# WASHINGTON

## Anacortes

Cavanaugh, Michael Everett *lawyer, arbitrator, mediator*
Felger, Ralph William *education educator, retired military officer*
Glein, Richard Jeriel, Sr. *lawyer*
Higgins, Robert (Robert Walter Higgins) *career officer, physician*
Hoffmann, Manfred Walter *consulting company executive*
Mc Cracken, Philip Trafton *sculptor*
Puglisi, Melany P. *marine chemical ecologist, researcher*
Randolph, Carl Lowell *chemicals executive*

## Arlington

Bullington, Gayle Rogers *writer, researcher*
Hedman, Zoe Ann *retired literature and language educator, artist*
Randall, Beatrice Janet *retired secondary school educator*

## Auburn

Butz, Gloria K. *elementary school educator*
Nazaire, Michel Harry *physician*
Sims, Marcie Lynne *language educator, writer*
Whitmore, Donald Clark *retired engineer*

## Bainbridge Island

Berg, Walter Louis *retired history professor*
Bowden, William Darsie *retired interior designer*
Carlson, Robert Michael *artist*
Fischer, Thomas Covell *law educator, consultant, writer*
Hart-Duling, Jean Macaulay *clinical social worker*
Johnson, Christine Vaughn *secondary school educator*
Skotheim, Robert Allen *botanist, educator*

## Battle Ground

Ezelle, Robert Eugene *diplomat*
Hansen, James Lee *sculptor*

## Belfair

Hager, Robert Worth *retired aerospace transportation executive*

## Bellevue

Andersen, James A. *retired state supreme court justice*
Armstrong, Ronald E. *corporate financial executive*
Arnold, Ronald Henri *nonprofit organization executive, consultant*
Berkley, James Donald *clergyman*
Carlson, Curtis Eugene *orthodontist, periodontist*
Christianson, Jeffrey A. *lawyer*
Clay, Orson C. *insurance company executive, director*
Cohen, Bram *web programmer*
Connors, John G. *former computer software company executive*
Day, Lawrence Elwood *technical manager*
George, Roger Allen *communications educator*
Graham, John Robert, Jr. *financial executive*
Hackett, Carol Ann Hedden *physician*
Hackett, John Peter *dermatologist*
Hall, Eleanor Williams *public relations executive*
Hannah, Lawrence Burlison *lawyer*
Kari, Donald G. *lawyer*
Marosan, George *plastic surgeon*
Morie, G. Glen *lawyer, manufacturing executive*
Myhrvold, Nathan P. *technology executive*
Olson, Robert William *writer, retired counselor*
Parks, Donald Lee *mechanical engineer, human factors engineer*
Phillips, Zaiga Alksnis *pediatrician*
Pigott, Charles McGee *transportation equipment manufacturing executive*
Pigott, Mark C. *automotive executive*
Plimpton, Thomas E. *automotive executive*
Pool, David *software executive*
Porad, Francine Joy *poet, painter*
Reynolds, Stephen Philip *utility company executive*
Rundell, Arden Grabke *musician*
Sebris, Robert, Jr. *lawyer*
Shifrin, Donald Lee *pediatrician*
Simonyi, Charles *software engineer*
Sweeney, David Brian *lawyer*
Tembreull, Michael A. *automotive executive*
Thompson, Winston Mark Obed *entomologist, consultant, writer*
Tian, Hongqi *application developer, researcher*
Valdman, Bertrand A. *utilities executive*
Walsmith, Charles Rodger *psychologist, educator*
Wang, Xing *power systems engineer*
Warren, James Ronald *retired museum director, journalist*
Wells-Henderson, Ronald John *investment counselor*
Westergaard, George Henry *secondary school educator*
Whatmore, George Bernard *research scientist, writer, internist*
Williamson, Charles R. *retired energy company executive*

## Bellingham

Anderson, David Bowen *lawyer*
Bourm, Roger Michael *real estate broker, investor, property manager*
Brakke, Myron Kendall *retired research chemist, educator*
Burdge, Rabel James *sociology educator*

Clark-Langager, Sarah Ann *curator, academic administrator*
Cox, David Jackson *biochemistry professor*
Cunningham, Mick H *education educator*
Feodorov, John *artist*
Hansen, Leonard Joseph *writer, journalist, editor, communications executive*
Howe, Warren Billings *physician*
Jansen, Robert Bruce *consulting civil engineer*
Livesay, Thomas Andrew *museum director, educator*
Madsen, Elizabeth Karlene *librarian*
Morse, Joseph Grant *chemistry educator*
Morse, Karen Williams *academic administrator*
Nelson, George Driver *astronomer, educator, former astronaut*
Packer, Mark Barry *lawyer, financial consultant, foundation official*
Raas, Daniel Alan *lawyer*
Ross, June Rosa Pitt *biologist, educator*
Whyte, Nancy Marie *performing arts educator*
Zech, Edward R. *cardiothoracic surgeon*

## Black Diamond

Walker, Minerva E. Gilara *poet, retail executive*

## Blaine

Miller, Ronald *journalist, critic*

## Bonney Lake

Aalbers-Selle, Laurie Lynn *music educator*

## Bothell

Anders, Harley Dillon, Sr. *retired federal agency administrator*
Constantino, Karen Marie *elementary school educator*
Gustafson, Alice Fairleigh *lawyer*
Hawthorne, Nan Louise *Internet company executive, consultant, web site designer, writer*
Kolker, Eugene *research scientist*
Watts, Linda Susan *humanities educator*
Wilds, Daniel O. *health products executive*

## Bremerton

Abel, Bob *physics professor, researcher*
Cunningham, Gary Allan *lawyer*
Fernandes, Phil *religious organization administrator, religious studies educator, philosophy educator, pastor*

## Brush Prairie

Edlich, Richard French *biomedical engineer, educator*
Zawodny, LaRae Jean *artist, secondary school educator*

## Burien

Burgess, Charles Orville *history professor*
Risse, Guenter Bernhard *physician, historian, educator*

## Burlington

Osborn, Kennethe C. *banker*

## Camano Island

Clowes, Garth Anthony *electronics executive, consultant*
de Vries, Rimmer *economist*
Hartley, Celia Love *nursing consultant, writer, retired nursing educator, nursing administrator*
O'Connor, Thomas Edward *petroleum geologist, management consultant*
Thayer, Thomas Manor, Jr. *artist*

## Camas

Conley, John F. *electrical engineer, researcher*
Kotsovos, Jerry Frank *retired secondary school educator*
Mancini, Richard Alan *music educator*

## Carnation

Beshur, Jacqueline E. *animal trainer, farmer, writer*

## Centralia

Buzzard, Steven Ray *lawyer*
Miller, James McCalmont *pediatrician*

## Chattaroy

Jordan, Marvin Evans, Jr. *record company executive, vocalist, actor, composer*

## Chehalis

Hunter, Glen Herbert *secondary school educator*

## Chelan

Curry, Michael W. *secondary school educator*

## Clarkston

Smith, Phyllis Mae *healthcare consultant, educator*
Torgerson, Linda Belle *music educator*

## Cle Elum

Galloway, Patricia Denese *civil engineer*

## Clinton

Powers, David Richard *educational administrator*

## Clyde Hill

Condon, Robert Edward *surgeon, educator, consultant*

## Colfax

Webster, Ronald B. *lawyer*

## College Place

Wiss, Gary Alan *language educator*

## Colville

Culton, Sarah Alexander *psychologist, educator*

## Coupeville

Lotzenhiser, George William *musician, educator, academic administrator, composer*
Mayhew, Eric George *medical researcher, educator, consultant*
Piercy, Gordon Clayton *bank executive*
Thom, Richard David *retired electronics executive*

## Deer Park

Mills, Robert Bruce (Bob Mills) *retired deputy county clerk*

## Des Moines

Tuell, Jack Marvin *superintendent, retired bishop*

## Dupont

Pettit, Ghery St. John *electronics engineer*

## Eastsound

de Boor, Carl-Wilhelm R. *mathematician*
Hoagland, Karl King, Jr. *lawyer*

## Edmonds

Bell, Nancy Lee Hoyt *real estate investor, middle school educator, volunteer*
Bondurant, Nancy Ruth *musician, music educator*
Monroe, James Walter *retired corporate financial executive*
Owen, John *retired newspaper editor*
Peckol, James Kenneth *consulting engineer*
Schmit, Lucien André, Jr. *retired structural engineer*
Thyden, James Eskel *diplomat, educator, lecturer*
Yoon, Jay Myoung *oncologist, hematologist, internist*

## Ellensburg

Carrothers, Carol Ann *special education services professional, educator*
Chachava, Maya *art educator*
Comstock, Dale Robert *mathematics professor*
Hoover, Amy Lynn *pilot, educator*
Kline, Celeste Marie *librarian*
Lindvig, Leona Mindell *librarian, educator*
McIntyre, Jerilyn Sue *academic administrator*
Panerio, Robert Major, Sr. *music educator, composer*
Ullrich, Dieter Claus *archivist*

## Endicott

Ray, Billy John, Jr. *music educator*

## Everett

Brown, Frederick Calvin *retired physics professor*
Constantine, Kevin *professional hockey coach*
Hundley, Ronnie *academic administrator*
Nelson, Carol Kobuke *bank executive*
Oliver, William Donald *orthodontist*
Olsen-Estie, Jeanne Lindell *golf course owner*
Ostergaard, Joni Hammersla *lawyer*
Smith, Thomas J. *surgeon, educator*
Valentine, Mark Conrad *dermatologist*
Walbesser, Henry Herman *computer science educator*

## Federal Way

Ballard, Ernesta *lumber company executive*
Corbin, William R. *wood products executive*
Cunningham, John Randolph *project manager*
Dooley, James H. *product company executive*
Dowdy, Robert Alan *lawyer, director*
Fulton, Daniel S. *corporate real estate executive*
Hanson, Richard E. *paper company executive*
Hogans, Mack L. *paper company executive*
Keller, James R. *manufacturing executive*
Ma, Zhenkui *remote sensing applications scientist, consultant*
McDade, Sandy D. *manufacturing executive*
Mersereau, Susan *information systems company executive, data processing executive*
Muzyka-McGuire, Amy *marketing professional, nutritionist, consultant*
Nance, John Joseph *lawyer, writer, air traffic controller, announcer, consultant*
Onustock, Michael R. *manufacturing executive*
Rogel, Edward P. *corporate human resources executive*
Rogel, Steven R. *forest products company executive*
Rossi, Ruth Harris *special education educator*
Taggart, Richard J. *corporate financial executive*
Taylor, Jack P. *lumber company executive*
Weyerhaeuser, George H., Jr. *paper manufacturing company executive*

## Freeland

Calio, Anthony John *research scientist, operations research specialist*

## Friday Harbor

Agosta, William Carleton *chemist, educator*
Daum, David Ernest *machinery manufacturing company executive*
Geyman, John Payne *physician, educator*
Hill, Ruth Beebe *editor, writer*
MacGinitie, Walter Harold *psychologist, educator*

## Gig Harbor

Bernard, Lowell Francis *retired academic administrator, educator*
Hunt, Leigh Raphael *playwright*
Minnerly, Robert Ward *retired headmaster*
Stover, Miles Ronald *management consultant*
Thompson, Ronald Edward *lawyer*

## Hansville

Blalock, Ann Bonar *evaluation researcher*

## Harrington

Nighswonger, David Glenn *music educator*

## Hoquiam

Kessler, Keith Leon *lawyer*

## Hunts Point

Ebsworth, Barney A. *retired travel company executive*

## Index

Davis, Pierre C. (Peter Pathfinder Davis) *priest*

## Issaquah

Barchet, Stephen *obstetrician, gynecologist, retired military officer*
Benoliel, Joel *lawyer*
Brotman, Jeffrey H. *wholesale distribution executive*
Cain, Coleen W. *writer, educator*

## Kelso

Janke, John Eric *secondary school educator*
McLain, Paul King *systems analyst*

## Kenmore

De Coster, Barbara Lou *retired technical services librarian*
Guy, Arthur William *electrical engineering educator, researcher*
Jennerich, Edward John *academic administrator, dean*
Sobolewski, John Stephen *computer scientist, director, consultant*
Sokol, Jennifer Marie *musician*

## Kennewick

Brewton, Wesley Hopkins (Wes Brewton) *retired chef, retired real estate manager*
Cobb, William Thompson *environmental and agricultural consultant*
Cochran, James Alan *mathematics professor, department chairman*
Hames, William Lester *lawyer*
Scott, Pamela J. *educational consultant*
Vickery, Byrdean Eyvonne Hughes (Mrs. Charles Everett Vickery Jr.) *retired library services administrator*

## Kent

Dumitrescu, Cristina M. *intensive care nurse*
Goo, Abraham Meu Sen *retired manufacturing executive*
Hebeler, Henry Koester *retired electronics executive, aerospace engineer*
Pierce, Danny Parcel *artist, educator*

## Keyport

Treacy, Gerald Bernard, Jr. *lawyer*

## Kirkland

Aikawa, Jerry Kazuo *internist, educator*
Alexander, Shaun *professional football player*
Argue, Don Harvey *college president, minister*
Barto, Deborah Ann *physician*
Brimhall, Dennis C. *hospital executive*
Chapple, John H. *telecommunications industry executive, former professional sports team executive*
Dunn, Jeffrey Edward *neurologist*
Holmgren, Mike *professional football coach*
McCaw, Craig O. *communications executive*
Mitchell, Joseph Patrick *architect*
Rich, Clayton *retired academic administrator, educator*
Ryles, Gerald Fay *investor, finance company executive*
Steinman, John Colburn *architect*
Szablya, Helen Mary *writer, language educator*
Teeley, Kevin *educational association administrator*
Tyllia, Frank Michael *academic administrator, educator*
Yamada-Fells, Mizue *music educator*

## La Conner

Garcia, John *psychologist, educator*
Knopf, Kenyon Alfred *economist, educator*
Robbins, Thomas Eugene *writer*

## Lacey

Breytspraak, John, Jr. *management consultant*
Louis, Glenn *music educator*
Ortmeyer, Carl Edward *retired demographer*
Siera, Steven G. *career planning administrator, educator*
Spangler, David Robert *academic administrator, educator, engineer*

## Lacrosse

Hagman, Betty Jo *elementary school educator*

## Lake Forest Park

Adams, Hazard Simeon *retired language educator, writer*

## Lake Stevens

Durden, Rome L. *aircraft manufacturing company executive*

## Lakebay

Schauer, Victoria Young *elementary school educator, writer*

## Lakewood

Cook, Anne Welsh *lumber company executive*
Oakes, DuWayne Earl *retired principal*
Owen, Thomas Walker *banker, portfolio manager*

## Langley

Le Roy, Robert Powell *retired minister, educator, writer*

## Longview

Uthmann, Richard W. *retired music educator*

## Lopez Island

Brownstein, Barbara Lavin *geneticist, educator, director*

## Lummi Island

Ewing, Benjamin Baugh *environmental engineer, educator, consultant*

## Lynden

Hibbs, Clair M. *retired pathologist*

## DiCerchio, Richard D. *wholesale distribution executive*
Drazdoff, Nola Gay *psychologist*
Galanti, Richard A. *wholesale business executive*
Matthews, John *human resources specialist, wholesale distribution executive*
Ptacek, William H. *library director*
Reid, John Mitchell (Jack Reid) *biomedical engineer, researcher, consultant*
Sinegal, James D. *wholesale distribution executive*
von Speyer, Jacques *financier*
Wainwright, Paul Edward Blech *construction company executive*
Wright, Theodore Otis *forensic engineer*

## Lynnwood

Bear, Gregory Dale *writer, illustrator*
Floten, Barbara Jean *educational dean*
Jenes, Theodore George, Jr. *retired military officer*
Lynch, Juneann M. *medical/surgical nurse, nursing educator*
Olsen, Kenneth Harold *geophysicist, astrophysicist, historian*
Tebbs, Carol Ann *secondary school educator, academic administrator*

## Mabton

Vannatter, David Alan *history educator, coach*

## Manchester

Fearon, Lee Charles *chemist*

## Manson

Stager, Donald K. *retired construction company executive*

## Maple Valley

Brown, Thomas Andrew *retired aircraft/weaponry manufacturing executive*
Willson, David Allen *retired reference librarian, writer*

## Marysville

Kell, Lyle Nicholas *retired minister, retired real estate broker*

## Mcchord Afb

Heim, Lori Joan *physician*

## Medical Lake

Grub, Phillip Donald *business educator*

## Medina

Dagnon, James Bernard *human resources executive*
Schlotterbeck, Walter Albert *manufacturing executive, lawyer*

## Mercer Island

Abi-Hashem, Naji *psychologist, educator*
Anderson, Peter MacArthur *retired lawyer*
Bridgforth, Robert Moore, Jr. *aerospace engineer*
Dawn, Clarence Ernest *historian, educator*
Dunner, David Louis *medical educator*
Dykstra, David Charles *management executive, consultant, accountant, author, educator*
Elgee, Neil Johnson *retired internist, endocrinologist, educator*
Gould, Alvin R. *manufacturing executive*
Kessler, Gale Suzanne *psychologist, educator*
Levenson, Robert Montie *retired physician*
Medved, Robert Allen *lawyer*
Noe, James Alva *retired judge*

## Mesa

Stevenson, Patricia Ann *elementary educator*

## Mill Creek

Latta, Diana Lennox *retired interior designer*
Stelzer, Gustav R. *retired automotive executive*

## Moses Lake

Palkovic, Francis Theodore *artist, educator*

## Mount Vernon

Klein, Henry *architect*
Moser, C. Thomas *lawyer*

## Mukilteo

Atal, Bishnu Saroop *retired speech research executive, educator*
Bohn, Dennis Allen *engineering executive*
Brown, Bruce Baden *accountant*
Liu, Hui (Robin Liu) *principal scientist, consultant, author*
White, Lowell Elmond, Jr. *retired medical educator*

## Naches

Assink, Nellie Grace *agricultural executive*

## Newcastle

Erxleben, William Charles *lawyer, data processing executive*
Patulot, Jun J. R. *insurance company executive*

## Nordland

Kramnicz, Rosanne *freelance writer*

## North Bend

Brumbaugh, Harley Aaron *retired music educator, conductor, composer, poet*
Kaplan, Donna Elaine *artist, educator*

## Oak Harbor

Daugherty, Kenneth Earl *research company executive, educator*
Meaux, Alan Douglas *retired computer technician, artist*
Miller, Robert Scott *social worker, hospital administrator*

## Ocean Park

Lee, Martha *artist, writer*

## Olympia

Alexander, Gerry L. *state supreme court justice*
Bergeson, Teresa *school system administrator*
Bloomquist, Rodney Gordon *geologist*
Boland, Winnifred Joan *retired librarian*
Bridge, Bobbe Jean *state supreme court justice*
Bruce, Robert Vance *historian, educator*
Carpenter, Stephen Hayes, Jr. *state attorney general*
Chambers, Thomas Jefferson *state supreme court justice*
Coontz, Stephanie Jean *history professor, writer*
Fairhurst, Mary E. *state supreme court justice*
Fisher, Nancy Louise *pediatrician, geneticist, retired nurse*
Gillispie, Mark A. *real estate broker*
Gregoire, Christine O. *governor, former state attorney general*
Haseltine, James Lewis *artist, consultant*
Haugen, Mary Margaret *state legislator*

Heilenday, Frank Tod *science educator*
Henderson, Bernadette Làkéy *educational association administrator*
Hutchins, Diane Elizabeth Rider *librarian*
Isaki, Lucy Power Slyngstad *lawyer*
Jackson, Thelma Harrison *educational consultant, researcher*
Johnson, Charles William *state supreme court justice*
Johnson, James Martin *state supreme court justice, lawyer*
Jun, Heesoon *psychology professor*
Long, Jeanine Hundley *retired state legislator*
Macduff, Ilone Margaret *music educator*
Madsen, Barbara A. *state supreme court justice*
McClelland, Craig Alexander *architect, educator, business owner*
McKenna, Rob *state attorney general, former councilman*
Myers, Sharon Diane *auditor*
Oberbillig, Molly Castleman *utilities executive*
Owen, Bradley Scott *lieutenant governor*
Owens, Susan *state supreme court justice*
Randlett, Mary Willis *photographer*
Reed, Sam *state official*
Roach, Pam *state legislator*
Roe, Charles Barnett *lawyer*
Sanders, Richard Browning *state supreme court justice*
Sesonske, Alexander *nuclear and chemical engineer*
Smith, Charles Z. *retired state supreme court justice*
Spanel, Harriet *state legislator*
Walkup, Hugh Robert *education administrator*
Wright, Constance Mohr *retired elementary school educator*

## Orcas

Greever, John *retired mathematics professor*

## Parkland

Johnson, LuAn K. *disaster management consultant*

## Pasco

Foley, Katherine Elizabeth *librarian*
Zacher, Irmagene *elementary school educator*

## Port Angeles

Brewer, John Charles *journalist*
McCormick, Karen Louise *savings and loan association executive*
Muller, Carolyn Rae *physical therapist, volunteer*
Muller, Willard C(hester) *writer*
Taylor, S. Brooke *lawyer*
Vermillion, Roy Alan *secondary school educator*

## Port Ludlow

Krugman, Stanley Lee *international management consultant*
Trzaska, Joyce Anne *publishing executive*

## Port Orchard

Thoman, Mark Edward *pediatrician*

## Port Townsend

Buhler, Jill Lorie *editor, writer*
Hiatt, Peter *retired library and information scientist*
Jones, John Wesley *entrepreneur*
Kooser, Ted (Theodore J. Kooser) *poet*
MacLean, Barbara Hutmacher *retired journalist, writer*
Merwin, William Stanley *poet*
Woolf, William Blauvelt *retired association executive*

## Poulsbo

Wayne, Kyra Petrovskaya *writer*

## Prosser

Cooper, Lynn Dale *retired minister, retired navy chaplain*
Proebsting, Edward Louis, Jr. *retired horticulturist*

## Pullman

Banas, Emil Mike *physicist, researcher*
Bates, Robert C. *academic administrator*
Bennett, Dick *college basketball coach*
Clement, Stephen Le Roy *agricultural researcher*
Condon, William Francis, Jr. *literature educator*
Croft, Vicki Faye *librarian*
Dobney, Fredrick John *academic administrator*
Folwell, Raymond Joseph *dean, economist, consultant*
Hinman, George Wheeler *physics professor*
Hosick, Howard Lawrence *cell biology professor, academic administrator*
Ibekwe, Abasiofiok Mark *soil scientist, educator*
Jenness, Valerie *sociologist, educator*
Johnson, Monica Kirkpatrick *sociologist, educator*
Kallaher, Michael Joseph *mathematics professor*
Kmec, Julie A. *sociologist, educator*
Kohler, Timothy A. *social sciences educator*
Laborie, Marie-Pierre Geneviève *education educator*
La Rue, George Sterling *electrical engineer, researcher, engineering educator*
Lewis, Norman G. *academic administrator, researcher, consultant*
McSweeney, Frances Kaye *psychology professor*
Medidi, Muralidhar *computer scientist, educator*
Morris, Lisa Kaplan *engineering educator, physics professor, mathematics professor*
Paznokas, Lynda Sylvia *elementary school educator*
Rawlins, V. Lane *academic administrator*
Ryan, Clarence Augustine, Jr. *biochemistry professor*
Savage, David William *lawyer*
Smith, Trenton Garry *education educator*
Sprunger, Leslie Karen *physiologist, educator*
Stock, David Earl *mechanical engineering educator*
Streamas, John *ethnic and American studies professor*
Swan, Susan Linda *history professor*
Thomashow, Linda Suzanne *microbiologist*
Warner, Dennis Allan *psychology professor*
Wright, John William *psychology educator*

Zlatos, Christy *librarian*

## Puyallup

Rink, Robert P. *secondary school educator*
Salak, Ann M. *literature and language professor, department chairman*

## Redmond

Ayala, Orlando *information technology executive*
Bach, Robert J. (Robbie Bach) *information technology executive*
Ballmer, Steven Anthony *computer software company executive*
Bradford, Joanne K. *computer software company executive*
Brakken, William *home improvement retail executive*
Burt, Thomas William *lawyer*
DelBene, Kurt *information technology executive*
DeVaan, Jon S. *information technology executive*
Driftmier, David King *data processing executive*
Fathi, Ben *information technology executive*
Flake, Gary William *computer software company executive*
Flessner, Paul *information technology executive*
Freedman, Michael Hartley *mathematician, educator*
Gates, Bill (William Henry Gates III) *computer software company executive*
Guday, Shai *program director*
Herzog, Eric Allen *marketing professional*
Heynssens, Paul Brian *lawyer, electrical engineer*
Hylbert, Paul *construction executive*
Johnson, Kevin *computer software company executive*
Kimmich, Jon Bradford *computer science program executive*
Leblond, Antoine *computer company executive*
Lee, Bryan *information technology executive*
Liddell, Christopher P. *computer software company executive*
Lomet, David Bruce *computer scientist*
Markezich, Ron *information technology executive*
Martinez, Maria *computer software company executive*
Mathews, Mich *computer company executive*
Meshii, Masahiro *materials science educator*
Muglia, Robert L. *information technology executive*
Mundie, Craig James *computers software company executive*
Nadella, Satya *information technology executive*
Oliver, Nuria *computer scientist*
Ozzie, Ray (Raymond E. Ozzie) *computer software company executive*
Shirley, Jon Anthony *software company executive*
Smith, Bradford Lee *information technology executive, lawyer*
Sobey, Edwin J. C. *museum director, consultant, oceanographer*
Sowder, Robert Robertson *architect*
Turner, Kevin (B. Kevin Turner) *information technology executive*
Valentine, Brian *information technology executive*
Vaskevitch, David *information technology executive*
Willard, H(arrison) Robert *electrical engineer*

## Renton

Greenwood, Loren *toy manufacturing executive*

## Republic

Chambers, Milton Warren *retired architect*

## Richland

Arm, Stuart Trevor *research engineer*
Bair, William J. *retired radiobiologist*
Bevelacqua, Joseph John *physicist, researcher*
Blumenkranz, David Benjamin *chemical engineer, consultant*
Brashear, Karen Kathleen *elementary school educator*
Chou, Charissa J. *staff scientist*
Corrales, Louis Rene *research scientist, director*
Elderkin, Charles Edwin *retired meteorologist*
Glennen, Robert Eugene, Jr. *retired academic administrator*
Kathren, Ronald Laurence *health physicist*
Madison, Jacqueline Edwina *librarian*
Miller, James Vince *university president*
Moore, Emmett Burris, Jr. *physical chemist, educator*
Murphy, Mark Kenneth *physicist, researcher*
Onishi, Yasuo *environmental researcher*
Peters, Leonard K. *environmental scientist*
Petrini, Fabrizio *computer scientist, researcher*
Powell, David Charles *music educator, meteorologist*
Roop, Joseph McLeod *economist*
Runkle, Robert Charles *physicist*
Shin, Yongsoon *research scientist*
Tsiklauri, Georgi Victor *physicist, researcher*

## Sammamish

Yocam, Eric Wayne *engineer*

## Seatac

Wells, Roger Stanley *software engineer*

## Seattle

Abbott, Robert Dean *psychology professor*
Alberg, Tom Austin *investment company executive, lawyer*
Albrecht, Richard Raymond *retired manufacturing executive, lawyer*
Alkire, John D. *lawyer, arbitrator, mediator*
Allen, Paul Gardner *computer company executive, professional sports team executive*
Allen, Ray *professional basketball player*
Alsdorf, Robert Hermann *lawyer*
Andersen, Niels Hjorth *chemistry professor, consultant, biophysicist, researcher*
Andrew, Lucius Archibald David III *bank executive*
Andrews, J. David *lawyer*
Andrews, Richard Otis *museum director*
Ausell, Julian S. *urologist, educator*
Appelbaum, Frederick Ray *oncologist*
Arnold, Robert Morris *banker*
Arthur, William Lynn *environmental and political program director*

Atwater, Brian F. *geologist*
Ayer, William S. *air transportation executive*
Babb, Albert Leslie *biomedical engineer, educator*
Bain, William James, Jr. *architect*
Baker, Roland Jerald *finance educator*
Baker-Johnson, Marcia J. *dental hygienist*
Bandrowski, Paul *information technology executive*
Banks, James Albert *educational research director, educator, researcher*
Barlow, Tani E. *history and women's studies professor*
Baruffi, Kumi Yamamoto *lawyer*
Bassingthwaighte, James Bucklin *physiologist, educator, medical researcher*
Bates, Charles Walter *human resources executive, lawyer*
Baum, William Alvin *astronomer, educator*
Beezer, Robert Renaut *federal judge*
Beighle, Douglas Paul *aerospace transportation executive*
Beirne, Owen Ross *dental educator, researcher*
Bell, William C. *foundation administrator*
Berger, Paul Eric *artist, photographer*
Berman, Steve William *lawyer, author*
Bernard, Eddie Nolan *oceanographer*
Berni, Rosemarian Rauch *rehabilitation and oncology nurse*
Beyers, William Bjorn *geography educator*
Bezos, Jeffrey Preston *multimedia company executive*
Bibaud, Rene *artist, performer, consultant*
Bichsel, Hans *physicist, consultant, researcher*
Bird, Sue (Suzanne Brigit Bird) *professional basketball player*
Birmingham, Richard Joseph *lawyer*
Bishop, Virginia Wakeman *retired librarian, retired humanities educator*
Blair, M. Wayne *lawyer*
Blake-Inada, Louis Michael *cardiologist, researcher*
Blase, Nancy Gross *librarian*
Bley, John L. *financial executive*
Blom, Daniel Charles *lawyer, investor, retired insurance company executive*
Blumenfeld, Charles Raban *lawyer*
Boardman, David *newspaper editor*
Bodansky, David *physicist, researcher*
Boeder, Thomas L. *lawyer*
Boersma, P. Dee *marine biologist, educator*
Boggs, Paula Elaine *lawyer*
Boman, Marc Allen *lawyer*
Borgatta, Edgar F. *sociologist, educator*
Bornstein, Paul *medical educator, biochemist*
Bosworth, Thomas Lawrence *architect, retired educator*
Boulware, Michael *professional football player*
Bowden, Douglas McHose *neuropsychiatric scientist, science foundation director*
Bowen, Jewell Ray *chemical engineering professor*
Bowes, Peter Joseph *priest, educator, director*
Boylan, Merle Nelson *librarian, educator*
Brammer, Lawrence Martin *psychologist, educator*
Bremner, William John *physician*
Breslow, Norman Edward *biostatistics educator, researcher*
Bridge, Herbert Marvin *retail executive*
Bridge, Jonathan Joseph *lawyer, retail executive*
Bringman, Joseph Edward *lawyer*
Brodsky, Anatol M. *research scientist*
Brooks, Terry *writer, former lawyer*
Brown, Michael Jay *lawyer*
Brown, Michael W. *former communications company executive*
Brown, Robert Alan *geophysicist, educator*
Brownlee, Donald Eugene, II, *astronomer, educator*
Bruner, Nancy J. *publishing executive*
Brunett, Alexander J. *archbishop*
Buck, Linda B. *medical educator*
Buckner, Philip Franklin *newspaper publisher*
Bufano, Ralph A. *retired museum executive*
Bunting, Kenneth Freeman *newspaper editor*
Burke, William Thomas *lawyer, educator*
Burns, Michael Joseph *operations and sales-marketing executive*
Burrows, Elizabeth MacDonald *religious organization executive, educator*
Butow, Robert Joseph Charles *historian, educator*
Campbell, Robert Hedgcock *investment banker, lawyer*
Card, Deborah Frances *orchestra administrator*
Carlson, Dale Arvid *retired university dean*
Carsberg, Scott *chef*
Carson, Scott E. *aerospace transportation executive*
Casey, M. Michael *food products executive*
Casey, Tom (Thomas W. Casey) *bank executive*
Catterall, William A. *pharmacology, neurobiology educator*
Chapman, Craig J. *finance company executive*
Chapman, Fay L. *lawyer*
Chapman, Larry Stephen *health science association administrator, consultant*
Char, Patricia Helen *lawyer*
Charlson, Robert Jay *atmospheric sciences educator*
Chatard, Peter Ralph Noel, Jr. *aesthetic plastic surgeon*
Choi, Jee Woong *research scientist*
Christian, Gary D. *chemistry professor*
Christiansen, Walter Henry *aerospace scientist, educator*
Claflin, Arthur Cary *lawyer*
Cline, Robert Stanley *retired air freight company executive*
Coburn, Robert Craig *philosopher, educator*
Cochran, Wendell Albert *science editor*
Coldewey, John Christopher *English literature educator*
Coldwell, Maria V. *performing arts association administrator*
Collette Breuner, Cora *pediatrician*
Collier, Tom Ward *musician, educator*
Coughenour, John Clare *federal judge*
Covington, Germaine Ward *municipal agency administrator*
Cox, Frederick Moreland *retired dean, social worker*

Creager, Joe Scott *geology and oceanography educator*
Crenshaw, Edward Lee, Sr. *aviation electronics technician*
Criminale, William Oliver, Jr. *applied mathematics professor*
Cross, Bruce Michael *lawyer*
Cullen, Jack Joseph *lawyer*
Cunningham, Janis Ann *lawyer*
Dale, David C. *physician, educator*
Dalzell, Rick *information technology executive*
Daniel, Thomas L. *zoology educator*
David, Daryl D. *finance company executive*
Davidson, Ernest Roy *chemist, educator*
Davidson, Robert William *not-for-profit executive*
Davis, Earl James *chemical engineering professor*
Davis, Jennie Sue *aerospace engineer*
Davis, John MacDougall *lawyer*
Davis, Stephen B. *Internet company executive, lawyer*
Dawson, Patricia Lucille *surgeon*
Day, Robert Winsor *preventive medicine physician, researcher*
De Alessi, Ross Alan *lighting designer*
Dear, Ronald Bruce *retired social work educator*
Dehmelt, Hans Georg *physicist, educator*
Deines, Katrina *architecture educator*
Demasi, Luciano *aerospace engineer, researcher*
Deming, Jody Wheeler *oceanography educator*
Denke, Conrad William *motion picture producer*
Denny, Brewster Castberg *retired university dean*
Desouza, Kevin Clyde *application developer*
de Tornyay, Rheba *nursing educator, retired dean*
DeVore, Paul Cameron *lawyer*
Dillard, Marilyn Dianne *property manager*
Dillow, John David *lawyer*
Dimmick, Carolyn Reaber *federal judge*
Dolan, Andrew Kevin *lawyer*
Donald, James L. *food service executive*
Dong, Nelson G. *lawyer*
Donlan, Dan Joseph *lawyer*
Doran, Charles Francis, Jr. *mathematician, mathematics professor*
Dorpat, Theodore Lorenz *psychoanalyst*
Dotten, Michael Chester *lawyer*
Duryee, David Anthony *management consultant*
Eastham, John D. *marketing executive*
Eigsti, Roger Harry *retired insurance company executive*
Eisenman, Robert N. *research scientist*
Elgin, Ron Alan *advertising executive*
Eller, Marlin *security firm executive*
Ellis, Georgiana Kehr *internist, oncologist*
Ellis, Stephen Charles *lawyer*
Ellison, Herbert Jay *historian, educator*
El-Moslimany, Ann Paxton *paleoecologist, educator, writer*
Elyn, Mark *retired vocalist*
Emmert, Mark Allen *academic administrator, educator*
Emory, Meade *lawyer*
Engel, Thomas *chemistry professor*
Epple, Steven *architectural firm executive*
Esbeck, Edward S. *retired education educator*
Eschbach, Joseph Wetherill *nephrology educator*
Estes, Kenneth William *history professor, military officer*
Evans, Bernard William *geologist, educator*
Fancher, Michael Reilly *editor, publishing executive*
Farbanish, Thomas *sculptor*
Farris, Jerome *federal judge*
Feigl, Eric Otto *physiology educator*
Feldman, Roger Lawrence *artist, educator*
Fidel, Raya *information science educator*
Fiedler, Fred Edward *retired organizational psychology educator, consultant*
Fihn, Stephan D. *internist, educator*
Fine, Arthur I. *philosopher, educator*
Fine, James Stephen *physician*
Finlayson, Bruce Alan *retired chemical engineering professor*
Fischer, Edmond Henri *biochemistry educator*
Fischer, Fred Walter *physicist, engineer, educator*
Fisher, Jeffrey L. *lawyer*
Fletcher, Betty Binns *federal judge*
Floss, Heinz G. *chemistry professor, researcher*
Fluke, Lyla Schram (Mrs. John M. (Lyla) Fluke Sr.) *publisher*
Forbes, David Craig *musician*
Foster, Barry Alan *cultural organization researcher, educator*
Fournier, R. E. Keith *biologist*
Fowler, David Covington *language educator*
Franklin, Jerry Forest *forest ecologist, educator*
Friend, Stephen H. *biotechnology company executive*
Frush, Curtis James *lawyer*
Gaffney, Joseph M. *lawyer*
Gardiner, John Jacob *writer, educator, philosopher*
Gardiner, T(homas) Michael *artist*
Garvens, Ellen Jo *art educator, artist*
Gates, Melinda French *foundation administrator*
Gates, Mimi Gardner *museum director*
Gates, R. Jordan *meteorologist*
George, Alexander Lawrence *political scientist, educator*
Gerberding, William Passavant *retired university president*
Gerhart, James Basil *physics professor*
Gerrard, Keith *lawyer*
Gerwick-Brodeur, Madeline Carol *marketing and timing professional*
Giarlo, Michael Joseph *librarian*
Giblett, Eloise Rosalie *retired hematologist*
Gilbert, Paul H. *engineering executive, consultant*
Giles, Robert Edward, Jr. *lawyer*
Gilleran, James E. *bank executive, former federal agency administrator*
Gillispie, Steven Brian *systems analyst, researcher*
Gittinger, D. Wayne *lawyer*
Glaser, Robert *communications executive*
Glover, Karen Elaine *lawyer*
Golston, Allan C. *foundation administrator*
Gonzalez, Carmen Gracia *law professor*
Goodkin, Robert *neurosurgeon, educator*
Goodlad, John Inkster *education educator, writer*
Gores, Thomas C. *lawyer*
Gormèzano, Keith *arbitrator, writer, web site designer*

Gorton, Slade (Thomas Slade Gorton III) *lawyer, former senator*
Gould, Ronald Murray *federal judge*
Gouldthorpe, Kenneth Alfred Percival *state official, editor*
Grace, Ryan Thomas *lawyer*
Gradel, James D. *lawyer*
Graham, Stephen Michael *lawyer*
Gray, Marvin Lee, Jr. *lawyer*
Green, Joshua III *foundation administrator, retired bank executive*
Green, William L. *lawyer*
Greenberg, E. Peter *microbiologist*
Greenwood, W. R. III *investment banker*
Grimley, Janet Elizabeth *newspaper editor*
Gross, Edward *retired sociologist*
Gross, Jeremy V. (Jerry Gross) *finance company executive*
Groudine, Mark Terry *oncologist*
Gunderson, Donald Raymond *fisheries educator and researcher*
Guntheroth, Warren Gaden *pediatrician, educator*
Gwinn, Mary Ann *newspaper reporter*
Halvarsson, Misha *business development strategist*
Halver, John Emil *nutritional biochemist*
Haman, Raymond William *retired lawyer*
Hampton, Shelley Lynn *hearing impaired educator*
Hands, Eric William *civil engineer, researcher*
Hansen, Richard Emory *psychologist*
Hansen, Thomas Nanastad *hospital administrator, pediatrician*
Hansen, Wayne W. *lawyer*
Hargrove, Mike (Dudley Michael Hargrove) *former professional baseball team manager*
Harmon, Daniel Patrick *classics educator*
Hartwell, Leland Harrison (lee hartwell) *geneticist, educator*
Hasl, Rudolph Carl *dean, law educator*
Hasselbeck, Matt *professional football player*
Hazelton, Penny Ann *law librarian, educator*
Hazzard, William Russell *geriatrician, educator*
Heath, George Ross *oceanographer*
Heath, Richard Raymond *retired investment company executive*
Heavey, Mike *judge*
Heer, Nicholas Lawson *language educator*
Heimfeld, Shelly *hematologist, immunologist, researcher*
Hellström, Ingegerd *medical researcher*
Hellström, Karl Erik *science educator, researcher*
Henderson, Maureen McGrath *medical educator*
Hendrickson, Anita Elizabeth *biology professor*
Henkel, Cathy *newspaper sports editor*
Henley, Ernest Mark *physics professor, retired dean*
Hermsen, James R. *lawyer*
Hill, Bob *professional basketball coach*
Hill, G. Richard *lawyer*
Hille, Bertil *physiology educator*
Hills, Regina J. *journalist*
Hilpert, Edward Theodore, Jr. *retired lawyer*
Himma, Kenneth Einar *philosophy educator*
Hineline, Curt Roy *lawyer*
Hinshaw, Mark Larson *architect, urban planner*
Hirschman, Charles, Jr. *sociologist, educator*
Hirschmann, Franz Gottfried *aerospace executive*
Hoffman, Allan Sachs *chemical engineer, educator*
Hollender, Lars Gösta *dental educator*
Holley, Rick R. *lumber company executive*
Hollinrake, John D., Jr. *lawyer*
Holmes, King Kennard *medical educator*
Holtan, Ramer B., Jr. *lawyer*
Hood, Leroy Edward *molecular biologist, educator*
Hornbein, Thomas Frederic *anesthesiologist*
Hornschemeier, Paul *graphic novelist*
Horsey, David *editorial cartoonist*
Hosken, Nancy Ann *research scientist*
Houston, Janeanne Currier *vocalist, educator*
Huston, John Charles *law educator*
Hutcheson, Mark Andrew *lawyer*
Ishimaru, Akira *electrical engineering educator*
Israel, Allen D. *lawyer*
Jackson, Lauren *professional basketball player*
Jacobson, Phillip Lee *architect, educator*
Jaffe, Robert Stanley *lawyer*
Jenkins, Speight *performing company executive, writer*
Jennerich, Elaine *librarian*
Jessen, Joel Anne *not-for-profit executive, art educator*
Johnson, Bruce Edward Humble *lawyer*
Johnston, Norman John *retired architecture educator*
Jonassen, James O. *architect*
Jones, Grant Richard *landscape architect*
Jones, Randal R. *lawyer*
Jonsson, Ted Wilbur *artist*
Judson, C(harles) James (Jim Judson) *lawyer*
Jurevicius, Joe *professional football player*
Kahn, Steven Emanuel *medical educator*
Kalet, Ira Joseph *medical computer scientist*
Kalina, Robert Edward *ophthalmologist, educator*
Kane, Alan Henry *lawyer*
Kaneko, Chris R.S. *research scientist*
Kaplan, Robert David *lawyer*
Kapur, Kailash Chander *industrial engineering educator*
Karr, James Richard *ecologist, educator, research director*
Karst, William B. *architectural firm executive*
Katon, Wayne J. *psychiatrist, researcher*
Katz, Treuman P. *health facility administrator*
Kaufman, Joel Daniel *medical educator, medical researcher*
Keegan, John E. *lawyer*
Kelly, Carolyn Sue *newspaper executive*
Kennedy, Mary Virginia *retired diplomat*
Kenny, George Edward *pathobiology educator*
Kevorkian, Jirair *aeronautics and astronautics engineering educator*
Keyt, David *philosophy and classics educator*
Khorasani, Leila *neurosurgeon*
Kido, Kenneth *bank executive*
Killinger, Kerry Kent *bank executive*
Kilpatrick, John Aaron *construction and development company executive*
Kimball, Harry Raymond *medical association administrator, medical educator*
King, Ivan Robert *astronomy educator*
King, Mary-Claire *geneticist, educator*

Kipness, Robert *painter*
Kirby, Ronald Eugene *fish and wildlife research administrator*
Kirschner, Marc Alan *neuroscientist*
Kittross, John Michael *retired communications educator*
Klausner, Richard D. *cell biologist, researcher*
Klebanoff, Seymour Joseph *medical educator*
Klee, Victor La Rue *mathematician, educator*
Klein, Jonathan D. *finance company executive*
Klein, Otto George III *lawyer*
Knechtges, David Richard *Chinese and East Asian studies educator*
Knight, W. H., Jr., (Joe Knight) *dean, law educator*
Kobayashi, Albert Satoshi *mechanical engineering educator*
Kocher, Cynthia *investment specialist*
Koegen, Roy Jerome *lawyer*
Koehler, Reginald Stafford III *lawyer*
Koh, Steve Y. *lawyer*
Kolb, Keith Robert *architect, educator*
Korg, Jacob *English literature educator*
Kraft, George Howard *physician, educator*
Kraft, James Allen *lawyer*
Krebs, Edwin Gerhard *biochemistry educator*
Krochalis, Richard F. *federal agency administrator*
Krohn, Kenneth Albert *radiologist, educator*
Kruckeberg, Arthur Rice *botanist, educator*
Kuhl, Patricia K. *science educator*
Kuhrau, Edward W. *lawyer*
Kunkel, Georgie Bright *freelance writer, retired counselor*
Kwiram, Alvin L. *physical chemistry professor, university official*
Lacitis, Erik *journalist*
Landefeld, Stewart M. *lawyer*
Larrabee, Wayne Fox, Jr. *facial plastic surgeon*
Larson, Anne M. *internist*
Larson, Eric B. *medical educator, director*
Law, Marcia Elizabeth *rehabilitation services professional*
Lazowska, Edward Delano *computer science educator*
Leale, Olivia Mason *small business owner, import marketing executive*
Lee, Cheegwan *environmental engineer, consultant*
Lee, Conrad S. *councilman*
Lee, John Marshall *mathematics professor*
Leitzell, Terry Lee *lawyer*
Leland, David D. *timber company executive*
Lemire, Ronald John *pediatrician, educator*
Lemly, Thomas Adger *lawyer*
Lidstrom, Mary E. *chemical engineering professor, microbiology professor*
Lincoln, Howard *manufacturing company and sports team executive*
Lindner, Karen Carr *psychologist, consultant*
Lisbakken, James Robert *lawyer*
Locke, Gary F. *lawyer, former governor*
Lombard, Kenneth T. *beverage company executive*
Longbrake, William Arthur *bank executive*
Losey, Beverley Brown *lawyer*
Lovett, Wendell Harper *architect, educator*
Loyer Nelson, Edith Merilynn *retired social worker*
Lubatti, Henry Joseph *physicist, researcher*
Lundin, Norman Kent *artist, educator*
MacLachlan, Douglas Lee *marketing educator*
Mahdaviani, Miriam *choreographer, educator*
Maier, Ronald Vitt *surgeon, educator*
Maleng, Norm *prosecutor*
Malins, Donald Clive *biochemist, researcher*
Mankoff, David Abraham *nuclear medicine physician*
Manning, J. Richard *lawyer*
Marchese, Lisa Marie *lawyer, educator*
Marshall, Donald E. *mathematics professor*
Martin, George Monroe *pathologist, gerontologist, educator*
Martínez, Yolanda R. *social services administrator*
Mason, Marilyn Gell *library administrator, writer, consultant*
Mason, Robert McSpadden *information scientist, educator, dean*
Matchett, William H(enry) *English literature educator*
Mathews, Sylvia Mary *foundation administrator*
Matsen, Frederick Albert III *orthopedic educator*
McCann, Richard Eugene *lawyer*
McConnell, J. Daniel *marketing and public relations professional*
McConney, Mary E. *information technology executive*
McCune, Philip Spear *lawyer*
McDermott, Susanne Finckh *fisheries biologist*
Mc Feron, Dean Earl *mechanical engineer, educator*
McHugh, Heather *poet*
McKay, John *prosecutor, lawyer*
McMillan, Nathaniel (Nate McMillan) *professional basketball coach*
Melo, Welton *professional soccer player*
Michael, Ernest Arthur *mathematics professor*
Migita, Russell *pediatrician, emergency physician*
Miles, Don Clifford *architect*
Miyata, Keijiro *culinary arts educator*
Monsen, Elaine Ranker *nutritionist, educator, editor*
Moore, Daniel Charles *retired anesthesiologist*
Motulsky, Arno Gunther *internist, geneticist, educator*
Moya, Cynthia Ann *small business owner, librarian*
Mugerauer, Robert W., Jr. *architecture educator*
Mukadam, Maya Shagufta *astronomer*
Mull, Robert W. *filmmaker, curator*
Mulroy, Michael Francis, II, *anesthesiologist*
Murdock, Tullisse Antoinette (Toni Murdock) *academic administrator*
Mussehl, Robert Clarence *lawyer*
Muy-Rivera, Martin *biochemist, researcher*
Nash, Cynthia Jeanne *journalist*
Nelson, Allen F. *proxy solicitation company executive*
Nelson, Arleen Bruce *social worker*
Nelson, James Alonzo *radiologist, educator*
Neukom, William H. *lawyer*
Newmeyer, Frederick Jaret *linguist, educator*
Nickels, Greg *mayor*

Niemi, Janice *retired lawyer, retired state legislator*
Ning, Xue-Han (Hsueh-Han Ning) *physiologist, researcher*
Nordstrom, Blake W. *retail executive*
Nordstrom, Bruce A. *department store executive*
Nutting, Maureen Murphy *historian, educator*
O'Brien, Kevin D. *medical educator*
Oehler, Richard William *lawyer*
Olmstead, Marjorie Ann *physics professor*
Olsen, Harold Fremont *lawyer*
Olson, David John *political science professor*
Olson, James William Park *architect*
Olstad, Roger Gale *science educator*
Oman, Henry *retired electrical engineer, engineering executive*
Overstreet, Karen A. *federal bankruptcy judge*
Ozaki, Nancy Junko *performance artist, performing arts educator*
Pace, David A. *human resources specialist, retail executive*
Paget, Joel Hathaway *lawyer*
Pagon, Roberta Anderson *pediatrician, educator*
Palmer, Douglas S., Jr. *lawyer*
Palmer, Earl Frank *minister*
Papayannopoulou, Thalia *hematologist, oncologist, educator*
Parikh, Jay R. *radiologist*
Parks, Michael James *editor*
Parks, Patricia Jean *lawyer*
Parris, Mark S. *lawyer, professional athletes consultant*
Patrick, Donald Lee *sociologist, educator*
Patton, Jody *management company executive*
Paul, Thomas Frank *lawyer*
Pearl, Nancy Linn *librarian*
Pedersen, Jamie D. *lawyer*
Perrin, Edward Burton *biomedical researcher, public health educator*
Perthou, Alison Chandler *interior designer*
Petrie, Gregory Steven *lawyer*
Phillips, Cheryl *reporter*
Phillips, William Robert *physician*
Pierson, David John *medical educator*
Piven, Peter Anthony *architect, management consultant*
Pizzorno, Joseph, Jr. *health products executive*
Plorde, James Joseph *physician, educator*
Plotnick, Robert David *economic consultant, educator*
Plough, Alonzo L. *city health department administrator*
Pocker, Yeshayau *chemistry and biochemistry educator*
Porter, Stephen Cummings *geologist, educator*
Prentke, Richard Ottesen *lawyer*
Pressly, Thomas James *history professor*
Price, John R. *lawyer, educator*
Prinster, Gordon D. *psychologist*
Pritchard, Llewelyn George *lawyer*
Pym, Bruce Michael *lawyer*
Rabinovitch, Benton Seymour *chemist, educator emeritus*
Ramsey, Paul Glenn *dean, internist*
Rankin, William Lee *air transportation scientist*
Rasic-Steben, Stephanie Ann *secondary school educator*
Rasmussen, Frederick Tatum *lawyer*
Ravenholt, Reimert Thorolf *epidemiologist, researcher*
Ray, Charles Kendall *retired university dean*
Redman, Eric *lawyer*
Reeg, Gloria D. *investment consultant*
Reese, Pokey *professional baseball player*
Reeves, Joan Hutchins *painter*
Reinhardt, William Parker *chemical physicist, educator*
Reskin, Barbara F. *sociologist*
Reynvaan, Michael Thomas *lawyer*
Riccobono, Richard M. *federal agency administrator*
Rice, Norman B. *bank executive, former mayor*
Riddiford, Lynn Moorhead *biologist, educator*
Rieke, Paul Victor *lawyer*
Ritter, Daniel Benjamin *lawyer*
Rivara, Frederick Peter *pediatrician, educator*
Rivera, Bavi Edna (Nedi Rivera) *bishop*
Robb, John Wesley *religion educator*
Roberts, Frank Alan *periodontist, researcher, dental educator*
Robertson, William Osborne *physician*
Robinson, Jeffrey P. *lawyer*
Rojas, Eddy M. *engineering educator*
Romm, Daniel F. *writer, retired computer technician*
Rondeau, George Charles, Jr. *lawyer*
Rose, Eric *physician, consultant*
Rose, Peter J. *delivery service executive*
Rosen, Jon Howard *lawyer*
Rosenblum, Jeffrey Ira *consulting economist*
Rotella, Stephen J. *bank executive*
Ruckelshaus, William Doyle *investment company executive, former federal agency administrator*
Ruddy, James W. *lawyer*
Rule, Ann *author*
Runte, Alfred *environmental historian, consultant*
Russell, Francia *ballet director, educator*
Russell, Robie George *lawyer*
Rutherford, Suzanne L. *geneticist*
Sale, George Edgar *pathologist*
Saneto, Russell Patrick *pediatric neurologist, epileptologist, neurobiologist*
Sarason, Irwin G. *psychology professor*
Sasaki, Tsutomu (Tom Sasaki) *real estate company executive, trade association administrator, consultant*
Sasenick, Joseph Anthony *consumer products company executive*
Sato, Norie *artist*
Saunders, Joseph W. *bank executive*
Sauter, Michael Joseph *real estate company executive*
Savage, Daniel Keenan *columnist, editor-in-chief*
Scheuerell, Mark David *researcher*
Schiffrin, Milton Julius *physiologist*
Schmidt, Peter Gustav *marine engineer*
Schneider, Harry H., Jr. *lawyer*
Schoenfeld, Walter Edwin *manufacturing executive*
Schultheis, Patrick Joseph *lawyer*
Schultz, Howard *beverage service executive, professional basketball team owner*

Schwab, Evan Lynn *lawyer*
Schwartz, Pepper Judith *sociologist, educator*
Scott, Cheryl M. *foundation administrator, healthcare educator*
Segal, Jack *mathematics professor*
Sellick, Kathleen A. *hospital administrator*
Severson, Gary R. *bank executive*
Sexson, Richmond Lockwood *professional baseball player*
Shirley, Donna *museum director, former aerospace engineer*
Sidbury, Robert *pediatrician*
Silver, Michael *education educator*
Sims, John Ernest *biologist, researcher*
Singer, Sarah Beth *poet*
Skirvin, Donald Murray *composer, writer*
Smith, Mary W. *secondary school educator, artist*
Smith, Orin C. *retired food products executive*
Smith, Orville Auverne *physiology educator*
Smith, Scott A. *lawyer*
Snow-Smith, Joanne Inloes *art history educator*
Soltys, John Joseph *lawyer*
Somerman, Martha J. *dean, dental educator*
Spafford, Michael Charles *artist*
Spindel, Robert Charles *electrical engineering educator*
Spitzer, Hugh D. *lawyer*
Spoor, Rhys *dentist*
Squires, William Randolph III *lawyer*
Stamatoyannopoulos, George *internal medicine educator*
Stamper, Norman H. *protective services official*
Staryk, Steven Sam *violinist, concertmaster, educator*
Stearns, Susan Tracey *lighting design company executive, lawyer*
Steichen, Randall R. *lawyer*
Steinberg, Kenneth Paul *medical educator*
Steiner, Robert Alan *neuroendocrinologist, educator*
Stenchever, Morton Albert *obstetrician, gynecologist*
Stern, Edward Abraham *physics professor*
Stoebuck, William Brees *law educator*
Stokke, Diane Rees *lawyer*
Stolov, Walter Charles *medicine physiatrist, educator*
Stonesifer, Patty (Patricia Q. Stonesifer) *foundation administrator*
Stowell, Kent *ballet director*
Strahilevitz, Meir *internet, researcher, psychiatry educator*
Stringer, William Jeremy *university official*
Sullivan, Daniel J. *artistic director*
Sundborg, Stephen V. *academic administrator*
Sutter, Joseph F. *aeronautical engineer, consultant, retired air transportation executive*
Suzuki, Ichiro *professional baseball player*
Szkody, Paula *astronomy educator, researcher*
Szkutak, Tom *corporate financial executive*
Takenaka, Toshiko *lawyer, educator*
Talachian, Reza *filmmaker*
Tall, Craig E. *finance company executive*
Tallman, Richard C. *federal judge, lawyer*
Tanzi, Ronald Thomas *artist, educator*
Taylor, Michael J. *shipbuilding company executive*
Terrell, William Glenn *university president emeritus*
Testy, Kellye *dean*
Thirlby, Richard Coller *surgeon*
Thomas, Edward Donnall *internist, hematologist, retired medical educator*
Thomas, Irv *writer, journalist*
Thomas, John Val *architect*
Thomas, Wendy Evelyn *biomedical engineer, educator*
Thorud, David B. *academic administrator*
Thouless, David James *retired physicist, educator*
Tift, Mary Louise *artist*
Tilden, Bradley D. *air transportation executive*
Tindall, Robert J. *architectural firm executive*
Todaro, George Joseph *pathologist, researcher*
Treiger, Irwin Louis *lawyer*
Trott, Nancy Roberts *editor*
True, William L. (Bill True) *retired real estate company executive*
Tschernisch, Sergei P. *academic administrator*
Tune, James Fulcher *lawyer*
Turnovsky, Stephen John *economics professor*
Tuthill, Oliver W., Jr. *psychologist, consultant*
Vallières, Eric *thoracic surgeon*
VanArsdel, Rosemary Thorstenson *English studies educator*
Vanasek, James George *commercial banker*
van den Berghe, Pierre Louis *sociologist*
Vander Ark, Tom *foundation administrator*
Van Lierop, John Henry, Jr. *music educator*
Vater, Youri L. *medical educator*
Vedder, Nicholas Blair *surgeon, researcher*
Vestal, Josephine Burnet *lawyer*
Vogel, David Seth *lawyer*
Vosk, Ted W. *lawyer*
Wagoner, David Everett *lawyer, arbitrator*
Wagoner, David Russell *writer, educator*
Walker, Walter Frederick *professional basketball team executive*
Walker, William O., Jr. *pediatrician*
Ward, Ronald R. *lawyer*
Washington, James Winston, Jr. *artist, sculptor*
Wasserman, Harriet M. *academic administrator*
Waterston, Robert Hugh *medical educator, researcher, medical geneticist, department chairman*
Weaver, Lois Jean *physician, educator*
Wechsler, Mary Heyrman *lawyer*
Weinberg, John Lee *federal judge*
Welk, Richard Andrew *plastic surgeon*
Wenk, Edward, Jr. *civil engineer, educator, writer, policy analyst*
White, Emily *epidemiologist, researcher*
Wilets, Lawrence *physicist, educator*
Wilke, Sabine *language educator*
Williams, J. Vernon *retired lawyer*
Williams, Nancy *lawyer*
Wilson, Jason *chef*
Wilson, L. Michelle *lawyer*
Wilson, Lizabeth Anne *dean, library director*
Wilson, Richard Randolph *lawyer*
Woods, James Sterrett *toxicologist*
Woods, Nancy Fugate *dean, women's health nurse, educator*

Wott, John Arthur *arboretum and botanical garden executive, horticulture educator*
Wright, Bagley *venture capitalist, entrepreneur, art collector*
Wurster, Charles Frederick *environmental scientist, educator*
Yarington, Charles Thomas, Jr. *surgeon, educator, health facility administrator*
Yashruti, Salah Hadi *retired surgeon*
Yuan, Chun *physicist, educator*
Yue, Agnes Kau-Wah *otolaryngologist*
Zager, Richard A. *medical educator, researcher*
Zilly, Thomas Samuel *federal judge*

**Seaview**
McNeil, Helen Jo Connolly *nursing educator, public health administrator*

**Sequim**
Beaton, Roy Howard *retired nuclear energy industry executive*
Huntley, James Robert *government official, international affairs scholar*
Jackson, Patrick Joseph *real estate company officer*
Kretschmer, Keith Hughes *investor*
Laube, Roger Gustav *retired banker*
Meacham, Charles Harding *federal agency administrator*

**Shelton**
Leverich, Denis *protective services official, educator*
McNabb, David E. *business educator, writer*
Milander, Henry Martin *educational consultant*

**Shoreline**
Dolacky, Susan K. *music educator*
Hanson, Kermit Osmond *business administration educator, retired dean*
Hutton, Winfield Travis *management consultant, educator*
Matesky, Nancy Lee *music educator*
Merendino, K. Alvin *surgeon, educator*

**Silverdale**
Balcomb, Mary Nelson *small business owner*
Shaw, Annita Louise *art educator*
Walske, M(ax) Carl, Jr. *physicist*

**Skamokawa**
Boentgen, Martha Mathilde *artist, small business owner, educator*
Martin, Irene Elizabeth *librarian, writer*

**Snohomish**
Bond, William *science educator*
Philpott, Larry La Fayette *horn player*

**Snoqualmie**
Coldwell, Douglas M. *radiologist*

**Spanaway**
Loete, Steven Donald *pilot*
McKinnon, James Buckner *real estate sales executive, writer, researcher*
Paris, Kathleen *secondary school educator*
Parker, Lynda Christine Rylander *secondary school educator*

**Spangle**
Anderson, Curtis Dale *music educator*

**Spokane**
Baugh, Bradford Hamilton *occupational and environmental health advisor*
Bender, Betty Wion *librarian*
Brock, Randall J. *poet*
Bunker, Nancy Ann *librarian, researcher*
Burton, Robert Lyle *accounting firm executive*
Bynagle, Hans Edward *library director, philosophy educator*
Cameron, Alex Brian *accountant, educator*
Carriker, Robert Charles *history professor*
Chamberlain, Barbara Kaye *small business owner, communications executive*
Chambers, Kevin Conrad *history professor*
Clarke, Judy *lawyer*
Cohen, Arnold Norman *gastroenterologist*
Connolly, Kenneth Thomas *lawyer*
Covey, Michael J. *forest products and real estate executive*
Cowles, William Stacey *newspaper publisher*
Crosby, Glenn Arthur *chemistry professor*
Danke, Virginia *educational administrator, travel consultant*
Edwards, James Robert *minister, educator*
Eliassen, Jon Eric *retired utilities executive, corporate financial executive*
Ely, Gary G. *utilities company executive*
Eymann, Richard Charles *lawyer*
Garrison, Mark W. *medical educator*
Harbaugh, Daniel Paul *lawyer*
Herzer, Marian Day *not-for-profit developer, educator*
Hilst, Glenn Rudolph *environmental sciences administrator, researcher*
Holbrook, Ryan F. *oncologist*
Horton, Susan Pittman *bank executive*
Houseman, Gerald L. *political science professor, writer*
Imbrogno, Cynthia *judge*
Inviolata, Maria *sister, educator*
Kafentzis, John Charles *journalist, educator*
Kovacevich, Robert Eugene *lawyer*
Kunkel, Richard Lester *public radio executive*
Lalonde, Stephen Duane *secondary school educator, writer*
Lane, Iris Mary *retired elementary school educator*
Lee, Hi Young *physician, acupuncturist*
Lee, Richard Francis James *evangelical clergyman, media consultant, lawyer*
Leighton, Jack Richard *small business owner, former educator*
Linn, Diana Patricia *retired elementary school educator*
May, Richard B. *psychology professor*
McCulloh, Thayne Martin *university administrator, consultant*

McDevitt, James A. *prosecutor, lawyer*
McManus, Patrick Francis *editor, educator, writer*
McWilliams, Edwin Joseph *banker*
Mielke, Clarence Harold, Jr. *hematologist*
Mobley, Karen Ruth *art director*
Moe, Orville Leroy *racetrack executive*
Murray, James Michael *librarian, lawyer*
Novak, Terry Lee *public information officer, educator, dean*
Polley, Harvey Lee *retired missionary, math and science educator*
Quackenbush, Justin Lowe *federal judge*
Robinson, Herbert Henry III *psychotherapist, educator*
Ruud, Clayton Olaf *engineering educator*
Siegel, Louis Pendleton *forest products executive*
Sines, Randy Dwain *retail executive*
Skylstad, William S. *bishop*
Spitzer, Robert J. *academic administrator*
Stackelberg, John Roderick *history professor*
Steadman, Robert K. *oral surgeon*
Steele, Karen Dorn *journalist*
Stirpe, Josh A. *sales executive*
Teets, Walter Ralph *accounting educator*
Tsutakawa, Edward Masao *management consultant*
Ueberroth, Peter Victor *former baseball commissioner*
Van Sickle, Frederick L. *federal judge*
Whaley, Robert Hamilton *judge*
Wirt, Michael James *library director*

**Stanwood**
Birkestol, Annabelle Mollie Elsie *retired elementary school educator*

**Stevenson**
Scherling, Bruce A. *civil engineer*

**Sumas**
Hemry, Larry Harold *former federal agency official, writer, inventor*

**Sunnyside**
Capener, Regner Alvin *minister, electronics engineer, writer*

**Tacoma**
Alatsis, Despina Katherine *music educator, director*
Anderson, Lynn L. *bank executive*
Archangelsky, Dmitry A. *application developer, researcher*
Bartlett, Norma Thyra *retired administrative assistant*
Baxter, Sheila R. *career military officer*
Bryan, Robert J. *federal judge*
Callan, Josi Irene *museum director*
Carlisle, Dale L. *lawyer*
Finn, Jerry *social sciences educator*
Fischer, Karen A. *librarian*
Flemming, Stanley Lalit Kumar *physician, mayor, state legislator*
Frantz, Dale Nelson *automobile import processing company executive*
George, Nicholas *lawyer, entrepreneur*
Gordon, Joseph Harold *lawyer*
Hilzendeger, Laura Kaye *business and marketing educator*
Holt, William E. *lawyer, department chairman*
Hudson, Edward Voyle *apparel executive*
Hutchings, George Henry *food company executive*
Krueger, James A. *lawyer*
Larhs, Anthony Emil *nuclear medicine physician*
Lent, Michael Stephen *artist, curator*
Liddle, Alan Curtis *retired architect*
Miller, Judson Frederick *lawyer, retired military officer*
Mowery, Gerald Eugene *publishing executive, writer*
Parikh, Neel *library director*
Ragan, Betty Sapp *artist, educator*
Reisberg, Leon Elton *education educator*
Sloan, Daniel Kay *electrical engineer*
Stuart, Jeffrey L. *mathematics professor, consultant*
Taylor, Peter van Voorhees *advertising and public relations consultant*
Thomas, Ronald Robert *English literature educator, writer*
Waldo, James Chandler *lawyer*
Wang, Arthur Ching-li *judge, law educator*
Wiegman, Eugene William *minister, academic administrator*
Wolf, Frederick George *management educator*

**Toppenish**
Ross, Kathleen Anne *academic administrator*

**Trout Lake**
Anderson, Douglas Del *retired music educator, recording industry executive*

**Tukwila**
Fitzpatrick, Thomas Mark *lawyer*
Robinson, Howard Arthur, Jr. *minister*
Talmadge, Philip Albert *retired judge, retired state senator*
Weidner, Mark *environment research executive*

**Tumwater**
Edmondson, Frank Kelley, Jr. *lawyer, legal administrator*

**University Place**
Bourgaize, Robert G. *economist*
Foster, Charles Carlton *physicist*
Henterly, Mary B. *biology educator*
Pliskow, Vita Sari *anesthesiologist*
Seiber, Richard Allan *retired minister*

**Vancouver**
Congdon, Roger Douglass *theology studies educator, minister*
Craven, James Michael (Omahkohkiaayo i'Poyi) *economist, educator*
Crews, William Odell, Jr. *religious organization administrator*
Donovan, Thomas John *humanities educator*
Gienger, Barbara J. *realtor, land developer*
Harris, Robert L(ee) *judge*

Hilligoss, Charles Adair *retired music educator*
Hulburt, Lucille Hall *artist, educator*
Hurst, Margaret Cheryl *elementary school educator, music educator*
Kodis, Mary Caroline *marketing consultant*
Kucer, Stephen Bradley *language educator, consultant*
Ogden, Daniel Miller, Jr. *public official, educator*
Ogden, Valeria Munson *management consultant, state representative*
Regan, Elizabeth Anne *bail bond agent*
Robertson, Joel Thomas *railroad executive*
Scott, Gary LeRoy *small business owner, photographer*
Smith, Linda A. *retired congresswoman*
Tuttle, Marcia *retired elementary school educator, music educator*
Warner, Matthew Douglas *executive recruiter*
Wharton, Penelope Lee (Penny Wharton) *music educator*

**Vashon**
Cushman, Karen Lipski *writer*

**Walla Walla**
Belay, Halefom *economist, educator*
Bridges, George S. *academic administrator, sociology educator*
Carlsen, James Caldwell *musicologist, educator*
Chaidarun, Sushela Songtanin *endocrinologist, researcher*
Hayner, Herman Henry *lawyer*
Lords, Traci Elizabeth (Nora Louise Kuzma) *actress, singer*
McIlvaine, Patricia Morrow *physician*
Perry, Louis Barnes *retired insurance company executive*
Potts, Charles Aaron *management executive, writer, publishing executive*
Rossi, Norbert Guido *music educator*
Simon, Nancy Lynn *performing arts educator, director*
Wade, Leroy Grover, Jr. *chemistry educator*
Yaple, Henry Mack *librarian*

**Washougal**
Gilbert, Patricia Lynn *music educator*
Guillory, Richard John *retired science educator*
Harness, William Edward *tenor*
Shoemaker, Cameron David James *retired dean*
Zimmerman, Loretta Ellen *history professor*

**Wenatchee**
Elfving, Don C. *horticulturist, educator*
Gotthold, William Eugene *emergency physician*
Knecht, Ben Harrold *surgeon*
Primm, Richard Kirby *physician*
Schrader, Lawrence Edwin *plant physiologist*
Williams, Keith Roy *museum director*

**Woodinville**
Alvarez, Bryan *newsletter editor, writer*
Couser, William Griffith *medical educator, academic administrator, nephrologist*
Cox, Catherine Nalan *psychologist*
Ericson, William B. *orthopedic hand surgeon*
Love, Keith Sinclair *communications executive*
Sanders, Richard Kinard *actor*

**Woodland**
Hansen, Walter Eugene *insurance executive*

**Yakima**
Halfmoon, Thomas William *history educator*
Jongeward, George Ronald *retired systems analyst*
Larson, Paul Martin *lawyer*
McDonald, Alan Angus *federal judge*
Meshke, George Lewis *drama and humanities educator*
Newland, Ruth Laura *small business owner*
Simonson, Susan Kay *hospital clinical care coordinator*
Suko, Lonny Ray *judge*
Walker, Lorene *retired elementary school educator*

# WEST VIRGINIA

**Athens**
Marsh, Joseph Franklin, Jr. *retired academic administrator*
Westbrook, Gary Wayne *music educator, consultant*

**Beckley**
Rehbein, Edward Andrew *minister, geologist, consultant*
Rhoades, Marye Frances *paralegal*
Wolfe, Carl Gundersen *adult education educator*

**Bethany**
Smith, G(odfrey) T(aylor) *college president*

**Beverly**
Pritt, Jeffrey Douglas *contractor, protective services official*

**Bluefield**
Moore, Robert E. *college president*
Reid, William James *mining executive*

**Bruceton Mills**
Butcher, Fred R. *biochemistry professor, academic administrator*

**Bunker Hill**
Marple, Thomas Franklin *columnist, reporter*

**Chapmanville**
Wilson, Terilyn Barrett *elementary school educator*

**Charles Town**
Graf, Virginia Lynch *retired education educator*
McDonald, Angus Wheeler *farmer*
Na, Tsung Shun (Terry Na) *Chinese studies educator, writer*
Starks, Doris N. *retired nursing educator, retired administrator*

## Charleston

Albright, Joseph P. *state supreme court justice*
Arrington, Carolyn Ruth *school system administrator, consultant*
Benjamin, Brent D. *state supreme court justice, lawyer*
Betts, Rebecca A. *lawyer*
Brown, James Knight *lawyer*
Chapman, John Andrew *retired chamber of commerce executive*
Chilton, Elizabeth Easley Early *newspaper executive*
Davis, Robin Jean *state supreme court chief justice*
DiPino, Raymond Kim *psychologist*
Dissen, James Hardiman *lawyer*
Faber, David Alan *federal judge*
Farley Raines, Krista Nicole *health facility administrator, healthcare educator*
Foster, Leska A. *elementary school educator*
Frostick, Robert Maurice *secondary school educator*
Gardner, Edward Tytus III *information technology executive*
Goodwin, Joseph Robert *judge*
Haught, James Albert, Jr. *journalist, editor*
Hechler, Ken *former state official, former congressman, writer, political science professor*
Hurt, Charles Edward *lawyer*
Ireland, Betty *state official*
King, Robert Bruce *federal judge*
Lamb, Patrick John *retired financial consultant, state official*
Lewis, Charles Raymond, II, *traffic engineer, consultant*
Love, Charles Marion III *lawyer*
Manchin, Joe, III, (Joseph Manchin III) *governor, former state official*
Maynard, Elliott E. *state supreme court justice*
McCabe, Brooks Fleming, Jr. *state legislator*
McCuskey, John F. *lawyer*
Mc Gee, John Frampton *communications company executive*
Mc Graw, Darrell Vivian, Jr. *state attorney general*
McHugh, Thomas Edward *state supreme court justice*
Mellert, Lucie Anne *writer, photographer*
Michael, M. Blane *federal judge*
Miller, Charles T. *prosecutor*
Neely, Richard *lawyer*
Paine, Steven L. *school system administrator*
Perdue, John D. *state official*
Richardson, Sally Keadle *academic administrator*
Robinson, E. Glenn *lawyer*
Rowe, Larry Linwell *lawyer, former state senator*
Rowe, Richard Edwin *lawyer*
Schott, Michael J. *library director*
Scott, Olof Henderson, Jr. *priest*
Stanley, Mary Elizabeth *judge*
Stanton, George Patrick, Jr. *lawyer*
Starcher, Larry Victor *state supreme court justice*
Taylor, Larry D. *lawyer*
Tomblin, Earl Ray *state legislator, lieutenant governor*
Ward, Ken, Jr. *journalist*
Zak, Robert Joseph *lawyer*

## Clarksburg

de la Pena, Cordell Amado *pathologist*
Keeley, Irene Patricia Murphy *federal judge*
Lapuz-De La Pena, Erlinda Laron *pathology professor*
Leuliette, Connie Jane *secondary school educator*
Sivakumaran, Kumaraswamy *civil engineer, consultant, lawyer*
Walmsley, James Naylor *hydroponic farming executive*
West, James C., Jr. *lawyer*

## Dunbar

Russell, James Alvin, Jr. *college administrator*
Young, Stephanie Angel *counseling administrator*

## Elizabeth

Lipps, Deloris Jean *secondary school educator*

## Elkins

Baxter, Phyllis *historian*
Maxwell, Robert Earl *federal judge*
Payne, Gloria Marquette *business educator*

## Enterprise

Morris, James Victor *secondary school educator*

## Fairmont

Aloi, Michael John *lawyer*
DeVito, Teresa Marie *artist*
Dudley-Eshbach, Janet *university president*
Fulda, Michael *political scientist, educator, space policy researcher*
Hardway, Wendell Gary *retired academic administrator*
Lach, Peter *humanities educator*
Swiger, Elizabeth Davis *chemist, educator*
Wang, Shen K. *orthopedist, surgeon*

## Fayetteville

Cook, Lewis Anderson *physician, anthropologist*

## Frankford

Mazzio-Moore, Joan L. *retired radiology educator, physician*

## Glenville

Tubesing, Richard Lee *library director*

## Greenville

Warner, Kenneth Wilson, Jr. *editor, publishing executive*

## Harpers Ferry

Boucher, Wayne Irving *policy analyst*
Callar, Donna Howe *counseling administrator, educator*

## Harrisville

Edwards, Tina Lou *school system administrator*

## Hedgesville

Boland, Gerald Lee *health facility administrator*

## Huntington

Anderson, Lorraine Pearson *dean*
Bagley, Charles Frank III *lawyer*
Cocke, William Marvin, Jr. *plastic surgeon, educator*
Culligan, Jenine Elizabeth *curator*
Fannin, Josephine Jewell *social services administrator*
Gould, Alan Brant *academic administrator*
Hayes, Robert Bruce *former college president, educator*
Jennings, Louis Brown *retired humanities educator*
Kent, Calvin Albert *academic administrator*
Lake, Esta Elizabeth *science educator*
McKown, Charles Henry *dean*
Miller, Stephen Blaine *plastic surgeon*
Molina, Rafael Evencio *retired urologist*
Mufson, Maurice Albert *infectious diseases physician, educator*
Nerhood, Robert Clarke *obstetrician, gynecologist*
Pratt, Mary Louise *librarian, writer*
Reynolds, Marshall Truman *printing company executive*
Taft, Edmund Morse *literature and language professor*
Underwood, Mark Forest *lawyer*
Welch, Lynne Brodie *nursing school dean*
Wenzel, Loren Alvin *finance educator*

## Hurricane

Hill, David Lawrence *lawyer, real estate agent*

## Institute

Miah, Mohammad Solaiman *economics professor, researcher*
Ruhnke, Timothy R. *zoologist, educator*

## Kearneysville

Biggs, Alan Richard *plant pathologist, educator*

## Keyser

Asonevich, Walter Jozef *English educator*
Falkowski, Theresa Gae *chemistry educator*

## Kingwood

Moyers, Sylvia Dean *retired medical librarian*

## Lewisburg

Ford, Richard Edmond *lawyer*
Hamra, Mary M. *medical educator, researcher*

## Lookout

Burdette, Charlotte *middle school educator*

## Martinsburg

Ayers, Anne Louise *small business owner, consultant, counselor*
Day, Michael Gordon *information technology executive, educator*
Dugger, Debra Martin *school counselor*
Hill, Philip Bonner *lawyer*
Martin, Clarence Eugene III *lawyer*
Rice, Lacy I., Jr. *lawyer*

## Montgomery

Minnich, Thomas Gayle *director*
Munasinghe, Ranjith Arachchige *mathematics professor, engineer*

## Morgantown

Albrink, Margaret Joralemon *medical educator*
Allamong, Betty Davis *retired academic administrator*
Attfield, Michael Deryck *research scientist*
Bajura, Richard Albert *academic administrator, mechanical engineer, educator*
Beattie, Diana Scott *biochemistry professor*
Bell, Lewis Clay *economics professor, government administrator*
Blakeman, Robyn L. *advertising executive, educator*
Blaydes, Sophia Boyatzies *English language educator*
Brown, Cheryl *agricultural studies educator, economist, educator*
Bryner, Randy *medical educator*
Bucklew, Neil S. *former academic administrator, educator*
Bush, Carletta Ann *art historian, educator*
Callejo, David Marcos *social sciences educator*
Chisholm, Lionel Donald John *ophthalmologist*
Clausell, Arlene Midget *retired elementary school educator*
Cochrane, Robert Lowe *biologist*
Collins, James William *health science association administrator, epidemiologist, mechanical engineer*
Cutlip, Robert Gregory *safety officer*
D'Alessandri, Robert M. *academic administrator, retired dean*
Dawley, David Daniel *finance educator*
De Vore, Paul Warren *technology educator*
D'Souza, Gerard Eugene *economist, educator*
Ducatman, Alan Marc *physician*
Fisher, John Welton, II, *lawyer, educator, academic administrator*
Fleming, William Wright, Jr. *pharmacology educator, department chairman*
Fusco, Andrew G. *lawyer*
Gladfelter, Wilbert Eugene *physiology educator*
Glover, Douglas Dennis *obstetrics, gynecology and pharmacology educator*
Guthrie, Hugh Delmar *chemical engineer*
Halabe, Udaya Bhatta *civil engineering educator, researcher*
Han, Runlin *biochemist, researcher*
Hardesty, David Carter, Jr. *academic administrator*
Hill, Ronald Charles *surgeon, educator*
Hudson, David M. *minister*
Jabbour, Nabil Milad *ophthalmologist*
Johnson, Michael David *dean, physiologist, educator*
Kim, Hong Nack *political science professor*
Kinsey, Donna Lee *music educator*
Koelbl, James J. *dean*
Koepke, Mark *physics professor*
Kuo, Ying Ying *instructional designer*
Martin, James Douglas *neurologist*
Mei, Betty Miuchi *director*

## Montgomery-Downs, Hawley Evelyn
Montgomery-Downs, Hawley Evelyn *psychologist, researcher*
Morris, William Otis, Jr. *lawyer, educator*
Moxley, Roy Anthony *early childhood educator*
Mucino-Quintero, Victor Hugo *mechanical engineering educator, consultant*
Murray, Gordon Franklin *medical educator*
Nath, Joginder *genetics and biology educator, researcher*
Park, Ju-Hyeong *environmental scientist, public health service officer*
Petsonk, Edward Lee *pulmonologist, researcher*
Pinheiro, Germania Araujo *physician, researcher*
Pyles, Rodney Allen *archivist, county official*
Rodriguez, Rich *college football coach*
Scudiere, Debra Hodges *lawyer*
Seehra, Mohindar Singh *physics professor, researcher*
Shekhawat, Dushyant *chemical engineer*
Shilaro, Priscilla Muronji *history professor*
Shumway, James M. *dean, medical educator*
Singer, Armand Edwards *foreign language educator*
Waller, Stacey *psychologist*
Wang, Desheng *cardiologist, physiologist, researcher*
Wenger, Sharon Louise *cytogeneticist, researcher, educator*
Wilson, Mary Alice *musician, educator*
Witt, Tom *economics researcher, educator*

## Moundsville

Wensyel, Mary Kathleen *elementary school educator*

## New Cumberland

Underwood, Elaine M. *elementary school educator*

## Oak Hill

Hamilton, Pat Ray *retired lawyer, state representative*

## Parkersburg

Branch, Michael Lee *social studies educator, consultant*
Childers, Robert Joseph *psychologist*
Dennis, James L. *history educator*
McKenzie, Lawrence J. *composition educator*
Nichols, Terry Jean *elementary school educator, music educator*
Rowland, Angela Kay *education educator, consultant*
Sperati, Carleton Angelo *retired chemist*
Wilson, Roberta Bush *retired psychotherapist, accountant*
Young III, Harmon Griffith *music educator*

## Pennsboro

Poling, Kermit William *minister*

## Princeton

Pauley, Michael Wetzel *director, school psychologist*
Pratt, Carolyn Kay *retired literature and language educator, retired mathematics educator*
Prudich, Gregory S. *lawyer*
Wall, Linda Amanda *economics educator*

## Pullman

Fearn, Noelle E. *criminologist, educator*

## Ranson

Rudacille, Sharon Victoria *medical technician*

## Reedsville

Williford, Drury Fisher, Jr. *historical researcher, writer, editor*

## Ripley

Riffe, Stacy Christine *secondary school educator*

## Romney

Saville, Royce Blair *lawyer*

## Ronceverte

Hooper, Anne Dodge *pathologist, educator*

## Saint Albans

Smith, Robert Carlisle *department administrator, welding educator*

## Salem

Raad, Virginia *pianist, educator*

## Shenandoah Junction

Showen, Donald Eugene, Jr. *music educator*

## Shepherdstown

Elliott, Jean Ann *retired library director*
Summerford, Ben Long *retired artist, educator*
Suttenfield, Diana *artist*

## Shinnston

Ford, Alma Regina *retired union official, educator*
Spears, Jae *state legislator*

## South Charleston

Atkins, Kenneth Earl *retired chemist*
Fishkin, Anne Sonya *retired special education educator*
Klimek, Deborah Lynn *ophthalmologist*

## Spencer

Parker, Theresa Ann Boggs *special education educator, music educator*

## Summit Point

Taylor, Harold Allen, Jr. *industrial minerals consultant*

## Teays

Lamb, Carl Vernon *writer, retired engineer*

## Triadelphia

McCullough, John Phillip *management consultant, educator*

## Weston

Billeter, Robert James *newspaper publisher*

## Wheeling

Bailey, John P. *lawyer*
Bradley, James G. *metals company executive*
Filben, Byron William *elementary school educator, director, secondary school educator, director*
Good, Laurance Frederic *hospital administrator*
Heceta, Estherbelle Aguilar *retired anesthesiologist*
Hill, Barry Morton *lawyer*
Johnston, Thomas E. *judge*
Phillis, Marilyn Hughey *artist*
Spencer, Catherine Ellen *academic administrator*
Thurston, Bonnie Bowman *religious studies educator, minister, poet*
Valdrini, Rita *prosecutor*

## White Sulphur Springs

Kleisner, Ted J. *hotel executive*

# WISCONSIN

## Algoma

Golomski, William Arthur Joseph *consulting company executive*

## Antigo

Fischer, Cindy L. *school system administrator*

## Appleton

Beck, Jill *academic administrator, dancer, educator*
Boldt, Oscar Charles *construction executive, director*
Boren, Clark Henry, Jr. *general and vascular surgeon*
Chaney, William Albert *retired history professor*
Froehlich, Harold Vernon *judge, retired congressman*
Geller, Scott A. *management consultant*
Goldgar, Bertrand Alvin *historian, educator*
Grayson, David S. *paper company executive*
Luther, Thomas William *retired dermatologist*
Malaney, Stephanie J. *reading specialist*
Maravolo, Nicholas C. *biology professor*
Petinga, Charles Michael *transportation executive*
Podair, Jerald E. *history professor*
Rippl, Frank George *retired music educator, retired organist*
Samson, Harvey Gilbert *lawyer*
Seifert, Kathi P. *manufacturing executive*
Spiegelberg, Harry Lester *retired paper company executive*
Stellmacher, Jon Michael *corporate financial executive*
Stringfellow, Julia *archivist*

## Argyle

Daley, Ron (Ronald Eugene Daley) *playwright, poet, theater director, theater producer*

## Ashland

Paruk, James David *biology professor*
Smith, Jane Schneberger *retired city administrator*

## Auburndale

Johnson, James T *secondary school educator*

## Baileys Harbor

Schultz, Richard Otto *ophthalmologist, educator*

## Balsam Lake

Mattson, Carol Linnette *social services administrator*

## Baraboo

Meine, Curt *biologist, writer*
Umhoefer, Aural M. *retired dean, educational consultant*
Wittstruck, Thorne Michael *physiologist*

## Barneveld

Kolb, Victoria L. *retired mathematics educator*

## Beaver Dam

Butterbrodt, John Ervin *real estate company officer*
Carnes, Jeneen A. *music educator*
Frank, Scott M. *mechanical engineer, consultant*
Jimenez, Juan F. *mathematician, educator*
Manthe, Cora De Munck *real estate company executive*
Mezei, Geoffrey D. *physiologist*

## Belgium

Sullivan, Patricia W. (Terry Sullivan) *real estate trainer*

## Beloit

Burris, John Edward *academic administrator, biologist, educator*
Davis, Harry Rex *political science professor*
Hendricks, Kenneth *wholesale distribution executive*
Knueppel, Henry W. *manufacturing executive*
Licary, Cheryl Ann *retired music educator, church musician*
Rosenthal, Timothy Mark *music educator*
Wheeler, Karla *education educator*

## Black Earth

Klug, Scott Leo *former congressman*

## Black River Falls

Lister, Thomas Edward *lawyer*

## Bowler

Bartholomaus, Brett William *small business owner*

## Brookfield

Bauer, Chris Michael *banker*
Curfman, Floyd Edwin *retired engineering educator*
Dillon, Donald F. *data processing executive*
Fibich, Howard Raymond *retired newspaper editor*
Jensen, Kenneth R. *data processing executive*
Lavender, Cheryl Ann *music educator, composer, writer*
Nickerson, Greg *public relations executive*

Guerin-Gonzales, Camille *history professor*
Guillery, Rainer Walter *anatomy educator*
Gustafson, David Harold *industrial engineering and preventive medicine educator*
Haller, Archibald Orben *sociologist, educator*
Hamerow, Theodore Stephen *historian, educator*
Hamers, Robert J. *chemistry educator, researcher*
Handelsman, Jo *plant pathologist, educator*
Hansen, W. Lee *economics professor*
Hanson, David James *lawyer*
Haq, Cynthia *physician, educator*
Hardie, Anthony D. *legislative staff member, social welfare administrator*
Harvey, William D. *utilities executive, lawyer*
Haslanger, Philip Charles *journalist*
Hassett, Dawnene Diane *education educator*
Heffernan, Nathan Stewart *retired state supreme court chief justice*
Hempe, A. Henry *labor relations specialist, labor arbitrator, lawyer*
Henderson, Arvis Burl *data processing executive, biochemist*
Heymann, S. Richard *lawyer*
Hickman, James Charles *finance educator, dean*
Hildebrand, Daniel Walter *lawyer*
Hill, Charles Graham, Jr. *chemical engineering educator*
Hinshaw, Molly A. *dermatologist*
Hokin, Lowell Edward *biochemist, educator*
Hopen, Herbert John *horticulture educator*
Hopson, James Warren *publishing executive*
Howell, Roberta F. *lawyer*
Hoyt, James Lawrence *journalism educator, writer*
Iltis, Hugh Hellmut *botanist, educator, environmental advocate*
Ives, Anthony Ragnar *ecologist*
Javid, Manucher J. *retired neurosurgery educator*
Jeanne, Robert Lawrence *entomologist, educator*
Jefferson, James Walter *psychiatrist, educator*
Johnson, Jean Elaine *nursing educator*
Johnson, Maryl Rae *cardiologist*
Johnson, Millard Wallace, Jr. *mathematics professor, engineering educator*
Johnson, Richard Arnold *statistics educator, consultant*
Kaesberg, Paul Joseph *virology researcher*
Kanskar, Manoj *physicist, engineering executive*
Karofsky, Peter Stuart *pediatrician, medical educator*
Kemnitz, Joseph William *physiologist, researcher*
Kiessling, Laura Lee *chemist, researcher*
Kim, Nam-Heon *engineering researcher*
Kingdon, Robert McCune *historian, educator*
Kitchen, Michael B. *bank executive*
Kleinhenz, Christopher *foreign language educator, researcher*
Knetter, Michael Mark *dean*
Knowles, Richard Alan John *language educator*
Knox, James C. *geologist, educator*
Krahn, Dean Dennis *psychiatrist, educator*
Krusick, Margaret Ann *state legislator*
K-Turkel, Judith Leah Rosenthal (Judi K-Turkel) *writer, editor, publisher*
Kulcinski, Gerald LaVerne *nuclear engineer, educator, dean*
Kurtz, Thomas Gordon *mathematics professor*
Kutler, Stanley Ira *historian, lawyer, educator*
Kutzbach, John E. *climate scientist*
Kuzuhara, Loren Wyatt *management consultant, educator*
Laessig, Ronald Harold *preventive medicine and pathology educator, state official*
La Follette, Douglas J. *state official*
Lagally, Max Gunter *physics professor*
Langer, Richard J. *lawyer*
Langer, Stanley Harold *chemical engineer, educator*
Lardy, Henry A. (Henry Arnold Lardy) *biochemistry professor*
Larson, John David *insurance company executive, lawyer*
Lasseter, Robert Haygood *electrical engineering educator, consultant*
Latta, Richard Allen *lawyer*
Lautenschlager, Peggy A. *state attorney general*
Lavers, Richard Marshall *lawyer*
Lawler, James Edward *physics professor*
Lawton, Barbara *lieutenant governor*
Lazarian, Alex *physics professor*
Lemanske, Robert F., Jr. *allergist, immunologist*
Lepczyk, Christopher Andrew *ecologist, biologist, ornithologist, research scientist*
Li, Kai *chemist, research scientist*
Lightfoot, Edwin Niblock, Jr. *retired chemical engineering educator*
Lillesand, Thomas Martin *engineer, educator*
Lin, Chun Chia *research physicist, educator*
Linstroth, Tod Brian *lawyer*
Linzer, Mark *medical educator, internist*
Little, George Daniel *clergyman*
Lovell, Edward George *mechanical engineering educator*
Lucey, Michael Ronan *gastroenterologist*
Luening, Robert Adami *retired agricultural studies educator*
Lund, Dennis Paul *surgeon*
Ma, Zhenqiang *education educator*
Macfarlane, Alastair Iain Robert *manufacturing executive*
MacKinney, Archie Allen *physician*
Maher, Louis James, Jr. *geologist, educator*
Maki, Dennis G. *epidemiology educator*
Malkus, David Starr *mathematician*
Malter, James Samuel *pathologist, educator*
Maravelias, Christos Theodoros *engineering educator*
Marlett, Judith Ann *nutritional sciences educator, researcher*
Marrett, Cora B. *science educator*
Martin, Robert David *judge, educator*
Mash, Donald J. *college president*
Mau, Bob *statistician*
McBride, Patrick Edward *medical educator, dean*
McCallum, Laurie Riach *state government lawyer*
McNelly, John Taylor *retired journalist, educator*
Mehta, Minesh P. *oncologist, educator*
Melli, Marygold Shire *law educator*
Miller, Paul Dean *breeding consultant, geneticist, educator*
Mohs, Frederic Edward *lawyer*
Moore, Lorrie *writer, English professor*

Morton, Stephen Dana *chemist, consultant*
Mowris, Gerald William *lawyer*
Mueller, Willard Fritz *economics professor*
Mukerjee, Pasupati *chemistry professor*
Nell, Herman *consumer products company executive*
Nevin, John Robert *business educator, consultant*
Newcomb, Eldon Henry *retired botany educator*
Ney, Peter Ernest *mathematician, educator*
Nice, Don *artist*
Nichols, Donald Arthur *economist, educator*
Noonan, Kenneth J. *pediatrician, surgeon, educator*
Nordby, Eugene Jorgen *orthopedic surgeon*
Novotny, Donald Wayne *electrical engineer, educator*
Odden, Allan Robert *education educator*
Olson, Norman Fredrick *food science educator*
Pella, Milton Orville *science educator*
Peters, Henry Augustus *neurologist*
Peterson, Erik Charles *prosecutor*
Petty, Brian E. *speech pathology/audiology services professional, opera singer, voice educator*
Pierce, Harvey R. *insurance company executive*
Piper, Odessa *chef*
Pitot, Henry Clement III *pathologist, educator*
Pondrom, Lee Girard *physicist, researcher*
Post, Jeffrey H. *insurance company executive*
Powell, Barry Bruce *classicist, educator*
Prange, Roy Leonard, Jr. *lawyer*
Pray, Lloyd Charles *geologist, educator*
Prosser, David Thomas, Jr. *state supreme court justice, former state legislator*
Protsch, Eliot G. *utilities executive, corporate financial executive*
Ragatz, Thomas George *lawyer*
Ranney, Joseph Austin *lawyer*
Reilly, Kevin P. *academic administrator*
Reynolds, Ernest West *retired internist, educator*
Rice, Joy Katharine *psychologist, education educator*
Rich, Daniel Hulbert *chemistry professor*
Rikkers, Layton Frederick *surgeon*
Riley, Jocelyn Carol *writer, television producer*
Ring, Gerald J. *real estate developer, insurance company executive*
Rinzel, Dennis Joseph *media specialist, director*
Roberts, Leigh Milton *psychiatrist*
Robinson, Stephen Michael *mathematician, educator*
Roessler, Carol Ann *state legislator*
Roggensack, Patience Drake *state supreme court justice*
Rosser, Annetta Hamilton *composer*
Rothschild, Matthew *editor*
Rowe, Marieli Dorothy *media literacy education consultant, organization executive*
Rowley, Howard A. *neurologist, radiologist, educator*
Rueckert, Roland Rudyard *retired virologist, educator*
Rusi, Eduard *engineering educator*
Russell, Jeffrey Scott *engineering educator*
Sack, Robert David *geography professor*
Sapiro, Virginia *academic administrator, political science professor*
Sauer, Jeff *university hockey coach*
Scherdin, Mary Jane Liskovec *retired librarian, researcher*
Scherer, Victor Richard *physicist, computer scientist, consultant, musician*
Scholz, John Karl *economist, educator*
Schott, Donald Karl *lawyer*
Schutta, Henry Szczesny *neurologist, educator*
Schwab, Donald Peter *finance educator*
Sewell, Richard Herbert *retired historian, retired educator*
Shabaz, John C. *judge*
Shafer, Byron Edwin *American government educator*
Shah, Dhavan Vinod *communications educator*
Shain, Irving *retired chemicals executive, academic administrator*
Sharkey, Thomas David *botanist, educator*
Shaw, Joseph Thomas *Slavic languages educator*
Shkel, Yuri M. *education educator, researcher*
Skiles, James Jean *electrical engineer, computer engineer, educator*
Skilton, John Singleton *lawyer*
Skinner, James Lauriston *chemist, educator*
Skochelak, Susan E. *dean*
Smith, Catherine Arnott *medical informatics educator, researcher*
Smith, Gary W.H. *retired sales executive*
Smith, Michael James *industrial engineering educator*
Sobkowicz, Hanna Maria *neurologist, researcher*
Sondel, Paul Mark *pediatric oncologist, educator*
Sonnedecker, Glenn Allen *pharmaceutical historian, educator*
Spear, Peter D. *retired academic administrator*
Spencer, Christopher S. *lawyer, insurance company executive*
Stein, James Howard *medical educator, researcher*
Steingass, Susan R. *lawyer*
Stewart, Warren Earl *chemical engineer, educator*
Stites, Susan Kay *writer, human resources specialist*
Strasbaugh, Joan Timmis *publishing executive*
Strier, Karen Barbara *anthropologist, educator*
Susman, Millard *geneticist, educator*
Sweeney, Timothy C. *lawyer*
Szybalski, Waclaw *geneticist, educator*
Temkin, Harvey L. *lawyer*
Thomas, J. Mark *sociologist, educator, minister*
Thompson, Barbara Storck *state official*
Thomson, James Alexander *molecular biologist, educator*
Tishler, William Henry *landscape architect, educator*
Tomé, Wolfgang Axel *physicist, researcher, educator*
Trubetskoy, Olga V. *medical researcher, educator*
Turner, Robert Lloyd *state legislator*
Turng, Lih-Sheng *education educator*
Underwood, Julie K. *dean, former law educator*
Vaughan, Michael Richard *lawyer*
Vaughan, Worth Edward *retired chemistry professor*
Voight, Jack C. *state official*

Vowles, Richard Beckman *literature educator*
Waldo, Robert Leland *retired insurance company executive*
Walker, Duard Lee *medical educator*
Walsh, David Graves *lawyer*
Webster, John Goodwin *biomedical engineering educator, researcher*
Weinbrot, Howard David *language educator*
Westman, Jack Conrad *child psychiatrist, educator*
Whiffen, James Douglass *surgeon, educator*
White, William Fredrick *lawyer*
Whitlow, Donna Sue *neuroscientist, researcher*
Wilcox, Jon P. *state supreme court justice*
Wiley, John D. *academic administrator*
Wilson, Franklin D. *sociology educator*
Wineke, William Robert *reporter, minister*
Wolfe, Barbara L. *economics professor, researcher*
Wood, Gary Stewart *dermatologist, researcher*
Workman, Jerome James, Jr. *chemist*
Wu, Chin H. *engineering educator*
Yavuz, Deniz Dervis *electrical engineer, researcher*
Young, Merwin Crawford *political science professor*
Young, Rebecca Mary Conrad *retired state legislator*
Yu, Hyuk *chemist, educator*
Zell, Josephine May *retired language educator*
Zimmerman, Howard Elliot *chemist, educator*
Zweifel, David Alan *newspaper editor*

## Manitowoc

Growcock, Terry D. *agricultural products executive*
Jones, Maurice D. *lawyer*
McBride, Craig Patrick *mathematics professor*
Nelson, Robert Louis *education educator, consultant*
Trader, Joseph Edgar *orthopedic surgeon*

## Marion

Gast, Timothy Alan *musician, educator, small business owner*

## Markesan

Chamberlain, Robert Glenn *retired tool manfacturing executive*
Kastenschmidt, Betty M. *elementary school educator, director*

## Marshfield

Hartwig, Randall Eugene *science educator*
Kuehner, Marvin Ernest *surgeon*
Vidaillet, Humberto J., Jr. *physician, administrator, researcher*

## Mauston

Curran, Paul Saether *lawyer*

## Mc Naughton

Bradshaw, Glenn Raymond *art educator*

## Menasha

Kneezel, Ronald D. *lawyer*
Streeter, Stephanie Anne *printing company executive*
Walter, Thomas Bernard *music educator, conductor*

## Menomonee Falls

Chicorel, Ralph *librettist, composer, playwright*
Hinnrichs-Dahms, Holly Beth *elementary school educator*
Janzen, Norine Madelyn Quinlan *clinical laboratory scientist*
Jeffries, Telvin *human resources specialist, retail executive*
Mansell, Kevin B. *retail executive*
Marshall, Jeffery M. *retail executive*
McDonald, Wesley S. *retail executive*
Montgomery, R. Lawrence *retail executive*
Schepp, Richard D. *lawyer, retail executive*

## Menomonie

Asthana, Rajiv *engineering educator, researcher*
Cutnaw, Mary-Frances *retired communications educator, writer, editor*
Lueder, Dianne Carol *library director*
Schmidt, Laura Jean *mathematics professor*
Sedlak, Robert *academic administrator*

## Mequon

Andritzky, Joseph George *law educator*
Bayne, Jay Stewart *information technology executive, consultant*
Berry, William Martin *financial consultant*
Bloom, James Edward *commodity trading and financial executive*
Braun, Michael Andrew *radiologist*
Dohmen, Mary Holgate *retired primary school educator*
Elias, Paul S. *retired marketing executive*
Ellis, William Grenville *academic administrator, management consultant*
Esselmann, Jesse J *education educator*
O'Shaughnessy, James Patrick *lawyer, consultant*
Petersen, Dorothy Virginia *investment company executive*
Sisney, Ned *education educator*
Terry, Leon Cass *neurologist, educator*
Whyte, George Kenneth, Jr. *lawyer*

## Merrill

Graham, Christopher A. *insurance company executive*
Whitburn, Gerald *insurance company executive*

## Middleton

Berman, Ronald Charles *lawyer, accountant*
Conaway, Jane Ellen *elementary school educator*
Gaub, Albrecht Friedrich *music editor*
Lee, Leslie Warren *marketing executive, educator*
Nora, Wendy Alison *lawyer*
O'Brien, James Aloysius *foreign language educator*
Piefer, Gregory Richard *information technology executive*

## Milton

Enlow, Donald Hugh *retired anatomist, dean*

Parker, Letitia *secondary school educator*

## Milwaukee

Abraham, William John, Jr. *lawyer*
Adami, Norman J. *brewery executive*
Aho, Eric *painter*
Allen, Bruce *physicist*
Alverson, William H. *lawyer*
Aman, Mohammed Mohammed *dean, library and information science professor*
Arbit, Bruce *direct marketing executive, consultant*
Babler, Wayne E., Jr. *lawyer*
Bader, Alfred Robert *chemist*
Bailey, Thomas Anthony *lawyer*
Ballman, Patricia Kling *lawyer*
Bannen, John Thomas *lawyer*
Barnes, Paul McClung *lawyer*
Barrett, Thomas M. *mayor, former congressman*
Barth, John M. *manufacturing executive*
Barth, Karl Luther *retired seminary president*
Beals, Vaughn Le Roy, Jr. *retired motorcycle manufacturing executive*
Becker, John Alphonsis *retired bank executive*
Behrendt, David Frogner *retired journalist*
Belazelkoska, Katerina *school system administrator*
Berdan, Robert J. *lawyer*
Berkoff, Marshall Richard *lawyer*
Biehl, Michael Melvin *lawyer, writer*
Biller, Joel Wilson *lawyer, retired diplomat*
Bishop, Charles Joseph *manufacturing executive*
Biskupic, Steven M. *prosecutor, lawyer*
Blasinski, Clare Marie *librarian*
Bleustein, Jeffrey L. *motorcycle company executive*
Boer, Ralf Reinhard *lawyer*
Boese, Gil Karyle *cultural organization administrator*
Bogut, Andrew *professional basketball player*
Bolger, T(homas) Michael *lawyer*
Braeger, Jessica Lynn *lawyer*
Branch, Joseph C. *lawyer*
Bremer, John M. *lawyer*
Bruce, Peter Wayne *lawyer, insurance company executive*
Burch, Thaddeus Joseph, Jr. *physics professor, director*
Busch, John Arthur *lawyer, educational association administrator*
Buss, Daniel Frank *environmental scientist*
Cannon, David Joseph *lawyer*
Carter, Charlene Ann *psychologist*
Carter, Curtis Lloyd *museum director*
Casey, John Alexander *lawyer*
Casper, Richard Henry *lawyer*
Chan, Carlyle Hung-lun *psychiatrist, educator*
Chandler, Edward William *communication systems engineer, electrical engineer, electrical engineering educator*
Chappell, Virginia *literature and language professor*
Cheatham, Wallace McClain *music educator*
Chokey, James A. *lawyer*
Christensen, Peter Glenn *literature educator, poet*
Christiansen, Keith Allan *lawyer*
Clark, James Richard *lawyer*
Cody, Christopher B. *secondary school educator*
Coffman, Terrence J. *retired academic administrator*
Colbert, Virgis W. *food products executive*
Colbert, Virgis William *food products executive*
Connelly, Mark *writer, educator*
Connolly, Gerald Edward *lawyer*
Cowley, Allen Wilson, Jr. *physiologist*
Crocker, Ray Dean *musician, musical director*
Culver, Curt S. *diversified financial services company executive*
Cutler, Richard W. *lawyer*
Daily, Frank J(erome) *lawyer*
Davidson, Rick *staffing company executive*
Davis, Don H., Jr. *multi-industry high-technology company executive*
Davis, Susan F. *human resources specialist*
Delfs, Andreas *conductor, musical director*
Demerdash, Nabeel Aly Omar *electrical engineer*
Dionisopoulos, George Allan *lawyer*
Dolan, Timothy Michael *archbishop*
Dunn, Michael J. *dean*
Emanuel, John F. *lawyer*
Evans, Terence Thomas *federal judge*
Farris, Trueman Earl, Jr. *retired newspaper editor*
Feinsilver, Donald Lee *psychiatry professor*
Feitler, Robert *shoe company executive*
Fellows, Gerald Lee *lawyer*
Fink, Jordan Norman *allergist, educator*
Florsheim, Richard Steven *lawyer*
Foldy, Seth Leonard *physician, educator*
Ford, T.J. *professional basketball player*
Frank, Dennis *psychotherapist, educator*
Fraser, Alexander Paul *lawyer*
Frauen, Kurt Herman *lawyer*
Frautschi, Timothy Clark *lawyer*
Friebert, Robert Howard *lawyer*
Friedman, James Dennis *lawyer*
Furlong, Mark F. *bank executive*
Gaggioli, Richard Arnold *mechanical engineering educator*
Gagliani, William Dennis *library director*
Gaines, Irving David *lawyer*
Galanis, John William *lawyer*
Gallagher, Richard Sidney *lawyer*
Gallop, Jane (Jane Anne Gallop) *women's studies educator, writer*
Garcia, Astrid J. *newspaper executive*
Gefke, Henry Jerome *lawyer*
Geilfuss, C. Frederick, II, *lawyer*
Gemignani, Joseph Adolph *lawyer*
Gershan, William M. *pediatrician, educator*
Geske, Janine Patricia *law educator*
Ghiardi, James Domenic *lawyer, educator*
Giacinti, Louis Anthony *educator, writer*
Gleason Heffron, Mary Ellen *education specialist*
Goodkind, Conrad George *lawyer*
Goodstein, Aaron E. *federal magistrate judge*
Gordon, David *museum director*
Graber, Richard William *lawyer, political organization worker*
Grabowski, Michael Joseph *financial executive*
Grade, Jeffery T. *manufacturing executive*
Graef, Luther William *civil engineer*
Greene, Victor Robert *history professor*
Greenstreet, Robert Charles *architect, educator*

Playfair, David Malcolm *vocalist, voice educator, researcher*
Robek, Mary Frances *business education educator*

**Sussex**
Losee, John Frederick, Jr. *manufacturing executive*
Stromberg, Gregory *printing ink company executive*

**Thiensville**
Roselle, William Charles *librarian*

**Thorp**
Alisky, Joseph Martin *physician, medical researcher*

**Three Lakes**
Bauknecht, Barbara Belle *retired pre-school educator*

**Tomah**
Neurohr, Shirley Ann *retired special education educator*

**Union Grove**
Dawson, Rose Dorothy *elementary school educator*
Stern, Walter Wolf III *lawyer*

**Verona**
White, Carolyn Louise *music educator*

**Wales**
Jaeger, Todd D. *music educator*

**Washburn**
Berg, Patricia J. *social studies educator*
Nutt, Sandra Kay *elementary school educator*

**Washington Island**
Raup, David Malcolm *paleontology educator*
Schweikert, Norman Carl *retired musician*

**Waterford**
Karraker, Louis Rendleman *retired corporate executive*

**Watertown**
Midcalf, Randall *language educator, director*

**Waukesha**
Cauley, James Robert *lawyer*
Falcone, Frank S. *academic administrator*
Franze, Robert Dennis *social studies educator*
Gola, Ralph H. *library and information scientist*
Graham, George Andrew, Jr. *psychologist, consultant*
Gustafson, Mardel Emma *secondary school educator, writer*
Helgert, Mark James *music educator*
Helland, Sherman M. *writer*
Hogan, Joseph M. *health products executive*
Lightfoot, Alfred J. *retired education educator*
Maas, Duane Harris *distilling company executive*
McCoy, John V. *lawyer*
Meyer, Debora Lynn *music educator*
Moran, Kevin Paul *lawyer*
Nettesheim, Timothy Alan *lawyer*
Ramirez, Agustin A (Gus Ramirez) *auto parts manufacturing company executive*
Redding, Kimberly Ann *history professor*
Stringham, Phyllis Joan *retired music educator*

**Waupaca**
Hansen, Louise Hill *music educator, retired application developer*

**Waupun**
Wendt, Thomas *finance company executive*

**Wausau**
Drengler, William Allan John *lawyer*
Etten, Stewart Louis *lawyer*
Gruling, Kay Ann *physician*
Loftus, Stephen Edward *elementary art educator*
Orr, San Watterson, Jr. *lawyer*
Veninga, James Frank *humanities educator, editor, writer*
Wadzinski, Mary Beth *administrative assistant*

**Wauwatosa**
Alexander, Robert Gardner *lawyer*
DeVillers, Ronald Joseph *retired music educator, musician*
Franke, Brent Douglas *real estate/insurance executive*
Heath, Robert F. *lawyer*
Hollister, Winston Ned *pathologist*
Kalogjera, Ikar Jaksa *psychiatrist, educator*
Mancuso, Joseph Edward *medical psychotherapist*
Savage, Thomas Ryan *lawyer*

**Wauzeka**
Acker, Terri G. *academic administrator, biology professor, healthcare educator, physical education educator*

**West Allis**
Roth, Terence Vincent *surgeon*
Wasick, Mary Ann *retired librarian*

**West Bend**
Gehl, William D. *manufacturing executive*
Murdy, Jill Maria *liturgy director, music director, educator*
VanBrunt-Kramer, Karen *business administration educator*

**West Salem**
Kindschy, Errol Roy *school system administrator*

**Wheeler**
Olson, Sheila J. *elementary school educator*

**Whitefish Bay**
Hawkins, Brett William *retired political science professor*

**Whitewater**
Baica, Malvina Florica *mathematician, educator, researcher*
Connor, James Richard *retired foundation administrator*
Greenhill, H. Gaylon *retired academic administrator*
Hsu, Maxwell K. *finance educator*
Jennings, Robert Lee *retired music educator*
Joseph, Stacey Ann McGraw *music educator, church choir director*
Kolb, Sharon Marie *education educator, director, consultant*
Nam, Ki-Bong *mathematics professor*
Saunders, Martha Dunagin *academic administrator*
Schroeder, Eileen Elizabeth *education educator*

**Williams Bay**
Hobbs, Lewis Mankin *astronomer*
Tobin, Dennis Michael *lawyer*

**Winneconne**
Hale, Donald Roy *music educator, musician*

**Wisconsin Rapids**
Engelhardt, LeRoy A. *retired paper company executive*
Olson-Hellerud, Linda Kathryn *elementary school educator*

**Wonewoc**
LaBansky, Gregory Allen *social studies educator*

**Woodruff**
Polasek, Edward John *retired electrical engineer, consultant*

## WYOMING

**Big Piney**
Walker, Joni Carol *secondary school educator*

**Buffalo**
Kirven, Timothy J. *lawyer*

**Casper**
Anderson, Kevin Stuart *archivist, librarian*
Bennion, Scott Desmond *physician*
Bovee, Debra Sue *elementary school educator*
Cotherman, Audrey Mathews *educational association administrator, management consultant*
Cottam, Keith M. *librarian, educator, administrator*
Davis, Lois Ann *computer specialist, educator*
Downes, William F. *federal judge*
Durham, Harry Blaine III *lawyer*
Elliott, Marian Kay *real estate manager*
Grussendorf, Steven Carl *music educator, director*
Keim, Michael Ray *dentist*
Kukes, Patrick J. *music educator*
Lowe, Robert Stanley *lawyer*
Ptasynski, Harry *geologist, oil industry executive*
Rickabaugh, René Lane *principal*
Searcey, Paul W. *music educator*
Stoval, Linda *political party official*
Stroock, Thomas Frank *oil and gas company executive*
Sullivan, Michael John *lawyer, former ambassador*
True, Jean Durland *entrepreneur, oil industry executive, gas industry executive*
Unruh, Eric W. *academic administrator, music educator*
Wildman, Peter Roberts *mathematics professor*
Wold, John Schiller *geologist, former congressman*

**Cheyenne**
Breen, Nathan David (Nate Breen) *historian, educator*
Brimmer, Clarence Addison *federal judge*
Brorby, Wade *federal judge*
Burke, E. James *lawyer, state supreme court justice*
Carlson, Kathleen Bussart *law librarian*
Catchpole, Judy *state official*
Crank, Patrick J. (Pat Crank) *state attorney general*
Freudenthal, Dave (David D. Freudenthal) *governor*
Freudenthal, Steven Franklin *lawyer, political organization worker*
Golden, T. Michael *state supreme court justice*
Hill, William U. *state supreme court justice, former state attorney general*
Joyce, Roger Gary *archivist, consultant*
Kite, Marilyn S. *state supreme court justice, lawyer*
Knight, Robert Edward *bank executive, educator*
Kunz, April Brimmer *state legislator, lawyer*
Lummis, Cynthia Marie *state official, lawyer*
McBride, James M. *school system administrator*
Mead, Matthew Hansen *prosecutor*
Meyer, Joseph B. *state official*
Mockler, Esther Jayne *state senator*
Moore, Dan Sterling *insurance executive, sales trainer*
Moore, Mary French (Muffy Moore) *potter, advocate*
Myers, Rolland Graham *investment counselor*
Newman, Steven David *psychologist, consultant*
Noe, Guy *retired social services administrator*
O'Brien, Terrence Leo *federal judge*
Palma, Jack D. *lawyer*
Pulse, Ronald H. *agricultural studies educator*
Sansonetti, Thomas L. *lawyer, former federal agency administrator*
Thomson, Thyra Godfrey *former state official*
Voigt, Barton R. *state supreme court chief justice*
Weigner, Brent James *secondary school educator*
Wilson-McKee, Marie *museum director*
Woodhouse, Gay Vanderpoel *former state attorney general, lawyer*

**Cody**
Donoghue, Ann Marie *museum administrator, consultant*
Garry, James B. *historian, naturalist, storyteller, writer*
Jackson, Harry Andrew *artist*

Price, B. Byron *historian*
Simpson, Alan K. *former US senator, lawyer*

**Douglas**
Daugherty, Sandra Gaye *artist*
Kilpatrick, Sherrill Lynn *elementary school educator*

**Dubois**
Glasser, Pamela Jean *musician, music educator*

**Ethete**
Tepper, Marcy Elizabeth *drug education director*

**Evanston**
Harris, Mark W. *mayor, lawyer*

**Gillette**
Bailey, Daniel B. *lawyer, entrepreneur*
Cummings, Judy Annette *retired secondary school educator*
Lubnau, Thomas Edwin, II *lawyer*
Michaels, Deborah Downey *lawyer*

**Glendo**
Burton, Eva Ella Mary *primary school educator*

**Glenrock**
Anderson, James *senator*

**Green River**
Albers, Dolores M. *secondary school educator*

**Jackson**
Cox, Paul Alan *ethnobotanist, educator*
Decker, Carol Arne *magazine publishing executive*
Furrer, John Rudolf *retired manufacturing executive*
Harris, Adam Duncan *curator*
Herrick, Gregory Evans *computer company executive*
Hessel, Marieluise *art collector*
Hirschfield, Alan James *entrepreneur*
Law, Clarene Alta *small business owner, retired state legislator*
Massy, William Francis *education educator, consultant*
Schuster, Robert Parks *lawyer*
Spence, Gerry (Gerald Leonard Spence) *lawyer, writer*

**Jackson Hole**
Farkas, Carol Garner *nurse, administrator*

**Kelly**
Harrice, Cy (Nicholas Psiharis) *announcer*
Knowles, William Standish *retired chemist*

**Lander**
Field, Francis Edward *electrical engineer, educator*
Raynolds, David Robert *buffalo breeder, writer*
Stevens, Sufjan *musician*

**Laramie**
Allen, John Logan *geographer, department chairman*
Arnold, Joseph Patterson *artist, small business owner*
Bagley, David Michael *environmental engineer, educator*
Boresi, Arthur Peter *writer, educator*
Chai, Winberg *political science professor, foundation administrator*
Chisum, Emmett Dewain *historian, researcher, archaeologist*
Cho, Jeasik *education educator*
Crocker, Thomas Dunstan *economics professor*
Darnall, Roberta Morrow *educational association administrator*
Dickman, Francois Moussiegt *former foreign service officer, educator*
Gill, George Wilhelm *anthropologist*
Grandy, Walter Thomas, Jr. *physicist, researcher*
Gray, Christine Ann Wittstock *psychologist*
Guerin, Charles Allan *museum director, artist*
Guzzo, Sandra Elizabeth *newspaper columnist, writer*
Hansen, Matilda *former state legislator*
Kelley, Robert Otis *medical educator, anatomist*
Kinney, Lisa Frances *lawyer*
Lauer, Warren *lawyer*
Maxfield, Peter Charles *state legislator, lawyer, educator*
Meyer, Edmond Gerald *energy scientist, retired chemistry professor, academic administrator, entrepreneur*
Mingle, John Orville *engineer, educator, lawyer, consultant*
Moldenhauer, Susan *museum director, curator*
Nye, Eric W. *English language and literature educator*
Rechard, Paul Albert *retired civil engineering company executive, consultant*
Reif, David (Frank David Reif) *artist, educator*
Ren, Jun *science educator, research scientist*
Roark, Terry Paul *astronomer, educator*
Sandeen, Eric John *history professor*
Shaffer, Sherrill Lynn *economist*
Shogren, Jason Fredrick *economics professor*
Spiegelberg, Emma Jo *business education educator, academic administrator*
Steiner, Joseph Francis *pharmacy educator*
Williams, Roger Lawrence *historian, educator*

**Lingle**
Gulisano, Cynthia Jo *elementary school educator*

**Lyman**
Turner, Del L. *social studies educator*

**Newcastle**
Engle, Kathleen Faye *elementary education educator*

**Pinedale**
Barlow, John Perry *writer, former rancher, advocate*

**Powell**
Dean, Patricea Louise *lawyer, law educator, small business owner*
Myers, Rex Charles *historian, educator, retired dean*
Patrick, H. Hunter *retired judge*
Sanders, Peggy Jean *artist*

**Riverton**
Bebout, Eli Daniel *oil industry executive*
Girard, Nettabell *lawyer*
Peck, Robert A. *publishing executive, state legislator*

**Sheridan**
Aguirre Batty, Mercedes *Spanish and English language educator, literature educator*
Dearinger, Tracy M. *business educator*
May, Peter Alan *biology educator*
Ryan, Michael Louis *controller*

**Teton Village**
Conrad, Donald Glover *insurance executive*

**Torrington**
Lewis, Mary Jane *retired elementary school educator*

**Wheatland**
Hunkins, Raymond Breedlove *lawyer, rancher*
Munari, Michael F. *music educator, small business owner*

**Wilson**
Breitenbach, Mary Louise McGraw *psychologist, chemical dependency counselor*
Chrystie, Thomas Ludlow *investor*
Gordon, Stephen Maurice *manufacturing company executive, rancher*
Harrell, Samuel Macy *agribusiness executive*
Sage, Andrew Gregg Curtin, II, *retired brokerage house executive*

**Worland**
Woods, Lawrence Milton *airline company executive*

# TERRITORIES OF THE UNITED STATES

## AMERICAN SAMOA

**Pago Pago**
Howland, Repeka Moata'a Isara *retired government community services administrator*
Kruse, F. Michael *judge*
Richmond, Lyle L. *judge*
Sunia, Aitofele Toese F. *lieutenant governor*
Togafau, Malaetasi M. (Sialega Malaetasi Mauga Togafau) *attorney general, judge*
Tuitele, Lui *school system administrator*
Tulafono, Togiola T.A. *governor*
Weitzel, John Quinn *bishop*

## FEDERATED STATES OF MICRONESIA

**Chuuk**
Samo, Amando *bishop*

**Pohnpei**
Falcam, Leo A. *former Micronesian government official*

## GUAM

**Hagatna**
Artero, Margaret T. *academic administrator, military officer*
Camacho, Felix Perez *governor*
Carbullido, F. Philip *judge*
Espaldon, Ernesto Mercader *plastic surgeon, former senator*
Gutierrez, Carl T. C. *former governor*
Leon-Guerrero, Jillette Torre *nonprofit organization executive, consultant, writer*
Manibusan, Joaquin V.E., Jr. *magistrate judge*
Maraman, Katherine Ann *judge*
Moylan, Douglas B. *attorney general*
Moylan, Kaleo *lieutenant governor*
Sablan, David J. *marketing professional, political organization worker*
Torres, Robert J., Jr. *judge*
Tydingco-Gatewood, Frances Marie *judge*
Unpingco, John Walter Sablan *chief federal judge*
Weeks, Janet Healy *retired supreme court justice*

**Mangilao**
Duenas, Laurent Flores *health and nursing consultant*
Inoue, Yukiko *educational research educator*
Strauch, Edward Hugo *writer, retired literature and language professor*

**Talofofo**
Taylor, James John *finance educator*

**Tamuning**
Aguigui, Ignacio Cruz *lawyer*
Rahmani, Kia M. *surgeon*

## NORTHERN MARIANA ISLANDS

**Saipan**
Castro, Alexandro C. *commonwealth supreme court justice*
Demapan, Miguel S. *commonwealth supreme court justice*
Fitial, Benigno Repeki *governor*
Inos, Rita Hocog *school system administrator*
Kaufer, Connie Tenorio *special education educator, researcher*

McNeill, John Hugh *pharmaceutical sciences educator*
McWhinney, Edward Watson *Canadian government legislator*
Mizgala, Henry F. *physician, consultant, retired medical educator*
Murray, Anne *singer*
Nemetz, Peter Newman *economist, researcher, policy analysis educator*
Newman, Murray Arthur *aquarium administrator*
Nonis, David *professional sports team executive*
Nosco, Peter Erling *humanities educator, consultant*
Overmyer, Daniel Lee *humanities educator*
Pacheco-Ransanz, Arsenio *language educator, historian, educator*
Penikett, Tony *mediator, negotiator, writer, political organization worker*
Peterson, Leslie Raymond *barrister*
Phillips, Anthony George *neurobiology researcher*
Phillips, John Edward *zoologist, educator*
Piternick, Anne Brearley *librarian, educator*
Rennie, Paul Steven *research scientist, surgeon*
Riedel, Bernard Edward *retired pharmaceutical sciences educator*
Rothstein, Samuel *librarian, educator*
Salcudean, Martha Eva *mechanical engineer, educator*
Saunders, Peter Paul *investor*
Saywell, William George Gabriel *business development and management consultant*
Shaw, Michael *biologist, educator*
Shearer, Ronald Alexander *economics professor*
Sinclair, Alastair James *geology educator*
Sion, Maurice *mathematics professor*
Sorensen, Poul Henrik Bredahl *physician, research scientist, pathologist*
Suedfeld, Peter *psychologist, educator*
Tate, Larenz *actor*
Tees, Richard Chisholm *psychology professor, researcher*
Unger, Richard Watson *history professor*
Vigneault, Alain *professional hockey coach*
Vogt, Erich Wolfgang *physicist, academic administrator*
Walker, Michael Angus *economist, director*
Wellington, William George *entomologist, ecologist, educator*
Yaffe, Barbara Marlene *journalist*
Young, Lawrence *electrical engineering educator*

**Victoria**
Antoniou, Andreas *electrical engineering educator*
Batten, Alan Henry *astronomer*
Best, Melvyn Edward *geophysicist*
Finlay, James Campbell *retired museum director*
Fuller, James Chester Eedy *retired chemical company executive*
Harvey, Donald *artist, educator*
Hollis, Reginald *archbishop*
Hutchings, John Barrie *astronomer, researcher*
Israel, Werner *physicist, educator*
Leffek, Kenneth Thomas *retired chemist, educator*
Manning, Eric *computer scientist, educator, dean, researcher*
Meadow, Charles *information scientist, writer*
Morton, Donald Charles *astronomer*
Nuttall, Richard Norris *management consultant, physician*
Richards, Vincent Philip Haslewood *retired librarian*
Shaw, Timothy Milton *political science professor*
Turpin, David Howard *biologist, educator, academic administrator*
Wiles, David McKeen *chemist*

**West Vancouver**
Copes, Parzival *economist, researcher*
Wynne-Edwards, Hugh Robert *geologist, educator, entrepreneur*

**Westbank**
Wedepohl, Leonhard Martin *electrical engineering educator*

## MANITOBA

**Winnipeg**
Alfa, Michelle Josephine *microbiologist, educator*
Anderson, David Trevor *law educator*
Burns, James William *financial executive*
Cohen, Albert Diamond *retail executive*
Cohen, Harley *engineering educator*
Curtis, Charles Edward *Canadian government official*
Edwards, Clifford Henry Coad *law educator*
Eyre, Ivan *artist*
Haworth, James Chilton *pediatrics educator*
Kuffel, Edmund *electrical engineering educator*
Lewis, André Leon *artistic director*
Liba, Peter Michael *Canadian provincial government official, retired communications executive*
MacKenzie, George Allan *medical products executive*
McCallum, John Stuart *finance educator, columnist*
Mufti, Aftab A. *civil engineering educator*
Persaud, Trivedi Vidhya Nandan *anatomy educator, researcher, consultant*
Poettcker, Henry *retired academic administrator*
Runnalls, David *think-tank executive*
Schacter, Brent Allan *oncologist, health facility administrator*
Schaefer, Theodore Peter *retired chemistry professor*
Schnoor, Jeffrey Arnold *lawyer*
Schultz, Harry *health science organization administrator*
Smith, Ian Cormack Palmer *biophysicist*
Turner, Robert Comrie *composer*
Watchorn, William Ernest *venture capitalist*

## NEW BRUNSWICK

**Fredericton**
Bray, Dale Irving *civil engineering educator*
Grotterod, Knut *retired paper company executive*
Kenyon, Gary Michael *gerontologist, educator*

Lumsden, Ian Gordon *art gallery director*
Strange, Henry Hazen *judge*

**Rothesay**
Fairweather, Robert Gordon Lee *retired lawyer*

**Saint Andrews**
Anderson, John Murray *operations research specialist, consultant, retired academic administrator*

**Saint John**
Condon, Thomas Joseph *university historian*

**Sussex**
Secord, Lloyd Douglas *health facility administrator*

## NEWFOUNDLAND AND LABRADOR

**Corner Brook**
Payne, Sidney Stewart *retired archbishop*

**Saint John's**
Clark, Jack Ivor *civil engineer, researcher*
Gibbons, Rex Vincent *geologist*
May, Arthur W. *retired academic administrator, educator*
Rochester, Michael Grant *geophysics educator*

**Torbay**
Dabinett, Diana Frances *artist*

## NORTHWEST TERRITORIES

**Yellowknife**
Blondin-Andrew, Ethel D. *Canadian government official*

## NOVA SCOTIA

**Bedford**
Birdsall, William Forest *retired librarian*
Hennigar, David John *portfolio manager, director*

**Chester Basin**
Parr-Johnston, Elizabeth *economist, consultant*

**Dartmouth**
Elliott, James A. *oceanographer, researcher*
Horrocks, Norman *librarian, educator, editor*
Mann, Kenneth Henry *marine ecologist*

**Halifax**
Carrigan, David Owen *history educator*
Casson, Alan Graham *thoracic surgeon, researcher*
Chowdhury, Dhiman *physician, consultant*
Dahn, Jeff Raymond *physics professor*
Dexter, Robert Paul *lawyer*
Fillmore, Peter Arthur *mathematician, educator*
Fowler, Charles Allison Eugene *retired architect, civil engineer*
Glube, Constance Rachelle *retired judge*
Gratwick, John *management consulting executive, writer, consultant*
Gray, James *English literature educator*
Hall, Brian Keith *biology professor, writer*
Hiltz, Arnold Aubrey *retired chemist*
Jaeger, Leslie Gordon *academic administrator*
Jones, William Ernest *chemistry professor*
Kulyk, Karen Gay *artist*
Langley, George Ross *medical educator*
LeValliant, Debbie *information technology executive*
Mann, David *energy and services company executive*
Murray, Thomas John (Jock Murray) *medical humanities educator, physician, neurologist*
Renouf, Harold Augustus *retired transportation executive*
Stairs, Denis Winfield *political science professor, department chairman*
Tonks, Robert Stanley *pharmacologist, educator, retired dean*

**Mahone Bay**
Collins, John Alfred *retired obstetrician, gynecologist, educator*

**North Sydney**
Nickerson, Jerry Edgar Alan *business executive*

**Stellarton**
Sobey, David Frank *food company executive*
Sobey, Donald Creighton Rae *real estate developer*

**Tatamagouche**
Roach, Margot Ruth *retired biophysicist, educator*

**Wolfville**
Ogilvie, Kelvin Kenneth *academic administrator, chemist, educator*

## NUNAVUT

**Kugaaruk**
Rodnunsky, Sidney *lawyer, educator*

## ONTARIO

**Aurora**
Cellucci, Paul (Argeo Paul Cellucci) *former ambassador, former governor*
Lanthier, Ronald Ross *retired manufacturing executive*

**Bowmanville**
Evans, Essi H. *research scientist*

**Bracebridge**
Evans, John David Daniel *judge*

**Brampton**
Bastian, Donald Noel *retired bishop*
Malhi, Gurbax Singh *Canadian government official*
Paikeday, Thomas M. *lexicographer, linguistic consultant*
Savoie, Leonard Norman *transportation company executive*

**Brantford**
Hanna, William Brooks *publishing executive, literary agent*

**Brockville**
Spalding, James Stuart *retired telecommunications industry executive*

**Burlington**
Harris, Philip John *engineering educator*

**Callander**
Haig, Susan *conductor*

**Cambridge**
MacBain, William Halley *minister, theology studies educator, academic administrator*
White, Joseph Charles *manufacturing and retailing company executive*

**Chatham**
McKeough, William Darcy *supply company executive*

**Collingwood**
Morley, Lawrence Whitaker *geophysicist, consultant*

**Concord**
Deveson, Gregory S. *automotive executive*

**Deep River**
Davies, John Arthur *retired physics professor, engineering educator, research scientist*
Milton, John Charles Douglas *nuclear physicist, researcher*

**Don Mills**
French, William Harold *retired newspaper editor*

**Dorchester**
Fanning, William James *professional sports team executive, commentator*

**Downsview**
Eggleton, Arthur C. *former Canadian government official, member of Parliament*
Forer, Arthur H. *biology professor, researcher, editor*

**Etobicoke**
Howe, James Tarsicius *retired insurance company executive*
McIntyre, John George Wallace *real estate developer, management consultant*
Scholefield, Peter Gordon *health facility administrator*

**Flamborough**
Lee, Alvin A. *literary educator, scholar, author*

**Freelton**
Sonnenberg, Hardy *data processing executive, researcher, electrical engineer*

**Gloucester**
Malouin, Jean-Louis *adult education educator*

**Greely**
Lister, Earle Edward *retired research executive*

**Guelph**
Beveridge, Terrance James *microbiology professor, researcher*
Bewley, John Derek *botany researcher, educator*
Dickinson, William Trevor *hydrologist, educator*
Kasha, Kenneth John *agriculturist, educator*
Land, Reginald Brian *library administrator*

**Hamilton**
Bandler, John William *electrical engineering educator, consultant*
Bienenstock, John *pathologist, educator, health facility administrator*
Campbell, Colin Kydd *electrical and computer engineering educator, researcher*
Crowe, Cameron Macmillan *chemical engineering professor*
Datars, William Ross *physicist, researcher*
Garland, William James *nuclear engineer, educator*
George, Peter James *economist, educator*
Gillespie, Ronald James *chemistry professor, researcher, writer*
McKay, Alexander Gordon *classics educator*
Mott, Rodney B. *metal products executive*
Roland, Charles Gordon *physician, medical educator, historian*
Ryan, Ellen Bouchard *psychology professor, gerontologist*
Spenser, Ian Daniel *chemistry professor*
Sprung, Donald Whitfield Loyal *physics professor*

**Holland Landing**
Dempster, Barry (Edward) *poet*

**Kanata**
Muckler, John *professional sports team executive*
Murray, Bryan Clarence *professional hockey coach*

**Kingston**
Akenson, Donald Harman *historian, educator*
Batchelor, Barrington de Vere *civil engineer, educator*
Campbell, Louis Lorne *mathematics professor*
Ewan, George Thomson *physicist, researcher*
Kaliski, Stephan Felix *economics professor*
Kaufman, Nathan *retired pathologist, educator*
Leggett, William C. *biology professor, academic administrator*

Low, James A. *physician*
MacKinnon, James Gordon *economist, educator*
Meisel, John *political scientist*
Spencer, John Hedley *biochemistry educator*
Stewart, Alec Thompson *physicist, educator*
Szarek, Walter Anthony *chemist, educator*
Wyatt, Gerard Robert *biology professor, researcher*

**Kitchener**
Coles, Graham *conductor, composer*
Eldred, Gerald Marcus *performing company executive*
Winger, Roger Elson *retired church administrator*

**London**
Bancroft, George Michael *chemical physicist, educator*
Bauer, Michael Anthony *computer scientist, educator*
Borwein, David *mathematics professor*
Cornies, Larry Alan *journalist, educator*
Davenport, Alan Garnett *civil engineer, educator*
Davenport, Paul *economics professor*
Dreimanis, Aleksis *emeritus geology educator*
Fyfe, William Sefton *geochemist, educator*
Gerber, Douglas Earl *classics educator*
Inculet, Ion I. *electrical engineer, educator, science association director, consultant*
Laidler, David Ernest William *economics professor*
Lala, Peeyush Kanti *research scientist, educator*
Livick, Stephen *fine art photographer*
Marotta, Joseph Thomas *medical educator*
Osbaldeston, Gordon Francis *finance educator, retired federal agency administrator*
Poole, Nancy Geddes *art gallery curator, writer*
Stewart, Harold Brown *biochemist*
Weijer, Charles *medical educator, researcher*
William, David *theater director, actor*
Wonnacott, Ronald Johnston *economics professor*

**Manotick**
Hobson, George Donald *retired geophysicist*
Osmond, Dennis Gordon *anatomist, researcher, medical educator*

**Markham**
Burns, H(erbert) Michael *healthcare executive, director*
Gulden, Simon *lawyer, management consultant, consultant*

**Mississauga**
Gupta, Rajesh *engineer, consultant*
Kennedy, John W. *health products executive*
Melnyk, Eugene N. *pharmaceutical company executive, professional sports team executive*
Palmer, Patrick Asa *retired bank executive, finance educator*

**Nepean**
Chudobiak, Walter James *electronics executive*
Kallmann, Helmut Max *musicologist, retired librarian*

**Niagara-on-the-Lake**
Nielsen-Jones, Ian Richard *lottery and gaming executive, consultant*
Olley, Robert Edward *economist, educator*

**Nobleton**
Embleton, Tony Frederick Wallace *retired Canadian government official*

**North York**
Adelman, Howard *philosophy educator*
Blundell, William Richard Charles *retired electric company executive*
Buzacott, John Alan *engineering educator*
Davey, Kenneth George *biologist, educator, academic administrator*
Flock, Howard *psychology professor*
Gasparrini-Etheridge, Claudia *publishing executive, research scientist, writer*
Regan, David *neuroscientist*
Thomas, Clara McCandless *retired literature educator*

**Ottawa**
Alper, Howard *chemistry professor*
Angus, W. David *Queen's Counsel*
Armstrong, Henry Conner *former Canadian government official, consultant*
Austin, Jacob (Jack Austin) *Canadian government official*
Baker, George S. *federal official*
Baum, Bernard Rene *research scientist*
Beare-Rogers, Joyce Louise *retired research and development executive*
Beatty, Perrin *business association executive*
Bélanger, Mauril *member of parliament*
Bélisle, Paul Charles *Canadian government official*
Bevilacqua, Maurizio *member of Canadian parliament*
Bozozuk, Michael *civil engineer*
Brooks, David Barry *resource economist*
Buchanan, John MacLennan *Canadian provincial official*
Carroll, Margaret Aileen *member of Canadian parliament*
Carty, Arthur John *science policy advisor, research administrator*
Catterall, Marlene *Canadian legislator*
Copps, Sheila *former Canadian government official*
Courtois, Bernard Andre *communications executive*
Csörgő, Miklós *mathematics and statistics educator*
d'Aquino, Thomas *lawyer, educator, entrepreneur*
Davey, Clark William *newspaper publisher*
Day, Stockwell Burt *government official*
de Bold, Adolfo J. *pathologist, educator, physiologist, researcher*
de Chastelain, A(lfred) John G(ardyne) D(rummond) *Canadian army officer, diplomat*
Dhaliwal, Herb (Harbance Singh) *legislator, former Canadian government official*
Dlab, Vlastimil *mathematics professor, researcher*
Dray, William Herbert *philosophy educator*
Efford, Reuben John (John Efford) *Canadian government official*

Fairbairn, Joyce *Canadian government official*
Fellegi, Ivan Peter *statistician*
Fitzpatrick, Brian *Canadian legislator*
Georganas, Nicolas D. *electrical engineering educator, academic administrator*
Gillingham, Bryan Reginald *music educator*
Gold, Lorne W. *Canadian government official*
Goodale, Ralph E. *Canadian government official*
Gordon, Steve *real estate company executive*
Graham, William C. *Canadian government official*
Griller, David *management consultant*
Guarnieri, Albina *Canadian legislator*
Hagen, Paul Beo *pharmacologist*
Halliday, Ian *astronomer*
Harb, Mac *Canadian government official*
Harington, Charles Richard *vertebrate paleontologist*
Holmes, John Leonard *chemistry professor*
Hughes, Stanley John *retired mycologist*
Hurteau, Gilles David *retired obstetrician, gynecologist, educator, dean*
Ingold, Keith Usherwood *chemist, educator*
Jordan, Joseph Louis *education educator, government official*
Kates, Morris *biochemist, educator*
Kilgour, David *Canadian member parliament*
Kingsley, Jean-Pierre *federal official*
Kroeger, Arthur *retired academic administrator, retired federal official*
Labarge, Margaret Wade *medieval history professor, historian, writer*
Lavoie, Lionel A. *physician, health science association administrator*
MacAulay, Lawrence A. *former Canadian government official, member of Parliament*
MacDonald, Flora Isabel *Canadian government official*
MacFarlane, John Alexander *retired federal agency administrator*
MacKay, William Andrew *judge*
Macklem, Michael Kirkpatrick *publisher*
Manley, John Paul *former Canadian government official*
Margeson, Theodore Earl *judge*
Maxwell, Judith *think-tank executive, economist*
McAvity, John Gillis *museum director, association executive, museologist*
McCallum, John *Canadian government official*
McGuire, Joseph *Canadian government official*
McLachlin, Beverley *Canadian supreme court chief justice*
McLure, John Douglas *management consultant, former Canadian government official*
Mills, Bob *member of Canadian parliament*
Minna, Maria *member of Canadian Parliament*
Murray, Larry *government agency administrator*
Murray, Lowell *Canadian senator*
O'Neil, Maureen *think-tank executive*
Penner, Keith *former Canadian government official*
Perry, Malcolm Blythe *biologist, researcher*
Peterson, James Scott (Jim Peterson) *Canadian government official*
Pettigrew, Pierre S. *Canadian government official*
Philogene, Bernard J. R. *academic administrator, science educator*
Plumptre, Tim *think-tank executive*
Prevost, Roxane Lise *music theory educator*
Ramsay, Donald Allan *physical chemist*
Regan, Geoff *Canadian government official*
Roland, Anne *registrar Supreme Court of Canada*
Ryan, William Francis *priest*
Saada, Jacques *legislator*
Scherrer, Helene Chalifour *Canadian government official*
Schneider, William George *chemist, research consultant*
Scott, Marianne Florence *retired librarian, educator*
Shiari, Behrouz *mechanical engineer, researcher*
Silverman, Ozzie *consulting strategist*
Squire, Anne Marguerite *retired humanities educator*
Staines, David McKenzie *language educator*
Stanford, Joseph Stephen *diplomat, lawyer, educator*
St-Onge, Denis Alderic *geologist, research scientist, educator*
Storey, Kenneth Bruce *biology professor*
Strayer, Barry Lee *retired judge*
Sylvestre, Jean Guy *former national librarian*
Tassé, Roger *lawyer, former Canadian government official*
Telegdi, Andrew *member of parliament*
Tellier, Henri *retired Canadian military officer*
Turcotte, Matheu *Olympic athlete*
Urie, John James *retired lawyer, former Canadian federal judge*
Valeri, Tony *Canadian government official, small business owner*
Vassilyadi, Michael *pediatric neurosurgeon*
Veizer, Ján *geology educator*
Vellacott, Maurice *legislator*
Volpe, Joseph *Canadian government official*
Wallot, Jean-Pierre *archivist, historian*
Whitehead, J. Rennie *science administrator, consultant*
Withers, Ramsey Muir *retired federal agency administrator*
Yalden, Maxwell Freeman *Canadian diplomat*
Yelich, Lynne *member of parliament*
Yeomans, Donald Ralph *Canadian government official, consultant*

## Owen Sound
Jones, Phyllis Edith *nursing educator*

## Paris
Hooper, Wayne Nelson *retired clergy member*

## Peterborough
Burwick, David *beverage company executive*
Davis, Gordon Richard Fuerst *retired biologist, translator*
Dumas, Michael Godfrey Joseph *artist*
Hutchinson, Thomas Cuthbert *ecology and environmental educator*
Theall, Donald Francis *retired university president*

## Red Lake
Zaikow, Larry J. James *painter*

## Richmond Hill
Garrison, Robert Frederick *astronomer, educator*

## Saint Catharines
Ayanso, Anteneh Wondimu *information systems educator*
Bergevin, V. Réal *customer relationship management executive*
Miller, John Peter (Jack Miller) *journalist*
Sivell, John Norman *language educator*
Stevenson, Garth *social sciences educator*

## Sault Sainte Marie
Ferris, Ronald Curry *bishop*

## Scarborough
Cetín, Anton *artist*
White, Calvin John *zoo executive, zoological association executive, financial manager*

## Stittsville
MacLeod, Robert Angus *microbiology educator, researcher*

## Thornhill
Lublinski, Michael *lawyer*

## Thorold
O'Mara, John Aloysius *retired bishop*

## Toronto
Ames, Steven *management consultant*
Angel, Aubie *endocrinologist, academic administrator*
Arthurs, Harry William *lawyer, educator, academic administrator*
Astman, Barbara Ann *artist, educator*
Augustine, Jerome Samuel *merchant banker*
Bandeen, Robert Angus *management consultant*
Bartleman, James K. *lieutenant governor*
Baxendale, Sonia A. *diversified financial services company executive*
Beckwith, John *musician, educator, composer*
Berezin, Sergei *professional hockey player*
Bhaduri, Ranjan *investment management professional*
Blewett, David Lambert *English literature educator*
Bloomberg, Lawrence S. *security firm executive, art appraiser*
Bohme, Diethard Kurt *chemistry professor*
Boland, Janet Lang *judge*
Bolley, Andrea *artist*
Braswell, Paula Ann *artist*
Brook, Adrian Gibbs *chemistry professor*
Bryant, Josephine Harriet *library executive*
Budrevics, Alexander *landscape architect*
Carder, Paul Charles *retired advertising executive*
Carlen, Peter Louis *neuroscientist, educator, science administrator, researcher*
Carrothers, Gerald Arthur Patrick *environmental and city planning educator*
Chandra, Ranjit Kumar *research scientist, educator, physician*
Chester, Simon George *lawyer*
Clark, Maura J. *oil and gas industry executive*
Clarkson, Adrienne *former Governor General of Canada*
Cleghorn, John Edward *bank executive*
Cockwell, Jack Lynn *finance company executive*
Colangelo, Bryan *professional sports team executive*
Colgrass, Michael Charles *composer*
Colombo, John Robert *poet*
Comper, Tony (F. Anthony Comper) *banker*
Connell, Philip Francis *food industry executive*
Cook, Stephen Arthur *mathematics and computer science educator*
Cook-Bennett, Gail *pension fund administrator*
Cunningham, Gordon Ross *finance company executive*
Curlook, Walter *management consultant*
Dale, Robert Gordon *investment company executive*
D'Alessandro, Dominic *financial executive*
Davis, Antonio Lee *professional basketball player*
Davis, William Grenville *lawyer, former Canadian government official*
Davison, Edward Joseph *electrical engineering educator*
Dean, Geoffrey *book publisher*
DeWitt, David B. *political scientist, educator, political organization worker*
Dickens, Bernard Morris *law educator*
Dimma, William Andrew *real estate executive*
Dobson, Wendy Kathleen *economics professor*
Dooher, Donna *chef*
Dubin, Charles Leonard *lawyer*
Dunlop, David John *geophysics educator, researcher*
Eagles, Stuart Ernest *real estate company officer*
Egoyan, Atom *film director*
Endrenyi, Janos *research engineer, educator*
Evans, John Robert *academic administrator, cardiologist*
Farkas, Leslie Gabriel *plastic surgeon*
Farley, Tom *real estate company executive*
Farquharson, Gordon MacKay *lawyer, director*
Fatt, William Robert *hotel executive*
Ferguson, John, Jr. *professional sports team executive*
Ferguson, Kingsley George *retired psychologist*
Fierheller, George Alfred *communications executive*
Fife, Edward H. *landscape architecture educator*
Finlay, Terence Edward *retired archbishop*
Fox, Wayne C. *stock exchange executive, corporate financial executive*
Fraser, William Neil *retired government agency administrator*
Friedlander, John Benjamin *mathematician, educator*
Fullerton, R. Donald *banker*
Furtado, Nelly Kim *vocalist*
Ganczarczyk, Jerzy Jozef *engineering educator, consultant*
Gilbert, Greg *professional hockey coach, retired professional hockey player*
Glaus, Troy *professional baseball player*
Godsoe, Peter Cowperthwaite *retired banker*

Goh, Chan Hon *ballerina*
Goldfarb, Martin *sociologist, researcher*
Goold, Douglas *think-tank executive*
Gordon, Harold Sonny *bank executive*
Goring, David Arthur Ingham *chemist, educator*
Gotlieb, Allan E. *former ambassador*
Gotlieb, Calvin Carl *computer scientist, educator*
Granatstein, Jack Lawrence *historian*
Grayson, Albert Kirk *social studies educator*
Greenwood, Lawrence George *banker*
Gregor, Tibor Philip *retired management consultant*
Halladay, Roy *professional baseball player*
Hayhurst, James Frederick Palmer *career and business consultant, inspirational speaker, writer*
Helleiner, Gerald Karl *economics professor*
Hillenbrand, Shea Matthew *professional baseball player*
Hodgkinson, Greta *dancer*
Hofmann, Theo *biochemist, educator*
Holyday, Douglas Charles *city councillor*
Hon Goh, Chan *dancer*
Hore, John Edward *commodity futures educator*
Hutchison, Andrew Sandford *archbishop*
Iacobucci, Frank *lawyer, judge, academic administrator*
Janischewskyj, Wasyl *electrical engineering educator*
Jaworska, Tamara *artist*
Johnson, Robert Eugene *historian, academic administrator*
Kain, Karen Alexandria *ballet dancer*
Kaufman, Donna S. *lawyer*
Kerr, David Wylie *utilities executive*
Klein, Gary *dentist*
Knowlton, Thomas A. *dean, retired food products executive*
Kooluris Dobbs, Linda Kia *artist, photographer*
Kramer, Burton *graphic designer, educator*
Kresge, Alexander Jerry *chemistry professor*
Kudelka, James *choreographer, artistic director*
Kushner, Eva *academic administrator, educator, author*
Landsberg, Michele *retired journalist*
Langer, Bernard *medical association administrator*
Lawson, Jane Elizabeth *retired bank executive*
Leech, James William *investment company executive*
Lindsay, Roger Alexander (Baron of Craighall) *investment executive*
Lindsay, William Kerr *surgeon*
Litherland, Albert Edward *physics professor*
Liversage, Richard Albert *cell biologist, educator*
Macdonald, Donald Stovel *public policy advisor*
Macdonald, Hugh Ian *economics professor, public policy professor, retired academic administrator*
MacDougall, Hartland Molson *retired bank executive*
MacLaren, Roy *retired Canadian government official*
MacLennan, David Herman *research scientist, educator*
Mann, George Stanley *diversified financial services company executive, real estate company officer*
Martin, Robert William *retired utilities executive*
Masui, Yoshio *zoology educator*
Maurice, Paul *professional hockey coach*
Mc Culloch, Ernest Armstrong *internist, educator*
Mckellar, Don *actor, screenwriter, filmmaker*
McMurtry, R. Roy *federal judge*
McWilliam, Joanne Elizabeth *retired theology studies educator*
Meagher, George Vincent *mechanical engineer*
Mercier, Eileen Ann *corporate financial executive*
Millgate, Michael (Michael Henry Millgate) *retired literature educator*
Mintz, Jack Maurice *think-tank executive, economics professor*
Moore, Carole Irene *librarian*
Moore, Christopher Hugh *writer*
Morey, Carl Reginald *musicologist*
Morneau, William *pension and benefits company executive*
Mulholland, William David, Jr. *retired bank executive*
Munk, Peter *mining executive*
Munro, John Henry Alexander *economics professor, writer*
Neligan, Peter C. *plastic surgeon*
Nesbitt, Richard *stock exchange executive*
Nguyen, San Duy *psychiatrist, educator*
Novak, David *theology studies educator, rabbi*
Ogilvie, Richard Ian *clinical pharmacologist*
Osler, Gordon Peter *retired utilities executive*
Ostry, Sylvia *academic administrator, economist*
Oundjian, Peter *conductor, music director*
Packham, Marian Aitchison *biochemistry professor*
Peacock, Molly *poet, educator*
Peca, Michael *professional hockey player*
Peterson, David Robert *lawyer, former Canadian government official*
Pinto, Maxwell Salustiano *management consultant*
Polanyi, John Charles *chemist, educator*
Poprawa, Andrew *diversified financial services company executive, accountant*
Pratt, Robert Cranford *political scientist, educator*
Price, Timothy R. *accountant*
Pritchard, Huw Owen *chemist, educator*
Rapoport, Anatol *humanities educator, biophysicist*
Rasky, Harry *producer, director, writer*
Ricciardi, J.P. *professional sports team executive*
Rogers, Edward Samuel *communications company executive*
Rooney, Paul George *mathematics professor*
Rose, Jeffrey Raymond *consultant, educator, public servant, trade unionist*
Salama, C. Andre Tewfik *electrical engineering educator*
Schramek, Tomas *ballet dancer, educator*
Schwartz, Gerald Wilfred *business executive*
Seiersen, Nicholas Steen *management consultant*
Semak, Michael William *photographer, educator*
Sessle, Barry John *adult education educator, researcher*
Shepherd, Gordon Greeley *space physics educator, researcher*
Silk, Frederick C.Z. *financial consultant*
Skvorecky, Josef Vaclav *literature educator, writer*
Slaight, Gary *broadcast executive*

Slemon, Gordon Richard *electrical engineering educator*
Sloan, David Edward *retired finance company executive*
Smith, Peter William Ebblewhite *electrical engineer, educator, research scientist, physicist*
Sole, Michael Joseph *cardiologist*
Stadelman, William Ralph *chemicals executive*
Staines, Mavis Avril *performing company executive*
Stoicheff, Boris Peter *physicist, researcher*
Storey, Susan *investment banker*
Stymiest, Barbara *stock exchange executive*
Sundin, Mats Johan *professional hockey player*
Tanenbaum, Joey *real estate developer*
Taylor, Allan Richard *retired banker*
Techar, Frank J. *bank executive*
Thall, Burnett Murray *retired newspaper executive*
Thomson, David K.R. *publishing executive*
Thomson, Richard Murray *retired bank executive*
Till, James Edgar *medical educator, researcher*
Tobe, Stephen Solomon *zoology educator*
Tolmie, Kenneth Donald *artist, writer*
Tsubouchi, David H. *Canadian provincial official*
Turnbull, John Cameron *retired pharmacist, consultant*
Turner, John Napier *former prime minister of Canada, legislator*
Turner, Robert Edward *psychiatrist, educator*
Van Der Wyst, Geon *dancer*
van Ginkel, Blanche Lemco *architect, educator*
Venetsanopoulos, Anastasios Nicolaos *electrical engineer, educator*
Verschuren, Annette *retail executive*
Volpé, Robert *endocrinologist, researcher, educator*
Waldman, Carol *dentist*
Webb, Anthony Allan *banker, director*
Weston, W. Galen, Sr., (Galen Weston) *diversified financial services company executive*
Wevers, John William *retired Semitic languages educator*
Whitfield, Simon *Olympic athlete*
Williams, Ricky (Errick Lynne Williams) *professional football player*
Wilson, Lynton Ronald *retired telecommunications industry executive*
Wilson, Michael Holcombe *investment banker, former Canadian government official*
Wleugel, John Peter *manufacturing executive*
Wonham, Walter Murray *electrical engineer, educator*
Zeng, Hong *audio system architect, researcher*

## Waterloo
Aczél, János Dezsö *mathematician*
Balsillie, Jim *information technology executive*
Berczi, Andrew Stephen *academic administrator, educator*
Falding, Harold Joseph *sociology educator*
Gladwell, Graham Maurice Leslie *mathematician, civil engineering educator*
Haworth, Lawrence Lindley *philosophy educator*
Hynes, Hugh Bernard Noel *biologist, educator*
Lazaridis, Mike *information technology executive, entrepreneur*
Morgan, Alan Vivian *geologist, educator*
Paldus, Josef *mathematics professor*
Penlidis, Alexander *chemical engineering professor*
Sedra, Adel Shafeek *engineering educator, academic administrator*
Smolin, Lee *physicist, researcher, writer*
Suits, Bernard Herbert *philosophy educator*
Urquhart, Tony *artist, educator*
Van Seters, John *retired biblical literature educator*
Vlach, Jiri *electrical engineering educator, researcher*
Warner, Barry Gregory *ecologist, educator*
Wen, Geyi *applied physics professor*
Wright, Douglas Tyndall *former university administrator*

## Willowdale
Goldberg, David Meyer *retired biochemist*
Irwin, John Wesley *publisher*
Kerner, Fred *book publisher, writer*
Sze, Michael Ming-Chih *actuary, consultant*
Winter, Frederick Elliot *fine arts educator*

## Windsor
Ferguson, John Duncan *medical research educator*
Hackam, Reuben *electrical engineering educator*
Kennedy, John Baptist *civil engineer*
La Rocque, Eugene Philippe *retired bishop*
Thibert, Roger Joseph *clinical chemist, educator*
Mohler, Brian Jeffery *diplomat*

## PRINCE EDWARD ISLAND

### Montague
Cregier, Don Mesick *historian, educator, researcher, consultant*

## QUEBEC

### Beaconsfield
Harder, Rolf Peter *graphic designer, painter*

### Beauharnois
Lebel, Robert *retired bishop*

### Gatineau
Wilson, Ian Edwin *cultural organization administrator, archivist*

### Ile Perrot
Lalonde, Marc *lawyer, former Canadian government official*

### Jonquière
Couture, Jean Guy *bishop*

### Laval
Baroudy, Bahige Mourad *biochemist, researcher*
Talbot, Pierre Joseph *microbiologist, researcher*

**Leclercville**

Morin, Pierre Jean *retired management consultant, social services administrator*

**Montpellier**

Poirier, Louis Joseph *neurology educator*

**Montreal**

Aguayo, Alberto Juan *neuroscientist*
Barrette, Jean *physicist, researcher*
Beauregard, Luc *public relations executive*
Beugnot, Bernard Andre Henri *literature educator*
Brecher, Irving *economics professor*
Brecher, Michael *political science professor*
Bruemmer, Fred *writer, photographer*
Burgess, John Herbert *cardiologist, educator*
Carbonneau, Guy *professional hockey coach, former professional hockey player*
Carroll, Robert Lynn *biology professor, paleontologist, curator, museum director*
Cedraschi, Tullio *investment company executive*
Chang, Thomas Ming Swi *research scientist, biotechnologist, educator*
Charney, Melvin *artist, architect, educator*
Clermont, Yves Wilfrid *anatomy educator, researcher*
Cruess, Richard Leigh *orthopedic surgeon, dean*
Cyr, J. V. Raymond *telecommunications industry executive*
Das Gupta, Subal *physics professor, researcher*
Davidson, Colin Henry *architect, educator*
Dealy, John Michael *chemical engineer, educator, holding company executive*
Eisenberg, Adi *chemist*
Ferguson, Michael John *electronics educator, communications educator*
Freedman, Samuel Orkin *university official*
Freeman, Carolyn Ruth *oncologist*
Gabbour, Iskandar *city and regional planning educator*
Gainey, Bob (Robert Michael Gainey) *professional sports team executive, retired professional hockey player*
Genest, Jacques *nephrologist, clinical scientist, science administrator*
Gibbs, Sarah Preble *biologist, educator*
Gillespie, Thomas Stuart *investment company executive*
Gillett, George Nield, Jr. *professional sports team executive, communications executive*
Girard, Francois *film director*
Gold, Phil *immunologist, educator, researcher*
Goldbloom, Victor Charles *pediatrician*
Goltzman, David *endocrinologist, educator, researcher*
Gonthier, Charles Doherty *retired judge*
Granger, Luc Marie *dean, psychologist*
Gratton, Robert *diversified financial services company executive*
Haccoun, David *electrical engineering educator*
Ikawa-Smith, Fumiko *anthropologist, educator*
Johnstone, Rose Mamelak (Mrs. Douglas Johnstone) *biochemistry educator*
Jolicoeur, Paul *molecular biologist*
Jones, Barbara Ellen *neurologist, educator*
Kinsley, William Benton *literature educator*
Koivu, Saku *professional hockey player*
Kovalev, Alexei *professional hockey player*
Kramer, Michael Stuart *pediatric epidemiologist*
Labadie, Bernard *performing company executive*
Lacombe, Jacques *conductor*
Lacoste, Paul *law educator, academic administrator*
Ladanyi, Branko *civil engineer, educator*
Lamarre, Bernard *engineering executive*
Large, John Andrew *library and information service professor*
Laurin, Pierre *finance company executive*
Leblond, Charles Philippe *anatomy educator, researcher*
Leroy, Claude *physics professor, researcher*
Levin, Richard I. *dean, cardiologist, researcher*
Lock, Edouard *performing company executive*
Mac Lean, Lloyd Douglas *surgeon*
Matziorinis, Kenneth N. *economist*
Melzack, Ronald *psychology professor*
Messing, Karen *occupational health researcher*
Michaud, Georges Joseph *physics professor*
Milic-Emili, Joseph *physiologist, educator*
Molson, Eric H. *brewery company executive*
Moser, William Oscar Jules *mathematics professor*
Moss, David *music company executive*
Mulder, David S. *cardiovascular surgeon*
Mulroney, Brian (Martin Brian Mulroney) *former Prime Minister of Canada*
Mysak, Lawrence Alexander *oceanographer, climatologist and mathematics educator*
Nadeau, Bertin Felix *holding company executive*
Nattel, Stanley *cardiologist, research scientist*
Nayar, Baldev Raj *political science professor*
Neveu, Jean *printing company executive*
Ngo, Van Tan (Tan Van) *financial planner, poet*
Normandeau, Andre Gabriel *criminologist, educator*
O'Neill, Daniel J. *brewery company executive*
Paidoussis, Michael Pandeli *mechanical engineering educator*
Pankov, Gradimir Krunislav *ballet artistic director*
Paul, T. V. *social sciences educator*
Perlin, Arthur Saul *chemistry professor*
Podgorsak, Ervin B. *medical physicist, educator, administrator*
Popovici, Adrian *law educator*
Pound, Richard William Duncan *lawyer, accountant*
Ramachandran, Venkatanarayana Deekshit *electrical engineering educator*
Raynauld, Andre *economist, educator*
Redfern, John D. *manufacturing executive*
Robb, James Alexander *lawyer*
Rochette, Louis *water transportation executive*
Rolland, Lucien Gilbert *paper company executive, director*
Saint-Pierre, Guy *engineering executive*
Scriver, Charles Robert *medical researcher, human geneticist, retired medical educator*
Selvadurai, Antony Patrick Sinnappa *civil engineer, educator, mathematician, consultant*
Sirois, Charles *communications executive*
Snell, Linda S. *internist, educator*

Solomon, Samuel *biochemistry educator, administrator*
Sourkes, Theodore Lionel *biochemistry professor*
Speirs, Derek James *diversified financial services company executive*
Stewart, Jane *psychology professor*
Suen, Ching Yee *computer scientist, educator, researcher*
Szabo, Denis *criminologist, educator*
Taras, Paul *physicist, researcher*
Thompson, John Douglas *corporate financial executive*
Torrey, David Leonard *investment banker*
Trigger, Bruce Graham *anthropology educator*
Turcotte, Jean-Claude Cardinal *archbishop*
Vaillancourt, Jean-Guy *sociology educator, researcher*
Vinet, Luc *physicist, educator*
Waller, Harold Myron *political science professor*
Webster, Norman Eric *journalist, foundation administrator*
Whitehead, Michael Anthony *chemistry professor*

**Mount Royal**

Elie, Jean André *investment banker*

**North Hatley**

Jones, Douglas Gordon *retired literature educator*

**Outremont**

Dufour, Jean-Marie *economist, statistician, educator*
Gulkin, Harry *arts administrator, film producer*
Levesque, Rene Jules Albert *retired physicist*

**Pointe-Claire**

Bachynski, Morrel Paul *physicist*
Lapointe, Lucie *research management executive*

**Quebec City**

Belanger, Gerard *economics professor*
Bonnelly, Claude *library director*
LeMay, Jacques *lawyer*
Morin, Louis *lawyer*
Potvin, Pierre *physiologist, educator*
Roy, Patrick *retired professional hockey player*
Stavert, Alexander Bruce *archbishop*
Theodorescu, Radu Amza Serban *mathematician, educator*
Verge, Pierre *legal educator*

**Rimouski**

Blanchet, Bertrand *archbishop*

**Rosemere**

Hopper, Carol *incentive program administrator, trade association administrator*

**Saint Jean Sur Richelieu**

Trudel, Marc J. *botanist, educator*

**Saint Laurent**

Dion, Stéphane *legislator*

**Saint-Adele**

Rousseau-Vermette, Mariette *artist*

**Saint-Sauveur**

Hanigan, Lawrence *retired rail transportation executive*

**Sainte Anne de Bellevue**

Broughton, Robert Stephen *engineering educator, consultant*

**Sainte-Foy**

Normand, Robert *retired lawyer*
Tremblay, Marc Adélard *anthropologist, educator*

**Sherbrooke**

Bourget, Edwin Robert *marine ecologist, educator*
Tremblay, André-Marie *physicist*

**Sillery**

Dinan, Robert Michael *lawyer*

**Varennes**

Bartnikas, Raymond *electrical engineer, educator*

**Verdun**

Gauthier, Serge Gaston *neurologist*
Lessard, Michel M. *finance company executive*

**Westmount**

Coolidge, Robert Tytus *deacon, historian, educator*
Fortier, L. Yves *barrister*
Kalaycioglu, Serdar *aerospace engineer, researcher*
Rothman, Melvin L. *retired judge*

**SASKATCHEWAN**

**Regina**

Barber, Lloyd Ingram *retired university president*
Bayda, Edward Dmytro *retired chief justice*
Haverstock, Lynda M. *lieutenant governor*
MacKay, Harold Hugh *lawyer*
Mollard, John Douglas *engineering and geology executive*
Phillips, Roger *retired steel company executive*
Symes, Lawrence Richard *computer science educator, university dean*

**Saskatoon**

Babiuk, Lorne Alan *virologist, immunologist, researcher*
Billinton, Roy *engineering educator*
Blakeney, Allan Emrys *Canadian government official, lawyer, educator*
Bornstein, Eli *artist, sculptor*
Hirose, Akira *physics professor, researcher*
Houston, C(larence) Stuart *radiologist, educator*
Huang, Pan Ming *soil science educator*
Ish, Daniel Russell *law educator, academic administrator*
Kartha, Kutty Krishnan *plant pathologist*
Kennedy, Marjorie Ellen *librarian*

Knott, Douglas Ronald *dean, agricultural sciences educator, researcher*
Smith, C. D. *civil engineering educator*
Sonntag, Bernard H. *agronomist, researcher, public information officer*

**YUKON TERRITORY**

**Whitehorse**

Couchman, Robert George James *foundation executive*

**Calgary**

Amonte, Tony (Anthony Lewis Amonte) *professional hockey player*
Maier, Gerald James *gas industry executive*
McCarty, Darren *professional hockey player*
Playfair, Jim *professional hockey coach*

**Halifax**

Matta, Chérif Farid *chemistry professor*

**Hamilton**

Ayers, Paul W. *chemistry professor*

**Montreal**

Bertrand, Luc *stock exchange executive*
Demers, Jacques *professional hockey team coach*
Jundi, Bilal *principal*
Loucks, Eric Barry *educator*
Lowy, Frederick Hans *academic administrator, psychiatrist*

**Niagara Falls**

Watson, George W. *energy executive*

**North Hatley**

Salt, Alfred Lewis *priest*

**Ontario**

Armstrong, Robin Louis *physics professor, physicist*
Warren, Jack Hamilton *retired diplomat, banker, trade policy advisor*

**Ottawa**

Axworthy, Lloyd *academic administrator, former Canadian government official*

**Sainte Anne de Bellevue**

Grant, William Frederick *geneticist, educator*

**Saskatoon**

Giesy, John Paul, Jr. *environmental scientist, educator*

**Sherbrooke**

Deslongchamps, Pierre *chemistry professor*

**Toronto**

Josselyn, Sheena A. *research scientist, educator*
Katchanovski, Ivan G. *political scientist, researcher*
Pollock, Bruce Godfrey *psychiatrist, educator*
Ryan, B.J. *professional baseball player*
Stanley, Deirdre *lawyer*
Urbach, David Robert *surgeon, educator*

**Vancouver**

Grant, Edward Robert *chemistry professor, science association executive*
Newtown, Thandie *actress*

**Waterloo**

Bernath, Peter *chemistry professor*
Fréchette, Louise *international organization official*
Shen, Xuemin Sherman *engineering educator, researcher*

**Whistler**

Rae, Barbara Joyce *employee placement company executive*

**Windsor**

Van Den Brande, Rene Albert *retired accountant*

**ARGENTINA**

**Buenos Aires**

Levy, Joseph Bruno *foundation administrator, educator*
Lopez-Murphy, Ricardo Hipolito *economist*
Montes, Leopoldo Feliciano *dermatologist, educator*

**ARMENIA**

**Yerevan**

Sargsyan, David *library director*

**ASCENSION**

**Claton**

Tonge, Bruce John *psychiatrist*

**AUSTRALIA**

**Altona**

Daniel-Dreyfus, Susan B. Russe *information technology executive*

**Armadale**

Neil, Sandra Eilleen Silverberg *psychologist*

**Australian National University**

Leigh, Andrew Keith *economist, researcher*

**Brighton**

Bellin, Howard *management consultant*

**Brighton Victoria**

Ogilvy, Geoff *professional golfer*

**Camberwell**

Base, Graeme Rowland *illustrator, author*
Peterson, Douglas Pete (Pete Peterson) *former ambassador, retired congressman*

**Cammeray**

Besley, Morrish Alexander (Tim Besley) *civil engineer*

**Canberra**

Taylor, Stuart Ross *geochemist, writer*

**Clayton**

Broadbear, Jillian Helen *medical researcher*

**Darlinghurst**

Davis, Judy *actress*

**Double Bay**

Guerin, Didier *magazine executive*
Peacock, Penne Korth *ambassador*

**Malanda**

Cooper, William Thomas *natural history artist*

**Melbourne**

Batrouney, Clive M. *finance company executive*
Browne, Jeffrey Francis *lawyer*
Searby, Richard Henry *academic administrator, lawyer*

**Milsons Point**

Foster, Milo George *manufacturing executive*

**Nedlands**

Marshall, Barry James *gastroenterologist*
Oxnard, Charles Ernest *anatomist, anthropologist, biologist, educator*

**Norfolk Island**

McCullough, Colleen *author*

**North Sydney**

Crowe, Russell *actor*
Scott, Brian Walter *management consultant*

**Paddington**

Keneally, Thomas Michael *author*

**Parkville**

Azer, Samy Aziz *gastroenterologist, medical educator*
Denton, Derek Ashworth *medical researcher, foundation administrator*
Metcalf, Donald *biomedical researcher*

**Perth**

Dow, Simon *artistic director, choreographer*

**Queensland**

Ho, Yik Hong *colon and rectal surgeon*

**Randwick**

Hall, Peter Francis *physiologist*

**Redfern**

Campion, Jane *film director, screenwriter*

**Springfield**

Spalvins, Janis Gunars *steamship company executive*

**Sydney**

Blakely, Edward James *economics professor*
Hora, Heinrich *physicist*
McLennan, Andrew M. *economics professor*
Packer, James Goodwin *library director, writer*
Selley, Michael L. *pharmaceutical company executive*
Bishop, Rosalinda Matubis *information manager*

**AUSTRIA**

**Graz**

Weisstein, Ulrich Werner *English literature educator*

**Grossgmain**

Mueller, Christa *radiologist*

**Vienna**

Higgins, William Woods *painter, art educator*
Pohl, Adolf Leopold *clinical chemist, quality assurance consultant*

**THE BAHAMAS**

**Nassau**

Dingman, Michael David *manufacturing executive, investor*
Harrison, Johnnie Sheppard *religious organization administrator*
Templeton, John Marks *investment counsel, financial analyst*

**BAHRAIN**

**Manama**

Sarhan, Mansoor Mohamed *library director*

**BANGLADESH**

**Dhaka**

Brooks, W. Abdullah *pediatrician, researcher*

**Kushtia**

Latifur Rahaman, Rasul Boaksh *legal association administrator*

## BELGIUM

**Antwerp**
Snyders, Dirk Johan *electrophysiologist and biophysicist educator*
Van Borm, Julien Ludovicus Adelia *library director*

**Brussels**
Baptiste, Thomas L. *career military officer*
Barnum, John Wallace *lawyer*
Bustin, George Leo *lawyer*
Buysse, Paul Henri Maria *manufacturing executive*
de Duve, Christian René *chemist, educator*
Freizer, Louis A. *radio producer*
Gray, C. Boyden (Clayland Boyden Gray) *ambassador, lawyer*
Horton, Linda Rae *lawyer*
Jadot, Jean Lambert Octave *clergyman*
Jones, James L., Jr. *career military officer*
Kempe, Frederick Schumann *newspaper editor, columnist*
Lewis, Jesse *editor*
Nuland, Victoria *US permanent representative to NATO*
Theyskens, Olivier *apparel designer*

**Diegen**
Dörken, Uwe R. *finance company executive*

**Genappe**
Williams, Jody *political organization administrator*

**Liège**
Mosora-Stan, Florentina Ioana *physics professor*

## BELIZE

**Belize City**
Brown, Sir George Noel *judge*

## BERMUDA

**Hamilton**
McCormick, Hugh Thomas *lawyer*

**Pembroke**
Freimark, Jeffrey Philip *corporate financial executive*
Stempel, Ernest Edward *insurance executive*

**St. George's**
Burchall, Leondra N. *history educator*

**Tuckers Town**
Heizer, Edgar Francis, Jr. *venture capitalist*

## BRAZIL

**Brasilia**
Amorim, Celso Luiz Nunes *Brazilian government official*
Cardoso, Fernando Henrique *former president of Brazil*

**Canoas**
Sluberski, Thomas Richard *international educator, journalist, theologian*

**Joinville**
Bernardini, Giovanni *electrical engineer*

**Sao Paulo**
Grellet-Tinner, Gerald *paleontologist*

**Sorocaba**
Martins, Nelson *physics professor*

## BRITISH VIRGIN ISLANDS

**Tortola**
Chalwell-Brewley, Lavon Patricia *biology educator*

## BULGARIA

**Blagoevgrad**
Stefanov, Stefan Minev *mathematics professor, researcher*

**Sofia**
Germanova-Krasteva, Diana *textile engineer, educator*

## CAMEROON

**Mutengene**
Raghunathan, Pratima Lalita *epidemiologist*

## CAYMAN ISLANDS

**Grand Cayman**
Abu-Ghazaleh, Mohammad *food products executive*

## CHANNEL ISLANDS

**Guernsey**
Schere, Jean *researcher*

## CHILE

**Santiago**
Wilkey, Malcolm Richard *retired ambassador, retired judge*

## CHINA

**Beijing**
Banister, Judith *demographer, educator*
Christianson, Jon L. *lawyer*
Jiabao, Wen *Chinese government official*
Lehman, Edward E. *lawyer*
Li, Zhaoxing *Chinese government official*
Ma, Mary (Mary Ma Xuezheng) *computer company executive*
Ren, Jiyu *library director*
Thomas, Robert Morton, Jr. *lawyer*
Thornton, John L. *former diversified financial services company executive*
Wei, Yuchuan *mathematician, electrical engineer, physicist, researcher*
Wu, Ying *telecommunications industry executive*
Yang, Chen Ning Franklin *physicist, educator*
Yang, Guangrong *physicist, researcher, educator*
Yao, Andrew Chi-Chih *engineering educator*
Zhou, Bang Rong *physicist, researcher*

**Chengdu**
Ma, Shijun *engineering educator*

**HangZhou**
Zhang, ZhiJian *engineering educator*

**Hong Kong**
Halperin, David Richard *lawyer*
Li, Ka-Shing *international entrepreneur*
Nelson, Steven Craig *lawyer*

**Shanghai**
Chueh, Chun Fei *import/export company executive*
Lin, Maria C. H. *lawyer*
Lu, Bao-Liang *computer scientist, educator*
Mao, Aiwu *physician, radiologist*
Prosser, Michael Hubert *communications educator*
Yun, Liang *marine engineer, educator*
Hsieh, Din-Yu *applied mathematics professor*

## COLOMBIA

**Bogota**
Botero, Alonso *physicist, educator*

## COSTA RICA

**San José**
Hoffman, Irwin *orchestra conductor*

## COTE D'IVOIRE

**Abidjan**
Perry, Cynthia Shepard *federal agency administrator*

## CROATIA

**Zagreb**
Štambuk, Nikola *research scientist*

## CYPRUS

**Nicosia**
Aloneftis, Andreas *business executive*
Elias, Kyriakides *electrical engineer, educator, electrical engineer, researcher*

## CZECH REPUBLIC

**Brno**
Klapka, Jindřich Ludvík *mathematician, research scientist*

**Prague**
Bubeník, Jan *cancer researcher, biology professor*
Čejka, Jiří *retired chemist, researcher*
Cusumano, James Anthony *filmmaker, vocalist, retired pharmaceutical executive, recording industry executive*
Holena, Martin *computer scientist*
Jungwirth, Tomas *physicist, researcher*
Kalkus, Stanley *librarian, administrator, consultant*
Kavan, Jan *Czech government official, former president UN General Assembly*
Kotrla, Miroslav *physicist*
Šebek, Michael *research scientist, entrepreneur*
Tuma, Stanislav Josef *radiologist*
Turková, Helga *librarian*
Zharikov, Alexander Nikolaevich *trade union federation executive*

**Zlaté Hory**
Plaček, Roman *cellist, composer, music educator*

## DENMARK

**Charlottenlund**
Garner, Fradley Hamilton *freelance/self-employed writer, editor*

**Copenhagen**
Elmer, Michael Bendik *legal administrator*
Kurrild-Klitgaard, Peter *political science professor*
Mottelson, Ben Roy *physicist*

Olgaard, Anders *economics professor*
Pethick, Christopher John *physicist*

**Farum**
Larsen, Poul Steen *retired library educator*

**Horsholm**
Sørensen, Erik *retired diversified financial services company executive*
Svensson, Sven Eilif *civil engineer, consultant*

**Nordborg**
Clausen, Jørgen Mads *engineering executive*

**Thisted**
Nordqvist, Erik Askbo *transportation executive*

## ECUADOR

**Quito**
Almeida, Francisco *telecommunications industry executive*

## EGYPT

**Cairo**
Elaraby, Nabil A. *judge, former diplomat*
Fahmy, Ibrahim Mounir *hotel executive*
Hawass, Zahi *archaeologist, educator, writer*
Lesch, Ann Mosely *political scientist, educator*

## EL SALVADOR

**Santa Tecla**
Acosta, Barbara Dole *language educator*

## ENGLAND

**Aberdeen**
Hill, Gregory Paul *oil industry executive*

**Askett Bucks**
Irons, Jeremy John *actor*

**Barnston Wirral**
Scragg, Thomas William *librarian, historian, solicitor*

**Bath**
Zalewska, Anna *economist, researcher*

**Beaconsfield**
Lindley, David *mechanical engineer*

**Beckenham**
Lader, Malcolm Harold *pharmaceutical consultant*

**Bedfordshire**
Gelman, Leonid Moiseevich *research scientist, educator*

**Berkshire**
Everitt-Newton, Katherine Evelyn *international management consultant*

**Beverley**
Edles, Gary Joel *lawyer, law educator*

**Bristol**
Box, Steve *animator, film director*

**Buckinghamshire**
Castell, Sir William Martin *health products executive*

**Cambridge**
Buckingham, Amyand David *chemistry professor*
Edwards, Sir Samuel Frederick *physicist, researcher*
Garrow, David Jeffries *historian, author*
Hawking, Stephen William *astrophysicist, mathematician*
Hawthorne, Sir William (Sir William Rede Hawthorne) *aerospace and mechanical engineer, educator*
Hogwood, Christopher Jarvis Haley *music educator*
Huxley, Sir Andrew (Sir Andrew Fielding Huxley) *physiologist, educator*
Kermode, Frank (John Kermode) *literary critic, educator*
Klug, Aaron *molecular biologist*
Mirrlees, Sir James Alexander *economics professor*
Rees, Martin John *astronomy educator*
Renfrew, Andrew Colin (Lord Renfrew of Kaimsthorn) *archaeologist, educator, director*
Richard, Alison Fettes *anthropology educator*
Steiner, George (Francis Steiner) *author, educator*

**Canterbury**
Holwell, Peter *management consultant*

**Charlbury**
Belkin, Boris David *violinist*

**Cheltenham Gloucestershire**
Winwood, Stephen Lawrence *musician, composer*

**Cheshunt Hertfordshire**
Leahy, Sir Terry *food products executive, marketing professional*

**Chiswick London**
Dyson, Tim *public relations executive*

**Coulsdon**
Vijayaratnam, Kanapathipillai *civil and environmental engineer, consultant, director, educator*

**Coventry**
Thomas, Howard *business educator*

**Dorset**
Randle, Peter *communications company executive*

**Durham**
Parman, Stephen Wayne *science educator*

**East Sussex**
Baker, James Barnes *architect*
Katin, Peter Roy *pianist*

**Essex**
Collins, Joan Henrietta *actress*

**Falmer**
Cornforth, Sir John Warcup *chemist*

**Hinxton Cambridge**
Stratton, Michael Rudolf *medical educator, researcher*

**Isle of Wight**
Stigwood, Robert Colin *film producer, television producer, radio producer, theater producer*

**Kent Cranbrook**
Hattersley-Smith, Geoffrey Francis *retired government research scientist*

**Lane End Bucks**
Blackton, Charles S(tuart) *history educator*

**Leavesden**
Watson, Emma *actress*

**Leeds**
Ichino, Yoko *ballerina*
Nixon, David *dancer*
Phillips, Oliver *tropical forest ecologist, researcher*
Pillay, Anand *education educator, researcher*
Slechta, Jiri *theoretical physicist*

**Leicester**
Harijan, Ram *technology transfer researcher*

**London**
Abu-Deeb, Kamal Mikha'il *humanities educator*
Alexeev, Dmitri Konstantinovich *pianist*
Amis, Martin Louis *author*
Andsnes, Leif Ove *concert pianist*
Arman Gelenbe, Deniz *concert pianist*
Ashkenazy, Vladimir Davidovich *concert pianist, conductor*
Assousa, George Elias *information technology executive, physicist, corporate executive*
Auerbach, Frank *artist*
Bailey, Christopher *apparel designer*
Baird, Dugald Euan *automotive executive*
Barnevik, Percy Nils *electrical company executive*
Beckinsale, Kate *actress*
Bell, Joshua *musician*
Berke, Joseph H. *psychotherapist*
Bertolucci, Bernardo *film director*
Binney, Robert Harry *bank executive*
Bloom, Orlando *actor*
Blunt, James Hillier *singer*
Bono, (Paul David Hewson) *singer, songwriter*
Bourne, Matthew *performing company executive, artistic director*
Bravo, Rose Marie *apparel executive*
Brennan, David R. *pharmaceutical executive*
Butler, Geezer (Terence Michael Joseph Butler) *musician*
Chadwick, Derek James *foundation administrator*
Chevalier, Tracy Rose *writer*
Clark, Cynthia Zang Facer *federal agency administrator*
Cleese, John Marwood *writer, comedian*
Codron, Michael Victor *theater producer*
Collins, Paul John *banker*
Conti, Tom *actor, theater director, writer*
Cope, Wendy *poet*
Cowell, Simon *television personality, music producer*
Curtis, Richard *author, screenwriter*
Dahrendorf, Lord Ralf Gustav *sociologist, educator*
Davis, Crispin *publishing company executive*
Day-Lewis, Daniel Michael Blake *actor*
Deighton, Len *author*
Delpy, Julie *actress*
DeMann, Freddy *film, play, television producer*
Desai, Nitin Dayalji *international organization official*
de Savorgnani, Adriane Aldrich *healthcare administrator, nurse*
Diamond, Robert E., Jr. *investment company executive*
Dohnányi, Christoph von *musician, conductor*
Douglas, Mary Tew *anthropology and humanities educator*
Drabble, Margaret *writer*
Duffy, Simon P. *telecommunications industry executive*
Duncan, Lindsay Vere *actress*
Edwards, Sylvia Ann *artist*
Elizabeth, II, (Elizabeth Alexandra Mary) *By the Grace of God of the United Kingdom of Great Britain and Northern Ireland and of Her Other Realms and Territories Queen, Head of the Commonwealth, Defender of the Faith*
Ellis, Claud M. Buddy *diversified financial services company executive*
Elson, Sarah Lee *art historian, consultant*
Enya, (Eithne Ni Bhraonain, Enya Brennan) *musician*
Eustace, Dudley Graham *diversified financial services company executive*
Fabricant, Arthur E. *lawyer, corporate financial executive*
Fine, Anne *writer*
Flint, Douglas J. *investment company executive*
Flor, Claus Peter *conductor*
Forsyth, Stephen A. *venture capitalist, department chairman*
Frayn, Michael *playwright*
Freud, Lucian Michael *painter*

Friis, Janus *Internet company executive, entrepreneur*
Fuller, Simon *music company executive, television producer*
Galloway, Janice *writer, editor*
Gardner, Jason P. *immunologist, biologist*
Gelenbe, Sami Erol *computer scientist, engineering educator*
Gervais, Ricky *actor, scriptwriter*
Glazer, Barry David *lawyer*
Glocer, Thomas Henry *publishing executive*
Goosen, Retief *professional golfer*
Gottesman, A(rthur) Edward *lawyer*
Graubard, Stephen Richards *historian, educator, editor*
Gray, Simon James Holliday *writer, educator*
Greener, Sir Anthony *telecommunications industry executive*
Habgood, Anthony John *wholesale distribution executive*
Haitink, Bernard J. H. *conductor*
Hall, Sir Peter Geoffrey *urban and regional planning educator*
Hallissey, Michael *retired management consultant*
Hare, David *playwright*
Harney, Kathryn Ann *opera singer*
Haubold, Samuel Allen *lawyer*
Hicks, Taylor Reuben *singer*
Hoskins, Bob (Robert William Hoskins) *actor*
Hudson, Manley O., Jr. *lawyer*
Hunsberger, Alice Chandler *religion educator, human rights activist, scholar*
Hunter Blair, Pauline Clarke *author*
Ioannou, Constantinos Elia *accountant*
Iommi, Tony (Frank Anthony Iommi) *musician*
James, P(hyllis) D(orothy) (Baroness James of Holland Park of Southwold in County of Suffolk) *author*
John, Sir Elton Hercules (Reginald Kenneth Dwight) *musician*
Jourdren, Marc Henri *investment banking company executive*
Junz, Helen B. *economist*
Kallakis, Achilleas Michalis S. *transportation executive, real estate company executive*
Kapranos, Alexander (Franz Ferdinand) *singer, musician*
Kingsley, Sir Ben *actor*
Kuper, Adam Jonathan *anthropologist, educator*
Leaf, Robert Stephen *public relations executive*
Lee, Janet *professional tennis player*
Leigh, Mike *film director*
Lessing, Doris (Doris May) *writer*
Lloyd Webber, Lord Andrew (Baron of Sydmonton) *composer, small business owner*
Lowenthal, David *historian, geographer*
MacClean, Walter Lee *dentist*
Mackerras, Sir Charles (Alan Maclaurin) *conductor*
Masur, Kurt *conductor, music director*
May, Robert McCredie (Lord May of Oxford) *biology educator*
McCowen, Alec *actor*
McDiarmid, Ian *actor, film director*
McGrath, Patrick *writer*
McGregor, Ewan Gordon *actor*
McKellen, Sir Ian *actor*
McPhee, Katharine Hope *singer*
Mendes, Sam (Samuel Alexander Mendes) *film director, theater director*
Meyer, Sir Christopher J.R. *former ambassador*
Miller, Jonathan Wolfe *theater and film director, physician*
Minton, Yvonne Fay *mezzo-soprano*
Montgomery, John Warwick (Baron of Kiltartan and Lord of Morris, Comte de St. Germain de Montgomery) *law educator, theologian*
Moody, Ron *actor, writer*
Mooney, James F. *telecommunications industry executive*
Morris, Desmond (John) *zoologist, writer, artist*
Morrison, William David *lawyer*
Moss, Kate *model*
Mosselmans, Carel Maurits *investment banker*
Muir-Taylor, Douglas James *ophthalmologist*
Murdoch, Elisabeth *media company executive*
Nagano, Kent George *conductor, music director*
Nagioff, Roger B. *investment company executive*
Nelson, Elizabeth Hawkins *not-for-profit association administrator*
Nelson, Walter Henry *communications consultant, author*
Newell, Mike *film director*
Oliver, Diane Frances *publisher, writer*
Oliver, Jamie *chef, television personality*
Oppenheimer, Deanna Watson *bank executive*
Ormsby, Eric Linn *writer, educator*
Palin, Michael Edward *actor, scriptwriter, writer*
Paton Walsh, Jill *writer*
Payne, Alexander *film director, writer*
Phocas, George J. *lawyer*
Plapinger, William A. *lawyer*
Polk, George Washington *telecommunications executive, entrepreneur*
Portes, Richard David *economics professor*
Powell, Sandy *costume designer*
Pryce, Jonathan *actor*
Quillen, Cecil Dyer III *lawyer*
Quint, David Paul *investment banking executive*
Radcliffe, Daniel *actor*
Ralston, Anthony *computer scientist, mathematician, educator*
Read, Piers Paul *author*
Rice, Sir Timothy Miles Bindon *lyricist*
Richardson, Ian William *actor*
Richardson, Miranda *actress*
Rickman, Alan *actor*
Rolle, Martha Collins (Martha Traudt Collins) *lawyer*
Roth, Richard *news correspondent*
Rowling, J.K. (Joanne Kathleen Rowling) *writer*
Rubin, Patricia Lee *art historian*
Rushdie, Salman *writer*
Rutter, Michael Llewellyn *child psychology educator*
Sarkis, Ziad Joseph *private equity executive*
Scardino, Dame Marjorie Morris *publishing executive*
Scott, Raymond Peter William *chemistry professor, writer*
Shankar, Ravi *composer, musician*

Sher, Sir Antony *actor, author*
Smith, Dame Maggie (Margaret Natalie Smith Cross) *actress*
Smith, Robert Michael *lawyer, mediator, arbitrator*
Smith, Zadie (Sadie Smith) *writer*
Spacey, Kevin *actor*
Spillane, Mary Catherine *television producer*
Staunton, Imelda (Imelda Mary Philomena Bernadette Staunton) *actress*
Stella, Frank Philip *artist*
Stelle, Kellogg Sheffield *physicist*
Stevens, Robert Bocking *lawyer*
Stojkovic, Dusan *lawyer*
Stopford, Philip *lawyer*
Stoppard, Tom (Tomas Straussler) *playwright*
Studzinski, John Joseph Paul *investment banking executive*
Taylor, Jim *scriptwriter, film director*
Thomas, Allen Lloyd *lawyer, private investor*
Tyson, Laura D'Andrea *dean, finance educator*
Uchida, Mitsuko *pianist*
van Hoften, James Dougal Adrianus *former astronaut, transportation executive*
Vanniasingham, Samuel Kanagasabapathy *accountant*
Verwaayen, Ben J.M. *communications company executive*
Walsh, Paul S. *food products executive*
Ward, Bill *musician*
Warner, Scott Dennis *investment banker*
Winner, Michael Robert *film director, film producer, writer*
Zennström, Niklas *Internet company executive, entrepreneur*
Zonana, Victor *lawyer, educator*

**Manchester**
de Silva, Eugene Lakshman *academic administrator, educator*
Wilson, Keith Dudley *media and music educator, consultant, dean*

**Middlesex**
Lynch, John Edward, Jr. *lawyer*

**Milton Keynes**
Throdahl, Mark Crandall *medical products executive*

**Newcastle-Upon-Tyne**
Valentine, Gary (Gary Lachman) *musician*

**North Wales**
Hands, Terence David (Terry Hands) *theater and opera director*

**Oxford**
Bullock, Peter Bradley *company director, consultant*
Carey, John *language educator, critic*
Halasyamani, P. Shiv *inorganic chemist, researcher*
Harvey, Paul H. *evolutionary biologist, researcher*
Raz, Joseph *philosophy educator, law educator*
Robinson, Mary *former United Nations official*
Shaw, Dennis Frederick *former library director, chartered physicist, consultant*
Vaisey, David George *librarian, archivist*
Varese, Federico *sociology professor*
Walker, Amber Michelle *military officer*

**Oxfordshire**
Gates, David Allen *physicist, researcher, educator*

**Poole**
Alsop, Marin *conductor, violinist, music director*

**Reading**
Dunning, John Harry *economics educator*
Spencer, David Anthony *geologist, researcher, educator*
Thacker, Charles P. *computer engineer, engineering executive*

**Redhill**
Donaldson, David *pathologist*

**Richmond**
Armfield, Diana Maxwell *artist, educator*

**Richmond-upon-Thames**
Smith, Norman Raymond *academic administrator*

**Saint Margaret's**
Attenborough, Baron Richard Samuel *actor, film director, film producer, ambassador*

**Southampton**
Brebbia, Carlos Alberto *engineering educator, consultant*
Spearing, Simon Mark *aeronautical engineer, educator*

**Stevenage**
Follett, Kenneth Martin *author*

**Stoke-on-Trent**
Burwood, Stephen Meredith *historian, educator*

**Stroud**
Robinson, John Beckwith *development management consultant*

**Surrey**
Els, Ernie (Theodore Ernest Els) *professional golfer*
Holm, Sir Ian *actor*
Immelman, Trevor *professional golfer*
Vere Hodge, Richard Anthony *pharmaceutical executive, consultant*
Weston, Sir John (Sir Philip John Weston) *company non-executive director, retired diplomat*

**Tunbridge Wells**
Howden, Frank Newton *priest, humanities educator*

**Westminster**
Broers, Lord Alec Nigel *engineering educator*

**Whitchurch**
Adams, Richard George *writer*

**Wiltshire**
Sherwin, James Terry *lawyer*
Ahrendts, Angela J. *apparel executive*
Aufhauser, David D. *lawyer, former federal agency administrator*

# ESTONIA

**Tallinn**
Köörna, Arno *economist, educator*

# ETHIOPIA

**Addis Ababa**
Huddleston, Vicki Jean *diplomat*

# FINLAND

**Helsinki**
Juhani, Erma *lawyer, former stock exchange executive*
Liewendahl, Bo Kristian *retired pathologist, nuclear medicine physician*

**Tampere**
Andriano, Kirk Patrick *pharmaceutical executive*

# FRANCE

**Aix-en-Provence**
Leskes, Andrea *academic administrator, educator*

**Antibes**
Fouillade, Jean-Paul Eric *management consultant*

**Arles**
Clergue, Lucien Georges *photographer*

**Armees**
Alliot-Marie, Michèle *French government official*

**Besancon**
Boillat, Guy Maurice Georges *mathematical physicist*

**Cedex**
Demers, Elizabeth Anne *education educator*

**Chatenay-Malabry**
Evesque, Pierre Henri *physics researcher*

**Collonges**
Morgenstern, Sheldon Jon *symphony orchestra conductor*

**Compiegne**
Dubuisson, Bernard Louis *science educator, administrator*

**Creteil**
Renoux, André *physicist, researcher*

**Draguignan**
Frame, Nancy Davis *lawyer*

**Gif-sur-Yvette**
Duplessy, Jean Claude *research scientist*

**Issy les Moulineaux**
de Pouzilhac, Alain Duplessis *advertising executive*

**Le Vesinet**
Fourt, Bernard-Francois P. *retired engineer*
Hillion, Pierre Théodore Marie *mathematical physicist*

**Levallois-Perret**
Filipacchi, Daniel *publishing executive*

**Lyon**
Bazin, Patrick *library director*
Robertson, David *conductor, music director*

**Malaucene Vaucluse**
Langenkamp, Mary Alice (M.A. Langenkamp) *artist, educator*

**Marseille**
Boutterin, Emmanuel *public relations executive*

**Noisy-le-Grand**
Le Quéré, Jean François Marie *scientific instrumentation researcher*

**Orleans**
Price, David Cecil Long *physicist, researcher*

**Orsay**
Friedel, Jacques *retired physics professor*

**Orvault**
Lorand, Cedric *information scientist, translator*

**Paris**
Alaïa, Azzedine *fashion designer*
Annaud, Jean-Jacques *film director, film producer, scriptwriter*
Barrows, Leland Conley *historian, educator, editor*
Baum, Axel Helmuth *lawyer*
Bergé, Pierre *apparel design executive*
Bujon de L'Estang, Francois *bank executive*
Burke, Michael *apparel executive*
Cagle, William Rea *retired librarian*
Cardin, Pierre *fashion designer*
Cherkaoui, Mohamed *sociologist*
Choay, Patrick Henri *pharmaceutical executive*

Collomb, Bertrand Pierre *cement company executive*
Constantin, Emilia *physicist, researcher*
Courtaud, Bernard Jean-Jacques *human resource consulting executive*
Courtois, Jean-Philippe *information technology executive*
Dean, John Gunther *diplomat*
de Gennes, Pierre-Gilles *physicist, educator*
de Havilland, Olivia Mary *actress*
Deneuve, Catherine (Catherine Dorleac) *actress*
Elbaz, Alber *apparel designer*
Fitoussi, Jean-Paul Samuel *economist, educator*
Ghesquière, Nicolas *apparel designer*
Gontier, Jean Roger *medicine and physiology educator*
Horovitz, Israel Arthur *playwright*
Jacob, François *biologist, educator*
Janicot, Daniel Claude Emmanuel *foundation administrator*
Jolas, Betsy *composer, educator*
Kourilsky, François Michel *research scientist*
Kouyaté, Lansana *economist, federal official, diplomat*
Lacroix, Christian Marie Marc *fashion designer*
Lagarde, Christine *French government official, lawyer*
Lagerfeld, Karl Otto *fashion designer*
Lehn, Jean-Marie Pierre *chemistry professor*
Marcus, Claude *advertising executive*
Myerson, Jacob Myer *retired diplomat*
Oliver, Louise V. *ambassador*
Payri, Joel *pharmaceutical marketing executive*
Piano, Renzo *architect*
Raharinaivo, André Léon *research scientist, educator*
Raimondi, Ruggero *opera singer*
Renouf, Edda *artist*
Ricol, Rene Jean *accountant*
Ross, Charles *artist*
Saint Laurent, Yves (Henri Donat Mathieu) *couturier*
Salans, Carl Fredric *lawyer*
Serre, Jean-Pierre *mathematician, scholar*
Vandame, Jean-Marie Richard *diversified financial services company executive*
Vuitton, Henry-Louis *designer*
Yuechiming, Roger Yue Yuen Shing *mathematics professor*

**Saint Ceols**
Saisselin, Remy Gilbert *fine arts educator*

**Saint Etienne**
Vergnaud, Jean-Maurice *science educator, researcher*

**Taninges**
Berger, John Peter *writer, painter, art critic*

**Valbonne**
Junker, Ulrich *computer scientist, researcher*

**Vandoeuvre-les-Nancy**
Blazy, Pierre François *science educator*

**Vence**
Polk, William Roe *historian*

**Villefranche-sur-Mer**
Legendre, Louis *oceanographer, educator, research scientist*

**Villeneuve d'Ascq**
Allain, Louis *literature educator*

# GEORGIA

**Tbilisi**
Urushadze, Levan Z. *political scientist, human rights activist*

# GERMANY

**Aachen**
Pinchuk, Anatoliy Oleksijovych *physicist*
Pischinger, Franz Felix *engineer, researcher, engineering educator*

**Apo**
Adams, Julian Timothy *psychologist*

**Augsburg**
Kunes, Jan *physicist*

**Bad Homburg**
Klatten, Susanne Quandt *pharmaceutical executive*

**Berlin**
Eichler, Hans Joachim *physics professor*
Jochmann, Frank *mathematician*
Köhler, Horst *President of Federal Republic of Germany*
Mantsch, Henry Horst *chemistry professor*
Nölting, Bengt *physicist, researcher*
Piper, Adrian Margaret Smith *philosopher, artist, educator*

**Bonn**
Albach, Horst *economist*
Rampacher, Hermann Hans *writer, consultant*

**Braunschweig**
Diethelm, Kai *mathematician, researcher*
Leseberg, Dieter Wolfgang Michael *mathematician*

**Bremen**
Fahle, Manfred *ophthalmology researcher*
Wells, Raymond O'Neil, Jr. *mathematics professor, researcher*

**Buchen**
Kiefer, Anselm Karl Albert *artist*

**Cologne**
Neisser, Horst *library director*

**Dortmund**
Vogt, Hartmut *education educator*

**Dresden**
Gluch, Steffen *company executive*
Schreier, Peter *tenor*

**Düsseldorf**
Andre, Carl *sculptor*
Schulz, Ekkehard *metal products executive*
Stuhl, Oskar Paul *scientific and regulatory consultant*

**Frankfurt**
Ammann, Jean-Christophe *art director*
Greiner, Walter Albin Erhard *physicist*
Michel, Hartmut *biochemist*
Papademos, Lucas *bank executive*
Simitis, Spiros *legal educator*
von Rosen, Rüdiger *stock exchange executive*

**Freiberg**
Zabecki, David Tadeusz *engineer, educator, military historian, military officer*

**Fulda**
Beckman, James Wallace Bim *management consultant, educator*

**Furth**
Rau, Magda *ophthalmologist*

**Garching**
Genzel, Reinhard *astrophysicist, educator*

**Göttingen**
Achtenhagen, Frank *economics professor*
Sheldrick, George Michael *chemistry professor, crystallographer*
Starck, Christian Walter *judge, retired law educator*
Toennies, Jan Peter *research chemical physicist*

**Halle**
Schmoll, Hans Joachim *hematology and oncology educator*
Thamm, Jochen Walter *library director*

**Hamburg**
Lüst, Reimar *foundation president*
Neumeier, John *choreographer, ballet company director*

**Heidelburg**
Yarvis, Jeffrey Scott *military officer, social worker*

**Karben**
Mansager, Erik Donn *adolescent counselor*

**Lübeck**
Fligge, Jörg *librarian, library director*

**Mannheim**
Solz, Hermann *plastic surgeon*

**Mayen**
Gartz, Rolf Fritz *foundation administrator*

**Munich**
Araiza, Francisco (José Francisco Araiza Andrade) *opera singer*
Bangle, Christopher Edward (Chris Bangle) *automotive company car designer*
Huber, Robert *biochemist, educator*
Schmidt, Stefan *mechanical engineer, economist*
Stoek, Thomas *management professional, sales professional*
Viermetz, Kurt F. *banker*
Whetten, Lawrence L. *international relations educator*

**Münster**
Spevack, Marvin *language educator*

**Neu Isenburg**
Hoare-Temple, Piers Howard *building maintenance executive*

**Nuremberg**
Doerries, Reinhard René *historian, educator*

**Obbornhofen**
Edwards, Grey Holt, Jr. *academic administrator, adult education educator*

**Ottilienstr**
Clarke, Ingrid Gadway *retired academic ombudsman, consultant*

**Paderborn**
Thim, Frank *physicist, astronomer*

**Regensburg**
Eisenmann-Klein, Marita *plastic surgeon*
Fichtner-Feigl, Stefan *surgeon, immunologist*
Jain, Manish *researcher*

**Schleusingen-Gethles**
Frank, Dieter *retired chemicals executive*

**Seeheim-Jugenheim**
Halama, Niels *physician, researcher*

**Seewiesen**
Huber, Franz *retired research director*

**Stutensee**
Barbian, Otto Alfred *physicist*

**Stuttgart**
Anderson, Reid Bryce *performing company executive*
Cardona, Manuel *physics professor*
Geh, Hans-Peter *retired library director, consultant*
von Klitzing, Klaus *research facility administrator, physicist*
Zetsche, Dieter *automotive executive*

**Tübingen**
Nüsslein-Volhard, Christiane *medical researcher*

**Walldorf**
Agassi, Shai *application developer, director*
Williams, Richard Charles *computer programmer, consultant*

**Weinheim**
Ostovic, Vlado *engineering educator, researcher*

**Witten**
Gaengler, Peter Wolfgang *dentist, researcher*

**Wuppertal**
Schubert, Guenther Erich *pathologist*
Richter, Gerhard *artist*

## GHANA

**Accra**
Oppey, Mark Ofusy *career officer*

**Legon**
Avorgbedor, Daniel Kodzo *music educator*

## GIBRALTAR

**Irishtown**
De Leon, Russ *Internet company executive*

## GREECE

**Athens**
Arnis, Efstathios Constantinos *mechanical engineer, space naval designer*
Boudoulas, Harisios *cardiologist, researcher, medical educator*
Brilakis, Harry Stylianos (Harilaos Stylianos Brilakis) *ophthalmologist*
Larounis, George Philip *manufacturing executive, director*
Miliotis, Demetrios *physics professor*
Papadakis, Panagiotis Agamemnon *corporate financial executive*

**Larisa**
Zacharoulis, Dimitris *surgeon, researcher*

**Mandra**
Panagopoulos, Panagiotis Nikos *physicist, researcher*

**Marousi**
Joannou, Dakis *hotel executive*

**Piraeus**
Papachristou, Costas John *physicist, researcher*

**Thessaloniki**
Koenig, John M. *ambassador*

## GRENADA

**St. George**
Jordan, Tiffany *finance educator*

## GUANA ISLAND

**Barrigada**
Perez, Annie Rivera *elementary school educator*

## GUATEMALA

**Antigua**
Rodgers, Frank *librarian*
Rosenthal, Gert *economist*

**Guatemala City**
Herrera-Llerandi, Rodolfo Eduardo *surgeon, educator*
Mayora-Alvarado, Eduardo Rene *lawyer, law educator*
Mishaan, Emilio *transplant surgeon, educator*

## HONG KONG

**Central**
Bing, Xu *artist*

**Cheung Sha Wan**
Dyer, David F. *apparel company executive*
Hilfiger, Tommy (Thomas Jacob Hilfiger) *fashion designer*

**Hong Kong**
Kao, Charles Kuen *electrical engineer, educator*
Laurie, James Andrew *broadcast executive, consultant, director, television executive producer, journalist*
Lee, Shau Kee *real estate developer*
Leung, Ka-Cheong *education educator*
Pacter, Paul Allan *accounting standards researcher*
Podd, Ann *newspaper editor*
Tse, Edmund Sze-Wing *insurance company executive*
Tsui, Lap-Chee *academic administrator, molecular genetics educator*

**Kowloon**
Cheng, Ping *engineering educator*
Chow, Yun-fat (Chow Yun-Fat) *actor*
Fung, Victor K. (Victor Fung Kwok King) *consumer products trading company executive*
Hung, Edward *research scientist*
Qiu, Larry Dongxiao *economics professor*

Wu, Daniel *actor*

**New Territories**
Lau, Lawrence Juen-Yee *academic administrator, economics professor, consultant*

**Pokfulam**
McNaughton, William Frank *translator, educator*

**South Horizons**
Chen, Concordia Chao *mathematician*

**Wanchai**
Iwasawa, Isoo (Francis Iwasawa) *accountant, management consultant*
Paulus, Michael John *government official, economist, bank executive*
Valente, Giorgio *finance educator*

## HUNGARY

**Budapest**
Fenyo, Jean-Pierre Ady *philosopher*
Poprády, Géza *librarian*
Rakos, Balázs *physicist, researcher*
Szigeti, János *physicist*

**Debrecen**
Csikai, Gyula *physicist, researcher*

**Sopron**
Sitkei, György *engineer, educator*

## INDIA

**Allahabad**
Aggarwal, Deepak *research engineer, educator*

**Bagalkot**
Chitme, Havagiray Revanappa *science educator*

**Balasore**
Talukdar, Atanu *electrical engineer*

**Bangalore**
Padhi, Radhakant *engineer*

**Bhubanesway**
Mohanty, Sitakanta *petroleum engineer*

**Calcutta**
Kothari, Hemraj *mechanical engineer, management consultant*

**Chennai**
Krishnani, Kishore Kumar *research scientist*

**Delhi**
Mitra, Asoke Nath *retired physicist, educator*

**Haryana Panchkula**
Naresh, Anubhav *dentist, educator*

**Hyderabad**
Das, Undurti Narasimha *endocrinologist, rheumatologist*

**Kanpur**
Joglekar, Satish Dinkar *physicist, educator*

**Kolkata**
Mazumder, Bijoy Singha *mathematician, educator, researcher*

**Lucknow**
Kumar, Raj *medical educator*

**Manipal**
Pai, Satish Upendra *publishing executive*

**Mirzapur**
Upadhyaya, Kripa Shankar *academic administrator, educator*

**Nagpur**
Modak, Jayant Pandurang *mechanical engineer, consultant*

**New Delhi**
Azad, Raj Vardhan *ophthalmologist, educator, surgeon, consultant*
Jain, Prem Chand *mechanical engineer*
Malone, David Michael *diplomat, educator*
Narain, Prem *agricultural scientist, educator, researcher*
Watson, Paul *photojournalist, correspondent*
Yadav, Hari Om *research scientist*

**Salem**
Thandapani, Ethiraj *mathematics professor*

**Varanasi**
Kumar, Vikas *neuropharmacologist, researcher*

**Warangal**
Peddaboina, Venkataiah *botanist, researcher*

## INDONESIA

**Jakarta**
Hsi, Edward Yang *lawyer, venture capitalist, industrialist*
Tilaar, Henry A.R. *social sciences educator*

## IRAN

**Tehran**
Ahmadinejad, Mahmoud (Mahmoud Ahmadinezhad) *President of Iran*
Jalali-Heravi, Mehdi *chemistry professor, researcher*

## IRELAND

**Cork**
Lyons, Nona Mary *adult education educator*

**County Kildare**
Kabdebo, Thomas George *library director*

**Donegal**
Friel, Brian (Bernard Patrick Friel) *author*

**Dublin**
Dooge, James Clement Ignatius *civil engineer, hydrologist*
McCauley, Kristina Akemi *project coordinator*
O'Reilly, Sir Anthony John Francis *media company executive, former food products company executive*
Sheridan, Jim *film director, screenwriter*

**Galway**
Hynes, Garry *theater director*

**Mullingar**
Donleavy, James Patrick *writer, artist*

## ISRAEL

**Arad**
Hollander, Samuel *economist, educator*

**Ashqelon**
Hansen, Peter *international organization executive*

**Be'er Sheva**
Brosilow, Coleman Bernard *chemical engineering educator*
Carmeli, Moshe *theoretical physicist*
Frenkel, David Arie *law professor*

**Gan Shlomo**
Tritter, Richard Paul *risk management consultant*

**Jerusalem**
Menses, Jan *artist, draftsman*
Olmert, Ehud *Prime Minister of Israel*
Rosenne, Meir *lawyer, federal agency administrator*
Rozett, Robert Bernard *library director, historian*
Shrensky, Don Steven *accountant, consultant*
Singer, Suzanne Fried *editor*

**Kiryat Shmone**
Gophen, Moshe *research scientist*

**Lod**
Gur, Joshua *optronics engineer, video engineer, consultant*

**Netanya**
Tsitverblit, Naftali Anatol *physicist, fluid mechanics engineer, researcher*

**Ra'anana**
Hayon, Elie M. *chemist, educator*

**Rehovot**
Sachs, Leo *geneticist, educator*
Zipori-Beckenstein, Pninit *business educator, researcher*

**Savyon**
Bushinsky, Jay (Joseph Mason) *journalist, news correspondent*

**Tel Aviv**
Gross, Joseph H. *lawyer, educator*
Jortner, Joshua *physical chemist, educator*

## ITALY

**Bologna**
Eco, Umberto *semiotics educator, author*
Lino, Marisa Rose *retired diplomat*

**Ciserano di Zingonia**
Vieri, Christian *professional soccer player*

**Como**
Casati, Fabio *engineer*
Casati, Giulio *theoretical physics professor*

**Cremia**
Malipiero, Victoria Schneider *vocalist*

**Florence**
Cecil, Charles Harkless *artist, educator*
Giannini, Frida *apparel designer*

**Maranello**
Schumacher, Michael *retired race car driver*

**Milan**
Berlusconi, Marina *publishing executive*
Cavalli, Roberto *fashion designer*
Dolce, Domenico *fashion designer*
Gabbana, Stefano *fashion designer*
Honegger, Federico *artist*
Prada, Miuccia Bianca *fashion designer*
Versace, Donatella *fashion designer*

**Naples**
Tarro, Giulio *virologist*

**Padua**
Onofrio, Roberto *physicist, researcher*
Shea, William Rene *historian, history and philosophy professor*

**Palermo**
Fiumara, Ettore *neurosurgeon*

**Pietrasanta Lucca**
Bugliani, Ann C. *international studies educator*

## ITALY

**Pisa**
Settis, Salvatore *archaeologist, art historian*

**Rieti**
Truini Palomba, Maria Giuseppina *supreme court lawyer, judge*

**Rome**
Benedict XVI, His Holiness Pope (Joseph Alois Ratzinger) *Pope of Roman Catholic Church, Bishop of Rome*
Gros-Pietro, Gian Maria *economics professor*
Hall, Tony P. *ambassador, retired congressman*
Kolvenbach, Peter Hans *priest, head of religious order*
Levada, William Joseph Cardinal *archbishop emeritus, cardinal*
Levi-Montalcini, Rita *neurobiologist, researcher*
Maraviglia, Bruno *physicist, researcher*
McGurn, William Barrett III *lawyer*
Scognamiglio Pasini, Carlo *economics and finance professor, senator*
Sisulu, Sheila Violet Makate *diplomat, international organization official*
Stigliano, Jose Maria *information technology executive, computer scientist*
Valentino, (Valentino Garavani) *fashion designer*
Westley, John Richard *economist*

**Treviso**
Bargnani, Andrea *professional basketball player*

**Turin**
Rossi, Guido A(ntonio) *mathematics professor, researcher*

**Vatican City**
Foley, John Patrick *archbishop*
Stafford, J. Francis Cardinal *archbishop*
Stafford, James Francis *cardinal*
Szoka, Edmund Casimir Cardinal *archbishop*

**Venice**
Pasinetti, Pier Maria *author*

**Verona**
Pozzo, Riccardo *philosophy educator*
Spogli, Ronald P. *ambassador*

## JAPAN

**Chiba**
Arai, Toshihiko *retired microbiology and immunology educator*
Hattori, Naozo *science educator*
Sakaguchi, Takehiro *healthcare educator, researcher*

**FPO**
Armendariz, Norma E. *preventive medicine technician*

**Fukuoka**
Ishibashi, Akira *mechanical engineer, educator*

**Gifu**
Hatada, Kazuyuki *mathematician, educator*

**Gunma**
Hironaka, Heisuke *mathematics professor, academic administrator*
Okada, Ryozo *medical educator, researcher*

**Gyoda**
Shibasaki, Yoshio *chemistry professor, researcher*

**Hachioji**
Kojima, Takeshi *law educator, arbitrator, writer*
Okada, Isamu *finance educator, researcher*

**Hamamatsu**
Kaneko, Masao *radiology educator, researcher, specialist*

**Hirakata**
Shigemitsu, Toshiro *ophthalmologist, researcher*

**Hiroshima**
Suzuki, Nobutaka *chemistry professor*

**Ibaraki**
Asanuma, Jun *engineering educator*
Kawano, Toshiaki *retired economics professor*
Urabe, Tohsuke *mathematics professor, researcher*

**Kanagawa**
Fukatsu, Tanefusa *retired classicist, educator*
Hoshino, Yoshiro *industrial relations specialist, educator*
Takeuchi, Tetsuya *materials engineer*

**Kashiwara**
Hori, Keiko *English literature educator*

**Kasugai**
Miyake, Yasuji *computer science educator*

**Kobe**
Inoue, Shun *sociologist*

**Kumatori**
Ohashi, Shoichi *business administration educator*

**Kushimoto**
Akura, Junsuke *ophthalmologist, researcher*

**Kyoto**
Tsuji, Toshizo *hospital administrator, educator*

**Machida**
Miyazaki, Koichi *economics professor*

**Mie**
Isshiki, Masayuki *sociologist, educator, dean*

**Minato**
Glauner, Frank J. *electronics executive*

**Mitaka**
Kazama, Toshio *humanities educator*

**Mito**
Kobayashi, Susumu *retired computer company executive*

**Nagoya**
Kajitani, Motohisa *sociology educator*
Sakai, Toshihiko *engineer*
Sendo, Takeshi *mechanical engineering educator, researcher, writer*

**Ohsu Shiga**
Matsuda, Wakoto *neurosurgeon, researcher*

**Okayama**
Morooka, Hiroshi *neurosurgeon*
Nii, Shiro *director, virologist, educator*
Okada, Shigeru *medical educator*
Ubuka, Toshihiko *biochemist, educator, academic administrator*

**Osaka**
Akase, Masako *humanities educator*
Horii, Reiichi *library director, educator*
Ikeda, Kazuyosi *physicist, poet*
Ishii, Sakae *retired physicist*

**Saitama**
Hozumi, Motoo *medical educator, researcher*

**Sapporo**
Asari, Eikichi *information sciences educator, researcher*
Nakagawa, Koji *endocrinologist, educator*
Sakai, Yu *pathologist*

**Shinjuku**
Shimada, Haruo *physical chemistry educator*

**Shizuoka**
Anma, So *engineer, consultant*

**Tochigi**
Honma, Koichi *pathologist, researcher*
Hyodo, Haruo *radiologist, educator*

**Tokorozawa**
Nakamura, Hiroshi *urology educator*

**Tokushima**
Kinno, Hitoshi *mechanical engineer, educator*

**Tokyo**
Akutsu, Yoshihiro *communications educator*
Baba, Isamu *construction company executive*
Chang, Steve *internet security company executive*
Chiba, Machiko *cooking advisor*
Connor, William Edwin, II, *finance company executive*
Dixon, Bonnie Lynn *lawyer*
Esaki, Leo (Esaki Leona) *physicist, foundation executive, university president*
Eto, Hajime *retired information scientist, educator*
Fujimoto, Junichiro *pathologist*
Fuketa, Toyojiro *physicist*
Fukuda, Atsuo *physicist, materials science researcher, educator*
Fukushima, Kiyohiko *economist*
Gyohten, Toyoo *economist*
Hakoshima, Shin-ichi *publishing executive*
Harada, Norio *software engineer, researcher, educator*
Hirayama, Eiji *psychologist, educator*
Hori, Yukio *engineering educator, scientific association administrator*
Iida, Shuichi *physicist, educator*
Iinuma, Hiroichi *finance educator*
Ishii, Akira *parasitologist, allergist, malariologist*
Kaneko, Isao *air transportation executive*
Kato, Shuichi *information scientist, educator*
Kobayashi, Noritake *business educator*
Krisher, Bernard *foreign correspondent*
Maki, Atsushi *economics professor*
Matsuda, Masatake *rail transportation executive*
Minier, Jean-Francois Raymond *investment banker*
Nakajima, Hiroshi *education educator*
Nishiyama, Chiaki *economist, educator*
Ohga, Norio *retired electronics executive*
Ohira, Kazuto *theatre company executive, writer*
Ozawa, Seiji *conductor, music director*
Petersen, Barry Rex *news correspondent*
Saba, Shoichi *electronics executive, director*
Sakurada, Yutaka *retired chemist*
Sakuta, Manabu *neurologist, educator*
Shirai, Shun *law educator*
Suzuki, Akira *physics professor*
Tanabe, Noriaki *library director*
Wakumoto, Yoshihiko *electronics company executive, grants executive*
Watanabe, Satoshi Patten *economist, researcher*
Yaku, Takeo T. *computer scientist, educator*

**Toyama**
Sumiyoshi, Tomiki *psychiatrist, researcher*

**Toyota**
Toyoda, Shoichiro *automotive executive*

**Tsukuba**
Hanaki, Nobuyuki *economics professor*
Shimizu, Kazuhiko *education educator*

**Utsunomiya**
Yorikawa, Hiroharu *physicist, researcher*

**Yokohama**
Ito, Noboru *electric power industry executive*
Kuroda, Yasumasa *political science professor, researcher*
Tokutani, Masao *risk management educator*
Taketomi, Susamu *physicist, researcher*

## JORDAN

**Irbid**
Al-Smadi, Adnan M. *dean*

El-Migdadi, Fayig *biochemist, educator, molecular biologist*

## KAZAKHSTAN

**Almaty**
Sadykova, Vera Philippovna *librarian, educator*

## KENYA

**Mombasa**
Harrell, Jerry DeWitt *ophthalmologist, director*

**Nairobi**
Maathai, Wangari *environmentalist, consultant*
Mignouna, Hodeba-Jacob Douwehan *geneticist, researcher*
Wamutiso, Kineene *humanities educator*

## LATVIA

**Riga**
Buholte, Agnese *library director*
Lācis, Aris *health facility administrator, cardiac surgeon*
Strautins, Vilnis *music educator, retired performing company executive*

## LEBANON

**Beirut**
Khatib, Rustom Atfat *gynecologist, researcher, endocrinologist, consultant, economist*
Moucharafieh, Ramzi Charif *orthopedist, surgeon*
Pederson, Patricia Velde *education educator, consultant*
Waterbury, John *academic administrator, political science professor, writer*

## LIBERIA

**Monrovia**
Johnson-Sirleaf, Ellen *President of Liberia, economist*

## LUXEMBOURG

**Kirchberg**
Leger, Philippe *legal administrator*

## MALAWI

**Lilongwe**
Eastham, Alan Walter, Jr. *foreign service officer, lawyer*

## MALAYSIA

**Perak**
Yussuf Izzuddim, Shah Ghafraullah Sultan *Sultan of Perak*

**Petaling Jaya**
Wong, Kuok-Shoong Daniel *research scientist*

**Serdang**
Soetedjo, Hariyadi *materials scientist, researcher*

## MALDIVES

**Male**
Habeeb, Habeeba Hussain *librarian*

## MEXICO

**Aguascalientes**
Godinez Flores, Ramon *bishop*

**Caolniatizapan**
Ramirez-Mireles, Fernando *electrical engineer*

**Colonia Cuauhtemoc**
Garza, Antonio O. *ambassador*

**Cuernavaca**
Bolivar Zapata, Francisco *biochemist*

**Distrito Federal**
de la Fuente Ramirez, Juan Ramon *academic administrator*

**Garza Garcia**
Alva, Salvador *food products executive*
Gustafson, Eric William *real estate investor, wildlife habitat conservationist*

**Jalisco**
Pordon, Grace *writer, poet, artist*

**Mexico City**
Aramburúzabála, Maria Asunción *food products executive*
Bruton, John Macaulay *trade association executive, consultant*
Creel Miranda, Santiago *Mexican government official*
De La Riva, Myriam Ann *artist*
Díaz, Francisco Gil *Mexican government official*
Gurria Trevino, José Angel *former Mexican government official*

Leon-Portilla, Miguel *historian, educator*
Nicholas, Ronald Wayde *business consultant*
Ortiz, Guillermo *banker*
Peyrot Gonzalez, Marco A. *secretary of the navy of Mexico*
Porraz, Mauricio Jimenez Labora *civil engineer, researcher*
Trevino, Guillermo Prieto *stock exchange executive*
Vargas Legaspi, Juan *manufacturing executive*

**Monterrey**
Amores, Jose E. *director*

**Reynosa**
Asomoza, Miguel A. *researcher, educator*

**Saltillo**
Anderson, Brooks Doran, II, *geologist, consultant*

**San Pedro Garza García**
Defiore, Perry Dennis *director, small business owner*
Carabias Lillo, Julia *government official*
Frenk, Julio Jose *minister of health for Mexico, health systems researcher, consultant*
Téllez Kuenzler, Luis *former government official, investment banker*

## MONACO

**Monte Carlo**
Lovett, Laurence Dow *retired real estate and steamship executive*

## MONGOLIA

**Ulaanbaatar**
Baasan, Ragchaa *diplomat*
Mandel, Leslie Ann *investment advisor, writer*

## MOROCCO

**Rabat**
Rafi, Mostafa *ophthalmologist*

## NETHERLANDS

**Amsterdam**
Kolko, Gabriel *historian, educator*
Rizzi, Joseph Vito *banker*
Vinken, Pierre Jacques *publishing executive*

**Haarlem**
Calhoun, David L. *information and media company executive*
Green, Zachary Gabriel *psychologist*

**Krimpen aan den Yssel**
Houtzager, Marianne Johanna (Marian de Boyen) *writer, artist, photographer*

**Maastricht**
Van Praag, Herman Meir *psychiatrist, educator, researcher*

**Rotterdam**
van Wachem, Lodewijk Christiaan *petroleum company executive*

**The Hague**
Aldrich, George Hoover *judge, arbitrator*
Allison, Richard Clark *judge*
Boed, Roman A. *legal administrator*
Buergenthal, Thomas *judge*
Cook, Linda Z. *utilities executive*
Higgins, Dame Rosalyn *judge*
Jiuyong, Shi *judge*
Kooijmans, Pieter Hendrik *judge*
Koroma, Abdul G. *judge*
Owada, Hisashi *judge*
Parra-Aranguren, Gonzalo *judge*
Rezek, Francisco *judge, former supreme court justice*
Shepard, Donald J. *insurance company executive*
Tomka, Peter *diplomat, arbitrator, judge, lawyer*

**Utrecht**
't Hooft, Gerardus (Gerard 't Hooft) *physicist, researcher*
Tielman, Rob A.P. *social sciences educator*

**Vlaardingen**
Smith, Arlan Robert *plastic and reconstructive surgeon*

## NEW ZEALAND

**Palmerston North**
Krone, Cheryl A. *research scientist, consultant*

**Wellington**
Jackson, Peter *film director*
Paquin, Anna *actress*
von Kohorn, Baron Ralph Steven *retired investment banker*
Wu, Lisa Maria *psychologist*
Gould, Wayne *application developer, retired judge*

## NIGERIA

**Anambra State**
Ekene, Anigwe Raphael *chemical engineer*

**Enugu**
Ozumba, Benjamin Chukwuma *obstetrician, gynecologist, educator*

Farman-Farmaian, Ghaffar *investment company executive*
Jacquesson, Alain L. *librarian*
Kim, Jim Yong *public health service officer, preventive medicine physician*
Maglacas, A. Mangay *nursing researcher, educator*
McDougall, Gay *lawyer*
Peskov, Vladimir Dmitrievich *physicist, consultant, physics professor*
Piot, Peter *international organization administrator*
Richter, Frank-Jürgen *economist, consultant*
Sidjanski, Dusan *economist, educator*
Sommaruga, Cornelio *foundation administrator, diplomat*
Steinberger, Jack *physicist, researcher*

**Hombrechtikon**
Landis, Floyd *professional cyclist*

**Lausanne**
Bloemsma, Marco Paul *investor*
Servien, Louis-Marc (Comte De Boisdauphin, Lord of Quendon) *finance company executive, import/export company executive*

**Lugano**
Badetti, Rolando Emilio *health science facility administrator*

**Meggen**
Galway, Sir James *flutist*

**Versoix**
Mahler, Halfdan Theodor *physician, health organization executive*

**Yverdon-les-Bains**
Egolf, Peter William *physicist*

**Zurich**
Binnig, Gerd Karl *physicist, educator*
Calatrava, Santiago *architect, structural engineer, artist*
Domingue, Gerald James *medical researcher, microbiologist, immunologist, educator, clinical bacteriologist*
Ernst, Richard Robert *chemist, educator*
Eschenmoser, Albert *chemist*
Hammesfahr, Robert Winter *lawyer*
Morari, Manfred *chemical engineer, educator*
Wassmer, Rudolf Andreas *entrepreneurial engineer*
Wüthrich, Kurt *molecular biologist, biophysicist, educator*
Zinkernagel, Rolf Martin *immunology educator*

## TAIWAN

**Hsinchu**
Wang, David *finance educator*

**Hualien**
Yiin, Lih-Ming *educator*

**Kaohsiung**
Chien, Yie W. *pharmaceutical science educator, academic administrator*
Lambert, Marianne T. *retired elementary school educator*
Wang, Gwo Jaw *orthopedic surgery educator*

**Pingtung**
Fan, Tai-Sheng Allen *social scientist in computer education and computing, educator*

**Taichung**
Liang, Chenju *engineering educator*
Lu, Shih-Peng *history professor*
Ou, Yen-Chuan *urologist*

**Tainan**
Chen, Chun-Jen *lawyer, educator*
Hsiao, Shih Wen *mechanical engineer, educator*
Huang, Ting-Chia *chemical engineering professor, researcher*
Lin, Jiin-Huey Chern *engineering educator*

**Taipei**
Chuang, Yii-Der *retired manufacturing executive, diplomat*
Dilley, Whitney Crothers *literature and language professor*
Lee, Yuan Tseh *chemistry professor*
Lo, Fu-chen *economist, educator, ambassador*
Tsung, Christine Chai-yi *financial executive, treasurer*
Yeh, Kuo Hsing *bank executive*

## TANZANIA

**Arusha**
Rapp, Stephen John *international prosecutor*

**Moshi**
Pomfret, David B. *medical educator, internist*

## THAILAND

**Bangkok**
Kornell, Ronald Frank *economist*
Kruck, Donna Jean *special education educator, consultant*
McMillion, Margaret Kim *foreign service officer*

**Bangsue**
Keeratiwintakorn, Phongsak Prasithsangaree *educator, consultant*

## TRINIDAD AND TOBAGO

**St Augustine**
Harris, Eon Nigel *dean, rheumatologist, internist*

## TUNISIA

**Carthage**
Sehili, Mahmoud *artist*

## TURKEY

**Adana**
Diler, Rasim Somer *psychiatrist, researcher*

**Ankara**
Gürkaynak, Refet S. *economist, consultant*
Kostakoglu, Lale *nuclear medicine educator, researcher*

**Istanbul**
Baksu, Alparslan *obstetrician, gynecologist, researcher*
Koyuncu, Ismail *engineering educator*
Ongan, Nilgün Erdal *interior designer, architect, artist*

**Kocaeli**
Sevilgen, Fatih Erdogan *computer scientist, educator*

## UKRAINE

**Odessa**
Vasiljev, Alexander Valerjovich *economist, metallurgical engineer*

## UNITED ARAB EMIRATES

**Abu Dhabi**
Sun, Yuefeng *research scientist, educator*
Taylor, Frederick William, Jr., (Fritz Taylor) *lawyer*

**Dubai**
Chohan, Gulshan-Naseem *office manager*
Khan, Waleed *auditor*

## UNITED STATES

**APO**
Carner, George *foreign service executive, economic strategist*

**San Juan**
Rodriguez-Velez, Rosa *prosecutor*

## VENEZUELA

**Caracas**
Eljuri, Elisabeth *lawyer*
Salas, Randall Nouel *automotive company executive*

## VIETNAM

**Ho Chi Minh City**
Israel, Barry John *lawyer*

## WALES

**Swansea**
Evans, Myron Wyn *physicist, researcher*

## ZAMBIA

**Nangoma**
Hansen, Florence Marie Congiolosi (Mrs. James S. Hansen) *social worker*

## ZIMBABWE

**Harare**
Salahuddin, Ahmad *civil engineer, educator*

## ADDRESS UNPUBLISHED

Aalberts, Nola Jean *social worker, administrator*
Aall, Christian Bergengren *entrepreneur*
Aamodt, Roger Louis *retired federal agency administrator*
Aatrapi, Marjane *writer, illustrator*
Abbas Borhan, Richat *medical association administrator*
Abbe, Elfriede Martha *sculptor, graphics designer*
Abbott, Robert Kennedy *artist, writer*
Abbott, Edward Leroy *finance executive*
Abbott, George Lindell *retired librarian*
Abbott, Kenneth Wayne *law educator*
Abbott, Lawrence E. *lawyer*
Abbott, Rebecca Phillips *art historian, consultant, photographer, director*
Abbott, Regina A. *neurodiagnostic technologist, consultant, business owner*
Abboud, Mara *artist*
Abdel-Monsef, Hani Ahmed *marketing professional*
Abdul-Jabbar, Kareem (Lew Alcindor, Lewis Ferdinand Alcindor) *professional basketball coach*
Abdulaev, Yalchin *neuroscientist, educator*
Abel, Barbara Ellen *photographer*
Abeles, Kim Victoria *artist*
Abeles, Sigmund M. *painter, sculptor, printmaker*
Abell, Anna Ellen *primary school educator*

Abell, Dawn Gabbitas *elementary school educator, secondary school educator, school system administrator*
Abelson, Harold *electrical engineer, educator*
Aberlin, Betty Kay *actress*
Abernathy, Ronald Fittz *pharmacist*
Abetti, Pier Antonio *electrical engineer, management consultant, educator*
Abid, Ann B. *art librarian*
Able, Kenneth Paul *biology professor*
Ablow, Keith Russell *writer*
Aboufakher, Rabeea *cardiologist*
Aboussie, Marilyn *retired judge*
Abraham, Katharine Gail *economics professor*
Abramowitz, Morton I. *former ambassador*
Abrams, Arthur Jay *retired physician*
Abrams, Jonathan *Internet company executive*
Abrams, Roz *newscaster*
Abrams Finger, Iris Dale *retired elementary school educator*
Abu-Khalaf, Murad *researcher*
Abu-Mostafa, Ayman Said *application developer, consultant*
Abu Qahouq, Jaber A. *electrical engineer, researcher*
Accordino, Frank Joseph *architect*
Acerra, Michele (Mike Acerra) *engineering and construction company executive*
Achauer, Bruce Michael *plastic surgeon*
Achord, James Lee *retired gastroenterologist*
Achorn, Robert Comey *retired newspaper publisher*
Ackerman, F. Duane (Duane Ackerman) *telecommunication industry executive*
Ackerman, Jack Rossin *investment banker*
Ackerman, Melvin *investment company executive*
Ackerman, Valerie B. *former sports association executive*
Ackermann, Bret Thomas *military officer, emergency physician*
Ackley, Robert Arthur *mathematics educator, retired military officer*
Adaikkalavan, Raman *computer scientist, educator*
Adaku, Chioma *non-profit organization administrator*
Adam, John, Jr. *insurance company executive emeritus*
Adam, Justine E. *psychologist*
Adams, Amy (Amanda Jessica Adams) *actress*
Adams, Arlin Marvin *lawyer, retired judge, arbitrator, mediator*
Adams, Brooke *actress*
Adams, Daniel Fenton *law educator*
Adams, David Parrish *historian, epidemiologist, educator*
Adams, Deanna Ruth *writer, educator*
Adams, Edwin Melville *retired diplomat, actor, writer*
Adams, James Charles *lawyer*
Adams, James Thomas *surgeon*
Adams, Joey Lauren *actress*
Adams, Kristin Anne *researcher*
Adams, Leocadia Donat *secondary school educator, writer*
Adams, Margaret Bernice *retired museum official*
Adams, Mignon Strickland *library director*
Adams, Patrick O. *career officer*
Adams, Peter Frederick *academic administrator, civil engineer*
Adams, Robert McCormick *anthropologist, educator*
AdamS, Sharon Butler *minister, philosopher, researcher*
Adams, Thomas Lynch, Jr. *lawyer*
Adams, Valencia I. *telecommunications industry executive*
Adams, Weston *former diplomat, military officer, lawyer*
Adamski, Mark Phillip *music educator*
Adamson, Dan Klinglesmith *retired science association executive*
Adamson, James B. *retail executive*
Adamson, Lynda G. *literature educator, writer*
Adams-Passey, Suellen S. *retired elementary school educator*
Addo, Charles Kwame *municipal official*
Adechi, Joel Wassi *international organization official*
Adelman, Rick (Richard Leonard Adelman) *former professional basketball coach*
Adkins, Thomas Samuel *library director*
Adkinson, Brian Lee *manufacturing executive*
Adler, Larry *marketing professional*
Adler, Nancy Elinor *psychologist, educator*
Adler, Raphael *retired humanities educator, speech pathology/audiology services professional*
Adler, Richard Melvin *architect, planner*
Adler, Samuel Hans *retired conductor, composer*
Adolph, Kathryn Ann *passenger service employee*
Adrean, Lee *communications executive*
Aduen, Javier Francisco *physician, researcher*
Adzick, Nick Scott *surgeon, educator*
Aehlert, Barbara June *health facility administrator*
Aelony, Yossef *retired physician*
Affleck, Ben *actor*
Africa, Colby Tait *information technology executive, poet*
Agee, Claudia *executive secretary, tax specialist*
Aghdashloo, Shohreh *actress*
Agne, Phyllis G. *artist, educator*
Agnew, Kathleen Dianne Crosbie *language educator*
Agrell, Jeffrey *musician*
Agresto, John Thomas *former college president, education consultant*
Aguilar-Bryan, Lydia *medical educator, researcher*
Aguinsky, Richard Daniel *electrical engineer, engineering executive*
Aguirregabiria, Victor *science educator*
Ahearne, John Francis *science foundation director, researcher*
Ahlqvist, Ola *educator*
Ahmad, Ali *research scientist, consultant*
Ahmad, Shahid *engineering educator*
Ahmed, Syed Z. *anthropologist*
Ahmed, Walid Khairy Mohamed *electrical engineer*
Ahn, Dong H *insurance company executive*
Ahrens, Franklin Alfred *veterinary pharmacology educator*

Aiken, Michael Thomas *former academic administrator*
Aikman, Albert Edward *lawyer*
Airoldi, Edoardo Maria *statistician, researcher, computer scientist, consultant*
Akerlind, Christopher *lighting designer, set designer*
Akhoury, Ravi *insurance company executive*
Akinci, Burcu *civil engineer, educator*
Akiyama, Cliff *forensic science educator, criminologist, researcher, consultant*
Akiyoshi, Toshiko *jazz composer, pianist*
Akridge, Steven L. *risk management consultant*
Aksen, Gerald *arbitrator, lawyer, educator*
Aladjem, Henrietta H. *writer*
Alba, Jessica *actress*
Albanese, Thomas *entrepreneur*
Albano, Michael J. *former mayor*
Albano, Pasquale Charles *finance educator, management consultant*
Alberger, William Relph *lawyer, retired government agency administrator*
Albers, Charles Edgar *retired investment company executive*
Alberti-Chappell, Roxana Dearing *psychologist*
Alberts, Renée Miller *counselor, alcohol/drug abuse services professional*
Albin, Barry G. *lawyer, rabbi*
Albrecht, Ronald Lewis *financial services executive*
Albritton, William Harold III *federal judge*
Alden, Ingemar Bengt *pharmaceuticals executive*
Alderfer, Clayton Paul *organizational consultant, writer*
Alderson, Sandy (Richard Lynn Alderson) *major league baseball executive*
Aldredge, Theoni Vachliotis *costume designer*
Aldrich, Franklin Dalton *medical researcher, consultant*
Aldrich, Patricia Anne Richardson *retired magazine editor*
Aldridge, Donald O'Neal *military officer*
Aldridge, Edward Cleveland, Jr., (Pete Aldridge) *former federal agency administrator*
Aldridge, Linda Ann *retired elementary school educator, retired librarian*
Aldrin, Buzz *retired astronaut*
Aleinikov, Andrei Grigoryevich *linguist, educator*
Alemu, Fitsum Achamyeleh *lawyer, researcher*
Alevizos, Susan Bamberger *lawyer, writer, musician*
Alexander, Ascencion (Cency) H. *school psychologist, educator*
Alexander, Barbara Toll *financial consultant*
Alexander, Danrick *mining engineer, educator*
Alexander, Donald G. *auditor, protective services official*
Alexander, Faith Dorothy *retired training services executive*
Alexander, James H. *industrial designer*
Alexander, Jessie Aronow *anesthesiologist*
Alexander, John Whitesides *musician, educator*
Alexander, Judd Harris *retired paper company executive*
Alexander, Marjorie Anne *artist, consultant*
Alexander, Mary Melson *secondary school educator*
Alexander, Nancy A. *information technology manager, consultant*
Alexander, Rebecca *library director, artist*
Alexander, Sheila A. *education educator, nurse, researcher*
Alexander, Thomas G. *chemist, researcher*
Alexiades-Armenakas, Macrene Renee *dermatologist, scientist, researcher, educator, consultant*
Alfano, Robert R. *science educator, engineering educator*
Alfaro, Victor *fashion designer*
Alfred, Stephen Jay *retired lawyer*
Algera, Henry F. *education educator*
Ali, Mohammed Zamshed *information technology executive, researcher*
Ali, Muhammad (Cassius Marcellus Clay) *retired boxer*
Aliber, Robert Z. *economist, educator*
Aliev, Eldar *former artistic director, choreographer, artist*
Alig, Frank Douglas Stalnaker *retired construction company executive*
Ali G, (Sacha Baron Cohen) *actor, comedian*
Alinder, Mary Street *writer, educator*
Alipio, Gary Glynn *writer, consultant*
Aljian, James Donovan *investment company executive*
Alker, Hayward Rose *political scientist, educator*
Allaire, Paul Arthur *former office equipment company executive*
Allard, Michael Alan *music educator, conductor*
Allbritton, Joe Lewis *diversified financial services company executive, director*
Allen, Bennie Carnel *employee relations specialist*
Allen, Bruce Templeton *retired economics professor*
Allen, Carol E. *retired elementary school educator*
Allen, Charles Eugene *university administrator, agriculturist, educator*
Allen, Charlotte *secondary school educator*
Allen, Claude Alexander *former federal official*
Allen, Donald Vail *investment company executive, musician*
Allen, Jacquelyn May *education educator, consultant*
Allen, Louis Alexander *management consultant*
Allen, Marilyn Myers Pool *theater director, video specialist*
Allen, Natalie *cable news anchor*
Allen, Philip *artist*
Allen, Richard Vincent *international business consultant, former national security advisor*
Allen, Roberta *writer, photographer, conceptual artist*
Allen, Toni K. *lawyer*
Allen, William Hayes *lawyer, educator*
Allen, William L. *editor*
Allen, William Sheridan *retired social sciences educator*
Allen, Woody (Allen Stewart Konigsberg) *director, actor, writer*
Alley, Kirstie *actress*
Allison, Andrew Marvin *church administrator*

Bowers, Richard Philip *manufacturing executive*
Bowes, Frederick III *publishing executive, consultant*
Bowes, Henry Edward *retired communications executive*
Bowles, Barbara Landers *investment company executive*
Bowlin, Patrick W. *secondary school educator*
Bowling, John C. *academic administrator*
Bowman, Bruce Alan *civil engineer*
Bowman, David Frederick *music educator*
Bowman, John J. *judge*
Bowne, Shirlee Pearson *credit manager*
Boxer, Alan Lee *accountant*
Boyatt, Thomas David *former ambassador*
Boyce, Joseph Nelson *retired journalist, consultant, educator*
Boyd, Claude Collins *educational specialist, consultant*
Boyd, John T. *engineering executive*
Boyd, Joseph Arthur, Jr. *lawyer*
Boyd, Kenneth R. *web programmer, mathematician*
Boyd, Mary Frances *retired school nurse, pastor*
Boyd, William Sprott *lawyer*
Boyda, Debora *advertising executive*
Boyer, Herbert Wayne *retired biochemist*
Boyer, Jeffrey N. *former retail executive*
Boyer, Lisa *basketball coach*
Boyer, Robert Allan *finance company executive*
Boykin, Robert Heath *retired banker*
Boyle, Lara Flynn *actress*
Boyle, Peter *actor*
Boyle, Richard John *art historian, author*
Boyle, Tatiana Gennadievna *research scientist*
Boyle, T.C. *writer, literature educator*
Boyle, Tim *apparel executive*
Boyles, James Kenneth *retired banker*
Boynes, Sean G. *dental anesthesiologist, researcher*
Boynton, Sandra Keith *illustrator, cartoonist, stationery products executive*
Boysen, Jonea Gene *marketing executive*
Braasch, John William *retired surgeon, consultant*
Brach, Paul Henry *artist*
Bracken, Peg *writer*
Brackett, Colquitt Prater, Jr. *judge, lawyer*
Bradbeer, Clive *biochemistry educator*
Braddock, Richard S. *internet company executive*
Braden, Thomas Wardell *news correspondent*
Bradford, Louise Mathilde *social work administrator*
Bradford, Marlene Kay *history educator, writer*
Bradford, Susan Anne *management consultant, writer*
Bradley, Amelia Jane *lawyer*
Bradley, Bill *former senator*
Bradley, Elizabeth Clay *financial planner, educator*
Bradley, Slater *artist*
Bradley, William Bryan *cable television regulator*
Bradsher, Keith Vinson *journalist*
Brady, Andrea Rassin *marketing executive*
Brady, Donna Elizabeth *sales executive, marketing executive, performing company executive*
Brady, Edward Thomas, Jr. *lawyer, writer*
Brady, Jean Stein *retired librarian*
Brady, M. Jane (Muriel Jane Brady) *judge, former state attorney general*
Brady, Mary Rolfes *music educator*
Brady, Wayne *actor*
Brady-Borland, Karen *retired reporter, columnist*
Braff, Zach *actor, director, scriptwriter*
Brafford, William Charles *lawyer*
Bragg, Lynn Munroe *trade association administrator, former federal commissioner*
Brahnam, Sheryl *computer scientist, researcher*
Brain, George Bernard *university dean*
Brainard, Melissa *accountant*
Brakebill, Jean Newton *military officer, nurse, educator*
Brakensiek, Jay Clemence *county official*
Bram, Leon Leonard *publishing company executive*
Bramhall, Debra A. *information technology manager, consultant*
Branagan, James Joseph *lawyer*
Branagh, Kenneth *actor, film director*
Brancato, Leo John *manufacturing executive*
Branch, Felicia Ann-Seldon *elementary school educator*
Brandon, Liane *filmmaker, educator*
Brandt, Robert Frederic III *retired editor, journalist*
Brandt, Ronald Stirling *retired editor, researcher*
Brandt-Soetermans, Valerie Louise *dancer, educator*
Brannon, Jean Estes *education educator*
Bransdorfer, Stephen Christie *retired lawyer*
Branson, Harley Kenneth *finance company executive*
Brant, William *surgeon, urologist*
Brantz, George Murray *retired lawyer*
Bratt, Nicholas *investment company executive, research and development company executive*
Bratton, William Edward *electronics executive, management consultant*
Braude, Edwin Simon *retired manufacturing executive*
Braude, Robert Michael *retired medical librarian*
Brauer, Rhonda Lyn *publishing executive, lawyer*
Braun, Amy M. *secondary school educator*
Braun, Jerome Irwin *lawyer*
Braun, Lilian Jackson *writer*
Braun, Mary Lucile Dekle (Lucy Braun) *physical therapist, consultant, counseling administrator, educator*
Braun, Stanley *orthodontist, educator*
Bravo, Paul *professional soccer player*
Braxton, Frederick *music educator*
Bray, Corey *intercollegiate athletics administrator*
Brazier, Don Roland *retired railroad executive*
Brazil, Aine M. *engineering company executive*
Breakstone, Kay Louise *public relations executive*
Breathed, Berkeley *cartoonist*
Breault, Robert Lee *music educator*
Bredehoft, John Michael *lawyer*
Bredfeldt, John Creighton *economist, financial analyst, retired military officer*
Breeden, Richard C. *investment company executive, former federal agency administrator*

Breeze, Philip Raley *director*
Brehl, James William *lawyer*
Brehm, Warren Gamaliel Harding *protective services official*
Breitman, Leo R. *banker*
Bremer, Paul (L. Paul Bremer, Lewis Paul Bremer III) *former diplomat*
Bremer, Ronald Allan *genealogist, editor*
Bremer Martino, Juan Jose *former ambassador*
Bremner, John McColl *agronomy and biochemistry educator*
Brenly, Bob *professional sports team executive, broadcaster*
Brennan, Donna Lesley *public relations company executive*
Brennan, Lawrence Edward *retired electronics engineer*
Brenneman, Russell Langdon *retired lawyer*
Brennen, Stephen Alfred *management consultant*
Brenner, David H. *marketing executive*
Brent, Robert Leonard *radiology and pediatrics educator*
Brett, Thomas Rutherford *federal judge*
Brettell, Richard Robson *art historian, museum consultant, educator*
Bretthauer, Erich Walter *chemist, educator*
Brewer, Barbara Bagdasarian *nursing administrator*
Brewer, Carey *retired academic administrator*
Brewer, Kelly Deanne *pharmaceutical sales specialist, oncological nurse*
Brewer, Lynn *energy executive*
Brewer, Roy Edward *lawyer*
Brewer, Summer M. *performing arts educator*
Brewer, Timothy Francis III *retired cardiologist*
Brewer, Wanda Eastwood *retired literature educator*
Brewster, Elizabeth Winifred *literature educator, poet, writer*
Brez, Dante (Mos Def) *musician, actor*
Brice, Jacqueline (Jackie Brice) *landscape artist*
Brickell, Charles Hennessey, Jr. *marine engineer, retired military officer*
Bricker, Harvey Miller *retired anthropology educator*
Bricker, Victoria Reifler *anthropologist, educator*
Bridger, Baldwin, Jr. *electrical engineer*
Bridges, Leonard Hal *retired history educator, writer*
Bridges-Kemp, Leslie LaVerne *administrative assistant*
Bridgewater, Albert Louis *retired science foundation administrator*
Briese, Michael W. *writer, deacon, inventor*
Briggle, Gary Lee *singer, actor, director, educator*
Briggs, James Henry, II, *electrical engineer*
Briggs, Philip *insurance company executive*
Briggs, Philip James *political science professor, writer*
Briggs, Thomas Henry *computer science educator*
Brightman, Sarah *singer, actress*
Briles, Judith *writer, consultant*
Brill, Kenneth C. *federal official, former ambassador*
Brim, Orville Gilbert, Jr. *former foundation administrator, writer*
Brinberg, Herbert Raphael *publishing executive*
Brindle, Lewis Carver *art association administrator, educator*
Briskman, Louis Jacob *lawyer*
Brister, Bill H. *lawyer, former bankruptcy judge*
Bristow, William Harvey, Jr. *psychiatrist*
Britt, John Roy *banker*
Britt, Rebecca Fae *communications executive*
Brizio-Molteni, Loredana *surgeon, educator*
Broaddus, John Alfred, Jr. *retired bank executive, economist*
Broadrick-Allen, Sandra Carol *retired city manager, civic worker, consultant*
Broadwater, James E. *publisher*
Brock, William Emerson *former secretary of labor*
Broderick, B. Michael, Jr. *state legislator, banker*
Broderick, James Allen *painter, art educator, etcher*
Broderson, Thelma Sylvia *retired marketing professional*
Brodhead, David Crawmer *lawyer*
Brodsky, Beverly Anne *writer, consultant, editor*
Brody, Adrien *actor*
Broek, Howard Windolph *real estate executive*
Brogliatti, Barbara Spencer *retired television and motion picture executive*
Brokaw, Tom (Thomas John Brokaw) *former network news anchor*
Brokke, Catherine Juliet *retired mission executive*
Bromwell, Linda Anne *librarian, writer*
Brondello, Sandy *professional basketball player*
Bronfine, Boris Isaakovich *surgeon*
Bronfman, Edgar Miles, Sr. *beverage company executive*
Bronkar, Eunice Dunalee *artist, educator*
Bronson, James B. *music educator*
Bronzi, Philip A. *retired social worker, educator*
Brook, Scott Jonathan Bradley *mayor, career consulting executive*
Brooke, Edward William *lawyer, retired senator*
Brooke, Francis John III *retired academic administrator*
Brooke, Ralph Ian *dental educator*
Brooker, Robert Elton, Jr. *retired manufacturing company executive*
Brookner, Anita *writer, educator*
Brookner, Jackie W. *sculptor, educator*
Brooks, Andrée Aelion *journalist, educator*
Brooks, Avery *actor, educator, musician*
Brooks, Babert Vincent *publisher*
Brooks, Deborah June *art educator*
Brooks, Garth (Troyal Garth Brooks) *musician, singer*
Brooks, Gary *crisis management and family business consultant*
Brooks, Geraldine *writer, reporter, news correspondent*
Brooks, Gerldine McGlothlin *music educator*
Brooks, Kathleen *journalist*
Brooks, Kenneth N. *forestry educator*
Brooks, Lorraine Elizabeth *retired music educator*
Brooks, Lynda Barbara *psychologist*
Brooks, Michael *music archivist*
Brooks, Michael Paul *retired urban planning educator*

Brooks Shoemaker, Virginia Lee *librarian*
Brooks-Turner, Myra *music educator*
Broome, Claire Veronica *epidemiologist, researcher*
Broome, Oscar Whitfield, Jr. *finance educator*
Brosda von Kupferberg, Baron Alexander Christian *investment banker*
Brosnan, Pierce *actor*
Brosz, Margaret Headley *pediatrics nurse*
Broth, Richard *perinatologist*
Brothers, John Alfred *retired oil company executive, chemicals executive*
Brotman, David Joel *architectural firm executive, consultant*
Brotman, Stuart Neil *management consultant, law educator, former museum administrator*
Brott, Walter Howard *retired cardiac surgeon, educator, retired military officer*
Broude, Ronald *music publisher*
Broughton, James Walter *real estate development executive, consultant*
Broughton, Phillip Charles *lawyer, director*
Browder, Felix Earl *mathematician, educator*
Brown, Alberta Mae *nurse*
Brown, Alice Elste *artist*
Brown, Alton C. *television personality, chef*
Brown, Amira Khalila *neuropsychologist, researcher*
Brown, Amy Christine *art educator*
Brown, April Schlea *pharmacist*
Brown, B. Andrew *lawyer*
Brown, Barbara June *hospital and nursing administrator*
Brown, Billye Jean *retired nursing educator*
Brown, Britt *retired publishing company executive*
Brown, Bruce Maitland *philanthropy consultant*
Brown, C Timothy *insurance company executive*
Brown, Carol Ann *librarian, director*
Brown, Carol Rose *artist*
Brown, Charles Dodgson *lawyer*
Brown, Dale Susan *retired federal agency administrator, academic administrator, consultant, writer*
Brown, David Richard *school system administrator, minister*
Brown, Deborah Eleanor *priest*
Brown, Denise *poet*
Brown, Donald Douglas *transportation executive, consultant, retired military officer*
Brown, Doug (Bryan Doug Brown) *career military officer*
Brown, Elizabeth Eleanor *retired librarian*
Brown, Geraldine *nurse, freelance writer*
Brown, Geraldine Reed *lawyer, management consultant*
Brown, Herbert Graham *entrepreneur*
Brown, Hershel M. *retired newspaper publisher*
Brown, J. E. (Buster Brown) *lawyer, consultant*
Brown, James Nelson, Jr. *retired accountant*
Brown, James W. *gastroenterologist*
Brown, Jeanette L. *environmental protection administrator*
Brown, Jeannette Elizabeth *retired science educator*
Brown, Jerry Milford *health products executive*
Brown, Jim (James Nathaniel Brown) *community activist, actor, retired professional football player*
Brown, John B. III *former federal agency administrator*
Brown, John Y. III *former state official*
Brown, June Gibbs *retired government official*
Brown, Kay (Mary Kathryn Brown) *retired state official, consultant, political organization worker*
Brown, Laima Adomaitis *art therapist, artist, writer*
Brown, Larry (Lawrence Harvey Brown) *professional basketball coach*
Brown, Lee Patrick *retired mayor, federal official, protective services official, educator*
Brown, Les (Lester Louis) *journalist*
Brown, Lora Alice *entertainment company executive, educator*
Brown, Margaret deBeers *lawyer*
Brown, Mary Ellen *former state legislator, accountant*
Brown, Michael DeWayne *former federal agency administrator, lawyer*
Brown, Michael Robert *healthcare corporation executive*
Brown, Pamela S. *former attorney general*
Brown, Peter Stewart *lawyer*
Brown, Richard Harris *former information technology executive*
Brown, Robert E. *transportation executive*
Brown, Robert Laidlaw *state supreme court justice*
Brown, Sandra *writer*
Brown, Stephen Hayze, Jr. *social worker*
Brown, Stephen S. *telecommunications industry executive*
Brown, Susan L. *internet and marketing services professional*
Brown-Barton, Grace Olive *music educator*
Browne, Frederick Douglas *physiologist, educator*
Browne, Jackson *singer, songwriter*
Browne, John Charles *physicist, researcher, lab administrator*
Browne, (Edmund) John Phillip (Lord Browne of Madingley) *oil industry executive*
Browne, Ray *congressman, insurance agent*
Brownell, Nora Mead *former commissioner*
Browning, Jane Louise *social services administrator*
Browning, Jennifer Anne *director*
Brown Leatherberry, Thomas Henry *performing company executive, clergyman*
Brownlee, Christine *elementary school educator*
Brownlee, Les (Romie Leslie Brownlee) *former civilian military employee*
Brownlee, Paula Pimlott *higher education consultant*
Brownrigg, Walter Grant *cartoonist*
Brown Spitzmueller, Janiece Marie *lawyer*
Broxmeyer, Lawrence *internist, researcher*
Broyles, William Dodson, Jr. *author, editor, scriptwriter*
Brozowski, Laura Adrienne *mechanical engineer*
Brubaker, Crawford Francis, Jr. *federal agency administrator, aerospace scientist, consultant*
Brubaker, James Edward *mechanical engineer*

Brubaker, William W., Jr. *federal agency administrator, civil engineer*
Bruce, David Lionel *retired anesthesiologist, educator*
Bruce, James Edmund *retired utilities executive*
Bruch, Virginia Irene Sullivan *librarian, writer*
Bruess, Charles Edward *lawyer*
Bruggeman, Terrance *biotechnology company executive*
Brugger, David John *media consultant*
Bruinsma, Gosse *research and development company executive*
Brumfield, Jack *communications executive*
Brunett, Emery Walter *pharmacist, educator*
Brungraber, Robert J. *civil engineer, educator*
Bruning, Earl H. *music educator*
Brunner, Kathleen Marie *humanities educator*
Bruno, Susan Elizabeth *retired secondary school educator*
Bruns, David Eugene *medical educator, researcher*
Brunt, Harry Herman, Jr. *psychiatrist*
Bruttomesso, Kathleen Ann *dean, nursing educator, researcher*
Bryan, Lawrence Dow *college president*
Bryant, Bertha Estelle *retired medical/surgical nurse*
Bryson, Nancy Southard *lawyer, former federal agency administrator*
Brzozowy, Kandy Doris *behavioral health writer*
Bubrick, Melvin Phillip *surgeon*
Bucci, Kathryn Klavas *pharmacist, consultant*
Buchanan, Carolee Horstman *special education educator, consultant*
Buchanan, John Lynn *retired broadcast executive*
Buchanan, Pat (Patrick Joseph Buchanan) *journalist, political commentator*
Buchanan, Theresa Carroll *judge*
Buchanan, William H., Jr. *retired lawyer, venture capitalist*
Buchholz, Todd *journalist, social sciences educator, consultant*
Buchin, Jean *psychologist, educator*
Buchmann, Alan Paul *lawyer*
Buchwald, Art *columnist, writer*
Buchwald, Naomi Reice *federal judge*
Buchwald, Nathaniel Avrom *retired physiologist professor*
Buck, Earl Wayne *private investigator, motel owner*
Buck, John E. *printmaker*
Buckelew, Larry C. *lab administrator*
Buckels, Marvin Wayne *savings and loan association executive*
Buckingham, Virginia *editor*
Buckler, Marilyn Lebow *school psychologist, educational consultant*
Buckley, Frederick Jean *lawyer*
Buckley, Kristy Loraine *lawyer, accountant*
Bucknum, Michael John *chemist, crystallographer, educator*
Buckwalter, Roger Jerome *editor, columnist*
Bucove, Arnold David *psychiatrist*
Bucy, J. Fred, Jr. *retired electronics company executive*
Buda, Thaddeus J., Jr. *retired lawyer*
Budd, Wayne A. *lawyer*
Budenz, Donald L. *ophthalmologist, educator*
Budnick, Ernest Joseph *recording industry executive*
Budnicki, Michael J. *nurse*
Budur, Nero *mathematician*
Buford, LaVerda Jo *director*
Bugental, James Frederick Thomas *retired psychologist, educator*
Bugliosi, Vincent T. *lawyer*
Buhagiar, Marion *editor, writer*
Buhain, Wilfrido Javier *medical educator*
Buhl, Cynthia Maureen *advocate, educator*
Buist, Neil Robertson MacKenzie *pediatric educator, medical association administrator*
Buitrón, Robert C. *artist, educator*
Buker, Robert Hutchinson, Sr. *army officer, thoracic surgeon*
Bulkley, Gregory Bartlett *cattle rancher, retired surgeon, research scientist, educator*
Bull, Bergen Ira *retired equipment manufacturing company executive*
Bulla, Clyde Robert *writer*
Bullard, Judith Eve *psychologist, systems engineer*
Bullock, Mary Brown *former academic administrator*
Bullock, Molly *retired elementary school educator*
Bullock, Sandra (Sandra Annette Bullock) *actress*
Bulow, Jack Faye *retired library director*
Bultas, William Fitzgerald *Internet company executive*
Bultman, Nils *musician, composer*
Bumgarner, Marlene Anne *editor, educator, writer*
Bunce, Christine A. *language educator*
Bunch, Jennings Bryan, Jr. *retired electrical engineer*
Buncke, Harry J. *retired plastic surgeon, retired educator*
Bundi, Renee *art director, graphics designer*
Bunker, Robert Duffield *protective services official, military officer*
Bunkowske, Eugene Walter *religious studies educator*
Bunyan, Ellen Lackey Spotz *retired chemist*
Burack, Michael Leonard *lawyer*
Burch, Annetta Jane *writer*
Burch, Lori Ann *obstetrics nurse*
Burcham, David W. *law educator*
Burchard, John Kenneth *retired chemical engineer*
Burchell, Kenneth Wayne *historian, appraiser*
Burchman, Leonard *federal official, journalist*
Burch-Martinez, Berkeley Alison *primary school educator*
Burden, Ordway Partridge *investment banker*
Burdette, Gary W. *music educator*
Burgdoerfer, Jerry J. *marketing and distribution executive*
Burge, Constance M. *television producer*
Burge, John Wesley, Jr. *management consultant*
Burgess, Marjorie Laura *retired protective services official*
Burghardt, Raymond Francis, Jr. *not-for-profit administrator, former ambassador*
Burhans, Frank Malcolm *mechanical engineer*
Burk, Raymond Franklin, Jr. *internist, educator, medical researcher*

Chang, Heng-Chia *communications engineer*
Chang, Runzi *electrical engineer*
Chang, Samuel Henry *computer scientist, educator*
Chang, Susan Marina *neuroscientist*
Chang, Victor Tsu-Shih *oncologist, researcher, educator*
Chang, Won *economist*
Chang, Ying Chih *engineering educator, researcher*
Chang, Yuan *neuropathologist, researcher, educator*
Channappayya, Sumohana *engineer, researcher*
Chansley, Deborah Lynn *education educator*
Chao, James Min-Tzu *architect*
Chao, Ruth *psychologist, researcher*
Chapman, Daniel P. *epidemiologist*
Chapman, Geneva Joyce *entrepreneur, educator, writer*
Chapman, Richard LeRoy *public affairs researcher*
Chapman, Robert Foster *federal judge*
Chapman, Thomas William *hospital executive*
Chapman, William *baritone*
Chappell, Annette M. *educational consultant, minister*
Chappell, Fred Davis *language educator, poet*
Charles, Elizabeth C. *administrative assistant*
Charles, George P. *religious studies educator*
Charles, Lola *interpreter*
Charles, Robert Bruce *lawyer, former federal agency administrator*
Charles, Walter *actor*
Charlton, Jesse Melvin, Jr. *retired management educator, lawyer*
Charlton, Shirley Marie *educational consultant*
Charnin, Jade Hobson *magazine executive*
Charwat, Andrew Franciszek *engineering educator*
Chase, Barbara Landis *headmaster*
Chase, Dawn Eileen *language educator*
Chase, Francis Marvin, Sr. *education educator, consultant*
Chase, Helen Louise *bank executive*
Chase, J. Vincent *property manager*
Chase, James Richard *retired college president*
Chase, Robin M. *entrepreneur*
Chase, William Robert *television executive*
Chaseman, Joel *communications consultant*
Chasin, Martin *art gallery director, consultant, educator*
Chassin, Jameson Lewis *retired surgeon*
Chassman, Leonard Fredric *retired labor union administrator*
Chast, Roz *cartoonist*
Chasteen, Beverly Joan *parochial school educator, elementary school educator*
Chatelain, Dalia de la Paz *elementary school educator, educational consultant*
Chatham, Rosemary Gail Moog *entrepreneur, musician, volunteer, composer*
Chati, Mandar Kalidas *operations research specialist*
Chavan Patil, Mahesh *research scientist*
Chave, Carol *arbitrator, retired lawyer*
Chaves-Carballo, Enrique *neuropediatrician*
Chaykin, Robert Leroy *manufacturing and marketing executive*
Cheatham, Jennifer *elementary school educator, consultant*
Cheatham, Robert William *retired lawyer*
Chebiam, Ramanan Venkata *computer engineer*
Checketts, Dave (David Wayne Checketts) *professional sports team executive*
Cheeger, Jeff *mathematics educator*
Cheek, Michael Carroll *lawyer*
Cheesman, John Michael *corporate financial executive*
Cheever, Susan *freelance/self-employed writer*
Chefitz, Joel Gerald *lawyer*
Chelle, Robert Frederick *electric power industry executive, educator*
Chen, Di *electronics executive, consultant, optical engineer*
Chen, Eric Yen-Po *accountant, consultant*
Chen, Julie *newscaster*
Chen, Kenichi *chef*
Chen, Qiang *engineer*
Chen, Shoei-Sheng *retired mechanical engineer*
Chen, Shuang *computer science professional*
Chen, Stephen S. F. *retired diplomat*
Cheng, Liang *video architect, researcher*
Cheng, Lili *research scientist*
Cheng, Richard *chemist*
Cheng, Yue *molecular geneticist, pathologist*
Cheong, Soonwuk *research scientist*
Chercover, Murray *television executive*
Cherin, Stephen J. *application developer, management consultant*
Chernichaw, Mark *broadcast executive, television producer, advertising executive, media consultant*
Cherovsky, Erwin Louis *lawyer, writer*
Cherry, Robert Steven III *municipal official*
Chesler, Doris Adelle *real estate broker*
Chesson, Michael Bedout *history professor, writer*
Chevalier, Paul Edward *retired retail executive, lawyer*
Chia, Pei-Yuan *bank executive*
Chiang, I-Ting *engineering educator*
Chiang, Michael Fred *physician*
Chiang, Mung *engineering educator, consultant*
Chiang, Wen-Chyuan *finance educator*
Chiaramonte, Christine Loren *elementary school educator*
Chiarelli, Peter W. *career military officer*
Chickamenahalli, Shamala A. *electronics engineer*
Chicorel, Marietta Eva *publishing company executive, consultant*
Childers, Charles Eugene *mining company executive*
Childers, Susan Lynn Bohn *special education educator, school system administrator, human resources and transition specialist, consultant*
Childs, John David *retired computer company executive*
Chilton, Lance Alix *pediatrician*
Chilvers, Derek *insurance company executive*
Chin, Peter S. *neurologist, researcher*
Chiplin, John *medical company executive*
Chirco, Jennifer B. *special education educator*
Chirico-Elkins, Ursula *retired librarian*
Chitnis, Ashay *research scientist*
Chiu, Dorothy *retired pediatrician*

Chiu, Felicia *finance company executive*
Chiussi, Fabio Massimo *research and development company executive*
Chmielinski, Edward Alexander *retired electronics company executive*
Cho, Alfred Yi *electrical engineer*
Cho, Margaret (Moran Cho) *comedienne, actress*
Choa, John Richard *architect*
Chodosh, Hyman Louis *neurologist*
Choi, Hack Sun *molecular biologist, researcher*
Choi, Ji Young *mathematics professor*
Choi, Kwang-Sik *adult education educator*
Choi, Youngok *information science educator*
Chong, James Tzeh-min *finance educator, researcher*
Chong, Kaman *osteopath*
Chopra, Samir *pharmaceutical executive, real estate company executive*
Chorpenning, Frank Winslow *retired immunology educator, researcher*
Chou, Chung-Kwang *bio-engineer*
Choueifati, Antoine (Tony Choueifati) *computer company executive*
Chouery, Farid Alexandre *electrical engineer, structural engineer, consultant*
Choukas-Bradley, Melanie *writer, photographer*
Chow, Jack C. *international organization administrator*
Chow, Judy *library and information scientist, educator*
Chow, Rita Kathleen *nursing consultant*
Chow, Timothy Yi-Chung *mathematician, systems engineer*
Chow, Winston *engineering executive*
Chretien, Jane Henkel *internist*
Chrétien, Raymond A.J. *retired ambassador*
Christensen, Karen Kay *lawyer*
Christensen, Madonna Dries *writer*
Christenson, Gregg Andrew *bank executive*
Christenson, Shen *editor*
Christian, James Wayne *economist*
Christian, Lori Coffelt *marketing professional*
Christiansen, David K. *health facility administrator*
Christiansen, Richard Dean *retired newspaper editor*
Christiansen, Richard Louis *orthodontist, educator, dean*
Christianson, Paul Alan *music educator*
Christin, Nicolas *computer scientist, researcher*
Christoffersen, Ralph Earl *chemist, researcher, director*
Christopher, Richard Scott *public relations executive, editor, advertising executive*
Christopher, Russell Lewis *baritone*
Christopher, Sharon A. Brown *bishop*
Christopherson, Dorothy Mae *musician*
Christopherson, Myrvin Frederick *college president*
Christy, Nicholas Pierson *physician*
Chrzanowski, David James *organist, accompanist*
Chu, Ellin Resnick *librarian, consultant*
Chu, Jack J. (Jack J. Zhu) *electrical engineer*
Chu, James *electronics executive*
Chu, Katherine K. *music educator*
Chu, Margaret S.Y. *former federal agency administrator*
Chu, Wai C. *engineer, researcher*
Chulack, Christopher M. *television director, television producer*
Chun, Asaph Y. *research scientist*
Chung, Caroline *marketing professional*
Chung, Doo-ri *apparel designer*
Chung, Jennifer M. *not-for-profit developer*
Chung, Wingyan *computer scientist, information scientist, educator*
Chung, Woo Cheol *electrical engineer*
Church, Charlotte *vocalist*
Church, Eugene Lent *physicist, consultant*
Churchill, Robert Wilson *state legislator, lawyer*
Churukian, George Allen *retired education educator*
Ciabattari, Mark *historian, writer*
Ciagala, Karencia Lucille *writer*
Cianci, Philip Joesph *broadcast engineer*
Ciccarelli, Chick *marketing professional*
Cicero, Carmen Louis *artist, educator*
Cicero, J. Deborah *management consultant*
Cichello, Samuel Joseph *architect*
Cicolani, Angelo George *research and development company executive, operating engineer*
Cifolelli, Alberta Carmella *artist, educator*
Cikovsky, Nicolai, Jr. *retired curator, art historian, educator*
Cilella, Salvatore George, Jr. *museum director*
Cinti, Sandro K. *internist, educator*
Ciofalo, Linda *vocalist, educator*
Ciraolo, Debra *sign language interpreter, consultant*
Citron, Diane *lawyer*
Citron, Richard Ira *management consultant*
Claes, Gayla Christine *writer, editor, consultant*
Claiborne, Liz (Elisabeth Claiborne Ortenberg) *fashion designer*
Clancy, Thomas L., Jr. *novelist, producer*
Clapp, Gordon *actor*
Clapper, James R., Jr. *retired military officer, former federal agency administrator*
Claridge, Elmond Lowell *retired engineering educator*
Clark, Alicia Garcia *political party official*
Clark, Beverly Ann *retired lawyer*
Clark, Beverly Jean *lawyer, mediator*
Clark, Caleb Morgan *political scientist, educator*
Clark, Donald Otis *lawyer*
Clark, Edgar Sanderford *insurance broker, consultant*
Clark, Eve Vivienne *linguist, educator*
Clark, James Covington *journalist, historian*
Clark, James Milford *retired college president*
Clark, Jason Allan *band director*
Clark, Jere Walton *economics professor, researcher*
Clark, Jim *communications executive*
Clark, Karen Heath *lawyer*
Clark, Mary Higgins *writer, communications executive*
Clark, Matt *writer*
Clark, Nancy Lucinda Brown *retired music educator*

Clark, Peter Bruce *retired publishing executive*
Clark, Philip Raymond *nuclear utility executive, engineer*
Clark, Richard Eugene *music educator*
Clark, Terri *country singer*
Clark, Thomas Carlyle *retired banker*
Clark, Vernon E. *retired military officer*
Clark, William, Jr. *professional society administrator*
Clarke, Sir Arthur Charles *author*
Clarke, Ciana Bernadine Bennett *education educator, researcher*
Clarke, Henry Lee *foreign service officer, ambassador*
Clarke, Janet Morrison *marketing executive*
Clarke, Jay A. *mathematics professor*
Clarke, Terence Michael *public relations and advertising executive*
Clarke, Victoria C. (Torie Clarke) *former federal agency administrator*
Clarkson, Patricia *actress*
Clausen, Jerry Lee *psychiatrist*
Claver, Robert Earl *television producer, director*
Clawson, John Addison *investment company executive, retired chemicals executive*
Clayton, David A(lvin) *biology professor*
Clayton, Julia B. *academic administrator, musician*
Clayton, Raymond Edward *municipal official*
Clayton, Richard Reese *retired diversified financial services company executive*
Claytor, Richard Anderson *retired federal agency administrator*
Cleary, Manon Catherine *artist, retired art educator*
Cleaver, James Edward *radiologist, educator*
Cleesattle, Jodi Lynn *lawyer*
Clemendor, Anthony Arnold *obstetrician, gynecologist, educator*
Clemens, Alvin Honey *insurance company executive*
Clement, Hope Elizabeth Anna *retired librarian*
Clement, John Edward Strausz *retired minister, retired religious organization administrator*
Clement, Kathryn B. *secondary school educator*
Clement, Yvonne Madeline *librarian*
Clements, Kimberly Dawne *school counselor*
Clementz, David M. *information technology executive*
Clemetson, Charles Alan Blake *physician*
Clemins, Patrick John *systems engineer, educator*
Clemmensen, Larry P. *former investment company executive*
Clemmons, Evelyn Yvonne *administrative assistant*
Clemons, Maggie Ruth *retired elementary school educator*
Clewett, Raymond Winfred *mechanical design engineer*
Cliff, Karen K. *music educator*
Clifford, Brother Peter *academic administrator, religious studies educator*
Clifton, Larry Stephen *theater educator*
Clifton, Russell B. *banking and mortgage lending consultant, retired mortgage company executive*
Clinkscale, Martha Novak *music educator, researcher*
Clogan, Paul Maurice *English language and literature educator*
Cloud, Bruce Benjamin, Sr. *construction company executive*
Clougher, Jaime Louise *director*
Clouston, Ross Neal *retired food and related products company executive*
Clubb, Bruce Edwin *retired lawyer*
Clymer, Adam *journalist, writer*
Cobb, John Boswell, Jr. *clergyman, educator*
Cobb, Miles Alan *retired lawyer*
Cobb, Ruth *artist*
Cobb, Virginia Horton *artist, educator*
Cobb-Myers, Janet Lea *music educator*
Cobey, Virginia Branum *artist, actress, art collector*
Coble, Yank David, Jr. *internist, endocrinologist*
Coburn, D(onald) L(ee) *playwright*
Coburn, Pamela Jane *opera singer, education educator*
Coburn, Steven D. *composer, musicologist, educator, pianist*
Cochetti, Roger James *international communications and internet company executive*
Cochran, Carolyn *library director*
Cochran, John P. *economics professor*
Cochran, Kathy Holcombe *music educator, conductor*
Cochran, Radeen M. *librarian*
Cochran, Robert Lee *music educator*
Cochrane, Lorna June *health science association administrator, consultant*
Cochrane, Walter E. *academic administrator, conductor, music supervisor, clarinet soloist*
Cockram, Suzanne M. *elementary school educator*
Cockrum, William Monroe III *investment banker, educator*
Codo, Christina *securities executive*
Cody, Aldus Morrill *retired editor, journalist, typographer*
Cody, Frank Joseph *education educator, educational consultant*
Cody, Judith *composer, writer*
Coe, Rodney Michael *medical educator*
Coffee, Joseph Denis, Jr. *retired college chancellor*
Coffey, Barbara Jane *psychiatrist*
Coffey, John Louis *federal judge*
Coffey, Paul *professional hockey player*
Coffin, Bertha Louise *retired telecommunications industry executive*
Cohane, Heather Christina *publishing executive, editor*
Cohen, Allan Richard *broadcast executive*
Cohen, Burton A. *radiologist*
Cohen, Carolyn A. *healthcare educator*
Cohen, Christopher B. *lawyer*
Cohen, Gloria Ernestine *elementary school educator*
Cohen, Jeffrey *lawyer*
Cohen, Joel J. *lawyer, investment banker*
Cohen, Jordan Jay *former medical association executive*
Cohen, Larry *film director, producer, screenwriter*

Cohen, Lawrence Alan *health facility administrator*
Cohen, Mark Herbert *broadcast executive*
Cohen, Michael Paul *retired statistician*
Cohen, Roberta Jane *think-tank associate*
Cohen, Sidney Mace *urologist*
Cohen, Stanley *retired biochemistry educator*
Cohen, William Nathan *radiologist*
Cohn, Avern Levin *district judge*
Cohn, Michael S. *investment company executive*
Cohn, Stephen M. *composer, music producer*
Cok, Ronald Steven *research scientist*
Coker, Christine E.H. *horticulturist, researcher*
Colacello, Bob (Robert John Colacello) *magazine editor, writer*
Colaianni, Joseph Vincent *judge*
Colangelo, Carmon *artist, printmaker, educator*
Colbern, Steven Garrett *chemist, researcher*
Cole, Carolyn *photojournalist*
Cole, David W. *information technology executive*
Cole, Nancy Stooksberry *educational research executive*
Cole, Nikki Jo *music educator*
Cole, Paula *pop singer, songwriter*
Coleman, Claire Kohn *public relations executive*
Coleman, Claudia L. *marketing executive*
Coleman, Dabney W. *actor*
Coleman, Earl Maxwell *publishing company executive*
Coleman, Gary William *elementary school educator*
Coleman, George Edward *musician*
Coleman, John Michael *lawyer, consumer products company executive*
Coleman, Mary Sue *academic administrator*
Coleman, Robert Lee *retired lawyer*
Coleman, Ronald Lee *insurance claims executive*
Coleman, William Thaddeus, Jr. *lawyer, former secretary of transportation*
Colescott, Robert Hutton *artist, educator*
Coletti, John Anthony *lawyer, retail executive, real estate company executive*
Colker, Edward *artist, educator*
Collier, Heather Elisha *psychometrist*
Collier, Herman Edward, Jr. *retired college president*
Collier, William Gayle *psychology professor, researcher*
Collins, Connie Sue *secondary school educator*
Collins, Douglas C. *hotel executive*
Collins, Douglas Patrick, Jr. *communications company executive, television producer*
Collins, Eileen Marie *astronaut*
Collins, Frank, Jr. *dentist, educator*
Collins, Harker *retired economist, retired manufacturing executive, retired publishing executive*
Collins, Irma Helen *music educator, consultant*
Collins, Izola E. *retired music educator*
Collins, J. Michael *retired public broadcasting executive*
Collins, Jean Katherine *language educator*
Collins, Joy *nurse, consultant, writer*
Collins, Kathleen Anne *artistic director*
Collins, Michael *aerospace consultant, astronaut*
Collins, Michael A. (Mac Collins) *former congressman*
Collins, Richard Stratton (Dick Collins) *retired public relations executive*
Collins, Theodore John *lawyer*
Collins, Walter Lloyd George *editor*
Collins, William J. (Billy Collins) *poet, educator*
Collischan, Judy Kay *art gallery director, museum director, critic, artist*
Collmer, Robert George *retired language educator*
Colodny, Edwin Irving *lawyer, retired air transportation executive*
Colombo, Rose Marie *freelance/self-employed newswriter, television personality*
Colon-Hernandez, Jeffrey *minister*
Colon Jimenez, Ely Xavier *mechanical engineer*
Colonnier, Marc Leopold *retired anatomist*
Colton, Mindy Zimmerman *artist, art director, consultant*
Colton, Sterling Don *retired lawyer, retired hotel executive*
Colwell, Bryan York *private investor, philanthropist*
Colwell, Rita Rossi *microbiologist, former federal agency administrator, medical educator*
Combs, Sean (Diddy) *record company executive, producer*
Comer, Evan Philip *manufacturing executive*
Comisky, Ian Michael *lawyer*
Compton, Allen T. *retired state supreme court justice*
Compton, Norma Haynes *retired dean, artist*
Compton, R. Brian *finance company executive*
Compton, Robert H. *lawyer*
Compton, W. Dale *physicist, researcher, engineer*
Compton, William F. *retired air transportation executive*
Compton, William Thomas *real estate investor*
Comtois, Marc Allen *engineer, historian*
Con, Adam Jonathan *choral conductor, music educator*
Conaway, Charles C. *former retail company executive*
Conaway, Margaret Grimes (Peggy Conaway) *library administrator*
Concialdi, Michael F. *secondary school educator, speech educator*
Condayan, John *foreign service officer*
Conde, Florentino T. *marketing executive, farmer*
Condit, Gary Adrian *former congressman*
Condon, Brody Kiel *computer graphics designer*
Condry, Robert Stewart *retired hospital administrator*
Congdon, Kelly Jo *mathematics educator*
Conger, Harry Milton *mining company executive*
Conklin, Eric Linwood *artist*
Conklin, Gayle F. *retired elementary school educator*
Conklin, William Frank *writer*
Conley, Helen Donovan *artist, poet*
Conley, Ned Leroy *lawyer*
Conn, Richard Lee *computer scientist, educator*
Connell, Carol Matheson *corporate communications specialist, consultant*
Connell, George Edward *retired academic administrator, research scientist*

D'Arbanville, Patti *actress*
Darby, Joseph M. *reservist*
D'Arcy, Paula *writer*
Darden, Lauretta *elementary school educator*
Dardick, Geeta *writer, psychotherapist*
Daren, Sylvia *poet*
Dargan, Pamela Ann *systems engineer, consultant*
Darien, Steven Martin *management consulting company executive*
Darling, Robert Edward *theater director*
Darrow, William Richard *retired pharmaceutical company executive, consultant*
Darsch, Nancy *former professional basketball coach*
Darvarova, Elmira *musician, concertmaster*
Daschle, Thomas Andrew *former senator*
Dash, Sanford Mark *aerospace scientist*
Dasso, Jerome Joseph *real estate educator*
Date, Elaine Satomi *physiatrist, educator*
Dattatreya, Galigekere Ramaswamy *engineering educator, consultant*
Dattilo, Thomas A. *retired manufacturing executive*
Daub, Hal (Harold John Daub Jr.) *lawyer*
Dauberman, Michelle L. *photography educator, design educator*
Daugherty, Frederick Alvin *federal judge*
Daughton, Donald *lawyer*
Davant, James Waring *investment banker*
Davatzes, Nickolas *retired broadcast executive*
Dave, Karen *computer scientist, author*
Davenport, Lawrence Franklin *academic administrator*
Davenport, Ray Charles *artist, lithographer*
DaVerne, Steven Richard *advertising director, artist, illustrator, behavior analyst*
Daves, Donald Rae *entertainment industry executive*
Daves, Glenn Doyle, Jr. *science educator, chemist, researcher*
David, Clive *events executive*
David, Larry *television scriptwriter, television producer, actor*
Davidheiser, Mark *social sciences educator, researcher*
Davidson, Anne Stowell *lawyer*
Davidson, Bonnie Jean *gymnastics educator, sports management consultant*
Davidson, Jeannie *costume designer*
Davidson, John Kenneth, Sr. *sociologist, educator, researcher, writer, consultant*
Davidson, Mark *writer, educator*
Davidson, Mayer B. *medical educator, endocrinologist, researcher*
Davie, Joseph Myrten *pathologist, immunologist, educator, science administrator*
Davies, Adam *artist, educator*
Dávila, Rafael Angel III *college counselor, educator*
Davion, Ethel Johnson *school system superintendent, curriculum specialist*
Davis, Anna Jane Ripley *elementary school educator*
Davis, C. VanLeer III *lawyer*
Davis, Cheryl K. *dean*
Davis, Clarence Clinton, Jr. *lawyer*
Davis, Darrell L. *retired automotive executive*
Davis, Gary L. *human resources professional*
Davis, Hiram Joe *public school administrator*
Davis, J. Alan *writer, film producer, television producer*
Davis, Jessica Hoffmann *education educator, researcher*
Davis, John F. III *travel company executive*
Davis (Jr.), John V. *newswriter, educator*
Davis, John Warren *real estate broker, consultant*
Davis, Johnny Reginald *former professional basketball coach*
Davis, Joseph Lloyd *academic administrator, consultant*
Davis, Kristin *actress*
Davis, Luther *writer, theater producer, motion picture producer*
Davis, Mamie (Denise Davis) *writer*
Davis, Mary Byrd *conservationist, researcher*
Davis, Mary Helen *psychiatrist, educator*
Davis, Natalie Zemon *retired history professor*
Davis, Osceola A. *opera singer*
Davis, Robert W. *computer company executive*
Davis, Roger Edwin *lawyer, retired retail executive*
Davis, Suzanne Spiegel *retired information specialist*
Davis, Taylor *sculptor*
Davis, Terrell *former professional football player*
Davis, Vivian *English language educator*
Davis, William Allison, II, *retired lawyer*
Davis, William L. *publishing company executive*
Davison, Helen Irene *secondary school educator, counseling administrator*
Davisson, Darrell Dean *art educator*
Daw, Lenore Estella *elementary school educator, librarian*
Dawdy, Doris Ostrander *writer*
Dawkins, Marva Phyllis *psychologist, educator*
Dawood, Khytam *psychologist, educator*
Dawson, Brandie *nurse, nursing consultant*
Dawson, Carol Gene *former commissioner, writer, consultant*
Dawson, Geraldine *medical educator, social worker*
Dawson, Howard W., Jr. *military officer*
Dawson, Janis Louise *music educator*
Dawson, Karen Oltmanns *forensic nurse, childbirth educator*
Dawson, Mary E. *lawyer*
Dawson, Virginia Sue *retired editor*
Day, Anthony *book critic, journalist*
Day, Brian Andrew *history educator*
Day, Donald Lee *retired engineering educator*
Day, John Denton *manufacturing executive, cattle and horse rancher, breeder, trainer, wrangler, actor, educator, entertainer*
Day, Joyce Cerejo *school psychologist*
Day, Kahlil Amyn *mediator, lawyer*
Day, Richard Allen *retired chemistry professor*
Day, Roland Bernard *retired judge*
Daza, Stephanie *anthropologist, educator*
Deacon, David Emmerson *advertising executive*
Deal, Ernest Linwood, Jr. *banker*
Deal, Gaye Follmer *writer*

Dean, Carole Lee *film company executive*
Dean, Denise Jane *elementary school educator*
Dean, Edwin Becton *entrepreneur*
Dean, Edwin Robinson *economist, educator, consultant*
Dean, John Wesley III *investment banker, former federal official*
Dean, Leslie Alan (Cap Dean) *international economic, social and political development consultant, defense analyst*
Dean, Michael M. *lawyer*
Dean, Thompson *diversified financial services company executive, investment banker*
De Angelis, Flavio *electrical engineer, researcher*
De Angelis, Rosemary Eleanor *actress*
De Antoni, Edward Paul *lab administrator*
Deats, Suzanne *writer, editor, artist*
DeBakey, Lois *science administrator, educator*
DeBakey, Michael Ellis *surgeon, educator*
DeBakey, Selma *communications educator, writer, editor*
De Blasi, Tony (Anthony Armando De Blasi) *artist*
de Blasis, James Michael *performing company executive, theater producer*
DeBock, Ronald Gene *real estate company executive*
De Both, Tanya *statistician*
Debroux, Douglas P. *secondary school educator*
DeBruce, Paul *agricultural food products company executive*
DeBuono, Barbara Ann *physician, state official*
Decatur, Raylene *former museum director*
Dechant, Virgil C. *retired fraternal organization administrator*
Dechar, Peter Henry *artist*
Deckard, Steve Wayne *science educator, academic administrator*
Decker, Michael H. *civilian military employee*
Decker, Walter Johns *toxicologist*
Dedman, Bill *journalist*
Deely, Maureen Cecelia *community health nurse*
Dees, Bowen Causey *retired institute executive*
De Felitta, Frank Paul *film producer, writer*
DeFeo, Philip D. *private equity firm executive*
DeFrancis, Suellen Maria *interior architect*
Degenhardt, Robert Allan *architectural firm executive, engineering executive*
De Gette, Diana Louise *congresswoman, lawyer*
DeGiulio, Lucas *artist*
Degryse, Bernard *cell biologist*
Deily, Linnet Frazier *former ambassador*
Deiro, Judith Anne *chemical dependency educator*
Dejammet, Alain *former diplomat*
DeJarnatt, Kitty M. *special education educator*
Deke, John *economist*
Dela Cruz, Jose Santos *retired commonwealth supreme court justice*
Delahanty, Rebecca Ann *school system administrator*
Delaney, John *protective services official*
Delany, Dana (Dana Welles Delany) *actress*
DeLapp, Tina Davis *retired nursing educator*
DeLaTorre, Phillip Eugene *law educator*
Delaty, Simone *retired language educator*
De Laurentiis, Giada *chef*
DeLay, Tom (Thomas Dale DeLay) *former congressman*
DelBello, Melissa P. *medical educator*
Delffs, Dudley J. *writer, educator*
Delgado, Roger Rodriguez *surgeon, educator*
Delgado Guay, Marvin Omar *internist, geriatrician*
Deliman, Robert Michael *surgeon*
De Line, Donald *former film company executive*
Dellagloria, John Castle *lawyer, educator*
De Lorenzo, William E. *retired foreign language educator*
de Lorimier, Alfred Alexandre *retired pediatric surgeon*
DelParigi, Angelo *research scientist*
Del Priore, Lucian V. *ophthalmologist, educator*
DeLuca, Anthony J. *civilian military employee*
De Lutis, Donald Conse *investment advisor, consultant*
Dely, Steven *retired aerospace company executive*
Demant, Hans Henrich *automotive executive*
Demant, Margaret H. *retired interior designer*
de Margitay, Gedeon *acquisitions and management consultant*
DeMartini, Richard Michael *retired bank executive*
de Matteo, Drea *actress*
de Medeiros, Ricardo Brilhante *immunologist, educator*
Demenchonok, Edward Vasilevich *philosopher, linguist, researcher, educator*
DeMille, Dale Esther *clinical educator*
DeMille, Nelson Richard *writer*
Deming, Rust M. *ambassador*
Demme, Jonathan *director, producer, writer*
Demyanovich, Karen Lee *language educator*
Dench, Judi *actress*
Denenberg, Katharine W. Hornberger (Tinka Denenberg) *artist, educator*
Denevan, William Maxfield *geographer, historical ecologist, educator*
Deng, Li *computer scientist, researcher*
Denious, Sharon Marie *retired publishing executive*
Denlinger, John Kenneth *journalist*
Denn, Cyril Joseph *retired financial advisor*
Dennehy, John Joseph *evolutionary biologist*
Dennis, Patricia Diaz *lawyer*
Densmore, Virginia Lee *music educator*
Denver, Eileen Ann *retired editor*
Deogaonkar, Milind S. *neurosurgeon, neuroscientist*
Deoul, Kathleen Boardsen *publishing executive*
De Palma, Brian Russell *film director, writer*
DePalma, Ralph George *surgeon, educator*
DePinto, David J. *public relations executive*
de Planque, E. Gail *physicist*
Derchin, Michael Wayne *portfolio manager and financial analyst*
Derden, Eugenia Gánez *entrepreneur, investor*
Dergarabedian, Paul *environmental services administrator, consultant*
Der-Houssikian, Haig *linguist, educator*
Dermanis, Paul Raymond *architect*
Dern, Laura *actress*

Deromedi, Roger K. *former food products company executive*
de Rossi, Portia *actress*
Derrick, Kathryn Thill *secondary school educator*
Derrickson, Keith Wayne *musician, educator*
Derrico, Georgia Santangelo *banker*
Deryuga, Vyacheslav O. *nuclear physicist*
Desai, Mukund N. *mathematician, researcher*
Desbarats, Peter Hullett *journalist, educator, academic administrator*
Descalzo de Blas, Alberto *humanities professor*
Desio, Delores Jean *writer, artist, retired elementary school educator*
DesJardins, J. Mark *writer*
De Sofi, Oliver Julius *data processing executive*
Desouza, Kevin *think-tank executive, researcher, academic administrator*
Despommier, Dickson Donald *microbiology educator, parasitologist*
Dessureault, Sophie *oncologist, surgeon, educator*
DeStefano, L. Timothy *music educator, conductor*
Detert, Miriam Anne *chemical analyst*
DeThomas, Joseph Michael *former ambassador*
Detweiler, David Kenneth *veterinary physiologist, educator*
Detwiler, Christina LeFevre *elementary school educator*
Deuel, Cassandra Lee *science educator*
Deutsch, Herbert Arnold *music educator*
Deutsch, James I. *curator*
Deutsch, John Ludwig *chemistry professor, researcher*
Deutsch, Kathleen Pilarcik *aquarist*
Deutsch, Peter R. *former congressman*
Deutschman, Louise Tolliver *curator*
DeVaris, Jeannette Mary *psychologist*
de Varona, Donna *sports reporter, former Olympic swimmer*
deVeer, Robert Kipp, Jr. *investment banker*
Devine, Donald C. *manufacturing executive*
Devine, John Martin *retired automotive executive*
de Vink, Lodewijk J. R. *healthcare consultant, former consumer pharmaceutical products company executive*
DeVivo, Ange *retired small business owner*
Devlin, Michael Coles *bass-baritone*
DeVore, Daun Aline *lawyer*
DeVore, Kimberly K. *healthcare executive*
DeVries, Robert Allen *foundation administrator*
DeVylder, Edgar Paul, Jr. *lawyer*
Dewald, William Guenthner *economist*
Dewar, James McEwen *marketing, aerospace and defense executive, developing nations consultant*
Dewees, Jennifer T. *lawyer*
Dewey, Arthur Eugene *former federal agency administrator*
deWilde, David Michael *management consultant, retired executive recruiter, lawyer, finance company executive*
Dews, P(eter) B(ooth) *retired pharmacology educator, physician*
Dexheimer, Larry William *advertising agency executive*
Dey, Moul *molecular biologist, researcher*
DeYoung, Marilyn Brant-Chandler *retired urban planner, farmer*
de Zegher, Catherine *museum director, curator*
Di, Francine *music educator, writer*
Diallo, Souleymane *research scientist, educator*
Diamant, Anita *writer*
Diamond, Gill *medical educator*
Diamond, Matthew Philip *performing arts association administrator, choreographer, dancer*
Diamond, Neil Leslie *singer, composer*
Diamond, Richard *retired educator*
Diamond, Robert Mach *higher education administrator*
Diamond, Stuart *lawyer, educator, business executive*
Diamond, Susan Zee *management consultant*
Dias, D. Stephen *secondary school educator*
Diaz, Cameron *actress*
Diaz, David *illustrator*
Diaz, Fernando Gustavo *neurosurgeon*
Diaz, Oscar, Jr. *voice educator, music institute director*
DiBattiste, Carol A. *military officer*
Di Benedetto, Stephen Anthony *performing arts educator*
Dibner, David Robert *architect, writer*
DiCandilo, Michael D *corporate financial executive, accountant*
DiCaprio, Leonardo *actor*
Di Cecco, James *real estate company executive*
Dick, James Cordell *concert pianist*
Dickens, Joyce Rebecca *addictions therapist, educator*
Dickens, Justin Kirk *nuclear physicist*
Dickerson, Cheryl Anne *counselor*
Dickerson, James Alan *psychologist*
Dickerson, John Robert *retired automotive engineer*
Dickeson, Robert Celmer *retired foundation administrator, management consultant*
Dickey, Joseph William *utilities executive, engineer*
Dickey, Linda Ann *learning center director*
Dickey, Robert Marvin (Rick Dickey) *property manager*
Dickey, Tommy D. *oceanographer, educator*
Dickinson, Donald Charles *library science professor*
Dickinson, Dwight *psychologist*
Dickinson, Gail Krepps *library science educator*
Dickman, James Bruce *photojournalist*
Dickman, James Earl *financial services executive*
Dickson, Constance Pierce *law librarian*
Dickson, James Francis III *surgeon*
Dickstein, Michael Ethan *mediator, arbitrator, lawyer*
Dickstein, Morris *language educator, writer*
diCorcia, Philip-Lorca *artist, photographer*
DiDomenico, Mauro, Jr. *communications executive*
Diefenderfer, Dan *filmmaker*
Diehl, Deborah Hilda *lawyer*
Diehl, Louis F. *hematologist*
Diehl, Stephen Anthony *human resources consultant*
Diem, Richard A. *social studies educator, educational consultant*

Diemer, Emma Lou *composer, educator*
Diener, Erwin *immunologist*
Diener, Royce *retired health products executive*
Dietler, Cortlandt S. *oil industry executive*
Dietrich, William Alan *reporter, writer*
Dietz, Arthur Townsend *investment counseling company executive*
DiFilippo, Armand *information technology executive*
DiFronzo, Francis G. *painter*
Di Giacomo, Fran *artist*
Di Giovanni, Anthony *retired coal mining company executive*
Diliberto-Macaluso, Kristen Ann *psychology professor*
Dill, Laddie John *artist*
Dillard, Teresa Mary *school counselor*
Dillenkoffer, Judith A. *music educator*
Dillingham, Katherine Hall *musician, educator*
Dillon, Francis Patrick *retired human resources executive*
Dillon, Matt *actor*
Dillon, Robert Sherwood *retired diplomat*
Dills, James Arlof *retired publishing executive*
Dimaira, Ann B. *medical/surgical nurse*
Di Massa, Rudolph J., Jr. *lawyer*
Dimitry, Theodore George *retired lawyer*
Dimopoulos, Linda J. *food service executive*
Dincecco, Jennie Elizabeth Williams Swanson *healthcare administrator, mentor, educator, volunteer*
Ding, Ai-Yue *conductor, music educator*
Ding, Jinwen *biomedical researcher*
Ding, Zhaohua *biomedical engineer, educator*
Dingle, Carol A. *state agency administrator, writer*
Dinkel, John George *automotive executive, consultant*
Dintrone, Charles Vincent *retired librarian*
Dion, Celine *musician*
Dionne, Richard M. *theater educator, theater director*
DiPaolo, Sonja Jean *retired nurse*
DiPiazza, Michael Charles *insurance company executive*
Dipko, Thomas Earl *retired minister, retired religious organization administrator*
DiPrima, Anne *elementary school educator*
DiPrima, Richard Joseph *neuropsychologist*
Dirksen, Robert Thomas *science professor*
Dirnt, Mike (Michael Ryan Pritchard) *musician, singer*
Dirvin, Gerald Vincent *retired consumer products company executive*
DiSanto, Lucille M. *special education educator, educator*
Dishy, Bob *actor*
Diskin, Charles J. *internist, researcher*
Disney, Roy Edward *broadcasting company executive*
Dispenza, Mary Catherine *director, educator, photographer*
DiStefano, Tony E. *communications executive*
Di Suvero, Mark *sculptor*
Ditka, Mike (Michael Keller Ditka Jr.) *sports commentator, former professional football coach*
Dittenhafer, Brian Douglas *banker, economist*
Ditter, J. William, Jr. *federal judge*
Diviney, Nancy Lynn *elementary school educator*
Dix, Samuel Morman *industrial engineer, economist, appraiser*
Dixon, Ben Harold *musician, educator*
Dixon, Gordon Henry *biochemist, educator*
Dixon, John Morris, Jr. *retired judge, lawyer*
Dixon, MacIntyre *actor*
Dixon, Paul Edward *lawyer, metal products executive, manufacturing executive*
Dixon, Tamecka *professional basketball player*
Dixon, William Robert *musician, educator*
Djang, David S.W. *physician*
Djordjevic, Dimitrije *historian, educator*
dKepner, Raechel L. *academic administrator*
Doan, Mary Frances *advertising executive*
Dobbs, Lou *television executive, editor*
Dobelle, Evan Samuel *academic administrator*
Doberenz, Alexander R. *retired nutrition educator, chemist*
Dobis, Charles, Jr. *systems administrator*
Dobler, Donald William *retired procurement and materials executive, retired dean*
Dobriansky, Lev Eugene *economics professor, diplomat*
Dobson, Dorothy Lynn Watts *retired elementary school educator*
Dobyns, Henry F(armer) *anthropology consultant, educator*
Dockery, J. Lee *retired medical school administrator*
Dockstader, Deborah Ruth *minister*
Doctor, Kenneth Jay *digital content consultant*
Dodds-Metts, Rebecca *wholesale company executive*
Dodge, Adriana *real estate investor, educator*
Dodge, R(alph) Edward, Jr. *physician*
Dodin, Ilya *research scientist*
Dodson, Daryl Theodore *ballet administrator, consultant*
Dodson, Samuel Robinette III *investment banker*
Doebler, Bettie Anne *language educator, researcher, poet*
Doell, Margaret J. *art educator*
Doerper, John Erwin *journal editor, publishing executive*
Dogançay, Burhan C. *artist, photographer, sculptor*
Dogoloff, Lee Israel *clinical social worker, psychotherapist, consultant*
Doherty, Charles Vincent *investment advisor*
Doherty, Evelyn Marie *data processing consultant*
Doherty, Peter Charles *immunologist*
Doherty, Shannen *actress*
Dohrmann, Russell William *manufacturing executive*
Dokurno, Anthony David *lawyer*
Dolan, Edward Francis *writer*
Dolan, Peter Brown *lawyer*
Dolan, Peter Robert *former pharmaceutical executive*
Dole, Arthur Alexander *former psychology professor, department chairman*
Dolenz, Mickey (George Michael Dolenz, Mickey Braddock) *entertainer, actor, television producer*

Elicker, Gordon Leonard *retired lawyer*
Eliot, Charles William John *former university president*
Eliot, Theodore Lyman, Jr. *former ambassador, consultant*
Elise, Kimberly (Kimberly Elise Trammel, Kimberly Elise Oldham) *actress*
Elisha, Larisa *musician, performer, educator*
Elix, Douglas Thorne *computer company executive*
Elizondo, Hector *actor*
Elkind, Mort William *management consultant*
Elkins, Robert N. *association executive*
Elledge, Stephen Joseph *medical educator*
Ellen, Martin M. *financial services executive*
Ellenberger, Jack Stuart *law librarian*
Ellenberger, Lon Karl *singer, music educator*
Ellett, Alan Sidney *real estate developer*
Ellickson, Donald Lien *retired economist, county official*
Ellig, Bruce Robert *retired personnel director*
Ellingsworth, Linda Benoit *freelance/self-employed writer*
Ellington, Mildred L. *librarian*
Elliot, Jared *financial management consultant*
Elliott, Bill *race car driver*
Elliott, Clark Albert *archivist, librarian, historian*
Elliott, David LeRoy *mathematician, educator, engineering educator*
Elliott, Edward *investment executive, financial planner*
Elliott, Kenneth Yates *theater educator*
Elliott, Stuart Jay *editor, journalist*
Elliott, Tommy *secondary school educator*
Ellis, Eric Shane *music educator*
Ellis, Janice Rider *nursing educator, consultant*
Ellis, John Hubert *retired history professor*
Ellis, Joseph John Michael III *historian, history professor*
Ellis, Lawrence Dobson *internist, educator*
Ellis, Robert Harry *retired broadcast executive, academic administrator*
Ellis, Steven George *public relations/corporate communications executive*
Ellis, William Ben *environmental educator, retired utility executive*
Ellison, Cynthia Kuehl *music educator, musician*
Ellner, Paul Daniel *retired microbiologist*
El-Mansy, Youssef A. *computer company executive*
El-Moursy, Magdy *electronics engineer*
Elpus, Kenneth *music educator, director*
Elrod, Deborah Lee *special education educator*
Else, Carolyn Joan *retired library director*
Elsey, George McKee *retired foundation administrator*
Elson, Edward Elliott *diplomat*
Elson, Gerald *automotive executive*
Eltayeb, Emil *pharmacist, researcher*
Elverum, Gerard William, Jr. *retired electronics executive, diversified financial services company executive*
Elway, John Albert *retired professional football player*
Elwood-Akers, Virginia Edythe *librarian, retired archivist*
Elzay, Richard Paul *retired dean, dental educator, department chairman*
Emano, Dennis M. *psychotherapist, educator*
Embry, Stephen Creston *lawyer*
Emek, Sharon Helene *risk management consultant*
Emerling, Carol G. *management consultant*
Emerson, Claudia *poet, language professor*
Emerson, Daniel Everett *retired communications company executive*
Emerson, Jamie *statistician, educator*
Emery, Alan Roy *scientist, museum administrator, business executive*
Emmett, James Robert *retired lawyer*
Emmett, Rita *professional speaker*
Emmons, Robert Duncan *diplomat*
Encarnación, Jose M. Izquierdo *construction executive, former Puerto Rico secretary of state*
Endicott, William F. *journalist*
Engel, Bernard Theodore *psychologist, educator*
Engel, Charles *economics professor*
Engel, Joan Marcia Lezar *psychologist, applied animal behaviorist*
Engel, Philip L. *retired insurance company executive*
Engel, Richard L. *career officer*
Engelbreit, Mary *art licensing entrepreneur*
Engelhardt, John Hugo *lawyer, bank executive*
Engelman, Rosalyn Ackerman *artist, marketing executive*
Engelmann, Rudolph Herman *electronics consultant, writer*
Engels, Beatrice Ann *artist, poet, retired real estate company executive*
Engels, Lawrence Arthur *retired metal products executive*
Enger, Edward Henry, Jr. *retired editor, writer*
Engle, Howard A. *retired pediatrician*
Engle, Mary Allen English *retired physician*
Engle, Steve Eugene *artist*
Engle, Steven B. *biotechnology company executive*
Engler, John M. *trade association administrator, former governor*
Englert, Helen Wiggs *writer*
English, Bruce Vaughan *environmentalist, consultant*
English, Floyd Leroy *telecommunications industry executive*
English, Patricia Dorzell *women's health nurse practitioner*
English-Anderson, San Dei *minister*
Angstrom, Marlene Mae *volunteer*
Eno, Amos Stewart *natural resource foundation administrator*
Eno, Woodrow E. *lawyer, retired insurance company executive*
Enoch, Craig Trively *retired judge*
Enomoto, Daisuke (Dice-K) *entrepreneur, investor*
Ensminger, Dale *retired mechanical engineer, retired electrical engineer*
Ensminger, John Jay *writer, poet, minister, counselor*
Entremont, Philippe *conductor, musician*
Epcar, Richard Michael *actor, writer, film director*
Epel, David *biologist, educator*
Ephron, Nora *writer*
Epp, Dianne Naomi *secondary school educator*

Epp, Eldon Jay *religion educator*
Eppolito, Mary *assistant principal, educator*
Epps, Charles Harry, Jr. *retired orthopaedic surgery educator, dean*
Epstein, Daniel E. *musician, educator*
Epstein, David M. *publishing executive*
Epstein, Judith Ann *judge*
Erb, Richard Louis Lundin *resort and hotel executive*
Erbay, Nazli *radiologist*
Erdely-Sayo, Sandrine *musician, educator*
Erdmann, Joachim Christian *retired physicist*
Erenstein, Alan *emergency nurse practitioner*
Erickson, Alan Eric *librarian*
Erickson, Carol Jean *literature and language professor*
Erickson, Dennis *professional football coach*
Erickson, Michae Ross *history educator*
Erickson, Stephanie Ann *psychologist*
Ericson, Jonathon Edward *environmental health science educator, researcher*
Ericson Cardell, Ede Anne *sculptor*
Eriksson, Steven *social studies educator*
Erkonen, William Edward *radiologist, medical educator*
Erlebacher, Arlene Cernik *retired lawyer*
Erlicht, Lewis Howard *broadcasting company executive*
Ernsberger, Donald Craig *professional society administrator*
Ernst, Daniel Pearson *lawyer*
Ernst, Edward Willis *retired electrical engineering educator*
Ernst-Fonberg, Mary Lou *biomedical researcher, educator*
Eron, Leonard David *psychology professor*
Erovenko, Igor V. *mathematics professor*
Erskine, Rodney D. *oil industry executive*
Ervin, Clark Kent *former federal agency administrator*
Ervin-Carr, Charlesetta Yvonne *secondary school educator*
Erwin, Donald Carroll *plant pathology educator*
Erwin, Elmer Louis *vintager, consultant*
Erwin, Linda McIntosh *retired librarian*
Escalante, Juan *performing company executive*
Escallón, Ana María *writer*
Escobar, Anthony *marketing professional, consultant*
Espenlaub, Margo Linn *women's studies educator, writer, artist*
Espinosa-Heidmann, Diego G. *ophthalmologist*
Espiricueta, Sylvia *counseling administrator*
Esquivel, Agerico Liwag *retired research physicist*
Esrey, William Todd *telecommunications company executive*
Essary, Andrew Charles *philosopher, educator, financial analyst*
Esser, James Mark *cardiovascular and interventional radiologist*
Essig, Mark G. *steel products company executive*
Essman, Susie *actress*
Estefan, Emilio, Jr. *music industry executive, producer, writer*
Estefan, Gloria Maria (Gloria Maria Milagrosa Fajardo) *singer, lyricist*
Esteller, Rosana *research scientist*
Esterly, Nancy Burton *retired physician*
Estes, Carl Lewis, II, *lawyer*
Estes, Elaine Rose Graham *retired librarian*
Estes, Mary Gwyn *art educator*
Estrin, Deborah Perry *human resources executive*
Estrin, Herbert Alvin *financial consultant, consultant, film company executive*
Estrin, Richard William *real estate broker*
Esty, John Cushing, Jr. *writer, educator, not-for-profit counsel*
Esunge, Julius Njome *mathematician, statistician*
Etheridge, Diana Carol *internet business executive*
Etra, Lionel *lawyer*
Ettinger, Harry Joseph *retired industrial hygiene engineer, retired consultant*
Ettinger, Joseph Alan *lawyer*
Ettore, Joseph R. *retired discount department store chain executive*
Etzel, Ruth Ann *pediatrician, epidemiologist, educator*
Eugster, Albrecht Konrad *veterinarian, laboratory director*
Eulau, Hank *actor*
Euster, Joanne Reed *retired librarian*
Eustis, Albert Anthony *lawyer, diversified financial services company executive*
Evangelista, Anita Loretta *freelance/self-employed writer, publishing executive, psychologist, nurse*
Evangelista, Nick Forrest *fencing master, writer, illustrator, publisher*
Evans, Barton, Jr. *analytical instrument company executive*
Evans, Bonita Dianne *education educator*
Evans, Christopher Lee *medical entomologist*
Evans, Dennis Hyde *chemist, educator*
Evans, Eric Alan *retired lawyer*
Evans, Frederick John *psychologist*
Evans, Gerald William *engineering educator, consultant*
Evans, Geraldine Ann *academic administrator*
Evans, Jack R. (J. Glenn Evans) *writer, poet*
Evans, James D., Jr. *retail executive*
Evans, James Handel *academic administrator, architect*
Evans, Karen Ann *social studies educator*
Evans, Lloyd Q. *psychologist, educator*
Evans, Margaret Utz *secondary school educator*
Evans, Marsha Johnson *former non-profit association administrator, retired military officer*
Evans, Richard Austin *education educator, consultant*
Evans, Robert George, Jr. *retail and mail order executive*
Evans, Rosemary Hall *civic worker*
Evans, Susan A. *chemist*
Evans, Wayne *obstetrician, perinatologist*
Evarts, Charles McCollister *orthopaedic surgeon*
Evdokimova, Eva *prima ballerina assoluta, director, producer, consultant, actress*
Everdell, William James *retired lawyer*
Everett, Rupert *actor*
Everett, Tom *actor*
Everhart, Gloria Elaine *music educator*

Evert, Chris (Christine Marie Evert) *retired professional tennis player*
Eviatar, Lydia *pediatrician, neurologist*
Ewald, Laura Anne *school librarian*
Ewen, H. I. *physicist*
Ewen, John A. *chemist*
Ewing, Elisabeth Anne Rooney *priest*
Ewing, James E. *priest*
Ewing, Raymond Charles *retired ambassador*
Exner, Frank Kepler *information scientist, indexer*
Eyler, John H., Jr. *retail toy and game company executive*
Faber, Michael Warren *lawyer*
Fabiano, Nicola *physicist, researcher*
Fabricatore, Carol Diane *artist, educator*
Fabunan, Ruben G. *physician, research scientist, inventor*
Fackler, Elizabeth *writer*
Fackler, Naomi Paula *retired librarian*
Fadiman, Anne *writer, educator*
Faenza, Michael M. *mental health association administrator*
Fager, Everett Dean *minister*
Fagin, David Kyle *gas industry executive*
Fahmy, Khaled *historian, educator*
Fahn, Larry *former environmental organization administrator*
Fahringer, Catherine Hewson *retired savings and loan association executive*
Fair, Jean Everhard *retired education educator*
Fairfield, Paula Kathleen *sound recording engineer*
Fairobent, Douglas Kevin *computer programmer*
Faiz, Alexandria *researcher, writer*
Falcon, Armando, Jr. *financial consultant, lawyer*
Falkowski, Paul Gordon *biological oceanographer*
Fan, Chien *aerospace engineer, researcher*
Fan, Cong *music educator*
Fan, Xuejun *research scientist*
Fan, Yong *research scientist*
Fanger, Robert D(woret) *retired finance company executive, management consultant*
Fanos, Kathleen Hilaire *osteopathic physician, podiatrist*
Fanwick, Ernest *lawyer*
Farabaugh, Christopher Scott *toxicologist, researcher*
Farah, Martha *psychology educator*
Farber, Zulima V. *former state attorney general, lawyer*
Fargo, Thomas Boulton *retired career military officer*
Farid, Farid O. *mathematics professor*
Faris, James Vannoy *cardiologist, educator, health facility administrator*
Fariss, Bruce Lindsay *endocrinologist, consultant*
Farkas, Daniel Frederick *food science and technology educator*
Farmakides, John Basil *lawyer*
Farmer, Christopher J. *political scientist, writer*
Farmer, Cornelia Griffin *lawyer, consultant, county hearings official*
Farmer, Crofton Bernard *atmospheric physicist*
Farmer, Kenneth Lloyd, Jr. *career military officer*
Farnsworth, Elizabeth *broadcast journalist*
Faron, Fay Cheryl *private investigator, writer*
Farquhar, Robin Hugh *educational consultant, former university president*
Farr, Barry Miller *physician, epidemiologist*
Farr, Ivanne Estelle *small business owner, consultant, artist, sculptor*
Farrar, Elaine Willardson *artist*
Farrar, John Edson, II, *finance company executive, consultant, investment advisor*
Farrell, Colin James *actor*
Farrell, Edward Wagner *retired dentist, educator*
Farrell, Mike *actor*
Farrell, Peg (Margaret Farrell) *former magazine publisher*
Farrell, Richard T. *human resources administrator*
Farrell, Suzanne (Roberta Sue Ficker) *ballerina*
Farrell, William Edgar *sales executive, management consultant, computer technician*
Farrelly, Peter John *screenwriter*
Farrington, Gregory C. *retired academic administrator*
Fasick, Adele Mongan *library and information scientist, educator*
Fast, Heinz Gerhard *music educator, conductor*
Fatemi, Faramarz Saifpour *history professor, political science professor, consultant*
Fattig, Elissa *school psychologist*
Faucett, Ralph E. *physician, surgeon*
Faucette, Gloria Marie *accountant, educator*
Faunce, Sarah Cushing *retired curator*
Faust, Vickie Lynn *secondary school educator*
Favero, Michele Maree *music educator, musician*
Fawcett, Farrah Leni *actress, model*
Fawcett, H. Daniel *nuclear medicine radiologist*
Fawcett, John Thomas *archivist*
Fawcett, Mary Louise *counselor, educator*
Faxon, Alicia Craig *art educator, department chairman*
Fay, Conner Martindale *retired marketing executive*
Fay, Peter Thorp *federal judge*
Fay, William Frederick *film producer*
Fazio, Evelyn M. *publisher, writer, agent, editor*
Feal, Gisele Catherine *foreign language educator*
Fearon, Charlene O'Brien *special education educator*
Fearrington, Ann Peyton *writer, illustrator, news correspondent*
Febbo, Phillip George *oncologist, researcher*
Federer, Roger *professional tennis player*
Federing, Eric N. *legislative staff member, public information officer*
Feeney, Maryann McHugh *not-for profit professional*
Feeney, Matthew Edward *linguist, educator*
Feigal, David W., Jr. *health science association administrator*
Feigenbaum, David Louis *lawyer*
Feigin, Barbara Sommer *marketing consultant*
Feigin, Ralph David *medical association administrator, pediatrician, educator*
Fein, Roger Gary *judge*
Fein, Seymour Howard *pharmaceutical executive*
Feinberg, Lynn Friss *gerontologist*
Feiner, Ava Sophia *public affairs consultant, management consultant, economist*
Feingold, Kenneth J. *artist*

Feinstein, Robert P. *dermatologist*
Feir, Dorothy Jean *entomologist, educator, physiologist*
Feisthammel, Audrey Marie *museum director, educator*
Feith, Douglas Jay *former federal agency administrator*
Feld, Carole Leslie *marketing executive*
Feldkamp, John Calvin *retired lawyer, educator*
Feldman, Eva Lucille *neurology educator*
Feldman, H. Larry *lawyer*
Feldman, Marc David *psychiatrist*
Feldman, Shirley Clark *retired psychology professor*
Feldshuh, Tovah S. *actress*
Feldstein, Eric A. *finance company executive*
Feldt, Gloria A. *social services administrator*
Felgar, Raymond Eugene *pathologist, educator*
Felicetti, Daniel A. *academic administrator*
Felix, Arthur Martin *chemistry educator, researcher*
Felix, Cheryl A. *air transportation executive*
Fella, Marie Ann *intelligence analyst, drug enforcement administration*
Feller, Lloyd Harris *lawyer*
Feller, Robert William Andrew *public relations executive, retired professional baseball player*
Fellman, Gerry Louis *lawyer, arbitrator*
Fellner, Eric *film producer*
Fels, Rendigs *economist, educator*
Felsted, Carla Martindell *librarian, writer, editor*
Felt, Mark (Deep Throat, W. Mark Felt Sr., William Mark Felt Sr.) *former federal agency administrator*
Felton, Helen Martin *retired adult education educator, writer*
Fenech, Craig E. *lawyer*
Fenech, Daniel Thomas *cartoonist*
Fenech, Joseph Charles *lawyer*
Fenimore, George Wiley *management consultant*
Fennema, Owen Richard *food chemistry educator*
Fenske, Marisa Lynn *elementary school educator*
Fenstersheib, Martin *city health department administrator*
Fenton, Thomas Trail *journalist*
Fenwick, James Henry *editor, writer, columnist*
Ferguson, Bradford Lee *lawyer*
Ferguson, Earl Wilson *cardiologist, medical executive, telemedicine consultant*
Ferguson, Emmet Fewell, Jr. *surgeon*
Ferguson, Gary Lee *public relations and security management executive*
Ferguson, Paul-Thomas *archivist, writer*
Fergusson, Dianne Smith *retired secondary school educator*
Fergusson, Frances Daly *former academic administrator*
Fernald, Harold Allen *publishing executive*
Fernandez, Antonio S. *investment company executive*
Fernandez, Fernando Lawrence *aeronautical engineer, research and development company executive*
Fernández-Velazquez, Juan Ramon *university chancellor*
Feroz, Ehsan Habib *accounting educator, researcher, writer*
Ferre, Antonio Luis *newspaper publisher*
Ferreira, Armando Thomas *sculptor, educator*
Ferreira, Jo Ann Jeanette Chanoux *management consultant, delivery service executive*
Ferrick, Kathleen Ann *elementary school educator, minister*
Ferry, Martha Morton *non-profit executive*
Festekjian, Jaco H. *plastic surgeon, educator*
Fetters, Norman Craig, II, *retired banker*
Feuer, Marshall Zev *import/export company executive*
Feuer-Stern, Barbie Shnider *elementary school educator, secondary school educator*
Fey, John Theodore *retired insurance company executive*
Fey, Willard *global environmental researcher, educator*
Fibiger, John Andrew *life insurance company executive*
Fichandler, Zelda *director*
Fiddick, Paul William *public official, broadcast executive*
Field, Arthur Norman *lawyer*
Field, Sally Margaret *actress*
Fields, Douglas Philip *building supply wholesale company executive*
Fields, Gail Baker *education educator*
Fields, Irving *pianist, composer, arranger, former band leader*
Fields, Jerri Lynn *foundation administrator*
Fields-Harris, Deborah Carol *mathematician, educator*
Fiennes, Ralph (Ralph Nathaniel Twisleton-Wykeham Fiennes) *actor*
Fife, Jonathan Donald *education educator*
Filardo, Thomas Wesley *physician*
Filchock, Ethel *education educator*
Filer, Emily Symington Harkins *retired foundation administrator, writer, non-profit consultant*
Filerman, Michael Herman *television producer*
Filippelli Marandola, Linda Patricia *school psychologist*
Filley, Christopher Mark *neurologist, researcher*
Fillmore, John Dillon *artist*
Finale, Frank L. *retired elementary school educator, writer*
Finauri, Graciela Maria *foreign service official*
Finch, Janet Buswell *musician*
Finch, Jennie *softball player*
Finckenauer, James O. *criminal justice educator, researcher*
Finder, Joseph Alan *writer*
Finder-Stone, Patricia Ann *nursing educator, volunteer*
Fine, David Jeffrey *hospital administrator, educator*
Fine, Jane Madeline *visual artist*
Fine, Lawrence B. *lawyer*
Finelsen, Libbi June *lawyer*
Finestone, Sheila *senator, retired legislator*
Finger, Harold Ben *nuclear energy industry executive, consultant, government agency administrator*
Fingerman, Milton *biologist, educator*

Gable, Carl Irwin *management consultant, writer, investor, retired lawyer*
Gable, Karen Elaine *healthcare educator*
Gabor, Zsa Zsa (Sari Gabor) *actress, cosmetics executive*
Gabor-Hotchkiss, Magda *research scientist, librarian*
Gabriel, Jeanette Hanisee *curator, art historian*
Gaddis, John Lewis *history professor*
Gaddy, Sidney Warren *government agency administrator*
Gadiesh, Orit *management consulting executive*
Gadomski, Robert Eugene *consulting executive, retired gas industry executive*
Gaffin, David Morris *meteorologist, researcher*
Gaffney, Mark Howard *writer*
Gaffney, Patricia Mounts *educational consultant*
Gaffney, Thomas *retired banker*
Gage, Patrick (Leonard Patrick Gage) *biotechnologist, pharmaceutical consultant*
Gahagan, Thomas Gail *obstetrician, gynecologist*
Gahan, David *singer*
Gaiber, Lawrence Jay *financial company executive*
Gaillard, George Siday III *architect*
Gaines, Boyd *actor*
Gaines, Brenda J. *retired financial services company executive*
Gaines, Cherie Adelaide *lawyer*
Gainey, Lilah Leigh *librarian*
Gainor, Thomas Edward *bank executive*
Gajl-Peczalska, Kazimiera J. *retired surgeon, pathologist, educator*
Galagan, Carol Anne *special education educator*
Galbraith, William Bruce *internist, educator*
Galda, Dwight William *finance company executive*
Gale, Stanley William *psychiatrist*
Gall, Mary Sheila *former federal agency administrator*
Gallagher, Cynthia *artist, educator*
Gallagher, Michael Robert *retired consumer products company executive*
Gallant, Stephen Laurie *librarian*
Galli, John Ronald *physicist, educator*
Galliano, Nessie Voisin *elementary school educator*
Gallimore, Margaret Martin *poet*
Galloway, Eilene Marie *space and astronautics consultant*
Galloway, Judy A. *deputy commissioner*
Galloway, Thomas D. *dean*
Galloway, William Rodney *military officer*
Gallucci-Breithaupt, Adrianne *psychologist, social worker*
Galvin, Christopher Brian *former electronics company executive*
Galvin, Matthew Reppert *psychiatry educator*
Galvis Assmus, Patricia *filmmaker, performing arts educator*
Galyon, James William *minister*
Gambari, Ibrahim Agboola *former international organization official*
Gambill, Jan-Michael Charles *professional tennis player*
Gamble, Desirata *artist, poet*
Gamble, E. James *lawyer, accountant*
Gambrell, Luck Flanders *corporate financial executive*
Gamer, Carlton Edwin *composer, music educator*
Gammon, Samuel Rhea III *association executive, former ambassador*
Gamroth, Arthur Paul *small business owner*
Gan, Chenny Quan *music educator, musician, artist*
Gan, Juis *interior designer*
Gand, Gayle *chef*
Gandolf, Raymond L. *media correspondent*
Ganelli, Giovanni *economist*
Ganesan, Raj *investment advisor, consultant*
Ganesh, Bikshandi *computer scientist, researcher*
Ganguly, Swaroop *research scientist*
Ganley, James Powell *retired ophthalmologist*
Gans, Curtis B. *think-tank executive*
Ganske, J. Greg *former congressman, plastic surgeon*
Gantz, Carroll Melvin *industrial design consultant, consumer product designer*
Ganz, Lowell *scriptwriter, television producer*
Garber, Aaron Matthew *performing company executive, music director*
Garber, Helen Kolikow *photographer, artist*
Garber, Victor *stage and film actor*
Garbers, Samantha *research scientist*
Garcia, Diego *finance educator*
Garcia, Eduardo *neurologist, consultant*
Garcia, Greg (Gregory Thomas Garcia) *writer*
Garcia, Julia Theresa *secondary school educator*
Garcia, Luis F. *photographer*
Garcia, Patricia *child development psychologist, researcher*
Garcia-Granados, Sergio Eduardo *portfolio manager, writer, historian*
Garcia y Carrillo, Martha Xochitl *pharmacist*
Gardin, Hershel *academic administrator, dean, management consultant*
Gardiner, Hobart Clive *petroleum company executive*
Gardner, Elizabeth Ann Hunt *artist, poet, genealogist*
Gardner, Emerson N., Jr. *military officer*
Gardner, Marvin Allen, Jr. *pastoral and clinical psychologist*
Gardner, Wilford Robert *physicist, researcher*
Gardom, Garde Basil *former lieutenant governor of British Columbia*
Gareau, Jean L. *application technology executive*
Garfield, Robert Edward *journalist*
Garfield-Woodbridge, Nancy *writer*
Garfinkle, Elaine Myra *writer*
Garland, James C. *retired academic administrator*
Garland, Robert Lee *secondary school educator, writer*
Garlin, Jeff *actor*
Garmany, Catharine Doremus *astronomer*
Garner, Algean, II, *healthcare company administrator, consultant*
Garner, Carlene Ann *not-for-profit fundraiser, consultant*
Garner, Doris Traganza *retired education educator*
Garner, James (James Scott Bumgarner) *actor*
Garner, Jay Montgomery *retired military officer*
Garner, Jennifer Anne *actress*

Garnet, Eva Desca *dance educator, choreographer*
Garniss, Joan Brewster *musician, educator*
Garofolo, Ronald Joseph *secondary education drafting and architecture educator*
Garrett, Brad *actor, comedian*
Garrett, Marshall Lee *anesthesiologist, educator*
Garriott, Owen Kay *astronaut, scientist*
Garrison, William Lloyd *retired cemetery executive*
Garruto, John Anthony *cosmetics executive*
Garruto, Ralph Michael *biomedical anthropologist, biologist, educator*
Gartenberg, Seymour Lee *retired recording industry executive*
Garth, Bryant Geoffrey *lawyer, educator*
Gartner, Lawrence Mitchell *pediatrician, medical educator*
Garwin, Richard Lawrence *physicist*
Garypie, Rudolph Renwick *library director*
Garza, Cutberto *nutrition educator*
Garzarella, Anthony *physicist, researcher*
Garzarelli, Elaine Marie *economist*
Gasper, Jo Ann *social services administrator, consultant*
Gasper, Kip Eric *secondary school educator*
Gasper, Ruth Eileen *real estate executive*
Gassaway, William Brooks *retired manufacturing executive, writer*
Gasser, Michael J. *consumer products company executive*
Gaston, Paul Morton *retired history professor*
Gatanas, Harry D. *career officer*
Gatch, Milton McCormick, Jr. *library director, clergyman, educator*
Gates, Susan Inez *magazine publisher*
Gatewood, Willard Badgett, Jr. *retired historian, writer*
Gathright, John Byron, Jr. *colon and rectal surgeon, educator*
Gatria, America I *retired writer*
Gattu, Balaji *information technology executive*
Gaultier, Jean-Paul *fashion designer*
Gaumer, Carol J. *marketing educator*
Gauss, John A. *former federal agency administrator, retired naval officer*
Gaustad, Edwin Scott *historian, educator*
Gavin, Mary Jane *retired medical/surgical nurse*
Gaviria Trujillo, Cesar *former international organization administrator, former President of Colombia*
Gavril, Jean (Jean Van Leeuwen) *writer*
Gay, David Edward Ryan *economist*
Gay, William Ingalls *veterinarian, retired health science association administrator*
Gaylin, Willard *physician, educator*
Geake, Raymond Robert *psychologist*
Geary, Stephen R. *engineer, educator, engineering executive*
Gebauer, Kurt Manfred *management executive*
Gebauer, Phyllis Victoria Feltskog *writer, educator*
Gebelein, Richard Stephen *judge, former state attorney general*
Gechtoff, Sonia *artist*
Geddes, Barbara Sheryl *communications executive, consultant*
Geddes, Robert *architect, educator*
Gedevanishvili, Shalva *materials scientist, researcher*
Gee, Robert Neil *law librarian*
Geib, Richard James *secondary school educator*
Geiger, Mark Watson *management educator*
Geiling, Louise Elizabeth *elementary school educator, secondary school educator*
Geisel, Harold Walter *diplomat*
Geissinger, Frederick Wallace *finance company executive*
Geistfeld, Ronald Elwood *retired dental educator*
Gelber, Robert Cary *law librarian*
Gelberg, Lillian *family medicine physician, educator*
Gelboin, Harry Victor *biochemistry educator, researcher*
Gellar, Sarah Michelle *actress*
Gelles, David Alexander *writer*
Gellis, Willard Leon *poet, language educator*
Geltzer, Sheila Simon *public relations executive*
Gemignani, Michael Caesar *clergyman, retired secondary school educator*
Genaro, Donald Michael *industrial designer*
Gencheva, Eugenia Svetoslavova *medical researcher*
Gendell, Gerald Stanleigh *retired public relations executive*
Gendron, George *magazine editor*
Genesoni, Jacqueline *mathematics educator*
Genêt, Barbara Ann *accountant, travel company executive*
Geng, Phil (Yiping Geng) *structural engineer*
Gengler, Richelle Ruth *musician, educator*
Gengler, Stephanie Jo *elementary school educator*
Genieser, Nancy Branom *radiologist*
Genis, Alice Singer *psychologist*
Genkins, Gabriel *physician*
Gennaro, Irene *sculptor*
Gens, Ralph Samuel *electrical engineering consultant*
Genser, Jared Matthew *lawyer*
Gentner, Joshua D. *lawyer*
George, Alfred L., Jr. *medical educator, researcher*
George, Gay *lawyer*
George, Gerald William *writer*
George, Jennifer M. *management professor, psychology professor*
George, Joey Russell *lawyer*
George, Kiranraj *electrical engineer, researcher*
George, Lynnane Ellis *military officer*
Georgescu, Peter Andrew *retired advertising executive*
Georgiev, Georgi Yordanov *physics professor*
Georgitis, John *allergist, educator*
Geraci, Richard V. *military officer, government agency administrator*
Gerald, Michael Charles *pharmacy educator, dean*
Gerard, Roy Dupuy *retired oil company executive*
Gere, James Monroe *civil engineering educator*
Gere, Richard *actor*
Gerges, Rafik Refaat Wessa *structural engineer*
Gerhardt, Carol *artist*
Gerlach, Douglas Eldon *internet developer, writer*
Gerlach, Jeanne Elaine *English language educator*

German, Randall Michael *materials scientist, educator*
Germond, Jack *retired columnist*
Germundsson, Roger *research scientist*
Gerou, Phillip Howard *architect*
Gerras, Stephen Joseph *military officer, psychologist*
Gerritsen, Mary Ellen *vascular and cell biologist*
Gerry, Debra Prue *psychotherapist, recording artist, writer*
Gershuny, Beth Suzanne *psychologist, educator*
Gerson, Darrin William *clinical psychologist*
Gerson, Donald Jerome *computer scientist, consultant, photographer, small business owner*
Gerstner, Jonathan Neil *religious studies educator*
Geschke, Charles M. *computer company executive*
Gessaman, Margaret Palmer *mathematician, educator, retired dean*
Getch, Lynne *social studies educator*
Gettleman, Marvin E. *retired history professor*
Getty, Estelle (Estelle Scher) *actress*
Getzendanner, Susan *lawyer*
Gewitz, Michael Harold *pediatric cardiologist*
Geyer, Wayne Rockwell *oceanographer*
Ghadry, Farid N. *political organization worker*
Ghausi, Mohammed Shuaib *retired dean, electrical engineer, educator*
Gherardi, Gherardo Joseph *pathologist*
Ghose, Anindya *finance educator*
Ghosh, Kartik C. *physics professor, researcher*
Ghovanloo, Maysam *engineer, educator*
Giamatti, Paul *actor*
Giampietro, Wayne Bruce *lawyer*
Gianturco, Delio Emanuele *management consultant, educator, author*
Gibb, Roberta Louise *lawyer, artist*
Gibbs, Leonard (Doc Gibbs) *musician*
Gibbs, Ronald Steven *obstetrician, gynecologist, educator*
Giblin, Patrick David *retired bank executive*
Gibran, Kahlil *sculptor*
Gibson, Lisette L. *elementary school educator, music educator*
Gibson, Mel *actor, film director, film producer*
Gibson, Milton Eugene *cardiologist*
Gibson, Pamela Hemenway *elementary school educator*
Gibson, Scott Russell *director*
Gibson, William Willard, Jr. *law educator*
Giebel, Miriam Catherine *librarian, genealogist*
Giesey, Ralph Edwin *retired historian*
Gieskes, Hans *information services and publishing executive*
Gifford, John Irving *retired agricultural equipment company executive*
Gifford, Marjorie Fitting *mathematician, educator, consultant*
Gift, James Joseph *aquatic toxicologist*
Gilani, Tariq Hasan *physics professor, researcher*
Gilbert, Elayne Rhoda *writer*
Gilbert, Frederick E. *development planner, Africanist, consultant*
Gilbert, Harriette Gurley *retired music educator*
Gilbert, Janice Rae *music educator*
Gilbert, Melissa *former actors guild executive, actress*
Gilbert, Ronald Rhea *lawyer*
Gilbert, Steven Jeffrey *venture capitalist, screenwriter*
Gilchrest, Thornton Charles *retired association executive*
Gilchrist, Gerald Seymour *pediatric hematologist, oncologist, educator*
Gilder, George Franklin *communications executive, writer*
Giles, Christopher Stewart *banker*
Giles, James Francis *financial executive*
Giles, William Elmer *editor*
Gilinsky, Victor *physicist*
Gill, Henry Herr *photojournalist*
Gill, Libby *television executive*
Gill, Thomas James III *pathologist, educator*
Gilleran, Peter Joseph *retired art educator*
Gillespie, Gary Don *physician*
Gillespie, Gerald Ernest Paul *comparative literature educator, writer*
Gillespie, Thomas William *retired academic administrator, religious studies educator*
Gillett, Mary Caperton *military historian*
Gilliam, Terry Vance *film director, actor, writer, illustrator*
Gillice, Sondra Jupin (Mrs. Gardner Russell Brown) *sales and marketing executive*
Gilman, J. Paul *former federal agency administration*
Gilmore, Angelo Scotty *physicist, systems engineer*
Gilmore, Kathi *former state treasurer*
Gilmore, Merle *diversified financial services company executive*
Gilpin, Jack *actor*
Gilroy, Frank Daniel *playwright*
Gim, Dong-Woo *display designer*
Ginsberg, Ernest *lawyer, banker*
Ginsburg, Iona Horowitz *psychiatrist*
Ginsburg, Lynn *writer*
Gintzler, Alan Scott *journalist*
Giordanengo, Sam Peter *history professor*
Giordano, Richard Vincent (Sir Richard Vincent Giordano) *chemicals executive*
Giovanni, Nikki (Yolanda Cornelia Giovanni) *poet, educator*
Giovinazzo, Vivian Curry *writer*
Girshick, Steven L. *engineering educator, researcher*
Gitelson, Susan Aurelia *corporate executive, philanthropist*
Gitner, Gerald L. *air transportation executive, investment banker*
Giuliano, Neil Gerard *civil rights organization executive, former mayor*
Giusti, Joseph Paul *retired academic administrator, consultant*
Givenchy, Hubert James Marcel Taffin de *fashion designer*
Gjerset, Ruth Anne *research scientist, educator*
Glacel, Barbara Pate *management consultant*
Gladden, Joseph Rhea, Jr. *lawyer*
Gladden, Vivianne Cervantes *healthcare consultant, writer*

Glasberg, Laurence Brian *investment company executive*
Glaser, Patricia L. *lawyer*
Glaser, Peter Edward *retired mechanical engineer, consultant, educator*
Glaser, Robert Joy *retired internist, foundation administrator*
Glashow, Sheldon Lee *physicist, researcher*
Glass, Dorothea Daniels *physiatrist, educator*
Glass, Ira *radio producer, radio personality*
Glass, Kenneth Edward *management consultant*
Glasser, Ira Saul *former civil liberties organization administrator*
Glasser, Norma Penchansky *sculptor*
Glassheim, Jeffrey Wayne *allergist, immunologist, pediatrician*
Glassick, Charles Etzweiler *foundation administrator*
Glassman, Cynthia A. *former commissioner*
Glasson, Lloyd *sculptor, educator*
Glatter, Rebecca Jan *secondary school educator*
Glauber, Robert R. *former financial regulatory service executive*
Glavic, Nancy Carol *finance educator*
Gleason, Kate *writer, educator, editor*
Gleaves, Leon Rogers *marketing executive, sales executive*
Gleijeses, Mario *holding company executive*
Glen, Niki *artist, sculptor*
Glendening, Terry Sky *psychologist*
Glenn, Roland Douglas *chemical engineer*
Glennon, Charles Edward *retired judge, lawyer*
Glick, J. Leslie *entrepreneur*
Glick, Ruth Burtnick *literature educator, writer*
Glindeman, Henry Peter, Jr. *real estate developer*
Glismann, Clementine *retired elementary school educator*
Glodt, Michelle Lee *literature and language educator*
Glogowski, Jeffrey Ronald *director, music educator*
Glosser, Jeffrey Mark *lawyer*
Glover, Janet Briggs *artist*
Glück, Louise Elisabeth *poet, educator*
Gluckstern, Robert Leonard *physics professor*
Gluys, Charles Byron *retired marketing management consultant*
Glynn, Carlin (Carlin Masterson) *actress*
Glynn, Edward *retired academic administrator*
Glynn, Peter Alexander Richard *health facility administrator, consultant*
Glysch, Randall Lee *research scientist*
Gobel, John Henry *lawyer*
Goble, Paul *writer, illustrator, artist*
Godager, Jane Ann *retired social worker*
Goddess, Lynn Barbara *real estate investor*
Godfrey, Donal Charles *priest*
Godfrey, Norman V. *plastic surgeon*
Godin, Seth Warren *video production executive, writer, entrepreneur, blog website writer*
Godinez, Joshua Ray *social sciences educator*
Godwin, Larry A. *protective services official*
Godwin, Pamela June *financial services executive*
Godwin, Ralph Lee, Jr. *real estate executive*
Goeltz, Richard Karl *finance company executive*
Goen, Bob *television show host*
Goering, Kevin W. *lawyer*
Goerz, Mary Elizabeth Larsen *civic worker*
Goetschius, James Brian *military officer, urban planner*
Goff, Renee Rosenstock *gifted and talented educator*
Gofferje, Hadwig *retired language educator*
Goffman, Thomas Edward *radiobiologist, oncologist*
Goforth, Jill Hastings *assistant principal*
Goggin, John R. *software engineer*
Gokulakrishnan, Ponnuthurai *chemical engineer*
Gold, Harold Arthur *lawyer*
Gold, Judith Hammerling *psychiatrist*
Gold, Leonard Singer *librarian, translator, curator*
Goldberg, David Alan *investment banker, lawyer*
Goldberg, David Theo *law educator, writer*
Goldberg, Edwin *rehabilitation specialist, consultant, interfaith clergyman*
Goldberg, Lee Winicki *furniture company executive*
Goldberg, Leonard *television and movie producer*
Goldberg, Lucianne *literary agent*
Goldberg, Mark Arthur *neurologist*
Goldberg, Martin *internist, educator*
Goldberg, Michael Ellis *neurologist, neuroscientist*
Goldberg, Samuel *retired mathematician, foundation administrator*
Goldberg, Victor Joel *retired data processing company executive*
Goldberg, Whoopi (Caryn Elaine Johnson) *actress, comedienne*
Goldberger, Arthur Earl, Jr. *information technology executive*
Goldberger, George Stefan *finance company executive*
Goldblum, Jeff *actor*
Golden, Charles Edward *retired pharmaceutical company executive*
Golden, David Edward *physicist*
Golden, Gerald Samuel *retired national medical board executive*
Golden, Joseph Aaron *lawyer*
Golden, Judith Greene *artist, educator*
Golden, Louis Joseph *retired editor, publishing executive*
Golden, Sheila S. *retired special education educator*
Goldfarb, Muriel Bernice *marketing consultant, advertising consultant*
Goldfarb, Ruth *poet, educator*
Goldin, Leon *artist*
Golding, Carolyn May *former government senior executive, consultant*
Golding, Terry David *engineering educator, researcher*
Goldman, Alan Ira *brokerage house executive*
Goldman, Alvin Ira *philosopher, educator*
Goldman, Judith *writer, editor, curator, consultant, publisher*
Goldman, William *writer, scriptwriter*
Goldmann, Morton Aaron *cardiologist, educator*
Goldner, Sheldon Herbert *retired import/export company executive*

Goldsborough, Robert Gerald *publishing executive, author*
Goldschmidt, Lynn Harvey *lawyer*
Goldsmith, Jeff Charles *management consultant*
Goldsmith, Robert Lewis *youth association magazine executive*
Goldspiel, Arnold Nelson *real estate executive*
Goldstein, Alfred George *consumer products company executive*
Goldstein, Avram *pharmacology educator*
Goldstein, Bernard *transportation executive, hotel executive*
Goldstein, Dora Benedict *pharmacologist, educator*
Goldstein, Irving Solomon *chemistry professor, consultant*
Goldstein, Jerome Arthur *mathematics professor*
Goldstein, Leonard Barry *dentist*
Goldstein, Michael *retail executive*
Goldstein, Norman Ray *international trading company executive, consultant*
Goldstein, Tamara Beth *musician*
Goldstein, Walter Elliott *biotechnology executive*
Goldston, Stephen Eugene *community psychologist, educator, consultant*
Goldthwait, Christopher E. *ambassador*
Goleman, Daniel Jay *psychologist, journalist*
Goll, Stephen E. *telecommunications executive*
Golon, Maryanne *photojournalist*
Golub, Sharon Bramson *retired psychologist, educator*
Gomatam, Rajesh Ranganathan *materials engineer, researcher*
Gomez, Melissa Mordell *trial consultant*
Gomez, Mirta *musician, educator*
Gomez-Uchida, Daniel *marine biologist, geneticist*
Gonnering, Russell Stephen *ophthalmic plastic surgeon*
Gonzales, Ernesto Luis B. *bank executive*
Gonzales, Richard Robert *counselor*
González, Bárbara Patricia *mathematics professor*
Gonzalez, Rose Marie Juarez *retired education educator*
Gonzalez-Alegre, Pedro *neurologist, researcher*
Good, Walter Raymond *investment company executive*
Goodacre, Jill *model*
Goodall, Jane *zoologist*
Goode, Stephen Hogue *publishing executive*
Goodenow, Robert W. *lawyer, former sports association administrator*
Goodfellow, Robin Irene *surgeon*
Goodkin, Michael Jon *publishing company executive*
Goodman, Bennett J. *hedge fund executive*
Goodman, Charles David *physicist, researcher*
Goodman, Elizabeth Ann *retired lawyer*
Goodman, Erika *dancer, actress*
Goodman, Robert Lee *nursing administrator*
Goodman, Stanley Leonard *advertising executive*
Goodreau, Robert Charles *surgeon*
Goodrich, Kenneth Paul *retired dean*
Goodsell, Charles True *public administration educator, researcher*
Goodwin, Alyson *psychiatrist*
Goodwin, Andrew Wirt, II, *radiologist*
Goodwin, Casey S. *music educator*
Goodwin, Irwin *journalist, writer*
Goodwin, Michael Mark *research scientist, electrical engineer, computer science engineer*
Goodwin, Richard Hale *botany educator*
Goodwyn, Betty Ruth *librarian*
Gopal, Kreshna *computer scientist, researcher*
Gopalakrishnan, Kasthurirangan *engineer*
Gora, Susannah Porter Martin *journalist, poet*
Gorbaty, Martin Leo *chemist, researcher*
Gordis, David Moses *academic administrator, rabbi*
Gordley, James Russell *law educator*
Gordon, Bruce Lowell *education educator, researcher*
Gordon, Douglas *artist*
Gordon, Ezra *architect, educator*
Gordon, George G. *lawyer*
Gordon, Leonard H(erman) D(avid) *history educator*
Gordon, Lonny Joseph *artist, educator, dean*
Gordon, Marc Stewart *pharmacist, research scientist*
Gordon, Marjorie *lyric-coloratura soprano, music educator, opera producer*
Gordon, Richard M. Erik *private investor, educator*
Gordon, Sharon Ann *mathematics educator, preschool education*
Gordon, William Edwin *physicist, educator, electrical engineer, academic administrator*
Gore, Al (Albert Arnold Gore Jr.) *former Vice President of the United States*
Gore, Andrew *editor-in-chief periodical*
Gore, Martin Lee *musician*
Gore, Tushar *marketing professional*
Gorea, Lucia-Iosefina *language educator, poet*
Gorence, Patricia Josetta *judge*
Gorey, Thomas C. *retail executive*
Gorin, Michael Bruce *ophthalmic molecular geneticist, educator*
Gorman, Charles Johnny *training services executive, retired human resources specialist*
Gorman, Joseph Tolle *retired automotive parts manufacturing executive*
Gorske, Robert H. *lawyer*
Gorski, Sue Musselwhite *retired school librarian*
Gorski, Waldemar *chemist, educator*
Gorsline, Stephen Paul *security specialist*
Gorsuch, Edward Lee *former chancellor*
Gosciewski, Robert Louis *logistician*
Goslin, Thomas B. *career officer*
Goss, Jerome Eldon *craftsman, retired cardiologist*
Goss, Joel Francis *writer*
Goss, Porter Johnston *former CIA director, former congressman*
Gossen, Emmett Joseph, Jr. *motel chain executive, lawyer*
Gottfried, Eugene Leslie *physician, educator*
Gottlander, Robert Jan Lars *dental company executive*
Gottlieb, Alan Merril *advertising, fundraising and broadcasting executive, writer*
Gottlieb, Gary L. *hospital administrator*
Gottlieb, Lynn *engineer*

Gottlieb, Robert Adams *editor, dance critic, writer*
Gottschalk, Charles M. *international energy consultant*
Gottwald, William M. *chemicals executive*
Gou, Jihua *engineering educator*
Gougar, Hans David *nuclear engineer, director*
Gould, Lewis F., Jr. *lawyer*
Gould, Martha Bernice *retired librarian*
Goulet, Charles Ryan *retired insurance company executive*
Goulet, Lorrie *sculptor*
Gourley, Greta Ann Kimbrough *pharmaceutical sciences educator*
Gourley, Sara J. *lawyer*
Gourvitz, Elliot Howard *lawyer*
Gouse, S. William, Jr. *mechanical engineering executive, researcher*
Govan, Gladys Vernita Mosley *retired critical care nurse, medical/surgical nurse*
Govindjee, *biophysics, biochemistry, and biology professor*
Gowans, Sir James Learmonth *science administrator, immunologist*
Gowler, Vicki Sue *newspaper editor, journalist*
Goyan, Jere Edwin *pharmaceutical executive, dean*
Goyol, Apollos Bitrus *education educator*
Gozon, Richard C. *retired paper distribution executive*
Graber, William Raymond *former pharmaceutical executive*
Grabstald, Harry *urologist, oncologist*
Grace, Marcia Bell *advertising executive*
Grachev, Mikhail Vladimirovich *business educator, researcher*
Grady, Lee Timothy *pharmaceutical chemist*
Grady, Sandra C. *minister, counselor*
Grady, Wayne Joseph *retired government official*
Graebner, James Herbert *transportation executive*
Graf, Deva *artist*
Graffam, Allen C. *secondary school educator, music educator*
Grafton, Beth P. *music educator*
Graham, Bob (Daniel Robert Graham) *former senator, former governor*
Graham, Cynthia Armstrong *banker*
Graham, David G. *preventive medicine physician, psychiatrist*
Graham, Howard Lee, Sr. *finance company executive*
Graham, James Herbert *retired dermatologist*
Graham, John Hamilton, II, *professional athletics manager*
Graham, K(athleen) M. (K. M. Graham) *artist*
Graham, Lanier *art historian, curator*
Graham, Laurie *editor, writer*
Graham, Olive Jane *retired medical/surgical nurse*
Graham, Steven Anthony *writer*
Graham, Stuart Edward *construction company executive*
Graham, Wallace Karl *chemicals executive*
Graham, William Henry *lawyer*
Gralla, Lawrence *publishing company executive*
Gralla, Milton *retired publisher*
Grambs, Jennifer *writer*
Grames-Lyra, Judith Ellen *artist, educator, municipal official*
Grandi, Attilio *engineering consultant*
Grann, Phyllis E. *editor, former publisher executive*
Granott, Nira *psychologist, researcher*
Grant, Alexander Marshall *retired ballet director*
Grant, Carmen Hill *psychologist, psychotherapist*
Grant, Daniel Gordon *information technology executive*
Grant, Frances Bethea *editor*
Grant, Isabella Horton *retired judge*
Grant, Leonard Tydings *clergyman*
Grant, Linda Hess *language educator*
Grant, Merrill Theodore *television producer*
Grant, Richard Earl *retired medical and legal consultant*
Grant, Walter Matthews *retired corporate financial executive, retired lawyer*
Graser, Alfred J. *airport terminal executive, director*
Grasserbauer, Doris *computer scientist, mathematician, educator*
Grasso, Dick (Richard A. Grasso) *former stock exchange executive*
Grattan, Patricia Elizabeth *retired art gallery director*
Gratz, Jay M. *steel company executive*
Grave de Peralta, Luis Ernesto *research scientist*
Graves, Joseph Scott *economist and management consultant*
Graves, Lorraine Elizabeth *dancer, educator, coach*
Graves, Todd Peterson *former prosecutor*
Graves, Wallace Billingsley *retired university executive*
Graves, William Preston *governor*
Gray, Charles Henry *actor, theater director*
Gray, David Lawrence *retired air force officer*
Gray, Francine du Plessix *writer*
Gray, Gloria Meador *librarian*
Gray, Gordon L. *communications educator*
Gray, Hazel Irene *retired special education educator, counselor, consultant*
Gray, Justin Y. *lawyer*
Gray, Mary Jane *retired obstetrician, gynecologist*
Gray, Richard Alexander, Jr. *retired chemical company executive*
Gray, Richard Arden *retired transportation executive*
Gray, Richard Moss *retired college president*
Gray, Thomas Stephen *writer*
Gray, William H. III *lawyer, former non profit association administrator, retired congressman*
Grayson, Edward Davis *lawyer, manufacturing executive*
Graziani, Leonard Joseph *pediatric neurologist, researcher*
Greaser, Constance Udean *retired automotive executive*
Greason, Walter David *history professor*
Grebstein, Sheldon Norman *academic administrator*
Grechanik, Jeffrey *operations research specialist*
Greco, Christopher Jon *musician, composer, educator*

Greeley, Andrew Moran *sociologist, writer*
Greeley, Jennifer Ann *military officer, educator*
Green, Anna Lucille *education educator*
Green, Barbara Marie *publisher, journalist, poet, writer*
Green, Carol H. *lawyer, educator*
Green, Carole L. *lawyer*
Green, David *hematologist*
Green, Grant S., Jr. *former federal agency administrator*
Green, Kevin Patrick *career officer*
Green, Louis Harry *retired surgeon*
Green, Michael Jay *medical educator*
Green, Patricia Pataky *school system administrator, consultant*
Green, Richard Calvin, Jr. *electric power and gas industry executive*
Green, Stanley E. *military officer*
Green, Thomas George *retired architect*
Green, Wilma Jane *writer*
Greenberg, Alan Courtney (Ace Greenberg) *securities trader*
Greenberg, Albert *art director*
Greenberg, Carolyn Phyllis *retired anesthesiologist*
Greenberg, Hinda Feige *library director*
Greenberg, Ira Arthur *psychologist*
Greenberg, Jack M. *former food products executive*
Greenberg, Maurice Raymond (Hank Greenberg) *retired insurance company executive*
Greenberg, Richard *playwright*
Greenberg, Ronald David *lawyer, educator*
Greenburg, Dan *author*
Greene, Alvin *management consultant*
Greene, Donald Richard *dermatologist, educator*
Greene, Enid *retired congresswoman*
Greene, Frank Sullivan, Jr. *investment company executive*
Greene, Howard E., Jr. *pharmaceutical executive*
Greene, John Colton *retired historian*
Greene, Margaret H. *telecommunications industry executive*
Greene, Robert Bernard, Jr., (Bob Greene) *news correspondent, journalist, writer*
Greene, Tracy A. *lawyer*
Greenebaum, Leonard Charles *retired lawyer*
Greenfield, Jason Michael *urologist*
Greenfield, Linda Sue *nursing educator*
Greenfield, Val Shea *ophthalmologist*
Greenspan, Alan *former Chairman of Federal Reserve System, economist*
Greenwald, Alice Marian *museum director*
Greenwald, John Edward *publishing executive, journalist*
Greenway, Joan M. *dean*
Greenwood, Janet Kae Daly *psychologist, academic administrator, marketing professional*
Greenwood, William Warren *news correspondent, journalist*
Greer, Carl Crawford *petroleum company executive*
Greer, Germaine *author*
Greer, K. Gordon *banker*
Greer, Kenneth E. *dermatologist*
Greer, Robert Bruce III *orthopedist, educator*
Greer, Suzanne Michelle *music educator*
Greever, Margaret Quarles *retired mathematics educator*
Gregerson, Daniel P. *retired computer company executive*
Gregg, David III *investment banker*
Greggs, Elanora *social worker*
Gregor, Ann *literature and language educator, reporter, application developer*
Gregor, Dorothy Deborah *retired librarian*
Gregory, Bettina Louise *retired journalist*
Gregory, Frederick Drew *federal agency administrator*
Gregory, James Alexander *editor, writer, film producer*
Gregory, Nelson Bruce *retired motel owner, retired naval officer*
Gregory, Peggy J. *music educator*
Grendell, James Henry *medical educator*
Grenier, Laura Margiotta *medical/surgical nurse*
Grenz, M. Kay *manufacturing executive*
Grey, Francis Joseph *accountant, educator*
Grey, Joel *actor*
Grey, Robert Dean *academic administrator, biology educator*
Gribbon, Deborah *museum director*
Grieb, Elizabeth *lawyer*
Griego, Linda *media executive*
Grier, David Alan *actor*
Griffin, Ward O., Jr. *surgeon, educator*
Griffin, Campbell Arthur, Jr. *retired lawyer*
Griffin, Carleton Hadlock *accountant, educator*
Griffin, James Anthony *bishop*
Griffin, Lawrence Russell, Sr. *management consultant*
Griffith, B. Herold (Bezaleel Herold Griffith) *retired plastic surgeon, retired educator*
Griffith, Melanie *actress*
Griffith, Rosita Denise *mathematics professor, chemistry professor*
Griffiths, Phillip A. *mathematician, retired academic administrator*
Griffiths, Rachel *actress*
Griffiths, Robert Budington *physics professor*
Griggs, Joyce L. *secondary school educator*
Griles, J. Steven (James Steven Griles, Steven Griles) *lobbyist, former federal agency administrator*
Grilley, Beryl H. *retired speech educator*
Grillo-López, Antonio J. *physician*
Grim, Patricia Ann *retired banker*
Grimaldi, David *financial advisor*
Grimaldi, Kathleen Galvin *literature and language educator, poet*
Grimes, James Gordon *geologist*
Griner, Paul Francis *physician*
Grinnell, Helen Dunn *musicologist, arts administrator*
Grinter, Donald W. *metal processing executive*
Grise-Owens, Erlene Y. *social worker, educator*
Grissom, J. David *private investor, bank executive*
Grissom, Marquis Deon *professional baseball player*
Gritter, Elizabeth *historian, researcher*
Grodsky, Jamie Anne *law educator*
Grody, Donald *actor, judge, lawyer*

Groenheim, Henri Arnold *psychologist, consultant*
Groetken, Troy Alan *lawyer, pharmacist*
Grolli, Frank Thomas *retired pharmacist*
Gromacki, Susan Jean *optometrist*
Gronniger, Jerome Timothy *financial analyst*
Grosbard, Ulu *film director*
Grosfeld, James *real estate development company executive*
Groskopf, Aubrey Bud *broadcast executive, lawyer*
Grosland, Emery Layton *retired banker*
Gross, Geoffrey Fries *systems architect*
Gross, Laura Ann *marketing and communications professional, herbalist, acupuncturist*
Gross, Pamela H. *editor*
Gross, Rachel N. *reading and instructional technology specialist*
Gross, Richard Benjamin *lawyer, film producer*
Grossman, Carolyn Sylvia Cort *retired elementary school educator*
Grossman, Cissy *curator, art historian*
Grossman, Edward Jerome *music educator, composer*
Grossman, Jerome Harvey *medical educator, medical association administrator*
Grossman, Joyce Renee *pediatrician, internist*
Grossman, Robert James *retired architect*
Grosso, Doreen Elliott *management consultant*
Grove, Richard Charles *retired power tool company executive*
Groves, B. C. *educational consultant, writer*
Groves, Bernice Ann *retired elementary and secondary school coordinator, educator*
Growick, Philip *advertising executive*
Grubb, Donald Hartman *paper industry company executive*
Gruber, Ira Dempsey *historian, educator*
Gruen, Margaret *actress*
Gruen, Shirley Schanen *artist*
Gruetzmacher, Nancy Lynn *middle schoool educator*
Grunder, Fred Irwin *industrial hygienist, consultant*
Grunder, Hermann A. *science administrator, director, research scientist*
Gruneich, Jeffrey Alan *biotechnologist, director*
Grunt, Jerome Alvin *retired pediatric endocrinologist*
Grushow, Sandy *broadcast executive*
Grutman, Jewel Humphrey *lawyer, writer*
Gruver, William Rolfe (Bill Gruver) *finance educator, retired investment banker*
Guare, John *playwright, educator*
Guarente, Leonard P. *medical geneticist, educator*
Gubbins, Keith Edmund *chemical engineering educator*
Guber, Peter *executive producer*
Gudell, Valerie M. *academic administrator, musician*
Gudenberg, Harry Richard *arbitrator, mediator*
Gudmundsson, Finnbogi *library administrator*
Guerra, Alma Del Rosario *music educator*
Guerrero, Lisa (Lisa Guerrero-Coles) *former sports reporter*
Guerrero, Vladimir *professional baseball player*
Guest, Linda Sand *education educator*
Guettel, Adam *lyricist, composer*
Gugel, Craig Thomas *advertising executive*
Guggenheim, Barbara Sue *art appraiser*
Guggisberg, Kristin Wilson *psychologist*
Guha, Hillol *hydrologist, researcher*
Guhr, Daniel Johannes *management consultant*
Gui, James Edmund *architect*
Guichard, Susan Weil *dietician, consultant*
Guikema, Seth David *civil engineer, researcher*
Guild, Jeffrey K. *mathematics professor*
Guiliano, Francis James *office products manufacturing company executive*
Guiliano, Mireille *consumer products company executive*
Guillermoprieto, Alma *journalist, non-fiction writer*
Guiterrez, Hector P. *surgeon*
Gulbrandsen, Patricia Hughes *physician*
Gulcher, Robert Harry *air transportation executive*
Gulledge, Sandra Smith *publishing executive, film producer*
Gullickson, JoAnne Lois *writer*
Gumpel, Hugh *artist*
Gumpert, Gustav *public relations executive*
Gund, Ann *art association administrator*
Gundersheimer, Werner Leonard *library director*
Gunderson, Carl Harmon *neurologist, educator*
Gunderson, Judith Keefer *golf association executive*
Gunderson, Ted Lee *security consultant*
Gunhus, Gaylord T. *military career officer*
Gunning, Carolyn Sue *dean, provost, nursing educator*
Gunsaulis, Linda C. *elementary school educator*
Gunter, William Dayle, Jr. *physicist, consultant*
Guo, Chao-Yu *statistician, educator*
Guo, Dongbai *application developer*
Guo, ZengKui *research scientist*
Gupta, Sanju *education educator, researcher*
Gurian, Mal *telecommunications executive*
Gurspan, Mitchell Scott *technology architect, writer*
Gurspan, Susan Judith *language educator*
Gurstel, Norman Keith *lawyer*
Gurwitch, Arnold Andrew *communications executive*
Guskin, Alan E. *university president*
Gussin, Robert Zalmon *retired health products executive*
Gussow, Sue Ferguson *artist, educator*
Gust, Anne Baldwin *former retail apparel company executive*
Gustafson, Craig Thomas *theater director, playwright, graphics designer*
Gustafson, Richard Alrick *retired university president*
Gutheinz, Jean *public relations executive*
Guthridge, Bill *university basketball coach*
Guthrie, Janet *professional race car driver*
Guthrie, Wallace Nessler, Jr. *naval officer*
Gutman, Richard Edward *lawyer*
Guy, Eleanor Bryenton *retired writer*
Guyer, Bernard *maternal and child health educator*
Guymon, Gary LeRoy *civil engineering educator*

Guynn, Jack (George C. Guynn) *retired bank executive*

Guyon, John Carl *retired university administrator*

Guzman, Carole L. *small business owner*

Gwalla-Ogisi, Nomsa *education educator*

Gyemant, Robert Ernest *diversified financial services company executive, merchant banker*

Ha, Chong Wan *information technology executive*

Haaland, Gordon Arthur *retired academic administrator*

Haar, Ana Maria Fernández *advertising executive, public relations executive*

Haas, Charlie *screenwriter*

Haas, Edward Lee *management consultant*

Haas, Frederick Carl *retired paper company executive, retired chemicals executive*

Haas, Holly Alice *set designer, small business owner*

Haas, Howard Green *retired bedding manufacturing company executive*

Haas, Suzanne Alberta *elementary school educator, secondary school educator*

Habecker, Eugene Brubaker *academic administrator*

Haber, Ralph Norman *psychology consultant, researcher, educator*

Haberman, Charles Morris *mechanical engineer, educator*

Habermann, Helen Margaret *botanist, educator*

Habiballa, Abdulgader A. *electrical engineer, computer engineer, educator*

Habicht, Frank Henry *retired manufacturing executive*

Hackbarth, Glenn M. *human services administrator*

Hackel-Sims, Stella Bloomberg *lawyer, former government official*

Hacker, Dean W. *mechanical engineer, educator*

Hackett, Robert John *lawyer*

Hackett, Wesley Phelps, Jr. *lawyer*

Hackman, Laura *theater director*

Hackney, Hugh Edward *lawyer*

Hackworth, Justin Scott *marketing executive, photographer*

Hadda, Janet Ruth *language educator, lay psychoanalyst*

Haddad, Edmonde Alex *public affairs executive*

Haddock, Raymond Earl *retired career officer*

Haddy, Theresa Brey *pediatrician, educator, hematologist, oncologist*

Haden, Clovis Roland *retired academic administrator, engineering educator*

Haden, Sara Chiara *psychologist*

Hadley, Leila Eliott-Burton (Mrs. Henry Luce III) *writer*

Hadley, William Melvin *retired dean*

Haeberle, Rosamond Pauline *retired music educator*

Haegele, John Ernest *metal products executive*

Haegerich, Tamara *behavioral scientist*

Hafemeister, Beverly Rae *consumer products company executive*

Haft, Gail Klein *pediatrician*

Hagan, Joseph Henry *educational consultant*

Hagel, John III *management consultant*

Hagel, Raymond Charles *publishing company executive, educator*

Hagelstein, Robert Philip *publisher*

Hageman, Richard Philip, Jr. *educational administrator*

Hagenlocker, Edward E. *retired automobile company executive*

Haggerty, Mary Elizabeth *retired elementary school educator*

Haggerty, Robert Johns *pediatrician, educator*

Haggis, Paul Edward *scriptwriter, television producer, television director*

Hah, Dooyoung *electrical engineer, educator*

Hah, Mina *psychiatrist*

Hahn, Frank Horace *economics professor*

Hahn, Helene B. *former motion picture company executive*

Hahn, James Kenneth *former mayor, lawyer*

Hahn, Karla Lynn *librarian*

Hahn, Mary Downing *writer*

Hahn, Virginia Lynn *reservations agent*

Hahn, Youngwon *mechanical engineer, researcher*

Haile, L. John, Jr. *journalist, publishing executive*

Haines, Dennis G. *military officer*

Haines, Richard Foster *retired psychologist*

Hait, Patrick David *music educator, elementary school educator*

Haithcock, William Dana, Jr. *physician*

Hajek, Robert J., Sr. *lawyer, real estate broker*

Hakala, Karen Louise *retired real estate specialist*

Hake, Ralph F. *former appliance manufacturing executive*

Hakim, Besim Selim *architecture and urban design educator, researcher, consultant, urban planner*

Hakimoglu, Ayhan *electronics executive*

Halasz, Stephen Joseph *retired optical engineer*

Halberstam, David *journalist, writer*

Halberstam, Heini *mathematics professor*

Haldeman, Joe William *writer*

Hale, Janet *federal agency administrator*

Hale, Wesley Raymond *research scientist, chemical engineer*

Haley, George Brock, Jr. *retired lawyer*

Halfen, David *retired publishing executive*

Halfvarson, Lucille Robertson *music educator*

Halitsky, Steve *data analyst, statistician, researcher*

Hall, Adrienne A. *international marketing communications executive, consultant, life balance coach*

Hall, Anthony Michael *actor*

Hall, Donald *poet*

Hall, Hansel Crimiel *communications executive*

Hall, James Evan *lawyer*

Hall, James Stanley *jazz guitarist, composer*

Hall, James William *university chancellor*

Hall, Jay *social psychologist*

Hall, Joan Torrens *lawyer*

Hall, John Hopkins *retired lawyer*

Hall, John Robert *psychiatrist*

Hall, Kathryn Marie *elementary school educator*

Hall, Kathryn Walt *ambassador*

Hall, Milton Reese *retired oil company executive, accountant, controller*

Hall, Monty *television producer, actor*

Hall, Peggy Craft *poet, retired secondary school educator*

Hall, Susan Laurel *artist, educator, writer*

Hall, Tom T. *retired country singer, songwriter*

Hall, William N. *lawyer*

Hall, Zach Winter *science administrator*

Hallacy, Don *telecommunications industry executive*

Halleck, Charles White *lawyer, photographer, former judge*

Haller, Jordan Daniel *cardiovascular surgeon*

Halliday, William Ross *retired physician, speleologist, writer*

Hallman, Cinda A. *management consultant*

Halpern, Alvin Michael *retired physicist, educator, consultant*

Halpern, James Bladen *lawyer*

Halpin, Daniel William *engineering educator, consultant*

Halverstadt, Robert Dale *mechanical engineer, metal products executive*

Ham, Sommy L. *publisher, writer*

Haman, Sarah Armstrong *librarian*

Hambidge, Douglas Walter *archbishop*

Hamblen, Lapsley Walker, Jr. *retired judge*

Hamblin, Terry Robert, Jr. *historian, educator*

Hambrecht, Patricia G. *retail executive*

Hamed, Martha Ellen *government administrator*

Hamel, Louis Reginald *systems analysis consultant*

Hamel, Rodolphe *retired lawyer, pharmaceutical executive*

Hamelin, Marcel *historian, educator*

Hamermesh, Bernard *physicist, researcher*

Hamill, (William) Pete *newspaper columnist, author, editor*

Hamilton, Darden Cole *construction management company executive*

Hamilton, David Eugene *minister, educator*

Hamilton, Jean *financial services executive, software executive*

Hamilton, Joe *communications company executive*

Hamilton, Judith Hall *computer company executive*

Hamilton, Laird John *professional surfer*

Hamilton, Thomas Michael *marketing executive*

Hamilton, Wendy J. *foundation administrator*

Hamister, Donald Bruce *retired electronics company executive*

Hamlen, Kevin William *computer scientist, educator*

Hamlin, Dan William *accountant, management consultant*

Hamlin, Harriett E. *educational consultant*

Hamlin, Sonya B. *communications specialist*

Hammad, Amir Youssef *electrical engineer, researcher*

Hammam, M. Shawky *electrical engineer, educator*

Hammann, Gregg C. *fitness equipment executive*

Hammer, Joyce Mae *gifted and talented educator*

Hammer, Wade Burke *retired oral and maxillofacial surgeon, educator*

Hammerschmidt, John Paul *retired congressman, lumber company executive*

Hammon, Paul Kenneth *engineering company executive, educator*

Hammond, Ann P. *retired elementary. high school and college educator, poet*

Hammond, Glenn Barry, Sr. *lawyer, electrical engineer*

Hammond, Graeme Lord *surgeon, educator*

Hammond, Harmony *artist, educator*

Hammond, Paul Young *political science professor*

Hampton, Kevin Michael *lawyer, real estate agent*

Hampton, Lori Beth *psychologist*

Hampton, Nanette Davina *private school educator, writer*

Hancock, Artemus Ward, Sr. *music educator*

Hancock, Patricia Ann *artist*

Hand, Herbert Hensley *finance educator, writer, entrepreneur*

Hand, Roger *physician, educator*

Handford, H. Allen *retired psychiatrist, medical educator*

Handler, Harold Robert *lawyer*

Handschu, Barbara Ellen *lawyer*

Handy, Edward Otis, Jr. *retired diversified financial services company executive*

Handy, Rollo Leroy *philosopher, researcher*

Hanes, Leigh B., Jr. *lawyer*

Hanford, George Hyde *retired educational association administrator*

Hangen, Terra *librarian, writer*

Hanket, Mark John *lawyer*

Hankins, Steven G. *retired food company executive*

Hankowsky, William P. *real estate company executive*

Hanks, Alan R. *chemistry professor*

Hanmer, Stephen Read, Jr. *retired federal official*

Hanna, Duke Ellsworth *retired neurological surgeon*

Hanna, Noreen Anelda *adult education educator, consultant*

Hannaman, Alberta Anna *artist*

Hanneman, Rodney Elton *metallurgical engineer*

Hanover, Donna Ann (Donna Ann Kofnovec) *radio personality, actress, journalist*

Hansell, John Royer *retired pathologist*

Hansen, Nick Dane *lawyer*

Hansen, Rex Cossey *mechanical engineer*

Hansen-Kyle, Linda L *counselor, nursing educator*

Hansen-Thomas, Holly Harbour *language educator*

Hanson, Harold Palmer *physicist, editor, academic administrator, government official*

Hanson, Jo *artist, educator, writer*

Hanson, John M. *civil engineering and construction educator*

Hanson, Paula *sports association executive*

Hanson, Tamara W. *accountant*

Hanson, Wendy Karen *retired chemical engineer*

Hantman, Barry G. *software engineer*

Hanushek, Eric Alan *economics professor*

Hapner, Mary Lou *securities trader, writer*

Harbaugh, Janice M. *counselor, consultant*

Harbert, Charles Armon *retired pharmaceutical executive, chemist, writer*

Hardage, Page Taylor *elementary school educator*

Hardaway, Robert Morris III *retired surgeon*

Hardcastle, Marcia E. (Marcia E. Temme) *retired journalist*

Harden, Mary Louise *human resources consultant, real estate broker, real estate appraiser*

Harden, Patrick Alan *journalist*

Harder, Robert Clarence *state official*

Hardie, James Hiller *retired lawyer*

Hardie, Michael Howard *mathematician, educator*

Hardin, Bridgette Everhart *educational research analyst*

Hardin, Hal D. *lawyer, judge, former US attorney*

Hardin, James Neal *language educator, writer*

Hardin, Paul III *law educator*

Harding, Marc Steven *lawyer*

Hardis, Stephen Roger *retired manufacturing company executive*

Hardwicke, Catherine Helen *film director, set designer*

Hardy, Chester Alfred *engineer*

Hardy, Clarence Earl, Jr. *government, nonprofit and corporate sector executive*

Hardy, Kathy L. *elementary school educator*

Hardy, Ralph W. F. *biochemist*

Hare, Norma Q. *retired school system administrator*

Harff, Charles Henry *retired lawyer, retired manufacturing executive*

Harford, Robert R. *dermatologist*

Hargadon, Bernard Joseph, Jr. *retired consumer goods company executive*

Haring, Ellen Stone (Mrs. E. S. Haring) *philosophy educator*

Hariton, Lorraine Jill *information technology executive*

Harkins, Edwin L. *musician, educator*

Harlan, Raymond Carter *special investigator, writer, retired communication executive, educator, and military officer*

Harlin, Marilyn Miler *marine botany educator, researcher, consultant*

Harlin, Renny (Renny Lauri Mauritz Harjola) *film director*

Harlow, Barbara Jean *publishing executive*

Harlow, Patricia Ann *retired elementary school educator*

Harman, Maryann Whittemore *artist, educator*

Harmel, Merel Hilber *anesthesiologist, educator*

Harms, Nancy Ann *nursing educator*

Harnack, Don Steger *retired lawyer*

Harnedy, Joan Catherine Holland *retired systems analyst*

Harper, Charles Michel *food products executive, director*

Harper, Conrad Kenneth *lawyer*

Harper, Henry H. *retired military officer*

Harper, James Weldon III *finance consultant*

Harper, Marsha Wilson *retired religious organization administrator*

Harper, Richard Henry *film producer, film director*

Harr, Lucy Loraine *public relations executive*

Harreld, Michael N. *bank executive*

Harrell, Henry Howze *tobacco company executive*

Harrell, Margaret Ann *workshop coordinator, editor*

Harrigan, Lori *Olympic athlete*

Harrigan, Rosanne Carol *medical educator*

Harriman, John Howland *retired lawyer*

Harrington, Herbert H. *accountant*

Harrington, Jean Patrice *academic administrator*

Harrington, John Tolan *medical educator, internist, nephrologist, retired dean*

Harrington, John Walter *pediatrician, medical researcher*

Harrington, Robert Dudley, Jr. *retired printing company executive*

Harris, Brandi Marie *theater educator*

Harris, Brian Joseph *psychologist, neuroscientist, educator*

Harris, Dale Hutter *retired judge*

Harris, Deanna Lynn *special education educator, writer*

Harris, Denise Michelle *advertising account executive*

Harris, Dolores M. *retired academic administrator, adult education educator*

Harris, Dudley Michael *film producer, film director, writer*

Harris, Elaine K. *medical consultant*

Harris, Eula Lee *retired photojournalist*

Harris, Harriet *actress*

Harris, Isiah, Jr. *telecommunications industry executive*

Harris, Joe Frank *former governor*

Harris, Marcelite Jordan *retired career officer*

Harris, Margaret T. *school system administrator*

Harris, Mark R. *film producer*

Harris, Mel *broadcast executive*

Harris, Merle Wiener *college administrator, educator*

Harris, Nicholas George *publisher*

Harris, Paul Smith *human resources professional*

Harris, Richard E. *neuroscientist, acupuncturist*

Harris, Richard Eugene Vassau *lawyer*

Harris, Robert A. *retired music educator*

Harris, Robert Norman *advertising executive, educator*

Harris, Rogers Sanders *bishop*

Harrison, Charles Maurice *retired lawyer, retired communications executive*

Harrison, Clifford *chef, small business owner*

Harrison, Ella Guidry *writer*

Harrison, John Raymond *foundation administrator, retired publishing executive*

Harrison, Judith Anne *human resources executive*

Harrison, Lynn Henry, Jr. *cardiovascular surgeon, educator, director*

Harrison, Nigel *musician*

Harrison, Thomas R. *music educator*

Harrison, William Burwell, Jr. *diversified financial services company executive*

Harrop, Daniel Smith III *psychiatrist*

Harshbarger, Richard B. *retired economics professor*

Harstad, Carolyn Audrey *writer, educator, photographer*

Hart, Arthur Alvin *historian, author*

Hart, Cecil William Joseph *otolaryngologist, surgeon*

Hart, Gary W. *retired senator, lawyer*

Hart, Howard Roscoe, Jr. *retired physicist*

Hart, James Warren *retired academic administrator, retired professional football player*

Hart, John *former professional sports team executive*

Hart, John H. *communications engineer*

Hart, Kitty Carlisle *performing arts association administrator*

Hart, Marnie R. *art educator*

Harte, Christopher McCutcheon *investment manager*

Hartford, Michael Wayne *health facility administrator*

Hartger, Barbara J. *marketing professional*

Hartley, James R. *musician, writer*

Hartman, Earl Kenneth *writer*

Hartmann, George Herman *retired manufacturing executive*

Hartmann, Robert Trowbridge *newspaperman, presidential counselor*

Hartnett, Edward J. *retired pharmaceutical executive*

Hartsock, Linda Sue *retired management consultant*

Hartstein, Harold Herman *psychology educator, consultant*

Hartwell, Carol L. *Spanish language educator, technical recruiter*

Hartzell, Karl Drew *retired dean, historian*

Harvey, Birt *retired pediatrician, educator*

Harvey, Glenn Francis *association manager*

Harvey, Louis-Charles *minister, seminary president, religion educator*

Harvey, Lynne Cooper *broadcast executive, civic worker*

Harvey, Marc S(an) *lawyer, historian, law educator*

Harvey, Nancy Melissa *media specialist, art educator*

Harvey, Richard Dudley *marketing consultant*

Harvey, Steven Patrick (Steve Harvey) *comedian, actor*

Harwell, Denise *researcher*

Harwell, William Earnest (Ernie Harwell) *retired commentator*

Haryono, Ignatius Wibisono *writer*

Hasen, Burton Stanley *painter*

Haskell, Molly *writer*

Hasko, Judith Ann *lawyer*

Haslett, Jared Wooddell *physicist, educator*

Hassan, Ibne *lawyer, diplomat, political philosopher, international strategist*

Hasse, John Edward *music curator*

Hasselmeyer, Eileen Grace *medical researcher*

Hasselmo, Nils *academic administrator, linguist, educator*

Hastings, L(ois) Jane *architect, educator*

Hatchell, Sylvia *basketball coach*

Hatfield, Jane Stauff *secondary school educator*

Hatfield, Julie Stockwell *journalist*

Hathcock, John Edward *vocalist*

Hathorne, Gayle Gene *musician, family historian*

Hatkoff, Craig Mitchell *real estate executive, educator*

Hattar, Jacqueline *lawyer*

Hauck, Frederick Hamilton *retired military officer, retired astronaut, retired aerospace executive*

Hauer, Erwin Franz *sculptor, educator*

Hauer, Jerome M. *city official*

Haug, Edward Joseph, Jr. *engineering educator, director*

Haugland, Susan Warrell *education educator, consultant*

Hauner, David *economist*

Hauptfuhrer, W. Barnes *bank executive*

Hauptmann, Randal Mark *biotechnologist*

Hausdorfer, Gary Lee *management consultant*

Hauser, Joyce Roberta *marketing professional*

Hauser, La Wayne *elementary school educator*

Hausman, Arthur Herbert *electronics company executive*

Hausman, Harriet Seceley *administrator*

Hausman, Marvin S. *research and development company executive*

Hautman, Pete (Peter Murray) *writer*

Hauver, Constance Longshore *lawyer*

Haver-Allen, Ann *communications director*

Hawes, Bess Lomax *retired folklorist*

Hawke, John Daniel, Jr. *former federal official*

Hawkes, Mary Newgeon *retired minister, educator*

Hawkins, Harold Stanley *pastor, school director, police chaplain*

Hawkins, Mary Ellen Higgins (Mary Ellen Higgins) *retired state legislator, public relations executive*

Hawthorne, Bruce N. *lawyer, former telecommunications industry executive*

Hawthorne, Douglas D. *medical association administrator*

Hawthorne, Enid Ruth *retired secondary school educator, social sciences educator*

Hawthorne, Roy John *retired music educator*

Hay, George Austin (Austin Hay) *actor, artist, musician, writer*

Hayakawa, Kan-Ichi *retired food scientist*

Hayes, Bernard M. *military officer, researcher*

Hayes, Byron Jackson, Jr. *retired lawyer*

Hayes, Charles Franklin III *retired museum director*

Hayes, Colleen Ballard *journalist, photographer, writer*

Hayes, Cynthia Ann (C.A. Hayes) *writer*

Hayes, David Ryan *mathematics professor*

Hayes, David Vincent *sculptor*

Hayes, Janet Gray *retired management consultant, retired mayor*

Hayes, John Patrick *retired manufacturing company executive*

Hayes, Jonathan *information technology executive, hardware and product designer*

Hayes, Patricia Thornton *music educator, retired director*

Hays, Kathleen *news correspondent*

Hays, Patrick Gregory *healthcare executive*

Hayton, Bernard Quentin, Jr. *library media specialist*

Haywood, H(erbert) Carl(ton) *psychologist, educator*

Hazard, Christopher Wedvik *international business executive*

Hazard, Geoffrey Cornell, Jr. *law educator*

Hollings, Fritz (Ernest Frederick Hollings) *former senator*
Holloran, Thomas Edward *business educator*
Holloway, Ernest Leon *retired university president*
Holloway, Ernest Robert III *historian, researcher*
Holloway, James Lemuel III *foundation executive, retired military officer*
Holly, Lauren (Lauren Michael Holly) *actress*
Holman, David Hughes *research scientist*
Holman, James J. *lawyer*
Holman, Tammi Sue *secondary school educator, department chairman*
Holmer, Alan Freeman *former trade association executive*
Holmes, Frederick Franklin *retired medical educator, physician, researcher*
Holmes, Henry Allen *diplomat*
Holmes, Michael Gene *lawyer*
Holmes, Michael L. *career officer*
Holmes, Samuel C. *music educator*
Holmes, Susan G. *music educator*
Holmstrom, Lynda Lytle *sociologist, educator*
Holt, Cheryl L. *medical educator*
Holt, George, Jr. *information technology executive*
Holt, Marjorie Sewell *lawyer, retired congresswoman*
Holt, Thaddeus *lawyer*
Holt, William Henry *retired physicist, researcher*
Holte, Debra Leah *investment company executive, financial analyst*
Holtkamp, Susan Charlotte *elementary school educator*
Holton, Grace Holland *accountant*
Holton, Winfred Byron III *writer*
Holtz, Laurence *artisan, photographer*
Holtzman, Robert Neil Nehemiah *neurosurgeon, neurologist*
Holtzschue, Karl Bressem *lawyer, author, educator*
Holub, Robert Frantisek *nuclear chemist, physicist*
Holyfield-Vega, Doretta Joyce *religious studies educator*
Holz, Carl Wayne *retired theologian*
Holz, George G., IV, *medical educator, research scientist*
Holzer, Edwin *advertising executive*
Holzer, Jenny *artist*
Holzkamp, Jane Strauss *business owner*
Holzman, D. Keith *management consultant, record company executive*
Hommel, Kevin Arthur *psychologist*
Honeystein, Karl *lawyer, media specialist*
Hong, Charles Sukki *tax specialist, consultant*
Hong, Ran-E *literature educator*
Honnold, John Otis *law educator*
Honour, Lynda Charmaine *research scientist, psychotherapist, educator*
Honsa, Thomas Patrick *secondary school educator, history professor*
Hood, Carra Leah *literature educator*
Hood, Glenda E. *former state official, former mayor*
Hood, William Boyd, Jr. *cardiologist, educator*
Hook, Jerry B. *pharmaceutical consultant*
Hooks, Earl J. *art educator, sculptor*
Hooper, Henry Olcott *retired academic administrator, physicist*
Hooper, Josh *advertising executive, writer, director*
Hooper, Robert Alexander *television producer, educator*
Hooper, Roger Fellowes *retired architect*
Hooper, Tom *film director, television director*
Hoover, Richard *set designer, art director, actor*
Hope, Carol J. *pharmacist, researcher, information technology manager*
Hope, Kathy Mitchell *social studies educator*
Hopkins, Brenda Luvenia *social sciences educator, minister*
Hopkins, Budd *artist, writer*
Hopkins, Daniel Nelson *materials engineer*
Hopkins, George Mathews Marks *retired lawyer, engineering executive*
Hopkins, Jan *journalist, newscaster*
Hopkins, Randal Alan *elementary school educator*
Hopkins, Robert Charles *chemistry and biophysics educator*
Hopp, Phillip Edward *gifted and talented educator*
Hoppensteadt, Frank Charles *mathematician, educator, dean*
Hopping, Richard Lee *retired academic administrator*
Horinko, Marianne Lamont *former federal agency administrator*
Horlick, Gary Norman *lawyer, educator*
Horlick, Ruth *photographer*
Horn, Howard M. *labor union administrator, consultant*
Horn, Stephen *retired congressman, political scientist*
Hornak, Thomas *retired electronics company executive*
Hornby, Kenneth Peter *information technology manager*
Hornby, Nick *writer*
Horner, Grace Ann *application developer*
Horner, Matina Souretis *retired academic administrator, corporate financial executive*
Hornyak, Roy Robert *music educator, minister*
Horowitz, Barry Martin *engineering company executive*
Horowitz, Kenneth A. *communications executive, entrepreneur*
Horowitz, Steve Michael *composer*
Horsager, Kent R. *former grain exchange executive*
Horsch, Kathleen Joanne *social services administrator, educator, consultant*
Horsley, Heidi *psychotherapist, educator, radio personality*
Horsman, David A. Elliott *writer, finance company executive, educator*
Horsman, Lenore Lynde (Eleanora Lynde) *voice educator, soprano, actress*
Horstmann, John F. *lawyer*
Horswill, C. Weir *retired obstetrician-gynecologist, photographer*
Horton, Finis Gene *real estate manager*
Horton, Kevin E. *music educator*
Horton, Patricia Mathews *artist, violist and violinist*
Horton, Robert Carlton *geologist*
Hortua, Giovanni *education educator, researcher*

Horwitz, Donald Paul *lawyer*
Horwitz, William J. *treasurer*
Hoskins, Alexander L. (Pete Hoskins) *retired zoological park administrator*
Hoskins, Carol Noll *nursing educator, researcher*
Hoskins, John Howard *retired urologist, educator*
Hosman, Sharon Lee *retired music educator*
Hosokawa, David *advertising executive*
Hotopp, Alice Claudine *music educator, soprano*
Houchin, Wanda Janice *counseling educator*
Hough, Thomas Henry Michael *retired lawyer, educator*
Houghtaling, Pamela Ann *communications professional, writer*
Houghton, Amory, Jr. *former congressman*
Houghton, Katharine *actress*
Houk, Irene Miller *dentist*
Hounsou, Djimon Gaston *actor*
House, Karen Elliott *former publishing executive, editor, journalist*
House, Stephen Eugene *information systems consultant*
Householder, Larry *state official, small business owner*
Houseman, Ann Elizabeth Lord *educational administrator*
Houston, Gloria *author, educator, consultant*
Houston, Whitney *vocalist, recording artist*
Houtz, Duane Talbott *hospital administrator*
Hovendick, James V. *retired business law educator, retired aerospace engineer*
Howard, David *ballet master, school administrator*
Howard, Dean Denton *electrical engineer, researcher, consultant*
Howard, Desmond Kevin *professional football player*
Howard, Donald Searcy *banker*
Howard, Florence Rostron *home economics educator*
Howard, Gary Scott *communications executive*
Howard, George, Jr. *federal judge*
Howard, H. William *information technology executive*
Howard, J. Timothy *former finance company executive*
Howard, James Joseph III *utility company executive*
Howard, James Kenton *academic administrator, journalist*
Howard, James Webb *brokerage house executive, engineer, lawyer*
Howard, Joseph Harvey *retired librarian*
Howard, Michael Eliot *historian, author*
Howard, Robert Elliott *former federal official, consultant, educator*
Howard, Robert Franklin *observatory administrator, astronomer*
Howard, Steve *mathematician, educator*
Howard, Terry Thomas *obstetrician, gynecologist*
Howard-Peebles, Patricia Nell *clinical cytogeneticist*
Howards, Stuart S. *urologist, educator*
Howe, John Prentice III *health facility administrator, physician*
Howell, Deborah S. *career officer*
Howell, Donald Lee *lawyer*
Howell, Joel DuBose *internist, educator*
Howell, Julius Ammons *retired plastic surgeon*
Howell, Margaret Joan (Margaret Howell Ashbaker) *psychology educator, secondary school educator*
Howell, Mary Jean *artist, administrative assistant*
Howell, William Page *real estate company executive*
Hower, Frank Beard, Jr. *retired banker*
Howes, Sophia DuBose *writer*
Howrey, Eugene Philip *retired economics professor, retired statistics professor*
Hoye, Robert Earl *systems science educator*
Hoyt, Mary Finch *writer, media consultant, retired federal official*
Hoyt, Robert F. *lawyer*
Hoyt, Roger Franklin *physicist*
Hricak, Hedvig *radiologist*
Hsieh, Tsui-Hsia *artist, educator*
Hsu, Emilie Tien-Jung *lawyer*
Hsu-Li, Magdalen *singer, poet, painter*
Hu, Esther Ming *astronomer, educator*
Hu, Genlin *biomedical researcher*
Hu, Hongde *mathematics professor*
Hu, Hua-ling Wang *historian*
Hu, Rose Qingyang *communications engineer, educator*
Hu, Weigang *software engineer*
Huang, Chuanyong *materials scientist, researcher*
Huang, Hong *bioinformatics specialist*
Huang, Shouhua *electronics engineer*
Huang, Verna D. *music educator*
Huang, Wei-Cho *research scientist*
Huang, Weihe *behavior analyst, educator*
Hubalek, Shirley Kay *music educator, art educator*
Hubbard, Elizabeth *actress*
Hubbard, Gregory Scott *physicist*
Hubbard, Marguerite *retired elementary school educator*
Hubbard, Thomas C. *former ambassador*
Hubbard, William Keith *former federal agency administrator*
Hubbe, Henry Ernest *financial forecaster, trading manager*
Hubbs, Violet Elizabeth Shamblin *retired filmmaker, retired photographer*
Huchton, Paul Joseph, Jr. *retired pediatrician*
Hudak, Thomas F(rancis) *finance company executive*
Huddle, Franklin Pierce, Jr. *diplomat*
Hudnut, Stewart Skinner *manufacturing executive, lawyer*
Hudson, Alan C.H. *music educator, tropical fruit farmer*
Hudson, Donald J. *stock exchange executive*
Hudson, Franklin Donald *manufacturing executive, consultant*
Hudson, Kate *actress*
Hudson, Katherine Mary *manufacturing executive*
Hudson, Stanton Harold, Jr. *public relations executive, educator, academic administrator*
Hudson, William Jeffrey, Jr. *manufacturing executive*
Huegel, Donna Marie *historian, writer, artist, archivist*

Huening, Christopher T. *music educator*
Huey, Constance Anne Berner *mental health counselor*
Huey, Ward L(igon), Jr. *retired media executive*
Huff, Michael *librarian*
Huffington, Anita *sculptor*
Huffman, Cady *actress*
Huffman, Durward Roy *academic administrator, electrical engineer*
Huffman, James Thomas William *oil industry executive*
Huffman, Janice Kay *education educator, retired elementary and middle school educator*
Huggins, Bob *former college basketball coach*
Hughes, Ann Hightower *retired economist, trade association administrator*
Hughes, Eugene Morgan *university president*
Hughes, Mary Alice *adult education educator, consultant*
Hughes, Michaela Kelly *actress*
Hughes, Patrick M. *federal agency administrator, retired military officer*
Hughes, Paul *elementary school educator*
Hughes, Sue Margaret *retired librarian*
Hughes, Thomas Parke *history professor*
Hughey, Richard Kohlman *writer, lawyer*
Hui, Sai-Hung *emergency medical professional*
Huie, Carol P. *information science educator*
Huja, Sarandeep *orthodontist, educator*
Hulet, Ervin Kenneth *retired nuclear chemist*
Hulett, Jonathon Spencer *investment company executive*
Hull, Edmund J. *former ambassador*
Hull, Jane Dee *former governor, former state legislator*
Hull, McAllister Hobart, Jr. *retired university administrator*
Hultstrand, Donald Maynard *bishop*
Humann, Richard *artist*
Humayun, Mark S. *ophthalmologist, educator*
Hume, Frederick Raymond *electronics executive*
Hume, Susan Rachel *finance educator*
Humenik, John M. *editor, publishing executive*
Humphreys, Robert Russell *lawyer, consultant, arbitrator*
Hundt, Reed Eric *management consultant, former federal agency administrator*
Hung, James Chen *engineering educator, consultant*
Hunnicutt, Victoria Anne Wilson *educational consultant*
Hunstad, Joseph Paul *plastic surgeon, educator*
Hunsucker, Robert Dudley *physicist, electrical engineer, educator, researcher*
Hunt, L. Susan *publishing executive*
Hunt, Mark D. *elementary school educator*
Hunt, Matthew David *music educator*
Hunt, William E., Sr. *retired state supreme court justice*
Hunter, Billy (G. William Hunter) *sports association administrator, lawyer*
Hunter, Frances Ellen Croft *music educator*
Hunter, Holly *actress*
Hunter, Jack Duval *retired lawyer*
Hunter, James Edward *chemist, consultant*
Hunter, J(ames) Paul *literature and language professor, literary critic*
Hunter, Juanita Walters *minister*
Hunter, Kenneth M. *business information systems educator*
Hunter, William David *education educator, consultant*
Hunterton, C. Stanley *lawyer*
Huntington, Lawrence Smith *investment banker*
Huntsman, Lee L. *former academic administrator, director*
Hunzicker, Warren John *retired cardiologist, medical educator, consultant, health facility administrator*
Huo, Bonnie Kwan *artist*
Huo, Jinshan *materials scientist*
Huppe, Alex *public relations executive*
Huras, William David *retired bishop*
Hurd, Byron Thomas *retired publishing executive*
Hurd, Jerrie *writer, photographer*
Hurd, Richard Nelson *pharmaceutical executive*
Hurley, Francis T. *retired archbishop*
Hurley, Kathy Lee *mental health services professional, director*
Huron, Roderick Eugene *minister, writer*
Hurst, Heather *illustrator*
Hurst, Leland Lyle *natural gas company executive*
Hurt, John Vincent *actor*
Hurttgam, Mark Howard *information technology manager*
Husarik, Stephen *music educator*
Husband, Terence J. (Casey Husband) *editor, writer*
Hushen, John Wallace *manufacturing executive*
Huston, Margo *journalist*
Hutcheon, Duncan Elliot *physician educator*
Hutcheon, Linda Ann *English language educator*
Hutchin, Nancy Lee *corporate business development executive*
Hutchins, James Leigh *quality assurance professional*
Hutchins, Mary Louise *retired library director*
Hutchins, Michael *non-profit scientific society administrator, conservation biologist*
Hutchins, Robert Ayer *architectural consultant*
Hutchinson, Michael Philip *education educator*
Hutchison, Barbara Bailey *singer, songwriter*
Huttenback, Robert Arthur *academic administrator, educator*
Hutter, Adolph Matthew, Jr. *cardiologist, educator*
Hutton, Carole Leigh *newspaper editor*
Hutton, Lauren (Mary Laurence Hutton) *model, actress*
Huvos, Andrew *internist, cardiologist, educator*
Huybrechts, Steven Marc *space system technologist*
Huynh, Phung Xuan *artist*
Hwang, Cordelia Jong *retired chemist*
Hwang, Huan-Sheng *engineer*
Hwang, Jason Kao *composer, violinist, music educator*
Hybl, William Joseph *lawyer, foundation administrator*
Hyde, Alan Litchfield *retired lawyer*
Hyde, Lawrence Henry, Jr. *manufacturing executive*

Hyde, M. Deborah *neurosurgeon*
Hyland, David Allen *performing company executive, actor*
Hyland, Geoffrey Fyfe *retired energy executive*
Iacono, James Michael *research and development company executive, nutrition educator*
Iamele, Richard Thomas *retired law librarian*
Iannuzzi Sucich, Michele F. *physician*
Iapalucci, Samuel H. *financial executive*
Iapicca, Kerri Anne *music educator*
Ibanez, Manuel Luis *academic administrator, biologist, educator*
Ichiishi, Tatsuro *economics and mathematics educator*
Idaszak, Jerome Joseph *economic journalist*
Idzik, Daniel Ronald *retired lawyer*
Ienner, Donald S. *former recording industry executive*
Ieyoub, Richard Phillip *lawyer, former state attorney general*
Igbineweka, Andrew Osabuohien *public administration, political science educator*
Iglesias, Maria Estrella *language educator, writer*
Ignagni, Karen *healthcare association executive*
Ignatiev, Alex *physics researcher*
Igoe, Thomas J., Jr. *lawyer*
Ihenacho, David Asonye *campus chaplain*
Ikeda, Tsuguo (Ike Ikeda) *retired social services administrator*
Iklé, Richard Adolph *lawyer*
Ilas, Germina *research scientist*
Iler, Robert *actor*
Illson, James Elias *management consultant*
Imesch, Joseph Leopold *bishop*
Immel, Barbara Kay Kephart *management consultant*
Impellizeri, John C. (Jack Impellizeri) *mathematics educator*
Impellizzeri, Anne Elmendorf *insurance company executive, non-profit executive*
Inci, Ahmet Can *finance educator*
Infante, Frank *musician*
Ingari, Frank A. *communications executive*
Ingberman, Sima *real estate company officer*
Ingersoll, Paul Mills *banker*
Ingle, M(orton) Blakeman *chemicals executive*
Ingraham, Cherie Ann *apparel designer, environmentalist, writer, educator*
Ingram, George Conley *judge*
Inlow, Rush Osborne *chemist*
Innis, Windsor Joe *artist, art educator*
Inouye, Wayne Ryo *computer company executive*
Insalaco-De Nigris, Anna Maria Theresa *middle school educator*
Insana, Arthur Gerard *writer, director*
Inscho, Jean Anderson *retired social worker, landscape artist*
Intilli, Sharon Marie *television director, small business owner*
Iovino, Pamela M. *federal agency administrator*
Ipsen, Grant Ruel *state legislator, insurance and investments professional*
Irish, Thomas Judson *retired plastic surgeon*
Irvin, Loretta Regan *elementary school educator*
Irvin, Michael Jerome *professional football player*
Irvine, John Alexander *lawyer*
Irvine, William Burriss *management consultant*
Irving, George Steven *actor*
Irving, Jeffrey Alan *management consultant, educator, lawyer*
Irving, John Winslow *writer*
Irving, Terry (Edward B. Irving III) *television producer*
Irwin, Bill *actor, clown*
Irwin, Elson Eugene *sportswriter, copy editor*
Irwin, Kenny *professional race car driver*
Irwin, Linda Belmore *public relations/marketing consultant*
Irwin, Mildred Lorine Warrick *library consultant, volunteer*
Isaac, Steven Richard *management consultant*
Isaac, Susan Victoria *literature and language professor, department chairman*
Isaacs, Susan *writer, scriptwriter*
Isenberg, Jane Frances *writer, retired language educator*
Iserson, Kenneth Victor *bioethicist, writer, medical educator*
Ishii, Yoshinori *environmental science educator, science writer*
Iskander, Sylvia Wiese *English literature educator*
Isley, Elizabeth C. H. *commercial display artist, interior designer*
Ismach, Arnold Harvey *retired journalism educator*
Isong, Enó *public health service officer*
Istock, Verne George *retired bank executive*
Itaketo, Umana Thompson *systems and control engineer*
Italiano, Daniel J. *music educator*
Itoh, William H. *former ambassador*
Ivanchenko, Lauren Margaret Dowd *pharmaceutical executive*
Ivanov, Vladimir V. *chemistry professor, researcher*
Ives, Colta Feller *museum curator, educator*
Ivester, M. Douglas (Melvin Douglas Ivester) *retired beverage company executive*
Ivey, Elizabeth Spencer *retired physicist, educator*
Ivey, Judith *actress*
Ivra, Augustine LaFranchiniax *pre-school educator*
Ivry, Alfred Lyon *philosophy educator, historian*
Ix, Robert Edward *food products executive*
Izenstark, Joseph Louis *retired radiologist, physician, educator*
Jabs, Aura Lee *minister, educator*
Jacir, Emily *photographer, conceptual artist*
Jack, Patricia Ann *assistant principal*
Jackman, Hugh *actor*
Jack-Moore, Phyllis *strategist, educational consultant*
Jackson, Brian Matthew *musician, educator*
Jackson, Charles Ian *writer, consultant*
Jackson, David Huntsman *retired cardiologist*
Jackson, Deborah Cheryl *mathematician*
Jackson, Eric Michael *marketing executive, writer, media specialist*
Jackson, Felicity Anne *performing arts organization administrator*
Jackson, Hunter *health products executive*

Kaplan, Jerry (S. Jerrold Kaplan) *former electronics company executive*
Kaplan, Leonard Eugene *accountant*
Kaplan, Phyllis *artist, composer*
Kaplan, Richard James *film producer, educator, film director, consultant, scriptwriter*
Kaplan, Rick (Richard N. Kaplan) *former broadcast executive*
Kaplan, Robert B. *linguistics educator, consultant, researcher*
Kaplan, Selna L. *medical educator*
Kaplowitz, Neil *gastroenterologist, educator*
Kapner, Lewis *lawyer*
Kapner, Lori *marketing professional*
Kapnick, Richard Bradshaw *lawyer*
Kapnick, Stewart *investment banker*
Kappner, Augusta Souza *academic administrator*
Kaprielian, Walter *advertising executive*
Kapur, Vishesh *medical educator, epidemiologist*
Karalekas, Anne *media executive*
Karalis, John Peter *computer company executive, lawyer*
Karayan, Ani A. *psychologist, consultant*
Karayanis, Plato Steven *opera company executive*
Kari, Daven Michael *English professor, religious studies educator*
Karim, Mohammed Rezaul *mathematics professor*
Karim, Muhammad Bazlul *political scientist, educator*
Karmaker, Haran *electronics engineer*
Karnaugh, Maurice *computer scientist, educator*
Karnazes, Dean (Constantine Karnazes) *endurance athlete, writer*
Karns, Elizabeth (Libby) A. *retired daycare administrator*
Karol, Michael Alan *editor*
Karp, Gerald Charles *biologist, educator, writer*
Karp, Naomi Katherine *United States government administrator*
Karp, Rosanne *oncology and women's health nurse*
Karplus, Paul Andrew *biochemistry educator*
Karr, Stephen William *retired judge*
Karson, Samuel *psychologist, educator*
Kartchner, Gayla L. *elementary school educator*
Kasami, Tadao *information science educator*
Kasdan, Lawrence Edward *film director, screenwriter*
Kaser, David *retired librarian, educator, consultant*
Kashnow, Richard A. *electronics executive*
Kasich, John R. *former congressman*
Kasick, Michele Lee *vocational school educator*
Kaskowitz, Edwin *social services executive*
Kaslow, Florence Whiteman *psychologist, educator, family business consultant*
Kaspar, Frances Wolf *music educator*
Kasperson, Roger *geographer, educator*
Kasprzak, Lucian Alexander *physicist, researcher, materials scientist*
Kass, David Norman *accountant, lawyer*
Kass, Jerome Allan *writer*
Kassewitz, Ruth Eileen Blower *retired public relations executive*
Kaster, Laura A. *lawyer*
Kastner, Marc Aaron *physics professor*
Kastor, Frank Sullivan *language educator*
Katen, Karen L. *pharmaceutical company executive*
Katinsky, Steven *communications company executive*
Kato, Tomiko *artist*
Katona, Peter Geza *biomedical engineer, educator*
Katz, Alex *artist*
Katz, Leandro *artist, filmmaker*
Katz, Marc D. *apparel executive*
Katz, Sanford Noah *lawyer, educator*
Katz, William Loren *author*
Katzenbach, Nicholas deBelleville *former United States attorney general*
Kauffman, David Lin *lawyer*
Kauffman, Marta *producer, writer*
Kaufman, David Joseph *lawyer*
Kaufman, Irving *retired engineering educator*
Kaufman, Stephen Lawrence *radiologist, educator*
Kaufmann, Charles Leonard *musician, composer*
Kaumeyer, Linda Louise *lawyer, educator*
Kavalek, Lubomir *chess expert*
Kavanaugh, Frank James *film producer, educator*
Kavner, Julie *actress*
Kavovit, Barbara *entrepreneur*
Kay, Aman B. *language educator, translator*
Kaye, Debra *composer, music educator*
Kaye, Judy *actress*
Kaye, Lori *actress, news reporter, producer*
Kaye, Stuart Martin *lawyer*
Kaylan, Howard Lawrence *musical entertainer, screenwriter, composer*
Kayser, Brian D. *retired psychologist, writer*
Kaz, Nathaniel *sculptor*
Kazan, Alexandra Khan *photographer, web site designer*
Ke, Yong *medical educator, researcher*
Keala, Francis Ahloy *security executive*
Kealey, Erin *philosopher*
Kean, Thomas Howard *former academic administrator, former governor*
Keane, Jeffry Robert *secondary school educator*
Kearns, James Joseph *artist*
Kearns, Richard P. *diversified financial services company executive*
Keating, Charles *actor*
Keatinge, Robert Reed *lawyer*
Keaton, John J. *artist*
Keaty, Robert Burke *lawyer, business consultant*
Keech, Elowyn Ann *interior designer*
Keegan, James Joseph *entrepreneur*
Keeler, James Leonard *food products executive*
Keeler, William Henry Cardinal *cardinal*
Keeley, Larry *innovation strategist*
Keeling, J(ohn) Michael *lawyer, trade association executive*
Keen, Constantine *retired manufacturing executive*
Keen, Victor F. *lawyer*
Keenan, Anthony Lee *trucking executive*
Keene-Burgess, Ruth Frances *military official*
Keengwe, Jared *education educator*
Keeter, Lynn Carpenter *language educator*
Keeton, Melinda Denise *music educator*
Keevil, Philip Clement *investment banker*
Kehlmann, Robert *artist, critic*

Kehn, Joann Suchocki *psychologist*
Keil, M. David *retired international association executive*
Keill, Stuart Langdon *psychiatrist*
Keim, Betty Lou *actress, literary consultant*
Keir, Gerald Janes *banker*
Keith, Brian Thomas *automotive executive*
Keith, Robert William *banker*
Keith, Toby (Toby Keith Covel) *country singer, songwriter, producer*
Keith, William Douglas *lawyer*
Kelalis, Barbara Anna Lisa *interior designer*
Kelleher, Timothy John *retired publishing company executive*
Keller, Paul *advertising executive, researcher*
Keller, Roberta Lynn *physician, researcher*
Keller, Thomas Collins Stevenson III *education educator*
Kelley, A. Benjamin *writer, educator, consultant*
Kelley, Edward Allen *publisher*
Kelley, James Francis *lawyer*
Kelley, Joseph E. *career officer*
Kelley, Kathryn B. *actress*
Kelley, Kevin H. *insurance company executive*
Kelley, Larry Dale *retired army officer*
Kelley, Patrick Alan *neurologist, educator*
Kelley, Sheila Seymour *public relations consultant*
Kellner, Irwin L. *economist*
Kellner, Jamie *broadcast executive*
Kellner, Lawrence W. (Larry Kellner) *air and aerospace transportation company executive*
Kellogg, Joseph K., Jr. *military career officer*
Kellogg, Peter R. *securities dealer*
Kelly, Anthony Odrian *textiles executive*
Kelly, Carol A. *travel company executive*
Kelly, Sister Dorothy Ann *academic administrator*
Kelly, James Andrew *former federal agency administrator, former policy research executive*
Kelly, Lucie Stirm Young *nursing educator*
Kelly, Michael Joseph, II, *publishing executive, investment company executive*
Kelly, Nancy Folden *art association administrator*
Kelly, Pamela B. *lawyer*
Kelly, Robert D *energy executive*
Kelly, Timothy E. *communications executive*
Kelly, Timothy Johnston *secondary school educator*
Kelm, Bonnie G. *art museum director, educator, art appraiser, consultant*
Kelso, John Hodgson *retired federal agency administrator*
Kelton, Elmer Stephen *novelist*
Kemper, John Dustin *mechanical engineering educator*
Kempf, Donald G., Jr. *retired lawyer*
Kempner, Maximilian Walter *dean, lawyer*
Kemprecos, Paul *writer*
Kendall, Charles Terry *librarian*
Kendall, Harry Wesley *playwright, writer*
Kenderian, Shant *engineer, consultant*
Kendig, William Lamar *retired federal official, accountant*
Kendrick, Budd Leroy *psychologist*
Kendrick, Kerry *military officer*
Kendzior, Robert Joseph *marketing executive*
Kenesson, Frank Girault *history educator, writer*
Kennedy, Charles *retired neuroscientist, retired medical educator*
Kennedy, Eugene Cullen *psychology professor, writer*
Kennedy, Harold Edward *lawyer*
Kennedy, Jerrie Ann Preston *public relations executive*
Kennedy, JoAnn *artist, educator*
Kennedy, Kevin Curtis *sports commentator, former professional baseball team manager*
Kennedy, Leo Raymond *engineering executive*
Kennedy, Linda Dale *music educator, musician*
Kennedy, Megan Catherine *music educator*
Kennedy, Thomas J. *lawyer*
Kennedy, William F. *retired military officer*
Kennerly, David Hume *photographer, writer, producer*
Kennett, Lee Boone, Jr. *historian, educator*
Kenney, John Michel *architect*
Kenny, Deborah *marketing professional, finance educator*
Kenny, Robert Wade *social sciences and humanities educator, writer*
Kenrich, John Lewis *retired lawyer*
Kenrick, Douglas Thomas *psychology professor, writer*
Kenseth, Matt *race car driver*
Kent, Donald Charles *retired physician*
Kent, Georgia L. *obstetrician, gynecologist, healthcare executive, educator*
Kent, Philip *communications executive*
Kenworthy, William Eugene *judge*
Kenyon, Daphne Anne *economist*
Keohane, Nannerl Overholser *political scientist, academic administrator*
Kerber, Ronald Lee *industrial corporation executive*
Kercher, David Max *retired mechanical engineer*
Kercheval, John William III *finance professor, aerospace and defense executive, vulture capitalist, former investment banker*
Kerdok, Amy Elizabeth *biomedical engineer, researcher*
Kerik, Bernard B. *former police commissioner*
Kerins, Francis Joseph *college president*
Kern, Charles William *retired academic administrator, chemist, educator*
Kern, Irving John *retired food company executive*
Kernan, Barbara Desind *federal official*
Kernan, Joseph Eugene III *former governor*
Kerney, Yolonda V. *music historian*
Kerns, Virginia B. *anthropologist, writer*
Kerr, Frederick Hohmann *retired health facility administrator, retired academic administrator*
Kerstann, Kimberly Fowler *epidemiologist, researcher*
Kertz, Hubert Leonard *telephone company executive*
Kerwin, Walter Thomas, Jr. *career officer, consultant*
Kesseler, Matthew John *librarian*
Kesselring, Debbie Anne *systems engineer*
Kessler, Keith *retired computer scientist*
Kessler, Roslyn Marie *financial analyst*
Ketchum, Irene Frances *library supporter*

Ketels, Gerhard H. *lawyer*
Kettel, Edward Joseph *retired oil industry executive*
Kettelkamp, Donald Benjamin *retired orthopedist*
Keune, Russell Victor *retired architect*
Kevles, Bettyann Holtzmann *writer, historian, educator*
Key, Ted *cartoonist*
Keyes, Alan L. *radio and talk show host, former federal government official*
Keyes, Joan Ross Rafter *education educator, writer*
Keys, John W. III *former federal agency administrator*
Khachemoune, Amor *physician*
Khan, Ahmed Mohiuddin *insurance company executive*
Khan, Arfa *radiologist, educator*
Khan, Aurangzeb *engineering educator*
Khan, Javed I. *engineering educator*
Khan, Navaid *pediatrician, researcher*
Kharbanda, Kusum K. *biologist, educator*
Khasawneh, Shadi Turki *computer scientist*
Khatib, Riad *infectious diseases physician, department head*
Khavari, Khalil Akhtar *psychology professor*
Khisti, Rahul Tryambak *neuropharmacologist, researcher*
Khiterer, Victoria M. *historian*
Khoury, Kenneth F. *lawyer*
Khuong, Loc Huu *corporate financial executive*
Khuri, Fadlo Raja *oncologist, educator*
Khvost-Vostrikova, Natalia S. *art educator, consultant*
Kibler, Samuel *music educator*
Kice, John Edward *engineer, educator, consultant*
Kidder, Margot (Margaret Ruth Kidder) *actress*
Kidder, Tracy (John Tracy Kidder) *writer*
Kiechle, Frederick Leonard *pathologist*
Kiefer, Renata Gertrud *epidemiologist, pediatrician, economist, management consultant*
Kienitz, LaDonna Trapp *lawyer, librarian, municipal official*
Kierscht, Marcia Selland *academic administrator, psychologist*
Kiesler, Charles Adolphus *psychologist, academic administrator*
Kilbane, Kathleen Ann *stage manager*
Kilborn, Toni Sweatt *insurance agent, consultant*
Kilbourn, William Douglas, Jr. *law educator*
Kilby, Sarah L. *mathematician, educator*
Kiley, Kevin C. *career military officer*
Killebrew, Betty Rackley *language educator*
Killeen, Michael John *lawyer*
Killeen, Thomas Francis *assistant principal*
Killian, William Paul *manufacturing executive*
Kilmann, Ralph Herman *business educator*
Kilpatrick, James Jackson, Jr. *columnist, writer*
Kilts, James M. *investment banker, former consumer products company executive*
Kim, Charles Wesley *microbiology educator*
Kim, Daniel Dae *actor*
Kim, Ellen Ye *music educator*
Kim, Hyunjoong *education educator*
Kim, Marianne Weiss *humanities educator*
Kim, Won Gyu *research scientist*
Kim, Wonsuk *mechanical engineer, researcher*
Kimball, Mary Holt *retired secondary school educator*
Kimball, Richard Arthur, Jr. *retired lawyer*
Kimbrell, Grady Ned *writer, educator, retired school system administrator*
Kimbrough, Pamela Seed *mathematics and chemistry professor, finance educator*
Kim-Farley, Robert James *epidemiologist, educator*
Kimmel, Mark *author, venture capital company executive*
Kin, Carol Joan (Ramaska) *elementary school educator*
Kincaid, Jamaica *writer*
Kincaid, Marilyn Coburn *medical educator*
Kincaid, Steven Randall *marketing professional*
Kindberg, Shirley Jane *pediatrician*
Kinder, David Allen *secondary school educator*
Kindseth, Anne *art educator, researcher*
King, Alfred Meehan *financial executive*
King, Algin Braddy *retired marketing educator*
King, Cynthia Bregman *writer*
King, David Alan *ecologist*
King, David Roy *lawyer*
King, Edward William *retired transportation executive*
King, Glen (Lenard Glen King) *broadcasting educator, composer*
King, Gundar Julian *retired dean*
King, Imogene M. *retired nursing educator*
King, James Calvin *mathematics educator*
King, James Forrest, Jr. *lawyer*
King, Jane Cudlip Coblentz *volunteer educator*
King, Jason Eric *medical educator, researcher*
King, Jeff *dog musher*
King, John Charles Peter *editor, writer*
King, John Ethelbert, Jr. *retired academic administrator*
King, Larry J. *communications educator*
King, Larry L. *playwright, actor*
King, Marva E. *environmental scientist*
King, Michael Howard *lawyer*
King, Patricia P. *music educator, director*
King, Rebecca J. *lawyer, consultant*
King, Regina *actress*
King, Renee Regan *music educator*
King, Robert Lucien *retired lawyer*
King, Rosalyn Mercita *social sciences educator, researcher, psychologist*
King, Sheldon Selig *health facility administrator, educator*
King, Susan Bennett *retired glass company executive*
King, William *sculptor*
King, William Collins *retired oil industry executive*
Kingera, Richard Nick *music educator*
Kingsbery, Walton Waits, Jr. *retired accounting firm executive*
Kingston, Maxine Hong *writer, educator*
Kingstein, Jonah *painter*
Kinnear, Greg *actor, film producer*

Kinney, Jeanne Kawelolani *English studies educator, writer*
Kinslow, Margie Ann *volunteer*
Kinzey, Bertram York, Jr.
Kinzie, Jeannie Jones *radiation oncologist, nuclear medicine physician*
Kipke, Michele Diane *education and social services administrator, former hospital director*
Kipniss, Robert *artist*
Kipniss MacDonald, Betty Ann *artist, educator*
Kipper, Barbara Levy *wholesale distribution executive*
Kirby, Odell *retired small business owner, newswriter, writer*
Kirchner, Lisa Beth *actress, vocalist*
Kirchner, Peter Thomas *nuclear medicine physician, educator, consultant*
Kirk, Carmen Zetler *data processing executive*
Kirk, Mark D. *biologist, educator*
Kirk, Rea Helene (Rea Helene Glazer) *special education educator*
Kirkby, Maurice Anthony *oil industry executive*
Kirkland, Geoffrey Alan *motion picture production designer*
Kirkland, Rebecca Trent *endocrinologist*
Kirkland, Richard Ide (Rik), Jr. *magazine editor*
Kirkland, Starr Melanie *librarian, writer*
Kirkland, Virgil Wayne *electrical engineer*
Kirkpatrick, Charles Harvey *immunologist, researcher*
Kirkpatrick, Garland Penn *retired pediatrician*
Kirkpatrick, James Joseph *psychologist*
Kirkwood, John *medical association administrator*
Kirsch, Roslyn Ruth *artist, educator, painter, printmaker*
Kirsch, Thorsten *cell biologist, educator*
Kirschenmann, Henry George, Jr. *management consultant, retired government official, accountant*
Kirshbaum, Jon Alan *systems analyst, consultant, retired systems administrator*
Kirshbaum, Laurence J. *literary agent, former publishing executive*
Kirshbaum, Lawrence G. *investment company executive*
Kirshenbaum, Kent *chemist, educator*
Kirsteuer, Ernst Karl Eberhart *biologist, curator*
Kiselik, Paul Howard *manufacturing executive*
Kiser, Nagiko Sato *retired librarian*
Kisiel, Ida Marie *education educator, writer*
Kiss, István Z. *chemist, researcher*
Kiss, Ronald K. *naval architect*
Kissinger, Henry Alfred *international consulting company executive, former secretary of state*
Kistiakowsky, Vera *physical researcher, educator*
Kiszka, Sonia Ann *nurse practitioner, educator*
Kitagawa, Audrey Emiko *retired lawyer*
Kitchen, Paul Howard *hockey historian*
Kitt, Eartha Mae *actress, singer*
Kitt, Walter *psychiatrist*
Kittredge, Nancy *artist*
Kivell, Wayne M. *music educator, choral conductor*
Kiziltas, Semiha *research scientist, engineer*
Klaehn, John R. *chemist, researcher*
Klaehne, Eberhard O.W. *pharmaceutical executive, chemist*
Klafter, Cary Ira *lawyer*
Klamon, Lawrence Paine *lawyer*
Klampe, Craig Allen *composer*
Klarich, David John *lobbyist, lawyer*
Klatell, Robert Edward *lawyer*
Klauberg, William Joseph *information technology executive*
Klauck, Judith Lynn *middle school educator*
Klaus, Charles *retired lawyer*
Klayman, Larry Elliott *lawyer, legal association administrator*
Kleczka, Gerald Daniel *former congressman*
Kleeman, Richard *mathematics professor*
Kleespies, Gavin W. *historian*
Kleiman, Alan Boyd *artist*
Kleiman, Bernard *lawyer*
Klein, Charlotte Conrad *public relations executive*
Klein, Charlotte Feuerstein *art consultant*
Klein, Chuck *retired private investigator, writer*
Klein, Edward *writer, producer*
Klein, Eugene *lawyer*
Klein, Ida *elementary school educator*
Klein, James Edgar *actor*
Klein, Linda Ann *lawyer*
Klein, Lynn Ellen *artist*
Klein, Mary Ann *special education educator*
Klein, Paul E. *lawyer*
Klein, Stephen Thomas *performing arts executive*
Klein, Susan Elaine *librarian*
Kleinberg, Howard J. *newswriter*
Kleiner, Janellyn Pickering *librarian*
Klein-Seetharaman, Judith *biochemist*
Kleinsorge, William Peter *metallurgical engineer*
Klema, Ernest Donald *nuclear physicist, educator*
Klement, Vera *artist*
Klemp, Barbara Anne *music educator*
Klett, Gordon A. *retired savings and loan association executive*
Kliebhan, Sister M(ary) Camille *academic administrator*
Kline, J. Peter *hotel executive*
Kline, Leona Ruth *nurse, volunteer*
Kline, Norman Douglas *retired judge*
Kline-Koenig, Barbara A. *medical/surgical nurse*
Kling, Vincent George *architect*
Klinger, Mary K. *performing company executive, educator*
Klinghoffer, Judith Apter *historian, consultant*
Klippert, Richard Hobdell, Jr. *engineering executive*
Kliszus, Edward A., Jr. *school system administrator*
Klitenic, Jason *lawyer*
Klohn, Earle Jardine *retired engineering company executive, consultant*
Klopfleisch, Stephanie Squance *social services agency administrator*
Klotman, Robert Howard *retired music educator*
Klott, David Lee *lawyer*
Klotter, Eleanor Irene *retired social worker*
Kloves, Steven *film director, scriptwriter*
Knake, Carina Ann *adult education educator*
Knapp, Howard Raymond *internist, clinical pharmacologist*

Lasser, Lawrence J. *former investment company executive*
Lassman, Adrienne *community volunteer*
Lasuchin, Michael *artist, retired art educator*
Lat, David B. *former assistant US attorney, online-journalist, editor, blogger*
Latham, Tamara Beryl *chemist, researcher*
Lathe, Garrett W. *music educator*
Lathrope, Daniel John *law educator*
Latimer, James Harold *musician, conductor, composer, music educator*
Latiolais, Minnie Fitzgerald *retired nurse, health facility administrator*
La Torre, Carissa Danitza *counselor*
Latta, George Haworth III *neonatal/perinatal nurse practitioner*
Latta, Jean Carolyn *financial analyst, chemist*
Lau, Joanna T. *information technology executive*
Lauber, Christine Anne *athletic trainer*
Lauderdale, Vance, Jr. *anesthesiologist*
Laudone, Anita Helene *lawyer*
Lauer, Jeanette Carol *dean, history educator, writer*
Lauer, Len J. *former telecommunications executive*
Laughlin, Daniel Charles *ecologist*
Laughlin, Louis Gene *economic analyst, consultant*
Lauper, Cyndi *musician*
Laurent, Pierre-Henri *history professor*
Laurenzo, Vincent Dennis *industrial management company executive*
Lauterbach, Edward Charles *psychiatric educator*
Lauterstein, Joseph *cardiologist*
LaVelle, Arthur *anatomy educator*
LaVerdiere, Claudette Marie *nun, head of religious order*
Lavey, Warren G. *lawyer*
Lavezzi, John Charles *retired art history educator, archaeologist*
Lavidge, Robert James *marketing research executive*
Lavin, Sylvia *architecture educator*
Lavin, Terrence J. *lawyer*
Lavington, Michael Richard *venture capital company executive*
Lavorato, Louis A. *retired state supreme court justice*
Lawer, Betsy *banker, small business owner, vintner, director*
Lawler, John A. *publishing executive*
Lawless, Michael Rhodes *pediatrics educator*
Lawless, Thomas William *lawyer*
Lawlor, LynnAnn Jennifer *reading educator*
Lawrence, David Long *radiologist*
Lawrence, Glenn Robert *arbitrator, mediator, lawyer*
Lawrence, John Patrick *statistician*
Lawrence, Margery H. (Margery Hulings Lawrence) *marketing consultant*
Lawrence, Mary Josephine (Josie Lawrence) *artist, retired library official*
Lawrence, Raymona Holloway *elementary school educator*
Lawrence, Ruth *writer, illustrator*
Lawrence, Sally Clark *retired academic administrator*
Lawrie, J. Michael *former software company executive*
Lawson, Carolina Donadio *language educator, translator*
Lawson, John Joseph *vocational educator, consultant*
Lawson, William Bradford *psychiatrist*
Lawton, Kelly Marie Lee *secondary school educator, performing arts educator*
Lax, Philip *land developer, space planner*
Layne, James Nathaniel *vertebrate biologist*
Layton, Robert Glenn *radiologist*
Layton, William George *retired management consultant, human resources executive, import/export company executive*
Lazar, Zoe L. *psychologist*
Lazaran, Frank *former retail executive*
Lazovsky, Lorna Deane *minister*
Lazzarini, Robert *sculptor*
Lea, Lorenzo Bates *lawyer*
Lea, Perry Victor *computer engineer*
Leach, Howard H. *former ambassador, former health care products company executive*
Leachman, Cloris *actress*
Leachtenauer, Jon Clark *optical scientist*
Leader, Joyce E. *ambassador*
Leahy, Jeannette (Jeannette Oliver Leahy Tinen Kaehler) *actress*
Leahy, T. Liam *business development and technology investor*
Lear, M. Kathleen *artist, music educator, small business owner*
Learned, Michael *actress*
Leary, Denis *actor, comedian*
Leary, Thomas Barrett *lawyer, former federal agency administrator*
Leath, Cheryl Lynn *retired pre-school educator, poet, painter*
Leath, Kenneth Thomas *plant pathologist, educator, agriculturist, consultant*
Leather, Victoria Potts *college librarian*
Leatherdale, Douglas West *insurance company executive*
Leavelle, Tommy Lee *mathematics professor*
Leavy, Herbert Theodore *publisher*
Leazer, William *retired biomedical consultant*
Lebbin, Carole Sue *artist*
Le Blanc, Alice Isabelle *academic administrator*
LeBlanc, Hugh Linus *political science professor, consultant*
LeBlanc, Jean Eva *writer, poet, educator*
LeBlanc, Leonard Joseph *retired electronics company executive*
LeBlanc, Matt (Matthew Steven LeBlanc) *actor*
LeBlond, Paul Henri *oceanographer, educator*
Lebon, Rachel L. *musician, educator*
LeBrecht, Thelma Jane Mossman *retired reporter*
le Carré, John (David John Moore Cornwell) *author*
Lecat, Robert J. *retired aeronautical engineer*
Lederer, Edith Madelon *journalist*
Lederer, Peter David *lawyer*
Lederman, Ira Seth *insurance company executive, lawyer*
Lederman, Leon Max *physicist, researcher*

Ledford, Brenda Kay *writer*
Ledford, Frank Finley, Jr. *retired surgeon, military officer*
Ledford, Janet Marie Smalley *real estate appraiser, consultant*
Ledogar, Stephen J. *retired diplomat*
Ledwig, Donald Eugene *association executive, consultant, retired broadcast executive, military officer*
Lee, Allen Michael *science educator*
Lee, Anita Combs *writer, speaker, consultant*
Lee, Bobby *actor, comedian*
Lee, Chava Cherta *psychotherapist, consultant*
Lee, Christopher Frank Carandini *actor, writer, singer*
Lee, Corinne Adams *retired English teacher*
Lee, Dai-Keong *composer*
Lee, Dan M. *retired state supreme court chief justice*
Lee, Donna A. *telecommunications industry executive*
Lee, Eunice *music educator*
Lee, Harrison Hon *librarian, consultant*
Lee, Jonathan Owen *financial services company executive, lawyer*
Lee, Joseph William *sales executive*
Lee, Magdalene *corporate financial executive*
Lee, Mordecai *political scientist, educator*
Lee, Pali Jae (Polly Jae Stead Lee) *retired librarian, writer*
Lee, Richard Kenneth *software company executive*
Lee, Ryan S. *dental association administrator*
Lee, Sandra Ann *investment company executive*
Lee, Sarena Jean *public health service officer*
Lee, Soh Yeong *music educator*
Lee, Soo-Hoon *human resources specialist*
Lee, Steve Chi Kong *bank executive*
Lee, Tamara Denise *health facility administrator, educator*
Lee, Thomas H. *investment company executive*
Lee, Tonïa Reneé *entertainer, former government agent, educator*
Lee, Wayne J. *lawyer*
Lee, William Franklin III *composer, musician*
Lee, Winnie Sita *dentist*
Lee, Won-Chan *psychometrician*
Leeds, Douglas Brecker *advertising executive, theater producer*
Leeds, Nancy Brecker *sculptor, lyricist*
Leeper, Kathleen Marie *elementary school educator*
Lefever, Bryce Edwin *psychologist*
Leff, Ilene J(afnel) *corporate executive, federal official*
Leff, Joseph Norman *yarn manufacturing company executive*
Lefferts, George *television producer*
Legge, Charles Alexander *federal judge*
Leggett, Roberta Jean (Bobbi Leggett) *retired social services administrator*
Lehman, Jeffrey Sean *former academic administrator*
Lehman, Joan Alice *real estate company executive*
Lehman, John F., Jr. *manufacturing executive*
Lehmann, Doris Elizabeth *retired elementary school educator*
Lehmann, (A) Spencer *retired chemist, retired chemical engineer*
Lehmkuhl, Lynn *publishing executive*
Lehner-Quam, Alison Lynn *library administrator*
Lehrer, Leonard *artist, educator*
Lehrer, Steven *health products executive*
Leiber, Judith Maria *designer, manufacturer*
Leibler, Kenneth Robert *finance company executive*
Leibowitt, Sol David *lawyer*
Leichtman, Maria Luisa *mental health services professional*
Leigh, Irene Wolff *psychologist*
Leigh, Richard E., Jr. *lawyer*
Leigh, Vincenta M. *health administrator*
Leijonhufvud, Axel Stig Bengt *economics professor*
Leimkuhler, Gerard Joseph *diversified financial services company executive*
Leininger, Madeleine Monica *nursing educator, consultant, retired anthropologist, editor, writer, theorist*
Leipzig, Arthur *photographer, retired educator*
Leitzel, Joan Ruth *retired academic administrator*
Lelyveld, Joseph Salem *former newspaper editor, news correspondent, writer*
LeMarbe, Edward S. *marketing executive, engineering executive*
Lemard, Glendene Anthea Nuala *research scientist*
Lemay, Gary B. *secondary school educator, psychologist, consultant*
Lembark, Connie Wertheimer *art consultant*
Lemesis, Guntis Victor *human resources specialist*
Lemke, James Underwood *physicist*
Lemke, Shawn G. *secondary school educator*
Lemlich, Robert *chemical engineer, educator*
Lenhart, Cynthia Rae *conservation organization executive*
Lennix, Harry Joseph III *actor*
Lennon, Joseph Luke *retired academic administrator, priest*
Lennox, Donald D(uane) *retired automotive and housing components company executive*
Lennox, William James, Jr. *retired military officer*
Leno, Jay (James Douglas Muir Leno) *talk show host, comedian, author*
Lenters, John Derick *geoscience educator*
Lenz, Henry Paul *management consultant*
León, Tania Justina *composer, music director, pianist*
Leonard, Hasse A. *psychologist, educator*
Leonard, J. Wayne *energy executive*
Leonard, James Kevin *mechanical engineer*
Leonard, Sugar Ray (Ray Charles Leonard) *retired professional boxer*
Leone, William J. *former prosecutor, lawyer*
Leong, Stephanie Mei *financial planner*
Leonhardt, Thomas Wilburn *librarian, library director*
Leoni, Tea (Elizabeth Tea Pantaleoni) *actress*
Leon Rivera, Aida I. *language educator*
Lepage, Robert *actor, playwright*
Lepeley, Maria-Teresa *educational association administrator*

L'Eplattenier, Nora Sweeny Hickey *nursing educator*
Lepley, Rick Allen *consumer products company executive*
Lepore, Dawn Gould *Internet company executive*
Leppard, Stephanie Jean *systems analyst, artist*
Lepping, Ronald P. *astrophysicist, researcher*
Lerner, Alan Charles *financial market economist, educator*
Lerner, Beth M. *non-profit consultant*
Lerner, Herbert J. *tax consultant*
Lerner, Laurence M. *college administrator*
Lerner, Vladimir Semion *computer scientist, educator*
LeRoy, G. Palmer *art dealer*
Leschly, Jan *retired consumer products company executive*
Lescroart, John Thomas *writer, composer, singer*
Le Shana, David Charles *retired academic administrator*
Lesher, John Lee, Jr. *consulting services company executive*
Lesiak, Karen Ann *librarian*
Lesko, Harry Joseph *transportation executive*
Leslie, Alfred *painter, filmmaker*
Leslie, John Webster, Jr., (Jack Leslie) *communications company executive*
Lester, Alicia Louise *financial analyst*
Lester, Julius B. *author*
Lester, Mark Charles *neurosurgeon*
Lester, Robin Dale *education educator, writer, former headmaster*
Lester, Susan E. *bank executive*
Lester, Virginia Laudano *academic administrator*
Lethem, Jonathan Allen *writer*
Leupold, Herbert August *physicist*
LeVasseur, Lee Allan *artist*
Levaux, Hugh Pierre *pharmaceutical executive, consultant*
Leveille, Gilbert Antonio *food products executive*
Level, Leon Jules *investor, director*
Leven, Linda *application developer, writer, actress, model, artist*
Levenback, Karen L. *librarian, archivist, educator, writer, editor*
Levens, Dorsey (Herbert Levens) *professional football player*
Levenson, Marc David *optics and lasers specialist, editor*
Leventhal, Ellen Iris *portfolio manager*
Leventhal, Ruth *retired parasitology educator, university official*
Levering, Arthur Chester *composer*
Levermore, Monique A. *psychologist, educator*
Levi, Josef Alan *artist*
Levick, Richard Scott *communications executive, lawyer, consultant, educator*
Levin, Alan Scott *pathologist, allergist, immunologist, lawyer*
Levin, Arnold Murray *social worker, psychotherapist, educator*
Levin, Gerald M. *former media and entertainment company executive*
Levin, Jack *physician, educator, biomedical investigator*
Levin, Michael Stuart *steel company executive*
Levin, Morton D(avid) *artist, printmaker, educator*
Levin, Roger Michael *lawyer*
Levine, Alan *lawyer*
Levine, Arthur Elliott *former academic administrator, educator*
Levine, Jack *artist*
Levins, John Raymond *investment advisor, educator, management consultant*
Levinsky, Frieda Libby *language educator*
Levinsohn, Gary *producer*
Levinson, Herbert Sherman *civil and transportation engineer*
Levinson, Kathy *former investment company executive, philanthropist*
Levinson, Kenneth S. *lawyer, corporate financial executive*
Levinson, Marina *information technology executive*
Levinson, Peter Joseph *retired lawyer*
Levitas, Miriam C. Strickman *documentary filmmaker*
Levitt, Seymour Herbert *radiologist, educator*
Levy, David *retired lawyer, insurance company executive, consultant*
Levy, Gad *atmospheric scientist, educator, statistician*
Levy, Leslie Ann *application developer*
Levy, Louis Edward *retired accounting firm executive*
Levy, Mark *art educator*
Levy, Robert Edward *retired management consultant*
Levy, Valery *publisher*
Lew, Roger Alan *manufacturing executive*
Lewie, Reva Goodwin *artist, educator*
Lewin, Tamar (Katherine Lewin) *reporter*
Lewinsky, Monica *handbag designer, television personality*
Lewis, Andrew Lindsay, Jr., (Drew Lewis) *former transportation and natural resources executive*
Lewis, Anthony *columnist, educator*
Lewis, Arthur Dee *aerospace transportation executive*
Lewis, Brian Kreglow *retired physiologist, computer scientist*
Lewis, Brock *investment company executive*
Lewis, Carl (Frederick Carlton Lewis) *Olympic track and field athlete*
Lewis, Charles Leonard *psychologist*
Lewis, Douglas *retired art historian*
Lewis, Emanuel Raymond *historian, psychologist, retired librarian*
Lewis, Floyd Wallace *former electric utility executive*
Lewis, George Ralph *consumer goods company executive*
Lewis, Hunter *investment advisor, writer*
Lewis, James Kevin *music educator*
Lewis, James Lee, Jr. *actuary*
Lewis, Leslie Joy *music company executive, consultant*
Lewis, Martin Edward *transportation executive, oil trader, foreign government concessionary*
Lewis, Martin R. *paper company executive, consultant*

Lewis, Ned Lehmon *secondary school educator*
Lewis, Perry Joshua *investment banker*
Lewis, Richard *actor, comedian*
Lewis, Rita Hoffman *plastic products manufacturing company executive*
Lewis, Russell T. *publishing executive*
Lewis, Samuel Winfield *retired federal agency administrator, retired diplomat*
Lewis, Sharyn Lee *sculptor*
Lewis, Suford *computer scientist, consultant*
Lewis, Victor Wayne *minister*
Lewitt, Miles Martin *computer engineering company executive*
Li, Gong *actress*
Li, Jian-Yang *research scientist*
Li, Lihong *electrical engineer, educator*
Li, Lihua *education educator*
Li, Mike Peng *information technology executive*
Li, Min *oncologist, educator*
Li, Qin *news anchor, reporter, television director, television producer*
Li, Tingye *electrical engineer*
Li, Xianchang *research engineer*
Li, Xiaojie *statistician, researcher*
Liang, Junxiang *retired aeronautics and astronautics engineer, educator*
Liang, Yanan *research scientist*
Libassi, Frank Peter *lawyer*
Liberati, Maria Theresa *lifestyle company executive, cooking expert, writer*
Liberman, Gail Jeanne *editor*
Libert, Cleo Patricia *computer scientist, consultant*
Libutti, Frank *information technology company executive, former federal agency administrator, retired military officer*
Lichten, William L. *retired physics professor*
Lichtenberg, Byron K. *futurist, consultant, manufacturing executive, pilot*
Lichtenstein, Harvey *performing arts association administrator*
Lichtman, Judith L. *lawyer, organization administrator*
Licke, Wallace John *lawyer*
Liddell, Mary Louisa *elementary school educator, computers educator*
Lidsky, Ella *retired law librarian*
Liebeler, Susan Wittenberg *lawyer*
Lieberfarb, Warren N. *digital media pioneer*
Lieberman, Anne Marie *retired financial executive*
Lieberman, Gail Forman *investment company executive*
Lieberman, Louis (Karl Lieberman) *artist*
Lieberman, Pamela Forbes *consumer products company executive*
Lieberson, Peter *composer*
Liebowitz, Daniel S.F. *retired medical educator*
Liebrandt, Paul *chef*
Lief, Beth *educational association administrator*
Lief, Thomas Parrish *sociologist, educator*
Lifschultz, Phillip *diversified financial services company executive, consultant, lawyer*
Lifson, Kalman Alan *retired retail executive, bank executive, portfolio manager*
Lifton, Paul Samuel *theater educator*
Light, Arthur Heath *bishop*
Lightman, Alan Paige *physics professor, writer*
Lightstone, Ronald *lawyer*
Likins, Peter William *retired academic administrator*
Li-lan, *artist*
Liljegren, Frank Sigfrid *art association administrator, artist, educator*
Lilley, William III *business executive, consultant*
Lilly, Edward Guerrant, Jr. *retired utilities executive*
Lilly, Thomas Gerald *retired lawyer*
Lilly-Hersley, Jane Anne Feeley *nursing researcher*
Limbaugh, Mark A. *federal agency administrator*
Limbrick, David D., Jr. *neurosurgeon, researcher*
Lin, Hamilton *investment banker, education educator*
Lin, Maya *architect, sculptor*
Lin, Qiuyun *education educator*
Lin, Ronghui *chemist, researcher*
Lincicome, David Richard *biomedical scientist, animal scientist*
Lind, Niels Christian *civil engineering educator*
Linda, Gerald *advertising executive, marketing executive*
Lindberg, Francis Laurence, Jr. *management consultant*
Linde, Maxine Helen *lawyer, corporate financial executive, investor*
Linde, Ronald Keith *investor*
Lindegren, Cecile Keyser *music educator*
Lindeman, Janet Claire *psychologist, educator*
Lindenberger, Herbert Samuel *writer, literature educator*
Lindenmayer, Elisabeth *international organization administrator*
Lindgren, William Dale *librarian*
Lindquist, Michael Adrian *career military officer*
Lindsay, Myranda J. *special education educator, military officer*
Lindsey, Ada Marie *dean, nursing educator*
Lindsey, James Harvey *surgeon*
Lindsey, Lawrence Benjamin *economist*
Lindsey, Roberta Lewise *music researcher, historian*
Lindstrom, Rosetta Arline *retired medical technician*
Linett, David *retired lawyer*
Ling, Bai *actor*
Lingle, Marilyn Felkel *journalist, columnist*
Lingle, Sarah Elizabeth *research scientist*
Lington, Aaron Joseph *music educator, musician*
Linhares, Judith Yvonne *artist, educator*
Link, David Thomas *dean, lawyer*
Link, George Hamilton *retired lawyer*
Link, Phyllida Korman *artist, educator*
Linklater, Richard *film director, actor, screenwriter*
Linn, Richard *federal judge*
Linton, Michael Alan *marketing executive*
Linz, Anthony James *osteopathic physician, consultant, educator*
Linzey, James Franklin *minister, military officer, vocalist*
Liotta, Lance Allen *pathologist*
Lipinski, Tara Kristen *retired professional figure skater*

Malphurs, Roger Edward *biomedical marketing executive*
Maltby, Florence Helen *library science educator*
Maltby, Richard Eldridge, Jr. *theater director, lyricist*
Mamula, Petar *gastroenterologist, director*
Manahan, Joan Elsie *health and physical education educator*
Manchester, Kenneth Edward *electronics executive, consultant*
Mandel, Adrienne Abramson *state legislator*
Mandyam, Giridhar Dhati *electronics engineer*
Maneker, Roberta S(ue) *public relations executive*
Manganaro, Francis Ferdinand *naval officer*
Mangasarian, Olvi Leon *education educator, research scientist*
Mangelsdorf, Thomas Kelly *psychiatrist, consultant*
Manglona, Ramona V. *judge, former attorney general*
Mangold, John Frederic *manufacturing executive, retired military officer*
Mangold, Sylvia Plimack *artist*
Mangual, Jesus A. *army officer*
Manika, John Francis *computer systems educator, computer information systems analyst*
Manion, Bonnie J. *volunteer, poet, composer*
Mankiewicz, Thomas Frank *screenwriter, director, producer*
Mankin, Robert Stephen *diversified financial services company executive*
Manley, Joan A(dele) Daniels *retired publishing executive*
Manley, John Hugo *computer company executive, educator*
Manley, Judith L. *director*
Mann, Clarence Charles *retired real estate company officer*
Mann, Donegan *lawyer*
Mann, Eric Louis *retired military officer, mathematics professor, researcher*
Mann, Joan Ellona *artist, editor*
Mann, Sally *photographer*
Manne, Henry Girard *lawyer, consultant, economist, educator, retired dean*
Mannelly, Patrick J. *former beverage company executive*
Mannes, Elena Sabin *film and television producer, television director*
Manning, James E. *social studies educator*
Manning, Lauren Forshay *financial service company executive*
Manning, Michael Nicholas *actor, singer, guitarist, broadcaster, journalist*
Manning, Nancy Christine *retired elementary school educator*
Manos, Christopher Lawrence *lawyer, mediator*
Mansfield, James E. *marketing professional, consultant*
Manson, Anne *music director*
Manuel, Jerry *former professional sports team manager*
Manuel, Ralph Nixon *retired private school executive*
Manuelian, Lucy Der *art historian, architecture educator*
Manyam, Bala Venkatesha *medical researcher, neurology educator*
Manzi, Jim P. *computer software company executive*
Mapes, Kimberly R. *biology educator*
Maplesden, Carol Harper *marriage and family therapist, music educator*
Mapp, Edward Charles *speech educator*
Maranchie, Jodi Kathleen *urologist, oncologist, researcher*
Marcdante, Karen Jean *medical educator*
Marceau, Yvonne *ballroom dancer, educator*
March, Michael F. *propulsion systems analyst, consultant*
Marchan, Marissa L. *social worker*
Marchese, Richard B. *manufacturing executive*
Marchi, Sergio Sisto *Canadian government official*
Marchiori, Massimo *computer scientist*
Marcinek, Margaret Ann *nursing education administrator*
Marco, Cura A. *medical educator*
Marcone, Angela T. *music educator*
Marcopoulos, George John *history professor*
Marcoux, Julia A. *midwife*
Marcus, Amy Dockser *reporter*
Marcus, Edward *economist, educator*
Marcus, Greil Gerstley *critic*
Marcus, Lee Evan *small business owner, consultant, accountant*
Marcus, Mitch *musician, composer*
Marcuse, Dietrich *retired physicist*
Marcy, Kevin Michael *film producer, lawyer*
Marée, Kathleen Nancy *retired language educator*
Margolis, Daniel Herbert *lawyer*
Margolis, David I(srael) *industrial manufacturing executive*
Margoshes, Miriam Kagan *information specialist*
Margules, Cecelia *composer, poet*
Mariconda, Nicholas Gerard *music educator, musician*
Marier, Robert L. *dean, hospital administrator*
Marin, Mona *epidemiologist*
Marinetti, Guido V. *biochemistry professor*
Marini, Frank Nicholas *political science and public administration educator*
Marinis, Thomas Paul, Jr. *lawyer*
Marino, Giovanni *surgeon*
Marion, John Louis *former fine arts auctioneer and appraiser*
Marion, Marjorie Anne *English language educator, educational consultant*
Mariucci, Steve *professional football coach, former college football player*
Mark, Hon Fong Louie *cytogeneticist*
Mark, Judi *actress, choreographer*
Mark, Mary Ellen *photographer*
Mark, Michael Laurence *retired music educator*
Marken, William Riley *editor-in-chief*
Marker, Marc Linthacum *lawyer, investor, entrepreneur*
Markey, Randolph David *marketing professional*
Markham, Charles Henry *neurologist*
Markle, Cheri Virginia Cummins *nurse*
Markman, Jon *business journalist*
Marko, Marlene *psychiatrist*

Markovich, Patricia H. *economist*
Marks, Bruce *performing company executive, choreographer*
Marks, John *engineer, consultant*
Marks, Marilyn *trailer company executive*
Marks, Martha Alford *writer*
Marks, Roberta Barbara *artist, educator*
Markus, Ramsey *dermatologist*
Marlow, Edward A. *former army officer*
Marlowe, Kathleen Scott *employment analyst*
Marlowe, Willie *artist, fine arts educator*
Marmer, Nancy *editor*
Marneros, Alexander Georg *physician, researcher*
Maroney, Jane Perkins *former state legislator, consultant*
Maroney, Thomas P. *lawyer, political party executive*
Maroni, Donna Farolino *biologist, researcher*
Marquis, Kathleen *librarian, archivist*
Marr, Carmel Carrington *retired state official*
Marr, Peter *actor, host, comedian*
Marrin, Charles Ainsworth Staveley *cardiovascular and thoracic surgeon, educator*
Marro, Anthony James *retired newspaper editor*
Marsalis, Branford *musician*
Marsalis, Wynton *musician*
Marse, Melissa J. *music educator, concert pianist*
Marsee, Susanne Irene *vocalist*
Marsh, Joan Knight *educational film, video and computer software company executive, publishing executive*
Marsh, Merrilyn Delano *sculptor, artist, painter*
Marshak, Robert Reuben *retired dean, medical educator, veterinarian*
Marshall, Charles Noble *rail transportation executive*
Marshall, John Paul *broadcast engineer*
Marshall, Jonathan *foundation administrator, journalist*
Marshall, Kathryn Sue *lawyer*
Marshall, Kenneth Robert *retired music educator*
Marshall, Robert Charles *computer company executive*
Marte-Bautista, Helen I. *retired performing arts educator*
Marti, Virgil *artist*
Martin, Albert Charles *manufacturing executive, lawyer*
Martin, Alice Howze *prosecutor*
Martin, Andrea Louise *actress, comedienne, writer*
Martin, Charles Fontaine *management consultant*
Martin, Clyde Verne *psychiatrist*
Martin, Daniel C. *surgeon, gynecologist, educator*
Martin, David Jerner *education educator*
Martin, Dianne Leslie *artist, educator*
Martin, Edwin Wilson *corporate director, columnist, educational consultant*
Martin, Elliot Edwards *theatrical producer*
Martin, George Raymond Richard *writer*
Martin, Gregory S. *air force officer*
Martin, Helen Loene *minister*
Martin, Helen Schatkowski *music educator, television producer*
Martin, James Kay *management consultant*
Martin, James Victor, Jr. *foreign service officer, writer*
Martin, Jean H. *retired interior designer*
Martin, Jesse Lamont *actor*
Martin, John Joseph *journalist*
Martin, John William, Jr. *retired lawyer, automotive executive*
Martin, Joseph Vinson *neuroscientist, educator*
Martin, Karen Siebenthal *community health nurse*
Martin, Lynn Morley *former secretary of labor*
Martin, Marilyn Mann *retired media specialist*
Martin, Noel *graphics designer, educator*
Martin, Paul *former Prime Minister of Canada*
Martin, Preston *finance company executive, consultant*
Martin, Raymond Bruce *plumbing equipment manufacturing company executive*
Martin, Renee Cohen *forensic document examiner, author, expert witness*
Martin, Robert D. *former hospital executive*
Martin, Robert Sidney *former museum director*
Martin, Trisa *education and human development educator*
Martin, William Edwin *lawyer*
Martineau, Robert John *retired law educator*
Martinez, Buck *baseball analyst*
Martinez, James Phillip *music educator*
Martinez, Matthew Gilbert *former congressman*
Martinez, Placido *energy executive*
Martinez-Maldonado, Manuel *academic administrator, dean, medical educator, physiology educator*
Martini, William J. *former congressman, state commissioner, judge*
Martin-Lowry, Beverly Anne *writer, columnist*
Martino, Joseph Paul *research scientist, researcher*
Martinson, Michael David *music educator, musician*
Mártonyi, Csaba Lászlo *retired ophthalmic photographer*
Martyl, (Mrs. Alexander Langsdorf Jr.) *artist*
Martyn, Evi *music educator, musician*
Martz, Judy Helen *former governor*
Maruoka, Jo Ann Elizabeth *retired information systems manager*
Maruyama, Magoroh *business educator, researcher, consultant*
Maruyama, Michelle *violinist*
Marx, Darrelyn Madonna *music educator, drama educator*
Marx, Michael William *language educator, writer*
Marx, Richard *vocalist, musician*
Maryks, Robert A. *history professor*
Masa, George John *retired bank executive*
Masagutov, Vakhid Erkinjonovich *application developer*
Masaki, Takahisa *translation company executive, educator*
Mascheroni, Eleanor Earle *marketing communications executive*
Mashnik, Stepan G. *physicist*
Masi, Robin *artist, writer, educator*
Masiello, Anthony M. (Tony Masiello) *former mayor*
Masiello, Rocco Joseph *air transportation executive, consultant*
Masket, Edward Seymour *television executive*

Maslanka, Daniel Chester *percussionist and music educator*
Maslanka, Sandra Karen *social worker, educator, educational consultant*
Mason, Connie Jeanne *writer*
Mason, Deirdre Dianne *secondary school educator*
Mason, Derrick *professional football player*
Mason, Emily *painter*
Mason, Frank Henry III *automotive executive, rental company executive*
Mason, George Henry *retired business educator*
Mason, Jackie *comedian, actor*
Mason, John Latimer *engineering executive*
Mason, John Oliver *freelance journalist, community activist, poet*
Mason, Linda *physical education educator, coach*
Mason, Lois E. (J. Day Mason) *painter, poet, actress, educator*
Mason, Marsha *actress, theater director, writer*
Mason, Rodney *performing arts educator*
Massad, Jordan Elias *mathematician*
Massad, Susan Moore *internist*
Massey, Robert Unruh *internist, educator, dean*
Massey, Stephen Charles *rare book dealer, consultant*
Massey, Thomas Benjamin *retired university president*
Massey, William Walter, Jr. *sales executive*
Massing, Michael *writer, media critic*
Massoudi, Bahram Barry *management consultant*
Masten, Jacqueline Gwendolyn *small business owner*
Masterson, Peter *actor, film producer*
Mastramico, Thomas J. *music educator*
Mastrian, Stacey Lynn *singer, educator*
Matarasso, Seth L. *dermatologic surgeon*
Matasar, Ann B. *retired dean, finance educator*
Matayoshi, Coralie Chun *lawyer, bar association executive*
Matema, Zsun-nee Kimball (Annette K. Miller) *social sciences educator*
Matera, Frances Lorine *elementary school educator*
Materia, Kathleen Patricia Ayling *nurse*
Materson, Richard Stephen *physician, educator*
Mates, Lawrence A., II, *medical company executive, consultant*
Mates, Robert Edward *mechanical engineering educator*
Mates, Susan Onthank *physician, educator, musician, writer*
Matheny, Adam Pence, Jr. *child psychologist, educator, consultant, researcher*
Mathes, Rachel Clarke *voice educator, singer*
Mathews, E. Anne Jones *retired library educator, academic administrator*
Mathewson, George Atterbury *retired lawyer*
Mathewson, Hugh Spalding *anesthesiologist, educator*
Mathieson, Garrett Alfred *insurance brokerage executive*
Mathieu, Georges Victor Adolphe *artist*
Mathieu, Michele Suzanne *grant writer, computer scientist, consultant*
Mathis, Sharon Bell *retired writer, librarian, curator*
Mathy, Robin Michelle *writer, researcher*
Matlin, Marlee *actress*
Matlock, Glen *musician*
Matlock, John Hudson *science administrator, materials engineer*
Matoax, Louise *mathematics professor, consultant*
Matschullat, Dale Lewis *lawyer, educator*
Matschullat, Robert W. *former consumer products company executive*
Matsen, John Martin *academic administrator, pathologist*
Matsko, Andrey B. *research scientist*
Matsuda, Fujio *retired academic administrator*
Mattar, Philip *writer*
Mattern, Joanne *writer, educator*
Matterson, Joan McDevitt *physical therapist*
Matthau, Charles Marcus *film director*
Matthew, Lyn *sales executive, consultant, marketing professional*
Matthews, Manyalibo Joseph *physicist, researcher*
Matthews, Norman Stuart *retail executive*
Matthews, William *health products executive*
Matthys, Dave *music educator*
Mattice, Howard LeRoy *education executive*
Mattingly, Mack Francis *former ambassador, former senator, entrepreneur*
Mattoli, Agostino Marron *management consultant*
Mattoon, Scott Alexander *private school educator*
Mattos Grell, Elizabeth *artist*
Mattox, Johnny Lynn *biologist, educator*
Mattrick, Donald A. *interactive entertainment software company executive*
Mattson, Stephen Joseph *retired lawyer*
Matz, Deborah *former federal agency administration*
Matzke, Jay *internist*
Mauch, Robert Carl *energy and financial services executive*
Maudlin, Robert V. *economics and government affairs consultant*
Maughan, Denita Rachelle *psychologist*
Maughan, Sir Deryck *former bank executive*
Maul, Kevin Jay *financial consultant, economist*
Maunder, Addison Bruce *agronomic research company executive*
Mauney, Thomas Lee *set designer*
Maurer, Evan Maclyn *museum director*
Mauskopf, Seymour Harold *history professor*
Maves, Michael Donald *medical association executive*
Maxey, Betty Jim *elementary school educator*
Maxfield, Louisa Fonda Gribble *executive secretary*
Maxwell, Jerome Eugene *corporate executive*
Maxwell, Joe (Joseph Edwin Maxwell) *former lieutenant governor*
Maxwell, Raymond Rogers *retired accountant*
Maxwell, Robert William *investment banker, financial analyst*
Maxwell, Sara (Sally) Elizabeth *psychologist, educator, speech pathology/audiology services professional, director*
May, Edgar *former state legislator*
May, Elaine *actress, theatre and film director*
May, Henry Stratford, Jr. *lawyer*

May, Ingrid Barbara *elementary school educator*
May, Phyllis Jean *financial executive*
Mayaram, Kartikeya *electrical engineer, educator*
Mayer, Allan *communications consultant, writer*
Mayer, Anthony John *investment company executive*
Mayer, James Joseph *retired corporate lawyer*
Mayer, Robert Anthony *retired college president*
Mayer, Steven T. *chemical engineer*
Mayer, Susan Martin *art educator*
Mayes, Michael Richard *research and development company executive, architect*
Mayfield, Robert Charles *academic administrator, geographer, educator*
Maynard, Robert Howell *retired lawyer*
Mayoras, Donald Eugene *corporate executive, writer, consultant, educator*
Mayro, Karl R. *realtor*
Mays, George Walter, Jr. *educational technology educator*
Mays, Jefferson *actor*
Mays, Jill Duncan *social services administrator, counselor*
Mayuga, Kenneth A. *cardiologist, researcher*
Mazankowski, Donald Frank *Canadian government official*
Mazza, David S. *pediatrician*
Mazzarelli, Debra Jean *real estate broker*
Mazzola, Mario *computer company executive*
McAleese Dube, Eileen Marie *retired secondary school educator*
McAllister, Singleton Beryl *lawyer*
McAmis, Edwin Earl *lawyer*
McAneny, Deborah H. *insurance company executive*
McAnuff, Des *artistic director*
McAuliffe, Terry (Terence Richard McAuliffe) *former political organization administrator*
McAvoy, John Joseph *lawyer*
McBride, Brian *professional soccer player*
McBride, Carol Bailey *science educator, consultant*
McBride, John P. *state commissioner*
McBride, Mildred Maylea *retired elementary school educator*
McBride, Thomas Dwayne *management consultant*
McBurney, Margot B. *retired librarian*
McCabe, Joseph, Jr. *telecommunications industry executive*
McCaffrey, Cindy *information technology executive*
McCaig, Jeffrey James *transportation company executive*
McCaleb, Neal A. *former federal agency administrator*
McCandless, Carolyn Keller *retired human resources specialist*
McCann, Diana Rae *secondary school educator*
McCann, Elizabeth Ireland *theater producer, television producer, motion picture producer*
McCann, June Vivian *retired physical education educator*
McCann, Margaret Ann *sister, educator*
McCann, Peter Paul *biology researcher, educator*
McCardell, John Malcolm, Jr. *history professor, academic administrator*
McCarlie, V. Wallace *dentist, researcher*
McCarrick, John F. *lawyer*
McCarrick, Theodore Cardinal *archbishop emeritus*
McCarthy, Daniel William *management consultant*
McCarthy, J. Thomas *lawyer, educator*
McCarthy, Karen P. *former congresswoman, former state legislator*
McCarthy, Nobu *actress, performing company executive, educator*
McCarthy, Paul Fenton *aerospace transportation executive, retired military officer*
McCarthy, Vincent Paul *lawyer*
Mc Carthy, Walter John, Jr. *retired utilities executive*
McCarthy-Allen, Mary Frances *medical foundation administrator, not-for-profit fundraiser, consultant*
McCartney, Sir Paul (James Paul McCartney) *musician*
McCarty, Thomas Joseph *publishing executive*
McCash, June Hall *writer, retired language educator*
McCaughey Ross, Elizabeth P. (Betsy McCaughey) *former lieutenant governor*
McCauley, Jane Reynolds *journalist*
McCausland, Peter *technology company executive*
McCausland, Thomas James, Jr. *retired brokerage house executive*
McClain, Lena Alexandria *protective services official*
McClain, Tim S. *lawyer*
McClanahan, Rue (Eddi-Rue McClanahan) *actress*
McClean, Lenora James *nursing educator, dean*
Mc Clellan, Catharine *anthropologist, educator*
McClellan, Larry Allen *minister, educator*
McClellan, Mark B. *former federal agency administrator*
McClellan, Robert Edward *civil engineer*
McClellan, Roger Orville *toxicologist*
McClellan, Scott K. *former White House press secretary*
McClendon, Irvin Lee, Sr. *business owner, editor*
Mc Clendon, William Hutchinson III *retired lawyer*
McClennen, Miriam J. *former state official*
McClinton, Donald George *retired diversified holding company executive*
McClinton, James Leroy *city administrator*
McCloskey, J(ohn) Michael *retired environmental services administrator*
McClure, Jack B. *retired thoracic surgeon*
Mc Collum, Ira William, Jr., (Bill Mc Collum) *former congressman*
McConnell, Dana Rae *psychologist*
McConnell, Edward Bosworth *legal association administrator, lawyer*
McConnell, Jack Baylor *retired corporate executive, physician*
McConnell, John William, Jr. *lawyer*
McConnell, Michael V. *medical educator, researcher*
Mc Cormack, Francis Xavier *lawyer, former oil company executive*

Milewski, Barbara Anne *pediatrics nurse, neonatal/perinatal nurse practitioner, critical care nurse*
Millane, Lynn *retired municipal official*
Millar, John Donald *physician, environmental services administrator, essayist, consultant, musician*
Millard, Charles Warren III *museum director, writer*
Millard, Donald Rex *financial executive*
Miller, Alan Jay *rare book dealer, author*
Miller, Anthony Bernard *physician, researcher*
Miller, Arjay *retired university dean*
Miller, Bernard Joseph, Jr. *advertising executive*
Miller, Beverly A(nn) *reference librarian*
Miller, Charles *investor, retired investment company executive*
Miller, Cheryl DeAnn *former professional basketball coach, broadcaster*
Miller, Darcy M. *publishing executive*
Miller, Diane Illian *cultural organization administrator*
Miller, Donald LeSessne *publishing executive*
Miller, Donald Muxlow *accountant*
Miller, Ellen S. *marketing executive*
Miller, Eunice A. *marriage and family therapist, sex therapist, foundation administrator*
Miller, Geoffrey *child neurologist*
Miller, Harold Edward *retired manufacturing conglomerate executive, consultant*
Miller, Jack David R. *radiologist, physician, educator*
Miller, Jacqueline Winslow *library director*
Miller, Jerry Huber *retired university chancellor*
Miller, John Eddie *lawyer*
Miller, Judith A. (Judy Miller) *retired journalist*
Miller, Linda Karen *retired secondary school educator, social studies educator, law educator*
Miller, Louis Howard *biologist, researcher*
Miller, Marilyn Lea *library and information scientist, educator*
Miller, Nidi R. *artist, sculptor, educator*
Miller, Norman Charles, Jr. *editor, reporter*
Miller, Patricia Louise *state legislator, nurse*
Miller, Patrick William *research scientist, educator*
Miller, Paul David *aerospace transportation executive, retired admiral*
Miller, Phillip Edward *environmental scientist*
Miller, Robert Joseph *lawyer, former governor*
Miller, Roberta Doris *elementary school educator*
Miller, Robin *chef, nutritionist, editor*
Miller, Ross Hays *retired neurosurgeon*
Miller, Ruth Ann *artist*
Miller, Sanford *car rental company executive*
Miller, Shannon *Olympic athlete*
Miller, Thomas J. *former ambassador*
Miller, Thormund Aubrey *lawyer*
Miller, Tracy Lynn *medical office administrator*
Miller, W. Kievit *writer*
Miller, Walter James *retired literature educator, writer*
Miller, Warren Lloyd *lawyer*
Miller, Wentworth *actor*
Milligan, Sister Mary *theology studies educator, consultant*
Milligan, Victor *consulting engineer*
Millikan, Clark Harold *physician*
Millimet, Erwin *lawyer*
Millman, Amy J. *government official*
Mills, Charles N. *healthcare supplies and products company executive*
Mills, Dale Douglas *journalist*
Mills, Douglas L. *physics professor*
Mills, Elizabeth Shown *historical writer, genealogist*
Mills, Eugene Sumner *academic administrator*
Mills, Garth Allen, Sr. *not-for-profit fundraiser, consultant*
Mills, Helene Audrey *retired education educator*
Mills, Kevin Lee *computer scientist, researcher*
Mills, Robert Lee *retired academic administrator*
Millsaps, Fred Ray *investor*
Millsaps, William Hobart, Jr. *retired editor*
Milner, Irvin Myron *retired lawyer*
Milnor, Hazel *nurse*
Milnor, William Robert *physician*
Milstein, Monroe Gary *retail executive*
Milsten, Robert B. *lawyer*
Milunas, J. Robert *health care organization executive*
Minahan, Daniel Francis *lawyer, retired manufacturing executive*
Minahan, Jessica Angela *special education services professional*
Mindlin, Paula Rosalie *retired reading educator*
Mingle, James John *lawyer*
Minikes, Stephan Michael *ambassador, lawyer, banker*
Minkoff, Hilda Bressler *secondary and adult education educator*
Minners, Howard Alyn *federal agency administrator, researcher, preventive medicine physician*
Minnix, Bruce Milton *television and theatre director*
Minshall, Greg *computer programmer*
Mintz, M. J. *lawyer*
Mintz, Morton Abner *writer, reporter*
Miquelon, Miriam F. *former prosecutor, lawyer*
Miracle, Doris Jean *retired medical/surgical nurse*
Miracle, Nancy *foundation administrator, writer*
Miranda-Levi, Jason *film producer, writer*
Mirk, Judy Ann *retired elementary school educator*
Misage, Mark Alan *physics educator*
Miscella, Maria Diana *humanities educator*
Mischke, Carl Herbert *retired religious association executive*
Miselson, Alex J. (Jacob Miselson) *portfolio manager, securities analyst, investment theorist*
Mishler, John Joseph *sculptor, art educator*
Miskus, Michael Anthony *electrical engineer*
Mislow, Kurt Martin *chemist, educator*
Misner, Charlotte Blanche Ruckman *retired community organization administrator*
Misner, Lorraine *lab administrator*
Misner-Elias, Michael Bryan *bank executive, consultant*
Misrach, Richard Laurence *photographer*
Mistry, Percy Shiavak *investment banker*

Mitau, Lee R. *lawyer, bank executive*
Mitch, William Evans *nephrologist*
Mitchard, Jacquelyn *writer*
Mitchell, Brian Stokes *actor*
Mitchell, Briane Nelson *lawyer*
Mitchell, David Benjamin *lawyer, arbitrator, mediator*
Mitchell, Gregory Alan *management consultant*
Mitchell, Jerry *choreographer, actor*
Mitchell, John Charles *marketing professional*
Mitchell, John Laurin Amos *biological science educator*
Mitchell, John W. *pharmaceutical executive*
Mitchell, Marcia Jeanne *writer*
Mitchell, Nicole Margaret *flutist, composer*
Mitchell, Rick *journalist, writer*
Mitchell, William Graham Champion *lawyer, corporate officer*
Mitelman, Bonnie Cossman *editor, writer*
Mitzner, Kenneth Martin *electrical engineer, consultant*
Miville, Marie Lucia *psychologist, educator*
Mize, David M. *marine corps officer*
Moazed, Khosrow L. *retired engineering educator*
Mobley, William Hodges *finance educator, researcher, writer*
Modesto, Victor L. *surgeon*
Modine, Matthew Avery *actor*
Moeck, Peter *crystallographer, materials scientist*
Moenssens, Sandra Birkelbach *marriage and family therapist, counselor, consultant*
Moffat, MaryBeth *consulting company executive*
Moffatt, Joyce Anne *performing company executive*
Moffatt, Katy (Katherine Louella Moffatt) *musician, lyricist, vocalist*
Moford, Craig S. *prosecutor*
Moglewer, Sarah Mana *music educator*
Mohaideen, A. Hassan *surgeon, consultant, health products executive*
Mohamed, Joseph, Sr. *real estate broker, real estate developer, farmer*
Mohan, Ram S. *chemistry professor*
Mohan, Tungesh Nath *television and film producer, film educator*
Mohanty, Saraju P. *computer scientist, educator*
Mohieldin, Ahmed Nader *electrical engineer*
Mohler, Ronald Rutt *electrical engineering educator*
Mohtadi, Hamid *economics professor, researcher*
Moley, Kevin Edward *ambassador*
Molholm, Kurt Nelson *retired federal agency administrator*
Molina, Jose *scriptwriter, television producer*
Molina, Josefa Maria *psychologist, marriage and family therapist*
Molinaro, Joseph Daniel *dentist*
Molini, Barbara Symonds *retired elementary school educator*
Molitor, Michael A. *entrepreneur, consultant*
Moll, David Carter *civil engineer*
Moll, Lloyd Henry *retired bank executive*
Moll, Maryann Elizabeth *education educator*
Mollenauer, Linn Frederick *retired physicist, writer*
Moller, Patricia Lynn *language educator*
Molloy, Sylvia *language educator*
Molmenti, Ernesto P. *surgeon*
Moloff, Alan Lawrence *retired military officer, physician*
Moloney, Daniel M. *electronics executive*
Molz, Redmond Kathleen *public affairs educator*
Momah, Ethel Chukwuekwe *retired women's health nurse*
Monacelli, Gianfranco *publishing executive*
Monaco, Anne Catherine *music educator*
Monaco, Chris *historian, writer, documentary filmmaker*
Monahan, Patrick *singer*
Monajemi, Pezhman *computer engineer*
Monck, Maureen F. *psychoanalyst*
Mondini-Ruiz, Franco *artist*
Moneo, José Rafael *architecture educator*
Moneskey, Tabitha Jean *assistant principal*
Monheit, Molly Jane *artist*
Monos, Dimitrios *medical educator, researcher*
Monroe, Frederick Fales *geologist, oceanographer*
Monson, David Carl *school system administrator, state legislator, farmer*
Montague, Rae-Anne *assistant dean*
Montanaro, Anthony *medical educator*
Monteith, Larry King *chancellor emeritus*
Montemarano, William J. *accountant*
Montgomery, Cliff Wilson *journalist, writer, researcher*
Montgomery, Hubert Theron, Jr. *physician, health care administrator*
Montgomery, John Richard *pediatrician, educator*
Montgomery, Larry Dale *biologist*
Montgomery, Roy Delbert *retired gas industry executive*
Montgomery, William D. *former ambassador*
Moody, Kathryn Currier *communications executive, educator*
Moody, Marilyn Dallas *retired librarian*
Moon, Barbara G. *lawyer*
Moon, David Turner, Jr. *history educator, researcher*
Mooney, James Hugh *newspaper editor*
Mooney, Michael Joseph *university professor*
Mooney, Thomas T. *history educator, geography educator*
Moore, Alma Stoner *writer, lyricist*
Moore, Betty Jo *legal assistant*
Moore, Daniel Alton, Jr. *retired state supreme court justice*
Moore, Deanna Cash *music educator, musician*
Moore, Donald Walter *retired academic administrator*
Moore, Helene Darlak *psychologist, consultant*
Moore, Jean E. *social worker, academic administrator, educator, radio personality*
Moore, John Ronald *manufacturing executive*
Moore, Juel Ann *retired elementary school educator*
Moore, Julie L. *bibliographer, librarian*
Moore, Malcolm Frederick *manufacturing executive*
Moore, Marsha Lynn *retired elementary school educator, counseling administrator*
Moore, Melba (Melba Hill) *actress, singer*

Moore, Oliver Semon III *publishing executive, consultant*
Moore, Patrick S. *epidemiologist, researcher, educator*
Moore, Richard Alan *landscape architect*
Moore, Robert Eric *artist*
Moore, Robert Henry *writer, editor, communications executive*
Moore, Robert Lowell, Jr., (Robin Moore) *author*
Moore, Robert William *professional organization executive*
Moore, Roy S. *former state supreme court chief justice*
Moore, Susanna *writer*
Moore, Thomas Andrew *former medical communications company executive*
Moore, Thomas David *academic administrator*
Moore, Thomas Paul *retired broadcast executive*
Moore, Tirin *neuroscientist, educator*
Moore, Tom *film and theater director*
Moore, William Leroy, Jr. *career officer, internist*
Moorhead, Glen W. (Wally) III *career officer*
Moorhead, Nancy B. *elementary school educator*
Moossy, John *neurologist, consultant, pathologist*
Mora, Antonio Gonzalez III *broadcast journalist*
Mora, Pat *writer, speech professional*
Moradi, Ahmad F. *software company executive*
Morahan, John Kelly *social studies educator*
Morales, Diane K. *former federal agency administrator*
Morales, Marcia Paulette Merry *language educator, archaeologist*
Moran, Charles A. *security firm executive, educator*
Moran, Thomas Harry *retired academic administrator*
Moran, Wendi K *biology educator*
Morano, Kevin R. *mining company executive*
Morden, John Reid *security-business intelligence consultant*
Morelan, Paula Kay *choreographer*
Morello, Joseph Albert *musician, educator*
Moresco, Robert *scriptwriter, film and television producer*
Moretti, August Joseph *pharmaceutical executive, lawyer*
Morfopoulos, V. *metallurgical engineer, materials engineer*
Morgan, Anne Marie G. *broadcast journalist, educator*
Morgan, Arlene Notoro *university administrator*
Morgan, Charles Russell *lawyer*
Morgan, Dennis Keith *lawyer*
Morgan, Edmund Sears *retired history professor*
Morgan, Evelyn Buck *retired nursing educator*
Morgan, James Durward *retired computer company executive*
Morgan, James John *environmental engineering educator*
Morgan, Jane Hale *retired library director*
Morgan, Linda Gail *theater producer*
Morgan, Lynn *sports association executive*
Morgan, M. Jane *computer systems consultant*
Morgan, Mary Lou *retired education educator, volunteer*
Morgan, Michael B. *retired music educator*
Morgan, Michael Lynn *music educator, foundation director*
Morgan, Owain David *investment company executive*
Morgan, Patricia *financial consultant, former Republican party chairman*
Morgan, Peter Monroe *religious organization administrator, minister*
Morgan, Robert Arthur *accountant*
Morgan, Ronald Brian *retired aerospace engineer, advocate, writer, lecturer*
Morgan, Ruth Prouse *academic administrator, educator*
Morgan, Thomas Rowland *retired marine corps officer*
Morgenroth, Earl Eugene *entrepreneur*
Morgenstein, William *shoe company executive*
Morgenstern, Kenneth E. *plastic surgeon*
Mori, Mariko *artist*
Moriarty, Donald William, Jr. *bank executive*
Morin, Lynn P. *music educator, director, secondary school educator*
Morioka, Brennon T. *engineering executive, political organization worker*
Moritz, Chad Henry *research scientist*
Morley, James Everitt, Jr., (Jay Morley Jr.) *retired academic administrator, former educational association administrator*
Morley, Martin L. *musician*
Morman, Dean Smith *accountant, consultant*
Morning, John *graphic designer*
Morphew, Dorothy Richards-Bassett *artist, real estate broker*
Morphy, James Calvin *lawyer*
Morrell, Gene Paul *gas industry executive, consultant*
Morrill, Penny Chittim *art historian*
Morris, Albert Jerome *health products executive*
Morris, Brenda Denise *music educator, director*
Morris, Donald George *engineering company executive*
Morris, G. Ronald *automotive executive*
Morris, Janine Elaine *psychologist*
Morris, John *composer, conductor, arranger*
Morris, John Woodland, II, *retired engineering consultant, retired military officer*
Morris, Martha Marnel *music educator*
Morris, Robert *songwriter, musician, music educator*
Morris, Robert Gemmill *retired foreign service officer*
Morris, Ronald Anthony *county official*
Morris, Scott Stephen *musician, educator*
Morrison, Cheryl Lynn *petroleum engineer, information technology manager*
Morrison, Donald William *lawyer*
Morrison, John James *lawyer*
Morrison, Martin *writer*
Morrison, Michael Gordon *academic administrator, clergyman, history professor*
Morrison, Robert Clifton *artist*
Morrison, Robert Scheck *former manufacturing executive, former food marketing processing company executive*
Morrison, Sarah Lyddon *author*

Morrison, Shelley *actress*
Morrison, Toni (Chloe Anthony Wofford) *writer, educator, editor*
Morrison, Van *musician, songwriter*
Morrissey, Edward T., II, *conservative political blogger, nationally-syndicated radio co-host, columnist*
Morrow, Barry Nelson *screenwriter, producer*
Morrow, Hubert W. *retired minister, retired theology studies educator, writer, educator*
Morrow, Rob *actor*
Morse, Robert Harry *lawyer*
Morse-McNeely, Patricia *poet, writer, retired secondary school educator*
Mortenson, Janice Gayle Mills *business owner, accountant*
Mortimer, Richard Walter *mechanical engineer, educator*
Morton, Donald John *librarian*
Mosallaei, Hossein *science educator*
Moseley, James R. *former federal agency administrator, farmer*
Moseley, Julia W. *music educator, preservationist*
Moser, Barry *artist*
Moser, Jeffery Richard *real estate manager*
Moser, Robert Lawrence *pathologist, health facility administrator*
Moses, Michael James *insurance company executive, small business owner*
Moses, Oral *music educator*
Moses, Sheila Johnson *nurse, bookkeeper*
Moses, Shelia P. *writer, poet, playwright, producer*
Mosiman, Rita Esther *music educator*
Moskal, Barbara M. *engineering educator, mathematics professor*
Moskovitz, Elisa McMillan *music educator, musician*
Moskovitz, Jackob *biology professor*
Mosner, Lawrence J. *retired financial administration company executive*
Mospaw, Kathan J. *retired social studies educator*
Mosqueira, Ignacio *astronomer, writer*
Moss, Carrie-Anne *actress*
Moss, Thomas Henry *science foundation director, physicist*
Mossawir, Harve H., Jr. *retired lawyer*
Mosteller, Robert P. *law educator*
Mott, Stewart Rawlings *food products executive, political organization worker*
Motto, Jerome Arthur *psychiatrist, educator*
Mottola, Tommy (Thomas D. Mottola) *recording industry executive*
Moulaison, Heather Lea *librarian, educator*
Moulder, Retha Ray *retired librarian, retired media specialist, freelance/self-employed educational consultant*
Moulitsas Zúniga, Markos *former military officer, blog writer*
Mountain, Clifton Fletcher *surgeon, educator*
Mourning, Alonzo *professional basketball player*
Mouttet, Jane Elizabeth *school librarian, educator*
Mow, Robert Henry, Jr. *lawyer*
Mow, Van C. *engineering educator, researcher*
Moya, Patrick Robert *lawyer*
Moyer, R. Charles *finance company executive, educator, retired dean*
Moynahan, John Daniel, Jr. *retired insurance executive*
Moyse, Hermann III *banker*
Mracky, Ronald Sydney *marketing executive, tourism consultant, media specialist*
Mrazek, Robert J. *writer, former congressman*
Mshana, Pamela Mariva *secondary school educator*
Muchmore, Don Moncrief *retired cultural organization administrator, retired museum director, foundation administrator*
Muckerman, Norman James *priest, writer*
Muczynski, Paul Frank *human resources specialist*
Mudavanhu, Blessing *research scientist*
Mudd, John O. *lawyer*
Mudd, Roger Harrison *newscaster, educator*
Mudd, S. Harvey *retired biochemist*
Mudry, Michael *pension and benefit consultant*
Muegge, Uwe *terminology professor*
Mueller, Gary Alfred *software engineer*
Mueller, Gerardine Lillian *art educator, artist*
Mueller, Paula Deutsch *retired music educator*
Mueller, Robert Louis *manufacturing executive*
Muhammad, Claudette Marie *religious organization administrator*
Muhlestein, Kerry *educator*
Muhn, Judy Ann *psychologist, genealogist, trainer*
Muir, Patricia Allen *professional association administrator*
Mujica, Mauro E. *architect*
Mukerjee, Shaibal *environmental scientist*
Mulcahy, Gabriel M. *pathologist*
Mulcahy, Robert Edward *management consultant*
Mulchahey, Terry S. *human resources executive, management consultant*
Mullan, Donald William *archbishop*
Mullen, William Joseph III *military analyst, retired army career officer*
Mullens, Delbert W. *automotive executive*
Muller, Henry Nicholas III *retired foundation administrator*
Muller, Peter *lawyer, film company executive, retail executive*
Muller, Scott William *lawyer*
Mullin, Leo Francis *airline executive*
Mullis, Gary Banks *biochemist*
Mulvee, Robert Edward *bishop*
Mumma, Albert Girard, Jr. *architect*
Mungekar, Hemant P. *process engineer, researcher*
Munger, Elmer Lewis *civil engineer, educator*
Munger, Kristen A. *school psychologist*
Munger, Paul R. *engineering educator*
Muñoz, Carlos Ramón *retired bank executive*
Munoz, Cheryl Ann *portfolio manager*
Munoz, Mario Alejandro *civil engineer, retired consultant*
Munro, Ralph Davies *former state official*
Munsell, Elsie Louise *retired lawyer*
Munsey, Virdell Everard, Jr. *retired utilities executive*
Munson, Lawrence Shipley *management consultant*
Munt, Janet Staples *state senator*
Munzner, Robert Frederick *biomedical engineer*

O'Connor, Shannon Leigh *psychologist*
Odar, Fuat *retired nuclear engineer*
O'Dell, Walden Wesley *manufacturing executive*
Oden, Jean P(hifer) *special education educator*
Oden, William Bryant *bishop, educator*
Odenigbo, Innocent Chukwunwike *linguist, writer, consultant*
Odermatt, Robert Allen *architect*
Odhiambo, Eucabeth A. *education educator*
Odom, Judy *software company executive*
Odom, Rod D., Jr. *telecommunications industry executive*
O'Donnell, John Michael *lawyer*
O'Donnell, Kathleen C. *artist*
O'Donnell, Kathleen Mary *social services administrator*
O'Donnell, Kevin *retired metal products executive*
O'Donnell, Rosie *television personality, actress, comedienne*
O'Donnell II, Brian A. *social studies educator*
O'Dowd, Sarah A. *lawyer*
Odya, Gregory Matthew *music educator, musician*
Oerter, Cynthia Lynn *medical technologist*
Oettinger, Julian Alan *lawyer, pharmaceutical executive*
Offen, Ronald Charles *retired school librarian*
Ofstad, Evelyn Larsen Boyl *retired primary school educator, radio personality, film producer*
Ogata, Katsuhiko *engineering educator*
Ogden, Benjamin *language educator*
Ogden, Maurice B. *retired minister, writer*
Ogdon, Michael William *minister, music educator*
Ogg, Wilson Reid *lawyer, retired judge, poet, publishing executive, educator*
Oginz, Richard J. *artist, sculptor*
Ogle, Edward Proctor, Jr. *investment advisor*
Oglesby, Elaine Sue *elementary school educator*
Ogliaruso, Michael Anthony *retired chemist, educator, actor*
O'Gorman, James Francis *art educator, writer*
O'Grady, Michael J. *federal agency administrator*
Ogunleye, Tolagbe Monuola *publishing executive, educator, small business owner, editor*
Oh, Jung Hun *computer engineer*
Oh, Mark Edward *minister*
Oh, Sandra *actress*
O'Hagan, Desmond Brian *artist*
O'Hara, Catherine *actress, comedienne*
O'Hara, Sabine U. *academic administrator, dean, economist, educator*
O'Hare, Dean Raymond *retired insurance company executive, director*
O'Hare, James Raymond *energy executive*
O'Hare, Joseph Aloysius *priest, editor-in-chief, former academic administrator*
Ohs, Karl *former lieutenant governor*
Oka, Takeshi *physicist, physical chemist, astronomer, educator*
Okada, Kazunori *research scientist*
O'Keefe, Edward Franklin *lawyer*
Okonedo, Sophie *actress*
Okoshi-Mukai, Sumiye *artist*
Okouchi-Guy, Alicia *performing arts educator*
Oksiloff, Christa *technologist, educator*
Olcyzk, Ed *professional athletics coach*
Oldenburg, Claes Thure *artist*
Oldman, Alfred Maurice *accountant, management consultant*
Olds, Jacqueline *psychiatrist, educator*
Olea, Hector *curator*
O'Leary, Dennis Sophian *accrediting body executive*
O'Leary, Sharon *obstetrician, gynecologist, researcher*
Oles, Paul Stevenson (Steve Oles) *architect, educator*
Olin, David Lind *conservator*
Olin, Lena Maria Jonna *actress*
Olins, Robert Abbot *communications research executive*
Olitski, Jules *artist*
Olive, David Michael *journalist, editor*
Oliver, Jerry Alton *former police chief*
Oliver, Matt *publishing executive*
Oliver, Ronald *retired medical technologist*
Oliver, Samuel William, Jr. *retired lawyer*
Olivos, Claudia *artist, educator*
Olkinetzky, Sam *artist, educator, retired museum director*
Olsen, David Alexander *insurance executive*
Olsen, Glen A. *church musician, educator*
Olshan, Judd David *environmental scientist*
Olson, Dale C. *public relations executive*
Olson, Harold Roy *computer company executive*
Olson, Margaret *music educator*
Olson, Phillip Roger *naval officer*
Olson, Robert Edward *coal mining executive*
Olsson-Hume, Irena *music educator*
Olszewski, Mark Eric *biomedical engineer, researcher*
O'Malley, Thomas D. *petroleum industry executive*
Omalu, Bennet Ifeakandu *physician, consultant*
Omasta, Matthew J. *artist, educator*
Omer, Margaret Vaughan (Peggy Omer) *retired computer technician, artist*
Omholt, Bruce Donald *product designer, mechanical engineer, consultant*
Onah, Ejembi John *chemist, researcher*
Ondrasik, John *singer, songwriter*
O'Neal, Tatum *actress*
O'Neal-Seralathan, Crescentia *advocate*
O'Neil, Carolyn *cable network executive, cable television host*
O'Neill, Harry William *retired research market and opinion company executive*
O'Neill, Kevin *professional athletics coach*
O'Neill, Mary Jane *not-for-profit administrator, consultant*
Ong, John Doyle *former ambassador, retired manufacturing executive*
Ongley, Lauri *mathematics professor*
Ono, Eiichi *engineering educator, researcher*
Onufriev, Alexey *science educator*
Onufrock, Richard Shade *retired pharmacist*
Onuigbo, Macaulay Amechi *nephrologist, internist*
Oort, Abraham Hans *meteorologist, researcher, educator*
Oppedahl, John Frederick *newspaper publisher, publishing executive*
Oppedahl, Phillip Edward *computer company executive*

Oral, Elif Arioglu *endocrinologist, researcher*
Oransky, Ivan *writer, editor*
Orbit, William (William Wainwright) *record producer*
Ordal, Caspar Reuben *retired cosmetics executive*
Ordonez, Christina Elizabeth *secondary school educator*
Orem, Cassandra Elizabeth (Sandra Orem) *small business owner, educator, holistic health consultant and practitioner*
Orkin, Jenna *writer*
Orlando, Lori Ann *medical researcher*
Orlebeke, William Ronald *retired lawyer, writer*
Ormasa, John *retired utilities executive*
Ormond, Julia *actress*
Orr, Frank Howard III *architect*
Orr, Jo Miller *music educator, voice educator*
Orr, Kenneth Bradley *academic administrator*
Orr, Richard Clayton *mathematician, retired securities trader*
Orr, Steven R. *health facility administrator*
Orrmont, Arthur *writer, editor*
Orsini, Eric Andrew *military officer*
Orszag, Steven Alan *applied mathematician, educator*
Ortego, Gilda Baeza *library director, educator*
Orth, David Nelson *endocrinologist, educator, sculptor, potter*
Ortiz, Angel Vicente *church administrator*
Ortiz, Felix W. *state legislator*
Ortiz, Mayra Zoe *psychologist*
Ortiz-Walters, Rowena *management educator*
Ortolano, Ralph J. *engineering consultant*
Orttung, William Herbert *chemistry professor*
Ory, Steven Jay *physician, educator*
Osberg, Gregory John *publishing company executive*
Osborn, Donna Marie *secondary school educator, mathematician*
Osborn, Kenneth Louis *financial executive*
Osborn, William George *savings and loan association executive*
Osborne, Barrie M. *motion picture producer*
Osborne, James Alfred *religious organization administrator*
Osborne, Joan (Elizabeth) *singer, songwriter*
Osborne, John L. *academic administrator, educator*
Osbourne, Ozzy (John Osbourne) *vocalist*
Ose, Douglas *former congressman*
O'Shea, Anna Belle Marie *music educator, liturgy administrator*
O'Shea, Catherine Large *marketing and public relations consultant*
O'Shea, Donald C. *physicist, educator, optical engineer*
O'Shields, Charlie *marketing professional*
Oshima, Junko *science educator, researcher*
Oshima, Michael W. *lawyer*
Oshita, John Takao *musician*
Osias, Richard Allen *corporate financial executive*
Osinski, Brenda Carol *music educator*
Oskin, JoEllen Ross *special education educator, school librarian*
Osmer-McQuade, Margaret *broadcast executive, journalist*
Osmond, Marie *singer*
Osowiec, Darlene Ann *clinical psychologist, educator, consultant*
Ossana, Diana Lynn *author, screenwriter*
Ostaszewski, Alyce Vitella *religion educator*
Ostberg, Henry Dean *marketing executive*
Oster, Lewis Henry *manufacturing executive, industrial engineer, consultant*
Osterhoff, James Marvin *retired telecommunications company executive*
Osterman, Catherine *Olympic athlete*
Ostlind, Dan A. *retired parasitologist*
Ostriker, Alicia Suskin *poet*
Ostrow, Joseph W. *advertising executive*
Ostrow, Stuart *theatrical producer, educator, author*
O'Sullivan, Judith Roberta *lawyer, writer, artist*
O'Sullivan, Lawrence Joseph *retired financial consultant*
O'Sullivan, Michael David *foundation executive*
O'Sullivan, Paul Kevin *management and instructional systems consultant*
Osvath, Ludovic Lajos *minister*
Otani, Yuriko L. (Charko) *artist*
Othman, Talat Mohamad *financial consultant, investment banker*
Otis, Jack *social work educator*
Otis, Lee (Sarah) Liberman *lawyer, educator*
Ott, Karl Otto *nuclear engineer, consultant*
Ott, Sharon *artistic director*
Outlaw, Lanny F. *gas company executive*
Ouyang, Norma M. *psychologist*
Ovadiah, Janice *not-for-profit developer, cultural organization administrator*
Overbey, Kellie Lyn *actress*
Owen, Claudia J. *academic administrator*
Owen, Paul *religious studies educator*
Owens, Birdie Murphy *retired music educator*
Owens, Charles Vincent, Jr. *pharmaceutical executive, consultant*
Owens, Rochelle *poet, playwright*
Owens, Sue Gaston *retired middle school educator*
Owens, Vicki Palmer *elementary school educator, academic coordinator*
Owens, William Arthur (Bill Owens) *telecommunications industry executive, retired military officer*
Owings, John R *corporate financial executive*
Oxnam, Philip Linton *small business owner*
Oxner, Catherine Cantrell *school psychologist, educator*
Özalp, Nesrin *mechanical engineer, research scientist*
Ozick, Cynthia *writer*
Ozkan, Betul C *education educator*
Ozturk, Ozcan *electrical engineer, researcher*
O'Brien-Amico, Leah *Olympic athlete*
Paarsch, Harry J. *economist, educator*
Pace, Charles Robert *psychologist, educator*
Pace, George W. *food products company executive*
Pacelle, Wayne *animal rights organization administrator*
Pacheco, Manuel Trinidad *retired academic administrator*
Pacheco, Susan *automotive executive*

Pacholski, Richard Francis *securities trader, consultant, financial consultant*
Pacifico, Albert Dominick *cardiovascular surgeon*
Pack, Michael *television producer, writer, director*
Packard, John Mallory *physician, researcher*
Packer, Matthew James *musician*
Pacor, Victor J. *diversified financial services company executive*
Padgett, Cynthia S. *artist*
Padian, Nancy *medical educator, epidemiologist*
Padilla, James Jerome (Jim Padilla) *retired automotive executive*
Paganelli, Charles Victor *physiologist, educator*
Pagano, Michelina Olimpia *art director, consultant, writer, scriptwriter*
Page, Barbara Rose *primary school educator*
Page, Jonathan Roy *portfolio manager*
Page, Patricia (Patty) Newton *real estate broker, real estate company executive*
Page, Patrick Joseph *art educator*
Page, Raymond *research and development company executive*
Paige, Vivian Jo-Ann *accountant*
Paine, Alan *poet*
Paino, Javier E. *physician*
Painter, Borden W. *former academic administrator*
Painter, Richard William *lawyer, educator*
Painter, Robert Lowell *surgeon, educator*
Painton, Russell Elliott *retired lawyer, retired mechanical engineer*
Pair, Jackson Jarrell *computer scientist, media consultant*
Pakala, James Cotton *library director, minister*
Pakenham, Rosalie Muller Wright *magazine and newspaper editor*
Pal, Prabir Kumar (Sunny Pal) *lawyer*
Pal, Pratapaditya *curator*
Palade, George Emil *research scientist, educator*
Paladino, Albert Edward *venture capitalist*
Paley, Russell Eliot *writer, small business owner*
Palileo, Hazel Valencia *videographer*
Palisi, Anthony Thomas *psychologist, educator*
Palmer, Charlotte Marie *writer*
Palmer, Dave Richard *retired military officer, academic administrator*
Palmer, Irene Sabelberg *retired dean, retired nursing educator, genealogist*
Palmer, Jocelyn Beth *volunteer*
Palmer, Marilyn Joan *English composition educator*
Palmer, Paul Richard *school librarian, archivist, curator*
Palmerlee, April Wahlestedt *management consultant*
Palmieri, Dora Ann *retired language educator*
Palms, Roger Curtis *writer, educator, minister*
Palter, Robert Monroe *humanities educator*
Palumbo, Matthew Aloysius *marketing executive*
Palumbo, Michael J. *air transportation executive*
Pan, Deming *chemistry professor*
Pan, Liang Ru *physicist, researcher*
Pan, Vivien L. *obstetrician, gynecologist*
Panagis, Pete *writer*
Panagotis, David Timothy *editor*
Pandel, Robin McEwan *elementary school educator*
Pandit, Vikram S. *investment banker*
Panetta, Michael Jon *retired state agency administrator, writer*
Panofsky, Wolfgang Kurt Hermann *physicist, researcher*
Pantoja, Juan Luis *hospital administrator, educator*
Panzer, Mary Caroline *historian, museum curator*
Paolozzi, Jennifer *elementary school educator*
Paolucci, Anne Attura *playwright, poet, literature educator, educational consultant*
Papa, Vincent T. *insurance company executive*
Papadakos, Nicholas Peter *retired state supreme court justice*
Papadonikolakis, Anastasios *orthopedist, surgeon*
Papakostas, Achilleas *telecommunications engineer, researcher*
Papalas, Mary Margaret *school psychologist*
Paparella, Leon Ralph *psychotherapist, consultant*
Papathomas, Georgia Nikolakopoulou *technology executive*
Pappas, Michael *former congressman*
Paps, Betty Lou *nursing educator*
Parameswaran, Raju *accountant*
Pardue, Dwight Edward *venture capitalist*
Paredes, James Anthony *anthropologist, educator*
Pareene, Alex E. *political blog editor*
Parent, Rodolphe Jean *retired Canadian air force officer, pilot*
Parham, Ellen Speiden *nutrition educator*
Parins, Robert James *professional football team executive, judge*
Paris, David Andrew *dentist*
Paris, Steven Mark *application developer*
Park, John Thornton *retired academic administrator*
Park, Myung Kun *medical educator*
Park, Penny Sheran *retired elementary school educator*
Park, Won Kuk *foundation administrator*
Parke, M. Leslie *artist*
Parke, Robert Leon *retired communications executive*
Parkel, James G. *former health association administrator*
Parker, Barbara Anne *education educator, social studies educator*
Parker, Brent Mershon *retired medical educator, internist, cardiologist*
Parker, Dawn Cassandra *social sciences educator*
Parker, Douglas Martin *retired lawyer, writer*
Parker, George Ernest *mathematics educator*
Parker, Gerald William *internist, health facility administrator, retired military officer*
Parker, James Francis *former air transportation executive, lawyer*
Parker, Joel Louise *nursing administrator*
Parker, John Francis *retired lawyer*
Parker, Marilla J. *school psychologist*
Parker, Mel *editor*
Parker, Michael D. *chemicals executive*
Parker, Robert Andrew *artist*
Parker, Susan Brooks *health facility administrator*
Parker, Towana D. *entrepreneur, director*
Parkinson, Dian *actress*
Parkison, Aimee Dawn *language educator, writer*

Parks, Jean Anne *retired acute care nurse*
Parks, Kizzy Marie *psychology professor*
Park Spencer, Karen Lynn *architect, apparel designer*
Parkyn, John William *editor, writer, columnist*
Parnell-Booth, Ruby Sheree *science educator*
Parode, Ann *lawyer*
Parr, Royse Milton *retired lawyer, writer*
Parrish, Stephen B. *psychotherapist*
Parrott, Wanda Sue *writer, journalist*
Parsons, Alexandra Clare *literature and language educator*
Parsont, Mina Rainès-Lambé *retired literature educator*
Partida, Gilbert A. *lawyer*
Partridge, Bruce James *lawyer, educator, writer*
Partridge, William J. *military officer, government agency administrator*
Pascale, Daniel Richard *lawyer*
Paschoud, François *classicist, educator*
Pasco, Hansell Merrill *retired lawyer*
Pascoe, B. Lynn *ambassador*
Pascoe, Patricia Hill *former state legislator*
Paskins, Janet Lynn *psychology professor, educational consultant*
Paskman, Andrea *dance specialist*
Pasqualoni, Paul *former college football coach*
Pasquier, Joël *music educator*
Passaro, Paul Charles *real estate company executive*
Pastorek, Paul G. *lawyer*
Pastrana, Travis *professional trick bike rider*
Pastula, Leah Lynn *mental health services professional*
Patankar, Ravindra *research scientist, educator*
Patch, Peter C. *psychologist*
Patchett, Arthur Allan *medicinal chemist, pharmaceutical executive*
Patchin, Rebecca J. *anesthesiologist, educator, administrator*
Pate, R. Hewitt (Robert Hewitt Pate III) *lawyer, former federal agency administrator*
Pate, William *telecommunications industry executive*
Patel, Uptal Dinesh *nephrologist, researcher*
Paterson, Robert E. *retail executive*
Patino-Brandfon, Sylvia *retired psychologist*
Patki, Kiran C. *pharmacologist, researcher*
Patmos, Adrian Edward *retired dean*
Patrick, Brenda Jean *educational consultant*
Patrick, Craig *former professional hockey team executive*
Patrick, Danica Sue *race car driver*
Patrick, Deval Laurdine *lawyer*
Patrick, Michele Mary *government official*
Patrick, Victor Phillip *lawyer*
Patterson, Collis Delano *secondary school educator*
Patterson, Dennis Joseph *management consultant*
Patterson, Elizabeth Johnston *retired congresswoman*
Patterson, Howard Yates *academic athletics administrator*
Patterson, Hubert Clifton *physician*
Patterson, James E. *economist, author, speaker*
Patterson, Marlene (None) *secondary school educator*
Patterson, Richard North *writer, lawyer*
Patterson, Ronald Paul *publishing executive, educator, minister*
Patterson, Samuel C. *retired political science professor*
Pattillo, Gary A. *beverage distribution executive*
Pattillo, Manning Mason, Jr. *academic administrator*
Patton, James Richard, Jr. *lawyer*
Patwardhan, Meenal B. *pathologist, researcher*
Pauken, Thomas Weir *venture capital executive, mediator*
Paul, Arthur *artist, illustrator, graphics designer, design consultant*
Paul, Eve W. *retired lawyer*
Paul, Kenneth *newspaper editor*
Paul, Richard Wright *lawyer*
Paul, Ronald Ernest *congressman*
Paul, Vivek *information technology executive*
Pauley, Jane *newscaster, journalist*
Paulsen, Brian Oliver *art educator, artist*
Paulsen, Frank Robert *college dean emeritus*
Pauly, John Edward *retired anatomist*
Paup, Martin Arnold *securities investor, real estate investor*
Pavarini, Peter Alfred *lawyer*
Pavel, Radu *mechanical engineer, researcher*
Payne, Barbara Ann *artist, educator*
Payne, Daniel Harold (Harold Payne) *real estate developer, small business owner*
Payne, Ladell *retired academic administrator*
Payne, Mary Libby *retired judge*
Payton, Donna S. *minister*
Payton, Thomas William *finance company executive*
Peach, Robert Westly *retired small business owner, engineer*
Peacock, Mary Willa *magazine editor, consultant*
Peapples, George Alan *retired automotive executive*
Pear, Charles E., Jr. *lawyer*
Pearce, Lisa Anne *composer, musician*
Pearce, Paul Francis *retired electronics executive, aerospace engineer*
Pearl, Laurence Dickson *retired federal government executive*
Pearlstein, Philip *artist*
Pearsall, Gloria W. *retired elementary school educator*
Pearson, Jennie Sue *retired government administrator*
Pearson, Paul Holding *insurance company executive*
Pearson, Richard Joseph *archaeologist, educator*
Pearson, W. Robert (William Robert Pearson) *former federal agency administrator, former ambassador*
Pease, Edward A. *former congressman*
Pease, Ron Dean *artist*
Pease-Pretty On Top, Janine B. *community college administrator*
Peck, Arthur John, Jr. *retired manufacturing executive, lawyer*
Peck, Paul Lachlan *minister*

Price, William James, IV, *investment banker*
Pride, Benjamin David *sales executive*
Pride, Dena Beth *small business owner*
Pridmore, Roy Davis *retired federal official*
Priest, Jessie Shaw *media specialist*
Priestley, Jason (Jason Bradford Priestley) *actor*
Prieto, Claudio R. *academic administrator, lawyer*
Primerano, Lavina S. *volunteer*
Primosch, James Thomas *music educator, composer, musician*
Prince, Andrew Steven *lawyer, retired government agency administrator*
Prince, Anna Lou *composer, music publisher, construction executive*
Prince, George Edward *retired pediatrician*
Prince, Richard *artist*
Principal, Victoria (Victoria Ree Principale) *actress, film producer, writer*
Prins, Robert Jack *retired academic administrator*
Priory, Richard Baldwin *former electric power industry executive*
Pritchard, Benjamin Chadwick *music educator*
Pritchard, Claudius Hornby, Jr. *retired university president*
Pritchard, Kathleen Jo *not-for-profit association administrator*
Proctor, Barbara Gardner *advertising agency executive, writer*
Proctor, John James *electrical engineer*
Proctor, Richard James *geologist, consultant*
Proctor, Robert Neel *history educator*
Profeta, Salvatore, Jr. *chemist, educator*
Prohovnik, Isak *medical educator*
Prokasy, William Frederick *academic administrator*
Prokopis, Emmanuel Charles *computer company executive*
Propp, Steven H. *legal analyst*
Propst, Harold Dean *retired academic administrator*
Propst, Michael Truman *pathologist*
Proulx, (Edna) Annie *writer*
Provensen, Alice *artist, writer*
Prucha, Ingmar R. *economist, educator*
Pruden, Ann Lorette *chemical engineer, researcher, management consultant*
Pruehsner, William Robert *biomedical engineer*
Pruett-Lawson, Jo Ann *marketing professional, special events coordinator*
Pruis, John J. *manufacturing executive*
Pruitt, Anne Loring *academic administrator, education educator*
Prusiner, Stanley Ben *neurologist, biochemist, virologist, educator*
Pruter, Robert Douglas *librarian*
Pruzan, Irene *musician, educator, public relations executive, art association administrator*
Pryor, Eric Jon *minister, writer*
Pryor, Harold S. *retired college president*
Pryor, Tommi Thornbury *marketing professional*
Przybylski, Sandra Marie *speech pathologist*
Puccinelli, Daniele *research scientist*
Puck, Wolfgang *chef*
Puetz, Pamela Ann *human resources executive*
Pulhamus, Marlene Louise *retired elementary school educator*
Pulitzer, Emily Rauh (Mrs. Joseph Pulitzer Jr.) *art historian, consultant*
Pullen, Penny Lynne *non-profit organization administrator, retired state legislator*
Pulling, Thomas Leffingwell *investment advisor*
Pullman, Philip Nicholas *writer, educator*
Pulte, Diane Marie *music educator*
Purcell, Bill *mayor*
Purcell, George Richard *artist*
Purcell, John Patrick, Jr. *writer, art educator*
Purcell, Philip James *retired diversified financial services company executive*
Purdy, Kevin Moore *estate planner*
Pursell, Carroll Wirth *history educator*
Pursey, Derek Lindsay *retired physics professor*
Purtle, Dorothy L. *religious studies educator*
Purtle, John Ingram *lawyer, former state supreme court justice*
Purvis, Gail *elementary school educator*
Purvis, George Frank, Jr. *life insurance company executive*
Puryear, James Burton *college administrator*
Puryear, Martin *artist, educator*
Pust, Ronald E. *physician, educator*
Puster, John C. *music educator*
Putman, Carol Jean *photographer, artist*
Putman, Mark *theater educator*
Putnam, Marlene Evans *artist*
Putnam, William Lowell *science association administrator*
Puzzo, Joseph Anthony, Jr. *middle school educator*
Pyatt, Kedar Davis, Jr. *research and development company executive*
Pyle, Donald Norris, II, *biologist*
Pylipow, Stanley Ross *retired manufacturing company executive*
Pytell, Robert Henry *retired lawyer, former judge*
Pytlinski, Jerzy Teodor *physicist, educator, research scientist*
Pytte, Agnar *physicist, retired academic administrator*
Qi, Xiaoning *electrical engineer, electronics engineer, researcher*
Qi, Zhigang *materials scientist, chemist*
Qiang, Xiao *advocate*
Qiu, Hai *research scientist*
Quade, Vicki *editor, writer, playwright, theater producer*
Quaid, Randy *actor*
Qualls, Robert L. *manufacturing executive, bank executive, educator, retired state official*
Quam, Teri *school psychologist*
Quant, Harold Edward *retired financial services company executive, rancher*
Quarles, James Linwood III *lawyer*
Quattlebaum, Robert Baskin *urologist*
Quattrone, Richard Douglas *physician, military officer*
Quattrone-Carroll, Diane Rose *clinical social worker*
Quay, Thomas Emery *lawyer*
Queen, James E. *automotive executive*
Quesnel-Vallée, Amélie *social sciences educator, medical educator*
Quiala, Maribel *psychotherapist, consultant*

Quigley, Leonard Vincent *lawyer*
Quillen, Cecil Dyer, Jr. *lawyer, consultant*
Quillen, Lloyd Douglas *oil and gas executive*
Quillen, William Tatem *retired judge, lawyer, educator*
Quinlan, Kathleen *actress*
Quinn, Charles Nicholas *journalist*
Quinn, Helen Rhoda Arnold *physicist*
Quinn, Mary M. *communications executive, marketing director*
Quinn, Pat (John Brian Patrick Quinn) *former professional hockey coach*
Quint Sehat, Arlene *art history educator, curator, museum administrator*
Quirino, Pedro *counselor*
Quirk, Kathleen L. *mining executive*
Quirk, Kenneth Paul *accountant*
Quirk, Raymond R *investment company executive*
Quuoquoi, Gadema K. *computer consultant*
Qutub, Amina Ann *biomedical researcher, entrepreneur*
Qutub, Musa Yacub *hydrogeologist, educator, consultant*
Rabideau, Marilyn Ann *elementary school educator*
Rabó, Jule Anthony *research scientist, consultant*
Rabon, William James, Jr. *architect*
Raborn, Marcia MacArthur *primary school educator*
Race, George Justice *pathology educator*
Racherla, Gopal *computer scientist, researcher*
Rada, Ruth Byers *retired dean*
Radcliffe, Redonia (Donnie Radcliffe) *journalist, writer*
Rader, Dotson Carlyle *writer, journalist*
Radford, R. S. *lawyer, law educator*
Radi, Zaher *pathologist*
Radlauer, Steve *freelance writer, journalist, producer*
Radmilovic, Velimir *materials scientist, researcher*
Radzik, Albin F. *military analyst, consultant*
Raeburn, Paul *editor, writer*
Raffegeau, Jean Michel *audit and consulting company executive*
Ragans, Rosalind Dorothy *writer, artist, retired educator*
Ragent, Boris *physicist*
Raghavan, Asuri *construction executive*
Ragheb, Samia *immunologist, educator*
Ragone, David Vincent *former university president*
Ragone, Tara Adams *lawyer*
Rahe, Maribeth Sembach *investment management executive*
Rahman, Abu Tayeb Rafiqur *former United Nations official*
Rahming, Etta Lorraine *social worker, consultant, psychotherapist, counseling administrator*
Raichle, Marcus Edward *radiology, neurology educator*
Railsback, Sherrie Lee *management consultant, educator*
Raimi, Samuel M. *film director*
Rainer, Rex Kelly *civil engineer, educator*
Raines, Franklin Delano *former finance company executive*
Raines, Howell Hiram *former newspaper editor, journalist*
Raines, Jeff *biomedical scientist, medical research director*
Rairdin, Craig Allen *software company executive, software developer*
Raitt, Bonnie Lynn *singer, musician*
Rajagopal, Chitra P. *engineering educator*
Rajagopalan, Dilip *pharmaceutical executive*
Rajani, Prem Rajaram *transportation company financial executive*
Rajendra, Kunwar *retired engineering educator, consultant*
Rajendran, Srividhya *computer scientist, researcher*
Rajput, Farzan *cardiologist*
Rajski, Peggy *film director, film producer*
Rajupalepu, Rahi K. *technologist, consultant*
Rakes, John Patrick *music educator*
Rako, Susan *psychiatrist, writer*
Rakove, Jack Norman *history professor*
Raley, Bennett William *former federal agency administrator*
Ram, Chitta Venkata *physician*
Ramadan, Nabih M. *pharmaceutical company official, educator*
Ramakrishnan, Kannan *mechanical engineer*
Rambo, Domingo H. *elementary school educator*
Ramey, Eudora Malois *minister*
Ramirez, Evangeline Rose *elementary school educator*
Ramírez, Felipe J. *musician, composer, artist, photographer*
Ramirez, Maria Eugenia *primary school educator*
Ramirez-Rivera, Jose *physician*
Ramis, Harold Allen *film director, screenwriter, actor*
Ramjee, Ramachandran *telecommunications industry executive, computer scientist*
Ramo, Virginia M. Smith *civic worker*
Ramos-Rinze, Jorge Rafael *computer scientist*
Rampone, Christie P. *professional soccer player*
Ramsay, J. Russell *psychologist*
Ramsay, Kalvin Kinsey *publisher, educator*
Rand, Calvin Gordon *art educator, educational consultant*
Rand, Joella Mae *retired nursing educator, counselor*
Rand, Robert Stephen *electrical engineer, physicist, statistician*
Randall, David John *physiologist, zoologist, educator*
Randall, Peter *retired plastic surgeon*
Randall, Richard Rainier *geographer*
Randazzo, Marisa Reddy *psychologist*
Randinelli, Tracey Anne *magazine editor*
Randolph, Donald Phillip *nurse anesthetist*
Randolph, Judson Graves *pediatric surgeon*
Randolph, Virgella *retired federal official*
Ranger, Mark J. *music educator*
Ranjan, Rahul *engineer, researcher*
Rankin, Douglas Houston *finance executive*
Rankin, Scott David *artist, educator*
Rann, Robert Kennedy *humanities educator*
Ranney, Helen Margaret *retired internist, hematologist, educator*

Ransom, Angela Dawn *nurse*
Ransom, Margaret Palmquist *public relations executive*
Ransom, Tasha Elana *news production assistant*
Ransome, Ernest Leslie III *retail executive*
Rao, Rama Krishna R. *pharmaceutical company executive*
Raouafi, Nour-Eddine *astrophysicist, researcher*
Raoufi, Azadeh *music educator*
Rapoport, Ronald Jon *journalist*
Rappaport, Irving S. *entrepreneur, lawyer, consultant*
Rappaport, James Wyant *lawyer, real estate developer*
Rashad, Phylicia *actress, singer, dancer*
Rasi, Humberto Mario *editor, educator*
Raskin, Fred Charles *retired transportation and utility holding company executive, educator*
Raskin, Michael A. *retail executive, director*
Rasor, Dina Lynn *journalist, private investigator*
Raspberry, Brenda *pre-school educator*
Rassman, Joel H. *home construction company executive*
Ratha, Dilip *economist, consultant*
Ratliff, Kimberlee Michelle *counselor*
Ratliff, Robert J. *retired farm equipment manufacturing executive*
Ratliff, William *former state senator, former lieutenant governor, civil engineer*
Ratnathicam, Chutta *transportation executive*
Ratner, Buddy Dennis *biomedical engineer, educator*
Ratner, Michael D. *lawyer*
Ratzenberger, John Deszo *actor, writer, film director*
Rau, David Edward *real estate consultant*
Rauch, Paul David *television producer*
Raucher, Herman *screenwriter, novelist*
Rausher, David Benjamin *internist, gastroenterologist*
Raven, Francis Harvey *mechanical engineer, educator*
Ravetch, Irving *screenwriter*
Ravinsky, Anthony *music educator*
Raviprakash, Kanakatte *molecular biologist*
Rawls, Frank Macklin *lawyer*
Rawnsley, Howard Melody *pathologist, educator*
Rawson, Richard J. *telecommunications industry executive, lawyer*
Ray, Amrit *pharmaceuticals strategist, company executive*
Ray, Carol Reneé *allied health professional*
Ray, Charles Aaron *ambassador*
Ray, Jane Zimrude *retired machine shop executive*
Ray, Marilyn Anne *nursing educator, researcher*
Ray, Rachael *chef, television personality*
Ray, Susan Elaine *principal*
Raymond, David Walker *lawyer*
Raymond, Lee R. *retired oil company executive*
Raymond, Ural Wayne *retired retail executive*
Rayner, William Alexander *retired newspaper editor, author*
Raziano, Amanda *environmental scientist*
Read, Richard Eaton *newspaper reporter*
Read, Tony John *management consultant*
Read, Virginia Hall *retired biochemistry professor*
Reader, George G. *retired internal-public health medicine educator*
Reagan, Nancy Davis (Anne Francis Robbins) *former First Lady of the United States, volunteer*
Reams, Patricia Lynn *retired elementary school educator*
Reardon, George Martin *lawyer*
Reath, George, Jr. *lawyer, mediator, arbitrator*
Reaves, Ray Donald *civil engineer*
Reavis, Charles Benton *choir director, educator*
Reay, Stefanie *application developer, educator*
Rebay, Luciano *language educator, literary critic*
Rebhun, Joseph *allergist, immunologist, medical educator*
Recchiuti, John Louis *history professor*
Rech, Lindsay Faith *writer*
Rechy, John Francisco *writer*
Reck, Elizabeth Torre *social worker, educator*
Redbord, Kelley Pagliai *dermatologist*
Redd, Scott (John Scott Redd) *federal official, retired military officer*
Redding, Rogers Walker *physics professor, academic administrator*
Reddy, Neelima G. *gastroenterologist, researcher*
Reddy, Ranga Vallela *anesthesiologist*
Redgrave, Vanessa *actress*
Redmon, Larry Allen *agronomist, educator*
Redmond, Arthur J. *insurance company executive*
Redmont, Bernard Sidney *dean, communications educator*
Reece, Karyn Lynn *small business owner, consultant*
Reece, Sheila Marlene *health facility administrator, writer*
Reece, Wanda G. *space station training engineer, writer*
Reed, Adam Victor *psychologist, engineer, information scientist*
Reed, Anne F. Thomson *management consultant*
Reed, Betty Jamerson *historian, educator*
Reed, David Patrick *information scientist*
Reed, Diane Marie *retired psychologist*
Reed, H. Owen *retired music educator*
Reed, James C., Jr. *lawyer*
Reed, Jean T. *retired archivist*
Reed, John Shedd *former railway executive*
Reed, John Shepard *former stock exchange executive*
Reed, Leon Samuel *photographer, writer*
Reed, Mary Carolyn Camblin *retired music educator, retired county official*
Reed, Rod A. *music educator, director*
Reeder, James Arthur *lawyer*
Reeder, Robert Harry *retired lawyer*
Rees, Raymond F. *military officer*
Reese, Angela Brooke *elementary school educator*
Reese, Hayne Waring *psychologist, educator*
Reese, Robert M. *retired lawyer*
Reeves, Daniel Edward *former professional football coach*
Reeves, Kathleen Walker *English language educator*
Reeves, Lucy Mary *retired elementary school educator*

Reeves, Richard *writer, historian*
Refai, Shahid *history professor*
Regan, Paul Jerome, Jr. *manufacturing company executive, consultant*
Regan, Peter Francis III *physician, medical educator*
Regel, Teresa Diamond *elementary school educator*
Regelbrugge, Roger Rafael *steel company executive*
Regenstreif, Herbert *lawyer*
Register, Karen *microbiologist, researcher*
Regnery, Russell Lawrence *microbiologist*
Reh, Sheila Natkins *humanities educator*
Rehak, James Richard *orthodontist*
Rehnke, Mary Ann *academic administrator*
Rehth, Ann *counselor*
Reich, Laurence *lawyer*
Reich, Otto Juan *political analyst, business consultant*
Reich, Robert Bernard *political economics educator, former secretary of labor*
Reiche, Frank Perley *lawyer, former federal commissioner*
Reichmanis, Elsa *chemist*
Reid, Debra Ann *history professor*
Reid, Geraldine Wold (Geraldine Reid Skjervold) *artist*
Reid, Helen Veronica *dean*
Reid, Katherine Lee *retired museum director, curator*
Reid, Orien *former medical association administrator*
Reid, Robert Lelon *engineering educator, dean*
Reid, Susan L. *conductor*
Reid, Tara *actress*
Reidy, Thomas Michael *financial executive*
Reilly, Charles Edmund, Jr. *communications executive*
Reilly, John C. *actor*
Reilly, Robert Joseph *counselor*
Reiman, Donald Henry *language educator*
Reimschuessel, Renate *pathologist*
Rein, Christopher M. *military officer*
Reinalda, David Anthony *elementary school educator*
Reinbold, Eric *social studies educator*
Reinhard, Diane L. *retired university president*
Reinhardt, John Edward *former international affairs specialist*
Reinhardt, Stephen Roy *federal judge*
Reiniche, Dominique *food products executive*
Reinike, Irma *retired writer, artist, poet, lyricist*
Reinke, Ralph Louis *retired academic administrator*
Reiser, Brian Sydney *economist, statistician*
Reiser, Richard Scott *lawyer*
Reisman, Judith Ann Gelernter *media communications executive, educator*
Reiss, Jerome *retired lawyer*
Reiss, Robert Francis *physician*
Reister, Ruth Alkema *lawyer, finance company executive*
Reiter, Glenn Mitchell *lawyer*
Remington, Mary *artist, author*
Remkus, Connie Elaine *nutritional consultant*
Ren, Xing Jian *physician*
Renaud, Bernadette Marie Elise *author*
Rendich, Ana *painter, collage artist*
Rendina, Salvatore N., Jr. *musician*
Rendl-Marcus, Mildred *artist, economist*
Rendu, Jean-Michel Marie *mining executive*
Renfro, Charles Gilliland *economist*
Renfro, Patricia Elise *library director, academic administrator*
Renfro, William Leonard *futurist, lawyer, inventor, entrepreneur*
Renkes, Gregg D. *former state attorney general*
Renne, Paul F. *retired food products executive*
Reno, Janet *former United States attorney general*
Renouf, Anne *corporate financial executive, consultant*
Renshaw, Jean Rehkop *management educator, consultant*
Rent, Clyda Stokes *academic administrator*
Renyi, Thomas A. *bank executive*
Repinski, Sara *library director*
Repp, Joan Mercedes *retired librarian*
Reppert, David Thomas *controller*
Reschke, Michael W. *real estate company officer*
Rescoe, Michael E. *computer company executive*
Resing, Maryloretto Rachel *guidance counseling administrator, elementary school educator, pastoral counselor*
Resnick, Kirsten Fay Markuson *history professor*
Resnick, Myron J. *retired insurance company executive, lawyer*
Ressom, Habtom W *education educator*
Retif, Thomas Newton *music educator*
Reuber, Grant Louis *banking insurance company executive*
Reuther, Ronald Theodore *museum director*
Reveal, Ernest Ira III *retired lawyer*
Revere, Virginia Lehr *psychologist*
Rew, Lawrence Boyd *lawyer*
Rewcastle, Neill Barry *neuropathologist*
Rey, Anamaria *psychologist*
Rey, Mark E. *federal agency administrator*
Reyes, Judy *actress*
Reyes, M. Jude *food products distribution executive*
Reynik, Robert John *materials scientist, consultant, science educator*
Reynolds, Clark Winton *economist, educator*
Reynolds, Devalyn L. *mathematician, educator*
Reynolds, Donald Martin *art historian, foundation administrator, educator*
Reynolds, Frank Miller *retired government agency administrator*
Reynolds, Fredric G. *broadcast executive*
Reynolds, Karen Ann *retired elementary school educator*
Reynolds, Lewis Dayton *pastor*
Reynolds, Patricia Ellen *artist*
Reynolds, Peggy Jean *elementary school educator*
Reynolds, Peter James *physicist*
Reynolds, Robert *artist, educator*
Reynolds, William Bradford *lawyer*
Reynolds, Wynetka Ann *academic administrator, educator*
Reza, Yasmina *author, playwright*

Ross, Darius Alexander *arbitrager and commodities trader, philanthropist*
Ross, Darrin *composer*
Ross, Edward *cardiologist*
Ross, Gloria Jean *artist*
Ross, Jeanne Nmi *psychologist*
Ross, Leonard Lester *anatomist, educator*
Ross, Michael Aaron *lawyer*
Ross, Michael Charles *lawyer*
Ross, Molly Owings *jewelry designer, sculptor, small business owner*
Ross, William Dee, Jr. *economist*
Rossello, Pedro *former governor*
Rossen-Knill, Deborah F. *academic administrator, language educator*
Rossetti, Armand John, Jr. *lawyer*
Rossi, Dino J. *former state legislator*
Rossi, Peter Henry *sociology educator*
Rossman, Ruth Scharff *artist, educator*
Rosten, Irwin *writer, producer, director*
Roswell, Robert H. *former federal agency administrator*
Roszkowski, Stanley Julian *retired federal judge*
Rotenberg, Marc Steven *advocate, lawyer*
Roth, Harvey Paul *retired publishing executive*
Roth, Jonathan Dean *music educator*
Roth, Michael *lawyer*
Roth, Philip Milton *writer*
Rothman, Howard Joel *lawyer*
Rothschild, Jennifer Ann *artist, educator*
Rothstein, Gerald Alan *investment consultant*
Rothwell, Timothy *pharmaceutical executive*
Rottenberg, Claire J. *writer, educator*
Rotunda, Adam Michael *dermatologist*
Roudebush, James Gordon *career military officer*
Roukema, Margaret Scafati *congresswoman*
Rouman, John Christ *classics educator*
Roumbos, Maria K. *elementary school educator*
Rourke, Mickey (Philip Andre Rourke Jr.) *actor*
Rouse, Roscoe, Jr. *retired librarian, educator*
Rouse, Terrie Suzitte *museum director*
Rousseau, Eugene Ellsworth *musician, music educator, consultant*
Routson, Clell Dennis *manufacturing executive*
Rowe, Audrey *paralegal*
Rowe, Bobby Louise *art educator*
Rowe, Hahn *composer*
Rowe, Richard R. *on-line information and management services company executive*
Rowe, William Davis *finance company executive*
Rowell, Barbara Caballero *retired academic administrator*
Rowell, Lester John, Jr. *retired insurance company executive*
Rowen, Henry Stanislaus *retired economist, former federal agency administrator*
Rowland, Allen R. *former retail executive*
Rowland, Pleasant T. *toy company executive, publisher*
Rowlands, Gena *actress*
Rowny, Michael J. *communications executive*
Roy, Michelle E. *musician, information technology consultant*
Royce, Paul Chadwick *healthcare administrator*
Roychowdhury, Abhijit *chemist, entrepreneur*
Rozario Stewart, Gwendolyn Michelle *elementary school educator*
Rozin, Boris *mathematician, writer*
Rozoff, Jonathan Mark *legal consultant*
Rubbert, Paul Edward *retired engineering executive*
Rubello, David Jerome *artist*
Ruben, Jeffrey M. *finance company executive, lawyer*
Rubenfeld, Stanley Irwin *lawyer, director, mediator, arbitrator*
Rubenstein, David Aaron *military officer, healthcare administrator*
Rubin, Ellen *educational coordinator*
Rubin, Martin N. *meeting planner, consultant*
Rubin, Phyllis Getz *health association executive*
Rubin, Richard Allan *lawyer*
Rubin, Robert Joseph *internist, consultant, nephrologist*
Rubin, Sandra Mendelsohn *artist*
Rubin, Vera Cooper *astronomer, researcher*
Rubin, Zick *psychology professor, writer, lawyer*
Rubinstein, Eva (Anna) *photographer*
Rubottom, George Milton *foundation administrator, chemist*
Rucci, Anthony Joseph *health care products and services executive*
Rudd, D(ale) F(rederick) *chemical engineering professor*
Ruder, Tia L. *music educator*
Rudick, A. Joseph *research and development company executive*
Rudin, Anne *retired mayor, nursing educator*
Rudley, Lloyd Dave *psychiatrist*
Rudner, Sara *dancer*
Rudolph, Heidi Anne Jantz *mathematician, educator*
Rudolph, James Robert *psychologist*
Rudolph, Maya *actress, comedienne*
Rudolph, Shay Jeanette *music educator, musician*
Rudolph, Wallace Morton *law educator*
Rudy, Raymond Bruce, Jr. *retired food company executive*
Ruedenberg, Klaus *theoretical chemist, educator*
Ruegg, Donald George *retired rail transportation executive*
Ruehl, Mercedes *actress*
Ruemmler, Kathryn H. *prosecutor*
Ruffin, David Aliston *secondary school educator, entertainer*
Ruffin, Herbert George, II, *history professor*
Ruffo, Michael *painter*
Rufus, Nancy G. *secondary school educator*
Rugaber, Walter Feucht, Jr. *retired publishing executive, academic administrator*
Ruggiero, David L. *music educator, accountant*
Ruggiero, Matthew John *bassoonist*
Ruggles, Rudy Lamont, Jr. *international security advisor*
Ruhm, Thomas Francis *retired lawyer*
Rui, Yong *research and development company executive*
Rukeyser, Robert James *manufacturing executive*
Ruland, Mildred Ardelia *retail executive, retail buyer*
Runkle, Ethel Mona *artist*

Runkle, Martin Davey *library director*
Runnells, Barbara Ann *technologist*
Ruoff, A. LaVonne Brown *language educator*
Rush, Jeffrey, Jr. *former federal agency administrator*
Rush, Julia Ann Halloran (Mrs. Richard Henry Rush) *artist, writer*
Rush, Norman *author*
Rush, Richard Henry *finance company executive, educator, writer*
Rushforth, Ann Fay *artist, art educator*
Rushforth, Brent N. *lawyer*
Rushnell, Squire Derrick *television executive, writer*
Rusie, Ruth Louise *special education educator*
Russ, Edmond Vincent, Jr. *marketing professional*
Russ, Joanna *author*
Russack, John A. *federal official*
Russell, Andrew Benjamin *historian, educator*
Russell, Attie Yvonne *academic administrator, pediatrics educator, dean*
Russell, Carol Ann *personnel service company executive*
Russell, Charles William III *communications executive, writer*
Russell, James Benjamin *microbiologist, educator, research scientist*
Russell, James Brian *broadcast executive, media consultant*
Russell, Theresa Lynn *actress*
Russell, Walter Dallas, Jr. *diversified financial services company executive*
Russo, Jose *pathologist*
Russo, Richard *writer*
Russo, Roy Lawrence *retired electronics engineer*
Russo, Vincent Joseph *surgeon*
Rutan, Charles R. *musician*
Rutgard, Lorraine Levin *hearing impaired educator*
Rutherford, John Sherman, III, (Johnny Rutherford) *professional race car driver*
Rutherford, Mary Louise Manlove *artist*
Rutledge, Mary Elizabeth *cultural organization administrator*
Rutsala, Vern A. *poet, writer, language educator*
Rutsky, Lester *retired textiles executive, writer*
Rutstein, Rebecca Anne *painter*
Ruviella-Knorr, Jeanne L. *music educator, consultant, clinician*
Ruzek, Sheryl Kendra Burt *healthcare educator, sociologist*
Ryan, Cynthia Rhoades *lawyer*
Ryan, Daniel John *university administrator*
Ryan, George William *manufacturing executive*
Ryan, James *insurance company executive*
Ryan, James C. *theater educator*
Ryan, Joan *food company executive*
Ryan, John Joseph *physician*
Ryan, John William *educational association administrator*
Ryan, Joyce Ethel *writer, artist*
Ryan, Leo Vincent *business educator*
Ryan, Marleigh Grayer *language educator*
Ryan, Timothy Patrick *investment company executive*
Ryan, William *executive*
Ryan-Halley, Charlotte Muriel *oncology clinical specialist, family practice nurse practitioner*
Rybak, Ilya A. *neuroscientist, biophysicist, educator*
Rybczyk, Joseph Anthony *physicist, researcher, writer, inventor*
Rydén, Bengt Gunnar *retired stock exchange executive*
Ryder, Donald J. *military career officer*
Ryder, Edmund Campion *art history professor*
Ryder, Tereasa Kai *retired protective services official*
Ryder, Winona (Winona Laura Horowitz) *actress*
Rydholm, Ralph Williams *advertising executive*
Rymar, Julian W. *manufacturing executive, director*
Ryskamp, Charles Andrew *museum director, educator*
Ryu, Jae *hydrologist*
Sa, Julie (Shia Ri Xiang) *former council woman, former mayor, real estate developer*
Sa, Ping *statistician, educator*
Saalfeld, Fred Erich *science educator, researcher*
Sabatini, David Domingo *cell biologist, biochemist*
Sabatini, Nelson John *healthcare executive*
Sabb, Annmarie Louise *retired chemist*
Sabbath, Joseph Waters *academic administrator*
Sabbatini, Marcello *journalist, motor sports weekly director*
Sabelhaus, Melanie R. *government agency administrator*
Sabin, Jorge A. *emergency physician, consultant*
Sacchetti, Susanne Louise *librarian*
Saccoccio, Jacqueline *artist*
Sacha, Robert Frank *osteopath, educator*
Sachatello-Sawyer, Bonnie Lynn *education educator, director*
Sachs, Sharona *internist, researcher*
Sack, Sylvan Hanan *lawyer*
Sackett, Susan Deanna *writer*
Sacks, Temi J. *public relations executive*
Sade, (Helen Folasade Adu) *singer, lyricist*
Sadinsky, Rachael *curator, art appraiser*
Sadoh, Godwin Simeon *music educator*
Sadow, Harvey S. *healthcare company executive*
Sadowski, Peter T. *lawyer*
Saeks, Richard Ephraim *engineering executive*
Saenz, Cecilia Sonia *education educator*
Safian, Shelley Carole *advertising executive*
Sagan, M. J. *architectural firm executive*
Sage, C. J. *literature and language professor, editor, writer*
Sager, Donald Jack *librarian, consultant, retired publishing executive*
Saha, Arun Kumar *engineering educator, researcher*
Sahelijo, Leonardo *geneticist, researcher*
Sahrakorpi, Seppo *physicist, researcher*
Saint, Eva Marie *actress*
St. Clair, Niké Eniko *music educator, conductor*
St. Clair, Thomas McBryar *mining and manufacturing company executive*
St. Claire, Frank Arthur *lawyer*
St. Germain, Fernand Joseph *retired congressman*

Saint-Girard, Christian *theater director, actor, educator, choreographer, theater producer*
Saint-Jacques, Bernard *linguistics educator*
St. John, Terry Noel *art educator*
St. Patrick, Matthew *actor*
Saito, Robert Shunichi *writer, poet*
Sajak, Pat *television game show host*
Sakai, Kiyoko *artist*
Saks, Gene *theater and film director, actor*
Saks, Judith-Ann *artist*
Saks, Stephen Howard *accountant, health organization executive*
Salamon, Rick *secondary school educator, department chairman*
Salamone, Joseph Charles *polymer chemistry professor*
Salat, Cristina *writer*
Saldanha, John *biologist, director*
Saleh, Brian Behrooz *aerospace transportation executive*
Salerno, Cherie Ann (C. S. Mau) *artist*
Salerno, Frederic V. *retired telecommunications company executive*
Salerno, Sister Maria *nursing educator, advanced practice nurse*
Salgado, Susana *musicologist, researcher, consultant*
Saliba, Jacob *manufacturing executive*
Saligman, Harvey *retired consumer products and services company executive*
Salinas, Tracie McLemore *mathematics professor*
Salis, Ari *radiologist*
Salisbury, Micheal Wayne *education educator*
Saliterman, Richard Arlen *lawyer*
Salkind, Michael Jay *science administrator, metallurgical engineer*
Salles, Felipe Weisz *musician*
Sallis, James *writer*
Salmon, Jerry Derr *federal air marshall*
Salo, Tommy *retired professional hockey player*
Salter, Claudia Joe *psychologist*
Saltzman, Philip *television producer, writer*
Salvanto, Maria *counselor*
Salvatore, Diane J. *editor-in-chief*
Salyers, Holly Amber *social studies educator*
Salzman, Arthur George *architect*
Samartzis, Dino *medical researcher, writer*
Samblis, Kelley C. *educator, researcher*
Sambora, Richie (Richard Stephen Sambora) *musician, singer, songwriter*
Samec, Diane Patricia *retired elementary school educator*
Samer, Bill Fred Carl *writer, cartoonist*
Sameroff, Arnold Joshua *developmental psychologist, educator, research scientist*
Samolyk, Keith Andrew *cardiovascular perfusionist, director*
Sampson, Clinton J. *director*
Sampson, David Synnott *lawyer*
Sampson, Robert Neil *professional society administrator, consultant*
Samra, Nicholas James *bishop*
Samson, Alvin *former distributing company executive, consultant*
Samuels, Marc *healthcare consultant*
Samuels, Maurice Andrew *French literature educator*
Samuelson, Robert Jacob *journalist*
Sanchez, Antonio Rodolfo, Jr. *oil industry executive*
Sanchez, Fausto H. *advertising executive*
Sanchez, Rafael Camilo *physician, educator*
Sanchez, Ricardo S. *career military officer*
Sandage-Mussey, Elizabeth Anthea *retired market research executive*
Sanders, Aaron Perry *radiation biophysics educator*
Sanders, Barry *retired professional football player*
Sanders, Charles Franklin *energy executive, consultant*
Sanders, Franklin D. *retired insurance company executive*
Sanders, Jay Olcutt *actor*
Sanders, Marlene *news correspondent, journalism educator*
Sanderson, James Richard *retired naval officer, financial consultant*
Sanderson, Janet A. *former ambassador*
San Diego, Armando Gonda *retired military officer, pathologist, consultant*
Sandler, Adam *actor*
Sandler, Norman *communications executive*
Sandlin, Max Allen, Jr. *former congressman*
Sandorsen, Cassiopeia *public health service officer*
Sands, Mark D. *musician, educator*
Sandstead, Auriel J. *retired secondary school educator, researcher, historian*
Sanfelippo, Peter Michael *thoracic surgeon*
Sanger, Frederick *retired molecular biologist*
San Jose, Angel Molina *surgeon*
Sankaran, Vinod *financial analyst*
San Miguel, Lolita *artistic director*
Sanquist, Nancy Johnson *real estate consultant, educator*
Sansbury, Olin Bennett, Jr. *retired university and orchestra administrator*
Santangelo, Gaspare Charles *education educator, retired principal*
Santiago, Jose E. *film producer, writer, director, educator*
Santina, Dalia *nutritionist, writer, skin care specialist*
Santini, Debrah Ann *art educator, artist*
Santman, Leon Duane *lawyer, former federal government executive*
Santomero, Anthony M. *retired bank executive, former public policymaker*
Santora, Ellen Durrigan *education educator*
Santos, Arthur Magno *thoracic cardiovascular surgeon*
Santos, Nicole Marie *elementary school educator*
Santoso, Irene *art director, graphics designer*
Santry, Barbara Lea *venture capitalist*
Sapienza, David Victor *social studies educator*
Sapoff, Meyer *retired electronics executive*
Sapp, John Raymond *lawyer*
Sapsowitz, Sidney H. *entertainment and media company executive*
Saracino, Dawn M. *physical therapist, educator*
Saravolatz, Louis Donald *epidemiologist, medical educator*

Sardisco, Karen Ann *artist, educator*
Sargent, Thomas Andrew *retired political science professor*
Sargent, William Winston *retired anesthesiologist*
Sari, Dita *labor union administrator*
Sarkisian, Pamela Outlaw *artist*
Sarkisov, Sergey Sergeyevich *engineering educator*
Sarma, Pallav *research scientist*
Sarofim, Louisa Stude *art patron, philanthropist*
Sarris, Andrew George *film critic*
Sarry, Christine *ballerina*
Saslekova, Lilia Emilianova *financial analyst*
Sass, Mary Martha *freelance writer, artist*
Sassa, Scott M. *former internet company executive*
Sassen, Saskia *urban planner, educator*
Sastrowardoyo, Teresita Manejar *nurse*
Satinover, Jeffrey B. *physicist, psychiatrist, writer*
Satterthwaite, Helen Foster *retired state legislator*
Sattler, Bruce Weimer *lawyer*
Sattler, Rolf *retired plant morphologist, educator*
Saucier, Gene Duane *retired state legislator, retired import/export company executive*
Saucier, Guylaine *corporate financial executive*
Sauerhaft, Stan *retired public relations executive, retired consultant*
Saul, Mark E. *secondary school educator, consultant*
Saunders, Lonna Jeanne *lawyer, newscaster*
Saunders, Stacy Dawn *secondary school educator, music educator, singer*
Saunders, Terry Rose *lawyer*
Sava, Vasyl *education educator*
Savage, Kim I. *academic administrator*
Savedra, Jeannine Evangeline *artist, educator*
Savela, Judith Gheldof *librarian*
Savercool, Susan Elisabeth *elementary school educator*
Savin, Ronald Richard *chemicals executive*
Savitz, Maxine Lazarus *aerospace transportation executive*
Sawai, Dahleen Emi *language educator*
Sawczuk, Ihor S. *urologist*
Sax, Joseph Lawrence *lawyer, educator*
Saxon, John David *lawyer, educator, policy analyst, educator*
Sayre, David *physicist*
Sayre, Donna *elementary school educator*
Sayre, Robert Freeman *language educator*
Scala, James *health facility administrator, consultant, writer*
Scales, Mauricco Lamont *history educator*
Scandary, E. Jane *special education educator, consultant*
Scanlan, John Douglas *retired ambassador*
Scanlon, Peter Redmond *retired accountant*
Scannell, Herb *broadcast executive*
Scarborough, Ann Barlow *secondary school educator*
Scarchuk, Lynn Nettleton *music educator*
Scardino, Peter T. *urologic oncologic surgeon*
Scarwid, Diana Elizabeth *actress*
Schabacker, Betty Barchet *artist*
Schadow, Karen E. *public speaking trainer, educator*
Schadt, James Phillip *investment and software executive*
Schaechter, Moselio *microbiology educator*
Schaefer, C. Barry *rail transportation executive, investment company executive*
Schaefer, William Goerman *lawyer*
Schall, Debra Jean *secondary school educator*
Schallert, William Joseph *actor*
Schanfield, Fannie Schwartz *community volunteer*
Scharf, Michael Paul *law educator*
Scharf, William *artist*
Scharlemann, Robert Paul *theology studies educator, minister*
Schatz, Wayne Ardale *district technology coordinator, educator*
Schauf, Victoria *pediatrician, educator*
Schaupp, Joan Pomprowitz *trucking executive, writer*
Schaut, Joseph William *retired bank executive*
Schear, Betty Z. *engineering executive, consultant*
Scheel, Nels Earl *corporate financial executive, accountant*
Scheele, Jennifer Joy *music educator*
Scheer, Teva Scheer *human resources specialist*
Scheiber, Stephen Carl *psychiatrist, director*
Scheiberg, Susan L. *librarian*
Schein, Edgar Henry *management educator*
Schell, Allan Carter *retired electrical engineer*
Schell, Melvin Frank, Jr. *real estate agent*
Schellenberger, Robert Earl *retired management educator, department chairman*
Schellman, John A. *chemistry professor*
Schenck, Jack Lee *retired electric utility executive*
Schenker, Leo *retired utilities executive*
Schenker, Marc Benet *preventive medicine physician, medical educator, department chairman*
Schenkkan, Robert Frederic *playwright, scriptwriter*
Schetky, Diane Heiskell *psychiatrist*
Schewe, Donald Bruce *archivist, library director*
Schexnayder, Brian Edward *vocalist, educator*
Schiaffino, S(ilvio) Stephen *retired medical association administrator*
Schiff, Martin *physician, surgeon*
Schiff, Stacy *writer*
Schiffer, Claudia *model*
Schiffer, Robert E. *former school system administrator*
Schillings, Karen Marie *elementary school educator*
Schirmer, Andrew L. *application developer*
Schlagel, Richard H. *retired philosophy educator*
Schlegel, John P. *academic administrator*
Schlein, Dov C. *banker*
Schlensker, Gary Chris *landscape company executive*
Schlesinger, Deborah Lee *retired librarian*
Schless, Phyllis Ross *investment banker*
Schley, Reeve III *artist*
Schlick, Austin C. *lawyer*
Schlieker, Janice Elaine Jones *campus minister*
Schlosser, Anne Griffin *librarian*
Schmalz, Carl Nelson, Jr. *artist, educator, art appraiser, printmaker*

Shinseki, Eric Ken *retired military officer*
Shipway, John Francis *retired career officer*
Shire, Talia Rose (Talia Rose Coppola) *actress*
Shirley, David Arthur *chemistry professor, science administrator*
Shirley-Quirk, John *singer, educator*
Shivers, Mitchell Everett *diplomat*
Shlapak, Fred *electronics executive*
Shockley, Edward Julian *retired air transportation executive*
Shoemaker, Bobby Jean (B.J. Foster) *writer*
Shohet, Stephen Byron *medical educator*
Shook, Ann Jones *lawyer*
Shoop, Glenn Powell *investment consultant*
Shore, Eleanor Gossard *retired medical school dean*
Shore, Robert *artist, educator*
Shore, Stephen *photographer*
Shorr, Harriet *artist*
Shotwell, Malcolm Green *minister*
Shoul, Melvin I. *retired surgeon*
Shoun, Ellen Llewellyn *retired secondary school educator*
Shrank, William H. *physician, researcher*
Shrembek, Carol Rose *claims consultant*
Shrestha, Anil *ecologist*
Shreve, Susan Richards *writer, educator*
Shriram, K. Ram *investment company executive*
Shriver, Eunice Mary Kennedy (Mrs. Robert Sargent Shriver Jr.) *foundation administrator, volunteer, social worker*
Shriver, Pamela H. *retired professional tennis player, sports analyst*
Shriver, Sargent (Robert Sargent Shriver Jr.) *lawyer*
Shrotriya, Vishal *research scientist*
Shrum, Robert Matthew *political strategist, educator, journalist*
Shteyngart, Gary *writer*
Shubb, William Barnet *judge*
Shuchart, Eugene Joseph *retired accountant*
Shugart, Jill *academic administrator*
Shuler, Jon Emmett *securities industry professional*
Shulgasser-Parker, Barbara *critic, writer*
Shull, Claire *documentary film producer, casting director*
Shulman, Mildred *artist*
Shulman, Yechiel *engineering educator*
Shultis, Robert Lynn *finance educator, consultant, retired professional society administrator*
Shultz, Delray Franklin (Lucky Shultz) *business coach, consultant*
Shultz, Stephen A. *secondary school educator*
Shumacker, Harris B., Jr. *retired surgeon, educator, author*
Shuman, Samuel Irving *lawyer, educator*
Shuman, Stanley S. *investment banker*
Shupe, Scott Marshall *engineering educator, consultant*
Shur, Michael *electrical engineer, educator, consultant*
Shuster, Bud *business executive, former congressman*
Shuster, Frederick *retired internist, gastroenterologist*
Shuster, Robert G. *electronics executive, consultant*
Shute, Richard Emil *federal agency administrator, engineer*
Shutler, Mary Elizabeth *academic administrator*
Shvo, Michael *real estate broker*
Shwartz, Sima M. *music educator*
Sibilla, Suzanne Rose *training and organizational development consultant*
Sibo, Elsa Lynette *secondary school educator*
Sibuma, Bernadette *educational consultant*
Sicart, Pierre-Alexandre Serge Henry *writer*
Siciliani, Alessandro Domenico *conductor*
Sicuro, Natale Anthony *academic and financial administrator, consultant*
Siddeeq, Baiyinah Nawal Rubye *secondary school educator*
Siddiqi, Javed *neurosurgeon*
Siddons, Anne Rivers (Sybil Anne Rivers Siddons) *writer*
Sidebottom, William George *communications executive*
Sides, Jack Davis, Jr. *lawyer*
Siebe, Carol Ann *retired elementary school educator*
Siebert, Thomas L. *lawyer, former ambassador*
Siefert-Kazanjian, Donna *corporate librarian*
Sieg, Kent G. *historian*
Siegal, Allan Marshall *journalist, consultant*
Siegal, Rita Goran *engineering company executive*
Siegel, George Henry *management consultant*
Siegel, Herbert Bernard *management consultant*
Siegel, Ira T. *publishing executive*
Siegel, Jack Morton *retired pharmaceutical executive*
Siegel, Mary Ann Garvin *writer*
Siegel, Vivian *biology editor*
Sielicki-Korczak, Boris Zdzislaw *political educator, investigative consultant*
Siemer, Deanne Clemence *lawyer*
Siems, Bennett A. *performing company executive*
Siena, James *artist*
Siffert, Robert Spencer *orthopedic surgeon*
Sifton, David Whittier *retired magazine editor*
Sigell, Leonard Trittack *pharmacologist, educator*
Sigety, Charles Edward *lawyer, financial planner*
Sigler, Jamie-Lynn *actress*
Sigmon, J. Lewis, Jr. *medical educator*
Sikes, Cynthia Lee *actress, children's advocate, singer*
Sikorska, Elzbieta Magdalena *artist*
Sikorski, James Alan *research chemist*
Sikorski, Lorena L. *secondary school educator*
Silano, Lawrence *music educator*
Silas, Paul *former professional basketball coach*
Silberman, Larry (Laurence Hirsch Silberman) *federal judge*
Silberstein, Alan Mark *financial services executive*
Silianoff, David *secondary school educator, educator, mathematics educator*
Siljak, Dragoslav D. *engineering educator, researcher*
Sillman, Amy *painter, art educator*
Sills, Richard Reynolds *scientist, educator*
Silva, Luis M. *marketing professional*

Silver, Lynn Leslie *research scientist, consultant*
Silver, Malcolm David *pathologist, educator*
Silverman, Burton Philip *artist*
Silverman, Ira Norton *news producer*
Silverman, Kenneth Eugene *language educator, writer*
Silverman, Matthew Adam *school system administrator*
Silverman, Stanley Wayne *chemical company executive*
Silverstein, Barbara Ann *conductor, artistic director*
Silverstein, Marc *TV host, reporter*
Silverthorn, Dee Unglaub *physiologist, educator*
Silvertooth, Carl Dennis *artist*
Silvestri, Alan Anthony *film composer*
Silvestri, Gina *lawyer*
Silvey, Anita Lynne *editor*
Simecka, Betty Jean *marketing executive*
Simendinger, Theodore John *writer, publishing executive*
Simeral, William Goodrich *retired chemical company executive*
Simmons, Deborah Jo *pharmacist, director*
Simmons, Deidre Warner *retired performing company executive, arts consultant*
Simmons, Geoffrey Stuart *physician, educator, writer*
Simmons, Lynda Merrill Mills *retired principal*
Simmons, Maya Tranemose *painter*
Simmons, Russell *recording industry executive*
Simms, Maria Ester *health facility administrator*
Simon, Bernece Kern *retired social worker*
Simon, Carly *singer, composer, author*
Simon, Donald John *financial planner, small business owner*
Simon, John Douglas *chemistry educator*
Simon, Leonard Samuel *banker*
Simon, Marc *communications executive*
Simon, Melvin I. *molecular biologist, educator*
Simon, Neil *playwright, screenwriter, television writer*
Simon, Nicholas J. III *medical products executive*
Simon, Norma Plavnick *psychologist*
Simon, Paul *musician, composer*
Simon, Peter E. *publishing executive*
Simon, Robert G. *lawyer*
Simon, Roger *newspaper columnist*
Simon, Ronald Isaac *financial executive*
Simon, William Leonard *scriptwriter, television producer, writer, film producer*
Simonds, Robert *producer*
Simonian, Simon John *surgeon, scientist, educator, health science association administrator*
Simons, Anneke Prins *artist, educator*
Simons, John Nelson *surgeon, consultant*
Simons, Lewis Martin *journalist*
Simons, Lynn Osborn *educational consultant*
Simons, Ryan William *urban planner*
Simons, Thomas W., Jr. *history professor*
Simonsen, Lorence B. *director*
Simonson, Lee Stuart *broadcast executive*
Simpkins, Annellen *author*
Simpson, Andrea Lynn *communications executive*
Simpson, Ashlee Nicole *vocalist, actress*
Simpson, Frederick James *retired science administrator*
Simpson, Hugh L. *news correspondent, newswriter*
Simpson, Jack Benjamin *medical technologist, business executive*
Simpson, John Noel (Virginia Simpson) *health facility administrator*
Simpson, Michael Marcial *science specialist, consultant*
Simpson, Murray *electrical engineer, consultant*
Simpson, Robert Homer *meteorologist, consultant*
Sims, Bennett Jones *minister, educator*
Sims, Elizabeth LaNeal *healthcare association executive*
Sims, Kent Otway *economist*
Sims, Pamela Jan (Cerussi) *writer, minister*
Sims Iannelli, Kimberly *writer*
Sinai, Allen Leo *economist, educator*
Sinclair, Cameron *architect*
Sinclair, Carol Ann *accountant, consultant*
Sinclair, Carole *publishing executive, editor*
Sincoff, Michael Z. *human resources and marketing executive*
Singer, David Michael *marketing executive, public relations executive*
Singer, Donna Lea *writer, editor, educator*
Singer, Markus Morton *retired trade association administrator*
Singer, S(iegfried) Fred *geophysicist, educator*
Singer-Chang, Gail Leslie *medical educator, consultant, social sciences educator*
Singh, Krishna Binod *obstetrician, gynecologist*
Singhal, Rajan *engineering executive, consultant*
Singletary, Patricia Ann *minister*
Singleton, John *director, screenwriter*
Singleton, Jonetta Williams *poet, retired special education educator*
Singleton, Robert Culton *academic administrator, theology studies educator*
Singleton-Wood, Allan James *communications executive*
Sinha, Rakesh Kumar *computer scientist, researcher*
Sinkford, Jeanne Craig *dental association administrator, retired dentist, retired dean, educator*
Sinning, Mark Alan *thoracic and vascular surgeon*
Sinnott, Stephen P. *prosecutor*
Sinor, Howard Earl, Jr. *lawyer*
Sirkeci Mergan, Birsen *electrical engineer, researcher*
Sirna, Gail Carolyn *artist, educator*
Sisk, Jane Elizabeth *economist, educator*
Siska, John Edward *foundation administrator, publishing executive*
Sisley, Emily Lucretia *psychologist, writer*
Sissel, George Allen *manufacturing executive, lawyer, engineer*
Sissman, Liron *artist, painter*
Sites, Kevin *news correspondent, journalist, web blogger*
Sitnyakovsky, Roman Emmanuil *scientist, writer, inventor, translator*
Sivill, Jason Ryan *music educator*
Sizemore, Joe R. *music educator, musician*
Sjostrand, Fritiof Stig *biologist, educator*

Skaba, Mark Paul *music educator*
Skaff, Joseph John *state agency administrator, retired military officer*
Skaggs, Bebe Rebecca Patten *college dean, clergywoman*
Skala, Gary Dennis *management consultant*
Skelland, Anthony Harold Peter *chemical engineering professor*
Skigen, Patricia Sue *lawyer*
Skinner, Daniel Thomas *language educator*
Skinner, Knute Rumsey *poet*
Skinner, Patricia Morag *state legislator*
Skinner, Thomas *broadcast executive*
Sklar, Holly L. *writer, columnist*
Skolnick, Lawrence *neonatal physician, medical association administrator*
Skolnik, Barnet David *retired lawyer*
Skoog, Andrew *music educator*
Skov, Arlie Mason *petroleum engineer, consultant*
Skowronski, Vincent Paul *musician, recording industry executive*
Skramstad, Harold Kenneth, Jr. *museum consultant*
Skromme, Lawrence H. *consulting agricultural engineer*
Skulski, Tia *human resources specialist*
Skwarczyński, Henryk Adam (Henryk Skwar) *writer*
Slachta, Gregory Andrew *urologist*
Slater, Brian (Raven Slate) *writer*
Slater, Eve E. *former federal agency administrator*
Slater, Lori Annette *project manager*
Slaughter, Djuanique Naté *healthcare analyst, project manager, consultant*
Slaughter, Freeman Cluff *retired dentist*
Slaughter, Vernon Leroy *recording industry consultant*
Slavens, Thomas Paul *library science professor*
Slavit, David Hal *otolaryngologist*
Slavitt, David Walton *retired lawyer*
Slayman, Carolyn Walch *geneticist, educator*
Sledge, Lela Bell *minister*
Sleeman, Donald George *construction executive, contractor*
Slezak, Erin Kathleen *elementary school educator*
Sloan, Michael Allan *neurologist*
Sloan, Robert D. *energy executive, lawyer*
Sloane, Neil James Alexander *mathematician, researcher*
Slobodnik, Ricci *mathematician, educator*
Slonaker, Norman Dale *lawyer*
Slosberg, Mike *advertising executive*
Slotkin, Marvin Bernard *surgeon*
Sloyan, Gerard Stephen *theology studies educator, priest*
Slusser, Eugene Alvin *electronics executive, consultant*
Smally, Donald Jay *consulting engineering executive*
Smardz, Zofia Jadwiga *editor, writer*
Smart, James Anthony *music educator*
Smart, Jill Bellavia *financial consultant*
Smaw, Shercoda Genee *research scientist*
Smeallie, Kevin Wayne *engineering company executive, consultant*
Smelser, Neil Joseph *sociologist*
Smeltzer, Debra Jean *botanist*
Smith, A. Robert *editor, author*
Smith, Adrian J.R. *management company executive*
Smith, Alan Michael *music educator, musician*
Smith, Alice Davis *retired biology educator, retired art educator*
Smith, Allan Laslett *research scientist, educator*
Smith, Anna Nicole (Vickie Lynn Hogan) *television personality, model*
Smith, Barbara Anne *health facility administrator, consultant*
Smith, Barbara Jeanne *retired librarian*
Smith, Carole Dianne *retired lawyer, editor, writer, product developer*
Smith, Catherine Marie *science educator*
Smith, Cathy Gaye *elementary school educator*
Smith, Charles Haddon *geologist, consultant, retired federal agency administrator*
Smith, Charlotte Reed *retired music educator*
Smith, Christopher T. *environmental health officer*
Smith, Cynthia S. *writer*
Smith, D(aisy) Mullett *publisher*
Smith, David Horton *retired social sciences educator*
Smith, Deborah L. *music educator, secondary school educator*
Smith, Debra A. *osteopath*
Smith, Denise Lorraine *accountant*
Smith, Diana Barker *music educator*
Smith, Edwin E. *aerospace transportation executive*
Smith, Fern M. *judge*
Smith, Floyd Leslie *insurance company executive*
Smith, Frederick Coe *retired manufacturing executive*
Smith, Frederick H. *archaeologist, educator*
Smith, George Drury *publishing executive*
Smith, George Patrick, II, *lawyer, educator*
Smith, Goff *industrial equipment manufacturing executive*
Smith, Gordon Ray *utilities executive*
Smith, H. Morgan *environmental scientist, educator*
Smith, Hamilton Othanel *molecular biologist, educator*
Smith, Harold Charles *pension fund administrator*
Smith, Howard I. *former insurance company executive*
Smith, James A. *lawyer*
Smith, Janet Marie *sports executive*
Smith, Jean Kennedy *former ambassador*
Smith, Kevin *film director, writer, actor*
Smith, Leila Hentzen *artist*
Smith, Leonore Rae *artist*
Smith, Leslie Roper *hospital administrator, health facility administrator*
Smith, Lois Arlene *actress, writer*
Smith, Marcia K. *government agency administrator*
Smith, Margaret Ann *retired art educator*
Smith, Margaret Taylor *volunteer*
Smith, Martin Bernhard *journalist*
Smith, Martin Cruz *author*
Smith, Martin Henry *retired pediatrician*

Smith, Michael L. *transportation company executive*
Smith, Michelle Rene *elementary school educator*
Smith, Mieko Kotake *education educator*
Smith, Nancy Angelynn *federal agency administrator*
Smith, Neil *former professional sports team executive*
Smith, Nick H. *former congressman, archivist, farmer*
Smith, Pamela Hyde *ambassador*
Smith, Patricia (Pat) Ann *elementary school educator*
Smith, Patricia Lynne *artist*
Smith, Paul Vergon, Jr. *retired gas industry executive*
Smith, Peter Walker *finance company executive*
Smith, Robert Hugh *retired engineering construction company executive*
Smith, Robert J., Jr. *real estate executive*
Smith, Robert Powell *former ambassador, retired foundation administrator*
Smith, Ruby Lucille *retired librarian*
Smith, Russell Francis *transportation executive*
Smith, Serafina Gangemi *artist*
Smith, Stuart Lyon *psychiatrist, corporate financial executive*
Smith, Susanna S. *school system administrator*
Smith, Sydney *elementary school educator*
Smith, Theodore Glenn *webmaster*
Smith, Thomas E. *social studies educator*
Smith, Thomas Eugene *investment company executive, financial consultant*
Smith, Todd Lee *protective services official*
Smith, V. Kerry *economics professor*
Smith, Vincent Milton *Feng Shui consultant, educator, writer*
Smith, Walton Napier *lawyer*
Smith, Wayne Calvin *chemical engineer, consultant*
Smith, Wendy Haimes *federal agency administrator*
Smith, Wendy L. *foundation executive*
Smith, Will *actor, rap artist*
Smith, William Charles *retired lawyer*
Smith, Yeardley *actress*
Smith, Yolanda Ippolito *law educator, researcher, writer*
Smith, Zannie O. *retired career officer*
Smith-Epstein, Mary Kathleen *dancer*
Smither, Howard Elbert *musicologist, educator*
Smith Fawzi, Mary C. *epidemiologist*
Smith-Singares, Eduardo *trauma surgeon, researcher*
Smits, Helen Lida *medical association administrator, educator*
Smock, Raymond William *historian*
Smoker, Roy Ellis *retired military officer*
Smoot, Oliver Reed, Jr. *lawyer, trade association administrator*
Smouse, H(ervey) Russell *lawyer*
Smukal, Michael William *music educator, composer, musician*
Smyth, Nicholas Patrick Dillon *surgeon*
Snare, Carl Lawrence, Jr. *retired accountant, financial planner*
Sneider, Joyce Pappachristou *dietician, educator*
Snelling, Barbara W. *retired state legislator*
Snelling, Robert Orren, Sr. *employment executive*
Snider, Gordon Lloyd *physician*
Snider, L. Britt *federal official*
Sniffen, Frances P. *artist*
Snipes, Wesley *actor, film producer*
Snodgrass, W. D. *writer, educator*
Snook, Paul *real estate company executive*
Snortland, Howard Jerome *financial consultant*
Snow, Claude Henry, Jr. *information services executive, consultant*
Snow, Gordon Raymond *composer, conductor, bass*
Snow, Jack (John William Snow) *former secretary of the treasury*
Snow, Joel Alan *research director*
Snow, Karl Nelson, Jr. *public management educator, academic administrator, retired state senator*
Snow, Marina *writer*
Snowden, Lawrence Fontaine *retired air transportation executive, retired military officer*
Snyder, Alan Carhart *finance company executive*
Snyder, Clarice Jane *music educator, musician*
Snyder, Colleen M. *music educator*
Snyder, Jean Maclean *lawyer*
Snyder, Joan *artist*
Snyder (Mackley), Louise Marie *speech pathology/audiology services professional, consultant*
Snyder, Marvin *neuropsychologist*
Snyder, Nathan *entrepreneur*
Snyder, Nathan Paul *music educator, musician*
Snyder, Stephen Edward *lawyer, mediator*
Snyder, William Burton *insurance company executive*
Snyderman, Ralph *medical educator, physician*
Snygg, John *mathematician, educator*
So, Jungmin *computer scientist, researcher*
Sobel, Dean *museum director, curator, artist*
Soble, Mark Richard *lawyer*
Sobol, Robert E. *medical company executive*
Sochynsky, Yaroslav *lawyer, arbitrator, mediator*
Socolow, Elizabeth Anne *poet, educator, artist, writer*
Soderbergh, Steven Andrew *filmmaker*
Sodums, Dzintars *writer*
Soeteber, Ellen *journalist, editor*
Sofair, Andre *epidemiologist, researcher*
Softic, Tanja *artist*
Sohn, Rayna Mayer *medical researcher, legal association administrator*
Sokal, Robert Reuven *biology professor, writer*
Sokol, Jan D. *lawyer*
Sokolowsky, Brian William *archivist, historian*
Solano, Julio Rafael *priest, educator*
Soliday, Michael David *secondary school and special educator*
Solivan, Neida M. *librarian, educator, school system administrator*
Solkoff, Jerome Ira *lawyer, educator*
Sollender, Joel David *management consultant, financial executive, accountant*
Solls, Mark A. *lawyer*

Stumpf, Heinrich Josef *psychometrician, research consultant*
Stupak, Mary Jo *psychotherapist, educator*
Sturr, James William, Jr. *bandleader, recording industry executive, clarinetist, saxophonist, small business owner*
Stutz, Pearl Hewlett *retired photojournalist*
Stutzman, Sandra Louise *advanced nurse practitioner*
Stuzin, James M. *plastic surgeon*
Styer, Denise Marie *psychologist*
Styron, William *writer*
Suber, Dianne Boardley *educational administrator*
Suber, Robin Hall *former medical and surgical nurse*
Sud, Pamela Rani *pulmonary and critical care physician, consultant*
Sudanowicz, Elaine Marie *government executive*
Sudarsky, Jerry M. *industrialist*
Suders, Joan Mary *elementary school educator*
Sueltz, Patricia C. *computer company executive*
Sugintas, Nora Maria *healthcare executive*
Suglia, Joseph Vincent *writer, educator*
Sukhatme, Jai *research scientist*
Sukopp, Karl Martin *sculptor, painter, graphic artist*
Sukumar, Sreenivas Rangan *operations research specialist, electrical engineer, computer engineer*
Sulc, Jean Luena (Jean L. Mestres) *lobbyist, consultant*
Sullivan, Charles *dean, educator, author*
Sullivan, Daniel Joseph *theater critic*
Sullivan, Dennis James, Jr. *retired hospitality and music executive*
Sullivan, Eugene John Joseph *manufacturing executive, director*
Sullivan, Eugene Raymond *judge*
Sullivan, G. Craig *household products executive*
Sullivan, George Edward *writer*
Sullivan, James Leo *organization executive*
Sullivan, John Dominic *theater producer, writer*
Sullivan, Kathryn D. *geologist, former astronaut, former science association executive*
Sullivan, Kathryn Meara *telecommunications industry executive*
Sullivan, Marissa M. *elementary school educator*
Sullivan, Mary Ann *artist*
Sullivan, Mary Rose *retired English language educator*
Sullivan, Mike *former professional hockey coach*
Sullivan, Nicholas G. *science educator*
Sullivan, Patricia *journalist*
Sullivan, Paul F. *career officer*
Sullivan, Roy Michael *aerospace engineer, researcher*
Sullivan, William Francis *lawyer*
Summar, Sharon Kay *elementary school educator*
Summerfield, John Robert *textile curator*
Summerlin, William Talley *allergist, immunologist, dermatologist*
Summers, Carol *artist*
Summers, Cathleen *film producer*
Summers, David Stewart *neurologist, consultant*
Summers, Lorraine Dey Schaeffer *retired librarian*
Summers, Marc *TV host, TV personality*
Summitt, Patricia Head *college basketball coach*
Sun, Chenghua *composer, music educator*
Sun, Keli *electrical engineer, researcher*
Sunde, Douglas *plastic surgeon*
Sunderman, Duane Neuman *chemist, research and development company executive*
Sundstrom, Aileen Lois *speech educator*
Sunia, Muagututia Fiti *former attorney general*
Suppes, Patrick *statistician, philosopher, psychologist, educator*
Suprun, Harry Zvi *pathologist*
Suput, Ray Radoslav *librarian*
Surface, James Louis, Sr. *trust officer, lawyer*
Surles, Richard Hurlbut, Jr. *retired law librarian*
Surplus, Robert Wilbur *retired music educator*
Susman, Morton Lee *lawyer*
Sussman, Barry *writer, demographer, editor*
Sussman, Howard Sivin *lawyer*
Sussman, Janet I. *social sciences educator*
Suter, Tracy A. *finance educator*
Sutherland, Deborah Alice *music educator*
Sutherland, Roger Collin *civil engineer, consultant*
Sutnick, Alton Ivan *medical educator, consultant, dean, internist, researcher*
Sutro, Edmund J. *secondary school educator, consultant*
Sutter, Eleanor Bly *retired diplomat*
Sutter, Laurence Brener *lawyer*
Suttie, John Weston *biochemist*
Sutton, Albert Philip *urologist*
Sutton, Dolores *actress, writer*
Sutton, Julia *musicologist, dance historian*
Sutton, Nancy Thurmond *music educator*
Sutton, Peter U. *military officer*
Sutton-Creech, Donna Lynn *gifted and talented educator*
Suzuki, Hidetaro *violinist*
Suzuki, Kunihiko *biomedical educator, researcher*
Svoboda, Janice June *nurse*
Swacker, Frank Warren *lawyer*
Swager, Cleo Marie *secondary school educator*
Swailes, William E. *counseling administrator*
Swalm, Thomas Sterling *aerospace transportation executive, retired military officer*
Swan, Annalyn *writer*
Swaner, Paula Margetts *clinical psychologist*
Swann, Charena Rai *psychotherapist, social worker*
Swann, Richard Rockwell *lawyer, banker*
Swanson (McNutt), Beverley Kay *special education educator*
Swanson, Carl D. *music educator, singer*
Swanson, Kurt *small business owner, artist*
Swanson, Patricia Klick *retired academic administrator, retired foundation administrator*
Swanstrom, Thomas Evan *economist*
Swartz, Jon David *psychologist, educator*
Swartz, Steven R. *publishing executive*
Sweeney, Deirdre Ann *lawyer*
Sweeney, Don Patrick *music coordinator, conductor*
Sweetland, Loraine Fern *librarian, educator*
Swensen, David Frederick *investment advisor*
Swenson, Shirley Ruth *retired elementary school educator*

Swerdlow, Martin Abraham *pathologist, educator*
Swett, Richard Nelson (Dick Swett) *diplomat, former congressman*
Swicklik, Mary Lou Marquardt *freelance/self-employed artist*
Swiecicki, Martin *retired neurosurgeon*
Swinburn, Carol Ditzler *retired state and municipal agency administrator*
Swinburn, Charles *rail transportation executive*
Switzer, Maurice Harold *journalist*
Swoap, David Bruce *government agency administrator, consultant, art director, state agency administrator*
Swoap, Thomas Frank, Jr. *history educator*
Swope, Donald Downey *retired banker*
Sykes, Kathryn Rosemarie *human resources specialist, consultant*
Sylvern, Craig *music educator*
Symchowicz, Samson *retired biochemist*
Synclair, Larry Ross *news correspondent, advocate*
Sypher, Francis J. *retired theology studies educator*
Sypolt, Diane Gilbert *retired judge*
Syverud, Kent Douglas *dean, law educator*
Sczublewski, Wendy Sue *small business owner, musician, freelance/self-employed writer*
Sze, Sarah *sculptor*
Sze, Sing-Hoi *science educator, researcher*
Szelenyi, Ivan *adult education educator*
Szep, Paul Michael *editorial cartoonist*
Szlam, Aleksander *manufacturing executive*
Szydlowski, Ralph *retired metal products executive*
Szymanski, Patrick Joseph *lawyer*
Szyszka, Roswita Evelyn *artist*
Taati, Poopak *media director*
Tabazadeh, Azadeh *environmental scientist, researcher*
Taber, Geoffrey Alexander *quality assurance professional*
Taboada, Javier Gustavo *neurologist*
Tabron, Wendy *paper company executive*
Tack, Theresa Rose *women's health nurse*
Tackett, Viti Lee *writer*
Taddei, Lois Annette Magowan *artist, interior designer*
Tadepalli, Srikanth *mechanical engineer, researcher*
Tadros, Fawzi M. *educator*
Tafoya, Michele *sports reporter*
Taft, Sheldon Ashley *retired lawyer*
Tagiuri, Consuelo Keller *child psychiatrist, educator*
Tagliabue, Paul John *retired national football league commissioner*
Tagliente, Josephine Marlene *artist*
Tague, John P. *air transportation executive*
Taishoff, Lawrence Bruce *publishing company executive*
Talamo, Jonathan Haskell *ophthalmologist, educator*
Talento-Miller, Eileen *psychometrician*
Talese, Nan Ahearn *freelance/self-employed publishing executive*
Tall, Sonia Terry *humanities educator, researcher*
Tallent, Hamlin B. *career officer*
Tallett, Elizabeth Edith *biopharmaceutical company executive*
Tallman, Ann Marie *lawyer*
Tallman, Renetta Deremer *music educator*
Talmage, David Wilson *retired microbiologist, retired educator, retired dean*
Tam, Sunny Wing Yee *physicist*
Tamborlane, William V., Jr. *pediatrician, educator*
Tambs, Lewis Arthur *diplomat, educator, historian*
Tammeus, William David *journalist, columnist*
Tamony, Katie *editor-in-chief*
Tan, Alson *computer scientist*
Tan, Maria (Mia Tan) *music educator*
Tan, Zixiang *education educator, researcher*
Tancer, Robert Stephen *prosecutor, educator*
Tancs, Linda Ann *lawyer*
Tandler, Bernard *cell biology educator*
Tandon, Rajiv *psychiatrist, educator*
Tane, Susan Jaffe *retired manufacturing company executive*
Tanenbaum, Jay Harvey *lawyer*
Tangherlini, Frank Robert *physics educator*
Tanguay, Jeanne Marie *social worker*
Tannenberg, Dieter E.A. *retired manufacturing executive*
Tanner, Laurel Nan *education educator*
Tanner, Lynn *actress*
Tanner, Peggy *retired nurse*
Tao, William K.Y. *retired education educator*
Taplett, Lloyd Melvin *human resources specialist, consultant*
Tapper, Leona (Leela) Siff *artist*
Taradash, Stacey *athletic trainer*
Taraki, Shirlee *librarian*
Taranta, Angelo (Visca Taranta) *physician, educator*
Tarantino, David A., Jr. *military officer, emergency physician*
Taranto, Maria Antoinette *psychology researcher and educator*
Tarbi, William Rheinlander *secondary education educator, curriculum consultant, educational technology researcher*
Tarbuck, Barbara Joan *actress*
Tarbutton, Lloyd T. *hotel executive, consultant*
Taren, James Arthur *neurosurgeon, educator*
Tarnopol, Michael Lazar *bank executive*
Tarr, Curtis W. *management consultant, educator*
Tarr, David Gerald *economist*
Tarr, Kenneth J. *retired investment company executive*
Tarrance, Vernon Lance, Jr. *research and development company executive*
Tarrant, Christine Gloria *music educator*
Tasman, Alice Lea Mast *not-for-profit fundraiser*
Tassone, Rebecca C. *elementary school educator*
Tata, Giovanni *publishing executive*
Tatavarthy, Aparna *biologist, researcher*
Tatlock, Anne M. *trust company executive*
Tatum, Arthur III *lexicographer, educator, pianist*
Tatum, Jerry Lee *researcher*
Tatum, Valorie *elementary school educator, pharmacist*
Taubman, A. Alfred *real estate developer*

Tauscher, Ellen O. *congresswoman*
Tavalin, Fern *educational consultant*
Tavares, Samia Costa *economics professor*
Tavella, Elise Shannon *librarian*
Tavrow, Richard Lawrence *lawyer*
Tayler, Irene *English literature educator*
Taylor, Alandya Natasha *elementary school educator*
Taylor, Ann *artist*
Taylor, Carson William *retired electrical engineer*
Taylor, Charles *law educator*
Taylor, Charles Henry *psychoanalyst, educator*
Taylor, Cora Hodge *social worker*
Taylor, Dave *former professional sports team executive, retired professional hockey player*
Taylor, David George *retired banker*
Taylor, Florietta *retired music educator, composer, retired social worker*
Taylor, Francis X. *former federal agency administrator, retired military officer*
Taylor, George Frederick *newspaper publisher, editor*
Taylor, George Peach, Jr. *career military officer*
Taylor, Hubert G. *lawyer*
Taylor, Job III *lawyer*
Taylor, John Brian *former federal agency administrator*
Taylor, John Calvin *dentist*
Taylor, John Jackson (Jay Taylor) *writer, retired diplomat*
Taylor, June Ruth *retired minister*
Taylor, Kathleen (Christine Taylor) *physical chemist, researcher*
Taylor, Margaret Turner *apparel designer, economist, writer, architectural designer*
Taylor, Nathalee Britton *retired nutritionist, freelance/self-employed writer*
Taylor, Peyton Troy, Jr. *oncologist, educator*
Taylor, Robert Morgan *electronics executive*
Taylor, Ronald Dean *retired psychologist, educator*
Taylor, Ronald Lewis *sociology educator*
Taylor, Roy Lewis *botanist, educator*
Taylor, Satomi Izumi *education educator*
Taylor, Sherri Joi *psychology professor*
Taylor, Steven D. *music educator*
Taylor, Timothy Joseph Andrew *social studies educator*
Taylor, William Colton *physician, educator*
Taylor, Wilson H. *retired diversified financial company executive*
Taylor-Anderson, Jill *reading specialist*
Taylor Claud, Andrea *retired educational consultant*
Taymor, Julie *theater, film and opera director and designer*
Teagan, John Gerard *publishing executive*
Teagle, David Bryan *manufacturing executive*
Teater, Dorothy Seath *retired county official*
Tebedo, MaryAnne *state legislator*
Tecco, Romuald Gilbert Louis Joseph *violinist, concertmaster*
Tedesco, Paul Herbert *humanities educator*
Teets, Peter B. *former civilian military employee*
Tegge, Patricia Ann *retired administrative assistant*
Tein, Jenn-Yun *psychologist, researcher*
Te Kanawa, Kiri *opera and concert singer*
Telnaes, Ann *cartoonist*
Temerlin, Liener *advertising executive*
Templeman, Lydia *retired assistant principal*
Templeton, Matt Aaron *art educator*
Templin, Kenneth Elwood *paper company executive*
TenHoeve, Thomas *academic administrator*
Tenney, Frank Putnam *marketing executive*
Teplow, Theodore Herzl *retired valve company executive*
Tepper, Lloyd Barton *preventive medicine physician, educator*
Ter Horst, Jerald Franklin *public affairs counselor*
Terp, Thomas Thomsen *lawyer*
Terpeluk, Peter G., Jr. *former ambassador*
Terr, Lenore Cagen *psychiatrist, writer*
Terracciano, Antonio *psychologist, researcher*
Terrell, G. Irvin *lawyer*
Terrell, Hellenna L. *education educator*
Terris, Susan *physician, cardiologist, researcher*
Terry, Carole Cosgrove *small business owner, historian, researcher*
Terry, Clifford Lewis *journalist*
Terry, Edwin Wellington *college librarian*
Terry, Elizabeth Hudson *personal care industry executive, realtor*
Terry, John Franklin, Jr. *secondary school educator*
Terry, Richard Edward *public utility holding company executive*
Terry, Robert Davis *neuropathologist, educator*
Tesarek, Dennis George *retired business consultant, writer, educator*
Tesseneer-Street, Susan *photographer, artist, writer*
Testaverde, Vincent Frank (Vinny Testaverde) *professional football player*
Tetteh, Emmanuel *director*
Tetzlaff, Christian *violinist*
Teuscher, Simon Hans *history professor, researcher*
Tevanian, Avadis, Jr. *information technology executive*
Tew, E. James, Jr. *management services company executive*
Textor, Robert Bayard *cultural anthropology educator, writer, consultant*
Thacker, Kirk David *secondary school educator*
Thackray, Arnold Wilfrid *historian, educator, foundation administrator*
Thackston, Edward Lee *civil engineering educator*
Thaler, Richard Winston, Jr. *investment banker*
Tharp, Twyla *dancer*
Tharpe, Frazier Eugene *journalist*
Theroux, Paul Edward *author*
Thewlis, David *actor*
Thie, Joseph Anthony *nuclear engineer*
Thiel, Philip *design educator*
Thiele, Gloria Day *librarian, small business owner*
Thiele, Howard Nellis, Jr. *lawyer*
Thiessen, Delbert Duane *psychologist*
Thomajan, Robert *lawyer, management consultant*
Thoman, Henry Nixon *lawyer*

Thomas, Adrian Wesley *research scientist, director, retired science educator*
Thomas, Betty *director, actress*
Thomas, Cheryl Shanks *public health service officer*
Thomas, Claudia Lynn *orthopedic surgeon*
Thomas, Donald Lee *construction technology educator*
Thomas, Frank M., Jr. *lawyer*
Thomas, Franklin Augustine *lawyer, consultant*
Thomas, Harry K., Jr. *former ambassador*
Thomas, James Edward, Jr. *brokerage house executive*
Thomas, Jo *journalist, educator*
Thomas, Joe Carroll *retired human resources director*
Thomas, John Howard *astrophysicist, mechanical engineer, educator*
Thomas, Kenneth Glyndwr *mining executive*
Thomas, Lee Muller *former paper company executive, former government offical*
Thomas, Patricia Anne *retired law librarian*
Thomas, Patricia Goodnow *journalist*
Thomas, Regena L. *former state official*
Thomas, Rob (Robert Kelly Thomas) *singer, songwriter*
Thomas, Stephen *retired industrial engineer*
Thomas, Steve *professional hockey player*
Thomas, Ted, Jr. *Drummer, producer, composer*
Thomas, Teresa Ann *microbiologist, educator*
Thomas, Tom *retired plastics company executive*
Thomas, William Scott *physician*
Thomas-Graham, Pamela *apparel executive*
Thompson, Alan Eric *economics professor*
Thompson, Andrea *television personality, retired newscaster, actress*
Thompson, Annie Laura (Laura Anne Thompson) *foreign language educator*
Thompson, Benjamin K.B. *financial analyst*
Thompson, Claire Louisa *nurse, educator, consultant*
Thompson, Craig Snover *corporate communications executive*
Thompson, David O'Neal *retired basketball player*
Thompson, Dean M., II *marketing executive*
Thompson, Didi Castle (Mary Bennett) *writer, editor*
Thompson, Dorothy Barnard *elementary school educator*
Thompson, Holley Marker *lawyer, consultant, marketing professional*
Thompson, J. Andy *bank executive*
Thompson, Jack Edward *mining company executive*
Thompson, Jennifer B. *Olympic swimmer*
Thompson, John Herd *history professor*
Thompson, Kenneth *software engineer*
Thompson, London (William London Evans-Thompson) *recording industry executive, publishing executive, sound recording engineer, executive film producer*
Thompson, Lorin Andrew III *chemist*
Thompson, Margie Ann *artist*
Thompson, Martin Christian *retired news executive*
Thompson, Mary Koleta *small business owner, not-for-profit developer*
Thompson, Philip C. *lawyer, investment advisor, educator*
Thompson, Ralph Newell *former chemical corporation executive*
Thompson, Richard Leon *pharmaceutical executive, lawyer*
Thompson, Richard Lloyd *retired pastor*
Thompson, Richard Stephen *management consultant*
Thompson, Sherwood *academic program director, consultant*
Thompson, Tina Marie *professional basketball player*
Thompson, Vetta Lynn Sanders *psychologist, educator*
Thomson, Caroline Helen *artist*
Thomson, Keith Stewart *biologist, author*
Thomson, Virginia Winbourn *humanities educator, writer*
Thongsak, Vajeeprasee Thomas *finance company executive*
Thoppil, Prasad *oceanographer, researcher*
Thoreen, Mary Louise *elementary school educator, consultant*
Thorhaug, Anitra L. *environmental scientist, educator*
Thorn, Terence Hastings *energy executive, consultant, writer*
Thornburg, Linda A. *writer*
Thorne, Stephen H. *research scientist*
Thornton, John Christopher *music educator*
Thornton, Kathryn C. *physicist, astronaut*
Thornton, Mary Leita *musician, educator*
Thornton, Ray *retired state supreme court justice, former congressman*
Thornton, Yvonne Shirley *obstetrician, writer, musician*
Thorp, Benjamin A. III *retired paper company executive*
Thorp, Steven Mark *music educator*
Thorsen, Marie Kristin *radiologist, educator*
Thorsen, Steven N. *mathematics professor, military officer*
Thorson, Connie Capers *library educator*
Thorstenberg, Laurence (John L. Thorstenberg) *oboe and English horn player*
Thrall, Richard Cameron, Jr. *broadcast executive*
Thrash, Rebecca C. *theater educator, theater director*
Threlkeld, Richard Davis *retired broadcast journalist*
Thrower, Daniel Nephi *musician, composer, educator*
Thueme, William Harold *secondary school educator, counselor, travel coordinator*
Thulean, Donald Myron *symphony conductor*
Thurmaier, Mary Jean *educational association administrator*
Thurman, JoAnn Truax *educational consultant*
Thurman, Karen L. *former congresswoman, lobbyist*
Thurmond, George Murat *judge*
Thurmond, J. Strom, Jr. *lawyer, former prosecutor*
Thurmond, John Peter, II *bank executive, rancher, archaeologist*

Verderber, Joseph Anthony *capital equipment company executive*
Verdery, David Norwood *broadcast programming executive*
Vergara, Camilo José *photographer*
Verhoff, Glen Charles *reading educator, choir director*
Verma, Surjit Kumar *retired school system administrator*
Vermeer, Donald Eugene *geography educator, retired*
Vermylen, Paul Anthony, Jr. *oil industry executive*
Vernon, Carl Atlee, Jr. *retired wholesale food distributor executive*
Veronis, George *geophysics educator*
Versch, Esther Marie *artist*
Vescovi, Jason D. *education educator*
Veselinovič, Draško *stock exchange executive*
Vessel, Amy Massey *education educator*
Vessey, John William, Jr. *military officer*
Vest, Charles Marstiller *engineering educator, former academic administrator*
Vest, Gayle Southworth *obstetrician, gynecologist*
Vest, R. Lamar *church administrator*
Vestal, Marilyn Anita *writer, researcher, educator*
Viamontes, George I. *psychiatrist, director*
Vichiola, Christopher Michael *writer, educator*
Vicino, Thomas Joseph *political science professor*
Viest, Ivan Miroslav *structural engineer, consultant*
Vieth, Christopher W. *former publishing executive*
Vila, Adis Maria *lawyer, business government executive*
Vilar, Alberto W. *investment company executive*
Villaire, Holly Hennen Hood *theater producer, director, actress, educator*
Villa-Komaroff, Lydia *molecular biologist, educator, academic administrator*
Villano, Mark Anthony *minister, educator*
Villarini, Awilda *musician, composer, music educator*
Villella, Edward Joseph *dancer, choreographer, performing arts association administrator*
Villforth, John Carl *engineer, health physicist*
Villoch, Kelly Carney *art director*
Viñas, Richard Roculan *non-commissioned officer*
Vincent, Charles Eagar, Jr. *sportswriter*
Vincent, Francis Thomas, Jr., (Fay Vincent) *former baseball commissioner*
Vincent, Hal Wellman *military officer, investor*
Vincent, James Louis *biotechnology company executive*
Vincent, Lynette Susanne *music educator*
Viner, Peter *communications executive*
Vines, John R. *career military officer*
Vinson, James Spangler *academic administrator*
Violenus, Agnes A. *retired school system administrator*
Viorst, Judith Stahl *writer*
Viorst, Milton *writer*
Virkhaus, Taavo *conductor*
Viscardi, Peter G. *risk management and environmental affairs executive*
Vishniac, Ethan Tecumseh *astronomy educator*
Vishnoi, Nisheeth Kumar *research scientist*
Visocki, Nancy Gayle *information services consultant*
Vita, Steven *poet*
Vitale, Dick *commentator, sports writer*
Vitt, David Aaron *health products executive*
Vittetoe, Marie Clare *retired clinical laboratory science educator*
Vlazny, John George *archbishop*
Voegtlin-Anderson, Mary Margaret *music educator, small business owner*
Voetsch, Barbara *neurologist, researcher*
Vogel, H. Victoria *psychotherapist, educator, writer, stress disorder and addiction recovery counselor*
Vogelzang, Alexa Ruth *music educator, opera singer*
Vohs, James Arthur *health facility administrator*
Voight, Jon *actor*
Voigt, Cynthia *writer*
Vojnovic, Igor Zoran *geographer, urban planner, educator*
Voketaitis, Arnold Matthew *bass-baritone, educator*
Volcker, Paul Adolph *economist, former Chairman of Federal Reserve System*
Volk, Austin N. *retired insurance company executive*
Volk, Patricia Gay *writer, essayist*
Volkhardt, John Malcolm *food products executive*
Volkman, Alvin *retired physician, research scientist, educator*
Volpe, Doris *artist*
Volpe, Edmond L(oris) *retired college president*
Volpe, Joseph *former opera company general manager*
Von Brandenstein, Patrizia *production designer*
Vonderbrink, Gerald William *retired academic administrator, real estate manager*
Vonderhaar, Steven Paul *counseling administrator*
von Furstenberg, Betsy *actress, writer*
von Furstenberg, Diane *fashion designer, writer, entrepreneur*
von Hoffman, Nicholas *writer, retired reporter*
von Kaenel, Howard J. *army officer*
von Sauers, Joseph F. *lawyer*
Vook, Frederick Ludwig *physicist, consultant*
Vorel, Stanislav R. *psychiatrist, neuroscientist*
Vosloo, Paul *public relations executive*
Voss, Omer Gerald *farm equipment executive*
Voss, Regis Dale *agronomist, educator*
Voss, William Charles *retired oil company executive*
Votaw, John Frederick, Sr. *educational association administrator, educator*
Voytek, Mary Sullivan *sculptor*
Vozzella, Thomas R. *musician, conductor, composer, organist*
Vu, Joseph Duong *financial educator*
Vydareny, Kay Herzog *radiologist, medical educator*
Vyn, Eleanor Mears *physical therapist*
Waaland, Irving T. *retired engineer*
Wachtell, Esther *non-profit management executive, consultant*
Wade, Daniel M. *recreational facility executive, hotel executive*

Wade, Ed *professional sports team executive*
Wade, June Booth *secondary school educator*
Wade, Suzanne L.C. *secondary school educator*
Wade, Thomas Edward *electrical engineering educator, academic administrator*
Wade, Wyn Craig *writer, educator*
Wadley, M. Richard *consumer products executive*
Waggoner, Kathleen Alice *psychotherapist*
Wagman, Robert John *journalist, writer*
Wagner, Arthur Ward, Jr. *lawyer*
Wagner, Cheri J. *business owner*
Wagner, Ellyn Santi *retired mathematics educator*
Wagner, Melinda *musician, composer*
Wagner, Paula *film producer*
Wagner, Richard *retired professional sports team executive, athletics consultant*
Wagoner, Brent Lee *director, coach*
Wahl, Donald J. *counseling administrator*
Wahlheim, Paul Steven *emergency physician*
Wahweah, Linda McNeil *insurance agent, writer*
Waite, Dennis Vernon *brokerage house executive, consultant*
Waite, Douglas John *chaplain*
Waitkus, Jay *writer*
Waitt, Theodore W. (Ted Waitt) *venture capitalist, former computer company executive*
Wakefield, Dan *writer, scriptwriter*
Waldera, Wanda Frances *artist*
Waldmeir, Peter Nielsen *retired journalist*
Waldrep, B. Dwain *education educator*
Walke, David Michael *business advisory, consulting and research executive*
Walken, Christopher *actor*
Walker, Annette *retired counseling administrator*
Walker, Beatriz Alem *language educator*
Walker, Craig Michael *lawyer*
Walker, Daniel Reuben *surgeon*
Walker, George Herbert III *former ambassador, retired investment banking company executive*
Walker, Gloria Lee *training services executive*
Walker, Gordon Davies *government official, writer, lecturer, consultant*
Walker, Henry Gilbert *health care executive, consultant*
Walker, Juanita Moffett *retired secondary school educator*
Walker, Kelley *painter*
Walker, Lorenzo Giles *surgeon, educator*
Walker, Mark A. *lawyer*
Walker, Michael Charles, Sr. *retired services executive*
Walker, Olene S. *former governor*
Walker, Richard Henry *lawyer*
Walker, Ronald Tracy *retired personnel director*
Walker, Roslyn Adele *retired museum director*
Walker, Valaida Smith *university administrator, retired*
Walker, Willa R. *performing arts association administrator*
Wall, Frederick Theodore *retired chemistry professor*
Wall, Jamie Lynn *elementary school educator*
Wall, M. Danny *finance company executive*
Wall, Matthew J., Jr. *surgeon, research scientist*
Wallace, Ardelia Leslene *elementary school educator*
Wallace, Arthur, Jr. *retired college dean*
Wallace, Carol *editor at large*
Wallace, Dee *actress*
Wallace, Desiree *investigational drug pharmacist, pharmacy educator*
Wallace, F. Blake *retired aerospace transportation executive, retired mechanical engineer*
Wallace, Jane House *retired geologist*
Wallace, Joyce Irene Malakoff *internist*
Wallace, Michele *writer, educator*
Wallace, Mike (Myron Leon Wallace) *newscaster, television personality*
Wallace, Nicolle (Nicolle Devenish) *former federal official*
Wallace, Robert Earl *geologist*
Wallace, Teresa Lynn *art educator*
Wallace De Cornwall, Clinton H. *media consultant*
Wallach, Patricia *councilman, retired mayor*
Wallack, Rina Evelyn *lawyer*
Waller, Eunice McLean *retired elementary school educator*
Wallerstein, Ralph Oliver *physician*
Wallingford, Anne *freelance/self-employed writer, marketing professional, consultant*
Wallington, Patricia McDevitt *computer company executive*
Wallis, Diana Lynn *artistic director*
Wallison, Frieda K. *lawyer*
Wallpher, Luis Antonio *small business owner, painter, writer*
Wallskog, Joyce Marie *nursing educator, retired psychologist*
Walmer, Edwin Fitch *retired lawyer*
Walmsley, Priscilla Helen *computer company executive*
Walsh, Dennis P. *federal agency administrator*
Walsh, Diane *pianist*
Walsh, Dolores Ann Gonczo (Lorry Walsh) *special education educator*
Walsh, George William *publishing company executive, editor, author*
Walsh, Joseph Thomas *law educator, retired state supreme court justice*
Walsh, M. Emmet *actor*
Walsh, Michael P. *mechanical engineer*
Walsh, Michael Thomas *historian, musician*
Walsh, Nan *artist, painter, sculptor, consultant*
Walsh, William Albert *management consultant, retired military officer*
Walsh Mitchell, Diana *school psychologist, consultant*
Walter, Carmel Monica *security firm executive, writer*
Walter, J. Jackson *management consultant, foundation administrator*
Waltermire, Thomas Allen *finance company executive*
Walters, Delores Maxine *anthropologist*
Walters, Glen Robert *retired banker*
Walters, Jean Marie *personal growth educator*
Walters, Matthew Paul *recreational facility executive, consultant*
Walters, Robert Ancil *physicist, mathematician*
Walther, Adriaan *retired physics professor*
Waltner, Beverly Ruland *artist*

Walton, Alice Louise *bank executive*
Walton, Andre *psychologist, consultant*
Walton, Christy R. *philanthropist*
Waltrip, Darrell Lee *race car driver*
Walumbwa, Fred Ochieng *business educator*
Wambaugh, Joseph A., Jr. *author*
Wan, Julia Chang *retired science educator*
Wan, Ming *computer scientist, researcher*
Wang, Chen-ku *retired library director*
Wang, Hong-Wei *biologist*
Wang, Nancy *pathologist, educator*
Wang, Perry G. *chemist, researcher*
Wang, Qigui *materials engineer, researcher*
Wang, Qin *computer engineer, researcher*
Wang, Ying *chemistry and physical science researcher*
Wang, Yinmin *materials scientist, educator*
Wang, Youcheng *information technology educator*
Wang-Birnbaum, Ruth Deborah *secondary school educator, director*
Wanger, Eugene Gilkison *retired lawyer*
Wannier, Mario Marc-Antoine *oil industry executive, multi-media specialist, director*
Wantland, William Charles *retired bishop, lawyer*
Wantz, Kathy Lynn Zepp *school nurse*
Warberg, Willetta *concert pianist, music educator*
Warble, Charles Edward *materials scientist*
Warch, Richard *former academic administrator*
Ward, Chester Lawrence *physician, consultant*
Ward (Bailey), Daisy Dale *writer*
Ward, Jonathan P. *former service company executive*
Ward, Monica *social sciences educator*
Ward, Thomas *research scientist*
Ward, William E. *career military officer*
Warder, Richard Currey, Jr. *dean, mechanical aerospace engineering educator*
Wardlow, Benjamin Franklin III *sales executive*
Ware, Brendan John *retired electrical engineer and utility executive*
Ware, D. Clifton *vocalist, educator*
Ware, Gwendolyn C. *retired counseling administrator*
Warfel, M(artha) Kay *speech pathology/audiology services professional*
Warner, Douglas Alexander III *banker*
Warner, Emily Hanrahan Howell *retired pilot, writer*
Warner, Karl K. *former prosecutor*
Warner, Mark Robert *former governor*
Warner, Tokesha L. *health facility administrator*
Warnock, William Reid *lawyer*
Warren, Alice Louise *artist*
Warren, David Hardy *psychologist, educator*
Warren, John William *professional society administrator*
Warren, Marie Antoinette *elementary school educator*
Warren, Rosanna *poet*
Warren, William Kermit *retired editor*
Warrior, Della C. *academic administrator, art educator*
Warshawsky, Isidore *physicist, consultant*
Wartluft, David Jonathan *retired librarian, minister*
Warwick, Dionne *singer*
Washburn, Donald Arthur *retired transportation executive, investor*
Washington, Denzel *actor*
Washington, Garrett Lloyd *language educator*
Washington, Kerry *actor*
Washington, Lawrence J., Jr. *chemicals executive*
Washington, Marcus D. *history educator*
Washington, Michele *educational consultant*
Wasmuth, Carl Erwin *retired physician, lawyer*
Wasson, James Walter *aircraft electronics manufacturing company executive*
Watanabe, Kyoichi A(loysius) *pharmacology educator, chemist*
Waterhouse, Keith *urologist, educator, retired surgeon*
Waters, Betty Lou *newspaper reporter, writer*
Waters, Lou *news correspondent*
Waters, Sylvia *dance company artistic director*
Waters, Timothy J. *lawyer*
Waters, William Carter III *retired internist, educator*
Watkins, Ann Esther *mathematics professor*
Watkins, Dean Allen *electronics executive, educator*
Watkins, Esther Sherrod *secondary school educator, school librarian*
Watkins, George Daniels *physics professor*
Watkins, James David *federal official, military officer*
Watkins, Wesley Wade *retired congressman*
Watley, Natasha *Olympic athlete*
Watne, Alvin L. *retired surgeon, educator*
Watrous, Robert Thomas *academic director*
Watson, Bernard Charles *foundation administrator, educator*
Watson, Catherine Elaine *journalist*
Watson, Donald Charles, Jr. *cardiothoracic surgeon, educator*
Watson, George Henry, Jr. *broadcaster, journalist*
Watson, Jenny *family and consumer sciences educator*
Watson, Kathy *political organization administrator*
Watson, Patricia Pullums *school system administrator*
Watson, Patty Jo *anthropology educator*
Watson, Robert Joe *retired health facility administrator, retired career officer*
Watt, Linda E. *former ambassador*
Watts, Anthony Lee *bank executive*
Watts, Ginny (Virginia C. Watts) *artist*
Watts, Helena Roselle *military analyst*
Watts, Mary Ann *retired elementary school educator*
Waud, Roger Neil *economist, educator*
Wavle, James Edward, Jr. *pharmaceutical company executive, lawyer*
Wax, Adam *biomedical engineer, educator*
Waxman, Ronald *computer engineer*
Way, Barbara Haight *retired dermatologist*
Way, Jacob Edson III *museum director*
Wayans, Damon *actor*
Wayans, Keenen Ivory *actor, producer*
Wayburn, Edgar *internist, environmentalist*
Wearn, Wilson Cannon *retired media executive*

Weathersby, George Byron *management company executive*
Weaver, Barbara Frances *librarian, consultant*
Weaver, Delbert Allen *retired lawyer*
Weaver, Franklin Thomas *retired newspaper executive*
Weaver, Howard C. *newspaper executive*
Weaver, Muriel Margaret *music educator*
Weaver, William Charles *manufacturing executive*
Weaver, William Schildecker *retired electric power industry executive*
Webb, Charles Franklin *computer engineer*
Webb, Lucy Jane *actress, film producer, consultant*
Webb, Maynard G., Jr. *retired Internet company executive*
Webb, O. Glenn *retired farm supplies company executive*
Webb, Wellington Edward *political organization administrator, former mayor*
Webb, William Timothy *mobile communications professional*
Weber, Bruce *photographer, filmmaker*
Weber, Bruce Edward *art historian*
Weber, Gloria Richie *retired minister, retired state legislator*
Weber, Idelle *artist, art educator*
Weber, John Walter *insurance company executive*
Weber, Jonathan *editor, journalist, educator*
Weber, Kenneth J. *hotel executive*
Weber, Mark *clothing company executive*
Weber, Sharalyn *graphics designer*
Webster, Christopher White *foreign service officer*
Webster, John Crosby Brown *minister, educator*
Webster, Larry Russell *artist*
Webster, Robert Kenly *lawyer*
Wechsler, Sergio *automotive executive, consultant*
Weddle, Laura Mildred Thomas *retired language educator*
Weeks, Clifford Myers *musician, academic administrator*
Weeks, William Rawle, Jr. *oil industry executive*
Wegman, Harold Hugh *management consultant*
Wegman, William George *artist*
Wegner, Lucy Siefert *information specialist*
Wehn, Karen Swaney *education educator, consultant*
Wei, Dong *technologist*
Wei, Yinghong *finance educator*
Weickert, Wanda Opal *child welfare and attendance counselor, psychotherapist, educator*
Weier, Carlton Timothy *retired mathematics professor*
Weigle, Peggy *information technology executive*
Weil, Lynne Amy *communications executive, writer*
Weil, Peter Henry *lawyer*
Weil, Randolph Allen *engineering executive*
Weil, Rolf Alfred *economist, retired university president*
Weil, Thomas P. *retired health services consultant*
Weinberg, Igor *clinical psychologist, researcher*
Weinberg, Steven *physics professor*
Weinberger, Arnold *retired electrical engineer*
Weiner, Anne Lee *social worker*
Weiner, Ferne *psychologist*
Weiner, Peter H. *lawyer*
Weiner, Richard *public relations executive*
Weiner-Heuschkel, Sydell *theater educator*
Weingand, Darlene Erna *librarian, educator*
Weingarten, Joseph Leonard *aerospace engineer*
Weinkauf, Mary Louise Stanley *retired clergywoman, educator*
Weinman, Connie Germann *banker, lawyer*
Weinman, Glenn Alan *lawyer*
Weinreb, Michael Philip *physicist*
Weinshenker, Naomi Joyce *clinical psychiatrist, educator, researcher*
Weinstein, Ali Anne *psychologist, researcher*
Weinstein, Bob (Robert Weinstein) *film company executive*
Weinstein, Harvey *film company executive, film producer*
Weinstein, Marta *packaging services company executive*
Weinstein, Mary Helen *musician, educator*
Weinstein, Michael P. *marine scientist, administrator*
Weinstein, Milton Charles *decision scientist, educator*
Weis, Margaret Edith *writer, editor*
Weisberg, Barbara *writer, editor*
Weisberg, David Charles *lawyer*
Weisbrod, John *former professional sports team executive*
Weisburger, Elizabeth Kreiser *retired chemist*
Weisenburger, Peter Dominic *theater educator, director*
Weiser, Dennis Charles *writer, philosopher*
Weisman, Lorenzo David *investment banker*
Weismantel, Gregory Nelson *management consultant, computer company executive*
Weiss, Alvin Harvey *chemical engineer, educator, research scientist, consultant*
Weiss, Bob (Robert William WEiss) *former professional basketball coach*
Weiss, Jerry Kenneth *sales executive, consultant, marketing professional*
Weiss, Joanne Marion *writer*
Weiss, Kenneth Andrew *lawyer, educator*
Weiss, Lyn Denise *physician*
Weiss, Michael Allen *retired retail executive*
Weiss, Scott Alan *commercial real estate consultant*
Weiss, Simona *retired paralegal*
Weiss, Steven Gary *physician*
Weissenburger, David Allen *psychologist, educator, consultant*
Weissman, Jack (George Anderson) *retired editor*
Weissman, Morris *printing company executive*
Weiswasser, Stephen *electronics executive*
Weisz, Paul B(urg) *physicist, researcher, chemical engineer*
Welburn, Edward T. *automotive executive*
Welch, Martin E. III *investor, retail executive*
Welch, Oliver Wendell *retired pharmaceutical executive*
Welch, Raquel *actress*
Weld, Bill (William Floyd Weld) *lawyer, former governor*
Weldon, Charles Jauverni *actor*
Weldon, Irene Elizabeth *music educator*

Wolfberg, Melvin Donald *optometrist, educational association administrator, consultant*
Wolfe, Charles Morgan *electrical engineering educator*
Wolfe, Gregory Baker *international relations educator*
Wolfe, Joan L. *non-profit organizations consultant*
Wolfe, Linda *writer*
Wolfensohn, James David *former diplomat, former President of the World Bank*
Wolff, Brian Richard *metal products executive*
Wolff, Eleanor Blunk *actress*
Wolff, Manfred Ernst *medicinal chemist, pharmaceutical executive*
Wolfgang, Jared Dale *music educator*
Wolfman, Ira Joel *editor, writer*
Wolford, Kathryn Frances *religious organization administrator*
Wolfram, David Anthony *information technology manager*
Wolfson, Michael George *retired lawyer*
Wollert, Gerald Dale *retired food products executive, securities trader*
Wolpert Richard, Chava *artist*
Woltering, Margaret Mae *retired educational association administrator*
Wonders, William Clare *geography educator*
Wong, Ah-San *planetary scientist, composer, writer*
Wong, B.D. *actor*
Wong, Colette L. *apparel designer, educator*
Wong, Deborah M. *science educator*
Wong, Elaine Dang *foundation executive*
Wong, Liliane *architect, educator*
Wong, Richard *music educator*
Wong, Suzanne Crawbuck *librarian*
Wong-Diaz, Francisco Raimundo *lawyer, educator*
Woo, Benson *financial executive*
Woo, Derek *electrical engineer, computer engineer*
Woo, Kenneth Roger *urologist*
Woo, Savio Lau-Yuen *bioengineering educator*
Wood, Corinne Gieseke *former lieutenant governor*
Wood, Dennis *communications executive*
Wood, Evan Rachel *actress*
Wood, Frances Diane *medical secretary, artist*
Wood, Frank *actor*
Wood, Janis Louise *retired assistant principal*
Wood, Jerilyn Ruth *literature and language professor, secondary school educator, interior designer*
Wood, Margaret *performing company executive*
Wood, Marian Starr *publishing executive*
Wood, Maurice *medical educator*
Wood, Robert Charles *lawyer, real estate developer*
Wood, Vivian Poates *mezzo soprano, educator*
Wood, William Preston *writer, lawyer*
Wood, Willis Bowne, Jr. *retired utilities executive*
Woodard, Catherine *arts patron*
Woodard, Joseph Lamar *law librarian, educator*
Woodard, Peter Clark *music educator, musician*
Woodbridge, John Dunning *history professor*
Woodburn, William A. *utilities executive*
Wooden, John Robert *former college basketball coach*
Woodford, Michael *economics professor*
Woodhouse, Helen Jackson *music educator*
Woodland, N. Joseph *retired optical engineer, retired mechanical engineer*
Woodrow, Kenneth B. *retired retail company executive*
Woodruff, Judy Carline *broadcast journalist*
Woodruff, Truman O(wen) *physicist, emeritus educator*
Woodruff, Virginia *broadcast journalist, writer*
Woodrum, Patricia Ann *librarian*
Woods, Cheryl *financial analyst*
Woods, David Lyndon *broadcast executive, former federal agency executive, publishing executive*
Woods, Gerald Wayne *lawyer*
Woods, Harriett Ruth *political organization worker, retired state official*
Woods, J. P. *religious organization administrator*
Woods, Phyllis Michalik *librarian*
Woods, Sandra Kay *real estate executive*
Woods, Susanne *academic administrator, educator*
Woodson, Darren Ray *retired professional football player*
Woodson, Jacqueline *writer*
Woodsworth, Anne *academic administrator, librarian*
Woodward, Ralph Barclay *music educator, small business owner*
Woodward, Thomas Morgan *actor*
Wooldridge, Stephen Craig *health facility administrator*
Wooldridge, William Charles *lawyer*
Woolston-Catlin, Marian *psychiatrist*
Woolworth, Susan Valk *primary school educator*
Woosnam, Ian Harold *professional golfer*
Wooster, Nicholas Wayne *band director*
Wooten, Carol G. *music educator, minister*
Wooten, Cecil Aaron *retired religious organization administrator*
Wooten, Frank Thomas *retired research facility executive*
Wooten, James Terrell *journalist*
Wooten, Joan Hedrich *minister*
Wooton, Joel *history professor, basketball coach*
Worboys, Roger Dick *retired communications executive*
Worenklein, Jacob Joshua *lawyer*
Workman, John Mitchell *chemist*
Workman, John P., Jr. *marketing professor*
Workman, Willard Allyn *association executive*
Worley, April Cole *artist, grant writer*
Worley, Debere *educational consultant*
Worley, Donald Lee *quality assurance professional*
Worley, Michelle Lynn *music educator*
Wormser, Sherri Lynne *pediatric physical therapist*
Worner, Theresa Marie *internist, educator*
Woronov, Mary Peter *actress*
Worrell, Richard Vernon *orthopedic surgeon, dean*
Worster, Ann Martin *historian*
Worth, Gary James *communications executive*
Woteki, Catherine Ellen *nutritionist*
Wozniak, Stephen Gary *computer scientist, philanthropist*

Wray, Peter *theater educator*
Wright, David L. *food and beverage company executive*
Wright, Dell *residential care and treatment facility executive*
Wright, Dixie Lee *special needs persons consultant*
Wright, Edward Thomas, Jr. *elementary school educator*
Wright, Franz Paul *poet, writer, translator*
Wright, Gladys Stone *music educator, writer, composer*
Wright, James David *social studies educator, writer*
Wright, Jan Carol *indexer*
Wright, Jason Chase *history educator*
Wright, Joan L. *artist*
Wright, Josephine Rosa Beatrice *musicologist, educator*
Wright, Julianne Clemmons *psychologist*
Wright, Kristopher *biology professor*
Wright, Lawrence George *writer*
Wright, Lori Dunkle *music educator, musician*
Wright, Mary James *senior education consultant*
Wright, Peggy Sue Espy *elementary school educator*
Wright, Randolph Earle *retired petroleum company executive*
Wright, Robert Payton *lawyer*
Wright, Steven *comedian*
Wright, Theodore Robert Fairbank *biologist, educator*
Wright, Virginia *art collector, curator*
Wrong, Dennis Hume *retired sociologist, educator*
Wruble, Bernhardt Karp *lawyer*
Wruble, Brian Frederick *investor*
Wu, Jeremy S. *federal official*
Wu, Min *computer and electrical engineer*
Wu, Xin *electrical engineer, researcher, educator*
Wu, Zheng Y. *hydroinformatics engineer, hydrologist, consultant*
Wuebbling, Donald J. *lawyer, insurance company executive*
Wuhl, Robert *actor*
Wulff, Lois Yvonne *retired librarian*
Wurth, Monty *information technology manager*
Wyatt, Lance B. *pharmaceutical executive*
Wyatt, Robert Lee, IV, *lawyer*
Wyche, Ruth Skyler *rehabilitation contractor, researcher*
Wyckoff, E. Lisk, Jr. *lawyer*
Wyeth, Andrew Newell *artist*
Wylan, Barbara *artist*
Wyman, Jane (Sarah Jane Fulks) *actress*
Wynar, Bohdan Stephen *retired librarian, writer, editor*
Wyngaarden, James Barnes *retired physician*
Wynn, Tracy Keenan *screenwriter*
Wynne, Benjamin Ray *history professor*
Wyrsch, Carolyn Irwin *historian, educator*
Wyrtki, Klaus *oceanography educator*
Wyse, Jason LaMar *music educator, director*
Wyse, Lois *advertising executive, writer*
Xi, Cecilia Q. *research scientist*
Xia, Guohua *scientist, psychiatrist, psychologist*
Xia, Yuni *information scientist, educator*
Xie, Minge *statistician, educator*
Xie, Song *musician, educator*
Xu, Shaohua *biochemist, researcher*
Xu, Yifang *engineer, researcher*
Xue, Yuan *engineering educator*
Yack, Patrick Ashley *editor*
Yackel, James William *mathematician, academic administrator*
Yackira, Michael William *electric power industry executive*
Yadrick, Robert Martin *occupational analyst*
Yaffe, Sumner Jason *pediatrician, educator, science administrator*
Yalam, Arnold Robert *allergist, immunologist, consultant*
Yale (Yeleyenide-Yale), Melpomene Fotine *researcher, anthropologist, archaeologist, art historian, conservator*
Yamaguchi, Kristi Tsuya *ice skater*
Yamamoto, Joe *retired psychiatrist, educator*
Yaman, Cevat *environmental engineer, educator*
Yampolsky, Phyllis *artist*
Yan, Su *mechanical engineer, researcher*
Yang, Bing-Shiang *biomedical engineer*
Yang, Chau-Jye (Jay) *management consultant*
Yang, Jidong *transportation engineer*
Yang, Jiong *education educator*
Yang, Tianyu *electrical engineer, educator*
Yannella, Donald *literature and language professor*
Yansouni, Cyril J. *computer company executive*
Yao, Jianan Johnny *research scientist, consultant*
Yao, Tessa Lorien *portfolio manager*
Yarbrough, Kathryn Davis *public health nurse*
Yarchoan, Robert *clinical immunologist, researcher*
Yarrow, Peter *folksinger*
Yashin, Alexei *professional hockey player*
Yates, David John C. *chemist, researcher*
Yates, John Robert, Jr. *civil engineering educator*
Yates, Mary Carlin *former ambassador*
Yates, Ronald Eugene *newspaper editor, educator, author, journalist*
Yates, Steven A. *curator, artist*
Yates, William Tennyson, II, *educational consultant, management consultant*
Yates-Riley, Veronica A. *mathematics educator*
Yau, Siu-Tung *physics professor*
Ybaben, Marc A. *psychologist, consultant*
Ye, Hua *electronics engineer*
Ye, Rick W. *microbiologist*
Yeager, Anson Anders *writer, retired editor, retired columnist*
Yeager, Jeana *aviator*
Yeager, Kurt Eric *research and development company executive*
Yeager, Mark Leonard *lawyer*
Yeager, Phillip Charles *transportation company executive*
Yeager, William Robert *musician, educator*
Yearwood, Trisha *country music singer, songwriter*
Yeend, Frances *soprano, music educator*
Yeh, Ying-Yu Emily *music educator*
Yemenidjian, Alex *former film company executive*

Yen, Bing Cheng *retired civil engineer, retired engineering educator*
Yeonas, George C. *real estate executive*
Yeosock, John John *military officer*
Yeric, Greg *electronics executive*
Yerrick, Randy Kregg *science educator*
Yershov, Andrei R. *computer scientist*
Yglesias, Rafael Jose *novelist*
Yielding, K. Lemone *physician*
Yilmaz, Bilge *chemical engineer, researcher*
Yim, Kang Sub *engineer*
Yingling, John A. *military officer*
Yingling, Phyllis Stuckey *writer*
Yiotis, Gayle *archivist, researcher, anthropologist, writer*
Yiu, Fang *structural engineer, researcher*
Yocam, Delbert Wayne *retired software products company executive*
Yodaiken, Ralph E. *pathologist, occupational health physician, educator*
Yoder, Jeffrey L. *music educator*
Yoder, Randall D. *music educator*
Yollick, Bernard Lawrence *otolaryngologist, surgeon*
Yong, Raymond Nen-Yiu *civil engineering educator*
Yontz, Kenneth Fredric *medical and chemical company executive*
Yood, Harold Stanley *retired internist*
Yood, James W. *art critic, historian, educator, writer*
Yoon, E. Yul *retired career officer*
Yopconka, Natalie Ann Catherine *executive secretary, computer specialist, educator, entrepreneur, small business owner*
York, Herbert Frank *physics professor*
York, Jerome B. *investment company executive, former computer retail executive*
Yost, William Albert *psychology professor*
Youmans, Julian Ray *neurosurgeon, educator*
Young, Amy Y. *librarian*
Young, Andrew Jackson, Jr. *civil rights leader, pastor, retired mayor, ambassador, retired congressman*
Young, Barry Harrison *retired mathematician, mechanical engineer*
Young, Burt *actor*
Young, C. Clifton *former state supreme court justice*
Young, Charles Edward *former academic administrator*
Young, David Nelson *media and communications consultant*
Young, Edwin S. W. *federal agency official*
Young, Elizabeth Bell *organization consultant*
Young, Frank Edward *retired federal agency administrator, religious organization administrator*
Young, Gail Diane *secondary school educator*
Young, James E. *real estate company executive, consultant, engineer*
Young, Jay Maitland *health products executive, consultant*
Young, Jennifer Baxendell *former federal agency administrator*
Young, John Hardin *lawyer*
Young, John Watts *retired astronaut*
Young, Judith Anne *animal conservationist*
Young, Lai-Sang *mathematician, educator*
Young, Patrick *editor, writer*
Young, Richard Alan *association executive*
Young, Ruth Brooks *retired elementary school educator*
Young, Steve G. *former labor union administrator*
Young, Teresa Gail Hilger *retired adult education educator*
Young, Thomas Lee *lawyer*
Young, Tzay Y. *electrical and computer engineering educator*
Young, Virgil Monroe *education educator*
Youngblood, Judy Ann *artist, educator*
Youngjohns, Robert H. *information technology executive*
Youngman, LuAnn L. *minister*
Youngs, Diane Campfield *learning disabilities specialist, educator*
Youngstrom, Paul Clarence *anesthesiologist*
Younker, Kathleen Teuber *pianist, music educator*
Youst, David Bennett *career development educator*
Yu, Hengyong *research scientist*
Yu, Jessica *director, producer, writer, editor*
Yu, Jun *biologist*
Yu, Shaocai *research scientist*
Yu, Tian-En *musician, music educator*
Yu, Wei *economist, researcher*
Yuan, Zeng-Guang *mechanical engineer, researcher*
Yuan, Zhaoxu *ophthalmologist, researcher*
Yue, Alfred Shui-Choh *metallurgical engineer, consultant*
Yue, Meng *electrical engineer*
Yuknis, Christina Marie *special education educator*
Yuksel, Murat *computer scientist, researcher*
Yun, James Kyoon *electrical engineer*
Yunis, Jorge Jose *anatomy, pathology, and microbiology educator*
Yurchuck, Roger Alexander *retired lawyer*
Yurechko, John Joseph *federal agency administrator, director*
Yuriko, (Yuriko Kikuchi) *dancer, choreographer*
Yusufi, Afifa *psychologist*
Yzaguirre, Raul Humberto *civil rights leader*
Zabilka, Ivan L. *secondary school educator*
Zabriskie, John L. *healthcare and agricultural products manufacturing company executive*
Zacharias, Donald Wayne *retired academic administrator*
Zachary, Je'Quita Yvette *elementary school educator, singer*
Zack, Daniel Gerard *library consultant*
Zaferson, William S. *philosophy educator, publisher*
Zagajewski, Adam *poet, writer*
Zagar, Robert John *psychologist, researcher*
Zagaski, Chester Anthony, Jr. *writer, researcher, consultant*
Zaghloul, Norann Amr *geneticist, research scientist*
Zahner Kraeft, Dorothy Simkin *elementary school educator, school librarian*

Zahran, Mohamed Mostafa *electrical engineer, educator*
Zais, Mitchell M. *career military officer*
Zajac, John *semiconductor equipment company executive*
Zakim, David *biochemist*
Zakim, Tom Edward *history professor*
Zaleski, Jan Franciszek *biochemist*
Zaleski, Jean *artist*
Zaltman, Mark Allen *federal agency administrator*
Zambrano, Eduardo Vicente *pathologist, researcher*
Zangen, Abraham *neuroscience researcher, consultant*
Zangwill, Steven *pediatrician, cardiologist*
Zanjacomo, Paulo Regis *engineering executive*
Zapf, Hermann *book and type designer*
Zappa, Gail *record producer*
Zappe, John Paul *city editor, educator, newspaper executive*
Zarb, Frank Gustave *investment company executive*
Zarins, Bertram *orthopedic surgeon*
Zaros, Wendy Cecilia *soprano, educator*
Zarro, Janice Anne *lawyer*
Zavadil, Martin R. *music educator, director, retired conductor*
Zawacki, Bruce Edwin *surgeon, educator, ethicist*
Zdanis, Richard Albert *academic administrator*
Zebi, Sandra *artist*
Zeffren, Eugene *cosmetics executive*
Zeglis, John D. *communications executive, lawyer*
Zehr, Norman Robert *retired association administrator*
Zehring, Karen *information executive*
Zeilberger, Doron *mathematics professor, researcher*
Zeilig, Nancy Meeks *writer, editor*
Zekman, Terri Margaret *graphic designer*
Zelasko, Eric Edward *music educator*
Zelek, Charles Andrew *program specialist, director*
Zelinski, Joseph John *engineering educator, consultant*
Zelinsky, Paul O. *illustrator, artist, writer*
Zell, Samuel *transportation leasing company executive*
Zeller, Joseph Paul *advertising executive*
Zelmanov, Efim Isaakovich *mathematician, educator*
Zelnick, Strauss *entertainment company executive*
Zemon, Stacy J. *disc jockey, writer, small business owner*
Zentz, Patrick James *artist, rancher*
Zerman, Melvyn Bernard *retired publishing executive, writer*
Zeta-Jones, Catherine *actress*
Zevon Tschacbasov, Irene Ann *artist, consultant, art historian*
Zgaljardic, Dennis Joseph *clinical neuropsychologist*
Zha, Gecheng *engineer, educator*
Zha, Xuan-Fang *engineering educator, researcher*
Zhang, Jinsong *chemistry professor*
Zhang, Li *engineer, researcher, educator*
Zhang, Ming *business and management consultant*
Zhang, Qingyu *education educator*
Zhang, Shu *statistician*
Zhang, Wei David *finance educator*
Zhang, Yanwen *research scientist*
Zhang, Zhongjian *research scientist*
Zhao, Tong *research scientist*
Zhao, Wei (Wayne) *materials scientist, researcher, transmission electron microscopist*
Zhao, Xueheng *research scientist*
Zhao, Zhen *music educator*
Zhao, Zhongshan *structural engineer, researcher*
Zhdanov, Boris *research scientist*
Zheng, Fawen *fluid mechanics engineer*
Zheng, Lingyi Albert *materials scientist, materials engineer, researcher*
Zheng, Lu *educator*
Zhou, Dayong *research scientist*
Zhou, Shao Man *chemist, researcher*
Zhu, Ben-Zhan *education educator, researcher*
Zhu, Carolyn Wei *healthcare educator*
Zhu, Yong *research scientist*
Ziegenhagen, David Mackenzie *retired health facility administrator, not-for-profit developer*
Ziegler, Jack (Jack Denmore) *cartoonist*
Ziegler, James L. *marketing executive*
Ziegler, William Alexander *lawyer*
Ziemba, Karen *actress*
Zierler, Neal *retired mathematician*
Ziese, Dennis Russell *retired protective services official, retired military officer*
Zilbert, Allen Bruce *education educator, computer scientist, consultant*
Zilkha, Ezra Khedouri *banker*
Zimet, Lloyd *sport psychologist, health educator, program planner and administrator*
Zimmerman, Harold Samuel *retired state legislator, publishing executive, state agency administrator*
Zimmerman, Helene Loretta *retired business educator*
Zimmerman, Jean *lawyer*
Zimmerman, Jo Ann *retired health science association administrator, educator, retired lieutenant governor*
Zimmerman, Marlin U., Jr. *chemical engineer*
Zimmerman, Myron *information technology executive*
Zimmerman, Phyllis Elaine *music educator, composer, director*
Zimmermann, Thomas Callander Price *retired historian, educator*
Zimmers, Vivian Eleanor *small business owner, consultant*
Zimny, Max *labor union administrator, lawyer, arbitrator*
Zinnen, Robert Oliver *management consultant, consultant*
Zischke, Douglas Arthur *foreign service officer*
Zitrin, Charlotte Marker *psychiatrist, educator, researcher*
Zizic, Thomas Michael *physician, educator*
Zoeller, Donald J. *lawyer*
Zografi, George *pharmacologist, educator*
Zohn, Andrew Eliot *musician, educator*
Zohn, Martin Steven *lawyer*

# Professional Index

## ALASKA

**Anchorage**
Maynard, Kenneth Douglas *architect*

## ARIZONA

**Green Valley**
Johnson, Charles Foreman *architectural firm executive*

**Payson**
Hershberger, Robert Glen *architect, educator*

**Phoenix**
Elmore, James Walter *architect, educator, retired dean*
Gwozdz, Kim Elizabeth *interior designer, furniture designer*
Hawkins, Jasper Stillwell, Jr. *architect*
Mireles, Jesse *architecture educator, department chairman, academic administrator*
Schiffner, Charles Robert *architect*

**Scottsdale**
Brown, Shirley Margaret Kern (Peggy Brown) *interior designer*
Sydnor, Douglas Bryan *architect, educator*
Wong, Joe Bing *retired architect*

**Sonoita**
Cook, William Howard *architect*

**Surprise**
Uhlmann, Elenore Arlene *interior designer, writer*

**Tucson**
Nelson, Edward Humphrey *architect*
Seehausen, Richard Ferdinand *architect*
Wallach, Leslie Rothaus *architect*

## ARKANSAS

**Little Rock**
Chilcote, Lugean Lester *retired architect, researcher*
Levy, Eugene Pfeifer *architectural firm executive, architect*
Truemper, John James, Jr. *retired architect*

**Winslow**
Burggraf, Frank Bernard, Jr. *landscape architect, retired educator*

## CALIFORNIA

**Bakersfield**
McAlister, Michael H. *architect*

**Belvedere**
Hugenberg, Patricia Ellen Petrie *product designer*

**Berkeley**
Brocchini, Ronald Gene *architect*
Cardwell, Kenneth Harvey *architect, educator*
Stoller, Claude *architect*
Walker, Peter *landscape architect*

**Chula Vista**
Weiss-Cornwell, Amy *interior designer*

**Corona Del Mar**
Jacobs, Donald Paul *architect*
Yeo, Ron *architect*

**Culver City**
Sussman, Deborah Evelyn *interior designer, small business owner*

**El Cerrito**
Burger, Edmund Ganes *architect*

**Fresno**
Darden, Edwin Speight, Sr. *architect*
Patnaude, William Eugene *architect*
Pings, Anthony Claude *architect*

**Highland**
MacQueen, Cherie K. *interior designer, retired newscaster, sportscaster*

**Indian Wells**
Munyon, William Harry, Jr. *architect*

**La Jolla**
Baesel, Stuart Oliver *architect*

**Laguna Niguel**
Axon, Donald Carlton *architect*

**Laguna Woods**
Badgley, John Roy *architect*

**Long Beach**
Pullman, Alan *architect*

**Los Angeles**
Bennett, Brent Jackson *architect*
Dworsky, Daniel Leonard *architect, educator*
Fickett, Edward Hale *architect, educator, arbitrator*
Gehry, Frank Owen *architect*
Johnson, Stephen *architectural firm executive*
Maltzan, Michael Thomas *architect*
Man, Lawrence Kong *architect, art dealer*
Moe, Stanley Allen *architect, consultant*
Neutra, Dion *architect*
Noble, Douglas *architecture educator*
Pfeiffer, Norman *architectural firm executive*
Phelps, Barton Chase *architect, educator*
Shelby, Carroll Hall *automotive designer*

**Manhattan Beach**
Blanton, John Arthur *architect, writer*

**Mill Valley**
D'Amico, Michael *architect, urban planner*

**Mojave**
Rutan, Burt (Elbert Leander Rutan) *aircraft designer, aircraft company executive*

**Mountain View**
Kobza, Dennis Jerome *architect*

**Newport Beach**
Bissell, George Arthur *architect*
Blankenship, Edward G. *architect*
Richardson, Walter John *architect*

**Novato**
Thompson, Peter Layard Hailey, Sr. *landscape and golf course architect, architectural firm executive*

**Ontario**
Endsley, Donal E. *architectural firm executive*
Gilliam, James L. *architectural firm executive*
Kain, Robert J. *architectural firm executive*

**Oxnard**
O'Connell, Hugh Mellen, Jr. *retired architect*

**Palo Alto**
Brown, Tim *product designer*
Lucente, Sam *industrial designer*

**Pasadena**
Goei, Bernard Thwan-Poo (Bert Goei) *architectural and engineering firm executive*
Thomas, Joseph Fleshman *retired architect*

**Pleasanton**
Fehlberg, Robert Erick *architect*

**Redondo Beach**
Shellhorn, Ruth Patricia *landscape architect*

**Riverside**
Deal, Kevin Paul *furniture designer*

**Sacramento**
Lionakis, George *architect*
Wasserman, Barry L(ee) *architect*

**San Diego**
Delawie, Homer Torrence *retired architect*
Naslund, Eric Christopher *architectural firm executive*
Paderewski, Sir Clarence Joseph *architect*
Quigley, Rob Wellington *architect*
Stepner, Michael Jay *architect*

**San Francisco**
Béhar, Yves *industrial designer*
Bull, Henrik Helkand *architect*
Campbell, Janet Coral *architect*
Del Campo, Martin Bernardelli *architect*
Ellis, John *urban designer*
Field, John Louis *architect*
Friedrichs, Edward Charles *architect*
Gensler, M. Arthur, Jr. *architect*
Halprin, Lawrence *landscape architect, urban planner*
Judd, Bruce Diven *architect*
Minar, Paul G. *interior designer, consultant*
Moris, Lamberto Giuliano *architect*
Parker, Derek *architectural firm executive*
Raeber, John Arthur *architect, construction consultant*
Thistlethwaite, David Richard *architect*
Warnecke, John Carl *architect*

**San Jose**
Tanaka, Richard Koichi, Jr. *architect, planner*

**San Luis Obispo**
Deasy, Cornelius Michael *retired architect*

**San Marcos**
Harmon, Harry William *architect, former university administrator*

**Santa Barbara**
Burgee, John Henry *architect*
Kruger, Kenneth Charles *architect*
Pochini, Judy Hay *interior designer, writer, editor*

**Santa Monica**
Koning, Hendrik *architect*
Mayne, Thom *architect*

**Santa Rosa**
Morris, Jack G. *architecture educator, writer*

**Sebastopol**
Drever, Richard Alston, Jr. *consulting architect*

**Shasta Lake**
Innes, Rob *product designer*

**Sonoma**
Woodbridge, John Marshall *architect, urban planner*

**South Pasadena**
Girvigian, Raymond *architect*

**Stanford**
Eustis, Robert Henry *design company executive, mechanical engineer*

**Sun City**
Holl, Walter John *architect, interior designer*

**Tarzana**
Smith, Mark Lee *architect*

**Thousand Oaks**
Smith-Kielland, Ingvald Alain *product designer*

**Turlock**
Shirvani, Sir Hamid *architect, educator, philosopher, writer, university president*

**Walnut Creek**
Costa, Walter Henry *architect*
Hassid, Sami *architect, educator*

**West Hollywood**
Joseph, J. Jonathan *interior designer*

## COLORADO

**Arvada**
Ball, Kenneth (Ken) Weston *landscape architect, sculptor*

**Boulder**
Carlson, Devon McElvin *architect, educator*

**Broomfield**
Williams, John James, Jr. *architect*

**Denver**
Abo, Ronald Kent *freelance/self-employed architect*
Anderson, John David *architect*
Bradburn, James Henry *architectural firm executive*
Brownson, Jacques Calmon *architect*
Dominick, Peter Hoyt, Jr. *architect*
Fentress, Curtis Worth *architectural firm executive*
Fogg, Janet *architectural firm executive*
Fuller, Robert Kenneth *architect, urban designer*
Hoover, George Schweke *architect*
Obermeier, Tom *architectural firm executive*
Prosser, John Martin *architecture educator*
Steenhagen, Robert Lewis *landscape architect, consultant*

**Fort Collins**
Grandin, Temple *industrial designer, science educator*

**Fort Garland**
Boyer, Lester Leroy, Jr. *architecture educator, consultant*

**Grand Junction**
Burdick, Margaret Seale (Marge Burdick) *interior designer*

**Littleton**
Shepherd, Donna Lou *interior designer*

**Vail**
Vosbeck, Robert Randall *architect*

## CONNECTICUT

**Centerbrook**
Grover, William Herbert *architect*
Harper, Robert Leslie *architect, educator*

**Cheshire**
Rowland, Ralph Thomas *retired architect*

**Hamden**
Roche, (Eamonn) Kevin *architect*

**Hartford**
Amatuli, Robert Alexander *architect*

**New Britain**
Mooney, Kenneth Frank *design educator*

**New Canaan**
Dean, Robert Bruce *architect*
Papp, Laszlo George *retired architect*
Risom, Jens *furniture designer, consultant, manufacturing executive*

**New Haven**
Chilton, William David *architect*
Newick, Craig David *architect*
Pelli, Cesar *architect*
Petit, Emmanuel J. *architecture educator*
Roth, Harold *architect*

**Niantic**
Butler, Jonathan Putnam *architect*

**Northford**
Gregan, Edmund Robert *landscape architect*

**Orange**
Miller, Henry Forster *architect*

**South Kent**
Baker, John Milnes *architect*

**Stonington**
Stoddard, Alexandra *interior designer, educator, writer*

**Trumbull**
Watson, Donald Ralph *architect, dean, writer, artist*

**Westport**
Ferris, Roger Patrick *architect*

## DELAWARE

**Newark**
Stick, Thomas Howard Fitchett *architect, construction litigation consultant*

## DISTRICT OF COLUMBIA

**Washington**
Bagnoli, David Christopher *architect*
Birnbaum, Charles A. *landscape architect*
Coffin, Beatriz de Winthuysen *landscape architect*
Cox, Warren Jacob *architect*
Gentner, Paul LeFoe *architect, consultant*
Greene, Thomas Hardy *architect*

Hartman, George Eitel *architect*
Hellmuth, George William *architect*
Holladay, Wilhelmina Cole *interior designer, museum director*
Jacobsen, Hugh Newell *architect*
Kulski, Julian Eugeniusz *architect, writer*
Lewis, Anne McCutcheon *architect*
Lewis, Roger Kutnow *architect, educator, author*
Liebenson, Gloria Krasnow *interior design executive, freelance writer*
Miller, Ewing Harry *retired architect*
Minkoff, Alice Sydney *interior designer stylist*
Murray, Christopher Charles III *architect*
Oehme, Wolfgang Walter *landscape architect*
Ramberg, Walter Dodd *architect*
Schlesinger, B. Frank *architect, educator*
Siegel, Lloyd Harvey *architect, real estate developer, consultant*
Woofter, Vivien Perrine *interior designer, consultant*
Yerkes, David Norton *architect*

## FLORIDA

**Bal Harbour**
Spiegel, Siegmund *architect*

**Boca Raton**
Harris, S. Buddy *architect, interior designer*

**Bonita Springs**
Trudnak, Stephen Joseph *landscape architect*

**Daytona Beach**
Amick, William Walker *golf course architect*

**Delray Beach**
Rippeteau, Darrel Downing *retired architect*

**Fort Myers**
Mair, Bruce Logan *interior designer, architectural firm executive*
Sappenfield, Charles Madison *architect, educator*

**Gainesville**
Hasell, Mary Joyce (Jo) *architecture educator*
Kohen, Martha *architecture educator*

**Indian River Shores**
Ahrens, William Henry *architect*

**Islamorada**
Shelton, Dorothy Aubinoe *interior designer*

**Jacksonville**
Morgan, William Newton *architect, educator*

**Longwood**
Gasperoni, Ellen Jean Lias *interior designer*

**Miami**
Arango, Jorge Sanin *architect*
Feito, Jose *architect*
Hampton, Mark Garrison *architect*
Spear, Laurinda Hope *architect*

**Miramar**
Stewart Simpson, Donnamay Angela *interior designer*

**Naples**
Jones, Richard Wallace *interior designer*
Lewis, Gordon Gilmer *golf course architect*
Lickhalter, Merlin *architect*

**Ormond Beach**
Cowley, Gerald Dean *architect*
Truitt, Richard byron *landscape architect*

**Oviedo**
Duda, Richard Frank *architect, engineering executive*

**Pensacola**
Bullock, Ellis Way, Jr. *architect*
Woolf, Kenneth Howard *architect*

**Saint Augustine**
Wilkes, Delano Angus *architect*

**Saint Petersburg**
Wedding, Charles Randolph *architect*

**Sebastian**
Lagin, Neil *landscape designer, consultant*

**Stuart**
Ankrom, Charles Franklin *golf course architect, consultant*

**Tallahassee**
Pugh, Thomas Doering *architecture educator, educator*

**Tampa**
Howey, John Richard *architect, writer*
Jennewein, James Joseph *architect*
Lashley, Keith Livingstone *architect, educator*

**West Palm Beach**
Marshall-Beasley, Elizabeth *landscape architect*
Ross, Edward Joseph *architect*

**Winter Haven**
Burns, Arthur Lee *architect*

## GEORGIA

**Alpharetta**
Walker, Thomas H. *industrial designer*

**Atlanta**
Bainbridge, Frederick Freeman III *architect*
Bull, Frank James *retired architect*
Cantley, Kevin Rilous *architectural firm executive*
Cooper, Jerome Maurice *architect*

Cupp, Robert Erhard *golf course architect, land use planner*
Diedrich, Richard Joseph *architect*
Eastman, Charles (Chuck) M. *architecture educator*
Guest, Rita Carson *interior designer*
Lewcock, Ronald Bentley *architect, educator*
Miller, Roger L. *architectural firm executive*
Muse, Gar *architectural firm executive*
Peponis, John *architect, educator*
Portman, John C., Jr. *architect, developer*
Pulgram, William Leopold *architect, space designer*
Scogin, Mack *architect, educator*
Sizemore, Michael Maynard *architectural firm executive*

**Augusta**
Woodhurst, Robert Stanford, Jr. *architect*

**Decatur**
Mc Intosh, James Eugene, Jr. *interior designer*

**Hiram**
Stevens, Charles Thomas, Sr. *drafting technology educator*

**Kingsland**
Huygens, Remmert William *architect*

**Macon**
Dunwody, Eugene Cox *architect*

**Rome**
Janowski, Thaddeus Marian *architect*

**Saint Simons Island**
Webb, Lamar Thaxter *architect*

**Savannah**
Yang, Dihua *architecture educator, researcher*

## HAWAII

**Honolulu**
Botsai, Elmer Eugene *architect, architecture educator, retired dean*
Hamada, Duane Takumi *architect*
Jensen, Barbara Wood *interior design business owner*
Yeh, Raymond Wei-Hwa *architect, educator*

**Waipahu**
Chang, Walter Tuck, Sr. *draftsman, real estate agent, religious studies educator*

## IDAHO

**Boise**
Hunsucker, Wayne (Carl Wayne Hunsucker) *architectural firm executive, educator*

## ILLINOIS

**Bloomington**
Switzer, Jon Rex *architect*

**Bolingbrook**
Caddy, Edmund H.H., Jr. *architect*

**Champaign**
Baker, Jack Sherman *architect, educator*
Boubekri, Mohamed *architecture educator*
Hopkins, Lewis Dean *architecture educator*
Riley, Robert Bartlett *landscape architect*

**Chicago**
Amstadter, Laurence *retired architect*
Ast, Bruno *architecture educator*
Balasi, Mark Geoffrey *architect*
Barney, Carol Ross *architect*
Belluschi, Anthony C. *architect*
Clark, Raymond S. *architectural firm executive*
Epstein, Sidney *architect, civil engineer*
Gold, Allan Harold *architect, structural engineer, educator*
Hackl, Donald John *architect*
Holabird, John Augur, Jr. *retired architect*
Kerbis, Gertrude Lempp *architect*
Legge Kemp, Diane *architect, landscape architect*
Mack, Alan Wayne *interior designer*
Matthei, Edward Hodge *architect*
McCullagh, Grant Gibson *retired architect*
McCurry, Margaret Irene *architect, educator, furniture designer, interior designer*
Phillips, Frederick Falley *architect*
Robertson, Donna Virginia *architect, educator, dean*
Rugo, Steven Alfred *architect*
Schroeder, Douglas Fredrick *architect*
Smith, Adrian Devaun *architect*
Tigerman, Stanley *architect, educator*
Torgersen, Torwald Harold *architect, consultant*
Valerio, Joseph Mastro *architectural firm executive, educator*
VanderBeke, Patricia K. *architect*
Vinci, John Nicholas *architect, educator*
Weber, Hanno *architect*
Weese, Benjamin Horace *architect*
Whitney, Patrick Foster *design educator*
Zheng, James *architectural firm executive*

**Deerfield**
Miller, Michael Thurman *architect*

**Evanston**
Grunsfeld, Ernest Alton III *architect*
Macsai, John *architect*

**Highland Park**
Dirsmith, Ronald *architect*
Dubin, Arthur Detmers *retired architect*
Tobin, Calvin Jay *retired architect*

**Hinsdale**
Unikel, Eva Taylor *interior designer*

**Kenilworth**
Schneider-Criezis, Susan Marie *architect*

**Lake Zurich**
Krolopp, Rudolph William *retired industrial designer, consultant*

**Mount Carroll**
Rogers, Ward Junior *retired industrial designer*

**Peoria**
Golan, Kim Marie *facility interior designer*

**Rockford**
Bradley, Charles MacArthur *retired architect*

**Schaumburg**
Otis, James, Jr. *architect*

**Skokie**
Siegal, Burton Lee *product designer, consultant, inventor*

**Tinley Park**
Lobes, Mark Robert *graphic design educator, coach*

**Wheaton**
Martin, Marcia Gray *retired architecture educator, artist, designer*

**Winnetka**
Piper, Robert Johnston *retired architect, urban planner*
Schlossman, John Isaac *architect*

## INDIANA

**Carmel**
Eden, Barbara Janiece *commercial and residential interior designer*
McLaughlin, Harry Roll *architect*

**Michigan City**
Manny, Carter Hugh, Jr. *architect, foundation administrator*

**Mishawaka**
Ponko, William Reuben *architect*
Troyer, LeRoy Seth *architect*

**Muncie**
Elvin, George *architecture educator*

**Notre Dame**
Stamper, John W. *architecture educator, academic administrator*

**South Bend**
Horsbrugh, Patrick *architect, educator, environologist*
Smith, Thomas Gordon *architect*

## IOWA

**Ames**
Lewis, Calvin Fred *architect, educator*
Palermo, Gregory Sebastian *architect*

**Clear Lake**
Broshar, Robert Clare *architect*

**Iowa City**
Neumann, Roy Covert *architect*

## KANSAS

**Lawrence**
Grabow, Stephen Harris *architecture educator*

**Manhattan**
Foerster, Bernd *architecture educator*

**Overland Park**
Cummings, Jan Norman *interior designer, educator*

**Topeka**
Katt, Gary Gene *retired architect*
Slemmons, Robert Sheldon *architect*

## KENTUCKY

**Lexington**
Romanowitz, Byron Foster *architect, engineer*

## LOUISIANA

**Baton Rouge**
Reich, Robert Sigmund *landscape architect*

**Bogalusa**
Gallaspy, Dixie *interior designer, innkeeper*

**New Orleans**
Bookhardt, Fred Barringer, Jr. *architect*
Frantz, Phares Albert *architect*
Klingman, John Philip *architect, educator*
Mathes, Edward Conrad *architect*

## MAINE

**Edgecomb**
Carlson, Suzanne Olive *architect*

**New Gloucester**
Jaccaci, August Thayer, Jr. *social architect, educator*

**New Harbor**
Fradley, Frederick Macdonell *retired architect*

**Seal Harbor**
Forbes, Peter *architect*

**York**
Lyman, William Welles, Jr. *retired architect*

## MARYLAND

**Annapolis**
Jansson, John Phillip *architect, consultant*
Miller, Richards Thorn *naval architect, engineer*

**Baltimore**
Adams, Harold Lynn *architect*
Brodie, Menasha J. (Jay Brodie) *architect, city planner, government executive*
Donkervoet, Richard Cornelius *architect*
Ford, John Gilmore *interior designer*
Snead, James Arrington *architect*

**Bethesda**
Popescu, Daniel *interior designer*

**Bowie**
Stone, Edward Harris, II, *landscape architect*

**Chevy Chase**
Auerbach, Seymour *architect*

**Montgomery Village**
Zabrek, Albert Samuel *architect*

**Olney**
Delmar, Eugene Anthony *architect*

**Rockville**
Morgan, William Bruce *naval architect*

**Severna Park**
Allison, John Langsdale *naval architect, marine engineer*

**Takoma Park**
DeVaris, Panayotis Eric *architect*

## MASSACHUSETTS

**Amherst**
Cornish, Geoffrey St. John *golf course architect*

**Bedford**
Payne, Harry Morse, Jr. *architect*
Shepley, Hugh *architect*

**Boston**
Collins, James H., Jr. *architectural firm executive*
Costa, Daniel Lawrence *architect*
Finegold, Maurice Nathan *architect*
Flansburgh, Earl Robert *architect*
Goody, Joan Edelman *architect*
Harkness, John Cheesman *retired architect*
Klema, Donald David *architect*
Mattox, Robert F. *architectural firm executive*
Pisani, Anthony Michael *architect*
Rawn, William Leete III *architect*
Stull, Donald LeRoy *architect*
Sullivan Stemberg, Maureen *interior designer*
Tappé, Albert Anthony *architect*
Twomey, Timothy *architect*
Wedge, Carole C. *architectural firm executive*

**Cambridge**
Anderson, Stanford Owen *architect, architectural historian, educator*
Bush, Michael *architectural firm executive*
Campbell, Robert *architect, writer*
Cohen, Preston Scott *architecture educator*
Gund, Graham *architectural firm executive*
Hamner, W. Easley *architect*
Jones, Mary M. *landscape architect*
Kobus, Richard Lawrence *architect*
Kruger, Kenneth *architect*
Mori, Toshiko *architecture educator*
Porter, William Lyman *architect, educator*
Ratti, Carlo Filippo *architect, researcher*
Rowe, Peter Grimmond *architecture educator, researcher*
Santos, Adele Naudé *architect, educator*
Tsoi, Edward Tze Ming *architect, urban planner, interior designer*

**Concord**
Brooker, Richard I. *architect*

**Edgartown**
Rosenfeld, Walter David, Jr. *architect, writer*

**Lexington**
Frey, John Ward *landscape architect*

**Marblehead**
Green, Richard John *architect*

**North Andover**
Goldstein, Charles Henry *architect, consultant*

**Springfield**
Engebretson, Douglas Kenneth *architect, interior designer*

**Waltham**
Notkin, Leonard Sheldon *architect*

**Wellesley**
Birkerts, Gunnar *architect*

**Weston**
Wood, Jeremy Scott *architect, urban designer*

**Woods Hole**
Newman, John Nicholas *naval architect educator*

## MICHIGAN

**Ann Arbor**
Beckley, Robert Mark *architect, educator*
Benford, Harry Bell *naval architect*
Fry, Richard E. *architectural firm executive*
Metcalf, Robert Clarence *architect, educator*
Turner, James A. *architecture educator*

**Chelsea**
Kendall, Kay Lynn *interior designer, consultant*
Paulsen, Serenus Glen *architect, educator*

**Detroit**
Francis, Edward D. *architect*
Frank, Richard Calhoun *architect*
Sims, Howard F. *architectural firm executive*

**Flint**
Tomblinson, James Edmond *architect*

**Kalamazoo**
Carver, Norman Francis, Jr. *architect, photographer*

**South Haven**
LaRocque, Linda Lou *interior designer, educator, playwright*

**Southfield**
Tuttle, Edward X. *architect, lawyer*

## MINNESOTA

**Chaska**
Olin, Peter Joel *landscape architect, educator*

**Duluth**
Salmela, David Daniel *architect*
Whiteman, Richard Frank *architect*

**Minneapolis**
Clemence, Roger Davidson *landscape architect, educator*
Fulop, Laszlo G. *architect*
Hollencamp, Greg *architectural firm executive*
Jacob, Bernard Michel *architect*
Martin, Roger Bond *landscape architect*
Moran, Lewis Terrill *architect*
Swenson, Mark Gregory *architect*
Tollefson, Lee *architect*

**Minnetonka**
Anderson, Tad Stephen *landscape architect, consultant, photographer*

**Northfield**
Sovik, Edward Anders *architect, consultant*

## MISSISSIPPI

**Biloxi**
Zocchi, Louis Joseph *product designer, game company executive*

**Columbus**
Kaye, Samuel Harvey *architect, educator*

**Jackson**
Burns, Robert, Jr. *retired architect, painter*
Dale, T.D. *architectural firm executive*

**Lumberton**
Wisznia, Walter *architectural firm executive*

**Mississippi State**
Martin, Edward Curtis, Jr. *landscape architect, educator*

**Starkville**
Ford, Robert MacDonald III *architect, educator*

## MISSOURI

**Branson**
Ownby, Jerry Steve *landscape architect, educator*

**Kansas City**
Seligson, Theodore H. *architect, interior designer, urban planner*

**Saint Louis**
Bextermiller, Theresa Marie *architect, computer engineer*
Cotton, W(illiam) Philip, Jr. *architect*
Lovelace, Eldridge Hirst *retired landscape architect, city planner*
Marti, Paul Edgar, Jr. *architect, educator*
Michaelides, Constantine Evangelos *architect, educator*
Thalden, Barry R. *architect*
Weese, Cynthia Rogers *architect, educator*

**Springfield**
Gardner, Steven *instructional designer*

**Weatherby Lake**
Hawkins, Geri Sue *interior designer, jewelry designer, realtor*

**Webster Groves**
Becker, Rex Louis *architect*

## MONTANA

**Bozeman**
DeHaas, John Neff, Jr. *retired architecture educator*

**Great Falls**
Davidson, David Scott *retired architect*

## NEBRASKA

### Lincoln
Mutunayagam, N. Brito *architecture educator*
Stange, James Henry *architect*
Steward, Weldon Cecil *architecture educator, architect, consultant*

### Omaha
Polsky, Donald Perry *architect*
Ryan, Mark Anthony *architect, lawyer*

## NEVADA

### Las Vegas
Marnell, Anthony Austin, II, *architect*

## NEW HAMPSHIRE

### Hanover
Brooks, H. Allen *architectural educator, author, lecturer*

## NEW JERSEY

### Bound Brook
Shive, Richard Byron *architect*

### Cape May Point
Jordan, Joe J. *architect*

### Colonia
Wiesenfeld, Bess G. *interior designer*

### East Orange
Fielo, Muriel Bryant *interior designer*

### Englewood
Schmidt, Ronald Hans *architect*

### Gillette
Knorr, Michael Jeffrey *architect*

### Haddon Heights
Westfield, Margaret Ann Hoyert *architect*

### Morristown
Nadaskay, Raymond *architect*

### Newark
Goldman, Glenn *architect, educator*

### Princeton
Allen, Stanley T. *architect, dean, educator*
Diller, Elizabeth E. *architect, educator, artist*
Ford, Jeremiah III *architect*
Graves, Michael *architect, educator*
Hillier, J(ames) Robert *architect*
Kehrt, Allan William *architect*

### Sussex
Hoyt, Earl Edward, Jr. *industrial designer*

### Upper Saddle River
Cappitella, Mauro John *architect*

## NEW MEXICO

### Albuquerque
Foster, Judi *interior designer, artist*
Gutierrez, Joni Marie *landscape architect, political organization worker*
Pirkl, James Joseph *industrial designer, educator, writer*
Pressman, Andy *architecture educator*
Schluntz, Roger *architecture educator*

### Corrales
Hooker, Van Dorn *architect, educator, artist*

### Santa Fe
Franzen, Ulrich J. *architect*
Leon, Bruno *architect, educator*

## NEW YORK

### Ardsley On Hudson
Guise, David Earl *architect, educator*

### Binghamton
Bearsch, Lee Palmer *architect, urban planner*

### Bronx
Gaveras, Harry *architect*

### Bronxville
Frost, A. Corwin *architect, consultant*

### Brooklyn
Katavolos, William *architecture educator, furniture designer*
Nadel, Monroe Stanley *retired architect, landscape architect*
Rice, John Thomas *architecture educator*

### Buffalo
Coles, Robert Traynham *architect*

### Cranberry Lake
Glavin, James Edward *landscape architect*

### Cross River
Thorn, Susan Howe *interior designer*

### Dobbs Ferry
Guggenheimer, Tobias Immanuel Simon *architect*

### East Hampton
Damaz, Paul F. *architect*
Delson, Sidney Leon *architect*

### Hastings On Hudson
Weinstein, Edward Michael *architect, consultant*

### Ithaca
Olpadwala, Porus *architecture educator, dean*

### Jamaica
Gati, William Eugene *architect, educator*

### Kew Gardens
Aldea, Patricia *architect*

### Locust Valley
Bentel, Carol Rusche *architect*
Bentel, Frederick Richard *architect, educator*
Bentel, Paul Louis *architect, educator*

### Long Island City
Sadao, Shoji *architect*

### Manhasset
Schiller, Arthur A. *architect, educator*

### Middletown
Fucci, Joseph Leonard *editor, college librarian*

### New Rochelle
Menzies, Henry Hardinge *architect*

### New York
Anderson, Ross S. *architectural firm executive*
Bader, Ian *architectural firm executive*
Baird, Penny Drue *interior designer*
Balmori, Diana *landscape designer*
Bartlett, Elizabeth Easton *interior designer*
Bergdoll, Barry G. *architectural historian, educator*
Bland, Frederick Aves *architect*
Bond, James Max, Jr. *architect, academic administrator*
Brennan, Henry Higginson *architect*
Buatta, Mario *interior designer*
Buttrick, Harold *architect*
Carlson, Richard A. *interior designer*
Chan, Lo-Yi Cheung Yuen *architect*
Charles, Michael Harrison *architectural interior designer*
Childs, David M. *architectural firm executive*
Cioppa, Robert *architectural firm executive*
Cobb, Henry Nichols *architect*
Cohn, Ian J. *architect*
Cutler, Laurence Stephan *architect, museum administrator, writer, advertising executive, educator*
Czajka, James Vincent *architect*
David, Theoharis Lambros *architect, educator*
Dennis, Diane Joy Milam *retired architect*
De Vido, Alfredo Eduardo *architect*
Djerejian, Robert Asbed *architect*
Edelman, Judith H. *architect*
Eisenman, Peter David *architect, educator*
Fowle, Bruce S. *architect*
Galan, Leonidez Vindollo *architect*
Gath, Jean Marie *architectural firm executive*
Gatje, Robert Frederick *architect, writer*
Ghaffari, Avideh Behrouz *interior designer*
Giddens-Jones, Emily Jane *architectural and interior designer, consultant*
Ginsberg, David Lawrence *architect*
Giurgola, Romaldo *architect, educator*
Gwathmey, Charles *architect*
Halsband, Frances *architect*
Hardy, Hugh *architect*
Hariri, Gisue *architect, educator*
Hayden, Richard Seth *architectural firm executive*
Hinz, Theodore Vincent *architect*
Holl, Steven Myron *architect, educator*
Holub, Martin *architect*
Ivy, Robert Adams, Jr. *architect, editor-in-chief*
Karlin, Susan *design company executive*
Kliment, Robert Michael *architect*
Kliment, Stephen Alexander *architect, editor, journalist*
Kohn, A. Eugene *architect*
Krebs, Carl F. *architectural firm executive*
Lefferts, Gillet, Jr. *architect*
Lewis, Paul *architecture educator*
Libeskind, Daniel *architect*
Liebman, Theodore *architect*
Masey, Jack *exhibition designer*
Meier, Richard Alan *architect*
Miller, George H. *architectural firm executive*
Minskoff, Edward *architectural firm executive*
Moss, Douglas *architectural firm executive*
Perkins, Lawrence Bradford, Jr. *architect*
Pokorny, Jan Hird *architect, educator*
Polshek, James Stewart *architect*
Pomeroy, Lee Harris *architect*
Prince-Ramus, Joshua *architect*
Quennell, Nicholas *landscape architect, educator*
Renfro, Charles *architect, educator*
Rockwell, David *architectural firm executive*
Slomanson, Lloyd Howard *architect, musician, photographer*
Smith-Miller, Henry Houck *architect*
Smotrich, David Isadore *architect*
Sono, Masayuki *architect, artist*
Stern, Robert Arthur Morton *architect, educator, writer*
Strasser, Robert *architectural firm executive*
Szeto, Yvonne *architectural firm executive*
Taylor, Marilyn Jordan *architectural firm executive*
Tschumi, Bernard *architect*
Varney, Carleton Bates, Jr. *interior designer, columnist, educator*
Viñoly, Rafael *architectural firm executive*
Voorsanger, Bartholomew *architect*
Wexler, Allan *architect, educator*
Wigley, Mark Antony *architecture educator*

### Northport
De Carolis, Philip Joseph *space designer, educator*

### Nyack
Degenshein, Jan *architect, planner*

### Penfield
Kraft, Donald Eugene *architecture and engineering company executive*

### Pleasantville
Annese, Domenico *retired landscape architect*

### Richfield Springs
Walters, Marjorie Anne *interior designer, consultant*

### Rye
Rolland, Peter George *landscape architect*

### Syracuse
Skoler, Louis *architect, educator*

### Tarrytown
Ladau, Robert Francis *architect, land use planner*

### Troy
Haviland, David Sands *retired architectural educator, researcher, administrator*

### Wappingers Falls
Johnson, Jeh Vincent *architect*

### Westhampton Beach
Flood, Angela *interior designer, artist*

## NORTH CAROLINA

### Asheville
King, Joseph Bertram *architect*

### Boone
Oelberg, Robert Nathan *landscape architect*

### Chapel Hill
Dixon, Frederick Dail *architect*
Godschalk, David Robinson *architect, urban development planner, educator*
Jordan, Janine *interior designer, consultant, small business owner*
Stipe, Robert Edwin *retired design educator*

### Charlotte
Ferebee, Stephen Scott, Jr. *architect*
Huberman, Jeffrey Allen *architect*
Montague, Edgar Burwell, III, (Monty Montague) *industrial designer*

### Davidson
Kamp, Barbara Ann *designer, poet, photographer, educator, artist*

### Kinston
Baker-Gardner, Jewelle *interior designer, consultant*

### Pisgah Forest
Albyn, Richard Keith *retired architect*

### Raleigh
Clarke, Lewis James *landscape architect*
Flournoy, William Louis, Jr. *landscape architect*
Malecha, Marvin John *architect, academic administrator*
Peele, Katherine N. *architect*

### Research Triangle Park
Atkins, John L. III *architect*

### Robbinsville
Ginn, Ronn *architect, urban planner, general contractor*

## OHIO

### Akron
Castronovo, Thomas Paul *architect, consultant*

### Berea
Tadych, Christopher Allen *architectural firm executive, architectural engineer*

### Celina
Fanning, Ronald Heath *architect, engineer*

### Cincinnati
Chatterjee, Jayanta *architecture and planning educator*
Glendening, Everett Austin *architect*
Goetzman, Bruce Edgar *architecture educator*
Luckner, Herman Richard III *interior designer*
Nielsen, George Lee *architect*
Preiser, Wolfgang Friedrich Ernst *architect, educator, consultant, researcher*
Schwartz, Robert Terry *industrial designer, director*
Senhauser, John Crater *architect*

### Cleveland
Bowen, Richard Lee *architect*
Eberhard, William Thomas *architect*
Gibans, James David *architect*
Kelly, John Terence *architect*
Madison, Robert Prince *architect*
Sande, Theodore Anton *architect, educator, foundation executive*
Zung, Thomas Tse-Kwai *architect*

### Columbus
Kirk, Ballard Harry Thurston *architect*
Tyne, Michael D. *architectural firm executive*
Voss, Jerrold Richard *architecture educator*
Warner, Charles Henry, Jr. *architect*

### Cuyahoga Falls
Haag, Everett Keith *architect*

### Marietta
McCreery, Jean Terrell *retired draftsman, editor*

### Oxford
Brown Manrique, Gerardo *architect, educator*

### Painesville
Filson, Ronald Coulter *architect, educator, dean*

### Reynoldsburg
Serraglio, Mario *architect*

### Toledo
Martin, Robert Edward *architect*

## OKLAHOMA

### Norman
Fillpot, Bob G. *architecture educator*
Henderson, Arnold Glenn *architect, educator*
Kudrna, James *architecture educator*
Sorey, Thomas Lester, Jr. *architect, educator*

### Oklahoma City
Halpin, Anna Marie *retired architect*

## OREGON

### Ashland
Mularz, Theodore Leonard *architect*

### Beaverton
Hatfield, Tinker L. *architect, apparel designer, product designer*

### Depoe Bay
Eaton, Leonard Kimball *retired architecture educator*

### Hillsboro
Dubrulle, Françoise M. *architect, painter, interior designer*
Koufaty, David *computer architect*

### Medford
Skelton, Douglas H. *architect*
Straus, David A. *architectural firm executive*

### Portland
Allen, Rex Whitaker *retired architect*

### Springfield
Lutes, Donald Henry *architect*

### Welches
Merrill, William Dean *retired architect, medical association administrator*

## PENNSYLVANIA

### Ambler
Clemmer, Leon *architect, space designer*

### Bethlehem
Spillman, Robert Arnold *architect*

### Camp Hill
Brandow, Theo *architect*

### Harrisburg
Knackstedt, Mary V. *interior designer*

### New Cumberland
Peters, Ralph Edgar *architectural firm executive, engineering executive*

### Philadelphia
Bower, John Arnold, Jr. *architect*
Brown, Denise Scott *architect, urban planner*
Dagit, Charles Edward, Jr. *architect, educator*
DeLong, David G. *architect, urban planner, educator*
Eiswerth, Barry Neil *architect, educator*
Hayes, John Freeman *architect*
Lawson, John Quinn *architect*
Magaziner, Henry Jonas *architect, writer*
Maxman, Susan Abel *architect*
Mertins, Detlef *architect, educator*
Olin, Laurie Dewar *landscape architect, educator*
Rauch, John Keiser, Jr. *architect*
Rybczynski, Witold Marian *architect, educator, writer*
Saylor, Peter M. *architect*
Trainer, Nancy Rogo *architect, planner*
Venturi, Robert *architect*

### Pittsburgh
Becherer, Richard John *architecture educator*
Damianos, Sylvester *architect, sculptor*
Hoglund, J. David *architectural firm executive*
Horowitz, Carole Spiegel *landscape contractor*
Rico-Gutierrez, Luis F. *architecture educator*

### State College
Haas, John C. *architect*

### University Park
Lindberg, Darla V. *architect, educator*

### Williamsport
Wittman, Brittany Lyn *design educator*

### Willow Grove
Suer, Marvin David *architectural consultant*

### York
Yourist, Sheldon Eric *product designer*

## RHODE ISLAND

### Bristol
Hendrix, John Shannon *architecture educator*

### Newport
Burgin, William Lyle *architect*

### Providence
Barnum, William Milo *architect*
Kagan, Marilyn D. *retired architect*
St. Florian, Friedrich Gartler *architect, educator*

---

**ARTS: LITERARY** *See also* **COMMUNICATIONS MEDIA**

---

**Phoenix**
Ellison, Cyril Lee *literary agent, retired publishing executive*

**Portal**
Williams, Jeanne *writer*

**Scottsdale**
Jarman, Beth S. *writer, educational consultant*
Taylor, James C. *writer*

**Sedona**
Gore, Willma Clarice *writer, educator*

**Tempe**
Raby, William Louis *writer, consultant*
Reyes, Guillermo Augusto *playwright, educator*

**Tucson**
Brett, Peter D. *writer*
Butcher, Russell Devereux *writer, photographer*
Martin, Marci *writer, former advertising specialist*
Stitt, Mari Leipper *poet*
Williams, Joy *writer*

## ARKANSAS

**Fayetteville**
Williams, Miller *retired poet, writer, translator*

**Hot Springs National Park**
Selix, Karen Elizabeth *writer, artist, vocalist*

**Little Rock**
Nunn, Patarica Dian *poet*

**Morrilton**
Lord, Penny *writer*
Lord, Robert *writer*

## CALIFORNIA

**Alameda**
Ngo, Tung Thanh *writer, photographer*
Rubin, Charles Alexis *writer*

**Altadena**
Burden, Jean Prussing *retired poet, editor*

**Aromas**
Fleischman, Paul *children's author*

**Atascadero**
Locke, Virginia Otis *writer*

**Berkeley**
Brooke, Tal (Robert Taliaferro) *writer*
Callenbach, Ernest *writer, editor*
Chetin, Helen Campbell *writer*
Katzen, Mollie *writer*
Kluger, Richard *writer, editor*
Knox, Helene Margrethe *poet, editor*
Masumoto, David Mas *writer, farmer*
Mukherjee, Bharati (Mrs. Clark Blaise) *writer, language educator*
Ruppenthal, Karl M. *author, educator*
Russell, Charlie L. *writer*
Soto, Gary *poet, writer*

**Beverly Hills**
Apatow, Judd *scriptwriter, television producer, film producer*
Ball, Alan *screenwriter*
Basichis, Gordon Allen *writer, scriptwriter, novelist, marketing consultant, media consultant*
Bass, Ronald *screenwriter*
Chase, David (David DeCaesare) *scriptwriter, television producer, television director*
Crowe, Cameron *screenwriter, film director*
Farrelly, Bobby (Robert Leo Rarrelly Jr.) *scriptwriter, film director, film producer*
Gaghan, Stephen *scriptwriter, film director*
Gelbart, Larry *scriptwriter, television producer, theater producer*
Groening, Matthew (Matthew Abram Groening) *writer, cartoonist*
Kaufman, Charlie *scriptwriter*
Lee, Whitney Fielding *literary agent*
Mandel, Babaloo *scriptwriter*
Pezzullo, Ralph Michael *writer, playwright*
Quinn, Patricia K. *literary agent*
Roth, Eric *screenwriter*
Schaffer, Akiva *writer, director*
Schulian, John (Nielsen Schulian) *screenwriter, author*
Shanley, John Patrick *playwright, screenwriter*
Sorkin, Aaron *scriptwriter, television producer, playwright*
Steinem, Gloria *writer, editor, advocate*
Taccone, Jorma *writer, director*
Ward, David Schad *scriptwriter, film director*

**Brea**
Curtis, James Richard *writer, editor*

**Calabasas**
Carner, Charles Robert, Jr. *screenwriter, director*

**Cameron Park**
Vorce-Tish, Helene R. *writer*

**Canoga Park**
Alexander, Sue *writer*

**Carson**
Delfin, Donna K. *writer, web programmer*

**Castro Valley**
Wycoff, Charles Coleman *writer, retired anesthesiologist*

**Cayucos**
Shahan, Sherry Jean *writer, educator*

**Chico**
Livingston, Myran Jay *author, film writer, director and producer*

**Chula Vista**
Nelson, Carl Alfred *writer, international business educator*
Ryan, Candace I. *writer, director, editor*

**Citrus Heights**
Daves, Sandra Lynn *poet, lyricist*

**Claremont**
Riley, Judith Merkle *writer, educator*
Tilden, Wesley Roderick *writer, retired application developer*
Wachtel, Albert *writer, educator*

**Clovis**
Shields, Allan Edwin *writer, photographer*

**Colton**
Allen, Blair Hamilton *writer, poet, artist, editor, photographer*

**Compton**
Shiloh, Allen *writer*

**Cotati**
Hill, Debora Elizabeth *writer, journalist, screenwriter*

**Cromberg**
Kolb, Ken Lloyd *writer*

**Cypress**
Edmonds, Ivy Gordon *retired writer*

**Dana Point**
Walker, Doris Isaak *writer, historian, educator*

**Davis**
Bunch, Richard Alan *writer, educator, poet, philosopher*
Major, Clarence Lee *writer, educator*

**Del Mar**
Morton, Frederic *author*

**Elk Grove**
Lichtman, Debbie *writer, secondary school educator*

**Fresno**
Garrison-Finderup, Ivadelle Dalton *writer, educator*
Lanter, Lanore *writer, educator*

**Garden Valley**
Price, Lew Paxton *writer, engineer*

**Glendale**
Spring, Carl Chaffee, Jr. *writer*

**Grass Valley**
Cheney, Margaret *writer, retired editor*
Washington, Allyn Jarvis *writer*

**Healdsburg**
Castellini, Mary Mercer *author*
Erdman, Paul Emil *author*
Myers, Robert Eugene *writer, educator*

**Hollywood**
Melchior, Ib Jorgen *scriptwriter, author, film director*

**Huntington Beach**
Flakes, Susan *playwright, scriptwriter, theater director*

**Inglewood**
King, J.L. *writer*

**Kensington**
Littlejohn, David *writer*

**La Jolla**
Antin, David *poet, critic*

**Laguna Beach**
Chevli, Lyn *writer*
Taylor, Theodore Langhans *retired author*

**Los Altos Hills**
Robbins, Doren Gurstein *poet, educator, artist*

**Los Angeles**
Basil, Douglas Constantine *writer, educator*
Baumbach, Noah *screenwriter*
Campbell, Bebe Moore *writer*
Carothers, A.J. *scriptwriter*
Cohen, Marcia Fan Baltimore *writer, psychologist*
Corwin, Norman *scriptwriter, film producer, film director*
Golden, Arthur *writer*
Good, Edith Elissa (Pearl Williams) *writer*
Horowitz, David Joel *author*
Kaplan, Nadia *writer*
Messerli, Douglas *writer, publisher*
Noguchi, Thomas Tsunetomi *writer, pathologist*
Patrick, Robert *playwright*
Schulberg, Budd *author*
Sedaris, Amy *writer, actress*
Shapiro, Mel *playwright, educator, theater director*
Sheldon, Sidney *writer, television director, television producer*
Sivertsen, Linda Joyce *writer, editor, publishing consultant*

**Menlo Park**
Heller, Esther A. *writer, educator*

**Modesto**
Norton, Max C. *writer, educator*

**Morgan Hill**
Singh, Loren Chan *writer, educator*

**Newport Beach**
Gould, Marilyn A. *writer, educator*
Wentworth, Diana von Welanetz *author*

**North Hollywood**
Campos, Luis *puzzle writer*

**Northridge**
Boberg, Dorothy Kurth *author*

**Oakland**
Foley, Jack (John Wayne Harold Foley) *poet, writer, editor-in-chief*
Haiman, Franklyn Saul *writer, communications educator*
Kivel, Paul *writer*
Schacht, Henry Mevis *writer, consultant*
Silverberg, Robert *writer*
Turner, Tom *writer, editor*
Zandvakili, Katayoon *writer*

**Oceano**
Scott, Donald Michael *writer, educator*

**Ontario**
Kloepfer, Marguerite Fonnesbeck *writer*

**Orinda**
Strong, Susan Clancey *writer, communications executive, editor*

**Pacific Grove**
Yep, Laurence Michael *author*

**Palm Springs**
Nelson, K. Bonita *literary agent*
Wouk, Herman *writer*

**Palo Alto**
Wright, Kirby Michael *writer, editor*

**Pasadena**
Brogden-Stirbl, Shona Marie *writer, researcher*
Yeager, Caroline Hale *writer, retired radiologist, consultant*

**Pebble Beach**
Peper, George Frederick *writer, retired publishing executive*

**Penngrove**
Haslam, Gerald William *writer, educator*

**Petaluma**
Hass, Robert L. *writer, literature educator*
Pronzini, Bill John (William Pronzini) *writer*
Rodriguez, Luis J. *writer*
Sebold, Alice *writer*
Spiegelman, Art *writer, cartoonist*

**Placerville**
Wilkinson, Rosemary Regina Challoner *poet, writer*

**Playa Del Rey**
McNeill, Daniel Richard *writer*

**Pomona**
Mezey, Robert *poet*

**Rancho Palos Verdes**
Zar, Judith L. (Mickey McBride) *writer*

**Rancho Santa Fe**
Byrd, Betty Rantze *writer*

**Rancho Santa Margarita**
Shusterman, Neal Douglas *writer, scriptwriter*

**Redondo Beach**
Battles, Roxy Edith *novelist, consultant, educator*

**Reedley**
Carey, Ernestine Gilbreth (Mrs. Charles E. Carey) *writer, educator*

**Richmond**
Ofteness, Ove (O.V. Michaelsen) *writer, musician*

**Ross**
Godwin, Sara *writer*

**Sacramento**
Gerringer, Elizabeth (The Marchioness de Roe Devon, Poet Julie de Vontine) *writer, lawyer*

**Saint Helena**
Wiggins, Rita Cassidy *poet*

**San Anselmo**
Harper Haines, Jan Frances *writer, educator*

**San Diego**
Brennan-Sparks, Jennifer Anne *writer*
Hammersmith, Nita Marie *writer*
Koppman, Mae Z. *writer, educator*
Krull, Kathleen *writer*
Lederer, Richard Henry *writer, educator, columnist*
Mahdavi, Kamal B. *writer, researcher*
Robbins, Tony (Anthony Robbins) *writer*
Sturman, George *poet*
Valdez, Jose Carbajal, Jr. *poet, lyricist*

**San Francisco**
Aslan, Madalyn *writer, educator*
Blaise, Clark Lee *writer, educator*
Emery, Vince *writer, educator*
Ferlinghetti, Lawrence *poet*
Ferris, Russell James, II, *writer*
Field, Carol Hart *writer, news correspondent, journalist*
O'Connor, Sheila Anne *freelance writer*
Ong, Lance Orion *writer*
Quick, William Thomas *writer, scriptwriter*
Rivlin, Gary *writer, reporter*
Rusher, William Allen *writer, commentator, columnist*
Sachs, Marilyn Stickle *writer, educator, editor*
Sterkina, Sofiya *writer*

**San Jose**
Loventhal, Milton *writer, playwright, lyricist*
Prestine, Joan Singleton *writer, educator, editor*
Wolverton, Edward Lee Allen *writer*

**San Luis Obispo**
Bunge, Russell Kenneth *writer, poet, editor*

**San Marcos**
Snow, Tiffany *writer, healer, composer*

**San Marino**
Sherwood, Midge *writer*

**San Rafael**
Nelson, James Carmer, Jr. *writer, editor, advertising executive*

**Santa Barbara**
Behrens, June Adelle *writer*
Canfield, Jack *writer, speaker, trainer*
Cunningham, Julia Woolfolk *author*
Kuczynski, John-Michael Maxime *writer*
Mitchell, Shawne Maureen *author*
Ramsay, William Charles *writer, composer*
Roddick, Hawley *writer, editor, personal historian*

**Santa Clara**
Simmons, Janet Bryant *writer, publishing executive*

**Santa Clarita**
Ayres, Glenn Alex *scriptwriter, film producer*

**Santa Cruz**
Davis, Angela Yvonne *political activist, educator, writer*

**Santa Monica**
Brainard, Cecilia Manguerra *writer*
Crichton, Michael (John Michael Crichton) *writer, film director*
Grubisich, Tom *screenwriter, editor, writer*
Huffington, Arianna (Arianna Stassinopoulos) *writer*
Leonard, Elmore John *writer, scriptwriter*
Lochte, Richard Samuel *writer*
Mora, Philippe *screenwriter, producer, director, painter*
Scott, Jill *poet, musician*
Shiffrin, Nancy *writer, educator*
Spataro, Janie Dempsey Watts *freelance/self-employed writer*

**Santa Rosa**
Guglielmino, Jude Patch *writer, humanitarian aid worker*

**Sausalito**
Hyde, Catherine Ryan *short story writer*

**Sebastopol**
Marler, Joan *writer, educator*

**Simi Valley**
Hochheiser, Marilyn *writer, actress*

**Somis**
Premack, Ann J. *writer*

**Sonoma**
Kizer, Carolyn Ashley *poet, educator*

**Stanford**
Conquest, Robert (George Robert Acworth Conquest) *writer, historian, poet*
Djerassi, Carl *writer, retired chemistry professor*
Steele, Shelby *writer, educator*
Wolff, Tobias (Jonathan Ansell Wolff) *writer*

**Studio City**
Parish, James Robert *writer, cinema historian*
Shavelson, Melville *scriptwriter, theater producer, director*

**Sugarloaf**
Black, Victoria Lynn *writer, artist*

**Sun Valley**
Casey, Paul Arnold *writer, producer, photographer, composer, director*

**Valencia**
Parks, Suzan Lori *playwright*

**Van Nuys**
Becker, Frawley *writer, dialogue director, location manager*

**Venice**
Eliot, Alexander *writer*

**Walnut Creek**
Chu, Valentin Yuan-ling *author*

**West Hollywood**
Peyton, Elizabeth Joy *writer, painter*
Slade, Bernard *playwright*

**Woodland Hills**
Lehr, Leslie Joyce *writer*

## COLORADO

**Boulder**
Conroy, Daniel Frederick *writer, playwright, poet, painter*

**Colorado Springs**
Van Ness, Lottye Gray *writer, genealogist*

**Crestone**
Thompson, William Irwin *writer, educator*

**Denver**
Avi, (Avi Wortis) *author*
Buckstein, Caryl Sue *writer*
Dallas, Sandra *writer*

Ducker, Bruce *writer, lawyer*
MacGregor, George Lescher, Jr. *freelance/self-employed writer, brokerage house executive*
Nemiro, Beverly Mirium Anderson *author, educator*
Osborn, Susan Chaney *writer, educator*

**Durango**
Korns, Leota Elsie *writer, mountain land developer, insurance broker*

**Englewood**
Hakim, Joy *writer*

**Greeley**
Willis, Connie (Constance E. Willis) *writer*

**Lakewood**
Peters, Julie Anne *writer*

**Lyons**
Spring, Kathleen *writer*

**Masonville**
Dubrovin, Vivian *writer*

**Montrose**
Gates, Viola R. *writer*

**Pueblo**
Shomaker, Gordon Alexander, Jr. *poet, writer*

**Westminster**
Lingle, JoLynn Fleishman *writer, educator*

**Wheat Ridge**
Morriss, Frank *writer, educator*

## CONNECTICUT

**Bethel**
Tesar, Jenny Elizabeth *freelance/self-employed writer, freelance/self-employed editor*

**Bolton**
Reyna, Magdalena Bessy *writer*

**Canton**
Jordan, Evora Ruth *writer, researcher, publishing executive*

**Chester**
Stark, Evelyn Brill *poet, musician*

**Clinton**
Adler, Peggy Ann *writer, illustrator, consultant, protective services official*

**Danielson**
Thibodeau, Joan Marie Serafin *writer, educator*

**Easton**
Maloney, John Joseph *writer*

**Fairfield**
Barone, Rose Marie Pace *writer, retired educator*

**Greenwich**
Ewald, William Bragg, Jr. *writer, consultant*
Hoberman, Mary Ann *author*
Wallach, Magdalena Falkenberg (Carla Wallach) *writer*

**Guilford**
Peters, William *writer, film producer, film director*

**Hartford**
Machado, Eduardo Oscar *playwright*

**Higganum**
DeBold, Richard Charles *writer*

**New Canaan**
Fredericks, Jeanne Maria Judson *literary agent*

**New Haven**
Phillips, Caryl *writer*
Scarf, Margaret (Maggie Scarf) *author*
Walbert, Kate *writer, educator*

**New London**
Espinosa, Resurreccion *playwright, theatre director, writer*

**Norwalk**
Bortolot, Gary *writer, educator*

**Roxbury**
Gurney, Albert Ramsdell *playwright, educator*

**Stamford**
Herlands, E. Ward *poet, printmaker*

**Storrs Mansfield**
Rimland, Lisa Phillip *writer, composer, lyricist*

**Suffield**
Sullivan, Edmund Bertram *writer*

**Waterford**
Commire, Anne *playwright, writer, editor*

**West Hartford**
Calip, Roger *writer, educator*

**Westbrook**
Fuller, Martha M. *poet*

**Weston**
Diforio, Robert George *literary agent*
Kilty, Jerome Timothy *playwright, theater director, actor*
Wiseman, Carter Sterling *writer, educator*

**Westport**
Hotchner, Aaron Edward *author*

## DISTRICT OF COLUMBIA

**Washington**
Alperovitz, Gar *author, educator*
Angell, Lois Louise *writer, comedienne, poet*
Arndt, Richard Tallmadge *writer, consultant, cultural administrator*
Atlas, Liane Wiener *writer*
Bennet, James *writer, editor*
Birnbaum, Norman *writer, humanities educator*
Brownstein, Elizabeth Smith *writer*
Burnham, David Bright *writer, educator*
Burns, David Mitchell *writer, retired diplomat*
Carroll, Andrew Patrick Keating *writer*
Coulter, Ann *writer, political columnist, lawyer*
Darr, Ann Russell *poet, educator*
Dunbar, Leslie Wallace *writer, consultant*
Easterbrook, Gregg Edmund *writer*
Furgurson, Ernest Baker, Jr., (Pat Furgurson) *writer*
Gallo, Anthony Ernest *playwright, economist*
Gioia, Dana (Michael Dana Gioia) *poet, critic, cultural organization administrator*
Hiebert, Ray Eldon *writer, educator*
Innis, Pauline *writer, publishing company executive*
Jasper, John A. *writer, lawyer*
Kosar, Kevin Richard *writer, consultant*
Kramer, Simon Paul *writer*
Leamer, Laurence Allen *writer*
Lynn, Karyl Charna (Karyl Lynn Kopelman Zietz) *writer, filmmaker, critic, television producer*
Mallon, Thomas *writer*
May, Stephen *writer, federal official, historian*
Merrell, Jesse Howard *writer*
Murphy, Joanne Becker *writer*
Nash, James Lee *poet, security official*
O'Sullivan, Michael *writer, art critic*
Park, Alice Mary Crandall *author, genealogist*
Robb, Lynda Johnson *writer*
Shaw, Russell Burnham *writer, journalist*
Smith, Stuart Seaborne *writer, government official, union official*
Tannen, Deborah Frances *writer*
Williams, Leaford Clemetson *writer, political scientist*

## FLORIDA

**Aventura**
Meltzer, Brad *writer*

**Babson Park**
Morrison, Kenneth Douglas *writer, columnist*

**Belleair Beach**
Fuentes, Martha Ayers *playwright*

**Boca Raton**
Keyes, Daniel *author*

**Bradenton**
Blanchard, Leonard Albert *writer, consultant, educator*

**Brandon**
Pantano, Daniele *poet, educator*

**Cape Canaveral**
Hess, Terry Lee *writer, educator, logistician*

**Cape Coral**
Hopkins, Lee Bennett *writer, educator*

**Clewiston**
Oeffner, Barbara Dunning *writer, educator, scriptwriter*

**Daytona Beach**
Mc Collister, John Charles *writer, minister, educator*

**Eustis**
Chorosinski, Eugene Conrad *writer, poet, author*

**Gainesville**
Carlson, David Edward *journalism educator, journalist, consultant*
Leahy, Thomas Melvin, Jr. *writer*
Smith, Jo Anne *writer, retired communications educator*

**Hallandale Beach**
Geller, Bunny Zelda *poet, writer, publisher, sculptor, artist*

**Hobe Sound**
Houser, Constance W. *writer, artist*

**Homosassa**
Carmichael, Roberta Kay *writer*

**Key Biscayne**
Clay, Cynthia Joyce *writer, editor-in-chief*

**Key West**
Congdon, Kirby *writer*
Mathews, Harry Burchell *poet, writer, educator*

**Leesburg**
Bayus, Lenore Weatherly *writer, public relations executive, consultant*

**Longboat Key**
Hazan, Marcella Maddalena *writer, educator, consultant*

**Melbourne**
Allington, Maynard *writer*

**Miami**
Alperin, Stanley I. *writer, editor, consultant*
Alschuler, Al *freelance/self-employed writer*
Benestante, Vincenzo *writer*
Goin-Harding, Cecilia Margaret *poet*
Goodman-Milone, Constance B. (Connie Malone) *writer*
Laje, Zilia L. *writer, publisher, translator*

Morgan, Marabel *writer*

**Milton**
Seaton, Carolle Carter *writer, educator*

**Naples**
Alpert, Hollis *writer*
Capelle-Frank, Jacqueline Aimee *writer*

**Niceville**
Hinze, Vicki Kay *writer, educator*

**North Miami**
McGrath, Campbell *poet, educator*

**Ocala**
Zink, Joan Wilson *writer, poet, composer*

**Orlando**
Powell, Elaine Marie *writer, educator*

**Palm Beach**
Javits, Joan (Zeeman) *writer, inventor*
Kay, Marcia Chellis *writer*

**Panama City**
Schafer, John Stephen *poet*

**Placida**
McClister, Michael *writer*

**Port Charlotte**
Wolff, Diane Patricia *writer, film and television producer*

**Saint Augustine**
Johnson, Timothy John *writer, educator*

**Saint Petersburg**
Linde, Shirley *writer, travel company executive*

**Sarasota**
Jones, Sally Daviess Pickrell *writer*
Kaminsky, Stuart M. *screenwriter, writer*
Kessler, Leonard *writer, illustrator*
Weeks, Albert Loren *writer, educator, journalist*
Wilson, Kenneth Jay *writer*

**Sebring**
DeWitt, Carol A. *writer*

**Tallahassee**
Bagley, James Robert *freelance writer*
Butler, Robert Olen *writer, educator*
Johnson, Margaret Anderson *writer, publishing executive, agricultural products executive*
Tourtet, Christiane Andrée *writer, photojournalist, reporter, advocate*

**Tampa**
Hanford, Grail Stevenson *writer*

**The Villages**
Oetjen, David L. (Jon David Douglas) *writer, film producer*

**Titusville**
Arnold, Arthur Joseph *writer, journalist*

**Vero Beach**
Massey, Howard Clayland *writer*
Proctor, William Gilbert, Jr. *writer*

**West Palm Beach**
Bergmann, Arthur M. *writer, retired journalist, retired county official*
Henry, Rene Arthur *writer, consultant*
Passy, Charles *writer*

**Winter Park**
Rooks, Linda *writer*

## GEORGIA

**Atlanta**
Cleage, Pearl Michelle *writer, playwright, journalist*
Edson, Margaret *playwright*
Potter, Polyxeni *writer, editor*

**Barnesville**
Brown, Angelia *poet*

**Columbus**
Cockrell, Pearl Hand *writer*

**Duluth**
Kramer, Edward E. *screenwriter, editor*

**Hephzibah**
Golphin, Elouise *writer, educator*

**Hoschton**
Campbell, Leslie Caine (Caine Campbell) *writer, historian*

**Kennesaw**
Stiles, Cheryl *writer, librarian, educator*

**Loganville**
Smelser, Thelma Ann *writer, tax specialist*

**Pine Mountain**
Bishop, Michael *writer*

**Saint Marys**
Berry, Stephen L. (Steve) *writer, lawyer*

**Savannah**
Coffey, Thomas Francis, Jr. *retired writer*
Thomas, Dwight Rembert *writer*

**Stone Mountain**
Allen (Irvin M.N.), Georgianne Lydia Christian *writer, poet*

**Woodstock**
Christmas, Bobbie Jaye *freelance/self-employed writer*

## HAWAII

**Honolulu**
Halloran, Richard Colby *writer, reporter, communications executive, editor*

**Kailua**
Bone, Robert William *writer*

**Waianae**
Holifield, Pearl Kam (Kam Holifield, Momi Kam Holifield) *poet*

## IDAHO

**Hailey**
Dolas, Evelyn Ann *poet, musician*

## ILLINOIS

**Belleville**
Pounds, Regina Dorothea *writer*

**Champaign**
Watson, Jessica Lewis *writer*

**Chicago**
Brown, Rosellen *writer*
Camper, Fred *freelance writer, educator*
Camper, John Jacob *writer, academic administrator*
Carroll, David *writer, illustrator*
Crane, R.H. *poet*
Felsenthal, Carol Judith *writer*
Hoover, Paul *poet*
Lach, Alma Elizabeth *food and cooking writer, consultant*
Lerner, Barbara *writer, researcher*
Madsen, Dorothy Louise (Meg Madsen) *writer*
Manelli, Donald Dean *scriptwriter, film producer*
Melnick, Jane Fisher *writer, educator, photographer*
Patner, Andrew *writer, art critic*
Plotnik, Arthur *writer, columnist*
Schultz, John L. *writer, educator*
Stacey, James Henry *writer, columnist*
Terkel, Studs (Louis Terkel) *writer, journalist*
Turow, Scott F. *writer, lawyer*
Urrea, Luis Alberto *writer*
Vowell, Sarah *writer, radio personality*
Winters, Anne *poet, educator*

**Crestwood**
Haggard, Edward (Ned) Roy *writer, consultant*

**East Peoria**
May, Janet Sue *playwright, lyricist*

**Evanston**
Gibbons, William Reginald, Jr. *poet, writer, translator, editor*
Holton, Lisa *writer, editor, researcher*
Kertész, Imre *writer*
Wright, Ellen *writing educator*

**Galesburg**
Metz, Robin O. *writer, educator, poet*

**Highland Park**
Greenblatt, Miriam *writer, editor, educator*

**Lake Forest**
Taylor, Barbara Ann Olin *writer, educational consultant*

**Marengo**
Mrkvicka, Edward Francis, Jr. *writer, finance company executive*

**Marshall**
Freeman, Charles E. *writer, musician*

**Morton Grove**
Vega, Steve *poet*

**Northfield**
Mamet, David Alan *playwright, theater producer*

**Oak Lawn**
Sullivan, Michael *writer, retired mathematics professor*

**Oakland**
Eriksen, Barbara Ann *writer, researcher*

**Ottawa**
Ballowe, James *writer, educator*

**Palatine**
Pohl, Frederik *freelance/self-employed writer*

**Peoria**
Grebner, Bernice Prill *author, astrological counselor*

**Prospect Heights**
Mooney, Timothy *playwright, actor, theater director*

**Rochester**
Petterchak, Janice A. *writer*

**South Barrington**
Kissane, Sharon Florence *writer, consultant, educator*

**Stoy**
Rhoten, Kenneth Dale *writer*

**University Park**
Patton, June Odessa *writer, consultant, educator, researcher*

**Urbana**
Dovring, Karin Elsa Ingeborg *writer, poet, playwright, media specialist*
Lieberman, Laurence *poet, educator*

**West Brooklyn**
Mays, K. J. *writer, musician*

**Wilmette**
Brindel, June Rachuy *writer*
Miripol, Jerilyn Elise *poet, writer, writing therapist*

**INDIANA**

**Bloomington**
Johnson-D'Alessio, Anna *writer, poet*

**Carmel**
Fadely, James Philip *writer, educator*

**Chesterton**
Petrakis, Harry Mark *author*

**Crawfordsville**
Karg, Thelma Aileen *writer*

**Elkhart**
Eddy, Darlene Mathis *poet, educator*

**Fort Wayne**
Frost, Helen Marie *writer*
Langhinrichs, Ruth Imler *playwright, writer*

**Frankfort**
Borland, Kathryn Kilby *writer*

**Howe**
Bowerman, Ann Louise *writer, secondary school educator, genealogist*

**Indianapolis**
Gregory, Valiska *writer*
Livers, Catherine McGhee *writer*

**Logansport**
Howland, Bette *writer*

**Morgantown**
Callon, Margaret Joann *writer, minister*

**Muncie**
Thornbro, William Graden *writer*

**Richmond**
Cooper, Jamie Lee *writer*

**Scottsburg**
Dockery, Linda *writer*

**IOWA**

**Cedar Falls**
Skaine, Rosemarie Keller *writer, consultant, publisher*

**Davenport**
Beguhn, Sandra E. *poet, writer*

**Iowa City**
Bell, Marvin Hartley *poet, language educator*
Johnson, Nicholas *writer, lawyer, educator*
Merrill, Christopher Lyall *writer*
Packer, ZZ (Zuwena) *writer, literature educator*
Stein, Robert A. *writer, educator, military officer*
Swensen, Cole *poet, educator*

**Leon**
Miller, Eleanora Genevieve *freelance/self-employed poet*

**Pella**
Muether, Charles Alexander *writer, educator*

**Sioux City**
Hassenger, James Michael *writer, retired small business owner*

**Windsor Heights**
Beadel, Stephen Jay *author*

**KANSAS**

**Leawood**
Garwood, Julie *writer*
Gray, Thomas Alva, Jr. *writer, minister, retired protective services official*

**KENTUCKY**

**Covington**
McQueen, Regenia *writer*

**Frankfort**
Embry, Michael Dale *writer, editor*

**Louisville**
Barnett, Joyce Lyndel *freelance/self-employed writer*
Oglesby, Joseph Woodson (Mike English) *writer, publishing executive*

**Madisonville**
May, Richard Warren *writer*

**Mayfield**
Murray, Helen *writer*

**LOUISIANA**

**Baton Rouge**
Madden, David *author*
Mueller, Lisel *writer, poet*
Sanders, Mary Elizabeth *writer, historian*

**Eunice**
Attole, Mary Bertha *writer*

**Gretna**
Kennedy, Maydra Jane Penisson (J.P. Kennedy) *poet*

**Lafayette**
Gaines, Ernest James *author*

**Metairie**
Grau, Shirley Ann (Mrs. James Kern Feibleman) *writer*

**New Orleans**
Friedmann, Patricia Ann *writer*
McFerren, Martha Dean *writer, librarian*

**MAINE**

**Allagash**
Hafford, Faye O'Leary *writer*

**Bangor**
King, Stephen Edwin *writer, scriptwriter*
King, Tabitha *author*

**Brewer**
Cote Robbins, Rhea Jeannine *writer, educator*

**Bristol**
Sabin, William Albert *writer*

**Dixmont**
Cummings, James William *poet*

**East Boothbay**
Ford, Richard *writer*

**Gardiner**
Dunbar, Robert Everett *writer, educator*

**Milbridge**
Enslin, Theodore Vernon *poet*

**New Harbor**
Carr, James Revell *writer, curator, retired museum director*

**Portland**
Neavoll, George Franklin *writer*
Weir, Anne *writer*

**Saco**
Morgan, Robin Evonne *poet, writer, journalist, editor*

**South Portland**
Manuel, Peter Jay *poet, librettist, literature and language professor*

**Stonington**
Pitts, Edgar Thurlow *writer, retired educator*

**Wayne**
Rosenkrantz, Roger Daniel *writer, educator*

**Wilton**
Emerson, Kathy *writer*

**MARYLAND**

**Annapolis**
Miller, John Grider *writer*

**Baltimore**
Barth, John Simmons *writer, educator*
Epstein, Daniel Mark *poet, dramatist, biographer*
Fisher, Alan Hall *guidebook writer*
Lederer, William Julius *author*
Schultheis, Patricia Ann *writer, editor*
Tyler, Anne (Mrs. Taghi M. Modarressi) *writer*
Van Riper, Robert Austin *writer, retired public relations executive*
Weisgal, Jeanne Nancy *writer*

**Bethesda**
Naylor, Phyllis Reynolds *writer*
Sanoff, Alvin Paul *writer, educational consultant*
Schaeffer, Charles Perry *writer, editor*

**Chevy Chase**
Atkin, Flora Blumenthal *playwright, theater director*
Bacon, Donald Conrad *writer, editor*

**College Park**
Whittemore, Edward Reed, II, *poet, retired educator*

**Fort Washington**
Cameron, Rita Giovannetti *writer, publishing executive*
Canlas, Luzano Pancho, Sr. *writer, researcher*

**Frederick**
Randall, Frances *technical writer*

**Fulton**
Hamlin, George L. *writer*

**Germantown**
Taylor, Douglas Howard *translator*
Weiner, Claire Muriel *freelance writer*

**Potomac**
Kessler, Ronald *author*
Pastan, Linda Olenik *poet*

**Rockville**
Madle, Robert Albert *writer*

**Saint Marys City**
Clifton, Lucille Thelma *author*

**Salisbury**
Booker, Betty Mae *poet*

**Severna Park**
Windsor, Patricia (Katonah Summertree, Perrin Winters, Anna Seeling) *author, educator, lecturer*

**Silver Spring**
Kellner, Mark Allen *writer*
Mitchum, Cassandra *poet, writer*
Sucher, Dorothy *writer, psychotherapist*
Whitten, Leslie Hunter, Jr. *writer, poet, reporter*

**MASSACHUSETTS**

**Amherst**
Sandweiss, Martha Ann *writer, history professor*
Tate, James Vincent *poet, English educator*

**Arlington**
Halperin, Helena Stacy *writer, educator*

**Barre**
Sullivan, James Edward *poet*

**Belmont**
McEvoy, Frances Jane Coman *writer, editor*
Rand, Peter *writer, editor, educator*

**Boston**
Angelou, Maya (Marguerite Annie Johnson) *writer, actress*
Appelbaum, Diana Karter *author*
Foer, Jonathan Safran *writer*
Knott, Bill *poet, literature educator*
Lahiri, Jhumpa (Nilanjana Sudeshna) *writer*
Lowry, Lois (Lois Hammersberg) *writer*
Martin, Jacqueline Briggs *writer*
Murray, Sabina *writer*
Say, Allen *writer, illustrator*
Schlosser, Eric *writer*
Shearer, Harry Julius *scriptwriter, actor, television director*
Simpson, Bennett *art critic, art museum curator*
Strothman, Wendy Jo *literary agent*
Terrill, Ross Gladwin *writer, educator*
Van Allsburg, Chris *writer, artist*
Wiesel, Elie *writer, educator*
Zelnick, Carl Robert *writer, educator*

**Brighton**
Valianti, Deborah L. *playwright*

**Byfield**
Kozol, Jonathan *writer*

**Cambridge**
DiCamillo, Kate *writer*
Dyck, Martin *literary theorist, mathematics historian*
Graham, Jorie *writer, educator*
Kaplan, Justin *author*
Ladd, Florence Cawthorne *writer*
Payack, Peter *poet, writer, artist, educator*
Rhoda, Janice Tucker *writer, educator, musician*
Yergin, Daniel Howard *writer, consultant*

**Chestnut Hill**
Valette, Jean Paul *writer*

**Cotuit**
Housewright, David W. *writer*

**Cummington**
Smith, William Jay *author*
Wilbur, Richard Purdy *writer, educator*

**Gardner**
Herrnkind, Hilda Marie *writer, military volunteer*

**Gloucester**
Junger, Sebastian *writer*

**Hatfield**
Yolen, Jane *writer*

**Lexington**
Kennedy, X.J. (Joseph Kennedy) *writer*

**Lincoln**
Donald, David Herbert *writer, history professor*

**Nantucket**
Philbrick, Nathaniel *writer*

**Newtonville**
Porter, Jack Nusan *writer, sociologist, educator, political organization worker*

**North Chelmsford**
Erkkila-Ricker, Barbara Howell *writer, photographer*

**Northampton**
Birdsall, Jeanne *writer, photographer*
Newman, Lesléa *writer*

**Pelham**
Fetler, Andrew *author, educator*

**Provincetown**
Oliver, Mary *poet*

**Revere**
Recupero-Faiella, Anna Antonietta *poet*

**Somerset**
Manchester, Steven Herbert *writer, educator*

**Southborough**
Mylotte, John Arnold *writer, educator*

**Wellesley**
Jacobs, Ruth Harriet *poet, playwright, sociologist, gerontologist*
Lloyd-Jones, Sir (Peter) Hugh (Jefferd) *writer*

**Wellfleet**
Piercy, Marge *poet, writer*

**West Newbury**
Dooley, Ann Elizabeth *freelance writers cooperative executive, editor*

**West Roxbury**
Ellenbogen, George *poet, educator*
Seltzer, Richard Warren, Jr. *writer, editor, consultant*

**Williamstown**
Pasachoff, Naomi *writer*

**Worcester**
Vick, Susan *playwright, educator, director, actress*

**MICHIGAN**

**Ann Arbor**
Gregerson, Linda Karen *poet, language educator, critic*
Perkins, George *writer, educator*

**Burton**
Farmer, Philip José *writer*

**Calumet**
Smith, Thomas Hugh (T. Kilgore Splake) *poet, writer, photographer*

**Canton**
Wiloch, Thomas *poet, editor*

**Detroit**
Madgett, Naomi Long *poet, editor, publisher, educator*

**East Lansing**
Perrin, Robert *writer, consultant*
Wakoski, Diane *poet, educator*

**Holland**
Nieuwsma, Milton John *writer, journalist*

**Idlewild**
Wooley, Geraldine Hamilton *poet, writer*

**Kalamazoo**
Light, Christopher Upjohn *freelance/self-employed writer, photographer*

**Mount Pleasant**
Smallwood, Carol *writer*

**Okemos**
Klunzinger, Thomas Edward *writer, actor, film director*

**Quinnesec**
Opolka, Jayme Lyn *medical writer, researcher*

**Republic**
Wixtrom, Donald Joseph *translator*

**Sodus**
Handy, Virginia Mae *writer*

**Sterling Heights**
Bohy, Ric *writer, commentator*

**West Bloomfield**
Brin, David *writer, astronomer*

**Ypsilanti**
Lottie, Adrian Jerome *writer, educator, consultant*

**MINNESOTA**

**Anoka**
Lindbergh, Reeve *writer, poet*

**Collegeville**
Hassler, Jon Francis *novelist*

**Edina**
Schwarzrock, Shirley Pratt *author, educator*

**Frontenac**
Hedin, Robert Alexander *writer*

**Maplewood**
St. Germain, Sharon Marie *writer*

**Minneapolis**
Baker, John Stevenson (Michael Dyregrov) *writer*
Erdrich, Louise (Karen Erdrich) *writer, poet*
Korotkin, Fred *writer, philatelist*

**Mounds View**
Wang, Aixue *translator, writer*

**New Hope**
Johnson, David Paul *writer, poet, publishing executive*

**Northfield**
Benkowski, Ann Marie *writer*

**Richfield**
Thompson, Steve Allan *writer*

**Rochester**
Hodgson, Harriet W. *health and wellness writer*

**Saint Paul**
Doermann, Humphrey *writer, consultant*
Havelin, Kate *writer, editor*
Keillor, Garrison Edward *writer, radio personality*

**Shakopee**
Gertis, Neill Allan *writer*

## MISSISSIPPI

**Ackerman**
Miller, Birthalene *writer*

**Hattiesburg**
Barthelme, Frederick (Rick) *writer, literature educator*

**Jackson**
McElvaine, Robert Stuart *writer, educator*

**Tupelo**
Parker, Jennifer Merri *writer, editor, educator*

**Vancleave**
Anthony, Geneva Jo *poet, writer*

## MISSOURI

**Bloomfield**
Ferrell, Paul Cleveland *writer*

**Blue Springs**
Baker, Jean Morrison *writer*

**Des Peres**
Sadlo, Kenneth Louis *poet, writer*

**Jefferson City**
McDaniel, Sue Powell *writer*

**Kansas City**
Kirch, Donald Allen *writer, composer*
Martin-Bowen, Lindsey *freelance writer*

**Knob Lick**
Kleinberg, Brenda Louise *writer, people's advocate*

**Lees Summit**
Payne, Roy A. *poet*

**Saint Louis**
Burgin, Richard Weston *writer, educator, editor*
Gass, William H. *writer, educator*
Lubbock, James Edward *retired writer, photographer, media consultant*
Lutz, John Thomas *author*
Miller, Judith Braffman *writer*
Phillips, Carl *poet, educator*
Schlafly, Phyllis Stewart *writer*
Smith, C. Grant *scriptwriter, film producer*
Swinson, Sara Hope *writer*

**Willow Springs**
Hinds, C. Robert (Bob) *retired writer*

## MONTANA

**Bigfork**
Wetzel, Betty Preat *writer*

**Bonner**
Smith, Annick *writer*

**Helena**
Benyus, Janine M. *writer*

**Missoula**
Haines, John Meade *poet, translator, writer*
Yee, Albert Hoy *writer, retired psychologist, educator*

## NEBRASKA

**Lincoln**
Magorian, James *poet, writer*

**Omaha**
Timmins, Lois Fahs *lecturer, writer, consultant*

## NEVADA

**Cold Springs**
Turner VanLydegraf, Claudia Beth *writer, researcher*

**Las Vegas**
Gardner, Grace Joely *writer, consultant, psychologist*
Palmer, Lynne *writer, astrologer*

## NEW HAMPSHIRE

**Brentwood**
Bunker, Dusty (Sandra Coby) *writer*

**Cornish**
Atkinson, James Blakely *writer, editor*

**Durham**
Ford, Daniel (Daniel Francis Ford) *writer*

**Etna**
Picoult, Jodi *writer*

**Keene**
Gooding, Judson *writer*

**Nashua**
Twedell, Terri Danni *writer, educator, artist*

**Peterborough**
Thomas, Elizabeth Marshall *writer*

**Richmond**
Rogers, Barbara Radcliffe *writer*

## NEW JERSEY

**Bergenfield**
Clark, Fred *writer, editor*
Davidson, Marilyn Copeland *writer, music educator, musician*

**Cape May Court House**
Cohen, Daniel Edward *writer*
Cohen, Susan Lois *writer*

**Cherry Hill**
Gardner, Joel Robert *writer, historian*

**Clementon**
Albee, Gloria *playwright*

**Edgewater**
Paci, Ruth A. *freelance/self-employed writer*

**Elizabeth**
Lucco, James Perry *writer*

**Hazlet**
Shea, James Bryan *writer*

**Highland Park**
Cheiten, Marvin Harold *playwright, manufacturing executive*

**Jackson**
Heck, Roberta M. *poet, writer*

**Lebanon**
Barto, Susan Carol *writer*

**Leonardo**
Bianchi, Hollis Dolce *writer, poet, artist*

**Long Branch**
Lagowski, Barbara Jean *writer, editor*
Stewart, Georgiana Liccione *writer*

**Manahawkin**
Turkot, Dorothy Regester Felton *writer, illustrator*

**Maplewood**
Lally, Michael David *writer, actor*

**Medford**
Henderson, Rita Elizabeth *literary agent, journalist*

**Metuchen**
Smyth, David *writer, editor*
Zatz, Arline *writer, photographer*

**Montclair**
Delgado, Ramon Louis *theater educator, author, director, playwright, lyricist*

**Mountainside**
Nielsen, Gwyn English *writer, illustrator, publishing executive, language educator*

**New Brunswick**
Jenkins, Alyce Mitchem *writer, educator*
Martínez, Tomás Eloy *writer, journalist*

**New Providence**
SanGiovanni, Mary Elizabeth *writer, freelance manager*

**Newark**
Dickson, Jim *writer, theater producer*

**Paramus**
Fader, Shirley Sloan *writer*

**Princeton**
Harford, James *writer*
Muldoon, Paul *poet, educator*
Williams, C(harles) K(enneth) *poet, educator, literature educator*

**Princeton Junction**
Norback, Craig Thomas *writer*

**Roosevelt**
Mallach, Alan *writer, consultant, city planner*

**South Orange**
Riordan, Rick *writer*

**Teaneck**
Wallmann, Jeffrey Miner *author*

**Toms River**
Fiore, Carmen Anthony *writer*

**Trenton**
Obed, Leonora Rita Villegas *writer*

**Warren**
Baxter, Nancy *medical writer*

**Wayne**
Liu, Timothy *poet, educator*

**Whippany**
Lemmo, Peter S. *writer, educational consultant*

**Whiting**
Willis, Ben *writer, artist*

## NEW MEXICO

**Albuquerque**
Anaya, Rudolfo *writer, educator*
Gahala, Estella Marie *writer, consultant*
Priem, Richard Gregory *writer, information technology executive*

**Chimayo**
Glendinning, Chellis *writer, psychologist*

**Las Cruces**
Medoff, Mark Howard *playwright, scriptwriter*

**Las Vegas**
Howard, Leland William *writer*

**Portales**
Williamson, Jack (John Stewart) *writer*

**Ranchos De Taos**
Dickey, Robert Preston *writer, educator, poet*

**Rio Rancho**
Stevens, Roger Templeton *writer*

**Santa Fe**
Bergé, Carol *writer*
Ferguson, Glenn Walker *writer, educator, retired ambassador*
Tarn, Nathaniel *poet, educator, translator*

**Silver City**
Charland, William A., Jr. *writer, educator, consultant*

## NEW YORK

**Albany**
Kennedy, William Joseph *novelist, educator*
Wildemann, Gregory Nylund *writer*

**Annandale On Hudson**
Achebe, Chinua *writer, humanities educator*
Manea, Norman *writer, educator*
Sourian, Peter *writer, language educator, educator*

**Ardsley On Hudson**
Lisle, Laurie *author*

**Astoria**
Griffin, Daniel Bernard, Jr. *writer, scriptwriter, lyricist*

**Averill Park**
Nevai, Lucia *writer*

**Ballston Spa**
Barba, Harry *writer, publisher, educator*

**Bay Shore**
Lindner, Deborah *writer, illustrator, photographer*

**Bedford Hills**
Fierstein, Harvey Forbes *playwright, actor*
Lustbader, Eric Van *writer*

**Briarcliff Manor**
Windham, Revish *poet*

**Brightwaters**
North, E(dward) Lee *retired writer, former aerospace company professional*

**Bronx**
Bingham, June *playwright*
Kornfeld, Robert Jonathan *playwright, photographer*

**Bronxville**
Morton, Brian *writer, editor*
Rosenthal, Lucy Gabrielle *writer, editor, educator*

**Brooklyn**
Bossert, Jill Audrey *author*
Chambers, William Edmond *writer*
Chernow, Ron *writer, journalist*
Cummings, Josephine Anna *writer, consultant, advertising executive*
Garrett, Nancy Fales *playwright, educator*
Gioseffi, Daniela (Dorothy Daniela Gioseffi) *poet, writer, playwright, critic*
Reynolds, Nancy Remick *writer, researcher, editor*
Rogers, Michael Alan *writer*
Williams, Edward Frank *poet, entertainment company executive*

**Buffalo**
Feldman, Irving *poet*
Muncomber, Debbie *writer*
Piazza, Kris A. *writer, editor*

**Cairo**
Ludwig, Laura Lonshein *poet*

**Camillus**
Albino, Joseph Xavier *writer, educator, photographer*

**Chappaqua**
George, Jean Craighead *author, illustrator*

**Chatham**
Kherdian, David *writer*

**Clinton**
Kay, Lois Jeanne *writer, educator*

**Copake**
Johnson, Paul Edward *poet, writer*

**Dobbs Ferry**
Fritz, Jean Guttery *writer*

**Dundee**
Tette, Sharan Flynn *writer*

**Flushing**
Goldsmith, Howard *writer, consultant*
Zinnes, Harriet Fich *poet, retired English educator, literary and art critic*

**Forest Hills**
Henley, Arthur *writer, editor*

**Fulton**
Long, Robert Emmet *author*

**Garden City**
Hecht, Jennifer Michael *poet, historian*

**Garnerville**
Evers, Gene *writer*

**Garrison**
Goggin, Dan Charles *playwright, composer, theater director*

**Great Neck**
Hurwitz, Johanna (Johanna Frank) *writer*

**Hamilton**
Berlind, Bruce Peter *poet, educator*

**Hartsdale**
Sundel, Alfred *retired medical writer*

**Henrietta**
Byfield, Bert A. *conservative humanitarian novelist*

**Highland**
Ratcliff, Carter Goodrich *writer, critic, poet*

**Highland Mills**
Gross, Mary Anne *author, educator*

**Interlaken**
Bleiler, Everett Franklin *writer, publishing company executive*

**Ithaca**
Morgan, Robert *writer, poet, educator*

**Katonah**
McCauley, Gerard Francis *literary agent*

**Larchmont**
Quigley, Martin Schofield *writer, educator*

**Latham**
Irwin, Heather May *writer, interior designer*

**Medusa**
Groom, Winston Francis, Jr. *writer*

**Millbrook**
Burbank, Kershaw *writer*

**Montauk**
Lavenas, Suzanne *writer, editor, consultant*

**Mount Kisco**
Hodara, Susan Mina *writer*

**Munnsville**
Carruth, Hayden *poet*

**New Paltz**
Robinson, Anthony Christopher *novelist, educator*

**New Rochelle**
Branch, William Blackwell *playwright, producer*
Saperstein, David *writer, film director, television personality*

**New York**
Albee, Edward Franklin *playwright, writer*
Allen, Oliver E. *writer*
Alvarez, Julia *writer*
Angell, Roger *writer, magazine editor*
Ashdown, Marie Matranga (Mrs. Cecil Spanton Ashdown Jr.) *writer, educator, cultural organization administrator*
Ashton, Dore *writer, educator*
Asimov, Janet Jeppson *writer, psychiatrist*
Atwood, Margaret Eleanor *writer*
Auster, Paul *writer*
Baitz, Jon Robin *playwright*
Baldacci, David *writer*
Balogh, Mary *writer*
Bank, Melissa S. *writer*
Bauer, Marion Dane *writer*
Bawden, Nina (Mary Bawden) *author*
Beattie, Ann *writer, educator*
Begley, Louis *writer, lawyer*
Beim, Norman *playwright, actor, theater director, writer*
Bell, Theodore Augustus, III, (Ted Bell) *writer, former advertising executive*
Benn, Theodore Alexander (Alec Benn) *writer*
Bentley, Eric *writer, playwright, literature educator*
Berendt, John Lawrence *writer, editor*
Berg, A. Scott (Andrew Scott Berg) *writer*
Berger, Thomas Louis *author*
Berkow, Ira Harvey *writer, journalist*
Birstein, Ann *writer, educator*
Block, Francesca Lia *writer*
Blount, Roy Alton, Jr. *freelance/self-employed writer*
Bluh, Bonnie *scriptwriter, actress, novelist, playwright*
Blume, Judy *author*
Bradbury, Ray Douglas *writer*
Bradford, Barbara Taylor *writer, journalist*
Bradley, Richard (Richard Blow) *writer*
Branch, Taylor *writer*
Brashares, Ann *writer*
Brathwaite, Edward Kamau (Kamau Brathwaite, Lawson Edward Brathwaite) *poet, educator*
Braudy, Susan Orr *writer*
Broad, William J. *science writer*
Brown, Dan *writer*
Brown, Rita Mae *writer*
Buchanan, Edna *writer, retired journalist*
Bujold, Lois McMaster *writer*
Burros, Marian Fox *writer*
Bynum, Sarah Shun-lien *writer, educator*
Cabalquinto, Luis Carrazcal *freelance writer*
Caldwell, Ian *writer*
Callo, Joseph Francis *writer*
Cameron, W. Bruce *writer*
Caputo, Philip Joseph *writer, journalist*

Card, Orson Scott (Byron Walley) *writer*
Carey, Peter Philip *writer*
Carlson, P(atricia) M(cElroy) *writer*
Castro, Jan Garden *writer, art educator, consultant*
Chabon, Michael *writer*
Cherryh, C. J. *writer*
Choldenko, Gennifer *writer*
Christopher, Nicholas *poet, writer*
Cisneros, Sandra *poet, short story writer, essayist*
Cleary, Beverly Atlee (Mrs. Clarence T. Cleary) *writer*
Coben, Harlan *writer*
Collins, Jackie (Jacqueline Jill Collins) *writer*
Collins, Max Allan, Jr. *writer*
Connelly, Michael *writer*
Conroy, Pat (Donald Patrick Conroy) *writer*
Coupland, Douglas Campbell *writer*
Cox, Ana Marie *writer, former political blogger*
Creech, Sharon *children's author*
Crittenden, Danielle Ann *writer, journalist*
Cronin, Doreen *writer, former lawyer*
Crouch, Stanley *writer, musician*
Curry, Jane Louise *writer*
Daheim, Mary Rene Richardson *writer*
Danto, Arthur Coleman *writer, philosopher, critic*
Davis, Patti *writer*
Decter, Midge *writer*
de Kretser, Michelle *writer*
DeLillo, Don *author*
Denker, Henry *playwright, author, director*
Deveraux, Jude (Jude Gilliam White) *writer*
Diamonstein-Spielvogel, Barbaralee *writer*
Dickey, Eric Jerome *writer*
Didion, Joan *writer*
Dillard, Annie *writer*
Dobell, Byron Maxwell *magazine consultant*
Doctorow, E.L. (Edgar Lawrence Doctorow) *writer, English educator*
Dolnick, Edward *writer*
Donaldson, Stephen Reeder *author*
Dowling, Danielle *writer*
Duffy, James Henry *writer, retired lawyer*
Duncan, Pearl Rose *writer*
Dunne, Dominick *writer*
Eckert, Allan Wesley *writer*
Eichenwald, Kurt *writer*
Eisenberg, Lee B. *writer*
Ellis, Bret Easton *writer*
Ellison, Nicholas Howell *literary agent*
Ellroy, James *writer*
Emerson, Ken *writer*
Ensler, Eve *playwright, actress*
Evanovich, Janet *writer*
Fagin, Dan *science and environmental writer, reporter*
Fargis, Alison K. *book developer, literary agent, consultant*
Fast, Julius *writer, editor*
Feinstein, John *writer, journalist*
Fielding, Helen *writer*
Fitch, Janet *writer*
Fleischman, Albert Sidney (Sid Fleischman) *writer*
Fowler, Karen Joy *writer*
Fox, Paula (Mrs. Martin Greenberg) *writer*
Frank, Elizabeth *writer, educator*
Franzen, Jonathan *writer*
Frazier, Charles Robinson *writer*
Frey, James *writer*
Friedman, B(ernard) H(arper) *writer*
Gaines, Steven S. *writer*
Gelb, Leslie Howard *writer, lecturer, consultant*
George, Elizabeth (Susan Elizabeth George) *writer*
George, Nelson *writer, film producer*
Gethers, Peter (Russell Andrews) *writer, publishing executive*
Giblin, James Cross *writer, publishing executive*
Gilbert, Jack *poet*
Gilman, Susan Jane *writer*
Gladwell, Malcolm *writer*
Goddard, Donald Letcher *writer, editor*
Goldman, Peter Louis *writer*
Golomb, Susan L. *literary agent*
Gonnerman, Jennifer *writer, journalist*
Goodman, George Jerome Waldo (Adam Smith) *writer, television journalist, consultant*
Gordon, David *playwright, theater director, choreographer*
Gordon, Mary Catherine *writer*
Goulden, Joseph Chesley *author*
Gourevich, Philip *writer, editor*
Grafton, Sue *novelist*
Grant, Cynthia D. *writer*
Greenwald, Sheila Ellen *writer, illustrator*
Grimes, Martha *author*
Grimm, David *playwright*
Grisham, John *writer*
Grogan, John *writer*
Hackbarth, Steven Lyle *writer, educator*
Hadas, Rachel *poet, educator*
Hague, William Edward *writer*
Haigh, Jennifer *writer*
Hamilton, Jane *writer*
Hamilton, Laurell K. *writer*
Handler, Daniel (Lemony Snicket) *writer*
Hardwick, Elizabeth *writer*
Harper, Karen *writer*
Harvey, La Verne Deborah *writer, theater producer, educator*
Hazzard, Shirley *author*
Heinemann, Larry C. *writer*
Hesse, Karen (Karen Sue Hesse) *writer, educator*
Heymann, C(lemens) David *author*
Hiaasen, Carl *writer, reporter*
Hilderley, Jeriann Gertrude *novelist, educator*
Hillenbrand, Laura *writer*
Hjortsberg, William Reinhold *writer*
Hoag, Tami *writer*
Hoffman, Alice *writer*
Horowitz, Joseph Irving *writer, educator*
Hotz, Robert Lee *writer, editor*
Howard, Richard (Joseph Howard) *poet, literary translator*
Humphreys, Josephine *writer*
Iles, Greg *writer*
Ishiguro, Kazuo *writer, scriptwriter*
Jacker, Corinne Litvin *playwright, writer*
Jacobs, Arnold Stephen *writer, commentator*
Jacoby, Coleman *scriptwriter*
Jakes, John *author*
Jannuzzi, Luigi *playwright, educator*
Jhabvala, Ruth Prawer *writer*

Johansen, Iris *writer*
Jones, Diana Wynne *writer*
Jong, Erica Mann *writer*
Josephson, Marvin *literary agent*
Kadohata, Cynthia *writer*
Kalich, Richard Barry *writer*
Karon, Jan (Janice Meredith Wilson) *writer*
Karr, Kathleen *writer*
Kauffmann, Stanley Jules *author*
Kaufman, Bel *author, educator*
Keene, Donald *writer, translator, language educator*
Kehret, Peg *writer*
Kellar, Charlotte Avrutis *writer*
Kellerman, Jonathan Seth *writer, pediatric psychologist, educator*
Kelley, Kitty *writer*
Kennedy, Adrienne Lita *playwright*
Klein, T(heodore) E(ibon) D(onald) *writer*
Klinkenborg, Verlyn *writer, educator*
Koch, Stephen Bayard *writer, language educator*
Koke, Richard Joseph *writer, curator*
Kostelanetz, Richard *writer, artist*
Kotlowitz, Robert *writer, editor*
Kotzwinkle, William *writer*
Krantz, Judith Tarcher *novelist*
Lamb, Wally *writer*
Lamm, Donald Stephen *literary agent*
Lapierre, Dominique *writer, historian, philanthropist*
Lashner, William Mark *writer*
Laurents, Arthur *playwright*
Lawson, Nigella *cookbook writer, celebrity chef*
Lee, Helie *writer*
Leepson, Marc *freelance/self-employed writer*
Lehane, Dennis *writer*
L'Engle, Madeleine (Mrs. Hugh Franklin) *writer*
Levin, Gail *writer, educator, photographer*
Levin, Ira *writer, playwright*
Levine, Gail Carson *writer*
Levoy, Myron *author*
Levy, Shawn Anthony *writer*
Lippman, Laura *writer*
Lorch, Maristella De Panizza *writer, educator*
Lord, M. G. *writer*
Lunardini, Christine Anne *writer, historian, school administrator*
Lurie, Alison *writer*
Macer-Story, Eugenia Ann *writer*
MacLachlan, Patricia *author*
Madden-Lunsford, Kerry Elizabeth *writer*
Maguire, Gregory *writer*
Manning, Martha Mary *writer, psychologist*
Mason, Bobbie Ann *writer*
Maupin, Armistead Jones, Jr. *writer*
McCarthy, Cormac (Charles Joseph McCarthy) *writer*
McCourt, Frank (Francis McCourt) *writer*
McCullough, David *writer, educator*
McDermott, Alice *writer*
Mcdonald, Gregory Christopher *author*
McInerney, Jay *writer*
McMurtry, Larry Jeff *author*
McNally, Terrence *playwright*
McQuown, Judith Hershkowitz *writer, consultant, financial planner*
Meltzer, Milton *author*
Menza, Claudia Marcella *literary agent*
Milazzo, Richard T. *writer*
Miller, Sue *writer*
Mitgang, Herbert *writer, journalist*
Moehringer, J. R. *writer*
Monk Kidd, Sue *writer*
Moody, Rick (Hiram Frederick Moody III) *writer*
Mooney, Richard Emerson *writer*
Morgan, Ted (Le Comte Sanche Armand Gabriel de Gramont) *writer*
Mosley, Walter *writer*
Munro, Alice *writer*
Munro, Eleanor *writer, lecturer*
Murphy, Cullen *writer, editor*
Nabokov, Peter Francis *writer*
Navarra, Tova *writer*
Nelson, Anne *playwright, former reporter*
Newberg, Esther *literary agent*
Nicol, Dominik *writer, photographer*
Noonan, Peggy *writer*
Oates, Joyce Carol *writer*
O'Doherty, Brian *writer*
Offit, Sidney *writer, educator*
Okrent, Daniel *writer*
Olafsson, Olafur Johann *writer, media company executive*
O'Nan, Stewart Smith *writer*
Osborne, Mary Pope *writer*
O'Toole, Patricia Ellen *writer, educator*
Packer, George *writer*
Pall, Ellen Jane *writer*
Palmer, Michael *poet*
Papell, Helen Gertrude *poet, retired librarian*
Paretsky, Sara N. *writer*
Park, Barbara *writer*
Parker, Robert Brown *writer*
Parkhurst, Carolyn *writer*
Patchett, Ann *writer*
Paterson, Katherine Womeldorf *writer*
Patterson, James Brendan, Jr. *writer, former advertising executive*
Perez-Firmat, Gustavo Francisco *writer, language educator*
Pérez-Rivera, Francisco (Frank Rivera) *writer*
Phillips, Reneé *writer*
Philp, Richard Nilson *writer, editor, journalist*
Pogrebin, Letty Cottin *writer, educator*
Polacco, Patricia *writer, illustrator*
Pollack, Barbara Grace *writer*
Pomerantz, Charlotte *writer*
Pool, Mary Jane *writer, editor*
Poole, William Daniel *writer, editor*
Price, Reynolds *writer, educator*
Quin-Harkin, Janet Elizabeth (Rhys Bowen) *writer*
Rapp, Adam *writer, playwright*
Rathmann, Peggy *writer, illustrator*
Reig, June Wilson *scriptwriter, television director, television producer*
Renehan, Edward John *writer*
Revkin, Andrew C. *writer, reporter*
Rhodes, Richard (Lee) *writer*
Rice, Luanne *writer*
Rich, Adrienne *poet*

Rigney, James Oliver, Jr., (Robert Jordan, Chang Lung, Reagan O'Neal, Jackson O'Reilly) *writer*
Roberts, Nora *writer*
Robinson, Kim Stanley *science fiction author*
Robinson, Marilynne *writer*
Robinson, Roxana Barry *writer, art historian*
Rollin, Betty *writer, television journalist*
Rollins, James (Jim Czajkowski, James Clemens) *writer, veterinarian*
Ronde, John Herman *writer, translator*
Root, William Pitt *poet, educator*
Rothenberg, Jerome *writer, literature educator*
Ruhl, Sarah *playwright*
Rumaker, Michael *writer, language educator*
Rylant, Cynthia *writer*
Sachar, Louis *writer*
Salinger, J(erome) D(avid) *author*
Salter, James *writer*
Salter, Mary Jo *poet*
Sanford, John (John Camp) *writer, journalist*
Sargent, Pamela *writer*
Saul, John Woodruff III *writer*
Schisgal, Murray *playwright*
Schjeldahl, Peter *poet, critic*
Schlesinger, Arthur, Jr., (Arthur Meier Schlesinger) *writer, educator, historian*
Seaman, Barbara (Ann Rosner) *author*
Segal, Lore *writer*
Sendak, Maurice Bernard *writer, illustrator*
Shaffer, Peter (Sir Peter Shaffer) *playwright*
Shao, Wei *writer, educator*
Shawn, Wallace *playwright, actor*
Sheehan, Susan *writer*
Shriver, Lionel (Margaret Ann Shriver) *writer*
Shulevitz, Uri *writer, illustrator*
Silbersack, John Walter *literary agent*
Silva, Daniel Joseph *writer*
Smith, Betty *writer, not-for-profit developer*
Smith, Warren Allen *writer, director, columnist*
Solnit, Rebecca *writer, critic*
Spencer-Fleming, Julia *writer*
Spoto, Donald *writer, educator*
Staples, Brent *writer, reporter*
Steel, Danielle Fernande *author*
Stevenson, William Henri *author*
Swann, Brian *writer, humanities educator*
Sykes, Plum *writer*
Talese, Gay *writer*
Tan, Amy Ruth *writer*
Taylor, Mildred D. *author*
Teachout, Terry *writer, critic*
Templeton, Fiona *poet, playwright, director, performance artist*
Thomason, Dustin *writer*
Tomkins, Calvin *writer*
Trillin, Calvin *writer, journalist*
Tuck, Lily *writer*
Urban, Amanda (Binky Urban) *literary agent*
Valdes-Rodriguez, Alisa *writer*
Vidal, Gore *writer*
Vollmann, William T. *writer*
Vonnegut, Kurt, Jr. *writer*
Walker, Alice *writer*
Wallace, Daniel *writer*
Waller, Robert James *writer*
Walter, Jess *writer*
Ward, Geoffrey Champion *writer, editor*
Wasserman, Steve *literary agent*
Watt, Douglas (Benjamin Watt) *writer, drama critic*
Weinberger, Eliot *literary essayist, poet, translator*
Wells, Rebecca *writer*
Wender, Phyllis Bellows *literary agent*
West, Paul Noden *writer, playwright*
White, Edmund Valentine *writer*
Whitney, Phyllis Ayame *author*
Whitty, Jeff *playwright, actor*
Wilds, Bonnie *writer, volunteer*
Williams, Ian George *writer*
Wolf, Naomi *writer*
Wolfe, Tom (Thomas Kennerly Wolfe Jr.) *writer, journalist*
Wolff, Virginia Euwer *writer*
Woods, Stuart *writer*
Wren, Gayden *playwright, theater director*
Wright, Douglas *playwright*
Wright, Gwendolyn *writer, architecture educator, historian*
Wright, Sarah Elizabeth *writer, poet*
Yaffe, James *writer*
Yglesias, Helen Bassine *author, educator*
Young, John Sacret *writer, film director, film producer*

**North Tonawanda**
Powers, Bruce Raymond *writer, language educator, consultant*

**Nyack**
Hendin, David Bruce *literary agent, writer, numismatist, educator*

**Olivebridge**
Osborne, Seward Russell *writer*

**Painted Post**
Kirk, Connie Ann *writer*

**Palisades**
Davis, Dorothy Salisbury *writer*

**Pawling**
Lester, Helen Doughty *writer*

**Plainview**
Nichter, Rhoda Samuels *writer, educator*

**Plandome**
Sherwood, James Webster III *writer*

**Port Jefferson**
Acker, Kathleen Alice Rusin *writer, editor, poet*

**Poughkeepsie**
Willard, Nancy Margaret *writer, educator*

**Purchase**
Phillips, Carly *writer*

**Red Hook**
Fitzpatrick, John *poet*

**Rhinebeck**
Sloane, Beverly LeBov *writer, consultant, writing instructor*

**Riverhead**
Banfelder, Robert Joseph *writer, literature educator*

**Rochester**
Hoch, Edward Dentinger *writer*
Rothberg, Abraham *writer*

**Rockville Centre**
Mazzucelli, Colette Grace Celia *author, educator*
Schwartz, Arthur *playwright, poet*

**Rye**
Hurwitz, Sol *writer, consultant*
Ketchum, William Clarence *author, educator*

**Sagaponack**
Cedering, Siv *poet, writer*

**Saratoga Springs**
Millhauser, Steven *writer*
Sainer, Arthur *writer, theater educator*

**Scarsdale**
Holmes, Rupert *playwright, singer, writer*
Topping, Seymour *writer*

**Sea Cliff**
Knudson, Rozanne Ruth *writer*

**Shady**
Malkine-Falvey, Fern Sylvie *writer, journalist, painter*

**Shelter Island**
Mayer, Martin Prager *writer*

**Shrub Oak**
Wald, Catherine *writer*

**Southold**
Cowley, Joseph Gilbert *writer*
Small, Bertrice W. *writer*

**Staten Island**
Foster, Paul *playwright*
Porter, Darwin Fred *writer*

**Tuckahoe**
Mariani, John F. *writer*

**Valley Stream**
Rachlin, Harvey Brant *writer*

**Vestal**
Cohen, Marvin A. *writer*

**Wainscott**
Herzog, Arthur III *author*

**Warwick**
Linnéa, Sharon *writer, playwright*

**West Nyack**
Pringle, Laurence Patrick *writer*

**Whitesboro**
O'Hara, Cynthia O'Connor *writer, columnist*

**Woodstock**
Godwin, Gail Kathleen *writer*

**Yonkers**
Baumel, Joan Patricia French *writer, educator*

## NORTH CAROLINA

**Chapel Hill**
Spencer, Elizabeth *writer*

**Charlotte**
Ethridge, Mark Foster III *writer, publishing executive, consultant*
Finley, Glenna *writer*

**Durham**
Anderson, Jean Bradley *writer*
Dorfman, Ariel *writer, educator*

**Flat Rock**
Bar-Sadeh, Madeleine Kay *writer*

**Greensboro**
Flynt, Candace Lambeth *writer*
Watson, Robert Winthrop *poet*

**Greenville**
Gilham, Hanna Kaltenbrunner *writer*

**Laurinburg**
Gilbert, Marie Rogers *poet*

**Midland**
Voncannon, Brian Everett *writer, scriptwriter, radio personality, naturopath*

**Raleigh**
Tucker, Helen Welch *writer*

**Southern Pines**
Kaufman, Bernhard Barken *writer, educator*

**Winston Salem**
Ehle, John Marsden, Jr. *writer*
Hanes, Frank Borden *writer, former business executive, farmer*

## OHIO

**Cincinnati**
Birmingham, Stephen *writer*

McAusland, Randolph Melville Neal *writer, art consultant*

**Cleveland**
Eagleeye-Lord, Amy *writer, editor*
Finn, Robert *writer, educator*
Kovel, Ralph Mallory *writer, antique expert*
Kovel, Terry Horvitz *writer, antiques authority*

**Cleveland Heights**
Sandburg, Helga *author*

**Columbus**
Hilliard, Andrea Leigh *writer*

**Dayton**
Heath, Mariwyn Dwyer *writer, legislative staff member*

**Glendale**
Strom, Kristina Chase *writer, consultant*

**London**
Harris, Lionel *writer, educator*

**Middletown**
McClain, Michael H. *writer*

**Napoleon**
Meekison, MaryFran *writer*

**Oberlin**
Taylor, Robert Larry *freelance/self-employed writer*

**Perrysburg**
Weaver, Richard L., II, *writer, educator*

**Stockport**
Winebrenner, William Patrick *writer*

**Stow**
Castillo, Katherine Lynn *writer, translator, business owner*

**Westerville**
Young, Bette Ann *writer*

**Worthington**
Vladem, Steven Allen *writer, film producer, motivational speaker*

**OKLAHOMA**

**Cleveland**
Anderson, Patricia Sue *writer*

**Oklahoma City**
Moore, Billy Don *scriptwriter, film producer*

**Shawnee**
Stoddard, Allan Lee *writer, musician*

**Tulsa**
Clark, Marian Wilson *writer*
Fielding, Peggy Lou Moss *writer*
Upton, Howard B., Jr. *writer, lawyer*

**OREGON**

**Beatty**
Nettelbeck, Fred Arthur *poet*

**Cannon Beach**
Hellyer, Constance Anne (Connie Anne Conway) *writer, musician*

**Culver**
Siebert, Diane Dolores *author, poet*

**Eugene**
Wilhelm, Kate (Katy Gertrude) *author*

**Klamath Falls**
Koch, Margaret Rau *writer, artist, historian*

**Newport**
Kennedy, Richard Jerome *writer*

**Portland**
Larson, Wanda Z. *writer, poet*
Porter, Elsa Allgood *writer, educator*
Tuska, Jon *writer, publishing executive*

**Shedd**
Ruurs, Margriet *writer*

**PENNSYLVANIA**

**Ambler**
Quinn, Colleen M. *reading specialist*

**Broomall**
Saunders, Sally Love *poet, educator*

**Drexel Hill**
Alexander, Lloyd Chudley *author*

**East Berlin**
Bamberger, Lauren R. *writer, photojournalist*

**Erie**
Silverthorn, Ann *writer*

**Flourtown**
Dressler, Mark Christopher *writer*

**Kennett Square**
Martin, George (George Whitney Martin) *writer*

**King Of Prussia**
Schumann, Paula M. L. *writer*

**Lancaster**
Shenk, Lois Elaine Landis *writer*

**Milford**
Le Guin, Ursula Kroeber *writer*

**Pen Argyl**
Martocci, Lewis Nicholas III *writer*

**Philadelphia**
Bernstein, Charles *poet, writer, educator*
Connor, Bernadette Yvonne *retired writer*
Fussell, Paul *writer, literature educator*
Givens, Janet Eaton *writer*
Hine, Thomas *writer*
Kinsella, Thomas *poet*
Paglia, Camille *writer, humanities educator*
Roisman, Lila *retired advertising writer*
Stewart, Susan *writer*
Wallace, Emily Mitchell *writer, editor, educator*

**Pottstown**
Hylton, Thomas James *author*

**Southampton**
Bendiner, Robert *writer, editor*

**Valley Forge**
Miller, Betty Brown *freelance writer*

**Wayne**
Burton, Betty Jane (B.J. Burton) *playwright*

**West Chester**
Baxter, Joan Anna Patten *technical writer*

**Windber**
Lee, James Alan *writer, editor*

**RHODE ISLAND**

**Barrington**
Deakin, James *writer*

**Bristol**
Braver, Adam *writer, educator*

**Johnston**
Merolla, Carol Ann *writer, consultant*

**Providence**
Coover, Robert *writer, scriptwriter, educator*
Eltringham, Dana Kristin *writer*
López-Morillas, Frances (Mapes) *translator*
Schevill, James Erwin *poet, playwright*
Steinbach, Meredith Lynn *writer, educator*
Vogel, Paula Anne *playwright*
Waldrop, Rosmarie *writer*

**SOUTH CAROLINA**

**Aiken**
Naifeh, Steven Woodward *writer*
Smith, Gregory White *writer*

**Anderson**
Kline, George Louis *writer, translator, retired philosophy and literature educator*

**Clover**
Montgomery, Connie Roger *writer*

**Columbia**
Newton, Rhonwen Leonard *writer, data processing executive, consultant*
Stamps, Laura Anne *writer, poet*

**Hilton Head Island**
Reed, Frances Boogher *writer, actress*

**Kiawah Island**
Harrigan, Anthony Hart *author*

**Lexington**
Wilkins, Robert Pearce *writer, lawyer*

**Rock Hill**
Bristow, Robert O'Neil *writer, educator*

**Summerville**
Reisman, Rosemary Moody Canfield *writer, humanities educator*

**SOUTH DAKOTA**

**Black Hawk**
Hudgens, Michael Thomas, Sr. *author, educator*

**TENNESSEE**

**Blaine**
Bull, James C. *poet*

**Cleveland**
Breuer, William Bentley *author*

**Knoxville**
Bell, Linda R. *writer, photographer*
Lammers, Laura Bea *writer, communications executive*

**Loudon**
Randall, Marilyn Mae *writer*

**Memphis**
Bausch, Richard Carl *writer, educator*
Quinn, Amelia Turner *writer*

**Nashville**
Alexander, Lora Kay *writer, composer*
Bird, Caroline *author*
Nichols, Tim *song writer, publisher*
Pearson, Sela *poet, speaker*

**Sisk**, Eileen Victoria *writer, journalist*
Smith, Agnes Eyvonda *writer*
Wiseman, Craig *song writer, publisher*

**Newport**
Dykeman, Wilma *writer, educator*

**Paris**
McFarlin, Shannon Dianne *writer, researcher*

**Sevierville**
Koff, Shirley Irene *writer*

**TEXAS**

**Alpine**
McBride, Elizabeth Anne Wilmore *writer*

**Amarillo**
Mojtabai, Ann Grace *author, educator*

**Austin**
Barnes, Thomas Joseph *writer*
Beazley, Hamilton *writer, educator*
Friedman, Kinky (Richard Friedman) *writer, musician*
Gustafsson, Lars Erik Einar *writer, educator*
Porter, Jenny Lind *writer*

**Boerne**
Price, John Randolph *writer*

**Canyon**
Roper, Beryl Cain *writer, retired library director, publishing executive*

**Cedar Hill**
Stowers, Carlton Eugene *writer*

**Chireno**
Mayhar, Ardath Frances (Frank Cannon, John Killdeer, Frances Hurst) *writer*

**Corpus Christi**
Foster, Bayard Everson *writer*

**Dallas**
Bartlett, Richard Chalkley *writer, conservationist*
Dee, Ronda *poet, photographer, small business owner, journalist*
Gillett, Grover *author*
Granowsky, Alvin *writer, educator*
Murphy, Randall Kent *writer, educator, consultant*
Phillips, Betty Lou (Elizabeth Louise Phillips) *writer, interior designer*
Sherrod, Danny Troy *writer, educator*

**Elgin**
Jordan, Charlene Hanson *writer*

**Fort Worth**
Lale, Cissy Stewart (Lloyd Lale) *freelance writer*
Munday, Stephen Dale *writer, artist*

**Georgetown**
Shelby, Roselle Price *writer, retired special education educator*

**Hereford**
Artho, Virginia Lou *writer, graphics designer*

**Houston**
Mallia, Marianne *medical writer*
Moser, Don *writer*
Parle, Bertha Ibarra *writer*
Pete, Eric E. *writer, claims representative*

**Kyle**
Atkinson, Valerie J. *writer, webmaster*

**Lubbock**
Craighead, Owen Lindsay *writer*

**Mansfield**
Parnell, Charles L. *speechwriter*

**Odessa**
Moseley, Clifford Wayne *writer, poet*

**Pasadena**
Thompson, Marian Nell *poetry, historical, non-fiction and fiction writer, educator, poet*

**San Antonio**
Ammann, Lillian Ann Nicholson *writer, editor, small business owner*
Fehrenbach, T.R. (Theodore Reed Fehrenbach) *writer*
Strojuy, Joan E. *writer*
Swiggett, Harold E. (Hal Swiggett) *writer, photographer*

**Smithville**
Clark, LaVerne Harrell *writer*

**Spring**
Jackson, Guida Myrl *writer, editor, literature educator*

**Springtown**
Marrs, James F., Jr., (Jim Marrs) *writer, journalist, educator*

**Stephenville**
Butler, Luther Dale *writer*

**Texarkana**
Presley, James Wright *writer, environmentalist*

**UTAH**

**Cedar City**
Modesitt, Leland Exton, Jr., (L.E. Modesitt Jr.) *writer, poet, consultant*

**Logan**
Hruby, George Geoffrey *writer, educator*

**Provo**
Hart, Edward LeRoy *poet, educator*

**Saint George**
Pearce, Carole Ann *poet*

**Salt Lake City**
Osherow, Jacqueline Sue *poet, English language educator*

**VERMONT**

**Bennington**
Bernard, April *poet, literature educator*
Godwin, Rebecca Thompson *writer, educator, editor*

**Burlington**
Hearon, Shelby *writer, educator*

**Chester**
Coleman, John Royston *writer*

**Johnson**
Rice, Rebecca Kynoch *writer, consultant, language educator*

**Marlboro**
Stevenson, Laura Caroline *writer, educator*

**Middlebury**
MacDonald, Kenneth R., Jr. *author, artist*

**Montpelier**
Dobbs, David *writer*

**Morrisville**
Besser, Gretchen Rous *writer, educator*

**South Royalton**
Powers, Thomas Moore *writer*

**Stamford**
Stevens, Lauren Rogers *writer, environmentalist*

**Thetford**
Paley, Grace *author, educator*

**VIRGINIA**

**Alexandria**
Malott, John Raymond *writer, consultant, not-for-profit executive*

**Arlington**
Callier, Maria Cecile *writer, journalist, radio producer, voice-over artist, actress*
England, Robert Stowe *writer*
Timperlake, Edward Thomas *writer*

**Ashburn**
Boyne, Walter James *writer, retired museum director*

**Charlottesville**
Casey, John Dudley *writer, language educator*
Dove, Rita Frances *poet, language educator*
McCrimmon, Barbara Smith *writer, librarian*

**Clifton**
Cavileer, Sharon E. *writer, public relations executive, consultant*

**Culpeper**
Rector, Donna Lynn *writer, photographer, vocalist*

**Fairfax**
Cosing, Arthur Paul, Jr. *writer, artist*

**Falls Church**
Leighton, Frances Spatz *writer, journalist*
Orben, Robert *scriptwriter, writer*
Whitehead, Kenneth Dean *writer, translator, retired federal agency administrator*

**Fort Belvoir**
Parrish, St. John, Florence Tucker *writer, retired federal agency administrator*

**Glen Allen**
Cornwell, Patricia Daniels *writer*

**Leesburg**
Budiansky, Stephen Philip *writer*
Johnson, Julia A. *writer*

**Lexington**
Stuart, Dabney *poet, language educator*

**Mc Lean**
Wallace, Barbara Brooks *writer*

**Meadowview**
Kingsolver, Barbara Ellen *writer*

**Portsmouth**
Mapp, Alf Johnson, Jr. *writer, historian, educator*
Nolen, Crystal Me'Kelle *poet, educator*

**Reston**
Smith, Ralph Lee *writer, musician*

**Richmond**
Morgan, Elizabeth Seydel *writer, educator, retired writer*
Reynolds, Sheri *writer*

**Roanoke**
Allen, Mike *writer*

**Stephenson**
Johnson, Eva Maria *retired translator*

**Sterling**
Bernal-Labrada, Emilio *writer, poet, interpreter, translator*

**Vienna**
Olshaker, Mark Bruce *scriptwriter, filmmaker*

**Virginia Beach**
Seward, William W(ard), Jr. *writer, educator*

**Williamsburg**
Smith, William Henry Preston *freelance/self-employed writer, editor, former telecommunications industry executive*

## WASHINGTON

**Arlington**
Bullington, Gayle Rogers *writer, researcher*

**Bellevue**
Olson, Robert William *writer, retired counselor*
Porad, Francine Joy *poet, painter*

**Bellingham**
Hansen, Leonard Joseph *writer, journalist, editor, communications executive*

**Black Diamond**
Walker, Minerva E. Gilara *poet, retail executive*

**Gig Harbor**
Hunt, Leigh Raphael *playwright*

**Issaquah**
Cain, Coleen W. *writer, educator*

**Kirkland**
Szablya, Helen Mary *writer, language educator*

**La Conner**
Robbins, Thomas Eugene *writer*

**Lynnwood**
Bear, Gregory Dale *writer, illustrator*

**Nordland**
Kramnicz, Rosanne *freelance writer*

**Port Angeles**
Muller, Willard C(hester) *writer*

**Port Townsend**
Kooser, Ted (Theodore J. Kooser) *poet*
Merwin, William Stanley *poet*

**Poulsbo**
Wayne, Kyra Petrovskaya *writer*

**Seattle**
Brooks, Terry *writer, former lawyer*
Gardiner, John Jacob *writer, educator, philosopher*
Kunkel, Georgie Bright *freelance writer, retired counselor*
McHugh, Heather *poet*
Romm, Daniel F. *writer, retired computer technician*
Rule, Ann *author*
Singer, Sarah Beth *poet*
Thomas, Irv *writer, journalist*
Wagoner, David Russell *writer, educator*

**Spokane**
Brock, Randall J. *poet*

**Vashon**
Cushman, Karen Lipski *writer*

## WEST VIRGINIA

**Charleston**
Mellert, Lucie Anne *writer, photographer*

**Teays**
Lamb, Carl Vernon *writer, retired engineer*

## WISCONSIN

**Argyle**
Daley, Ron (Ronald Eugene Daley) *playwright, poet, theater director, theater producer*

**Brookfield**
Schmitz, John J. *writer, educator*

**Elkhorn**
Dunn, Walter Scott, Jr. *writer, museum director, consultant*

**Green Bay**
Erickson, Ruth Alice *poet, artist*

**Kaukauna**
Rice, Ferill Jeane *writer*

**Madison**
Grajkowski, Michelle A. *literary agent*
K-Turkel, Judith Leah Rosenthal (Judi K-Turkel) *writer, editor, publisher*
Moore, Lorrie *writer, English professor*
Riley, Jocelyn Carol *writer, television producer*
Stites, Susan Kay *writer, human resources specialist*

**Milwaukee**
Connelly, Mark *writer, educator*

**Oshkosh**
Alderson, Jo Bartels *writer, poet*

**Racine**
Wright, Betty Ren *children's book writer*

**Saukville**
Gulan, Bonnie Marion *writer, researcher*

**Shawano**
Mutter, John J., Jr. *writer, researcher*

**Waukesha**
Helland, Sherman M. *writer*

## WYOMING

**Laramie**
Boresi, Arthur Peter *writer, educator*

**Pinedale**
Barlow, John Perry *writer, former rancher, advocate*

## TERRITORIES OF THE UNITED STATES

### GUAM

**Mangilao**
Strauch, Edward Hugo *writer, retired literature and language professor*

## CANADA

### BRITISH COLUMBIA

**Heriot Bay**
Bringhurst, Robert *poet*

**Vancouver**
Bowering, George Harry *writer, consultant, language educator*
Cohen, Leonard (Norman Cohen) *poet, writer, musician*

### ONTARIO

**Holland Landing**
Dempster, Barry (Edward) *poet*

**Toronto**
Colombo, John Robert *poet*
Moore, Christopher Hugh *writer*
Peacock, Molly *poet, educator*

### QUEBEC

**Montreal**
Bruemmer, Fred *writer, photographer*

## MEXICO

**Jalisco**
Pordon, Grace *writer, poet, artist*

## AUSTRALIA

**Norfolk Island**
McCullough, Colleen *author*

**Paddington**
Keneally, Thomas Michael *author*

## DENMARK

**Charlottenlund**
Garner, Fradley Hamilton *freelance/self-employed writer, editor*

## ENGLAND

**Cambridge**
Steiner, George (Francis Steiner) *author, educator*

**London**
Amis, Martin Louis *author*
Chevalier, Tracy Rose *writer*
Cleese, John Marwood *writer, comedian*
Cope, Wendy *poet*
Curtis, Richard *author, screenwriter*
Deighton, Len *author*
Drabble, Margaret *writer*
Fine, Anne *writer*
Frayn, Michael *playwright*
Galloway, Janice *writer, editor*
Gray, Simon James Holliday *writer, educator*
Hare, David *playwright*
Hunter Blair, Pauline Clarke *author*
James, P(hyllis) D(orothy) (Baroness James of Holland Park of Southwold in County of Suffolk) *author*
Lessing, Doris (Doris May) *writer*
McGrath, Patrick *writer*
Ormsby, Eric Linn *writer, educator*
Paton Walsh, Jill *writer*
Read, Piers Paul *author*
Rowling, J.K. (Joanne Kathleen Rowling) *writer*
Rushdie, Salman *writer*
Smith, Zadie (Sadie Smith) *writer*
Stoppard, Tom (Tomas Straussler) *playwright*
Taylor, Jim *scriptwriter, film director*

**Stevenage**
Follett, Kenneth Martin *author*

**Whitchurch**
Adams, Richard George *writer*

## FRANCE

**Paris**
Horovitz, Israel Arthur *playwright*

**Taninges**
Berger, John Peter *writer, painter, art critic*

## GERMANY

**Bonn**
Rampacher, Hermann Hans *writer, consultant*

## IRELAND

**Donegal**
Friel, Brian (Bernard Patrick Friel) *author*

**Mullingar**
Donleavy, James Patrick *writer, artist*

## ITALY

**Venice**
Pasinetti, Pier Maria *author*

## NETHERLANDS

**Krimpen aan den Yssel**
Houtzager, Marianne Johanna (Marian de Boyen) *writer, artist, photographer*

## SWITZERLAND

**Bern**
Carlson, Dale Bick *writer*

## ADDRESS UNPUBLISHED

Aatrapi, Marjane *writer, illustrator*
Adams, Deanna Ruth *writer, educator*
Aladjem, Henrietta H. *writer*
Alinder, Mary Street *writer, educator*
Alipio, Gary Glynn *writer, consultant*
Allen, Roberta *writer, photographer, conceptual artist*
Aloff, Mindy *writer*
Alterman, Eric Ross *writer, journalist*
Andersen, Kurt Byars *writer*
Andreasson, Kim J. *writer, consultant*
Anselmo, Robert Louis *writer*
Anshaw, Carol *writer*
Anton, Barbara *writer*
Antonelli, Rosemary *writer*
Apple, Gary Winston *writer, educational consultant*
Apps, Jerold Willard *writer*
Argers, Helen *writer, playwright*
Arlen, Michael J. *writer*
Ash, Jennifer Gertrude *writer, editor*
Ashanti, Baron James *poet, educator*
Avery, Stephen Neal *playwright, writer*
Ayre, Florence Collel *retired writer*
Bahr, Jane Marie *writer, retired language educator*
Bailey, Blake *writer*
Bailey, William Waddell *writer, communications executive*
Bakeman, Carol Ann *travel writer, singer*
Baker, Mark Allen *writer, art historian*
Baldrige, Letitia *writer, management consultant*
Balliett, Whitney *writer, critic*
Barney, Donna Nadyne *writer*
Barrett, Katherine *writer, columnist, television producer*
Barzun, Jacques *writer, literary agent*
Bassett, Elizabeth Ewing (Libby Bassett) *writer, editor, consultant*
Baum, Roger S. *writer*
Beatts, Anne Patricia *writer*
Bel Geddes, Joan *writer*
Benedict, Stewart H. *writer, playwright*
Berg, Darla Gaye *writer*
Bertram, Jean DeSales *writer*
Biddle, Judith Ann *retired writer*
Black, David *writer, educator*
Blake Ramos, Debra Barbara *writer*
Bloch, Lucienne S. *writer*
Block, Lawrence *writer*
Blos, Joan W. *writer, critic, educator*
Bly, Elizabeth Ann *writer*
Bochco, Steven *screenwriter, television producer*
Bodsworth, Fred *writer, ecologist*
Bova, Benjamin William *writer, editor*
Bowden, Mark Robert *writer*
Boyle, T.C. *writer, literature educator*
Bracken, Peg *writer*
Braun, Lilian Jackson *writer*
Briese, Michael W. *writer, deacon, inventor*
Briles, Judith *writer, consultant*
Brodsky, Beverly Anne *writer, consultant, editor*
Brookner, Anita *writer, educator*
Brooks, Geraldine *writer, reporter, news correspondent*
Brown, Denise *poet*
Brown, Sandra *writer*
Brzozowy, Kandy Doris *behavioral health writer*
Bulla, Clyde Robert *writer*
Burch, Annetta Jane *writer*
Burke, Doug *writer*
Bush, Yvonne *writer, counselor*
Butterworth, William Edmund, III, (W.E.B. Griffith) *writer*
Cáceres, Franklin Thomas *retired writer*
Caldwell-Smith, Gaetana Lee *writer*

Caletti, Deb L. *writer*
Calore, Paul *writer, retired government agency administrator*
Campanelli, Michele Wallace *writer, singer*
Campbell, Addison James, Jr. *writer*
Carcaterra, Lorenzo Gabriel *writer*
Carlisle-Frank, Pamela L. *writer, researcher, consultant*
Carlyon, David James *writer, theater director*
Carroll, Mary Patricia *writer*
Casey, Barbara Louise *writer, consultant*
Cecil, Elizabeth Jean *writer*
Cheever, Susan *freelance/self-employed writer*
Choukas-Bradley, Melanie *writer, photographer*
Christensen, Madonna Dries *writer*
Ciagala, Karencia Lucille *writer*
Claes, Gayla Christine *writer, editor, consultant*
Clancy, Thomas L., Jr. *novelist, producer*
Clark, Mary Higgins *writer, communications executive*
Clark, Matt *writer*
Clarke, Sir Arthur Charles *author*
Coburn, D(onald) L(ee) *playwright*
Collins, William J. (Billy Collins) *poet, educator*
Conklin, William Frank *writer*
Cook, Robin *writer*
Cooper, Jane Todd (J. C. Todd) *poet, writer, educator*
Corey, Elizabeth B. *poet, writer*
Cowan, Andrew Glenn *television writer, producer, performer*
Croswell, Katrina Antoinette *writer*
Curtis, Dolores Rogers *writer*
Cussler, Clive Eric *author*
Cutler, Karan Davis *writer, columnist*
Dagstine, Lawrence *writer, artist*
Dailey, Janet *writer*
D'Arcy, Paula *writer*
Dardick, Geeta *writer, psychotherapist*
Daren, Sylvia *poet*
David, Larry *television scriptwriter, television producer, actor*
Davidson, Mark *writer, educator*
Davis, J. Alan *writer, film producer, television producer*
Davis, Luther *writer, theater producer, motion picture producer*
Davis, Mamie (Denise Davis) *writer*
Dawdy, Doris Ostrander *writer*
Deal, Gaye Follmer *writer*
Deats, Suzanne *writer, editor, artist*
Delffs, Dudley J. *writer, educator*
DeMille, Nelson Richard *writer*
Desio, Delores Jean *writer, artist, retired elementary school educator*
DesJardins, J. Mark *writer*
Diamant, Anita *writer*
Dolan, Edward Francis *writer*
Donnally, Patricia Broderick *writer*
Druffel, Ann Bernice *researcher, writer*
Dworzan, Helene Liberman *writer, poet, playwright*
Eckhart, TammyJo *writer*
Eglee, Charles Hamilton *scriptwriter, film producer, television producer*
Ehrenreich, Barbara *writer*
Ellingsworth, Linda Benoit *freelance/self-employed writer*
Emerson, Claudia *poet, language professor*
Englert, Helen Wiggs *writer*
Ensminger, John Jay *writer, poet, minister, counselor*
Ephron, Nora *writer*
Escallón, Ana María *writer*
Esty, John Cushing, Jr. *writer, educator, not-for-profit counsel*
Evangelista, Anita Loretta *freelance/self-employed writer, publishing executive, psychologist, nurse*
Evans, Jack R. (J. Glenn Evans) *writer, poet*
Fackler, Elizabeth *writer*
Fadiman, Anne *writer, educator*
Farrelly, Peter John *screenwriter*
Fearrington, Ann Peyton *writer, illustrator, news correspondent*
Finder, Joseph Alan *writer*
Fitzgerald, Timothy K. *writer, political organizer, non-profit administrator*
Fleming, Thomas James *writer*
Fletcher, Donald Rodgers *writer, religious studies educator*
Foote, Horton *playwright, scriptwriter*
Fraser, Kathleen Joy *poet, creative writing professor*
Freedman, Russell Bruce *author*
French, Marilyn *writer, critic, historian*
Fryer, Thomas Waitt, Jr. *writer*
Frymer, Murry *writer, film critic, theater critic*
Fuentes, Carlos *writer, retired ambassador*
Fuller, Jack William *writer, retired publishing executive*
Gaffney, Mark Howard *writer*
Gallimore, Margaret Martin *poet*
Ganz, Lowell *scriptwriter, television producer*
Garcia, Greg (Gregory Thomas Garcia) *writer*
Garfield-Woodbridge, Nancy *writer*
Garfinkle, Elaine Myra *writer*
Gatria, America I *retired writer*
Gavril, Jean (Jean Van Leeuwen) *writer*
Gebauer, Phyllis Victoria Feltskog *writer, educator*
Gelles, David Alexander *writer*
Gellis, Willard Leon *poet, language educator*
George, Gerald William *writer*
Gilbert, Elayne Rhoda *writer*
Gilroy, Frank Daniel *playwright*
Ginsburg, Lynn *writer*
Giovanni, Nikki (Yolanda Cornelia Giovanni) *poet, educator*
Giovinazzo, Vivian Curry *writer*
Gleason, Kate *writer, educator, editor*
Glück, Louise Elisabeth *poet, educator*
Goble, Paul *writer, illustrator, artist*
Goldberg, Lucianne *literary agent*
Goldfarb, Ruth *poet, educator*
Goldman, Judith *writer, editor, curator, consultant, publisher*
Goldman, William James *scriptwriter*
Goss, Joel Francis *writer*
Graham, Steven Anthony *writer*
Grambs, Jennifer *writer*
Gray, Francine du Plessix *writer*
Gray, Thomas Stephen *writer*

Green, Wilma Jane *writer*
Greenberg, Richard *playwright*
Greenburg, Dan *author*
Greer, Germaine *author*
Guare, John *playwright, educator*
Gullickson, JoAnne Lois *writer*
Guy, Eleanor Bryenton *retired writer*
Haas, Charlie *screenwriter*
Hadley, Leila Eliott-Burton (Mrs. Henry Luce III) *writer*
Haggis, Paul Edward *scriptwriter, television producer, television director*
Hahn, Mary Downing *writer*
Haldeman, Joe William *writer*
Hall, Donald *poet*
Hall, Peggy Craft *poet, retired secondary school educator*
Harrison, Ella Guidry *writer*
Harstad, Carolyn Audrey *writer, educator, photographer*
Hartman, Earl Kenneth *writer*
Haskell, Molly *writer*
Hautman, Pete (Peter Murray) *writer*
Hayes, Cynthia Ann (C.A. Hayes) *writer*
Helprin, Mark *author*
Hemon, Aleksander *writer*
Hendra, Tony *writer, comedian, actor*
Herman, George Adam *writer, literature educator*
Herman, Hank *writer*
Herman, Michelle *writer*
Higbee, Donna Good *writer, researcher*
Higdon, Pamela Leis *writer*
Hill, Donna Marie *writer, retired librarian*
Hill, Laban Carrick *writer*
Hillenburg, Stephen *writer, television producer, animator*
Hillerman, Tony *writer, journalist, educator*
Himmelfarb, Gertrude (Mrs. Irving Kristol) *writer, educator*
Hitchcock, Jane Stanton *playwright, novelist*
Hoagland, Tony *writer*
Hoff, Benjamin Lloyd *writer, scriptwriter*
Hoffman, William *writer*
Hollander, Anne *writer*
Holton, Winfred Byron III *writer*
Hornby, Nick *writer*
Horsman, David A. Elliott *writer, finance company executive, educator*
Houston, Gloria *author, educator, consultant*
Howes, Sophia DuBose *writer*
Hoyt, Mary Finch *writer, media consultant, retired federal official*
Hu, Hua-ling Wang *writer, historian*
Hughey, Richard Kohlman *writer, lawyer*
Hurd, Jerrie *writer, photographer*
Insana, Arthur Gerard *writer, director*
Irving, John Winslow *writer*
Isaacs, Susan *writer, scriptwriter*
Isenberg, Jane Frances *writer, retired language educator*
Jackson, Charles Ian *writer, consultant*
Jacobs, Nancy Carolyn Baker *writer*
Jaffee, Annette Williams *novelist*
Johnsen, Barbara Parrish *writer*
Johnson, Angela *children's book author*
Jones, Edward Paul *writer, editor*
Jones, Renee Maureen *writer*
Jones, Thomas Claburn *poet, educator*
Jorden, William John *writer, retired diplomat*
Just, Ward Swift *author*
Kanin, Fay *screenwriter*
Kass, Jerome Allan *writer*
Katz, William Loren *author*
Kelley, A. Benjamin *writer, educator, consultant*
Kelton, Elmer Stephen *novelist*
Kemprecos, Paul *writer*
Kendall, Harry Wesley *playwright, writer*
Kevles, Bettyann Holtzmann *writer, historian, educator*
Kidder, Tracy (John Tracy Kidder) *writer*
Kimbrell, Grady Ned *writer, educator, retired school system administrator*
Kimmel, Mark *author, venture capital company executive*
Kincaid, Jamaica *writer*
King, Cynthia Bregman *writer*
King, Larry L. *playwright, actor*
Kingston, Maxine Hong *writer, educator*
Kirshbaum, Laurence J. *literary agent, former publishing executive*
Klein, Edward *writer, writer*
Knobloch, Marcia M. (Marta Knobloch) *writer*
Knotts, Robert Spencer (Bob Knotts) *writer, playwright*
Koepp, David *screenwriter*
Kohn, Alfie *writer, educator*
Konigsburg, Elaine Lobl *writer*
Krauds, Dean Ray *writer*
Kossman, Nina *writer, translator*
Kotlowitz, Alex *writer, journalist*
Kramer, Larry *playwright, writer*
Kruger, Mollee Coppel *writer*
Krupat, Kitty Weiss *writer, educator*
Kumin, Maxine Winokur *poet, writer*
Kushner, Tony *playwright, scriptwriter*
Lambert, LeClair Grier *writer, lecturer, consultant, former state government public information administrator*
Lambert, Richard Bowles, Jr. *freelance writer*
Lapine, James Elliot *playwright, director*
Larkin, Joan *poet, literature and language educator*
Larsdotter, Anna-Lisa *retired translator, artist*
Lawrence, Ruth *writer, illustrator*
LeBlanc, Jean Eva *writer, poet, educator*
le Carré, John (David John Moore Cornwell) *author*
Ledford, Brenda Kay *writer*
Lescroart, John Thomas *writer, composer, singer*
Lester, Julius B. *author*
Lethem, Jonathan Allen *writer*
Lindenberger, Herbert Samuel *writer, literature educator*
Lippard, Lucy Rowland *writer, educator, critic, curator*
Little, Charlotte Louise *poet, writer*
Lober, Lionel M. *scriptwriter, film producer*
Locke, J. Duane *poet, painter, photographer*
Long, Elaine *writer, editor*
Lopez, Barry Holstun *writer*
Lubell, Ellen *writer*

Luben, Delma *writer, poet, editor*
Luhn, Robert Kent *writer, magazine editor*
Lunsford, Carol Anne *writer, artist, retired special education educator*
Lynds, Gayle Hallenbeck *writer*
Macaulay, David Alexander *author, illustrator*
Madison, Deborah Leafy *writer, chef*
Mailer, Norman Kingsley *writer*
Mankiewicz, Thomas Frank *screenwriter, director, producer*
Marks, Martha Alford *writer*
Martin, George Raymond Richard *writer*
Martin-Lowry, Beverly Anne *writer, columnist*
Mason, Connie Jeanne *writer*
Massing, Michael *writer, media critic*
Mathieu, Michele Suzanne *grant writer, computer scientist, consultant*
Mathis, Sharon Bell *retired writer, librarian, curator*
Mathy, Robin Michelle *writer, researcher*
Mattar, Philip *writer*
Mattern, Joanne *writer, educator*
McCash, June Hall *writer, retired language educator*
McCoy, Dorothy Eloise *writer, educator*
McDonald, April D. *writer*
McFall, Catherine Gardner *poet, critic, educator*
McGee, Harold James *writer*
McIntier, Russell J. *retired writer*
McMichaels, Susan Bishop Winship *writer, educator*
McMillan, Terry L. *writer, educator*
McPhee, John Angus *writer*
McPherson, James Alan *writer, educator*
McWhorter, Diane *writer*
McWilliams, Michael *writer, publisher*
Mead, Loren Benjamin *writer, consultant*
Mendoza, George *poet, author*
Merrill, Jean Fairbanks *writer*
Miller, W. Kievit *writer*
Mills, Elizabeth Shown *historical writer, genealogist*
Mintz, Morton Abner *writer, reporter*
Mitchard, Jacquelyn *writer*
Mitchell, Marcia Jeanne *writer*
Molina, Jose *scriptwriter, television producer*
Moore, Robert Henry *writer, editor, communications consultant*
Moore, Robert Lowell, Jr. (Robin Moore) *author*
Moore, Susanna *writer*
Mora, Pat *writer, speech professional*
Moresco, Robert *scriptwriter, film and television producer*
Morrison, Martin *writer*
Morrison, Sarah Lyddon *author*
Morrison, Toni (Chloe Anthony Wofford) *writer, educator, editor*
Morrow, Barry Nelson *screenwriter, producer*
Morse-McNeely, Patricia Jane *poet, writer, retired secondary school educator*
Moses, Shelia P. *writer, poet, playwright, producer*
Mrazek, Robert J. *writer, former congressman*
Murphy, Jim *writer*
Muson, Howard Henry *writer, consultant*
Myers, Sophia M. *writer, researcher, artist, cartographer, translator*
Myers, Walter Dean *young adult book author*
Narbon, Lilian *writer*
Neely, Mark Edward, Jr. *writer*
Nelson, Richard John *playwright, film director, screenwriter*
Nesbit, Lynn *literary agent*
Nichols, Mike Thomas *writer*
Noëldechen, Joan Marguerite *writer*
Nova, Craig *writer*
Nurick, Carl J. *writer, consultant, poet*
O'Brien, Charles Harold *writer, priest*
O'Brien-Palmer, Michelle Ann *educational writer, consultant*
Oransky, Ivan *writer, editor*
Orkin, Jenna *writer*
Orrmont, Arthur *writer, editor*
Ossana, Diana Lynn *author, screenwriter*
Ostriker, Alicia Suskin *poet*
Owens, Rochelle *poet, playwright*
Ozick, Cynthia *writer*
Paine, Alan *poet*
Paley, Russell Eliot *writer, small business owner*
Palmer, Charlotte Marie *writer*
Panagis, Pete *writer*
Paolucci, Anne Attura *playwright, poet, literature educator, educational consultant*
Parrott, Wanda Sue *writer, journalist*
Patterson, Richard North *writer, lawyer*
Penn, Zachary Owen *screenwriter*
Percival, Nora Lourie *writer, retired editor*
Perry, Tyler *playwright, actor, theater director, theater producer*
Persico, Joseph Edward *writer, historian*
Pettigrew, Dawn Karima *writer*
Phillips, Jill Meta *writer, critic, astrologer*
Phillips, Susan Leslie *writer*
Pierce, Tamora *writer*
Polite, Carlene Hatcher *writer, educator*
Pollitt, Katha *writer, educator, poet*
Porter, Margaret Evans *novelist, lecturer, historian*
Poundstone, William Nicholas, Jr. *writer*
Powell, Alma Johnson *writer, advocate, foundation administrator*
Prescott, Richard Chambers *writer*
Proulx, (Edna) Annie *writer*
Pullman, Philip Nicholas *writer, playwright*
Purcell, John Patrick, Jr. *writer, art educator*
Rader, Dotson Carlyle *writer, journalist*
Ragans, Rosalind Dorothy *writer, artist, retired educator*
Raucher, Herman *screenwriter, novelist*
Ravetch, Irving *screenwriter*
Rech, Lindsay Faith *writer*
Rechy, John Francisco *writer*
Reeves, Richard *writer, historian*
Reinike, Irma *retired writer, artist, poet, lyricist*
Renaud, Bernadette Marie Elise *author*
Reza, Yasmina *author, playwright*
Rheingold, Howard *technology writer, virtual community expert*
Rhymer, Scott Campbell *writer, historian*
Rice, Anne *writer*
Richardson, Mozelle Groner *author*
Richter, W.D. *screenwriter, director, producer*
Riehecky, Janet Ellen *writer*

Riley, Robert Shean *writer, publishing executive, retired army officer*
Rimel, Ira Wesley *writer, US Navy supply officer, real estate specialist, real estate appraiser, real estate broker*
Ringel, Judy G. *writer*
Robinson, David Bradford *writer, poet*
Rogers, David *playwright, actor*
Rooney, Andrew Aitken *writer, journalist*
Rosen, Norma *writer*
Rosenblatt, Roger *writer*
Rosenfeld, Albert Hyman *science and medical writer*
Roth, Philip Milton *writer*
Rottenberg, Claire J. *writer, educator*
Rush, Norman *author*
Russ, Joanna *author*
Russo, Richard *writer*
Rutsala, Vern A. *poet, writer, language educator*
Ryan, Joyce Ethel *writer, artist*
Sackett, Susan Deanna *writer*
Saito, Robert Shunichi *writer, poet*
Salat, Cristina *writer*
Sallis, James *writer*
Samer, Bill Fred Carl *writer, cartoonist*
Schenkkan, Robert Frederic *playwright, scriptwriter*
Schiff, Stacy *writer*
Schnackenberg, Gjertrud Cecelia *poet*
Schneider, Phyllis Leah *writer, editor*
Schueler, Gerald Joseph *writer, systems analyst, consultant*
Schwartz, Lynne Sharon *freelance/self-employed writer*
Scott, Dorothy *writer*
Scott, Joyce *writer*
sDerksen, Mary Lou *writer, retired secondary school educator*
Seamans, William *writer, retired reporter, commentator*
Sedaris, David Raymond *writer*
Seidel, Frederick Lewis *poet*
Severin-Hansen, Jeanne Anne *poet*
Severo, Richard *writer*
Sevilla, Emerita Nepomuceno *writer*
Shagan, Steve *scriptwriter, film producer*
Shapiro, Harvey *poet*
Sheldon, Edith Louise Thach *writer*
Shelley, Lore *writer, small business owner, realtor*
Shepard, Sam (Samuel Shepard Rogers) *playwright, actor*
Shoemaker, Bobby Jean (B.J. Foster) *writer*
Shreve, Susan Richards *writer, educator*
Shteyngart, Gary *writer*
Sicart, Pierre-Alexandre Serge Henry *writer*
Siddons, Anne Rivers (Sybil Anne Rivers Siddons) *writer*
Siegel, Mary Ann Garvin *writer*
Simendinger, Theodore John *writer, publishing executive*
Simon, Neil *playwright, screenwriter, television writer*
Simon, William Leonard *scriptwriter, television producer, writer, film producer*
Simpkins, Annellen *author*
Sims, Pamela Jan (Cerussi) *writer, minister*
Sims Iannelli, Kimberly *writer*
Singer, Donna Lea *writer, editor, educator*
Singleton, Jonetta Williams *poet, retired special education educator*
Skinner, Knute Rumsey *poet*
Sklar, Holly L. *writer, columnist*
Skwarczyński, Henryk Adam (Henryk Skwar) *writer*
Slater, Brian (Raven Slate) *writer*
Smith, Cynthia S. *writer*
Smith, Martin Cruz *author*
Snodgrass, W. D. *writer, educator*
Snow, Marina *writer*
Socolow, Elizabeth Anne *poet, educator, artist, writer*
Sodums, Dzintars *writer*
Solomon, Andrew Wallace *author*
SoRelle, Ruth Doyle *writer, journalist*
Spada, James *writer, photographer, publishing executive*
Sparks, Nicholas *writer*
Spiegel, Marcia Cohn *writer*
Spies, Karen Bornemann *writer, educational consultant*
Stashower, Daniel Meyer *writer*
Steele, Judith McConnell *writer*
Stepak, Asa Martin *writer, linguist*
Stern, Richard Gustave *writer*
Stevens, Shane *novelist*
Stine, R(obert) L(awrence) *children's book author*
Stone, John Timothy, Jr. *writer*
Stone, Sandra *writer, artist*
Strand, Mark *poet*
Straub, Peter Francis *novelist*
Strong, Virginia Wilkerson *freelance writer, former special education educator*
Stroud, Patricia Tyson *writer*
Strouse, Jean *writer*
Stuart, Kiel *writer*
Styron, William *writer*
Suglia, Joseph Vincent *writer, educator*
Sullivan, George Edward *writer*
Sussman, Barry *writer, demographer, editor*
Swan, Annalyn *writer*
Tackett, Viti Lee *writer*
Tatum, Arthur III *lexicographer, educator, pianist*
Taylor, John Jackson (Jay Taylor) *writer, retired diplomat*
Theroux, Paul Edward *author*
Thompson, Didi Castle (Mary Bennett) *writer, editor*
Thornburg, Linda A. *writer*
Thurner, Henry *retired writer*
Todd, Catherine Jackson *writer*
Toibin, Colm *writer, journalist*
Tower, Mollie Gregory *writer, educator, consultant*
Towler, Katherine *writer*
Tran, Lan P. *writer, performer*
Trubo, Richard M. *writer*
Truman, Margaret *writer*
Tucker, Jack William Andrew *writer, film editor, film producer*
Twichell, Chase *poet*
Ucko, Barbara Clark *writer*
Ulin, David Lawrence *writer, editor, educator*

Unger, Barbara *poet, retired educator*
Updike, John Hoyer *writer*
Valdes, Gina *writer*
Valentine, Jean *poet, educator, writer*
Vestal, Marilyn Anita *writer, researcher, educator*
Vichiola, Christopher Michael *writer, educator*
Viorst, Judith Stahl *writer*
Viorst, Milton *writer*
Vita, Steven *poet*
Voigt, Cynthia *writer*
Volk, Patricia Gay *writer, essayist*
von Hoffman, Nicholas *writer, retired reporter*
Wade, Wyn Craig *writer, educator*
Waitkus, Jay *writer*
Wakefield, Dan *writer, scriptwriter*
Wallace, Michele *writer, educator*
Wallingford, Anne *freelance/self-employed writer, marketing professional, consultant*
Wambaugh, Joseph A., Jr. *author*
Ward (Bailey), Daisy Dale *writer*
Warren, Rosanna *poet*
Weis, Margaret Edith *writer, editor*
Weisberg, Barbara *writer, editor*
Weiser, Dennis Charles *writer, philosopher*
Weiss, Joanne Marion *writer*
Whalen, Charles William, Jr. *writer, retail executive, congressman, educator*
Whalin, W. Terry *writer, editor*
Whelchel, Sandra Jane *writer*
White, Daphne Milbank *writer*
Wiehe, Fred *writer*
Wilbur, Marcia Kaoru *writer*
Wilkinson, Claude Henry *writer, artist, English literature educator*
Will, Roland Tracy, II, *writer, editor, journalist, publisher, actor*
Willett, Richard *writer, editor*
Williams, Darcel Patrice *writer, editor*
Williams, Niama Leslie JoAnn *writer, educator*
Wilson, Colin Henry *writer*
Wilson, Lanford *playwright*
Wilson, Roberta Louise *writer, editor, journalist, activist*
Winter, Terence *writer*
Wolf, Elizabeth Ann *writer*
Wolfe, Linda *writer*
Wood, William Preston *writer, lawyer*
Woodson, Jacqueline *writer*
Wright, Franz Paul *poet, writer, translator*
Wright, Lawrence George *writer*
Wynn, Tracy Keenan *screenwriter*
Yeager, Anson Anders *writer, retired editor, retired columnist*
Yglesias, Rafael Jose *novelist*
Yingling, Phyllis Stuckey *writer*
Zagajewski, Adam *poet, writer*
Zagaski, Chester Anthony, Jr. *writer, researcher, consultant*
Zeilig, Nancy Meeks *writer, editor*
Zulauf, Sander (Sander William Zulauf) *poet, educator, editor*

---

# ARTS: PERFORMING

## UNITED STATES

### ALABAMA

**Adamsville**
Wright, Carlton Jeffery *music educator, conductor*

**Auburn**
Cornelius, Larry *band director*
Turner, Louise (Lee) Kreher *retired dance educator*
Vasquez, Ramon Francisco *music educator*

**Auburn University**
Lyda, Robert Louis *music educator*

**Birmingham**
Johnson, Allison T. *music educator*
Mitchell, Lynn Hatfield *music educator, director, musician*
Mosteller, Darla Brooks *singer*
Reynolds, Jeffrey Warren *music educator*
Tyler, Ashley Suzanne *music educator*

**Daleville**
Nichols, Mark A. *music educator*

**Demopolis**
Bonds, Philippe Dale *music educator*

**Elberta**
Kauffman, Carl Herbert *music educator*

**Fairhope**
Mozer, Martha K. *music educator*

**Florence**
Lee, Soojeong *music educator, soprano*

**Foley**
Pearce, Stephen Ferron *music educator*

**Fort Payne**
Cook, Jeffrey Alan *musician*

**Gadsden**
Gagliardo, Michael Robert *music educator, conductor*

**Headland**
Taylor, John Paul *music educator, minister*

**Homewood**
Tucker, Rhonda Reneé *music educator*

**Huntsville**
Conran, Michael Artemus *voice educator, director*
Contreras, Frank R. *musician*
Hall, Doris Spooner *music educator*

Lyles, Brian M. *music educator*

**Jacksonville**
Gossett, Jeffrey David *music educator*

**Leeds**
Smith, Robert K. *music educator, director*

**Mentone**
Herndon, Mark Joel *musician*

**Millbrook**
Boartfield, Ernest William *music educator*

**Millport**
Fowler, William Ralph *music educator*

**Montgomery**
Copeland, Jacqueline Turner *music educator*
Petty, Willie Clifford *musician, composer, educator*

**Pinson**
Lawley, Perry Edward *music educator*

**Pleasant Grove**
Miller, Robert Ward *music educator*

**Point Clear**
Englund, Gage Bush *dancer, educator*

**Talladega**
Lanier, Anita Suzanne *musician, educator*
McKinney, John Paul *performing company executive*

**Thomasville**
Shewmake, Bridgett Loree *project specialist*

**Troy**
Allard, Catherine *music educator, musician*

**Tuscaloosa**
Boyd, J. Thomas *music educator*
Cleino, Edward H. *music educator*

**Wadley**
Caldwell, Ann B. *music educator*

**Weaver**
Holland, Jared Andrew *music educator*

**ALASKA**

**Anchorage**
DeLap, Miriam Anne *music educator*
Gazaway, Barbara Ann *music educator, art educator*

**Auke Bay**
d'Armand, John Berger *music educator*

**Eagle River**
Lange, Ron Q. *music educator*

**Indian**
Wright, Gordon Brooks *musician, conductor, educator*

**Juneau**
Clark, Jocelyn Collette *musician*

**ARIZONA**

**Benson**
Eggleston, Adam Thomas *chorus educator, drama educator, composer*

**Chandler**
Carpenter, Ron D. *music educator*
Faust, Donny D. *music educator*
Simon, Diane Rose *music educator, writer, poet*

**Flagstaff**
Ellis, Cathryn G. *theater educator, costume designer*
Hanson, Lloyd William *music educator*
Moore, Kent Ross *music educator*
Poen, Kathryn Louise *music educator, performing arts association administrator*
Riddle, Douglas S *music educator*

**Fountain Hills**
Tyl, Noel Jan *retired vocalist, astrologer, writer*

**Glendale**
Cotton, Sally Jean *retired music educator*
Mahoney, Jill Elizabeth *music educator*
Pang, Darren *hockey analyst, retired professional hockey player*

**Holbrook**
Schoeing, Benjamin Samuel *music educator, conductor*

**Mesa**
Powelson, John Jay *music educator*
Skoldberg, Phyllis Linnea *music educator, musician*

**Nogales**
Cochran, James Randall *music educator*

**Phoenix**
Andersen, Ib *performing company executive*
Anderson, Gary Gene *music educator*
Baldasano, Laura May *music educator, director*
Cooper, Alice (Vincent Damon Furnier) *popular musician*
Hayward, Kevin Andrew *music educator, director*
Hooper, Daniel Lee *music educator, composer*
Kirkland, Joseph *voice educator*
Long, Michael Alan *musician, writer*
Nijinsky, Tamara *actress, puppeteer, author, librarian, educator*
Schaefer, Gregory Lauren *music professor*
Sucato, Robert Alan *filmmaker, director*

Thomas, Jim Gus *music educator*
Walker, Thomas Carlton *music educator*
Werner, Leo C. *music educator, consultant*
Wheaton, Marilyn *musician*

**Prescott Valley**
Shelley, Bonnie J. *voice educator*

**Sahuarita**
Albertson, Paulette Smith *music educator*

**Scottsdale**
Baack, Paula D. *music educator*
Burley, John M. *music educator*
Como, Ed *theater educator, set designer*
Farney, Charlotte Eugenia *musician, educator*
Newman, Ursula Irene *music educator*
Peterson, John Willard *composer, publishing executive*
Westmoreland, Preston *radio personality*

**Sedona**
Bays, Theresa *music director, liturgist*

**Sierra Vista**
Boughan, Zanetta Louise *music educator*

**Surprise**
Eastman, Donna Kelly *composer*

**Tempe**
Barker, David *actor, educator*
Bradford, Steven Paul *film educator, department chairman*
Humphreys, Jere Thomas *music educator, consultant*
Lombardi, Eugene Patsy *retired conductor, musician, educator*
Marshall, Kimberly *music educator, musician*
Nagrin, Daniel *dancer, educator, choreographer, writer*

**Tucson**
Ashby, Garmon J.N. *music educator, director*
Aurand, Charles Henry, Jr. *music educator*
Cullen, Shawn L. *music educator*
Dickey, Jerry R. *theater educator*
Ostromencki, Nancy Lee *music educator*
Seaman, Arlene Anna *retired musician*
Walsh, Craig T. *composer, educator*
Wyatt, Roland Gratts *music educator, voice educator, consultant*

**Vail**
Cardieri, Alexander M. *music specialist, music educator*

**Yuma**
Straley, Forrest Alvin Chip *theater educator, director, actor*

**ARKANSAS**

**Bella Vista**
Zehring, Lawrence Edward *music educator*

**Fayetteville**
Jackson, Barbara Ann Garvey *music educator*

**Fort Smith**
Momand, Elizabeth Blanton *singer, music educator*

**Gravette**
Legler, Kristin M. *music educator*

**Greers Ferry**
Robbins, Etta Jo *music educator*

**Harrison**
Rickman, William Thomas *choral director*

**Jonesboro**
Bartee, Neale *music educator, musician, conductor*
Groves, Mark *music director*
Schaefer, Kelly Marie *theater educator, costume designer*

**Little Rock**
Buehling, Cynthia Gwynne *music educator*
Davis, Suanna Jeanette *music educator, mezzo-soprano*
Groesbeck, Rolf Alfred *music history and ethnomusicology educator*
Metzler, James Robert *musician*
Raney, Miriam Day *actress*
Raphael, Jay E. *theater educator, director, actor*

**Russellville**
Herrick, Nita Marie *music educator*

**Siloam Springs**
Wubbena, Jan Helmut *music professor*

**West Memphis**
Peoples, Johnny Ray *music educator*

**CALIFORNIA**

**Agoura Hills**
Curiale, Joseph James *composer, writer*

**Alameda**
LaRose, Katherine Stencel *music educator*

**Albany**
Boris, Ruthanna *dancer, educator, choreographer, dance therapist*

**Altadena**
Klages, Karen Louise *music educator, musician*

**Anaheim**
Schubert, Joseph Edward *music educator*

**Antioch**
Adams, Liliana Osses *music performer, harpist*
Molina, Ron Joseph *music educator*

**Arcadia**
Chih, Luke *music educator, conductor*
Guo, Xin *music educator, editor*

**Artesia**
Costa, David Lourenco *music educator, conductor*

**Atwater**
Ryan, Kelli Lorraine *ballerina, educator*

**Bakersfield**
Kempf, Robert Louis *theater educator, theater director*
Provencio, Roberto Enrique *music educator, music minister*
Reed, James Michael *music educator, singer*

**Bellflower**
de Thouars, Victor Ivan Charles *performance artist, educator*

**Belmont**
Musmann, Lois S. *conductor, music educator*

**Berkeley**
Campion, Edmund Joseph *composer, educator*
Dudley, Anna Carol *singer, voice educator*
Hagar, Sammy *musician, vocalist, composer*
Imbrie, Andrew Welsh *composer, educator*
Medak, Susan Lee *performing company executive*
Reid, Frances Evelyn Kroll *freelance/self-employed cinematographer, film director, communications executive*
Walton, Ortiz Montaigne *musician, sociologist*
Zaentz, Saul *film producer, former record company executive*

**Beverly Hills**
Abdul, Paula (Paula Julie Abdul) *singer, dancer, choreographer*
Abrams, J.J. (Jeffrey Jacob Abrams) *television producer, scriptwriter*
Alexander, Jason (Jay Scott Greenspan) *actor*
Allen, Debbie *actress, choreographer, dancer, television director*
Allen, Joan *actress*
Allen, Ted *television personality*
Allen, Tim (Timothy Allen Dick) *actor, comedian*
Ambrose, Lauren (Lauren Anne D'Ambruoso) *actress*
Anderson, Pamela Denise *actress*
Anderson, Wes (Wesley Wales Anderson) *film director*
Ann-Margret, (Ann-Margret Olsson) *actress, performer*
Arnold, Tom *actor, comedian, television producer*
Arquette, Patricia *actress*
Avary, Roger Roberts (Frank Brauner) *film director, producer, writer*
Aykroyd, Daniel Edward *actor, writer*
Bacon, Kevin *actor*
Badham, John MacDonald *motion picture director*
Banderas, Antonio *actor*
Barclay, Paris *television director, television producer*
Barkin, Ellen *actress*
Barrymore, Drew *actress*
Barton, Mischa *actress*
Bateman, Jason *actor*
Bates, Kathy *actress*
Bay, Michael Benjamin *film director*
Beatty, Warren *actor, film director, film producer*
Bello, Maria Elana *actress*
Belushi, James A. *actor*
Bening, Annette *actress*
Berenger, Tom (Thomas Michael Moore) *actor*
Berg, Jeffrey Spencer *talent agency executive*
Berkus, James *talent agent*
Biel, Jessica *actress, model*
Bisset, Jacqueline *actress*
Black, Jack (Thomas Black) *actor*
Blaine, David *magician*
Blanchett, Cate (Catherine Elise Blanchett) *actress*
Bogdanovich, Peter *film director, writer, producer, actor*
Bonham-Carter, Helena *actress*
Bosworth, Kate *actress*
Bratt, Benjamin *actor*
Braun, Zev *motion picture and television producer*
Brenneman, Amy *actress*
Bridges, Jeff *actor*
Brillstein, Bernie J. *producer, talent manager*
Broderick, Matthew *actor*
Brokaw, Norman Robert *talent agency executive*
Buckland, Marc *television director*
Burnett, Carol *actress, comedienne, singer*
Burnham, John Ludwig *agent*
Burstyn, Ellen (Edna Rae Gillooly) *actress*
Busfield, Timothy *actor*
Bush, Sophia *actress*
Bymel, Suzan Yvette *talent manager, film producer*
Byrne, Gabriel *actor*
Campbell, Neve *actress*
Capshaw, Kate (Kathy Sue Nail) *actress*
Carpenter, John Howard *director, producer, screenwriter*
Carradine, Keith Ian *actor, singer, composer*
Carrere, Tia (Althea Rae Duhinio Janairo) *actress*
Carrey, Jim *actor*
Carter, Lynda *actress, entertainer*
Caruso, David *actor*
Castellaneta, Dan (Daniel Louis) *actor*
Castle-Hughes, Keisha *actress*
Caton-Jones, Michael *film director, film producer*
Cattrall, Kim *actress*
Caviezel, James Patrick *actor*
Channing, Carol *actress*
Chappelle, Dave (David Chappelle) *actor, comedian*
Cheadle, Don *actor*
Christensen, Hayden *actor*
Chritton, George A. *theater producer*
Church, Thomas Hayden *actor*
Clooney, George *actor*
Close, Glenn *actress*
Coen, Ethan *film director, writer*

Coen, Joel *film director, writer*
Collette, Toni *actress*
Columbus, Chris *film director, screenwriter*
Condon, Tom *sports agent*
Condon, William (Bill) *director, writer, producer*
Congdon, Amanda *actress, web video blogger, writer*
Connelly, Jennifer *actress*
Connery, Sir Sean (Thomas Sean Connery) *actor*
Cook, Dane (Dane Jeffrey Cook) *comedian, actor*
Corbett, John *actor*
Corbin, Barry *actor, writer*
Cox Arquette, Courteney *actress*
Craig, Daniel *actor*
Cristofer, Michael *actor, writer, playwright, scriptwriter*
Croll, Tony *cinematographer, television director*
Cronenberg, David *film director*
Cruz, Penelope *actress*
Culkin, Macaulay *actor*
Curry, Tim *actor*
Curtis, Jamie Lee *actress*
Cusack, Joan *actress*
Cusack, John *actor*
Daly, Tyne *actress*
Daniels, Jeff *actor, playwright*
Davis, Geena (Virginia Davis) *actress*
DeGeneres, Ellen *actress, comedienne, talk show host*
Delaney, Kim *actress*
De Niro, Robert *actor, film producer, film director, restaurant owner*
Dennehy, Brian *actor*
Depp, Johnny *actor*
Dern, Bruce MacLeish *actor*
DeVito, Danny Michael *actor, film director*
Diesel, Vin (Mark Vincent) *actor*
Donaldson, Roger *film director, film producer*
Donner, Richard *film director, producer*
Dooley, Paul *actor, writer*
Dorff, Stephen *actor*
Dotrice, Roy Louis *actor*
Dourdan, Gary *actor*
Drescher, Fran *actress*
Dreyfuss, Richard Stephan *actor*
Duchovny, David *actor*
Duke, Patty (Anna Marie Duke) *actress*
Duncan, Michael Clarke *actor*
Duvall, Robert (Robert Selden Duvall) *actor*
Duvall, Shelley *actress*
Eastwood, Clint (Clinton Eastwood Jr.) *actor, film director, film producer*
Eikenberry, Jill *actress*
Elfman, Jenna (Jennifer Mary Butala) *actress*
Elliott, Sam *actor*
Elwes, Cary *actor*
Emanuel, Ari (Ariel Z. Emanuel) *talent agent*
Emmerich, Roland *director, producer, writer*
Epps, Omar *actor*
Eyre, Chris *film director*
Falco, Edie *actress*
Fallon, Jimmy *actor*
Favreau, Jon *actor, film director, film producer*
Fellowes, Julian *actor*
Ferguson, Craig *actor*
Ferrell, Conchata Galen *actress, performing arts educator*
Ferrell, Will (John William Ferrell) *actor*
Fey, Tina *actress*
Filicia, Thom *television personality, interior designer*
Flaum, Marshall Allen *television producer, writer, director*
Flockhart, Calista *actress*
Foch, Nina *actress, creative consultant, film director, educator*
Fonda, Jane *actress*
Forsythe, William *actor*
Fox, Michael J. *actor*
Fox, Vivica *actress*
Foxworth, Robert Heath *actor, film director*
Foxx, Jamie (Eric Bishop) *actor, comedian*
Franken, Al (Alan Stuart Franken) *comedian, writer, actor*
Fraser, Brendan *actor*
Frears, Stephen *film director*
Gandolfini, James *actor*
Garofalo, Janeane *actress, comedienne*
Garr, Teri (Ann) *actress*
Getty, Balthazar *actor*
Gilpin, Peri *actress*
Glover, John *actor*
Glover, Savion *actor, dancer*
Gooding, Cuba, Jr. *actor*
Goodman, John *actor*
Gosnell, Raja *film editor, film director*
Graham, Heather *actress*
Graham, Lauren *actress*
Grant, Hugh *actor*
Grenier, Adrian *actor*
Griffin, Kathy *comedienne, actress*
Griffin, Merv Edward *former entertainer, television producer, entrepreneur*
Griffith, Andy (Andrew Samuel Griffith) *actor*
Grodin, Charles *actor, writer, theater director*
Guest, Christopher *actor, director, screenwriter*
Gugino, Carla *actress*
Gyllenhaal, Jake *actor*
Gyllenhaal, Maggie *actress*
Hackford, Taylor *film director*
Hackman, Gene (Eugene Alden Hackman) *actor*
Hallstrom, Lasse *film director*
Hamilton, Linda *actress*
Hanks, Tom *actor, film producer, film director*
Hannah, Daryl *actress*
Hanson, Curtis *film director, scriptwriter*
Harden, Marcia Gay *actress*
Harmon, Angie (Angie Sehorn) *actress*
Harrelson, Woody *actor*
Harris, Mel (Mary Ellen Harris) *actress*
Harris, Neil Patrick *actor*
Hart, Melissa Joan Catherine *actress*
Hartnett, Josh *actor*
Haskell, Peter Abraham *actor, director*
Hathaway, Anne *actress*
Hawke, Ethan Green *actor*
Hawn, Goldie *actress*
Hayek, Salma *actress*
Haysbert, Dennis *actor*
Heasley, Thomas Allen *composer, musician*
Heaton, Patricia *actress*

Heder, Jon *actor*
Hershey, Barbara (Barbara Herzstein) *actress*
Heston, Charlton (John Charlton Carter) *actor*
Hewitt, Jennifer Love *actress, singer*
Hill, Walter *film director, writer, producer*
Hoffman, Dustin Lee *actor*
Holmes, Katie (Katherine Noelle Holmes) *actress*
Hopkins, Sir Anthony (Philip) *actor*
Hopkins, Stephen *film director, producer*
Hopper, Dennis *actor, writer, photographer, film director*
Howard, Ron *film director*
Howard, Terrence Dashon *actor*
Hughes, John W. *film producer, screenwriter, film director*
Hunt, Bonnie *actress*
Hunt, Helen (Helen Elizabeth Hunt) *actress*
Hunt, Linda *actress*
Hurd, Gale Anne *film producer*
Hurley, Elizabeth *actress, model, film producer*
Hurt, William *actor*
Huston, Anjelica *actress*
Hutton, Timothy *actor*
Idle, Eric *actor, scriptwriter, film producer, lyricist*
Imperioli, Michael *actor*
Jackson, Janet (Janet Damita Jo Jackson) *vocalist, dancer*
Janseen, Famke *actress*
Jenkins, Patty *film director, scriptwriter*
Johansson, Scarlett *actress*
Jolie, Angelina *actress*
Jones, Cherry *actress*
Jonze, Spike *film director*
Jordan, Glenn *film director, television director, theater director*
Jordan, Neil Patrick *film director, writer*
Josephson, Nancy *talent agency executive*
Judd, Ashley *actress*
Keaton, Diane *actress*
Keaton, Michael *actor, comedian*
Keener, Catherine *actress*
Keitel, Harvey *actor*
Keith, David Lemuel *actor*
Kelly, Moira *actress*
Kerns, Joanna de Varona *actress, writer, director*
Khan, Chaka (Yvette Marie Stevens) *singer*
Kidman, Nicole *actress*
Kilmer, Val *actor*
King, Charles *agent*
Kingston, Alex (Alexandra Kingston) *actress*
Klum, Heidi *model, actress*
Knoxville, Johnny (Philip John Clapp) *actor*
Krause, Peter *actor*
Kravitz, Lenny *singer, guitarist*
Kressley, Carson *television personality*
Lahti, Christine *actress*
Lake, Ricki (Ricki Pamela Lake) *talk show host, actress*
Lane, Nathan (Joseph Lane) *actor*
Langella, Frank *actor*
Lansbury, Angela Brigid *actress*
LaPaglia, Anthony *actor*
Law, Jude (David Jude Law) *actor*
Lawrence, Martin *actor, comedian*
Lear, Norman Milton *producer, writer, director*
Leder, Mimi *television director, film director, film producer*
Lee, Ang *film director*
Lee, Jason *actor*
Leguizamó, John *actor, comedian*
Leigh, Jennifer Jason (Jennifer Leigh Morrow) *actress*
Leonard, Robert Sean *actor*
Levant, Brian *film director*
Levinson, Barry L. *film director*
Levy, Eugene *actor, film director, screenwriter*
Lewis, Juliette *actress*
Limato, Edward Frank *agent*
Lindo, Delroy *actor*
Linney, Laura *actress*
Liotta, Ray *actor*
Liu, Lucy *actress*
Lloyd, Christopher *actor*
Lohan, Lindsay *actress*
Lord, Marjorie *actress*
Lovett, Richard *talent agency executive*
Lowe, Rob *actor*
Lucas, Josh (Josh Maurer) *actor*
Mac, Bernie *actor, comedian*
MacLaine, Shirley *actress*
Macy, William H. *actor*
Madsen, Michael *actor*
Maher, Bill *television personality, comedian, television producer*
Malick, Terrence (David Whitney II) *film director*
Malkovich, John *actor*
Malone, Jena *actress*
Mandel, Howie *actor, comedian*
Manheim, Camryn *television and film actress*
Mann, Michael Kenneth *film director, film producer*
Mantello, Joseph *theater director*
Margulies, Julianna *actress*
Marsden, James (James Paul Marsden) *actor*
Marshall, Penny (C. Marshall, Carole Penny Marshall) *director, actress*
Martin, Steve *actor, comedian*
Martinson, Constance Frye *television personality, television producer*
Masterson, Mary Stuart *actress*
Mastrantonio, Mary Elizabeth *actress*
Mathis, Samantha *actress*
Mazar, Debi *actress*
McAdams, Rachel *actress*
McCarthy, Jenny *actress*
McDermott, Dylan *actor*
McGovern, Elizabeth *actress*
Meirelles, Fernando *film director*
Mendes, Eva *actress*
Messing, Debra *actress*
Metcalf, Laurie (Lauren Ophelia Metcalfe) *actress*
Meyer, Breckin *actor*
Milius, John Frederick *film writer, director*
Miller, Bennett *film director*
Miller, Sienna *actress*
Mol, Gretchen *actress*
Molina, Alfred *actor*
Moore, Demi (Demi Guynes, Demetria Gene Guynes) *actress*
Moore, Julianne (Julie Anne Smith) *actress*

Moore, Mandy (Amanda Leigh Moore) *actress, singer*
Moore, Mary Tyler *actress*
Moore, Michael *film director, writer*
Mortensen, Viggo *actor*
Morton, Samantha *actress*
Mullally, Megan *actress*
Mulroney, Dermot *actor*
Muniz, Frankie (Francisco James Muniz IV) *actor*
Murphy, Cillian *actor*
Murray, Bill *actor, writer*
Najimy, Kathy *actress*
Neill, Sam *actor*
Neville, Aaron *musician*
Nicita, Rick *agent*
Nixon, Cynthia *actress*
O'Donnell, Chris *actor*
Olmos, Edward James *actor*
Olyphant, Timothy *actor*
Owen, Clive *actor*
Pacino, Al (Alfredo James Pacino) *actor, film director, film producer*
Palminteri, Chazz *actor*
Paltrow, Gwyneth *actress*
Pantoliano, Joe *actor*
Parker, Alan (William) (Sir Alan Parker) *film director, writer*
Parker, Mary-Louise *actress*
Parker, Sarah Jessica *actress*
Patinkin, Mandy *actor, singer*
Patric, Jason *actor*
Paxton, Bill *actor, film director*
Paymer, David *actor*
Peet, Amanda *actress*
Pepper, Barry *actor*
Perlman, Rhea *actress*
Petersen, Wolfgang *film director*
Phillippe, Ryan *actor*
Piscopo, Joseph Charles *actor*
Pitt, Brad *actor*
Piven, Jeremy *actor*
Platt, Oliver *actor*
Plummer, Christopher (Orme) (Arthur Plummer) *actor*
Polanski, Roman *film director, writer, actor*
Pollack, Sydney *film director*
Pompeo, Ellen *actress*
Portman, Natalie *actress*
Posey, Parker *actress*
Pullman, Bill *actor*
Quaid, Dennis *actor*
Quinn, Aidan *actor*
Rai, Aishwarya *actress*
Reese, Della (Deloreese Patricia Early) *singer, actress*
Reeves, Keanu *actor*
Reiner, Carl *director, actor, writer*
Reiner, Rob *film director, actor*
Reynolds, Kevin *film director, writer*
Rhames, Ving (Irving) *actor*
Rhys-Meyers, Jonathan *actor*
Ricci, Christina *actress*
Richardson, Patricia *actress*
Riley, Jack *actor, writer*
Ringwald, Molly *actress*
Rivers, Joan *entertainer*
Roberts, Julia Fiona *actress*
Rodriguez, Robert *filmmaker*
Rogers, Mimi *actress*
Romero, George A. *film director*
Rossellini, Isabella *actress, model*
Ruffalo, Mark *actor*
Rush, Geoffrey *actor*
Russell, Keri *actress*
Russell, Kurt Von Vogel *actor*
Russo, Anthony *film director*
Russo, Joe *film director*
Ryan, Meg (Margaret Mary Emily Ann Hyra) *actress, film producer*
Sagal, Katey *actress*
Saget, Bob *actor, comedian, writer, television director*
Samberg, Andy *actor*
Sambery, Andy *actor*
Sandrich, Jay H. *television director*
Sarsgaard, Peter *actor*
Sayles, John Thomas *film director, writer, actor*
Scacchi, Greta *actress*
Schneider, Rob *actor*
Schroder, Rick *actor*
Scott, Ridley *film director*
Scott-Thomas, Kristin *actress*
Sedgwick, Kyra *actress*
Sellecca, Connie *actress*
Sevigny, Chloë *actress*
Sewell, Rufus *actor*
Seymour, Jane *actress*
Shadyac, Thomas *film director, producer*
Shalhoub, Tony *actor, television producer*
Shatner, William *actor*
Short, Martin *actor, comedian, film critic*
Shue, Elisabeth *actress*
Shuler Donner, Lauren *film producer*
Shyamalan, M. Night (Manoj Nelliyattu Shyamalan) *film director*
Silverman, Jonathan *actor*
Silverman, Sarah *actress, comedian, writer*
Simmons, Gene (Chaim Witz, Gene Klein) *musician*
Simpson, Jessica Ann *vocalist, actress*
Simpson, Mike *talent agent*
Singer, Bryan *film producer, director, writer, actor*
Sinise, Gary *actor*
Skerritt, Tom *actor*
Slater, Christian *actor*
Smith, Jaclyn *actress*
Sommers, Stephen *film director, scriptwriter, film producer*
Sonnenfeld, Barry *director, cinematographer*
Sorvino, Mira *actress*
Sorvino, Paul *actor*
Spacek, Sissy (Mary Elizabeth Spacek) *actress*
Spader, James *actor*
Spelling, Tori (Victoria Davey Spelling) *actress*
Spheeris, Penelope *film director*
Spielberg, Steven (Steven Allan Spielberg) *film director, film producer*
Stahl, Nick *actor*
Stamos, John *actor*
Statham, Jason *actor*
Steenburgen, Mary *actress*

Stern, Sandor *film director, writer*
Stiers, David Ogden *actor, conductor*
Stiles, Julia *actress*
Stoltz, Eric *actor*
Streep, Meryl (Mary Louise Streep) *actress*
Sutherland, Donald *actor*
Sutherland, Kiefer *actor*
Suvari, Mena *actress*
Swank, Hilary Ann *actress*
Swayze, Patrick *actor, dancer*
Swofford, Beth *agent*
Sykes, Wanda *comedienne, actress*
Tamblyn, Amber Rose *actress*
Tambor, Jeffrey *actor, theater director, educator*
Taylor, Christine *actress*
Taylor, Lili *actress*
Theron, Charlize *actress*
Thompson, Emma *actress*
Thompson, Larry Angelo *film and television producer, lawyer, motivational speaker, writer*
Thurman, Uma Karuna *actress*
Tierney, Maura *actress*
Tilly, Jennifer *actress*
Tom, Lauren *actress, singer*
Tomei, Marisa *actress*
Travolta, John *actor*
Tripplehorn, Jeanne *actress*
Tucci, Stanley *actor*
Turlington, Christy *model*
Turner, Kathleen *actress*
Turturro, Nicholas *actor*
Tyler, Liv *actress*
Underwood, Blair *actor, television producer*
Underwood, Ronald Brian *director, producer*
Van Dyke, Dick *actor, comedian*
Van Zandt, Steven *actor, musician, radio personality*
Vardalos, Nia *actress, screenwriter*
Vaughn, Vince *actor*
Verhoeven, Paul *film director*
Visnjic, Goran *actor*
Wachowski, Andy *film director*
Wachowski, Larry *film director*
Wagner, Lindsay Jean *actress*
Ward, Sela *actress*
Waters, John *film director, writer, actor*
Watts, Naomi *actress*
Wayans, Marlon *actor, film producer, writer*
Wayans, Shawn *actor, film producer, writer*
Weaver, Sigourney (Susan Alexandra Weaver) *actress*
Weir, Peter Lindsay *film director*
Weisz, Rachel *actress*
Whaley, Frank *actor*
White, Betty *actress, comedienne*
White, Meg (Megan Martha White) *musician, vocalist*
Whitford, Bradley *actor*
Wiatt, James Anthony *theatrical agency executive*
Wilkinson, Tom *actor*
Williams, Michelle *actress*
Willis, Walter Bruce (Bruce Willis) *actor, vocalist*
Wilson, Luke *actor*
Wilson, Owen *actor*
Winger, Debra *actress*
Winkler, Henry Franklin *actor, film producer, director*
Winters, Dean *actor*
Wirtschafter, David *talent agency executive*
Witherspoon, Reese (Laura Jean Reese Witherspoon) *actress*
Wood, Elijah *actor*
Woods, James *actor*
Wright, Jeffrey *actor*
Wright Penn, Robin *actress*
Wu, Yusen (John Woo) *film director*
Zane, Billy *actor*
Zanuck, Lili Fini *film director, producer*
Zellweger, Renee *actress*

**Bonita**

Ling, Jahja Wang-Chieh *conductor*

**Brentwood**

Semtner, Emma Margarette *music educator*

**Brisbane**

Baadh, Valerie *choreographer, movement educator, theater producer, production designer*

**Burbank**

Baker, Rick *make-up artist*
Bender, Jack *television producer, television director, actor*
Berman, Bruce *entertainment company executive, television producer*
Big Boy, (Kurt Alexander) *radio personality, actor*
Bloomberg, Stu *television producer*
Branch, Michelle *musician*
Bublé, Michael *singer*
Burk, Bryan *television producer*
Bush, Billy *television personality*
Cher, (Cherilyn Sarkisian) *singer, actress*
Clapton, Eric *musician*
Clark, Dick *performer, producer*
Connelly, Mary *television producer*
Crane, David *producer*
de Ravin, Emilie *actress*
Eubanks, Kevin *jazz guitarist*
Feltenstein, George *film producer, entertainment company executive*
Fishburne, Laurence III *actor*
Fogerty, John Cameron *musician, composer*
Franco, James *actor*
Garcia, Jorge *actor*
Glavin, Edward P. *television producer*
Handel, William Wolf *radio personality*
Henley, Don *singer, drummer, songwriter*
Higgins, Jean *television producer*
Howard, James Newton *composer*
Jovovich, Milla (Natasha Militza Jovovich) *model, actress*
Kilgariff, Karen *television producer*
Lang, K. D. (Katherine Dawn Lang) *country music singer, composer*
Lanois, Daniel *record producer, musician, popular*
Lassner, Andy *television producer*
Lindelof, Damon *television producer, scriptwriter*
McGraw, Tim *country music singer*
Mc Vie, Christine Perfect *musician*
McVie, John *musician*

Mitchell, Joni (Roberta Joan Anderson) *singer, songwriter*
Murphy, Michael George *actor*
Navarro, Dave (David Michael Navarro) *musician, recording artist*
Neill, Ve *make-up artist*
O'Dell, Nancy *television personality*
O'Quinn, Terry (Terrance Quinn) *actor*
Petty, Tom (Thomas Earl Petty) *musician, composer*
Piddock, James Anthony *actor*
Remini, Leah *actress*
Renfroe, Owen *television director*
Rhimes, Shonda *producer, director, writer*
Rimes, LeAnn *country music singer*
Rivera, Miluka *actress, journalist, poet*
Rzeznik, Johnny *singer, musician*
Schiff, Richard *actor*
Schumacher, Joel *film director, scriptwriter*
Shore, Howard Leslie *composer*
Silver, Joel *film producer*
Stewart, Rod (Roderick David Stewart) *singer*
Watros, Cynthia *actress*
Weiskopf, Wanda *mezzo soprano, writer, poet*
Wells, John Marcum *producer, writer*
Wonder, Stevie (Steveland Hardaway Judkins, Stevland Morris) *musician*
Young, Neil *musician, songwriter*
Zimmer, Hans Florian *composer*

**Calabasas**

Levy, Dena Christine *television producer, director*
Phillips, Teddy Steve, Sr. *conductor, saxophone player, production company executive*

**Canoga Park**

Taesch, Richard Edmond *music educator*

**Carlsbad**

Missett, Judi Sheppard *dancer, jazzercise company executive*

**Carmel**

Gordon, David Jamieson *tenor*

**Castro Valley**

West, Doyle Thomas *retired music educator*

**Chatsworth**

Cassar, Jon Francis *television director, film director*

**Claremont**

Cramer, Alfred William *musician, educator*
Huang, Hao H. *music educator, department chairman*

**Clovis**

Badgley, Clifford W. *music educator*
Kawashima, Hope Nozomi *musician*
van der Paardt, Tamara Ann *music educator*

**Concord**

Accatino, Steven C. *instrumental music educator, orchestra conductor*
Blair, Virginia Devoto *music educator*

**Corona Del Mar**

Morisseau, Nan Kruger *television personality*

**Costa Mesa**

Chambers-Belida, Candace R. *radio personality, writer, television producer, educator*
Mumford, Lawrence R. *composer, educator*

**Covina**

Wilkerson, Andrea Leta *musician, educator*

**Culver City**

Brooks, James L. *film producer, director*
Brooks, Mel *film producer, actor, film director, scriptwriter*
Chaffin, Cean *producer*
Evans, Linda (Linda Evanstad) *actress*
Finkelman Cox, Penney *film producer*
Fisher, Lucy *film producer*
Hall, Barbara *television producer*
James, Kevin III *actor*
Kaufman, Richard Stuart *conductor*
Marshall, Garry K. (Garry Kent Marsciarelli) *film producer, director, writer*
Sakai, Richard *motion picture and television executive, producer*
Shamberg, Michael *film producer*
Thomas, Marlo (Margaret Julia Thomas) *actress*
Tisch, Steven Elliot *television and movie producer*
Trebek, Alex *television game show host*
Wick, Douglas *producer*
Ziskin, Laura *television producer, film producer*

**Davis**

Bauer, Ross *composer, music educator*

**Diamond Bar**

Snoop Dogg, (Calvin Broadus) *vocalist, actor*

**Downey**

Achon, Raquel Andrea *music educator, consultant*

**El Centro**

Gaede, Robert Matthew *music educator*

**El Cerrito**

Ma, L. Eve Armentrout *television producer, educator*
Tayler, David S. *musician*

**El Monte**

Mestas, Luis Herrera *theater educator, dancer*

**Emeryville**

Bird, Brad *film director, writer, animator*

**Encinitas**

Litvin, Inessa Elizabeth *piano educator*

**Encino**

Bright, Kevin S. *producer*
Ingels, Marty *agent, broadcast executive*
Shire, David Lee *composer*

Taylor, Renee *actress, writer*
Westmore, Michael George *make-up artist, writer*
Wilder, Gene *actor, film director, writer*

**Escondido**
Rockwell, Elizabeth Goode *dance company director, consultant, educator*

**Eureka**
Cox, Christopher Mark *music educator*

**Fort Bragg**
Gjerde, Rosalie Carolyn *music educator, conductor*

**Fortuna**
Souza, Jonathan Raymond *music educator, conductor*

**Fountain Valley**
Treadway-Dillmon, Linda Lee *actress, stuntwoman, dancer, dispatcher*

**Fremont**
Yamamoto, Masako *music educator*

**Fresno**
Kristensen, Allan Erik *music educator*

**Fullerton**
Frost, Jacqueline Beth *cinematographer, educator*
Wiley, David Cole *television producer*

**Glendale**
Gibbons, Leeza *television and radio talk show host, entertainment reporter*
O'Day, Anita Belle Colton *entertainer, musician, vocalist*
Robinson, Smokey (William Robinson) *singer, composer*
Sotelo, Eduardo (El Piolín) *radio personality*
Sprosty, Joseph Patrick *film producer, writer, motion picture weapons specialist*
Thallander, Mark Alan *music educator*

**Glendora**
Prukcsatonkul, Kamol *music educator*

**Granada Hills**
Paton, John Glenn *voice educator*

**Grass Valley**
Lynn, David Lawrence *music educator*

**Hat Creek**
Shepard, David Haspel *film restoration specialist*

**Highland**
Gordon, Stewart Lynell *musician, educator*

**Hollywood**
Adams, William James, Jr., (Will.i.am) *rap artist*
Berryman, Guy *musician*
Buckland, Jon *musician*
Calva, Robert Baraquiel *music educator*
Cannell, Stephen Joseph *television writer, producer, director, actor*
Champion, Will *musician*
Fergie, (Stacy Ann Ferguson) *singer*
Gomez, Jaime Luis (Taboo) *rap artist*
Greenwood, Jonathan Richard Guy (Jonny Greenwood) *musician*
Helm, Levon *musician, actor*
LaMontaine, John M. *composer*
Lindo, Allen Pineda (Apl.de.ap) *rap artist*
Lynne, Shelby (Shelby Lynn Moorer) *country singer*
Martin, Chris *vocalist*
Miles, Joanna *actress, playwright, director*
Minnelli, Liza *singer, actress*
Warren, Diane *lyricist*
Yorke, Thomas Edward *musician, vocalist*

**Huntington Beach**
Amen, Thomas Eugene, II, *theater director, educator*
Pieper, Michael Joseph *television producer, actor, talk show host*

**Irvine**
Avzaradel, Bob *music educator*
McKayle, Donald Cohen *choreographer, director, writer, dance educator*
Ruyter, Nancy Lee Chalfa *dance educator*

**Kentfield**
Halprin, Anna Schuman (Mrs. Lawrence Halprin) *dancer*

**La Crescenta**
Purcell, Lee (Lee Jeune Williams) *actress, film producer*

**La Habra Heights**
Agajanian, Gilda *pianist*

**La Jolla**
Reynolds, Roger Lee *composer, educator*

**La Palma**
Levy, Elaine Ann *music educator*

**La Quinta**
Hull, Kathryn Blomquist *music educator, composer, consultant*
Knoblauch, Mary Reilly (Mary Louise Reilly) *retired music educator, writer*

**La Verne**
Kent, Steven Kyle *theater director, educator*

**Laguna Beach**
Englund, Robert *actor, director, producer*

**Laguna Woods**
McClure, Hal H. *film producer*

**Lake Forest**
Blackley, Daniel John *theater educator, theater director*

**Lakeside**
Seaberg, Eric Dayle *audio engineer*

**Lancaster**
Bell, Gary Lynn *owner production company, video and audio producer*
Wooster, Larry D. *music educator*

**Livermore**
Darter, Thomas Eugene, Jr. *composer, musician, writer*

**Lodi**
Tan, Robert C. *music educator*

**Lompoc**
Belisle-Foreman, Karen *music educator*
Lyra, Jon Robert *music educator, artist*

**Long Beach**
Engle, Robert Irwin *music educator, translator*

**Los Altos**
Davies, Paul Anthony *composer, music educator*

**Los Altos Hills**
Archibeque, Charlene Paullin *retired music educator*

**Los Angeles**
Archer, Anne *actress*
Arkin, Adam *actor*
Arnett, Will *actor*
Arquette, Rosanna (Rosanna Lauren Arquette) *actress*
Bacharach, Burt *composer, conductor*
Bain, Conrad Stafford *actor*
Ballard, Glen *composer*
Banks, Tyra (Tyra Lynne Banks) *retired model, television personality*
Bardem, Javier *actor*
Barker, Robert William (Bob Barker) *television personality*
Beck, (Beck Hansen) *musician, songwriter*
Begley, Ed, Jr. *actor*
Bell, Lee Phillip *television personality, television producer*
Bell, William J., Jr. *television producer*
Benatar, Pat (Pat Andrzejewski) *rock singer*
Bergman, Marilyn Keith *lyricist, writer*
Berman, Richard Keith *television producer, film producer*
Biggs, Jason *actor*
Bing, Steve *film producer*
Black, Lewis *comedian, actor*
Bloom, Claire *actress*
Bologna, Joseph *actor*
Bosley, Tom *actor*
Brolin, James (James Brunderlin) *actor*
Brown, Carol *make-up artist*
Brown, Jason Robert *composer, arranger*
Burnett, T-Bone (Henry John Burnett) *music producer, musician*
Burrows, James *television and motion picture director, producer*
Burton, Brian Joseph (Danger Mouse) *sound recording engineer, musician*
Burton, Tim (Timothy William Burton) *film director*
Buzzi, Ruth *comedienne*
Caine, Michael *actor*
Campbell, Glen *singer, entertainer*
Campbell, Martin *film director, producer, writer*
Carlin, George Denis *comedian, actor*
Carrillo, Elpidia *actress*
Cassavetes, Nick *film director, actor*
Catanzarite, David M. *theater educator, director*
Cates, Gilbert *television producer, theater director, film producer*
Cee-Lo, (Thomas DeCarlo Callaway) *singer*
Champlin, Charles Davenport *television personality, critic, writer*
Chapman, Carolyn *broadcasting director*
Chiklis, Michael *actor*
Chow, Stephen (Sing-Chi Chow) *actor*
Cohen, Aryell *music educator*
Combs, Holly Marie *actress*
Cooper, Chris *actor*
Corman, Roger William *film director*
Coston, Suzanne *television producer*
Cox, Brian *actor*
Crockett, Donald Harold *composer, music educator*
D'Accone, Frank Anthony *music educator*
Dale, Jim *actor*
Davidson, Gordon *theater producer, theater director*
Davis, John A. *film producer*
Dawson, Rosario *actress, singer*
Dee, Ruby (Ruby Dee Davis) *actress, writer, film director*
Del Toro, Benicio *actor*
Dempsey, Patrick *actor*
Diehl, Dolores *performing company executive*
Donahue, Ann M. *television producer*
Dr. Dre, (Andre Young) *rapper, record producer*
Duke, Margaret Joyce *sound recordist, broadcast engineer*
DuMont, James Kelton, Jr. *actor, theater producer*
Dunst, Kirsten *actress*
Duritz, Adam *musician*
Eckhart, Aaron *actor*
Edwards, Blake *film director*
Eliel, Ruth Louise *performing company executive*
Elrod, Lu *retired music educator, actress*
Elswit, Robert *cinematographer*
Engvall, Bill *comedian, actor*
Fairchild, Morgan (Patsy McClenny) *actress*
Farrell, Joseph *film producer, financial analyst, film company executive, sculptor, writer*
Feinstein, Michael Jay *singer, pianist, musicologist, educator*
Fincher, David *film director, film producer*
Flanagan, Fionnula Manon *actress, writer, theater director*
Fleischmann, Ernest Martin *performing arts executive, consultant*
Foster, Sutton *actress*
Franz, Dennis *actor*
Garrett, Spencer *actor, writer, director*

Gifford, Kathie Lee *television personality, vocalist*
Gondry, Michel *film director*
Gordon, Allen Barry *musician, composer*
Gosling, Ryan (Ryan Thomas Gosling) *actor*
Grammer, Kelsey *actor*
Greenberg, Barry Michael *talent executive*
Gronnier, Henry Maurice *violinist, educator*
Hancock, Herbert Jeffrey (Herbie Hancock) *composer, pianist, publisher*
Hart, Mary *television talk show host*
Hayes, Reggie *actor*
Heigl, Katherine Marie *actress*
Helms, Ed *comedian, actor*
Henderson, Florence *actress, singer*
Henkel, Kathy *composer*
Hirabayashi, Keith Cooke *actor, martial arts instructor*
Hoff, Christian *actor*
Hoffman, Philip Seymour *actor*
Horovitz, Adam (King Adrock) *recording artist*
Hurwitz, Mitchell *television producer, writer*
Ice-T, (Tracy Marrow) *rap artist, actor*
Ireland, Kathy *actress, apparel designer*
Jagger, Sir Mick (Michael Philip Jagger) *singer, musician*
Johnson, Charles Floyd *television executive, producer*
Jones, Sir Tom (Thomas Jones Woodward) *singer*
Keith, David *symphony orchestra conductor*
Kellerman, Sally Claire *actress*
Kelley, David E. *producer, writer*
Kelley, Malcolm David *actor*
Kimmel, Jimmy (James Christian Kimmel) *television personality*
Klauss, Kenneth Karl *composer, music educator*
Kyles, Cedric Antonio (Cedric the Entertainer) *comedian, actor*
Landers, Audrey *actress, singer*
Larry the Cable Guy, (Daniel Lawrence Whitney) *comedian, radio personality*
LeBeau, Mary Delle *dancer, educator, writer*
Ledger, Heath *actor*
Leeves, Jane *actress*
Lennon, Sean Taro Ono *musician*
Lightfoot, Peter *music educator, baritone*
Linkletter, Arthur Gordon *radio and television broadcaster*
London, Andrew Barry *film editor*
Lopez, George *actor, comedian*
Lunden, Joan *television personality*
MacLachlan, Kyle *actor*
Maguire, Tobey (Tobias Vincent Maguire) *actor*
Malden, Karl (Malden Sekulovich) *actor*
Malone, Nancy *actress*
McConaughey, Matthew *actor*
McCormick, Carolyn *actress*
McQueen, Justice Ellis (L. Q. Jones) *actor, television director*
McRaney, Gerald *actor*
Milchan, Arnon *film producer*
Moore, Shemar *actor*
Moreno, Rita (Rosita Dolores Alverio) *actress*
Morissette, Alanis Nadine *singer*
Morton, Joe *actor*
Mueller, Carl Richard *theater arts educator, author*
Muldaur, Diana Charlton *actress*
Newhart, Bob (George Robert Newhart) *entertainer*
Newman, Randy *singer, songwriter, musician*
Nicholson, Jack *actor*
Noble, James Wilkes *actor*
Nyman, Michael Lawrence *composer*
O'Brien, Pat *television personality*
Ohlmeyer, Donald Winfred, Jr. *film and television producer*
Oldham, Granville Murl, Jr. *conductor, educator*
Oldman, Gary *actor*
Olsen, Ashley Fuller *actress*
Olsen, Mary-Kate *actress*
Pare, Michael *actor, singer*
Peña, Elizabeth *actress*
Penn, Sean *actor*
Phillips, Todd *film director, film producer*
Phoenix, Joaquin Raphael *actor*
Pritzker, Jean *film producer*
Rando, John *theater director*
Reynolds, Burt *actor, film director*
Richmond, Rocsan *television executive producer, small business owner*
Rickles, Donald Jay *comedian, actor*
Rodriguez, Daniel *tenor, former protective services official*
Rogers, Wayne M. *actor, investor, investment strategist, businessman*
Rohrer, Susan Earley *film producer, film director, scriptwriter*
Rosenberg, Alan *actors guild executive*
Ross, Marion *actress*
Roth, Tim *actor*
Rowell, Victoria *actress*
Rubin, Stanley Creamer *television producer, film producer*
Ruskin, Joseph Richard *actor, director*
Russo, Rene *actress*
Samaha, Elie *producer, film company executive, business owner*
San Giacomo, Laura *actress*
Santaolalla, Gustavo *musician, composer, record producer*
Sargent, Joseph Daniel *motion picture and television director*
Sawyer, Toni *actress*
Schott, Robert W. (Bob Schott) *film producer, actor, film director*
Schulman, Cathy *film producer*
Scott, Tony *film director*
Selleck, Tom *actor*
Shay, Anthony Victor *choreographer, dance historian*
Sheedy, Ally (Alexandra Elizabeth Sheedy) *actress*
Smiley, Tavis *radio talk show host*
Smits, Jimmy *actor*
Stamp, Terence Henry *actor*
Stanton, Harry Dean *actor*
Stapleton, Jean (Jeanne Murray) *actress*
Stevenson, Robert Murrell *music educator*
Streisand, Barbra Joan *singer, actress, film director*
Takei, George Hosato *actor*

Thomas, John David *composer, musician, compact disc artist, photographer, music and arts business owner*
Tomlin, Lily *actress*
Trembly, Dennis Michael *musician*
Ullman, Tracey *actress, singer*
Valentine, Dean *film producer*
Waits, Thomas Alan *composer, actor, singer*
Washington, Isaiah *actor*
Waterston, Samuel Atkinson *actor*
Watson, Emily *actress*
Whitaker, Forest *actor, film producer, director*
Winters, Barbara Jo *musician*
Wyle, Noah *actor*
Yoakam, Dwight *country western musician*
York, Michael (Michael York-Johnson) *actor*
Zemeckis, Robert L. *film director*
Ziesmer, Jerry H. *film director*

**Los Osos**
Kreitzer, Jacalyn Bower *vocalist, voice educator*

**Malibu**
Almond, Paul *film director, film producer, scriptwriter, writer*
Bush, Kristian *musician*
Emelio, M. Melanie *music educator, singer*
Gail, Maxwell Trowbridge, Jr. *actor, musician*
Harris, Ed (Edward Allen Harris) *actor*
Keach, Stacy, Jr. *actor, theater director, theater producer, musician, composer*
LaChanze, (R. LaChanze Sapp, Rhonda Sapp) *actress*
Nettles, Jennifer *singer*
Shapiro, Alex *composer*
Vereen, Ben *actor, singer, dancer*

**Manteca**
Kanary, Regina *music educator*

**Marina Del Rey**
Hasselhoff, David *actor*

**Martinez**
George, Julianne Mary *music educator, conductor*

**Menlo Park**
Baez, Joan Chandos *vocalist*

**Mill Valley**
Padula, Fred David *filmmaker*

**Modesto**
Jones, Mary Cunningham *music educator*
Rogers, Wanda Faye *vocalist*

**Monrovia**
Brown, Gwendolyn Williams *music educator*

**Moorpark**
Kessner, Dolly Eugenio *music educator, concert pianist*

**Mountain View**
Isaacs, Nicholas Stephen *music educator, director*

**Murrieta**
Cloud, Mark F. *film director, film editor, film producer, musician*

**Nevada City**
Clausen, Jeanne Lorraine *musician*
Hersh, Howard Douglas *composer, conductor, writer*

**Newport Beach**
Landau, Martin *actor*
Steinberg, Leigh William *sports agent*

**North Hollywood**
Cottrell, David Milton *sound recording engineer, producer, singer, songwriter*
Fanning, Dakota *actress*
Holmes, Michael *performing company executive, performing arts educator*
McMartin, John *actor*
Meat Loaf, (Marvin Lee Aday) *popular musician, actor*
Newton-John, Olivia *singer, actress*
Reynolds, Debbie (Mary Frances Reynolds) *actress*
Smothers, Tom *actor, singer*
Stone, Sharon *actress*
Thomas, Tony *producer*
Toplitt, Gloria H. *music educator, actress, vocalist*
Toussieng, Yolanda *make-up artist*

**Northridge**
Cartwright, Nancy *actress, television producer*
Loudon, Craig Michael *video specialist*

**Oakland**
DeFazio, Lynette Stevens *dancer, educator, choreographer, violinist, actress*
Glover, Danny *actor*
Lake, Suzanne *singer, music educator*
Zschau, Marilyn *singer*

**Oceanside**
Swoger, James Wesley *magician*

**Ojai**
Paxton, Glenn Gilbert *composer*

**Orange**
Atherton, Peter L. *music educator, singer*
Matthews, Joseph Virgil *musician, music educator*

**Oxnard**
Druckman, Joel Isadore *musician, educator*

**Pacific Palisades**
Ritter, Jason *actor*

**Pacifica**
Latham, Benjamin Erwin *music educator*

**Palm Springs**
Dean, Mary Young *musician*

## Palo Alto
Lo, Yee On *composer*

## Palos Verdes Estates
Hayter, Karyn Leanne *theater educator*

## Palos Verdes Peninsula
Julien, Gail Leslie *model, public relations professional*

## Pasadena
Halsted, Margo *music educator, carillonneur*
Horak, Jan-Christopher *filmmaker, educator, curator*
Karlin, Jan M. *violinist, performing company executive*
Menefee, John William III *cinematographer, film producer*

## Petaluma
Bailey, Preston Edward *music educator*
Klemenok, Kevin John *music educator*

## Port Hueneme
Schneider, Arthur Paul *retired videotape and film editor, author*

## Redondo Beach
Richards, Denise *actress*

## Redwood City
Hoy, Linda Jo *theater educator, actress*

## Reedley
Walter, Burl Leroy, Jr. *retired music educator*

## Reseda
Wagner, Robert *actor*

## Sacramento
Mazzaferro, James Joseph *music educator*
McCann, Kim Lou M. *theater educator, director*
Nice, Carter *conductor*
Piper, Jami Kathleen *music educator, composer, musician*
Rainwater, Eric *composer, music educator*
Welter, Paula Joy *singer, songwriter*
Wilmer, Robin Louise *music educator*

## Salinas
Rosen, Jacqueline I. *musician, educator*

## San Diego
Adler, Christopher Alan *composer, educator*
Bates-Romeo, Delores Alvenia *music educator, consultant*
Campbell, Ian David *opera company director*
Crill, Alice Eileen *music educator*
Crump-Pace, Jacqueline Anita *music educator*
Flettner, Marianne *opera administrator*
Herriman, Darleen Ann *music educator*
O'Brien, Jack George *artistic director*
Overton, Marcus Lee *performing arts association administrator, actor, writer*
Pagan, Keith Areatus *music educator, academic administrator*
Payne, September Anne *music educator*
Pfiffner, Patrick Meehan *musician, educator*
Stein, Franklin Joseph *music educator*
Ward-Steinman, David *composer, music educator, pianist*

## San Francisco
Anastacia, (Anastacia Lyn Newkirk) *singer*
Caniparoli, Val William *choreographer, dancer*
Cisneros, Evelyn *dancer*
Etheridge, Melissa Lou *singer, lyricist*
Gockley, David (Richard David Gockley) *opera director*
Gregory, Sara Susan (Sudie) *musician, singer, lyricist, poet, recording industry executive, sound recording engineer, archivist*
Griggs, Lewis Brown *executive producer, speaker, trainer*
Hastings, Edward Walton *theater director*
Jenkins, Margaret Ludmilla *choreographer, dancer*
Jolly, Todd B. *music educator, minister*
Katz, Jeff *television personality*
Lau, Jenny Kwok Wah *theater educator, consultant, film educator, consultant*
LeBlanc, Tina *dancer*
Lee, Iara *filmmaker*
Maffre, Muriel *ballet dancer*
McGuire, Kathleen Alison *conductor*
Mohli, David M. *music educator, writer*
Muren, Dennis E. *special effects expert*
Osborne, Donald Eugene *performing company executive*
Owens, Ronald Stephen (Ronn Owens) *radio talk show host*
Perloff, Carey *performing company executive, theater director, playwright*
Philipps, Kinga (Szpakiewicz) *TV show host*
Pierson, Jay Arthur *music educator*
Rosenberg, Betsy *radio personality, environmentalist*
Rosenberg, Pamela *opera director, conductor*
Runnicles, Donald *conductor*
Shorenstein Hays, Carole *theater producer*
Straw, Lee *music educator, actor*
Tomasson, Helgi *dancer, choreographer, dance company executive*
Van Dyck, Wendy *dancer*
Wang, Wayne *film director*
Williamson, Laird *theater director, actor*

## San Jose
Brooks, Allison Ruth *music educator*
Carstens, Marilynn *freelance/self-employed music educator*
Collins, Alison *opera singer, music educator*
Dalis, Irene *mezzo soprano, performing arts association administrator*
Nahat, Dennis F. *performing company executive, choreographer*
Near, Timothy *theater director*
Sultanov, Namig, 2d Baronet, *musician, music educator*

## San Juan Bautista
Wolfe, Michael Bramson *film producer, writer*

## San Marcos
Houk, Benjamin Noah *performing company executive, choreographer*

## San Mateo
Burton, Al *television producer, television director, writer*
Davis, Troy Edward *music educator*

## San Rafael
Brubeck, David Warren *musician*
Lesh, Philip Chapman *musician, composer*
Lucas, George Walton, Jr. *film director, film producer, scriptwriter*
Marsh, Marian E. *voice educator*
Santana, Carlos *guitarist*

## San Ramon
Harris, Philip III *movie theater executive, lawyer*

## Santa Ana
Donchey, Sheryl Diane *theater educator, department chairman*
Payne, Steven M. *musician, director*

## Santa Barbara
Ben-Dor, Gisselle *conductor, musician*
Brodhead, James E(aston) *actor, writer*
Feigin, Joel *composer, educator*
Horne, Marilyn Berneice *mezzo-soprano*
Sebastian, Suzie *television producer*

## Santa Clara
Cachopo, Patricia Ann *music educator*

## Santa Clarita
Feldman Nebenzahl, Bernardo *composer, educator*
Plew, Paul Timothy *music educator, dean*

## Santa Cruz
Carson, Benjamin Leeds *composer, educator*
Martinez, Alma R. *actress, theater director, educator*
Winston, George *solo pianist, guitarist, harmonica player*

## Santa Monica
Adams, Ryan (David Ryan Adams) *musician*
Almqvist, Pelle *singer*
Angel, Steven *musician*
Apple, Fiona (Fiona Apple Maggart) *singer, songwriter*
Benjamin, Stuart *film producer*
Bruckheimer, Jerry *producer*
Burrell, Orville Richard (Shaggy) *popular musician*
Cameron, James *film director, screenwriter, producer*
Carrabba, Christopher Ender *singer*
Curran, Leigh *actress, playwright*
Eminem, (Marshall Mathers III) *rap artist*
Eve, (Eve Jihan Jeffers) *rap artist, actress*
Frot-Coutaz, Cecile *television producer*
Grace, Maggie *actress*
Hannigan, Alyson *actress*
Hu, Kelly *actress*
Jewison, Norman Frederick *film producer, director*
Kanin, Josh David *film studies educator*
Katina, Elena Sergejevna *singer*
Kennedy, Kathleen *film producer*
Leaf, Paul *film producer, writer*
Li, Jet (Li Lian Jie, Lei Lin-Git) *actor*
Lohner, Henning *composer, filmmaker*
Louis-Dreyfus, Julia *actress*
Marshall, Frank W. *film producer, director*
McMahon, Julian *actor*
Minghella, Anthony *film director, screenwriter*
Peña, Michael Anthony *actor*
Redford, Robert (Charles Robert Redford) *actor, film director*
Reznor, Trent *musician*
Roberts, Tony (David Anthony Roberts) *actor*
Simpson, India.Arie *musician*
Smith, Anna Deavere *actress, educator, playwright*
Stewart, Patrick *actor*
Stone, Oliver *film director, film producer, scriptwriter*
Summer, Donna (La Donna Adrian Gaines) *singer, songwriter, actress*
Suschitzky, Peter *cinematographer*
The Edge, (David Howell Evans) *musician*
Watanabe, Ken *actor*
Watson, Dee (Arthel Lane Watson) *vocalist, guitarist, banjoist, recording artist*

## Sherman Oaks
Bakula, Scott *actor*
Blair, Linda Denise *actress*
Clark, Susan (Nora Goulding) *actress*
Elfman, Danny *composer*
Gibbs, Antony (Tony Gibbs) *film editor*
Heffner, Daniel Jason *film producer*
Jordan, Bonita Adele *television producer*
Karras, Alex *actor, retired professional football player*
Norwood, Brandy Rayana (Brandy) *singer, actress*
Sabella, Ernie *actor*
Schlessinger, Laura *radio talk show host*
Taylor, Elizabeth (Dame Elizabeth Rosemond Taylor) *actress*

## South Lake Tahoe
Williams, Mark Didrik *music educator, composer*

## Stanford
Cohen, Albert *musician, educator*

## Stevenson Ranch
Krainin, Julian Arthur *film director, film producer, cinematographer, writer*

## Stockton
Wilcox, Helena Marguerita (Rita) *music educator*

## Studio City
Basinger, Kim (Kimila Ann Basinger) *actress*
Boyett, Joan Reynolds *performing company executive*
Devane, William *actor*

## San Marcos

Gallardo, Sandra Silvana *television producer, actress*
Grace, Topher *actor*
Kenney, H. Wesley, Jr., (Harry Wesley Kenney Jr.) *television producer, television director*
King, Carole (Carole Klein) *lyricist, singer*
Najee, (Jerome Najee Rasheed) *musician*
Rogers, Suzanne C. *actress*
Sinbad, (David Adkins) *actor, comedian*
Steinberg, Roy Bennett *television producer, director, educator*
Werner, Tom *television producer, professional baseball team executive*

## Sunnyvale
Garner, Shirley Imogene *retired music educator*
Lanaro, Clara Marrama *music educator, writer*

## Sylmar
Foster, Dudley Edwards, Jr. *musician, educator*

## Tarzana
Richman, Peter Mark *actor, painter, film producer*

## Temecula
Ojeda, Nelson A., II, *musician*

## Templeton
Girolo, Nella Sue *retired voice educator*

## Thousand Oaks
Loren, Sophia *actress*
Rooney, Mickey (Joe Yule Jr.) *actor*
Sloane, J.P. *television producer, theologian, entertainer, writer*

## Toluca Lake
Beal, John Everett *composer, conductor*
Morton, Hugh Wesley *television producer, television director*

## Tracy
Hammer, (Stanley Kirk Burrell) *musician*

## Turlock
Sutherland, Andrew C. *actor, educator*

## Ukiah
Lind, Leslie J. *music educator*

## Universal City
Bowen, Andrea *actress*
Chavira, Ricardo Antonio *actor*
Cross, Marcia *actress*
Denton, James *actor*
Hatcher, Teri *actress*
Huffman, Felicity (Flicka Huffman) *actress*
Lawless, Lucy (Lucille Francis Ryan) *actress*
Longoria, Eva (Eva Jacqueline Longoria, Eva Longoria Christopher) *actress*
McCormack, Eric *actor*
Merkerson, S. Epatha *actress*
Reitman, Ivan *film director, producer*
Savant, Doug *actor*
Sheridan, Nicolette *actress*
Strong, Brenda *actress*
Wolf, Dick (Richard A. Wolf) *television producer*
Woodard, Alfre *actress*

## Valencia
Klahr, Lewis *film director*
Millar, Michael William *musician*
Windsor, William Earl *consulting engineer, sales representative*

## Valley Center
Camp, Joseph Shelton, Jr. *film producer, director, writer*

## Valley Village
Barkin, Elaine Radoff *composer*
Diller, Phyllis (Phyllis Ada Driver Diller) *actress, writer*

## Van Nuys
Boone, Deborah Ann (Debby Boone) *singer*
Walsh, Thomas Francis, Jr. *producer, writer, director*

## Venice
Bill, Tony *producer, director*
Chartoff, Robert Irwin *film producer*

## Ventura
Hoffman, Kenneth *music educator*
Lawson, Robert Earl *music educator, conductor*
Turturro, John *actor*

## Visalia
Carrillo, Melchor Paul *voice educator*
Porterfield-Pyatt, Chaumonde R. *music educator, advocate*

## Walnut
Karr, Joanne Fern *theater educator*

## Watsonville
Dehner, David Anthony *music educator, voice educator*

## Weed
Schaefer, M. Elaine *music educator, conductor*

## West Hills
Smith, Chad A. *band director*

## West Hollywood
Annakin, Kenneth Cooper *film director, writer*
Arnaz, Lucie Desiree *actress*
Bassett, Angela *actress*
Baxter, Meredith *actress*
Berry, Halle Maria *actress*
Burke, Clem *musician*
Cage, Nicolas (Nicolas Coppola) *actor*
Cole, Natalie Maria *singer*
Deschanel, Caleb *cinematographer, film director*
Destri, Jimmy *musician*
Franklyn, Audrey Pozen *talent promoter, television personality*
Harper, Robert *actor*

## Whittier

Harry, Deborah Ann *singer*
Hayes, Sean (Sean Patrick Hayes) *actor, comedian*
Holloway, Josh *actor*
Jackson, Randy *music producer, television personality, musician*
Krabbe, Jeroen Aart *actor*
Presley, Priscilla (Pricilla Ann Wagner, Priscilla Beaulieu Presley) *actress*
Romijn, Rebecca *actress, model*
Sackett, Barnard (Barney) *actor, film producer, director, scriptwriter*
Stein, Ben (Benjamin Jeremy Stein) *television personality, writer, lawyer, economist*
Stein, Chris *musician*
Tarantino, Quentin Jerome *film director, scriptwriter*
Thornton, Billy Bob *actor, film producer*

## Whittier
Korf, Jean Prinz *retired theater educator*

## Woodland Hills
Chiodini, John Allen *musician, composer*
O'Connor, Brian D. A. *music educator, French horn musician*

# COLORADO

## Arvada
Bett, Robert Scott *music educator*

## Aspen
Berkeley, Edward *performing arts association administrator, music educator*
Tsontakis, George *composer, conductor*

## Aurora
Farmer, Keith Allen *music educator*
Roberts-Ramsbotham, Hazel Ruth *piano educator*

## Boulder
Bernstein, Giora *artistic director*
Fink, Robert Russell *music educator, retired dean, music theorist*
Kotter, Rita Joan *theatre educator, design consultant*
Mooney, William Piatt *actor*
Sable, Barbara Kinsey *retired music educator*
Sarson, John Christopher *television producer, director, writer*

## Broomfield
Gill, Michael Gerard *music educator*
Stacks, Karen Beth *music educator*

## Centennial
Heath, Jayne Marie *music educator*

## Colorado Springs
Ansorge, Iona Marie *musician, educator, real estate agent*
Ashcraft, Vernon Arthur *music educator*
Coker, Carolyn Ann *music educator*
Scott, Carla Anne *music educator, musician*

## Crawford
Cocker, Joe *popular musician*

## Denver
Bricker Janzen, Donna Lee *music educator*
Burshtan, John Willis *television producer*
Ceci, Jesse Arthur *violinist*
Fredmann, Martin *ballet company artistic director, educator, choreographer*
Hammond, Dave Andrew *music educator, musician*
Hockman, Lorraine Frances *music educator*
Kuzma, John Joseph *church musician*
McClinton, David Anthony *performing company executive*
Morales, John Paul *television services producer*
Robinson, Cleo Parker *artistic director*

## Elizabeth
Brownson, Sue McPherson *music educator*

## Fort Collins
Kraus, David (Dirk) Bruce *musician, educator*
Pluth, Joseph, Jr. *music educator*

## Fort Morgan
Overton, Larry Dean *music educator, musician*

## Grand Junction
Phillips, Ruth Amelia *retired music educator, artist*

## Greeley
Copley, R. Evan *music educator*
Murray, Robert Patrick *music educator, musician*
Womble, Ken *theater educator, film director, writer, actor*

## Greenwood Village
Walter, Heath Allen *music educator*

## Highlands Ranch
Fiess, Stephen Charles Edward *musician, music educator*
Snell, Michael Steven *music educator*

## Littleton
Alykova, Valentina *musician, music educator*
Day, Susan Marie *music educator, composer*
Johansson, Alicia Barbara *musician*
Keats, Donald Howard *composer, educator*
Reinker, Mary Stefanich *musician, music educator*
Wolfer, Dale *retired music educator*
Zwilling, Mark C. *music director*

## Loveland
Balsiger, David Wayne *television director, writer, television producer, television director, researcher*
Kreutz, Robert A. *music educator, musician*

## Manitou Springs
Hopwood, Brian Keith *music educator, musician*

**Montrose**
Davis, Christopher Thomas *music educator, musician*

**Monument**
Hutchison, Jon McKee *music educator*

**Niwot**
Buss, Kathleen E. *music educator*

**Northglenn**
Kappler, Karen L. *music educator, musician*

**Pritchett**
Hall, Carol Ann *music educator*

**Pueblo**
Brown, Courtney Allison *composer, writer, singer*
Genova, Wayne D. *music educator, consultant*

**Thornton**
Parker, Alice Jeanne *music educator*

**U S A F Academy**
Galema, Joseph M. *music director*

**Westminster**
Kopperud, Marilyn Sue *music educator*
White, John David *composer, musician*

**Woodland Park**
Critchlow, Bryan Douglas *music educator*

## CONNECTICUT

**Bloomfield**
Boltes, Carlos *musician, educator*
Mamlok, Walter Joseph *music educator, musician*
Santanella, Richard Charles, Jr. *music educator*

**Branford**
Smith, Richard Emerson (Dick Smith) *make-up artist*

**Bridgeport**
Richard, Ellen *theater executive*
Sheehan, Geoffrey *theater educator*

**Bristol**
Jaworski, Ron *sports analyst*
Levy, Steve *sports anchor, studio host*
Mayne, Kenny *sports anchor*
Mortensen, Chris *sports analyst, reporter*
Paolantonio, Sal *sports correspondent*

**Canaan**
Thorne, Francis *composer*

**Canton**
Richardson, Dana Roland *technology consultant*

**Chaplin**
Wood, Wendy Deborah *filmmaker*

**Colchester**
Bartkowski, Kathleen Susan *musician*

**Danbury**
Hirshfield, Louis Russell *music educator, musician*
Nelson, Willie Hugh *musician, lyricist*

**East Haddam**
Borton, John Carter, Jr., (Terry Borton) *theatrical producer*
Frost, Susan Beth *theater producer*

**Fairfield**
Upton, Barbara M. *music director*

**Greenwich**
Shimchick, Marie *music educator*

**Hartford**
Mardinly, Susan J. *musician, music educator*
Mills, Corinne C. *music educator*

**Ledyard**
Hammond, Russell Paul *music educator*

**Meriden**
Zak, Stephanie B. *music educator*

**Middlefield**
Friedman, Adam R. *performing company executive, educator*

**Monroe**
Freas, Thomas A. *music professor*

**Mystic**
Bobruff, Carole Marks *radio producer, radio personality*

**New Haven**
Andrew, Dudley *film and comparattive literature professor*
Bresnick, Martin *composer, educator*
Bundy, James Abbott *performing company executive*
Feldman, Grace A. *music educator*
Martignetti, Frank Anthony III *music educator, church music director*
Nolan, Victoria *theater director*
Tirro, Frank Pascale *music educator, composer, writer*
Warshaw, Marvin D. *conductor, educator, musician*

**New Preston**
Grizzard, George *actor*

**Newington**
Anderson, Kathryn Parks *music educator*
Bell, Kenneth Leman, Jr. *music educator, musician*
Cohen, Fern K. *music educator*

**North Windham**
Careau, James Thomas *music educator*

**Norwalk**
Eagan, Sherman G. *producer, communications executive*

**Oakville**
Carroll, Constance Marie *piano educator, organist, director*

**Old Greenwich**
Walton, Constance Williams *music educator*

**Ridgefield**
Kantor, James Graham *music educator, composer*
Taylor, Edwin R. *music director*

**Rocky Hill**
Burnett, Claire Conklin *music educator*

**Southbury**
Bergen, Polly *actress*

**Southport**
Walker, Charles Dodsley *conductor, organist*

**Stamford**
Clement, Bill *hockey analyst*
Karp, Steve *agent*
Macurdy, John Edward *bass*

**Storrs Mansfield**
Rose, Dale A.J. *performing arts educator*

**Washington Depot**
Pendleton, Moses Robert Andrew *dancer, choreographer*
Tracy, Michael Cameron *choreographer, educator*

**West Cornwall**
Engel, Jeffrey Mark *musician, music educator*

**West Hartford**
Braus, Ira L. *music educator, researcher*

**Weston**
Fredrik, Burry *theater producer, theater director*

**Westport**
Feliciano, José *entertainer*
Newman, Paul *actor, food products executive, race car driver*
Smith, Andrew James Thomas *music educator*
Solum, John Henry *flutist, educator, author*

**Willimantic**
Brodie, Ellen Faith *theater educator, director*

**Winsted**
Atkins, Adam Preston *music educator, singer*

## DELAWARE

**Bear**
Hudson, Kelly Marie *music educator*

**Camden Wyoming**
Pfeuffer, Robert John *musician*

**Greenville**
Parets, Paul L. *music educator*

**Lewes**
Neal, Carole Elkins *music educator*

**Middletown**
Harney, Edward Gary *music educator*

**Millville**
Zinman, David Joel *conductor*

**Newark**
Robinson, Marie Hadley *voice educator*

**Wilmington**
Amado, David *conductor*
Glanden, William Donald *pianist, music educator, composer*
Wesler, Ken *performing arts company executive*

## DISTRICT OF COLUMBIA

**Washington**
Ames, Frank Anthony *musician, film producer*
Anderson, Mary Ann Grasso *theater association executive*
Bahn, Lina Y. *musician*
Battis, Emery John *actor*
Begala, Paul Edward *television personality, political scientist, consultant*
Crawford-Mason, Clare Wootten *television producer, journalist*
Damjanovich, Chaslav M. (Casey Diamond) *filmmaker, television producer, writer*
Day, Doris (Doris von Kappelhoff) *singer, actress*
Dhue, Stephanie *television producer, reporter*
Domingo, Placido *tenor*
Donlon, Claudette *performing company executive*
Doty, Shayne Taylor *organist*
Dukert, Betty Cole *television producer*
Elliott, Graham John *music educator, director*
Fischer, Elizabeth (Betsy) *television producer*
Gersh, Darren *television correspondent*
Hamlisch, Marvin *composer, conductor, musician, entertainer*
Harpham, Virginia Ruth *violinist*
Kahn, Michael *stage director*
Kaiser, Michael M. *performing company executive*
Kaltchev, Ivo *musician, educator*
Kendall, Peter Landis *television news executive*
Massey, Jeanne Kelly *performing company executive*
Rostropovich, Mstislav Leopoldovich *conductor, musician, music director*

Royle, David Brian Layton *television producer, journalist*
Russell, Mark *comedian*
Schwarz, Gerard *conductor, musician, music director*
Slatkin, Leonard Edward *conductor, musician, music director*
Smith, Molly D. *theater director*
Stamberg, Susan Levitt *radio personality*
Steiner, Ruth *music educator*
Stone, Florence Smith *film producer, consultant*
Walsh, John *television show host, missing children and victims' rights advocate*
Webre, Septime *ballet company artistic director, choreographer*
Weidenfeld, Sheila Rabb *television producer, writer*
Winans, Cece *gospel vocalist*
Wolff, Karen Lias *music educator*

## FLORIDA

**Apopka**
Reinecke, William T. *conductor, educator*

**Bayonet Point**
Errington, Norman *television producer, photographer*

**Boca Raton**
Dower Gold, Catherine Anne *music history educator*

**Bradenton**
Smith-Gonzalez, April Renee *music educator*

**Cantonment**
Coakley, William Travis *music educator*

**Cape Coral**
Wendel, Joan Audrey *music educator*

**Clearwater**
Cross, Beverly Jean *music educator*

**Clermont**
Kemp, Gretchen Laurel *choral director, music educator*
Sides, I. Ruth S. *retired music educator*

**Coral Gables**
Asmus, Edward Paul *music educator*
De Sena, Ferdinando *composer, educator*
Williams, Lowell E. *theater educator*

**Coral Springs**
Kristofferson, Kris *singer, lyricist, actor*

**Davie**
Walkinshaw, Nicole M. *performing arts educator*

**Daytona Beach**
Dumm, Robert Wayne *musician, educator, writer*
Kuiper, Dirk *performing arts educator, writer*
Poitier, Constance Rena *music specialist, educator*

**Deerfield Beach**
Allaire, Gaston George *music educator, researcher*

**Deland**
Musco, Lynn Ann *music educator*
Niemann, Chester S., Jr. *retired band director, customer service administrator*

**Delray Beach**
Spyker, Harry A. III *music educator*

**Dunedin**
Huffman, Thomas David *church music director, organist*

**Fort Lauderdale**
Kilgus, Edward Chip *singer, actor, writer, poet*
LeRoy, Miss Joy *model, apparel designer*
Mathis, Donald Raymond *music educator*
Putnam, Gene Chumley *music educator*
Randi, James (Randall James Hamilton Zwinge) *magician, educator*
Stayton, James Michael *music educator*
Webster, Ernest Wesley *musician, educator*

**Fort Myers**
Canham, Pruella Cromartie Niver *music educator*
Renfroe, W. Douglas *musician, conductor, music educator*

**Gainesville**
DesForges, Deborah Waln *music educator*
Jones, Gregory R. *theater educator*

**Graceville**
Moon, Kimberle Irene *voice educator*

**Green Cove Springs**
Davidson, Joy Elaine *retired mezzo soprano*

**Hallandale**
Vaserstein, Ludmila *music educator*

**Jacksonville**
Duke, Andrea K. *music educator*
Homsley, Denise Louise *music educator*
Huber, Mary Susan *music educator*
Laymon, April Marie *music educator*
Page, Willis *conductor*
Smith, Stephen Mark *music educator*
Stanley, Helen Camille *composer, musician*
Stewart, Sandra Kay *music educator*
Taylor, Gavin Hall *music educator*

**Jupiter**
Kobylarski, Rebecca Lee *music educator*

**Key West**
Buffett, Jimmy (James William Buffett) *vocalist, songwriter, writer*

**Kissimmee**
Weaver, Russell *music educator*

**Lady Lake**
Rosene, Paul Earl *music educator*

**Lake Helen**
Finn, Stephen Martin *film producer, venture capitalist*

**Lake Wales**
Walton, Madalyn Carol *music educator*

**Lakeland**
Buckmaster, Matthew Tobe *music educator, musician, small business owner*
Jacobson, Barbara Dinger *music educator*

**Largo**
Benoit, Christopher Louis *music educator*
Szalkowski, Deborah *music educator*

**Lecanto**
Max, Buddy (Boris Max Pastuch) *musician*
Wheatley, Deborah A. *music educator*

**Manalapan**
Hyatt, Susan Marie *theater educator, director, actress*

**Mary Esther**
McTyeire, Robert Adams *sound engineer, music company executive, consultant*

**Melbourne**
Kreines, Joseph Melvin *conductor*
Savickis, Rodney Fredrick *theater educator, theater director*

**Merritt Island**
Yoh, William Harry, Jr. *music educator*

**Miami**
Allen, Charles Norman *television, film and video producer*
Berman, Mona S. *actress, playwright, theater director, theater producer*
Diez, Oliver *music educator*
Di Liddo, Michael *music educator, musician*
Feinberg, Wendie *television producer*
Galatas, Ruth Ann *musician, publishing executive, educator*
Guzman, Iris Vila *music educator*
Harmon, Monica Renee *music educator*
Heuer, Robert Maynard, II, *opera company executive*
Kahn, Jack Merrill *television producer*
Kingman, Barbara *music educator*
Madurga, Gonzalo F. *performing company executive, actor, singer*
Marley, Damian Robert Nesta (Jr. Gong) *reggae artist*
Mauch, Diane Farrell *music educator*
McCall, Anthony *filmmaker*
Pilafian, Audrey Kalenian *music educator*
Remek, Robert Thomas *music educator, church musician*
Saralegui, Cristina Maria *Spanish language television personality, journalist*
Walkley, Mary L. *voice and music educator*
Walz, Leo R. *conductor*

**Miami Beach**
Gardiner, Pamela Nan *performing company executive*
Lawson, Eve Kennedy *dancer*
Rosenhaus, Drew *professional sports agent*

**Milton**
Arnold, Margaret Morelock *music educator, soprano*
Losee, Michael Patrick *music director*

**Montverde**
Perry, Douglas Skip Dale *music educator*

**Naples**
Kirby, Charles William, Jr. *dancer, choreographer*
White, Roy Bernard *performing arts association administrator*

**Neptune Beach**
Palmer, Jane G. *music educator*

**Niceville**
Fitzpatrick, James Thomas *music educator*

**North Miami**
Stills, Stephen *musician, vocalist, composer*

**North Palm Beach**
Hayman, Richard Warren Joseph *conductor*

**Ocala**
Lowe, John Thomas, Jr. *church and concert musician*

**Orange Park**
Layton, Jim Alan *music educator, director*

**Orlando**
Beckner, Cynthia Byrd *music educator, elementary school educator*
Harris, Lani M. *theater educator*
Haxton, David *filmmaker, photographer*
McMahon, Ed *television and radio personality*
Pyle, Artimus (Thomas Delmar Pyle) *musician*
Shirk, Christine Louise *music educator*
Weaver, Earl D. *theater educator*
Yonetani, Ayako *music educator, entertainer*

**Ormond Beach**
Hodkinson, Sydney Phillip *composer, educator, musician, conductor*

**Oviedo**
Backel, Michelle P. *theater educator*

**Palm Harbor**
Katzen-Guthrie, Joy *performance artist, engineering executive*
Krawczynski, Tony Edward *music educator*

**Panama City**
Fejer, T. William *musician, composer, architect, furniture designer*

**Pensacola**
Jaffe, Alberto P. *musician, educator*
Rubardt, Peter Craig *conductor, educator*

**Pinellas Park**
Benedict, Gail Cleveland *music educator*

**Port Richey**
Fry, Ronald Sylvan *music educator, director*

**Port Saint Lucie**
Rothschild, Mary Ann *music educator*

**Punta Gorda**
Kitson, Don E. *music educator*
Stratas, Teresa (Anastasia Strataki) *soprano*

**Ruskin**
Dickson, Tim *music educator, marine life administrator*

**Saint Augustine**
Danielson, Reva Annette *pianist, music educator*
Gilmore, H. James *film producer, educator*

**Saint Petersburg**
Carroll, Charles Michael *music educator*

**Sarasota**
Allen, Charles Franklin *music educator*
Carstens, Charlene B. *composer, music educator*
Edwards, Michael Donald *artistic director, drama educator*
Faron, Sally Rogers *performing arts association administrator, consultant*
McCollum, John Morris *tenor*
McMaster, Gloria (Gloria Bugni Juhn) *mezzo-soprano, educator*
Mizer, Joyce Taylor *music educator*
Sarakatsannis, Leonidas Nicholas *musician, concert pianist, music educator, composer, conductor*
Schwartz, Francis *music educator, composer*
Stewart, Donald George *musician, composer, music industry executive*
Vasilaki, Linda Boozer *music educator*

**Stuart**
Kooluris, Hortense Dolan *performing arts educator, consultant, dancer*

**Summerfield**
Lynne-O'Brien, Vincent *theater director, actor*

**Tallahassee**
Coleman, Robert H. *theater educator*
Corzine, Jennifer Jean *music educator*
Harrison, Luvada A. *voice educator, singer*
Harsanyi, Janice *retired soprano, educator*
Scott, Marcus Lewis Elliot *music educator*
Shaftel, Matthew Robert *music educator, tenor, conductor*
Stebleton, Michelle Marie *music educator, musician*
Streem, James Kenneth *musician, educator*
Zwilich, Ellen Taaffe *composer*

**Tampa**
Dupuis, John James *music educator, composer*
Edberg, Judith Florence *music educator*
Hankenson, E(dward) Craig, Jr. *performing arts executive*
Hankins, Phillip R. *music educator*
Leopold, Blake *music educator*
Nichols, Nancy Diane *music educator*
Scialdo, Mary Ann *music educator, musician*
Stefanov, Ivanka *music educator*

**Temple Terrace**
Barlar, Rebecca Nance *music educator*

**Treasure Island**
Dunn, Craig Andrew *entertainer, conductor, writer, composer, educator*

**Valparaiso**
Merritt, Phyllis June *music educator, director*

**Venice**
Gabriele, Charles *composer, educator*
Tausan, Carol A. *music educator*

**West Palm Beach**
Hale, Marie Stoner *artistic director*
Phillips, Kenneth Wayne *music educator*
Robinson, Raymond Edwin *conductor, music educator, writer*

**Winter Garden**
Ellis, Missie Lynne *music educator*

**Winter Park**
Beute, Brian Arthur *music educator*
LaCognata, John Patrick *music educator*
Wallace, Curtis Wilbern, Jr. *music director, organist*
Wrancher, Elizabeth Ann *music educator, opera singer*
Zivot, Eric *actor, educator*

## GEORGIA

**Albany**
Rodriguez, Sergio Raul *music educator, conductor*
Young, Scott Christopher *music educator, musician*

**Athens**
Staub, August William *theater producer, educator*

Stipe, Michael *musician, film producer*

**Atlanta**
Alexander, Alonzo III *music educator, composer*
Austin, Johnta *musician*
Fifty Cent, (Curtis James Jackson) *rap artist*
Flannery, James William *performing arts educator, theater director, singer*
Fletcher, Kathy Jordan *music educator*
Gibson, Michael Allen *music educator*
Grant, Susan *television executive*
Hanthorn, Dennis Wayne *performing arts association administrator*
Lil Jon, (Jonathan Smith) *hip hop artist, recording industry executive*
McFall, John *artistic director*
McKnight, Terrance Thales *music educator*
Raymond, Usher, IV, (Usher) *vocalist, actor*
Slade, Scott *radio personality*
Spano, Robert *conductor, music director*
Vulgamore, Allison *performing arts association administrator*
Wallace, Peter Marsden *radio producer, commentator, writer*
Watkins, Tionne (T-Boz) *singer*
Wesley, Nicole Leigh *dancer, choreographer*
Woodard, Diane E. *music educator*
Wylly, Barbara Bentley *performing arts association administrator*

**Austell**
Pope, Jacqueline Privette *music educator*
Smiley, Jacquelyn *voice educator*

**Barnesville**
Robbins, Dan S. *theater educator, theater director*

**Bethlehem**
Sass, Joshua Lee *music educator*

**Blue Ridge**
Watkins, Nancy Ann *music and art educator*

**Brunswick**
Douglas, Christopher Thomas *music educator, musician*

**Calhoun**
Milam, Ben William *music educator*

**Carrollton**
Bleuel, John Stephen *music educator*
Holcombe, Brenda Sue *performing arts educator*

**Chamblee**
Pearson-King, Lynn *music educator, director*

**Cleveland**
Durden, Julie Mariann *music educator*

**Columbus**
Golden, Joseph David *music educator*
Hiatt, Florence Ellen *musician*
Musgrove, Katherine E. *theater educator*
Rumbelow, Robert Wesley *composer, conductor, director*

**Conyers**
Waters, Roger Allen *music educator*

**Cordele**
Bell, Andrew C. *music educator*
Helms, Bobby Gillespie *music educator, consultant*
Partin, Stephen Andrew *music educator*

**Dallas**
Erwin, Patrick Michael *music educator*

**Dawsonville**
Carroll, Martha Lynn *music educator, church pianist, editor, writer, illustrator*

**Decatur**
Hamilton, Frank Strawn *musician, composer, educator*
Ray, Amy *vocalist, guitarist*
Saliers, Emily *singer, musician*
Strain, Michael L. *music director, performing company executive*

**Duluth**
Gilcrist, Kathy Ann *theater educator*
McClung, Samuel Brenton *music educator, consultant*

**East Point**
Bridgewater, Herbert Jeremiah, Jr. *radio personality*

**Fayetteville**
Hood, Barbara W. *musician, educator*

**Fitzgerald**
Newsome, John David, Jr. *music educator*

**Flowery Branch**
Congdon, Jon Harvey *music educator*

**Griffin**
Lindsey, James Robert, II, *music educator, director, secondary school educator*

**Guyton**
Murray, Anthony David *music educator, director*

**Hartwell**
Rushing, Tonnie Austin Page *musician, educator*

**Kennesaw**
Adams, Dean (Lewis Adams) *theater director*
Kruger, Harry *retired conductor, retired music educator*
Sherr, Laurence E. *music educator, composer*

**Lagrange**
Gittinger, Laurie Ellen *music educator, elementary school educator*

**Lawrenceville**
Folds, Frank Elliott *music educator*

**Leesburg**
Hilley, Mary Kay *music educator*

**Loganville**
McGonigle, Terry L. *theater educator, consultant*

**Lookout Mountain**
Brown, Jeanell S. *music educator*

**Louisville**
Abdich, Robert Nicholas *band director, musician*

**Marietta**
Fletcher, Carlos Alfredo Torres *video and film production company executive*
Morisco, Jerid Simon *music educator, conductor*
Poor, Andrew Ford *music educator*
Roach, Carole Hyde *music educator*

**Martinez**
Meyers, Nicholaus *music educator*

**Mcdonough**
Wilson, Russell Edward *music educator*

**Milledgeville**
Ragan, Charlotte Ann *music educator*

**Mount Berry**
Davis, John Edward *music educator, musician*

**Mount Vernon**
Bowdidge, Mark *music educator*

**Nashville**
Cosson, Mary Gwendolyn *music educator*

**Norcross**
Koperniak, Matthew Ryan *music educator, director, secondary school educator*

**Oakwood**
Phillips, Ernie Howard *music educator*

**Peachtree City**
Day, Annette J. *music educator*

**Rome**
Davis, Susan Lynn *music educator, musician*

**Roswell**
Bridges, Chris (Ludacris) *musician, actor*
Siepi, Cesare *opera singer*
Welch, Robert Bennett *retired music educator, retired conductor*

**Savannah**
Court, Stacie Lorraine *musician, tax specialist*
Holland, Robert D. *music educator*
Hutchinson, Michael E. *music educator, conductor*

**Smyrna**
Dean, Martha Elizabeth *music educator*
Rife, Elizabeth *musician, music educator*

**Statesboro**
Whitaker, Mical Rozier *theater director, educator*

**Stockbridge**
Sanders, Curtis Arra *music educator*

**Stone Mountain**
Fairweather, Daniel Edward *music educator*

**Suwanee**
Harriman, John *music educator*

**Sylvania**
Harper, Michael Christopher *music educator*

**Sylvester**
Kroll, Francis Scott *music educator*

**Tifton**
Robinson, John Christopher *music educator*

**Toccoa Falls**
Council, Thomas Maurice *music educator*

**Tucker**
Hardy, Michael C. *performing arts administrator*

**Union City**
Bryant, Curtis *composer, educator*

**Valdosta**
McLendon, Richard Charles *music educator*

**Waleska**
Muzyka, Pola Marie *film producer, artist*

**Young Harris**
Richardson, Vernal Edward *retired music educator*
Wolfersteig, Eloise Smith *retired music educator*

## HAWAII

**Ewa Beach**
Lewis, Mary Jane *film producer, film director, scriptwriter*

**Honolulu**
Abe, Gregg Koyei *music educator*
Akinnuoye-Agbaje, Adewale *actor*
Andrews, Naveen William Sidney *actor*
Ho, Don (Donald Tai Loy Ho) *entertainer, singer*
Langhans, Edward Allen *drama and theater educator*
Pauka, Kirstin *theater educator, director*
Tanner, Jerré E. *composer, retired publishing executive*

**Kaneohe**
Poliahu, George *retired music educator*

Young-Pohlman, Colette Lisa *music educator*

**Kapolei**
Dudley, Doris S. *music educator, small business owner*

**Laie**
Gorman, Vicki Pfluger *voice educator*

## IDAHO

**Arco**
Jardine, Cindy M. *music educator*

**Boise**
Aitken, Paul Arthur *composer, conductor*
Hofflund, Mark *theater director*
Holt, Isabel Rae *radio program producer*
Kent, E(verett) Allen *performing arts association administrator, theater producer*

**Heyburn**
Barson, Ross J. *music educator, assistant principal*

**Idaho Falls**
Finnigan, Bernard Keith *filmmaker, writer*

**Nampa**
Johnson, Daniel D. *music educator*

**Preston**
Seare, Paul Dearden *music educator*

**Rexburg**
Barrus, Charles LaMar, Jr. *music educator*

## ILLINOIS

**Algonquin**
Gnutek, Anthony Edward *music educator*
Wise, Jack Ronald *music educator*

**Aurora**
Daugherty, Diane Ruth *music educator*
Gregson, Timothy Howard, II, *music educator, musician, singer*
McCarthy, Mary Elizabeth (Beth) Constance *conductor, music educator*
Pappas, Margene *retired music educator*

**Barrington**
Carter, Jeanie *performing company executive*

**Belleville**
Jones, Donald Leigh *retired music educator*

**Bloomington**
Brown, Jared *theater director, educator, writer*
Cook, Richard Kent *music educator, musician*
Moham, Carren *music educator, singer*
Vayo, David Joseph *composer, music educator*

**Bourbonnais**
Dalton, Martha Gomer *music educator*

**Buffalo Grove**
Kosobayashi, Kevan Takashi *music educator*

**Carbondale**
Townsend, Gregory Williams *music educator*

**Champaign**
Fredrickson, L(awrence) Thomas *composer*
Morrissette, Jason William *theater educator, actor, director*
Mueller, Rodney Alan *music educator*
Reedy, Frances Starr *music educator, cellist*

**Charleston**
Daum, John LaVern *retired band director, educator*
Dulaney, John Robert *music educator*
Fine, Elaine Sarah *composer, musician*

**Chicago**
Ahern, Joseph James, Jr. *television station executive*
Arpino, Gerald Peter *performing company executive*
Basden, Cameron *ballet mistress, dancer*
Black, Robert Durward *television producer*
Brauer, Sasha Gerritson *church musician, music educator*
Corrin, Dean C. *theater educator, playwright*
Dabrowski, Edward John *television technical director*
Daniel, T. *mime performer, theater director, choreographer*
Eisenberg, Daniel *filmmaker*
Falls, Robert Arthur *artistic director*
Farina, Dennis *actor*
Florine, Jane L. *musicology educator*
Gulbrandsen, Norman Ralph *retired music educator*
Heider, Anne Harrington *music educator*
Janners, Erik Nikolas *music educator, conductor*
Kritz, Robert
Lazar, Ludmila *concert pianist, music educator*
Letts, Tracy *actor, playwright*
Mason, William *opera company director*
May, Aviva Rabinowitz *music educator, musician, linguist*
McIntyre, Sarah Elizabeth *vocalist*
Padberg, Helen Swan *violinist*
Pollak, Lisa *radio producer*
Ran, Shulamit *composer*
Renard, Paul Steven *music educator*
Robinson, Reginald R. *musician*
Rosenberg, Thomas B. *film producer, real estate company executive*
Savage, Terry *television personality, journalist, stockbroker*
Scott, Stephen Brinsley *theater producer*
Sedelmaier, John Josef *filmmaker*
Slyde, Jimmy (James T. Godbolt, King of Slides) *tap dancer*
So, Kevin *singer*

Springer, Jerry *television talk show host, radio personality*
Stratman, Deborah *filmmaker, film and video educator*
Taylor, Koko *singer*
Teolis, Michael Francis *music educator, musician, conductor, composer*
Vincent, Jim *performing company executive*
Wang, Albert James *violinist, educator*
Wasson, Jeffrey *music educator*
Winfrey, Oprah *television talk show host, actress, television producer*
Wooten, Robert E. *music educator*
Yost, Emery Joseph *music industry producer, educator*
Yu, Linda *newswoman, television anchorwoman*
Zajicek, Jeronym *retired music educator*

**Chicago Heights**
Reed, Scott C. *music educator, writer*

**Country Club Hills**
McClelland, Helen *music educator*

**Crystal Lake**
Faulds, Marguerite Zita *music educator*

**Decatur**
Coryell, Sandra Kay *music educator*
Stafford, John H., II, *composer, music educator*

**Deerfield**
Tashjian, Beatrice Charmian *composer, educator*

**Dekalb**
Gelman, Alexander *theater director, educator*
Goldenberg, William Bruce *music educator, musician*

**Dixon**
Hertel, William John *music educator*

**Downers Grove**
Hornish, Ronald Frederick *music educator*
Piekarz, Frank Jeffrey *music educator*
Roselieb, Craig Alan *band director*
Tedeschi, Thomas E., Jr. *music educator*

**East Peoria**
Twitty, Susan Kay *music educator*
Wadsworth Walker, Cherilee *music educator*

**Edwardsville**
Anderson, Mary Jane *music educator*
Anop, Lenora-Marya *violinist, music educator*
Claudson, William Dolan *music educator*
Schultz, Norbert J. *retired music educator*

**Effingham**
Wallace, Bradford F. *music educator*

**Evanston**
Eberley, Helen-Kay *opera singer, recording industry executive, poet*
Hall, Bruce A. *music educator*
Hemke, Frederick L. *academic administrator*
Kujala, Walfrid Eugene *musician, educator*
McDonough, Bridget Ann *music theatre company director*
Peters, Gordon Benes *retired musician*
Zimmerman, Mary Alice *performing arts educator*

**Flanagan**
Keck, Gerald Ray *music educator*

**Flossmoor**
Day, Gregory Lynn *music educator*

**Forreston**
Braker, William Paul *music educator*
Harn, Amy Helen *music educator, director*

**Frankfort**
Coughlin, Kimberly Ann *music educator*

**Franklin Park**
Miller, Bryan Michael *music educator*

**Galesburg**
Polay, Bruce *music educator, conductor*
Ridlon, Kathleen *dancer, educator*

**Geneva**
Klenke, Deborah Ann *band and choral director, department chairman*

**Glen Carbon**
Jarabak, Phyllis A. *music educator*

**Granite City**
Roberds, Wyatt Kayne *music educator*

**Grayslake**
Cayari, Christopher *music educator*

**Griggsville**
Evans, H. Todd *music educator*

**Gurnee**
Myren, Allen W(illiam) *retired music educator*

**Herscher**
Van Meter, LeRoy Ray *music educator*

**Highland Park**
Hobson, Stephen Gilbert *conductor, music educator*

**Jacksonville**
Hayter, John Eldon *retired music educator*
Walters, Christopher Matchette *music director*

**La Grange**
Zethmayr, Ellen Lolakos *music educator, writer*

**Lake Zurich**
Juknelis, Nick *music educator*
Thompson, Joshua M. *music educator*

**Lincolnshire**
Boyton, Rick *theater director, actor*

**Lincolnwood**
Akos, Francis *retired violinist, conductor*

**Lockport**
Whyte, Kelly Ann *music educator*

**Lombard**
Lindsay, Diane Miller *music educator*

**Loves Park**
Dixon, John James *music educator*

**Macomb**
Bean, Matt *theater educator*
Kim, Chung-Ha *music educator*
Solomonson, Glen Terrance *music educator, musician*
Thompson, James Lynn *music educator*
Walker, Tammie Leigh *music educator*
Woods, Jeannie Marlin *theater educator*

**Mattoon**
Black, Todd Ronald *music educator*

**Mokena**
Wright, Chely *country singer*

**Moline**
Stodt, F. Chloe *piano educator*

**Niles**
Foster, Martha Mitchell *television director, writer*
Kessell, Charles Arthur *music educator, musician*
Martinez, Euri Anthony *music educator, small business owner*

**Northbrook**
Slattery, James Joseph (Joe Slattery) *actor*

**O Fallon**
Fairchild, David Lawrence *music educator*
Lang, Matthew *music educator*

**Oak Forest**
Aukes, Matthew H. *band educator*

**Oak Lawn**
Martin, Charles E. *music educator*

**Park Forest**
Billig, Etel Jewel *theater director, actress*

**Park Ridge**
Barnett, Patrick Shawn *music educator*

**Pekin**
Rimington, James Earl *music educator, consultant*

**Plainfield**
Serna, Phillip Woodrow *music educator, musician*

**Prophetstown**
Bohms, Stephanie A. *music educator, director*

**River Forest**
Bogojevich, Natasha *composer, educator*

**Rock Island**
Hand, Angela Rene *singer*

**Saint Charles**
Stovall, April Leanne *music educator*

**Saint Jacob**
Carter, Dennis R. *music educator, band director, musician*

**Schaumburg**
Dodohara, Jean Noton *music educator*
Janssen, Carron Joyce *music educator*
Riffel, Karen Sheffer *music educator*

**Shabbona**
Feken, John E. *music educator, director*

**Skokie**
Gregerman, Daniel P. *choral director*

**South Holland**
Anderson, Paul Martin *music educator, musician*

**Springfield**
Johnson, Paul Harold *music director*

**Sterling**
McCord, Julie Ann *retired conductor*

**Urbana**
Hedlund, Ronald *baritone*
Hicks, Darren Scott *music educator*
Keys, Henson *theater educator, actor, theater director*
Schleis, Thomas Henry *music educator, organist*

**Vernon Hills**
Sundell, Randy *music educator*

**Villa Park**
Antonelli, Joseph K. *musician, music educator*

**Virginia**
Webster, Kim S. *music educator*

**Waterloo**
Hoffmann, Mary Jukich *voice educator*

**Waukegan**
Houle, Jeanne Larson *retired music educator*

**West Chicago**
Noonan, Josette Marie *music educator*

**Wheaton**
Lim, Cheryl Cheon-Ae *music educator*

**Williamsville**
Pruitt, David R. *music educator, musician*

**Wilmette**
Hurley, Andrew John *musician*
Jampole, Michael *music educator, composer*
Merrier, Helen *actress, writer*
Stump, Patrick Martin *musician*
Wentz, Peter (Peter Lewis Kingston Wentz III) *musician*

**Winnetka**
Ladd, David Scott *music educator*

## INDIANA

**Anderson**
Rouintree, James Paul *retired music educator*

**Bedford**
Freeman, Beth Ellen *music educator, real estate agent*

**Bloomington**
Brown, Keith *musician, educator*
Effron, David Louis *conductor, performing company executive*
Jorgensen, Estelle Ruth *music educator*
Kiesgen, Paul *music educator*
Mac Watters, Virginia Elizabeth *singer, music educator, actress*
Murphy, Otis *music educator*
Phillips, Harvey G. *musician, educator, performing arts educator*
Spera, Dominic Gregorio *music educator, writer*
Strommen, Linda Sue *music educator, musician*
Svetlova, Marina *ballerina, retired choreographer*
Tsutsumi, Tsuyoshi *musician, educator*

**Boonville**
Meyer, Dana Lynn *music educator*

**Brownsburg**
Prather, Deborah A. *music educator*

**Brownstown**
Brock, Stephanie Ann *music educator*

**Carmel**
Peterson, James Michael *drama educator*

**Chandler**
Hooper, Venita *piano educator, accompanist*

**Columbia City**
Cremeans, Hersel John *music educator*

**Crown Point**
Shaffer, Peggy S. *music educator*

**Elkhart**
Carnall, Timothy W. *music educator*

**Evansville**
Matthews, Steven Dee *retired music educator, pilot, educator*
Reed, R. Douglas *music educator*

**Fort Wayne**
Peterson, Wayne Howard *musician*

**Greenwood**
Fritz, Samuel *music educator*

**Hammond**
Hansen, Jack Winsor *musician, educator*

**Hanover**
Batchvarova, Madlen Todorova *music educator, conductor*

**Indianapolis**
Baldwin, Keith L. *music educator, secondary school educator*
Belt, Kenneth A. *music educator*
Burgomaster, Frederick *music director*
Coomer, Steven Robert *music educator, musician*
Crookall, Simon *performing company executive*
DeCaro, James L. *band director*
Everly, Jack *conductor*
Gibbs, David Richard *musician, journalist, photographer, writer*
Ilgen, Dorothy L. *arts foundation executive*
Moratz, Karen Evans *musician*
Murphy, Meissa Bleu *music educator, behaviorist*
Pockrass, Joseph Craig *music educator*
Rees, Fred Joseph *music educator*
Schmid, John A. *musician, voice educator*
Sorley, Rebecca Ellen *music educator*
Venzago, Mario *conductor, music director*
Westra, Mitzi Sue *music educator*

**Jeffersonville**
Morgan, Roberta Diane *music educator*

**Kokomo**
Highlen, Larry Wade *music educator, piano rebuilder, tuner*

**Marion**
Maher, John Gene *music educator, musician*
Miller, Peter Karl *music educator*

**Michigan City**
Wiegand, Elizabeth *musician, educator*

**Mishawaka**
Kendall, Michael Jay *music educator, musician*
Klopfenstein, Reginald Lee *music educator*

**Mount Summit**
Bales, James Lavon *music educator*

**Muncie**
Ballard, Jeffrey Dale *music educator, tenor*
Maurer, Kathleen Marie *music educator, vocalist*
Roothaan, John *music educator, jazz pianist*

**Portage**
Williams, Susan Marie *music educator*

**Salem**
Davis, Duane L. *music educator, vocalist*

**South Bend**
Muniz, Jorge *composer, music educator*

**Trail Creek**
Nagle, Ronald K. *music educator*

**Valparaiso**
Pritchett, Daniel R. *music educator*

**Waterloo**
Johnson, George Axil III *television producer*

**Zionsville**
Garfunkel, Art *singer, actor*

## IOWA

**Algona**
Aboud, John Anthony *music educator*

**Ames**
Rodde, James F. *music educator*
Work, George Paul *cellist*

**Bettendorf**
Schulz, Sally Ann *pastoral musician, conductor, educator*

**Cedar Falls**
Chesnutt, Rod Martin *music educator*
Fanelli, Michael Paul *musician, educator, writer*
Glockner, Richard Peter *theater educator, actor, theater director*

**Cedar Rapids**
Rohr, Carol Ann *composer, music educator*

**Cherokee**
Gordon, Roma Dianne *music educator*

**Clinton**
Engelson, Robert Allen *music educator*

**Council Bluffs**
Kurt, Johnny Thomas *music educator*
Lippoldt, Vaughn Arthur *retired music educator*

**Davenport**
Dcamp, Charles Barton *music educator*

**Des Moines**
Butz, John Newton *theater educator, actor*

**Dubuque**
Barland, Charles John *music educator*
Patterson, David *music educator*

**Fort Dodge**
Cassady, Daniel Bennet *music educator*

**Hubbard**
Wessel, Gregory James *music educator*

**Indianola**
Croskery, Virginia *music educator, vocalist*
Larsen, Robert LeRoy *artistic director*
Mace, Jerilee Marie *performing arts association administrator*
Poulsen, James Viggo III *music educator, composer*

**Iowa City**
Kottick, Edward Leon *musician, educator*
Mather, Roger Frederick *retired music educator, writer*
Preucil, Doris Bogen *music educator*

**Le Mars**
Hallberg, Theodore Forest *music educator*
Niebuhr, Paul David *music educator*

**Mason City**
Backlin, William Wayne *music educator, composer*
Slaven, Timothy William *theater educator, set designer*

**Mount Pleasant**
Crane, Frederick Baron *retired music educator*
Edwards, Jason Ray *music educator, musician*
Larsen, Christopher Svend *music educator*

**Muscatine**
Phillips, Janet K. *music educator*

**Newton**
Brostrom, Dennis Alan *music educator*

**Ogden**
Bardole, Richard Allen *music educator*

**Ottumwa**
Wormhoudt, Pearl Shinn *voice educator, writer*

**Pella**
Hartman, Mark LeRoy *music educator, musician*

**Pleasant Valley**
Myatt, William Howard *theater educator, director, actor*

**Sheffield**
VanHorn, Bradley Kent *musician*

**Sheldon**
St. Clair, Clifford Mark *music educator*

**Sully**
Fopma, Mary Louise *music educator*

**Tipton**
Farwell, Walter Maurice *vocalist, educator*

**Washington**
Buchholz, Lee William (Leroy William Buchholz) *retired music educator*

## KANSAS

**Chanute**
Smith, David *music educator*

**El Dorado**
Garber, Ronald Lee *music educator*

**Emporia**
Bartruff, Jim *theater educator, director*

**Garden City**
Wright, J. Clayton *music educator*

**Gem**
Ziegelmeier, Patricia Kay *music educator, executive secretary*

**Great Bend**
Gaunt, Glenna Sue *voice educator*

**Hugoton**
Kelling, Sherry Lee *music educator, interior designer, educator*

**Hutchinson**
Brewer, William Thomas *theater educator, theater director*
Widener, Charlene *theater director, educator*

**Iola**
Tebbets, Gary Duane *music educator*

**Lawrence**
Castle, Joyce *mezzo soprano*
Hilding, Jerel Lee *music and dance educator, retired dancer*
Pozdro, John Walter *retired music educator, composer*
Smith, Henry Heller *music educator, director*
Tsubaki, Andrew Takahisa *theater director, educator*

**Lenexa**
Warenskjold, Dorothy *singer, educator*
Williams, Larry R. *music educator*

**Lindsborg**
Mahraun, Daniel Allen *musician, director*

**Manhattan**
Mortenson, Kristin Oppenheim *musician*

**Marion**
Beckham, Dwight Russel, Sr. *music educator, composer*

**Morganville**
Clark, Anne Louise *music educator, musician*

**Olathe**
Mathews, Valinda Gail *theater educator, gifted and talented educator*

**Ottawa**
Davidson, Medora Lea *dance educator*
Forrest, Daniel Ernest *composer, music educator*

**Overland Park**
Lamb, Gordon Howard *music educator*
Pretzel, Mark William *musician*

**Parsons**
Walker, Robert R. *music educator*

**Shawnee Mission**
Watts, Carl Douglas *music educator*

**Topeka**
Dunning, John Wilson, II, *voice educator, director*
Gamboa, Norman Armando *conductor, educator*
Kellim, Kevin D. *music educator*
Schultz, LeAnne *violinist, performer, music educator*

**Wichita**
Cress, Jerry W. *music educator*
Johnson, C. Nicholas *dance company executive*
Maust, Ezma Minnie *music educator*
Weber, W. David *music educator*

## KENTUCKY

**Albany**
Sell, James Douglas *music educator*

**Bowling Green**
Berry, Mark Sean *music educator*
Sexton, Timothy Curt *music educator*

**Burkesville**
Burris, Larry Brent *music educator, director*

**Burlington**
Mitchell, Timothy Lynn *music educator*

**Calvert City**
Madison, Vicki DiAnne *retired music educator*

**Campbellsville**
Gaddis, John Robert *music educator*
Martin, J(ames) Kenneth *music educator*
McArthur, Lisa R. *music educator, musician*

**Clarkson**
Day, John Nelson *music educator*

**Frankfort**
Fletcher, Winona Lee *theater educator*

**Georgetown**
Hall, Sara Y. *retired music educator*

**Greenville**
Beaty, Ted Hugh *music educator*

**Hopkinsville**
Wilkinson, Daniel Melvin *music educator*

**Lancaster**
Taylor, Senica Duwayne *music educator*

**Lexington**
Cameron-Mickens, Vertrelle Diane *singer, conductor, voice educator*
O'Hurley, John *actor*
Zack, George J. *conductor*

**London**
Felts, Garnet A. *voice educator*
McFadden, David Michael *music educator, director*

**Louisville**
Atz, Sarah J. *music educator*
Fenner, Chris *music educator*
Greer, Ginger Dell *music educator*
Hernandez, John E. *musician, music educator*
Kirkpatrick, G. Leon *music educator*
Marks-Morgan, Linda Lee *music educator*
Mowery, Ward Franklin *retired music educator*
Sherman, Mildred Mozelle *music educator, vocalist, actress, opera director*

**Maysville**
Trimble, Garnet O'Cull *retired music educator*

**Monticello**
Sexton, Scotty Eugene *music educator, gifted and talented educator*

**Morehead**
Detweiler, Greg Jeffrey *music educator*

**Murray**
Hill, Todd Edwin *band director*

**Owensboro**
Stovall, Beth Roop *music educator*

**Richmond**
Machado-Echezuria, Marianella Perpetua *composer, writer, educator*

**Russell Springs**
Floyd, Christopher Chad *music educator, director*

**Russellville**
Sauerbrunn, Mark Aaron *music educator*

**Stanford**
Underwood, Ray Stuart *music educator*

## LOUISIANA

**Baton Rouge**
Buchmann, Molly O'Banion *choreographer, educator*
Burt, Vickie P. *theater educator, theater director*
Hartzog, Elizabeth Windham *music educator*
Hirst, Edwin Timothy *music educator*
Mathews, Sharon Walker *performing company executive, secondary school educator*
McCoy, Wesley Lawrence *musician, educator, conductor*
Nave, J. L. *performing company executive*
Norem, Richard Frederick, Sr. *musician, educator*
Smith, Richard James *retired music educator*
Tandberg, Gerilyn Gay *theater educator, costume designer*
Torns, David Loren *conductor, director, musician*
Yarbrough, Martha Cornelia *music educator*

**Hammond**
Ratliff, Joy *music educator, singer*

**Houma**
Adams, Richard David *music educator*

**Iowa**
Kuykendall, Richard G. *music educator*

**Lafayette**
Daniel, Margaret Hagen *music and voice educator*
Lim, Chan Kiat *music educator*
Stravinska, Sarah *dance educator*

**Mandeville**
Genevay, Kelly Elizabeth *music educator*

**Metairie**
Grotkowski, Edward Michael *music educator, director*
Pizzo, Andrew Joseph *music educator*
Villia, Morris Sabastian *music producer, publishing executive, writer*

**Monroe**
Huntington, Lisa Lynee *music educator*
Trapp, A.C. *retired music educator*

**Natchitoches**
Anzaldua, Lori Anne *music educator*

**New Orleans**
St. Julien, Thais Mary *soprano, musician*
Williams, Anthony Ervin *music educator*

**Norco**
Munch, Christopher Joseph *music educator*

**Ruston**
Crook, Paul B. *performing arts educator, director*

**Scott**
Richardson, Cindy Guidry *voice educator, music educator, religious education administrator*

**Shreveport**
Jenkins, Clifford *music educator*
Tinker, Paul David *music educator*

**Slidell**
Larson, Sandra Pauline *music educator*

**Sulphur**
Fuller, Betty Stamps *music educator*

**Westlake**
Ecker, John J. *music educator*
Yarbrough, Frances Carole *music educator*

## MAINE

**Brunswick**
Schwartz, Elliott Shelling *composer, writer, music educator*

**Castine**
Davis, Peter Frank *filmmaker, writer*

**Gorham**
Chaulet, (Frédérique) Emmanuelle *performing company executive, actress, educator*
Lehmann, Robert Alexander *conductor, musician, director*

**Hancock**
Blasi, Antonio *music educator*

**Old Town**
Priest, Jeffrey Arnold *music educator*

**Orono**
Cox, Dennis Keith *music educator, conductor*

**Portland**
Bucci, Thomas Vincent *music educator, pianist, composer*
Miller, Buffy *dancer*

**Southwest Harbor**
Drummond, Carol Cramer *voice educator, lyricist, writer, artist*

**Sullivan**
Davis-Wexler, Ginia *singer, director*

**Waterville**
Benissan, Jordan Messan *music educator*

**West Baldwin**
Simmonds, Rae Nichols *musician, composer, educator*

## MARYLAND

**Annapolis**
Kolmus, Ryan Francis *music educator*
Seep, Dorothy M. *music educator*

**Arnold**
Marder, Barbara Hermling *theater educator, department chairman*

**Baltimore**
Constantine, Andrew *conductor*
Harrison, Michael *opera company director*
Huggins, Amy Branum *music educator*
Jacobson, Katherine Louise *musician, music educator*
Maw, Nicholas *composer, music educator*
Otal, Monica D. *music educator*
Ruppert, Joseph Alphonsus *music educator, language educator*
Skirpan, Richard Michael *conductor, music educator*

**Bethesda**
Burkhalter, Susan Shively *music educator, organist*

**Bowie**
Hillsman, Joan Rucker *music educator*

**Brandywine**
Briggs, John Harold, Sr. *music educator*

**Cambridge**
Rihanna, (Robyn Rihanna Fenty) *singer*

**Chestertown**
Clarke, Garry Evans *composer, educator, academic administrator, musician*

**Columbia**
Kearns, Ronald Edwin *music educator*
Weems, Helen Rachel *music educator, musician*

**Crofton**
Mahaffey, Redge Allan *movie producer, director, writer, actor, scientist, business executive*

**Elkton**
Moon, William Neal *music educator*

**Ellicott City**
Wann, Michael Stephen *music educator*

**Emmitsburg**
Fields, Victor Lee *music educator*

**Friendsville**
Biser-Rinard, Kendra May *music educator*

**Frostburg**
Bauman, Jon Ward *retired music educator*
Horner, Ronald George *music educator, musician*

**Great Mills**
Bufis, Matthew Peter *music educator*

**Gwynn Oak**
Hughes, Catherine L. (Cathy Hughes) *radio personality, broadcast executive*

**Jarrettsville**
Brennan, Molly B. *music educator*

**Kensington**
Forrest, Sidney *clarinetist, music educator*

**La Plata**
Herdman-Fisher, Carolyn A. *music educator*

**Largo**
Martin, Flora Y. *music educator*

**Owings Mills**
Swartz, Eugene Robert, Jr. *music educator, minister*

**Potomac**
Sirotin, Peter *musician, educator*

**Reisterstown**
Stefano, Toni Amanda *voice educator*

**Rosedale**
Gretz, Ronald John *music educator, conductor*

**Saint Marys City**
Froom, David *composer, music educator*

**Salisbury**
Bowden, Derek Thomas *orchestra director, educator*
Schoyen, Jeffrey Gerald *music educator, conductor*

**Silver Spring**
Brandt, Elsa Lund Erickson *music educator*
Secular, Sidney *actor, writer, fundraiser, consultant*

**Towson**
Crawford, Leneida Marie *singer, educator*
Decker, Michael John *music educator, musician*
Dzbinski, Alex J. *music educator*
Forrest, Juliet *dancer, educator, choreographer*
Jothen, Michael Jon *music educator, composer, conductor*

**Westminster**
Rogers, Jeffery Paul *music educator*

## MASSACHUSETTS

**Allston**
Spencer, Lara *television personality, journalist*

**Amherst**
Donohue, Therese Brady *artistic director, choreographer, costume and set designer*
Spratlan, Lewis *composer, educator*

**Auburn**
Giannini, Antoinette Frances *music educator, researcher*

**Belmont**
Goolkasian Rahbee, Dianne *musician, composer, music educator*

**Boston**
Anderson, Jewelle Lucille *musician, educator*
Bacon, A. Smoki *television host*
Barker, Edwin Bogue *musician*
Beatty, Carl *music educator*
Bourque, Laurie *film director, film instructor*
Brackeen, JoAnne M. *pianist, composer, educator*
Carlberg, Frank Thomas *composer, musician*
Craig, Patricia *voice educator, opera singer*
Deal, Kerry Lynn *music educator, soprano*
Del Sesto, Janice Mancini *opera company executive*
Durham, Gary Daniel *music educator, singer*
Firth, Everett Joseph *timpanist*
Fortunato, D'Anna E. *voice educator, mezzo soprano*
Goldstein, Sara *music educator*
Harvey, Mark Sumner *composer, educator, retired minister, musician*
Hoffman, Stanley Marc *composer, editor*
Hoyt, Herbert Austin Aikins *television producer*
Jochum, Veronica *pianist*
Katz, Paul *musician, music educator*
Lesser, Laurence *musician, educator*
Liotta, Jeanne *film direction, film instructor*
Lockhart, Keith Alan *conductor, music director*
Lowell, Richard Lee *music educator, musician*
Lublin, Robert Ian *theater educator*
MacCombie, Bruce Franklin *composer, college administrator*
Marsh, Milton R.W. *composer*
Martinborough, Samuel Neil *music educator, conductor, musician*
McPhee, Jonathan *music director, conductor, composer, interim artistic coordinator*
Mitchell, Jon Ceander *music educator, conductor*
Moriarty, John *opera administrator, artistic director*
Nettles, Barrie L. *music educator*
Nissinen, Mikko Pekka *dancer, performing arts company executive, artistic director*
Rochinski, Stephen James *musician, educator*
Schwartz, Lloyd *music critic, poet*
Sonnenschein, David *music educator, composer, conductor*
Veloudos, Spiro V. *performing company executive, theater educator*
Vila, Robert Joseph *television personality, real estate developer, space designer*
Wheeler, W(illiam) Scott *composer, conductor, music educator*
Williams, John Towner *composer, conductor*
Woodard, Fredrick James, Jr. *music educator, musician*
Young, Laura *dance educator, choreographer*

**Braintree**
Hallenbeck, Rachel Kirsten *music educator, director*

**Brewster**
Johnson, Jill Ann *lyricist, actress*

**Cambridge**
Cleary, David Michael *composer, critic, library assistant*
Connick, Harry, Jr. *musician, actor, vocalist, composer, lyricist*
de Varon, Lorna Cooke *choral conductor*
Gibbons, Joe *filmmaker*
Harbison, John *composer*
Holmberg, Arthur Carl *performing arts educator, director, theater critic*
Kraus, Rozann B. *performing company executive*
Orchard, Robert John *theater producer, educator*
Pinkham, Daniel *composer*
Sims, Ezra *composer*
Wood, Pamela Sharon *music educator, soprano*

**Concord**
Bethell, Charlyn *music educator*
Gomberg, Sydelle *dancer educator*
Gorny, Marina Dubinsky *music educator*

**Dedham**
Magner, Jerome Allen *performing company executive*

**Dorchester**
Jackson, Jimmie L. *retired music educator, retired organist*

**Fall River**
Brenner, Rylan *theater educator, director*

**Falmouth**
Brock, Nancy Jeanne *composer, writer, music educator*

**Foxboro**
Kennedy, Susan Marie *music educator*

**Framingham**
Bogard, Carole Christine *soprano*
Struyk, Pieter M. *music educator*

**Great Barrington**
Curtin, Phyllis *music educator, dean, vocalist*

**Hingham**
Noel, Barbara Hughes McMurtry *retired music educator*

**Hopkinton**
Moran, Wendy Jacqueline *music educator, musician*

**Hyannis**
Capparella (Muller), Nancy Lisa *music educator*

**Lincoln**
Giles, Allen *pianist, composer, music educator*
Hawkins, Malcolm *music educator, composer*

**Lynnfield**
Hodgkins, Douglas Wendell *music educator*

**Marblehead**
Kennedy, Elizabeth Mae *musician*

**Mashpee**
Jamison, John L. *music educator, musician*

**Mattapoisett**
Ellis, Stanley Weston *musician, educator*

**Medford**
Kouguell, Susan *film educator*

**Melrose**
Burnim, Kalman Aaron *retired theater educator*

**Methuen**
Lattini, James Tufic *music educator*

**Nantucket**
Rorem, Ned *composer, writer*

**Needham**
Di Domenica, Robert Anthony *musician, composer*

**Newton**
Li, Fan *pianist, music educator*
Osborne, Charles David *singer, composer, conductor*
Wahlberg, Mark *actor*

**Newton Center**
Schuller, Gunther Alexander *composer*

**North Adams**
McConnell, Matthew Stephen *composer*

**Northampton**
Jakuc, Monica *music educator, pianist, fortepianist*
Levy, Ralph Jacob, Jr. *retired theater educator*
Naegele, Philipp Otto *musician, educator*

**Norton**
Crutcher, Ronald Andrew *music educator, academic administrator*

**Norwood**
Bermani, Eric J. *musician, conductor*

**Plymouth**
Gregory, Dick *comedian, volunteer*

**Provincetown**
Sturner, Lynda *performing company executive*

**Salem**
Melby, John B. *composer, educator*

**Sandisfield**
Burtis, Herbert *musician*

**Somerville**
Suhrstedt, Barbara Lynn *concert pianist, voice educator*

**Southbridge**
Rutanen, Roy Stewart *producer, television personality*

**Vineyard Haven**
Breuer, Joann Green *theater director*

**Waltham**
Boykan, Martin *composer, music educator*
Wyner, Yehudi *composer, educator, pianist, conductor*

**Wellesley**
Matthews, Andrea Morgan *soprano, educator*

**Westborough**
Stillitano, Joseph Michael *music educator*

**Weston**
Tenney, Sarah G. *music educator*

**Williamstown**
Jaffe, Andrew William *music educator, composer*

**Woburn**
Guo, Ling *musician, consultant*

**Worcester**
Corbin, Frank Wayne *music educator*
Curran, Louis Jerome, Jr. *choral master*
Delorey, John Francis *music educator*
Falco, Richard Gerard *music educator*
Hagar, Richard Joseph *music educator, musician*
Hatfield, Renee S.J. *music educator*

## MICHIGAN

**Adrian**
Dodson, John Thomas *orchestra conductor*
Warner, Joanne Marie *theater educator*

**Allendale**
Bazany, Ted Bruce *music educator*
Campbell, Arthur J. *music educator*

**Ann Arbor**
Peng Chen, Hsiu-Hui *music educator*
Scavarda, Donald Robert *composer, artist*
Westlake, E. J. *performing arts educator*

**Battle Creek**
Matthews, Wyhomme S. *retired music educator, academic administrator*

**Belleville**
Van Tassel, Michael L. *music educator*

**Berrien Springs**
Ritzenthaler, Beatriz Augusta *musician, educator*
Wiltse, Richard Arthur *music educator*

**Bloomfield Hills**
Haidostian, Alice Berberian *concert pianist, volunteer, not-for-profit fundraiser*
Swift, Jonathan *television personality, educator*

**Brighton**
Wolf, Robert John *music educator*

**Burton**
Johnson, Jolene Carole *music educator*

**Dearborn**
Popovich, George Lee *theater educator*

**Detroit**
Bryant, Marchelle Dionne *performing arts educator*
Di Chiera, David *opera company director*
Duensing, Dorothy Jean *music educator, vocalist*
Dworkin, Aaron *violinist, educator*
Parsons, Anne *performing company executive*
Risner, Doug S. *performing arts educator, researcher*
Scott, Nina Elizabeth Ray *music educator*

**East Lansing**
Kirk, Edgar Lee *retired musician, educator*
Robinson, Mitchell *music educator*

**Farmington Hills**
Goslin, Gerald Hugh *concert pianist, educator*
Tedrick, Deborah Lynne *singer, actress, educator*

**Ferndale**
Purtan, Dick (Paul Purtan) *radio personality*

**Frankfort**
Storrer, William Allin *theater educator, consultant*

**Grand Blanc**
Byerly, Carl Wesley *music educator, academic administrator*

**Grand Rapids**
Biser, Larry *music educator, director*
Horn, Joyce Elaine *music educator*
Schwanda, Grace Elaine *music educator*
Taylor, Mark Lyman *music educator*
Webb, Mark Russell *music educator*

**Hillsdale**
Knecht, Melissa *music educator, musician*

**Holland**
De Jong, James Edward *conductor*

**Jackson**
Nugent, Ted (Theodore Anthony Nugent) *musician*

**Kalamazoo**
Kasdorf, Thomas Roger *music educator*
Ratner, Carl Joseph *opera stage director, baritone*
Webber, John Charles *composer, music educator*

**Lansing**
Hetrick, Esther *music educator*

Howard, David L. *conductor, baritone*

**Lincoln**
Martinico, Jennifer Marie *music educator*

**Mason**
Yoakam, Lynn Kelly *harpist, educator*

**Monroe**
Nuechterlain, James Howard *music educator*

**Mount Pleasant**
Orlik, Christina Bear *music educator*

**Northport**
Scripps, Douglas Jerry *music educator, conductor*

**Plainwell**
Mundo, Paul L. *music educator*

**Redford**
Hoge, Ann Cancilla *music educator*

**Rochester Hills**
Eisenhower, Laurie *performing company executive*
Parker, Catherine L. *theater educator*

**Romeo**
Tsukamoto, Daniel *piano instructor, church organist*

**Saginaw**
Coughlin, Jeannine Marie *music educator*
Eschmann, Paul David *music educator, mathematics educator*

**Swartz Creek**
Russell, Charles Harry *music educator, restaurant manager*

**Traverse City**
Faulmann, Roger Ray *retired music educator*

**Warren**
Cutter, Jeffrey S. *music educator*

**Wyoming**
Nelson, Tami Sue *music educator*

**Ypsilanti**
Bengtsson, Erling Blöndal *musician, retired music educator*

## MINNESOTA

**Anoka**
Chamberlain, Sonja Kay *music educator*

**Bemidji**
Wold, Kenneth Jon *music educator*

**Benson**
Duncan, J. Brock *music educator*

**Big Lake**
Fillafer, Richard *music educator*

**Blaine**
Olson, Bruce Van *music educator*

**Bloomington**
Ohnsorg, Brian Gregory *music educator, singer*
Smith, Henry Charles III *symphony orchestra conductor*

**Caledonia**
Kranz, Eliott Gregory *music educator*
Kranz, Kimberly Renee *elementary music educator*

**Chanhassen**
Prince, (Prince Rogers Nelson) *musician, actor*

**Circle Pines**
Lahann, Jon Clifford *music educator*

**Coon Rapids**
Vogel, Scott Charles *music educator*
Wilson, Sylvia Alyce *musician, educator*

**Duluth**
Morath, Max Edward *entertainer, composer, writer*

**Edina**
Markgraf, Cheryl Lee *church musician, conductor*
Pauley, Marlene Joan *musician, conductor*

**Golden Valley**
Spake, Mary Barbara *music educator*

**Madison**
Omland, Kim Marie *music educator, department chairman*

**Marshall**
Meffert, Robert Lee *music educator*

**Milaca**
Wig, Robert Curtis *retired music educator, conductor*

**Minneapolis**
Crabtree, Vicki Gail *musician*
Fetler, Paul *retired composer*
Foreman, Edward Vaught *voice educator, book publisher, writer, translator, composer, singer*
Hyslop, David Johnson *retired arts administrator*
Kaess, John Philip *music educator, director*
Monson, Cindy Lou *music educator*
Severinsen, Doc (Carl H. Severinsen) *conductor, musician*
Vanska, Osmo *music director*
Williams, Yolanda Yvette *music educator*
Wollan, Curtis Noel *theater producer, theater director*
Zahler, Noel Barry *composer, music educator*

**Minnetonka**
Bell, William Robert *music educator*

**Monticello**
Krohn, Brett Duane *music educator*

**Moorhead**
Eyler, David Paul *music educator*
Rothlisberger, Rodney John *music educator*

**Morris**
Kleinwolterink, John Evan *music educator*

**Mound**
Whaley, Roger Glenn *music educator*

**New Brighton**
Carlson, Kaye Lilien *retired music educator*

**New Ulm**
Moldenhauer, Kermit Gene *music educator*
Schubkegel, Joyce Catherine *music educator, composer*

**North Branch**
Zumwalde, Barry *music educator*

**Plymouth**
Trump, Stephanie *music educator, director*

**Saint Cloud**
Martinson, Jody Marie *voice educator*

**Saint James**
Ferdig, Jerald Jim *music educator*

**Saint Paul**
Coppock, Bruce *orchestra executive*
Dahlberg, Eric Ross *music educator*
McGegan, Nicholas *music director*
Ollmann, Brad Eric *music educator*
You, Yali *music educator*

**Vadnais Heights**
Martinez, Kathryn Marie *music educator*

**Wayzata**
Skrowaczewski, Stanislaw *conductor, composer*

**Winona**
Bures, Ruth Ellen *music educator, composer*

**Woodbury**
Sandberg, Steve Jason *music educator*

## MISSISSIPPI

**Amory**
Bending, Martha King *music educator*

**Cleveland**
Wojcik, John Casimir *music educator, director*

**Goodman**
King, Kathy Cooper *music educator*

**Greenwood**
Horn, Lawrence Charles *retired music educator*

**Hattiesburg**
De Chiaro, John Paul *music educator*
Malone, Mark Hugh *music educator*

**Jackson**
Girtman, Paxton M *music educator*
Guise, Linda Jackson *music educator*
Smith, Carnice *music educator, director*

**Mccomb**
Chamberlin, Mary Ellen *music educator*

**Natchez**
Wynn, Bobbye Faye *music educator*

**Southaven**
Dale, Randy Neil *music educator*

**Sumrall**
Downey, James Cecil *retired music educator, retired humanities educator*

**University**
Dor, George W. K *music educator*
Pulliam, Rene E. *performing arts educator*
Willson, David E. *music educator*

## MISSOURI

**Alton**
Scott, Lori Denise *music educator, musician*

**Blue Springs**
Washburn, Gladys Haase *retired church musician, educator, director*

**Bolivar**
Tarrant, James Richard III *music educator*

**Bowling Green**
Bruce, Judith Esther *retired music educator, elementary school educator*

**Butler**
Turner, Vicky Jo *music educator*

**Carl Junction**
Wostal, Holly Ann *music educator*

**Chillicothe**
Kapono, Francie Napuaonalani Josie *music educator*

**Columbia**
Burgoyne, Suzanne *theater educator, writer*
Dolbashian, Edward John *conductor*

**Creve Coeur**
Faust, John Joseph, Jr. *performing arts educator, theater director*
Randle, Bernadette *musician, composer, graphics designer*

**De Soto**
Jackson, Candine Lee *performing arts educator, English and speech educator*

**Dearborn**
McInnis, Robin Lynn *voice educator*

**Eldon**
Hannah, Melody Lorraine *music educator, elementary school educator*

**Eureka**
Baker, Donna Kay *music educator, director*

**Fayette**
Vandelicht, Roy Dean *music educator*

**Festus**
Auchly, Christopher M *music educator*

**Fulton**
McClain, Cindy Dunstan *music educator*

**Graham**
Svoboda, Robert Ray *music educator*

**Hannibal**
Corkern, David E. *music educator*

**Harrisonville**
Mathew, Kip *music educator*

**Herculaneum**
Smelser, Douglas Martin *music educator*

**House Springs**
Grassino, Sandra Smith *theater educator, language educator*

**Independence**
Pinick, Sariah Kay *music educator*
Pointer, Rosanne Elise *music educator*

**Kansas City**
Ibsen, Van *theater director*
Kuenn, Marjorie Asp *music educator*
Londré, Felicia Mae Hardison *theater educator*
Parcell, John Cleo *music educator*
Robertson, Kenneth Carl *music educator*
Whitener, William Garnett *dancer, choreographer*

**Kirksville**
Gooch, Warren Peter *composer, music educator*
Weerts, Richard Kenneth *music educator*

**La Plata**
Christy, Victor Joseph *music educator*

**Lexington**
Crosson, Timothy J. *music educator*

**Liberty**
Harriman, Richard Lee *performing arts association administrator, educator*

**Marshall**
Sayer, Ronald J. *composer, educator*

**Maryville**
Kling, Carl Andrew *music educator*
Schultz, Patricia Bowers *vocal music educator, conductor*

**Moberly**
Werner, Karen Elaine *music educator*

**Monett**
White, Danika Elaine *music educator*

**Nixa**
Huneycutt, David Jason *music educator*

**Pacific**
Hogan, Kurt Avery *music educator*

**Platte City**
Bonsignore, Matthew Harold *music educator*
Jones, Jay Robert *music educator*

**Point Lookout**
Gerlach, Bruce Alan *music educator, department chairman, composer*

**Poplar Bluff**
Bonk, Rachael Louise *music educator*

**Republic**
Edwards, Craig C. *music educator*

**Riverside**
Bell, John *music educator*

**Rogersville**
Hover, Tryphena Michael *music educator*

**Saint Charles**
Bobrowski, Leonard Stephen *music educator, director*
Grooms, Pamela Gayle *music educator*
Quiggins, Larry Dale *theater educator*
Wallace, Brian Mark *music educator*
Wieberg, Karey Rose *music educator, director*

**Saint Clair**
Israel, John Martin *music educator, musician*

**Saint James**
Stevens, Helen Jean *music educator*

**Saint Joseph**
Smith, Thomas Patrick *music director*

**Saint Louis**
Di Bisceglie, Laureen Gail *pianist, accompanist, educator*
Friz, Gayle Peycke *music educator*
Haley, Johnetta Randolph *music educator*
Ladd, Debbie K. *theater educator, director*
Onovwerosuoke, Fred *music educator, musicologist*
Schindler, Laura Ann *piano teacher, accompanist*
Schweizer, Gregory Paul *music educator*
Stewart, John Harger *music educator*
Turner-Richard, Lana R. *musician, director, composer*
Woolf, Steven Michael *artistic director*

**Springfield**
Breon, April Michelle *music educator*
Dissmore, Larry David *music educator, conductor, musician*
Dove, Michael Karl *music educator, director*
Hawkins, Kevin Andrew *music educator*
Moulder, T. Earline *musician*
Salisbury, Marie Joyce (Marie Joyce Alberti) *musician, educator*
Spicer, Holt Vandercook *retired theater educator*

**Warrensburg**
Smith, Richard Bernard *music educator*
Wood, Kenneth Edward *music educator, tenor*

**Waynesville**
Sabatasso, Jared Ray *music educator*

**Wentzville**
Berry, Chuck (Charles Edward Anderson Berry) *musician, composer*
Gerard, Dawn M. *theater educator*

**Wright City**
Schaffer, William D. *music educator, alderman*

## MONTANA

**Baker**
Whiteman, Jill Karen *music educator*

**Big Timber**
Bratvold, James *music educator*

**Billings**
Barnea, Uri N. *conductor, musician*
Corey, Scott D. *music educator*

**Bozeman**
Langford, Chad *music educator, composer*
Vick, Jeffrey Harrison *music educator, musician*

**Butte**
Clark, Gloria A. *music educator*

**Eureka**
Atherton, Michael Ward *music educator*
Kessler-Hodgson, Lee Gwendolyn *actress, performing company executive*

**Great Falls**
Johnson, Gordon James *performing company executive, composer*
Voss, Lisa Marie *music educator*

**Kalispell**
Slater, Allen J. *music educator*

**Whitefish**
DeFranco, Boniface Ferdinand Leonard (Buddy DeFranco) *clarinetist, bandleader*

## NEBRASKA

**Bellwood**
Lunde, Keith A. *music educator, animal breeder*

**Cairo**
Wiebe-Brown, Beverly *music educator*

**Columbus**
Antholz, Marty *music educator*

**Crete**
Fahrlander, Eric *music educator*

**Gering**
Raines, Robert Randle *music educator*

**Hooper**
Poessnecker, Myron *music educator*

**Kearney**
Buckner, Nathan Andrew *music educator, musician*
Schnoor, Neal Henry *music educator*

**Leigh**
Welsch, Kevin Eugene *music educator*

**Lincoln**
Blanke, Henry H., Jr. *retired theater educator*
Collier, Nathan Morris *musician, educator*
Dixon, Wheeler Winston *film and video studies educator, writer*
Dyrland, Jonathan David Ellis *music educator, tenor*
Falcone, Anthony M. *music educator*
Hanrahan, Kevin *music educator*
Monson, Larry Lee *music educator*
White, Tyler Goodrich *composer, conductor*

**Lyons**
Rose, Dwight Dean *music educator*

**Mc Cook**
Regier, Bryan L. *music educator*
Watts, Susan Helene *theater educator*

**Norfolk**
Luellen, James Arthur *music educator*

**North Platte**
Mueller, Wayne Dennis *music educator*

**Omaha**
Abrahams, Daniel *music educator*
James, Jeffrey R. *music educator*
Johnson, James David *concert pianist, organist, educator*
Keiser, Catherine Ann *band director*
McCandless, Michael J. *theater educator, director*
McKean, Howard Curtis *music educator, composer*
Seitz, Carole Jane *composer, educator*

**Sidney**
Zigweid, Richard Neil *music educator*

**Wayne**
Weber, Bradley R. *music educator*

**Wilber**
Vrbka, Judith Mary *music educator*

## NEVADA

**Boulder City**
Schultheis, Adam John *music educator, consultant*

**Elko**
Lovell, Walter Benjamin *music educator, radio personality*

**Henderson**
Dehart, Susan Marie *music educator*
Riske, William Kenneth *producer, cultural services consultant*
Travers, Andrew Robert *music educator, musician*

**Indian Springs**
Dvorak, DeLyle Dennis *music educator, consultant, early childhood educator*

**Las Vegas**
Anton, Susan *actress*
Baker, Anita *singer*
Bernstein, Maureen Ann *theater educator, director*
Borovicka, Marsha Lorraine *music educator*
Dragone, Franco *performing company executive*
Fleischer, Eric Matthew *music educator*
Frances, Marie Cecilia *theater producer, television producer*
Goulet, Robert Gerard *entertainer*
Jackson, Charles Anthony *music educator, radio personality*
Kendell, Ken *music educator*
Knight, Gladys (Gladys Maria Knight) *singer*
Lewis, Jerry (Joseph Levitch) *comedian*
Muhlenbruck-Fleischer, Deborah Lynn *music educator*
Sakugawa, June Elizabeth *music educator*
Sulich, Vassili *artistic director*
Wiemer, Robert Ernest *film and television producer, writer, director*

**North Las Vegas**
Talley, Brenda S. *performing arts center director, theatrical light designer*

**Reno**
Aldrich, Gary O. *singer, educator*
Daniels, Ronald Dale *conductor*
Lee, H. Helen *music educator*
Smith, Catherine Parsons *music educator*

**Sandy Valley**
Viscuglia, Jenny Lou *music educator*

## NEW HAMPSHIRE

**Alstead**
Holloway, Robert Charles *musician, composer*

**Durham**
Kaye, David Julian *theater educator*

**Hanover**
Dong, Kui *music educator, composer*
Ehrlich, David Gordon *film director, educator*

**Holderness**
Butler, George Tyssen *film director, producer, photographer, writer*

**Manchester**
Marchesseault, Anita *music educator*

**Orford**
Karol, John J., Jr. *producer, filmmaker*

**Walpole**
Burns, Kenneth Lauren *filmmaker, historian*

## NEW JERSEY

**Allendale**
Ruth, Rodney *musician, music consultant, contractor, educator*

**Allentown**
Sulyok, Paul David *music educator, composer*

**Bayville**
Worth, Katherine Marie *retired vocalist*

**Belleville**
Resciniti, John William *music educator, protective services official*

**Bergenfield**
Glazer, Gilda F. *musician, educator*
Marciano, Lisa Oggioni *musician, music educator*

**Bogota**
McCann, Barry John *music educator*
Oakland, Ron *violinist*

**Cherry Hill**
Clauser, Donald Roberdeau *musician*
Rabic, James William *music educator, personal trainer*

**Cinnaminson**
Edwin, Robert *voice educator*

**Clayton**
Bertenshaw, William Howard III *radio and television producer*

**Cliffside Park**
Perhacs, Marylouise Helen *musician, educator*

**Colts Neck**
Borisov, George P. *music educator*

**Delanco**
Lane, Carrie Belle (Hairston) *retired music educator*

**Denville**
Veech, Lynda Anne *musician, educator*

**East Brunswick**
Savio, Frances Margaret Cammarotta *music educator*

**East Hanover**
Iovel, Alla *music educator, writer*

**East Windsor**
Park, Hyosang *music educator*

**Edison**
Chen-Maxham, Li-Chan *soprano*
Fan, Shirley Tsui-Yu *music educator*

**Egg Harbor Township**
Nelson, Edward R. *pianist, composer, educator, consultant*

**Elizabeth**
de la Viña-Sierra, Diana Maria *music educator*

**Englewood**
Svezia, Vera Tisheff *concert pianist*

**Far Hills**
Burns, Amy Margaret *music educator*

**Fords**
Brown, James *singer, broadcasting executive*

**Fort Lee**
Amara, Lucine *vocalist*
Morozova, Irina *musician, music educator*
Thomopoulos, Michael *music educator*

**Freehold**
Cheng, Grace Zheng-Ying *music educator*

**Hackettstown**
Berrie, Marily Monteith *music educator*

**Highlands**
Saunders Furda, Denise Elizabeth *music educator*
Skidmore, Nancy Lynne *music educator, pre-school educator*

**Hoboken**
Upchurch, Leslie Purcell *music educator*

**Jackson**
McCormick, Harold J. *music educator*

**Jersey City**
Hayes, Isaac *rhythm and blues singer, composer*
Queen Latifah, (Dana Owens) *recording artist, actress*
Warren, Maredia Delois *music educator*

**Leonia**
Deutsch, Nina *pianist, vocalist*
Dondysh, Victoria *pianist*

**Lincroft**
Benham, Helen *music educator*

**Madison**
Moffa, Bonnie J. *performing arts company executive, director, educator*

**Mahwah**
Morneweck-Fuld, Lynn E. *music educator*

**Manasquan**
Barr, Ted Walker *music educator*

**Matawan**
Updegraff, Steven Phillip *music educator*

**Medford**
Sheffer, James Thomas *music educator, elementary school educator*

**Middletown**
Vitalo, Sandra Lynn Liddy *music educator, singer*

**Monmouth Junction**
Lien, Ting-Ting *music educator*

**Montclair**
Cioffi, Patrizia *soprano, voice educator, arts consultant*
Walker, George Theophilus, Jr. *composer, music educator, pianist*

**New Brunswick**
Gambino, Anthony Thomas *music educator, musician*
Trautman, Mark Allen *conductor*

**Newark**
Macal, Zdenek *conductor, music director*

**Newton**
Boulware, Bobbie L. *music educator*

**North Caldwell**
Boronow, John David *music educator*
Imhof, David Charles *music educator*

**North Plainfield**
Parrcott, Dorian Lee, II, *music educator*

**Northfield**
McNeal, Jane Erskine *music educator, musician*

**Oakland**
DeFreest, Kevin Albert *music educator*

**Ocean Grove**
Perwo, George Edward *music educator*

**Paramus**
Gordon, Scott (Harry Scott Buehlmeier) *entertainer, actor*
Marcel-Calderon, Linda *music educator*
Saltzman, Jared *performing arts educator, lighting designer*

**Park Ridge**
Popolizio, Rick *music educator*

**Parsippany**
Iapicca, Michael Alfonso *music educator*
Reed, Howie *music educator, minister*

**Pennsville**
Ludlam, James Brian *music educator*

**Perth Amboy**
Richardson-Melech, Joyce Suzanne *music educator, singer*

**Princeton**
Branker, Anthony Daniel John *music educator, researcher, composer*
Kawarsky, Jay A. *music educator, conductor, composer*
Levy, Kenneth *music educator*
Lustig, Graham *artistic director*
Orphanides, Nora Charlotte *ballet educator*

**Ramsey**
Gipple, Douglas John *theater educator, literature and language educator*

**Raritan**
Bower, David Norman *music educator, director*

**Ridgefield**
Tracey, Matthew Sean *music educator, musician*

**Rivervale**
Moderacki, Edmund Anthony *music educator, conductor*

**Roosevelt**
Zuckerman, Mark Alan *composer, consultant*

**Salem**
Brauer, Shaun Michael *music educator*

**Scotch Plains**
Kraemer, Ira B. *symphony conductor*

**Secaucus**
Diggs, Taye (Scott Diggs) *actor*

**Sicklerville**
Simpson, Eugene Thamon *music educator, singer*

**Skillman**
Hackel, Adam William *music educator*

**Somerset**
DeMonic, Betty Lee *music educator*

**South Orange**
Nowik, John David *music educator, musician*

**Sparta**
Jacobs-Quam, Vivien Marie *retired music educator*
McMeen, Elmer Ellsworth III *musician, retired lawyer*

**Summit**
Falletta, Jo Ann *conductor*
Kahmann, Chesley *composer, music educator, pianist*

**Teaneck**
Bullough, John Frank *musician, educator*
Carter, Regina *jazz violinist*
Graham, Janet Lorraine *music educator*

**Tenafly**
Tall, Susan Porter *music educator*

**Trenton**
Cole, Richie Thomas *musician, composer, educator*
Demitry, Elpis Hope *music educator*

**Warren**
Maull, George Marriner *conductor, educator*

**Wayne**
DeRosa, Richard Jerome *composer, musician, educator*
Sullivan, Glenn D. *music educator*

**West Orange**
Atkins, Richard Bart *film, television producer*
Mazur, Thomas A. *music educator*

**Westfield**
Schlosberg, Theodore K. *music educator*

**Wildwood Crest**
Carey, Steven Everett *music educator*

**Woodbridge**
Qiu, Li-Hui *music educator, actress*

**NEW MEXICO**

**Albuquerque**
Jewell, Donna Louise *choreographer, educator*
Kierst, Debra B. *theater educator, theater director*
Liotta, William A. *theater educator*
Mock, Joan Bodet *music educator*
Neel, Sandra Laureen *voice educator, vocalist*
Poole, David Evans *music educator, composer*
Rasmussen, Kerrie L. *theater educator*
Sanks, John Clement *music educator*
Steinbach, Falko *pianist, composer, educator*
Tiano, Anthony Steven *television producer, publishing executive*

**Artesia**
Jensen, Eric Reinhard *music educator*

**Belen**
Jolly, Jeffrey Russell *music educator, musician*

**Corrales**
Radcliffe, Glena Eloise *lyricist, poet, composer*

**Edgewood**
Hamilton, Jerald *musician*

**Hobbs**
Wong, Yau-Sun *music educator, conductor, composer*

**Las Cruces**
Fitzgearld, Gayl *music educator, musician*

**Portales**
Carr, Tracy A. *musician, educator*
Dal Porto, Mark Daniel *music educator*
Mancusi, Roberto Francesco Costantino *vocalist, educator*
Wozencraft-Ornellas, (Betty) Jean *singer, music educator*

**Roswell**
Hedin, Edna Jenks *musician, educator*

**Santa Fe**
Ballard, Louis Wayne *composer*
Gaddes, Richard *opera company director*
Gilbert, Alan *conductor*
Knight, Kenneth Hugh *conductor*
Ovitsky, Steven Alan *musician, symphony orchestra executive*
Rubenstein, Bernard *orchestra conductor*
Snider, Richard Douglas *music educator, director*
Zlatoff-Mirsky, Everett Igor *violinist*

**Tesuque**
MacGraw, Ali *actress*

**NEW YORK**

**Addison**
Vona, John David *music educator*

**Albany**
Marschilok, Edward *music educator, musician*

**Amherst**
Biddle, Paul Daniel *music educator*
Marone, James Matthew *music educator*

**Annandale On Hudson**
Miyagawa, Chiori *theater educator, playwright*
Tower, Joan Peabody *composer, educator*

**Astoria**
Francesca, Mike *radio personality*
Russo, Chris *radio personality*
Sirignano, Monica Ann *performing company executive, playwright*

**Attica**
Rogers, Donald L. *music educator, department chairman, animal breeder*

**Babylon**
Kroll, Brian Walter Thomas *music educator*

**Baldwinsville**
Bowen, Jonathan L. *music educator, consultant*

**Bayside**
Zinn, William *musician, composer*

**Bedford**
Chase, Chevy (Cornelius Crane Chase) *comedian, actor, writer*

**Binghamton**
Powell, Barbara Ann *music educator, voice educator*
Silverberg, Carol Eve *theater educator*
Wildoner, Nancy Schamu *music educator, fine arts department chairman*

**Blasdell**
Smith, Robin E. *music educator*

**Bloomington**
Culver, Michael Patrick *music educator, composer*

**Boiceville**
Thomas, David Clifton *music educator*

**Briarcliff Manor**
Wheeler, Margaret Jane *actress, soprano, voice educator*

**Brightwaters**
Zayas, Elinor Abrams *music educator*

**Brockport**
McGhee, Diane Baumann *dance instructor, consultant*

**Bronx**
Ask-Nanko, Lorraine Charlotte *music educator*
Coyote, Peter (Peter Cohon) *actor*

De Luca, Eva *vocalist, writer, composer, entrepreneur, inventor*
Doyle, Brian Leahy *theater educator, director*
Fletcher, Judith Ellen *music educator*
Lemos, Arthur *retired music educator*
Mittler, Diana (Diana Mittler-Battipaglia) *music educator, pianist*
Rubensky, Mitchell *band director*
Sherman, Judith Dorothy *theater producer, engineer, recording industry executive*

**Bronxville**
Biscardi, Chester *composer, educator*

**Brookhaven**
Desiderio, Joseph Gerard *music educator*

**Brooklyn**
Douglas, Jerry *bluegrass musician, dobro player*
Gatten, David *filmmaker*
Hopkins, Karen Brooks *performing arts executive*
Lazar, Paul Alan *actor*
Lee, Spike (Shelton Jackson Lee) *film director, film producer*
McQuiggan, John A. *theater producer, writer*
Mitcheltree, Dennis *musician, educator*
Morris, Mark William *choreographer*
Niesen, James Louis *theater director*
Richmond, Eero *composer, music librarian*
Ruane, Krista *TV food stylist*
Sahlene, *singer*
Slonczewski, Craig (Craig Slon) *composer*
Smith, Bernadine M. *radio personality, filmmaker, writer, film producer, film director*
Streb, Elizabeth A. *choreographer, dancer*
Vidal, Maureen Eris *theater educator, actress*

**Brookville**
Sugar, Joseph Robert *music educator, conductor, musician*

**Buffalo**
Boyar, Benjamin *music educator*
DiFranco, Ani *music executive, musician*
Lombardo Appleby, Linda Rose *music educator*
Manes, Stephen Gabriel *concert pianist, educator*
Reed, Janet *dance educator, choreographer*
Wagner, Barbara Lee *musician*

**Caledonia**
Walker, Todd A. *music educator, football coach*

**Canton**
Halstead, Ann Marie G. *performing arts educator*

**Carthage**
Mosher, Daniel Lee *music educator*

**Central Islip**
Voigt, Philip Kenneth *music educator*

**Chester**
Munsch, Martin John III *sound recording engineer, music producer*

**Cicero**
Pink, (Alecia B. Moore) *singer*

**College Point**
Mullany, Kevin Fergus *music educator, director*

**Commack**
Ohman, Franklin Eric *ballet educator, choreographer*

**Corning**
Peters, Linda S. *musician, educator*

**Crugers**
Norman, Jessye *soprano*

**Deer Park**
Amend, Stephen J. *musician*
Chapman, Ronald Thomas *musician, educator*

**Delmar**
Beck, David Christopher *music educator, conductor*

**Derby**
Cuomo, Rivers *singer, songwriter*

**Dix Hills**
Mymit, Chuck W. *music educator, musician*

**Dobbs Ferry**
Briskin, Efrem *music educator*
Sherin, Edwin *theater director, film director, television director, actor*

**East Greenbush**
Quenelle, Susannah Sherman *music educator*

**East Hampton**
Dello Joio, Norman *composer*
Nelson, Mark D. *music educator, arts education administrator*

**East Patchogue**
McAleese, Alice S. *music educator*

**Elmont**
Kolb, Lisa Marie *music educator*

**Elmsford**
Price, Richard Galen *sound recording engineer, music producer, conductor*

**Endicott**
Gleason, James Perley *music educator*

**Farmingdale**
Facchiano, Patricia A. *music educator*

**Fayetteville**
Larson, Lori Geralyn *music educator, singer*

**Flushing**
Cesarano, Michael Ferdinand *theater educator, actor*
Evens, Lucie Ann *music educator*
Smaldone, Edward Michael *composer*

**Forest Hills**
Mathieu Byers, Deborah Anne *performing company executive*
Polakoff, Abe *baritone*

**Freeport**
Zurcher, Zean William *retired music educator, musician*

**Fulton**
Jennings, Meghan Young *music educator*

**Garden City**
Boquiren, Sidney Marquez *composer, educator*
Einenkel, Robert Herbert *theater educator, actor, director*
Gray, Phil R. *band director, musician*
Moravec, Paul *composer*
Pereira, John William Miller *theater educator*
Wetherill-Smith, Linda Marie *music educator, musician, performing arts association administrator*

**Germantown**
Farberman, Harold *conductor, composer*
Rollins, Sonny (Theodore Rollins) *composer, musician*

**Grahamsville**
Pilc, Jean-Michel *composer, musician*

**Great Neck**
Schwartz, Michael Robert *music educator, department chairman*

**Greenlawn**
Lelyveld, Gail Annick *actress*

**Greenvale**
Senft, Mason George *musician*
Watt, Stephanie Denise *musician, educator, department chairman*

**Hancock**
Geer, Paul DeWitt *music educator*

**Harpursville**
Cline, Nicole Elizabeth *music educator*

**Hastings On Hudson**
D'Antoni, Philip *television producer*
Sharpe, Robert Kent *writer, director, producer, photographer*
Wolfe, Stanley *composer, educator*

**Hempstead**
Coleman, Benjamin Joseph *music educator*
Graffeo, Mary Thérèse *music educator, performer*
Heuermann-Nowik, Patricia Calhoun *theater director*
Schechtman, Saul *conductor*

**Hicksville**
Garner, Beth L. *music educator*
Kronowitz, Pamela Renee *music educator*

**Highland**
Ratick, Randie H. *music educator, elementary school educator*

**Homer**
Bull, Beverly Jane *piano and voice educator*

**Howard Beach**
Leiter, Samuel L. *theater educator*

**Hudson**
Loder, Randolph James *music educator*

**Hunter**
Khanzadian, Vahan *tenor*

**Huntington**
Masear, Claude *music educator, musician*
Oler, Kim *voice educator*

**Hyde Park**
Beckmann, Kathleen Ann *music educator*

**Islip**
Ramsden, Virginia Ann *retired music educator*

**Ithaca**
Arquit, Nora Harris *retired music educator, writer*
Husa, Karel *composer, conductor, educator*

**Jackson Heights**
Morrow, Nana Kwasi Scott Douglas *choreographer, director, writer, filmmaker, educator*
Stevenson, Amanda (Sandy Stevens) *librettist, composer, songwriter*

**Jamaica**
Lee, Joseph *musician, educator*

**Johnson City**
De Angelo, Jan Joseph *music educator*

**Katonah**
Brownlee, Delphine *actress, musician*

**Kenmore**
Kuhn, William Andrew *music educator*

**Kew Gardens**
Chen, Yuanlin *composer*

**Lancaster**
Meides, Holly Sue *music educator*

**Lindenhurst**
Snider, Dee (David Daniel Snider) *rock singer, composer, radio personality*

**Long Beach**
Gach, Jay Anthony *composer*

**Long Eddy**
Hoiby, Lee *composer, concert pianist*

**Long Island City**
Convery, Robert *composer, educator*
Giaimo, Kathryn Ann *performing arts company executive*

**Manhasset**
Brand, Oscar *folk singer, writer, educator*
Sirooni, Anahid Alice *composer*

**Massapequa**
Turk, Elizabeth Ann *music educator*

**Melville**
Pinto, Janet Sue *music educator*
Sobol, Elise Schwarcz *music educator*

**Merrick**
Sardo, Sanford *music educator*

**Millbrook**
Flexner, Josephine Moncure *musician, educator*

**Millerton**
Hastings, Donald Francis *actor, writer*

**Monroe**
Furman-Markowitz, Joanna Florence *dance educator*

**Montgomery**
Teutul, Paul, Sr. *television personality, mechanic*

**Mount Morris**
Leyerle, William Dean *music educator, publishing executive*

**Nanuet**
Hurd, David Gary *music educator, actor, musician*

**Narrowsburg**
Krause, Gloria Rose *music educator*

**New Hartford**
Weiss, Holly Anne *music educator, singer*

**New York**
Adams, Bryan *vocalist, composer, photographer*
Adams, John Coolidge *composer, conductor*
Adler, Richard *composer, lyricist*
Aguilera, Christina *vocalist*
Ahrens, Lynn *lyricist*
Alda, Alan *actor, film director, scriptwriter*
Alexander, Jane (Jane Quigley) *actress, theater educator, writer*
Allen, Betty (Mrs. Ritten Edward Lee III) *mezzo-soprano*
Alt, Carol A. *actress, model, entrepreneur, writer*
Altman, Robert (Robert Bernard Altman) *film director, writer, producer*
Amos, Tori *musician, singer*
Anagnost, Dino *artistic director*
Anania, Vincent Jay *film director, educator*
Ananiashvili, Nina *ballerina*
Andersen, Mark *musician*
Andrade, Andres *vocalist, educator*
Armitage, Karole *dancer*
Arroyo, Martina *soprano*
Asakawa, Takako *dancer, educator, choreographer, director*
Ashanti, (Ashanti Shequoiya Douglas) *vocalist*
Asner, Edward *actor*
Atkins, John *concert pianist, voice educator, model*
Bacall, Lauren (Betty Joan Perske) *actress*
Bana, Eric *actor*
Barber, Russell Brooks Butler *television producer*
Barbour, Catherine Jean *actress, set designer, director, mime*
Barrett, Herbert *performing company executive, management consultant*
Bart, Roger *actor*
Bashkow, Jack Simon *musician*
Beauford, Carter *musician*
Bednar, Rudy *television producer, director*
Bee, Samantha *comedian, actress*
Beeson, Jack Hamilton *composer, educator, writer*
Behar, Joy *television personality*
Behrendt, Greg *comedian*
Belzer, Richard *actor, comedian*
Benjamin, Andre Lauren (Dre, André 3000) *vocalist, actor*
Bergman, Lowell *television news producer*
Besterman, Douglas *composer, orchestrator*
Bikel, Theodore *actor, singer*
Birkenhead, Thomas Bruce *theater producer, educator*
Björk, (Björk Guðmundsdóttir) *singer, composer*
Bledel, Alexis (Kimberly Alexis Bledel) *actress*
Bolton, Michael *singer, songwriter*
Boston, Gretha *actress, vocalist*
Boxill, Edith Hillman *music therapist, educator, writer*
Bracco, Lorraine *actress*
Brant, Henry *composer*
Breakstone, Joshua Scott *musician, educator, composer*
Brinkley, Christie *model, spokesperson, designer*
Brohn, William David *conductor, orchestrator, arranger*
Brothers, Joyce Diane *television personality, psychologist*
Brown, Chris (Christopher Maurice Brown) *singer*
Brown, David *motion picture producer, writer*
Brown, Trisha *dancer*
Bucchino, John *composer*
Bundchen, Giselle *model*
Burke, Delta *actress*
Bush, Lauren *model*
Butler, Kerry *actress*
Byer, Diana *performing company executive*

Caldwell, L. Scott *actress*
Campbell, Alan *actor*
Cantrell, Lana *actress, lawyer, singer*
Capalbo, Carmen *theater director, producer*
Caples, Richard James *performing company executive, lawyer*
Carell, Steve *comedian, actor*
Carlson, Marvin Albert *theater educator*
Carmichael, Jesse Royal *musician*
Carmona, Wayne *television producer*
Carney, Michael *orchestra leader*
Carter, Elliott Cook, Jr. *composer*
Cash, Rosanne *singer, songwriter*
Castel, Nico *tenor, educator*
Cazeaux, Isabelle Anne Marie *retired music educator*
Cesar, Kamala *dancer, educator*
Chang, Marian S. *filmmaker, composer*
Channing, Stockard (Susan Antonia Williams Stockard) *actress*
Chappell, Wallace *performing company executive*
Chase, Will *actor*
Chenoweth, Kristin *actress*
Christensen, Dieter *ethnomusicologist*
Chusid, Martin *musicologist, educator*
Ciara, (Ciara Princess Harris) *R&B performer*
Clark, Victoria *actress*
Clarkson, Kelly Brianne *singer*
Colbert, Stephen *comedian, actor*
Collins, Phil (Philip David Charles Collins) *singer, songwriter, drummer, record producer*
Conway, Kevin *actor, performing company executive*
Corddry, Rob *comedian, actor*
Corigliano, John Paul *composer*
Corsaro, Frank Andrew *theater director*
Coughlin, Brian Edward *musician*
Crystal, Billy *comedian, actor*
Cunningham, Merce *dancer*
Curry, Adam Clark *television personality, radio personality, computer programmer, computer technology company executive*
Curtin, Jane Therese *actress, writer*
Curtis, Paul James *performance artist*
Dakin, Christine Whitney *dancer, educator*
Daltrey, Roger *musician*
Danitz, Marilynn Patricia *choreographer, video specialist*
Dano, Linda *actress*
Danza, Tony *actor*
David, Hal *lyricist*
Davidovsky, Mario *retired composer*
Deen, Paula H. *television personality, restaurant owner, chef*
de Kenessey, Stefania Maria *composer*
DePreist, James Anderson *conductor*
DeWoody, Beth Rudin *film producer*
DiBiasio, Adolf R. *entertainment company executive*
Di Vittorio, Salvatore *composer, conductor*
Domino, Fats (Antoine Domino) *pianist, singer, songwriter*
Douglas, Kyan *television personality*
Downs, Hugh Malcolm *retired radio and television broadcaster*
Doyle, John *artistic director, designer*
Dratch, Rachel *comedienne, actress*
Drukman, Steven Charles *theater educator, playwright*
Duchin, Peter Oelrichs *musician*
Duff, Hilary Ann *actress, singer*
Dukakis, Olympia *actress*
Dulaine, Pierre *ballroom dancer*
Du Prez, John *composer*
Durang, Christopher *actor, playwright*
Dusick, Ryan Michael *musician*
Dylan, Bob (Robert Allen Zimmerman) *singer, composer*
Earle, Eugenia *music educator*
Ebersole, Christine *actress*
Eisler, Edith *music educator*
Ellin, Doug *film producer, television producer, television director, writer*
Elliott, Missy (Melissa Arnette Elliot) *musician*
Ellis, Scott *theatrical director*
Ellis, Terry *vocalist*
Emme, (Emme Aronson) *model, apparel designer*
Epstein, Matthew *opera company director*
Eschenbach, Christoph *conductor, musician, music director*
Estes, Simon Lamont *opera singer, bass-baritone*
Eustis, Oskar (Paul Jefferson Eustis) *performing company executive*
Evans, Faith *singer*
Fantasia, (Fantasia Monique Barrino) *singer*
Farino, Julian *television director, film director, television producer*
Farley, Carole *soprano*
Feit, Barberi Paull *composer, lyricist, psychotherapist, writer*
Feld, Eliot *dancer, choreographer, performing company executive*
Fields, Felicia P. *actress*
Filarski Hasselbeck, Elizabeth *television host/personality*
Fisher, Joely *actress*
Fisk, Eliot H. *musician*
Flack, Roberta *singer*
Fleming, Renée L. *opera singer*
Flowers, Brandon Richard *singer*
Fogel, Henry *orchestra administrator*
Fogler, Dan *actor*
Fontana, Thomas Michael *television producer, scriptwriter*
Foreman, Richard *theater director, playwright*
Formento, Daniel *radio company executive, writer*
Fowler, Beth *actress*
Fox, Matthew *actor*
Friedman, Debbie *singer, songwriter, religious studies educator*
Garcia, Andy *actor*
Gazzara, Ben *actor*
Gelb, Peter *performing company executive*
Gibney, Alex *producer, film director, writer*
Gillinson, Sir Clive Daniel *performing company executive, former musician*
Giraldi, Robert Nicholas *film director*
Glass, Philip *composer, musician*
Goines, Leonard *music educator, consultant*
Goldsmith, Merwin *actor, theater director*
Goldston, James *television producer*

Goto, Midori *classical violinist*
Graff, Randy *actress*
Greenberg, Mark *television producer*
Grenrock-Woods, Stacey *comedian, actress*
Greyson, Ann S. *choreographer, theater producer*
Griffel, L. Michael *music educator, researcher*
Griffiths, Jem *singer*
Griffiths, Richard *actor*
Groban, Josh *vocalist*
Grohl, David Eric *musician*
Gunn, Nathan *baritone*
Haggerty, Luane Ruth Davis *theater director, educator, actress*
Haimes, Todd *artistic director*
Hall, Michael C. *actor*
Halmi, Robert, Sr. *film producer, television producer*
Hammett, Kirk Lee *musician*
Hammond, Darrell *actor*
Hargitay, Mariska Magdolina *actress*
Harmon, Jane *theater producer*
Harrell, Ray Evans *performing company executive, conductor, educator*
Harris, Julie (Julie Ann Harris) *actress*
Hartley, Hal *film director*
Hartwick, Gary Glenn *entertainment company executive*
Hastings, Deborah *bass guitarist*
Hawkins, Oliver Taylor (Taylor Hawkins) *musician*
Heald, Anthony *actor*
Hebert, Bliss Edmund *opera director*
Helm, Lenora Zenzalai *musician, music educator*
Herrera, Paloma *dancer*
Herron, Cindy *actress, vocalist*
Herzog, Werner (Werner Stipetic) *film director*
Hetfield, James *singer*
Ho, Betty Juenyü Yülin *retired music educator, physiologist, educator*
Holmes, Anna-Marie *ballerina*
Houghton, James *performing company executive*
Hourigan, Jacqueline (Jack Hourigan) *television personality*
Hughes, Doug *theater director*
Hurlin, Dan *theater director*
Hutchinson, Lynda Ronette (Billie Holiday Jr., Princess of Jazz, Munchie) *vocalist, musician, comedian, actress*
Hyman, Earle *actor, educator*
Hytner, Nicholas *theatrical director*
Imus, Don (John Donald Imus Jr.) *radio personality*
IRIA, (Irja Leino) *model, artist, painter*
Ivanov, Kalin Hristov *music educator, musician*
Ivory, James Francis *film director*
Jackson, Anne (Anne Jackson Wallach) *actress*
Jacobs, Jim *actor, composer, librettist, playwright*
Jacobs, Paul A. *music educator*
Jaffe, Susan *ballerina*
James, Christopher Lewis *composer*
Jamison, Judith *dancer*
Jason, Kyle *radio personality, musician*
Jay-Z, (Shawn Corey Carter) *rap artist, music company executive*
Jean, Wyclef *musician, recording industry executive*
Jefferson, Denise *dance school director*
Jett, Joan (Joan Larkin) *musician*
Jones, Bill T. *dancer, choreographer*
Jung, Doris *soprano*
Kahane, Jeffrey *conductor, pianist*
Kamen, D. Jonathan *film producer*
Kamlot, Robert *performing arts executive*
Kanakaredes, Melina *actress*
Karchin, Louis Samuel *composer, educator*
Kassel, Virginia Weltmer *television producer, scriptwriter*
Keating, Isabel *actress*
Kellogg, Paul *opera company director*
Kelly, R. (Robert Sylvester Kelly) *musician, recording industry executive*
Kenny, Tom *actor*
Kent, Julie *dancer, actress, model*
Kent, Linda Gail *dancer*
Kenwright, Bill *theatrical producer*
Keys, Alicia (Alicia Augello Cook) *vocalist, musician, songwriter*
Kid Rock, (Robert James Ritchie) *singer*
Kilik, Jon *film producer*
Kimball, Chad *actor*
Kinberg, Judy *television producer, television director*
King, B.B. (Riley B. King) *singer, guitarist*
Kirle, Bruce *theater educator*
Kitahata-Sporn, Amy *movement educator*
Klein, Robert *comedian, actor*
Kline, Kevin Delaney *actor*
Kozak, Harley Jane *actress, writer*
Kudisch, Marc *actor*
Kurman, Juta *music educator*
La Barbara, Joan Linda *composer, musician, singer*
LaBelle, Patti (Patricia Louise Holte) *singer, entertainer*
Laderman, Ezra *composer, educator, college dean*
Lane, Kenneth Robert *producer, distributor*
Lane, Louis *musician, conductor*
Lang, Pearl *dancer, choreographer*
Lang, Stephen *actor*
Lange, Jessica Phyllis *actress*
Lanpher, Katherine *radio personality, columnist*
Lansbury, Edgar George *theatrical producer*
Lansner, Gabrielle *choreographer, dancer, performing company executive, actress*
Lauer, Matt *television personality*
Leach, Robin *producer, writer, television host*
Lee, Amy *singer*
Legend, John (John Stephens) *musician*
Legrand, Michel Jean *composer*
Lenox, Adriane *actress*
Leppard, Raymond John *conductor, musician*
Leritz, Lawrence R. *choreographer, singer, dancer*
Lessard, Stefan *musician*
Letterman, David *talk show host, producer, comedian, writer*
Levine, Adam Noah *singer*
Levine, James *conductor, music director, pianist*
Levinson, Stephen *television producer*
Lewis, Jerry Lee *country-rock singer, musician*
Libin, Paul *theater producer, theater executive*
LiBretto, John Charles *television director*

Lilly, Evangeline *actress*
Lima, Adriana Francesca *model*
Limbaugh, Rush Hudson III *radio talk show host*
Lipton, James *television personality*
Loeb, Lisa *singer, lyricist*
Loney, Glenn Meredith *theater educator*
Lopez, Robert *composer, lyricist*
Losier, Marie *film director*
Love, Shirley *mezzo-soprano*
Lubovitch, Lar *dancer, choreographer*
Lucas, James E(vans) *operatic director*
Lucci, Susan *actress*
Lunn, Kitty Elizabeth *actress*
LuPone, Patti *actress*
Lyman, Peggy *artistic director, dancer, choreographer, educator*
Ma, Yo-Yo *cellist*
Maazel, Lorin *conductor, composer, violinist, music director*
Madden, Mickey *musician*
Maddow, Rachel *radio personality, political activist*
Malakhov, Vladimir *dancer*
Malkin, Barry *film editor, consultant*
Malloy, Michael Dennis *radio personality*
Mamlok, Ursula *composer, educator*
Manilow, Barry (Barry Alan Pincus) *singer, composer*
Mann, Aimee *singer, songwriter*
Mansouri, Lotfollah (Lotfi Mansouri) *retired performing company executive*
Mantegna, Joe Anthony *actor, playwright*
Maraynes, Allan Lawrence *filmmaker, television producer*
Mardirosian, Tom *actor, playwright*
Margolis, Mark Neal *actor*
Marino, Dan *sports broadcaster, retired professional football player*
Maron, Marc *radio personality, comedian, actor, writer*
Marshall, Kathleen *choreographer, theater director*
Marshall, Robert *film director, television director, theater director, choreographer*
Martin, Ricky (Enrique Martin Morales IV) *vocalist, actor*
Martini, Richard K. *theatrical producer*
Martins, Peter *ballet master, choreographer, dancer*
Marx, Jeff *composer, lyricist, lawyer, writer*
Mason, Marshall W. *theater director, educator, author*
Matthews, Dave *singer, musician*
Maxwell, Carla Lena *dancer, choreographer, educator*
Mayer, John *musician*
Mays, Linda *performing arts association administrator*
Maysles, Albert H. *filmmaker*
Mazzo, Kay *ballet dancer, educator*
Mazzola, John William *retired performing company executive, consultant*
McCall, Brendan *dancer, educator*
McClure, Lee *musician, composer, educator*
McDonald, Audra Ann *actress, vocalist*
McGrady, Phyllis *television producer*
McKagan, Duff (Michael Andrew McKagan) *bassist*
McKenzie, Kevin Patrick *artistic director*
McKeown, Allan John *television producer, theater producer*
Mc Lean, Don *singer, instrumentalist, composer*
Meadow, Lynne (Carolyn Meadow) *theater producer*
Mehta, Zarin *performing company executive*
Mekas, Jonas *filmmaker, poet*
Mellencamp, John (John Cougar) *singer, lyricist*
Mendel, Nate (Nathan Gregor Mendel) *musician*
Merchant, Natalie Anne *musician, singer*
Meunier, Monique *dancer*
Michaels, Lorne *television writer, producer*
Miller, Beth McCarthy *television director*
Miller, Dennis *comedian*
Mintz, Shlomo *conductor, violist*
Mitchell, Arthur *dancer, choreographer, performing company executive, educator*
Moby, (Richard Melville Hall) *musician*
Monaghan, Dominic *actor*
Monk, Debra *actress*
Monk, Meredith Jane *artistic director, composer, choreographer, filmmaker*
Moore, Leroi *musician*
Moore, Michael Watson *motion picture editor*
Moore, Rachel Suzanne *performing company executive, dancer*
Morano, Frank *radio producer, talk show host*
Moyers, Judith Davidson *television producer*
Muller, Jennifer *choreographer, dancer*
Muradian, Vazgen *violist, composer*
Murphy, Carolyn *model*
Murphy, Donna *actress*
Murphy, Rosemary *actress*
Nair, Mira *film director, film producer*
Nederlander, James Morton *theater executive*
Nelly, (Cornell Haynes Jr.) *rap artist*
Nugent, Nelle *theater, film and television producer*
O'Brien, Conan *talk show host, writer, performer*
O'Neal, Hank *theater producer, small business owner*
Oremus, Stephen *composer*
Oz, Frank (Frank Richard Oznowicz) *entertainer, film director*
Parker, Alice *composer*
Parsons, Estelle *actress, director, theater producer*
Patton, Antwan Andre (Big Boi) *vocalist*
Paul, Les *entertainer*
Pavarotti, Luciano *lyric tenor*
Payton-Wright, Pamela *actress*
Pendleton, Austin *actor, theater director*
Perlman, Itzhak *violinist*
Perlmutter, Alvin Howard *television and film producer*
Perrineau, Harold *actor*
Perry, Douglas *opera singer*
Peters, Bernadette (Bernadette Lazzara) *actress*
Peters, Roberta *soprano*
Phair, Liz *vocalist*
Philbin, Regis (Regis Francis Xavier Philbin) *television personality*
Plant, Robert Anthony *singer, composer*
Poehler, Amy *comedienne, actress*

Poor, Peter Varnum *television producer, television director*
Posin, Kathryn Olive *choreographer*
Powers, Scott *television producer, actor*
Previn, André (Andre Ludwig Prewin) *composer, conductor, pianist*
Price, Leontyne (Mary Violet Leontyne Price) *retired concert and opera singer, soprano*
Prince, Harold *theatrical director, producer*
Pulos, Virginia Kate *actress, consultant*
Queler, Eve *conductor*
Quivers, Robin *radio personality*
Ramirez, Sara *actress*
Ramirez, Tina *artistic director*
Randolph, David *conductor*
Read, William Tim *musician*
Redgrave, Lynn *actress*
Reeves, Dianne *singer*
Reeves, Jennifer Todd *filmmaker*
Reich, Steve *composer*
Reinhart, Charles Lawrence *performing company executive*
Reinking, Ann H. *dancer, actress*
Renick, Kyle *artistic director*
Reuben, Gloria *actress, singer*
Rhodes, Randi *radio personality*
Rhodes, Samuel *violist, educator*
Richards, Martin *theatrical producer*
Rifkin, Ron *actor*
Rigg, Dame Diana *actress*
Riley, Mark *radio personality, political scientist*
Ripa, Kelly Maria *television personality, actress*
Rivera, Chita (Conchita del Rivero) *actress, singer, dancer*
Rivera, Geraldo *television personality, journalist*
Rizer, Maggie *model*
Robbins, Tim (Timothy Francis Robbins) *actor, film director*
Roberts, Denise (Denise Roberts Hurlin) *dancer*
Robison, Paula Judith *flutist*
Rodriguez, Freddy *actor*
Ronstadt, Linda Marie *singer*
Rosen, Nathaniel Kent *cellist*
Ross, Diana (Diana Ernestine Earle Ross) *singer, actress, entertainer, fashion designer*
Roth, Daryl *theater producer*
Rothfeld, Michael B. *theatrical producer, investor*
Rothschild, Amalie Randolph *filmmaker, film producer, film director, photographer*
Rouse, Christopher Chapman III *composer, educator*
Rubin-Vega, Daphne *actress*
Rudel, Julius *conductor*
Rudin, Scott *film and theatre producer*
RuPaul, (Andre Charles) *model, singer*
Russell, David O. *film director, film producer, scriptwriter*
Saddler, Donald Edward *choreographer, dancer*
Salerno-Sonnenberg, Nadja *violinist*
Salonen, Esa-Pekka *conductor, music director*
Salonga, Lea *actress, singer*
Santiago-Hudson, Ruben *actor*
Sarandon, Susan Abigail *actress*
Schafer, Milton *composer, pianist, educator*
Schechner, Richard *theater director, educator*
Scheeder, Louis *theater producer, director, educator*
Schoenfeld, Gerald *performing company executive*
Schorer, Suki *ballet teacher*
Schwantner, Joseph *composer, educator*
Scott, Campbell *actor*
Seal, *musician*
Sean Paul, (Sean Paul Henriques) *singer*
Seary, Lawrence Anthony *cinematographer, editor*
Seidler, Alan Richard *composer, musician, music company executive*
Seldes, Marian *actress*
Seltzer, Leo *cinematographer, educator*
Serebrier, José *musician, composer, conductor*
Severs, William Floyd *actor*
Shaffer, Paul *musician, bandleader*
Shakira, Isabel Mebarak Ripoll) *musician*
Sheik, Duncan *singer, songwriter*
Shelley, Carole *actress*
Sherman, Arthur *theater educator, writer, actor, composer, sculptor*
Shiflett, Chris *musician*
Shuman, Earl Stanley *songwriter, music publisher*
Siegel, Marc Monroe *television producer, scriptwriter, director*
Sills, Beverly (Mrs. Peter B. Greenough) *performing company executive, singer*
Silver, Joan Micklin *film director, screenwriter*
Silvers, Sally *choreographer, performing company executive*
Simkin, Toby James *theater producer, consultant*
Simmons, Joseph (Run Simmons, Reverend Run) *musician*
Sirico, Genaro *actor*
Sitomer, Sheila Marie *television producer, television director*
Slash, (Saul Hudson) *guitarist*
Sliwa, Curtis *radio personality, volunteer*
Smith, Malcolm Sommerville *bass*
Soley, David Benjamin *composer*
Solomons, Gus, Jr. (Gustave Martinez) *choreographer, dancer, writer*
Somerhalder, Ian Joseph *actor*
Sorum, Matt *drummer*
Soyer, David *cellist, music educator*
Spears, Britney *singer*
Speller, Robert Ernest Blakefield, Jr. *choreographer*
Spinney, Caroll *entertainer, educator*
Sporn, Michael V. *producer, director*
Stang, Arnold *actor, writer, film director*
Stang, Rolf Kristian *vocalist, educator, actor, advertising executive, writer*
Stern, Howard Allan *radio personality, television show host*
Stevens, Risë *performing arts association administrator*
Stewart, Ellen D. *theater producer*
Stewart, Jon (Jonathan Stewart Leibowitz) *comedian, actor*
Stiefel, Ethan *dancer, performing company executive*
Sting, (Gordon Matthew Sumner) *musician, songwriter, actor*
Stoltzman, Richard Leslie *clarinetist*
Storch, Arthur *theater director*

Strasfogel, Ian *stage director, playwright*
Stroman, Susan *choreographer, theater director*
Stucky, Steven (Edward) *composer, conductor*
Studdard, Ruben (Christopher Ruben Studdard) *singer*
Subkoff, Tara *actress, apparel designer*
Swan, William *actor*
Talmi, Yoav *conductor, composer*
Taylor, Paul B. *choreographer*
Taylor, Regina *actress*
Tepper Madover, Arielle *theater producer*
Tesori, Jeanine *composer*
Thomas, Richard *actor*
Thompson, Donald Raymond *film producer, playwright*
Thompson, Jewel Taylor *music educator*
Tilson Thomas, Michael *conductor, music director*
Timberlake, Justin *vocalist*
Tinsley, Boyd Calvin *musician*
Torres, Dalys E. *music educator, consultant*
Travis, Sarah *orchestrator*
Trecartin, Ryan *filmmaker*
Tree, Michael *violinist, violist, educator*
Trujillo, Robert *musician*
Trump, Ivanka (Ivana Marie Trump) *model, real estate company executive*
Uggams, Leslie *entertainer*
Ulrich, Lars *drummer*
Underwood, Carrie Marie *singer*
Valentine, James Burgon *musician*
Valletta, Amber *actress, model*
Van Halen, Eddie (Edward Lodewijk Van Halen) *musician*
Varone, Douglas Joseph *choreographer*
Vaughn, Dona D. *performing company executive*
Vega, Suzanne *singer, songwriter*
Vieira, Meredith *television personality*
Wagner, Alan Cyril *television and film producer, consultant, performing arts educator*
Walden, Shelton Harrison *radio personality, educator*
Wallach, Eli *actor*
Waxman, Anita *theater producer*
Wedgeworth, Ann *actress*
Weiland, Scott Richard *singer*
Weinberg, Max *musician*
West, Kanye *rap artist*
Wexler, Peter John *artist, photographer, theater designer*
Wheeldon, Christopher *dancer, choreographer*
White, George Cooke *theater director, foundation administrator*
White, Jack (John Anthony Gillis) *musician, producer*
White, Lillias *actress*
Wilcox, T.J. *filmmaker*
Wile, Joan *composer, lyricist, singer*
Wiley-Hart, Debra *musician, educator*
Williams, Montel *television talk show host*
Williams, Vanessa (Vanessa Lynn Williams) *recording artist, actress*
Wilson, Cassandra *singer*
Wilson, Edwin *theater director*
Wittstein, Edwin Frank *theater director, set designer*
Wolf, Peter *singer, composer*
Wolfe, George C. *theater director, producer, playwright*
Wood, Ronald *musician*
Woodward, Joanne Gignilliat *actress*
Woodward, Kirk *theater director*
Wuorinen, Charles Peter *composer*
Yamaguchi, Masaya *musician, educator*
Young, John Lloyd *actor*
Zhang, Xian *conductor*
Zirinsky, Susan *television producer*
Zombie, Rob (Robert Cummings) *musician, filmmaker*
Zorn, John *composer, musician*
Zosike, Joanie Fritz *theater director, actress*
Zucker, Stefan *tenor, writer, editor, commentator*
Zukerman, Pinchas *concert violinist, violist, conductor*

**Newcomb**
Chatzky, Herbert *music educator*

**Niagara Falls**
DiVita-Frommert, Angela Marie *music educator*

**Norwich**
Mayo, Mary E. *music educator, conductor*

**Oceanside**
Bider, Bruce Evan *music educator, director*

**Oneonta**
Pignato, Joseph Michael *composer, music educator, musician*

**Orchard Park**
Carducci, Donald Joseph *music educator*
Mayo, Cynthia Gould *music educator*

**Oswego**
Rial, Joseph J. *theater educator, set designer*

**Oyster Bay**
Joel, Billy (William Martin Joel) *musician*

**Pawling**
Jones, James Earl *actor*
Utter, Donald L. *music educator*

**Peekskill**
Black, Carolyn Rebecca *music educator*

**Penn Yan**
Stempien, Joseph Jeffrey *music educator*

**Pine Bush**
Prokopchak, Peter A. *music educator*

**Port Washington**
Feuss, Judith Farrar *music educator, musician*
Starr, Ringo (Richard Starkey) *musician, actor*
van Schenkhof, Carol Dougherty (Carol Dovan) *soprano, music educator*

**Potsdam**
Lanz, Christopher Charles *conductor*

**Poughkeepsie**
Wilson, Richard Edward *composer, music educator, pianist*

**Purchase**
Magaziner, Elliot Albert *musician, conductor, educator*
McElwaine, James William *music educator*

**Queensbury**
Cirillo, James John *music educator*

**Red Hook**
Gudenzi-Ruess, Ida Carmen V. *music educator, artist*

**Rego Park**
Cheng, Iris Yi-Chen *music educator*

**Rochester**
Bohrer, Brian E. *music educator*
Gauldin, Robert L. *music educator, composer*
Günter-McCoy, Jane Hutton *singer*
Kaupa, Mike *music educator, musician*
Kissel, Lynn Anne *music educator*
Macpherson, Daniel Craig *music educator*
Scotto, Ciro Gerard *composer, educator*

**Rocky Point**
Knapp, Craig Brian *music educator, musician*

**Ronkonkoma**
Saladino, Frank S. *music educator*

**Rosendale**
Goldpaugh Brown, Bethany J. (Beverly) *theater educator, writer, costume designer*

**Roslyn**
Rosegarten, Rory *personal manager, television producer, theater producer, film producer*

**Sag Harbor**
Immerso, John Joseph *music educator*

**Saint James**
Kalabza-Balsamo, Debra Alyce *music educator*

**Saint Regis Falls**
O'Bryan, Margaret Sundberg *music educator*

**Saratoga Springs**
Porter, David Hugh *musician, classicist, academic administrator, music educator*

**Sayville**
Grizzaffi, Kimberly Anne *music educator, secondary school educator*

**Schenectady**
Hermance, Myron E., Jr. *conductor, educator*
Rice, Ruth Elaine *music educator*
Szokody, Aniko *pianist, educator*

**Schroon Lake**
Pendell, Zhanna I. *music educator*
Williams, Wayne M. *music educator*

**Sea Cliff**
Anders, Gerald Randolph *music educator*
Popova, Nina *dancer, choreographer, director*

**Slate Hill**
Izzo, I. Victor III *music educator*

**Smithtown**
Ariosto-Oill, Lynn Carol *music educator*

**Sparkill**
Dahl, Arlene *actress, writer, designer, cosmetics executive*

**Sparrow Bush**
Murray, William Bruce *opera singer*

**Staten Island**
Aurelia, Alan C. *performing company executive, music director*
Fusco, Jo Ellen *music educator*
Trogan, Roland Bernard *composer, educator*

**Suffern**
Ralph, Stanley Lee *performing arts educator, musician*

**Sunnyside**
Gil Orrios, Angel *theater director, lighting designer, translator*

**Syracuse**
Elms, Ben *actor, theater director*
Flaver, John Anthony *retired music educator*
Lazarow, Victor *theater educator*
Orentlicher, John *video research educator, artist*
Wolff, Catherine Elizabeth *opera company executive*

**Uniondale**
Sanchez, Laura Ann *music educator*

**Valhalla**
Fachnie, H(ugh) Douglas *film manufacturing company official*

**Walden**
Murphy, Pamela Ann *music educator, actress, musician*

**Wallkill**
Strauser, Susan Parkyn *performing arts educator, singer*

**Walton**
Bolton, Theresa M. *music educator*

**Wantagh**
Berk, Adele L. *composer, music educator*

**Warwick**
English, Dennis *music educator*

**Washingtonville**
Marcialis, Angelo Vincent *music educator, musician*

**West Chazy**
Slosson, Constance Sweet *retired music educator*

**West Hurley**
Martucci, Vincent James *composer, pianist*

**West Point**
Williams, Craig Stewart *organist, music educator, director*

**White Plains**
Ramos, Paul-John *composer, writer*
Sedelmaier, J. J. *filmmaker*
Wedge, Chris *animation director, studio executive*

**Williamsville**
Whitcomb, James Stuart *videographer, photographer, production company executive*

**Willow**
Bley, Carla Borg *composer*

**Yonkers**
Baumel, Herbert *violinist, conductor*
Senator, Ronald Paul *composer, writer, retired music educator*

## NORTH CAROLINA

**Asheville**
Thompson, Charles Spurgeon *retired music educator, retired conductor*

**Black Mountain**
Belue, Janie A. *music educator*

**Boiling Springs**
Lahaie, L. Scot *theater educator*

**Carolina Beach**
Mansbery, Sarah Huntsman *music educator*

**Chapel Hill**
Hammond, David Alan *stage director, educator*
Neff, Severine *music educator*
Powell, Carolyn Wilkerson *retired music educator*

**Charlotte**
Belflowers, Timothy Dion *organist, choir director*
Herring, Rebecca Royce *music educator, consultant*
Hough, Michael Brady *music educator*
Iley, Martha Strawn *music educator*
Metz, Catherine Taylor *performing arts educator*
Michalski, Stanley Franklin *music educator, conductor*
Mills, Stacey Webster *music educator, musician*
Reese, Annette Evelyn *music educator*
Thompson, Jocelyn Pharr *organist, director, music educator*

**Cullowhee**
Beam, Richard Squires *theater educator*
Lormand, Paul Edward *performing company executive*

**Davidson**
Sprague, Raymond *music educator*

**Durham**
Daw, Amy W. *music educator*
Faris, Marc R *composer, education educator*
Krakowski, Jane *actress*
Nakarai, Charles Frederick Toyozo *music educator*
Ward, Robert *composer, educator, conductor*

**Elizabeth City**
Weaver, Michael Alan *music educator*

**Elon**
Artley, Malvin Newton *music educator, composer*

**Fayetteville**
Barnicle, Mary Anne *music educator, piano accompanist*
Curtis, Marvin Vernell *music educator*
Fakhouri, Fouad Kifah *composer, conductor*
Jackson, Johnny Loretta *music educator*
Jones, Villie *music educator*
Richardson, James Bernard *music educator*

**Franklinton**
Elmore, Cenieth Catherine *music educator*

**Gastonia**
Fayssoux, Patricia Ann Paysour *music educator*

**Greensboro**
Cornelius, Polly Butler *voice educator, soprano*
Deere, James Dickson *voice and music educator, writer*
Drye, Jonathan Reed *voice educator*
Haas, Christopher Eric *theater educator*
Horton, Gregory Jerome *theater educator, costume designer*
Locke, John R. *music educator, director*
Middleton, Herman David, Sr. *retired theater educator*
Nolker, David Brett *music educator*
Owen, Lindsay Alexander *music director*
Russell, Peggy Taylor *soprano, educator*
Vulpi, Frank Joseph *music educator*
Waters, Robert Francis, Jr. *music educator, writer*

**Greenville**
Bath, Joanne McMath *music educator*
Riley, Rhonda Wingate *music educator*

**Hendersonville**
Tatsch, Jacki Lynn *music educator, diversified financial services company executive*

**Hickory**
Schlagenhauf, Sherry Denise *music educator*

**Indian Trail**
Brewer, James Timothy *music educator, director*

**Iron Station**
Wise, Kimberly Anne (Schillaci) *music educator, musician*

**Jacksonville**
Brooks, Joli *music educator*

**Lake Junaluska**
Markey, James Ian *music educator, tenor*

**Leicester**
Entzi, Karen Russell *orchestra educator*

**Lexington**
Mabe, Walter Lee *music educator*

**Louisburg**
Miller, Brian Daniel *music educator, organist*

**Lumberton**
Carter, Angela Barnhill *music educator*

**Mars Hill**
Greene, Tena Lorraine *singer, educator, actor*
Newton, Paul George *musician, retired librarian*

**Matthews**
Fox, Beth A. *music educator*
Judge, Joseph Donald *music educator*

**Monroe**
Casstevens, Charles Franklin, Jr. *music educator, minister*
Reynolds, Jeffrey Michael *music educator*

**Mooresville**
Faires, Ian Matthew *music educator*

**North Wilkesboro**
Shumaker, Tara L. *performing arts educator*

**Pembroke**
Stevens, Robyn Anne *music educator*

**Pittsboro**
Cottrell, Eugene Paul *band director*

**Raleigh**
Aiken, Clay (Clayton Holmes Aiken) *singer*
Batson, Jonathon Kingsley *composer, singer*
Evans, Margaret Griffin *music educator*
Garriss, Phyllis Weyer *music educator, performer*
Herrmann, John C. *music educator, church musician*
Huff, Ann Linnea *music educator*
Hynus, Anita Eileen *music educator*
Poe, Terry Lynn *music educator*
Thompson Cornwall, Lonieta Aurora *music educator, consultant*

**Reidsville**
Covington, Bennie Mell, Jr. *music educator*

**Rich Square**
Baugham, Samuel McCoy *actor, painter*

**Roseboro**
Cobb, Katherine Simon *theater educator*

**Salisbury**
Higbee, Dale (Strohe) *musician, retired psychologist*

**Southern Pines**
Ward, Susan Sprinkle *organist*

**Swannanoa**
Whittington, Lorin Dale *music educator*

**Taylorsville**
Payne, Ronald Dean, II, *music educator, director*

**Todd**
Cole, Susan Stockbridge *retired theater educator*

**Wake Forest**
Thompson, Christina Elizabeth *music educator, musician*

**Wilmington**
Cameron, Kay *conductor, composer*
Duarte, Hugo *composer*
Leutze, James Richard *television producer, former academic administrator*

**Winston Salem**
Bulluck, Matthew Heyer *performing arts educator*
DeMaio Caprilli, Barbara Jean *music educator*
Grillo, Henry R. *theater educator, technical director*
Mitchener, John Edward *music educator, musician*
Mueller, John S. *music educator*
Mueller, Margaret S. *musician, educator*
Trautwein, George William *conductor, violinist, educator*

**NORTH DAKOTA**

**Bismarck**
Gray, Arlene *music educator, musician*
Lundberg, Susan Ona *musical organization administrator*
Seil, Michael James *music educator*
Tornow, L. William *musician*

**Grand Forks**
Burgess, Gaye Margaret *theater educator*
Gallo, Sergio Roberto *music educator, researcher*
Towne, Gary Spaulding *music educator*

**OHIO**

**Ada**
Henkels, Scott *theater director, educator*

**Akron**
Barlowe Bodman, Amy *violinist, composer*
Czarnecki, Rita Marie *music educator, pianist*
LaNasa, Patricia Jeanne *music educator*
Migid, Adel A. *theater educator, set designer, consultant*
Rouvas, Sakas *singer, gymnast*

**Amelia**
Hill, Diane L. *music educator*

**Athens**
Crist, Richard Le Roy *voice educator*

**Bay Village**
Berry, Edgar Allen *music educator*

**Beloit**
Barnett, Robert James *music educator, musician*

**Berea**
Barth, Daniel M. *music educator*
Fralick, J. R. *music educator*
Sanders, Phyllis May *musician*
Uniatowski, Joanne M. *singer, educator*
Zeitlin, Louise R. *music educator*

**Boardman**
Pavalko, Robert A., II, *music educator*

**Bowling Green**
Pelletier, Andrew John *music educator*
Thayer, Robert Wilcox *music educator*
Wolcott, Vernon *music educator, musician*

**Cambridge**
Marks, Robert Gale *music educator*

**Canal Winchester**
Aho, Eric Ward *music educator, conductor*

**Canfield**
Scurich, Kelly Lemos *music director*

**Canton**
Bridges, Cynthia Lynn *music educator*

**Cedarville**
Spencer, Mark William *music educator, minister, announcer*

**Chagrin Falls**
Shakley, Elaine M. *organist, department chairman*

**Chardon**
Orcino, Leonard Anthony *composer, conductor*

**Cincinnati**
Browning, Robert David *music educator*
Burkhead, Phillip Lee *musician, educator*
Costigan-Kerns, Louise E. *musician*
Gardner, Adam Daniel *music educator*
Geis, Stephen Anthony *music educator*
Gilbert, Jay *radio personality*
Gottlieb, Kenneth Allen *music educator*
Griffiths, Kenneth Ross *music educator, voice educator*
Hale, Nathan Kelly *music educator, artist*
Jarvi, Paavo *conductor, music director*
Morgan, Victoria *performing company executive, choreographer*
Paavo, Jarvi *conductor*
Roderer, Joshua A. *music educator*
Scott, Jim *radio personality*
Sies, Timothy Ray *music educator*
Tocco, James *pianist*
Torbush, Rodney Kristian *music educator*
Winfrey, Marcellene Sedetta *music educator, church musician*

**Cleveland**
Erb, Donald *composer*
Gladden, Dean Robert *arts administrator, educator, consultant*
Gould, Eric David *musician, educator*
Ingram, Lori Ruth *performing arts association administrator*
Manson, Marilyn (Brian Hugh Warner) *musician*
Matthews, Eric Joddy *film director*
Morris, Thomas William *symphony orchestra administrator*
Stanziano, Stephen *music educator*
Warner, Carolyn G. *musician, music educator*
Weir, Dame Gillian Constance *musician*
Welser-Möst, Franz *conductor, music director*

**Cleveland Heights**
Baker, Brett E. *music educator*
Pease, Robin A. *performing company executive, actress*

**Columbia Station**
Yearley, Barbara Ellen *music educator*

**Columbus**
Allen, Lois Arlene Height (Mrs. James Pierpont Allen) *musician*
Barlow-Ware, Jacqueline Sue *music educator*
Charles, Gerard *performing company executive, choreographer*
Collins, Caron Lee *music educator*
Drvota, Mojmir *retired cinema educator, author*
Ensign, Joel Francis *musician*
Harris, Donald *composer*
Hirokami, Junichi *conductor, music director*
Renshler, Rosemary P. *retired music educator*
Rosenstock, Susan Lynn *orchestra administrator*
Satoh, Yuko *music educator*
Wang, Tianshu *music educator, musician*
Wild, Earl *composer*

**Cuyahoga Falls**
Paulis, Brian E. *conductor, composer*

**Dayton**
Carrier, Rachel Esther *music educator, director*
Hanna, Marsha L. *artistic director*
Richmond, Allen *conductor, educator*
Walters, Jefferson Brooks *musician, retired real estate broker*
Wasson, Barbara Hickam *music educator*
Wasson, Steven *music educator, piano technician*

**Delaware**
Gardner, Bonnie Milne *theater educator, playwright*
Jamison, Roger W. *pianist, educator*

**Doylestown**
Morton, Sallie W. *music educator*

**Dublin**
Santanello, Patricia Jane *theater educator*

**Elida**
Roach, Bradley Charles *music educator*

**Findlay**
Hanson, David Alan *music educator*
Mattis, Tim *music educator*
Thomas, Zachary Adam *music director, educator*

**Geneva**
Carrel, Marianne Eileen *music educator*

**Granville**
Gander, Robert D *theater director, education educator*

**Hamilton**
Glass, Robert Edward *retired music educator*
Kerestan, Kitty Wilde *music educator*
Moore, Michael Robert *music educator, band director*

**Hilliard**
Pyles, Selma Broadway *music educator*

**Hiram**
Bane, James Wallace *music educator*

**Holland**
Conlin, Thomas *conductor*

**Independence**
Lanigan, John *radio personality*
Malone, Jimmy *radio personality*

**Kettering**
Meckstroth, Wilma Jean *piano educator, accompanist, music company executive*
Reynolds, Joan Lorelle *music educator*

**Kirtland**
Petrone, John R. *retired music educator, composer*

**Lewis Center**
Lutz, Michael Edward *music educator*

**Lima**
Shaw, Sue Ann *church organist*

**Lisbon**
Yonchak, Michael Stephen *music educator*

**Lorain**
Murrell, Jill Pongracz *music educator, director*

**Mansfield**
Sturts, Donna Jean *music educator*

**Marion**
Barker, Tamara Elizabeth *music educator*
Schwartz, Lance *music educator*

**Medina**
Holliday, Keith Alan *music educator, musician*

**Mentor**
Herschman, Terry DiFranco *music educator*
Michaels, Edward G. *music educator, musician*

**Millersport**
Harkabus, Noelle Marie *music educator*

**North Olmsted**
Janson, Patrick *vocalist, educator, actor*

**Oak Harbor**
Sievert, Vicki Lee *retired music educator*

**Oberlin**
Crawford, Henry Gerald *music educator*
Hoffmann, Richard *composer, educator*
Mumford, Jeffrey *composer, educator*
Rutstein, Sedmara Zakarian *piano educator, concert pianist*

**Orwell**
Carlson, Timothy A. *music educator*

**Oxford**
Thomas, Robert Jay *music educator, musician*

**Parma**
Indovina, Cynthie Lynn *music educator*
Musat, Katherine Gadus *retired music educator*

**Perry**
Godfrey, W. Robert *music educator, singer, actor*

**Pickerington**
Lang, Lisa Ann *music educator*

**Port Clinton**
Peitz, Todd Adam *music educator*

**Portsmouth**
Brehm, Shawn Lamar *band director*

**Powell**
O'Neal, R. Douglas *music educator, musician*

**Rocky River**
Cronquist, Robert Lee *conductor*

**Springfield**
Faber, Trudy *music educator*
Todd, Carol *music educator*

**Toledo**
Chambers, Virginia Anne *music educator*
Finkbeiner, Carlton S. (Carty Finkbeiner) *radio personality, former mayor*
Girgis-Hanna, Mary Fahim *music educator*

**Twinsburg**
Bensie, Lori Anne *music educator*

**Urbana**
Pencil, Faith Ann *music educator*

**Vincent**
Foster, Christopher Robert *music educator*

**Wapakoneta**
Wirth, Tamara L. *music educator*

**Warren**
Rollo, Richard James *music educator*

**West Unity**
Miller, Nancy Celesta *music educator, director*

**Whitehouse**
Boyle, Daniel Robert *musician, delivery service executive*

**Wickliffe**
Barnes, Lili Darnelle *music educator, director*
Graves, Pamela Kay *music educator*

**Willoughby**
Baker, Charles Stephen *music educator*
Linsenmeier, Carol Vincent *music educator*

**Wooster**
Fries, Thomas Anthony *music educator*

**Wyoming**
Jablonsky, Atarah *retired music educator*

**Youngstown**
Summers, Michael Edward *music educator*

**Zanesville**
Brown, Karen Rima *orchestra manager, Spanish language educator*
McLaughlin, James Lee *musician, director*

**OKLAHOMA**

**Ada**
Baggech, Melody A. *music educator*

**Altus**
Carson, Kirk *music educator*

**Bethany**
Whitsett, Eleanor Watkins *musician, educator, composer*

**Broken Arrow**
Smith, Jeffrey Andrews *musician, educator, sound recording engineer*

**Davenport**
Walker, Sandra Kay *theater educator*

**Durant**
Daniels-Ayers, Dana Sue *musical theater educator, singer, actress*

**Inola**
Paul, Gary Wayne *music educator*

**Lawton**
Baldwin, Larry Todd *voice educator*
Detweiler, Stanley Bruce *music educator*
Underwood, Kirsten Fedje *musician, educator*

**Miami**
George, Barbara M. *theater educator, department chairman, actor, director*

**Mounds**
Fellows, Esther Elizabeth *musician, music educator*
Halsey, James Albert *entertainer, theater producer*

**Muskogee**
Ehlers, Deborah Layne *theater director*

**Mustang**
Olson, Jon Philip *music educator, director, voice educator, actor*

**Norma**
Hartel, Austin Stewart *performing arts educator, choreographer*

**Norman**
Ambrosini, Armand Anthony *music educator*
Herstand, Theodore *retired theatre artist, retired educator*

**Oklahoma City**
Holeman, Lora White *music educator*
Matlock, Gina Rae *music educator*
Payne, Gareld Gene *vocal music educator, medical transcriptionist*
Price Boday, Mary Kathryn *choreographer, small business owner, educator*
Ragsdale, Frank Wayne *voice educator, singer*
Schimek, John Bradley *music educator, musician*

**Owasso**
Murray, Todd Anthony *performing company executive*

**Sapulpa**
Claussen, Alex *music educator*

**Shawnee**
Clark, Don Eugene *voice educator, vocalist*
Watson, Kimberly *music educator, pianist*

**Tulsa**
Angelini, Marcello *artistic director*
Liggitt, Lonnie Robert *music educator, researcher*
Owens, Jana Jae *entertainer*
Sowell, Laven *retired music educator*
Weinstock Rad, Katheryn Louise *music educator*
Womack, Lee Ann *country musician*

**Vinita**
Lollman, Matthew Tobias *music educator*

**Wayne**
Purdy, Mary Rosiland *music educator*

**Wynnewood**
Huitt, Keith David *music educator, history educator*

## OREGON

**Bend**
Seed, Brian Bruce *music educator*

**Brookings**
Shepherd, William Michael *music educator, musician*

**Eugene**
Bailey, Exine Margaret Anderson *soprano, educator*
Bergquist, Peter *retired music educator*
Bossuat, Judy Weigert *music educator*
Johnson, David Paul *music educator*

**La Grande**
Espinosa, Leandro *composer, conductor, educator*

**Milton Freewater**
Agidius, Michael Gregory *music educator*

**Milwaukie**
Averill, Corey Douglas *music educator*
Walker, Scott Allen *theater and language arts educator, theater director*

**Monmouth**
Oberst, Sharon Stokes *dancer, educator, choreographer*

**Mount Angel**
Petrik, F. A. *music educator*

**Pendleton**
Muller, Steven John *music educator*

**Portland**
Bailey, Robert C. *opera company executive*
Berentsen, Kurtis George *music educator, conductor*
Huggett, Monica *performing company executive, musician*
Jackson, Roberta Q. *music educator*
Kohne, Heidi Ann *church musician*
Love, Edith Holmes *theater producer*
Mittelstaedt, Janet Rugen *music educator, composer*
Ryberg, William A. *orchestra executive*
Stowell, Christopher R. *artistic director, choreographer, retired dancer*
Tolon, Michael Oded *music educator, director*
Voglar, Inés Ana *musician, educator*
York, David Pierce *music educator, composer, performing company executive*

## PENNSYLVANIA

**Akron**
Leithmann, David Edward *music educator*

**Aliquippa**
Forringer, Letitia Marie *music educator*

**Allentown**
Beltzner, Gail Ann *music educator*
Mealey, Grace Eleanor *music educator*

**Annville**
Condran, Cynthia Marie *gospel musician*

**Arendtsville**
Cope, Jamie H. *music educator*

**Armagh**
Gongaware, Acey M. *music educator*

**Bangor**
Long, Joshua Eric *music educator, small business owner*
Paine, Marlin Craig *band director*

**Beaver Falls**
Copeland, Robert Marshall *music educator, department chairman*

**Bessemer**
Bonnar, Jason *music educator*

**Bethlehem**
Diggs, David B. *music educator*
Schumacher, Stanley E. *composer, musician*
Simons, Audrey Kay *music educator*
Warfield, William Leonard *musician, composer, educator*

**Bloomsburg**
Hower, Eileen M. *music educator*

**Boswell**
Croft, Daniel Thomas *music educator*

**Bradford**
Ewert, Kevin *theater educator*

**Brodheadsville**
Snyder, Nadine Eldora *music educator*

**Bryn Mawr**
Goutman, Lois Clair *retired drama educator*

**Butler**
Crytzer, Lynn Carol *music educator*

**Center Valley**
Wehr, Matthew *music educator*

**Chadds Ford**
Swensson, Evelyn Dickenson *conductor, composer, librettist*

**Chalfont**
Ashley, Kathleen Labonis *music educator*

**Clarks Summit**
Maxwell, Brian T. *theatre and communications professor*

**Cresson**
Rosensteel Way, Nancy Ann *music educator*

**Delta**
Withrow, James A *music educator*

**Derry**
Baltzer, Cynthia Louise *music educator*

**Dillsburg**
Riley, R. Douglas *music educator*

**Dover**
Apgar, Andrew R. *music educator*
Moul, Brian E. *music educator*

**Doylestown**
Maxwell, Clair D. *musician, director, educator*
Solly, Richard Peter *music educator*

**Drexel Hill**
Martino, Michael Charles *entertainer, musician, actor*

**East Stroudsburg**
Miller, Robert W. *music educator, musician*

**Easton**
DeGrandis, Ronald Wayne *music educator*

**Edgemont**
Davis, Scott Charles *music educator, political activist*

**Edinboro**
Howell, Allen C. *music educator, choir director*

**Elizabeth**
Cornelius, David Frederick *band director*
Maurer, Mark Carey *music educator*

**Elizabethtown**
Kitchen, Otis Dorsey *music educator*

**Elizabethville**
McCartney, Chad Edward *music educator*

**Emmaus**
Denmead, Bruce Palmer *music educator*

**Emporium**
Sensenig, Daniel Scot *music educator*

**Ephrata**
Reed, Galen K. *music educator*

**Erie**
Collura, Frank Charles *conductor*
Santillano, Mark Ramon *dancer, educator*
Wilson, Shirley Willink *music educator, musician*

**Everett**
Whetstone, Joni Lee *music educator*

**Fairless Hills**
Vodicka, Jason Douglas *music educator*

**Ford City**
Cramer, Dennis F. *music educator, freelance/self-employed musician*

**Fort Washington**
Pezick, Patricia *music educator*

**Franklin**
Johnston, Steven Roy *music educator*

**Fredericksburg**
Daubert, Harlan Aaron *music educator, director*

**Galeton**
Bull, Inez Stewart *retired music educator, curator, director, singer, writer, musician*

**Gettysburg**
Bowman, Christopher Todd *music educator, football coach*
Hansen, Mark R. *music educator*

**Greencastle**
Wertime, Timothy Ray *music educator*

**Hamburg**
Pietsch, Douglas K. *music educator*

**Hatboro**
Carroll, Lucy Ellen *theater director, educator*

**Hazleton**
DeMelfi, (Ronald) Daniel *music educator, director*

**Hershey**
Gingrich, Shawn M. *music educator, church administrator*

**Horsham**
Schopp, David L. *music educator*

**Hughesville**
Boyer, Mark A. *music educator*

**Hunker**
Springer, Robert Wade *music educator*

**Huntingdon Valley**
Sadoff, Joan Handleman *film producer, social worker*

**Imperial**
Peters, Raymond Andrew *music educator*

**Indiana**
Salser, Scott A. *music educator*

**Johnstown**
McCleester, Frank Raymond *music educator*

**Kennett Square**
Litzenberg, G. Scott *music educator, director*

**King Of Prussia**
Helmetag, Diana *music educator*
Liebermann, Lowell *composer, conductor, pianist*

**Kingston**
Weisberger, Barbara *artistic director, advisor, educator*

**Lancaster**
Heil, Paul Samuel *radio producer*

**Langhorne**
Isensee, Paul Ralph *music educator, minister*

**Lansdowne**
Geist, Lorraine Pinnelli *music educator, director*

**Latrobe**
Tourre, Marc Louis *music educator*

**Lebanon**
Fox, Wayne Charles *music educator*

**Lewisburg**
Muller, Riana Ricci *musician, educator*

**Liberty**
Nelson, Thomas John *music educator, musician*

**Line Lexington**
Kuehne, Tracy Elizabeth *music educator*

**Lititz**
Fulginiti, Todd E. *music educator*

**Loysburg**
Stuckey, Ellen Mae *music educator*

**Mc Alisterville**
Milliken, Kevin David *music educator*

**Milford Square**
Sewell, Gloriana *music educator*

**Monroeville**
Read, Robert Allen *music educator*

**Montoursville**
Carpenter, Dennis Eugene *music educator*

**Mount Pleasant**
Collins, Frederick George *music educator, secondary school educator*

**Natrona Heights**
Koharchik, Thomas David *music educator*

**New Castle**
Zumpella, Thomas Joseph *music educator*

**New Milford**
Burkett, Jeffrey O'Hara *music educator*

**New Oxford**
Rohrbaugh, Nova R. *retired music educator*

**New Wilmington**
Moser, Jonathan R. *music educator*

**Newtown**
Hoffman, Michael Bruce *music educator, composer*
Maholic, Julie Lynn *music educator, elementary school educator*
Nowak, Jerry (Gerald C. Nowak) *music educator, musician, writer*
Sheridan, John J. *musician, music educator*

**North Versailles**
Winkleblech, Jerry A. *band director*

**Oakmont**
Billings, David Arthur *music educator*

**Pen Argyl**
Cortez, Rita *music educator*

**Philadelphia**
Blavat, Jerry (Gerald Joseph Blavat) *television personality, actor*
Colson, Rosemary *music educator*
Crumb, George Henry *composer, educator*
Daugherty, F(rancis) Mark *music educator, conductor, theater director*
Davis, Paige (Mindy Paige Davis) *television personality and host*
Driver, Robert Baylor, Jr. *opera company administrator*
Garonzik, Sara Ellen *stage producer*
Gilbert, Charles *performing arts educator, writer*

Greenbaum, Matthew Jonathan *composer*
Harris, Rennie *choreographer*
Ingolfsson-Fassbind, Ursula G. *music educator*
Jenkins, Marc Delano *music educator*
Kaiser, Roy *artistic director*
Morrison, Alan *musician, educator*
Myers Brown, Joan *performing company executive*
Prischmann Gryniewicz, Deborah Anne *voice educator, vocalist*
Sawallisch, Wolfgang *conductor*
Scaglione, Louis III *music educator, conductor*
Smith, Lloyd *musician*
Stallman, Robert *flutist, editor, recording artist, arranger*
White, Nicholas John *musician, director, composer*

**Pipersville**
Block, Caryn S. *composer*

**Pittsburgh**
Ban, Janet F. *music educator*
Bardyguine, Patricia Wilde *dancer, performing company executive*
Cardenes, Andres Jorge *musician, educator*
Desiree, Laura *dancer*
Greciano, Sandra Eames *voice educator*
Harth, Sidney *musician, educator*
Hollingsworth, Samuel Hawkins, Jr. *bassist*
Keeling, Kenneth Augustus, Sr. *music educator*
Orr, Terrence S. *dancer, ballet master, artistic director*
Posvar, Mildred Miller *opera singer*
Stolarevsky, Kathryn Fell *music educator*

**Pottstown**
Speca, Vivian E. *music educator, researcher*

**Reading**
Uhler, Kathryn L. *music educator*
Zug, Elizabeth E. *concert pianist, educator*

**Reedsville**
Garner, Douglas *music educator*

**Rimersburg**
Rush, Kevin Arland *music educator*

**Royersford**
Jennings, Kris *music educator*

**Saegertown**
Ralph, NancyJo *retired music educator*

**Schuylkill Haven**
Evans, Christopher Jay *music educator*

**Selinsgrove**
Viker, Erik *theater educator*

**Shippensburg**
Cart, Jon Robert *music educator, musician*

**Sidman**
Coco, Samuel Louis *music educator, musician, composer*

**Slippery Rock**
Smiley, Laura Cicely *theater educator, performing company executive*

**Spring City**
Britcher, Michael *music educator*

**Strattanville**
Taylor, Kristie Leigh *performing arts educator, actor*

**Swarthmore**
Devin, Lee (Philip Lee Devin) *dramaturg, author*
Redden, Taylor Tilghman *musician*

**Swiftwater**
Brooks, Joyce Maria *music educator*

**Throop**
Moran, Leslie Mason *music educator*

**Tunkhannock**
Zellner, Ryan Matthew *music educator*

**Upper Darby**
Kahler, Nancy J. *music educator, director*

**West Chester**
Albert, Kristen Ann *music educator*
Burton, John Bryan *music educator*
Gingery, Philip Alvah *music educator*
Pennington, Robert Edgar *music educator*

**Wexford**
Stefan, Todd Robert *music educator*

**Whitehall**
Anonia, Francis *music educator*

**Wilkes Barre**
Baranoski, Joseph Thomas *music educator*

**Williamsburg**
Lewis, David P. *music educator*

**Willow Hill**
Dorand, Freda J. *music educator*

**York**
Sier, Ruth Elaine *music educator*
Worley, Richard Alan *music educator*

**Youngsville**
Montgomery, Christina Lynn *music educator*

**Youngwood**
Duvall, Hollie Jean *music educator*

## RHODE ISLAND

**Chepachet**
Jubinska, Patricia Ann *ballet instructor, choreographer, artist, anthropologist, archaeologist*

**Cranston**
Burge, David Russell *concert pianist, composer, music educator*
Lachance, Philip Roland *music educator*

**Cumberland**
Rossi, Joseph Anthony *film and television make-up artist, educator*

**Hope**
Stadtmueller, Claire Louise *soprano, performing arts educator*

**Johnston**
Torelli, Anthony-Alexander *music educator, conductor, musician*

**Lincoln**
Marsden, Herci Ivana *classical ballet artistic director*

**Newport**
Englander, Roger *television producer, director*
Malkovich, Mark Paul III *musician, performing company executive*
Raum, Mary Beth *performing arts educator*
Roos, Casper *actor*

**Pawtucket**
Orson, Barbara Tuschner *actress*

**Providence**
Barnhill, James Orris *theater educator*
Dempsey, Raymond Leo, Jr. *radio and television producer, moderator, writer*
Faraone, Philip *organist, director, consumer products company executive*
Ruth, Sebastian A. *performing company executive*
Toro, Stephen Ralph *music educator*

**Smithfield**
Seabra, James Joseph *music educator, musician*

**Warwick**
Swenson, Susie Doris A. *music educator*

## SOUTH CAROLINA

**Aiken**
Snyder, Robert Ellis *retired music educator, minister*

**Anderson**
Powell, Richard A. *music educator*

**Charleston**
Cantwell, Don *artistic director*
Gunn, Morey Walker, Jr. *music educator, director, musician*
Jones, Benjamin Preston *music educator*
Jones, Vivian Eilene *music educator*

**Clemson**
Li-Bleuel, Linda *musician, educator*

**Clinton**
Fleury, Wilbert Leigh *music director, educator*
Roth, Dale Davis *music educator, religious organization administrator*

**Clover**
Lenard, Daniel Hardy *music educator*

**Columbia**
Ezell, Elizabeth Anne *music educator*
Olenchak, Frank Richard *music educator, musician*
Robbins, Emmalee Elizabeth *theater director, speech professional*
Rucker, Darius *musician*
Starrett, William *dancer, artistic director*

**Edisto Island**
Van Metre, Margaret Cheryl *performing company executive, dancer, educator*

**Florence**
Foster, Jackie Green *voice educator*
Wurster, Abigail Michelle *theater educator, costume designer*

**Fort Mill**
Dickey, Martin *music educator*

**Gaffney**
Hill, Harry Hoffman, Jr. *musician, educator*

**Goose Creek**
Vogt, Kathleen Cunningham *musician, music educator*

**Greenville**
Ballou, Kathryn Jeanne *performing arts educator*
Parker, David G. *music educator, music publisher*
Rice, Michael V. *voice educator*
Ringenberg, Donna Lou *music educator, conductor*
Schoonmaker, Gail Graham *voice educator, director*

**Greenwood**
Hughes, Christopher Adam *conductor, educator*

**Hilton Head Island**
Balkin, Alfred *music educator, composer*
Brock, Karena Diane *dancer, educator*
Selvy, Barbara *dance instructor*

**Johnston**
Jackson, Tracey L *music educator*

**Lexington**
Calloway, Gary R. *choral director, music director*

**Loris**
Whisnant, Stephen Labron *music educator*

**Moore**
King, Tamara Powers *music educator, musician*

**Mount Pleasant**
Royall, Mary-Julia C. *church organist, historian*
Scott, Jeffrey Ryan *music educator*

**Newberry**
McGinnis, Barry Eugene *music educator, musician*

**Orangeburg**
Lee, Donald Ray, Jr. *music educator*

**Pendleton**
Landreth, James Mack *elementary school music educator*

**Rock Hill**
Malambri, William F., Jr. *music educator, consultant*

**Roebuck**
Baier, Susan Lovejoy *music educator*
Smith, Alan Wade *music educator*

**Spartanburg**
Bolton, Calvin *music educator*
Lucktenberg, Jerrie Čadek *music educator*
McCraw, William Gary *music educator, director, musician*
Vaneman, Christopher M. *music educator, musician*

**Summerville**
Capps, Phillip Lewis *music educator*

**Walterboro**
Meshach, Joseph Robert *music educator*

## SOUTH DAKOTA

**Aberdeen**
Manhart, Grant Lee *music educator*
Zaidan, Raouf George *music educator*

**Armour**
Weidenbach, Mary E. *music educator*

**Dell Rapids**
Mitchell, Wayne Antoine *retired music educator*

**Emery**
Klassy, David L. *organist, accompanist, performing company executive, music educator*

**Mitchell**
Almjeld, Paul F. *conductor, music educator*
Mahlen, Tatum L. *voice educator*

**Sioux Falls**
Bennett, Thomas *orchestra executive*
Hoffman, Steven A. *performing arts association administrator*
Krause, Thomas Henry *music educator, composer*
Schmidt, Brian Arnold *composer, conductor*

**Vermillion**
Curry, James Nixon *music educator*
Rognstad, Richard L. *music educator, cellist*
Thomson, John Alistair *music educator*

## TENNESSEE

**Alexandria**
Thomas, Deona Lee *music educator*

**Antioch**
Ely, Joe *musician*

**Brentwood**
Grant, Amy *singer, songwriter*
Taylor, Nicole Renée (Niki Taylor) *model, shop owner*
Tucker, Tanya Denise *singer*
Walker Bonner, Linda Carol *music educator*

**Chattanooga**
Schow, Thomas Albert *music educator, educator, military officer*

**Clarksville**
Lee, Bob D. *music educator, consultant*

**Cleveland**
Thomas, Phillip *music educator, department chairman, musician*
Wittenburg, Michael Shane *concert pianist, music educator*

**Columbia**
Scheusner, Ronald L. *music educator*

**Cookeville**
Chang, Wei Tsun *music educator*
Dugle, Jon Richard *music educator*

**Cordova**
Cheatham, Wanda M. *music educator*
Johnson, Lori D. *voice educator, director*
Pugh, Dorothy Gunther *artistic director*

**Dayton**
Luther, Sigrid *music educator*

**Franklin**
Haseltine, Dan *christian rock musician*

**Gallatin**
Ritter, Renee O. *theater educator*

**Germantown**
Legett, Benjamin J. III *choral director, composer*

**Greenbrier**
Ault, Andrew Jared *music educator, disc jockey*

**Hermitage**
Thompson, Fred Dalton *actor, former senator*

**Huntland**
Burton, Janet Ruth Wisner *music educator*

**Jackson**
Dale, Karen McCall *music educator*
McRoberts, Terry Allan *music educator*

**Jamestown**
Holt, Lesley Lea *music educator*

**Jefferson City**
Robertson, Everett B. *performing arts educator, consultant*

**Johnson City**
Jenrette, Thomas Shepard, Jr. *music educator, choral director*
Stewart, Frank Graham *composer, clarinetist*

**Kingsport**
Brown, Richard E. *music educator*

**Knoxville**
Boling, Mark Edward *music educator*
Eleazer, Alan Garrett *church musician, music educator*
MacLean, Calvin A. *theater educator, department chairman, theater director*
Moore, Marvelene C. *music educator*
Speas, Bruce Orburn *theater educator*

**Lawrenceburg**
Hayes, Sylvia Richmond *music educator*

**Lebanon**
Daniels, Charlie *musician, lyricist*

**Livingston**
Dingwall, Gregory Scot *music educator*

**Madisonville**
Pereira, Hoffmann Urquiza *music educator*

**Martin**
Wade, Reba *musician, educator*

**Maryville**
Taddie, Daniel Lawrence *music educator*

**Memphis**
Chester, James A. *music educator*
Ching, James Michael *performing company executive, composer, conductor*
McRee, Celia *composer, singer, actress, writer, producer*
Nemec, Christopher E. *music educator*
Ouzts, David Perry *church music director, organist*
Owen-Leinert, Susan Huff *voice educator, vocalist*
Philipp, Karla Ann *music educator, conductor, musician*
Presley, Lisa Marie *singer*
Williams, David Russell *retired music educator*

**Milligan College**
Major, Richard *theater educator, actor, director*

**Millington**
Ducey, Edward Michael *musician*

**Morristown**
Rowland, Kyla Faye *musician*

**Murfreesboro**
Gregory, Brenda Kay *music educator*

**Nashville**
Arnold, Eddy *singer*
Bales, Barry *bluegrass musician*
Balzary, Michael Peter (Flea) *musician, recording artist, actor*
Bentley, Dierks *country singer, songwriter*
Block, Ron *musician*
Brooks, Kix (Leon Eric Brooks) *musician*
Chesney, Kenny *country singer, songwriter*
Demarcus, Jay (Stanley Demarcus) *country musician, songwriter*
Dunn, Ronnie Gene *musician*
Estrin, Kari (Karen Ruth Estrin) *theater producer, agent, consultant*
Evans, Sara *country singer, songwriter*
Fleck, Bela *country musician*
Frusciante, John Anthony *musician*
Gentry, Teddy Wayne *country musician*
Giles, Joe W. *music educator*
Griffith, Nanci *singer, songwriter*
Harris, Emmylou *singer*
Hill, Faith *musician*
Jackson, Alan *musician, lyricist*
Kasper, Jocelyn A. Alaimo *music educator, musician*
Kiedis, Anthony *vocalist, recording artist, actor*
King, Ed *musician*
Krauss, Alison *country musician*
Lawrence, Tracey *country singer, songwriter*
Levox, Gary (Gary Wayne Vernon Jr.) *country/rock singer*
Maguire, Martie (Martha Elenor Erwin Maguire) *musician*
Maines, Natalie Louise *musician*
Mandrell, Barbara Ann *singer, entertainer, actress, producer, writer*
McBride, Martina *vocalist*
McDonald, Reginald Adrian *musician, educator*
Montgomery, Dillard Brewster *musician, educator*
Owen, Randy Yeuell *country musician, cattle rancher*
Paisley, Brad *musician*
Powell, Billy *musician*
Richey, Kimberly Kay *singer, actress, composer*
Robison, Emily Burns *musician*
Rooney, Joe Don *country musician*
Rossington, Gary *musician*
Sartor, David P. *composer*
Smith, Chad Gaylord *musician, recording artist*

Twain, Shania (Eilleen Regina Edwards) *musician*
Urban, Keith *country singer, songwriter*
Valentine, Alan Darrell *performing company executive, conductor*
Waters, Karen Rigsby *music educator*
Watkins, Sara *musician*
Williams, Hank, Jr. (Randall Hank Williams) *country singer, songwriter*
Wilson, Gretchen *vocalist*
Wonders, Pamela Kim *music educator*

**Oak Ridge**
Crawford, Arlene Joanne *music educator, director*

**Pigeon Forge**
Parton, Dolly Rebecca *singer, composer, actress*

**Powell**
Roach, Janet Ann *music educator*

**Ripley**
Ammons, H. Ray *band director*

**Sparta**
Klughart, Toni Anne *music educator, musician, singer*

## TEXAS

**Abilene**
Ashford, Kecia A. *voice educator, vocalist*
Pender, Martha Helen *retired singer*

**Alice**
Taylor, Bryce B *music educator, consultant*

**Alpine**
Sawyer, Jay M. *theater educator*

**Amarillo**
Busch, Mildred Moorman *music educator*
Faulkner, Charles L. *music educator*
Tatum, David Alan *music minister*

**Arlington**
Jordan, Robert Randy *music educator*
Thomas, Lois C. *musician, educator, religious organization administrator, composer*

**Aubrey**
Pizzamiglio, Albert Theodore (Al Pierson) *conductor*

**Austin**
Antokoletz, Elliott Maxim *music educator*
Aubery, Stephen Royston Edmund *film producer*
Brockett, Oscar Gross *theater educator*
Choi, Anna JeeHee *music educator*
Coltman, Felicity Ann *music educator*
Hancock, Gerre Edward *musician, educator*
Henley, Paul Thomas *music educator, researcher*
Hinojosa, Tish (Leticia Hinojosa) *vocalist*
Lary, Banning Kent *film producer, writer*
Leare, Bobbie Jean *musician, educator*
Mills, Stephen *artistic director*
Morris, Quinton Ilando *music educator, director*
Mueller, Peggy Jean *dance educator, choreographer, rancher*
Ruiz, Cookie *performing company executive*
Shea, Andrew Brendan *film director, film producer*
Williamson, Barry Scott *conductor, performing arts educator*
Young, Phyllis Casselman *music educator*
Zlateva, Maria *music educator*

**Baytown**
Harrison, Paula Jean *church musician*

**Beaumont**
Brailsford, June Evelyn *musician, educator*
Wheatley, Randall *theater educator, theater director, playwright*

**Belton**
Jones, Deborah Fuchs *music educator*
Wood, Connie Garrison *music educator*

**Borger**
Strecker, Judy Ellen *music educator*

**Brownwood**
Banks, Patricia Anne *music educator, minister*

**Carrollton**
Fisher, Ryan Austin *choral director*

**Carthage**
Brumley, Larry Gene *music educator*

**Conroe**
Zwick, Robert A. *music educator, conductor*

**Corpus Christi**
Allison, Joan Kelly *music educator, pianist*
Hanna, Fahed Essa *music educator*
Jonker, Margaret N. *music educator*

**Dallas**
Antioco, John F. *entertainment company executive*
Bloom, John (Joe Bob Briggs) *comedian, writer*
Brandt, Carole *theater educator, department chairman*
Croskell, Madelon Byrd *music educator, classical vocalist*
Dederich-Pejovich, Susan Russell *harpist*
Elliott, Dorothy Gail *music educator, writer*
Etgen, Ann *performing arts educator, choreographer*
Franklin, Janice L. *music educator*
Franklin, Kirk *singer*
Johnson, Mary Elizabeth *music educator, musician*
Joyner, Tom *radio personality*
Litton, Andrew *conductor, music director*
Palmer, Christine (Clelia Rose Venditti) *vocalist, educator, musician*
Palmer, Larry Garland *music educator, writer, musician*

Pell, Jonathan Laurence *performing company executive*
Pelletier, Sho-mei *musician, educator*
Sallee, Wanda Jean *music educator*
Stone, Karen *opera company director*
Stuart, Frances Deaderick *retired music educator*
Thomas, Paul Lindsley *composer, musician, director*
Thomas, Sarah Elaine *music educator*

**Deer Park**
Wester, R. Glen *music educator, director*

**Denton**
McTee, Cindy *classical musician, educator*
Peters, Juanita Teal *music educator*
Wodnicki, Adam Juliusz *pianist, educator*

**Edinburg**
Munn, Vivian Carole *music educator, conductor*

**El Lago**
Chase, Jeanette Knapp *music educator*

**Falfurrias**
Cantu, Imelda M. *theater educator*

**Fort Worth**
Alford, Michele T. *theater educator*
Castro-Balbi, Jesús *musician, educator*
Cliburn, Van (Harvey Lavan Cliburn Jr.) *concert pianist*
Dressler, Oscar H. *music educator*
Dunleavy, Willa Gill *music educator, director*
Faherty, David Miles *musical instrument repairman*
Harth-Bedoya, Miguel *conductor*
Lipkin, Seymour *musician, conductor, educator*
Piedt, David Lawrence *musician*
Raessler, Kenneth Ray *music educator, university administrator, writer*
Stevenson, Ben *artistic director*
Yacante, Maria Lucy *music educator, researcher*

**Garland**
Fain, Thomas Alton, Jr. *music educator*

**Gonzales**
Ince, Laurel T. *music educator*

**Granbury**
Aten, Tammy Liegh *music educator*
Bogner, Beauen Andrew *theater educator, elementary school educator*

**Helotes**
Yamin, Sonya *music educator, voice educator*

**Houston**
Adams, Yolanda Yvette *singer*
Anderson, Lela M *music educator, composer*
Beyoncé, (Beyoncé Giselle Knowles) *singer*
Boyd, Gregory *theater director*
Brown, Glenda Ann Walters *ballet director*
Cupp, Aneta Joan *music educator*
Englesmith, Tejas *actor, television producer, curator*
Freud, Anthony Peter *opera director*
Girouard, Peggy Jo Fulcher *ballet educator*
Graf, Hans *conductor, music director*
Hazelip, Linda Ann *musician, small business owner, executive assistant*
Hescht, Billy Wade *theater educator*
Jackson, Donna Ann *musician, piano teacher*
Jones, Florence M. *music educator*
Krajewski, Michael *conductor*
Norris, Chuck (Carlos Ray) *actor*
Parish, Sharon Denise *music educator, director*
Rigdon, Kevin Leigh *theater educator, lighting designer, set designer*
Roewe, Robin Hughes *music educator, artist, musician*
Rose, Beatrice Schroeder (Mrs. William H. Rose) *harpist, educator*
Rowland, Kelly (Kelendria Trene Rowland) *singer*
Runnels, Brian David *music educator*
Sharpley, Norma Geraldine *music educator*
Simpson, Robert Louis *music educator*
Talbert, Arthur Thomas *music educator*
Welch, Stanton *performing company executive*
Wenk, Bridget Kelly *music educator, musician*
Williams, Michelle (Tenetria Michelle Williams) *singer*

**Huntsville**
Russell, George Haw *video production company executive*

**Ingram**
Riedel, Holly *theater director*

**Irving**
Decker, Tristan Quinn *technical director, lighting designer, set designer*
D'Spain, Michael Fraser *music educator*

**Keene**
Doroftei, Mugur Gideon *music educator, conductor, composer, musician*

**Keller**
King, Chi-Chi Wong *choir director*

**Killeen**
Bryan, Arthur Lee *music educator*

**Kingwood**
Hagen, Barbara C. *music educator*

**Kirbyville**
Gaspard, James M. *music educator, musician*

**La Feria**
Zamarripa, Victor Manuel *sound recording engineer, purchasing agent*

**Laredo**
Sosa, Francisco Javier *music educator, consultant*
Soto, Gilberto D. *music educator*

**Liberty**
Davis, Freida J. *music educator*

**Lubbock**
Aker, Suzanne Deverse *physical movement educator*
Arnold, Sue *music educator*
Chung, Ya-Li *music educator*
Gilbert, John Haspel *music educator*
Hartwell, William Gersham III *retired music educator*
Wray, Robert Theodore *music educator*

**Magnolia**
Bryant, Kimberly Dawn *theater educator, actor*

**Marshall**
Branscome, Eric Eugene *music educator, writer*
Farmer, T. Brent *music educator*

**Mcallen**
Huber, Melba Stewart *dance educator, dance studio owner, historian, retailer*

**Mesquite**
Marin, Jackie Willis *music educator, pianist*
Nye, Randall Wayne *music educator*

**Midland**
Celia, George *composer, writer*
Pysh, Gregory M. *music educator*

**Midlothian**
Patty, Patricia Kae *music educator*

**Mineral Wells**
Warfield, Gerald Alexander *composer, writer*

**Mission**
Holkup, Linda Patricia *music educator*

**Missouri City**
Rathnau, Heather Hearn *music educator, writer*

**Monahans**
Jones, Evelyn Rojean *theater educator, theater director*

**Nacogdoches**
Jacobsen, Jeffrey Richard *music educator*

**North Richland Hills**
Dvorak, Mark Anthony *music educator*
Shier, Elizabeth M. *music educator*

**Pampa**
Willingham, Jeanne Maggart *performing arts educator, performing company executive*

**Pasadena**
Austin-Goza, Pamela Kay *voice educator*
Gilley, Mickey Leroy *musician*
Rocha, Brenda Duvall *theater educator*

**Pearland**
Johnson, Hugh James *retired music educator*

**Plano**
Mick, James Paul *music educator*

**Quitaque**
Herrington, Patsy Jean Stark *music educator*

**Richardson**
Long, Allen Floyd *music educator, minister*

**Rio Grande City**
Lung, Auristela R. *music educator*

**Robert Lee**
Myers, Sterling *choir director*

**Rockwall**
Tucker, Kimberly Joan *music educator*

**San Antonio**
Hornsby, David McMillan *musician, music educator*
Oppenheim, Martha Kunkel *pianist, educator*
Peters, Richard Spencer *musician*
Robertson, Sterling Clifton *music educator, musician*
Sharpley, Robert Louis *performing arts educator, language educator*
Silantien, John Joseph *music educator*
Watson, Ronald Lynn *theater educator*
Wilkins, Christopher Putnam *conductor*

**San Marcos**
Schmidt, John Charles *music educator*

**Sherman**
Cutler, Timothy Spence *music educator, composer*

**Shiner**
Burnett, Vida C. *music educator*

**Spring**
Englert, David John *music educator*

**Sugar Land**
Lester, Jason *singer, music educator*
Martinez, Antonio *choir director, art director*
Victor, Ann Michele *musician, educator*

**Tahoka**
Bennett, Hazel Connolly *music educator, small business owner*

**Temple**
Pinno, John Walter *musician, educator*

**Texas City**
Adams, Mark *theater director*

**The Colony**
Mitchell, Melvin Clifford *music educator*

**The Woodlands**
Holter, Mark E. *musician, educator*

**Tyler**
Baker, Rebecca Louise *musician, music educator, consultant*
Rogers, Cheryl Lynn *music and dance educator*
Rumbley, Philip Lee *music educator, musician, photographer*
Wright, Mary Ellen *theater educator*

**Van**
Lockwood, Kelly *music educator*

**Waco**
Albrecht, Karen Elizabeth *voice educator, theater director*
McKinney, Timothy Richmond *music educator*

**Weatherford**
Banks, Michael Pat *music educator, director*
Bradle, Sue E. *music educator, editor*

**Wharton**
George, Lila Gene Plowe Kennedy *music educator*

**Wichita Falls**
Scherler, Kathy Louise *music educator, researcher*

## UTAH

**Cedar City**
Modesitt, Carol Ann *vocalist, music educator, opera director*

**Clearfield**
Satterthwaite, Shawn Briscoe *musician, educator*

**Kaysville**
Eads, Penni Daun *music educator*
Houtz, Randy L. *music educator*

**Lindon**
Osmond, Donald Clark (Donny Osmond) *singer*

**Park City**
Becker, William Watters *theater producer*

**Provo**
Mendenhall, Cory J. *music educator, conductor*

**Salt Lake City**
Curry, Robert A. *music educator*
Dynak, David Michael *theater educator*
Emerson, Norene Rogers *music educator*
Ewers, Anne *opera company director*
Fogle, Sheryl Kay *voice educator, music educator*
Johnson, Xan Stuart *performing arts educator*
Kåge, Jonas *performing company executive*
Roens, Steven Thomas *music educator, associate dean*
Romney-Manookin, Elaine Clive *retired music educator, composer*
Walker Neve, Diana *singer, voice educator*
Wilberg, Mack J. *conductor, composer*

**Spanish Fork**
Lunt, Rick A. *music educator*

**Woods Cross**
Blackley, Cheryl Ann *freelance/self-employed music educator, musician*
Hendriksen, Neil Evan *music educator*

## VERMONT

**Burlington**
Tamarkin, Kate *conductor*

**Colchester**
Peters, Troy Clark *conductor, composer*

**Johnson**
Whitehill, Angela Elizabeth *artistic director*

**Marlboro**
Brelsford, Edmund Munger III *musician, educator*

**Norwich**
Stetson, Eugene William III *film producer, environmentalist, consultant*

**West Glover**
Weaver, John Borland *musician, department chairman, composer*

**Weston**
Stettler, Stephen F. *performing company executive*

## VIRGINIA

**Alexandria**
Eluhow, Ljiljana Skoric *musician, educator*

**Arlington**
Cadby, Carol *theater educator, theater director*
Hamilton, Anthony *singer*
Mc Donald, Gail Faber *musician, educator*
Southern, Hugh *retired performing arts manager*
Whitfield, Margaret Denny *retired music educator*

**Ashburn**
Baber, Leonard William *music educator, musician*
Haymon, Chadron Zonelle *music educator, minister*

**Bealeton**
Neidich, Patrick C. *music educator, director*

**Blacksburg**
Sipes, Theodore Ward *music educator, singer*

**Bristol**
Harman, Raejean Ann *music educator*

**Burke**
Holder, Roy Cecil *music educator*

**Chantilly**
Ross, Drew *music educator*

**Charlottesville**
Chapel, Robert Clyde *theater director, educator*
Ross, Walter Beghtol *music educator, composer*
Sibert, Polly Lou *conductor, music educator*
Tornello, Vincent Joseph *music educator*

**Chesapeake**
Dixon, Timothy Kaine *music educator*
Hayslett-Wallace, Jeanette *music educator*

**Chesterfield**
Shaffer, Earl E., Jr. *music educator*

**Dublin**
Billaud, Louise Ann *musician, educator*

**Fairfax**
Mann, Laura Ann *soprano*
Miller, Patricia A. *music educator, opera and concert artist*
Siddons, Joy Garbee *music educator*
Wenner, Debby Linn *mezzo soprano, educator*

**Falls Church**
Schoonover, Stanley R. *music educator, consultant*

**Glen Allen**
McCullough, James *composer, writer, retired art association administrator, writer*

**Gloucester Point**
Sandridge, Donald Otis *music educator*

**Hampton**
Buchanan, Alvin Douglas *music educator*
Harris, Carl G. *music educator*
Tomassetti, Benjamin *music educator*

**Harrisonburg**
Choi, In Dal *music educator*
Wingard, Christine *music educator*

**Herndon**
Walker, Lawrence Howard, Jr. *music educator, department chairman*

**Lebanon**
Fuller, Wrenda Sue *music and secondary school educator*

**Leesburg**
Hamman, William Lesley *music educator*
Herrmann, Herbet George, IV, *music educator*
Mahood, Ken *music educator*

**Lexington**
Young, Bruce Kenneth *film director*

**Lorton**
Celentano, Suzanne *movement educator*

**Lynchburg**
Howell, Peggy Haas *musician*
Seay, Marlaina Joan *theater educator, set designer*

**Manassas**
Livingston, Jo Ellen Brooks *music educator*
Martin, Anna Marie *music educator*
Schlechte, Deborah Whitley *music educator*

**Mc Lean**
Hudson, William L. *conductor*
Morlan, Merwyn Eugene *retired music educator*

**Monterey**
Akaike, Hiroko *music educator, conductor*

**Newport News**
Lenwell, John D. *music educator*
Rossettini, Timothy James *music educator, director*
Snider, Diane Meier *organist, choir director, music educator*

**Norfolk**
Klein, Nancy Kirkland *choral music educator*
Mark, Peter *performing company executive, conductor*
Musgrave, Thea *composer, conductor*
Nixon, Patricia Saunders *music educator, actress*
Thompson, VeRita Jean *music educator*

**Oak Hill**
Ritter, Elza K. *music educator*

**Radford**
James, Clarity (Carolyne Faye James) *mezzo soprano*

**Reston**
Esh, Laura Rae *music educator*
Higgs, Joey L. *music educator*

**Richmond**
Carlton, Buzz (Clyde Gordon Carlton Jr.) *singer, songwriter, entertainer, recording artist*
Doss, Marilyn Ruth *music educator*
Erb, James Bryan *music educator, conductor, musicologist*
Freeman, Edward Carl, Jr. *music minister*
Kennedy, Patricia Berry *retired music educator*
Melcher, Elizabeth *musician*
Winslett, Stoner *artistic director*

**Roanoke**
Bradshaw, James R. *music educator*

**Sandston**
Manson, Zynora Davis *music educator, minister*

**Spotsylvania**
Peters, Joanna Eilene *music educator*

**Springfield**
Kimball, Steven Paul *music educator*

**Staunton**
Balsley, Philip Elwood *entertainer*

**Sterling**
Basham, Michael Eric *music educator, director*
Jefferson, Sandra Traylor *choreographer*
Lacey, Aaron Michael *actor, director, film producer, scriptwriter*

**Stuarts Draft**
Taylor, James A. *music educator*

**Suffolk**
Bollinger, Michael *artistic director*

**Vienna**
Kinsolving, Sylvia Crockett *musician, educator*

**Virginia Beach**
Adams, David Franklyn *music educator*
Dixon, John Spencer *performing arts association administrator*
Forbes, Cynthia Ann *music educator*
Garcia, Franc C. *music educator, director*
Lutsyshyn, Oksana *concert pianist, organist*
Panoff, Stephen Edward *music educator*
Prescott, David L. C., Jr. *music educator*
Snead, David N. *music educator*
Tuskey, Laura Jeanne *music educator, pharmacologist*
Ventura, Roland P. *music educator*
Watkins, Brenda L. *music educator*

**Williamsburg**
Gavaler, Joan Susan *dance educator*

**Winchester**
Aiosa, Charlotte Nelson *music educator*

**Wise**
Seay, Joseph Daniel *music educator*

**Woodbridge**
Brittain, Lara Michelle *music educator*

**Woodstock**
Mrosko, Matthew L. *music educator*

**Yorktown**
Kirsch, Darren Matthew *music educator*

**WASHINGTON**

**Bellevue**
Rundell, Arden Grabke *musician*

**Bellingham**
Whyte, Nancy Marie *performing arts educator*

**Bonney Lake**
Aalbers-Selle, Laurie Lynn *music educator*

**Camas**
Mancini, Richard Alan *music educator*

**Clarkston**
Torgerson, Linda Belle *music educator*

**Coupeville**
Lotzenhiser, George William *musician, educator, academic administrator, composer*

**Edmonds**
Bondurant, Nancy Ruth *musician, music educator*

**Ellensburg**
Panerio, Robert Major, Sr. *music educator, composer*

**Endicott**
Ray, Billy John, Jr. *music educator*

**Harrington**
Nighswonger, David Glenn *music educator*

**Kenmore**
Sokol, Jennifer Marie *musician*

**Kirkland**
Yamada-Fells, Mizue *music educator*

**Lacey**
Louis, Glenn *music educator*

**Longview**
Uthmann, Richard W. *retired music educator*

**North Bend**
Brumbaugh, Harley Aaron *retired music educator, conductor, composer, poet*

**Olympia**
Macduff, Ilone Margaret *music educator*

**Richland**
Powell, David Charles *music educator, meteorologist*

**Seattle**
Card, Deborah Frances *orchestra administrator*
Coldwell, Maria V. *performing arts association administrator*
Collier, Tom Ward *musician, educator*
Denke, Conrad William *motion picture producer*
Elyn, Mark *retired vocalist*
Forbes, David Craig *musician*
Houston, Janeanne Currier *vocalist, educator*
Jenkins, Speight *performing company executive, writer*
Mahdaviani, Miriam *choreographer, educator*
Mull, Robert W. *filmmaker, curator*
Ozaki, Nancy Junko *performance artist, performing arts educator*
Russell, Francia *ballet director, educator*

**Skirvin**, Donald Murray *composer, writer*
Staryk, Steven Sam *violinist, concertmaster, educator*
Stowell, Kent *ballet director*
Sullivan, Daniel J. *artistic director*
Talachian, Reza *filmmaker*
Van Lierop, John Henry, Jr. *music educator*

**Shoreline**
Dolacky, Susan K. *music educator*
Matesky, Nancy Lee *music educator*

**Snohomish**
Philpott, Larry La Fayette *horn player*

**Spangle**
Anderson, Curtis Dale *music educator*

**Tacoma**
Alatsis, Despina Katherine *music educator, director*

**Trout Lake**
Anderson, Douglas Del *retired music educator, recording industry executive*

**Vancouver**
Hilligoss, Charles Adair *retired music educator*
Wharton, Penelope Lee (Penny Wharton) *music educator*

**Walla Walla**
Lords, Traci Elizabeth (Nora Louise Kuzma) *actress, singer*
Rossi, Norbert Guido *music educator*
Simon, Nancy Lynn *performing arts educator, director*

**Washougal**
Gilbert, Patricia Lynn *music educator*
Harness, William Edward *tenor*

**Woodinville**
Sanders, Richard Kinard *actor*

**WEST VIRGINIA**

**Athens**
Westbrook, Gary Wayne *music educator, consultant*

**Morgantown**
Kinsey, Donna Lee *music educator*
Wilson, Mary Alice *musician, educator*

**Parkersburg**
Young III, Harmon Griffith *music educator*

**Salem**
Raad, Virginia *pianist, educator*

**Shenandoah Junction**
Showen, Donald Eugene, Jr. *music educator*

**WISCONSIN**

**Appleton**
Rippl, Frank George *retired music educator, retired organist*

**Beaver Dam**
Carnes, Jeneen A. *music educator*

**Beloit**
Licary, Cheryl Ann *retired music educator, church musician*
Rosenthal, Timothy Mark *music educator*

**Brookfield**
Lavender, Cheryl Ann *music educator, composer, writer*

**Bryant**
Sutherland, Marion Ida *music educator*

**Colgate**
Earl, Marcia Hunt *music educator, director*

**Delavan**
Lepke, Charma Davies *musician, educator*

**Dodgeville**
Dentinger, Ronald Lee *comedian, speaker, freelance writer*

**Dunbar**
Habing, Brett William *music educator*

**Eau Claire**
Schwartzhoff, Gary R. *music educator*

**Franklin**
Booth, Ronald Eugene *music educator*

**Greenfield**
McKillip, Patricia Claire *operatic soloist*

**Horicon**
Gasner, Donn Allan *music educator*

**Kenosha**
Kinchen, James Benjamin, Jr. *music educator, choral conductor*

**Kimberly**
Gall, Craig F. *music educator*

**La Crosse**
Bina, Steven J. *music educator*
Luckner, Brian William *choir director, organist, composer*

**Lake Mills**
Klotz, Bradley Alan *music educator, musician*

**Madison**
Bartley, Linda L. *musician, music educator*
De Main, John *opera company director*
Faulkner, Julia Ellen *opera singer*
Furumoto, David John *theater educator*
Rosser, Annetta Hamilton *composer*

**Marion**
Gast, Timothy Alan *musician, educator, small business owner*

**Menasha**
Walter, Thomas Bernard *music educator, conductor*

**Menomonee Falls**
Chicorel, Ralph *librettist, composer, playwright*

**Middleton**
Gaub, Albrecht Friedrich *music editor*

**Milwaukee**
Cheatham, Wallace McClain *music educator*
Crocker, Ray Dean *musician, musical director*
Delfs, Andreas *conductor, musical director*
Harris, Christine *dance company executive*
Pink, Michael *performing company executive*
Samson, Richard Max *theater director, investment company executive*
Uecker, Bob *actor, radio announcer, former baseball player, television personality*

**Mosinee**
Dul, Carla Marie *music educator*

**Neenah**
Orm, Sally S. *music educator, consultant*

**New Berlin**
Belich, Kay S. *music educator*

**Oconomowoc**
Bleke, Diane K. *music educator, director*

**Platteville**
Alcalay, Eugene Christian *pianist*

**Pleasant Prairie**
Clark, William Henry *retired music educator*

**Racine**
Schoening, Ruth Irene *retired music educator, musician*

**Reedsburg**
Miotke, David Roy *music educator*

**Rice Lake**
Hoch, Matthew Ryan *music educator*

**River Falls**
Hedahl, Gorden Orlin *theater educator, dean*

**Rudolph**
Heywood, Gail Anne *music educator, musician*

**Saint Francis**
Wurgler, Timothy Raymond *music educator*

**Shell Lake**
Aderman, Oscar Darrell *retired music educator*

**Shorewood**
Bowers, Jane Meredith *retired music educator*

**South Milwaukee**
Thompson, Peter John *music educator, director*

**Spring Green**
Day, Sarah Jane *actor*

**Superior**
McKnight, Patricia Gayle *musician, artist, writer, educator*
Playfair, David Malcolm *vocalist, voice educator, researcher*

**Verona**
White, Carolyn Louise *music educator*

**Wales**
Jaeger, Todd D. *music educator*

**Washington Island**
Schweikert, Norman Carl *retired musician*

**Waukesha**
Helgert, Mark James *music educator*
Meyer, Debora Lynn *music educator*
Stringham, Phyllis Joan *retired music educator*

**Waupaca**
Hansen, Louise Hill *music educator, retired application developer*

**Wauwatosa**
DeVillers, Ronald Joseph *retired music educator, musician*

**Whitewater**
Jennings, Robert Lee *retired music educator*
Joseph, Stacey Ann McGraw *music educator, church choir director*

**Winneconne**
Hale, Donald Roy *music educator, musician*

**WYOMING**

**Casper**
Grussendorf, Steven Carl *music educator, director*
Kukes, Patrick J. *music educator*
Searcey, Paul W. *music educator*

**Dubois**
Glasser, Pamela Jean *musician, music educator*

**Lander**
Stevens, Sufjan *musician*

**Wheatland**
Munari, Michael F. *music educator, small business owner*

**TERRITORIES OF THE UNITED STATES**

**PUERTO RICO**

**Bayamon**
Ortiz, William *composer, music educator*

**San Juan**
Daddy Yankee, (Raymond Ayala) *musician*
López, Ilca *music educator, mezzo soprano*

**CANADA**

**ALBERTA**

**Calgary**
Grand-Maitre, Jean *performing company executive*
Monk, Allan James *baritone*
Raeburn, Andrew Harvey *performing arts consultant, recording industry executive*

**BRITISH COLUMBIA**

**Vancouver**
Esposito, Jennifer *actress*
Fichtner, William *actor*
Jones, Norah *vocalist, musician*
Lavigne, Avril *singer*
McLachlan, Sarah *musician, composer*
Murray, Anne *singer*
Tate, Larenz *actor*

**MANITOBA**

**Winnipeg**
Lewis, André Leon *artistic director*
Turner, Robert Comrie *composer*

**ONTARIO**

**Callander**
Haig, Susan *conductor*

**Kitchener**
Coles, Graham *conductor, composer*
Eldred, Gerald Marcus *performing company executive*

**London**
William, David *theater director, actor*

**Ottawa**
Gillingham, Bryan Reginald *music educator*
Prevost, Roxane Lise *music theory educator*

**Toronto**
Beckwith, John *musician, educator, composer*
Colgrass, Michael Charles *composer*
Egoyan, Atom *film director*
Furtado, Nelly Kim *vocalist*
Goh, Chan Hon *ballerina*
Hodgkinson, Greta *dancer*
Hon Goh, Chan *dancer*
Kain, Karen Alexandria *ballet dancer*
Kudelka, James *choreographer, artistic director*
Mckellar, Don *actor, screenwriter, filmmaker*
Oundjian, Peter *conductor, music director*
Rasky, Harry *producer, director, writer*
Schramek, Tomas *ballet dancer, educator*
Staines, Mavis Avril *performing company executive*
Van Der Wyst, Chan *dancer*

**QUEBEC**

**Montreal**
Girard, Francois *film director*
Labadie, Bernard *performing company executive*
Lacombe, Jacques *conductor*
Lock, Edouard *performing company executive*
Pankov, Gradimir Krunislav *ballet artistic director*

**Vancouver**
Newtown, Thandie *actress*

**AUSTRALIA**

**Darlinghurst**
Davis, Judy *actress*

**North Sydney**
Crowe, Russell *actor*

**Perth**
Dow, Simon *artistic director, choreographer*

**Redfern**
Campion, Jane *film director, screenwriter*

**BELGIUM**

**Brussels**
Freizer, Louis A. *radio producer*

## COSTA RICA

**San José**
Hoffman, Irwin *orchestra conductor*

## CZECH REPUBLIC

**Prague**
Cusumano, James Anthony *filmmaker, vocalist, retired pharmaceutical executive, recording industry executive*

**Zlaté Hory**
Plaček, Roman *cellist, composer, music educator*

## ENGLAND

**Askett Bucks**
Irons, Jeremy John *actor*

**Cambridge**
Hogwood, Christopher Jarvis Haley *music educator*

**Charlbury**
Belkin, Boris David *violinist*

**Cheltenham Gloucestershire**
Winwood, Stephen Lawrence *musician, composer*

**East Sussex**
Katin, Peter Roy *pianist*

**Essex**
Collins, Joan Henrietta *actress*

**Isle of Wight**
Stigwood, Robert Colin *film producer, television producer, radio producer, theater producer*

**Leavesden**
Watson, Emma *actress*

**Leeds**
Ichino, Yoko *ballerina*
Nixon, David *dancer*

**London**
Alexeev, Dmitri Konstantinovich *pianist*
Andsnes, Leif Ove *concert pianist*
Arman Gelenbe, Deniz *concert pianist*
Ashkenazy, Vladimir Davidovich *concert pianist, conductor*
Beckinsale, Kate *actress*
Bell, Joshua *musician*
Bertolucci, Bernardo *film director*
Bloom, Orlando *actor*
Blunt, James Hillier *singer*
Bono, (Paul David Hewson) *singer, songwriter*
Bourne, Matthew *performing company executive, artistic director*
Butler, Geezer (Terence Michael Joseph Butler) *musician*
Codron, Michael Victor *theater producer*
Conti, Tom *actor, theater director, writer*
Cowell, Simon *television personality, music producer*
Day-Lewis, Daniel Michael Blake *actor*
Delpy, Julie *actress*
DeMann, Freddy *film, play, television producer*
Dohnányi, Christoph von *musician, conductor*
Duncan, Lindsay Vere *actress*
Enya, (Eithne Ní Bhraonain, Enya Brennan) *musician*
Flor, Claus Peter *conductor*
Gervais, Ricky *actor, scriptwriter*
Haitink, Bernard J. H. *conductor*
Harney, Kathryn Ann *opera singer*
Hicks, Taylor Reuben *singer*
Hoskins, Bob (Robert William Hoskins) *actor*
Iommi, Tony (Frank Anthony Iommi) *musician*
John, Sir Elton Hercules (Reginald Kenneth Dwight) *musician*
Kapranos, Alexander (Franz Ferdinand) *singer, musician*
Kingsley, Sir Ben *actor*
Leigh, Mike *film director*
Lloyd Webber, Lord Andrew (Baron of Sydmonton) *composer, small business owner*
Mackerras, Sir Charles (Alan Maclaurin) *conductor*
Masur, Kurt *conductor, music director*
McCowen, Alec *actor*
McDiarmid, Ian *actor, film director*
McGregor, Ewan Gordon *actor*
McKellen, Sir Ian *actor*
McPhee, Katherine Hope *singer*
Mendes, Sam (Samuel Alexander Mendes) *film director, theater director*
Miller, Jonathan Wolfe *theater and film director, physician*
Minton, Yvonne Fay *mezzo-soprano*
Moody, Ron *actor, writer*
Moss, Kate *model*
Nagano, Kent George *conductor, music director*
Newell, Mike *film director*
Palin, Michael Edward *actor, scriptwriter, writer*
Payne, Alexander *film director, producer*
Pryce, Jonathan *actor*
Radcliffe, Daniel *actor*
Rice, Sir Timothy Miles Bindon *lyricist*
Richardson, Ian William *actor*
Richardson, Miranda *actress*
Rickman, Alan *actor*
Shankar, Ravi *composer, musician*
Sher, Sir Antony *actor, author*
Smith, Dame Maggie (Margaret Natalie Smith Cross) *actress*
Spacey, Kevin *actor*
Spillane, Mary Catherine *television producer*
Staunton, Imelda (Imelda Mary Philomena Bernadette Staunton) *actress*
Uchida, Mitsuko *pianist*
Ward, Bill *musician*
Winner, Michael Robert *film director, film producer, writer*

**Manchester**
Wilson, Keith Dudley *media and music educator, consultant, dean*

**Newcastle-Upon-Tyne**
Valentine, Gary (Gary Lachman) *musician*

**North Wales**
Hands, Terence David (Terry Hands) *theater and opera director*

**Poole**
Alsop, Marin *conductor, violinist, music director*

**Saint Margaret's**
Attenborough, Baron Richard Samuel *actor, film director, film producer, ambassador*

**Surrey**
Holm, Sir Ian *actor*

## FRANCE

**Collonges**
Morgenstern, Sheldon Jon *symphony orchestra conductor*

**Lyon**
Robertson, David *conductor, music director*

**Paris**
Annaud, Jean-Jacques *film director, film producer, scriptwriter*
de Havilland, Olivia Mary *actress*
Deneuve, Catherine (Catherine Dorleac) *actress*
Jolas, Betsy *composer, educator*
Raimondi, Ruggero *opera singer*

## GERMANY

**Dresden**
Schreier, Peter *tenor*

**Hamburg**
Neumeier, John *choreographer, ballet company director*

**Munich**
Araiza, Francisco (José Francisco Araiza Andrade) *opera singer*

**Stuttgart**
Anderson, Reid Bryce *performing company executive*

## GHANA

**Legon**
Avorgbedor, Daniel Kodzo *music educator*

## HONG KONG

**Kowloon**
Chow, Yun-fat (Chow Yun-Fat) *actor*
Wu, Daniel *actor*

## IRELAND

**Dublin**
Sheridan, Jim *film director, screenwriter*

**Galway**
Hynes, Garry *theater director*

## ITALY

**Cremia**
Malipiero, Victoria Schneider *vocalist*

## JAPAN

**Tokyo**
Ohira, Kazuto *theatre company executive, writer*
Ozawa, Seiji *conductor, music director*

## LATVIA

**Riga**
Strautins, Vilnis *music educator, retired performing company executive*

## NEW ZEALAND

**Wellington**
Jackson, Peter *film director*
Paquin, Anna *actress*

## REPUBLIC OF KOREA

**Seoul**
Han, Oksoo *musician, music director*
Jeong, Ji-Hoon (Rain) *singer*

## RUSSIA

**Moscow**
Kogan, Pavel *conductor*

**Saint Petersburg**
Temirkanov, Yuri Khatuevich *conductor, music director*

## SPAIN

**Madrid**
Almodovar, Pedro *filmmaker*
Frühbeck de Burgos, Rafael *conductor*

## SWITZERLAND

**Geneva**
Barenboim, Daniel *conductor, pianist, music director*

**Meggen**
Galway, Sir James *flutist*

## ADDRESS UNPUBLISHED

Aberlin, Betty Kay *actress*
Adams, Amy (Amanda Jessica Adams) *actress*
Adams, Brooke *actress*
Adams, Joey Lauren *actress*
Adamski, Mark Phillip *music educator*
Adler, Samuel Hans *retired conductor, composer*
Affleck, Ben *actor*
Aghdashloo, Shohreh *actress*
Agrell, Jeffrey *musician*
Akiyoshi, Toshiko *jazz composer, pianist*
Alba, Jessica *actress*
Alexander, John Whitesides *musician, educator*
Aliev, Eldar *former artistic director, choreographer, educator*
Ali G, (Sacha Baron Cohen) *actor, comedian*
Allard, Michael Alan *music educator, conductor*
Allen, Marilyn Myers Pool *theater director, video specialist*
Allen, Woody (Allen Stewart Konigsberg) *director, actor, writer*
Alley, Kirstie *actress*
Allison, Glorietta Travis *music educator, soprano*
Allston, Charita Capers *music educator*
Amenabar, Alejandro *film director, film producer, actor*
Amgott, Madeline *television producer, consultant*
Amstutz, Curtis J. *music educator*
Anderson, Beth Aimee *music educator*
Anderson, Gillian *actress*
Anderson, Lynn (Rene Anderson) *singer*
Anderson, PT (Paul Thomas IV) *film director*
Anderson, Robin Louise *music educator*
Andreu, Helene C. *dancer, educator*
Andrews, Dame Julie (Julia Elizabeth Wells) *actress, singer*
Anger, Kenneth *director, filmmaker, author*
Aniston, Jennifer *actress*
Annis, Francesca *actress*
Anthony, Marc (Marco Antonio Muniz) *singer, composer, actor*
Apel, Harry James *music producer, entertainer, composer*
Apel, Robert William *actor*
Applegate, Christina *actress*
Apted, Michael David *film director*
Arenal, Julie (Mrs. Barry Primus) *choreographer*
Arkin, Alan Wolf *actor*
Armstrong, Billie Joe *singer, musician*
Armstrong, Holly Lopez *music educator*
Arnold, Mary Spears *retired music educator*
Arnold, Tichina *actress, singer*
Arthur, Beatrice *actress*
Arthurs, Chase Amber *music educator*
Astin, Sean Patrick *actor, film director, film producer, writer*
Authement, Patty Lynn *music educator*
Auwarter, Douglas D. *music educator*
Azaria, Hank *actor*
Bach, Jan Morris *composer, educator*
Bach, Jane Ella *music educator*
Bader, Diedrich *actor*
Badu, Erykah *singer, songwriter*
Baerwald, Susan Grad *television broadcasting company executive producer*
Baker, Kathy Whitton *actress*
Balaban, Bob *actor, film director*
Baldwin, Alec (Alexander Rae Baldwin III) *actor*
Bale, Christian *actor*
Ball, Marcia *vocalist*
Balser, Robert Edward *animation film producer, director*
Baranski, Christine *actress*
Barber, Elizabeth Jean *vocalist, educator, artist*
Barbera, Joseph *motion picture and television producer, cartoonist*
Barnes, Phil *music educator*
Barranger, Milly Slater *theater educator, writer*
Barrio, Soledad *dancer*
Barsalona, Frank Samuel *retired theatrical agent*
Bartlett, Jeremiah Seth *music educator*
Bartoli, Cecilia *soprano*
Baryshnikov, Mikhail *ballet dancer, actor*
Bassett, Leslie Raymond *composer, educator*
Bateman, Thomas Anthony *music educator, musician*
Baxter, Elizabeth Palm *music educator*
Bayolo, Armando Jesús *composer, music educator*
Bazar, Jill A. *music educator*
Beach, Gary *actor*
Becker, Wendy Jeanne *music educator, lyricist, educator*
Behlmer, Rudy H., Jr. *retired director, writer, film educator, entertainer*
Behrens, Jason Lynn *music educator*
Belafonte, Harry (Harry George Belafonte Jr.) *singer, concert artist, actor*
Beloff, Zoe *filmmaker, educator, photographer*
Belzberg, Edet *filmmaker*
Bencini, Sara Haltiwanger *concert pianist*
Benjamin (Rector), Jennifer Danielle *music educator, director, voice educator*
Benner, Timothy L. *theater director, actor*
Bennett, Sharon Kay *music educator*
Bennett, Tony (Anthony Dominick Benedetto) *entertainer*
Benning, James *film director*
Benson, Jeanne P. *music educator*
Benton, Robert *film director, screenwriter*
Beresford, Bruce *film director*
Berezin, Tanya *acting coach, educator, actress*
Bergen, Candice *actress, writer, photojournalist*
Berger, Phil *musician*
Bergeron, Earleen Fournet *actress*
Berlind, Roger Stuart *stage and film producer*
Berlinger, Warren *actor*
Berman, Sanford Solomon *motion picture sound designer, composer, arranger, artist*
Berman, Shari Springer *film director, scriptwriter*
Bernhard, Sandra *actress, comedienne, singer*
Bersegeay, Cecile Maite *singer*
Besson, Luc *film director, film producer*
Bethke, Louise Virginia *music educator, writer*
Bevan, Tim *film producer*
Bielawa, Herbert Walter *composer, pianist, educator*
Binoche, Juliette *actress*
Bishop, Kelly (Carole Bishop) *actress*
Bissell, James Dougal III *motion picture production designer*
Biziou, Peter *cinematographer*
Black, Lisa Hartman *actress, singer*
Blackburn, Royce Franklin *vocalist, educator*
Blackstone, Dara *music educator*
Blethyn, Brenda Anne *actress*
Blige, Mary Jane *recording artist*
Blomquist, Alan Charles *film producer*
Bloom, Frances Virginia *retired music educator*
Bloomquist, Kenneth Gene *music educator, director*
Bloomquist, Paul Frederick *music educator, director, secondary school educator, musician*
Blossom, Beverly *choreographer, educator*
Boardman, Eunice *retired music educator*
Boatwright, Helen Strassburger *voice educator*
Bobbie, Walter *theatrical director*
Bock, Janine Schmelzer *music educator*
Boe, David Stephen *musician, educator, dean*
Bogosian, Eric *actor, writer*
Bohrman, David Ellis *television news producer*
Bonazzi, Elaine Claire *mezzo soprano*
Bond, Victoria Ellen *conductor, composer*
Bonet, Lisa (Lilakoi Moon, Lisa Michelle Boney) *actress*
Bonifati, Louis M. *music educator*
Bon Jovi, Jon (John Francis Bongiovi Jr.) *musician, singer, songwriter, actor, professional sports team executive*
Bonnard, Raymond *theater director*
Borden, David *composer, educator*
Borkowski, Francis Thomas *music educator*
Boroski, Will *actor, educator*
Bosco, Philip Michael *actor*
Boulez, Pierre *composer, conductor*
Bowers, Norma Jean *music educator*
Bowman, David Frederick *music educator*
Boyle, Lara Flynn *actress*
Boyle, Peter *actor*
Brady, Mary Rolfes *music educator*
Brady, Wayne *actor*
Braff, Zach *actor, director, scriptwriter*
Branagh, Kenneth *actor, film director*
Brandon, Liane *filmmaker, educator*
Brandt-Soetermans, Valerie Louise *dancer, educator*
Braxton, Frederick *music educator*
Breault, Robert Lee *music educator*
Brewer, Summer M. *performing arts educator*
Brez, Dante (Mos Def) *musician, actor*
Briggle, Gary Lee *singer, actor, director, educator*
Brightman, Sarah *singer, actress*
Brody, Adrien *actor*
Bronson, James B. *music educator*
Brooks, Avery *actor, educator, musician*
Brooks, Garth (Troyal Garth Brooks) *musician, singer*
Brooks, Gerldine McGlothlin *music educator*
Brooks, Lorraine Elizabeth *retired music educator*
Brooks, Michael *music archivist*
Brooks-Turner, Myra *music educator*
Brosnan, Pierce *actor*
Brown, Alton C. *television personality, chef*
Brown, Lora Alice *entertainment company executive, educator*
Brown-Barton, Grace Olive *music educator*
Browne, Jackson *singer, songwriter*
Brown Leatherberry, Thomas Henry *performing company executive, clergyman*
Broyles, William Dodson, Jr. *author, editor, scriptwriter*
Bruning, Earl H. *music educator*
Bullock, Sandra (Sandra Annette Bullock) *actress*
Bultman, Nils *musician, composer*
Burdette, Gary W. *music educator*
Burge, Constance M. *television producer*
Burke, Brooke *actress, model*
Burmester, Leo (Leo Burmeister) *actor*
Burnett, Mark *television producer*
Burns, Edward J., Jr. *actor, film director*
Burrell, Pamela *actress*
Buscemi, Steve *actor*
Bush, Betty J. *music educator, elementary school educator*
Bush, Eileen Shanin *voice educator*
Bush, Ellen D. *music educator*
Bush, Kate (Catherine Bush) *singer, songwriter*
Butler, Brett *comedienne, actress*
Butt, Sameer *filmmaker, writer*
Button, Richard Totten *television producer, ice skater*
Butz, Norbert Leo *actor*
Bynes, Amanda *actress*
Byrd, Debra Ann *actor, theater producer, performing company executive*
Caan, James *actor, director*
Caldwell, Joshua *filmmaker*
Calegari, Maria *ballerina*
Calissi, Jeffrey Luke *music educator*
Calman, Craig David *actor, writer*
Campbell, Monna Kay *music educator*
Campbell, Neal Franklin *music educator*
Cannavale, Bobby (Roberto Cannavale) *actor*
Cannon, Dyan *actress*
Carey, Drew *actor*
Carey, Mariah *vocalist, songwriter*
Carley, Kurt *actor*

Irving, Terry (Edward B. Irving III) *television producer*
Irwin, Bill *actor, clown*
Italiano, Daniel J. *music educator*
Ivey, Judith *actress*
Jackman, Hugh *actor*
Jackson, Brian Matthew *musician, educator*
Jackson, Felicity Anne *performing arts organization administrator*
Jackson, Kate *actress*
Jackson, Michael Joseph *musician*
Jackson, Nagle *stage director, playwright*
Jackson, Samuel L. *actor*
Jackson, Victoria Lynn *actress, comedienne*
Jacobi, Bonnie Schaffhauser *music teacher, pianist*
Jacobi, Derek George *actor*
Jacobs, Annette M. *music educator*
Janis, Conrad *actor, musician, art dealer*
Janney, Allison *actress*
Janney, Kay Print *retired performing arts educator, theater director*
Jaquette, William C. *music educator*
Jarmusch, Jim *film director, actor*
Jarve, Dawna N. *music educator*
Jarvi, Neeme *conductor, music director*
Jefferson, Marvin Kazembe *actor, theater educator*
Jeffreys, Joe E. *theater educator, writer*
Jenkin, James Thomas *video editor*
Jenkins, Richard Dale *actor, theater director*
Jennings, Ken (Kenneth Wayne Jennings III) *Jeopardy champion, software engineer*
Jensen, Nancy Daggett *music educator*
Jeter, James Yandell *freelance/self-employed musician*
Jewel, (Jewel Kilcher) *folk singer, songwriter*
Joanou, Phil *film director*
Joel, Katie (Katie Lee Joel, Katherine Lee) *television personality*
Johnson, Dennis Ira *theater educator, playwright*
Johnson, Jeanne Jordan *music educator, department chairman*
Johnson, Timothy D. *music educator, composer, poet*
Jones, Constance Coralie *retired music educator*
Jones, Shirley *actress, singer*
Jones, Steve *musician*
Jones, Tommy Lee *actor*
Joosten, Kathryn (Kathryn Joostyn) *actress*
Jordan, Jeremy Robert *music educator*
Kaczmarek, Jane *actress*
Kaisershot, A. Kevin *composer*
Kalmar, Carlos *music director*
Kamerin, Kim K. *music educator*
Kane, Carol *actress*
Kaplan, Richard James *film producer, educator, film director, consultant, scriptwriter*
Karayanis, Plato Steven *opera company executive*
Kasdan, Lawrence Edward *film director, screenwriter*
Kaspar, Frances Wolf *music educator*
Kauffman, Marta *producer, writer*
Kaufmann, Charles Leonard *musician, composer*
Kavanaugh, Frank James *film producer, educator*
Kavner, Julie *actress*
Kaye, Debra *composer, music educator*
Kaye, Judy *actress*
Kaye, Lori *actress, news reporter, producer*
Kaylan, Howard Lawrence *musical entertainer, screenwriter, composer*
Keating, Charles *actor*
Keeton, Melinda Denise *music educator*
Keim, Betty Lou *actress, literary consultant*
Keith, Toby (Toby Keith Covel) *country singer, songwriter, producer*
Kelley, Kathryn B. *actress*
Kennedy, Linda Dale *music educator, musician*
Kennedy, Megan Catherine *music educator*
Keyes, Alan L. *radio and talk show host, former federal government official*
Kibler, Samuel *music educator*
Kidder, Margot (Margaret Ruth Kidder) *actress*
Kilbane, Kathleen Ann *stage manager*
Kim, Daniel Dae *actor*
Kim, Ellen Ye *music educator*
King, Patricia P. *music educator, director*
King, Regina *actress*
King, Renee Rogman *music educator*
Kingera, Richard Nick *music educator*
Kinnear, Greg *actor, film producer*
Kirchner, Lisa Beth *actress, vocalist*
Kirkland, Geoffrey Alan *motion picture production designer*
Kitt, Eartha Mae *actress, singer*
Kivell, Wayne M. *music educator, choral conductor*
Klampe, Craig Allen *composer*
Klein, James Edgar *actor*
Klein, Stephen Thomas *performing arts executive*
Klemp, Barbara Anne *music educator*
Klinger, Mary K. *performing company executive, educator*
Klotman, Robert Howard *retired music educator*
Kloves, Steven *film director, scriptwriter*
Knight, Shirley *actress*
Knightley, Keira *actress*
Knowles, William Leroy (Bill Knowles) *television news producer, journalism educator*
Koepke, Allen Henry *music educator, composer*
Kokkeler, Fay Esther *music educator*
Kollias, Jim Harry *music educator*
Kolojejchick, Andrew J. *music educator*
Komlos, Peter *violinist*
Kong, Mingshan *music educator*
Kopelson, Arnold *film producer*
Koplowitz, Stephan *choreographer*
Krabbe, Thomas Joseph *music educator*
Kraus, Lisa Marie Wasko *music educator, composer, musician*
Kriegsman, Sali Ann *performing arts executive, consultant, writer*
Kringer, Micheal Dale *music educator, director, voice educator*
Kroll, Robert Ronald *music educator*
Kudrow, Lisa (Lisa Marie Diane Kudrow) *actress*
Kunstman, D. Bryan *choral director, vocalist*
Kuo, Michelle Chen (Chou-hsia Chen) *musician, educator*
Kuriansky, Judy *television personality, radio personality, reporter, clinical psychologist, writer, educator*
Kurtz, Swoosie *actress*

Kutcher, Ashton (Christopher Ashton Kutcher) *actor*
Kutrzeba, Joseph S. *theater producer, director*
Kwiram, Bernard Rudolph Alvin *music educator, conductor*
Lachey, Nick (Nicholas Scott Lachey) *singer, actor*
Ladd, Diane *actress*
Lambert, John Walton *music educator*
Lane, Diane *actress*
Lane, Patrice Ellen *music educator*
Lane, Ted A. *music educator, musician*
Lang, Dennis Alan *music educator*
Larsen, Lone *music educator, conductor*
Larson, Joan Isbell *musician, educator*
LaRue, Eva Marie *actress*
LaSalle, Eriq *actor, film director*
Lathe, Garrett W. *music educator*
Latimer, James Harold *musician, conductor, composer, music educator*
Lauper, Cyndi *musician*
Leachman, Cloris *actress*
Leahy, Jeannette (Jeannette Oliver Leahy Tinen Kaehler) *actress*
Learned, Michael *actress*
Leary, Denis *actor, comedian*
LeBlanc, Matt (Matthew Steven LeBlanc) *actor*
Lebon, Rachel L. *musician, educator*
Lee, Bobby *actor, comedian*
Lee, Christopher Frank Carandini *actor, writer, singer*
Lee, Dai-Keong *composer*
Lee, Eunice *music educator*
Lee, Soh Yeong *music educator*
Lee, William Franklin III *composer, musician*
Lefferts, George *television producer*
Lennix, Harry Joseph III *actor*
Leno, Jay (James Douglas Muir Leno) *talk show host, comedian, writer*
León, Tania Justina *composer, music director, pianist*
Leoni, Tea (Elizabeth Tea Pantaleoni) *actress*
Lepage, Robert *actor, playwright*
Levering, Arthur Chester *composer*
Levinsohn, Gary *producer*
Levitas, Miriam C. Strickman *documentary filmmaker*
Lewis, James Kevin *music educator*
Lewis, Richard *actor, comedian*
Li, Gong *actress*
Lichtenstein, Harvey *performing arts association administrator*
Lieberson, Peter *composer*
Lifton, Paul Samuel *theater educator*
Lindegren, Cecile Keyser *music educator*
Lindsey, Roberta Lewise *music researcher, historian*
Ling, Bai *actor*
Lington, Aaron Joseph *music educator, musician*
Linklater, Richard *film director, actor, screenwriter*
Lipton, Bob *music educator, composer*
Lithgow, John Arthur *actor, film director*
Little Richard, (Richard Wayne Penniman) *musician, lyricist, minister*
LL Cool J, (James Todd Smith) *rap artist, actor*
Lo, Welby Joseph *music educator*
Locklear, Heather *actress*
Lockwood, Paul Timothy *actor, writer, film director*
Locricchio, Matthew *actor, writer*
Loker, Robin Lee *music educator*
Lonchyna-Lisowsky, Maria *music educator*
Long, Shelley (Shelley Lee Long) *actress*
Lopez, Jennifer *actress, singer, dancer*
Lopez, Soledad *actress*
Loring, Gloria Jean *vocalist*
Loughlin, Lori *actress*
Love, Courtney *singer, actress*
Love, Laura *singer, songwriter*
Loveless, Patty (Patty Ramey) *country music singer*
Lovitz, Jon *actor, comedian*
Lubin, Steven *concert pianist, musicologist*
Luckey-Aukerman, Daisy S. *music educator*
Ludwig, Christa *retired mezzo soprano*
Lueth, Martin S. *music educator*
Lukasiewicz, Paul Manus *music educator*
Lumet, Sidney *film director*
Lupri, Matthias Albrecht *composer*
Lupu, Radu *pianist*
Lydon, John Joseph (Johnny Rotten) *musician*
Lyford, Ronald Lee *music educator*
Lyne, Adrian *film director*
Lynn, Loretta Webb (Mrs. Oliver Lynn Jr.) *singer*
MacDowell, Andie (Rose Anderson MacDowell) *actress*
Macpherson, Elle *model*
Madeira, Francis King Carey *conductor, educator*
Madonna, (Madonna Louise Veronica Ciccone) *singer, actress, producer*
Madsen, Peter *music educator, musician*
Madsen, Virginia *actress*
Maffia, Roma *actress*
Magor, Louis Roland *conductor*
Mahoney, John *actor*
Mainhart, Robert *music educator*
Mallory, Benjamin Wade *music educator*
Malm, Mia *actress*
Maltby, Richard Eldridge, Jr. *theater director, lyricist*
Mannes, Elena Sabin *film and television producer, television director*
Manning, Michael Nicholas *actor, singer, guitarist, broadcaster, journalist*
Manson, Anne *music director*
Marceau, Yvonne *ballroom dancer, educator*
Marcone, Angela T. *music educator*
Marcus, Mitch *musician, composer*
Marcy, Kevin Michael *film producer, lawyer*
Margules, Cecelia *composer, poet*
Mariconda, Nicholas Gerard *music educator, musician*
Mark, Judi *actress, choreographer*
Mark, Michael Laurence *retired music educator*
Marks, Bruce *performing company executive, choreographer*
Marr, Peter *actor, host, comedian*
Marsalis, Branford *musician*
Marsalis, Wynton *musician*
Marse, Melissa J. *music educator, concert pianist*
Marsee, Susanne Irene *vocalist*

Marsh, Joan Knight *educational film, video and computer software company executive, publishing executive*
Marshall, Kenneth Robert *retired music educator*
Marte-Bautista, Helen I. *retired performing arts educator*
Martin, Andrea Louise *actress, comedienne, writer*
Martin, Elliot Edwards *theatrical producer*
Martin, Helen Schatkowski *music educator, television producer*
Martin, Jesse Lamont *actor*
Martinez, Buck *baseball analyst*
Martinez, James Phillip *music educator*
Martinson, Michael David *music educator, musician*
Martyn, Evi *music educator, musician*
Maruyama, Michelle *violinist*
Marx, Darrelyn Madonna *music educator, drama educator*
Marx, Richard *vocalist, musician*
Maslanka, Daniel Chester *percussionist and music educator*
Mason, Jackie *comedian, actor*
Mason, Marsha *actress, theater director, writer*
Mason, Rodney *performing arts educator*
Masterson, Peter *actor, film producer*
Mastramico, Thomas J. *music educator*
Mastrian, Stacey Lynn *singer, educator*
Mathes, Rachel Clarke *voice educator, singer*
Matlin, Marlee *actress*
Matlock, Glen *musician*
Matthau, Charles Marcus *film director*
Matthys, Dave *music educator*
May, Elaine *actress, theatre and film director*
Mays, Jefferson *actor*
McAnuff, Des *artistic director*
McCann, Elizabeth Ireland *theater producer, television producer, motion picture producer*
McCarthy, Nobu *actress, performing company executive, educator*
McCartney, Sir Paul (James Paul McCartney) *musician*
McClanahan, Rue (Eddi-Rue McClanahan) *actress*
McCready, Sam *theater educator, actor, theater director*
McDermott, Patricia (Tricia McDermott) *theater director, educator*
McDormand, Frances *actress*
McDowell, Malcolm *actor*
McEntire, Reba Nell *musician, actress*
McGlothen, Steven Raymond *motion picture producer*
McGowan, Rose *actress*
McGrath, Kimberly Kay *music educator*
McKendrick, Ryan Parker *music educator, conductor*
McMaster, Brian John *artistic director*
McNeal, James E. *music educator*
McNown, Edythe S. *music educator*
McShane, Ian *actor*
Meara, Anne *actress, playwright, writer*
Meharg, Karen *music educator*
Meisels, Judith A. *pianist, music educator*
Melhuse, Peder Nyhagen *actor, educator*
Melillo, Joseph Vincent *theater producer*
Mellits, Marc Andrew *composer*
Melton, William Everett *retired music educator*
Mendelsohn, Carol S. *television producer*
Menzel, Idina *actress, singer*
Meredith, Wendi Sue *music educator*
Meyer, Christopher Lee *music educator*
Meyerink, Victoria Paige *film producer, actress*
Mezacapa, Edna S. *music educator, elementary school educator*
Midler, Bette *singer, entertainer, actress*
Mikulas, Dana Cameron *voice educator, music educator*
Mikulay, Mark P. *music educator*
Milano, Alyssa *actress*
Miller, Wentworth *actor*
Minnix, Bruce Milton *television and theatre director*
Miranda-Levi, Jason *film producer, writer*
Mitchell, Brian Stokes *actor*
Mitchell, Jerry *choreographer, actor*
Mitchell, Nicole Margaret *flutist, composer*
Modine, Matthew Avery *actor*
Moffatt, Joyce Anne *performing company executive*
Moffatt, Katy (Katherine Louella Moffatt) *musician, lyricist, vocalist*
Moglewer, Sarah Anne *music educator*
Mohan, Tungesh Nath *television and film producer, film producer*
Monaco, Anne Catherine *music educator*
Monahan, Patrick *singer*
Moore, Deanna Cash *music educator, musician*
Moore, Melba (Melba Hill) *actress, singer*
Moore, Tom *film and theater director*
Morelan, Paula Kay *choreographer*
Morello, Joseph Albert *musician, educator*
Morgan, Linda Gail *theater producer*
Morgan, Michael B. *retired music educator*
Morgan, Michael Lynn *music educator, foundation director*
Morin, Lynn P. *music educator, director, secondary school educator*
Morley, Martin L. *musician*
Morris, Brenda Denise *music educator, director*
Morris, John *composer, conductor, arranger*
Morris, Martha Marnel *music educator*
Morris, Robert *songwriter, musician, music educator*
Morris, Scott Stephen *musician, educator*
Morrison, Shelley *actress*
Morrison, Van *musician, songwriter*
Morrow, Rob *actor*
Moseley, Julia W. *music educator, preservationist*
Moses, Oral *music educator*
Mosiman, Rita Esther *music educator*
Moskovitz, Elisa McMillan *music educator, musician*
Moss, Carrie-Anne *actress*
Mueller, Paula Deutsch *retired music educator*
Murphy, Brittany *actress*
Murphy, Eddie *comedian, actor*
Murphy, Timothy W. *music educator*
Murray, Carla Mary *sound effects artist, artist*
Murray, Richard Russell *music educator*
Murray, Stephen Sanford *composer, lyricist, playwright*

Murray Shaw, Juleen *actress*
Musante, Tony (Anthony Peter Musante Jr.) *actor*
Myers, Angela Michelle *music educator, department chairman*
Myers, Jeffrey Daniel *concert pianist, music educator*
Myers, Margaret Jane (Dee Dee Myers) *television personality, editor*
Myers, Mike *actor, scriptwriter, film producer*
Myerson, Alan *television director, film director*
Nagra, Parminder *actress*
Namath, Joseph William *entertainer, former professional football player*
Narita, Hiro *cinematographer*
Narofsky, Rebecca *music educator*
Naughton, James *actor*
Neary, Patricia Elinor *ballet director*
Neblett, Carol *soprano*
Nederlander, James Laurence *theater producer*
Neeson, Liam *actor*
Neil, Katharine Currie *soprano, director*
Nelms, Sharon Dee *music educator*
Nelson, Craig T. *actor*
Nelson, Ron *composer, educator, conductor*
Néron, Martin *musician*
Nesbitt, Mitzi Evalee *voice educator, director*
Ness, Bernice Hagie *retired music educator*
Neubauer, John M. *music educator, consultant*
Neuwirth, Bebe (Beatrice Neuwirth) *dancer, actress*
Neville, Phoebe *choreographer, dancer, educator*
Nevins, Sheila *television producer*
Newmar, Julie Chalane *actress, dancer, real estate businesswoman*
Newton, Wayne (Carson Wayne Newton) *entertainer, actor, recording industry executive*
Nichols, James Walker *retired music educator*
Nichols, Mike *stage and film director*
Nicolaides, Steve *film producer*
Nielsen, Leslie *actor*
Nigro, Kenneth Michael *music educator, musician*
Niguidula, Kathleen Ann *music educator, musician*
Nixon, Marni *singer*
Noll, Jeanne C. *retired music educator*
Nolte, Nick *actor*
Norton, Edward *actor*
Nowak, Andrew *music educator*
O'Boyle, Maureen *television show host*
O'Brien, Orin Ynez *musician, educator*
O'Connor, Jim *television host*
O'Donnell, Rosie *television personality, actress, comedienne*
Odya, Gregory Matthew *music educator, musician*
Oh, Sandra *actress*
O'Hara, Catherine *actress, comedienne*
Okonedo, Sophie *actress*
Okouchi-Guy, Alicia *performing arts educator*
Olin, Lena Maria Jonna *actress*
Olsen, Glen A. *church musician, educator*
Olson, Margaret *music educator*
Olsson-Hume, Irena *music educator*
Ondrasik, John *singer, songwriter*
O'Neal, Tatum *actress*
Orbit, William (William Wainwright) *record producer*
Ormond, Julia *actress*
Orr, Jo Miller *music educator, voice educator*
Osborne, Barrie M. *motion picture producer*
Osborne, Joan (Elizabeth) *singer, songwriter*
Osbourne, Ozzy (John Osbourne) *vocalist*
O'Shea, Anna Belle Marie *music educator, liturgy administrator*
Oshita, John Takao *musician*
Osinski, Brenda Carol *music educator*
Osmond, Marie *singer*
Ostrow, Stuart *theatrical producer, educator, author*
Ott, Sharon *artistic director*
Overbey, Kellie Lyn *actress*
Owens, Birdie Murphy *retired music educator*
Pack, Michael *television producer, writer, director*
Packer, Matthew James *musician*
Palileo, Hazel Valencia *videographer*
Parkinson, Dian *actress*
Paskman, Andrea *dance specialist*
Pasquier, Joël *music educator*
Pearce, Lisa Anne *composer, musician*
Pedersen, Keith Ernest *music educator*
Pendergrass, Teddy (Theodore D. Pendergrass) *musician*
Percy, Lee Edward *motion picture film editor*
Perkins, Leeman Lloyd *music educator, musicologist*
Perle, George *composer*
Perry, Luke (Coy Luther Perry III) *actor*
Perry, Matthew *actor*
Persoff, Nehemiah *actor, artist*
Pesci, Joe *actor*
Peterson, Anne Elizabeth Wallace *music educator, composer*
Peterson, Clark C. *announcer, writer, poet, speaker*
Peterson, David Lars *music educator*
Petrie, Nancy Sue Yenshaw *music educator*
Pettibon, Raymond *video artist*
Pfeiffer, Michelle *actress*
Phillips, Michelle Gilliam *actress, writer*
Phillips, Winifred Patricia *radio producer, composer*
Pick, Ryan Thomas *music educator*
Pierce, David Hyde *actor*
Pierce, Ponchitta Ann *TV host, television producer, journalist, writer, consultant*
Pinckney, Sandra *TV host*
Pinkerton, A. Louise *vocalist, music educator*
Pinkett-Smith, Jada *actress*
Pinkins, Tonya *actress*
Planeta, Kathleen M. *music educator*
Plant, Linda R. *music educator*
Plimpton, Martha *actress*
Plimpton, Peggy Lucas *trustee*
Plummer, Amanda *actress*
Pohlhaus, Tess *theater educator*
Pohlmann, Evelyn Gawley *music educator, consultant*
Poitier, Sidney *actor, film director*
Polchinski, Alysa R. *music educator, artist*
Poledouris, Basil K. *composer*
Poll, Martin Harvey *film producer*
Pollak, Kevin *actor*
Pop, Iggy (James Newell Osterberg) *composer, singer, musician*

Wyse, Jason LaMar *music educator, director*
Xie, Song *musician, educator*
Yarrow, Peter *folksinger*
Yeager, William Robert *musician, educator*
Yearwood, Trisha *country music singer, songwriter*
Yeend, Frances *soprano, music educator*
Yeh, Ying-Yu Emily *music educator*
Yoder, Jeffrey L. *music educator*
Yoder, Randall D. *music educator*
Young, Burt *actor*
Younker, Kathleen Teuber *pianist, music educator*
Yu, Jessica *director, producer, writer, editor*
Yu, Tian-En *musician, music educator*
Yuriko, (Yuriko Kikuchi) *dancer, choreographer*
Zappa, Gail *record producer*
Zaros, Wendy Cecilia *soprano, educator*
Zavadil, Martin R. *music educator, director, retired conductor*
Zelasko, Eric Edward *music educator*
Zemon, Stacy J. *disc jockey, writer, small business owner*
Zeta-Jones, Catherine *actress*
Zhao, Zhen *music educator*
Ziemba, Karen *actress*
Zimmerman, Phyllis Elaine *music educator, composer, director*
Zohn, Andrew Eliot *musician, educator*
Zsigmond, Vilmos *cinematographer, film director*
Zucker, David *film director*
Zurick, John *consultant, former dance company director*
Zvacek, Bret *music educator*

---

# ARTS: VISUAL

## UNITED STATES

### ALABAMA

**Alexander City**
Towery, Sarah Carlisle *artist, retired art educator*

**Auburn**
Hatfield, Donald Gene *retired art educator*
Ross, Conrad Harold *art educator, writer*

**Birmingham**
Keller, Armor *artist, arts advocate*
Maddox, Martha Lacey Gardner *artist*

**Fairfield**
McCaslin, LaTanya *art educator*

**Florence**
Chanin, Natalie *costume designer, apparel designer*
Knight, Karen Anne McGee *artist, educator, educational research administrator*
Marone-Cinzano, Enrico *apparel designer*

**Fort Payne**
Curington, Thomas Franklin III *photographer, writer*

**Guntersville**
Jones, Valerie Marie *art educator*

**Huntsville**
Dasher, Glenn *art educator, department chairman*

**Marion**
Street, Deborra Lynn *fine arts director*

**Mobile**
Clausell, Deborah Deloris *artist*
Conlon, James Edward *retired art educator, sculptor*
White, Richard Dean *art conservator*

**Tuscaloosa**
Meester, Donna Jean *costume designer, educator*

### ALASKA

**Cordova**
Bugbee-Jackson, Joan *sculptor, educator*

**Fairbanks**
Nakoneczny, Michael Martin *artist*

### ARIZONA

**Benson**
Erden, Sybil Isolde *artist*

**Bisbee**
McQuerry, Patricia Ann *painter, retired secondary school educator*
Stiles, Knute *retired artist*

**Casa Grande**
Zivic, William Thomas *artist, sculptor, art gallery owner*

**Cave Creek**
Garcia, Steve Joseph *artist, small business owner*

**Chinle**
Coor, Caren Barbara *art educator*

**Clarkdale**
Eide, Joel Sylvester *art consultant, appraiser*

**Green Valley**
de Soto, Ernest Frank *artist, writer*

**Lake Montezuma**
Burkee, Irvin *artist*

**Mesa**
Kim, Kai Y. *art educator, artist*

**Oracle**
Rush, Andrew Wilson *artist*

**Paradise Valley**
McCall, Robert The *artist*
Quinn, Brian Grant *art educator, sculptor*

**Patagonia**
La Noue, Terence David *artist, educator*

**Peoria**
Falk, Eugene Henry *artist*

**Phoenix**
Stone, Hazel Anne Decker *artist*

**Scottsdale**
Afsary, Cyrus *artist*
Berman, Gizel *sculptor*
Schutzky, Marilyn Horsley *artist*
Yares, Riva *art dealer, writer, publishing executive*

**Sedona**
Coleman, M.L. (Michael Lee) *artist*

**Sun City**
Blanchet, Jeanne Ellene Maxant *artist, educator, performer*

**Tempe**
Sol'Sax, *artist, educator*

**Tucson**
Conant, Howard Somers *artist, educator*
Crooks, Roselyn June *artist, writer*
Goltz, Pat *artist, web site designer*
Lascelles, Susan *artist*
Matthew, Neil Edward *artist, educator*
McNamara, Michael *lighting designer, educator*

### ARKANSAS

**Ashdown**
Edmonson, Phyllis Denty *artist*

**Berryville**
Brown, Frances Louise (Grandma Fran) *artist, art gallery director*

**Fayetteville**
Wilson, Charles Banks *artist*

**Newport**
Hembrey, Shea *artist*

**Palestine**
Taylor, Barbara Mae Helm *artist, educator*

### CALIFORNIA

**Alta Loma**
Maloof, Sam *woodworker*

**Anaheim**
Bennett, Genevieve *artist*
Nelipovich, Sandra Grassi *artist*

**Arcata**
Land-Weber, Ellen *photography professor*

**Auburn**
Rothwell, Elaine B. *artist*

**Bakersfield**
Reep, Edward Arnold *artist*

**Berkeley**
Bendix, Jane *artist, writer, illustrator*
Genn, Nancy *artist*
Hartman, Robert Leroy *artist, educator*
Miyasaki, George Joji *artist*
Polos, Iris Stephanie *artist*
Simpson, David William *artist, educator*

**Beverly Hills**
Ferretti, Dante *display designer*
Ford, Tom *apparel designer, apparel executive*
Yedidsion, Meira *computer artist, sculptor*

**Bolinas**
Harris, Paul *sculptor*
Okamura, Arthur Shinji *artist, educator*

**Camarillo**
Bowman, Bruce *art educator*
d'León, Omar *artist*

**Cambria**
Harden, Marvin *artist, educator*

**Carmel**
Hobbs, C. Fredric *artist, filmmaker, writer*
Jacobs, Ralph, Jr. *artist*

**Carson**
Hirsch, Gilah Yelin *artist, writer*

**Chatsworth**
Strieby, B. Lorraine *artist*

**Chico**
Hornaday, Richard H. *artist, retired art educator*

**Citrus Heights**
Walker, Ronald Craig *artist, educator*

**Claremont**
Benjamin, Karl Stanley *artist, art educator*
Blizzard, Alan *artist*
Dunye, Cheryl *artist, filmmaker*
Gonzales-Day, Kenneth Robert *artist, educator*
Rankaitis, Susan *artist*
Zehr, Connie *sculptor, art educator*

**Corona Del Mar**
Delap, Tony *artist*

**Costa Mesa**
Muller, Jerome Kenneth *photographer, art director, editor*

**Culver City**
Grant, Joan Julien *artist*
Simmons, Kimora Lee *apparel designer, television personality, model*

**Daly City**
Kennedy, Gwendolyn Debra *artist, scriptwriter, playwright*

**Davis**
DePaoli, Geri M. (Joan DePaoli) *artist, art historian*

**Desert Hot Springs**
Laws, Maurice Wesley *set decorator, museum exhibit designer*

**Elmira**
Montoya, Malaquias *art educator, artist*

**Encino**
Kempisty, Michael *artist, writer, actor*

**Escondido**
Carey, Catherine Anita *artist, art educator*

**Fair Oaks**
Potter, George Kenneth *artist*

**Fallbrook**
Ragland, Jack Whitney *artist*

**Flintridge**
Johnston, Oliver Martin, Jr., (Ollie Johnston) *animator*

**Garberville**
Nyokka, Suzette *artist, natural health educator*

**Gilroy**
Wu, Wayne Wen-Yau *artist*

**Glen Ellen**
Haslag, Karen Christine *art educator, musician*

**Healdsburg**
Wunderlich, Alfred Leon *artist, art educator*

**Idyllwild**
Gawecki, Marcia Elizabeth *artist, writer*

**Indio**
Porter, John Paul *artist, educator*
Zorick, Nancy Lee *artist, actress*

**Irvine**
Marootian, Dorothy *artist*

**La Jolla**
Hawkinson, Tim *sculptor*
Hester, Perrietta Burke *artist, educator*
Imana, Jorge Garron *artist*
Low, Mary Louise (Molly Low) *documentary photographer*
Merrim, Louise Meyerowitz *artist, actress*
yLang, Lenore Schulman *visual artist*

**La Puente**
Vetter, Lawrence Anthony *art educator, consultant*

**Lafayette**
Shurtleff, Akiko Aoyagi *artist, consultant*

**Laguna Beach**
Foote, Kay Rebber *artist*

**Lagunitas**
Holman, Arthur Stearns *artist*

**Lakewood**
Marthell, Yvette Jessica *photographer, educator, filmmaker*

**Lincoln**
Johnson, Ursula Anne *artist*

**Long Beach**
Barron, (Mary Lou) Slater *artist, retired art educator*
Bowen, Fern Chambers *artist, educator*
Braunstein, Terry Malikin *artist*
Viola, Bill *artist, writer*

**Los Angeles**
Apple, Jacki (Jacqueline B. Apple) *artist, educator, writer*
Apt, Charles *artist*
Barth, Uta *artist, educator*
Bas, Hernan *artist*
Brendel, Bettina *abstract artist*
Caroompas, Carole Jean *artist, educator*
Collier, Anna *photographer*
Curran, Darryl Joseph *photographer, educator*
Dallmeyer, Robert Frederick *art educator, writer*
De Larios, Dora *artist*
Durant, Sam *artist*
Gadal, Louis Stephen *artist*
Gillespie, Craig *art director*
Grinnan, Katie *artist*
Grotjahn, Mark *painter*
Hamilton, Patricia Rose *art dealer*
Hess, Frederick Scott *artist*
Hockney, David *artist*
Johnston, Ynez *artist, educator*
Judge, Mike *animator*
Kiley, Katie *printmaker, painter*
Klausen, Raymond *theatre set designer, television production designer, sculptor*
Kupper, Ketti *artist*
Layton, Harry Christopher *art director*

Zornes, Milford *artist*

**Los Gatos**
Carson, Sol Kent *artist, educator*

**Los Osos**
Kreitzer, David Martin *artist*

**Malibu**
Freeman, K. Genevieve *art and design educator, artist*

**Manhattan Beach**
Matranga, Frank Peter *art educator, artist*

**Mariposa**
Bruce, John Anthony *artist*
Rogers, Earl Leslie *artist, educator*

**Menlo Park**
Gard, Toby *computer graphics designer*

**Mission Viejo**
Mc Afee, Margaret Anne *retired art educator*

**Moraga**
O'Brien, Bea Jae *artist*

**Morgan Hill**
Freimark, Robert (Bob Freimark) *artist*

**Mountain View**
Hwang, Dennis (Dennis Hwang-Jung-moak) *graphic computer artist*

**Newbury Park**
Violano, Stella Marie *artist*

**Newport Beach**
Belić Weiss, Zoran *artist, design educator, director*
Halmos, Jeff *apparel designer*
Lamberto-Egan, Josia *apparel designer*
Shipley, Sam *apparel designer*
Spitz, Barbara Salomon *artist*
Whitledge, John *apparel designer*

**North Hollywood**
Miller, Philip Gray *artist*

**Northridge**
Bassler, Robert Covey *artist, educator*

**Novato**
McNamara, John Stephen *artist, educator*

**Oakdale**
Saletta, Mary Elizabeth (Betty Saletta) *sculptor*

**Oakhurst**
Cantwell, Christopher William *artist*

**Oakland**
Beasley, Bruce Miller *sculptor*
Gonzalez, Arthur Padilla *artist, educator*
Rath, Alan T. *sculptor*
Saunders, Raymond Jennings *artist, educator*

**Orange**
Banning, Donna Rose *art educator*
Felisky, Barbara Rosbe *artist*
Torres, Rudy Arnold *artist*

**Orinda**
Epperson, Stella Marie *artist*

**Pacific Grove**
Tanguy-Tracey, Sheila Anne *artist, poet*

**Pacific Palisades**
Chesney, Lee Roy, Jr. *artist*
Helfgott, Gloria Vida *artist*

**Pacifica**
Galindo, Donald Vernon *artist*

**Palm Desert**
Anderson, R. Christian *art designer, artist, director, media consultant*
Kaufman, Charlotte King *artist*

**Palm Springs**
Brasier, Robert Cress *art educator, artist*

**Palo Alto**
Christiansen, Susan Putnam *artist, educator, consultant*
Richardson, Tom (Edward Thompson Richardson) *artist*

**Palo Cedro**
Aust, Elizabeth Ann (Betty) *artist*

**Palos Verdes Estates**
Sharp, Jane Shriver *artist*

**Panorama City**
Janis, Elinor Raiden *artist, educator*

**Pasadena**
Pashgian, Margaret Helen *artist*

**Pebble Beach**
Mortensen, Gordon Louis *artist, printmaker*

**Penn Valley**
Sands, Sharon Louise *art director, publishing executive, artist*

**Petaluma**
McChesney, Robert Pearson *artist*
Skalagard, Hans Martin *artist*

**Pomona**
Fetterly, Barbara Louise *artist*
Wilson, Stanley Charles *artist, educator, curator, art gallery director, consultant*

**Quartz Hill**
McAllister, Bruce Richard *art educator*

**Rancho Mirage**
Novak, Joe *artist*

**Redlands**
Ristau, Jacob Robert *art educator, graphics designer*

**Richmond**
Wessel, Henry *photographer*

**Riverside**
Bell, Helen Lavin *artist*
Smith, Dorothy Ottinger *apparel designer, volunteer*

**Rosemead**
Jin, Jing Yi *photographer, film director*

**Roseville**
Smith, Kaye Train *artist*

**Sacramento**
Allan, William George *artist, educator*
Harvey, Ian *artist, educator*
Kondos, Gregory *painter, art educator*
Piskoti, Carol Lee *art educator*

**Salinas**
Puckett, Richard Edward *artist, consultant, former recreation executive*

**San Carlos**
Oliver, Nancy Lebkicher *artist, retired elementary school educator*

**San Clemente**
Butler, Russell *artist*

**San Diego**
Caldwell, Joan Marie *artist, educator*
D'Agostino, Claudio *sculptor*
Moore, Linda Anderson *art dealer, curator*
Nelson, Kadir *illustrator, artist*
Nevius, Cynthia Nell *artist, educator*

**San Francisco**
Babcock, Jo *artist, educator*
Barber, Malcolm *auction house executive*
Beall, Dennis Ray *artist, educator*
Bechtle, Robert Alan *artist, educator*
Chaet, Vicky Isabel *visual artist*
Chin, Sue Soone Marian (Suchin Chin) *artist, photojournalist*
DeSoto, Lewis Damien *art educator, artist*
Dickinson, Eleanor Creekmore *artist, educator*
Donnelly, Trisha *artist*
Elder, Muldoon *artist, poet, film producer*
Eurich, Judith *art appraiser, printmaker*
Goldstein, Sydney Rachel *photographer, writer, radio producer*
Goldstine, Stephen Joseph *art educator*
Honig, Al *artist*
Howard, David F. *artist*
Lieber, Tom Alan *painter*
Martin, Fred *artist, academic administrator*
McClintock, Jessica *fashion designer*
Muranaka, Hideo *artist, educator*
Petersen, Roland *artist, printmaker*
Pfaff, Laura King *auction house executive*
Presniakov, Alexander *artist, sculptor, inventor, writer*
Raciti, Cherie *artist*
Roehrman, Todd Frederick *costume designer, educator*
Sherratt, Holly *art appraiser*
Smith, Jennie *artist*
Stermer, Dugald Robert *designer, writer, consultant, illustrator*
Tantum, James Kent *artist, publisher*
Ternar, Mine Y. *artist, art educator*
Thiebaud, Wayne Morton *artist*
Toney, Anita Karen *printmaker*
Wonner, Paul John *painter*

**San Jose**
Dowd, Susan Carol *art educator*
Ellner, Michael William *art educator*
Estabrook, Reed *artist, educator*
Purpura, Grace *artist, retired art educator*

**San Juan Bautista**
Nutzle, Futzie (Bruce John Kleinsmith) *artist, writer, animator*

**San Juan Capistrano**
Ealy, Cynthia Pike *artist, real estate agent*

**San Mateo**
Huxley, Mary Atsuko *artist*

**San Pedro**
Parkhurst, Violet Kinney *artist*

**Santa Barbara**
Corbani, Candace Bedford *antiques broker, political campaign consultant, researcher*
Eguchi, Yasu *artist*
Hayward, Jean *artist, musician, interior designer, performance artist*
Rosenthal, Earl Edgar *art history educator, artist*
Sudbrack, Eli (assume vivid astro focus) *artist*

**Santa Clara**
Lane, Holly Diana *artist*

**Santa Cruz**
Russell, Laura Wimberly *artist*

**Santa Monica**
Alexander, Peter Houston *artist*
Bosman, Richard *artist, printmaker*
Giannulli, Mossimo *designer, apparel business executive*
Haroon, Nasreen *artist*
Masucci, Michael James *artist*

**Sausalito**
Wiley, William T. *artist*

**Sebastopol**
Worthington, Nancy G. *sculptor, multi-media artist*

**Shadow Hills**
Bangs, Cate (Cathryn Margaret Bangs) *film production designer, interior designer*

**Sierra Madre**
Converse, Elizabeth *artist, writer*

**Solvang**
Rymer, Ilona Suto *artist, retired art educator*

**Somis**
Kehoe, Vincent Jeffré-Roux *photographer, cosmetics executive*

**Sonoma**
Fellows, Alice Combs *artist*

**South Pasadena**
Askin, Walter Miller *artist, educator*
Sverdlove, Zolita *artist, painter, printmaker*
Yett, Sally Pugh *art educator, consultant*

**Stanford**
Corn, Wanda Marie *art educator*

**Stinson Beach**
Schwarm, Harold Chambers *artist*

**Stockton**
Oak, Claire Morisset *artist, educator*
Sumida, Gregory Zio *artist, photographer, musician, astronomer*
Wright, Evelyn Louise *artist*

**Studio City**
Brommer, Gerald Frederick *artist, writer*
Easterson, Sam *artist*
Manders, Susan Kay *artist*

**Sun Valley**
Sweet, Harvey *set designer, lighting designer*

**Sunnyvale**
Daltchev, Ana Ranguel *sculptor*

**Sunset Beach**
Anderson, William (Bill) Maxwell *artist, educator*

**Sylmar**
Scheib, Gerald Paul *art educator*

**Templeton**
Foster-Wells, Karen Margaret *artist*

**Thousand Oaks**
Heyer, Carol Ann *illustrator*

**Torrance**
Everts, Connor *artist*

**Tustin**
Mazzucato, Carla Carli *artist*

**Universal City**
Bismuth, Pierre *artist*

**Van Nuys**
Graham, Roger John *photography professor, journalism professor*
Vasilyeva, Anna *artist, writer*

**Venice**
Adams, Lisa Kay *artist*
Alf, Martha Joanne *artist*
Binns, Tom *jewelry designer*
Chipman, Jack *artist*
Eversley, Frederick John *sculptor, engineer*

**Walnut Creek**
Reimann, Arline Lynn *artist*

**West Hills**
Duzy, Merrilyn Jeanne *artist, educator*

**West Hollywood**
Barker, Clive *artist, film director, film producer, scriptwriter*
Currin, John *artist*

**Westlake Village**
Weiss, Barbara G. *artist*

**Yucca Valley**
Dockendorff, Robert Lawrence *computer graphics designer*

**COLORADO**

**Arvada**
Halley, Diane Esther *artist*

**Aspen**
Fischl, Eric *artist*
Mitchell, Karen Frances *artist, jewelry designer*
Soldner, Paul Edmund *artist, ceramist, educator*

**Aurora**
D'Amico, Sandra Hathaway *art educator*

**Boulder**
Bolomey, Roger Henry *sculptor*
Matthews, Eugene Edward *artist*
Schleiner, Anne-Marie *computer graphics designer*
Wolfe, Lynn Robert *art educator*

**Colorado Springs**
Goehring, Kenneth *artist*

**Cortez**
Kristin, Karen *artist*

**Delta**
Lowell, Lauretta Jane *craftsman, poet*

**Denver**
Daniels, Martha K. *artist*
Froula, Barbara Sue *artist, architect*
Graham, Pamela Smith *artist, educator*
Shwayder, Elizabeth Yanish *sculptor*
Witold, Kaczanowski *painter, sculptor*

**Dolores**
Rice, Wayne *artist, educator, small business owner*
Winterer-Schulz, Barbara Jean *graphics designer, writer*

**Durango**
Balas-Whitfield, Susan *artist*

**Englewood**
Gilboy, Margaretta *artist, educator*

**Greeley**
Miccio, Elizabeth Petrick *artist*

**La Veta**
Schneider, Kenny *artist, educator*
Zehring, Peggy Johnson *artist*

**Lake George**
Norman, John Barstow, Jr. *graphics designer, educator*

**Laporte**
Riba, Shirley *artist*

**Loveland**
Bierbaum, Janith Marie *artist*
Lundeen, George Wayne *artist*
Weresh, Thelma Faye *sculptor*

**Montrose**
Radovich, Donald *painter, illustrator, retired art educator*

**Paonia**
Noonan, Robert Harry *art and music educator*

**Salida**
Strawn, Melvin Nicholas *artist, educator*

**Woodland Park**
Cockrille, Stephen *art director, business owner*

**CONNECTICUT**

**Brookfield**
Gerstein, Mordicai *illustrator, writer*

**Brooklyn**
McIlvane, Edward James *stained glass artist, educator*

**Cos Cob**
Kane, Margaret Brassler *sculptor*

**Darien**
Anderson, Robert Alexander *portrait artist*
Ossi, James Matthew *artist*

**Fairfield**
Bullard, Roger Perrin *artist*

**Falls Village**
Cronin, Robert Lawrence *painter*

**Gaylordsville**
Dunn, Virginia *artist*

**Georgetown**
Julian, Alexander, II, *menswear designer*

**Greenwich**
Perless, Robert L. *sculptor*

**Guilford**
Pease, David Gordon *artist, educator*

**Hartford**
Hammer, Alfred Emil *artist, educator*
Martin, Ionis B. *artist, educator*

**Meriden**
Bertolli, Eugene Emil *sculptor, consultant*
Tamburine, Jean Helen *sculptor, painter, illustrator*

**Milford**
Curt, Denise Morris *painter, photographer*

**Mystic**
Hoie, Claus *artist*
Rooney, Maria Dewing *photographer*

**Naugatuck**
Mannweiler, Mary-Elizabeth *painter*

**New Canaan**
Kovatch, Jak Gene *artist*

**New Haven**
Bailey, William Harrison *artist, educator*
Chaet, Bernard Robert *artist, educator*
Fairbanks Harris, Theresa Louise *art educator, restorer*
Feinstein, Rochelle *artist, educator*
Grausman, Philip *sculptor*
Johnson, Lester Fredrick *artist*
Lindroth, Linda (Linda Hammer) *artist, writer, curator*
Pronin, Anatoly *photographer*
Reed, Robert James, Jr. *painter, art educator*
Reynolds, Jock *artist, curator, art gallery director*
Yeargan, Michael *scenic designer*

**Newtown**
Cottingham, Robert *artist*

**North Grosvenordale**
Kornbluth, Frances Helen Schachter *artist*

**Norwalk**
Babcock, Catherine Evans *artist, educator*
Perry, Charles Owen *sculptor*

**Old Lyme**
Chandler, Elisabeth Gordon (Mrs. Laci De Gerenday) *sculptor, musician*
Osborne, Judith Barbour *artist*

**Old Saybrook**
Neal, Irene Collins *artist, educator*

**Sharon**
Johns, Jasper *artist*

**Stamford**
Babson, Jane Frances *artist, writer*
Cassidy, Denis Andrew *artist, architect*
Rudman, Joan Eleanor *artist, educator*

**Storrs Mansfield**
Crossgrove, Roger Lynn *art educator*
Saternow, Tim *set designer, lighting designer, theater educator, painter*

**Unionville**
Dublac, Robert Revak *artist*

**Voluntown**
Caddell, Foster *artist*

**Wallingford**
Lauttenbach, Carol *artist*
Neff, John Adam *artist*

**Washington**
Grimes, Margaret Whitehurst *artist, educator*

**West Cornwall**
Simont, Marc *artist*

**West Hartford**
Boothe, Power *visual artist, filmmaker, set designer*
Keller, Dorothy Bosch *art educator*
Wessel, Frederick Warner *artist, educator*

**Weston**
Bleifeld, Stanley *sculptor*

**Westport**
Chernow, Ann Levy *artist, educator*
Fisher, Leonard Everett *artist, educator, writer*
Reilly, Nancy (Anne Caulfield Reilly) *painter*
Siff, Marlene Ida *artist, space designer*
Weiss, Harvey *artist, educator*

**DELAWARE**

**Dagsboro**
Hanna, Anne Marie *artist*

**Greenville**
Reynolds Cooch, Nancy D. (Mrs. Edward W. Cooch Jr.) *sculptor*

**Lewes**
Costigan, Constance Frances *artist, educator*

**New Castle**
Almquist, Don *illustrator, artist*

**Newark**
Brown, Hilton *artist, educator, writer*
Chapman, H. Perry *art educator*
Homer, William Innes *art history educator, art expert, writer*
Rowe, Charles Alfred *artist, graphics designer, educator*

**Wilmington**
Bounds-Seemans, Pamella J. *artist*

**DISTRICT OF COLUMBIA**

**Washington**
Baughman, J. Ross *photographer, writer, educator*
Blair, James Pease *freelance photographer*
Bowman, Dorothy Louise *artist*
Brown, Pamela Wedd *artist*
Carroll, M(argaret) Lizbeth Carr *art educator, graphics designer, photographer*
Clark, Michael *artist*
Colton Skolnick, Judith A. *artist*
DiPerna, Frank Paul *photographer, educator*
Fall, Dorothy *artist, art director, art association administrator*
Forrester, Patricia Tobacco *artist*
Fujimara, Makota *painter*

Gilliam, Sam *artist*
Gumpert, Gunther *artist*
Hogan, Felicity *artist*
Ihrie, John Richard III *art educator*
Jecklin, Lois Underwood *art corporation executive, consultant*
Kahn, Deborah *artist, educator*
Kapikian, Catherine Andrews *artist*
Kimes, Don Mark *artist, educator*
Koller, Shirley Leavitt *sculptor*
Kushnir, Andrei *artist, consultant*
O'Callaghan, Thomas Aloysius *artist, librarian*
Parish, Norman *artist, art gallery director*
Rose, Deedie Potter *arts patron*
Steadham, Richard Lynn *magazine art director*
Stovall, Lou *printmaker*
Tacha, Athena *sculptor, artist, educator*
Wasko-Flood, Sandra Jean *artist, educator*

**FLORIDA**

**Atlantic Beach**
Gartland, Alice Johnson *artist*

**Aventura**
Johnson, Ray R. *artist*

**Beverly Hills**
Larsen, Erik *retired art history educator*

**Boca Grande**
Carlson, Jane Cartwright *painter*

**Boca Raton**
Fineman, Geraldine Gottesman *artist*
Fishenfeld, Grace *artist, educator*

**Bradenton**
Voorhees, Stephanie Robin Faught *retired art educator*

**Clearwater**
Slade, Roy *artist, college president, museum director*

**Clermont**
Cox, Margaret Stewart *photographer*

**Crawfordville**
Siamis, Janet Neal *painter*

**Dania Beach**
Satin, Claire Jeanine *sculptor, artist*

**Davie**
Schwab, Judith *artist, educator, sculptor*

**Daytona Beach**
Alvarez, Marianne *artist, photographer, educator*
Dalia, Vesta Mayo *artist*
Samuelson, Fred Binder *artist, educator*

**Debary**
Pelosi, Haydee *sculptor*

**Delray Beach**
Mills, Agnes Eunice Karlin *artist*
St. George, Elaine *art educator*

**Edgewater**
Michajlow, Eustachy Iom *artist*
Schubert, Jeanne *artist*

**Fort Lauderdale**
Duke, James T *art educator, consumer products company executive*

**Fort Myers**
Schwartz, Carl Edward *artist, printmaker*

**Fort Pierce**
Jefferson, Zanobia Bracy *art educator, artist*
Swenson, Ada Perez *artist*

**Gainesville**
Favini, Paul Furey *costume designer, educator*
Harley, Ruth *artist, educator*
Navab, Aphrodite Desiree *artist, educator, writer*

**Hobe Sound**
Houser, Jim (James Cowing Houser Jr.) *artist*

**Hollywood**
Sadowski, Carol Johnson *artist*

**Indian Harbor Beach**
Traylor, Angelika *stained glass artist*

**Jacksonville**
Eden, F. Brown *artist*

**Jensen Beach**
Aho, Paul Richard *artist, art educator*

**Key Biscayne**
de la Cruz, Rosa *art collector*

**Key Largo**
Kennedy, Mary Sussock *artist*

**Key West**
McIntosh, Jon Charles *illustrator, graphics designer, painter*

**Kissimmee**
McCann, Jean Friedrichs *artist, educator*

**Lake Buena Vista**
Cerri, Robert Noel *photographer*

**Lake Mary**
Bachmann, Bill *photographer*
Reagan, Bettye Jean *artist*

**Lakeland**
Rogers, James Gordon, Jr. *art educator*
Stark, Bruce Gunsten *artist*

**Land O Lakes**
O'Connell, Carmela Digristina *appraisal executive, consultant*

**Melbourne**
King, Virginia Shattuck *painter, retired school nurse, educator*

**Miami**
Bannard, Walter Darby *artist, art critic*
Chambers, Elenora Strasel *artist*
Falagan, Margarita Martinez *art educator*
Kislak, Jean Hart *art director*
Moran, Kate *sculptor, photographer*
Pelton, Margaret Marie Miller *retired art educator, academic administrator, artist*
Pietrocarlo, Nick *artist, consultant, information technology manager*
Salinas, Baruj *artist, architect*
Sparkman, Barry Steven *artist, art educator, museum administrator*
Steinbaum, Bernice *art dealer*

**Miami Beach**
Carnase, Thomas Paul *graphics designer, consultant*
Lehr, Mira Tager *artist*
Rut, Wanda E. *artist, educator, writer*

**Mount Dora**
Kirton, Jennifer Myers *artist*
Langgood, Judith Ann *art educator*

**Naples**
Birdsall, Stephanie E. *artist*
Eldridge, David Carlton *art and antique appraiser*
Vickery, Robert Remsen *painter*
Vickrey, Robert Remsen *artist*
York, Tina *painter*

**North Palm Beach**
Kaplan, Muriel Sheerr *sculptor*

**Orange Park**
Hunt, J(ulian) Courtenay *artist*

**Orlando**
Warren, Dean Stuart *artist*

**Palatka**
Slanina, Lynnsey D. *costume designer, educator*

**Palm Beach Gardens**
Samuels, Fern Jacqueline *artist, educator*

**Plantation**
Cher Killigan, Beatriz M. *art educator*

**Ponte Vedra Beach**
Draper, J(osiah) Everett *artist, author, educator*

**Port Saint Lucie**
Staub, Carol Anne *artist*

**Punta Gorda**
Pollard, Herschel Newton *artist, psychologist*

**Rockledge**
Ollie, Pearl Lynn *artist, singer, lyricist*

**Rotonda West**
Durham, Olga Kalapaca *retired art educator, volunteer*

**Safety Harbor**
Banks, Allan Richard *artist, art historian, researcher*

**Sarasota**
Chase, Jeanne Norman *artist, educator*
Fulton Ross, Gale *artist, actor*
Goodacre, Glenna *sculptor*
Harmon, Foster (Loren Foster Harmon) *arts consultant*
Lengyel, Alfonz *art history educator, archeology educator, museology educator*

**Satellite Beach**
Rains, Baxter Smith *sculptor, consultant*

**Sebastian**
Pieper, Patricia Rita *artist*

**Spring Hill**
Whyte, Raymond A. *artist*

**Tallahassee**
Greene, Daniel E. *pastel artist*
Thompson, Omar *art educator, artist*
Weale, Mary Jo *artist*

**Tamarac**
Baron-Malkin, Phyllis *artist, art educator*

**Tampa**
Cardoso, Anthony Antonio *artist, educator*
de Lama, Alberto *artist*
O'Brien, Mary Ellen Christina *artist, educator*
Sopher, Vicki Elaine *appraiser*
Wujcik, Theo Frank *artist*

**Venice**
Girman, Dee-Marie *artist, singer*

**Vero Beach**
David, Ivo *artist, poet, real estate broker*
Ferrell, Catherine K. *sculptor, painter*

**West Palm Beach**
Gronlund, Robert B. *art collector, fund raising consultant*
Longhofer, Gordan Allen *art educator, performance artist*
Lozito, Gilda Lelia *artist, painter*

**Weston**
Napp, Gudrun F. *artist*

**Winter Haven**
Schepis, Anthony Joseph *artist, educator*

**Winter Springs**
San Miguel, Manuel *painter, writer*

**Zephyrhills**
Anderson, Lisa D. *graphics designer, educator*

**GEORGIA**

**Alpharetta**
Bolton, Robin Jean *artist, painter*

**Athens**
DeZurko, Edward Robert *art educator*
Dunham, Richard E. III *lighting designer, consultant, set designer, educator*
Harshman, Melissa Ann *art educator*
Herbert, James Arthur *retired art educator, artist, filmmaker*
Kaufman, Glen Frank *art educator*
Olsen, Richard James *artist, educator*
Paul, William Dewitt, Jr. *retired art educator, photographer, videographer, museum director*
Smith, Susan Carlton *artist, illustrator*

**Atlanta**
Bawa, Avantika *artist, educator*
Greco, Anthony Joseph *artist, educator, dean*
Grumet, Priscilla Hecht *fashion specialist, consultant, writer*
Guberman, Sidney *painter, writer*
James, Rose Victoria *sculptor, poet*
Laxson, Ruth Knight *artist*
Malone, James Hiram *graphics designer, journalist, writer*
McLean, James Albert *artist, educator*
Milner, Carolyn Rose *artist, educator*
Parrish, Carl E. *artist, educator*
Riley, Raquel *photographer*
Rodríguez, Rocío *artist*

**Augusta**
Hand, Maryanne Kelly *artist, educator*
Schultz, Nancy Jansson *artist*

**Avondale Estates**
Carroll, Jane Hammond *artist, writer, poet*

**Blairsville**
Sterling, Colleen *artist*

**Cave Spring**
Morrow, Winifred Bryant *artist, educator*

**Cochran**
Agnew, Charlie Martin *art educator, artist*

**Cordele**
Mitchell, James Marshall, Jr. *artist, educator*

**Hawkinsville**
Whipple, Woodrow Thomas *artist, educator*

**Hiawassee**
Davis, Nighta J. *photographer, artist*

**Macon**
Reitnauer, Otto Charles *fine arts director*

**Marietta**
Lahtinen, Silja Liisa *artist*

**Mount Berry**
Mew, Thomas Joseph, III, (Tommy Mew) *artist, educator*

**Rome**
Hodges, Thomas C. *art educator*

**Roswell**
Christopher, Lin *artist*
Rayburn, Boyd Dale *artist*

**Savannah**
Aja-Herrera, Marie *fashion designer, educator*
Aquadro, Jeana Lauren *graphic designer, educator*
Field, Jonathan David *art educator*
Fischer, Thomas Jeffrey *art educator*
Foley, Marilyn Lorna *artist*
Hung, Chin-Cheng *art educator, artist*
Shanken, Edward A. *art educator, design educator*

**Valdosta**
Lindsay, LeVonne D. *costume designer, educator*

**Wildwood**
Dombrowski, Bob *artist, writer*

**HAWAII**

**Hilo**
Grabar, Andrew *art educator, artist*

**Honolulu**
Betts, Barbara Stoke *artist, educator*
Chun, Jacqueline Clibbett *artist, educator*
Guthrie, Edgar King *artist*
Pickens, Frances Jenkins *artist, educator*
Uhl, Philip Edward *artist, photographer, cinematographer*

**Kapaau**
Jankowski, Theodore Andrew *artist*

**IDAHO**

**Gooding**
Larson, Lynn Wood *artist, musician*

**Harrison**
Carlson, George Arthur *artist*

**Osburn**
Bardelli, Frederick Ketchell *artist, art educator*

**Sandpoint**
Schultz, Stephen W. *art educator*

**Yellow Pine**
Auth, Robert Ralph *art educator*

**ILLINOIS**

**Bourbonnais**
Wilkey, Elmira Smith *illustrator, artist, writer, educator*

**Champaign**
Kotoske, Roger Allen *artist, educator*
Young, Paul *graphic designer, edcator*

**Chicago**
Alcantara, Anita Luisa *community arts administrator*
Amft, Robert Ernest *artist, photographer*
Anderson, Craig Allen *retired art educator, artist*
Aubin, Barbara Jean *artist*
Bowman, Leah *fashion designer, consultant, photographer, educator*
Burroughs, Margaret Taylor Goss *artist*
Castillo, Mario Enrique *artist, educator*
Coffey, Susanna Jean *art educator, artist*
Crane, Barbara Bachmann *photographer, educator*
Crnkovich, Ruth Anne *art appraiser, museum director*
Dunning, Jean *artist*
Edelstein, Teri J. *art educator, art director, consultant*
Fotopoulos, James *artist*
Gniech, Charles *art educator, artist*
Gunning, Tom *art educator*
Hannum, Terence J. *artist, director, art critic*
Himmelfarb, John David *artist*
Hindman, Leslie Susan *auction company executive*
Hunt, Richard *sculptor*
Kearney, John Walter *sculptor, painter*
Kenney, Estelle Koval *artist, educator*
King, Andre Richardson *architectural graphic designer*
Krantz, Claire Wolf *artist, freelance critic, curator*
Marshall, Kerry James *artist*
McElheny, Josiah G. *sculptor*
McGrail, Jeane Kathryn *artist*
Michod, Susan Alexander *artist, painter*
Paterakis, Angela Gregory *art educator, writer*
Postiglione, Corey M. *artist, critic, art educator*
Stack, Michael *artist*
Steele, Eric Henry *sculptor, lawyer*
Steinberg, Rubin *retired art educator, artist*
Tessing, Louise Scire *graphic designer*
Thall, Robert *photographer, educator*
Wharton, Margaret Agnes *artist*
Wiens, Ann *artist, writer, editor, art critic*

**Cissna Park**
McCullough, Edward L. *artist, educator*

**Des Plaines**
Banach, Art John *retired graphic artist*

**Dixon**
Huber, Marianne Jeanne *art dealer, art appraiser*

**East Dundee**
Simons, Gail S. *artist, educator, librarian*

**Edwardsville**
Hampton, Phillip Jewel *artist, educator*
Malone, Robert Roy *artist, art educator*

**Elgin**
Carl, Jeffery *art educator*

**Eureka**
Wells, Christopher Lindell *art educator, football coach, baseball coach*

**Evanston**
Altman, Edith G. *sculptor*
Conger, William Frame *artist, educator*
Schiff, Molly Jeanette *artist, researcher*

**Forest Park**
Poplawska, Anna *artist, educator, art critic*

**Glencoe**
Siske, Regina *artist*

**Glenview**
Hough, Winston *artist*

**Highland Park**
Humay, Priscilla *artist*
Slavick, Ann Lillian *retired art educator*

**Hudson**
Mills, Frederick VanFleet *art educator, watercolorist*

**Lake Forest**
Weston, Dawn Thompson *artist, researcher*

**Lombard**
Ahlstrom, Ronald Gustin *artist*

**Mchenry**
Chisu, Ioan *artist*

**Mount Prospect**
Eliason, Birdell *painter, educator*

**North Aurora**
Sabey, Richard Homer *retired graphics designer*

**Oak Lawn**
Jachna, Joseph David *photographer, educator*

**Peoria**
Davis, Charisse Maria *doll maker, folk artist*

**Rockford**
Heflin, Tom Pat *artist*

**Rolling Meadows**
Bauer, Lorain *art educator*

**Romeoville**
Mitchell, Paul *computer graphics designer, educator*

**Saint Charles**
Malinowski, Maryellen *photographer, artist*

**Table Grove**
Thomson, Helen Louise *retired artist*

**Techny**
Vanderstappen, Harrie Albert *art educator*

**Vermont**
Datcu, Ioana *artist*

**Waukegan**
Miller, Helen Elizabeth *art educator, adult education educator, artist*

**Willowbrook**
Burrows, Donald Albert *artist, painter, photographer, dean*

**Winnetka**
Plowden, David *photographer*

**Woodridge**
Rathke, Barbara Joanne Andrews *art educator*

**Woodstock**
Trausch, Thomas Vincent *art educator, artist*

**Yorkville**
Freese, Carolyn Lee *art educator*

**INDIANA**

**Bloomington**
Connally, Sandra Jane Oppy *retired art educator, artist*
O'Hearn, Robert Raymond *stage designer*
Stines, Betty Irene Parham *artist*

**Evansville**
Baker, Gloria Marie *artist*
Nagy, Ann M. *art educator, music educator*

**Greensburg**
Black, Marsha Jean *art educator, writer*

**Indianapolis**
Rutledge, Joanne *artist, consultant*

**Muncie**
Fillwalk, John Alfred *art educator, artist*
Hunter, Miriam Eileen *artist, educator*

**Notre Dame**
Sandusky, Billy Ray *art educator, artist*

**South Bend**
Larkin, Eugene David *artist, educator*

**Terre Haute**
Lamis, Leroy *artist, retired art educator*

**Valparaiso**
Olson, Lynn *sculptor, painter, writer*

**West Lafayette**
Ichiyama, Dennis Yoshihide *art educator, educational association administrator*

**Winamac**
Ligocki, Gordon Michael *artist, educator*

**Winona Lake**
Swartzentruber, Don Michael *artist, educator*

**IOWA**

**Ames**
Bruene, Barbara Jane *artist, educator*

**Ankeny**
Stahr, Curtis Brent *photographer, art association administrator, educator*

**Cedar Falls**
Blakesley, Kimberly Kay *art educator, consultant*
Golczewski, Artur *art history educator*

**Cedar Rapids**
Gilmor, Jane Ellen *artist, educator*

**Des Moines**
Holland, Brent Andrew *art educator, painter*
Reece, Maynard Fred *artist, writer*

**Indianola**
Kazmerzak, Richard Anthony *art educator*

**Iowa City**
Lasansky, Mauricio *artist*
Myers, Virginia Anne *art educator*
Schmidt, Julius *sculptor*
Scott, John Beldon *art history educator, writer*
Young, Laura Elizabeth *artist*

**Marshalltown**
Bousum, Julie Kaye *art educator*

**KANSAS**

**Dodge City**
Sewell, Carol Ann *artist*

**Hays**
Kuksi, Kris M. *artist*

**Junction City**
Heesch, Marcella B. *art educator*

**Lawrence**
Brejcha, Vernon L. *artist, art educator*
Dooley, Patrick John *graphic designer, design educator*

**Manhattan**
Kren, Margo *artist, educator*

**Ottawa**
Howe, William Hugh *artist*

**Overland Park**
Amundson, Beverly Carden *artist*

**Pittsburg**
Krug, Harry E. *art educator, artist*

**Topeka**
Peters, Barbara Waterman *artist, educator*

**KENTUCKY**

**Fort Thomas**
Lutz, Mark *computer graphics designer, art educator*

**Fort Wright**
Sullivan, Connie Castleberry *artist*

**Franklin**
Law, Jerriann Marcella *artist, poet, writer*

**Jeffersontown**
Williams, Petra Schatz *antiquarian, director*

**Lexington**
Girard, C. Jack *art educator, artist*
Sandoval, Arturo Alonzo *artist, educator*

**Murray**
Guy, Sallie T. *artist*

**Wickliffe**
Frueh, Deborah K.A. (Debi Frueh) *artist, poet*

**Winchester**
Snowden, Ruth O'Dell Gillespie *artist*

**LOUISIANA**

**Bastrop**
Bonsall, Vicki J. *art educator*

**Baton Rouge**
Baron, Stuart *artist, art educator, director*
Goodell, Rosemary Wilson *artist, educator*
Rutledge, Katherine Burck *artist*

**Cecilia**
Girouard, Tina *artist, curator*

**Choudrant**
Ford, John Charles *artist*

**Covington**
Flattmann, Alan Raymond *artist, educator*

**Lafayette**
Clark, Elsa Myriam *artist*

**Metairie**
Casselli, Henry Calvin, Jr. *artist, painter*
Crosby, Deborah Berry *artist*

**Natchitoches**
Moreau, Robert Daniel, Jr. *art educator*

**New Orleans**
Bailey, Barry Stone *sculptor, educator*
Ernest, Tabi Elise *art educator, photographer*
Thornell, Jack Randolph *photographer*

**Ruston**
Bukowski, Marie Diane *artist, educator*

**Shreveport**
Hughes, Mary Sorrows *artist*

**Westwego**
Brehm, Loretta Persohn *retired art educator, librarian, consultant*

**Zachary**
Mills, Elizabeth Jennings *art educator*

**MAINE**

**Camden**
Etter, Howard Lee *artist*

**Cape Elizabeth**
Materson, Edward Arthur *sculptor, artist*

**Cushing**
Magee, Alan *artist*

**Gorham**
Chen, Ray Gow Hwei *art educator, department chairman, artist*

**Kennebunk**
Betts, Edward *artist*

**New Harbor**
Lyford, Cabot *sculptor*

**Ogunquit**
West, Norman Ellsworth *artist*

**Raymond**
Sinclair, Louis *artist, writer*

**Searsport**
Barnes, Robert Myrrdyn *artist, educator*

**South Portland**
Huntoon, Abby Elizabeth *artist, educator*

**Vinalhaven**
Indiana, Robert (Robert Clark) *artist*

**Wiscasset**
Leslie, Seaver *artist*

**York**
Hallam, Beverly (Beverly Linney) *artist*
Roché, Robert Richard *artist*

**MARYLAND**

**Annapolis**
Fry, Virginia Milne *artist, poet*
Markman, Ronald *artist, educator*
Thoms, Josephine Bowers *artist*

**Baltimore**
Duncan, Lionel Sebastian *artist, educator*
Klitzke, Theodore Elmer *arts consultant, retired college dean*
Reinsel, Joseph Thomas *art educator, artist*
Tucker, James L., Jr. *art educator, artist*
Yates, Sharon *artist*

**Bethesda**
Benson, Elizabeth Polk *art specialist*
Dignac, Geny (Eugenia M. Bermudez) *sculptor*
Elliott, George Armstrong III *artist, journalist*
Fleming, Patricia Stubbs (Patsy Fleming) *artist*
Sarnoff, Lili-Charlotte (Lolo Sarnoff) *artist*

**Boyds**
Bu, Rulei *artist, educator*

**Brentwood**
Kaskey, Raymond John *sculptor*

**Chestertown**
Amos, James Lysle *photographer*

**Chevy Chase**
Kranking, Margaret Graham *retired artist, educator*

**College Park**
Richardson, W.C. *painter*

**Denton**
Doster, Rose Eleanor Wilhelm *artist*

**Galena**
Hunsperger, Elizabeth Jane *art and design consultant, educator*

**Glen Echo**
Stevenson, A. Brockie *retired artist*

**Glenelg**
Niese, Henry Ernst *artist, educator*

**Hyattsville**
Shinolt, Eileen Thelma *artist*

**Lothian**
Messenger, Barbara Beall *artist*

**Olney**
Hails, Barbara Geldermann *artist*

**Silver Spring**
Aranya, Gwendalin Qi *painter, priest, educator*
Fitzgerald, Joseph Patrick *artist*
Frassrand, Pete *art educator*
Peiperl, Adam *sculptor, photographer*

**Towson**
Brooks, Gavin *artist*
Kissel, William Thorn, Jr. *sculptor*

**Trappe**
Burns-Bowie, Maureen Elizabeth *sculptor*

**Westminster**
Pearson, Steven Robert *artist, art educator*

**Woodbine**
Nuss, Barbara Gough *artist*

**MASSACHUSETTS**

**Amherst**
Anderson, Ronald Trent *artist, educator*
Dabrowski, Thaddeus E. *art educator, art consultant, painter*
Lasch, Pat *artist, educator*
Liebling, Jerome *photographer, educator*
Reed, Daphne Stevenson *artist*
Yarde, Richard Foster *art educator*

**Arlington**
Dahill, Thomas Henry *artist, educator*
Tollen, Cynthia Joyce *photographer, writer*

**Belmont**
Colón, Ernie *comic book artist*

**Beverly**
Bartnick, Harry William *artist, art educator*
Gilby, Dena *art educator*
Manning, William Frederick *retired photographer*
Roy, Robert William *artist, educator*

**Bolton**
Keane, Karen M. *auction house executive*

**Boston**
Ablow, Joseph *artist, educator*
Ablow, Roz Karol (Roselyn Karol Ablow) *painter, curator*
Aso, Kaji *artist*
Fesko, Colleene *art appraiser*
Fletcher, Stephen L. *art appraiser*
Goldstein, Nathan *artist, writer*
Hershey, Nona *artist, printmaker, educator*
Hurwitz, Sidney *printmaker*
Kotting, Joey *artist*
McIlvain, Isabel *sculptor, art educator*
Parker, Olivia *photographer*
Wiesner, David *illustrator, children's writer*

**Brewster**
Stoltenberg, Donald Hugo *artist, writer*

**Brookline**
Barron, Ros *artist*
Burns, Ikuko Kawai *artist*
Rubin-Katz, Barbara *sculptor, human services manager*
Swirnoff, Lois *artist, educator*

**Cambridge**
Ackerman, James *fine arts educator*
Alcalay, Albert S. *artist, design educator*
Bakanowsky, Louis Joseph *artist, educator, architect*
Brackett, Prilla Smith *artist, educator*
Chandler, Fay Martin *artist*
Dobson, Parrish *photographer, educator*
Feininger, Theodore Lux *artist*
Jacob, Wendy *artist, educator*
Jonas, Joan (Joan Amerman Edwards) *artist*
Kelsey, Robin E. *art history educator*
Maeda, John *graphics designer, artist, computer scientist*
Mazur, Michael *artist*
Mc Kie, Todd Stoddard *artist*
Slosburg-Ackerman, Jill Rose *artist, educator*
Wodiczko, Krzysztof *artist, architect, educator*

**Canton**
Hayes, Michelle Christine *artist, educator*

**Concord**
Ihara, Michio *sculptor*
MacNeill, Frederick Douglas *artist*

**Dennis**
Cetto, Teresa *art educator*

**East Orleans**
Burkert, Robert Randall *artist*

**Easthampton**
Lake, Shelley *artist*

**Fall River**
Andrade, Manuela Pestana *art educator*
Wilner, Marion Leonard *art educator*

**Framingham**
Aronson, Benjamin *artist*
Feldman, Nan Hass *artist, educator*

**Gloucester**
Steele-Goetemann, Judith Ann *artist, educator, art gallery owner*
White, Lucette Darby *painter, sculptor*

**Granville**
Brown, Stephen Pat *artist*

**Harwich**
Steward, Aleta Joanna *fine artist, digital artist*

**Haverhill**
Newman, Rochelle Joyce *artist, educator, writer*

**Jefferson**
Parham, Valerie deForest Byron *artist*

**Leominster**
Zephir, Jeanne Yvonne *artist*

**Lexington**
Coleman, Loring W. *artist*

**Lynn**
Farris, Robert Harold, Jr. *artist, educator*
Petchkis, Anthony James *artist*

**Marblehead**
Heins, Esther *artist, illustrator*

**Medford**
Simpson, Theodore Brian *set designer, educator*

**Medway**
Burnett, Calvin *artist, educator*

**Natick**
Geller, Esther (Bailey Geller) *artist*

**Needham**
Branfman, Steven Jay *artist, educator*
Celli, Paul *art educator*

**Newton**
Jencks, Penelope *sculptor*

**Newtonville**
Polonsky, Arthur *artist, educator*

**North Adams**
Sloan, Julie L. *stained glass artist, consultant*

**Northampton**
Rupp, Sheron Adeline *photographer, educator*
Schneider, Katy *painter, educator*
Schuleit, Anna *artist*

**Norwell**
Brett, Jan Churchill *illustrator, author*

**Orleans**
Baird, Julian Thompson, Jr. *art dealer*

**Provincetown**
Collins, Larry Richard *artist, educator, art gallery director*
Hutchinson, Peter Arthur *artist*

**Reading**
Frey, Joanne Alice Tupper *art educator*
Nordstrand, Nathalie Elizabeth Johnson *artist*

**Rockport**
Mosher, Donald Allen *artist*
Nicholas, Thomas Andrew *artist*
Whitcomb, Kay *artist*

**Sharon**
Edmonds, Nick *sculptor*

**Shrewsbury**
Kranich, Margaret Mansley *artist*

**Somerville**
Yu, Shan *artist*

**South Boston**
Crump, Walter M. *artist, art educator*

**South Hadley**
Hall, Lee *artist, educator, writer*

**Sudbury**
Aronson, David *artist, retired art educator*

**Vineyard Haven**
Ortlip, Paul Daniel *artist*

**Wakefield**
Fioravanti, Jeff *artist*

**Waltham**
Hodes, Suzanne Ruth *artist*

**Wayland**
Dergalis, George *artist, educator*

**Wellesley**
Copplestone, David Wesley *artist, small business owner*
McGibbon, Phyllis Isabel *art educator, artist*

**Westfield**
Conant, Patricia Carol *printmaker, educator*

**Westwood**
Liberman, Judith *artist*

**Williamstown**
Blair, Phyllis E. *artist*

**Winchester**
Ferrara, Lee *graphics designer, artist, educator*
Neuman, Robert Sterling *art educator, artist*

**Woburn**
DeCrosta, Susan Elyse *graphic designer*

**Worcester**
Hovsepian, Leon *artist, designer*

## MICHIGAN

**Ann Arbor**
Curtin, Joseph *violinmaker*
Eisenberg, Marvin Julius *retired art history educator*
Rogers, Bryan Leigh *artist, art educator*
Stewart, Paul Leroy *art educator, printmaker*

**Auburn Hills**
Mandiberg, David Michael *sculptor*

**Birmingham**
Kozlow, Richard *artist*

**Camden**
Falls, Kathleene Joyce *photographer*

**Capac**
Wagner, Dorothy Marie *retired senior creative designer, artist*

**Dearborn**
Cape, James Odies E. *fashion designer*

**Detroit**
Abt, Jeffrey *art educator, art historian, artist, writer*
DuMouchelle, Ernest J. *art appraiser*
DuMouchelle, Lawrence F. *art appraiser*
Johnson, Lester Larue, Jr. *artist, educator*
Moldenhauer, Judith A. *graphic design educator*
Spoutz, Eric I. *art dealer, conservator, curator, investor, consultant*

**Flint**
Chaney, Carol A. *multimedia artist*
Davidek, Stefan *artist*
Smith, Catherine Jean *artist, educator*

**Grand Rapids**
Bolt, Eunice Mildred DeVries *artist*
Jackoboice, Sandra Kay *artist*

**Grosse Ile**
Stump, M. Pamela *sculptor*

**Grosse Pointe Farms**
Krentzin, Earl *sculptor, silversmith*

**Hillsdale**
Frudakis, Anthony Parker *sculptor, educator*

**Holland**
Van Noord, Diane C. *artist, educator*

**Holly**
Stolpin, William Roger *printmaker*

**Howell**
Watkins, Curtis WinthroP *artist*

**Jenison**
Frye, Della Mae *portrait artist*

**Kalamazoo**
Light, John Richard *sculptor*
Vander Weg, Phillip Dale *art educator, academic administrator, sculptor*

**Midland**
Belton, Betty Kepka *retired art educator, artist*

**Monroe**
Pixley, Sylvia Kay *artist*

**Mount Pleasant**
Traines, Rose Wunderbaum *sculptor, educator*

**Novi**
Maniscalco, Joseph *artist, educator*

**Petoskey**
Switzer, Carolyn Joan *artist, educator*

**Plymouth**
Moore-Viculin, Charlotte Anne *artist, musician*

**Port Huron**
Rowark, Maureen *fine arts photographer*

**Riverdale**
Kirby, Kent Bruce *artist, educator*

**Skandia**
Johnson, Judy M. *artist, writer*

**Watersmeet**
Freund, William Frederick *retired art educator, artist*

**Ypsilanti**
Fairfield, Richard Thomas *art educator*

## MINNESOTA

**Bemidji**
Skinner, Jauneth *art educator, graphic artist*

**Brooklyn Park**
Kiland, Lance Edward *art educator*

**Harmony**
Webster, Jeffrey Leon *graphic designer*

**Mankato**
McCarl, David *costume designer, educator*

**Minneapolis**
Christopherson, Howard M. *artist*
Hallman, Gary L. *photographer, educator*
Holen, Norman Dean *art educator, artist*
Marling, Karal Ann *art history educator, social sciences educator, curator*
Preuss, Roger Emil *artist*
Ramalho-Ahrndt, Maria Gabriela *art educator*
Rose, Thomas Albert *artist, educator*
Rowan, Herman T. *art educator, artist*
Slettehaugh, Thomas Chester *retired art educator*
Stone, Harold B. *artist, educator*

**Newport**
Yelland, Mary Virginia *artist*

**Oakdale**
Nagdimon, Ellen Tara *artist, educator*

**Saint Cloud**
Specht-Jarvis, Roland Hubert *fine arts educator, humanities educator, dean*

**Saint Paul**
Burke, Mary Griggs (Mrs. Jackson Burke) *art collector*
Lasansky, Leonardo *artist, educator*
Matteson, Clarice Chris *artist, educator*
Tylevich, Alexander V. *sculptor, architect*

## MISSISSIPPI

**Brandon**
Schoolar, Laurel Ann *artist, educator*

**Clinton**
Cook, Stephen Day *art educator*
Gore, Samuel Marshall *art educator, sculptor*

**Columbus**
Summer, Emily Eugenia *artist, art educator*

**Hattiesburg**
McRaney, Joan Katherine *artist*

**Jackson**
Stanton, Sylvia Doucet *artist, art gallery owner*

**Ridgeland**
Long, Roger Leonard *artist*

**University**
Wicker, Nancy Lynn *art history educator*

## MISSOURI

**Ballwin**
Geis, Milton Arthur *painter, writer*

**Bolivar**
Gott, Wesley Atlas *art educator*

**Columbia**
Stack, Frank Huntington *painter, retired art educator*

**Conway**
Maxwell, Quentin D. *art educator*

**Hermann**
Mahoney, Catherine Ann *artist, educator*

**Hollister**
Canfield, Cindy Sue *art educator*

**Independence**
Willett, Teri Kay *art educator*

**Jefferson City**
Craver, Charles Henry *illustrator*

**Kansas City**
Johnston, Lynn Beverley *animator*
Lee, Margaret Norma *artist*
Mast, Kande White *artist*
Schaffer, Sandra Sue *artist, educator*

**Lamar**
Bowling, Gary R. *art educator*

**Lewistown**
Terpening, Virginia Ann *artist*

**Platte City**
Kalin, D. Jean (Dorothy Jean Kalin) *artist, educator*

**Saint Joseph**
Niewald, Wilbur *artist*

**Saint Louis**
Buggs, Dwayne Andre *fine arts coordinator, music educator*
Fondaw, Ronald Edward *artist, educator*
Hansman, Robert G. *art educator, artist*
Metcalfe, Elizabeth Brokaw *art educator*
Ward-Brown, Denise *sculptor, educator*
Zonia, Dhimitri *artist*

**Sibley**
Morrow, Elizabeth Hostetter *sculptor, museum director, farmer, educator*

**Springfield**
Armstrong, Bill Howard *artist, educator*

**Stover**
Reynolds, Sallie Blackburn *artist, volunteer*

**Webster Groves**
Gergeceff-Cooper, Lorraine *artist, consultant*
Osver, Arthur *artist*

## MONTANA

**Billings**
Jones, Doris Logan *artist, art educator*

## NEBRASKA

**Gering**
Peters, Gretchen J. *artist, educator*

**Lincoln**
Howard, Dan F. *retired art educator, artist*
Kunc, Karen *artist, educator*

**Norfolk**
Lynch, Michael L. *art educator*
Timmer, Margaret Louise (Peg Timmer) *art educator*

**Ogallala**
Cerny, Allen Terry *art educator*

**Omaha**
Bradshaw, Laurence James *artist, educator*
Buchanan, Sidney A. *sculptor*

## NEVADA

**Las Vegas**
Goldblatt, Hal Michael *photographer, accountant*

**Reno**
Goin, Peter Jackson *art educator*
Harder, Kelsie T. *artist, educator*
McLeod, Carolyn Louise *artist*

## NEW HAMPSHIRE

**Amherst**
Johnson, Daryl Diane *painter*

**Concord**
Resnick, Kenneth *photography director*

**Durham**
McConnell, Michael *art educator*

**Francestown**
Milton, Peter Winslow *artist*

**Hancock**
Pollaro, Paul Philip *artist*

**Hanover**
Boghosian, Varujan Yegan *sculptor, educator*
Moss, Ben Frank III *art educator, painter*
Walp, Susan Jane *illustrator, educator*

**Jaffrey**
Press, Fred *artist*

**Newport**
Gayvoronsky, Ludmila *artist, educator*

**Portsmouth**
Bourgeault, Ronald *art appraiser*
McCann, Margaret Hazel *artist, educator*

**Stratham**
Green, Catherine Cooper *artist*
Terry, Elizabeth Hays *artist, small business owner*

**Wolfeboro**
Bonin, Suzanne Jean *artist*

## NEW JERSEY

**Asbury**
Hannay, Janneka Evans *artist*

**Atlantic City**
Pullman, Jennifer King *art educator, artist*

**Atlantic Highlands**
Tice, George A(ndrew) *photographer*

**Belmar**
Swett, Stephen Frederick, Jr. *artist, educator*

**Bernardsville**
Coheleach, Guy Joseph *artist*
Spofford, Sally (Sally Hyslop) *artist*

**Blairstown**
Bean, Bennett *artist*

**Bordentown**
Barker, Al C. (Albert Charles Barker) *artist*

**Bridgewater**
Glesmann, Sylvia-Maria *artist*
Patton, Diana Lee Wilkoc *artist, educator, illustrator*

**Caldwell**
Palombo, Lisa *artist*

**Califon**
Rosen, Carol Mendes *artist*

**Cresskill**
Smyth, Craig Hugh *fine arts educator*

**East Orange**
Jones-Gregory, Patricia *art educator*

**Egg Harbor Township**
Schreiber, Eileen Sher *artist*

**Englewood**
Anuszkiewicz, Richard Joseph *artist*
Dallas, Dorothy Benz *painter, printmaker*

**Fair Lawn**
Hurewitz, Florence *painter, educator*

**Flemington**
Jacobsen, Betty *artist, art educator*

**Franklin Lakes**
Baker, Cornelia Draves *artist*

**Glassboro**
Murashima, Kumiko *artist, educator*
Wasserman, Burton *artist, educator*

**Hackensack**
Parisi, Cheryl Lynn *art educator*

**Hackettstown**
Lamour, Kenol *artist, educator*

**Hightstown**
Drotch, Eric Jay *artist, educator, researcher*

**Hoboken**
Erbe, Gary Thomas *artist*

**Holmdel**
Slovik, Sandra Lee *retired art educator*

**Jersey City**
Altamura, Mauro A. *artist, educator*
Gurevich, Grigory *visual artist, educator, mime*

**Keasbey**
Hari, Kenneth Stephen *painter, sculptor, writer*

**Lakewood**
Pilgram, Suzanne *artist, art educator*

**Lambertville**
Thorstensen, Shelley M. *artist, educator*

**Laurel Springs**
Roma, Aida Clara *artist*

**Linwood**
Chernoff, Deborah Shelley *art educator*

**Livingston**
Beerman, Herbert *art educator*

**Long Branch**
Tesser, Dorothy *artist*
Woolwich, Madlyn-Ann Crawford *artist, educator*

**Manasquan**
Nardone, Vincent Joseph *artist, educator*

**Maplewood**
Woods, Krystyna Janina *artist, pharmacist*

**Medford**
Mayer, Joyce Harris *artist*

**Metuchen**
Arbeiter, Joan *artist, educator*

Stummer, Helen M. *photographer*

**Montclair**
Goldring, Nancy Deborah *artist, educator*
Williamson, Philemona *artist*

**Moorestown**
Missel, Esther Barbara *artist*

**New Vernon**
Bross, Albert Louis, Jr. *artist*

**Newton**
Hollander, Roslyn *artist, educator*

**North Plainfield**
Delgyer, Leslie Amelia *artist*

**Oakland**
Dressel, Margaret Jane *artist, art educator*

**Oradell**
Struck, Norma Johansen *artist*

**Paramus**
Jacobs, Helen Nichols *artist*

**Passaic**
Sebek, Miklós László *sculptor, educator*

**Paterson**
Gaydos, Tim J. *artist*

**Penns Grove**
Reilley, James Clark *artist, cartoonist, small business owner*

**Phillipsburg**
Richards, Jay Claude *photographer, publishing executive, historian*

**Picatinny Arsenal**
Zulauf, Madeline Ruth *photographer, artist*

**Piscataway**
Mizrahi, Isaac *fashion designer*
Rosalsky, Barbara Ellen *artist, community health nurse*

**Pompton Plains**
Kettlewood, Bea Card *artist, retired educator*

**Princeton**
Bois, Yve-Alain *art educator, curator*
Boretz, Naomi Messinger *artist, educator*
Bunnell, Peter Curtis *retired art educator, curator*
George, Thomas *artist*
Grabar, Oleg *retired art educator*
Johnson, Margaret Kennard *artist, educator*
Mc Vicker, Charles Taggart *artist, educator*
Seawright, James L., Jr. *sculptor, educator*

**Rahway**
Dolinich-Matuska, Christine *artist*

**Red Bank**
Terris, Albert *metal sculptor*

**Ringwood**
Barbour, Arthur J. *artist*

**Rutherford**
Petrie, Ferdinand Ralph *illustrator, artist*

**South Bound Brook**
Weir, Sonja Ann *artist*

**South Orange**
Leshnoff, Susan Kriegel *art educator, artist*

**Sparta**
Rosser, Alvin Raymon *artist*

**Springfield**
Marino, Natalie Marie *artist*

**Stockton**
Mahon, Robert *photographer*
Schoenherr, John (Carl) *artist, illustrator*

**Summit**
Baker, Alden *artist*
Rousseau, Irene Victoria *artist*

**Tenafly**
Koons, Irvin Louis *graphics designer, consultant, marketing professional*

**Toms River**
Unger, Howard Albert *artist, photographer, educator*

**Trenton**
Leipzig, Melvin *art educator*
Miller, Ruane *artist, educator*

**Ventnor City**
Robbins, Hulda Dornblatt *artist, printmaker*

**Verona**
Ayaso, Manuel *artist*

**Wayne**
Cetrulo, Jerry *artist, sculptor*
Garcia, Ofelia *art educator, department chairman*

**Williamstown**
Ash, Donna Joan-Stillwell *art educator*

**Wyckoff**
Oberndorf, Mark Robert *artist*

**NEW MEXICO**

**Abiquiu**
Botts, Gregory *artist*
Hamburger, Sydney K. *sculptor*

**Albuquerque**
Antreasian, Garo Zareh *artist, lithographer, art educator*
Barry, Steve *sculptor, educator*
Coleman, Barbara McReynolds *artist*
Hahn, Betty *artist, photographer, educator*
Hovel, Esther Harrison *art educator*
Miera, Lucille Catherine Miera *artist, retired art educator*
Multhaup, Merrel Keyes *artist*
Nelson, Mary Carroll *artist, writer*
Phillips, Ronald Edward *artist, sales executive*
Qualley, Charles Albert *art educator*
Ré, Paul Bartlett *artist, writer*
Sisson, Laurence P. *artist*
Steider, Doris *artist*
Truby, Betsy Kirby *artist, illustrator, photographer*
Williams, Juanita Rosalie *artist*
Witkin, Joel-Peter *photographer, poet*

**Alto**
Zeitelhack, Gloria Jeanne *artist*

**Arroyo Hondo**
Davis, Ronald *artist, printmaker*

**Belen**
Chicago, Judy *artist*

**El Prado**
Nes, Margaret Isabel *artist*

**Gallup**
Cattaneo, Jacquelyn Annette Kammerer *artist, educator*

**Hobbs**
Garey, Patricia Martin *artist*

**Nogal**
Moeller, Susan Elaine *artist*

**Penasco**
Marx, Nicki Diane *sculptor, painter*

**Roswell**
Peterson, Dorothy Hawkins *artist, educator*
Wiggins, Kim Douglas *artist, appraiser, dealer*

**Santa Fe**
Blakemore, Sally Gay *graphic designer*
Dean, Nat *artist, designer, educator*
Evans, Dick *artist*
Harroun, Dorothy Sumner *artist*
Horndeski, Gregory Walter *artist, mathematics educator*
Karp, Diane R. *art educator*
Peña, Amado Maurilio, Jr. *artist, curator, educator*
Sloan, Jeanette Pasin *artist*
Sloane, Phyllis Lester *artist*

**Taos**
Beck, Ursula *art educator, artist*
Bell, Larry Stuart *artist*
Harmon, Barbara Sayre *artist*
Smith, Dinah Maxwell *painter, photographer*

**NEW YORK**

**Albany**
Carson, JoAnne *art educator, artist*
Lawton, Nancy *artist*

**Alfred**
Fei, Jun *art educator, graphics designer*
Higby, Wayne (Donald Higby) *artist, educator*
Scheer, Joseph H. *artist, education educator*

**Amagansett**
Seelbach, Anne Elizabeth *artist*

**Amenia**
Hale, Nathan Cabot *sculptor, artist, poet*

**Amityville**
Walker, Lois Virginia *multimedia designer, educator, poet, editor*

**Ancram**
Blechman, R. O. *artist, filmmaker*

**Ancramdale**
Weinstein, Joyce *artist*

**Annandale On Hudson**
LÊ, An-My *photographer, educator*
Pfaff, Judy *artist*

**Bay Shore**
Baradzi, Amelia *stained glass artist, restorationist*

**Beacon**
Siejka, George John *artist*

**Bearsville**
Hera, *sculptor*

**Bellerose**
Stecher, Pauline *painter, educator*

**Binghamton**
Sokolowski, Linda Robinson *artist, educator*

**Briarcliff Manor**
Lew, Leslie *artist*

**Bronx**
Adams, Alice *sculptor*
Bacarella, Flavia *artist, educator*
Basile, Philip John Anthony *multimedia designer*
Behnken, William Joseph *art educator, artist*
Gonzalez, Rose A-Navarro *artist*
Juszczyk, James Joseph *artist*
Kassoy, Hortense (Honey Kassoy) *artist, sculptor, painter*
Kitt, Olga *artist*
Korman, Barbara *sculptor*

**Brookhaven**
Grucci Butler, Donna *fireworks company executive*

**Brooklyn**
Amendola, Sal John *artist, educator, writer*
Amrhein, Joe *artist*
Anderson, Lennart *artist*
Andrews, Benny *artist*
Armstrong, L. C. *artist*
Bates, Leo James *artist*
Bui, Phong *painter*
Carlile, Janet Louise *artist, educator*
Costello, Jeffrey *apparel designer*
Diamond, Jessica *artist*
Dinnerstein, Harvey *artist*
Dinnerstein, Simon Abraham *artist, educator*
Dubnau, Jenny *artist*
Estern, Neil Carl *sculptor*
Fischer, R. M. *sculptor*
Gianlorenzi, Nona Elena *art dealer, painter*
Gisolfi, Diana (Diana Gisolfi Pechukas) *art history educator*
Grado, Angelo John *artist*
Haber, Ira Joel *artist, art educator*
Jemisin, Noah *artist, educator*
Jones, Susan Emily *fashion educator, administrator, educator emeritus*
Kemp, James William *graphic artist*
Kjok, Sol *artist, art educator*
Lieberman, Zachary *artist*
Nii, Yuko *artist*
Otterness, Tom *artist*
Padovano, Anthony John *fine arts educator, artist*
Pearlstein, Seymour *artist*
Peker, Elya Abel *artist*
Piene, Chloe *artist, filmmaker*
Pitynski, Andrzej Piotr *sculptor*
Rauschenbusch, Stephanie *artist, educator, poet*
Rocco, Ron *artist*
Schaefer, Marilyn Louise *artist, writer, educator*
Shaw, Kendall (George Shaw) *artist, educator*
Tagliapietra, Robert *apparel designer*
Whitman, Fargo Deborah *artist*
Zakanitch, Robert Rahway *artist*
Zweig, Janet *artist*

**Brookville**
Ceraso, Steven *art educator*

**Buffalo**
Houseknecht, Stephen *artist, educator*
Janiga, Mary Ann *art educator*
McKibbin, William Alex *artist*

**Buskirk**
Johanson, Patricia Maureen *artist, architect*

**Campbell Hall**
Greenly, Colin *artist*

**Canaan**
Walker, William Bond *painter, retired librarian*

**Cazenovia**
Wyckoff, Sylvia Spencer *art educator, artist*

**Cold Spring**
Hodes, Barney *artist*

**Corning**
Buechner, Thomas Scharman *artist, museum director, retired glass manufacturing company executive*

**Cortlandt Manor**
Rosenberg, Marilyn Rosenthal *artist, poet*

**Croton On Hudson**
Johann, Anne Dorothy *visual artist, painter, graphic artist*
Wandel, Sharon Lee *sculptor*

**Cutchogue**
Dank, Leonard Dewey *medical illustrator, audio-visual consultant*

**Dix Hills**
Fouladvand, Hengameh *artist*

**Dobbs Ferry**
Andreadis, Constantine *art educator, art therapist*

**Dryden**
Alsdorf-Sprout, Elizabeth Ruth *art educator*

**East Hampton**
Jaudon, Valerie *artist*
Riley, Cheryl *artist, educator*
Scott, Rosa Mae *art educator, artist*

**East Meadow**
Harrison, Robert L. *photographer, writer, retired transportation executive, poet, playwright*

**East Setauket**
Badalamenti, Fred Leopoldo *artist, educator*
Tuttle, Anne Palmer *artist, education educator*

**Eastchester**
Stern, Louise *artist*

**Elmira**
Miran, Patricia Marie *art educator*

**Fayetteville**
Hadyk-Wepf, Sonia Margaret *artist, real estate manager*

**Flushing**
Carlson, Cynthia Joanne *artist, educator*
Trachuk, Arina George *artist, educator*
Yeo, Kim Eng *artist*

**Fly Creek**
Dusenbery, Walter Condit *sculptor*

**Forest Hills**
Morgan, Jacqui *illustrator, painter, art educator, writer*

**Franklin Square**
Indiviglia, Salvatore Joseph *artist, retired military officer*

**Freeport**
Golici, Nicolae *sculptor*

**Great Neck**
Seidler, Doris *artist*

**Greenlawn**
Popren, Valerie *artist*

**Hartsdale**
McMann, Edith Brozak (Edith Brozak) *performing and visual artist*

**Herkimer**
Durham, Jeanette Randall *artist, educator*

**Hudson**
Bothma, Stef-Albert *artist*

**Huntington**
Benny, Sandra Marie *artist*
Tar, Laszlo *artist*

**Huntington Station**
Nagin, Mary Deborah *artist*

**Irvington**
Lippmann, Janet Gurian *artist, art gallery owner*

**Ithaca**
Garrison, Elizabeth Jane *artist*
Grippi, Salvatore William *artist*
McCue, Arthur Harry *artist, educator*
Mikus, Eleanore Ann *artist*
Poleskie, Stephen Francis *retired art educator, artist, writer, publisher*
Schuler, Mary Callaghan *artist, educational association administrator*
Squier, Jack Leslie *sculptor, educator*

**Jackson Heights**
Dacey, Paul *artist*

**Jamaica**
Cade, Walter III *artist, actor, musician, vocalist*

**Jefferson**
Sullivan, Jim *artist*

**Jeffersonville**
Craft, Douglas Durwood *artist*
Harms, Elizabeth Louise *artist*

**Johnson City**
McMillen, Marieta Louise *art educator*

**Katonah**
Giobbi, Edward Giacchino *artist*

**Kenoza Lake**
Baumgardner, Matthew Clay *artist*

**Lake Peekskill**
Cutrone, Ronnie Blaise *artist*

**Lawrence**
Henriquez, Allen *artist*

**Little Falls**
Veeder, Donna Clark *artist*

**Long Island City**
Goodwin, Guy *artist, retired art educator*
McCoy, Ann *artist*
Young, Aaron *conceptual artist*

**Mahopac**
Gonzalez-Tornero, Sergio *artist*

**Manhasset**
Stevens, Thelma Kaplan *artist, educator*

**Marcellus**
Baker, Bruce Roy *artist, illustrator*

**Merrick**
Cariola, Robert Joseph *artist*

**Millbrook**
Della-Volpe, Ralph Eugene *artist*
Duesberry, Joellyn Toler *artist*

**Mount Vernon**
Sherrill, Milton Lewis *sculptor, painter*

**New Hampton**
Sinnard, Elaine Janice *painter, sculptor*

**New Paltz**
Azank, Roberto *artist*

**New Rochelle**
Slotnick, Mortimer H. *artist*

**New York**
Abboud, Joseph M. *fashion designer*
Abish, Cecile *artist*
Abramovic, Marina *artist*
Acra, Reem *apparel designer*
Adams, Dennis Paul *artist*
Adri, (Adri Steckling Coen) *fashion designer*
Adrian, Barbara (Mrs. Franklin C. Tramutola) *artist*
Aitken, Doug *artist*
Ali, Laylah *artist*
Allard, Linda Marie *fashion designer*
Alpert, William Harold (Bill Alpert) *artist, painter*
Altmejd, David *artist*
Amelan, Bjorn G. *sculptor, set designer*
Amenoff, Gregory *artist, educator*
Anastasi, William Joseph *artist*
Antezzo, Matthew J. *artist*
Anthony, William Graham *artist*
Antonakos, Stephen *sculptor*
Aptekar, Ken *painter*

Arcangel, Cory *artist, computer technician*
Armani, Giorgio *fashion designer*
Arms, Anneli (Anna Elizabeth Arms) *artist, educator*
Arnold, Ann *artist, illustrator*
Azara, Nancy Jean *sculptor, book designer, educator*
Badgley, Mark *fashion designer*
Baechler, Donald *painter*
Baldessari, John Anthony *artist*
Banerjee, (Bimal Banerjee) *artist, educator*
Banker, Amy Beth Cohen *artist, writer, educator, curator, actress, poet*
Barlow, Lou *painter*
Barnes, Gregg *costume designer*
Barnet, Will *artist, educator*
Barnett, Will *painter*
Bartlett, Jennifer Losch *artist*
Bartlett, John *fashion designer*
Baxter, Violet Diane *artist*
Beal, Jack *artist*
Becker, Jonathan *photographer*
Beckman, Ericka *artist, filmmaker*
Belag, Andrea Susan *artist*
Ben-Haim, Zigi *artist*
Berlind, Robert Elliot *artist, educator*
Berman, Ariane R. *artist*
Bernheimer, G. Max *art appraiser*
Berthot, Jake *artist, educator*
Bethel, Denise *art appraiser*
Bhavsar, Natvar Prahladji *artist*
Bialler, Nancy *art appraiser*
Biddle, Flora Miller *art patron, museum administrator*
Billington, Ken *lighting designer*
Birmelin, Robert *artist*
Blair, Dike *sculptor, painter*
Blake, Jeremy *artist*
Boardman, Seymour *artist*
Bochner, Mel *artist*
Bonino, Fernanda *art dealer*
Bourgeois, Louise *sculptor*
Boutis, Tom *artist, painter, printmaker*
Bradshaw, Dove *artist*
Brett, Nancy Heléne *artist*
Brody-Lederman, Stephanie *artist*
Brown, Cecily *artist*
Browne, Thom *apparel designer*
Bruder, Harold Jacob *artist, educator*
Brychtova, Jaroslava *sculptor*
Bunts, Frank Emory *artist*
Burckhardt, Tom *artist*
Butterly, Kathy *sculptor*
Byron, Eric Howard *sculptor, museum researcher and administrator*
Caivano, Ernesto *artist*
Cajori, Charles Florian *artist, educator*
Campbell, Ronald Neil *retired graphics designer*
Canonero, Milena *costume designer*
Cappellazzo, Amy *art appraiser, writer*
Cardile, Paul Julius *fine arts dealer*
Carpenter, James *glass innovator*
Castoro, Rosemarie *sculptor*
Cattelan, Maurizio *artist*
Chamberlain, John Angus *sculptor*
Chambers, William McWillie *artist, art dealer*
Chermayeff, Ivan *graphics designer*
Chin, Mel *sculptor*
Chinn, Yuen Yuey *art educator, painter*
Christensen, Anne *art director*
Chwast, Seymour *graphic artist*
Clemente, Francesco *artist*
Close, Chuck (Charles Thomas Close) *artist*
Coe, Sue *artist, journalist*
Coffin, Anne Gagnebin *arts administrator, editor*
Cogger, Cassia Žamecki *painter*
Cohen, Cora *artist*
Colburn, Martha *animator, filmmaker, artist*
Cole, Willie *artist*
Colen, Dan *artist*
Colp, Norman Barry *artist, curator*
Conelli, Maria Ann *art educator, dean, architect*
Cooper, Paula *art dealer*
Coraggio, Linus *sculptor, consultant*
Cortor, Eldzier *artist, printmaker*
Costa, Francisco *fashion designer*
Cowles, Charles *art dealer*
Cox, Peter *artist*
Craft, Liz *artist*
Crile, Susan *artist*
Crowley, Bob *scenic designer, costume designer, director*
Crown, Roberta *artist, educator*
Cucullo, Santiago *artist*
Cunningham, Francis *artist*
Cutler, Amy *artist*
Cutler, Ronnie *artist*
Dana, F(rank) Mitchell *theatrical lighting designer*
Davidson, Nancy Brachman *artist, educator*
Davis, Lisa Corinne *artist*
DeBeers, Sue *photographer*
DeBellevue, Lucky *sculptor*
Deem, George *artist*
de la Renta, Oscar *fashion designer*
DeLuccia, Paula *artist*
DeMonte, Claudia Ann *artist, educator*
Dennis, Donna Frances *artist, educator*
Di Meo, Dominick *artist, sculptor, painter*
Di Mitri, Piero *fashion designer*
Dine, Jim *artist*
Dobbs, John Barnes *artist, educator*
Dodd, Lois *artist, art educator*
Dole-Recio, Lecia *artist*
Dolman, Edward James *auction house executive*
Donneson, Seena Sand *artist*
Doonan, Simon *window dresser, creative director*
Dowell, James Thomas *artist, filmmaker*
Drucker, Mort *commercial artist*
Drum, Sydney Maria *artist*
Dubrow, John *artist*
Duff, John Ewing *sculptor*
Dunbar, Leila *antiques appraiser, auction house executive*
Dunkelman, Loretta *artist*
Dyyon, Mario (LeRoy Frazier) *artist*
Edelson, Mary Beth *artist, educator*
Egielski, Richard *illustrator*
Eins, Stefan *artist, curator, science researcher, writer*
Eisenberg, Marc S. *artist, sculptor*
Eisenberg, Sonja Miriam *artist*

Enders, Elizabeth McGuire *artist*
Engelberg, Gail May *fine arts patron*
Estes, Richard *artist*
Fasnacht, Heide Ann *artist, educator*
Fausel, Alan *art appraiser*
Feigen, Richard L. *art dealer, collector, writer*
Feltus, Alan Evan *artist*
Fernández, Teresita *sculptor*
Feuerman, Carole A. *sculptor, artist*
Field, Patricia *apparel designer*
Finch, Spencer *artist*
Findlay, Michael Alistair *art dealer, poet*
Finkelstein, Henry *artist*
Fischer, Carl *photographer, graphic designer, actor*
Fischer, Rob *sculptor*
Fisher, Vernon *artist, educator*
Florin, Sharon *artist*
Foulkes, Llyn *artist, educator*
Frankenthaler, Helen *artist*
Freedberg, David Adrian *art educator, art historian*
Frehm, Lynne *painter*
Fujimura, Makoto *artist*
Furnas, Barnaby *painter*
Gage, Beau *artist*
Gagosian, Larry *art dealer*
Gallagher, Ellen *artist*
Gallo, David *scenic designer*
Garrett, Wendell *antiques appraiser, historian, editor*
Geissbuhler, Stephan *graphics designer*
Gerard, Barbara *visual artist, educator*
Gerdts, William Henry *art history educator*
Gertjejansen, Doyle *artist, educator*
Gibson, Ralph H(olmes) *photographer*
Gibson, Sandra *painter, filmmaker*
Gimblett, Maxwell Harold *artist, art educator*
Ginsberg, Elizabeth *artist, educator*
Ginzel, Andrew H. *artist*
Glaser, Milton *graphics designer, illustrator*
Gold, Sharon Cecile *artist, educator*
Golici, Ana *artist*
Gonzalez-Falla, Sondra Gilman *art collector*
Goodnough, Robert Arthur *artist*
Gourevitch, Jacqueline *artist*
Graham, Robert *sculptor*
GrandPré, Mary *illustrator, pastel artist*
Grannan, Katy *photographer*
Greely, Hannah *artist*
Greenberger, Bette Jo *retired art educator*
Griefen, John Adams *artist, educator*
Grooms, Red (Charles Rogers Grooms) *artist*
Grossman, Barbara *artist, educator*
Grossman, Nancy *artist*
Gursky, Andreas *artist*
Gutman, Robert William *retired art educator*
Guyton, Wade *artist*
Guzman, Kathleen McFadden *antiques appraiser, auctioneer*
Haacke, Hans Christoph Carl *artist, educator*
Haas, Richard John *artist*
Haessle, Jean-Marie Georges *artist*
Hagin, Nancy *printmaker, painter*
Halaby, Samia Asaad *painter, educator, writer*
Hall, Joan *artist*
Hamoy, Carol *artist*
Handforth, Mark *artist*
Harrison, Rachel *artist*
Hay, Alex *painter, sculptor*
Heinemann, Peter *artist, educator*
Heintz, Florent M. *art appraiser*
Henkes, Kevin *illustrator, writer*
Henry, Robert S. *art educator*
Henselmann, Caspar Gustav Fidelis *sculptor*
Herman, Stan *fashion designer*
Hernandez, Lazaro *apparel designer*
Herrera, Arturo *artist*
Herrera, Carolina *fashion designer*
Herring, Oliver *artist*
Highstein, Jene Abel *sculptor*
Hodges, Jim *artist*
Holder, Donald *lighting designer*
Holstad, Christian *artist*
Holton, William *artist*
Horn, Roni *artist*
Horsfield, Craigie *artist*
Hort, Michael *art collector*
Hort, Susan *art collector*
Horvat, Olga *artist*
Houghtelling, Ayres *artist, architectural engineer*
Howard, Mildred *sculptor*
Hull, Cathy *artist, illustrator*
Hurwitz, Adam *painter*
Incandela, Gerald Jean-Marie *artist*
Ireland, Patrick *artist*
Iturbide, Graciela *photographer*
Jackson, Henry Nathaniel *clothing designer*
Jacobs, Marc *fashion designer*
Jacquette, Yvonne Helene *artist*
Jenkins, Paul *artist*
Jensen, Bill *artist*
Johnson, Betsey Lee *fashion designer*
Johnson, Harmer Frederik *art appraiser*
Joo, Michael *artist, educator*
Judge, Mary Frances *artist*
Jurinko, Andy Floyd *artist*
Kahn, Wolf *artist*
Kaish, Luise Clayborn *sculptor, painter, educator*
Kaish, Morton *artist, educator*
Kamali, Norma *fashion designer*
Kan, Diana Artemis Mann Shu *painter, art educator, writer*
Karan, Donna (Donna Faske) *fashion designer*
Keller, Marthe *artist, painter*
Kelley, Mike *artist*
Kelly, Ellsworth *painter, sculptor*
Kelly, Mary *sculptor*
Kemper, Randy *fashion designer*
Keno, Leigh R. *antiques dealer, appraiser*
Keno, Leslie B. *antiques dealer, appraiser*
Kepets, Hugh Michael *artist*
Khalil, Mohammad Omer *artist, educator*
Khedoori, Toba *artist*
Kidd, Chip *book designer, writer*
Kim, Atta *photographer*
Kinstler, Everett Raymond *artist*
Klein, Calvin Richard *fashion designer*
Klein, Cynthia *art appraiser*
Klotz, Florence *costume designer*
Knerr, Theodore *artist, photographer*

Koons, Jeff *artist*
Koppelman, Chaim *artist, educator*
Koppelman, Dorothy Myers *artist, consultant*
Korot, Beryl *artist*
Kozloff, Joyce *artist*
Kramarsky, Werner H. *art collector*
Kramer, Harry *artist*
Krementz, Jill *photographer, author*
Kroell, Devi *accessories designer*
Kruger, Barbara *artist, art critic*
Kurahara, Ted Naomi *artist, painter*
Kusmierski, Janet Louise *painter, graphics designer, illustrator*
Kutosh, Sue *artist*
Lam, Derek *apparel designer*
Lamagna, Carlo M. *art educator*
Lane, Kenneth Jay *jewelry designer*
Lange, Liz *apparel designer and executive*
Lanyon, Ellen (Mrs. Roland Ginzel) *artist, educator*
Lash, Stephen Sycle *auction company executive*
Lasker, Jonathan Lewis *artist*
Lasker, Joseph L. *artist, illustrator*
Lauren, Ralph *fashion designer*
Leandre, Juan (Joan Leandre) *computer graphics designer, artist*
Lee, Catherine *sculptor, painter*
LeGrady, George *photographer, educator*
Leiber, Gerson August *artist*
Leibovitz, Annie *photographer*
Lekberg, Barbara *sculptor*
Lepore, Nanette *apparel designer*
Lerner, Sandra *artist*
Levine, David *artist*
Lewin, Betsy R. *illustrator*
LeWitt, Sol *artist*
Liden, Hanna *photographer*
Lipsky, Pat *artist*
Loengard, John Borg *photographer, editor*
Loring, John Robbins *artist, writer*
Lou, Liza *artist*
Louizos, Anna Alexandra *set designer*
Lovell, Whitfield *artist*
Lowry, George S. *art appraiser*
Lowry, Nicholas D. *art appraiser*
Lutz, Tina *apparel designer*
Maione, Donna *fashion designer*
Manglano-Ovalle, Inigo *sculptor*
Mangold, Robert Peter *artist*
Mann, Frank Bert *artist, educator*
Mann, Katinka *artist*
Marco, Mitchell *artist*
Marcus, Gwen Ellen *sculptor*
Marden, Brice *artist*
Margolin, Jean Spielberg *artist*
Martin, Cameron *artist*
Masnyj, Yuri *painter, sculptor*
Mason, Frank Herbert *artist, educator*
Maury, Richard *painter*
Mayer, Rosemary *artist*
Mayle, Jane *apparel designer*
McCollough, Jack *apparel designer*
McCoy, Jennifer *artistic collaborator, educator*
McCoy, Kevin *artistic collaborator, educator*
McCredie, James Robert *fine arts educator*
McDarrah, Fred William *photographer, editor, writer*
McElhinney, James Lancel *artist, educator*
McEwen, Adam *artist*
Mc Gowin, William Edward *artist*
McHugh, Caril Eisenstein Dreyfuss *art dealer, art gallery director, consultant*
McKenzie, Mary Beth *artist*
McKinley-Haas, Mary *artist*
Meckseper, Josephine *sculptor*
Metzger, Evelyn Borchard *artist*
Meyer, Tobias *auction house executive*
Meyers, Dale (Mrs. Mario Cooper) *artist*
Miano, Louis Stephen *arts advisor*
Milder, Jay *artist*
Miller, Nicole Jacqueline *fashion designer*
Miller, Richard Kidwell *artist, actor, educator*
Milonas, Minos *artist*
Mingwei, Lee *artist*
Mir, Aleksandra *artist*
Mischka, James *fashion designer*
Miyake, Issey *fashion designer*
Monahan, Matthew *artist*
Morley, Malcolm A. *artist*
Mozenter, Cyrilla *artist*
Murphy, Catherine *painter*
Murray, Elizabeth *artist*
Nama, George *artist*
Nauman, Bruce *artist*
Neiman, LeRoy *artist*
Neshat, Shirin *artist*
Neumann, Andrew *artist*
Ney, Alexander *artist, sculptor*
Nick, George *painter*
Nickson, Graham *artist*
Nigo, *fashion designer*
Niven, James Graham *auctioneer, art appreciator, philanthropist*
Norsten, Todd *artist*
Nozkowski, Thomas *painter*
O'Bryan, C. Jill *visual artist, writer*
Ocampo, Manuel *artist*
O'Connor, Chuck (Charles O'Connor) *painter*
Ohlson, Douglas Dean *artist, educator*
Okuhara, Tetsu *artist, photographer*
Oldenburg, Richard Erik *auction company executive*
Oldham, Todd *fashion designer*
Olshan, Bernard *artist*
O'Neil, Robyn *artist*
Opie, Catherine *photographer*
Orozco, Gabriel *artist*
Ortman, George Earl *artist*
Osorio, Pepon *artist*
Ostermann, Curt *lighting designer, educator*
Pace, Stephen Shell *artist, educator*
Paik, Younhee *artist*
Panzera, Anthony *artist*
Parker, Trey *animator*
Pask, Scott *set designer*
Passlof, Pat *artist, educator*
Patmos, Marcia *apparel designer*
Peckolick, Alan *painter, graphics designer, photographer*
Perlis, Donald M. *artist*
Picasso, Paloma *fashion designer*

Pierson, Jack *artist*
Pilati, Stefano *apparel designer*
Pionk, Richard Cletus *artist, educator*
Plavinskaya, Anna Dmitrievna *artist*
Polsky, Cynthia Hazen *artist, art collector, philanthropist*
Poons, Larry *artist*
Porter, Liliana Alicia *artist, photographer, painter, printmaker, filmmaker*
Porter, Marc Bennett *auction house executive*
Portnow, Marjorie *painter*
Pozzi, Lucio *artist, educator*
Prieto, Monique N. *artist*
Priore, Christopher Anselmo *artist*
Pujol, Ernesto *artist*
Quackenbush, Robert Mead *artist, writer, psychoanalyst*
Quinson, Bruno Andre *painter, retired publishing executive*
Quisgard, Liz Whitney *artist, sculptor*
Raab, Gail Barbara *painter, educator*
Rathbone, Peter B. *art appraiser*
Rauschenberg, Robert *artist*
Reddy, Krishna Narayana *artist, educator*
Reese, Tracy *fashion designer*
Reininghaus, Ruth *retired artist*
Remington, Deborah Williams *artist*
Resika, Paul *artist*
Ricco, Donna *fashion designer*
Richards, Bill Arthur *artist, educator*
Rifka, Judy *artist, educator*
Ringgold, Faith *artist*
Rodriguez, Narciso *fashion designer*
Rogers, Jenny *artist, interior designer, consultant*
Roi, Alice (Alice Roy Blumenthal) *apparel designer*
Romano, Clare *artist*
Rose, Herman *artist*
Rosenberg, Alex Jacob *art appraiser, art dealer*
Rosenberg, Terry *artist*
Ross, John T. *artist, educator*
Rotolo, Susan (Suze) *artist*
Rovner, Michal *video artist, photographer*
Rowley, Cynthia *apparel designer*
Rubinfien, Leo H. *photographer, filmmaker*
Ruscha, Edward *artist*
Russell, Maryanne *photographer*
Russotto, Paul *artist, educator*
Ryman, Robert Tracy *artist*
Samaras, Lucas *artist, photographer*
Sanders, Rhea *artist*
Sandler, Lucy Freeman *art history educator*
Santore, Joseph *painter*
Sarafpour, Behnaz *apparel designer*
Schapiro, Miriam *artist*
Schnabel, Julian *artist*
Schneider, JoAnne *artist*
Schuselka, Elfi *artist*
Schwalb, Susan Amelia *artist, educator*
Scofidio, Ricardo *artist, educator, architect*
Seborovski, Carole *artist*
Seliger, Charles *artist*
Serra, Richard *sculptor*
Shahn, Jonathan *sculptor*
Shamask, Ronaldus *fashion designer*
Shambroom, Paul *artist, photographer*
Shapiro, Joel Elias *artist*
Sharp, Anne Catherine *artist, educator*
Shatter, Susan Louise *artist*
Shaw, Jim *painter*
Shechet, Arlene J. *artist*
Sherman, Sarai *sculptor, painter*
Sherrod, Philip Lawrence *artist, composer, painter, poet*
Sibley, David Allen *illustrator, writer, ornithologist*
Sibony, Gedi *sculptor*
Sigal-Ibsen, Rose *artist*
Sikander, Shahzia *artist*
Simmons, Danny, Jr. *artist, poet, art gallery director, foundation administrator*
Simonds, Charles Frederick *artist*
Singer, Barbara Helen *photographer*
Sirena, Antonia M. Fanara *artist*
Sis, Peter *illustrator, children's book writer, filmmaker, artist*
Sisto, Elena *artist, educator*
Slavin, Arlene *artist*
Sleigh, Sylvia *artist, educator*
Slitkin, Barbara Ann *artist*
Sloat, Richard Joel *artist*
Slone, Sandi *artist*
Slonem, Hunt *artist*
Smith, Clare *art appraiser*
Smith, Kiki *artist*
Smith, Shirley *artist*
Smith, Zak *artist*
Snow, Dash *photographer*
Solomon, Richard Hugh *art dealer, publishing executive*
Som, Peter *apparel designer*
Sone, Yutaka *artist*
Sonneman, Eve *artist*
Sopanen, Jeri Rainer *photography director*
Soth, Alec *photographer*
Spade, Kate (Katherine Noel Spade) *apparel designer*
Spence, Sique (Mary Stewart Spence) *art dealer*
Sperakis, Nicholas George *artist*
Spikol, Eileen *artist*
Stainrook, Harry Richard *photographer, retired bank executive*
Starr, Steven Dawson *photographer*
Stefanelli, Joseph James (Joe Stefanelli) *artist*
Steffe, Cynthia *fashion designer*
Stewart, Jack *artist, educator, writer*
Stoloff, Carolyn *artist, educator, poet*
Stone, Caroline Fleming *artist*
Stuart, Jill *apparel designer*
Stuart, Michelle Rae *artist*
Sugarman, George *artist*
Sui, Anna *fashion designer*
Sultan, Altoon *artist*
Swain, Robert *artist*
Swartz, Julianne *artist*
Sweeney, Spencer *artist*
Swenson, Erick *painter, artist*
Tansey, Mark *painter*
Thomasos, Denyse *artist*
Tobin, Steve Robert *artist*
Toi, Zang *apparel designer*

Toledo, Isabel *apparel designer*
Tomaselli, Fred *artist*
Tooker, George *artist*
Tribe, Lee *sculptor, educator*
Tsao, Vivian J. *artist, educator*
Tscherny, George *graphics designer*
Tuttle, Richard *artist*
Upright, Diane Warner *art dealer*
Van Tran, Tam *painter*
Violette, Banks *painter, sculptor*
Vollbracht, Michael *apparel designer, illustrator*
Wagner, Robin Samuel Anton *stage and set designer*
Wald, Sylvia *artist*
Walgren, Frances J. *art appraiser*
Walker, Kara *artist*
Walton, Anthony John (Tony Walton) *set designer, illustrator, writer*
Wang, Vera *fashion designer*
Washburn, Phoebe *artist*
Waxman, Wendy *set designer*
Wechsler, Gil *lighting designer*
Weems, Carrie Mae *photographer*
Weil, Rex *artist, art critic*
Weiner, Lawrence Charles *artist*
Weinstock, Rose *artist*
Weissman, Walter *artist, photographer*
Wesley, Eric *sculptor, artist*
Wesley, John Mercer *artist*
Westman, Barbara *artist*
Westphalen, Olav *artist, sculptor*
Weyman, Todd D. *art appraiser*
Widing, Eric P. *auction specialist*
Williams, Christopher *photographer*
Williams, Sue *artist*
Wolfson, Jordan *artist*
Woo, Alex *jewelry designer*
Wright, Faith-dorian *artist*
Wunderman, Jan Darcourt *artist*
Wurmfeld, Sanford *artist, educator*
Wyeth, James Browning *artist*
Yu, Jean *apparel designer*
Zacharias, Athos *artist*
Zackheim, Michele *artist*
Zimmerman, Elyn *artist*
Zittel, Andrea *painter, sculptor*

**Niagara Falls**
Schifano, Kath M. *artist, educator*

**North Bellmore**
Trigoboff, Sybelle *artist, educator*

**North Blenheim**
Rotterdam, Paul Zwietnig *artist, retired art educator*

**North White Plains**
Erla, Karen *artist, painter, collagist, printmaker*

**Northport**
Hohenberger, Patricia Julie *fine arts and antique appraiser, consultant*

**Nyack**
Chien, Jennie *sculptor*

**Old Westbury**
Adams, Mac *art educator, sculptor*

**Oneonta**
Freckelton, Sondra *artist*
Wyshock, Michael Thomas *artist, educator*

**Ossining**
Sadan, Mark *photographer, film producer, artist*

**Oswego**
Fox, Michael David *retired art educator*

**Oyster Bay**
Mooney, James David, Jr. *aerial photographer*
Prey, Barbara Ernst *artist*

**Palisades**
Knowlton, Grace Farrar *sculptor, photographer*
Porta, Siena Gillann *sculptor, educator*

**Piermont**
Berkon, Martin *artist*

**Pound Ridge**
Schwebel, Renata Manasse *sculptor*

**Purchase**
Zimiles, Murray *artist, educator*

**Rhinebeck**
Ewald, Wendy Taylor *photographer, writer, educator*

**Riverhead**
Gilhooley, Dan *artist, psychoanalyst*

**Rochester**
Gong, Nancy Y. *artist, small business owner*
Merritt, Howard Sutermeister *retired art educator*
Singer, Alan Daniel *artist*
Wygant, Patricia Bryans *artist*

**Roslyn**
Finke, Leonda Froehlich *sculptor, educator*

**Roslyn Heights**
Newmark, Marilyn *sculptor*

**Ruby**
Cole, Max *artist*

**Sag Harbor**
Rizzle, Dan *artist*

**Sagaponack**
Van de Bovenkamp, Hans *artist*

**Saint Bonaventure**
Pierce, Constance Laundon *artist, educator*

**Saratoga Springs**
Stake, Peter *art educator, artist*
Upton, Richard Thomas *artist*

**Scarsdale**
Newman, Stacey Clarfield *artist, curator*
Ries, Martin *artist, educator*

**Shelter Island Heights**
Culbertson, Janet Lynn *artist*

**Skaneateles**
Torrey, Linda A. *art educator*

**Snyder**
Breverman, Harvey *artist*

**Southampton**
Kanovitz, Howard *artist, educator*
Swift, Mary Lou *art dealer, financial consultant*
Tuma, Mym *sculptor, painter, educator*

**Spencerport**
Wolsky, Jack *retired art educator*

**Staten Island**
Adler, Barbara Arlene *artist*

**Stony Brook**
Levine, Martin *printmaker, art educator*
Pekarsky, Melvin Hirsch *artist*
Pindell, Howardena Doreen *artist*

**Sugar Loaf**
Endico, Mary Antoinette *artist*

**Syosset**
Greene, Christine Elizabeth *artist*

**Syracuse**
Belfort-Chalat, Jacqueline *art educator, sculptor*
Forbes, Peter Edwin *sculptor*
Phillips, Larry Arthur *artist*
Thomas, Sidney *fine arts educator, researcher*

**Tappan**
Dell, Robert Christopher *sculptor, art educator*
Golbert, Sandra *artist*

**Utica**
Fiori-Blanchfield, Joan *artist, art historian*

**Vestal**
Adour, Colleen McNulty *artist, educator*

**Wainscott**
Russo, Alexander Peter *artist, educator*

**Wallkill**
Koch, Edwin Ernest *artist, interior designer*

**Wantagh**
Forman, Anne *artist*
Glaser, David *painter, sculptor*

**White Plains**
Machover, Carl *computer graphics designer, consultant, computer engineer*

**Wilmington**
Leary, Daniel *artist*

**Woodmere**
Ginsburg, Estelle *artist*
Winick, Bernyce Alpert *artist, photographer*

**Woodstock**
Banks, Rela *sculptor*
Currie, Bruce *artist*
Jordan, John Lester (Gaudeamus) *artist*

**Yonkers**
Speirs, Greg *artist*

**NORTH CAROLINA**

**Asheville**
Tynes, Robert Dick *artist, educator*

**Brevard**
Dillon, Doris (Doris Dillon Kenofer) *artist, art historian, educator, interior designer*

**Burnsville**
Bernstein, William Joseph *glass artist, educator*
Doyle, John Lawrence *artist*

**Cary**
O'Meallie, Kitty *artist*

**Chapel Hill**
Stevens, Phyllis A. *conceptual artist*

**Charlotte**
Bonnefoux, Jean-Pierre *art director, choreographer, dancer*
D'Amato, Frances Louise *art educator, psychology professor*
Walker, John Seibels *artist*

**Cornelius**
Connor, Michael Donnell *art educator, writer, artist*

**Davidson**
Grosch, Laura Dudley *artist, educator*
Jackson, Herb *artist, educator*

**Durham**
Chicquor, Isabel *art educator, artist*
Liles, Joseph Marshall III *artist, educator*

**Franklin**
Kinard, Cynthia Cochran *artist, writer*

**Gastonia**
Easter, Willie, Jr. *artist, writer*

Patterson, Elaine Wilcox *art educator*

**Goldsboro**
Turlington, Patricia Renfrew *artist, educator*

**Greensboro**
Stratton, Jack *artist, art educator, curator, conservator*
Watson, Betty *artist*

**Greenville**
Wallin, Leland Dean *artist, educator*

**Hendersonville**
Tatreau, (Dolores) Maxine *artist*

**Huntersville**
Nowlin, Connie Blackwell *artist*

**Landis**
Lynch, Samuel Curlee, Jr. (Sir Sami Lynch) *painter*

**Leland**
Karch, Jacqueline *artist*

**Lexington**
Frontz, Leslie Kay *art educator*

**Mount Airy**
Vaughn, Frances Austin *art educator*

**Pittsboro**
Kachergis, Joyce W. *book designer*

**Raleigh**
Robinson, Charlotte Hill *artist*

**Rockingham**
Perkins, Susan Lammonds *art educator*

**Sanford**
Higgins, George Edward *sculptor*

**Winston Salem**
Faccinto, Victor Paul *artist, gallery administrator*

**Zebulon**
Ruffing, Anne Elizabeth *artist*

**NORTH DAKOTA**

**Mandan**
Hodge, Ann Linton *artist*

**OHIO**

**Akron**
Borowiec, Andrew *art educator, photographer*
Korow, Elinore Maria *artist, educator*

**Ashtabula**
Morisue, Glenn T. *graphics designer*

**Athens**
Kortlander, William Clark *painter*
Lazuka, Robert *artist, art educator*

**Aurora**
Lawton, Florian Kenneth *artist, educator*

**Bowling Green**
Mueller, Greg Lester *artist, educator*
Ocvirk, Otto George *artist*

**Cincinnati**
Bollen, Sharon Kesterson *artist, educator*
Brady, Darlene Ann *artist, designer, architect*
Brod, Stanford *graphics designer, educator*
Florez, Mary A. *artist*
Lynch, Matthew *artist, art educator*
Shoenberger, Barbara Frances *artist, educator*
Wygant, Foster Laurance *art educator*

**Cleveland**
Adams, Henry *art educator*
Cassill, Herbert Carroll *artist*
Deming, David Lawson *art educator*
Fallon, Pat *artist, educator*
Taylor, Nellie Ruby *artist, poet*

**Columbus**
Chafetz, Sidney *art educator*
Fraser, Pamela *artist*
Leeman, Stacy N. *artist, education educator*
Russell, Nas'Naga R. *illustrator*
Simson, Bevlyn *artist*
Sullivan, Billy *artist*
Sunami, John Soichi *designer*
Wagner, Robert Walter *photographer, communications educator, educator, film producer, consultant*
Yancey-Jones, Floristine Darlene *artist, educator*
Zex, Damon *artist*

**Dayton**
Leland, Nita Ellen Shannon *artist, writer*
Wikstrom, Loretta Wermerskirchen *artist*
Zahner, Mary Anne *art educator*

**Defiance**
Yeager, Bobbi Ann *visual arts educator, artist*

**Euclid**
Adrine-Robinson, Kenyette *art educator, poet, artist, photographer*
Howson, James G. *photographer*

**Garfield Heights**
Shafer, John Eric *art educator*

**Georgetown**
Ruthven, John A. *wildlife artist*

**Greenville**
Alexander, Paul Richard *illustrator*

Foureman, Nancy Lee *artist*

**Hamilton**
Luther, Elissa Meredith *art educator*

**Hilliard**
Cupp, David Foster *photographer, journalist*

**Hudson**
Carducci, Judith Weeks Barker *artist, retired social worker*

**Kent**
Ozanich, Ruth Shultz *artist, poet, retired elementary school educator*

**Kirtland**
Armstrong, Mary Ogden *artist, graphics designer*

**Marietta**
Schultheis, Rita Virginia *artist*

**Miamisburg**
Michaelis, Betty Jane *sculptor, retired small business owner*

**Oxford**
Ewing, Susan R. *art educator, artist*

**Pandora**
Williams, Mark Ellis *artist, educator*

**Perrysburg**
Autry, Carolyn *artist, art history educator*
Catalano, Dominic *art educator, illustrator*

**Powell**
Mitchell, Cathy (C.C.) Christine *art educator*

**Seven Hills**
Stanczak, Julian *artist, educator*

**Springfield**
Humphries, Jimmy *set designer, educator*

**Strongsville**
Myers, Jack Fredrick *artist, educator, writer*

**Swanton**
Perry, Nadine Margaret *retired art educator, artist*

**Toledo**
Brower, James Calvin *graphic artist, painter*
Cousino, Joe Ann *sculptor*
McGlauchlin, Tom *artist*

**Troy**
DeHart, Karen Trautmann *artist, educator*

**Wadsworth**
Neumann, Jeffrey Jay *photographer, minister*

**West Carrollton**
Rabold, Barbara Ann *artist, writer, systems analyst*

**Willoughby**
Vokic, Heather Maureen *artist, educator*

**Wilmington**
Moore, Timothy Isaac *photographer, protective services official*

**Youngstown**
Pernotto, James Angelo *artist*

**OKLAHOMA**

**Ada**
West, Mildred Marie *art educator*

**Depew**
Cooper, Wayne *conceptual artist*

**Lawton**
Mays, Quincy *art educator*

**Midwest City**
Gonzalez, Richard Theodore *photographer*
Thomas, Suzanne Charise *artist, educator*

**Norman**
Caldwell, Susan Havens *art educator*
Wood, Betty Jean *conceptual artist, art educator*

**Oklahoma City**
Alaupovic, Alexandra Vrbanic *artist, educator*
Boston, Billie *costume designer, costume history educator*
Whitener, Carolyn Raye *artist*

**Tulsa**
Frazier, Mary Ann *artist*
Hess, Stanley O. *retired art educator*
Valero, Maria Teresa *photographer, art educator*

**Weatherford**
Jeong, EunKyung *artist, educator*

**OREGON**

**Bandon**
Handley, Louise Patricia *artist*
Lindquist, Louis William *artist, researcher, writer*

**Bend**
Brooke, Sandra Lee *painter*

**Cannon Beach**
Greaver, Harry *artist*

**Depoe Bay**
Blacketer, James Richard *artist*

**Medford**
Schubert, Ruth Carol Hickok *artist, educator*

**Newberg**
Keith, Pauline Mary *artist, illustrator, writer*

**Newport**
Gilhooly, David James III *artist*

**Portland**
Boutwell, Anne Dielschneider *retired artist*
Lorenz, Nancy *artist*
Mazzola, Michael *lighting designer*
Ramsby, Mark Delivan *lighting designer, consultant*
Street, Terri M. *artist, educator*

**Sutherlin**
Gugel, Merilynn Sue *artist*

## PENNSYLVANIA

**Abington**
Goldfine, Beatrice *artist*

**Allentown**
Kocsis, James Paul *artist*

**Annville**
George, Katherine Elizabeth *artist, educator*

**Ardmore**
Levy, Rochelle Feldman *artist*

**Bethlehem**
Travers, Jason Eric *art educator, artist*

**Blakeslee**
Negri, Rocco Antonio *artist, illustrator*

**Blue Bell**
Martino, Babette *artist*

**Camp Hill**
Rowe, Michael Duane *artist*

**Cochranville**
Sazegar, Morteza *artist*

**Easton**
Bellissimo, Mary E. *art educator*

**Elkins Park**
Erlebacher, Martha Mayer *artist, educator*
Stinnett, Hester Ann *artist, educator, art school administrator*

**Fairview**
Krider, Margaret Young *art educator*

**Glen Mills**
Turner, Janet Sullivan *painter, sculptor*

**Glenshaw**
Guentner, James Francis, Jr. *art educator, artist*

**Glenside**
Medel, Rebecca Rosalie *artist*
Rawlins, W. Scott *art educator*

**Glenwillard**
Milne, Christopher McQuiston Wilmoth *photographer, journalist, educator*

**Greensburg**
Fajt, Karen Elaine *art educator*

**Haverford**
Williams, William Earle *artist, educator, curator*

**Indiana**
LaRoche, Lynda *artist, educator*

**Jim Thorpe**
Meneeley, Edward Sterling *artist*

**Kimberton**
Williams, Lawrence Soper, Jr. *photographer*

**Kutztown**
Summer, Evan D. *artist, art educator*

**Lancaster**
Kermes, Constantine John *artist, industrial designer*
Poser, Joan Rapps *artist, writer*

**Levittown**
Marable, Simeon-David *artist*

**Lewisburg**
Seybold, David James *artist*

**Lincoln University**
Benson, Heidi Lam *art educator*

**Lititz**
Buccilla, Brenda Klugh *art educator*

**Lumberville**
Katsiff, Bruce *artist*

**Marshalls Creek**
Svoboda, Joanne Dzitko *artist, educator*

**Media**
Turner, Letitia Rhodes *artist*

**Millersville**
Hay, Teri B. *artist, educator*

**Philadelphia**
Camp, Donald Eugene *experimental photographer, educator*
Creedon, Dennis William *arts education administrator, consultant*
Di Falco, Gerard A. *artist*
Goodman, Sidney *artist*
Granger, Randy William *art educator, consultant*
Le Clair, Charles George *artist, retired dean*

Lewis, E(arl) B(radley) *artist, illustrator*
Miraglia, Peter F. *artist, photographer*
Miyamori, Keiko *artist*
Newman, Libby *painter, printmaker, curator*
Oh, Alice *art educator*
Paone, Peter *artist*
Seyler, Monique Georgina *artist*
Spandorfer, Merle Sue *artist, educator, writer*
Tileston, Jackie *artist, educator*
Warner, Deborah Courtney *artist, educator*
Willet, E. Crosby (Everett Crosby Willet) *artist*
Yaros, Constance Greenberg *painter, sculptor*

**Pittsburgh**
Burgess, David Lowry *artist*
Carr, Winifred Walker *artist, historian*
Cooley, Cynthia Furber *artist*
Herrington, Howard Ray *artist*
Levin, Golan *artist, composer, engineer*
Wilkins, David George *fine arts educator*

**Pottstown**
Mitchell, Eric Ehrman *photographer, stock broker*

**Reading**
Garrison, Matthew Moore *artist, educator*

**Richboro**
Burtt, Larice Annadel Roseman *artist*

**Schwenksville**
Zucker, Barbara J. *artist, educator*

**Shamokin Dam**
Connolly, Elma Troutman *artist, muralist, art gallery owner*

**Solebury**
Anthonisen, George Rioch *sculptor, artist*

**Swarthmore**
Hungerford, Constance Cain *art educator*

**University Park**
Garoian, Charles Richard *artist, educator*

**Upper Black Eddy**
Sherr, Ronald Norman *artist*

**Washington Crossing**
Wells, Charles *sculptor, printmaker*

**Wellsboro**
Driskell, Lucile G. *artist*

**West Chester**
Brasfield, Andrew McCollum *artist*

**West Grove**
Allman, Margo Hutz *sculptor, painter*

## RHODE ISLAND

**Charlestown**
Rohm, Robert Hermann *sculptor, educator*

**Jamestown**
Worden, Katharine Cole *sculptor*

**Newport**
Jae, (Jae French) *sculptor*

**Providence**
Campbell, Bolaji Victor *art history educator, artist, critic*
Corkery, Timothy James *painter, educator*
Feldman, Walter Sidney *artist, educator*
Golden, Hal *artist, consultant*
Heyman, Lawrence Murray *printmaker, painter*
Howes, Lorraine de Wet *fashion designer, educator*
Lee, Eugene *theatrical set designer*
McSheehy, Cornelia Marie *artist, educator*
Sgouros, Thomas *artist*
Townley, Hugh *sculptor, educator*

**Wakefield**
Leete, William White *retired artist*

## SOUTH CAROLINA

**Cordova**
Hallman, Catherine Owens *art educator*
Sellers, LaBron E. *art educator, minister*

**Greenville**
Dreskin, Jeanet Steckler *painter, medical artist, educator*

**Hilton Head Island**
Shepard, Steve *graphic artist, painter*

**Inman**
D'Ambrosio, Jody (Gigi) Lynn *art educator*

**Irmo**
Branham, Jennie Jones *artist*

**Orangeburg**
Hunter, Terry Keith *artist, educator, art association administrator, consultant*
Kozachek, Janet Lynne *artist, educator*
Staley, Alvin *artist, educator*
Staley, Bretta *artist, educator*

## SOUTH DAKOTA

**Mission**
MacKichan, Margaret Anna *artist, art educator*

**Yankton**
Clatworthy, Catherine Lynn *educational trainer, graphics designer*

## TENNESSEE

**Chattanooga**
Martin, Chester Y. *sculptor, painter*
Mills, Olan, II, *photography company executive*
Parks, Susan Jane *artist*

**Johnson City**
Lyle, Valarie Gay *art educator, artist*

**Kingsport**
Crockett, Frank McClung *arts educator, retired music educator*

**Knoxville**
Drinnon, Janis Bolton *artist, poet, volunteer*
Markert, Cynthia Allin *artist*

**Memphis**
McPherson, Larry Eugene *photographer, educator*
Riss, Murray *photographer, educator*

**Murfreesboro**
Reed, Angelica Denise *sculptor, writer, illustrator*

**Nashville**
Chandler, Nettie Johnson *artist*
Creasy, Charles L. *creative director*
LeQuire, Alan Russell *sculptor, educator*

**Oak Ridge**
Regan-Stanton, Christa Maria *artist*
Runtsch, Clarence Frederick *sculptor*

## TEXAS

**Arlington**
Evans, Kathryn Miller *art educator, department chairman*
Munoz, Celia Alvarez *artist*

**Austin**
Armstrong, Nak *jewelry designer*
Bucknall, Malcolm Roderick *artist*
Camargo, Anthony *jewelry designer*
Charles, Michael Ray *artist*
Curtis, Mary Louise *artist, educator*
Daly, Stephen Jeffrey *art educator*
Fearing, William Kelly *art educator, artist*
Guerin, John William *artist*
Hatgil, Paul Peter *artist, sculptor, educator*
High, Timothy Griffin *artist, educator, curator, writer*
Sawyer, Margo Lucy *artist, educator*
Scott, David Winfield *artist, museum administrator*
Smith, Jeffrey Chipps *art educator*
Weismann, Donald Leroy *artist, educator, filmmaker, writer*

**College Station**
Martin, Carol Jacquelyn *artist, educator*

**Corpus Christi**
Crane, Frances Hawkins *artist, educator*

**Crosby**
King, Vernon Dale *art educator*

**Dallas**
Basden, John William *artist*
Dealey, Lynn Townsend *artist*
Lawrence, Annette *artist*
Nelson, Pamela Hudson *artist, educator*
Norman, Bobby Don *artist, writer, research scientist*

**Denton**
Austin, Jerry L. *art educator*
Bertine, Dorothy Wilmuth *artist, educator, accountant, genealogist, poet, writer*
McMath, Elizabeth Moore *graphic artist*

**Dublin**
Collins, Roy Dale *illustrator, writer*

**Euless**
Leding, Anne Dixon *artist, educator*

**Fort Worth**
Allen, William Marion III *retired graphics designer, artist*
Brown, George Edward, Jr. *visual arts educator, soccer coach*
Gorman, Rhonda Renee *costume designer, educator*
Hixon, Karen J. *art and environmental patron*
Stevenson, Ruth Carter *art patron*

**Friendswood**
Moore, Alicia Jane *art educator*

**Georgetown**
Aguillon, Charles Christopher *art director*

**Houston**
Anderson, Dawolu Jabari *illustrator*
Blakemore, Amy *photographer*
Cyrus, Jamal *artist*
Davenport, Bill *sculptor*
Evans, Kenya *artist*
Hamilton, Jacqueline *arts consultant*
Honeycutt, George Leonard *retired photographer*
Kagle, Joseph Louis, Jr. *artist, arts administrator, art historian, educator*
Mehretu, Julie *artist*
Orr, Carole *artist*
Pruitt, Robert A. *artist*
Randolph, Lynn Moore *artist*
Reid, Katherine Louise *artist, educator, writer*
Thummel, Rosa *artist*
Twombly, Cy (Edwin Parker Twombly Jr.) *artist*

**Huntsville**
Hanssen, Kristina Schirm *costume designer, educator*
Lea, Stanley E. *artist, educator*

**Irving**
Sigurdson, Mike James *visual art educator*
Strunck, Juergen *printmaker*

**Kerrville**
Burt, Allen Daniel *artist*
Chance, F. Earlayne *artist*
Frudakis, Evangelos William *sculptor*

**Lakehills**
Spears, Diane Shields *art director, elementary school educator*

**Longview**
Statman, Jan B. *artist*

**Lubbock**
Doyle, Laurie Ellen *art educator*

**Mc Kinney**
Wright, Thomas Parker *artist*

**Mission**
Nichols, Edward Edson *artist*

**Murchison**
Taweel, Janice M. *artist, art educator*

**Port Aransas**
Van Baalen, Donna Gale *artist, retired pharmacist*

**Post**
Killian, Lawrence Harding, II, (Larry H. Killian) *sculptor*

**Rosenberg**
Haygood, Eithel Marinella *artist, educator*

**San Antonio**
Nigro, R. Lisa *artist, foundation administrator, director*

**Waco**
Askins, Sally Lynn *costume designer, educator*
Chatmas, John Thomas *art educator, artist*

**Wimberley**
McCoy, John Denny *artist*

## UTAH

**Castle Valley**
Zavada, Barbara Johanna *artist, educator*

**Logan**
Rasmuson, Brent J. *photographer, small business owner*

**Provo**
Fielding, Eric *set designer, educator*

**Rush Valley**
Pierce, Diane Jean *artist*

**Salt Lake City**
Wassmer, Theodore Milton *artist*

## VERMONT

**Bennington**
Lum, Mary *artist, art educator*

**Brattleboro**
Abrams, Jackie *artist, educator*

**Charlotte**
Robinson, Sally Winston *artist*

**Dorset**
Marron, Pamela Anne *artist*

**East Montpelier**
Christiansen, Andrew P. *website designer, historic archives digitilizer*

**Enosburg Falls**
Svendsen, Alf *artist, art educator*

**Middlebury**
Bumbeck, David *artist, retired educator*

**Newbury**
McGarrell, James *artist, educator*

**North Pomfret**
Shepherd, Gaal *artist*

**Pittsfield**
Wacker, Susan Regina *graphics designer, consultant*

**Reading**
Dike, Rad (Edward Conrad Dike) *artist*

**West Burke**
Van Vliet, Claire *artist*

**Weston**
Kasnowski, Chester Nelson *artist, educator*

**Williston**
Essman, Robert Norvel *artist, graphics designer*

## VIRGINIA

**Alexandria**
Kim, Sook Cha *artist*
Lopatin, Carol Keesler *artist*
Whitson, Elizabeth Temple *graphics designer*

**Arlington**
Bass, Judy Marsha *artist, educator*
Dunlap, William *artist, art educator, art critic, lecturer*

## POLAND

**Warsaw**
Abakanowicz, Magdalena *artist, sculptor*

## SPAIN

**Seville**
Sanchez, Leonedes Monarrize Worthington (His Royal Highness Duke de Leonedes of Spain Sicily Greece) *fashion designer*

## SWEDEN

**Bralanda**
Emilson, Henry Bertil *artist*

## TUNISIA

**Carthage**
Sehili, Mahmoud *artist*

## ADDRESS UNPUBLISHED

Abbe, Elfriede Martha *sculptor, graphics designer*
Abbett, Robert Kennedy *artist, writer*
Abboud, Mara *artist*
Abel, Barbara Ellen *photographer*
Abeles, Kim Victoria *artist*
Abeles, Sigmund M. *painter, sculptor, printmaker*
Agne, Phyllis G. *artist, educator*
Akerlind, Christopher *lighting designer, set designer*
Aldredge, Theoni Vachliotis *costume designer*
Alexander, Marjorie Anne *artist, consultant*
Alfaro, Victor *fashion designer*
Allen, Philip *artist*
Ancona, George Efrain *photographer, author*
Andersson, Helen Demitrous *artist*
Andrade, Edna *artist, art educator*
Annus, John Augustus *artist*
Antin, Eleanor *artist*
Arifi, Fatana Baktash *artist, educator*
Arnone, John *set designer*
Aronson, Marc *artist*
Arrott, Patricia Graham *artist, educator*
Asato, Evan Masami *artist, architect, designer*
Aschheim, Eve Michele *artist, educator*
Atkinson, Tracey Blake *artist, art educator*
Atwood, Colleen *costume designer*
Atwood Pinardi, Brenda *artist, educator*
Azarian, Mary *illustrator*
Badgett, Steven *artist*
Barnes, Robert Vincent *retired elementary and secondary school art educator*
Barone, Angela Maria *artist, researcher*
Barrow, Thomas Francis *artist, educator*
Barth, Frances *artist*
Bateman, Robert McLellan *artist*
Battie, David Anthony *art appraiser*
Baxter, Robert James *artist*
Behr, Marion Ray *artist*
Bell, Patricia Ann *photographer, artist, writer*
Benzle, Curtis Munhall *artist, art educator*
Berkowitz, Terry *artist, fine arts educator*
Bernard, David Edwin *artist*
Berns, Pamela Kari *artist, publisher*
Berridge, Mary Lloyd *photographer*
Bierman, Sandra *artist*
Bingham, Marian *artist, printmaker*
Binkley, Howell *lighting designer*
Binkley, Timothy *computer graphics designer, educator*
Birchard, Catherine Suzanne Sieh *artist*
Blackwell, Lois Moore *fashion designer, educator, visual artist*
Blondheim, Linda Kalb *artist*
Bloom, Hyman (Chaim Melamed) *artist*
Bohary, James *artist*
Bohrman, Catherine Leuchs *sculptor*
Boldovitch, Gerri *art educator*
Borges, Rozie D. *artist*
Bornoff, David Tai *artist*
Bowen, Ginger Ann *artist*
Bowen-Forbes, Jorge Courtney *artist, poet*
Bowers, Andrea *artist*
Boynton, Sandra Keith *illustrator, cartoonist, stationery products executive*
Brach, Paul Henry *artist*
Bradley, Slater *artist*
Broderick, James Allen *painter, art educator, etcher*
Bronkar, Eunice Dunalee *artist, educator*
Brookner, Jackie W. *sculptor, educator*
Brooks, Deborah June *art educator*
Brown, Alice Elste *artist*
Brown, Amy Christine *art educator*
Brown, Carol Rose *artist*
Buck, John E. *printmaker*
Buitrón, Robert C. *artist, educator*
Bundi, Renee *art director, graphics designer*
Burns, Leslie Kaye *artist*
Burns, Toni Anthony *artist*
Burr, Tom *artist*
Burtley, Calvin *art director*
Bustos, Rey *art educator, artist*
Butler Yank, Leslie Ann *artist, writer, editor*
Butterfield, Deborah Kay *sculptor*
Byrd, Marc Robert *display designer*
Cabot, Hugh III *painter, sculptor*
Cady, Dennis Vern *painter, printmaker, sculptor*
Cain, David Paul *art educator*
Calamar, Gloria *artist*
Campbell, Demarest Lindsay *artist, writer, interior designer*
Campello, Florencio Lennox *artist, art critic*
Carone, Nicolas *artist*
Carpenter, Pearl Elizabeth *artist*
Carraher, Mary Lou Carter *art educator*
Carroll, Marie-Jean Greve *retired art educator, artist*
Carter, Nanette Carolyn *artist*
Casanova, Aldo John *sculptor*

Caseiras, Jo Ann Striga *artist, educator*
Cassara, Frank *artist, educator, printmaker*
Catlett, Elizabeth *sculptor, educator, printmaker*
Cavaleri, Judith Ann *art educator*
Celentano, Francis Michael *artist, art educator*
Chung, Doo-ri *apparel designer*
Cicero, Carmen Louis *artist, educator*
Cifolelli, Alberta Carmella *artist, educator*
Claiborne, Liz (Elisabeth Claiborne Ortenberg) *fashion designer*
Cleary, Manon Catherine *artist, retired art educator*
Cobb, Ruth *artist*
Cobb, Virginia Horton *artist, educator*
Cobey, Virginia Branum *artist, actress, art collector*
Colangelo, Carmon *artist, printmaker, educator*
Colescott, Robert Hutton *artist, educator*
Colker, Edward *artist, educator*
Colton, Mindy Zimmerman *artist, art director, consultant*
Condon, Brody Kiel *computer graphics designer*
Conklin, Eric Linwood *artist*
Conley, Helen Donovan *artist, poet*
Conroy, Tamara Boks *artist, special education educator, retired nurse*
Coon, Cheryl A. *artist, art educator, curator*
Cooper, Elva June *artist*
Cooper, Rebecca *art dealer*
Cornell, Thomas Browne *artist, educator*
Couper, James Maxwell *painter, educator*
Craw, Freeman (Jerry) *graphic artist*
Crocker, Suzanne *painter*
Cumming, Robert Hugh *artist, photographer*
Cummings, David William *artist, educator*
Cunningham, Kathy *art educator, artist*
Curnutte, Mary E. *artist*
Currie, Steven Ray *artist*
Curtis, Thomas Pelham, II, *artist, educator, small business owner*
Dahse, Kenneth William *photographer, writer, educator*
Dailey, Daniel Owen *artist, educator, product designer*
D'Alessio, Valaida Corrine *artist, consultant*
Dallmann, Daniel F. *artist, educator*
Dangremond, David W. *art history educator*
Dani, *sculptor, painter*
Dauberman, Michelle L. *photography educator, design educator*
Davenport, Ray Charles *artist, lithographer*
Davidson, Jeannie *costume designer*
Davies, Adam *artist, educator*
Davis, Taylor *sculptor*
Davisson, Darrell Dean *art educator*
De Blasi, Tony (Anthony Armando De Blasi) *artist*
Dechar, Peter Henry *artist*
DeGiulio, Lucas *artist*
Denenberg, Katharine W. Hornberger (Tinka Denenberg) *artist, educator*
Diaz, David *illustrator*
diCorcia, Philip-Lorca *artist, photographer*
DiFronzo, Francis G. *painter*
Di Giacomo, Fran *artist*
Dill, Laddie John *artist*
Di Suvero, Mark *sculptor*
Doell, Margaret J. *art educator*
Dogançay, Burhan C. *artist, photographer, sculptor*
Dominguez, Eddie *artist*
Downes, Rackstraw *artist*
Doyle, Tom *sculptor*
Drasler, Gregory John *artist*
Drummond, Sally Hazelet *artist*
Duong, Anh *artist, actress*
Durham, Jimmie *artist, poet*
Duval-Carrié, Edouard *artist*
Earney, Michael Patrick *artist*
Eddy, Don *artist*
Edmo, Jean Umiokalani *artist, poet*
Egas, Eric *artist*
Elcik, Elizabeth Mabie *fashion illustrator*
Engelman, Rosalyn Ackerman *artist, marketing executive*
Engels, Beatrice Ann *artist, poet, retired real estate company executive*
Engle, Steve Eugene *artist*
Ericson Cardell, Ede Anne *sculptor*
Estes, Mary Gwyn *art educator*
Fabricatore, Carol Diane *artist, educator*
Farrar, Elaine Willardson *artist*
Faxon, Alicia Craig *art educator, department chairman*
Feingold, Kenneth J. *artist*
Ferreira, Armando Thomas *sculptor, educator*
Fillmore, John Dillon *artist*
Fine, Jane Madeline *visual artist*
Finley, Harry *artist, museum director*
Fiore, Joseph Albert *artist*
Fish, Janet Isobel *artist*
Fish, Jeanne Spencer *artist, retired lawyer*
Fisher, Kim *artist*
Fisher, Neal Foster *artist, writer*
Fitzgerald, Joan V. *artist*
Francis, Karen *painter, television producer*
Frank, Dana *photographer, small business owner*
Franklin, Patt *artist, educator*
Frasconi, Antonio *artist, educator*
Frederick, Elizabeth Eleanor Tatum *watercolor artist, retired educator*
Freilicher, Jane *artist*
Freyermuth, Virginia Karen *art educator*
Friday, Katherine Orwoll *artist*
Friedlander, Lee N. *photographer*
Friedman, Marcia L. *photographer, writer, artist*
Fromboluti, Sideo *artist*
Frost, Sue Emmons *art educator*
Frudakis, Zenos Antonios *sculptor, artist*
Fugate-Wilcox, Tery *artist*
Furth, Alan J. *artist*
Gallagher, Cynthia *artist, educator*
Gamble, Desirata *artist, poet*
Garber, Helen Kolikow *photographer, artist*
Garcia, Luis F. *photographer*
Gardner, Elizabeth Ann Hunt *artist, poet, genealogist*
Gaultier, Jean-Paul *fashion designer*
Gechtoff, Sonia *artist*
Gennaro, Irene *sculptor*
Gerhardt, Carol *artist*

Gibran, Kahlil *sculptor*
Gilleran, Peter Joseph *retired art educator*
Gim, Dong-Woo *display designer*
Givenchy, Hubert James Marcel Taffin de *fashion designer*
Glasser, Norma Penchansky *sculptor*
Glasson, Lloyd *sculptor, educator*
Glen, Niki *artist, sculptor*
Glover, Janet Briggs *artist*
Golden, Judith Greene *artist, educator*
Goldin, Leon *artist*
Gordon, Douglas *artist*
Gordon, Lonny Joseph *artist, educator, dean*
Goss, Jerome Eldon *craftsman, retired cardiologist*
Goulet, Lorrie *sculptor*
Graf, Deva *artist*
Graham, K(athleen) M. (K. M. Graham) *artist*
Grames-Lyra, Judith Ellen *artist, educator, municipal official*
Greenberg, Albert *art director*
Gruen, Shirley Schanen *artist*
Guggenheim, Barbara Sue *art appraiser*
Gumpel, Hugh *artist*
Gussow, Sue Ferguson *artist, educator*
Haas, Holly Alice *set designer, small business owner*
Hall, Susan Laurel *artist, educator, writer*
Hammond, Harmony *artist, educator*
Hancock, Patricia Ann *artist*
Hannaman, Alberta Anna *artist*
Hanson, Jo *artist, educator, writer*
Harman, Maryann Whittemore *artist, educator*
Hart, Marnie R. *art educator*
Hasen, Burton Stanley *painter*
Hauer, Erwin Franz *sculptor, educator*
Hayes, David Vincent *sculptor*
Head, Melva Ann *artist*
Heiss, Mary Wynne *artist*
Heller, Jules *artist, educator, writer*
Helpern, Joan (Joan Marshall) *designer, business executive*
Hemmerdinger, William John *artist*
Hendricks, James Powell *artist*
Henes, Donna *artist, writer*
Henry, Dale *artist*
Hepper, Carol *artist, educator*
Herley, Daveen Dorothy *art educator, artist*
Herman, Joni Marie-Victor *artist*
Herzberg, Thomas *artist, educator, illustrator*
Hill, Clinton *artist*
Hilton, Nicky (Nicholai Olivia Hilton) *apparel designer*
Hiuni, Dahn *art educator, artist*
Hogle, Ann Meilstrup *painter, art educator*
Holbrow, Gwendolyn Jane *artist, writer*
Holden, Donald *artist, writer*
Hollerbach, Serge *artist*
Holtz, Laurence *artisan, photographer*
Holzer, Jenny *artist*
Hooks, Earl J. *art educator, sculptor*
Hoover, Richard *set designer, art director, actor*
Hopkins, Budd *artist, writer*
Horlick, Ruth *photographer*
Horton, Patricia Mathews *artist, violist and violinist*
Howell, Mary Jean *artist, administrative assistant*
Hsieh, Tsui-Hsia *artist, educator*
Huffington, Anita *sculptor*
Humann, Richard *artist*
Huo, Bonnie Kwan *artist*
Hurst, Heather *illustrator*
Huynh, Phung Xuan *artist*
Ingraham, Cherie Ann *apparel designer, environmentalist, writer, educator*
Innis, Windsor Joe *artist, art educator*
Isley, Elizabeth C. H. *commercial display artist, interior designer*
Jacir, Emily *photographer, conceptual artist*
Jackson, Matthew Day *assemblage artist*
Jamison, Philip *artist*
Jansen, Angela Bing *artist, educator*
Jay, Norma Joyce *artist*
Jeswald, Joseph *artist*
Johnson, Elaine Lucille *artist, director*
Jones, Carter Ruthven, Jr. *sculptor, educator*
Jones, John Harding *photographer*
Jones, Lindsey *art appraiser*
Josephson, Kenneth Bradley *artist, retired art educator*
Jung, Kwan Yee *artist*
Kabakov, Ilya *artist*
Kahn, Cecily *painter*
Kahn, Susan *artist*
Kalina, Richard *artist*
Kaplan, Phyllis *artist, composer*
Kato, Tomiko *artist*
Katz, Alex *artist*
Katz, Leandro *artist, filmmaker*
Kaz, Nathaniel *sculptor*
Kazan, Alexandra Khan *photographer, web site designer*
Kearns, James Joseph *artist*
Keaton, John J. *artist*
Kehlmann, Robert *artist, critic*
Kennedy, JoAnn *artist, educator*
Kennerly, David Hume *photographer, writer, producer*
Khvost-Vostrikova, Natalia S. *art educator, consultant*
Kindseth, Anne *art educator, researcher*
King, William *sculptor*
Kingstein, Jonah *painter*
Kipniss, Robert *artist*
Kipniss MacDonald, Betty Ann *artist, educator*
Kirsch, Roslyn Ruth *artist, educator, painter, printmaker*
Kittredge, Nancy *artist*
Kleiman, Alan Boyd *artist*
Klein, Charlotte Feuerstein *art consultant*
Klein, Lynn Ellen *artist*
Klement, Vera *artist*
Knodt, Jean Sausele *artist, educator*
Knox, Susan *artist*
Koch, Philip Frederick *artist*
Koch, Virginia Greenleaf (Virginia M. Greenleaf) *painter*
Komar, Vitaly *artist*
Kors, Michael (Karl Anderson Jr.) *fashion designer*
Kozak, Rosemary *artist, educator*
Kraft, Yvette *art educator*

Kriesberg, Irving *painter*
Krukowski, Samantha H. *art educator, artist*
Krulik, Barbara S. *prodution manager, curator, art director, writer*
Kulicke, Robert M. *artist*
Kusama, Yayoi *sculptor, painter*
Kwong, Eva *artist, educator*
Kyle, Gene Magerl *merchandise presentation artist*
Laderman, Gabriel *artist*
Ladewig Goodman, Jeanne Margaret *artist*
Laessig, Robert H. *artist*
Lai, Feng-Qi *instructional designer and educator*
Landau, Emily Fisher *art collector, foundation administrator*
Langland, Harold Reed (Tuck) *sculptor, educator*
La Rocca, Isabella *artist, educator*
Lasuchin, Michael *artist, retired art educator*
Lavezzi, John Charles *retired art history educator, archaeologist*
Lawrence, Mary Josephine (Josie Lawrence) *artist, retired library official*
Lazzarini, Robert *sculptor*
Lear, M. Kathleen *artist, music educator, small business owner*
Lebbin, Carole Sue *artist*
Leeds, Nancy Brecker *sculptor, lyricist*
Lehrer, Leonard *artist, educator*
Leiber, Judith Maria *designer, manufacturer*
Leipzig, Arthur *photographer, retired educator*
Lembark, Connie Wertheimer *art consultant*
LeRoy, G. Palmer *art dealer*
Leslie, Alfred *painter, filmmaker*
LeVasseur, Lee Allan *artist*
Levi, Josef Alan *artist*
Levin, Morton D(avid) *artist, printmaker, educator*
Levine, Jack *artist*
Levy, Mark *art educator*
Lewie, Reva Goodwin *artist, educator*
Lewinsky, Monica *handbag designer, television personality*
Lewis, Sharyn Lee *sculptor*
Lieberman, Louis (Karl Lieberman) *artist*
Li-lan, *artist*
Linhares, Judith Yvonne *artist, educator*
Link, Phyllida Korman *artist, educator*
Lisk, Penelope Tsaltas *artist*
Litchfield, Heidi *photographer, photojournalist*
Littleton, Harvey Kline *artist*
Lobdell, Frank *artist*
Lockhart, Sharon *artist*
Longo, Robert *artist, film director*
Longo, Vincent *art educator, painter, printmaker*
Lopez Heredia, Hubert *artist*
Lord, Carolyn Marie *artist*
Lorelli, Elvira Mae *artist, art educator*
LoSchiavo, Francesca *set designer*
Lucchesi, Bruno *sculptor*
Ludwig, Allan Ira *photographer, educator, artist, writer*
Lutes, Jim G. (James Lutes) *artist*
Lyman, Dorothy Grace *artist, writer, arts and crafts shop executive*
Lynch, Mary Jean *art educator, consultant*
Lynd, Phyllis *art educator*
Mager, Ingrid Irina *artist*
Mahmud, Shireen Dianne *photographer*
Mahoney, Shawn Patrick *artist*
Mangold, Sylvia Plimack *artist*
Mann, Joan Ellona *artist, editor*
Mann, Sally *photographer*
Marion, John Louis *former fine arts auctioneer and appraiser*
Mark, Mary Ellen *photographer*
Marks, Roberta Barbara *artist, educator*
Marlowe, Willie *artist, fine arts educator*
Marsh, Merrilyn Delano *sculptor, artist, painter*
Marti, Virgil *artist*
Martin, Dianne Leslie *artist, educator*
Martin, Noel *graphics designer, educator*
Mártonyi, Csaba László *retired ophthalmic photographer*
Martyl, (Mrs. Alexander Langsdorf Jr.) *artist*
Masi, Robin *artist, writer, educator*
Mason, Emily *painter*
Mason, Lois E. (J. Day Mason) *painter, poet, actress, educator*
Mathieu, Georges Victor Adolphe *artist*
Mattos Grell, Elizabeth *artist*
Mauney, Thomas Lee *set designer*
Mayer, Susan Martin *art educator*
McCully, Emily Arnold *illustrator, writer*
McCurdy, Michael Charles *illustrator, author*
McFarren, Naza *artist*
McKay, Renee *artist*
McKnight, Thomas Frederick *artist*
McMillen, Elizabeth Cashin *artist*
McPeters, Sharon Jenise *artist, writer*
Meagher, Sandra Krebs *artist*
Menefee, Linnea-Norma *antique dealer*
Mercer, Frances deCourcy *artist, educator*
Meret, Alexandru Sasha *artist, illustrator*
Merritt, Eleanor Lynette *artist, educator*
Middaugh, Robert Burton *artist*
Middleman, Raoul Fink *artist*
Milana Panopoulos, Maria *artist*
Miller, Nidi R. *art, sculptor, educator*
Miller, Ruth Ann *artist*
Mishler, John Joseph *sculptor, art educator*
Misrach, Richard Laurence *photographer*
Mondini-Ruiz, Franco *artist*
Monheit, Molly Jane *artist*
Moore, Robert Eric *artist*
Mori, Mariko *artist*
Morning, John *graphic designer*
Morphew, Dorothy Richards-Bassett *artist, real estate broker*
Morrison, Robert Clifton *artist*
Moser, Barry *artist*
Mueller, Gerardine Lillian *art educator, artist*
Murray, Robert Gray *sculptor*
Myers, Dorothy Roatz *artist*
Myers, Sue Bartley *artist*
Nagy, Elizabeth Garver *artist*
Nasseripour, Mohammad Michel *artist, architect*
Negron, Jesús (Bubu) *artist*
Neri, Manuel *sculptor, educator*
Neville, Elizabeth Egan *artist, educator*
Newell, Shirley Ann Cecil *retired art dealer, artist*
Newman, Muriel Kallis Steinberg *art collector*
Nichols, Iris Jean *retired illustrator*

---

## ASSOCIATIONS AND ORGANIZATIONS *See also* specific fields

## UNITED STATES

**Long Beach**
Fischler, Sandy Lynn *charitable and informational organization executive*

**Los Altos**
Larson, Carol S. *foundation administrator, lawyer*
Wilbur, Colburn Sloan *foundation consultant and trustee, former executive*

**Los Angeles**
Alvarado, Pablo *day laborer organizer & immigrant rights activist*
Daly, Robert Anthony *international relief organization executive, former professional sports team executive, retired film company executive*
Erichsen, Peter Christian *foundation administrator*
Gomez, Elizabeth M. *community organization administrator*
Grant, Mark Antonio *organization administrator*
Hernandez, Antonia *foundation administrator, lawyer*
Horowitz, David Charles *consumer advocate, radio and television commentator, newspaper columnist, director*
Ibarra, Irene M. *foundation administrator*
Im, Hyepin Christine *not-for-profit developer*
Lindley, F. Haynes, Jr., (Francis Haynes Lindley Jr.) *foundation executive, lawyer*
Lizarraga, David C. *non-profit community development corporation administrator*
Mack, James Curtis, II, *cultural organization administrator*
Powell, James Lawrence *educational association administrator, museum director, geologist*
Prewitt, Jean *not-for-profit organization executive*
Racklin, Barbara Cohen *fundraising consultant*
Ross, Robert K. *foundation administrator, physician*
Shakely, John Bower (Jack Shakely) *foundation executive*
Smith, Jean Webb (Mrs. William French Smith) *civic worker*
Wells, Bradley W. *foundation administrator*
Williams, James M. *foundation administrator*
Wilson, Phill *foundation administrator*
Wlaschin, Ken *cultural organization administrator, writer*

**Marina Del Rey**
Bearzi, Maddalena *not-for-profit developer, writer*
Heath, Berthann Jones *educational association administrator*

**Menlo Park**
Altman, Drew E. *foundation executive*
Brown, Charles Dickson *not-for-profit fundraiser, consultant*
Collins, Nancy Whisnant *foundation administrator*
Gimon, Eleanor Hewlett *philanthropist*
Pallotti, Marianne Marguerite *foundation administrator*
Smith, Marshall Savidge *foundation executive*

**Mill Valley**
Schreyer, Chara *foundation administrator, art collector*

**Modesto**
Mattos, William Harold *trade association administrator, publishing executive*
Whiteside, Carol Gordon *foundation executive*

**Montclair**
Boyd, Mary H. (Mary H. Merrill) *social services administrator*

**Mountain View**
Bills, Robert Howard *political party executive*

**Napa**
Loar, Peggy Ann *foundation administrator, museum administrator*

**Novato**
Peters, Thomas *foundation administrator*

**Oakland**
Cohen, Larry *not-for-profit developer, social services administrator*
Hawkins, Robert B. *think-tank executive*
Lazar, John Edward *social services administrator, not-for-profit developer*
Macmeeken, John Peebles *foundation executive, educator*
Miller, Maurice Lim *cultural organization administrator*
Widener, Mary Lee *non-profit financial executive*

**Oceanside**
Roberts, James McGregor *retired trade association administrator*

**Oxnard**
Tolmach, Jane Louise *community activist, municipal official*

**Pacific Palisades**
Caster, Jacqueline Jacobs *not-for-profit executive*
Hubbs, Donald Harvey *foundation executive*
Snowhook, Ann Laferty *social services administrator*

**Palm Springs**
Ellsworth, Frank L. *not-for-profit executive*

**Palmdale**
Phillips, Ruthanne *special education administrator*

**Palo Alto**
Lee, Virginia Fern *community volunteer*
Nichols, William Ford, Jr. *foundation administrator, educator, health science association administrator*
Skoll, Jeffrey S. *philanthropist, former internet company executive*

**Pasadena**
Chen, Sandra Yi-Ting *political organization worker*

Staehle, Robert L. *foundation executive*

**Placentia**
Cash, Jeanie Maritta *educational association administrator*

**Rancho Mirage**
Wyatt, Lenore *civic worker*

**Rancho Palos Verdes**
Vanderlip, Elin Brekke *professional society administrator, volunteer*

**Redding**
Potter, James Vincent *association executive*

**Redwood City**
Spangler, Nita Reifschneider *volunteer*

**Riverside**
Bosse, Mark Thomas *social services administrator*
Peterson, Arthur Laverne *foundation administrator*
Smith, Richard Charles *not-for-profit administrator, educator, consultant, advocate*

**Sacramento**
Greene, Richard *association executive*
McFarland, Kevin John *foundation administrator*
Munitz, Barry *former arts and foundation administrator*
Ross, Jean M. *think-tank executive*
Vixie Sandy, Mary Dolores *educational association administrator*

**Salinas**
Chester, Lynne *foundation administrator, artist*

**San Andreas**
Breed, Allen Forbes *social services administrator*

**San Diego**
Ballinger, Charles Edwin *educational association administrator*
Grosser, T.J. *not-for-profit fundraiser*
Krejci, Robert Harry *not-for-profit developer, consultant*
Lane, Gloria Julian *foundation administrator*
Sheldon, Lois Elizabeth *social services administrator*
Van Schoik, D. Rick *think-tank executive*

**San Francisco**
Barzelatto, Jose S. *social welfare organization executive*
Bereuter, Douglas Kent *foundation administrator, former congressman*
Bitterman, Mary Gayle Foley *foundation executive*
Canales, James Earl, Jr. *foundation president*
Chang, Patti *foundation administrator*
Delaney, Martin *not-for-profit developer*
Eastham, Thomas *retired foundation administrator*
Egan, Patricia Jane *foundation administrator, retired director*
Fisher, Robert Morton *foundation administrator, academic administrator*
Gimon, Juliette *foundation administrator, volunteer*
Giovinco, Joseph *non profit agency administrator, writer*
Goldman, Richard N. *foundation administrator*
Guillermo, Tessie *foundation administrator*
Guttentag, Lucas *advocate, lawyer*
Kamm, John *non-profit organization administrator, human rights activist*
Liu, Hanmin *foundation administrator*
Martinez Tucker, Sara *educational association administrator*
Masaoka, Jan *not-for-profit executive*
Mattern, Douglas James *think-tank executive*
Meader, Keith Alan *social services administrator*
Mitchell, Theodore Reed *educational association administrator, former academic administrator*
Moore, Kenneth G. *foundation administrator, former manufacturing executive*
Moore, Steven E. *foundation administrator*
Penhoet, Edward *foundation administrator, former biochemicals company executive, former dean*
Pipes, Sally C. *think-tank executive*
Pope, Carl *environmental organization administrator*
Renstrom, Lisa *environmental organization administrator*
Soler, Esta *foundation administrator*
Steele, Shari *think-tank executive*
Tripp, Alan H. *educational association administrator, consultant*

**San Mateo**
Saldinger, Anne Grenn *cultural organization administrator, psychologist*

**San Rafael**
Burks, Rocky Alan *disability access coordinator, consultant*

**Santa Barbara**
McCoy, Lois Clark *retired social services administrator, retired county official, editor*
Rehm, Susan J. *social services professional*

**Santa Clarita**
Boyer, Carl III *not-for-profit developer, retired mayor, municipal official, secondary school educator*

**Santa Monica**
Baer, Walter S. *think-tank executive*
Foley, Jane Deborah *foundation executive*
Klowden, Michael Louis *think-tank executive*
Milken, Michael R. *think-tank executive, philanthropist*
Rich, Michael David *think-tank executive, lawyer*
Siart, William Eric Baxter *non-profit education organization administrator*
Thomson, James Alan *think-tank executive*

**Sherman Oaks**
Leighton, Carolyn *foundation administrator*

**Stanford**
Lyman, Richard Wall *foundation administrator, academic administrator, historian*

**Stinson Beach**
Metz, Mary Seawell *retired foundation administrator, retired academic administrator*

**Stockton**
McCarthy, Beverly Fitch *retired civic leader, educator*

**Studio City**
Frumkin, Simon *political organization worker, writer*

**Sylmar**
Froelich, Beverly Lorraine *foundation administrator*

**Temecula**
Betz, Martin G. *art association administrator*

**Valencia**
Anguiano, Lupe *advocate*

**Woodside**
Blum, Richard Hosmer Adams *foundation administrator, educator*

**Yorba Linda**
Stavropoulos, Rose Mary Grant *community activist, volunteer*

## COLORADO

**Aspen**
Bucksbaum, Melva *foundation administrator*

**Boulder**
Hayes, Richard Johnson *association executive, retired lawyer*
Heath, Josephine Ward *foundation administrator*
Hess, John Warren *professional society administrator*
Johnston, Laurance Scott *foundation director*
Johnstone, Sally Mac *educational association administrator, psychology educator*

**Broomfield**
Flanders, Eleanor Carlson *community volunteer*

**Centennial**
Bryan, A(lonzo) J(ay) *retired service club official*

**Colorado Springs**
Coppock, Richard Miles *retired not-for-profit administrator*
Hawley, Nanci Elizabeth *professional society administrator*
Killian, George Ernest *retired educational association administrator*
Miller, Zoya Dickins *civic worker, consultant*

**Denver**
Childears, Linda *foundation administrator*
Fujioka, Jo Ann Ota *educational association administrator, consultant*
Gates, Chris *not-for-profit developer, political organization worker*
Halaby, Theodore S. *political organization worker, retired lawyer*
Hogan, Curtis Jule *labor union administrator, industrial relations specialist, consultant*
Ittelson, Lane *foundation administrator*
Knaus, Tim *political organization administrator*
Low, Merry Cook *civic worker*
McConnell, John *environmental activist, founder of Earth Day*
Waak, Patricia Ann *political organization administrator, environmental association executive*

**Englewood**
Gloss, Lawrence Robert *fundraising executive*
Keesling, Ruth Morris *foundation administrator*
Lessey, Samuel Kenric, Jr. *foundation administrator*
Neiser, Brent Allen *foundation executive, public information educator, finance educator*

**Fort Collins**
Eddy, Gladys Louise *educational administrator*

**Greeley**
Bond, Richard Randolph *foundation administrator, legislator*
Schrenk, Gary Dale *foundation executive*

**Lakewood**
Isely, Henry Philip *association executive, integrative engineer, writer, educator*

**Littleton**
Keogh, Heidi Helen Dake *advocate*

**Loveland**
Rodman, Alpine C. *arts and crafts company executive, photographer*

**Mancos**
Brown, Joy Alice *social services administrator*

## CONNECTICUT

**Avon**
Griggs, Julie Hinds *foundation administrator, marriage and family therapist*

**Branford**
Resnick, Idrian Navarre *foundation administrator*

**Bridgeport**
Pagano, Celeste Ann *social services coordinator*

**Danbury**
Meyers, Abbey S. *foundation administrator*

**Darien**
Penrose, Charles, Jr. *professional society administrator*

**East Hartford**
Chatell, Roger Armand *youth agency executive, camp director*

**Fairfield**
Shelton, Carolyn Johnson *professional society administrator*

**Falls Village**
Toomey, Jeanne Elizabeth *animal activist*

**Greenwich**
Bjornson, Edith Cameron *foundation administrator, communications consultant*
Kovner, Kathleen Jane *civic worker, portrait artist*
Russell, William Edwards, IV, *educational association administrator, researcher*
Stauffer, Valerie Vilas *civic volunteer*

**Groton**
Kennedy, Evelyn Siefert *foundation executive, textiles executive*

**Guilford**
Stevens, Lydia Hastings *community volunteer*

**Hartford**
Apruzzese, Philip John *educational association administrator, educator*
Decko, Kenneth Owen *trade association administrator*
Dumond, Mara Germaine *educational administrator, literacy facilitator*
Eshoo, Barbara Anne Rudolph *non-profit administrator*

**Meriden**
Larson, Alvin Frederick *educational association administrator, researcher*

**New Canaan**
Brakeley, George Archibald, Jr. *fundraising consultant*
Giusti, Kathy *foundation administrator*
McNamara, Francis Joseph, Jr. *retired foundation executive, lawyer*

**New Haven**
Anderson, Carl Albert *fraternal organization administrator, lawyer, dean*
Singer, Jon Douglas *foundation administrator, writer*

**Newington**
Sumner, David George *association executive*

**Newtown**
Forger, Robert Durkin *retired professional association administrator*

**North Branford**
Houghton, Alan Nourse *educational association administrator, consultant*
Logan, John Arthur, Jr. *retired foundation executive*

**Riverside**
Coulson, Robert *retired professional society administrator, arbitrator, writer*

**Roxbury**
Styron, Rose *human rights activist, poet, journalist*

**Stamford**
Chisholm, Andrea Lynne *trade association administrator, foundation administrator*
Peterson, Elizabeth Holly *art association administrator*
Stillings, Irene Ella Grace Cordiner *retired foundation executive*

**Trumbull**
Norcel, Jacqueline Joyce Casale *educational association administrator*

**Vernon Rockville**
Roden, Jon-Paul *retired educator, labor union organizer, educational consultant*

**Waterbury**
Harper, Barbara Clara *educational program administrator, counselor*

**Westport**
MacCormack, Charles Frederick *international relief organization executive*

**Wilton**
Kaskell, Peter Howard *professional society administrator, lawyer*

## DELAWARE

**Lewes**
Spence, Sandra *retired professional society administrator*
Warden, Richard Dana *government labor union official*

**Rehoboth Beach**
Magazine, Alan Harrison *association executive, consultant*

**Wilmington**
Emmert, Richard Eugene *retired industrial and professional association executive*
Fleming, Blanche Miles *educational association administrator*

**Palm Beach**
Elson, Suzanne Goodman *social services administrator*
Hope, Margaret Lauten *retired civic worker*
Levine, Audrey Pearlstein *foundation administrator*
Rinker, Ruby Stewart *foundation administrator*

**Palm Beach Gardens**
Falk, Bernard Henry *trade association executive*

**Palm Coast**
Boyer, Kaye Kittle *association management executive*
Cook, Gloria Houston *civic leader*

**Ponte Vedra Beach**
Slayton, Gus *foundation administrator*
Watson, John Lawrence III *former trade association executive*

**Port Orange**
Collyer, Robert B. *trade association administrator*

**Saint Petersburg**
Allshouse, Merle Frederick *educational organization administrator*
Benham, Emily *fundraiser*

**Sanibel**
Ball, Armand Baer *former association executive, consultant*

**Sarasota**
Boersma, Lawrence Allan (Larry Allan) *animal welfare administrator, photographer*
Culkin, Charles Walker, Jr. *retired trade association administrator*

**Sun City Center**
Kochanski, Lois Whidden *foundation administrator*

**Tallahassee**
Humphrey, Louise Ireland *civic worker, equestrienne*
Turnbull, Marjorie Reitz *foundation executive, retired state legislator*
Yecke, Cheri Pierson *educational researcher, administrator, columnist, writer*

**Tampa**
Milito, Connie Marie *education administrator, government relations administrator*

**West Palm Beach**
Coppock, Mark Stephen *not-for-profit executive*

**Wilton Manors**
Kaufmann, Vicki Marie *social services administrator*

**Winter Park**
Kaston, Lisa Marsha *social services administrator*
Olsson, Nils William *former association executive*

**GEORGIA**

**Americus**
Palmer, Edward Kent *charitable organization executive*

**Athens**
Algeo, John Thomas *association executive, retired educator*

**Atlanta**
Anthony, Barbara Cox *foundation administrator*
Bankoff, Joseph R. *art association administrator*
Birdsong, Alta Marie *volunteer*
Copenhaver, John Barns *not-for-profit executive, lawyer*
Dotson, Albert *not-for-profit fundraiser*
Finley, Michael Valton *foundation executive*
Goizueta, Olga (Olga Casteleiro de Goizueta) *foundation administrator, philanthropist*
Hopping, Janet Melinda *educational association administrator*
Hough, Leslie Seldon *educational association administrator*
King, Dexter Scott *foundation administrator*
Lynch, Kevin Anthony *educational association administrator*
McTier, Charles Harvey *foundation administrator*
Spillett, Roxanne *social services administrator*
Steele, Charles, Jr. *civil rights association executive, former state legislator*
Tillman, Mary Norman *urban affairs consultant*
Weatherly, Alvis Morrison, Jr. *retired association developer*

**Decatur**
Grace, George H. *not-for-profit fundraiser*
Wheelan, Belle S. *educational association administrator*

**Macon**
Knight Olson, Beverly *foundation administrator*

**Marietta**
Anderson, Vanessa Alferea *educational association administrator*
Kelly, William Watkins *educational association executive*

**Peachtree City**
Nix, Kemie Richards *educational association administrator, editor*

**Roswell**
Polatty, Rose Jackson *civic worker*

**Saint Simons Island**
Bell, Ronald Mack *university foundation administrator, consultant*

**Savannah**
Gillespie, Daniel Curtis, Sr. *retired not-for-profit developer*

**HAWAII**

**Honolulu**
Cooke, Mary Moragne *volunteer*
Hack, Randolph C. *advocate, educator, counselor*
Morrison, Charles E. *think-tank executive*
Ogburn, Nancy Wrenn *civic volunteer*
Ramler, Siegfried *foundation administrator*
Robinson, Robert Blacque *foundation administrator*
White, Emmet, Jr. *retirement community administrator*

**Kailua Kona**
Iolana, Patricia Elvira *foundation administrator, consultant*

**Kapolei**
Moriyama, Karen Ito *educational association administrator*

**Naalehu**
Carroll, Mary Colvert *not-for-profit developer, consultant*

**Volcano**
Nicholson, Marilyn Lee *arts administrator*

**IDAHO**

**Boise**
Boyce, Carolyn *political organization administrator*

**Moscow**
Fiske, Janet Morray *volunteer, elementary school educator, researcher*

**ILLINOIS**

**Barrington**
Worrell, Sharyn Dianne *volunteer, retired flight attendant*

**Belvidere**
Luhman, William Simon *community development administrator*

**Carlinville**
Bellm, Joan *civic worker*

**Chicago**
Becker, Heather Shawn *art association administrator, artist*
Berkson, Sadie *volunteer*
Bourdon, Cathleen Jane *professional society administrator*
Brown, Elizabeth McCarthy *social services administrator*
Chacko, Samuel *association official*
Craine, Thomas Knowlton *not-for-profit developer*
Dolan, Thomas Christopher *professional society administrator*
Dull, Charles C. *educational association administrator*
Fanton, Jonathan Foster *foundation administrator*
Fleming, Brian Elliott *social services administrator*
Froetscher, Janet *social services administrator*
Heineman, Natalie (Mrs. Ben W. Heineman) *civic worker*
Hodge, Linda M. *former educational association administrator*
Hurd, Jennifer Jacoby *not-for-profit executive*
Jackson, Jesse Louis *political organization worker, clergyman*
Johnson, Gary Thomas *cultural organization administrator*
Jones, Mary Laura *not-for-profit developer*
Kelly, Jerry Bob *social services administrator*
King, Quintin L. *trade association administrator, lobbyist*
Knapp, Paul Raymond *think-tank executive*
Lies, Valerie Sharp *foundation administrator*
MacDougal, Gary Edward *corporate board member, foundation trustee*
Mazany, Terry *foundation administrator*
McDonald, William Brice *educational association administrator*
Minow, Josephine Baskin *civic volunteer*
Olsen, Rex Norman *trade association executive*
Richman, Harold Alan *social welfare policy educator*
Scherer, Karla *foundation executive, venture capitalist*
Shanahan, Betty *professional society administrator*
Sigmon, Joyce Elizabeth *professional society administrator*
Simmons, Adele Smith *foundation executive, former educator*
Strauss, Deborah *foundation administrator*
Thomas, Barbara L. *not-for-profit executive*
Weselak, Anna Marie Schmidt *educational association administrator, media consultant*
White, Linda Marie *former fraternal organization administrator*
Wilson, Cleo Francine *foundation administrator*

**Clarendon Hills**
Choice, Priscilla Kathryn Means (Penny Choice) *retired educational association administrator*

**Crystal Lake**
Chamberlain, Charles James *railroad labor union executive*

**Evanston**
Gordon, Julie Peyton *foundation administrator*
Lewis, Charles A. *foundation administrator*
Rielly, John Edward *educational association administrator*

**Thrash**, Patricia Ann *retired educational association administrator*

**Galena**
Sipiera, Paul P., Jr. *foundation administrator, retired geology and astronomy professor*

**Hazel Crest**
Freed, Melvyn Norris *retired educational association administrator, writer*

**Jacksonville**
Mathews, Jack Sherman *foundation administrator, retired insurance company executive*

**Lake Forest**
Morell, William Nelson, Jr. *foreign trade association executive, government agency administrator*

**Matteson**
Garrett-Wilson, Shirlyn Maria *social services administrator*

**Northbrook**
Siegal, Judy A. *social services administrator*

**Oak Brook**
John, Richard C. *enterprise development organization executive*

**Ottawa**
Thornton, Edmund B. *philanthropist*

**Rosemont**
Good, William Allen *professional society executive*

**Schaumburg**
Little, Bruce Washington *professional society administrator*
Tompson, Marian Leonard *professional society administrator*

**Skokie**
Gleason, John Patrick, Jr. *trade association executive*
Polus Gerstner, Lillian *educational association administrator, director*
Weidmann, K. Timothy *not-for-profit fundraiser, writer*

**Sterling**
Fitzgerald, Carol J. *foundation administrator, not-for-profit organization administrator*

**Sycamore**
Stone, Van Courtright *not-for-profit developer*

**Waukegan**
Drapalik, Betty R. *volunteer, artist, educator*

**Wilmette**
Brink, Marion Francis *trade association administrator*

**INDIANA**

**Bloomington**
Brinkman, Paul Del(bert) *retired foundation administrator, journalist, educator*
Mobley, Tony Allen *foundation administrator, former dean, recreation educator*
Wells, Kimberly K. *not-for-profit organization executive*

**Fort Wayne**
Walda, John D. *educational association administrator, lawyer*

**Indianapolis**
Alvarez, Thomas *foundation administrator, writer, consultant, film producer*
Barcus, Robert Gene *retired educational association administrator*
Braun, Robert Clare *retired association and advertising executive*
Finley, Katherine Mandusic *professional society administrator*
Lilly, Ruth E. *philanthropist*
Matthews, Dewayne *foundation administrator*
Mutz, John Massie *foundation administrator, former state official, former energy executive*
Robbins, N. Clay *foundation administrator*
Sweezy, John William *political party official*
Tempel, Eugene Raymond (Gene Tempel) *foundation administrator, speaker, researcher*
Vereen, Robert Charles *retired trade association administrator*

**Lawrenceburg**
Edwards, Marie D. *social services administrator*

**North Manchester**
Mason, Stephen Olin *not-for-profit developer*

**Terre Haute**
Aldridge, Sandra *civic volunteer*

**West Lafayette**
Baumgardt, Billy Ray *professional society administrator, agriculturist*

**IOWA**

**Cedar Rapids**
Arnold-Olson, Helen B. *not-for-profit consultant*
Whipple, William Perry *foundation administrator*

**Des Moines**
McGuire-Riggs, Sheila *Democratic party chairman*

**Fairfield**
Hagelin, John Samuel *political organization administrator, theoretical physicist*

**Holstein**
Soseman, Eleanor Douglass *volunteer*

**Sioux City**
Waller, Ephraim Everett *retired association executive*

**KANSAS**

**Kansas City**
Jones, Charles W. *labor union executive*

**Lawrence**
Wiechert, Allen LeRoy *educational association administrator*

**Shawnee**
Wilson, Eugene Rolland *retired foundation executive*

**Shawnee Mission**
Green, John Lafayette, Jr. *educational association administrator*

**Topeka**
Frahm, Sheila *association executive, academic administrator, former government official*
Perry, Nancy *foundation administrator*

**Wichita**
Rueb, Sheree A. *social services administrator*
Vliet, Marni *foundation administrator*

**Winfield**
Gray, Ina Turner *fraternal organization administrator*

**KENTUCKY**

**Corbin**
Barton-Collings, Nelda Ann *political organization worker, bank executive*

**Florence**
Gorman, Gayla Marlene Osborne *consumer affairs executive*

**Lexington**
Lewis, Robert Kay, Jr. *fundraising executive*
Sexton, Robert Fenimore *educational organization executive*

**Louisville**
Appleberry, James Bruce *educational association administrator*
Early, Jack Jones *foundation executive*
Zepeda, Susan Ghozeil *foundation administrator*

**LOUISIANA**

**Baton Rouge**
Davis, Carol *educational association administrator, educator*

**Mandeville**
Landry, Joseph L., Jr. *retired affirmative action specialist*

**New Orleans**
Mbadugha, Loretta Nkeiruka Akosa *social services administrator, consultant*
Teamer, Charles Carl, Sr. *former fraternal organization administrator*

**MAINE**

**Augusta**
Gervais, Paul Nelson *foundation administrator, psychotherapist, writer, public relations executive*

**Bangor**
Coffman, Michael S. *international organization official, ecologist*

**Falmouth**
Hathaway, Lynn McDonald *education advocate, administrator*

**Georgetown**
Chapin, Maryan Fox *civic worker*

**Portland**
Haddad, Freddie Duke, Jr. *not-for-profit fundraiser, consultant*

**South Portland**
Harris, Penny Smith *fundraising consultant*

**Topsham**
Rosser, Richard Franklin *educational association administrator, consultant*

**Waterford**
Stockwell, William F. *not-for-profit fundraiser, consultant*

**York**
Smart, Mary-Leigh Call (Mrs. J. Scott Smart) *civic worker*

**MARYLAND**

**Annapolis**
Erskine, Janis *educational association administrator*

**Baltimore**
Brock, Roslyn McCallister *association executive*
Coleman, Carolyn Quilloin *association executive*
Fuentealba, Victor William *professional society administrator*

Gordon, Bruce S. *civil rights organization executive, former telecommunications company executive*
Hayes, Dennis Courtland *civil rights association executive, lawyer*
Leonard, Joseph Howard *staff specialist*
Mfume, Kweisi *civil rights association executive, former congressman*
Nelson, Douglas W. *foundation administrator*
Pinkard, Anne Merrick *foundation administrator*

**Bel Air**
Thursfield, Fred Falconer, II, *foundation administrator*

**Belcamp**
Tapp, Mamie Pearl *educational association administrator*

**Bethesda**
Beall, Robert Joseph *foundation executive*
Cleary, Timothy Finbar *professional society administrator*
Day, Robert Dwain, Jr. *foundation administrator, lawyer*
Dulin, Maurine Stuart *volunteer*
Grau, John Michael *trade association executive*
Kavanaugh, Everett Edward, Jr. *trade association executive*
Metzger, Henry *federal research institution administrator*
Reed, Berenice Anne *cultural organization administrator, educator, artist*
Salisbury, Tamara Paula *foundation executive*
Saunders, Charles Baskerville, Jr. *retired association executive*
Sprott, Richard Lawrence *foundation administrator, researcher*
Stone, Jeremy Judah *professional society administrator*

**Bowie**
Caire, Kaleem (Michael) Steven *not-for-profit fundraiser*
Littlefield, Roy Everett III *association executive, law educator*

**California**
Powell, Melchior Daniel *educational administrator, lawyer*

**Chevy Chase**
Hunt, Frederick Talley Drum, Jr. *association executive*

**College Park**
Brazile, Donna *advocate*
Khoury, Bernard V. *educational administrator*
Murdoch, Amelia Clara *educational association administrator*
Stover, Carl Frederick *foundation executive*

**Columbia**
Gray, Kirk Lamond *social investment firm executive, anthropologist*
Purcell, James Nelson, Jr. *cultural organization administrator*
Rogers, Thomas Francis *foundation administrator*

**Crofton**
Ross, E(dwin) Clarke *association executive, educator*

**Damascus**
Nelligan, William David III *professional association executive*

**Derwood**
Crawford, Stephen *think tank executive*

**Gambrills**
Messner, Howard Myron *professional association executive*

**Greenbelt**
Matthews, Darryl R., Sr. *not-for-profit fundraiser*
Miller, Alwin Vermar *educational association administrator, consultant*

**Kensington**
Mintz, Suzanne *association executive*

**Largo**
Ryan, Carol J. *educational administrator*

**Lusby**
Sprague, Edward Auchincloss *retired professional society administrator, economist*

**Mitchellville**
Ball, Robert M(yers) *retired social security, welfare and health policy specialist, writer, lecturer*

**North Bethesda**
Sherman, Deane Murray *culture organization administrator*

**Potomac**
Ingram, Richard Thomas *retired educational association executive, consultant*
Johnson, Anne Hale *educational association administrator, director*
Keefe, Arthur Thomas III *non-profit fund raising executive*
Rosenberg, Sarah Zacher *retired cultural organization administrator*

**Rockville**
Bardack, Paul Roitman *cultural organization administrator*
Futrovsky, Cheryl Jean *foundation administrator, performing company executive*
Grandy, Fred *foundation administrator, former congressman, former actor*
Kline, Raymond Adam *professional organization executive*
Marcuccio, Phyllis Rose *retired educational association administrator, editor*

**Severna Park**
Hall, Marcia Joy *non-profit organization administrator*

**Silver Spring**
Baskerville, Lezli *educational association administrator*
Fockler, Herbert Hill *foundation executive*
Fustero, Robert Raymond *retired political organization worker*
Gandy, Kim Allison *feminist organization executive, lawyer*
Hayman, Harry *professional society administrator, electrical engineer*
Hong Duc, Duong *economic development company executive*
Smedley, Lawrence Thomas *retired organization executive*
Winston, Michael Russell *foundation executive, historian*

**Stevenson**
Middendorf, Alice Carter *volunteer*

**Stevensville**
Engel, Bradford Charles *educational association administrator, secondary school educator*

**Upper Marlboro**
Buffenbarger, Thomas (R. Thomas Buffenbarger, Robert Thomas Buffenbarger) *labor union administrator*

**Waldorf**
Raiman, Rosemary A. *advocate*

## MASSACHUSETTS

**Amherst**
MacKnight, Carol Bernier *educational association administrator*

**Belmont**
Harris, William Wolpert *foundation administrator*

**Boston**
Cabot, Louis Wellington *foundation trustee*
Deissler, Mary Alice *foundation executive*
DiGiustini, Antonetta Anna *educational association administrator, educator*
Grogan, Paul Stanley *foundation administrator*
Katsoulomitis, Georgia *foundation administrator, lawyer*
Knight, Norman *volunteer, retired broadcast executive*
Meisner, Mary Jo *foundation administrator, former newspaper editor*
Trumbull, David Lewis Kitchen *trade association executive*

**Brookfield**
Couture, Ronald David *art association administrator, web site designer, consultant*

**Cambridge**
Berlowitz, Leslie *cultural organization administrator*
Lee, Barbara *political activist, foundation administrator*
Rensberger, Boyce *science journalism fellowship program administrator*
Shaheen, C. Jeanne *political organization administrator, former governor*
White, Shelby *art association administrator*

**Dedham**
Frazier, Ronald F. *non-profit association administrator*

**Dorchester**
Smith, Survilla Marie *social services administrator, artist, poet*

**Framingham**
Harrington, Joseph Francis *educational company executive, history educator*

**Greenfield**
Hutcheson, Thomas Worthington *trade association administrator*

**Groton**
Anthony, Sylvia *social welfare organization executive*

**Hull**
Anderson, Timothy Christopher *educational association administrator*

**Ipswich**
Munro, Donald William, Jr. *non-profit organization executive*
Wilson, Doris H. *volunteer*

**Lexington**
Garing, Ione Davis *civic worker*

**Malden**
Guild, Richard Samuel *trade association management company executive*

**Marion**
McPartland, Patricia Ann *educational association administrator, health educator*

**Medfield**
Phillips, Marion Grumman *civic volunteer, writer*

**New Bedford**
Bullard, John Kilburn *educational association administrator*

**Pittsfield**
Wenner, Gene Charles *arts management executive*

**Quincy**
Holway, David J. *labor union administrator*

Wilson, Blenda Jacqueline *foundation administrator*

**Sharon**
Reilley, Dennen *research agency administrator, educator*

**Southborough**
Warren, John Coolidge *educational administrator*

**Wayland**
Humphrey, Diana Young *fundraiser*

**Wellesley**
Fuccillo, Ralph *foundation administrator, consultant*

**Weston**
Daly, Charles Ulick *foundation executive*

**Winchester**
Reno, John F. *foundation administrator*

## MICHIGAN

**Ann Arbor**
Diana, Joseph A. *retired foundation executive*
Elliott, Cheryl *foundation president*
Guardo, Carol J. *association executive*
Kennedy, David Boyd *foundation executive, lawyer*
Ware, Richard Anderson *foundation executive*

**Battle Creek**
Bowser, Shirley *volunteer*
Davis, Laura Arlene *retired foundation administrator*
Speirn, Sterling K. *foundation administrator*

**Belmont**
Powers, Linda S. *art association administrator*

**Detroit**
Cooke, William Nelson *labor management professor, consultant*
Gettelfinger, Ron *labor union administrator*
Neithercut, Mark Edward *foundation consultant*
Noland, Mariam Charl *foundation executive*

**Dowagiac**
Murphy, Ellis *association management executive*

**Flint**
Belcher, Max *social services administrator, dean*
Maynard, Olivia P. *foundation administrator*
Munerlyn, Lorraine *foundation administrator*
White, William Samuel *foundation executive*

**Grand Haven**
Johnson, Dorothy A. *foundation administrator*

**Grand Rapids**
Jones, Ora McConner *retired foundation administrator*
Paterson, Hattie P *philanthropist*
Sieger, Diana R. *foundation administrator*

**Kalamazoo**
Petersen, Anne C. (Cheryl Petersen) *foundation administrator, educator*

**Mount Clemens**
Gielniak, Michael Gerard *non-profit executive, education consultant*

**Saint Clair Shores**
Smith, Frank Earl *retired trade association administrator*

**Sterling Heights**
Fleming, Mac Arthur *retired labor union administrator*

**Traverse City**
Bullis, Jo Louise *social services administrator, educator*

**Troy**
Marshall, John Elbert III *foundation executive*
Rapson, Richard (Rip Rapson) *foundation administrator*

**Waterford**
Laing, James Thomas *retired not-for-profit developer*

**Ypsilanti**
Peoples, Alice Leigh *not-for-profit executive*

## MINNESOTA

**Lake Lillian**
Marquardt, Steve Robert *advocate*

**Minneapolis**
Binger, Erika L. *foundation administrator*
Birk, Peggy J. *foundation administrator*
Herbison, Priscilla Joan *social services administrator, law educator*
Johnson, John Warren *retired professional society administrator*
Leuchovius, Deborah *advocate, special education services professional, consultant*

**Rochester**
Riggs, Jeanette Templeton *civic worker*

**Saint Cloud**
Prout, Robert Stephen *higher education consultant, law enforcement consultant*

**Saint Paul**
Eibensteiner, Ron *political organization administrator, venture capitalist*
Kurtz, Harold Paul *foundation executive*
Pampusch, Anita Marie *foundation administrator*

Pratt, Jon *not-for-profit executive*
Skillingstad, Constance Yvonne *social services administrator, educator*
Stauber, Karl Neill *foundation administrator*

**White Earth**
Vizenor, Erma J. *Native American tribal leader*

## MISSISSIPPI

**Clarksdale**
Lucy, William (Bill Lucy) *labor union administrator*

**Crystal Springs**
Bates, Lura Wheeler *retired trade association administrator*

**Fayette**
La Salle, Arthur Edward *historic foundation executive*

**Jackson**
Hendrix, Albert Randel *social services administrator*
Risley, Rod Alan *educational association administrator*
Sullivan, Bettye Yarborough *foundation administrator*

**Tougaloo**
Whittington, Felicia Trenise *social services administrator, educator*

## MISSOURI

**Ballwin**
Pallozola, Christine *not-for-profit executive*

**Bridgeton**
Kenison, Raymond Robert *fraternal organization administrator, director*

**Chesterfield**
Diamandis, Peter H. *foundation administrator*

**Columbia**
Brushwood, Mack Lewis *labor union administrator*
Dreier, Keith Lynn *not-for-profit fundraiser*
McDermott, Dennis Michael *trade association executive*

**Earth City**
Anderhalter, Oliver Frank *educational organization executive*

**Kansas City**
Bugher, Robert Dean *professional society administrator*
Schramm, Carl J. *foundation administrator*
Vowell, Karma *arts organization fundraiser*

**Lees Summit**
Carter, William Gerald *non-profit corporation executive*

**Moline Acres**
Hinton, Velecia Ann *social welfare administrator*

**Rolla**
Bagnall, Lindsay Lomax *not-for-profit executive*

**Saint Louis**
Bascom, C. Perry *retired foundation administrator*
Brauer, Camilla Thompson (Kimmy Thompson Brauer) *civic leader*
Duhme, Carol McCarthy *civic worker*
Fletcher, Bill, Jr. *political organization executive, activist*
Hunter, Earle Leslie III *retired professional association executive*
Kimmey, James Richard, Jr. *foundation administrator*
Pope, Robert E(ugene) *fraternal organization administrator*
Winter, Mildred M. *educational administrator*

**Springfield**
O'Block, Robert *association executive, publishing executive*

## MONTANA

**Billings**
Sample, Joseph Scanlon *foundation executive*

**Browning**
Thomas, Patrick *Native American tribal leader*

**Manhattan**
Sanddal, Nels Dodge *foundation executive, consultant*

## NEBRASKA

**Harrison**
Coffee, Virginia Claire *civic worker, former mayor*

**Lincoln**
Hardin, Martha Love Wood *civic leader*
Rosenow, John Edward *foundation executive*

**Omaha**
Strawhecker, Paul Joseph *fundraising consultant*

## NEVADA

**Carson City**
Ayres, Janice Ruth *social services administrator*
Gates, Bermira *not-for-profit developer, director*

**Henderson**
Freyd, William Pattinson *not-for-profit fundraiser, director*

**Incline Village**
Johnston, Bernard Fox *foundation executive, writer*

**Las Vegas**
Carnes, Zandy *trade association administrator*
Manley, Edward Harry, Jr. *professional association administrator, food products executive, retired military officer*
Martinez, Adriana *political organization worker, photographer*
Nicholson, R. Stephen *former cultural organization administrator*
Spencer, Carol Brown *retired educational association administrator*

**NEW HAMPSHIRE**

**Concord**
Chaney, Michael Parker *not-for-profit developer, writer*

**Dover**
Nelson, Michael Underhill *educational association administrator*

**Peterborough**
Eppes, William David *arts and humanities advocate*

**Pike**
Teschner, Douglass Paul *project administrator*

**NEW JERSEY**

**Atlantic City**
Jamieson, John Edward, Jr. *social services administrator, minister*

**Basking Ridge**
Probert, Edward Whitford *foundation executive, volunteer*

**Bernardsville**
Cooperman, Saul *retired educational association administrator*

**Glen Ridge**
Pendley, Donald Lee *association executive*

**Glen Rock**
D'Angelo, Thomas J. *not-for-profit developer, financial consultant*

**Highland Park**
Kolodzei, Natalia A. *art association administrator, art historian, curator*

**Millburn**
Tinning, Herbert Peter *association executive*

**Montclair**
Campbell, Stewart Fred *foundation administrator, consultant*

**New Brunswick**
Bunch, Charlotte *advocate*

**New Vernon**
Dugan, John Leslie, Jr. *foundation executive*

**Paramus**
Noguere, Suzanne *trade association administrator, poet*

**Paterson**
Radke, Stephen Lewis *social services administrator*

**Pennington**
Calvo, Roque John *professional society administrator*

**Plainfield**
Limpert, John H., Jr. *fund raising executive*

**Princeton**
Balch, Stephen Howard *professional society administrator*
Bland, Calvin *foundation administrator*
De Lung, Jane Solberger *independent sector executive*
Hughes, Robert G. *foundation administrator*
Jeffers, Beverly Maynard *volunteer*
Johnson, Barbara Piasecka *volunteer, art historian, investor*
Kassof, Allen H. *foundation administrator*
Kenyon, Regan Clair *educational research executive*
Landgraf, Kurt M. *educational association administrator*
Pechura, Constance Mary *foundation administrator*
Plaks, Livia Basch *foundation executive*
Silverman, Jane Aresty *not-for-profit organizational consultant*

**Red Bank**
Hearth, Blair Anthony *fundraiser, clergyman*

**Rumson**
Brenner, Theodore Engelbert *retired trade association administrator*
Swartz, Renee Becker *civic volunteer*

**Shiloh**
Garrison, John Raymond *organization executive*

**Skillman**
Rhett, Haskell Emery Smith *educational association administrator*

**Summit**
D'Alessandro, Mari Angelina *art association administrator*

**Trenton**
Binder, Elaine Kotell *associations consultant*

**Union Beach**
Gilmartin, Clara T. *volunteer*

**West Caldwell**
Giblin, Thomas Patrick *labor union administrator, political organization administrator*

**West Orange**
Rinsky, Judith Sue Lynn *foundation administrator, educator consultant*

**NEW MEXICO**

**Bernalillo**
Paisano, Stuwart *Native American tribal leader*

**Rio Rancho**
Norman, Phyllis B. *volunteer*

**Santa Fe**
Miller-Engel, Marjorie *foundation administrator, commissioner, small business owner*

**NEW YORK**

**Akwesasne**
Ransom, James W. *Native American tribal leader*

**Albany**
Huxley, Carole Frances Corcoran *educational association administrator*

**Amherst**
Clark, Donald Malin *professional association executive*

**Bayside**
Madden, Joseph Daniel *trade association executive*

**Briarcliff Manor**
Read, John Conyers *non-profit company executive*

**Brooklyn**
Horowitz, Sara *labor organizer*
Morgan, Mary Louise Fitzsimmons *fund raising executive, lobbyist*
Pickens, Schanica Lynn *homefinding supervisor, online educator*
Werner, Judith *not-for-profit developer, literature educator*
Wilson, Robert Warne *philanthropist*

**Buffalo**
Clarkson, Elisabeth Ann Hudnut *volunteer*
Ezzo, David Alber *not-for-profit developer, anthropologist*
Harvey, Steven John *not-for-profit developer*
Hunt, Jane Helfrich *volunteer*
Spengler, Paul Albert *grants and foundation administrator*

**Centereach**
Chassman, Karen Moss *educational association administrator*

**Clarence**
Stringer, Gretchen Engstrom *consulting volunteer administrator*

**Commack**
Price, Amelia Ruth *not-for-profit foundation president, artist, small business owner*

**Corning**
Cicerchi, Eleanor Ann Tomb *not-for-profit fundraiser*

**Dobbs Ferry**
Sutton, Francis Xavier *social services administrator, consultant*

**Flushing**
Fichtel, Rudolph Robert *retired association executive*
Li, Hongzhi *foundation administrator, writer*

**Freeport**
Walker, Lula Noriega *educational association administrator*

**Glenmont**
Bellizzi, John J. *law enforcement association administrator, pharmacist, educator*

**Harrison**
Wadsworth, Frank Whittemore *foundation administrator, literature educator*

**Hastings On Hudson**
Cassella, William Nathan, Jr. *retired not-for-profit organization executive*

**Hudson**
Miner, Jacqueline *political consultant*

**Irving**
Snyder, Barry E., Sr. *Native American tribal leader*

**Larchmont**
Hinerfeld, Ruth G. *civic organization executive*

**Lewiston**
Henry, Leo R. *Native American tribal leader*

**Manhasset**
Foerst, John George, Jr. *retired fundraising executive*

**Montauk**
Butler, Thomas William *retired health and social services administrator*

**New Rochelle**
Black, Page Morton *civic worker, vocalist, musician*

**New York**
Acevedo Marte, Matin *political organization worker*
Ackerman, Lisa Marilyn *foundation administrator, consultant*
Alex, Paula Ann *foundation administrator*
Anderson, Richard Theodore *trade association administrator, urban planner*
Annan, Kofi A. *Secretary General of the United Nations*
Ashley, Dwayne *not-for-profit fundraiser*
Atkins, Veronica *philanthropist*
Baird, Zoë *foundation administrator, lawyer*
Beardsley, Theodore S(terling), Jr. *professional society administrator*
Belknap, Norton *foundation administrator*
Bergman, Charles Cabe *foundation executive*
Berman, Greg *think-tank executive*
Berresford, Susan Vail *not-for-profit developer*
Bischoff, Theresa Ann *not-for-profit association executive*
Bolton, John Robert *international organization official, former federal agency administrator*
Bowen, William Gordon *foundation administrator, economist*
Brown, Mark Malloch *international organization official*
Brown, Terrence Charles *art association executive, researcher, lecturer*
Brownstein, Alan P. *health foundation executive, consultant*
Buckman, Thomas Richard *foundation executive, educator*
Burnham, Christopher Bancroft *international organization official, former federal agency administrator*
Cahan, Cora *not-for-profit developer*
Calhoun, Craig Jackson *social scientist, educator*
Canada, Geoffrey *social welfare administrator, writer*
Caputo, Lucio *trade company executive*
Carlson, Donna *art association administrator, director*
Cassullo, Joanne Leonhardt *foundation administrator*
Catley-Carlson, Margaret *not-for-profit executive*
Cavanagh, Richard Edward *non-profit executive*
Chapin, Schuyler Garrison *retired cultural organization administrator, retired dean*
Chen, Lucia *foundation administrator*
Christensen, Kathleen Elizabeth *foundation administrator*
Conarroe, Joel Osborne *foundation administrator, educator, editor*
Connor, W. Robert (Walter Robert Connor) *foundation administrator, classicist, educator*
Cox, Larry *human rights organization executive*
Dajani, Virginia *art association administrator*
Dauer, Sheila A. *human rights program director*
Davis, Kathryn Wasserman *foundation executive, educator, writer*
de La Sabliere, Jean-Marc *international organization official*
Dennis, Everette Eugene, Jr. *foundation executive, educator, writer*
DeVita, M. Christine *foundation administrator*
Diggins, Peter Sheehan *arts administrator*
Dykstra, Gretchen *foundation administrator*
Easum, Donald Boyd *consultant, educator, former institute executive, diplomat*
Elliott, Eleanor Thomas *foundation executive, volunteer*
Ellis, Ross *non-profit organization executive*
Fehr, Donald M. *baseball union executive*
Flicker, John *foundation executive*
Fontaine, John C. *foundation administrator, lawyer, former newspaper company executive*
Fox, Daniel Michael *foundation executive, writer*
Frost, William Lee *foundation executive*
Gallagher, Edward Peter *foundation administrator*
Giuliani, Judith *not-for-profit executive*
Goodwin, Michael *labor union administrator*
Grayer, Jonathan *education company executive*
Green, Micah S. *trade association administrator*
Gregorian, Vartan *foundation administrator*
Grimaldi, Nicholas Lawrence *fundraising executive*
Guehenno, Jean Marie *international organization official*
Haase, Leif Wellington *foundation administrator*
Harris, David Alan *not-for-profit organization executive*
Hedgpeth, Kim Roberts *trade association administrator*
Henry, Frederick B. *foundation administrator*
Hesselbein, Frances Richards *foundation administrator, writer, editor*
Heyzer, Noeleen *international organization official*
Hill, Janine *think-tank associate*
Hoffman, Linda R. *social services administrator*
Howard, David *retired association administrator*
Innis, Roy Emile Alfredo *foundation executive*
Iselin, John Jay *foundation president*
Jackson McCabe, Jewell *not-for-profit developer*
Jacobsen, Theodore H. (Ted H. Jacobsen) *labor union administrator, secondary school educator*
Jones, David R. *not-for-profit executive*
Kaggen, Lois Sheila *non-profit organization executive, advocate*
Kasirer, Suri *lobbyist*
Katzowitz Shenfield, Lauren *philanthropy consultant*
Keithley, Carter *trade association administrator*
Kopp, Wendy *educational association administrator*
Kriegel, Jay L. *Olympic organizing committee executive, public relations executive*
Kuyper, Joan Carolyn *foundation administrator*
Labunski, Stephen Bronislaw *professional society administrator*
Larberg, John Frederick *retired social welfare executive, wine consultant, educator*

Lauder, Jo Carole *art association administrator*
Laurence, Michael Marshall *foundation administrator*
Lawson-Johnston, Peter Orman *foundation executive*
Lee, David Hee-Don *trade association administrator, educator*
Lee, Thomas F. *art association administrator*
Leet, Mildred Robbins *social welfare administrator, consultant*
Leffler, Marvin *foundation administrator, writer*
Luckman, Sharon Gersten *arts administrator*
Luks, Allan Barry *executive director*
Mahoney, Margaret Ellerbe *foundation executive*
Maynard, Virginia Madden *foundation administrator*
McCrary, Eugenia Lester (Mrs. Dennis Daughtry McCrary) *civic worker, writer*
McNamara, Mary Ellen *not-for-profit executive*
McNeil, Wendy Lawson-Johnston *foundation administrator*
Michel, Nicolas *international organization administrator*
Milbank, Jeremiah *foundation executive*
Miller, Harvey S. Shipley *foundation trustee, philanthropist*
Moran, Martin Joseph *fundraising company executive*
Morial, Marc Haydel *association executive, former mayor*
Motoc, Mihnea Ioan *international organization official*
Muse, Martha Twitchell *foundation executive*
Neidich, Brooke Garber *foundation administrator, art patron*
Newman, Eileen *not-for-profit organization executive*
Nicolau, Siobhan *cultural organization administrator*
O, Cao K. *cultural organization administrator*
Orr, James F. III *foundation administrator*
Osborn, Frederick Henry III *foundation executive*
Otunnu, Olara A. *childrens organization official*
Oxnam, Robert Bromley *trust company advisor*
Peresman, Joel *foundation administrator*
Peters, Elizabeth *media organization director*
Polin, Jane L. *foundation official*
Randel, Don Michael *foundation administrator, former academic administrator, musicologist*
Raynor, Bruce S. *labor union administrator*
Rodin, Judith Seitz *foundation administrator, former academic administrator, psychologist, educator*
Roney, Carley *wedding company executive, writer*
Rose, Joanna Semel *volunteer*
Rosenthal, Joel Howard *think-tank executive*
Roth, Kenneth *human rights advocate*
Rover, Edward Frank *foundation administrator, lawyer*
Rupp, George Erik *international relief organization executive*
St. Martin, Charlotte *trade association administrator*
Sanchez, Manuel *retired social services administrator, writer*
Sard, Susannah Ellen *non-profit executive*
Sayres, Edwin J., Jr. *animal welfare organization administrator*
Schlesinger, Stephen Cannon *think-tank executive*
Senese, Daniel *professional society administrator*
Sidamon-Eristoff, Anne Phipps *not-for-profit developer*
Slutsky, Lorie A(nn) *foundation executive*
Smith, Barry Hamilton *foundation administrator, physician*
Spatz, Andre *international organization executive*
Spero, Joan Edelman *foundation administrator*
Spindler, James Andrew *not-for-profit executive*
Steedman, Doria Lynne Silberberg *foundation administrator*
Straus, Oscar S., II, *foundation executive*
Sullivan, Mary Brosnahan *advocate, social services administrator*
Sussman, Leonard Richard *foundation executive*
Symonette, Lys *foundation executive, musician, writer*
Tenenbaum, Ann G. *art association administrator*
Tharoor, Shashi *international organization official*
Tobin, Eugene Marc *foundation administrator, retired academic administrator*
Tofel, Richard Jeffrey *foundation administrator*
Toussaint, Roger *labor union administrator*
Traverse, Lyn D. *not-for-profit fundraiser, communications executive*
Trump, Blaine (Martha Lindley Blaine Beard Trump) *philanthropist*
Ungaro, Susan Kelliher *foundation administrator, former magazine editor*
Van de Bovenkamp, Sue Erpf *foundation administrator*
Veneman, Ann Margaret *international organization executive, former secretary of agriculture*
Walker, Jennie Louise *not-for-profit fundraiser, consultant*
Wang, John *not-for-profit company executive*
Wanner, Eric *foundation executive*
Wattleton, Faye (Alyce Faye Wattleton) *educational association administrator, advocate*
Weeks, David Frank *foundation administrator*
Weingarten, Rhonda (Randi Weingarten) *labor union administrator, lawyer*
Wenegrat, Saul S. *art association administrator*
Wilson, Marie C. *foundation administrator*
Wucker, Michele *educational association administrator, writer*
Wylde, Kathryn S. *business organization executive*

**Niagara Falls**
Hawkins De Golier, Danielle *political activist*

**Oneida**
Halbritter, Ray (Arthur Raymond Halbritter) *Native American tribal leader*

**Pawling**
Peale, Ruth Stafford (Mrs. Norman Vincent Peale) *not-for-profit executive*

**Pleasant Valley**
Becofsky, Arthur Luke *arts administrator, writer*

**Riverdale**
Yale (Yeleyenide-Yale), Serina *philanthropist, apparel designer*

**Rochester**
Klinke, Louise Hoyt *volunteer*
Lebman, Robert Richard *social services administrator*
Pacala, Leon *retired professional society administrator*
Robbins, Nancy Slinker *volunteer*

**Saranac**
Smith, J. Kellum, Jr. *foundation administrator, lawyer*

**Saratoga Springs**
Carovano, John Martin *not-for-profit developer*

**Scarsdale**
Bruck Lieb Port, Lilly *retired advocate, columnist, commentator*

**Schenectady**
Hull, Roger Harold *foundation administrator, former academic administrator*

**Seneca Falls**
Luisi-Potts, Billie *not-for-profit executive*

**Staten Island**
Lutkenhouse, Anne *non-profit executive*

**Stony Brook**
Brandwein, Ruth Ann *social welfare educator, social services administrator, writer*

**Stony Creek**
La Grasse, Carol Winter *property rights activist, retired civil engineer*

**Syracuse**
Furze, Edward William *fundraising consultant*
Irwin, Peter C. *not-for-profit fundraiser*

**Tarrytown**
Bergson, Henry Paul *professional society administrator*

**Tonawanda**
Glickman, Marlene *non-profit organization administrator*

**Troy**
Geddis, Carol J. *educational association administrator*

**Watertown**
Henderson, Gladys Edith *retired social welfare examiner*

**Watkins Glen**
Spencer, Dawn Joyce *animal advocate*

**White Plains**
Howse, Jennifer Louise *foundation administrator*

**Yonkers**
Neal, Leora Louise Haskett *social services administrator*

## NORTH CAROLINA

**Asheville**
Gray, Robert Ward *art association administrator*

**Cary**
Bryant, Mynora Joyce *not-for-profit fundraiser*
Martin, William Royall, Jr. *retired professional society administrator*

**Chapel Hill**
Ferris, William Reynolds *humanities organization administrator, folklore educator*
Kenan, Thomas Stephen III *philanthropist*
Krasno, Richard Michael *foundation executive, educator*

**Charlotte**
Cochrane, Eugene W., Jr. *foundation administrator*
Locke, Elizabeth Hughes *retired foundation administrator*
McClure, Howard Jean, Jr. *advocate*
Spiro, Robert Harry, Jr. *foundation and business executive, educator*

**Clinton**
Griffin, Betty Lou *not-for-profit developer, educator*

**Durham**
Bevan, William *retired foundation executive*
Semans, Mary Duke Biddle Trent *foundation administrator*

**Greensboro**
Kornegay, Horace Robinson *trade association administrator, congressman, lawyer*
Revell, Henry, Jr. *social services administrator, retired education educator*

**New Bern**
Danjczek, Michael Harvey *social services administrator*

**Pembroke**
Goins, Jimmy (James Ernest Goins) *Native American tribal leader*

**Pinehurst**
Linville, Ray Pate *educational association administrator, retired military officer, editor, writer*

**Raleigh**
Daubert, Erik Joseph *organization administrator, consultant*

**Lee, Howard N.** *educational association administrator*
McKinney, Carolyn *educational association administrator, educator*
Orr, Robert F. *not-for-profit administrator, retired state supreme court justice*

**Waynesville**
Cole, James Yeager *foundation administrator*

**Wilson**
McCain, Betty Landon Ray (Mrs. John Lewis McCain) *political party official, state official*

**Wingate**
Dodd, John Robert *non-profit organization administrator*

**Winston Salem**
Jones, F(rancis) Whitney *fund raising executive, consultant*

## NORTH DAKOTA

**Bismarck**
Stoller, Rose *think-tank executive*

**Fargo**
Thompson, Vern *political organization executive*

**Grand Forks**
Jones, Arthur Frederick *art university administrator, educator*

**Minot**
Moe, Vida Delores *civic worker*

**Williston**
Yockim, James Craig *foundation administrator*

## OHIO

**Akron**
Collier, Alice Elizabeth Becker *retired social services administrator*
Frank, John V. *foundation administrator*

**Berlin Center**
Haynali, Carolyn Ann *social services administrator*

**Canton**
Fernandez, Kathleen M. *cultural organization administrator*
McIlwain-Massey, Nadine *retired foundation administrator*

**Chagrin Falls**
Ostendorf, Joan Donahue *fund raiser, volunteer*
Vail, Iris Jennings *civic worker*

**Cincinnati**
Hill-Cook, Patricia Ann *social services administrator*
Motch, Marjorie McCullough *service organization executive*
Ray, Glenn *art association administrator*
Sowder, Fred Allen *foundation administrator, alphabet specialist*

**Cleveland**
Boyd, Byron A. *labor union administrator*
Calkins, Hugh *foundation executive*
Carter, John Dale *organizational development coordinator*
Distelhorst, Garis Fred *trade association administrator*
FallCreek, Stephanie Jean *non-profit organization executive*
Hartley, Duncan *fundraising executive*
Kolda, Thomas Joseph *non-profit organization executive*
Pike, Kermit Jerome *cultural organization administrator*
Smith, Jerome *not-for-profit developer, film producer, writer*
Thompson, Paul C. *labor union administrator*

**Columbus**
Akers, Saundra Ruth *retired disability rights advocate*
Newman, Diana S. *foundation administrator, consultant*
Ritchey, Kenneth William *educational association administrator*
Selby, Diane Ray Miller *fraternal organization administrator*
Sharp, Paul David *institute administrator*
Trent, Elton Roger *educational assessment administrator, writer*

**Coshocton**
Freund, Carol Louise *social services consultant*

**Dayton**
Daley, Robert Emmett *retired foundation executive*
Thomas, Marianna *volunteer community activist, writer, speaker*
Williams, Walker Richard, Jr. *social services administrator*

**Dublin**
Needham, George Michael *association executive*

**Fairview Park**
Fordyce, James Stuart *non-profit organization executive*

**Hamilton**
Gruenwald, James Howard *association executive, consultant*

**Hilliard**
Riggle, Blair Andrew *educational association administrator, consultant, psychologist, educator*

**Lewis Center**
Heinlen, Daniel Lee *alumni organization administrator*

**Oberlin**
Reinoehl, Richard Louis *social services administrator, scholar*

**Oxford**
Miller, Robert James *educational association administrator*

**Richfield**
Lewis, Sylvia Davidson *foundation executive*

**Silver Lake**
Cantor, Arnold *labor relations official*

**Springfield**
Pitzer, Betty Braun *retired social services administrator*

**Sylvania**
Garrison, Linda *retired foundation administrator*

**Worthington**
Luck, James I. *foundation executive*

## OKLAHOMA

**Ardmore**
Cawley, Michael A. *foundation administrator, lawyer*

**Durant**
Pyle, Gregory E. *Native American tribal leader*

**Enid**
McCobb, Allan Paul *not-for-profit organization executive*

**Lawton**
Hooper, Roy B. *lobbyist*

**Oklahoma City**
Brooks, Gene (Leslie Gene Brooks) *cultural organization administrator*
Gumerson, Jean Gilderhus *health foundation executive*
Kerr, Lou C. *foundation administrator*
Parmley, Jay *political organization administrator*
Reneau, Brenda *trade association executive*

**Okmulgee**
Ellis, A.D. *Native American tribal leader*

**Tahlequah**
Smith, Chad Corntassel *Native American tribal leader*

## OREGON

**Ashland**
Kreisman, Arthur *higher education consultant, retired humanities educator*

**Bend**
Evers-Williams, Myrlie Beasley *advocate, cultural organization administrator*

**Corvallis**
Wilkins, Caroline Hanke *advocate, political organization worker*

**Lake Oswego**
Bruce, John Allen *retired foundation executive, educator*

**Portland**
Buckstein, Steve *think-tank executive*
Collins, Maribeth Wilson *retired foundation administrator*
Hudson, Jerry E. *foundation administrator*
Patterson, Beverly Ann Gross *not-for-profit fundraiser, consultant, social services administrator, writer*
Pine, William Charles *foundation executive*
Brooks, Charlee S. *foundation administrator*
Showalter, Marilyn Grace *trade association administrator, director*
Wilson, Thomas Dale *not-for-profit fundraiser*

**Salem**
Frank, Gerald Wendel *advocate, journalist*

**Summerville**
Hopkins, Gerald Frank *trade association administrator*

## PENNSYLVANIA

**Bryn Mawr**
Cooney, Patricia Ruth *civic worker*

**Carlisle**
Anderson, Howard Wayne, Jr. *training company executive*

**Columbia**
Stuckert, Caroline Morris *retired non-profit executive, anthropologist*

**Dillsburg**
Bowers, Glenn Lee *retired professional society administrator*

**Drexel Hill**
Schiazza, Guido Domenic (Guy Schiazza) *educational association administrator*

**Elkins Park**
Pak, Hyung Woong *community advocate*

**Fogelsville**
Flores, Robin Ann *geriatric program and service consultant*

**Gibsonia**
Haas, Eileen Marie *homecare advocate*

**Glenside**
Block, Isaac Edward *professional society administrator*

**Harrisburg**
Breslin, Michael Joseph III *social services administrator, educator*
Zwifka, David Alan *not for profit executive, consultant*

**Havertown**
Wing, Kennard Thompson *educational organization official*

**Hazleton**
Kraynak, Marcelle Georgeann *not-for-profit developer*

**Kingston**
Friedman, Pauline Poplin *civic worker, consultant*

**Lewisburg**
Neuman, Nancy Adams Mosshammer *civic leader*

**Macungie**
Nenstiel, Susan Kisthart *fundraising professional*

**Mechanicsburg**
Gibbons, Miles Joseph, Jr. *foundation administrator*

**Monroeville**
Skolnick, Marilyn *civic worker*

**Philadelphia**
Bailin, Michael A. *foundation administrator*
Hamilton, Samuel C. *not-for-profit fundraiser*
Makous, Bruce B. *fundraiser, writer*
Mallery, David *education association executive, consultant*
Meyerson, Margy Ellin *urbanist, civic volunteer*
Reed, Sally Gardner *cultural organization administrator*
Sicherman, Harvey *think-tank executive*
Vredenburgh, Judy *youth organization executive*

**Pittsburgh**
Boyce, Doreen Elizabeth *foundation administrator, educator*
Constant, Louay *policy analyst*
Fox, Debra L. *educational association administrator, business owner*
Gerard, Leo W. *labor union executive*
Gibson, Samuel Norris *educational association administrator, retired clergyman*
King, Maxwell E. P. *foundation administrator*
McDaniel, Sharon Toliver *social welfare administrator, foundation administrator*
Petersen, Jean Snyder *educational association administrator*
Scaife, Richard Mellon *philanthropist*
Ziegler, Arthur P., Jr. *foundation executive*

**Reading**
LaSorsa, Vincent John *think-tank executive, psychologist*

**Rydal**
Fernberger, Marilyn Friedman *not-for-profit developer, consultant, volunteer*

**State College**
Book, Edward Raymond *retired trade association administrator*
Phillips, Janet Colleen *retired educational association administrator, editor*

**Villanova**
Friend, Theodore Wood III *foundation executive, historian, writer*

**Warrendale**
Rumbaugh, Max Elden, Jr. *professional society administrator*

**Wayne**
Annenberg, Leonore A. *foundation administrator*
Etris, Samuel Franklin *trade association research consultant*

**Wynnewood**
Meyers, Mary Ann *foundation administrator, consultant, writer*

**York**
Foster, Timothy Edward *educational association administrator*
Wiles, Lessley Decker *foundation administrator, preservationist*

## RHODE ISLAND

**Kingston**
Molloy, David Scott, Jr. *labor relations educator*

## SOUTH CAROLINA

**Aiken**
Ely, Duncan Cairnes *social services administrator*

**Anderson**
Bailey, Jake Schultz *volunteer, retired electrical engineer*

**Charleston**
Ferguson, Esther B. *volunteer*
Hughes, Blake *retired professional society administrator, retired publishing executive*

**Chester**
Cox, Kevin Monterey *educational association administrator*

**Clemson**
Zielinski, Paul Bernard *grant program administrator, civil engineer*

**Columbia**
Bjontegard, Arthur Martin, Jr. *foundation executive*

**Green Pond**
Ittleson, H(enry) Anthony *foundation executive*

**Hilton Head Island**
Ostergard, Paul Michael *philanthropy consultant*

**Lancaster**
Bundy, Charles Alan *retired foundation executive*

**Saint Helena Island**
Tarr-Whelan, Linda *policy center executive*

**Woodruff**
Childers, Bob Eugene *educational association executive*

**SOUTH DAKOTA**

**Eagle Butte**
Frazier, Harold Clay (Tahunska Luta) *Native American tribal leader*

**Sioux Falls**
Piper, Kathleen *former political organization administrator*

**TENNESSEE**

**Knoxville**
Froula, James DeWayne *honor society administrator*

**Memphis**
Jalenak, Peggy Eichenbaum *volunteer*
Tibbs, Martha Jane Pullen *civic worker, retired social worker*

**Nashville**
Benson, Edwin Welburn, Jr. *trade association executive*
Henderson, Milton Arnold *professional society administrator*
McIntyre, Edward Patrick, Jr. *not-for-profit executive*
Policinski, Eugene Francis *foundation administrator, editor, radio personality, television personality, television producer*
Snyder, Barbara Lou *retired educational association administrator*
Turk, Thomas Liebig *cultural organization administrator*

**Whites Creek**
Coleman, John Daniel *political strategist*

**TEXAS**

**Amarillo**
Berry, Jacob Obadiah *not-for-profit developer, rancher*
Crain, Mary Tom *volunteer*

**Arlington**
Eudaly, Olivia Coggin *not-for-profit executive, educator*

**Austin**
Banks, Virginia Anne (Ginger Banks) *association administrator*
Bonjean, Charles Michael *foundation executive, sociologist, educator*
Cleaves, Peter Shurtleff *foundation administrator*
Houston, Ron *professional society administrator*
Kolar, Mary Jane *trade and professional association executive*
Long, Teresa Lozano *foundation administrator, educator*
Mc Kinney, Michael Whitney *trade association executive*
Middleton, Harry Joseph *foundation administrator*
Romero, Jesse Charles *political consultant*
Stoner, James Lloyd *retired foundation administrator, clergyman*

**Beaumont**
Davis, Gloria Whittie *educational association administrator*

**Breckenridge**
Jones, Karen Annette *civic volunteer*

**Cedar Park**
Love, Ben Howard *retired organization executive*

**Corpus Christi**
French, Dorris Towers Bryan *volunteer*

**Dallas**
Braun, Susan J. *foundation administrator*
Brinker, Nancy Goodman *social services administrator, former ambassador*
Bucker, Robert *educational fundraiser*
Cockerham, Sidney Joe *professional society administrator*
Dell, Susan *foundation administrator, apparel designer*
Friedheim, Jan V. *educational association administrator*
Goodman, John C. *think-tank executive*
Santos, Charles Daniel *cultural organization administrator*

**El Paso**
Goodman, Gertrude Amelia *civic worker*

**Fort Worth**
Wilson-Webb, Nancy Lou *educational association administrator*

**Fulton**
Lamb, Richard *cultural organization administrator*

**Galveston**
Baker, Robert Ernest, Jr. *retired foundation executive*

**Georgetown**
Busfield, Roger Melvil, Jr. *retired trade association executive, educator*

**Houston**
Bailey, Kelley *foundation administrator*
Bennett, Olga Salowich *civic worker, graphic arts researcher, consultant*
Charnveja, Pat S. *civic leader, former oil and gas industry executive*
Faulkner, Larry Ray *foundation administrator, former academic administrator*
Foss, Michelle Michot *think-tank executive, economist*
Ifft, Lewis George III *company administrator*
Issa, Mariam *volunteer, cultural organization administrator*
Owen, Jane Dale *non-profit organization executive*
Tarlov, Alvin Richard *foundation administrator, physician, educator*

**Irving**
Birch, Glynn R. *non-profit organization administrator*
Olson, Herbert Theodore *trade association executive*
Wilkerson, H. Dean, Jr. *association and organization executive*
Williams, Roy L. *fraternal organization administrator*

**Mcallen**
Spyker, Leola Edith *missionary*

**Plano**
Carver, Rita *not-for-profit fundraiser, consultant*

**Richardson**
Atkins, Howard Gray, Jr. *social services administrator*
Smith, Mark P. *foundation administrator*

**Round Rock**
Mountain, Janet *foundation administrator, former computer company executive*

**San Antonio**
Crichton, Flora Cameron *volunteer, foundation administrator*
Dunlap, Kathryn Sharp *educational association administrator*
Gonzalez, Antonio *voter registration project executive*
Loeffler, Tom (Thomas Gilbert Loeffler) *lobbyist, former congressman*

**Sugar Land**
Hosley, Marguerite Cyril *civic worker*

**Texarkana**
Malcolm, Molly Beth *political organization worker, counselor*

**UTAH**

**Bountiful**
Burningham, Kim Richard *educational association administrator, former state legislator*

**Salt Lake City**
Clark, Deanna Dee *volunteer*
Cofield, Philip Thomas *educational association administrator*
Julander, Paula Foil *foundation administrator*

**VERMONT**

**Brattleboro**
Bellamy, Carol *international organization administrator*

**Middlebury**
Geier, Philip Otto III *foundation executive, consultant, director, academic administrator*

**Montpelier**
Barbieri, Christopher George *professional society administrator*

**Peacham**
Barnes, Harry G., Jr. *advocate, consultant*

**Shelburne**
Ryerson, William Newton *non profit organization executive*

**VIRGINIA**

**Alexandria**
Baker, Brent Harold *foundation executive*
Baroody, Michael Elias *trade association executive*
Bolger, Robert Joseph *retired trade association administrator*
Bryant, Anne Lincoln *educational association executive*
Carter, Gene Raymond *professional association executive*
Cooper, David Earl Kaleoikaika *foundation executive*
Crane, Stephen Charles *professional society administrator*
Engler, Brian David *professional society administrator*

**Foster**, Serrin Marie *non-profit organization executive*
Gould, Charles W. *foundation administrator, lawyer*
Greenstein, Ruth Louise *think-tank executive, lawyer*
Kratovil, Jane Lindley *think tank associate, not-for-profit developer*
Lachance, Janice Rachel *professional association administrator, retired federal agency administrator, lawyer*
Lendsey, Jacquelyn L. *association administrator*
Lenz, Edward Arnold *trade association administrator, lawyer*
Lusk, Cody *auto association executive*
Maehara, Paulette V. *fundraising executive*
Rabun, John Brewton, Jr. *criminal justice agency executive*
Rector, John Michael *pharmaceutical association executive, lawyer*
Schubert, Richard Francis *social services administrator, consultant*

**Arlington**
Bond, Phillip J. *technology association executive, former advertising executive*
Buchanan, Louise *political organization worker, consultant*
Chafuen, Alejandro Antonio *think-tank executive*
Chattman, Raymond Christopher *association executive*
Futrell, John William *environmental agency executive, lawyer*
Herbst, Robert LeRoy *organization executive*
Hunter, J(ohn) Robert *insurance consumer advocate*
Langworthy, Everett Walter *professional society administrator, natural gas exploration company executive*
Lightfoot, David William *foundation administrator, linguistics educator*
McCurdy, David Keith *trade association administrator, former congressman*
McKinnon, Russell F. *professional society administrator*
O'Day, Paul Thomas *trade association executive*
Palmer, Larry Leon *foundation administrator, former ambassador*
Powell, Edward A., Jr., (Ned Powell) *nonprofit organization executive*
Raizen, Senta Amon *educational association administrator, researcher*
Shannon, Thomas Alfred *retired educational association administrator emeritus*
Stangroom, Tom M. *non-profit organization administrator*
Swetnam, Michael S. *think-tank executive*

**Brookneal**
Watson, Jason Bradley *not-for-profit developer*

**Bumpass**
Hoyt, John Arthur *cultural organization administrator, minister*

**Burke**
Woodruff, C(harles) Roy *retired professional association executive, consultant*

**Chantilly**
Sroka, John Walter *trade association executive*

**Charlottesville**
Johnston, Margaret Schuster *volunteer, retired language educator*
Jordan, Daniel Porter, Jr. *foundation administrator, historian, educator*
Thompson, Kenneth W(infred) *educational association administrator, writer, editor, social sciences educator*

**Earlysville**
Brownell, Blaine Allison *educational association administrator, former academic administrator, history professor*
Rotherham, Andrew J. *not-for-profit administrator, consultant*

**Fairfax**
Hollans, Irby Noah, Jr. *retired trade association administrator*
LaPierre, Wayne R., Jr. *lobbyist*
Lomax, Michael Lucius *non-profit association administrator*
Roberts, Cecil Edward, Jr. *labor union administrator*
Robinson, Kayne B. *lobbyist, former political organization officer*

**Falls Church**
McGinly, William C. *healthcare association executive*

**Flint Hill**
Dietel, William Moore *former foundation executive*

**Franktown**
Kellam, Caramine *volunteer*

**Garrisonville**
Emely, Charles Harry *trade association executive, consultant*

**Great Falls**
DiBona, Charles Joseph *retired trade association administrator*

**Herndon**
Woerth, Duane E. *labor union administrator*

**Leesburg**
De Barbieri, Mary Ann *not-for-profit developer, management consultant*

**Louisa**
Small, William Edwin, Jr. *association and recreation executive*

**Lynchburg**
Craddock, Mary Spencer Jack *volunteer*
Johnson, Robert Bruce *historic preservationist, director, small business owner*

**Mc Lean**
Calhoun, John Alfred *social services administrator*
McInerney, James Eugene, Jr. *trade association executive*
Stackpole, Kerry Clifford *association executive*

**Middleburg**
Sodolski, John *retired professional society administrator*

**Mount Vernon**
Belden, David Leigh *professional society administrator, engineering educator*

**Newport News**
Hightower, John Brantley *arts administrator, educator*
Mazur, Rhoda Himmel *community volunteer*

**Norfolk**
Magee, Kathleen S. *foundation executive*

**Reston**
Ancell, Robert Manning *leadership organization executive*
Brennan, Norma Jean *professional society administrator, director*
Gates, James David *retired professional society administrator*
Hope, Samuel Howard *accreditation organization executive*
Madry-Taylor, Jacquelyn Yvonne *educational association administrator*
Minton, Joseph Paul *retired safety organization executive*
Mogge, Harriet Morgan *educational association executive*
Natale, Patrick J *professional society administrator*

**Richmond**
Bankos, Jean *educational association administrator, educator*
Brackenridge, N. Lynn *not-for-profit developer*
Framme, Lawrence Henry III *political organization administrator, lawyer*

**Roanoke**
Manns, Essie Jeanette Delaney *advocate*

**Spotsylvania**
Clower, William Dewey *retired trade association executive*

**Springfield**
Bartlow, Gene Steven *professional society administrator, retired military officer*
Larson, Reed Eugene *foundation administrator*

**Sterling**
Chavez, Linda *civil rights organization executive*

**Vienna**
Jones, Terrence Dale *foundation executive, consultant*

**Virginia Beach**
Weber, Alban *professional society administrator, lawyer*

**White Stone**
Sparks, Kenneth R. *association executive*

**Williamsburg**
Campbell, Colin Goetze *foundation president*
Chandler, Kimberley Lynn *educational association administrator*

**Woodbridge**
Garon, Richard Joseph, Jr. *political organization worker*

**WASHINGTON**

**Bellevue**
Arnold, Ronald Henri *nonprofit organization executive, consultant*

**Kirkland**
Teeley, Kevin *educational association administrator*

**Olympia**
Henderson, Bernadette Läkéy *educational association administrator*

**Port Townsend**
Woolf, William Blauvelt *retired association executive*

**Seattle**
Arthur, William Lynn *environmental and political program director*
Bell, William C. *foundation administrator*
Davidson, Robert William *not-for-profit executive*
Foster, Barry Alan *cultural organization researcher, educator*
Gates, Melinda French *foundation administrator*
Golston, Allan C. *foundation administrator*
Green, Joshua III *foundation administrator, retired bank executive*
Jessen, Joel Anne *not-for-profit executive, art educator*
Martínez, Yolanda R. *social services administrator*
Mathews, Sylvia Mary *foundation administrator*
Scott, Cheryl M. *foundation administrator, healthcare educator*
Stonesifer, Patty (Patricia Q. Stonesifer) *foundation administrator*
Vander Ark, Tom *foundation administrator*

**Spokane**
Herzer, Marian Day *not-for-profit developer, educator*

Lamel, Linda Helen *professional society executive, retired insurance company executive, lawyer, arbitrator, retired college president*
Landon, Susan N. *humanitarian, arts and environmental advocate, poet*
LaPidus, Jules Benjamin *educational association administrator*
Lassman, Adrienne *community volunteer*
Ledwig, Donald Eugene *association executive, consultant, retired broadcast executive, military officer*
Leggett, Roberta Jean (Bobbi Leggett) *retired social services administrator*
Lenhart, Cynthia Rae *conservation organization executive*
Lepeley, Maria-Teresa *educational association administrator*
Lerner, Beth M. *non-profit consultant*
Lichtman, Judith L. *lawyer, organization administrator*
Lief, Beth *educational association administrator*
Liljegren, Frank Sigfrid *art association administrator, artist, educator*
Lindenmayer, Elisabeth *international organization administrator*
Luckey, Doris Waring *civic volunteer*
MacCarthy, Talbot Leland *civic volunteer*
Mahoney, Ann Dickinson *fundraiser*
Makepeace, Mary Lou *foundation administrator, former mayor*
Malek, Marlene *foundation administrator*
Manion, Bonnie J. *volunteer, poet, composer*
Maroney, Thomas P. *lawyer, political party executive*
Marshall, Jonathan *foundation administrator, journalist*
Mays, Jill Duncan *social services administrator, counselor*
McAuliffe, Terry (Terence Richard McAuliffe) *former political organization administrator*
McDonald, Douglas Robert *non profit agency executive*
McFate, Kenneth Leverne *trade association administrator*
McFate, Patricia Ann *foundation executive, science educator*
McWethy, Patricia Joan *educational association administrator*
Melanson, Dorothy *political organization administrator*
Mende, Robert Graham *retired engineering association executive*
Menzel, Marybelle Proctor *volunteer*
Metcalf, Karen *retired foundation executive*
Meyer, Rachel Abijah *foundation administrator, artist, poet*
Michel, Elizabeth Cheney *social reform consultant*
Miller, Diane Illian *cultural organization administrator*
Mills, Garth Allen, Sr. *not-for-profit fundraiser, consultant*
Miracle, Nancy *foundation administrator, writer*
Misner, Charlotte Blanche Ruckman *retired community organization administrator*
Moore, Robert William *professional organization executive*
Muchmore, Don Moncrief *retired cultural organization administrator, retired museum director, foundation administrator*
Muir, Patricia Allen *professional association administrator*
Muller, Henry Nicholas III *retired foundation administrator*
Murphy-Pilon, Monica *cultural organization administrator*
Nelson, Florence Ely *civic leader*
Niemiec, Edward Walter *retired professional association executive*
Oaks, Sunny *child and family advocate, consultant, lyricist*
O'Connor, Doris Julia *not-for-profit fundraiser, consultant*
O'Donnell, Kathleen Mary *social services administrator*
O'Neal-Seralathan, Crescentia *advocate*
O'Neill, Mary Jane *not-for-profit administrator, consultant*
O'Sullivan, Michael David *foundation executive*
Ovadiah, Janice *not-for-profit developer, cultural organization administrator*
Pacelle, Wayne *animal rights organization administrator*
Palmer, Jocelyn Beth *volunteer*
Park, Won Kuk *foundation administrator*
Parkel, James G. *former health association administrator*
Poole, Thomas Richard *endowment capital campaign director, fund raising counsel*
Porter, John Wilson *educational association administrator, director*
Powell, Dana Lindsley *art association administrator, consultant*
Prejean, Sister Helen Theresa *human rights advocate, writer, lecturer*
Primerano, Lavina S. *volunteer*
Pritchard, Kathleen Jo *not-for-profit association administrator*
Pullen, Penny Lynne *non-profit organization administrator, retired state legislator*
Qiang, Xiao *advocate*
Ramo, Virginia M. Smith *civic worker*
Rheinfrank, Sally Lyman *volunteer*
Richardson, Veta Teresa *professional society administrator, lawyer*
Richardson, William Chase *retired foundation administrator*
Ridings, Dorothy Sattes *former association executive*
Rimel, Rebecca Webster *foundation administrator*
Riordan, John Thomas *trade association executive, consultant*
Riskin, Victoria *former trade association administrator*
Roberson, James O. *foundation executive*
Robinson, David Zav *not-for-profit consultant*
Rotenberg, Marc Steven *advocate, lawyer*
Rubottom, George Milton *foundation administrator, chemist*
Rutledge, Mary Elizabeth *cultural organization administrator*

Ryan, John William *educational association administrator*
Sampson, Robert Neil *professional society administrator, consultant*
Sari, Dita *labor union administrator*
Schanfield, Fannie Schwartz *community volunteer*
Schulz, William Frederick *human rights scholar and advocate*
Schumacher, Philip Gerard *fundraising executive*
Schuster, Elaine *retired civil rights professional*
Schwartz, John J. *association executive, consultant*
Schweiker, Richard Schultz *former trade association administrator, former secretary of health & human services, former senator*
Scott, Jacqueline Delmar Parker *educational association administrator, consultant*
Scott, Karen Elizabeth *advocate*
Scott, Sandra J. *not-for-profit executive*
Seggerman, Anne Crellin *foundation executive*
Seiff, Gloria Louise *volunteer*
Seldman, Neil Norman *cultural organization administrator*
Shackelford, Lottie Holt *civic worker, former mayor*
Shriver, Eunice Mary Kennedy (Mrs. Robert Sargent Shriver Jr.) *foundation administrator, volunteer, social worker*
Singer, Markus Morton *retired trade association administrator*
Siska, John Edward *foundation administrator, publishing executive*
Smith, Margaret Taylor *volunteer*
Smith, Wendy L. *foundation executive*
Solo, Joyce Rubenstein *volunteer*
Spaulding, Helen Bowdoin *former foundation administrator*
Spencer, Lonabelle (Kappie Spencer) *political agency administrator, lobbyist*
Stanley, George Joel *social services administrator, advocate*
Stearns, Stewart Warren *charitable association executive*
Steele, Jamie Keys *social services executive, consultant*
Steelman, Sara Gerling *retired art association administrator*
Stellar, Arthur Wayne *educational association administrator*
Stevens, Sheila Maureen *retired teachers union administrator*
Stobb, Mary Jean *retired association administrator*
Stokes, Kaleda Maryum *educational association administrator*
Sulc, Jean Luena (Jean L. Mestres) *lobbyist, consultant*
Sullivan, James Leo *organization executive*
Tasman, Alice Lea Mast *not-for-profit fundraiser*
Thurmaier, Mary Jean *educational association administrator*
Tipping, William Malcolm *social services administrator*
Tisch, Wilma Stein *foundation administrator*
Tobin, Gary Allan *cultural and community organization educator*
Towle, Alexis Charles (Lex Towle) *education advocate*
Transou, Lynda Lou *advertising art administrator*
Trinchero, Agnes Theresa *social services consultant, administrator, educator*
Van Etten, Peter Walbridge *foundation executive*
Votaw, John Frederick, Sr. *educational association administrator, educator*
Wachtell, Esther *non-profit management executive, consultant*
Walton, Christy R. *philanthropist*
Warren, John William *professional society administrator*
Watson, Bernard Charles *foundation administrator, educator*
Watson, Kathy *political organization administrator*
Webb, Wellington Edward *political organization administrator, former mayor*
White, Rebecca E. *advocate*
Wilson, Kathy Kay *former foundation administrator, consultant*
Wirth, Timothy Endicott *foundation administrator, retired senator*
Wise Masters Hughes, Janice Ann *school social worker*
Wolfe, Joan L. *non-profit organizations consultant*
Woltering, Margaret Mae *retired educational association administrator*
Wong, Elaine Dang *foundation executive*
Woods, Harriett Ruth *political organization worker, retired state official*
Wooten, Frank Thomas *retired research facility executive*
Workman, Willard Allyn *association executive*
Young, Andrew Jackson, Jr. *civil rights leader, pastor, retired mayor, ambassador, retired congressman*
Young, Elizabeth Bell *organization consultant*
Young, Richard Alan *association executive*
Young, Steve G. *former labor union administrator*
Yzaguirre, Raul Humberto *civil rights leader*
Zehr, Norman Robert *retired association administrator*
Zimny, Max *labor union administrator, lawyer, arbitrator*

## ATHLETICS

### UNITED STATES

#### ALABAMA

**Auburn**
Housel, David *retired athletic director*
Tuberville, Tommy *college football coach*

**Tuscaloosa**
Shula, Mike *college football coach*

#### ALASKA

**Eagle River**
Cotten, Samuel Richard *fisheries consultant, former state legislator, consultant*

#### ARIZONA

**Glendale**
Barnett, Michael *professional sports team executive*
Doan, Shane *professional hockey player*
Fuhr, Grant *professional hockey player*
Gretzky, Wayne Douglas *retired professional hockey player, professional hockey coach*
Nolan, Owen *professional hockey player*
Roenick, Jeremy *professional hockey player*

**Phoenix**
Bidwill, William V. *professional football executive*
Boldin, Anquan *professional football player*
Colangelo, Jerry John *professional sports team executive*
D'Antoni, Mike *professional basketball player*
Fitzgerald, Larry *professional football player*
Garagiola, Joe, Jr. *baseball team executive*
Gillom, Jennifer *professional basketball player*
Grant, Brian Wade *professional basketball player*
Green, Dennis *professional football coach*
Green, Shawn *professional baseball player*
James, Edgerrin Tyree *professional football player*
Leinart, Matt *professional football player*
Lemieux, Claude *former professional hockey player, professional sports team executive*
Marion, Shawn *professional basketball player*
Melvin, Bob *professional baseball player*
Mulholland, Terence John (Terry Mulholland) *professional baseball player*
Nash, Steve *professional basketball player*
Smith, Emmitt J. III *retired professional football player*
Stoudemire, Amare Carsares *professional basketball player*
Taurasi, Diana *college basketball player*
Ward, Charlie *professional basketball player*

**Tempe**
Koetter, Dirk *college football coach*
Warner, Kurt (Kurtis Warner) *professional football player*

**Tucson**
Kearney, Joseph Laurence *retired athletic conference administrator*

#### CALIFORNIA

**Alameda**
Brooks, Aaron Lafette *professional football player*
Davis, Allen *professional football team executive*
Herrera, John *professional football team executive*
Jordan, LaMont *professional football player*
Moss, Randy *professional football player*
Sapp, Warren Carlos *professional football player*
Shell, Art (Arthur Shell Jr.) *professional football coach*

**Aliso Viejo**
Cohen, Sasha (Alexandra Pauline Cohen) *ice skater*

**Anaheim**
Anderson, Garret *professional baseball player*
Burke, Brian *professional sports team executive*
Carlyle, Randy *professional hockey coach, retired professional hockey player*
Green, Travis *professional hockey player*
Moreno, Arturo (Arte Moreno) *major league baseball team owner, former advertising executive*
Niedermayer, Scott *professional hockey player*
Pronger, Chris *professional hockey player*
Selanne, Teemu *professional hockey player*

**Berkeley**
Tedford, Jeff *college football coach*

**Beverly Hills**
Johnson, Magic (Earvin Johnson Jr.) *professional sports team executive, development company executive, former professional basketball coach and player*

**Camarillo**
Bryan, Bob *professional tennis player*

**Carson**
Cienfuegos, Mauricio *professional soccer player*
Del Prado, Sergio *professional soccer team executive*
Lalas, Alexi (Panayotis Alexander Lalas) *professional sports team executive, retired professional soccer player*
Ruiz Gutierrez, Carlos Humberto *professional soccer player*
Schmid, Sigi *professional soccer coach*

**Coronado**
Axelson, Joseph Allen *professional sports team executive, publishing executive*

**Danville**
Wisniewski, Stephen Adam *professional football player*

**El Segundo**
Bryant, Kobe *professional basketball player*
Buss, Jeanie *professional sports team executive*
Divac, Vlade *professional basketball player*
Jackson, Philip Douglas *professional basketball coach*
Leslie, Lisa DeShaun *professional basketball player*
Milton-Jones, DeLisha *professional basketball player*
Odom, Lamar Joseph *professional basketball*

Toler, Penny *former professional basketball player, sports team executive*
Weatherspoon, Teresa Gaye *professional basketball player*

**La Jolla**
Bavasi, Peter Joseph *sports management executive*

**Lake Forest**
Cranmer, Scotty *professional trick bike rider*

**Los Angeles**
Barry, Brent Robert *professional basketball player*
Baylor, Elgin Gay *professional basketball team executive*
Blake, Rob *professional hockey player*
Brand, Elton *professional basketball player*
Brown, Kwame *professional basketball player*
Carroll, Pete *college football coach*
Cassell, Samuel James *professional basketball player*
Cechmanek, Roman *professional hockey player*
Colletti, Ned *professional sports team executive*
Crawford, Marc *professional hockey coach*
Dantzscher, Jamie *gymnast*
De La Hoya, Oscar *boxer*
Dorrell, Karl *college football coach*
Drew, J.D. *professional baseball player*
Dunleavy, Mike, Sr. *professional basketball coach*
Floyd, Tim *men's college basketball coach, former professional basketball coach*
Furcal, Rafael *professional baseball player*
Gagne, Eric *professional baseball player*
Garciaparra, Nomar (Anthony Nomar Garciaparra) *professional baseball player*
Hextall, Ron *professional sports team executive, former professional hockey player*
Hopkins, Bernard *professional boxer*
Howland, Ben *men's college basketball coach*
Kent, Jeffrey Franklin *professional baseball player*
Kittles, Kerry *professional basketball player*
Lasorda, Thomas Charles (Tommy Lasorda) *professional baseball team manager*
Lavin, Stephen Michael *university basketball coach*
Little, William Grady (Grady Little) *professional baseball coach*
Lombardi, Dean *professional sports team executive*
Maddux, Gregory (Gregory Alan Maddux) *professional baseball player*
Maloney, Kristen *gymnast*
Mobley, Cuttino Rashawn *professional basketball player*
Olivier, Kathy Ricks *college basketball coach*
Penny, Brad *professional baseball player*
Robitaille, Luc *retired professional hockey player*
Scates, Allen Edward *coach*
Torchetti, John *former professional hockey coach*

**Monrovia**
Stevens, Gary *retired jockey*

**Northridge**
Jumonville, Felix Joseph, Jr. *physical education educator, real estate company officer*

**Oakland**
Boggan, Daniel, Jr. *sports association administrator*
Chavez, Eric *professional baseball player*
Cohan, Christopher J. *professional sports team executive*
Davis, Baron *professional basketball player*
Fisher, Derek *professional basketball player*
Kendall, Jason Daniel *professional baseball player*
Kotsay, Mark Steven *professional baseball player*
Montgomery, Mike *professional basketball coach*
Nelson, Donald Arvid (Nellie Nelson) *former professional basketball coach*
Richardson, Jason Anthoney *professional basketball player*
Street, Huston *professional baseball player*
Thomas, Frank Edward *professional baseball player*
Zito, Barry *professional baseball player*

**Rancho Cucamonga**
Okoye, Christian Emeka *professional football player*

**Riverside**
Everett, Carl *professional baseball player*

**Sacramento**
Abdur-Rahim, Shareef (Julius Shareef Abdul-Rahim) *professional basketball player*
Artest, Ron (Ronald William Artest Jr.) *professional basketball player*
Bibby, Mike *professional basketball player*
Griffith, Yolanda Evette *professional basketball player*
Musselman, Eric *professional basketball coach*
Totton, Gayle *professional sports team executive*

**San Diego**
Bochy, Bruce *professional sports team manager, coach*
Gates, Antonio *professional football player*
Giles, Brian Stephen *professional baseball player*
Hoffman, Trevor William *professional baseball player*
Klesko, Ryan *professional baseball player*
Lucchino, Lawrence *sports team executive, lawyer*
Moores, John *professional sports team executive*
Park, Chan Ho *professional baseball player*
Piazza, Mike (Michael Joseph Piazza) *professional baseball player*
Schottenheimer, Marty (Martin Edward Schottenheimer) *professional football coach*
Spanos, Dean A. *professional sports team executive*
Tomlinson, LaDainian *professional football player*
Wells, David Lee *professional baseball player*

**San Francisco**
Alou, Felipe Rojas *professional baseball manager*
Bonds, Barry Lamar *professional baseball player*
Cepeda, Orlando *retired professional baseball player*

Durham, Ray *professional baseball player*
Magowan, Peter Alden *professional sports team executive, retail executive*
Schmidt, Jason *professional baseball player*
Vizcaino, Jose Luis Pimental *professional baseball player*
Vizquel, Omar Enrique *professional baseball player*

**San Jose**
Carle, Matt *professional hockey player*
Cheechoo, Jonathan *professional hockey player*
Thornton, Joe *professional hockey player*
Wilson, Douglas Frederick *professional sports team executive, retired professional hockey player*
Wilson, Ronald Lawrence *professional hockey coach*

**Santa Clara**
Chastain, Brandi Denise *professional soccer player*
DeBartolo-York, Denise *sports team executive*
Dilfer, Trent *professional football player*
Nolan, Mike *professional football player*
Plummer, Ahmed *professional football player*
Smith, Alex *professional football player*
Turner, Norv (Norval Eugene Turner) *professional football coach*

**Sausalito**
Casals, Rosie *retired professional tennis player*

**Solvang**
Roberts, Monty *horse trainer, writer*

**Stockton**
Murphy, Jeremiah T. *professional sports team executive, construction executive*

**Valley Village**
Bench, Johnny Lee

**Vista**
Hawk, Tony *professional skateboarder*
Way, Danny *professional skateboarder*

## COLORADO

**Boulder**
Neinas, Charles Merrill *sports association executive, consultant*

**Colorado Springs**
Beard, Amanda *swimmer, Olympic athlete*
Bobek, Nicole *professional figure skater*
Cash, Swin (Swintayla Marie Cash) *professional basketball player*
Cheek, Joey *Olympic athlete*
Clay, Bryan Ezra *Olympic track and field athlete*
Coughlin, Natalie *Olympic athlete*
Crocker, Ian *Olympic athlete*
Gardner, Rulon E. *Olympic athlete*
Gatlin, Justin *Olympic track and field athlete*
Granato, Catherine (Cammi Granato) *Olympic athlete*
Hall, Gary, Jr. *Olympic athlete*
Hamilton, Tyler *professional cyclist, Olympic athlete*
Hamm, Morgan *Olympic athlete*
Hayes, Joanna *Olympic track and field athlete*
Hughes, Sarah *figure skater*
Krayzelburg, Lenny *Olympic athlete*
Kupets, Courtney *Olympic athlete*
Kwan, Michelle Wing *professional figure skater*
Ligety, Ted *Olympic athlete*
May, Misty *Olympic athlete*
McCool, Courtney *Olympic athlete*
McDonough, Ann Patrice *ice skater*
Nikodinov, Angela *professional figure skater, Olympic athlete*
Ogrean, David William *sports association executive*
Pappas, Tom *Olympic track and field athlete*
Patterson, Carly *Olympic athlete*
Phelps, Michael *Olympic athlete*
Quann, Megan *Olympic athlete*
Riley, Ruth Ellen *professional basketball player*
Schultz, Richard Dale *national athletic organization executive*
Teter, Hannah *Olympic athlete*
Torres, Dara *Olympic athlete*
Tueting, Sarah *professional hockey player*
Walsh, Kerri Lee *Olympic athlete*
Wariner, Jeremy *Olympic track and field athlete*

**Denver**
Anthony, Carmelo F. *professional basketball player*
Apodaca, Bob *professional baseball coach*
Balboa, Marcelo *professional soccer player*
Camby, Marcus D. *professional basketball player*
Giguere, Francois *professional sports team executive*
Hankinson, Tim *soccer coach*
Helton, Todd *professional baseball player*
Hurdle, Clint *professional athletics manager*
Karl, George *professional basketball coach*
Martin, Kenyon *professional basketball player*
Miller, Andre *professional basketball player*
Quenneville, Joel *professional hockey coach*
Sakic, Joe (Joseph Steve Sakic) *professional hockey player*
Smith, C. Lamont *sports association executive, lawyer*
Theodore, Jose *professional hockey player*

**Englewood**
Bailey, Champ *professional football player*
Lynch, John Terrence *professional football player*
Plummer, Jason Steven (Jake Plummer) *professional football player*
Shanahan, Mike *professional football coach*
Smith, Rod *professional football player*

**U S A F Academy**
DeBerry, Fisher *college football coach*

## CONNECTICUT

**Bristol**
Corso, Lee *former football coach, football analyst*
Flutie, Doug (Douglas Richard Flutie) *retired professional football player*
Gwynn, Anthony Keith (Tony Gwynn) *former professional baseball player*
Kruk, John Martin *retired professional baseball player, sportscaster*
Piniella, Louis Victor *professional baseball team manager*
Sutcliffe, Rick (Richard Lee Sutcliffe) *professional baseball player*
Theismann, Joseph Robert (Joe Theismann) *former professional football player, announcer*
Wynalda, Eric *professional soccer player*

**Cos Cob**
Leamy, Nancy M. *professional athletics coach*

**Farmington**
DiCicco, Tony *soccer coach*

**Litchfield**
Kennedy, Susan Orpha *physical education educator, consultant, sports official*

**Simsbury**
Yagudin, Alexei *Olympic athlete, ice skater*

**South Windsor**
Baretta, Marsha Motyl *elementary school physical education educator*

**Stamford**
Goldsmith, Donna *sports association executive*
Johnson, Dwayne Douglas (The Rock) *professional wrestler, actor*
McMahon, Linda E. *sports association executive*
McMahon, Vince (Vincent Kennedy McMahon) *sports entertainment company executive*
Valentine, Bobby (Robert John Valentine) *professional baseball manager*

**Storrs Mansfield**
Auriemma, Geno *women's college basketball coach*
Calhoun, Jim *men's college basketball coach*

**Uncasville**
Lobo, Rebecca *professional basketball player*

**West Haven**
Hatch, Annia *gymnast*

## DELAWARE

**Newark**
Wilson, Deborrah *physical education educator*

## DISTRICT OF COLUMBIA

**Washington**
Adu, Freddy *professional soccer player*
Arenas, Gilbert *professional basketball player*
Castilla, Vinivio Soria *professional baseball player*
Cordero, Wilfredo Nieva *professional baseball player*
Cruz, Deivi *professional baseball player*
Hanlon, Glen *professional hockey coach*
Hernandez, Livan Eisler *professional baseball player*
Holdsclaw, Chamique Shaunta *professional basketball player*
Jamison, Antawn *professional basketball player*
Jordan, Eddie *professional basketball coach*
Kolzig, Olaf *professional hockey player*
McPhee, George *professional sports team executive*
Moreno, Jaime *professional soccer player*
O'Malley, Susan *professional basketball team executive*
Ovechkin, Alexander *professional hockey player*
Patrick, Richard M. *professional hockey team executive*
Robinson, Frank *professional baseball manager, retired professional baseball player*
Saunders, Alan Keith *professional football coach*
Shriver, Timothy Perry *sports association executive*
Soriano, Alfonso Guilleard *professional baseball player*
Stanley, Marianne *professional athletics coach*
Thomas, Etan *professional basketball player, poet*
Upshaw, Gene (Eugene Upshaw) *sports association executive*

## FLORIDA

**Bradenton**
Haas, Tommy (Thomas Mario Haas) *professional tennis player*

**Carol City**
Cabrera, Miguel *professional baseball player*
Girardi, Joseph Elliott (Joe Girardi) *professional baseball manager, former professional baseball player*

**Clermont**
Richardson, Dot (Dorothy Gay) *former Olympic softball player, physician*

**Coral Gables**
Harriell, Kysha *athletic trainer, educator*

**Coral Springs**
Singh, Vijay *professional golfer*

**Davie**
Boston, David *professional football player*
Capers, Dom (Dominic Capers) *professional football coach*
Culpepper, Daunte *professional football player*

Harrington, Joey *professional football player*
Mularkey, Mike *professional football coach*
Saban, Nick *professional football coach*
Taylor, Jason Paul *professional football player*
Thomas, Zach Michael *professional football player*

**Daytona Beach**
Ahn, Shi Hyun *professional golfer*
Andrews, Donna L. *professional golfer*
Baena, Marisa *professional golfer*
Barrett, Tina *professional golfer*
Bodine, Geoff *race car driver*
Creamer, Paula *professional golfer*
Davies, Laura *professional golfer*
DeLuca, Annette *professional golfer*
Doolan, Wendy *professional golfer*
France, Brian Z. *sports association executive*
France, James C. *professional sports executive*
France, William Clifton, Jr. *professional sports executive*
Gordon, Jeff *race car driver*
Han, Hee-Won *professional golfer*
Hurst, Patricia Ann *professional golfer*
Inkster, Juli *professional golfer*
Jang, Jeong *professional golfer*
Kane, Lorie *professional golfer*
Kerr, Cristie *professional golfer*
Kim, Christina *professional golfer*
Kim, Mi Hyun *professional golfer*
King, Betsy *professional golfer*
Klein, Emilee *professional golfer*
Kung, Candie *professional golfer*
Lincicome, Brittany *professional golfer*
Mallon, Meg *professional golfer*
Mears, Casey *race car driver*
Neumann, Liselotte *professional golfer*
Ochoa, Lorena *professional golfer*
Pak, Se Ri *professional golfer*
Park, Grace *professional golfer*
Park, Hee-Jung (Hee Jong Park) *professional golfer*
Robbins, Kelly *professional golfer*
Rosales, Jennifer *professional golfer*
Rudd, Ricky *race car driver*
Saiki, Kim *professional golfer*
Sheehan, Patty *professional golfer*
Sorenstam, Annika *professional golfer*
Steinhauer, Sherri *professional golfer*
Stupples, Karen *professional golfer*
Teske, Rachel *professional golfer*
Votaw, Ty M. *golf association commissioner*
Webb, Karrie *professional golfer*
Whitworth, Kathrynne Ann *professional golfer*
Wie, Michelle Sung *professional golfer*

**Deerfield Beach**
King, Don *boxing promoter*

**Fort Lauderdale**
Mahan, Mary Hoyle *retired physical educator*

**Gainesville**
Donovan, Billy *men's college basketball coach*
Meyer, Urban *college football coach*
Peck, Carolyn *basketball coach*

**Hollywood**
King, Alma Jean *retired physical education educator, healthcare educator*

**Jacksonville**
Campo, Dave *professional football coach*
Del Rio, Jack *professional football coach, former professional football player*
Leftwich, Byron Antron *professional football player*
Taylor, Fred *professional football player*
Washington, MaliVai *retired professional tennis player, foundation administrator*

**Jupiter**
Vanatta, Bob *athletic administrator*

**Key West**
Keenan, Mike (Micheal E. Keenan) *former professional sports team executive*

**Lady Lake**
Hartzler, Genevieve Lucille *physical education educator*

**Miami**
Coker, Larry *college football coach*
Loria, Jeffrey H. *sports team executive*
Martin, Jacques *professional hockey coach, professional sports team executive*
O'Neal, Shaquille Rashaun *professional basketball player*
Payton, Gary Dwayne *professional basketball player*
Riley, Patrick James *professional basketball coach*
Wade, Dwyane *professional basketball player*
Williams, Jason Chandler *professional basketball player*
Willis, Dontrelle *professional baseball player*

**Miami Beach**
Shula, Don Francis *retired professional football coach, professional sports team executive*

**Naples**
Frazer, John Howard *tennis association executive, retired manufacturing executive*

**Navarre**
Bare Grounds, Patricia Kelly *personal trainer, alcohol/drug abuse services professional, medical products executive*

**North Palm Beach**
Nicklaus, Jack William *professional golfer*

**Orlando**
Hardaway, Penny (Anfernee Deon Hardaway) *professional basketball player*
Hill, Brian *professional basketball team coach*
Hill, Grant *professional basketball player*
Price, (William) Mark *professional basketball player*

Redick, J.J. (Jonathan Clay Redick) *college basketball player*

**Ormond Beach**
Wendelstedt, Harry Hunter, Jr. *umpire*

**Palm Beach Gardens**
Ames, Stephen *professional golfer*
Couples, Frederick Steven *professional golfer*
Daly, John Patrick *professional golfer*
Duval, David Robert *professional golfer*
Furyk, James Michael (Jim Furyk) *professional golfer*
Haas, Jay *professional golfer*
Hamilton, Todd *professional golfer*
Mickelson, Phil (Philip Alfred Mickelson Jr.) *professional golfer*
Verplank, Scott Rachal *professional golfer*
Wadkins, Lanny Lanston *professional golfer*
Woods, Tiger (Eldrick Woods) *professional golfer*

**Palm City**
Mc Hale, John Joseph *baseball club executive*

**Ponte Vedra Beach**
Agassi, Andre Kirk *retired professional tennis player*
Blake, James Riley *professional tennis player*
Campbell, Chad *professional golfer*
Cink, Stewart *professional golfer*
Coria, Guillermo *professional tennis player*
Curtis, Ben Clifford *professional golfer*
DiMarco, Christian *professional golfer*
Ferrero, Juan Carlos *professional tennis player*
Finchem, Tim *sports association executive*
Garcia, Sergio *professional golfer*
Gaudio, Gaston *professional tennis player*
Ginepri, Robby (Robert Louis Ginepri) *professional tennis player*
Grosjean, Sebastien Rene *professional tennis player*
Langer, Bernard *professional golfer*
Moya, Carlos *professional tennis player*
Nalbandian, David *professional tennis player*
Novak, Jiri *professional tennis player*
Pavin, Corey Allen *professional golfer*
Rodriguez, Chi Chi (Juan Rodriguez) *professional golfer*
Weir, Mike *professional golfer*
Wilson, Dean *professional golfer*

**Saint Petersburg**
Clijsters, Kim *professional tennis player*
Coetzer, Amanda *professional tennis player*
Craybas, Jill *professional tennis player*
Dementieva, Elena *professional tennis player*
Granville, Laura *professional tennis player*
Hunsicker, Gerry *sports association executive*
Kuznetsova, Svetlana *professional tennis player*
Maddon, Joe *professional baseball coach*
Myskina, Anastasia *professional tennis player*
Sharapova, Maria *professional tennis player*
Shaughnessy, Meghann *professional tennis player*
Zimmer, Donald William *former professional baseball coach, former professional baseball manager*

**Sunrise**
Belfour, Ed *professional hockey player*
Larionov, Igor *professional hockey player*
Odelein, Lyle *professional hockey player*
Offerdahl, John Arnold *former professional football player, food service executive*

**Tallahassee**
Bowden, Bobby *college football coach*
Yerg, Beverly Johnson *physical education educator, researcher*

**Tampa**
Alstott, Michael Joseph (Mike Alstott) *professional football player*
Andreychuk, David *professional hockey player*
Brooks, Derrick Dewan *professional football player*
Burke, Sean *professional hockey player*
Feaster, Jay *professional sports team executive*
Galloway, Joe *professional football player*
Glazer, Malcolm *professional sports team executive*
Gruden, Jon *professional football coach*
Lecavalier, Vincent *professional hockey player*
Richards, Brad *professional hockey player*
St. Louis, Martin *professional hockey player*
Tortorella, John *professional hockey coach*

**Valrico**
Hess, Bonnie B. *physical education educator, volleyball coach*

**West Palm Beach**
Floyd, Raymond Loran *professional golfer*
Scott, Adam *professional golfer*

## GEORGIA

**Athens**
Richt, Mark *college football coach*

**Atlanta**
Aaron, Hank (Henry L. Aaron) *professional baseball team executive*
Bellamy, Walter *professional basketball player*
Braine, David Thomas *university athletic director*
Cox, Bobby (Robert Joe Cox) *professional baseball manager*
Douglas, Lee (Charles Douglas) *basketball team executive*
Gailey, Chan, Jr., (Thomas Chandler Gailey) *college football coach*
Hartley, Bob *professional hockey coach*
Hewitt, Paul Harrington *basketball coach*
Hudson, Tim *professional baseball player*
Jones, Andruw Rudolf *professional baseball player*
Jones, Chipper (Larry Wayne Jones Jr.) *professional baseball player*
Kovalchuk, Ilya *professional hockey player*
Renteria, Edgar *professional baseball player*

Rucchin, Steve *professional hockey player*
Schuerholz, John Boland, Jr. *professional baseball executive*
Smoltz, John Andrew *professional baseball player*
Thompson, Wallace Reeves III *physical education educator*
Waddell, Don *professional sports team executive*
Woodson, Mike *professional basketball coach*

**Fairburn**
Holyfield, Evander *professional boxer*

**Flowery Branch**
Abraham, John *professional football player*
Blank, Arthur M. *professional sports team executive, retired lumber company executive*
Crumpler, Alge *professional football player*
Dunn, Warrick *professional football player*
Hall, DeAngelo *professional football player*
McKay, Richard James *professional sports team executive*
Mora, Jim, Jr. *professional football coach*
Vick, Michael (Michael Dwayne Vick) *professional football player*

**Marietta**
Devigne, Karen Cooke *retired amateur athletics executive*

**Morrow**
Totty, Totty Okoro *soccer coach*

## ILLINOIS

**Alsip**
Fournier, Maureen Mary *physical education educator*

**Chicago**
Albright, Chris *professional soccer player*
Baines, Harold Douglass *retired professional baseball player, baseball bench coach*
Baker, Dusty (Johnnie B. Baker Jr.) *professional baseball team manager*
Baumgardt, Justi Michelle *professional soccer player*
Beasley, DaMarcus Lamont *professional soccer player*
Berhalter, Gregg *professional soccer player*
Bocanegra, Carlos *professional soccer player*
Buehrle, Mark *professional baseball player*
Burnitz, Jeromy *professional baseball player*
Cherdunolo, Steve *professional soccer player*
Ching, Brian *professional soccer player*
Conrad, Jimmy *professional soccer player*
Convey, Bobby (Robert Francis Convey) *professional soccer player*
Dempsey, Clinton (Clint) Drew *professional soccer player*
Dempster, Ryan Scott *professional baseball player*
Donovan, Landon *professional soccer player*
Dudley, Rick (Richard C. Dudley) *professional sports team executive*
Dye, Jermaine *professional baseball player*
Erkes, Jason *sports association executive*
Fawcett, Joy Lynn *retired professional soccer player*
Foudy, Julie Maurine *retired professional soccer player, Olympic athlete*
Gabarra, Carin Leslie *professional soccer player, professional soccer coach*
Gervais, Mark G. *physical education educator*
Gordon, Ben *professional basketball player*
Guillen, Ozzie (Oswaldo Jose Barrios Guillen) *professional baseball team manager*
Hahnemann, Marcus *professional soccer player*
Hamm, Mia (Mariel Margaret Hamm) *retired professional soccer player*
Heinrichs, April *soccer coach*
Howard, Tim *professional soccer player*
Hucles, Angela Khalia *professional soccer player*
Johnson, Eddie *professional soccer player*
Jones, Cobi *professional soccer player*
Keller, Kasey *professional soccer player*
Khabibulin, Nikolai *professional hockey player*
Konerko, Paul *professional baseball player*
Kreis, Jason *professional soccer player*
Lee, Derrek Leon *professional baseball player*
Lewis, Eddie *professional soccer player*
Lilly, Kristine Marie *professional soccer player*
MacMillan, Shannon Ann *professional soccer player*
Mastroeni, Pablo *professional soccer player*
Milbrett, Tiffeny Carleen *professional soccer player*
Myernick, Glenn *professional soccer coach*
O'Brien, John *professional soccer player*
Olsen, Ben *professional soccer player*
Onyewu, Oguchi *professional soccer player*
O'Reilly, Heather Ann *Olympic athlete*
Parlow, Cynthia Maria *professional soccer player*
Pizer, Howard Charles *sports and entertainment executive*
Pope, Eddie *professional soccer player*
Prior, Mark *professional baseball player*
Ralph, Damani *professional soccer player*
Ramirez, Aramis *professional baseball player*
Reddick, Catherine Anne (Cat Reddick) *Olympic athlete*
Reinsdorf, Jerry Michael *professional sports team executive, real estate company executive, accountant, lawyer*
Reyna, Claudio *professional soccer player*
Roberts, Tiffany Marie *former soccer player*
Schwartz, Alan Gifford *sport company executive*
Scurry, Briana Collette *professional soccer player*
Selolwane, Diphetogo (Dipsy Selolwane) *professional soccer player*
Skiles, Scott Allen *professional basketball coach*
Sobrero, Kate (Kathryn Michele Sobrero) *professional soccer player*
Tallon, Dale *professional sports team executive*
Thomas, Tim *professional basketball player*
Thome, Jim *professional baseball player*
Venturini, Tisha Lea *professional soccer player*
Wallace, Ben *professional basketball player*
Wambach, Abby (Mary Abigail Wambach) *Olympic athlete*
Wolff, Josh *professional soccer player*

Wood, Kerry *professional baseball player*
Yawney, Trent *professional hockey coach, retired professional hockey player*

**Evanston**
Davis, Shani *Olympic athlete*

**Glenview**
King, Billie Jean Moffitt *retired professional tennis player*

**Lake Forest**
Benson, Cedric *professional football player*
Griese, Brian *professional football player*
McCaskey, Michael B. *professional football team executive*
Muhammad, Mushin *professional football player*
Orton, Kyle *professional football player*
Smith, Lovie *professional football coach*
Urlacher, Brian *professional football player*

**Libertyville**
Trzyna, Chris *physical education educator*

**Lincolnshire**
Schauble, John Eugene *physical education educator*

**Mahomet**
Thompson, Margaret M. *physical education educator*

**Springfield**
Hicks, David Eric *retired sports association executive*

**Westmont**
Tricase, Elizabeth *gymnast*

## INDIANA

**Bloomington**
Sampson, Kelvin Dale *college basketball coach*

**Granger**
Thomas, Debi (Debra J. Thomas) *ice skater*

**Indianapolis**
Bird, Larry Joe *professional athletics manager, former professional basketball coach*
Carlisle, Rick *professional basketball coach*
Catchings, Tamika Devonne *professional basketball player*
Croshere, Austin *professional basketball player*
Dawes, Dominique *Olympic athlete*
Dungy, Tony *professional football coach*
Fortner, Nell *professional athletics coach*
Freeney, Dwight *professional football player*
Greene, Maurice *Olympic athlete, track and field athlete*
Harrison, Marvin *professional football player*
Irsay, James Steven *professional football team owner*
Jackson, Stephen *professional basketball player*
Jones, Marion *track and field athlete*
Keflezighi, Mebrahtom *professional marathon runner*
Manning, Peyton Williams *professional football player*
Montoya, Juan Pablo *professional race car driver*
O'Neal, Jermaine *professional basketball player*
Taylor, Angelo *Olympic athlete*
Vinatieri, Adam Matthew *professional football player*
Wilkinson, Laura *Olympic athlete*
Williams, Bernard *Olympic athlete*

**Muncie**
Lynch, Bill *university football coach*

**Notre Dame**
Weis, Charlie *college football coach*

**West Lafayette**
Sims-Curry, Kristy *women's college basketball coach*

## IOWA

**Ames**
Fennelly, William *basketball coach*

**Davenport**
Foster, James Franklin *professional sports management executive*

**Iowa City**
Bowlsby, Bob *athletic director*
Ferentz, Kirk *college football coach*

**Riverside**
Rew, Ken E. *physical education educator, healthcare educator, coach*

## KANSAS

**Manhattan**
Patterson, Deb *women's college basketball coach*

**Mission**
Trevino, Lee Buck *professional golfer*
Watson, Thomas Sturges *professional golfer*

**Saint Marys**
Byers, Walter *athletic association executive*

**Yates Center**
Stockebrand, Larry Dean *physical education educator, director*

## KENTUCKY

**Lexington**
Prado, Edgar *horse racing jockey*
Smith, Michael Earl *jockey*

Zito, Nick *horse trainer, breeder*

**Louisville**
Petrino, Bobby *college football coach*
Pitino, Richard *collegiate basketball coach, former professional basketball coach*

**Richmond**
Inman, Larry Joe *basketball coach*

## LOUISIANA

**Baton Rouge**
Chatman, Dana (Pokey Chatman) *women's college basketball coach*
Miles, Les *college football coach*

**Grambling**
Robinson, Eddie Gay *college football coach*

**Metairie**
Brees, Drew *professional football player*
Bush, Reggie *professional football player*
Payton, Sean *professional football coach*

**New Orleans**
Scelfo, Chris *university football coach*

**Shreveport**
Shemwell, Mary Anne *adapted physical education specialist*
Sutton, Hal Evan *professional golfer*

## MAINE

**Bangor**
Kelley, Barbara Bannin *physical education educator*

**Kingfield**
Wescott, Seth *Olympic athlete*

**Portland**
Blair, Bonnie Kathleen *former professional speedskater, former Olympic athlete*
Chow, Amy *gymnast, Olympic athlete*
Powers, Ross *Olympic athlete*

## MARYLAND

**Baltimore**
Angelos, Peter G. *professional sports team executive, lawyer*
Bedard, Erik *professional baseball player*
Benson, Kris *professional baseball player*
Duquette, Jim *professional sports team executive*
Fassel, Jim (James E. Fassel) *professional football coach*
Lewis, Jamal *professional football player*
Lewis, Ray *professional football player*
McNair, Steve LaTreal *professional football player*
Ogden, Jonathan *professional football player*
Palmeiro, Rafael Corrales *professional baseball player*
Robinson, Brooks Calbert, Jr. *former professional baseball player, sports commentator, business consultant*
Sanders, Deion Luwynn *professional football player*
Tejada, Miguel *professional baseball player*

**College Park**
Frese, Brenda *women's college basketball coach*

**Owings Mills**
Billick, Brian *professional football coach*
Newsome, Ozzie *professional sports team executive*

**Rockville**
Greenberg, Jerrold Selig *health education educator*

## MASSACHUSETTS

**Boston**
Ainge, Danny Ray *professional basketball coach*
Allen, Tony *professional basketball player*
Beckett, Joshua Patrick *professional baseball player*
Blendon, Robert Jay *health policy educator*
Cherington, Ben *professional sports team executive*
Chiarelli, Peter *professional sports team executive*
Crisp, Coco (Covelli Crisp) *professional baseball player*
DiSarcina, Gary Thomas *retired professional baseball player, sportscaster*
Duquette, Daniel F. *professional baseball team executive*
Epstein, Theo N. *professional sports team executive*
Foulke, Keith Charles *professional baseball player*
Francona, Terry Jon *professional baseball manager*
Gomes, Ryan *professional basketball player*
Gonzalez, Juan (Alberto Vazquez) *professional baseball player*
Grousbeck, Wyc *professional sports team executive*
Henry, John W. *professional sports team executive*
Hoyer, Jed *professional sports team executive*
Leetch, Brian Joseph *professional hockey player*
Lewis, Dave *professional hockey coach, former professional hockey player*
Loretta, Mark *professional baseball player*
Lowell, Mike *professional baseball player*
Neely, Cameron Michael *former professional hockey player*
Ortiz, David (David Americo Ortiz Arias) *professional baseball player*
Papelbon, Jon *professional baseball player*
Pierce, Paul *professional basketball player*
Ramirez, Manuel Aristides (Manny Ramirez) *professional baseball player*

Rivers, Glenn Anton (Doc Rivers) *professional basketball coach*
Schilling, Curtis Montague *professional baseball player*
Sinden, Harry *professional sports team executive*
Szczerbiak, Wally *professional basketball player*
Timlin, Mike *professional baseball player*
Varitek, Jason *professional baseball player*
Wakefield, Timothy Stephen (Tim Wakefield) *professional baseball player*
Walker, Antoine Devon *professional basketball player*

**Chestnut Hill**
O'Brien, Tom *college football coach*

**Foxboro**
Belichick, Bill (William Stephen Belichick) *professional football coach*
Brady, Tom (Thomas Edward Patrick Brady Jr.) *professional football player*
Bruschi, Tedy *professional football player*
Dillon, Corey *professional football player*
Kraft, Robert K. *professional sports team executive*

**Lynnfield**
Kerrigan, Nancy *professional figure skater, retired Olympic athlete*

**Newbury**
Vilma, Jonathan Polynice *professional football player*

**North Brookfield**
McNeaney, Lee Anne *physical education educator*

**Springfield**
Hagan, Clifford O. *retired basketball player*

**Whitman**
Daley, James L. *coach, director*

## MICHIGAN

**Allen Park**
Kitna, Jon *professional football player*
Marinelli, Rod *professional football coach*
Millen, Matt *professional sports team executive*
Pollard, Marcus *professional football player*
Williams, Roy *professional football player*

**Ann Arbor**
Carr, Lloyd *college football coach*
Ray, Elise *gymnast*

**Auburn Hills**
Billups, Chauncey *professional basketball player*
Dumars, Joe III *retired professional basketball player*
Hamilton, Richard Clay *professional basketball player*
McDyess, Antonio *professional basketball player*
Palmer, Wendy *professional basketball player*
Saunders, Flip (Philip D. Saunders) *professional basketball coach*
Wallace, Rasheed *professional basketball player, marketing professional*

**Detroit**
Babcock, Mike *professional hockey coach*
Bing, David *retired professional basketball player, metal products executive*
Bowman, William Scott (Scotty Bowman) *professional hockey coach*
Chelios, Christos K. *professional hockey player*
Datsyuk, Pavel *professional hockey player*
Devellano, James Charles *professional hockey manager, baseball executive*
Hasek, Dominik *professional hockey player*
Holland, Ken *professional sports team executive*
Ilitch, Marian *professional hockey team executive, food service executive*
Ilitch, Michael *professional hockey team executive, food products executive*
Lidstrom, Nicklas *professional hockey player*
Martz, Mike *former professional football coach*
Monroe, Craig *professional baseball player*
Ordonez, Magglio *professional baseball player*
Osgood, Chris *professional hockey player*
Rodriguez, Ivan Torres *professional baseball player*
Yzerman, Steve (Stephen Gregory Yzerman) *professional sports team executive, retired professional hockey player*

**East Lansing**
Izzo, Thomas *college basketball coach*

## MINNESOTA

**Eden Prairie**
Childress, Brad *professional football coach*
Johnson, Brad *professional football player*
McCombs, Billy Joe (Red McCombs) *professional football team executive*
Smoot, Fred *professional football player*
Woods, Gary V. *professional football team executive, former professional basketball team executive, automotive executive*

**Minneapolis**
Augustus, Seimone *professional basketball player*
Boone, Bret Robert *professional baseball player*
Casey, Dwane *professional basketball player*
Gardenhire, Ronald Clyde *professional athletics manager*
Garnett, Kevin *professional basketball player*
Hudson, Troy *professional basketball player*
Kelly, Tom (Jay Thomas Kelly) *retired professional sports team manager*
Lehman, Tom (Thomas Edward Lehman) *professional golfer*
Mauer, J *professional baseball player*
McConnell Serio, Suzie Theresa *former professional basketball player, professional basketball coach*

McHale, Kevin Edward *professional sports team executive, retired professional basketball player*
Monson, Dan *college basketball coach*
Nanne, Louis Vincent *professional hockey team executive*
Nevin, Phillip *professional baseball player*
Olowokandi, Michael *professional basketball player*
Santana, Johan Alexander *professional baseball player*
Smith, Katie (Katherine May Smith) *professional basketball player*
Sprewell, Latrell Fontaine *professional basketball player*

**Saint Paul**
Lemaire, Jacques *professional hockey coach*
Risebrough, Doug *professional sports team executive*

## MISSISSIPPI

**Itta Bena**
Wax, Benjamin *physical education educator, consultant*

**Mississippi State**
Croom, Sylvester *football coach*

## MISSOURI

**Bridgeton**
Faulk, Marshall William *professional football player*

**Earth City**
Bulger, Marc *professional football player*
Chandler, Christopher Mark (Chris Chandler) *professional football player*
Coakley, Dexter *professional football player*
Holt, Torry *professional football player*

**Kansas City**
Allen, Marcus *retired professional football player*
Brett, George Howard *baseball executive, former professional baseball player*
Cunningham, Gunther *professional football coach*
Edwards, Herman *professional football coach*
Gansler, Robert *professional soccer coach*
Gonzalez, Tony *professional football player*
Green, Trent Jason *professional football player*
Holmes, Priest *professional football player*
Hunt, Lamar *professional football team executive*
Johnson, Larry, Jr. *professional football player*
Moore, Dayton *professional sports team executive*
Shields, Will Herthie *professional football player*

**Saint Louis**
Carpenter, Chris *professional baseball player*
Davidson, John *professional sports team executive, former hockey analyst*
Demitra, Pavol *professional hockey player*
Devers, Gail *track and field athlete*
Eckstein, David *professional baseball player*
Edmonds, James Patrick (Jim Edmonds) *professional baseball player*
Grudzielanek, Mark James *professional baseball player*
Guerin, Bill *professional hockey player*
Haslett, Jim *professional football coach*
Joyner Kersee, Jackie (Jacqueline Joyner Kersee) *retired track and field athlete*
Kitchen, Mike *professional hockey coach, retired professional hockey player*
Lalime, Patrick *professional hockey player*
La Russa, Tony, Jr., (Anthony La Russa Jr.) *professional baseball manager*
Linehan, Scott *professional football coach*
Morris, Matthew Christian *professional baseball player*
Pace, Orlando Lamar *professional football player*
Pleau, Lawrence Winslow *professional sports team executive*
Pujols, Albert *professional baseball player*
Rolen, Scott Bruce *professional baseball player*
Smith, Ozzie (Osborne Earl Smith) *retired professional baseball player*
Tkachuk, Keith *professional hockey player*
Weight, Doug *professional hockey player*

## NEBRASKA

**Hastings**
Katen, Troy William *basketball coach, academic administrator*

**Lincoln**
Callahan, Bill *college football coach*
Mulvaney, Mary Jean *retired physical education educator*

**Seward**
Madsen, Aaron Jeffrey *athletic trainer*

## NEVADA

**Las Vegas**
Schneiter, George Malan *professional golfer, real estate developer*

## NEW HAMPSHIRE

**Newmarket**
Jernigan, David Bruce *men's college basketball coach*

## NEW JERSEY

**Branchville**
Pasvolsky, Richard Lloyd *retired parks, recreation, and environment educator*

**Cherry Hill**
Erving, Julius (Julius Winfield Erving II) *retired professional basketball player, business executive*
Trotter, Jeremiah *professional football player*

**East Orange**
Tarver, Antonio *professional boxer*

**East Rutherford**
Accorsi, Ernest William, Jr. *professional football team executive*
Arrington, LaVar *professional football player*
Brodeur, Martin *professional hockey player*
Burress, Plaxico *professional football player*
Carter, Vince *professional basketball player*
Cartwright, James William (Bill Cartwright) *professional basketball coach, retired professional basketball player*
Coughlin, Tom *professional football coach*
Elias, Patrik *professional hockey player*
Frank, Lawrence *professional basketball coach*
Gionta, Brian *professional hockey player*
Gomez, Scott *professional hockey player*
Guevara, Amado *professional soccer player*
Jefferson, Richard *professional basketball player*
Julien, Claude *professional hockey coach*
Kidd, Jason *professional basketball player*
Lamoriello, Louis Anthony *professional sports team executive*
Langenbrunner, Jamie *professional hockey player*
MacLean, John *professional hockey coach, former professional hockey player*
Manning, Eli (Elisha Nelson Manning) *professional football player*
Mashburn, Jamal *professional basketball player*
Mogilny, Alexander *professional hockey player*
Robinson, Clifford *professional basketball player*
Shockey, Jeremy Charles *professional football player*
Stevens, Scott *retired professional hockey player*
Strahan, Michael Anthony *professional football player*
Toomer, Amani *professional football player*
Umenyiora, Osi *professional football player*
Vanderbeek, Jeffrey *professional sports team executive*

**Fort Lee**
Baiul, Oksana *former figure skater, clothing designer*

**Jersey City**
Thor, Ira P. *sports director*

**Little Falls**
Berra, Yogi (Lawrence Peter Berra) *former professional baseball player, coach and manager*

**New Brunswick**
Dougherty, Neil Joseph *physical education educator, consultant*

**Secaucus**
Arena, Bruce *professional soccer coach*
Bradley, Bob *professional soccer coach*
Meola, Tony *professional soccer player, actor*
Sakiewicz, Nick *professional sports team executive*
Sanders, Summer *Olympic athlete, news correspondent, newscaster*
Silver, Adam *sports association executive*

**Stone Harbor**
Koss, Rosabel Steinhauer *retired health and physical education educator*

**Union**
Darden, Joseph Samuel, Jr. *health educator*

## NEW MEXICO

**Abiquiu**
Howlett, Phyllis Lou *retired athletics conference administrator*

## NEW YORK

**Brentwood**
Burgess, John Thomas *physical education educator, consultant*

**Brockport**
Smith, Daniel Elon *physical education educator*

**Bronx**
Abreu, Bobby *professional baseball player*
Afterman, Jean *professional sports team executive*
Cashman, Brian *professional sports team executive*
Damon, Johnny *professional baseball player*
Giambi, Jason Gilbert *professional baseball player*
Jeter, Derek Sanderson *professional baseball player*
Johnson, Randy (Randall David Johnson) *professional baseball player*
Lienert, Christoph *physical education educator*
Martinez, Tino *professional baseball player*
Matsui, Hideki *professional baseball player*
Mazzilli, Lee *professional baseball manager*
Mussina, Michael Cole *professional baseball player*
Olerud, John Garrett *professional baseball player*
Pena, Antonio Francisco (Tony Pena) *professional athletics coach*
Posada, Jorge Rafael *professional baseball player*
Rivera, Mariano *professional baseball player*
Rodriguez, Alex (Alexander Emmanuel Rodriguez) *professional baseball player*
Sheffield, Gary Antonian *professional baseball player*
Steinbrenner, George Michael III *professional baseball team executive, shipbuilding company executive*
Torre, Joe (Joseph Paul Torre) *professional baseball team manager*
Widger, Chris *professional baseball player*

Williams, Bernie (Bernabe Figueroa Williams) *professional baseball player*

**Brooklyn**
Lentini, Francine *physical education educator*
Ratner, Bruce C. *professional sports team executive, real estate developer*

**Buffalo**
Drury, Chris *professional hockey player*
Kelly, Jim (James Edward Kelly) *former professional football player*
Regier, Darcy John *professional sports team executive*
Ruff, Lindy *professional hockey coach*

**Cooperstown**
Mays, Willie Howard, Jr., (Say Hey Kid) *former professional baseball player*
Sutter, Bruce (Howard Sutter) *retired professional baseball player*

**Flushing**
Beltran, Carlos *professional baseball player*
Delgado, Carlos Juan *professional baseball player*
Glavine, Tom (Thomas Michael Glavine) *professional baseball player*
Martinez, Pedro Jaime *professional baseball player*
Minaya, Omar *professional sports team executive*
Randolph, Willie Larry *professional baseball manager*
Reyes, Jose *professional baseball player*
Wagner, Billy *professional baseball player*
Wright, David *professional baseball player*

**Garden City**
Berka, Marianne Guthrie *health and physical education educator*

**Hempstead**
Bradway, Terry *professional sports team executive*
Coles, Laveranues *professional football player*
Dyson, Andre *professional football player*
Ferguson, D'Brickashaw *professional football player*
Fiedler, Jay *professional football player*
Mangini, Eric *professional football coach*
Martin, Curtis *professional football player*
Tannenbaum, Mike (Michael Tannenbaum) *professional sports team executive*

**Lake Placid**
Grimmette, Mark *Olympic athlete*
Martin, Brian *Olympic athlete*
Rossi, Ronald Aldo *sports association administrator, Olympic athlete*

**Mamaroneck**
McEnroe, Patrick *former professional tennis player, sports commentator*

**New Hyde Park**
Esiason, Boomer (Norman Julius Esiason) *professional football player*

**New York**
Adubato, Richard Adam (Richie Adubato) *professional basketball coach*
Bettman, Gary Bruce *National Hockey League Commissioner*
Blazejowski, Carol A. *professional sports team executive, retired professional basketball player*
Brown, James Kevin (Kevin Brown) *professional baseball player*
Brown, Renee *sports association executive*
Canseco, Jose *retired professional baseball player*
Capriati, Jennifer Maria *professional tennis player*
Colon, Bartolo *professional baseball player*
Cook, Traci *sports association executive*
DuPuy, Bob (Robert A. DuPuy) *major league baseball executive*
Francis, Steve *professional basketball player*
Frye, Channing *professional basketball player*
Garber, Donald *Major League Soccer commissioner*
Goodell, Roger *national football league commissioner*
Granik, Russ (Russell T. Granik) *sports association executive*
Gulati, Sunil *sports administrator*
Hernandez, Keith *retired professional baseball player*
Houston, Allan Wade *professional basketball player*
Jackson, Reggie (Reginald Martinez Jackson, Mr. October) *former professional baseball player*
Jagr, Jaromir *professional hockey player*
Johnson, Vickie *professional basketball player*
Leiter, Al (Alois Terry Leiter) *retired professional baseball player*
Louganis, Greg E. (Gregory Efthimios Louganis) *retired Olympic athlete, actor*
Lundqvist, Henrik *professional hockey player*
Marbury, Stephon *professional basketball player*
Mariner, Jonathan D. *major league baseball executive*
Martin, Michael Townsend *sports association executive, marketing professional, consultant*
Nusum, John Barry *professional soccer player*
Orender, Donna *sports association executive*
Ozolinsh, Sandis *professional hockey player*
Phillips, Tari *professional basketball player*
Renney, Tom *professional hockey coach*
Rose, Jalen *professional basketball player*
Ruta, Thomas V. *professional sports team executive, accounting professional*
Sampras, Pete *retired professional tennis player*
Sather, Glen Cameron *professional hockey team executive, coach*
Scott, Dale Allan *major league umpire*
Selig, Bud (Alan H. Selig) *major league baseball commissioner*
Shanahan, Brendan Frederick *professional hockey player*
Steinfeld, Allan *sports association administrator*
Stern, David Joel *National Basketball Association Commissioner*
Thomas, Isiah Lord III *professional basketball coach, professional sports team executive, retired professional basketball player*

Ward, Aaron *professional hockey player*
Watson, Robert Jose *professional sports team executive*
Zahndt, Richard H. *sports association executive, lawyer*

**North Tonawanda**
Zimmerman, Bonnie Elizabeth *physical education educator*

**Orchard Park**
Jauron, Dick (Richard M. Jauron) *professional football coach*
Levy, Marv (Marvin Daniel Levy) *professional sports team executive, former professional football coach*
McGahee, Willis *professional football player*
Spikes, Takeo Gerard *professional football player*

**Plainview**
Zhitnik, Alexei *professional hockey player*

**South Salem**
Schindler, Teri *sports association executive*

**Syracuse**
Boeheim, Jim *college basketball coach*

**Uniondale**
DiPietro, Rick *professional hockey player*
Kozlov, Viktor *professional hockey player*
Milbury, Mike *professional sports team executive, former professional hockey coach*
Nolan, Ted (Theodore John Nolan) *professional hockey coach*
Snow, Garth *professional sports team executive, former professional hockey player*
Trottier, Bryan John *professional sports team executive, former professional hockey player and coach*
Wang, Charles B. *professional sports team executive, former computer company executive*

**West Point**
Ross, Robert Joseph (Bobby Ross) *college football coach*

**White Plains**
Davenport, Lindsay *professional tennis player*
Frazier, Amy *professional tennis player*
Garrison-Jackson, Zina *retired professional tennis player*
Gilbert, Bradley *professional tennis coach, former professional tennis player, former Olympic athlete*
Gimelstob, Justin *professional tennis player*
Morariu, Corina *professional tennis player*
Raymond, Lisa *professional tennis player*
Rubin, Chanda *professional tennis player*
Williams, Serena *professional tennis player, apparel designer*
Williams, Ted Vaughnell *physical education educator*
Williams, Venus *professional tennis player*

## NORTH CAROLINA

**Biltmore Lake**
Steele, Russell Loren *football coach*

**Carrboro**
Generous, William Thomas, Jr., (Tom Generous) *coach, educator*

**Chapel Hill**
Smith, Dean Edwards *retired men's college basketball coach*
Williams, Roy *college basketball coach*

**Charlotte**
Bickerstaff, Bernie *professional basketball player*
Davis, Stephen *professional football player*
Delhomme, Jake Christopher *professional football player*
Fox, John *professional football coach*
Johnson, Jimmie *race car driver*
Lacey, Trudi *professional athletics coach*
Okafor, Emeka *professional basketball player*
Peppers, Julius *professional football player*
Proehl, Ricky *professional football player*
Smith, Steve *professional football player*
Staley, Dawn Michelle *professional basketball player*
Stinson, Andrea Maria *professional basketball player*
Weinke, Chris *professional football player*
Whitfield, Fred, Jr. *professional sports team executive*

**Concord**
Busch, Kurt *race car driver*
Smith, Ollen Bruton *sports association executive*

**Conover**
Jarrett, Dale *race car driver*

**Durham**
Case, Richard W. *sports association executive*
Goestenkors, Gail *basketball coach*
Krzyzewski, Mike *university athletic coach*
Rennie, John *soccer coach*

**High Point**
Burton, Ward *professional race car driver*

**Huntersville**
Stewart, Tony *professional race car driver*

**Mooresville**
Earnhardt, Dale, Jr. *race car driver*
Edwards, Carl *race car driver*
Elder, Christian *race car driver*
Martin, Mark *race car driver*
Münter, Leilani Maaja *race car driver*
Newman, Ryan *race car driver*
Waltrip, Michael *professional race car driver*

**Raleigh**
Brind'Amour, Rod *professional hockey player*
Cole, Erik *professional hockey player*
Hedican, Bret *professional hockey player*
Irbe, Arturs *professional hockey player*
Laviolette, Peter *professional hockey coach*
Lowe, Sidney *professional basketball coach*
Rutherford, Jim *professional sports team executive*
Staal, Eric *professional hockey player*
Stillman, Cory *professional hockey player*
Tverdovsky, Oleg *professional hockey player*
Ward, Cam *professional hockey player*
Wesley, Glen *professional hockey player*
Whitney, Ray *professional hockey player*

**Randleman**
Petty, Richard *retired race car driver*

**Statesville**
Kahne, Kasey *race car driver*
Mayfield, Jeremy *race car driver*

**Welcome**
Sauter, Johnny *race car driver*

## OHIO

**Aurora**
Eakin, Thomas Capper *sports promotion executive*

**Berea**
Crennel, Romeo *professional football coach*
Davis, Butch (Paul Hilton Davis) *former professional football coach*

**Canton**
Carson, Harry *retired professional football player*
Mack, Tom *retired professional football player*
Moon, Warren *professional football player*
Shaw, Billy *retired professional football player*
Wright, Rayfield *professional football player*

**Cincinnati**
Chambliss, Carroll Christopher *professional baseball coach*
Dunn, Adam *professional baseball player*
Griffey, Ken, Jr. (George Kenneth Griffey Jr.) *professional baseball player*
Johnson, Chad *professional football player*
Lewis, Marvin *professional football coach*
Narron, Jerry *professional baseball manager*
Palmer, Carson *professional football player*

**Cleveland**
Appleby, Stuart *professional golfer*
Brown, Mike *professional basketball coach*
Elarton, Vincent Scott *professional baseball player*
Gooden, Drew *professional basketball player*
Henman, Tim *professional tennis player*
Ilgauskas, Zydrunas *professional basketball player*
James, LeBron *professional basketball player*
Jones, Damon *professional basketball player*
Lopez, Nancy *retired professional golfer*
Moceanu, Dominique *retired Olympic athlete*
Pierce, Mary *professional tennis player*
Seles, Monica *professional tennis player*

**Columbus**
Bartels, Robert Louis *retired physical education educator, coach*
Fedorov, Sergei *professional hockey player*
Gallant, Gerald *professional hockey coach, retired professional hockey player*
Hamm, Paul *Olympic athlete*
MacLean, Doug *professional sports team executive*
Modin, Fredrik *professional hockey player*
Tressel, Jim *college football coach*

**Fairfield**
Robertson, Oscar Palmer (Big O Robertson) *chemical company executive, former professional basketball player*
Sheehan, Samantha *gymnast*

**Oxford**
Pont, John *football coach, educator*

**Westlake**
Ohno, Apolo Anton *Olympic athlete*
Parra, Derek *Olympic athlete*

## OKLAHOMA

**Norman**
Stoops, Bob *college football coach*

**Oklahoma City**
Binning, Bette Finese (Mrs. Gene Hedgcock Binning) *athletic association official*
Fernandez, Lisa *softball player*
Paul, Chris *professional basketball player*
Scott, Byron Alton *professional basketball coach, retired professional basketball player*

## OREGON

**Bend**
Nosler, Robert Amos *sports association executive*

**Corvallis**
Casey, Pat *college baseball coach*

**Eugene**
Sisley, Becky Lynn *physical education educator*

**Portland**
Patterson, Steve *professional basketball team executive*
Van Exel, Nickey Maxwell *professional basketball player*

## PENNSYLVANIA

**California**
Cramer Roh, Joni Lee *physical education educator*

**Clifton Heights**
Pagano, Richard Donald *physical education educator, researcher*

**Easton**
Holmes, Larry, Sr. *retired boxer*

**Grove City**
Lyle, Donald L. *physical education educator, department chairman*

**King Of Prussia**
Rubin, Michael G. *sports internet company executive*

**Philadelphia**
Akers, David *professional football player*
Brown, Dave *professional sports team executive*
Cashman, Wayne *professional athletics coach*
Cheeks, Maurice Edward *professional basketball coach, retired professional basketball player*
Clarke, Robert Earle (Bobby Clarke) *professional sports team executive*
Desjardins, Eric *retired professional hockey player*
Dunphy, Fran *men's college basketball coach*
Forsberg, Peter *professional hockey player*
Gagné, Simon *professional hockey player, Olympic athlete*
Gillick, Patrick
Hitchcock, Ken *professional hockey coach*
Howard, Ryan *professional baseball player*
Iverson, Allen Ezail *professional basketball player*
Kearse, Jevon *professional football player*
Lurie, Jeffrey *professional sports team executive*
Manuel, Charlie (Charles Fuqua Manuel Jr.) *professional baseball manager*
McNabb, Donovan *professional football player*
Primeau, Keith *retired professional hockey player*
Reid, Andy *professional football coach*
Rollins, James Calvin (Jimmy Rollins) *professional baseball player*
Rowand, Aaron *professional baseball player*
Ryan, Ron *former professional sports team executive, consultant*
Sanderson, Geoff *professional hockey player*
Smith, L.J. *professional football player*
Snider, Edward Malcolm *professional hockey club executive*
Utley, Chase *professional baseball player*
Warren, Christopher Collins *professional football player*
Webber, Chris, III, (Mayce Edward Christopher Webber) *professional basketball player*
Westbrook, Brian *professional football player*

**Pittsburgh**
Berenato, Agnus McGlade *women's college basketball coach*
Cowher, Bill (William Laird Cowher) *professional football coach*
Crosby, Sidney *professional hockey player*
Faneca, Alan *professional football player*
LeBeau, Dick *professional football coach, retired professional football player*
LeClair, John Clark *professional hockey player*
Lemieux, Mario *professional sports team executive, retired professional hockey player*
Littlefield, David *professional sports team executive*
Malkin, Evgeni *professional hockey player*
McClatchy, Kevin S. *professional sports team executive*
Mesa, Jose Ramon *professional baseball player*
Polamalu, Troy *professional football player*
Recchi, Mark *professional hockey player*
Roethlisberger, Ben *professional football player*
Rooney, Daniel M. *professional football team executive*
Shero, Ray (Rejean Shero) *professional sports team executive*
Therrien, Michel *former professional hockey coach*
Tracy, Jim (James Edward Tracy) *professional baseball manager*
Wannstedt, David Raymond *college football coach, former professional football coach*
Ward, Hines, Jr. *professional football player*

**Reading**
Hornish, Sam, Jr. *race car driver*

**Springfield**
Heath, Michael R. *physical education educator*

**University Park**
Paterno, Joe (Joseph Vincent Paterno) *college football coach*

**Villanova**
Wright, Jay *men's college basketball coach*

**Youngstown**
Palmer, Arnold Daniel *professional golfer*

## RHODE ISLAND

**Cranston**
Perna, Marie Immaculate *retired physical education educator*

**Providence**
Russell, Bill *former professional basketball team executive, former professional basketball player*

## SOUTH CAROLINA

**Clemson**
Bowden, Tommy *college football coach*

**Columbia**
Spurrier, Steve (Steven Orr Spurrier) *college football coach*

**Myrtle Beach**
Berry, James W. *athletic trainer, secondary school educator*

**Rock Hill**
Ford, Mary (Polly) Wylie *retired physical education educator*

## TENNESSEE

**Knoxville**
Fulmer, Phillip *university football coach*

**Memphis**
Battier, Shane *professional basketball player*
Calipari, John *men's college basketball coach*
Fratello, Mike (Michael Robert Fratello) *professional basketball coach*
Gould, Rebecca Susan *sports association executive*
West, Jerry Alan *professional basketball team executive*

**Mount Juliet**
Hamilton, Bobby *professional race car driver*
Lester, Bill (William Alexander Lester) *race car driver*

**Nashville**
Arnott, Jason *professional hockey player*
Collins, Kerry *professional football player*
Fisher, Jeff *professional football coach*
George, Eddie (Edward Nathan George) *former professional football player*
Kariya, Paul *professional hockey player*
Leipold, Craig L. *professional sports team executive*
Poile, David Robert *professional sports team executive*
Snoddy, Chris Raymond *athletic trainer*
Trotz, Barry *professional hockey coach*
Young, Vince Paul, Jr. *professional football player*

## TEXAS

**Arlington**
Lee, Carlos *professional baseball player*
Millwood, Kevin *professional baseball player*
Rogers, Kenny (Kenneth Scott Rogers) *professional baseball player*
Showalter, Buck (William Nathaniel Showalter III) *major league baseball team manager*
Teixeira, Mark *professional baseball player*
Young, Michael *professional baseball player*

**Austin**
Armstrong, Lance *professional cyclist*
Barnes, Richard Dale (Rick Barnes) *men's college basketball coach*
Blake, Jeff *professional football player*
Brown, Mack *college football coach*
Conradt, Jody *basketball coach*
Crenshaw, Ben *professional golfer*
Stapleton, Bill *sports and entertainment agent*

**Carrollton**
Lieberman-Cline, Nancy *sports commentator, former professional basketball coach, former player*

**Coppell**
Aikman, Troy *former professional football player*

**Dallas**
Cuban, Mark *professional sports team executive, Internet company executive*
Dir, Dave *professional soccer coach*
Hamilton, David Lee *sports association administrator, retired environmental company executive*
Hatchell, Steven James *collegiate sports association executive*
Hedrick, Chad *Olympic athlete*
Hudel, Chestella Alvis *athletics educator*
Johnson, Avery *professional basketball coach, retired professional basketball player*
Laettner, Christian Donald *professional basketball player*
Stackhouse, Jerry *professional basketball player*
Van Horn, Keith *professional basketball player*

**Fort Worth**
Patterson, Gary *college football coach*

**Frisco**
Armstrong, Doug *professional sports team executive*
Hicks, Thomas O. *professional sports team executive, real estate developer*
Lindros, Eric *professional hockey player*
Lites, James R. *professional hockey team executive*
Modano, Mike (Michael Modano) *professional hockey player*
Tippett, Dave *professional hockey coach*

**Galveston**
Foster, William Edwin (Bill Foster) *nonprofessional basketball coach*

**Houston**
Alexander, Leslie Lee *professional sports team owner*
Baker, Vincent Lamont *professional basketball player*
Berkman, Lance *professional baseball player*
Carr, David *professional football player*
Chancellor, Van *professional basketball coach*
Clemens, Roger (William Roger Clemens) *professional baseball player*
Ewing, Patrick Aloysius *professional basketball coach*
Garner, Phil *professional athletics coach*
Hayes, Elvin Ernest *retired basketball player*
Howard, Juwan *professional basketball player*
Kubiak, Gary *professional football coach*
Lamont, Gene *professional baseball coach, former professional baseball team manager*
Lidge, Brad *professional baseball player*
McGrady, Tracy *professional basketball player*
Ming, Yao *professional basketball player*
Moulds, Eric Shannon *professional football player*

**Irving**
Allen, Larry Christopher *professional football player*
Bledsoe, Drew *professional football player*
Glenn, Terry *professional football player*
Jones, Jerry (Jerral Wayne Jones) *professional football team executive*
Jones, Julius *professional football player*
Owens, Terrell Eldorad *professional football player*
Parcells, Bill (Duane Charles Parcells) *professional football coach*
Vanderjagt, Mike *professional football player*
Witten, Jason (Christopher Jas Witten) *professional football player*

**Leander**
Erickson, Ralph D. *retired physical education educator, small business owner, consultant*

**Lubbock**
Knight, Bobby (Robert Montgomery Knight) *college basketball coach*
Leach, Mike *college football coach*

**Round Rock**
Ryan, Nolan *former professional baseball player*

**San Antonio**
Artemov, Vladimir Nikolaevich *gymnastics coach*
Azzi, Jennifer L. *professional basketball player*
Bowen, Bruce *professional basketball player*
Brown, Devin *professional basketball player*
Duncan, Tim *professional basketball player*
Finley, Michael *professional basketball player*
Ginobili, Manu *professional basketball player*
Holt, Peter M. *professional sports team executive, agricultural products executive*
Horn, Joe *professional football player*
Johnson, Shannon *professional basketball player*
Ludzik, Steve *professional hockey coach*
Massenburg, Tony *professional basketball player*
Mohammed, Nazr *professional basketball player*
Nesterovic, Rasho *professional basketball player*
Parker, Tony *professional basketball player*
Popovich, Gregg *professional basketball coach*
Robinson, David Maurice *professional basketball player*
Robinson, Glenn *professional basketball player*

## UTAH

**Park City**
Mancuso, Julia *skier, Olympic athlete*
Miller, Bode *skier*
Shea, Jim *Olympic athlete*
White, Shaun Roger *Olympic athlete, professional snowboarder, professional skateboarder*
Young, Steven *retired professional football player*

**Salt Lake City**
Boozer, Carlos Austin, Jr. *professional basketball player*
Miller, Larry H. *professional sports team executive, auto dealer, broadcast executive*
Sloan, Jerry (Gerald Eugene Sloan) *professional basketball coach*
Witty, Christine (Chris Witty) *speed skater*

## VIRGINIA

**Alexandria**
Singletary, Michael *retired professional football player, motivational speaker*

**Arlington**
Smith, Stanley Roger *retired professional tennis player*

**Ashburn**
Brunell, Mark Allen *professional football player*
Gibbs, Joe (Joseph Jackson Gibbs) *professional football coach*
Moss, Santana *professional football player*
Portis, Clinton *professional football player*
Snyder, Daniel *professional sports team executive, communications executive*

**Blacksburg**
Beamer, Frank *college football coach*

**Dublin**
Clark, Shelia Roxanne *sports association executive, legislative analyst*

**Fairfax**
Larranaga, Jim *men's college basketball coach*

**Mc Lean**
Chang, Michael *professional tennis player*
Hewitt, Lleyton *professional tennis player*

**Reston**
Kasten, Stanley Harvey *professional sports team executive*

## WASHINGTON

**Carnation**
Beshur, Jacqueline E. *animal trainer, farmer, writer*

Mutombo, DiKembe (Dikembe Mutombo Mpolondo Mukamba Jean Jacque Wamutombo) *professional basketball player*
Oswalt, Roy E. *professional baseball player*
Pettitte, Andrew Eugene (Andy Pettitte) *professional baseball player*
Sandman, Bradford Aaron *coach, educator*
Smith, Rick *professional sports team executive*
Swoopes, Sheryl Denise *professional basketball player*
Van Gundy, Jeff *professional basketball coach*
Williams, Mario *professional football player*

Vincent, Francis Thomas, Jr. (Fay Vincent) *former baseball commissioner*
Wade, Ed *professional sports team executive*
Wagner, Richard *retired professional sports team executive, athletics consultant*
Waltrip, Darrell Lee *race car driver*
Watley, Natasha *Olympic athlete*
Weisbrod, John *former professional sports team executive*
Weiss, Bob (Robert William WEiss) *former professional basketball coach*
Westphal, Paul *professional basketball coach*
Whitsitt, Bob (Robert James Whitsitt) *former professional football team executive*
Williams, Jimy *professional athletics manager*
Wilpon, Fred *professional sports team executive*
Wilson, Ralph Cookerly, Jr. *professional football team executive*
Wooden, John Robert *former college basketball coach*
Woodson, Darren Ray *retired professional football player*
Woosnam, Ian Harold *professional golfer*
Yamaguchi, Kristi Tsuya *ice skater*
Yashin, Alexei *professional hockey player*

---

**BUSINESS** *See* **FINANCE: INDUSTRY**

---

**COMMUNICATIONS** *See* **COMMUNICATIONS MEDIA; INDUSTRY: SERVICE**

---

**COMMUNICATIONS MEDIA** *See also* **ARTS: LITERARY**

---

# UNITED STATES

## ALABAMA

**Birmingham**
Allen, Christopher C. *publishing executive*
Bozzelli, Richard *publishing executive*
Crichton, Douglas Bentley *editor, writer*
Culpepper, Mary Kay *publishing executive*
Griffin, Eleanor *publishing executive, editor*
Hanson, Victor Henry, II, *newspaper publisher*
Kennedy, Joe David, Jr., (Joey Kennedy) *editor*
Powell, Larry *communications educator*
Scarritt, Thomas Varnon *newspaper editor*
Seitz, Karl Raymond *editor*
Smyth, Rich *publishing executive*
Stephens, James T. (J.T. Stepehens) *publishing executive*

**Dothan**
Pearson, Deborah Faye *newscaster*

**Hueytown**
Nelson, Susan Rhodes *media specialist, educator*

**Trussville**
Jacobson, James Edmund *retired newspaper editor*

**Tuscaloosa**
Reinhart, Kellee Connely *journalist*
Ross, Daniel J.J. *publishing executive*

## ALASKA

**Anchorage**
Pearson, Larry Lester *journalism educator*
Tobin, William Joseph *newspaper editor*

## ARIZONA

**Carefree**
Mangouni, Norman *publishing executive*

**Chandler**
Goyer, Robert Stanton *retired communications educator and administrator*

**Gilbert**
Kenney, Thomas Frederick *broadcast executive*

**Lake Montezuma**
Loveland, John Bigelow *editor, writer*

**Marana**
Steckler, Larry *publishing executive, writer*

**Mesa**
Tindle, Charles Dwight Wood *broadcast executive*

**Phoenix**
Bushee, Ward III *newspaper editor*
Dickey, Robert J. *publishing executive*
Edens, Gary Denton *broadcast executive*
Joseph, Gregory Nelson *media critic, writer, actor, advocate*
Leach, John F. *editor, director, journalist, educator*
Lovely, Randy *editor*
Moyer, Alan Dean *retired newspaper editor*
Pyle, Thomas Alton *broadcast executive*
Steckler, Phyllis Betty *publishing consultant*
Turi, Louis *publishing executive*
Zidich, John M. *publishing executive*

**Prescott**
Anderson, Parker Lynn *columnist, playwright*

**Scottsdale**
Johnson, Micah William *television newscaster, director*
Weil, Louis Arthur III *retired newspaper publishing executive*

**Sedona**
Sasmor, James Cecil *publishing representative, educator*

**Tempe**
Rankin, William Parkman *communications educator, academic administrator*
Richards, Gale Lee *communications educator*

**Tucson**
Davis, Cathy *publishing executive*
Hale, William Bryan, Jr. *newspaper editor*
Hayt, Therese D. *newspaper executive*
Martin, June Johnson Caldwell *journalist*

## ARKANSAS

**Fayetteville**
Chung, Donghun *communications educator*

**Hot Springs Village**
Smith, W. Preston *publishing executive, educator, real estate broker*

**Little Rock**
Greenberg, Paul *editor*
Parkhurst, Ted A. *publishing executive*
Portis, Charles McColl *reporter, writer*
Smith, Griffin *editor*

**Star City**
Scifres, Teresa Ellen *reporter, educator*

## CALIFORNIA

**Agoura Hills**
Teresi, Joseph *publishing executive*

**Alameda**
Billings, Thomas Neal *computer and publishing executive, management consultant, entrepreneur, journalist, writer*

**Alhambra**
Duke, Donald Norman *publishing executive*

**Alpine**
Greenberg, Byron Stanley *newspaper and business executive, consultant*

**Alta Loma**
Straka, Laszlo Richard *retired publishing consultant*

**Arcadia**
Belnap, David F. *journalist*

**Atascadero**
Rios, Evelyn Deerwester *columnist, musician, artist, writer*

**Bayside**
Pennekamp, Peter Henk *public radio executive, arts administrator*

**Belvedere Tiburon**
Kramer, Lawrence Stephen *journalist*
Rosenthal, Robert Jon *newspaper editor, journalist*

**Berkeley**
Bagdikian, Ben Haig *journalist, educator*
Browne, G.M. Walter Shawn *journalist, publisher*
Helson, Henry Berge *publisher, educator, retired mathematician*
Hertelendy, Paul *critic, writer, poet*
Lesser, Wendy *editor, writer, consultant*
Pfeiffer, Phyllis Kramer *publishing executive*
Susskind, Teresa Gabriel *publishing executive*
Taylor, Matthew Alan *publishing executive, editor, mediator*

**Beverly Hills**
Berney, Bob *film company executive*
Bradshaw, Terry (Terry Paxton Bradshaw) *sports announcer, former professional football player*
Corwin, Stanley Joel *book publisher*
Filosa, Gary Fairmont Randolph V., II, *columnist, theater producer, film producer*
Friedman, Robert Lee *film company executive*
Gabler, Elizabeth Brand *film company executive*
Ganis, Sidney *film company executive, producer*
Grazer, Brian *film company executive*
Heller, Paul Michael *film company executive, film producer*
Hill, David *broadcast executive*
Israel, David *journalist, scriptwriter, film producer*
Lond, Harley Weldon *editor, publishing executive*
Schneider, Charles Ivan *newspaper executive*
Shapiro-Mathes, Angela *broadcast executive*
Sherwood, Kehela (Karen Kehela Sherwood) *broadcast executive*
Utley, Nancy *film company executive*
Wolper, David Lloyd *motion picture and television executive*
Zanuck, Richard Darryl *motion picture company executive*

**Brisbane**
Daniels, Caroline *publishing executive*

**Burbank**
Ancier, Garth Richard *television broadcast executive*
Aviv, Oren R. *film company executive*
Barber, Gary *motion picture company executive*
Cook, Richard W. (Dick Cook) *film company executive*
DiBonaventura, Lorenzo *film company executive*
Fleishman, Susan Nahley *entertainment company executive*
Hoffman, Mark *broadcast executive*

Horn, Alan F. *film company executive*
Iger, Robert Allen *entertainment company executive*
Janollari, David *television broadcasting executive, cable producer, television producer*
Kaye, Jhani *radio station executive, television producer, television director*
Kroll, Sue *broadcast executive*
Kwan-Rubinek, Veronika *broadcast executive*
Lee, Paul *broadcast executive*
Letterie, Kathleen *broadcast executive*
Madison, Paula *broadcast executive*
Marinelli, Janice *broadcast executive*
McPherson, Stephen *broadcast executive*
Meyer, Barry Michael *motion picture executive*
Michel, Donald Charles *editor*
Nelson, Diane W. *broadcast executive*
Pedowitz, Mark *broadcast executive*
Robinov, Jeff *film company executive*
Ross, Rich *broadcast executive*
Schumacher, Thomas *film company executive*
Sklar, Marty (Martin A. Sklar) *entertainment company executive*
Staggs, Thomas O. *entertainment company executive*
Sweeney, Anne M. *cable television company executive*
Taubin, Dawn *film company executive*
Welinsky, Howard Steven *film distribution executive*
Younger, Laurie *broadcast executive*
Zucker, Jeffrey *broadcast executive*

**Burlingame**
Mendelson, Lee M. *film company executive, film producer, film director, writer*

**Calabasas**
Rubin, Rick (Frederick Jay Rubin) *record producer*

**Carlsbad**
Howard, Robert Staples *newspaper publisher*
Owen, Charles Theodore *journalist, publishing executive*
Sperling, Irene R. *publishing executive*

**Carmel**
Koeppel, Gary Merle *publishing executive, art gallery owner, writer*
Mollman, John Peter *publishing executive*

**Chula Vista**
Blankfort, Lowell Arnold *newspaper publisher*

**Costa Mesa**
Gottlieb, Jeffrey Paul *journalist*

**Culver City**
Blake, Jeff *film company executive, lawyer*
Landau, Yair *film company executive*
Lynton, Michael *film company executive*
Pascal, Amy Beth *film company executive*
Russell, Robin J. *broadcast executive*
Van Galder, Valerie *broadcast executive*
Vollack, Lia *broadcast executive*
Wigan, Gareth *film company executive*

**Daly City**
Batlin, Robert Alfred *retired newspaper editor*

**Del Mar**
Kaye, Peter Frederic *columnist*

**Downey**
Wayman, Joseph McKelden *editor, researcher*

**El Segundo**
Carey, Chase (Charles G. Carey) *broadcast executive*
Palkovic, Michael W. *broadcast executive*

**Emeryville**
Bax, Simon Tristan *film company executive*
Catmull, Edwin E. *film company executive, computer graphics engineer*
Lasseter, John A. *film company executive, computer animator*
Palmer, Craig *digital music and media company executive*
Roberts, Dale (Ty) *digital music and media company executive*
Roth, Joe *motion picture company executive*

**Encino**
Glickman, Daniel Robert *motion picture association executive, former congressman*
Rawitch, Robert Joe *journalist, educator*

**Escondido**
Ehrhart, Joseph Edward *retired broadcast technician*

**Fresno**
Morales, Hugo *broadcast executive*
Wilson, James Ross *communications educator, broadcast executive*

**Fullerton**
Lewandoski, Robert Henry *editor, publisher*

**Glendale**
Coleman, Lewis Waldo *film company executive, former bank executive*
Daly, Ann Michelle *broadcast executive*
DeLuca, Michael *film company executive*
Enrico, Roger A. *film company executive, retired soft drink company executive*
Geffen, David Lawrence *film company executive, former recording company executive*
Katzenberg, Jeffrey *film company executive*
MacDonald, Laurie *film company executive*
Parkes, Walter F. *film company executive*
Snider, Stacey *film company executive*
Uhrich, Kevin Patrick *editor*

**Glendora**
Thornburg, Lee Ellis *film executive, director*

**Gold River**
Shaw, Eleanor Jane *newspaper editor*

**Greenbrae**
Cohn, Bruce *film and television company executive*
Freedman, Albert Z. *publishing executive*

**Hollywood**
McAdams, Frank Joseph III *communications educator*
Perth, Rod *network entertainment executive*
Salzman, David Elliot *entertainment industry executive*

**Inglewood**
Sludikoff, Stanley Robert *publisher, writer*

**Irvine**
Bartkus, Richard Anthony *magazine publisher*
Kaplan, Arline Ray *editor, writer*
Lesonsky, Rieva *editor-in-chief*
Power, Francis William *newspaper publisher*
Siegel, Barry *journalist, writer, literature educator*
Stein, M(eyer) L(ewis) *journalist, editor, writer*

**La Jolla**
Copley, David C. *newspaper publishing company executive*
Freedman, Jonathan Borwick *journalist, writer, educator*
Hallin, Daniel Clark *communications educator*
Harris, T. George *editor*

**Long Beach**
Adler, Jeffrey D. *media consultant, management consultant*
Yousef, Fathi Salaama *communications educator, management consultant*

**Los Altos**
Collins, Gordon Dent *recording industry executive*

**Los Angeles**
Archerd, Army (Armand A. Archerd) *columnist, retired commentator*
Baquet, Dean Paul *newspaper editor*
Barberie, Jillian *newscaster, meteorologist*
Bart, Peter Benton *editor, film producer, writer*
Battista, Richard *entertainment company executive*
Berman, Gail *film company executive*
Boyle, Barbara Dorman *film company executive*
Charen, Mona *columnist*
Churgin, Amy *publishing executive*
Clarke, Peter *communications and health educator*
Cohn, Gary Dennis *journalist*
Cole, K.C. *journalist, writer*
Delugach, Albert Lawrence *journalist*
Demick, Barbara *journalist*
Dolan, Mary Anne *journalist, columnist*
Dwyre, William Patrick *journalist*
Edmonds, Tracey E. *film company executive*
Fein, Irving Ashley *television and motion picture executive*
Field, Ted (Frederick Field) *film company executive, recording industry executive*
Fields, Robin *reporter*
Findley, John Allen, Jr. *publishing executive*
Firstenberg, Jean Picker *film institute executive*
Flanigan, James J(oseph) *journalist*
Gelber, Danielle Arna *broadcast executive*
Gianopulos, Jim *film company executive*
Gross, Larry Paul *communications educator*
Harbert, Ted (Edward W. Harbert III) *broadcast executive*
Harvey, Randy *editor, reporter*
Hefner, Hugh Marston *editor-in-chief*
Herzog, Doug *broadcast executive*
Hiltzik, Michael *journalist*
Iovine, Jimmy *recording industry executive*
Ivins, Molly (Mary Tyler Ivins) *columnist, writer*
Johnson, Jeffrey M. *publishing executive*
Jones, Quincy *producer, composer, arranger, conductor, trumpeter*
Knapp, Cleon Talboys *publishing executive*
Kraft, Scott Corey *news correspondent*
Kristof, Kathy M. *journalist*
Langguth, Arthur John *journalist, educator, writer*
Larrubia, Evelyn *reporter*
Lazarus, Mell *cartoonist*
Lee, Kwan Min *communications educator, consultant*
Lee, Stan (Stanley Martin Lieber) *cartoon publisher, writer*
Leonard, Jack *reporter*
Levine, Pamela *film company executive*
Liguori, Peter *film company executive*
Litewka, Albert Bernard *publishing executive, entertainment executive*
Lopez, Steve *journalist*
Lowenthal, Abraham Frederic *international relations educator*
Lozano, Monica Cecilia *publishing executive*
Malkin, Michelle *syndicated columnist*
Maltin, Leonard *commentator, writer*
McFarling, Usha Lee *newswriter*
Miles, Jack (John Russiano) *journalist, educator*
Millauer, Liselotte *journalist*
Moss, Jerome (Jerry) S. *recording industry executive*
Neil, Daniel *journalist*
North, Oliver Laurence (Ollie North) *syndicated columnist, retired military officer*
O'Neil, William Scott *publishing executive*
Ostroff, Dawn T. *broadcast executive*
Parks, Michael Christopher *journalist, educator*
Perenchio, Andrew Jerrold *film and television executive*
Petersen, Robert E. *magazine publishing executive*
Phillips, Geneva Ficker *academic editor*
Piller, Charles Leon *journalist*
Plate, Thomas Gordon *columnist, educator*
Raksin, Alex *reporter, writer*
Ramos, Jorge *newscaster*
Rich, Alan *film critic, writer*
Rosenzweig, Richard Stuart *publishing company executive*
Rosett, Daniel J. *film company executive*
Rush, Herman E. *television executive*
Rust, Patricia Joan *television executive*

Saltzman, Joseph *journalist, educator, television producer*
Sands, Rick (Richard Sands) *film company executive*
Sarnoff, Thomas Warren *television executive*
Sella, Anthony *film company executive*
Shuster, Alvin *journalist, reporter*
Shuster, Beth *editor*
Sigband, Norman Bruce *communications educator*
Singleton, Joan Vietor *publishing executive, writer, film producer*
Sloan, Harry Evans *film company executive*
Stephens, Loren M. *publishing executive, writer*
Tassler, Nina *broadcast executive*
Taylor, Daniel J. *film company executive*
Tellem, Nancy Reiss *broadcast executive*
Thompson, Anne Kathleen *entertainment journalist*
Trembly, Cristy *television executive*
Turner, Craig *editor, journalist*
Van Buren, Abigail (Jeanne Phillips) *columnist, educator*
Walden, Dana *broadcast executive*
Ward, Leslie Allyson *journalist, editor*
Yari, Bob *film company executive, film producer*
Zacchino, Narda *newspaper editor*

**Los Gatos**
Hastings, Reed *film company executive, educational association administrator*

**Marina Del Rey**
Lindheim, Richard David *broadcast executive, director*

**Mill Valley**
Leslie, Jacques Robert, Jr. *journalist*
McNamara, Stephen *newspaper executive*

**Modesto**
Smith, Chester *broadcast executive*

**Monterey**
Goldstein, Kenneth F. *entertainment company executive, publishing executive*

**Monterey Park**
Stapleton, Jean *journalism educator*

**National City**
Beauchamp, Miles Philip *editor, columnist, consultant*

**Newport Beach**
Bryant, Thomas Lee *magazine editor*
Dean, Paul John *magazine editor*
Steelberg, Chad *broadcast advertising company executive*
Steelberg, Ryan *broadcasting advertising company executive*

**Northridge**
Dart, John Seward *journalist, editor*

**Oakland**
Dailey, Garrett Clark *publisher, lawyer*
George, Donald Warner *online columnist and editor, freelance writer*
McKinney, Judson Thad *broadcast executive*
Mott, Frederick B., Jr. *publishing executive*
Schrag, Peter *editor, writer*
Wood, Larry (Mary Laird) *journalist, writer, public relations executive, educator, environmental consultant*

**Oceanside**
Beck, Marilyn Mohr *columnist*

**Ontario**
Rappaport, Michael Paul *columnist*

**Pacific Grove**
Davis, Robert Edward *retired communications educator*

**Pacific Palisades**
Hadges, Thomas Richard *media consultant*
Kirkgaard, Valerie Anne *media group executive, radio host, writer, radio producer, consultant*
Price, Frank *motion picture and television company executive*

**Pacifica**
Cole, David Macaulay *journalist, consultant*
Kelly, Kevin *editor*

**Palm Desert**
Ayling, Henry Faithful *editor, consultant, journalist, poet*

**Palm Springs**
Atkins, Robert *art critic, art educator, art historian, journalist, editor*
Gerard, James Wilson *publishing consultant*

**Palo Alto**
Hamilton, David Mike *publishing executive*

**Pasadena**
Matthews, Mildred Shapley *freelance/self-employed editor*
Spector, Phil *record company executive*

**Paso Robles**
Brown, Benjamin Andrew *retired journalist*

**Petrolia**
Cockburn, Alexander *journalist*
St. Clair, Jeffrey *editor*

**Placentia**
Zweifel, Donald Edwin *editor, lobbyist, consultant*

**Playa Del Rey**
Cairns, Diane Patricia *motion picture executive*

**Rancho Palos Verdes**
Hillinger, Charles *journalist, writer*

**Redlands**
Heiss, David James *editor*

**Redondo Beach**
Kich, Rolf *communications scientist, consultant*

**Riverside**
James, Etta (Jamesetta Hawkins) *recording artist*
McLaughlin, Leighton Bates, II, *journalist, educator, retired reporter*
Russo, Marisa N. *media consultant*
Sokolsky, Robert Lawrence *journalist*

**Rolling Hills Estates**
Conrad, Paul Francis *cartoonist*

**Sacramento**
Henson, Glenda Maria *newswriter*
Lundstrom, Marjie *editor, columnist*
Philip, Tom *reporter*
Pruitt, Gary B. *publishing company executive*
Shriver, Maria Owings *news correspondent*
Walsh, Denny Jay *reporter*
Walters, Daniel Raymond *political columnist*

**San Diego**
Breen, Stephen P. *editorial cartoonist*
Cervantes, Danielle Christina *journalist, news analyst*
Da Rosa, Alison *travel editor*
Fike, Edward Lake *newspaper editor*
Humes, Edward *journalist, writer*
Kaufman, Julian Mortimer *broadcasting company executive, consultant*
Kim, Lee Ann *reporter, newscaster*
Klein, Herbert George *newspaper editor*
Krulak, Victor Harold *newspaper executive*
Kyle, Robert Campbell, II, *publishing executive*
Olshevsky, George *editor*
Pincus, Robert Lawrence *art critic, historian*
Rowe, Peter A. *columnist*
Steen, Paul Joseph *retired broadcasting executive*
Winner, Karin E. *editor*

**San Francisco**
Bentley, Lisa *publisher*
Blackwell, Savannah Rose *journalist*
Bronstein, Phil *publishing executive*
Cameron, Heather Anne *publishing executive*
Cohn, Roger *editor*
Davidson, Keay *newswriter*
Dickey, Glenn Ernest, Jr. *sportswriter*
Duncan, David Ewing *editor, writer*
Duscha, Julius Carl *journalist*
Fainaru-Wada, Mark *journalist*
Falk, Steven B. *newspaper publishing executive*
Fitzmaurice, Deanne *photojournalist*
Fox, Steve *editor-in-chief*
Garchik, Leah Lieberman *journalist*
German, William *newspaper editor*
Graysmith, Robert *political cartoonist, author*
Hafner, Katie *reporter*
Hale, Cecil *communications educator, business educator*
Hamilton, Joan Nice *editor-in-chief*
Klein, Marc S. *editor, publishing executive*
Lazarus, David *journalist*
Markoff, John *reporter*
McCracken, Harry *journalist*
Minor, Halsey *multimedia company executive*
Newmark, Craig Alexander *communications executive*
Oxarart, Frank *broadcast executive*
Pazour, Don *publishing executive*
Perlman, David *journalist*
Pimentel, Benjamin Impelido *journalist*
Quittner, Josh *editor*
Richtel, Matt (Theron Heir) *reporter, cartoonist*
Rosenheim, Daniel Edward *journalist, television news director*
Rubenstein, Steven Paul *newspaper columnist*
Russell, Sabin *newswriter*
Sansweet, Stephen Jay *journalist, writer, marketing executive*
Schwarz, Glenn Vernon *newspaper editor*
Singh, Jai *online news executive*
Thompson, Adam Clay *reporter*
Vega, Frank J. *newspaper publishing executive*
Walsh, Joan *editor-in-chief*
Williams, Lance *journalist*
Winn, Steven Jay *critic*

**San Jose**
Carey, Peter Kevin *reporter*
Ceppos, Jerome Merle (Jerry Ceppos) *newspaper editor*
Diamond, Diana Louise *editor, journalist*
Goldberg, Susan *editor*
Harris, Jay Terrence *communications educator*
McDonald, Susan *publishing executive*
Mendoza, Martha *reporter*
Migielicz, Geralyn *photojournalist*
Nardi, Glen *publishing executive*
Ridder, P. Anthony (Paul Anthony Ridder) *newspaper company executive*
Rossi, Steven B. *newspaper publishing company executive*

**San Pedro**
Bowling, Lance Christopher *recording industry executive*

**San Rafael**
Blakeslee, Helen P. *columnist*
Morgan, Michael Brewster *publishing executive*

**Santa Ana**
Anderson, N. Christian III *newspaper publisher*
Balzer, Robert Lawrence *journalist*
Brusic, Ken *editor*
Katz, Tonnie *newspaper editor*

**Santa Barbara**
Ackerman, Marshall *publishing executive*
Brilliant, Ashleigh Ellwood *cartoonist, writer*
Brown, J'Amy Maroney *journalist, media consultant, investor*
Campbell, William Steen *publishing executive, writer, chaplain*
Dubroff, Henry Allen *editor, journalist*

Jackson, Beverley Joy Jacobson *columnist, educator*
McCaw, Wendy Petrak *publishing executive*

**Santa Monica**
Alpert, Herb *composer, recording artist, producer, painter*
Anthony, Polly *broadcast executive*
Feltheimer, Jon *entertainment company executive*
Horowitz, Zachary I. *entertainment company executive*
Littlefield, Warren *television executive*
Morgenstern, Joe *film critic*
Rifkin, Arnold *film company executive*
Vrabeck, Kathy *videogame publishing executive*
Williams, Kenneth Scott *entertainment company executive*

**Santa Rosa**
Callum, Myles *magazine editor, writer*
Person, Evert Bertil *retired newspaper and radio executive*
Swofford, Robert Lee *editor, journalist*

**Sausalito**
Battelle, John *journalist, educator, writer, entrepreneur*
Hansen, Charles Morton *editor, retired military officer*

**Seaside**
May, James Harvey *communications educator*

**Sebastopol**
O'Reilly, Tim *computer book publishing company executive, open sourcer advocate*

**Sherman Oaks**
Drudge, Matt *journalist*

**Sonoma**
Beckmann, Jon Michael *publishing company executive*

**South Pasadena**
Mantell, Suzanne Ruth *editor*

**Stanford**
Andreopoulos, Spyros George *writer*
Baker, Patricia Ann *publishing executive*
Roberts, Donald Frank, Jr. *communications educator*
Suppes, Christine Johnson *publishing executive*

**Studio City**
Kelley, Jan *publishing executive, musician*

**Summerland**
Cannon, Louis Simeon *journalist, writer*

**Sunland**
Nepales, Ruben Viado *journalist*

**Sunnyvale**
Coleman, Gregory G. *former magazine publisher*

**Sylmar**
Valdez, Denise *newscaster*

**Tehachapi**
Mitchell, Betty Jo *publishing executive, writer*

**Thousand Oaks**
Albertson, Marty P. *music company executive*
Ferber, Samuel *publishing executive*

**Toluca Lake**
Ragan, Ann Talmadge *media and production consultant, actor*

**Torrance**
Adelsman, Jean (Harriette Adelsman) *newspaper editor*

**Tujunga**
Loehwing, Lord Rudi Charles *publicist, radio broadcasting executive, journalist*

**Universal City**
Bromstad, Angela *broadcast executive*
Finkelstein, Rick *film company executive*
Hammer, Bonnie *broadcast executive*
Langley, Donna *film company executive*
Linde, David *film company executive*
Menendez, Belinda *broadcast executive*
Meyer, Ron *film company executive*
Parent, Mary *film company executive*
Randall, Karen *film company executive*
Rocco, Nikki *film company executive*
Schulz, Diana *film company executive*
Shmuger, Marc *film company executive*
Stuber, Scott *film company executive*

**Ventura**
Gallagher, Timothy J. *newspaper editor*
Greig, William Taber, II, *publishing company executive*
Howry, Joe R. *newspaper editor*

**Vista**
Linhart, Letty Lemon *editor*

**Walnut**
Tan, Colleen Woo *communications educator*

**Walnut Creek**
Satz, Louis K. *publishing executive*
Trousdale, Stephen Richard *newspaper editor*

**West Hollywood**
Grey, Brad *film company executive*
Huntsberry, Frederick D. *film company executive*
Shaye, Robert Kenneth *film company executive*
Shearmur, Alli *broadcast executive*

**West Los Angeles**
Hirschhorn, Charles *media company executive*

**Wilton**
Harrison, George Harry, III, (Hank Harrison) *publishing executive, author*

**Woodland Hills**
Deters, Thomas C. *publishing executive, educator*
Harris, Barbara S. *publishing executive, editor-in-chief*
Jacobson, Sidney *editor*
McCluggage, Kerry *film and television executive*
Rafter, Tracy *publishing executive*
Russell, Anne M. *editor-in-chief*

**Yreka**
Smith, Vin *editor, small business owner, writer*

## COLORADO

**Aspen**
Hayes, Mary Eshbaugh *editor, writer*
Thomas, William Daniel *journalist*

**Berthoud**
Davis, Donald Alan *news correspondent, writer, lecturer*

**Boulder**
Clos, Lynne Mobley *magazine publisher, paleontologist*
El Mallakh, Dorothea Hendry *editor, publishing executive*
Ritzel, Brent Paul *publishing executive, consultant*

**Brighton**
Wagner, Samuel Albin Mar *recording industry executive, educator*

**Centennial**
Ulevich, Neal Hirsh *photojournalist*

**Cherry Hills Village**
Stapleton, Katharine Hall (Katie Stapleton) *commentator, writer*

**Colorado Springs**
Zapel, Arthur Lewis *book publishing executive*

**Denver**
Barbour, Alton Bradford *retired human communication studies educator*
Brom, Libor *journalist, educator*
Chavez, Jeanette *editor*
Clark, Gary R. *newspaper editor*
Dance, Francis Esburn Xavier *communications educator*
Drake, Sylvie (Jurras Drake) *theater critic*
Elliman, Donald M., Jr. *magazine company executive*
Engdahl, Todd Philip *editor*
Heisler, Todd *photojournalist*
Kasper, Shirley Elaine *journalist, writer, researcher*
Kim, Jinah *reporter*
LaMendola, Walter Franklin *technology educator, technology business executive*
Landess, Mike (Malcolm Lee Landess III) *newscaster*
McDonald, Kirk *publishing executive*
Moore, Gregory L. *editor*
Rothman, Paul Alan *publishing executive*
Saltz, Howard Joel *newspaper editor*
Sheeler, Jim *journalist*
Singleton, William Dean *publishing executive*
Willbanks, Roger Paul *publishing and book distributing company executive*
Woerner, Robert Eugene *editor, writer*
Wolman, Jonathan Paley *journalist*
Zimmer, Larry William, Jr. *sports announcer*

**Durango**
Ballantine, Morley Cowles (Mrs. Arthur Atwood Ballantine) *editor*
Van Mols, Brian *publishing executive*

**Englewood**
Burnett, George A. *directory publishing executive*

**Evergreen**
Dobbs, Gregory Allan *journalist*

**Georgetown**
Stern, Mort(imer) P(hillip) *communications educator, editor, reporter, consultant*

**Golden**
Baron, Robert Charles *publishing executive*

**Granby**
Johnson, William Potter *publishing executive, director*

**Gunnison**
Gelwicks, James M. *retired communications educator*

**Highlands Ranch**
Harris, Douglas Clay *retired newspaper executive*

**Littleton**
Bennett, Janice Lynn *publisher, educator*
Udevitz, Norman *publishing executive*

**Morrison**
Myers, Harry J., Jr. *retired publisher*

## CONNECTICUT

**Bethel**
Shepard, Jean Heck *retired publishing consultant*

**Bridgeport**
Simoneau, Cynthia Lambert *editor, educator*

**Bridgewater**
Crooke, Robert Andrew *media consultant, writer, educator*

## Bristol
Berman, Chris *sportscaster*
Bodenheimer, George *broadcast executive*
Brantley, Jeffrey Hoke *baseball analyst, retired professional baseball player*
Driessen, Christine F. *broadcast executive*
Gammons, Peter *columnist, commentator*
Greenberg, Mike *sportscaster*
Olney, Robert Stanbury III *sportswriter and baseball analyst*
Scott, Stuart *sports anchor*
Simmons, Bill *sportswriter*
Tirico, Mike *sportscaster*

## Chester
Frost-Knappman, (Linda) Elizabeth *publishing executive, editor, writer*

## Cos Cob
Hauptman, Michael *broadcasting company executive*

## Danbury
Burns-DeMelo, Heather Ellsworth *publishing executive*
Lagardere, Arnaud *publishing executive*
Reynolds, Jean Edwards *publishing executive*

## Darien
Brooke, Avery Rogers *publisher, writer*
Workman, Sharon Joy *journalist*

## Deep River
Cobb, Hubbard Hanford *magazine editor, writer*

## Easton
Enos, Randall *cartoonist, illustrator*
Lorenz, Lee Sharp *cartoonist*

## Fairfield
Hodgkinson, William James *publishing executive*
Kaff, Albert Ernest *reporter, writer*

## Greens Farms
Deford, Frank *sportswriter, commentator, writer*

## Greenwich
Brant, Peter M. *magazine publishing executive, real estate developer*
Landau, Jon *music producer, manager*
Moffly, John Wesley, IV, *magazine publishing executive*
Welling, Kathryn Marie *editor*

## Hartford
Davis, Jack Wayne, Jr. *publishing executive*
Harden, Jon Bixby *publishing executive*
Noel, Don Obert, Jr. *retired editor, columnist*
Pach, Peter Barnard *columnist, editor*
Yardley, Bill *journalist*

## Ivoryton
Bendig, William Charles *editor, artist*

## Kensington
Murphy, Thomas John *publishing executive*

## Lakeville
Estabrook, Robert Harley *journalist*

## Madison
Egbert, Emerson Charles *retired publisher*

## Middletown
Balay, Robert Elmore *editor, librarian*

## Milford
Henderson, Albert Kossack *publishing executive, consultant, food products executive*

## Moodus
Cumming, Robert Emil *editor, writer*

## New Britain
Martin, Vivian Bonita *journalist, educator*

## New Canaan
Allen, Joseph Henry *retired publishing company executive*

## New Haven
Fuchs, Elinor *film critic, playwright, educator*
Leeney, Robert Joseph *newspaper editor*
McClatchy, J. D. *editor, writer, educator*

## Norwalk
DeCesare, Donald E. *broadcast executive*

## Old Greenwich
Dixon, John Morris *magazine editor*

## Old Saybrook
Purcell, Bradford Moore *publishing company executive*

## Rocky Hill
Powers, Helen *columnist, writer*

## Sharon
Gordon, Nicholas *broadcast executive, performing arts executive*

## Shelton
Kantrowitz, Jonathan Daniel *publishing executive, educator, lawyer*

## Sherman
Cowley, Robert William *editor, writer, consultant, lecturer*

## Stamford
Britt, Glenn Alan *media company executive*
Fein, Ronnie *journalist, writer*
Harrington, Richard J. *information business executive*
Kisseberth, Paul Barto *retired publishing executive*
Lane, Hana Umlauf *editor*
Pardue, Bill *publishing executive*
Tow, Leonard *television executive*

## Stonington
Elliott, Osborn *journalist, educator, retired dean*

## Storrs Mansfield
Croteau, Maureen Elizabeth *journalism educator*
Maier, Romulus *journalist*

## Waterbury
Pape, William James, II, *newspaper publisher*

## Westport
Kramer, Sidney B. *publishing executive, literary agent, lawyer*
McCormack, Donald Paul *newspaper consultant*
Stern, Robert D. *publishing executive*

## Wethersfield
Osborne, Louise *publishing executive*

## Wilton
Bair, Tom *publishing executive*
Binder, Steven F. *publishing executive*
Frank, Robert Allen *media consultant*
Seitz, Nicholas Joseph *editor, journalist*
Tarde, Jerry (Gerard Tarde) *magazine executive*

## Woodbridge
Menchaca, Frank *editorial director*

# DELAWARE

## Dover
Smyth, Joel Douglas *newspaper executive*

## New Castle
Cansler, Leslie Ervin *retired newspaper editor*

## Newark
DeVivo, Sal J. *newspaper executive*
Jackson, Marvin Dennis *journalism educator, writer*

# DISTRICT OF COLUMBIA

## Washington
Adams, Robert Edward *journalist*
Affens, Steven Charles *television photojournalist*
Aguirre-Baca, Francisco *publisher, consultant*
Allam, Hannah *journalist*
Allen, Henry Southworth *journalist, critic*
Andrews, John Frank *editor, author, educator*
Angier, Natalie Marie *science journalist*
Apple, Raymond Walter, Jr., (R.W. Apple, Jr.) *journalist*
Applebaum, Anne *journalist, writer*
Arana, Marie *editor, writer*
Archibald, George *reporter*
Arena, Kelli *news correspondent*
Arnovitz, Benton Mayer *editor*
Asker, James Robert *magazine editor*
Atlas, Terry *journalist*
Bailey, Charles Waldo, II, *journalist, writer*
Balz, Daniel John *newspaper editor, journalist*
Barber, Ben Bernard Andrew *journalist*
Barnes, Frederic Wood, Jr. *journalist, political analyst*
Barnes, Julian E. *editor*
Barone, Michael D. *political correspondent, writer, editor*
Bennett, Philip *editor*
Bern, Paula Ruth *columnist*
Bird, Kai *journalist, historian*
Birnbaum, Jeffrey *columnist, political correspondent*
Blitzer, Wolf *news correspondent*
Boo, Katherine *newswriter*
Boyce, Clayton Winfred *strategic communications consultant, transportation industry expert, journalist*
Bradlee, Benjamin Crowninshield *former editor*
Branegan, James Augustus III *journalist*
Brock, Gregory E. *editor*
Broder, David Salzer *reporter, writer*
Brown, John Patrick *publishing executive, financial consultant*
Bruzelius, Nils Johan Axel *journalist*
Buzbee, Sally Streff *news correspondent*
Cameron, Carl (Karl Lamberg-Karlovsky) *political correspondent*
Cannon, Carl M. *reporter*
Centanni, Steve *national news correspondent*
Chen, Joie *news correspondent*
Clift, Eleanor *news correspondent, writer*
Coll, Stephen Wilson *journalist*
Cook, David *editor*
Cooper, Matthew *journalist*
Copeland, Peter *editor*
Corbett, Rebecca *editor*
Cosgrove, John Patrick *editor*
Covault, Craig *editor*
Cowan, Edward *journalist, editor*
Crenshaw, Albert Burford *journalist*
Curtiss, Richard Holden *magazine editor, writer*
Cutler, Bernard Joseph *editor-in-chief, writer*
Dawson, Jessica *art critic*
Day, Charles Williamson *commentator*
de Borchgrave, Arnaud *editor, writer, lecturer*
Deeb, Mary-Jane *editor, educator*
DeFrank, Thomas Michael *journalist*
Dillin, John Woodward, Jr. *retired editor, reporter*
Dionne, E. J., Jr. *columnist*
Dixon, Glenn *art critic*
Doan, Michael Frederick *editor*
Donaldson, Samuel Andrew *journalist*
Donohoe, Cathryn Murray *journalist*
Dorn, James Andrew *editor*
Dowd, Maureen *columnist*
Downie, Leonard, Jr. *editor, writer*
Drew, Elizabeth *commentator, journalist, writer*
Duffy, Brian P. *editor*
Dujack, Stephen Raymond *editor*
Dyer, Susan Kristine *editor, librarian*
Eaton, Sabrina Catherine Elizabeth *journalist*
Edsall, Thomas Byrne *reporter*
Edwards, Bob (Robert Alan Edwards) *radio news anchor*
Elfin, Mel *magazine editor*

Elsasser, Glen Robert *journalist*
Engel, Margaret *journalist*
Entman, Robert Mathew *communications educator, consultant*
Faherty, Robert Louis *publishing executive*
Fahey, John M., Jr. *book publishing executive*
Feld, Karen Irma *columnist, journalist, commentator, speech professional*
Fields, Suzanne Bregman *syndicated columnist*
Fineman, Howard David *news correspondent*
Finkel, David *journalist*
Fleming, Lee Virginia *art critic, writer, curator*
Foer, Franklin *editor*
Forgey, Benjamin Franklin *architecture and art critic*
Franzen, Byron T. (John Franzen) *media specialist*
Friedman, Thomas Loren *foreign correspondent, writer*
Galloway, Joseph Lee, Jr. *writer, journalist*
Garrels, Anne *news correspondent*
Gelernter, David H. *critic, painter, educator*
Geyer, Georgie Anne *columnist, educator, commentator, writer*
Gibson, Florence Anderson *talking book company executive, narrator*
Givhan, Robin Deneen *journalist*
Glass, Andrew James *newspaper editor*
Glassman, James Kenneth *editor, writer, publishing executive*
Goldberg, Jonah Jacob *political columnist*
Goler, Wendell *political correspondent*
Gopnik, Blake *art critic*
Gorman, Patricia Jane *editor*
Graham, Donald Edward *publishing company executive*
Greene, Marcia Slacum *editor*
Greenhouse, Linda Joyce *journalist*
Griffin, Paul L. *publishing executive, fraternal organization administrator*
Grimaldi, James V. *journalist*
Grosvenor, Gilbert Melville *journalist, educator, publishing executive*
Gutman, Roy William *reporter*
Guzy, Carol *photojournalist*
Gwaltney, Corbin *publishing executive, editor*
Halsey, Ashley III *newspaper editor*
Hammond, Allen Lee *editor, consultant, former broadcaster, non-profit policy research center executive*
Harrison, Patricia de Stacy *broadcast executive, former federal agency administrator*
Hartman, Carl (Howard Carl Hartman) *reporter*
Havemann, Joel *editor*
Headden, Susan M. *editor*
Hecht, Marjorie Mazel *editor*
Henry, Ed *news correspondent*
Henry, John Cooper *journalist*
Herman, Andrea Maxine *newspaper editor*
Herridge, Catherine *political correspondent*
Hiatt, Fred *journalist*
Higham, Scott *reporter*
Hileman, Bette *journalist*
Hills, Stephen P. *publishing executive*
Hinden, Stanley Jay *newspaper editor*
Hoagland, Jimmie Lee *newspaper editor*
Hoyt, Clark Freeland *journalist, editor*
Hulse, Carl *newspaper executive*
Hume, Brit (Alexander Britton Hume) *journalist*
Hunt, Albert R. *editor*
Ijaz, Mansoor *news correspondent*
Jacobson, Louis Alan *journalist*
James, Bruce Richard *publishing executive*
Jehl, Douglas *news correspondent*
Johns, Christopher George *photojournalist, editor*
Johnson, Richard Kent *publishing executive*
Jones, Boisfeuillet, Jr., (Bo Jones) *publishing executive*
Joo, Douglas D.M. *newspaper and video production and aviation executive*
Joyce, Anne Raine *editor*
Kammer, Jerry *reporter*
Karl, Jonathan David *television journalist*
Kilian, Pamela Reeves *journalist, writer*
King, Colbert Isaiah *editor*
King, Larry (Larry Zeiger) *broadcaster, radio personality*
King, Llewellyn Willings *publishing executive, educator, commentator, writer*
Kinsley, Michael E. *newspaper columnist*
Kiplinger, Knight Austin *journalist, publishing executive*
Kirk, Donald *journalist*
Kirkpatrick, David D. *news correspondent*
Klose, Kevin *broadcast executive*
Knight, Athelia Wilhelmenia *journalist*
Kondracke, Morton Matt *journalist*
Kurtz, Howard *journalist, author*
Labaton, Stephen *journalist, lawyer*
Lamb, Brian Patrick *broadcast executive*
Lambro, Donald Joseph *columnist*
Lardner, George, Jr. *journalist, writer*
Larson, George Charles *magazine editor, writer*
Lasseter, Tom *journalist*
Lawson, Jennifer *broadcast executive*
Lee, Debra Louise *cable television company executive*
Leeds, Charles Alan *publishing executive*
Lehrman, Margaret McBride *broadcast executive, television producer*
Leubsdorf, Carl Philipp *publishing executive*
Levey, Robert Frank *columnist, not-for-profit fundraiser*
Lewis, Charles Joseph *journalist*
Liasson, Mara *news correspondent*
Lichtblau, Eric *journalist*
Loker, Elizabeth St. John *newspaper executive*
Longaker, Mark *gallery critic, writer*
Loo, Beverly Jane *publishing executive*
Lubar, Jeffrey Stuart *journalist, trade association executive*
Mankiewicz, Frank F. *journalist, writer*
Marash, David *television news correspondent*
Marimow, William K. *editor*
Marshall, Joshua Micah *publisher, blog writer, columnist, editor, political journalist*
McBee, Susanna Barnes *retired journalist*
McCarthy, Maura *critic, editor*
McCormally, Kevin Jay *editor*
McFeatters, Ann Carey *journalist*
McKinnon, John D. *reporter*

McLaughlin, John J. *broadcast executive, television producer, journalist, political commentator*
Melendy, David Russell *newscaster, reporter*
Messiah-Jiles, Sonceria *publishing executive*
Meyerson, Harold *journalist*
Miller, Nicole *art columnist*
Mitchell, Andrea *journalist*
Moran, Terry *news correspondent*
Moss, Madison Scott *editor*
Murphy, Caryle Marie *foreign correspondent*
Novak, Robert David Sanders *columnist, commentator*
O'Brien, Soledad *news anchor*
O'Brien, Timothy Andrew *journalist, writer, lawyer, educator*
Ohanian, Bernard Jay *writer, editor*
Oka, Takashi *journalist, consultant, educator*
Ong, Laureen E. *broadcast executive*
Pace, David *journalist*
Padden, Preston *broadcast executive*
Page, Clarence E. *columnist*
Page, Tim *music critic, writer, producer*
Palmer, Stacy Ella *periodical editor*
Panero, Hugh Edward *broadcast executive*
Parsons, Gary M. *broadcast executive*
Peck, Louis Moses *editor*
Peirce, Neal R. *journalist*
Pelham, Ann *publishing executive, department chairman*
Penniman, Nicholas *editor*
Peretz, Martin *publishing executive, educator*
Perkins, Lucian *photographer*
Perl, Peter *editor*
Phalen, Patricia Frances *media specialist, educator*
Pincus, Walter Haskell *news editor*
Pinkerton, James Pearson *columnist, political analyst*
Porges, Lawrence Michael *editor*
Pratt, Carin *television executive*
Pratt, Dana Joseph *publishing consultant*
Priest, Dana *journalist*
Prina, L(ouis) Edgar *journalist*
Putzel, Michael *journalist, editor*
Rankin, Robert Arthur *journalist*
Raspberry, William James *journalist*
Ratner, Ellen Faith *news analyst, news correspondent, writer*
Ravenal, Earl Cedric *international relations educator, writer*
Rice, Susan Elizabeth *foreign policy analyst, former federal agency administrator*
Ridgeway, James Fowler *journalist*
Riechmann, Deb *reporter*
Risen, James E. *journalist*
Roberts, Cokie (Corinne Boggs Roberts) *newscaster*
Roberts, John *news anchor*
Rosen, Gerald Robert *editor*
Russert, Timothy John *broadcast journalist, broadcast executive*
Safire, William *journalist, foundation administrator*
Salant, Jonathan D. *reporter*
Samsot, Robert Louis *editor, consultant*
Scheibel, Kenneth Maynard *journalist*
Schieffer, Bob *newscaster*
Schmidt, Susan *journalist*
Schram, Martin Jay *journalist*
Scoblic, J. Peter *magazine editor*
Seidman, L(ewis) William *television commentator, publisher*
Semas, Philip Wayne *editor*
Shadid, Anthony *journalist*
Shales, Thomas William *television and film critic, writer, journalist*
Shanks, Hershel *editor, writer*
Shannon, Donald Hawkins *retired editor*
Shapiro, Walter Elliot *columnist*
Shaw-Eagle, Joanna *art critic*
Sheehan, Neil *reporter, writer*
Shenon, Philip *journalist*
Siegel, Robert Charles *broadcast journalist*
Silver, Brian Quayle *broadcast journalist, musician, educator*
Simpson, Cam *reporter*
Slafka, Kristi Lynne *journalist*
Slater, Jim *sportswriter, journalist*
Smith, Cara *editorial executive*
Smith, John B. *publishing executive*
Smith, R. Jeffrey *reporter*
Smith, Stephen Grant *journalist*
Stephanopoulos, George Robert *political reporter*
Stephens, Joe Alan *investigative reporter*
Stern, Carl Leonard *retired news correspondent, federal official*
Stern, Kenneth P. *broadcast executive*
Stern, Marcus A. *journalist*
Stolberg, Sheryl Gay *journalist*
Stossel, Scott Hanford *editor, writer*
Sullivan, Andrew M. *online journalist, editor, news blogger*
Taubman, Philip *publishing executive*
Terzian, Philip Henry *journalist*
Thomasson, Dan King *newspaper executive, columnist*
Tiede, Tom Robert *journalist*
Tierney, John Marion *journalist, columnist, reporter*
Tischler, Gary *critic, journalist*
Toedtman, James Smith *journalist, editor*
Tolchin, Martin *journalist, writer*
Toledano, Ralph de *columnist, writer, poet*
Toles, Thomas Gregory *editorial cartoonist*
Totenberg, Nina *journalist*
Trafford, Abigail *columnist, editor, writer*
Turner, Ted (Robert Edward Turner) *retired broadcast company executive, philanthropist*
Waldman, Amy *journalist*
Walker, Martin Alan *journalist*
Weisman, Steven Roger *newspaper editor*
Weiss, Rick *reporter*
Whitworth, William A. *magazine editor*
Wilkison, David *editor*
Will, George Frederick *editor, journalist, commentator*
Williams, Juan *news correspondent*
Winfrey, Carey Wells *journalist, editor*
Winter, Thomas Swanson *publishing executive*
Woodward, Bob (Robert Upshur Woodward) *newspaper reporter, writer*

Yardley, Jonathan *journalist*
Zahn, Paula *newscaster*

## FLORIDA

### Aventura
Perkel, Robert Simon *photojournalist, educator*

### Boca Raton
Handel, Morton Emanuel *film company executive, management consultant*
Levine, Irving R. *commentator, dean, writer, educator*
McQueen, Scott Robert *broadcast executive*
Perel, David *editor*

### Boynton Beach
Jacobs, Wendy *editor, realtor*
Klein, Bernard *publishing executive*

### Braden River
Wilkerson, Janet Stafford *publishing executive, educator*

### Bradenton
Crouthamel, Thomas Grover, Sr. *editor, consultant*
Heffernan, John William *retired journalist*
McFarland, Richard Macklin *retired journalist*
White, Dale Andrew *journalist*

### Clearwater
VanMeer, Mary Ann *publishing executive, writer, webmaster*

### Coconut Grove
Alarcon, Raul, Jr. *broadcast executive*

### Coral Gables
Roberts, Samuel Smith *television news executive*

### Daytona Beach
Davidson, Herbert M., Jr., (Tippen Davidson) *newspaper owner*

### Delray Beach
Salsberg, Arthur Philip *publishing executive*

### Dover
Pearson, Walter Donald *editor, columnist*

### Fort Lauderdale
Fleetwood, Clifford Gene ("The Father of Philosophical Art" Fleetwood) *recording industry executive, publishing executive*
Hartz, Deborah Sophia *editor, writer*
Markus, Robert Michael *retired journalist*
Packer, Billy *sports announcer (broadcast)*
Ruffner, Frederick G., Jr. *book publisher*
Schulte, Frederick James *newpaper editor*
Williamson, William Paul, Jr. *journalist*

### Fort Myers
Barbour, William Rinehart, Jr. *retired book publisher*

### Gainesville
Barber, Charles Edward *publishing executive, journalist*
Holland, Norman Norwood *critic*
Kaid, Lynda Lee *communications educator*
Kaplan, John *photojournalist, educator, consultant*
Logan, William *poetry critic, literature and language professor, poet*

### Gulfport
Andrisani, John Anthony *editor, writer*
Beary, Jack *journalist, educator, county official*

### Hallandale
Schatken, Nancy Leah *medical editor*

### Heathrow
Argirion, Michael *editor*

### Hialeah
Browne, Donald Victor *broadcast executive*
Hernandez, Roland *broadcast executive*

### Hillsboro Beach
Gibbons, Celia Victoria Townsend (Mrs. John Sheldon) *editor, publisher*

### Hollywood
Lopez, Filemon *broadcast executive*

### Jacksonville
Barrow, Sally Settle *media specialist, librarian*
Bedell, Elizabeth Snyder (Betty Bedell) *editor-in-chief, marketing professional*
Cannon, Carl N. *publishing executive*
Davis, Fred *journalist, educator*
Hartmann, Frederick William *newspaper editor*
Lehmbeck, John Pierce *journalist, writer*
Vincent, Norman Fuller *broadcast executive*

### Key Biscayne
Pope, John Edwin *editor, columnist*

### Lake Worth
Pecker, David J. *magazine publishing company executive*

### Lakeland
MacDonald, Susan Priest *media specialist, writer*

### Lutz
Kolb, Richard Maurice *sports writer, sportscaster*

### Melbourne
Mikolajczyk, Mark S. *publishing executive*

### Melrose
Burt, Alvin Victor, Jr. *journalist*

### Miami
Black, Creed Carter *newspaper executive*
Chapman, Alvah Herman, Jr. *retired newspaper executive*

---

de Leon, Lidia Maria *magazine editor*
Fichtner, Margaria *journalist*
Fiedler, Tom *editor-in-chief*
Fisher, Ann *recording industry executive, lawyer*
Hampton, John Lewis *retired newspaper editor*
Harrison, Stanley L. *editor, educator, writer*
Lawrence, David, Jr. *journalist*
Lew, Salvador *radio station executive*
Lewis, John Milton *cable television company executive*
O'Bryon, Linda Elizabeth *broadcast executive*
Pitts, Leonard Garvey, Jr. *columnist, writer*
Russell, James Webster, Jr. *editor, columnist*
Salinas, María Elena *newscaster, columnist*
Savage, James Francis *editor*
Tsai, John Jengshyong *publishing executive*
Wax, William Edward *photojournalist*
Wilson, Dave *editor*

### Mount Dora
Trundle, W(infield) Scott *publishing executive, newspaper, lawyer*

### Naples
Blevins, Charles Russell *publishing executive*
Burdick, Robert W. *newspaper editor*
Clapp, Roger Howland *retired publishing executive*
Clarke, John Patrick *retired newspaper publisher*
Cobb, Brian Eric *broadcast executive*
Jones, Philip Howard *broadcast journalist*
Mills, Dorothy Jane (Dorothy Z. Seymour) *editor, consultant*
Penniman, Nicholas Griffith, IV, *retired newspaper publisher*

### Niceville
Warren, J. Richard *editor, retired humanities educator*

### North Palm Beach
Lavine, Alan *columnist, writer*

### North Port
Coe, Laurie Lynne Barker *photojournalist, artist*

### Orlando
Dunn, William Bruna III *journalist*
Hall, Charlotte Hauch *editor*
Healy, Jane Elizabeth *newspaper editor*
Maupin, Elizabeth Thatcher *theater critic*
Pierce, Jerry Earl *publishing executive*
Reese, Charles Edgar *columnist*
Waltz, Kathleen M. *publishing executive*
Waltz, Kathy *publishing executive*

### Palm Bay
Pattyn, Sue *publishing executive*

### Palm Beach
Monath, Norman *publishing company executive*
Pryor, Hubert *editor, writer, consultant*

### Palm Coast
Afflick, Gilbert Leslie *editor, journalist*

### Palm Harbor
Barker, Larry Lee *communications educator*
Jones, Winona Nigels *retired media specialist*

### Parrish
Wood, Benton *retired editor, priest*

### Pensacola
Bowden, Jesse Earle *editor, writer, cartoonist, journalist, educator*

### Pompano Beach
Roen, Sheldon R. *publishing executive, psychologist*

### Port Saint Lucie
Sommers, Robert Thomas *editor, writer*

### Punta Gorda
Miles, Frank Charles *retired newspaper executive*

### Saint Augustine
Nolan, Joseph Thomas *journalism educator, communications consultant*

### Saint Petersburg
Barnes, Andrew Earl *former newspaper executive*
Belich, John Patrick, Sr. *journalist, private investigator*
Corty, Andrew P. *publishing executive*
Dennis, Brady *journalist*
Haiman, Robert James *editor, journalist, educator, media consultant, critic*
Hooker, Robert Wright *journalist*
Jenkins, Robert Norman *reporter, editor*
Johnson, Edna Ruth *editor*
Naughton, James Martin *journalist*
Patterson, Eugene Corbett *retired editor, publishing executive*
Pittman, Robert Turner *retired newspaper editor*
Tash, Paul Clifford *editor, publishing executive*

### Sanford
Scott, Mellouise Jacqueline *retired media specialist*

### Sanibel
Ray, Charles Albert *photojournalist*

### Sarasota
Hughes, Allen *music critic*
Jackel, Lawrence *publishing executive*
Leidel, Katherine *journalist, newscaster*
Marino, Eugene Louis *publishing executive, director*
North, Marjorie Mary *columnist*
Proffitt, Waldo, Jr. *newspaper editor*
Stevens, Elisabeth Goss (Mrs. Robert Schleussner Jr.) *journalist, writer, graphic artist*

### Tallahassee
Dadisman, Joseph Carrol *retired newspaper executive*

---

Morgan, Lucy Ware *news correspondent, journalist*
Pettijohn, Fred Phillips *retired publishing executive*

### Tamarac
Froehlich, Fritz Edgar *communications educator, telecommunications scientist*

### Tampa
Friedlander, Edward Jay *journalist, educator*
Huey, Peggy J. *communications educator, performing company executive*
Jacobus, Mary *publishing executive*
Palmer, Denise E. *publishing executive*
Reed, Donna Marie *editor*
Schueler, John R. *newspaper executive*
Thelen, Gil *publishing executive*
Tully, Darrow *newspaper publisher*
Weaver, Janet S. *editor*

### Tarpon Springs
Leisner, Anthony Baker *publishing company executive*

### Venice
Cool, Kim Patmore *editor, publishing executive, retail executive*
Corrigan, William Thomas *retired broadcast news executive*

### Vero Beach
Binney, Jan Jarrell *publishing executive, marketing professional*

### West Palm Beach
Johnson, Martin Allen *publishing executive, artist*
Rukeyser, M.S., Jr. *television consultant, writer*
Sears, Edward Milner, Jr. *newspaper editor*

### Winter Haven
Benton, Obie Folsom *publishing executive, writer*

## GEORGIA

### Athens
Feldman, Edmund Burke *art critic*
Fink, Conrad Charles *journalist, educator, communications executive, consultant*
Soloski, John *journalism and communications educator*
Thomas, Patricia Joanne *journalist, writer*

### Atlanta
Alleyne, Mark Dacosta *communications educator, journalist*
Amanpour, Christiane *news correspondent*
Anstrom, Decker *broadcast executive*
Austin, Dallas *record company executive, producer*
Berry, Dennis (G. Dennis Berry) *publishing executive*
Bisher, James Furman *journalist, writer*
Chambers, Anne Cox *publishing executive, former diplomat*
Connelly, Terrence John, Sr. *television and cable station executive*
Dobson, Bridget McColl Hursley *television executive, writer*
Fortin, Judy *cable news anchor*
Hayes, Jimmy W. *media company executive*
Howell, George *art critic*
Jones, Joe Kenley *journalist*
Kennedy, James Cox *publishing and media executive*
Kintzel, Roger S. *publishing executive*
Klein, Jonathan *broadcast executive*
Kloer, Philip Baldwin *critic*
Luckovich, Mike *cartoonist*
Mellott, John *publishing executive*
Merdek, Andrew Austin *publishing and media executive, lawyer*
Morant, Brenda White *publishing executive, small business owner, investor*
Neil, Robert F. *broadcast executive*
Polk, James Ray *journalist*
Puckett, Susan *newspaper editor*
Robelot, Jane *anchor*
Roberts, Chuck *cable news anchor*
Sanchez, Ricardo *broadcast executive*
Sansone, Victor *broadcast executive*
Scott, Marian Alexis *journalist*
Seal, Manuel, Jr. *music company executive, composer*
Simao, Paul *news agency executive*
Sloan, Mary Jean *retired media specialist*
Teepen, Thomas Henry *editor, journalist*
Toner, Michael F. *journalist*
Tucker, Cynthia Anne *journalist*
Wallace, Julia Diane *newspaper editor*
Walton, Jim *news network executive*
Whitt, Richard Ernest *reporter*
Wilson, Debora J. *broadcast executive*
Wussler, Robert Joseph *broadcast executive, media consultant*

### Augusta
Denton, Frank M. *publishing executive*

### Decatur
Knight, Walker Leigh *publishing executive, minister*
Shaw, Jeanne Osborne *editor, poet*

### Fayetteville
Turnipseed, Barnwell Rhett III *journalist, public relations consultant*

### Fort Valley
Archer, Lloyd Daniel *communications educator*

### Georgetown
Briggs, Niwana Page *editor, writer*

### Jekyll Island
Bentley, James Luther *former journalist*
McKinley, Douglas Webster (Webb McKinley) *consultant*

---

### Kennesaw
Kinnick, Katherine Neil *communications educator, academic administrator*

### Mableton
Rowe, Bonnie Gordon *music company executive*

### Marietta
Dunwoody, Kenneth Reed *magazine and book editor*
Hays, Robert William *communications educator, consultant, writer*
Opre, Thomas Edward *retired editor, retired film company executive*
Williamsen, Dannye Sue *publishing executive, writer*

### Oxford
Sitton, Claude Fox *newspaper editor*

### Richmond Hill
Budde, Neil Frederick *publishing company executive, editor, publisher*

### Roswell
Peterson, Donald Robert *editor, vintage automobile consultant*

### Savannah
Smith, David Lee *retired editor*

### Statesboro
Adhikari, Dharma Nanda *journalist, writer, educator*

### Watkinsville
Williams, Vivian (Vinnie) Marie *publishing executive, editor, writer*

## HAWAII

### Honolulu
Chung, Kea Sung *television broadcasting executive*
Keyes, Saundra Elise *newspaper editor*
Platte, Mark *editor*
Rexner, Romulus *publishing executive*
Simonds, John Edward *retired newspaper editor*
Sparks, Robert William *retired publishing executive*

### Kaneohe
McGlaughlin, Thomas Howard *publishing executive, retired military officer*

### Pahoa
Lewis, Jack (Cecil Paul Lewis) *publishing executive, editor*

### Waipahu
Look, Pauwilo *media specialist, architectural engineer*

## IDAHO

### Boise
McLuskie, Ed *communications educator*

### Idaho Falls
Harris, Darryl Wayne *publishing executive*

### Mccall
Romano, Michael *publishing executive, consultant*

### Sandpoint
Bowne, Martha Hoke *editor, consultant*

## ILLINOIS

### Addison
Klemens, Thomas Lloyd *editor*

### Arlington Heights
Baumann, Daniel E. *publishing executive*
Lampinen, John A. *newspaper editor*
Ray, Douglas Kent *newspaper executive*

### Berwyn
Forst, Edmund Charles, Jr. *communications educator, administrator, consultant*

### Buffalo Grove
Kuennen, Thomas Gerard *journalist*
Samors, Neal *publishing executive, writer*
True, Michelle Ailene *editor, writer*

### Burr Ridge
Wyatt, Robert Odell *journalism educator*

### Carol Stream
Bemis, Mary Ferguson *magazine editor*
Franzen, Janice Marguerite Gosnell *magazine editor*

### Champaign
Dulany, Elizabeth Gjelsness *editor*
Hansen, Kathryn Gertrude *editor, retired state official*
Kroner, Fred L. *journalist*
McCulloh, Judith Marie *editor*
Meyer, August Christopher, Jr. *broadcast executive, lawyer*
Turquette, Frances Bond *editor*
Watts, Robert Allan *publisher, lawyer*

### Charleston
Coutant, Mary McElwee *retired editor*

### Chicago
Anderson, Karl Stephen *editor*
Artner, Alan Gustav *art critic, journalist*
Baca, Stacey *newscaster*
Barr, Emily L. *broadcast executive*
Barron, John *editor*

Beaudet-Francès, Patricia Suzanne *photography editor*
Bleifuss, Joel *journalist*
Breen, Neil Thomas *publishing executive*
Broadhead, Glenn J. *communications educator, consultant*
Brock, Kathy *newscaster*
Brotman, Barbara Louise *journalist, writer*
Brumback, Charles Tiedtke *retired newspaper executive*
Bulka, Micheal *art critic*
Burns, Diann *newscaster*
Burton, Cheryl *newscaster*
Cappo, Joseph C. *journalist, writer*
Chapman, Stephen James *columnist*
Childers, Mary Ann *newscaster*
Ciezadlo, Janina A. *art critic, educator*
Cook, Bruce Lawrence *editor*
Cooke, Michael *editor-in-chief, publishing executive*
Cross, Robert Clark *journalist*
Cruickshank, John Douglas *publishing executive*
Curwen, Randall William *journalist, editor*
Darby, Edwin Wheeler *retired columnist*
Dee, Ivan Richard *book publisher*
DeLong, Ray *editor*
Dold, Robert Bruce *journalist*
Ebert, Roger Joseph *film critic*
Essex, Joseph Michael *visual communication planner*
Feder, Robert *columnist*
Ferguson, Renee *news correspondent, reporter*
Ferrara, Annette *editor, educator*
Fetridge, Clark Worthington *publishing executive*
FitzSimons, Dennis Joseph *broadcast executive, publishing executive*
Fontanarosa, Phil Bernard *medical journal executive editor, emergency physician, educator*
Forbes, Dorsey Connors *commentator, journalist*
Francuch, Paul Charles *broadcast journalist*
Gomez, Sylvia *newscaster*
Grossman, Kate Nadia *journalist*
Guillen, Alita (Alita Haytayan) *newscaster*
Hallinan, Joseph Thomas *journalist, reporter*
Hardin, Terrence Armstrong *former radio broadcasting manager*
Harrelson, Ken *sports broadcaster*
Harvey, Paul *commentator, writer, columnist*
Hefner, Christie Ann *publishing executive*
Hill, Darlene *newscaster*
Hiller, David Dean *publishing executive*
Hooper, Brad *editor, librarian*
Hsu, Judy *newscaster*
Huebner, Jeff *art journalist, freelance writer*
Huntley, Robert Stephen *newspaper editor*
Idol, Anna Catherine *magazine editor*
Jones, Linda *communications educator*
Jordan, Karen *newscaster*
Judge, Bernard Martin *editor, publishing executive*
Kamyszew, Christopher D. *film executive, educator, curator*
Keller, Julia *reporter*
Kelly, Curtis Hartt *retired publishing executive*
Kim, Danial *publishing executive*
Kisor, Henry Du Bois *editor, columnist, critic, writer*
Klapthor, James *news media relations specialist*
Klatt, Wayne Roy *editor, writer*
Klaviter, Helen Lothrop *editor-in-chief, magazine editor*
Krashesky, Alan *newscaster*
Krueger, Bonnie Lee *editor, writer*
Larson, Roy *journalist, publishing executive*
Lipinski, Ann Marie *publishing executive*
Loesch, Katharine Taylor *communication and theatre educator*
Longworth, Richard Cole *journalist*
Loo, Nancy *newscaster*
Lythcott, Marcia A. *newspaper editor*
Martinez, Natalie *newscaster*
McDaniel, Charles-Gene *journalism educator, writer*
McNally, Andrew, IV, *publishing executive, director*
Migala, Lucyna J. *journalist, broadcast executive, artistic director*
More, José *photojournalist*
Nash, Jessie Madeleine *journalist, science writer*
Nault, William Henry *publishing executive*
O'Shea, James *managing editor*
Paris, Gordon A. *publishing executive*
Peerman, Dean Gordon *magazine editor*
Pender, Nancy *newscaster*
Peres, Judith May *journalist*
Perez, Sylvia *newscaster, reporter*
Plotnick, Harvey Barry *publishing executive*
Pope, Kerig Rodgers *retired magazine executive*
Primm, Earl Russell III *publishing executive*
Rice, Linda Johnson *publishing executive*
Rice, William Edward *journalist*
Robinson, Robin *newscaster*
Roeper, Richard *columnist*
Roth, Robert A. *newspaper executive*
Roy, Kevin *newscaster*
Rynkiewicz, Stephen Michael *journalist*
Scanlan, Thomas Cleary *publishing executive, editor*
Seaman, Donna Jean *editor, writer*
Shebel, Heather A. *editor*
Smith, Sam *columnist, writer*
Stoklosa, Gregory A. *publishing executive*
Suchomel, Mark *publishing executive*
Ullrich, Polly *art critic*
Veres, Bob *editor*
von Rhein, John Richard *music critic, journalist, writer*
Weinberg, Lila Shaffer *editor, writer*
Weintraub, Joseph Barton *publishing executive*
Wier, Patricia Ann *publishing executive, consultant*
Wille, Lois Jean *retired editor*
Winnecke, Joycelyn *editor*
Wolfe, Sheila A. *journalist*
Workman, Michael *editor-in-chief, publishing executive, art critic*
Youngman, Owen Ralph *newspaper executive*
Zwecker, William Rene, Jr., (Bill Zwecker) *newspaper columnist, television reporter*

**Crystal Lake**
Keller, William Francis *publishing consultant*

**Des Plaines**
Clapper, Marie Anne *magazine publisher*

**Elgin**
Jakle, Kenneth Richard *broadcast executive*
Turnquist, Jerry L. *communications educator, journalist*

**Elmhurst**
Pruter, Margaret Franson *editor*

**Evanston**
Borcover, Alfred Seymour *journalist*
Deming, Thomas Edward *publishing executive*
Felknor, Bruce Lester *publishing executive, consultant, writer*
Galvin, Kathleen Malone *communications educator*
Ghiglione, Loren Frank *journalism professor*
Hixson, Kathryn *art critic*
Jacobs, Norman Joseph *publishing executive*
Jones, Robert Russell *retired magazine editor*
Kuenster, John Joseph *editor*
McCarron, John Francis *editor*
Otwell, Ralph Maurice *retired newspaper editor*
Peck, Abraham *editor, writer, educator, media consultant*
Wilhelm, Frank L. *publisher, writer*
Ziomek, Jonathan S. *journalist, educator*

**Glenview**
Martin, James Frederick *media consultant*

**Greenville**
Flowers, Creole Duane *publishing executive*

**Highland Park**
Hawkins, Margaret *art critic, writer, educator*
Johnson, Curtis Lee *publishing executive, editor, writer*
Pattis, S. William *publishing executive*
Rutenberg-Rosenberg, Sharon Leslie *retired journalist*

**Huntley**
Balk, Alfred William *journalist*

**Itasca**
Porter, Ethel Mae *publishing executive*

**Kenilworth**
Cook, Stanton R. *media company executive*
Hayes, M. M.M. *publishing executive*

**Lake Bluff**
Marozsan, John Robert *retired publishing company executive*
Schreiber, George Richard *publishing executive, writer*
Snader, Jack Ross *publishing company executive*

**Lake Forest**
Schulze, Franz, Jr. *critic, educator*

**Lake In The Hills**
Kay, Dennis Matthew *retired publishing company official*

**Libertyville**
True, Raymond Stephen *editor, writer*

**Mount Vernon**
Withers, W. Russell, Jr. *broadcast executive*

**Northbrook**
Pesmen, Sandra (Mrs. Harold William Pesmen) *editor, educator*

**Oak Brook**
Biedron, Theodore John *publishing executive, advertising executive*

**Oregon**
Haynes, Gary Allen *photojournalist, editor*

**Orland Park**
Saubert, Nicole J. *communications educator, social studies educator*

**Pekin**
Dancey, Charles Lohman *retired newspaper executive*

**Peoria**
McConnell, John Thomas *publishing executive*
Murphy, Sharon Margaret *retired communications educator*

**Peru**
Carus, Milton Blouke *children's periodicals publisher*

**Prospect Heights**
Robinson, Martin (Marty Robinson) *television and radio broadcaster, media consultant*

**Rantoul**
Weber, Rochelle Irene *editor, writer*

**River Forest**
Valauskas, Edward Justin *librarian, editor, Internet consultant*

**Rockford**
Fleming, Thomas J. *editor, publishing executive*
Jacobi, Fredrick Thomas *newspaper publisher*

**Schaumburg**
Spada, Alfred Thomas *publishing executive*

**Springfield**
Carmichael, Buff *publishing executive*

**Urbana**
Christians, Clifford Glenn *communications educator*
Dash, Leon DeCosta, Jr. *journalist*
Ono, Kent Alan *communications educator*

Sandvig, Christian Edward *communications educator, researcher*

**Villa Park**
Gordon, Rachel Singer *editor*

**Wheaton**
Taylor, Mark Douglas *publishing executive*

**Wilmette**
Boyle, Antonia Barnes *writer, editor*
Trohman, Joseph Mark *editor*

**Winnetka**
Burke, John Edward *communications editor*
Quaal, Ward Louis *broadcast executive*

## INDIANA

**Anderson**
Clanin, Douglas Edward *editor, researcher*

**Bloomington**
Jacobi, Peter Paul *journalism educator, writer*
Lee, Don Yoon *publishing executive, academic administrator, writer*
Pedersen, Paul Mark *sportswriter, educator, columnist*
Schurz, Scott Clark *journalist*
Walling, Donovan Robert *editor, writer*

**Fort Wayne**
Inskeep, Richard Glenn *publishing executive*
Klugman, Stephan Craig *newspaper editor*

**Franklin**
Nuwer, Henry Joseph (Hank Nuwer) *journalist, educator*

**Greencastle**
Hall, David *newspaper editor*

**Indianapolis**
Coffey, Charles Moore *communication research professional, writer*
Fine, Pamela B. *newspaper editor*
Garmel, Marion Bess Simon *retired arts journalist*
Hall, Emily Marie *editorial assistant*
Henry, Barbara Ann *publishing executive*
McKeand, Patrick Joseph *newspaper publisher, educator*
Russell, Frank Eli *retired newspaper publishing executive*
SerVaas, Cory *editor-in-chief*
Wheeler, Daniel Scott *management executive, editor*
Wright, David Burton *retired newspaper publishing company executive*

**Inglefield**
James, Marion Ray *retired publishing executive, editor*

**Knightstown**
Richardson, Shirley Maxine *editor*

**Kokomo**
Hockney, Dean Wesley *editor, writer*

**Lafayette**
Renzetti, Phyllis Jean *retired technical editor*

**Martinsville**
Kendall, Robert Stanton *newspaper editor, journalist, automotive executive*

**Michigan City**
Varro, Barbara Joan *retired editor*

**Muncie**
Bell, Stephen Scott (Steve Bell) *journalist, educator*

**Munster**
Potempa, Philip Matthew *journalist, columnist, communications educator*

**South Bend**
Smith, E. Berry *television and radio consultant*

**Terre Haute**
Vincent, Richard C. *communications educator, researcher*

## IOWA

**Ames**
Alumbaugh, JoAnn McCalla *magazine editor*

**Cedar Falls**
Skaine, James C. *retired communications educator*

**Cedar Rapids**
Keller, Eliot Aaron *broadcast executive*

**Des Moines**
Butler, Gayle *editor-in-chief*
DeWulf Nickell, Karol *editor-in-chief*
Gartner, Michael Gay *editor, baseball executive, television executive*
Graham, Diane E. *newspaper editor*
Kerr, William T. *publishing executive, broadcasting executive*
Lacy, Stephen M. *publishing and broadcasting executive*
Leach, Dave Francis *editor, musician*
Myers, Mary Kathleen *publishing executive*
Stier, Mary P. *publishing executive*
Van Zante, Shirley M(ae) *magazine editor*
Witke, David Rodney *retired newspaper editor, consultant*

**Holy Cross**
Ross, Christine Marie *media coordinator, small business owner, disc jockey, educator*

**Iowa City**
Gronbeck, Bruce Elliot *communications educator*

**Mason City**
Collison, Jim *publishing executive*

**Moville**
Baker, Kent Alfred *broadcasting executive, publishing company executive*

**Red Oak**
Higdon, Hal *sportswriter*

**Waterloo**
Green, Nancy Loughridge *publishing executive*

**West Des Moines**
Dooley, Donald John *retired publishing executive*

## KANSAS

**Halstead**
Orr, Jim (James D. Orr) *editor, writer, publishing executive*

**Hutchinson**
Baumer, Beverly Belle *journalist*
Buchanan, Bruce *publishing executive*
Buzbee, Richard Edgar *retired newspaper editor*

**Iola**
Lynn, Emerson Elwood, Jr. *retired newspaper editor/publisher*

**Lawrence**
Dickinson, William Boyd, Jr. *media consultant*
Hale, Richard Lee *magazine editor*
Simons, Dolph Collins, Jr. *publishing executive, editor*

**Manhattan**
Seaton, Edward Lee *editor, publishing executive*

**Marion**
Meyer, Bill *publishing executive, editor*

**Mission Hills**
Rose, Stephen F. *columnist*

**North Newton**
Snider, Marie Anna *syndicated columnist*

**Olathe**
Dodd, James B. *internet executive*

**Overland Park**
Christian, Shirley Ann *journalist, author*
Wornall, Ilah Ruth (Ruthie) *publishing executive, educator*

**Salina**
Entriken, Robert Kersey, Jr. *editor, writer*

**Shawnee Mission**
Martin, Donna Lee *retired publishing company executive*

**Wichita**
Hatteberg, Larry Merle *photojournalist*

## KENTUCKY

**Fort Knox**
Barnes, Larry Glen *journalist, editor, educator*

**Fort Mitchell**
Silvers, Gerald Thomas *retired publishing executive*

**Glasgow**
Knicely, Carroll Franklin *publishing executive*

**Goshen**
Strode, William Hall III *photojournalist*

**Greenville**
Walters, Sue Fox *broadcast executive, accountant*

**Lexington**
Cross, Alvin Miller (Al Cross) *journalist*
Donohew, Robert Lewis, Sr. *communications educator*
Keeling, Larry Dale *journalist*
Kelly, Timothy Michael *newspaper publisher*
Kissling, Fred Ralph, Jr. *publishing executive, insurance agency executive*

**Louisville**
Hawpe, David Vaughn *editor, journalist*
Towles, Donald Blackburn *retired publishing executive*

**Paducah**
Stice, Dwayne Lee *broadcasting company executive*

**Pewee Valley**
Gill, George Norman *newspaper publishing company executive*

## LOUISIANA

**Alexandria**
Smith, Joe Dorsey, Jr. *retired newspaper executive*

**Baton Rouge**
Finney, Clifton Donald *publishing executive*
Gilmore, Clarence Percy *editor-in-chief, writer*

**La Place**
Fiffie Proctor, JoAnn *media and technology specialist*

**Lake Charles**
Beam, James Carroll (Jim Beam) *retired newspaper editor*
Stacey, Truman *journalist, consultant*

**Monroe**
Mickel, Ruth Phelps *commentator, librarian*

**New Orleans**
Amoss, Walter James, III, (Jim Amoss) *editor*
Ball, Millie (Mildred Porteous Ball) *editor, journalist*
Clark, Joshua Maker *publishing executive*
Crumley, David Oliver *publishing executive, writer, corporate executive*
Ferguson, Charles Austin *retired newspaper editor*
Phelps, Ashton, Jr. *newspaper publisher*
Pope, John Marvin *journalist*
Roesler, Robert Harry *media consultant*

**Shreveport**
Lazarus, Allan Matthew *retired newspaper editor*
Robinson, Garry Lewin *television news executive*

**Slidell**
Lovell, Emily Kalled *retired journalist*

**MAINE**

**Belfast**
Griffith, Patricia King *journalist*

**Camden**
Kidder, Rushworth Moulton *journalist*

**Cape Elizabeth**
Rich, John Hubbard, Jr. *news correspondent*

**Castine**
Bernstein, Lester *editorial consultant*

**Chebeague Island**
Traina, Albert Salvatore *publishing executive*

**Damariscotta**
Blake, Bud (Julian Watson) *cartoonist*

**East Boothbay**
Gibson, Barry Joseph *editor*

**Kennebunkport**
Ray, Virginia H. S. *columnist, writer*

**Lincoln**
Kneeland, Douglas Eugene *retired newspaper editor*

**Penobscot**
dePaolo, Ronald Francis *editor-in-chief, writer*

**Sedgwick**
Schroth, Thomas Nolan *editor*

**MARYLAND**

**Adelphi**
Monroe, Bryan *publishing executive, trade association administrator*

**Annapolis**
Finerty, Martin Joseph, Jr. *editor, military officer*

**Baldwin**
Kiper, Mel, Jr. *sports commentator*

**Baltimore**
Broening, Walter Stephens, Jr. *journalist, history educator*
Donovan, Dianne Francys *journalist*
Dorsey, John Russell *journalist*
Franklin, Timothy A. *editor*
Hirsh, Allan T. III *book publisher*
Hirsh, Allan Thurman, Jr. *publishing executive*
Matthews, Rondra J. *publishing executive*
McNatt, Glenn *art critic*
Murphy, Frances Louise, II, *retired newspaper publisher*
Rodricks, Daniel John *columnist, television commentator*
Rouguol, J. Wynn *theater critic*
Sanders, Julius Ray *music company executive*
Shannon, Joe *art critic, painter*
Sterne, Joseph Robert Livingston *editor, educator*

**Bethesda**
Chronister, Gregory Michael *newspaper editor*
Cornish, Edward Seymour *magazine editor*
English, Michela *entertainment company executive*
Frank, Richard Sanford *retired magazine editor*
Herman, Edith Carol *journalist*
Johnson, Robert Louis *broadcast executive, professional sports team executive*
Kaplan, Marjorie *broadcast executive*
Kempster, Norman Roy *journalist*
Lannan, Maura Anne Kelly *reporter*
Larrabee, Donald Richard *publishing executive*
McHale, Judith A. (Judith Ottalloran) *broadcast executive, lawyer*
Nelson, John Howard (Jack Howard Nelson) *journalist*
Olson, Lynn *editor*
Pickerell, James Howard *photojournalist*
Wagner, Cynthia Gail *editor, writer*

**Cheverly**
Miller, Mark Karl *journalist, editor*

**Chevy Chase**
Adler, James Barron *publishing executive*
Bruno, Harold Robinson, Jr. *retired journalist, writer*
Cowen, Eugene Sherman *broadcast executive*
Glaser, Vera Romans *journalist*
Kilborn, Peter Thurston *journalist*
Kriegsman, Alan M. *arts critic*
Shipler, David Karr *journalist, writer*
Shogan, Robert *news correspondent*

Smith, Hedrick Laurence *journalist, television producer*
Sperling, Godfrey, Jr. *retired journalist*
Toth, Robert Charles *retired journalist*

**College Park**
Beasley, Maurine Hoffman *journalism educator, historian*
Gomery, Douglas *communications educator, writer*
Grunig, James Elmer *communications educator, researcher, public relations consultant*
Johnson, Haynes Bonner *journalist, writer, commentator*

**Columbia**
Greyson D'Otazzo, Meaghan Regina *literary critic*

**Easton**
Wilson, Laura Ann *newspaper editor*

**Galesville**
Whaley, Garwood *music company executive*

**Garrett Park**
Kornberg, Warren Stanley *journalist*

**Havre De Grace**
Wetter, Virginia Forwood Patc *broadcast executive*

**Landover**
Maduka, Chikezie *journalist*

**Lanham**
Godwin, Mary Jo *editor, librarian, consultant*
Lyons, James Edward (Jed) *publishing executive*

**Lutherville Timonium**
Cedrone, Louis Robert, Jr. *retired critic*

**Monkton**
Parker, Robert M., Jr., (Bob Parker) *wine critic, writer*

**North Potomac**
Lide, David Reynolds *editor-in-chief*

**Owings Mills**
Holdridge, Barbara *book editor, writer, consultant*

**Perryville**
Quesenbery, Erika Lynn *media specialist, curator*

**Potomac**
Christian, John Kenton *publishing executive, marketing professional, consultant*
Fox, Arthur Joseph, Jr. *editor*
Karnow, Stanley *journalist, writer*
Sundick, Sherry Small *journalist, writer, poet*

**Rockville**
Kohlmeier, Louis Martin, Jr. *newspaper reporter*
Miller, Claire Ellen *editor, educator, writer*

**Salisbury**
Heller, R. Andrew *communications educator, theater educator, director*
Kleiman, Gary Howard *broadcast, advertising and cellular communications consultant*

**Silver Spring**
Bennett, Carol(ine) Elise *retired reporter, actress*
Carson, Steven Lee *newspaper publisher*
Eiserer, Leonard Albert Carl *publishing executive*
Koppel, Ted *newscaster*
Kurata, Phillip Cedomir *journalist*
Rodgers, Johnathan *broadcast executive*
Truitt, Gordon Edward *editor, writer*
Vernon, Weston, III, (Wes Vernon) *broadcaster, writer, actor*
Whitaker, Joel *publishing executive, public official*

**Street**
Spangler, Ronald Leroy *retired television executive, aircraft executive, automobile consultant*

**Sunderland**
Franklin, Jon Daniel *writer, journalist, educator*

**University Park**
Beckenstein, Myron *journalist*

**MASSACHUSETTS**

**Allston**
Becton, Henry Prentiss, Jr. *broadcast executive*

**Bedford**
Goodman, William Beehler *editor, literary agent*

**Boston**
Baron, Martin *editor*
Bennett, Clay *cartoonist*
Bergenheim, Richard C. *editor*
Caldwell, Gail *book critic*
Carroll, Jill *freelance journalist*
Cohen, Rachelle Sharon *journalist*
Convey, Kevin R. *editor*
Cook, Gareth *reporter*
Donovan, Helen W. *newspaper editor*
Eichler, Jeremy *music critic*
Feeney, Mark *journalist*
Flaherty, Lois Talbot *editor, psychiatrist, educator*
Flockhart, Barbara Townsley *publishing executive*
Foreman, Judy *journalist*
Godine, David Richard *publishing executive*
Golden, Daniel *journalist*
Hillery, Thomas Hungiville *journalist, financial consultant*
Hostetter, Amos Barr, Jr. *cable television executive*
Jacoby, Jeff *journalist, commentator*
James, Bill *baseball writer, statistician*
Kennedy, Louise Avery *theater critic, newspaper editor, writer*
Kilbourne, Jean *media analyst, educator*
Kimball, George Edward III *sports columnist*
King, Nick *newspaper editor*
Klarfeld, Jonathan Michael *journalism educator*

Kotz, Nathan Kallison (Nick Kotz) *news correspondent, author*
Krakoff, Robert Leonard *publishing executive*
Kuttner, Robert Louis *editor, writer, columnist*
Larkin, Michael John *editor, journalist*
Lawrence, Merloyd Ludington *editor*
Lee, Donald Young (Don Lee) *publishing executive*
Leland, Timothy *retired newspaper executive*
Loth, Renée *editor*
Mason, Charles Ellis III *magazine editor*
Norment, Eric Stuart *newspaper editor*
Purcell, Patrick Joseph *newspaper publisher*
Rodman, Sarah *music critic*
Schulz, John Joseph *communications educator*
Seglin, Jeffrey L. *columnist, educator*

**Bridgewater**
Holton, Susan A. *communications educator*

**Brighton**
Holley, Michael *sportswriter, sportscaster*

**Brookline**
Bourne, Katherine Day *journalist, educator*

**Cambridge**
Aronson, Michael Andrew *editor*
Giles, Robert Hartmann *journalist, educator*
Goodman, Ellen Holtz *journalist*
Jones, Alex S. *reporter, writer*
Lenger, John Richard *journalism educator*
MacKinnon, Rebecca *media consultant, researcher*
Negroponte, Nicholas *media specialist, educator*
Nordell, Hans Roderick *journalist, retired editor*
Wilcox, Maud *editor*

**Chestnut Hill**
Smith, Richard Alan *publishing and specialty retailing executive*

**Cohasset**
Replogle, David Robert *publishing executive*

**Concord**
Heinle, Beverly Diane *publishing executive*

**Dedham**
Redstone, Sumner Murray *broadcast executive, lawyer*

**Edgartown**
MacDonald, Duncan *broadcaster, writer, communications consultant*

**Framingham**
Levy, Joseph Louis *publishing company executive*
Twombly, Stephen Doane *magazine publisher*

**Franklin**
Maril, David C. *editor*

**Hingham**
Menzies, Ian Stuart *newspaper editor*
Pallai, David Francis *publishing executive*

**Hudson**
Osoff, Jeffrey Arlin *media company executive*

**Leeds**
Deane, James Garner *editor, conservationist*

**Lexington**
Davis, Robert J. *internet company executive*

**Lincoln**
Nenneman, Richard Arthur *retired publishing executive*

**Marblehead**
Quigley, Stephen Howard *executive editor*

**Natick**
Darehshori, Nader Farhang *publishing sales executive*

**Needham**
Greenway, Hugh Davids Scott *journalist*

**Needham Heights**
Salhany, Lucille S. (Lucy Salhany) *broadcast executive*

**Newton**
Hume, Ellen Hunsberger *media analyst, educator, journalist*
Knez, Brian J. *publishing executive*

**North Adams**
Thurston, Donald Allen *broadcast executive*

**North Chelmsford**
Kotelly, George Vincent *editor, writer, electrical engineer*

**Pittsfield**
Rich, Philip Dewey *publishing executive*

**Plymouth**
Flood, H. Gay (Hulda Gay Flood) *editor, consultant*

**Quincy**
Lippincott, Joseph P. *photojournalist, educator*

**Rockport**
Bissell, Phil (Charles P. Bissell) *cartoonist*

**Siasconset**
Smith, Harrison Harvey *journalism consultant*

**South Easton**
Keith, Michael Curtis *communication educator, writer*

**South Hadley**
Cowan, Wayne Harper *editor, writer*
Elleman, Barbara *editor*

**Springfield**
Starr, David *editor, publisher*

**Vineyard Haven**
Lovewell, Mark Alan *journalist*

**Wayland**
Huff, William Braid *retired publishing company executive*

**Wellfleet**
Limpitlaw, John Donald *publishing executive, minister*

**West Falmouth**
King, Richard Hood *retired newspaper executive*

**West Tisbury**
Méras, Phyllis Leslie *journalist*

**Weston**
Sanzone, Donna S. *publishing executive*

**Westport**
Gormley, Robert John *retired publishing executive*

**Westwood**
Borgman, George Allan *journalist*

**Winchester**
Ockerbloom, Richard C. *newspaper executive*

**Woburn**
Lundquist, Eric *editor-in-chief*

**Worcester**
Bennett, Bruce S. *publishing executive*

**MICHIGAN**

**Ann Arbor**
Beaver, Frank Eugene *critic, historian*
Bedard, Patrick Joseph *editor, writer, consultant*
Csere, Csaba *magazine editor*
Driscoll, John *publishing executive*
Eisendrath, Charles Rice *journalism educator, farmer, consultant*
Hessler, David William *information and multimedia systems educator*
Houghtlin, Robert *publishing executive*
Lewis, Robert Enzer *editor, educator*

**Baroda**
Reckline, Sigmund Joseph *publishing executive, editor*

**Bay City**
Hiner, John Patrick *newspaper editor*

**Bloomfield Township**
Brown, Lynette Ralya *journalist, publicist*

**Dearborn**
Hogan, Brian Joseph *editor*
Kiska, Timothy Olin *communications educator, radio producer*

**Detroit**
Albom, Mitch David *sports columnist*
Alpert, Daniel *broadcast executive*
Andrews, Caesar *editor*
Anger, Paul *newspaper editor*
Bennett, Grace *publishing executive*
Blomquist, David Wels *journalist*
Burzynski, Susan Marie *newspaper editor*
Butler, David J. *newspaper editor*
Colby, Joy Hakanson *critic*
DeRamus, Betty Jean *columnist*
Fladung, Thom *managing editor*
McTyre, Robert Earl *publishing executive*
Parry, Dale D. *newspaper editor*
Smyntek, John Eugene, Jr. *editor*
Taylor, Jeff *reporter, editor*

**East Lansing**
Freedman, Eric *journalist, educator, writer*
Greenberg, Bradley Sander *communications educator*
Ralph, David Clinton *communications educator*

**Farmington**
Bryfonski, Dedria Anne *publishing executive*

**Grand Rapids**
Bolinder, Scott W. *publishing company executive*
Bytwerk, Randall Lee *communication educator*
Kaczmarczyk, Jeffrey Allen *journalist, music critic, dance critic*
Mayo, David Wayne *sportswriter*

**Grosse Pointe**
Hill, Draper *editorial cartoonist*
Whittaker, Jeanne Evans *retired journalist*

**Grosse Pointe Farms**
Christian, Edward Kieren *broadcasting station executive*

**Grosse Pointe Park**
Elsila, David August *editor*

**Grosse Pointe Woods**
McWhirter, Glenna Suzanne (Nickie McWhirter) *retired columnist*

**Lansing**
Brown, Nancy Field *editor*

**Manistee**
Trussell, Charles Tait *columnist*

**Mount Pleasant**
Petrick, Michael Joseph *journalism educator*

**Saginaw**
Chaffee, Paul Charles *newspaper editor, publisher*

**Sault Sainte Marie**
Balfantz, Gary Leonard *communications and drama educator*

**Southfield**
Catallo, Heather *newscaster*
Gayle, Monica *broadcast journalist*
Makupson, Amyre Porter *broadcast executive*
Margolis, Sherry *newscaster*
Stinger, Fanchon *newscaster*
Thomas, Judy Janet *reporter, public health service officer*
Timmons, Robbie *news anchor*

**Sturgis**
Hair, Robert Eugene *editor, writer, historian*

**Waterford**
James, William Ramsay *broadcast executive*

**Ypsilanti**
Evans, Gary Lee *communications educator, consultant*
Okafor, Victor O. *journalist, educator*

## MINNESOTA

**Bloomington**
Larson, Michael Len *newspaper editor, hospital administrator, publishing executive*

**Duluth**
Latto, Lewis M. *broadcast executive*

**Eden Prairie**
Carver, Gloria Jean *documentation specialist*
Thompson, Sally Ann *editor*

**Edina**
Bisping, Bruce Henry *photojournalist*

**Minneapolis**
Cope, Lewis *journalist*
Cowles, John, Jr. *publishing executive, women's sports promoter, philanthropist*
Crosby, Jacqueline Garton *newspaper editor, journalist*
Flanagan, Barbara *journalist*
Gyllenhaal, Anders *publishing executive, editor*
Johnson, Gary L. *publishing executive*
Knatterud, Mary E. *editor, educator, writer*
Laing, Karel Ann *magazine publishing executive*
Lerner, Harry Jonas *publishing executive*
McGuire, Tim *editor*
Meador, Ron *newspaper editor, writer*
Miller, Alan M. *editor, writer, educator, television host*
Moyer, J. Keith *publishing executive*
Murphy, Joseph Edward, Jr. *broadcast executive*
Randall, Roger David *publishing executive*
Scallen, Thomas Kaine *broadcast executive*
Smetana, Mary Jane *reporter*
Steinberg, Michael *music critic, educator*
Werner, Lawrence H. *editor*
White, Robert James *retired columnist*

**Minnetonka**
Weisman, Eric *music company executive*

**Rochester**
Shampo, Marc Anthony *retired editor*

**Saint Joseph**
Rowland, Howard Ray *mass communications educator*

**Saint Louis Park**
Kalman, Marc *radio station executive*

**Saint Paul**
Amidon, Paul Charles *publishing executive*
Bree, Marlin Duane *publisher, author*
Feinberg, David Erwin *publishing executive*
Hubbard, Stanley Stub *broadcast executive*
Kling, William Hugh *broadcast executive*
Lofquist, Vicki L. *journalist*
Wehrwein, Austin Carl *freelance/self-employed reporter*
Weschcke, Carl Llewellyn *publishing executive*

**West Saint Paul**
Cento, William Francis *retired newspaper editor*

## MISSISSIPPI

**Gulfport**
Biffle, Tony *editor*

**Hattiesburg**
Hickman, Ronald Lee *media broker, broadcast executive*

**Jackson**
Lindsay, Arnold Arness *reporter*
Mitchell, Jerry *reporter*

**Kosciusko**
Shoemaker, William C. *journalist*

**Natchez**
Kirk, Susanne Smith *editor*

## MISSOURI

**Carthage**
McAfee, Diana Mae *media specialist, music educator*

**Chesterfield**
Gietschier, Steven Philip *journalist, historian*

**Clayton**
Costas, Bob (Robert Quinlan Costas) *sportscaster*

**Columbia**
Benoit, William Lyon *communication educator*
Chambers, Glenn Darrell *film company executive, art director*
Kramer, Michael W. *communications educator*
Loory, Stuart Hugh *journalist*
Sanders, Keith Page *journalism educator*

**Hannibal**
Katsion, John Roy *communications educator*

**Jefferson City**
Brown, Vicki Knasel *newswriter*

**Joplin**
Massa, Richard Wayne *retired communications educator*

**Kansas City**
Allen, John L., Jr. *journalist, writer*
Batiuk, Thomas Martin *cartoonist*
Brisbane, Arthur Seward *newspaper publisher*
Busby, Marjean (Marjorie Jean Busby) *retired journalist*
Davis, James Robert *cartoonist*
Gallagher, Maggie *columnist*
Gray, Helen Theresa Gott *editor*
Gusewelle, Charles Wesley *journalist, writer*
Lindenbaum, Sharon *publishing executive*
McGruder, Aaron *cartoonist*
Mc Meel, John Paul *newspaper syndicate and publishing executive*
McSweeney, William Lincoln, Jr. *retired publishing executive*
Oliphant, Patrick *cartoonist*
Palmer, Cruise *newspaper editor*
Thornton, Thomas Noel *publishing executive*

**Marshall**
Berry, Karen Ann *communications educator*

**Saint Louis**
Boddie, Don O'Mar *recording industry executive*
de Chasca, Edmund *editor, writer*
Ehrlich, Ava *broadcast executive*
Elkins, Ken Joe *retired broadcast executive*
Engelhardt, Thomas Alexander *editorial cartoonist*
Fanetti, Mary-June *writer, editor*
Gauen, Patrick Emil *news correspondent*
Goldberg, Norman Albert *music publisher, writer*
Green, Joyce *book publishing company executive*
Hays, Howard H. (Tim Hays) *editor, publisher*
Holt, Glen Edward *editor*
Killenberg, George Andrew *publishing executive, consultant, retired editor*
Martínez-Solís, Luis Fernando *journalist, writer, historian*
Pollack, Joe *retired columnist, critic, writer*
Randolph, Jennings, Jr. (Jay Randolph) *sportscaster*
Rice, Patricia Jane *journalist*
Waters, Richard *retired publishing executive*

**Springfield**
Champion, Norma Jean *communications educator, state legislator*
Glazier, Robert Carl *publishing executive*

## MONTANA

**Billings**
Larsen, Kimbert E. *journalist*

**Bozeman**
Stohr, Kate (Katherine A. Stohr) *freelance journalist*

**Missoula**
Borrie, William Thomas *communications educator*

## NEBRASKA

**Friend**
De Bevoise, Lee Raymond *editor, writer*

**Lincoln**
Dyer, William Earl, Jr. *retired newspaper editor*
McKee, James Lee *publishing executive*
Raz, Hilda *editor-in-chief, language educator*

**Omaha**
Batchelder, Anne Stuart *retired publishing executive, political organization worker*
Casper, Peggy Wiedman *court reporter*
Derrick, Deborah Ball *editor, writer*
King, Larry *editor*

## NEVADA

**Henderson**
Kelley, Michael John *newspaper editor*
Wills, Robert Hamilton *retired publishing executive*

**Las Vegas**
Frigard, Monique Denise *journalist*
Miller, Valerie Carol *journalist*
Scherf, Dietmar *publishing executive, artist, minister*
Tash, Martin Elias *publishing company executive*
Wooten, Glen Donovan *media consultant*

**Reno**
Hengstler, Gary Ardell *publisher, editor, lawyer*
Weniger-Phelps, Nancy Ann *media specialist, photographer*

**Sparks**
Boyer, Patricia W. *publishing executive, editor*

## NEW HAMPSHIRE

**Concord**
Brown, Tom Christian *newspaper publishing executive*

Laughlin, Larry *communications media executive*

**Dublin**
Hale, Judson Drake, Sr. *publishing executive, editor, writer*

**Exeter**
Wicklein, John Frederick *journalist, educator*

**Keene**
Salcetti, Marianne *newswriter, educator*

**Lebanon**
Linnell, Robert Hartley *editor-in-chief*

**Lyme**
Dwight, Donald Rathbun *publishing executive, corporate communications specialist*

**Manchester**
Perkins, Charles III *newspaper and website editor*

**Nashua**
Wright, Elizabethada Amanda *communications educator*

**Portsmouth**
Hopkins, Jeannette Ethel *book publisher, editor*

**Salem**
Smith, Laurence Roger *journal editor*

## NEW JERSEY

**Allendale**
DiBlasi, Dianne Clark *editor*

**Belleville**
Salvini, Emil Robert *publishing executive, writer, historian*

**Bloomfield**
Glasser, Stephen Andrew *publishing executive, lawyer*

**Caldwell**
Mann, Robert Christopher *communications educator, television producer, television personality*

**Cape May**
Fox, Matthew Ignatius *publishing executive*

**Chatham**
Kane, Cynthia M. *editor, writer*
Meagher, James Proctor *editor*

**Cherry Hill**
Rudman, Solomon Kal *magazine publisher*

**Cranbury**
Yoseloff, Julien David *publishing company executive*

**Cranford**
Bodian, Nat G. *publishing and marketing consultant, author, lecturer, lexicographer, historian*

**Deal**
Becker, Richard Stanley *music publisher*

**Dover**
Kassell, Paula Sally *editor, publisher*

**East Brunswick**
Meningall, Evelyn L. *retired educational media specialist*

**Edison**
Hunter, Michael *publishing executive*

**Englewood Cliffs**
Dobrzynski, Judith Helen *journalist, commentator*
Haltiwanger, Robert Sidney, Jr. *book publishing executive*
Insana, Ronald Gerard *newscaster*
Saible, Stephanie Irene *magazine editor*

**Flemington**
Thomas, Anne Moreau *former newspaper owner*
Zulker, Charles Bates *broadcasting company executive*

**Fords**
Blond, Stuart Richard *magazine editor*

**Fort Lee**
Orman, Suze *news correspondent, writer*
Stuart, Carole *publishing executive*

**Garwood**
Jannotti, Gene Patrick *business consultant, telecommunications professional*

**Gillette**
Nathanson, Linda Sue *publishing executive, writer*

**Glen Ridge**
Addison, Herbert John *consulting editor, writer*

**Hackensack**
Ahearn, James *columnist*
Borg, Malcolm Austin *publishing executive*
Margulies, James Howard *editorial cartoonist*

**Hackettstown**
Scalza, Margaret T. *publishing executive*

**Hamilton**
Gideon, Richard Walter *broadcasting management consultant*

**Highland Park**
Fogiel, Max *publishing executive*

**Hillsborough**
Yuster-Freeman, Leigh Carol *broadcast executive*

**Hoboken**
Chapman, Natalie Prichard *publishing executive*
Hakki, Ayesha *editor-in-chief*
Spring, Michael *editor, writer*
Tardiff, Jill Alexandria *publishing executive, photographer*
Ubell, Robert Neil *editor, educator, publishing executive, consultant*

**Jersey City**
Hitchcock, John C. *communications media executive*
Ingrassia, Paul Joseph *publishing executive*
Lipschutz, Neal S. *editor*
Stine, Rick D. *editor*

**Lakewood**
Forbes, Gordon Maxwell *sportswriter, commentator*

**Lawrenceville**
Ben-Asher, Daniel Lawrence *photojournalist, retired legislative staff member*

**Leonia**
Greenwald, Martin *publishing company executive*

**Lindenwold**
Jackson, Yocontalie Ann *entertainment company executive*

**Madison**
Goodman, Michael B(arry) *communications educator*

**Millburn**
Wagenheim, Kal *journalist, editor*

**Monmouth Junction**
Prestbo, John Andrew *editor, writer, journalist*

**Monroe Township**
Reichek, Morton Arthur *retired magazine editor, writer*

**Montclair**
Delbourgo, Joëlle Lily *publishing executive*
Gollob, Herman Cohen *retired publishing executive*

**Montvale**
Politi, Beth Kukkonen *publishing services company executive*

**Montville**
Teubner, Ferdinand Cary, Jr. *retired publishing executive*

**Mountainside**
Holton, Carlotta *editor-in-chief, writer*
Horner, Shirley Jaye *columnist, writing and publishing consultant*
Slabe, James F. *publishing executive*

**Neptune City**
Axelrod, Glen Scott *publishing executive, pet product company executive*

**New Brunswick**
Horowitz, Irving Louis *publisher, educator*
Katz, James E. *communications educator*

**New Providence**
Barnes, Sandra Henley *retired publishing company executive*

**Newark**
Aregood, Richard Lloyd *editor*
Arwady, George E. *publishing executive*
Cave, Damien *journalist*
Dauth, Frances Kutcher *journalist, editor*
Gettleman, Jeffrey *journalist*
Izenberg, Jerry *sportswriter, columnist, author*
Kelley, Tina *journalist*
McGurk, Christopher J. *former film company executive*
Newhouse, Mark William *publishing executive*
Nutt, Amy Ellis *journalist*
Smothers, Ronald *journalist*
Steinbaum, Robert S. *publishing executive, lawyer*
Willse, James Patrick *newspaper editor*

**Nutley**
To, Stephen Edward *editor, writer*

**Oldwick**
Snyder, Arthur *publishing executive*

**Paterson**
Deffaa, Chip *jazz critic*

**Pitman**
Reinfeld, George *retired communications educator*

**Plainfield**
Allen, Stuart (Stuart Allen Sup) *film and television company executive*
Johnson, Lonnie L., Jr. *information specialist*

**Pleasantville**
Applewhite, Kim *music company executive, educator*

**Princeton**
Crawford, Franklin David *publishing executive*
Dubrovsky, Gertrude Wishnick *journalist, researcher*
Green, Claude *information company executive*
Hanks, Richard *information company executive*
Levine, Richard James *publishing executive*
Lincoln, Anna *publishing executive, language educator*
Lippincott, Walter Heulings, Jr. *retired publishing executive*
Nied, Thomas Herman *retired media specialist*

Centrello, Gina *publishing executive*
Chan, Janet *editorial director*
Chang, Jeannette *publishing executive*
Chang, Laura *editor*
Charney, Marc D. *editor*
Chernoff, Allan *correspondent*
Chesnutt, Jane *publishing executive*
Chestnut, Colette *broadcast executive*
Chira, Susan *editor*
Chirico, Anthony (Tony) *publishing executive*
Chopey, Nicholas P. *editor*
Cieply, Michael *editor, writer*
Clagett, Leslie Plummer *editor, writer*
Clark, Joan Hardy *retired journalist*
Clayton, Joseph P. *broadcast executive*
Clines, Francis X. *journalist*
Cobb, James G. *editor*
Coen, Jessica *blog writer, editor*
Cohen, Adam *reporter, lawyer*
Cohen, Betty L. *broadcast executive*
Cohen, Claudia *journalist, television reporter*
Cohen, Lyor *recording industry executive*
Cohen, Patricia *editor, critic*
Cohen, Richard Martin *journalist*
Coles, Joanna *magazine editor-in-chief*
Collins, Gail *editor*
Collins, Richard Lawrence *editor*
Colmes, Alan *political commentator, radio personality*
Cona, Louis *publishing executive*
Conde, Yvonne M. *freelance journalist*
Confessore, Nicholas *journalist*
Connolly, John Joseph *publishing executive*
Cooney, Joan Ganz *broadcast executive, director*
Cooper, Anderson Hays *news correspondent, cable news anchor*
Cooper, Gloria *editor, press critic*
Cooper, Helene *editor*
Cooper, Michael *journalist*
Corcoran, David *newspaper editor*
Corn, David *editor, political correspondent*
Cornwell, W. Don *broadcasting executive*
Corporon, John Robert *broadcast executive*
Cortina, Betty *magazine editor*
Cotter, Holland *art critic, writer*
Couric, Katie (Katherine Anne Couric) *newscaster, journalist*
Coyne, Judith *editor*
Crain, Rance *publishing company executive*
Cramer, Douglas Schoolfield *broadcasting executive*
Crandell, Susan *magazine editor*
Creswell, Julie *reporter*
Crier, Catherine *newscaster*
Crist, Judith *film and drama critic*
Croce, Arlene *critic*
Cronin, Anne *editor*
Cronkite, Walter *radio and television news correspondent*
Cross, Theodore Lamont *publisher, author*
Crovitz, Louis Gordon *journalist, lawyer*
Crowdus, Gary Alan *film company executive*
Crystal, J. Scott *publishing executive*
Culhane, John William *journalist, writer, film historian*
Cuomo, Chris (Christopher Cuomo) *newscaster, lawyer*
Cuozzo, Steven David *newspaper editor*
Curley, Thomas *newspaper executive*
Curry, Ann *correspondent, anchor*
Dahl, Jonathan *magazine editor-in-chief*
Daley, Suzanne *editor*
D'Angelo, Joseph Francis *publishing executive*
Danziger, Lucy *editor*
Dargis, Manohla *film critic*
Darnton, John Townsend *journalist*
Dauman, Philippe P. *broadcast executive*
Dauten, Dale Alan *newspaper columnist*
Davis, Clive Jay *record company executive*
Day, James *television executive*
De Angelis, Judy *anchorwoman*
DeCesare, John *publishing executive*
Denby, David *film critic*
Denson, J. Russell *publishing executive*
Derow, Peter Alfred *publishing company executive*
Desiato, Michael *editor-in-chief*
Deull, Charles Brian *publishing executive, lawyer*
Deutsch, Claudia *reporter*
Deutsch, Martin Bernard Joseph *editor, publishing executive*
DeVoe, David, Sr. *publishing executive*
Dierdorf, Daniel Lee (Dan Dierdorf) *sports commentator, football analyst, former professional football player*
Dikkers, Scott *editor*
Diller, Barry *broadcast executive*
Disney, Anthea *publishing executive*
Dodge, Geoffrey A. *magazine publisher*
Doe, Willo *critic, writer, artist*
Dolan, Michael J. *broadcast executive*
Donnelly, Patrick L. *broadcast executive, lawyer*
Dooley, Thomas E. *broadcast executive*
Dormann, Henry O. *magazine publisher*
Dotson, Robert Charles (Bob Dotson) *news correspondent*
Downes, Lawrence *editor*
Dozier, Kimberly *news correspondent*
Drasner, Fred *newspaper publishing executive*
Duffy-King, Jan (John Mitchell Maver Wallace) *journalist, media consultant*
Dukmejian, Michael *publishing executive*
Dunn, Martin *editor-in-chief*
Dunning, Jennifer *dance critic, reporter*
Dwyer, Jim *reporter, columnist*
Eaker, Sherry Ellen *editor*
Ebersol, Dick (Duncan Dickie Ebersol) *television broadcasting executive*
Ebony, David *editor, arts critic*
Eckman, Fern Marja *journalist*
Edgerley, Susan *editor*
Edidin, Peter *editor*
Edmiston, Mark Morton *publishing company executive*
Egen, Maureen Mahon *publishing executive*
Elder, Janet *editor*
Ellerbee, Linda (Linda Jane Smith) *reporter*
Ellingwood, Susan *editor*
Ellis, Rosemary *editor-in-chief*
Elsen, Jon *editor*
Emmerich, Toby *film company executive*
Emmrich, Stuart J. *editor*

Enberg, Dick *sportscaster*
Engstrom, Erik *publishing executive*
Esposito, Richard Joseph *journalist, executive*
Esterow, Milton *publishing executive*
Evans, Sir Harold Matthew *editor, publisher, writer*
Evans, Linda Kay *publishing executive*
Fabrikant, Geraldine *journalist*
Fager, Jeffrey *broadcast executive*
Fahim, Kareem *journalist*
Falco, Randy *broadcast executive*
Fallows, James Mackenzie *journalist*
Farber, David *editor*
Farrell, Patrick *editor*
Fears, Linda *editor-in-chief*
Feder, Barnaby *reporter*
Federle, Michael *publishing executive*
Feldman, Helaine *editor, public relations associate*
Fell, M. Ann *publishing executive*
Feniger, Jerome Roland, Jr. *broadcast executive*
Ferguson, Tim Wayne *editor, journalist*
Fertig, Howard *publishing executive*
Feyer, Thomas *editor*
Filkins, Dexter Price *newspaper reporter*
Finder, Alan *reporter*
Fine, Michael Joseph *publishing executive, communications executive*
Finkelstein, James A. *media executive*
Finn, Edwin Anthony, Jr. *publishing executive*
Finn, Peter Michael *broadcast executive*
Fiori, Pamela *publishing executive, writer*
Fireman, Kenneth Howard *journalist*
Firestone, David E. *editor*
Fisher, Arthur *magazine editor*
Flanagan, Sean Patrick *publishing executive*
Flom, Jason *music company executive*
Florio, Steven T. *magazine executive*
Florio, Thomas A. *magazine publisher*
Foley, Ann *broadcast executive*
Forbes, Steve (Malcolm Stevenson Forbes Jr.) *publishing executive*
Forbes, Timothy Carter *publishing executive*
Ford, Mark Patrick *publishing executive*
Forden, Diane Claire *magazine editor*
Forsberg, Myra *editor*
Foster, Gary *publishing executive, information technology executive*
Fox, Margalit (Eve) *journalist, editor, writer*
Fox, Mitchell B. *magazine publisher*
Fox, Sylvan *journalist, educator*
Fraguela, James *publishing executive*
Frankel, Max *retired journalist*
Franks, Martin Davis *broadcast executive*
Frear, David J. *broadcast executive*
Freeland, Chrystia *editor, director*
Freudenheim, Milton B. *journalist*
Freyre, Fabio *publishing executive*
Friedman, Jane *publishing executive*
Friedman, Sam *editor*
Fuentez, Tania Michele *journalist*
Fuller, Bonnie *editor-in-chief*
Gabriel, Trip (Bertram Gabriel III) *editor*
Gabrielson, Charles *publishing executive*
Gaffney, Elizabeth Mallory *editor, writer, literature educator, translator*
Gainsburg, Roy Ellis *publishing executive*
Gallo, William Victor *cartoonist*
Ganz, Axel *publishing executive*
Ganzi, Victor Frederick *publishing executive*
Gardino, Vincent Anthony *broadcast executive*
Gardner, Janet Paxton *journalist, film producer*
Garrett, Laurie *journalist, global health scholar*
Geary, Hilary R. *society editor*
Geddes, John M. *editor*
Gehringer, Richard George *publishing executive*
Geiser, Elizabeth Able *publishing company executive*
Gerth, Jeff *journalist*
Gewirtz-Friedman, Gerry *editor*
Geyer, Thomas Powick *newspaper publisher*
Gharib, Susie *newscaster*
Giannetti, Stephen P. *publishing executive*
Gibney, James S. *editor*
Gibson, Charles DeWolf *newscaster*
Gibson, John *news anchor, correspondent*
Gigot, Paul Anthony *editor*
Gilbert, Rose Bennett *journalist*
Giordano, Mary Ann *editor*
Girard, Judy *broadcast executive*
Gissler, Sigvard Gunnar, Jr. *journalist, educator, retired editor*
Gladstone, Bernard *columnist*
Gladstone, Rick *editor*
Glanze, Walter D. *editor, writer, lexicographer, publishing consultant*
Glater, Jonathan D. *reporter*
Glusman, John Alan *editor, writer*
Goldberg, Danny *recording industry executive*
Golden, Michael *publishing executive*
Golin, Mark *editor*
Goodstein, Laurie Beth *journalist*
Goodstein, Les *newspaper publishing executive*
Gotti, Victoria *columnist, writer, actress*
Gottlieb, Robert *publishing executive*
Gourevitch, Philip *editor*
Grace, Nancy A. *news correspondent, former prosecutor*
Graham, Alma Eleanor *editor, writer, educational consultant*
Graham, Fred Patterson *news correspondent, journalist*
Granath, Herbert A. *television industry executive*
Graustark, Barbara *editor*
Graves, Earl G., Jr., (Butch Graves) *publishing executive*
Graves, Earl Gilbert *publishing executive*
Gray, Jerry *editor*
Green, Dan *publishing executive*
Green, George Joseph *publishing executive*
Green, Lauren *news anchor and correspondent, concert pianist*
Greenberg, Stephen D. *broadcast executive*
Greene, Richard H. *journalist, writer, policy analyst*
Greenfield, Jeff (Henry Jeff Greenfield) *news analyst*
Greenman, Josh *editor*
Greenstein, Scott *broadcast executive*
Greenwald, Julie *recording industry executive*
Grenquist, Peter Carl *publishing executive, consultant*

Griffith, William Henry (Bill Griffith) *cartoonist*
Grimes, Suzanne *publishing executive*
Grimes, William *critic*
Grose, William Rush *publishing executive*
Gross, Amy *editor-in-chief*
Gross, Judy E. *publishing executive*
Grune, Steven Bryan *publishing executive*
Guiher, James Morford, Jr. *publisher, writer*
Haberman, Clyde *columnist*
Hackett, George *editor*
Haegele, Patricia *publishing executive*
Hagerty, Patrick K. *publishing executive*
Hall, Lisa Gersh *broadcast executive, lawyer*
Hall, Trish *editor*
Hansell, Saul Henry *reporter*
Hanson, Jane *newscaster*
Harrow, Nancy (Mrs. Jan Krukowski) *editor-in-chief, composer, singer*
Hart, Clare *information company executive*
Harty, Thomas H. *publishing executive*
Haubegger, Christy *media consultant, publishing executive*
Hauser, Gustave M. *broadcast executive*
Headlam, Bruce *editor*
Hearst, George Randolph, Jr. *publishing executive, real estate company executive*
Heartney, Eleanor *art critic*
Heekin-Canedy, Scott H. *publishing executive*
Heffernan, Virginia *television critic*
Held, Ivan *publishing executive*
Helliker, Kevin *journalist*
Henican, Ellis *columnist, political correspondent*
Henriques, Diana Blackmon *journalist*
Herbert, Bob *columnist*
Herman, Mindy *broadcast executive*
Herring, Hubert B. *editor*
Hersh, Seymour Myron *journalist, writer*
Herszenhorn, David *journalist*
Hertz, Leon *publishing executive*
Hesser, Amanda Lea *journalist, chef*
Hicklin, Aaron *editor-in-chief*
Hicks, Jonathan P. *journalist*
Hicks, Tyler Gregory *publishing company executive, writer*
Hilchey, Tim *editor*
Hill, Brian Eugene *music publishing executive, musician, educator*
Hippeau, Eric *book publishing executive*
Hirsch, Faye *editor, art critic*
Hirschman, David S. *editor*
Hochfield, Sylvia *arts editor*
Hodge, Roger D. *editor*
Hoffman, Jared *music company executive*
Hoge, Warren M. *editor*
Holden, Stephen *film critic*
Holland, Bernard Peabody *music critic*
Holland, Rebecca Lloyd *publishing executive*
Hollander, Joel L. *broadcast executive*
Holliday, Guy D. "Doc" *publishing executive*
Holt, Sidney Clark *journalist*
Holton, Lisa *publishing executive*
Hondros, Chris *photojournalist*
Horyn, Cathy *newspaper editor*
Hu, Winnie *journalist*
Huckshorn, Kristin *journalist*
Hudlin, Reginald Alan *broadcast executive, film director, writer*
Huey, John Wesley, Jr. *editor*
Hughes, Brigid *former editor*
Hunsinger, Peter *publishing executive*
Hurley, Cheryl Joyce *book publishing executive*
Hutchins, Traver *publishing executive*
Huxtable, Ada Louise *architecture critic*
Imperato, Anthony Peter *publishing executive*
Impoco, Jim *editor*
Ingrassia, Lawrence *editor*
Ireland, Jay *broadcast executive*
Irish, George Butler *media company executive*
Isenberg, Steven Lawrence *retired publishing executive*
Isherwood, Charles *theater critic*
Jackson, Keith MacKenzie *retired sports commentator*
Jacobs, Lawrence A. *media company executive, lawyer*
Jamieson, Wendell *editor*
Jamison, Jayne *publishing executive*
Jannot, Mark Allen *magazine publishing executive*
Jaroff, Leon Morton *magazine editor*
Jarrell, Tim *travel guide publishing executive*
Jarvis, Jeff *journalist, former critic, news blogger*
Jefferson, Margo L. *journalist*
Jellinek, George *broadcast executive, music educator, writer*
Jesselli, Steve *journalist*
Johnson, Brooke Bailey *broadcast executive*
Johnson, Richard *editor*
Johnston, David Cay Boyle *journalist*
Jolly, Thomas Alan *journalist*
Jones, Laurie Lynn *magazine editor*
Jones Reynolds, Star (Starlet Marie Jones) *television host, lawyer, former prosecutor*
Kadden, Jack *editor*
Kagan, Julia Lee *magazine editor*
Kahn, Joseph F. *journalist*
Kakutani, Michiko *critic*
Kalajian-Lagani, Donna *publishing executive*
Kalech, Marc *newspaper editor*
Kaminer, Ariel *journalist*
Kandel, Myron *newscaster, columnist*
Kann, Peter Robert *publishing executive, journalist*
Kanner, Bernice *columnist*
Kaplan, Jill Rebecca *publishing executive*
Kaplan, Peter W. *editor-in-chief*
Kaplan, Robert David *journalist*
Karlgaard, Rich *publishing executive*
Karmazin, Mel *broadcast executive*
Karpel, Craig S. *journalist, editor*
Karr, Jane *editor*
Kaufman, Jason Edward *art critic, reporter, editor*
Kaufman, Victor A. *broadcast executive, retired film company executive*
Kayse, Kathleen *publishing executive*
Keagy, Dorothy (Dotti Keagy) *copy director*
Keane, Bil *cartoonist*
Keenan, Terry *anchor, correspondent*
Keiser, Lauren Keith *publishing executive, composer*
Keller, Bill *editor*
Kelly, James *editor*
Kennedy, James M. *editor*

Keppler, Herbert *publishing executive*
Keteyian, Armen *news correspondent*
Khan, Sura *film company executive*
Kiechel, Walter III *editor*
Kimball, Roger *editor, writer, publishing executive*
Kimmelman, Michael Simon *art critic*
Kirschbaum, Laurence J. *publishing executive*
Kislik, Richard William *publishing executive*
Kissel, Howard William *drama critic*
Kisselgoff, Anna *dance critic*
Klein, Jason Evan *publishing executive*
Klein, Laura Colin *publishing executive*
Klein, Naomi *journalist*
Klingensmith, Michael *publishing executive*
Klipper, Mitchell S. *book publishing executive*
Kluger, Jeffrey *reporter, author*
Kneale, Dennis Randall *publishing executive*
Knopf, Alfred, Jr. *retired publisher*
Koepp, Stephen *editor*
Koerner, Brendan I. *columnist*
Kolata, Gina *journalist*
Kolatch, Myron *magazine editor*
Kolson, Ann J. *editor*
Koplos, Janet *editor, art critic*
Koppelman, Charles A. *record company executive*
Korda, Michael Vincent *retired publishing company executive, writer*
Korvin, Catherine Madeleine *editor*
Koslow, Sally *editor-in-chief*
Koster, Elaine *publishing executive*
Koteff, Ellen *periodical editor*
Koten, John F. *editor-in-chief*
Kozinn, Allan *music critic, reporter*
Kramer, Marc Z. *publishing executive*
Kramon, Glenn *newspaper business editor*
Kravitz, Lee *editor*
Kristof, Nicholas Donabet *journalist*
Kroft, Steve *news correspondent, editor*
Kulish, Nicholas *reporter*
Kupper, William P., Jr. *publishing executive*
Kushner, Jared C. *publishing executive, real estate developer*
Lack, Andrew R. *music company executive*
Lagani, Daniel *publishing executive*
Lagani, Joseph A. *publishing executive*
Lamont, Lansing *journalist, writer, foundation administrator*
Landau, Sidney Ivan *lexicographer*
Landman, Jonathan *editor*
Lapham, Lewis Henry *editor, television personality, writer*
Larsen, Jonathan Zerbe *journalist*
Lawhon, Charla *editor*
Lawrence, Nina *publishing executive*
Laybourne, Geraldine B. *broadcast executive*
Leach, Bryan *music company executive*
Leahey, Lynn *editor-in-chief*
Leahy, Michael Joseph *retired newspaper editor*
Lee, Bruce *editor, writer*
Lee, Frances Helen *editor*
Lee, Jennifer B. *journalist*
Lee, Sally A. *editor-in-chief*
Lees, Alfred William *former magazine editor, writer*
Lehmann-Haupt, Christopher Charles Herbert *book reviewer*
Leighty, Keith *editor*
Leive, Cynthia *editor-in-chief*
Levin, Alan M. *television journalist*
Levin, Martin P. *publishing executive, lawyer*
Levine, Ellen R. *editor-in-chief*
Levinson, Warren Mitchell *broadcast journalist*
Levitz, Paul Elliot *publishing executive*
Levy, Clifford J. *reporter*
Lewis, Edward T. *publishing executive*
Liberman, Megan Rose *editor*
Liftin, Joan R. *photojournalist, educator*
Liles, Kevin *music company executive*
Lingeman, Richard Roberts *editor-in-chief, writer*
Linz, Werner Mark *international publishing executive*
Lipscomb, Thomas Heber III *media company executive*
Lipson, Allen S. *entertainment company executive, lawyer*
Lloyd, Kenneth L. *columnist*
Loeb, Marshall Robert *journalist*
Logan, Don *publishing executive*
Lohr, Steve *reporter*
Longley, Marjorie Watters *newspaper executive*
Longobardi, David *editor-in-chief*
Loomis, Carol J. *journalist*
Louderback, Jim *editor-in-chief*
Loughlin, John P. *publishing executive*
Louis, Sean *broadcast executive*
Lowry, Rich *editor*
Lundberg, George David, II, *medical editor-in-chief, pathologist*
Luo, Michael *journalist*
Lurie, Ranan Raymond *political cartoonist, artist, journalist*
Lynne, Michael *film company executive*
Lyons, Nick *publishing executive*
MacArthur, John Roderick C. G. (Rick MacArthur) *magazine publisher, journalist*
MacBain, Louise T. Blouin *publishing executive*
MacGowan, Sandra Firelli *publishing executive, consultant*
Mack, Stan *cartoonist*
Maclin, Amy *editor*
Macri, Theodore William *book publisher*
Madden, John *sportscaster, retired professional football coach*
Maidment, Paul *publishing executive*
Mapes, Glynn Dempsey *newspaper editor*
Margolick, David *journalist, writer*
Marks, Ed *editor*
Marlette, Douglas Nigel *editorial cartoonist, comic strip creator*
Marriott, Michel *reporter*
Marsh, Michele *former newscaster*
Marshall, Tom *publishing executive*
Martin, Judith Sylvia *journalist*
Martin, Paul Ross *editor*
Maryles, Daisy *editor*
Marzorati, Gerald *editor*
Maslin, Janet *critic*
Mason, Linda *broadcast executive*
Mason, Paul *broadcast executive*
Mathews, Jack Wayne *journalist, film critic*
Mathis, Catherine J. *publishing executive*

Kaidy, Mitchell *retired journalist, legislative staff member*
Lank, Edith Handleman *journalist, educator*
Magnuson, Karen M. *editor*
Moore, Matthew Scott *publishing executive, advocate, writer*
Pitoniak, Scott Michael *sportswriter*

**Rye**
Nelson, Vita Joy *editor, publisher*

**Sag Harbor**
Brody, Jacqueline *editor*
Epstein, Jason *publishing company executive*

**Sagaponack**
Graham, Howard Barrett *publishing company executive*

**Saratoga Springs**
Powell, Louie J. *editor-in-chief, engineer, consultant*

**Scarsdale**
Erbsen, Claude Ernest *retired journalist*
Goodman, Jordan Elliot *journalist*
Heese, William John *retired music publishing company executive*
O'Neill, Michael James *editor, author*
Pope, Leavitt Joseph *broadcast company executive*
Topping, Audrey Ronning *photojournalist*

**Selkirk**
Christoph, Peter Richard *historical editor, archivist*

**Sleepy Hollow**
Flynn-Connors, Elizabeth Kathryn *reporter, editor*
Melvin, Russell Johnston (Jay Melvin) *magazine publishing consultant*
Neill, Richard Robert *retired publishing executive*

**Somers**
Cohn, Howard *retired magazine editor*

**South Setauket**
Poli, Kenneth Joseph *editor, writer, photographer*

**Staten Island**
Dennery, Linda *newspaper publishing executive*
Kahn, Jim *former magazine publisher*
Newhouse, Donald E. *newspaper publishing executive*
Newhouse, Samuel Irving, Jr., (Si Newhouse Jr.) *publishing executive*
Prince, Danforth *publishing executive, journalist*

**Stony Brook**
Harvey, Christine Lynn *publishing executive*

**Syracuse**
Blakely, Caroline Miller *retired editor*
Bunn, Timothy David *newspaper editor*
Obbie, Mark Joseph *communications educator*
Wrigley, Brenda Jean *communications educator*

**Tarrytown**
Stein, Sol *publishing executive, writer*

**Troy**
Friedman, Sue Tyler *technical publications executive*

**Waccabuc**
Krefting, Robert J(ohn) *publishing company executive*

**Wainscott**
Henderson, William Charles *editor*

**Warwick**
Simon, Dolores Daly *copy editor*

**White Plains**
Davies, Matt *cartoonist*
Foderaro, Lisa *reporter*
Leish, Kenneth William *retired publishing company executive*

**Williamsville**
Levite, Laurence A. *publishing executive*

**Willsboro**
Reuther, David Louis *retired children's book publisher, writer*

**Wyandanch**
Weber, Carl *publishing executive, retail bookstore executive, writer*

**Yonkers**
Fyle, Clifford Nelson *publishing executive, educator*
McKean, Kevin S. *publishing executive, writer*
Slade, Margot S. *editor*
Westphal, Carol Jean *media specialist*

**Yorktown Heights**
Wade, James O'Shea *editor, writer*

## NORTH CAROLINA

**Brevard**
Phillips, Euan Hywel *publishing executive*

**Chapel Hill**
Bailey, Herbert Smith, Jr. *retired publisher*
Bowers, Thomas Arnold *journalism educator, dean*
Cole, Richard Ray *communications educator, former dean*
Lauder, Valarie Anne *editor, educator*
Meyer, Philip Edward *journalism educator*
Ravenel, Shannon *book publishing professional*

**Charlotte**
Armstrong, James David *editor, educator, minister*
Barrows, Frank Clemence *journalist*
Bauroth, Nancy Ann *journalist, former marketing executive*

Gotta, Joseph D. *music company executive*
Haines, Kenneth H. *sports television broadcasting and marketing executive*
Thames, Rick *publishing executive, editor*
Williams, Edwin Neel *newspaper editor*

**Denver**
Detter, Carla Renee *media specialist*

**Durham**
Cayne, Bernard Stanley *editor*
Cohn, Stephen Andrew *publishing executive*
Fiske, Edward B. *editor, educator, journalist, consultant*
Harrell, Carlton (Benjamin Carlton Harrell) *retired editor, writer*
Hawkins, William E. N. *newspaper editor*
Rossiter, Alexander, Jr. *publishing executive, editor*

**Greensboro**
Blackwell, William Ernest *broadcast executive*
Gill, Evalyn Pierpoint *editor, writer, publisher*
Jellicorse, John Lee *communications and theatre educator*

**Harrisburg**
Economaki, Chris Constantine (Christopher Economaki) *publishing executive*

**Jefferson**
Franklin, Robert McFarland *book publisher*

**Pembroke**
Curtis, Anthony R. *communications educator*
Curtis, Judith Genevicz *communications educator*

**Raleigh**
Brown, William Harris *editor*
Crisp, Fred *retired publishing executive*
Effron, Seth Alan *editor, journalist*
Evans, Janet *publishing executive*
Harrison-Jervay, Evelyn Yvonne *publishing executive*
McKinney, Donald Lee *magazine editor*
Parker, Joseph Mayon *retired publishing executive*
Pittman, James Morris (Jack Pittman) *cartoonist, illustrator, character designer, consultant*
Reeves, Ralph Bernard III *publishing executive*
Wilson, Sue *newspaper editor*

**Research Triangle Park**
Greenwell, Arnold *editor, photographer*

**Saluda**
McCutcheon, John Tinney, Jr. *retired journalist*

**Southport**
Pepper, Jeffrey Mackenzie *publishing executive*

**Winston Salem**
Graybeal, Barbara *editor, writer*
King, Wayne Edgar *journalist, educator*
Price, Henry Escoe *broadcast executive*
Zagoria, Sam D(avid) *reporter, educator, federal agency administrator*

**Wrightsville Beach**
Mc Ilwain, William Franklin *newspaper editor, writer*

## NORTH DAKOTA

**Fargo**
Littlefield, Robert Stephen *communications educator, training consultant*
Marcil, William Christ, Sr. *publisher, broadcast executive*

**Grand Forks**
Glassheim, Eliot Alan *editor, state legislator*

## OHIO

**Akron**
Burbach, Mike *editor*
Simmons, Debra Adams *editor*

**Athens**
Metters, Thomas Waddell *sportswriter*
Scott, Charles Lewis *retired photojournalist*
Stempel, Guido Hermann III *journalism educator*

**Avon Lake**
Pascarella, Perry James *editor, writer*

**Cincinnati**
Beckwith, Barbara Jean *journalist*
Burleigh, William Robert *newspaper executive*
Burroughs, Thomas, Jr. *media consultant*
Callinan, Tom *editor*
Campbell, Dell *publishing executive*
Church, Robert Arthur *retired publishing executive*
Davis, Robin *publishing executive*
Flanagan, Martha Lang *publishing executive*
Fox, Joan Friedlander *restaurant critic*
Irwin, Miriam Dianne Owen *publishing executive, writer*
Lowe, Kenneth W. *multimedia executive*
McMullin, Ruth Roney *retired publishing executive*
Mechem, Charles Stanley, Jr. *retired broadcast executive*
Petty, Priscilla Hayes *columnist, television producer*
Whipple, Harry M. *newspaper publishing executive*

**Cleveland**
Bellamy, Gail Anne Ghetia *magazine editor, author, speaker*
Brandt, John Reynold *editor, journalist*
Clifton, Douglas C. *newspaper editor*
Conrad, Robert David *broadcast executive, educator*
Giannetti, Louis Daniel *film critic, educator*
Jensen, Kathryn Patricia (Kit) *broadcast executive*

Jindra, Christine *editor*
Kanzeg, David George *radio station executive*
Machaskee, Alex *newspaper publishing company executive*
Molyneaux, David Glenn *newspaper travel editor*
O'Hara, Thomas Patrick *managing editor*
Schultz, Connie *reporter*

**Columbus**
Barry, James P(otvin) *editor, writer*
Brower, Patricia Ann *music company executive*
Cox, Mitchel Neal *editor*
Dervin, Brenda Louise *communications educator*
Dimmick, John W. *communications educator*
Gribble, Charles Edward *editor, language educator*
Grossberg, Michael Lee *film critic, writer*
Kefauver, Weldon Addison *publishing executive*
Lowe, Clayton Kent *radio film critic, educator*
Sherrill, Thomas Boykin III *retired newspaper publishing executive*

**Dayton**
Matheny, Ruth Ann *editor*

**Lakewood**
Condon, George Edward *journalist*

**Mason**
Smith, C. LeMoyne *retired publishing executive*

**Oxford**
Sanders, Gerald Hollie *communications educator*

**Pepper Pike**
Vail, Thomas Van Husen *retired publishing executive*

**Seaman**
Cartaino, Carol Ann *editor*

**Sidney**
Stevens, Robert Jay *magazine editor*

**Toledo**
Block, John Robinson *newspaper publisher*
Block, William K., Jr. *media executive*
Mahr, Joe *journalist*
Royhab, Ronald *journalist, editor*
Sallah, Michael D. *journalist*
Weiss, Mitch *journalist*

**Westerville**
DeVassie, Terry Lee *publishing executive*

**Wooster**
August, Robert Olin *retired journalist*
Schreiber, Clare Adel *journalist*

**Yellow Springs**
Cawood, Albert McLaurin (Hap Cawood) *retired newspaper editor*

## OKLAHOMA

**Ada**
Jones, Bret Austin *communications educator, writer*

**Allen**
Deaton, Janice Ann *media specialist, elementary school educator*

**Chouteau**
Sasser, Charles Wayne *journalist, educator, writer*

**Durant**
Hendricks, John Allen *communications educator*

**Norman**
Drayton, John N. *publishing executive*

**Oklahoma City**
Gourley, James Leland *editor, publishing executive*
Gourley, Vicki Clark *publishing executive*
Hale, Sue A. *editor*
Hutson, Lindel G. *newspaper editor*
Triplett, E. Eugene *editor*

**Terlton**
Bender, John Henry, Jr., (Jack Bender) *editor, cartoonist*

**Tulsa**
Haring, Robert Westing *newspaper editor*
Jones, Jenk, Jr. *editor, educator*
Ma, Xiaomin *communications educator*
Nyikos, Stacy Ann *publishing executive*

**Warr Acres**
Engle, Richard Victor *publishing executive*

**Wewoka**
Trimble, Vance Henry *retired newspaper editor*

## OREGON

**Albany**
Wood, Kenneth Arthur *retired editor, writer*

**Ashland**
Risser, James Vaulx, Jr. *journalist, educator*

**Corvallis**
Hall, Don Alan *editor, writer, educator*
Klingeman, Nancy Woodruff *editor, researcher, volunteer*

**Eugene**
Baker, Alton Fletcher III *editor, publishing executive*
Baker, Bridget *publishing executive*
Tykeson, Donald Erwin *broadcast executive*

**Milton Freewater**
Gipson, Stephen Richard *journalist, construction executive*

**Portland**
Attig, Rick *editor*
Bates, Doug *editor*
Bhatia, Peter K. *editor, journalist*
Bunza, Linda Hathaway *editor, writer, composer, director*
Dolan, William J. *media company executive*
Graves, Earl William, Jr. *journalist*
Jaquiss, Nigel *reporter*
Johnston, Virginia Evelyn *retired editor*
Rowe, Sandra Mims *publishing executive*
Stickel, Frederick A. *publishing executive*

**Salem**
Mainwaring, William Lewis *publishing company executive, author*

**Wallowa**
Wizard, Brian *publisher, author*

**Wilsonville**
Giesbrecht, F. Bruce *entertainment company executive*

## PENNSYLVANIA

**Bellwood**
Broadwater, Robert Paul *publishing executive, writer*

**Bensalem**
Kang, Benjamin Toyeong *journalist, minister*

**Butler**
Hawk, Kathleen Patricia *broadcast consultant*

**Carlisle**
Fish, Chester Boardman, Jr. *retired editor*

**Easton**
Stitt, Dorothy Jewett *journalist*

**Emmaus**
Bricklin, Mark Harris *magazine editor, publisher*
Favorule, Denise *publishing executive*
Rodale, Ardath Harter *publishing executive*
Vaccariello, Liz *editor-in-chief*

**Felton**
Shoemaker, Eleanor Boggs *television production company executive*

**Flourtown**
Lee, Adrian Iselin, Jr. *journalist*

**Gettysburg**
Gritsch, Ruth Christine Lisa *editor*

**Greenville**
Root, Brian K. *journalist*

**Harleysville**
Smagalski, Carolyn M. *publishing executive, webmaster, director*

**Harrisburg**
Antoun, Annette Agnes *editor, publisher*
DeKok, David *writer, reporter*
Gover, Raymond Lewis *retired newspaper executive*

**Havertown**
Hendrickson, Paul Joseph *journalist, writer, educator*

**Honesdale**
Clark, Christine May *editor, author*

**Jenkintown**
Booker, Alvin Eugene *publishing executive, consultant*

**Kennett Square**
Landstrom, Elsie Hayes *retired editor*

**King Of Prussia**
Broido, Arnold Peace *music publishing company executive*

**Lancaster**
Shaw, Charles Raymond *journalist*

**Mechanicsburg**
Juditz, Lillian Mickley *retired communications educator*
Stouffer, Nancy Kathleen *publishing company executive*

**Monaca**
Chapin, John R. *communications educator*

**Moon Township**
Lawson, John DuVal *communications educator*

**Philadelphia**
Alchin, John Reginald *cable company executive*
Bennett, Amanda *editor*
Carey, Arthur Bernard, Jr. *editor, columnist*
Cooper, Richard Lee *newspaper editor, journalist*
Days, Michael *editor*
Gordon, Anne Kathleen *editor*
Halpern, Eric Franklin *university publishing director*
Hatch, Denny (Alden Denison) *publishing executive, writer*
Jackson, Harold *journalist*
Klein, Julia Meredith *freelance journalist*
Leiter, Robert Allen *journalist, editor, writer*
Lent, John Anthony *journalist, educator*
Parry, Lance Aaron *publishing executive*
Pedersen, Darlene Delcourt *publishing executive, writer, psychotherapist*
Porter, Jill *journalist*
Price, Vincent *communications educator, department chairman*
Rorer, John Whiteley *publisher, consultant*
Vitez, Michael *reporter*
Wilkinson, Signe *cartoonist*

**Pittsburgh**
Apone, Carl Anthony *journalist*
Getz, Jan Mason *announcer, educator*
Leo, Peter Andrew *columnist, educator*
Lopes, Jerry *broadcast executive*
Roof, Robert L. *broadcast executive, sales executive*
Shribman, David Marks *editor*

**Saint Davids**
Denenberg, Herbert Sidney *journalist, lawyer, educator, retired state official*

**Scranton**
Lynett, William Ruddy *publishing executive, broadcast executive*

**Sewickley**
Swann, Lynn Curtis *sportscaster, former professional football player*

**State College**
Coppersmith Fredman, Marian Ungar *magazine publisher*

**Warrington**
Ward, Hiley Henry *journalist, educator*

**Washington Crossing**
Roche, Gail Connor *editor*

**Wayne**
Fabbri, Anne R. *critic, curator*

**West Chester**
Gallagher, Terrence Vincent *editor*
Mahoney, William Francis *editor, writer*

**West Conshohocken**
Lenfest, Harold FitzGerald *former cable television executive, lawyer*

**Williamsport**
Rosebrough, Carol Belville *cable television company executive*

**Worcester**
Curtis, Alton Kenneth *film company executive, clergyman*

**Wynnewood**
Bernfeld, Gerald E. *editor, writer, retired nursing educator*

## RHODE ISLAND

**Charlestown**
Ungaro, Joseph Michael *newspaper publishing executive, consultant*

**Cranston**
Parravano, Amelia Elizabeth (Amy Beth Parravano) *recording industry executive*

**Pawtucket**
Daya, Jackie *publishing company executive*

**Portsmouth**
Needham, Richard Lee *magazine editor*
Parker, Nancy Knowles (Mrs. Cortlandt Parker) *publishing executive*

**Providence**
Dujardin, Richard Charles *journalist*
Farmer, Susan Lawson *retired broadcast executive, former secretary of state*
Rosenberg, Alan Gene *editor*

**Wakefield**
Wyman, James Vernon *retired publishing executive*

**Warwick**
Halperson, Michael Allen *publishing executive*

**Woonsocket**
Eno, Paul Frederick *editor, writer*

## SOUTH CAROLINA

**Bennettsville**
Kinney, William Light, Jr. *editor, publishing executive*

**Blackstock**
King, Robert Thomas *editor, writer*

**Cayce**
McElveen, William Lindsay *broadcasting executive, lecturer*

**Charleston**
Schreadley, Richard Lee *newswriter, retired editor*
Tarleton, Larry Wilson *editor*
Williams, Barbara Stambaugh *editor*

**Columbia**
Breedin, Berryman Brent *journalist, consultant, historian, public relations executive*
Dickey, Elizabeth Brown *retired journalism educator*
Kendler, Bernhard *retired editor*
McNeely, Patricia Gantt *communications educator*

**Easley**
Failing, George Edgar *editor, clergyman, educator*

**Greenville**
Hipp, William Hayne *broadcast executive*

**Orangeburg**
Sims, Edward Howell *editor, writer*

**Simpsonville**
Kanzler, George *journalist, music critic*

## SOUTH DAKOTA

**Huron**
Groth, Charles William *journalist, historian*

**Rapid City**
Wishard, Della Mae *former newspaper editor*

**Sioux Falls**
Garson, Arnold Hugh *publishing executive*
Masters, Lee *broadcast executive*

## TENNESSEE

**Chattanooga**
Lutgen, Robert Raymond *newspaper editor*

**College Grove**
Battle, William Robert (Bob Battle) *retired publishing executive*

**Johnson City**
Daly, Conrad C. *editor*

**Kenton**
Jenkins-Brady, Terri Lynn *publishing executive, journalist*

**Knoxville**
Aguilar, Julia Shell *publishing executive*
Howard, Herbert Hoover *broadcasting and communications educator*
Rukeyser, William Simon *journalist*
Teeter, Dwight Leland, Jr. *journalism educator*
Ziegler, Dhyana *broadcasting educator, academic administrator*

**La Vergne**
Chandler, James E. *publishing executive*

**Maryville**
Bradford, Tutt Sloan *retired publisher*

**Memphis**
Stokes, Henry Arthur *journalist*

**Murfreesboro**
Flanagan, Van Kent *journalist*
Walker, David Ellis, Jr. *communications educator, minister, consultant*

**Nashville**
Boyd, Theophilus Bartholomew III *publishing company executive*
Green, Lisa Cannon *online editor*
Mayhew, Aubrey *music industry executive*
Shaw, Carole *editor, publisher*
Sherborne, Robert *editor*
Stone, Lawrence Mynatt *publishing executive*

## TEXAS

**Abilene**
Armstrong, Randy Lee *communications educator*
Boyll, David Lloyd *broadcast executive*

**Amarillo**
Robertson, Pauline Durrett *publishing executive*

**Austin**
Allison, Stephen Galender *broadcast executive*
Conine, Ernest *columnist*
Hankins, Michael James-Edwin *broadcast executive*
Knapp, Mark Lane *communications educator, consultant*
Mayes, Wendell Wise, Jr. *former broadcasting company executive*
Olasky, Marvin *journalist, educator, editor*
Stout, Patricia A. *communications educator*
Williamson, Thomas Arnold *publishing executive*
Wilson, Michael Joseph *newspaper executive*

**Bacliff**
Kahn, Kathleen Pica *photojournalist, arbitrator, mediator*

**Beaumont**
Baker, Mary Alice *communications educator, consultant*
Roth, Lane *communications educator*

**Crockett**
Gibbs, James Howard *broadcast executive*

**Dallas**
Bailon, Gilbert *newspaper executive*
Blessen, Karen Alyce *freelance/self-employed journalist, artist*
Blumenthal, Karen *newspaper executive*
Brown, Colleen *broadcast executive*
Burns, Scott *columnist*
Cantrell, Scott *newspaper music critic*
Decherd, Robert William *newspaper and broadcasting executive*
Diaz Meyer, Cheryl *photojournalist*
Dillon, David Anthony *editor, educator*
Dufner, Edward Joseph *editor*
Glines, Carroll Vane, Jr. *magazine editor*
Holmes, Bert Otis E., Jr. *retired editor*
Kutner, Janet *art critic, book reviewer*
Lesson, David *photojournalist*
Lumpkin, John O. *news organization executive*
McPherson, Gail *publishing and real estate executive*
Mong, Robert William, Jr. *publishing executive*
Moroney, James M. III *publishing executive*
Osborne, Burl *publishing executive, editor*
Proud, Robert Donald (Robert Payton) *broadcast executive*
Smith, Nancy Woolverton *journalist, real estate agent, antique appraiser*
Smith, Sue Frances *newspaper editor*
Wilk, Stuart *publishing executive*

**Euless**
Steffen, Tina Marie *journalist, home economist, elementary school educator*

**Fort Worth**
Hunt, Dianna *editor*
Peipert, James Raymond *journalist*
Price, Michael Howard *journalist, critic, composer*
Record, Phillip Julius *journalist*
Turner, Wesley R. *publishing executive*
Witt, Jim *editor*

**Houston**
Anderson, Nick *editorial cartoonist*
Barlow, Jim B. *retired columnist, writer*
Bischoff, Susan Ann *newspaper editor*
Cohen, Jeff *editor, publishing executive*
Donnelly, John Thomas *editor*
Downing, Margaret Mary *newspaper editor*
George, Deveral D. *editor, journalist, advertising consultant*
Gray, Robert Steele *publishing executive, editor, writer*
Hawes, William Kenneth *communication educator, author*
Heinsen, Lindsay *newspaper editor*
Hobby, William Pettus *retired broadcast executive*
Holmes, Ann Hitchcock *journalist*
Hutchison, Brady Lee *editor, history professor*
Jetton, Steve *newspaper editor*
Kientz, Renee *newspaper editor*
Marek, Joycelyn *publishing executive*
McDavid, George Eugene (Gene Mc David) *retired newspaper executive*
Oren, Bruce Clifford *editor, artist*
Pederson, Tony Weldon *newspaper editor*
Read, Michael Oscar *editor, consultant*
Roberts, Charles Murray *retired publishing executive, writer*
Schott, Sally Maria *music publisher, arts education consultant*
Summerlin, Deborah Lynn *theater technician, video technician*
Sweeney, Jack *publishing executive*
Taylor, James Sheppard *communications educator*
Wagner, Charlene Brook *secondary school educator*
Walls, Martha Ann Williams (Mrs. B. Carmage Walls) *publishing executive*
Ward, David Henry (Dave Ward) *television news reporter, anchorman*
Wilburn, John *editor*

**Irving**
Halter, Jon Charles *magazine editor, writer*
Young, J. Warren *magazine publisher*

**Jacksonville**
Thrall, Gordon Fish *publishing executive*

**Kerrville**
Dozier, William Everett, Jr. *publishing executive, editor-in-chief*

**Kyle**
Saunders, Patricia Gene Knight *freelance writer, editor*

**La Marque**
Bernard, Lora Marie *journalist, public relations and development specialist*

**Longview**
Udy, Rae *columnist, writer*

**Lubbock**
Punyanunt-Carter, Narissra *communications educator*

**Richardson**
Senderling, Jon Townsend *journalist, public relations executive, consultant*

**San Antonio**
Clark, Robert Phillips *editor, consultant*
Cotae, Paul *communications educator*
Davis, Jolene Bryant *magazine publishing executive consultant*
Foster, Nancy Haston *columnist, writer*
Gwathmey, Joe Neil, Jr. *broadcast executive*
Heloise, *columnist, writer*
Hogan, John *broadcast executive*
Lenke, Joanne Marie *publishing executive*
Mays, L(ester) Lowry *broadcast executive*
Michaels, Willard A. (Bill Michaels) *retired broadcasting executive*
Winik, Joanne *broadcast executive*

**San Marcos**
Keeley, Maureen Patricia *communications educator, writer*
Stovall, Frances Middagh *journalist, preservationist*

**Spring**
Randazzo, Gary Wayne *newspaper executive*

**The Woodlands**
Cagle, Melinda Reeves *editor*
Logan, Mathew Kuykendall *journalist*

**Tyler**
Brock, Dee Sala *television executive, educator, writer, consultant*

**Wharton**
Jackson, Larry C. *publishing executive*

## UTAH

**Ogden**
Coleman, Robert D. *music critic, educator*
Thornburg, Ron *editor*

**Park City**
Baumgardner, Barbara Borke *publishing consultant*

Gallivan, John William *retired publishing executive*

**Provo**
Bartlett, Leonard Lee *retired communications educator, advertising executive*
Holbrook, Jay Mack *publishing company executive*
Willes, Mark Hinckley *media specialist*

**Salt Lake City**
Conway, Nancy Ann *newspaper editor*
Fehr, John William *newspaper editor*
Gregersen, R(oald) George *newspaper publishing executive*
Hatch, George Clinton *television executive*
Hughes, (Robert) John *journalist, educator*
Paulsen, Vivian *editor*
Sillars, Malcolm Osgood *communications educator*
Smith, Donald E. *broadcast engineer*

## VERMONT

**Hartland Four Corners**
Brady, Upton Birnie *editor, literary agent*

**Hinesburg**
Carlson, Stephen *publishing executive*

**Lincoln**
Kompass, Edward John *consulting editor*

**North Pomfret**
Crowl, John Allen *retired publishing company executive*

**Norwich**
Paine, Walter Cabot *journalist, consultant*

**Weathersville**
Harris, Christopher *editor, writer*

**Woodstock**
Goulazian, Peter Robert *retired broadcasting executive*

## VIRGINIA

**Alexandria**
Arundel, John Howard *journalist, publisher*
Fleming, Douglas Riley *journalist, publishing executive, consultant*
Heil, Alan Lewis, Jr. *retired radio broadcast executive, writer*
Hobbs, Michael Edwin *broadcast executive*
Kerger, Paula Arnold *broadcast executive*
Salinas, Rodney Jay C. *media company executive*
Shosky, John Edwin *media consultant, speechwriter*
Yoder, Edwin Milton, Jr. *columnist, educator, editor, writer*

**Annandale**
Freeman, Baba Foster *editor*

**Arlington**
Arnold, Gary Howard *film critic*
Clayton, James Edwin *journalist*
Elsberg, John William *publishing executive, writer*
Fleischman, Phil *radio news executive*
French, Mary B. *editor, photographer, poet, retired literature educator*
Goodman, Mark *journalist, educator*
Holovaty, Adrian *editor, web site designer*
Ifill, Gwen *moderator, political reporter*
Lehrer, James Charles *reporter, journalist*
MacDougall, William Lowell *magazine editor*
MacNeil, Robert Breckenridge Ware *retired journalist, writer*
McWethy, John Fleetwood *journalist*
Neikirk, William Robert *journalist*
Neuharth, Allen Harold *newspaper publisher*
Quinn, John Collins *publishing executive, editor*
Regnery, Alfred Scattergood *publishing executive*
Reiss, Susan Marie *editor, writer*
Rockefeller, Sharon Percy *broadcast executive*
Simonson, David C. *retired newspaper association executive*
Tyrell, Robert Emmett, Jr. *editor in chief, writer*

**Ashburn**
Sanfelici, Arthur H(ugo) *editor, writer*

**Basye**
Amolsch, Arthur Lewis *publishing executive*

**Charlottesville**
Forrest, Patricia Anne *publishing executive, editor*
Kaiserlian, Penelope Jane *publishing executive*
Thornhill, Arthur H., Jr. *retired publishing executive*
Wood, James Arthur *cartoonist*

**Chester**
Gray, Frederick Thomas, Jr., (Rick Gray) *journalist, actor, educator*

**Dulles**
Desmond, Ned *editor, writer*

**Fairfax**
Kieffer, Jarold Alan *publishing executive, writer*
McAllister, William Howard III *newspaper reporter, columnist, public affairs consultant*

**Fairfax Station**
Randell, Cortes W. *news service executive*

**Falls Church**
Aukofer, Frank Alexander *journalist*
Cromley, Allan Wray *retired journalist*
Kaplow, Herbert Elias *journalist*

**Great Falls**
Garrett, Wilbur (Bill Garrett) *magazine editor*

**Hampton**
Brauer, Harrol Andrew, Jr. *broadcast executive*

**Herndon**
Berry, Fred Clifton, Jr. *editor, writer*
Miller, Donald Lane *publishing executive*

**Leesburg**
Petranek, Stephen Lynn *editor*

**Lexington**
Luecke, Pamela *editor, educator*

**Luray**
Burzynski, Norman Stephen *editor*

**Manassas**
Bahner, Sue (Florence Suzanna Bahner) *broadcast executive*

**Marion**
Elledge, Glenna Ellen Tuell *journalist*

**Mason Neck**
Mc Curdy, Patrick Pierre *editor*

**Mc Lean**
Clark-Johnson, Susan *publishing executive*
Dubow, Craig A. *publishing executive*
Feller, Mimi A. (Millicent Feller) *newspaper publishing executive*
Gallagher, Brian *editor-in-chief*
Giallombardo, Leslie *publishing executive*
Gniewek, Raymond Louis *newspaper editor*
Martore, Gracia *publishing company executive*
Mathews, Linda McVeigh *newspaper editor*
Mazzarella, David *editor*
McCorkindale, Douglas Hamilton *publishing executive*
Moon, Craig A. *publishing executive*
Moore, Dennis *news correspondent*
Parshall, Gerald *journalist*
Paulson, Kenneth Alan *editor*
Prichard, Peter S. *newspaper editor*
Ritter, Hal *newspaper editor*
Ullmann, Owen *journalist*
Weiss, Susan *newspaper editor*
Williams, John A. (Jack Williams) *newspaper publishing executive*

**Midlothian**
Chapman, Gilbert Whipple, Jr. *publishing executive*
Crutchfield, George Thomas *journalism educator*

**Norfolk**
Addis, Kay Tucker *newspaper editor*
Barry, Richard Francis III *publishing executive*
Batten, Frank *newspaper publisher, cable broadcaster*
Sizemore, William Howard, Jr. *journalist*

**Paeonian Springs**
Sloyan, Patrick Joseph *journalist*

**Reston**
Carey, Jack H. *publishing executive*
Powell, Anne Elizabeth *editor-in-chief*

**Richmond**
Bryan, John Stewart III *newspaper publisher*
Henry, Robert Randolph Ran *newswriter, educator*
Seals, Margaret Louise Crumrine *managing editor*

**Springfield**
Myers, Elissa Matulis *publishing executive, professional society administrator*

**Stanardsville**
Anns, Arlene Eiserman *publishing company executive*

**Staunton**
Sorrells, Nancy Taylor *publishing executive, writer, historian*
Thompson, George Fletcher *editor, publishing executive*

**Vienna**
Mc Arthur, George *journalist*
McElveen, Joseph James, Jr. *journalist, writer, newscaster, educator*

**Virginia Beach**
Goffigan, Christopher Wayne *research associate*
Robertson, Pat (Marion Gordon Robertson) *religious broadcasting executive, university president and chancellor*

**Warrenton**
Brimelow, Peter *journalist*

**Winchester**
Byrd, Harry Flood, Jr. *publishing executive, retired senator*

**Woodbridge**
Binder, L. James *retired magazine editor, journalist*

## WASHINGTON

**Bellevue**
George, Roger Allen *communications educator*

**Blaine**
Miller, Ronald *journalist, critic*

**Chattaroy**
Jordan, Marvin Evans, Jr. *record company executive, vocalist, actor, composer*

**Edmonds**
Owen, John *retired newspaper editor*

**Friday Harbor**
Hill, Ruth Beebe *editor, writer*

**Port Angeles**
Brewer, John Charles *journalist*

**Port Ludlow**
Trzaska, Joyce Anne *publishing executive*

**Port Townsend**
Buhler, Jill Lorie *editor, writer*
MacLean, Barbara Hutmacher *retired journalist, writer*

**Seattle**
Boardman, David *newspaper editor*
Bruner, Nancy J. *publishing executive*
Buckner, Philip Franklin *newspaper publisher*
Bunting, Kenneth Freeman *newspaper editor*
Cochran, Wendell Albert *science editor*
Fancher, Michael Reilly *editor, publishing executive*
Grimley, Janet Elizabeth *newspaper editor*
Gwinn, Mary Ann *newspaper reporter*
Henkel, Cathy *newspaper sports editor*
Hills, Regina J. *journalist*
Hornschemeier, Paul *graphic novelist*
Horsey, David *editorial cartoonist*
Kelly, Carolyn Sue *newspaper executive*
Kittross, John Michael *retired communications educator*
Lacitis, Erik *journalist*
Nash, Cynthia Jeanne *journalist*
Parks, Michael James *editor*
Phillips, Cheryl *reporter*
Savage, Daniel Keenan *columnist, editor-in-chief*
Strahilevitz, Meir *inventor, researcher, psychiatry educator*
Trott, Nancy Roberts *editor*

**Spokane**
Cowles, William Stacey *newspaper publisher*
Kafentzis, John Charles *journalist, educator*
Kunkel, Richard Lester *public radio executive*
McManus, Patrick Francis *editor, educator, writer*
Steele, Karen Dorn *journalist*

**Tacoma**
Mowery, Gerald Eugene *publishing executive, writer*

**Woodinville**
Alvarez, Bryan *newsletter editor, writer*

## WEST VIRGINIA

**Bunker Hill**
Marple, Thomas Franklin *columnist, reporter*

**Charleston**
Chilton, Elizabeth Easley Early *newspaper executive*
Haught, James Albert, Jr. *journalist, editor*
Ward, Ken, Jr. *journalist*

**Greenville**
Warner, Kenneth Wilson, Jr. *editor, publishing executive*

**Parkersburg**
McKenzie, Lawrence J. *composition educator*

**Weston**
Billeter, Robert James *newspaper publisher*

## WISCONSIN

**Appleton**
Malaney, Stephanie J. *reading specialist*

**Brookfield**
Fibich, Howard Raymond *retired newspaper editor*

**Fond Du Lac**
Witte, Dale Andrew *choral director, educator*

**Green Bay**
Daley, Arthur James *retired magazine publisher*

**Greendale**
Kaiser, Ann Christine *magazine editor*
Pohl, Kathleen Sharon *editor*

**Iola**
Krause, Chester Lee *publishing executive*

**Janesville**
Fitzgerald, James Francis *broadcast executive*

**Madison**
Burgess, James Edward *publishing executive*
Burns, Elizabeth Murphy *media executive*
Foley, Ellen Madaline *journalist*
Gruber, John Edward *editor, historian, photographer*
Haslanger, Philip Charles *journalist*
Hopson, James Warren *publishing executive*
Hoyt, James Lawrence *journalism educator, writer*
McNelly, John Taylor *retired journalist, educator*
Rinzel, Dennis Joseph *media specialist, director*
Rothschild, Matthew *editor*
Rowe, Marieli Dorothy *media literacy education consultant, organization executive*
Shah, Dhavan Vinod *communications educator*
Strasbaugh, Joan Timmis *publishing executive*
Wineke, William Robert *reporter, minister*
Zweifel, David Alan *newspaper editor*

**Menomonie**
Cutnaw, Mary-Frances *retired communications educator, writer, editor*

**Milwaukee**
Behrendt, David Frogner *retired journalist*
Farris, Trueman Earl, Jr. *retired newspaper editor*
Garcia, Astrid J. *newspaper executive*
Kritzer, Paul Eric *publishing executive, lawyer*
Leonard, Richard Hart *journalist, educator*
Mykleby, Kathy *newscaster, reporter*
Otto, Jean Hammond *journalist*

Spore, Keith Kent *newspaper executive*

**Pewaukee**
Lee, Jack (Jim Sanders Beasley) *broadcast executive*

**Racine**
Miller, Yolanda *publisher, writer*

## WYOMING

**Jackson**
Decker, Carol Arne *magazine publishing executive*

**Kelly**
Harrice, Cy (Nicholas Psiharis) *announcer*

**Laramie**
Guzzo, Sandra Elizabeth *newspaper columnist, writer*

**Riverton**
Peck, Robert A. *publishing executive, state legislator*

## TERRITORIES OF THE UNITED STATES

### PUERTO RICO

**Bayamon**
Berio, Blanca *editor*

**San Juan**
Casiano, Kimberly *publishing executive*
Sepúlveda, Sandra *communications educator*

### VIRGIN ISLANDS

**St John**
Walker, Ronald R. *editor, educator, writer*

## CANADA

### ALBERTA

**Edmonton**
Hughes, Linda J. *newspaper publisher*

### BRITISH COLUMBIA

**Vancouver**
Yaffe, Barbara Marlene *journalist*

### ONTARIO

**Brantford**
Hanna, William Brooks *publishing executive, literary agent*

**Don Mills**
French, William Harold *retired newspaper editor*

**London**
Cornies, Larry Alan *journalist, educator*

**North York**
Gasparrini-Etheridge, Claudia *publishing executive, research scientist, writer*

**Ottawa**
Davey, Clark William *newspaper publisher*

**Saint Catharines**
Miller, John Peter (Jack Miller) *journalist*

**Toronto**
Dean, Geoffrey *book publisher*
Landsberg, Michele *retired journalist*
Slaight, Gary *broadcast executive*
Thall, Burnett Murray *retired newspaper executive*
Thomson, David K.R. *publishing executive*

**Willowdale**
Kerner, Fred *book publisher, writer*

### QUEBEC

**Montreal**
Moss, David *music company executive*
Webster, Norman Eric *journalist, foundation administrator*

## AUSTRALIA

**Double Bay**
Guerin, Didier *magazine executive*

## BELGIUM

**Brussels**
Kempe, Frederick Schumann *newspaper editor, columnist*
Lewis, Jesse *editor*

## CHINA

**Shanghai**
Prosser, Michael Hubert *communications educator*

## ENGLAND

**Cambridge**
Kermode, Frank (John Kermode) *literary critic, educator*

**London**
Davis, Crispin *publishing company executive*
Fuller, Simon *music company executive, television producer*
Glocer, Thomas Henry *publishing executive*
Murdoch, Elisabeth *media company executive*
Oliver, Diane Frances *publisher, writer*
Roth, Richard *news correspondent*
Scardino, Dame Marjorie Morris *publishing executive*

## FRANCE

**Levallois-Perret**
Filipacchi, Daniel *publishing executive*

## HONG KONG

**Hong Kong**
Laurie, James Andrew *broadcast executive, consultant, director, television executive producer, journalist*
Podd, Ann *newspaper editor*

## INDIA

**Manipal**
Pai, Satish Upendra *publishing executive*

**New Delhi**
Watson, Paul *photojournalist, correspondent*

## IRELAND

**Dublin**
O'Reilly, Sir Anthony John Francis *media company executive, former food products company executive*

## ISRAEL

**Jerusalem**
Singer, Suzanne Fried *editor*

**Savyon**
Bushinsky, Jay (Joseph Mason) *journalist, news correspondent*

## ITALY

**Milan**
Berlusconi, Marina *publishing executive*

## JAPAN

**Tokyo**
Akutsu, Yoshihiro *communications educator*
Chang, Steve *internet security company executive*
Hakoshima, Shin-ichi *publishing executive*
Krisher, Bernard *foreign correspondent*
Petersen, Barry Rex *news correspondent*

## NETHERLANDS

**Amsterdam**
Vinken, Pierre Jacques *publishing executive*

## QATAR

**Doha**
Pedrosa, Veronica *journalist*

## REPUBLIC OF KOREA

**Seoul**
Park, Myungkark *publishing company owner*
Yoon, Hyung-Doo *publisher, educator*

## SOUTH AFRICA

**Johannesburg**
Berk, Philip Woolf *journalist*

## SWITZERLAND

**Alpnach**
Bocker, Hans Jurgen *editor-in-chief, consultant, finance educator*

## ADDRESS UNPUBLISHED

Abrams, Roz *newscaster*
Achorn, Robert Comey *retired newspaper publisher*
Aldrich, Patricia Anne Richardson *retired magazine editor*
Allen, Natalie *cable news anchor*
Allen, William L. *editor*

Martin, John Joseph *journalist*
Martin, Marilyn Mann *retired media specialist*
Masket, Edward Seymour *television executive*
Mason, John Oliver *freelance journalist, community activist, poet*
McCarty, Thomas Joseph *publishing executive*
McCauley, Jane Reynolds *journalist*
McCormick, Susan Konn *retired publishing executive*
McDarrah, Gloria Schoffel *editor, writer*
McGinnis, Marcy Ann *broadcast executive*
McGuirk, Terrence *former broadcasting company executive*
McIntyre, Bruce Herbert *media consultant, marketing professional*
McLucas, Kate *magazine editor*
McManus, Jason Donald *retired editor-in-chief*
McManus, Sean Joseph *broadcast executive*
McMichael, Jessica Leigh *journalist, writer, poet*
McNally, Connie Benson *magazine editor, publisher, antiques dealer*
McNamara, James M. *broadcast executive*
McNeil, Jan Torbet *communications educator*
Means, Marianne *columnist*
Mears, Walter Robert *journalist*
Medavoy, Mike *film company executive, film producer*
Medina, Kathryn Bach *book editor*
Mellema, Donald Eugene *retired radio news reporter and anchor*
Melody, Michael Edward *publishing company executive*
Mercado-Valdes, Frank *broadcast executive*
Mesrobian, Arpena Sachaklian *publishing executive, consultant, editor*
Mestres, Ricardo A. III *film company executive*
Metoyer, Pamela Paradis *scientific editor, writer*
Meyer, Andrew W. *retired publishing executive*
Meyer, Pucci *editor*
Meyers, John Allen *magazine publisher*
Michaels, Marion Cecelia *newswriter, editor, news syndicate executive*
Miller, Darcy M. *publishing executive*
Miller, Donald LeSessne *publishing executive*
Miller, Judith A. (Judy Miller) *retired journalist*
Miller, Norman Charles, Jr. *editor, reporter*
Mills, Dale Douglas *journalist*
Millsaps, William Hobart, Jr. *retired editor*
Mitchell, Rick *journalist, writer*
Monacelli, Gianfranco *publishing executive*
Montgomery, Cliff Wilson *journalist, writer, researcher*
Mooney, James Hugh *newspaper editor*
Moore, Oliver Semon III *publishing executive, consultant*
Moore, Thomas Paul *retired broadcast executive*
Mora, Antonio Gonzalez III *broadcast journalist*
Morgan, Anne Marie G. *broadcast journalist, educator*
Mottola, Tommy (Thomas D. Mottola) *recording industry executive*
Mudd, Roger Harrison *newscaster, educator*
Murphy, Ann Pleshette *magazine editor-in-chief*
Murphy, Kim *newspaper bureau chief*
Mysel, Randy Howard *publishing company executive*
Nachman, Gerald Weil *columnist, critic, writer*
Neff, Donald Lloyd *news correspondent, writer*
Neill, Rolfe *retired newspaper executive*
Nelson, Martha Jane *magazine editor*
Newbauer, John Arthur, Jr. *editor*
Newman, Rachel *editor*
Novick, Julius Lerner *theater critic, educator*
Nye, Dorothy Mae *freelance journalist, educator*
Oakley, Andrew Arthur *journalist, educator*
Obermayer, Herman Joseph *newspaper publisher*
Ochs, Michael *editor, librarian, music educator*
Ogunleye, Tolagbe Monuola *publishing executive, educator, small business owner, editor*
Olive, David Michael *journalist, editor*
Oliver, Matt *publishing executive*
O'Neil, Carolyn *cable network executive, cable television host*
Oppedahl, John Frederick *newspaper publisher, publishing executive*
Osberg, Gregory John *publishing company executive*
Osmer-McQuade, Margaret *broadcast executive, journalist*
Pakenham, Rosalie Muller Wright *magazine and newspaper editor*
Panagotis, David Timothy *editor*
Pareene, Alex E. *political blog editor*
Parker, Mel *editor*
Parkyn, John William *editor, writer, columnist*
Patterson, Ronald Paul *publishing executive, educator, minister*
Paul, Kenneth *newspaper editor*
Pauley, Jane *newscaster, journalist*
Peacock, Mary Willa *magazine editor, consultant*
Penney, Alexandra *magazine editor-in-chief, writer*
Pepper, Jonathon L. *media executive*
Perkins, Anthony B. *editor-in-chief, writer, educator*
Perry, Michael C. *theatre publisher, educator*
Peterson, Kevin Bruce *newspaper editor, publishing executive*
Phillips, Glynda Ann *editor*
Picower, Warren Michael *editor*
Pi-González, Amaury Francisco *announcer, journalist*
Pletcher, Eldon *retired cartoonist*
Pomeranz, Michael *newscaster*
Poster, Meryl *film company executive*
Povich, Lynn *journalist, internet executive*
Powell, Ardal *music company executive, editor*
Preddy, Raymond Randall *retired newspaper publisher, educator*
Press, Aida Kabatznick *retired editor, poet, writer*
Price, Nelson (John Nelson Price) *author, journalist*
Price, Tom *journalist*
Priest, Jessie Shaw *media specialist*
Quade, Vicki *editor, writer, playwright, theater producer*
Quinn, Charles Nicholas *journalist*
Radcliffe, Redonia (Donnie Radcliffe) *journalist, writer*
Radlauer, Steve *freelance writer, journalist, producer*
Raeburn, Paul *editor, writer*

Raines, Howell Hiram *former newspaper editor, journalist*
Ramsay, Karin Kinsey *publisher, educator*
Randinelli, Tracey Anne *magazine editor*
Rapoport, Ronald Jon *journalist*
Rasi, Humberto Mario *editor, educator*
Rasor, Dina Lynn *journalist, private investigator*
Rayner, William Alexander *retired newspaper editor, author*
Read, Richard Eaton *newspaper reporter*
Reynolds, Fredric G. *broadcast executive*
Richman, Alan *magazine editor, educator*
Rierson, Robert Leak *retired broadcast executive, scriptwriter*
Riggs, Michael David *editor, writer*
Righini, Marilou Mausteller *editor, consultant*
Rinearson, Peter Mark *journalist, writer, software executive*
Rivard, Robert *newspaper executive*
Roberts, David Lowell *journalist, educator*
Roberts, Delmar Lee *editor*
Roberts, Edwin Albert, Jr. *editor, journalist*
Roberts, Margaret Harold *editor, publisher*
Rodrigue, George P. *newpaper executive*
Rojany, Lisa Adrienne *publishing company executive, writer*
Rollins, Edward Tyler, Jr. *retired newspaper executive*
Roosevelt, Phil *periodical editor*
Rooth, Signe Alice *editor, consultant*
Rosenberg, Shirley Sirota *publications executive*
Rosenthal, Arthur Jesse *publishing executive*
Roth, Harvey Paul *retired publishing executive*
Rugaber, Walter Feucht, Jr. *retired publishing executive, academic administrator*
Rushnell, Squire Derrick *television executive, writer*
Russell, James Brian *broadcast executive, media consultant*
Sabbatini, Marcello *journalist, motor sports weekly director*
Salvatore, Diane J. *editor-in-chief*
Samuelson, Robert Jacob *journalist*
Sanders, Marlene *news correspondent, journalism educator*
Sapsowitz, Sidney H. *entertainment and media company executive*
Sarris, Andrew George *film critic*
Scannell, Herb *broadcast executive*
Schneider, Howard Stewart *former newspaper editor*
Schorr, Daniel Louis *broadcast journalist, author, lecturer*
Schrand, Richard Henry *broadcast executive, educator*
Schuch, Beverly *anchor*
Schurenberg, Eric *magazine editor*
Sciolino, Elaine *reporter*
Sedlacek, Sarah Lynn *publishing executive*
Seligman, Nicole K. *broadcast executive, lawyer*
Seminara, Lynda Anne *editor*
Shacter, James Detmers *editor, writer*
Shapiro, Richard Charles *publishing executive, sales executive, marketing professional*
Shelledy, James Edwin III *newspaper editor*
Shelton, Stephani *broadcast journalist, consultant*
Shulgasser-Parker, Barbara *critic, writer*
Siegal, Allan Marshall *journalist, consultant*
Siegel, Ira T. *publishing executive*
Siegel, Vivian *biology editor*
Sifton, David Whittier *retired magazine editor*
Silverstein, Marc *TV host, reporter*
Silvey, Anita Lynne *editor*
Simmons, Russell *recording industry executive*
Simon, Peter E. *publishing executive*
Simon, Roger *newspaper columnist*
Simons, Lewis Martin *journalist*
Simonson, Lee Stuart *broadcast executive*
Simpson, Hugh L. *news correspondent, newswriter*
Sinclair, Carole *publishing executive, editor*
Sites, Kevin *news correspondent, journalist, web blogger*
Skinner, Thomas *broadcast executive*
Slaughter, Vernon Leroy *recording industry consultant*
Smardz, Zofia Jadwiga *editor, writer*
Smith, A. Robert *editor, author*
Smith, George Drury *publishing executive*
Smith, Martin Bernhard *journalist*
Soeteber, Ellen *journalist, editor*
Speerstra, Karen M. *former publishing executive*
Spence, James Robert, Jr. *broadcast executive, educator*
Stahl, Lesley R. *news correspondent*
Stall, William Read *retired newswriter*
Stamaty, Mark Alan *cartoonist, writer, artist*
Stanley, Scott, Jr. *editor*
Stanton, John Jeffrey *editor, director, journalist, government agency administrator, educator*
Stauderman, Albert Philip, Jr. *media consultant*
Stennett, William Clinton (Clint Stennett) *television station executive, state legislator*
Stephens, Edward Carl *communications educator, writer*
Stephenson, Toni Edwards *publishing executive, investment company executive, communications executive*
Steptoe, Sonja *journalist*
Stevens, Mark *publishing executive*
Stiff, Robert Martin *newspaper editor*
Stock, Stephen Michael *broadcast journalist*
Storm, Hannah *newscaster*
Strothman, James Edward *editor-in-chief*
Stuart, Nancy Rubin (Nancy Zimman Stetson) *journalist, writer, television producer*
Stutz, Pearl Hewlett *retired photojournalist*
Sullivan, Daniel Joseph *theater critic*
Sullivan, Dennis James, Jr. *retired hospitality and music executive*
Sullivan, Patricia *journalist*
Swartz, Steven R. *publishing executive*
Switzer, Maurice Harold *journalist*
Synclair, Larry Ross *news correspondent, advocate*
Szep, Paul Michael *editorial cartoonist*
Taati, Poopak *media director*
Tafoya, Michele *sports reporter*
Taishoff, Lawrence Bruce *publishing company executive*
Talese, Nan Ahearn *freelance/self-employed publishing executive*

Tammeus, William David *journalist, columnist*
Tamony, Katie *editor-in-chief*
Tata, Giovanni *publishing executive*
Taylor, George Frederick *newspaper publisher, editor*
Teagan, John Gerard *publishing executive*
Telnaes, Ann *cartoonist*
Terry, Clifford Lewis *journalist*
Tharpe, Frazier Eugene *journalist*
Thomas, Jo *journalist, educator*
Thomas, Patricia Goodnow *journalist*
Thompson, London (William London Evans-Thompson) *recording industry executive, publishing executive, sound recording engineer, executive film producer*
Thompson, Martin Christian *retired news executive*
Thrall, Richard Cameron, Jr. *broadcast executive*
Threlkeld, Richard Davis *retired broadcast journalist*
Tiedge-Lafranier, Jeanne Marie *editor*
Tierney, Brian Patrick *publishing executive, former advertising and public relations executive*
Timbaland, (Timothy Z. Mosley) *recording industry executive, rap artist*
Toay, Thelma M. *columnist, poet*
Tobias, Andrew Previn *columnist, educator*
Todd, Jay Marlyn *retired editor*
Torgerson, Katherine P. *media consultant, corporate communications specialist*
Toussaint, Allen Richard *recording studio executive, composer, pianist*
Triece, Anne Gallagher *magazine publisher*
Trudeau, Garretson Beekman (Garry Trudeau) *cartoonist*
Trueman, William Peter Main *broadcaster, columnist*
Tugend, Alina Nurit *journalist*
Turek, Sonia Fay *journalist*
Turnley, David Carl *photojournalist*
Twigg-Smith, Thurston *newspaper publisher*
Tyrity, Kathy Milica *reporter, editor*
Ucciardo, Frank Joseph *journalist, reporter*
Urbano, Juan Antonio *broadcast executive, television producer, television director*
Urchak, Jill Danielle *commentator*
Urdang, Laurence *editor, publishing executive*
Valenti, Jack Joseph *former motion picture executive*
Vaughan, Samuel Snell *editor, writer, publishing executive*
Verdery, David Norwood *broadcast programming executive*
Vieth, Christopher W. *former publishing executive*
Vincent, Charles Eagar, Jr. *sportswriter*
Vitale, Dick *commentator, sports writer*
Wagman, Robert John *journalist, writer*
Waldmeir, Peter Nielsen *retired journalist*
Wallace, Carol *editor at large*
Wallace, Mike (Myron Leon Wallace) *newscaster, television personality*
Wallace De Cornwall, Clinton H. *media consultant*
Walsh, George William *publishing company executive, editor, author*
Warren, William Kermit *retired editor*
Waters, Betty Lou *newspaper reporter, writer*
Waters, Lou *news correspondent*
Watson, Catherine Elaine *journalist*
Watson, George Henry, Jr. *broadcaster, journalist*
Wearn, Wilson Cannon *retired media executive*
Weaver, Franklin Thomas *retired newspaper executive*
Weaver, Howard C. *newspaper executive*
Weber, Jonathan *editor, journalist, educator*
Weinstein, Bob (Robert Weinstein) *film company executive*
Weinstein, Harvey *film company executive, film producer*
Weissman, Jack (George Anderson) *retired editor*
Welsh, Dorothy Dell *columnist, writer*
Welsome, Eileen *journalist, writer*
Werman, Thomas Ehrlich *record producer*
West, Betsy *broadcast executive*
Weymouth, Elizabeth (Lally) Graham *editor, columnist*
Whipple, Judith Roy *retired editor*
Whitaker, Mark Theis *editor*
White, Keith Brandon (Babe) *music company executive, songwriter, actor, producer, author*
Whitesell, John Edwin *retired motion picture company executive*
Whittell, Polly (Mary Kaye Whittell) *editor, journalist*
Whittemore, Brian *media consultant, advertising executive*
Wies, Barbara *publishing executive, editor*
Wiessler, David Albert *news correspondent*
Wilkerson, Isabel *journalist, writer*
Wille, Wayne Martin *retired editor*
Williams, Anita Marie *publishing executive, writer*
Williams, Brown F *media specialist, consultant*
Willis, Clayton *broadcaster, former government official, educator, arts consultant*
Wilson, James Reid, Jr. *publishing executive*
Windhauser, John William *retired journalism educator, consultant*
Winston-Macauley, Marnie *columnist, writer*
Winter, Judy Elaine *freelance/self-employed journalist, speaker*
Witcover, Jules Joseph *columnist, writer*
Woestendiek, John, Jr., (William John Woestendiek) *newspaper reporter*
Woldt, Harold Frederick, Jr. *newspaper publishing executive*
Wolfman, Ira Joel *editor, writer*
Wood, Marian Starr *publishing executive*
Woodruff, Judy Carline *broadcast journalist*
Woodruff, Virginia *broadcast journalist, writer*
Woods, David Lyndon *broadcast executive, former federal executive, publishing executive*
Wooten, James Terrell *journalist*
Yack, Patrick Ashley *editor*
Yates, Ronald Eugene *newspaper editor, educator, author, journalist*
Yemenidjian, Alex *former film company executive*
Yood, James W. *art critic, historian, educator, writer*
Young, David Nelson *media and communications consultant*
Young, Patrick *editor, writer*
Zappe, John Paul *city editor, educator, newspaper executive*

Zerman, Melvyn Bernard *retired publishing executive, writer*
Ziegler, Jack (Jack Denmore) *cartoonist*

---

## EDUCATION *See also* specific fields for postsecondary education

## UNITED STATES

### ALABAMA

**Albertville**
Pollard, Wanda Meadows *primary school educator*

**Alexander City**
Chapman, Mary Kathryn *elementary school educator*

**Auburn**
Galbraith, Ruth Legg *retired dean, home economist*
Groccia, James Edward *education educator*
Jones, Allen *history educator, archivist*
Miller, Wilbur Randolph *academic administrator*
Osei, Joseph *education educator, minister*
Philpott, Harry Melvin *former university president*
Voitle, Robert Alan *dean, physiologist*
Zallen, Harold *academic administrator, chemist*

**Auburn University**
Dodge, Timothy de K. *school librarian*
Richardson, Edward R. *academic administrator*

**Birmingham**
Berte, Neal Richard *academic administrator*
Deal, William Brown *medical school dean, physician, educator*
Fambrough, Reinhard Eugene *director, music educator*
Garrison, Carol Z. *academic administrator*
Hnizdil, Paul J. *secondary school educator*
Katiyar, Santosh Kumar *education educator*
Koomullil, Roy Paulose *mechanics and engineering educator*
Kreisberg, Robert A. *dean, medical educator*
Mc Callum, Charles Alexander *academic administrator*
Morrisey, Michael A. *health economics educator*
Pollick, G. David *academic administrator, philosopher*
Thomas, Huw Francis *dean, dental educator*
Ward, Perry W. *college president*
Westmoreland, Andrew *academic administrator*

**Brilliant**
Franks, Gracie G. *elementary school educator*

**Coosada**
Reynolds, Linda Ann *elementary school educator*

**Crossville**
Blessing, Maxine Lindsey *secondary school educator*

**Cullman**
Ivey, Mona Kay *secondary school educator, educational association administrator, consultant*

**Decatur**
Julich, Nancy C. *secondary school educator*
Smith, Trina *academic administrator*

**Dothan**
Fleming, Jennie M *retired education educator*
Flowers, V. Anne *retired academic administrator*
Phillips, Kenneth Edward *history educator, writer*

**Eufaula**
Bush, Billie Faye *mathematics educator*
Conniff, Alexandra Acosta *secondary school educator*

**Eutaw**
Merritt, Edith Bradford *elementary school educator*

**Fairhope**
Gwin, John Michael *retired education educator, consultant*

**Florence**
Williams, Joyce Hall *secondary school educator*

**Grand Bay**
Taylor, Anne Wilkerson *elementary school educator*

**Grant**
Segler, Lynn Cchandler *elementary school educator*

**Guntersville**
Burroughs, Julie M. *elementary school educator*

**Huntsville**
Burko, Lior M. *physics educator*
Foster, Deborah Simmons *elementary school educator*
Franz, Frank Andrew *academic administrator, physicist, educator*
Hawley, Harold Patrick *educational consultant*
Krueger, Kathleen Susan *special education administrator*
Lundquist, Charles Arthur *academic administrator*
Moore, Ann Roy *school system administrator*
Morgan, Beverly Hammersley *elementary school educator, artist*
Ratchford Merchant, Betty Jo *retired elementary school educator*

**Jacksonville**
Dunaway, William Preston *retired school system administrator*

**Jasper**
Morgan, Holly Guthrie *elementary school educator*
Rowland, David Jack *retired academic administrator*
Sparkman, Brandon Buster *secondary school educator, consultant, writer*

**Leeds**
Wilson, Maggie Isabelle Lovell *secondary school educator, literature educator*

**Livingston**
Green, Asa Norman *university president*
Padgett, Christine Elizabeth King *education educator*
Smith, Louis Roycraft, Jr. *guidance and counseling educator, administrator*

**Madison**
Brannan, Eulie Ross *educational consultant*
Gibson, John Thomas *academic administrator, consultant*
Jones, Christine Regina *secondary school educator*

**Marion**
Cleveland, Willie Mae *elementary school educator*

**Maylene**
Copes, Marvin Lee *academic administrator*

**Mobile**
Bullard, Bettie Catherine Posey *adult education educator*
Clarke, Ulma Leverna *retired elementary school educator*
Parden, Cindy Maria *elementary school educator*
Phan, Anh-Vu *adult education educator, researcher*
Rewak, William John *retired academic administrator, clergyman*
Sumlin, Margaret Brown *special education educator*

**Montevallo**
McChesney, Robert Michael, Sr. *academic administrator*

**Montgomery**
Gravatt, Lincoln Edmund *history educator*
King, Andrea S. *secondary school educator*
May, Cecil Richard, Jr. *academic administrator*
Morton, Joseph *school system administrator*
Smiley, Virginia A. *elementary school educator*
Tennimon, Dannie Earl *academic administrator, educator*

**Muscle Shoals**
Smith, Harry Delano *education administrator*

**Pell City**
Wright, Lauren Noelle *elementary school educator, music educator*

**Seale**
Harris-Stokes, Joyce A. *secondary school educator*

**Sumiton**
Rizzo, Stephen Wayne Burton *secondary school educator, music minister*

**Troy**
Davidson, Barry Sheldon *academic administrator, comparative and adult education educator*

**Tuscaloosa**
Fields, Ruth Kinniebrew *secondary and elementary educator, consultant*
Hughey Surman, Stacy Leigh *education educator*
McNealey, Ernest *college president*
Randall, Kenneth C. *dean, law educator*
Thomas, Joab Langston *retired academic administrator, biologist, educator*
Witt, Robert E. *academic administrator*

**Tuscumbia**
Hutchens, Eugene Garlington *academic administrator*

**Tuskegee**
Green, Elbert P. *retired academic administrator*
White, Mildred Virginia *secondary school educator, retired counseling administrator*

**Webb**
Knowles, Julie Nall *secondary school educator*

**ALASKA**

**Anchorage**
Byrd, Milton Bruce *academic administrator*
Comeau, Carol Smith *school system administrator*
Davis, Bettye Jean *school system administrator, state legislator*
Maimon, Elaine Plaskow *university chancellor*
Thurber, Sharon Lee *elementary resource educator*
Zandman-Zeman, Ronald Edwin *elementary school educator, minister*

**Barrow**
Blankenship, Trent *school system administrator, educator*

**Bethel**
Turner, Kathy Ann *special education educator*

**Eagle River**
Sparks, Jack Norman *dean*

**Fairbanks**
Alexander, Vera *dean, marine science educator*
Doran, Timothy Patrick *academic administrator*
Hamilton, Mark R. *academic administrator*
Kilbourn, Aldean Gae *secondary school educator*

Reichardt, Paul Bernard *academic administrator, chemist, educator*

**Juneau**
Pugh, John Robert *academic administrator, educator, retired state official*
Sampson, Roger *school system administrator*

**Kotzebue**
O'Brien, Annmarie *education educator*

**Tuntutuliak**
Daniel, Barbara Ann *retired elementary school educator*

**Wrangell**
Miller, Jennifer L. *elementary school educator, small business owner*

**ARIZONA**

**Arizona City**
Donovan, Willard Patrick *retired elementary school educator*

**Bullhead City**
Regan, Noelle Kristin *middle school educator*

**Chandler**
Casteel, Camille *school system administrator*
Fons, Margaret E. *elementary school educator*
Miller, Patricia Ann *secondary school educator*
Rowe, Ernest Ras *education educator, academic administrator*

**Douglas**
Nicodemus, Karen A. *college president*

**Flagstaff**
Baron, Patricia Burrell *university director*
Haeger, John Denis *academic administrator*

**Fort Mohave**
Roy, Christopher Marvin *elementary school educator*

**Fountain Hills**
Sorenson, Gretchen Hartley *elementary school educator*
Wright, C. T. Enus *former academic administrator*

**Gilbert**
Crandall, Sharon *elementary school educator*

**Glendale**
Cota, Lisa Foley *secondary school educator*
Kleissle, Karyn *chemistry educator, biology educator*
Staczek, John Joseph *academic administrator, consultant*

**Goodyear**
Molina, Tanya E. *school librarian*

**Green Valley**
Fuer-Davis, Beverly Jean *retired elementary school educator*
Smith, Raymond Lloyd *former university president, consultant*

**Kingman**
Stephens, Anne Catherine *special education educator*

**Lakeside**
Mack, Ina Leah *secondary school educator, pre-school administrator*
Seely, Dennis M. *secondary school educator*

**Mesa**
de Masi, Kenneth Forrest *secondary school educator*
Dillenberg, Jack *dean*
Duvall, Debra *school system administrator*
Molina-Walters, Debi Ann *education educator*
Philbrick, Douglas Robert *principal, librarian, educator, mental health professional*
Pullenza, Patricia *English educator, writer, designer*
Ramirez, Janice L. *assistant school superintendent*

**Oro Valley**
Meredith, Keith Edward *retired academic administrator, educator*

**Palo Verde**
Aldridge, Robert *principal*

**Phoenix**
Coor, Lattie Finch *university president*
Coyle, Linda Marie *elementary school educator*
Culnon, Sharon Darlene *special education educator, reading specialist*
Edwards, Vicki Ann *director*
Erwin, Barbara F. *school system administrator*
Fleenor, Geneva Lucille *retired elementary school educator*
Lee, Barbara S. *special education educator*
McConnell, Albert Lynn *director*
Noone, Laura Palmer *academic administrator, lawyer*
Pritchard Wood, Grace Ruth *elementary school educator*
Saggio, Joseph John *dean*
Sperling, John Glen *education company executive, educator*
Taylor, Amanda Deanne *elementary school educator*
Udall, Vesta Hammond *special education educator*
Yamamoto, Alice M. *secondary school educator*

**Pinetop**
Gilbert-Tiegs, Marion Ann *gifted and talented educator, consultant*

**Prescott**
Waterer, Bonnie Clausing *retired secondary school educator*

**Rio Verde**
Vanselow, Neal Arthur *retired academic administrator, retired internist*

**Scottsdale**
Hill, Louis Allen, Jr. *retired dean, civil engineer, consultant*
Lillestol, Jane Brush *educational consultant*
Phillips, Wanda Charity *secondary school educator, writer*
Stone, Alan Jay *retired academic administrator*

**Sun Lakes**
Thompson, Loring Moore *retired college administrator, writer*

**Surprise**
Bradford, Mariah *elementary school educator, consultant*
Brahms, Katheryn Ann *early childhood educator*
Neuman, Isabel *mathematics educator*
Stevenson, Norma Ann *elementary school educator, real estate agent, property manager*

**Tempe**
Barnhill, Robert E. *university administrator, educator*
Colgate, Catharine Pamella *secondary school educator*
Crow, Michael M. *academic administrator*
Guo, Hongbin *education educator*
Haggerson, Nelson Lionel, Jr. *education educator*
Peck, Ernest James, Jr. *academic administrator*
Tabbara, Hadi *director, researcher*
Thor, Linda M. *college president*
Wang, Ning *education educator*
White, Patricia Denise *dean, law educator*
Wills, J. Robert *academic administrator, theater educator, writer*
Winter Chaser, Vivian Janice *elementary school educator*

**Tucson**
Aguilar, Darla J. *adult education educator*
Arenas, Alberto *education educator*
Bootman, J. Lyle *pharmacy educator*
Coakley, Stephanie Joy *museum educator*
Deal, Mike Gary *educator*
Giberti, Tina Shereen *principal*
Johnson, John Gray *retired university chancellor*
Johnstone, Craig S. *elementary school educator*
Kaltenbach, C(arl) Colin *dean, educator*
Manning, Laura Shelton *assistant principal*
Martinez Sanchez, Mary Ann *academic administrator*
Massaro, Toni Marie *dean, law educator*
Nachman, Michael William *education educator*
Portney, Paul Rogers *dean*
Raab, Diane *special education educator*
Ramirez, Raul *academic administrator*
Shelton, Robert Neal *academic administrator, physics professor, researcher*
Soto, Angela C. *elementary school educator*
Stoffle, Carla Joy *university library dean*
Thomson, Donald Arthur *education educator*

**ARKANSAS**

**Arkadelphia**
Dunn, Charles DeWitt *academic administrator*
Elrod, Ben Moody *academic administrator*
Futrell, Alvin *director*
Grant, Daniel Ross *retired academic administrator*

**Bald Knob**
Barber, Leah Adrianne *elementary school educator, literacy educator*

**Blytheville**
Edmonds, Revis L., Jr. *history educator*
Fulling, Sharon S. *college nursing program director*

**Camden**
Bradshaw, Otabel *retired primary school educator*

**Clarksville**
Stone, George Clifford *education educator, researcher*

**Conway**
Cloyd, J. Timothy *academic administrator*
Thompson, Winfred Lee *academic administrator, lawyer*

**Farmington**
Schoppmeyer, Martin William, Jr. *school system administrator*

**Fayetteville**
Ferritor, Daniel E. *retired chancellor*
Jones, Louis, Jr., (Bucky Jones) *academic administrator*
Mosebach, Michael *education educator*
Schoppmeyer, Martin William *education educator*
Sears, Derek William George *education educator, researcher*
Smith, Robert Victor *academic administrator, educator*

**Fort Smith**
Gooden, Benny L. *school system administrator*

**Hardy**
Jones, Shirley J. *elementary school educator*

**Harrison**
Street, Susan Lee *elementary school educator*

**Hindsville**
Peirce, Carole *elementary school educator*

**Hot Springs National Park**
Farris, Jefferson Davis *university administrator*

**Jonesboro**
Frego, Georgia Kaye *elementary school educator*
Malinsky, Marci Ann *education educator*

Smith, Eugene Wilson *retired academic administrator, education educator*

**Little Rock**
Bass, Evelyn Elizabeth *elementary school educator*
Coffman, Deborah Kay *director*
Cothren, Martha Rose *history educator*
Fribourgh, James Henry *retired university administrator*
Hathaway, Charles E. *academic administrator*
James, T. Kenneth *school system administrator*
McIntyre, Nina M. *counseling administrator*
Reece, E. Albert *dean, obstetrician, gynecologist, perinatologist*
Smith, Paula Yvette *education educator*
Truex, Dorothy Adine *retired university administrator*
Wilson, I. Dodd *dean*
Xu, Xiaowei *education educator, researcher*

**Magazine**
Cleveland, Jared Allen *superintendent*

**Magnolia**
Harrison, Betty Carolyn Cook *retired education educator, administrator*

**Mountainburg**
Roper, Paul Kirk *elementary school educator*

**Nashville**
Couch, Holly G. *secondary school educator*

**Osceola**
Young, Marilyn Virginia *elementary school educator*

**Pangburn**
Roe, Sandy C. *gifted and talented educator*

**Pearcy**
Burch, Bobby Joe *secondary school educator*

**Pine Bluff**
Bock, Joe Ann *educational examiner*
Davis, Lawrence A., Jr. *academic administrator*

**Prairie Grove**
Dunn, Anne Ewald Nefflen *retired elementary school educator*

**Rogers**
Nunneley, Janelle Annette *education educator*
Spainhower, James Ivan *retired college president*

**Russellville**
Eidson, Martha Head *elementary school educator*
Morris, Lois Lawson *retired education educator*

**Searcy**
Burks, David Basil *academic administrator, educator*

**Springdale**
Cordell, Beulah Faye *retired special education educator*

**Van Buren**
Peer, Diana Kay *principal*

**White Hall**
Scott, Vicki Sue *school system administrator*

**CALIFORNIA**

**Agoura Hills**
Kuzmanovic, Jane Violet *academic administrator*

**Alameda**
Verrill, Kathleen Wills *special education educator*

**Alhambra**
Austin, Elizabeth Ruth *retired elementary school educator*
Suzuki, Bob H. *retired academic administrator*

**Aliso Viejo**
Carroll, Adeline F. *special education educator*

**Alta Loma**
Campbell, Ellen Feyk *elementary school educator*
Haskvitz, Alan Paul *elementary school educator, consultant*

**Anaheim**
Barry, Sandra *school system administrator*
Goodspeed, Kathryn Ann *pre-school educator*
Guajardo, Elisa *counselor, educator*
Unan, George Vincent *adult education educator*

**Aptos**
Bohn, Ralph Carl *educational consultant*
Hirsch, Bette G(ross) *academic administrator, language educator*

**Arcadia**
Baltz, Patricia Ann (Pann Baltz) *retired elementary school educator*
Matsuura, Kenneth Ray *counseling administrator*

**Arcata**
McCrone, Alistair William *retired academic administrator*

**Atherton**
Lane, Joan Fletcher *academic administrator*

**Azusa**
Liegler, Rosemary Menke *dean*
Pacino, Maria Antonieta *education educator, department chairman*
Parham, Thomas David *education educator*

**Bakersfield**
Davisson, Scott Louis *secondary school educator*
Fuller, Jean *school system administrator*
Hancock, Tapp *elementary school educator*

Zarra, Ernest Joseph III *secondary school educator, researcher*

**Barstow**
Gibbon, Mary-Lynn *special education educator*
Gregg, Donna Lynn *mathematics educator*

**Beaumont**
Youngren, Delvana Hope *secondary school educator*

**Belmont**
Huber, Margaret Ann *former college president*

**Berkeley**
Azarpay, Guitty *education educator*
Bacchetta, Paola *education educator*
Birgeneau, Robert Joseph *academic administrator, physicist, researcher*
diSessa, Andrea A. *education educator*
Doyle, Fiona Mary *dean, metallurgical engineer, educator*
Freedman, David Amiel *statistics educator, consultant*
Freedman, Sarah Warshauer *education educator*
Gray, Paul Russell *academic administrator, electrical engineering educator*
Heathcock, Clayton Howell *chemistry educator, researcher*
Johnson, Mary Katherine (Katie Johnson) *elementary school educator*
Leonard, Thomas *dean, librarian*
Linn, Marcia Cyrog *education educator*
Lipps, Jere Henry *biology educator, geology educator*
Lyons, Richard Kent *dean, finance educator*
Miles, Raymond Edward *retired dean, organizational behavior and industrial relations educator*
Pearson, P. David *dean*
Shortell, Stephen Michael *dean, health services researcher*
Staff, Virgil Clinton *retired history educator*

**Bermuda Dunes**
Eppert, Luana Kyle *retired secondary school educator, sculptor, writer*

**Beverly Hills**
Grant, Michael Ernest *educational administrator, management educator*

**Bloomington**
Lawrence, William, Jr. *retired elementary school educator*

**Brentwood**
Groseclose, Wanda Westman *retired elementary school educator*

**Browns Valley**
Stevens, Aileen *retired secondary school educator*

**Buena Park**
Carcich, Ronald A. *secondary school educator*

**Burbank**
Neumann, Nancy Ruth *private school educator*

**Calabasas**
Walker, Larry A. *secondary school educator*

**Camarillo**
Arthington, Carol Ann *elementary school educator*
Rush, Richard R. *academic administrator*

**Capitola**
Jackson, Kingsbury Temple *educational consultant, financial consultant*
Stobbe, Colleen Sue *elementary school educator, consultant*

**Carlsbad**
Golding, Brage *university president*
Rodak, Sharon Lorraine *elementary school educator, researcher*

**Carmel**
Faul, June Patricia *education specialist*
Freed, Sharon Lou *retired principal*

**Carmichael**
O'Leary, Marion Hugh *retired dean, chemist*

**Carpinteria**
Williams, Benjamin, IV, *headmaster, history educator*

**Carson**
Brassell, Danny *education educator*
Fisher, Farah Lee *education educator*
Mori, Allen Anthony *academic administrator, consultant*
Stuart, Nancy Giovinazzo *secondary school educator*

**Cathedral City**
Sexton, Douglas Robert *education educator*

**Ceres**
Carrico, Kimberly Anne *elementary school educator*
Wedlake, Philip Russell, Jr. *school system administrator*

**Cerritos**
Rosenberg, Steve *secondary school educator*

**Chico**
Bernhardt, Victoria L. *director, researcher*
Esteban, Manuel Antonio *academic administrator, language educator*
Hyde, Geraldine Veola *retired secondary school educator*
Zingg, Paul Joseph *academic administrator*

**Chino**
Lopez, Sonja *education educator*

**Chino Hills**
Kim, Kenny H. *secondary school educator*

**Claremont**
Alexander, John David, Jr. *college administrator*
Bekavac, Nancy Yavor *academic administrator, lawyer*
Gann, Pamela Brooks *academic administrator*
Kates, Gary *academic administrator*
Klawe, Maria Margaret *academic administrator, engineering and computer science educator*
Liggett, Thomas Jackson *retired seminary president*
Maguire, John David *academic administrator, educator, writer*
Oxtoby, David William *academic administrator, chemistry professor*
Platt, Joseph Beaven *former college president*
Skandera Trombley, Laura Elise *academic administrator, literature educator*
Stanley, Peter William *former academic administrator*
Strauss, Jon Calvert *retired academic administrator*

**Clayton**
Bower, Fay Louise *academic administrator, nursing educator*

**Coachella**
Gonzales, Martha *school administrator*

**Corte Madera**
Dalpino, Ida Jane *retired secondary school educator*

**Costa Mesa**
Fones, Monty Garth *secondary school educator*

**Covina**
Baker, Elenora Frances *retired elementary school educator*

**Culver City**
Geiselman, LucyAnn *college president*

**Cupertino**
Lyon, Mary Lou *retired secondary school educator*

**Cypress**
Henrickson, Leslie Ann *educational consultant, researcher*
Turbow, David Joseph *education educator, musician*

**Danville**
Harks, Helene Louise *elementary school educator*

**Davis**
Biggart, Nicole Woolsey *dean*
Cannon, William Bernard *retired academic administrator*
Eastin, Delaine Andree *education educator*
Faller, Roland *education educator*
Hinshaw, Virginia *academic administrator*
Perschbacher, Rex Robert *dean, law educator*
Pritchard, William Roy *former university systems administrator*
Springer, Sally Pearl *university administrator*
Tanno, John W. *university librarian*
Vanderhoef, Larry Neil *academic administrator*

**Diamond Bar**
Domeño, Eugene Timothy *elementary education educator, principal*

**Downey**
Brooks, Lillian Drilling Ashton (Lillian Hazel Church) *adult education educator*
Robles, Darline P. *school system administrator*
Takagi, Carol *educational consultant*

**Dublin**
King, Suzanne Dampier *chemistry educator*

**El Cajon**
Anthony, Roy Sanford, Jr. *secondary school educator*
Ostermeyer, Maryann *secondary school educator, writer*
Thomas, Esther Merlene *elementary and adult education educator*

**El Dorado Hills**
Tierney, Kevin Allen *elementary school educator*

**Elk Grove**
Moe, Janet Anne *elementary school educator, church organist*

**Encino**
Church, Kathy Lynn *education educator, consultant*

**Escondido**
Moore, Marc Anthony *retired academic administrator, writer, retired military officer*
Sanders, Adrian Lionel *retired educational consultant*
Walker, Patricia Ann *special education educator*

**Fair Oaks**
Hutton, Essex Clark, Sr. *adult education educator*
Lemke, Herman Ernest Frederick, Jr. *retired elementary school educator, consultant*

**Fairfield**
Herring, Lynne D. *secondary school educator*

**Folsom**
Sarraf, Shirley A. *secondary school educator*

**Fountain Valley**
Otto, Marie (Bertha Otto) *educational administrator, educational consulting company executive*

**Fremont**
Berman Salot, Jeannette Goldberg *retired elementary school educator*
Venturini, Judith Anne *education educator*

**Fresno**
Cornish, Bonita Clark *retired secondary school educator*
Genini, Ronald Walter *retired history educator, historian*
Misakian, Jo Ellen Priest *school librarian, dean*
Ortiz, John Michael *provost*
Rojeski, Hallie E. *elementary school educator*
Tudman, Cathi Graves *elementary school educator*
Welty, John Donald *academic administrator*

**Fullerton**
Donoghue, Mildred Ransdorf *education educator*
Fischer, Robert Blanchard *academic administrator, researcher*
Smith, Ephraim Philip *academic administrator*

**Garden Grove**
Lichty, Jolene Jennings *elementary school educator*
Schwalm, Laura *school system administrator*

**Gardena**
Harvey, Cyril Leslie *education educator*
Hite, Janet Sue *elementary school educator*
Hume-Dawson, Rodney Babatune *education educator*

**Glendale**
Blackwell, Linda Jane *elementary school educator*
Hong, Christian Sang *history educator*
Whalen, Lucille *retired academic administrator*

**Glendora**
Schiele, Paul Ellsworth, Jr. *retired academic administrator, writer*

**Goleta**
Everhart, Thomas Eugene *retired academic administrator, engineering educator*
Gilbert, Richard Keith *education educator, researcher*

**Granada Hills**
Pulido-Ragus, Elisa S. *secondary school educator, department chairman*

**Hanford**
Hazen, William A. *secondary school educator*

**Harbor City**
Dingman, Linda Susan *special education educator*

**Hawthorne**
Brann, Donald Lewis, Jr. *school superintendent*

**Hayward**
Guo, Jiansheng *language and psychology educator*
Rees, Norma S. *academic administrator*

**Hermosa Beach**
Zartman, Patrick Joseph *secondary school educator*

**Hesperia**
Du Lac, Lois Arline *retired secondary school educator, writer*

**Huntington Beach**
Agadjanyan, Michael Grant *education educator*
Davidson-Shepard, Gay *secondary school educator*
Ramphal, Julie Frances *retired secondary school educator*
Yglesias, Kenneth Dale *college president*

**Indio**
Houghton, Robert Charles *secondary school educator*
Lawson, Charles Derrick *principal, educator*

**Inglewood**
Cato, Gloria Maxine *retired secondary school educator*

**Irvine**
Bryant, Susan V. *academic administrator*
Castellanos, Jeanett *education educator*
Drake, Michael V. *academic administrator, ophthalmologist, educator*
Fleischer, Everly Borah *academic administrator, department chairman*
Jorion, Philippe *education educator*
McCubbin, Sharon A. *elementary school educator*
Munoff, Gerald J. *university librarian*
Policano, Andrew J. *dean, finance educator*
Rothman, Barbara I. *elementary school educator*
Schaefer, Ronald Dean *secondary school educator*
Walton, Lars Timothy *director, consultant*

**Kentfield**
Jones, David Alonzo *education educator, choreographer*

**La Canada Flintridge**
Lamson, Robert Woodrow *retired school system administrator*

**La Jolla**
Atkinson, Richard Chatham *academic administrator, cognitive scientist*
Cavenee, Webster K. *director*
Chandler, Marsha *academic administrator, educator*
Foxe, Marye Anne *academic administrator*
Henig, Suzanne *retired academic administrator, editor, writer*
Holmes, Edward Warren *dean, medical educator*
Khan, Imran *education educator*
Mah, Silvia Armitano *director, educator*
Miller, David R. *academic administrator*
Penner, Stanford Sol *director*
Savoia, Maria Christina *vice dean*
Schottlaender, Brian E.C. *university librarian*
Sullivan, Robert S. *college dean*

**La Mesa**
Browne, Juanita Maria *academic administrator, social sciences educator*
Charleton, Margaret Ann *child care administrator, consultant*
Kinzel, David L. *elementary school educator*

**La Verne**
Fleck, Raymond Anthony, Jr. *retired academic administrator*
Morgan, Stephen Charles *academic administrator*

**Lake Elsinore**
Druskoff, Barbara Therese *elementary school educator*

**Lakewood**
Baptista, Arnaldo D. *secondary school educator*

**Live Oak**
Spilman, Janet Lynne *special education educator*

**Livermore**
Fong, Nelson S. *secondary school educator*

**Lodi**
Bishop-Graham, Barbara *secondary school educator, journalist*
Reinold, Christy Diane *school counselor, consultant*
Siler, Virginia Carlisle *retired elementary school educator*

**Loma Linda**
Goodacre, Charles J. *dean, academic administrator*
Kyle, James Lewis *dean, physician*

**Long Beach**
Alexander, F. King *academic administrator*
Burnett, Ella M. Glenn *education educator*
Collins, Aristide J., Jr. *academic administrator*
Duran, Matias Martin *retired adult education educator*
Fleming, Jane Williams *retired elementary school educator, writer*
Gahungu, Prosper *mathematics educator*
Lathrop, Irvin Tunis *retired dean*
Lauda, Donald Paul *dean*
Reed, Charles Bass *chief academic administrator*
Reichard, Gary Warren *academic administrator, historian, educator*
Rutherford, Vicky Lynn *special education educator*
Singhal, Meena *education educator*
Springer, Wilma Marie *retired elementary school educator*
Withers, Aldina *educational consultant*
Vollmer, Richard Dietrich *statistics and operations research educator*

**Los Angeles**
Abrams, Norman *academic administrator, law educator*
Alkin, Marvin C. *education educator*
Armstrong, Lloyd, Jr. *academic administrator, physics professor*
Bernstein, Leslie *academic administrator, biostatistician, epidemiologist*
Bice, Scott Haas *dean, law educator*
Carnesale, Albert *former academic administrator*
Chapman Collins, Janice *school system administrator*
Cheeseboro, Margrit *retired economics educator*
Cortines, Ramon C. *former school superintendent*
Cowan, Marie Jeanette *dean, nurse, medical educator*
Dewey, Donald Odell *dean, academic administrator*
Diehl, Kristin *education educator*
Ellenberg, Marcia Stamler *retired elementary school educator*
Erdos, Joanna E. *school counselor, secondary school educator*
Fitz-Carter, Aleane *retired elementary school educator, composer*
Geller, Debra F. *academic administrator, educator*
Gilligan, Thomas W. *dean, finance educator*
Gothold, Stuart Eugene *school system administrator, education educator*
Gupta, Yash *dean*
Haight, G. Timothy *academic administrator, consultant*
Haley, Roslyn Trezevant *educational program director*
Harvey, James Gerald *educational consultant, researcher*
Henderson, Brian Edmond *dean, physician, educator*
Hill, Millicent E. *English educator*
Hoi, Samuel Chuen-Tsung *academic administrator*
Hubbard, John Randolph *retired academic administrator, department chairman, diplomat*
Jin, Yan *adult education educator*
Kleingartner, Archie *dean, educator, academic administrator*
Levey, Gerald Saul *dean, internist, educator*
Lieber, David Lee *university president*
Lynch, Beverly Pfeifer *education and information studies educator*
Malone, Carolyn Lucia Marino *education educator*
Mandel, Joseph David *academic administrator, lawyer*
Martin, Shane Patrick *education educator, consultant*
Martinez, Maritza Araceli *elementary school educator*
McGregor, Judith Ann *education educator*
Morin, JoyAnn Hauge *education educator*
Moriuchi, K. Derek *secondary school educator*
Nakanishi, Don Toshiaki *Asian American studies educator, writer*
Needleman, Jack *education educator, researcher*
Oakes, Jeannine *education educator*
Ordonez, Fernando Ivan *adult education educator*
Park, No-Hee *dean, academic administrator*
Petak, William John *systems management educator*
Pierskalla, William Peter *dean, finance educator, engineering educator*

Prager, Susan Westerberg *academic administrator, law educator*
Reagins-Lilly, Soncia Rae *dean*
Rosenstock, Linda *dean, medical educator*
Rosser, James Milton *academic administrator*
Sample, Steven Browning *academic administrator*
Schill, Michael H. *dean, law educator*
Schuetze-Coburn, Marje *university librarian*
Shideler, Ross Patrick *literature and language educator, writer, translator, poet*
Slavkin, Harold Charles *dean, biologist*
Taylor, Leigh Herbert *dean*
Torres-Gil, Fernando M. *academic administrator*
Tribble, Denise Hall *registrar*
Vredevoe, Donna Lou *academic administrator, microbiologist, educator, biomedical researcher*
Wagner, Ruth Joos *elementary school educator*
Wagner, William Gerard *dean, information scientist, consultant, physicist, investment manager*
Waterman, Christopher *dean*
Wesel, Richard D. *education educator, researcher*
Wexler, Robert *academic administrator*
Wilkerson, LuAnn *dean, medical educator*
Willison, Bruce Gray *dean*
Zexter, Eleanor M. *secondary school educator*

**Los Banos**
Flores-Ramirez, Jessica *resource educator*

**Los Gatos**
Rachlin, Jeanne-Marie *mathematics educator*

**Malibu**
Benton, Andrew Keith *academic administrator, lawyer*
Davenport, David *academic administrator, lawyer, educator*
Phillips, Ronald Frank *academic administrator*
Raine, Melinda L. *school librarian*
Starr, Kenneth Winston *dean, lawyer*
Warder, Michael Young *academic administrator*

**Marina Del Rey**
Swartout, William R. *education educator, director*

**Menifee**
Balow, Irving Henry *retired education educator*

**Menlo Park**
Zercher, Craig Allen *special education educator, researcher*

**Merced**
Tomlinson-Keasey, Carol Ann *academic administrator*

**Milpitas**
Ogawa, Joichi Raphael *director, consultant*

**Modesto**
Price, Robert William *school superintendent, consultant*

**Montebello**
Lopez, Donald Robert *parochial school educator, writer*

**Moreno Valley**
Marshall, Debra Lynn *secondary school educator*
Moulthrop, Rebecca Lee Stilphen *retired elementary school educator*

**Morgan Hill**
Horning, Barbara Hortense Scheer *retired elementary school educator*

**Murrieta**
deVries-White, Donna Lynn *education educator, consultant*

**Napa**
Schmidt, Hollie *secondary school educator*

**National City**
Quigley, Deborah Hewitt *adult education educator*

**Needles**
Thomas, Michael J. *secondary school educator*

**Norco**
Hamilton Boone, Jeanmarie *director*
Tuttle, Timothy Joseph *secondary school educator*

**North Hills**
Deets, Richard M. *secondary school educator, consultant*

**North Hollywood**
Chang, Wung *academic administrator, investment advisor, educator*

**Northridge**
Ackermann, Sue Ann *mathematics educator*
Curzon, Susan Carol *academic administrator*
Koester, Jolene *academic administrator*
Mitchell, James Andrew *education educator*

**Norwalk**
Duffee, Beverly Ann *secondary school educator*

**Novato**
Jaeger, Patsy Elaine *retired secondary school educator, artist*
Patterson, W. Morgan *college president*

**Oakland**
Diaz, Sharon *education administrator*
Dibble, David Van Vlack *visually impaired educator, lawyer*
Dynes, Robert C. *academic administrator, physicist*
Gomes, Wayne Reginald *academic administrator*
Griffin, Betty Jo *elementary school educator*
Holmgren, Janet L. *college president*
Isaac Nash, Eva Mae *secondary school educator*
Krause, Marcella Elizabeth Mason (Mrs. Eugene Fitch Krause) *retired secondary school educator*
Stewart, John Lincoln *university administrator*

**Oceanside**
Johnson, Karen Elaine *secondary school educator, tax preparer*
Wright, Darcy Laureen *leadership educator, writer*

**Ojai**
Mulligan, Michael K. *headmaster*
Shagam, Marvin Hückel-Berri *private school educator*

**Olivehurst**
Green, Tim M. *mathematics educator*

**Ontario**
McGehee, Sharon *school system administrator*

**Orange**
Cooper, Steven Harold *education educator*
Hamilton, Harry Lemuel, Jr. *academic administrator, science educator*
Kraft, Arthur *dean*

**Orinda**
Counelis, James Steve *education educator*

**Orland**
Wainio, Marsha Dianne *school system administrator*

**Oxnard**
Decker, Robert Charles Morgan *literature and language educator*

**Pacific Grove**
Longman, Anne Strickland *special education educator, consultant*

**Pacific Palisades**
Outcalt, David Lewis *academic administrator, mathematics professor, consultant, musician*

**Palm Desert**
Baxter, Betty Carpenter *academic administrator*
Bratrud, Linda Kay *secondary school educator*
Owings, Thalia Kelley *elementary school educator*

**Palm Springs**
Hartman, Rosemary Jane *retired special education educator*

**Palo Alto**
Bohrnstedt, George William *educational researcher*
Chace, William Murdough *former university administrator, literature educator*
Dugger, Marguerite J. *retired special education educator*
Heneveld-Story, Christy Jean *educational researcher*

**Palos Verdes Estates**
Lazzaro, Anthony Derek *academic administrator*

**Paradise**
Barr, Donald Roy *statistics and operations research educator, statistician*

**Paramount**
Williams, Vivian Lewie *retired counseling administrator*

**Pasadena**
Arnold, Frances Hamilton *chemistry educator*
Baltimore, David *former academic administrator, microbiologist, educator*
Chameau, Jean-Lou *academic administrator*
Douglas, Kimberly *university librarian*
Gilman, Richard Carleton *retired college president*
Koshalek, Richard *academic administrator, former museum director, consultant*
Lingenfelter, Sherwood Galen *academic administrator, retired anthropologist*
Siemon-Burgeson, Marilyn M. *education administrator*
Stolper, Edward Manin *secondary school educator*

**Penn Valley**
Longan, Suzanne M. *retired elementary school educator*

**Petaluma**
DeLaurenti McClure, Tracy *elementary school educator*
O'Hare, Sandra Fernandez *education educator*
Thomas, Nancy Hinckley *special education educator*

**Placerville**
Wessels-McCoy, Denise Wendy *pre-school administrator, consultant*

**Pleasant Hill**
Bastrenta, Brigitte Elisabeth *school administrator*
Nelson, Bette Sturr *secondary school educator*

**Pleasanton**
Roshong, Dee Ann Daniels *dean, educator*

**Pomona**
Ambrose, William Wright, Jr. *dean, educator, academic administrator*
Dishman, Rose Marie Rice *academic administrator, researcher*
Stallones, Jared Reuel *education educator*
Trotter, F(rederick) Thomas *retired academic administrator*

**Porterville**
Hayes, Shirley Ann *special education educator*
Miller, Gary Lee *secondary school educator*

**Poway**
Conant, Kim Untiedt *retired elementary school educator*

**Quartz Hill**
Nettelhorst, Robin Paul *academic administrator, writer*

**Ramona**
Van Zant, Susan Lucille *principal*

**Rancho Cucamonga**
Buckley, Lawrence G. *dean*

**Rancho Palos Verdes**
McFadden, Thomas *academic administrator*

**Red Bluff**
Kennedy, James William, Jr., (Sarge Kennedy) *special education administrator, consultant*

**Redlands**
Salmon, Catherine Anne *education educator*
Simnjanovski, Riste *counseling administrator*
Wilson, Lois Fair *retired school system administrator*

**Rialto**
Gilbert, Joanne Toone *director, educator*

**Richmond**
Paré, Jocelyn Marie *elementary school educator, consultant*

**Ridgecrest**
Finholm, Scott Robert *secondary school educator*

**Riverside**
Boldt, William Gregory *academic administrator, consultant*
Chen, Wilfred *education educator*
Córdova, France Anne-Dominic *academic administrator, astrophysicist*
Day, Renee Noelle *secondary school educator, special education educator*
Fontana, Sandra Ellen Frankel *special education educator*
Geraty, Lawrence Thomas *academic administrator, archaeologist, educator*
Prosser, Michael Joseph *college librarian*
Rainey, Susan J. *school system administrator*
Suyenaga, Elsie Sakae *retired elementary school educator*
Yacoub, Ignatius I. *dean*

**Rohnert Park**
Arminana, Ruben *academic administrator, educator*
Babula, William *dean, writer*
Nowak, Linda Ilene *education educator*

**Sacramento**
Amezcua, Esther Hernandez *elementary school educator*
Barankin, Joseph Paul *director, consultant*
Bass de Martinez, Bernice *academic administrator, consultant*
Block, Alvin Gilbert *academic administrator*
Clover, Haworth Alfred *elementary school educator, historian*
Drummond, Marshall Edward (Mark Drummon) *academic administrator*
Gerth, Donald Rogers *retired university president, educator*
Gosfield, Margaret *secondary school educator, school system administrator, consultant, editor*
Heym, Roger H. *literature and language educator*
Jelinek, David *education educator, writer*
Lam, Siuwa Monica *education educator, consultant*
O'Connell, Jack *school system administrator*
Opperman, Rosanna Resendez *vice principal*
Parker, Elizabeth Rindskopf *dean, law educator*
Sanborn, Kathy *career planning administrator, consultant*
Silva, Joseph, Jr. *dean, medical educator*
Zaidi, Emily Louise *retired elementary school educator*

**Salinas**
Bernhard, Nancy Lynn *secondary school educator*

**San Anselmo**
Crawley, Cheryl K. *school system administrator*

**San Bernardino**
Aylmer, Francoise *academic administrator*

**San Diego**
Blas, Marlene Jambaro *academic administrator, educator*
Early, Teri Wilson (Denise Wilson) *elementary school educator, educator*
Idos, Margarita de Leon *elementary school educator*
Jellison, Beverly Irene *literature and language educator*
Lyons, Mary E. *academic administrator*
Mayer, George Roy *education educator*
Meno, Lionel R. *academic administrator*
Rodenberg, Johanna Kristine *education educator, consultant*
Rodriguez, Daniel B. *dean, law educator*
Schwartz, Alfred *former dean*
Thorud, Jeffrey Scott *director, lawyer*
Walker, Donald Ezzell *retired academic administrator*
Weber, Stephen Lewis *academic administrator*

**San Francisco**
Abbott, Richard Lee *academic administrator*
Ackerman, Arlene *school system administrator*
Addiego, Russell Francis *middle school educator*
Bertolami, Charles Nicholas *dean, dental educator, oral surgeon*
Brand, Jeffrey S. *dean, law educator*
Bratton, Christopher Alan *academic administrator, videographer, art educator*
Clifford, Geraldine Joncich (Mrs. William F. Clifford) *retired education educator*
Corrigan, Robert Anthony *academic administrator*
Davis, Patricia Margaret Alice *psychology educator, religion educator*
Dracup, Kathleen Anne *dean, nursing educator*
Dugoni, Arthur A. *dean, orthodontics educator*
Fleishhacker, David *school administrator*
Holland, April Anne *elementary school educator*

**Kane**, Mary Kay *academic administrator, law educator*
Kessler, David Aaron *dean, medical educator*
Kozloff, Lloyd M. *dean, microbiologist, educator*
LaBelle, Thomas Jeffrey *research executive, academic administrator*
Lane, Mary B. *education educator, writer*
Murdoch, Colin *academic administrator*
Newton, Nell Jessup *dean, law educator*
Oberman, Ida *research and evaluation director, consultant*
Peterson, Linda Lou *special education educator*
Privett, Stephen A. *academic administrator, priest*
Roth, Michael S. *academic administrator, art educator*
Sakamoto, Katsuyuki *retired academic administrator, psychologist, educator*
Stauffer, Thomas Michael *former university president*
Stephens, Elisa *college president*
Vercruysse, Raymond James *director*
Warner, Rollin Miles, Jr. *economics educator, real estate broker*

**San Jacinto**
Hert, Theresa M. *mathematics educator*

**San Jose**
Arvizu, Charlene Sutter *elementary school educator*
Boac, Thelma Blantucas *principal*
Fleck, Andrew J *education educator*
Haycock, Kenneth Roy *academic administrator, educator, academic administrator, consultant*
Holyer, Erna Maria *adult education educator, writer, artist*
Lobig, Janie Howell *special education educator*
Okerlund, Arlene Naylor *academic administrator, writer*
Taylor, Richard Cordia *mathematics educator*
Wesson, Kenneth Alan *educational consultant*
Yu, Paul *academic administrator*

**San Juan Capistrano**
Larwood, Susan Elizabeth *elementary school educator*

**San Leandro**
Dolgin, Stephen Mark *secondary school educator, retired social worker*

**San Luis Obispo**
Aiello, Michael Benjamin *secondary school educator*
Baker, Warren J(oseph) *university president*
Ericson, Jon Meyer *academic administrator, language educator*
Gardebring, Sandra S. *academic administrator*
Haile, Allen Cleveland *academic administrator*

**San Marcos**
Lilly, Martin Stephen *retired university dean*

**San Marino**
Footman, Gordon Elliott *educational administrator*

**San Pedro**
Gaines, Jerry Lee *retired secondary school educator*

**San Rafael**
Adcock, Muriel W. *special education educator*
Fink, Joseph Richard *academic administrator*
Thomas, Mary Ann McCrary *counselor, school system administrator*

**Santa Ana**
Lawson, Barbara Slade *elementary school educator, artist*
Moore, David Gene *academic administrator*

**Santa Barbara**
Auston, David Henry *former academic administrator, electrical engineer, educator*
Boyan, Norman J. *retired education educator*
Castro, Joseph Isaac *academic administrator, educator*
Cirone, William Joseph *educational administrator*
Lucas, Gene *academic administrator*
Murdoch, Helen Claire *secondary school educator*
Norris, Virginia Oakley *secondary school educator*
O'Dowd, Donald Davy *retired university president*
Sinsheimer, Robert Louis *retired academic administrator, educator*
Yang, Henry T.Y. *chancellor, educator*

**Santa Clara**
Atkinson, Darren C. *education educator*
Haskell, Timothy O. *academic administrator*
Ling, Nam *dean*
Locatelli, Paul Leo *academic administrator*
Moberg, Dennis *director*
Polden, Donald *dean, law educator*
Rozman, James D. *school system administrator, minister*

**Santa Clarita**
Lavine, Steven David *academic administrator*

**Santa Cruz**
Blumenthal, George *academic administrator, astronomy and astrophysics professor*
Delaney, Margaret L. *academic administrator*
Garcia-Luna-Aceves, J.J. *education educator*
Rothwell, Wendy *biology educator*

**Santa Maria**
Armstrong, James D. *school system administrator, musician*

**Santa Monica**
Henderson, Rosemary C. *elementary school educator*
Sohaili, Monira *retired special education educator*
Soloff, Laura J. *academic administrator*

**Santa Rosa**
Webb, Charles Richard *retired university president*

## Saratoga

Barna, Lillian Carattini *school system administrator*
Houston, Elizabeth Reece Manasco *correctional education consultant*

## Seal Beach

Pipes, Doris Perry *secondary school educator, consultant*

## Seaside

Anderson, David Louis *academic administrator, history professor*
Paget, Ruth Pennington *academic administrator, educator, writer*

## Signal Hill

Vandament, William Eugene *retired academic administrator*

## Silverado

Mamer, James Michael *secondary school educator*

## Solana Beach

Beck-von-Peccoz, Michele *retired secondary school educator, writer*

## South Pasadena

Fuller, Kathy J. *special education educator, consultant, researcher*

## Stanford

Anderson, Theodore Wilbur *statistics educator*
Barron, Brigid *education educator*
Boaler, Jo *education educator*
Cuban, Larry *education educator, researcher*
Eisner, Elliot W. *education educator*
Etchemendy, John *academic administrator, educator*
Evers, Williamson Moore *education policy analyst, political scientist*
Hennessy, John L. *academic administrator*
Henriksen, Thomas Hollinger *academic administrator*
Hilton, Ronald *international relations educator*
Joss, Robert L. *dean*
Kamil, Michael *education educator*
Kays, William Morrow *academic administrator, mechanical engineer*
Kramer, Larry *dean, law educator, lawyer*
Laughlin, Robert B. *academic administrator, physics professor*
Loeb, Susanna *education educator*
Long, Sharon Rugel *dean, molecular biologist, educator*
Lotan, Rachel *education educator*
Palm, Charles Gilman *academic administrator*
Pea, Roy *education educator*
Perry, William James *education educator, former secretary of defense*
Raisian, John *academic administrator, economist*
Riggs, Henry Earle *academic administrator, engineering educator*
Shavelson, Richard *education educator*
Spence, Andrew Michael (A. Michael Spence) *former dean, finance educator*
Stipek, Deborah Jane *dean, education educator*
Stone, William Edward *academic administrator, consultant*
Strober, Myra Hoffenberg *education educator, consultant*
Veinott, Arthur Fales, Jr. *university educator*
Whitney, Rodger Franklin *academic administrator*
Wotipka, Christine Min *education educator*

## Stanton

Zabel-Durham, Martha L. *retired secondary school educator*

## Stockton

Cobb, Judy Lynn *elementary school educator*
DeRicco, Lawrence Albert *retired college president*
Derosa, Donald V. *academic administrator*
Fish, Tom *special education educator, vocational school educator*
Gilbertson, Philip *academic administrator*
Haines, Joybelle *retired elementary school educator*
Kareem, A'isha *educational consultant, counselor*
Ren, Jianhua *education educator*
Sorby, Donald Lloyd *dean*

## Sun Valley

Mayhue, Richard Lee *dean, minister, writer*

## Sunnyvale

Schwartz, Eleanore Anita *retired elementary school educator, small business owner*

## Tehachapi

Sprinkle, Martha Clare *elementary school educator*

## Temecula

Cherrington, Pamela Jo *special education educator*

## Thousand Oaks

Sladek, John R., Jr. *academic administrator, neurobiology and anatomy educator*
Venable, Diane Dailey *retired elementary school educator*

## Torrance

Kuc, Joseph A. *research scientist*

## Trinidad

Conant, Ralph Wendell *retired academic administrator, writer, educator*

## Turlock

Burns, James W. *academic administrator, researcher, consultant*

## Twentynine Palms

Clemente, Patrocinio Ablola *secondary school educator*

## Union City

Lindsey, Tommie *secondary school educator*

---

Muñoz, Eduardo Rafael *elementary school educator*

## Upland

Hawks, Wesley Howard *retired director, music educator*
Kennedy, Mark Alan *secondary school educator*

## Vallejo

Wilson, Carrie Lee Stroud *principal*
Zingale, Donald Paul *academic administrator, educator*

## Valley Center

Arciniega, Tomas Abel *university president*

## Van Nuys

Wright, Judith Ann *elementary school educator*

## Venice

Beery-Polglase, Penelope (Pixie) *education educator*

## Victorville

Scott, Deborah Elizabeth *school system administrator, poet*
Toner, Stephen J. *education educator*

## Visalia

Garcia, William L. *academic administrator*

## Walnut Creek

Lilly, Luella Jean *retired academic administrator*

## Watsonville

Desimone, Richard Louis *principal*

## Weimar

Kerschner, Lee R(onald) *academic administrator, political scientist, educator*

## Westlake Village

Gleim, Frances Hollearn *elementary school educator*

## Whittier

Drake, E. Maylon *academic administrator*
Rahiman, Karla Molina *school counselor*
Rinard, Arthur Calvin *secondary school educator*

## Wilmington

Smith, Samantha Denice Akers *primary school educator*

## Woodland

Gray, Sue *elementary school educator*

## Woodland Hills

Valladares-Barbush, Lisette Marie *mathematics educator*
Zeitlin, Herbert Zakary *college administrator, real estate consultant, writer*

## Yorba Linda

Lunde, Dolores Benitez *retired secondary school educator*

# COLORADO

## Arvada

Bindel, Thomas Herbert *chemistry educator*
Krohnfeldt, Gretchen Ann *secondary school educator, genealogist*

## Aurora

Sorenson, Katherine Ann *elementary school educator*
Tovani, C. Cristine *literature and language educator, writer*

## Bayfield

Horton, Frank Elba *academic administrator, geographer, educator*

## Boulder

Anderson, Ronald Delaine *education educator*
Borko, Hilda *education educator*
Brown, Hank *academic administrator, former senator*
DiStefano, Philip *academic administrator*
Hawkins, Brian Lee *academic administrator, educator*
Landesman, Howard M. *retired academic administrator*
Peterson, G. P. (Bud Peterson) *academic administrator*
Roberts, Pamela Ranger *secondary school educator*
Williams, James Franklin, II, *dean, librarian*
Wilson, M. Roy *academic administrator, medical educator*
Wolzien, Charles Frederick *dean, music educator, musician*

## Brighton

Bacon, Melvin Leon *secondary school educator*

## Calhan

Henderson, Freda LaVerne *elementary school educator*

## Centennial

Galaznik, Judith Ann *elementary school educator*

## Colorado Springs

Adams, Bernard Schroder *retired college president*
Bartalo, Theresa Marie *elementary school educator*
Burdo, Amy *elementary school educator*
Celeste, Richard F. *academic administrator, retired ambassador, retired governor*
Fielden, C. Franklin III *early childhood education consultant*
Hinkle, Betty Ruth *retired academic administrator*
Schulzki, Anton G. *history educator*
Shockley-Zalabak, Pamela Sue *academic administrator*

---

## Cortez

Skinner, Eulalia Ardith *retired secondary school educator*

## Denver

Albino, Judith Elaine Newsom *university president*
Bosworth, Bruce Leighton *school administrator, educator, consultant*
Burrows, Bertha Jean *retired academic administrator*
Byyny, Richard Lee *academic administrator*
Carbone, Rocco William III *elementary school educator*
Chu, Roderick Gong-Wah *academic administrator*
Coombe, Bob (Robert D. Coombe) *academic administrator*
Driggs, Margaret *private school educator*
Emmet, Thomas Addis, Jr. *college administrator, consultant*
Eriksson, Steven Bret *elementary school educator*
Fulkerson, William Measey, Jr. *college president*
Hegarty, George John *academic administrator, literature educator*
Jarles, Ruth Sewell *education educator*
Jordan, Stephen M. *academic administrator*
Kourlis, Rebecca Love *director, former state supreme court justice*
Kraus, Joseph Roland *school librarian*
Moloney, William J. *school system administrator*
Pointer, Marsha G. *principal*
Ritchie, Daniel Lee *former academic administrator*
Rubin, Cathy Ann *retired secondary school educator*
Sumner, Stephen C. *academic administrator*
Waterman, Ellen K. *director*

## Dove Creek

Buffington, Jimmy Glen *history educator*

## Durango

Barter, Mary F. *academic administrator*
Jones, Joel Mackey *academic administrator*
Ware, Charlotte Ethel *retired elementary school educator*
Webb, Troy Hooker *education educator*

## Eagle

Lammers, Monica *elementary school educator*

## Elizabeth

Travis, Mitchell G. *secondary school educator*

## Englewood

Corson, Jeff Gordon *history educator*
Kubik, Timothy Robert White *director, history educator*
Macdonald, Patricia Lynn *gifted and talented educator*
Shields, Marlene Sue *elementary school educator*

## Erie

Nichols, Janet Hildreth *elementary school educator, childbirth and parenting educator*

## Estes Park

Calden, Diane Dorothy *reading educator*

## Fort Collins

Baldwin, Lionel Vernon *retired university president*
Colbert, Debora A. *director*
Harper, Judson Morse *retired university administrator, consultant, educator*
Maher, Thomas George *academic administrator, producer, media educator*
Penley, Larry Edward *academic administrator, finance educator*
Ricard, Virginia Belle *adult education educator*

## Golden

Bickart, Theodore Albert *university president emeritus*
Shea, Dion Warren Joseph *academic administrator, fundraiser*
Truly, Richard H. *academic administrator, retired pilot, retired federal agency administrator*

## Grand Junction

Armstrong, Alden Arthur *retired elementary school educator, photographer, writer*
Scott, Pamela Sue *middle school educator*

## Greeley

Duff, William Leroy, Jr. *retired dean, finance educator*
Jackson, Patricia Anne *primary school educator, consultant*

## Greenwood Village

Lesh-Laurie, Georgia Elizabeth *academic administrator, biology professor, medical researcher*

## Gunnison

Javernick, Amy Sue *special education educator*

## Joes

Crawford, Dorothy Hill *retired secondary school educator*

## Johnstown

French, Irene Wagdy *special education educator*

## La Veta

Emsden, Katharine Nicely *retired history educator, writer*

## Lakewood

Joy, Carla Marie *history educator*
McBride, Guy Thornton, Jr. *college president emeritus*
Nelson, Deborah Jane *family and consumer science educator*
Reed, Joan-Marie *special education educator*
Stromberg, Patricia Roberts *retired school librarian*

## Lamar

Banker, Carol Anne *elementary school educator*

---

## Littleton

Bush, Stanley Giltner *secondary school educator*
Greenberg, Elinor Miller *director, consultant*
Grounds, Vernon Carl *seminary administrator*
Tucker, James Raymond *primary school educator*

## Louisville

Stahler, Joyce Ann *history educator*

## Mancos

Whitehead, Linda Sue *English, American history, and special education educator*

## Nederland

Lutz, Frank Wenzel *education administration educator*
Morrison, K. Jaydene *education counseling firm executive*

## Norwood

Brantingham, Andrya J. *special education educator*

## Ordway

Fosdick, Jacque Janelle *literature and language educator, theater educator*

## Pueblo

Mara, Patrick Scott *mathematics educator*
Ramirez, Monica E. *education educator, consultant*
Sisson, Ray L. *retired dean, author*
Werner, Betty Ann *academic administrator*

## Snowmass Village

DiBiaggio, John A. *university president*

## Towner

Fees, Ruth Anna *secondary school educator*

## U S A F Academy

Born, Dana H. *dean, career military officer*
Regni, John F. *academic administrator, career military officer*

## Walden

Ary, Bonnita Ellen *registrar, federal official*

## Walsh

Lancaster, Robert Carl *secondary school educator*

## Westminster

Eaves, Stephen Douglas *high school and vocational administrator, educator, consultant*

## Windsor

Schumacher, Tara *biology educator*

# CONNECTICUT

## Avon

Behrend, Donald Fraser *academic administrator, educator*

## Beacon Falls

Feige, Mary S *literature and language educator*

## Bloomfield

Baccus, R. Eileen Turner *retired academic administrator*
Young, Albert Frederick Antonio *director*

## Branford

Johnson, Eva Jo *educational consultant*

## Bridgeport

Lanci, Janet Mead *academic administrator, educator*

## Bristol

LaGanga, Donna Brandeis *dean*
Mielcarz, Sharon Marie *assistant principal*

## Canterbury

Yaworski, James John III *elementary school educator*

## Colchester

Latman, Joel *history educator*

## Danbury

Hawkes, Carol Ann *academic administrator*

## Enfield

Doty, Victoria Skower *elementary school educator*

## Fairfield

Howell, Karen Jane *private school educator*
Miles, Leland Weber *retired academic administrator*
Paolini, Claire Jacqueline *dean, educator*

## Falls Village

Purcell, Mary Louise Gerlinger *retired adult education educator*

## Farmington

Deckers, Peter John *dean*
Ford, Burch Tracy *headmaster*
Melekote, Swathanthra Kumar *education educator*
Robinson, Peter J. *dean, periodontal educator, pathologist*

## Groton

English, James Fairfield, Jr. *former college president*

## Guilford

Speth, James Gustave *dean, environmental studies educator, lawyer*

## Hamden

Brown, Jay Marshall *retired secondary school educator*
Hines, Haywoodene *elementary and middle school educator*
Robson, Carol Ann Shaffner *retired secondary school educator*

**Hartford**
Brown, W. Miller *faculty dean*
Cibes, William Joseph, Jr. *retired academic administrator*
Frost, James Arthur *former university president*
Jones, James Fleming, Jr. *academic administrator, language educator*
Reynolds, Scott Walton *academic administrator*
Sternberg, Betty J. *school system administrator*

**Killingworth**
Strain, Harriet Rice *retired secondary school educator*

**Lakeville**
Mattoon, Robert H., Jr., (Skip Mattoon) *headmaster*

**Manchester**
Campbell, Katherine Marie Langrehr *elementary and secondary education educator*
Daube, Jonathan Mahram *academic administrator*
Fiano, Darcy Anne Fillmore *elementary school educator, consultant*

**Meriden**
Angeli, Robert Joseph *principal*

**Middletown**
Bennet, Douglas Joseph, Jr. *academic administrator*
Brown, Judith *academic administrator*

**Monroe**
Lipeles, Enid Sandra *chemistry educator*

**New Britain**
Boyea, Ruthe W. *retired education educator*
Miller, John Winston *academic administrator*

**New Haven**
Alpern, Robert J. *dean, medical educator*
Benson, Richard *dean, photographer*
Birnbaum, Irwin Morton *educational consultant, lawyer*
Degutis, Linda Christine *adult education educator, epidemiologist, researcher*
Greene, Liliane *literature and language educator, editor*
Hennah, Vivian Lisa *school system administrator*
Koh, Harold Hongju *dean, law educator*
Kronman, Anthony Townsend *dean, law educator*
Lamar, Howard Roberts *academic administrator, historian*
LaPalombara, Joseph *political science educator, industrial management educator*
Levin, Rick (Richard Charles Levin) *academic administrator, economist*
Lorimer, Linda Koch *university educator*
McNamara, Julia Mary *academic administrator, foreign language educator*
Norton, Cheryl J. *academic administrator*
Pagani, Mark *education educator, researcher*
Podolny, Joel M. *dean, management educator*
Schleifer, Alison Pedicord *educational consultant*
Seilacher, Adolf *special education educator*
Sommers, Alexis Nigel *academic administrator, engineering educator*

**New London**
Hammond, Ulysses Bernard *academic administrator*
Higdon, Leo Ignatius, Jr., (Lee Higdon) *academic administrator*

**North Branford**
Gasparine, Barbara Ellen *elementary school educator*

**North Haven**
Fuggi, Gretchen Miller *education educator*
Hudson, Richard L. *retired adult education educator, minister*

**North Stonington**
Keane, John Patrick *retired secondary school educator*

**Norwalk**
Johnson, Robert James *psychology educator*

**Plainfield**
Barfield, Kem *director, educator*

**Redding**
Macintyre, Malcolm Scott *retired secondary education educator*

**Ridgefield**
Brewster, Carroll Worcester *former academic administrator*
Lindsay, Dianna Marie *educational administrator*

**Southbury**
Rine, Maureen S. *elementary school educator*

**Southport**
Cappeto, Michael Arnold *university dean*

**Storrs**
Baxter, Donald Leon Murray *education educator*

**Storrs Mansfield**
Austin, Philip Edward *academic administrator*
Farr, William Joseph *secondary school educator*
Kerr, Kirklyn M. *academic administrator, veterinarian, pathologist*
MacDonald, John Thomas *school system administrator*
Nicholls, Peter J. *academic administrator*
Price, Glenda Delores *dean, college president*
Wang, Guiling *education educator, researcher*
Woods, David G. *dean*

**Taconic**
Medvecky, Patricia *retired elementary school educator*

**Terryville**
Doughty-Jenkins, Bonnie-Marie *middle school educator*

**Torrington**
Marshall, Kathleen Ann *elementary school educator*

**Trumbull**
Lang, James Richard *education consultant*
Nevins, Lyn (Carolyn A. Nevins) *school disciplinarian*

**Wallingford**
Shanahan, Edward J. *headmaster*

**Waterbury**
Brown, Lillian Hill *retired academic administrator*
Lang, Christine JoAnn *elementary school educator*
Mador, Jonathan Mark *director, education educator*
Martone, Eric Anthony Domenic *history educator*
Sanders, Richard L. *academic administrator*

**Watertown**
Watson, Michael Thomas *biology educator*

**West Hartford**
Coleman, Winifred Ellen *academic administrator*
Harrison, Walter Lee *university president*
Malone, Thomas Francis *academic administrator, meteorologist*
Markham, Claire Agnes (M. Clare Markham) *retired chemistry educator, consultant*
Tonkin, Humphrey Richard *academic administrator, educator*

**West Redding**
Rhodes, Stanley Williams *retired secondary school educator*

**Westport**
Freedman, Judith Greenberg *retired elementary school educator, state legislator*
Warner, Kerstin Julianna *gifted and talented educator*

**Willimantic**
Barbuto, Leah M. *early childhood and technology educator, consultant*
Carter, David George, Sr. *academic administrator*
Singh, Delar K. *education educator*
Wilson, Margaret Sullivan *retired executive dean, consultant*

**Wilton**
Grunewald, Donald *former college president, educator*
Reilly, Kathleen C. *director, retired secondary school educator*

**Windsor**
Weigel, Russell H. *headmaster*

**Windsor Locks**
Coelho, Sandra Signorelli *secondary school educator, consultant*

**Woodbridge**
Malloy, Ina Arlene *secondary school educator, photographer*

## DELAWARE

**Bear**
Stewart, Shirley Anne *elementary school educator*

**Dover**
Braverman, Ray Howard *secondary school educator*
Sessoms, Allen Lee *academic administrator, physicist, educator, retired diplomat*
Sorenson, Liane Beth McDowell *director, state legislator*

**Georgetown**
Orlando, John D. *elementary school educator*

**Hockessin**
Suwin, Nancy Churchman *educational consultant*

**Laurel**
Selby, Cora Norwood *retired elementary school educator*

**Middletown**
Roach, Daniel T., Jr., (Tad Roach) *headmaster*

**Milton**
Lindsay, Joyce W. *secondary school educator*

**New Castle**
Brownson, Kenneth C. *dean*
Guidry, A. Gail *secondary school educator*
Rolland, Kathy Ann *elementary school educator*
Sanderson, Devon Lee *elementary school educator*

**Newark**
Bailey, Daniel Carl *higher education administrator*
Dybowski, Cecil *chemistry educator*
Mitchell, Peter Kenneth *educational consultant*
Roselle, David Paul *academic administrator, mathematician, educator*

**Wilmington**
Fullerton, Ann Elizabeth *retired biology educator*
Higgins, Roxanne Snelling *educational consultant*

## DISTRICT OF COLUMBIA

**Washington**
Alatis, James Efstathios *university dean emeritus*
Aleinikoff, Thomas Alexander *dean, law educator*
Arnez, Nancy Levi *educational leadership educator*

Barrett, Richard David *university director, consultant, retired bank executive*
Boggs, George Robert *academic administrator*
Brzezinski, Zbigniew *political science educator, writer, former national security advisor*
Burgin, Walter Hotchkiss, Jr. *retired academic administrator*
Buser, Carolyn Elizabeth *adult education educator*
Carrier, Warren Pendleton *retired university chancellor, writer*
Churchill, John Hugh *college academic administrator*
Clewell, Beatriz Chu *director, researcher*
Convey, John J. *academic administrator*
Covington, Eileen Queen *secondary school educator*
Crane, Edward Harrison III *academic administrator, financial analyst*
Curris, Constantine William *university president*
Daly, George Garman *dean*
DeGioia, John J. *academic administrator*
DePaul, Christina *dean, artist*
Dixon, Michel L. *educational administrator*
Duffey, Joseph Daniel *academic administrator*
Dunn, Michael M. *academic administrator, career military officer*
Elliott, Emerson John *education consultant, policy analyst*
Feder, Judith *dean*
Fisher, Miles Mark, IV, *education educator, religious studies educator, minister*
Flaherty, Sister Mary Jean *dean*
Fox, William F. *dean, law educator*
French, Roderick Stuart *university chancellor*
Fusco, Aurilla Marie *director*
Garrison, Gwen E. *educational researcher, consultant*
Gibson, Cecelia Anne *registrar*
Goodman, Valerie Rene *secondary school educator*
Grossman, Claudio M. *dean, law educator*
Jarvis, Charlene Drew *academic administrator, former scientist*
Jaskot, Richard D. *academic administrator, career military officer*
Jones, Alice Samuels *elementary education educator, reading specialist*
Jones, Judith Miller *director*
Jordan, Irving King *university president*
Kamras, Jason *mathematics educator*
Keaney, Thomas Addis *academic administrator, management consultant, educator, military officer*
Keeley, Robert Vossler *retired academic administrator, ambassador*
Kerwin, Cornelius Martin *academic administrator, educator*
Kienzl, Gregory Stephen *education researcher*
Kim, Mikyong Minsun *education educator*
Kirk, Artemis G. *university librarian*
Lord, Jerome Edmund *education administrator, writer*
Luttwak, Edward Nicolae *academic administrator, policy and business consultant*
Malveaux, Floyd Joseph *dean*
Manley, Audrey Forbes *retired academic administrator, pediatrician, retired military officer*
McDowell-Craig, Vanessa Dennise *supervisor, consultant*
Milman, Natalie *education educator*
Mohrman, Kathryn j. *academic administrator*
Muller, Steven *international studies educator, academic administrator*
Nastal, David Thomas *secondary school educator*
Nwagbaraocha, Joel Onukwugha *academic administrator, educator*
O'Connell, David M. *academic administrator, priest*
O'Donovan, Leo Jeremiah *former academic administrator, priest, theologian*
Phillips, Susan Meredith *academic administrator, economist*
Ranck, Edna Runnels *academic administrator, researcher*
Reddel, Carl Walter *academic administrator*
Rouse, Leo E. *dean, dental educator*
Schmoke, Kurt L. *dean, former mayor*
Smith, Abbie Oliver *college administrator, educator*
Smith-Smith, Peola *principal, not-for-profit executive*
Stewart, Debra Wehrle *academic administrator*
Swygert, Haywood Patrick *academic administrator*
Thomas-Razza, Constance *retired elementary school educator*
Trachtenberg, Stephen Joel *academic administrator*
Trangsrud, Roger H. *dean, law educator*
Tucker, Marc Stephen *education policy analyst, author*
Van Ummersen, Claire A(nn) *academic administrator, biologist, educator*
Vargas-Baron, Emily *educational development specialist*
Ward, David *academic administrator, educator*
Weiss, Charles, Jr. *educator*
Wheeler, Stephen Anthony *biology educator*
Williams, Ella Marilyn *mathematics educator*
Wise, Lorraine E. *educational consultant*

## FLORIDA

**Babson Park**
Reeb, W. Suzanne *retired elementary and middle school educator and nurse*

**Bartow**
Logan, Heidi Christine *elementary school educator*

**Boca Raton**
Arden, Eugene *retired university provost*
Boykin, Anne Jane *dean*
Brogan, Frank T. *academic administrator, former lieutenant governor*
Connor, Frances Partridge *retired education educator*
Hunter, Barry C. *secondary school educator*

Miller, Eugene *academic administrator, finance educator*
Ross, Kevin McAndrew *academic administrator*
Russ, Fenee L. *principal, consultant*
Tennies, Robert Hunter *headmaster*
Warshaw, Carole Klein *education educator, consultant*

**Bokeelia**
Judd, Jacqueline Vogel *retired middle school educator*

**Bonita Springs**
Becker, Richard Charles *retired college president*
Johnson, Franklyn Arthur *academic administrator*
McManigal, Shirley Ann *retired dean*

**Bradenton**
Moore, John Hampton *academic administrator*
Pillot, Gene Merrill *retired school system administrator*
Wolf, John Michael *adult education seminar consultant*

**Cape Coral**
Graham, Dorothy E. *elementary school educator*

**Clearwater**
Coraggio, James Thomas *educational measurement consultant, researcher*

**Cocoa**
Gamble, Thomas Ellsworth *academic administrator*

**Coconut Creek**
Brenner, Egon *academic administrator, education consultant*

**Cooper City**
Garrard, Patricia Renick *elementary school educator*

**Coral Gables**
Mangravite, Ronald *education educator, writer*
Prilleltensky, Isaac *dean*
Shalala, Donna Edna *academic administrator, former secretary of health and human services*
Wiles, David Ernest *academic administrator*

**Dania**
Fernander, Karen Geneine *secondary school educator*

**Daytona Beach**
Foushee-Higgs, Rosa *elementary school educator, artist*
Green, Betty Nielsen *education educator, consultant*

**Debary**
Coble, Alicia Sharon *retired elementary school educator, retired secondary school educator*

**Deland**
Dascher, Paul Edward *dean, accounting educator*
Langston, Paul T. *dean, composer, music educator*
Lee, Howard Douglas *academic administrator*
Mendez, Elsie Noemi *elementary school educator*
Wittich, John Jacob *retired academic administrator, finance company executive*

**Delray Beach**
Hofman, Elizabeth Elveretta *retired mathematics educator, guidance counselor, dean*
Leeds, Susanne *special education educator, writer*
Ross, Donald Edward *former academic administrator*

**Deltona**
Marrett, Caroline Denise *special education educator*

**Dunnellon**
Fonseca, Julio *retired secondary school educator*

**Estero**
Brush, George W. *college president*

**Fort Lauderdale**
Edmund, Norman Wilson *educational researcher*
Fischler, Abraham Saul *retired academic administrator, educator*
Hanbury, George Lafayette, II, *academic administrator*
McCan, James Lawton *education educator*
McIntyre, Jennifer Noel *academic administrator*
Sanderson, Rita Marye *history educator*
Trubey, Lillian Priscilla *retired secondary school educator*
Uchin, Robert Allen *dean, endodontist*
Valdes, Arlene H. *assistant principal*
Wilbur, Colleen Patricia *elementary school educator, principal*

**Fort Mc Coy**
Cromer, Don M. *secondary school educator, music educator*

**Fort Myers**
Colgate, Doris Eleanor *sailing school owner, administrator*
Shafer, Barbara Hough *retired secondary school educator*

**Fort Pierce**
Massey, Edwin R. *college president*
Roberts, Owen A *school system administrator, researcher*
Schwenger, Wilbur John *mathematics educator, mathematics professor*

**Fort Walton Beach**
Hicks, Patricia J. *secondary school educator*

**Gainesville**
Bashirullah, Rizwan *education educator, researcher*
Brodeur, Michael Stephen *dean*
Brown, Myra Suzanne *school librarian*

Bryan, Robert Armistead *academic administrator, educator*
Challoner, David Reynolds *academic administrator, endocrinologist*
Chambers, Robert Hunter III *academic administrator, consultant, historian, educator*
Cheek, Jimmy Geary *academic administrator, agricultural studies educator*
Colburn, David R. *academic administrator*
Dolan, Teresa A. *dean, educator, researcher*
Fouke, Janie M. *academic administrator, educator*
Jerry, Robert Howard, II, *dean, law educator*
Lowenstein, Ralph Lynn *university dean emeritus*
Machen, James Bernard *academic administrator*
Maple, Marilyn Jean *educational media coordinator*
Marshall, Kevin A. *director*
Mills, Jon *dean, law educator*
Phillips, Winfred Marshall *university administrator, mechanical engineer, educator, biomedical researcher*
Popescu, Mihaela *elementary school educator, researcher*
Rosenberger, Margaret Adaline *retired elementary school educator, writer*
Saucerman, Alvera Adeline *elementary school educator*
Viessman, Warren, Jr. *dean, civil engineering educator*
York, E. Travis *retired academic administrator*

**Glen Saint Mary**
Bales, Mary Catherine *gifted and talented educator*

**Goulds**
Taylor, Millicent Ruth *elementary school educator*

**Graceville**
Kinchen, Thomas Alexander *college president*

**Greenacres**
Romick, Joyce Trudeau *elementary school educator*

**Hialeah**
Palacios, Olga *director*

**Hobe Sound**
Blumengarten, Jerry *educational consultant*

**Hollywood**
Clark, Deborah A. *secondary school educator*

**Homestead**
Davis, Scott Michael *director, music educator*
Whitehorton, Thelma *educational administrator*

**Indialantic**
Scrivener, Lois Doing *principal, educator*

**Inverness**
Cross, Sandra Kay *primary school educator*

**Jacksonville**
Bruns, Robert A. *history educator*
Cagle, Margaret Broughton *retired parochial school educator*
Delaney, John Adrian *academic administrator*
Fanniel, Ronald Noel, Sr. *educational consultant*
Fine, Cory R. *education educator, consultant*
Hughes, Carolyn Wright *elementary school educator, director*
Jamrich, John Xavier *retired university administrator*
Kinne, Frances Bartlett *academic administrator*
Leonard, Thomas Michael *university program director, educator*
Main, Edna Dewey (June Main) *education educator*
Olin, Marilyn *secondary school educator*
Osborn, Marvin Griffing, Jr. *educational consultant*
Sandercox, Robert Allen *academic administrator, minister*

**Jensen Beach**
Kraynak, Helen *special education consultant*

**Kennedy Space Center**
Feldman, Stephen *academic administrator*

**Kissimmee**
Haynes, Ulric St. Clair, Jr. *retired dean*
Norris, Marty Todd *elementary school educator*
Toothe, Karen Lee *elementary and secondary school educator*

**Lake Worth**
Carlisle, Ervin Frederick *university provost, educator*
Taylor, Clifford Otis *retired principal*

**Lakeland**
Ashmore, Kathryn Louise *education educator*
Boyer, Naomi Rose *education educator, director*
Holland, Leland Norman, Jr. *dean, educator*
Matheny, Pamela Bemko *secondary school educator*
Washington, Gloria Dunn *secondary school educator*

**Land O Lakes**
Mallon, Kellie Jane *special education educator*
Quackenbush, Roger E. *retired secondary school educator*

**Largo**
Bentz, Laura Marie *supervisor*
Osborne, Mary Gagliardi *elementary school educator, director*

**Leesburg**
Bolden, Kristin Elizabeth *secondary school educator*
Smith, Kathy L. *elementary school educator, cosmetics executive, consultant*

**Longwood**
Johnson, Nancy Plattner *secondary school educator*

**Lynn Haven**
Durden, Paul Alan *mathematics educator, mathematics professor*

**Madison**
Steen, Morris Grissom, Jr. *academic administrator, retired military officer*

**Marianna**
Duffee, Betty B. *biology educator*

**Melbourne**
Catanese, Anthony James *academic administrator*
Fox, Thomas George *academic administrator*
Weaver, Lynn Edward *academic administrator, consultant, editor*
Zabel, Dianne Donnelly *retired elementary school educator*

**Merritt Island**
McClanahan, Leland *university director*
Young, Nancy Mayer *retired secondary school educator, artist*

**Miami**
Armstrong, Pamela Kay *principal*
Banas, Suzanne *middle school educator*
Brooten, Dorothy *retired dean, nursing educator*
Brown, Judith Oropallo *academic administrator, political science professor*
Clarkson, John G. *academic administrator, ophthalmologist*
Fish, Stanley Eugene *dean, language educator*
Foote, Edward Thaddeus, II, *academic administrator, lawyer*
Germain, Marie-Line *education educator*
Horner, Diane L. *dean*
Jones, Janice Cox *elementary school educator, writer*
Kaplan, Betsy Hess *retired school board member*
Katz, Sandra *educational consultant, psychologist, education educator*
Lee, J. Patrick *academic administrator*
Maidique, Modesto Alex *academic administrator*
McCabe, Robert Howard *college president*
McLaughlin, Margaret Brown *adult education educator, writer*
Revis-Pyke, Robin Lynn *director*
Rodriguez, Josefa Nieves *special education educator, language educator*
Rodriguez-Walling, Matilde Barcelo *special education educator*
Rose-Singh, Judith Angella *elementary school educator*
Stiehm, Judith Hicks *director, political scientist, educator*
Vielot, Alain J. *elementary school educator*
Wated, Guillermo *psychology educator*

**Miami Beach**
Danzis, Rose Marie *emeritus college president*
Gitlow, Abraham Leo *retired dean*

**Miami Gardens**
Conley, James W. *English language educator, language arts educator*
Wilson, Isabel Gomez *elementary school educator, consultant*

**Miami Shores**
Raphael, Amy Beth *director*

**Mount Dora**
Scharfenberg, Margaret Ellan *retired elementary school educator*

**Naples**
Mahalawich, Anne Mary *retired mathematics educator*
Wedel-Cowgill, Millie Redmond *secondary school educator, performing arts educator, communications educator, education educator*

**Nokomis**
Lockledge, Jack E. *retired principal*

**North Miami Beach**
Clanton, Wendy McCarley *elementary school educator, assistant principal*
Foote, Gwendolyn Sue *middle school educator, artist*

**Ocala**
Boyd, Donald Cameron *education educator, history educator*
Delozier, Doris M. *retired secondary school educator*
Hayashi, Adam *education educator*

**Ocoee**
Godsell, Richard Vernon *elementary school educator*

**Okeechobee**
Egolf, James Edward *history educator*

**Opa Locka**
Agrawal, Piyush C. *school system administrator*

**Orange City**
Brakeman, Louis Freeman *retired university official*

**Orange Park**
Combs, Diane Louise *elementary school educator, music educator*

**Orlando**
Clinton, Stephen Michael *academic administrator*
Colbourn, Trevor *retired academic administrator, historian*
Connolly, Joseph Francis, II, *academic administrator, government consultant*
Gill, Michele Gregoire *education educator*
Guzman, Marie Elvira *school guidance counselor*
McFerren, Tina JoAnn *secondary school educator*
Profitt, Donald Ralph *secondary school educator*
Vaughn, Rosalyn Mae *academic administrator*
Wilson, Brenda Marie *secondary school educator*

**Ormond Beach**
Ebbs, George Heberling, Jr. *university executive*

**Osprey**
Weathermon, Sidney Earl *elementary school educator*

**Oviedo**
Gendron, Mary W. *retired educator*
MacKenzie, Charles Sherrard *academic administrator*
Sciaino, Maria Ann *counseling administrator*

**Palatka**
Davis, Craig Anderson *secondary school educator*
Embree, Mary Evelyn *retired secondary school educator*

**Palm Bay**
Colman, Charles Kingsbury *academic administrator, criminologist*

**Palm Beach Gardens**
Más, Beverley Berlin *career planning advisor, counseling advisor*
Orr, Joseph Alexander *educational administrator*
Peck, Maryly VanLeer *retired academic administrator, chemical engineer*

**Palm City**
Harvin, Kay Kerce *retired elementary school educator*

**Palm Harbor**
Hewitt, Sarah Nichole *educational consultant, researcher*
Perkins, Robert Edward *retired secondary school educator*

**Pembroke Pines**
Embergher, Mary Louise *elementary school educator*

**Pensacola**
Dorman, Jo-Anne *elementary school educator*
Holloway, Barbara Jean Chambers *retired secondary school educator*
Mueller, Susan Jones *school system administrator*

**Plantation**
Treible, Kirk *retired academic administrator, foundation administrator*
Young, William Benjamin *retired special education educator*

**Pompano Beach**
Johnson, Dorothy Curfman *elementary school educator*
Williams, Cloretta Mae *retired elementary school educator*

**Ponte Vedra Beach**
Patterson, Oscar III *academic administrator*
Tyler, Diane Lazzelle *elementary school educator*

**Port Charlotte**
Hill, Richard Earl *academic administrator*
Norris, Dolores June *elementary school educator*

**Port Orange**
Chesnut, Nondis Lorine (Angel Love) *education educator, writer, learning specialist, scriptwriter*
Johnson, Susan F. *elementary school educator*

**Port Saint Lucie**
Earley, Deborah Loraine *education educator, researcher*
Guglielmino, Lucy Margaret Madsen *education educator, researcher, consultant*
Guglielmino, Paul Joseph *educator*

**Punta Gorda**
Klarik, Bela William James Clark *retired school system administrator*
Spaulding, Mar *retired special education educator*

**Saint Augustine**
Banton, Theodore Daniel *school system administrator*
Proctor, William Lee *college chancellor*
Sappington, Sharon Anne *retired school librarian*

**Saint Leo**
Hammond, Bruce Ray *academic administrator, consultant*

**Saint Petersburg**
Armacost, Peter Hayden *academic administrator*
Dinsdale, Carol Ellen *special education educator*
Nussbaum, Leo Lester *retired college president, consultant*
Sebastien, Anya Celita *academic administrator, consultant*
Smith, Betty Robinson *elementary school educator*
Southworth, William Dixon *retired education educator*

**Sarasota**
Atwell, Robert Herron *academic administrator*
Cleland, Sherrill *college president*
Martia, Dominic Francis *academic administrator*
St. John, Terri *secondary school educator*
Scanlon, Janice Lynn *retired gifted and talented educator*
Thompson, Annie Figueroa *retired academic administrator*

**Sebastian**
Mauke, Otto Russell *retired college president*

**Seffner**
Jackson, Greg L. *academic administrator*

**Seminole**
Schmitz, Dolores Jean *primary school educator*

**South Daytona**
Fernández, Lianne *elementary school educator, consultant*

**Spring Hill**
Post, Wendy *elementary school educator*
Wood, Shelton Eugene *education educator, minister, consultant*

**Stuart**
Stocks, Donna Brandenburg *school system administrator*

**Sugarloaf**
Greenberg, Linda Garrett *education educator, volunteer, singer*

**Sun City Center**
Chapman, Lenora Rosamond *day care provider, social service organization director*

**Tallahassee**
Bailey, Theresa L. *director, consultant*
Blaber, Michael *education educator*
Burkman, Ernest, Jr. *education educator*
Bye, Raymond Erwin, Jr. *academic administrator*
Ervin, Charles Phifer, Jr. *education educator, retired military officer*
Grant, Sydney R. *education educator, consultant*
Humphries, Frederick S. *former university president*
Kickliter, Raymond Lawton *retired secondary school educator*
Lick, Dale Wesley *educational leadership educator*
Losh, Susan Carol *education educator, researcher*
Mills, Belen Collantes *early childhood education educator*
Mooney, Krista Michele *academic administrator*
Morgan, Robert Marion *educational research educator*
Scott, Fran *adult education educator*
Sliger, Bernard Francis *academic administrator, economist, educator*
Waas, Harriet Issner *elementary school educator*
Washington, Cecile Fernando *career planning administrator*
Weidner, Donald J. *dean, law educator*
Wetherell, Thomas Kent *academic administrator*
Winn, John L. *school system administrator*
Yang, Xiaojun *education educator*

**Tampa**
Barrow, Frederica Harrison *education educator, social worker*
Bruner, Darlene York *education educator, consultant*
Erickson, Linda E. *retired academic administrator*
Hegarty, Thomas Joseph *academic administrator, history educator*
Jones, Franklin Ross *academic administrator*
Kruschwitz, Walter Hillis *retired physics educator*
Leto, Sharon Ann *secondary school educator, consultant*
Luddington, Betty Walles *school library media specialist*
Meisels, Gerhard George *academic administrator, chemist, educator*
Sanchez, Mary Anne *retired secondary school educator*
Sbramaniam, Chitra P. *educational consultant*
Young, William Henry *education educator, writer, consultant*

**Tarpon Springs**
Byrne, Richard Hill *counselor, educator*

**The Villages**
Behrendt, Richard Louis *academic administrator*
Phillips, Patricia Jeanne *retired school system administrator*

**Titusville**
O'Sullivan, Patricia Ann *principal, writer*
Robinson, Christina Anne *secondary school educator*

**Valrico**
McCrystal, Jennifer Cross *elementary school educator*

**Venice**
Finlay, Susan Sparling *education educator*

**Vero Beach**
Hardie, James Carl *academic administrator, consultant*
Harris, Nancy Lee *special education educator, behavior analyst*

**West Palm Beach**
Benavides, Christopher *special education educator*
Maktouf, Samir *education company executive*
Pingpank, Robert Charles *retired mathematics educator*

**Wewahitchka**
de Abreu, Sue *elementary school educator*
Stryker, Terence Wayne *secondary school educator*

**Wimauma**
Shober, Amy *education educator*

**Winter Garden**
Gillet, Pamela Kipping *special education educator*

**Winter Park**
Carpan, Ann Carolyn *school librarian, educator*

**Zephyrhills**
Barron, Ilona Eleanor *secondary school educator, consultant*

**GEORGIA**

**Albany**
Carmichael, Ann Louise *elementary school educator*
Forsyth, Rosalyn Moye *middle school educator*
Jenkins, Patricia Ann *early childhood educator*
Johnson, Debra Pope *education educator*

Keith, Carolyn Austin *secondary school counselor*
Shields, Portia Holmes *academic administrator*
Wooden, Ontario Sherrod *academic administrator*

**Alpharetta**
Filliat, Elizabeth Hartley *retired secondary school educator*

**Americus**
Capitan, William Harry *university president emeritus*
Stanford, Henry King *college president*

**Athens**
Adams, Michael Fred *academic administrator, political scientist, educator*
Andrews, Grover Jene *adult education educator, administrator*
Benson, P. George *dean, finance educator*
Castenell, Louis Anthony *academic administrator*
Crowley, John Francis III *university dean*
Power, Chandra Lynn *elementary school educator*
Smagorinsky, Peter *education educator*
Toma, J. Douglas *education educator*
White, Rebecca Hanner *dean, law educator*
Wraga, William Gerard *education educator*

**Atlanta**
Aaberg, Thomas Marshall, Sr. *academic administrator*
Affonso, Dyanne D. *dean*
Alexander, Cecil Abraham *academic administrator, consultant, retired architect*
Arthur, Thomas Carlton *former dean, law educator*
Bellamy, Ivory *elementary school educator, consultant*
Benveniste, Lawrence M. *dean*
Betts, Jennifer Leah *secondary school educator*
Blum, Terry C. *dean*
Brice Ross, Carla Yvette *school counselor*
Bright, David Forbes *academic administrator, classicist, educator*
Broadnax, Walter D. *university president, educator*
Cilella, Mary Winifred *director*
Clough, Gerald Wayne (Wayne Clough) *academic administrator*
Cox, Kathy *school system administrator*
Curry, Toni Griffin *counseling center executive, consultant*
Davis, Erroll Brown, Jr. *academic administrator, former utilities executive*
Day, Janet S. *academic administrator*
Denmark, Darron B. *academic administrator*
Edmondson, Earnest Eugene *secondary school educator*
Ferris, James Leonard *academic administrator*
Hall, Beverly L. *school system administrator*
Henry, Ronald James Whyte *academic administrator, physicist, educator*
Henry, Thomas Reid *education educator, researcher*
Hogan, John Donald *retired college dean, finance educator*
Hunter, Howard Owen *academic administrator, law educator*
Ignatonis, Sandra Carole Autry *special education educator*
Jefferson, Jonathan Kenneth *dean*
Jolley, Samuel Delanor, Jr. *academic administrator*
Kaminshine, Steven J. *dean, law educator*
Langston, Sheila Annette *special education educator, consultant*
Lawley, Thomas Joseph *dean, medical educator*
Lee, Hamilton H. *education educator*
Lewis, Earl *academic administrator*
Liang, Steven Yuehsan *education educator*
Long, Leland Timothy *retired geophysics educator, seismologist*
Lovewell, Marjorie Klingensmith *secondary school educator*
Lucas, M. Frances *university administrator*
Luce, Richard *university librarian*
Meredith, Thomas C. *academic administrator*
Meyer, Ellen L. *academic administrator*
Meyer, Richard W. *school librarian*
Mogabgab, Rose-Warren Berryman *academic administrator, writer*
Nentwich, Michael Andreas Erhart *director*
Orenstein, Walter Albert *director*
Patton, Carl Vernon *academic administrator, educator*
Rogers, Brenda Gayle *educational administrator, educator, consultant*
Rojas, Carlos *literature and language educator*
Towslee, Janet L. *special education educator*
Wagner, James Warren *academic administrator, engineering educator*
Yancey, Carolyn Dunbar *academic administrator*

**Augusta**
Drisko, Connie Lee Hastings *dean, dental educator*
Jackson, Rosa M. *retired elementary school educator*
Osborne, James B., Sr. *academic administrator*
Puryear, Joan Copeland *academic administrator*
Tedesco, Francis Joseph *retired academic administrator, medical educator*

**Bainbridge**
Miley, Jenna Yvonne *education educator, consultant*

**Baxley**
Williams, David Alfred *elementary school educator*
Williams, Sonia Kay *retired secondary school educator*

**Bishop**
Bower, Douglas William *counseling administrator, psychotherapist, clergyman*

**Brooklet**
McCormick, Paula Shurling *elementary school educator*

**Brunswick**
Pittman, Catherine Sylvia *secondary school educator*

Spencer, Shirley Ann *secondary school educator, speech educator, literature educator*

**Camilla**
Daniels, Deloria *elementary school educator*

**Canton**
Harrison, David E. *secondary school educator*
Horton, Delories Epps *gifted and talented educator*

**Carrollton**
Hynes, Thomas John *academic administrator*
Sethna, Beheruz Nariman *academic administrator, educator, management consultant*

**Cartersville**
DiMassimo, Thomas *secondary school educator, military officer*
Wheeler, Susie Weems *retired school system administrator*

**Cataula**
Averill, Ellen Corbett *retired secondary education science educator, administrator*

**Cedartown**
Burgess, Peggy Biggers *special education educator*

**Chatsworth**
Howard, Timothy Ray *elementary school educator, historian*

**Cleveland**
Kendrick, Brenda Cloyd *school counselor*

**College Park**
Bradley, Lynn Hecht *school librarian*

**Columbus**
Beall, Charles Donald *former special education educator*
Duncan, Frances Murphy *retired special education educator*
Ingram, Rhea *education educator*
Jinright, Noah Franklin *vocational school educator, security firm executive*
Montgomery, Anna Frances *elementary school educator*
Riggsby, Dutchie Sellers *education educator*

**Conyers**
Grider, Rhonda Patriece *elementary school educator, writer*

**Covington**
Fallings, Gloria Vondell *special education educator*
Norwood, Brandi Aisha *middle school educator*

**Dahlonega**
Potter, David L. *academic administrator*

**Dallas**
Coley, Linda Marie *retired secondary school educator*

**Dalton**
Ford, Katherine Michelle *special education educator*

**Decatur**
Kiss, Elizabeth *academic administrator, philosophy educator*

**Demorest**
Rogers, Elizabeth (Betty) Carlisle *education educator, consultant*

**Douglasville**
Yates, Brenda H. Carroll *secondary school educator*

**Duluth**
Guillory, Barbara Ann *elementary school educator*
Koch, Linda Marie *elementary school educator*

**Eatonton**
Thompson, Laura Kay *school system administrator*

**Evans**
McCorkle, Pamela Loveridge *elementary school educator*
Stout, Elva Carolyn Fraser *elementary school educator*

**Fairburn**
Milam, Lynne Morgan *special education educator*

**Fayetteville**
Borders, Donna Turner *elementary school educator*

**Flowery Branch**
Coll, Edward Girard, Jr. *university president*

**Gainesville**
Burd, John Stephen *retired academic administrator, music educator*
Floyd, Hazel McConnell *special education educator*
Thrasher, Karen Hewell *counseling administrator*

**Griffin**
Phillips, Audrey Patricia (Pat Phillips) *secondary school educator*

**Hiram**
Crutchfield, Veda Maria Sharp *elementary school educator*

**Ila**
Greene, Sheree' Jeane *elementary school educator, consultant*

**Jeffersonville**
Capece, Michelle René *elementary school educator*
Hawthorne, Sarah Beck *reading educator*

**Kennesaw**
Siegel, Betty Lentz *university president*

**Lagrange**
Ault, Ethyl Lorita *special education educator, consultant*

**Lake Park**
Blanton, Vallye J. *elementary school educator*
Carpenter, Paula Jo *elementary school educator*

**Lawrenceville**
Crain, Mary Ann *elementary school educator*

**Lexington**
Newsome, Christa Anne *elementary school educator*

**Lilburn**
Bendelius, Bonnie Sue *elementary school educator*
Frapwell, Sharon Ann *mathematics educator*
Jamie, Parker Scott *elementary school educator, music educator, director*

**Macon**
Davis, David Scott *academic administrator, chemistry professor*
Floyd, Daisy Hurst *dean, law educator*
Pilcher, Christie W. *special education educator*
Steeples, Douglas Wayne *retired university dean, consultant, researcher*

**Marietta**
Houston, Dorothy Middleton *elementary school educator*
Rivers, Alma Faye *secondary school educator*
Rossbacher, Lisa Ann *academic administrator*
Shaw, Judith Ann *secondary school educator, human resources specialist, consultant*

**Mcdonough**
Mauney, Brandi Savage *special education diagnostician*

**Metter**
Farmer, DeWayne Mark *director, photographer*

**Moultrie**
Newberry, Daniel M. *elementary school educator*

**Newnan**
Royal, Nancy B. *primary school educator*

**Norcross**
Hellyer, Christine Frances *secondary school educator, art educator*

**Peachtree City**
Barnes, Marylou Riddleberger *retired academic administrator*

**Perry**
Giles, Lisa Lanette *elementary school educator*

**Powder Springs**
Drawdy, Larry Wayne *elementary school educator*

**Riverdale**
Lambert, Ethel Gibson Clark *secondary school educator*

**Rockmart**
Vinson, Victoria Dean *middle school educator*

**Rome**
Slack, Clemontene *education educator*

**Roopville**
Huckeba, Emily Causey *retired elementary school educator*

**Saint Marys**
Hall, Lois Bremer *secondary school educator, volunteer*
Keating, Mary Tucker *retired school system administrator*

**Saint Simons Island**
Mathis, Luster Doyle *academic administrator, political scientist, educator*

**Savannah**
Brown, Carlton E. *college president*
Chong, Bruce Simon *dean, broadcast executive*
Dirlam, David Kirk *education educator*
Felcyn, Diane Annette *museum educator*
Houngues, Desire Mensanh *dean*
Leighton, Richard Frederick *retired dean*
Polite, Evelyn C. *retired elementary school educator, evangelist*
Rowan, Richard G. *academic administrator*
Thompson, Larry James *retired gifted and social studies education educator*
Wallace, Paula S. *academic administrator*

**Statesboro**
Li, Xiezhang *education educator*
Olvey, Pamela Hagan *elementary school educator*

**Stone Mountain**
Brown, Rhonda Jean *special education educator*
Dees, Julian Worth *retired academic/research administrator*
Torbush, Deborah Nickels *psychology educator*
Warthan, Helen Patricia *retired secondary school educator*

**Suwanee**
Stanley, Gwen G. *elementary school educator*

**Thomasville**
Williams, Gerald Arnett *academic administrator*

**Tiger**
Ring, Yvonne Ann *special education educator*

**Toccoa Falls**
Gardner, Donna Rae (Diehl) *education educator*

**Tucker**
Stewart, Connie Ward *retired academic administrator*

**Union City**
Drake-Hamilton, Lillie Belle *retired secondary school educator*

**Valdosta**
Bailey, Hugh Coleman *university president*
Burnette, Ada M. Puryear *program coordinator*
Warrick, Emory Lawrence *retired education educator*

**Vidalia**
Findley, LaRee *history educator*

**Watkinsville**
Leathers, Joyce Carol *secondary school educator*

**West Point**
Albarado, Rebecca Hill *elementary school educator*

**Whitesburg**
Nicholson, Diane M. *special education educator*

**Woodstock**
Moses, Marjorie *elementary school educator*

## HAWAII

**Aiea**
Manabe, Shari A *education educator*

**Hilo**
Pezzuto, John Michael *dean, pharmacology educator*
Tseng, Rose *academic administrator*

**Honolulu**
Chock, Raelene *school system administrator*
Englert, Peter *academic administrator, director*
Fale, Kim Kimball *secondary school educator, director*
Gee, Chuck Yim *dean*
Gonsalves, Margaret Leboy *elementary school educator*
Hamamoto, Patricia *school system administrator*
Higa, D. Puanani *secondary school educator*
Hu, Ching Yuan *academic administrator*
Ingersoll, Caroline Yee *director*
Johnson, Katherine Marie *elementary school educator*
Keith, Kent Marsteller *academic administrator, writer, lawyer, recreational facility executive*
Konan, Denise *academic administrator, economics professor*
McClain, David Stanley *academic administrator, business and management professor*
Migimoto, Fumiyo Kodani *retired secondary school educator*
Osborne, Larry Norman *dean, consultant*
Perkins, Frank Overton *academic administrator, marine biologist*
Pickens, Alexander Legrand *retired education educator*
Plourde, William E. *secondary school educator*
Roley, V. Vance *dean, finance educator*
Schneider, Niklas *educator*
Silva, Mary Barnes *retired elementary school educator*
Soifer, Aviam *dean, law educator*
Wee, Christine Dijos *elementary school educator*
Wright, Chatt Grandison *academic administrator*

**Kailua**
Tubbs, Mary S. *curriculum coordinator*

**Kailua Kona**
Clewett, Kenneth Vaughn *academic administrator*
Diama, Benjamin *retired secondary school educator, artist, composer, writer*
Spitze, Glenys Smith *retired teacher and counselor*

**Kaneohe**
Ashley, Elizabeth *dean, educator*
LaMarchina, Marilynne May *elementary school educator*
Maeshiro, Mitzi (Mikilani) *literature and language educator*

**Laie**
Miller, Ronald Mellado *education educator*
Shumway, Eric *academic administrator*

**Wailuku**
DeVey, Graham Richard *secondary school educator, retired engineering executive*

## IDAHO

**Boise**
Andrus, Cecil Dale *academic administrator*
Ansbach, Thomas M. *academic administrator*
Griffin, Sylvia Gail *reading specialist*
Howard, Marilyn *state school system administrator*
Maloof, Giles Wilson *academic administrator, author*

**Burley**
Vargas, Teresa Marie Bradley *elementary school educator*

**Caldwell**
Hendren, Robert Lee, Jr. *academic administrator*
Hoover, Robert Allan *university president*

**Cottonwood**
Wicks, Dwight Earl *elementary school educator*

**Hagerman**
Roberts, Ronald John *education educator, director*

**Lewiston**
Branting, Steven D. *gifted and talented consultant*
Marshall, Josie *secondary school educator*
Thomas, Dene Kay *academic administrator, educator*

**Meridian**
Ascuena, Vikki Pepper *secondary school educator*

**Moscow**
Abraham, Terry *school librarian*
Jankowska, Maria Anna *school librarian, educator*
White, Timothy Peter *academic administrator, physical education educator*

**Mountain Home**
Jett, Sandra *elementary school educator*

**Ola**
Farr, Reeta Rae *special education administrator*

**Pocatello**
Berrey, Eleanor G. *elementary school educator*
Lawson, Jonathan Nevin *academic administrator, educator*
Robinson, Evelyn Etta *principal*

**Rexburg**
Clark, Kim Bryce *academic administrator*

**Sun Valley**
Cassell, William Comyn *retired college president*

**Twin Falls**
Mathews, Donna Mae *special education educator*
Williams, Ashlee Jean *English educator, psycho-social rehabilitation specialist*

## ILLINOIS

**Alexander**
Eck, Gail Ann *elementary school educator*

**Alton**
Boyle, Ann M. *dean, dental educator*

**Argonne**
Vivio, Frank Michael *education educator, researcher*

**Arlington Heights**
Kopielski, Camille Ann *counseling administrator, volunteer*

**Athens**
Curry, John Wesley *retired secondary school educator*

**Aurora**
Daugherty, Patricia Ann *retired elementary school educator*
Easley, Pauline Marie *retired elementary school educator*
Keutzer, Ronald Eugene *mathematics educator*
Porzio, Donald Timmis *mathematics educator*

**Batavia**
Kosek, Wayne Richard *retired secondary school educator*

**Beecher**
Dettmer, Janet Kay *retired elementary school educator*
Squier, Victoria (Vicki) J. *mathematics educator*

**Belleville**
Hilgenbrink, Robert J. *academic administrator*
Stone, William David *secondary school educator, consultant*

**Bement**
Vezina, Vicky Lynne *middle school educator*

**Berwyn**
Wunderlich, Dorothy Anastasia *superintendent*

**Bloomington**
Wilson, Richard F. *academic administrator*

**Blue Island**
Tisch, Carrie Catherine *elementary school educator*

**Bourbonnais**
Rezba, Patricia Louise *middle school educator*

**Braidwood**
Zolecki-Browning, Diana M. *middle school educator*

**Bridgeview**
Henson, Sheila J. *elementary school educator, assistant principal*

**Broadview**
Bland, Pamela June *special education educator*

**Bushnell**
Cortelyou, Cynthia Ann *elementary school educator*

**Byron**
Love, LeeAnn *elementary school educator*

**Carbondale**
Baker, Clora Mae *education educator*
Dixon, Billy Gene *academic administrator, educator*
Poshard, Glenn (Glendal W. Poshard) *academic administrator, former congressman*

Quisenberry, Nancy Lou *academic administrator, educator*
Scott, Shirley Clay *dean*
Snyder, Carolyn Ann *education educator, librarian, director*

**Carlinville**
Witham, Craig Ray *biology and chemistry educator*

**Carol Stream**
Mollet, Emily A. *secondary school educator*

**Cerro Gordo**
Gilpin, Vicky Sue *literature and language educator, principal*

**Champaign**
Becker, Lawrence Paul *educator*
Bernhardt, Mark Daniel *economics educator*
Ghosh, Avijit *dean*
Herman, Richard H. *academic administrator*
Hurd, Heidi M. *dean, humanities educator, law educator*
Ikenberry, Stanley Oliver *education educator, director, former university president*
Loeb, Jane Rupley *academic administrator, educator*
McConkie, George Wilson *education educator*
Schnarre, Thomas Dale *education educator*
Spodek, Bernard *early childhood educator*
Summerfield, Gale *director, educator*

**Charleston**
Eberly, Charles *counseling and student development educator*
NeSmith, Richard A. *education educator, consultant*
O'Rourke, Kathleen Ann *education educator*
Rives, Stanley Gene *retired academic administrator*
Surles, Carol D. *academic administrator*
Thornburgh, Daniel Eston *retired university administrator, journalism educator*

**Chebanse**
McLaughlin, Barbara Lyn *elementary school educator*

**Chicago**
Adelman, Pamela Bernice Kozoll *education educator*
Bailey, Nettie Whitney *retired elementary school educator, retired assistant principal*
Baley, Joan Marie *elementary school educator*
Beane, Marjorie Noterman *academic administrator*
Bigg, Susan Jeanette *educational consultant*
Bindenagel, James Dale *university executive*
Binion, Celious *retired parochial school educator*
Buniak, Raymond *educational professional*
Cafferty, Pastora San Juan *education educator*
Collens, Lewis Morton *academic administrator, law educator*
Cottone, Dominic Patrick *director*
Crockett, George Ephriam *secondary school educator*
Cueto, Rochelle E. *elementary school educator*
Culp, Kristine Ann *dean, theology studies educator*
Daniel, Elnora D. *academic administrator*
Davis, Addie L. *mathematics educator*
Davros, Michael George *education educator*
Driskell, Claude Evans *college director, educator, dentist*
Feig, Barbara Krane *elementary school educator, author*
Freehling, Daniel Joseph *dean, law educator*
Gabelnick, Helene S. *education educator*
Garanzini, Michael J. *academic administrator, priest*
Garber, Philip Robert *academic administrator, researcher*
Graham, Bruce S. *dean, educator*
Gross, Theodore Lawrence *university administrator, author*
Hamada, Robert S(eiji) *dean, educator, economist, entrepreneur*
Harris, Rodney *education educator, researcher*
Harris, Shirley *elementary school educator, secondary school educator, adult education educator*
Hawkins, Loretta Ann *retired secondary school educator, playwright*
Hayes, Alice Bourke *academic administrator, biologist, researcher*
Heydecker, Jeanne-Elise Marie *school district coordinator, traditional and web marketing executive*
Holliday, Patricia A. *elementary school educator*
Holtschneider, Dennis H. *academic administrator, priest*
Hunter Harris, Phyllis Irene *retired secondary school educator*
Jarrett, Tukoi Demarco *director*
Johnson, Mary Ann *vocational school owner*
Jones, Tony *academic administrator*
Keiderling, Timothy Allen *chemistry educator, researcher*
Khan, M. Wasiullah *academic administrator*
Krent, Harold J. *dean, law educator*
Kubistal, Patricia Bernice *educational consultant*
Kuner, Charles *secondary school educator*
Landerholm, Elizabeth Jane *early childhood education educator*
Landsberg, Lewis *dean, endocrinologist, medical researcher*
Leonard, Sister Anne C. *school system administrator*
Levandowski, Barbara Sue *education educator*
Levmore, Saul *dean, law educator*
Lusk, Peggy June *retired counseling administrator*
Madara, James Lee *dean, pathologist, educator, epitheliologist*
Mason, Gregory Wesley, Jr. *secondary school educator*
McCrank, Lawrence J. *dean, school librarian*
McCray, Curtis Lee *academic administrator*
McMath, Lula Wray *retired elementary school educator, realtor*
McPherson, Michael Steven *academic administrator, economist*

Mindes, Gayle Dean *education educator*
Minogue, John P. *academic administrator, educator, priest*
Mirza, Leona Lousin *elementary school educator, director*
Nadler, Judith *school librarian*
O'Brien, Gregory Michael St. Lawrence *academic administrator*
O'Reilly, Charles Terrance *university dean*
Pando, Jesus *education educator*
Panko, Jessie Symington *education educator*
Petitan, Debra Ann Burke *elementary school educator, counselor, design engineer, writer*
Powers, William Bryan *academic administrator*
Reilly, Anne Huedepohl *university educator, researcher*
Restivo, Charles L. *academic administrator*
Rhone, Elvie Sue *educational administrator*
Richardson, John Thomas *academic administrator, clergyman*
Royster, Lynn Christine *academic administrator, educator*
Schieser, Hans Alois *education educator*
Schubert, William Henry *curriculum studies educator*
Sessions, Joan T. *director, educator*
Shaver, Joan Louise Fowler *dean, women's health nurse*
Sinha, Raj P. *education educator, researcher*
Snyder, Edward Adams *dean, economics professor*
Standberry, Herman Lee *school system administrator, educational consultant*
Steinberg, Salme Elizabeth Harju *academic administrator, historian*
Stovall-Brooks, Patricia *elementary school educator, writer*
Sulkin, Howard Allen *academic administrator*
Swanson, Don Richard *university dean*
Van Zandt, David E. *dean, law educator*
Wasan, Darsh Tilakchand *academic administrator, chemical engineer, educator*
Wham, David Buffington *secondary school educator*
White, C. Vanessa *director*
Wittbrodt, Elizabeth Stratton *education educator*
Yandle, Stephen Thomas *dean*
Young, Lauren Sue Jones *education educator*
Zimmer, Robert J. *academic administrator, mathematician, educator*

**Chicago Heights**
Buishas, Kristin Maureen *elementary school educator*
Nowocin, Debra Terese *gifted and talented secondary education educator*

**Cisne**
White, Sharon *elementary school educator*

**Collinsville**
Daugherty, Phyllis Lyn *secondary school educator*

**Country Club Hills**
Scott, Earline *school system administrator*

**Davis**
Fulfer, Matrona Penny *retired school librarian, columnist*

**Decatur**
Munoz, Joseph Mark *education educator, consultant*

**Deerfield**
Wrobbel, Karen *education educator, consultant*

**Dekalb**
Legg, J. Ivan *academic administrator*
Monat, William Robert *university official*
Splansky, Sandra J. *director*

**Des Plaines**
Canfield, Jinhee *mathematics educator*
Coburn, James LeRoy *academic administrator*
Lee, Margaret Burke *college president, language educator*

**Dolton**
Hahn, Gerald Eugene *industrial education educator*

**Dow**
Schuler, Dorothy R. *education educator, consultant, retired elementary school educator*

**Downers Grove**
Punt, Leonard Cornelis *educational services company executive*

**Du Quoin**
Ibendahl, Jean Ayres *retired elementary and secondary educator*

**East Alton**
DiPaolo, Marcella Kay *elementary school educator*

**East Dubuque**
Kussmaul, Donald *academic administrator*

**East Saint Louis**
Wright, Katie Harper *educational administrator, journalist*

**Edwardsville**
Banks, Ronald Dwayne *academic administrator, industrial engineer, educator*
Kuba, Joan Carol *special education educator*

**Effingham**
Lewis, Linda Sue *retired elementary school educator*

**Elgin**
Mao, Ruixuan (Rick Mao) *dean*
Puotinen, Arthur Edwin *college president, minister*

**Elmhurst**
Pollack, Judy Barbara *special education educator*
Sample, Steven Dale *secondary school educator*

**Elmwood**
Vaughan, Patricia Ann *elementary school educator*

**Eureka**
Staudenmeier, William John, Jr. *academic administrator, dean, sociology professor*

**Evanston**
Bienen, Henry Samuel *academic administrator, political scientist, educator*
Boye, Roger Carl *academic administrator, journalism educator*
Brown, Eric Ricardo *biology educator*
Christian, Richard Carlton *dean, former advertising agency executive*
Dumas, Lawrence B. *academic administrator*
Jacobs, Donald P. *retired dean, banking and finance educator*
Jain, Dipak Chand *dean, marketing educator, consultant*
Lewis, Dan Albert *education educator*
Peterson, Penelope Loraine *dean, education educator*
Power, Peggy Ann *elementary school educator*
Sheldon, Mark *assistant dean*
Weber, Arnold Robert *academic administrator*

**Galesburg**
Haywood, Bruce *retired academic administrator*
Taylor, Roger Lee *academic administrator, lawyer*

**Glen Carbon**
Lazerson, Earl Edwin *retired academic administrator*

**Glen Ellyn**
Bollendorf, Robert Fredrick *retired education educator, psychologist*
King, Peggy Marsha *special education educator, researcher*
Maciejewski, Nora Jean *elementary school educator*
Neurauter, Elizabeth Strain *secondary school educator*
Patten, Ronald James *university dean*

**Glenview**
Corley, Jenny Lynd Wertheim *elementary school educator*

**Granite City**
Humphrey, Owen Everett *retired education administrator*

**Gurnee**
Halsne-Baarda, Alana Michelle *secondary school educator*

**Highland Park**
Hershenson, Martha Bradford *history educator*
Tribbey, Fern *mathematics educator*

**Hillsboro**
Doss, JoAnn Trauernicht *retired elementary school educator*

**Hinsdale**
Taylor, T(homas) Roger *educational consultant, educator*

**Hoffman Estates**
Larson, John M. *educational consultant*

**Jacksonville**
Anderson, Michael R. *elementary school educator, writer*
Chaffee, James *academic administrator*
Johns, Beverley Anne Holden *special education administrator*

**Kankakee**
Roy, Sudipta D. *education educator*

**Lake Forest**
Gayle, Carol *history educator, educational association administrator*
Herron, Orley R. *college president*

**Lake Villa**
Kastor, Matthew Anton *secondary school educator, music educator*

**Lincolnshire**
Martin, John Driscoll *school administrator*

**Lincolnwood**
Greenblatt, Deana Charlene *elementary school educator*

**Lombard**
Benning, Joseph Raymond *principal*

**Macomb**
Goldfarb, Alvin *academic administrator*
Hayes, Paul Robert *retired field and clinical experiences coordinator*
Kyllonen Rose, Julie Frances *college program administrator*

**Madison**
Purdes, Alice Marie *retired adult education educator*

**Malta**
Ragan, Dennis M. *mathematics educator*

**Markham**
Majeski, Susan Saxer *elementary school educator*
Peacock, Marilyn Claire *primary school educator*

**Marseilles**
Nellett, Gaile H. *adult education educator*

**Maywood**
Lid, Glenn David *chemistry educator*

**Mchenry**
Carson, Linda Marie *elementary school educator*

**Metamora**
Harbers, Rebecca Ann *physical education educator*

**Mokena**
Lighty, Michelle McCowan *secondary school educator*

**Moline**
Mitchell, Lucille Anne *retired elementary school educator*

**Monmouth**
Bruce, Mary Hanford *academic administrator, educator, writer*

**Monroe Center**
Coulahan, Mike J. *principal*

**Morton**
Corey, Judith Ann *retired elementary school educator*

**Naperville**
Briseno, Kathleen *education educator*
Florence, Ernest Estell, Jr. *special education educator*
Rosenthal, Edward Leonard *secondary school educator*
Wilde, Harold Richard *college president*

**New Baden**
Gregov, Maria Irma Pott *retired elementary school educator*

**New Lenox**
Hesser, Christa E. *secondary school educator*

**Normal**
Bowman, C. Alvin *academic administrator*
Buller, Chrysalis Chablis *director*
Hickrod, George Alan Karnes Wallis *educational administration educator*
Miller, Wilma Hildruth *education educator*
Musick, Marilyn Irene *retired secondary school educator*
Presley, John Woodrow *academic administrator*
Temple, Mark Allen *adult education educator, consultant*

**Northbrook**
Ben-Arie, Ronit Peleg *elementary school educator*
Rosenberg, Auria Eleanor *secondary school educator*
Ruter, Allan J. *literature and language educator*

**O Fallon**
Ritzel, Tracey L. *special education educator*

**Oak Brook**
Hoffmann, Joan Carol *retired academic dean*

**Oak Lawn**
Jandes, Kenneth Michael *superintendent of schools*

**Oak Park**
Adelman, William John *retired academic administrator, industrial relations specialist*
Venerable, Shirley Marie *retired gifted and talented educator*
Young, Jessica S.E. *secondary school educator*

**Oakbrook Terrace**
Levine, Norman M. *academic administrator*
Overbye, David Lawrence *dean, researcher*
Taylor, Ronald Lee *academic administrator*

**Orland Park**
Ritchey, Lauretta Marie *secondary school educator*

**Palatine**
Wilk, Pamela June *elementary school educator*

**Palos Hills**
Crawley, Vernon Obadiah *academic administrator*
McGarel-Warkocki, Lynn M. *history educator*

**Park Forest**
Orr, Marcia *pre-school administrator, consultant*

**Pecatonica**
Duncan, Linda M. *elementary school educator*

**Pekin**
White, Richard Lee, Jr. *secondary school educator*

**Peoria**
Kelly, Grace Dentino *secondary school educator*
Sanderson, Kenneth Jerome *school system administrator, consultant*
Sattler, Joan Linda *education educator, dean*

**Peotone**
Kanosky, Albert Leo *history educator, small business owner*

**Quincy**
Tomczak, Patricia Ann *dean, archivist*

**Richton Park**
Pierce, Mary E. *retired elementary school educator, public relations consultant*
Piucci, Virginio Louis *academic administrator*

**River Forest**
Carroll, Donna M. *academic administrator*
Coe, Donald Kirk *retired academic administrator*
Heggerty, Michael *school system administrator, consultant, writer*

**Robinson**
Wolfe, Ellen Darlene *school librarian, elementary school educator*

**Rock Island**
Bahls, Steven Carl *academic administrator, educator*

Clay, Carol Sue *reading specialist*
Hendrickx, Irene S. *elementary school educator*
Horstmann, James Douglas *retired academic administrator*

**Rockford**
Hartz, Linda M. *elementary school educator*
Howard, John Addison *retired academic administrator*
Steele, Carl Lavern *academic administrator*
Steely, Allen Merle *secondary school educator*

**Rolling Meadows**
Bassi, Suzanne Howard *retired secondary school educator, volunteer*
Yerkan, Robert R. *educational consultant*

**Rossville**
Tracy, Christina L. *secondary school educator*

**Round Lake Beach**
Harold, Kathleen T. *elementary school educator*

**Sandwich**
Meier, Carolyn K. *elementary school educator*

**Schaumburg**
Maluchnik, Rosemary Pellicore *elementary school educator*
Westlund, Maribeth *secondary school educator*

**South Chicago Heights**
Misdom, Amanda Michelle *elementary school educator, music educator*

**South Holland**
Doty, Brandon S. *history educator*

**Springfield**
Aiello, Elizabeth Blackwell *secondary school educator*
Dunn, Randy J. *school system administrator*
Kocis, Janet Kay *elementary school educator*
Poorman, Robert Lewis *retired academic administrator*
Schroeder, Raymond Ernest *educational administrator*
Turner, Sharon Lou Willson *elementary and gifted education educator*

**Sycamore**
Johnson, Yvonne Amalia *elementary school educator, consultant*

**Tinley Park**
Cox, Carrie Lee *secondary school educator*

**Troy**
Perkins, Sandra Laird *biology educator*

**Tuscola**
Henderson, E. Suzanne *elementary school educator*

**University Park**
Keys, Paul Ross *academic administrator, educator*

**Urbana**
Foulonneau, Muriel *education educator*
Knobloch, Neil A. *education educator*
Stukel, James Joseph *academic administrator, mechanical engineer, educator*

**Villa Park**
Russo, Cheryl Jean *elementary school educator, special education educator*

**Washington**
Schupp, Joyce Elaine *elementary school educator*

**Waukegan**
Akouris, Dianne Frances *school system administrator*

**Wayne City**
Staggs, Teresa Laverne *special education educator*

**Wheaton**
Litfin, A. Duane *academic administrator*

**Wheeling**
Jackson, Carolyn M. *school librarian*

**Wilmette**
Ballard, Patricia Jo *elementary school educator*
Mandel, Judith Lynn *primary school educator*
Smutny, Joan Franklin *academic director, educator*

**Winnetka**
Bundy, Blakely Fetridge *pre-school administrator*
Huggins, Charlotte Susan Harrison *retired secondary school educator, writer, travel company executive*
Johnson, Julie West *secondary school educator, writer*
McKee, Judith Nelson *elementary school educator, educational consultant*

**Wood River**
Shelton, Michael Patrick *principal*

**INDIANA**

**Anderson**
Nicholson, Robert Arthur *college president*

**Bicknell**
Ford, Andrea Michelle *mathematics educator*

**Bloomington**
Alderson, Arthur Stancliff III *education educator*
Arnove, Robert Frederick *education educator*
Barnes, A. James *dean*
Bornholdt, Laura Anna *academic administrator*
Chafel, Judith Ann *education educator*
Chaifetz, Marshal Lawrence *educational consultant, educator*

Herbert, Adam William, Jr. *academic administrator, educator*
Louis, Kenneth R.R. Gross *academic administrator*
Lucas, Judith Ann *secondary school educator*
Mehlinger, Howard Dean *education educator*
Robel, Lauren *dean, law educator*
Robinson, Jennifer Meta *academic administrator, consultant*
Ryan, John William *academic administrator*
Smith, Carl Bernard *education educator*
Smith, Daniel C. *dean, finance educator*
Steele, Patricia Ann *dean, librarian*
Webb, Charles Haizlip, Jr. *retired university dean*

**Bluffton**
Whitehead, Wendy Lee *special education educator*

**Brookville**
Barker, Norman Glen *mathematics educator, physics educator*

**Brownsburg**
Griffin, Mike *history educator*

**Butler**
Bowman, Connie Jo *secondary school educator*

**Carmel**
Rand, Leon *academic administrator*
Vargas-Williams, Traci Junelle *special education educator*

**Connersville**
Newton, Cindy Lynn *elementary school educator*

**Crawfordsville**
Ford, Andrew Thomas *former academic administrator*
White, Patrick E. *academic administrator*

**Demotte**
Mitchell, Timmy J. *principal*

**East Chicago**
Fortenberry, Delores B. *dean*

**Elwood**
Sipe, Dena G. *elementary school educator*

**Evansville**
Jennings, Stephen Grant *academic administrator*

**Fort Wayne**
Dahl, John Clarence, Jr. *academic administrator*
Longsworth, Susan Kay *elementary school educator*
Robinson, Wendy Y. *school system administrator*
Wartell, Michael Alan *academic administrator*

**Franklin**
Stone, Mary Ann *literature and language educator*

**Gary**
Smith, Vernon G. *education educator, state legislator*

**Goshen**
Meyer, Albert James *educational researcher*

**Granger**
Morgan, Ardys Nord *school improvement consultant*

**Greencastle**
Bottoms, Robert Garvin *academic administrator*
Erb, Thomas Owen *education educator*

**Hammond**
Delph, Donna Jean (Donna Maroc) *education educator, consultant, academic administrator*
Fehring, Mary Ann *secondary school educator*

**Huntington**
Burson, Susan Jewel *early childhood educator, elementary school educator*
Priddy, Evelyn J. *education educator*

**Indianapolis**
Bepko, Gerald Lewis *retired academic administrator, law educator*
Brater, Donald Craig *dean, educator*
Brenner, Mark Lee *academic administrator, physiologist, educator*
Broome, Marion *dean*
Clark, Charles M., Jr. *medical school administrator*
Dai, Yuan-Shun *education educator*
Floyd, James M., Jr. *adult education educator*
Goldblatt, Lawrence I. *dean, educator, researcher*
Gooldy, Patricia Alice *retired elementary school educator*
Hardin, Boniface *academic administrator*
Harrold, John Andrew *education educator, consultant*
Holigrocki, Richard *educator*
Keaton, Margaret-Ann Coleman *education educator*
Kennedy, Russell Edward *academic administrator*
Malone, Jean Hambidge *educational consultant*
Mead, Susanah M. *dean*
Najjar, Diana *elementary school educator*
Pitts, Beverley J. *academic administrator*
Reed, Suellen Kinder *school system administrator*
Slocum, Judith Ann *retired elementary school educator*
Solomon, Marilyn Kay *primary school educator, consultant, small business owner*
Speth, Gerald Lennus *educational consultant, management consultant*
Stoker, Daniel J. *academic administrator*
Strauss, Diane Jayne *retired elementary and secondary school educator, small business owner*
Sullender, Joy Sharon *retired elementary school educator*
Woody, John Frederick *retired secondary school educator*

**Jeffersonville**
Phillips, Arlene Marie *retired secondary school educator*

**Kentland**
Hiatt, Tony John *biology educator, director*

**La Porte**
Johnson, Bruce Ross *elementary school educator*

**Lafayette**
Mitchell, Pamela Lee *elementary school educator*
Roush, Nadine Marie *elementary school educator*
Troutner, Joanne Johnson *director, consultant, secondary school educator*

**Lagrange**
Roth, Gayle Yvonne *elementary school educator*

**Leopold**
Spence, Rodney Glen *education educator, coach*

**Lizton**
King, Richard Gene *superintendent*
Rauch, Eric *biology educator*

**Lowell**
Stewart, Bradley Mitchell *secondary school educator*

**Madison**
Williams, Carole Lee *secondary school educator*

**Marion**
Lawson, Diane Sue *elementary school educator*

**Middlebury**
Dickey, Lucy Jane *elementary school educator*

**Mishawaka**
Kummeth, Beth A. *elementary school educator*

**Modoc**
Shore, Randy *secondary school educator*

**Muncie**
Amman, E(lizabeth) Jean *academic administrator*
Dickson, Nancy Starr *retired elementary school educator*
Gora, JoAnn M. *academic administrator*
Kitchens, Frederick Lynton III *education educator, researcher*
Klotz, Ann Marie *director*
Lawhead, Victor Bernard *education educator*
Stewart, Rita Joan *academic administrator*

**New Albany**
Riehl, Jane Ellen *education educator*

**New Harmony**
Rice, David Lee *university president emeritus*

**New Haven**
Powelson, Gale Dawn *elementary school educator*

**Newburgh**
Culiver, Elizabeth Ann *elementary school educator*

**North Manchester**
Switzer, Jo Young *college president*

**Notre Dame**
Burish, Thomas Gerard *academic administrator, psychology professor*
Crosson, Frederick James *retired dean, humanities educator*
Jenkins, John I. *academic administrator*
Malloy, Edward Aloysius *academic administrator*
Marmion, Daniel Keith *school librarian*
Maziar, Christine M. *academic administrator*
O'Hara, Patricia Anne *dean, law educator*
O'Meara, Onorato Timothy *academic administrator, mathematician*
Scheidt, W. Robert *chemistry educator, researcher*
Woo, Carolyn Yauyan *dean*
Younger, Jennifer A. *university librarian*

**Richmond**
Bennett, Douglas Carleton *academic administrator*
Routson, Susan Hutchins *secondary school educator, consultant, peer counseling specialist*

**Roanoke**
Cutshall-Hayes, Diane Marion *elementary school educator*
Geyer, Catherine S. *elementary school educator*

**Russiaville**
Berry, Patricia A. *elementary school educator*
Suffield, Judith Kreutz *secondary school educator*

**South Bend**
Cerny, William *retired education educator, musician*
Doyle, Colleen Elizabeth *secondary school educator*
Fitzpatrick, Eileen Theresa *chemistry educator*
Harriman, Gerald Eugene *retired business administrator, retired economics professor*
Storin, Matthew Victor *academic administrator, educator, retired editor*

**Spencerville**
Clark, Donna M. *retired elementary school educator*

**Tell City**
Arterberry, Patricia *retired elementary school educator*

**Terre Haute**
Betts, Katherine Helen *academic administrator, educator*
Dando, William Arthur *academic administrator, geography and geology educator*
Hunt, Effie Neva *retired dean, literature educator*
Leach, Ronald George *education educator, librarian*

Malooley, David Joseph *electronics and computer technology educator*
Mellor, J. P. *education educator*
Olsen, Christopher John *education educator*

**Upland**
Kesler, Jay Lewis *retired academic administrator*

**Valparaiso**
Hillila, Bernhard Hugo Paul *retired education educator*
Mundinger, Donald Charles *retired college president*
Schnabel, Robert Victor *retired academic administrator*
Taylor, Heather Marie *director*

**Versailles**
Perry, Donna Sue *special education educator*

**Walton**
Krug, Don L. *secondary school educator, director*

**Wanatah**
Moser, Sandra Kay *secondary school educator*

**Warsaw**
Utter, Brenda Lu *adult education educator*

**West Lafayette**
Asher, J. William *education educator, psychology professor*
Beering, Steven Claus *academic administrator, medical educator*
Cosier, Richard A. *dean, finance educator*
Dyrenfurth, Michael John *education educator, academic administrator*
Gennett, Timothy *academic administrator*
Jang, SooCheong (Shawn) *education educator*
Jischke, Martin C. *academic administrator*
Mauer, Lisa *education educator*
Moyars-Johnson, Mary Annis *retired history professor*
Newby, Timothy James *education educator, researcher*
Reckowsky, Michael J. *academic administrator*
Ringel, Robert Lewis *academic administrator*
Rud, Anthony Gordon, Jr. *education educator*
Savaiano, Dennis Alan *education educator, dean*
Shertzer, Bruce Eldon *education educator*
Silva, Tony *education educator, editor*
VanFossen, Phillip J. *academic administrator*

**Westfield**
Bradbury, Betty Marie *history educator, music educator*

## IOWA

**Ames**
Allen, Benjamin J. *academic administrator*
Bugeja, Michael Joseph *director, educator, writer*
Crabtree, Beverly June *retired dean*
Ebbers, Larry Harold *education educator*
Geoffroy, Gregory L. *academic administrator, educator*
Jackson, George Arthur *dean, educator*
Manatt, Richard *retired education educator*
Mattila, Mary Jo Kalsem *elementary and art educator*

**Anita**
Stender, Julia Mae *mathematics educator*

**Belmond**
Martinek, Cynthia L. *principal*

**Bettendorf**
Hengst, Herbert Randall *retired adult education educator*

**Camanche**
DeLacy, Gary Richard *principal*
Fuglsang, Steven M. *principal*

**Cedar Falls**
Lettow, Lucille Jane *school librarian, education educator*

**Cedar Rapids**
Brighi, Robert J. *principal*
Urbanowski, Melena Haskovec *elementary school educator*

**Cherokee**
Henke, Marcia Ann *secondary school educator*
Rice, Christina Lynn Bochtler *literature and language educator*

**Clarinda**
Boysen, Katharine *school system administrator, director*

**Creston**
Dillenburg, Carolyn Eva Lauer *retired secondary school educator*

**Davenport**
Hudson, Celeste Nutting *education educator, consultant, reading clinic administrator*
Meyer, Jane Mary *elementary school educator*

**Des Moines**
Gaines, Ruth Ann *secondary school educator*
Jeffrey, Judy *school system administrator*
Maxwell, David E. *academic executive, educator*
Paterik, Frances Sue *secondary school educator, actress*

**Dubuque**
Haugen, Jane S. *elementary school educator*
Lickteig, Mary Joan *elementary school educator*
Toale, Thomas Edward *school system administrator, minister*

**Epworth**
Boice, Daniel Gene *college librarian*

**Forest City**
Tillman, Joseph Edward *elementary school educator*

**Fort Madison**
Moon, Julie Ann *elementary school educator*

**Grinnell**
Osgood, Russell King *academic administrator*

**Harlan**
Sondag, Mary Jo *elementary school educator, education educator*

**Indianola**
Dyer, Cynthia Myers *school librarian, archivist*

**Iowa City**
Barrera, Susan Cristina *secondary school educator*
Boyd, Willard Lee *academic administrator, educator, lawyer, museum director*
Brennan, Robert Lawrence *educational director, psychometrician*
Buckwalter, Kathleen C. *academic administrator, educator*
Dreher, Melanie Creagan *dean, nursing educator*
Feldt, Leonard Samuel *academic administrator, educator*
Gray, George Trumon *test development professional*
Hogan, Michael *academic administrator*
Ingram, Beth F. *academic administrator*
Johnsen, David C. *dean, dental educator*
Jones, Carolyn *dean, law educator*
Kurtz, Alice Kaufman *elementary school educator*
Plapp, Bryce Vernon *biochemistry educator*
Robillard, Jean Eugene *dean, academic*
Roe, Gerald Bruce *director, writer*
Spriestersbach, Duane Caryl *academic administrator, speech pathology/audiology services professional, educator*

**Johnston**
Hattel, Carson Matthew *elementary school educator*

**Keokuk**
Wendt, David Allen *literature and language educator*

**Le Grand**
Ryan, Deloris Kay *elementary school educator*

**Marion**
Ritchie, Ronald Thomas *history educator*

**Marshalltown**
Price, Bernice Irene *retired elementary school educator*
Weidenaar, Bradley William *literature and language educator*

**Monticello**
Balster, Barbara Ann *elementary school educator*

**Mount Vernon**
Will, Frederic *university administrator, writer*

**Muscatine**
Mowl, Linda *special education educator*

**New Hampton**
Herman, Claudia Bernice *elementary school educator*

**Newton**
Ward, Doree Maxine *secondary school educator*

**Oelwein**
Flaucher-Falck, Velma Ruth *retired special education educator*

**Oskaloosa**
Burrow, Paul Irving *secondary school educator*

**Ottumwa**
Lechner, Jane Ann *mathematics educator*
Newquist, Judy Lynne Roos *elementary school educator, education educator*
Stannard, Natalie Marie *secondary school educator*
Vasconez, Dennis Cornelius *secondary school educator, voice educator*

**Parkersburg**
Schmitz, Marianina Alice *literature and language educator*

**Rock Valley**
Bulthuis, Sidney Aaron *secondary school educator*
Ortman, Don L. *principal*

**Seymour**
Horton, Laura Kaye *special education educator*

**Sheldon**
Gifford, Carla J. *education educator*

**Sioux City**
Mounts, Nancy *secondary school educator*
Rants, Carolyn Jean *academic administrator, educator*
Young, Janet Marie *secondary school educator*

**Urbandale**
Hoyt, Kenneth Boyd *education educator, writer*

**Vinton**
Ramsey, Ardeth Jane *retired elementary school educator*

**Waterloo**
Kober, Arletta Refshauge (Mrs. Kay L. Kober) *supervisor*

**Waverly**
Rose, Mary Mabel *retired elementary school educator*

**Wever**
Hardy, Julia Irene *elementary school educator*

## KANSAS

**Baldwin City**
Baker, Margaret Moore-Fritz *retired school librarian, retired humanities educator*
Long, Patricia N. *academic administrator*
Rosenthal, Dan *retired director*

**Caney**
Wilmoth, Marsha Hope *elementary school educator*

**Clearwater**
Taverner, Pamela Johnson *secondary school educator*

**Coffeyville**
DeRosa, Michael L. *elementary school educator, artist*
Partridge, Sharon Sue *secondary school educator*

**Cottonwood Falls**
Dodez, Diane M. *principal*

**Emporia**
Fowler, Barbara J. *elementary school educator*
Wenger, James L. *education educator*

**Eureka**
Ditko, Pamela Ann *physical education educator, coach*

**Frontenac**
Wilson, Donald Wallin *academic administrator, communications educator*

**Garden City**
Hauschild, Barbara A. *principal*
Tidwell, Russell Murray *secondary school educator*

**Great Bend**
Rittenhouse, Nancy Carol *elementary school educator*

**Hays**
Budig, Jeanette *special education educator*
Harbin, Calvin Edward *retired educator*

**Horton**
Radford, Virginia Rodriguez *retired secondary school educator, librarian*

**Hoyt**
Morris, Sandra N. *elementary school educator*

**Independence**
Wright, Tami LaDonna *pre-school educator*

**Kansas City**
Atkinson, Barbara F. *dean, medical educator, executive vice chancellor*
Burke, Thomas Richard *community college administrator*
Clifton, Thomas E. *academic administrator, minister*
Miller, Karen L. *dean, nursing educator*
Warne, Alan M. *adult education educator, consultant*

**Lawrence**
Berry, James Lee *retired military educator*
Frederickson, Horace George *retired academic administrator, humanities educator*
Gaumer Erickson, Amy Sue *special education educator*
Hemenway, Robert E. *academic administrator, language educator*
Lariviere, Richard Wilfred *academic administrator, educator*
Locke, Carl Edwin, Jr. *academic administrator, engineer, educator*
McAllister, Stephen Robert *dean, law educator*
McDiarmid, Diane *education educator, researcher*
Peterson, Nancy *special education educator*
Turnbull, Ann Patterson *special education educator, consultant, research director*

**Leawood**
Talley, Melvin Gary *academic administrator*

**Liberal**
Hicks, Linda Reona *elementary school educator*
Smothermon, Reba Maxine *elementary school educator*

**Manhattan**
Coffman, James Richard *academic administrator, veterinarian, educator*
Muir, William Lloyd III *academic administrator*
Wefald, Jon *academic administrator*
White, Warren John *education educator*

**Meade**
Brannan, Cleo Estella *retired elementary school educator*

**Mission**
Merrill, Donna *special education educator*

**Moundridge**
Clark, Rustin *school system administrator*

**North Newton**
Ediger, Marlow *education educator*

**Ogden**
Armendariz, Jim *principal*

**Olathe**
Anderson, Peggy C. *elementary school educator*
Menke, Diana Lynn *elementary school educator*
Obenhaus, Steven Lee *secondary school educator*
Roller, Robert H. *academic administrator, finance educator*

Stevens, Diana Lynn *elementary school educator*

**Overland Park**
Damron, Nancy Lynn *secondary school educator*
Gerson, Steven Marc *technology writing professor, consultant*
Hodgell, Murlin Ray *university dean*
Plese, Joseph Marshall *education educator, actor*
Voska, Kathryn Caples *consultant, facilitator*
Whelan, Richard J. *retired academic administrator*

**Oxford**
Browning, Terri L. *secondary school educator*

**Pittsburg**
Runyan, Charles Kent *education educator*

**Pomona**
Gentry, Alberta Elizabeth *elementary school educator*

**Pratt**
Hart, Don Lee *academic administrator, writer*

**Russell**
Branick, Terry Lynn *secondary school educator*

**Shawnee Mission**
Allen, Janet Lee *special education educator*
Barton, Betty Louise *school system administrator*
Black, Lisa Zahn *elementary school educator*
Sweeney, Leo Joseph *university administrator*

**Sublette**
Myers, Connie Lanine *elementary school educator*
Swinney, Carol Joyce *secondary school educator*

**Topeka**
Corkins, Bob *school system administrator*
Eubank, Steven Eugene *secondary school educator*
Farley, Jerry B. *academic administrator*
McFarland, William Joseph (Joe McFarland) *academic administrator*
Wilson, Peggy Jo *secondary school educator*

**Wichita**
Philson, Richard Michael *academic administrator*
Platt, George Milo *university administrator*
Powell, Shirley Theressa *elementary school educator*
Vaughn, Kerri Lynn *elementary school educator*

**Yates Center**
Edwards, Mary Lee *retired secondary school educator, home economist*

## KENTUCKY

**Benton**
Pagel, Andrew W. *history educator*

**Berea**
Krug, John Carleton (Tony Krug) *academic administrator, library director, consultant*

**Bowling Green**
Atwell, Nedra Wheeler *education educator, consultant*
Burch, Barbara G. *academic administrator*
Butts, Vanessa Oldham *secondary school educator*
Haynes, Robert Vaughn *retired academic administrator, historian*

**Buckner**
Thompson, Deborah J. *mathematics educator*

**Campbellsville**
Spurling, Teresa Phillips *education educator*

**Covington**
Berg, Lorine McComis *retired guidance counselor*

**Danville**
Breeze, William Hancock *academic administrator*
Kennan, Elizabeth Topham *academic administrator, retired historian*
Roush, John A. *academic administrator*

**Fort Knox**
Olive, Karl William *elementary education educator, secondary educator*
Tucker, Brenda Brunette *elementary school educator*

**Fort Thomas**
Clinkenbeard, Janelle Darlene *retired elementary school educator*

**Frankfort**
Reid, George Willis *college president*
Shabazz, David Lorenzo *vocational school educator*
Sias, Mary *university president*

**Grethel**
Hughes, Cindi Baker *special education educator*

**Guston**
Yundt, Betty Brandenburg *elementary school educator*

**Hardin**
Morrow, Bruce William *academic administrator, management consultant*

**Harlan**
Greene, James S. III *school administrator*

**Hartford**
Taylor, David Michael *elementary school educator*

**Hickman**
Black, David A. *secondary school educator*

**Lexington**
Allison, Jonathan Mackinnon *university professor, researcher*

Burris, Ashley Paige *director, educator*
Calderhead, William John *special education educator, researcher*
Cole, Henry Philip *educational psychology educator*
Gill, Karen V. *secondary school educator, consultant*
Guskey, Thomas Robert *education educator*
Leaumont, Anne Parlanti *special education educator*
Norman, Charlene Wilson *secondary school educator*
Sullivan, Patrick Giles *education educator, researcher*
Todd, Lee Trover, Jr. *academic administrator, electrical engineer*
Turner, Sharon P. *dean, dentist, educator*
Vestal, Allan W. *dean, law educator*
Wethington, Charles T., Jr. *academic administrator*

**Louisville**
Cecil, Bonnie Susan *elementary school educator*
Choi, Namok *education educator*
Goldstein, Irvin L. *elementary school educator*
Greaver, Joanne Hutchins *mathematics educator, writer*
Jenne, Sue Oak *secondary school educator*
Kaplan, Joel A. *academic administrator*
Karwowski, Waldemar *adult education educator*
Mohler, Richard Albert, Jr. *academic administrator, theologian*
Oates, Thomas R. *university executive*
Rothstein, Laura *dean, law educator*
Swain, Donald Christie *retired academic administrator, historian, educator*
Wagoner, Ruth R *education coach*

**Madisonville**
Deger, Robert John, Jr. *college dean*

**Middlesboro**
Owens, Chuck *secondary school educator, broadcast technician*

**Morehead**
Klecker, Beverly McCauley *academic administrator*

**Mount Sterling**
Aileen-Donohew, Phyllis Augusta *educational consultant*
Johnston, Jacqueline Anne *school administrator, director*

**Newport**
Clinkenbeard, James Howard *principal*

**Nicholasville**
Armstrong, Marcy Lynn *literature and language educator, special education educator*
Burton, Malinda Daugherty *school librarian*
Midkiff, Dinah Lee *retired elementary and middle school educator*

**Owensboro**
Cinnamond, Robert E. *education educator, writer*
Humphreys, Daniel James *elementary school educator*
Roberts, Brian Wayne *middle school educator, minister*

**Pikeville**
Smith, Harold Hasken *university administrator*

**Princeton**
Earnest, Melissa Webb *education educator*
Faughn, Dale *biology educator*

**Richmond**
Blanchard, Paul *academic administrator, educator*

**Shelbyville**
Hedrick, William David *secondary school educator, musician*

**Shepherdsville**
Austin, Jim E. *secondary school educator*

**Somerset**
Pennington, Aubrey El *director*

**Versailles**
Taylor, Elizabeth *secondary school educator*

**LOUISIANA**

**Alexandria**
Fletcher, Keith Merril *mathematics educator*
Maples, Mary Lou *elementary school educator*
Wesse, David Joseph *higher education administrator, consultant*

**Baton Rouge**
Bensman, Stephen J. *school librarian, researcher*
Boyce, Bert Roy *university dean emeritus, library and information science educator*
Caffey, Horace Rouse *academic administrator, agricultural company executive*
Harper, Sandra Stecher *academic administrator*
Harrelson, Clyde Lee *retired secondary school educator*
Jenkins, William L. *academic administrator*
Mc Cameron, Fritz Allen *retired university administrator*
Ngandu, Pius Nkashama *education educator*
O'Keefe, Sean Charles *academic administrator, former federal agency administrator*
Okeil, Ayman M. *educator*
Perkins, Huel Davis *retired academic administrator*
Picard, Cecil *school system administrator*
Prestage, James Jordan *university chancellor*
Risinger, Beth N. *elementary school educator*
Smith, Michael *academic administrator*

**Benton**
Hudson, Marguerite W. *secondary school educator*

**Bunkie**
Laborde, Terry James *secondary school educator*

**Centerville**
Mancuso, Monica Laughlin *educational administrator*

**Crowley**
Privat, Ruby (Ruby Thibodeaux) *elementary school educator*

**Elm Grove**
Turner, Steven Jay *director*

**Franklin**
Fairchild, Phyllis Elaine *school counselor*

**Glenmora**
Burns, Linda D. *elementary school educator*

**Grambling**
Francis, Norman C. *academic administrator*
Judson, Horace Augustus *academic administrator, chemistry educator*
Porter, Wilma Jean *retired educational consultant*

**Hammond**
Parker, Clea Edward *retired university president*
Valverde, Roldan Arturo *education educator, researcher*

**Harvey**
Weekley, Judy Liddington *special education educator*

**Houma**
Dagenhardt, Glynn Anthony *secondary school educator*

**Lacombe**
Hendricks, Donald Duane *retired school librarian*

**Lafayette**
Authement, Ray Paul *college president*
Colbert-Cormier, Patricia A. *secondary school educator*
Dasgupta, Subrata *director*
Fekih, Afef *education educator*
Oller, John W., Jr. *educator, writer*
Petry, Ruth Vidrine *retired principal*
Redding, Evelyn A. *dean*
Rieck, William Albert *education educator, academic administrator*

**Lake Charles**
Fields-Gold, Anita *retired dean*
Hebert, Robert D. *academic administrator*

**Mandeville**
Arrowsmith, Marian Campbell *elementary school educator, supervisor, educator*

**Metairie**
Blunt, Joyce Omega *special education educator*
Chambers, Thomas Edward *academic administrator, psychologist*
Crosby, Marena Lienhard *retired academic administrator*
St. John, Bridgette Alayne *secondary school educator*

**Monroe**
Cofer, James Erwin *academic administrator*
Foreman, Teresa *educational consultant, educator*
Profit, Loretha Spurs *retired elementary school educator*

**Natchitoches**
Findley, James Lee *academic administrator, history professor*
Lacina, Lorna J. *education educator*
Wolfe, George Cropper *retired private school educator, artist, writer*

**New Iberia**
Hockless, Mary Fontenot *educational consultant*

**New Orleans**
Bennett-Johnson, Earnestine Rose *education educator, consultant*
Cody, Wilmer St. Clair *educational policy researcher*
Cowen, Scott S. *academic administrator*
Gordon, Joseph Elwell *university official, educator*
Hovland, Eric Jeffrey *dean, endodontics educator*
Kelly, Eamon Michael *university president emeritus*
McCall, John Patrick *college president, educator*
Novakov, George John, Jr. *gifted and talented educator, consultant, administrative assistant*
Paradise, Louis Vincent *education educator, dean*
Peoples, Gerald C. *college president*
Ponoroff, Lawrence *dean, law educator, consultant*
Query, Lance D. *dean, university librarian*
Sherman, Edward Francis *dean, law educator*

**Newllano**
Boren, Lynda Sue *gifted education educator*

**Opelousas**
Underwood, Lorainne Ballard *literature and language educator*

**Pineville**
Lott, Johnnye Jo *elementary school educator, writer*
Smith, Mabel Hargis *retired secondary school educator, musician*

**Ruston**
Barron, Brian Richard *education educator*
Freasier, Aileen W. *special education educator*
Maxfield, John Edward *retired university dean*
Nassar, Raja *statistics educator, researcher, consultant*
Taylor, Foster Jay *retired university president*
Zhu, Huiguang *research educator*

**Saint Martinville**
Fournet, Patricia Sibley *retired secondary school educator*

**Shreveport**
Amin, Helen Jewitt *special education educator*

**Slidell**
Dabdoub, Paul Oscar *academic administrator*
Fincher, Margaret Ann *retired secondary school educator*
Marton, Kathryn Widman *secondary school educator*

**Sorrento**
Welch, Joe Ben *academic administrator*

**Springhill**
Thomas, Faye Evelyn J. *elementary and secondary school educator*

**Tallulah**
Gilbert, Rochelle Wilhelmina *education educator, consultant*

**Thibodaux**
Breaux, Annette Lalande *education educator, writer*
Harris, Rose M. *academic administrator*
Hulbert, Stephen Thompson *academic administrator*

**West Monroe**
Ford, Mary Ann *secondary school educator, educator*
North, Sherri L. *elementary school educator*

**Westlake**
Grantham, Camille Renee Theriot *high school librarian, media specialist*

**MAINE**

**Acton**
Cunningham, Joyce Wentworth *retired secondary school educator*

**Augusta**
Crosby, Nathaniel Howard *elementary school educator*
Gendron, Susan Ann *school system administrator*
Randall, Richard J. *academic administrator*

**Bangor**
MacTaggart, Terrence Joseph *professor, former university chancellor*
McKinnon, Carolyn Ann *child care center director*

**Bar Harbor**
Krevans, Julius Richard *academic administrator, internist*
Swazey, Judith Pound *academic administrator, science educator*

**Bremen**
Wilson, Linda Smith *retired academic administrator*

**Brunswick**
Greason, Arthur LeRoy, Jr. *retired university administrator*
McEwen, Craig A. *dean*
Mills, Barry *academic administrator, lawyer*

**Corea**
Harward, Donald West *retired academic administrator*

**Fairfield**
Martin, James *retired education educator*

**Farmington**
Kalikow, Theodora June *academic administrator*

**Fort Kent**
Cost, Richard Willard *academic administrator, educator*

**Islesboro**
Rogers, William Raymond *retired academic administrator, psychologist, educator*

**Kennebunk**
Rollerson, Marnie Loreen *secondary school educator, art educator*

**Kennebunkport**
Featherman, Sandra *academic administrator, political science professor*

**Lewiston**
Hansen, Elaine Tuttle *academic administrator*
Reich, Jill *dean*

**North Yarmouth**
Fecteau, Rosemary Louise *educational administrator, educator, consultant*

**Old Orchard Beach**
Day, Marlene E. *elementary school educator*

**Old Town**
Alex, Joanne DeFilipp *elementary school educator*

**Orono**
Estler, Suzanne E. *education educator*
Innis, Daniel Eugene *dean, consultant*
Kennedy, Robert Alan *educational administrator*
Rice, Edward Perry *secondary school educator*
Szymanski, Edna Mora *dean*
Townsend, David W. *director*
Wiersma, G. Bruce *dean, forester, educator*

**Portland**
Dill, William Rankin *college president*
Khoury, Colleen A. *dean*
Lyons, Charles M. *education educator, former academic administrator*

**Saco**

Pattenaude, Richard Louis *university administrator*
Vincent, Christine *academic administrator*

**Presque Isle**
Burgher, Karl E. *academic administrator*

**Skowhegan**
Ross, James Owen *education educator, researcher*

**South Thomaston**
Buffington, Audrey Virginia *elementary school educator, writer*

**Waterville**
Adams, William D. *academic administrator*
Cook, Susan Farwell *director*

**Yarmouth**
Bischoff, David Canby *retired university dean*
Hart, Loring Edward *academic administrator*

**York**
Minard, Maryann Johnson *elementary school educator, secondary school educator, director*

**MARYLAND**

**Accident**
Nicklin, Shawn Douglas *history educator*

**Accokeek**
Kutchi, Judith Ann *elementary school educator*

**Adamstown**
Church, Martha Eleanor *retired academic administrator*

**Adelphi**
Heeger, Gerald Arthur *university president*
Walker, Mamie Odena *retired secondary school educator*

**Annapolis**
Bowen, Linnell R. *director*
Jacobs, Linda Joan *secondary school educator*
Miller, William Charles *academic administrator, retired naval officer*
Stern, Margaret Bassett *retired special education educator, author*

**Arnold**
Smith, Martha A. *academic administrator*

**Baltimore**
Allan, Janet D. *dean*
Arrindell, Nicholas J. *academic administrator, educator*
Ball, Gregory Francis *biological psychology educator*
Ball, Marion Jokl *academic administrator*
Bradford, Peter Durgin *elementary school educator*
Brody, William Ralph *academic administrator, radiologist, educator*
Browne, Lovetie W. *special education educator, small business owner*
Ellis, Brother Patrick (H. J. Ellis) *academic administrator*
Gifford, Donald George *dean, law educator*
Gleichmann, Frances Evangeline *retired elementary school educator*
Grasmick, Nancy S. *school system administrator*
Guler, Osman *education educator, researcher*
Haddaway, Heather Michelle *elementary school educator, music educator*
Heller, Barbara R. *former dean, nursing educator*
Isable, Alisha *elementary school educator*
Jackson, Stanley Edward *retired special education educator*
Keller, George Charles *higher education consultant, writer*
Kenyatta, David Roger Joseph *director, lawyer*
Lazarus, Fred, IV, *academic administrator*
Lewis, Edwin Augustus Stevens *physics educator*
McPartland, James Michael *academic administrator*
Oji, Pauline E. *secondary school educator*
Reid, Lauretta Glasper *retired principal*
Robinson, Retiana Cecelia *secondary school educator*
Ruby, Mary Lorraine *special education educator*
Ross, Richard Starr *retired medical school dean, cardiologist, educator*
Rothenberg, Karen H. *dean, law educator*
Scales, Robert H., Jr. *former academic administrator, retired army officer*
Seurkamp, Mary Pat *college president*
Simmons, Howard L. *education educator*
Stohler, Christian S. *dean, dental educator*
Tiefenwerth, William Philip *university program director*
Tillapaugh, Daniel Weston *academic administrator*
Wadsworth, Julie Bell *secondary school educator*

**Beltsville**
Bruckner, Daniel Raymond *history educator*

**Bethesda**
Bulger, Roger James *academic administrator*
Corn, Milton *dean, physician, consultant*
Hamilton, J-Mauri *academic administrator*
Hemming, Val G. *retired dean, educator*
Musil, Robert Kirkland *educator*
Solomon, Henry *university dean*

**Bowie**
Lowe, Calvin W. *university president*

**Cambridge**
Tenanty, Jane Elizabeth *secondary school educator*

**Chestertown**
Tipson, (Lynn) Baird *academic administrator, religious studies educator*

**Chevy Chase**
Rayburn, Wendell Gilbert, Sr. *educational consultant*

Towsner, Cynthia Merle *academic administrator, educator*

**College Park**
Bernstein, Melvin *provost*
Destler, William W. *academic administrator*
Dieter, George Elwood, Jr. *academic administrator*
Frank, Howard *dean, information technology executive*
Hey, Nancy Henson *educational administrator*
Ingold, Catherine White *academic administrator*
Jabaji, Ramsey George *academic administrator*
Langenberg, Donald Newton *retired academic administrator, physicist*
Mote, Clayton Daniel, Jr. *academic administrator, mechanical engineer, educator*
Strickland, Lee Stephen *educator, consultant*
Toll, John Sampson *retired academic administrator, physics professor*

**Columbia**
Duncan, Mary Ellen *academic administrator*
Jones-Wilson, Faustine Clarisse *retired education educator*
Whiting, Albert Nathaniel *former university chancellor*

**Damascus**
Splete, Marilyn Detweiler *retired secondary school educator*

**Easton**
Behm, Mark Edward *academic administrator, consultant*

**Ellicott City**
Bruley, Duane Frederick *academic administrator, consultant, engineer*
Wheltle, Margaret Maie *retired secondary school educator*

**Emmitsburg**
Houston, George R., Jr. *college president*

**Essex**
Bunn, Wm. Jeffrey *secondary school educator, director*

**Federalsburg**
Kennedy-Milligan, Diana Lynne *secondary school educator*

**Fort Washington**
Bull, Sharon Kay *elementary school educator*

**Frederick**
Brauer, Ethel May *secondary school educator*
Burkhard, Fred (Bud) *academic administrator*
Marx, Patricia Anne *education educator*
Pastoor, Robertus Antonius *academic administrator*

**Frostburg**
Gibralter, Jonathan C. *academic administrator*
Gira, Catherine Russell *retired academic administrator*
Root, Edward Lakin *education educator, academic administrator*

**Gaithersburg**
Bremenstuhl, David P. *elementary school educator*

**Greenbelt**
Bernstein, Kenneth J. *secondary school educator*

**Hagerstown**
Warner, Charles David III *academic administrator*

**Havre De Grace**
Alegi, Marc Patrick *middle school educator*

**Hollywood**
Freeman, Michael Anthony *academic administrator, educational consultant*

**Indian Head**
Price, Teresa Annette *elementary school educator*

**Joppa**
Bates, Martha Copenhaver *elementary school educator*

**Kensington**
Ellwanger, Albert Thompson III *secondary school educator*
Holloway, William Jimmerson *retired education educator*

**Keymar**
Meakin, Matthew *director*

**Lanham**
Ingraham, Cynthia Louise Johnson *educational consultant*

**Laurel**
Dorsey, John Wesley, Jr. *retired academic administrator, economist*
Hunter, Edwina Earle *elementary school educator*
Stumpff, Robert Thomas *retired academic administrator*
Williams, Barbara Ivory *educational researcher*

**Lusby**
Ladd, Culver Sprogle *secondary school educator*

**Marion Station**
Handy, Mary Thomas *retired elementary school educator*

**North Potomac**
Busche, Leon Frank *secondary school educator*

**Ocean Pines**
Crawford, Norman Crane, Jr. *academic administrator, consultant*

**Odenton**
Lambert, Vickie Ann *retired dean, nursing consultant*

**Owings**
Oring, Stuart August *audio-visual specialist, writer, photographer, researcher*
Redmond, John Andrew *elementary school educator*

**Owings Mills**
Earnhardt, David Lu *retired literature and language educator, writer, musician*

**Pittsville**
Richards, Samuel J. *secondary school educator*

**Potomac**
Kuykendall, Crystal Arlene *educational consultant, lawyer*

**Princess Anne**
Thompson, Thelma Barnaby *university president, classical languages educator*

**Rockville**
Kowalchick, Edward M. *headmaster*
Sparks, David Stanley *academic administrator*
Stansfield, Charles W. *educational administrator*

**Saint Marys City**
O'Brien, Jane Margaret *academic administrator*

**Saint Michaels**
Feisel, Lyle Dean *retired dean, electrical engineer, educator*

**Salisbury**
Gorrow, Teena Ruark *education educator*

**Silver Spring**
Burgos-Sasscer, Ruth *chancellor emeritus*
Camphor, James Winky, Jr. *educational administrator*
Coles, Anna Louise Bailey *retired dean, nurse*
Cooper, Nannie Coles *education educator, consultant*
Haynes, Leonard L. III *director*
Latson, Richard Charles *retired audio-visual specialist*
Miller, Karla Patricia *elementary school educator*
Oliver, Kimberly *Teacher of the Year*
Whalen, John Philip *retired academic administrator, priest, lawyer*

**Stevenson**
Manning, Kevin James *academic administrator*

**Swanton**
Cummins, Delmer Duane *academic administrator, historian*

**Towson**
Caret, Robert Laurent *academic administrator*
Hoch, David Allen *athletic director*

**Union Bridge**
Hannah, Judy Challenger *private education tutor*

**Westminster**
McKay, Gretchen Kreahling *dean, educator, director*
Rosenthal, Michael Ross *academic administrator, consultant*

## MASSACHUSETTS

**Amherst**
Adrion, William Richards *academic administrator, computer and information sciences educator, writer*
Bradley, Raymond Stuart *education educator, researcher*
Call, Gregory S. *academic administrator, mathematics professor*
Hartwell, Alfred Stedman *international relations educator, consultant*
Immerman, Neil *academic administrator, computer science educator*
Lombardi, John V. *academic administrator, historian*
Marx, Anthony W. *academic administrator*
May, Ernest Dewey *academic administrator, musician*
Muriel, Ana *education educator*
Prince, Gregory Smith, Jr. *retired college president*
Seymour, Charlena *academic administrator*

**Andover**
Loschi, Richard Paul *middle school educator*

**Arlington**
Fulmer, Vincent Anthony *retired college president*

**Ashfield**
Bannister, Geoffrey *academic administrator, geographer*

**Bedford**
White, Alan Frederick *academic administrator*

**Beverly**
Eastman, W. Dean *secondary school educator*
Towner, Mark A. *dean, visual artist*

**Boston**
Alden, Vernon Roger *academic administrator*
Aoun, Joseph *academic administrator, linguistics educator, researcher*
Beer, Michael *education educator, researcher*
Berk, Lee Eliot *academic administrator*
Bloom, Barry R. *dean, medical educator*
Brown, Robert Arthur *academic administrator, chemical engineering professor*
Brown, Roger H. *academic administrator*
Caldwell, Ann Wickins *academic administrator*
Chang, Shan Nan *education educator, academic administrator*

Chou, Laisheng *education educator*
Cox, Malcolm *academic administrator, medical educator*
DePaola, Dominick Philip *academic administrator*
Dienstag, Jules Leonard *dean, hepatologist, medical researcher*
Dluhy, Deborah Haigh *dean*
Doyle, Mathias Francis *academic administrator, political scientist, educator*
Elasmar, Michael *director, educator*
Fertitta, Angela *dean*
Frankl, Spencer Nelson *dean, dentist*
Garber, Carol Ewing *physiology educator*
Gibson, Nigel C. *education educator*
Grant, Barbara Hurwitz *history educator*
Harris, Andrew Michael *director*
Hedlund, Ronald David *academic administrator, researcher, educator*
Keusch, Gerald Tilden *academic administrator*
Kirkpatrick, Edward Thomson *retired academic administrator, retired mechanical engineer*
Koh, Howard Kyongju *academic administrator, educator, former public health commissioner*
Landsmark, Ted *academic administrator*
Lataif, Louis Edward *dean*
Le Quesne, Philip William *chemistry educator, researcher*
Maganzini, Brother John Bernard *academic administrator*
Martin, Joseph Boyd *dean, neurologist, educator*
Mehra, Pushkar *director, educator*
Meissner, Walt *dean*
Myers, Robert K. III *director, musician, composer*
Norris, Lonnie Harold *dean*
O'Rourke, Maureen A. *dean, law educator*
Penney, Sherry Hood *academic administrator, consultant*
Piscatelli, Nancy Kelley *elementary school educator*
Reede, Joan Yvonne *academic administrator, medical educator, pediatrician*
Ronayne, Michael Richard, Jr. *academic dean*
Scrimshaw, Susan Crosby *academic administrator*
Silber, John Robert *retired academic administrator, law educator, philosophy educator*
Simmons, Sylvia Jeanne Quarles (Mrs. Herbert G. Simmons Jr.) *academic administrator, educator*
Sloan, Katherine (Kay Sloan) *college president*
Spieler, Emily A. *dean, law educator*
Van Domelen, John Francis *academic administrator*
Xu, Xiping *adult education educator, director*
Zungolo, Eileen H. *dean*

**Bridgewater**
Tinsley, Adrian *former college president*

**Byfield**
Doggett, John Martin, Jr., (Marty Doggett) *headmaster*

**Cambridge**
Bane, Mary Jo *dean, political science professor*
Champion, Hale (Charles Hale Champion) *academic administrator, lecturer, government official, consultant*
Clay, Phillip L. *academic administrator*
Conway, Jill Kathryn Ker *former academic administrator, writer*
Ellwood, David Tabor *dean, public policy educator*
Elmore, Richard F. *education educator*
Emanuel, Kerry Andrew *academic administrator, meteorologist, oceanographer, educator*
Eurich, Nell P. *education educator*
Fischer, Kurt Walter *education educator*
Fox, John Bayley, Jr. *university dean*
Graham, Patricia Albjerg *education educator*
Gray, Paul Edward *academic administrator*
Hockfield, Susan *academic administrator, medical educator*
Howitt, Arnold Martin *academic administrator, educator*
Hyman, Steven Edward *academic administrator, physiatrist, educator*
Jacobs, Vicki Ann *education educator*
Johnson, Howard Wesley *retired academic administrator, finance company executive*
Kagan, Elena *dean, law educator*
Kelman, Steven Jay *education educator*
Khoury, Philip S. *academic administrator*
Kirby, William C. *dean, history professor*
Lagemann, Ellen Condliffe *history and education educator, former dean*
Lawrence-Lightfoot, Sara *education educator, sociologist*
McCartney, Kathleen *dean, education educator*
McKenna, Margaret Anne *academic administrator*
Mitchell, William J. *academic administrator, architecture educator*
Putnam, Robert D. *education educator*
Reif, L. Rafael *academic administrator, engineering educator*
Rowe, Mary P. *organizational ombudsman, management educator*
Schmalensee, Richard Lee *dean*
Shinagel, Michael *dean, English literature educator*
Smith, David Julian *educational consultant*
Sollors, Werner *literature and language educator*
Summers, Lawrence Henry *former academic administrator, former secretary of the treasury educator*
Thiemann, Ronald Frank *dean, religious studies educator*
Tirman, John *academic research director*
Whitlock, Charles Preston *former university dean*

**Cheshire**
Vincent, D. Christopher *history educator*

**Chestnut Hill**
Altbach, Philip *director, educator*
Bando, Patricia Alice *academic administrator*
Beaton, Albert Eugene *education educator*
Deese, David Allen *education educator, researcher*
Gaiser, Ted Joseph *academic administrator, minister*
Gow, Peter *secondary school educator, writer*
Keating, Patrick J. *academic administrator*
Leahy, William Patrick *academic administrator, historian, educator*

Nemerowicz, Gloria *academic administrator*

**Concord**
Dresden, Jacob A. *headmaster*
Giles, Kathleen C. *headmaster*

**Danvers**
Beauregard, John *college librarian, consultant*
Clark, Sharon Jackson *private school administrator*

**Dartmouth**
Nieviedgal, Carol Belmarce *elementary school educator*

**Deerfield**
Widmer, Eric *headmaster*

**Devens**
Sizer, Theodore R. *education educator*

**Dighton**
Buote, Rosemarie Boschen *retired special education educator*

**Douglas**
Bachelder, Beverly Brandt *secondary school educator, assistant principal, director*

**Duxbury**
Swanson, Richard Oscar *history educator, department chairman*
Thrasher, Dianne Elizabeth *mathematics educator, computer scientist, consultant*

**Easton**
Barrett, Mary Kathleen *secondary school educator*

**Everett**
Blake, Margaret Mary *director*

**Fiskdale**
Costello, Christine Ann *fine arts director, church organist*

**Framingham**
Flanagan, Timothy James *academic administrator, criminal justice educator*
Heineman, Helen L. *retired academic administrator*
Hodgins, Beatrice Davis *retired elementary school educator, primary school educator*
Lucci, Dorothy Ann *educational consultant, psychologist*

**Franklin**
Benjamin, Bernard Edward *school system administrator, director*

**Granby**
Mucha, Sister Marlene M. *secondary school educator*

**Groton**
Commons, Richard B. *headmaster*
Wiggins, D. Scott *headmaster*

**Haydenville**
Shallcross, Doris Jane *education educator*

**Holden**
O'Neil, William Francis *academic administrator*

**Hubbardston**
Marceau, Judith Marie *retired elementary school educator, small business owner*

**Hyannis**
O'Brien, Kathleen L. *special education educator*

**Hyde Park**
Harris, Emily Louise *special education educator*

**Indian Orchard**
Daley, Veta Adassa *educational administrator*

**Ipswich**
Dion Faust, Debra *secondary school educator*
Lombardo, Ann Marie *special education educator, writer, artist*

**Lakeville**
Ledwith, Edward J *elementary school educator*

**Lexington**
Collins, Allan Meakin *education educator*
McFarland, Philip James *secondary school educator, writer*

**Longmeadow**
Ezrin, Myer *retired director*
Katz, Barbara Stein *special education educator*
Leary, Carol Ann *academic administrator*

**Lowell**
McAloon, Noreen Marie *elementary school educator*
Ting, John M. *dean, engineering educator*
Zhang, Xiaoqi *education educator*

**Lynn**
Astuccio, Sheila Margaret *educational administrator*
Ryder, Edward Francis *secondary school educator*

**Malden**
Driscoll, David P. *school system administrator*
Jonker, Jean Elizabeth *educational consultant*

**Marion**
Latham, Christopher Robert *alumni and development director*

**Marstons Mills**
Martin, David Standish *education educator*

**Medford**
Bacow, Lawrence Seldon *academic administrator, environmental scientist, educator*

Bharucha, Jamshed *academic administrator*
Bosworth, Stephen Warren *dean, former ambassador*
Glaser, James M. *dean, political science professor*
Sternberg, Robert Jeffrey *dean, psychology professor, researcher*

**Middleton**
Stanley, (Malchan) Craig *school system administrator, consultant, psychologist, researcher*

**Mill River**
Dunsay, Charles William *elementary school educator*

**Milton**
Robertson, Robin Alayne *headmaster, anthropologist*
Wengler, Marguerite Marie *counseling administrator*

**Natick**
Sullivan, Brianne May *history educator, educational program director*

**Needham**
Kossuth, Joanne M. *academic administrator*
Miller, Richard Keith *academic administrator, engineering educator*
Zambone, Alana Maria *special education educator, consultant*

**New Bedford**
Matsumoto, Carolee Setsuko *researcher, education developer and administrator*

**Newburyport**
Robinson, Joyce McPeake *academic administrator*

**Newton**
Matteson, Carol J. *academic administrator*
O'Connell, Sister Virginia M. *school librarian*
Peterson, Lloyd, Jr. *academic administrator, consultant*

**Newton Center**
Garvey, John Hugh *dean, law educator*

**North Adams**
Newby, Kelli *education educator*

**North Andover**
Becker, Lawrence Wilfred *headmaster*

**North Easton**
Churchill, Jean Frances *secondary school educator, finance educator*

**Northampton**
Christ, Carol Tecla *academic administrator*
Mahoney, Maureen A. *academic administrator*

**Northfield**
Stevens, Donald John *secondary school educator*

**Norton**
Marshall, Dale Rogers *academic administrator, political scientist, educator*

**Norwood**
Reilley, Margaret Randall *secondary school educator*

**Peabody**
Generazzo, Arlene Diamond *retired elementary school educator*

**Pittsfield**
Norris, Jeannie *headmaster*
Page, Daniel Bennett *dean, musician*
Wood, Elizabeth Ann *special education educator*

**Plymouth**
Woodburn, Norma Denman *biology educator*

**Plympton**
Smith, Robert Rutherford *dean, communications educator*

**Quincy**
Adams, Ronald G. *elementary school educator*
Chisholm, Maureen *academic administrator*

**Salem**
Doran, Kathleen Brewer *dean, consultant*

**Scituate**
Spangler, Stanley Eugene *international relations educator*

**Sharon**
Johnson, Addie Collins *secondary school educator, retired dietician*

**Shrewsbury**
Haig, Barbara Frances *elementary school educator*
Onorato, Nicholas Louis *retired program director, economist*

**Somerville**
Austill, Allen *dean emeritus*

**South Dartmouth**
Ward, Richard Joseph *university dean, educator, author*

**South Deerfield**
Fritz, Nancy H. *retired educational researcher, administrator*

**South Hadley**
Bowie, Lee *academic administrator, philosopher, educator*
Creighton, Joanne Vanish *academic administrator*

**South Yarmouth**
Stewart, Virginia Haken *elementary school educator*

**Southampton**
Salomao, Cheryl May Labrie *elementary school educator*

**Southborough**
Hill, Antony J. deV. *headmaster, history educator*
Hill, Elsa N. *headmaster, literature and language educator, lawyer*
Stubbart, David James *elementary school educator*

**Southbridge**
Vasey, Ann L. *pre-school administrator, counselor*

**Spencer**
Higgins, Jane Edgington *secondary school educator*
Robinson, Evelyn Edna *secondary school educator*

**Springfield**
Caprio, Anthony S. *academic administrator*
Cleland, Thomas Edward, Jr. *secondary school educator*
Cook, Kathryn Anne *secondary school educator*
Cremonini, Michael P. *English educator, acting educator*
Mantoni, Philip Joseph *retired principal, education educator*
Scibelli, Andrew M. *academic administrator*

**Sudbury**
Aldrich-Bennett, Florence Anne *elementary school educator*

**Waltham**
Adamian, Gregory Harry *academic administrator*
Edmiston, Scott *academic administrator, educator*
Krauss, Marty Wyngaarden *academic administrator*
Reinharz, Jehuda *academic administrator, history educator*
Rinehart, Kenton W. *academic administrator*
Sullivan, Mary E. *retired secondary educator, past state legislator*
Wawrzaszek, Susan V. *university librarian*

**Watertown**
Tompkins, Curtis Johnston *retired academic administrator*

**Webster**
Loosemore, Paula M. *literature and language educator*

**Wellesley**
Auerbach, Jerold S. *academic administrator, educator*
Cuba, Lee *dean*
Heartt, Charlotte Beebe *university official*
Walsh, Diana Chapman *academic administrator, sociologist, educator*

**West Roxbury**
Roach, Maureen S. *primary school educator*

**Westford**
Antón-Oldenburg, Mary Felice *principal*

**Williamstown**
Chandler, John Wesley *educational consultant*
Niemeyer, Peter Eduard *history educator*
Schapiro, Morton Owen *academic administrator*

**Winchester**
Irving, Gitte Nielsen *secondary school educator*
Rahmeier, Lynne Jillson *primary school educator, secondary school educator*

**Woburn**
Tramonte, Michael Robert *education educator*
Winson, Ellen-Marie (Macone) *school system administrator, reading specialist*

**Woods Hole**
Farrington, John William *academic administrator, dean, research scientist*

**Worcester**
Bassett, John E. *academic administrator, language educator*
Berkey, Dennis Dale *university president*
Brooks, John Edward *college president*
Harding, Beth Ann *middle school educator*
Indic, Premananda *education educator, researcher*
Lazare, Aaron *dean, psychiatrist*
Mardilovich, Ivan P. *education educator, researcher*
McFarland, Michael C. *academic administrator*
Palmer, John Anthony III *secondary school educator, music educator, language educator*
Vellaccio, Frank *academic administrator*

**Yarmouth Port**
Hall, James Frederick *retired college president*

## MICHIGAN

**Adrian**
Caine, Stanley Paul *college administrator*
Yehuda, Simone Naomi *education educator*

**Akron**
Wright, Michelle Denise *elementary school principal*

**Algonac**
Paquet, Gary Lee *elementary school educator*

**Allendale**
Haas, Thomas Joseph *academic administrator, chemistry educator*

**Alma**
Swanson, Robert Draper *college president*
Tracy, Saundra J. *academic administrator*

**Ann Arbor**
Ball, Deborah Loewenberg *dean, education educator*

Beutler, Suzanne A. *retired secondary school educator, artist*
Bigelow, Wilbur Charles *retired education educator*
Bryant, Barbara Everitt *academic administrator, researcher, retired marketing professional, retired federal agency administrator*
Caminker, Evan H. *dean, law educator*
Chin, Chen Ooi *dean*
Dolan, Robert J. *dean*
Fleming, Suzanne Marie *academic administrator, freelance/self-employed writer*
Hilton, James L. *university librarian*
Im, Hong Geun *educator*
Kalbfleisch, John David *statistics educator*
Kelch, Robert Paul *former dean, pediatric endocrinologist*
Omenn, Gilbert Stanley *academic administrator, internist*
Paul, Ara Garo *university dean*
Polverini, Peter J. *dean, dental educator*
Potempa, Kathleen M. *dean, nursing educator*
Raman, Lakshmi *education educator*
Rogers, Bryan L. *dean*
Schacht, Jochen Heinrich *biochemistry educator*
Stern, Alexandra Minna *education educator*
Sullivan, Thomas Patrick *academic administrator*
Warner, Kenneth E. *dean, public health educator, consultant*
Warner, Robert Mark *dean, archivist, historian*
Xie, Yu *adult education educator*

**Armada**
Kummerow, Arnold A. *superintendent of schools*

**Benton Harbor**
Lundgren, Colleen Bowling *elementary school educator, consultant*
Yoder, Dale Roy *history educator*

**Berrien Springs**
Lesher, William Richard *retired academic administrator*
Lundgren, Dennis David *elementary school educator, secondary school educator*

**Big Rapids**
Ryan, Ray Darl, Jr. *academic administrator*
Westman, Craig Ellery *academic administrator*

**Birch Run**
Thompson-Christie, Heather Marie *adult education educator*

**Bloomfield Hills**
Rumbell, Mary Beth *secondary school educator*

**Byron Center**
VanderJagt, Kathleen Sue *parochial school educator*

**Carleton**
Ely, Deborah D. *elementary school educator*

**Caro**
Hile, Michele Vera *middle school educator*

**Commerce Township**
Smith, Barbara Kathryn *retired elementary school educator*

**Dearborn**
Beyer, Roberta *dean, education educator, writer, researcher*
Henderson, Stanley Elwood *academic administrator, consultant*
Zhu, Qiang *education educator*

**Dearborn Heights**
Carter, Julia Marie *secondary school educator*
Johns, Diana *secondary school educator*

**Delton**
Collier-Horn, Mary Eliza *literature and language educator*

**Detroit**
Anderson, Thomas Caryl *dean*
Barrett, Nancy Smith *academic administrator*
Booth, Betty Jean *retired daycare administrator, poet*
Bridge, Patrick David *education educator*
Buncich, Wanda Jacqueline *elementary school educator*
Corbitt, Eumiller Mattie *special education educator*
Edelstein, Tilden Gerald *academic administrator, historian, educator*
Fay, Sister Maureen A. *university president*
Green, Charles Adam *retired education educator, psychologist*
Mitchell, Connie *director*
Smith, Gary Richard *technology educator*
Speegle, Laura Ann *elementary school educator*
Steiman, H. Robert *dean, dental educator*
Whittum-Hudson, Judith Anne *education educator, researcher*

**East Lansing**
Brophy, Jere Edward *education educator, researcher*
Byerrum, Richard Uglow *college dean*
Cheng, Betty Hsiao-Chih *education educator, researcher*
Harrison, Jeremy Thomas *dean, law educator*
Honhart, Frederick Lewis III *academic director*
Petropoulos, Evangelos *former health institute director, educator, researcher*
Rothert, Marilyn L. *dean, nursing educator*
Saint Arnault, Denise Marie *education educator, researcher*
Simon, Lou Anna Kimsey *academic administrator*
Snoddy, James Ernest *education educator*
Strampel, William Derkey *dean, medical educator*
Unsworth, Michael Edward *university librarian*
Velicer, Janet Schafbuch *retired elementary school educator*
Yang, Lijian *educator*
Young, Raymond James *retired education educator*

**Elk Rapids**
Thompson, Richard Thomas *academic administrator*

**Essexville**
Gabil, Diane Rapson *retired special education educator*

**Farmington Hills**
Barry, Essie Marilyn *elementary school educator, writer*
Faxon, Jack *headmaster*
Hagerty, Robert E. *academic administrator*

**Ferndale**
Pennock, Peggy Ann *secondary school educator*

**Flint**
Marcinkoski, Annette Marie *retired elementary school educator*
Simmons, Robert Randolph *principal*

**Franklin**
Reinhart, Anne Christine *special education educator, consultant*

**Fremont**
Edwards, Loren Allan *secondary school educator*

**Grand Rapids**
Diekema, Anthony J. *college president, consultant*
Kelly, Ruth Ellen *elementary school educator*
Lake, Veronica *director*
Lubbers, Arend Donselaar *retired academic administrator*
Maupin, Karin Louise *secondary school educator*
VanHarn, Gordon Lee *academic administrator*

**Grayling**
Lasby, Terri Darlene *adult education educator*

**Gwinn**
Lasich, Vivian Esther Layne *secondary school educator*

**Hale**
Lixey, Elizabeth Voulgarakis *secondary school educator*

**Harbor Springs**
Cappel, Constance *educational consultant, writer*

**Haslett**
Warrington, Willard Glade *retired university official*

**Holland**
Nyenhuis, Jacob Eugene *academic administrator*
Schieringa, Paul Kenneth *special education educator, entertainer*
Van Wylen, Gordon John *former college president*

**Holt**
Wood, Mary Elizabeth *retired secondary school educator, church musician*

**Houghton**
Hungwe, Kedmon Nyasha *education educator, researcher*
Wray, Kent *academic administrator*

**Interlochen**
Kimpton, Jeffrey S. *academic administrator*

**Jackson**
Wingblade, Loren Charles *education educator*

**Kalamazoo**
Bailey, Judith Irene *academic administrator, consultant*
Burns, James W. *education educator*
Dahlinger, Martha Louise *elementary school educator*
Evans, Oliver H. *college administrator*
Haenicke, Diether Hans *academic administrator emeritus, educator*
Hueng, Chiayang James *educator*
Palchick, Bernard S. *academic administrator, art educator*
Showalter, Shirley H. *academic administrator*

**Lake Orion**
Bernia, John Charles, Jr. *secondary school educator*
Leonard, Jacquelyn Ann *retired elementary school educator*

**Lakeview**
Clingan, Nancy Beth *secondary school educator*

**Lanse**
Augustine, Henry Joseph *secondary school educator*

**Lansing**
Flanagan, Michael P. *school system administrator*
Straus, Kathleen Nagler *academic administrator, educator*

**Lawrence**
Applewhaite, Carlisle S. *special education educator, consultant*
Bourg, Louise Janette *retired secondary school educator*

**Livonia**
Kujawa, Sister Rose Marie *academic administrator*
McDowell, Richard William *academic administrator*

**Ludington**
Puffer, Richard Judson *retired college chancellor*

**Macomb**
Farmakis, George Leonard *retired education educator*

**Marine City**
Robinson, Michelle A. *elementary school educator*

**Marquette**
Manning, Robert Hendrick *retired audio-visual services executive*

**Marshall**
Hammond, Jane Pamela *adult education educator*

**Mesick**
Johnson, David Allen *history and English educator*

**Midland**
Barker, Nancy Lepard *university official*
Grzesiak, Katherine Ann *primary school educator*

**Mount Pleasant**
Scott, Renay Marie *academic administrator, educator*

**Northville**
Sawyer, Harriet Behner *retired secondary school educator*

**Okemos**
Edwards, Caryn Louise *educational consultant, special education educator*

**Ossineke**
Larson, Ilene Kay *elementary school educator*

**Pentwater**
Noffke, Frank Edward *educational planner, writer, educator*

**Plymouth**
Bain, Elaine Rugienius *secondary school educator*

**Pontiac**
Hatten, Angela *secondary school educator*
Love, Sharon Irene *elementary school educator*

**Portage**
Taylor, Karen Lynn *biology educator*

**Redford**
Behen, Daniel James *elementary school educator*
Hoeft, Stacy *principal*
Schnuell-Ruth, Karen D. *elementary school educator*

**Riverview**
Wilczynski, Christie Louise *secondary school educator, counselor*

**Rochester**
Kleimola, Sharon Leigh *retired elementary school educator*
Packard, Sandra Podolin *education educator, consultant*
Russi, Gary D. *academic administrator*

**Rogers City**
Lamp, Brenda S. *elementary school educator*

**Roseville**
Lane, Debra Lillian *secondary school educator*

**Royal Oak**
Pike, Charlene Helen *retired secondary school educator*
Pricer, Wayne Francis *counseling consultant*

**Saginaw**
Scharffe, William Granville *academic administrator, educator*
Shinaver, Alan L. *educator*

**Saint Clair Shores**
Skoney, Sophie Essa *educational administrator*

**Saint Joseph**
Rommel, James Joseph *elementary school educator*

**Sault Sainte Marie**
Youngblood, Betty J. *academic administrator*

**Scottville**
Pollock, Kevin Alexander *academic administrator*

**Shelby Township**
Luz, Kyle Stuart *physics educator*

**South Haven**
Llorens, Merna Gee *elementary school educator, retired music educator*

**South Lyon**
Palmer, Kimberly Anne *director*

**Southfield**
Chambers, Charles MacKay *academic administrator, lawyer, consultant*
Dean, Kelly A. *principal*
Lee, James Edward, Jr. *educational consultant*

**Spring Lake**
Bussard, Janice Wingeier *retired secondary school educator*

**Taylor**
Coleman, Fay *literature and language educator, director*
Gusky, Stacy L *private school educator*
Hunt, Brian Keith *special education educator*

**Traverse City**
Alzuny, Thomas *secondary school educator*
Czarny, Thomas Gerard *secondary school educator*
Zimmerman, Paul Albert *retired academic administrator, minister*

**Trenton**
Cicotte, Melony *elementary school educator*

Wukovits, John Francis *secondary school educator, writer*

**University Center**
Boyse, Peter Dent *academic administrator*
Gilbertson, Eric Raymond *academic administrator, lawyer*

**Walled Lake**
Remer, Deborah Jane *elementary school educator*

**Waterford**
Anderson, Francile Mary *secondary school educator*

**West Bloomfield**
Simpson, Robert Lee *academic administrator, department chairman, biologist, educator*

**West Branch**
Krzyminski, MaryAnn Marie *literature and language educator*

**Williamston**
Johnson, Tom Milroy *dean, physician, educator*

**Wyoming**
Couch, Katrina Denise *elementary school educator*

**Yale**
Hedge, Janice Faye *secondary school educator*

**Ypsilanti**
Harris, Michael *academic affairs administrator, public policy and administration educator*
Kramer, Catherine Ann *elementary school educator*
Lewis-White, Linda Beth *elementary school educator*
Reifel Werner, Melody Ann *academic administrator*
Robbins, Jerry Hal *educational administration educator*
Willis, Craig Dean *academic administrator*

## MINNESOTA

**Ada**
Sillerud, Arlen Roger *retired secondary school educator*

**Austin**
Schmid, Harald Heinrich Otto *biochemistry educator, academic administrator*

**Bemidji**
Sterbenk-Lund, Jacquelyn Marie *chemistry educator, biology educator*

**Chisholm**
Fleming, Jennifer Renee *history educator, coach*

**Coleraine**
Jones, Gail *elementary school educator*

**Collegeville**
Reinhart, Dietrich Thomas *academic administrator, social studies educator*

**Cottage Grove**
Russell, Christopher John *secondary school educator, music educator*

**Duluth**
Stauber-Johnson, Elizabeth Jane *retired elementary school educator*
Ziegler, Richard J. *dean, educator*

**Eagan**
Sievwright, Julia Ann *elementary school educator*

**Eden Prairie**
Knickerbocker, Vicky Ann *academic administrator*

**Elmore**
Kortgard, Karen Marie *special education educator, counselor*

**Ely**
Sagen, Harry Bradley *education educator*

**Faribault**
Collins, Ruth Ann *principal*

**Glenwood**
Tessman, Wes *secondary school educator*

**Grand Rapids**
Hall, Frieda Atlas *history educator*
King, Sheryl Jayne *secondary school educator, counselor*

**Inver Grove Heights**
Howarth, Mark Evans *secondary school educator*

**Little Falls**
Morgan, Mary Jo *school system administrator*
Perfetti, Robert Nickolas *educational consultant*

**Mankato**
Nickerson, James Findley *retired education educator*

**Maple Grove**
Kirpes, Anne Irene *elementary school educator*

**Marine On Saint Croix**
Gavin, Robert Michael, Jr. *educational consultant*

**Marshall**
Bonnstetter, Rhonda S. *education educator*
Danahar, David C. *academic administrator, historian, educator*
Van Overbeke, Debbie Ann *education educator*

**Minneapolis**
Atwood, John Brian *dean*
Bowie, Norman Ernest *university official, educator*

Bruininks, Robert H. *academic administrator, psychologist, educator*
Chapman, David Wilfred *education educator*
DiGangi, Frank Edward *academic administrator*
Edwardson, Sandra *dean, nursing educator*
Jacobs, Benjamin M *education educator*
Johnson, Alex Moore *dean, law educator*
Johnson, David Chester *academic administrator, sociologist, educator*
Krause, Timothy Gilbert *academic administrator, web strategist*
Lindell, Edward Albert *academic administrator, religious organization administrator*
Lloyd, Patrick M. *dean, dental educator*
Maruyama, Geoffrey *academic administrator, educator*
Mengler, Thomas M. *dean*
Montgomery, Lynn Marie *educational consultant*
O'Keefe, Michael *academic administrator, physicist*
O'Keefe, Thomas Michael *academic administrator*
Osander, John *secondary school educator*
O'Toole, Stephen Joseph *special education educator*
Schuh, G(eorge) Edward *dean, agricultural economist*
Sullivan, Alfred Dewitt *academic administrator*
Svendsbye, Lloyd August *academic administrator, theologian, educator*
Tuckson, Reed V. *academic administrator*
Veldey, Bonnie *special education educator*
Warring, Douglas Franklin *education educator, psychologist, director*
Wilhelm, Gretchen *retired secondary school educator, volunteer*

**Minnetonka**
Wigfield, Rita L. *elementary school educator*

**Moorhead**
Dille, Roland Paul *college president*
Treumann, William Borgen *university dean*

**Morris**
Kim, Jong-Min *education educator*

**New Brighton**
Hankes, Margaret Ellen *parochial school educator, consultant*

**New Ulm**
Sprung, William *school system administrator*

**Northfield**
Boardman, Shelby J. *academic administrator*
Oden, Robert A., Jr. *academic administrator*

**Osseo**
Anya, Adamma Chukwudi *special education educator*

**Park Rapids**
Novak, Larry Ray *secondary school educator, music educator, director*

**Plymouth**
Gauger, Beth Lynn *literature and language educator*
Vieth, William Chapman *secondary school educator*

**Richfield**
Devlin, Barbara Jo *school district administrator*
Reilly, Jill Marlene *school system administrator*

**Rochester**
Stockwell, Linda M. *principal*

**Roseville**
Seagren, Alice *school system administrator, former state legislator*

**Rushford**
Stras, Penny Lynn *director*

**Saint Bonifacius**
Ingolfsland, Dennis Eldon *school librarian, religious studies educator*

**Saint Cloud**
Wertz, John Alan *retired secondary school educator*

**Saint Paul**
Bauer, Jean Warner *educator*
Brushaber, George Karl *academic administrator, minister*
Dybvig, Mary McIlvaine *educational consultant, psychologist*
Dykstra, Robert *retired education educator*
Gorski, Paul Cameron *education educator, consultant*
Hanna, Kathryn Lura *university administrator*
Harvey, Patricia A. *school system administrator*
Hornbach, Daniel J. *academic administrator, biologist, educator*
Huber, Sister Alberta *academic administrator*
King, Jack Burge *academic librarian*
Kurzer, Mindy Susan *adult education educator*
Lee, Andrea Jane *academic administrator, nun*
McCormick, James Harold *academic administrator*
Rosenberg, Brian C *academic administrator*
Vecoli, Rudolph John *retired history educator, director*

**Sleepy Eye**
Jirak, Sarah Reed *secondary school educator*

**Waseca**
Frederick, Edward Charles *university official*

**Winona**
Beyer, Mary Edel *primary education educator*
Franz, Craig Joseph *academic administrator, biology professor*
Krueger, Darrell William *academic administrator*
Nasstrom, Roy Richard *educational consultant*

## MISSISSIPPI

**Ackerman**
Coleman, Frances McLean *secondary school educator*

**Alcorn State**
Wyatt, Helen J. *special education educator*

**Amory**
Llewellyn, Charles Ray *secondary school educator*

**Biloxi**
Brown, Sheba Ann *elementary school educator*
Manners, Pamela Jeanne *secondary school educator*

**Cleveland**
Lane, Randy James *education educator, consultant*

**Ecru**
Mounce, Carolyn P. *retired school librarian*

**Enterprise**
McCarty, Margaret Jane *retired elementary school educator*

**Ethel**
Glaskox, Anna C *secondary school educator*

**Gulfport**
Opel, Pamela Lynn *elementary school educator*

**Hattiesburg**
Bedenbaugh, Angela Lea Owen *chemistry educator, researcher*
Bower, Janie Pittman *mathematics educator*
Griffith, Jerry A. *environmental science educator*
Gunther, William David *academic administrator, economics professor*
Henry, Myron *academic administrator*
Lucas, Aubrey Keith *retired university president*
Noonkester, James Ralph *retired college president*
Shin, Jae-Hwa *educator*
Sulbaran, Tulio *education educator, researcher*

**Holly Springs**
Beckley, David Lenard *academic administrator*

**Itta Bena**
Ahanonu, Chukwuma Smart *education educator*

**Jackson**
Anglin, Linda McCluney *retired elementary school educator*
Bounds, Hank M. *school system administrator*
Broome, Kathryn *secondary school educator*
Collins, Deloris Williams *secondary school educator*
Hupp, James R. *dean, dental educator*
Luse, Lender *biology educator*
Mayeaux, Anne Russell *education educator*

**Leakesville**
Hollinghead, Juanita Green *elementary school educator*

**Madison**
Watts, Thomas Parrish *history educator, consultant*

**Meridian**
Leewer, William George, Jr. *education educator*

**Minter City**
Mitchell, Patsy Malier *religious school founder, administrator*

**Mississippi State**
Foglesong, Robert H. *academic administrator, career military officer*
Rabideau, Peter Wayne *dean, chemistry professor, educator*

**Nettleton**
Cherry, Jeffrey Lynn *history educator*

**Ocean Springs**
Parrott, Linda Susan *chemistry educator*

**Olive Branch**
Leary, Frances Elizabeth Cooper *secondary school educator*
McRae, Carol Reeves *secondary school educator, theater director*

**Oxford**
Carter, Gail Marie *special education educator*
Moorhead, Sylvester Andrew *retired education educator*
Walton, Gerald Wayne *retired university official*

**Philadelphia**
Montgomery, Kathryn Suzainne *elementary school educator*

**Ridgeland**
Harmon, George Marion *academic administrator*

**Senatobia**
Latham, Amy Moore *academic administrator*

**Starkville**
Mabry, Donald Joseph *retired academic administrator, history professor*
Martin, Theodore Krinn *former university administrator*

**Tupelo**
Cleveland, Mary Heloise *elementary school educator*
Hawkins, Bridgett Burnett *elementary school educator*

**University**
Davis, Samuel Marion *dean, law educator, researcher*
Stephens, Earnest B. *academic administrator*

## Vicksburg
Keulegan, Emma Pauline *special education educator*

## MISSOURI

## Arnold
Kasey, Arthur R. III *secondary school educator*
Miller, Pamela Sue *elementary school educator*

## Aurora
Lyon, Lucy *school system administrator*

## Bakersfield
Barnes, Sandra Lynn *special education educator*

## Belton
Hoye, Linda Lee *special education educator*
Short, Joel Barton *secondary school educator, department chairman*

## Bethel
Coonrod, Delberta Hollaway (Debbie Coonrod) *retired elementary school educator, consultant*

## Blue Springs
Hiles, Barbara Lynn *retired elementary school educator*
Hochgrebe, Nolan Robards *secondary school educator*

## Cape Girardeau
King, Cynthia Rose *literature and language educator, theater arts director*

## Carl Junction
Pulliam, Frederick Cameron *educational administrator*

## Chillicothe
Logan, Janet Louise *retired elementary school educator*

## Clayton
Rogers-Beard, Donna Jane *history educator*

## Columbia
Crist, William Miles *dean, pediatrician, educator*
Deaton, Brady J. *academic administrator*
Dessem, R. Lawrence *dean, law educator*
Flinn, Mark van Doren *education educator*
George, Melvin Douglas *retired university president*
Hanrahan, Timothy Ryan *elementary school educator*
Janda, Mark William *history educator*
Libby, Wendy B. *academic administrator*
Maxcy, Brendan David *education educator*
McKinley, Lori *education educator*
Miller, Paul Ausborn *adult education educator*
Pittman, Von Veron *education educator*
Triplett, Gregory Edward *educator, researcher*

## Conway
Day, Sandy J. *gifted and talented educator, tax specialist*

## Ewing
Lueckenhoff, Mark Albert *elementary school educator*

## Fayette
Inman, Marianne Elizabeth *academic administrator*

## Florissant
James, Dorothy Louise King *special education educator*
Kralemann, William Joseph *retired chemistry educator*
Linn, Dale E. *secondary school educator*

## Forsyth
Klinefelter, Sarah Stephens *retired dean, broadcast executive*

## Fulton
Forsythe, George Barnett *academic administrator, dean*
Lamkin, Fletcher M., Jr. *academic administrator*

## Granby
Sparkman, Lyle Bruce *academic administrator, education educator*

## Grandview
Ferguson, Cathy Lynne *elementary school educator*

## Green City
Bender, Patricia Ann *secondary school educator*

## Hazelwood
O'Reilly, Mary Catherine *elementary school educator*

## Independence
Franklin, J. Richard *principal*
Rees, Elaine *chemistry educator*
Starks, Carol Elizabeth *retired principal*

## Jefferson City
Bardwell, Rosemary Ann *elementary school educator*
King, D. Kent *school system administrator*
Mahoney, Carolyn Ray *academic administrator*
Novotney, Donald Francis *superintendent of schools*

## Jennings
Jansen, Michele R. *curriculum and instruction specialist*

## Kansas City
Byers-Pevitts, Beverley *college administrator, educator*
Caulfield, Joan *director, educator*

Chambers, Gina *school system administrator, education educator*
Churchman, Michael Steele Bright *educational consultant, educator*
Collins, Kathleen *academic administrator, art educator*
Eubanks, Eugene Emerson *education educator, consultant*
Guilliland, Martha W. *academic administrator*
Hamilton, Richard Alfred *academic administrator, marketing executive*
Jonas, Harry S. *medical education consultant*
Judd, Barbara Anne *history educator, counselor*
Lenz, Jacquelyn I. *literature and language educator*
McCollum, Clifford Glenn *college dean emeritus*
Pyle, Matthew Jared *secondary school educator*
Schuchman, Philip Melchor *education educator*
Snelling, Troy Wayne *history educator*
Suni, Ellen Y. *dean, law educator*
Trotter, Betty Lou *retired secondary school educator*
Willsie, Sandra Kay *provost, dean, internist, educator*

## Kirksville
Dixon, Barbara Bruinekool *academic administrator*

## Kirkwood
Cooksey, Robert Lee *school system administrator*

## Lees Summit
Linder, Beverly L. *elementary school educator*

## Liberty
Tanner, Jimmie Eugene *retired dean*
Winkler, Douglas J. *secondary school educator*

## Maryville
Hubbard, Dean Leon *academic administrator*
Smith, Keith Allen *secondary school educator*

## Mexico
Cortez, Robert Victor *secondary school educator, music educator*

## Neosho
Allman, Margaret Ann Lowrance *counseling administrator*

## Nevada
Schulze, Cheryl Ranea *secondary school educator*

## New Bloomfield
Luebbert, Terry Lynne *elementary school educator*

## Nixa
Roman, Alfred Victor *science education educator*

## North Kansas City
Jackson, Randal Lynn *secondary school educator*

## O Fallon
Reid, Lorene Frances *middle school educator*

## Parkville
Breckon, Donald John *academic administrator*

## Poplar Bluff
Milligan, Laura Ann Kassing *director*

## Prairie Home
Bacon, Sherri Leah *elementary school educator*

## Raytown
Hodson, Cynthia Lou *elementary school educator*
MacLeod, Linda Ann *secondary school educator*
Morrill, Kelli Rae *secondary school educator*

## Richmond
Solomon, Patty Jo *elementary school educator*

## Richmond Heights
Chandler, James Barton *international education consultant*

## Rolla
Carney, John F. III *academic administrator*
Shah, Y. T. *academic administrator*
Warner, Don Lee *dean emeritus*

## Saint Charles
LaRosa, Thomas J. *director*
Nagle, Linda Marie *elementary school educator*
Parker, Marsha Marie *dean, actress*
Segelhorst, Cindy Marie *pre-school educator*
Stone, Mary Sainz *elementary school educator*

## Saint Louis
Baker, Shirley Kistler *academic administrator*
Biondi, Lawrence *academic administrator, priest*
Blasingame, David Thomas *academic administrator*
Cain, James Nelson *arts school and concert administrator*
Danforth, William Henry *retired academic administrator, physician*
Dodge, Paul Cecil *academic administrator*
Duncan-Hewitt, Wendy Carolyn *dean, medical educator*
Freiling, Marianne *principal*
Fritz, Tarren Denise *elementary school educator*
George, Thomas Frederick *academic administrator*
Gilligan, Sandra Kaye *private school director*
Hicks, Shirley E. *director*
Hunt, Norma Jean *retired elementary school educator*
Kalyanaraman, Ramki *education educator, researcher*
Kennelly, Sister Karen Margaret *retired academic administrator, church administrator, nun*
Koff, Robert Hess *academic administrator, adult education educator*
Krasney, Rina Susan *school librarian*
Lackey, Kayle Diann *elementary school educator*
Leavitt, Lynda *school system administrator, educator*
Lederle, Kenneth Joseph *director, secondary school educator*

Leonard, Judith Price *educational advisor*
Lewis, Jeffrey E. *dean, law educator*
Lewis, Jodi A. *secondary school educator, theater educator*
Mahan, David James *retired academic administrator*
Mitchell, Louise Tyndall *special education educator*
Monteleone, Patricia L. *dean*
O'Neill, Sheila *principal*
Ramming, Michael Alexander *retired school system administrator*
Rebmann, Terri *director*
Scheffing, Dianne Elizabeth *special education educator*
Schejbal, Nancy Kay *secondary school educator*
Sproule, James Michael *dean, communications educator*
Walker, Doretta Anita *director*
Weiss, Robert Francis *retired academic administrator, religious organization administrator, consultant*
Welch, Michael John *chemistry educator, researcher*
Williamson, Marilyn *retired secondary school educator*
Woodward, Mary Lou *retired elementary school educator*
Wrighton, Mark Stephen *academic administrator, chemistry professor*

## Saint Peters
Caples, Linda Griffin *retired secondary school educator*

## Sainte Genevieve
Crouther, Michele Jean *history educator, literature and language educator*

## Salem
Will, Anne Marilyn *retired elementary school educator*

## Savannah
Bales, Eugene Hamlin *retired secondary school educator, retired elementary school educator*

## Springfield
Ames, Jimmy Ray *education educator*
Castleberry, Joseph L. *academic administrator*
Reed, Robert Allen *elementary school educator*
Thompson, Kip Russell *education educator, researcher*
Toste, Anthony Paim *chemistry educator, researcher*

## Sullivan
Schuler, Juanita Louise *education educator*

## Troy
Lawrence, John R. *academic administrator*

## Warrensburg
Lamirande, Maria *elementary school educator*

## Warsaw
Campbell, Anita Louise *literature and language educator, speech educator*

## Washington
Chambers, Jerry Ray *school system administrator, consultant*

## Waynesville
Campbell, Sonya Beth *elementary school educator*

## Webb City
James, Kathryn A. *secondary school educator*

## West Plains
Melissa, Huff Ann *secondary school educator*

## Wheatland
Nickel, Karen June *secondary school educator*

## Windyville
Condron, Daniel Ralph *academic administrator, metaphysics educator*

## MONTANA

## Billings
Mace, Michael R. *academic administrator, real estate development consultant, mortgage executive*

## Bozeman
Buonamici, April Graham *elementary school educator, music educator*
Gamble, Geoffrey *academic administrator*

## Butte
Gilmore, W. Franklin (Frank Gilmore) *academic administrator*
Haugen, Margaret Ellen *daycare administrator*
L'heureux, Richard Allen *academic administrator, consultant*
Spear, Terry M *education educator, consultant*

## Dayton
Catalfomo, Philip *retired university dean*

## Helena
McCulloch, Linda *school system administrator*
Stearns, Sheila MacDonald *academic administrator*
Trebon, Thomas *academic administrator*

## Lodge Grass
Rockabove, Magdalene M. *special education educator*

## Lolo
Stewart, JoAnne *retired director*

## Missoula
Brown, Perry Joe *dean*
Dennison, George Marshel *academic administrator*

Latino, Chad Gregory *history educator*
Vogelsberg, Ross Timm *education educator, researcher*

## Wolf Point
Ulrickson, Virginia Gayle *elementary school educator, librarian*

## NEBRASKA

## Arlington
Moskus, Jerry Ray *retired academic administrator*

## Aurora
Lockmon, Nancy *mathematics educator*

## Bellevue
Dorsey, Jacquelyn A. *secondary school educator*
Kayne, Jon Barry *academic administrator, psychologist*
Muller, John Bartlett *university president*
Stohlman, Bruce Richard *secondary school educator*

## Cedar Bluffs
Fleischman, Brian William *mathematics educator*

## Chadron
Stack, Robert Vernon *dean, mathematics professor*

## Columbus
Thoms, Christopher Michael *elementary school educator*

## Grand Island
Weseman, Vicki Lynne *elementary school educator*

## Gretna
Druliner, Marcia Marie *education educator*

## Hebron
Dunback, M. Kathleen Meyer *literature and language educator*

## Kearney
Johnston, Gladys Styles *university official*

## Kimball
Walker, Judy Lou *special education educator, director*

## Lincoln
Bradley, Richard Edwin *retired academic administrator*
Christensen, Douglas D. *school system administrator*
Grady, Marilyn L. *education educator*
Grew, Priscilla Croswell *academic administrator, geologist, educator*
Martin, Charity Kay *academic librarian, educator*
Milligan, Cynthia Hardin *dean, lawyer*
Nelson, Darrell Wayne *academic administrator, research scientist*
Perlman, Harvey Stuart *academic administrator*
Reinhardt, John W. *dean, dental educator*
Smith, L. Dennis *former academic administrator*
Willborn, Steven L. *dean, law educator*

## Norfolk
Mortensen-Say, Marlys *retired school system administrator*

## Omaha
Belck, Nancy Garrison *dean, educator*
Bruckner, Martha *academic administrator*
Gerteis, Christopher *history educator*
Greenwald, Catherine Diane *elementary school educator*
Kinney, B. Dale *secondary school educator*
Louis, Virgie Lee *retired secondary school educator*
Newton, John Milton *academic administrator, psychologist, educator*
Pamies, Rubens John *dean*
Ryan, Sheila A. *retired dean, nursing educator*
Wang, Guangshun *educator*

## Papillion
Wynn, Kevin D. *secondary school educator, coach*

## Waverly
Jensen, Daniel *history educator*

## Winnebago
Bauer-Sanders, Katherine Ann *primary school educator*

## NEVADA

## Carson City
Brant, James William *educational consultant, mathematician, educator*
Eftimoff, Anita Kendall *educational consultant*
Rheault, Keith W. *school system administrator*
Wadman, William Wood III *educational director, technical research executive, consulting company executive*

## Elko
Lesbo, Paula Mae *elementary and secondary education educator*
Sethaler, Bernard A. *secondary school educator*

## Ely
Petersen, Lisa Rae *elementary school educator*

## Henderson
Andolina, Nancy Jean *middle school educator, dancer, English and language arts educator*
Holmes, BarbaraAnn Krajkoski *retired secondary school educator*
Keene, Richard Brian *school system administrator, educational consultant*
Maryanski, Fred J. *academic administrator*
Thomas, James Patrick *special education educator*

## Las Vegas

Ananias, José *retired school system administrator*
Ashley, David B. *academic administrator, engineering educator*
Baloglu, Seyhmus *hospitality and tourism educator*
DeBusk, Lorraine *elementary school educator*
Ernst, Suzanne *academic administrator, educator*
Ferrillo, Patrick J., Jr. *dean, endodontist*
Gaspar, Anna Louise *retired elementary school educator, consultant*
Hall, Gene E. *education educator*
Hamby, Jennifer Lynne *elementary school educator*
Morgan, Richard J. *dean, law educator*
Phillips, Karen *secondary school educator*
Pierce, Thresia Korte (Tish Pierce) *primary school educator*
Rieckenberg, Desiree *academic administrator*
Shuman, R. Baird *academic administrator, consultant, language educator, writer*
Singer, Clifford *mathematics educator, artist*

## North Las Vegas

Davis, Jennifer Ann *elementary school educator*
Kelly, Christopher Pat *dean, educator*

## Reno

Burnett, John A. *director*
Cathey-Gibson, Sharon Sue Rinn *principal, academic administrator*
Dietrich, Dean Forbes *academic administrator*
Glick, Milton Don *academic administrator, chemist*
Herzog, Serge *academic administrator, researcher*
Perry, Jean Louise *retired dean, academic administrator*

## Silver Springs

O'Malia, Mary Frances *special education educator*

## NEW HAMPSHIRE

### Alton

Stevens, Thomas D., Jr. *secondary school educator, music educator*

### Colebrook

Bernard, Susan Shattuck *retired secondary school educator*

### Concord

Blankenstein, Elizabeth M. *director, educator*
Jillette, Arthur George, Jr. *school system administrator, educator*
Matthews, William R., Jr., (Bill Matthews) *headmaster*
Tracy, Lyonel B. *school system administrator*

### Dover

Pelletier, Marsha Lynn *secondary school educator, poet*

### Durham

DeMitchell, Todd Allan *education educator*
Farrell, William Joseph *university chancellor*
Mallory, Bruce *academic administrator*
Newman, J. Bonnie *academic administrator, former government official*
Shea, Christine M. *education educator*

### Exeter

Tingley, Tyler C. *headmaster*

### Gilford

Wool, Alan D. *mathematics educator*

### Hanover

Danos, Paul *dean, accounting educator*
Green, Ronald Michael *bioethics educator*
Hennessey, John William, Jr. *academic administrator, educator*
Spielberg, Stephen Paul *dean, educator*
Wright, James Edward *academic administrator, historian, educator*

### Henniker

Nitschke-Shaw, Debra Ann *education educator, dean*

### Manchester

Joshuah, Richard Totten-Greenwood *elementary school educator*

### Meredith

Fahey, Mary Crane *elementary school educator*
Nyhan, Mary E. *literature and language educator*

### Middleton

Feyler, Carrie A. *elementary school educator*

### Milford

Queeney, Deborah Ann *special education educator*

### Nashua

Arthur, Rose Ann Horman *dean*
Mitsakos, Charles Leonidas *education educator, consultant*
Provencher, Jeanne Stansfield *secondary school educator*

### New London

Ponder, Anne *academic administrator*

### Plaistow

Goddu, Kevin Albert *secondary school educator*
Wilder, Dwight Safford *academic administrator*

### Raymond

Benz, Marilyn Christine *elementary school educator*

### Rindge

Martin, Frederick Nichols *school system administrator*

### Salem

Courtois, Michael G. *biology educator*

## Somersworth

Dahms, Bruce John *secondary school educator*

## Tilton

Found, Sandra Thrall *mathematics educator, mathematics professor*

## West Lebanon

Halperin, George Bennett *education educator, retired military officer*

## NEW JERSEY

### Asbury Park

Avella, John Thomas *educational administrator*

### Basking Ridge

Besch, Lorraine W. *special education educator*

### Belleville

Shuhan, Janice-Lynn Nazziola *secondary school educator*

### Berkeley Heights

Shaffer, Gail Dorothy *secondary school educator*

### Bernardsville

Robinson, Maureen Loretta *retired secondary school educator*

### Blairstown

Fechisin, Wendy Leigh *mathematics educator*

### Brick

Tozer, Jean Frame *gifted and talented educator*

### Bridgewater

Hart, Karen Jean *special education educator*

### Brigantine

Kickish, Margaret Elizabeth *elementary school educator*

### Browns Mills

Rakes, Randi Lee *elementary school educator, test developer*

### Butler

Abdelsalam, Sylvia Claire *secondary school educator*

### Caldwell

Savage, Joseph George *academic administrator*
Werner, Patrice (Patricia Ann Werner) *academic administrator*

### Camden

Brooks, Gail Denise *school system administrator, consultant*
Daniels, Albertina Diana *secondary school educator*
Gordon, Walter Kelly *retired academic administrator, retired language educator*
Solomon, Rayman Louis *dean, law educator*

### Cherry Hill

Marrella-Davis, Christy Elizabeth *history educator*

### Cinnaminson

Lorenz, Betsy M. *elementary school educator*

### Colts Neck

Crowder-Pagano, Linda Louise *special education educator*

### Columbia

Timcenko, Lydia Teodora *secondary school educator, biochemist*

### Cresskill

Marion, Winifred Zenorini *retired elementary school educator*

### Denville

Doane, Eileen Maloney *learning disabilities teacher consultant*

### East Brunswick

Kish, John R. *secondary school educator, music educator*

### East Hanover

Tamburro, Peter James, Jr. *secondary school educator*

### Egg Harbor City

Farris, Vera King *former college president*

### Englewood

DeJarnett, Rodney *headmaster*

### Englewood Cliffs

Kim, Jae Taik *adult education educator*

### Ewing

Gitenstein, Donna M. *academic administrator*

### Flanders

Kuzma, Deborah J. *vice principal, music educator*

### Flemington

Wolfson, Barbara Libensperger *guidance counselor*

### Fords

Ayers, Christopher James *special education educator*

### Fort Lee

Sugarman, Alan William *educational consultant*

### Glassboro

D'Augustine, Robert *academic administrator, lawyer*
Gephardt, Donald Louis *academic administrator*

## Glen Gardner

Orfe, N. Michael *secondary school educator*

## Green Brook

Balsamello, Melissa (Marley) *elementary school educator*

## Hackensack

Williamson, (Eulah) Elaine *elementary school educator*

## Hightstown

Elliott, Frank Nelson *retired college president*
Green, John F. *headmaster*
Miller, Mary Kathleen *secondary school educator*
Szarawarski, Carollee *special education educator*

## Hillside

Dickerson, Martin Lee *principal*

## Hoboken

Raveché, Harold Joseph *academic administrator*

## Jackson

Ranone, John Louis *school board executive*

## Jersey City

Farrior, Evan Bell *special education educator, writer*
Morales, Carlos *director, educator*
Shamburg, Christopher *education educator*
Soo Hoo, Tsung (Bill) Yao *security studies educator, consultant*

## Kendall Park

DeLollis-Fitzgerald, Heather A. *special education educator*

## Lakewood

Conklin, Jack L. *education educator*
Williams, Barbara Anne *retired academic administrator*

## Lanoka Harbor

Lake, William Robert *school district administrator*

## Lawrenceville

Jordan, Mildred Rice Loretta *education educator*
Lackie, Robert Jonathan *university librarian, educator, consultant*
Rozanski, Mordechai *academic administrator*
Stehle, Edward Raymond *secondary education educator, school system administrator*
Tharney, Leonard John *education educator, consultant*

## Layton

Seely, Maribeth Walsh *elementary school educator*

## Lincroft

Ruiz Madas, Yesenia *educational counselor*

## Linden

Bedrick, Bernice *retired principal, science educator*

## Linwood

Sutman, Francis Xavier *university dean*

## Little Ferry

Hayes, Lynda Margaret *elementary school educator*

## Madison

Bull, Vivian Ann *retired academic administrator, educator*
Mertz, Francis James *university president*
Weisbuch, Robert Alan *academic administrator*
Wojtaszek, Kevin Joseph *director, video editor*

## Mahwah

Davis, Henry Vance *education educator*

## Manahawkin

Barton, Noreen Duffy *secondary school educator*

## Maplewood

Ennis, Boyce *art facilitator, music director*

## Marlton

Cheney, Eleanora Louise *retired secondary school educator*

## Marmora

Johnson, Joyce Ann *elementary school educator*

## Martinsville

Raby, John Cornelius *secondary school educator*

## Matawan

Liggett, Twila C. *academic administrator, broadcast executive, educator*

## Mays Landing

May, John T. *college president*

## Mendham

Allen-Scerbo, Susan Lynn *secondary education educator, counselor*
Bennett, Nancy Evans *secondary school educator*
Posunko, Barbara *retired elementary school educator*
Sagurton, Wilma *retired secondary school educator, musician, historian*

## Metuchen

Lasz, Anais *school librarian*
Massey, Eleanor Nelson *school librarian, media specialist*

## Middlesex

Hilliard, Robert Allan *secondary school educator*

## Montclair

Cole, Susan A. *academic administrator, language educator*
Robila, Stefan Alexandru *education educator*

## Montville

Birkett, Norman Myles *private school educator, writer*

## Morristown

Prisco, Dorothy DeSteno *academic administrator*
Venezia, William Thomas *school system administrator, counseling consultant*

## Mount Holly

Hersh, David William *director*

## New Brunswick

Chatterjee, Indrani *history educator, researcher*
Durnin, Richard Gerry *education educator*
Greenberg, Michael Richard *urban studies and community health educator*
McCormick, Richard Levis *academic administrator*
Nelson, Jack Lee *education educator*
Stanley, Jason *education educator*
Stauffer, George B. *dean, music historian, musician, consultant*
Strawderman, William E. *statistics educator*
Strickland, Dorothy *education educator*
Tanner, Daniel *education educator*

## New Monmouth

Santos, Sharon Lee *parochial school educator*

## New Providence

Blessing, Leonard C. *secondary school educator*
Hirsch, Maxine K. *special education educator, councilman*

## Newark

Altenkirch, Robert A. *academic administrator*
Arbuckle, Peggy Trawick *educational consultant, special education educator*
Bergen, Stanley Silvers, Jr. *retired academic administrator*
Bloom, Joel S. *academic administrator*
Bolden, Marion A. *superintendent*
Chavis, Janet Daugett *school system administrator*
Czumaj, Artur *education educator*
Docarmo, Jerry Soares *academic administrator*
Feldman, Cecile Arlene *dean, dental educator*
Fenster, Saul K. *retired academic administrator*
Griffith, Hurdis M. *dean*
Hobbs, Patrick Esmond *dean, law educator*
Joffe, Russell T. *former dean*
Kennedy, Leslie W. *dean*
Petillo, John J. *former academic administrator, former priest*
Shiffrar, Margaret Mary *education educator*
Slaton, Gwendolyn Childs *academic administrator*
Vincenti, Gene A. *director, consultant*
Vladeck, Bruce Charney *academic administrator, healthcare educator*

## Newton

MacMurren, Margaret Patricia *secondary school educator, consultant*

## Norwood

Murburg, Thelma D. *retired elementary school educator*

## Orange

Maynard, Estelle L. *pre-school educator, director*

## Paramus

Agresta, Anthony John *academic administrator, educational consultant, language educator*
Hadaller, David Lawrence *academic administrator*
LaMothe, Catherine A. *elementary school educator*

## Parsippany

Smay, Connie R. *educational media specialist, educator*

## Passaic

Johnson, Myrtle Alice Harris *elementary and secondary school educator*

## Paterson

Fields, Marvin Leon *secondary school educator*

## Pennington

Rigg, Lyle D. *headmaster*

## Piscataway

Colaizzi, John Louis *dean*
Dill, Ellis Harold *university dean*
Schuler, Randall Steve *education educator, writer*
Trontell, Marie Celestine *dean*

## Plainfield

Reeder, Hubert *elementary school educator*
Ruiz, Pedro Javier *education educator*

## Pleasantville

London, Charlotte Isabella *secondary school educator*

## Pompton Plains

Pischl, Adolph John *school administrator*

## Princeton

Cooper, Michael R. *dean*
Goddard, Peter *academic administrator, mathematical physicist*
Hollander, Toby Edward *education educator*
Malkiel, Nancy Weiss *dean, historian, educator*
Pimley, Kim Jensen *financial training consultant*
Slaughter, Anne-Marie *dean*
Tilghman, Shirley Marie *academic administrator, biology professor*

## Rahway

Freedman, Stanley Lewis *assistant principal*

## Randolph

Ghosh, Ajit Kumar *daycare administrator*

## Ridgewood

Blakely, Jane McCarthy *secondary school educator*

**Robbinsville**
Biondi, Linda Ann *elementary school educator*

**Rockaway**
Allen, Dorothea *secondary school educator*

**Roselle**
Di Marco, Barbaranne Yanus *principal*

**Roselle Park**
Scarpelli, Vito *retired adult education educator, small business owner*

**Seabrook**
Damiano, Beth Carole *special education educator*

**Short Hills**
Robbins-Wilf, Marcia *educational consultant*

**Sicklerville**
Miller, Audrey Thornton *retired vice principal*

**Skillman**
Cummings, Peggy Ann *counseling administrator*

**Somerville**
Gorton-Horan, Ann Hilbert *vice principal*
Weisblatt, Barbara Ann *secondary school educator*

**South Amboy**
Moskal, Anthony John *retired dean, management consultant, educator*

**South Hackensack**
Wille, Rosanne Louise *educational consultant*

**South Orange**
Hanbury, Kevin M. *dean, priest*
Stringile, Marie Elizabeth *educational administrator*
Toy, Tasha Chantey *academic administrator, educator*

**Sparta**
Stickney, Carol Jean *special education educator, consultant*

**Summit**
Starks, Florence Elizabeth *retired special education educator*

**Teaneck**
Dewey, Ralph Jay *school system administrator*
Smith, Susan Elizabeth *guidance administrator*
Walker, Lucy Doris *secondary school educator, writer*

**Tinton Falls**
Ostar, Allan William *educational consultant*

**Toms River**
D'Alessandro-Fernandez-Phillips, Gina *elementary school educator*

**Trenton**
Brown, Peggy Lee *academic administrator, consultant, singer*
Davy, Lucille E. *school system administrator*
Depuglio, Joseph *physics educator*
Grossman, David Michael *academic administrator, educator*
Pruitt, George Albert *college president*
Riccards, Michael Patrick *academic administrator*
Scheiring, Michael James *college official*
Smallwood, Robert Albian, Jr. *retired secondary education educator*

**Union**
Applbaum, Ronald Lee *academic administrator*
Lederman, Susan Sturc *public administration professor*

**Union City**
Bozoyan, Sylvia *elementary school educator*
Englese, Damon Joseph *director*
Sullivan, Kathleen Ann *secondary school educator*

**Vernon**
Ryan, John Michael *secondary school educator*

**Vineland**
Vaden, Sandra Drake *academic administrator*

**Waldwick**
Lynch, Carol *special services director, psychologist*

**Wall**
Gaona, Arlene *secondary school educator*
Petrovich, Dorothy *elementary school educator*

**Warren**
Hennings, Dorothy Grant (Mrs. George Hennings) *education educator*

**Wayne**
Connell, Joseph F. *academic administrator*
Speert, Arnold *academic administrator, chemistry educator*

**West Long Branch**
Ensor, Linda Lineberger *literature and language educator*
Gaffney, Paul Golden, II, *academic administrator, retired military officer*
Lutz, Francis Charles *dean, civil engineering educator*
Pearson, Thomas Spencer *academic administrator*

**West Milford**
Goerig, Marianne *elementary school educator*

**West Orange**
Bojsza, Joan E. *elementary school educator*
Connolly, Mark A. *biology educator*
Pollara, Joanne *learning disabilities educator, consultant*
Thomas, Gary L. *retired academic administrator*

**Westfield**
Balsamello, Jason Reed *principal, educator*

**Wildwood**
DiMedio, Michael Joseph *secondary school educator*

**Williamstown**
Heidemark, George John *elementary school educator*

**Willingboro**
Denslow, Deborah Pierson *primary school educator*
Jenerette, Joyce Williams *elementary school educator, educational consultant*

**Woodbridge**
Warren, Arthur Lee *secondary school educator, school system administrator*

**Yardville**
Lauricella, Margaret Pierce *school system administrator*

## NEW MEXICO

**Alamogordo**
McFadin, Helen Lozetta *retired elementary school educator*
VanAlstine, Rick G. *secondary school educator*

**Albuquerque**
Beiler, Holly Anne *education educator*
Caldera, Louis Edward *academic administrator, former federal official*
Caplan, Edwin Harvey *retired dean, retired finance educator*
de Gouvea, Raul *educator, consultant*
DelCampo, Robert Gregory *education educator*
Everitt, Elizabeth M. *school system administrator*
Frias, Shirlee N. *elementary school educator*
Garcia, F. Chris *academic administrator, political scientist, educator*
Graff, Pat Stuever *secondary school educator*
Greene, Linda Kay *retired secondary school educator*
Hansen, Harold B., Jr. *elementary school educator, assistant principal*
Hopfinger, Anton Joseph *education educator, consultant*
Lambert, Jeffrey Scott *secondary school educator*
Lattman, Laurence Harold *retired academic administrator*
Pabisch, Peter Karl *director, literature educator, humanities educator*
Qi, Huaqing *special education educator*
Roth, Paul Barry *dean, educator, emergency medicine physician*
Scarnecchia, Suellyn *dean, law educator*
Stuart, Cynthia Morgan *retired academic administrator*
Trunk, James Francis *secondary school educator*
Zink, Lee Berkey *retired academic administrator, economist, educator*

**Carlsbad**
Pinching, Deborah Anne Odell *special education educator*

**Clovis**
Ingram, Peggy Joyce *secondary school educator*

**Farmington**
Anderson, Evelyn Louise *elementary school educator*
Young, Patricia Anne *secondary school educator, writer*

**Hagerman**
Denning, Dink *special education educator*

**Laguna**
Ray, Rebecca Ann *elementary school educator*

**Las Cruces**
Cothrun, Thomas Keith *secondary school educator*
Evans, Eloise Swick *retired secondary school educator, writer*
Hoger, Herbert King *education educator*
López, Eric Joseph *psychology educator, consultant*

**Lordsburg**
Clem, Sarah Lynn *special education educator*

**Placitas**
Watson-Boone, Rebecca A. *dean, researcher, library and information scientist, educator*

**Portales**
Cobb, Jeanne Beck *education educator, researcher, consultant*
Frost, Everett Lloyd *academic administrator, anthropologist*
Howard, Carolyn F. *elementary school educator*
Terry, Michael W. *elementary school educator*

**Roswell**
Odom, William Greg *secondary school educator, music educator*

**Santa Fe**
Cerny, Charlene Ann *director*
Enos, Anya Dozier *academic administrator, director*
Gallegos, Mary Ellen *education educator, department chairman*
Garcia, Veronica *school system administrator*
Harcourt, Robert Neff *educational administrator, genealogist, journalist*
Primozic, Daniel Thomas *dean*
Sandoval, Isabelle Medina *education educator*

**Shiprock**
Atcitty, Fannie L. *elementary school educator, education educator*

Austin-Garrison, Martha A. *education educator, researcher*

**Silver City**
Snedeker, John Haggner *university president*

**Tucumcari**
Barry, Phillip Owen *college president*

## NEW YORK

**Albany**
Brademas, John *retired academic administrator, former congressman*
Covington, Sim Jonathan, Jr. *counseling administrator, director*
Ebert, Loretta Caren *university librarian*
Mills, Richard Paul *school system administrator*
Mumpower, Jeryl L. *academic administrator*
Robbins, Cornelius (Cornelius Van Vorse) *educational administration educator*
Ryan, John R. *academic administrator, career military officer*
Salins, Peter D. *academic administrator*
Verdile, Vincent Paul *dean, emergency physician*

**Alfred**
Hunter, John Orr *college president*

**Amityville**
Fischer, Stacey Kim *principal*
Palumbo, Anthony *education educator*
Wright, Nannie Bell *retired secondary school educator*

**Angola**
Ross, Sue Hoisington *elementary school educator, music educator*

**Annandale On Hudson**
Botstein, Leon *academic administrator, conductor, historian*

**Aurora**
Ryerson, Lisa M. *academic administrator*

**Babylon**
Mastrandrea, Patricia *elementary school educator, consultant*
Schwarz, Barbara Ruth Ballou *elementary school educator*
Vaswani, Sheila Ann *secondary school educator*

**Batavia**
Steiner, Stuart *college president*

**Bellmore**
Feldman, Harriet Ruth *dean*

**Bellport**
Schultheis, Edwin Milford *dean, business educator*

**Bemus Point**
Erickson, Susan Phillians *secondary school educator*

**Binghamton**
DeFleur, Lois B. *academic administrator*
Jenkins, David Mark *educator*
Meador, John Milward, Jr. *dean*
Swain, Mary Ann Price *university official*

**Bohemia**
Schwartz, Laurie *special education educator*

**Boiceville**
Boms, Michael *secondary school educator*

**Brentwood**
Auguste, Gabriel Joseph *retired mathematics educator*

**Brockport**
Gemmett, Robert J. *dean, English language educator*

**Bronx**
Antwi, Ebenezer Yaw *education educator*
Baranin, Rosemarie *elementary school educator*
Bowers, Francis Robert *educational consultant, literature educator*
Hauser, Bernice Worman *director*
Keating, Tedd Michael *adult education educator*
Kelley, Aloysius Paul *academic administrator, priest*
Kelly, Thomas M. *headmaster*
McShane, Joseph Michael *academic administrator, priest*
Nathanson, Melvyn Bernard *academic administrator, mathematician, educator*
Ortiz Ruiz, Aida M. *university administrator, educator*
Purpura, Dominick P. *dean, neuroscientist*
Ramsey, Doris Theresa *elementary school educator*
Rothstein, Anne Louise *academic administrator, educator*
Scanlan, Thomas Joseph *college president, educator*
Socol, Sheldon Eleazer *university official*
Spiegel, Allen Michael *dean, internist*
Wertheim, Mary Danielle *educational coordinator*

**Bronxville**
Myers, Michele Tolela *academic administrator*

**Brooklyn**
Alleva, Paula Savino *principal, elementary school educator*
Arcuri, Leonard Philip *elementary school educator*
Birenbaum, William M. *former university president*
Bugliarello, George *academic administrator, educator*
Chung, Ping Tsai *education educator*
Dealy, Michael Thomas *psychology educator*
D'Elia, Nicholas *secondary school educator*

Douglass, Melvin Isadore *school system administrator, humanities educator, composer*
Feigelson, Eugene B. *dean*
Frisch, Ivan Thomas *academic administrator, educator, computer and communications company executive*
Greene, Gladstone Fitzpatrick *education educator, consultant*
Hero, George A. *history educator*
Hill, Elizabeth Anne *academic administrator, lawyer*
Ierardi, Eric Joseph *school system administrator*
Isaac-Emmons, Merlyn Hulda *academic administrator, educator*
Kimmich, Christoph Martin *academic administrator, educator*
McLaughlin, (Patricia) Tricia Marie *education educator, artist*
Mc Clenney, Byron Nelson *community college administrator*
O'Connor, Sister George Aquin (Margaret M. O'Connor) *academic administrator, educator*
Panwar, Shivendra Singh *education educator, researcher*
Remsen, James F., Jr. *biology educator*
Rosario-Olmedo, Carmen Gloria *principal*
Shivcharran, Jaigobin *secondary school educator, consultant*
Simons, Barbara *retired elementary school educator*
Taylor, Ian Logan *dean*
Witherspoon, Maria Bernarda Pena *principal*
Wolfe, Ethyle Renee (Mrs. Coleman Hamilton Benedict) *academic administrator*

**Brookville**
Goubeaud, Karleen R. *education educator*
Rhee, Jeong-eun *education educator*
Swaner, Lynn E *education educator*

**Buffalo**
Anker, Beverly Elaine *retired elementary school educator*
Buchanan, Richard N. *dean, dental educator*
Cathey, Patrice Antoinette *secondary school educator, director*
Gielow, Kathleen Louise *career planning administrator, consultant, special education educator*
Grant, S. G. *education educator*
Holm, Bruce Allen *academic administrator, researcher*
Lee, Jaekyung *education educator, researcher*
McClary, Glen David *educator*
Meshlovitz, Mary E. *educational consultant, special education educator*
Milazzo, David Anthony *mathematics educator*
Olsen, R. Nills *dean, law educator*
Owens, Cecelie Ann *elementary school educator*
Schmidli, Keith William *vocational education administrator, educator, researcher*
Silverman, Robert Mark *education educator, researcher*
Simpson, John Barclay *academic administrator*
Triggle, David John *dean, pharmacist, consultant*
Tucker, Melvin Jay *education educator, researcher*
Veronica, Debra Clarisse *principal*
Wagle, A. Tina *education educator, researcher*
Wang, Jui Hsin *biochemistry educator*

**Camillus**
Deegan, Robert *secondary school educator*

**Canandaigua**
Love, Robert Lyman *retired education educator, consultant*
Schwartz, Adam J. *elementary school educator*

**Canton**
Sullivan, Daniel F. *academic administrator, sociologist, educator*

**Cato**
Labeille, Claudine *elementary school educator*

**Central Valley**
Regan, Richard Felix *secondary school educator, musician, conductor*

**Chazy**
Ratner, Gayle *special education educator*

**Churchville**
Balch, Glenn McClain, Jr. *academic administrator, minister, writer*

**Cicero**
Crabtree, Robert Allen *elementary school educator*

**Clarence**
Johnston, Joan Lawler *director, consultant*

**Clifton Springs**
Spoto, Carl Alexander, Jr. *history educator*

**Clinton**
Paris, David C. *academic administrator, political scientist, educator*
Stewart, Joan Hinde *academic administrator*

**Cohoes**
Davey, Mark Christopher *assistant principal*

**Cold Spring**
Posniack, Lee Joseph *secondary school educator*

**Corfu**
Cavanaugh, Michael John *history educator*
Walker, Barbara Hills *secondary school educator*

**Corning**
Wilson, Cecilia Ann *special education educator*

**Cornwall On Hudson**
Peirce, Karen Patricia *education educator*

**Cross River**
Gilarde-Green, Michela M. *secondary school educator*

**Delmar**
Houghton, Raymond Carl, Jr. *education educator*

**Derby**
McKeating, Thomas Francis *secondary school educator*

**Dobbs Ferry**
Postman, Robert Derek *dean, mathematics educator*

**Douglaston**
Palatnick, Frank Sidney *educational consultant*

**Dryden**
Powell, Marsha *director, educator, pathologist*

**Dunkirk**
Burlett, Helen Marie *elementary school educator*

**East Aurora**
Woodard, Carol Jane *educational consultant*

**East Greenbush**
Thornton, Thomas E. *literature and language educator*

**East Hampton**
Osterweil, Adam Matthew *elementary school educator, writer*
Schetlin, Eleanor M. *retired associate dean*

**East Islip**
Donohue, Claire P. *retired school librarian*

**East Northport**
Rose, Richard *secondary school educator*

**East Setauket**
Maffia, Christina *elementary school educator, consultant*

**East Syracuse**
McGlynn, Sean *secondary school educator*

**Eastchester**
Cherry, Theresa Cotrone *principal*
Kravath, Alan Wolfe *education evaluator*

**Elmira**
Meier, Thomas Keith *academic administrator, language educator*

**Endicott**
Goodwin, Charles Hugh *technology education educator*

**Fairport**
DeMay, Michael F. *secondary school educator, director*
Englert, John F. *secondary school educator, coach*
Marshall, Julie Arnitz *biology educator*

**Far Rockaway**
Sussman, Laureen Glicklin *elementary school educator*

**Flushing**
Anderson, Michelle J. *dean, law educator*
Rosenberg, Deborah A. *special education educator*
Totakura, Satyanarayana Raju *secondary school educator*

**Forest Hills**
Buhks, Ephraim *college administrator, technology educator*
D'Addario, Alice Marie *retired school system administrator*

**Fort Montgomery**
Butler, Patricia Claire *retired history educator*

**Fredonia**
Croxton, Jack Sanders *director, consultant*
Horvath, Virginia Schaefer *academic administrator*

**Freeport**
Martorana, Barbara Joan *secondary school educator*

**Garden City**
Dods, Stuart C. *mathematics educator*
Scott, Robert Allyn *academic administrator*
Shuart, James Martin *retired academic administrator*
Wickiewicz, Jessica-Lauren Charlotte *academic administrator*

**Glen Cove**
Olsen, Robert C., Jr. *academic administrator, military officer*

**Glen Head**
Martin, David S. *retired secondary school educator, administrator*

**Great Neck**
Fried, Belle Warshavsky *education educator*
Marcus, Philip *dean*

**Greenport**
Monsell, Thomas Oliver *secondary school educator, writer*

**Greenvale**
Regazzi, John James III *dean, publishing executive*
Shenker, Joseph *academic administrator*
Steinberg, David Joel *academic administrator, historian, educator*

**Guilderland**
Escobar, Deborah Ann *gifted and talented educator*

**Hamburg**
Gorline, Lynda Ruth *elementary school educator*
Meissner, Anita Cohoon *retired elementary school educator*

**Hamilton**
Chopp, Rebecca S. *academic administrator*
Johnston, Michael (William Johnston) *political science educator, university administrator*
Pagano, Jo Anne *education educator*

**Harrison**
Northcutt, Marie Rose *elementary school educator, special education educator*

**Harrisville**
Seelman, Jannet Genevieve *secondary school educator*

**Hartsdale**
Aker, Susan K. *elementary school educator, assistant principal*
Lightburn, Anita Louise *dean, social work educator*

**Hauppauge**
Reid, Margaret Elizabeth *elementary school educator, secondary school educator*

**Hempstead**
Berliner, Herman Albert *academic administrator, economist, educator, dean*
Salten, David George *academic administrator*
Watford, Dolores *elementary school educator*

**Henrietta**
Wolcott, Kyle B, *secondary school educator*

**Herkimer**
Lowery, Kathleen Ann *elementary school educator*

**Hewlett**
Mahoney, Eileen Heron *secondary school educator*

**Hicksville**
Noll, Amy *secondary educator*

**Holland**
Loockerman, William Delmer *retired educational administrator*

**Horseheads**
Andrake, Nancy Carolyn *retired secondary school educator*
Clark, Judy Ann *elementary school educator*

**Houghton**
Chamberlain, Daniel Robert *college president*
Luckey, Robert Reuel Raphael *retired academic administrator*

**Huntington**
Roberts, Elizabeth Anne Stephens *educational consultant*

**Huntington Station**
Stevens, Susan Seltenreich Cirillo *special education educator*

**Hurley**
Opdahl, Viola Elizabeth *secondary school educator*

**Ithaca**
Erickson, David *educator*
Firebaugh, Francille Maloch *academic administrator*
Green, Edward Thomas, Jr. *education educator*
Halpern, Bruce Peter *academic administrator, researcher, educator*
Lovelace, Richard Van Evera *education educator, research scientist*
McConkey, James Rodney *literature and language educator, writer*
Norton, Mary Beth *history educator, writer*
Rhodes, Frank Harold Trevor *academic administrator, geologist*
Schwab, Stewart Jon *dean, law educator*
Scott, Norman Roy *academic administrator, agricultural engineer, educator*
Skorton, David Jan *academic administrator*
Stycos, Maria Nowakowska *adult education educator*
Swieringa, Robert Jay *dean, accounting educator*
Williams, Peggy Ryan *academic administrator*

**Jamaica**
Bartilucci, Andrew Joseph *university administrator*
Bunshaft, Charles Edward *elementary school educator, consultant*
Carey, Elaine *education educator, historian*
Cline, Janice Claire *education educator*
Daly, Mary C. *dean, law educator*
Davis-Jerome, Eileen George *educational consultant, principal*
Faust, Naomi Flowe *education educator*
Harrington, Donald James *university president*
Kaplan, Carolyn Sue *elementary school educator*
Keizs, Marcia V. *academic administrator*
Pratt-Johnson, Yvonne Karen *education professor*
Sciame, Joseph *university administrator*
Skirde, Edward George *academic administrator, consultant*

**Jamestown**
Bogey, Brian Allen *secondary school educator, music educator, director*

**Katonah**
Carlson, Karen Beth *elementary school educator*

**Kendall**
Rak, Linda Marie *elementary school educator, consultant*

**Kings Point**
Mazek, Warren F(elix) *dean, economics professor*

**Lake Peekskill**
Bloom, Janet K *audio-visual specialist, poet*

**Lake Placid**
Pappalardo, Rosa Gloria *secondary school educator*

**Reiss**, Paul J. *academic administrator*

**Lewiston**
Sheeran, Maureen Flynn *retired secondary school educator*

**Lockport**
Leader, Bruce Robert *secondary school educator*

**Long Beach**
Shahda Geraci, Carole Anne *elementary school educator*

**Long Island City**
Dromm, Daniel Patrick *elementary school educator*
Lieberman, Janet Elaine *academic administrator*
Lucca, Louis Anthony *academic administrator*
Roberts, Kathleen Joy Doty *secondary school educator*

**Loudonville**
Toal, James Francis *academic administrator*

**Mahopac**
McCluskey, Frank Bryce *director*

**Mamaroneck**
Martin, Roger Harry *retired college president*

**Manlius**
Booth, Patricia Vogt (Trish Booth) *educational consultant*

**Massapequa Park**
Blake, Diane Patricia *elementary school educator*

**Merrick**
Fleischman, Francine D. *secondary school educator*
Garfinkel, Lawrence Saul *academic administrator, educator, television producer*
Harrison, Marjorie Freeman *secondary education educator, librarian*
Howard, Joyce Anne *elementary school educator*

**Middle Village**
Katz, Harvey I. *secondary school educator*

**Montgomery**
Moore, Virginia Lee Smith *elementary school educator*

**Montrose**
Matthias, George Frank *retired secondary school educator*

**Mount Morris**
Mistretta, Theresa Mary *retired elementary school educator*

**New Hartford**
Boyle, William Leo, Jr. *educational consultant, retired academic administrator*

**New Paltz**
Emanuel-Smith, Robin Lesley *special education educator*
Flanagan Kelly, Anne Marie *academic administrator*
Poskanzer, Steven Gary *academic administrator, lawyer*

**New Rochelle**
Cohen, Saul Bernard *retired academic administrator, geographer*
Frankl, Evan Stewart *secondary school educator*
Gallagher, John Francis *education educator*
Reddington, Mary Jane *retired secondary school educator*
Sweeny, Stephen Jude *academic administrator*

**New Windsor**
MacLeod, Mary Frances *mathematics educator*

**New York**
Adler, Norman Tenner *psychology educator, dean*
Alfano, Michael Charles *academic administrator*
Arndt, Cynthia *educational administrator*
Baslaw-Finger, Annette *education educator, consultant*
Benhabib, Jess *adult education educator*
Bess, James Lawrence *academic administration educator*
Bloomgarden, Karenne Jo *elementary school educator, small business owner*
Bollinger, Lee Carroll *academic administrator, law educator*
Boylan, Elizabeth Shippee *academic administrator, biologist, educator*
Brabeck, Mary Margaret *dean, psychology professor*
Brinkley, Alan David *provost, historian*
Brooks, Mark J. *academic administrator*
Brown, Joyce F. *academic administrator*
Buckley, Robert John *academic administrator, researcher*
Burgess, Clara Skipwith *retired principal*
Burns, Red *academic administrator*
Campbell, Mary Schmidt *dean*
Caputo, David Armand *academic administrator, political scientist, educator*
Carnabuci, Frank J. III *headmaster*
Clapp, Stephen Henry *dean, violinist*
Claster, Jill Nadell *academic administrator, history educator*
Consagra, Sophie Chandler *academic administrator*
Cooley, Thomas F. *dean, economist, educator*
Cureton, Nadia *academic administrator*
Danielson, John M. *educational consultant, former federal agency administrator*
Davidson, Anthony R. *education educator, consultant*
Durkin, Dorothy Angela *university official*
Essandoh, Hilda Brathwaite *primary school educator*
Evarts, Helen Coleman *secondary school educator*
Fabian, Larry Louis *academic administrator*

Finegold, Amy Beth *elementary school educator, consultant*
Fischbach, Gerald D. *dean, neurobiology educator*
Fuhrman, Susan H. *academic administrator, education educator*
García, Mildred *academic administrator*
Gatto, John Taylor *educational consultant, educator*
Gerety, Tom *academic administrator, lawyer, educator, philosopher*
Germano, William Paul *dean, former publishing executive*
Gibson, Arlene Joy *headmaster*
Gillespie, John Thomas *retired university administrator*
Goldberger, Paul Jesse *dean, architecture critic, writer*
Goldstein, Matthew *academic administrator*
Gottschalk, Alfred *retired academic administrator, museum administrator*
Grant, Sonia Vivienne *secondary school educator*
Haffner, Alden Norman *academic administrator*
Halperin, Jonathan L. *medical school administrator*
Hansen, William D. *educational consultant, former federal agency administrator*
Hassebo, Yasser Youssef *education educator, researcher*
Hoffner, Marilyn *university administrator*
Hood, Donald Charles *academic administrator, psychologist, educator*
Horowitz, Frances Degen *academic administrator, psychology educator*
Hubbard, R. Glenn (Robert Glenn Hubbard, Glenn Hubbard) *academic administrator, former federal official*
Ilchman, Warren Frederick *academic administrator, foundation administrator, educator*
Istomin, Marta Casals *retired school president, performing company executive*
Jansky, Jeannette Jefferson *learning disabilities specialist*
Jelinek, Vera *dean*
Jeynes, Mary Kay *college dean*
Joel, Richard Marc *academic administrator, law educator, dean*
Kase, Nathan Ginden *dean*
Kerrey, Bob (J. Robert Kerrey) *academic administrator, former senator*
Klein, Joel Irwin *school system administrator*
Lamm, Norman *academic administrator, rabbi*
Lamster, Ira Barry *dean, academic administrator*
Lange, Phil C. *retired education educator*
Levine, Naomi Bronheim *academic administrator*
Lloyd, Jean *retired early childhood educator*
Lowengrub, Morton *academic administrator*
Macchiarola, Frank Joseph *academic administrator, educator*
Marcuse, Adrian Gregory *academic administrator*
McGarry, Robert Alan *university administrator*
McLaughlin, David *academic administrator, mathematics professor, neural science educator*
Morreale, Joseph Constantino *academic administrator, educator, economist, consultant*
Ness, Pamela Miller *elementary school educator*
Nissim, Shai *special education educator, consultant*
Nurse, Sir Paul M. *academic administrator*
Oliva, Lawrence Jay *retired academic administrator, history professor*
Paige, Roderick Raynor *educational consultant, former secretary of education*
Parkin, Gerard Francis Ralph *chemistry educator, researcher*
Pawliczko, George Ihor *academic administrator*
Polisi, Joseph William *academic administrator*
Pulanco, Tonya Beth *special education educator*
Rabb, Harriet Schaffer *academic administrator, lawyer*
Reutter, Eberhard Edmund, Jr. *education and law educator*
Revesz, Richard Luis *dean, law educator*
Rhodes, David *academic administrator*
Roche, John Edward *college administrator, human resources specialist, educator*
Rowland, Esther E(delman) *retired dean*
Rubini, Gail *education director*
Rubino, Victor Joseph *academic administrator, lawyer*
Rudenstine, Neil Leon *former academic administrator, educator*
Scaffidi, Judith Ann *academic administrator*
Schaller-Demers, Debra Susan *academic administrator coordinator*
Schizer, David Michael *dean, law educator*
Sclafani, Susan K. *educational consultant, former federal agency administrator*
Seitz, Frederick *former university administrator*
Selby, Cecily Cannan *dean, science educator*
Sexton, John Edward *academic administrator, law educator*
Shapiro, Judith R. *academic administrator, anthropology educator*
Shaw, Lacy *education consultant*
Shields, James Joseph *academic administrator, educator, writer*
Silverman, Martin Morris Bernard *secondary school educator*
Sims, William Jack *secondary school educator*
Snyder, Jon David *dean*
Sobol, Thomas *education educator*
Southworth, Robert Alexander, Jr. *education researcher, educator*
Steiner, David M. *dean*
Summerfield, Judith Pearl *dean, English language educator*
Takamura, Jeanette Chiyoko *dean*
Thompson, William C., Jr. *school system administrator*
Travis, Jeremy *academic administrator*
Waren, Stanley Arnold *academic administrator, performing company executive*
Weinstein, Sidney *retired university program director*
Wylie, James Malcolm *adult education educator*
Yee, Kenton K. *educator*
Yu, Pauline Ruth *former dean, educational association administrator*

**Newburgh**
Sakac, Sister Ann *academic administrator*

**Newport**
West, Susan R. *elementary school educator, consultant*

**Niagara University**
Denig, Stephen Joseph *education educator*

**North Collins**
Cataldo, John *principal*

**North Salem**
Mittelstadt, Beverly Anne *elementary school educator*

**Ogdensburg**
Smith, Carol Ann *academic administrator*

**Old Westbury**
Christofides, Fotine *parochial school educator*
van Wie, Paul David *secondary school educator, historian*

**Orangeburg**
Filippelli, James Anthony *literature and language educator*
Filoramo, Dorothy Christine *academic administrator*

**Orchard Park**
Gloss, Wendy *principal*

**Oriskany**
Jacobson, Karen *retired elementary school educator*

**Oswego**
Garruto, John *counseling administrator*
White, Kevin J. *education educator, consultant*

**Ozone Park**
Bellamy, Renee Adele *secondary school educator*
Peeples, Thelma J. *elementary school educator*

**Palmyra**
Rose, Donna Marie *secondary school educator, farmer*

**Paul Smiths**
Mills, John W. *academic administrator*

**Pittsford**
Barker, Julie A. *school system administrator*
Bernstein, Paul *retired academic dean*
Green, Martin Lincoln *retired academic administrator*
Sproull, Robert Lamb *retired academic administrator, physicist, director*
Thompson, Brian John *academic administrator, optics scientist, educator*

**Plattsburgh**
Withrow, Gregory B. *director, accountant*

**Pleasantville**
Loase, John *education educator*

**Pomona**
Frelow, Robert Dean *retired school system administrator, writer*

**Port Jefferson Station**
Shockley, Alonzo Hilton, Jr. *school system administrator*
Spahr, Clinton S., Jr. *retired elementary school educator*

**Port Washington**
Gordon-Tennant, Jennifer Jay *secondary school educator*

**Portville**
Welty, Inga Ann *mathematics educator*

**Potsdam**
Collins, Anthony G. *academic administrator*
Ha, Andrew Kwangho *education educator*
Kim, Eugene *education educator*
Rudiger, Lance Wade *secondary school educator*
Schwaller, John Frederick *academic administrator, historian, educator*
Scott, Jean A. *university president*

**Poughkeepsie**
Brakas, Nora Jachym *education educator*
Conklin, Donald David *academic administrator*
Hill, Catharine Bond (Cappy Hill) *academic administrator, economics professor*
Jackson, Judy Faye *academic administrator*
Opdycke, Leonard Emerson *retired elementary school educator, publishing executive, writer*
Parker, Raymon Philip *dean*
Taylor, Patricia *director*

**Purchase**
Lacy, Bill *academic administrator, architect*
Putman, Jeffrey Scott *academic administrator*
Vardin, Patricia Anne *education educator*

**Rexford**
Schmitt, Roland Walter *retired academic administrator*

**Rochester**
Adams, Carol H. *dean*
Blanda-Holtzberg, Marianne Lourdes *education educator, consultant*
Chiverton, Patricia Ann *dean, nursing educator*
Christensen, Sonya Marie *school librarian*
Cohen, Jules *former dean, internist, educator*
Dam, Lee Addison *vice principal*
Everett, Claudia Kellam *retired special education educator*
Garwood, Naomi Fuji *education educator*
Griswold, Kathy Ann King *academic administrator*
Guzick, David S. *dean, educator*
Jackson, Thomas Humphrey *former academic administrator*

Joynt, Robert James *academic administrator, physician*
Kirschenbaum, Howard *education educator*
Larson, Joanne Caroline *educator*
Munson, Harold Lewis *education educator*
Seligman, Joel *academic administrator*
Shirley, Bonnie J. *retired elementary school educator*
Smith, David Harry Watrous *retired secondary school educator*
Sottile, Joseph James *elementary school educator, poet*
Surace, Theresa *special education educator*
Tucker, Jeffrey Allen *education educator*
Velletri, Thomas Joseph *elementary school educator, artist*
Zupan, Mark A. *dean, business professor*

**Rocky Point**
Falcone, David J. *elementary school educator*

**Roosevelt**
Adams, Mary A. *retired assistant principal*

**Roslyn**
Stracher, Dorothy Altman *education educator, consultant*

**Saint Bonaventure**
Dembele, Gaston *adult education educator*

**Saint James**
Kelly, Michael Joseph *academic administrator, consultant*

**Saint Regis Falls**
Johnson, Karleen A. *retired primary school educator*

**Sanborn**
Godell, Lori B. *elementary school educator*
Michalak, Janet Carol *childhood education educator, coordinator*
Nowak (Jarosz), Linda Therese *special education educator, consultant*
Pogel, Alan Fred *history educator*

**Sands Point**
Cullinan, Bernice Ellinger *education educator*

**Saratoga Springs**
Glotzbach, Philip A. *academic administrator, philosopher, educator*
Greco, Joseph Angelo *supervisor*

**Sayville**
Vigliotta, Margaret D. *secondary school educator, art educator, artist*

**Schenectady**
Ainlay, Stephen Charles *academic administrator, educator*
Hartkern, Danielle Anne *elementary school educator*
Turin, Lars *secondary school educator, artist*

**Selden**
Connors, William Francis, Jr. *academic administrator*

**Seneca Falls**
Norman, Mary Marshall *academic administrator, alcohol/drug abuse services professional, educator*

**Shirley**
Harper, Catherine B. *primary school educator*

**Silver Creek**
Kurzawa, Marilyn Taylor *educational consultant*

**Smithtown**
Felice, Lisa M. *special education educator*
Haskins, Debra May *academic administrator, educator*

**Sparkill**
Solomon, Pearl Gold *education educator, consultant*

**Spencerport**
Broussard, Allison M. *secondary school educator, artist*

**Spring Valley**
Johnson, Judith A. *educational administrator*

**Staten Island**
Brady, Christine Ellen *education coordinator*
Springer, Marlene *university administrator, educator*
Wilson, Alice McAteer *secondary school educator*

**Sterling**
Anderson, Nancy Marie Greenwood *special education educator*

**Stony Brook**
Barnett, Jeffrey Adam *academic administrator*
Cochran, James Kirk *dean, oceanographer, educator, geochemist*
Kenny, Shirley Strum *academic administrator*
Rifkin, Barry R. *dean, dental educator, researcher*
Shamash, Yacov *dean, electrical engineering educator*
Tewarson, Reginald Prabhakar *retired mathematics educator, consultant*

**Syracuse**
Arterian, Hannah R. *dean, law educator*
Cantor, Nancy *academic administrator*
Castro, Alfonso Peter *education educator, consultant*
Chickadonz, Grace Harlow *dean*
Freund, Deborah A. *academic administrator*
Krathwohl, David Reading *retired education educator*
Milač, Metod M. *retired school librarian*
Miles, Kenneth Ontario *academic program director*

Murphy, Cornelius B., Jr. (Neil Murphy) *academic administrator*
Scheinman, Steven Jay *dean, medical educator*
Taylor, Robert Saxton *retired dean*
Thorin, Suzanne E. *dean, university librarian*
Wallerstein, Mitchel Bruce *dean, educator*
Ware, Bennie *academic administrator*

**Tarrytown**
Marcus, Sheldon *school policy and administration educator*

**Thiells**
Ziotis, Josephine *elementary school educator, restaurant owner*

**Tonawanda**
Vacanti, Mary Parisi *director, consultant*

**Troy**
Jackson, Shirley Ann *academic administrator, physicist*
Kahl, William Frederick *retired academic administrator*
Luraas, Sandra *elementary school educator, secondary school educator*
Mayo, Robert Raymond *university librarian*
Neff, Jeanne Henry *academic administrator*
Wait, Samuel Charles, Jr. *academic administrator, educator*

**Uniondale**
Impagliazzo, Jenette Celeste *elementary school educator*

**Utica**
Baber, Bob *dean*
Hockey, Christopher Lawrence *academic administrator*

**Valhalla**
Hankin, Joseph Nathan *college president*
O'Connell, Ralph Anthony *dean, psychiatrist, educator*

**Valley Stream**
Rodgers, John Joseph III *educational administration consultant, educator*
Wood, Catherine T. *special education educator*

**Webster**
Powers, Richard Gerard *history educator*

**West Babylon**
Ford, Clara S. *retired secondary school educator*

**West Point**
Finnegan, Patrick *dean, military officer, lawyer*

**West Seneca**
Beehler, Mark *director*
Tanski, Sarah Piatko *mathematics educator*

**Westbury**
Greenberger, Roni Susan *elementary school educator*
Marks, Debra Jane *special education educator*
Ross-Lee, Barbara *dean, educator*

**Westhampton Beach**
Perez, Dawn Marie *elementary school educator*

**White Plains**
Ottinger, Richard Lawrence *dean emeritus*
Szolnoki, John Frank *special education educator, administrator*

**Williamsville**
Huff, Kenneth L. *elementary school educator*

**Woodmere**
Seyfert, Wayne George *secondary education educator, anatomy educator*

**Yonkers**
Boveroux, Lorie Ann Hansen *secondary school educator, graphics designer*
Lee, Claudia S. *retired elementary school educator*
Liggio, Jean Vincenza *adult education educator, artist*
Wooton, Francine Evans *secondary school educator*

**Yorktown Heights**
Schiller, Barbara *retired special education educator*

**NORTH CAROLINA**

**Asheville**
Brown, David G. *academic administrator*
Merrill, Deane Whitney, Jr. *secondary school educator, consultant*
Pfeiffer, William Sanborn *education educator, writer*

**Bakersville**
Buchanan, Robin Byington *school system administrator*

**Belmont**
Ratchford, Melinda Eudy *education educator*

**Boone**
Austin, Roberta Jones *elementary school educator*
Duke, Charles Richard *dean*
Durham, Harvey Ralph *academic administrator*
Harbinson, William Grady *dean, composer*
Lugo, Emil J. *retired secondary school educator*
McGaha, Cindy *education educator*

**Buies Creek**
Johnson, George Lloyd *education educator, consultant, writer*
Wiggins, Norman Adrian *academic administrator, law educator*

**Burlington**
Phillips, Ruth Ann *retired secondary school educator*

**Cary**
Rahmani, Carol Hipp *school system administrator, psychologist*
Summers, Suzanne Frances Hemenway *elementary school educator*

**Chapel Hill**
Broad, Margaret Corbett (Molly Broad) *academic administrator*
Carroll, Roy *retired academic administrator*
Cronenwett, Linda Houk *dean, nursing educator*
Edwards, Richard LeRoy *dean, social sciences educator, management consultant*
Folkerts, Jean *dean, journalism educator*
Fordham, Christopher Columbus III *dean, academic administrator, medical educator*
Freund, Cynthia M. *dean*
Ganley, Oswald Harold *retired director*
Hughes-Hassell, Sandra *education educator*
Jones, W. S. (Steve Jones) *dean*
Levine, Madeline Geltman *literature and language educator, translator*
Magill, Samuel Hays *academic administrator, consultant*
Mc Kean, John Rosseel Overton *university dean*
Michalak, Sarah C. *university librarian*
Moeser, James Charles *academic administrator*
Roper, William Lee *dean, preventive medicine physician, health facility administrator*
Salgado, Maria Antonia *education educator*
Sanders, John Lassiter *retired academic administrator*
Stearns, Sally Clark *education educator*
Ware, William Brettel *education educator*
Wescott, Joseph Warren, II, *academic administrator, education educator*
Williams, John N. *dean, dental educator*
Wolfenden, Richard Vance *biochemistry educator*

**Charlotte**
Bhatnagar, Abha *school system administrator, department chairman*
Bowles, Erskine B. *academic administrator, former White House chief of staff*
Britt, Julia Moody *secondary school educator*
Croker, Brent Allen *counseling administrator*
Dubois, Philip Leon *academic administrator, political scientist, educator*
Eppley, Frances Fielden *secondary school educator, writer*
Fretwell, Elbert K., Jr. *retired university chancellor, consultant*
Hutchings-Hoffman, Cathy Jo *early childhood educator*
McAfee, Larry W. *chemistry educator*
Mercer, Evelyn Lois *retired counseling administrator*
Peterson, Evonne Stewart *elementary school educator*
Smith, Samantha June *literature and language educator*
Tyson, Cynthia Haldenby *academic administrator*
Woodward, James Hoyt *retired academic administrator, retired engineering educator*
Wright, Bonnie H. *elementary school educator*
Yancy, Dorothy Cowser *college president*

**Chocowinity**
Castle, William Eugene *retired academic administrator*

**Cullowhee**
Bardo, John William *academic administrator*
Carlisle, James Steven, Jr. *dean, actor*
Coulter, Myron Lee *retired academic administrator*
Kauffman, N. Leroy *academic administrator*
Reed, Alfred Douglas *retired academic administrator*

**Dallas**
Brown, Pearlie Murray *school librarian*

**Davidson**
Vagt, Robert F. *academic administrator*

**Durham**
Bartlett, Katharine Tiffany *dean, law educator*
Breeden, Douglas Tower *dean, financial consultant*
Brodhead, Richard H. *academic administrator*
Denlinger, Ann T. *school system administrator*
Dennis, Helen Oldham *elementary school educator*
Dowell, Earl Hugh *dean, aerospace and mechanical engineering educator*
Huestis, Charles Benjamin *former academic administrator*
Jakubs, Deborah *university librarian*
Jeffreys, Arcelia Taylor *education educator*
Kuniholm, Bruce Robellet *academic administrator, educator*
Lange, Peter *academic administrator*
Parker, William *education educator*
Roger, Edwin Mclendon *education educator*
Schmalbeck, Richard Louis *dean, lawyer*
Williams, Robert Sanders (Sandy Williams) *dean, academic administrator, educator, researcher*

**Elizabeth City**
Banerjee, Hirendra Nath *educator*
Luton, John Willis *education educator*

**Elon**
Tolley, Jerry Russell *academic administrator*

**Fairview**
Brown, Gregory Neil *academic administrator, forester, educator*
Godard, Jerry Holton Caris *retired dean, psychology and literature professor*

**Fayetteville**
Hagans, Valerie Mae Gee *special education educator*

Jordan, Karla Salge *retired primary school educator*

**Flat Rock**
Oliver, Ann Breeding *secondary school educator, art dealer*

**Fort Bragg**
Stafford, C. Stewart *educational consultant, educator*

**Franklin**
Earhart, Eileen Magie *retired elementary school educator, retired child and family life educator*
Maki, Joan Owen *gifted and talented educator*

**Gastonia**
Crissman, Katherine Kolb *counseling administrator*

**Greensboro**
Bynum, Magnolia Virginia Wright *retired secondary school educator*
Cole, Johnnetta Betsch *academic administrator, educator*
French, Lenny Sue *elementary school educator*
Hajek, Ellen *elementary school educator*
Linster, Michelle Lynn *education educator, consultant*
Miller, Robert Louis *dean, chemistry professor*
Oliver, Donna H. *academic administrator, secondary school educator*
Perkins, Mark L. *university chancellor*
Saul, Connie Cline *secondary school educator*
Schunk, Dale Hansen *dean*
Simmons, Michelle Holschuh *school librarian, educator*
Sullivan, Patricia A. *academic administrator*
Williams, Ereka Rochelle *education educator*
Zopf, Evelyn LaNoel Montgomery *retired guidance counselor*

**Greenville**
Anderson, Patricia Jean *elementary school educator*
Ballard, Steven C. *academic administrator*
Bearden, James Hudson *university official*
Drought, Michael Hall *academic administrator*
Eakin, Richard Ronald *academic administrator, mathematics educator*
Pawlak, Roman Maciej *education educator*
Rouse, William Arthur, Jr. *education educator*

**Hamlet**
Ewing, Viola P. *elementary school educator*

**Harrisburg**
Patchen, Kelly A. *elementary school educator*

**Hillsborough**
Adams, Rex *dean*

**Holly Springs**
Booth, Penelope Partridge *secondary school educator, writer, principal*

**Hope Mills**
McBryde, Cecilia Collins *secondary school educator*

**Indian Trail**
Hinson, Robert Wayne *education educator*

**Kernersville**
Miller, Helen *history educator*

**Kings Mountain**
Randall, Susan *education educator*

**Kinston**
Petteway, Samuel Bruce *college president*

**Lake Junaluska**
Martinson, Jacob Christian, Jr. *academic administrator*
Stanton, Donald Sheldon *academic administrator*

**Laurinburg**
Deegan, John, Jr. *academic administrator, educator, researcher*

**Louisburg**
Foth, Rodney Stephen *academic administrator, science educator*

**Maxton**
Ellis, Hubert Lee *retired secondary school educator*

**Monroe**
Griffin, Cathy McWhorter *elementary school educator*

**Montreat**
Struble, Dan *academic administrator*

**Morven**
Lowe, David Wayne *elementary school educator, education educator*

**Mount Olive**
Beck, Julie Renee *academic administrator*
Raper, William Burkette *retired college president*

**Murfreesboro**
White, Martin Christopher *academic administrator*

**Murphy**
Deslauriers, Suzanne Dawsey *secondary school educator, artist*

**Nashville**
Penick, Angela Lucas *elementary school educator*

**Pilot Mountain**
Smith, Richard Jackson *elementary school educator*

**Raleigh**
Atkinson, June *school system administrator*
Baker, Stanley Beckwith *education educator*
Barnhardt, Robert Alexander *dean*
Bruck, Robert Ian *education educator*
Burris, Craven Allen *retired college administrator, educator*
Davis, Janice *school system administrator*
Dolce, Carl John *education administration educator*
Drew, Nancy McLaurin Shannon *counselor, consultant*
Fedewa, Michael Joseph *school system administrator*
Hartford, Maureen A. *academic administrator*
Jarrett, Polly Hawkins *retired secondary school educator*
Li, Bailian *academic administrator*
Mac Cormac, Earl Ronald *retired education educator*
Maidon, Carolyn Howser *director*
Memory, Jasper Durham *academic administrator, physics professor*
Nelson, Larry A. *statistics educator, consultant*
Oblinger, James L. *academic administrator*
Parramore, Barbara Mitchell *education educator*
Penick, John E. *education educator*
Petters, Robert M. *education educator*
Robinson, Prezell Russell *academic administrator*
Scott, Stephen Carlos *academic administrator*
Whetzel, Julie Anne *special education educator*
Whitaker, Bruce Ezell *college president*
Winstead, Nash Nicks *academic administrator, plant pathologist*
Wynne, Johnny Calvin *dean, plant pathologist, researcher*

**Ramseur**
Coward, Pamela Kinney *elementary school educator*

**Red Springs**
Jacobs, Kimberly Ann *elementary school educator*

**Research Triangle Park**
Call, Douglas William *university official, naval officer*

**Robbins**
Smith, Janet Brewer *secondary school educator*

**Rockingham**
Robertson, Ralph S. *secondary school principal*

**Rocky Mount**
Nelsen, William Cameron *educational consultant*

**Ronda**
Somers, Shelley Allen *elementary school educator*

**Rougemont**
Holeman, Betty Jean *counseling administrator*

**Salisbury**
Freeman, Algeania Warren *academic administrator*
Jenkins, Jimmy Raymond *academic administrator*
Troxler, Willie Thomasene *retired elementary school educator*

**Seven Lakes**
Reilly, David Henry *retired university dean*

**Shelby**
Edgar, Ruth R. *retired elementary school educator*

**Smithfield**
Madern, Laurene Patricia *secondary school educator*

**Southport**
Spain, Sheryl Scarbrough *school counselor, educator*

**Statesville**
Allred, Susan G. *school system administrator*

**Thomasville**
Mintz, Donna Pierce *elementary school educator*

**Wadesboro**
Hamby, Kristie Lynne *director*

**Wake Forest**
Buchanan, Edward A. *education educator*

**Walstonburg**
Beaman, Joyce Proctor *retired secondary and elementary school educator, writer*

**Warrenton**
Kearney, Irene Spruill *elementary school educator*

**Waxhaw**
Lubs, Lori Deanne *elementary school educator*

**Weaverville**
Hall, Linda *secondary school educator*

**Wilmington**
Hancock, Robert Douglas *educator*
Moallem, Mahnaz *educational researcher*

**Winston Salem**
Applegate, William Brown *dean, researcher, medical educator, department chairman*
Cahill, Eileen Mary *secondary school educator*
Constantinidis, Christos *education educator*
Gordon, William Charles *academic administrator*
Hatch, Nathan Orr *academic administrator*
Hearn, Thomas K., Jr. *academic administrator*
Patel, Ajay *dean*
Roth, Marjory Joan Jarboe *special education educator*
Walsh, Robert K. *dean*
Wilson, Van Cedric *academic administrator*
Zubov, Lynn *special education educator, researcher*

**Woodland**
Wilson, Lloyd Lee *registrar, educator*

**Woodleaf**
Nelson, Jennifer *elementary school educator*

## NORTH DAKOTA

**Bismarck**
Evanson, Barbara Jean *middle school education educator*
Joersz, Fran Woodmansee *secondary school educator*
Potts, Robert Leslie *academic administrator*
Sanstead, Wayne Godfrey *school system administrator*

**Bottineau**
Hagen, Mavis Arlo *elementary school educator*

**Cooperstown**
Surerus, Dorothea Kae *elementary school educator*

**Crystal**
Bradshaw, Glorianne Marie *elementary school educator*

**Edgeley**
Jolin, Diane Louise *elementary school educator*

**Elgin**
Hintz, Pam K. *secondary school educator, science educator*

**Ellendale**
Schlieve, Hy C. J. *school administrator*

**Fargo**
Meester, Holly *elementary school educator, music educator, sales executive*
Morey, Charlotte Ann *elementary school educator, music educator*

**Gackle**
Wittmier, Denise Donelle *elementary school educator*

**Grand Forks**
Aune, Adonica Schultz *education educator, consultant*
Kupchella, Charles Edward *academic administrator, author, educator*
Milavetz, Barry *academic administrator, molecular biologist*
Mondry, Diane *secondary school educator*
Nordlie, Robert Conrad *biochemistry educator*
Olson, Myrna Raye *education educator*
Page, Sally Jacquelyn *university official, management educator*

**Hunter**
Nyberg, Anne Marie *secondary school educator*

**Mayville**
Pederson, John Martin *education educator*

**Minot**
Jermiason, John Lynn *elementary school educator, farmer, rancher*

**Oakes**
German, Susan Lee *secondary school educator*

**Rolla**
Seehafer, Brenda Ann *elementary school educator*

**Valley City**
Rogers, Patricia Louise *education educator, consultant*

## OHIO

**Ada**
Baker, Kendall L. *academic administrator*

**Akron**
Barker, Harold Kenneth *former university dean*
Buzzelli, Charlotte Grace *special education educator*
Duan, Zhong-Hui *education educator, researcher*
Ichilov, Nehemia *principal, consultant*
Linberger, Peter *school librarian*
von Spiegel, Janice Krieger *mathematics educator*

**Amelia**
Kahles, Cheryl Mary *elementary school educator*

**Athens**
Bruning, James Leon *academic administrator, educator*
Crowl, Samuel Renninger *retired dean, language educator*
Hogan, Terrence James *academic administrator, consultant*
Krendl, Kathy *dean*
McDavis, Roderick J. *academic administrator*
Tymas-Jones, Raymond *dean*

**Aurora**
Ross, Violet Bica *retired elementary school educator, retired psychologist*

**Bay Village**
Gorman, Elias John *history educator*

**Berea**
Durst, Richard Wayne *academic administrator*
Tomlin-Houston, Lisa *higher education administrator, director*

**Bexley**
Verde, Brian James *secondary school educator*

**Blanchester**
Coates, Pamela Marie *principal*

**Bluffton**
Liu, Kejing *education educator*

**Campbell**
Peltz, Ruby *elementary school educator*

**Canfield**
Le Brun, John Leo *education educator, tax specialist*

**Canton**
Broniak, Lynn Marguerite *gifted and talented educator, technology educator*
Peck, Douglas Caton *dean, educator*
Tullys, Marilyn Steen *retired elementary school educator*

**Chagrin Falls**
Brown, Jeanette Grasselli *retired director*
Deihl, Charles L. *former college president*
Indriolo, Johna Marie *elementary school educator*
Robertson, Linda F. *educational administrator*

**Chardon**
Horvath, Madelon Toft *secondary school educator*

**Chillicothe**
Cunningham, Susan Kathryn *retired secondary school educator*

**Chippewa Lake**
Javorek, Richard Alan *history educator, consultant*

**Cincinnati**
Ates, Delories *retired counseling administrator*
Briggs, Henry Payson, Jr. *headmaster*
Cain, Linda Joanne *retired academic administrator*
Clifford, Joel Patrick *secondary school educator*
Dionysiou, Dionysios Demetriou *adult education educator, researcher*
Dugan, Timothy P. *director, philosopher, educator*
Greengus, Samuel *academic administrator, theology studies educator*
Harrison, Donald Carey *academic administrator, cardiologist, educator*
Kelz, Rochelle Shelle K. *academic administrator*
Kessinger, Thomas Anthony *education educator, consultant, social studies educator*
Kutch, Keith Dwayne *academic administrator, dean*
Lindell, Andrea Regina *dean, nurse*
Martin, William Joseph, II, *dean, educator*
Nagy, Donna M. *dean, law educator*
Nester, William Raymond, Jr. *retired academic administrator*
Rahnfeld, Vincent D. *counseling administrator*
Smith, Gregory Allgire *academic administrator*
Stern, David Mark *dean, educator*
Sublett, Roger H. *academic administrator*
Teeters, Linda Marie *retired secondary school educator*
Urso, Julie Ann *secondary school educator*
Wagner, Thomas Edward *academic administrator, educator*
Winkler, Henry Ralph *retired academic administrator, historian*
Woods, Carol Smith *private school educator*
Zimpher, Nancy Lusk *academic administrator*

**Circleville**
Conley, John Wallace *academic administrator*

**Cleveland**
Arndt, Charles Richard *dean*
Boboc, Marius *education educator*
Byrd-Bennett, Barbara *school system administrator*
Cerone, David *academic administrator*
Eastwood, Gregory Lindsay *academic administrator*
Eustis, Joanne D. *university librarian*
Goldberg, Jerold S. *dean*
Hundert, Edward M. *former academic administrator, educator*
Johnson, Victoria Houston *elementary school educator, poet*
McArdle, Richard Joseph *retired academic administrator*
McCullough, Joseph *retired academic administrator*
Nickerson, Gary Lee *educational consultant*
Powell, Carl R. *academic administrator*
Queen, Joyce *elementary school educator*
Quigney, Theresa Ann *special education educator*
Simson, Gary Joseph *dean, law educator*
Tary-Lehmann, Magdalena *education educator*
Thomas, David Manning *secondary school educator*
Topol, Eric Jeffrey *academic administrator, cardiologist, educator*
Weidenthal, Maurice David (Bud Weidenthal) *academic administrator, journalist*
Wertheim, Sally Harris *director, academic administrator, dean, education educator, consultant*
Wykle, May L. *dean, educator, researcher*

**Cleveland Heights**
Close, Carole Lynne *education educator, consultant*

**Columbia Station**
Goll, Paulette Susan *education educator*

**Columbus**
Alutto, Joseph Anthony *dean, management educator*
Armes, Walter Scott *retired vocational school administrator*
Ash, Thomas Phillip *school system administrator*
Balkrishnan, Rajesh *education educator*
Beck, Paul Allen *dean, political science professor*
Bell, Karen A. *dean*
Bina, Melvina Jean Humpal *elementary school educator*
Cocchi, Wayne Paul *special education educator*
Cole, Charles Chester, Jr. *academic administrator*
Cole, Clarence Russell *college dean*
Culbertson, Jack Arthur *education educator*
Fields, Henry William *college dean*

Gonzalez, Karen Eileen *middle school educator*
Griffith, Dennison W. *academic administrator, art educator, artist*
Holbrook, Karen Ann *academic administrator, biologist*
Koenigsknecht, Roy A. *dean*
Kronmiller, Jan E. *dean, academic administrator*
Lisko (Dozer), Bonnie Lee *education educator*
Mrozek, Lawrence James *director*
O'Hanlon, Nancyanne *school librarian, educator*
Otte, Paul John *academic administrator, consultant*
Parent, Richard Earl *education educator, consultant*
Racke, Michael Karl *academic administrator*
Rogers, Nancy Hardin *dean, law educator*
Sanfilippo, Alfred Paul *dean, medical educator, pathologist*
Sedmak, Daniel D. *academic administrator*
Snyder, Barbara Rook *academic administrator*
Stephens, Thomas M(aron) *education educator*
Stull, Elizabeth Crosby *retired education educator*
Stull, Gary Evan *secondary school educator, writer*
Turner, Elvin L. *retired school system administrator*
Warmbrod, Catharine Phelps *educational researcher, consultant*
Willke, Thomas Aloys *academic administrator, statistician, educator*
Zelman, Susan Tave *school system administrator*

**Coshocton**
Boyce, Stanley Edman *retired secondary school educator*

**Dayton**
Carson, Dora A. *secondary school educator*
Curran, Daniel J. *academic administrator, sociologist, educator*
Dermody, Diana Dorothy *elementary school educator*
Goldenberg, Kim *academic administrator, internist*
Hopkins, David R. *academic administrator, educator*
Lasley, Thomas J., II, *education educator*
Part, Howard Mitchell *dean*
Pestello, Fred P. *academic administrator*
Potter, Dan R. *history educator*

**De Graff**
Fleming, Lucinda Marie *secondary school educator*

**Delaware**
Pettigrew, Carolyn Landers *academic administrator, minister*

**Delta**
Miller, Beverly White *former college president, educational consultant*

**Dublin**
Bordelon, Carolyn Thew *elementary school educator*
Meek, Violet Imhof *retired dean*
Sanner, Myrna Joyce *elementary school educator*
Souch, Mary Pauline *gifted and talented educator*

**Edon**
Hruska, Bradley J. *elementary school educator*

**Fairfield**
Glass, Linda L. *elementary school educator*
Hubbard, Michele Masanek *secondary school educator, soccer coach*

**Fairview Park**
Flynn, Patricia M. *director, special education educator, gifted and talented educator*

**Findlay**
Freed, DeBow *academic administrator*
Nissley, M. John *dean, educator*
Young, Brian A. *academic administrator*

**Fredericktown**
Ackerman, Loretta Ann *retired secondary school educator*

**Fremont**
Johnson, Laurence F. *college executive*
Ruble, Amanda L. *elementary school educator*

**Gambier**
Nugent, S. Georgia *academic administrator*
Spaid, Gregory P. *academic administrator, art educator*

**Georgetown**
Fite, Tom W. *retired mathematics educator, farmer*

**Green**
Davidson, Dale Alan *secondary school educator, director*
Long, Kathy Jean *special education educator*

**Greenville**
Darmer, Ellen Suzanne *school system administrator*

**Hamilton**
Zahner-Krach, Anne Colette *preschool educator*

**Hemlock**
Johnson, George Warner *gifted and talented educator, consultant*

**Hudson**
Goheen, Janet Moore *counseling administrator, sales executive*
Hallenbeck, Linda S. *elementary school educator*
Lambacher, Kathleen Hartwell *education educator*
Schneider, Rudolph F. *education educator*

**Ironton**
Curry, Estella Roberta *education educator, school psychologist, consultant*

**Kent**
Buttlar, Rudolph Otto *retired college dean*

Cartwright, Carol Ann *retired academic administrator*
Gaston, Paul Lee *academic administrator, language educator*
Gosnell, Davina J. *dean, nursing educator*
Lefton, Lester Alan *academic administrator, psychology professor*
Phillips, Matthew Todd *history educator*

**Lewis Center**
Thomason, Sandra Lee *elementary school educator*

**Lima**
MacBenn, Joseph Vernon *director*

**Lorain**
Wittlinger, Cheryl A. *elementary school educator*

**Mansfield**
Gregory, Deirdre Dianne *secondary school educator*
Olinger, Angela Marie *adult education educator*
Riedl, John Orth *retired university dean*

**Marietta**
Francis, Lynne Ann *elementary school educator, music educator*
Fredericks, Margaret Matterson *elementary school educator*

**Marion**
Iams, Denise Zucker *retired mathematics educator*

**Massillon**
Eckhart, Marylouise Christine Santilli *pre-school educator*

**Mc Donald**
Daigle, Barbara Dianne *elementary school educator*

**Medina**
Feola, David Craig *secondary school administrator*
Timco, Joseph Justin *elementary school educator*

**Mentor**
Hale, Jeffrey L. *economics educator*

**Miamiville**
Franz, Iris Vivian (Vivian Franz) *dean, director*

**Middleburg Heights**
Kosar, James Joseph *secondary school educator*

**Morristown**
Tucker, Betty J. *literature and language educator*

**Mount Vernon**
Shriver, William Russell *secondary school educator*
Strouse, Debra J. *director*

**Napoleon**
Bevelhymer, Darlene Pearl *secondary school educator, lawyer*

**New Concord**
Boggs, Bennett Gibson *academic administrator*

**New Holland**
Reeves, Nancy Rapp *elementary school educator*

**New Lexington**
Harper, Toni Jane *secondary school educator*

**New Philadelphia**
Doughten, Mary Katherine (Molly Doughten) *retired secondary school educator*

**Newark**
Kaiser, Judith Arlene *retired elementary school educator*

**North Canton**
Kairis, Rob *school librarian, consultant*

**Oak Harbor**
Randels, David George *retired secondary school educator*
Whitaker, Mary Jane *retired elementary school educator*

**Oberlin**
Brown, John Lott *former university president, retired educator*
Dye, Nancy Schrom *academic administrator, historian, educator*
Koppes, Clayton R. *academic administrator*
Sepkoski, Dara Henning *museum educator*

**Orrville**
Beyeler, Julia *academic administrator*
Hennell, Robert William III *secondary school educator*
Warner, Patricia Ann *secondary school educator*

**Oxford**
Hodge, David Charles *academic administrator, geography professor*
Shriver, Phillip Raymond *academic administrator*
Thompson, Bertha Boya *retired education educator*

**Painesville**
Davis, Barbara Snell *education educator*

**Parma**
Brennan, Sean Patrick *secondary school educator, municipal official*
McCarthy, Carrie Ann *secondary school educator, director*
Scheffel, Donna Jean *elementary school educator*
Tener, Carol Joan *retired secondary school educator, consultant*

**Patriot**
Riggle, Patricia Carol *special education educator*

**Peninsula**
Sigler, Theresa Jane *school system administrator*

**Pepper Pike**
Stano, Sister Diana *academic administrator*

**Perrysburg**
Bohleke, Henry Charles *academic administrator, educator*

**Pickerington**
Collins, Arlene *secondary school educator*

**Plymouth**
Hartman, Ruth Campbell *director, educator*

**Port Clinton**
Ewersen, Mary Virginia *retired school system administrator, poet*

**Portsmouth**
Baker, Donna L. *history educator*

**Rio Grande**
Hatfield, Barbara Scott *academic administrator*

**Saint Marys**
Anderson, Tracy *literature and language educator*
VanderHorst, Monica S. *physical education educator*

**Sandusky**
Coffey, Deborah S. Findley *elementary school educator*

**Sardinia**
Evans, C(aroline) Sue *education educator*

**Shaker Heights**
Brachna, Gabor (Samuel) *elementary school educator*
Trefts, Joan Landenberger *retired principal*

**Sidney**
Seitz, James Eugene *retired college president, freelance writer*

**Solon**
Williams, Jeffery Lynn *secondary school educator, consultant*

**South Euclid**
Hall-Chambers, Kymberly Renee *elementary school educator*

**Springfield**
Dominick, Charles Alva *college official*
Kinnison, William Andrew *retired university president*
Lowe-Hoover, Steven C. *history educator*

**Steubenville**
McGrath, Dennis Michael *secondary school educator*

**Stow**
Mangrum, Richard Lee *flight educator*

**Streetsboro**
Cielec, Greg J. *literature and language educator*
Cravcenco, Ludmila *academic administrator*

**Sylvania**
Bond, Suzanne Mary *gifted and talented educator*
Helmer, Robert C. *academic administrator*
Masten, Barbara Jean *education educator, department chairman*
Sampson, Earldine Robison *education educator*
Weinblatt, Charles Samuel *retired academic administrator*

**Toledo**
Closius, Phillip J. *dean, law educator*
Gutteridge, Thomas G. *academic administrator, consultant, arbitrator*
Harter, James Lester *academic administrator, consultant*
Hasan, Bassam *education educator*
Knuth, Marya Danielle *special education educator*
Konwinski, Jacqueline Marie Koralewski *secondary school educator*
Perz, Sally *academic administrator, former state legislator*
Pham, David Lan *secondary school educator, writer*
Rabideau, Margaret Catherine *retired media center director*
Reichert, Christine Edwards *academic administrator*
Romanoff, Marjorie Reinwald *retired education educator*
Seubert, Lori A. *elementary school educator*
Skaff, Anita L. *secondary school educator*
White, Kathy Jean *educator*

**University Heights**
Seaton, Shirley Smith *academic administrator, consultant*
Whelan, John Joseph *education educator*

**Upper Arlington**
Conley, Diana Jean Montenaro *elementary school educator*

**Valley View**
Miller, Susan Ann *retired school system administrator*

**West Milton**
Mahaney, Kellie Rose *elementary school educator, consultant*

**Westerville**
DeVore, C. Brent *college president, educator*
Husarik, Ernest Alfred *educational administrator*
Kerr, Thomas Jefferson, IV, *academic administrator*

**Wickliffe**
Wainio, Melody F. *registrar*

**Wilberforce**
Williamson, Vikki Lyn *university official, financial executive*

**Willoughby**
Grossman, Mary Margaret *elementary school educator*
Pennington, John Robert *biology educator, department chairman*

**Youngstown**
Theall, Michael *education educator, director*
Zorn, Robert Lynn *education educator*

## OKLAHOMA

**Alva**
Knedler, Mike *academic administrator*

**Bartlesville**
Baker-Morris, Kay *special education educator*

**Bethany**
Crabtree, John Michael *academic administrator, consultant*

**Bixby**
Hawthorne, Karen Lee *school librarian, educator*
Walker, Jerald Carter *academic administrator, minister*

**Broken Arrow**
Loper, Jana Sue *secondary school educator*

**Chickasha**
Willoughby-Smith, Dolores Anne *elementary school educator, consultant*

**Choctaw**
Uselton, Bill W. *secondary school educator*

**Davis**
Patterson, Lyn *director*

**Disney**
Hamilton, Carl Hulet *retired academic administrator*

**Edmond**
Harryman, Rhonda L. *special education educator*
Myster, Randall Walton *education educator, researcher*
Sibley, William Arthur *academic administrator, physics professor, consultant*

**El Reno**
Hawkins, Anita Lynne *primary school educator*

**Enid**
Camp, Robinson Eugene *chemistry educator*

**Gage**
Fiel, Irene Kay *secondary school educator*

**Kingfisher**
Allen, Vicky L. *secondary school educator*

**Langston**
Haysbert, JoAnn Wright *academic administrator*

**Lawton**
Smiley, Frederick Melvin *education educator, consultant*
Smith, Michelle *education educator*

**Midwest City**
Cook, James Junior *academic administrator*

**Moore**
Chiles, Mary Jane *secondary school educator*

**Muskogee**
Fulbright, Denise Nichole *education educator*
Swanson, Jacqueline V. *academic administrator, educator, women's health nurse practitioner*

**Norman**
Boren, David Lyle *academic administrator, former senator*
Croft, Janet Brennan *academic librarian*
Landers, Thomas Lee *dean, educator*
Mergler, Nancy L. *academic administrator*
Nelson, Donna Jean *chemistry educator, researcher*
Pappas, James Pete *university administrator*
Pedersen, Jon Erle *education educator, dean*
Provine, Lorraine *retired mathematics educator*
Sharp, Paul Frederick *retired academic administrator, educational consultant*
Van Horn, Richard Linley *academic administrator*
Zapffe, Nina Byrom *retired elementary school educator*
Zhai, Yan *education educator, researcher*

**Oklahoma City**
Coats, Andrew Montgomery *dean, lawyer, former mayor*
Cotton, Anita L. *secondary school educator*
Dunham, Dennis Paul *dean, educator*
Garrett, Sandy Langley *school system administrator*
Gathright, Julie L. *primary school educator*
Graves, Virginia Beth *elementary school educator*
Hageman, Dale *alternative staffing company executive*
Howland, Ellenmarie Myers *retired elementary school educator*
Jackson, Michael Wayne *academic administrator, researcher*
Kraker, Deborah Schovanec *special education educator*
Kriesel, Deanna Jean *education educator*
Lavender, Maxine Knight *special education educator*

O'Neal, Mike *secondary school educator, state representative*
Risser, Paul Gillan *academic administrator, botanist*
Seljeseth, Carol H. *physics educator*
Shelite, Leslie Michelle *vocational school educator*
Voth, Douglas W. *dean, educator*
Weigel, Paul Henry *biochemistry educator educator, researcher, consultant*
Williamson, Marvel *dean, nursing administrator, sexologist, educator, writer*
Woods, Pendleton *college director, author*
Young, Stephen K. *dean, academic administrator*

**Piedmont**
DeLozier, Joshua Mark *history educator*

**Ponca City**
Gallagher, Gary W(ayne) *educational services executive*
Rice, Sue Ann *retired dean, psychologist*

**Pryor**
Titsworth, Tobie Richard III *academic administrator*

**Sand Springs**
Sedlack, Kashannia Lynn *history educator*

**Shawnee**
Sharp, Ron *secondary school educator*

**Stillwater**
Chung, Jong-Moon *education educator*
Halligan, James Edmund *academic administrator, chemical engineer*

**Tahlequah**
Edwards, Terri Lyn Wilmoth *education educator*

**Tulsa**
Buthod, Mary Clare *school administrator*
Donaldson, Robert Herschel *university administrator, educator*
Lawless, Robert William *academic administrator*
Roger, Jerry Lee *academic administrator*
Thornton, Charlie Mae *secondary school educator*
Trennepohl, Gary Lee *academic administrator, finance educator*
Upham, Steadman *academic administrator, anthropologist, educator*
Wood, Emily Churchill *special education educator, social studies educator, consultant*

**Wilburton**
Morgan, Linda F. *director*

**Woodward**
Hicks, LaDawn Ann *elementary school educator*
Johnson, Gregory B. *secondary school educator*

## OREGON

**Ashland**
Baird, Susan Elizabeth *secondary school educator, writer*
Battistella, Edwin L. *dean*
Cullinan, Mary Patricia *academic administrator, literature and language professor*
Zinser, Elisabeth Ann *academic administrator*

**Beaverton**
de Sá e Silva, Elizabeth Anne *secondary school educator*
Duncan, Richard Fredrick, Jr. *secondary school educator, consultant*
Frank, Sister Ruth M. *principal, educator*

**Clackamas**
Woods, Dennis Oliver *headmaster, market and political research analyst*

**Corvallis**
Byrne, John Vincent *educational consultant*
Davis, John Rowland *academic administrator*
Langworthy, William Clayton *college official*
Verts, Lita Jeanne *academic administrator*
Young, Roy Alton *university administrator, educator*

**Dallas**
Brown, James Chandler *retired university administrator*

**Days Creek**
Andreiux, Alfred Hermon *secondary school educator*

**Eugene**
Frohnmayer, David Braden *academic administrator*
Gall, Meredith Damien (Meredith Mark Damien Gall) *education educator, writer*
Moseley, John Travis *academic administrator, physicist, researcher*
Pickett, Stephen Wesley *academic administrator, consultant*
Womack, James Errol *college president*

**Grants Pass**
Murdock, Doris Dean *special education educator, program developer*

**Gresham**
Light, Betty Jensen Pritchett *retired dean*
Vela, Joel E. *college president*

**Hillsboro**
Cook, Mandy Lee Hill *education educator*

**Joseph**
Gilbert, David Erwin *academic administrator, physicist*

**Klamath Falls**
Dow, Martha Anne *academic administrator, biology professor*

Krowen, Duane E. *elementary school educator*

**La Grande**
Woodward, Ralph Frederick, Jr. *elementary school educator, consultant, education educator*

**Lowell**
Boyle, John Howard *history educator*

**Mcminnville**
Walker, Charles Urmston *retired university president*

**Medford**
Dixon, Andrew Derart *retired academic administrator*

**Milton Freewater**
Piefer, Thomas R. *history educator*

**Monmouth**
Dantas-Whitney, Maria E. *education educator*
Dunn, Doris Marjory *retired secondary school educator, volunteer*

**Newberg**
Johnson, Thomas Floyd *former academic administrator, educator*

**Oceanside**
Wadlow, Joan Krueger *retired academic administrator, retired construction executive*

**Ontario**
Gaskill, John William *secondary school educator*

**Portland**
Bartlett, Thomas Alva *retired educational administrator*
Bodin, Kate *dean*
Bragdon, Paul Errol *retired academic administrator, educator*
Braun, Stephen Baker *academic administrator*
Clinton, Jack W. *dean*
Diver, Colin S. *academic administrator, educator*
Harris, Cynthia Viola *principal*
Haug-Chin, Christine Anna *secondary school educator*
Hochstettler, Thomas John *academic administrator, historian*
Koblik, Steven S. *academic administrator*
Kohler, Peter Ogden *academic administrator, internist, educator*
Leupp, Edythe Peterson *retired education educator*
McClave, Donald Silsbee *academic administrator*
Njoku, Scholastica Ibari *retired college librarian, writer*
Phillips, Vicki L. *school system administrator*
Silverstein, Paul Adam *education educator, researcher*
Sylvester, Robert *dean, musician*
Unger, Karen Virginia *director*
Whitlow, Lillian *retired elementary school educator, poet*

**Roseburg**
Tilson, Daniel *elementary school educator*

**Salem**
Castillo, Susan *school system administrator*
Hoff, Reno R. *academic administrator*
Page, Cheryl Miller *elementary school educator*
Pelton, M. Lee *academic administrator*
Tamura, Linda Gayle *education educator*
Yoder, Jonathan Paul *secondary school educator*

**The Dalles**
Hayden, I. Jill *secondary school educator*

**Yachats**
Robeck, Mildred Coen *education educator, writer*

## PENNSYLVANIA

**Aliquippa**
Drobac, Nikola (Nick Drobac) *education educator, consultant*

**Allentown**
Canfield, Cindy Kay Raup *elementary school educator*
Haddon, Eva W. *principal*
Pavelich, Judith *secondary school educator*

**Annville**
McGill, William James, Jr. *academic administrator, writer*

**Ashland**
Fey, Tammey Lynn *elementary school educator*

**Avonmore**
Smith, Luella Margaret *special education educator*

**Bala Cynwyd**
Oswald, James Marlin *education educator, researcher*

**Beaver**
Strock, Robert S. *retired education educator*

**Bensalem**
O'Toole, Michael Anthony *academic administrator*

**Bentleyville**
Blasko, Barbara Ann *secondary school educator*

**Berwick**
Pasukinis, Cheryl Renee *elementary school educator*
Spencer, Allison Ann *biology educator*

**Bethlehem**
Gast, Alice Petry *academic administrator, chemical engineering educator*
Stehney, Ann Kathryn *academic administrator, mathematician, educator*

Story, Bernard J *academic administrator*

**Bloomsburg**
Kozloff, Jessica S. *academic administrator*

**Blue Bell**
Brendlinger, LeRoy R. *academic administrator*

**Boyertown**
Kulakowsky, Barry L. *elementary school educator*
Mauger, Cynthia Carroll *secondary school educator*

**Broomall**
DiRosa, Steven Joseph *primary school educator, secondary school educator*

**Brownsville**
Martin, Richard H. *principal*

**Bryn Mawr**
Baird, John Absalom, Jr. *retired academic administrator*
Frank, Edward David, II, *history educator*
Kinney, Dale *dean, art history educator*
Kuncl, Ralph *provost*
Opendak, Irene *academic administrator*
Vickers, Nancy J. *academic administrator*

**Canonsburg**
Mascetta, Joseph Anthony *principal*

**Carlisle**
Asimakakis, Panagiota *mathematics educator*
Burgett, Gordon P., Jr. *physics educator*
Durden, William G. *academic administrator*
McConnaughay, Philip J. *dean, law educator*

**Center Valley**
Gambet, Daniel G(eorge) *academic administrator, minister*

**Chambersburg**
Malmont, Andrea G. *education educator*

**Chester**
Harris, James Thomas III *college administrator, educator*

**Coatesville**
Krug, Lee Allen *chemistry educator, coach*

**Collegeville**
Strassburger, John Robert *academic administrator*

**Connellsville**
Brady, Marsha McCandless *secondary school educator*
Humbert, Kimberly Ramsay *secondary school educator*

**Conshohocken**
Sigafoos, Thomas W., Jr. *principal*

**Cooperstown**
Hogg, James Henry, Jr. *retired education educator*

**Coudersport**
Kuratomi, Ernie Kazuo *principal*

**Dallas**
Goss, Sheryl E. *director*

**Dimock**
Rezykowski, Catherine R. *secondary school educator*

**Douglassville**
Schwarz, Kathryn J. *gifted and talented educator*

**Downingtown**
Romanosky, LuAnn *elementary school educator*
Valentin, Joan Marie *secondary school educator*

**Doylestown**
Thomas, Ellen Louise *school system administrator*

**Drexel Hill**
Turnbull, Mary Regina *secondary school educator*

**Dunmore**
Bochicchio, Kim *literature and language educator*
Parmar, Parminder *education educator*

**East Petersburg**
Walker, Sue Albertson *retired school system administrator, educational consultant*

**East Stroudsburg**
Amirian, Susan *adult education educator*
Braithwaite, Barbara Jo *retired secondary school educator*
Kansfield, Norman J. *former seminary president*

**Easton**
Teboh-Ewungkem, Miranda Ijang *education educator*
Weiss, Daniel H. *academic administrator, former dean*

**Edwardsville**
Lukas, Edward Michael *retired secondary school educator*

**Elizabethtown**
Garber, Margaret Mary *elementary school educator*
Gordon, Laurie Anne *academic director*
Ritsch, Frederick Field *academic administrator, historian*
Sample, Frederick Palmer *former college president*

**Elverson**
Sakoian, Lorraine J. *secondary school educator*

**Emlenton**
Berg, Janice Carol *elementary school educator*

**Erie**
Breckenridge, James G. *dean, consultant*
Henry, Martin Daniel *university president*
Zelazny, Catherine *elementary school educator*

**Exeter**
Flickinger, Donald E. *elementary school educator, mathematics educator*
Stocker, Joyce Arlene *retired secondary school educator*

**Fairfield**
Westfall, Terri Lee *kindergarten educator*

**Fairless Hills**
Hess, Frances Elizabeth *retired secondary school educator, retired director*
Steckroat, Patricia A. *special education educator*

**Fairview**
Stern, Marilyn Jean *special education educator*

**Flourtown**
Cooke, Sara Mullin Graff *daycare provider, kindergarten educator, medical assistant*

**Fort Washington**
Trombley, Edward Francis III *registrar*

**Franklin**
Sauer, Mary Julia *special education educator*

**Gettysburg**
Boritt, Gábor Szappanos *history educator*
Will, Katherine Haley *academic administrator*

**Gladwyne**
Castetter, William Benjamin *retired education educator, educational director*

**Greensburg**
Neff, Mary Ellen Andre *retired elementary school educator*

**Greenville**
Cooper, Brandon Pearce *director*

**Gwynedd Valley**
Owens, Kathleen C. *academic administrator*

**Hanover**
Clark, Sandra Marie *school administrator*

**Harleysville**
Hauber, Dorothy Marie *elementary school educator*

**Harmony**
O'Shea, Patrick Alan *elementary school educator*

**Harrisburg**
Batts, Barbara Jean *academic administrator, director*
Brown, John Walter *vocational education supervisor*
Burns, Rebecca Ann *elementary school educator, librarian*
Hample, Judy G. *academic administrator*
Popnik, Marlene Alita *retired school librarian*
Zahorchak, Gerald Lee *school system administrator, executive secretary*

**Harrison City**
McWilliams, Samuel Robert *secondary school educator*

**Hatfield**
Jesberg, Robert Ottis, Jr. *educational consultant, science educator*

**Haverford**
Bean, Philip Albert *dean, historian*
Dawson, John David *academic administrator, religious studies educator*
Tritton, Thomas Richard *academic administrator, biologist, educator*

**Hawley**
Genello, Denise M. *special education educator*

**Hershey**
Cook, Christine *elementary school educator*
Jones, Marshall Bush *education educator, researcher*

**Homestead**
King, Richard Wayne *principal*

**Honesdale**
Barbe, Walter Burke *education educator*

**Huntingdon**
Kepple, Thomas Ray, Jr. *college administrator*

**Immaculata**
Fadden, Sister R. Patricia *academic administrator, nun*

**Indiana**
Atwater, Tony *university president*
Barbor, Gretchen Kunst *secondary school educator, theater educator, director*
Cogar, Theodore Monroe *director*
Janicak, Christopher A. *academic administrator, educator*
Pettit, Lawrence Kay *university president*
Pidgeon, John Anderson *headmaster*
Thibadeau, Eugene Francis *education educator, consultant*

**Irwin**
Perich, Terry Miller *retired secondary school educator*

**Jefferson Hills**
Smith, Leslie Edgar *vocational school administrator*

**Jenkintown**
Oh, Soojin Susan *elementary school educator*

**King Of Prussia**
Martini, Perry James *educational consultant*

**Kintnersville**
Barnes, Francis V. *school system administrator*

**Knox**
Rupert, Elizabeth Anastasia *retired dean*

**La Plume**
Boehm, Edward Gordon, Jr. *college administrator, educator*

**Lafayette Hill**
Delacato, Carl Henry *education educator*
Delacato, Janice Elaine *special education educator, consultant*

**Lancaster**
Ebersole, Mark Chester *emeritus college president*
Fry, John Anderson *academic administrator*
Grube, Rebecca Sue *elementary school educator, consultant*
Kneedler, Alvin Richard (Richard Kneedler) *former academic administrator*

**Langhorne**
Neff, Amy Hancock *elementary school educator*

**Latrobe**
Porembka, Michael Richard *assistant principal, supervisor*
Towey, Jim (H. James Towey) *academic administrator, former federal official*
Will, James Fredrick *academic administrator, former steel company executive*

**Lebanon**
Balthaser, Gerda Haas *elementary school educator*

**Leesport**
Schmeck, Deborah M. *literature and language educator*

**Lehman**
Novrocki, Michael W. *secondary school educator*
Williams, Thomas Alan *elementary school educator, small business owner*

**Levittown**
Walker, Patricia Ann Dixon *retired elementary school educator, real estate rehabilitator*

**Lewisburg**
Huffines, Marion Lois *academic administrator, language and linguistics educator*
Laszewski, Ronald Thomas *college official*
Mitchell, Brian Christopher *academic administrator*

**Lewistown**
Porpotage-Sigler, Marylou M. *academic administrator*
Varner, Vance Sieber *principal*

**Lincoln University**
Nelson, Ivory Vance *academic administrator*
Norris, Jo Anne Wareham *intervention specialist, consultant*
Van Dover, James Kenneth *education educator*

**Lititz**
Hudelson, Judith Giantomass *elementary school educator*
McGlynn, James Francis *chemistry educator, chemical engineer*

**Little Meadows**
Staby, Dorothy Louise *elementary school educator*

**Lock Haven**
Almes, June *retired education educator, librarian*

**Loretto**
Shipman, Donald George *academic administrator*

**Macungie**
Rubin, Arthur Herman *retired academic administrator*

**Malvern**
Bash, Tamela Sue *educational consultant*

**Manheim**
Saylor, Carol Hannah *school system administrator, educator*

**Mansfield**
Benjamin, Woan-Jue Jane *education educator, researcher*
Loeschke, Maravene S. *academic administrator, theater educator*

**Maple Glen**
Weaver-Stroh, Joanne Mateer *education educator, consultant*

**Martinsburg**
Neff, Robert Wilbur *academic administrator, educator, minister*

**Mc Elhattan**
Garner, Charles William *retired educational administration educator, consultant*

**Meadville**
Dixon, Armendia Pierce *school program administrator*
Fait, Cinda Ruth McGill *elementary school educator*

**Mechanicsburg**
Feaser, Deborah Ellen *mathematics educator*
Hoffman, Diane Mae *special education educator*

**Media**
Jackson, Katherine Church *retired elementary school educator, literature educator*

**Mercersburg**
Tompkins, Christopher Robin *director, educator*

**Milford**
Reynolds, Edwin Wilfred, Jr. *retired secondary education educator*

**Millerton**
Kipferl, Christiana A. *special education educator*

**Monaca**
Pinchot, Daniel J. *director*

**Monroeville**
Furman, L. Robert *principal, music educator*

**Montgomeryville**
Detwiler, Christine Wendler *special education educator*

**Montoursville**
Hunter, Corey Ryan *secondary school educator*

**Moosic**
Joyce, Patrick Francis *secondary school educator*

**Morgantown**
Dierwechter, David C. *retired elementary school educator, theater director*

**Morrisdale**
Yontosh, Sharlene Mary *principal*

**Mount Pleasant**
Dangelo, Eugene Michael *elementary school educator*

**Nanticoke**
Donohue, Patricia Carol *academic administrator*

**Nelson**
Kyofski, Bonelyn Lugg *retired education educator*

**Nescopeck**
Shultz, Jack Ellsworth *education educator*

**New Castle**
Blaskewicz, Nancy Jane *elementary school educator*

**New Freedom**
Spicer, Barbara Jean Wentz *elementary school educator*

**New Kensington**
Kalavar, Jyotsna Mirle *education educator*

**New Oxford**
Martin, Sandra Ann *special education educator, writer*

**New Paris**
Stoner, Lois Carole *biology educator*

**Newtown**
Booraem, Hendrik, V, *education educator, historian*
Duncan, Stephen Robert *elementary school educator*

**Oil City**
Sabousky, Richard Anthony *adult education educator*

**Pen Argyl**
Kovaleski, Diane Marie *secondary school educator*

**Perkasie**
Ferry, Joan Evans *school counselor*

**Philadelphia**
Aversa, Dolores Sejda *educational administrator*
Bass, Aaron *school system administrator*
Bates, James Earl *academic administrator*
Beachem, Michael T., IV, *academic administrator, counseling administrator*
Brown, Lawrence David *statistics professor*
Brucker, Paul C. *academic administrator, physician*
Capers, Gregg *secondary school educator, musician*
Caplan, Arthur Leonard *university program director, educator*
Cline, Celeste Ann *primary school educator*
Cohen, David Walter *academic administrator, educator, periodontist*
Cooperman, Barry S. *academic administrator, chemist, educator*
Corzo, Miguel Angel *academic administrator*
Donnelly, Gloria Ferraro *university dean*
Dunn, Mary Maples *academic administrator*
Fernandez, Happy Craven (Gladys Fernandez) *academic administrator*
Fitts, Michael Andrew *dean, law educator*
Giegengack, Robert *university administrator*
Goon, Arthur David *academic administrator, educator*
Graffman, Gary *academic administrator, pianist, music educator*
Grassie, William John *academic administrator*
Gutmann, Amy *academic administrator, political science and philosophy educator*
Hack, Gary Arthur *dean*
Hart, Ann Weaver *academic administrator*
Houshmand, Ali A. *academic administrator*
Jeffcoat, Marjorie K. *dean, dental educator*
Johnson, Shari *elementary school educator*
Kraft, Amber Dawn *education program developer*
Liacouras, Peter James *academic administrator, educator, lawyer, arbitrator*
Lowry, Ralph James, Sr. *retired history educator*
Marchetti, Michael Joseph *director*
McCafferty, Eileen Patricia *elementary school educator*

Means, John Barkley *director, language educator*
Meyerson, Martin *academic administrator, urban planner*
Moon, Richard Eugene *secondary school educator*
Nasca, Thomas Joseph *dean*
Nelson, Genevieve Murphy *secondary school educator*
Oliver, Florence Beatrice *secondary school educator*
Onley, Sister Francesca *academic administrator*
Padulo, Louis *university administrator*
Papadakis, Constantine N. *academic administrator, civil engineer, educator*
Reinstein, Robert J. *dean, law educator*
Rogers, Carton (H. Carton Rogers III) *school librarian, academic administrator*
Romer, Daniel *university official, psychologist, educator*
Roper, Nicole Elizabeth *history educator*
Rosato, Jennifer L. *dean, law educator*
Rubenstein, Arthur Harold *academic administrator, educator, dean, internist*
Rudczynski, Andrew B. *academic administrator, medical researcher*
Shupp, Matthew Ryan *director, educator*
Sibolski, Elizabeth Hawley *academic administrator*
Tansy, Martin F. *dean*
Tucho, Admasu Etafa *education educator*
Wachman, Marvin *retired academic administrator*
Wiley, James Dee *retired history and biology educator, national park service ranger*

**Phoenixville**
McClure, A. Glenn *education educator, department chairman*

**Pittsburgh**
Braun, Thomas W. *dean, academic administrator*
Cho, Sung K. *education educator*
Cohon, Jared L. *academic administrator*
Davis, Larry E. *academic administrator*
Dougherty, Charles John *academic administrator*
Dunn, Kenneth B. *dean*
Eckert, Jean Patricia *elementary school educator*
Geibel, Sister Grace Ann *university president*
Heitzenroder, Wendy Roberta *elementary school educator*
Herring, David John *dean, law educator*
Hunker, Jeffrey *dean*
Kamlet, Mark *provost*
Kupfer, David J. *psychiatry professor*
Lehoczky, John Paul *statistics educator*
Livi, Ivan David *retired educational administrator*
Miller, Ronald Lynn *director*
Mowrey, Kimberly Allison *school system administrator, editing consultant*
Nordenberg, Mark Alan *academic administrator, law educator*
Packard, Rochelle Sybil *elementary school educator*
Praytor, Kent Dwayne *career planning administrator*
Rago, Ann D'Amico *academic administrator, public relations executive*
Richard, Jean-Francois *education educator, consultant*
Ross, Madelyn Ann *academic administrator, newspaper editor*
Shank, Gary D. *education educator*
Smartschan, Glenn Fred *educational consultant*
Sobehart, Helen C. *academic administrator, educator*
Van Dusen, Albert Clarence *academic administrator*
Walls Perry, J(oyce) Lorraine *elementary school educator*
Weidman, John Carl, II, *education and sociology educator, consultant*

**Pocono Summit**
Buffington, Amy Lynn *secondary school educator*
Yorke-Viney, Sally Anne *elementary school educator*

**Pottsville**
Schwenk, Sandra Mates *secondary school educator*
Silberling, Sherrill Jean *literature and language educator*

**Quarryville**
Armerding, Hudson Taylor *retired college president, consultant*

**Reading**
Bowles, Patricia Mary *secondary school educator*
Pumariega, JoAnne Buttacavoli *mathematics educator*
Yoder, James Dale *adult education educator*

**Sandy Lake**
Lengauer, Mary Irene *elementary school educator*

**Schuylkill Haven**
Sarno, Patricia Ann *biology educator*

**Scottdale**
Lee, John Lawrence, Jr. *educational administrator*

**Scranton**
Panuska, Joseph Allan *retired academic administrator*
Passon, Richard Henry *retired academic administrator, language educator*

**Selinsgrove**
Lemons, L. Jay *academic administrator*

**Sharon**
Kovac, Shirley Ann *retired elementary school educator*

**Shippensburg**
Basler, Linda Gerber *retired elementary school educator*
Bej, Emil *retired dean*
Ceddia, Anthony Francis *university administrator*

**Shohola**
Hess, Judith A. *secondary school educator*

**Slippery Rock**
Mraz, Mark *education educator, researcher*

**Souderton**
Rosenberger, Janet Thuma *retired elementary school educator*

**Southampton**
Gniewek, Debra Lyman *school librarian, consultant*

**Spring Mills**
Songer, Susan Kay *secondary school educator*

**State College**
Dupuis, Victor Lionel *retired curriculum and instruction educator*
Link, Phoebe Forrest *education educator, writer, social worker, poet*
Remick, Forrest Jerome, Jr. *former university official*

**Swarthmore**
Bloom, Alfred Howard *academic administrator, educator*

**Thorndale**
Ryan, Francis William *history educator, coach, dean*

**Titusville**
Campasino, Ellen Marie *elementary school educator*

**University Park**
Antle, Charles Edward *statistics educator*
Askov, Eunice May *adult education educator*
Dugda, Mulugeta Tuji *education educator*
Gurgevich, Elise *academic administrator*
Hammond, J. D. *retired academic administrator*
Olian, Judy D. *dean*
Semali, Ladislaus *education educator*
Spanier, Graham Basil *academic administrator*
Yoder, Edgar Paul *education educator*
Zabel, Diane Marion *school librarian*
Zatsiorsky, Vladimir Moiseevich (Michailovich) *biomechanics educator, researcher*

**Upper Darby**
Crouse, Carol K. Mavromatis *elementary school educator*
Hudiak, David Michael *academic administrator, lawyer*
Leiby, Bruce Richard *secondary school educator, writer*

**Vandergrift**
Lizik, Andrea Noreen *elementary school educator*

**Verona**
Bruno, Louis Vincent *principal*

**Villanova**
Dobbin, Edmund J. *academic administrator*
Fitzpatrick, M. Louise *dean, nursing educator*
Heitzmann, Ray *education educator, athletic coach*
Sargent, Mark A. *dean, law educator*

**Warminster**
Ciabarra, Louise *secondary school educator, medical/surgical nurse*
Ciao, Frederick J. *school system administrator, educator*
Vietri, Linda Smith *gifted and talented educator*

**Washington**
Haring-Smith, Tori *academic administrator*

**Weatherly**
Sipler, Barbara Marie *secondary school educator*

**West Chester**
Bove, Patrice Magee *elementary school educator*

**West Grove**
Olson, Leroy Calvin *retired educational administration educator*

**West Mifflin**
Migliorato, Lynne Gyurisin *elementary school educator*

**Whitehall**
O'Connor, M. Carol *private school educator*

**Wilkes Barre**
Horoszy, Albert John *mathematics educator*

**Williamsport**
Garner, Ronald A. *automotive technology educator*
Weaver, Lucille Mae *retired elementary school educator, radiological technician*

**Willow Grove**
Burtt, Anne Dampman *special education educator*

**Wyalusing**
Kusmierz, Ann Marie Dorothy *elementary school educator*

**Yardley**
Breitenfeld, Frederick, Jr. *retired educational consultant, broadcast executive*

**Yatesville**
Roberts, Anne Marie Gabrielle *chemistry educator*

**York**
Andrews, Jennifer Lee *secondary school educator*
Caffrey, Lynn Regina *education educator*
Musone, Amy Lynn *elementary school educator*

**Youngwood**
Henry, Candy A. *education educator, writer*

**RHODE ISLAND**

**Jamestown**
Tinker, Thomas Eaton *retired headmaster*
Ullrich, Robert Albert *academic administrator*

**Kingston**
Carothers, Robert Lee *academic administrator*
Seitsinger, Anne M. *education educator*

**Middletown**
Jackson, John Edward *adult education educator, retired military officer*
Peterson, Eric F. *headmaster*

**Newport**
Ellsworth, James Byron *national security educator*
Mooshagian, Mark Nishan *education educator*
Shuford, Jacob L. *academic administrator, career military officer*
Wood, Berenice Howland *retired secondary school educator*

**Pawtucket**
Lepore, Lisa *principal*

**Providence**
Alfonso, Mariana *education educator, researcher*
Bowlby, Raynna R. *school librarian*
Deal, Joseph Maurice *academic administrator, art educator, photographer*
Greer, David Steven *dean, educator, physician*
Kertzer, David Israel *academic administrator, anthropology educator, writer*
Kestin, Randi Miriam *educational analyst*
Mandle, Earl Roger *academic administrator, former museum director*
McWalters, Peter *school system administrator*
Robert, Stephen *academic administrator*
Simmons, Ruth J. *academic administrator*
Stout, John Wilson *academic administrator*

**Saunderstown**
Donovan, Gerald Alton *retired academic administrator, retired dean*

**Warwick**
Izzi, John *mathematics educator, writer, actor*

**Westerly**
Crowley, Cynthia Warner Johnson *secondary school educator*

**Woonsocket**
Stubbs, Donald Clark *retired secondary school educator*
Walker, Suzanne Ross *mathematics and education educator*

## SOUTH CAROLINA

**Allendale**
Fennell, Linda Maynor *pre-school educator*

**Anderson**
Karanfil, Tanju *educator, consultant*

**Andrews**
Scott, Veronica L. *middle school educator*

**Bamberg**
Cockrell, Clarice *education specialist*

**Batesburg**
Hallman, Jenny C. *education educator*

**Beaufort**
Parisi, Leah Evans *dean, nursing educator, lawyer*
Walter, Deborah *elementary school educator*

**Blythewood**
Daniels, James Douglas *retired academic administrator*

**Camden**
Woolard, Gilbert Garland, Jr. *educational consultant*

**Charleston**
Appleget, Terri Lynn *elementary school educator*
Egelson, Pauline C. *director*
Festa, Conrad *academic administrator*
Greenberg, Raymond Seth *academic administrator, educator, health facility administrator*
Poole, Roger Cliff *academic administrator, finance educator, retired military officer*
Rosa, John William *academic administrator, career military officer*
Schachte, Margaret Pringle *director*

**Clemson**
Barker, James F. *academic administrator*
Felder, Frankie Ottowiess *academic administrator*
Helms, Doris R. *academic administrator*
Kelly, John William, Jr. *academic administrator*
Sluss, Dorothy Louise *education educator, researcher*

**Clinton**
Griffith, John Vincent *academic official*

**Columbia**
Bedenbaugh, Allyn Purvis *retired elementary school educator*
Carter, Kathryn Gibson *education educator, consultant*
Cofield, Virginia Riley *elementary school educator, piano teacher*
Crain, Linda Eargle *retired elementary school educator*
Crews, Tena B. *educational director*
Fletcher, Madilyn Mae *academic administrator, director*
Friedman, Myles Ivan *education educator*
Gillespie Stewart, Ellyn Marie *mathematics educator*
Guy, Cheryl Jenkins *secondary school educator, consultant*
Odom, Jerome D. *academic administrator*
Outin, Mary Louise *business, multi-cultural history and geneology educator*
Palms, John Michael *academic administrator, physicist*

Rekers, George Alan *education educator, clinical psychologist*
Schoen-Giddings, Linda N. *science assessment specialist, science education consultant*
Sinclair, Linda Drumwright *educational consultant*
Sorensen, Andrew Aaron *academic administrator*
Sproat, Ruth C. *retired director, consultant*
Tenenbaum, Inez Moore *school system administrator*

**Denmark**
Bendidi, Rachid *dean, educator*
Dawson, Leonard E. *college president*

**Florence**
Carter, Luther Fredrick *university president*

**Fort Mill**
Honeycutt, Brenda *secondary school educator*

**Gaffney**
Griffin, Walter Roland *academic administrator, historian, educator*

**Gilbert**
Padget, Barbara Johnson *elementary school educator*

**Greenville**
Dobson, Karen Coogler *elementary school educator*
Jones, Bob III *academic administrator*
Jones, Robert Thaddues *principal*
Payne, George Frederick *academic administrator*
Shi, David E. *academic administrator, historian*
Sleeman, Anita Marie *education educator, academic administrator, director*
Smith, Philip Daniel *academic administrator, education educator*

**Greenwood**
Epps, Susie Rebecca Smith *secondary school educator*
Jackson, Larry Artope *retired college president*
Marino, Sheila Burris *education educator*

**Hartsville**
Rubinstein, Joseph Harris *education educator*

**Hemingway**
Sumlin, Peggy McDonald *elementary school educator*

**Holly Hill**
Shuler, Karen Bull *elementary school educator*

**Kershaw**
Wall, Kathy Elliott *secondary school educator*

**Kiawah Island**
Warren, Russell Glen *educational consultant*

**Landrum**
Smith, Constance *retired elementary school educator*

**Lexington**
Morrison, Sherrie Crawford *secondary school educator*

**Marion**
Kirkpatrick, Donald Robert *secondary school educator*

**Mount Pleasant**
Allen, Louise Anderson *education educator*
Gilbert, James Eastham *academic administrator*

**Myrtle Beach**
Parker, Donna Tully *elementary school educator, department chairman*

**Okatie**
Edwards, Nancy Jo *gifted and talented educator, consultant*

**Pawleys Island**
Proefrock, Carl Kenneth *academic medical administrator*

**Pelzer**
Veres, Tanis *elementary school educator*

**Pickens**
Hardin, Janet Becker *gifted and talented educator, music educator*

**Prosperity**
Kinard, Ira Hubert, Jr. *biology educator*

**Ridge Spring**
Livingston, Kimberly R. *elementary school educator*

**Rock Hill**
Roddey, Cynthia Plair *education educator*

**Spartanburg**
Caldwell, Steven Douglas *education educator, consultant*
Dunlap, Benjamin Bernard *academic administrator*
McGehee, Larry Thomas *retired academic administrator*
Rush, Kathy Lynn *education educator*
Stephens, Bobby Gene *college administrator, consultant*
Teague, Charles Porter *academic administrator*

**Sumter**
Mingo, Joe Louis *elementary school educator*

**Taylors**
Porter, Jean McRae *counselor*

**Varnville**
Kelly, Twyla LaKesha *elementary school educator*

## SOUTH DAKOTA

**Aberdeen**
Maier, Karen Marie *school librarian*

**Armour**
Schneider, Mary Ek *literature and language educator*

**Brookings**
Miller, Peggy Gordon Elliott *academic administrator*
Vanderpan, Norma *retired elementary school educator*

**Garretson**
Mohr, Becky J. *elementary school educator*

**Groton**
Nelson, Dorene *retired secondary school educator*

**Huron**
Mittelstedt, Sarah Anna *elementary school educator*

**Lead**
Hoff, James Hans *elementary school educator*

**Mitchell**
Padrnos, Diane E. *language arts educator*
Russell, Annika Renee *secondary school educator, financial consultant*

**Murdo**
Ball, Bev Ann *secondary school educator*

**Nemo**
Price, Georgianna Thrower *elementary school educator*

**Pierre**
Melmer, Rick *school system administrator*

**Rapid City**
Ankrum, Dorothy Darlene *elementary school educator*
Hughes, William Lewis *retired dean, electrical engineer*
Johnson, Rosemary S. *elementary school educator*
Schleusener, Richard August *college president*

**Sioux Falls**
Ashworth, Julie *elementary school educator*
Balcer, Charles Louis *college president emeritus, educator*
Swier, Janet Kay *secondary school educator*
Talley, Robert Cochran *academic administrator, cardiologist*
Wagoner, Ralph Howard *academic administrator*

**Vermillion**
Avoseh, Mejai Bola Mike *adult education educator, researcher*
Kephart, Helen Jean Orr *retired secondary school educator*

**Yankton**
Foster, James Caldwell *dean, historian*

## TENNESSEE

**Allardt**
Copeland, Patricia Ruth *elementary school educator*

**Antioch**
Arthur, Christon George *academic administrator, educator*
Feris, Ryan Walker *elementary school educator*
Mattice, Debora J. *special education educator, consultant*

**Bluff City**
Arnold, SaBrina Nicole *secondary school educator*

**Brentwood**
Oonk, Marian Bernice *elementary school educator*

**Bristol**
Johnson, Opal Burton *retired elementary school educator*

**Chattanooga**
Obear, Frederick Woods *academic administrator*
Stacy, Bill Wayne *academic administrator*

**Chuckey**
Brown, Anne Million *retired elementary school educator*

**Clarksville**
Deitrich, Margaret Alice *education educator*
Hoppe, Sherry Lee *academic administrator*
Newby, Earl Fernando *education educator*
Stoddard, Peter Hawkins *education educator, consultant*

**Cleveland**
Harper, James Edward, Jr. *academic administrator*
Suits, Janice Crye *elementary school educator*

**Collierville**
Boswell, Rupert Dean, Jr. *retired academic administrator, mathematician, educator*
Culley, J.P. *education educator*

**Columbia**
Cantrell, Sharron Caulk *principal*
Storey, Pamela T. *elementary school educator*

**Cookeville**
Greeson, James Emerson *educational consultant, educator*
Volpe, Angelo Anthony *retired academic administrator, chemist, educator*

**Covington**
Wright, Bonnie Shankle *assistant principal, choir director*

**Dresden**
Maddox, Mark Lee *academic administrator*

**Dyersburg**
Robertson, Wanda Sue *secondary school educator*

**Farragut**
Riley, Ray Allan *biology educator*

**Goodlettsville**
Vatandoost, Nossi Malek *art school administrator*

**Henderson**
Gardner, Elmer Claude *academic administrator*

**Hendersonville**
Kinney, Betty Caudill *elementary school educator*

**Jackson**
Agee, Bob R. *academic administrator, educator, minister*
Weaver, Terry L. *special education educator, writer*

**Johnson City**
Alfonso, Robert John *university administrator*
Beeler, Marsha Colleen *education educator*
Franks, Ronald Dwyer *dean, psychiatrist, educator*
Tollefson, Terrence Alfred *education educator, consultant*

**Kingsport**
Groseclose, Clara Rita *retired secondary school educator*
McKee, Denise Michelle *history educator*

**Kingston**
Lannom, Julie Conway Hudson *secondary school educator*

**Knoxville**
Boling, Edward Joseph *retired academic administrator*
Creasia, Joan Catherine *dean, nursing educator*
Garrison, Arlene Allen *academic administrator, engineering educator*
Hatton, Barbara R. *academic administrator*
Heppding, Fred, Jr. *history educator, department chairman*
Jones, Sherman J. *academic administrator, investment company executive, educator*
Levy, Robert A. *academic administrator*
Mankel, Francis Xavier *retired principal, priest*
McRae, John Malcolm *dean, educator, architect*
Minkel, Clarence Wilbert *university official*
Petersen, John D. *academic administrator*
Romeo, Joanne Josefa Marino *mathematics educator*
Russell, Rodney E. *school system administrator*
South, Stephen A. *academic administrator*

**Lafayette**
Pagan, Vicki *biology educator*

**Lebanon**
Eaton, Harvill Carlton *academic administrator*

**Manchester**
Westberry, Anita Parrish *education educator*

**Maryville**
Briggs, Geraldine Hackworth *reading specialist, eduator*

**Memphis**
Dunathan, Harmon Craig *college dean*
Gilpatrick, Russell O. *dean, dental educator*
Gourley, Dick R. *college dean*
Grant, Michael M. *education educator*
Nance, Libba L. *elementary school educator*
Nesin, Jeffrey David *academic administrator*
Owen, William Franklin *academic administrator, former research and development company executive*
Raines, Shirley Carol *academic administrator*
Sharon, Momany *retired elementary school educator, retired music educator*
Troutt, William Earl *academic administrator*

**Millington**
Gray, Barbara L. *assistant principal, tax specialist*

**Murfreesboro**
Baker-Templeton, Angie Auburn *elementary school educator*
Doyle, Delores Marie *retired principal*
Hemby-Grubb, Virginia *education educator, consultant*

**Nashville**
Benbow, Camilla Persson *dean, psychology professor*
Brigham, Nicolette Bainbridge *educational consultant*
Butler, William Blaine *dean, dental educator*
Clinton, Barbara Marie *director, social worker*
Collins, Joe Lena *retired secondary school educator*
Cyrus, Cynthia J. *dean, music educator*
Farran, Dale Clark *education educator*
Gabbe, Steven Glenn *dean, educator, obstetrician, gynecologist*
Gee, Elwood Gordon *academic administrator*
Gherman, Paul M. *university librarian*
Guha, Sujata *education educator*
Hazelip, Herbert Harold *academic administrator*
Hefner, James A. *academic administrator*
Johnson, Melvin N. *academic administrator, economist*
Longhurst, Robert Russell *retired secondary school educator*
Manning, Charles W. *university chancellor*
Maupin, John E., Jr. *college president*
McKerley, Annette Elizabeth *school system administrator*
McMurry, Idanelle Sam *educational consultant*

Mitchell, Angela Carol *elementary school educator*
Moon, Fletcher Froe *college librarian, multi-media artist, minister*
Morton, Linda June *academic administrator*
O'Leary, Hazel R. *academic administrator, retired federal official, lawyer*
Pierce, Patricia Ann *university administrator*
Pitz, Robert Wendell *professor mechanical engineering*
Porter, Andrew Calvin *academic administrator, psychologist, educator*
Ramer, Hal Reed *academic administrator*
Reschly, Daniel J. *education administrator, psychologist*
Rivera, Maximiano Marquez *academic administrator, educator, researcher, writer*
Royal, Brenda Campbell *biology educator*
Seivers, Lana C. *school system administrator*
Seligson, Mitchell Allan *political science educator*
Woodruff, Linda Gyjuan *mathematics educator*
Zepos, Nicholas S. *academic administrator*

**Newport**
Ball, Travis, Jr. *school administrator, editor*

**Pleasant Hill**
Hull, Charles William *retired special education educator*

**Pleasant View**
Hampton, Margaret Ann Barnes *elementary school educator*

**Pulaski**
Murrell, James Thomas *academic administrator, botanist*

**Rockwood**
Metcalfe, Christopher Lee *secondary school educator, music educator*

**Savannah**
Flanagan, Judy *director, special events consultant*

**Sewanee**
Croom, Frederick Hailey *academic administrator, mathematician, educator*
Cunningham, Joel Luther *academic administrator*
Patterson, William Brown *dean, history professor*

**Telford**
Mashburn, Donald Eugene *education educator*

**TEXAS**

**Abilene**
Christopher, Mary M. *education educator, consultant*
Flores, Kathryn Louise *mathematics educator*
McCaleb, Gary Day *university official*
Specht, Alice Wilson *university libraries dean*
Turner, Willard Craig *academic administrator*

**Allen**
Fornadel, Martha Sue *elementary school educator*

**Alpine**
Cullins, Robert Carlton *academic administrator*

**Amarillo**
Carter, Edythe (Edie) L. *mathematics educator*
McClure, Caleb J. *associate principal*
Mueller, Vicki Lynn *elementary school educator*

**Argyle**
Duncan, Laura Ann *mathematics educator, department chairman*

**Arlington**
Butler, Donald *educator*
Fleming, Ralph Don *secondary school educator*
Graca, Thomas John *education educator*
Han, Chien-Pai *statistics educator*
Jaramillo, Jorge Fernando *educator*
Joohi, Lee *early childhood educator*
Pomerantz, Martin *chemistry educator, researcher*

**Austin**
Armstrong, Neal Earl *academic administrator*
Ayres, Robert Moss, Jr. *retired university president*
Bordin, Cristina Stanley *academic administrator*
Brewer, Thomas Bowman *retired university president*
Carleton, Don Edward *academic administrator, writer*
Cunningham, William Hughes *retired academic administrator, marketing professional, educator*
Doluisio, James Thomas *dean, pharmacy educator*
DuBose, Gaylan Ray *elementary school educator, musician, writer*
Dubose, Kathryn Michaud *secondary school educator*
Fair, Harry David *academic administrator, physicist*
Fonté, Richard W. *university administrator*
Gau, George W. *dean*
Gonzalez-Gerth, Miguel *literature and language educator, writer*
Harris, Ben M. *education educator*
Jordan, Bryce *retired university president*
Kelley, Henry Paul *academic administrator, psychology educator*
Lenoir, Gloria Cisneros *secondary school educator, computer scientist, educator*
Livingston, William Samuel *academic administrator, political scientist, educator*
Matthews, Charles R. *academic administrator*
May, Robert George *dean, accounting educator*
McKeown-Moak, Mary Park *educational consultant*
Neeley, Shirley *school system administrator*
Powers, William Charles, Jr. *academic administrator, law educator*
Roueche, John Edward, II, *education educator, director*
Royal, Darrell K. *university official, retired football coach*
Sands, Dolores S. *dean*

Shilling, Roy Bryant, Jr. *academic administrator*
Springer, David William *dean, social sciences educator*
Wurzbach, Linda *educational consultant*
Yudof, Mark George *academic administrator, law educator, federal agency administrator*

**Bastrop**
Carpenter, Delbert Stanley *educational administration educator*

**Baytown**
Casey, Carole Lynn *elementary school educator, music educator*

**Beaumont**
Brentlinger, William Brock *college dean*
Comick, Terrence Christopher *principal*
Gagne, Mary *academic administrator*
Martin, Quincy III *career planning administrator*
Maxey, Debra S. *secondary school educator*
Payne, Elton Curtis, Jr. *adult education educator*
Ward, Debra Yvette *elementary school educator*

**Bellaire**
Crayton, Arnell *secondary school educator*

**Boerne**
Goode, Bobby Claude *retired secondary school educator*

**Bonham**
Gerner, Leonard Arthur *elementary school educator, minister*

**Booker**
Doerrie, Bobette *educational consultant, secondary school educator*

**Brownsville**
Garcia, Juliet Villarreal *academic administrator*
Santa-Coloma, Bernardo *secondary school educator, consultant*

**Bryan**
Fields, Sheila Crain *elementary school educator*
Hanks, Clay David *academic administrator*
Richmond, Dina Rae *retired secondary school educator*

**Burkburnett**
Avens, Brad *literature and language educator*

**Canyon**
Long, Russell Charles *academic administrator*

**Carrizo Springs**
Saldana, Manuel E., Jr. *school system administrator*

**Cedar Hill**
Jackson, Robert Roscoe *education educator*
Lowe, Cynthia Ann *director*

**Cedar Park**
Ragan, Amy K. *secondary school educator*

**Cisco**
Johnson, Cynthia Zuckernick *history educator*

**Clyde**
Roberts, Cynthia Jeanne *history educator*

**Coldspring**
Brister, Frank Lutz III *secondary school educator*

**College Station**
Adkisson, Perry Lee *university system chancellor*
Bowen, Ray Morris *academic administrator, engineering educator*
Calhoun, John C., Jr. *academic administrator*
Cocanougher, Arthur Benton *academic administrator*
Dasgupta, Sumantra *education educator, researcher*
Davis, Edwin Paul *history educator*
Dickey, Nancy Wilson *chancellor, dean, physician*
Erlandson, David Alan *education administration educator*
Gates, Robert Michael *academic administrator, former CIA director*
Hooton, James G. *academic administrator*
Lynn, Laurence Edwin, Jr. *academic administrator, educator*
McTeer, Robert D., Jr. *academic administrator, former bank executive*
Murano, Elsa A. *academic administrator, former federal agency administrator*
Prior, David B. *academic administrator*
Sandlin, Jennifer April *education educator*
Strawser, Jerry R. *dean*

**Colmesneil**
LaFaye, Teri Kirkham *literature and language educator, writer*

**Commerce**
Justice, Madeline Carol *education educator*
Schmidt, L. Lee, Jr. *retired university official*
Scott, Joyce Alaine *academic administrator*
Vornberg, James Alvin *education educator*

**Coppell**
Witt, Kim Lou *elementary school educator*

**Corpus Christi**
Abdelsamad, Moustafa Hassan *dean*
Beller, Stephen Mark *retired academic administrator*
Cassidy, Jack *academic administrator, educator*
Furgason, Robert Roy *academic administrator, director, retired engineering educator*
Killebrew, Flavius Charles *academic administrator, biology professor*
Reynolds, Z. Paul *academic administrator*
Vegh, Linda Libasci *secondary school educator*

**Crane**
Hugendubler, Richard Thomas *secondary school educator*

**Crockett**
LaClair, Patricia Marie *physical education director, paramedic*

**Cross Plains**
Swanson, Janet M. *retired secondary school educator*

**Cypress**
Bishop, Dawn Marie *elementary school educator*

**Dallas**
Abdo, Virginia Richie *secondary school educator*
Attanasio, John Baptist *dean, law educator*
Ballesteros, Victor Hugo *dean*
Blankenbaker, Zarina *adult education educator, consultant*
Cho, Ho Soon Michelle L. *adult education educator*
Cirilo, Amelia Medina *educational consultant*
Cole, James S. *dean, dental educator*
Cook, Gary Raymond *academic administrator, minister*
Dumerer, Lorraine JoAnne Lori *secondary school educator, consultant*
Friedheim, Stephen Bailey *educational consultant*
Giggleman, Gene Felton *academic administrator, veterinarian*
Haayen, Richard Jan *academic administrator, insurance company executive*
Harrison, Frank *former university president*
Hester, Linda Hunt *retired dean, counseling administrator, sociology educator, health and physical education educator*
Karns, Phyllis J. Spear *dean*
McCartor, Sheila Smith *secondary school educator*
Mitchell, Richard R. *principal*
Moran, Rebecca Ann *secondary school educator*
Richardson, Don L. *secondary school educator*
Shambaugh, Irvin Calvin, Jr. *aptitude test firm executive*
Turner, Robert Gerald *academic administrator*
Williams, Michael Edward, Sr. *dean*
Wrucke-Nelson, Ann C. *elementary school educator*

**Denton**
Austin, Zan *assistant principal*
Bataille, Gretchen *academic administrator*
Greenlaw, Marilyn Jean *retired adult education educator*
Kiraly, Mark Andrew *mathematics educator*
Lee, Jeong-Mee *education educator*
McCaslin, Richard Bryan *history educator*
McDonald-West, Sandi MacLean *director, consultant*
Smith, Howard Wellington *education educator, retired dean*
Turner, Philip Michael *academic administrator, writer*

**Dripping Springs**
Smith, Ellis Carlton *history educator, consultant*

**Edinburg**
Arriola, Roland S. *academic administrator*

**Egypt**
Wynn, John Thomas *retired academic administrator, farming executive, economic consultant, oil and gas producer*

**El Paso**
Casas, Martha *education educator*
Curie, Roger Kent *adult education educator, consultant*
Erskine, William Crawford *retired academic administrator, accountant, health facility administrator*
Hernandez, Roberto Reyes *secondary school educator*
Howell, Norman Glen *elementary school educator*
Jarvis, Richard S. *academic administrator*
Kilbourne, Bruce Deane *history educator*
Natalicio, Diana Siedhoff *academic administrator*
Oliva, Maricela *education educator*
Riter, Stephen *academic administrator, electrical engineer*
Small, Ray *university administrator*
Torres, Richard *literature and language educator*
Vojta-Oswald, Clarice Gertrude *educational diagnostician*
Yanar, Maria Luisa (Tita) *director*

**Elgin**
Shelby, Nina Claire *special education educator*

**Farmers Branch**
Reyes, Czarina Suzanne *mathematics educator*

**Fort Worth**
Blanck, Ronald Ray *academic administrator, internist, military officer*
Boschini, Victor John, Jr. *academic administrator*
Chambers, Ima Louise *secretarial skills educator, executive secretary*
Currier, Mike *elementary school educator, writer*
Donovan, Nowell *academic administrator*
Johnson, Melody *school system administrator*
Kankel, Courtneye Ayn *history educator*
Saenz, Michael *college president*
Simmons, Jean Byers *academic administrator, director*
Slater, Carmen Rochelle *elementary school educator*
Tucker, William Edward *academic administrator, minister*

**Franklin**
Perry, Anne Marie Litchfield *secondary school educator*

**Fredericksburg**
Chase, John David *retired dean, retired internist*

**Freeport**
Baskin, William Gresham *counselor, vocalist, music educator*

**Galveston**
Langston, Sue H. *secondary school educator, director*
Parisi, Valerie Marie *dean, medical educator*
Stobo, John David *dean, educator, physician*

**Garland**
Quinn, Peggy Armstrong *elementary school educator, writer*

**Georgetown**
Brody, Gerald David *academic administrator*
Lovin, Keith Harold *retired academic administrator, philosopher, educator*
Schrum, Jake Bennett *academic administrator*

**Giddings**
Walker, Hershel O. *history educator*

**Graham**
Lovell, Lisa Inez *special education educator*

**Granbury**
Curl, Samuel Everett *retired dean, agriculturist, consultant*

**Grand Prairie**
Allen, Thomas Raymond *physics educator, music educator*
Puckett, Mary Alice *primary school educator, consultant*

**Grapevine**
Hirsh, Cristy J. *principal*

**Hale Center**
Courtney, Carolyn Ann *school librarian*

**Hardin**
Ringer, Paula Denise Hollenshead *elementary school educator*

**Hawkins**
Holmes, Lorene Barnes *academic administrator*

**Hereford**
Gilbert, Connie Fay *secondary school educator*
Yavornik, Barbara Ann *pre-school educator*

**Houston**
Adair, Wendy Hilty *university official*
Alfini, James Joseph *dean, educator, lawyer*
Anderson, Claire W. *gifted and talented educator*
Autry, Cheryl Renee *special education educator*
Beckingham, Kathleen Mary *education educator, researcher*
Benefield, Janis Wilson *school librarian, media specialist*
Bott, Simon Gregory *chemistry educator, researcher*
Brooks, Philip Russell *chemistry educator, researcher*
Bui, Khoi Tien *college counselor*
Butler, William Thomas *academic administrator, physician, educator*
Caram, Dorothy Farrington *educational consultant*
Cazenave, Anita Washington *secondary school educator*
Djerejian, Edward Peter *academic administrator, retired diplomat*
Elliott, Douglas S. *secondary school educator*
Flaitz, Catherine M. *dean, dental educator*
Gaelens, Albert Robert *director, educational administrator, priest*
Godine, Marion Cecilia *adult education educator*
Gonzalez, Antonio *academic administrator, educator, title company executive*
Goodwin, Heather Marie *educational consultant*
Hoffman, Philip Guthrie *former university president*
Hughes, Eloise Stapp *education educator*
Jackson, Wanda Britton *secondary school educator*
Johnson, Ronald *academic administrator*
Kneese, Carolyn Calvin *retired education educator*
Leebron, David Wayne *academic administrator, law educator*
Lin, Hong *science and technology educator*
Madrid, Michael John *director*
Malki, Heidar A. *dean*
Mansell, Joyce Marilyn *retired special education educator*
Mariotto, Marco Jerome *dean, psychology educator, researcher*
Matthews, Kathleen Shive *biochemistry educator*
McDonald, Marilyn A. *academic assistant*
Oakes, Pamela R. *retired elementary school educator*
O'Rourke, Marylyn Kay *counseling administrator, consultant*
Paul, Alida Ruth *elementary school educator*
Pickering, James Henry III *academic administrator, educator*
Ruban, Lilia *education educator, researcher*
Saavedra, Abelardo *school system administrator*
Silver, Jonathan *private school administrator*
Smith, Arthur Kittredge, Jr. *academic administrator, political scientist, educator*
Smith, James M. *dean*
Stephenson, Hunter W. *writing educator*
Stripling, Kaye *school system administrator*
Sullivan-Szuts, Betty Anne *academic administrator, educator*
Thomson, Donna R *primary school educator, researcher*
Urbina, Febe Gloria *elementary school principal*
Verwers, Jody Ann *mathematics educator*
Wacker-B., Deborah *secondary Spanish and special education educator*
Wagner, Paul Anthony, Jr. *education educator*
Webb, Marty Fox *principal*
Whiting, Martha Countee *retired secondary school educator*
Wiley, Shirley Winona Walters *adult education educator, artist*
Williames, Lee John *academic administrator, history professor*

**Huntsville**
Marks, Bobby Kees *academic administrator*
Payne, David Emer *university administrator*

Ward, Richard Hurley *director, dean, writer*

**Hutto**
Hamilton, Elizabeth Ann *elementary school educator*

**Iola**
Nelson, John Harrison *mathematics educator*

**Irving**
Martin, Thomas Lyle, Jr. *academic administrator*

**Joaquin**
Gill, Madeline Kay *school and youth counselor*

**Johnson City**
Pollock, Margaret Landau Peggy *elementary school educator*

**Keller**
Smith, Eleanor Jane *retired university chancellor, consultant*

**Kerrville**
Freeny, Katherine H. *adult education educator, chemist, researcher*

**Kilgore**
Turpin, Michael Hunter *academic administrator*

**La Porte**
Svambera, Beatrice Alice *secondary school educator*

**Laredo**
Black, Clifford Merwyn *academic administrator, sociologist, educator*
Greybeck, Barbara Jean *education educator*
Heimes, Charmaine Marie *elementary school educator, poet, writer*
Reuthinger, Georgeanne *special education educator*
Shepherd, Terry Lynn *special education educator*

**League City**
Cherry, Jeffrey Allen *secondary school educator*

**Llano**
Wilson, Dena Suzette *elementary school educator*

**Longview**
Gentry, Vernessa Diana *principal, consultant*

**Lubbock**
Allcorn, Seth Ford *dean, academic administrator*
Conover, William Jay *statistics educator*
Haragan, Donald Robert *academic administrator, geologist, educator*
Hart, Melanie A. *secondary school educator*
Quinn Trank, Christine *education educator*
Repman, Judith Lavine *educator*
White, Alice Virginia *academic administrator*

**Marfa**
Chambers Tucker, Johnnie L. *elementary school educator, rancher*

**Maxwell**
Peters, Carol Ann *secondary school educator*

**Mcallen**
Gonzalez, Rolando Noel *secondary school educator, theology studies educator, photographer*
Millan, Brett Jorge *education educator*
Ramirez, Leo Armando, Sr. *mathematics educator*
Truitt, Rodgers Paul *educator*

**Mclean**
Riley, Jacqulyn (Jacque) Diane *English educator, theater educator*

**Megargel**
Robertson, John *principal*

**Mesquite**
Gant, Linda Gayle *elementary school educator*
Holt, Mildred Frances *special education educator*
Vaughan, Joseph Lee, Jr. *education educator, consultant*
Wenrich, John William *college president*

**Mico**
McDonald, Mary Helen *special education educator*

**Midland**
Bridges, Judy Cantrell *gifted and talented education educator*
Dempsey, Christina Marie *reading educator*
Eustace, Natalie Bencowitz *elementary school educator*

**Midlothian**
Alderman, Amy Joy Spigel *elementary school educator*

**Morton**
Black, Rebecca J. *secondary school educator*

**Mount Pleasant**
Kirkpatrick, Jim C. *secondary school educator*

**New Braunfels**
Barragán, Celia Silguero *elementary school educator*
Oestreich, Charles Henry *retired university president*

**Odessa**
Braswell, Jody Lynn *gifted and talented educator*

**Orange**
Odom, Sarah Bernice *elementary school educator*

**Paige**
Trevino, Jerry Rosalez *retired secondary school principal*

**Palestine**
Akin, Charles S. *academic administrator*

**Paris**
McCuen, Maureen E. *history educator*

**Pasadena**
Blue, Monte Lynn *college president*

**Plano**
Rhodes, Doris Chaney *freelance/self-employed secondary school educator*

**Port Arthur**
Goza, Jim *chemistry educator*

**Randolph Afb**
Brennan-Bergmann, Bridget Catherine *special education educator*

**Red Oak**
Dulworth, Rhonda Rencé *secondary school educator*

**Richardson**
Daniel, David Edwin *academic administrator, civil engineer*
Heath, Mary Ann *elementary school educator*

**Rockwall**
Cates, Sue Sadler *educational diagnostician*

**Rosenberg**
Lefler, Sherry LynettE *elementary school educator*
Smith, October *elementary school educator*
White, Gretchen Nance *education educator, writer*

**Rowlett**
Bell, Ronald *secondary school educator*

**San Angelo**
Davison, Elizabeth Jane Linton *education educator*
Smith, Karen B. *educational consultant*

**San Antonio**
Arce, Arturo Galvan *military programs instructor*
Barnes, Helen Joyce *elementary school educator*
Bennett, Sister Elsa Mary *retired secondary school educator*
Davis, Marlon Quinn *assistant principal*
Dyas, Anna Marie *gifted and talented educator*
Escobar, Irma *secondary school educator*
Faules, Barbara Ruth *retired elementary school educator*
Gibbons, Robert Ebbert *university official*
Graf, Dorothy Jo *elementary school educator*
Hale, Nancy Annette Bills *kindergarten educator*
Henderson, Dwight Franklin *dean, educator*
Hudspeth, Almetra Kavanaugh *retired elementary school educator*
Kalkwarf, Kenneth Lee *dean, dental educator*
Madrid, Olga Hilda Gonzalez *retired elementary school educator, school system administrator*
Maxwell, Diana Kathleen *education educator, primary school educator*
McSorley, Rita Elizabeth *adult education educator*
Menchaca, Robert *elementary school educator*
Nichols, Sharon Louise *educator, researcher*
Noriega, Elizabeth Govea *elementary school educator*
Orange, Carolyn *education professor*
Palacios, Lisa May *academic administrator*
Recker, Patricia Bullion *secondary school educator*
Route, Candace *elementary school educator*
Sanchez, Susie Riojas *elementary school educator*
Schoenfeld, Lawrence Steven *psychology educator*
Wells, Ross R. *secondary school educator, writer*
Wright, Wayne E. *education educator*
Young, James Julius *academic administrator, retired military officer*

**San Juan**
Guzmán, Belinda F. *elementary school educator*

**San Marcos**
Erwin, Warner Scott, Sr. *academic administrator, consultant*
Lee, Kathryn S. *education educator, counseling administrator*

**Sherman**
Page, Oscar C. *academic administrator*

**Spring**
Lewis, Amy Marie *secondary school educator, music educator*
Schweiger, Peggy *physics educator*

**Stephenville**
Albrecht, Annette C. *education educator, consultant*
Dougherty, Thomas Michael *education educator*

**Sugar Land**
Matney, Judy McCaleb *secondary school educator*

**Sulphur Springs**
Gibson, Jannette Poe *educational consultant*

**Temple**
Dostal, David Eugene *education educator, researcher*
Fairlie, Thomas Andrew *director*
Meshack, Geneva Tucker *retired elementary school educator*

**Texarkana**
Austin, Sandra Jenelle *school librarian, language educator*
Tate, Nancy Jane *secondary school educator*

**Trenton**
Yeager, Evan Todd *academic administrator, small business owner*

**Tyler**
Davidson, Jack Leroy *academic administrator*

Peters, Robert K. *dean, newscaster, newswriter, journalist*
Prater, Emma Lou *retired academic administrator*
Sanchez, Heliodoro Torres, Jr. *education educator*
Waller, Wilma Ruth *retired secondary school educator, retired librarian*

**Uvalde**
Vela, Joel E. *academic administrator*

**Waco**
Belew, John Seymour *academic administrator, chemist*
Bennighof, James Malcolm *academic administrator*
Brooks, Roger Leon *retired academic administrator*
Emanuel, Gloria Page *retired secondary school educator*
Lilley, John Mark *academic administrator*
Lindsey, Jonathan Asmel *academic administrator, school librarian, educator*
Reynolds, Herbert Hal *university administrator*
Sloan, Robert Bryan, Jr. *academic administrator*
Toben, Bradley J. B. *dean, law educator*

**Weatherford**
Colton, James Patrick *academic administrator*

**Whitewright**
Summers, Bertie Jean *secondary school educator*

**Wichita Falls**
Hancock, Carole Patricia *academic administrator*
Lowrance, Muriel Edwards *retired educational specialist*

**Wimberley**
Jennett, Joseph Charles *retired academic administrator, engineering educator*

**Windcrest**
Froiland-Baker, Mary Lou *assistant principal*

**Winters**
Reagan, Brilla Jane *principal*

**UTAH**

**Cedar Hills**
Ashton, Dawne Belinda *retired secondary school educator*

**Draper**
Walz, Angela *retired secondary school educator*

**Holladay**
McKell, Cyrus M. *retired dean, plant physiologist, consultant*

**Logan**
Albrecht, Stan LeRoy *academic administrator, sociologist, educator*
Shaver, James Porter *retired education educator, dean*

**Ogden**
Bedford, Daniel Peter *educator*

**Orem**
Jackman, Roderick Victor *distance learning educator*
Sederburg, William Albert *academic administrator, former state senator*
Stevens, Lori Ann LaBeau *school librarian, educator*

**Park City**
Rude, Lara Peirce *special education educator*

**Provo**
Boyter, Scott M. *academic administrator*
Bradshaw, Jerald Sherwin *chemistry educator, researcher*
Bullough, Robert Vernon, Jr. *educational studies professor*
Densley, Colleen T. *principal*
Fleming, Joseph Clifton, Jr. *dean, law educator*
Hill, Ned Cromar *dean, finance educator, consultant*
Prater, Mary Anne *education educator, researcher*
Samuelson, Cecil O., Jr. *academic administrator*
Worthen, Kevin *dean, law educator*

**Riverton**
Littell, Lon Andrews *elementary school educator*

**Saint George**
Wiltsey, Susan A. *secondary school educator, priest*

**Salt Lake City**
Bassis, Michael Steven *academic administrator*
Bennion, John Warren *urban education educator*
Drew, Clifford James *dean, psychologist, educator*
Fukuta, Norihiko *professor emeritus in meteorology, researcher*
Harrington, Patti *school system administrator*
Keefe, Maureen Ruth *dean*
Liu, Gang *education educator, researcher*
Markham, Reed B. *education educator, consultant*
McCleary, Lloyd E(verald) *education educator*
West, Jason Brossard *education educator, consultant*
Wolfinger, Nicholas H. *educator*
Young, Michael Kent *academic administrator, law educator*

**West Jordan**
Betenson, Gaye Brinton *secondary school educator*

**VERMONT**

**Bennington**
Coleman, Elizabeth *college president*

**Brandon**
Dwyer, Michael Francis *secondary school educator*

**Burlington**
Allard, Judith Louise *secondary school educator*
Fogel, Daniel Mark (Daniel Mark Kahn-Fogel) *academic administrator, literature educator, writer*
Kelly, Sister Marie *school system administrator*
Murthy, Sanjeeva N. *education educator, materials scientist*
Thompson, Ellen Ann *elementary school educator*

**East Montpelier**
Gannon, Robin Bickford *elementary school educator*

**Essex Junction**
Bisson, Roger *middle school educator*

**Fairfield**
Lazarnick, Sylvia *retired secondary school educator*

**Lyndonville**
Moore, Carol A. *academic administrator*

**Middlebury**
Liebowitz, Ronald D. *academic administrator*
O'Brien, George Dennis *retired academic administrator*

**Montpelier**
Cate, Richard H. *school system administrator*
Muncy, Tina Gray *educator, educational coordinator*

**Morrisville**
Lamphere, Leigh Ann *elementary school educator, music educator*

**Plainfield**
Jervis, Jane Lise *academic administrator, historian*

**Poultney**
Fingon, Joan Carroll *education educator*
Pentkowski, Raymond J. *principal*

**Shelburne**
Myers, David Alan *middle school music educator*

**South Royalton**
Doria, Anthony Notarnicola *college dean, educator*

**Strafford**
Williams, William Magavern *headmaster*

**Swanton**
Suitor, Dorcas P. *elementary school educator*

**Vergennes**
Lewis, Elizabeth R. *director*

**White River Junction**
Kobe, Alexander *biology educator, department chairman*

**Whiting**
Jacobson, Edward *retired elementary school educator, retired principal*

**Wolcott**
Houston, Nioka Heath *elementary school educator*

**VIRGINIA**

**Alexandria**
Bartlett, Elizabeth Susan *audio-visual specialist*
Blanchette, Theresa Marie *elementary school educator*
Dubin, Martin Steven *principal*
Jenkins, John Smith *retired dean, lawyer*
Patel, Manu V. *physics educator*
Rae, Jeneanne *new product development and innovation development consultant, educator*
Schiff, Charlene *adult education educator*

**Amherst**
Campbell, Catherine Lynn *elementary school educator*

**Arlington**
Finta, Frances Mickna *secondary school educator*
Freeman, Peter A. *computer science educator, dean*
Gee, David E. *academic administrator*
Haggett, Rosemary Romanowski *academic administrator*
Helm, Brett *history educator*
Houston, Paul David *school association administrator*
McTique, Maurice P. *director*
Peck, Malcolm Cameron *educational exchange specialist*
Polsby, Daniel D. *dean, law educator*
Price, Donald Ray *academic administrator, researcher, agricultural engineer*
Rogers, Sharon J. *education consultant*
Sharp, Barry J. *school system administrator*
Shepherd, Mildred Roof *retired secondary school educator, art restorer*
Thompson, Barbara Ann *principal, educator*
Violand-Sanchez, Emma Natividad *school administrator, educator*
Whittier, Barbara J (Bobbie) *retired biology educator, retired chemistry educator*

**Ashburn**
Alwani, Ahmed J. *dean, consultant*

**Bedford**
Day, Mark Ronald *history educator, director*

**Blacksburg**
Barksdale, Mary Alice *education educator*

Blanchard, Dorothy Hardt *academic administrator, volunteer*
Campbell, Joan Virginia Loweke *secondary school educator, language educator*
Hawkins, Larry Edward *biology educator*
McNamee, Mark *academic administrator*
Steger, Charles William *academic administrator*
Torgersen, Paul Ernest *academic administrator, educator*

**Boones Mill**
Johnson, Georginea Angell *elementary school educator*

**Charlottesville**
Ayers, Edward *dean*
Biltonen, Rodney Lincoln *biochemistry educator, pharmacology educator*
Brodrick, Sheri Mary-Ann *secondary school educator*
Casteen, John Thomas III *academic administrator*
Garson, Arthur, Jr. *dean, medical educator*
Jeffries, John Calvin, Jr. *dean, law educator*
Smith, Clyde Ray *dean*
Wittenborg, Karin *university librarian*

**Chesapeake**
Hill, Deborah Nixon *elementary school educator, minister*
Kohns, Jonathan Wesley *secondary school educator*
Lewter, Helen Clark *retired elementary school educator*
Notti, Donna Betts *special education educator*
Webb, Julia Jones *elementary school educator, minister*

**Chester**
Law, Thomas Melvin *academic administrator*

**Chesterfield**
Weldon, Thérèse Hemler *secondary school educator, art educator*

**Clifton**
Latt, Pamela Yvonne *school system administrator*

**Dale City**
Baxter, Ruth Howell *educational administrator, psychologist*

**Danville**
Aaron, Larry Gene *secondary school educator, writer, minister*
Pfau, Richard Anthony *university president*

**Dublin**
Wall, Jennifer Grey *assistant principal*

**Fairfax**
Carty, Rita Mary *dean, nurse*
Crissey, Rebecca Lynn *special education educator*
Fox, Donna M. *dean, biology professor*
Longin, Thomas Charles *retired academic administrator*
Nicogossian, Anrauld E.T. *education educator*
Rendine, Maria Farese *retired secondary school educator*
Silcox, Gordon Bruce *executive coach*

**Fairfax Station**
Cantu, Jennifer St. John *gifted and talented educator*

**Falls Church**
Aziz, Afzal *biology educator*
Johnson, William David *retired academic administrator*
Todd, Shirley Ann *school system administrator*
Waylonis, Jean Lynnette *elementary school educator*

**Farmville**
Cormier, Patricia Picard *academic executive*
Kitchie, Matthew Anthony *director*

**Floyd**
Bosniak, Murray Eli *educational consultant*

**Fort Lee**
Simmonds, Robert Maurer *education educator*

**Fredericksburg**
Schlegelmilch, Margaret Ann *elementary school educator*

**Front Royal**
Stevens, Loretta Marie *special education educator*

**Gainesville**
Tuck, Russell R., Jr. *college president emeritus*

**Great Falls**
Andrews, Betty Bauserman *retired secondary school educator, real estate manager*

**Hampden Sydney**
Wilson, Samuel V. *academic administrator*

**Hampton**
Fox, Margaret Louise *retired secondary school educator*
Goode, Constance Loper *elementary school principal*
Harvey, William Robert *university president*

**Harrisonburg**
Carrier, Ronald Edwin *academic administrator, director*
Pappas, Eric Charles *director*

**Herndon**
Jones, Reba (Becki) Pestun *elementary school educator, music educator*

**Kilmarnock**
Blake, Robin Bell *middle school educator*

**Lawrenceville**
Frye, Gary E. *elementary school educator*
Hardy, Sandra Vanessa *elementary school educator*

**Lexington**
Partlett, David F. *dean, law educator*
Ruscio, Kenneth Patrick *academic administrator, political science professor*
Williams, H. Thomas (Tom Williams) *academic administrator, physicist, educator*

**Lovettsville**
Ryan-Griffith, Mary Kate *special education educator*

**Lynchburg**
Alcindor, Esther *education educator*
Armstrong, Barry K. *education educator*
Bowman, Kathleen Gill *academic administrator*
Herndon, Merle Puckette *school system administrator*
Mabry, Cynthia Callands *secondary school educator*
Proffitt, John Daniel, Jr. *education educator*
Ross, Jeffrey C. *mathematics educator, department chairman*

**Marion**
Groseclose, Joanne Stowers *special education educator*

**Mc Dowell**
Harkleroad, Jo-Ann Decker *special education educator*

**Mc Gaheysville**
Kemper, Diana Mede *history educator*

**Mc Lean**
Jackson, Juanita Wallace *educational consultant*
Percival, Meghan Jeanne *secondary school educator*

**Mechanicsville**
Watkins, Carol A. *special education educator*

**Melfa**
Harmon, Patricia Marie *retired special education educator*

**Midlothian**
Lamont-Gordon, Melissa Lynne *orchestra director, music educator*

**Newport News**
Eastman, John Robert *education educator*
McDonald, Karis Jeanine *elementary school educator, adult education educator*

**Norfolk**
Bourie, Elizabeth Conley *gifted resource specialist*
Bucher, Katherine Toth *education educator, librarian*
Combs, Charles Donald *academic administrator*
Hu, Fang Q. *adult education educator*
Koch, James Verch *academic administrator, economist*
McDemmond, Marie Valentine *academic administrator, consultant*
McKinney, Sueanne E. *education educator*
Meyers, Carolyn Winstead *academic administrator, mechanical engineer, educator*
Miller, Khadijah Olivia *education educator*
Runte, Roseann *academic administrator*
Sharpe, Martha Anne Smith *academic administrator, consultant*
Sirjani, Mojtaba B. *education educator*
Steele, James Eugene *retired school system administrator*
Young, Joy W. *gifted and talented educator*

**Oakton**
Condit, Robert B. *counselor*

**Petersburg**
Benn, Candace Marilea *elementary school educator*
Watson, Samuel Ray *academic administrator*

**Portsmouth**
Rampersaud Lundy, Sheryll *special education educator*

**Powhatan**
Robertson, Penetha Browning *secondary school educator*

**Quantico**
Stout, Mary Webb *dean*

**Radford**
Kyle, Penelope Ward *academic administrator*

**Reston**
Keefe, James Washburn *educational writer, researcher, consultant*
Lynch, Monique Christine *mathematics educator*

**Richmond**
Aristides, Sismanis *education educator, department chairman*
Brown, Marilyn Branch *retired educational administrator*
Budd, Richard Wade *academic administrator, dean, priest*
Cooper, William Edwin *academic administrator, psychologist, linguist, educator*
Corona, Rosalie *psychology educator*
DeMary, Jo Lynne *school system administrator, elementary school educator*
Drain, Cecil B. *dean, nursing educator, retired military officer*
Fleisher, Paul *retired elementary school educator*
Hamel, Dana Bertrand *academic administrator*
Harris, Barbara McDaniel-Wolfe *retired elementary school educator*
Hunt, Ronald J. *dean, dental educator*
Jewell-Sherman, Deborah *school system administrator*
Johnson, Patricia Lee *mathematics educator*

Jones, Jeanne Pitts *pre-school administrator*
Kalmanson, Daniel Patrick *academic administrator*
Langston, Nancy Sue Friedrich *dean*
McGee, Henry Alexander, Jr. *academic administrator*
Newsome, Heber H., Jr. *retired academic administrator*
Salley, John Jones *retired academic administrator, oral pathologist*
Selden, Jane Tibbs *biology educator*
Smolla, Rodney Alan *dean, law educator*
Spindler, Judith Tarleton *elementary school educator*
Toscan, Richard Eric *dean, theater educator*
Trani, Eugene Paul *university president, educator*
Whitehurst, Lucinda Snyder *school librarian*

**Rockbridge Baths**
Glidden, Robert Burr *academic administrator, consultant, music educator*

**Rose Hill**
Lane, Mary Winston *secondary school educator*

**Salem**
Day, John T. *academic administrator, dean*
Fisher, Charles Harold *chemistry educator, researcher*
Sailer, Rachel Ann *secondary school educator*

**Shenandoah**
Atkins, Denise Beth *elementary school educator*

**Spring Grove**
Davis, Shirley Stancil *retired elementary education educator*

**Springfield**
Kurth, Ronald James *retired academic administrator, retired military officer*

**Stafford**
Garrison, Anne-Marie Dickinson *middle school educator*

**Sterling**
Steffens, Brian Douglas *elementary school educator, director*

**Suffolk**
Brown, Alvenice Hortense Bryan *educator*

**Sweet Briar**
Muhlenfeld, Elisabeth S. *academic administrator, literature educator, writer*

**Tazewell**
Clayter, Katherine W. Moss *secondary school educator*

**Victoria**
McLaughlin, Sally Crump *elementary school educator*

**Vienna**
Hock, Randolph Edward *adult education educator, writer*
Kropp, Edward H. *education educator, consultant*
Marx, Gary Dean *educational consultant, futurist, think-tank executive*

**Virginia Beach**
Gardner, Karen High *special education educator*
Jones, Robert Clair *middle school educator*
Melvin, Carole Ramey *educational consultant*
Morgan, Raymond Franklin *education educator*
Poe, Kenneth Donovan *secondary school educator*
Selig, William George *academic administrator*
Von Mosch, Wanda Gail *middle school educator*
Ziegler, Rochelle Elizabeth *special education educator*

**Waynesboro**
Dillon, William Henry *retired secondary school educator*
Wade, Dianne Elizabeth *secondary school educator*

**Williamsburg**
Abiona-Lipot, Priscilla Roono *retired elementary school educator*
Calver, Richard Allen *retired dean*
Eliason, Nancy Carol *education consultant*
Hight, Orian Langley *retired education educator*
McCarthy, Connie Kearns *university librarian*
Nichol, Eugene R. *academic administrator*
Nichol, Gene Ray, Jr. *academic administrator, law educator*
Reveley, Walter Taylor III *dean, law educator*

**Wise**
Smiddy, Joseph Charles *retired academic administrator*

**Woodberry Forest**
Campbell, Dennis Marion *academic administrator, educator, theologian*

**Yorktown**
Douthat, Rebecca Arlene *retired secondary school educator*
Goetz, Kevin Edward *instructional specialist*
Lee, Veverlyn A. *history educator*

# WASHINGTON

**Anacortes**
Felger, Ralph William *education educator, retired military officer*

**Arlington**
Hedman, Zoe Ann *retired literature and language educator, artist*
Randall, Beatrice Janet *retired secondary school educator*

**Auburn**
Butz, Gloria K. *elementary school educator*

**Bainbridge Island**
Johnson, Christine Vaughn *secondary school educator*

**Bellevue**
Westergaard, George Henry *secondary school educator*

**Bellingham**
Cunningham, Mick H *education educator*
Morse, Karen Williams *academic administrator*

**Bothell**
Constantino, Karen Marie *elementary school educator*

**Camas**
Kotsovos, Jerry Frank *retired secondary school educator*

**Chehalis**
Hunter, Glen Herbert *secondary school educator*

**Chelan**
Curry, Michael W. *secondary school educator*

**Clinton**
Powers, David Richard *educational administrator*

**Des Moines**
Tuell, Jack Marvin *superintendent, retired bishop*

**Ellensburg**
McIntyre, Jerilyn Sue *academic administrator*

**Everett**
Hundley, Ronnie *academic administrator*

**Federal Way**
Rossi, Ruth Harris *special education educator*

**Gig Harbor**
Bernard, Lowell Francis *retired academic administrator, educator*
Minnerly, Robert Ward *retired headmaster*

**Kelso**
Janke, John Eric *secondary school educator*

**Kenmore**
Jennerich, Edward John *academic administrator, dean*

**Kennewick**
Scott, Pamela J. *educational consultant*

**Kirkland**
Argue, Don Harvey *college president, minister*
Rich, Clayton *retired academic administrator, educator*
Tyllia, Frank Michael *academic administrator, educator*

**Lacey**
Siera, Steven G. *career planning administrator, educator*
Spangler, David Robert *academic administrator, educator, engineer*

**Lacrosse**
Hagman, Betty Jo *elementary school educator*

**Lakebay**
Schauer, Victoria Young *elementary school educator, writer*

**Lakewood**
Oakes, DuWayne Earl *retired principal*

**Lynnwood**
Floten, Barbara Jean *educational dean*
Tebbs, Carol Ann *secondary school educator, academic administrator*

**Mabton**
Vannatter, David Alan *history educator, coach*

**Mesa**
Stevenson, Patricia Ann *elementary school educator*

**Olympia**
Bergeson, Teresa *school system administrator*
Jackson, Thelma Harrison *educational consultant, researcher*
Walkup, Hugh Robert *education administrator*
Wright, Constance Mohr *retired elementary school educator*

**Pasco**
Zacher, Irmagene *elementary school educator*

**Port Angeles**
Vermillion, Roy Alan *secondary school educator*

**Pullman**
Bates, Robert C. *academic administrator*
Dobney, Fredrick John *academic administrator*
Folwell, Raymond Joseph *dean, economist, consultant*
Laborie, Marie-Pierre Geneviève *education educator*
Lewis, Norman G. *academic administrator, researcher, consultant*
Paznokas, Lynda Sylvia *elementary school educator*
Rawlins, V. Lane *academic administrator*
Smith, Trenton Garry *education educator*

**Puyallup**
Rink, Robert P. *secondary school educator*

**Richland**
Brashear, Karen Kathleen *elementary school educator*
Glennen, Robert Eugene, Jr. *retired academic administrator*

Miller, James Vince *university president*

**Seattle**
Banks, James Albert *educational research director, educator, researcher*
Carlson, Dale Arvid *retired university dean*
Cox, Frederick Moreland *retired dean, social worker*
Denny, Brewster Castberg *retired university dean*
Emmert, Mark Allen *academic administrator, educator*
Esbeck, Edward S. *retired education educator*
Gerberding, William Passavant *retired university president*
Goodlad, John Inkster *education educator, writer*
Hampton, Shelley Lynn *hearing impaired educator*
Hasl, Rudolph Carl *dean, law educator*
Knight, W. H., Jr., (Joe Knight) *dean, law educator*
Murdock, Tullisse Antoinette (Toni Murdock) *academic administrator*
Pocker, Yeshayau *chemistry and biochemistry educator*
Ramsey, Paul Glenn *dean, internist*
Rasic-Steben, Stephanie Ann *secondary school educator*
Ray, Charles Kendall *retired university dean*
Silver, Michael *education educator*
Smith, Mary W. *secondary school educator, artist*
Somerman, Martha J. *dean, dental educator*
Stringer, William Jeremy *university official*
Sundborg, Stephen V. *academic administrator*
Terrell, William Glenn *university president emeritus*
Testy, Kellye *dean*
Thorud, David B. *academic administrator*
Tschernisch, Sergei P. *academic administrator*
Wasserman, Harriet M. *academic administrator*
Wilson, Lizabeth Anne *dean, library director*
Woods, Nancy Fugate *dean, women's health nurse, educator*

**Shelton**
Milander, Henry Martin *educational consultant*

**Spanaway**
Paris, Kathleen *secondary school educator*
Parker, Lynda Christine Rylander *secondary school educator*

**Spokane**
Danke, Virginia *educational administrator, travel consultant*
Lalonde, Stephen Duane *secondary school educator, writer*
Lane, Iris Mary *retired elementary school educator*
Linn, Diana Patricia *retired elementary school educator*
McCulloh, Thayne Martin *university administrator, consultant*
Spitzer, Robert J. *academic administrator*

**Stanwood**
Birkestol, Annabelle Mollie Elsie *retired elementary school educator*

**Tacoma**
Reisberg, Leon Elton *education educator*

**Toppenish**
Ross, Kathleen Anne *academic administrator*

**University Place**
Henterly, Mary B. *biology educator*

**Vancouver**
Hurst, Margaret Cheryl *elementary school educator, music educator*
Tuttle, Marcia *retired elementary school educator, music educator*

**Walla Walla**
Bridges, George S. *academic administrator, sociology educator*

**Washougal**
Shoemaker, Cameron David James *retired dean*

**Yakima**
Halfmoon, Thomas William *history educator*
Walker, Lorene *retired elementary school educator*

**WEST VIRGINIA**

**Athens**
Marsh, Joseph Franklin, Jr. *retired academic administrator*

**Beckley**
Wolfe, Carl Gundersen *adult education educator*

**Bethany**
Smith, G(odfrey) T(aylor) *college president*

**Bluefield**
Moore, Robert E. *college president*

**Chapmanville**
Wilson, Terilyn Barrett *elementary school educator*

**Charles Town**
Graf, Virginia Lynch *retired education educator*

**Charleston**
Arrington, Carolyn Ruth *school system administrator, consultant*
Foster, Leska A. *elementary school educator*
Frostick, Robert Maurice *secondary school educator*
Paine, Steven L. *school system administrator*
Richardson, Sally Keadle *academic administrator*

**Clarksburg**
Leuliette, Connie Jane *secondary school educator*

**Dunbar**
Russell, James Alvin, Jr. *college administrator*
Young, Stephanie Angel *counseling administrator*

**Elizabeth**
Lipps, Deloris Jean *secondary school educator*

**Enterprise**
Morris, James Victor *secondary school educator*

**Fairmont**
Dudley-Eshbach, Janet *university president*
Hardway, Wendell Gary *retired academic administrator*

**Harpers Ferry**
Callar, Donna Howe *counseling administrator, educator*

**Harrisville**
Edwards, Tina Lou *school system administrator*

**Huntington**
Anderson, Lorraine Pearson *dean*
Gould, Alan Brant *academic administrator*
Hayes, Robert Bruce *former college president, educator*
Kent, Calvin Albert *academic administrator*
McKown, Charles Henry *dean*
Welch, Lynne Brodie *nursing school dean*

**Keyser**
Falkowski, Theresa Gae *chemistry educator*

**Lookout**
Burdette, Charlotte *middle school educator*

**Martinsburg**
Dugger, Debra Martin *school counselor*

**Montgomery**
Minnich, Thomas Gayle *director*

**Morgantown**
Allamong, Betty Davis *retired academic administrator*
Bajura, Richard Albert *academic administrator, mechanical engineer, educator*
Bucklew, Neil S. *former academic administrator, educator*
Clausell, Arlene Midget *retired elementary school educator*
D'Alessandri, Robert M. *academic administrator, retired dean*
Hardesty, David Carter, Jr. *academic administrator*
Johnson, Michael David *dean, physiologist, educator*
Koelbl, James J. *dean*
Mei, Betty Miuchi *director*
Moxley, Roy Anthony *early childhood educator*
Shumway, James M. *dean, medical educator*

**Moundsville**
Wensyel, Mary Kathleen *elementary school educator*

**New Cumberland**
Underwood, Elaine M. *elementary school educator*

**Parkersburg**
Dennis, James L. *history educator*
Nichols, Terry Jean *elementary school educator, music educator*
Rowland, Angela Kay *education educator, consultant*

**Princeton**
Pauley, Michael Wetzel *director, school psychologist*
Pratt, Carolyn Kay *retired literature and language educator, retired mathematics educator*
Wall, Linda Amanda *economics educator*

**Ripley**
Riffe, Stacy Christine *secondary school educator*

**Saint Albans**
Smith, Robert Carlisle *department administrator, welding educator*

**South Charleston**
Fishkin, Anne Sonya *retired special education educator*

**Spencer**
Parker, Theresa Ann Boggs *special education educator, music educator*

**Wheeling**
Filben, Byron William *elementary school educator, director, secondary school educator, director*
Spencer, Catherine Ellen *academic administrator*

**WISCONSIN**

**Antigo**
Fischer, Cindy L. *school system administrator*

**Appleton**
Beck, Jill *academic administrator, dancer, educator*

**Auburndale**
Johnson, James T *secondary school educator*

**Baraboo**
Umhoefer, Aural M. *retired dean, educational consultant*

**Barneveld**
Kolb, Victoria L. *retired mathematics educator*

**Beloit**
Burris, John Edward *academic administrator, biologist, educator*
Wheeler, Karla *education educator*

**Coleman**
Brady, Jeremy B. *secondary school educator*

**De Forest**
O'Neil, J. Peter (James Peter O'Neil) *elementary school educator, computer scientist*

**Eau Claire**
Field, Barbara Kay *elementary school educator*
Hulke, Kevin Lee *mathematics educator, researcher*
Ripp, Kenneth Leon *secondary school educator*

**Elkhart Lake**
Harper, Carrie Lynn *school counselor*

**Elkhorn**
Reinke, Doris Marie *retired elementary school educator*

**Ellsworth**
McCoy, Jeanne M. *principal*

**Fish Creek**
Abegg, Martin Gerald *retired academic administrator*

**Fort Atkinson**
Schumacher, Mabel G. *director, consultant*

**Fountain City**
Zurbuchen, John Frederic *principal*

**Glendale**
Schenker, Eric *university dean, economist*

**Grafton**
Mathews, Nikki *mathematics educator, science educator*

**Green Bay**
Hardy, Deborah Lewis *dean, educator, dental hygienist*
Shepard, W. Bruce *academic administrator*
Weidner, Edward William *academic administrator, political scientist*

**Hales Corners**
Herman, Ellen Rombs *literature and language educator*

**Hartford**
Falkenstein, Sara André *retired elementary school educator*

**Hartland**
Desotell, Laurence D. *history and political science educator*

**Holmen**
Meyer, Karl William *retired university president*

**Hudson**
Dahle, Carol Jo *secondary school educator, director*
Dahle, Johannes Upton *retired academic administrator*

**Kenosha**
Campbell, F(enton) Gregory *academic administrator, historian*
Groleau, Thomas G. *academic administrator*
Iaquinta, Leonard Phillip *academic administrator, writer, consultant, not-for-profit fundraiser*

**La Crosse**
Medland, William James *university chancellor*

**Loyal**
Anderson, Joseph Bennett *elementary school educator*

**Madison**
Burmaster, Elizabeth *school system administrator*
Busby, Edward Oliver *retired dean*
Davis, Kenneth Boone, Jr. *dean, law educator*
Frazier, Kenneth L. *university librarian*
Goldrick, Sara Youcha *higher education educator*
Hamers, Robert J. *chemistry educator, researcher*
Hassett, Dawnene Diane *education educator*
Johnson, Richard Arnold *statistics educator, consultant*
Knetter, Michael Mark *dean*
Ma, Zhenqiang *education educator*
Mash, Donald J. *college president*
Odden, Allan Robert *education educator*
Reilly, Kevin P. *academic administrator*
Sapiro, Virginia *academic administrator, political science professor*
Shkel, Yuri M. *education educator, researcher*
Skochelak, Susan E. *dean*
Spear, Peter D. *retired academic administrator*
Turng, Lih-Sheng *education educator*
Underwood, Julie K. *dean, former law educator*
Wiley, John D. *academic administrator*

**Manitowoc**
Nelson, Robert Louis *education educator, consultant*

**Markesan**
Kastenschmidt, Betty M. *elementary school educator, director*

**Menomonee Falls**
Hinnrichs-Dahms, Holly Beth *elementary school educator*

**Menomonie**
Sedlak, Robert *academic administrator*

**Mequon**
Dohmen, Mary Holgate *retired primary school educator*
Ellis, William Grenville *academic administrator, management consultant*
Esselmann, Jesse J *education educator*
Sisney, Ned *education educator*

**Middleton**
Conaway, Jane Ellen *elementary school educator*

**Milton**
Parker, Letitia *secondary school educator*

**Milwaukee**
Aman, Mohammed Mohammed *dean, library and information science professor*
Barth, Karl Luther *retired seminary president*
Belazelkoska, Katerina *school system administrator*
Cody, Christopher B. *secondary school educator*
Coffman, Terrence J. *retired academic administrator*
Dunn, Michael J. *dean*
Feinsilver, Donald Lee *psychiatry professor*
Giacinti, Louis Anthony *educator, writer*
Gleason Heffron, Mary Ellen *education specialist*
Kearney, Joseph D. *dean, law educator*
Keshvala, Seelpa H *secondary school educator*
Lobb, William K. *dean, dental educator*
Nowack, James Albert *education educator*
Peng, Zhong-Ren *education educator*
Read, Sister Joel *academic administrator*
Rheams, Annie Elizabeth *education educator*
Rindler, Robert *academic administrator*
Sankovitz, James Leo *retired development director, lobbyist*
Schroeder, John H. *university chancellor*
Toumanoff, Peter George *educator*
Velez, William *education educator*
Vento-Bente, Chris *director, department chairman*
Wake, Madeline Musante *academic administrator, nursing educator*
Waller, Mary Bellis *educational consultant, researcher*
Weiner, Wendy L(ou) *elementary school educator, writer*
Wild, Robert Anthony *academic administrator*

**Mount Horeb**
Nemec, Eileen Carla *elementary school educator, consultant*

**Nekoosa**
Ramirez, Mary Catherine *retired secondary school educator*

**New London**
Fitzgerald, Laurine Elisabeth *university dean, educator*

**Oconto**
Seidl, Susan Kathryn *secondary school educator*

**Oneida**
Engel, Pamela Marie *associate principal, trainer*

**Oshkosh**
Buser, Rose M. *elementary school educator*
Earns, Lane Robert *academic administrator, historian, educator*
Olejniczak, Bernard Charles *education educator*
Ristow, Thelma Frances *retired elementary school educator*

**Rhinelander**
Conlin, Judith *retired director*

**Rice Lake**
Seymour, Michelle Gene *elementary school educator*

**Ripon**
Jeffries, Paul Franklin *philosophy educator*

**River Falls**
Thibodeau, Gary Arthur *academic administrator*

**Sheboygan**
Fritz, Kristine Rae *retired secondary school educator*

**Shorewood**
Lietz, Jeremy Jon *educational administrator, writer*

**Sparta**
Steward, Thomas James *school system administrator*

**Stevens Point**
Bunnell, Linda Hunt *academic administrator*

**Sun Prairie**
Schmidt, Glenn Norbert *special education educator*

**Superior**
Bowden, Laura Ann *retired secondary school educator, retired counselor*
Erlenbach, Julius E. *academic administrator, musician*
Jacobs, Laura Elizabeth *school librarian, educator, archivist*
Morden, Annette Sonja Knudson *retired education educator*

**Three Lakes**
Bauknecht, Barbara Belle *retired pre-school educator*

**Tomah**
Neurohr, Shirley Ann *retired special education educator*

**Union Grove**
Dawson, Rose Dorothy *elementary school educator*

**Washburn**
Nutt, Sandra Kay *elementary school educator*

**Waukesha**
Falcone, Frank S. *academic administrator*
Gustafson, Mardel Emma *secondary school educator, writer*
Lightfoot, Alfred J. *retired education educator*

## Wauzeka
Acker, Terri G. *academic administrator, biology professor, healthcare educator, physical education educator*

## West Salem
Kindschy, Errol Roy *school system administrator*

## Wheeler
Olson, Sheila J. *elementary school educator*

## Whitewater
Greenhill, H. Gaylon *retired academic administrator*
Kolb, Sharon Marie *education educator, director, consultant*
Saunders, Martha Dunagin *academic administrator*
Schroeder, Eileen Elizabeth *education educator*

## Wisconsin Rapids
Olson-Hellerud, Linda Kathryn *elementary school educator*

## WYOMING

## Big Piney
Walker, Joni Carol *secondary school educator*

## Casper
Bovee, Debra Sue *elementary school educator*
Rickabaugh, René Lane *principal*
Unruh, Eric W. *academic administrator, music educator*

## Cheyenne
McBride, James M. *school system administrator*
Weigner, Brent James *secondary school educator*

## Douglas
Kilpatrick, Sherrill Lynn *elementary school educator*

## Gillette
Cummings, Judy Annette *retired secondary school educator*

## Glendo
Burton, Eva Ella Mary *primary school educator*

## Green River
Albers, Dolores M. *secondary school educator*

## Jackson
Massy, William Francis *education educator, consultant*

## Laramie
Cho, Jeasik *education educator*

## Lingle
Gulisano, Cynthia Jo *elementary school educator*

## Sheridan
May, Peter Alan *biology educator*

## Torrington
Lewis, Mary Jane *retired elementary school educator*

## TERRITORIES OF THE UNITED STATES

## AMERICAN SAMOA

## Pago Pago
Tuitele, Lui *school system administrator*

## GUAM

## Hagatna
Artero, Margaret T. *academic administrator, military officer*

## Mangilao
Inoue, Yukiko *educational research educator*

## NORTHERN MARIANA ISLANDS

## Saipan
Inos, Rita Hocog *school system administrator*
Kaufer, Connie Tenorio *special education educator, researcher*

## PUERTO RICO

## Guaynabo
Cancel, Carmen Iliana *biology educator*

## Ponce
Gonzalez, Bertha Irene *counseling administrator, mediator*

## Ramey
Aponte, Abraham *secondary school educator*

## San German
Mojica, Agnes *academic administrator*

## San Juan
Carreras, Francisco José *retired academic administrator, foundation administrator*
Joglar, Francisco *academic administrator*
Jorge, Juan Carlos *education educator, researcher*
Matheu, Federico Manuel *university chancellor*
Rey-Hernandez, Cesar A. *school system administrator*

## VIRGIN ISLANDS

## Frederiksted
Birbahadur, Dindial *secondary school educator*

## St Thomas
DePass-Creque, Linda Ann *educational consultant association executive, former education commissioner*
Michael, Noreen *school system administrator*

## MILITARY ADDRESSES OF THE UNITED STATES

## EUROPE

## APO
Knudsen, Gene Arthur *school system administrator*

## CANADA

## ALBERTA

## Calgary
Neale, Ernest Richard Ward *retired university official, consultant*
Smith, Rowland James *educational administrator*
Watanabe, Mamoru *internist, researcher*
White, Terrence Harold *academic administrator, sociologist*

## Edmonton
Kratochvil, Byron George *chemistry educator, researcher*
Tyrrell, D. Lorne J. *university dean*

## BRITISH COLUMBIA

## Cobble Hill
Cox, Albert Reginald *retired dean, retired cardiologist*

## Surrey
Lee, Jeong-Kyu *education educator*

## Vancouver
Finnegan, Cyril Vincent *retired dean, zoology educator*

## MANITOBA

## Winnipeg
Poettcker, Henry *retired academic administrator*

## NEWFOUNDLAND AND LABRADOR

## Saint John's
May, Arthur W. *retired academic administrator, educator*

## NOVA SCOTIA

## Halifax
Carrigan, David Owen *history educator*
Jaeger, Leslie Gordon *academic administrator*

## Wolfville
Ogilvie, Kelvin Kenneth *academic administrator, chemist, educator*

## ONTARIO

## Gloucester
Malouin, Jean-Louis *adult education educator*

## Kingston
Spencer, John Hedley *biochemistry educator*

## Ottawa
Jordan, Joseph Louis *education educator, government official*
Kroeger, Arthur *retired academic administrator, retired federal official*
Philogene, Bernard J. R. *academic administrator, science educator*

## Peterborough
Theall, Donald Francis *retired university president*

## Saint Catharines
Ayanso, Anteneh Wondimu *information systems educator*

## Toronto
Evans, John Robert *academic administrator, cardiologist*
Hayhurst, James Frederick Palmer *career and business consultant, inspirational speaker, writer*
Knowlton, Thomas A. *dean, retired food products executive*
Kushner, Eva *academic administrator, educator, author*
Ostry, Sylvia *academic administrator, economist*
Sessle, Barry John *adult education educator, researcher*

## Waterloo
Berczi, Andrew Stephen *academic administrator, educator*
Wright, Douglas Tyndall *former university administrator*

## QUEBEC

## Montreal
Freedman, Samuel Orkin *university official*
Granger, Luc Andre *dean, psychologist*
Levin, Richard I. *dean, cardiologist, researcher*

## SASKATCHEWAN

## Regina
Barber, Lloyd Ingram *retired university president*

## Saskatoon
Knott, Douglas Ronald *dean, agricultural sciences educator, researcher*

## Montreal
Jundi, Bilal *principal*
Loucks, Eric Barry *educator*
Lowy, Frederick Hans *academic administrator, psychiatrist*

## Ottawa
Axworthy, Lloyd *academic administrator, former Canadian government official*

## MEXICO

## Distrito Federal
de la Fuente Ramirez, Juan Ramon *academic administrator*

## Monterrey
Amores, Jose E. *director*

## San Pedro Garza García
Defiore, Perry Dennis *director, small business owner*

## AUSTRALIA

## Melbourne
Searby, Richard Henry *academic administrator, lawyer*

## BERMUDA

## St. George's
Burchall, Leondra N. *history educator*

## BRITISH VIRGIN ISLANDS

## Tortola
Chalwell-Brewley, Lavon Patricia *biology educator*

## ENGLAND

## Leeds
Pillay, Anand *education educator, researcher*

## London
May, Robert McCredie (Lord May of Oxford) *biology educator*
Tyson, Laura D'Andrea *dean, finance educator*

## Manchester
de Silva, Eugene Lakshman *academic administrator, educator*

## Oxford
Varese, Federico *sociology professor*

## Richmond-upon-Thames
Smith, Norman Raymond *academic administrator*

## FRANCE

## Aix-en-Provence
Leskes, Andrea *academic administrator, educator*

## Cedex
Demers, Elizabeth Anne *education educator*

## GERMANY

## Dortmund
Vogt, Hartmut *education educator*

## Obbornhofen
Edwards, Grey Holt, Jr. *academic administrator, adult education educator*

## Ottilienstr
Clarke, Ingrid Gadway *retired academic ombudsman, consultant*

## Seewiesen
Huber, Franz *retired research director*

## GUANA ISLAND

## Barrigada
Perez, Annie Rivera *elementary school educator*

## HONG KONG

## Hong Kong
Leung, Ka-Cheong *education educator*

Tsui, Lap-Chee *academic administrator, molecular genetics educator*

## New Territories
Lau, Lawrence Juen-Yee *academic administrator, economics professor, consultant*

## INDIA

## Mirzapur
Upadhyaya, Kripa Shankar *academic administrator, educator*

## IRELAND

## Cork
Lyons, Nona Mary *adult education educator*

## JAPAN

## Okayama
Nii, Shiro *director, virologist, educator*

## Tokyo
Nakajima, Hiroshi *education educator*

## Tsukuba
Shimizu, Kazuhiko *education educator*

## JORDAN

## Irbid
Al-Smadi, Adnan M. *dean*

## LEBANON

## Beirut
Pederson, Patricia Velde *education educator, consultant*
Waterbury, John *academic administrator, political science professor, writer*

## PHILIPPINES

## Quezon City
Lee-Chua, Queena N. *mathematics educator*

## POLAND

## Gdansk
Mokrzecki, Lech Marian *history of education educator*

## REPUBLIC OF KOREA

## Seoul
Lee, Sungho H. *education educator, consultant, academic administrator*
Sohn, Jungyul *education educator*

## Suwon
Choi, Cheol Yong *educator, researcher*

## SCOTLAND

## Saint Andrews
Dover, Sir Kenneth James *chancellor, retired classicist*

## SWEDEN

## Uppsala
Champion, Margrét Gunnarsdóttir *literature and language educator*

## TAIWAN

## Hualien
Yiin, Lih-Ming *educator*

## Kaohsiung
Lambert, Marianne T. *retired elementary school educator*

## THAILAND

## Bangkok
Kruck, Donna Jean *special education educator, consultant*

## Bangsue
Keeratiwintakorn, Phongsak Prasithsangaree *educator, consultant*

## TRINIDAD AND TOBAGO

## St Augustine
Harris, Eon Nigel *dean, rheumatologist, internist*

## ADDRESS UNPUBLISHED

Abell, Anna Ellen *primary school educator*

Abell, Dawn Gabbitas *elementary school educator, secondary school educator, school system administrator*
Abrams Finger, Iris Dale *retired elementary school educator*
Ackley, Robert Arthur *mathematics educator, retired military officer*
Adams, Leocadia Donat *secondary school educator, writer*
Adams, Peter Frederick *academic administrator, civil engineer*
Adams-Passey, Suellen S. *retired elementary school educator*
Agresto, John Thomas *former college president, education consultant*
Ahlqvist, Ola *educator*
Aiken, Michael Thomas *former academic administrator*
Aldridge, Linda Ann *retired elementary school educator, retired librarian*
Alexander, Mary Melson *secondary school educator*
Alexander, Sheila A. *education educator, nurse, researcher*
Algera, Henry F. *education educator*
Allen, Carol E. *retired elementary school educator*
Allen, Charles Eugene *university administrator, agriculturist, educator*
Allen, Charlotte *secondary school educator*
Allen, Jacquelyn May *education educator, consultant*
Allred, Dawn Peterman *adult education educator*
Almore-Randle, Allie Louise *special education educator, academic administrator*
Altman, Heidi Zimmerhanzel *educational administrator educator, educational specialist*
Amir, Koubaa *academic administrator*
Amos, Linda K. *academic administrator*
Anderson, Gregory Thomas *secondary school educator, researcher, historian*
Anderson, Joan R. *secondary school educator*
Anderson, Marilyn June *retired secondary school educator*
Anderson, Monica Luffman *school librarian, educator, real estate broker*
Anderson, Paul Wayne *assistant principal*
Anderson, Shawn Renee *director*
Anspacher, Stephen John *university official*
Appleton, Kevin *academic administrator*
Araeipour, Mohammad Reza *education educator*
Archer, Lillian Patricia *academic administrator, dean*
Armacost, Mary-Linda Sorber Merriam *retired academic administrator*
Armstrong, Jacque *pre-school educator*
Armstrong, Marian Louise *secondary school educator*
Armstrong, Marsha Susan *elementary school educator*
Armstrong-Law, Margaret *school administrator*
Arndt, Laura Bodeen *mathematics educator*
Arnett, Edward McCollin *chemistry educator, researcher*
Arnold, P. A. *special education educator*
Arp, Arlene *elementary school educator*
Ascher, William *program and policy educator*
Ashcraft, David John *secondary school music educator*
Atherton, Barbara Klein *elementary school educator*
Babbitt, Samuel Fisher *retired university official*
Bain, Linda L. *academic administrator*
Baker, Robert M.L., Jr. *academic administrator, research scientist*
Baldwin, Marie Hunsucker *retired secondary school educator*
Ball, Brenda Joyce Sivils *retired secondary school educator*
Banks, Carolyn Duty *retired history educator*
Barboro, Paul C. *elementary school educator*
Barkley, Terrell Wayne *retired school librarian, archivist, curator*
Barr, Adam *biology educator*
Barrett, Evelyn Carol *retired secondary school educator*
Bartel, Arthur Gabriel *retired principal, alderman, culinary arts instructor*
Basham, Garlyn Argabright *retired academic administrator*
Bathke, Douglas Allen *secondary school educator*
Baxter, Cecil William, Jr. *retired college president*
Beadle, Elizabeth Ahrens *retired elementary school educator*
Beamish, Mark Richard *secondary school educator*
Beard, Christina Evette *French educator*
Beatty, Marilyn Barton *special education educator*
Beck, Barbara Nell *elementary school educator*
Beck, Irene Clare *educational consultant, writer*
Becker, Allienne R. *education educator, writer*
Becker, Dorothy Loretta *education educator, librarian*
Becker, Roger *school system administrator*
Belcher, Charles William *education educator*
Bell, Loretta Mae *elementary school educator*
Benedict, Barry Arden *university administrator*
Bentley, Charmaine Clark O'Fallon *secondary school educator*
Berendes, Theresa Marie *mathematics educator*
Berge, Zane Lee *education educator, consultant*
Berger, Barbara *special education educator, educational consultant*
Bergeron, Patricia Ann *retired education educator, consultant*
Bergman, Hermas John (Jack Bergman) *retired college administrator*
Berkhoudt, Thomas Walter *director*
Bernstein, I. Melvin *dean, materials scientist*
Berra-Marfisi, Eleanore-Lucia *retired secondary school educator*
Bert, Clara Virginia *retired secondary school educator, retired school system administrator*
Berthiaume, Gayle *elementary school educator*
Bess, Robin Patrick *history educator*
Beston, Rose Marie *retired academic administrator*
Biddle, Kimberly Sue *primary school educator*
Bigelow, Sharon Lee *elementary school educator*
Bingham, Gloria Futrell *retired secondary school educator*
Birr, Cynthia Ruth *special education educator*

Bishop, Charles Edwin *academic administrator, economist, educator*
Bishop, Sue Marquis (Ina Sue Marquis Bishop) *retired dean*
Black, Recca Marcele *elementary school educator*
Blackledge, David William *retired academic administrator*
Blanco, Maria Alejandra *educational consultant, researcher*
Blood, Peggy A. *academic administrator*
Bloodworth, Gladys Leon *elementary school educator*
Boesch, Diane Harriet *retired elementary school educator*
Bogacz, Dolores Rosalie Marie *retired elementary school educator, paralegal*
Boise, Audrey Lorraine *retired special education educator*
Boltz, Carol Hofmann *retired reading specialist*
Bondi, Joseph Charles, Jr. *education educator, consultant*
BonHomme, Kevin Peter *mathematics educator*
Boothe, Leon Estel *academic administrator emeritus, consultant*
Bourque, Boyd D. *secondary school educator*
Bowen, Richard Lee *retired academic administrator, political scientist, educator*
Bowens, Gloria Furr *educational administrator*
Bowlin, Patrick W. *secondary school educator*
Bowling, John C. *academic administrator*
Boyd, Claude Collins *educational specialist, consultant*
Bradford, Marlene Kay *history educator, writer*
Brain, George Bernard *university dean*
Branch, Felecia Ann-Seldon *elementary school educator*
Brannon, Jean Estes *education educator*
Braun, Amy M. *secondary school educator*
Breeze, Philip Raley *director*
Brewer, Carey *retired academic administrator*
Brooke, Francis John III *retired academic administrator*
Brown, David Richard *school system administrator, minister*
Browning, Jennifer Anne *director*
Brownlee, Christine *elementary school educator*
Brownlee, Paula Pimlott *higher education consultant*
Bruno, Susan Elizabeth *retired secondary school educator*
Bruttomesso, Kathleen Ann *dean, nursing educator, researcher*
Bryan, Lawrence Dow *college president*
Buchanan, Carolee Horstman *special education educator, consultant*
Buckler, Marilyn Lebow *school psychologist, educational consultant*
Buford, LaVerda Jo *director*
Bullock, Mary Brown *former academic administrator*
Bullock, Molly *retired elementary school educator*
Burch-Martinez, Berkeley Alison *primary school educator*
Burke, Joseph C. *former university official*
Burns, Kathleen Adley *educational consultant*
Burrell, E. William *retired university adminstrator, educator*
Burton, Bruce Arthur *education educator*
Burton, Lavon D. *education educator*
Bush, Janice *principal*
Butler, Andrew John *education educator, researcher*
Butler, Debra Yvonne *special education educator, small business owner*
Byerly, Steven Lee *educational consultant*
Cacciatore, Sharen Wendy *educational administrator*
Cady, Michael *academic administrator*
Cafiero, Jennifer Annette *academic administrator, educator*
Cahill, Charles L. *retired academic administrator, chemistry professor*
Calkins, Diane Kay *retired elementary school educator, musician, golfer*
Callaghan, Thomas H. *secondary school educator*
Cameron, Lucille Wilson *retired dean*
Cañedo, Marion *school system administrator*
Canelli, Jeanne *early childhood educator*
Cannon, Lena Ferrara (Lee) *retired education educator*
Cardona, Julio Jose *academic administrator, researcher*
Carlin, Betty *education educator*
Carlin, John William *educator, retired governor*
Carlin, Marian P. *secondary school educator*
Carlson, M. Susan *education educator*
Carpenter, Rosalie T. *education educator, consultant*
Carter, Herbert Edmund *retired university official*
Casesa, Margret (Peggy) Muriel *special education educator*
Cassidy, Christine Cathryn *secondary school educator*
Castellanos-Brandon, Alba G. *secondary school educator*
Castiglia, Patricia Anne Thorson *dean, nursing educator*
Catlett, Terrye Denise *elementary school educator*
Chak, Ambreen Isra *secondary school educator*
Chalk, Kirsten K. *elementary school educator, music educator*
Chandler, Alice *retired academic administrator, educational consultant*
Chansley, Deborah Lynn *education educator*
Chappell, Annette M. *educational consultant, minister*
Charlton, Shirley Marie *educational consultant*
Chase, Barbara Landis *headmaster*
Chase, Francis Marvin, Sr. *education educator, consultant*
Chase, James Richard *retired college president*
Chasteen, Beverly Joan *parochial school educator, elementary school educator*
Chatelain, Dalia de la Paz *elementary school educator, educational consultant*
Cheatham, Jennifer *elementary school educator, consultant*
Chiaramonte, Christine Loren *elementary school educator*

Childers, Susan Lynn Bohn *special education educator, school system administrator, human resources and transition specialist, consultant*
Chirco, Jennifer B. *special education educator*
Choi, Kwang-Sik *adult education educator*
Christopherson, Myrvin Frederick *college president*
Churukian, George Allen *retired education educator*
Clark, James Milford *retired college president*
Clarke, Ciana Bernadine Bennett *education educator, researcher*
Clayton, Julia B. *academic administrator, musician*
Clement, Kathryn B. *secondary school educator*
Clements, Kimberly Dawne *school counselor*
Clemons, Maggie Ruth *retired elementary school educator*
Clifford, Brother Peter *academic administrator, religious studies educator*
Clougher, Jaime Louise *director*
Cochrane, Walter E. *academic administrator, conductor, music supervisor, clarinet soloist*
Cockram, Suzanne M. *elementary school educator*
Cody, Frank Joseph *education educator, educational consultant*
Coffee, Joseph Denis, Jr. *retired college chancellor*
Cohen, Gloria Ernestine *elementary school educator*
Cole, Nancy Stooksberry *educational research executive*
Coleman, Gary William *secondary school educator*
Coleman, Mary Sue *academic administrator*
Collier, Herman Edward, Jr. *retired college president*
Collins, Connie Sue *secondary school educator*
Compton, Norma Haynes *retired dean, artist*
Concialdi, Michael F. *secondary school educator, speech educator*
Congdon, Kelly Jo *mathematics educator*
Conklin, Gayle F. *retired elementary school educator*
Connell, George Edward *retired academic administrator, research scientist*
Conquest, Claire M. *secondary school counselor*
Constant, William C. *special education educator*
Cook, Edward Joseph *college president*
Cook, Sister Mary Mercedes *school system administrator, director*
Cooper, James Michael *education educator*
Cooper, Kathleen Bell *dean, former federal agency administrator*
Copeland, Bonnie S. *former school system administrator*
Copeland, Henry Jefferson, Jr. *former college president*
Copeland, Phillips Jerome *retired academic administrator, retired military officer*
Corts, Thomas Edward *academic administrator*
Cothran, Anne Jennette *academic administrator*
Cox, Lakawthra Monique *academic administrator*
Crabtree, Jacquelynn Kay *elementary school educator*
Cramer, Robert Vern *retired college administrator, consultant*
Crawford, Kenneth Charles *retired academic administrator*
Crean, Jason James *biology educator, consultant*
Crehan, Jacquelyn R. *retired dean*
Cronholm, Lois S. *academic administrator*
Cronin, Thomas Edward *former academic administrator*
Cross, Kathryn Patricia *education educator*
Crotts, Carolyn Pearl *school librarian*
Crum, Karen Sanzo *principal, educator*
Cruz-Connerton, Mayra *elementary school educator*
Csaky, Pamela E. *secondary school educator, department chairman*
Cuevas, Kimberly Lynette *secondary school educator*
Culver, Mona Capricia *retired elementary school educator*
Cummings, Patricia Ann *elementary school educator*
Cunningham, Lynne Anne *elementary school educator*
Cupolo, Nancy *education educator, department chairman*
Curnyn, Kathleen Marie *elementary school educator*
Dady, Nadege J. *director*
Daniels, Edgar Roth *education educator, consultant*
Daniels, Mary P. *academic administrator, technologist*
Darden, Lauretta *elementary school educator*
Davenport, Lawrence Franklin *academic administrator*
Dávila, Rafael Angel III *college counselor, educator*
Davion, Ethel Johnson *school system superintendent, curriculum specialist*
Davis, Anna Jane Ripley *elementary school educator*
Davis, Cheryl K. *dean*
Davis, Hiram Joe *public school administrator*
Davis, Jessica Hoffmann *education educator, researcher*
Davis, Joseph Lloyd *academic administrator, consultant*
Davison, Helen Irene *secondary school educator, counseling administrator*
Daw, Lenore Estella *elementary school educator, librarian*
Day, Brian Andrew *history educator*
Dean, Denise Jane *elementary school educator*
Debroux, Douglas P. *secondary school educator*
DeJarnatt, Kitty M. *special education educator*
Delahanty, Rebecca Ann *school system administrator*
Derrick, Kathryn Thill *secondary school educator*
Detwiler, Christina LeFevre *elementary school educator*
Diamond, Richard *retired educator*
Diamond, Robert Mach *higher education administrator*
Dias, D. Stephen *secondary school educator*
Dickey, Linda Ann *learning center director*
Dillard, Teresa Mary *school counselor*

DiPrima, Anne *elementary school educator*
DiSanto, Lucille M. *special education educator, educator*
Dispenza, Mary Catherine *director, educator, photographer*
Diviney, Nancy Lynn *elementary school educator*
dKepner, Raechel L. *academic administrator*
Dobelle, Evan Samuel *academic administrator*
Dobson, Dorothy Lynn Watts *retired elementary school educator*
Dockery, J. Lee *retired medical school administrator*
Donahoo, Saran *education educator*
Donaldson, Wilma Crankshaw *elementary school educator*
Donegan, Darlene Chavon *history educator*
Donoff, R. Bruce *dean, oral surgeon, dental educator*
Doody, William E. *secondary school educator*
Dorr, Aimee *dean, education educator*
Dorsey, John Kevin *dean*
Doviak, Ingrid Ellinger *elementary school educator*
Drake, Evelyn Downie *retired secondary school educator*
Drake, George Albert *retired academic administrator, retired historian, educator*
Dresbach, Mary Louise *state educational administrator*
Drum, Alice *academic administrator, educator*
Dryfoos, Walter Gallatin *academic administrator*
DuBose, Mike Stanley *ethnic studies educator, literature and language professor*
Duderstadt, James Johnson *academic administrator, engineering educator*
Duffy, Ann Patricia *elementary school educator*
Duffy, John Joseph *retired academic administrator, historian, educator*
Dumas, Rhetaugh Etheldra Graves *retired university official*
Duminuco, Vincent Joseph *academic administrator, educator*
Duncan, Kevin A. *history educator*
Duncan, Robert Bannerman *dean, strategy and organizations educator*
Dunn, Helen Elizabeth *retired secondary school educator*
Duplessis, Audrey Joseph *school system administrator*
Dutson, Thayne R. *dean*
Dwinell, Ann Jones *retired special education educator*
Dycus, Elizabeth Rasmussen *academic administrator*
Dzombak, Agnes Marie (Jo) *secondary school educator*
Earenfight, Theresa Marie *education educator*
Eddy, Kelly J. *history educator*
Edelman, Norman Herman *dean, medical educator, academic administrator*
Edmundson, Lorna Duphiney *academic administrator*
Edwards, Ardis Lavonne Quam *retired elementary education educator*
Edwards, Mark U., Jr. *academic administrator, history professor, writer*
Edwards, Robert Hazard *retired college president*
Edwards-Mitchum, Lillian (Red the Poet) *secondary school educator, writer*
Einoder, Camille Elizabeth *retired secondary school educator*
Eliot, Charles William John *former university president*
Elliott, Tommy *secondary school educator*
Elrod, Deborah Lee *special education educator*
Elzay, Richard Paul *retired dean, dental educator, department chairman*
Epp, Dianne Naomi *secondary school educator*
Eppolito, Mary *assistant principal, educator*
Erickson, Michae Ross *history educator*
Ervin-Carr, Charlesetta Yvonne *secondary school educator*
Espiricueta, Sylvia *counseling administrator*
Evans, Bonita Dianne *education educator*
Evans, Geraldine Ann *academic administrator*
Evans, James Handel *academic administrator, architect*
Evans, Margaret Utz *secondary school educator*
Evans, Richard Austin *education educator, consultant*
Ewald, Laura Anne *school librarian*
Fair, Jean Everhard *retired education educator*
Farquhar, Robin Hugh *educational consultant, former university president*
Farrington, Gregory C. *retired academic administrator*
Faust, Vickie Lynn *secondary school educator*
Fearon, Charlene O'Brien *special education educator*
Felicetti, Daniel A. *academic administrator*
Felix, Arthur Martin *chemistry educator, researcher*
Felton, Helen Martin *retired adult education educator, writer*
Fenske, Marisa Lynn *elementary school educator*
Fergusson, Dianne Smith *retired secondary school educator*
Fergusson, Frances Daly *former academic administrator*
Fernández-Velazquez, Juan Ramon *university chancellor*
Ferrick, Kathleen Ann *elementary school educator, minister*
Feuer-Stern, Barbie Shnider *elementary school educator, secondary school educator*
Fields, Gail Baker *education educator*
Fife, Jonathan Donald *education educator*
Filchock, Ethel *education educator*
Finale, Frank L. *retired elementary school educator, writer*
Finckenauer, James O. *criminal justice educator, researcher*
Fink, Holly Berman *elementary school educator*
Fishburn, Janet Forsythe *dean*
Fleetwood, Mary Annis *education association executive*
Fletcher, Brady Jones *vocational education career specialist*
Fleury, Paul Aimé *dean, physicist*
Foesch, Kimberli Ann *elementary school educator*

Manuel, Ralph Nixon *retired private school executive*
Mapes, Kimberly R. *biology educator*
Marier, Robert L. *dean, hospital administrator*
Marshak, Robert Reuben *retired dean, medical educator, veterinarian*
Martin, David Jerner *education educator*
Martinez-Maldonado, Manuel *academic administrator, dean, medical educator, physiology educator*
Mason, Deirdre Dianne *secondary school educator*
Massey, Thomas Benjamin *retired university president*
Matasar, Ann B. *retired dean, finance educator*
Matera, Frances Lorine *elementary school educator*
Matsen, John Martin *academic administrator, pathologist*
Matsuda, Fujio *retired academic administrator*
Mattice, Howard LeRoy *education educator*
Mattoon, Scott Alexander *private school educator*
Maxey, Betty Jim *elementary school educator*
May, Ingrid Barbara *elementary school educator*
Mayer, Robert Anthony *retired college president*
Mayfield, Robert Charles *academic administrator, geographer, educator*
McAleese Dube, Eileen Marie *retired secondary school educator*
McBride, Mildred Maylea *retired elementary school educator*
McCann, Diana Rae *secondary school educator*
McClean, Lenora James *nursing educator, dean*
McCosham, Joyce L. *secondary school educator*
McCoy, Mary Jane *retired principal*
McDaniel, Sara Sherwood (Sally McDaniel) *trainer, consultant*
McDonough, Patrick Dennis *academic administrator*
McDowell, Laura Oneita *secondary school educator*
McGee, Harold Johnston *former academic administrator*
McGinn, Kathleen M. *mathematics educator*
McGowan, Susan *gifted and talented educator*
McGuinn, Brenda Beck *mathematics educator*
McHoes, Ann McIver *academic administrator, computer engineer*
McIntyre, Virgie M. *elementary school educator*
McKinney, Kay Griffin *elementary school educator*
McMains, Donald Paul *education educator*
McMillan, Jenny Hill *elementary school educator*
McNamara, Brenda Norma *retired secondary school educator*
Mecham, Steven Ray *school system administrator*
Medley, Donald Matthias *retired education educator*
Meek, Linda Duke (Linda Bullion Meek) *elementary school educator, writer*
Megginson, Laura Irene *secondary school educator*
Megna, Steve Allan *retired secondary school educator*
Melton, Emma Alexander *educational consultant, retired elementary school educator*
Meltzer, E. Alyne *elementary school educator, social worker, volunteer*
Mendon, Karen Jeanette *elementary school educator*
Mendonca, Wayne D. *history educator*
Mendoza, Karen Lynn *special education educator*
Menges, Martha *special education educator*
Merriweather, Freda E. *education educator*
Meskill, Victor P. *academic administrator, educator*
Messer, Donald Edward *academic administrator, theology studies educator*
Metzler, Ruth Horton *genealogical educator*
Meyer, Frances Margaret Anthony *educational consultant*
Michael, Robert *history educator*
Miller, Arjay *retired university dean*
Miller, Jerry Huber *retired university chancellor*
Miller, Linda Karen *retired secondary school educator, social studies educator, law educator*
Miller, Roberta Doris *elementary school educator*
Mills, Eugene Sumner *academic administrator*
Mills, Helene Audrey *retired academic administrator*
Mills, Robert Lee *retired academic administrator*
Minkoff, Hilda Bressler *secondary and adult education educator*
Mirk, Judy Ann *retired elementary school educator*
Misage, Mark Alan *physics educator*
Molini, Barbara Symonds *retired elementary school educator*
Moll, Maryann Elizabeth *education educator*
Moneskey, Tabitha Jean *assistant principal*
Monson, David Carl *school system administrator, state legislator, farmer*
Montague, Rae-Anne *assistant dean*
Monteith, Larry King *chancellor emeritus*
Moon, David Turner, Jr. *history educator, researcher*
Mooney, Michael Joseph *university professor*
Mooney, Thomas T. *history educator, geography educator*
Moore, Donald Walter *retired academic administrator*
Moore, Juel Ann *retired secondary school educator*
Moore, Marsha Lynn *retired elementary school educator, counseling administrator*
Moore, Thomas David *academic administrator*
Moorhead, Nancy B. *elementary school educator*
Moran, Thomas Harry *retired academic administrator*
Moran, Wendi K *biology educator*
Morgan, Arlene Notoro *university administrator*
Morgan, Mary Lou *retired education educator, volunteer*
Morgan, Ruth Prouse *academic administrator, educator*
Morley, James Everitt, Jr., (Jay Morley Jr.) *retired academic administrator, former educational association administrator*
Morrison, Michael Gordon *academic administrator, clergyman, history professor*
Mouttet, Jane Elizabeth *school librarian, educator*
Mshana, Pamela Mariva *secondary school educator*

Muhlestein, Kerry *educator*
Murphy, Thelma Arabella *elementary school educator, photographer*
Musa, Samuel Albert *university executive*
Musselwhite, Beneta Jo *mathematics educator*
Nadelman, Martin Hershel *college president*
Nalty, Keisha Janice *secondary school educator*
Nance, Mary Joe *retired secondary school educator*
Neal, Dennis Melton *elementary school educator*
Neftci, Salih Nur *educator, writer*
Neilon, Patrick Daniel *special education educator*
Nelson, Carol Evelyn *retired pre-school educator*
Nelson, JoAnn *secondary school educator, educational consultant*
Nereng, Linda Rae *elementary school educator*
Neunzig, Carolyn Miller *elementary, middle and high school educator*
Nevin, Ann Irene *education educator*
New, Rosetta Holbrock *retired secondary school educator, retired department chairman, retired nutrition consultant*
Ngu, Anne HeeHiong *education educator, researcher*
Nichols, Waunell B. *elementary school educator*
Nieh, Jason *educator*
Niemiec, Margaret G. *elementary school educator*
Nixon, Sandra L. *retired registrar*
Noble, John Henry, Jr. *education educator, researcher*
Noblin, Elizabeth *elementary school educator*
Noddings, Nel *education educator, writer*
Noel, Amy Sue *elementary school educator*
Noffsinger, Nancy Leigh *special education educator*
Nohr, Barbara J. *secondary school educator*
North, Ann R. *secondary school educator*
Nye, Linda Purcell *secondary school educator*
Ochoa, Vanessa Jeanette *academic administrator*
O'Connell, William Raymond, Jr. *educational consultant, retired academic administrator*
Oden, Jean P(hifer) *special education educator*
Odhiambo, Eucabeth A. *education educator*
Offen, Ronald Charles *retired school librarian*
Ofstad, Evelyn Larsen Boyl *retired primary school educator, radio personality, film producer*
Oglesby, Elaine Sue *elementary school educator*
O'Hara, Sabine U. *academic administrator, dean, economist, educator*
Ordonez, Christina Elizabeth *secondary school educator*
Orr, Kenneth Bradley *academic administrator*
Osborn, Donna Marie *secondary school educator, mathematician*
Osborne, John L. *academic administrator, educator*
Oskin, JoEllen Ross *special education educator, school librarian*
Owen, Claudia J. *academic administrator*
Owens, Sue Gaston *retired middle school educator*
Owens, Vicki Palmer *elementary school educator, academic coordinator*
Ozkan, Betul C *education educator*
Pacheco, Manuel Trinidad *retired academic administrator*
Page, Barbara Rose *primary school educator*
Painter, Borden W. *former academic administrator*
Palmer, Irene Sabelberg *retired dean, retired nursing educator, genealogist*
Palmer, Paul Richard *school librarian, archivist, curator*
Pandel, Robin McEwan *elementary school educator*
Paolozzi, Jennifer *elementary school educator*
Park, John Thornton *retired academic administrator*
Park, Penny Sheran *retired elementary school educator*
Parker, Barbara Anne *education educator, social studies educator*
Parker, George Ernest *mathematics educator*
Parsons, Alexandra Clare *literature and language educator*
Patmos, Adrian Edward *retired dean*
Patrick, Brenda Jean *educational consultant*
Patterson, Collis Delano *secondary school educator*
Patterson, Howard Yates *academic athletics administrator*
Patterson, Marlene (None) *secondary school educator*
Pattillo, Manning Mason, Jr. *academic administrator*
Paulsen, Frank Robert *college dean emeritus*
Payne, Ladell *retired academic administrator*
Pearsall, Gloria W. *retired elementary school educator*
Pease-Pretty On Top, Janine B. *community college administrator*
Pederson, Donald Otis *academic administrator, physicist, educator*
Peduzzi, Claudia Claire *elementary school educator*
Penney, Nancy Sanford *retired special education educator*
Peoples, John Arthur, Jr. *former university president, consultant*
Perger, Donna Spagnoli *retired secondary school mathematics educator*
Perkins, Edward A., Jr. *elementary school educator*
Perry, Jean *elementary school educator*
Perry, Joyce Fitzwilliam *secondary school educator*
Perz, Erva Kay *retired elementary school educator*
Pescatore-Shirey, Hope Jean *middle school reading educator*
Peterson, Walter Fritiof *retired academic administrator*
Pettigrew, L. Eudora *retired academic administrator*
Pewitt, James Dudley *academic administrator*
Phillips, Richard A. *English educator*
Phillips, Tikera Monique *elementary school educator*
Phipard, Nancy Midwood *retired special education educator, poet*
Pierce, Susan Resneck *academic administrator, literature educator, consultant*
Pinto, Rosalind *retired secondary school educator, volunteer*

Pitta, Janine Rose *elementary school educator*
Pizzuro, Salvatore Nicholas *special education educator*
Plants, Walter Dale *retired elementary school educator, minister*
Platis, James George *secondary school educator*
Podeschi, Amanda Landacre *director, educator*
Pointer, Michelle Phillips *counselor, educator, consultant*
Polimeni, Rebecca H. *special education educator*
Pollack, Marsha *secondary school educator*
Ponitz, David H. *former academic administrator*
Porreca, Anne Agnes *secondary school educator, counseling administrator*
Post, Kelly Marie *elementary school educator*
Powell, Dava Annette *computer educator, grant writer*
Power, Carolyn Porter *elementary school educator, principal*
Prieto, Claudio R. *academic administrator, lawyer*
Prins, Robert Jack *retired academic administrator*
Pritchard, Claudius Hornby, Jr. *retired university president*
Prokasy, William Frederick *academic administrator*
Propst, Harold Dean *retired academic administrator*
Pruitt, Anne Loring *academic administrator, education educator*
Pryor, Harold S. *retired college president*
Pulhamus, Marlene Louise *retired elementary school educator*
Purvis, Gail *elementary school educator*
Puryear, James Burton *college administrator*
Puzzo, Joseph Anthony, Jr. *middle school educator*
Rabideau, Marilyn Ann *elementary school educator*
Raborn, Marcia MacArthur *primary school educator*
Rada, Ruth Byers *retired dean*
Ragone, David Vincent *former university president*
Rambo, Domingo H. *elementary school educator*
Ramirez, Evangeline Rose *elementary school educator*
Ramirez, Maria Eugenia *primary school educator*
Raspberry, Brenda *pre-school educator*
Ray, Susan Elaine *principal*
Reams, Patricia Lynn *retired elementary school educator*
Redmont, Bernard Sidney *dean, communications educator*
Reese, Angela Brooke *elementary school educator*
Reeves, Lucy Mary *retired elementary school educator*
Regel, Teresa Diamond *elementary school educator*
Rehnke, Mary Ann *academic administrator*
Reid, Helen Veronica *dean*
Reinalda, David Anthony *elementary school educator*
Reinhard, Diane L. *retired university president*
Reinke, Ralph Louis *retired academic administrator*
Rent, Clyda Stokes *academic administrator*
Resing, Maryloretto Rachel *guidance counseling administrator, elementary school educator, pastoral counselor*
Ressom, Habtom W *education educator*
Reynolds, Karen Ann *retired elementary school educator*
Reynolds, Peggy Jean *elementary school educator*
Reynolds, Wynetka Ann *academic administrator, educator*
Rice, Dale R. *education educator*
Rice, Gary Russell *retired special education educator*
Rice, Jerry Allen *educational consultant*
Rice, Patricia Oppenheim Levin *special education educator, consultant*
Richards, Patty *secondary school educator*
Richardson, Kelly Christopher *literature and language educator, writer*
Ricketson, Mary E. *dean, lawyer*
Ridge, Davy-Jo Stribling *school librarian*
Ridout, Susan Ramp *education educator*
Rief, Michelle M. *cultural studies educator*
Rivers, Nancy Lee *retired elementary school educator*
Roaden, Arliss Lloyd *retired academic administrator*
Roark, Ian R. *school system administrator*
Rob, Mohammad Abdur *education educator, researcher*
Roberts, Judith Ann *secondary school educator*
Roberts, Kathleen Mary *retired school system administrator*
Roberts, Margaret A. *elementary school educator*
Roberts, Patricia Lee *education educator*
Roberts, Roxann Mae *secondary school educator*
Robertson, Thomas Sinclair *academic administrator*
Robertson, Wyndham Gay *university official, journalist*
Robinson, James Alfred *middle school educator*
Robinson, Nancy Nowakowski *academic administrator*
Robles, Rosalie Miranda *elementary school educator*
Rochelle, Lugenia *academic administrator*
Rochon, Thomas Richard *academic administrator*
Rodgers, Lois Eve *secondary school educator*
Rogers, Dorothea May *education educator*
Rogers, Paula McGivern *secondary school educator*
Rogers, Steffen H. *retired academic administrator*
Rojas, Victor Hugo Macedo *retired vocational education educator*
Roller, Pamela Jo *elementary school educator*
Roosevelt, Mary Winskill *elementary school educator*
Rosenberg, Raymond David *special education educator, consultant*
Rosenblum, Estelle H. *retired dean, nursing educator*
Rossen-Knill, Deborah F. *academic administrator, language educator*
Roumbos, Maria K. *elementary school educator*
Rowell, Barbara Caballero *retired academic administrator*
Rozario Stewart, Gwendolyn Michelle *elementary school educator*

Rubin, Ellen *educational coordinator*
Ruffin, David Aliston *secondary school educator, entertainer*
Rufus, Nancy G. *secondary school educator*
Rusie, Ruth Louise *special education educator*
Russell, Attie Yvonne *academic administrator, pediatrics educator, dean*
Rutgard, Lorraine Levin *hearing impaired educator*
Ryan, Daniel John *university administrator*
Sabbath, Joseph Waters *academic administrator*
Sachatello-Sawyer, Bonnie Lynn *education educator, director*
Saenz, Cecilia Sonia *education educator*
Salamon, Rick *secondary school educator, department chairman*
Salisbury, Micheal Wayne *education educator*
Samblis, Kelley C. *educator, researcher*
Samec, Diane Patricia *retired elementary school educator*
Sampson, Clinton J. *director*
Sandstead, Auriel J. *retired secondary school educator, researcher, historian*
Santangelo, Gaspare Charles *education educator, retired principal*
Santora, Ellen Durrigan *education educator*
Santos, Nicole Marie *elementary school educator*
Saul, Mark E. *secondary school educator, consultant*
Saunders, Stacy Dawn *secondary school educator, music educator, singer*
Sava, Vasyl *education educator*
Savage, Kim I. *academic administrator*
Savercool, Susan Elisabeth *elementary school educator*
Sayre, Donna *elementary school educator*
Scales, Mauriceo Lamont *history educator*
Scandary, E. Jane *special education educator, consultant*
Scarborough, Ann Barlow *secondary school educator*
Schall, Debra Jean *secondary school educator*
Schiller, Robert E. *former school system administrator*
Schillings, Karen Marie *elementary school educator*
Schlegel, John P. *academic administrator*
Schmidt, Ruth Ann *retired academic administrator*
Schneider, Carolyn Alice Brauch *elementary school educator*
Schneider, Mary Louise *retired elementary school educator*
Schofield, Barbara Curtright *retired principal*
Schowalter, William Raymond *college dean, educator*
Schrage, Rose *retired academic administrator*
Schumacher, Cynthia Jo *retired elementary and secondary education educator*
Schure, Alexander *university chancellor*
Schuster, Carol Joyce *special education educator, consultant*
Schwalbe, Lowell D *secondary school educator*
Schwartz, Eleanor Brantley *academic administrator*
Scott, Gloria Randle *former college president*
Seo, Byung-In *literature and language educator*
Sestini, Virgil Andrew *retired biology educator*
Shaffer, Shirley Pollack *secondary school educator, sales executive*
Shapiro, Dianna J. *school librarian*
Shapiro, Rose *elementary school educator*
Shavender, Marilyn Faye *retired elementary school educator*
Shaw, Talbert O. *university president*
Sheldon, Thomas Donald *academic administrator*
Shellman-Lucas, Elizabeth C. *special education educator, researcher*
Shepard, Anna Richardson *elementary school educator*
Shepard, Christy J. *special education educator*
Sherrer, Charles David *dean, clergyman*
Sherrick, Rebecca Louise *academic administrator*
Shields, Cynthia Rose *college administrator*
Shore, Eleanor Gossard *retired medical school dean*
Shoun, Ellen Llewellyn *retired secondary school educator*
Shugart, Jill *academic administrator*
Shultz, Stephen A. *secondary school educator*
Shutler, Mary Elizabeth *academic administrator*
Sibo, Elsa Lynette *secondary school educator*
Sibuma, Bernadette *educational consultant*
Sicuro, Natale Anthony *academic and financial administrator, consultant*
Siddeeq, Baiyinah Nawal Rubye *secondary school educator*
Siebe, Carol Ann *retired elementary school educator*
Sikorski, Lorena L. *secondary school educator*
Silianoff, David *secondary school educator, educator, mathematics educator*
Silverman, Matthew Adam *school system administrator*
Simmons, Lynda Merrill Mills *retired principal*
Simons, Lynn Osborn *educational consultant*
Simonsen, Lorence B. *director*
Singleton, Robert Culton *academic administrator, theology studies educator*
Skaggs, Bebe Rebecca Patten *college dean, clergywoman*
Slezak, Erin Kathleen *elementary school educator*
Smith, Alice Davis *retired biology educator, retired art educator*
Smith, Cathy Gaye *elementary school educator*
Smith, Michelle Rene *elementary school educator*
Smith, Mieko Kotake *education educator*
Smith, Patricia (Pat) Ann *elementary school educator*
Smith, Susanna S. *school system administrator*
Smith, Sydney *elementary school educator*
Snelling, Robert Orren, Sr. *employment executive*
Soliday, Michael David *secondary school and special educator*
Solmssen, Peter *retired academic administrator*
Sonnek, Karla Jean *secondary school educator*
Sonnenschein, Hugo Freund *academic administrator, writer, economist, educator*
Sorber, Charles Arthur *academic administrator*
Spencer, Lisa Ann *special education educator*
Spencer, Rex LeRoy *retired secondary school educator*

# ENGINEERING

## UNITED STATES

Slack, Donald Carl *agricultural engineer, educator*
Smerdon, Ernest Thomas *engineering educator*
Venkata, Subrahmanyam Saraswati *engineering educator, researcher*
Wyant, James Clair *engineering company executive, educator*

**Williams**
Erickson, Edward Grant *electrical engineer*

## ARKANSAS

**Conway**
Peeples, James Thomas *computer engineer, musician*

**Fayetteville**
Andrews, John Frank *retired civil and environmental engineering educator*
Gaddy, James Leoma *chemical engineer, educator*
White, John Austin, Jr. *engineering educator, academic administrator*

**Fort Smith**
Timmons, William Todd *chemical engineer, educator*

## CALIFORNIA

**Aliso Viejo**
Boeckmann, Alan L. *engineering company executive, construction management company executive*

**Alpine**
Roberts, Dwight Loren *engineering consultant, writer*

**Altadena**
Coles, Donald Earl *retired engineering educator*

**Anaheim**
McNulty, James Francis *engineering executive*
Watson, Oliver Lee III *aerospace engineer, manufacturing executive*

**Atherton**
Lowry, Larry *engineering company executive*

**Berkeley**
Bajcsy, Ruzena *computer engineer*
Bea, Robert G. *civil engineering educator*
Birdsall, Charles Kennedy *electrical engineer*
Bogy, David B(eauregard) *mechanical engineering educator*
Cairns, Elton James *chemical engineering professor*
Derenzo, Stephen E. *electrical engineering and computer science educator, researcher*
Dornfeld, David Alan *engineering educator*
Fenves, Gregory L. *engineering educator*
Frisch, Joseph *mechanical engineer, educator, consultant*
Fuerstenau, Douglas Winston *mineral engineering educator*
Garrison, William Louis *civil engineering educator*
Hsu, Chieh Su *applied mechanics engineering educator, researcher*
Hu, Chenming *electrical engineering educator*
Kastenberg, William Edward *engineering educator, science educator*
Kuh, Ernest Shiu-Jen *electrical engineering educator*
Leitmann, George *mechanical engineer, educator*
Lewis, Edwin Reynolds *biomedical engineering educator, academic administrator*
Liepmann, Dorian *engineering educator*
Monismith, Carl Leroy *civil engineering educator*
Muller, Richard Stephen *electrical engineer, educator*
Newton, Arthur Richard (Richard Newton, A. Richard Newton) *engineering educator*
Ott, David Michael *engineering company executive*
Pagni, Patrick John *mechanical engineering science educator, safety engineer, researcher*
Penzien, Joseph *structural engineering educator*
Pigford, Thomas Harrington *nuclear engineering educator*
Pister, Karl Stark *engineering educator*
Polak, Elijah *engineering educator, computer scientist*
Prausnitz, John Michael *chemical engineer, educator*
Sastry, Sosale Shankara *electrical engineer, computer scientist, educator*
Schultz, E. Eugene, Jr. *computer engineer*
Varaiya, Pravin P. *electrical engineer*
Wiegel, Robert Louis *consulting engineering executive*
Wright, Paul Kenneth *mechanical engineering educator*
Yeung, Ronald Wai-Chun *engineering educator, researcher*

**Berry Creek**
Miller, Joseph Arthur *manufacturing engineer, consultant, educator*

**Bishop**
Archer, James Orville *retired aeronautical engineer*

**Boonville**
Hanes, John Ward *civil engineer, sculptor, rancher, director*

**Brea**
Brown, Ronald Malcolm *engineering corporation executive*

**Buellton**
Porter, Bruce Jackman *computer engineer, application developer, portfolio manager, civil engineer*

**Burbank**
Tourapis, Alexandros *signal processing engineer, researcher*

**Campbell**
Ross, Hugh Courtney *electrical engineer*

**Canoga Park**
Hajela, Gyaneshwar P. *systems engineer, educator*

**Carmel**
Alsberg, Dietrich Anselm *electrical engineer, consultant*
Youngdahl, Paul Frederick *mechanical engineer*

**Carson**
Mende, Howard Shigeharu *mechanical engineer*

**Chatsworth**
Gunn, Stanley Veerin *retired engineer*

**Chico**
Allen, Charles William *mechanical engineer, educator*

**Claremont**
Dym, Clive Lionel *engineering educator*
Kucij, Timothy Michael *engineer, minister, musician*
Molinder, John Irving *engineering educator, consultant*
Monson, James Edward *electrical engineer, educator*
Tanenbaum, Basil Samuel *engineering educator*

**Clovis**
Brahma, Chandra Sekhar *civil engineering educator*

**Concord**
Crandall, Ira Carlton *electrical engineer, consultant*

**Costa Mesa**
Brady, John Patrick, Jr. *electronics educator, consultant*
Sharpe, Constantine *engineer, consultant, mathematics professor*

**Coto De Caza**
Sheehy, Jerome Joseph *electrical engineer*

**Covina**
Paulson, Raymond Arnold *engineering executive*

**Culver City**
Mann, Michael Martin *engineering executive*

**Cupertino**
Edson, William Alden *retired engineering educator, researcher*
Haskell, Barry Geoffry *computer engineer, researcher*

**Davis**
Al-Asaad, Hussain *electrical engineer, educator*
Barakat, Abdul I. *engineering educator*
Bombardelli, Fabián Alejandro *hydraulic engineer, researcher*
Chancellor, William Joseph *agricultural engineering educator*
Cheney, James Addison *civil engineering educator*
Gates, Bruce Clark *chemical engineer, educator*
Marino, Miguel Angel *engineering educator*
Pan, Ning *engineering educator*
Wang, Shih-Ho *electrical engineer, educator*

**Del Mar**
Wilkinson, Eugene Parks *nuclear engineer, director*

**Dinuba**
Leps, Thomas MacMaster *civil engineer, consultant*

**Downey**
Baumann, Theodore Robert *aerospace engineer, consultant, military officer*

**El Cajon**
Summers, Stanley Eugene *mechanical engineer*

**El Segundo**
Abbassian-Kashi, Mandana *industrial engineer, systems engineer*
Brekke, John Peters *aerospace engineer*
Daughaday, Douglas Robert *computer engineer*
Oei, Lok S. *digital communications systems and DSP engineer, researcher*
Webb, Darryl Willard *systems engineer*

**Emerald Hills**
Chao, Kwang-Chu *chemical engineer, educator*

**Emeryville**
Zwoyer, Eugene Milton *retired consulting engineering executive*

**Encinitas**
Kim, Kyehee *environmental engineer, consultant*

**Encino**
Friedman, George Jerry *aerospace engineer, engineering executive*
Knuth, Eldon Luverne *engineering educator*

**Escondido**
Kennedy, Robert Philip *civil engineer*

**Fallbrook**
Harsha, Philip Thomas *retired aerospace engineer*

**Folsom**
Ryu, Woong Hwan *electrical engineer*

**Fremont**
Chen, Wai-Kai *electrical engineering and computer science educator, consultant*
Duan, Xiaodong *engineer*

Henry, Leo G. *engineer, consultant*
Le, Thuy Trong *nuclear engineer, educator*
Wu, James Chen-Yuan *aerospace engineering educator*

**Fullerton**
Chaudhry, Maqsood Ahmed *electrical engineer, educator*
Rubin, Arthur Leonard *systems engineer, mathematician*

**Glendale**
Dallas, Saterios (Sam Dallas) *aerospace engineer, researcher, consultant*

**Glendora**
Haile, Benjamin Carroll, Jr. *retired chemical engineer, retired mechanical engineer*

**Goleta**
Sensiper, Samuel *electrical engineer*

**Hacienda Heights**
Love, Daniel Joseph *consulting engineer*

**Hayward**
Kimbell, Marion Joel *retired engineer*

**Hollywood**
Nalbandyan, Ashot *engineer*

**Huntington Beach**
Grooms, Henry Randall *civil engineer*
Leveton, Ian Sinclair *civil engineer*
Nguyen, Han Van *mechanical engineer*

**Indian Wells**
Jorgensen, Gordon David *retired engineering company executive*

**Irvine**
Alexopoulos, Nicolaos George *electrical engineering educator*
Ang, Alfredo Hua-Sing *civil engineering educator*
Chelapati, Chunduri Venkata *civil engineering educator*
Kazemitabar Amirkolaie, Seyed Javad *engineer, researcher*
Samueli, Henry *electrical engineer, educator, entrepreneur*
Schoendorfer, Donald W. *engineer*
Sirignano, William Alfonso *aerospace and mechanical engineer, educator*
Sklansky, Jack *electrical and computer engineering educator, researcher*
Stubberud, Allen Roger *electrical engineering educator*
Ting, Albert Chia *biomedical engineer, researcher*

**Kensington**
Oppenheim, Antoni Kazimierz *mechanical engineer*

**La Canada Flintridge**
Macmillan, Robert Smith *electronics engineer*

**La Jolla**
Asaro, Robert J. *engineering educator*
Chang, William Shen Chie *electrical engineering educator*
Chien, Shu *physiology and bioengineering educator*
Fung, Yuan-Cheng Bertram *bioengineering educator, writer*
Karbhari, Vistasp M. *engineering educator, researcher*
Karin, Sidney *computer science engineering educator*
Levy, Ralph *engineering executive, consultant*
Milstein, Laurence Bennett *electrical engineering educator, researcher*
Nahavandi, Amir Nezameddin *retired engineering firm executive*
Najmabadi, Farrokh *engineering educator*
Nemat-Nasser, Sia *engineering educator, researcher*
Rudee, Mervyn Lea *engineering educator, researcher*
Saldivar, Enrique *bioengineer, researcher*
Schmid-Schoenbein, Geert Wilfried *biomedical engineer, educator, researcher*
Seible, Frieder *structural engineer, educator*
Telengator, Alexander M. *engineer*
Zhongren, Cao *electrical engineer, researcher*

**La Verne**
Lou, Yiming *chemical engineer*

**Lafayette**
Krueger, Robert Edward *mechanical engineer, manufacturing executive*

**Laguna Hills**
Hammond, R. Philip *chemical engineer*

**Lake Forest**
Fahim, Amr *electrical engineer*
Schroeder, John A. *systems engineering consultant, educator*

**Lancaster**
Hodges, Vernon Wray *mechanical engineer*

**Livermore**
Banerjee, Souvik *process engineer, researcher*
Goodwin, Bruce T. *engineer*
Johnson, Roy Ragnar *electrical engineer, researcher*
King, Ray John *electrical engineering educator, engineering company executive*
Reyes, Susana *nuclear engineer*

**Lomita**
Balcom, Orville *engineer*

**Lompoc**
Means, James Andrew *engineer*

**Long Beach**
Davis, Mark Hezekiah, Jr. *electrical engineer*

de Soto, Simon *mechanical engineer*
Dillon, Michael Earl *engineering executive, mechanical engineer, educator*
Kumar, Rajendra *electrical engineering educator*
Wagdy, Mahmoud Fawzy *engineering educator*

**Los Alamitos**
Eckelman, Richard Joel *engineering specialist*

**Los Altos**
Gough, William Cabot *engineer*
Peterson, Victor Lowell *aerospace engineer, consultant*
Sharpe, Roland Leonard *structural engineer, consultant*

**Los Altos Hills**
Fondahl, John Walker *civil engineering educator*

**Los Angeles**
Buffington, Gary Lee Roy *safety engineer, construction executive*
Chang, Jane P. *chemical engineering educator*
Chen, Francis F. *physics and engineering educator*
Cheng, Tsen-Chung *electrical engineering educator*
Chew, Elaine *engineering educator, musician*
Chobotov, Vladimir Alexander *aerospace engineer, educator*
Crombie, Douglass Darnill *aerospace communications system engineer*
Danziger, Bruce Edward *structural engineer*
Dhir, Vijay K. *mechanical engineering educator*
Didkovsky, Leonid V *engineer*
Dorman, Albert A. *engineering executive, consultant, architect*
Dragan, Alexandra *mechanical engineer, consultant, environmental engineer, researcher, engineering educator*
Friedlander, Sheldon Kay *chemical engineering professor*
Geller, Michael D. *engineering educator*
Hashemi, Hossein *engineering educator*
Hovanessian, Shahen Alexander *electrical engineer, educator, consultant*
Itoh, Tatsuo *engineering educator*
Jacobson, Marcus J. *retired mechanical engineer*
Ju, Jiann-Wen *mechanics educator, researcher*
Kelly, Robert Edward *engineer, educator*
King-Ning, Tu *materials science and engineering educator*
Kuehl, Hans Henry *electrical engineering educator*
Madni, Asad Mohamed *engineering executive*
Marmarelis, Vasilis Zissis *engineering educator, writer, consultant*
Martin, J(ohn) Edward *architectural engineer*
Mataric, Maja J. *engineering educator*
Maxworthy, Tony *mechanical and aerospace engineering educator*
Mendel, Jerry Marc *electrical engineering educator*
Min, Taegee *aerospace engineer, researcher, mechanical engineer*
Muntz, Eric Phillip *aerospace and mechanical engineering educator, consultant*
Newman, Richard G. *engineering company executive*
Nikias, Chrysostomos L. (Max Nikias) *engineering educator*
Nobe, Ken *chemical engineering professor*
Okrent, David *engineering educator*
O'Neill, Russell Richard *engineering educator*
Parente, Robert Bruce *electrical engineer, consultant*
Perrine, Richard Leroy *environmental engineer, educator*
Ramo, Simon *retired engineering executive*
Robson, Glenn R. *engineering and design company executive*
Roychowdhury, Vwani *electrical engineer, educator*
Rubinstein, Moshe Fajwel *engineering educator*
Russell, Joseph Allen *engineer, consultant*
Safadi, M. Oussama *engineering educator*
Safonov, Michael George *electrical engineering educator, consultant*
Scholtz, Robert Arno *electrical engineering educator*
Settles, F. Stan, Jr. *engineering educator, manufacturing executive*
Sewell, William George III *electronics engineer, writer*
Sugar, Ronald D. *aerospace executive*
Swamikannu, Xavier *environmental engineer, state official*
Synolakis, Costas E. *engineering educator*
Taciroglu, Ertugrul *civil engineer, educator*
Toumari, Arman *environmental engineer, chemistry professor*
Udwadia, Firdaus Erach *engineering educator, consultant*
Wagner, Christian Nikolaus Johann *materials engineering educator*
Welch, Lloyd Richard *electrical engineer, educator, communications engineer, consultant*
Willner, Alan Eli *electrical engineering educator*
Yablonovitch, Eli *electrical engineering educator*
Yang, Fan *electrical engineer, researcher*
Yen, Teh Fu *civil and environmental engineering educator*

**Los Gatos**
Kazan, Benjamin *electrical engineer, researcher*
Rosenheim, Donald Edwin *electrical engineer*

**Malibu**
Bedrosian, Edward *retired electrical engineer*

**Marina Del Rey**
Abebe, Henok *engineer, researcher*

**Martinez**
Sepulveda, Eduardo Solideo *chemical engineer*

**Menifee**
Morshed, Moqbul Monty *civil and environmental engineer*

Sorstokke, Susan Eileen *systems engineer*

**Tustin**
Prasad, Birendra (Brian) *mechanical engineer*

**Ventura**
Gaynor, Joseph *chemical engineer, management consultant*

**Victorville**
Sedeño, Eugene Raymond *electrical engineer, consultant*

**Walnut**
Cheng, Shide *engineer, researcher*

**Walnut Creek**
Hanson, Robert Duane *engineering educator*

**Watsonville**
Brown, Alan Charlton *retired aeronautical engineer*

**Westlake Village**
Caligiuri, Joseph Frank *retired engineering executive*

**Westminster**
Armstrong, Gene Lee *systems engineer, consultant, retired aerospace transportation executive*

**Wilmington**
Hatch, Ronald Ray *engineer*

**Woodland Hills**
Hokana, Gregory Howard *engineering executive*
Piersol, Allan Gerald *mechanical engineer*

**Yorba Linda**
Lynch, Frank Thomas *aeronautical engineer, consultant*
Porcello, Leonard Joseph *engineering research and development executive*

## COLORADO

**Arvada**
Ferguson, Lloyd Elbert *retired manufacturing engineer*

**Aurora**
Heller, Austin Norman *chemical and environmental engineer*
Robertson, James Mueller *civil engineer, educator*

**Bayfield**
Collins, William Leroy *retired telecommunications engineer*

**Boulder**
Anseth, Kristi S. *tissue engineer, engineering educator*
Barnes, Frank Stephenson *electrical engineer, educator*
Buck, Michael Charles *electrical engineer, researcher*
Corotis, Ross Barry *civil engineer, educator, academic administrator*
Davis, Robert Heater *chemical engineering educator*
Hanna, William Johnson *electrical engineering educator*
Hauser, Ray Louis *engineer, researcher, entrepreneur*
Hill, David Allan *electrical engineer*
Jin, Xiaoying *electrical engineer, computer engineer, researcher*
Joy, Edward Bennett *electrical engineer, educator, consultant*
Mulhern, Martin Robert *engineer*
Murnane, Margaret Mary *engineering and physics educator*
Nordgren, Ronald Paul *engineering educator, researcher*
Reitsema, Harold James *aerospace engineer*
Sani, Robert LeRoy *chemical engineering professor*
Shanahan, Eugene Miles *flow measurement instrumentation company executive*
Smith, Ernest Ketcham *electrical engineer*
Timmerhaus, Klaus Dieter *chemical engineering professor*
Uberoi, Mahinder Singh *aerospace engineer, researcher*
Zable, Jack Louis *mechanical engineer, educator*

**Broomfield**
Drouillard, Thomas F., II, *aerospace engineer*

**Centennial**
Goughnour, Roy Robert *civil engineer, educator*
Grant, Paul *chemical engineer, real estate broker, lawyer*

**Colorado Springs**
Adnet, Jacques Jim Pierre *astronautical and electrical engineer, consultant*
Heilman, John Edward *engineering consultant*
Morris, Steven Lynn *engineering consultant, retired military officer*
Watts, Oliver Edward *engineering company executive*
Ziemer, Rodger Edmund *electrical engineering educator, consultant*

**Columbine Valley**
Gagin, Lawrence Vincent *ceramics engineer, consultant*

**Denver**
Bialasiewicz, Jan Tadeusz *electrical engineering educator*
Chamberlain, Adrian Ramond *transportation engineer*
Colvis, John Paris *aerospace engineer, mathematician, research scientist*

Fay, Richard James *mechanical engineer, engineering executive, educator*
Long, Francis Mark *retired electrical engineer*
Matin, Mohammad Abdul *electrical engineer, educator*
McCandless, Bruce, II, *aerospace engineer, retired astronaut*
Porter, J. Reid *engineering executive*
Reshotko, Eli *aerospace engineer, educator*
Scott, Gregg Alan *civil engineer*
Smith, William French, II, *safety engineer*

**Englewood**
Haliw, Jerome Michael *civil engineer*
Olcer, Nuri Yelman *engineering researcher, educator*
Peterson, Ralph Randall *engineering executive*

**Estes Park**
Ojalvo, Morris *civil engineer, educator*
Webb, Richard C. *engineering company executive*

**Fort Collins**
Abt, Steven R. *civil engineer, educator*
Barbezat, Eugene LaVar *computer engineer, retired military officer*
Cermak, Jack Edward *engineer, educator*
Chong, Edwin K. P. *engineering educator*
Matthies, Frederick John *civil and environmental engineer*
Richardson, Everett Vern *hydraulic engineer, educator, administrator, consultant*
Roesner, Larry August *civil engineer*

**Golden**
Keyser, Matt *transportation engineer*
Myers, Daryl Ronald *engineer*
Sloan, Earle Dendy, Jr. *chemical engineering educator*
Spurck, Richard Francis *materials engineer*

**Grand Junction**
Agapito, J. F. T. *mining engineer, mineralogist*

**Greenwood Village**
Arvizu, Dan Eliab *mechanical engineer*

**Highlands Ranch**
Brierley, Corale L. *geological and biomining engineer*
Eberhard, Jacob John *software engineer*

**Longmont**
Doyle, James Thomas *electronics engineer*

**Loveland**
Fleischer, Gerald Albert *industrial engineer, educator*

**Superior**
Middlebrooks, Eddie Joe *environmental engineer*

**U S A F Academy**
Musselman, Randall L. *electrical engineer, educator*
Post, Martiqua Leigh *engineering educator*

**Wheat Ridge**
Scherich, Erwin Thomas *civil engineer, consultant*

## CONNECTICUT

**Bethany**
Barnes, Richard Barton *mechanical engineer, musician*

**Bloomfield**
Cornell, Robert Witherspoon *engineer, consultant*
De Maria, Anthony John *electrical engineer*
Kissa, Karl Martin *electrical engineer*

**Bolton**
Banas, Conrad Martin *mechanical engineer, chief scientist*

**Branford**
Sipprell, George Sidney *aerospace engineer, consultant*
Wegener, Peter Paul *engineering educator, writer*

**Colchester**
Huzmezan, Mihai *aerospace engineer*

**Darien**
Forman, J(oseph) Charles *chemical engineer, consultant, writer*

**East Hartford**
Cao, Ming *mechanical engineer*
Jacobson, Clas A. *engineering educator, director*
Staroselsky, Alexander *mechanical engineer, materials scientist*

**Enfield**
Oliver, Bruce Lawrence *retired information systems educator*

**Hartford**
Boman, Paul Eric *engineering executive*
Bronzino, Joseph Daniel *electrical engineer*
Gieras, Jacek Franciszek *engineering educator, research scientist*

**Jewett City**
Pucel, Robert Albin *electronics engineer, researcher*

**Milford**
Bubencik, John William, II, *civil engineer, consultant, transportation engineer*

**Mystic**
Thompson, Robert Allan *aerospace engineer*

**New Britain**
Kurkovsky, Stan A. *engineering educator*

**New Haven**
Narendra, Kumpati Subrahmanya *electrical engineer, educator*
Saltzman, W. Mark *engineering educator*

**Norwalk**
Bays, John Theophanis *consulting engineer*
Swift, Richard J. *engineering company executive*
Wilks, Paul Almy, Jr. *engineering executive*

**Old Lyme**
Doersam, Charles Henry, Jr. *engineer, educator, entrepreneur, writer*

**Orange**
Lobay, Ivan *mechanical engineering educator*

**Ridgefield**
McConnell, John Edward *retired electrical engineering company executive*

**South Windsor**
Hobbs, David Ellis *mechanical engineer*

**Storrs Mansfield**
Bzymek, Zbigniew Marian *engineering educator*
Pitkin, Edward Thaddeus *aerospace engineer, consultant*
Shaw, Montgomery Throop *chemical engineering professor*
Stephens, Jack Edward *civil engineer, consultant*
Zhang, Yuwen *mechanical engineer, researcher*

**Stratford**
Blair, Sylvia H. *aerospace engineer*

## DELAWARE

**Camden Wyoming**
Jones, Jay Paul *environmental engineer*

**Lewes**
Beaufait, Frederick W(illiam) *retired engineering educator*

**Newark**
Allen, Herbert Ellis *environmental chemistry educator*
Boncelet, Charles George *engineering educator*
Byrne, John Michael *energy and environmental educator*
Cha, Daniel K. *environmental engineer, educator*
Kim, Hee June *engineer*
Ritter, William Frederick *civil and agricultural engineering educator, consultant*
Russell, Thomas William Fraser *chemical engineer, educator*
Sandler, Stanley Irving *chemical engineering educator*
Sarkar, Kausik *acoustical engineer, educator*
Wagner, Norman Joseph III *chemical engineering educator, researcher*

**Rehoboth Beach**
Bischoff, Kenneth Bruce *chemical engineering educator*

**Wilmington**
Naylor, Craig G. *engineering company executive*

## DISTRICT OF COLUMBIA

**Washington**
Anthony, Donald Barrett *engineering executive*
Arkilic, Galip Mehmet *mechanical engineer, educator*
Bainum, Peter Montgomery *aerospace engineer, consultant*
Blanchard, Bruce *civil engineer, federal official*
Bonk, Stephen Francis *electrical engineer*
Bresee, James Collins *chemical engineer*
Burton, William Joseph *engineering executive*
Chen, Ho-Hong H.H. *industrial engineering executive, educator*
Cleave, Mary L. *environmental engineer, former astronaut*
Deason, Jonathan Pierce *environmental engineer, federal agency administrator*
Deland, Michael Reeves *engineering company executive*
Della Torre, Edward *electrical engineer, educator*
Eisner, Howard *engineering educator, engineering executive*
Giallorenzi, Thomas Gaetano *optical engineer*
Hershey, Robert Lewis *mechanical engineer, management consultant*
Kao, Timothy Wu *civil engineering educator*
Kaufman, Roger E. *engineering educator*
Khozeimeh, Issa *electrical engineer, educator*
Mooney, John Joseph *chemical engineer*
Pickholtz, Raymond Lee *electrical engineering educator, consultant*
Rust, William David, Jr. *retired structural engineer*
Savage, Nora F. *environmental engineer*
Skinner, Robert Earle, Jr. *civil engineer, engineering executive*
Skolnik, Merrill I. *electrical engineer*
Townsend, Marjorie Rhodes *aerospace engineer, engineering executive*
Wang, John Cheng Hwai *communications engineer, researcher*
Weiner, Edward *civil engineer, federal agency administrator*
Whitworth, Horace Algernon *mechanical engineer*
Williamson, Carl Augustus *engineering executive*

**Washington Navy Yard**
Campbell, Regan Helen *engineer*

## FLORIDA

**Amelia Island**
Lilly, Wesley Cooper *marine engineer*

**Aventura**
Wolfenson, Azi U. *electrical, mechanical and industrial engineer, consultant*

**Boca Raton**
Lin, Yukweng M. *engineer, educator*
Mussenden, Georg Antonio *electronics engineer*

**Bonita Springs**
Katzen, Raphael *consulting chemical engineer*

**Bradenton**
Garvick, Kenneth Ryan *broadcast engineer, announcer, educator*

**Brandon**
Stephens, Robert David *environmental engineering executive*

**Brooksville**
Lauer, Harry Curtis *retired civil engineer*

**Cocoa**
Block, David L. *solar engineering executive*

**Coral Gables**
Rew, William Edmund *civil engineer*
Saffir, Herbert Seymour *structural engineer, consultant*
Sumanth, David Jonnakoty *industrial engineer, educator*

**Davie**
Upadhiaya, Umesh Chandra *engineer, consultant*

**Daytona Beach**
Dhainaut, Jean-Michel Maurice *engineering educator*
Helfrick, Albert Darlington *electronics engineering educator, consultant, department chairman*

**Deerfield Beach**
Nieto, Mario *civil engineer*

**Deland**
Freeman, Ronald Eugene *environmental engineer*
Rattman, William John *electronics and electro-optic engineer*

**Delray Beach**
Smith, Charles Oliver *retired engineer*

**Dunedin**
Goodale, Arthur Worthington *civil engineer, researcher*

**Eglin Afb**
Franzen, Larry William *aerospace electronics engineer*

**Fort Myers**
Moeschl, Stanley Francis *electronics engineer, electrical engineer, management consultant*
Scott, Kenneth Elsner *mechanical engineering educator*

**Gainesville**
Abbaschian, Reza *materials science and engineering educator*
Alptekinoglu, Aydin *engineering educator, management educator*
Anderson, Timothy J. *chemical engineering professor*
Blanch, Paul Bradford *biomedical engineer, researcher*
Capehart, Barney Lee *industrial engineer, systems engineer, educator*
Cristescu, Nicolaie Dan *engineering educator*
Delfino, Joseph John *environmental engineering sciences educator*
Fossum, Jerry George *electrical engineering educator*
Fregly, B. J. *engineering educator*
Hollien, Harry Francis *communications engineer*
Huang, Jinhua *mechanical engineer, researcher*
Isaacs, Gerald William *retired agricultural engineering educator, consultant*
Khargonekar, Pramod Prabhakar *engineering educator*
Kurzweg, Ulrich Hermann *engineering science educator*
Law, Mark Edward *electrical engineer, educator*
Lee, Won Suk *engineering educator*
O, Kenneth Kyongyop *engineering educator*
Sadrameli, Mojtaba Seyed *chemical engineer, researcher*
Sah, Chih-Tang *electrical and computer engineering educator*
Schmertmann, John Henry *civil engineer, educator, consultant*
Sherif, S. A. *engineering educator*
Slavickas, Rimas Anthony *industrial engineer, educator*
Verink, Ellis Daniel, Jr. *metallurgical engineering educator, consultant*
Wang, Jianlin *civil engineering educator*
Xie, Huikai *engineering educator*

**Indialantic**
Godfrey, Raymond Michael *information systems consultant*

**Jacksonville**
Arbogast, Gordon Wade *systems engineer, educator, consultant , retired military officer*
Costin, Rea-Silvia *civil engineer*
Mueller, Edward Albert *retired transportation engineer*
Vasana, Susan (Chun-Ye) *engineering educator*

**Jupiter**
Migliaro, Marco William *electrical engineer*
Wolff, Edward Alvin *electronics engineer*

**Kennedy Space Center**
Hancock, Randy A. *safety engineer*
Tang, Philip W. *engineer, educator*

**Keystone Heights**
Ohanian, Mihran Jacob *nuclear engineer, educator, dean, researcher*

**Kissimmee**
Sherwood, Jack Robert *quality engineer, logistics consultant*

**Lady Lake**
Granger, Robert Alan *mechanical and aerospace engineering educator*

**Lake Mary**
Nagda, Durga Shanker *environmental engineer, researcher*

**Lake Worth**
Copeland, Richard Loyd *electrical engineer*

**Lauderhill**
Swisher, Charles Francis *electrical engineer, consultant*

**Longboat Key**
Gollobin, Leonard Paul *chemical engineer*
Workman, George Henry *structural engineering consultant*

**Lutz**
Anderson, Karl Franklin *systems engineer, researcher*

**Melbourne**
Maloratsky, Leo G. *electrical engineer*

**Miami**
Ajamil, Luis *civil engineer*
Ayala, Melvin *electrical engineer, researcher*
Candocia, Frank *computer engineer, educator*
Chang-Mota, Roberto *electrical engineer*
Levy, Cesar *mechanical engineer, educator*
Veziroglu, Turhan Nejat *mechanical engineering educator, researcher*

**Naples**
Lynn, Larry (Verne Lauriston Lynn) *engineering executive*
Sowman, Harold Gene *ceramics engineer, researcher*
Suziedelis, Vytautas A. *retired engineering corporation executive*
Thampi, Mohan Varghese *environmental health and civil engineer*
Williams, George Earnest *retired engineer, retired corporate financial executive*

**Nokomis**
Beck, George William *retired industrial engineer*
Novak, Robert Louis *civil engineer, pavement management consultant*

**North Palm Beach**
Sooy, William Ray *information technology executive*

**Orlando**
Carroll, Ginger Christine *software engineer*
Delfyett, Peter *engineering educator*
DeMara, Ronald Francis *computer engineer, educator*
Ha, Yonggang *optical engineer*
Rosenbach, Leopold *engineer, consultant*
Yu, Chuanzhao *electrical engineer, researcher*
Zhai, Yun *electrical engineer, researcher*

**Osprey**
Boldt, Heinz *aerospace engineer*
Jones, George Yovicic *civil engineer*

**Palm Beach**
Callahan, Edward William *chemical engineer, retired manufacturing executive*

**Palm Beach Gardens**
Gillette, Frank C., Jr. *retired mechanical engineer*

**Panama City**
D'Arcy, Gerald Paul *engineering executive, consultant*

**Pensacola**
Matteo, Daniel Patrick *aerospace engineer, consultant*
Olsen, Richard Galen *biomedical engineer, consultant*
Rashid, Muhammad Harunur *electrical engineering educator*

**Plantation**
Alisetti, Edwin Luis *engineer, corporate financial executive*
Hsu, Jiun-Jia *engineering educator, transportation engineer*

**Port Charlotte**
Kok, Hans Gebhard *consulting engineer*

**Port Orange**
Millar, Gordon Halstead *mechanical engineer, agricultural products executive*

**Saint Augustine**
Lund, Frederick Henry *aerospace and electrical engineer*

**Saint Cloud**
Everett, Woodrow Wilson *electrical engineer, educator*

**Saint Petersburg**
Cardenas-Valencia, Andres Manuel *chemical engineer, researcher*
Collins, Carl Russell, Jr. *industrial engineer*

**Sarasota**
Deutsch, Sid *biomedical engineer, educator*
Long, Robert Radcliffe *fluid mechanics engineer, educator*
Metzger, Sidney *retired communications engineer*

Oldshue, James Y. *chemical engineering consultant*
Ross, Gerald Fred *electrical engineering executive, researcher*

**Satellite Beach**
Clark, John F. *space systems engineering educator*
Van Arsdall, Robert Armes *engineer, retired military officer*

**Sun City Center**
Edwards, Paul Beverly *retired science and engineering educator*
Jeffries, Robert Joseph *retired engineer, information technology executive, educator*

**Tallahassee**
AbdelRazig, Yassir A. *engineering educator*
Coloney, Wayne Herndon *civil engineer*
Das, Himangshu Shekhar *civil engineer*
Dea, David Young Fong *electrical engineer, consultant*
De Forest, Sherwood Searle *agricultural engineer, agricultural products executive*
Hall, Houghton Alexander *electrical engineer, municipal official*
Lee, Peter John *research engineer*

**Tampa**
Carnahan, Robert Paul *civil engineer, educator, researcher, consultant*
Ghiu, Silvana Melania Stefania *process and development engineer*
Hunter, Larry Lee *retired electrical engineer*
Zayas-Castro, José *engineering educator, researcher*

**Venice**
Przemieniecki, Janusz Stanislaw *engineering executive, former government senior executive and college dean*
Slate, Floyd Owen *retired engineering educator*

**West Palm Beach**
Aaron, M. Robert *electrical engineer*
Davis, Paul B. *retired mechanical engineer, civil engineer*

**Winter Haven**
Johnson, Gordon Selby *consulting electrical engineer*

**Winter Park**
Figner, William James *computer engineer*
Granberry, Edwin Phillips, Jr. *safety engineer, consultant*

## GEORGIA

**Albany**
Marbury, Ritchey McGuire III *engineering executive, surveyor*

**Alpharetta**
Yeatman, Henry Clay *mechanical engineer*

**Athens**
Abdel-Hadi, Ali Ismail *engineer, educator*
Annis, Patricia Anne *textile engineer, educator*
McCutcheon, Steven Clifton *ecological and environmental engineer, hydrologist*
Nelson, Stuart Owen *agricultural engineer, researcher, educator*

**Atlanta**
Abdel-Khalik, Said Ibrahim *nuclear and mechanical engineering educator*
Bao, Gang *biomedical engineer, educator*
Barksdale, Richard Dillon *civil engineer, educator*
Bellanca, Joseph Paul *engineering construction executive*
Burdell, George P. *retired mechanical engineer*
Cressler, John David *electrical engineering educator*
Eckert, Charles Alan *chemical engineering educator*
Ellingwood, Bruce Russell *structural engineer, educator*
Forney, Larry J. *chemical engineer, educator*
Giddens, Don Peyton *engineering educator, researcher*
Hanagud, Sathyanaraya V. *aerospace engineer, educator*
Harrison, George Brooks *engineer, researcher, retired military officer*
Hodges, Dewey Harper *aerospace engineer, educator*
Johnson, Eric N. *engineering educator, researcher*
Loven, Andrew Witherspoon *environmental engineering company executive*
McIntire, Larry Vern *biomedical engineering educator*
Nair, Sankar *chemical engineer, educator*
Nerem, Robert Michael *engineering educator, consultant*
O'Kon, James Alexander *engineering company executive*
Papapolymerou, John *engineering educator*
Price, Edward Warren *aerospace engineer, educator*
Rahnema, Farzad *engineering educator, department chairman*
Rouhani, Shahrokh *civil engineering environmental educator, consultant*
Sadr, Reza *mechanical engineer, educator*
Salant, Richard Frank *mechanical engineer, educator*
Stacey, Weston Monroe, Jr. *nuclear engineer, physicist, educator*
Su, Kendall Ling-Chiao *engineering educator*
Tentzeris, Emmanouil Manos *engineering educator, researcher*
Thuesen, Gerald Jorgen *industrial engineer, educator*
Tincher, Wayne Coleman *engineering educator*
Vachon, Reginald Irenee *mechanical engineer*
Vito, Raymond P. *engineering educator, researcher*
Winer, Ward Otis *mechanical engineer, educator*
Yavari, Arash *engineering educator*

Yoganathan, Ajit Prithiviraj *biomedical engineer, educator*

**Avondale Estates**
Bastin, Clinton *retired chemical engineer, retired nuclear energy industry executive*

**Big Canoe**
Bendelius, Arthur George *engineering firm executive*

**Columbus**
Gibbons, Dona Alden Coe *electrical engineer, director*
Haneman, Vincent Siering, Jr. *consulting engineer, educator, dean*
Sweeney, Robert David *retired communications engineer*

**Doraville**
Wempner, Gerald Arthur *engineering educator*

**Duluth**
Colwell, Gene Thomas *engineering educator*
Luger, Donald R. *engineering company executive*

**Fairburn**
Johnston, Carolyn Judith *construction engineer*

**Flowery Branch**
Reynolds, George Anthony, Jr. *engineering executive*

**Gainesville**
Jones, William Benjamin, Jr. *retired electrical engineering educator*

**Jasper**
Wiltse, James Cornelius *retired electrical engineer*

**Kennesaw**
Petersen, David M. *electrical engineer*

**Lagrange**
Bledsoe, L. Bernard, Jr. *retired textile engineer*

**Macon**
Aldridge, Melvin Dayne *engineering educator*
Hails, Robert Emmet *retired aerospace engineer, manufacturing executive, retired military officer*
Leonard, Michael Steven *industrial engineering educator*

**Marietta**
Eggersman, Denise *computer engineer, educator*
Fitzgerald, John Edmund *retired civil engineering educator*
Miles, Thomas Caswell *aerospace engineer*

**Norcross**
Harrison, Gordon Ray *engineering executive, consultant, research scientist*

**Robins Afb**
Manley, Nancy Jane *environmental engineer*

**Savannah**
Hsu, Ming-Yu *engineering educator*

**Sky Valley**
Geer, Ronald Lamar *mechanical engineer, consultant, retired oil industry executive*

**Smyrna**
Tripp, Victor K. *electrical engineer, researcher*

**Stone Mountain**
Bacon, Louis Albert *retired consulting civil engineer*

**Townsend**
Hicks, Harold Eugene *chemical engineer*

**Warner Robins**
DePriest, C(harles) David *engineering executive, retired military officer*

## HAWAII

**Honolulu**
Chen, Wai-Fah *civil engineering educator*
Cox, Richard Horton *civil engineering executive*
Ghasemi Nejhad, Mehrdad N. *mechanical engineering educator*
Koide, Frank Takayuki *electrical engineering educator*
Ma, Kougen *engineering educator, researcher*
Ogburn, Hugh Bell *chemical engineer, consultant*
Wang, Jaw-Kai *bioengineering educator*
White, Gary Richard *electrical engineer*

**Kapaau**
McFee, Richard *electrical engineer, physicist*

**Kapolei**
Adachi, Athan Ken *civil engineer*

**Wahiawa**
Camery, John William *computer engineer*

## IDAHO

**Boise**
Cory, Wallace Newell *retired civil engineer*
Zarges, Thomas H. *engineering executive*

**Idaho Falls**
Miller, Gregory Kent *structural engineer*
Riemke, Richard Allan *nuclear engineer*

**Inkom**
Ambrose, Tommy W. *chemical engineer, engineering executive*

**Moscow**
DeShazer, James Arthur *biological engineer, educator, administrator*

**Pocatello**
Jacobsen, Richard T. *mechanical engineering educator*
Leung, Solomon W. *engineering company executive, researcher*
Valentine, Ralph Schuyler *chemical engineer, director*

## ILLINOIS

**Argonne**
Ahmed, Shabbir *chemical engineer*
Chang, Yoon Il *nuclear engineer*
Kim, Yeon Soo *nuclear engineer, researcher*
Kumar, Romesh *chemical engineer*
Reed, Claude Brinton *systems engineer*

**Aurora**
Koopman, Richard Nelson *engineer, consultant*

**Belleville**
Thien-Stasko, Vicki Lynn *civil engineer*

**Bloomington**
Pannell, Thierry Edgard *engineer, information technology manager*

**Burr Ridge**
Parker, James John *engineer, marketing professional*

**Carbondale**
Mohanty, Manoj K. *mineral engineer, educator*

**Champaign**
Korst, Helmut Hans *mechanical engineer, educator*
Rose, Walter Deane *retired engineering educator*

**Chicago**
Babcock, Lyndon Ross, Jr. *environmental engineer, educator*
Banerjee, Prashant *industrial engineer, educator, computer scientist*
Chung, Paul Myungha *mechanical engineer, educator*
Darabi, Houshang *engineering educator*
Dix, Rollin C(umming) *mechanical engineering educator, consultant*
Dutta, Mitra *engineer, educator*
Epstein, Raymond *engineering and architectural executive*
Gerstner, Robert William *structural engineering educator, consultant*
Gupta, Krishna Chandra *mechanical engineering educator*
Guralnick, Sidney Aaron *engineering educator*
Hartnett, James Patrick *engineering educator*
Ivanov, Kamen Petkov *engineering educator*
Kennedy, Lawrence Allan *mechanical engineering educator*
Lin, James Chih-I *biomedical engineer, electrical engineer, educator*
Linden, Henry Robert *chemical engineer, researcher*
Miller, Irving Franklin *chemical engineer, educator, biomedical engineer, academic administrator*
Miller, Verne William *computer engineer, consultant*
Minkowycz, W. J. *mechanical engineering educator*
Murata, Tadao *engineering and computer science educator*
Omosheyin, Rotimi *electronics engineer, real estate company executive*
Perez-Luna, Victor Hugo *chemical engineer, educator*
Rikoski, Richard Anthony *electrical engineering executive*
Wong, Thomas Tang Yum *engineering educator*

**Chicago Heights**
Kavis, George *engineer, photographer*

**Clarendon Hills**
Moritz, Donald Brooks *mechanical engineer, consultant*

**Darien**
Hanson, Martin Philip *mechanical engineer, farmer*

**Decatur**
Koucky, John Richard *metallurgical engineer, manufacturing executive*

**Deerfield**
Saida, Toyoyasu *chemical and biochemical engineer*

**Dekalb**
Kong, Xuan *electrical engineer, educator*

**Des Plaines**
Lyu, Seung Won *metallurgical engineer, environmental scientist*
Relwani, Nirmal Murlidhar (Nick Relwani) *mechanical engineer*

**Downers Grove**
Choudhury, A. N. M. Masum *optical engineer*

**Evanston**
Backman, Vadim *biomedical engineer, educator*
Bazant, Zdenek Pavel *engineering educator*
Belytschko, Ted *engineering educator*
Bobco, William David, Jr. *consulting engineering company executive*
Carr, Stephen Howard *materials engineer, educator*
Colgate, J. Edward *mechanical engineering educator*
Daskin, Mark Stephen *engineering educator*

Fessler, Raymond R. *metallurgical engineering consultant*
Fine, Morris Eugene *materials engineer, educator*
Frey, Donald Nelson *industrial engineer, educator, retired manufacturing executive*
Goldstick, Thomas Karl *biomedical engineering educator*
Keer, Leon Morris *engineering educator*
Krizek, Raymond John *engineering educator, consultant*
Liang, Chuang *optical engineer, researcher*
Murphy, Gordon John *electrical engineer, educator*
Ottino, Julio Mario *engineering educator*
Schofer, Joseph Landy *civil engineer, educator*
Shah, Surendra Poonamchand *engineering educator*
Smith, Spencer Bailey *engineering and business educator*
Sobel, Alan *electrical engineer, physicist*
Taflove, Allen *electrical engineer, educator, researcher, consultant*
Van Ness, James Edward *electrical engineering educator*
Weertman, Julia Randall *materials engineering educator*
Zhou, Hai *engineering educator*

**Forsyth**
Graf, Karl Rockwell *nuclear engineer*

**Gilman**
Ireland, Herbert Orin *retired engineering educator*

**Glencoe**
Dean, H. Clark *retired civil engineer, genealogist*

**Glendale Heights**
Rawal, Darshan Lal *civil engineer, structural engineer, consultant*

**Glenview**
Panarese, William C. *civil engineer*
Speer, David Blakeney *industrial executive*
Van Zelst, Theodore William *civil engineer, engineering company executive*

**Gurnee**
Sommerlad, Robert Edward *environmental research engineer*

**La Grange**
Mehlenbacher, Dohn Harlow *civil engineer, consultant*

**Lake Forest**
Lambert, John Boyd *chemical engineer, consultant*

**Libertyville**
Szini, Istvan Janos *electronics engineer*

**Lisle**
Hayes, Richard J., Jr. *engineering company executive*

**Moline**
Taylor, Byron Keith *industrial engineer*

**Naperville**
Crawford, Raymond Maxwell, Jr. *nuclear engineer*
Joyce, William H. *engineering company executive, chemical engineer*
Vora, Manu Kishandas *chemical engineer, consultant*

**Norridge**
Petrakis, Myron Titos *retired mechanical engineer*

**Northbrook**
Adler, Robert *electronics engineer*
Boettcher, Robert Walter *civil engineer*

**Oak Forest**
Kogut, Kenneth Joseph *engineer, consultant*

**Oak Park**
Clark, John Peter III *engineer, consultant*

**Palatine**
Kieft, Gerald Nelson *mechanical engineer*

**Park Forest**
Williams, Jack Raymond *civil engineer*

**Peoria**
Hindi, Riyadh *engineering educator, researcher*
Kroll, Dennis Edwards *industrial engineering educator*

**Plainfield**
Chakrabarti, Subrata Kumar *marine research engineer*

**Quincy**
Centanni, Ross J. *engineering executive*

**Rockford**
Eliason, Jon Tate *electrical engineer*

**Rolling Meadows**
Eckel, James J. *aerospace engineer*

**Schaumburg**
Aryanfar, Farshid *electrical engineer, electronics engineer*
Kornowski, Robert Richard *engineer, science educator*

**Skokie**
Corley, William Gene *engineering research executive*

**Sycamore**
Ballee', Shawn Alexander *engineering educator*

**Urbana**
Bergeron, Clifton George *engineer, educator*
Blahut, Richard Edward *electrical and computer engineering educator*

Braatz, Richard Dean *chemical engineer*
Buckius, Richard O. *mechanical engineer, educator*
Chao, Bei Tse *mechanical engineering educator*
Chato, John Clark *mechanical and bioengineering educator*
Coleman, James J. *electrical engineer, educator*
Conry, Thomas Francis *mechanical engineering educator*
Do, Minh N. *engineering educator*
Eden, James Gary *electrical engineer, educator, physicist, researcher*
Garcia, Marcelo Horacio *engineering educator, consultant*
Hall, William Joel *retired civil engineer, educator*
Hannon, Bruce Michael *engineering educator*
Hess, Karl *electrical and computer engineering educator*
Holonyak, Nick, Jr. *electrical engineering educator*
Huang, Thomas Shi-Tao *electrical engineering educator, researcher*
Jacobson, Sheldon Howard *engineering educator*
Kumar, Panganamala Ramana *electrical and computer engineering educator*
Loui, Michael Conrad *engineering educator*
Mayes, Paul Eugene *engineering educator, consultant*
Miley, George H. *nuclear and electrical engineering educator, plasma engineer, energy conversion scientist*
Park, Jae Hyun *mechanical engineer, researcher*
Rao, Nannapaneni Narayana *electrical engineer*
Snoeyink, Vernon L. *civil engineer, educator*
Strano, Michael *chemical engineer*
Wah, Benjamin Wan-Sang *electrical and computer engineering educator*
Walker, William Hamilton *civil engineer, educator*

**Westchester**
Tutins, Antons *electrical and audio engineer*

**Wheaton**
Hambley, Douglas Frederick *geological and environmental engineer*

**Wilmette**
Muhlenbruch, Carl W. *civil engineer*
Wadden, Richard Albert *environmental engineer, educator, science administrator, consultant*

## INDIANA

**Carmel**
Fisher, Mark Leighton *software engineer*
Walsh, John Charles *metallurgical engineer, director*

**Evansville**
Black, Gary William *industrial engineer*
Swenty, Brian Jay *civil engineer, educator*

**Fort Wayne**
Lyons, Jerry Lee *mechanical engineer*
Streeter, Robert Davenport *electrical engineer, consultant*

**Hammond**
Pierson, Edward Samuel *engineering educator, consultant*
Zhou, Chenn Qian *mechanical engineer, department chairman*

**Indianapolis**
Akbari, Pezhman *aerospace engineer, researcher*
Anwar, Sohel *engineering educator*
Griffith, Roy Lloyd *design engineer*
Poinsette, Donald Eugene *engineering executive, management consultant*
Ramos, Jose A. *engineering educator*
Smith, Kenneth Dale *civil engineer, consultant*

**Kokomo**
Miller, Robert Frank *retired electronics engineering educator*

**Lafayette**
Caldwell, Barrett Scott *industrial engineering educator*
Etzel, James Edward *environmental engineering educator*
Fox, Robert William *mechanical engineering educator*
Geddes, Leslie Alexander *engineering educator, forensic engineer, physiologist*
Liley, Peter Edward *retired engineering educator*
Osborn, John Robert *retired engineering educator*
Pipes, Robert Byron *mechanical engineer, educator*

**Muncie**
Seymour, Richard Deming *technology educator*

**Noblesville**
Monical, Robert Duane *engineering company executive*

**Notre Dame**
Gray, William Guerin *engineering educator*
Incropera, Frank Paul *mechanical engineering educator*
Merz, James Logan *electrical and materials engineering educator, researcher*
Michel, Anthony Nikolaus *electrical engineering educator, researcher*
Ovaert, Timothy Christopher *mechanical engineering educator*
Schmitz, Roger Anthony *chemical engineer, educator, academic administrator*
Stadtherr, Mark A. *chemical engineer, educator*

**Rockport**
Smith, Mary Lee *civil engineer, technician*

**Terre Haute**
Badar, M. Affan *engineering educator*

**Warsaw**
Mroczkowski, Matthew *biomedical engineer*

**West Lafayette**
Albright, Lyle Frederick *chemical engineering educator*
Altschaeffl, Adolph George *retired civil engineering educator*
Andres, Ronald Paul *chemical engineer, educator*
Barany, James Walter *industrial engineering educator*
Buckmaster, Dennis Rene *agricultural engineer, educator*
Cohen, Raymond *mechanical engineer, educator*
Delleur, Jacques William *retired engineering educator*
Drnevich, Vincent Paul *engineering educator*
Irudayaraj, Joseph M. *engineering educator*
Jackson, Mark James *engineering educator*
Katehi, Linda P.B. *engineering educator*
Ladisch, Michael R. *engineering educator*
Landgrebe, David Allen *electrical engineer*
Lin, Pen-Min *electrical engineer, educator*
Marshall, Francis Joseph *aerospace engineer*
Naik, Sameer Vijaykumar *mechanical engineer, educator*
Ong, Chee-Mun *engineering educator*
Peroulis, Dimitrios *engineering educator, consultant*
Ramkrishna, Doraiswami *chemical engineering educator, researcher*
Salvendy, Gavriel *industrial engineer, educator*
Schwartz, Richard John *electrical engineering educator, researcher*
Taber, Margaret Ruth *retired engineering technology educator*
Thomas, Marlin Uluess *industrial engineer, educator, academic administrator*
Varma, Arvind *chemical engineering educator, researcher*
Viskanta, Raymond *mechanical engineering educator*
Wankat, Phillip Charles *chemical engineering educator*
Williams, Theodore Joseph *engineering educator*
Yao, Bin *mechanical engineering educator*

## IOWA

**Ames**
Anderson, Robert Morris, Jr. *electrical engineer*
Baumann, Edward Robert *environmental engineering educator*
Black, James Robert *industrial engineer*
Brown, Robert C. *engineering educator*
Buchele, Wesley Fisher *retired agricultural engineering educator*
Chimenti, Dale E. *engineering educator*
Larsen, William Lawrence *engineering educator*
Okiishi, Theodore Hisao *mechanical engineering educator*
Sanders, Wallace Wolfred, Jr. *civil engineer*
Wilder, David Randolph *retired materials engineer*

**Bettendorf**
Heyderman, Arthur Jerome *engineer, civilian military employee*

**Cambridge**
Colvin, Thomas Stuart *agricultural engineer, farmer*

**Cedar Rapids**
Smith, Bruce Vaughn *electrical engineer*

**Clear Lake**
Brown, Robert Grover *engineering educator*

**Coralville**
Dong, Jun *mechanical engineer, researcher*

**Davenport**
Chowdhury, Ali Asraf *electrical engineer, researcher*
Gehl, Eugene Patrick *aerospace engineer*
Pedersen, Karen Sue *electrical engineer*

**Emmetsburg**
Farnsworth, Steven Robert *safety engineer*

**Iowa City**
Dove, Edwin L. *engineering educator*
Marshall, Jeffrey Scott *mechanical engineer, educator*
Park, Joon Bu *biomedical engineer, researcher, educator*
Patel, Virendra Chaturbhai *mechanical engineer, educator*
Sonka, Milan *electrical and computer engineering educator*
Yang, Jingzhou *engineer, educator*

**Madrid**
Handy, Richard Lincoln *civil engineer, educator*

**Muscatine**
Stanley, Richard Holt *consulting engineer*
Thomopulos, Gregs G. *consulting engineering company executive*

**Sioux Center**
De Boer, Douglas F. *engineering educator*

**West Des Moines**
Conner, William Bruce *facilty engineer*

## KANSAS

**Emporia**
Alshare, Khaled A. *information systems educator*

**Garden City**
Alam, A.N.M. Mahbub Ul *engineer, educator*

**Hays**
Purvis, Karen R. *sanitary engineer*

**Lawrence**
Benjamin, Bezaleel Solomon *architectural engineer, educator*

Darwin, David *engineering educator, consultant*
Green, Don Wesley *chemical and petroleum engineering educator*
Moore, Richard Kerr *electrical engineering educator*
Muirhead, Vincent Uriel *retired aerospace engineer*
Roskam, Jan *aerospace engineer*
Rowland, James Richard *electrical engineering educator*

**Leawood**
Karmeier, Delbert Fred *engineer, consultant, realtor*

**Manhattan**
Das, Sanjoy *engineering educator, researcher*
Dissanayake, Sunanda *engineering educator*
Hagen, Lawrence Jacob *agricultural engineer*
Johnson, William Howard *retired agricultural engineer, retired educator*
Lee, E(ugene) Stanley *engineering educator*
Motipalli, V. V. Satish Kumar *mechanical engineer, researcher*
Simons, Gale Gene *nuclear and electrical engineer, educator*

**Overland Park**
Daniel, Karen *engineering and design company executive*
Rodman, Leonard C. *engineering and construction executive*
Tubbs, David Eugene *mechanical engineer, marketing professional*
Vaughan, Brad *engineering and design company executive*

**Topeka**
Nason, Barry Mark *systems engineer, mathematician, educator*

**Wichita**
McKee, George Moffitt, Jr. *civil engineer, consultant*
Wilhelm, William Jean *civil engineering educator*

## KENTUCKY

**Bowling Green**
Xing, Guangming *engineering educator*

**Campton**
Drake, David Lee *electronics engineer*

**Georgetown**
Caroland, William Bourne *structural engineer*

**Lexington**
Baker, Merl *engineering educator*
Brock, Louis Milton, Jr. *engineering educator, researcher*
Chen, Zhi *electrical engineering educator*
Drake, Vaughn Paris, Jr. *electrical engineer*
Holsapple, Clyde Warren *decision and information systems educator*
Male, Alan Thomas *engineering educator, foundation administrator*
Omar, Mohammed A. *engineering educator, consultant*

**Louisville**
Cornelius, Wayne Anderson *electrical and computer engineering consultant*
Garcia, Rafael Jorge *retired chemical engineer*
Kantardzic, Mehmed M. *engineering educator*
Tran, Long Trieu *industrial engineer*

**Murray**
Ferreyra, Rafael Andres *agricultural and biological engineer, consultant, researcher*

**Winchester**
Studebaker, John Milton *utilities engineer, consultant, educator*

## LOUISIANA

**Baker**
Cross, James Edward *electrical engineering educator*

**Baton Rouge**
Alam, Mohammmad Shah *engineering educator, researcher*
Bernhard, James M., Jr. *engineering executive*
Chen, Peter Pin-Shan *engineering educator, computer science and internet/web educator, data processing executive*
Corripio, Armando Benito *chemical engineering professor*
Deng, Zhi-Qiang *civil and environmental engineering educator, researcher*
Gammon, Malcolm Ernest, Sr. *surveying and engineering executive*
Khonsari, Michael M. *mechanical engineering educator*
Moody, Gene Byron *engineering executive, small business owner, minister*
Mugnier, Clifford John *engineering educator, consultant*
Pike, Ralph Webster *chemical engineer, educator, academic administrator*
Sinclair, Glenn Bruce *mechanical engineering educator, researcher*
Tsai, Frank Tsung-Chen *engineering educator, researcher*
Tumay, Mehmet Taner *geotechnical engineering educator, researcher*

**Dubach**
Straughan, William Thomas *engineering educator, structural engineering consultant*

**Elm Grove**
Livingston, John H. *retired engineer, retired military officer*

**Hammond**
Parish, Richard Lee *engineer, consultant*

**Harvey**
Simon, Keith R. *safety engineer, petroleum engineer, radio personality*

**Kenner**
Hallila, Bruce Allan *welding engineer*

**Lafayette**
Domingue, Emery *retired consulting engineering company executive*
Fang, Cheng-Shen *chemical engineering professor*
Marshak, Alan Howard *electrical engineer, educator*
Rickey, Horace B., Jr. *retired civil engineer, retired architectural engineer*

**Lake Charles**
Levingston, Ernest Lee *engineering company executive*

**Metairie**
Nicoladis, Michael F. *engineering company executive*

**Napoleonville**
Blanchard, Donald Pierre, Jr. *petroleum engineer*

**New Orleans**
Lannes, William Joseph III *electrical engineer*
Lintinger, Gregory John *electrical engineer, educator*
Wang, Ting *mechanical engineering educator*

**Ruston**
Sterling, Raymond Leslie *civil engineering educator, researcher, consultant*

**Shreveport**
Foreman, John Patrick *electrical engineer*

**Slidell**
Stuart, Charles Edward *electrical engineer, oceanographer*
Tewell, Joseph Robert, Jr. *retired electrical engineer*

## MAINE

**Falmouth**
Rohsenow, Warren Max *retired mechanical engineer, educator*

**Scarborough**
Raisbeck, Gordon *systems engineer, consultant*

**Waterville**
Laurence, Robert Lionel *chemical engineering professor*

## MARYLAND

**Aberdeen Proving Ground**
Clayton, John Daniel *mechanical engineer, researcher*
Cozby, Richard Scott *electronics engineer, military officer*

**Adelphi**
Bayne, Stephen B. *electronics engineer, researcher*
Podlesak, Thomas F. *electronics engineer*
Young, S. Susan *electrical engineer, researcher*

**Annapolis**
Johnson, Bruce *engineering educator*
Rogers, David Freeman *aerospace engineering educator*
Salem, Thomas Eric *electrical engineer, educator*
Trescott, Sara Lou *water resources engineer*

**Baltimore**
Abd-Elmoniem, Khaled Zakarya *biomedical engineer, researcher*
Apsel, Alyssa *electrical engineer, computer engineer*
Gracias, David H. *chemical engineer, educator*
Jelinek, Frederick *electrical engineer, educator*
Jones, Nicholas P. *civil engineering educator*
Kaliel, Bheem Prakash *engineering educator, consultant*
Katz, Joseph Louis *chemical engineer, educator*
Lerner, Andrew Charles *engineer, economist*
Nathanson, Harvey Charles *electrical engineer*
Rene, Vidal *electrical engineer, educator*
Thakar, Nitish Vyomesh *biomedical engineering educator*
Wang, Tza-Huei (Jeff Wang) *engineering educator*
Washington, Strother Lee, Jr. *mechanical engineer, design engineer*
Yue, Wusi *computer engineer, researcher*
Zaveri, Jigish Shirish *chemical engineer, educator*

**Bethesda**
Burbage, Tom *aeronautical engineer*
Burdeshaw, William Brooksbank *engineering executive*
Camardo, Michael F. *engineering company executive*
Freedman, Joseph *retired sanitary and public health engineering consultant*
Kemelhor, Robert E(lias) *mechanical engineer*
Kinsey, John Allen *systems engineer, technical director*
Kutemeyer, Peter Martin *industrial engineering executive*
Saville, Thorndike, Jr. *coastal engineer*

**Chevy Chase**
Cheng, David Keun *engineering educator*
Lebow, Irwin Leon *communications engineering consultant*
Rockwell, Theodore *nuclear engineer*

**College Park**
Anderson, John David, Jr. *aerospace engineer*

Ayyub, Bilal M. *engineer, educator, engineering executive, researcher*
Barbe, David Franklin *electrical engineer, educator*
Faria, Jose Alberto *engineering educator, consultant*
Farvardin, Nariman *engineering educator*
Granatstein, Victor Lawrence *electrical engineer, educator*
Gupta, Ashwani Kumar *mechanical engineering educator*
Kang, Kyeongpyo *transportation engineer, researcher*
Lathan, Corinna Elisabeth *aerospace engineer*
Levine, William Silver *electrical engineer, educator*
Marcus, Steven Irl *electrical engineering educator*
Newcomb, Robert Wayne *electrical engineer educator*
Orloff, Jonathan Harris *engineering educator*
Qi, Jianwei *mechanical engineer, researcher*
Radhakrishnan, Anand *aerospace engineer, researcher*
Skibniewski, Miroslaw Jan *engineering educator*
Smidts, Carol *mechanical engineer, educator*
Tabatabaee, Vahid *architectural engineer, researcher*
Taylor, Leonard Stuart *engineering educator, consultant*

**Columbia**
Cheng, Jian-Yu *mechanical engineer, researcher, application developer*
Saini, Simarjeet Singh *electronics engineer*
Straja, Sorin Radu *chemical engineer, mathematician, computer programmer*

**Crofton**
Freeman, Ernest Robert *engineering executive*
Laurenson, Robert Mark *mechanical engineer*

**Easton**
Kerr, James Wilson *engineer*

**Frostburg**
Teker, Kasif *engineering educator*

**Gaithersburg**
Cookson, Alan Howard *electrical engineer, researcher*
Ferrell, Charles Madison *nuclear engineer, physicist*
Kibira, Deogragias *electronics engineer, educator*
Levine, Robert Sidney *chemical engineer, consultant*
Madhavan, Raj *electrical engineer, electronics engineer*
Reddy, Thikkavarapu Ramachandra *electrical engineer*
Schlenoff, Craig *mechanical engineer*
Wright, Richard Newport III *retired engineering executive, engineering educator*

**Germantown**
Sorensen, John Noble *retired mechanical and nuclear engineer*

**Greenbelt**
Al-Bassyiouni, Moustafa *engineering company executive, engineering educator*
Amato, Deborah Douglass *aerospace engineer*
Bryant, Paul T. *electronics engineer*
Jeong, Seong-Il *aerospace engineer, researcher*
Vranish, John Michael *electrical engineer, researcher*

**Hagerstown**
Ksienski, Aharon Arthur *retired electrical engineer*

**Hunt Valley**
Kinstlinger, Jack *engineering executive, consultant*

**Indian Head**
Latimer, Paul Jerry *industrial engineer*

**La Plata**
Zinn, Michael Wallace *aerospace engineer*

**Lanham**
Criscimagna, Ned Henry *engineer*
Reupke, William Albert *engineer*

**Lanham Seabrook**
Hogie, Keith *systems engineer, computer engineer*

**Laurel**
Damarla, Thyagaraju *electronics engineer*
Eaton, Alvin Ralph *aeronautical engineer, electronics executive, systems engineer*
Land, H. Bruce III *electronics engineer, aerospace engineer*
Land, Henry Bruce III *electronics engineer, researcher*
Levitt, Gerald Steven *engineering executive*
Weerackody, Vijitha *electrical engineer, researcher*

**Linthicum Heights**
Skillman, William Alfred *consulting engineering executive*

**Lutherville**
Parekh, Dhirajlal Gokaldas *electrical engineer*

**Millersville**
DiAiso, Robert Joseph *civil engineer*

**Parkville**
Jensen, Arthur Seigfried *retired engineering executive, physicist, consultant*

**Patuxent River**
Stroup, Darryl Ray *systems engineer*

**Potomac**
Pietzsch, Jan Benjamin *engineering company executive*

**Queenstown**
Corn, Morton *environmental engineer, educator*

**Rockville**
Abron, Lilia A. *chemical engineer*
Ashar, Hansraj G. *structural engineer, nuclear regulator*
Burdick, William MacDonald *biomedical engineer*
Davies-Venn, Christian *environmental engineer*
Geem, Zong Woo *engineer*
McDonald, Capers Walter *biomedical engineer, manufacturing executive, entrepreneur, educator*
Paulhus, Norman Gerard, Jr. *aerospace engineer*
Seagle, Edgar Franklin *environmental engineer, consultant*
Zhao, Xiaoliang *mechanical engineer, researcher*

**Severna Park**
Davis, John Adams, Jr. *electrical engineer, research and development company executive*

**Silver Spring**
Koltnow, Peter Gregory *engineer, consultant*
Mok, Carson Kwok-Chi *structural engineer*
Okigbo, Franklin C. *engineering company executive*
Scipio, L. Albert, II (Louis Albert Scipio II) *retired aerospace science engineering educator, historian*
Shalowitz, Erwin Emmanuel *civil engineer*
White, Edmund William *chemical engineer*

**Suitland**
Brooks, Richard C. *electrical engineer, federal official*

**West Bethesda**
Sevik, Maurice *acoustical engineer, researcher*

## MASSACHUSETTS

**Acton**
Hicks, Walter Joseph *electrical engineer*

**Amherst**
Franks, Lewis E. *electrical and computer engineering educator, researcher*
Nash, William Arthur *civil engineer, educator*
Swift, Calvin Thomas *electrical and computer engineering educator*
Vogl, Otto *polymer science and engineering educator*
Winter, Horst Henning *chemical engineer, educator*

**Andover**
Agassounon, William B. G. *engineer, researcher*
Jakes, William Chester *electrical engineer*

**Bedford**
An, Hong *engineer*
Fante, Ronald Louis *engineer*
Jelalian, Albert V. *electrical engineer*
Linden, Kurt Joseph *electronics engineer*
Riopka, Taras P. *computer engineer*
Winter, David Louis *retired systems engineer, human factors scientist*

**Belmont**
Merrill, Edward Wilson *chemical engineering professor*

**Billerica**
Kinsman, Robert Preston *biomedical plastics engineer*

**Boston**
Baillieul, John Brouard *aerospace engineering and applied mathematics educator*
Choo, Arthur C.S. *structural engineer, consultant*
De Luca, Carlo John *biomedical engineer, educator*
Frank-Kamenetskii, Maxim D. *biomedical engineer*
Fraser, Donald C. *engineering executive, educator*
Gardner, Timothy S. *biomedical engineer, educator*
Giles, Roscoe C. *engineering educator*
Jain, Rakesh K. *chemical engineering educator, tumor biology educator*
Karpovsky, Mark Girsh *computer engineering educator, research laboratory director*
Langer, Robert Martin *retired chemical engineering company executive, consultant*
McSweeney Woodfall, Irene Frances *civil engineer, director*
Moore, Richard Lawrence *structural engineer, consultant*
Novotny, Vladimir *engineering educator, consultant*
Pierce, Allan Dale *engineering educator, researcher, editor*
Serafim, Philip E. *electrical engineer, computer engineer*
Teich, Malvin Carl *electrical engineering educator*

**Burlington**
Angle, Colin *electrical engineer, robotic company executive*
Greiner, Helen *mechanical engineer*
Rhee, Sokwoo *mechanical engineer*

**Cambridge**
Abernathy, Frederick Henry *mechanical engineering educator*
Apostolakis, George E. *engineering educator, researcher*
Barnhart, Cynthia *engineering educator, researcher*
Battin, Richard Horace *aeronautical engineer*
Beér, János Miklós *engineering educator*
Belcher, Angela *engineering educator*
Ben-Akiva, Moshe Emanuel *civil engineering educator*
Benedict, Manson *retired chemical engineer, educator*
Beranek, Leo Leroy *acoustical engineer, consultant*
Bras, Rafael Luis *engineering educator*
Brenner, Howard *chemical engineering educator*
Bulovic, Vladimir *engineering educator*
Caplice, Christopher *engineering educator*

Chen, Sow-Hsin *nuclear engineering educator, researcher*
Chung, Soon-Jo *engineer, researcher*
Clifford, Gari David *engineering educator, biomedical engineer*
Cohen, Robert Edward *chemical engineering professor, consultant*
Colton, Clark Kenneth *chemical engineering professor*
Covert, Eugene Edzards *aerospace engineer, aeronautics professor*
Crandall, Stephen Harry *engineering educator*
Crawley, Edward Francis *aerospace engineering educator*
de Neufville, Richard Lawrence *engineering educator*
de Weck, Oliver *engineering educator, researcher*
Dewey, Clarence Forbes, Jr. *engineering educator*
Drake, Elisabeth Mertz *chemical engineer, consultant*
Duffy, Robert Aloysius *aeronautical engineer*
Dugundji, John *aeronautical engineer*
Eagleson, Peter Sturges *civil engineer, environmental engineer, educator*
Fay, James Alan *mechanical engineering educator*
Flemings, Merton Corson *engineering educator, materials scientist*
Frey, Daniel D. *engineering educator, researcher*
Fujimoto, James G. *electrical engineering educator*
Gallager, Robert Gray *electrical engineering educator*
Griffith, Linda G. (Linda Griffith-Cima) *biomedical engineer, chemical engineer, educator*
Gyftopoulos, Elias Panayiotis *mechanical and nuclear engineering educator*
Hansen, Kent Forrest *nuclear engineering educator*
Harris, Wesley L. *aeronautical engineer, educator*
Hastings, Daniel *aeronautical engineer, educator*
Heywood, John Benjamin *mechanical engineering educator*
How, Hoton *electrical engineer*
Hunter, Ian W. *engineering educator, researcher*
Ippen, Erich Peter *electrical engineer, educator, physicist*
Kazimi, Mujid Suliman *nuclear engineer, educator*
Kerwin, Justin E. *naval engineer, educator*
Ladd, Charles Cushing III *civil engineer, educator*
Lagace, Paul Alfred *aeronautical engineering educator*
Langer, Robert Samuel, Jr. *chemical, biomedical engineering educator*
Lee, Se-Hee *electrical engineer, researcher*
Leveson, Nancy G. *aeronautical engineer*
Magee, Christopher L. *systems engineer*
Marini, Robert Charles *environmental engineering executive*
Markey, Winston Roscoe *aeronautical engineering educator*
Marks, David Hunter *civil engineering educator*
Mei, Chiang Chung *civil engineer, educator*
Mikaelian, Tsoline *aerospace engineer*
Milgram, Jerome H. *marine and ocean engineer, educator*
Mindell, David A. *engineering educator*
Moavenzadeh, Fred *engineering educator*
Munguia Tapia, Emmanuel *electrical engineer, researcher, computer scientist*
Newman, Dava Jean *aerospace engineering educator, director*
Nightingale, Deborah Seifert *systems engineer, consultant*
Penfield, Paul Livingstone, Jr. *electrical engineering educator*
Pian, Theodore Hsueh-Huang *engineering educator, consultant*
Powell, Adam Clayton *engineering educator, consultant*
Probstein, Ronald Filmore *mechanical engineering educator*
Rivest, Ronald L. *engineer*
Rogers, Peter Phillips *environmental engineer, educator, urban planner*
Roos, Daniel *engineering educator*
Rose, Robert Michael *materials engineering educator*
Ruina, Jack Philip *electrical engineer, educator*
Russell, Kenneth Calvin *metallurgical engineering educator*
Samson, Leona D. *biological engineering educator, research center director*
Sarma, Sanjay E. *electronics engineer, educator*
Sheffi, Yossi *engineering educator, researcher*
Smith, Amy B. *mechanical engineer, engineering educator*
Smith, Kenneth Alan *chemical engineer, educator*
Staelin, David Hudson *electrical engineering educator, consultant*
Stevens, Kenneth Noble *electrical engineer, educator*
Suh, Nam Pyo *mechanical engineering educator*
Suresh, Subra *materials engineer, educator*
Sussman, Joseph *engineering educator, researcher*
Tarokh, Vahid *engineering educator*
Todreas, Neil Emmanuel *nuclear engineering educator*
Triantafyllou, Michael Stefanos *engineering educator*
Trilling, Leon *aeronautical engineering educator*
Ungar, Eric Edward *mechanical engineer*
Vander Velde, Wallace Earl *aeronautical and astronautical engineering educator*
White, David Calvin *electrical engineer, educator, energy executive, consultant*
Whitman, Robert Van Duyne *civil engineering educator*
Williams, James Henry, Jr. *mechanical engineer, educator, consultant*
Wittrup, Karl Dane *chemical engineer, educator*
Wuensch, Bernhardt John *ceramic engineering educator*
Young, Laurence Retman *biomedical engineer, educator*
Zhang, Shuguang *biomedical engineer*

**Carlisle**
Drew, Philip Garfield *retired engineering company executive, consultant*

## Charlestown
Ntziachristos, Vasilis *bioengineer*

## Concord
Davidson, Frank Paul *retired macroengineer, retired lawyer*
Villers, Philippe *mechanical engineer*
Woll, Harry J. *electrical engineer*

## Dartmouth
Notaros, Branislav M. *electrical engineer, educator*

## Fall River
Alam, Akm A. *ceramics engineer*

## Foxboro
Pierce, Francis Casimir *civil engineer*

## Framingham
Crossley, Frank Alphonso *retired metallurgical engineer*
Kendall, Julius *consulting engineer*
Lindsay, Leslie *packaging engineer*

## Hampden
Joubert, Raymond Ernest *retired electrical engineer*

## Holbrook
Crandlemere, Robert Wayne *engineering executive*

## Lexington
Aldrich, Nancy Cook *engineer*
Aronin, Lewis Richard *metallurgical engineer*
Bailey, Fred Coolidge *retired engineering consulting company executive*
Benitz, Gerald Robert *electrical engineer*
Beusch, John Ulrich *engineer, researcher*
Bussgang, Julian Jakub *electronics engineer, consultant*
Dinneen, Gerald Paul *electrical engineer, retired federal official*
Freed, Charles *engineering consultant, researcher*
Garrelick, Joel Marc *acoustical scientist, consultant*
Gelb, Arthur *electrical and systems engineering executive*
Keicher, William Eugene *electrical engineer*
Morrow, Walter Edwin, Jr. *electrical engineer, lab administrator*
Zayhowski, John J. *electrical engineer, researcher*

## Lincoln
Kerrebrock, Jack Leo *aeronautics and astronautics engineering educator, department chairman*

## Longmeadow
Lemnios, Andrew Zachery *aerospace engineer, educator, researcher*

## Lynn
Chow, Humphrey Wai *mechanical engineer*

## Lynnfield
Meyer, Piotr Jan *electronics engineer*

## Marlborough
Bennett, C. Leonard *electrical engineer*

## Medford
Abriola, Linda Marie *civil engineer, environmental engineer*
Greif, Robert *mechanical engineering educator*
Uhlir, Arthur, Jr. *electrical engineer, academic administrator*

## Medway
Hoag, David Garratt *retired aerospace engineer*

## Nantucket
Kales, Paul Albert *engineering educator, cartoonist*

## Natick
Berglund, Larry Glenn *mechanical engineer, educator*
Latanision, Ronald Michael *materials science and engineering consultant*
Pokorny, Joseph Wenceslaus III *engineer*

## Newton
Lev-Ari, Hanoch *electrical engineering educator*
Marrone, Philip A. *chemical engineer*
Sheridan, Thomas Brown *mechanical engineering and applied psychology educator, researcher, consultant*

## Norwood
Sheingold, Daniel H. *electrical engineer*

## Paxton
Clarke, Edward Nielsen *engineering science educator*

## Peabody
McDonald, Michael Perry *retired transportation engineer, musician*
Peters, Leo Francis *environmental engineer*

## Pittsfield
Feigenbaum, Armand Vallin *systems engineer, information technology executive*
Shammas, Nazih Kheirallah *environmental engineer, consultant, engineering educator*

## Quincy
Colgan, Sumner *manufacturing engineer, chemical engineer*

## Shutesbury
Abbott, Douglas Eugene *engineering educator*

## Somerset
Bower, John *retired fluid mechanics engineer, commissioner*

## Stoughton
Graber, Samuel David *environmental and water resources engineer, consultant*

## Sudbury
Fowler, Charles Albert *electronics engineer*

## Swampscott
Kaufman, William Morris *electrical engineer, consultant*

## Tewksbury
Faccini, Ernest Carlo *mechanical engineer*

## Waban
Christian, John Thomas *civil engineer*
Mark, Melvin *mechanical engineering educator, consultant*

## Waltham
Guerra, John Michael *optical engineer*
Gumpertz, Werner Herbert *structural engineering company executive*
Pralle, Martin Ulrich *materials engineer, director*

## Wellesley
Weil, Thomas Alexander *retired electronics engineer*

## Weston
Katz, William Emanuel *retired chemical engineer*

## Winchester
Hansen, Robert Joseph *civil engineer*
Koppel, Lowell B. *chemical engineer*

## Worcester
Gaudette, Glenn R. *biomedical engineer, educator*
Katz, Robert Nathan *ceramics engineer, educator*
Lou, Wenjing *engineering educator*
Parrish, Edward Alton, Jr. *electrical and computer engineering educator, academic administrator*

## Wrentham
Bittenbender, Brad James *environmental engineer*

# MICHIGAN

## Ann Arbor
Adriaens, Peter *environmental engineer, consultant*
Becher, William Don *retired electrical engineer, engineering educator, writer*
Bilello, John Charles *engineering educator, director*
Chaffin, Don Brian *industrial engineering educator, research director*
Depcik, Christopher David *mechanical engineer, researcher*
England, Anthony Wayne *engineering educator, dean, science educator*
Friedmann, Peretz Peter *aerospace engineer, educator*
Gibala, Ronald *metallurgical engineering educator*
Gilbert, Elmer Grant *engineering educator, control theorist*
Hayes, John Patrick *electrical engineering and computer science educator, consultant*
Kammash, Terry *nuclear engineering educator*
Koren, Yoram *mechanical engineering educator*
Kozma, Adam *electrical engineer*
Lian, Jie *engineering educator, researcher*
Martin, William Russell *nuclear engineering educator*
Meitzler, Allen Henry *electrical engineering educator, automotive scientist*
Merte, Herman, Jr. *mechanical engineering educator*
Meyer, John Frederick *engineering educator*
Petrick, Ernest Nicholas *mechanical engineer, researcher*
Pollock, Stephen Michael *operations research engineer, educator, consultant*
Powell, Kenneth Grant *aerospace engineering educator*
Root, William Lucas *electrical engineering educator*
Savari, Serap Ayse *engineering educator, researcher*
Senior, Thomas Bryan A. *electrical engineering educator, researcher, consultant*
Shyy, Wei *aerospace and mechanical engineering researcher, educator*
Steel, Duncan Gregory *engineering educator*
Wilson, Richard Christian *engineering firm executive*
Wojcik, Laura A. *engineer, consultant*
Young, Edwin Harold *chemical and metallurgical engineering educator*

## Auburn Hills
Liu, C. Q. *engineer*

## Battle Creek
Risukhin, Vladimir Nikolayevich *aeronautical engineer, educator*

## Bingham Farms
Gratch, Serge *retired mechanical engineering educator*

## Bloomfield
Gabriel, Martin George *engineering consultant*

## Bloomfield Hills
Stivender, Donald Lewis *mechanical engineering consultant*

## Dearborn
Cairns, James Robert *mechanical engineering educator*
Chou, Clifford Chi Fong *research engineering executive*
Gandhi, Haren S. *chemical engineer*
Jie, Min *mechanical engineering educator, researcher*
Little, Robert Eugene *engineering educator*
Mi, Chunting Chris *engineering educator*
Shim, Taehyun *mechanical engineer*

Thai-Tang, Hau *automotive engineer*
Yang, Guangbin *engineer*

## Detroit
Kummler, Ralph H. *chemical engineer, educator, dean*
Lee, Joon Sang *engineering educator*
McWhorter, Sharon Louise *engineering executive, inventor, consultant*
Rathod, Mulchand *mechanical engineering educator*
Rivin, Evgeny Izrailevich *mechanical engineer, consultant*
Taraza, Dinu *engineering educator, researcher*

## East Lansing
Andersland, Orlando Baldwin *engineering educator*
Chen, Kun-Mu *electrical engineering educator*
Cutts, Charles Eugene *retired engineering educator*
Foss, John Frank *mechanical engineering educator*
Goodman, Erik David *engineering educator*
Lloyd, John Raymond *mechanical engineering educator*
Pierre, Percy Anthony *engineering educator*
Saul, William Edward *engineering educator*
Uludag, Umut *electrical engineer, researcher*
von Bernuth, Robert Dean *agricultural engineering educator, consultant*
Von Tersch, Lawrence Wayne *engineering educator, dean*

## Eastport
Tomlinson, James Lawrence *mechanical engineer*

## Farmington
Neyer, Jerome Charles *consulting civil engineer*

## Farmington Hills
Hurd, Mary K. *civil engineer, writer*

## Flint
Echempati, Raghu *mechanical engineering educator, consultant*

## Flushing
Bain, William David *electronics engineer, writer*

## Grand Blanc
Riley, Ronald Jim *industrial engineer, consultant*

## Grand Rapids
Garver, Frederick Merrill *industrial engineering executive*
Keller, Fred P. *engineering company executive*

## Greenbush
Paulson, James Marvin *retired engineering educator*

## Grosse Pointe
Beltz, Charles Robert *retired engineering executive*

## Grosse Pointe Shores
Holness, Gordon Victor Rix *engineering executive, mechanical engineer*

## Holland
Stynes, Stanley Kenneth *retired chemical engineer, educator*

## Houghton
Crittenden, John Charles *engineering educator*
Heckel, Richard Wayne *metallurgical engineering educator*
Huang, Eugene Yuching *civil engineer, educator*
Mishra, Piyush *computer engineer, researcher, educator*
Narain, Amitabh *aerospace and mechanical engineering educator*
Welch, Eric D. *electrical engineer, consultant*
You, Zhanping *civil engineer, educator*

## Kalamazoo
Litynski, Daniel Mitchell *engineering educator, retired military officer*

## Lansing
Shirtum, Earl Edward *retired civil engineer*

## Leland
Soutas-Little, Robert William *mechanical engineer, educator*

## Livonia
Uicker, Joseph Bernard *retired engineering company executive*

## Mattawan
Greene, Timothy James *industrial engineering educator*

## Midland
Meister, Bernard John *retired chemical engineer*

## Niles
Marshall, Gerald Francis *optical engineer, consultant, physicist*

## North Branch
Stevenson, James Laraway *engineering company executive, electronics engineer, computer engineer, communications engineer, engineering educator*

## Pontiac
Hampton, Philip Michael *consulting engineering company executive*
Wang, Yucong *engineering executive*

## Rochester
Haskell, Richard Edmund *engineering educator*
Loh, Robert N. K. *engineering educator*
Polis, Michael Philip *engineering educator*
Yang, Lianxiang *optical engineer, educator*

## Royal Oak
Fragomeni, James Mark *mechanical engineer, educator*

## Shelby Township
Aukland, Neil Ralph *electronics engineer, researcher*
Nagy, Louis Leonard *engineering executive, researcher*

## Southfield
Battah, Hammam Jamil *civil engineer, utilities executive*
McKeen, Alexander C. *retired engineering executive, foundation administrator*
Song, Xubin *mechanical engineer, researcher*

## Sterling Heights
Lane, Wendall Chenney, Jr. *automotive engineer*

## Troy
Nefske, Donald Joseph *engineer*
Zhenyu, Kong *industrial engineer*

# MINNESOTA

## Bloomington
Ouyang, Jun *electrical engineer, researcher*
Tsu, I-Fei *materials engineer*

## Brooklyn Park
DeBusk, Charles Richard *engineer, consultant*

## Eden Prairie
Higgins, Robert Arthur *electrical engineer, educator, consultant*

## Grand Marais
Napadensky, Hyla Sarane *engineering consultant*

## Lakeville
Setterholm, Jeffrey Miles *systems engineer*

## Madison
Husby, Donald Evans *engineering company executive*

## Maple Plain
Erdmann, John Baird *environmental engineer*

## Minneapolis
Abi-Ghanem, Georges Victor *civil engineer, environmental engineer*
Anderson, John Edward *mechanical engineering educator*
Ariyur, Kartik Balasubramanian *control systems engineer, researcher*
Cussler, Edward Lansing, Jr. *chemical engineer, educator*
Davis, Howard Ted *engineering educator*
Galambos, Theodore Victor *civil engineer, educator*
Gulliver, John Stephen *civil engineering educator*
Hayes, Caroline Clark *engineering educator*
Hillstrom, Thomas Peter *engineering executive*
Johnson, Walter Kline *civil engineer*
Joseph, Daniel Donald *aeronautical engineer, educator*
Keller, Kenneth Harrison *engineering educator*
Kvalseth, Tarald Oddvar *mechanical engineer, educator*
Lambert, Robert Frank *electrical engineer, educator, consultant*
Levinson, David Matthew *engineering educator, civil engineer*
Oriani, Richard Anthony *metallurgical engineer, educator*
Parhi, Keshab Kumar *electrical and computer engineering educator*
Persson, Erland Karl *electrical engineer, engineering executive*
Pfender, Emil *mechanical engineering educator*
Sadraie, Hamid Reza *civil engineer, researcher*
Scriven, L. E(dward) *engineering educator*
Srirangarajan, Seshan *electrical engineer, researcher*

## Minnetonka
Johnson, Lennart Ingemar *materials engineering consultant*

## Saint Paul
Mlinar, John R. *mechanical engineer*

## Woodbury
Beck, Warren Randall *retired glass technologist*

# MISSISSIPPI

## Bay Saint Louis
Corbin, James H. *engineering executive, meteorologist, oceanographer*

## Biloxi
Brinsmade, Akbar Fairchild *chemical engineering consultant*

## Gulfport
LaBorde, Oriel *civil engineer*

## Jackson
Eldek, Abdelnasser A. *engineering educator, researcher*

## Kiln
Mathur, Abhinav *research engineer*

## Mississippi State
Babski-Reeves, Kari *industrial and systems engineering educator*
Eksioglu, Burak *engineering educator*
Janus, Jonathan Mark *aerospace engineer, educator*
Potimiche, Gabriel Petru *mechanical engineer, researcher*
Shah, Vijay Pravin *electrical engineer, researcher*

Thompson, Joe Floyd *aerospace engineer, researcher*
Truax, Dennis Dale *civil engineer, educator, consultant*

**Ridgeland**
Ghirmai, Tadesse *engineering educator, researcher*

**Starkville**
Jacob, Paul Bernard, Jr. *electrical engineering educator*
Liu, Qingyun *thermal and mechanical research engineer*

**University**
Cheng, Alexander Hung-Darh *engineering educator, consultant*
Matalgah, Mustafa Muhammad *engineering educator, researcher*
Smith, Allie Maitland *engineering educator*
Yakovlev, Alexander B. *electrical engineer, educator*

**West Point**
Cliett, Charles Buren *retired aeronautical engineer, retired educator, retired academic administrator*

**MISSOURI**

**Ballwin**
Cornell, William Daniel *mechanical engineer*

**Columbia**
Creighton, Donald Louis *mechanical engineer, consultant*
Day, Cecil LeRoy *agricultural engineering educator*
Edgington, Bobbie George *communications engineer, consultant*
Frisby, James Curtis *retired agricultural engineering educator*
Gu, Zhimang *engineer*
Keyvan, Shahla *nuclear engineer, educator*
Kirawanich, Phumin *electrical engineer*
O'Connor, John Thomas *civil engineering educator*
Pringle, Oran Allan *mechanical and aerospace engineering educator*
Retzloff, David George *engineering educator*
Shende, Rajesh V. *chemical engineer, materials scientist, researcher*

**Florissant**
Stevens, Robert Edward *engineering company executive*

**Fortuna**
Ramer, James LeRoy *civil engineer*

**Four Seasons**
Bivins, Susan Steinbach *systems engineer*

**Kansas City**
Acheson, Allen Morrow *retired engineering executive*
Davis, (Francis) Keith *civil engineer*
Green, Frank Earl *civil engineer*
Leigh, Cheri J. *engineering consulting executive*

**Kirkwood**
Holsen, James Noble, Jr. *retired chemical engineer*

**North Kansas City**
Hild, Travis Robert *network engineer*

**Rolla**
Chen, Genda *civil engineer, educator*
Chowdhury, Badrul *engineering educator*
Day, Delbert Edwin *ceramic engineering educator*
Liou, Fue-Wen Frank *engineering educator*
Rao, Vittal Srirangam *electrical engineering educator*
Saperstein, Lee Waldo *mining engineering educator*
Sauer, Harry John, Jr. *mechanical engineer, educator, academic administrator*
Sedigh Sarvestani, Sahra *engineering educator*
Venayagamoorthy, Ganesh Kumar *electrical engineer, computer engineer, educator*
Yu, Wei-Wen *retired engineering educator*

**Saint Charles**
Haas, Daniel Louis *structural engineer*

**Saint Louis**
Antonacci, Anthony Eugene *retired engineer*
Balint, David Lee *engineering company executive*
Briggs, William Benajah *retired aerospace engineer*
Byrnes, Christopher Ian *engineering educator*
Dreifke, Gerald Edmond *electrical engineering educator*
Dudukovic, Milorad P. *chemical engineering educator, consultant*
Goldstein, Julius Lester *biomedical engineer, consultant*
Gould, Phillip Louis *engineering educator, department chairman*
Husar, Rudolf Bertalan *mechanical engineering educator*
Izuchukwu, John Ifeanyichukwu *industrial engineer, mechanical engineer*
McKelvey, James Morgan *chemical engineering educator, retired dean*
Orton, George Frederick *aerospace engineer*
Peters, David Allen *mechanical engineering educator, consultant*
Ross, Monte *electrical engineer, researcher*
Rudy, Yoram *biomedical engineer, biophysicist, educator*
Shrauner, Barbara Wayne Abraham *electrical engineer, educator*
Stepanek, Curtis E *electrical engineer*
Sutera, Salvatore Philip *mechanical engineer, educator*
Szabo, Barna Aladar *engineering educator*
Zurheide, Charles Henry *consulting electrical engineer*

**Springfield**
Maples, Jimmie Kay *mechanical engineer*

**University City**
McVey, Francis Daniel *mechanical engineer, software developer, educator*
Winter, David Ferdinand *electrical engineering educator, consultant*

**MONTANA**

**Bozeman**
Cokelet, Giles Roy *biomedical engineering educator*
Mandell, John F. *chemical engineer, educator*
Mian, Ahsan *engineering educator, mechanical engineer*
Nehrir, M. Hashem *electrical engineer, educator*
Sanks, Robert Leland *environmental engineer, retired educator*
Stanislao, Joseph *engineering educator, consultant*

**Great Falls**
Walker, Leland Jasper *civil engineer*

**Harlem**
Brekke, Alan Lee *industrial engineer*

**Kalispell**
Freiberg, Robert Jerry *engineering executive*

**Pony**
Anderson, Richard Ernest *agricultural engineer, consultant, rancher*

**NEBRASKA**

**Clay Center**
Hahn, George LeRoy *agricultural engineer, biometeorologist*

**Lincoln**
Burnham, Stephen John *civil engineer*
Edison, Allen Ray *electrical engineer, educator*
Edwards, Donald Mervin *systems engineer, educator, dean*
Splinter, William Eldon *agricultural engineering educator*
Sundaram, Murali M. *manufacturing engineer, researcher*
Wang, Lijun *chemical engineer, educator*
Woollam, John Arthur *electrical engineering educator, physics professor*

**Omaha**
Houser, Kevin *engineering educator*
Tunnicliff, David George *civil engineer, consultant*

**NEVADA**

**Boulder City**
Wyman, Richard Vaughn *engineering educator, engineering company executive*

**Dayton**
Clements, Linda L. *materials engineer, educator, journalist*

**Henderson**
Wennerstrom, Arthur John *aeronautical engineer*

**Incline Village**
Merdinger, Charles John *civil engineer, educator, military officer, academic administrator*
Thompson, David Alfred *industrial engineer*

**Las Vegas**
Culp, Gordon Louis *consulting engineer, management consultant*
Haas, Robert John *aerospace engineer*
Hashem, Zouheir Anwar *engineering company executive, educator*
Herzlich, Harold J. *chemical engineer*
Liu, Qunli *engineering educator, researcher*
Massier, Paul Ferdinand *mechanical engineer*
Mc Elroy, John Harley *electrical and industrial engineering educator*
Messinger, George Clement *engineering executive, consultant*
Neumann, Edward Schreiber *transportation engineering educator*
Ramos, Albert A. *electrical engineer*

**Minden**
Bently, Donald Emery *electrical engineer*

**Reno**
Carr, James Russell *engineering educator*
Danko, George *engineering educator*
Fuerstenau, M(aurice) C(lark) *metallurgical engineer*
Je, Chung-Hwan *engineering educator, researcher*
Kleppe, John Arthur *electrical engineer, educator, engineering executive*
Mandl, William John *electronics engineer, researcher*
Vasquez, Victor R. *chemical engineering educator*

**Sparks**
Lagasse, Bruce Kenneth *retired structural engineer*

**NEW HAMPSHIRE**

**Farmington**
Panek, William Dominick *systems engineer executive*

**Hanover**
Lotko, William *engineering educator*
Queneau, Paul Etienne *metallurgical engineering educator*

**Hudson**
Ainley, David James *systems engineer, electrical engineer*

**Laconia**
Parthasarathy, Vinod *manufacturing engineer, consultant*

**Manchester**
Hower, Philip Leland *semiconductor device engineer*
Kamen, Dean *biomedical engineer*
Pochampally, Kishore K. *engineering educator*

**Nashua**
Woodruff, Thomas Ellis *electronics consulting executive*
Yannone, Ronald Matthew *systems engineer, researcher*

**New London**
Crane, Robert Kendall *engineering educator, researcher, consultant*

**Portsmouth**
Baumann, Hans D. *engineering executive*

**Warner**
Hunt, Everett Clair *engineering educator, researcher, consultant*

**NEW JERSEY**

**Absecon**
Cartlidge, Edward Sutterley *mechanical engineer*

**Basking Ridge**
Drewry, Don Neal *fire protection engineer*

**Bedminster**
David, Edward Emil, Jr. *electrical engineer, engineering executive, management consultant*

**Camden**
Madan, Deepak S. *engineering executive*

**Cherry Hill**
Batterman, Steven Charles *engineering mechanics and bioengineering professor, consultant*

**Cinnaminson**
Hanejko, Francis Gary *metallurgical engineer, metallurgist*

**Clinton**
Bosch, Robert John, Jr. *mechanical engineer*

**Columbus**
Litman, Bernard *electrical engineer, consultant*

**East Brunswick**
Daniel, Charles Timothy *transportation engineer, consultant*

**Englewood**
Deresiewicz, Herbert *retired mechanical engineering educator, retired academic administrator*

**Ewing**
Brunda, Daniel Donald *retired aerospace engineer, consultant, inventor, writer*

**Florham Park**
Rexford, Jennifer *communications engineer*

**Fort Lee**
Treskov, Yakov Maks *engineer*

**Fort Monmouth**
Perlman, Barry Stuart *electrical engineer, researcher*

**Freehold**
Christ, Duane Marland *retired computer systems engineer*

**Glassboro**
Dahm, Kevin *chemical engineer, educator*
Slater, C. Stewart *chemical engineering educator*

**Haddonfield**
Chu, Horn Dean *chemical engineer*

**Harrison**
Srinivasan, Purushothaman *electrical engineer, researcher*

**Helmetta**
Gabay, Eleonora V. *mechanical engineer, educator*

**Hewitt**
Selwyn, Donald *engineering administrator, researcher, inventor, educator*

**Highland Park**
Spencer, Herbert Harry *structural engineer, researcher, computer analyst*

**Hillsborough**
Sun, Wei *electrical engineer*

**Hoboken**
Boesch, Francis Theodore *electrical engineer, educator*
Chassapis, Constantin *mechanical engineer, educator*
Griskey, Richard George *chemical engineering professor*
Lawrence, Victor B. *computer engineer, systems engineer*
Savitsky, Daniel *retired structural engineer, retired educator*
Sisto, Fernando *mechanical engineering educator*
Voloshin, Yury *chemical engineer*
Xing, Yiping *electrical engineer, researcher*
Yao, Yu-Dong *electrical engineer, educator, electrical engineer, researcher*

**Holmdel**
Lang, Howard Lawrence *electrical engineer*
Papadias, Constantinos Basil *electrical engineer*

**Hopatcong**
Ferderber-Hersonski, Boris Constantin *process engineer*

**Jackson**
Tague, Charles Francis *retired engineering company executive, real estate company executive, construction executive*

**Jersey City**
Vasmatzidis, Ioannis *systems engineer*

**Kinnelon**
Haller, Charles Edward *engineer, consultant*

**Lakewood**
Fanuele, Michael Anthony *retired electronics engineer, research engineer*

**Little Falls**
Viil, Heino *retired engineer*

**Livingston**
Daman, Ernest Ludwig *mechanical engineer*
Stevens, William Dollard *mechanical engineer, consultant*

**Madison**
Chang, Darwin Ray *civil engineer*

**Mahwah**
Rakotobe-Joel, Thierry *engineering educator, researcher, department chairman*

**Manasquan**
Abate, John E. *electrical engineer, consultant*

**Matawan**
Fennessy, James Gerard *retired engineer*

**Montclair**
Eager, George Sidney, Jr. *electrical engineer, engineering executive*

**Morris Plains**
Bennett, John Charles *former engineering and construction executive*

**Morristown**
Kittelberger, Larry E. *engineering executive*
Lieberman, Lester Zane *engineering company executive*
Rainal, Attilio Joseph *retired electronics engineer*

**Neptune**
Zurick, Jack *electrical engineer, consultant*

**New Brunswick**
Jaluria, Yogesh *mechanical engineering educator, department chairman*
Weng, George Jueng-Cious *engineering educator*

**New Providence**
Fleming, James William *ceramics engineer*

**Newark**
Bar-Ness, Yeheskel *electrical engineer, educator*
Dhawan, Atam Prakash *engineering educator, dean*
Friedland, Bernard *engineer, educator*
Hanesian, Deran *chemical engineer, educator, environmental scientist, consultant*
Hrycak, Peter *retired engineering educator*
Pfeffer, Robert *chemical engineer, academic administrator, educator*
Rosato, Anthony Dominick *mechanical engineer, educator*
Spillers, William Russell *civil engineering educator*
Vaidya, Jaideep Shrikant *engineering educator*
Van Buskirk, William Charles *engineering educator*

**Newfoundland**
Van Winkle, Edgar Walling *retired electrical engineer*

**North Brunswick**
Frenkiel, Richard Henry *retired systems engineer, consultant*

**Ocean**
Reich, Bernard *communications engineer*

**Oradell**
Roe, W. Barton *engineering executive*

**Parsippany**
Theiss, Richard Edward *electrical engineer, applications engineer*

**Pennington**
Zhang, Hong (Rick) *design engineer, researcher*

**Pennsauken**
Alday, Paul Stackhouse, Jr. *retired mechanical engineer*

**Piscataway**
Balaguru, Perumalsamy *civil engineering educator*
Flanagan, James Loton *electrical engineer, researcher, engineering educator*
Linke, Richard A. *optical engineer*
Poses, Frederic M. *engineering company executive*
Salkind, Alvin J. *engineering educator, dean, consultant*
Shanefield, Daniel Jay *ceramic engineering educator*
Sincoskie, W. David *computer engineer*
Welkowitz, Walter *biomedical engineer, educator*
Zhang, Dajun *biomedical engineering educator*

**Princeton**
Bartolini, Robert Alfred *electrical engineer, researcher*

Billington, David Perkins *civil engineering educator*
Debenedetti, Pablo Gaston *chemical engineering professor*
Gillham, John Kinsey *chemical engineering professor*
Gmachl, Claire *electrical engineer, educator*
Lechner, Bernard Joseph *consulting electrical engineer*
Leonard, Naomi Ehrich *aerospace engineer, engineering educator*
Liu, Bede *electrical engineering educator*
Miles, Richard Bryant *mechanical and aerospace engineering educator*
Palomar, Daniel Perez *electrical engineer*
Poor, Harold Vincent *electrical engineering educator*
Russel, William Bailey *engineering educator*
Saville, Dudley Albert *chemical engineering educator*
Socolow, Robert Harry *engineering educator*
Song, Zhen *electrical engineer, researcher*
Stengel, Robert Frank *engineering and applied science educator*
Tsui, Daniel C. *electrical engineer, physicist*
VanMarcke, Erik Hector *civil engineer, educator*
Verdu, Sergio *engineering educator*
Wei, James *chemical engineering professor, academic dean*

**Princeton Junction**
Bair, William Alois *engineer*
Denlinger, Edgar Jacob *electronics engineering executive, researcher*
Haddad, James Henry *chemical engineer, consultant*
Lull, William Paul *engineering consultant*
Vahaviolos, Sotirios John *electrical engineer, researcher, engineering executive*

**Rancocas**
Rowan, Henry M. *electrical engineer*

**Ridgewood**
Farrell, Gregory Alan *biomedical engineer*

**Rumson**
Rowe, Harrison Edward *electrical engineer*

**Sea Bright**
Plummer, Dirk Arnold *chemical, electrical, and electronics engineer*

**Secaucus**
Lynch, Joseph Michael *engineer, consultant*

**Short Hills**
Wharton, Lennard *engineering company executive*

**Skillman**
Brill, Yvonne Claeys *engineer, consultant*

**South Plainfield**
Kennedy, John William *engineering company executive*

**Sparta**
Truran, William Richard *electrical engineer*

**Stratford**
Daguisan, Janel *biomedical engineer, electronics and computer educator, music producer*

**Summit**
Fukui, Hatsuaki *retired electrical engineer, art historian*
Rosensweig, Ronald Ellis *chemical engineer, consultant*

**Swedesboro**
Lovell, Theodore *electrical engineer, consultant*

**Teaneck**
Ehrlich, Ira Robert *mechanical engineering consultant*
Reinish, Gloria Brooks *electrical engineer, educator*

**Titusville**
Cooper, Paul *retired mechanical engineer, science association director, researcher*

**Union**
Newman, Stephen Alexander *chemical engineer*

**Upper Saddle River**
Wallace, William III *engineering executive*

**Voorhees**
Siskin, Edward Joseph *engineering company executive, construction company executive*

**Watchung**
Michaelis, Paul Charles *engineering physicist executive*
Tornqvist, Erik Gustav Markus *chemical engineer, research scientist, consultant*

**Wayne**
Geiger, David E *engineer*
Schmidt, Barnet Michael *communications and electronic engineer*

**West Caldwell**
Piel, Emil J. *retired engineering educator*

**West New York**
Gruenberg, Elliot Lewis *electronics engineer and company executive*

**Westfield**
Bhagat, Phiroz Maneck *mechanical engineer*

**NEW MEXICO**

**Alamogordo**
Ernst, James Allan *safety engineer, consultant*

**Albuquerque**
Anderson, Lawrence Keith *electrical engineer, consultant*
Ardelean, Emil Valentin *mechanical engineer, researcher*
Baum, Carl Edward *electrical engineer, researcher*
Brinker, Charles Jeffrey *chemistry and chemical engineering educator*
Cornelius, Chris James *chemical engineer, researcher*
Dorato, Peter *electrical and computer engineering educator*
Finch, Robert Jonathan *communications engineer, consultant*
Hall, Jerome William *research engineering educator*
Herrera, Gilbert Victor *engineering executive*
Mansell, Justin Dennis *optical engineer, consultant*
Mitchelhill, James Moffat *retired civil engineer*
Moulds, William J. *retired aeronautical engineer*
Peck, Ralph Brazelton *civil engineering educator, consultant*
Sebesta, Henry R. *engineering executive, researcher*
Urgessa, Girum Solomon *structural engineer, researcher*

**Belen**
Toliver, Lee *mechanical engineer*

**Carlsbad**
Piper, Lloyd Llewellyn, II, *engineer, government and service industry executive*

**Cedar Crest**
Meinel, Carolyn Pettit *industrial engineer, writer*

**Cerrillos**
Lutz, Raymond Price *retired industrial engineer, educator*

**Cloudcroft**
Hadfield, Michael James *electrical engineer*

**Embudo**
Rogers, Benjamin Talbot *mechanical engineer, consultant*

**Farmington**
Lewis, Homer Dick *retired nuclear engineer*

**Kirtland Afb**
Pham, Khanh Dai *aerospace engineer, researcher*
Prather, William Doyle *electronics engineer, researcher*

**Las Cruces**
Deng, Shuguang *chemical engineer, educator*
Ford, Clarence Quentin *mechanical engineer, educator*

**Los Alamos**
Chang, Chong Hyuck *engineer*
Dudziak, Donald John *nuclear engineer, educator*
Jackson, James F. *nuclear engineer, educator*
Mortensen, Fred N. *engineer*
Stoddard, Stephen Davidson *ceramics engineer, retired state senator*
Wohlberg, Brendt *electrical engineer, researcher*

**Placitas**
Hidy, George Martel *chemical engineer, engineering executive*

**Santa Fe**
Goorley, John Timothy *nuclear engineer*
Kaman, Helen S. *retired aerospace engineer, artist*
Morrison, Malcolm Cameron *engineering management professional*

**NEW YORK**

**Albany**
Alberski, Tadeusz Czeslaw *civil engineer, researcher*
Fanuele, Frank John *engineering executive, electrical engineer*
Happ, Harvey Heinz *electrical engineer, educator*
Roy, Rob J. *biomedical engineer, anesthesiologist, educator*

**Amherst**
Govindaraju, Venu *computer engineer, educator*
Kutsin, Leonid *engineering educator, researcher*

**Astoria**
Unsal-Tunay, Nuran *geological engineer, researcher*

**Bethpage**
Conti, James Joseph *retired chemical engineer, educator*

**Big Flats**
Orsillo, James Edward *computer engineer, information technology executive*

**Binghamton**
Yu, Ming *engineering educator, researcher*

**Brewster**
Nadel, Norman Allen *civil engineer*

**Briarcliff Manor**
Chou, Chun-Ting *engineer, researcher*

**Bronxville**
Brunale, Vito John *aerospace engineer*

**Brooklyn**
Armenakas, Anthony Emmanuel *aerospace engineering educator*
Birenbaum, Leo *retired engineering educator*
Crânganu, Constantin *engineer*
Das, Nirod K. *engineering educator*
Haralick, Robert Martin *electrical engineering educator*
Helly, Walter Sigmund *engineering educator*

Hussein, Osama *computer engineer, educator*
Iskander, Magued *engineering educator, consultant*
Knizhnik, Leonid *engineering educator*
McLean, William Ronald *retired electrical engineer, consultant*
Parlamis, Michael Frank *civil engineer, construction executive*
Shaw, Leonard Glazer *retired electrical engineering educator, consultant*
Wei, Xinzhou *engineering educator*

**Buffalo**
Cartwright, Alexander N. *electrical engineer, educator*
Chang, Ching Ming (Carl Chang) *engineering executive, mechanical engineer, educator, writer*
Karwan, Mark Henry *engineering educator*
Meredith, Dale Dean *civil engineering educator*
Neelamegham, Sriram *chemical engineer, educator, researcher*
Pados, Dimitris A. *electrical engineer, educator*
Reismann, Herbert *engineer, educator*
Ruckenstein, Eli *chemical engineering professor*
Sarjeant, Walter James *electrical and computer engineering educator*
Shaw, David Tai-Ko *electrical and computer engineering educator, academic administrator*
Tsai, Christina W. *civil engineer, educator*
Weber, Thomas William *chemical engineering professor*
Weller, Sol William *chemical engineering professor*
Zirnheld, Jennifer L. *engineering educator, researcher*

**Cato**
Sheckler, Ross David *engineering executive*

**Chappaqua**
Pomerene, James Herbert *retired computer engineer*

**Cheektowaga**
Wozniak, Richard Anthony *computer engineer*

**Clarence**
Greatbatch, Wilson *biomedical engineer*

**Clifton Park**
Sun, Zuo *mechanical engineer, researcher*

**Clinton**
Pagani, Albert Louis *aerospace system engineer*

**Cold Spring**
Pugh, Emerson William *electrical engineer*

**Corning**
Beall, George Halsey *ceramics engineer*

**Dix Hills**
Braun, Ludwig *retired engineering educator*

**East Norwich**
Rosen, Meyer Robert *chemical engineer*

**Farmingdale**
Bandyopadhyay, Amitabha *engineering educator*

**Flushing**
Birnstiel, Charles *consulting engineer*
Goldenshteyn, Vladimir Lev *civil engineer*
Kopp, Ilya Zinovij *engineering educator*
Stahl, Frank Ludwig *civil engineer*

**Franklin Square**
Cantilli, Edmund Joseph *safety engineer, educator, translator, writer, consultant*

**Glenville**
Anderson, Roy Everett *retired electrical engineer*

**Greenlawn**
Bachman, Henry Lee *electrical engineer, engineering company executive*

**Hauppauge**
Buckley, Robert Matthew *electrical engineer*

**Hawthorne**
Lavenberg, Stephen S. *electrical engineer, researcher*

**Hempstead**
Goldstein, Stanley Philip *engineering educator*

**Huntington**
Christiansen, Donald David *electrical engineer, editor, publishing executive, consultant*
LaTourrette, James Thomas *retired electrophysics, electrical engineering and computer science educator*

**Huntington Station**
Agosta, Vito *mechanical and aerospace engineering educator*

**Ithaca**
Carlin, Herbert J. *electrical engineering educator, researcher*
De Boer, Pieter Cornelis Tobias *mechanical and aerospace engineering educator*
Dick, Richard Irwin *environmental engineer, educator*
Eastman, Lester Fuess *electrical engineer, educator*
Fuchs, W. Kent *engineering educator*
Haith, Douglas A. *engineering educator, researcher*
Leibovich, Sidney *engineering educator*
Loucks, Daniel Peter *environmental systems engineer*
Maxwell, William Laughlin *retired industrial engineering educator*
McGuire, William *civil engineer, educator*
Meyburg, Arnim Hans *transportation engineer, educator, consultant*
O'Rourke, Thomas Denis *civil engineer, educator*
Phelan, Richard Magruder *mechanical engineer*
Rodríguez, Ferdinand *chemical engineer, educator*

Smith, Julian Cleveland, Jr. *chemical engineering professor*

**Jericho**
Shinners, Stanley Marvin *electrical engineer*

**Katonah**
Bashkow, Theodore Robert *electrical engineering consultant, former educator*

**Kew Gardens**
Chipkin, Frederick *textile designer, consultant, artist, writer*

**Lansing**
Emelett, Stephen John *electrical engineer, researcher*

**Liverpool**
Hamlett, James Gordon *electronics engineer, management consultant, educator*

**Melville**
Bongiorno, Joseph John, Jr. *electrical engineering educator*
Bultan, Aykut *communications systems engineer*
Olesen, Robert Lind Ole *electrical engineer*
Schmid, Charles Ernest *acoustical engineer, academic administrator*
Taub, Jesse J. *electrical engineering researcher*

**Mohegan Lake**
Paik, John Kee *structural engineer*

**Morrisville**
Shayya, Walid H. *natural resources engineer*

**Mount Kisco**
Green, Paul Eliot, Jr. *retired optical engineer*

**Mount Sinai**
Kopp, Richard Edgar *electrical engineer*

**New Hyde Park**
Hyman, Abraham *electrical engineer*

**New Paltz**
Chikwendu, Sunday C. *engineering educator, mathematician*

**New York**
Acrivos, Andreas *chemical engineering professor*
Ahmad, Jameel *civil engineer, researcher, educator*
Boley, Bruno Adrian *engineering educator*
Bove, John Louis *chemistry and environmental engineering educator, researcher*
Brazinsky, Irv(ing) *chemical engineering educator, department chairman*
Briskman, Robert David *engineering executive*
Chen, Tak-Ming *retired civil engineer, consultant*
Chevray, Rene *engineering educator*
Chowdhury, Md. Shoaib *engineer*
Cowin, Stephen Corteen *biomedical engineering educator, consultant*
DiMaggio, Frank Louis *civil engineering educator*
Fawcett, Christopher Babcock *civil engineer, construction and water resources company executive*
Fogel, Irving Martin *consulting engineer*
Galil, Zvi *engineering educator*
Girard, Anouck *engineering educator*
Grunes, Robert Lewis *engineering executive, consultant*
Guo, Linfeng *communications engineer, researcher*
Habib, Ibrahim Wahby *computer engineer, educator*
Hennessy, John Francis III *engineering executive, mechanical engineer*
Hielscher, Andreas Helmut *biomedical engineer*
Jarvik, Robert Koffler *biomedical research scientist*
Kim, Se Jung *civil engineer*
Kraft, Robert *computer network engineer, publishing executive*
Lai, W(ei) Michael *mechanical engineer, educator*
Lammie, James Louis *engineering executive, retired military officer*
Laufer, Mark Vladimir *retired engineering educator*
Manassah, Jamal Tewfek *electrical engineer, educator, management consultant*
Masri, Safwan Malek *industrial engineer, educator*
Mynbaev, Djafar K. *engineering physics educator*
O'Neill, Thomas J. (Tom O' Neill) *engineering company executive*
Osgood, Richard Magee, Jr. *electrical engineering professor, researcher*
Paaswell, Robert Emil *civil engineer, educator*
Rubenstein, Leonard *engineering company executive*
Rumschitzki, David Sheldon *chemical engineering educator*
Sadegh, Ali M. *mechanical engineering educator, researcher, consultant*
Schoenfeld, Robert Louis *biomedical engineer*
Schwartz, Mischa *electrical engineering educator*
See, SawTeen *structural engineer*
Seinuk, Ysrael A. *architectural engineer*
Shinnar, Reuel *engineering educator, consultant*
Smith, Gordon H. *civil engineer, consultant, forensic engineer consultant*
Subak-Sharpe, Gerald Emil *electrical engineer, educator*
Sullivan, Kenneth Wayne *engineer*
Tamaro, George John *consulting engineer*
Tsividis, Yannis P. *electrical engineering educator*
Vogelman, Joseph Herbert *scientific engineering company executive*
Watkins, Charles Booker, Jr. *mechanical engineering educator*
Weinstein, Herbert *chemical engineer, educator*
Wilson, Daniel H. *robotics engineer, writer*
Yao, David Da-Wei *engineering educator*
Yegulalp, Tuncel M. *mining engineer, educator*

**Niakayuna**
Lu, Hai *electrical engineer, physicist*

**Niskayuna**
Fatić, Vuk Marko *electrical engineer, educator, researcher*

Feitelberg, Alan S. *chemical engineer*
Hu, Qingying *optical engineer*
Kapur, Ajay *systems engineer*
Qu, Ronghai *electrical engineer*
Sanborn, Stephen D. *systems engineer*

**Northport**
Weber, Ray Everett *engineering executive, consultant*

**Norwich**
Koon, Thomas Robert *engineering educator, consultant*

**Norwood**
Church, Richard Dwight *electrical engineer, scientist*

**Owego**
Zendle, Howard Mark *systems engineer, researcher*

**Oxford**
Ryan, Kenneth Eugene *engineer*

**Phoenix**
Ackerman, Roger G. *ceramics engineer*

**Plattsburgh**
Treacy, William Joseph *electrical and environmental engineer*

**Pleasantville**
Pike, John Nazarian *optical engineering consultant*
Urban, Joseph Jaroslav *engineer, consultant*

**Potsdam**
Chin, Der-Tau *chemical engineer, educator*
Rengaswamy, Raghunathan *chemical engineering researcher, educator*
Zamankhan, Parsa *mechanical engineer*

**Poughkeepsie**
Buti, Taqi N. *electrical engineer*
Chu, Richard Chao-Fan *mechanical engineer*
Ellsworth, Michael Joseph, Jr. *mechanical engineer*
Logue, Joseph Carl *electronics engineer, consultant*
Padegs, Andris *electrical engineer, engineering company executive*
Simons, Robert Edward *mechanical engineer, consultant*

**Rego Park**
Nakanishi, Yuko Julie *engineering educator, consultant*

**Rochester**
Anthamatten, Mitchell Lewis *chemical engineer, educator*
Carstensen, Edwin Lorenz *retired biomedical engineer, retired biophysicist*
Coumou, David J. *electrical engineer, consultant*
Joos, Felipe Miguel *mechanical engineer, researcher*
Kurdziel, Michael Thomas *engineering executive*
Niznik, Carol Ann *electrical engineer, educator, consultant*
Parker, Kevin James *electrical engineer, educator*
Smoral, Vincent J. *electrical engineer*
Stratton, John Alfred *electrical engineer, educator*
Tavli, Bulent *communications engineer, researcher*
Xia, Tongsheng *electrical engineer*

**Rye**
Lehman, Lawrence Herbert *consulting engineering executive*

**Scarsdale**
Borg, Robert Frederic *civil engineer*

**Schenectady**
Andresen, Peter Louis *materials engineer*
Larsen, Einar V. *electrical and systems engineer, consultant*
Mikata, Yozo *mechanical engineer, application developer*
Ringlee, Robert James *consulting engineering executive*
Sutherland, Peter Edward *electrical engineer*

**Setauket**
Levine, Sumner Norton *industrial engineer, educator, editor, writer, financial consultant*

**Smithtown**
Rockensies, John William *mechanical engineer*

**Somers**
Anderson, John Erling *chemical engineer*

**Stony Brook**
Bennett, Tyrone LaMont *engineer, director*
Chiang, Fu-Pen *mechanical engineering educator, researcher*
Gambino, Richard Joseph *materials engineer, educator*
White, Henry J. *engineering educator, consultant*
Zemanian, Armen Humpartsoum *electrical engineer, mathematician*

**Suffern**
Coronel, Victor Felipe *engineering educator*

**Syracuse**
Fawcett, James Walter *computer engineer, educator*
Kim, Yong-Woo *engineer, educator, consultant*
Sargent, Robert George *engineering educator*
Yanjun, Yan *electrical engineer, statistician*

**Tappan**
Cardenas, Raul Rodolfo, Jr. *engineering executive, educator, consultant*

**Tonawanda**
Drozdziel, Marion John *aeronautical engineer*

**Troy**
Bergles, Arthur Edward *mechanical engineering educator*
Block, Robert Charles *nuclear engineering educator*
Dobry, Ricardo *engineering educator*
Dvorak, George J. *mechanics and materials engineering educator*
Freyssinier Nova, Jean Paul *electrical engineer, educator*
Gerhardt, Lester A. *engineering educator, dean*
Gill, William Nelson *chemical engineering professor*
Glicksman, Martin Eden *materials engineering educator*
Haddock, Jorge *industrial engineering educator, consultant*
Hsu, Cheng *decision sciences and engineering systems educator*
Kane, Ravi *biomedical engineer*
Lahey, Richard Thomas, Jr. *nuclear engineer, fluid mechanics engineer*
Littman, Howard *chemical engineer, educator*
McDonald, John Francis Patrick *electrical engineering educator*
Messac, Achille *mechanical engineer, aerospace engineer*
Nelson, John Keith *electrical engineer, educator*
Sanderson, Arthur Clark *engineering educator*
Shephard, Mark Scott *civil and mechanical engineering educator*
Shuey, Richard Lyman *engineering educator, consultant*
Woods, John William *electrical, computer and systems engineering educator, consultant*
Zimmie, Thomas Frank *civil engineer, educator*

**Upton**
Foerster, Conrad Louis *project engineer*
Mahajan, Devinder *chemical engineer, chemistry professor*
Steinberg, Meyer *chemical engineer*

**Valatie**
Smith, Albert Aloysius, Jr. *electrical engineer, consultant*

**Valhalla**
Goldowsky, Michael Philip *mechanical engineer*

**Watervliet**
Bishop, Aisha Suzette *materials engineer*
Elrahman, O. Abd *environmental and transportation engineer, educator*

**Webster**
McWilliams, C. Paul, Jr. *engineering executive*

**West Kill**
Dwon, Larry *retired electrical engineer, educator, consultant*

**White Plains**
Arimilli, Ravi K. *computer engineer*
Foster, John Horace *consulting environmental engineer*
Freed, Arthur *civil engineer*
Haines, Daniel Webster *engineering consultant, engineering educator*
Huang, Han *systems engineer*
Mitchell, Robert Dale *engineer, consultant*

**Williamsville**
Kim, Jung Taek *electrochemical engineer*
Metzger, Ernest Hugh *aerospace engineer, research scientist*

**Yorktown Heights**
Dennard, Robert Heath *engineering executive, scientist*
Kim, Keunwoo *electrical engineer, researcher*
Kosonocky, Stephen V. *electrical engineer, computer graphics designer, researcher*
Terman, Lewis Madison *retired electrical engineer, researcher, director*

## NORTH CAROLINA

**Cary**
Conrad, Hans *materials science and engineering educator*
Duan, Jiwen *chemical engineer*
Hauser, John Reid *electrical engineering educator*
Vick, Columbus Edwin, Jr. *retired civil engineering design firm executive*

**Chapel Hill**
Marchionini, Gary Joseph *information science educator*
McKinney, Ross Erwin, Sr. *civil engineering educator*
Okun, Daniel Alexander *environmental engineering educator*

**Charlotte**
Cooke, Steven John *chemical engineer, consultant, scientist*
Elanayar, Sunil K. *research and development engineer*
Fang, Hongbing *engineering educator, researcher*
Fitzpatrick, James Ward, Jr. *engineering educator*
Jordan, Robert Sands *electrical engineer*
Norris, William Robert *engineer, researcher*
Valasquez, Joseph Louis *industrial engineer*

**Columbus**
Brooks, Jerry Claude *safety engineer, educator*

**Concord**
Sheppard, Douglas G. *manufacturing project engineer*

**Durham**
Bejan, Adrian *mechanical engineering educator*
Carter, Calvin H., Jr. *materials engineer*
Casey, H(orace) Craig, Jr. *electrical engineering educator*

D'Amato, Victor Arthur *environmental engineer, consultant*
Goodwin, Frank Erik *materials engineer*
Petroski, Henry *engineering educator, writer*
Plonsey, Robert *electrical and biomedical engineer*
Stiff-Roberts, Adrienne D. *electrical engineer, educator*
Utku, Senol *civil engineer, computer science educator*
Vatavuk, William Michael *chemical engineer, writer*

**Elizabeth City**
Rawat, Kuldeep S. *engineering educator*

**Granite Falls**
Humphreys, Kenneth King *engineer, educator, professional society administrator*

**Greensboro**
Fujino, Michimasa *aeronautical engineer*
Oliver, Terry James *electronics engineer, educator, communications engineer*

**Hendersonville**
Kingsbury, Carolyn Ann *aerospace engineer, craftsman, writer*

**Murphy**
Kerr, Walter Belnap *retired electrical engineer, language researcher, consultant*

**New Bern**
Moeller, Dade William *environmental engineer, educator*
Painter, Jack Timberlake *civil engineer*
Whitehurst, Brooks Morris *chemical engineer*

**Raleigh**
Agamloh, Emmanuel B. *systems engineer, consultant*
Barrett, Rolin Farrar, Jr. *mechanical engineer, consultant*
Beatty, Kenneth Orion, Jr. *chemical engineer, educator*
Bitzer, Donald Lester *electrical engineer, educator, retired lab administrator*
Doorn, Michiel Roelof Jan *environmental engineer, consultant*
Gardner, Robin Pierce *engineering educator*
Gorga, Russell E *polymer engineer*
Holton, William Coffeen *electrical engineering executive*
Kolbas, Robert Michael *electrical engineering educator*
Larsen, Ralph Irving *environmental research engineer*
Loboa, Elizabeth Grace *biomedical engineer, educator*
Lyons, Kevin M. *engineering educator*
Masnari, Nino Antonio *electrical engineer, educator*
Odum, Jeffery Neal *mechanical engineer*
Ozturk, Mehmet Cevdet *engineering educator*
Sneed, Ronald Ernest *retired project engineer, engineering educator*
Turinsky, Paul Josef *nuclear engineering educator*
Wehring, Bernard William *nuclear engineering educator*
Whitaker, Thomas Burton *agricultural engineer, educator*
Williams, Hugh Alexander, Jr. *retired mechanical engineer, consultant*
Zorowski, Carl Frank *engineering educator, academic administrator*

**Research Triangle Park**
Baumann, Karsten *engineer, researcher*
Everett, LaTonya Michelle *computer engineer*
Isler, Raymond Earl *engineer*
Johnson-Payton, Lori Renee *systems engineer*
Lemieux, Paul *chemical engineer, researcher*

**Sunset Beach**
Mattson, Clarence Russell *safety engineer*

**Swannanoa**
Stuck, Roger Dean *electrical engineering educator*

**Washington**
Hackney, James Acra III *industrial engineer, consultant, retired manufacturing executive*

**Whispering Pines**
Kuhn, Matthew *retired engineering company executive*

**Whiteville**
Harrelson, Bob Fitzgerald *engineering company executive*

**Winston Salem**
Bourne, Henry Clark, Jr. *electrical engineer, educator, retired academic administrator*

## NORTH DAKOTA

**Fargo**
Reitan, Daniel Kinseth *electric and computer engineering educator*
Yadav, Om Prakash *reliability engineer, educator*

## OHIO

**Ada**
Srinivasa, Vemuru R. *engineering educator, researcher*

**Akron**
Brown, David Rupert *engineering executive*
Isayev, Avraam Isayevich *polymer engineer, educator*
Jana, Sadhan C. *engineering educator, researcher*

**Athens**
Irwin, Richard Dennis *electrical engineering educator*

Matolak, David William *engineering educator*
Robe, Thurlow Richard *engineering educator, dean*

**Aurora**
Kirchner, James William *retired electrical engineer*

**Barberton**
Kitto, John Buck, Jr. *mechanical engineer*

**Berea**
Atchinson, Kenneth *engineering educator*

**Cambridge**
Beldyk, Richard Michael *mechanical engineer*

**Cincinnati**
Agrawal, Dharma Prakash *engineering educator*
Bahr, Donald Walter *retired chemical engineer*
Cabezas, Heriberto *chemical engineer, researcher*
Greenberg, David Bernard *chemical engineering educator*
Hodge, Bobby Lynn *mechanical engineer, manufacturing executive*
Hwang, Sun-Tak *chemical engineering educator*
Kowel, Stephen Thomas *electrical engineer, educator*
Madson, Philip Ward *engineering executive, consultant*
Morgan, William Richard *mechanical engineer*
Ratliff, Thomas Asbury, Jr. *retired engineer*
Sinha, Sunil K. *aerospace engineer, consultant*
Toftner, Richard Orville *engineering executive*
Weisman, Joel *retired engineering educator*
Wisler, David Charles *aerospace engineer*

**Cleveland**
Abramson, Alexis R. *engineering educator*
Angus, John Cotton *chemical engineering educator*
Burghart, James Henry *electrical engineer, educator*
Deissler, Robert George *fluid dynamics researcher*
DellaCorte, Christopher *engineer*
Hardy, Richard Allen *mechanical engineer, engineering executive*
Ko, Wen-Hsiung *electrical engineering educator*
Madden, James D. *forensic engineer*
Plachta, David W. *aerospace engineer*
Saada, Adel Selim *civil engineer, educator*
Savinell, Robert Francis *engineering educator*
Wilson, Jack *aeronautical engineer*

**Columbus**
Adeli, Hojjat *engineer, educator, computer scientist*
Alexander, Carl Albert *ceramics engineer, educator*
Altan, Taylan *engineering educator, director*
Bechtel, Stephen E. *mechanical engineer, educator*
Bhushan, Bharat *mechanical engineer*
Brodkey, Robert Stanley *chemical engineering educator*
Cruz, Jose Bejar, Jr. *engineering educator*
Fan, Liang-Shih *chemical engineering educator*
Fenton, Robert Earl *electrical engineering educator*
Harris, Ronald David *chemical engineer*
Houser, Donald Russell *mechanical engineering educator, consultant*
Miller, Don Wilson *nuclear engineering educator*
Moulton, Edward Quentin *civil engineer, educator*
Ozkan, Umit Sivrioglu *chemical engineering professor*
Peters, Leon, Jr. *engineering educator*
Rapp, Robert Anthony *metallurgical engineering educator*
Rojas, Roberto G. *electrical engineer*
Sebo, Stephen Andrew *electrical engineer, educator, researcher, consultant*
Sertel, Kubilay *engineer, researcher*
Taiganides, E. Paul *agricultural and environmental engineer, consultant*
Wang, Chaoli *electronics engineer*
Zakin, Jacques Louis *chemical engineering educator*
Zhu, Xiankui *mechanical engineer, researcher*

**Dayton**
Ballal, Dilip Ramchandra *mechanical engineering educator*
Houpis, Constantine Harry *retired electrical engineering educator*
Mukhopadhyay, Sharmila Mitra *materials engineer, educator*
Phillips, Chandler Allen *biomedical engineer*
Schmitt, George Frederick, Jr. *materials engineer*

**Dublin**
Singh, Rajendra *mechanical engineering educator*

**Farmdale**
Grove, Rebecca Irene *mechanical engineer*

**Gahanna**
Majtenyi, Steven Istvan *retired civil engineer, consultant*

**Gates Mills**
Enyedy, Gustav, Jr. *chemical engineer*

**Hamilton**
Speckert, Robert E. *engineering educator*

**Lakeside Marblehead**
Haering, Edwin Raymond *chemical engineering educator, consultant*

**Mansfield**
Sheridan, Mark William *mechanical engineer, financial planner*

**Mayfield Heights**
Chaffee, Mark Anthony *engineer*
Grants, Valdis *engineering manager*

**Medina**
Rog, Joseph W. *engineering company executive*

**Middletown**
Newby, John Robert *metallurgical engineer*

**North Olmsted**
Bluford, Guion Stewart, Jr. *engineering company executive*

**Oxford**
Koo, Jeong-Hoi *engineering educator*
Ward, Roscoe Fredrick *engineering educator*

**Poland**
Murphy, Thomas Michael *civil engineer*

**Shaker Heights**
Siegel, Robert *heat transfer engineer*

**Springboro**
Saxer, Richard Karl *metallurgical engineer, retired military officer*

**Toledo**
Berhan, Lesley Michelle *mechanical engineering educator*
Elahinia, Mohammad H. *engineering educator, researcher*
Koo, Benjamin Hai Chang *structural engineer, educator*
Wolff, Edwin Ray *retired construction engineer, consultant*

**West Chester**
Arasakesari, Subramaniam *chemical engineer, research scientist, consultant*
Tanov, Romil R. *mechanical engineer, researcher*

**Wooster**
Hodgson, David B. *safety engineer, science educator*

**Worthington**
Compton, Ralph Theodore, Jr. *electrical engineering educator*

**Wright Patterson Afb**
Palazotto, Anthony N. *aerospace engineering educator*
Rodrigues, Stanley John *materials engineer, researcher*

**Yellow Springs**
Trolander, Hardy Wilcox *engineering executive, consultant*

**Youngstown**
Cernica, John N. *engineering educator, civil engineer, consultant*
Fok, Thomas Dso Yun *civil engineer*

## OKLAHOMA

**Lawton**
Krishnaiyer, Krishnan *industrial engineer*

**Muskogee**
Henry, Rickey Roy *electrical contractor, educator*

**Norman**
Bert, Charles Wesley *mechanical and aerospace engineer, educator*
Campbell, John Morgan *retired chemical engineer*
Gollahalli, Subramanyam Ramappa *engineering educator*
Ibrahim, Tamer Selim *engineering educator*
MacFarland, Miriam Katherine (Mimi MacFarland) *computer engineer, consultant, writer, educator*
Morris, Richard Ides *retired petroleum engineer, science educator*
Zelby, Leon Wolf *electrical engineer, educator, consultant*

**Oklahoma City**
Coll, Mario M *engineering company executive*
Miller, Herbert Dell *petroleum engineer*

**Ponca City**
Gong, Xiaoyi *engineer*

**Stillwater**
Case, Kenneth Eugene *industrial engineering educator*
Maddox, Robert Nott *chemical engineer, educator*
Madihally, Sundararajan V. *engineering educator*
Mize, Joe Henry *industrial engineer, educator*
Oliveira, Carlos *engineering educator*
Rajamani, Vignesh *electrical engineer*
Ramakumar, Ramachandra Gupta *electrical engineering educator*
Thompson, David Russell *engineering educator, dean*

**Tulsa**
Azar, J. J. *engineering educator*
Simionescu, Petru-Aurelian *engineering educator, researcher*
Williams, John Horter *civil engineer, energy industry executive*
Yu, Mengjiao *petroleum engineer, educator*

## OREGON

**Beaverton**
Chartier, Vernon Lee *electrical engineer*

**Corvallis**
Byers, William D *engineering executive*
Engelbrecht, Rudolf *electrical engineering educator*
Kornilovitch, Pavel *device engineer*
Temes, Gabor Charles *electrical engineering educator*

**Florence**
Ericksen, Jerald Laverne *retired science engineering educator*

**Hillsboro**
Ahsan, Akm Ariful *electrical engineer, researcher*
Hiranandani, Manish Ashok *electrical engineer*
Kocharyan, Varuzhan *electrical engineer, engineering educator, researcher*

**John Day**
Tuttle, Kenneth Lewis *retired engineering educator, consultant, researcher*

**Klamath Falls**
Woodall, David Monroe *engineer, researcher, dean*

**Lake Oswego**
Gehrig, Edward Harry *electrical engineer, consultant*

**Myrtle Point**
Walsh, Don *engineer, consultant*

**Portland**
Al-Rabadi, Anas Naser Essa *electrical engineer, computer engineer*
Hall, Howard Pickering *engineering and mathematics educator*
Kennedy, R(obert) Evan *engineering executive, consultant, retired structural engineer*
Kocaoglu, Dundar F. *engineering management educator, industrial engineer, civil engineer*
Pham, Kinh Dinh *electrical engineer, educator, engineering executive*

**Salem**
Butts, Edward Perry *civil engineer, environmental consultant*

**Sunriver**
Clough, Ray William, Jr. *civil engineering educator*

**Woodburn**
Oliver, Madison E. *retired engineering executive, mechanical engineer*

## PENNSYLVANIA

**Allentown**
Foster, Edward Paul (Ted Foster) *process industries executive*
Gewartowski, James Walter *retired electrical engineer*
Hansel, James Gordon *engineer, educator*
Weir, Bonnie E. *reliability engineer*

**Allison Park**
Lagnese, Joseph F. *environmental engineer*

**Ashland**
Polyakov, Yuriy Sergeyevich *engineer, researcher*

**Bala Cynwyd**
Staley, Kenneth Bernard *civil engineer*

**Bethel Park**
Korchynsky, Michael *metallurgical engineer*

**Bethlehem**
Durkee, Jackson Leland *civil engineer*
El-Aasser, Mohamed S. *engineering educator, academic administrator*
Fisher, John William *civil engineering educator*
Pense, Alan Wiggins *metallurgical engineer, academic administrator*
Tuzla, Kemal *mechanical engineer, researcher*

**Boalsburg**
Gettig, Martin Winthrop *retired mechanical engineer*

**Bridgeport**
Lee, Robert *engineer*

**Bryn Mawr**
Hegedus, L. Louis *chemical engineer, retired research and development company executive*

**Chadds Ford**
Isakoff, Sheldon Erwin *chemical engineer*

**Cheltenham**
Weinstock, Walter Wolfe *systems engineer*

**Cheswick**
Nair, Bala Radhakrishnan *engineer*

**Clearfield**
Singh, Shiwendra Prasad *civil engineer*

**Coopersburg**
Bolle, Donald Martin *retired engineering educator*
Peserik, James E. *electrical engineer, consultant, safety engineer, computer engineer*
Siess, Alfred Albert, Jr. *engineering executive, management consultant*

**Coraopolis**
Kay, George Paul *environmental engineer*

**Easton**
Radisavljevic-Gajic, Verica *mechanical engineer, educator*

**Erie**
Dockstader, Emmett Stanley *civil engineer, construction executive*
Wu, Yi *mechanical engineer*

**Glen Mills**
Churchill, Stuart Winston *chemical engineering educator*

**Greensburg**
Amari, Suprasad V. *mechanical engineer*
Ference, Edward W. *engineering executive, structural engineer*
Langer, Alois *biomedical engineer*

**Hershey**
Lim, Jung Yul *biomedical engineer*

**Homestead**
Mandel, Herbert Maurice *civil engineer*

**Huntingdon Valley**
West, A(rnold) Sumner *chemical engineer*

**Irwin**
Kuhn, Howard Arthur *engineering executive, educator*

**Jamison**
Touhill, C. Joseph *environmental engineer*

**Jenkintown**
Haythornthwaite, Robert Morphet *civil engineer, educator*

**Johnstown**
Depra, Alan Jay *mechanical engineer*

**Lancaster**
Ebersole, J. Glenn, Jr. *engineering, marketing, management, public relations and strategic planning executive*
Graffis, Leister F. *retired engineering executive*

**Lansdale**
Hargens, Charles William III *electrical engineer, consultant*

**Lewisburg**
Aldrich, Robert Adams *agricultural engineer, consultant*
Raymond, Timothy Michael *engineering educator*

**Meadville**
Gilles, Bruce Carlson *civil engineer*

**Mercer**
Zellers, Robert Charles *materials engineer, consultant, speaker*

**Moon Township**
Rabosky, Joseph George *engineering consulting company executive*

**Murrysville**
Yang, Wen-Ching *chemical engineer*

**New Kensington**
Jarrett, Noel *chemical engineer, researcher*

**Newtown**
Rao, Sudhakar *aerospace engineer, researcher*

**Newtown Square**
Murphy, Arthur Thomas *systems engineer, consultant*
Perrone, Nicholas *engineering company executive*

**Philadelphia**
Bilgutay, Nihat Mustafa *engineering educator, associate dean*
Bordogna, Joseph *engineering educator, former science foundation executive*
Cohen, Ira Myron *retired aeronautical and mechanical engineering educator*
Daryoush, Afshin Samimi *electrical engineer, educator*
Director, Stephen William *electrical and computer engineering educator, academic administrator*
El-Sherif, Mahmoud A. *electrical engineering educator, engineering executive*
Falkie, Thomas Victor *mining engineer, mining executive*
Fegley, Kenneth Allen *systems engineering educator*
Glandt, Eduardo Daniel *chemical engineering educator*
Jaron, Dov *biomedical engineer, educator*
Lauer, Richard Thomas *biomedical engineer*
Lawley, Alan *materials engineer, educator*
Lewin, Peter Andrew *electrical engineer, educator*
Litt, Mitchell *chemical engineer, educator, bioengineer*
Mao, Weidong *communications engineer, technology executive*
Mattia, Davide *materials engineer, researcher*
Morlok, Edward Karl *engineering educator, consultant*
Mulford, Richard Albert *mechanical engineer, professional society administrator*
Noh, Hongseok *engineering educator*
Popovics, Sandor *civil engineer, educator, researcher*
Quinn, John Albert *chemical engineering professor*
Walker, Allen Lyon *engineer*
Winston, Flaura K. *engineering researcher*
Zhang, Ruifeng *engineering educator*

**Pittsburgh**
Biegler, Lorenz Theodor *chemical engineering educator*
Bloom, William Millard *furnace design engineer*
Casasent, David Paul *electrical engineer, educator, data processing executive*
Charap, Stanley Harvey *electrical engineering educator*
Choset, Howie *engineering educator, researcher*
Cotchen, J. Kevin *metallurgical engineer, writer*
Desai, Niranjan A. *chemical engineer*
Dzombak, David Adam *environmental engineering educator*
Hendrickson, Chris Thompson *civil and environmental engineering educator, researcher*
Hoburg, James Frederick *electrical engineering educator*
Hollis, Ralph L. *engineering educator*
Jordan, Angel Goni *electrical and computer engineering educator*
Khosla, Pradeep Kumar *engineering educator*
Lejeune, Miguel *engineering educator*
Leney, George Willard *retired consulting engineer*
Li, Ching-Chung *electrical engineering educator*
McAvoy, Bruce Ronald *engineer, consultant*
McNamee, Rebecca Landes *engineering educator, researcher*

Mickle, Marlin Homer *electrical engineer, educator*
Milnes, Arthur George *electrical engineer, educator*
Neuman, Charles P. *electrical and computer engineering educator*
Nielsen, Paul Douglas *engineering executive, retired military officer*
O'Donnell, William James *engineering executive*
Ozdoganlar, Burak *mechanical engineer, educator*
Peterson, Robert Scott *electrical engineer*
Petrovic, Bojan *nuclear engineer, educator*
Pettit, Frederick Sidney *metallurgical engineering educator, department chairman*
Rohrer, Gregory Scott *materials engineer, educator*
Ruh, Edwin *ceramic engineer, consultant, researcher*
Samonds, Jason Michael *biomedical engineer*
Savvides, Marios *electrical engineer, computer engineer, research scientist*
Sharma, Nawal K. *bioengineering educator, researcher*
Sheikhi, M. Reza H. *engineering educator*
Simaan, Marwan *electrical engineering educator*
Stahl, Laddie L. *engineering company executive*
Westerberg, Arthur William *retired chemical engineering professor*
Whittaker, William L. (Red Whittaker) *engineering educator, research scientist*
Wickert, Jonathan Adam *engineering educator*
Yu, Jie *communications engineer*

**Reading**
Moriarty, John Klinge *electrical engineer, consultant*

**Sewickley**
Fells, Charles Dayton *civil engineer, educator*

**State College**
Albright, Gifford Harry *retired architectural engineering educator, consultant*
Barnoff, Robert Mark *civil engineering educator*
Brown, John Lawrence, Jr. *electrical engineering educator*
Foderaro, Anthony Harolde *nuclear engineering educator*
Grimes, Dale Mills *physics and electrical engineering educator*
Hettche, L. Raymond *engineering educator, retired research scientist*
Olson, Donald Richard *mechanical engineering educator*
Shaikh, Nazrul Islam *industrial engineer, researcher*
Sinha, Sunil K. *engineer, educator*
Swanson, David Carl *engineering educator, researcher*

**Swarthmore**
Krendel, Ezra Simon *systems and human factors engineering consultant*

**University Park**
Ayala, Luis F. *engineering educator*
Bose, Nirmal Kumar *electrical engineer, mathematics educator*
Chehab, Ghassan R. *civil engineer, educator*
Cross, Leslie Eric *electrical engineering educator*
Davids, Norman *engineering educator, researcher*
Duda, John Larry *chemical engineering educator*
Elliott, Herschel *agricultural engineer, educator*
Hogg, Richard *process engineer*
Holl, John William *engineering educator*
Irwin, Mary Jane *engineering educator*
Jeong, Jae-Weon *architectural engineer, educator*
Kabel, Robert Lynn *chemical engineering professor*
Knott, Kenneth *industrial engineering educator, consultant*
Lai, Chieh-Ping *engineer, researcher*
Liu, Zi-Kui *materials engineer, educator*
Manbeck, Harvey B. *agricultural and biological engineer, educator*
McCormick, Barnes Warnock *aerospace engineering educator*
Mentzer, John Raymond *electrical engineering educator*
Ramani, Raja Venkat *engineering educator*
Scanlon, Andrew *structural engineering educator*
Thompson, William, Jr. *engineering educator*
Tittmann, Bernhard Rainer *engineering science and mechanics educator*
Todd Copley, Judith A. *engineering educator*
Vannice, M. Albert *chemical engineering professor, researcher*
Vrentas, James Spiro *chemical engineering professor*
Witzig, Warren Frank *nuclear engineer, educator*
Wysk, Richard A. *engineering educator, researcher*
Zhang, Qiming *engineering educator, researcher*

**Villanova**
McLaughlin, Philip VanDoren, Jr. *mechanical engineering educator, researcher, consultant*
Tomlinson, J. Richard *retired engineering services company executive*

**Waynesboro**
Martin, Harold G. *engineering consultant*

**West Mifflin**
Ardash, Garin *mechanical engineer*

**West Point**
Buckland, Barry Christopher *chemical engineer*

**Williamsport**
Albert, Eric *engineering educator*

**Yardley**
Hochreiter, Joseph Christian, Jr. *engineering company executive*

**York**
Chervil, Rudy *mechanical engineer*
Horn, Russell Eugene *engineering executive, consultant*

Horn, Russell Eugene, Jr. *engineering executive*
Kennedy, Christopher Robin *ceramics engineer, director*

## RHODE ISLAND

**Bristol**
Danzberger, Alexander Harris *retired chemical engineer, consultant*

**Middletown**
Ellison, William Theodore *marine engineer*

**Newport**
Ruffa, Anthony Armand *mechanical engineer*

**Portsmouth**
Becken, Bradford Albert *engineering executive*

**Providence**
Freund, Lambert Ben *engineering educator, researcher, consultant*
Glicksman, Maurice *engineering educator, retired dean, retired provost*
Hazeltine, Barrett *electrical engineer, educator*
Needleman, Alan *mechanical engineering educator*
Richman, Marc Herbert *engineer, forensic specialist, educator*
Skasanna, Rey *industrial engineer, department chairman*
Weiner, Jerome Harris *mechanical engineering educator*

**Wakefield**
Boothroyd, Geoffrey *industrial and manufacturing engineering educator*

## SOUTH CAROLINA

**Aiken**
Hootman, Harry Edward *retired nuclear engineer*

**Beaufort**
Pinkerton, Robert Bruce *mechanical engineer*

**Bluffton**
Jerger, Edward William *engineering educator, dean*

**Blythewood**
Falcone, Anthony *mechanical engineer*

**Camden**
Sindler, Allan Jay *chemical engineer, sculptor, educator*

**Charleston**
Fei, James Robert *engineering executive, consultant*
Haemmerich, Dieter *biomedical engineer*

**Clemson**
Greenstein, Joel Sandor *industrial engineering educator*
Jalili, Nader *mechanical engineer, educator*
Luo, Jian *engineering educator, researcher*
Pursley, Michael Bader *engineering educator, communications systems researcher, consultant*
Rangaraju, Prasada Rao *engineering educator, researcher*
Zumbrunnen, David Arnold *mechanical engineering and materials science educator, consultant*

**Columbia**
Baskin, C. R. *civil engineer*
Gibbons, Joseph Harrison *engineering educator, farmer*
Graulty, Robert Thomas *engineer, consultant*
Koudymov, Alexei N. *electrical engineer, researcher*
Monnier, John R. *chemical engineering educator*

**Edisto Island**
Cannon, David C. *mechanical engineer, consultant*

**Greer**
Hu, Yiping *metallurgical engineer*

**Hartsville**
Menius, Espie Flynn, Jr. *electrical engineer*

**Hilton Head Island**
Bruun, Per Moller *civil engineer, consultant*
Huckins, Harold Aaron *chemical engineer*
Windman, Arnold Lewis *retired mechanical engineer*

**Orangeburg**
Basher, Hasanul A. *electrical engineer*
Hong, Jae-Dong *industrial engineering educator*

**Salem**
Darnell, William Headen *chemical engineer, medical/surgical nurse, nursing educator*

## SOUTH DAKOTA

**Brookings**
Ropp, Michael E. *engineering educator*

**Rapid City**
Pillay, Gautam *chemical engineer, chemist, academic administrator*
Ramakrishnan, Venkataswamy *civil engineer, educator*
Scofield, Gordon Lloyd *mechanical engineer, educator*

**Spearfish**
Addy, Alva Leroy *mechanical engineer*

## TENNESSEE

**Arnold Afb**
Davis, John William *government science and engineering executive*

**Brentwood**
Clevenger, William Thomas *electrical engineer*

**Chattanooga**
Hensley, Marble John, Sr. *civil engineer, consultant*

**Cookeville**
Chowdhuri, Pritindra *electrical engineer, educator*
Sissom, Leighton Esten *engineering educator, dean, consultant*
Velu, Yogeshwar Karunakaran *industrial engineer, researcher*
Wang, Chunsheng *chemical engineer, educator*

**Crossville**
Bell, Charles Eugene, Jr. *retired industrial engineer*

**Greenbrier**
Newell, Paul Haynes, Jr. *engineering educator*

**Jackson**
Cole, John Frankland *electrical engineer, educator*

**Kingsport**
Siirola, Jeffrey John *chemical engineer*
Tant, Martin Ray *chemical engineer, biomedical engineer*

**Knoxville**
Alexeff, Igor *retired electrical engineering educator*
Bose, Bimal Kumar *electrical engineering educator*
Cliff, Steven Burris *engineering executive*
Du, Hongtao *systems engineer*
Edwards, Brian J. *chemical engineer, educator*
Irick, David Kim *engineering educator, consultant*
Koschan, Andreas F. *computer engineer, educator*
Mc Dow, John Jett *biosystems engineering educator*
Mise, Jesse Sherden *structural engineer, consultant*
Naoumov, Viatcheslav I. *mechanical engineer, educator*
Prados, John William *engineering educator*
Richards, Stephen Harold *engineering educator*
Roth, John Reece *electrical engineer, educator, researcher, inventor*
Schuler, Theodore Anthony *retired civil engineer*
Uhrig, Robert Eugene *nuclear engineer, educator*
Wu, Jie *electronics engineer, educator*

**Martin**
Wheeler, Edward *engineering educator*

**Maryville**
Oakes, Lester Cornelius *retired electrical engineer, consultant*

**Memphis**
Born, Robert Heywood *consulting civil engineer*
Hewitt, Robert Warren *engineering educator, consultant*
Lin, L. Yu *civil engineer, educator*
Madhavan, Kunchi *engineering educator*
Rue, Douglas Michael *solutions engineer*
Russomanno, David James *electrical engineer, educator*
Williams, Edward F(oster) III *environmental engineer*
Yang, Yunzhi *biomedical engineer*

**Nashville**
Galloway, Kenneth Franklin *engineering educator*
Hahn, George Thomas *materials engineering educator, researcher*
Harris, Thomas Raymond *biomedical engineer, educator*
LeVan, Martin Douglas *chemical engineering professor*
McCabe, Clare *chemical engineer, educator*
Schnelle, Karl Benjamin, Jr. *chemical engineering professor, consultant, researcher*
Speece, Richard Eugene *civil engineer, educator*

**Oak Ridge**
Ally, Moonis R. *chemical engineer*
David, Stanislaus Anthony *metallurgical engineer*
Pannala, Sreekanth *aerospace engineer*
Wang, Hong *engineer, researcher*

**Winchester**
Masters, George Windsor, Jr. *electrical engineer, educator*

## TEXAS

**Alpine**
Kittlitz, Rudolf Gottlieb, Jr. *chemical engineer, researcher*

**Amarillo**
Mechenbier, Catherine *engineering educator*
Von Eschen, Robert Leroy *electrical engineer, consultant*

**Arlington**
Clark, Dayle Meritt *civil engineer*
Liang, Qilian *engineering educator*
Liu, Hanli *biomedical engineer, educator*
Rollins, Albert Williamson *civil engineer, consultant*
Stevens, Gladstone Taylor, Jr. *retired industrial engineer, retired educator*
Yeung, Kai S. *engineering educator*

**Austin**
Abraham, Jacob A. *computer engineering educator, consultant*

Akins, Vaughn Edward *retired engineering company executive*
Al-Omari, Ra'ed M. *computer engineer, consultant, computer scientist, researcher*
Baker, Lee Edward *biomedical engineering educator*
Brannon-Peppas, Lisa *chemical engineer, researcher*
Breen, John Edward *civil engineer, educator*
Brock, James Rush *chemical engineering professor*
Bronaugh, Edwin Lee *retired electrical engineer*
Burns, Ned Hamilton *civil engineering educator*
Carlton, Donald Morrill *retired research, development and engineering executive*
Chen, Shaochen *mechanical engineer, educator*
Cywar, Adam Walter *engineering executive*
Dougal, Arwin Adelbert *electrical engineer, educator*
Fair, James Rutherford, Jr. *engineering educator, consultant*
Ganesan, Venkat *engineering educator*
Goodenough, John Bannister *engineering educator, physicist, researcher*
Harris, Richard Lee *engineering executive, retired military officer*
Haznedar, Haldun *electronics engineer*
Himmelblau, David Mautner *chemical engineer*
Hixson, Elmer L. *retired engineering educator*
Howell, John Reid *mechanical engineering educator, director*
Hughes, Thomas J.R. *mechanical engineering educator, consultant*
Hull, David George *aerospace engineering educator, researcher*
Jensen, Paul Allen *mechanical engineer*
Johnson, Sandra K. *electrical engineer*
Koen, Billy Vaughn *mechanical engineering educator*
Lamb, Jamie Parker, Jr. *retired mechanical engineer*
Loo, Lynn (Yueh-Lin) *chemical engineer*
Marya, Manuel Paul Claude *metallurgical and materials engineer*
Mc Ketta, John J., Jr. *chemical engineering professor*
Nichols, Steven Parks *mechanical engineer, educator, lawyer, academic administrator*
Oden, John Tinsley *engineering educator, mathematician, consultant*
Peppas, Nicholas Athanassiou *chemical and biomedical engineering educator, consultant*
Reese, Lymon Clifton *civil engineering educator*
Richards-Kortum, Rebecca Rae *biomedical engineering educator*
Rylander, Henry Grady, Jr. *mechanical engineering educator*
Sanchez, Isaac Cornelius *chemical engineer, educator*
Sandberg, Irwin Walter *retired electrical and computer engineering educator*
Schechter, Robert Samuel *chemical engineer, educator*
Sciance, Carroll Thomas *chemical engineer, educator*
Steinfink, Hugo *chemical engineering professor*
Stokoe, Kenneth H., II *civil engineer, educator*
Streetman, Ben Garland *electrical engineering educator*
Swartzlander, Earl Eugene, Jr. *engineering educator, former electronics company executive*
Tapley, Byron Dean *aerospace engineer, educator*
Thurston, George Butte *mechanical and biomedical engineering educator*
Tucker, Richard Lee *civil engineer, educator*
Walton, Charles Michael *civil engineering educator*
Welch, Ashley James *engineering educator*
Willson, C. Grant *chemical engineering and chemistry professor*

**Baird**
Rodenberger, Charles Alvard *aerospace engineer, consultant*

**Beaumont**
Aung, Kendrick Than *mechanical engineer, educator*
Hopper, Jack Rudd *chemical engineering professor*
Koehn, Enno *engineering educator, researcher*
Morales, Emmitt *mechanical engineer, consultant*

**Beeville**
Littlejohn, John Joseph *petroleum engineer*

**Bryan**
Bigham, Robert Eric *engineer*
Samson, Charles Harold, Jr., (Car Samson) *retired engineering educator, consultant*

**Bushland**
Howell, Terry Allen *agricultural engineer*

**Canyon Lake**
Stachiw, Jaroslaw (Jerry) Drahomyr *mechanical engineer, consultant*

**Channelview**
Dunn, Donald Glenn *electrical engineer, consultant*

**College Station**
Bennett, G(eorge) Kemble *engineering educator*
Buchanan, Walter Woolwine *electrical engineer, educator, academic administrator*
Creasy, Terry Steven *materials engineer, educator*
Ehsani, Mehrdad (Mark Ehsani) *electrical engineering educator, consultant*
Ewing, Richard Edward *mathematics, chemical and petroleum engineering educator*
Fletcher, Leroy Stevenson *mechanical engineer, educator*
Hall, Kenneth Richard *chemical engineering professor, consultant*
Hann, Roy William, Jr. *civil engineer, educator*
Holland, Charles Donald *chemical engineer, educator*
Hsieh, Jen-Shan *fluid mechanics engineer, researcher*
Kehtarnavaz, Nasser *electrical engineering educator*

Kuhn, Beverly Thompson *transportation engineer*
Lee, William John *petroleum engineering educator, consultant*
Lu, Mi *computer engineer, educator*
Lytton, Robert Leonard *civil engineer, educator*
Mathewson, Christopher Colville *engineer, geologist, educator*
Ntaimo, Lewis *engineering educator, researcher*
Page, Robert Henry *retired engineering educator, researcher*
Painter, John Hoyt *engineer*
Patton, Alton DeWitt *electrical engineering consultant*
Radovic, Miladin *engineering educator, researcher*
Reddy, J. N. *mechanical engineering educator*
Richardson, Herbert Heath *mechanical engineer, educator, dean*
Riskowski, Gerald Lee *engineering educator*
Ullman, Gerald Lee *transportation engineer*
Vierow, Karen *mechanical nuclear engineer, researcher*
Weese, John Augustus *mechanical engineer, educator*
Xiong, Zixiang *engineering educator, researcher*

**Corpus Christi**
Fulkerson, Amber Rhea *sanitary engineer*

**Dallas**
Doty, Elmer *aeronautical engineer*
Eberhart, Robert Clyde *biomedical engineering educator, researcher*
Fontana, Robert Edward *electrical engineer, educator, retired military officer*
Francisco, Glen Leif *engineer, engineering executive*
Huang, Yen Ti *civil engineer*
Kovacevic, Radovan *mechanical engineering educator*
McLane, William Delano *mechanical engineer*
Rainwater, R. Steven *systems engineer*
Schulze, Richard Hans *environmental engineering executive*
Sengupta, Chaitali *computer engineer*
Szygenda, Stephen A. *electrical and computer engineering educator, researcher*
Waheed, Khurram *electrical engineer, electronics engineer, educator*
Williams, Charles Edward *engineer*
Xiu, Liming *electrical engineer*
Zhou, Desheng *petroleum engineer*

**El Paso**
Heide, John Wesley *engineering executive*
Pan, Rong *engineering educator*
Reznik, Leonid Carlovich *engineering and information technology educator, researcher*

**Fort Worth**
Astrup, Jens Leo *retired civil engineer*
Cunningham, Atlee Marion, Jr. *aeronautical engineer*
Nichols, James Richard *civil engineer, consultant*
Palmer, Jeffery Dean *systems engineering manager, consultant*
Teichgraeber, Richard D. *electrical engineer, researcher*

**Frisco**
Lim, Jae Doeg *systems engineer, researcher*
Mihm, John Clifford *chemical engineer*

**Galveston**
Otis, John James *civil engineer*

**Garland**
Zimmerman, S(amuel) Morton (Mort Zimmerman) *engineering executive*

**Georgetown**
Moore, Pat Howard *engineering and construction executive, educator*

**Houston**
Antalffy, Leslie Peter *mechanical engineer*
Athanasiou, Kyriacos A. *biomedical engineer*
Balakotaiah, Vemuri *engineering educator, researcher, consultant*
Bomba, John Gilbert *civil engineer, consultant*
Bovay, Harry Elmo, Jr. *retired engineering company executive*
Bueno, Pablo Cesar *aeronautical engineer, educator*
Burrus, Charles Sidney (Sidney Burrus) *electrical engineering educator*
Chapman, Alan Jesse *engineering educator*
Cheatham, John Bane, Jr. *retired mechanical engineering educator*
Duerr, David *civil engineer*
Ehlig-Economides, Christine A. *petroleum engineer*
Focht, John Arnold, Jr. *engineer*
Fossati, Humberto Mario *electrical engineer, researcher*
Frank, Karen Denise *aerospace engineer*
Halas, Naomi J. *nanoscale science and engineering educator*
Hasen, Michael *engineering company executive, civil engineer*
Henley, Ernest Justus *chemical engineering professor*
Hirasaki, George Jiro *chemical engineer, educator*
Horton, Thomas Edward, Jr. *mechanical engineering educator*
Hsu, Thomas Tseng-Chuang *civil engineering educator*
Huang, Hsien-Lu *electrical engineer*
Hutchens, Harry Price, Jr. *engineer*
Kavandi, Janet Lynn *aerospace power engineer, chemist*
Kennedy, Ken *computer science educator*
Kobayashi, Riki *retired chemical engineer, educator*
Krishen, Kumar *research technologist*
Lienhard, John Henry, IV, *mechanical engineer, educator*
Litvinov, Dmitri *engineering educator*
Luss, Dan *chemical engineering professor*
Matthews, Charles Sedwick *petroleum engineer, consultant*

Miele, Angelo *engineering educator, researcher, consultant, author*
Morris, Owen Glenn *engineering corporation executive*
O'Geary, Dennis Traylor *retired engineering company executive*
Peng, Liang-Chuan *mechanical engineer*
Powell, Alan *engineering educator, research scientist*
Prats, Michael *petroleum engineer, educator*
Qiao, Fengxiang *transportation engineer, educator*
Rhodes, Allen Franklin *engineering executive*
Sneider, Robert M. *petroleum exploration engineer*
Talapatra, Dipak Chandra *retired aerospace engineer*
Tsai, Tom Chunghu *chemical engineer*
Vazquez, Luis *electronics engineer*
Wren, Robert James *aerospace engineering manager*
Yelich, Louis James *engineering executive*

**Irving**
Abu-Suleiman, Amr *industrial engineer, researcher*
McCormack, Grace Lynette *civil engineering technician*
Pascal, Tracey Michele *software engineer, director*
Walley, James Marvin, Jr. *engineering executive, management consultant, real estate company executive*

**Katy**
Chavez, Victor Manuel *petroleum engineer, utilities executive*

**Kilgore**
Gosalia, Keyoor Chetan *electrical engineer*

**League City**
Kanuth, James Gordan *chemical engineer*

**Livingston**
Hayes, Gordon Glenn *civil engineer*

**Lubbock**
Archer, James Elson *engineering educator*
Dudek, Richard Albert *engineering educator*
Karp, Tanja Nicolette *electrical engineer, educator*
Kiesling, Ernst Willie *civil engineering educator, dean*
Kristiansen, Magne *electrical engineer, educator*

**Mc Kinney**
Gill, David bRIAN *electrical engineer, educator*

**Mineral Wells**
Mei, Anhua *mechanical engineer, researcher*

**Pasadena**
Martinez, Fernando V. *civil engineer*

**Port Aransas**
Lehmann, William Leonardo *electrical engineer, educator*

**Prairie View**
Qian, Lijun *electrical engineer, educator*

**Rockport**
Minor, Joseph Edward *civil engineer, educator*

**San Antonio**
Abramson, Hyman Norman *engineering and science research executive*
Akopian, David *engineering educator*
Atchley, Curtis Leon *mechanical engineer*
Franke, Ernest A. *electrical engineer, educator*
Glawe, Dawn *engineering educator*
Weinbrenner, George Ryan *aeronautical engineer*

**San Diego**
Sankar, Hari *communications engineer*

**San Marcos**
Asiabanpour, Bahram *engineering educator*
Fischer, Joyce Faye *engineering educator*

**Spring**
Szymczak, Edward Joseph *mechanical engineer*
Woodward, Clifford Edward *chemical engineer*

**Sugar Land**
Effendi, Wajih Tariq *petroleum engineer*

**Temple**
Wang, Xiuying *agricultural engineer, researcher*

**The Woodlands**
Evans, Walter Reed *retired engineering executive, consultant*
Griffith, James William *systems engineer, consultant*

**Tyler**
Sathyamoorthy, Muthukrishnan *engineering educator, dean*

**Waco**
Bradley, Walter Lee *mechanical engineer, educator, researcher, consultant*
Farison, James Blair *electrical biomedical engineer, educator*

**Warda**
Kunze, Otto Robert *retired agricultural engineering educator*

**Webster**
Kobayashi, Herbert Shin *electrical engineer*


## UTAH

**Bluffdale**
Bliss, Rick Wayne *engineer*

**Dugway**
Benson, Morgan *energy engineer, retired military officer*

**Holladay**
Silver, Barnard Joseph Stewart *mechanical and chemical engineer, consultant, inventor*

**Ivins**
Theurer, Byron W. *aerospace engineer, business owner*

**Logan**
Bowles, David Stanley *engineering educator, consultant*
Hargreaves, George Henry *civil and agricultural engineer, researcher*
Keller, Jack *agricultural engineering educator, consultant*
Ren, Wei *control systems educator*
Subprasom, Kitti *civil engineer*

**Manti**
Funk, William Henry *retired environmental engineering educator*

**Murray**
Volberg, Herman William *electronics engineer, consultant*

**Ogden**
Davidson, Thomas Ferguson *retired chemical engineer*

**Provo**
Comer, David John *engineering educator*
Jensen, Michael Allen *engineering educator*
Smoot, Leon Douglas *chemical engineer, educator, retired dean*

**Salt Lake City**
Anderson, Charles Ross *civil engineer*
Bamberg, Eberhard *engineering educator*
Barney, Kline Porter, Jr. *engineering company executive, consultant*
Call, Charles H., Jr. *civil engineer*
DeVries, Kenneth Lawrence *mechanical engineer, educator*
Gandhi, Om Parkash *electrical engineer*
Ghosh, Sambhunath (Sam Ghosh) *civil engineering educator, environmental engineer*
Sandquist, Gary Marlin *engineering educator, researcher, consultant, writer, military officer*
Sohn, Hong Yong *chemical engineer, metallurgical engineer, educator*
Stringfellow, Gerald B. *engineering educator*

**West Jordan**
Huang, Ming-Huang *engineer, materials scientist*


## VERMONT

**Burlington**
Outwater, John Ogden *mechanical engineering educator*
Pinder, George Francis *engineering educator, research scientist*

**Essex Junction**
Jin, Zhenrong *electrical engineer, researcher*

**Jericho**
Bolin, Henry Robert *retired engineer*

**Shelburne**
Anderson, Richard Louis *electrical engineer*


## VIRGINIA

**Afton**
Stefanovic, Victor R *electrical engineer, consultant*

**Alexandria**
Cook, Charles William *aerospace engineer, consultant, educator*
Glynn, Ernest B. *civil engineer, environmental engineer*
Gould, Phillip *engineer*
Hesterberg, Larry Allen *aerospace engineer*
Lasser, Howard Gilbert *chemical engineer, consultant*
MacLaren, William George, Jr. *engineering executive*
Mandil, I. Harry *nuclear engineer*
Murray, Russell, II, *aeronautical engineer, security consultant*
Poehlein, Gary Wayne *retired chemical engineering professor*
Weisberg, Leonard R. *retired engineering executive, researcher*
Wilcox, David Eric *electrical engineering educator, consultant*

**Annandale**
Ochs, Walter J. *civil engineer, consultant*

**Arlington**
Allen, David *systems engineer*
Brighton, John A. *mechanical engineer, academic administrator*
Cox, Henry *engineer, researcher*
Hall, Carl William *agricultural and mechanical engineer*
Hazelrigg, George Arthur, Jr. *systems engineer, educator*
Heineken, Frederick George *biochemical engineer*
Kumar, Srikanta Ponnathpur *electrical engineer, researcher*
Lala, Jaynarayan Hotchand *computer engineer*
MacDonald, Paul Edward *electrical engineer*
Rahman, Muhammad Abdur *mechanical engineer*
Reagan, Lawrence Paul, Jr. *engineering executive, consultant*
Ren, Chiang H. *aerospace engineer*
Salmon, William Cooper *mechanical engineer, engineering company executive*
Shortal, Terence Michael *systems company executive*
Stevens, Donald King *retired aeronautical engineer, consultant*

**Ashburn**
Nickle, Dennis Edwin *electronics engineer, consultant, deacon*

**Bedford**
Ramsey, Forrest Gladstone, Jr. *retired engineering company executive*

**Blacksburg**
Agah, Masoud *electrical engineer, educator*
Aref, Hassan *fluid mechanics engineer, educator*
Batra, Romesh Chander *engineering educator, researcher*
Brown, Gary Sandy *electrical engineering educator*
Diplas, Panayiotis *civil engineering educator*
Disney, Ralph L. (Ralph Lynde Disney) *retired industrial engineering educator*
Glasser, Wolfgang Gerhard *chemical engineering wood science researcher, educator*
Gray, Festus Gail *electrical engineer, educator, researcher*
Hanowski, Richard Joseph *transportation engineer, director*
Ibrahim, Jihad *electrical engineer*
Lee, Fred C. *electrical engineering educator*
Librescu, I. Liviu *acoustical engineer, mechanical engineer, researcher*
Ma, Lili *engineering educator*
Mishra, Amitabh *computer engineer, educator*
Mitchell, James Kenneth *civil engineer, educator*
Phadke, Arun G. *engineering educator*
Price, Dennis Lee *industrial engineer, educator*
Randall, Clifford Wendell *civil engineer, educator*
Schetz, Joseph Alfred *aerospace engineer, educator*
Squires, Arthur Morton *chemical engineer, educator*

**Blue Ridge**
Elmore, Walter A. *electrical engineer, consultant*

**Burke**
Lynch, Charles Theodore, Sr. *materials science engineering researcher, consultant, educator*

**Chantilly**
Austin, Wanda Murry *systems engineer*

**Charlottesville**
Aylor, James Hiram *engineering educator*
Berger, Toby *electrical engineer, educator*
Braiman, Mark Stephen *biomedical educator, researcher*
Brewer, Philip Warren *retired civil engineer*
Gaden, Elmer Lewis *retired engineering educator*
Garber, Nicholas Jack *civil engineer, educator*
Hoel, Lester A. *civil engineering educator, department chairman*
Hudson, John Lester *chemical engineering professor*
Inigo, Rafael Madrigal *retired electrical engineering educator*
Kent, Richard W. *mechanical engineer*
Krzysztofowicz, Roman *systems engineering and statistical science educator, consultant*
Lee, Jen-shih *biomedical engineering educator*
Louis, Garrick E. *systems engineer, educator*
Pierce, Shayn *biomedical engineer, educator*
Reynolds, Albert Barnett *nuclear engineer, educator*
Theodoridis, George Constantin *biomedical engineering educator, researcher*
Townsend, Miles Averill *aerospace and mechanical engineering educator*

**Edinburg**
Trindal, Wesley Steele *mechanical engineer*

**Fairfax**
Boone, James Virgil *retired engineering executive, researcher*
Chen, Chun-Hung *engineering educator*
Cook, Gerald *electrical engineering educator*
Felsburg, David F. *engineering executive, educator*
Ganesan, Rajesh *industrial engineer, researcher*
Gertler, Janos John *electrical engineer, educator*
Houck, Mark Hedrich *engineering educator*
Palmer, James Daniel *information technology educator*
Sage, Andrew Patrick, Jr. *systems engineering and management educator*
Villarreal, Carlos Castañeda *engineering executive*

**Fairfax Station**
Duff, William Grierson *electrical engineer, educator*

**Falls Church**
Hibbs, Ernest G. *engineering executive*
Jones, Russel Cameron *civil engineer, educator*
Klopfenstein, Rex Carter *electrical engineer*
Lorenzo, Michael *engineer, real estate broker, government official*
Tether, Anthony John *aerospace executive*

**Fredericksburg**
Hasenfus, Harold Joseph *retired mechanical engineer, naval technical director*
Medding, Walter Sherman *retired environmental engineer*

**Hampton**
Bartels, Robert Edwin *aerospace engineer*
Bradley, Arthur Thomas *electrical engineer*
Joshi, Suresh Meghashyam *engineer, researcher*
McAdaragh, Raymon Michael *aerospace engineer, researcher*
Refaat, Tamer F. *electrical engineer, researcher*
Sobieski, Jaroslaw *aerospace engineer*
Sun, Rensheng *electrical engineer, educator*
Zhu, Weiying *engineering educator*

**Harrisonburg**
Choi, Yong-Seok *communications engineer, researcher*

**Kilmarnock**
Ibañez, Alvaro *patent design company executive*

**Lynch Station**
Skeen, David Ray *systems engineer, consultant, engineering executive, educator*

**Lynchburg**
Wang, Kaihong *mechanical engineer, researcher*

**Manassas**
Haddad, Nadim Fawzi *engineer, researcher*
Marshall, Joseph Roman, Jr. *electrical engineer*

**Mc Lean**
Carnicero, Jorge Emilio *aeronautical engineer, transportation executive*
Dobson, Donald Alfred *retired electrical engineer*
Kappaz, Michael H. *engineering and energy executive*
McCambridge, John James *civil engineer*
Rosenbaum, David Mark *engineering executive, consultant, educator*
Schauer, Franz Peter *civil and nuclear engineer, educator*
Stine, John Andrew *communications engineer, researcher*

**Middleburg**
Langley, Rolland Ament, Jr. *engineering and management consultant*

**Montross**
Fountain, Robert Roy, Jr. *retired engineering company executive, farmer, military officer*

**Newport News**
Donaldson, Coleman duPont *retired aeronautical engineer, aerospace engineer, consultant*
Hubbard, Harvey Hart *aeroacoustician, noise control engineer, consultant*
Whitesides, John Lindsey, Jr. *aerospace engineering educator, researcher*

**Norfolk**
Dhali, Shirshak Kumar *engineering educator*
Karim, Mohammad Ataul *electrical engineering educator, researcher*
Rabadi, Ghaith *engineering educator, consultant*
Samuels, John M., Jr. *industrial engineer*
Seow, Ming-Jung *computer engineer, researcher*
Wei, Benjamin Min *engineering educator*
Wiltse, James Clark *civil engineer*

**Penhook**
Coar, Richard John *mechanical engineer, aerospace transportation executive, consultant*

**Reston**
Choi, Michael Kamwah *aerospace engineer, mechanical engineer, researcher*
Kahn, Robert E. *electrical engineer*

**Richmond**
Aiken, Peter Haynes *systems engineer, educator, architect, consultant, data engineer*
Compton, Olin Randall *consulting electrical engineer, researcher*
Karahaliloglu, Koray *electrical engineer, educator*
Lingerfelt, Alan Thomas *civil engineer, real estate company executive*
Mattauch, Robert Joseph *retired electrical engineering educator, retired dean*
Morkoç, Hadis *electrical engineer, educator*
Sprinkle, William Melvin *acoustical engineer, engineering executive*

**Roanoke**
Landis, John William *retired engineering executive, consultant, government advisor*

**Salem**
Shaffner, Patrick Noel *retired architectural engineering executive*

**Springfield**
Casazza, John Andrew *electrical engineer, energy executive*
Meikle, Philip G. *engineer, retired government agency executive*
Sonnemann, Harry *electrical engineer, consultant*

**Suffolk**
Noblitt, Nancy Anne *aerospace engineer*

**Vienna**
Keiser, Bernhard Edward *engineering executive, communications engineer, consultant*
Salah, Sagid *retired nuclear engineer*
Woodward, Kenneth Emerson *retired mechanical engineer*

**Virginia Beach**
Bradshaw, Denis James *engineer, graphic designer*
Spivak, Maurice Sidney *civil engineer, consultant*

**Wallops Island**
Krause, David John *aerospace engineer, director*

**Warrenton**
Gullace, Marlene Frances *systems engineer, consultant*
Uygur, Mustafa Eti *engineering educator*

**Waynesboro**
Lane, Lawrence Jubin *retired electrical engineer, consultant*

**Williamsburg**
Aaron, Bertram Donald *engineering executive, management consultant*

**Woodbridge**
Kreipke, Merrill Vincent *civil engineer, consultant*


## WASHINGTON

**Auburn**
Whitmore, Donald Clark *retired engineer*

**Bellevue**
Parks, Donald Lee *mechanical engineer, human factors engineer*
Wang, Xing *power systems engineer*

**Bellingham**
Jansen, Robert Bruce *consulting civil engineer*

**Brush Prairie**
Edlich, Richard French *biomedical engineer, educator*

**Camas**
Conley, John F. *electrical engineer, researcher*

**Cle Elum**
Galloway, Patricia Denese *civil engineer*

**Dupont**
Pettit, Ghery St. John *electronics engineer*

**Edmonds**
Peckol, James Kenneth *consulting engineer*
Schmit, Lucien André, Jr. *retired structural engineer*

**Issaquah**
Reid, John Mitchell (Jack Reid) *biomedical engineer, research consultant*
Wright, Theodore Otis *forensic engineer*

**Kenmore**
Guy, Arthur William *electrical engineering educator, researcher*

**Lummi Island**
Ewing, Benjamin Baugh *environmental engineer, educator, consultant*

**Mercer Island**
Bridgforth, Robert Moore, Jr. *aerospace engineer*

**Mukilteo**
Bohn, Dennis Allen *engineering executive*

**Olympia**
Sesonske, Alexander *nuclear and chemical engineer*

**Pullman**
La Rue, George Sterling *electrical engineer, researcher, engineering educator*
Morris, Lisa Kaplan *engineering educator, physics professor, mathematics professor*
Stock, David Earl *mechanical engineering educator*

**Redmond**
Willard, H(arrison) Robert *electrical engineer*

**Richland**
Arm, Stuart Trevor *research engineer*
Blumenkranz, David Benjamin *chemical engineer, consultant*

**Sammamish**
Yocam, Eric Wayne *engineer*

**Seattle**
Babb, Albert Leslie *biomedical engineer, educator*
Bowen, Jewell Ray *chemical engineering professor*
Davis, Earl James *chemical engineering professor*
Davis, Jennie Sue *aerospace engineer*
Demasi, Luciano *aerospace engineer, researcher*
Finlayson, Bruce Alan *retired chemical engineering professor*
Gilbert, Paul H. *engineering executive, consultant*
Hands, Eric William *civil engineer, researcher*
Hoffman, Allan Sachs *chemical engineer, educator*
Ishimaru, Akira *electrical engineering educator*
Kapur, Kailash Chander *industrial engineering educator*
Kevorkian, Jirair *aeronautics and astronautics engineering educator*
Kobayashi, Albert Satoshi *mechanical engineering educator*
Lee, Cheegwan *environmental engineer, consultant*
Lidstrom, Mary E. *chemical engineering professor, microbiology professor*
Mc Feron, Dean Earl *mechanical engineer, educator*
Oman, Henry *retired electrical engineer, engineering executive*
Rojas, Eddy M. *engineering educator*
Schmidt, Peter Gustav *marine engineer*
Spindel, Robert Charles *electrical engineering educator*
Sutter, Joseph F. *aeronautical engineer, consultant, retired air transportation executive*
Thomas, Wendy Evelyn *biomedical engineer, educator*
Wenk, Edward, Jr. *civil engineer, educator, writer, policy analyst*

**Spokane**
Ruud, Clayton Olaf *engineering educator*

**Stevenson**
Scherling, Bruce A. *civil engineer*

**Tacoma**
Sloan, Daniel Kay *electrical engineer*

**WEST VIRGINIA**

**Charleston**
Lewis, Charles Raymond, II, *traffic engineer, consultant*

**Clarksburg**
Sivakumaran, Kumaraswamy *civil engineer, consultant, lawyer*

**Morgantown**
Cutlip, Robert Gregory *safety officer*
De Vore, Paul Warren *technology educator*
Guthrie, Hugh Delmar *chemical engineer*

**Halabe**, Udaya Bhatta *civil engineering educator, researcher*
Mucino-Quintero, Victor Hugo *mechanical engineering educator, consultant*
Shekhawat, Dushyant *chemical engineer*

**WISCONSIN**

**Beaver Dam**
Frank, Scott M. *mechanical engineer, consultant*

**Brookfield**
Curfman, Floyd Edwin *retired engineering educator*
Thomas, John *mechanical engineer, artist*

**Green Bay**
Panchalavarapu, Poornachandra Rao *industrial engineer, consultant*

**Hartford**
Aubuchon, Richard E. *engineering executive*

**La Crosse**
Davy, Michael Francis *civil engineer, consultant*

**Madison**
Beachley, Norman Henry *mechanical engineer, educator*
Bird, Robert Byron *chemical engineering educator, author*
Boyle, William Charles *engineering educator*
Dietmeyer, Donald Leo *retired electrical engineering educator*
Emmert, Gilbert Arthur *retired engineering educator*
Grogan, Paul J. *retired engineering educator*
Gustafson, David Harold *industrial engineering and preventive medicine educator*
Hill, Charles Graham, Jr. *chemical engineering educator*
Kim, Nam-Heon *engineering researcher*
Kulcinski, Gerald LaVerne *nuclear engineer, educator, dean*
Langer, Stanley Harold *chemical engineer, educator*
Lasseter, Robert Haygood *electrical engineering educator, consultant*
Lightfoot, Edwin Niblock, Jr. *retired chemical engineering educator*
Lillesand, Thomas Martin *engineer, educator*
Lovell, Edward George *mechanical engineering educator*
Maravelias, Christos Theodoros *engineering educator*
Novotny, Donald Wayne *electrical engineer, educator*
Rusi, Eduard *engineering educator*
Russell, Jeffrey Scott *engineering educator*
Skiles, James Jean *electrical engineer, computer engineer, educator*
Smith, Michael James *industrial engineering educator*
Stewart, Warren Earl *chemical engineer, educator*
Webster, John Goodwin *biomedical engineering educator, researcher*
Wu, Chin H. *engineering educator*
Yavuz, Deniz Dervis *electrical engineer, researcher*

**Menomonie**
Asthana, Rajiv *engineering educator, researcher*

**Milwaukee**
Chandler, Edward William *communication systems engineer, electrical engineer, electrical engineering educator*
Demerdash, Nabeel Aly Omar *electrical engineer*
Gaggioli, Richard Arnold *mechanical engineering educator*
Graef, Luther William *civil engineer*
Heinen, James Albin *electrical engineering educator*
Reyer, Steven E. *engineering educator*
Stemper, Brian D. *biomedical engineer*
Valencia Lavao, Jesus M. *electrical engineer, consultant*
Widera, Georg Ernst Otto *mechanical engineering educator, consultant*
Yeh, Chia-Chou *electrical engineer, researcher*

**Oconomowoc**
Dupies, Donald Albert *retired civil engineer*

**Platteville**
Li, Wei *engineering educator, researcher*

**Richland Center**
Heinen, John Timothy *environmental engineer*

**Soldiers Grove**
Ewing, Brian Kim *retired engineering executive, writer*

**Spooner**
Frey, Paul Howard *chemical engineer, engineering consultants company executive*

**Stevens Point**
Drew, Richard Allen *retired electrical engineer*

**Woodruff**
Polasek, Edward John *retired electrical engineer, consultant*

**WYOMING**

**Lander**
Field, Francis Edward *electrical engineer, educator*

**Laramie**
Bagley, David Michael *environmental engineer, educator*
Mingle, John Orville *engineer, educator, lawyer, consultant*

Rechard, Paul Albert *retired civil engineering company executive, consultant*

**TERRITORIES OF THE UNITED STATES**

**PUERTO RICO**

**Mayaguez**
Suarez, Luis Edgardo *civil engineering educator*
Virella, Juan Carlos *civil engineer, researcher*

**VIRGIN ISLANDS**

**St Croix**
Lee, Sidney Phillip *chemical engineer, state senator*

**CANADA**

**ALBERTA**

**Calgary**
Glockner, Peter G. *civil and mechanical engineering educator*
Lam, Galen Ka-Ron *electrical engineer*
Malik, Om Parkash *electrical engineering educator, researcher*
McDaniel, Roderick Rogers *petroleum engineer, consultant*

**Edmonton**
Lock, Gerald Seymour Hunter *retired mechanical engineering educator*
Offenberger, Allan Anthony *electrical engineering educator*
Otto, Fred Douglas *chemical engineering professor*
Zuo, Ming Jian *industrial engineering educator*

**BRITISH COLUMBIA**

**Burnaby**
Thomas, Howard Paul *civil engineer, consultant*

**Lake Country**
Muggeridge, Derek Brian *engineering executive, consultant*

**Vancouver**
Salcudean, Martha Eva *mechanical engineer, educator*
Young, Lawrence *electrical engineering educator*

**Victoria**
Antoniou, Andreas *electrical engineering educator*

**Westbank**
Wedepohl, Leonhard Martin *electrical engineering educator*

**MANITOBA**

**Winnipeg**
Cohen, Harley *engineering educator*
Kuffel, Edmund *electrical engineering educator*
Mufti, Aftab A. *civil engineering educator*

**NEW BRUNSWICK**

**Fredericton**
Bray, Dale Irving *civil engineering educator*

**NEWFOUNDLAND AND LABRADOR**

**Saint John's**
Clark, Jack Ivor *civil engineer, researcher*

**ONTARIO**

**Burlington**
Harris, Philip John *engineering educator*

**Hamilton**
Bandler, John William *electrical engineering educator, consultant*
Campbell, Colin Kydd *electrical and computer engineering educator, researcher*
Crowe, Cameron Macmillan *chemical engineering professor*
Garland, William James *nuclear engineer, educator*

**Kingston**
Batchelor, Barrington de Vere *civil engineer, educator*

**London**
Davenport, Alan Garnett *civil engineer, educator*
Inculet, Ion I. *electrical engineer, educator, science association director, consultant*

**Mississauga**
Gupta, Rajesh *engineer, consultant*

**North York**
Buzacott, John Alan *engineering educator*

**Ottawa**
Bozozuk, Michael *civil engineer*
Georganas, Nicolas D. *electrical engineerning educator, academic administrator*
Shiari, Behrouz *mechanical engineer, researcher*

**Toronto**
Davison, Edward Joseph *electrical engineering educator*
Endrenyi, Janos *research engineer, educator*
Ganczarczyk, Jerzy Jozef *engineering educator, consultant*
Janischewskyj, Wasyl *electrical engineering educator*
Meagher, George Vincent *mechanical engineer*
Salama, C. Andre Tewfik *electrical engineering educator*
Slemon, Gordon Richard *electrical engineering educator*
Smith, Peter William Ebblewhite *electrical engineer, educator, research scientist, physicist*
Venetsanopoulos, Anastasios Nicolaos *electrical engineer, educator*
Wonham, Walter Murray *electrical engineer, educator*
Zeng, Hong *audio system architect, researcher*

**Waterloo**
Penlidis, Alexander *chemical engineering professor*
Sedra, Adel Shafeek *engineering educator, academic administrator*
Vlach, Jiri *electrical engineering educator, researcher*

**Windsor**
Hackam, Reuben *electrical engineering educator*
Kennedy, John Baptist *civil engineer*

**QUEBEC**

**Montreal**
Dealy, John Michael *chemical engineer, educator*
Ferguson, Michael John *electronics educator, communications educator*
Haccoun, David *electrical engineering educator*
Ladanyi, Branko *civil engineer, educator*
Lamarre, Bernard *engineering executive*
Paidoussis, Michael Pandeli *mechanical engineering educator*
Ramachandran, Venkatanarayana Deekshit *electrical engineering educator*
Saint-Pierre, Guy *engineering executive*
Selvadurai, Antony Patrick Sinnappa *civil engineer, educator, mathematician, consultant*

**Sainte Anne de Bellevue**
Broughton, Robert Stephen *engineering educator, consultant*

**Varennes**
Bartnikas, Raymond *electrical engineer, educator*

**Westmount**
Kalaycioglu, Serdar *aerospace engineer, researcher*

**SASKATCHEWAN**

**Regina**
Mollard, John Douglas *engineering and geology executive*

**Saskatoon**
Billinton, Roy *engineering educator*
Smith, C. D. *civil engineering educator*

**Waterloo**
Shen, Xuemin Sherman *engineering educator, researcher*

**MEXICO**

**Caolniatizapan**
Ramirez-Mireles, Fernando *electrical engineer*

**Mexico City**
Porraz, Mauricio Jimenez Labora *civil engineer, researcher*

**AUSTRALIA**

**Cammeray**
Besley, Morrish Alexander (Tim Besley) *civil engineer*

**BRAZIL**

**Joinville**
Bernardini, Giovanni *electrical engineer*

**BULGARIA**

**Sofia**
Germanova-Krasteva, Diana *textile engineer, educator*

**CHINA**

**Beijing**
Yao, Andrew Chi-Chih *engineering educator*

**Chengdu**
Ma, Shijun *engineering educator*

**HangZhou**
Zhang, ZhiJian *engineering educator*

**Shanghai**
Yun, Liang *marine engineer, educator*

## CYPRUS

**Nicosia**
Elias, Kyriakides *electrical engineer, educator, electrical engineer, researcher*

## DENMARK

**Horsholm**
Svensson, Sven Eilif *civil engineer, consultant*

**Nordborg**
Clausen, Jørgen Mads *engineering executive*

## ENGLAND

**Beaconsfield**
Lindley, David *mechanical engineer*

**Cambridge**
Hawthorne, Sir William (Sir William Rede Hawthorne) *aerospace and mechanical engineer, educator*

**Coulsdon**
Vijayaratnam, Kanapathipillai *civil and environmental engineer, consultant, director, educator*

**Reading**
Thacker, Charles P. *computer engineer, engineering executive*

**Southampton**
Brebbia, Carlos Alberto *engineering educator, consultant*
Spearing, Simon Mark *aeronautical engineer, educator*

**Westminster**
Broers, Lord Alec Nigel *engineering educator*

## FRANCE

**Le Vesinet**
Fourt, Bernard-Francois P. *retired engineer*

## GERMANY

**Aachen**
Pischinger, Franz Felix *engineer, researcher, engineering educator*

**Freiberg**
Zabecki, David Tadeusz *engineer, educator, military historian, military officer*

**Munich**
Schmidt, Stefan *mechanical engineer, economist*

**Weinheim**
Ostovic, Vlado *engineering educator, researcher*

## GREECE

**Athens**
Arnis, Efstathios Constantinos *mechanical engineer, space naval designer*

## HONG KONG

**Hong Kong**
Kao, Charles Kuen *electrical engineer, educator*

**Kowloon**
Cheng, Ping *engineering educator*

## HUNGARY

**Sopron**
Sitkei, György *engineer, educator*

## INDIA

**Allahabad**
Aggarwal, Deepak *research engineer, educator*

**Balasore**
Talukdar, Atanu *electrical engineer*

**Bangalore**
Padhi, Radhakant *engineer*

**Bhubanesway**
Mohanty, Sitakanta *petroleum engineer*

**Calcutta**
Kothari, Hemraj *mechanical engineer, management consultant*

**Nagpur**
Modak, Jayant Pandurang *mechanical engineer, consultant*

**New Delhi**
Jain, Prem Chand *mechanical engineer*

## IRELAND

**Dublin**
Dooge, James Clement Ignatius *civil engineer, hydrologist*

## ISRAEL

**Be'er Sheva**
Brosilow, Coleman Bernard *chemical engineering educator*

**Lod**
Gur, Joshua *optronics engineer, video engineer, consultant*

## ITALY

**Como**
Casati, Fabio *engineer*

## JAPAN

**Fukuoka**
Ishibashi, Akira *mechanical engineer, educator*

**Ibaraki**
Asanuma, Jun *engineering educator*

**Kanagawa**
Takeuchi, Tetsuya *materials engineer*

**Nagoya**
Sakai, Toshihiko *engineer*
Sendo, Takeshi *mechanical engineering educator, researcher, writer*

**Shizuoka**
Anma, So *engineer, consultant*

**Tokushima**
Kinno, Hitoshi *mechanical engineer, educator*

**Tokyo**
Hori, Yukio *engineering educator, scientific association administrator*

## NIGERIA

**Anambra State**
Ekene, Anigwe Raphael *chemical engineer*

## PAKISTAN

**Lahore**
Rai, Maqbool Ahmad *civil engineer, consultant*

## PHILIPPINES

**Mondaluyong City**
Abiera, Roberto *mechanical engineer*

## POLAND

**Szczecin**
Wierzcholski, Wunschik Christoph *mechanical engineer, mathematician, information scientist*

**Warsaw**
Klemens, Rudolf Henryk *mechanical engineer*

**Wrocław**
Golinski, Joseph Antoni *mechanical engineer*

## PORTUGAL

**Algés**
Horta, José Carlos de Oliveira Sousa *civil engineering consultant*

**Lisbon**
Portela, Antonio Gouvea *retired mechanical engineer, researcher*

## REPUBLIC OF KOREA

**Cheonan**
Shin, Hyun Joon *industrial engineer*

**Daejeon**
Kang, Kyungin *electronics engineer, researcher*
Park, Seok-Kyun *civil engineer, educator*

**Incheon**
Cho, Chongdu *mechanical engineer, educator*

**Pusan**
Ha, Chang Sik *polymer science educator*

**Seoul**
Cha, Suk Won *engineering educator, researcher*
Zi, Goangseup *engineering educator*

**Yuseung**
Lee, Kwangil *electrical engineer, researcher*

## RUSSIA

**Ivanovo**
Ramenskaya, Ludmila Mikael *chemical engineer, researcher*

**Moscow**
Kirpilenko, Grigory Grigor'Evich *engineer, researcher*
Krikalev, Sergei Konstantinovich *flight engineer, cosmonaut, researcher*

## SINGAPORE

**Singapore**
Soon, Boon Yi *engineer*
Zhou, Wei *engineer, educator*

## SWEDEN

**Lund**
Massey, James Lee *electrical engineering educator*

## SWITZERLAND

**Zurich**
Morari, Manfred *chemical engineer, educator*

## TAIWAN

**Taichung**
Liang, Chenju *engineering educator*

**Tainan**
Hsiao, Shih Wen *mechanical engineer, educator*
Huang, Ting-Chia *chemical engineering professor, researcher*
Lin, Jiin-Huey Chern *engineering educator*

## TURKEY

**Istanbul**
Koyuncu, Ismail *engineering educator*

## ZIMBABWE

**Harare**
Salahuddin, Ahmad *civil engineer, educator*

## ADDRESS UNPUBLISHED

Abelson, Harold *electrical engineer, educator*
Abetti, Pier Antonio *electrical engineer, management consultant, educator*
Abu Qahouq, Jaber A. *electrical engineer, researcher*
Aguinsky, Richard Daniel *electrical engineer, engineering executive*
Ahmad, Shahid *engineering educator*
Ahmed, Walid Khairy Mohamed *electrical engineer*
Akinci, Burcu *civil engineer, educator*
Alexander, Danrick *mining engineer, educator*
Amann, Charles Albert *mechanical engineer, researcher*
Amundson, John Kay *electrical engineer*
Anderson, John Gaston *electrical engineer, consultant*
Arcot, Prakash Kumar B *engineer, consultant*
Armaingaud, Franck *engineer*
Arsalan, Qamar H. *electrical engineer*
Asadorian, Diana C. *electrical engineer, educator*
Atilgan, Timur Faik *retired structural engineer*
Awwal, Abdul Ahad Sami *engineer, educator*
Axford, Roy Arthur *nuclear engineering educator*
Azar, Fred S. *biomedical engineer, researcher*
Bae, Seongtae *electrical engineer*
Bakht, Baidar *civil engineer, researcher, educator*
Baktir, Selcuk *electrical engineer, computer engineer, researcher*
Baltazzi, Evan Serge *engineering research consulting company executive*
Banerjee, Kaustav *electrical and computer engineering educator*
Bar-Cohen, Avram *mechanical engineering educator*
Bare, Jane Crum *chemical engineer*
Barrett, Michael Henry *civil engineer*
Bartlett, Desmond William *engineering company executive*
Bauer, Richard Carlton *nuclear engineer*
Baum, Eleanor *electrical engineering educator*
Beach, Harry Lee, Jr. *mechanical engineer, aerospace engineer*
Beard, Leo Roy *retired civil engineer*
Beckjord, Eric Stephen *nuclear engineer, researcher*
Belt, Cynthia K. *mechanical engineer*
Berry, Patrick Lowell *chemical engineer*
Bers, Abraham *electrical engineering and physics educator*
Bershad, Neil Jeremy *electrical engineering educator*
Bertin, John Joseph *aeronautical engineer, educator, researcher*
Besio, Walter G. *engineering educator*
Beumer, Richard Eugene *retired engineering executive*
Bhardwaj, Sarvesh *electrical engineer*
Bhatia, Rajan *engineer, physicist, researcher*
Bhattacharyya, Arun Kumar *antenna engineer*
Bier, Karla *chemical engineer, educator*
Binkley, David Martin *engineering educator*
Blagojevic, Goran *electrical engineer, consultant*
Blakesley, Wayne Lavere, Jr. *retired production engineer*
Bloch, Erich *retired electrical engineer, science foundation director*
Blunt, Shannon David *electrical engineer, researcher*
Boch, David Paul *engineering technical specialist*
Bornhorst, Kenneth Frank *electromagnetics and systems engineer*
Borroni-Bird, Christopher E. *transportation engineer*
Bowman, Bruce Alan *civil engineer*
Boyd, John T. *engineering executive*
Brazil, Aine M. *engineering company executive*
Brennan, Lawrence Edward *retired electronics engineer*

Brickell, Charles Hennessey, Jr. *marine engineer, retired military officer*
Bridger, Baldwin, Jr. *electrical engineer*
Briggs, James Henry, II, *electrical engineer*
Brozowski, Laura Adrienne *mechanical engineer*
Brubaker, James Edward *mechanical engineer*
Brungraber, Robert J. *civil engineer, educator*
Bunch, Jennings Bryan, Jr. *retired electrical engineer*
Burchard, John Kenneth *retired chemical engineer*
Burhans, Frank Malcolm *mechanical engineer*
Button, Donald D. *electrical engineer*
Buyurgan, Nebil *engineering educator, researcher*
Byrd, Lloyd Garland *retired civil engineer*
Byun, Gwibo *engineer, researcher*
Carey, Stephanie L. *systems engineer, educator*
Carlson, Robert Codner *industrial engineering educator*
Carnahan, Brice *chemical engineer, educator*
Cerny, Louis Thomas *civil engineer, transportation engineer, consultant*
Cha, Soyoung Stephen *mechanical engineer, educator*
Chadwell, Charles B. *civil engineer, educator*
Chandra, Abhijit *engineering educator*
Chang, Heng-Chia *communications engineer*
Chang, Runzi *electrical engineer*
Chang, Ying Chih *engineering educator, researcher*
Channappayya, Sumohana *engineer, researcher*
Charwat, Andrew Franciszek *engineering educator*
Chebiam, Ramanan Venkata *computer engineer*
Chen, Qiang *engineer*
Chen, Shoei-Sheng *retired mechanical engineer*
Chiang, I-Ting *engineering educator*
Chiang, Mung *engineering educator, consultant*
Chickamenahalli, Shamala A. *electronics engineer*
Cho, Alfred Yi *electrical engineer*
Chou, Chung-Kwang *bio-engineer*
Chouery, Farid Alexandre *electrical engineer, structural engineer, consultant*
Chow, Winston *engineering executive*
Chu, Jack J. (Jack J. Zhu) *electrical engineer*
Chu, Wai C. *engineer, researcher*
Chung, Woo Cheol *electrical engineer*
Cianci, Philip Joesph *broadcast engineer*
Claridge, Elmond Lowell *retired engineering educator*
Clemins, Patrick John *systems engineer, educator*
Clewett, Raymond Winfred *mechanical design engineer*
Collins, Michael *aerospace consultant, astronaut*
Colon Jimenez, Ely Xavier *mechanical engineer*
Comtois, Marc Allen *engineer, historian*
Conway, Richard Ashley *environmental engineer*
Corallo, N. Ralph *retired health care products design engineer*
Cromer, Donald L. *aerospace and electrical engineer*
Cruikshank, Thomas Henry *energy services and engineering executive*
Cui, Hongliang *engineering company executive, researcher*
Cummins, Nancyellen Heckeroth *electronics engineer*
Dally, James William *mechanical engineering educator, consultant*
Daly, Donald F. *retired engineering company executive*
Dargan, Pamela Ann *systems engineer, consultant*
Dattatreya, Galigekere Ramaswamy *engineering educator, consultant*
Day, Donald Lee *retired engineering educator*
De Angelis, Flavio *electrical engineer, researcher*
Dickerson, John Robert *retired automotive engineer*
Ding, Zhaohua *biomedical engineer, educator*
Dix, Samuel Morman *industrial engineer, economist, appraiser*
Donohue, George L. *mechanical engineer, educator*
Donohue, Marc David *chemical engineering professor*
Dorning, John Joseph *nuclear engineering, physics, and applied mathematics educator*
Douglas, Karin Nadja *engineer*
Drucker, Alan Steven *mechanical engineer*
Dukhan, Nihad *mechanical engineer, educator*
Dull, William Martin *retired engineering executive*
Dunbar, Bonnie J. *engineer, astronaut*
Dupuis, Russell Dean *electrical engineer, researcher*
Durrani, Sajjad Haidar *aerospace engineer, consultant, communications engineer*
Dyer, Ira *ocean engineering educator, consultant*
Eaglet, Robert Danton *electrical engineer, aerospace scientist, consultant, retired military officer*
Eberstein, Arthur *former biomedical engineering educator, researcher*
Eden, Murray *electrical engineer, emeritus educator*
Edgar, Thomas Flynn *chemical engineering professor*
Edwards, Victor Henry *chemical engineer*
Eissmann, Robert Fred *retired manufacturing engineer*
Elam, Matthew *industrial engineer, educator*
El-Moursy, Magdy *electronics engineer*
Engelmann, Rudolph Herman *electronics consultant, writer*
Ensminger, Dale *retired mechanical engineer, retired chemical engineer*
Ernst, Edward Willis *retired electrical engineering educator*
Ettinger, Harry Joseph *retired industrial hygiene engineer, retired consultant*
Evans, Gerald William *engineering educator, consultant*
Fan, Chien *aerospace engineer, researcher*
Fernandez, Fernando Lawrence *aeronautical engineer, research and development company executive*
Finkelstein, Maynard Joel *retired mechanical engineer*
Fishman, Bernard *mechanical engineer*
Flick, Carl *electrical engineer, consultant*
Foley, Gary J. *chemical engineer, researcher, computer scientist, federal agency administrator*
Folsom, Tyler Cleveland *computer engineer, educator*

Wilson, Gary Thomas *engineering executive*
Wilson, Leland Earl *retired petroleum engineer*
Wilson, Melvin Edmond *retired civil engineer*
Wintle, Rosemarie *biomedical electronics engineer*
Wolfe, Charles Morgan *electrical engineering educator*
Woo, Derek *electrical engineer, computer engineer*
Woo, Savio Lau-Yuen *bioengineering educator*
Woodland, N. Joseph *retired optical engineer, retired mechanical engineer*
Wu, Min *computer and electrical engineer*
Wu, Xin *electrical engineer, researcher, educator*
Wu, Zheng Y. *hydroinformatics engineer, hydrologist, consultant*
Xu, Yifang *engineer, researcher*
Xue, Yuan *engineering educator*
Yaman, Cevat *environmental engineer, educator*
Yan, Su *mechanical engineer, researcher*
Yang, Bing-Shiang *biomedical engineer*
Yang, Jidong *transportation engineer*
Yang, Tianyu *electrical engineer, educator*
Yates, John Robert, Jr. *civil engineering educator*
Ye, Hua *electronics engineer*
Yen, Bing Cheng *retired civil engineer, retired engineering educator*
Yilmaz, Bilge *chemical engineer, researcher*
Yim, Kang Sub *engineer*
Yiu, Fang *structural engineer, researcher*
Yong, Raymond Nen-Yiu *civil engineering educator*
Young, Tzay Y. *electrical and computer engineering educator*
Yuan, Zeng-Guang *mechanical engineer, researcher*
Yue, Alfred Shui-Choh *metallurgical engineer, consultant*
Yue, Meng *electrical engineer*
Yun, James Kyoon *electrical engineer*
Zahran, Mohamed Mostafa *electrical engineer, educator*
Zanjacomo, Paulo Regis *engineering executive*
Zelinski, Joseph John *engineering educator, consultant*
Zha, Gecheng *engineer, educator*
Zha, Xuan-Fang *engineering educator, researcher*
Zhang, Li *engineer, researcher, educator*
Zhao, Zhongshan *structural engineer, researcher*
Zheng, Fawen *fluid mechanics engineer*
Zimmerman, Marlin U., Jr. *chemical engineer*

# FINANCE: BANKING SERVICES
*See also* **FINANCE: INVESTMENT SERVICES**

## UNITED STATES

### ALABAMA

**Birmingham**
Banton, Julian Watts *banker*
Buckner, Heath *investment banker*
Dick, John R. *bank executive*
Horsley, Richard David *banker*
Jones, D. Paul, Jr. *bank executive, lawyer*
Marks, Charles Caldwell *retired investment banker, retired manufacturing executive*
Moore, Jackson Watts *bank executive*
Morgan, Hugh Jackson, Jr. *retired bank executive, retired energy executive*
Northen, Charles Swift III *retired bank executive*
Page, Ruffner *bank executive*
Powell, William Arnold, Jr. *retired bank executive*
Weatherly, Robert Stone, Jr. *banker*

**Dothan**
Peterson, Roger *community bank executive, retired international investment banker, retired manufacturing executive, retired air force officer*

**Montgomery**
Hoffman, Richard William *retired banker*
Taylor, Watson Robbins, Jr. *investment banker*

### ALASKA

**Anchorage**
Cuddy, Daniel Hon *bank executive*
Rasmuson, Edward Bernard *banker*
Reed, Frank Metcalf *bank executive, director*

**Fairbanks**
Heckman, Jyotsna (Jo) L. *bank executive*

### ARIZONA

**Paradise Valley**
Unruh, James Arlen *bank executive*

**Phoenix**
Jungbluth, Connie Carlson *banker*
Ralston, Barbara Jo *banker*
Richardson, Judy McEwen *investment banker, consultant, cartoonist*

**Scottsdale**
Garfield, Ernest *bank executive, consultant*
Leonard, George Edmund *bank executive, credit manager, marketing professional*

**Surprise**
Koessel, Donald Ray *retired bank executive*

**Tucson**
Bernmúdez, Carmen *trust company executive*
Markman, Sherman *investment banker, venture capitalist, financial consultant*

### ARKANSAS

**Bentonville**
Walton, Jim Carr *bank executive*

**Little Rock**
Green, Johnnie D. *loan officer*
Gulley, Wilbur Paul, Jr. *retired savings and loan association executive*

### CALIFORNIA

**Bakersfield**
Sawyer, Nelson Baldwin, Jr. *credit union executive*

**Beverly Hills**
Balash, Jeffrey Linke *investment banker*
Goldsmith, Bram *banker*
Israel, Richard Stanley *investment banker*
Walker, William Tidd, Jr. *investment banker*

**Calabasas**
Presland-Byrne, Peter *mortgage company executive*

**Carmel**
Barton, Hugh Perry *bank executive*
Dobey, James Kenneth *banker*

**Cathedral City**
Poppe, Eugene Dale *banker*

**City Of Industry**
Contreras-Sweet, Maria *bank executive*

**Costa Mesa**
Giannini, Valerio Louis *investment banker*

**Encinitas**
Ford, William Francis *retired bank holding company executive*

**Escondido**
Newman, Barry Ingalls *retired bank executive*

**Fresno**
Smith, Richard Howard *banker*

**Glendale**
Cross, Richard John *bank executive*

**Irvine**
Jamshidipour, Yousef *bank executive, economist, financial advisor*
Rady, Ernest S. *thrift and loan association executive*

**La Jolla**
Bower, Christopher James *investment banker*

**La Mesa**
Schmidt, James Craig *retired bank executive, savings and loan association executive*

**Lafayette**
Dethero, J. Hambright *banker*

**Laguna Beach**
Matzdorff, James Arthur *investment banker, internet marketing professional*

**Lake Arrowhead**
Fitzgerald, John Charles, Jr. *investment banker*

**Long Beach**
Hancock, John Walker III *banker*
Keller, J(ames) Wesley *credit union executive*

**Los Angeles**
Barren De Serres, Bruce Willard (H.R.H. The Duke Bruce Willard Barren de Serres) *merchant banker*
Cohee, Kevin *bank executive*
Coulter, David A. *investment banker*
Riordan, George Nickerson *investment banker*
Thompson, Elizabeth *bank executive*

**Malibu**
DeMieri, Joseph L. *retired bank executive*

**Manhattan Beach**
Magner, Rachel Harris *retired banker*

**Menlo Park**
Chamberlain, Paul Edward *investment banker*
Grimes, Michael D. *investment banker*
Hazen, Paul Mandeville *banker*
Schmidt, Chauncey Everett *banker, director*

**Newport Beach**
Casey, Thomas Clark *retired trust company executive, investment advisor*
Prince, Thomas E. *bank executive*

**Oakland**
Kettell, Russell Willard *banker*
Nelson, Shirley W. *bank executive*
Sandler, Herbert M. *bank executive*
Sandler, Marion Osher *bank executive*

**Oceanside**
Rosier, David Lewis *retired investment banker*

**Orinda**
Trowbridge, Thomas, Jr. *mortgage company executive*

**Pasadena**
Keys, Scott *bank executive*
Patton, Richard Weston *retired mortgage company executive*
Perry, Michael W. *bank executive*

**San Diego**
Reinhard, Christopher John *merchant banker, venture capitalist, biotechnologist, director*
Wiesler, James Ballard *retired banker*

**San Francisco**
Atkins, Howard Ian *bank executive*
August-deWilde, Katherine *banker*
Baumhefner, Clarence Herman *retired bank executive*
Bee, Robert Norman *banker*
Callahan, Patricia R. *bank executive*
Dellas, Robert Dennis *investment banker*
Demarest, David Franklin, Jr. *banker, retired government official*
Edwards, C. Webb *bank executive*
Gillette, Frankie Jacobs *retired savings and loan association executive, federal agency administrator, social worker*
Ho, Doreen Woo *bank executive*
Hoyt, David A. *bank executive*
Kovacevich, Richard M. *bank executive*
Lee, Pamela Anne *bank executive, accountant, financial analyst*
Matthews, Gilbert Elliott *investment banker*
McGettigan, Charles Carroll, Jr. *investment banker*
McGrath, Don John *bank executive*
Munio, David J. *bank executive*
Oman, Mark C. *bank executive*
Ostler, Clyde W. *banker*
Stumpf, John G. *bank executive*
Tolstedt, Carrie L. *bank executive*
Warner, Harold Clay, Jr. *banker, investment company executive*
Yellen, Janet Louise *bank executive*

**San Jose**
Hall, Robert Emmett, Jr. *investment banker, realtor*

**San Marino**
Gouw, Julia Suryapranata *bank executive*
Ng, Dominic *bank executive*

**San Rafael**
Djordjevich, Miroslav-Michael *bank executive*

**Santa Barbara**
Anderson, Donald Meredith *bank executive*
Tilton, David Lloyd *savings and loan association executive*

**Santa Monica**
Davis, Stephen Edward Folwell *banker*
Heimbuch, Babette E. *bank executive*

**Tarzana**
Weil, Leonard *banker*

**Upland**
Horton, Michael L. *mortgage company executive, publishing executive*

**Walnut Creek**
Rhody, Ronald Edward *bank executive, communications executive*
Saavedra, Charles James *retired banker*

### COLORADO

**Castle Rock**
Corboy, James McNally *investment banker*

**Denver**
Grant, William West III *banker*
Imhoff, Walter Francis *investment banker*
Kemper, J. Mariner *bank executive*
Nicholson, Will Faust, Jr. *bank executive*
Orullian, B. LaRae *bank executive*

**Englewood**
Rosser, Edwin Michael *mortgage company executive*

**Estes Park**
Piper, Mark Harry *retired banker*

**Greeley**
Smith, Jack Lee *bank executive*

**Greenwood Village**
Davidson, John Robert (Jay) *bank executive*
Sims, Douglas D. *bank executive*

**Lakewood**
Fugate, Ivan Dee *banker*

**Palisade**
Barnewall, Marilyn MacGruder *retired banker*

**Vail**
Hoover, Gary Lynn *banker*

### CONNECTICUT

**Cos Cob**
Kane, Jay Brassler *banker*

**Darien**
Mapel, William Marlen Raines *retired bank executive*

**Essex**
Miller, Elliott Cairns *retired bank executive, lawyer*

**Fairfield**
Brett, Arthur Cushman, Jr. *banker*
Cooper, L.E., Jr. *bank executive, lawyer, writer*

**Greenwich**
Bedrosian, Gregory Ronald *investment banker*
de Visscher, Francois Marie *investment banker*
Long, Thomas Michael *investment banker*
Nevin, Crocker *investment banker*
Smith, Phillips Guy *banker*
Stockman, David Alan *investment banker*
Swarz, Jeffrey Robert *investment banker, biotechnologist, neuroscientist*

**Hartford**
Fiszel, Geoffrey Lynn *investment banker, investment advisor*

**New Canaan**
MacEwan, Nigel Savage *retired merchant banker*

**New Haven**
Patterson, Peyton R. *bank executive*

**Norwalk**
Piper, Thomas Laurence III *banker*

**Ridgefield**
Mesznik, Joel R. *investment banker*

**Stamford**
Mayer, John Anton, Jr. *bank executive*

**Waterbury**
Smith, James Copenhaver *bank executive*

**Weston**
Zimmerman, Bernard *investment banker*

**Westport**
Donaldson, James Neill *banker*
Kelly, Paul Knox *investment banker*

**Windsor**
Ferraro, John Francis *investment banker*

### DELAWARE

**Wilmington**
Cecala, Ted Thomas, Jr. *banker, accountant*
Cochran, John R. III *bank executive*
Krulak, Charles Chandler *bank executive*
St. Clair, Jesse Walton, Jr. *retired savings and loan association executive*
Wright, Vernon Hugh Carroll *bank executive*

### DISTRICT OF COLUMBIA

**Washington**
Bernanke, Ben Shalom *Chairman of Federal Reserve System*
Bies, Susan Schmidt *bank executive*
Carson, Thomas Bode *bank executive, consultant*
Conlin, Linda Mysliwy *bank executive, former federal agency administrator*
Couper, William *bank executive*
Decker, Brett M. *bank executive*
Douglas, Leslie *investment banker*
Graham, William Pierson *investment banker, entrepreneur*
Guenther, Jack Donald *banker*
Holbrooke, Richard Charles Albert *investment banker, former ambassador*
Kohn, Donald L. *bank executive, economist*
Kroszner, Randall Scott *bank executive, economics professor*
Lambright, James H. *bank executive*
Mathias, Edward Joseph *merchant banker*
McNamara, Robert Strange *former President of the World Bank, former Secretary of Defense*
Mishkin, Frederic Stanley *bank executive, economics educator*
Morales, Hector E., Jr. *bank executive, lawyer*
Pollock, Alexander John *banker*
Relch, John *banker, federal agency administrator*
Rotberg, Eugene Harvey *investment banker, lawyer*
St. John, Julie *mortgage company executive*
Tomlinson, Alexander Cooper *investment banker, consultant*
Warsh, Kevin Maxwell *bank executive*
Weatherstone, Sir Dennis *retired bank executive*
Wolfowitz, Paul Dundes *President of the World Bank, former federal agency administrator*

### FLORIDA

**Boca Grande**
de Saint Phalle, Thibaut *investment banker, financial consultant*

**Boca Raton**
Andrews, Holdt *investment banker*
Frankel, Charles James III *banker*
Goldberger, Melvin Tobias *bank executive*

**Coral Gables**
Brownell, Edwin Rowland *banker, civil engineer, land surveyor*

**Destin**
Blossman, Alfred Rhody, Jr. *banker*

**Dunedin**
Rosa, Raymond Ulric *retired banker*

**Englewood**
Simis, Theodore Luckey *investment banker, information technology executive*

**Fort Lauderdale**
Leach, Ralph F. *banker*
Thayer, Charles James *investment banker*

**Highland Beach**
Lane, James McConkey *retired investment banker*

**Jacksonville**
Hovey, Charles William *mortgage company executive*

**Key Biscayne**
Wilson, Robert Gordon *investment banker*

**Lantana**
Barrett, Robert James III *investment banker*

**Marco Island**
Cooper, Thomas Astley *bank executive*

## Miami
Aguirre-Sacasa, Francisco Xavier *international banker, diplomat*
Lopez, Miriam *bank executive, department chairman*

## Naples
Kley, John Arthur *banker*
Kvetko, Colleen M. *bank executive*
Martinuzzi, Leo Sergio, Jr. *banker*

## Nokomis
Hawley, Phillip Eugene *investment banker*

## North Miami Beach
Kropp, James Herbert, Sr. *investment manager*

## North Palm Beach
Lynch, William Walker *banker*

## Orlando
Hoepner, Theodore John *banker*
Shirek, John Richard *retired savings and loan executive*

## Palm Beach
Coleman, Denis Patrick, Jr. *investment banker*

## Pensacola
Stuart, Walter Bynum III *retired banker*

## Pompano Beach
Calatchi, Ralph Franklin *investment banker, writer*
Kester, Stewart Randolph *banker*

## Ponte Vedra Beach
de Selding, Edward Bertrand *retired bank executive*
O'Brien, Raymond Vincent, Jr. *banker*

## Punta Gorda
Haswell, Carleton Radley *banker*

## Saint Petersburg
Godbold, Francis Stanley *investment banker, security firm executive*

## Sarasota
Geithner, Paul Herman, Jr. *retired banker*
Phillips, Howard William *investment banker*

## Tampa
Michaels, John Patrick, Jr. *investment banker, media broker*

## Tarpon Springs
Johnson, Randall Clyde *mortgage company executive*

## Temple Terrace
Rink, Wesley Winfred *retired bank executive*

## Tequesta
Turrell, Richard Horton, Sr. *banker*

## Tierra Verde
Stewart, John Murray *retired bank executive*

## Vero Beach
Crosby, John Griffith *investment banker*
Sheehan, Charles Vincent *investment banker*

## Wellington
Guillama-Alvarez, Noel Jesus *merchant banker, healthcare executive*

## West Palm Beach
Addison, Ferguson Lofton Lightbourne *retired bank executive*

# GEORGIA

## Alpharetta
Freeman, Douglas K. *bank executive*

## Atlanta
Barron, Patrick Kenneth *bank executive*
Biggins, J. Veronica *bank executive*
Chapman, Hugh McMaster *banker*
Chau, Pin Pin *bank executive*
Dowling, Roderick Anthony *investment banker*
Hollis, Timothy Martin *bank executive*
Humann, L. Phillip *bank executive*
Long, Robert Richard *banker*
McNabb, Dianne Leigh *investment banker, accountant*
Reed, William R., Jr. *bank executive*
Wells, James M. III *bank executive*
Williams, James Bryan *banker*
Young, James E. *banker*

## Columbus
Anthony, Richard E. *bank executive*
James, Elizabeth R. (Lee Lee James) *bank executive*
Prescott, Thomas W. *bank executive*

## Flowery Branch
Monroe, Melrose *retired bank executive*

## Kennesaw
Whittingham, Harry Edward, Jr. *retired banker*

## Savannah
Clemmons, John B. *bank executive, director, retired mathematics educator*

## Stockbridge
Grimes, Richard Allen *banker, educator*

# HAWAII

## Honolulu
Johnson, Lawrence M. *retired bank executive*
Midkiff, Robert Richards *trust company executive, finance company executive, consultant*

Tanoue, Donna A. *bank executive, former federal agency administrator*
Wolff, Herbert Eric *banker, former army officer*

# IDAHO

## Ketchum
McElhinny, Wilson Dunbar *banker*

# ILLINOIS

## Blue Island
Yager, Vincent Cook *retired bank executive*

## Burr Ridge
McCormack, Robert Cornelius *investment banker*

## Chicago
Adams, Austin A. *bank executive*
Bakwin, Edward Morris *banker*
Bartter, Brit Jeffrey *investment banker*
Blair, Edward McCormick *investment banker*
Bobins, Norman R. *banker*
Bobrinskoy, Charles Kellogg *investment banker*
Citera, Peter M *mortgage company executive*
Dancewicz, John Edward *investment banker*
Fenton, Clifton Lucien *investment banker*
Glickman, Robert Jeffrey *bank executive*
Lyon, Charles Herbert Randolph *investment banker*
Montgomery, Charles Howard *retired bank executive*
Moskow, Michael H. *bank executive*
Reilly, Robert Frederick *investment banker*
Roberts, Theodore Harris *banker*
Scharf, Charles W. *bank executive*
Schulte, David Michael *investment banker*
Scully, John Edward, Jr. *banker*
Stevens, Mark *banker*
Stirling, James Paulman *investment banker*
Swift, Edward Foster III *investment banker*
Theobald, Thomas Charles *banker*
Weston, Roger Lance *banker*

## Dundee
Weck Farrag, Kristin W. *bank executive*

## Evanston
Scholten, Menno Nico *mortgage banker*

## Fox River Grove
Abboud, Alfred Robert *banker, consultant, investor, director*

## Highwood
Brown, Lawrence Haas *retired banker*

## Kenilworth
Corrigan, John Edward, Jr. *retired banker, lawyer*

## Lake Forest
Ross, Robert Evan *bank executive*
Seaman, Irving, Jr. *banker*

## Mattoon
Horsley, Jack Everett *bank executive, writer, lawyer*

## Melrose Park
Giancola, James J. *bank executive*

## Northbrook
Gratalo, John, Jr. *banker, small business owner*
Keehn, Silas *retired bank executive*

## Oak Brook
Iles, Eileen Marie *bank executive, risk management consultant*
Khoshabe, Steven Y. *mortgage company executive*

## Palatine
Hershenhorn, Robert Gene *bank executive*

## Prospect Heights
Derickson, Sandy *bank executive*

## Wilmette
Griffiths, Robert Pennell *banker*

## Winnetka
Klapperich, Frank Lawrence, Jr. *investment banker*

# INDIANA

## Columbus
Abts, Henry William *retired banker*

## Greenwood
Broscoe, Peter A. *mortgage company executive, consultant*

## Muncie
Anderson, Stefan Stolen *retired banker*
Bower, Connie Ilene *bank executive*

## South Bend
Jones, Wellington Downing III *banker*

# IOWA

## Cedar Rapids
Wax, Nadine Virginia *retired bank executive*

## Clinton
Kearney, Michael John *banker*

## Des Moines
Heiden, Cara *mortgage company executive*

## Maquoketa
Tubbs, Edward Lane *banker*

## Mason City
Rodamaker, Marti Tomson *bank executive*

# KANSAS

## Coldwater
Adams, Elizabeth Herrington *banker*

## Liberal
Richard, Loren Dru *bank executive*

## Olathe
Roby, Brian L. *bank executive*

## Pratt
Loomis, Howard Krey *banker, director*

## Shawnee Mission
McEachen, Richard Edward *banker, lawyer*

## Topeka
Bunten, William Daniel *retired banker*

# KENTUCKY

## Louisville
Guillaume, Raymond Kendrick *banker*
Thompson, Kathy C. *bank executive*

## Shepherdsville
Pike, Burlyn *retired bank director, lawyer*

# LOUISIANA

## Lafayette
Hail, Karen L. *bank executive*

# MAINE

## Bangor
Bullock, William Clapp, Jr. *banker*

## Cape Elizabeth
Cotter, Joseph Francis *retired bank executive, hotel executive*

# MARYLAND

## Annapolis
Berg, Gordon Hercher *banker*
McGuirk, Ronald Charles *retired bank executive, economic advisor*
Schleicher, Nora Elizabeth *bank executive, treasurer, accountant*

## Baltimore
Baldwin, Henry Furlong *banker*
Barnhill, Gregory Hurd *investment banker*
Hopkins, Samuel *retired investment banker*
Jacobs, Richard James *banker, educator*
Kent, Edgar Robert, Jr. *investment banker*
Liberto, Joseph Salvatore *retired bank executive*
Massey, Garnetta D. *bank executive*
Schaefer, Robert Wayne *banker*

## Bethesda
Rosenbaum, Greg Alan *merchant banker, consultant*
Saul, B. Francis, II, *bank executive, director*

## Centreville
Griffith, Alan Richard *retired banker*

## Columbia
DeRosa, Thomas J. *investment banker, investment company executive*

## Darnestown
Lightner, Gene Cleek *investment banker*

## North East
Goldbach, Jennifer DeBerdine *bank executive*

## Owings Mills
Sanner, George Bradley *bank executive*

## Rockville
Meyer, F. Weller *bank executive*

# MASSACHUSETTS

## Andover
Yannalfo, Brett Conlon *bank executive*

## Boston
Aquilino, Daniel *banker*
Berstein, Robert L. *investment banker*
Brown, William L. *banker*
Finnegan, Neal Francis *retired banker*
Gifford, Charles K. *banker*
Hill, Richard Devereux *retired banker*
Minehan, Cathy Elizabeth *bank executive*
Phillips, Daniel Anthony *trust company executive*
Pline, Jennifer Alice *trust company executive*
Vermilye, Peter Hoagland *banker*

## Cambridge
Edgerly, William Skelton *banker*

## Dover
Aldrich, Frank Nathan *banker*

## Longmeadow
Lo Bello, Joseph David *bank executive*

## Newton
Teig, Marlowe Gilman *investment banker*

## Pittsfield
Fawcett, Gayle P. *bank executive*

## Reading
Burbank, Nelson Stone *investment banker*

## Wellesley
Small, Parker Adams III *investment banker*

## West Wareham
Worrell, Cynthia Lee *bank executive*

## Westport
Nichols, C. Walter III *retired trust company executive*

## Westwood
Riley, Henry Charles *banker*

## Winchester
Brennan, Francis Patrick *banker*

## Worcester
Hunt, John David *retired bank executive*

# MICHIGAN

## Bay City
Van Dyke, Clifford Craig *retired bank executive*

## Dearborn
Musson, Warren R. *investment banker*

## Detroit
Babb, Ralph W., Jr. *bank executive*
Beran, John R. *banker*
Buttigieg, Joseph J. *bank executive*
Jeffs, Thomas Hamilton, II, *retired bank executive*
Piper, William Howard *bank executive*

## Frankfort
Foster, Robert Carmichael *banker*

## Grand Rapids
Van Dyke, Michelle *bank executive*

## Grosse Pointe
Mengden, Joseph Michael *retired investment banker*

## Grosse Pointe Farms
Surdam, Robert McClellan *retired banker*

## Livonia
Gilbert, Daniel *mortgage company executive*

## Saginaw
Evans, Harold Edward *banker*

## Southfield
Shields, Robert Emmet *merchant banker, lawyer*

## Waterford
Houston, E(rnest) James, Jr. *banker, consultant*

# MINNESOTA

## Chanhassen
Severson, Roger Allan *bank executive*

## Eden Prairie
Hanson, Dale S. *retired bank executive*

## Edina
Campbell, James Robert *retired bank executive*

## Minneapolis
Carlson, Jennie Peaslack *bank executive*
Cooper, William Allen *bank executive*
Davis, Richard K. *bank executive*
Griffith, Sima Lynn *investment banker, consultant*
Grundhofer, Jerry A. *bank executive*
Grundhofer, John F. *bank executive*
Moffett, David McKenzie *bank executive*
Morrison, John M. *bank executive*
Pohlad, Carl R. *bank executive, professional sports team executive*
Stern, Gary Hilton *bank executive*

## Saint Paul
Rothmeier, Steven George *merchant banker, investment company executive*

## Wayzata
Brown, Bull W. *bank executive*
Nagorske, Lynn A. *bank executive*
Rich, Willis Frank, Jr. *banker*

# MISSISSIPPI

## Gulfport
Thatcher, George Robert *banker, writer, journalist, columnist*

## Tupelo
Ramage, Martis Donald, Jr. *banker*

# MISSOURI

## Bridgeton
Brunngraber, Eric Henry *banker*

## Clayton
Kemper, David Woods, II, *banker*

## Independence
Barker, Keith Rene *investment banker*

## Kansas City
Green, Jerry Howard *investment banker*
Hoenig, Thomas M. *bank executive*
Kemper, Rufus Crosby, Jr. *retired bank executive*

## Saint Charles
Gross, Charles Robert *bank executive, state senator*

## Saint Louis
Barksdale, Clarence Caulfield *retired banker*

Bealke, Linn Hemingway *banker*
Blake, Allen H. *bank executive*
Bryant, Ruth Alyne *banker*
Costigan, Edward John *retired investment banker*
Dierberg, James F. *bank executive*
Joyner, Dee Ann *bank executive*
Maurer, Frederic George III *bank executive*
Rasche, Robert Harold *banker, retired economics educator*
Stann, John Anthony *investment banker*
Stoecker, David Thomas *banker*

**Saint Peters**
Beckmann, Bill *mortgage company executive*
Pring, Robert Bradford *banker, financial consultant*

**Springfield**
Budzinsky, Armin Alexander *investment banker*
McCartney, N. L. *investment banker*

**Walker**
Martin, Phillip Dwight *bank consulting company executive, mayor*

## NEBRASKA

**Lincoln**
Lundstrom, Gilbert Gene *bank executive, lawyer*

**Sutton**
Johnson, Michael Randy *bank executive*

## NEVADA

**Logandale**
Smiley, Robert William, Jr. *investment banker*

**Reno**
Binns, James Edward *retired banker*

## NEW HAMPSHIRE

**Sanbornville**
Berg, Warren Stanley *retired bank executive*

**Silver Lake**
Tregenza, Norman Hughson *investment banker*

## NEW JERSEY

**Bay Head**
O'Brien, Robert Brownell, Jr. *banker, consultant, yacht broker, opera company executive*

**Chatham**
Leonett, Anthony Arthur *banker*

**Cherry Hill**
Hill, Vernon W., II, *bank executive*

**Cliffside Park**
Goldstein, Howard Bernard *investment banker*

**Hamilton**
Blohm, Robert *investment banker, economist, statistician*

**Jersey City**
Goldberg, Arthur *merchant banker, financial consultant, educator*
Kramer, Helene *banking executive*
Tang, C. Mark *investment banker, venture capitalist*

**Little Falls**
Casey, Karen Anne *banker*

**Madison**
Armstrong, Richard William *bank executive, management consultant*

**Morristown**
Kearns, William Michael, Jr. *investment banker*
Moore, Milo Anderson *banker*

**Newton**
Case, Tammy *bank executive*

**Parsippany**
Jones, Charles Hill, Jr. *banker*

**Princeton**
Ganoe, Charles Stratford *banker, consultant*
Mills, Bradford *merchant banker*

**Ridgewood**
Hayes, Michael Joseph *investment banker, entrepreneur, retail executive*

**Short Hills**
Bartels, Stanley Leonard *investment banker*

**Shrewsbury**
Feeney, John Robert *banker*

**Spring Lake**
D'Luhy, John James *investment banker*

**Summit**
Lewis, Donald Emerson *banker*
Mueller, Paul Henry *retired bank executive*
Singleterry, Gary Lee *investment banker*

**Tenafly**
Bernstein, William Robert *banker*

## NEW MEXICO

**Deming**
Rogers, Alice Louise *retired bank executive, writer, researcher*

**Santa Fe**
Clyde, Larry Forbes *banker*
Dreisbach, John Gustave *investment banker*
Morrissey, Michael Joseph *investment banker*

## NEW YORK

**Bedford**
Philip, Peter Van Ness *former trust company executive*

**Briarcliff Manor**
Oakley, Richard Putney *investment banker*

**Brooklyn**
Bottiglia, Frank Robert *bank executive*
Cohen, Alan *investment banker*
Singer, Eric T. *investment banker*

**Buffalo**
Sadler, Robert E., Jr. *bank executive*
Wilmers, Robert George *bank executive*

**De Witt**
Belden, Sanford Adams *banker*

**East Hampton**
Good, Allen Hovey *investment banker, real estate broker*

**Elmont**
Cusack, Thomas Joseph *retired banker*

**Great Neck**
Katz, Edward Morris *banker*

**Greenwich**
Smethurst, E(dward) William, Jr. *investment banker*

**Hartsdale**
Katz, John *investment banker*

**Larchmont**
Kaufmann, Henry Mark *mortgage banker*

**Locust Valley**
Comfort, William Twyman, Jr. *banker*

**Long Island City**
Markus, Maura *bank executive*

**Melville**
Kanas, John Adam *bank executive*

**New Paltz**
Smith, Kathleen Tener *bank executive*

**New York**
Adams, John Brett *investment banker, pharmaceutical executive*
Agostinelli, Robert Francesco *investment banker*
Alemany, Ellen R. *bank executive*
Allen, Claxton Edmonds III *investment banker*
Bagatelle, Warren Denis *investment banker*
Bains, Leslie Elizabeth *banker*
Ballard, Charles Alan *investment banker*
Barry, Nancy Marie *bank executive*
Beim, David Odell *investment banker, educator*
Bellanger, Serge René *bank executive*
Bermudez, Jorge Alberto *bank executive*
Biglari, Hamid *investment banker*
Boardman, D. Dixon (Dennie Dixon Boardman) *investment banker*
Braunstein, Douglas *bank executive*
Bravo, Luis Fernando *investment banker*
Brody, Kenneth David *investment banker*
Burke, James Joseph, Jr. *investment banker*
Calello, Paul *banker*
Carey, William Polk *investment banker*
Castle, John Krob *merchant banker*
Cavanagh, Michael J. *bank executive*
Cephas, Derrick D. *bank executive, lawyer*
Chalsty, John Steele *investment banker*
Chammah, Walid A. *investment banker*
Childs, John Farnsworth *retired bank executive*
Christodoulou, Marilena *investment banker, finance company executive*
Clifford, Stewart Burnett *banker, director*
Cohen, Jonathan Little *investment banker*
Collins, Adriana *banker*
Corrigan, E(dward) Gerald *investment banker*
Crockett, Andrew Duncan *bank executive*
Cromwell, Oliver Dean *investment banker*
Darst, David Martin *trust company executive, investment banker*
David-Weill, Michel Alexandre *retired investment banker*
Davin, James Manson *investment banker*
Davis, George Linn *banker*
Deans, Patricia Herrmann *investment banker*
Debs, Richard A. *investment banker*
DelliBovi, Alfred A. *bank executive*
Deutsch, David Neil *investment banker*
Djeddah, Richard Nissim *investment banker*
Dooley, Douglas John *bank executive*
Douglass, Robert Royal *bank executive, lawyer*
Drew, Ina R. *bank executive*
Dwek, Cyril S. *banker*
Enders, Anthony Talcott *banker*
Erdoes, Mary Callahan *investment banker*
Eshleman, Diane Varrin *bank executive*
Farley, Terrence Michael *banker*
Feder, Harry Simon *bank executive*
Fischer, Stanley *bank executive*
FitzPatrick, Daniel M. *trust company executive, lawyer*
Flaherty, Pamela Potter *bank executive*
Flowers, J. Christopher *investment banker*
Frank, Frederick *investment banker*
Fredericks, Ivy Lindstrom *investment banker*
Friedberg, Barry Sewell *investment banker*
Fruitman, Frederick Howard *investment banker*
Furman, Roy Lance *investment banker, theater producer*
Gamble, Theodore Robert, Jr. *investment banker*
Gant, Donald Ross *investment banker*
Garner, Albert Headden *investment banker*

Garrett, Robert *investment banker, director*
Geithner, Timothy F. *bank executive*
Gellert, Michael Erwin *investment banker*
Godridge, Leslie V. *bank executive*
Gold, Jeffrey Mark *investment banker*
Goldmark, Peter Francis *banker*
Gonzalez, Eugene Robert *investment banker*
Gossett, Robert Francis, Jr. *merchant banker*
Greenhill, Robert Foster *investment banker*
Greenstein, Abraham Jacob *mortgage company executive, accountant*
Greenthal, Jill A. *investment banker*
Haddon, James Francis *banker*
Hakala, Thomas John *private banker, financial planner, accountant*
Halpern, Merril Mark *investment banker*
Hamdan, Lawrence Anise *investment banker, lawyer*
Harlan, Leonard Morton *merchant banker*
Harrison, Gilbert Warner *investment banker*
Heimann, John Gaines *investment banker*
Herregat, Guy-Georges Jacques *retired banker*
Hersch, Dennis Steven *bank executive, lawyer*
Hill, J(ames) Tomilson *investment banker*
Horowitz, Gedale Bob *investment banker*
Hricik, Lorraine E. *bank executive*
Hultquist, Timothy Allen *investment banker*
Hurley, Dean C. *bank executive, lawyer*
Jack, Bradley H. *investment banker*
Janiak, Anthony Richard, Jr. *investment banker*
Johansson, Jerker Mats *investment banker*
Johnson, Scott Stuart *merchant banker*
Johnson, Thomas Stephen *banker*
Kaufman, Mark Steiner *banker, director*
Kennedy, John Joseph *bank financial officer*
Kindler, Robert Alan *investment banker*
Kirdar, Nemir Amin *banker*
Krawcheck, Sallie L. *bank executive*
Krimendahl, Herbert Frederick, II, *investment banker*
Lawrence, Christopher Rueckert *investment banker*
Layton, Donald Harvey *retired banker*
Lazio, Rick Anthony (Enrico Anthony Lazio) *bank executive, former congressman*
LeBlond, Richard Knight, II, *banker*
Leighton, Lawrence Ward *investment banker*
Leung, Firman *investment bank executive*
Lincoln, Edmond Lynch *investment banker*
Lipper, Kenneth *investment banker, film producer, writer*
Lucander, Henry *investment banker*
Manges, James Horace *investment banker*
Maurer, Jeffrey Stuart *trust company executive*
Maxwell, Anders John *investment banker*
McClelland, W. Carter *bank executive*
McDonald, Stephen Douglas *banker*
McFarland, Alan Roberts *investment banker*
Mc Gillicuddy, John Francis *retired banker*
McGuire, Raymond J. *investment banker*
McMullan, William Patrick III *investment banker*
Meachin, David James Percy *investment banker*
Mendoza, Roberto G., Jr. *banker*
Menschel, Robert Benjamin *investment banker*
Merriss, Philip Ramsay, Jr. *banker*
Miller, Garfield Lankard III *investment banker*
Milstein, Howard P. *bank executive*
Mintz, Norman Nelson *investment banker, educator, retired academic administrator*
Myerberg, Marcia *investment banker*
Nasser, Jacques *banker, former automotive company executive*
Needham, George Austin *investment banker*
Newbold, John Lowe *retired banker, financial consultant*
Nolan, William Joseph III *banker*
Obolensky, Ivan *investment banker, foundation administrator, writer*
Ogunlesi, Adebayo O. *investment banker*
Ostrander, Thomas William *investment banker*
Peetz, Karen B. *bank executive*
Perella, Joseph Robert *investment banker*
Peretsman, Nancy B. *investment banker*
Perlmutter, Louis *investment banker, lawyer*
Petrie, Donald Joseph *banker*
Poll, Robert Eugene, Jr. *bank executive*
Pote, Harold William *banker*
Prizzi, Jack Anthony *investment banking executive*
Purse, Charles Roe *investment banker*
Putney, Mary Lynn *bank administrator, educator*
Rainis, Eugene Charles *bank executive*
Rattner, Steven Lawrence *investment banker*
Rhodes, William Reginald *banker*
Roach, John Hendee, Jr. *bank executive, investment banker, financial services executive*
Roberts, Donald Munier *retired banker, trust company executive*
Rockefeller, David *banker*
Roosevelt, Theodore, IV, *investment banker*
Rose, Robert Neal *investment banker*
Ross, Wilbur Louis, Jr. *investment banker*
Rubin, Robert Samuel *investment banker*
Safra, Joseph *bank executive*
Sandelman, Jonathan E. (Jon) *investment banker*
Saunders, Thomas A. III *investment banker*
Scaturro, Philip David *investment banker, academic administrator*
Schiff, David Tevele *investment banker*
Schumacher, Robert Denison *banker*
Schupak, Donald *merchant banker, lawyer, strategic planner*
Schwarzman, Stephen Allen *investment banker*
Scott, Margaret Simon *retired mortgage broker*
Senior, Enrique Francisco *investment banker*
Sevilla-Sacasa, Frances Aldrich *bank executive*
Shanks, Eugene Baylis, Jr. *banker*
Shipley, Walter Vincent *retired bank executive*
Sidwell, David H. *bank executive*
Slusser, William Peter *investment banker*
Smith, Hilary Cranwell Bowen *investment banker*
Smith, Raymond W. *investment banking executive*
Smith, W. Keith *bank executive*
Spangler, Arnold Eugene *investment banker*
Spielvogel, Sidney Meyer *investment banker*
Stein, Howard S. *retired banker, investment advisor, consultant*
Stern, James Andrew *investment banker*
Storper, David H. *bank executive*
Straton, John Charles, Jr. *investment banker*
Sulimirski, Witold Stanislaw *banker*
Suskind, Dennis A. *investment banker*
Svenson, Charles Oscar *investment banker*

Tagliaferri, Lee Gene *investment banker*
Tanner, Harold *investment banker*
Taylor, Richard William *investment banker, portfolio manager*
Thornburgh, Richard Edward *bank executive*
Towbin, A(braham) Robert *investment banker*
Trachtenberg, Matthew J. *trust company executive*
Van Dine, Vance *investment banker*
van Hengel, Maarten *banker*
Viniar, David *investment banker*
von Fraunhofer-Kosinski, Katherina *bank executive, advertising executive*
Wadsworth, John (Jack) Spencer, Jr. *investment banker*
Walters, Milton James *investment banker*
Warner, Miner Hill *investment banker*
Wasserstein, Bruce *investment banker*
Webster, Lesley Daniels *bank executive*
Weil, Frank A. *investment banker, lawyer*
Weinberg, John Sidney *investment banker*
Weinberg, Peter Amory *investment banker*
Weiner, Walter Herman *bank executive, lawyer*
Weintz, Jacob Frederick, Jr. *retired investment banker*
Wellin, Keith Sears *investment banker*
Whiting, Gordon James *investment banker*
Whittemore, Laurence Frederick *bank executive*
Wigmore, Barrie Atherton *investment banker*
Wilson, Don Matthew III *corporate banking executive*
Winkelried, Jon A. *investment banker*
Winters, William Thomas *bank executive*
Wit, Harold Maurice *retired investment banker, lawyer*
Woetzel, Kurt D. *banking executive*
Wolff, William F. III *investment banker*
Wolitzer, Steven Barry *investment banker*
Wright, Deborah C. *bank executive*
Yancey, Richard Charles *investment banker*
Young, George Haywood III *investment banker*
Young, Robert Craig *banker*

**Oyster Bay**
Schwab, Hermann Caspar *banker*
Walsh, Charles Richard *retired banker*

**Quogue**
Hines, William Eugene *banker*

**Ridgewood**
Jones, Harold Antony *banker*

**Rochester**
Hanson, Karen Noble *financial holding company executive*
Wayland-Smith, Robert Dean *retired banker*

**Rye**
Gambee, Robert Rankin *investment banker*

**Saratoga Springs**
Wait, Charles Valentine *banker*

**Scarsdale**
Abbe, Colman *investment banker*

**Shelter Island**
Dowd, David Joseph *banker, construction executive*

**Southampton**
Brokaw, Clifford Vail III *investment banker*

**Stamford**
Bergleitner, George Charles, Jr. *investment banker*

**Syracuse**
Gray, Charles Augustus *banker*

**Tonawanda**
Haller, Calvin John *banker*

**Uniondale**
Reddy, Gerard Anthony *consumer banker*

**West Harrison**
Verano, Anthony Frank *retired banker*

**White Plains**
Bober, Lawrence Harold *retired banker*
Bushkin, Merle Jerome *investment banker*

**Wyandanch**
Newman, Samuel *retired trust company executive*

**Yonkers**
Philipps, Edward William *former banker, real estate appraiser*
Singer, Cecile Doris *bank executive, former state legislator*

## NORTH CAROLINA

**Charlotte**
Alphin, J. Steele *bank executive*
Bessant, Cathy (Catherine Pombier Bessant) *bank executive, marketing professional*
Brinkley, Amy Woods *bank executive*
Brown, Edward J III *bank executive*
Browning, Roy Wilson III *former mortgage banking executive*
Clark, Ranjana B. *bank executive*
Davis, Jean E. *bank executive*
de Molina, Alvaro G. *bank executive*
Desoer, Barbara J. *bank executive*
Fox, William J. *bank executive, former federal official*
Hammonds, Bruce L. *bank executive*
Hance, James Henry, Jr. *bank executive*
Jones, Milton H., Jr. *bank executive*
Lewis, Kenneth D. *bank executive*
McFayden, Shannon W. *bank holding company executive*
McGee, Liam E. *bank executive*
Migoya, Carlos *bank executive*
Nichols, Debra *bank executive*
Oken, Marc D. *retired bank executive*
Sutton, Cecilia (Cece Sutton) *bank executive*

Oppenheimer, Deanna Watson *bank executive*
Quint, David Paul *investment banking executive*
Studzinski, John Joseph Paul *investment banking executive*
Warner, Scott Dennis *investment banker*

## FRANCE

**Paris**
Bujon de L'Estang, Francois *bank executive*

## GERMANY

**Frankfurt**
Papademos, Lucas *bank executive*

**Munich**
Viermetz, Kurt F. *banker*

## JAPAN

**Tokyo**
Minier, Jean-Francois Raymond *investment banker*

## NETHERLANDS

**Amsterdam**
Rizzi, Joseph Vito *banker*

## NEW ZEALAND

**Wellington**
von Kohorn, Baron Ralph Steven *retired investment banker*

## SCOTLAND

**Tighnabruaich**
Reisinger, Ronald Busch (Baron of Inneryne, Laird of Ascog Castle, Laird of Eilean Na Beithe) *bank executive*

## SPAIN

**Madrid**
Botín, Ana Patricia *bank executive*

## TAIWAN

**Taipei**
Yeh, Kuo Hsing *bank executive*

### ADDRESS UNPUBLISHED

Ackerman, Jack Rossin *investment banker*
Alper, Andrew Michael *former investment banker*
Alvord, Joel Barnes *retired bank executive*
Andreas, David Lowell *retired banker*
Aninat, Eduardo *international banking official*
Armacost, Samuel Henry *bank executive*
Arnhold, Henry H. *investment banker*
Ashton, Thomas Walsh *investment banker*
Atkins, Victor Kennicott, Jr. *private investor*
Baker, Henry S., Jr. *investment banker*
Bansak, Stephen A., Jr. *investment banker, financial consultant*
Baramova, Irina Antonova *investment banker*
Barr, Michael Charles *banking consultant, lawyer*
Barrow, Charles Herbert *investment banker*
Baxter, Nevins Dennis *bank consultant*
Bibby, Douglas Martin *mortgage association executive*
Birky, John Edward *banker, financial consultant*
Boykin, Robert Heath *retired banker*
Boyles, James Kenneth *retired banker*
Breitman, Leo R. *banker*
Britt, John Roy *banker*
Broaddus, John Alfred, Jr. *retired bank executive, economist*
Brosda von Kupferberg, Baron Alexander Christian *investment banker*
Buckels, Marvin Wayne *savings and loan association executive*
Burden, Ordway Partridge *investment banker*
Busse, Leonard Wayne *banker, financial consultant*
Cawley, Charles M. *retired bank executive*
Chase, Helen Louise *bank executive*
Chia, Pei-Yuan *bank executive*
Christenson, Gregg Andrew *bank executive*
Clark, Thomas Carlyle *retired banker*
Clifton, Russell B. *banking and mortgage lending consultant, retired mortgage company executive*
Cockrum, William Monroe III *investment banker, educator*
Cook, Charles Wilkerson, Jr. *bank executive, retired municipal official*
Cooney, John Thomas *retired banker*
Cottrell, Mary-Patricia Tross *bank executive*
Craighead, Rodkey *banker, director*
Crawford, Stephen S. *investment banker*
Curry, John Michael *investment banker*
Czarnecki, Gerald Milton *investment banker, venture capitalist*
Davant, James Waring *investment banker*
Deal, Ernest Linwood, Jr. *banker*
Dean, John Wesley III *investment banker, former federal official*
DeMartini, Richard Michael *retired bank executive*
Derrico, Georgia Santangelo *banker*
deVeer, Robert Kipp, Jr. *investment banker*
Dittenhafer, Brian Douglas *banker, economist*
Dodson, Samuel Robinette III *investment banker*

Doyle, L. F. Boker *retired trust company executive*
Dublon, Dina *former bank executive*
Duke, Betsy (Elizabeth A. Duke) *bank executive*
Dunn, Richard Joseph *retired investment banker*
Eaton, Curtis Howarth *banker, lawyer*
Fahringer, Catherine Hewson *retired savings and loan association executive*
Fetters, Norman Craig, II, *retired banker*
Finocchiaro, Alfonso G. *bank executive*
Fisher, Richard Welton *bank executive*
Fishman, Alan H. *bank executive*
Fitzgerald, William Allingham *savings and loan association executive, director*
Fix, John Neilson *banker*
Freedman, Charles *retired bank executive*
Freeman, Ralph Carter *investment banker, management consultant*
Gaffney, Thomas *retired banker*
Gainor, Thomas Edward *bank executive*
Giblin, Patrick David *retired bank executive*
Giles, Christopher Stewart *banker*
Goldberg, David Alan *investment banker, lawyer*
Gonzales, Ernesto Luis B. *bank executive*
Graham, Cynthia Armstrong *banker*
Greenspan, Alan *former Chairman of Federal Reserve System, economist*
Greer, K. Gordon *banker*
Gregg, David III *investment banker*
Grim, Patricia Ann *retired banker*
Grissom, J. David *private investor, bank executive*
Grosland, Emery Layton *retired banker*
Guynn, Jack (George C. Guynn) *retired bank executive*
Harreld, Michael N. *bank executive*
Hauptfuhrer, W. Barnes *bank executive*
Helfer, Ricki Tigert *banking consultant*
Hess, Dennis John *investment banker*
Hetland, James Lyman, Jr. *banker, lawyer, educator*
Hickey, Joseph Michael *investment banker*
Hogan, Robert Henry *trust company executive*
Howard, Donald Searcy *banker*
Hower, Frank Beard, Jr. *retired banker*
Huntington, Lawrence Smith *investment banker*
Ingersoll, Paul Mills *banker*
Istock, Verne George *retired bank executive*
Jeffers, Michael Bogue *mortgage company executive, lawyer*
Jennings, Joseph Ashby *banker*
Jensen, Edmund Paul *retired bank holding company executive*
Jepson, Robert Scott, Jr. *bank executive*
Jones, Richard Melvin *bank executive, director, former retail executive*
Kaiser, Suzanne Billo *investment banker*
Kane Hittner, Marcia Susan *bank executive*
Kapnick, Stewart *investment banker*
Keevil, Philip Clement *investment banker*
Keir, Gerald Janes *banker*
Keith, Robert William *banker*
Kilts, James M. *investment banker, former consumer products company executive*
Klett, Gordon A. *retired savings and loan association executive*
Kooken, John Frederick *retired bank holding company executive*
Kotler, Steven *investment banker*
Kulenovic, Dzafer Jeff *bank executive, advocate*
Kulesha, Kevin John *investment banker*
Lagomasino, Maria Elena *retired bank executive*
Larr, Peter *retired bank executive*
Larsen, Terrance A. *retired bank holding company executive*
Lawer, Betsy *banker, small business owner, vintner, director*
Lee, Steve Chi Kong *bank executive*
Lester, Susan E. *bank executive*
Lewis, Perry Joshua *investment banker*
Lin, Hamilton *investment banker, education educator*
MacCallum, David Hopper *investment banker*
MacWilliams, Kenneth Edward *investment banker*
Magner, Marjorie *former bank executive*
Malone, Wallace D., Jr. *retired bank executive*
Masa, George John *retired bank executive*
Maughan, Sir Deryck *former bank executive*
Maxwell, Robert William *investment banker, financial analyst*
McGough, Brian Edward *investment banker, lawyer*
McGuinn, Martin Gregory *retired bank executive, lawyer*
McMennamin, Michael J. *savings and loan executive, investment banker*
Meeker, Guy Bentley *banker*
Mehta, Shailesh J. *banker*
Menaker, Ronald Herbert *retired bank executive*
Meyer, Henry Lewis III *bank executive*
Misner-Elias, Michael Bryan *bank executive, consultant*
Mistry, Percy Shiavak *investment banker*
Moll, Lloyd Henry *retired bank executive*
Moriarty, Donald William, Jr. *bank executive*
Moyse, Hermann III *banker*
Muñoz, Carlos Ramón *retired bank executive*
Nuzzo, Anthony Gerald *bank executive*
O'Brien, Thomas Henry *former bank holding company executive*
Osborn, William George *savings and loan association executive*
Pandit, Vikram S. *investment banker*
Pefley, Norman Gordon *bank executive*
Perrotta, Antonio *trust company executive*
Peters, Ralph Frew *investment banker*
Pett, John Lyman *banker*
Place, Janey *banking consultant, former bank executive*
Poehner, Raymond Glenn *retired bank executive*
Pontius, Stanley N. *bank holding company executive*
Poole, William *bank executive*
Porter, Walter Thomas, Jr. *retired bank executive*
Price, William James, IV, *investment banker*
Renyi, Thomas A. *bank executive*
Reuber, Grant Louis *banking insurance company executive*
Rice, Joseph Albert *retired bank executive*
Rishel, Richard Clinton *retired bank executive*
Robards, Thomas Frederick *banker*
Roby, Joe Lindell *investment banker*
Romero-Rainey, Rebeca *bank executive*

Santomero, Anthony M. *retired bank executive, former public policymaker*
Schaut, Joseph William *retired bank executive*
Schlein, Dov C. *banker*
Schless, Phyllis Ross *investment banker*
Searle, Philip Ford *banker*
Seeds, Sharon Lynn *bank processor*
Semrod, T. Joseph *banker*
Shelton, James Douglas *banker*
Shinn, George Latimer *investment banker, consultant, finance educator*
Shuman, Stanley S. *investment banker*
Simon, Leonard Samuel *banker*
Solomon, Jack David *investment banker*
Sorgenfrei, Robert L. *retired trust company executive*
Stansell, Ronald Bruce *retired investment banker*
Stegenga, James Jay *bank examiner, director*
Stephenson, Herman Howard *retired banker*
Stewart, Carleton M. *retired bank executive, director*
Stotter, Harry Shelton *banker, lawyer*
Surface, James Louis, Sr. *trust officer, lawyer*
Swope, Donald Downey *retired banker*
Tarnopol, Michael Lazar *bank executive*
Tatlock, Anne M. *trust company executive*
Taylor, David George *retired banker*
Thaler, Richard Winston, Jr. *investment banker*
Thompson, J. Andy *bank executive*
Thurmond, John Peter, II, *bank executive, rancher, archaeologist*
Tily, Stephen Bromley III *retired bank executive*
Trafton, Stephen J. *bank executive*
Tyagarajan, Krishna Carthik *investment banker*
Tyrrell, Gerald Gettys *banker*
Tyson, H. Michael *retired bank executive*
Urkowitz, Michael *banker*
Vennat, Michel *former bank executive, lawyer*
Walters, Glen Robert *retired banker*
Walton, Alice Louise *bank executive*
Warner, Douglas Alexander III *banker*
Watts, Anthony Lee *bank executive*
Weinman, Connie Germann *banker, lawyer*
Weisman, Lorenzo David *investment banker*
West, Rexford Leon *retired bank executive*
Whitehead, John Cunningham *former bank executive*
Whitney, Edward Bonner *retired investment banker*
Williams, Jeffrey P. *investment banker*
Zilkha, Ezra Khedouri *banker*

---

## FINANCE: FINANCIAL SERVICES

### UNITED STATES

### ALABAMA

**Birmingham**
Coyne, Edward James, Sr. *international business educator*
Gibson, Sloan D., IV, *corporate financial executive*
Hendley, Dan Lunsford *retired finance company executive*
Holloway, Betsy Bugg *marketing educator*
Jordan, D. Bryan *corporate financial executive*
Newton, Don Allen *economic development consultant*
Nowlan, Charles F. *controller*
Ritter, C. Dowd *diversified financial services company executive*

**Decatur**
Michelini, Sylvia Hamilton *auditor*
Talley, Richard Woodrow *accountant*

**Dothan**
Cross, Steven Jasper *finance educator*

**Huntsville**
Graves, Benjamin Barnes *business administration educator*
Stewart, Verlindsey Laquetta *accounting educator*

**Montgomery**
Smith, Larry Steven *financial analyst, accountant, farmer*

**Tuscaloosa**
Gup, Benton Eugene *banking educator*
Mayer, Morris Lehman *marketing educator*
Ray, Nelda Howton *financial consultant*

### ALASKA

**Anchorage**
Ashcraft, Charles Olin *business educator*
Riendl, Robin Wendy *financial planning specialist, financial advisor*
Rylander, Robert Allan *financial service executive*

### ARIZONA

**Carefree**
Smoot, David Paul *finance company executive*

**Chino Valley**
Norton, Douglas Ray *former auditor general*

**Flagstaff**
Everett, Judith *merchandising educator*

**Goodyear**
Eppen, Gary Dean *business educator*

**Mesa**
Linxwiler, Louis Major, Jr. *retired finance company executive*

**Paradise Valley**
Chrisman, William Herring *tax specialist, consultant*

**Phoenix**
Clark, John *corporate financial executive*
Cole, John *controller*
Hovis, John *corporate financial executive*
Kunkel, Joe Carroll *finance company executive*
Lemon, Leslie Gene *retired diversified financial services company executive, lawyer*
Mullen, Daniel Robert *finance company executive*
Upson, Donald V. *retired corporate financial executive*
Van Fleet, David Dominic *management educator*

**Scottsdale**
Hansen, Donald W. *diversified financial services company executive, consultant*
Shower, Robert Wesley *corporate financial executive*
Washburn, Jerry Martin *accountant, corporate executive*

**Sun City West**
Schrag, Adele Frisbie *business education educator*

**Surprise**
Miller, James Rumrill III *finance educator*

**Tempe**
Kaufman, Herbert Mark *finance educator*
Pany, Kurt Joseph *finance educator, consultant*
Poe, Jerry B. *financial educator*
Reckers, Philip Merle *accountant, educator*

**Tucson**
Cain, Vernon *retired diversified financial services company executive*
Carleton, Willard Tracy *retired finance educator*
Fajardo, Sarah Elizabeth Johnson *financial consultant*
Hellon, Michael Thomas *financial analyst, political organization worker*
Horne, William McHenry *finance educator*
Ruscher, Charles B. *finance educator, consultant*
Smith, Kenneth Rodger *finance educator*

**Wickenburg**
Daniel, James Richard *accountant, corporate financial executive*

### ARKANSAS

**Arkadelphia**
Webster, Robert Lee *accounting educator, researcher*

**Batesville**
Stephens, Anna Jo *finance educator*

**Conway**
Horton, Joseph Julian, Jr. *economics and finance educator*
McNew, Bennie Banks *retired finance educator*

**Fayetteville**
Burton, Scot *finance educator*
Hay, Robert Dean *retired management educator*
Rosenberg, Leon Joseph *marketing educator*

**Little Rock**
Bell, Joseph R. *finance educator*
Goodner, Norman Wesley *governmental relations specialist*
Scivally, Bart Murnane *accountant, auditor*

**Mena**
Wiles, Betty Jane *accountant*

**Pine Bluff**
Brown-King, Kimberly Kaye *finance educator*

**Sherwood**
George, James Edward *accountant*

### CALIFORNIA

**Anaheim**
Lano, Charles Jack *retired financial executive*

**Bakersfield**
Bacon, Leonard Anthony *accounting educator*

**Bell Canyon**
Labbett, John Edgar *financial analyst*

**Berkeley**
Berk, Jonathan Bryan *finance educator*
Bucklin, Louis Pierre *business educator, consultant*
Rippe, Lynn E. *portfolio manager*
Staubus, George Joseph *finance educator*

**Beverly Hills**
Griffith, Clark Dexter *corporate financial executive*
McGagh, William Gilbert *financial consultant*
McMorrow, William J. *finance company executive*

**Brea**
Oh, Tai Keun *business educator, consultant*

**Buena Park**
Kristy, James E. *financial consultant, consultant*

**Burbank**
Gold, Stanley Phillip *diversified investments executive*
Thornton, Cameron Mitchell *financial planner*

**Calabasas**
Goldfield, Emily Dawson *finance company executive, artist*
McLaughlin, Thomas Keith *diversified financial services company executive*

Mozilo, Angelo R. *diversified financial services company executive*
Sambol, David E. *diversified financial services company executive*
Samuels, Sandor Eli *diversified financial services company executive, lawyer*
Sieracki, Eric P. *diversified financial services company executive*

**Campbell**
Vincent, David Ridgely *financial consultant*

**Carmel**
de Vos, Paula Francesca *finance company executive, investment advisor, consultant*

**Chico**
Van Auken, Stuart *marketing educator*

**Chula Vista**
Sullivan, Patrick Allen *strategic management educator*

**Claremont**
Christian, Suzanne Hall *financial planner*

**Corona Del Mar**
Indiek, Victor Henry *finance corporation executive*

**Coronado**
Baumer, Edward Ferdinand *finance company executive*

**Costa Mesa**
Metzger, Vernon Arthur *management educator, consultant*

**Crestline**
Douglas, Cindy Holloway *financial consultant*

**Culver City**
Eckel, James Robert, Jr. *financial planner*

**Fairfield**
Schunke, Hildegard Heidel *accountant*

**Fallbrook**
Freeman, Harry Lynwood *retired accountant*

**Foster City**
Coghlan, John Philip *corporate financial executive*

**Fremont**
Jensen, Paul Edward Tyson *business educator, consultant*
Lyons, Irving (Bud) III *corporate financial executive*

**Fresno**
Harris, Breck Anthony *business educator, writer, researcher*
Tellier, Richard Davis *management educator*

**Fullerton**
Foote, Paul Sheldon *business educator, administrator, consultant*

**Hayward**
Kohl, John Preston *finance educator, consultant*
McKenzie, Brian Bruce *finance educator*

**Huntington Beach**
Hamilton, Allen Philip *financial advisor*

**Irvine**
Alch, Mark Lee *finance educator, researcher*
Cole, Robert K. *diversified financial services company executive*
Farrar, Donald Keith *retired finance company executive*
Feldstein, Paul Joseph *management educator*
Gillis, Christine Diest-Lorgion *financial planner, stockbroker*
Madden, Thomas A. *finance educator*
Morrice, Brad A. *diversified financial services company executive*
Parnes, Andrew H. *financial executive*
Premchand, Arigapudi *retired financial consultant*
Rankin, James *finance company executive*
Vines, Henry Ellsworth III *accountant, lawyer, financial planner*

**Laguna Niguel**
Bauer, Barbara A. *financial consultant*

**Lakewood**
Bogdan, Carolyn Louetta *financial specialist, retired small business owner*

**Larkspur**
Aster, Richard (Rick) F., Jr. *diversified financial services company executive*

**Lincoln**
Dorn, Mary Ann *retired auditor*

**Los Altos**
Scifres, Donald Ray *finance company executive*
Yu, Oliver Shukiang *corporate executive, educator, technology strategist*

**Los Angeles**
Allen, Sharon *accounting firm executive*
Allen, Suzanne *financial planning executive, insurance agent, writer, educator*
Anderson, John Edward *diversified holding company executive, lawyer*
Bennis, Warren Gameliel *business administration educator*
Berman, Geoffrey Louis *diversified financial services company executive*
Beyer, Robert D. *corporate financial executive*
Borsting, Jack Raymond *business administration educator*
Broad, Eli *finance company executive, art collector*
Brown, Kathleen *diversified financial services company executive*
Chan, David Ronald *tax specialist, lawyer*

Day, Robert Addison, Jr. *investment management company executive*
Goedde, Alan George *financial company executive*
Leach, Anthony Raymond *financial executive*
Lowy, Peter *corporate financial executive*
McElyea, Jacquelyn Suzanne *accountant, real estate consultant*
Mock, Theodore Jaye *finance educator*
More, Philip Harvey Birnbaum *business administration educator*
Morrison, Donald Graham *business educator, consultant*
Morrow, Winston Vaughan *financial executive*
Mosich, Anelis Nick *accountant, writer, educator, consultant*
O'Toole, James Joseph *business educator*
Ownbey, Vance Scott *corporate financial executive*
Ramer, Lawrence Jerome *corporation executive*
Resnick, Lynda *corporate financial executive*
Stancill, James McNeill *finance educator, consultant*
Stewart, David Wayne *marketing educator, psychologist, consultant*
Taylor, Peter J. *diversified financial services company executive*
Udvar-Hazy, Steven F. *leasing company financial executive*
Walendowski, George Jerry *accounting and business educator*
Westerfield, Randolph W. *finance educator, former dean*
Weston, John Frederick *business educator, consultant*
Williams, Julie Ford *retired finance company executive, economist*

**Malibu**
Baskin, Otis Wayne *business educator*

**Manhattan Beach**
Allmon, Michael Bryan *financial consultant*
Pettersen, Thomas Morgan *accountant, corporate financial executive*

**Menlo Park**
McDonald, Warren George *accountant, consultant, mortgage company executive, savings and loan association executive*
Messmer, Harold Maximilian, Jr., (Max Messmer) *financial services executive*
Scholes, Myron S. *financier, former law and finance educator*

**Mill Valley**
Bull, George E. III *finance company executive*
Mumford, Christopher Greene *corporate financial executive*

**Milpitas**
Ligan, Warren J. *corporate financial executive*

**Montecito**
Burford, Jerrad Dalon *corporate financial executive, writer*

**Moraga**
Tom, Randolph L. *corporate financial executive*

**Napa**
Gillespie, Marcia Lou *tax specialist, accountant, musician*
Hennings, Dorothy Ann *financial advisor*
Hess, Donald Marc *diversified financial services company executive*

**Newport Beach**
Bron, Guillermo (Bill Bron) *lending company executive*
Bruggeman, Terrance John *corporate financial executive*
Gross, William H. (Bill Gross) *financial analyst, investment company executive*

**Northridge**
Roberts, Teri Alane *finance educator, volunteer*

**Novato**
Bibeault, Donald Bertrand *corporate financial executive, investor*

**Oakland**
Lee, Jong Hyuk *accountant*
Tyndall, David Gordon *business educator*

**Oceanside**
Garfin, Louis *retired actuary*

**Pacific Palisades**
Hagenbuch, Rodney Dale *financial consultant*

**Palo Alto**
Herrick, Tracy Grant *fiduciary*
Horngren, Charles Thomas *finance educator*

**Palos Verdes Peninsula**
Manning, Christopher Ashley *finance educator, consultant*

**Pasadena**
Axelson, Charles Frederic *retired accounting educator, food products executive*
Hunt, Hazel Analue Stanfield *retired accountant*

**Pittsburg**
Williams-Thomas, Elizabeth A. *financial planner, consultant*

**Pleasanton**
Edwards, Robert L. *corporate financial executive*

**Pollock Pines**
Johnson, Stanford Leland *finance educator*

**Pomona**
Lin, Lianlian *management educator*
Patten, Thomas Henry, Jr. *finance educator, personnel director*

**Poway**
Mueller, Gerhard Gottlob *retired financial accounting standard setter, retired educator*
Uke, Alan Kurt *finance company executive*

**Rancho Cucamonga**
Jones, Nancy Langdon *financial planning practitioner*

**Rancho Mirage**
Steele, Charles Glen *retired accountant*

**Redlands**
Pick, James Block *business professor, writer*

**Rocklin**
Dwyer, Darrell James *finance company executive*

**Sacramento**
Betts, Bert A. *retired treasurer, accountant*
Gardner, Jerry Lee *financial consultant*
Parker, Dennis Rey *finance educator*

**Salinas**
Stevens, Wilbur Hunt *accountant*

**San Clemente**
Petruzzi, Christopher Robert *business educator, consultant*

**San Diego**
Buska, Sheila Mary *controller, writer, columnist*
Crisci, Mathew G. *corporate financial executive, writer*
Gengor, Virginia Anderson *financial planning executive, educator*
Jeub, Michael Leonard *financial consultant*
Markowitz, Harry Max *finance and economics educator*
Riedy, Mark Joseph *finance educator*
Stambaugh, Larry G. *finance company executive*
West, James Harold *finance company executive*

**San Francisco**
Barlow, William Pusey, Jr. *accountant*
Bauch, Thomas Jay *financial consultant, retired lawyer, retired apparel executive*
Carr-Ruffino, Norma *management educator*
Cuggino, Michael Joseph *financial executive*
Dodds, Christopher V. *finance company executive*
Friedman, Tully Michael *corporate financial executive*
Fuller, James William *financial planner*
Graw, LeRoy Harry *diversified financial services company executive*
Herringer, Frank Casper *diversified financial services company executive*
Im, Subin *marketing educator*
Johns, Christopher P. *corporate financial executive*
MacNaughton, Angus Athole *finance company executive*
McKeever, Michael Pierce, Sr. *economics and business educator*
Moe, Michael *diversified financial services company executive*
Palmer, William Joseph *accountant*
Paterson, Richard Denis *corporate financial executive*
Richey, Ellen *credit card company executive*
Sasaki, Robert J. *financial services executive*
Silverman, Victoria Lillian *consultant, fundraiser, cultural organization administrator*
Uri, George Wolfsohn *accountant*
Vuoto, Anthony *corporate financial executive*
Weihrich, Heinz *management educator*

**San Jose**
Berman, Shawn L. *finance educator*
Effren, Gary Ross *financial executive*
Jiang, William Yuying *business educator, consultant, researcher*
Landis, Kevin *diversified financial services company executive*
Morrison, William Fosdick *business educator, retired electrical company executive*
Smith, David Eugene *business administration educator*

**San Luis Obispo**
Blakeslee, Diane Pusey *financial planner*
Thatcher, Janet Solverson *financial advisor, writer*

**San Marcos**
He, Shaoyi *information systems educator*
Kagan, Stephen Bruce (Sandy Kagan) *corporate financial executive*

**San Marino**
Grantham, Richard Robert *financial consultant*

**San Mateo**
Baio, James R. *diversified financial services company executive*
Bhatia, Sandeep *financial services company executive*
Johnson, Charles Bartlett *corporate financial executive*
Johnson, Gregory E. *diversified financial services company executive*
Johnson, Rupert Harris, Jr. *finance company executive*

**San Ramon**
Crowe, Stephen J. *comptroller*
Vaughn, John Rolland *auditor*

**Santa Ana**
Kennedy, Parker S. *finance company executive*
Ricketts, James F. *treasurer*

**Santa Barbara**
Abbinante, Christopher *finance company executive*
Egan, Susan Chan *securities analyst, writer*
Maudsley, Ronald R. *finance company executive*

**Santa Clara**
McGowan, Stephen T. *corporate financial executive*
Yee, Keith Philip *finance company executive, accountant*

**Santa Monica**
Markoff, Steven C. *finance company executive*
Moses, Samuel B. *accountant, consultant*

**Santa Rosa**
Biderman, Charles Israel *diversified financial services company executive*

**Sherman Oaks**
Hein, Todd Jonathan *accountant*

**Sonora**
Wheeler, Elton Samuel *financial executive*

**Stanford**
Holloway, Charles Arthur *public and private management educator*
McDonald, John Gregory *financial investment educator*
Montgomery, David Bruce *marketing educator*
Paté-Cornell, Marie-Elisabeth Lucienne *finance educator, engineering educator*
Pfeffer, Jeffrey *business educator*

**Stockton**
Ballot, Michael Harvey *business administration educator, consultant*
Taylor, Francis Michael *auditor, municipal official*
Weick, Cynthia Wagner *business educator*

**Sunnyvale**
Merrill, Wendy Jane *financial services company executive*

**Tarzana**
Firestone, Morton H. *finance company executive*
Goldberg, Harvey *corporate financial executive*

**The Sea Ranch**
Carter, Richard Duane *management educator*

**Torrance**
Bell, Scott Andrew *financial consultant*

**Upland**
Barden, Shirley Ramsey *credit union executive*
Cullen, Robert John *financial planner, investment advisor*

**Valley Springs**
Vitrac, Jean-Jacques Charles *international business consultant*

**Visalia**
O'Leary, Deanna Kay *benefits compensation analyst, consultant*

**Vista**
Dyson, Brian G. *business consulting company executive, former beverage company executive*
Ferguson, Margaret Ann *tax specialist, consultant*

**Walnut**
Budzak, Stephen Howard *tax specialist, consultant*

**Walnut Creek**
McCauley, Bruce Gordon *financial consultant*

**West Sacramento**
Anderson, William Wallace *financial executive*

**Westlake Village**
Detterman, Robert Linwood *financial planner*
Erdelyi, Eileen Edith *financial planner, financial advisor*

**Woodland Hills**
Babayans, Emil *financial planner*
Piszel, Anthony S. *corporate financial executive*
Tuthill, Walter Warren *accountant, management consultant*

## COLORADO

**Boulder**
Bangs, F(rank) Kendrick *former business educator*
Kuhn, Timothy R. *finance educator*
Melicher, Ronald William *finance educator*
Stanton, William John, Jr. *marketing educator, author*

**Broomfield**
Seabrook, Raymond J. *corporate financial executive*

**Centennial**
Milliken, Douglas Gordon *financial consultant, municipal official*

**Clifton**
Konola, Claudette June *finance company executive, consultant*

**Conifer**
Boese, Michelle Lynne *accountant, consultant*

**Denver**
Clark, Suzanne *accountant*
Cook, Albert Thomas Thornton, Jr. *financial advisor*
Gimbel, Alfred Adolf *employee benefits professional*
Hall, Richard Murray, Jr. *finance executive, consultant*
Hughes, Bradley Richard *finance company executive*
Levinson, Shauna T. *finance company executive*
Lincoln, Alexander III *financial analyst, lawyer, private investor*
Seiple, John W., Jr. *corporate financial executive*

**Dillon**
Townsend, James Douglas *accountant*

**Erie**
Alpers, John Hardesty, Jr. *financial planner, retired military officer*

**Fort Collins**
Ewing, Jack Robert *accountant*
Kinnison, Robert Wheelock *retired accountant*

**Grand Junction**
Freeman, Neil *accounting executive, computer consulting firm executive*

**Henderson**
Reibold, Dorothy Ann *accountant, researcher*

**Lakewood**
Axley, Hartman *retired financial planner, underwriter*
Hadley, Marlin LeRoy *financial planner, consultant*
Nichols, Vicki Anne *financial consultant, librarian*

**Littleton**
Wittbrodt, Edwin Stanley *financial planner, consultant, retired military officer*

**Longmont**
Sandler, Thomas R. *accountant, director*

**Monte Vista**
Rausch, Paul Matthew *financial executive*

**Monument**
McIver, Deborah Kay *tax specialist, entrepreneur, small business owner*

**Nederland**
Thomas, Daniel Foley *retired diversified financial services company executive*

**Steamboat Springs**
Potter, William Bartlett *diversified financial services company executive*

**Twin Lakes**
Homan, Ralph William *finance company executive*

**Wheat Ridge**
Gerlick, Helen J. *tax practitioner, accountant*

## CONNECTICUT

**Avon**
Mazur, Edward John, Jr. *financial planner*

**Bethel**
Tomasko, Edward A. *financial planner*

**Cos Cob**
Halvorsen, Ole Andreas *financier*

**Danbury**
Moskowitz, Stanley Adam *finance company executive*
Proctor, Richard Jerome, Jr. *business educator, expert witness, accountant*

**Darien**
Lim, Ralph Wei Hsiong *finance educator*
Schell, James Munson *finance company executive*

**East Hartford**
Barredo, Rita M. *auditor*

**Fairfield**
Booth, George Keefer *corporate financial executive*
Neal, Michael A. *corporate financial executive*

**Farmington**
Centofanti, Joseph *accountant*

**Greenwich**
Hewitt, Dennis Edwin *financial executive*
Horton, Jared Churchill *retired diversified financial services company executive, metal products executive*
Macaulay, William Edward *financial executive*
Mandel, Stephen, Jr. *financier*
Smith, Rodger Field *financial executive*
Tarantino, Dominic A. *retired professional services firm executive*

**Hamden**
He, Xiaohong *finance educator*

**Hartford**
Bennett, Alan M. *corporate financial executive*
Campbell, Timothy Reid *financial services company executive*
Geisler, James E. *corporate financial executive*
Johnson, David M. *finance company executive*
Olejiniczak, Ronald M *corporate financial executive*
Price, Robert J *corporate financial executive*
Quirk, Alfred P, Jr. *corporate financial executive*
Souza, Diane D *corporate financial executive*

**Litchfield**
Kenagy, Robert Coffman *planning consulting company executive*
Martin, R. Keith *business and information systems educator, consultant*

**Madison**
James, John Whitaker, Sr. *finance company executive*

**Mystic**
Nolf, David M. *financial consultant*

**New Canaan**
Kamerschen, Robert Jerome *retired business executive, private investor, consultant*

**New Haven**
Abdelsayed, Wafeek Hakim *accounting educator*
Garten, Jeffrey E. *finance educator*

**Norwalk**
Chesser, Leicle E. *corporate financial executive*
Peppet, Russell Frederick *accountant*

Scheinman, Stanley Bruce *corporate financial executive*
Tropin, Kenneth G. *fund management executive*

**Old Lyme**
Fairfield-Sonn, James Willed *management educator, consultant*

**Prospect**
Powell, Raymond William *financial planner, school administrator*

**Redding**
Campbell, Joseph John *retired finance company executive*

**Stamford**
Azam, Zeshan Raza *diversified financial services company executive*
Gonnelli, Patrick M. *finance company executive*
Jason, J. Julie *portfolio manager, writer, lawyer*
Lessin, Andrew Richard *accounting executive*
Loh, Arthur Tsung Yuan *finance company executive*
Mactas, Mark V. *diversified financial services company executive*
Mahony, Edward B. *corporate financial executive*
Morgan, William J. *accounting company executive*
Pansini, Michael Samuel *financial analyst, tax specialist*
Rand, A. Barry *financial services executive*
Reardon, Michael J. *finance company executive*
Williams, Reba White *corporate financial executive, writer, researcher*
Wilson, Mark *corporate financial executive*

**Trumbull**
Ewing, Anna M. *stock exchange executive*

**West Hartford**
Detmar-Pines, Gina Louise *business strategy and policy educator*

**West Haven**
Boronico, Jess Stephen *management science educator, dean*
Ellis, Lynn Webster *retired finance educator, retired telecommunications consultant*
Haley, George Thomas *marketing educator*
Haley, Usha C.V. *international business educator*

**Westport**
McKane, David Bennett *business executive*
Ready, Robert James *finance company executive*

**Wilton**
Hersh, Ira Paul *tax specialist, financial consultant*
Wright, Joseph Robert, Jr. *corportate executive*

## DELAWARE

**Dover**
Kim, Dae Ryong *management information systems educator*

**Newark**
Gehrlein, William Vincent *business professor*
Sawyer, John Edward *management educator*
Velury, Uma *finance educator, researcher*

**Wilmington**
Copeland, Tatiana Brandt *accountant*
Griffin, Jo Ann Thomas *retired financial planner, tax specialist*
Mand, Martin Gary *financial executive*
Rogoski, Patricia Diana *corporate financial executive*
Vecchione, Kenneth A. *corporate financial executive*

## DISTRICT OF COLUMBIA

**Washington**
Aggarwal, Reena *finance educator*
Armstrong, Alexandra *financial planner*
Arnold, G. Dewey, Jr. *accountant*
Belt, Bradley Deck *financial services executive*
Blakely, Robert T. *financial executive*
Chambers, Letitia Pearl Caroline *consulting firm executive*
Collamore, Thomas Jones *corporate financial executive*
Coneway, Peter Richard *retired diversified financial services company executive*
Crosby, David S. *finance educator, consultant*
DiGanci, Todd T. *stock exchange executive*
Droms, William George *finance educator, investment advisor*
Finneran, John Patrick, Jr. *finance company executive, educator*
Flügelman, Máximo Enrique *financier, composer*
Johnson, James A. *finance company executive*
Krueger, Anne *finance company executive, economist*
Larsen, Richard Gary *finance company executive*
Levin, Robert J. *finance company executive*
Levy, Michael B. *business educator*
Ludwig, Eugene Allan *financial consultant, lawyer, former US Comptroller of the Currency*
Malek, Frederic Vincent *finance company executive*
Mayo, John W. *finance educator*
Merrifield, Dudley Bruce *finance educator, federal official*
Morris, Robert Crane *management training executive*
Morse, John B., Jr. *corporate financial executive*
Mudd, Daniel H. *finance company executive*
Niemeier, Charles D. *accountant*
Pane, Natalia *policy and research analyst, strategic planner*
Parde, Duane Arthur *association executive*
Rieser, Joseph A., Jr. *tax specialist*
Schapiro, Mary L. *financial regulatory service executive*
Sweeney, Richard James *finance professor*

Szamosfalvi, Jozsef *corporate financial executive, consultant*
Taylor, David Kerr *international business educator, consultant*
Tsuji, Takako *financial analyst*
Walker, David Alan (David Alan Walker) *finance educator*
Zoeller, Jack Carl *finance company executive*

## FLORIDA

**Aventura**
Fishel, Peter Livingston *finance company executive*
Kliger, Milton Richard *diversified financial services company executive*

**Belleair Bluffs**
Sexton, Donald Lee *retired business administration educator*

**Belleview**
Bellis, Arthur Albert *financial executive, government official*

**Boca Raton**
Babbar, Sunil *finance educator*
Miles, Jesse Mc Lane *retired accounting company executive*
Rosenberg, Lee Evan *financial planner*
Sigel, Marshall Elliot *financial consultant*

**Boynton Beach**
Bartholomew, Arthur Peck, Jr. *accountant*
Mittel, John J. *diversified financial services company executive, economist*

**Bradenton**
Hashmi, Sajjad Ahmad *finance educator, dean*

**Clearwater**
Campolettano, Thomas Alfred *international contract manager*
Crites, Richard Ray *financial planner, finance company executive, investment advisor*
Feldman, Marvin Herschel *financial consultant*

**Cocoa Beach**
Wirtschafter, Irene Nerove *tax specialist, consultant, military officer*

**Coral Springs**
Sommerer, John *accountant, former mayor*

**Crestview**
Scott, George Gallmann *accountant*

**Davie**
Morris, Joseph Raymond *finance educator*

**Deerfield Beach**
Moran, Patricia Genevieve *corporate financial executive*
Siegel, Steven L. *finance company executive, consultant*

**Deland**
Plane, Donald Ray *retired management science educator*

**Delray Beach**
McKay, Patricia A. *corporate financial executive*

**Fort Lauderdale**
Bamberg, Louis Mark *wealth planning and business insurance specialist*
Cobb, David Keith *accountant*
Feldman, Les J. *finance educator*
Pohlman, Randolph A. *business administration educator, dean*
Seyoum, Belay *business educator*
Shoemaker, William Edward *corporate financial executive*
Vasquez, William Leroy *business educator, consultant*

**Highland Beach**
Rosner, M. Norton *diversified financial services company executive*

**Hobe Sound**
Caspersen, Finn Michael Westby *diversified financial services company executive*

**Hollywood**
Harkin, Daniel John *controller*

**Jacksonville**
Adams, Scott Leslie *accountant*
Edwards, Marvin Raymond *investment counselor, economical consultant*
Fortado, Bruce *management educator*
Patel, Vinod Motibhai *accountant*
Tomlinson, William Holmes *management educator, retired military officer*
Vane, Terence G., Jr. *finance company executive, lawyer*

**Jupiter**
De George, Lawrence Joseph *diversified financial services company executive*

**Lady Lake**
Di Benedetto, Ann Louise *retired accounting administrator*

**Lake Mary**
Cosler, Steven Douglas *diversified financial services company executive*

**Lake Wales**
Connor, John Thomas, Jr. *portfolio manager*
Luing, Gary Alan *financial management educator*

**Lakeland**
Plastow, Edward George *business administration educator*

**Largo**
Shillinglaw, Gordon *retired finance educator*

**Lutz**
Hacker, Michelle Wendy *auditor, researcher, finance educator*

**Melbourne Beach**
Harrington, Peter Tyrus *emergency management company executive, public relations executive, consultant, writer, photographer*
Harris, Jack Howard, II, *financial consultant, director*

**Miami**
Capraro, Franz *accountant*
Forgione, Dana Anthony *accounting educator*
Ibler, Gerold *finance company executive, consultant*
Kregg, Judith Lynne *accountant*
Natoli, Joseph T. *financial administrator, former publishing executive*
Nunez-Lawton, Miguel G. *financial analyst*
Pomeranz, Felix *accounting educator*

**Miami Beach**
Cohen, Philip Herman *accountant*
Howard, Melvin *financial executive*

**Miami Shores**
Diener, Betty Jane *business educator*

**Naples**
Hansen, Claire V. *financial executive*
Madigan, Joseph Edward *financial executive, director, consultant*
Ordway, John Danton *retired pension fund administrator, lawyer, accountant*

**New Port Richey**
Deasy, Theresa *finance company executive, accountant*

**Niceville**
Litke, Donald Paul *acquisition executive, retired military officer*

**North Miami**
Tate, Stanley G. *diversified business executive, expert witness*

**North Palm Beach**
Frevert, James Wilmot *retired financial planner, investment advisor*
Higgins, Jay F. *diversified financial services company executive*

**Orlando**
Bearman, David *corporate financial executive*
Kellison, Stephen George *actuarial consultant*

**Oviedo**
Drummer, Donald Raymond *diversified financial services company executive, educator*

**Palatka**
Ginn, John Arthur, Jr. *financial consultant*

**Palm Beach**
Banks, Russell *financial planner, consultant*
Harper, Mary Sadler *financial consultant*

**Pensacola**
Apap, Antonio *finance educator, portfolio manager*

**Riverview**
Ingersoll, Ronald J. *corporate financial executive*

**Saint Augustine**
DeLaughter, Thomas Glenn *business administration educator, consultant*

**Saint Petersburg**
Bryant, Timothy Clark *investment brokerage executive*
Freeman, Corinne *financial analyst, retired mayor*
Godwin, Benjamin Braxton *finance company executive*
Meyer, Robert Allen *finance educator*
Naimoli, Vincent Joseph *diversified financial services company executive*
Putnam, J. Stephen *corporate financial executive*
Shuck, Robert F. *financial consultant*
Wasserman, Susan Valesky *accountant, artist, yoga instructor*

**Sarasota**
Arreola, John Bradley *financial planner*
Bailey, Robert Elliott *financial executive*
Dryce, H. David *accountant, consultant*
Miles, Arthur J. *financial planner, consultant*
Morris, Gordon James *finance company executive, consultant*
Schmalzried, Marvin Eugene *financial consultant*

**Sun City Center**
Gummere, Walter Cooper *finance educator, consultant*
Malkin, Moses Montefiore *retired employee benefits administration company executive, diversified financial services company executive*

**Tallahassee**
Ashler, Philip Frederic *international trade and development advisor*
Cronin, Jerome Joseph, Jr. *marketing educator, consultant*
Lamont, Bruce Thomas *management educator*
Rushing, John Alan *business educator*

**Tampa**
Abdelrahman, Talaat Ahmad Mohammad *financial executive*
Aldrich, David Alan *accountant, consultant*
Alexander, William Olin *finance company executive*
Barnett, Michael L. *strategic management educator*
DeVane, Mindy Klein *financial planner*

Gaska, Christine *accountant*
Henard, Elizabeth Ann *controller*
Hernandez, Gilberto Juan *accountant, auditor, management consultant*
Hlavay, Jay Alan *financial analyst*
Lebouitz, Martin Frederick *diversified financial services company executive, consultant*
Murthy, Uday *accountant, educator*
Nord, Walter Robert *business administration educator, researcher, consultant*
Plumeri, Joseph James, II, *financial executive*

**Venice**
Meyerhoff, Jack Fulton *corporate financial executive*

**Vero Beach**
Conway, Earl Cranston *business educator, retired manufacturing company executive, educator*
Koontz, Alfred Joseph, Jr. *financial analyst, consultant*
Riefler, Donald Brown *financial consultant*
Satuloff, Barth *accountant, dispute resolution professional, investment strategist, publishing executive, rancher*

**Wesley Chapel**
Mendelsohn, Louis Benjamin *financial analyst*

**West Palm Beach**
Doto, Paul Jerome *retired accountant*
Herrick, John Dennis *financial planner, consultant, retired food products executive*
Livingstone, John Leslie *accountant, economist, management consultant, educator*

**Weston**
Holtzman, Gary Yale *retired diversified financial services company executive*

**Winter Haven**
Goodman, Karen Lacerte *financial services executive*

**Winter Park**
Gray, Anthony Rollin *retired finance company executive*
Starr, Martin Kenneth *management educator*
Therrien, Francois Xavier, Jr. *business and tax consultant*

## GEORGIA

**Alpharetta**
Corby, Francis Michael, Jr. *finance company executive*
Kurtz, Robert Arthur *finance company executive*

**Athens**
Miller, Herbert Elmer *accountant*
Zinkhan, George Martin III *marketing educator*

**Atlanta**
Appeadu, Charles Edward *finance educator, researcher*
Benston, George James *accountant, economist*
Chambers, Robert William *diversified financial services company executive*
Cook, John M. *retired finance company executive*
Dakhli, Mourad *finance educator*
Davis, D. Scott *corporate financial executive*
Douglas, William W. *corporate financial executive*
Fanning, Thomas Andrew *corporate financial executive*
Hanna, Frank Joseph, Jr. *credit company executive*
Hudson, Dean *tax accountant*
Johnson, Phillip Murray *treasurer, paper company executive, consumer products company executive*
Lobb, William Atkinson *financial services executive*
Lurie, Nicholas H. *marketing educator*
Lustig, Michael A. *finance company executive*
Malhotra, Naresh Kumar *marketing educator*
Mamrack, William H. *tax specialist*
Parsons, Leonard Jon *marketing educator, consultant*
Perdue, David A., Jr. *finance company executive, consultant*
Reece, Richard Kent *finance executive*
Smith, Richard F. *financial services company executive*
Terrel, James E. *controller*
Tome, Carol B. *corporate financial executive*
Villwock, Kenneth James *management company executive*
Zhang, Guoqiang *finance educator*

**Augusta**
Parish, Michael J. *controller*

**Carrollton**
Cochran, J. Guyton, Jr. *corporate financial executive*

**Columbus**
Blanchard, James Hubert *finance company executive*

**Conyers**
Spearman, Maxie Ann *financial analyst, administrator*

**Hinesville**
Wise, Carl Stamps *accounting educator*

**Kennesaw**
Robinson, Kenneth Charles *management educator*

**Macon**
Kitchens, William Charlie *accountant*
Rigsby, Sheila Goree *accounting firm executive*

**Marietta**
Aronoff, Craig Ellis *business educator, consultant*
Edwards, Charles Mundy III *financial consultant*
Kiger, Ronald Lee *retired contract negotiator*

**Milledgeville**
Engerrand, Doris Dieskow *retired business educator*

**Oakwood**
Martin, Johnny Benjamin *accountant*

**Savannah**
Smith, Elizabeth Mackey *retired financial consultant*

**Statesboro**
Murkison, Eugene Cox *finance educator*
Stewart, Lewis Moore *finance educator*

**Thomasville**
Stepanek, David Leslie *financial services company executive*

**Woodstock**
Austin, John David *retired financial executive*

## HAWAII

**Honolulu**
Agrusa, Jerome *tourism studies educator*
Betts, James William, Jr. *financial analyst, consultant*
Fukushima, Barbara Naomi *financial advisor*
Haig, David M. *diversified financial services company executive*
Hirai, Craig Kazuo *accountant*
Hook, Ralph Clifford, Jr. *business educator*
Ng, Wing Chiu *accountant, educator, application developer, lawyer, advocate*
Palia, Aspy Phiroze *marketing educator, researcher, consultant*
Rhee, Mooweon *business educator*
Solidum, James *finance and insurance executive*
Sterrett, James Melville *accountant, consultant*
Stockholm, Charles M. *diversified financial services company executive*

**Princeville**
Taylor, James Walter *business and management educator*

## IDAHO

**Boise**
Juetten, George H. *company executive*

**Meridian**
Bach, William Kenneth, Jr. *financial consultant, director*

## ILLINOIS

**Aurora**
Wear, Jean Ann *accountant*

**Barrington**
Furst, Warren Arthur *retired corporate executive*

**Batavia**
Morefield, Michael Thomas *financial executive*

**Belleville**
Fietsam, Robert Charles *accountant*

**Bellwood**
Miller, Denyce Karlina *tax specialist*

**Buffalo Grove**
Johnson, Craig Theodore *portfolio manager*
Leonetti, Michael Edward *financial planner*

**Cahokia**
Healy, Steven Michael *accountant, city official*

**Carbondale**
Mathur, Ike *finance educator*

**Champaign**
Brighton, Gerald David *retired finance educator*
Perry, Kenneth Wilbur *finance educator*
Schoenfeld, Hanns-Martin Walter *finance educator*
Spice, Dennis Dean *financial consultant*

**Chicago**
Barré, Laura *finance company executive*
Blake, Aileen *finance company executive*
Campbell, William Henry, Jr. *financial consultant, former federal agency administrator*
Chapman, Alger Baldwin *finance company executive, lawyer*
Christianson, Stanley David *finance company executive*
Chromizky, William Rudolph *accountant*
Fensin, Daniel *diversified financial service company executive*
Fischer, Paul *corporate financial executive*
Fitzgerald, Robert Maurice *financial executive, retired bank executive*
Fleming, Richard H. *finance executive*
Forbes, John Edward *retired financial consultant*
Fregetto, Eugene Fletcher *marketing educator*
Goodman, Robert Stanley *management educator*
Heineman, Ben Walter *corporation executive*
Ibbotson, Roger G. *financial educator*
Kalt, David *diversified financial services company executive*
Kamerick, Eileen Ann *corporate financial executive, lawyer*
Krause, James R. *stock exchange executive*
Kudish, David J. *financial executive*
Kullberg, Duane Reuben *accounting firm executive*
Kurish, James Brian *finance executive*
Landan, Henry Sinclair *financial and business consultant*
Landeck, Carl *corporate financial executive*
Lorch, Robert K. *corporate financial executive*
Mallory, Robert Mark *controller, finance company executive*

Mayer, Raymond Richard *business administration educator*
McDonnell, David Croft *diversified financial services company executive*
McGrath, Michael G. *finance company executive*
Miglis, Thomas G. *financial services company executive*
Mitchell, J. Barry *corporate financial executive*
Nusbaum, Edward E. *accounting company executive*
Pavelich, Daniel L. *retired account and tax management consulting executive*
Pritzker, Nicholas J. *diversified financial services company executive*
Rasin, Rudolph Stephen *corporate financial executive*
Reed, M. Scott *accounting company executive*
Ryan, Patrick G. *diversified financial services company executive, director*
Schornack, John James *accountant*
Schueppert, George Louis *financial executive*
Schumann, William Henry III *corporate financial executive*
Sullivan, Bernard James *accountant*
Verschoor, Curtis Carl *business educator, consultant*
Vitale, Gerald Lee *finance company executive*
Weil, Roman Lee *finance educator*
Wittenberg, Jon Albert *accountant*
Young, Scott Thomas *business management educator*

**Deerfield**
Boyd, Joseph Don *diversified financial services company executive*
Heiman, Marvin Stewart *finance company executive*
Park, Jeffrey Bryan *controller*

**Elmhurst**
Choyke, Phyllis May Ford (Mrs. Arthur Davis Choyke Jr.) *management executive, editor, poet*

**Evanston**
Corey, Gordon Richard *financial advisor, former utilities executive*
Dranove, David Stuart *business educator, consultant, economist*
Kotler, Philip *marketing educator, writer*
Malthouse, Edward Carl *finance educator*
Prince, Thomas Richard *accountant, educator*
Sawhney, Mohanbir S. *finance educator*
Scott, Walter Dill *management educator*
Stern, Louis William *marketing educator, consultant*
Weber, Klaus *finance educator*

**Geneva**
Young, Jack Allison *financial executive*

**Glendale Heights**
Cook, Doris Marie *retired accountant, educator*

**Glenview**
Levin, Donald Robert *business and finance executive, motion picture producer, professional sports team owner*

**Greenville**
Filby, Ivan Leonard *management educator*

**Gurnee**
Hall, Terry *accountant*

**Highland Park**
Afterman, Allan B. *accountant, educator, financial consultant, researcher*

**Hinsdale**
Urbik, Jerome Anthony *financial consultant*

**Itasca**
Civgin, Don *corporate financial executive*

**Kenilworth**
Bott, Harold Sheldon *accountant, management consultant*

**La Grange Park**
Perkins, William H., Jr. *retired finance company executive*

**Lisle**
Ruyle-Hullinger, Elizabeth Smith (Beth Ruyle) *municipal financial advisor, consultant*

**Lombard**
Garrett, Paul James *financial planner*

**Macomb**
Bauerly, Ronald John *marketing educator*

**Mount Prospect**
Epstein, Stephen Roger *financial executive*

**Naperville**
Calamos, Nick P. *diversified financial services company executive*
Tan, Li-Su Lin *accountant, insurance company executive, consultant*

**Northbrook**
Feibel, Frederick Arthur *financial consultant*
Hale, Danny Lyman *diversified financial services company executive*
Mandel, Karyl Lynn *accountant*

**Northfield**
Shillestad, John Gardner *diversified financial services company executive*

**Oak Brook**
Ciccarone, Richard Anthony *financial executive*
Koufis, John Theodore *accountant*

**Oakbrook Terrace**
Catalano, Gerald *accountant*
Keller, Dennis James *management educator*

**Palatine**
Butler, John Musgrave *financial consultant*
Spinner, Lee Louis *accountant*

**Park Ridge**
Russell, William Steven *treasurer*

**Peoria**
Burritt, David B. *corporate financial executive*
Vaughan, David John *corporate financial executive*

**Prospect Heights**
Aldinger, William F. III *diversified financial services company executive*
Armishaw, Andrew C. *financial services company executive*
Harvey, Kenneth M *corporate financial executive*

**Quincy**
Mallory, Troy L. *accountant*

**Rockford**
Wallem, Paul Sigurd *financial planner*

**Rolling Meadows**
Cangemi, Michael Paul *accountant, author, consultant*

**Schaumburg**
Devonshire, David W. *financial executive*
Hanna, Nessim *marketing educator*

**Springfield**
Morris, Donald *tax specialist*
Travis, Lawrence Allan *accountant*

**Sugar Grove**
Norris, Blanche Lee *business consultant, educator*

**Wheaton**
Holman, James Lewis *financial consultant, management consultant*

**Wilmette**
Wishner, Maynard Ira *retired finance company executive, lawyer*

## INDIANA

**Bloomington**
Belth, Joseph Morton *retired business educator*
Bonser, Charles Franklin *public administration educator*
Dalton, Dan R. *finance educator, former dean*
DeHayes, Daniel Wesley *business educator*
Gordon, Paul John *management educator*
Hustad, Thomas Pegg *marketing educator*
Perkins, William Clyde *business educator*
Wentworth, Jack Roberts *business educator, consultant*

**Carmel**
Mahoney, Margaret Ellis *accountant*
Pickens, Robert Bruce *retired accountant*

**Columbus**
Miller, William Irwin *finance company executive*

**Evansville**
Gaither, John Francis *accountant, consultant*

**Fort Wayne**
Gutreuter, Jill Stallings *financial consultant, financial planner*

**Hobart**
Arand, Frederick Francis *accountant, finance company executive*

**Indianapolis**
Amonett, Larry *accountant*
Carey, Edward Marshel, Jr. *accountant*
Fisher, Gene Lawrence *controller, accountant*
Furlow, Mack Vernon, Jr. *retired chief financial officer, treasurer, financial analyst*
Goodwin, William Maxwell *financial executive*
Kaufman, Barton Lowell *financial services company executive*
Long, Clarence William *accountant*
Onochie, Florence N *accountant*

**La Porte**
Casey, Keith Allen *accountant*

**Lafayette**
Helmuth, Ned D. *financial planner*

**Muncie**
Smith, Van P. *diversified financial services company executive*

**Notre Dame**
Reilly, Frank Kelly *business educator*
Shannon, William Norman III *finance educator, food service executive*
Vecchio, Robert Peter *business management educator*

**Portage**
Schroeder, Marvis Lynn *accountant, artist*

**South Bend**
Agbetsiafa, Douglas Kofi *financial consultant, management consultant*
Cohen, Ronald S. *accountant*

**Terre Haute**
Steinbaugh, Robert P. *management and finance educator*

**Warsaw**
Leno, Sam R. *corporate financial executive*

**West Lafayette**
Brey, Eric Trent *hospitality and tourism educator*
Cooper, Arnold Cook *management educator, researcher*

Lewellen, Wilbur Garrett *management educator, consultant*
Moskowitz, Herbert *management educator*

## IOWA

**Ames**
Hunger, J(ohn) David *business educator*
Kaufmann, Jeffrey Baer *finance educator*

**Cedar Falls**
Rajendran, Kadiampatti Natarajan *marketing educator*
Shimp, Karen Ann *accountant, corporate financial executive*

**Davenport**
Nagle, John E. *accountant*

**Des Moines**
Scholten, Gary P. *finance company executive*
Smith, Diana Marie *business educator*
Vaughan, Therese Michele *insurance educator*

**Iowa City**
Collins, Daniel W. *accountant, educator*
Riesz, Peter Charles *marketing educator, consultant*

**Johnston**
Poppe, Pamela J. *accountant*

**Ottumwa**
Lang, Janelle J. *accountant*

**Waterloo**
Mathys, Gordon D. *accountant, educator*

**West Des Moines**
Henderson, Jason Craig *financial advisor*

## KANSAS

**Lawrence**
Beedles, William LeRoy *finance educator, financial consultant*
Conard, John Joseph *finance company executive*

**Leawood**
Dykes, Archie Reece *finance company executive*
White, Shanon Kathleen *accountant, consultant*

**Lenexa**
Russo, Guy J. *financial services company executive*

**Lindsborg**
Fisk, Irwin Wesley *financial investigator*

**Manhattan**
Sheu, Chwen *finance educator*
Swanson, Diane L. *business management and economics educator, researcher*

**Mission**
Churchill, James Garton *retired finance company executive*

**Overland Park**
Guckenheimer, Daniel Paul *financial advisor*
Stem, Carl Herbert *business educator*
Zinke, Michael Duane *finance and accountancy manager*

**Shawnee Mission**
Johnson, Bradford McClure *financial consultant, investor*

**Wichita**
Sullivan, Mitzi *accountant*

## KENTUCKY

**Franklin**
Baldock, Brian F. *corporate financial executive*

**Louisville**
McKim, Ruth Ann *financial planner*
Morell, Michael John *actuary*
Simpson, David Michael *financial planner, educator*
Taylor, Robert Lewis *finance educator*

**Madisonville**
Kington, Barry Clark *investor, consultant*

**Masonic Home**
Coryell, Glynn Heath *financial services executive*

## LOUISIANA

**Baton Rouge**
Bedeian, Arthur George *business educator*
Crumbley, Donald Larry *accounting educator, writer*
DeVille, Donald Charles *accountant*
Thomas, Jeffrey Cone *financial executive, consultant*

**Covington**
Doody, Louis Clarence, Jr. *retired accountant*
Files, Mark Willard *business and financial consultant*

**Kenner**
McShan, Clyde Griffin, II, *diversified financial services company executive*

**Mandeville**
Aaron, Shirley Mae *retired tax specialist*

**Metairie**
Gereighty, Andrea Saunders *diversified financial services company executive, poet*

**New Orleans**
Barach, Jeffrey Alvan *management educator*
Cook, Victor Joseph, Jr. *finance educator, consultant*
McFarland, James W. *finance educator*
Zhang, Jun *finance educator*

**Pineville**
Conway, Evelyn Atkinson *accountant, financial analyst*

**Ruston**
Mesak, Hani Ibrahim *marketing educator*
Phillips, Thomas J., Jr. *accountant, educator*

**Shreveport**
Burton, George Aubrey, Jr. *accountant*
Goodman, Sylvia Klumok *film center executive*

## MAINE

**Camden**
Dyer, Barbara F. *retired accountant, writer*

**Cumberland Foreside**
Martin, Joseph Robert *retired corporate financial executive*

**Friendship**
MacIlvaine, Chalmers Acheson *retired financial executive, former association executive*

**Hampden**
Scroggins, M. Suzanne Paonessa *budget analyst*

**Topsham**
Palesky, Carol East *tax accountant*

**Waterville**
Chapman, James R. *business and technology educator*

## MARYLAND

**Adelphi**
Sutherland, Alan Roy *business educator*

**Annapolis**
Ames, Steven Reede *financial planner*
DiPentima, Renato Anthony *corporate financial executive*
Gavian, Peter Wood *securities analyst*

**Baltimore**
Kues, Irvin William *financial planner*
Langmead, Joseph Michael *accountant, consultant, educator*
Legum, Jeffrey Alfred *holding company executive*
Mason, Raymond Adams *finance company executive*
Quinn, Michael Desmond *diversified financial services company executive*
Rogers, Brian Charles *portfolio manager, investment company executive*
Roupe, James Paul *accountant*
Smith, E. Follin *corporate financial executive*

**Bethesda**
Castelli, Alexander Gerard *accountant*
Gould, W. Scott *financial administrator*
Palumbo, James Fredrick *finance company executive*
Schwarz, Louis Jay *financial advisor*

**Chevy Chase**
Linowes, David Francis *finance educator, corporate financial executive*

**College Park**
Fu, Michael C. *management science educator*
Sims, Henry P., Jr. *management educator*
Souza, Gilvan Castro *operations and management educator*

**Columbia**
Kurlander, Neale *accountant, law educator*

**Gaithersburg**
Johnson, George H. *finance company executive*
Ruth, James Perry *financial planner*

**Glyndon**
Colhoun, Howard Post *financial executive*

**Greenbelt**
Jenkins, Norman *accountant*

**Hyattsville**
Lovick, Norman *accountant*

**Potomac**
Rhode, Alfred Shimon *finance educator*

**Princess Anne**
Sharma, Dinesh Kumar *management science educator*

**Rockville**
Burt, Marvin Roger *financial advisor, investment manager*
Edwards, Bert Tvedt *accountant*
Kamerow, Martin Laurence *accountant*

**Silver Spring**
Yasher, Michael *retired accountant*

**Stevenson**
Hilgenberg, John Christian *corporate financial executive, consultant*

**Trappe**
Blades, G(ene) Granville *accountant*

**Upper Marlboro**
Symlar, Jesse Lee *finance executive*

**Wye Mills**
Schnaitman, William Kenneth *retired finance company executive*

## MASSACHUSETTS

**Allston**
Mills, Daniel Quinn *business educator, consultant, author*

**Amherst**
Manz, Charles Craig *management educator*
Roberts, Chris *strategy and finance educator, researcher*

**Ashfield**
Gabriel, Peter Paul *business educator*

**Ashland**
Pettinella, Nicholas Anthony *corporate financial executive*

**Barnstable**
Temkin, Robert Harvey *accountant*

**Belmont**
Rich, Sharon Lee *financial planner*

**Boston**
Aber, John William (Jack) *finance educator, consultant*
Akin, Steven Paul *finance company executive*
Antonellis, Joseph C. *financial services company executive*
Baker, Charles Duane *business administration educator*
Bavaria, Joan *finance company executive*
Black, Scott M. *diversified financial services company executive*
Boyd, David Preston *business educator*
Brooke, Peter A. *corporate financial executive*
Brunel, Frederic F. *marketing educator, researcher*
Bruns, William John, Jr. *business administration educator*
Canback, Staffan *corporate advisor*
Carmany, George Walter III *finance company executive, consultant*
Cash, James Ireland, Jr. *retired business educator*
Christenson, Charles John *retired business educator*
Cole, Shawn *finance educator*
Cripps, Richard E. *diversified financial services company executive*
Curran, Michael J. *finance company executive*
Davis, Christopher C. *diversified financial services company executive*
Deshpandé, Rohit *business educator*
Domini, Amy Lee *portfolio manager*
Eddleston, Kimberly Ann *management educator*
Elfner, Albert Henry III *retired portfolio manager*
Fetter, Thomas *portfolio manager*
Fox, Edward A. *retired finance company executive*
France, Joseph David *financial analyst*
Gifford, Nelson Sage *finance company executive*
Gormley, Pamela D. *controller*
Hardy, Victoria Elizabeth *finance educator*
Hayes, Robert Herrick *technology management educator*
Hayes, Samuel Linton III *business educator*
Ives, J. Atwood *financial executive*
Kaplan, Robert S. *business educator, former investment banker*
Kaufmann, Patrick J. *business educator*
Langwell, Dennis J. *corporate financial executive*
Lodge, George C(abot) *business administration educator*
Logue, Ronald E. *finance company executive*
Marshall, Martin Vivan *business administration educator, consultant*
Maxwell, J. B. *financial consultant, marketing professional, consultant*
McArthur, John Hector *business educator*
McCraw, Thomas Kincaid *business history educator, editor, writer*
McFarlan, Franklin Warren *business administration educator*
Miller, Bill (William H. Miller III) *diversified financial services company executive*
Murphy, John Vincent *accountant*
Park, William H(erron) *finance company executive*
Pitts, James Atwater *finance company executive*
Reiling, Henry Bernard *business educator*
Shemin, Barry L. *actuary*
Shepherdson, James A. (Jamie) *diversified financial services company executive*
Sloane, Carl Stuart *corporate executive, educator, management consultant*
Spooner, John D. *financial planner, writer*
Vatter, Paul August *business administration educator, dean*
Young, David William *management educator*

**Boxboro**
Parmese, Gabriel J. *corporate financial executive*

**Brookline**
Reedy, Harry Lee *financial services executive*

**Cambridge**
Allen, Thomas John *finance educator*
Chatterjee, Sharmila *marketing educator*
Hauser, John Richard *marketing and management science educator*
Langerman, John W. R. *financial services company executive*
Leonard, Herman Beukema (Dutch Leonard) *public finance, management, and leadership educator*
Magnanti, Thomas L. *management educator, engineering educator*
Malone, Thomas W. *business educator, researcher*
Mohamed, Mustafa A. *management educator*
Pounds, William Frank *management educator*
Steel, Robert K. *former diversified financial services company executive*
Stevenson, Howard Higginbotham *business educator*
von Hippel, Eric Arthur *innovation educator*
Watts, Ross Leslie *finance educator*

**Chestnut Hill**
Bartunek, Jean Marie *management educator*
Safizadeh, M. Hossein *finance educator*

**Concord**
Weiss, James Michael *financial analyst, portfolio manager*

**Foxboro**
Bush, Raymond T. *accountant, architectural firm executive*
Karelitz, Richard Alan *treasurer, lawyer*

**Framingham**
Komola, Christine T. *corporate financial executive*

**Hopkinton**
Teuber, William J, Jr. *corporate financial executive*

**Leominster**
Ford, John Stephen *treasurer*

**Lexington**
Klein, Lawrence Allen *finance educator*

**Lowell**
Teague, Bernice Rita *accountant*

**Marblehead**
Snow, George Bartlett *accountant, city manager*

**Pittsfield**
Zelka, Sandra Lynn *finance company executive*

**Plainville**
Zani, Frederick Caesar *retired financial consultant*

**Quincy**
Britt, Margaret Mary *finance educator*

**South Hadley**
Fisher, William Thomas *business administration educator*

**Sudbury**
Meltzer, Donald Richard *retired treasurer*

**Swansea**
Hjerpe, Edward Alfred III *finance and banking executive*

**Tewksbury**
Black, Richard Bruce *corporate executive, consultant*

**Waltham**
Ackerman, Robert Wallace *private equity manager*
Curnan, Susan P. *social policy and management educator, consultant*
Farb, Thomas Forest *financial executive*
Kasputys, Joseph Edward *corporate financial executive, economist*
McClary, Loretta Mary *accountant*
O'Connell, Jeanne *financial planner, insurance broker*
Porter, Biggs C. *corporate financial executive*

**Watertown**
Saraidaridis, Susan Bridget *taxonomist*

**Wellesley**
Tofias, Allan *retired accountant*

**Westfield**
Niles, DeBorah Olive *benefits compensation analyst*

**Weston**
Valente, Louis Patrick (Dan Valente) *financial planner, director*

**Worcester**
Greenberg, Nathan *accountant*

## MICHIGAN

**Ann Arbor**
Elger, William Robert, Jr. *accountant*
Foster, Alan Herbert *diversified financial services company executive, educator*
Kim, E. Han *financial analyst, educator*
Prahalad, C.K. *finance educator, corporate strategist*
Seyhun, Hasan Nejat *finance educator, department chairman*
Wilhelm, Edward W. *corporate financial executive*

**Auburn Hills**
Knight, Jeffrey Alan *finance executive*

**Belleville**
Palmer, James F. *corporate financial executive*

**Benton Harbor**
Templin, Roy *corporate financial executive*

**Berrien Springs**
Maguad, Ben Abrico *management educator*

**Birmingham**
McCuen, John *finance and tooling company executive, columnist, educator*

**Bloomfield Hills**
Cuffe, Stafford Sigesmund *business, technology, manufacturing and management consultant*
Poth, Stefan Michael *retired diversified financial services company executive*

**Clarkston**
Kruzan, James Brendan *financial planner*

**Dearborn**
Bannister, Michael E. *corporate financial executive*
Lee, Hei Wai *finance educator, researcher*

**Detroit**
Butler, Timothy W. *business educator*
Datta, Sudip *finance educator*
Higby, Mary A. *marketing executive, educator*
Kahalas, Harvey *business educator*

**East Lansing**
Kang, Jun-Koo *finance educator*
Luccock, Thomas Nelson *auditor, director*
Miracle, Gordon Eldon *advertising educator*
Wilson, R. Dale *marketing educator*

**Farmington**
Itin, Thomas William *merchant, investment banker, consultant*

**Farmington Hills**
Smith, Isabel Francis *financial planner*

**Flint**
Stone, Pamela Ann *accountant*

**Frankfort**
Schmidt, Robert Charles, Jr. *finance company executive*

**Grand Rapids**
Carpenter, John R. *finance educator*
Mavima, Paul *finance educator*
Staples, David M. *corporate financial executive*

**Grosse Pointe Farms**
Fromm, Joseph L. *financial consultant*
Weingart, Robert Paul *financial consultant*

**Harper Woods**
Barba, Lance Elliott *financial consultant, investment advisor*

**Lansing**
Feight, Theodore J. *financial planner*

**Livonia**
McHard, James Lorin *corporate financial executive, freelance/self-employed composer, writer*
Valerio, Michael Anthony *diversified financial services company executive*

**Maple City**
Duff, James George *retired finance company executive, automotive executive*

**Marquette**
Camerius, James Walter *marketing educator, corporate researcher*

**Midland**
Merszei, Geoffrey E. *corporate financial executive*

**Mount Pleasant**
Garver, Michael Scott *finance educator*

**Oxford**
Smith, Jay Lawrence *financial planning company executive*

**Portage**
Zhang, Charles C. *financial planner*

**Southfield**
Boyce, Daniel Hobbs *finance company executive*
Rawden, David *financial services company executive*
Vandenberghe, James H. *financial executive*

**Troy**
Dellinger, Robert J. *corporate financial executive*

**University Center**
Hall, David McKenzie *business and management educator*

**Utica**
Egan, Ron *corporate financial executive*

**Waterford**
Gulda, Edward James *diversified financial services company executive*

**West Bloomfield**
Rauwerdink, William Jay *accountant*

**MINNESOTA**

**Bloomington**
Kuntz, Lila Elaine *business educator*

**Duluth**
Nelson, Dennis Lee *finance educator*

**Eden Prairie**
Johnson, Howard Arthur, Jr. *corporate executive, operations analyst, financial officer*

**Golden Valley**
Harrison, David D. *corporate financial executive*

**Minneapolis**
Avella, Joseph Ralph *business professor*
Berry, David J. *former financial services company executive*
Berryman, Robert Glen *finance educator, consultant*
Campbell, Jon R. *diversified financial services company executive*
Cracchiolo, James M. *diversified financial services company executive*
Elm, Dawn Rae *management educator*
Goldberg, Luella Gross *diversified financial services company executive*
Hoffmann, Thomas Russell *business management educator*
Kinney, Earl Robert *mutual funds company executive*
Mohanty, Sunil K. *finance educator, researcher*
Montgomery, Henry Irving *financial planner*

Moore, Cornell Leverette *financial services executive, lawyer*
Reha, Rose Krivisky *retired finance educator*
Rudelius, William *marketing educator*
Schwartz, Howard Wyn *business and marketing educator, consultant*

**Nevis**
Stibbe, Austin Jule *retired accountant*

**Saint Cloud**
Supanvanij, Janikan *finance educator*

**Saint Paul**
Bessette, Andy F. *diversified financial services company executive*
Fishman, Jay Steven *financial services executive*
Heyman, William Herbert *financial services executive*
Wheelock, Pam *financial executive*

**MISSISSIPPI**

**Brandon**
Cooper, Cynthia F. *accountant, consultant*

**Hattiesburg**
Doty, Duane Harold *business educator*

**Meridian**
Havard, Jeanne S. *finance educator*

**Mississippi State**
Chrisman, James Joseph *management educator*
Vance, David A. *information systems educator*

**Starkville**
Thomas, Garnett Jett *accountant*

**Tupelo**
Nash, Henry Warren *marketing educator*

**MISSOURI**

**Ballwin**
Bond, Dennis Earl *auditor*

**Carthage**
Skaggs, Ronald Lee *controller, history professor, religious studies educator*

**Columbia**
Arunpachalam, V. *accountant, educator*
Cunningham, Billie M. *accounting educator*
Lansford, Raymond William *retired finance educator*
Micheas, Athanasios Christou *finance educator*
Nikolai, Loren Alfred *accounting educator*

**Ellisville**
Henry, Roy Monroe *financial planner*

**Fenton**
Powers, James G. *corporate financial executive*

**Jefferson City**
McCaskill, Claire *auditor*

**Kansas City**
Bloch, Henry Wollman *diversified financial services company executive*
Boysen, Melicent Pearl *finance company executive*
Brandmaier, Jeff *diversified financial services company executive*
Ernst, Mark A. *diversified financial services company executive*
Ingraham, James H. *diversified financial services company executive*
Pruitt, Stephen Wallace *finance educator*
Rowland, Landon Hill *diversified holding company executive*
Stevens, James Hervey, Jr. *retired financial planner*

**Kirksville**
Mun, Kyung Chun *finance educator, researcher*

**Lees Summit**
Foudree, Charles M. *financial consultant*

**Maryland Heights**
Stiften, Edward J. *corporate financial executive*

**O Fallon**
Hull, James E. *financial services company executive*
McElhatton, Jerry *credit card company executive*

**Saint Charles**
Chilton, Kenneth Wayne *business research director, educator*

**Saint Louis**
Armstrong, Theodore Morelock *corporate financial executive*
Brockhaus, Robert Herold, Sr. *business educator, consultant*
Carlson, Arthur Eugene *accounting educator*
Crider, Robert Agustine *international financier, protective services official*
Fitch, Rachel Farr *health policy analyst*
Folz, Carol Ann *benefits compensation analyst*
Liggett, Hiram Shaw, Jr. *retired diversified financial services company executive*
Lock, Albert Larry, Jr. *finance company executive*
Malone, Rich L. *financial services company executive*
Rich, Harry Earl *corporate financial executive*
Shepperd, Thomas Eugene *accountant*
Snyder, William W. *corporate financial executive*
Tei, Takuri *accountant*
Till, Brian D. *finance educator, consultant*
Wiggins, Dewayne Lee *financial executive*
Winter, Richard Lawrence *diversified financial services company executive*
Zhou, Guofu *finance educator*

**Springfield**
Denton, D. Keith *management educator*

**MONTANA**

**Billings**
Stapleton, Corey *financial planner*

**Bozeman**
Davis, Nicholas Homans Clark *finance company executive*

**Helena**
Craig, Mary Lauri *accountant*
Toole, Joan Trimble *financial consultant*

**Rollins**
Greer, Willis Roswell, Jr. *finance educator*

**Troy**
Sherman, Signe Lidfeldt *portfolio manager, former research chemist*

**NEBRASKA**

**Boys Town**
DiBacco, T. Jay *financial services executive, retired military officer*

**Fremont**
Dunklau, Rupert Louis *financial planner, consultant*

**Lincoln**
Byrd, Lorelee *state treasurer*
Digman, Lester Aloysius *management educator*
Lienemann, Delmar Arthur, Sr. *accountant, real estate developer*
Nadkarni, Sucheta *finance educator*

**Omaha**
Bartlett, Jerry *financial services company executive*
Fairfield, Bill L. *finance company executive*
Heasley, Philip *financial services company executive*
Jaksich, Daniel J. *controller*
Munger, Charles T. *diversified company executive*
Reiter-Palmon, Roni *finance educator*
Sklarsky, Frank S. *corporate financial executive*

**Wayne**
Paxton, John Ray *management educator*

**NEVADA**

**Las Vegas**
Duva-Mikhail, Donna Marie *financial executive*
Hobbs, Guy Stephen *financial executive*
Rodgers, Steven Edward *tax practitioner, educator*
Stark, S. Daniel, Jr. *diversified financial services company executive*
Williams, Mary Irene *business education educator*

**NEW HAMPSHIRE**

**Amherst**
Atwater, Verne Stafford *finance educator*

**Bedford**
Steadman, David Rosslyn Ayton *corporate financial executive, director*

**Goffstown**
Martel, Eva Leona *accountant*

**Hanover**
Anthony, Robert Newton *retired management educator*
French, Kenneth Ronald *finance educator*
Govindarajan, Vijay *finance educator*
Logue, Dennis Emhardt *finance educator, consultant, dean, writer, banker*
Murdza, Peter John, Jr. *actuary*
Peteraf, Margaret Ann *strategic management and organization educator*

**Manchester**
Maloney, Simone *accountant*
Merideth, Susan Carol *business administration educator*

**Meredith**
Lovett, Miller Currier *retired management educator, minister, educator*

**Nashua**
Hemming, Walter William *financial consultant*

**Peterborough**
Day, John Sidney *management sciences educator*

**West Swanzey**
Faulkner, Mary E. *treasurer*

**NEW JERSEY**

**Avon By The Sea**
Bruno, Grace Angelia *accountant, retired educator*

**Bloomfield**
Conta, Richard Vincent *actuary*

**Chatham**
Earle, Jean Buist *finance company executive, computer company executive*

**Cranbury**
Kemmerer, Peter Ream *financial executive*

**Edison**
Hecht, William David *accountant*

**Pedescleaux-Muckle**, Gail *retired business analyst, writer, artist*

**Egg Harbor City**
Earl, Donald W. *treasurer, executive secretary*

**Ewing**
McCarty, John Albert *management educator*

**Fairfield**
Byer, Theodore Scott *accountant*
Sangiuliano, Barbara Ann *tax consultant*

**Florham Park**
Bossen, Wendell John *retired financial planner*

**Fort Lee**
Armellino, Michael Ralph *retired portfolio manager*
Soejima, Daisuke *diversified financial services company executive, economist*
Weinstock, George David *financial services company executive*

**Franklin Lakes**
Reed, JoAnn A. *corporate financial executive*

**Galloway**
Newell, Eric James *financial planner, retired insurance company executive*

**Hackettstown**
Quade, Robert Thomas *finance educator*

**Hightstown**
Darr, Walter Robert *financial analyst*

**Ho Ho Kus**
Deupree, Marvin Mattox *financial consultant*

**Iselin**
Accardi, Joseph Ronald *accountant*
Sperduto, Michael A. *corporate financial executive*

**Jackson**
Cohen, Walter Stanley *financial consultant*
Hagberg, Carl Thomas *financial executive*

**Jersey City**
Balter, Leslie Marvin *business communications educator*
Laski, John N. *finance educator*

**Little Falls**
Birnberg, Jack *financial executive*

**Livingston**
Hallman, Thomas B. *finance company executive*
Leone, Joseph M. *finance company executive*
Peek, Jeffrey M. *corporate financial executive*

**Marlton**
Gorenberg, Charles Lloyd *finance company executive*
Laubach, Roger Alvin *accountant*

**Medford**
Micko, Alexander S. *corporate financial executive, educator, treasurer*

**Monmouth Beach**
Herbert, LeRoy James *retired accounting firm executive*

**Montclair**
Luftglass, Murray Arnold *corporate financial executive*

**Montville**
Klapper, Byron D. *finance company executive*

**Morganville**
Sternfeld, Marc Howard *finance educator*

**Morristown**
Anderson, David J. *corporate financial executive*
Flynn, Marie Cosgrove *portfolio manager, corporate financial executive*

**Mount Laurel**
Mann, Louis Eugene *financial planner*

**New Brunswick**
Foley, Eugene Arthur *accountant, consultant*
Mills, George Marshall *financial consultant*
Onwuchekwa, Michael O. *accountant, educator*

**Newark**
Arabie, Phipps *marketing educator, researcher*
Clymer, Brian William *diversified financial services company executive, retired state official*
Contractor, Farok *business and management educator*

**Parsippany**
Wechter, Ira Martin *tax specialist, financial planner*

**Plainsboro**
Schreyer, William Allen *retired finance company executive*

**Princeton**
Ait-Sahalia, Yacine *finance educator*
Goldfarb, Irene Dale *retired financial planner*
Harvey, Norman Ronald *retired finance company executive*

**Princeton Junction**
Cohen, Florence Emery *retired financial services executive*

**Red Bank**
Daidone, Lewis Eugene *finance company executive*
Oberst, Robert John *financial analyst*
Rose, Arthur Royal *financial planner, tax consultant*
Watson, Charles M. *financial consultant*

**Ridgefield Park**
Denning, Karen Craft *finance educator*

**River Edge**
Gass, Manus M. *accountant, construction executive*

**Rivervale**
Becker, Murray Leonard *corporate financial consultant, actuary*

**Rochelle Park**
Gaer, Michael Ira *financial planner*

**Roseland**
Golden, Robert Charles *finance company executive*

**Short Hills**
Alesio, Steven W. *financial services company executive*
Gibson, William Lee *financial consultant*
Mebane, William Black *controller, financial consultant*
Price, Michael F. *money management executive*

**Skillman**
Liro, Joseph R. *diversified financial services company executive*

**South Orange**
Amar, A. D. *business educator, management consultant*

**Spring Lake**
O'Connor, Francis X. *financial executive*

**Teaneck**
Chandrashekaran, Rajesh *marketing educator*
Daddario, Richard *chief financial officer, accountant*

**Thorofare**
Andrews, Raymond Douglas *financial executive*

**Warren**
Hartman, David G. *actuary*
O'Reilly, Michael *corporate financial executive*

**Wayne**
Li, Fuan *marketing educator, researcher*

**West Orange**
Zimmerman, David Carl *controller, corporate financial executive*

**Woodbridge**
Ayub, Yacub *financial consultant*

**NEW MEXICO**

**Albuquerque**
Kaehele, Bettie Louise *accountant*
Leach, Richard Maxwell, Jr., (Max Leach Jr.) *corporate professional, consultant*

**Las Cruces**
Bell, M. Joy Miller *financial planner, real estate agent*
Cochrun, John Wesley *financial consultant*
Constantini, Louis O. *financial consultant, stockbroker*
Peterson, Robin Tucker *marketing educator*

**Portales**
Brunsen, William Henry *finance educator, consultant*

**Santa Fe**
Thornburg, Garrett, Jr. *finance company executive*
Watkins, Stephen Edward *accountant, publishing executive*

**Taos**
Brown, David Warfield *management educator, lawyer, academic administrator*

**NEW YORK**

**Albany**
Blount, Stanley Freeman *marketing educator*

**Amherst**
Jen, Frank Chifeng *finance and management educator*

**Baldwinsville**
Wilson, Harold Batting *treasurer*

**Binghamton**
Kim, Yong Jin *finance educator*
Zhou, Nan *finance educator*

**Brockport**
Keiser, John Dougherty *business educator*

**Bronx**
Lee, Dong Hwan *business administration educator*
Meyer, Edward Henry *business and economics educator, lawyer*
Osborne, Claudina Rosetta *financial analyst*

**Brooklyn**
Arseneau, Jospeh Arseneau *financial consultant*
Evans, John T. *finance educator, consultant, social sciences educator, researcher*
Fischman, Myrna Leah *accountant, educator*
Hechtman, Howard *financial analyst*

**Buffalo**
Bennett, Shirley Ann *business technology educator*
Carlson, Bruce William *diversified holding company executive*
Gruen, David Henry *financial analyst*
Jacobs, Jeremy Maurice, Sr. *diversified financial services company executive, professional sports team executive*

Oliver, Dominick Michael *business educator*
Shick, Richard Arlon *finance educator*
Zaffram, Robert *finance educator*

**Canton**
Pollard, Fred Don *finance company executive, director*

**Central Islip**
McCrain, Michael William *accountant, financial planner*

**Chittenango**
Cassell, William Walter *retired accounting operations consultant*

**Commack**
Kurtz, Joel Barry *finance executive*

**Croton On Hudson**
Lewins, Steven *financial analyst, investment company executive, legislative staff member, retired military officer*

**East Greenbush**
Mucci, Patrick John *financial consultant, realtor, commercial loan broker*

**East Meadow**
Cymbler, Murray Joel *corporate financial executive*

**East Rochester**
Murray, James Doyle *accountant, educator*

**Eden**
Thomas, Jimmy Lynn *retired treasurer*

**Flushing**
Sanborn, Anna Lucille *pension fund administrator, consultant*

**Fredonia**
Aghazadeh, Seyed-Mahmoud *finance educator*

**Geneseo**
Lim, Seong Bae *business educator*

**Glen Head**
Stack, Edward William *diversified financial services company executive*

**Greenvale**
Rao, Srikumar Srinivas *marketing educator*

**Hempstead**
Aaron, Merik Roy *financial executive, educator, lawyer*
Barak, Benny *marketing and business educator, department chairman*
Lee, Keun Sok *business educator, consultant*
Roble, Carole Marcia *accountant*

**Hicksville**
Stein, Melvin A. *accountant*

**Highland**
Kells, Albert John *mergers and acquisitions consultant*

**Hopewell Junction**
Donovan, Andrew Joseph *financial consultant*

**Huntington**
Slutsky, Leonard Alan *finance executive, consultant*

**Ithaca**
Daouk, Hazem *finance educator*
Dyckman, Thomas Richard *accountant, educator*
Kimes, Sheryl Elaine *business educator*
Lesser, William Henri *marketing educator*

**Jericho**
Spatafore, Anthony R. *financial executive*

**Lakewood**
Deppas, Louis Anthony *financial adviser*

**Lewiston**
LoTempio, Julia Matild *retired accountant*

**Little Neck**
Overton, Rosilyn Gay Hoffman *finance company executive*

**Manhasset**
Pitti, Donald Robert *financial consultant*

**Medford**
Saunders, Audrey J. *tax specialist, writer*
Snyder, Mark Jeffrey *financial planner, actuary*

**Mineola**
McGonigle, James Gregory *financial consultant*

**Monroe**
Fontana, John Arthur *employee benefits specialist*
Winslow, DeLana Lynn *business educator*

**New City**
Borelli, Francis J(oseph) (Frank Borelli) *diversified financial services company executive*

**New York**
Albano, David Warren *financial executive, business analyst*
Altfest, Lewis Jay *financial planner*
Anderson, Theodore Wellington *portfolio strategist*
Assael, Henry *marketing educator*
Audet, Paul L. *diversified financial services company executive*
Banga, Ajay *diversified financial services company executive*
Barse, David M. *financial services executive*
Bartlett, Richard Allan *finance company executive*
Bateman, Paul *diversified financial services company executive*
Bennett, Paul B. *stock exchange executive*

Berger, Stephen *finance company executive*
Berkowitz, Brad Alan *financial analyst*
Berman, Walter S. *treasurer*
Bernstein, Phyllis J. *financial consultant*
Bibliowicz, Jessica M. *financial analyst*
Bisignano, Frank *diversified financial services company executive*
Black, Steven D. *diversified financial services company executive*
Blankfein, Lloyd C. *diversified financial services company executive*
Bleser, Philip F. *diversified financial services company executive*
Bovin, Denis Alan *finance company executive*
Bowden, Linda *diversified financial services company executive*
Boykin, Richard A. *tax specialist*
Bradley, John Francis *financial services company executive*
Brand, Jason *diversified financial services company executive*
Braunstein, Lancelot Michael (Lance Braunstein) *financial services company executive*
Brown, Clifford Bryant *financial consultant*
Browning, Candace *corporate financial executive*
Brustein, Lawrence *finance company executive*
Buller, Steven E. *diversified financial services company executive*
Burton, John Campbell *accounting educator, former dean*
Buttner, Jean Bernhard *diversified financial services company executive*
Caffrey, Patricia *diversified financial services company executive*
Calio, Nicholas E. *diversified financial services company executive*
Canes, Brian Dennis *benefits compensation analyst*
Caputo, Lisa M. *finance company executive*
Carter, Peyton Franklin III *accountant*
Cashin, Richard M., Jr. *diversified financial services company executive*
Chang, Joyce *corporate financial executive*
Chenault, Kenneth Irvine *finance company executive*
Claire, Thomas Andrew *financial executive, consultant, educator, writer*
Clark, Howard Longstreth, Jr. *finance company executive, director*
Clark, Michael K. *diversified financial services company executive*
Clark, Robert Henry, Jr. *finance company executive*
Cockrell, Sanford Alonza III *accountant*
Cogliano, Dan *tax specialist, accountant*
Cohn, Bertram Josiah *portfolio manager*
Cohn, Gary D. *diversified financial services company executive*
Conway, E. Virgil *financial consultant, lawyer*
Corbet, Kathleen A. *financial information company executive*
Coughlin, Christopher J. *financial executive*
Craig, Charles Samuel *marketing educator*
Cramer, Jim (James J. Cramer) *financial information executive*
Crane, Charles Grant *financial analyst*
Crittenden, Gary Lewis *diversified financial services company executive*
Cruz, Zoe *diversified financial services company executive*
Cumming, Ian M. *holding company executive*
Cummings, John W. *diversified financial services company executive*
De Lisi, Nancy *corporate financial executive*
Devlin, Robert Manning *diversified financial services company executive*
Dimon, James L. (Jamie Dimon) *diversified financial services company executive*
DiPiazza, Samuel A., Jr. *finance company executive*
Domowitz, Ian *finance company executive*
Dougan, Brady W. *diversified financial services company executive*
Duch, Stephen *corporate financial executive*
Edsparr, Patrik L. *diversified financial services company executive*
Edward, Jeffrey N. *diversified financial services company executive*
Edwards, Jeffrey N. *diversified financial services company executive*
Elmer, Russell S. *diversified financial services company executive, lawyer*
Engel, Amy J. *corporate financial executive*
Englander, Israel A. *financier*
Engle, Robert F. *finance educator*
Evans, Mary Johnston *corporate director*
Fakahany, Ahmass L. *finance company executive*
Falk, Charles H. (Harry Falk) *stock exchange executive*
Fink, Laurence D. *diversified financial services company executive*
Finn, Brian D. *financial services executive*
Fleming, Gregory J. *finance company executive*
Flynn, Timothy P. *finance company executive*
Fowler, John M. *finance company executive*
Freiberg, Steven J. *diversified financial services company executive*
Fridson, Martin Steven *finance company executive*
Frye, Clayton Wesley, Jr. *finance company executive*
Gallo, Martha J. *diversified financial services company executive*
Gardner, H. McIntrye (Mac Gardner) *diversified financial services company executive*
Gilligan, Edward P. *diversified financial services company executive*
Golden, William Theodore *trustee, corporate director*
Goldstein, Jeffrey Alan *corporate financial executive*
Goldstein, Steve *corporate financial executive*
Goodman, Roy Matz *corporate financial executive, former state senator*
Gorman, James P. *finance company executive*
Graf, John A. *finance company executive*
Graf, Peter Gustav *accountant, lawyer*
Grebow, Edward *finance company executive*
Groves, Ray John *accountant*
Guillaume, Juanita Connor *financial analyst, minister*
Harris, Ethan S. *diversified financial services company executive*

Hayes, John D. *diversified financial services company executive*
Heleniak, David William *diversified financial services company executive, lawyer*
Hensel, Katherine Ruth *portfolio manager, investment advisor*
Hines, Walter James *stock exchange executive*
Hopkins, Deborah C. *diversified financial services company executive*
Horan, Anthony J. *diversified financial services company executive*
Hornstein, Mark *financial executive*
House, David C. *diversified financial services company executive*
Isaacs, Jeremy M. *finance company executive*
James, Hamilton Evans (Tony James) *private equity executive*
Johnson, Clarke Courtney *financial consultant, educator*
Johnson, J. Chester *corporate financial executive, consultant, writer*
Johnson, Suzanne M. Nora *diversified financial services company executive, lawyer*
Jones, Thomas Wade *financial services company executive*
Joseph, Michael Sarkies *accountant*
Joynt, Stephen W. *financial services company executive*
Kapito, Robert S. *diversified financial services company executive*
Kaplan, Todd P. *diversified financial services company executive*
Karpen, Marian Joan *financial executive*
Karr, Robert A. *financier*
Kaufman, Henry *diversified financial services company executive*
Kaye, Walter *corporate financial executive*
Keegan, Peter W. *diversified financial services company executive*
Kellner, George *financial analyst*
Kelly, Alfred F., Jr. *diversified financial services company executive*
Kenneally, Michael E. *diversified financial services company executive*
Kennedy, Kevin W. *finance company executive*
Kennedy, Thomas Patrick *financial executive*
Kessinger, Kevin M. *diversified financial services company executive*
Kessler, Stuart *accountant, financial planner*
Kirsch, Donald *financial consultant*
Kirsh, Michael Alan *financial estate planner*
Knapp, Ellen M. *financial company executive*
Knerr, Anthony David *financial consultant*
Koeppel, Noel Immanuel *financial planner, securities and real estate broker*
Kopelman, Richard Eric *management educator*
Kozlowski, Cheryl M. *fixed income analyst*
Kraus, Peter Steven *diversified financial services company executive*
Ladjevardi, Hamid *portfolio manager*
Lamb, Robert Boyden *finance and management educator*
Langford, Laura Sue *corporate financial executive*
Laue, Bruce Antonio *financial consultant, writer*
Leibowitz, Martin L. *financial services company executive*
Lessing, Brian Reid *actuary*
Lessing, Stephen M. *finance company executive*
Leven, Ann Ruth *financial consultant*
Lilien, Robert Jarrett *diversified financial services company executive*
Linen, Jonathan S. *diversified financial services company executive*
MacDonald, Alan S. *diversified financial services company executive*
MacDonald, Ronald Francis *diversified financial services company executive*
Mack, John J. *diversified financial services company executive*
MacLellan, Steve *diversified financial services company executive*
Maclin, Samuel Todd *diversified financial services company executive*
Madden, Michael Daniel *finance company executive*
Maher, Jonathan Bannon *finance executive*
Malernee, James Kent, Jr. *financial consultant*
Mandelbaum, Harold Neil *accountant*
Mandelbaum, Jay *diversified financial services company executive*
Marlas, James Constantine *diversified financial services company executive*
Masterson, Ellen Hornberger *accountant*
McCall, H. Carl *financial services executive, former state comptroller*
McCormack, Richard Thomas Fox *diversified financial services company executive, former ambassador*
McCree, Donald Hanna III *diversified financial services company executive*
McCutchen, William Walter, Jr. *management educator*
McDaniel, Raymond W., Jr. *financial information company executive*
Meehan, Sandra Gotham *corporate financial executive, consultant, writer*
Merin, Mitchell M *corporate financial executive*
Meyer, Fred Josef *finance company executive*
Meyer, Pearl *compensation executive consultant*
Miller, Heidi G. *diversified financial services company executive*
Morgan, Frank Edward, II, *corporate financial executive*
Mosse, Peter John Charles *financial services executive*
Moyles, Philip Vincent, Jr. *financial services company executive*
Mulligan, John J. *corporate financial executive*
Murphy, John B. *portfolio manager*
Nally, Dennis Mathew *finance company executive*
Nickell, Frank (Nick) T. *diversified financial services company executive*
Nides, Thomas Richard *diversified financial services company executive*
Norman, Stephen Peckham *finance company executive*
Oler, Wesley M., IV, *portfolio manager*
O'Neal, E. Stanley (Stanley O'Neal) *diversified financial services company executive*
Openshaw, Jennifer *finance company executive*
Ostling, Paul James *corporate financial executive*
Paddock, Anthony Conaway *financial consultant*

Palion, Peter Thaddeus *financial planner*
Palmer, Jessica *diversified financial services company executive*
Papps, Bruce William *financial analyst, investment company executive*
Parrett, William G. *accounting company executive*
Pincus, Lionel I. *financial executive, entrepreneur*
Powell, Scott *diversified financial services company executive*
Presby, J. Thomas *financial advisor, director, arbitrator*
Prince, Charles O., III, (Chuck Prince) *diversified financial services company executive*
Puth, David W. *diversified financial services company executive*
Quigley, James B. *diversified financial services company executive*
Quigley, James H. *finance company executive*
Radin, Amy Janine *financial services company executive*
Ramirez, Maria Fiorini *financial consultant*
Randich, Steven J. *financial services company executive*
Reiss, Dale Anne *corporate financial executive*
Richardson, Alfonso Austin *accountant, financial services executive*
Rielly, John P. (J.P. Rielly) *corporate financial executive*
Ritch, Kathleen *diversified financial services company executive*
Roethenmund, Otto Emil *finance company executive, bank executive*
Rohatyn, Felix George *diversified financial services company executive, former ambassador*
Rosenberg, Alan David *accountant*
Rowe, David Lee *financial advisor*
Rubin, Robert Edward *diversified financial services company executive, former secretary of the treasury*
Rutherfurd, John *financial information company executive*
Saint-Donat, Bernard Jacques *finance company executive*
Salom, Roberto *financial executive*
Salzberg, Barry *finance company executive*
Salzman, Robert Jay *accountant*
Savas, Emanuel S. *finance educator, public official*
Schaefer, John H. *finance company executive, security firm executive*
Schick, Thomas *diversified financial services company executive*
Schlein, Michael Edward *diversified financial services company executive*
Schlosstein, Ralph L. *diversified financial services company executive*
Schoenhut, Frederick W. *stock exchange executive*
Schubert, Scott E. *corporate financial executive*
Schueneman, Diane L. *diversified financial services company executive*
Schwartz, Bart *diversified financial services company executive*
Schwartz, Robert *finance educator*
Sclafani, Joseph L. *diversified financial services company executive*
Scully, Robert William (Bob Scully) *diversified financial services company executive*
Segal, Martin Eli *retired actuarial and consulting company executive*
Shallcross, Deanne J. *finance company executive*
Sharp, J(ames) Franklin *finance educator, portfolio manager*
Shaw, David Elliot *financial executive*
Shenkman, Mark Ronald *investment and finance executive*
Showalter, David Scott *accounting executive*
Siegel, Arthur Herbert *finance company executive*
Siguler, George William *diversified financial services company executive*
Simmons, John Derek *retired financial consultant*
Simmons, Robert J. *treasurer*
Slazberg, Barry *corporate financial executive*
Slotkin, Todd *diversified financial services company executive*
Soros, George *pension fund administrator*
Speziale, Richard Salvatore *financial executive*
Sprayregen, James H.M. *diversified financial services company executive, lawyer*
Srednicki, Richard J. *diversified financial services company executive*
Staley, James E. *diversified financial services company executive*
Stein, Elliot, Jr. *business executive*
Steinhardt, Michael H. *diversified financial services company executive*
Stranese, Michael T. *corporate financial executive*
Stross, Randall E. *business history professor, columnist*
Sutton, Mark B. *diversified financial services company executive*
Tavel, Mark Kivey *finance company executive, economist*
Tchoumak, Adelina *corporate financial executive*
Thoman, G. Richard *corporate financial executive*
Tiesi, Joseph A. *corporate financial executive*
Tillman, Vickie A. *financial information company executive*
Tisch, James Solomon *diversified holding company executive*
Toy, Stephen J. *corporate financial executive*
Trinkaus, John William *management educator*
Tuft, Thomas E. *diversified financial services company executive*
Turley, James S. *corporate financial executive*
Turner, Patrick Noel Waddington *portfolio manager*
Updike, Helen Hill *financial advisor*
Volk, Norman Hans *financial executive*
Volk, Stephen Richard *diversified financial services company executive, investment banker, lawyer*
Voss, Linda I. *finance company executive*
Warren, David P. *stock exchange executive*
Weill, Sanford I. (Sandy Weill) *former diversified financial services company executive*
Weinberger, Mark Alan *corporate financial executive, former federal agency administrator*
Weingrow, Howard Louis *finance company executive*
Whiting, Anthony *executive search consultant*
Whitman, Martin J. *portfolio manager*
Wickens, Drew C. *finance director*

Wyss, David Alen *diversified financial services company executive*
Yastine, Barbara A. *diversified financial services company executive*
Yeung, Bernard Yin *finance educator*
Zand, Dale Ezra *business management educator*
Zoellick, Robert Bruce *diversified financial services company executive, former federal agency administrator*

**Niagara Falls**
Askins, Arthur James *accountant, auditor*

**North Tonawanda**
Greenberg, Michael Jay *accountant*

**Orchard Park**
Keenan, John Paul *leadership and management educator, consultant, director, psychologist*

**Pearl River**
Bryant, Karen Worstell *financial advisor, investment company executive*

**Pine Plains**
Trapp, Peter Jarl Rudolf *portfolio manager, farmer*

**Pittsford**
Snyder, Donald Edward *finance company executive*

**Plainview**
Feller, Benjamin E. *actuary*

**Pleasant Valley**
Odescalchi, Edmond Péry *international financial consultant, author*

**Pomona**
Landau, Lauri Beth *accountant, consultant*

**Poughkeepsie**
Hansen, Karen Thornley *accountant*
Klingenberg, Beate *management educator, director*

**Pound Ridge**
Darcy, Keith Thomas *finance company executive, educator*

**Purchase**
Selander, Robert W. *finance company executive*
Xiao, Shuyi *finance company executive*

**Rego Park**
Thomas, James Edward *accountant*

**Rochester**
Ashley, Stephen B. *finance company executive*
Cameros, Alan Lee *finance company executive*
DuBrin, Andrew John *management educator, writer, behavioral sciences educator, writer*
Giglio, Mary Ann *executive*
Golisano, B. Thomas *financial services company executive, professional sports team executive*
Goyer, Virginia L. *accountant*
Judge, Jonathan J. *financial services company executive*
Marriott, Marcia Ann *business and economics educator, health facility administrator*
Schwert, G(eorge) William III *finance educator*

**Rye**
Gabelli, Mario J. *diversified financial services company executive*

**Rye Brook**
Berk, Alan S. *accountant*

**Saratoga Springs**
Dickinson, Richard Henry *accountant*

**Scarsdale**
Gladstone, William Louis *accountant*
Gollin, Stuart Allen *accountant*
O'Brien, Edward Ignatius *corporate financial executive, director, investor, lawyer*

**Shelter Island**
Shaw, Alan Roger *retired finance company executive, finance educator*

**Staten Island**
Clark, Sylvia Dolores *business educator*
Gelbein, Jay Joel *accountant*

**Syracuse**
Marcoccia, Louis Gary *accountant, academic administrator*

**Tarrytown**
Ferrari, Robert Joseph *finance educator, retired bank executive*
Hyman, Leonard Stephen *financial consultant, economist, writer*

**Troy**
Phan, Phillip Hin Choi *business educator, consultant*

**Uniondale**
Guerrera, Lisa E. *financial planner*

**Valhalla**
Christesen, John D. *business educator*

**Valley Stream**
Ellis, Bernice *financial planner, investment advisor*

**Waccabuc**
Tognino, John Nicholas *diversified financial services company executive*

**Wappingers Falls**
Hogan, Edward Robert *financial services executive*

**Water Mill**
Kreimer, Michael Walter *financial planner, investment company executive*

**Waterloo**
Schreck, Richard Thomas *accountant*

**Webster**
McCormack, Stanley Eugene *financial consultant*
Nicholson, Douglas Robert *accountant*

**Westbury**
Mondello, John Paul *financial consultant*

**White Plains**
Kroner, Arnold Friedrich *financial consultant, economist*
Prabhu, Vasant *corporate financial executive*
Sacco, John Michael *accountant*
Zuckerman, Marc Abraham *finance educator*

**Williamsville**
Mack, Gregory John *financial executive and consultant*

**Windsor**
Warner, Roberta Arlene *retired accountant, financial services executive*

**Woodbury**
Barnett, Rochelle *accountant*

**Woodside**
Hofmann, Herbert C. *diversified financial services company executive*

**Yonkers**
Herman, Martin H. *retired accountant*
Johansen, Robert Joseph *consulting actuary*

**York**
Coleman, David Cecil *financial executive*

## NORTH CAROLINA

**Asheville**
Horwitz, Bertrand Nathan *finance educator*
Letzig, Betty Jean *financial consultant*

**Chapel Hill**
Perreault, William Daniel, Jr. *business administration educator*
Rosen, Benson *business administration educator*
Ross, Coleman DeVane *accountant, insurance company executive*
Whybark, David Clay *business educator, researcher*

**Charlotte**
Anderson, Gerald Leslie *finance company executive*
Burke, Peggy Hudgins (Margaret Hudgins Burke) *auditor*
Campbell, J(ohn) Jette *corporate finance executive*
Goodwin, William H., Jr. *diversified financial services company executive*
Halas, Paul Anthony, Jr. *business appraisal and valuation specialist, consultant*
Mancuso, Michael John *retired corporate financial executive*
Moynihan, Brian T. *finance company executive*
Parmelee, William Douglas *financial executive, accountant*
Schulz, Walter Kurt *accountant, information technology consultant*
Stepp, James Michael *finance company executive*

**Clemmons**
Taquey, Antony *accountant*

**Durham**
Bettman, James Ross *management educator*
Rondinelli, Dennis A(ugust) *business administration educator, researcher*

**Flat Rock**
Daubert, Madeline J. *finance educator*

**Greensboro**
Englar, John David *finance educator, textiles executive, lawyer*
Jones, Thomas Owen, Jr. *finance educator, military officer*
Lloyd, Lila G. *business educator*
Lowe, Kevin Brian *finance company executive*

**Morganton**
Hartley, Helen Rosanna *business educator*

**New Bern**
Phipps, Patsy Duncan *retired auditor*

**Pittsboro**
Cotter, Michael William *finance educator, retired ambassador*

**Raleigh**
Aldridge, Adrienne Yingling *accountant, financial analyst, writer*
Gibson, Ronald P. *finance company executive*
Hergeth, Helmut H. *finance educator, educator*
Hritz, Pamela Lynne *accountant*
Jessen, David Wayne *accountant*
Lenard, Mary Jane *finance educator*
Sangkil, Moon *finance educator*
Stevenson, Denise L. *diversified financial services company executive, consultant, realtor*

**Salisbury**
Tseng, Howard Shih Chang *business educator, investment company executive, economics professor*

**Tryon**
Flynn, Kirtland, Jr. *accountant*

**Wilkesboro**
Thomas, David Lloyd *accountant, consultant*

**Winston Salem**
Mecimore, Charles Douglas *retired accounting educator*

## NORTH DAKOTA

**Grand Forks**
Carlson, Steven J. *finance educator*
Haskins, James P. *finance educator, consultant*
Patton, Gregory Kenneth *management educator*

**Mayville**
Skean, Mark Edgar *finance educator, consultant*

## OHIO

**Ada**
Cooper, Ken Errol *retired management educator*

**Akron**
Kramer, Richard J. *corporate financial executive*

**Amelia**
Hayden, Joseph Page, Jr. *finance company executive*

**Avon Lake**
Wilson, W. David *corporate financial executive*

**Bowling Green**
Lunde, Harold Irving *retired management educator*
Nicolaou, Andreas I. *finance educator, consultant*

**Chagrin Falls**
Pierson, Marilyn Ehle *financial planner*

**Cincinnati**
Anderson, Jerry William, Jr. *diversified financial services company executive, educator*
Bell, Sandra Elizabeth *corporate financial executive*
Conaton, Michael Joseph *diversified financial services company executive*
Dougherty, Charlotte Anne *financial planner, insurance and securities representative*
Gyuro, Paula Candice *financial planner*
Huenefeld, Thomas Ernst *financial consultant, retired banker*
Krishnan, Hema A. *finance educator*
Lawson, Randall Clayton, II, *finance company executive*
Lintz, Robert Carroll *retired diversified financial services company executive*
Mantel, Samuel Joseph, Jr. *management educator, consultant*
McMullen, W. Rodney *financial officer*
Miles, John Bill *retired accountant, retired tax specialist*
Schiff, John Jefferson, Jr. *finance company executive*
Siekmann, Donald Charles *accountant*
Wulker, Laurence Joseph *portfolio manager, educator, financial planner*

**Cleveland**
Boyle, Kammer *financial planner, investment advisor, research analyst, options trader*
Chester, Russell Gilbert, Jr. *accountant, auditor*
Holland, Brian Joseph *corporate financial executive*
Key, Helen Elaine *accountant, educator, consulting company executive*
Koch, Charles John *credit agency executive*
Lerner, Randolph D. *finance company executive*
Mayne, Lucille Stringer *finance educator*
Neu, Richard W. *credit agency executive*
Pidert, Sandy Kristin *finance educator*
Previts, Gary John *finance educator, consultant*
Quinlan, Mark *credit agency executive*
Seaton, Robert Finlayson *retired finance company executive*
Stratton-Crooke, Thomas Edward *financial consultant*
Weiss, Zev *corporate financial executive*

**Columbus**
Anand, Jaideep *management educator, consultant*
Berry, William Lee *business administration educator*
Collier, David Alan *management educator*
Kreager, Eileen Davis *financial consultant*
LaLonde, Bernard Joseph *finance educator*
Raabe, William Alan *tax writer, business educator*
Rouholt, Robert A. *financial executive*
Sestina, John E. *financial planner*

**Cuyahoga Falls**
Moses, Abe Joseph *financial planner, consultant*

**Dayton**
Bocian, Pete *corporate financial executive*
Hoge, Franz Joseph *accounting firm executive*
Singhvi, Surendra Singh *financial consultant*
White, Lawrence Edward *treasurer, financial executive*

**Dublin**
Henderson, Jeffrey W. *corporate financial executive*

**East Liverpool**
Baumgardner, Edward *financial company executive*
Gailey, Joan Dale *retired finance educator*

**Fairfield**
Stecher, Kenneth W. *financial corporation executive*

**Geneva**
Clement, Daniel Roy, IV, *accountant*

**Harrison**
Kocher, Juanita Fay *retired auditor*

**Holland**
Sacksteder, Thomas Michael *corporate financial executive, entrepreneur, writer*

**Kent**
Ryans, John Kelley, Jr. *marketing educator*

**Kettering**
Kankey, Roland Doyle *finance educator*

**Mansfield**
Shah, James M. *actuary*

**Maumee**
Risley, David Milo *controller*

**Nelsonville**
DiLiberto, Sam Michael *business educator*

**Oxford**
Cronley, Maria Lynn *marketing educator*
Goodell, George Sidney *retired finance educator*

**Shaker Heights**
Donnem, Sarah Lund *financial analyst, non-profit consultant, political organization consultant*
Krulitz, Leo Morrion *financial planner, publishing executive, director*

**Shandon**
Wilson, James Ray *international business educator*

**Springboro**
Walden, James William *accountant, educator*

**Strongsville**
Pinkerton, Richard LaDoyt *retired management educator*

**Toledo**
Geisler, Nathan David *financial consultant*
Hiltz, Kenneth A. *corporate financial executive*

**University Heights**
Murphy, Paul Regis, Jr. *business educator*

**Warren**
Robbins, Robert Marvin *accountant*

**Wilberforce**
Omolewu, Gabriel Adebayo *business educator, researcher*

**Youngstown**
Edirisooriya, Gunapala *finance educator*

## OKLAHOMA

**Lawton**
Davis, Ellen Marie *business educator*

**Moore**
Lee, Myung Woo *accountant, financial secretary*

**Oklahoma City**
Crites, Carl D. *auditor*
Vaughn, William T *corporate financial executive*

**Okmulgee**
Mitcham, Julius Jerome *accountant*

**Stillwater**
Anderson, Cokie Gaston *finance educator, computer educator, humanities educator*
Chakraborty, Goutam *marketing educator*
Jadlow, Janice Wickstead *finance educator*
Mowen, John C. *business educator*

**Tahlequah**
Carment, Thomas Maxwell *accounting educator, consultant, researcher*

**Tulsa**
Hough, Jill Renee *business professor*
Jones, Michael Lynn *financial consultant, branch operations manager*
Kaiser, George B. *corporate financial executive*
Wilson, Carol Sue Maples *business administration educator*
Witt, Edward Joseph, Jr. *tax specialist, accountant*

## OREGON

**Eugene**
Lindholm, Richard Theodore *economics and finance educator*
Miner, John Burnham *industrial relations educator, writer*

**Grants Pass**
Smith, Barnard Elliot *management educator*

**Lake Oswego**
Mylnechuk, Larry Herbert *financial executive*

**Portland**
Bosch, Samuel Henry *diversified financial services company executive*
Dow, Mary Alexis *auditor*
Epperson, Eric Robert *finance executive, film producer*
Finley, Lewis Merren *financial consultant*
Marker, Carl W. *diversified financial services company executive*
McMahon, Paul Francis *finance company executive*
Parsons, Eric E. *financial company executive*
Stewart, Marlene Metzger *financial planning practitioner, insurance agent*
Watne, Donald Arthur *retired accountant, educator*
Weber, George Richard *financial and internet marketing executive, writer*
White, Roberta Lee *financial analyst*
Workman, Norman Allan *accountant, management consultant*

**Talent**
Farrimond, George Francis, Jr. *management educator*

**West Linn**
Luchterhand, Ralph Edward *financial advisor*

## PENNSYLVANIA

**Allentown**
Heitmann, George Joseph *business educator, consultant*

**Allison Park**
LaDow, C. Stuart *financial consultant*

**Ardmore**
Waetzman, Larry Samuel *diversified financial services company executive*

**Bala Cynwyd**
Cohen, Rachel Rutstein *financial planner*
McGill, Dan Mays *insurance business educator*
Miller, L. Martin *accountant, financial planner*

**Bethlehem**
Barsness, Richard Webster *management educator, academic administrator*
Hobbs, James Beverly *business administration educator, writer, academic administrator*
Stella, John Anthony *financial executive*

**Blue Bell**
Haugen, Janet B. *corporate financial executive*

**Braddock**
Slack, Edward Dorsey III *financial systems professional, consultant*

**Bryn Mawr**
Giese, William Herbert *tax accountant*
Moyer, F. Stanton *financial executive, pharmaceutical executive*

**Callery**
Frydryk, Karl Allen *financial executive*

**Camp Hill**
Burry, Peter Ross *finance company executive*
Custer, John Charles *portfolio manager*

**Canton**
Sutton, Carl *finance educator*

**Carlisle**
Robinson, Ronald Michael *financial executive, financial consultant*

**Chester**
Saad, Germaine H. *business management educator, researcher*

**Danville**
Currid, Michael *finance educator, consultant, real estate developer*

**Du Bois**
Forsythe-Adamson, Velma Brown *accountant, consultant, literature educator*

**Eddystone**
Fredrick, Susan Walker *tax company manager*

**Flourtown**
Christy, John Gilray *diversified financial services company executive*

**Glenside**
Ralston, Steven Philip *portfolio manager, financial analyst*

**Greencastle**
Horst, Carolyn Diane *accountant*

**Greensburg**
Foreman, John Daniel *financial executive*

**Harrisburg**
Rooke, Ben G. *finance company executive, lawyer*

**Havertown**
Brinker, Thomas Michael *finance company executive*

**Hermitage**
Gurgovits, Stephen J. *financial executive*

**Horsham**
Harrison, Deborah Lynn *accountant, consultant*

**Indiana**
Falcone, Thomas William *finance educator*

**Kennett Square**
Bell, Philip Wilkes *accountant, economist, educator*

**King Of Prussia**
Filton, Steve G. *corporate financial executive*

**Kutztown**
Ogden, James Russell *marketing educator, consultant, lecturer, writer*

**Lancaster**
Freeman, Clarence Calvin *retired diversified financial services company executive*

**Lebanon**
McMindes, Roy James *aggregate company executive*

**Macungie**
Moore, Joyce Kristina *financial planner, director*

**Newtown Square**
Mestre, Oscar Luis *financial consultant*

**Oaks**
West, Alfred Paul, Jr. *financial services executive*

**Philadelphia**
Alexander, Elmore Rosebur III *business educator, dean*
Alexander, William Herbert *business educator, former construction executive*

Anderson, Rolph Ely *finance educator*
Babbel, David Frederick *finance and insurance educator*
Blume, Marshall Edward *finance educator*
Booth, Anna Belle *accountant*
DiTrolio, Joseph *controller*
Donaldson, Thomas *finance educator*
Hayden, Yvonne Meddling *retired accountant, small business owner*
Hindelang, Thomas Joseph *finance educator, dean*
Kimberly, John Robert *management educator, consultant*
Kotabe, Masaaki *finance educator*
Ksansnak, James Edward *diversified financial services company executive, accountant*
Lodish, Leonard Melvin *finance educator, entrepreneur*
Mazzarella, James Kevin *business administration educator*
Michel-Kerjan, Erwann O. *finance educator*
Netessine, Serguei *finance educator*
Rose, Jane A. *financial planner*
Rosenbloom, Bert *marketing educator, consultant, writer*
Rowan, Richard Lamar *business management educator*
Sanyour, Michael Louis, Jr. *diversified financial services company executive*
Saul, Ralph Southey *diversified financial services company executive*
Selles, Robert Hendrikus *retired actuary*
Siegel, Jeremy James *financial analyst, educator*
Summers, Anita Arrow *finance educator*
Tegtmeyer, Jordan Michael *financial analyst*
Wachter, Susan Melinda *finance educator, educator*
Webber, Ross Arkell *management educator*
Ziegler, Donald Robert *accountant*

**Pittsburgh**
Demchak, William S. *corporate financial executive*
Franklin, Kenneth Ronald *diversified financial services company executive, consultant*
Gu, Zhaoyang *finance educator*
Guyaux, Joseph C. *corporate financial executive*
Haggerty, Gretchen R. *accounting and finance executive*
Haley, Roy W. *finance company executive*
Ijiri, Yuji *finance educator*
Johson, Michael Pennington *finance educator, consultant*
King, William Richard *business educator, consultant*
Kriebel, Charles Hosey *management sciences educator*
McGuire, Timothy William *economics and management educator, dean*
Means, Dwight Bardeen, Jr. *financial consultant, educator*
Rohr, James Edward *diversified financial services company executive*
Saykiewicz-Sajkiewicz, Jan Napoleon *marketing educator*
Stevens, William Talbert *financial services executive*
Thorne, John Reinecke *finance educator, venture capitalist*
Wagner, Lawrence M. *diversified financial services company executive*
Zoffer, H. Jerome *business educator, dean*

**Plymouth Meeting**
Personius, Kevin T. *financial analyst*

**Portland**
Groff, Arthur M. *controller*

**Reading**
McCullough, Eileen (Eileen McCullough LePage, Elli McCullough) *financial consultant, writer, editor, educator*

**Richboro**
Higginbotham, Kenneth James *finance company executive*

**Saint Davids**
Bertsch, Frederick Charles III *finance company executive*

**Scranton**
Eckersley, Richard Laurence *accountant*

**Sewickley**
Bly, James Charles, Jr. *finance company executive*
Jehle, Michael Edward *financial advisor, lawyer*

**Slippery Rock**
Mukherjee, Pracheta *management educator, researcher, consultant*

**University Park**
Enis, Charles Richard *accountant, educator*
McKeown, James Charles *finance educator, consultant*

**Valley Forge**
Phelizon, Jean Francois *finance company executive*

**Villanova**
Nawrocki, David Norman *finance educator*

**Wayne**
Sims, Robert John *financial planner*

**West Chester**
Blasiotti, Robert Vincent *accountant, consultant*
Cox-Klaczak, Karen Michelle *finance educator, computer company executive*
Handzel, Steven Jeffrey *accountant*

**West Conshohocken**
Worley, Richard B. *financial consultant*

**Wilkes Barre**
McHale, Maureen Bernadette Kenny *controller*

**Wynnewood**
Robinson, Robert L. *retired diversified financial services company executive, lawyer*

**Yardley**
Gilmour, D(avid) James *financial analyst, systems analyst*

**York**
Day, Ronald Richard *retired financial executive*
Kornblatt, David *corporate financial executive*
Wise, Charles William III *financial advisor*

## RHODE ISLAND

**Barrington**
Mihaly, Eugene Bramer *diversified financial services company executive, consultant*

**Bristol**
Bosco, Susan M. *management professor*

**Cranston**
Langlois, Michael A. *financial consultant*

**East Providence**
Tripp, Michael Windsor *accountant*

**Kingston**
Mazze, Edward Mark *marketing educator, consultant*

**Providence**
McNeil, Paul Joseph, Jr. *financial analyst*

## SOUTH CAROLINA

**Charleston**
Lader, Philip *corporate financial executive, lawyer, academic administrator, diplomat*
Prewitt, William Chandler *finance company executive*

**Columbia**
Hollis, Charles Eugene, Jr. *finance company executive*
Monahan, Thomas Paul *accountant*
Pritchett, Samuel Travis *finance and insurance educator, researcher, consultant*

**Due West**
Haselden, Gregory W. *accountant, educator*

**Fort Mill**
Park, John *financial consultant*

**Greenville**
Oxner, Glenn Ruckman *financial executive*
Porter, Charles Michael (Mike Porter) *business consultant, executive*

**Pawleys Island**
Bischoff, Frederick Christopher III *retired accountant*

**Rock Hill**
Cornick, Michael F(rederick) *accounting educator*

**Seneca**
Fairleigh, Marlane Paxson *retired management educator*

**Sumter**
Blakely, Delores Phinella *financial consultant, business advisor, evangelist*
Van Bulck, Hendrikus Eugenius *accountant*

**West Columbia**
Byars, Merlene Hutto *accountant, artist, writer*

## SOUTH DAKOTA

**Mitchell**
Uecker, Grant Gordon *financial consultant*

**Platte**
Pennington, Beverly Melcher *financial services company executive*

**Sioux Falls**
Rogers, David Hughes *banking and financial service professor, dean, real estate company executive*

## TENNESSEE

**Alamo**
Finch, Evelyn Vorise *financial planner*

**Chattanooga**
Russe, Conrad Thomas Campbell *accountant*

**Cleveland**
Rhodes, Arthur Delano *benefits administrator*

**Cordova**
Haslam, Edward T. *finance company executive*
Isaacson, Bond R. *finance company executive*
Kiphart, Richard P. *finance company executive*
Labry, Edward A. III *finance company executive*
Palmer, Dan M. *finance company executive*

**Crossville**
Lansford, Edwin Gaines *accountant*

**Jackson**
Nance, William R., Jr. *finance educator*

**Knoxville**
Kahn, Kenneth B. *finance educator, consultant*
Lindeman, Barry James *internal auditor, nurse, minister*
Naoumova, Irina Yevgenievna *business educator, consultant*

**Madison**
Hadley, John Livingston, V, *management executive, writer*

**Mc Kenzie**
Blasick, James David *finance educator*

**Memphis**
Brandon, Elvis Denby, Jr. *financial planner*
Brandon, Elvis Denby III *financial planner*
Brandon, Raymond Wilson *financial planner, securities principal*
Horn, D. Ralph *corporate financial executive*
Iles, Roger Dean *business educator*
Umholtz, Clyde Allan *financial analyst*

**Nashville**
Brophy, Jeremiah Joseph *retired finance company executive, retired military officer*
Christie, William Gary *finance educator*
Clemens, Peter J., IV, *corporate financial executive*
Doyle, William Robert *finance educator*
Evans, Franklin Bachelder *finance educator, consultant*
Ford, Gerald J. (Jerry) *finance company executive*
Freudenthal, Ernest Guenter *technology and business educator*
Gore, Steven Lowell *accountant*
Hazen, Samuel N *finance educator*
Masulis, Ronald *finance educator*
Rutherford, William B. *corporate financial executive*
Shallcross, Richard *corporate financial executive*
Ullestad, Merwin Allan *tax specialist, director*
Weingartner, H(ans) Martin *finance educator*

**Rockford**
Nesbit, Sandi Michelle *corporate financial executive*

**Soddy Daisy**
Randall, Kay Temple *accountant, retired real estate agent*

**TEXAS**

**Addison**
Rinehart, Neil *financial consultant*

**Aledo**
Reilly, Michael Atlee *finance company executive, venture capital investor*

**Amarillo**
Strickland, Anita Maurine *retired business educator, librarian*

**Argyle**
Pettit, John Douglas, Jr. *management educator*

**Arlington**
de Jong, Pieter Johannes *finance educator, physical therapist*
Sabherwal, Sanjiv *finance educator*
Swanson, Peggy Eubanks *finance educator*

**Austin**
Alpert, Mark Ira *marketing educator*
Anderson, Urton Liggett *accounting educator*
Crum, Lawrence Lee *banking educator*
Cundiff, Edward William *retired marketing educator*
Granof, Michael H. *finance educator, department chairman*
Jastrow, Kenneth M. *financial executive*
Kimberlin, Sam Owen, Jr. *financial consultant*
Larson, Kermit Dean *finance educator*
Parrino, Robert *finance educator*
Peterson, Robert Allen *marketing educator*
Titman, Sheridan *finance educator*

**Boerne**
Tom, James Robert *accountant*

**Breckenridge**
DuBose, Sandra Lynn *finance educator*

**Brownwood**
Bell, Mary E. Beniteau *accountant*
DeHay, Jerry Marvin *business educator, small business owner*

**Burton**
Knauss, Robert Lynn *corporate financial executive*

**Cleburne**
Gorman, Charlotte A. *business executive*

**College Station**
Mahajan, Arvind *finance educator*
Spanjol, Jelena *finance educator*
Wichern, Dean William *business educator*

**Dallas**
Bishop, Gene Herbert *corporate financial executive*
Coldwell, Philip Edward *financial consultant*
Eads, John A. *accountant*
Grant, Joseph Moorman *finance company executive*
Guthrie, M. Philip *corporate financial executive*
Hay, Jess Thomas *retired finance company executive*
Howland, Grafton Dulany *financial counselor*
Jimenez, Mercy *business educator*
Jobe, Larry Alton *finance company executive*
Moore, Thomas Joseph *finance company executive*
Morgan, Gregory Paul *financial investment advisor*
Pullen, Timothy L. *corporate financial executive*
Rossel, Cary *corporate financial executive*
Shimer, Daniel Lewis *finance company executive*
Skinner, James E. *corporate financial executive*
Smerge, Raymond G. *finance company executive*
Smith, Patsy Juanita *financial executive*
Walker, Gordon Beverley Moore, Jr. *business educator*

**Denton**
Brock, Horace Rhea *finance educator*
Evangelopoulos, Nicholas E. *finance educator*
Newell, Charldean *public administration educator*

**Edinburg**
Kaynak, Hale *finance educator, researcher*

**El Paso**
Cadena, Frederico Eduardo *finance company executive*
Kelley, Sylvia Johnson *financial services firm executive*

**Fort Worth**
Bass, Robert Muse *financier*
Berce, Daniel Eugene *financial services company executive, accountant*
Clark, Emory Eugene *diversified financial services company executive*
Dominiak, Geraldine Florence *retired accounting educator*
Karnes, Keith Dale *portfolio manager*
Pappas-Speairs, Nina *financial planner, educator*
Rainwater, Richard Edward *financial consultant, investor*
Waller, Gary Wilton *administration educator, minister*

**Frisco**
Bloskas, John D. *retired finance company executive*

**Galveston**
Selig, Oury Levy *port financial consultant*

**Garland**
Lord, Jacqueline Ward *accountant, photographer, artist*
McGill, Maurice Leon *corporate financial executive*

**Georgetown**
Sellers, Fred Evans *accounting educator*

**Grand Prairie**
Ebozue, Benson Obian *financial analyst*

**Hockley**
Williams, James Lee *finance company executive*

**Houston**
Braden, John Alan *accountant*
Clark, Janet F. *corporate financial executive*
Cloninger, Dale Owen *finance educator*
Crispin, Andre Arthur *diversified financial services company executive*
D'Agostino, James Samuel, Jr. *corporate financial executive*
Elkins, James Anderson III *financial consultant*
Getz, Lowell Vernon *financial advisor*
Harris, Venita Van Caspel *retired financial planner*
Horvitz, Paul Michael *finance educator*
Janssens, Joe Lee *controller*
Jones, Eli III *marketing and sales educator*
Karnes, John Herbert, Jr. *corporate financial executive, lawyer*
Larkin, William Vincent, Jr. *corporate financial executive*
Mahadeva, Manoranjan *financial executive, accountant*
McEachern, Stephen Mathew *accountant*
Rawson, Jim Charles *finance company executive*
Reese, Albert Leslie, Jr. *financial executive*
Salam, Debera Jean *accounting company executive*
Sarofim, Fayez Shalaby *finance company executive*
Simpson, Robert G. *corporate financial executive*

**Huntsville**
Sower, Victor Edmund *management educator*

**Hurst**
Moore, Herff Leo, Jr. *management educator*

**Irving**
Ashby, Elizabeth Sybil *marketing analyst*
Brown, Linda Harper *bookkeeping company executive*
Massah, Cherilyn *auditor*

**Laredo**
Ortiz, Jaime *business educator*

**Lubbock**
Wolfe, Verda Nell *pension consultant, financial planner*

**Mc Kinney**
Kessler, John Paul, Jr. *financial planner*

**Mcallen**
Roney, Glen E. *finance company executive*

**Midland**
Groce, James Freelan *financial consultant*

**Nacogdoches**
Stetz, Phil E. *management educator, entrepreneur*

**Normangee**
Cox, Jack Ronald, Jr. *finance educator*

**Pampa**
Crow, Donna Gayle *business educator*

**Pasadena**
Scott, William Floyd *accountant*

**Plano**
Bravard, Jean-Louis *diversified financial services company executive*
Day, Kevin Thomas *retired business executive, retired investment banker, retired foundation administrator*

**Prairie View**
De Luna-Gonzalez, Elma *accountant, academic administrator*

**Richland Hills**
Haynes, Ruth Elaine *accountant*

**Richmond**
Dholakia, Utpal M. *management educator, consultant*

**Rosharon**
Jenkins, Judith Alexander *bank consultant*

**Round Rock**
Puri, Rajendra Kumar *business and tax specialist, consultant*

**San Antonio**
Fuhrmann, Charles J., II, *financial consultant*
Jones, James Richard *business administration educator*
Lalwani, Ashok K. *marketing educator*
Messina, Paul Francis *finance educator*
Stevens, Dennis Max *auditor*
Weber, William Wesley *accountant*

**San Marcos**
Darling, John Rothburn *business educator*
Palmer, Roger Raymond *finance educator*
Taylor, Ruth Arleen Lesher *marketing educator*

**Spring**
Kehoe, John Kimball *finance educator, consultant*

**Stafford**
Pate, John Gillis, Jr. *financial consultant, educator*

**Stephenville**
Collier, Boyd Dean *finance educator, management consultant*

**Sugar Land**
Keefe, Carolyn Joan *tax accountant*

**Waco**
Rose, John Thomas *finance educator*

**Wichita Falls**
Hamlin, Don Auer *financial executive*

**Wimberley**
Skaggs, Wayne Gerard *retired diversified financial services company executive*

**UTAH**

**Logan**
Kannan, Vijay R. *business educator*

**Orem**
Hunt, H(arold) Keith *retired business management educator, marketing consultant*

**Salt Lake City**
Alter, Edward T. *treasurer*
Brady, Rodney Howard *diversified financial services company executive, broadcast executive, director, retired academic administrator, retired federal official*
Elkins, Glen Ray *retired diversified management services company executive*
Johnson, Auston Gilbert III *auditor*
Nelson, Roger Hugh *finance educator, corporate financial executive, consultant*
Nicolatus, Stephen Jon *financial consultant*

**VERMONT**

**Brandon**
Konwin, Thor Warner *financial executive*

**Quechee**
Vitty, Roderic Bemis *retired financial planner, publishing executive*

**Rutland**
Norris, Richard Anthony *accountant, waste management administrator*

**VIRGINIA**

**Abingdon**
Jones, Mary Trent *endowment fund trustee*

**Alexandria**
Bellon, Venetia Rochelle *financial consultant, educator*
Inman, Stephen Eugene *finance officer*

**Annandale**
Connair, Stephen Michael *financial analyst*
Hulbert, Mark J. *financial analyst, columnist*
Jones, David Charles *international financial and management consultant*

**Arlington**
Caplan, Mitchell H. *diversified financial services company executive*
Florida, Richard Louis *finance educator*
Page, Harry Robert *business administration educator*

**Blacksburg**
Moore, Laurence John *business educator*
Patterson, Douglas MacLennan *finance educator*

**Chantilly**
Carlson, Robert Charles *financial planner, writer*
Young, M. Dendy *finance company executive*

**Charlottesville**
Davis, Edward Wilson *business administration educator*
DeMong, Richard Francis *finance and investments educator*
Harris, Robert Shields *finance educator*
Minehart, Jean Besse *tax accountant*
Sahr, Morris Gallup *financial planner*

**Shenkir**, William Gary *business educator*
Sihler, William Wooding *finance educator*

**Charlottesvle**
Haigh, Robert William *business professor*

**Chesapeake**
Barnes, Stacy Ray *finance educator, researcher*

**Chester**
Roane, David James, Jr. *information technology auditor*

**Fairfax**
Burnett, Michael Bruce *benefits compensation analyst*
Meamber, Laurie Ann *marketing educator*

**Falls Church**
Bruck, Bill *finance company executive*
Nason, Charles Tuckey *retired diversified financial services company executive*
Purvis, Ronald Scott *financial planner, real estate company officer*

**Harrisonburg**
Ramsey, Jackson Eugene *management educator*

**Keswick**
Pochick, Francis Edward *financial consultant*

**Lexington**
Cline, Philip Lee *business and economics educator*
DeVogt, John Frederick *management science and business ethics educator, consultant*

**Luray**
Bell, Michael Joseph *business and information technology educator*

**Mc Lean**
Bailar, Gregor S. *finance company executive*
Bitsberger, Timothy S. *finance company executive, former federal agency administrator*
Blazer, Randolph C. *diversified financial services company executive*
Boyd, Ralph F., Jr. *finance company executive, former federal agency administrator*
Fairbank, Richard D. *diversified financial services company executive*
Fritz, Thomas Vincent *business executive*
Goktepe, Janet Rose *retired financial analyst*
Kautt, Glenn Gregory *financial planner, consultant*
McQuade, Eugene M. *finance company executive, former bank executive*
Stowe, Alexis Mariani *accountant, consultant*
Syron, Dick (Richard Francis Syron) *finance company executive, economist*

**Mineral**
Mayo, Louis Allen *diversified financial services company executive*

**Newport News**
Le Mons, Kathleen Ann *securities company executive, portfolio manager, investment officer*

**Norfolk**
McKee, Timothy Carlton *taxation educator*

**North Garden**
May, Eleanor Goddard *retired business administration educator*

**Reston**
Fitzpatrick, Thomas J. (Thomas J. Fitzpatrick) *finance company executive*
Lister, Harry Joseph *financial company consultant*
Lord, Albert L. *finance company executive*
Polemitou, Olga Andrea *accountant*

**Richmond**
Austin, John D. *corporate financial executive*
King, Robert Leroy *business administration educator*
Krug, Jeffrey Alan *international business educator*
Mann, Stephen Ashby *financial consultant*
Neal, Stu M. *finance educator, writer*
Palmer, Robert J. *corporate financial executive*
Ritter, Robert T. *diversified financial services company executive*
Scott, Sidney Buford *finance company executive*
Wagner, Jody M. *treasurer*

**Sterling**
Hough, Lawrence A. *former financial organization executive*

**Vienna**
Kumar, Verinder *accountant, financial executive*
Townsend, Irene Fogleman *accountant, tax specialist*

**Weems**
Martin, William Raymond *retired financial manager*

**Williamsburg**
Ainscough, Thomas Lee, Jr. *business educator, internet marketing consultant*
Gottfried, Mark Ellis *accountant, consultant*
Holstein, William Kurt *business administration educator*
Kottas, John Frederick *business administration educator*
McLennan, Barbara Nancy *tax specialist*
Messmer, Donald Joseph *business management educator, marketing consultant*
O'Connell, William Edward, Jr. *retired finance educator*
Paige, Hilliard Wegner *corporate financial executive, consultant*
Pearson, Roy Laing *business administration educator*

**Woodbridge**
Denison, Cynthia Lee *accountant, tax specialist*

## WASHINGTON

**Bellevue**
Armstrong, Ronald E. *corporate financial executive*
Graham, John Robert, Jr. *financial executive*

**Edmonds**
Monroe, James Walter *retired corporate financial executive*

**Federal Way**
Taggart, Richard J. *corporate financial executive*

**Issaquah**
von Speyer, Jacques *financier*

**Medical Lake**
Grub, Phillip Donald *business educator*

**Mukilteo**
Brown, Bruce Baden *accountant*

**Olympia**
Myers, Sharon Diane *auditor*

**Seattle**
Baker, Roland Jerald *finance educator*
Chapman, Craig J. *finance company executive*
David, Daryl D. *finance company executive*
Gross, Jeremy V. (Jerry Gross) *finance company executive*
Klein, Jonathan D. *finance company executive*
MacLachlan, Douglas Lee *marketing educator*
Szkutak, Tom *corporate financial executive*
Tall, Craig E. *finance company executive*

**Shelton**
McNabb, David E. *business educator, writer*

**Shoreline**
Hanson, Kermit Osmond *business administration educator, retired dean*

**Spokane**
Burton, Robert Lyle *accounting firm executive*
Cameron, Alex Brian *accountant, educator*
Teets, Walter Ralph *accounting educator*

**Tacoma**
Hilzendeger, Laura Kaye *business and marketing educator*
Wolf, Frederick George *management educator*

## WEST VIRGINIA

**Charleston**
Lamb, Patrick John *retired financial consultant, state official*

**Elkins**
Payne, Gloria Marquette *business educator*

**Harpers Ferry**
Boucher, Wayne Irving *policy analyst*

**Huntington**
Wenzel, Loren Alvin *finance educator*

**Morgantown**
Dawley, David Daniel *finance educator*

## WISCONSIN

**Appleton**
Stellmacher, Jon Michael *corporate financial executive*

**Eau Claire**
Rusch, Gerald Allen *financial consultant*
Weil, D(onald) Wallace *business administration educator*

**Franklin**
Schutte, Richard David *diversified financial services company executive*

**Madison**
Aldag, Ramon John *management and organization educator*
Hickman, James Charles *finance educator, dean*
Nevin, John Robert *business educator, consultant*
Schwab, Donald Peter *finance educator*

**Mequon**
Berry, William Martin *financial consultant*

**Milwaukee**
Culver, Curt S. *diversified financial services company executive*
Grabowski, Michael Joseph *financial executive*
McDonald, R. Bruce *corporate financial executive*
Poliner, Gary A. *corporate financial executive*
Schnoll, Howard Manuel *financial consultant, investment company executive*
Schwister, Jay Edward *portfolio manager*
Simoneau, Daniel Robert *accountant, educator, artist*
Szwarc, Wlodzimierz *operations research professor*
Zore, Edward John *financial services executive*

**New Berlin**
Gebhard, LaVerne Elizabeth *retired accounting educator*

**Oconomowoc**
Kneiser, Richard John *accountant*

**Stevens Point**
Dombeck, Michael P. *finance educator, conservationist*

**Superior**
Robek, Mary Frances *business education educator*

**Waupun**
Wendt, Thomas *finance company executive*

**West Bend**
VanBrunt-Kramer, Karen *business administration educator*

**Whitewater**
Hsu, Maxwell K. *finance educator*

## WYOMING

**Laramie**
Spiegelberg, Emma Jo *business education educator, academic administrator*

**Sheridan**
Dearinger, Tracy M. *business educator*
Ryan, Michael Louis *controller*

## TERRITORIES OF THE UNITED STATES

### GUAM

**Talofofo**
Taylor, James John *finance educator*

### PUERTO RICO

**Mayaguez**
Ruiz-Vargas, Yolanda *finance educator*

**San Juan**
Rosso de Irizarry, Carmen (Tutty Rosso de Irizarry) *finance executive*

## MILITARY ADDRESSES OF THE UNITED STATES

### PACIFIC

**Fpo**
Tarpeh-Doe, Linda Diane *controller*

## CANADA

### ALBERTA

**Calgary**
Agarwal, James *marketing educator*

### BRITISH COLUMBIA

**Vancouver**
Mattessich, Richard Victor (Alvarus) *business administration researcher*

### MANITOBA

**Winnipeg**
Burns, James William *financial executive*
McCallum, John Stuart *finance educator, columnist*

### NOVA SCOTIA

**Bedford**
Hennigar, David John *portfolio manager, director*

### ONTARIO

**London**
Osbaldeston, Gordon Francis *finance educator, retired federal agency administrator*

**Ottawa**
Beatty, Perrin *business association executive*

**Toronto**
Baxendale, Sonia A. *diversified financial services company executive*
Cockwell, Jack Lynn *finance company executive*
Cook-Bennett, Gail *pension fund administrator*
Cunningham, Gordon Ross *finance company executive*
Hore, John Edward *commodity futures educator*
Mann, George Stanley *diversified financial services company executive, real estate company officer*
Mercier, Eileen Ann *corporate financial executive*
Morneau, William *pension and benefits company executive*
Poprawa, Andrew *diversified financial services company executive, accountant*
Price, Timothy R. *accountant*
Schwartz, Gerald Wilfred *business executive*
Silk, Frederick C.Z. *financial consultant*
Sloan, David Edward *retired finance company executive*
Stymiest, Barbara *stock exchange executive*
Weston, W. Galen, Sr., (Galen Weston) *diversified financial services company executive*

**Willowdale**
Sze, Michael Ming-Chih *actuary, consultant*

### QUEBEC

**Montreal**
Desmarais, Paul *diversified management and holding company executive*
Gratton, Robert *diversified financial services company executive*
Laurin, Pierre *finance company executive*
Nadeau, Bertin Felix *holding company executive*
Ngo, Van Tan (Tan Van) *financial planner, poet*
Speirs, Derek James *diversified financial services company executive*
Thompson, John Douglas *corporate financial executive*

**Verdun**
Lessard, Michel M. *finance company executive*

**Windsor**
Van Den Brande, Rene Albert *retired accountant*

## AUSTRALIA

**Melbourne**
Batrouney, Clive M. *finance company executive*

## BELGIUM

**Diegen**
Dörken, Uwe R. *finance company executive*

## BERMUDA

**Pembroke**
Freimark, Jeffrey Philip *corporate financial executive*

## CHINA

**Beijing**
Thornton, John L. *former diversified financial services company executive*

## CYPRUS

**Nicosia**
Aloneftis, Andreas *business executive*

## DENMARK

**Horsholm**
Sørensen, Erik *retired diversified financial services company executive*

## ENGLAND

**Coventry**
Thomas, Howard *business educator*

**London**
Ellis, Claud M. Buddy *diversified financial services company executive*
Eustace, Dudley Graham *diversified financial services company executive*
Ioannou, Constantinos Elia *accountant*
Sarkis, Ziad Joseph *private equity executive*
Vanniasingham, Samuel Kanagasabapathy *accountant*

**Oxford**
Bullock, Peter Bradley *company director, consultant*

## FRANCE

**Paris**
Ricol, Rene Jean *accountant*
Vandame, Jean-Marie Richard *diversified financial services company executive*

## GREECE

**Athens**
Papadakis, Panagiotis Agamemnon *corporate financial executive*

## GRENADA

**St. George**
Jordan, Tiffany *finance educator*

## HONG KONG

**Hong Kong**
Pacter, Paul Allan *accounting standards researcher*

**Wanchai**
Iwasawa, Isoo (Francis Iwasawa) *accountant, management consultant*
Valente, Giorgio *finance educator*

## ISRAEL

**Jerusalem**
Shrensky, Don Steven *accountant, consultant*

**Rehovot**
Zipori-Beckenstein, Pninit *business educator, researcher*

## JAPAN

**Hachioji**
Okada, Isamu *finance educator, researcher*

**Kumatori**
Ohashi, Shoichi *business administration educator*

**Tokyo**
Connor, William Edwin, II, *finance company executive*
Iinuma, Hiroichi *finance educator*
Kobayashi, Noritake *business educator*

**Yokohama**
Tokutani, Masao *risk management educator*

## PORTUGAL

**Lisbon**
Santos Gomes, Maria da Conceicao Fialho *financial services executive*

## SAUDI ARABIA

**Riyadh**
Olayan, Lubna S. *finance company executive*

## SCOTLAND

**Dundee**
Lee, Thomas Alexander *accountant, educator*

## SPAIN

**Zaragoza**
Yadav, Prashant *finance educator*

## SWITZERLAND

**Lausanne**
Servien, Louis-Marc (Comte De Boisdauphin, Lord of Quendon) *finance company executive, import/export company executive*

## TAIWAN

**Hsinchu**
Wang, David *finance educator*

**Taipei**
Tsung, Christine Chai-yi *financial executive, treasurer*

## UNITED ARAB EMIRATES

**Dubai**
Khan, Waleed *auditor*

## ADDRESS UNPUBLISHED

Abbott, Edward Leroy *finance executive*
Albano, Pasquale Charles *finance educator, management consultant*
Albrecht, Ronald Lewis *financial services executive*
Alexander, Barbara Toll *financial consultant*
Alexander, Donald G. *auditor, protective services official*
Allbritton, Joe Lewis *diversified financial services company executive, director*
Almeida, Richard Joseph *finance company administrator*
Alper, Merlin Lionel *corporate financial executive*
Alvare, Charles Daguerre *financial advisor, educator*
Amaldoss, Wilfred *marketing educator*
Anaya, Richard Alfred, Jr. *financial consultant*
Arenberg, Julius Theodore, Jr. *retired accounting company executive*
Ashby, Franklin Charles, Jr. *corporate financial executive, educator*
Atcheson, Sue Hart *business educator*
Atwood, Donna Elaine *retired financial manager*
Austin, Carlton Joseph *finance company executive*
Awazu, Yukika *corporate executive*
Bagwill, John Williams *retired pension fund administrator*
Baier, Lucinda *corporate financial executive*
Bains, Harrison MacKellar, Jr. *retired finance company executive*
Bákér, J. A., *executive management advisor and consultant, monetary architect, financial engineer emeritus*
Balakrishnan, P. V. (Sundar) (P.V. Sundar Balakrishnan) *marketing educator*
Balzan, Ronald Dean *diversified financial services company executive*
Bartkus, Barbara R. *management educator*
Bartlett, Shirley Anne *accountant*
Baumann, Martin F. *former finance company executive*
Bechkoff, Jennifer "Kat" *business educator*
Beller, Luanne Evelyn *retired accountant*
Bellows, Howard Arthur, Jr. *corporate financial executive*
Belluomini, Frank Stephen *accountant*
Bennett, Peter Dunne *retired marketing educator*
Benson, Donald Erick *finance company executive*

## FINANCE: INSURANCE

### UNITED STATES

#### ALABAMA

**Anniston**
Currie, Larry Lamar *insurance agent*

**Birmingham**
Coleman, Gary L. *insurance company executive*
Hudson, C. B., Jr. *insurance company executive*
Johns, John D. *insurance company executive, lawyer*

Ritchie, Allen W. *insurance company executive*

## ALASKA

### Anchorage
Trevithick, Ronald James *underwriter*

## ARIZONA

### Paradise Valley
Tyner, Neal Edward *retired insurance company executive*

### Rio Verde
Harding, John Hibbard *retired insurance company executive*

### Scottsdale
Vairo, Robert John *insurance company executive*
Williams, Margaret M. (Meg Williams) *insurance company executive*

### Sun City
Reynolds, John Francis *insurance company executive*

### Tucson
Haney, Robert Locke *retired insurance company executive*
Ziehler, Tony Joseph *insurance agent*

## ARKANSAS

### Cherokee Village
Payne, Howard James *retired insurance company executive*

### Pine Bluff
Bradford, Jay Turner *insurance company executive, state legislator*

## CALIFORNIA

### Alameda
Leong, Jonathan R. *insurance company executive*

### Auburn
Jeske, Howard Leigh *retired insurance company executive, lawyer*

### Calabasas
Christensen, Donn Wayne *insurance executive*

### Cupertino
Knapp, George Griff Prather *retired insurance executive*

### Encino
Parrott, Dennis Beecher *retired insurance company executive*

### Fullerton
Woods, Betty *insurance company executive*

### Garden Grove
Williams, J(ohn) Tilman *insurance company executive, real estate agent, municipal official*

### Irvine
Matros, Richard K. *insurance company executive*

### Los Altos
Zebroski, Edwin Leopold *risk management consultant*

### Los Angeles
Hostovich, Teena Maria *insurance brokerage executive*
Houston, Ivan James *insurance company executive*
Inman, James Russell *claims consultant*
Johnson, E. Eric *insurance company executive*
Joseph, George *insurance company executive*

### Menifee
Roark, Robert Cameron *insurance agent*

### Newark
Dong, Weimin *risk management consultant*
Gupta, Anju *risk management consultant*

### Newport Beach
Marcoux, Carl Henry *insurance company executive, writer, historian*
Morris, James T. *insurance company executive*
Sutton, Thomas C. *insurance company executive*
Tran, Khanh T. *insurance company executive*

### Novato
Carendi, Jan R. *insurance company executive*

### Oakland
Halvorson, George Charles *healthcare insurance company executive*

### Orange
Godeke, Raymond Dwight Cook *insurance company executive, accountant*

### Paso Robles
Webster, David Arthur *retired life insurance company executive*

### Rancho Mirage
Fromm, Erwin Frederick *retired insurance company executive*

### San Diego
Baxter, Robert Hampton *insurance company executive*
Purcifull, Robert Otis *insurance company executive*
Rotter, Paul Talbott *retired insurance executive*

### San Francisco
Enfield, Donald Michael *insurance company executive*
Lamberson, John Roger *insurance company executive*
Martinez, Belinda *health insurance company executive*
Stewart, Richard Edwin *insurance consulting company executive*

### San Juan Capistrano
Gardner, Carol Ann *insurance company executive*

### San Rafael
Keegan, Jane Ann *insurance executive, consultant*

### Santa Ana
DeRoy, Craig I. *title insurance company executive, lawyer*
Klemens, Thomas A. *insurance company executive*

### Santa Monica
Schaeffer, Leonard David *health insurance company executive*

### Sherman Oaks
Holden, William Willard *insurance executive*
Milgrim, Darrow A. *insurance company executive*

### Thousand Oaks
Herman, Joan Elizabeth *health insurance company executive*
Valdez, Josh *health insurance company executive*

### Woodland Hills
Clarey, Patricia T. *health insurance company executive, former state official*
Helwig, David S. *healthcare insurance company executive*

### Woodside
Freitas, Antoinette Juni *insurance company executive*

## COLORADO

### Aurora
Nelson, Marvin Ray *retired life insurance company executive*

### Englewood
Hardy, Wayne Russell *insurance and investment broker*
Manley, Richard Walter *insurance company executive*

### Fort Collins
Schendel, Winfried George *insurance company executive*

### Littleton
Volpe, Richard Gerard *insurance accounts executive, consultant*

### Superior
Forshee, Gladys Marie *insurance agent, writer*

## CONNECTICUT

### East Hartford
Lautzenheiser, Barbara Jean *insurance company executive*

### Essex
Miller, Walter Neal *insurance company consultant*

### Greenwich
Berkley, William Robert *insurance holding company executive*
Clements, Robert *insurance executive*
Fuller, Theodore *retired insurance executive*

### Hampton
Roenigk, Martin Allen *insurance company executive*

### Hartford
Ayer, Ramani *insurance company executive*
Bermel, John J *insurance company executive, corporate financial executive*
Bertolini, Mark T. *insurance company executive*
Bolton, Roger *insurance company executive*
Brennan, Troyen A. *insurance company executive, medical educator, lawyer*
Casazza, William James *insurance company executive, lawyer*
Cheng, Wei-Tih *insurance company executive*
Elliott, Eric S *insurance company executive*
Entrekin, David W *insurance company executive*
Geyer, James A *insurance company executive*
Haylon, Michael E. *insurance company executive*
Hebert, Paul B *insurance company executive*
Mullane, Denis Francis *insurance company executive*
Popik, William C *insurance company executive*
Roth, William H *insurance company executive*
Rowe, John Wallis (Jack Rowe) *insurance company executive, health facility administrator*
Sargent, Joseph Denny *insurance executive*
Scully, John Carroll *life insurance marketing research company executive*
Wilde, Wilson *insurance company executive*
Williams, Ronald A. *health insurance company executive*
Wise, Richard Evans *corporate executive*
Wright, Elease *insurance company executive*
Young, Dona Davis Gagliano *insurance company executive, lawyer*
Zwiener, David K. *insurance company executive*

### Middletown
Bohan, Lawrence Stewart *retired insurance company executive*

### New Canaan
Burns, John Joseph, Jr. *financial and insurance holding company executive*

Cohen, Richard Norman *insurance executive*
Ylvisaker, James William *insurance executive*

### Stamford
Chickering, Howard Allen *insurance company executive, lawyer*
Hudson, Harold Jordon, Jr. *retired insurance executive*
Schiff, Jayne Nemerow *underwriter*

### Trumbull
Berg, Charles G. *insurance company executive*

### Vernon Rockville
Wolff, Gregory Steven *insurance company executive*

### West Hartford
Wilder, Michael Stephen *former insurance company executive*

### Weston
Thompson, N(orman) David *insurance company executive*

## DELAWARE

### Wilmington
Nottingham, Robinson Kendall *insurance company executive*

## DISTRICT OF COLUMBIA

### Washington
Haley, John *risk management consultant*
Martin, Julie A. *retired insurance company executive*
Nicely, Olza M. (Tony) *insurance company executive*
Pitt, Harvey Lloyd *risk management consultant, former federal agency administrator*
Schiller, Harvey W. *risk management company executive*
Simpson, Louis A. *insurance company executive*

## FLORIDA

### Atlantic Beach
Preble, Robert Curtis, Jr. *insurance executive*

### Boca Raton
Kaye, Barry *insurance company executive*
Richardson, R(oss) Fred(erick) *insurance company executive, consultant*

### Boynton Beach
Bryant, Donald Loyd *insurance company executive*

### Daytona Beach
Adams, John Carter, Jr. *insurance executive*

### Fort Lauderdale
Hull, Richard Franklin *insurance brokerage executive*
Lilley, Mili Della *insurance company executive, entertainment management consultant*

### Fort Myers
Mc Queen, Robert Charles *retired insurance executive*

### Gainesville
Boothroyd, Herbert J. *insurance company executive*

### Holiday
Peterson, George Folke *retired insurance company executive, writer*

### Jacksonville
Lyon, Wilford Charles, Jr. *insurance executive*

### Juno Beach
Holmes, Melvin Almont *insurance company executive*

### Key Largo
Daenzer, Bernard John *insurance company executive, consultant*

### Lake Mary
Swonger, Thomas K. H., Jr. *insurance company executive*

### Miami
Gabor, Frank *insurance company executive*
Heggen, Arthur William *insurance company executive*
Martinez, Carlos *insurance agent*
Shusterman, Nathan *underwriter, financial consultant*
Van Wyck, George Richard *insurance company executive*

### New Port Richey
Hanahan, James Lake *retired insurance executive*

### Oldsmar
Caronis, George John *insurance executive*

### Ormond Beach
Burt, Wallace Joseph, Jr. *insurance company executive*

### Oviedo
Brethauer, William Russell, Jr. *claim investigator*

### Ponte Vedra Beach
MacKowski, John Joseph *retired insurance company executive*

### Punta Gorda
McDaniel, Norwood Allan *insurance agent*

### Redington Beach
Alpert, Barry Mark *insurance company and banking executive*

### Saint Petersburg
Fraser, John Wayne *insurance executive, consultant, underwriter*

### Sarasota
Bushey, Alan Scott *retired insurance holding company executive*

### Spring Hill
Vanderburg, Paul Stacey *insurance executive, consultant*

### Tampa
Bishopric, Karl *insurance company executive, retired investment banker, real estate company executive, retired advertising executive*
Campos, Jackie C. *insurance agent*
Sullivan, Joseph Peter *risk and insurance management consultant*

### Winter Park
Kraft, Kenneth Houston, Jr. *insurance agency executive*

## GEORGIA

### Alpharetta
Fowler, Vivian Delores *insurance company executive*
Smith, Derek V. *risk management consultant*

### Atlanta
Black, Kenneth, Jr. *retired insurance company executive*
Gregory, Mel Hyatt, Jr. *retired insurance company executive*
Hilliard, Robert Glenn *insurance company executive, lawyer*
Hubbell, Fred Shelton *insurance company executive*

### Columbus
Amos, Daniel Paul *insurance company executive*
Cloninger, Kriss III *insurance company executive*
Lester, James D. III *insurance company executive*
Loudermilk, Joey M. *insurance company executive, lawyer*

### Lagrange
Hudson, Charles Daugherty *insurance executive*

### Norcross
Atkinson, A. Kelley *insurance company executive*

### Savannah
Dodge, William Douglas *risk management consultant*

## HAWAII

### Honolulu
Kanehiro, Kenneth Kenji *insurance educator, risk analyst, consultant*
Noguchi, Hideo *insurance company executive*

## IDAHO

### Twin Falls
Startin, W. Lane *insurance agent*

## ILLINOIS

### Bloomington
Blackburn, John D. *insurance company executive*
Brunner, Kim M. *insurance company executive, lawyer*
Curry, Alan Chester *insurance company executive*
Rust, Edward Barry, Jr. *insurance company executive, lawyer*
Tipsord, Michael L. *insurance company executive*
Trosino, Vincent Joseph, Sr. *insurance company executive*

### Chicago
Adams, John S. *insurance company executive*
Bartholomay, William C. *insurance brokerage company executive, professional baseball team executive*
Beemster, Joseph Robert *risk management consultant*
Bradley, Thomas A. *insurance company executive*
Case, Gregory C. *insurance company executive*
Chang, Yi-Cheng *insurance agent*
DeMoss, Jon W. *insurance company executive, lawyer*
Draut, Eric J. *insurance company executive*
Fernandez, Geno *insurance company executive*
Hughes, Martin P. *insurance company executive*
Jerome, Jerrold V. *retired insurance company executive*
Lerner, Alexander Robert *insurance company executive*
Lorenz, Hugo Albert *retired insurance executive, consultant*
McCaskey, Raymond F. *insurance company executive*
Parcells, Frederick R. *underwriter*
Peponis, Harold Arthur *insurance agent, portfolio manager*
Rodgers, James Foster *insurance research executive, economist*
Southwell, Donald G. *insurance company executive*
Tyree, James C. *insurance company executive*
Vie, Richard Carl *insurance company executive*
Zucaro, Aldo Charles *insurance company executive*

### Darien
Bland, Robert S. *insurance company executive*

**Des Plaines**
Pannke-Smith, Peggy *insurance company executive*

**Galena**
Crandall, John Lynn *retired insurance company executive, consultant*

**Gilberts**
Barilich, Thomas Anthony *risk management consultant*

**Hinsdale**
Denton, Ray Douglas *insurance company executive*

**Itasca**
Gallagher, J. Patrick, Jr. *insurance company executive*

**Moline**
Middleton, Marc Stephen *corporate insurance risk manager*

**Naperville**
Desch, Theodore Edward *retired insurance company executive, lawyer*
Dombeck, Harold Arthur *insurance company executive*

**Northbrook**
Cruikshank, John W. III *insurance agent*
Liddy, Edward M. *insurance company executive*
McCabe, Michael J. (Mick) *insurance executive, lawyer*
Pike, Robert William *insurance company executive, lawyer*
Wilson, Thomas Joseph *insurance company executive*

**Park Ridge**
Ewald, Robert Frederick *insurance company executive, consultant*

**Rock Island**
Lardner, Henry Petersen (Peter Lardner) *insurance company executive*

**Skokie**
Hoopis, Harry Peter *insurance executive, entrepreneur*

**Springfield**
Dodge, Edward John *retired insurance company executive*
Simpson, William Arthur *insurance company executive*

## INDIANA

**Carmel**
Hohmann, James E. *insurance company executive*
Husman, Catherine Bigot *retired insurance company executive, consultant*
Prieur, C. James *insurance company executive*

**Columbus**
Osborn, DeVerle Ross *insurance company executive*

**Fort Wayne**
Dunsire, P(eter) Kenneth *insurance company executive*

**Indianapolis**
Boxer, Mark L. *healthcare insurance company executive*
Dorr, Marjorie W. *healthcare insurance company executive*
Faller, Keith *healthcare insurance company executive*
Gaunce, Michael Paul *insurance company executive*
Glasscock, Larry Claborn *health insurance company executive*
Lewis, Randall J. *healthcare insurance company executive*
Lytle, L(arry) Ben *insurance company executive, lawyer*
McCarthy, Harold Charles *retired insurance company executive*
McKinney, E. Kirk, Jr. *retired insurance company executive*
Nussbaum, Samuel *healthcare insurance company executive, medical educator*
Rosenblatt, Alice F. *healthcare insurance company executive*
Stocker, Michael Aubrey *health insurance company executive*
Watts, John S., Jr. *insurance company executive*

**Schererville**
Jarrett, Alexis *insurance agent, lawyer*

## IOWA

**Des Moines**
Brooks, Roger Kay *insurance company executive*
Gersie, Michael H. *insurance company executive*
Godlasky, Thomas C. *insurance company executive*
Griswell, J. Barry *insurance company executive*
Kalainov, Sam Charles *insurance company executive*
Kelley, Bruce Gunn *insurance company executive, lawyer*
Williams, Carl Chanson *insurance company executive*

**Oskaloosa**
Mangold, Archie Wayne, II, *insurance agent*

## KANSAS

**De Soto**
Strubbe, Thomas R. *insurance industry executive*

**Eudora**
Miller, David Groff *insurance agent*

## KENTUCKY

**Louisville**
Jones, David A., Jr. *insurance company executive*
LeClaire, Brian P. *health benefits company executive*
McCallister, Michael B. *insurance company executive*
McCormick, Steven Thomas *insurance company executive*
Rosky, Theodore Samuel *insurance company executive*

**Owensboro**
Webb, Otis D. *retired underwriter*

## LOUISIANA

**Kenner**
Kuebler, David Wayne *insurance company executive, private investigator*

**New Orleans**
Marks, Charles Dennery *insurance consultant*

**Shreveport**
Harbuck, Edwin Charles *insurance agent*

## MAINE

**Portland**
Buckley, Paul Richard, Sr. *insurance executive*
Candage, Howard Everett *insurance management consultant, agent, broker*

## MARYLAND

**Baltimore**
Goodman, William Richard *insurance adjusting company executive*
Hecht, Alan Dannenberg *insurance executive*
Tocco, Elaine Kay *insurance agent*

**Brandywine**
Jaffe, Morris Edward *insurance executive*

**Chester**
Dabich, Eli, Jr. *insurance company executive*

**Elkton**
Jasinski-Caldwell, Mary L. *insurance company executive*

**Mitchellville**
Ball, Robert M. *social security and health insurance specialist*

**Parkton**
Cummins, Paul Zach, II, *insurance company executive*

**Reisterstown**
Tirone, Barbara Jean *retired health insurance administrator*

## MASSACHUSETTS

**Boston**
Aborn, Foster Litchfield *insurance company executive*
Brown, Stephen Lee *retired insurance company executive*
Bunker, Beryl H. *retired insurance company executive, volunteer*
Condrin, J. Paul *insurance company executive*
Enfanto, Frank W. III *health insurance company executive*
Kelly, Edmund Francis *insurance company executive*
Morton, Edward James *insurance company executive*
Van Faasen, William C. *health insurance company executive*

**Duxbury**
Wangler, William Clarence *retired insurance company executive*

**Maynard**
Pastore, William M. *insurance company executive*

**Needham**
Rodman, Sumner *insurance company executive*

**North Attleboro**
Koussa, Harold Alan *insurance account executive*

**North Chatham**
O'Brien, Robert Emmet *insurance company executive*

**North Dighton**
Silvia, David Alan *insurance broker*

**Quincy**
Moran, James Joseph, Jr. *insurance company executive*

**South Orleans**
Hale, Margaret Smith *insurance company executive, educator*

**Springfield**
Burkett, Lawrence V. *retired insurance company executive, lawyer*
Gunton, Howard E. *insurance company executive*
Johnson, Robert Allison *life insurance company executive*
Reese, Stuart Harry *insurance company executive*

**Tewksbury**
Shea, William J. *former insurance company executive*

**Waltham**
Roosevelt, James, Jr. *insurance company executive, lawyer*

**Webster**
Fels, Gerald *insurance company executive*

**Wellesley**
Baker, Charles D. *health insurance company executive*

**West Hyannisport**
Gingold, George Norman *insurance company executive, lawyer*

**Worcester**
Angelini, Michael P. *insurance company executive*
Eppinger, Frederick H., Jr. *insurance company executive*

## MICHIGAN

**Detroit**
Schwartz, Michael Robinson *insurance company executive*
Whitmer, Richard E. *insurance company executive*

**Kalamazoo**
Curry, John Patrick *insurance company executive, management consultant*

**Lansing**
Arends, Herman Joseph *former insurance company executive*
Fisher, John W. *insurance company executive*
Looyenga, Roger L. *insurance company executive*

## MINNESOTA

**Bemidji**
Bridston, Paul Joseph *strategic management consultant*

**Coon Rapids**
Bordner, Patricia Anne *insurance agent, writer*

**Edina**
Anderson, Gregory Shane *insurance executive*

**Hibbing**
Calligan, William Dennis *retired life insurance company executive*

**Minneapolis**
Anderson, Richard H. *health insurance company executive, former air transportation executive*
Feldman, Nancy Jane *insurance company executive*
Keets, John David, Jr. *insurance company executive*
McGuire, William W. *health insurance company executive*
Munsell, William A. *healthcare insurance company executive*
Nicholson, Bruce J. *insurance company executive*
Turner, John Gosney *insurance company executive, director*

**Minnetonka**
Dapper, L. Robert *healthcare insurance company executive*
Los, Cornelis Albertus *risk analyst, economist, finance educator*
Rivet, Jeannine M. *insurance company executive*
Robbins, Orem Olford *insurance company executive*
Sheehy, Robert J. *insurance company executive*

**Owatonna**
Annexstad, Albert T. *insurance company executive*

**Saint Paul**
Benet, Jay S. *insurance company executive*
Johnson, James Erling *insurance executive*
Lipp, Robert I. *insurance company executive*
Jenkler, Robert L. *insurance company executive*
Yessman, Timothy *insurance company executive*
Zuraitis, Marita *insurance company executive*

## MISSISSIPPI

**Clinton**
Montgomery, Keith Norris, Sr. *insurance agent, military officer*

## MISSOURI

**Chesterfield**
Mirza, Azam A. *insurance company executive*

**Maryland Heights**
Buselmeier, Bernard Joseph *insurance company executive*

**Saint Louis**
Bryant, Donald L., Jr. *insurance and benefits company executive*
Mullens, William Reese *retired insurance company executive*

**Sikeston**
Cartner, David Steven *claims representative, retired military officer*

## NEBRASKA

**Holdrege**
Hendrickson, Bruce Carl *life insurance company executive*

**Omaha**
Hamburg, Marc D. *insurance company executive*
Haney, J. Terrence *retired insurance consultant*
Jetter, Arthur Carl, Jr. *insurance company executive*
Lechowicz, Lisa Marie *retired insurance company executive*
Neary, Daniel P. *insurance company executive*

## NEVADA

**Henderson**
Johnson, Joan Bray *insurance company consultant*

## NEW HAMPSHIRE

**Hanover**
Kemp, Karl Thomas *insurance company executive*

**Manchester**
Ehrlich, Charles Gordon *insurance company executive, lawyer*

**Rochester**
Dworkin, Gary Steven *insurance company executive*

## NEW JERSEY

**Branchville**
Murphy, Gregory E. *insurance company executive*

**Glen Rock**
Mc Elrath, Richard Elsworth *retired insurance company executive*

**Jersey City**
Coyne, Frank J. *insurance industry executive*

**Madison**
Parker, Henry Griffith III *insurance executive*

**New Vernon**
McCormack, John Joseph, Jr. *insurance company executive*

**Newark**
Banta, Vivian L. *insurance company executive*
Blount, Susan L. *insurance company executive, lawyer*
Carbone, Richard J. *insurance executive*
Marino, William J. *insurance executive*
Ryan, Arthur Frederick *insurance company executive*
Winters, Robert Cushing *insurance company executive*

**Paramus**
Crow, Lynne Campbell Smith *insurance company representative*

**Plainfield**
Krump, Paul J. *insurance company executive*

**Princeton**
Sandman, Peter M. *risk management consultant*

**Ridgewood**
O'Leary, Paul Gerard *retired insurance company executive*

**Short Hills**
MacKinnon, Malcolm D(avid) *retired insurance company executive*

**Spring Lake**
Bonhag, Thomas Edward *insurance company executive, financial planner, financial consultant*

**Warren**
Finnegan, John D. *insurance company executive*

**Whitehouse Station**
Fiscus, Philip Wayne *underwriter*

**Wyckoff**
Munson, William Leslie *insurance company executive*

## NEW MEXICO

**Albuquerque**
Liss, Norman Richard *insurance executive*
Roseman, Steven A. *insurance company executive, lawyer*
Wainio, Mark Ernest *insurance company consultant*

## NEW YORK

**Albany**
Cole, John Adam *insurance executive*

**Amityville**
Imbert, Richard Conrad *insurance company executive, real estate developer*

**Armonk**
Brown, Joseph W., Jr., (Jay Brown) *insurance company executive*
Dunton, Gary C. *insurance company executive*
Ferguson, Roger Walter, Jr. *reinsurance company executive, former bank executive*

**Ballston Spa**
Popham, Todd Gordon *insurance company executive*

**Bemus Point**
Ross, Roderic Henry *retired insurance company executive*

**Binghamton**
Best, Robert Mulvane *insurance company executive*

**Bronx**
Elkins, Alfred David *insurance company executive*

**Brooklyn**
Faison, Seth Shepard *retired insurance broker*

**Cobleskill**
Wilson, Lewis Lansing *insurance executive*

**Cohocton**
Sarfaty, Wayne Allen *insurance agent, financial planner*

**Dryden**
Baxter, Robert Banning *insurance company executive*

**Lindenhurst**
Hungerford, Gary A. *insurance executive, columnist, writer, editor*

**Long Island City**
Henrikson, C. Robert *insurance company executive*
Rein, Catherine Amelia *insurance company executive, lawyer*

**Merrick**
Cherry, Harold *insurance company executive*

**Mineola**
Miller, Loring Erik *insurance agent, broker*

**New Rochelle**
Leaf, Robert Jay *dental insurance consultant*

**New York**
Bartley, Matthew B. *insurance company executive*
Bensinger, Steven J. *insurance company executive*
Biggs, John Herron *retired insurance company executive*
Blevins, Jennifer Lynn *insurance company executive*
Cabiallavetta, Mathis *insurance company executive*
Callahan, Dennis S. *insurance company executive*
Campbell, Judith E. *retired insurance company executive*
Cherkasky, Michael G. *insurance company executive*
Clayton, Jon Kerry *insurance company executive*
Crystal, James William *insurance company executive*
Davis, Karen *insurance company executive, educator*
Dolan, Raymond Bernard *insurance company executive, director*
Flynn, William Joseph *insurance company executive*
Frenkel, Jacob Aharon *insurance company executive*
Harris, David Henry *retired life insurance company executive*
Hartwig, Robert Paul *insurance institute executive, economist*
Hildebrand, Phillip J. *insurance company executive*
Hohn, Harry George *retired insurance company executive, lawyer*
Hutchings, Peter Lounsbery *retired insurance company executive, director*
Kandarian, Steven A. *insurance company executive*
Kaplan, Keith Eugene *insurance company executive, lawyer*
Kaplan, Theodore Norman *insurance company executive*
Knapp, Amy K. *insurance company executive*
Lassiter, Phillip B. *insurance company executive*
Launer, Leland C., Jr. *insurance company executive*
Manning, Dennis J. *insurance company executive*
Martens, Erwin W. *risk management consultant*
Matthews, Edward E. *retired insurance company executive*
McCarthy, Gloria M *insurance company executive*
Melone, Joseph James *retired insurance company executive*
Moran, Thomas J. *insurance company executive*
Murray, Richard Maximilian *insurance company executive*
Piligian, Georgette A. *insurance company executive*
Pollock, Robert B. *insurance company executive*
Procope, Ernesta Gertrude *insurance company executive*
Remshard, John W. *insurance company executive*
Sandler, Robert Michael *insurance company executive*
Savage, Frank *insurance executive*
Schwartz, Robert George *retired insurance company executive*
Scott, Bertram *insurance company executive*
Sguerra, Jaime *insurance company executive*
Sievert, Frederick J. *insurance company executive*
Somers, John Arthur *insurance company executive*
Sproule, Michael E. *insurance company executive*
Sternberg, Seymour *insurance company executive*
Sullivan, Martin J. *insurance company executive*
Teleanu, Florin I. *risk management consultant, financial analyst*
Toppeta, William John *insurance company executive, lawyer*
Vidal, David Jonathan *insurance company executive, journalist*
Washington, Clarence Edward, Jr. *insurance company executive*
Weber, Lisa M. *insurance company executive*
Wendlandt, Gary E. *insurance company executive*
Wheeler, William J. *insurance company executive*
Willumstad, Robert B. *insurance company executive, retired bank executive*
Wintrob, Jay S. *insurance company executive*
Wisner, Frank George *insurance company executive, former ambassador*
Yalen, Gary N. *retired insurance company executive*

**Northport**
Miller, Philip John *insurance agent, consultant*

**Pound Ridge**
Bennett, Edward Henry *reinsurance executive*

**Saratoga Springs**
Ford, Dexter *retired insurance company executive*

**Scarsdale**
Decaminada, Joseph Pio *retired insurance company executive*

**Schenectady**
Murray, Edward Rock *insurance broker*

**Staten Island**
Gavrity, John Decker *retired insurance company executive*

**Syosset**
Kniffin, Paula Sichel *insurance sales executive*

**Yonkers**
Wolfson, Irwin M. *insurance company executive*

## NORTH CAROLINA

**Camden**
Hammond, Roy Joseph *reinsurance company executive*

**Chapel Hill**
Clark, Arthur Watts *insurance company executive*
Fine, J(ames) Allen *insurance company executive*
Szejniuk, Nathan M. *disaster preparedness coordinator, health care preparedness consultant*

**Winston Salem**
Beardsley, Charles Mitchell *retired insurance company executive*

## NORTH DAKOTA

**Grand Forks**
Wogaman, George Elsworth *insurance company executive, financial consultant*

## OHIO

**Amelia**
Campbell, John G. *insurance company executive*

**Canton**
Schauer, Thomas Alfred *insurance company executive*

**Chillicothe**
Copley, Cynthia Sue Love *insurance adjuster*

**Cincinnati**
Barrett, John F. *insurance company executive*
Horrell, Karen Holley *insurance company executive, lawyer*
Klein, Jerry Emanuel *insurance and financial planning executive*
Klinedinst, Thomas John, Jr. *insurance agency executive*
Lindner, Carl H. III *insurance company executive*
Lindner, Carl Henry, Jr. *insurance company executive, professional sports team executive*
Lindner, S. Craig (Stephen Craig Lindner) *insurance company executive*
Runk, Fred J. *retired insurance company executive*
Scheineson, Irwin Bruce *insurance and investment company executive*

**Cleveland**
Clapp, Kent W. *insurance company executive*
Lewis, Peter Benjamin *insurance company executive*
Renwick, Glenn M. *insurance company executive*

**Columbus**
Duryee, Harold Taylor *insurance consultant*
Jurgensen, William G. *insurance company executive*
Shisler, Arden L. *insurance and transportation company executive*

**Fairfield**
Carmichael, Dan R. *insurance company executive*

**Mayfield**
Forrester, W. Thomas, II, *insurance company executive*
Jarrett, Charles Elwood *insurance company executive, lawyer*

**Powell**
Emanuelson, James Robert *retired insurance company executive*

## OKLAHOMA

**Oklahoma City**
Case, Bill *insurance agent, state representative*
Ille, Bernard Glenn *insurance company executive, director*
Jenkins, Sherry L. *state insurance program administrator*
Schille, John R. *insurance company executive*

**Tulsa**
Hoe, Richard March *insurance and securities consultant, writer*

## OREGON

**Portland**
Galbraith, John Robert *insurance company executive*

## PENNSYLVANIA

**Bala Cynwyd**
Shepard, Geoffrey Carroll *insurance company executive*

**Berwyn**
McIntyre, James Owen *insurance executive*

**Bushkill**
Garretto, Leonard Anthony, Jr. *insurance company executive*

**Camp Hill**
Mead, James Matthew *insurance company executive*

**Elkins Park**
Hart, William C. *underwriter, educator, writer*

**Erie**
Garcia, Philip A. *insurance company executive*
Hirt, F. William *insurance company executive*
Ludrof, Jeffrey A. *insurance company executive*

**Harleysville**
Browne, Michael L. *insurance company executive*

**Hatboro**
Quigley, Robert Charles *insurance industry consultant*

**King Of Prussia**
Katz, Arnold Martin *insurance brokerage firm executive*
Volpe, Ralph Pasquale *retired insurance company executive*

**Newtown Square**
Staats, Dean Roy *retired reinsurance executive*

**Philadelphia**
Bell, Michael W. *insurance company executive*
Glass, Dennis Robert *insurance company executive*
Hanway, H. Edward *insurance company executive*
Kim, John Y. *insurance company executive*
Murabito, John *insurance company executive*
Stonecipher, David A. *insurance company*

**Pittsburgh**
Melani, Kenneth R. *insurance company executive*

**Ridgway**
Aiello, Gennaro C. *insurance company executive*

**Wayne**
Yoskin, Jon William, II, *insurance company executive*

## RHODE ISLAND

**Johnston**
Hurley, Brian J. *insurance company executive*
Subramaniam, Shivan Sivaswamy *insurance company executive*

**Lincoln**
DiMuccio, Robert A. *insurance company executive*

## SOUTH CAROLINA

**Columbia**
Averyt, Gayle Owen *retired insurance executive*

**Georgetown**
Schumaker, William Thomas *retired insurance company executive*

## SOUTH DAKOTA

**Aberdeen**
Stoia, Viorel G. *life underwriter*

## TENNESSEE

**Athens**
Trent, Henry Gibson, Jr. *insurance company executive, educator*

**Chattanooga**
Copeland, Floyd Dean *insurance company executive, lawyer*
Greving, Robert C. *insurance company executive*
Watjen, Thomas Ros *insurance company executive*

**Nashville**
Howell, John Floyd *insurance company executive*

**Seymour**
Steele, Ernest Clyde *retired insurance company executive*

## TEXAS

**Austin**
Mullen, Ron *insurance company executive*
Payne, Tyson Elliott, Jr. *retired insurance executive*
Watson, Brenda Bennett *insurance company executive*

**Dallas**
Cline, Bobby James *insurance company executive*
Madden, Teresa Darleen *insurance agency owner*
Rinne, Austin Dean *retired insurance company executive*
Weakley, Clare George, Jr. *insurance company executive, theologian, entrepreneur*

**Fort Worth**
Blackburn, Wyatt Douglas *insurance executive*
Mitchell, Robert Joseph *insurance executive*

**Galveston**
Moody, Robert Lee *insurance company executive*

**Hillsboro**
Haddaway, James David *retired insurance company official*

**Houston**
Couch, Jesse Wadsworth *retired insurance company executive*
Davis, Rex Lloyd *insurance company executive*
Dean, Robert Franklin *insurance company executive*
Hook, Harold Swanson *former management consulting executive*
Lindsey, John H. *insurance agency executive*
Lyons, Phillip Michael, Sr. *insurance accounting and real estate executive*
Morris, Stewart, Jr. *title insurance company executive*
Saraf, Sanjeev R. *safety and risk management consultant, researcher*
Way, Stephen L. *insurance company executive*

**Lake Jackson**
Elbert, James Peak *independent insurance agent, minister*

**Livingston**
Stovall, Jerry (Coleman Stovall) *insurance company executive*

**Mc Kinney**
McAndrew, Mark S. *insurance company executive*

**North Richland Hills**
Gedwed, William J. *insurance company executive*

**Plano**
Jensen, Ronald L. *insurance company executive*

**San Antonio**
Colyer, Kirk Klein *insurance executive, real estate investment executive*
Davis, Robert G. *insurance company executive*
Robles, Josue, Jr. *insurance company executive*
Wellberg, Edward Louis, Jr. *insurance company executive*

**Tyler**
Guin, Don Lester *insurance company executive*

## UTAH

**Ogden**
Buckner, Elmer La Mar *retired insurance company executive*

## VIRGINIA

**Chesterfield**
Tate, Wendy K. *risk management specialist*

**Glen Allen**
Kirshner, Alan I. *insurance company executive*
Rogal, Andrew L. *insurance company executive*

**Lynchburg**
McRorie, William Edward *retired insurance company executive*

**Norfolk**
Dungan, William Joseph, Jr. *insurance agent, educator, economist*

**Penhook**
Hahn, John William *retired insurance company executive*

**Richmond**
Fraizer, Michael D. *insurance company executive*

**Williamsburg**
Herrmann, Benjamin Edward *former insurance executive*

## WASHINGTON

**Bellevue**
Clay, Orson C. *insurance company executive, director*

**Newcastle**
Patulot, Jun J. R. *insurance company executive*

**Seattle**
Eigsti, Roger Harry *retired insurance company executive*

**Walla Walla**
Perry, Louis Barnes *retired insurance company executive*

**Woodland**
Hansen, Walter Eugene *insurance executive*

## WISCONSIN

**Madison**
Anderson, David R. *insurance company executive*
DuRose, Stanley Charles, Jr. *retired insurance company executive*
Eldridge, James Francis *insurance company executive, lawyer*
Larson, John David *insurance company executive, lawyer*
Pierce, Harvey R. *insurance company executive*
Post, Jeffrey H. *insurance company executive*
Waldo, Robert Leland *retired insurance company executive*

**Merrill**
Graham, Christopher A. *insurance company executive*
Whitburn, Gerald *insurance company executive*

**Milwaukee**
Johannes, Kay L. *insurance company executive*
Piehler, Barbara F. *insurance company executive*
Trytek, David Douglas *insurance company executive*

**Nashotah**
Vincent, Norman L. *retired insurance company executive*

**Stevens Point**
Schuh, Dale R. *insurance company executive*

## WYOMING

**Cheyenne**
Moore, Dan Sterling *insurance executive, sales trainer*

**Teton Village**
Conrad, Donald Glover *insurance executive*

## CANADA

### NOVA SCOTIA

**North Sydney**
Nickerson, Jerry Edgar Alan *business executive*

### ONTARIO

**Etobicoke**
Howe, James Tarsicius *retired insurance company executive*

**Toronto**
D'Alessandro, Dominic *financial executive*

## BERMUDA

**Pembroke**
Stempel, Ernest Edward *insurance executive*

## HONG KONG

**Hong Kong**
Tse, Edmund Sze-Wing *insurance company executive*

## ISRAEL

**Gan Shlomo**
Tritter, Richard Paul *risk management consultant*

## NETHERLANDS

**The Hague**
Shepard, Donald J. *insurance company executive*

## SOUTH AFRICA

**Cape Town**
Cleary, Sean Michael *risk management executive*

## ADDRESS UNPUBLISHED

Adam, John, Jr *insurance company executive emeritus*
Ahn, Dong H *insurance company executive*
Akhoury, Ravi *insurance company executive*
Akridge, Steven L. *risk management consultant*
Armstrong, F(redric) Michael *retired insurance company executive, consultant*
Becker, JoAnn Elizabeth *retired insurance company executive*
Bergquist, Sandra Lee *claims consultant*
Bertrand, Frederic Howard *retired insurance company executive*
Borda, Richard Joseph *retired insurance company executive*
Boscia, Jon Andrew *insurance company executive*
Briggs, Philip *insurance company executive*
Brown, C Timothy *insurance company executive*
Burns, Carroll Dean *insurance company executive*
Chilvers, Derek *insurance company executive*
Clark, Edgar Sanderford *insurance broker, consultant*
Clemens, Alvin Honey *insurance company executive*
Coleman, Ronald Lee *insurance claims executive*
Conroy, Thomas Francis *insurance company consultant*
Cooper, Charles Gordon *retired insurance company executive*
Countryman, Gary Lee *retired insurance company executive*
D'Alessandro, David Francis *insurance company executive*
D'Allesandro, David F. *insurance company executive*
DiPiazza, Michael Charles *insurance company executive*
Duckworth, Tara Ann *insurance company executive*
Earls, Kevin Gerard *insurance company executive*
Emek, Sharon Helene *risk management consultant*

Engel, Philip L. *retired insurance company executive*
Fey, John Theodore *retired insurance company executive*
Fibiger, John Andrew *life insurance company executive*
Fisher, Russell D *insurance company executive*
Foley, William Patrick, II, *title insurance company executive*
Goulet, Charles Ryan *retired insurance company executive*
Greenberg, Maurice Raymond (Hank Greenberg) *retired insurance company executive*
Heard, William Robert *retired insurance company executive*
Hinds, Edward Dee *insurance and investment professional, financial planner*
Impellizzeri, Anne Elmendorf *insurance company executive, non-profit executive*
Jacobson, James Bassett *retired insurance company executive, retired savings and loan association executive*
Johnson, Glendon E. *retired insurance company executive*
Jones, Frank Joseph *insurance company executive*
Jones, Lupe Sirena *insurance agent*
Kelley, Kevin H. *insurance company executive*
Khan, Ahmed Mohiuddin *insurance company executive*
Kilborn, Toni Sweatt *insurance agent, consultant*
Lacey, Cloyd Eugene *retired insurance company executive*
Ladd, Joseph Carroll *retired insurance company executive*
Langer, Ray Fritz *retired insurance executive*
Leatherdale, Douglas West *insurance company executive*
Lederman, Ira Seth *insurance company executive, lawyer*
Maatman, Gerald Leonard *insurance company executive*
Maginn, John Leo *retired insurance company executive*
Maloney, Therese Adele *insurance company executive*
Mathieson, Garrett Alfred *insurance brokerage executive*
McAneny, Deborah H. *insurance company executive*
McGavick, Michael S. *former insurance and financial services company executive*
McKenna, Terence Patrick *retired insurance company executive*
McLaughlin, Michael John *retired insurance company executive*
Metcalf, Wayne C. III *retired insurance company executive*
Moses, Michael James *insurance company executive, small business owner*
Moynahan, John Daniel, Jr. *retired insurance executive*
Mutz, Gregory Thomas *insurance company executive*
Nagler, Stewart Gordon *retired insurance company executive*
Newman, Steven Harvey *insurance company executive, director*
Norris, Darell Forest *retired insurance company executive*
O'Hare, Dean Raymond *retired insurance company executive, director*
Olsen, David Alexander *insurance executive*
Papa, Vincent T. *insurance company executive*
Pearson, Paul Holding *insurance company executive*
Peters, Douglas Alan *risk management consultant*
Porter, Dixie Lee *insurance company executive, consultant*
Purvis, George Frank, Jr. *life insurance company executive*
Redmond, Arthur J. *insurance company executive*
Resnick, Myron J. *retired insurance company executive, lawyer*
Rich, Bradford Whitman *retired insurance executive, lawyer*
Rockwood, Frederick Whitney *insurance company executive*
Rodino, Vincent Louis *insurance company executive*
Romasco, Robert G. *insurance company executive*
Rowell, Lester John, Jr. *retired insurance company executive*
Ryan, James *insurance company executive*
Sanders, Franklin D. *retired insurance company executive*
Shrembek, Carol Rose *claims consultant*
Smith, Floyd Leslie *insurance company executive*
Smith, Howard I. *former insurance company executive*
Snyder, William Burton *insurance company executive*
Soltz, Judith E. *insurance company executive, retired lawyer*
Steadman, Paul Willis *insurance company executive*
Stewart, Gordon Curran *insurance association executive*
Strong, John David *insurance company executive*
Tringale, Anthony Rosario *insurance company executive*
Underhill, Jacob Berry III *retired insurance company executive*
Van Houten, James Forester *former insurance company chief executive, educator, consultant*
Vasholz, Lothar Alfred *retired insurance company executive*
Viscardi, Peter G. *risk management and environmental affairs executive*
Volk, Austin N. *retired insurance company executive*
Wahweah, Linda McNeil *insurance agent, writer*
Weber, John Walter *insurance company executive*
Wentz, Sidney Frederick *insurance company executive, foundation administrator*
Westervelt, James Joseph *retired insurance company executive*
Whiteley, Benjamin Robert *retired insurance company executive*
Williams, Arthur L., Jr. *retired insurance company executive*
Wills, William Ridley, II, *retired insurance company executive, historian*

Zupsic, Matthew Michael *insurance company executive*

# FINANCE: INVESTMENT SERVICES

## UNITED STATES

### ALABAMA

**Birmingham**
Comer, Donald III *investment company executive*
Morgan, Allen B., Jr. *securities executive*
Tucker, Thomas James *retired investment company executive*

**Montgomery**
Blount, Winton Malcolm III *investment executive*

### ALASKA

**Anchorage**
Jay, Christopher Edward *stockbroker*

### ARIZONA

**Phoenix**
Franke, William Augustus *investor*
Stern, Richard David *investment company executive*
Taylor, Elizabeth Jane *investment advisor, real estate company executive, marketing executive*

**Scottsdale**
Doede, John Henry *investment company executive*
Getz, Bert Atwater *investment company executive*

**Tucson**
Lomicka, William Henry *investor*
Schannep, John Dwight *brokerage house executive*

### ARKANSAS

**Little Rock**
Good, Mary Lowe (Mrs. Billy Jewel Good) *investment company executive, educator*
Light, Jo Knight *stockbroker*
Whiteside, Charles B. III *investment company executive*

### CALIFORNIA

**Alamo**
Bouret, Pierre George *brokerage house executive*

**Anaheim**
Frank, Judith Ann (Jann Frank) *retired entrepreneur, small business owner*

**Antioch**
Archuleta, Keith Anthony *entrepreneur, business and management consultant*

**Atherton**
Sollman, George Henry *venture capitalist*
Walsh, William Desmond *investor*

**Belvedere Tiburon**
Rayner, Arno Alfred *investment company executive, consultant*

**Berkeley**
Blume, James Beryl *investment advisor*

**Beverly Hills**
Covitz, Carl D. *investment company executive, federal official, state official*
Evans, Louise *investor, retired psychologist*
Gordy, Berry *entrepreneur, film producer, recording industry executive*
Gores, Tom T. *investment company executive*
Kerkorian, Kirk *investor, former motion picture company executive, consultant*
Seidel, Joan Broude *securities dealer, investment advisor*

**Camarillo**
Sullivan, Michael Evan *investment company executive*

**Carmel**
Hamilton, Beverly Lannquist *investment executive*
Lockton, David Ballard *entrepreneur, information technology executive*

**Coronado**
Smith, Albert Cromwell, Jr. *investment company executive, writer*

**Costa Mesa**
Kiang, Assumpta (Amy Kiang) *brokerage house executive*

**Fresno**
Dauer, Donald Dean *investment company executive*

**Irvine**
Jones, Joie Pierce *entrepreneur, educator, acoustician, writer*

**La Jolla**
Stone, Donald Diamond *investment and sales executive*

**Los Altos**
Carsten, Jack Craig *venture capitalist*

**Los Angeles**
Angeloff, Dann Valentino *brokerage house executive*
Ashwell, Rachel *entrepreneur, interior designer*
Barrack, Thomas J., Jr. *real estate investor, lawyer*
Bernstein, Arthur Harold *venture capital executive*
Binder, Gordon M. *venture capitalist*
Gores, Alec E. *venture capitalist*
Holly, Krisztina J. *entrepreneur, academic administrator*
Hurt, William Holman *investment management company executive*
Larkin, Thomas Ernest, Jr. *investment management company executive*
Leff, Daniel V. *venture capitalist*
Mann, Nancy Louise (Nancy Louise Robbins) *entrepreneur*
Nogales, Luis Guerrero *investment company executive*
Reed, George Ford, Jr. *investment executive*
Saban, Haim *investment company executive, television producer*
Trumbull, Stephen Michael *entrepreneur, musician*

**Menlo Park**
Bowes, William K., Jr. *venture capital investment company executive*
Copeland, Eric *venture capital company executive*
Davies, Paul Lewis III *venture capitalist*
Doerr, John (L. John Doerr) *venture capitalist*
Fenton, Noel John *venture capitalist*
Joy, Bill (William Nelson Joy) *venture capitalist, former computer software company executive*
Khosla, Vinod *investment company executive*
Kramlich, C(harles) Richard (Dick) *venture capitalist*
Lucas, Donald Leo *investor*
Lynch, Charles Allen *investment company executive, director*
Marquardt, David F. *venture capitalist*
McNamee, Roger B. *venture capitalist, musician*
Perkins, Tom (Thomas James Perkins) *venture capital company executive*
Roberts, George R. *investment banking company executive*
Wolfson, Mark Alan *investor, educator, dean*

**Newport Beach**
Durand, Robert Matthew *investment company executive*
Thorp, Edward Oakley *investment management company executive*

**Oakland**
Al Malik, Amir Isa *entrepreneur, consultant, musician*
Fletcher, Mark *entrepreneur*

**Orange**
Tuggle, Francis Douglas *entrepreneur, consultant, management educator, scientist*

**Palo Alto**
Avis, Gregory M. *venture capitalist*
Breyer, James William *venture capitalist*
Haque, Promod *venture capitalist*
Kawasaki, Guy *venture capitalist, investment banker, evangelist, entrepreneur, blog writer, writer*

**Palos Verdes Estates**
Mennis, Edmund Addi *investment management consultant*

**Pasadena**
Arnott, Robert Douglas *investment company executive*
Fredericks, Ward Arthur *venture capitalist*
Villanueva, Daniel L., Jr. *investment company executive*

**Rancho Santa Fe**
Kessler, A. D. *investment advisor, consultant, commentator*

**Roseville**
Grant, Barbara *venture capitalist*

**San Diego**
Brandes, Charles H. *investment company executive*
Dunn, David Joseph *investment company executive*
Ellsworth, Robert Fred *investment executive, former government official*
Wadlington, W. M. *retired commodity futures trader, financial engineer*

**San Francisco**
Buckner, John Knowles *investor*
Draper, William Henry III *venture capitalist*
Dunn, Patricia Cecile *investment company executive*
Hagenbuch, John Jacob *investor*
Halliday, John Meech *investment company executive*
Hellman, F(rederick) Warren *investor*
James, George Barker, II, *investment company executive*
Levine, Alison *entrepreneur, leadership development consultant, adventurer*
Mahoney, Michael James *investment company executive*
Marduel, Alix *venture capitalist*
Nedelman, Adam *entrepreneur*
Redo, David Lucien *investment company executive*
Rock, Arthur *venture capitalist*
Rowen, Harvey Allen *investment company executive*
Schwab, Charles R. *brokerage house executive*
Shansby, John Gary *investor*
Siebel, Kenneth *investment advisor*
Steyer, Thomas Fahr *investment company executive*
Thiel, Peter A. *investment company executive*
Turner, Ross James *investment company executive*
Weisel, Thomas W. *investment company executive*
Winblad, Ann *investment company executive*

**San Mateo**
Krikorian, Blake *entrepreneur, consumer electronics company executive*

Strohm, David *venture capitalist*

**Santa Ana**
Martinez, Rueben *entrepreneur*

**Santa Barbara**
Bartlett, James Lowell III *investment company executive*
Emmeluth, Bruce Palmer *investment company executive, venture capitalist*
Lovelace, Jon (Jonathan Bell Lovelace) *investment management company executive*

**Santa Clara**
Dave, Tushar A. *Indo-US venture capital company executive*
Dham, Vinod K. *Indo-US venture capitalist company executive*

**Santa Monica**
Calacanis, Jason McCabe *internet entrepreneur, blogger*
Casso, Jesse, Jr. *investment company executive, investment advisor*
Lederman, Bruce Randolph *investment company executive, retired lawyer*
Unterman, Thomas *venture capitalist, lawyer*

**Sausalito**
Apatoff, Michael John *entrepreneur*

**Tarzana**
Lauter, James Donald *retired stockbroker*
Neece, Olivia Helene Ernst *investment company executive, consultant*

**Thousand Oaks**
Gregory, Calvin *real estate investor*

**Torrance**
Enright, Stephanie Veselich *investment company executive, financial consultant*

**Valencia**
Wolfson, Jeremy *investment advisor*

**Westlake Village**
Feiman, Thomas E. *investment company executive*

**Woodside**
Fisher, Kenneth Lawrence *investment management firm executive*

**COLORADO**

**Arvada**
Glodava, Mila Garcia *entrepreneur, educator, consultant*
Weitzel, Ginger M. *entrepreneur, critical care nurse*

**Aurora**
Ton, Paul *investor, educator*

**Boulder**
Mehalchin, John Joseph *entrepreneur, finance company executive*

**Cherry Hills Village**
Van Loucks, Mark Louis *venture capitalist, financial planner*

**Denver**
Black, Gary D. *investment company executive*
Case, Steve (Stephen M. Case) *healthcare investment company executive, former media and entertainment company executive*
Eppler, Jerome Cannon *investment advisor*
Scheid, Steven L. *investment company executive*
Wagner, Judith Buck *investment firm executive*

**Englewood**
Guggenheim-Boucard, Alan Andre Albert Paul Edouard *international consultant*

**Evergreen**
Jackson, William Richard *entrepreneur*

**Grand Junction**
Skogen, Haven Sherman *investment company executive*

**Littleton**
Lode, Trygve Tennyson *entrepreneur, actor*
Sutton, Robert Edward *investment company executive*

**CONNECTICUT**

**Collinsville**
Whitney, Carol Marie *securities trader*

**Darien**
Koontz, Carl Lennis, II, *investment counselor*

**Fairfield**
Gad, Lance Stewart *investment advisor, lawyer, private investor*

**Greenwich**
Duff, Philip *investment company executive*
Ford, William E. *investment company executive*
Ganek, David Kent *investor*
Jones, Paul Tudor, II, *investment executive*
Lampert, Edward *investment company executive*
Marram, Ellen R. *investment company executive*
Pados, Frank John, Jr. *investment company executive*
Reeves, Michael Spencer *investment company executive*
Schneider, John Arnold *investor*
Tournillon, Nicholas Brady *investment company executive*
Winkler, Charles Howard *investment company executive*

**Hartford**
Giamalis, John N *investment company executive*
Marra, Thomas M *investment company executive*
O'Keefe, James William, Jr. *investment manager and banker*
Znamierowski, David M *investment company executive*

**Litchfield**
Booth, John Thomas *private investor*
Sherva, Dennis G. *retired investment company executive*

**New Canaan**
Bisbee, Gerald Elftman, Jr. *investment company executive*
Pike, William Edward *retired investment company executive*
Stadther, Michael Jon *entrepreneur, writer, publisher*

**Norwalk**
Hathaway, Carl Emil *investment company executive*

**Sharon**
Learsy, Raymond J. *private investor*

**Simsbury**
Borges, Francisco Lopes *venture capitalist*

**South Kent**
Keehner, Michael Arthur Miller *investment banking executive*

**Southport**
Wilbur, E. Packer *investment company executive*

**Stamford**
Cohen, Steven A. *investment company executive*
Hawley, Frank Jordan, Jr. *venture capital executive*
La Penta, Robert Vincent *venture capitalist*

**West Hartford**
Bigler, Harold Edwin, Jr. *retired investment company executive*

**Westport**
O'Keefe, John David *brokerage house executive*
Rudd, Nicholas *investor, consultant*
Samberg, Arthur J. (Art Samberg) *investment company executive*
Stewart, Martha Kostyra *entrepreneur, lecturer, author*
Walton, Alan George *venture capitalist*

**DELAWARE**

**Millsboro**
Lasher, Hiram Nelson *entrepreneur, consultant*

**Wilmington**
Kalil, James, Sr. *investment executive*

**DISTRICT OF COLUMBIA**

**Washington**
Ansary, Cyrus A. *investment company executive, lawyer*
Applegarth, Paul Vollmer *investment and development executive*
Burris, Howard L. *investment company executive*
Coreth, Joseph Herman *investment advisor*
Darman, Richard *investor, former federal official*
Farr, Michael Keogh *investment company executive*
Fisher, Robert Dale *stockbroker, retired naval officer*
Furash, Edward Elliott *investment company executive, banker, educator, writer, theater producer*
Gibson, Paul Raymond *international trade and investment development company executive*
Gilburne, Miles R. *venture capitalist*
Hartwell, Stephen *investment company executive*
Johnson, Sheila Crump *entrepreneur*
Kent, Jill Elspeth *entrepreneur, art appraiser, lawyer*
McCaul, Elizabeth *investment advisor, former state agency administrator*
McGreevey, Lisa S. *investment company executive*
Mosbacher, Robert A. *investment company executive*
Nordlinger, Gerson *investor*
Powell, Michael Kevin *investment company executive, former federal official*
Selin, Ivan *entrepreneur*
Shrier, Adam Louis *investment company executive, consultant*
Simon, John A. *investment company executive*
Tanous, Peter Joseph *investment advisor*
Van de Water, Mark E. *investment company executive*
Wheeler, Thomas Edgar *private equity executive*

**FLORIDA**

**Alva**
Darlow, George Anthony Gratton *investor*

**Boca Raton**
Barbarosh, Milton Harvey *merchant banking executive*
Batmasian, Marta Tersakian *investment company owner*
Bell, Marc H. *investment company executive*
Chestnov, Richard Franklin *private investor*
Land, Judith Broten *stockbroker*

**Boynton Beach**
Allison, Dwight Leonard, Jr. *investor*
Frankenberger, Bertram, Jr. *investor, consultant*

**Coral Gables**
Nunez-Portuondo, Ricardo *investment company executive*

Steinberg, Alan Wolfe *investment company executive*

**Fort Lauderdale**
Berrard, Steven R. *investment company executive, former automotive retail company executive*
Horvitz, David W. *investment company executive*
Huizenga, H. Wayne *entrepreneur, professional sports team executive*
Knight, Kenneth Vincent *entrepreneur, venture capitalist*
Sanders, Howard *investment company executive*
Vladem, Paul Jay *investment advisor*

**Fort Myers**
Pouliot, Assunta Gallucci *retired business school owner, director, consultant*

**Gainesville**
Oliver, Robert Bruce *retired investment company executive*

**Hobe Sound**
Parker, H. Lawrence *investor, retired rancher, retired investment banker*

**Jacksonville**
Monsky, John Bertrand *investment company executive*
Schultz, Frederick Henry *investor, former government official*

**Jupiter**
Kulok, William Allan *entrepreneur, venture capitalist*

**Lake Placid**
Viater, John Ronald *investment company executive*

**Marco Island**
Pettersen, Kjell Will *securities trader, consultant*

**Miami**
Arison, Shari *investment company executive*
Batcheller, Joe Ann *entrepreneur*
Dorion, Robert Charles *entrepreneur, investor*
Ferré, Maurice Antonio *entrepreneur*

**Naples**
Fogg, Joseph Graham III *investment company executive*
Frantzen, Henry Arthur *retired investment company executive*

**North Palm Beach**
Dreyfoos, Alexander W., Jr. *investor, research scientist*

**Palm Beach**
Bagby, Joseph Rigsby *financial investor*
Johnson, Theodore Mebane *brokerage house executive*
McCarter, Thomas Nesbitt III *investment company executive, consultant*
Quick, Thomas Clarkson *brokerage house executive*

**Palm Beach Gardens**
Kleinberg, Lawrence H. *investor, consultant*
Mergler, H. Kent *investment counselor*

**Pompano Beach**
Grossman, Daniel V *investor*
Rifenburgh, Richard Philip *investment company executive*

**Punta Gorda**
Presley, Brian *investment company executive*

**Saint Petersburg**
Emerson, William Allen *retired investment company executive*
James, Thomas A. *investment company executive*
Nichols, Katie *investment company executive*
Short, James F. *investment company executive*

**Sarasota**
Balliett, John William *entrepreneur, real estate company executive*

**Tampa**
Hanford, Agnes Rutledge *retired investment advisor*
Schultz, Barbara Marie *investment advisor*
Sigety, Charles Birge *investment company executive*

**Tierra Verde**
Gaffney, Thomas Francis *private investor*

**Village Of Golf**
Birle, James Robb *investor*

**West Palm Beach**
Rhoads, B. Eric *entrepreneur, artist*

**GEORGIA**

**Atlanta**
Banks, Marvin R., Jr. *investment company executive*
Green, Holcombe Tucker, Jr. *investment company executive*
Keough, Donald Raymond *investment company executive, former beverage company executive*
McMahon, Donald Aylward *investor, corporate director*
Mitchell, Stephen Milton *investment company executive*
Roberts, Thomasene Blount *entrepreneur*
Wheeler, Chris D. *investment company executive*

**Austell**
Orr, Zellie *entrepreneur, educator, writer, researcher*

**Columbus**
Diaz-Verson, Salvador, Jr. *investment advisor*

**Cumming**
Drew, Paul S. *entrepreneur*

**Marietta**
Lee, Raymond William III *institutional stockbroker*

**Saint Simons Island**
Turbidy, John Berry *investor, management consultant*

**HAWAII**

**Hilo**
Dinges, Richard Allen *entrepreneur*

**Honolulu**
Cooke, Samuel Alexander *retired brokerage house executive*
Haight, Warren Gazzam *investor*
Lee, Lorrin L. *internet marketing entrepreneur, architect, writer*
Leyden, Michael Joseph, II, (Lei Jie Ming) *entrepreneur, writer*

**Kaneohe**
Talbert, Geal Fukumoto *investment representative*

**ILLINOIS**

**Alton**
Greenwood, John E. *investment advisor*

**Arlington Heights**
Leon, Edward *investor*

**Chicago**
Barr, John W. *investment company executive, foundation administrator*
Bergonia, Raymond David *venture capitalist*
Block, Philip Dee III *retired investment company executive*
Brodsky, William J. *investment company executive*
Carey, Charles P. *commodities exchange executive*
Case, Donni Marie *investment company executive*
Chaleff, Carl Thmas *investment company executive*
Claeys, Jerome Joseph III *investment company executive*
Cloonan, James Brian *investment company executive*
Colker, David A. *stock exchange executive*
Cressey, Bryan Charles *venture capitalist*
Crown, James Schine *investment company executive*
Cupps, Andrew S. *investment company executive*
Dan, Bernard W. *commodities exchange executive*
Donohue, Craig S. *mercantile exchange executive*
Duffy, Terrence A. *mercantile exchange executive*
Fossett, Steven (J. Steven Fossett) *retired investor, adventurer*
Gilbert, Debbie Rose *entrepreneur*
Goldstein, William A. *investment counsel*
Gorchow, Bruce D. *investment company executive*
Gordon, James A. *investment company executive*
Griffin, Kenneth C. *investment company executive*
Herron, David A. *stock exchange executive*
Hickey, Jerome Edward *investment company executive*
Hobson, Mellody *investment company executive*
Kelly, Arthur Lloyd *investment company executive*
Kneen, John W. *venture capitalist*
Leszinske, William O. *investment company executive*
Lurie, Ann LaSalle *investment company executive, foundation administrator*
Marcovici, Michael *investment company executive*
Miner, Thomas Hawley *entrepreneur*
Oliver, Harry Maynard, Jr. *retired brokerage house executive*
Osborn, William A. *investment company executive*
Palumbo, Michael *investment company executive*
Phillips, Don *investment research company executive*
Pritzker, Penny *investor*
Renslow, Charles George *entrepreneur*
Rogers, John W., Jr. *investment company executive*
Rosenberg, Sheli Z. *investment company executive*
Rutledge, Edward K. *mortgage broker*
Shuman, Ann *investment company executive*
Slansky, Jerry William *investment company executive*
Stearns, Neele Edward, Jr. *investment company executive*
Underwood, Robert Leigh *venture capitalist*
Vroman, Kendal *investment company executive*
Walter, Mark R. *investment company executive*
Wasendorf, Russell R., Sr. *brokerage house executive*
Weinberg, David B. *investor*
Weiner, Gerald Arne *stockbroker*
Whitney, Kent R.E. *securities trader*
Wilhelm, David C. *investment company executive*
Wilmouth, Robert K. *commodities trader*

**Decatur**
Decker, Charles Richard *investment company executive, educator*

**Deerfield**
Howell, George Bedell *investment company executive*

**Highland Park**
Uhlmann, Frederick Godfrey *securities trader*

**Hinsdale**
Peckenpaugh, Robert Earl *investment advisor*

**Itasca**
Balasa, Mark Edward *investment consultant*

**Lake Forest**
Young, Ronald Faris *commodities trader*

**Lisle**
Skweres, Thomas W. *entrepreneur, writer, poet, investor, consultant, advertising executive*

**Naperville**
Calamos, John Peter, Sr. *brokerage house executive*
Penisten, Gary Dean *entrepreneur*
Vanagas, Rimantas (Ray) Andrius (Ray Vanagas) *entrepreneur, real estate developer, real estate company executive*

**Northbrook**
Colburn, David Dunton *investment advisor*
Edelson, Ira J. *venture capitalist*

**Oak Brook**
Spohr, Earl Clyde *retired investment advisor, retired military officer*

**Oakbrook Terrace**
Tang, George Chickchee *investment company executive*

**Park Ridge**
Albert, Elizabeth Franz (Mrs. Henry B. Albert) *investor, artist, conservationist*

**River Forest**
Wirsching, Charles Philipp, Jr. *retired brokerage house executive, securities trader*

**Riverwoods**
Hochschild, Roger C. *investment company executive*

**Vernon Hills**
Krasny, Michael P. *investment company executive*

**Westmont**
Warner, H. Ty *entrepreneur, manufacturing executive*

**Wheaton**
Back, Robert Wyatt *investment company executive, pharmaceutical executive, consultant*

**Willow Springs**
Jashel, Larry Steven (L. Steven Rose) *entrepreneur, media consultant*

**Wilmette**
Albright, Townsend Shaul *brokerage house executive, consultant*

**INDIANA**

**Bloomington**
Kuratko, Donald F. *entrepreneur, educator, consultant*

**Evansville**
Brill, Alan Richard *entrepreneur*
Frary, Charles O., III, (Chuck Frary) *venture capitalist*

**Fort Wayne**
Herrick, Mark Anthony *entrepreneur*

**Greenwood**
Grube, Elizabeth *investment company executive*

**Indianapolis**
Sheehan, Kevin Edward *venture capitalist*

**West Lafayette**
Phillips, Terry LeMoine *investment advisor*

**IOWA**

**Bettendorf**
Rathje, James Lee *broker*

**Des Moines**
Pappajohn, John G. *venture capitalist*

**KANSAS**

**Holton**
Cripe, Elizabeth Ann (Betty Cripe) *investment company executive*

**Shawnee Mission**
Braude, Michael *commodities trader, researcher*

**Topeka**
Hedrick, Lois Jean *investment company executive, state official*

**KENTUCKY**

**Bowling Green**
Buntzman, Gabriel Franklin *investor, educator*

**Louisville**
Saunders, Robert Samuel *venture capitalist*

**Murray**
Boston, Betty Lee *investment company executive, financial consultant, financial planner*

**LOUISIANA**

**Monroe**
Hawley, Jeffrey Lance *investments executive, accountant*

**New Orleans**
Dahlberg, Carl Fredrick, Jr. *entrepreneur*
Doley, Harold Emanuel, Jr. *securities company executive*
Flower, Walter Chew III *investment counselor*

**Ruston**
Marbury, Virginia Lomax *insurance and investment executive*

**Shreveport**
Makishi, Yasuko *securities trader, writer*

**MAINE**

**Bryant Pond**
Conary, David Arlan *investment company executive*

**MARYLAND**

**Baltimore**
Berghuis, Brian *investment company executive*
Bowman, Donald Eugene *investment advisor*
Brown, Eddie C. *investment company executive*
Curley, John Francis, Jr. *mutual fund executive*
Himelfarb, Richard Jay *investment company executive*
Riepe, James Sellers *investment company executive*
Roche, George Augustine *investment management executive*

**Bethesda**
Allmon, Charles W. *investment advisor*
Biddle, Albert George Wilkinson, III, (Jack Biddle) *venture capitalist*
Koonce, Calvin Scott *brokerage firm executive, physicist*
Meakem, Carolyn Soliday *investment executive, financial planner, money manager, consultant*

**Bowie**
Gourdine-Tyson, Natachia *investment company executive, writer*

**Columbia**
Moore, Darla D. *investment company executive*

**Hagerstown**
Baer, John Metz *entrepreneur*

**Lutherville Timonium**
Cappiello, Frank Anthony, Jr. *investment advisor*

**Rockville**
Jacques, Joseph William *investment advisor*

**Towson**
McManus, Walter Leonard *brokerage house executive*

**MASSACHUSETTS**

**Acton**
Boghani, Ashok Balvantrai *entrepreneur, management consultant*

**Belmont**
Lloyd, Boardman *investment company executive*

**Beverly**
Holberton, Philip Vaughan *entrepreneur, educator*

**Boston**
Bennett, George Frederick *retired investment company executive*
Benson, James M. *investment company executive*
Beyerl, Scott Alan *investment company executive*
Boden, Mark Emmanual *investment company executive, investment advisor*
Bressler, Richard J. *investment company executive, former entertainment company executive*
Cantella, Vincent Michele *securities trader, director*
Carey, John Andrew *investment company executive*
Curran, Michael J. *stock exchange executive*
de Burlo, Comegys Russell, Jr. *investment company executive, educator, retired treasurer*
Ebsworth, William Robert *investment company executive*
El-Erian, Mohamed A. *investment manager*
Estin, Hans Howard *retired brokerage house executive*
Gononsky, Edwin O. O. *investment broker*
Haldeman, Ed (Charles Edgar Haldeman Jr.) *investment company executive*
Johnson, Abigail Pierrepont *investment company executive*
Johnson, Edward Crosby, III, (Ned Johnson) *investment company executive*
Jonas, Stephen P. *investment company executive*
Lange, Harry W. *investment company executive*
Lee, David Stoddart *retired investment company executive*
McColgan, Ellyn *investment company executive*
McCullen, Joseph T., Jr. *venture capitalist*
Morby, Jacqueline *venture capitalist*
Morrison, Gordon Mackay, Jr. *investment company executive*
Morton, William Gilbert, Jr. *stock exchange executive*
Oates, William Armstrong, Jr. *investment company executive*
Peckham, John Munroe III *investment executive, author, lecturer*
Pozen, Robert Charles *investment company executive*
Price, Steven *venture capitalist, communications executive, lawyer*
Scott, Black *investment company executive*
Voss, Peter S. *investment company executive*
Waite, Charles Prescott *entrepreneur*

**Cambridge**
Alexander, Seth *investment company executive*
Anquetil, Patrick Armond *investment company executive, researcher*
Goldberg, Marc Evan *biotechnology venture capitalist*

**Carlisle**
Fohl, Timothy *investment company executive*

**Concord**
Schiller, Pieter Jon *retired venture capital executive*
Wickfield, Eric Nelson *investment company executive*

**Manchester**
Porter, Henry Homes, Jr. *investor*

**Medford**
Goldberg, Pamela Winer *entrepreneur, educator*

**Newton**
Saffran, Kalman *entrepreneur, venture capitalist*

**Pepperell**
Holmes, Jean Louise *real estate investor, humanities educator*

**Prides Crossing**
Crate, Darrell W. *investment company executive, political organization administrator*

**Siasconset**
Albani, Thomas J. *investor*

**South Dartmouth**
Greene, William Caswell *investment company executive*

**Southborough**
Chryssis, George Christopher *entrepreneur*

**Taunton**
Ricciardi, Louis Michael *brokerage house executive*

**Waltham**
Cox, Howard Ellis, Jr. *venture capitalist*
Metcalfe, Robert M. *venture capitalist, former engineer-scientist, former publishing executive, writer*
Spoon, Alan Gary *venture capital company executive*

**Wellesley**
Tierney, Thomas J. *social entrepreneur*

**West Roxbury**
Lovell, Francis Joseph *retired investment company executive*

**Weston**
Alcock, George Lewis, Jr., (Peter Alcock) *investor, business strategist*

**Westwood**
Gillette, Hyde *retired brokerage house executive*

**MICHIGAN**

**Farmington Hills**
Ellmann, Sheila Frenkel *investment company executive*

**Flint**
Acuff, A. Marshall, Jr. *retired investment company executive*

**Kalamazoo**
Truesdell, Timothy L. *private investor*

**Madison Heights**
Janke, Kenneth *investment consultant*

**Trenton**
Tang, Cyrus *investment company executive*

**West Bloomfield**
Mamut, Mary Catherine *retired entrepreneur*

**MINNESOTA**

**Edina**
Bean, Glen Atherton *entrepreneur*

**Minneapolis**
Bagan, Mark G. *grain exchange executive*
Cowles, John Jay III *investment company executive, entrepreneur*
Dale, John Sorensen *investment company executive, portfolio manager*
Fauth, John J. *venture capitalist*
Lindau, Philip *commodities trader*
Piper, Addison Lewis *securities executive*

**Minnetonka**
Pillsbury, George Sturgis *retired investment advisor*

**Stillwater**
Horsch, Lawrence Leonard *venture capitalist, corporate financial executive*

**Waubun**
Christensen, Marvin Nelson *venture capitalist*

**Wayzata**
Wyard, Vicki Shaw *investment and insurance company executive*

**MISSOURI**

**Kansas City**
Morgison, F. Edward *investment broker*
Stowers, James Evans, Jr. *investment company executive*

**Lees Summit**
Korschot, Benjamin Calvin *retired investment company executive*

**Saint Louis**
Anagnostopoulos, Constantine Emmanuel *venture capitalist, former company executive*

Bagby, Robert L. *investment company executive*
Bernstein, Donald Chester *brokerage house executive, lawyer*
Bickel, Floyd Gilbert III *investment counselor*
Keffler, Karl Joseph *investment company executive, lawyer*
Skrainka, Alan Frederick *securities analyst*

**MONTANA**

**Helena**
Lindgren, Robert Kemper *securities investor, auditor*

**NEBRASKA**

**Omaha**
Buffett, Warren Edward *entrepreneur, investment company executive*
Cross, Walter Thomas *investment company executive*
Moglia, Joseph H. *brokerage house executive*
Ricketts, John Joe *securities company executive*

**NEVADA**

**Boulder City**
Stephenson, Arthur Emmet, Jr. *investment company executive*

**Las Vegas**
Kasama, Hideto Peter *international business and investment advisor*
Roberts, Lia *investor, political organization worker*

**Reno**
Harsh, Antoinette Mollett *investor*

**Sparks**
Holder, Harold Douglas, Sr. *investor, hotel executive*

**NEW HAMPSHIRE**

**Derry**
Sapareto, Frank Vincent, II, *investment advisor, state legislator*

**Dover**
Parks, Joe Benjamin *entrepreneur, retired state legislator*

**NEW JERSEY**

**Avenel**
Berg, Louis Leslie *investment executive*

**Basking Ridge**
Tamarelli, Alan Wayne *venture capitalist*

**Bridgewater**
Lowman, Tyrone David *entrepreneur*

**Brookside**
Fairchild, Samuel Wilson *investor, retired federal agency administrator, financial services executive*

**Chatham**
Tepper, David A. *hedge fund manager*

**Cresskill**
Uehling, Gordon Alexander, Jr. *investment company executive*

**East Brunswick**
Hurst, Gregory Squire *investment company executive, theater director, theater producer*

**Englewood**
Kramer, Orin Stuart *investment services company executive*

**Fort Lee**
Lippman, William Jennings *investment company executive*

**Hackensack**
Heilborn, George Heinz *investor*

**Jersey City**
Ezrati, Milton Joseph *investment manager, economist, writer*

**Lincoln Park**
Sichuk, George *entrepreneur, quantum biochemist, educator*

**Little Falls**
Shern, Stephanie Marie *investment company executive, accountant*

**Mendham**
Kirby, Allan Price, Jr. *investment company executive*
Pierson, Robert David *investor*

**Morristown**
Kirby, Jefferson W. *investment company executive*

**New Brunswick**
Mills, Dorothy Allen *investor*

**Newark**
O'Flynn, Thomas M. *investment company executive*

**Park Ridge**
Giovannoli, Joseph Louis *entrepreneur, lawyer*

**Parsippany**
Moch, Kenneth Ian *entrepreneur*

**Pennington**
Gundeck, Caroline Nyklewicz *investment company executive*

**Princeton**
Chamberlin, John Stephen *investor, consumer products company executive*
Doll, Robert C. *investment company executive*
Fernholz, Erhard Robert *investment executive*
Gund, Gordon *venture capitalist, investment company executive*
Johnston, Robert Fowler *venture capitalist*
Treu, Jesse Isaiah *venture capitalist*

**Red Bank**
Hertz, Daniel Leroy, Jr. *entrepreneur*

**Rumson**
Strong, George Hotham *private investor, consultant*

**Short Hills**
Howe, James Everett *investment company executive*

**Skillman**
Tenenbaum, Bernard Hirsh *entrepreneur, educator*
Wheelock, Keith Ward *retired investment company executive, educator*

**Summit**
Malin, Robert Abernethy *investment company executive*

**Totowa**
Tuthill, Jay Dean, II, *investment executive*

**Upper Saddle River**
Oolie, Sam *manufacturing and investment company executive*

**Watchung**
Cox, Archibald, Jr. *investment company executive*


**NEW MEXICO**

**Santa Fe**
Colvin, Greta Wilmoth *entrepreneur*


**NEW YORK**

**Albany**
Leichman, Kenneth William *investment executive*

**Babylon**
Brackett, Ronald E. *investment company executive, lawyer*

**Ballston Spa**
Wages, Robert Coleman *equity investor*

**Bay Shore**
Williams, Tonda *entrepreneur, consultant*

**Bedford Corners**
Singer, Craig *entrepreneur, inventor, investor, consultant*

**Blue Point**
Owen, Thomas Llewellyn *investment company executive*

**Brooklyn**
Ross, Randolph Ernest *investor*

**Buffalo**
Irwin, Robert James Armstrong *investment company executive*
Littlewood, Douglas Burden *brokerage house executive*

**Glen Cove**
Pettersen, Kevin Will *investment company executive*

**Glens Falls**
Pearsall, Glenn Lincoln *brokerage house executive*

**Goshen**
DeMueller, Lucia *investment consultant*

**Great Neck**
Appel, Gerald *investment advisor*
Hampton, Benjamin Bertram *brokerage house executive*

**Hempstead**
Sodano, Salvatore F. *former stock exchange executive*

**Ithaca**
Hojnowski, Jules Austin *entrepreneur*

**Manhasset**
Calvin, Donald Lee *stock exchange official*
Gardner, Robert *financial services executive*

**Maspeth**
Blitz, Nelson, Jr. *entrepreneur*

**Merrick**
Poppel, Seth Raphael *entrepreneur*

**Mount Kisco**
Eastburn, John S., Jr. *venture capitalist*
Frieder, Samuel P. *venture capitalist*
Kohlberg, James A. *venture capitalist*
Kohlberg, Jerome, Jr., (Jerry Kohlberg) *venture capitalist, lawyer*
Lacovara, Christopher *venture capitalist*
Romeyn, Prescott C. *venture capitalist*
Wildstein, Evan *venture capitalist*

**New Hyde Park**
Richards, Bernard *investment company executive*

**New York**
Allen, Herbert Anthony, Jr. *investment company executive*
Allison, Herbert Monroe, Jr. *investment company executive*
Alliton, Vaughn *brokerage executive*
Andersen, K(ent) Tucker *investment executive*
Aronson, Edgar David *venture capitalist*
Attwood, James Albert, Jr. *investment company executive*
Baha, Christian J. *investment company executive*
Bailey, Jerome H. (Jerry Bailey) *mercantile exchange executive*
Barry, Thomas Corcoran *investment advisor*
Beinecke, Frederick William *investment company executive*
Beldock, Donald Travis *investor*
Bell, Martin Allen *investment company executive*
Bellas, Albert Constantine *investment executive*
Benton, Daniel C. *investment company executive*
Bernard, Lewis W. *foundation executive, former finance company executive*
Bewkes, Eugene Garrett, Jr. *investment company executive, consultant*
Birkelund, John Peter *investment company executive*
Blalock, Sherrill *investment advisor*
Blavatnik, Leonard *investment company executive*
Bricklin, Malcolm *automotive entrepreneur*
Brine, Kevin R. *investment company executive*
Britz, Robert G. *stock exchange executive*
Britz Lotti, Diane Edward *investment company executive*
Brody, Alan Jeffrey *investment company executive*
Brotman, Steven *venture capitalist*
Brown, Ronald *retired stockbroker*
Bruce, Duncan Archibald *investor, writer*
Brunie, Charles Henry *investment manager*
Buckles, Robert Howard *retired investment company executive*
Butte, Amy S. *brokerage house executive*
Carter, Marshall Nichols *stock exchange executive*
Castellano, Michael John *investment company executive*
Cayne, James E. (Jimmy Cayne) *securities trader, diversified financial services company executive*
Cecil, Donald *retired investment company executive*
Chai, Nelson J. *stock exchange executive*
Chapin, Samuel R. *investment company executive*
Chapman, Max C., Jr. *investment company executive*
Chen, Philip Minkang *brokerage house executive*
Cheng-Kingdon, Anla *venture capitalist*
Chunilal, Damian *investment company executive*
Clark, Mayree Carroll *investment banking executive*
Clay, John Peter *investment company executive*
Clemente, Lilia Calderon *capital company executive*
Cohen, Abby Joseph *investment company executive*
Cohen, Alan M. *investment company executive*
Cohen, Claire Gorham *investment company executive*
Cole, Carolyn Jo *brokerage house executive*
Condron, Christopher M. (Kip Condron) *investment company executive*
Considine, Jill M. *securities trader*
Conway, Richard Francis *investment company executive*
Cooperman, Leon G. *investment company executive*
Cortez, Ricardo Lee *investment management executive*
Curry, Boykin (Ravenel Boykin Curry IV) *investment manager*
Dallen, Russell Morris, Jr. *investment company executive, lawyer, publishing company executive*
Davis, J. Morton *investment company executive, venture capitalist, economist*
Davis, Jordan S. *venture capitalist*
Dehn, James Keith *investment company executive*
de Nicola, Anthony J. *investment company executive*
de Oliveira, Ramon *investment company executive*
Dias Griffin, Anne *investment advisor*
Diker, Charles M. *investment advisor*
Di Palma, Joseph Alphonse *investment company executive, lawyer*
Dorsett, Burt *investment company executive*
D'Souza, Rohit *investment company executive*
Dumler, Richard J. *venture capitalist*
Einiger, Carol Blum *investment company executive*
Elliman, Christopher J. (Kim Elliman) *investment company executive*
Elvey, Malcolm *venture capitalist*
Ercklentz, Alexander Tonio *investment company executive*
Evnin, Anthony Basil *venture capital investor*
Fahey, James Edward *brokerage house executive*
Fahour, Ahmed *investment company executive*
Feldberg, Meyer *investment advisor, university dean emeritus*
Findakly, Hani K. *investment company executive*
Fiorilla di Santa Croce, John Leopoldo *investment company executive, lawyer*
Fisher, Peter R. *investment company executive, former federal agency administrator*
Flinn, Michael de Vlaming *investment company executive*
Forst, Edward C. *investment company executive*
Forstmann, Theodore J. *investment firm executive*
Friedenberg, Daniel Meyer *investor, writer*
Friedman, Robert Laurence *investment company executive*
Fuld, Richard Severin, Jr., (Dick Fuld) *investment banking executive*
Gavin, Paula Lance *investment company executive*
Gelband, Michael *investment company executive*
Genader, Robert J. *investment company executive*
Gero, Anthony George *securities and commodities trader*
Goelet, Robert G. *investment company executive*
Goldfarb, David *investment banking executive*
Goodman, Edwin A. *venture capitalist*
Gottesman, David Sanford *investment company executive*

Grano, Joseph J., Jr. *securities industry executive*
Gray, Farrah *entrepreneur, writer*
Gray, James L. *investment company executive*
Greenblatt, Joel *investment company executive, finance educator, writer*
Gregory, Joseph M. *investment company executive*
Greifeld, Robert A. *stock exchange executive*
Gruss, Martin David *investor*
Gubert, Walter Alexander *investment company executive*
Gutfreund, John Halle *investment company executive, consultant*
Handler, Richard B. *investment company executive*
Hansmann, Ralph Emil *investment executive, director*
Harris, Carla Ann *investment company executive*
Harris, Charles E. *venture capital investment executive*
Hart, Gurnee Fellows *investment counselor*
Haskell, John Henry Farrell, Jr. *investment company executive*
Helsby, Keith R. *stock exchange executive*
Herrmann, Lacy Bunnell *investment company executive, entrepreneur, venture capitalist*
Hertog, Roger *investment company executive*
Hilton, Andrew Carson *investment company executive, retired manufacturing company executive, management consultant*
Hodges, Deborah *investment company executive*
Holland, Michael Francis *investment company executive*
Horn, Karen Nicholson *investment company executive, former bank executive*
Howard, Nathan Southard *brokerage house executive, lawyer*
Hyman, Morton Peter *private equity investment company executive*
Ilacqua, Rosario Salvatore *securities analyst*
Jackson, Ann Williams *private equity investment executive*
James, Marc Stephen *brokerage house executive*
Jamison, Douglas W. *venture capitalist*
Janney, Stuart Symington III *investment company executive*
Janulis, Theodore P. *investment company executive*
Jenrette, Richard Hampton *investment and insurance company executive*
Jepson, Hans Godfrey *investment company executive, director*
Jones, Abbott C. *investment company executive*
Jordon, John W., II, *investment company executive*
Kehoe, John P. *investor relations executive*
Kelly, William Michael *investment company executive*
Ketchum, Richard G. *stock exchange executive, lawyer*
Kim, Dow *investment company executive*
Kinney, Catherine R. *stock exchange executive*
Kinney, Gilbert Hart *investor*
Klein, Jeffrey Peter *investor*
Kovner, Bruce *investment company executive*
Kraemer, Harry M. Jansen, Jr. *investment company executive, former medical products executive*
Kravis, Henry R. *venture capitalist*
Kreitman, James E. *securities trader*
Kressel, Henry *venture capitalist*
LaBranche, Michael (George M.L. LaBranche IV) *securities trader*
Lackritz, Marc E. *securities industry association executive*
Lamle, Hugh Roy *investment advisor, consultant*
Lamport, Anthony Matthew *venture capitalist*
Lang, Everett Francis, Jr. *brokerage house executive*
Langone, Kenneth G. *investment company executive*
Lasser, Joseph Robert *investment company executive*
Lauder, Ronald Stephen *investor*
Lawrence, Bryan Hunt *investment company executive*
Lawson-Johnston, Peter, II, *investment company executive*
Lebenthal, Alexandra *investment firm executive*
Levitt, Arthur, Jr. *investment company executive, former federal agency administrator*
Loeb, John Langeloth, Jr. *investment counselor, consultant*
Lubin, Daniel C. *venture capitalist*
Luke, Douglas Sigler *investment company executive*
Lutnick, Howard William *brokerage house executive*
Lynch, Gary G. *investment company executive, lawyer*
MacAllaster, Archie *investment company executive*
Mager, Ezra Pascal *investment company executive*
Marron, Donald Baird *venture capitalist*
Mayer, William Emilio *investor*
McCann, Robert J. *investment company executive*
McDade, Herbert H. III *investment company executive*
McDonald, James S. *investment company executive*
McGee, Hugh E. III *investment company executive*
McGlynn, William Charles *brokerage house executive*
McKay, Geoff *private equity investor*
McNulty, James J. *former mercantile exchange executive*
Meeker, Mary G. *brokerage house executive*
Mehiel, Dennis *investment company executive*
Metz, Emmanuel Michael *investment company executive, lawyer*
Millard, Robert B. *investment company executive*
Miller, Corbin Russell *investment company executive*
Mindich, Eric *investment company executive*
Minicucci, Robert A. *investment company executive*
Mnuchin, Steven T. *investment company executive*
Molinaro, Samuel L. *investment company executive*
Morris, William Charles *investor*
Morse, Robert Parker *investment company executive*
Murray, Eileen K. *investment company executive*
Nabi, Stanley Andrew *brokerage house executive*
Nazem, Fereydoun F. *venture capitalist, entrepreneur*

Newsome, James E. *mercantile exchange executive*
Niemiec, David Wallace *investment company executive*
Offit, Morris Wolf *investment company executive*
O'Grady, Beverly Troxler *investment executive, counselor*
Olinger, Chauncey Greene, Jr. *investment company executive, editorial consultant*
O'Meara, Christopher M. *investment company executive*
Pappas, Milton J. *venture capitalist*
Paul, Andrew Mitchell *investment advisor*
Peterson, Peter George *investment company executive*
Pietri, Todd T. *venture capitalist*
Pittman, Robert Warren *investor*
Pollack, Stephen J. *stockbroker*
Pouschine, John Laurence *private equity investment executive*
Proctor, Georganne C. *investment company executive*
Putnam, Jerry (Gerald D. Putnam) *stock exchange executive*
Queally, Paul B. *venture capitalist*
Quick, Peter *stock exchange executive*
Quirk, John James *investment company executive*
Rand, Lawrence Anthony *investor, finance company executive*
Rizzuto, Richard Peter *entrepreneur*
Robinson, James D. III *venture capitalist*
Rogers, James Beeland, Jr., (Jim Rogers) *retired investment company executive*
Rogers, Theodore Courtney *investment company executive*
Rosenbloom, Daniel *investment advisor, lawyer*
Rosenfeld, Gerald *investment company executive, financial analyst*
Salomon, Richard E. *investment company executive*
Sapir, Tamir *entrepreneur*
Saul, Andrew M. *investment company executive*
Schaeffer, Richard *mercantile exchange executive*
Schafer, Oscar S. *investment company executive*
Schick, Harry Leon *investment company executive*
Schiff, Frank *investment company executive*
Schiff, Marlene Sandler *entrepreneur*
Scott, William Clement III *investor*
Sender, Adam D. *investment company executive, art collector*
Shalom, Liliane Winn *investment company executive, consultant*
Shapiro, Robert Frank *investment company executive*
Sharp, Rob *investment company executive*
Shavin, Helene B. *venture capital company executive*
Sheffery, Michael B. *investment company executive*
Shrut, Arlene R. *entrepreneur, director*
Siebert, Muriel (Mickie) *brokerage house executive, retired bank executive*
Simpkins, Neil P. *investment company executive, automotive executive*
Smith, Malcolm Bernard *investment company executive*
Sorte, John Follett *investment firm executive*
Spector, Warren J. *investment company executive*
Stein, David Fred *investment company executive*
Sterling, Robert Lee, Jr. *investment company executive*
Stern, Walter Phillips *investment company executive*
Stewart, E(dward) Nicholson *investment management executive*
Suhler, John Stuart *investor*
Tamke, George William *venture capitalist*
Tananbaum, Steven Andrew *investment consultant*
Tendler, David *investment company executive*
Thain, John A. *stock exchange executive*
Thomson, Todd Stuart *investment company executive*
Tizzio, Thomas Ralph *brokerage house executive*
Tozer, W. James, Jr. *investment company executive*
Train, John *investment advisor, federal official*
Ule, Guy Maxwell, Jr. *stockbroker*
Valbuena, Vivian *brokerage house executive*
Virtue, Ted *investment company executive*
Walker, Jeffrey Clemens *venture capitalist*
Wareham, Raymond Noble *brokerage house executive*
Williams, Christopher *investment company executive*
Williams, Dave Harrell *investment company executive*
Wolf, Peter Michael *investment manager, consultant, writer*
Wolkoff, Neal L. *stock exchange executive*
Wood, Jerry *investment company executive*
Yetman, Gary *investment company executive*
Zachem, Tyler *investment company executive*
Zeitlin, Jide James *investor*
Zeuschner, Erwin Arnold *brokerage house executive*
Zwickler, Allen *investment advisor, educator*

**Purchase**
Black, Leon David *private investment company executive*
Wachenheim, Edgar III *investment company executive*

**Riverhead**
Orben, Jack Richard *investment company executive, director*

**Rochester**
Rulison, Joseph Richard *investment advisor*

**Rye**
Crawford, R. George *investment company executive, educator, filmmaker*

**Sag Harbor**
Brody, Eugene David *investment company executive*

**Southampton**
Culp, Michael Bronston *investor, writer, publisher*

**Tuxedo Park**
Davis, Shelby Moore Cullom *investment company executive, consultant*

**Wantagh**
Zinder, Newton Donald *investment advisor, consultant*

**Westbury**
Lorber, Howard Mark *investments executive*

**White Plains**
Gottlieb, Lester M. *entrepreneur*

**Woodstock**
Ober, Stuart Alan *investment advisor, writer*

**Yonkers**
Smith, Aldo Ralston, Jr. *brokerage house executive*

## NORTH CAROLINA

**Charlotte**
Cummings, Stephen Emery *investment banking executive*
Grimaldi, James Thomas *investment fund executive*
Ragan, Robert Allison *private investment executive, financial consultant*

**Greensboro**
Johnson, Marshall Hardy *investment company executive*

**Murphy**
Pezzella, Jerry James, Jr. *investment company executive, real estate company executive*

**Raleigh**
Krallinger, Joseph Charles *entrepreneur, consultant, writer*

## NORTH DAKOTA

**Fargo**
Tallman, Robert Hall *investment company executive*

**Grand Forks**
Gjovig, Bruce Quentin *entrepreneur, consultant*

## OHIO

**Alpha**
James, Francis Edward, Jr. *investment advisor*

**Bay Village**
Hook, John Burney *investment company executive*

**Brunswick**
Reed, Jane Garson *entrepreneur*

**Bryan**
Oberlin, Earl Clifford III *securities brokerage company executive*

**Cincinnati**
Anning, Robert Doan Hopkins *brokerage company executive*
Klein, Sophia H. *entrepreneur*
Lucke, Robert Vito *investment company executive*

**Cleveland**
Brentlinger, Paul Smith *venture capital executive*
Charnas, Michael (Mannie Charnas) *investment company executive*
Morgenthaler, David Turner *venture capitalist*
Summers, William B., Jr. *brokerage house executive*

**Columbus**
Barthelmas, Ned Kelton *brokerage house executive*

**Dayton**
Mitakides, Louella Jane *entrepreneur*

**Holland**
Batt, Nick *property and investment executive*

**Strongsville**
Cameron, David Ronald *entrepreneur, historian, researcher*

**Westerville**
Barr, John Michael *investor, management consultant*

## OKLAHOMA

**Bethany**
McGowan, Bernard Wayne (Bernie McGowan) *venture capitalist, writer*

**Lawton**
Carraher, Shawn Michael *investment company executive, management educator*

**Muskogee**
Kang, Heesam *investment analyst, educator*

**Tulsa**
Neas, John Theodore *investment company executive*

**Woodward**
Riffel, Loren Darrel *retired entrepreneur*

## OREGON

**Chiloquin**
Reed, David George *entrepreneur*

**Medford**
Hennion, Carolyn Laird (Lyn Hennion) *investment executive*

**Portland**
Corbett, Alice Catherine *investor*
Milton, Catherine Higgs *entrepreneur*
Rutherford, William Drake *investment executive*
Stott, Peter Walter *investment company executive*

## PENNSYLVANIA

**Bala Cynwyd**
Gleklen, Donald Morse *investment company executive*

**Berwyn**
Hambrecht, William R. *investment banking firm executive*

**Blue Bell**
Giordano, Nicholas Anthony *brokerage house executive*

**Clarks Summit**
Janoski, Henry Valentine *investment advisor, former banker*

**Lafayette Hill**
King, Leon *investment advisor*

**Lancaster**
Carlisle, James Patton *entrepreneur*

**Ligonier**
Mellon, Seward Prosser *brokerage house executive*

**Mechanicsburg**
Owen, Tony Quinn *investment company executive, horse trainer*

**Media**
Hemphill, James S. *investment management executive, financial advisor*

**Murrysville**
Maurer, Richard Michael *investment company executive*

**New Hope**
Sergey, John Michael, Jr. *investment company executive, consultant*

**Newtown Square**
Lewis, James Earl *investor*

**Paoli**
Denny, William Murdoch, Jr. *investment management executive*

**Philadelphia**
Frucher, Meyer S. (Sandy Frucher) *stock exchange executive*
Gowa, Andrew *investor, lawyer*
Neff, P(aul) Sherrill *venture capitalist*
Palmer, Russell Eugene *investment company executive, retired dean*
Savitz, Samuel J. *actuarial consulting firm executive*
Simpson, Carol Louise *investment company executive*
Woosnam, Richard Edward *venture capitalist, lawyer*

**Pittsburgh**
Bernt, Benno Anthony *entrepreneur, investor*
Donahue, John Francis *investment company executive*
Druckenmiller, Stanley F. *investment company executive*
Hillman, Henry Lea *investment company executive*
Walton, James Mellon *investment company executive*

**Radnor**
Buck, James Mahlon, Jr. *venture capitalist*

**Valley Forge**
Bogle, John Clifton *investment company executive*
Brennan, John Joseph *mutual fund company executive*

**Wexford**
Stover, Richard L. *investor*

**Williamsport**
McDonald, Peyton Dean *brokerage house executive*

**York**
White, Timothy Paul *brokerage house executive*

## RHODE ISLAND

**Newport**
Higgins, Harriet Pratt *investment advisor*
Stone, Edward Luke *investor, realtor*

**Providence**
Hall, Almon C. III *investment company executive*
Joukowsky, Artemis A. W. *private investor*

**Wakefield**
Mason, Scott MacGregor *entrepreneur, inventor, consultant*

## SOUTH CAROLINA

**Columbia**
Brockelsby, Jeffrey Lind *investment executive*

**Johns Island**
Cameron, Thomas William Lane *investment company executive*

**Orangeburg**
Dalton, Cheryl Renee *entrepreneur*

**Sullivans Island**
Romaine, Henry Simmons *retired investment company executive, consultant*

## TENNESSEE

**Hixson**
Kemp, Robert Bowers, Jr. *investment manager*

**Memphis**
Reaves, Charles Durham *investment company executive, lawyer*

**Nashville**
Bradford, James C., Jr. *brokerage house executive*
Byrd, Andrew Wayne *investment company executive*
Hanselman, Richard Wilson *entrepreneur*
Kuhn, Paul Hubert, Jr. *investment advisor*
Nelson, Edward Gage *brokerage house executive, bank executive, consultant*
Roberts, Kenneth Lewis *investor, lawyer, foundation administrator*

## TEXAS

**Addison**
Smith, Cece *venture capitalist*

**Austin**
Baumgartner, Robert *investment company executive, consultant*
Yacktman, Stephen *investment company executive*

**Corpus Christi**
Hepner, Jon R. *investment company executive*

**Corsicana**
Dyer, James Mason, Jr. *investment company executive*

**Dallas**
Bayne, James Elwood *investor*
Brown, Benjamin A. *investment advisor*
Byrne, Susan M. *investment company executive*
Crockett, Dodee Frost *brokerage house executive*
Durham, Michael Jonathan *investment professional*
Lynch, William Wright, Jr. *investment company executive, engineer*
Muse, John R. *investment company executive*
Owen, Daniel Thomas *entrepreneur, venture capitalist*
Rachofsky, Howard *retired investor, art collector, patron*
Stoffel, Paul T. *investment company executive*
Tucker, Keith A. *investment company executive*

**Duncanville**
Cooley, Robert Daniel *investor, real estate company executive*

**El Paso**
Prendergast, Thomas A. *investments consultant, management consultant*

**Fort Worth**
Bass, Sid Richardson *investment company executive*
Bonderman, David *investment company executive, lawyer*

**Groveton**
Pyle, Benjamin Malrey *investor*

**Horseshoe Bay**
Anderson, Kenneth Ward *investor, consultant*

**Houston**
Barrere, Clem Adolph *business brokerage company executive*
Duncan, Charles William, Jr. *investor, retired federal official*
O'Connor, Ralph Sturges *investment company executive*
Richards, Leonard Martin *investment executive, consultant*
Vaughan, Eugene H. *investment company executive*
Wells, Damon *investment company executive*
Williams, Edward Earl, Jr. *entrepreneur, educator*

**San Antonio**
McClane, Robert Sanford *entrepreneur, bank executive*
Terracina, Roy David *entrepreneur*

## UTAH

**Salt Lake City**
Meldrum, Peter Durkee *venture capitalist, biotechnology company executive*

## VERMONT

**Middlebury**
Pardee, Scott Edward *securities dealer*

**Quechee**
DeRouchey, Beverly Jean *investment company executive*

## VIRGINIA

**Alexandria**
Boisi, Geoffrey T. *investment company executive*
Rahming, John Christopher *investment company executive, consultant*

**Arlington**
Choksi, Mary *investment company executive*
Drayton, Bill (William Drayton) *social entrepreneur, lawyer, management consultant*
Scarborough, Robert Henry, Jr. *entrepreneur*

**Charlottesville**
Gunter, Bradley Hunt *capital management executive*

**Dutton**
Washburn, John Rosser *entrepreneur*

**Falls Church**
Isaac, William Michael *brokerage house executive, retired government agency administrator*

**Herndon**
Burns, Patrick Owen *venture capital company executive*

**Middleburg**
Parkinson, James Thomas III *investment consultant*

**Orange**
Thompson, Louis Milton, Jr. *investment company executive, consultant*

**Reston**
Icahn, Carl Celian *investor*
Mitchell, Ellen Clabaugh *investment executive*

**Richmond**
Phillips, Thomas Edworth, Jr. *investment company executive, consultant*

**Stanardsville**
Anns, Philip Harold *brokerage house executive, pharmaceutical executive*

**Suffolk**
Holloway, Christopher Matthew *brokerage house executive*

**Virginia Beach**
Melsheimer, Mel P(owell) *venture capitalist*

**Williamsburg**
Gordon, Baron Jack *stockbroker*
Hargrove, Roy Belmont III *stockbroker*
Roberson, Robert S. *investment company executive*

## WASHINGTON

**Bellevue**
Wells-Henderson, Ronald John *investment counselor*

**Kirkland**
Ryles, Gerald Fay *investor, finance company executive*

**Port Townsend**
Jones, John Wesley *entrepreneur*

**Seattle**
Alberg, Tom Austin *investment company executive, lawyer*
Heath, Richard Raymond *retired investment company executive*
Kocher, Cynthia *investment specialist*
Nelson, Allen F. *proxy solicitation company executive*
Reeg, Gloria D. *investment consultant*
Ruckelshaus, William Doyle *investment company executive, former federal agency administrator*
Wright, Bagley *venture capitalist, entrepreneur, art collector*

**Sequim**
Kretschmer, Keith Hughes *investor*

## WISCONSIN

**Mequon**
Bloom, James Edward *commodity trading and financial executive*
Petersen, Dorothy Virginia *investment company executive*

**Milwaukee**
O'Neill, James Martin *venture capitalist*

## WYOMING

**Casper**
True, Jean Durland *entrepreneur, oil industry executive, gas industry executive*

**Cheyenne**
Myers, Rolland Graham *investment counselor*

**Jackson**
Hirschfield, Alan James *entrepreneur*

**Wilson**
Chrystie, Thomas Ludlow *investor*
Sage, Andrew Gregg Curtin, II, *retired brokerage house executive*

## TERRITORIES OF THE UNITED STATES

## PUERTO RICO

**Hato Rey**
Ferrer, Miguel Antonio *brokerage house executive*

## CANADA

### ALBERTA

**Calgary**
Cumming, Thomas Alexander *brokerage house executive*

### BRITISH COLUMBIA

**Vancouver**
McCaw, John E., Jr. *investment company executive, professional sports team executive*
Saunders, Peter Paul *investor*

### MANITOBA

**Winnipeg**
Watchorn, William Ernest *venture capitalist*

### ONTARIO

**Toronto**
Bhaduri, Ranjan *investment management professional*
Dale, Robert Gordon *investment company executive*
Fox, Wayne C. *stock exchange executive, corporate financial executive*
Leech, James William *investment company executive*
Lindsay, Roger Alexander (Baron of Craighall) *investment executive*
Nesbitt, Richard *stock exchange executive*

### QUEBEC

**Montreal**
Cedraschi, Tullio *investment company executive*
Gillespie, Thomas Stuart *investment company executive*
Bertrand, Luc *stock exchange executive*

## MEXICO

**Mexico City**
Trevino, Guillermo Prieto *stock exchange executive*

## THE BAHAMAS

**Nassau**
Templeton, John Marks *investment counsel, financial analyst*

## BERMUDA

**Tuckers Town**
Heizer, Edgar Francis, Jr. *venture capitalist*

## CHINA

**Hong Kong**
Li, Ka-Shing *international entrepreneur*

## ENGLAND

**London**
Diamond, Robert E., Jr. *investment company executive*
Flint, Douglas J. *investment company executive*
Forsyth, Stephen A. *venture capitalist, department chairman*
Jourdren, Marc Henri *investment banking company executive*
Nagioff, Roger B. *investment company executive*

## GERMANY

**Frankfurt**
von Rosen, Rüdiger *stock exchange executive*

## MONGOLIA

**Ulaanbaatar**
Mandel, Leslie Ann *investment advisor, writer*

## NORWAY

**Oslo**
Heyerdahl, Jens P. *investment company executive*

## SAUDI ARABIA

**Riyadh**
Alsaud, Prince Alwaleed Bin Talal Bin AbdulAziz *investment company executive, investor, entrepreneur*

## SWITZERLAND

**Baar**
Rich, Marc David *commodities trader*

**Geneva**
Farman-Farmaian, Ghaffar *investment company executive*

**Lausanne**
Bloemsma, Marco Paul *investor*

**Zurich**
Wassmer, Rudolf Andreas *entrepreneurial engineer*

## UNITED ARAB EMIRATES

**Dubai**
Chohan, Gulshan-Naseem *office manager*

## ADDRESS UNPUBLISHED

Aall, Christian Bergengren *entrepreneur*
Ackerman, Melvin *investment company executive*
Albanese, Thomas *entrepreneur*
Albers, Charles Edgar *retired investment company executive*
Aljian, James Donovan *investment company executive*
Allen, Donald Vail *investment company executive, musician*
Anderson, Paulette Elizabeth *investment company executive, retired elementary school educator*
Arbuckle, John Finley, Jr. *retired investment advisor*
Aurin, Robert James *entrepreneur*
Bacharach, Melvin Lewis *venture capitalist*
Bacon, Caroline Sharfman *investor, consultant*
Bailey, Rita Maria *investment advisor, psychologist*
Balsamo, Stephen *brokerage house executive*
Bantry, Bryan *entrepreneur, air transportation executive, television director, television producer*
Beitler, Stephen *investment company executive, venture capitalist*
Bell, Michael A. *investment company executive*
Berkley, Stephen M. *entrepreneur, investor*
Berlin, Howard Richard *investment company executive, retired portfolio manager*
Beyman, Jonathan Eric *investment company executive*
Blackwell, Michael Sidney *broker, financial services executive*
Bowles, Barbara Landers *investment company executive*
Bratt, Nicholas *investment company executive, research and development company executive*
Breeden, Richard C. *investment company executive, former federal agency administrator*
Brown, Herbert Graham *entrepreneur*
Burks, Jack D. *investment executive*
Callard, David Jacobus *investment company executive*
Camplin, Peter M., Sr. *entrepreneur, writer*
Carr, Harold Noflet *investment company executive*
Casson Madden, Chris *entrepreneur, interior designer*
Chapman, Geneva Joyce *entrepreneur, educator, writer*
Chase, Robin M. *entrepreneur*
Chatham, Rosemary Gail Moog *entrepreneur, musician, volunteer, composer*
Clawson, John Addison *investment company executive, retired chemicals executive*
Clemmensen, Larry P. *former investment company executive*
Codo, Christina *securities executive*
Cohn, Michael S. *investment company executive*
Cormie, Donald Mercer *investment company executive*
Crawford, Richard Eben, Jr. *retired investment advisor*
Cunningham, Ronnie Walter *venture capitalist*
Dean, Edwin Becton *entrepreneur*
De Lutis, Donald Conse *investment advisor, consultant*
Derden, Eugenia Gánez *entrepreneur, investor*
Dietz, Arthur Townsend *investment counseling company executive*
Doherty, Charles Vincent *investment advisor*
Drake, Rodman Leland *investment company executive, consultant*
Dreman, David Nasaniel *investment counselor, security analyst*
Duarte, Prospero Villacin *retired entrepreneur*
Dunbar, Prescott Nelson *investment company executive*
Dunn, John Raymond, Jr. *stockbroker*
Elliott, Edward *investment executive, financial planner*
Engelbreit, Mary *art licensing entrepreneur*
Enomoto, Daisuke (Dice-K) *entrepreneur, investor*
Fernandez, Antonio S. *investment company executive*
Fitts, Catherine Austin *investment advisor*
Fiumefreddo, Charles A. *brokerage house executive*
Freed, Eva Praeger *investment advisor*
Ganesan, Raj *investment advisor, consultant*
Gilbert, Steven Jeffrey *venture capitalist, screenwriter*
Glasberg, Laurence Brian *investment company executive*
Glick, J. Leslie *entrepreneur*
Godwin, Pamela June *financial services executive*
Goldman, Alan Ira *brokerage house executive*
Good, Walter Raymond *investment company executive*
Goodman, Bennett J. *hedge fund executive*
Gordon, Richard M. Erik *private investor, educator*
Grasso, Dick (Richard A. Grasso) *former stock exchange executive*
Greenberg, Alan Courtney (Ace Greenberg) *securities trader*
Greene, Frank Sullivan, Jr. *investment company executive*
Hapner, Mary Lou *securities trader, writer*
Harte, Christopher McCutcheon *investment manager*
Hinshaw, Ernest Theodore, Jr. *private investor, retired Olympic team official, retired finance company executive*

Hintz, Scott Raymond *investor, financial consultant*
Hochheimer, Frank Leo *brokerage and financial industry executive*
Holte, Debra Leah *investment company executive, financial analyst*
Horsager, Kent R. *former grain exchange engineer, lawyer*
Howard, James Webb *brokerage house executive, engineer, lawyer*
Hudson, Donald J. *stock exchange executive*
Hulett, Jonathon Spencer *investment company executive*
Kahn, Herta Hess (Mrs. Howard Kahn) *retired investment company executive*
Kavovit, Barbara *entrepreneur*
Keegan, James Joseph *entrepreneur*
Kellogg, Peter R. *securities dealer*
Kirshbaum, Lawrence G. *investment company executive*
Knapp, J. Barclay *entrepreneur*
Knox, Lance Lethbridge *venture capitalist*
Kreitzer, Lois Helen *investor*
Kwitek, Benjamin Joseph *entrepreneur, consultant*
Lally, John Patrick *investment company executive*
Landsman, Richard *investment company executive, finance educator*
Lasser, Lawrence J. *former investment company executive*
Lavington, Michael Richard *venture capital company executive*
Leahy, T. Liam *business development and technology investor*
Lee, Sandra Ann *investment company executive*
Lee, Thomas H. *investment company executive*
Level, Leon Jules *investor, director*
Levins, John Raymond *investment advisor, educator, management consultant*
Levinson, Kathy *former investment company executive, philanthropist*
Lewis, Brock *investment company executive*
Lewis, Hunter *investment advisor, writer*
Lieberman, Gail Forman *investment company executive*
Linde, Ronald Keith *investor*
Logan, Dan *investor, writer*
Logan, Kent *retired securities industry executive*
Lovoy, Joseph T. *investment advisor*
Lynch, Thomas Peter *retired investment company executive*
Malik, Om *former venture capitalist, blog website company executive, journalist*
Mayer, Anthony John *investment company executive*
McCausland, Thomas James, Jr. *retired brokerage house executive*
McNeill, Robert Patrick *investment advisor*
Mikeska, Noel Rhea *entrepreneur, health advocate*
Mikitka, Gerald Peter *brokerage house executive, consultant*
Miller, Charles *investor, retired investment company executive*
Miller, Robert Warren *entrepreneur*
Millsaps, Fred Ray *investor*
Molitor, Michael A. *entrepreneur, consultant*
Morgan, Owain David *investment company executive*
Morgenroth, Earl Eugene *entrepreneur*
Nadel, Elliott *investment company executive*
Niehoff, Karl Richard Besuden *brokerage house executive*
Nordley, Gerald David *investor, writer*
Nunnelly, Mark Edward *investor*
Ogle, Edward Proctor, Jr. *investment advisor*
Pacholski, Richard Francis *securities trader, consultant, financial consultant*
Paladino, Albert Edward *venture capitalist*
Pardue, Dwight Edward *venture capitalist*
Parker, Towana D. *entrepreneur, director*
Pauken, Thomas Weir *venture capital executive, mediator*
Paup, Martin Arnold *securities investor, real estate investor*
Peterson, Dawn Michelle *entrepreneur, writer*
Pham, Duc *entrepreneur, engineering executive, researcher*
Pinkney, D. Timothy *investment company executive*
Pottruck, David Steven *brokerage house executive*
Pulling, Thomas Leffingwell *investment advisor*
Quirk, Raymond R *investment company executive*
Rahe, Maribeth Sembach *investment management executive*
Rappaport, Irving S. *entrepreneur, lawyer, consultant*
Reed, John Shepard *former stock exchange executive*
Ridgway, Rozanne LeJeanne *investment company executive, retired ambassador*
Roberts, David Glen *prospector, investor*
Rondeau, Doris Jean *entrepreneur, consultant*
Ross, Darius Alexander *arbitrager and commodities trader, philanthropist*
Rothstein, Gerald Alan *investment consultant*
Ryan, Timothy Patrick *investment company executive*
Rydén, Bengt Gunnar *retired stock exchange executive*
Santry, Barbara Lea *venture capitalist*
Sells, Boake Anthony *private investor*
Shriram, K. Ram *investment company executive*
Shuler, Jon Emmett *securities industry professional*
Smith, Thomas Eugene *investment company executive, financial consultant*
Snyder, Nathan *entrepreneur*
Steen, Carlton Duane *private investor, retired food products executive*
Steinhause, Mitchell *former mercantile exchange executive*
Stephens, Donald R(ichards) *investor*
Stewart, Thomas Clifford *investment company executive*
Stiles, Thomas Beveridge, II, *retired investment company executive*
Street, David Hargett *investment company executive*
Stuart, Gerard William, Jr. *investment company executive, alderman, city official*
Swensen, David Frederick *investment advisor*

Tarr, Kenneth J. *retired investment company executive*
Thomas, James Edward, Jr. *brokerage house executive*
Trongale, Nicholas Albert *entrepreneur, researcher*
Tull, C. Thomas *investment advisor*
Urciuoli, J. Arthur *brokerage house executive*
Uys, Jurgen Peter Brinker *securities analyst*
Valentine, Gene C. *securities dealer*
Veselinović, Draško *stock exchange executive*
Vilar, Alberto W. *investment company executive*
Waite, Dennis Vernon *brokerage house executive, consultant*
Waitt, Theodore W. (Ted Waitt) *venture capitalist, former computer company executive*
Welch, Martin E. III *investor, retail executive*
Whelan, James Robert *investor, import/export company executive*
Wilson, Robert James Montgomery *investment company executive*
Wolf, Christopher Robin *investment executive*
Wruble, Brian Frederick *investor*
York, Jerome B. *investment company executive, former computer retail executive*
Zarb, Frank Gustave *investment company executive*
Zwerling, Gary Leslie *retired investment company executive*

# GOVERNMENT: AGENCY ADMINISTRATION

## UNITED STATES

### ALABAMA

**Auburn University**
Owens, Melvin *public safety administrator, minister*

**Birmingham**
Wheeler, Cathy Jo *federal agency administrator*

**Clanton**
Baughman, Bruce Prentiss *state agency administrator*

**Cullman**
Little, Phyllis A. *protective services official*

**Huntsville**
Schumann, J. Paul *retired federal agency administrator*

**Mobile**
Bostwick, Robert Otis *government agency administrator*
Cunningham, Julian Antonia *retired protective services official*

**Montgomery**
Baker, Jimmy H. *former state finance administrator*
Mandry, Christine M. *public information officer*

**Wedowee**
Frank, Vincent Stephan, Jr. *federal agency administrator, human resources specialist*

### ALASKA

**Anchorage**
Burke, Marianne King *state agency administrator, finance company executive, consultant*

**Juneau**
Usera, Vincent L. *state agency administrator*

### ARIZONA

**Goodyear**
Carlson, Norman A. *retired federal agency administrator*

**Phoenix**
Chavez, Nelba R. *state agency administrator, former federal agency administrator*
Harris, Jack F. *police chief*
Houseworth, Richard Court *retired state agency administrator*
Karnas, Fred G., Jr. *urban policy advisor*
Peters, Mary E. *former federal agency administrator*

**Scottsdale**
Redden, Persefini Kore Anne *protective services official*

**Tucson**
Emerson, Kirk *government agency administrator*
Patla, John Michael *protective services official*
Walker, Franklin Curtis *federal agency administrator*

### ARKANSAS

**Little Rock**
Greene, Tristan Dorian *state agency administrator*

### CALIFORNIA

**Alpine**
Oliverio, Ponzio *protective services official, educator*

**Bakersfield**
Bernard, Alexander *protective services official*

**Beverly Hills**
Snowden, David L. *protective services official*

**Chico**
Hanton, E. Michael *public information officer, consultant*

**City Of Industry**
Cavanaugh, Janis Lynn *protective services official, educator*

**El Centro**
Steensgaard, Anthony Harvey *federal agency administrator*

**Fowler**
Bowman, Joseph Paul *protective services official, writer, retired military officer*

**Fresno**
Rank, Everett George *federal agency administrator*

**Irvine**
Rogan, James Edward *former federal agency administrator, former congressman*

**La Jolla**
Whaley, Storm Hammond *retired federal agency administrator*

**Los Angeles**
Bamattre, William *fire chief*
Bratton, William J. *police chief, former police commissioner*
Robinson, James W. *fire captain*

**Norco**
McNeal, Phyllis Paulette *parole agent*

**Pasadena**
Parker, Robert Allan Ridley *federal agency administrator, astronaut*
Rinaldi, James J. *federal agency administrator*

**Rancho Cucamonga**
Donaldson, Kelley Lynnae *fire prevention specialist*

**Sacramento**
Bersin, Alan Douglas *state agency administrator, lawyer*
Campbell, Tom *state agency administrator, dean, former congressman*
Marin, Rosario *state agency administrator, former federal agency administrator*
Metzer, Laren Wayne *government agency administrator, archivist*
Myrrdin, Terry A. *state agency administrator*
Patino, Douglas Xavier *government agency administrator, academic administrator*
Roberts, Paul Dale *state agency administrator, writer*

**San Diego**
Butterfield, Alexander Porter *government agency administrator, air transportation executive*
Lansdowne, William M. *police chief*

**San Francisco**
Tarnoff, Peter *federal agency administrator, consultant*

**San Jacinto**
Willis, Ralph Walker *retired firefighter*

**San Jose**
Davis, Robert *police chief*

**San Ysidro**
Schneider, Christine Lynn *customs inspector*

**Santa Barbara**
Aylesworth, Owen Roy *retired firefighter, genealogist, philanthropist*

**Santa Monica**
Timmer, Barbara *state agency administrator*

**Soledad**
Casillas, Jesse Diaz *protective services official*

**Stanford**
Krasner, Stephen David *federal agency administrator, political science educator*

**Stockton**
Jackson, Jewel *retired state agency administrator*

**Westlake Village**
Seymour, Jeffrey Alan *governmental relations consultant*

**COLORADO**

**Arvada**
Kurth, Suzanne M. *criminalist*

**Centennial**
Councell, Randall Eugene *protective services official*

**Commerce City**
Colon, Alan Brian *protective services official, federal agency administrator*

**Denver**
Adkins, Jeanne M. *state agency administrator*
Logan, James Scott, Sr. *federal agency administrator*
Mencer, Sue (Constance Suzanne Mencer) *former federal agency administrator*

**Eldorado Springs**
Lovins, L. Hunter *public policy institute executive, consultant, educator*

**Englewood**
McGraw, Jack Wilson *federal agency administrator*

**Pueblo**
Deasy, Irene M. *retired protective services official*

**Vail**
McGee, Michael Jay *protective services official, educator*

**CONNECTICUT**

**Bloomfield**
Shimelman, Susan Fromm *state agency administrator*

**Hamden**
Leddy, James Francis *protective services official*

**Hartford**
McNallen, James Berl *federal agency administrator, marketing professional, educator*

**Southbury**
Foxworth, Johnnie Hunter *retired state agency administrator*

**Suffield**
Hanzalek, Astrid Teicher *public information officer, consultant*

**DELAWARE**

**Dover**
Britt, Maisha Dorrah *protective services official*
Woodruff, Valerie *state agency administrator*

**Newark**
Le Min, Thomas Francis *law enforcement official, educator*

**DISTRICT OF COLUMBIA**

**Pentagon**
Dominguez, Michael L. *federal agency administrator, former civilian military employee*

**Washington**
Adams, A. John Bertrand *public affairs consultant, director*
Adams, Timothy D. *federal agency administrator*
Allen, Charles E. *federal agency administrator*
Andersen, Margo K. *federal agency administrator*
Andrew, James M. *federal agency administrator*
Andrews, Terrence Michael *senior policy advisor*
Aoki, Steven *federal agency administrator*
Apple, Daina Dravnieks *federal agency administrator*
Atkinson, George H. *federal agency administrator, chemistry professor*
Azar, Alex Michael, II, *federal agency administrator, lawyer*
Badger, Doug *federal agency administrator*
Baginski, Maureen A. *federal agency administrator*
Bair, Sheila Colleen *federal agency administrator, former education educator*
Baker, Stewart Abercrombie *federal agency administrator*
Barnett, Thomas O. *federal agency administrator*
Barrett, Thomas J. *federal agency administrator, retired military officer*
Bartuska, Ann *government official, biologist*
Baruah, Sandy K. (Santanu Kumar Baruah) *federal agency administrator*
Basham, W. Ralph *federal agency administrator*
Bateman, Paul William *federal agency administrator*
Battle, Michael A. *federal agency administrator, former prosecutor, lawyer*
Baxter, Sandra L. *government agency administrator*
Beato, Cristina V. *government agency administrator*
Bergner, Jeffrey Thomas *federal agency administrator*
Bernardi, Roy A. (Romolo Albert Bernardi) *federal agency administrator*
Berrios, Wilbert *public information officer*
Blackwill, Robert D. *former federal agency administrator*
Blakey, Marion Clifton *federal agency administrator*
Blazy, Louis Joseph III *federal agency administrator*
Boardman, Joseph H. *federal agency administrator*
Bodine, Susan P. *federal agency administrator*
Bohigian, David Steele *federal agency administrator*
Bosworth, Dale N. *federal agency administrator*
Boucher, Richard A. *federal agency administrator*
Bourgeois, Douglas J. *government agency administrator*
Boyer, Jan E. *federal agency administrator*
Boykin, William G. (Jerry Boykin) *federal agency administrator, career military officer*
Bradbury, Steven G. *federal agency administrator*
Bradley Gardner, Janice *federal agency administrator*
Brailer, David J. *federal agency administrator, health information technology executive*
Brand, Rachel L. *federal agency administrator, lawyer*
Brenner, Joel F. *federal agency administrator*
Briggs, Ethel DeLoria *federal agency administrator*
Brooks, Linton Forrestall *federal agency administrator*
Brouillette, Dan R. *former federal agency administrator*
Brown, Dana A. *federal agency administrator*
Brown, Harold *former secretary of defense*
Brown, Reginald Jude *federal agency administrator*

Brown-Hruska, Sharon *federal agency administrator*
Buchanan, Gale Arlon *federal agency administrator, former dean*
Buford, James A. *city health department administrator*
Burgess, Ronald L., Jr. *federal agency administrator, career military officer*
Burns, R. Nicholas (Robert Nicholas Burns) *federal agency administrator, former ambassador*
Cabaniss, Dale *government agency administrator*
Cabrera, Orlando J. *federal agency administrator*
Cambone, Stephen Anthony *federal agency administrator*
Campanelli, Richard M. *federal agency administrator*
Capka, J. Richard (Joseph Richard Capka) *federal agency administrator, retired military officer*
Carbonell, Josefina G. *federal agency administrator*
Cartwright, Brian Grant *federal agency administrator, lawyer*
Chellaraj, Rajkumar *federal agency administrator*
Cherry, Schroeder *federal agency administrator*
Christopherson, Charles R., Jr. *federal agency administrator*
Chu, David S.C. *federal agency administrator, economist*
Chun, Shinae *federal agency administrator*
Ciccoella, Charles S. (Chick) *federal agency administrator*
Clark, Kathryn *government agency administrator*
Clark, Michell C. *federal agency administrator*
Clarke, Kathleen Burton *federal agency administrator*
Clement, Paul D. *federal agency administrator, lawyer*
Clerihue, Randolph James *federal agency administrator*
Cohen, Jay M. *federal agency administrator, retired military officer*
Cole, Bruce Milan *federal agency administrator, art historian*
Connaughton, Sean Thomas *federal agency administrator*
Conner, Charles F. *federal agency administrator*
Conway, John Thomas *federal agency administrator, lawyer, engineer*
Cooper, Daniel L. *federal agency administrator*
Corts, Paul Richard *federal agency administrator*
Couch, Robert M. *federal agency administrator*
Cox, Christopher (Charles Christopher Cox) *federal agency administrator, former congressman*
Cox, Courtland *minority business administrator*
Cox, John W. *federal agency administrator*
Creel, Harold Jennings, Jr. *federal commission administrator, lawyer*
Cresanti, Robert Charles *federal agency administrator*
Crumpton, Henry A. (Hank Crumpton) *federal agency administrator*
Curry, Thomas J. *federal agency administrator, former state agency administrator*
Curtis, Charles B. *former federal agency administrator*
D'Agostino, Thomas Paul *federal agency administrator*
Dale, Shana L. *federal agency administrator*
Daniels, Stephen M. *government official*
Dempsey, Joan *federal agency administrator*
DeSutter, Paula A. *federal agency administrator*
DeTrani, Joseph *federal agency administrator*
Devaney, Earl E. *federal agency administrator*
Dhillon, Uttam *federal agency administrator*
Diaz, Alphonso Vincent *federal agency administrator*
Diaz, Nils Juan *federal agency administrator*
Doan, Lurita Alexis *federal agency administrator*
Dobriansky, Paula Jon *federal agency administrator*
Domenech, Edgar A. *government agency administrator*
Donnelly, Shaun Edward *government agency administrator*
Dorfman, Cynthia Hearn *government agency administrator*
Dorr, Thomas C. *federal agency administrator*
Downie, Richard Duncan *government agency administrator, retired military officer*
Dreeben, Michael R. *federal agency administrator*
Dugan, John Cunningham *federal agency administrator, lawyer*
Dunne, Patrick W. *federal agency administrator, retired military officer*
Duvall, Tyler Davis *federal agency administrator*
Edelman, Eric Steven *federal agency administrator, former ambassador*
Eggenberger, Andrew Jon *federal agency administrator*
Ellis, Joe W. *federal agency administrator*
England, Gordon Richard *federal agency administrator*
Engleman Connors, Ellen G. *federal agency administrator*
Everson, Mark Whitty *federal agency administrator*
Felix, Larry R. *federal agency administrator*
Figueroa, Orlando *federal agency executive*
Fine, Glenn A. *federal agency administrator*
Finley, James I. *federal agency administrator*
Fisher, Alice S. *federal agency administrator, lawyer*
Flory, Peter Cyril Wyche *federal agency administrator*
Fong, Phyllis Kamoi *federal agency administrator, lawyer*
Ford, Cecilia Sparks *federal agency administrator*
Fore, Henrietta Holsman *federal agency administrator*
Foresman, George W. *federal agency administrator*
Fort, Randall Martin *federal agency administrator*
Foulke, Edwin Gerhart, Jr. *federal agency administrator, lawyer*
Fox, James Edward, Jr. *federal agency administrator*
Franco, Omar *government agency administrator*
Fratto, Tony (Salvatore Antonio Fratto) *federal agency administrator*

Frawley Bagley, Elizabeth *government advisor, ambassador*
Frazer, Jendayi Elizabeth *federal agency administrator, former ambassador*
Freeman, Catherine E. *government policy advisor*
Freeman, Chas W., Jr. *federal agency administrator, writer, ambassador*
Freeman, Sharee M. *federal agency administrator*
Fried, Daniel *federal agency administrator, former ambassador*
Fromer, Kevin *federal agency administrator*
Gallagher, Patricia E. *government agency administrator*
Gambatesa, Donald Anthony *federal agency administrator*
Garman, David Kline *federal agency administrator*
Garnette, Cheryl Petty *government agency administrator*
Gatons, Anna-Marie Kilmade *government official*
Gearan, Mark D. *former federal agency administrator*
Gillis, John W. *federal agency administrator*
Glasbrenner, Karl Christian *federal agency administrator*
Goldin, Daniel S. *former federal agency administrator*
Goldway, Ruth Y. *federal agency administrator*
Gonzalez, Emilio T. *federal agency administrator*
Gorn, Janet Marie *government official*
Grandmaison, J. Joseph *federal agency administrator*
Gray, George M. *federal agency administrator*
Gray, Lyons *federal agency administrator*
Greaux, Cheryl Prejean *federal agency administrator*
Gregor, Clark R. *public information officer*
Griffin, David D. *federal agency administrator, aerospace scientist*
Griffin, Richard J. *federal agency administrator*
Grimes, John Grayson *federal agency administrator*
Grossman, Marc Issaiah *former federal agency administrator*
Gruenberg, Martin J. *federal agency administrator, lawyer*
Guard, Patricia J. *federal agency administrator*
Gulliford, James B. *federal agency administrator*
Hager, John Henry *federal agency administrator, former lieutenant governor*
Halaska, Terrell *federal agency administrator*
Hall, Dale (H. Dale Hall) *federal agency administrator*
Hanley, Allison Anne *federal agency administrator*
Hart, Sarah V. *federal agency administrator*
Harting, Harry Lloyd, Jr. *government agency administrator, retired military officer*
Hatfield, Fred *federal agency administrator*
Hayden, Michael Vincent *CIA Director, career military officer*
Hayes, Paula Freda *federal agency administrator*
Heddell, Gordon S. *federal agency administrator*
Helgerson, John Leonard *federal agency administrator*
Henke, Robert Joseph *federal agency administrator*
Henke, Tracy Ann *federal agency administrator*
Henry, Emil W., Jr. *federal agency administrator*
Herbst, John Edward *federal agency administrator, former ambassador*
Hersman, Deborah A. P. *federal agency administrator*
Hess, Michael Edward *federal agency administrator*
Hevel, Gary Francis *public information officer, consultant*
Higgins, Bradford R. *federal agency administrator*
Higgins, Kathryn O'Leary (Kitty O'Leary Higgins) *federal agency administrator, former consulting firm executive*
Hill, Christopher R. *federal agency administrator, former ambassador*
Hill, John H. *federal agency administrator*
Hill, Kent Richmond *federal agency administrator*
Hillen, John Francis *federal agency administrator*
Hobbs, Ira *federal agency administrator*
Horn, Sharon K. *government agency administrator*
Horn, Wade Frederick *federal agency administrator*
Horner, Constance Joan *federal agency administrator*
Howard, John *federal agency administrator*
Hughes, Karen Parfitt *federal agency administrator*
Huhtala, Marie Therese *federal agency administrator, former ambassador*
Hungar, Thomas G. *federal agency administrator, lawyer*
Hunt, Earl Stephen *federal agency administrator*
Hutchison, Claude B., Jr. *federal agency administrator*
Iverson, Kristine Ann *federal agency administrator*
Jackson, Beverly Roberson *state agency administrator, consultant*
Jackson, Darryl W. *federal agency administrator*
Jackson, Michael P. *federal agency administrator, former engineering company executive*
Jarrett, Jeffrey D. *federal agency administrator*
Jeffery, Reuben III *federal agency administrator*
Jenson, William G. *federal agency administrator*
Johnson, Charles E. *federal agency administrator*
Johnson, Henry Louis *federal agency administrator, former school system administrator*
Johnson, Kelly A. *federal agency administrator*
Jonas, Tina Westby *federal agency administrator*
Joseph, Robert G. *federal agency administrator*
Justesen, Troy Ralph *federal agency administrator*
Kappes, Stephen R. *federal agency administrator*
Karsner, Andy (Alexander Armand Karsner) *federal agency administrator*
Kaveeshwar, Ashok G. *federal agency administrator*
Kearney, Stephen Michael *federal agency administrator*
Keisler, Peter Douglas *federal agency administrator, lawyer*
Kelly, Paul Vincent *federal agency administrator*
Kendrick, Kim *federal agency administrator*

Kennedy, Patrick F. *federal agency administrator, former ambassador*
Kesselman, Marc L. *federal agency administrator*
Kilgore, Edwin Carroll *retired federal agency administrator*
Kim, Wan J. *federal agency administrator, lawyer*
Kimmitt, Robert Michael *federal agency executive, former business executive*
Kincannon, Louis (Charles Louis Kincannon) *federal agency administrator*
Kirsanow, Peter N. *federal agency administrator*
Klepner, Jerry D. *federal agency administrator*
Kneedler, Edwin S. *federal agency administrator*
Knight, Bruce Irving *federal agency administrator*
Korb, Donald L. *federal agency administrator, lawyer*
Krieg, Kenneth J. *federal agency administrator*
Kringen, John A. *federal agency administrator*
Krongard, Howard J. *federal agency administrator, lawyer*
Kussman, Michael J. *federal agency administrator*
Lampl, Peggy Ann *public information officer*
Langfeld, Stanley Chaitt *government executive*
Lappin, Harley G. *federal agency administrator*
LaSpada, Carmella *government agency administrator*
Lastowka, James Anthony *former federal agency administrator, lawyer*
Lautenbacher, Conrad Charles, Jr. *federal agency administrator, retired naval officer*
Lavin, Franklin Leo *federal agency administrator, former ambassador*
Law, Steven J. *federal agency administrator*
Lebryk, David A. *federal agency administrator*
Ledbetter, Kenneth W. *federal agency administrator*
Levey, Stuart A. *federal agency administrator*
Levinson, Daniel Ronald *federal agency administrator, lawyer*
Lewis, Dennis M. *federal agency administrator, former hospital administrator*
Liebman, Wilma B. *government agency administrator*
Likins, Rose Marie *federal agency administrator, former ambassador*
Livingood, Wilson S. *protective services official*
Lloyd, James D. *federal agency administrator*
Lockhart, James Bicknell III *federal agency administrator*
Lowenkron, Barry Frederick *federal agency administrator*
Lowery, Clay *federal agency administrator*
Loy, James Milton *former federal agency administrator, retired coast guard officer*
MacFarlane, Cathy M. *federal agency administrator*
Madden, Darryl Jay *federal agency administrator*
Maddox, Lauren M. *federal agency administrator*
Magwood, William D. *federal agency administrator*
Mainella, Fran (Frances P. Mainella) *federal agency administrator*
Mansfield, Gordon Hall *federal agency administrator*
Martin, Jack *federal agency administrator*
Martin, Kevin J. *federal agency administrator*
Maxwell, David Ogden *federal agency administrator, mortgage company executive*
Mc Afee, William *government official*
McCormack, Sean Ian *federal agency administrator*
McCormick, David H. *federal agency administrator*
McCutchen, Tammy Dee *federal agency administrator*
McDonald, Frances D. *government official, editor, lawyer*
McGee, James M. *federal agency administrator*
McKay, Margo Marquita *federal agency administrator, lawyer*
McKee, Margaret Jean *federal agency administrator*
McMurray, Claudia Anne *federal agency administrator, lawyer*
McNulty, Paul J. *federal agency administrator, former prosecutor*
McPherson, Ted R. (Edward Russell McPherson) *federal agency administrator*
McQueary, Charles E. (Chuck McQueary) *federal agency administrator*
Mehlman, Bruce P. *former federal agency administrator, trade association administrator*
Meisburg, Ronald Edward *federal agency administrator, lawyer*
Merritt, Carolyn *government agency administrator*
Miller, John *federal agency administrator, former news correspondent*
Moe, Ronald Chesney *public administration researcher*
Mok, Samuel Tinsing *federal agency administrator*
Mondello, Lisette McSoud *federal agency administrator*
Monroe, Jane D. *federal agency administrator*
Monroe, Stephanie Johnson *federal agency administrator*
Montanez-Johner, Nancy *federal agency administrator*
Montelongo, Michael *federal agency administrator, military officer*
Moore, Powell Allen *former federal agency administrator*
Morgan, Linda Joan *former federal agency administrator*
Morrissey, Patricia A. *federal agency administrator*
Moschella, William Emil *federal agency administrator*
Moy, Edmund C. *federal agency administrator*
Mueller, Robert Swan III *FBI Director*
Munson, Richard Jay *government agency administrator*
Muris, Timothy Joseph *former federal agency administrator, lawyer, educator*
Murphy, Frances M. *federal agency administrator*
Myers, Julie L. *federal agency administrator*
Nakayama, Granta Y. *federal agency administrator, lawyer*
Nason, Nicole R. *federal agency administrator*
Neal, Darwina Lee *federal agency administrator*
Nelson, Keith A. *federal agency administrator*

Nethery, John Jay *government official, military officer*
Nitze, William Albert *government official, lawyer, not-for-profit developer, energy executive*
Norquist, David L. *federal agency administrator*
Obering, Trey (Henry A. Obering) *federal agency administrator, career military officer*
O'Brien, Patrick Michael *federal agency administrator*
O'Connor, Eileen J. *federal agency administrator*
Ohl, Joan Eschenbach *federal agency administrator*
Oliver, LeAnn Michelle *government official*
Olsen, Jody (Josephine K. Olsen) *federal agency administrator*
Omass, George A. *federal agency administrator*
Opfer, George J. *federal agency administrator*
Orbach, Raymond Lee *federal agency administrator, physicist, researcher*
O'Sullivan, Stephanie L. *federal agency administrator*
Owsley, Douglas W. *forensic osteologist, researcher, anthropologist*
Patenaude, Pamela Hughes *federal agency administrator*
Patrick, Susan D. *federal agency administrator*
Patterson, Anne Woods (Anne Brevard Woods Patterson) *federal agency administrator, former ambassador*
Paul, Jerald S. *federal agency administrator, former state representative, lawyer*
Paulison, R. David (Robert David Paulison) *federal agency administrator*
Peacock, Marcus C. *federal agency administrator*
Perle, Richard Norman *former federal agency administrator*
Pistole, John S. *federal agency administrator*
Pittman, R. Allen *federal agency administrator*
Pizzella, Patrick *federal agency administrator*
Polito, Robert J. *federal agency administrator*
Potter, Jack (John E. Potter) *federal agency administrator*
Powell, Benjamin Albond *federal agency administrator, lawyer*
Powell, Dina Habib *federal agency administrator*
Preston, Steven C. *federal agency administrator, former service company executive*
Prosper, Pierre-Richard *federal agency administrator*
Quarles, Randal Keith *federal agency administrator, lawyer*
Quello, James Henry *government official*
Ramsey, Charles H. *police chief*
Rato y Figaredo, Rodrigo *international banking official*
Rees, Nina Shokraii *federal agency administrator*
Reich, John M. *federal agency administrator*
Ressel, Teresa Mullett *federal agency administrator*
Reynolds, Jerry (Gerald A. Reynolds) *federal agency administrator*
Riccini, Kenneth A. *government agency administrator*
Richlen, Scott Lane *federal government program administrator*
Riggs, Barbara *federal agency administrator*
Rodley, Carol A. *federal agency administrator*
Rodman, Peter Warren *federal agency administrator*
Rosenfeld, Ronald Allen *federal agency administrator*
Rosenker, Mark Victor *federal agency chairman*
Rottman, Ellis *public information officer*
Runge, Jeffrey William *federal agency administrator*
Rutherford, Boyd Kevin *federal agency administrator*
Rutledge, Peter J. *federal agency administrator*
Sampson, David Allan *federal agency administrator*
Sauerbrey, Ellen Elaine Richmond *federal agency administrator, former ambassador*
Scarlett, Lynn (Patricia Lynn Scarlett) *federal agency administrator*
Schafer, Jacqueline Ellen *federal agency administrator*
Schaitberger, Harold *protective services official, labor union administrator*
Schaumber, Peter Carey *federal agency administrator*
Scheinberg, Phyllis F. *federal agency administrator*
Schieck, Frederick W. *federal agency administrator*
Schneider, Ann Imlah *federal agency administrator, education consultant*
Schoettle, Enid C.B. *federal agency administrator*
Schofield, Regina Brown *federal agency administrator*
Sedgwick, Jeffrey Leigh *federal agency administrator, political science professor*
Sell, Clay (Jeffrey Clay Sell) *federal agency administrator*
Shane, Jeffrey Neil *federal agency administrator, lawyer*
Shannon, Thomas A., Jr. *federal agency administrator*
Shearer, Paul Scott *federal agency administrator, trade association administrator*
Shiner, Josette Sheeran *federal agency administrator*
Sigal, Jill L. *federal agency administrator*
Simon, Raymond Joseph *federal agency administrator, former school system administrator*
Simonson, Stewart Gerard *retired federal agency administrator*
Simpson, James S. *federal agency administrator*
Sirri, Erik R. *federal agency administrator, economist*
Sizemore, Richard Tom III *government agency administrator*
Skinner, Richard L. *federal agency administrator*
Skinner, Thomas V. *federal agency administrator*
Smith, Dennis G. *federal agency administrator*
Smith, Dorrance (J. Dorrance Smith) *federal agency administrator*
Sontag, Ed *former federal agency administrator*
Spooner, David M. *federal agency administrator, lawyer*

Sproat, Edward F., III, (Ward Sproat) *federal agency administrator*
Spurgeon, Dennis Ray *federal agency administrator, former manufacturing executive*
Stanley, Daniel Raymond, Sr. *federal agency administrator*
Staples, George McDade *federal agency administrator, former ambassador*
Steele, Ana Mercedes *retired federal agency administrator*
Stevenson, Katherine Holler *federal agency administrator*
Stoner, John Richard *federal agency administrator*
Strachan, Linda Avery *federal agency administrator*
Strasser, Richard Joseph, Jr. *federal agency administrator*
Stroup, Sally *federal agency administrator*
Suboleski, Stanley C. *federal agency administrator, mining engineer*
Sullivan, Daniel J. *federal agency administrator*
Sullivan, James M. *federal agency administrator*
Sullivan, Mark J. *federal agency administrator*
Talbert, Kent Dean *federal agency administrator, lawyer*
Tamargo, Mauricio J. *federal agency administrator*
Tamillow, Michael *federal agency administrator*
Thompson, Lawrence Hyde *federal agency official*
Thomsen, Linda Chatman *federal agency administrator*
Thorson, Eric M. *federal agency administrator*
Timmons, William Evan *business executive*
Tinsley, Nikki Lee Rush *federal agency administrator*
Tobey, William Hayward *federal agency administrator, former investment banker*
Tobias, Randall Lee *federal agency administrator, retired pharmaceutical company executive*
Truscott, Carl J. *federal agency administrator*
Tuerk, William F. *federal agency administrator, lawyer*
Vaughn, Gladys Gary *federal agency administrator, researcher, not-for-profit executive*
Venkayya, Rajeev V. *federal agency administrator, biomedical researcher, educator*
Ventimiglia, Vincent J., Jr. *federal agency administrator*
Wainstein, Kenneth L. *federal agency administrator, former prosecutor*
Warder, Lawrence A. *federal agency administrator*
Watson, Harlan L(eroy) *federal agency administrator, physicist, economist*
Watson, Peter S. *federal agency administrator*
Watson, Rebecca Wunder *federal agency administrator, lawyer*
Weems, Kerry N. *federal agency administrator*
Weimer, Thomas R. (R. Thomas Weimer) *federal agency administrator*
Weiner, Robert Stephen *federal agency administrator*
Welch, C. David *assistant secretary of state, former ambassador*
Wells, Linton, II, *federal agency administrator*
Werner, Robert William *federal agency administrator*
Whitaker, Scott *former federal agency administrator, lobbyist*
White, John W. *federal agency administrator, lawyer*
Williams, Darlene F. *federal agency administrator*
Williams, Julie Lloyd *federal agency administrator, lawyer*
Winkenwerder, William, Jr. *federal agency administrator*
Wolanin, Thomas Richard *federal agency administrator, educator*
Wolff, Otto J. *federal agency administrator*
Wooldridge, Sue Ellen *federal agency administrator, lawyer*
Wright, Sylvia *government agency administrator*
Wu, Benjamin H. *federal agency administrator, lawyer*
Young, Donald Alan *federal agency administrator*
Young, John Jacob, Jr. *federal agency administrator*
Zaleski, Gary George *federal agency administrator, accountant*

## FLORIDA

### Delray Beach
Schenkel, Suzanne Chance *retired natural resource specialist*

### Fort Myers
Lounsbury, David Arthur *protective services official, educator*

### Fort Pierce
Belcher, Dorothy S. *state correctional department administrator*

### Gulf Stream
Nalen, Craig Anthony *federal agency administrator*

### Jacksonville
Rutherford, John *sheriff*

### Jensen Beach
Peterson, David Frederick *retired government agency administrator*

### Labelle
Pratt, Donald Dwayne *protective services official*

### Lake City
Gay, John Marion *retired federal agency administrator, financial analyst*

### Lakeland
Mahr, Aaron Lee *government agency administrator*

### Niceville
Crawford, Jackie R. *retired federal agency administrator*

### Sun City Center
Hottinger, Joseph Earle *retired government agency administrator*

### Tallahassee
Braswell, Jackie Boyd *state agency administrator*
Buford, Barbara Fest *retired state agency administrator*
Gunnarsson, Roy *government agency administrator, consultant*
Thomas, James Bert, Jr. *retired federal agency administrator*

## GEORGIA

### Atlanta
Aiken, Vernoy Fred *government agency administrator*
Butler, Richard J. *federal agency administrator, consultant*
Gerberding, Julie Louise *federal agency administrator*
Jaffe, Harold W. *federal agency administrator*
McGowan, Angela Kay *government agency administrator, researcher*
Mecke, William Moyn *public information officer*
Pennington, Richard J. *police chief*

### Augusta
Cheng, Wu C. *retired patent examiner*

### Brunswick
Moran, John Bernard *retired government official*

### Cumming
Nelson, Dennis Stephen *protective services official*

### Jonesboro
Colburn, Donald Eugene *protective services official*

### Morrow
Culver, Dan Louis *federal agency administrator*

### Peachtree City
Ebneter, Stewart Dwight *utility industry management consultant*

## HAWAII

### Honolulu
Chapman, Duane Lee (Dog) *bail enforcement agent*
Devaney, Donald Everett *law enforcement official*
Keogh, Richard John *firearms and explosives consultant*
Saiki, Patricia (Mrs. Stanley Mitsuo Saiki) *federal agency administrator, congressman*

### Mililani
Hunkele, Lester Martin III *retired federal agency administrator*

### Oahu
Moose, Charles A. *former protective services official*

## IDAHO

### Boise
Schultz, Richard H. *state agency administrator*
Smith, Marsha H. *state agency administrator, lawyer*

### Idaho Falls
Rydalch, Ann *federal agency administrator*

## ILLINOIS

### Chicago
Dickman, Martin J. *federal agency administrator*
Kuczwara, Thomas Paul *federal agency administrator, lawyer*
Nash, Donald Gene *federal investigator, economist*
Ruder, David Sturtevant *government official, lawyer, educator*
Thomas, Cherryl T. *former federal agency administrator*
Van Pelt, Robert Irving *retired firefighter*

### Flora
Shrum, John *equal rights officer*

### Northlake
Haack, Richard Wilson *retired police officer*

### Springfield
Phelps, David Dwain *state agency administrator, former congressman*
Schroeder, Joyce Katherine *state agency administrator, research analyst*

## INDIANA

### Columbus
Hicks, Gregory Steven *government agency administrator*

### East Chicago
Ramos, John C., Jr. *protective services official, educator*

### Gary
Isla, Exu Reidemer Quero *protective services official, lawyer, writer*

### Indianapolis
Gerdes, Ralph Donald *fire safety consultant*
Landis, Larry Seabrook *state agency administrator*

**Schererville**
Opacik, Milan *protective services official, musician*

**South Bend**
Hellyer, Timothy Michael *protective services officer*

## IOWA

**Council Bluffs**
Guttau, Michael K. *state agency administrator, banker*

**Des Moines**
Brickman, Kenneth Alan *state agency administrator*
Martens, Harvey Arthur *retired government worker, academic administrator*
Nelson, Charlotte Bowers *public administrator*

**Kellogg**
Anderson, Dale C. *state agency professional, travel consultant*

## KANSAS

**Overland Park**
McCann, Vonya B. *federal agency administrator, telecommunications industry executive*

**Wichita**
Etter, Gregg Wayne, Sr. *police officer, educator*

## KENTUCKY

**Bowling Green**
Wells, Jerry *protective services official*

**Lexington**
Calvert, C. Emmett *former state agency administrator*

**Louisville**
Adams, Robert Waugh *state agency administrator, economist, educator*

## LOUISIANA

**Baton Rouge**
Harper, Robert D. *state agency administrator*
Parks, James William, II, *public facilities executive, lawyer*

**New Orleans**
Collins, Harry David *forensic engineer, mechanical engineer, nuclear engineer, claims consultant*

## MAINE

**Saco**
Mason, Nancy Tolman *retired state agency administrator*

## MARYLAND

**Annapolis**
Galvin, Michael Francis *state agency administrator, arborist*

**Baltimore**
Abrams, Rosalie Silber *retired state agency official*
Barnhart, Jo Anne B. *federal agency administrator*
Corley, Rose Ann McAfee *government official*
Crawford, Fred Lee *public information officer*
Gooden, Eric *government agency administrator, real estate agent*
Rzepkowski, James Edward *state agency administrator*
Uhl, Scott Mark *state agency administrator*

**Del Air**
O'Bryon, James Fredrick *defense conusltant*

**Beltsville**
Tso, Tien Chioh *federal agency administrator, researcher, agronomist*

**Bethesda**
Abrams, David B. *federal agency administrator*
Alexander, Duane Frederick *federal agency administrator, pediatrician, researcher*
Alving, Barbara *federal agency administrator, hematologist*
Barros, Colleen *federal agency administrator*
Battey, James F., Jr. *federal agency administrator, neurologist*
Berg, Jeremy Mark *federal agency administrator, biochemist, researcher*
Buetow, Kenneth H. *federal agency administrator*
Coates, Paul M. *government agency administrator*
Collins, Francis S. *federal agency administrator, geneticist, physician*
Doroshow, James Halpern *federal agency administrator, oncologist*
Fauci, Anthony Stephen *federal agency administrator, allergist, immunologist*
Fefferman, Hilbert *government official, lawyer*
Fraumeni, Joseph Francis, Jr. *federal agency administrator, epidemiologist*
Grady, Patricia A. *federal agency administrator*
Harford, Joe B. *federal agency administrator*
Hodes, Richard J. *federal agency administrator, immunologist, researcher*
Hrynkow, Sharon Hemond *federal agency administrator, neuroscientist, researcher*
Insel, Thomas R. *federal agency administrator, psychiatrist*
Jones, John Franklin, Jr., (Jack F. Jones) *federal agency administrator*

Joyce, Bernita Anne *retired federal agency administrator*
Katz, Stephen Ira *federal agency administrator*
Landis, Story Cleland *federal agency administrator, neurobiologist*
Larrabee, Barbara Princelau *retired intelligence officer*
Millstein, Richard Allen *federal agency administrator*
Morgan, John Davis *government agency administrator, consultant*
Murrett, Robert B. *federal agency administrator, career military officer*
Niederhuber, John Edward *federal agency administrator, oncologist, surgeon, immunologist*
O'Callaghan, Jerry Alexander *federal agency administrator*
Ostrander, Elaine A. *federal agency administrator, geneticist*
Penn, Audrey S. *federal agency administrator*
Pettigrew, Roderic I. *federal agency administrator, radiologist, researcher*
Pinn, Vivian W. *federal agency administrator, pathologist*
Rabson, Alan Saul *federal agency administrator, pathologist, educator*
Richardson, John *retired international relations executive*
Ruffin, John *federal agency administrator, researcher*
Ruiz-Bravo, Norka *federal agency administrator*
Sieving, Paul A. *federal agency administrator, ophthalmologist, educator*
Singer, Dinah S. *federal agency administrator, immunologist, researcher*
Springfield, Sanya A. *federal agency administrator*
Stanfield, Brent B. *federal agency administrator*
Straus, Stephen Ezra *federal agency administrator, biomedical researcher*
Tabak, Lawrence A. *federal agency administrator, dentist*
White, Jeffrey D. *federal agency administrator*
Zerhouni, Elias Adam *federal agency administrator*

**Chevy Chase**
Broide, Mace Irwin *public information officer*
Pitofsky, Robert *federal agency administrator, law educator*
Reilly, Edward Francis, Jr. *federal agency administrator, former state senator*

**Columbia**
Privitera, Joseph F. *retired foreign service official, writer, researcher*

**Easton**
Colton, Elizabeth Wishart *government agency administrator*

**Fort George G Meade**
Alexander, Keith B. *federal agency administrator, career military officer*
Black, William B., Jr. *federal agency administrator*

**Frederick**
Baker, Joanne Evelyn *retired government agency administrator*
Wiltrout, Robert H. *federal agency administrator*

**Gaithersburg**
Hertz, Harry Steven *government official*
Jeffrey, William Alan *federal agency administrator, physicist*
Semerjian, Hratch Gregory *federal agency administrator*

**Greenbelt**
Weiler, Edward J. *federal agency administrator*

**Kensington**
Rosenthal, Alan Sayre *government official, lawyer*
Suraci, Charles Xavier, Jr. *retired federal agency administrator, air transportation executive, consultant*

**Laurel**
Chrismer, Ronald Michael *federal agency administrator*

**Madison**
Hoffman, Alicia Coro *retired federal executive*

**Rockville**
Clark, Harry Westley *federal agency administrator*
Croyle, Robert T. *federal agency administrator, psychologist, educator*
Curie, Charles G. *federal agency administrator*
Dal Pan, Gerald J. *federal agency administrator*
Davis, Beverly Watts *federal agency administrator*
Duke, Elizabeth M. *federal agency administrator*
Epstein, Jay Stuart *federal agency administrator*
Gray, Paulette Styles *federal agency administrator, biologist*
Grim, Charles W. *federal agency administrator*
Hawk, Ernest T. *federal agency administrator*
Klein, Dale Edward *federal agency administrator, engineering educator*
Lumpkin, Murray M. *federal agency administrator*
Manderscheid, Ronald William *program administrator*
Power, A. Kathryn *federal agency administrator*
Reyes, Luis A. *federal agency administrator*
Shekar, Sam S. *federal agency administrator*
Strausberg, Robert L. *federal agency administrator*
Telesetsky, Walter *federal agency administrator*
Uhl, Kathleen *federal agency administrator*
van Dyck, Peter Cuyler *federal agency administrator*
von Eschenbach, Andrew C. *federal agency administrator, oncologist, urologic surgeon*
Whitescarver, Jack Edward *federal agency administrator*

**Silver Spring**
Dunnigan, John H. *federal agency administrator*
Johnson, David L. *federal agency administrator, retired military officer*

Kline, Jerry Robert *retired administrative judge, ecologist*
Maas, Joe (Melvin Joseph Maas) *retired federal agency administrator*
Mahoney, James R. *federal agency administrator*
Ware, Thaddeus Van *retired government official*
Williams, Paul *retired federal agency administrator*

## MASSACHUSETTS

**Boston**
Crimlisk, Jane Therese *probation officer*

**Cambridge**
Carter, Ashton Baldwin *former federal agency administrator*
Donahue, John David *federal agency administrator, educator*
Hunt, Swanee G. *public policy educator, former ambassador*

**Lexington**
Thernstrom, Abigail *federal agency administrator, writer*

**Westborough**
Horwitz, Eleanor Catherine *public information officer*

## MICHIGAN

**Detroit**
Bully-Cummings, Ella M. *police chief*
Dale, Shirley Marie *protective services official*
Gee, Ramondo Reginald *internal revenue service territory manager*
Moss, Leslie Otha *homeland security specialist*

**Hastings**
Yarger, James Richard *protective services official, director*

**Houghton**
Fink, William Orman *retired federal agency administrator, management consultant*

**Jackson**
Copeland, Eric *protective services official*

**Lansing**
Couto, C. Douglass *state agency administrator*

**Midland**
Adams, Thomas Walton *corrections official*

**New Haven**
Shaw, Charles Rusanda *retired government investigator*

**Southfield**
Gleichman, John Alan *protective services official*

**Wyandotte**
Kaurin, Douglas Edward *protective services official*

## MINNESOTA

**Brainerd**
Peterson, Donn Neal *forensic engineer, engineering company executive*

**Elk River**
Richardson, Mark P. *protective services official, educator*

**Saint Paul**
Boudreau, Lynda L. *state agency administrator*

## MISSISSIPPI

**Clarksdale**
Schmidt, John Frederick III *government agency administrator, consultant*

**Pearl**
Latham, Robert Richard, Jr. *retired state agency administrator*

**Vicksburg**
Houston, James R. *government agency administrator*

## MISSOURI

**Anderson**
Coble, Mary Gloria *protective services official, rancher*

**Clayton**
Davenport, Dennis Lynn *protective services official*

**Kansas City**
Parker, Dennis Gene *former sheriff, martial arts instructor*

**Saint Louis**
King, Joseph, Jr. *federal agency administrator*

**Wheeling**
Roe, Mary Ann *postmaster*

## NEBRASKA

**Lincoln**
Fleharty, Mary Sue *government agency administrator*

**Omaha**
Hansen, James Allen *state agency administrator*

Mactier, Ann Dickinson *state agency administrator*

## NEVADA

**Henderson**
Perkins, Richard D(ale) *protective services official, state legislator*

**Las Vegas**
Lally, Norma Ross *retired federal agency administrator*
Smith, Jimmy Wayne, Sr. *forensic specialist*

**Reno**
Svahn, John Alfred *federal agency administrator*

## NEW HAMPSHIRE

**Bedford**
Pasquerreli, Shawna *forensic specialist*

**Concord**
Mevers, Frank Clement *state agency administrator, archivist*

**Goffstown**
Day, Russell Clover *state agency administrator*

**Hanover**
Koop, C. Everett (Charles Everett Koop) *former Surgeon General of the United States, educator*

## NEW JERSEY

**Adelphia**
Carter, Harry Robert *fire protection consultant*

**Camden**
Uhler, Walter Charles *government official, writer*
Venegas, Arturo, Jr. *protective services official*

**Cape May Court House**
Pierson, Jeffrey Lynn *protective services officer*

**East Orange**
Ilogienboh, Caroline O. *protective services official, publishing executive*

**Kenilworth**
Gen, Martin *protective services executive*

**Maplewood**
Rabadeau, Mary Frances *protective services official*

**Mountainside**
Weigele, Richard Sayre *police officer*

**New Brunswick**
Coscia, Anthony R. *state agency administrator, lawyer*

**Princeton**
Whipple, William, Jr. *government policy consultant, writer*

**Tabernacle**
DiBella, Russell Thomas *federal investigator*

**Toms River**
Moran, Jeffrey W., Jr. *county surrogate*

**Trenton**
Bauer, Virginia S. *state agency administrator*
Caspersen, Sidney J. *state agency administrator*
Socolow, David Jacob *state agency administrator*

## NEW MEXICO

**Albuquerque**
Gutierrez, Sidney M. *federal agency administrator*
Jaramillo, Mari-Luci *retired federal agency administrator*
Varela, Alan Mark *government agency administrator, lawyer*
Williams, Marion Lester *government official*

**Kirtland Afb**
Tritten, James John *federal agency administrator, educator*

**Santa Fe**
Johnson, Eric B. *police chief*

## NEW YORK

**Albany**
Bradley, Edward James *state official, computer programmer and analyst*
Cross, Robert Francis *commissioner*
Eristoff, Andrew S. *state agency administrator*
Mulholland, Nancy W. *state agency administrator*

**Bayside**
Tovar-Mengibar, Salvador *retired government agency administrator*

**Bronx**
Conlon, Edward *police officer, writer*

**Chappaqua**
Laun, Louis Frederick *government official*

**Garden City**
Laureano, Mari *government agency administrator, writer*

**Huntington**
Kirwin, Barbara Rosa *forensic specialist*

**Kirkwood**
Skinner, Christopher G. *protective services official, farmer*

**New York**
Beausoleil, Doris Mae *retired federal agency housing specialist*
Cuomo, Andrew Mark *former secretary of housing and urban development*
Falkenrath, Richard A. *protective services official*
Hirsch, Charles S. *city health department administrator*
Kelly, Raymond Walter *police commissioner*
Noble, Ronald Kenneth *Secretary General of Interpol*
Ringler, Kenneth J., Jr. *state agency administrator*
Sheehan, Michael Andrew *former protective services official, former federal agency administrator*
Sorensen, Gillian Martin *United Nations official*
Stewart, Ruth Ann *public policy educator*
Talbot, Phillips *retired Asian affairs specialist*
Turso, Vito Anthony *government agency administrator, public information officer*

**Rochester**
Phillips, Harold John III *protective services official, consultant*
Sexstone, Brian Thomas *protective services official*

**Romulus**
Ostrander, Robert Edwin *retired United Nations interregional advisor, petroleum company executive*

**Valhalla**
Czarnecki, Anthony J. *correction administrator, educator*

## NORTH CAROLINA

**Canton**
Roberts, Bill Glen *retired protective services official*

**Chapel Hill**
Andrews, Richard Nigel Lyon *public information officer, educator, environmental services administrator*
Umminger, Bruce Lynn *government agency administrator, research scientist, educator, consultant*

**Charlotte**
Swecker, Chris (Christophe E. Swecker) *protective services official, former federal agency administrator*

**Greensboro**
Ward, Charles A. *federal agency administrator*

**Jackson**
Brown, Gary *economic development agency executive*

**Lillington**
Cole, Raymond Eugene *public information officer*

**Raleigh**
Dornan, John Neill *public policy center professional*
Freeman, Franklin Edward, Jr. *government agency administrator*
Neenan, Peter Anthony *state agency administrator*
Sanford, Jo Anne *state agency administrator*

**Research Triangle Park**
Schwartz, David A. *federal agency administrator*

## OHIO

**Akron**
Shane, Sandra Kuli *postal service administrator*

**Columbus**
Gillmor, Karen Lako *state agency administrator*
Kearns, Merle Grace *state agency administrator*
McInturff, Floyd M. *retired state agency administrator*
Rucker, Richard Neal *retired protective services official, emergency medical technician, director*
Taylor, Joel Sanford *government agency administrator*

**Delaware**
Ciochetty, John Bryan *protective services official*

**Hiram**
Chema, Thomas V. *government official, consultant, academic administrator, lawyer*

**Monroe**
Homer, Gregory C. *protective services official*

**Montpelier**
Deckrosh, Hazen Douglas *retired state agency educator and administrator*

**Newark**
Barner, Bruce Monroe *retired state agency administrator, not-for-profit developer*
Billy, Gerry Dee *protective services official*

**Pomeroy**
Brockert, Joseph Paul *government executive, writer, editor, designer*

**Zanesville**
Istok, Christine Markward *retired executive director social service agency, consultant*

## OKLAHOMA

**Oklahoma City**
Bush, William Arden *federal agency administrator*
Wheeler, Jane Frances *protective services official*

**Tinker Afb**
Penn, Vernita Lynn *government agency administrator*

**Tulsa**
Deihl, Michael Allen *federal agency administrator*

**Wagoner**
Hadley, Charline A. *protective services official*

## OREGON

**Corvallis**
Bamberger, Michael *protective services official*

**Eugene**
Jiler, Linda Cerise *retired fire and aviation program support specialist, fire emergency dispatcher, consultant, researcher, writer*

## PENNSYLVANIA

**Bangor**
Schiavone, John *state agency administrator*

**Campbelltown**
Jurell, William D. *protective services official*

**Gettysburg**
Roach, James Clark *federal agency administrator*

**Hanover Township**
Ginyard, Caleb Nathaniel III *government agency administrator*

**Harrisburg**
Wentzel, Paul H., Jr. *state agency administrator*

**Philadelphia**
Hackney, Sheldon *former federal agency administrator, history educator*
Hairston, Harold B. *protective services official*

**Unionville**
De Marino, Donald Nicholson *federal agency administrator, diversified financial services company executive*

**Wallingford**
Cook, Harvey Carlisle *law enforcement official*

## RHODE ISLAND

**Providence**
Hedlund, Ellen Louise *state agency administrator, educator*

**Saunderstown**
Knauss, John Atkinson *retired federal agency administrator, oceanographer, educator, retired dean*

## SOUTH CAROLINA

**Swansea**
Inabinet, George Walker, Jr. *retired state agency administrator*

## SOUTH DAKOTA

**Pierre**
Duhamel, Judith Reedu Olson *public information officer, former state senator*

## TENNESSEE

**Knoxville**
Harris, Skila *government agency administrator*

**Memphis**
Knight, H. Stuart *law enforcement official, consultant*

**Mount Juliet**
Chester, Thomas Wayne *state agency administrator*

**Smithville**
Morris, Howard Henderson *protective services official*

## TEXAS

**Arlington**
Kassen, Alan Neil *protective services official*

**Austin**
Ashworth, Kenneth Hayden *public information administrator*
Combs, Susan *state agency administrator*
James, Randall S. *state banking department commissioner*

**Baytown**
Leiper, Robert Duncan *local government official*

**Bryan**
Owens, Harold B. *former state agency consultant*

**Dallas**
Garreans, Leonard Lansford *protective services official, criminal justice professional*
Kunkle, David M. *police chief*
Mathis-Thorton, Dianna Dawn *protective services official, writer, publishing executive, not-for-profit developer*

**Duncanville**
Fewel, John Gerrard *government agency administrator, director*

**Fort Worth**
Jackson, Stephen Eric *public speaker, life strategist*

**Houston**
Asher, Jerry L. *retired federal agency administrator*
Dillon, Jimi *protective services official*

**Kingsland**
Watson, Elizabeth Marion *protective services official*

**San Antonio**
McManus, William Paul *police chief*

**Wylie**
Flores, Noe Cortez *protective services official*

## UTAH

**Salt Lake City**
Sparks, Mildred Thomas *state agency administrator, educator*

## VERMONT

**Springfield**
Putnam, Paul Adin *federal agency administrator*

## VIRGINIA

**Alexandria**
Cabral, Sam A. *protective services official, labor union administrator*
Hale, Robert Fargo *federal association executive*
Hark, William Henry *retired federal agency administrator, aerospace physician*
Hughes, Grace-Flores *federal agency administrator*
Johnson, JoAnn Mardelle *federal agency administrator*
Knowlton, William Allen *federal agency administrator, educator*
Leestma, Robert *retired federal agency administrator, educational association administrator*
Leonhart, Michele Marie *federal agency administrator*
Tandy, Karen P. *federal agency administrator*
Widner, Ralph Randolph *retired public administrator*

**Annandale**
Christianson, Geryld B. *government agency administrator, consultant*
Gioconda, Thomas F. *government program administrator, retired military flag officer*

**Arlington**
Askey, Thelma J. *federal agency administrator*
Bune, Karen Louise *state agency administrator*
Clark, John F. *federal agency administrator*
Covington, James Edwin *government agency administrator, psychologist*
Dudas, Jonathan W. *federal agency administrator*
Farr, Jesse F. *federal agency administrator*
Hawley, Edmund S. (Kip Hawley) *federal agency administrator*
McDonald, Bernard Robert *retired federal agency administrator*
Meadows, Vickers B. *federal agency administrator*
Metz, Craig Huseman *government relations executive*
Moore, Guy Will *retired public information officer, historian, writer*
Rymer, Jon T. *federal agency administrator*

**Boydton**
Hoyle, Harvey Alvin *protective services official*

**Chantilly**
Fitzgerald, Dennis D. *federal agency administrator*
Kerr, Donald MacLean, Jr. *federal agency administrator, physicist*

**Charlottesville**
Roseberry, Edwin Southall *retired state agency administrator*

**Danville**
Reaves, Joseph Shane *protective services official*

**Fairfax**
Jones, George Fleming *international consultant*

**Flint Hill**
Williamson, Richard Hall *federal agency administrator*

**Fort Belvoir**
Keeney, Leah M. *government agency administrator*
Tegnelia, James A. *federal agency administrator*

**Fredericksburg**
Kusserow, Richard Phillip *federal agency administrator, corporate financial executive*

**Great Falls**
Turner, Stansfield *former CIA director, retired military officer*

**Hampton**
Dunn, Keith A. *government agency administrator, consultant*
Roe, Lesa B. *federal agency administrator*

**Herndon**
Bridges, Roy Dubard, Jr. *former federal agency administrator*

**Leesburg**
Ink, Dwight A. *government agency administrator*

**Mc Lean**
Burke, Sheila P. *federal agency administrator*
Cannon, Mark Wilcox *retired government official*
Doyle, Frederick Joseph *retired government research scientist*
Lion, Linda N. *retired federal agency administrator*
Mahan, Clarence *federal agency administrator, writer*
Malley, Raymond Charles *retired foreign service official, industrial executive*
Spaulding, Wallace Holmes *retired federal agency professional*
Yancik, Joseph John *retired government official*

**Mineral**
Donald, James Robert *federal agency administrator, writer, economist*

**Oakton**
Entzminger, John Nelson, Jr. *federal agency administrator, electrical engineer*

**Quantico**
Mangan, Terence Joseph *retired federal agency administrator*

**Reston**
Myers, Mark D. *federal agency administrator, geologist*
Pasternack, Robert Harry *former federal agency administrator*
Rosendhal, Jeffrey David *federal agency administrator, educator, astronomer*
Shelton, Hugh (Henry Hugh Shelton) *former Chairman of the Joint Chiefs of Staff*

**Richmond**
Blake, Peter *state agency administrator*
Face, E. Joseph, Jr. *state agency administrator*

**Spotsylvania**
Hill, Jimmie Dale *retired federal agency administrator*

**Upperville**
Johnson, Manuel Holman, Jr. *government official, economics educator, business executive*

**Williamsburg**
Flanders, Raymond Alan *dentist, governmental health agency administrator*
Gentry, James William *retired state agency administrator*

## WASHINGTON

**Bothell**
Anders, Harley Dillon, Sr. *retired federal agency administrator*

**Seattle**
Krochalis, Richard F. *federal agency administrator*
Riccobono, Richard M. *federal agency administrator*
Stamper, Norman H. *protective services official*

**Sequim**
Huntley, James Robert *government official, international affairs scholar*
Meacham, Charles Harding *federal agency administrator*

**Shelton**
Leverich, Denis *protective services official, educator*

**Spokane**
Novak, Terry Lee *public information officer, educator, dean*

**Vancouver**
Ogden, Daniel Miller, Jr. *public official, educator*

## WISCONSIN

**Madison**
Dies, David C. *government agency administrator*

**Sturtevant**
Marschke, Sean M. *police captain, emergency management director*

## TERRITORIES OF THE UNITED STATES

## AMERICAN SAMOA

**Pago Pago**
Howland, Repeka Moata'a Isara *retired government community services administrator*

## PUERTO RICO

**San Juan**
Luna, Jesus *protective services official*

## VIRGIN ISLANDS

**St Thomas**
Baker, Harold M. *government agency administrator, retired military officer*

## MILITARY ADDRESSES OF THE UNITED STATES

### EUROPE

#### APO

Ohman, Diana J. *government agency administrator, former state official*

### CANADA

#### ONTARIO

**Ottawa**

MacFarlane, John Alexander *retired federal agency administrator*
Murray, Larry *government agency administrator*
Withers, Ramsey Muir *retired federal agency administrator*

**Toronto**

Fraser, William Neil *retired government agency administrator*
Macdonald, Donald Stovel *public policy advisor*
Tsubouchi, David H. *Canadian provincial official*

### COTE D'IVOIRE

#### Abidjan

Perry, Cynthia Shepard *federal agency administrator*

### ENGLAND

#### London

Clark, Cynthia Zang Facer *federal agency administrator*

### HONG KONG

#### Wanchai

Paulus, Michael John *government official, economist, bank executive*

### MALAWI

#### Lilongwe

Eastham, Alan Walter, Jr. *foreign service officer, lawyer*

### UNITED STATES

#### APO

Carner, George *foreign service executive, economic strategist*

#### ADDRESS UNPUBLISHED

Aamodt, Roger Louis *retired federal agency administrator*
Akiyama, Cliff *forensic science educator, criminologist, researcher, consultant*
Aldridge, Edward Cleveland, Jr., (Pete Aldridge) *former federal agency administrator*
Alvarez, Aida M. *former federal agency administrator*
Amorello, Matthew John *former state agency administrator, former state senator*
Anderson, David Wayne *former federal agency administrator*
Anderson, Wayne Carl *public information officer, retired corporate financial executive*
Armitage, Richard Lee *former federal agency administrator*
Baquet, Charles R. III *former federal agency administrator, international studies educator*
Barca, James Joseph *fire department administrative services executive*
Barram, David J. *federal agency administrator*
Bayer, Robert Edward *retired federal agency administrator*
Bell, Phillip Jackson *federal agency administrator*
Benton, Marjorie Craig *federal agency administrator*
Bey, Joan S. *retired public information officer*
Bishop, C. Diane *state agency administrator, educator*
Blix, Hans Martin *retired intergovernmental agency administrator*
Bowen, Nicholas Robert *state agency administrator*
Brehm, Warren Gamaliel Harding *protective services official*
Brown, Dale Susan *retired federal agency administrator, academic administrator, consultant, writer*
Brown, John B. III *former federal agency administrator*
Brown, Michael DeWayne *former federal agency administrator, lawyer*
Brubaker, Crawford Francis, Jr. *federal agency administrator, aerospace scientist, consultant*
Brubaker, William W., Jr. *federal agency administrator, civil engineer*
Bunker, Robert Duffield *protective services official, military officer*
Burgess, Marjorie Laura *retired protective services official*
Bush, Frederick Morris *former federal agency administrator*
Campbell, Arthur Andrews *retired federal agency administrator*

Canterbury, Charles *protective services official, labor union administrator*
Cantu, Jose Francisco *retired postal worker*
Carmona, Richard Henry *former Surgeon General of the United States*
Chapman, Richard LeRoy *public affairs researcher*
Chu, Margaret S.Y. *former federal agency administrator*
Clarke, Victoria C. (Torie Clarke) *former federal agency administrator*
Claytor, Richard Anderson *retired federal agency administrator*
Cornish, Richard Joseph *international affairs consultant, retired diplomat*
Coye, Molly Joel *state agency administrator*
Crane, Barry D. *former federal agency administrator*
Crawford, Lester Mills, Jr. *former federal agency administrator*
Crowell, Craven H., Jr. *retired state agency administrator*
Delaney, John *protective services official*
Dewey, Arthur Eugene *former federal agency administrator*
Dingle, Carol A. *state agency administrator, writer*
Doret, Peter *state agency administrator, lawyer*
Dunne, Mary Maguire *federal agency administrator, lawyer*
Ervin, Clark Kent *former federal agency administrator*
Feiner, Ava Sophia *public affairs consultant, management consultant, economist*
Feith, Douglas Jay *former federal agency administrator*
Fella, Marie Ann *intelligence analyst, drug enforcement administration*
Felt, Mark (Deep Throat, W. Mark Felt Sr., William Mark Felt Sr.) *former federal agency administrator*
Finauri, Graciela Maria *foreign service official*
Fisher, David Russel *government executive*
Fisher, Linda J. *former federal agency administrator*
Forbes-Richardson, Helen Hilda *state agency administrator*
Frazier, Henry Bowen III *retired federal agency administrator*
Friday, Elbert Walter, Jr. *federal agency administrator, meteorologist*
Gaddy, Sidney Warren *government agency administrator*
Gall, Mary Sheila *former federal agency administrator*
Gauss, John A. *former federal agency administrator, retired naval officer*
Gilman, J. Paul *former federal agency administration*
Godwin, Larry A. *protective services official*
Golding, Carolyn May *former government senior executive, consultant*
Goss, Porter Johnston *former CIA director, former congressman*
Green, Grant S., Jr. *former federal agency administrator*
Gregory, Frederick Drew *federal agency administrator*
Hale, Janet *federal agency administrator*
Helms, J. Lynn *retired federal agency administrator*
Henkin, Josh *federal agency administrator, consultant*
Hensley, Ralph Henry III *federal agency administrator*
Hernandez, Israel *federal agency administrator*
Heyman, Ira Michael *federal agency administrator, law educator, museum executive*
Hickok, Eugene Welch *former federal agency administrator*
Hodsoll, Francis Samuel Monaise *government official*
Horinko, Marianne Lamont *former federal agency administrator*
Hubbard, William Keith *former federal agency administrator*
Hughes, Patrick M. *federal agency administrator, retired military officer*
Iovino, Pamela M. *federal agency administrator*
James, Kay Coles *former federal agency administrator*
Jameson, Patricia Marian *government agency administrator*
Jen, Joseph Jwu Shun *former federal agency administrator*
Karp, Naomi Katherine *United States government administrator*
Kelly, James Andrew *former federal agency administrator, former policy research executive*
Kelso, John Hodgson *retired federal agency administrator*
Kerik, Bernard B. *former police commissioner*
Keys, John W. III *former federal agency administrator*
Kott, Alan *state agency administrator*
Kutscher, Ronald Earl *retired federal agency administrator*
Kwame, Guy Allen *protective services official*
LaBarre, Carl Anthony *retired federal agency administrator*
Lancaster, Karine R. *retired city health department administrator*
Larson, Alan Philip *former federal agency administrator*
Lat, David B. *former assistant US attorney, online-journalist, editor, blogger*
Lee, Tonia Reneé *entertainer, former government agent, educator*
Lewis, Samuel Winfield *retired federal agency administrator, retired diplomat*
Limbaugh, Mark A. *federal agency administrator*
Lofca, Izzet *protective services official, researcher*
Lokmer, Stephanie Ann *international business development consultant*
Lovelace, Rose Marie Sniegon *federal space agency administrator*
Lovell, Malcolm Read, Jr. *public information officer, educator, retired trade association administrator, retired federal official*
Loy, Frank Ernest *retired federal agency administrator*
Lu, Natalie *federal agency administrator*

Luce, Thomas Warren III *former federal agency administrator*
Magaw, John W. *former federal agency administrator*
Matz, Deborah *former federal agency administration*
McCaleb, Neal A. *former federal agency administrator*
McClain, Lena Alexandria *protective services official*
McClellan, Mark B. *former federal agency administrator*
McCormick, David Harold *government agency administrator*
McCormick, Robert Junior *former federal agency administrator*
McDowell, Elaine *retired federal government executive, educator*
McHale, Paul F., Jr. *federal agency administrator, former congressman*
McLaughlin, John Edward *former federal agency administrator*
McLean, Walter Franklin *government agency administrator, business consultant, legislator, minister*
McTaggart, Timothy Robert *state agency administrator, lawyer*
Mehan, George Tracey III *former federal agency administrator*
Meyer, Donald Robert *state agency administrator, lawyer*
Millman, Amy J. *government official*
Minners, Howard Alyn *federal agency administrator, researcher, preventive medicine physician*
Molholm, Kurt Nelson *retired federal agency administrator*
Molz, Redmond Kathleen *public affairs educator*
Morales, Diane K. *former federal agency administrator*
Moseley, James R. *former federal agency administrator, farmer*
Murr, James Coleman *retired federal agency administrator*
Newman, Constance Berry *federal agency administrator*
Nyquist, Maurice Otto *retired federal agency administrator, scientist*
O'Brien, Odessa Louise *protective services official*
O'Grady, Michael J. *federal agency administrator*
Oliver, Jerry Alton *former police chief*
Panetta, Michael Jon *retired state agency administrator, writer*
Pearson, Jennie Sue *retired government administrator*
Pearson, W. Robert (William Robert Pearson) *former federal agency administrator, former ambassador*
Perkins, Raymond Lamont *retired government official*
Peterson, E. Anne *former federal agency administrator*
Peterson, Katherine H. *federal agency administrator, former ambassador*
Philippus, Al A. *former police chief*
Plame, Valerie Elise *former intelligence agent*
Powell, Donald E. *federal agency administrator*
Raley, Bennett William *former federal agency administrator*
Rey, Mark E. *federal agency administrator*
Reynolds, Frank Miller *retired government agency administrator*
Rhodes, Karren *public information officer*
Ricciardi, Steven Drew *protective services official*
Ridgway, James Mastin *retired government agency administrator*
Rodgers, Bruce Alan *government agency administrator, psychologist*
Rosenberg, Alison P. *public information officer*
Roswell, Robert H. *former federal agency administrator*
Rush, Jeffrey, Jr. *former federal agency administrator*
Ryder, Tereasa Kai *retired protective services official*
Sabelhaus, Melanie R. *government agency administrator*
Schoenberg, Mark George *government agency administrator*
Schoenberger, James Edwin *retired federal agency administrator*
Schur Kaufman, Susan *retired public affairs consultant*
Schwartz, Carol Levitt *government official*
Schweitzer, Theodore Gottlieb III *government agency administrator*
Schwoch, Robert William *public affairs director*
Scoppetta, Nicholas *fire commissioner*
Scott, Jeffrey Lyle *protective services official*
Shasteen, Donald Eugene *government official*
Shute, Richard Emil *federal agency administrator, engineer*
Skaff, Joseph John *state agency administrator, retired military officer*
Slater, Eve E. *former federal agency administrator*
Smith, Marcia K. *government agency administrator*
Smith, Nancy Angelynn *federal agency administrator*
Smith, Todd Lee *protective services official*
Smith, Wendy Haimes *federal agency administrator*
Sorter, Bruce Wilbur *federal program administrator, educator, consultant*
Spinrad, Richard William *former federal agency administrator, oceanographer*
Stagliano, Vito Alexander *federal agency administrator, utilities executive, writer*
Stenbit, John Paul *former federal agency administrator*
Stone, David M. *former federal agency administrator, retired career military officer*
Swinburn, Carol Ditzler *retired state and municipal agency administrator*
Swoap, David Bruce *government agency administrator, consultant, art director, state agency administrator*
Taylor, Francis X. *former federal agency administrator, retired military officer*
Taylor, John Brian *former federal agency administrator*

Ter Horst, Jerald Franklin *public affairs counselor*
Towle, Leland Hill *retired federal agency administrator*
Truesdale, John Cushman *federal agency administrator, lawyer*
Turner, John Freeland *former federal agency administrator, retired state legislator*
Umpenhour, Ken Eugene *protective services official*
Vandiver, Sara Elizabeth Sharp Rankin *retired postmaster*
Walsh, Dennis P. *federal agency administrator*
Wendt, E. Allan *international affairs consultant*
Whitman, Christine Todd *former federal agency administrator, former governor*
Williams, B. John, Jr. *retired federal agency administrator, lawyer*
Williams, Steven A., Jr. *former federal agency administrator*
Williams, Sue M. *federal agency administrator, writer*
Winn, Morris X. *former federal agency administrator*
Winter, Roger Paul *former federal agency administrator*
Winterowd, Norman Wadell *government agency administrator*
Withrow, Mary Ellen *federal agency administrator*
Young, Edwin S. W. *federal agency official*
Young, Frank Edward *retired federal agency administrator, religious organization administrator*
Young, Jennifer Baxendell *former federal agency administrator*
Yurechko, John Joseph *federal agency administrator, director*
Zaltman, Mark Allen *federal agency administrator*
Ziese, Dennis Russell *retired protective services official, retired military officer*

## GOVERNMENT: EXECUTIVE ADMINISTRATION

### UNITED STATES

#### ALABAMA

**Birmingham**

Boomershine, Donald Eugene *bureau executive, development official*

**Montgomery**

Baxley, Lucy *lieutenant governor*
Ivey, Kay Ellen *state official*
King, Troy *state attorney general*
Riley, Bob (Robert Renfroe Riley) *governor*
Worley, Nancy L. *state official*
Young, Caron L *county official*

#### ALASKA

**Anchorage**

Brown, Dean Naomi *state official, geologist*
Knowles, Tony *former governor*
Leman, Loren Dwight *lieutenant governor, civil engineer*

**Juneau**

Márquez, David W. *state attorney general*
Murkowski, Frank Hughes *governor*

**Kodiak**

Selby, Jerome M. *mayor*

#### ARIZONA

**Anthem**

MacMillan, Hoke *former state attorney general*

**Mesa**

Hawker, Keno *mayor, trucking company executive*

**Phoenix**

Brewer, Janice Kay *state official*
Dobronski, Mark William *judge, justice of the peace*
Goddard, Terry *state attorney general*
Gordon, Philip Bruce *mayor*
Meeks, Jacquelynn *city health department administrator*
Napolitano, Janet Ann *governor*

**Scottsdale**

Quayle, Dan (James Danforth Quayle) *former vice president United States*
Quayle, Marilyn Tucker *wife of former United States vice president, lawyer*

**Sun Lakes**

Sharpless, Joseph Benjamin *retired county official*

**Tucson**

Walkup, Robert E. *mayor*

#### ARKANSAS

**Bella Vista**

Medin, Myron James, Jr. *city manager*

**Heber Springs**

Rawlings, Paul C. *retired government official*

**Little Rock**

Beebe, Mike *state attorney general*
Cheek, James Richard *ambassador*
Daniels, Charlie *state official*
Fisher, Jimmie Lou *state official*
Huckabee, Michael Dale *governor*

Priest, Sharon Devlin *retired state official, not-for-profit developer*
Weiss, Richard A. *state official*

## CALIFORNIA

### Anaheim
Pringle, Curt *mayor*

### Benicia
von Studnitz, Gilbert Alfred *state official*

### Berkeley
Hamilton, Randy Haskell *city manager*
Taylor, John Lockhart *retired municipal official*

### Carson
Oropeza, Jenny *state official*

### Claremont
Pedersen, Richard Foote *diplomat, academic administrator*

### Coronado
Hostler, Charles Warren *retired ambassador, international affairs consultant*

### Felicity
Istel, Jacques Andre *mayor*

### Fresno
Autry, Alan *mayor, actor, former professional football player, film company executive*

### Grass Valley
Cassella, Dennis Gene *retired county official*

### La Jolla
Davidow, Jeffrey *former ambassador to Mexico*
Shakespeare, Frank *ambassador*

### Laguna Woods
Hussey, William Bertrand *retired diplomat*

### Long Beach
O'Neill, Beverly Lewis *mayor, former college president*
Sato, Eunice Noda *former mayor, consultant*

### Los Angeles
Antonovich, Michael Dennis *county official*
Ash, Roy Lawrence *former federal official*
Davis, Michael Rico *county official*
Fielding, Jonathan Evan *city health department administrator, pediatrician*
Helm, Robert Wilbur *federal official*
Molina, Gloria *municipal official*
Toman, Mary Ann *federal official*
Villaraigosa, Antonio R. *mayor*

### Marina
Mettee-McCutchon, Ila *municipal official, retired military officer*

### Menlo Park
Lane, Laurence William, Jr. *retired ambassador, publisher*

### Monrovia
Mountjoy, Dennis Lee *state official*

### Montebello
Calderon, Ronald *state official*

### Monterey Park
Smith, Betty Denny *county official, administrator, fashion executive*

### Moreno Valley
White, Charles R. *former mayor*

### Napa
Battisti, Paul Oreste *retired municipal official*

### Oakland
Brown, Jerry (Edmund Gerald Brown Jr.) *mayor, former governor*

### Oceanside
Lyon, Richard *retired mayor, retired military officer*

### Ontario
Dastrup-Hamill, Faye Myers *city official*

### Oroville
Curry, William Sims *county official*

### Palo Alto
Schnabel, Rockwell Anthony *former ambassador*

### Pasadena
Bogaard, William Joseph *mayor, lawyer, educator*

### Rancho Cucamonga
Dutton, Robert D. *state official*

### Rancho Mirage
Ford, Gerald Rudolph, Jr. *38th President of the United States*

### Redlands
Hanson, Gerald Warner *retired county official*

### Richmond
Corbin, Rosemary MacGowan *former mayor*

### Sacramento
Bettenhausen, Matthew Robert *state official, lawyer*
Bustamante, Cruz M. *lieutenant governor*
Dunnett, Dennis George *retired state official*
Fargo, Heather *mayor*
Hunter, Patricia Rae (Tricia Hunter) *state official*
Lockyer, Bill (William Lockyer) *state attorney general*
McPherson, Bruce A. *state official, former state legislator*

Schwarzenegger, Arnold Alois *governor*
Wyland, Mark *state official*

### San Diego
Bliesner, James Douglas *municipal/county official, consultant*
Golding, Susan G. *former mayor*
Sanders, Jerry *mayor, former social services executive*
Shepard, Jean M. *city health department administrator*

### San Francisco
Hewitt, Conrad W. *former comissioner, accountant*
Katz, Mitchell H. *city health department administrator*
Newsom, Gavin *mayor*
Reilly, William Kane *former government official, educator, lawyer, conservationist*

### San Jose
Gonzales, Ron *mayor, former county supervisor*

### San Luis Obispo
Shlaudeman, Harry Walter *retired diplomat*

### Santa Ana
Daly, Tom *county official*
Wellborn, Michael *county official*

### Santa Monica
Aaron, David L. *diplomat, author*

### Seaside
Panetta, Leon Edward *former White House chief of staff, former congressman*

### Solana Beach
Gildred, Theodore E. *former diplomat, real estate developer*

### Stanford
Abraham, Spencer (Edward Spencer Abraham) *former Secretary of Energy*

### Stockton
Meissner, Katherine Gong *municipal official*

### Tracy
Waziri, Ghaus Ghulam *diplomat*

### Walnut Creek
Walston, Roderick Eugene *federal official*

### Yuba City
Kemmerly, Jack Dale *retired state official*

## COLORADO

### Aurora
Sheffield, Nancy *city agency administrator*

### Colorado Springs
Rivera, Lionel *mayor*
Swihart, James W., Jr. *diplomat*

### Denver
Brown, Keith Lapham *retired ambassador*
Cohen-Vader, Cheryl Denise *municipal official*
Dennis, Gigi (Ginette E. Dennis) *state official, former state legislator*
Hickenlooper, John W. *mayor*
Muja, Kathleen Ann *state official, consultant*
Norton, Jane E. (Jane Bergman) *lieutenant governor*
Owens, Bill *governor*
Suthers, John William *state attorney general, former prosecutor*

### Pueblo
Occhiato, Michael Anthony *municipal official*

## CONNECTICUT

### Canton Center
Humphrey, Samuel Stockwell *town official, physicist*

### Easton
Meyer, Alice Virginia *state official*

### Hartford
Blumenthal, Richard *state attorney general*
Bysiewicz, Susan *state official*
Nappier, Denise L. *state official*
Perez, Eddie A. *mayor*
Rell, M. Jodi *governor*
Sullivan, Kevin B. *lieutenant governor, former state legislator*

### New Haven
Zedillo Ponce de León, Ernesto *former president of Mexico*

### Northford
James, William Hall *former state official, educator*

### Stamford
Dennies, Sandra Lee *city official*
Farren, J. Michael *former government official, lawyer*
Malloy, Dannel Patrick *mayor*

## DELAWARE

### Dover
Carney, John C., Jr. *lieutenant governor*
Minner, Ruth Ann *governor*
Windsor, Harriet Smith *state official*

### Newark
Woo, S. B. (Shien-Biau Woo) *retired state official, physicist, educator*

### Wilmington
Danberg, Carl Christian *state attorney general*

## DISTRICT OF COLUMBIA

### Washington
Abdenur, Roberto Mameri Pinto *ambassador*
Abell, Charles S. *federal official*
Abell, Richard Bender *federal judicial officer, lawyer*
Abrams, Elliott *federal official*
Abshire, David Manker *former ambassador, research executive*
Addington, David S. *federal official, lawyer*
Adelstein, Jonathan Steven *commissioner*
Aguirre, Eduardo, Jr. *ambassador, former federal agency administrator*
Ahmad, Syed Hasan *ambassador*
Albright, Madeleine Korbel *former secretary of state*
Allgeier, Peter Frederick *ambassador*
Almaguer, Frank *ambassador*
Andersen, Robert Allen *retired federal official*
Angula, Helmut Kangulohi *Namibian government official*
Aranoff, Shara L. *federal official*
Arietti, Michael Ray *ambassador*
Arnall, Roland E. *ambassador*
Atherton, Charles Henry *federal commission administrator*
Atkins, Paul S. *commissioner*
Ayalon, Daniel *ambassador*
Ayele, Kassahun *ambassador*
Ayres, Mary Ellen *federal official*
Azcuenaga, Mary Laurie *government official*
Badlishah, Abdul Halim Mu'adzam Shah *Sultan of Kedah*
Bagley, Grant P. *federal official, physician*
Baicker, Katherine (Kate Baicker) *federal official, economics professor*
Baker, Douglas B. *federal official*
Bandler, Donald Keith *international consultant, former ambassador*
Barbosa, Rubens Antonio *former ambassador*
Bartlett, Dan (Daniel J. Bartlett) *federal official*
Bassin, Jules *foreign service officer*
Becker, Brenda L. *federal official*
Berger, Sandy (Samuel R. Berger) *former national security advisor*
Beyrle, John R. *ambassador*
Bhatia, Karan K. *ambassador*
Blahous, Charles P. *federal official*
Blanchard, James Johnston *ambassador, retired governor*
Bodman, Samuel Wright III *secretary of energy, former specialty chemicals and materials company executive*
Bolten, Joshua Brewster *White House chief of staff*
Bost, Eric M. *ambassador, former federal agency administrator*
Boswell, Eric J. *federal official*
Boyce, Ralph L. *ambassador*
Brazeal, Aurelia Erskine *former ambassador*
Breathitt, Linda K. *energy advisor, former federal energy commissioner*
Brewster, Robert Charles *diplomat, consultant*
Brotodiningrat, Soemadi Djoko Moerdjono *ambassador*
Browning, Steven Alan *ambassador*
Burns, William Joseph *ambassador, former federal agency administrator*
Burson, Charles W. *former federal official, former state attorney general, lawyer*
Bush, George Walker *43rd President of the United States*
Bush, Laura Welch *First Lady of United States*
Bushnell, Prudence *diplomat, former management consultant, trainer*
Butenis, Patricia A. *ambassador*
Cain, James P. *ambassador, lawyer*
Campbell, John *ambassador*
Campos, Roel C. *commissioner*
Carson, Johnnie *former ambassador, academic administrator*
Casey, Kathleen L. *commissioner*
Cason, James Caldwell *ambassador*
Chao, Elaine Lan (Hsiao Lan Chao) *secretary of labor*
Cheney, Dick (Richard Bruce Cheney) *Vice President of the United States*
Chertoff, Michael *secretary of homeland security, former federal judge*
Chien, Nguyen Tam *ambassador*
Chorba, Timothy A. *former ambassador to Singapore*
Cino, Maria *Secretary of Transportation*
Cleland, Joseph Maxwell (Max Cleland) *federal official, former senator*
Cloud, John Albert, Jr. *ambassador*
Collins, James Franklin *retired ambassador*
Collins, Keith *federal executive*
Combs, Linda Morrison *federal official*
Connaughton, James L. *federal official*
Cook, Michael Blanchard *government executive*
Copps, Michael Joseph *commissioner*
Corbin, Michael *diplomat*
Crocker, Chester Arthur *diplomat, federal agency administrator*
Crocker, Ryan C. *ambassador*
Cropp, Linda W. *city official*
Crouch, Jack Dyer, II, (J.D. Crouch) *federal official, former ambassador*
Crowder, Richard Thomas *ambassador*
Cusick, Robert Irwin *federal official, lawyer*
Cutler, Walter Leon *diplomat, foundation executive*
Danilovich, John J. *federal official, former ambassador*
Davidson, Donetta Lea *federal official, former state official*
de Icaza Gonzalez, Carlos Alberto (Carlos de Icaza) *ambassador*
Dellums, Ronald Vernie *mayor-elect, retired congressman*
del Rosario, Albert F. *ambassador*
Denett, Paul Alfred *federal official*
Diatta, Joseph *Nigerian diplomat*
Dominguez, Cari M. *federal official*
Donilon, Thomas E. *federal official*
Dorn, Jennifer Lynn *federal official*

Duemling, Robert Werner *diplomat, museum director*
Duffy, Michael F. *commissioner*
Dunn, David B. *ambassador*
Dunn, Michael V. *commissioner*
Dybul, Mark Richard *ambassador*
Dye, Rebecca Feemster *commissioner*
Eagleburger, Lawrence Sidney *former secretary of state*
Earp, Naomi Churchill *federal official, lawyer*
Eaton, William A. *ambassador, former federal agency administrator*
Eddy, John Joseph *diplomat*
El-Nakib, Hesham Moussa *diplomat*
Elwood, Patricia Cowan *district secretary, political consultant, international relations education specialist*
Ely-Raphel, Nancy *diplomat*
Ensenat, Donald Burnham *ambassador, lawyer*
Escobedo Cabral, Anna *federal official*
Fahmy, Nabil *ambassador*
Fingar, Thomas *federal official*
Fleisher, Eric Wilfrid *retired foreign service officer*
Foley, Tom (Thomas Stephen Foley) *former ambassador, former congressman*
Ford, Charles A. *ambassador*
Francke, Rend Rahim *ambassador*
Franklin, Barbara Hackman *former government official*
Fritsche, Claudia *diplomat, ambassador*
Garthoff, Raymond Leonard *retired diplomat, diplomatic historian, researcher*
Gati, Toby T. *international advisor*
Gessaman, Donald Eugene *retired government executive*
Giffin, Gordon D. *former ambassador, lawyer*
Gilliom, Judith Carr *federal official*
Ginsberg, Marc Charles *former diplomat, investment company executive*
Glendening, Parris Nelson *former governor, political science educator*
Gnehm, Edward W., Jr. *ambassador*
Golkiewicz, Gary J. *federal official*
Gonzales, Alberto R. *United States Attorney General, former state supreme court justice*
Gregorian, Raffi *diplomat*
Griffin, Christine M. *commissioner*
Grove, Brandon Hambright, Jr. *diplomat*
Guhin, Michael A. *ambassador*
Gutierrez, Carlos M. *secretary of commerce, former grocery manufacturing company executive*
Hachana, Mohamed Nejib *ambassador*
Hadley, Stephen John *national security advisor*
Hagin, Joseph Whitehouse, II, *federal official*
Hale, David M. *ambassador*
Hannah, John P. *federal official*
Harbour, Pamela Jones *commissioner, lawyer*
Harrop, William Caldwell *retired ambassador*
Hastings, George L. *federal official*
Hays, Dennis K. *former ambassador*
Hein, Jay F. *federal official*
Herbold, Patricia Louise *ambassador*
Hillman, Jennifer Anne *federal official*
Hodges, Heather M. *ambassador*
Hoffman, Alfred, Jr. *ambassador, real estate developer*
Hooks, Aubrey *ambassador*
Horowitz, Herbert Eugene *retired diplomat*
Hubbard, Allan Brooks *federal official, former chemical company executive*
Hume, Cameron R. *ambassador*
Hunter, Michael James *state government official, lawyer, educator*
Ischinger, Wolfgang *ambassador, diplomat*
Ishimaru, Stuart Jon *commissioner, former federal agency administrator*
Iskandar, Harris *attache*
Jackson, Alphonso Roy *secretary of housing and urban development*
Jackson, Jeanine E. *ambassador*
Jacobson, Tracey Ann *ambassador*
Jarque, Carlos M. *former federal official*
Jiechi, Yang *ambassador*
Johanns, Michael Owen *secretary of agriculture, former governor*
Johnson, Brenda LaGrange *ambassador*
Johnson, Clay III *federal official*
Johnson, David Timothy *diplomat*
Johnson, Jennifer J. *federal official*
Johnson, Stephen L. *federal official*
Jones, James Robert *ambassador, retired congressman, lawyer*
Jones, Richard Henry *ambassador*
Kaiser, Philip Mayer *retired diplomat*
Kaplan, Joel David *federal official*
Kato, Ryozo *ambassador*
Kauzlarich, Richard Dale *retired ambassador, political scientist, consultant*
Keating, Francis Anthony, II, *retired governor, lawyer*
Keevey, Richard Francis *federal official, state official, educator*
Kelliher, Joseph T. *commissioner*
Kelly, John Joseph, Jr. *federal official*
Kelly, Suedeen G. *commissioner*
Kempthorne, Dirk Arthur *secretary of the interior, former governor*
Kenney, Kristie Anne *ambassador*
Killgore, Andrew Ivy *former ambassador*
Kolb, Charles Edward Mealey *federal government official, lawyer*
Koplan, Stephen *federal official*
Koskinen, John Andrew *foundation executive*
Kostelnik, Michael Charles *commissioner, retired military officer*
Kovacic, William Evan *commissioner, law educator*
LaFleur, Christopher J. *ambassador*
Lake, Anthony (W. Anthony Lake) *former national security advisor*
Lane, Charlotte R. *federal official, lawyer*
Langdale, Mark *ambassador, former hotel executive*
Lazear, Edward Paul *federal official, economics professor*
Leavitt, Michael Okerlund *secretary of health and human services*
Leibowitz, Jon *commissioner*
Levitte, Jean-David *ambassador*
Levy, Leah Garrigan *federal official*

Lewis, Ann Frank *former government official*
Libby, Lewis (I. Lewis Libby, Scooter Libby) *former federal official*
Loftis, Robert G. *ambassador*
Lowe, Mary Frances *federal official*
Lowenstein, James Gordon *former diplomat, international consultant*
Lucas, James Walter *federal official*
Luedtke, Thomas *associate administrator procurement for NASA*
Lukken, Walt(er) *commissioner*
Lundsager, Margrethe (Meg Lundsager) *federal official*
Madras, Bertha Kalifon *federal official, neuroscientist*
Magee, Charles Thomas *international consultant, retired diplomat*
Maisto, John F. *ambassador*
Majoras, Deborah Platt *commissioner*
Manning, David Geoffrey *ambassador*
Marburger, John Harmen III *federal official*
Marcus, Kenneth L. *federal official*
Marine, Michael W. *ambassador*
Martinez, Carmen Maria *ambassador*
Masekela, Barbara Joyce Mosima *ambassador*
McCallum, Robert Davis, Jr. *ambassador, former federal agency administrator*
McCaw, Susan Rasinski *ambassador*
McCormick, William Paul *ambassador*
McDowell, Robert M. *commissioner*
McEldowney, Nancy *ambassador*
McKenna, Frank Joseph *ambassador, lawyer*
McLarty, Thomas F., III, (Mack McLarty) *former governement advisor, business executive*
McMillin, Stephen S. *federal official*
McPhie, Neil Anthony Gordon *federal official*
Meece, Roger A. *ambassador*
Meyerrose, Dale William *federal official, retired military officer*
Miers, Harriet Ellan *federal official, lawyer*
Milam, William Bryant *former ambassador, senior policy scholar*
Miller, William Green *former ambassador*
Mineta, Norman Yoshio *former secretary of transportation, management consultant*
Moeller, Philip D. *commissioner*
Mombouli, Serge *ambassador*
Montgomery, Brian D. *commissioner*
Myaing, U. Linn *ambassador*
Nardi Riddle, Clarine *chief of staff*
Natsios, Andrew Stephen *diplomat, former federal agency administrator*
Nazareth, Annette LaPorte *commissioner, lawyer*
Negroponte, John Dimitri *Director of National Intelligence, former ambassador*
Newman, Sherryl Hobbs *former district secretary*
Nicholson, Jim (Robert James Nicholson) *secretary of veterans affairs, former ambassador*
Norland, Donald Richard *retired foreign service officer*
Oberwetter, James C. *ambassador*
Obiozor, George Achulike *ambassador*
Okun, Deanna Tanner *federal official*
Olson, Lyndon Lowell, Jr. *ambassador*
Orr, Bobette Kay *diplomat*
Owen, Henry *former ambassador, consultant*
Parris, Mark Robert *former ambassador, policy advisor*
Pascual, Carlos *ambassador*
Passage, David *diplomat*
Patron, June Eileen *former government official*
Paulson, Hank (Henry Merritt Paulson Jr.) *secretary of the treasury, former diversified financial services company executive*
Pearce, Drue *federal official, former state legislator*
Pearson, Daniel R. *federal official*
Pendleton, Miles Stevens, Jr. *diplomat*
Perino, Dana Marie *federal official*
Phillips, James D. *retired diplomat*
Piccininno, Anthony Ray *government administrative executive*
Pionk, Jerome Lee *federal official, trade association administrator*
Piromya, Kasit *ambassador*
Placke, James Anthony *retired diplomat*
Polt, Michael C. *ambassador*
Portman, Robert Jones *federal official, former ambassador, former congressman*
Powell, Nancy Jo *federal official, former ambassador*
Quainton, Anthony Cecil Eden *diplomat*
Railton, W. Scott (William Scott Railton) *commissioner*
Randt, Clark Thorp, Jr. *ambassador, lawyer*
Ranneberger, Michael E. *ambassador*
Reed, John Hathaway *former ambassador*
Reznik, Mykhailo B. *ambassador*
Ricciardone, Francis Joseph, Jr. *ambassador*
Rice, Condoleezza *secretary of state, former national security advisor*
Richardson, Scott *federal official, researcher, writer*
Roberts, Walter Ronald *retired diplomat*
Rogers, Thomasina Venese *federal commissioner*
Rogowsky, Robert Arthur *federal official, educator*
Rooney, Francis *ambassador*
Rosch, John Thomas (Tom Rosch) *commissioner, lawyer*
Rose, Mary McNally *federal official*
Rosenfeld, Arthur F. *federal official, lawyer*
Ross, Dennis B. *former diplomat*
Rove, Karl Christian *federal official*
Rumsfeld, Donald Henry *secretary of defense*
Sanders, Jackie Wolcott *ambassador*
Sayre, Robert Marion *ambassador*
Schieffer, John Thomas *ambassador, former professional baseball team executive*
Schlicher, Ronald Lewis *ambassador*
Schneider, Cynthia Perrin *former ambassador, political science professor*
Schneider, Mark Lewis *foreign policy executive, retired government agency administrator*
Schulte, Gregory L. *ambassador*
Schwab, Susan Carroll *ambassador, former academic administrator*
Scowcroft, Brent *former national security advisor, retired military officer*
Seck, Mamadou Mansour *ambassador, military officer*

Sellin, Theodore *diplomat, consultant*
Shaw, Theresa S. (Terri Shaw) *federal official*
Shinn, David Hamilton *former diplomat, educator, writer*
Shirzad, Faryar *federal official*
Silverman, Leslie E. *commissioner*
Simmons, Anne L. *federal official*
Slaughter, Matthew J. *federal official, economics professor*
Slutz, Pamela Jo Howell *ambassador*
Smalley, Robert Manning *diplomat*
Smith, Elaine Diana *foreign service officer*
Smith, Patricia Grace *federal official*
Sobel, Clifford M. *ambassador*
Solberg, Mary Ann *federal official*
Sonnenfeldt, Helmut *former government official, educator, consultant, writer*
Spagnoletti, Robert J. *attorney general*
Spector, Melbourne Louis *retired foreign service officer*
Spellings, Margaret LaMontagne *secretary of education*
Spitzer, Marc Lee *commissioner, former state legislator*
Springer, Linda M. *federal official*
Stadtler, Walter Edward *diplomat*
Stapleton, Craig Roberts *ambassador*
Stock, Ann *federal official*
Sullivan, Kevin F. *federal official*
Sumwalt, Robert Llewellyn III *commissioner, pilot*
Suro-Bredie, Carmen Cecilia *federal official*
Tarrants, William Eugene *federal official*
Tate, Deborah Taylor *commissioner*
Taubman, Nicholas F. *ambassador*
Taylor, William B., Jr. *ambassador*
Teare, Richard Wallace *retired foreign service officer*
Tefft, John F.
Thawley, Michael *diplomat*
Thomas, Ralph Charles III *federal official*
Thompson, Horace A., III, (Topper Thompson) *commissioner, lawyer*
Timken, William R., Jr., (William Robert Timken Jr.) *ambassador, former manufacturing executive*
Townsend, Fran (Frances Fragos Townsend) *federal official*
Ushakov, Yury Viktorovich *ambassador*
Van de Water, Read *federal official*
van Voorst, Carol *ambassador*
Varney, Christine A. *federal official*
Vento, Sergio *ambassador*
Vershbow, Alexander R. *ambassador*
Verville, Elizabeth Giavani *federal official*
Villarosa, Shari *ambassador*
Walker, David Michael *federal official*
Walker, Edward S., Jr. *former ambassador*
Walters, John P. *federal official*
Wang, Kim *commissioner, librarian*
Ware, Marilyn *ambassador, former utilities company executive*
Watson, Arthur Dennis *federal official*
Wayne, Earl Anthony *ambassador, former federal agency administrator*
Wayne, Stephen J. *government educator, writer*
Wellinghoff, Jon *commissioner*
Wexler, Anne *government relations and public affairs consultant*
Whitney, Benson K. *ambassador*
Wilkins, David Horton *ambassador, former state legislator*
Williams, Anthony A. *mayor*
Wilson, Ross *ambassador*
Wise, Bob (Robert Ellsworth Wise Jr.) *former governor, former congressman*
Wolf, John S. *ambassador, former federal agency administrator*
Wolff, Candida (Candi Wolff) *federal official*
Wolters, Curt Cornelis Frederik *foreign service officer*
Wood, Michael M. *ambassador*
Yanai, Shunji *former diplomat*
Zarate, Juan Carlos *federal official*
Zelikow, Philip David *federal official, public policy educator*
Ziman, Barry Russell *government relations executive*
Zinmeister, Karl *federal official*

## FLORIDA

### Aventura
Garcia, Marc Anthony *diplomat*

### Boynton Beach
Polinsky, Janet Naboicheck *retired state official, retired state legislator*
Warshaw, Stanley Irving *federal official, consultant*

### Brooksville
Anderson, Richard Edmund *city manager, management consultant*

### Fernandina Beach
Smeeton, Thomas Rooney *government affairs consultant*

### Fort Lauderdale
Atkinson, Christopher Lee *county official*
Burleigh, A. Peter *ambassador*
Gunzburger, Suzanne Nathan *municipal official, social worker*
Johnson, Mary Margaret Dickens *governmental and commercial researcher, consultant*

### Fort Myers
Lamach, Bernard D. *professional engineer, county commissioner*

### Gainesville
Heflin, Martin Ganier *diplomat, political scientist*

### Hollywood
Giulianti, Mara Selena *mayor*

### Jacksonville
Goldhagen, Jeffrey Lee *city health department administrator*

### Miami
Carey-Shuler, Barbara *county commissioner*
Cefaratti, Anthony Joseph *retired diplomat*
Diaz, Manuel A. *mayor*
Magrath, Kathleen Barry *retired municipal official*
Pinder, Renee Monique *diplomat*

### Orlando
Schoettger, Theodore Leo *city official*

### Palmetto
Angulo, Charles Bonin *foreign service officer, lawyer*

### Ponte Vedra Beach
Soderberg, Nancy *former court official, writer*

### Punta Gorda
Smith-Mooney, Marilyn Patricia *city government official, management consultant*

### Sarasota
Morrow, William Earl *retired government official, retired law educator*

### Tallahassee
Bush, Jeb (John Ellis Bush) *governor*
Cobb, Sue McCourt *state official, former ambassador*
Crist, Charles (Charlie Crist) *state attorney general*
Hetrick, Charles Brady *retired county official*
Jennings, Toni *lieutenant governor*
Mortham, Sandra Barringer *former state official*
Ramsey, Sally Ann Seitz *retired state official*

### Tampa
Freedman, Sandra Warshaw *former mayor*
Iorio, Pam *county official*
Platt, Jan Kaminis *former county official*

## GEORGIA

### Atlanta
Baker, Thurbert E. *state attorney general*
Carter, Jimmy (James Earl Carter Jr.) *39th President of the United States*
Cox, Cathy *state official*
Dean, James Edward *retired state official*
Franklin, Shirley Clarke *mayor*
Howard, Pierre *former state official*
Laney, James Thomas *former ambassador, educator*
Perdue, George (Sonny Perdue) *governor, former state legislator*
Scott, Donald Lavern *city manager, former army officer*
Taylor, Mark *lieutenant governor*

### Brunswick
Patrick, Connie L. *federal official*

### Conyers
Kelly, John Hubert *diplomat*

### Saint Simons Island
Douglas, William Ernest *retired commissioner*

### Tucker
Streeb, Gordon Lee *diplomat, economist*

## HAWAII

### Honolulu
Aiona, James R., Jr. *lieutenant governor*
Bennett, Mark J. *state attorney general*
Bronster, Margery S. *retired state attorney general, lawyer*
Hannemann, Mufi *mayor*
Harris, Jeremy *former mayor*
Lingle, Linda *governor*
Okimoto, Glenn Michiaki *state official*

### Mililani
Olsen, Harris Leland *diplomat, writer, real estate company executive, educator*

## IDAHO

### Boise
Benham, James H. *state official*
Ricks, Mark G. *lieutenant governor, former state senator*
Risch, James E. *governor, former lieutenant governor, former state legislator*
Terteling-Payne, Carolyn Ann *city official*
Wasden, Lawrence *state attorney general*
Wilson, Jack Fredrick *retired federal government official*
Ysursa, Ben T. *state official*

### Idaho Falls
King, Ronald Amos *federal official, retired communications professional*

## ILLINOIS

### Carbondale
Cole, Brad *mayor*

### Champaign
Semonin, Richard Gerard *retired state official*

### Chicago
Balanoff, Clem *county election director*
Craig, John Bruce *former ambassador, air transportation executive*
Daley, Richard Michael *mayor*
Dempsey, Mary A. *commissioner, lawyer*
Enenbach, Mark Henry *community action agency executive, educator*
Harris, Gregory Scott *municipal official*
Lee, Yoon Mo *state official*
Madigan, Lisa *state attorney general*

### Miami (right column)
Mason, Terry *city health department administrator, urologist*
Natarus, Burton F. *municipal legislator, lawyer*
Olk, Frederick James *county official, legal assistant*
Quinn, Patrick *lieutenant governor*
Robbins, Audrey *county official*
Stroger, John H., Jr. *county official*
Topinka, Judy Baar *state official, political organization worker*
Trotter, Cortez *city official, former fire commissioner*
Walker, Thomas Ray *city aviation commissioner*
Wood, Patrick Henry III *former federal official*

### Downers Grove
Jacklin, William Thomas *retired county official, educator*

### Glenview
Olson, Roy Arthur *retired government official*

### Hinsdale
Mehuron, William Otto *retired federal official*

### Machesney Park
Vaughn, Linda Marie *municipal official*

### Quincy
Points, Roy Wilson *municipal official*

### Springfield
Blagojevich, Rod R. *governor, former congressman*
White, Jesse *state official*

### Urbana
Edgar, Jim *former governor*
Prussing, Laurel Lunt *mayor, economist*

### Wheeling
Kenny, James Casey *ambassador, construction company executive*

## INDIANA

### Fort Wayne
Lee, Timothy Earl *international agency executive, paralegal*

### Indianapolis
Caine, Virginia A. *city health department administrator*
Carter, Steve *state attorney general*
Daniels, Mitchell Elias, Jr. *governor, former federal official*
Peterson, Bart *mayor*
Rokita, Todd *state official*
Skillman, Becky Sue *lieutenant governor, former state legislator*

### La Porte
Morris, Leigh Edward *mayor, retired health facility administrator*

### New Castle
Nipp, Tom *mayor, protective services official, artist*

### South Bend
Davis, Katherine Lyon *former lieutenant governor*

## IOWA

### Creston
Nurnberg, Roger C. *county official*

### Des Moines
Anderson, Eric Anthony *city manager*
Bergman, Bruce E. *municipal official*
Corning, Joy Cole *retired state official*
Culver, Chester J. (Chet Culver) *state official, educator*
Deluhery, Patrick John *state official*
Gronstal, Tom *commissioner, bank executive*
Huser, Geri D. *state official*
Jacobs, Libby Swanson *state official*
Kramer, Mary Elizabeth *ambassador, former state legislator*
Miller, Thomas J. *state attorney general*
Pederson, Sally *lieutenant governor*
Vilsack, Thomas *governor*

### Marion
Pate, Paul Danny *mayor*

### Oelwein
McFarlane, Beth Lucetta Troester *retired mayor*

### Rockwell City
Erkenbrack, Lori Jean *county official*

### West Burlington
Trousil, Hans Kurt *mayor*

## KANSAS

### Arkansas City
Bruton, Rebecca Ann *mayor, commissioner*

### Coffeyville
Garner, Jim D. *state official, lawyer*

### Garden Plain
Stovall, Carla Jo *former state attorney general*

### Hutchinson
Kerr, Dave *state official, marketing professional*

### Pittsburg
Trent, Darrell M. *ambassador, academic administrator*

**Topeka**
Jenkins, Lynn M. *state official, former state legislator*
Kline, Phillip D. *state attorney general*
Moore, John Eddy *lieutenant governor*
Sebelius, Kathleen Gilligan *governor*
Thornburgh, Ron E. *state official*

**Wichita**
Knight, Robert G. *mayor, investment banker*

## KENTUCKY

**Frankfort**
Fletcher, Ernie (Ernest Lee Fletcher) *governor, former congressman*
Grayson, Trey (C.M. Grayson) *state official*
Pence, Stephen Beville *lieutenant governor*
Sonego, Ian G. *assistant attorney general*
Stumbo, Gregory D. *state attorney general*

**Lexington**
Isaac, Teresa Ann *mayor, lawyer*
Miller, Pamela Gundersen *mayor*

**Versailles**
Farish, William S. *former ambassador, horse breeder*

## LOUISIANA

**Baton Rouge**
Ater, Al *state official*
Blanco, Kathleen Babineaux *governor*
Foti, Charles C., Jr. *state attorney general*
Landrieu, Mitchell Joseph *lieutenant governor*
Mc Call, Jerry Chalmers *retired federal official*

**New Orleans**
Nagin, Ray (Clarence Ray Nagin Jr.) *mayor*
Stansbury, Harry Case *state commissioner*

**Slidell**
Dearing, Reinhard Josef *city official*

## MAINE

**Augusta**
Baldacci, John Elias *governor, former congressman*
Dunlap, Matthew Gordon *state official, former state legislator*
McCormick, Dale *state official*
Rowe, G. Steven *state attorney general*

**Belfast**
Worth, Mary Page *mayor*

**Brunswick**
King, Angus S., Jr. *former governor*

## MARYLAND

**Annapolis**
Andrews, Archie Moulton *retired federal official*
Clagett, Virginia Parker *state official*
Ehrlich, Robert L., Jr. *governor, former congressman*
Kane, Mary Deely *state official*
Kopp, Nancy Kornblith *state official*
Schaefer, William Donald *state official, former governor*
Steele, Michael *lieutenant governor*

**Baltimore**
Aumann, R. Karl *commissioner, former state official*
Curran, J. Joseph, Jr. *state attorney general*
Jones, Raymond Moylan *strategy and public policy educator*
O'Malley, Martin Joseph *mayor, lawyer, retired councilman*
Sharfstein, Joshua M. *city health department administrator, pediatrician*
Willis, John T. *former secretary of state*

**Bethesda**
Bowsher, Charles Arthur *retired government official, financial executive*
Dennin, Joseph Francis *former government official, lawyer*
Gude, Gilbert *former federal official, former state official, nurseryman, writer*
Hempstone, Smith, Jr. *diplomat, journalist*
Kawazoe, Robin Inada *federal official*
Kirby, Harmon Elwood *retired ambassador*
Laingen, Lowell Bruce *diplomat*
MacKay, Charles Robert *federal official, consultant*
Morrison, Bruce Andrew *federal official, public information officer*
North, William Haven *foreign service officer*
Rowell, Edward Morgan *retired foreign service officer, educator*
Stoddard, Philip Hendrick *foreign affairs analyst, consultant, writer*
Vest, George Southall *retired diplomat*

**Cabin John**
Ingraham, Edward Clarke, Jr. *retired foreign service officer*

**Chevy Chase**
Albright, Raymond Jacob *federal official*
Lukens, Alan Wood *retired ambassador, retired federal official*

**Cockeysville**
Barnes, Peter *federal official*

**College Park**
Benedick, Richard Elliot *diplomat*
Gansler, Jacques Singleton *public policy educator*

**Columbia**
Lok, Joan Mei-Lok *community affairs specialist, artist*
Scates, Alice Yeomans *retired federal official*

**Ellicott City**
Galinsky, Deborah Jean *county official*

**Fort Washington**
Smoot, Burgess Howard *federal official*

**Gaithersburg**
French, Judson Cull *federal official*

**Hollywood**
Newhouse, Alan Russell *retired federal official*

**North Bethesda**
Szabo, Daniel *federal official*

**Oxford**
Shepard, William Seth *diplomat, writer*

**Potomac**
Roesser, Jean Wolberg *state official*

**Rockville**
Chiogioji, Melvin Hiroaki *retired federal official, entrepreneur*
Jaczko, Gregory Bela *commissioner, physicist*
Klosson, Michael *foreign service officer*
Lyons, Peter B. *commissioner*
McGaffigan, Edward, Jr. *commissioner*
Merrifield, Jeffrey S. *commissioner*
Woodcock, Janet *federal official*

**Severna Park**
Meima, Ralph Chester, Jr. *retired diplomat, real estate company executive*

**Silver Spring**
Bassett, William, Jr. *regional analyst*
Ewing, Blair Gordon *federal official*

**West Bethesda**
Vogelgesang, Sandra Louise *former ambassador, writer, consultant*

## MASSACHUSETTS

**Boston**
Auerbach, John M. *city health department administrator*
Fishman, Len *state commissioner*
Galvin, William Francis *state official*
Healey, Kerry Murphy *lieutenant governor*
Menino, Thomas M. *mayor*
Reilly, Thomas F. *state attorney general*
Romney, Mitt (Willard Mitt Romney) *governor*
Shattuck, John *diplomat, civil rights lawyer, educator*

**Bridgewater**
Heffernan, Peter John *state official*

**Brockton**
Sullivan, Brendan Paul *state official, consultant, communications educator*

**Cambridge**
Gergen, David Richmond *federal official, magazine editor*
Porter, Roger Blaine *federal official, educator*
Ramcharan, Bertrand *former international organization official*

**Canton**
Fuchs, Lawrence Howard *federal official, educator*

**Dartmouth**
Connors, Robert Leo *city official*

**Roslindale**
Sullivan, Dorothy Rona *state official*

**Sherborn**
Kennedy, Chester Ralph, Jr. *retired state official, art director*

**Worcester**
Murray, Timothy P. *mayor*

**Yarmouth Port**
Nichols, Robert Lyman *retired foreign service officer, lecturer*

## MICHIGAN

**Ann Arbor**
Ford, Betty Ann (Elizabeth Ann Ford) *former First Lady of the United States, health facility executive*
Funk, Sherman Maxwell *former government official, writer, consultant*
Sheldon, Ingrid Kristina *retired mayor, controller*

**Battle Creek**
Baldwin, Susan Olin *commissioner, management consultant*

**Cadillac**
Walker, Dale Maxwell *city official*

**Detroit**
Bell Wilson, Carlotta A. *state official, consultant*
Kilpatrick, Kwame Malik *mayor*
Maseru, Noble A.W. *city health department administrator*

**Dowagiac**
Ott, C(larence) H(enry) *ambassador, accounting professor*

**Fennville**
Kamman, Curtis Warren *retired ambassador*

**Flint**
Conyers, Jean Louise *chamber of commerce executive*

**Grand Rapids**
Logie, John Hoult *former mayor, lawyer*
Posthumus, Richard Earl *former lieutenant governor, farmer*

**Lansing**
Cherry, John D., Jr. *lieutenant governor*
Christian, Sandra Svec *retired state official*
Cox, Mike *state attorney general*
Granholm, Jennifer Mulhern *governor*
Kleine, Robert J. *state official*
Land, Terri Lynn *state official*

**Montague**
Davis, Robert Leach *retired federal official*

**Muskegon**
Roy, Paul Emile, Jr. *county official*

**Warren**
Kolakowski, Diana Jean *county commissioner*

## MINNESOTA

**Chisholm**
Peterson, Marjorie *former mayor*

**Golden Valley**
Leppik, Margaret White *municipal official*

**Minneapolis**
Carlson, Arne Helge *former governor*
Mondale, Joan Adams *wife of former Vice President of United States*
Mondale, Walter Frederick *former Vice President of United States, lawyer, diplomat*
Rybak, R. T. *mayor*

**Northfield**
Levin, Burton *diplomat*

**Saint Paul**
Hatch, Mike *state attorney general*
Kiffmeyer, Mary *state official*
Molnau, Carol *lieutenant governor*
Pawlenty, Timothy J. *governor*

## MISSISSIPPI

**Jackson**
Barbour, Haley Reeves *governor*
Clark, Eric C. *state official*
Hood, Jim *state attorney general*
Moore, Mike *former state attorney general*
Tuck, Amy *lieutenant governor*
Winter, William Forrest *retired governor, lawyer*

## MISSOURI

**Jefferson City**
Blunt, Matt (Matthew Roy Blunt) *governor, former state official*
Carnahan, Robin *state official*
Farmer, Nancy *state official*
Kinder, Peter D. *lieutenant governor, former state legislator*
Nixon, Jeremiah W. (Jay Nixon) *state attorney general*

**Kansas City**
Barnes, Kay *mayor*
Danner, Kathleen Frances Steele *federal official*
Davis, Richard Francis *city government official*
Price, Charles H., II, *former ambassador*
Stroup, Kala Mays *former education commissioner, educational alliance administrator*

**Saint Louis**
Brauer, Stephen Franklin *diplomat, manufacturing company executive*
Holden, Robert (Bob Holden) *former governor*

## MONTANA

**Billings**
Larsen, Richard Lee *city manager, consultant, retired mayor, arbitrator*

**Clancy**
Ekanger, Laurie *retired state official, consultant*

**Helena**
Bohlinger, John C. *lieutenant governor, former state legislator*
Cooney, Mike *former secretary of state*
Johnson, Brad *state official*
Mazurek, Joseph P. *lawyer, former state legislator*
McGrath, Mike *state attorney general*
Schweitzer, Brian *governor*

**Missoula**
Brown, Bob (Robert Joseph Brown) *former state official*

## NEBRASKA

**Lincoln**
Beermann, Allen J. *former state official*
Bruning, Jon Cumberland *state attorney general*
Gale, John A. *state official*
Heineman, David Eugene *governor*
Novoa, Yanira *diplomat*
Seng, Coleen Joy *mayor*
Sheehy, Rick *lieutenant governor*

**Omaha**
Fahey, Mike *mayor*

Moore, Scott *former state official*

## NEVADA

**Carson City**
Chanos, George J. *state attorney general*
Guinn, Kenny C. *governor*
Heller, Dean *state official*
Hunt, Lorraine T. *lieutenant governor*

**Henderson**
McKinney, Sally Vitkus *state official*

**Las Vegas**
Goodman, Oscar Baylin *mayor, lawyer*

## NEW HAMPSHIRE

**Auburn**
Herman, William George *municipal official*

**Concord**
Ayotte, Kelly A. *state attorney general*
Gardner, William Michael *state official*
Hill, Donald S. *state commissioner*
Lynch, John H. *governor*

**Dover**
Denaco, Parker Alden *state official, lawyer, arbitrator*

**Goffstown**
Holden, Carol Helen *county official*

**Nashua**
Pignatelli, Debora Becker *state official*

## NEW JERSEY

**Caldwell**
Lukabu Khabouji N'Zaji, *diplomat*

**Cape May Point**
Fraser, Malcolm Cavanagh *mayor*

**Egg Harbor Township**
Polillo, Ronald R. *federal official*

**Elizabeth**
Bollwage, J. Christian *mayor*

**Irvington**
Paden, Harry *municipal official*

**Jersey City**
Healy, Jerramiah *mayor*

**Kearny**
John, Ricky *state official*

**Morristown**
Healey, Thomas J. *former government official, brokerage house executive*

**Newark**
Booker, Cory Anthony *mayor, lawyer*
Pryor, Stefan I. *city manager, real estate developer*

**Princeton**
Kurtzer, Daniel Charles *former ambassador*
Matlock, Jack Foust, Jr. *diplomat*

**Sea Isle City**
Tull, Theresa Anne *retired diplomat*

**Somerset**
Soaries, DeForest B., Jr. *former state official*

**Trenton**
Abelow, Bradley *state official*
Corzine, Jon Stevens *governor, former senator*
Martin, James Hanley *state attorney general*
Palmer, Douglas Harold *mayor*
Rabner, Stuart Jeff *state attorney general, lawyer*
Wells, Nina Mitchell *state official*

## NEW MEXICO

**Albuquerque**
Giller, Edward Bonfoy *retired government official, retired military officer*

**Clovis**
Bradley, Walter D. *lieutenant governor, real estate broker*

**Mesilla**
Lewis, Delano Eugene *ambassador, retired broadcast executive*

**Santa Fe**
Coss, David *mayor*
Denish, Diane D. *lieutenant governor*
Eaton, Robert Crutcher *federal official*
Madrid, Patricia A. *state attorney general*
Richardson, Bill (William Blaine Richardson) *governor*
Vigil-Giron, Rebecca *state official*

## NEW YORK

**Albany**
Clarey, Donald Alexander *government affairs consultant*
Donohue, Mary *lieutenant governor*
Hevesi, Alan G. *state official, former city manager*
Jacobs, Christopher L. *state official*
Jennings, Gerald D. (Jerry Jennings) *mayor*
Novello, Antonia Coello *state health commissioner, pediatric nephrologist, former Surgeon General of the United States*
Pataki, George E. *governor*

Spitzer, Eliot Laurence *state attorney general*
Toren, Mark *state official, statistician*

**Armonk**
Wago, Mildred Hogan *retired municipal official*

**Brewster**
Bates, Barbara J. Neuner *retired municipal official*

**Bronx**
Carrion, Adolfo, Jr. *city manager*
Mendez, Ruben Policarpio *diplomat, educator, economist*

**Brooklyn**
Evans-Tranumn, Shelia *commissioner, former literature and language educator*
Markowitz, Marty (Martin Markowitz) *city manager*

**Buffalo**
Brown, Byron W., Jr. *mayor, former state legislator*
Giambra, Joel Anthony *municipal official*

**Canandaigua**
Barden, George V. *county official, watershed specialist*

**Kew Gardens**
Marshall, Helen M. *city manager*

**Lawrence**
Berman, Carol *retired commissioner*

**Manlius**
Cotter, William Donald *retired commissioner, retired editor*

**Mineola**
O'Connell, Maureen C. *county official, former state legislator*

**Nedrow**
Lyons, Oren *Native American chieftain, conservationist*

**New York**
Abe, Nobuyasu *ambassador, international organization administrator*
Andjaba, Martin *diplomat*
Ataeva, Aksoltan *diplomat*
Ayafor, Martin Chungong *ambassador*
Baja, Lauro Liboon, Jr. *diplomat*
Berruga-Filloy, Enrique *ambassador*
Blinken, Donald *ambassador, investment banker*
Bloomberg, Michael Rubens *mayor*
Boykin, Keith O. *former government official, writer*
Brown, Carroll *retired diplomat, association executive, consultant*
Buissonnière, Marine *international organization administrator; physician*
Chaves, Jose Maria *diplomat, lawyer, foundation administrator, educator*
Clarke, Richard Alan *former federal official*
Clinton, Bill (William Jefferson Clinton) *42nd President of the United States*
Cosgrave, Paul J. *commissioner*
Curiel, Carolyn *former ambassador*
Curley, Walter Joseph Patrick *diplomat, investment banker*
Daniels, Randy A. *former state official*
Davis, Richard Joel *former government official, lawyer*
Doctoroff, Daniel L. *municipal official*
Doyle, Michael W. *international official, educator*
Durrant, M. Patricia *diplomat*
Egeland, Jan *international organization official*
Eisenstadt, G. Michael *diplomat, writer, educator, researcher*
Ferguson, Sarah *The Duchess of York*
Fields, C. Virginia *city manager*
Frieden, Thomas R. *city health department administrator, epidemiologist*
Friedman, Stephen *former federal official, former diversified financial services executive*
Gardner, Richard Newton *diplomat, lawyer, educator*
Gaspar-Martins, Ismael Angelina *diplomat, former government minister, business executive*
Gelb, Bruce Stuart *city commissioner, consultant*
Gotbaum, Betsy *municipal official*
Haass, Richard Nathan *federal official*
Ilkin, Baki *diplomat, Turkish government official*
Katz, Abraham *retired foreign service officer*
Levin, Herbert *retired diplomat, foundation administrator*
Lewis, Stephen H. *diplomat*
Løj, Ellen Margrethe *ambassador*
Mbanefo, Arthur Christopher Izuegbunan *diplomat*
McFarland, Kathleen Troia (KT McFarland) *government defense consultant*
Moleko, Lebohang Kenneth *ambassador*
Moutari, Ousmane *permanent representative to UN Niger*
Muñoz, Heraldo (Heraldo Muñoz Valenzuela) *diplomat*
Murphy, Richard William *retired diplomat*
Ney, Edward N. *ambassador, advertising executive, public relations executive*
Nussbaum, Bernard W. *federal official, lawyer*
Okun, Herbert Stuart *diplomat, educator*
Phillips, David L. *diplomat, mediator, foundation executive*
Platt, Nicholas *retired ambassador*
Pleuger, Guenter *diplomat*
Prendergast, Sir Kieran *former international organization official*
Qazi, Ashraf Jehangir *ambassador*
Raab, Jennifer J. *city commissioner*
Rabiu, Badru I.O. *federal official*
Ranald, Ralph Arthur *former government official, educator*
Rapoport, Miles S. *former state offical*
Rock, Allan Michael *ambassador, former Canadian government official*
Ryan, Richard *ambassador*
Sadik, Nafis *United Nations administrator*

Snow, Tony *White House press secretary, political commentator, analyst*
Streator, Edward *retired diplomat, management consultant*
Stringer, Scott M. *city manager, former state legislator*
Swing, William Lacy *ambassador*
Taylor, Diana Lancaster *state official*
Urroz-Rapold, Patricia Julia S. *retired diplomat, writer*
Wang, Guangya *ambassador, international organization official*
Wibisono, Makarim *diplomat*
Williamson, Richard Salisbury *ambassador*
Wolff, Alejandro Daniel *ambassador*
Wyzner, Eugeniusz *diplomat*
Yishan, Zhang *ambassador*
Zackheos, H.E. Sotirios *ambassador*

**Staten Island**
Molinaro, James P. *city manager*

**Syracuse**
Barclay, H(ugh) Douglas *ambassador, lawyer*
Driscoll, Matthew J. *mayor, real estate developer, small business owner*
Levitsky, Melvyn *former ambassador*
Ortiz, Fernando, Jr. *commissioner*

**Troy**
McDermott, Robert J. *commissioner*

**Watertown**
Coe, Benjamin Plaisted *retired state official*

**Williamsville**
Danni, F. Robert *town official*

## NORTH CAROLINA

**Chapel Hill**
Schoonover, Brenda B. *ambassador*

**Charlotte**
Brynn, Edward Paul *former ambassador*
McCrory, Patrick *mayor*

**High Point**
Pate, William Patrick *city manager*
Phillips, Earl Norfleet, Jr. *diplomat, financial services executive*

**Merritt**
de Vos, Peter Jon *ambassador*

**Mill Spring**
Saunders, Barry Wayne *state official*

**New Bern**
Linkonis, Suzanne Newbold *retired probation officer, retired counselor*

**Pittsboro**
Doenges, Byron Frederick *former government official, finance educator*

**Raleigh**
Cooper, Roy Asberry III *state attorney general*
Easley, Michael F. *governor*
Joyner, Lorinzo Little *commissioner*
Marshall, Elaine Folk *state official*
Perdue, Beverly Eaves *lieutenant governor, geriatric consultant*

**Southern Pines**
Toon, Malcolm *former ambassador*

**Wilson**
Wyatt, Edward Avery, V, *city manager*

## NORTH DAKOTA

**Bismarck**
Dalrymple, Jack *lieutenant governor*
Hoeven, John *governor*
Jaeger, Alvin A. (Al Jaeger) *state official*
Stenehjem, Wayne Kevin *state attorney general, lawyer*

**Minot**
Watne, Darlene Claire *county official*

## OHIO

**Cincinnati**
Mallory, Mark L. *mayor, former state legislator*
Qualls, Roxanne *mayor*

**Cleveland**
Campbell, Jane Louise *former mayor*
Jackson, Frank G. *mayor*

**Columbus**
Blackwell, J. Kenneth (John Kenneth Blackwell) *state official*
Bradley, Jennette B. *state official, former lieutenant governor*
Coleman, Michael Bennett *mayor*
Hogan, Michael F. *state official*
Johnson, Bruce E. *lieutenant governor, former state legislator*
Lashutka, Gregory S. *mayor, lawyer*
Long, Teresa C. *city health department administrator*
Montgomery, Betty Dee *state auditor, former state attorney general, former state legislator*
Petro, James Michael *state attorney general*
Speck, Samuel Wallace, Jr. *state official*
Taft, Bob *governor*
Walcher, Kathleen *state official*

**Dayton**
Lashley, William Bartholomew *county official*
McLin, Rhine Lana *mayor, former state legislator*

**Martins Ferry**
Douglas, Leslie A. *municipal official*

**Medina**
Ballard, John Stuart *retired mayor, lawyer, educator*

**Toledo**
Carroll, William J. *municipal official*

## OKLAHOMA

**Ada**
Anoatubby, Bill *governor of Chickasaw Nation*

**Norman**
Corr, Edwin Gharst *ambassador*

**Oklahoma City**
Cornett, Mick *mayor*
Edmondson, Drew (William Andrew Edmondson) *state attorney general*
Fallin, Mary Copeland *lieutenant governor*
Henry, Brad (C. Brad Henry) *governor*
Savage, Susan M. *state official, former mayor*

**Park Hill**
Mankiller, Wilma Pearl *retired tribal leader*

**Tulsa**
Madison, Eddie Lawrence, Jr. *public relations consultant, editor, writer*
Rooney, Laurence Francis III *ambassador to the Vatican, construction executive*
Taylor, Kathy *mayor*

## OREGON

**Eugene**
Bascom, Ruth F. *retired mayor*
Collas-Dean, Angela G. *retired commissioner, small business owner*

**Lake Oswego**
Campbell, Colin Herald *former mayor*

**Portland**
Katz, Vera *former mayor, former college administrator, state legislator*
Kitzhaber, John Albert *former governor, emergency physician, former state senator*
Potter, Tom *mayor*

**Salem**
Bradbury, William Chapman, III, (Bill Bradbury) *state official*
Kulongoski, Ted (Theodore Ralph Kulongoski) *governor, former state supreme court justice*
Myers, Hardy *state attorney general*

## PENNSYLVANIA

**Donora**
Todd, Norma Ross *retired government official*

**Easton**
Murphy, Bruce Allen *government educator, law educator, writer*

**Glen Mills**
Dunion, Celeste Mogab *municipal official, consultant, foundation administrator*

**Harrisburg**
Baker Knoll, Catherine *lieutenant governor*
Corbett, Thomas Wingett, Jr. *state attorney general, lawyer*
Cortés, Pedro *state official*
Hafer, Barbara *state official*
Koken, M. Diane *state commissioner*
Pizzingrilli, Kim *state official*
Rendell, Edward Gene *governor, retired mayor, lawyer*
Wolfe, Gary Donald *retired commissioner, librarian*

**Newtown**
Brennan, Thomas John *city and state official, consultant, educator*

**Norristown**
Biondi, Anthony *municipal official*

**Philadelphia**
Godley, Joanne *city health department administrator*
Harris, Raymond Jesse *retired federal official*
Houstoun, Feather O'Connor *state official*
O'Connor, Charles Edward, Jr. *state government official, lawyer*
Schweiker, Mark S. *former governor*
Street, John F. *mayor*

**Pittsburgh**
Kerber, Frank John *retired diplomat*
Mitchell, George Charles *diplomat, international consultant, mediator, educator, writer*
O'Neill, Paul Henry *former secretary of the treasury*
Ravenstahl, Luke R. *mayor*
Simpson, Daniel H. *ambassador*

**State College**
Lamb, Robert Edward *retired diplomat, retired professional society administrator*

**York**
Wiles, William Wharton *retired federal government official*

## RHODE ISLAND

**Kingston**
Sundlun, Bruce *former governor*

**Providence**
Brown, Matthew A. *state official*
Carcieri, Donald L. *governor*
Fogarty, Charles Joseph *lieutenant governor*
Lynch, Patrick C. *state attorney general*
Pine, Jeffrey Barry *lawyer, former state attorney general*

## SOUTH CAROLINA

**Columbia**
Bauer, R. Andre *lieutenant governor*
Hammond, Mark *state official*
Hao, Shiqi *state official*
McMaster, Henry Dargan *state attorney general*
Page, Randall *state official*
Sanford, Marshall (Mark Sanford) *governor, former congressman*

**Lexington**
Morris, Earle Elias, Jr. *retired state official*

**Spartanburg**
Barnet, William III *mayor, textiles executive*

## SOUTH DAKOTA

**Gettysburg**
Burge, Steven Donald *city administrator*

**Pierre**
Daugaard, Dennis M. *lieutenant governor*
Larson, Vern L. *state official*
Long, Larry *state attorney general*
Nelson, Chris A. *state official*
Rounds, Michael *governor*

## TENNESSEE

**Athens**
Guy, Joe Danny *mayor, historian*

**Brownsville**
Banks, Webb Follin *mayor*

**Dyersburg**
Revell, Bill *mayor*

**Memphis**
Herenton, Willie W. *mayor*
Madlock, Yvonne *city health department administrator*

**Nashville**
Bailey, Stephanie B.C. *city health department administrator*
Bredesen, Philip Norman *governor*
Darnell, Riley Carlisle *state official, lawyer*
Gore, Tipper (Mary Elizabeth Gore) *wife of the former vice president of the United States*
Summers, Paul G. *state attorney general*
Thomas, Hazel Beatrice *state official*
Wadley, Fredia Stovall *state commissioner*
Wilder, John Shelton *lieutenant governor*

**Oak Ridge**
Holloway, Jacqueline *county commissioner*

**Townsend**
Sundquist, Don *retired governor, retired congressman, sales executive*

## TEXAS

**Arlington**
Wilson, Cheryl Reneé *municipal official*

**Austin**
Abbott, Greg *state attorney general, former state supreme court justice*
Connor, Geoffrey Scott *former state official, lawyer*
Cooke, Carlton Lee, Jr. *mayor*
Dewhurst, David *lieutenant governor*
Gates, Charles Woodley, Sr. *city official*
Johnson, Lady Bird (Mrs. Claudia Alta Taylor Johnson) *former First Lady of the United States*
Perry, Rick *governor*
Williams, Roger *state official*
Wynn, Will *mayor*

**Beaumont**
Lord, Evelyn Marlin *mayor*

**Brenham**
Pipes, Paul Ray *county commissioner*

**Dallas**
Lake, Joseph Edward *ambassador*
Miller, Laura *mayor, journalist*
Thompson, Zachary *city health department administrator*

**El Paso**
Cook, John *mayor*
Wardy, Joe *former mayor*

**Fort Worth**
Moncrief, Michael Joseph *mayor, former state legislator*

**Harlingen**
Matz, James Richard *municipal official*

**Houston**
Baker, James Addison, III, (Jim Baker) *ambassador, lawyer, former secretary of state*
Bush, George Herbert Walker *41st President of the United States*
Chang, Helen T. *municipal official*
Marcotte, Michael Steven *municipal official*
White, William H. *mayor*

**La Feria**
Philip, Sunny Koipurathu *municipal official*

**Lubbock**
Stuart, Frank Adell *county official*

**Mineola**
Stevenson, David Wayne *municipal official*

**New Braunfels**
Krueger, Robert Charles *former ambassador, former congressman, former senator*

**Plano**
Evans, Pat *mayor*

**San Antonio**
Catto, Henry Edward *former government official, retired ambassador*
Daley, William M. *former federal government official*
Garza, Ed *former mayor*
Hardberger, Phillip Duane *mayor, judge, lawyer, journalist*
Henderson, Connie Chorlton *retired city planner, artist, writer*
Peak, Howard W. *former mayor*

**UTAH**

**North Salt Lake**
Johnson, Frank *educator, retired state official*

**Salt Lake City**
Allen, Ronald Carl *commissioner, former state senator, former computer company executive, consultant, artist*
Anderson, Ross Carl *mayor, lawyer*
Herbert, Gary Richard *lieutenant governor*
Huntsman, Jon Meade, Jr. *governor, former federal agency administrator*
Leary, G. Edward *state financial commissioner*
Quinn, Eugene Frederick *diplomat, minister*
Shurtleff, Mark L. *state attorney general*

**VERMONT**

**Burlington**
Kunin, Madeleine May *former ambassador to Switzerland, former governor*

**Montpelier**
Douglas, Jim (James Holley Douglas) *governor*
Dubie, Brian E. *lieutenant governor*
Markowitz, Deborah Lynn *state official*
Pelham, Tom *commissioner*
Sorrell, William H. *state attorney general*

**Peacham**
Engle, James Bruce *ambassador*

**South Londonderry**
Spiers, Ronald Ian *diplomat*

**VIRGINIA**

**Alexandria**
Byrne, John Edward (JEB Byrne) *retired federal official*
Connell, Mary Ellen *diplomat*
Costagliola, Francesco *retired government official*
Fitton, Harvey Nelson, Jr. *former government official*
Gwadosky, Dan A. *former state official, federal agency administrator*
Havens, Harry Stewart *retired federal official, management consultant*
Helman, Gerald Bernard *diplomat*
McNicol, David Leon *retired federal official*
Nesbitt, Wanda L. *ambassador*
Powell, Colin Luther *former secretary of state, former Chairman of the Joint Chiefs of Staff*
Pringle, Robert Maxwell *diplomat*
Tucker, Alvin Leroy *retired government official*

**Annandale**
Rogers, Stephen Hitchcock *retired ambassador*

**Arlington**
Aggrey, Orison Rudolph *former ambassador, consultant, academic administrator*
Bolster, Archie Milburn *retired foreign service officer*
Edmondson, William Brockway *retired foreign service officer*
Galloway, William Jefferson *retired foreign service officer*
Haig, Alexander Meigs, Jr. *former secretary of state, retired military officer*
Heivilin, Donna Mae *retired government executive*
Katzen, Jay Kenneth *retired diplomat, state legislator, government agency administrator*
Krys, Sheldon Jack *retired diplomat*
Mc Donald, John Warlick *diplomat*
Ochmanek, David Alan *defense analyst*
Pendleton, Mary Catherine *retired foreign service officer*
Sundquist, Alexandra (Alix Sundquist) *diplomat, consultant*
Winter, Harvey John *retired government official*
Wood, Heidi *commissioner*

**Charlottesville**
Newsom, David Dunlop *ambassador, educator*

**Chesapeake**
Myrick, Bismarck *diplomat*

**Crozet**
Reswick, James Bigelow *former government official, biomedical engineer*

**Dulles**
Jacobs, Janice Lee *ambassador*
Mathieu, Gail Dennise *ambassador*

**Mulford**, David Campbell *ambassador, former finance company executive*
Skodon, Emil Mark *ambassador*

**Fairfax**
Haskett, Dianne Louise *retired mayor, lawyer, consultant*
Pyatt, Everett Arno *federal official*

**Falls Church**
Beyer, Donald Sternoff, II, *former state offical*
Bingman, Charles Franklin *government executive, educator*
Ward, George Frank, Jr. *international programs executive, ambassador*

**Fredericksburg**
Jones, Harry Edward *diplomat, writer*

**Haymarket**
Doolittle, Warren T. *retired federal official*

**King George**
Newhall, David III *retired federal official*

**Lynchburg**
Stephens, Bart Nelson *former foreign service officer*

**Manassas**
Storing, Paul Edward *retired foreign service officer*

**Manassas Park**
Wolle, William Down *foreign service officer*

**Mathews**
Busby, Morris D. *former ambassador*

**Mc Lean**
Cahill, Harry Amory *diplomat, educator*
Healy, Theresa Ann *retired ambassador*
Russell, Theodore Emery *diplomat*
Smith, Russell Jack *diplomat, consultant*
Trout, Maurice Elmore *diplomat*

**Newington**
Clark-Bourne, Kathryn Orpha *consul*

**Norfolk**
Andrews, Mason Cooke *mayor, obstetrician, gynecologist, educator*
Griffith, Charles Dee, Jr. *state official*

**Richmond**
Bolling, Bill (William T. Bolling) *lieutenant governor, former state senator*
Hanley, Katherine Keith *state official*
Kaine, Timothy Michael *governor*
LeBlanc, Daniel G. *state official*
McDonnell, Bob (Robert Francis McDonnell) *state attorney general, former state legislator*
Petera, Anne Pappas *state official*
Wilder, L(awrence) Douglas *mayor, former governor*

**Spotsylvania**
Hardy, Dorcas Ruth *business and government relations executive*

**Springfield**
Stottlemyer, David Lee *federal official*

**Stafford**
Williams, Carlisle M., Jr. *municipal official, insurance company executive*

**Stanardsville**
Keel, Alton Gold, Jr. *ambassador*

**Susan**
Ambach, Dwight Russell *retired foreign service officer*

**The Plains**
Gibbons, John Howard (Jack Gibbons) *federal official, physicist*

**Vienna**
DeWitt, Charles Barbour *federal official*

**Virginia Beach**
Friedman, Andrew Mitchell *director housing and neighborhood preservation*
Oberndorf, Meyera E. *mayor*

**Winchester**
Ojeda Eiseley, Jaime de *former Spanish ambassador, educator*

**Woodbridge**
Noorbakhsh, Masood *county official*

**WASHINGTON**

**Battle Ground**
Ezelle, Robert Eugene *diplomat*

**Deer Park**
Mills, Robert Bruce (Bob Mills) *retired deputy county clerk*

**Edmonds**
Thyden, James Eskel *diplomat, educator, lecturer*

**Olympia**
Carpenter, Stephen Hayes, Jr. *state attorney general*
Gregoire, Christine O. *governor, former state attorney general*
McKenna, Rob *state attorney general, former councilman*
Owen, Bradley Scott *lieutenant governor*
Reed, Sam *state official*

**Seattle**
Covington, Germaine Ward *municipal agency administrator*

**Gouldthorpe**, Kenneth Alfred Percival *state official, editor*
Kennedy, Mary Virginia *retired diplomat*
Nickels, Greg *mayor*
Plough, Alonzo L. *city health department administrator*

**Sumas**
Hemry, Larry Harold *former federal agency official, writer, inventor*

**WEST VIRGINIA**

**Charleston**
Hechler, Ken *former state official, former congressman, writer, political science professor*
Ireland, Betty *state official*
Manchin, Joe, III, (Joseph Manchin III) *governor, former state official*
Mc Graw, Darrell Vivian, Jr. *state attorney general*
Perdue, John D. *state official*

**WISCONSIN**

**Ashland**
Smith, Jane Schneberger *retired city administrator*

**Franklin**
Wheaton, Douglas B. *city manager, lawyer*

**Madison**
Bauman, Susan Joan Mayer *mayor, lawyer, commissioner*
Doyle, Jim (James Edward Doyle) *governor*
Earl, Anthony Scully *retired governor, lawyer*
La Follette, Douglas J. *state official*
Lautenschlager, Peggy A. *state attorney general*
Lawton, Barbara *lieutenant governor*
Thompson, Barbara Storck *state official*
Voight, Jack C. *state official*

**Milwaukee**
Barrett, Thomas M. *mayor, former congressman*

**Pewaukee**
Farrow, Margaret Ann *former lieutenant governor*

**WYOMING**

**Cheyenne**
Catchpole, Judy *state official*
Crank, Patrick J. (Pat Crank) *state attorney general*
Freudenthal, Dave (David D. Freudenthal) *governor*
Lummis, Cynthia Marie *state official, lawyer*
Meyer, Joseph B. *state official*
Thomson, Thyra Godfrey *former state official*
Woodhouse, Gay Vanderpoel *former state attorney general, lawyer*

**Evanston**
Harris, Mark W. *mayor, lawyer*

**Laramie**
Dickman, Francois Moussiegt *former foreign service officer, educator*

## TERRITORIES OF THE UNITED STATES

**AMERICAN SAMOA**

**Pago Pago**
Sunia, Aitofele Toese F. *lieutenant governor*
Togafau, Malaetasi M. (Sialega Malaetasi Mauga Togafau) *attorney general, judge*
Tulafono, Togiola T.A. *governor*

**FEDERATED STATES OF MICRONESIA**

**Pohnpei**
Falcam, Leo A. *former Micronesian government official*

**GUAM**

**Hagatna**
Camacho, Felix Perez *governor*
Gutierrez, Carl T. C. *former governor*
Moylan, Douglas B. *attorney general*
Moylan, Kaleo *lieutenant governor*

**NORTHERN MARIANA ISLANDS**

**Saipan**
Fitial, Benigno Repeki *governor*
Villagomez, Timothy P. *lieutenant governor*

**PALAU ISLAND**

**Palau**
Remengesau, Thomas, Jr. *Palauan government official*

**PUERTO RICO**

**San Juan**
Acevedo-Vilá, Aníbal *governor, former congressional representative*
Andujar, Norma Burgos *former state official*

**Bonilla**, Fernando J. *Puerto Rican government official*
Sanchez-Ramos, Roberto J. *attorney general*
Santini, Jorge *mayor*

**VIRGIN ISLANDS**

**Charlotte Amalie**
Stapleton, Marylyn Alecia *diplomat*

**St Thomas**
Drue, Kerry Erica *attorney general*
Richards, Vargrave A. *lieutenant governor*
Turnbull, Charles Wesley *governor*

## MILITARY ADDRESSES OF THE UNITED STATES

**ATLANTIC**

**Apo**
Brownfield, William R. *ambassador*

**EUROPE**

**APO**
Cejas, Paul L. *diplomat, executive*
Khalilzad, Zalmay *ambassador*
Korologos, Tom Chris *ambassador*
Marshall, Brian Laurence *federal official*
Morella, Constance Albanese *ambassador, former congresswoman*
Neumann, Ronald Eldredge *ambassador*
Untermeyer, Charles Graves (Chase Untermeyer) *ambassador, diplomat*
Wagner, Ann Louise *ambassador, former political organization executive*
Yates, John Melvin *retired ambassador*

**FPO**
Benedict, Lawrence Neal *foreign service officer*
Gadsden, James Irvin *ambassador*
Tuttle, Robert Holmes *ambassador, former federal official*

## CANADA

**MANITOBA**

**Winnipeg**
Curtis, Charles Edward *Canadian government official*
Liba, Peter Michael *Canadian provincial government official, retired communications executive*

**NORTHWEST TERRITORIES**

**Yellowknife**
Blondin-Andrew, Ethel D. *Canadian government official*

**ONTARIO**

**Aurora**
Cellucci, Paul (Argeo Paul Cellucci) *former ambassador, former governor*

**Brampton**
Malhi, Gurbax Singh *Canadian government official*

**Downsview**
Eggleton, Arthur C. *former Canadian government official, member of Parliament*

**Nobleton**
Embleton, Tony Frederick Wallace *retired Canadian government official*

**Ottawa**
Angus, W. David *Queen's Counsel*
Armstrong, Henry Conner *former Canadian government official, consultant*
Austin, Jacob (Jack Austin) *Canadian government official*
Baker, George S. *federal official*
Bélisle, Paul Charles *Canadian government official*
Bevilacqua, Maurizio *member of Canadian parliament*
Buchanan, John MacLennan *Canadian provincial official*
Copps, Sheila *former Canadian government official*
Day, Stockwell Burt *government official*
Efford, Reuben John (John Efford) *Canadian government official*
Fairbairn, Joyce *Canadian government official*
Fitzpatrick, Brian *Canadian legislator*
Gold, Lorne W. *Canadian government official*
Goodale, Ralph E. *Canadian government official*
Graham, William C. *Canadian government official*
Guarnieri, Albina *Canadian legislator*
Harb, Mac *Canadian government official*
Kilgour, David *Canadian member parliament*
Kingsley, Jean-Pierre *federal official*
MacAulay, Lawrence A. *former Canadian government official, member of Parliament*
MacDonald, Flora Isabel *Canadian government official*
Manley, John Paul *former Canadian government official*
McCallum, John *Canadian government official*
McGuire, Joseph *Canadian government official*
Mills, Bob *member of Canadian parliament*
Minna, Maria *member of Canadian Parliament*

Penner, Keith *former Canadian government official*
Peterson, James Scott (Jim Peterson) *Canadian government official*
Pettigrew, Pierre S. *Canadian government official*
Regan, Geoff *Canadian government official*
Roland, Anne *registrar Supreme Court of Canada*
Scherrer, Helene Chalifour *Canadian government official*
Stanford, Joseph Stephen *diplomat, lawyer, educator*
Valeri, Tony *Canadian government official, small business owner*
Volpe, Joseph *Canadian government official*
Yalden, Maxwell Freeman *Canadian diplomat*
Yeomans, Donald Ralph *Canadian government official, consultant*

**Toronto**
Bartleman, James K. *lieutenant governor*
Clarkson, Adrienne *former Governor General of Canada*
Gotlieb, Allan E. *former ambassador*
Holyday, Douglas Charles *city councillor*
MacLaren, Roy *retired Canadian government official*
Turner, John Napier *former prime minister of Canada, legislator*
Mohler, Brian Jeffery *diplomat*

**QUEBEC**

**Montreal**
Gabbour, Iskandar *city and regional planning educator*
Mulroney, Brian (Martin Brian Mulroney) *former Prime Minister of Canada*

**SASKATCHEWAN**

**Regina**
Haverstock, Lynda M. *lieutenant governor*

**Saskatoon**
Blakeney, Allan Emrys *Canadian government official, lawyer, educator*

**Ontario**
Warren, Jack Hamilton *retired diplomat, banker, trade policy advisor*

## MEXICO

**Colonia Cuauhtemoc**
Garza, Antonio O. *ambassador*

**Mexico City**
Creel Miranda, Santiago *Mexican government official*
Díaz, Francisco Gil *Mexican government official*
Gurria Trevino, José Angel *former Mexican government official*
Peyrot Gonzalez, Marco A. *secretary of the navy of Mexico*
Carabias Lillo, Julia *government official*
Frenk, Julio Jose *minister of health for Mexico, health systems researcher, consultant*
Téllez Kuenzler, Luis *former government official, investment banker*

## AUSTRALIA

**Camberwell**
Peterson, Douglas Pete (Pete Peterson) *former ambassador, retired congressman*

**Double Bay**
Peacock, Penne Korth *ambassador*

## BELGIUM

**Brussels**
Gray, C. Boyden (Clayland Boyden Gray) *ambassador, lawyer*
Nuland, Victoria *US permanent representative to NATO*

## BRAZIL

**Brasilia**
Amorim, Celso Luiz Nunes *Brazilian government official*
Cardoso, Fernando Henrique *former president of Brazil*

## CHILE

**Santiago**
Wilkey, Malcolm Richard *retired ambassador, retired judge*

## CHINA

**Beijing**
Jiabao, Wen *Chinese government official*
Li, Zhaoxing *Chinese government official*

## CZECH REPUBLIC

**Prague**
Kavan, Jan *Czech government official, former president UN General Assembly*

## ENGLAND

**London**
Elizabeth, , II, (Elizabeth Alexandra Mary) *By the Grace of God of the United Kingdom of Great Britain and Northern Ireland and of Her Other Realms and Territories Queen, Head of the Commonwealth, Defender of the Faith*
Meyer, Sir Christopher J.R. *former ambassador*

**Oxford**
Robinson, Mary *former United Nations official*

## ETHIOPIA

**Addis Ababa**
Huddleston, Vicki Jean *diplomat*

## FRANCE

**Armees**
Alliot-Marie, Michèle *French government official*

**Paris**
Dean, John Gunther *diplomat*
Lagarde, Christine *French government official, lawyer*
Myerson, Jacob Myer *retired diplomat*
Oliver, Louise V. *ambassador*

## GERMANY

**Berlin**
Köhler, Horst *President of Federal Republic of Germany*

## GREECE

**Thessaloniki**
Koenig, John M. *ambassador*

## INDIA

**New Delhi**
Malone, David Michael *diplomat, educator*

## IRAN

**Tehran**
Ahmadinejad, Mahmoud (Mahmoud Ahmadinezhad) *President of Iran*

## ISRAEL

**Jerusalem**
Olmert, Ehud *Prime Minister of Israel*

## ITALY

**Bologna**
Lino, Marisa Rose *retired diplomat*

**Rome**
Hall, Tony P. *ambassador, retired congressman*
Sisulu, Sheila Violet Makate *diplomat, international organization official*
Spogli, Ronald P. *ambassador*

## LIBERIA

**Monrovia**
Johnson-Sirleaf, Ellen *President of Liberia, economist*

## MALAYSIA

**Perak**
Yussuf Izzuddim, Shah Ghafraullah Sultan *Sultan of Perak*

## MONGOLIA

**Ulaanbaatar**
Baasan, Ragchaa *diplomat*

## NETHERLANDS

**The Hague**
Tomka, Peter *diplomat, arbitrator, judge, lawyer*

## PERU

**Lima**
Struble, James Curtis *ambassador*

**Miraflores Lima**
Kuczynski, Pedro-Pablo *Prime Minister of Peru*

## PHILIPPINES

**Makati**
Mabilangan, Felipe Hugo, Jr. *diplomat*

## REPUBLIC OF THE CONGO

**Kinshasa Gombe**
Sanders, Robin Renee *ambassador*

## SPAIN

**Canary Islands**
Wells, Melissa Foelsch *ambassador*

**Madrid**
Aznar, José María *former prime minister of Spain, political organization official*
Vural, Volkan *Turkish diplomat*

## SWEDEN

**Lidingö**
Crapon de Caprona, Count Noël François Marie *retired senior United Nations official*

**Stockholm**
Wachtmeister, Count Wilhelm H.F. *diplomat*

## SWITZERLAND

**Bern**
Gonzalez, Guillermo Enrique *diplomat*

**Geneva**
Brown, Kent Newville *ambassador*

## THAILAND

**Bangkok**
McMillion, Margaret Kim *foreign service officer*

## ADDRESS UNPUBLISHED

Abramowitz, Morton I. *former ambassador*
Adams, Edwin Melville *retired diplomat, actor, writer*
Adams, Weston *former diplomat, military officer, lawyer*
Addo, Charles Kwame *municipal official*
Albano, Michael J. *former mayor*
Allen, Claude Alexander *former federal official*
Almond, Lincoln *retired governor, retired lawyer*
Amato Chiaramonte Bordonaro, Baron Carlo Camillo *ambassador, consultant*
Anzai, Earl I. *former state attorney general*
Arcos, Cresencio S. *ambassador*
Armstrong, Anne Legendre (Mrs. Tobin Armstrong) *retired ambassador*
Atwater, Phyllis Y. *municipal official*
Babauta, Juan Nekai *former governor, former congressional representative*
Baca, Jim *mayor*
Baker, James Edward *city planner*
Baldyga, Leonard J. *retired diplomat, consultant*
Bandar, Prince bin Sultan bin Abd al-Aziz Al Saud *former ambassador*
Baptista, Robert Charles, Jr. *federal official, lawyer*
Battle, Vincent M. *former ambassador*
Bayless, Betsey *state official*
Beard, Ann Southard *diplomat, oil industry executive*
Beasley, David Muldrow *former governor, consultant*
Benavente, Diego Tenorio *former lieutenant governor*
Benson, Craig Robert *former governor*
Benson, Joanne E. *retired lieutenant governor*
Bernstein, Stuart A. *former ambassador*
Betti, John Anso *federal official, retired automotive executive*
Binsfeld, Connie Berube *former state official*
Bishop, Oliver Richard *retired state official*
Black, Shirley Temple (Mrs. Charles A. Black) *retired ambassador, retired actress*
Blanco Mendoza, Herminio Alonso *former Mexican government official*
Blankenship, J. Richard *former ambassador*
Bliss, Donald Tiffany, Jr. *ambassador*
Boardman, Connie *former mayor, biologist, educator*
Bolen, David Benjamin *former ambassador*
Botelho, Bruce Manuel *mayor, retired state attorney general*
Boudria, Don *Canadian government official*
Bowen, Otis Ray *former secretary of health and human services, former governor*
Boyatt, Thomas David *former ambassador*
Brakensiek, Jay Clemence *county official*
Bremer, Paul (L. Paul Bremer, Lewis Paul Bremer III) *former diplomat*
Bremer Martino, Juan Jose *former ambassador*
Brill, Kenneth C. *federal official, former ambassador*
Broadrick-Allen, Sandra Carol *retired city manager, civic worker, consultant*
Brock, William Emerson *former secretary of labor*
Brook, Scott Jonathan Bradley *mayor, career consulting executive*
Brown, John Y. III *former state official*
Brown, June Gibbs *retired government official*
Brown, Kay (Mary Kathryn Brown) *retired state official, consultant, political organization worker*
Brown, Lee Patrick *retired mayor, federal official, protective services official, educator*
Brown, Pamela S. *former attorney general*
Brownell, Nora Mead *former commissioner*
Burchman, Leonard *federal official, journalist*
Bush, Barbara Pierce *former First Lady of the United States, volunteer*
Calderón, Sila Maria *former governor*
Calland, Albert M. III *federal official, career military officer*

Card, Andy (Andrew Hill Card Jr.) *former White House chief of staff*
Carlucci, Frank Charles III *former secretary of defense*
Carpenter, David Erwin *retired county official, land use planner*
Carter, Rosalynn Smith (Eleanor Rosalynn Carter) *former First Lady of the United States*
Cauchon, Martin *former Canadian government official*
Cayetano, Benjamin Jerome *former governor, former state senator and representative*
Chen, Stephen S. F. *retired diplomat*
Cherry, Robert Steven III *municipal official*
Chrétien, Raymond A.J. *retired ambassador*
Clarke, Henry Lee *foreign service officer, ambassador*
Clayton, Raymond Edward *municipal official*
Condayan, John *foreign service officer*
Coop, Frederick Robert *retired city manager*
Coppie, Comer Swift *retired state official*
Corkery, James Caldwell *retired Canadian government executive, mechanical engineer*
Cornell, Robert Arthur *federal official*
Cosman, Francene Jen *former government official*
Cunningham, James Blair *ambassador*
Daglis, Lisa Genine *deputy attorney general*
Dalsimer, Anthony Stearns *retired foreign service officer, educator*
Daly, Paul Sylvester *former mayor, retired academic administrator, management consultant*
Dawson, Carol Gene *former commissioner, writer, consultant*
Deily, Linnet Frazier *former ambassador*
Dejammet, Alain *former diplomat*
Deming, Rust M. *ambassador*
DeThomas, Joseph Michael *former ambassador*
Dillon, Robert Sherwood *retired diplomat*
Dornbush, K. Terry *former ambassador, consulting company executive, educator*
Egan, Wesley William *former ambassador*
Eisenhower, John Sheldon Doud *former ambassador, writer*
Eliot, Theodore Lyman, Jr. *former ambassador, consultant*
Elson, Edward Elliott *diplomat*
Emmons, Robert Duncan *diplomat*
Ewing, Raymond Charles *retired ambassador*
Farber, Zulima V. *former state attorney general, lawyer*
Fenstersheib, Martin *city health department administrator*
Fiddick, Paul William *public official, broadcast executive*
Fischer, David J. *retired mayor*
Ford, Christopher Ashley *federal official, lawyer*
Ford, Ford Barney *retired federal official*
Fowler, Wyche, Jr. *ambassador*
Fraser, Donald MacKay *retired mayor, retired congressman*
Galloway, Judy A. *deputy commissioner*
Gardom, Garde Basil *former lieutenant governor of British Columbia*
Gaviria Trujillo, Cesar *former international organization administrator, former President of Colombia*
Geisel, Harold Walter *diplomat*
Gilmore, Kathi *former state treasurer*
Glassman, Cynthia A. *former commissioner*
Goldthwait, Christopher E. *ambassador*
Gore, Al (Albert Arnold Gore Jr.) *former Vice President of the United States*
Grady, Wayne Joseph *retired government official*
Graves, William Preston *governor*
Hahn, James Kenneth *former mayor, lawyer*
Hall, Kathryn Walt *ambassador*
Hamed, Martha Ellen *government administrator*
Hanmer, Stephen Read, Jr. *retired federal official*
Harder, Robert Clarence *state official*
Harris, Joe Frank *former governor*
Hauer, Jerome M. *city official*
Hawke, John Daniel, Jr. *former federal official*
Hazeltine, Joyce *former state official*
Hecklinger, Richard E. *ambassador*
Heed, Peter W. *former state attorney general*
Heimbold, Charles Andreas, Jr. *former ambassador*
Hennemeyer, Robert Thomas *diplomat*
Henry, Sherrye P. *political advisor, radio personality*
Henry, Stephen Lewis *retired lieutenant governor, orthopedic surgeon, educator*
Hester, Nancy Elizabeth *county government official*
Hirono, Mazie Keiko *former lieutenant governor*
Holiday, Edith Elizabeth *former presidential adviser, cabinet secretary*
Holmes, Henry Allen *diplomat*
Hood, Glenda E. *former state official, former mayor*
Householder, Larry *state official, small business owner*
Howard, Robert Elliott *former federal official, consultant, educator*
Hubbard, Thomas C. *former ambassador*
Huddle, Franklin Pierce, Jr. *diplomat*
Hull, Edmund J. *former ambassador*
Hull, Jane Dee *former governor, former state legislator*
Itoh, William H. *former ambassador*
Jacobsen, Diane DeMell *foreign policy specialist*
Javits, Eric Moses *ambassador, lawyer*
Jeter, Howard F. *former ambassador*
Johnson, Darryl Norman *retired ambassador*
Jordan, Mary Lucille *commissioner*
Katzenbach, Nicholas deBelleville *former United States attorney general*
Kendig, William Lamar *retired federal official, accountant*
Kernan, Barbara Desind *federal official*
Kernan, Joseph Eugene III *former governor*
Kobluk, Michael Daniel *retired municipal official*
Kulstad, Guy Charles *public works official*
Leach, Howard H. *former ambassador, former health care products company executive*
Leader, Joyce E. *ambassador*
Ledogar, Stephen J. *retired diplomat*
Loiello, John Peter *diplomat, international consultant*
Luti, Bill (William Joseph Luti) *federal official, retired military officer*

Macedo de la Concha, Rafael *former Mexican government official*
Mack, Earle Irving *former ambassador, former real estate company executive*
Maestrone, Frank Eusebio *diplomat*
Marchi, Sergio Sisto *Canadian government official*
Marr, Carmel Carrington *retired state official*
Martin, Lynn Morley *former secretary of labor*
Martin, Paul *former Prime Minister of Canada*
Martz, Judy Helen *former governor*
Masiello, Anthony M. (Tony Masiello) *former mayor*
Mattingly, Mack Francis *former ambassador, former senator, entrepreneur*
Maxwell, Joe (Joseph Edwin Maxwell) *former lieutenant governor*
Mazankowski, Donald Frank *Canadian government official*
McBride, John P. *state commissioner*
McCaughey Ross, Elizabeth P. (Betsy McCaughey) *former lieutenant governor*
McClellan, Scott K. *former White House press secretary*
McClennen, Miriam J. *former state official*
McClinton, James Leroy *city administrator*
Mc Coy, Tidal Windham *former government official*
McDonald, Jackson *ambassador*
McDougall, Donald Blake *retired provincial official, librarian*
McGowan, Gerald S. *diplomat*
McGreevey, Jim (James Edward McGreevey) *former governor*
McKeachnie, Gayle F. *former lieutenant governor*
McLellan, A. Anne *Canadian government official*
McMichael, Guy H. III *federal official*
McNamara, Ted (Thomas Edmund McNamara) *federal official, former ambassador*
Mercado-Ramos, Ferdinand *former Puerto Rican government official*
Miles, Richard *former ambassador*
Millane, Lynn *retired municipal official*
Miller, Thomas J. *former ambassador*
Minikes, Stephan Michael *ambassador, lawyer, banker*
Moley, Kevin Edward *ambassador*
Montgomery, William D. *former ambassador*
Morris, Robert Gemmill *retired foreign service officer*
Morris, Ronald Anthony *county official*
Munro, Ralph Davies *former state official*
Murphy, Gerald *retired federal official*
Murphy, Thomas J., Jr. *former mayor*
Navarrete, Jorge Eduardo *ambassador*
Nelson, Norman Daniel *government official*
Nemfakos, Charles Panagiotis *defense industry executive, strategic consultant*
Ness, Susan *federal official*
Norquist, John Olaf *former mayor*
Norton, Gale Ann *former secretary of the interior*
Obermann, Richard Michael *governmental technology and policy analyst*
Ohs, Karl *former lieutenant governor*
Ong, John Doyle *former ambassador, retired manufacturing executive*
Pascoe, B. Lynn *ambassador*
Pearl, Laurence Dickson *retired federal government executive*
Peeler, Bob *lieutenant governor*
Petrequin, Harry Joseph, Jr. *foreign service officer*
Peyton, John *mayor*
Pirsch, Carol McBride *retired county official, state senator, community relations manager*
Plaisted, Joan M. *diplomat*
Pont Marchese, Marisara *former Puerto Rican government official*
Powers, John T., Jr. *former mayor*
Pridmore, Roy Davis *retired federal official*
Purcell, Bill *mayor*
Rahman, Abu Tayeb Rafiqur *former United Nations official*
Randolph, Virgella *retired federal official*
Ratliff, William *former state senator, former lieutenant governor, civil engineer*
Ray, Charles Aaron *ambassador*
Reagan, Nancy Davis (Anne Francis Robbins) *former First Lady of the United States, volunteer*
Redd, Scott (John Scott Redd) *federal official, retired military officer*
Reinhardt, John Edward *former international affairs specialist*
Renkes, Gregg D. *former state attorney general*
Reno, Janet *former United States attorney general*
Rickert, Jonathan Bradley *retired foreign service officer*
Ridge, Tom (Thomas Joseph Ridge) *former secretary of homeland security*
Ries, Charles P. *ambassador*
Rimler, Anita A. *former state official*
Rimsza, Skip *former mayor*
Riordan, Richard J. *former state official, former mayor*
Rivers, Beverly D. *former district secretary*
Robinson, Laurie Overby *former assistant attorney general*
Rocca, Christina B. *ambassador, former federal agency administrator*
Rocha, V. Manuel *former diplomat, international trade consultant*
Rogers, Joe *former lieutenant governor*
Rosenthal, Helen Nagelberg *county official, advocate*
Rosenthal, James D. *retired federal official, retired ambassador*
Ross, Christopher Wade Stelyan *diplomat*
Rossello, Pedro *former governor*
Rudin, Anne *retired mayor, nursing educator*
Russack, John A. *federal official*
Sa, Julie (Shia Ri Xiang) *former council woman, former mayor, real estate developer*
Salmon, Jerry Derr *federal air marshall*
Sanderson, Janet A. *former ambassador*
Scanlan, John Douglas *retired ambassador*
Schoettler, Gail Sinton *former ambassador*
Sembler, Melvin F. *former ambassador, real estate developer*
Shea, Gwyn *former state official*
Shelley, Kevin Francis *former state official*
Sherrer, Gary *former state lieutenant governor, bank executive*

Shivers, Mitchell Everett *diplomat*
Smith, Jean Kennedy *former ambassador*
Smith, Pamela Hyde *ambassador*
Smith, Robert Powell *former ambassador, retired foundation administrator*
Snider, L. Britt *federal official*
Snow, Jack (John William Snow) *former secretary of the treasury*
Sotirhos, Michael *ambassador*
Stanton, William Anthony *diplomat*
Stewart, Jane *former Canadian government minister*
Stridiron, Iver Allison *former attorney general*
Stumpe, Warren Robert *county official, retired engineering executive*
Sudanowicz, Elaine Marie *government executive*
Sunia, Muagututia Fiti *former attorney general*
Sutter, Eleanor Bly *retired diplomat*
Swett, Richard Nelson (Dick Swett) *diplomat, former congressman*
Tambs, Lewis Arthur *diplomat, educator, historian*
Teater, Dorothy Seath *retired county official*
Terpeluk, Peter G., Jr. *former ambassador*
Thomas, Harry K., Jr. *former ambassador*
Thomas, Regena L. *former state official*
Tienken, Arthur T. *retired foreign service officer*
Towell, Timothy Lathrop *foreign service officer*
Townsend, Kathleen Kennedy *former lieutenant governor*
Ulmer, Frances Ann *retired state official*
Underwood, Cecil Harland *retired governor, diversified financial services company executive*
Van Cleave, Michelle Kim *former federal official*
Vasquez, Gaddi H. *ambassador, former federal agency administrator*
Ventura, Jesse (James James) *former governor*
Walker, George Herbert III *former ambassador, retired investment banking company executive*
Walker, Gordon Davies *government official, writer, lecturer, consultant*
Walker, Olene S. *former governor*
Wallace, Nicolle (Nicolle Devenish) *former federal official*
Warner, Mark Robert *former governor*
Watkins, James David *federal official, military officer*
Watt, Linda E. *former ambassador*
Webster, Christopher White *foreign service officer*
Weld, Bill (William Floyd Weld) *lawyer, former governor*
Whelan, Susan *former Canadian government official*
Wilson, Joseph Charles, IV, *former ambassador*
Windom, Stephen Ralph *former lieutenant governor, lawyer*
Wolf, Dale Edward *state official*
Wolfensohn, James David *former diplomat, former President of the World Bank*
Wood, Corinne Gieseke *former lieutenant governor*
Wu, Jeremy S. *federal official*
Yates, Mary Carlin *former ambassador*
Zischke, Douglas Arthur *foreign service officer*

# GOVERNMENT: LEGISLATIVE ADMINISTRATION

## UNITED STATES

### ALABAMA

**Birmingham**
Allen, Maryon Pittman *former senator, clothing designer, journalist*
Hilliard, Earl Frederick *congressman, lawyer*

**Mobile**
Edwards, Jack *congressman, lawyer*

**Montgomery**
Dixon, Larry Dean *state legislator*

### ALASKA

**Anchorage**
Sturgulewski, Arliss *state legislator, director*

**Juneau**
Kohring, Victor H. *state legislator*
McGuire, Lesil L. *state representative*
Stevens, Gary Lee *state senator*

**North Pole**
James, Jeannette Adeline *state legislator, accountant, small business owner*

### ARIZONA

**Paradise Valley**
Salmon, Matt *former congressman, communications company executive*

**Phoenix**
Brown, Jack A. *state representative, rancher, real estate broker*
Kyl, Jon Llewellyn *senator*

**Tucson**
Bartlett, David Carson *state legislator*

**Waddell**
Turner, Warren Austin *state legislator*

### ARKANSAS

**Dumas**
Schexnayder, Charlotte Tillar *state legislator*

**Greenwood**
Walters, Bill *retired state senator*

### CALIFORNIA

**Bakersfield**
Ashburn, Roy *state senator*

**Compton**
Dymally, Mervyn Malcolm *retired congressman*

**Long Beach**
Karentte, Betty *state legislator*

**Martinez**
Canciamilla, Joseph *state legislator*

**Monterey**
Browder, John Glen *former congressman, educator*

**Ontario**
Soto, Nell *state senator*

**Sacramento**
Chu, Judy May *assemblywoman*
Kuehl, Sheila James *state legislator*
Liu, Carol *state representative*
McCarthy, Kevin *state representative*
Morrow, Bill *state legislator*
Pavley, Fran J. *state representative*
Strickland, Anthony *state representative*
Tran, Van Thai *state legislator*
Yee, Leland Y. *state legislator*

**San Mateo**
Mullin, Gene *state legislator*

**Stockton**
Singleton, Marvin Ayers *state legislator, otolaryngologist*

**West Covina**
Torres, Esteban Edward *congressman, trade association administrator*

### COLORADO

**Colorado Springs**
Sinclair, William Donald *state legislator, retired church official*

**Denver**
Anderson, Norma V. *retired state legislator*
Faatz, Jeanne Ryan *councilman*
Meiklejohn, Alvin J., Jr. *state legislator, lawyer, accountant*
Takis, Stephanie *retired state senator*
Williams, Suzanne *state senator*

**Fort Collins**
Schaffer, Robert (Bob Schaffer) *former congressman*

**Grand Junction**
Bishop, Tilman Malcolm *retired state legislator*

### CONNECTICUT

**Branford**
Gejdenson, Sam *former congressman*

**Glastonbury**
Googins, Sonya Forbes *state legislator, retired banker*

**Hartford**
Fahrbach, Ruth C. *state legislator*
Mushinsky, Mary M. *state legislator*

**Ledyard**
McGrattan, Mary K. *state legislator*

**New Haven**
Dyson, William R. *state legislator, educator*

**Riverside**
Powers, Claudia McKenna *state legislator*

### DELAWARE

**Dover**
Amick, Steven Hammond *state legislator, lawyer*
Spence, Terry R. *state legislator*

**Newark**
Neal, James Preston *state senator, project engineer*

### DISTRICT OF COLUMBIA

**Washington**
Abercrombie, Neil *congressman*
Ackerman, Gary Leonard *congressman*
Aderholt, Robert B. *congressman, lawyer*
Akaka, Daniel Kahikina *senator*
Akin, Todd (William Todd Akin) *congressman, former state legislator*
Alexander, Lamar (Andrew Lamar Alexander) *senator, former secretary of education, former governor, lawyer*
Alexander, Rodney M. *congressman*
Allard, Wayne (Alan Wayne Allard) *senator, veterinarian*
Allen, George Felix, Jr. *senator, former governor*
Allen, Thomas H. *congressman, lawyer*
Andrews, Robert Ernest *congressman, lawyer*
Baca, Joe *congressman*
Bachus, Spencer T. III *congressman, lawyer*
Backlin, Jim *legislative staff member*
Baird, Brian N. *congressman*
Baker, Richard Hugh *congressman*
Baldwin, Tammy *congresswoman, lawyer*
Barrett, James Gresham *congressman*
Barrow, John J. *congressman, lawyer*
Bartlett, Roscoe G. *congressman*
Barton, Joe Linus *congressman*
Bass, Charles Foster *congressman*

Baucus, Max Sieben *senator*
Bayh, Evan (Birch Evan Bayh III) *senator, former governor*
Bean, Melissa *congresswoman*
Beauprez, Bob *congressman*
Becerra, Xavier *congressman, lawyer*
Bennett, Robert F. *senator*
Berkley, Shelley (Rochelle Levine Berkley) *congresswoman, lawyer*
Berman, Howard Lawrence *congressman, lawyer*
Berry, Marion *congressman*
Biden, Joseph Robinette, Jr. *senator*
Biggert, Judith Borg *congresswoman, lawyer*
Bilbray, Brian Patrick *congressman*
Bilirakis, Michael *congressman, lawyer, corporate financial executive*
Bingaman, Jeff, Jr., (Jesse Francis Bingaman) *senator*
Bishop, Rob *congressman*
Bishop, Sanford Dixon, Jr. *congressman, lawyer*
Bishop, Timothy H. *congressman*
Blackburn, Marsha *congresswoman*
Bliley, Thomas Jerome, Jr. *former congressman*
Blumenauer, Earl *congressman*
Blunt, Roy D. *congressman*
Boehlert, Sherwood Louis *congressman*
Boehner, John Andrew *congressman*
Bond, Christopher Samuel (Kit Bond) *senator, lawyer*
Bonilla, Henry *congressman, broadcast executive*
Bonner, Josiah Robins, Jr., (Jo Bonner) *congressman*
Bono, Mary Whitaker *congresswoman*
Boozman, John *congressman*
Bordallo, Madeleine Mary (Mrs. Ricardo Jerome Bordallo) *congresswoman*
Boren, Daniel David *congressman*
Boswell, Leonard L. *congressman*
Boucher, Rick (Frederick C. Boucher) *congressman, lawyer*
Boustany, Charles W., Jr. *congressman, surgeon*
Boxer, Barbara *senator*
Boyd, F. Allen, Jr. *congressman, farmer*
Bradley, Jeb (Joseph E. Bradley) *congressman*
Brady, Kevin Patrick *congressman*
Brady, Robert A. *congressman*
Brown, Corrine *congresswoman*
Brown, Henry E., Jr. *congressman*
Brown, Sherrod Campbell *congressman, retired state official*
Brownback, Sam Dale *senator, lawyer*
Bunning, Jim (James Paul David Bunning) *senator, former professional baseball player*
Burgess, Michael C. *congressman*
Burns, Conrad Ray *senator*
Burr, Richard M. *senator, former congressman*
Burton, Dan L. *congressman*
Butterfield, George Kenneth, Jr. *congressman, former state supreme court justice*
Buyer, Steven Earle *congressman, lawyer*
Byrd, Robert Carlyle *senator*
Calvert, Ken *congressman*
Camp, David Lee *congressman, lawyer*
Campbell, John B. T. III *congressman, former state senator*
Cannon, Christopher Black *congressman, lawyer*
Cantor, Eric I. *congressman, lawyer*
Cantwell, Maria E. *senator*
Capito, Shelley Moore *congresswoman*
Capps, Lois Ragnhild Grimsrud *congresswoman, former school nurse*
Capuano, Michael Everett *congressman, lawyer*
Cardin, Benjamin Louis *congressman, lawyer*
Cardoza, Dennis *congressman*
Carnahan, Russ (John Russell Carnahan) *congressman, lawyer*
Carper, Thomas Richard *senator, former governor*
Carr, Bob *congressman, lawyer*
Carson, Julia M. *congresswoman*
Carter, John Rice *congressman, lawyer*
Case, Edward E. *congressman, lawyer*
Castle, Michael N. *congressman, lawyer*
Chabot, Steven Joseph *congressman, lawyer*
Chafee, Lincoln D. *senator*
Chambliss, Saxby (C. Saxby Chambliss) *senator*
Chandler, Ben (Albert Benjamin Chandler III) *congressman, former state attorney general*
Chocola, Chris *congressman, lawyer*
Christian-Christensen, Donna Marie *congresswoman*
Clay, William Lacy, Jr. *congressman*
Cleaver, Emanuel, II, *congressman, former mayor, minister*
Clinton, Hillary (Hillary Diane Rodham Clinton) *senator, lawyer, former First Lady of United States*
Clyburn, James Enos (Jim Clyburn) *congressman*
Coble, Howard (John Howard Coble) *congressman, lawyer*
Coburn, Tom (Thomas Allen Coburn) *senator*
Cochran, Thad (William Thad Cochran) *senator*
Cole, Tom *congressman*
Coleman, Norman, Jr. *senator, former mayor*
Collins, Susan Margaret *senator*
Conaway, Mike *congressman*
Conrad, Kent (Gaylord Kent Conrad) *senator*
Conyers, John, Jr. *congressman*
Cooper, James Hayes Shofner (Jim Cooper) *congressman, lawyer*
Cornyn, John III *senator*
Costa, Jim *congressman*
Costello, Jerry F., Jr. *congressman, former county official*
Craig, Larry Edwin *senator*
Cramer, Robert E., Jr., (Bud Cramer) *congressman, lawyer*
Crapo, Michael Dean *senator, former congressman, lawyer*
Crenshaw, Ander *congressman, lawyer*
Crowley, Joseph *congressman*
Cubin, Barbara Lynn *congresswoman*
Cuellar, Henry *congressman, lawyer*
Culberson, John Abney *congressman, lawyer*
Cummings, Elijah E. *congressman*
Davis, Artur *congressman, lawyer*
Davis, Danny K. *congressman*
Davis, Geoff *congressman*
Davis, Jim *congressman, lawyer*
Davis, Jo Ann S. *congresswoman*
Davis, Lincoln *congressman*
Davis, Susan A. *congresswoman*

Young, Bill (Charles William Young) *congressman*
Young, Donald E. *congressman*

## FLORIDA

**Bradenton**
Woodson-Howard, Marlene Erdley *former state legislator*

**Dade City**
Brown-Waite, Virginia (Ginny Brown-Waite) *congresswoman*

**Ormond Beach**
Lynn, Evelyn Joan *state senator, consultant*

**Osprey**
Smith, Robert Clinton *former senator*

**Tallahassee**
Blanton, Faye Wester *legislative official*

**Tampa**
Davis, Helen Gordon *retired state senator*

## GEORGIA

**Americus**
Hooks, George Bardin *state legislator, insurance and real estate company executive*

**Athens**
McBee, Mary Louise *retired state legislator, retired academic administrator*

**Atlanta**
Butler, Gloria Singleton *state legislator*
Coleman, Terry Lewis *state legislator*
Miller, Zell Bryan *former senator, former governor*
Orrock, Nan *state legislator*
Stanley, Pamela Aurelia *state legislator*

**Columbus**
Harbison, Ed *state legislator, broadcast journalist, motivational speaker*

**Decatur**
Majette, Denise *former congresswoman*

**Rincon**
Purcell, Ann Rushing *state legislator, human services manager*

**Savannah**
Johnson, Eric B. *state legislator*

**Smyrna**
Atkins, William Austin, Sr., (Bill Atkins) *former state legislator*

## HAWAII

**Honolulu**
Baker, Rosalyn Hester *state senator*
Magaoay, Michael Y. *state representative*
Sakamoto, Norman Lloyd *state legislator, civil engineer*
Takumi, Roy Mitsuo *state legislator*

**Kailua**
Young, Jacqueline Eurn Hai *former state legislator, consultant*

## IDAHO

**Boise**
Black, Pete *retired state legislator, educator*
Keough, Shawn *state legislator*
Lodge, Patti Anne *state senator*

**Jerome**
Bell, Maxine Toolson *state legislator, librarian*

## ILLINOIS

**Chicago**
Berman, Arthur Leonard *retired state legislator*
Doherty, Brian Gerard *alderman*
Jones, Emil, Jr. *state legislator*

**Jacksonville**
Findley, Paul *former congressman, author, educator*

**Lake Forest**
Frederick, Virginia Fiester *state legislator*

**Pontiac**
Ewing, Thomas William *congressman, lawyer*

**Springfield**
Collins, Annazette R. *state representative*
Currie, Barbara Flynn *state legislator*
Daniels, Lee Albert *state representative*
Hannig, Gary L. *state representative*
Jefferson, Charles E. *state representative*
Klingler, Gwendolyn Walbolt *state representative*
Kosel, Renée *state representative*
Martinez, Iris *state senator*
Pankau, Carole *state senator*
Parke, Terry Richard *state representative*

**Sycamore**
Burzynski, James Bradley *state legislator*

**Westchester**
Lightford, Kimberly A. *state legislator*

## INDIANA

**Columbus**
Garton, Robert Dean *state legislator*

**Indianapolis**
Austin, Terri Jo *state representative*

**Shoals**
Boyd, Earl E., Jr. *councilman*

**West Lafayette**
Scholer, Sue Wyant *retired state legislator*

## IOWA

**Des Moines**
Boettger, Nancy J. *state legislator*
Bukta, Polly *state representative*
Jochum, Pam *state representative*
Ragan, Amanda *state senator*
Szymoniak, Elaine Eisfelder *retired state senator*

**Sioux City**
Andersen, Leonard Christian *former state legislator, real estate investor*
Doyle, Donald Vincent *retired state legislator, lawyer*

## KANSAS

**Clay Center**
Braden, James Dale *former state legislator*

**Hutchinson**
O'Neal, Michael Ralph *state legislator, lawyer*

**Overland Park**
Vratil, John Logan *state legislator, lawyer*

**Prairie Village**
Newton, Dean *state representative*

**Salina**
Horst, Deena Louise *state legislator*

**Shawnee Mission**
Sader, Carol Hope *former state legislator*

**Topeka**
Carlin, Sydney *state representative*
Dan, Johnson *state representative*
Gordon, Lana G. *state representative*
Kirk, Nancy A. *state legislator, nursing home administrator*
Merrick, Raymond F. *state representative*
Petty, Marge D. *state senator*
Saville, Pat *state senate official*
Schmidt, Derek *state senator*
Storm, Suzanne *state representative*

**Wichita**
Pottorff, Jo Ann *state legislator*

## KENTUCKY

**Frankfort**
Marcotte, Paul Henry *state representative*
Palumbo, Ruth Ann *state legislator*
Pullin, Tanya *state representative*
Richards, Jody *state legislator, communications educator, small business owner*
Stine, Katie Kratz *state legislator*

**Shelbyville**
Miller, Mary Helen *retired state government administrator*

## LOUISIANA

**Lake Charles**
Mount, Willie Landry *state legislator*

**New Orleans**
Irons, Paulette Riley *state legislator, lawyer*

## MAINE

**Augusta**
Edmonds, Beth *state legislator, lieutenant governor*
Martin, John Lewis *state legislator*

**Belgrade Lakes**
Kany, Judy C(asperson) *retired state senator*

**Brunswick**
Pfeiffer, Sophia Douglass *retired state legislator, lawyer*

## MARYLAND

**Annapolis**
Barve, Kumar P. *state legislator*
Busch, Michael *state legislator*
Doory, Ann Marie *legislator*
Hollinger, Paula Colodny *state legislator*
Kelley, Delores Goodwin *state legislator*
Lee, Susan C. *state legislator, lawyer*
Love, Mary Ann E. *state legislator*
Madden, Martin Gerard *former state legislator*
Ruben, Ida Gass *state senator*

**Bethesda**
Reed, Miriam Bell *legislative staff member*

**Frederick**
Byron, Beverly Butcher *retired congresswoman*

**Rockville**
Petzold, Carol Stoker *state legislator*

## MASSACHUSETTS

**Boston**
Canavan, Christine Estelle *state legislator*
Creedon, Geraldine *state legislator*
Creem, Cynthia Stone *state legislator, lawyer*
Jehlen, Patricia D. *state legislator*
Peisch, Alice Hanlon *state legislator*
Rogeness, Mary Speer *state legislator*
Walrath, Patricia A. *state legislator*
Wolf, Alice Koerner *state legislator, former mayor*

**Gardner**
Hawke, Robert Douglas *retired state legislator*

**Newton Highlands**
Hummel, Margaret P. *state representative*

**Springfield**
Melconian, Linda Jean *state senator, lawyer, educator*

## MICHIGAN

**Lansing**
Hoffman, Philip Edward *legislative consultant*
Hopgood, Hoon-Yung *state representative*

**Livonia**
McCotter, Thaddeus George *congressman*

**Troy**
Hillegonds, Paul *former state legislator*

## MINNESOTA

**Brainerd**
Samuelson, Donald B. *former state legislator*

**Eden Prairie**
Luther, William P. *former congressman*

**Minneapolis**
Greenfield, Lee *state legislator*
Mickelson, Stacey *state legislator*
Oliver, Edward Carl *retired state legislator, retired insurance company executive, small business owner*
Reichgott Junge, Ember Darlene *retired senator, lawyer, writer, broadcast commentator, radio personality*
Spear, Allan Henry *state legislator, historian, educator*
Wejcman, Linda *retired state legislator*

**Ottertail**
Anderson, Bob *state legislator, retired small business owner*

**Saint Paul**
Chaudhary, Satveer *state senator*
Minge, David *former congressman, lawyer, law educator*
Pappas, Sandra Lee *state senator*
Wohlman, Matthew Jerry *legislative staff member*

**South Saint Paul**
Metzen, James P. *state legislator, bank executive*

## MISSISSIPPI

**Jackson**
Coleman, Mary H. *state legislator*

## MONTANA

**Butte**
Harrington, Dan William *state senator*

**Cut Bank**
Roush, Glenn A. *state senator*

**Dillon**
Tash, Bill *state senator*

**Helena**
Hill, Richard (Rick) Allan *former congressman*
Mahlum, Dale Duane *state legislator, small business owner*

**Medicine Lake**
Nelson, Linda J. *state legislator*

**Winifred**
Butcher, Edward Bernie *state senator*

## NEBRASKA

**Lincoln**
Kristensen, Douglas Allan *former state legislator*
Preister, Donald George *state legislator, greeting card manufacturer*
Redfield, Pamela A. *state legislator*
Schimek, DiAnna Ruth Rebman *state legislator*
Stuhr, Elaine Ruth *state legislator*

## NEVADA

**Las Vegas**
Wall, Clarence Vinson *state legislator*
Wiener, Valerie *state senator, writer, communications executive*

**Reno**
Raggio, William John *state legislator*

## NEW HAMPSHIRE

**Concord**
Clemons, Jane Andrea *state legislator*
Cote, David Edward *state legislator*

Eaton, Thomas R. *state legislator*
Ferland, Brenda L. *state representative*
Flora, Kathleen M. *retired state representative*
Foster, Linda Timberlake *state legislator*
Francoeur, Sheila T. *state representative*
Gatsas, Ted (Theodore L. Gatsas) *state legislator*
Ginsburg, Ruth *state representative*
Hager, Elizabeth Sears *state legislator, social services administrator*
Kaen, Naida *state representative*
Larsen, Sylvia B. *state legislator*
Norelli, Terie Thompson *state legislator*
Nowe, Ronald John *state legislator, small business owner*
Pilliod, James P. *state legislator, physician*
Richardson, Barbara Hull *state legislator, social worker*
Stickney, Nancy Carver *state legislator*
Thompson, Rob Roy *legislator, writer*

**Derry**
Katsakiores, George Nicholas *state legislator, retired food service executive*

**Dover**
Pelletier, Arthur Joseph *state legislator, data processing executive, educator*

**Durham**
Wheeler, Katherine Wells *retired state legislator*

**Hanover**
Copenhaver, Marion Lamson *retired state legislator*
Crory, Elizabeth Lupien *retired state legislator*

**Lancaster**
Pratt, Leighton Calvin *retired state legislator*

**Manchester**
Arnold, Barbara Eileen *state legislator*

**Moultonborough**
Patten, Betsey Leland *state legislator*

**Randolph**
Bradley, Paula E. *former state legislator*

**Windham**
Arndt, Janet S. *former state legislator, educator*

## NEW JERSEY

**Edison**
Barnes, Peter J., Jr. *assemblyman*

**Flemington**
Lance, Leonard *state legislator*

**Hillside**
Franks, Robert D. (Bob Franks) *former congressman*

**Matawan**
Thompson, Samuel Donald *assemblyman*

**Montclair**
Gill, Nia H. *state legislator*

**Ocean City**
Hughes, William John *former congressman, diplomat*

**Plainfield**
Green, Gerald B. *state legislator*

**Rosemont**
Torricelli, Robert G. *former senator*

**Short Hills**
Ogden, Maureen Black *retired state legislator*

**Somerville**
Biondi, Peter J. *assemblyman*

**South Orange**
Hackett, Mims, Jr. *state legislator*

**Teaneck**
Weinberg, Loretta *state legislator*

**Trenton**
Codey, Richard James *state senator, former governor*

## NEW MEXICO

**Albuquerque**
Rutherford, Thomas Truxtun, II, *state legislator, municipal official*
Sanchez, Raymond G. *former state legislator*
Stewart, Miriam Kay (Mimi Stewart) *state legislator, educator*

**Hobbs**
Reagan, Gary Don *state legislator, lawyer*

**Sandia Park**
Beffort, Sue Wilson *state legislator*

**Santa Fe**
Vaughn, Gloria C. *state representative*

## NEW YORK

**Albany**
Bruno, Joseph L. *state legislator*
Jacobs, Rhoda S. *state legislator*
Paterson, David Alexander *state legislator*
Smith, Ada LaVerne *state legislator*
Stavisky, Toby Ann *state legislator*
Volker, Dale Martin *state legislator, lawyer*

**Brooklyn**
Holmes, Robert Eugene *legislative staff member, journalist*

**Derby**
Pordum, Francis J. *former state legislator, educator, marketing professional*

**Ithaca**
Lifton, Barbara *state legislator, secondary school educator*

**Jamaica**
Flake, Floyd Harold *former congressman*

**New York**
Abate, Catherine M. *retired state legislator*
Quinn, Christine Callaghan *councilwoman*
Silver, Sheldon *state legislator, lawyer*
Wachs, Joel *former city councilman, foundation administrator*

**Ossining**
Galef, Sandra Risk *state legislator, educator*

**Port Chester**
Oppenheimer, Suzi *state legislator*

**Rochester**
John, Susan V. *state representative*

**Syracuse**
DeFrancisco, John Anthony *state legislator, lawyer*

## NORTH CAROLINA

**Advance**
Cochrane, Betsy Lane *former state senator*

**Burlington**
Holt, Bertha Merrill *state legislator*

**Chapel Hill**
Edwards, John Reid *former senator, lawyer*
Kinnaird, Eleanor Gates *state legislator, lawyer*

**Charlotte**
Clodfelter, Daniel Gray *state legislator, lawyer*

**Greensboro**
Shaw, Robert Gilbert *retired state legislator, food service executive*

**Hickory**
Ballenger, Cass (Thomas Cass Ballenger) *former congressman, retired plastics company executive*

**Raleigh**
Lancaster, H(arold) Martin *congressman, academic administrator*
Stevens, Richard Yates *state senator*
Sutton, Ronnie Neal *state legislator, lawyer*

**Southern Pines**
Funderburk, David Britton *retired congressman, ambassador, consultant*

**Wilmington**
Nelson, Tannis Flynn *parliamentarian, retired music educator*

## NORTH DAKOTA

**Ashley**
Kretschmar, William Edward *state legislator, lawyer*

**Bismarck**
Nelson, Carolyn *state legislator*

**Edgeley**
Schimke, Dennis J. *former state legislator*

**Minot**
Tollefson, Ben C. *state legislator, retired utilities executive*

## OHIO

**Akron**
Seiberling, John Frederick *retired congressman, lawyer, educator*

**Cleveland**
Drake, Grace L. *retired state senator, cultural organization administrator*
Oakar, Mary Rose *congresswoman*

**Columbus**
Buehrer, Stephen *state representative*
Dann, Marc *state senator*
Glenn, John Herschel, Jr. *former senator, former astronaut*
Miller, Ray *state senator*
Setzer, Arlene J. *state representative, retired secondary school educator*
Smith, Shirley A. *state legislator, state representative*
Wachtmann, Lynn R. *state legislator*

**Tiffin**
Galipeau, Peter Armand *councilman*

## OKLAHOMA

**Oklahoma City**
Ford, Charles Reed *state legislator*
Jones, Tad *state representative*
Mass, Michael Don *state legislator*
Riley, Nancy C. *state legislator*
Staggs, Barbara Annette *state representative*

## OREGON

**Albany**
Oakley, Carolyn Le *state legislator, city manager, director*

**Marylhurst**
Hatfield, Mark Odom *former senator*

**Mcminnville**
Nelson, Donna Gayle *state representative*

**Portland**
Furse, Elizabeth *retired congressman, small business owner*
Gordly, Avel Louise *state legislator, political organization worker*
Lang, Philip David *retired state legislator, insurance company executive*

**Salem**
Anderson, Laurie Monnes *state senator*
Burdick, Ginny Marie *state senator*
Minnis, Karen *state representative*
Qutub, Eileen *state legislator, real estate appraiser*
Tomei, Carolyn *state representative*
Wirth, Kelley K. *state representative*
Yih, Mae Dunn *state legislator*

## PENNSYLVANIA

**Chalfont**
Wilson, Jean Louise *retired state legislator*

**Harrisburg**
Crahalla, Jacqueline R. *state representative*
Herman, Lynn Briggs *state legislator*
Miller, Sheila *state legislator*
Vance, Patricia H. *state senator*
Williams, Constance *state senator*

**Lewisberry**
Smith, Bruce I. *state legislator*

**Philadelphia**
Jacobs, Jonathan Mark *parliamentary consultant*
Josephs, Babette *legislator*
Roebuck, James Randolph, Jr. *state legislator*

**Wayne**
Rubley, Carole A. *state legislator*

## RHODE ISLAND

**Providence**
Ajello, Edith H. *state legislator*
Algiere, Dennis Lee *state legislator*
Gibbs, June Nesbitt *state senator*

**Warwick**
Revens, John Cosgrove, Jr. *state legislator, lawyer*

## SOUTH CAROLINA

**Columbia**
Courson, John Edward *state legislator, insurance company executive*
Leatherman, Hugh Kenneth, Sr. *state legislator, engineering executive*
McConnell, Glenn F. *state legislator, lawyer, art gallery director*

**Greenville**
DeMint, Jim (James Warren DeMint) *senator, former congressman*
Manly, Sarah Letitia *retired state legislator, ophthalmic photographer, angiographer*
Mann, James Robert *former congressman*

## SOUTH DAKOTA

**Miller**
Morford, JoAnn (JoAnn Morford-Burg) *state senator, investment company executive*

**Mud Butte**
Ingalls, Marie Cecelie *former state legislator, retail executive*

**Pierre**
Pederson, Gordon Roy *state legislator, retired military officer*

## TENNESSEE

**Memphis**
Ford, Harold Eugene *retired congressman*

**Nashville**
Person, Curtis S., Jr. *state legislator, lawyer*

## TEXAS

**Austin**
Denny, Mary Craver *state legislator, business owner*
Giddings, Helen *state representative, personnel management director*
Shapiro, Florence *state legislator, advertising executive, public relations executive*
Wong, Martha Jee *state representative*

**Beaumont**
Brooks, Jack Bascom *former congressman*
Lampson, Nicholas V. *former congressman*

**Garland**
Driver, Joe Luther *state legislator, consultant, insurance agent*

**Laredo**
Zaffirini, Judith *state legislator, small business owner*

## UTAH

**Corinne**
Ferry, Miles Yeoman *state legislator*

**Provo**
Valentine, John Lester *state legislator, lawyer*

**Salt Lake City**
Black, Wilford Rex, Jr. *retired state legislator*
Carnahan, Orville Darrell *retired state legislator, retired academic administrator*
Shepherd, Karen *retired congresswoman*
Walker, Carlene Martin *state senator*

**West Valley City**
Peterson, Millie M. *state senator*

## VERMONT

**Middlebury**
Nuovo, Betty A. *state representative*

**Milton**
Rivero, Marilyn Elaine Keith *state legislator*

**Montpelier**
Paquin, Edward H., Jr. *retired state legislator, not-for-profit developer*

**Rutland**
Ferraro, Betty Ann *retired state senator*

**Saint Albans**
Keenan, Kathleen *state legislator*

## VIRGINIA

**Alexandria**
Collins, Cardiss *retired congresswoman*

**Arlington**
Murat, William M. *legislative staff member*

**Fairfax**
Miller, Emilie F. *former state senator, consultant*

**Leesburg**
Mims, William Cleveland *state legislator, lawyer*

**Mc Lean**
Callahan, Vincent Francis, Jr. *state legislator, publishing executive*
Gibbons, Sam Melville *retired congressman, government agency administrator*
Paul, Andrew Robert *defense and legislative consultant*

**Newport News**
Trible, Paul Seward, Jr. *former United States senator*

**Richmond**
Devolites, Jeannemarie Aragona *state legislator*
McQuigg, Michele Berger *state legislator*

**Vienna**
Higginbotham, Wendy Jacobson *legislative staff member, writer*

## WASHINGTON

**Olympia**
Haugen, Mary Margaret *state legislator*
Long, Jeanine Hundley *retired state legislator*
Roach, Pam *state senator*
Spanel, Harriet *state legislator*

**Seattle**
Lee, Conrad S. *councilman*

**Vancouver**
Smith, Linda A. *retired congresswoman*

## WEST VIRGINIA

**Charleston**
McCabe, Brooks Fleming, Jr. *state legislator*
Tomblin, Earl Ray *state legislator, lieutenant governor*

**Shinnston**
Spears, Jae *state legislator*

## WISCONSIN

**Black Earth**
Klug, Scott Leo *former congressman*

**Fort Atkinson**
Lorman, Barbara K. *retired state senator*

**Madison**
Albers, Sheryl Kay *state legislator*
Barish, Lawrence Stephen *nonpartisan legislative staff administrator*
Darling, Alberta Helen *state legislator, art gallery director, marketing professional*
Hardie, Anthony D. *legislative staff member, social welfare administrator*
Krusick, Margaret Ann *state legislator*
Roessler, Carol Ann *state legislator*
Turner, Robert Lloyd *state legislator*
Young, Rebecca Mary Conrad *retired state legislator*

**Nashotah**
Neumann, Mark W. *former congressman, real estate developer*

## WYOMING

**Cheyenne**
Kunz, April Brimmer *state legislator, lawyer*
Mockler, Esther Jayne *state senator*

**Cody**
Simpson, Alan K. *former US senator, lawyer*

**Glenrock**
Anderson, James *senator*

**Laramie**
Hansen, Matilda *former state legislator*
Maxfield, Peter Charles *state legislator, lawyer, educator*

# TERRITORIES OF THE UNITED STATES

## VIRGIN ISLANDS

**St Thomas**
Berry, Lorraine Ledee *state senator*

# CANADA

## BRITISH COLUMBIA

**Vancouver**
McWhinney, Edward Watson *Canadian government legislator*

## ONTARIO

**Ottawa**
Bélanger, Mauril *member of parliament*
Carroll, Margaret Aileen *member of Canadian parliament*
Catterall, Marlene *Canadian legislator*
Dhaliwal, Herb (Harbance Singh) *legislator, former Canadian government official*
Murray, Lowell *Canadian senator*
Saada, Jacques *legislator*
Telegdi, Andrew *member of parliament*
Vellacott, Maurice *legislator*
Yelich, Lynne *member of parliament*

## QUEBEC

**Saint Laurent**
Dion, Stéphane *legislator*

## ADDRESS UNPUBLISHED

Armey, Richard Keith (Dick Armey) *former congressman*
Bard, Ellen Marie *former state legislator, retired small business owner*
Bassano, C. Louis *state legislator, fuel oil company executive*
Beals, Nancy Farwell *former state legislator*
Bilbray, James Hubert *retired congressman, lawyer, consultant*
Binienda, John J. *state legislator*
Blanchard, MaryAnn N. *state legislator*
Bonsack, Rose Mary Hatem *state legislator, physician*
Bradley, Bill *former senator*
Broderick, B. Michael, Jr. *state legislator, banker*
Brown, Mary Ellen *former state legislator, accountant*
Browne, Ray *congressman, insurance agent*
Burns, Max *former congressman*
Callahan, Sonny (H.L. Callahan) *former congressman*
Campbell, Ben Nighthorse *former senator*
Carnahan, Jean *former senator*
Carpenter, Robert C. *state legislator, retired banker*
Carson, Brad Rogers *former congressman*
Carstairs, Sharon *legislator*
Chan, Wilma *state legislator*
Churchill, Robert Wilson *state legislator, lawyer*
Collins, Michael A. (Mac Collins) *former congressman*
Condit, Gary Adrian *former congressman*
Coyne, William Joseph *former congressman*
Culp, Faye Berry *state legislator*
Danner, Patsy Ann *former congresswoman*
Daschle, Thomas Andrew *former senator*
De Gette, Diana Louise *congresswoman, lawyer*
DeLay, Tom (Thomas Dale DeLay) *former congressman*
Duniphan, J. P. *state legislator, small business owner*
Dunlap, Patricia C. *state legislator*
Dunn, Jennifer Blackburn *former congresswoman*
Federing, Eric K. *legislative staff member, public information officer*
Finestone, Sheila *senator, retired legislator*
Fitzgerald, Peter Gosselin *former senator, lawyer*
Forbes, Michael Patrick *former congressman*
Foust, Robert Schmertz *retired legislative staff member*
Fox, Galen W. *state representative*
Ganske, J. Greg *former congressman, plastic surgeon*
Graham, Bob (Daniel Robert Graham) *former senator, former governor*
Greene, Enid *retired congresswoman*
Hammerschmidt, John Paul *retired congressman, lumber company executive*

Hart, Gary W. *retired senator, lawyer*
Hawkins, Mary Ellen Higgins (Mary Ellen Higgins) *retired state legislator, public relations executive*
Hearn, Joyce Camp *retired state legislator, educator, consultant*
Helms, Jesse *retired senator*
Hickey, Win E(spy) *former state legislator, social worker*
Hill, Baron Paul *former congressman*
Holliday, Robert Kelvin *retired state legislator, publishing executive*
Hollings, Fritz (Ernest Frederick Hollings) *former senator*
Horn, Stephen *retired congressman, political scientist*
Houghton, Amory, Jr. *former congressman*
Ipsen, Grant Ruel *state legislator, insurance and investments professional*
James, Sharpe *state senator, former mayor*
Johnson, Jay Withington *former congressman*
Kasich, John R. *former congressman*
Kleczka, Gerald Daniel *former congressman*
Konnyu, Ernest Leslie *former congressman*
La Falce, John Joseph *former congressman, lawyer*
Lipinski, William Oliver *former congressman*
Maloney, James Henry *former congressman, real estate developer*
Mandel, Adrienne Abramson *state legislator*
Maroney, Jane Perkins *former state legislator, consultant*
Martinez, Matthew Gilbert *former congressman*
Martini, William J. *former congressman, state commissioner, judge*
May, Edgar *former state legislator*
McCarthy, Karen P. *former congresswoman, former state legislator*
Mc Collum, Ira William, Jr., (Bill Mc Collum) *former congressman*
McGovern, George Stanley *former senator*
Meshel, Harry *former state senator, political party official*
Metcalf, Jack *former congressman, retired state senator*
Meyers, Jan *retired congresswoman*
Miller, Patricia Louise *state legislator, nurse*
Munt, Janet Staples *state senator*
Nielsen, Linda Miller *councilman*
Oakland, Suzanne N.J. Chun *state legislator*
Ortiz, Felix W. *state legislator*
Ose, Douglas *former congressman*
Pappas, Michael *former congressman*
Pascoe, Patricia Hill *former state legislator*
Patrick, Michele Mary *government official*
Patterson, Elizabeth Johnston *retired congresswoman*
Paul, Ronald Ernest *congressman*
Pease, Edward A. *former congressman*
Pell, Claiborne *former senator*
Perricone, Charles *former state legislator*
Pettis-Roberson, Shirley McCumber *retired congresswoman*
Pevear, Roberta Charlotte *retired state legislator*
Pressler, Larry *former senator, lawyer*
Rodriguez, Ciro Davis *former congressman*
Rossi, Dino J. *former state legislator*
Roukema, Margaret Scafati *congresswoman*
St. Germain, Fernand Joseph *retired congressman*
Sandlin, Max Allen, Jr. *former congressman*
Satterthwaite, Helen Foster *retired state legislator*
Saucier, Gene Duane *retired state legislator, retired import/export company executive*
Searle, Rodney Newell *state legislator, farmer, insurance agent*
Shuster, Bud *business executive, former congressman*
Skinner, Patricia Morag *state legislator*
Smith, Nick H. *former congressman, archivist, farmer*
Snelling, Barbara W. *retired state legislator*
Stickney, Jessica *former state legislator*
Strauss, Paul *shadow senator*
Tauscher, Ellen O. *congresswoman*
Tebedo, MaryAnne *state legislator*
Thurman, Karen L. *former congresswoman, lobbyist*
Toomey, Patrick Joseph *former congressman*
Treppler, Irene Esther *retired state senator*
Vellenga, Kathleen Osborne *retired state legislator*
Wallach, Patricia *councilman, retired mayor*
Watkins, Wesley Wade *retired congressman*
Wolf, Katie Louise *state legislator*
Zimmerman, Harold Samuel *retired state legislator, publishing executive, state agency administrator*

---

## HEALTHCARE: DENTISTRY

### UNITED STATES

### ARIZONA

**Glendale**
Manhold, John Henry *dental educator, consultant*

**Mesa**
Winkler, Sheldon *dentist, educator*

**Tucson**
Hawke, Robert Francis *dentist*

### CALIFORNIA

**Arcadia**
Gamboa, George Charles *retired oral surgeon, educator*

**Berkeley**
Bernstein, Josh *dentist*

**Beverly Hills**
Sands, Kevin B. *dentist*

Shlosberg, Stuart R. *prosthodontist*

**Hollywood**
Hoesli, Hanna *dentist*

**Los Angeles**
Dorfman, William M. *dentist*
Dummett, Clifton Orrin *dentist, educator*
Yen, Stephen L. *orthodontist, researcher*

**Manteca**
Tonn, Elverne Meryl *pediatric dentist, dental benefits consultant, forensic odontologist*

**Monterey Park**
Sekiguchi, Eugene *dentist*

**Northridge**
Logan, Lee Robert *orthodontist*

**Pasadena**
Mc Carthy, Frank Martin *oral surgeon, educator*

**San Diego**
Grossman, Michael Samuel *periodontist*

**San Francisco**
Bensinger, David August *dentist, dean*
Gekelman, Diana *dentist, dental educator, researcher*
Greenspan, Deborah *dental educator*
Khosla, Ved Mitter *oral and maxillofacial surgeon, educator*
Olsen, Steven Kent *dentist*
Wescott, William Burnham *oral maxillofacial pathologist, educator*

**San Jose**
Lee, Stanley Tak *dentist*
Sraon, Dilber S. *dentist*
Yoshizumi, Donald Tetsuro *dentist*

**San Mateo**
Fletcher, Vernon Jerome *dental association administrator, director*

**San Rafael**
Greene, John Clifford *dentist, retired dean*
Gryson, Joseph Anthony *orthodontist*

**Scotia**
Hise, Mark Allen *dentist*

**Ventura**
Shifman, Ruth Miri *dentist*

### CONNECTICUT

**Avon**
Weiss, Robert Michael *dentist*

**Brookfield**
Cohen, Mark Steven *dentist*

**Farmington**
Hall, Robert Stevens *dentist*
Ioannidou, Efthimia *periodontist, educator*

**Southbury**
Hopf, Frank Rudolph *retired dentist*

**Vernon Rockville**
Putnam, Richard *dentist, educator*

### DISTRICT OF COLUMBIA

**Washington**
Calhoun, Noah Robert *oral maxillofacial surgeon, educator*
Richeson, James Grady, Jr. *dentist*

### FLORIDA

**Bay Harbor Islands**
Rosenbluth, Morton *periodontist, educator*

**Boca Raton**
Armstrong, Edward Bradford, Jr. *oral and maxillofacial surgeon, educator*

**Bradenton**
Engelman, Melvin Alkon *retired dentist, dental products executive*

**Fort Lauderdale**
Oliet, Seymour *endodontics educator, dean, dentist*
Siegel, Michael Alan *dental educator*

**Fort Myers**
Laboda, Gerald *oral and maxillofacial surgeon*

**Gainesville**
Catalanotto, Frank A. *dentist*

**Jacksonville**
Halil, Susan Terrell *dental hygienist*

**Jupiter**
Nessmith, H(erbert) Alva *dentist*

**Largo**
Frantzis, Theodosios George *periodontist*

**Madison**
Shaw, Roderick Kirkpatrick III *dentist*

**Melbourne**
Elder, Stewart Taylor *dentist, retired military officer*

**Miami**
Higley, Bruce Wadsworth *orthodontist*
Iver, Robert Drew *dentist*

**Tamarac**
O'Neil, Thomas *dentist*

**Tampa**
Pasetti, Louis Oscar *retired dentist*
Perret, Gerard Anthony, Jr. *orthodontist*

**Winter Park**
McKean, Thomas Wayne *dentist, retired military officer*

### GEORGIA

**Atlanta**
Freedman, Louis Martin *dentist*

**Augusta**
Baker, Philip Steven *dentist, educator*
Rogers, Michael Bruce *orthodontist*

**Fort Gordon**
Windhorn, Richard J. *dentist*

**Macon**
Walton, DeWitt Talmage, Jr. *dentist*

### HAWAII

**Honolulu**
Nishimura, Pete Hideo *oral surgeon*

**Pearl City**
Sue, Alan Kwai Keong *dentist*

### ILLINOIS

**Chicago**
Barr, Sanford Lee *dentist*
Bramson, James B. *dentist, dental association administrator*
Glenner, Richard Allen *dentist, dental historian*
Graber, Thomas M. *orthodontist, researcher*
Hardaway, Ernest, II, *oral and maxillofacial surgeon, public health service officer*
Santangelo, Mario Vincent *retired dentist*
Yale, Seymour Hershel *dental radiologist, educator, gerontologist, dean*

**Lake Forest**
Jones, Gordon Kempton *dentist*

**Naperville**
Grimley, Jeffrey Michael *dentist*

**Park Ridge**
Kenney, John Patrick *dentist*

**Riverwoods**
Douglas, Bruce Lee *oral and maxillofacial surgeon, occupational and geriatric health educator, consultant*

**Westmont**
Schefdore, Ronald L. *dentist*

### INDIANA

**Evansville**
Fritz, Edward Lane *dentist*
Raibley, Parvin Rudolph *dentist*

**Gary**
Stephens, Paul Alfred *dentist*

**Indianapolis**
Christen, Arden Gale *dental educator, researcher, consultant*
Hartsfield, James Kennedy, Jr. *orthodontist, geneticist*

**Terre Haute**
Roshel, John Albert, Jr. *orthodontist*

### IOWA

**Ankeny**
Weigel, Ollie J. *dentist, former mayor*

**Iowa City**
Bishara, Samir Edward *orthodontist*
Olin, William Harold *orthodontist, educator*

### KANSAS

**Topeka**
Fyler, Carl John *dentist*

### KENTUCKY

**Brandenburg**
Bowen, Patricia Lederer *dental educator*

**Danville**
Morris, Alvin Leonard *retired dentist, academic administrator*

**Lexington**
Okeson, Jeffrey Paul *dental educator, director*

**Louisville**
Parkins, Frederick Milton *dental educator, dean*

### MAINE

**Kennebunkport**
Mulvihill, James Edward *periodontist, educator*

### MARYLAND

**Baltimore**
Grant, Leslie Edwina *dentist, dental association administrator*

**Bethesda**
Kruger, Gustav Otto, Jr. *retired oral surgeon, educator, department chairman*

**Columbia**
Rovelstad, Gordon H. *dentist, researcher*

**Potomac**
Cotton, William Robert *retired dentist*

**Rockville**
Chohayeb, Aida A. *dentist, educator*

**Simpsonville**
Altschuler, Bruce Robert *research dentist*

### MASSACHUSETTS

**Boston**
Friedman, Paula Konowitch *dentist, academic administrator*
Johansen, Erling *retired dental educator, dean*
Sachdeo, Amit *dentist, researcher*
Zawaideh, Samer K. *orthodontist*

**Hanover**
Lonborg, James Reynold *dentist, former professional baseball player*

### MICHIGAN

**Ann Arbor**
Ash, Major McKinley, Jr. *dentist, educator*
Brown, William Ernest *dentist*

**Dearborn Heights**
Abramson, Marc A. *dentist*

### MINNESOTA

**Mankato**
Dumke, Melvin Philip *dentist*

**Minneapolis**
Doroschak, John Z. *dentist, consultant*
Shapiro, Burton Leonard *dentist, geneticist, educator*

### MISSISSIPPI

**Flowood**
Byrd, Joyce Marie *dentist*

### MISSOURI

**Chesterfield**
Selfridge, George Dever *retired dentist, retired military officer*

**Kansas City**
Reed, Michael John *dentist, dean, oral biology educator*

### NEBRASKA

**Fremont**
Roesch, Robert Eugene *dentist*

**Lincoln**
Sullivan, Robert Emmett *pediatric dentist, educator*

**Omaha**
Lynch, Benjamin Leo *oral surgeon, educator*
Zaiman, K(oichi) Robert *dentist*

### NEW JERSEY

**Chatham**
Hurley, Allyson Kingsley *dentist*

**Fair Haven**
Di Turi, Christopher *dentist, educator*

**Freehold**
Greenstein, Gary *periodontist, dental educator*

**Hackettstown**
Wiedemann, Charles Louis *dentist*

**Ho Ho Kus**
Van Slooten, Ronald Henry Joseph *dentist*

**Manalapan**
Mamoun, John Sami *dentist*

**Maple Shade**
Gordon, Paul *retired dentist, artist*

**Newark**
Bikofsky, Veronica M. *dentist*

**Oakland**
Maccario, Maurice Malcolm *oral and maxillofacial surgeon, consultant*

**Voorhees**
Lampert, S. Henry *retired dentist*
Piermatti, Jack *dentist*

**Woodbridge**
Galkin, Samuel Bernard *orthodontist*

## NEW MEXICO

**Farmington**
Graham, Warren Kirkland *dentist*

## NEW YORK

**Bellmore**
Lederman, Gary *dentist*

**Brooklyn**
Lish, Bruce Jared *dentist*
Schweikert, Edgar Oskar *dentist*

**Camillus**
Caryl, William R., Jr. *orthodontist*

**Glen Cove**
Woodman, Edward *dentist*
Woodman, Ryan *dentist*

**Grand Island**
Hennigar, William Grant, Jr. *dentist*

**Great Neck**
Elkowitz, Lloyd Kent *dental anesthesiologist, dentist, pharmacist*

**Huntington**
Sforza, Alfred Vincent *dentist, educator, writer*

**New York**
Arvystas, Michael Geciauskas *orthodontist, educator*
Denmark, Stanley Jay *orthodontist*
Glassman, Debra *dentist*
Glassman, Steven *dentist*
Kahn, Norman *dental educator, pharmacologist*
Kaslick, Ralph Sidney *dentist, educator*
Lituchy, Gregg *dentist*
Lowenberg, Marc Gregory *dentist*
Mandel, Irwin Daniel *dentist*
Marder, Michael Zachary *dental educator, researcher*
Mitchell, Dennis Anthony *dentist, educator*
Rosenthal, Larry *cosmetic dentist*
Rozenberg, Lana *cosmetic dentist*
Scarola, John Michael *dentist, educator*
Sendax, Victor Irven *dentist, educator, dental implant researcher*
Smigel, Irwin *dentist*
Wank, Gerald Sidney *periodontist, educator*

**Ossining**
Maloney, William James *dentist, educator*

**Schenectady**
Andreen, Aviva Louise *dentist, researcher, academic administrator, educator*
DeLuke, Dean M. *oral surgeon*

**Troy**
Medicus, Hildegard Julie *retired dentist, orthodontist, educator*

**Yonkers**
Torrese, Dante Michael *prosthodontist, educator*

## NORTH CAROLINA

**Boone**
Warren, Robert Lee *dentist, educator*

**Chapel Hill**
Arnold, Roland R. *dental educator, researcher*
Proffit, William Robert *orthodontics educator*
Stamm, John William Randolph *dentist, educator*
White, Raymond Petrie, Jr. *dentist, educator, dean*

**Charlotte**
Hufanda, Joseph *dentist*
McClelland, Richard Lee *dentist*
Twisdale, Harold Winfred *dentist*
Yaste, Christian *dentist*

## OHIO

**Beachwood**
Robertson, Edward Neil *dentist*

**Cincinnati**
Lytle, James DeVore *retired dentist*

**Columbus**
Jolly, Daniel Ehs *dental educator*

**Cuyahoga Falls**
Barsan, Robert Blake *dentist*

**Lancaster**
Burns, Glenn Richard *dentist*

**Milford**
Creath, Curtis Janssen *pediatric dentist*

**Pepper Pike**
Goodman, Donald Joseph *dentist*

**Sylvania**
Kastner, Michael James *dentist*

**Toledo**
McVicker, Michael C. *dentist*

## OKLAHOMA

**Claremore**
Winters, Kevin L. *dentist*

**Oklahoma City**
Shillingburg, Herbert Thompson, Jr. *dental educator*

**Tulsa**
Letcher, William *dentist*

## OREGON

**Portland**
Bartley, Murray Hill *retired dental educator*

## PENNSYLVANIA

**Bryn Mawr**
Bedrick, Anthony Edward *oral surgeon, educator*

**Chambersburg**
Scarlata, Paul Anthony *oral surgeon*

**Clarion**
Foreman, Thomas Alexander *dentist*

**Collegeville**
Sharifi, Azalea A. *orthodontist and general dentist*

**Lansdale**
Strohecker, Leon Harry, Jr. *orthodontist*

**New Holland**
West, Daniel Charles *dentist*

**Newtown**
Paghdiwala, Abid F *dentist*

**Norristown**
Steinberg, Arthur Irwin *periodontist, educator*

**Philadelphia**
Fielding, Allen Fred *oral and maxillofacial surgeon, educator*
Pappas, Charles Nicholas III *dentist, educator*
Vanarsdall, Robert Lee, Jr. *orthodontist, educator*

**Pittsburgh**
Collins, Bobby McManus, II, *dental educator*
Ismail, Yahia Hassan *dentist, educator*

**Willow Grove**
Ohama, Gary Louis *dental ceramist*

## RHODE ISLAND

**Warren**
Mehlman, Edwin Stephen *endodontist*

## SOUTH CAROLINA

**Charleston**
Cordova, Maria Asuncion *dentist*

**West Columbia**
Witherspoon, Walter Pennington, Jr. *orthodontist, volunteer*

## TENNESSEE

**Knoxville**
McGuire, John Albert *dentist*

**Memphis**
Butts, Herbert Clell *retired dentist, educator*
Cannon, Joe Louis *retired orthodontist*
Harris, Edward Frederick *orthodontics educator*

**Nashville**
Conley, Richard Scott *orthodontist, educator*
Martin, James Larence *dentist, educator*

## TEXAS

**Corpus Christi**
Fashemo, Dds, Mph, Deji V. *orthodontist*

**Flower Mound**
Kolodny, Stanley Charles *oral surgeon, retired military officer*

**Houston**
Kiat-amnuay, Sudarat *prosthodontist, educator*
Shetty, Kishore V. *dentist, director*

**Lackland Afb**
Dunn, William Jackson *dental educator, researcher*

**Livingston**
Davidson, John Robert *retired dentist*

**Missouri City**
Chang, Jeffrey Chai *dentist, educator, researcher*

**Mount Pleasant**
McCauley, Dan Paul *dentist*

**Plano**
Taylor, Paul Peak *pediatric dentist, educator*

**San Antonio**
Cochran, David L. *periodontist, dental educator, department chairman*
Langland, Olaf Elmer *retired dental educator*
Schmitz, John Phillip *maxillofacial surgeon, researcher*

## VIRGINIA

**Falls Church**
Chaffin, Jeffrey G. *dentist*

**Richmond**
Laskin, Daniel M. *oral and maxillofacial surgeon, educator*

**Virginia Beach**
Lowe, Cameron Anderson *dentist, endodontist, educator*

## WASHINGTON

**Bellevue**
Carlson, Curtis Eugene *orthodontist, periodontist*

**Everett**
Oliver, William Donald *orthodontist*

**Seattle**
Baker-Johnson, Marcia J. *dental hygienist*
Beirne, Owen Ross *dental educator, researcher*
Hollender, Lars Gösta *dental educator*
Roberts, Frank Alan *periodontist, researcher, dental educator*
Spoor, Rhys *dentist*

**Spokane**
Steadman, Robert K. *oral surgeon*

## WISCONSIN

**New Glarus**
Sippy, David Dean *dentist*

**Shawano**
Swetlik, William Philip *orthodontist*

## WYOMING

**Casper**
Keim, Michael Ray *dentist*

# CANADA

## ONTARIO

**Toronto**
Klein, Gary *dentist*
Waldman, Carol *dentist*

# ENGLAND

**London**
MacClean, Walter Lee *dentist*

# GERMANY

**Witten**
Gaengler, Peter Wolfgang *dentist, researcher*

# INDIA

**Haryana Panchkula**
Naresh, Anubhav *dentist, educator*

## ADDRESS UNPUBLISHED

Anderson, Vera Strong *retired dentist*
Barkmeier, Wayne W. *dentist, researcher, educator*
Beagrie, George Simpson *dentist, educator, retired dean*
Bentley, Kenneth Chessar *oral and maxillofacial surgeon, educator*
Birtcil, Robert Franklin, Jr. *dental educator*
Braun, Stanley *orthodontist, educator*
Brooke, Ralph Ian *dental educator*
Carroll, La Shun La Rue *endodontist*
Christiansen, Richard Louis *orthodontist, educator, dean*
Collins, Frank, Jr. *dentist, educator*
Connell, Judson T. *dentist*
Crawford, Felix Conkling *retired dentist*
Daniels, Elizabeth *retired dentist*
Farrell, Edward Wagner *retired dentist, educator*
Geistfeld, Ronald Elwood *retired dental educator*
Goldstein, Leonard Barry *dentist*
Hammer, Wade Burke *retired oral and maxillofacial surgeon, educator*
Herman, David Jay *orthodontist*
Hoffman, Jerry Irwin *retired dental educator*
Houk, Irene Miller *dentist*
Huja, Sarandeep *orthodontist, educator*
Lee, Ryan S. *dental association administrator*
Lee, Winnie Sita *dentist*
Löe, Harald *retired dentist, educator, researcher*
Lorton, Lewis *dentist, researcher*
McCarlie, V. Wallace *dentist, researcher*
Meffert, Roland Matthew *periodontist, educator*
Mele, Joanne Theresa *dentist*
Molinaro, Joseph Daniel *dentist*
Newbrun, Ernest *oral biology and periodontology educator*
Paris, David Andrew *dentist*
Rehak, James Richard *orthodontist*
Riley, Cheryl M. *prosthodontist, military officer*
Rippert, Eric Theodore *oral and maxillofacial surgeon, healthcare consultant*
Sinkford, Jeanne Craig *dental association administrator, retired dentist, retired dean, educator*
Slaughter, Freeman Cluff *retired dentist*

Taylor, John Calvin *dentist*

---

## HEALTHCARE: HEALTH SERVICES

# UNITED STATES

## ALABAMA

**Auburn**
Barker, Kenneth Neil *pharmacy administration educator*

**Birmingham**
Cooper, Karen René *health facility administrator, nursing administrator*
Crittenden, Martha A. *rehabilitation services professional*
Grinney, Jay *health facility company executive*
Herzig, Terrell W *health facility administrator, educator*
Hoidal, David *health facility administrator*
Holmes, Suzanne McRae *nursing supervisor*
Hullett, Sandral *hospital administrator, health facility administrator*
Lowman, John D., Jr. *physical therapist, researcher*
Perry, Helen *medical/surgical nurse, secondary school educator*
Pickett, Stephen Alan *hospital administrator*
Roth, William Stanley *hospital foundation executive*
Snow, Michael D. *health facility administrator*
Terry, Patricia Hart *dietician, educator*

**Daphne**
Curreri, Peter William *health facility administrator, consultant*

**Decatur**
Mardis, Elizabeth Williams *occupational health nurse*

**Florence**
Foote, Dorothy Gargis *nursing educator*

**Huntsville**
Ingram, Shirley Jean *social worker*

**Lafayette**
Woody, Mary Florence *nursing educator, academic administrator*

**Mobile**
Clark, Jack *retired health facility administrator*
Wisner, Pamela L. *social worker*

**Montgomery**
Williamson, Donald Ellis *public health service officer, state agency administrator*

**Opelika**
Smith-Sanders, Carol Ann *physical therapist, music therapist, psychologist*

**Ozark**
DuBose, Elizabeth (Bettye DuBose) *community health nurse*

**Pelham**
Lee, James A. *health facility finance executive*

**Talladega**
Swain, Mary Magdalene Dickerson *pediatrics nurse*

**Tuscaloosa**
Farahat, Medhat S. *researcher*
Orcutt, Ben Avis *retired social work educator*

**Tuskegee Institute**
Paris, Deidre Eileen *artificial intelligence researcher, educator*

## ALASKA

**Anchorage**
Freedman, F. Kenneth *psychotherapist*
Gottlieb, Katherine *health facility administrator*

**Fairbanks**
Nottingham, Juanita C. *medical/surgical nurse*

**Kotzebue**
Dakai, Steven Henry *alcohol/drug abuse services professional*

**Palmer**
Young-Campbell, Laura L. *speech pathology/audiology services professional*

**Soldotna**
Moore, Hubert, Jr. *retired addictions counselor, consultant*

## ARIZONA

**Casa Grande**
McGillicuddy, Joan Marie *psychotherapist, consultant*
Stanley, Charles L. *alcohol/drug abuse services professional*

**Chandler**
Graham, Anita Louise *correctional and legal nurse consultant, community health nurse*

**Flagstaff**
Poff, Boris *medical technician*

**Hereford**
Schenk, Quentin Frederick *retired social work educator, psychologist, mayor*

**Mesa**
Ahearn, Geraldine *medical/surgical nurse, writer, poet*
Boyd, Leona Potter *retired social worker*
David, Susan Holcombe *child and family therapist*

**Parker**
Grazier, Diana Lynn *community health nurse, medical/surgical nurse, writer*

**Payson**
Lasys, Joan *medical/surgical nurse, educator*

**Peoria**
Nelson, Mary Kathryn *bilingual counselor, small business owner, real estate agent, artist, singer*

**Phoenix**
Day, Sharon Hoelscher *healthcare educator*
Golio, John Michael *technologist, engineering executive, writer*
Hunt, Linda *hospital administrator*
Johnson, Elizabeth Misner *health services executive*
Kivlahan, Coleen *public health officer*
Mitchell, Wayne Lee *retired health facility administrator*
Mulheron, MariLynn *family practice nurse practitioner*
Norris, John Steven *healthcare company executive*

**Rio Verde**
Ramsey, David Selmer *retired health facility administrator*

**San Carlos**
DJangi, Ahmad Reza *health facility administrator*

**Scottsdale**
Brown, Frederick Lee *health facility administrator*
Heilman, Raymond L. *health facility administrator*
Meyers, Marlene O. *retired hospital administrator*
Pelham, Judith *health system administrator*
Summerhill, Ronald Raymond *psychotherapist, psychologist*
Timmons, Evelyn Deering *pharmacist*
Weaver, Linda Marie *pharmacist, education educator*

**Sun City West**
Holloway, Diane Elaine *psychotherapist, consultant, writer*

**Tucson**
Arcus, Sam George *social worker, educator, writer*
Díaz, Elena R. *community health nurse*
Dyer-Raffler, Joy Ann *retired special education diagnostician, educator*
Hanson, Thor *retired health agency executive, retired naval officer*
Shropshire, Donald Gray *hospital executive*
Thompson, Kathleen Shambaugh *marriage and family counselor*
Yuan, Nicole Patricia *healthcare educator*

**Yuma**
Houggard, Santa Carol Hall *family nurse practitioner, consultant*
Kiley, Thomas *rehabilitation counselor*
Rush, Dorie Mae *nursing educator*

## ARKANSAS

**Eureka Springs**
McCullough, V. Beth *pharmacist, educator*

**Fayetteville**
Banks, David Russell *former health care executive*
Farley, Roy Carl *counselor educator*

**Fort Smith**
Churchey, Randy L. *health facility administrator*

**Little Rock**
Brown, Larry Douglass *research consultant, writer*
Elders, Joycelyn (Minnie Jocelyn Elders, Minnie Joycelyn Lee) *public health service officer, endocrinologist, former Surgeon General of the United States*
Thomas, Lestene *nurse*

**State University**
Barredo, Ronald De Vera *physical therapist, educator*

## CALIFORNIA

**Agoura Hills**
Merchant, Roland Samuel, Sr. *health facility administrator, educator*

**Albany**
Daniels, Lydia M. *health care administrator*

**Alhambra**
Ly, Allan Q. *medical technician*

**Anaheim**
Gregg, James R. *optometrist, educator*
Lee, Donna Jean *retired nurse*

**Arleta**
Kelley, Frances A. *occupational therapist, consultant*

**Berkeley**
Bissell, Mina J. *lab administrator, biochemist*
Carpenter, Kenneth John *nutrition educator*
Enoch, Jay Martin *optometrist, educator, research scientist*
Eyoum, Marie-Ange Naida *researcher*
Gilbert, Neil Robin *social work educator, writer, consultant*

**Harris**, Michael Gene *optometrist, educator, lawyer*
Hill, Lorie Elizabeth *psychotherapist*
Lashof, Joyce Cohen *public health service officer, educator*
Tutashinda, Kweli (Brian P. Altheimer) *chiropractic physician, educator*
Westheimer, Gerald *optometrist, educator*

**Beverly Hills**
Seizer, Fern Victor *retired mental health services administrator*

**Canoga Park**
Meier, Sue A. *marriage and family therapist, director*

**Carlsbad**
Benjamin, Theresa Mary *retired psychotherapist*
Craig, Jenny *human services manager*

**Carmel**
Reamy, Michaelin *marriage and family therapist, educator, consultant*

**Cathedral City**
Berry, Ester Lorée *vocational nurse*

**Cerritos**
Woodson-Glenn, Yolanda *social worker*

**Chico**
Akimoto, Martin Wayne *mental health services professional*

**Claremont**
Martin, Jay Herbert *psychoanalyst, language professor, political science professor*

**Clovis**
Von Prince, Kilulu Magdalene *retired occupational therapist, sculptor*

**Commerce**
Crabtree, James Robert *nursing educator*

**Crockett**
Silverman, Mervyn F. *health science association administrator, consultant*

**Cypress**
Scott, Gregory W. *health care company executive*

**Davis**
Schneeman, Barbara Olds *nutritionist, educator*
Stern, Judith Schneider *nutritionist, researcher, educator*
Stroeve, Pieter *chemical engineering researcher, educator*
Turnlund, Judith Rae *nutritionist*

**Desert Hot Springs**
Zarres, Sharon L. *marriage and family therapist, health facility administrator*

**Duarte**
Riggs, Arthur D. *health facility administrator, research scientist*

**Dublin**
Lloyd, Leonard Edward *marriage and family therapist, consultant*

**Encino**
House, Karen Sue *nursing consultant*
Vogel, Susan Carol *nursing administrator*

**Escondido**
Bakko, Orville Edwin *retired health facility administrator*
Dannenberg, Otto Doyle *retired optometrist*

**Fontana**
Ferreri, Michael Victor *optometrist*

**Frazier Park**
Edwards, Sarah Anne *social worker, psychologist*

**Fresno**
Corless, Dorothy Alice *nursing educator*
De La Cruz-Reyes, Pilar L. *nursing administrator*

**Fullerton**
Montgomery, Thom Mathew *health program administrator, counselor*

**Glendale**
Ebert, Gerard (Gerry Ebert) *hypnotherapist, freelance/self-employed writer*

**Glendora**
Lasko, Allen Howard *pharmacist*

**Hanford**
DeCarvalho, Lorie T. *mental health services professional, director*

**Hawthorne**
Fila, John Charles *psychoanalyst*

**Highland**
Tacal, Jose Vega, Jr. *retired public health official, veterinarian*

**Inglewood**
Epstein, Marsha Ann *public health service officer, physician*

**La Jolla**
Best, Brookie Manning Dugan *pharmacist*
Harrison, Larry J. *health facility administrator*
Ledermann, Robert Joseph *social worker, psychotherapist*

**Laguna Beach**
Arnold, John David *management counselor*
Bernstein, Jean Newman *retired public health information officer*

**Laguna Woods**
Leonard, Elizabeth Adney *social worker*

**Lake Elsinore**
Young, Patricia Janean *speech pathology/audiology services professional*

**Lake Forest**
Boccia/Stacy, Judy Elaine *home health agency executive, consultant*
Goldsmith, David L. *health facility administrator*

**Lemoore**
Barnes, Kirsten Aileen *school counselor*

**Lincoln**
Helzer, James Dennis *retired health facility administrator*

**Loma Linda**
Bullock, Weldon Kimball *health facility administrator, pathologist, educator*
Llerandi Phipps, Carmen Guillermina *nutritionist and dietitian*
Molnar, Violet *mental health nurse*

**Lompoc**
Wagner, Geraldine Marie *nursing educator, consultant*

**Long Beach**
Brown, Lester B. *social worker, educator*
Mathieu, Susan Leifer *recreational therapist, educator*
Mullins Berg, Ruth Gladys *nurse*
Welch, Ronnie Scott *health facility administrator*

**Los Altos**
Spiller, Gene Alan *nutritionist, health facility administrator*

**Los Angeles**
Andersen, Ronald Max *health services researcher, educator*
Baron, Melvin Farrell *pharmacy educator*
Boswell, James Douglas *medical research executive*
Breslow, Lester *public health physician, educator*
Brodwin, Martin George *counselor, educator*
Carson, Margaret *human services administrator*
Compton, William Henry, Jr. *mental health services professional*
Cordova, Richard D. *hospital administrator*
de la Rocha, Castulo *health services executive*
Harrison, Gail G. *public health educator*
Horowitz, Ben *health facility administrator*
Koeffler, H. Phillip *health facility administrator*
Lloyd-Jones, Dadiva Bocobo *nursing assistant, writer*
Looney, Claudia Arlene *health facility administrator*
McCabe, Edward R. B. *hospital administrator, educator, physician*
Nield, Margaret *nursing researcher*
Priselac, Thomas M. *health facility executive, educator*
Rice, Thomas Howard *healthcare educator*
Roberts, Robert Winston *social worker, educator, dean*
Rosenthal, J. Thomas *hospital administrator, medical educator*
Silverstein, Suzanne *art therapist*
Stoughton, W. Vickery *healthcare executive*
Territo, Mary C. *health facility administrator, hematologist, educator*
Thompson, Judith Kastrup *nursing researcher*
Utz, Sarah Winifred *nursing educator*
van Dam, Heiman *psychoanalyst*
Ver Steeg, Donna Lorraine Frank *nurse, sociologist, educator*
White-Whitfield, Lisa Denise *social worker*

**Lower Lake**
Garcia, Beatrice Maude *social worker, director*

**Marysville**
Myers, Elmer *psychiatric social worker*

**Menlo Park**
Holmquest, Donald Lee *health organization director, nuclear medicine physician, lawyer, retired aerospace engineer*

**Modesto**
Smith, Heather Lynn *psychotherapist, recreational therapist*

**Monterey**
Robinson, Marla Holbrook *community care nurse*

**Moorpark**
Young, Victoria E. *occupational health nurse, lawyer*

**Moraga**
Allen, Richard Garrett *healthcare educator*

**Morro Bay**
LaLanne, Jack (François Henri LaLanne) *physical fitness specialist, entrepreneur*

**Novato**
Kratka-Schneider, Dorothy Maryjohanna *psychotherapist*

**Oakland**
Crane, Robert Meredith *health facility administrator*
Hafey, Joseph Michael *health association executive*
Miller, Barry *researcher, psychologist*
Sartor, Vivian Juanita *nursing administrator*

**Oceanside**
Downer, William John, Jr. *retired health facility administrator*

**Ontario**
Fangerow, Kay Elizabeth *nurse*

**Hanner**, Jean P. *retired nursing administrator, art gallery owner, religious organization administrator*

**Orange**
Karnes, Frances Rozelle *counselor, educator*
Williams, Benjamin R. *health facility administrator*

**Pasadena**
Brotman, Richard Dennis *counselor*
Chu, Benjamin K. *hospital administrator*
Holmes, Louis Ira *physician assistant, educator, photojournalist*
Lu, Thomas T. *lab administrator, information technology executive*

**Pomona**
Barsugli, Jesse Benjamin *lab administrator*
Okamoto, Mark P. *pharmacist, educator, dean*

**Rancho Cordova**
Kasch, Mary Courteol *occupational therapist*

**Redlands**
Coleman, Arlene Florence *retired pediatrics nurse*

**Riverside**
Chang, Sylvia Tan *health facility administrator, educator*

**Rohnert Park**
Johnson, Herman Leonall *retired research nutritionist, researcher*

**Roseville**
Netto, Paul V. *critical care nurse*

**Sacramento**
Chason, Robert *health facility administrator*
Dager, William Erling *pharmacist, educator*
Drachnik, Catherine Meldyn *recreational therapist, artist, counselor*
von Friederichs-Fitzwater, Marlene Marie *researcher*

**San Andreas**
Prema, Nitya *marriage and family therapist, artist*

**San Bernardino**
Harter-Speer, Joan E. *human services educator*

**San Diego**
Astroth, Margo Foltz *mental health nurse, nurse psychotherapist*
Bennett, Andrew David *alcohol/drug abuse services professional*
Doan, Tai Danh *social worker, director*
Francisco, Edith Gaba *medical/surgical nurse*
Jenkins, Adrienne *women's health nurse*
Larson, Vernon Dale *audiologist, researcher*
Paupp, Terrence Edward *researcher*
Schmidt, Terry L. *healthcare executive*

**San Francisco**
Eng, Catherine *health facility administrator, physician*
Harlan, Neil Eugene *retired health facility administrator*
Kirincic, Paul E. *human services administrator*
Laret, Mark R. *health facility executive*
Mahley, Robert W. *health facility administrator*
Rosales, Suzanne Marie *hospital coordinator*
Speidel, John Joseph *public health professional, educator*
Young, Lowell Sung-yi *health facility administrator, medical educator*

**San Jose**
Ha, Kiet Tuan *hospital administrator*
Song, Jessica Chuyunn *pharmacist, educator*

**San Marcos**
Ball, Betty Jewel *retired social worker, consultant*

**San Rafael**
Amada, Gerald *retired psychotherapist*
Friesecke, Raymond Francis *health company executive, director*
Malifrando, Frank *healthcare executive, theater producer, consultant, film producer, international real estate investor, publisher*

**Santa Barbara**
Salotti, Kathryn E. *marriage and family therapist*

**Santa Monica**
Archambault, Nicole Marie *speech pathology/audiology services professional, consultant*
Brook, Robert Henry *public health service officer, internist, educator*
McGlynn, Elizabeth A. *health policy analyst*
Rice, Donald Blessing *biotechnology executive, former federal official*
Rice, Pamela Ann *marriage and family therapist*

**Santa Rosa**
Borglum, Keith Carsten *health care business consultant*

**Santee**
Schenk, Susan Kirkpatrick *nursing educator, consultant, small business owner*

**Seal Beach**
Cunningham, Terence Thomas III *hospital administrator*

**Sherman Oaks**
Krueger, Kenneth John *nutritionist, educator*

**Simi Valley**
Erzinger, Kathy McClam *nursing educator*

**Sonoma**
Markey, William Alan *health facility administrator, consultant*

**South San Francisco**
Lee, Leonard S. *health facility administrator*

**Stanford**
Marsh, Martha H. *hospital administrator*
Mc Namara, Joseph Donald *researcher, retired protective services official*
Muendermann, Annegret *researcher*
Strena, Robert Victor *lab administrator, director*

**Tarzana**
Rinsch, Maryann Elizabeth *occupational therapist*

**Thousand Oaks**
Stephens, Diana L. *counselor, educator*

**Torrance**
Ebeling, Vicki *marriage and family therapist, psychotherapist, writer*

**Travis Afb**
Wible, Julie Lynn *human services administrator, military officer*

**Truckee**
Todd, Linda Marie *nutrition researcher, circulation manager, financial consultant, pilot*

**Tustin**
Kim, Han Pyong *researcher*

**Upland**
Likens, John David *rehabilitation services professional*

**Vallejo**
Crosley-Mayers, Diane *social worker*
Toms, Kathleen Moore *nurse*

**Van Nuys**
Dea, Fay Suey *counselor, educator*
Greene, Albert Lawrence *healthcare executive*

**Visalia**
Gray, Kris Diane *nursing consultant, forensic specialist*

**Walnut Creek**
Nolan, Janiece Simmons *health facility administrator*
Schneider, Gisela Helga *medical technician*

**Westlake Village**
Dimitriadis, Andre C. *health care executive*

**Woodland**
Bauer, Cynthia Renae *nurse*

**Woodland Hills**
Greaves, Roger F. *health maintenance organization executive*
Pettit, John W. *health facility administrator*
Putman, John A. *biofeedback practitioner, consultant*
Rich, Marvin P. *health association executive*
Yates, Gary L. *marriage and family therapist*

**Yuba City**
Price, Ardythe Bernadeane *nurse*

## COLORADO

**Aurora**
Morrow, Caroline Donovan *retired social worker*

**Boulder**
Holdsworth, Janet Nott *women's health nurse*
Kirshbaum, Daniel Joseph *researcher*
Middleton-Downing, Laura *psychiatric social worker, artist, small business owner*
Princeton, Joy Carol *retired nursing educator*

**Centennial**
Frame, Roger Everett *mental health counselor*

**Colorado Springs**
Cameron, Paul Drummond *health facility administrator*
Driscoll, David Lee *chiropractor*
Elias, John *lab administrator*
Haas, Julian L. *researcher, educator*
Lamont, Mary *nurse*
Strickland, Sylvia Raye *social worker*

**Denver**
Edelman, Joel *health facility administrator*
Plummer, Ora Beatrice *nursing educator, consultant*
Rael, Henry Sylvester, Sr. *retired health administrator, financial and management consultant*
Taussig, Lynn Max *healthcare administrator, pulmonologist, pediatrician, educator*
Thompson, Cathy Joanne *nursing educator, consultant, critical care nurse*
Witt, Catherine Lewis *neonatal nurse practitioner, writer*

**Fort Collins**
Savage, Eldon Paul *retired environmental health educator*

**Georgetown**
Etcheson, Christopher Carlyle *public health service officer*

**Grand Junction**
Hoagland, Christina Gail *occupational therapist, industrial drafter*

**Greenwood Village**
Evans, Nola Lea *healthcare specialist*

**Longmont**
Jones, Beverly Ann Miller *nursing administrator, retired patient services administrator*

**Louisville**
Shively, Merrick Lee *pharmaceutical scientist, consultant*

**Meeker**
Omer, Robert Wendell *hospital administrator*

**Peyton**
Dunn, Doris *retired critical care nurse, artist, rancher*

**Steamboat Springs**
Hanlon, Dean William *physical therapist*

**Yuma**
Hertneky, Randy Lee *optometrist*

## CONNECTICUT

**Avon**
Odenheimer, Robert W. *health care services company executive*
Shulman, Steven J. *health services company executive*

**Bloomfield**
Thorpe, James *retired researcher*

**Bridgeport**
King, Sister Eleace *special education services professional*
Macdonald, Karen Crane *occupational therapist, geriatrics services professional*
Trefry, Robert J. *health facility administrator*

**Cheshire**
Condon, Thomas Brian *retired hospital executive*

**East Haven**
Vermette, Raymond Edward *retired health facility administrator*

**Glastonbury**
Cassotto, Mary Lou Grace *counselor, educator, lawyer*

**Greenwich**
Krauser, Robert Stanley *health care executive*

**Groton**
Daniel, J. Christopher *health facility executive, family medicine physician, military officer*

**Hamden**
Cole-Schiraldi, Marilyn Bush *occupational therapist, educator*

**Hartford**
Gryskiewicz, Kristen Alta *pharmacist*

**Milford**
Muth, Eric Peter *optician, consultant*

**New Haven**
Armbruster, Paula *social worker, director, child mental health educator*
Benfer, David William *hospital administrator*
De Rose, Sandra Michele *psychotherapist, educator, administrator*
Fleischman, Gary Franklin *acupuncturist*
Grey, Margaret *nursing educator*
Jones, Katherine R. *nursing educator*
Krauss, Judith Belliveau *nursing educator*
Lord, Ruth *retired researcher, philanthropist, writer*
McCorkle, Ruth *oncological nurse, educator, researcher*
Stiber, Julie Anne *social worker*

**North Branford**
Womer, Charles Berry *retired hospital executive, management consultant*

**Old Lyme**
Algiere, Scott G. *health facility administrator*

**Redding**
Benyei, Candace Reed *psychotherapist*

**Simsbury**
Long, Ann Marle *health facility administrator*

**Southbury**
Bowen, Christopher Edward *researcher, director*

**Stafford Springs**
Zeldes, Benjamin *retired optometrist*

**Stamford**
Bostin, Marvin Jay *hospital and health services consultant*
Scott, Gregory Alan *pharmacist, writer*

**Storrs**
Petrovic, Kimberly Ann *nursing researcher, nursing educator*

**Stratford**
Spodick, Pearl Blegen *counselor, medical psychotherapist*

**Suffield**
Bianchi, Maria *critical care nurse, acute care nurse practitioner*

**Waterbury**
Lum, Johnny *physician assistant, consultant*

**West Haven**
Lisi, Anthony James *chiropractor, educator*

## DELAWARE

**Hockessin**
Croyle, Barbara Ann *health facility administrative executive*

**Lewes**
Fried, Jeffrey Michael *health care administrator*

**Wilmington**
Schmerling, Erwin Robert *counselor, retired physicist*
Wallace, Jesse Wyatt *pharmaceutical scientist*

## DISTRICT OF COLUMBIA

**Washington**
Alleyne, Sir George A.O. *public health administrator, educator*
Alward, Ruth Rosendall *nursing consultant*
Angotti, Catherine Marie *occupational health director*
Arling, Donna Dickson *social worker*
Auerbach, Judith Diane *public health service officer*
Baigis, Judith Ann *nursing educator, academic administrator*
Baird, Donna Selma *counselor, educator*
Behney, Clyde Joseph *health policy researcher*
Brown, Lawrence George *medical director*
Burris, James Frederick *federal healthcare administrator, educator*
Chalk, Rosemary Anne *health science association administrator*
Corrigan, Janet M. *health science association administrator*
Davies, J. Clarence (Terry Davies) *researcher, public information officer*
Delbanco, Suzanne F. *human services administrator*
Delgado, Jane *health policy executive, writer, psychologist*
DeParle, Nancy-Ann Min *former federal agency administrator, lawyer*
Eckenhoff, Edward Alvin *health facility administrator, educator*
Fineberg, Harvey Vernon *medical institute administrator*
Fitzgerald, Helen Teresa *social worker, writer*
Gaynor, Suzanne Marie *healthcare executive, researcher*
Ginsburg, Paul B. *health facility administrator*
Golden, Olivia Ann *human services administrator*
Gray, Bradford Hitch *health service researcher*
Grob, George Frederick *health science association administrator*
Hager, Mary Hastings *nutritionist, educator, consultant*
Harling, Barbara Jean *social worker*
Hartmann, Robert Sankey *health facility administrator, not-for-profit fundraiser*
Higgins, Paul John *medical director, career military officer*
Jones, Stanley Boyd *retired researcher*
Kelley, Patrick W. *health science association administrator, preventive medicine physician*
Lewis, Benjamin Pershing, Jr. *pharmacist, retired public health service officer*
Lombardo, Fredric Alan *pharmacist, educator*
Martinez, Rose Marie *health science association administrator*
Meehan, Shirley *human services administrator*
Michnich, Marie E. *health policy analyst, consultant, educator*
Mitchell, Ruthie Yvette *human services administrator, director*
Nightingale, Stuart Lester *public health service officer*
Pierce, John Randall *medical inspector, pediatrician*
Pollack, Ronald Frank *healthcare organization executive, lawyer*
Pope, Andrew *health science association administrator*
Porter, John Weston *counselor, consultant, administrator*
Raju, Minnie M. *nursing administrator, critical care nurse*
Rios, Elena *health association administrator*
Rowland, Diane *health facility administrator, researcher*
Salisbury, Dallas L. *researcher, director*
Sanchez-Way, Ruth Dolores *public health administrator*
Satcher, David *public health service officer, former Surgeon General of the United States*
Southby, Richard McKellar Fairfax *health services educator, consultant*
Stoiber, Susanne A. *health science organization administrator*
Tipre, Dnyanesh Nishikant *pharmacist, researcher*
Walker, Audrey Thayer *social worker, psychotherapist*
Wesberry, James Pickett, Jr. *anti-corruption specialist, management consultant*
Wootan, Margo G. *nutritionist, director*
Wuzor, Geoffrey Onyema *psychotherapist*
Yarwood, Bruce *health science association administrator*

## FLORIDA

**Altamonte Springs**
LeBlanc, Janet M. *addictions and relationship counselor*

**Boca Raton**
Baumgarten, Diana Virginia *gerontological nurse*
Richman, Joseph Herbert *retired public health service officer*
Rothberg-Blackman, June Simmonds *retired nursing educator, psychotherapist*

**Chattahoochee**
Carrasco, José Aníbal *recreational therapist*

**Clearwater**
Barry, Joyce Alice *dietician, consultant*
Halsey, Jean Michele *nursing educator*
Vasilyadis, Leon *retired social worker*

**Daytona Beach**
Cardwell, Harold Douglas, Sr. *retired rehabilitation services professional*

**Deerfield Beach**
Gambino, S(alvatore) Raymond *lab administrator, educator*
Solomon, Barry Jason *human services administrator, consultant*

**Delray Beach**
Ellsweig, Phyllis Leah *retired psychotherapist*

**Deltona**
Bondinell, Stephanie *counselor, academic administrator*

**Ellenton**
Edson, Herbert Robbins *retired foundation and hospital executive, retired military officer*

**Fernandina Beach**
Kurtz, Myers Richard *retired hospital administrator*

**Fort Lauderdale**
Adams, Nancy R. *nurse, retired military officer*
Alpert, Martin Jeffrey *chiropractic physician*
Kornblau, Barbara L. *physical therapist, educator*
Rentoumis, Ann Mastroianni *psychotherapist*

**Fort Myers**
Nugent, Timothy Scott *alcohol/drug abuse services professional*
Thurman, Cynthia Denise *human services administrator*
Woodbridge, Norma Jean *nurse, writer*

**Gainesville**
Acholonu, Wilfred W., Jr. *clinical pharmacy specialist, educator*
Bzoch, Kenneth Rudolph *speech and language educator, department chairman*
Doering, Paul Louis *pharmacist, educator*
Kersey, Talana S. *mental health counselor*
Small, Natalie Settimelli *retired pediatric mental health counselor*

**Hialeah**
Perez, Leyanee C. *nutritionist, consultant*

**Hillsboro Beach**
Marshall, Jo Taylor *social worker*

**Hollywood**
Harris, Jacqueline Myers *speech pathology/audiology services professional*

**Jacksonville**
Cruz, Theresa Lavaina *mental health services professional, educator*
Davis, Linda Lennon McConnell *critical care nurse*
O'Connor, R. D. *retired health services administrator*
Pavlick, Pamela Kay *nurse, consultant*
Scarborough, Marion Nichols *nutritionist, recreational facility executive*
Watkins, Julia Anne *healthcare educator, researcher*
Williams, Leola Wilkerson *social worker, writer*

**Jensen Beach**
Gamble, Raymond Wesley *retired marriage and family therapist, clergyman*

**Kennedy Space Center**
DiBiase, Catherine Priscilla *nurse*

**Kissimmee**
Goode, Betty Ruth *retired social worker*

**Largo**
Bush, Debra W. *occupational health nurse*
Hamlin, Robert Henry *public health service officer, educator, management consultant*

**Melbourne**
Hughes, A. N. *psychotherapist*

**Miami**
Auerbach, Ethel Louise *healthcare facility administrator*
Cekauskas, Cynthia Danute *social worker*
Dann, Oliver Townsend *psychoanalyst, psychiatrist, educator*
Embden, Dawn Terris *medical/surgical nurse, writer*
Hernandez, Marie *nurse*
Himburg, Susan Phillips *dietician, educator*
Kaiser, Gerard A. *hospital administrator*
Kelley, Michael James *medical services executive, author*
Kooima, Linda Kay *neonatal and pediatrics nurse*
Newton, Terry Fernando *health facility specialist, writer*
Osinski, Martin Henry *healthcare consultant*
Rozek, Thomas M. *health facility administrator*
Saland, Deborah *psychotherapist, educator*
Schafer, Marie *nurse, educator*
Schor, Olga Seemann *mental health counselor, real estate broker*

**Mount Dora**
Crone, Eugene N. *addictions specialist, retired educator*

**Naples**
Cotrone, Janice Lynne *nursing consultant*
Farnham, Robert E. *health facility administrator*
Vumbacco, Joseph V. *health services executive*

**New Port Richey**
Charters, Karen Ann Elliott *critical care nurse, health facility administrator*

**New Smyrna Beach**
Faherty, Sandra Lee *social worker, psychotherapist*

**Orange Park**
Rice, Ronald James *hospital administrator*

**Orlando**
Eastmond-Robinson, June Patricia *nursing educator*
Leuner, Jean D'Meza *nursing educator, director*
Pande, Anurag *researcher*
Shaoulov, Vesselin *technologist*
Sharp, Christina Krieger *retired nursing educator*

**Palm Beach Gardens**
Holloway, Edward Olin *human services manager*
Schurtz, Ora Sears *hypnotist, educator*
Sonnier, Joseph A. *lab administrator, physician*

**Panama City**
Reedy-Dewey, Madeline Anne *retired occupational therapist*

**Panama City Beach**
Nelson, Edith Ellen *dietician*

**Pensacola**
Appleyard, Diane Paige *human service administrator*
Maygarden, Jerry Louis *health care foundation executive*
Shimmin, Margaret Ann *women's health nurse*
Wright, Shannon Marie *psychotherapist, counselor*

**Plant City**
Henry, J. Myrle *pharmacist*

**Plantation**
Gonshak, Isabelle Lee *nurse, volunteer*

**Poinciana**
Spero, Barry Melvin *retired health facility administrator*

**Pompano Beach**
Dunn, Eston Robert *healthcare educator, director*

**Port Charlotte**
Kidd, A. Paul *health facility administrator, government agency administrator*

**Port Saint Lucie**
Beatrice, Ruth Hadfield *hypnotherapist, retired elementary school educator, financial administrator*

**Rockledge**
Means, Michael David *hospital administrator*

**Saint Petersburg**
Jordan, William Reynier, Sr. *retired therapist, poet*

**Sarasota**
Carr, Patricia Ann *community health nurse*
Harris, Judith Ann White *occupational health nurse, educator*
Middleton, Norman Graham *social worker, psychotherapist*

**Stuart**
Cocoves, Anita Petzold *psychotherapist*

**Tallahassee**
Blair, Maudine *psychotherapist, communications executive, management consultant*
Weaver, Thomas Harold *health facility administrator*

**Tamarac**
Krause, John L. *retired optometrist*

**Tampa**
Berarducci, Adrienne *nursing educator, researcher*
Boutros, Linda Nelene Wiley *medical/surgical nurse*
Castellano, Josephine Massaro *medical records specialist*
Mahan, Charles Samuel *public health educator*
Roberts, Jill Carolyne *researcher, educator*

**Trenton**
Ivey, James Frederick, Jr. *health facility administrator, physician*

**Venice**
Barritt, Evelyn Ruth Berryman *nurse, educator, dean*

**West Palm Beach**
Bernhardt, Marcia Brenda *mental health counselor*

**Weston**
Gordon, Lori Heyman *psychotherapist, author, educator*

**Winter Park**
Haendiges, Anne R. *marriage and family therapist*
Jernigan, Donald *hospital administrator*

**Zephyrhills**
Walton, Shirley Dawn *retired medical technician*

**GEORGIA**

**Albany**
Wernick, Joel *health facility administrator*

**Alpharetta**
Mock, Melinda Smith *orthopedic nurse specialist, consultant*

**Atlanta**
Anderson, Barbara Allen *alcohol/drug abuse services professional, archivist*
Baird, Marianne Saunorus *critical care clinical nurse specialist, administrator*
Bales, Virginia Shankle *health science association administrator*
Barker, William Daniel *hospital administrator*
Chandler, Robert Charles *healthcare consultant*
Foege, William Herbert *public health administrator, educator*
Fox, John T. *health facility administrator*
Henry, John Dunklin, Sr. *hospital executive*

**Honaman**, J. Craig *health facility administrator*
Hopkins, Donald Roswell *public health physician*
Johnson, Carl Frederick *marriage and family therapist*
Martin, David Edward *health sciences educator*
Polhamus, Barbara *nutritionist, educator*
Salmon, Marla E. *nursing educator, dean*
Seffrin, John Reese *health science association administrator, educator*
Walton, Carole Lorraine *clinical social worker*
Weed, Roger Oren *rehabilitation services professional, educator*
Wong, Faye Ling *public health service officer*

**Augusta**
Gillespie, Edward Malcolm *hospital administrator*
Logan, Betty Mulhern *human services specialist*
Phillips, Marjorie Shaw *pharmacist, educator*

**Brunswick**
Herndon, Alice Patterson Latham *public health nurse*

**Columbus**
Simmons, Lynda Teel *nurse, healthcare executive*

**Decatur**
Barrs, Thomas Jackson III *pharmacist*
Gregory, Sharon E. *neonatal clinical nurse specialist, nurse practitioner*
Hinman, Alan Richard *public health physician, epidemiologist*
Kelly, Karen Deloris *addiction counselor, administrator*
Nease, Judith Allgood *marriage and family therapist*
Rosenberg, Mark L. *health facility administrator*

**Evans**
Feldman, Elaine Bossak *medical nutritionist, educator*

**Fayetteville**
Cokuslu, Lynda Elizabeth McCord *medical assistant*

**Jasper**
Ledford, Shirley Louise *practical nurse*

**Keysville**
Cartwright, Maggie B. *retired nurse*

**Lawrenceville**
Swanson, Lynnette Sue *special olympics coordinator, special education educator*

**Macon**
Patterson, Kenneth *nurse*

**Marietta**
McEntire, Betty *health facility administrator*
Moscato, Joseph Louis, Jr. *health facility administrator, military officer*

**Rome**
Borchardt, Marc *nurse anesthetist*

**Roswell**
Herron, Harriette A. *retired occupational health nurse*

**Savannah**
DiClaudio, Janet Alberta *health information administrator*

**Snellville**
Dodd, Violet M. *nursing educator, recreational therapist, counselor*

**Statesboro**
Bartels, Jean Ellen *nursing educator*

**HAWAII**

**Honolulu**
Cadman, Edwin Clarence *health facility administrator, retired medical educator*
Fischer, Joel *social work educator*
Kadohiro, Jane K. *nurse, educator, consultant*
Kaholokula, Joseph Keaweaimoku *mental health services professional, researcher*
Kennedy, Faye *retired social worker, author*
Lum, Jean Loui Jin *nursing educator*
Titchenal, Charles Alan *nutrition educator*
Wilson, William James *healthcare executive*

**Kailua**
Lundquist, Dana Richard *health facility administrator*

**IDAHO**

**Boise**
Brownson, Mary Louise *counselor, educator, artist*

**Bonners Ferry**
McClintock, William Thomas *health care administrator*

**Coeur D' Alene**
Flygare, Richard Andrew *physician assistant*

**Meridian**
Thorsted, V. Darleene *neonatal/perinatal nurse, community health nurse*

**Pocatello**
Eichman, Charles Melvin *counselor*

**Post Falls**
Soss, Daniel Lee *social work educator*

**ILLINOIS**

**Alton**
Kessler, William Eugene *healthcare executive*

**Argonne**
John, Charles J. *public health service officer, educator*

**Arlington Heights**
Baptist, Allwyn J. *healthcare consultant*
Telleen, Judy *counselor*

**Belleville**
Andersen, Barbara Jo *technologist, educator*
Shim, Sang Koo *mental health services professional*

**Berwyn**
Hudik, Martin Francis *hospital administrator, educator, consultant, writer*

**Bolingbrook**
Day, Mary Ann *medical/surgical nurse*
Price, Theodora Hadzisteliou *individual, child and family therapist*

**Buffalo Grove**
Rai, Rajat *health facility administrator*

**Carbondale**
Kawewe, Saliwe Moyo *social work educator, researcher*

**Centralia**
Whitten, Mary Lou *nursing educator*

**Champaign**
May, Linda Karen Cardiff *occupational health nurse, safety engineer, consultant*

**Chatham**
Chew, Keith Elvin *health facility administrator*

**Chicago**
Andreoli, Kathleen Gainor *nurse, educator, dean*
Berman, Laura *sex therapist*
Brakel, Samuel Jan *public safety executive, law educator*
Chereska, Steven Edward *counselor, paralegal*
Giachello, Aida L. *social worker*
Goldsmith, Ethel Frank *medical social worker*
Goodman, Larry J. *health facility administrator*
Gulati, Martha *health facility administrator, cardiologist*
Hardy-Evans, Gloria Gean *healthcare educator*
Heltne, Paul Gregory *researcher, museum director*
Hill, Barbara Benton *healthcare executive*
Lal, Anil *health facility administrator*
Lerner, Wayne M. *healthcare executive*
Logemann, Jerilyn Ann *speech pathologist, educator*
Meccia, Francis (Frank) Anthony *physician assistant*
Mecklenburg, Gary Alan *hospital executive*
Reed, Vastina Kathryn (Tina Reed) *child and adolescent psychotherapist*
Riordan, Michael C. *hospital administrator*
Scheetz, Marc Howard *pharmacist*
Scott, Nancy L. *health facility administrator, consultant*
Shannon, Iris Reed *health facility administrator, consultant*
Spergel, Irving Abraham *social worker, researcher*
Tambur, Anat *lab administrator*
Tanabe, Paula *nursing educator, researcher*
Thomas, Leona Marlene *healthcare educator*
Trifilio, Steven Michael *pharmacist, educator*
Watson, Easter Jean *psychotherapist, financial program consultant*
Wilhelm, John L. *health facility administrator*

**Darien**
Jordan, Ronald P. *pharmacist, pharmaceutical executive, consultant*

**Deerfield**
Nitzki-George, Diane M. *pharmacist, medical writer*
Shakno, Robert Julian *hospital and social services administrator*

**Dekalb**
Crosser, Carmen Lynn *marriage and family therapist, social worker, consultant*
Shi, Lin *marriage and family therapist, educator*

**Des Plaines**
D'Anca, John Arthur *psychotherapist, educator*

**Downers Grove**
Wristen, Edward L. *health facility administrator*

**East Saint Louis**
Lane-Trent, Patricia Jean *social worker*

**Edwardsville**
Douglas, Thomas John *healthcare educator*
Gupchup, Gireesh Vijay *pharmacist, educator*

**Elgin**
Barnett, Sue *nurse*
Beyer, Karen Haynes *social worker*

**Elmhurst**
Moffitt, Ray *social worker, consultant*

**Evanston**
Hughes, Edward F. X. *healthcare educator, preventive medicine physician*
Neaman, Mark Robert *hospital administrator*

**Freeport**
Weaver, Michael Glenn *pharmacist*

**Galena**
Alexander, Barbara Leah Shapiro *clinical social worker*

**Glen Ellyn**
Cummings, Joan E. *health facility administrator, educator*

**Glenview**
Coulson, Elizabeth Anne *physical therapist, educator, state representative*

**Harrisburg**
Rushing, Philip Dale *retired social worker*

**Hillside**
Savic, Jelena *technologist, educator*

**Hinsdale**
Kim, Micaela *speech pathology/audiology services professional*

**Ingleside**
D'Andrea, Dana M. *medical/surgical nurse, lawyer*

**Lemont**
Hayes, Randy Alan *family therapist*

**Lincolnshire**
Fradin, Russell P. *human resources company executive, former computer company executive*

**Litchfield**
Deaton, Beverly Jean *nursing administrator, educator*

**Macomb**
Hopper, Stephen Rodger *hospital administrator*

**Matteson**
van der Hoek, Sherry A. *counselor*

**Maywood**
Barbato, Anthony L. *hospital administrator, medical educator*

**Moline**
Gleich, Carol S. *health professions education executive*

**Mount Prospect**
Rueggeberg, Erna M. *nursing consultant, nursing administrator, researcher*

**Naperville**
Spunt, Avery L. *pharmacist*

**Northbrook**
Kahn, Sandra S. *psychotherapist*
Mulhall, Kimberly A. *business manager*
Noeth, Carolyn Frances *speech and language pathologist*

**Northfield**
Lubawski, James Lawrence *healthcare consultant*

**Oak Brook**
Bower, Barbara Jean *nurse, consultant*
Skogsbergh, James H. *health facility administrator*

**Oak Lawn**
Wiechert, Barbara Theresa *school nurse practitioner*

**Oak Park**
Varchmin, Thomas Edward *public health service officer*

**Palos Hills**
Healy, Judith Ann *social worker*

**Park Forest**
Steinmetz, Jon David *health facility administrator, psychologist*

**Park Ridge**
Campbell, Bruce Crichton *hospital administrator*
Pippen, Jennifer Lynn *therapist, consultant*

**Peoria**
McCollum, Jean Hubble *medical technician*
Walker, Philip Chamberlain, II, *health facility administrator*

**Peotone**
Hilsenhoff, Robert Dean *retired pharmacist*

**Plainfield**
Schinderle, Robert Frank *retired hospital administrator*

**Quincy**
Reynolds, Judith Amy *nutritionist, consultant, animal scientist, educator*

**Rockton**
Pennell, Danny Joe *social worker*

**Romeoville**
Sprovieri, Bridgette Ann *social worker, school system administrator*

**Round Lake**
Abdullah, Bashar Y. *pharmacist, researcher*

**Saint Anne**
Holtzman, Michael *alcohol abuse professional*

**Savoy**
Bednar, Susan Gail *social worker, consultant, social sciences educator*

**Silvis**
Bobb, Harold Daniel *chiropractor, consultant*

**Skokie**
Guillermo, Linda *clinical social worker*
Langguth, Margaret Witty *health facility administrator*
McCarthy, Michael Shawn *health care company executive, lawyer*

**Springfield**
Schroyer, Michael Kevin *healthcare consultant, hospital executive*

**Tinley Park**
Daniels, Kurt R. *speech and language pathologist*

**Urbana**
Baker, David Hiram *nutritionist, educator*
Eddy-Johnson, Deanna M. *home health care advocate*
Erdman, John W. *nutritionist, educator*
Visek, Willard James *nutritionist, animal scientist, physician, educator*

**Walnut**
Meisenheimer, Sharon Lee *nurse*

**Westchester**
Clarke, Richard Lewis *health science association administrator*

**Wheaton**
Pape, Patricia Ann *social worker, consultant*

**Wilmette**
Ellis, Helene Rita *social worker*

## INDIANA

**Anderson**
Bracken, Linda Darlene *medical/surgical nurse*

**Bluffton**
Brockmann, William Frank *retired health facility administrator*

**Carmel**
Rushing, Debra Farrow *pharmacist*

**East Chicago**
Psaltis, Helen *medical/surgical nurse*

**Fort Wayne**
Freeman, Sharon Elizabeth *psychiatric clinical nurse specialist*
Wooten, Marc *hospital administrator, medical educator*

**Granger**
Harmelink, Ruth Irene *marriage and family therapist, writer*

**Indianapolis**
Buhner, Byron Bevis *health science facility administrator*
Colby, David C. *healthcare management company executive*
Corley, William Edward *hospital administrator*
Davis, Edgar Glenn *public health service officer, educator*
Handel, David Jonathan *health facility administrator*
Harden, Anita Joyce *nurse*
Hitchens, William Randolph (Randy Hitchens) *healthcare executive*
McCall-Rodriguez, Leonor *healthcare services company executive, entrepreneur*
Moelhman, Amy Jo *social worker*
Pishchalnikov, Yuri A. *researcher*
Rhoad, Richard E. *healthcare executive*
Riegsecker, Marvin Dean *pharmacist, state senator*
Shi, Lizheng *health economist*
Storm, Janet S. *psychiatric social worker*
Warner, Joanne Rains *nursing educator, associate dean*

**Jeffersonville**
Walburn, John Clifford *mental health services professional*

**Kokomo**
Coppock, Janet Elaine *mental health nurse*

**Lafayette**
McBride, Angela Barron *nursing educator*

**Linden**
Eutsler, Therese Anne *physical therapist*

**Logansport**
Healun, Kathy E. *nursing educator, nursing administrator*
Walter, Patricia L. *psychotherapist, consultant*

**Mishawaka**
Haley, David Alan *healthcare executive*

**Muncie**
Hoffman, Mary Catherine *retired nurse, anesthetist*
Popovich, Karen *health facility administrator*

**New Albany**
Rhodes, Betty Fleming *rehabilitation services professional, nurse*

**Rockport**
Davis, Karen Sue *hospital nursing supervisor*

**Tell City**
Thrasher, Mary Ahlf Marcroft *educator, social worker*

**West Lafayette**
Belcastro, Patrick Frank *pharmacist, researcher*
Christian, John Edward *health science association administrator, educator*
Kirksey, Avanelle *nutrition educator*
Peck, Garnet Edward *pharmacist, educator*
Shaw, Stanley Miner *pharmacist, educator*

## IOWA

**Cedar Rapids**
Stephens, Ralph Renne *massage therapy educator*
Ziese, Nancylee Hanson *social worker*

**Council Bluffs**
Alley, Mary Lou Vande Woude *retired medical/surgical nurse*

**Davenport**
MacNaughton, Neil Scot *nursing educator*

**Decorah**
Lord-Dinan, Elizabeth Ann *nursing administrator, director*

**Des Moines**
Dukes, Vanessa Johnson *dietician*
Marsh, Wendy K. *pharmacist, lawyer*
Wallace, Samuel Taylor *health system administrator*

**Dubuque**
Barker, Barbara Yvonne *nursing home administrator*
Frommelt, Molly Kathleen *nursing educator*

**Glenwood**
Campbell, William Edward *mental hospital administrator*

**Iowa City**
Anderson, Rachel L. *healthcare educator, researcher*
Craft-Rosenberg, Martha Jane *nursing educator, researcher*
Densen, Paul Maximillian *retired health facility administrator*
Herman, Ronald Alton *pharmacokineticist, educator*
Katen-Bahensky, Donna *health facility administrator*
Muir, Ruth Brooks *alcohol/drug abuse services professional, consultant*
Nesbitt, John Arthur *recreational therapist, writer, educator, researcher*
Wurster, Dale Erwin *pharmacist, educator, retired dean*

**Spirit Lake**
Quaday-Gray, Ailene Diann *retired speech pathology/audiology services professional*

**Walford**
Brooks, Debra L. *healthcare executive, neuromuscular therapist*

**West Des Moines**
Matthews, Alexander *health facility administrator*

## KANSAS

**Colby**
Morrison, James Frank *optometrist, state legislator*

**Hays**
Bustos, Rudolph R. *health facility administrator*
Caprez, Judith V. *social worker, director*

**Humboldt**
Finney, Paul *acupuncturist, Chinese herbologist, entrepreneur*

**Hutchinson**
Davis, Mary Elizabeth *speech pathologist, educator, counselor*

**Kansas City**
Godwin, Harold Norman *pharmacist, educator*
Jerome, Norge Winifred *nutritionist, anthropologist, educator*
Sanders-Hall, Patricia E. *health facility administrator*

**Lawrence**
Mc Coin, John Mack *social worker*

**Manhattan**
Shanklin, Carol W. *dietician, educator*

**Newton**
Rogers, Rita Doris Luck *family nurse practitioner*

**North Newton**
Goering, Jacob D. *retired psychoanalyst*

**Shawnee Mission**
Breen, Katherine Anne *speech and language pathologist*

**Topeka**
Osinski, Kay *nursing educator, medical/surgical nurse*
Varner, Charleen LaVerne McClanahan *nutritionist, educator, dietician*

**Wichita**
Da'Luz Vieira-Jones, Lorraine Christine C. *acupuncturist, researcher*
Dorr, Stephanie Tilden *psychotherapist*
Fitch, Diane K. *human services administrator*
Guthrie, Diana Fern *nursing educator*
Manske, Robert C. *physical therapist, educator*

## KENTUCKY

**Brooksville**
Dorton, Truda Lou *medical/surgical nurse, geriatrics nurse*

**Calvert City**
Butler, Sheila Morris *occupational health nurse*

**Frankfort**
Fleming, Juanita Wilson *nursing educator, academic administrator*

**Grayson**
Hunt, Andrea Wheaton *nurse*

**Harrodsburg**
Herman, Alice Gertrude *retired nursing educator*

**Henderson**
Logan, John A. III *hospital administrator*

**Lexington**
Bennett, Victoria Elizabeth *rehabilitation nurse, dialysis technician*
DeLuca, Patrick Phillip *pharmacist, educator, medical association administrator*
Farrar, Donna Beatrice *health facility administrator*
Fedorchuk, Mary Kathrine *social worker*
Garman, Ray Fillmore *occupational physician, director*
Karpf, Michael *medical administrator*
Martin, Craig Allen *infectious diseases pharmacist*
Mudd, Angela *social worker*
Rowe, Melinda Grace *public health service officer*

**Louisville**
Bloem, James H. *managed health care executive*
Carlisle, Douglas R. *health facility administrator*
Hanson, Dennis Michael *retired health facility administrator*
Hathcock, Bonita Catherine (Bonnie Hathcock) *managed health care company executive*
Kuntz, Edward Lawrence *healthcare executive*
Lofton, Kevin Eugene *medical facility administrator*
Lunsford, W. Bruce *health facility administrator, health products executive*
Mather, Elizabeth Vivian *healthcare executive*
Mountz, Wade *retired healthcare executive*

**Murray**
Keller, Randal Joseph *toxicology educator*

**Pikeville**
Hunter, Trudy Pearl *surgical nurse*

**Radcliff**
Cole, Jessie Mae *nursing assistant, freelance/self-employed writer*

**Richmond**
Hall, Kathy *health facility administrator*

**Russellville**
Harper, Shirley Fay *nutritionist, educator, consultant, lecturer*

**Warsaw**
Davis, Michael L. *guidance counselor*

## LOUISIANA

**Alexandria**
Slipman, Ronald (Samuel Slipman) *hospital administrator*

**Baton Rouge**
Broussard, Malcolm Joseph *pharmacist, consultant*
Morvant, Barbara L. *nursing administrator*

**Fort Polk**
Lubbers, Alice Dianne *operating room nurse*

**Gretna**
Layman, Kim Florinda Marie *pharmacist, writer*

**La Place**
Lodwick, Judith Lynne *nursing educator*

**Leesville**
Gutman, Lucy Toni *social worker, educator*

**Mandeville**
Treuting, Edna Gannon *retired nursing administrator, educator*

**Metairie**
Evans, Carol Rockwell *nursing administrator*

**Natchitoches**
Egan, Shirley Anne *retired nursing educator*

**New Orleans**
Culbertson, Richard Allen *healthcare educator, health facility administrator*
Howard, Richard Ralston, II, *medical health advisor, researcher, financial consultant*

**Pearl River**
Thiel, David Brian *physician assistant*

**Ruston**
Bourgeois, Patricia McLin *women's health and pediatrics nurse, educator*
Kim, B. J. *technologist, educator*

**Shreveport**
Heacock, Donald Dee *social worker*
Hummel, Kay Jean *physical therapist*

**Ville Platte**
Patsicostas, Susan Joanna *mental health services professional, psychotherapist*

## MAINE

**Augusta**
Dakivich, Brian Alan *hospital administrator, psychologist*

**Bangor**
Ballesteros, Paula Mitchell *nurse*

**Brooklin**
Schmidt, Lynda Wheelwright *psychotherapist*

**Dresden**
Iserbyt, Charlotte Thomson *researcher, consultant, writer, educator*

**East Boothbay**
Eldred, Kenneth McKechnie *acoustician, consultant*

**Fort Fairfield**
Shapiro, Joan Isabelle *lab administrator, medical/surgical nurse*

**Freeport**
Cushman, Margaret Jane *herbalist, nurse*

**Old Town**
Nelligan, Annette Frances *social worker*

**Portland**
Wipfler, William John *health facility administrator*

**Westbrook**
Larochelle, Patricia Anne *technologist*

## MARYLAND

**Adamstown**
Munson, John Christian *acoustician*

**Annapolis**
Goldwater, Marilyn R(ubin) *medical/surgical nurse, state legislator*
Klejnot, Getha Jean *school nurse practitioner, music educator*
Levin, Gilbert Victor *biotechnology company executive*

**Baltimore**
Beilenson, Peter Lowell *former public health official*
Bridges, John Francis Patrick *healthcare educator, researcher*
Campbell, Jacquelyn C. *community health nurse*
Englar, Nancy Ellen *nurse, consultant, nursing educator*
Harris, Yael *health policy educator*
Henderson, Donald Ainslie *public health service officer*
Hsueh, Mingkai *researcher*
Kaplan, Abner J. *social worker, public relations executive*
Kumin, Libby Barbara *speech language pathologist, educator*
Lawson, Edward Earle *neonatal/perinatal nurse practitioner*
Meltzer, Arthur Adam *researcher, researcher*
Morford, Thomas *health facility administrator*
Njie, Veronica P.S. *clinical nurse, educator*
Peterson, Ronald R. *health service administrator*
Sachs, Murray B. *audiologist, educator*
Townsend, John Cunningham *optometrist*

**Bethesda**
Gaarder, Marie *speech pathologist*
Govern, Frank Stanley *health facility and research administrator, healthcare educator, writer*
Graeff, Alan S. *health association executive*
Hausman, Steven Jack *health science association administrator*
Hsu, S. Dana *technologist*
Jonas, Gary Fred *healthcare executive*
Koslow, Stephen Hugh *health science association administrator, pharmacologist*
McCray, Alexa T. *health science association administrator, director*
McDonough, Thomas P. *health facility administrator*
Monjan, Andrew Arthur *health facility administrator*
Nakamura, Richard *mental health services professional*
Obrams, Gunta Iris *clinical research administrator*
Oddis, Joseph Anthony *health associations executive*
Polsby, Gail K. *psychotherapist*
Pospisil, George Curtis *health science administrator*
Robinson, Sharon Beth *health science association administrator*
Rumbaugh, John R. *health facility administrator, military officer*
Stover, Ellen L. *health scientist, psychologist*
Taylor, Lindsay David, Jr. *healthcare executive, bank executive, federal agency administrator*
Tracy, Thomas Miles *international health organization official*
Wise, Allen F. *health care administrator*
Wolf, Dale B. *health facility administrator, corporate financial executive*

**Bowie**
Speller-Brown, Barbara Jean *pediatric nurse practitioner*

**Chevy Chase**
Pedersen, Wesley Niels M. *public relations and public affairs counselor*

**Clarksville**
Hung, Mei-Jong Chow *social worker*

**Columbia**
Canahuati, Judy *lactation consultant*
Pacifico, Joseph Carl *counselor*
Piou-Brewer, Magalie *psychotherapist, educator, small business owner*

**Damascus**
Styer, Joanne Louise *retired dietician*

**Frederick**
Devineni, Mohan *pharmacist*

**Gaithersburg**
Dowd, Carolyn Lay *social worker*
Gloyd, Rita A. *retired social worker*
Quraishi, Mohammed Sayeed *retired health facility administrator, research scientist*

**Greenbelt**
Morris, Joseph Anthony *retired health science association administrator*

**Hagerstown**
Harrison, Lois Smith *hospital executive, educator*

**Laurel**
Landis, Donna Marie *nursing administrator, women's health nurse*

**Lutherville**
Goodman, Valerie Dawson *psychiatric social worker*

**Marriottsville**
Strange, Donald Ernest *healthcare company executive*

**Mitchellville**
Kendall, Katherine Anne *social worker*

**Owings Mills**
Ryan, Judith W. *geriatrics nurse, educator*

**Potomac**
Gaston, Marilyn Hughes *health facility administrator*
Wolman, Eric *health care consultant*

**Rockville**
Barbera, Thomas P. *health care company executive*
Dodgen, Daniel W. *health policy advisor, psychologist*
Groban, Mark D. *health care company executive*
Howard, Lee Milton *international health consultant*
Long, Cedric William *health facility administrator*
McCormick, Kathleen Ann Krym *geriatrics nurse, computer information specialist, federal agency administrator*
O'Donnell, James Francis *retired health scientist administrator*
Parham-Hopson, Deborah *health programs administrator*
Peele, Roger *hospital administrator*
Scully, Martha Seebach *speech and language pathologist*

**Salisbury**
Romanowski, Autumn Dawn *health facility administrator*

**Severna Park**
Daly, Charles Arthur *health facility administrator*
Rheinstein, Peter Howard *healthcare company executive, physician, lawyer*

**Silver Spring**
Blakeney, Barbara A. *public health service officer*
Young, Jay Alfred *chemical safety and health consultant, editor, writer*

**Takoma Park**
Stephenson, Patricia Ann *public health researcher, educator*

**Upper Marlboro**
Wesley, Ruby LaVerne *nursing educator, administrator, researcher*

## MASSACHUSETTS

**Acton**
Buck-Moore, Joanne Rose *nursing administrator, educator*

**Arlington**
Junger, Miguel Chapero *retired acoustics researcher*
Zimmer, Anna Held *social worker*

**Attleboro**
Bischoff, Marilyn Brett *clinical social worker, personal life coach, psychotherapist*

**Auburndale**
Kibrick, Anne *retired nursing educator, dean*

**Belmont**
Kargman, Marie Witkin *marriage and family therapist*

**Boston**
Bebo, Joseph Anthony *counselor, educator*
Berkman, Lisa F. *public health educator*
Blumenthal, David *health policy expert*
Bungay Massaro, Kathleen *pharmacist, researcher, medical educator*
Cohen, Alan Barry *researcher, educator*
Dwyer, Johanna Todd *nutritionist, educator*
Fowler, Floyd Jackson, Jr. *researcher*
Frank, Richard G. *healthcare educator*
Gura, Kathleen Marie *pediatric pharmacist, educator*
Kane, Daniel E. *nurse*
Levy, Paul Finanque *health facility administrator*
Lowenstein, Arlene Jane *nursing educator, health facility administrator*
Mandell, James *health facility executive, urologist, educator*
Mongan, James John *healthcare system administrator*
Nigrin, Daniel J. *hospital administrator, endocrinologist, medical educator*
Noble, Mildred M. *retired social worker*
Ratilal, Purnima *acoustician*
Reinherz, Helen Zarsky *social worker, researcher*
Shin, Sunny Hyucksun *social worker, educator*
Slavin, Peter L. *hospital administrator*
Stevens, Joyce West *social worker, educator, researcher*
Szumita, Paul Michael *pharmacist*
Watanabe, Mark David *pharmacist, educator*
Wizwer, Phillip *pharmacist, consultant*
Zaleznik, Abraham *psychoanalyst, management specialist, educator*

**Boxford**
Siegert, Barbara (Barbara Marie Siegert) *health care administrator*

**Boylston**
Larson, Roland Elmer *health facility administrator*

**Brockton**
Moore, Mary Johnson *nurse*

**Buzzards Bay**
Cirillo, Jeannine L. *pharmacist*

**Cambridge**
Botkin, James W. *leadership and executive coach*
Burns, Virginia *social worker*
Chodorow, Nancy Julia *psychotherapist, educator*
Narayanamurti, Venkatesh *health science association administrator*
Orfield, Antonia Marie *optometrist, researcher*
Sabeti, Pardis Christine *researcher*

**Canton**
Bihldorff, John Pearson *hospital director*
Sawtelle, Carl S. *psychiatric social worker*

**Centerville**
Condon, Ann Blunt *psychotherapist*

**Chatham**
O'Connell, Brian *public health service officer, educator, writer*

**Chestnut Hill**
Burgess, Ann Wolbert *nursing educator*
Munro, Barbara Hazard *nursing educator, dean, researcher*

**Chicopee**
Dame, Catherine Elaine *acupuncturist*

**Framingham**
Austin, Sandra Ikenberry *nursing educator, consultant*

**Georgetown**
Ramseur, T. Michael *social worker*

**Great Barrington**
Frye-Moquin, Marsha Marie *social worker*

**Greenfield**
Curtiss, Carol Perry *health facility administrator, consultant, nurse*

**Hyannis**
Nicholson, Ellen Ellis *clinical social worker*

**Lexington**
Bombardieri, Merle Ann *psychotherapist*

**Lowell**
Collins, Sean Michael *physical therapist, educator*

**Ludlow**
Budnick, Thomas Peter *social worker*

**Medford**
Almedom, Astier M. *healthcare educator, researcher*

**Needham**
Ryan, Una Scully *health science association administrator, medical educator*

**New Bedford**
LaPorte, Adrienne Aroxie *nursing administrator*

**Newton**
Mullen, Maureen Ann *social worker*

**Northampton**
Nehring, Fletcher Aldrich *pharmacist*

**Rockland**
Dunne, Myra Schley *nurse, consultant*

**Southbridge**
Mangion, Richard Michael *health facility administrator*

**Sudbury**
Ames, Lois Winslow Sisson *social worker, educator, writer*
Henderson, Ernest III *healthcare executive*

**Taunton**
Anderson, Peter D. *pharmacist, forensic specialist*

**Tewksbury**
Herlihy-Chevalier, Barbara Doyle *retired mental health nurse*
Tabea, Emile Victor *health facility administrator*

**Walpole**
Chapell, Robin L. *public health service officer*

**Waltham**
Wallack, Stanley S. *healthcare administrator*

**Wareham**
Gayoski, Kathleen Mary *counselor, minister*

**Watertown**
Pellegrom, Daniel Earl *health and development executive*
Rudman, Ilene H. *psychotherapist*

**Wellesley Hills**
Carroll, Deirdre Holden *psychiatric nurse practitioner, educator, medical researcher*

**Woods Hole**
Speck, William T. *former physician, health facility administrator*

**Worcester**
Harper, Doreen C. *nursing educator*

**Yarmouth Port**
Phelps, Judson Hewett *health facility administrator, marketing professional*

## MICHIGAN

**Allen Park**
Kirby, Dorothy Manville *social worker*

**Ann Arbor**
Allen-Meares, Paula G. *social work educator, dean*
Bashshur, Rashid L. *health facility administrator, educator*
Beeton, Alfred Merle *lab administrator, director, biologist, educator, environmentalist*
Funnell, Martha Mitchell *diabetes research administrator*
Griffith, John Randall *health facility administrator, educator*
Hinshaw, Ada Sue *nursing educator, former dean*
Howard, Matthew Owen *social worker, educator*
Ketefian, Shaké *nursing educator*
McLaughlin, Catherine G. *healthcare educator*
Oakley, Deborah Jane *public health service officer, nursing educator*
Romani, John Henry *health science association administrator, educator*
Rosenberg, Jerry C. *lab administrator, surgeon*
Rupp, Ralph Russell *retired audiologist, educator, author*
Sung, Kyu-Taik *social worker, educator, gerontologist, researcher*

**Benton Harbor**
Watkins, M(artha) Anne *family practice nurse practitioner*

**Dearborn**
Beauford, Sandra *nurse, data processing executive*

**Detroit**
Barnhart, Mary C. *health facility administrator*
Duggan, Michael E. *health facility administrator*
Krouse, Helene June *nursing educator*
Moses, Gregory H., Jr. *health services administrator*
Redman, Barbara Klug *nursing educator*
Schlichting, Nancy Margaret *hospital administrator*
Warden, Gail Lee *healthcare executive*

**Dexter**
Hanamey, Rosemary T. *nursing educator*

**East Lansing**
Noel, Mary Margaret *nutritionist, educator*

**Flint**
Williams, Veronica Myres *psychotherapist, social worker*

**Franklin**
Sax, Mary Randolph *speech and language pathologist*

**Grand Haven**
Disbrow, Sidney Arden, Jr. *chiropractor*

**Grand Ledge**
Evert, Sandra Florence (Sandra Wheeler) *medical/surgical nurse, consultant*

**Grosse Pointe**
Marshall, Douglas William *health research administrator, educator*

**Grosse Pointe Park**
Knapp, Mildred Florence *retired social worker*

**Holland**
Franken, Darrell *counselor, writer, publishing executive*

**Holly**
Evans Snowden, Audra Lynn *counselor*

**Ionia**
Ulmer, Evonne Gail *health science association administrator*

**Kalamazoo**
Bennett, Arlie Joyce *clinical social worker*
Lander, Joyce Ann *retired nursing educator, retired medical/surgical nurse*
Ortiz-Button, Olga *social worker*

**Laingsburg**
Collins, Mary Alice *psychotherapist, social worker*

**Lansing**
Nicholas, Caroline Jean *retired nurse, consultant*
Reason, Elizabeth M. *health facility administrator*

**Livonia**
Gepford, Barbara Beebe *retired nutrition educator*

**Muskegon**
Cusick Reimink, Ruth Elizabeth *community health nurse*

**Pontiac**
Beemer, Dawn Marie *public health service officer*

**Rochester Hills**
Romero, Josefino Tabernilla *nurse anesthetist*

**Saginaw**
Moyer, Genevieve J. *counselor*

**Southfield**
Martin, Marcella Edric *retired community health nurse*
Saidi, Reza F *researcher*
Sedler, Rozanne Friedlander *social worker, educator*

**Traverse City**
Frick, James Carlton *physician assistant, director*
VanderKolk, Mary DeDecker *nursing educator*

**Troy**
Arking, Lucille Musser *nurse, epidemiologist*

Potts, Anthony Vincent *optometrist, orthokeratologist*
White, James, Jr. *psychiatric, mental health nurse, consultant*

**Warren**
Bell, Julie Marie *health facility administrator, consultant*

**Ypsilanti**
Fox, Diane Porretta *nursing educator*

## MINNESOTA

**Bemidji**
Martinson, Ida Marie *medical/surgical nurse, educator, physiologist*

**Bloomington**
Nichols, Donna Mardell *nurse anesthetist*

**Burnsville**
Foss, Emma Thoren *retired social worker*

**Circle Pines**
Davis, Richard Carlton *rehabilitation services administrator*

**Elysian**
Thayer, Edna Louise *health facility administrator*

**Grand Marais**
Dupre, Lonnie *arctic explorer, writer, photographer*

**Minneapolis**
Croll, Jillian Kathleen *dietician, researcher*
DeNavaez, Denny *health facility administrator*
Drake, Dallas Sumner *researcher*
Gerdner, Linda Ann *nursing researcher, educator*
Hemsley, Stephen J. *healthcare company executive*
Kane, Robert Lewis *public health service officer, educator*
Kilbourne, Barbara Jean *health and housing executive*
Larson, Sheryl Ann *social worker, researcher*
Shemchuk, Mary Elizabeth *occupational therapist*
Sprenger, Gordon M. *hospital administrator*
Steen-Hinderlie, Diane Evelyn *social worker, musician*
Suryanarayanan, Raj Gopalan *pharmacist, researcher, consultant, educator*
Taylor, Frederick R. *health facility administrator*
Tomlinson, Patricia Short *nursing scientist, educator*
Van Ryn, Michelle *healthcare educator*

**Minnetonka**
Pearson, Kevin *health facility administrator*
Penshorn, John S. *health facility administrator*
Quam, Lois *healthcare company executive*

**New Brighton**
Appel, William Frank *pharmacist*

**Robbinsdale**
Anderson, Scott Robbins *hospital administrator*

**Rochester**
Cortese, Denis A. *healthcare executive, medical educator*
DeBoer, Stephen W. *dietician*
Gervais, Sister Generose *hospital consultant*
Prendergast, Franklyn G. *health facility administrator, medical educator*
Robbins, Thomas Landau *researcher, editor*

**Saint Paul**
Barry, Anne M. *public health officer*
Braun, Richard J. *lab administrator*
Bruhn, JoAnn Marie *radiologic technologist, writer, speaker*
Haertl, Kristine Lynn *occupational therapist, educator*
Owens, B. Mitchell *lab administrator*
Schoonover, James A. *lab administrator*
Shepherd, Terry L. *health facility administrator*
Weisberg, David Steven *healthcare consultant*
Wiersma, Kevin *lab administrator*

## MISSISSIPPI

**Jackson**
Rawson, John Elton *neonatologist, medical educator*
Tchounwou, Paul Bernard *environmental health specialist, toxicologist, educator*

**Mc Cool**
Miller, Charlotte Faye *speech pathology/audiology services professional*

**Mississippi State**
Hosie, Thomas Walsh *counselor, educator*

**Moss Point**
Bolton, Betty J. *medical/surgical nurse, poet*

**Ocean Springs**
Lee, Kathleen Mary *health facility administrator, nursing executive*

**Pass Christian**
Henrion, Rosemary Provenza *psychotherapist, educator*

**Shaw**
Garner, Mable Tecola *health facility administrator*

## MISSOURI

**Arcadia**
Davis, Jo *nurse, writer, professional speaker, small business owner, photographer*

**Cape Girardeau**
Langenfeld, Mark E. *healthcare educator*

**Chesterfield**
Ashworth, Ronald Broughton *health facility executive, accountant*

**Columbia**
Gysbers, Norman Charles *counselor, educator*
Hensley, Elizabeth Catherine *nutritionist, educator*

**Festus**
Baker, Marycarol Germaine *physical therapist, educator*

**Hollister**
Herron, Gayle Ann *health facility administrator, forensic psychotherapist, consultant*

**Jefferson City**
Bussabarger, Mary Louise *retired mental health services professional*

**Kansas City**
Eddy, Charles Alan *chiropractor*
Fetsch, Susan Hackler *nursing administrator, educator*
Krieg, Nancy Kay *social worker, poet, musician*
Oliver, Thornal Goodloe *retired health facility administrator*
Wade, John Cornelius *healthcare system administrator*

**Liberty**
Samuel, Robert Thompson *optometrist*

**Rolla**
Sin, Yong Wook *researcher, educator*

**Saint Charles**
Tabaka, Sandra Lee *retired medical/surgical nurse*

**Saint Louis**
Baum, M(ary) Carolyn *occupational therapist*
Borders, John Gillespie *psychotherapist, retired corporate financial executive*
Brockhaus, Joyce Patrica Dees *counselor, family therapist, consultant, family business consultant*
Ezenwa, Josephine Nwabuoku *social worker*
Foy, Betsy D. *health facility administrator, educator*
Hancock, Camilla Ann *pharmacist*
Molloff, Florence Jeanine *speech and language therapist*
Payne, Pauline Maria *retired medical/surgical nurse*
Pryor, David Bram *health science association administrator*
Ryan, Sister Mary Jean *health facility executive*
Schoenhard, William Charles, Jr. *health facility administrator*
Smith, Gladys Ann *counselor, military medic*
Stretch, John Joseph *social worker, educator, management consultant*

**Sedalia**
Gingerich, Naomi R. *emergency room nurse*

**Springfield**
Cornelius-White, Jeffrey H. *counselor, education educator*
Holloway, Wanda Kaye *psychotherapist, consultant*
Woomer, David Lee *pharmacist*

**Walnut Shade**
McCall, Charles Barnard *health facility administrator, educator*

## MONTANA

**Billings**
Zulkowski, Karen *nursing educator, researcher*

**Victor**
Davenport, Anne Marilyn *dietitian*

## NEBRASKA

**Broken Bow**
Bigbee, Darlene Mae *retired medical/surgical nurse*

**Kearney**
Squires, Allison P. *nursing educator*

**Lincoln**
Drullinger, Leona Pearl Blair *obstetrics nurse*
Steffan, Judy Mae *medical/surgical nurse*

**Omaha**
Baldwin, Jeffrey Nathan *pharmacy educator*
Hachten, Richard Arthur, II, *health facility administrator*
Thompson, Cheryl Bagley *nursing educator, director*

## NEVADA

**Las Vegas**
Duncombe, Patricia Warburton *retired social worker*
Francis, Timothy Duane *chiropractor*
Gilchrist, Ann Roundey *medical/surgical nurse*
Marlon, Anthony M. *healthcare company executive, cardiologist*
Meiner, Sue Ellen Thompson *adult nurse practitioner, consultant, gerontologist*
Michel, Mary Ann Kedzuf *nursing educator*

**Reno**
Cornell, Annie Aiko *nurse, administrator, retired military officer*
Middlebrooks, Deloris Jeanette *retired nursing educator*

Pinson, Larry Lee *pharmacist, state agency administrator*

## NEW HAMPSHIRE

**Amherst**
Buff, Margaret Anne *psychiatric nurse practitioner*

**Concord**
McCall, Junietta Baker *psychotherapist, minister*
White, Jeffrey George *healthcare consultant*

**Franklin**
Galloway, Jeanne Marie *public health service officer, consultant*

**Lebanon**
Dillon Rydman, Linda Gay *nurse, consultant*

**Londonderry**
Parten, Priscilla M. *medical and psychiatric social worker, educator*

**Manchester**
Bolduc, Diane Eileen Mary Buchholz *psychotherapist*

**Meriden**
Brent, Patricia Lee *health facility administrator, writer*

**Plymouth**
Gorin, Stephen H. *social worker, educator*

**Salem**
Stone, Patricia A. *special education services professional, consultant*

## NEW JERSEY

**Basking Ridge**
McNamee, James M. *lab administrator*

**Bedminster**
Delehanty, Martha *human services administrator*

**Belle Mead**
Sarle, Charles Richard *health facility executive*

**Belvidere**
Walsh, John Alfred *retired social worker*

**Boonton**
Lunt, Alan Nicholas *rehabilitation services professional*

**Burlington**
Britt, Donna Marie *school nurse*
Rowlette, Henry Allen, Jr. *social worker, counseling psychologist*

**Chatham**
Murphy, Joseph James *chiropractic physician*

**Cherry Hill**
Berman, Steven Eric *audiologist*
Blakney, Juanita Mosley *psychotherapist*
Grado-Wolynies, Evelyn (Evelyn Wolynies) *nursing educator*

**Deptford**
Johns, Michael Douglas *healthcare executive, medical device executive, former federal government official*

**East Orange**
Hudson-Zonn, Eliza *nurse, psychologist*

**East Rutherford**
Cathey, Gertrude Brown *retired medical/surgical nurse*

**Edgewater Park**
Mednick, Sheldon Ira *pharmacist*

**Edison**
Islam, Naushad 3 *pharmacist, government agency administrator*
Winter, Robin Okner *health facility administrator*

**Elizabeth**
Pompey-Plummer, Danielle Nicole *counselor*
Rauh, Linda Ann *rehabilitation services professional, counselor*

**Elmwood Park**
Grodman, Marc D. *lab administrator, physician, medical educator*

**Englewood**
Gulko, Edward *healthcare executive, consultant*

**Erial**
Browna, Jo McIntyre *nurse*

**Fair Lawn**
Carrera, Jaganath *acupuncturist, yoga educator*

**Flemington**
Van Ost, Lynn *physical therapist, Olympic team official*

**Franklin Lakes**
McGill, Kenneth, Jr. *mental health services professional*

**Green Brook**
Spoeri, Randall Keith *healthcare company executive*

**Hackensack**
Ferguson, John Patrick *health facility administrator*

**Hamilton Square**
Ridolfi, Dorothy Porter Boulden *nurse, real estate broker*

**Highland Park**
Blum, Lisa Carrie *social worker, researcher*
Grady, Joyce (Marian Joyce Grady) *psychotherapist, consultant*
McGoldrik, Monica *marriage and family therapist, researcher*

**Kenilworth**
Yang, Tsong-Toh (T.T.) *pharmacist, researcher*

**Kinnelon**
Preston, Andrew Joseph *pharmacist, drug company executive*

**Livingston**
Adelsberg, Harvey *hospital administrator*

**Madison**
Ellenbogen, Leon *nutritionist, biochemist, retired pharmaceutical executive*

**Mahwah**
Hailparn, Diana Finnegan *psychotherapist, writer*

**Manasquan**
Kelman, Marybeth *retired health care consultant, health policy analyst*

**Matawan**
Nolan, Sharon Theresa *nurse, educator*

**Metuchen**
Macarin-Mara, Lynn *psychotherapist, consultant*

**Montville**
Leeson, Lewis Joseph *pharmacist, researcher*

**Moorestown**
McDaniel, Joanava B. *nurse*

**Morristown**
Prince, Leah Fanchon *lab administrator, executive secretary*
Stiskal, Joseph Alexander *neonatologist*

**Neptune**
Hersh, Steven Lance *hypnotherapist, writer*

**New Brunswick**
Findley, Patricia Ann *social worker, health services researcher, educator*
Huhmann, Maureen Brigitte *dietitian, researcher*
Ma, Jun *researcher*
Prince, Jonathan D. *social worker, educator*

**New Providence**
Ring, Timothy Michael *human services administrator, pharmaceutical executive*

**Newark**
Mercado, Lillian Amensina *counselor*
Mital, Dinesh Prakash *healthcare educator, consultant*

**Newfield**
Dreher, Frank H., Jr. *retired optician*

**Paterson**
Daniels, Cheryl Lynn *pediatrics nurse*

**Perth Amboy**
Cruz, Nelson Xavier *healthcare executive*

**Piscataway**
Agrawal, Shruti *researcher*

**Plainfield**
Holdorf, Harry Hulbert *health facility administrator*

**Plainsboro**
Dezii, Christopher Michael *medical/surgical nurse, medical researcher*

**Princeton**
Gu, Henry Hongsheng *pharmacist, researcher*
Kelly, Paul J. *lab administrator, physician, researcher*
Logue, Judith Felton *psychoanalyst, educator*
Marks, James S. *public health service administrator*
Spicer, Michael E. *lab administrator*

**Red Bank**
Brown, Valerie Anne *psychotherapist, social worker, educator*
Carmody, Margaret Jean *retired social worker*
Gutentag, Patricia Richmand *social worker, family counselor, occupational therapist*

**Ridgewood**
Clements, Lynne Fleming *marriage and family therapist, application developer*

**Roseland**
Malafronte, Donald *health facility administrator*

**Rutherford**
Suarez, Sally Ann Tevis *health facility administrator, nurse, consultant*

**Saddle Brook**
Clifton, Nelida *social worker*

**South Orange**
Budin, Wendy C. *nursing educator, researcher*
Hanifin, Christopher James *physician assistant, educator*
Hansell, Phyllis Shanley *nursing educator, administrator, researcher, consultant*
Hecht, Marion B. *counselor*

**Teaneck**
Alperin, Richard Martin *social worker, psychoanalyst*

**Teterboro**
Freeman, Kenneth W. *laboratory executive*
Hagemann, Robert A. *health facility administrator*
Mohapatra, Surya N. *laboratory executive*
Prevoznik, Michael E. *health facility administrator, lawyer*

**Trenton**
Miller, Velvet G. *health science association administrator*

**Wanamassa**
McTague-Dougherty, Amy Elizabeth *speech pathology/audiology services professional*

**Warren**
Kozberg, Donna Walters *rehabilitation services professional*

**West Caldwell**
Schiff, Robert *healthcare consulting company executive*

**West New York**
Schmidt, Nancy Anne *psychotherapist*

**West Orange**
Bornstein, Lester Milton *retired health facility administrator*
De Lisa, Joel Alan *rehabilitation physician, research executive*
Shapiro, Jared *freelance/self-employed emergency medical technician*

**Willingboro**
Bevels, Esther Marie *medical technician, director*

**Wyckoff**
Metrey, George David *social work educator, retired academic administrator*

## NEW MEXICO

**Alamogordo**
Patch, Lisa E. *health services director, nurse*

**Albuquerque**
Davidge, K. Genevieve *clinical social worker*
Erickson, Sue Alice *health educator, consultant, nurse*
Gordon, Larry Jean *environmental health educator*
Gurney, Burke *physical therapist, educator*
White, Jennifer Phelps *counselor*

**Farmington**
Thompson, Joseph T., Jr. *health facility administrator*

**Las Cruces**
Little, Karen J. *counselor*

**Roswell**
Davis, Margaret Thacker *retired critical care, medical and surgical nurse*

**Santa Fe**
Melnick, Alice Jean (AJ Melnick) *counselor*

**Truth Or Consequences**
Rush, Domenica Marie *health facilities administrator*

## NEW YORK

**Albany**
DeNuzzo, Rinaldo Vincent *pharmacy educator*
Gellis, Zvi Dan *healthcare educator*

**Amherst**
Brogan, Michael Spencer *physical therapist, educator*

**Astoria**
Matheson, Linda *retired social worker*

**Bayside**
Kennedy, Mary Theresa *mental health services professional*

**Bronx**
Hilliard, Carol *nurse, educator, consultant, researcher*
Iezza, Anita Kay *physician assistant*
Megalli, Maguid Ramzi *health facility administrator*

**Brooklyn**
Abraham, Teena *pharmacist, educator*
Eliasi, Jennifer Rebecca *dietician, consultant*
Gonsalves, Patricia E. *surgical nurse*
Gross, Stephen Mark *pharmacist, dean*
Gustin, Mark Douglas *healthcare executive*
Hawkins, Vivian Agatha *mental health nurse, educator*
Horvath, Annette *home care administrator*
Landau, Joel *health services administrator*
Lockey, James Peter *public health service officer*
Morales, Jose *psychotherapist, writer*
Murillo-Rohde, Ildaura Maria *marriage and family therapist, consultant, educator, retired dean*
Peters, Mercedes *psychotherapist*
Phillips, Gretchen *social worker*
Pine, Bessie Miriam *social worker, columnist*
Samuel, Carren C. *hospital administrator*
Suarez, Maria C. *health care plan company executive*
Toranzo, Nilsa Caridad *special education services professional*
Wrotten, Marylean *medical coordinator, counselor*

**Buffalo**
Ahmed, Jamil *rehabilitation service physician*
Blane, Howard Thomas *alcohol/drug abuse services professional, researcher*
Hoffman, Faith Louise *social worker*
Nielsen, Nancy H. *health organization executive*
Saab, Maureen Wilson *social worker, consultant*

Schentag, Jerome John *pharmacy educator*

**Chappaqua**
Boal, Lyndall Elizabeth *social worker*

**Corinth**
Bein, Edward C. *chiropractor, educator*

**Cortland**
Brush, Florence Clapham *kinesiologist, exercise physiologist, physical education educator*

**Cropseyville**
Makowiec, Judith A. Neilson *family nurse practitioner*

**East Amherst**
Fleming, Renee Rizzo *pharmacist*

**Eastchester**
Giuliano, Robert Paul *pharmacist*

**Fairport**
Mierswa, Ruth Mildred *counselor, writer*

**Flushing**
Kim, Sun-Hae *retired medical/surgical nurse, writer, retired nurse midwife, retired physical therapist*

**Fulton**
Ludington, Janice Fay *speech pathology/audiology services professional*

**Garden City**
Scollard, Patrick John *hospital executive*

**Glenmont**
Haizlip, Viola *medical/surgical nurse*

**Glens Falls**
Vitvitsky, Jack *physician assistant*

**Great Neck**
Feldman, Gary Marc *nutritionist, consultant*

**Hartsdale**
Schweitzer, Caren S. *social worker*

**Hastings On Hudson**
Stillman, Jeanne Betsock *public health administrator, consultant*

**Haverstraw**
Eidelman, Sharon (Sherry) R. *marriage and family therapist*

**Holley**
Ruck, Rosemarie Ulissa *retired social worker, freelance/self-employed writer*

**Hornell**
Piper, W. Stephen *healthcare educator*

**Huntington Station**
Williams, Una Joyce *psychiatric social worker*

**Hurley**
Petruski, Jennifer Andrea *speech and language pathologist*

**Hyde Park**
Rider, Kathleen Mary *dietician*

**Ithaca**
Clune, JoAnn Guardalibene *retired nurse*
Oh, HyungSeon *power systems researcher*
Wills, Michael Stephen *nutritionist, quality assurance professional*

**Jackson Heights**
Chang, Lydia Liang-Hwa *social worker, educator*

**Jamaica**
Geffner, Donna Sue *speech pathology/audiology services professional, audiologist, educator*

**Johnstown**
Gibson, Jahnn Hansen Swanker *mental health nurse*

**Lewiston**
Moraca-Sawicki, Anne Marie *oncology nurse*

**Marcellus**
Pirozzi, Mildred Jean *retired nursing administrator*

**Medford**
Brower, Robert Charles *rehabilitation counselor, small business owner*
Lieberman, Carol *healthcare marketing communications consultant*

**Middletown**
Ojeda, Joseph A. *psychotherapist*
Radeboldt-Daly, Karen Elaine *retired medical/surgical nurse*

**Mineola**
Christiansen, Colleen M. *physician assistant*

**Mount Vernon**
NelsonWilliams, Cecelia Elaine *dietician, nutritionist*

**New Berlin**
Tyler, Jean M. *special education services professional*

**New York**
Aigen, Betsy Paula *psychotherapist*
Alves, Flavio P. *researcher, director*
Bailey, Darlyne *social worker, educator*
Barnum, Barbara Stevens *retired nursing educator, writer*
Barrett, Elizabeth Ann Manhart *psychotherapist, consultant, educator*
Batavia, Mitchell *physical therapist, educator*

Bendor, Susan Julia *social worker, educator*
Berardi, Loretta A. *human services manager*
Berman, Michael Allen *hospital administrator, pediatric cardiologist*
Billig, Robert Emanuel *psychiatric social worker*
Boufford, Jo Ivey *health administrator, educator*
Breslow, Jan Leslie *scientist, educator, physician*
Brodie-Baldwin, Helen Sylvia *retired college and human services administrator*
Brownell, Patricia Jane *social worker, educator*
Buehler, Thomas *psychotherapist, expressive therapist, artist*
Burns, M. Michele *human resources company executive*
Byrne, Mary Woods Woods *pediatric nurse practitioner*
Camp, Sharon L. *reproductive health organization administrator*
Cardinale, Kathleen Carmel *retired health facility administrator*
Clemens, Rosemary A. *health facility administrator, foundation administrator*
Cook, Sarah Sheets *women's health nurse*
Corcoran, Joseph P. *health facility administrator*
Corwin, Steven *hospital administrator*
Cox, Carole Beth *social worker, educator*
Daniel, Samuel J. *hospital administrator, medical educator*
Dehn, Cathleen Patterson *health facility administrator*
Dinerman, Miriam *social work educator*
Donald, Arnold W. *health science association administrator, former food products executive*
Dorn, Sue Bricker *retired hospital administrator*
Drayer, Burton Paul *hospital administrator, neuroradiologist*
Ethan, Carol Baehr *psychotherapist, psychoanalyst*
Fagin, Claire Mintzer *nursing educator, nursing administrator*
Fenchel, Gerd Hermann *psychoanalyst*
Fink, Matthew E. *health facility executive, educator*
Flynn, Laurie M. *social worker*
Forbes, Sally *researcher, editor, curator*
Forese, Laura Lee *hospital administrator, orthopedist*
Franciosa, Joseph Anthony *healthcare consultant*
Gangwisch, James Edward *social worker, researcher*
Giordano, Bill A. *psychotherapist*
Glickman, Robert Morris *health facility administrator, dean*
Goff, Robert Edward *healthcare executive, insurance company executive*
Gold, William Elliott *health care management consultant, educator*
Goodwin, Beatrice *nursing educator, consultant*
Green, Barbara Strawn *psychotherapist*
Kamerman, Sheila Brody *social work educator*
Kapoor, Neera *optometrist, research scientist*
Kassan, Lee D. *psychotherapist, writer*
Kassel, Catherine M. *community, maternal, and women's health nurse, consultant*
Kent, Deborah Warren *hypnotherapist, consultant, lecturer*
Khan, Shahnawaz *pharmacist, director*
Kuttler, Judith Esther *retired psychotherapist*
Lawrence, Lauren *psychotherapist, writer*
Leitman, I. Michael *health facility administrator*
Levinson, Rascha *psychotherapist*
Lopez, Pedro Felipe *social worker, educator, playwright, writer*
Mattson, Marlin Roy Albin *health facility administrator, psychiatry educator*
Mayeux, Richard *hospital administrator, neurologist*
McGonagle, Duncan Francis *mental health nurse, substance abuse counselor*
Moskowitz, Randi Zucker *nurse*
Mulvihill, William J. *former health science association administrator*
Mundinger, Mary O'Neil *nursing educator*
Murphy, Stacia *health service association executive*
Nam, Heekyung Biya *rehabilitation therapist*
Neubauer, Peter Bela *psychoanalyst*
Ossenberg, Hella Svetlana *psychoanalyst*
Packer, Linda S. *psychotherapist*
Pakter, Jean *maternal and child health consultant*
Pandolfi, Frances *health facility administrator*
Pardes, Herbert *health facility executive, psychiatrist, educator*
Paulson, Loretta Nancy *psychoanalyst*
Pennisi, Liz *women's health nurse*
Piombino, Nicholas *psychotherapist*
Rackow, Eric C. *hospital administrator*
Radwin, Jerome J. *health service officer*
Redlener, Irwin Elliot *health facility administrator, educator*
Resnick, Rhoda Brodowsky *psychotherapist*
Reynolds, John R. *hospital executive*
Richards, Cecile *healthcare network executive*
Rothenberg, Eleanore *psychotherapist*
Saffar, Jean-Marc *healthcare consultant*
Scott, Mimi Koblenz *psychotherapist, actress, journalist, playwright*
Sharoff, Leighsa *nursing educator, researcher*
Silber, Steven A. *lab administrator, physician*
Simmons, Richard Milton Teagle *physical fitness specialist, television personality*
Sochet, Mary Allen *psychotherapist, educator, writer*
Solomon, Libertina *pharmacist, educator*
Trent, Charles H., *social work educator*
Ungvarski, Peter J. *nursing administrator*
Varmus, Harold Eliot *health science administrator, educator, science researcher*
Watson, Anthony L. *health facility executive*
Whyatt, Robin M. *healthcare educator*
Woods, Joycelyn Sue *alcohol/drug abuse services professional*
Yadeka, Theophilus Adeniyi *hospital administrator*
Yohay, Steven Jacob *healthcare company executive, consultant*
Yoshiuchi, Ellen Haven *healthcare educator, clinical counselor*

**Ossining**
Robinson, Karen Vajda *dietician*

**Ozone Park**
Catalfo, Betty Marie *public health service officer, nutritionist, writer*

**Patchogue**
Lamberta, Gail Carol *recreational therapist, physical education educator*
McPherson, Sherry Lynn *social worker*

**Plattsburgh**
Fowler, Alyce Milton *health facility administrator*

**Pomona**
Downey, Bruce L. *medical company executive, lawyer*

**Poughkeepsie**
Deiters, Sister Joan Adele *psychoanalyst, nun, chemistry professor*
Heller, Mary Bernita *psychotherapist*

**Rochester**
Aydelotte, Myrtle Kitchell *retired nursing administrator*
Braley, Oleta Pearl *community health nurse, writer*
Hurlbut, Robert Harold *health care services executive*
Huston, Samuel Richard *health facility executive*
Nace, Morton Oliver, Jr. *human services manager*

**Roslyn**
Weinberg-Aptekar, Doris Mae *psychotherapist, school psychologist, hypnotherapist*

**Rye**
Davis, Samuel *hospital administrator, educator, consultant*
Newburger, Howard Martin *psychoanalyst*
Wilmot, Irvin Gorsage *former hospital administrator, educator, consultant*

**Saranac Lake**
Caguiat, Carlos Jose *health facility administrator, priest*

**Scarborough**
Mohl, Allan S. *social worker*

**Schenectady**
Oliker, David William *healthcare management administrator*

**Shelter Island**
Nicklin, George Leslie, Jr. *psychoanalyst, educator, physician, writer*

**Staten Island**
Lazzara, Margo Valentine *counselor, writer*
Martin, Frances Lee *nursing educator*
Nadler, Nona Jean *social worker*
Spada, Dominick *pharmacist*

**Suffern**
Raven, Luisa Antonia *psychotherapist, nurse*

**Syracuse**
Allis, Damian Gregory *technologist, chemist, consultant*
Fitzgerald, Harold Kenneth *social work educator, consultant*
Swartz, Michael Frederick *physician assistant*

**Tarrytown**
Safian, Keith Franklin *hospital administrator*

**Troy**
Fusfeld, Herbert Irving *research management and public policy executive*

**Valhalla**
Iatropoulos, Michael John *health research executive, pathology educator*

**Westbury**
Cohen, Abraham Ezekiel *retired health care company executive*

**White Plains**
Fowlkes, Nancy Lanetta Pinkard *social worker*
Hariton, Jo Rosenberg *psychotherapist, educator*
Leung, Betty Brigid *nursing administrator*

**Williamsville**
Perry, J. Warren *health facility administrator, educator*

**Yonkers**
Roberson, Doris Jean Herold *retired social worker*

**Yorktown Heights**
Chen, Jia *science and technology researcher*

## NORTH CAROLINA

**Buies Creek**
Wright, Mary P. *counselor*

**Burlington**
King, David Paul *health services executive, lawyer*
MacMahon, Thomas P. *healthcare company executive*
Powell, James Bobbitt *health facility administrator, pathologist*

**Chapel Hill**
Baker, Edward L., Jr. *public health physician*
Gordon-Larsen, Penny *nutritionist, educator, researcher*
Murray, Michael Dennis *pharmacist*
Rimer, Barbara K. *health facility administrator, educator, dean*
Soltys, Florence Gray *social worker*
Zeisel, Steven H. *nutritionist, scientist, educator*

**Charlotte**
Casey, John T. *hospital administrator*
Slaton, Charles R. *hospital administrator*

**Dunn**
Hill, Susan Beasley *recreational therapist*

**Durham**
Brantley, Jeffrey Garland *health science association administrator*
Fulkerson, William *hospital administrator, pulmonologist*
Gilliss, Catherine Lynch *nursing educator*
Holzworth, Donald A. *lab administrator*
LeGrand, Chris *lab administrator*
Pericak-Vance, Margaret A. *health facility administrator*
Wu, Li-Tzy *alcohol/drug abuse services professional, researcher*
Yu, Bing *researcher*

**Elizabeth City**
Griffin, Gladys Bogues *critical care nurse, educator*

**Fairmont**
Spencer, Melissa Johanna *psychotherapist, special education educator*

**Fayetteville**
Jansen, Michael John *health facility administrator*
MacRae, Elizabeth (Elizabeth MacRae Halsey) *counselor, actor*

**Goldsboro**
Cannon, Alice Grace *counselor*

**Greensboro**
Acheampong, Joseph Kofi *pharmacist, researcher*
Allen, Jesse Owen III *organizational behavior specialist*
Evans, Jonathan Christopher *social worker*
Harris-Offutt, Rosalyn Marie *counselor, consultant, mental health nurse, writer*
Knesel, Ernest Arthur, Jr. *health facility administrator, chemicals executive*
McDaniel, James Mark, Jr. *health care executive*
Mozell, Herbert Lee *mental health services professional*
Penley, Virginia Long *social worker*
Schwenn, Lee William *retired health facility administrator*

**Hendersonville**
Deskin, William C. *healthcare educator*
Heil, Mary Ruth *retired counselor*

**High Point**
Gripper, James Kaiser *mental health services professional, consultant*
Scearse, Patricia Dotson *nursing educator, dean*

**Lake Waccamaw**
Spaulding, Lila Bernice *marriage and family counselor*

**Mooresville**
Atlas, Marilyn S. *social worker*

**Newland**
Lustig, Susan Gardner *occupational therapist*

**Pembroke**
Meadors, Allen Coats *health facility administrator, educator, academic administrator*

**Raleigh**
Bailey, Mary Beatrice *retired health science association administrator*
Geller, Janice Grace *nurse*
Johnson, Mary Pauline (Polly Johnson) *nursing administrator*

**Rockingham**
Evans, Patricia McCormick *psychotherapist*

**Rutherfordton**
Crummie, Ann Vaughn *mental health services professional*

**Salisbury**
Ward, Brenda Robinson *social worker*

**Shelby**
Blanton, Madge Brantley *family practice nurse practitioner*

**Wilmington**
Maness, Eleanor Palmer *researcher*

**Winston Salem**
Hwang, Wenke *public health researcher*
Preslar, Len Broughton, Jr. *hospital administrator*

## NORTH DAKOTA

**Fargo**
Rice, Jon Richard *health facility administrator, physician*

**Grand Forks**
Nielsen, Forrest Harold *research nutritionist*
Ransom, Michael T. *counselor*

**Valley City**
Stillings, Dennis Otto *research association administrator, consultant*

## OHIO

**Akron**
Komorny, Kenneth Michael *pharmacist*
West, Michael Alan *retired hospital administrator*

**Ashland**
Gearhart, Randall F. *healthcare educator*

**Bucyrus**
Cooper, April Helen *family practice nurse practitioner*

## Canton
Bartlette, Donald Lloyd *social worker, consultant, counselor, educator*

## Cincinnati
Bacher, Susan Lorraine *nursing educator*
Besier, James Louis *pharmacist, educator*
Derstadt, Ronald Theodore *health facility administrator*
Goldstein, Sidney *pharmacist*
Henney, Jane Ellen *health facility administrator, educator, oncologist*
Hensgen, Herbert Thomas *medical technologist*
Lang, Jackie Ann *nursing consultant*
Lewis, Lonnie Howard *psychotherapist, educator*
Lichtin, Leon (Judah Leon Lichtin) *pharmacist*
Patel, Nick C. *pharmacy professor, psychiatry professor*
Scherer, Ronald Callaway *voice scientist, educator*
Schubert, William Kuenneth *hospital medical center executive*
Stinson, Mary Florence *retired nursing educator*

## Cleveland
Baker, Melvin *pharmacist*
Blum, Arthur *social worker, educator*
Cosgrove, Delos M. (Toby Cosgrove) *health facility administrator, surgeon*
Curran, Phyllis Marie *counselor*
Kalina, Eunice Goldstein *human services director*
Rothstein, Fred C. *health facility administrator*
Womack, John W. *pharmacist*
Wood, Paul F. *national health agency executive*

## Columbus
Anderson, Carole Ann *nursing educator, academic administrator*
Banasik, Robert Casmer *health facility administrator, educator*
Duckworth, Winston Howard *researcher*
Farfan, Erika Marissa *social science researcher*
Fawcett, Sherwood Luther *lab administrator*
Guglielmi, Rhonda E. *nursing administrator*
Kulp, Marjean A.T. *optometrist, educator*
Meezan, William Alan *social work educator, consultant*
Schuller, David Edward *cancer center administrator, otolaryngologist*
Sims, Richard Lee *retired hospital administrator*

## Dayton
Gladden, Robert Wiley *healthcare executive*
Nixon, Charles William *acoustician*

## Dover
Haggis, Mary Ripley *nurse, genealogist*

## Dublin
Ford, Brendan A. *health facility administrator*
Labrum, Ronald K. *health facility administrator*
Thomas, Stephen S. *health facility administrator*
Troup, Gordon A. *health facility administrator*

## Elyria
Myers, John T. *physical therapist, educator*

## Findlay
Stephani, Nancy Jean *social worker, journalist*

## Gnadenhutten
Wolf, Joan Mangon *nursing educator*

## Independence
Van Kirk, Robert John *nursing case manager, educator*

## Kettering
Peres, Frank J. *healthcare administrator*

## Lancaster
Varney, Richard Alan *health facility administrator*

## Little Hocking
Corbin, David P. *counselor*

## Mason
Clements, Michael Craig *health services consulting executive, retired renal dialysis technician*

## Mayfield Heights
Billick, Steven M. *emergency medical technician*

## Middletown
Gordon, Sandy Gale Combs *medical/surgical nurse*

## Olmsted Falls
Semple, Jane Frances *health facility director*

## Owensville
Seifert, Caroline Hamilton *community health nurse*

## Pataskala
Thrasher, Rose Marie *critical care nurse, community health nurse*

## Ravenna
Turcotte, Margaret Jane *retired nurse*

## Sebring
Kelley-Hall, Maryon Hoyle *retired social worker*

## Sidney
Leffler, Carole Elizabeth *retired mental health nurse, women's health nurse*

## Tallmadge
Kaul, Mohan Lal *social worker, educator*

## Toledo
Borovicka, Mary Catherine *pharmacist, educator*
Cavanaugh, Steven M. *healthcare company executive*
Francis, Barbara Joan *nurse, paralegal*
Lessick, Mira Lee *nursing educator*
Ormond, Paul A. *healthcare company executive*
Weikel, Malcolm Keith *healthcare company executive*

## Westlake
Schroth, Joyce Able *social worker*

## Worthington
Bernhagen, Lillian Flickinger *retired school health consultant*
Lentz, Edward Allen *consultant, retired health administrator*

## Yellow Springs
Graham, Jewel Freeman *social worker, lawyer, educator*

## Youngstown
Miller, Kenneth Lee *counselor, educator*

# OKLAHOMA

## Ada
Davenport, Ann Adele Mayfield *retired home care agency administrator*

## Bethany
Alexander, Patrick Byron *hospital administrator, consultant*
Arbuckle, Averil Dorothy (Cookie Arbuckle) *healthcare facility administrator*

## Broken Arrow
Muller, Patricia Ann *nursing administrator, educator*

## Muskogee
Heck, Jennifer Leigh *neonatal/perinatal nurse practitioner, educator*

## Norman
Hoang, Trung Q. *researcher*

## Oklahoma City
Bronson, William Cavolt, Jr. *retired counselor*
Church, Chelsea O. *pharmacist, educator*
Forni, Patricia Rose *nursing educator*
Jones, Renee Kauerauf *health facility administrator*
McClellan, Mary Ann *pediatric nurse practitioner*
Mustion, Alan Lee *pharmacist*
Spencer, Melvin Joe *retired health facility administrator, retired lawyer, retired consultant*

## Tulsa
Buker, William James *psychotherapist, educator*
Carpenter, Nancy J. *health science association administrator*
Cherry, Andrew Lawrence, Jr. *social work educator, researcher*
Gray, Karen Kay *counselor*
Jurgensen, Monserrate *clinical nurse, consultant*

# OREGON

## Ashland
Masters, Robert Edward Lee *psychotherapist, sexologist*

## Bend
Irwin, Kerri Lynne *pharmacist, writer, small business owner*

## Central Point
Brown, Christopher Patrick *health care administrator, educator*

## Corvallis
Givertz, Michelle Dora *healthcare educator*
Oldfield, James Edmund *retired nutrition educator*

## Cove
Kerper, Meike *family violence, sex abuse and addiction educator, consultant*

## Eugene
Acker, Martin Herbert *psychotherapist, educator*
Camp, Delpha Jeanne *counselor*
Weiss, Marianna Shrenger *psychotherapist*

## Florence
Van Horn, O. Frank *retired counselor, consultant*

## Lebanon
Griswold, Elaine C. *nurse, consultant*

## Milwaukie
Orloff, Barbara-Lee Marguerite Hewitt *social worker*

## Pendleton
Smiley, Richard Wayne *researcher*

## Portland
Korb, Christine Ann *music therapist, researcher, educator*
Shireman, Joan Foster *social work educator*

## Redmond
Dey, Charlotte Jane *retired community health nurse*

## Salem
Dettwyler, William Karl *medical technologist*
Edge, James Edward *health care administrator*
Zumwalt, Roger Carl *hospital administrator*

## Sandy
Jensen, Judy Dianne *psychotherapist, consultant*

# PENNSYLVANIA

## Acme
Babcock, Marguerite Lockwood *addictions treatment therapist, educator, writer*

## Allentown
Jebitsch, Jenna Lynn *clinician*
Sadr, Ann *psychotherapist, educator*

## Bethlehem
Anderson, David Martin *environmental health consultant*

## Bloomsburg
Guschel, Timothy James *pharmacist*

## Camp Hill
Crider, Rudyard Lee *psychotherapist*

## Canonsburg
Prost, Mary Jane *school nurse*

## Coatesville
Zarychta, William Alex *physician assistant*

## Collegeville
Dunstan, Russ Frank *psychological services professional*

## Davidsville
Pepoy, Marya Alexandra *healthcare educator, coach*

## Doylestown
Meyer, Diane Christine *social worker*

## East Stroudsburg
Henley, Richard James *health facility administrator*

## Easton
Pysher, Zane Kermit *retired counselor*

## Elkins Park
Verma, Satya Bhushan *optometrist, educator*

## Erie
Sensor, Mary Delores *health facility administrator, consultant*

## Grantham
Kreamer, Carolyn Lee *nursing educator, community health nurse*

## Hamburg
Schappell, Abigail Susan *retired speech, language and hearing specialist, massage therapist, Reiki master*

## Hanover
Conway, Samuel Anthony *retired chiropractor*

## Harrisburg
Bailey, Diandrea Michelle *rehabilitation services professional*
Cadieux, Roger Joseph *geriatrics services professional*

## Havertown
Garrahan-Masters, Mary Patricia *retired social worker, writer*

## Hershey
Christensen, Dawn Michelle *family practice nurse practitioner, consultant*
Moskowitz, Jay *health science association administrator, educator, dean*
Paz, Harold Louis *hospital administrator, internist, educator*

## Hopwood
Syphers, James Edgar *retired social worker*

## Hulmeville
Jackson, Mary L. *health services executive*

## Huntingdon Valley
Cohen, Michael R. *health facility administrator, pharmacist*
Isard, Phillip Isaac *medical nutritionist, consultant*

## Kennett Square
Hager, George V., Jr. *health services executive*

## King Of Prussia
Miller, Alan B. *hospital management executive*

## Lancaster
Brunner, Lillian Sholtis *nurse, writer*

## Lansdale
Bierman, Arnold *optometrist*

## Lawrenceville
Chua, Frank *researcher, educator*

## Lititz
Hartz, Brian David *physical therapist, educator, small business owner*

## Mc Keesport
Lodor, Marci Ann *dietitian*

## Meadville
Steen, John *health policy company executive, consultant*

## Mechanicsburg
Ortenzio, Rocco Anthony *health facility administrator*

## Mifflinburg
Miller, Mary Lynn *nurse*

## Newtown Square
Garthwaite, Thomas Leonard *medical officer*

## Orwigsburg
Mason, Joan Ellen *nurse*

## Philadelphia
Altschuler, Steven M. *health facility executive, pediatrician, gastroenterologist*
Broytman, Vladislav I. *hygenist*
Butler, Marie Gladys *nursing educator*
Charney, Natalie J. *mental health services professional, educator, researcher*

Clarkin, John Francis *health care management executive*
Freeman, Ellen Wood *research professor*
Holman, Larry Dean *retired healthcare administrator*
Kumanyika, Shiriki K. *nutrition epidemiology researcher, educator*
Macauley, Karen Elizabeth *nursing administrator, emergency nurse practitioner*
Marino, Ralph J. *rehabilitation services professional*
McFadden, Cori Erin *psychotherapist, educator*
Mohamed, Feroze B. *radiology professor, director*
Muller, Ralph W. *hospital administrator*
Niederdeppe, Jeffrey David *researcher*
Peck, Susan Nell *pediatric nurse*
Potter, Alice Catherine *medical technician*
Rogers, Joseph A. *mental health association administrator*
Shillingsburg, Cynthia Lynn *medical technician, educator*
Williams, Sankey Vaughan *health services researcher, internist*
Zurakowski, Tamara Lee *gerontological nurse practitioner, nursing educator*

## Pittsburgh
Calabrisi, Robert R. *health facility administrator, educator*
George, John Anthony *health corporation executive*
Goldstein, Bernard David *public health service officer, educator*
Kuehm, Julie K. *nurse, educator*
Moore, Pearl B. *nursing educator*
Pennell, Daniel Mark *researcher*
Petracchi, Helen E. *social worker, educator*
Romoff, Jeffrey Alan *healthcare executive*
Rudy, Ellen Beam *nursing educator*
Shin, Sungjae *nutritionist*
Smith, Ryan Arthur Harold *mental health services professional, writer*
Wilson, Frances Helen *retired occupational therapist*
Zanardelli, John Joseph *healthcare organization executive*

## Port Matilda
Holt, Frieda M. *nursing educator, retired academic administrator*

## Pottstown
Coulter, Kathleen Marie *psychotherapist, consultant*

## Reading
Bell, Frances Louise *medical technologist*
Gordon, Mildred Harriet Gross *hospital executive*
Sauer, Elissa Swisher *nursing educator*
Shultz, Lois Frances Casho *nursing supervisor*

## Richboro
Maholic, Nancy L. *nurse*

## Scranton
McKenna, Ann K. *nutritionist, educator*
West, Daniel Jones, Jr. *health care consultant, educator*

## Spring House
van Steenwyk, John Joseph *healthcare plan consultant*

## Trevose
Quinn, Holli Jo Bardo *social worker, educator, librarian*

## University Park
Guthrie, Helen A. *nutritionist, educator, dietician*
Liu, Yongjun *researcher*
Mayers, Stanley Penrose, Jr. *public health service officer, educator*

## Villanova
Haynor, Patricia Manzi *nursing educator, consultant*

## Washington Boro
Snyder, John Jacob *researcher*

## West Chester
Cinelli, Bethann *school health educator*

## West Mifflin
Skonsky, Caroline Treschow *marriage and family therapist*

## Wilkes Barre
Daniel, Longyhore S. *pharmacist, educator*
Legg, Timothy James *nursing educator*

## Williamsport
Saka, Tuna *technology educator*

## Willow Street
Keiser, Paul Harold *retired hospital administrator*
Wesbury, Stuart Arnold, Jr. *health science association administrator, educator*

## Wynnewood
Anyanwu, Chukwuma Uchenna *clinical pharmacist, biomedical researcher*

## York
Alcon, Sonja L. *retired medical social worker*
Bartels, Bruce Michael *health facility administrator*
Rosen, Raymond *health facility executive*
Thomas, Tracey Williams *researcher*

# RHODE ISLAND

## Cranston
Wilson, Valerie Petit *health science association director*

## Newport
Cicilline, J. Clement *mental health services professional, state legislator*

Woods, Donald E. *healthcare executive*

**Providence**
Kenna, George Anthony *pharmacist, researcher*
Monteiro, Lois Ann *nursing educator*
Recupero, Patricia Ryan *hospital president, psychiatrist, lawyer, health facility executive*

**Warwick**
Horn, Donna M. *pharmacist, medical association administrator*
Richards, Priscilla Ann *medical/surgical nurse*

**SOUTH CAROLINA**

**Aiken**
Wright, G. Todd *lab administrator, director*

**Bishopville**
Miller, Blondell Stephenson *social worker, minister*

**Charleston**
Anthony, Margaret Louise *nurse*
Cosby, Stephanie Bennett *health services professional*
Smith, Thurston Sinclair *mental health services professional, consultant, community activist*

**Columbia**
Amidon, Roger Lyman *public health service officer, educator*
Eleazer, G. Paul *geriatrics services professional, educator*
Ettel, Zita Moak *nursing administrator, food service executive*
Ruffin, Julian Edward *marriage and family therapist, educator*
Seigler, Ruth Queen *college nursing administrator, educator, consultant, nurse*

**Easley**
Howe, Linda Arlene *nursing educator, writer*

**Florence**
Waddill, Cynthia Kay *nurse*

**Gaffney**
Griffin, Penni Oncken *social worker, educator*

**Hilton Head Island**
Wesselmann, Glenn Allen *retired health facility administrator*

**Holly Hill**
Anderson, LaShawn Ecleasha *rehabilitation technician*

**Hopkins**
Garrett, Robin Scott *health facility administrator*

**Lyman**
Morgan, Leon Terrell *environmental health services specialist*

**Marion**
Inabinet, Lawrence Elliott *retired pharmacist*

**Spartanburg**
Jones, William Osborne, II, *physician assistant*

**Summerville**
Burke, Rhonda Williams *counselor*
Deavers, James Frederick *optometrist, clinical nutritionist*

**SOUTH DAKOTA**

**Pierre**
Weyer, Dianne Sue *health facility administrator*

**Rapid City**
Corwin, Bert Clark *optometrist*

**Sioux Falls**
McMillin, Joan Austin *social worker*
Richards, LaClaire Lissetta Jones (Mrs. George A. Richards) *social worker*
VanDemark, Michelle Volin *critical care, neuroscience nurse*

**Vermillion**
Sevening, Diane Kay *alcohol/drug abuse studies educator, researcher*

**TENNESSEE**

**Antioch**
Brown, Katherine Yvonne *occupational therapist, educator*

**Bartlett**
Huffman, D. C., Jr. *pharmacist, educator, health science association administrator*

**Brentwood**
Carpenter, William F. III *hospital management company executive, lawyer*
Chapdelaine, Perry Anthony, Jr. *public health service officer, preventive medicine physician, educator*
Smith, Wayne Thomas *healthcare company executive*

**Clarksville**
Staivisky, Jeanne Louise *counselor, alcohol/drug abuse services professional*

**Cleveland**
Preston, Forrest L. *healthcare executive*

**Clinton**
Seib, Billie McGhee Rushing *nursing administrator, consultant*

**Cookeville**
Reynolds, Barbara C. *retired mental health educator, dean*

**Crossville**
Sower, Milene A. *nursing educator*

**Dickson**
Surji, Kemal M. *health facility administrator, consultant*

**Franklin**
Miller, Dennis Edward *health medical executive*

**Friendsville**
Dees, Linda Jo *nurse, educator*

**Germantown**
Nolly, Robert J. *pharmacist, health facility administrator, educator*

**Goodlettsville**
Harper, Jewel Benton *pharmacist*

**Harriman**
Vann, Lillie Mae *retired nurse*

**Hendersonville**
Davis, Robert Norman *hospital administrator*

**Jellico**
Hausman, Keith Lynn *health facility administrator, physical therapist*

**Knoxville**
Matteson, Karla J. *health science association administrator*
McGuire, Sandra Lynn *nursing educator*
Mc Hargue, Carl Jack *lab administrator*
Trout, Monroe Eugene *health facility administrator*

**La Follette**
Watson, S. Michele *school nurse*

**Linden**
Mitchell, Elizabeth Marelle *family practice nurse practitioner, medical/surgical nurse, nursing educator*

**Memphis**
Bargagliotti, Lillian Antoinette *nursing educator*
Boucher, Bradley Albert *pharmacist, educator*
Carter, Michael Allen *nursing educator*
Diggs, Walter Whitley *health science facility administrator*
Kun, Larry E. *health facility administrator, clinical investigator*
Mahato, Ram Ishwar *pharmacist, educator*
Oliver, Guillermo *hospital administrator, researcher*
Shulkin, Barry *health facility administrator*

**Morristown**
Harmon, David Eugene *optometrist, geneticist*

**Murfreesboro**
Jernigan, Nathan Scott *psychotherapist*

**Nashville**
Bolian, George Clement *healthcare executive, psychiatrist*
Brown, Tommie Florence *social work educator*
Brukardt, Gary A. *health facility administrator*
Cannon, Sharon M. *health facility administrator*
Carlson, Robert Marshall *health facility administrator*
Dalton, James Edgar, Jr. *health facility administrator*
Frist, Thomas Fearn, Jr. *hospital management company executive*
Goldberg, Larry M *hospital administrator*
Johnson, R. Milton *healthcare executive*
Johnston, William P. *health facility administrator*
Kaiser, Allen Bernard *health facility administrator*
McNally, James Rand (Randy McNally) *pharmacist, state legislator*
Perlin, Jonathan Brian *health services company executive, former federal agency administrator*
Sergent, John Stanley *hospital administrator, medical educator*
Urmy, Norman B. *hospital administrator*

**Oak Ridge**
Jones, Virginia McClurkin *retired social worker*
Slusher, Kimberly Goode *researcher*

**Saulsbury**
Jacobs, Henry Madison, Jr. *researcher, writer*

**Sevierville**
Heldman, Betty Lou Faulkner *retired health facility administrator*

**Somerville**
Macdonald, Sally Polk Bowers *retired addictions therapist*

**TEXAS**

**Amarillo**
Simpson, Chad W. *pharmacist, educator*

**Arlington**
Adams, Phyllis C. *nursing educator*
McCuistion, Robert Wiley *hospital administrator, management consultant, lawyer*

**Austin**
Attal, Gene (Fred Eugene Attal) *hospital executive*
Barrera, Elvira Puig *retired counselor, academic administrator*
Davis, Donald Robert *nutritionist, researcher, consultant*
Durbin, Richard Louis, Sr. *health facility administrator, consultant*
Easley, Christa Birgit *nurse, researcher*
Fleming, Francine Faye *legal nurse consultant*

**Cedar Hill**
Findley, Milla Jean *nutritionist*
Warren, Shirley M. *respiratory therapist*

**Chillicothe**
Brock, Helen Rachel McCoy *retired mental health and community health nurse*

**College Station**
Pal, Ranadip *researcher*

**Colleyville**
Donnelly, Barbara Schettler *retired medical technologist*

**Conroe**
Sowers, Amelia Barnet *speech and language pathologist*

**Dallas**
Anderson, Ron Joe *health facility administrator, internist, educator*
Arbique, Debbie Anita *emergency nurse practitioner*
Bradley, John Andrew *health facility administrator*
Brown, Stephen F. *health facility administrator*
Farber, Stephen D. *health facility administrator*
Fetter, Trevor *healthcare industry executive*
France, Newell Edwin *retired health facility administrator*
Goldmann, James Allen *healthcare consultant*
Harris, Hazel Lynn *medical/surgical nurse*
Hitt, David Hamilton, Sr. *retired health facility administrator*
Johnson, Murray H. *optometrist, researcher, consultant, lecturer*
Kangas, Edward A. *healthcare company executive, former diversified financial services company executive*
Lyne, Kevin Peter *technologist*
Madzik, Elizabeth May *hospital administrator*
Miller, Jo Carolyn Dendy *family and marriage counselor, manager*
Richardson, Dennise Marie *physician assistant*
Schecter, Arnold Joel *public health physician, researcher*
Schochet, Barry P. *health care executive*
Smith, William Randolph (Randy Smith) *health facility administrator*
Solomon, Risa Greenberg *clinical social worker, child and family therapist, former entertainment industry executive*
Taulbee, Thomas Lester *psychotherapist, educator*
Timpa, Vicki Ann *government health program administrator*
Wassenich, Linda Pilcher *retired health facility administrator*
Wheeler, M. Cass *health science association administrator*
Young, Melodie S. *adult nurse practitioner*

**Denton**
Kwon, Junehee *dietician, educator*
Olim, August Souza *counselor*
Surprise, Juanee *chiropractor, nutrition consultant*

**Dyess Afb**
Chester, Linnes Lee, Jr. *healthcare association administrator*

**Edinburg**
Wilson, Bruce Keith *men's health nurse*

**El Campo**
Abshire, Mary Young *dietitian, small business owner*

**El Paso**
Edmonds, Velma McInnis *nursing educator*
Flores, Yolanda *speech pathology/audiology services professional, consultant*
Hedrick, Wyatt Smith *pharmacist*
Juarez, Antonio *psychotherapist, consultant, counselor, educator*
Mitchelll, Paula Rae *nursing educator, dean*
Moya, Eva M. *health services executive*

**Fort Sam Houston**
Gordon, Ella Dean *nursing educator, women's health nurse*
Nelson, James Harold *health sciences administrator*

**Fort Worth**
Adams, Lavonne Marilyn Beck *critical care nurse, educator*
Brockman, Leslie Richard *social worker*

**Galveston**
Hargraves, Martha Ann *health services administrator, researcher*
Munsell, Debra S. *physician assistant, educator*
Rogers, Helen Lynch *physical therapist, educator*

**Georgetown**
Smitheram, Margaret Etheridge *health facility administrator, director*

**Grand Prairie**
Solomon, Arthur Charles *pharmacist*

**Hayes, Patricia Ann** *health facility administrator*

Kirk, Lynda Pounds *biofeedback therapist, neurotherapist, counselor*
Lansford, James Lowell *technologist*
Larkam, Beverley McCosham *social worker, marriage and family therapist*
McClintic, James A. *lab administrator*

**Brenham**
Zander, Jeanne Marie *healthcare educator*

**Bryan**
Buckley, John Joseph, Jr. *healthcare executive*
Guitry, Loraine Dunn *community health nurse*

**Carrollton**
Withrow, Lucille Monnot *nursing home administrator*

**Harlingen**
Miller, Rodney D. *health facility administrator, consultant*

**Helotes**
Rojo, Ruth M. *nutritionist, consultant, director*

**Houston**
Aitken, Iam *health facility administrator*
Altman, William Carl *health facility administrator, industrial relations specialist, investment company executive, consultant*
Andrae, Richard M. *health club administrator*
Arafat, Raouf Raafat *public health service officer*
Arcilla, Demetrio Ballares, Jr. *health facility administrator, rehabilitation services professional, writer, genealogist*
Arcilla, Juanita R. *physical therapist*
Callender, Norma Anne *counselor, public relations executive*
Calvin, Amy Olivier *nursing educator, researcher*
Caskey, Caroline T. *lab administrator*
Chima, Felix O. *social work educator*
Davis-Lewis, Bettye *nursing educator*
Demory-Luce, Debby Kay *dietician, consultant*
Felleman, Daniel Jay *healthcare educator, science educator*
Florian-Lacy, Dorothy *social worker, educator*
Golinkin, Webster Fowler *healthcare executive, media consultant*
Gunn, Joan Marie *health facility administrator*
Hanrahan, Lawrence Martin *healthcare consultant*
Hawkins, Barbara Reed *mental health nurse*
Hempfling, Linda Lee *nurse*
Holmes, Harry Dadisman *health care consultant*
Montgomery, Denise Karen *nurse*
Moore, Lois Jean *health science facility administrator*
Peabody, Arlene L. Howland Bayar *retired enterostomal therapy nurse*
Potluri, Venkateswara Rao *medical facility administrator*
Reed, Kathlyn Louise *occupational therapist, educator*
Revere, Frances Lee *healthcare educator*
Rives, Terry Edward *public health service officer, researcher, epidemiologist*
Robbins, Susan Paula *social work educator*
Sawh, Ravi-Persad *lab administrator, researcher*
Spikes, Patricia White *medical technologist*
Tervalon, Josephine M. *psychotherapist, social worker*
Tsui, Stephen Alan *researcher*
Vassilopoulou-Sellin, Rena *researcher*
Wagener, Christine Elizabeth *psychotherapist, educator*
Wallace, Mark Allen *hospital administrator*
Wilkinson, Miles Frome *healthcare educator, researcher*
Wilson, Gerald Everette *funeral services company executive*
Wissel-Littmann, Jeffrey G. *health facility executive*

**Irving**
Hicks, Allen Morley *retired hospital administrator*
Jorden, Yon Yoon *health services company executive*

**Karnes City**
Davis, Troy Arnol *reflexologist, hypnotherapist*

**Kerrville**
Denke, Margo A. *nutritionist, researcher, endocrinologist*

**Kingsville**
Bleidt, Barry Anthony *pharmacy educator*

**La Porte**
Fotsch, George Bernard III *chemical addiction counselor*

**Lackland Afb**
Beck, William Joseph *health facility administrator, geophysicist*

**Lubbock**
Feola, Mario *researcher*
Parks, Katie Mae *human services manager*
Yoder-Wise, Patricia Snyder *nursing educator*

**Midland**
Syed, Elizabeth Chance *health facility administrator, critical care nurse*

**Mount Pleasant**
Giddens, Martha Lynn *health science association administrator, educator*

**Normange**
Rector, M. Eugene *community pharmacist*

**Panhandle**
Sherrod, Lloyd Bruce *retired nutritionist*

**Pasadena**
Kenagy, Cheri Lynn *nurse*

**Plano**
Hightower, David R. *environmental health specialist, educator*
Parsons, Michael J. *health facility administrator*
Shelton, James D. (Denny Shelton) *hospital management company executive*

**Port Arthur**
Vinecour, Oneida Agnes *nurse*

**Red Oak**
Jones, Genia Kay *critical care nurse, consultant*

**Richardson**
Krauss, Henry Frederick, Jr. *optometrist*

**Rockwall**
Johnston, Nicklett Rose *research nurse, clinical perfusionist*

**San Antonio**
Accountius, Patricia L. *dietician, consultant*
Avant, Patricia Kay *nursing educator*
Champion, Michael Edward *physician assistant, clinical perfusionist*
Crabtree, Ben C. *neuromuscular therapy clinic director*
Dacbert-Friese, Sharyn Varhely *social worker, evangelist*
Davis, Sarah Jane *health facility administrator*
DeNice, Marcella Louise *counselor*
Eyer, Julia Arlene *speech pathology/audiology services professional, educator*
Gonzalez, Hector Hugo *nursing educator*
Grabinski, Jodi *pharmacist, researcher*
Lancaster, Malcolm Clayton *retired hospital administrator*
Lin, Ai-Ling *researcher*
Murphy, Sharon B. *health facility administrator*
Pysher, Alan Guy *retired nurse anesthetist*
Robertson, Samuel Luther, Jr. *psychotherapist, educator*
Somlo, Valeska Barbara *medical/surgical nurse*
Swansburg, Russell Chester *nursing educator, consultant, health facility administrator*
Triplitt, Curtis Lee *pharmacist, medical educator, researcher*
Van de Putte, Leticia *pharmacist, state senator*
Walsh, Nicolas Eugene *rehabilitation services professional, educator*

**San Marcos**
Chavkin, Nancy Feyl *social worker, educator*
Shaw, Donald Keith *physical therapist, educator*

**Spur**
Warren, Jennifer Elizabeth *family nurse practitioner*

**Sugar Land**
Chatterjee, Nilesh *researcher*
Heitzenrater, James F *hospital administrator*
Kajander, Judy Elaine *social worker*
Wagner, Donald Bert *health facility administrator*

**Taylor Lake Village**
Jenicek, Alicia Joanne *nursing consultant*

**Temple**
Frost, Juanita Corbitt *retired hospital foundation coordinator*
Hoffer, John Lee *health facility administrator, medical educator*

**Texarkana**
Bertrand, Betty Harleen *nurse*

**Waco**
Scott, Richard Elton *health facility administrator*

**Weatherford**
Scott, Geneva Lee Smith *nursing educator*

**Zephyr**
Lancaster, Carroll Townes, Jr. *health services executive*

**UTAH**

**Centerfield**
Parkin, Fern Agnes Marvel *medical/surgical nurse, nursing educator*

**North Logan**
Boyer, Albert Bruce *optometrist, educator*

**Ogden**
Jones, Galen Ray *physician assistant*

**Saint George**
Chilow, Barbara Gail *social worker*

**Salt Lake City**
Kjeldsberg, Karl R. *lab administrator, physician, educator*
Melton, Arthur Richard *public health administrator*
Weiss, Ronald L. *lab administrator*

**South Jordan**
Wirthlin, Richard Bitner *researcher*

**VERMONT**

**Brattleboro**
Bussino, Melinda Holden *human services administrator*

**East Thetford**
Cummings Rockwell, Patricia Guilbault *psychiatric nurse*

**Hyde Park**
Roberts, Carolyn C. *former hospital administrator*

**Shelburne**
Mead, Philip Bartlett *healthcare administrator, educator, retired obstetrician*

**Winooski**
Higgins, Margaret Ann *medical/surgical nurse*

**VIRGINIA**

**Alexandria**
Gormley, Dennis Michael *research scholar*
Grachek, Marianna Kern *healthcare administrator*
Mallon, Francis J. *health science association administrator*
Pastin, Mark Joseph *health science association administrator, educator*
Penrose, Cynthia C. *retired health care consultant*

**Annandale**
Abdellah, Faye Glenn *retired public health service executive*

**Arlington**
Guirguis, Raouf Albert *health science association administrator*
Hannett, Frederick James *healthcare consulting company executive*
Kerns, Wilmer Lee *researcher*

**Centreville**
Malouff, Frank Joseph *health care association executive*

**Charlottesville**
Howell, Robert Edward *hospital administrator*
Wiggins, Barbara Sue *pharmacist, educator*

**Colonial Heights**
Morgan, Barbara M. *psychotherapist, educator*

**Crozet**
Detmer, Don Eugene *health informatics, management and policy researcher*

**Culpeper**
Goddard, Frances Byrd *clinical social worker*

**Fairfax**
Drenkard, Karen Neil *nursing administrator*
Knee, Ruth Irelan (Mrs. Junior K. Knee) *social worker, health care consultant*
Mattson, Joy Louise *oncological nurse*
Meyer, David Lavon *health administration executive*

**Fairfax Station**
Barringer, Joan Marie *counselor, educator, artist, writer*

**Falls Church**
Klingman, Charles David *health facility administrator*

**Farmville**
Terry, Wayne Gilbert *healthcare educator, hospital administrator*

**Fort Lee**
Wicker, Christopher Eugene *public health service officer*

**Locust Grove**
Walsh, Geraldine Frances *nursing administrator*

**Lynchburg**
Pursley, Frank James *retired personal development specialist*

**Mc Lean**
Walsh, Marie Leclerc *nurse*

**Newport News**
Warren, Daniel Churchman *health facility administrator*

**Norfolk**
Davis, Russell Haden *psychotherapist, consultant*
Hartman, Deanna Mears *retired family counselor, addiction counselor*

**Portsmouth**
Hammond, Robie Lee *health science association administrator*

**Reston**
Di Trapani, Marcia A. *health facility administrator, community health nurse, educator*
Eldridge, Gloria Nicole *health care policy expert, researcher, financial consultant*
Gearheart, Galen Grant *pharmacist, educator*

**Richmond**
Balster, Robert Louis *alcohol/drug abuse services professional*
Barker, Thomas Carl *retired health facility administrator*
Bovender, Jack Oliver, Jr. *hospital management company executive*
Freund, Emma Frances *technologist*
Gandy, Gerald Larmon *rehabilitation counseling educator, psychologist, writer*
Massenburg, Johnnye Smith *speech pathology/audiology services professional, minister*
Neal, Gail Fallon *physical therapist, educator*
Northrop, Mary Ruth *retired mental health nurse*

**Roanoke**
Kinzie, Brenda Asburry *counselor*
Klein, Deborah Rae *nurse*

**Ruther Glen**
Unison-Pace, Wendy Jane *nursing professor*

**Springfield**
Dake, Marcia Allene *retired nursing educator, dean*
Williams, Cecilia Lee Pursel *optometrist*

**Vienna**
Kader, Nancy Stowe *nursing consultant, bioethicist, philosopher*
Welters, Anthony *health services executive*

**Virginia Beach**
Denzler, James Wyatt *pharmacist*
McDonald, Linda L. *massage therapist*
McWaters, Jeffrey L. *healthcare executive*

**Weyers Cave**
Wright, James Nash *healthcare educator, psychologist*

**Williamsburg**
Farrar, John Thruston *health facility administrator*
Ringlesbach, Dorothy Louise *retired nurse, writer*

**Winchester**
Havrda, Dawn E. *pharmacist, educator*
Kidd, Robert Scott *pharmacist, educator*
Lin, Susan Hamady *occupational therapist, educator*
Pulliam Plummer, Joyce *medical technician*

**Woodbridge**
Flori, Anna Marie DiBlasi *health facility administrator, nurse, anesthesiologist*
McMahon, Janet Mankiewich *critical care nurse*
Monaco, Anthony John *retired health facility administrator, writer*
Phillips-LeSane, Fay M. *mental health professional*

**WASHINGTON**

**Bainbridge Island**
Hart-Duling, Jean Macaulay *clinical social worker*

**Camano Island**
Hartley, Celia Love *nursing consultant, writer, retired nursing educator, nursing administrator*

**Clarkston**
Smith, Phyllis Mae *healthcare consultant, educator*

**Ellensburg**
Carrothers, Carol Ann *special education services professional, educator*

**Kent**
Dumitrescu, Cristina M. *intensive care nurse*

**Kirkland**
Brimhall, Dennis C. *hospital executive*

**Lynnwood**
Lynch, Juneann M. *medical/surgical nurse, nursing educator*

**Mukilteo**
Atal, Bishnu Saroop *retired speech research executive, educator*

**Oak Harbor**
Miller, Robert Scott *social worker, hospital administrator*

**Port Angeles**
Muller, Carolyn Bue *physical therapist, volunteer*

**Seattle**
Berni, Rosemarian Rauch *rehabilitation and oncology nurse*
Chapman, Larry Stephen *health science association administrator, consultant*
Dear, Ronald Bruce *retired social work educator*
de Tornyay, Rheba *nursing educator, retired dean*
Dorpat, Theodore Lorenz *psychoanalyst*
Hansen, Thomas Nanastad *hospital administrator, pediatrician*
Katz, Treuman P. *health facility administrator*
Law, Marcia Elizabeth *rehabilitation services professional*
Loyer Nelson, Edith Merilynn *retired social worker*
Monsen, Elaine Ranker *nutritionist, educator, editor*
Nelson, Arleen Bruce *social worker*
Sellick, Kathleen A. *hospital administrator*

**Seaview**
McNeil, Helen Jo Connolly *nursing educator, public health administrator*

**Spokane**
Baugh, Bradford Hamilton *occupational and environmental health advisor*
Robinson, Herbert Henry III *psychotherapist, educator*

**Yakima**
Simonson, Susan Kay *hospital clinical care coordinator*

**WEST VIRGINIA**

**Charles Town**
Starks, Doris N. *retired nursing educator, retired administrator*

**Charleston**
Farley Raines, Krista Nicole *health facility administrator, healthcare educator*

**Hedgesville**
Boland, Gerald Lee *health facility administrator*

**Morgantown**
Collins, James William *health science association administrator, epidemiologist, mechanical engineer*

**Parkersburg**
Wilson, Roberta Bush *retired psychotherapist, accountant*

**Ranson**
Rudacille, Sharon Victoria *medical technician*

**Wheeling**
Good, Laurance Frederic *hospital administrator*

**WISCONSIN**

**Burlington**
Oestmann, Mary Jane *retired health science association administrator*

**Columbus**
Brinkman, Michael Owen *health care consultant, educator*

**Eau Claire**
Brill, Donald Maxim *researcher, educator*

**Fond Du Lac**
Christie, Jacqueline Ann *nurse*

**Franklin**
Stenzel, Mary Francis *social worker*

**Green Bay**
McIntosh, Elaine Virginia *nutrition educator*

**Madison**
Berven, Norman Lee *counselor, psychologist, educator*
Brower, Aaron Mitchell *social worker, educator*
Derzon, Gordon M. *hospital administrator*
Johnson, Jean Elaine *nursing educator*
Marlett, Judith Ann *nutritional sciences educator, researcher*
Petty, Brian E. *speech pathology/audiology services professional, opera singer, voice educator*

**Milwaukee**
Frank, Dennis *psychotherapist, educator*
Howe, G. Edwin *healthcare executive*

**Oshkosh**
Brooks, Scott J. *rehabilitation services professional, writer*

**River Falls**
Hayden, Paul Allan *speech pathology educator, consultant, researcher*

**Seymour**
Lentz, Cherie Lynn *nurse*

**Wauwatosa**
Mancuso, Joseph Edward *medical psychotherapist*

**WYOMING**

**Ethete**
Tepper, Marcy Elizabeth *drug education director*

**Jackson Hole**
Farkas, Carol Garner *nurse, administrator*

# TERRITORIES OF THE UNITED STATES

**GUAM**

**Mangilao**
Duenas, Laurent Flores *health and nursing consultant*

**PUERTO RICO**

**Fajardo**
Millan, Alvin *speech pathology/audiology services professional, educator*

**Mayaguez**
Dika, Sandra Loree *researcher*

**VIRGIN ISLANDS**

**Charlotte Amalie**
Garfield, Winifred L. *nursing administrator*

**Christiansted**
Christian, Cora L.E *health facility administrator, physician*

# CANADA

**ALBERTA**

**Edmonton**
Fields, Anthony Lindsay Austin *health facility administrator, oncologist, educator*

**BRITISH COLUMBIA**

**Sidney**
Mann, Cedric Robert *retired health facility administrator, oceanographer*

**MANITOBA**

**Winnipeg**
Schultz, Harry *health science organization administrator*

**NEW BRUNSWICK**

**Sussex**
Secord, Lloyd Douglas *health facility administrator*

**ONTARIO**

**Etobicoke**
Scholefield, Peter Gordon *health facility administrator*

**Markham**
Burns, H(erbert) Michael *healthcare executive, director*

**Owen Sound**
Jones, Phyllis Edith *nursing educator*

**Toronto**
Turnbull, John Cameron *retired pharmacist, consultant*

## QUEBEC

**Montreal**
Messing, Karen *occupational health researcher*

## MEXICO

**Reynosa**
Asomoza, Miguel A. *researcher, educator*

## CHANNEL ISLANDS

**Guernsey**
Schere, Jean *researcher*

## ENGLAND

**London**
Berke, Joseph H. *psychotherapist*
de Savorgnani, Adriane Aldrich *healthcare administrator, nurse*

## GERMANY

**Karben**
Mansager, Erik Donn *adolescent counselor*

**Regensburg**
Jain, Manish *researcher*

## JAPAN

**Chiba**
Sakaguchi, Takehiro *healthcare educator, researcher*

**FPO**
Armendariz, Norma E. *preventive medicine technician*

**Kyoto**
Tsuji, Toshizo *hospital administrator, educator*

## LATVIA

**Riga**
Lācis, Aris *health facility administrator, cardiac surgeon*

## REPUBLIC OF KOREA

**Seoul**
Yoo, Vak Yeong *health facility administrator*

**Taegu**
Kim, Doohie *retired public health educator*

## RUSSIA

**Moscow**
Trelewicz, Jennifer Q. *researcher*

## SWITZERLAND

**Geneva**
Kim, Jim Yong *public health service officer, preventive medicine physician*
Maglacas, A. Mangay *nursing researcher, educator*

**Lugano**
Badetti, Rolando Emilio *health science facility administrator*

## ZAMBIA

**Nangoma**
Hansen, Florence Marie Congiolosi (Mrs. James S. Hansen) *social worker*

## ADDRESS UNPUBLISHED

Aalberts, Nola Jean *social worker, administrator*
Abbott, Regina A. *neurodiagnostic technologist, consultant, business owner*
Abernathy, Ronald Fittz *pharmacist*
Abu-Khalaf, Murad *researcher*
Adams, Kristin Anne *researcher*
Aehlert, Barbara June *health facility administrator*
Alberts, Renée Miller *counselor, alcohol/drug abuse services professional*
Alton, N. Kirby *health facility administrator*
Alvarez-Galloso, Roberto C. *mental health professional*
Ambersound, Rochelle Lillian *retired social worker*
Anderson, Andrea R. *health facility administrator*
Anderson, Jack Roy *healthcare company executive*
Anyanwu, Chukwukre *alcohol/drug abuse services professional*

Aon, Frank Joseph Garcia *lab administrator, materials scientist*
Arnold, Janet Nina *health facility administrator, consultant*
Austan, Frank Acosta *clinician, educator*
Austin, John H. *health care administrator*
Babao, Donna Marie *retired community health and psychiatric nurse, educator*
Babitzke, Theresa Angeline *health facility administrator*
Baier, Edward John *retired public health service officer, industrial hygiene engineer, consultant*
Bailey, Margaret Elizabeth *nurse, retired military officer*
Bailey, Suzanne Lynne *nursing educator*
Baldwin, William Russell *optometrist, foundation administrator*
Ball, John Robert *healthcare executive*
Barker, Virginia Lee *nursing educator*
Barry, Camille T. *health and human services director*
Bass, Lynda D. *retired medical/surgical nurse, nursing educator*
Baymiller, Lynda Doern *social worker*
Bear, Geraldine M. *nursing assistant, poet*
Becker, Nancy May *nursing educator*
Beckford, Omar Marien *researcher*
Bell, Rebecca *psychotherapist, journalist*
Bell, Susan Jane *nurse*
Benefield, Emily Anne *nurse, human services manager*
Bennett, Geraldine Eudora (Jerrie Bennett) *mental health services professional, nursing educator*
Bennett-Williams, Sharon K. *mental health services professional, writer*
Berger, Miriam Roskin *dance therapist, educator*
Berman, Richard Angel *health facility administrator*
Bertram, Susan *rehabilitation services professional*
Biegel, David Eli *social worker, educator*
Blair, Kathie Lynn *social worker*
Bland, Deborah Shaffer *nurse*
Blomstrand, Doreen Kathryn *retired physician assistant*
Blonz, Edward Robert *nutritionist, biochemist*
Blumberg, Mark Stuart *health service researcher, scientist, director*
Bockius, Ruth Bear *nursing educator*
Bohanon, Kathleen Sue *neonatologist*
Bollinger, Sharon Moore *psychotherapist*
Boone, Donna Clausen *physical therapist, statistician, researcher*
Borg, Ruth I. *home nursing care provider*
Bosma, Jennifer *nursing association administrator*
Boyd, Mary Frances *retired school nurse, pastor*
Braun, Mary Lucile Dekle (Lucy Braun) *physical therapist, consultant, counseling administrator, educator*
Brewer, Barbara Bagdasarian *nursing administrator*
Bronzi, Philip A. *retired social worker, educator*
Brosz, Margaret Headley *pediatrics nurse*
Brown, Alberta Mae *nurse*
Brown, April Schlea *pharmacist*
Brown, Barbara June *hospital and nursing administrator*
Brown, Billye Jean *retired nursing educator*
Brown, Geraldine *nurse, freelance writer*
Brown, Laima Adomaitis *art therapist, artist, writer*
Brown, Michael Robert *healthcare corporation executive*
Brown, Stephen Hayze, Jr. *social worker*
Brunett, Emery Walter *pharmacist, educator*
Bryant, Bertha Estelle *retired medical/surgical nurse*
Bucci, Kathryn Klavas *pharmacist, consultant*
Buckelew, Larry C. *lab administrator*
Budnicki, Michael J. *nurse*
Burch, Lori Ann *obstetrics nurse*
Büsch, Annemarie *retired mental health nurse*
Butler, Shawna Marie *medical/surgical nurse*
Campbell, Edward Wallace *nutritionist*
Campbell, Reginna Gladys *medical/surgical nurse*
Carpentieri, Sarah C. *neuropsychologist, researcher, clinical psychologist*
Carrington, Arese U. *medical doctor, public health consultant*
Carson, Regina E. *healthcare administrator, pharmacist, educator, geriatric specialist*
Carter, Melva Jean *retired medical technician*
Castleman, Breaux Ballard *health management company executive*
Cauthorne-Burnette, Tamera Dianne *family practice nurse practitioner, consultant*
Cawood, Jenny Lind *social worker, poet*
Centafont, Lucy Ann Alexander *occupational therapist, consultant*
Chait, Fay Klein *health administrator*
Chambers-Steinberg, Wanda *researcher*
Chang, Debbie I-Ju *health programs and research executive, director*
Chapman, Thomas William *hospital executive*
Chow, Rita Kathleen *nursing consultant*
Christiansen, David K. *health facility administrator*
Cochrane, Lorna June *health science association administrator, consultant*
Cohen, Carolyn A. *healthcare educator*
Cohen, Lawrence Alan *health facility administrator*
Collins, Joy *nurse, consultant, writer*
Condry, Robert Stewart *retired hospital administrator*
Conte, Julie Villa *nurse, administrator*
Cooper, Eugene Bruce *speech pathology/audiology services professional, educator*
Couch, Daniel Michael *healthcare executive*
Cox, John Curtis *health facility administrator*
Crispin, Patricia Lynnette *social worker*
Crocker, Barbara Jean *clinical nurse specialist*
Croft, Kathryn Delaine *social worker, consultant*
Cromwell, Florence Stevens *occupational therapist*
Culton, Paul Melvin *retired counselor, educational administrator, interpreter*
Daly, Janis J. *physical therapist, researcher*
Dawson, Brandie *nurse, nursing consultant*
Dawson, Karen Oltmanns *forensic nurse, childbirth educator*
De Antoni, Edward Paul *lab administrator*

Deely, Maureen Cecelia *community health nurse*
Deiro, Judith Anne *chemical dependency educator*
DeLapp, Tina Davis *retired nursing educator*
DeVore, Kimberly K. *healthcare executive*
Dickens, Joyce Rebecca *addictions therapist, educator*
Dickerson, Cheryl Anne *counselor*
Dimaira, Ann B. *medical/surgical nurse*
Dincecco, Jennie Elizabeth Williams Swanson *healthcare administrator, mentor, educator, volunteer*
DiPaolo, Sonja Jean *retired nurse*
Doberenz, Alexander R. *retired nutrition educator, chemist*
Dogoloff, Lee Israel *clinical social worker, psychotherapist, consultant*
Dorman, Arthur *optometrist, state legislator*
Doucette, Betty *public and community health and geriatrics nurse*
Douglas, Janice Green *physician, educator*
Drews, Jürgen *pharmaceutical researcher*
Duel, Ward Calvin *retired healthcare consultant*
Duffy, Mary Kathleen *neonatal nurse*
Dumas, Sandra Lee *medical technician, microbiologist*
Durkee, Dianna *medical/surgical nurse*
Dyer, Wayne Walter *psychologist, writer, radio and television personality*
Dy-Liacco, Gabriel S. *psychotherapist*
Eaton, Shirley M. *medical/surgical nurse*
Edelsberg, Sally Comins *physical therapist, educator*
Edelstein, Rosemarie (Rosemarie Hublou) *medical/surgical nurse, educator, geriatrics nurse*
Elkins, Robert N. *association executive*
Ellis, Janice Rider *nursing educator, consultant*
Eltayeb, Emil *pharmacist, researcher*
Emano, Dennis M. *psychotherapist, educator*
English, Patricia Dorzell *women's health nurse practitioner*
Erenstein, Alan *emergency nurse practitioner*
Faiz, Alexandria *researcher, writer*
Fawcett, Mary Louise *counselor, educator*
Feigal, David W., Jr. *health science association administrator*
Finder-Stone, Patricia Ann *nursing educator, volunteer*
Fine, David Jeffrey *hospital administrator, educator*
Finley, Sarah Maude Merritt *retired social worker*
Fischer, Carl Robert *retired health facility administrator*
Fleksher, Cassandra C. *psychology and research rehabilitation professional*
Floyd, William R. *former health facility administrator*
Fogelman, Ann Florence *nutrition consultant, educator, researcher*
Fondiller, Shirley Hope Alperin *nursing educator, journalist, historian*
Ford-Reed, Lillie Mae *geriatrics services professional*
Forest, Eva Brown *health facility administrator, composer*
Forsyth, George Lionel *psychotherapist, author*
Fountain, Linda Kathleen *health science association executive*
Fralix Gold, Carolyn M. *medical/surgical nurse, educator, consultant*
Franklin-Griffin, Cathy Lou Hinson *nursing educator*
Fuke, Dawn C. *clinical pharmacy specialist*
Fuller, Richard Kenneth *retired alcohol/drug abuse services professional*
Gable, Karen Elaine *healthcare educator*
Garcia y Carrillo, Martha Xochitl *pharmacist*
Garner, Algean, II, *healthcare company administrator, consultant*
Garza, Cutberto *nutrition educator*
Gavin, Mary Jane *retired medical/surgical nurse*
Gerry, Debra Prue *psychotherapist, recording artist, writer*
Gladden, Vivianne Cervantes *healthcare consultant, writer*
Glynn, Peter Alexander Richard *health facility administrator, consultant*
Godager, Jane Ann *retired social worker*
Goldberg, Edwin *rehabilitation specialist, consultant, interfaith clergyman*
Gonzales, Richard Robert *counselor*
Goodman, Robert Lee *nursing administrator*
Gordon, Marc Stewart *pharmacist, research scientist*
Gottlieb, Gary L. *hospital administrator*
Govan, Gladys Vernita Mosley *retired critical care nurse, medical/surgical nurse*
Graham, Olive Jane *retired medical/surgical nurse*
Grant, Richard Earl *retired medical and legal consultant*
Greenfield, Linda Sue *nursing educator*
Greggs, Elanora *social worker*
Grenier, Laura Margiotta *medical/surgical nurse*
Grise-Owens, Erlene Y. *social worker, educator*
Grolli, Frank Thomas *retired pharmacist*
Gromacki, Susan Jean *optometrist*
Guichard, Susan Weil *dietician, consultant*
Hackbarth, Glenn M. *human services administrator*
Hansen-Kyle, Linda L *counselor, nursing educator*
Harbaugh, Jeanne M. *counselor, consultant*
Hardin, Bridgette Everhart *educational research analyst*
Harms, Nancy Ann *nursing educator*
Hartford, Michael Wayne *health facility administrator*
Harwell, Denise *researcher*
Hays, Patrick Gregory *healthcare executive*
Healy, Patricia Colleen *social worker*
Heatherley, James Lawrence *psychotherapist, educator*
Henneman, Stephen Charles *psychotherapist*
Henry, Sue *social worker, educator*
Hertz, Kenneth Theodore *healthcare executive*
Hickman, Lucille *physical therapist*
Hines, Colleen M. *clinical nurse specialist*
Hoeffer, Beverly *nursing educator, researcher*
Hofmann, Paul Bernard *healthcare consultant*
Hope, Carol J. *pharmacist, researcher, information technology manager*

Horsley, Heidi *psychotherapist, educator, radio personality*
Hoskins, Carol Noll *nursing educator, researcher*
Houtz, Duane Talbot *hospital administrator*
Howe, John Prentice III *health facility administrator, physician*
Huey, Constance Anne Berner *mental health counselor*
Hui, Sai-Hung *emergency medical professional*
Hurley, Kathy Lee *mental health services professional, director*
Ignagni, Karen *healthcare association executive*
Inscho, Jean Anderson *retired social worker, landscape artist*
Isong, Enó *public health service officer*
Jackson-Tkac, Stephanie Ann *nurse*
Jacobs, Arthur Dietrich *health services executive, educator, researcher*
Jacobson, Harry Rudolf *hospital administrator, physician*
Jacoby, Erika *social worker*
Janke, Norma E. *nursing consultant*
Jarvis, Irene *retired medical/surgical nurse*
Jennings, Kathryn Mary *alcohol/drug abuse services professional*
Jensen, Eva Marie *medical/surgical nurse*
Jessup, R. Judd *health science association administrator*
Johnson, Doris Jean *social worker*
Johnson, June Alexis *counselor, social worker*
Johnson, Nichole Sharese *school nurse practitioner, basketball coach*
Johnson, Sally A. *nurse, educator*
Johnson, Summer *researcher, policy administrator*
Johnson, Van R. *health facility administrator*
Johnson-Moran, Kelly Kathleen *health facility administrator, writer*
Jones, David Allen *retired health benefits company executive*
Jones, Jolene Rebecca *medical transcriptionist, educator*
Jones, Lisa Maria Draper *counselor*
Jones Tergeoglou, Beverly Gloria *special education services professional*
Jordan, Deovina Nasis *nursing administrator*
Joseph, Eleanor Ann *health science association administrator, consultant*
Kadoguchi, Susan Sanaye *retired technologist, retired cytotechnologist*
Kahol, Kanav *researcher*
Kaiser, Nina Irene *health care consultant*
Karp, Rosanne *oncology and women's health nurse*
Kelly, Lucie Stirm Young *nursing educator*
Kerr, Frederick Hohmann *retired health facility administrator, retired academic administrator*
Kim, Eunyoung *researcher*
King, Imogene M. *retired nursing educator*
King, Sheldon Selig *health facility administrator, educator*
Kiszka, Sonia Ann *nurse practitioner, educator*
Kline, Leona Ruth *nurse, volunteer*
Kline-Koenig, Barbara A. *medical/surgical nurse*
Klotter, Eleanor Irene *retired social worker*
Knies, Robert Carl, Jr. *critical care nurse*
Kohn, Jean Gatewood *retired health facility administrator, pediatrician*
Kopec-Garnett, Linda *nursing administrator, researcher*
Kott, Alexander *technologist, researcher*
Kretchmar, Leslie *medical/surgical nurse*
Kruger, Nancy R. *university program director, nurse*
Kuhler, Deborah Gail *grief therapist, retired state legislator*
Kuo, Chun-Fang Frank *counselor, educator*
Lamberton, Jacquelyn Edmunds *retired psychotherapist*
Langenkamp, Sandra Carroll *retired human services administrator*
Larson, Richard Everett *lab administrator*
Lass, Diane *counselor*
Latiolais, Minnie Fitzgerald *retired nurse, health facility administrator*
La Torre, Carissa Danitza *counselor*
Latta, George Haworth III *neonatal/perinatal nurse practitioner*
Lee, Chava Cherta *psychotherapist, consultant*
Lee, Sarena Janeen *public health service officer*
Lee, Tamara Denise *health facility administrator, educator*
Leichtman, Maria Luisa *mental health services professional*
Leigh, Vincenta M. *health administrator*
Leininger, Madeleine Monica *nursing educator, consultant, retired anthropologist, editor, writer, theorist*
L'Eplattenier, Nora Sweeny Hickey *nursing educator*
Levin, Arnold Murray *social worker, psychotherapist, educator*
Lilly-Hersley, Jane Anne Feeley *nursing researcher*
Lindstrom, Rosetta Arline *retired medical technician*
Lippincott, Jonathan Ramsay *healthcare executive*
Loarie, Thomas Merritt *healthcare executive*
Logan, David Bruce *health facility administrator, nurse*
Loop, Floyd D. *retired healthcare executive*
Lubic, Ruth Watson *health facility administrator, nurse midwife*
Luce, Donald Sanders *social worker*
Lyngbye, Jørgen *hospital advisor, researcher*
Lynn, Julia Carolyn *school nurse practitioner*
Lyons, Anthony Patrick *acoustician, acoustical engineer, researcher*
Lysne, Allen Bruce *laboratory director*
Mackay, Leo Sidney, Jr. *healthcare company executive, former federal agency administrator*
MacKenzie, Donald Murray *health facility administrator*
Magill, Rosalind May *psychotherapist*
Maiolini, Gloria J. *nursing case manager, poet, writer*
Majors, Nelda Faye *physical therapist*
Malin, Harold Martin, Jr. *sexologist, educator*
Malks, Betty F. *social worker*
Maplesden, Carol Harper *marriage and family therapist, music educator*
Marchan, Marissa L. *social worker*

Marcinek, Margaret Ann *nursing education administrator*
Marcoux, Julia A. *midwife*
Markle, Cheri Virginia Cummins *nurse*
Martin, Karen Siebenthal *community health nurse*
Maslanka, Sandra Karen *social worker, educator, educational consultant*
Materia, Kathleen Patricia Ayling *nurse*
Mates, Lawrence A., II, *medical company executive, consultant*
Matterson, Joan McDevitt *physical therapist*
McCuistion, Peg Orem *retired health facility administrator*
McEvoy, Lorraine Katherine *oncology nurse*
McNulty, Kathleen Anne *social worker, consultant, psychotherapist*
Medina, Sandra *social worker, educator*
Mestel, Sherry Y. *social worker, school psychologist, art therapist*
Mewani, Rajshree R.(amchand) *researcher*
Michael, Jerrold Mark *public health service officer, educator, retired dean*
Micozzi, Marc Stephen *health executive, physician, educator*
Milewski, Barbara Anne *pediatrics nurse, neonatal/perinatal nurse practitioner, critical care nurse*
Miller, Eunice A. *marriage and family therapist, sex therapist, foundation administrator*
Milnor, Hazel *nurse*
Milunas, J. Robert *health care organization executive*
Minahan, Jessica Angela *special education services professional*
Miracle, Doris Jean *retired medical/surgical nurse*
Misner, Lorraine *lab administrator*
Moenssens, Sandra Birkelbach *marriage and family therapist, counselor, consultant*
Momah, Ethel Chukwuekwe *retired women's health nurse*
Monck, Maureen F. *psychoanalyst*
Moore, Jean E. *social worker, academic administrator, educator, radio personality*
Morgan, Evelyn Buck *retired nursing educator*
Moses, Sheila Johnson *nurse, bookkeeper*
Murphy, Margaret A. *nursing educator, adult nurse practitioner*
Murray, Julia Kaoru (Mrs. Joseph E. Murray) *occupational therapist*
Myer, Mary Elizabeth *researcher*
Nakagawa, Allen Donald *radiologic technologist*
Nardozzi, Peter Michael *pharmacist, clinical educator, lecturer, entrepreneur*
Nashif, Taysir N. *researcher, writer*
Nelson, Alice Carlstedt *retired nursing educator*
Neumann, Forrest Karl *retired health facility administrator*
Newton, Elizabeth Purcell *counselor, consultant, writer*
Nichols, Elizabeth Grace *nursing educator, dean*
Nichols, Laurie I. *nurse*
Nickel, Janet Marlene Milton *retired geriatrics nurse*
Nidetz, Myron Philip *health care delivery systems consultant*
Nisbet, Toma A. *nursing administrator*
Norbeck, Jane S. *retired nursing educator*
Norkin, Cynthia Clair *retired physical therapist*
O'Baire-Kark, Marika *nurse, educator, poet, writer*
Oerter, Cynthia Lynn *medical technologist*
Oksiloff, Christa *technologist, educator*
Oliver, Ronald *retired medical technologist*
Onufrock, Richard Shade *retired pharmacist*
Orr, Steven R. *health facility administrator*
Pantoja, Juan Luis *hospital administrator, educator*
Paparella, Leon Ralph *psychotherapist, consultant*
Paps, Betty Lou *nursing educator*
Parham, Ellen Speiden *nutrition educator*
Parker, Joel Louise *nursing administrator*
Parker, Susan Brooks *health facility administrator*
Parks, Jean Anne *retired acute care nurse*
Parrish, Stephen B. *psychotherapist*
Pastula, Leah Lynn *mental health services professional*
Penachio, Anthony Joseph, Jr. *psychotherapist, hypnotherapist, behavioral therapist*
Peringian, Lynda Ann *dietician, writer*
Peters, Carol Ann Dudycha *counselor*
Phanstiel, Howard G. *managed healthcare company executive*
Phillipe, Chester Tolleson *alcohol/drug abuse services professional, educator*
Phillips, Caroline L. *lab administrator*
Pieknik, Rebecca Anne *technologist, educator*
Pilous, Betty Scheibel *medical/surgical nurse*
Pipchick, Margaret Hopkins *advance practice psychiatric nurse, marriage and family therapist*
Plauche, Nancy Caroline *retired counselor*
Poe, Laura *nursing educator, administrator*
Poepping-Faulkner, Michele Ann *pharmacist, educator*
Poulos, Clara Jean *nutritionist*
Price, Alicia Hemmalin *retired psychotherapist, alcohol/drug abuse services professional*
Price, Donna B. *special education services professional*
Przybylski, Sandra Marie *speech pathologist*
Quattrone-Carroll, Diane Rose *clinical social worker*
Quiala, Maribel *psychotherapist, consultant*
Quirino, Pedro *counselor*
Rahming, Etta Lorraine *social worker, consultant, psychotherapist, counseling administrator*
Rajupalepu, Rahi K. *technologist, consultant*
Rand, Joella Mae *retired nursing educator, counselor*
Randolph, Donald Phillip *nurse anesthetist*
Ransom, Angela Dawn *nurse*
Ratliff, Kimberlee Michelle *counselor*
Ray, Carol Reneé *allied health professional*
Ray, Marilyn Anne *nursing educator, researcher*
Reck, Elizabeth Torre *social worker, educator*
Reece, Sheila Marlene *health facility administrator, writer*
Rehth, Ann *counselor*
Reilly, Robert Joseph *counselor*
Remkus, Connie Elaine *nutritional consultant*
Richburg, Billy Keith *healthcare manager, consultant, entrepreneur*
Rigan, Karwyn E. *speech pathology/audiology services professional*

Ritter, Elise Dawn *therapist, clinical social worker, writer, artist, photographer*
Robinson, Gail Patricia *retired mental health counselor*
Rodriguez, Donna Jeanne Anglin *dietician, writer*
Rogers, Elizabeth London *retired geriatrics services professional*
Rollins, Diann Elizabeth *occupational health nurse, primary school educator*
Romano, Joseph Anthony *healthcare education and marketing consultant*
Royce, Paul Chadwick *healthcare administrator*
Rubin, Phyllis Getz *health association executive*
Runnells, Barbara Ann *technologist*
Ruzek, Sheryl Kendra Burt *healthcare educator, sociologist*
Ryan-Halley, Charlotte Muriel *oncology clinical specialist, family practice nurse practitioner*
Sabatini, Nelson John *healthcare executive*
Sadow, Harvey S. *healthcare company executive*
Salerno, Sister Maria *nursing educator, advanced practice nurse*
Salvanto, Maria *counselor*
Samolyk, Keith Andrew *cardiovascular perfusionist, director*
Samuels, Marc *healthcare consultant*
Sandorsen, Cassiopeia *public health service officer*
Santina, Dalia *nutritionist, writer, skin care specialist*
Saracino, Dawn M. *physical therapist, educator*
Sastrowardoyo, Teresita Manejar *nurse*
Scala, James *health facility administrator, consultant, writer*
Schneider, Catherine Chemin *occupational therapist, consultant*
Schumann, Gay Lee *special education services professional, consultant*
Schutzer, Karen Ann *nurse*
Sears, Sandra Jones *medical/surgical nurse, consultant*
Seelman, Katherine Dolores *institute administrator*
Shannon, Mary Lou *adult health nursing educator*
Sheehan, Sophia Ann *marriage and family therapist, director*
Shen, Shihui *research assistant*
Shiao, Shyang-Yun Pamela K. *nursing educator*
Simmons, Deborah Jo *pharmacist, director*
Simms, Maria Ester *health facility administrator*
Simon, Bernece Kern *retired social worker*
Simpson, Jack Benjamin *medical technologist, business executive*
Simpson, John Noel (Virginia Simpson) *health facility administrator*
Sims, Elizabeth LaNeal *healthcare association executive*
Slaughter, Djuanique Naté *healthcare analyst, project manager, consultant*
Smith, Barbara Anne *health facility administrator, consultant*
Smith, Leslie Roper *hospital administrator, health facility administrator*
Sneider, Joyce Pappachristou *dietician, educator*
Snyder (Mackley), Louise Marie *speech pathology/audiology services professional, consultant*
Somes, Joan Marie *critical care nurse*
Sommerfeld, Marianna *retired social worker, writer*
Sondik, Edward J. *health science administrator*
Souza, Lawrence M. *health facility administrator*
Speer, Nancy Girouard *health facility administrator*
Stack, Robert Timothy *health facility administrator*
Stancil, Irene Mack *family counselor*
Stark, Altreca *admissions counselor*
Stash, Susan Michele *critical care nurse*
Steed, Airica Danita *medical/surgical nurse, consultant*
Stopler, Tracy *dietician, educator*
Storm, J. Reni *nurse, consultant*
Stoutenburg, Jane Sue Williamson *nurse practitioner, fund raiser, actress*
Stratton, Mariann *retired military nursing executive*
Stupak, Mary Jo *psychotherapist, educator*
Stutzman, Sandra Louise *advanced nurse practitioner*
Suber, Robin Hall *former medical and surgical nurse*
Sugintas, Nora Maria *healthcare executive*
Svoboda, Janice June *nurse*
Swann, Charena Rai *psychotherapist, social worker*
Tack, Theresa Rose *women's health nurse*
Talento-Miller, Eileen *psychometrician*
Tanguay, Jeanne Marie *social worker*
Tanner, Peggy *retired nurse*
Tatum, Jerry Lee *researcher*
Taylor, Cora Hodge *social worker*
Taylor, Nathalee Britton *retired nutritionist, freelance/self-employed writer*
Thomas, Cheryl Shanks *public health service officer*
Thompson, Claire Louisa *nurse, educator, consultant*
Tingstrum, Nancy Ash *dietitian*
Tolliver, Glenda Reeder *social worker*
Tompkins, Christopher Paul *researcher*
Tracy, Susanne Mary *nursing researcher, educator*
Trejos, Franklin Anthony *retired physician assistant*
Tripodi, Tony *retired social worker, retired dean, editor, writer*
Tyson, Lucille R. *health facility administrator, geriatrics nurse*
Udrys, Almis Gerardas *health policy consultant*
Van de Bogart, Debra Scherwerts *medical/surgical nurse, researcher*
Vogel, H. Victoria *psychotherapist, educator, writer, stress disorder and addiction recovery counselor*
Vohs, James Arthur *health facility administrator*
Vyn, Eleanor Mears *physical therapist*
Waggoner, Kathleen Alice *psychotherapist*
Walker, Henry Gilbert *health care executive, consultant*
Wallace, Desiree *investigational drug pharmacist, pharmacy educator*
Wallskog, Joyce Marie *nursing educator, retired psychologist*

Wantz, Kathy Lynn Zepp *school nurse*
Warfel, M(artha) Kay *speech pathology/audiology services professional*
Warner, Tokesha L. *health facility administrator*
Watson, Robert Joe *retired health facility administrator, retired career officer*
Wei, Dong *technologist*
Weickert, Wanda Opal *child welfare and attendance counselor, psychotherapist, educator*
Weil, Thomas P. *retired health services consultant*
Weiner, Anne Lee *social worker*
Weng, Daniella *pharmacist, researcher*
Westberry, Paula I. *nursing administrator*
White, Eugene Vaden *retired pharmacist*
White, Sarah Jowilliard *retired counselor*
Wickham, Dianne *nursing administrator*
Wiebe, Leonard Irving *pharmacist, educator*
Wieland, William Dean *healthcare consulting executive*
Williams, Betty Jean *medical/surgical nurse*
Williams, Elizabeth *human services administrator*
Williams, Shannon Renee *mental health services professional*
Williams Maddox-Brown, Janice Helen *nurse*
Wish, LeslieBeth Berger *psychotherapist, writer, management consultant*
Wolfberg, Melvin Donald *optometrist, educational association administrator, consultant*
Wooldridge, Stephen Craig *health facility administrator*
Wormser, Sherri Lynne *pediatric physical therapist*
Woteki, Catherine Ellen *nutritionist*
Wright, Dell *residential care and treatment facility executive*
Wyche, Ruth Skyler *rehabilitation contractor, researcher*
Yadrick, Robert Martin *occupational analyst*
Yale (Yeleyenide-Yale), Melpomene Fotine *researcher, anthropologist, archaeologist, art historian, conservator*
Yarbrough, Kathryn Davis *public health nurse*
Zhu, Carolyn Wei *healthcare educator*
Ziegenhagen, David Mackenzie *retired health facility administrator, not-for-profit developer*
Zimmerman, Jo Ann *retired health science association administrator, educator, retired lieutenant governor*

## HEALTHCARE: MEDICINE

### UNITED STATES

### ALABAMA

**Alexander City**
Tyler, Eric Owen *pediatrician*

**Auburn**
Parsons, Daniel Lankester *pharmaceutics educator*

**Birmingham**
Ambalavanan, Namasivayam *neonatologist, educator*
Andrews, James R. *orthopedic surgeon*
Bittner, Vera *cardiologist*
Briggs, Dick Dowling, Jr. *physician, educator*
Bueschen, Anton Joslyn *physician, educator*
Caulfield, James Benjamin *pathologist, educator*
Childs, Alex Joseph *gynecologist*
Clayton, Orville Woolford *surgeon*
Cooper, Max Dale *pediatrician, researcher*
Curtis, John J. *medical educator*
Diethelm, Arnold Gillespie *surgeon*
Elewski, Boni Elizabeth *dermatologist, educator*
Finley, Wayne House *medical educator*
Fleming, William Cary *retired physician, retired consultant*
Gaston, Robert Samuel *internist, nephrologist, consultant*
Greene, Ernest Rinaldo, Jr. *anesthesiologist, chemical engineer*
Griffin, Charles Roland *surgeon*
Hirschowitz, Basil Isaac *physician*
Johnston, Carden *emergency physician, pediatrician, educator*
Kimberly, Robert Parker *medical educator*
Kingsley, John Raymond *surgeon*
Kirby, Russell Stephen *epidemiologist, researcher, geographer*
Kirchner, John Shirk *orthopedic surgeon*
Koopman, William James *medical educator, internist, immunologist*
Meezan, Elias *pharmacologist, educator*
Oakes, Walter Jerry *pediatric neurosurgeon*
Omura, George Adolf *medical oncologist*
Oparil, Suzanne *cardiologist, researcher, educator*
Pittman, Constance Shen *endocrinologist, educator*
Pittman, James Allen, Jr. *endocrinologist, educator*
Rich, Robert Regier *physician, medical educator, immunologist*
Russell, Richard Olney, Jr. *cardiologist, educator*
Sauer, Paul Frederick *plastic surgeon*
Schmitt, Lee Aubrey *surgeon*
Shehi, Lyle Edward, Jr. *psychiatrist*
Siegel, Herrick Jove *orthopedic surgeon*
Stevenson, Edward Ward *retired otolaryngologist, surgeon*
Trigg, Jack Walden, Jr. *retired physician*
Volanakis, John Emmanuel *immunologist, rheumatologist*

**Cullman**
Morris, Sylvia June Burbank *retired physician*

**Fairhope**
Mozley, Paul David *retired obstetrics and gynecology educator*

**Huntsville**
Dunegan, Deason C. *plastic surgeon*
Huber, Donald Simon *physician*
Johnson, John D., Jr. *neurosurgeon*
Nuessle, William Raymond *surgeon*

Tietke, Wilhelm *gastroenterologist, educator*

**Mobile**
Atkinson, William James, Jr. *retired cardiologist*
Brogdon, Byron Gilliam *radiologist, educator*
DeBakey, Ernest George *physician, surgeon*
Hariadi, John Wesley *otolaryngologist, surgeon*
Littleton, Jesse Talbot III *radiology educator*
Rodning, Charles Bernard *surgeon*
Scantlebury, Velma Patricia *surgeon*
Smith, Jesse Graham, Jr. *dermatologist, educator*
Wertelecki, Wladimir *pediatrician, educator*

**Montgomery**
Adams, Robert Barry *pathologist*
Frazer, David Hugh, Jr. *allergist*
Myers, Ira Lee *physician*

**Opelika**
Lightfoote, William Edward *neurologist*

**Orange Beach**
Conrad, Marcel Edward *hematologist, educator*

**Spanish Fort**
Benjamin, Regina Marcia *physician, administrator*

**Tuscaloosa**
Keeton, J. E. *retired psychiatrist*
Pieroni, Robert Edward *internist, educator, military officer*
Sinclair, Robert Ewald *retired physician*

**Tuskegee Institute**
Casimire-Etzioni, Athema Louise *veterinary pathologist*

**Vestavia**
Nuckols, Frank Joseph *psychiatrist*

### ALASKA

**Anchorage**
Christensen, Ronald E. *physician*
Mills, William James, Jr. *orthopedist, surgeon, researcher*

### ARIZONA

**Carefree**
Hook, William Franklin *radiologist*

**Green Valley**
Moser, Robert Harlan *internist, educator, writer*

**Mesa**
Cooley, Jack Crain *surgeon, cardiologist*
Hagen, Nicholas Stewart *medical educator, consultant*

**Paradise Valley**
Burkholder, Peter Miller *retired physician, educator*
Hale, Harry William *retired surgeon, educator*
Lorenzen, Robert Frederick *ophthalmologist*
Targovnik, Selma E. Kaplan *retired dermatologist*

**Phoenix**
Ammon, John Richard *anesthesiologist*
Charlton, John Kipp *pediatrician*
Friedman, Shelly Arnold *cosmetic surgeon*
Guerra, Aldo Benjamin *plastic surgeon, cosmetic surgeon*
Hendin, Barry Allen *physician*
Khan, Mohammed Yousuf *physician, consultant*
Laufer, Nathan *cardiologist*
Lovett, William Lee *surgeon*
Modny, Cynthia Jean *dermatologist*
Reed, Wallace Allison *anesthesiologist*
Sage, Webster LeGene, Jr. *ophthalmologist*
Singer, Jeffrey Alan *surgeon*
Stern, Stanley *psychiatrist*
Teague, Robert Cole *physician*
Underwood, Paul Lester *cardiologist*
Von Hoff, Daniel Douglas *oncologist*
Wright, Richard Oscar III *pathologist, educator, clinical ethicist*
Zerella, Joseph T. *retired pediatric surgeon*

**Prescott**
Garcia-Buñuel, Luis *neurologist*

**Rio Verde**
Culligan, John Austin *thoracic surgeon*

**Scottsdale**
Chaurasia, Vishal *physician, writer*
Chikly, Bruno Jacques *osteopath physician*
Dahl, Mark Victor *dermatologist, educator*
Daniel, William Walter, Jr. *radiologist*
Evans, Tommy Nicholas *obstetrician, gynecologist, educator*
Gibney, John *plastic surgeon, consultant, medical researcher*
Gregory, Robert Erb *surgeon*
Harrison, Nedra Joyce *surgeon*
Hecht, Frederick *pediatrician, medical geneticist, researcher, consultant, writer, editor*
Heppell, Jacques Philippe *surgeon, educator*
Kinney, Carolyn *physician*
Leighton, William D. *plastic and reconstructive surgeon*
Levin, Warren Mayer *family practice physician*
Lewis, John Christopher *allergist*
Morrison, Donald Nick *surgeon*
Orford, Robert Raymond *physician, consultant*
Parish, James Michael *medical educator*
Patel, Naresh Pratap *medical educator, physician, consultant*
Reznick, Richard Howard *pediatrician*
Roarke, Michael Charles *medical educator, nuclear medicine physician*
Roberts, Catherine C. *radiologist, educator*
Sanderson, David R. *physician*
Shors, Clayton Marion *retired cardiologist*
Steier, Jeffrey David *neurologist*
Tazelaar, Henry Dale *physician, educator*

**Sedona**
Briney, Allan King *retired radiologist*
Hawkins, David Ramon *psychiatrist, writer, researcher, spiritual teacher*
Metzner, Richard Joel *psychiatrist, psychopharmacologist, educator*

**Sun City**
Chokshi, Parag H. *gastroenterologist, internist*
Nicchi, Vincent, Jr. *cardiologist*

**Tempe**
Anand, Suresh Chandra *physician*
Herald, Cherry Lou *medical researcher, educator*
Playford, Nancy Jean *medical association administrator*
Schneller, Eugene Stewart *health administration and policy educator*

**Tonopah**
Pallin, Samuel Lear *ophthalmologist, educator, medical director*

**Tubac**
Pardue, A. Michael *retired plastic and reconstructive surgeon*

**Tucson**
Ablin, Richard Joel *immunologist, educator*
Alpert, Joseph Stephen *cardiologist, educator*
Capp, Michael Paul *pediatrician, educator*
Corrigan, James John, Jr. *pediatrician, educator, dean*
Dalen, James Eugene *cardiologist, educator*
DeLuca, Dominick *medical educator, researcher*
Ewy, Gordon Allen *cardiologist, researcher, educator*
Favre, Kelly Ann *surgeon*
Graham, Anna Regina *pathologist, educator*
Hattery, Robert Ralph *radiologist, educator*
Hoffert, Paul Washington *surgeon*
Houser, Harold Byron *epidemiologist*
Hughes, John Harold *surgeon, educator*
Katakkar, Suresh Balaji *hematologist, oncologist*
King, Joseph Willet *child psychiatrist*
Kischer, Clayton Ward *human embryologist, educator*
Levenson, Alan Ira *psychiatrist, physician, educator*
Marchalonis, John Jacob *immunologist, educator*
Marcus, Frank Isadore *cardiologist, educator*
Martin, Loren Winston *allergist*
Meislin, Harvey Warren *emergency healthcare physician, professional society administrator*
Quan, Stuart Fun *internist, educator*
Rogers, Lee Frank *radiologist*
Russell, Findlay Ewing *physician*
Ryan, Kenneth J. *immunologist, educator*
Sibley, William Austin *neurologist, educator*
Weil, Andrew Thomas *physician, educator*
Woolfenden, James Manning *nuclear medicine physician, educator*
Woosley, Raymond *pharmacologist, educator*

**Vail**
Reichlin, Seymour *endocrinologist, educator*

**Yuma**
Anderson, John Albert *physician*

## ARKANSAS

**El Dorado**
Tommey, Charles Eldon *retired surgeon*

**Fayetteville**
Fink, William James *retired surgeon*

**Fort Smith**
Coleman, Michael Dortch *nephrologist*
Howell, James Tennyson *allergist, immunologist, pediatrician*
Snider, James Rhodes *radiologist*

**Helena**
Kontos, George John, Jr. *surgeon*

**Jonesboro**
Jones, Kenneth Bruce *surgeon*

**Little Rock**
Bruce, Thomas Allen *physician, educator*
Campbell, Gilbert Sadler *surgeon, educator*
Hart, Ronald Wilson *radiobiologist, educator, toxicologist, business adviser*
Hough, Aubrey Johnston, Jr. *pathologist, physician, educator*
Jansen, G. Thomas *dermatologist*
Jaquiss, Robert Douglas Benjamin *pediatric cardiac surgeon*
Lang, Nicholas Paul *surgeon*
Liem, Pham H. *geriatrician*
Lucy, Dennis Durwood, Jr. *neurologist, educator*
Mrak, Robert Emil *neuropathologist, educator*
O'Brien, Mark Stephen *pediatric neurosurgeon*
Olden, Kevin William *medical researcher*
Raza, Asim *psychiatrist*
Safirstein, Robert Louis *nephrologist, medical educator, medical researcher*
Sotomora-von Ahn, Ricardo Federico *pediatrician, educator*
Ward, Harry Pfeffer *hematologist, retired academic administrator*

**North Little Rock**
Clothier, Jeffrey Lane *neuropsychiatrist, educator*

**Scranton**
Uzman, Betty Ben Geren *retired pathologist*

**Springdale**
Rosenschein, Guy Raoul *pediatric and visceral surgeon, airline pilot*

## CALIFORNIA

**Agoura Hills**
deCiutiis, Alfred Charles Maria *oncologist, television producer*

**Alameda**
Chen, Arthur *physician, hospital administrator*
Whorton, M. Donald *physician, epidemiologist*

**Aliso Viejo**
Kizer, Kenneth Wayne *emergency physician, medical educator, physician executive*

**Anaheim**
Glazer, Sidney *physician, director*

**Arroyo Grande**
Grisez, James Louis *physician, plastic surgeon*

**Auburn**
Henrikson, Donald Merle *forensic pathologist*

**Bakersfield**
Prunes, Fernando *plastic surgeon, educator*
Sio, Jimmy Ong *embryologist*

**Baldwin Park**
Feng, Mark I. *urologist, surgeon*

**Belvedere**
Wallerstein, Robert Solomon *retired psychiatrist*

**Belvedere Tiburon**
Behrman, Richard Elliot *pediatrician, dean*
Fishman, Robert Allen *retired neurologist, educator, department chair*
Hoffman, Julien Ivor Ellis *pediatrician, educator, cardiologist*

**Berkeley**
Abel, Carlos Alberto *immunologist*
Buffler, Patricia Ann *epidemiologist, educator, dean*
Coffin, Grange Simons *pediatrician*
Diamond, Marian Cleeves *anatomist, educator*
Duhl, Leonard J. *psychiatrist, educator*
Grossman, Elmer Roy *pediatrician*
Reingold, Arthur Lawrence *epidemiologist, educator*
Tempelis, Constantine Harry *immunologist, educator*
Troxel, David B. *pathologist*
Winkelstein, Warren, Jr. *physician, educator*

**Beverly Hills**
Arieff, Allen Ives *physician*
Bao, Katherine Sung *pediatric cardiologist*
Caster, Andrew Ian *ophthalmologist*
Catz, Boris *endocrinologist, educator*
Fein, William *ophthalmologist*
Fisher, Garth (Donald Garth Fisher) *plastic surgeon*
Golshani, S. Daniel *plastic surgeon*
Haworth, Randal Digby *plastic surgeon*
Hofbauer, John D. *ophthalmologist*
Karpman, Harold Lew *cardiologist, educator, writer*
Klein, Arnold William *dermatologist*
Kotler, Robert *cosmetic surgeon*
Markman, Ronald Abraham *psychiatrist, lawyer*
Marshak, Harry *plastic surgeon*
Menkes, John Hans *pediatric neurologist*
Moelleken, Brent Roderick Wilfred *surgeon*
Nackel, John George *medical association administrator*
Palmer, Francis Roger III *plastic surgeon*
Perlman, Jon Arthur *plastic surgeon*
Rey, Robert M. *plastic surgeon*
Rosenthal, Richard Jay *psychiatrist*
Ryan, Frank Harry *plastic surgeon*
Seiff, Stephen S. *ophthalmologist*
Semel, George Herbert *plastic surgeon*

**Borrego Springs**
Strong, John Oliver *plastic surgeon, educator*

**Burbank**
Renner, Andrew Ihor *surgeon*

**Canyon Lake**
Sparks, Dale Boyd *allergist, health facility administrator*

**Carlsbad**
Chopra, Deepak *preventive medicine physician, writer*
Fox, Roger Edwin *retired physician*

**Carmel**
Felch, William Campbell *internist, editor*

**Carmel Valley**
Chapman, Robert Galbraith *retired hematologist, administrator*

**Cerritos**
Shavelle, Robert *medical researcher, consultant*

**Chatsworth**
Stephenson, Irene Hamlen *biomedical researcher, consultant, editor, educator*

**Chula Vista**
Cohen, Elaine Helena *pediatrician, cardiologist, educator*

**Claremont**
Johnson, Jerome Linné *cardiologist, educator*

**Corona**
Silva, A. R. *surgeon, educator*

**Corona Del Mar**
Tobis, Jerome Sanford *physician*

**Coronado**
Mock, David Clinton, Jr. *internist*

**Daly City**
Sun, Edward Chih-Yu *surgeon, orthopedist*

**Davis**
Bauer, Herbert *retired physician*
Cardiff, Robert Darrell *pathology educator*
Gardner, Murray Briggs *pathologist, educator*
Jensen, Hanne Margrete *pathologist, educator*
Jones, Edward George *neuroscience educator, neurologist*
Palmer, Philip Edward Stephen *radiologist*
Pessah, Isaac Ness *pharmacology and toxicology educator*
Rhode, Edward Albert *veterinary medicine educator, veterinary cardiologist*
Richman, David Paul *neurologist, educator, researcher*

**Del Mar**
Scherger, Joseph Edward *family physician, educator*

**Delano**
Salmassi, Sadegh *physician*

**Downey**
Gong, Henry, Jr. *internist, researcher, educator*
Perry, Jacquelin *orthopedist, surgeon*
Shapiro, Richard Stanley *physician*
Victoroff, Jeff *neurology professor, psychology professor*

**Duarte**
Bhatia, Smita *epidemiologist, researcher, pediatric oncologist, educator*
Mojica, Pablo *surgeon*

**East Palo Alto**
Vaughan, Winston C. *otolaryngologist, surgeon*

**El Dorado Hills**
Sparks, Robert Dean *medical administrator, gastroenterologist*

**El Macero**
Stowell, Robert Eugene *pathologist, retired educator*

**Eldridge**
Schain, Richard *neurologist, consultant*

**Elk Grove**
Forbes, Kenneth Albert Faucher *urologist, retired surgeon*

**Emeryville**
Fields, Howard Lincoln *neurologist, physiologist, educator*
Hurst, Deborah *pediatric hematologist*
Teufel, William Lockwood *emergency physician*

**Encino**
Lesavoy, Malcolm Alan *plastic surgeon*

**Escondido**
McCarberg, Bill Harold *physician*

**Folsom**
Anderson, Jeffrey Lee *physician, anesthesiologist, consultant*
Ewing, Russell Charles, II, *physician*

**Fontana**
Afagh, Arman *physician*
Johna, Samir *surgeon*

**Fountain Valley**
Kieu, Quynh Dinh *pediatrician, not-for-profit developer*

**Fremont**
Clarke, Christina *epidemiologist, educator*

**Fresno**
Cunningham, Mark Alan *surgeon*
Leigh, Hoyle *psychiatrist, educator, writer*
Patton, Jack Thomas *family practice physician*
Welch, Jack Hamill *retired internist*

**Fullerton**
Baugh, William Preston *dermatologist*
Monty, Louis Harold *psychiatrist*
Sugarman, Michael *physician, rheumatologist*

**Goleta**
Zuk, Carmen Veiga *psychiatrist*

**Grass Valley**
Ely, Parry Haines *dermatologist, educator*

**Greenbrae**
Parnell, Francis William, Jr. *otolaryngologist*

**Gualala**
Ring, Alice Ruth Bishop *retired preventive medicine physician*

**Half Moon Bay**
Robertson, Abel L., Jr. *pathologist*

**Hanford**
Gamboa, Lucito G. *pathologist*

**Hayward**
Bachicha, Joseph Alfred *physician, educator*

**Hemet**
Mata, David Joseph *physician*

**Hillsborough**
Kraft, Robert Arnold *retired medical educator, physician*
Packard, Peter *retired internal medical educator*

**Hollywood**
Sanders, Bill *medical educator*

**Huntington Beach**
Pineda, Anselmo *neurosurgery educator*

**Indian Wells**
Hrabal, Antonin *physician, educator*

**Inglewood**
Dorr, Lawrence D. *orthopedic surgeon*

**Irvine**
Friedenberg, Richard Myron *radiologist, educator, physician*
Gupta, Sudhir *immunologist, educator*
Kim, Moon Hyun *endocrinologist, educator*
Lipkin, Steven Monroe *medical educator, oncologist*
McEligot, Archana Jaiswal *epidemiologist, educator*
Miledi, Ricardo *neurobiologist*
Nalcioglu, Orhan *radiologist, educator*
Ory, Caron *biomedical researcher*
Pal, Sukumar *immunologist, researcher*
Quilligan, Edward James *retired obstetrician, gynecologist, educator*
Smith, Andrew Donald *plastic surgeon*
van-den-Noort, Stanley *neurologist, educator*
Werlin, Lawrence B. *obstetrician, gynecologist, endocrinologist*
Wong, Nathan Donald *medicine and epidemiology researcher, educator*
Zhou (Syuu), Wei (Yi) *medical researcher, educator*

**Kentfield**
German, Donald Frederick *physician*
Schmid, Rudi (Rudolf Schmid) *retired internist, educator, academic administrator*

**La Canada Flintridge**
Byrne, George Melvin *physician*

**La Crescenta**
Riccardi, Vincent Michael *pediatrician, educator, entrepreneur*

**La Jolla**
Akiskal, Hagop Souren *psychiatric researcher, educator*
Atai, Manucher *surgeon*
Bailey, David Nelson *pathology educator, dean, academic administrator*
Barrett-Connor, Elizabeth Louise *epidemiologist, educator*
Beutler, Ernest *physician, research scientist*
Blanchard, Daniel G. *cardiologist*
Bloom, Floyd Elliott *internist, neuroscientist*
Bottini, Massimo *medical researcher*
Bucko, Carroll Dennis *plastic surgeon*
Carmichael, David Burton *physician*
Chisari, Francis V. *pathologist*
Cleveland, Don W. *biomedical researcher*
Dalessio, Donald John *internist, neurologist, educator*
Dandan, Randa Hilal *pharmacologist, researcher*
Dimsdale, Joel Edward *psychiatry educator*
Dixon, Frank James *pathologist, educator*
Edginton, Thomas S. *pathologist, educator, molecular biologist, vascular biologist*
Edwards, Charles Cornell *surgeon, medical association administrator*
Friedmann, Theodore *physician*
Garland, Cedric Frank *epidemiologist, educator*
Gill, Gordon N. *medical educator*
Glatt, Stephen Joseph *psychiatry educator*
Haddad, Gabriel G. *pediatrician, educator*
Hamburger, Robert N. *pediatrician, educator, consultant*
Han, Jiahuai *medical researcher*
Hofmann, Alan Frederick *biomedical researcher, educator*
Horner, Anthony Adam *pediatrician, educator*
Kaback, Michael *medical educator*
Katzman, Robert *neurologist, medical educator*
Klonoff-Cohen, Hillary Sandra *epidemiologist*
Mendoza, Stanley Atran *pediatric nephrologist, educator*
Moossa, A. R. *surgeon, educator*
Nakamura, Robert Motoharu *pathologist*
Nyhan, William Leo *pediatrician, educator*
Rearden, Carole Ann *clinical pathologist, educator*
Reed, John C. *physician, researcher*
Rubin, Lewis J. *physician, researcher*
Schneider, Gerald L. *plastic surgeon*
Seagren, Stephen Linner *oncologist*
Silver, Dee Edward *physician, neurologist*
Singer, Robert *plastic surgeon*
Steinberg, Daniel *preventive medicine physician, educator*
Swain, Judith Lea *cardiologist, educator*
Tan, Eng Meng *immunologist, biomedical researcher*
Taupenot, Laurent *medical educator, researcher*
Taylor, Palmer W. *pharmacology educator*
Thompson, Charlotte Ellis *pediatrician, educator, writer*
Tsuang, Ming Tso *psychiatrist, educator*
Walker, Richard Hugh *orthopaedic surgeon*
Yen, Samuel S(how)-C(hih) *obstetrician, gynecologist, educator, endocrinologist*

**La Mesa**
Boghairi, Anoushiravan *cardiologist*

**La Quinta**
Calvin, James Willard *thoracic and vascular surgeon*
Pitkin, Roy Macbeth *retired obstetrician, educator*

**Laguna Beach**
Dana, Edward Runkle *retired physician*

**Laguna Hills**
Widyolar, Sheila Gayle *dermatologist*

**Laguna Woods**
Berk, Jack Edward *gastroenterologist, educator*
Ross, Mathew *medical educator*

**Lemoore**
Gerhard, H. John *orthopaedic surgeon, military officer*

**Welsh**, William Daniel *geriatric medicine family practice physician*

## Lincoln
Chong, Vernon *retired surgeon, retired military officer*
Rockwell, Don Arthur *retired psychiatrist*

## Loma Linda
Bailey, Leonard Lee *surgeon*
Behrens, Berel Lyn *physician, academic administrator, health facility administrator*
Bull, Brian Stanley *pathologist, educator*
Chan, Philip J. *medical educator*
Coggin, Charlotte Joan *cardiologist, educator*
Condon, Stanley Charles *gastroenterologist*
Dayes, Lloyd Albert *neurosurgeon, minister*
Herrmann, Paul C. *physician, chemist*
Llaurado, Josep G. *nuclear medicine physician, researcher*
Mace, John Weldon *pediatrician*
Slater, James Munro *radiation oncologist*
Strother, Allen *biochemical pharmacologist, researcher*
Wareham, Ellsworth Edwin *cardiothoracic surgeon, educator*

## Long Beach
Kwaan, Jack Hau Ming *retired physician*
Macer, George Armen, Jr. *orthopedic hand surgeon*
Molina, Joseph Mario (Mario Molina) *medical administrator*
Stemmer, Edward Alan *surgeon, educator*
Wells, James H. *plastic surgeon*
Worcester, Howard Lester *internist*
Wu, Sing-Yung *physician, researcher*

## Los Alamitos
Lee, Jhemon Hom *physician*

## Los Altos
Orman, Nanette Hector *psychiatrist*

## Los Angeles
Aberle, Denise Ru *radiologist, researcher*
Alkalay, Arie L. *pediatrician*
Alkon, Ellen Skillen *physician*
Apt, Leonard *physician*
Apuzzo, Michael Lawrence John *neurological surgeon*
Aronowitz, Joel Alan *plastic and reconstructive surgeon*
Averbook, Beryl David *retired surgeon*
Basak, Saroj Kumar *medical researcher*
Beart, Robert W., Jr. *colon and rectal surgeon, educator*
Bernstein, Sol *cardiologist, educator*
Bessman, Samuel Paul *pediatrician, educator, biochemist*
Bhidayasiri, Roongroj *neurologist, researcher*
Biles, John Alexander *pharmacologist, chemist, educator*
Bindingnavele, Vijay Krishna *plastic surgeon*
Blahd, William Henry *physician, nuclear medicine physician, director*
Bodey, Bela *immunologist, pathologist, oncologist*
Bondareff, William *psychiatrist, educator*
Borenstein, Daniel Bernard *psychiatrist, educator*
Brackmann, Derald E. *otolaryngologist*
Braunstein, Glenn David *physician, educator*
Catlin, Don H. *molecular pharmacologist, educator*
Chandor, Stebbins Bryant *pathologist*
Cherry, James Donald *pediatrician*
Chopra, Inder Jit *endocrinologist*
Clemente, Carmine Domenic *anatomist, educator*
Coates, Thomas J. *medical association administrator*
Cook, Ian Ainsworth *psychiatrist, researcher, educator*
Cote, Richard James *pathologist, researcher*
Cunneen, Scott Anthony *surgeon*
Danoff, Dudley Seth *surgeon, urologist*
Davidson, Ezra C., Jr. *obstetrician, gynecologist, educator, academic administrator*
Detels, Roger *epidemiologist, retired dean*
Dignam, William Joseph *obstetrician, gynecologist, educator*
Edgerton, Bradford Wheatly *plastic surgeon*
Enstrom, James Eugene *epidemiologist*
Eo, SuRak *plastic surgeon, educator*
Ettenger, Robert Bruce *physician, pediatric nephrologist*
Feig, Stephen Arthur *pediatrician, educator, preventive medicine physician, hematologist, oncologist*
Fodor, Peter Bela *plastic surgeon*
Fonkalsrud, Eric Walter *pediatric surgeon, educator*
Francis, Charles K. *medical educator*
Gabriel, Ronald Samuel *child neurologist*
Gatti, Richard A. *medical educator, medical geneticist*
Geller, Stephen Arthur *pathologist, educator*
Gewertz, Bruce Labe *surgeon, educator*
Goin, Marcia Kraft *physician*
Gonick, Harvey Craig *nephrologist, educator*
Goodwin, Scott Craig *interventional radiologist*
Gorney, Roderic *psychiatrist, educator*
Grody, Wayne William *physician*
Haywood, L. Julian *cardiologist, educator*
Henriksen, Eva Hansine *retired anesthesiology educator*
Hirai, Denitsu *surgeon*
Hirsch, Anthony Terry *physician*
Hoang, Duc Van *pathologist*
Hollander, Daniel *gastroenterologist, medical educator*
Horwitz, David A. *rheumatologist, educator*
House, John William *otolaryngologist*
Huerta, Sergio *physician, researcher*
Hyde, Manly Richard *thoracic surgeon*
Ignarro, Louis J. *pharmacology educator*
IsHak, Waguih William *psychiatrist*
Itabashi, Hideo Henry *medical educator, consultant, coroner, pathologist*
Jadvar, Hossein *nuclear medicine physician, biomedical engineer*
Jalali, Behnaz *psychiatrist, educator*
Johnson, Cage Saul *hematologist, educator*
Kamil, Elaine Scheiner *pediatric nephrologist, educator*
Katz, Ronald Lewis *physician, educator*

Kaufman, Francine R. *pediatric endocrinologist*
Kaunitz, Jonathan Davidson *physician*
Kelly, Arthur Paul *physician*
Kelly, Daniel *neurosurgeon*
Kim, Kwang-Jin *medical educator*
Kleeman, Charles Richard *medical educator, nephrologist, researcher*
Kramer, Barry Alan *psychiatrist, educator*
Lawrence, Sanford Hull *physician, immunochemist, author*
Lazareff, Jorge Antonio *neurosurgeon, researcher*
Lechago, Juan *pathologist, educator*
Li, Andrew J. *gynecologist, oncologist*
Liberman, Robert Paul *psychiatry educator, researcher, writer*
Linsman, Joseph F. *retired radiologist*
Macavinta-Tenazas, Gemorsita *physician*
Maloney, Robert Keller *ophthalmologist, medical educator*
Marjoram, Paul *medical educator, researcher*
Maronde, Robert Francis *internist, pharmacologist*
Martinez, Miguel Acevedo *urologist, consultant, lecturer*
McKenna, Robert Joseph, Jr. *thoracic surgeon*
Mellinkoff, Sherman Mussoff *medical educator*
Mihan, Richard *retired dermatologist*
Miller, Timothy Alden *plastic and reconstructive surgeon*
Miranda, M. Jeanne *psychiatrist*
Mondino, Bartly J. *ophthalmologist*
Morgan, Elizabeth *plastic surgeon*
Moxley, John Howard III *internist*
Moy, Ronald Leonard *dermasurgeon*
Murphree, A. Linn *ophthalmologist*
Nael, Kambiz *radiologist, researcher*
Natarajan, Sathima *pathologist*
Nathwani, Bharat N. *pathologist, educator*
Nelson, Marvin Dale, Jr. *radiologist, educator*
Nissenson, Allen Richard *physician, educator*
Noble, Ernest Pascal *pharmacologist, biochemist, educator*
Parmelee, Arthur Hawley, Jr. *pediatric medical educator*
Pi, Edmond Hsin-Tung *psychiatry educator*
Pohost, Gerald Michael *cardiologist, medical educator*
Qiao, Jian-Hua *pathologist, researcher*
Rachelefsky, Gary Stuart *medical educator*
Rasgon, Natalie Luzina *psychiatrist*
Rassman, William R. *plastic surgeon*
Rimoin, David Lawrence *medical geneticist*
Roven, Alfred Nathan *surgeon*
Roy-Burman, Pradip *molecular biology and virology educator*
Rubin, Robert Terry *psychiatrist, researcher, educator*
Rudkin, George Henry *plastic surgeon*
Ryan, Stephen Joseph, Jr. *ophthalmologist, educator*
Sarma, Radha J. *cardiologist, educator*
Sarnat, Bernard George *plastic surgeon, educator, researcher*
Scheibel, Arnold Bernard *psychiatrist, educator, research director*
Schelbert, Heinrich Ruediger *nuclear medicine physician*
Schwarz, Ernst Ruediger *cardiologist, researcher*
Shahinian, Hyrayr K. *surgeon*
Shen, Wei-Chiang *medical educator*
Sherman, Randolph *plastic and reconstructive surgeon, educator*
Shields, William Donald *physician, educator*
Siegel, Michael Elliot *nuclear medicine physician, educator*
Siegel, Sheldon C. *pediatrician, immunologist, allergist*
Siegel, Stuart Elliott *pediatric oncologist, educator*
Skaggs, David L. *orthopedist, educator*
Solnik, Meir Jonathon *gynecologist, director*
Solomon, David Harris *geriatrician, educator*
Speigel, Brennan Mason Ross *internist, gastroenterologist, researcher*
Stein, James Eric *pediatric surgeon*
Stevanovic, Milan V. *surgeon*
Stiehm, E. Richard *pediatrician, educator*
Straatsma, Bradley Ralph *ophthalmologist, educator*
Sullivan, Stuart Francis *anesthesiologist, educator*
Sultan, Wafa *psychiatrist*
Sutterby, Larry Quentin *internist*
Talner, Lee k. Norman Donald *psychiatrist, educator*
Tolo, Vernon Thorpe *orthopedist, educator*
Toluie, Kamran *cardiologist, electrophysiologist*
Wallach, Howard Frederic *psychiatrist*
Wasterlain, Claude Guy *neurologist*
Weiner, Leslie Philip *neurology educator, researcher*
Weiss, Martin Harvey *neurosurgeon, educator*
Wells, Kenneth Brooks *medical educator, researcher*
Whybrow, Peter Charles *psychiatrist, educator, director, author*
Wilkinson, Alan Herbert *nephrologist, educator*
Wilson, Miriam Geisendorfer *retired physician, educator*
Wincor, Michael Z. *psychopharmacology educator, clinician, researcher*
Withers, Hubert Rodney *radiotherapist, radiobiologist, educator*
Wong, Wing-Yen *hematologist, educator*
Woodley, David Timothy *dermatology educator*
Yamauchi, Paul Steven *dermatologist, researcher*
Yao, Mingzhong *medical researcher, educator*
Yersiz, Hasan *medical educator*
Zalavras, Charalampos *orthopedic surgeon*
Ziering, Craig L. *osteopath*

## Malibu
Morgenstern, Leon *surgeon*

## Manhattan Beach
Lin, Henry C. *physician, researcher*

## Menlo Park
Harris, Edward Day, Jr. *physician*
Hoffman, Thomas Edward *dermatologist*
Kovachy, Edward Miklos, Jr. *psychiatrist, consultant*
McQuillen, Michael Paul *neurologist, educator*

## Mill Valley
Harris, Jeffrey Saul *physician, consultant, health facility administrator*
Kolb, Felix Oscar *physician*

## Mission Hills
Strazzeri, James C. *orthopedist, surgeon, health facility administrator*

## Mission Viejo
Berger, William Ezial *allergist, director*

## Modesto
Jacisin, John James *psychiatrist*
Khanna, Kanwal *rheumatologist*
Suntra, Charles Ratapol *surgeon, educator*

## Monrovia
Comings, David Edward *medical geneticist*

## Monterey
Black, Robert Lincoln *pediatrician, educator*
Lehr, Jeffrey Marvin *immunologist, allergist*

## Mountain View
Abel, Elizabeth Ann *dermatologist*
Brilliant, Larry (Lawrence Brilliant) *preventive medicine physician, epidemiologist, technology pioneer, writer, educator, entrepreneur, social venture capitalist*
Urman, Jeffrey David *physician, educator*
Warren, Richard Wayne *obstetrician, gynecologist*

## Napa
Bogdan, Michael Andrew *plastic surgeon*
Morgese, Vincent John *neurosurgeon*
Pickett, Justus Cunningham *medical association administrator*

## Newbury Park
Bleiberg, Leon William *surgeon, podiatrist*

## Newhall
Stein, Karl N. *plastic and reconstructive surgeon*

## Newport Beach
Amyes, Edwin Westby *neurosurgeon*
Chiu, John Tang *physician*
Connolly, John Earle *surgeon, educator*
Shamoun, John Milam *plastic surgeon*
Solmer, Richard *physician*
Viehe, Richard B. *podiatrist*

## Northridge
Sarka, George *medical educator*

## Novato
Kassel, Arthur David *retired orthopaedic surgeon*

## Oakland
Brindis, Ralph *cardiologist, consultant, medical educator*
Cary, Alice Shepard *retired physician*
Collen, Morris Frank *retired medical association administrator, retired physician, retired researcher, consultant*
Hoffinger, Scott A. *pediatric orthopedic surgeon*
Killebrew, Ellen Jane (Mrs. Edward S. Graves) *cardiologist, educator*
Klatsky, Arthur Louis *cardiologist, epidemiologist*
Kupers, Terry Allen *psychiatrist, educator*
Le Noir, Michael A. *allergist*
Magloire, Alix J. (Magloire) *internist*
Ng, Lawrence Ming-Loy *pediatrician*
Sharpton, Thomas *physician*
Weinmann, Robert Lewis *neurologist*

## Oceanside
Curtin, Thomas Lee *ophthalmologist*

## Orange
Ahlering, Thomas Edward *urologist, surgeon, researcher*
Amin, Alpesh N. *internist*
Armstrong, David Ligon *psychiatrist*
Barr, Ronald Jeffrey *dermatologist, pathologist*
Borghei, Peyman *medical researcher*
Chang, Jae Chan *hematologist, oncologist, educator*
Crumley, Roger Lee *surgeon, educator, otolaryngologist*
DiSaia, Philip John *obstetrician, gynecologist, radiology educator*
Fischel, Richard Jeffrey *thoracic surgeon*
Fisher, Mark Jay *neurologist, neuroscientist, educator*
Hubbell, Floyd Allan *internist, educator*
Kanofsky, Myron Ross *physician*
Lee, Yee-Lean *biomedical researcher*
Lott, Ira Totz *pediatric neurologist*
Meier, Steven W. *orthopedist, surgeon, consultant*
Morgan, Beverly Carver *pediatrician, educator*
Rowen, Marshall *radiologist*
Simjee, Aisha *ophthalmologist, educator*
Smith, Ronald Edward *ophthalmologist*
Vaziri, Nosratola Dabir *internist, educator, nephrologist*
Wong, Brian Jet-Fei *surgeon*
Yu, Jen *medical educator*
Zi, Xiaolin *epidemiologist, medical researcher*

## Pacific Palisades
Beck, John Christian *physician, educator*
Cailliet, René *retired medical educator*
Claes, Daniel John *physician*
Daniels, John R. *oncologist, educator*
Love, Susan Margaret *surgeon, educator, writer*
Tourtellotte, Wallace William *neurologist, educator*

## Palm Desert
Widran, Jerrold Joseph *urologist*

## Palm Springs
Gaede, James Ernest *physician, medical educator*

## Palo Alto
Adamson, Geoffrey David *endocrinologist, surgeon*
Albers, Gregory W. *neurologist*

Ashford, John Wesson, Jr. *psychiatrist, researcher*
Bagshaw, Malcolm A. *radiation oncologist, educator*
Blessing-Moore, Joann Catherine *allergist, pulmonologist*
Britton, M(elvin) C(reed), Jr. *rheumatologist*
Chen, Stephen Shi-hua *pathologist, biochemist*
Dement, William Charles *medical researcher, educator*
Fajardo, Luis Felipe *pathologist, educator, director*
Fries, James Franklin *internal medicine educator*
Galel, Susan Alpert *transfusion medicine physician*
Hays, Marguerite Thompson *nuclear medicine physician, educator*
Holman, Halsted Reid *medical educator, physician*
Kaye, Ronald Lee *physician, educator*
Keeffe, Emmet Britton *medical educator*
Lane, Alfred Thomas *medical educator*
Michie, Sara H. *pathologist, educator*
Moss, Richard B. *pediatrician*
Needleman, Philip *cardiologist, pharmacologist*
Peng, Stanford Lee-Yu *physician*
Pizzo, Philip A. *pediatrician, educator, dean*
Raffin, Thomas A. *physician*
Salvatierra, Oscar, Jr. *transplant surgeon, urologist, educator*
Schendel, Stephen Alfred *surgeon, educator*
Schurman, David Jay *orthopedic surgeon, educator*
Shuer, Lawrence Mendel *neurosurgery educator*
Silverman, Norman Henry *cardiologist, educator*
Strober, Samuel *immunologist, educator*
Sunshine, Philip *pediatrician*
Tune, Bruce Malcolm *pediatrics educator, renal toxicologist*
Urquhart, John *medical researcher, educator*
Weng, Wen-Kai *oncologist, medical researcher*
Yuan, Nanci *pediatrician, pulmonologist, educator*

## Palos Verdes Peninsula
Narasimhan, Padma Mandyam *physician*
Thomas, Claudewell Sidney *psychiatrist, educator*
Van Der Meulen, Joseph Pierre *neurologist*

## Panorama City
Bass, Harold Neal *pediatrician, medical geneticist*
Sue, Michael Alvin *allergist*

## Paradise
Haws, Hale Louis *medical association administrator, consultant*

## Pasadena
Buchwald, Jed Zachary *environmental health researcher, science history educator*
Glovsky, Myron Michael *medical educator*
Harvey, Joseph Paul, Jr. *orthopedist, educator*
Jones, Lawrence Wager *physician, researcher*
Lake, Kevin Bruce *medical association administrator*
Opel, William *medical research administrator*
Shaw, Anthony *pediatric surgeon, retired educator*
Short, Elizabeth M. *internist, educator, retired federal agency administrator*
Wong, Raymond Shiu-Loong *radiologist*

## Piedmont
Montgomery, Theodore Ashton *physician*
Reich, Stanley Benjamin *radiologist, medical educator*

## Pinole
Naughton, James Lee *internist*

## Pleasant Hill
Hollister, Arthur Clair, Jr. *epidemiologist, consultant, retired public health service officer*

## Pomona
Gambone, Joseph Charles *medical educator, consultant*
Vo, Huu Dinh *pediatrician, educator*

## Portola Valley
Fogarty, Thomas James *surgery educator*
Hafkenschiel, Joseph Henry, Jr. *cardiologist, educator*

## Rancho Mirage
Chuang, Tsu-Yi *dermatologist, epidemiologist, educator*
Cone, Lawrence Arthur *medical educator*
Weil, Max Harry *internist, cardiologist, educator, medical researcher*

## Rancho Palos Verdes
Kwan, Benjamin Ching Kee *ophthalmologist*
Neilan, Aidan Joseph *radiologist*

## Rancho Santa Fe
Affeldt, John Ellsworth *retired physician*
Carr, David Turner *physician*
Nadler, Henry Louis *pediatrician, educator, geneticist*
Rockoff, S. David *radiologist, physician, educator*

## Rancho Santa Margarita
Bunkis, Juris *plastic surgeon*

## Redding
Nwangburuka, Okechukwu Nkem *psychiatrist*
Renard, Ronald Lee *allergist*

## Redlands
Bangasser, Ronald Paul *physician, director*

## Redwood City
Ellis, Eldon Eugene *surgeon*
Sweet, Victoria *medical educator, physician*

## Rialto
Alav, Faramarz *cardiologist, internist*

## Richmond
Arnon, Stephen Soulé *physician, research scientist*

## Riverside
Bricker, Neal S. *physician, educator*
Evangelista, Allan *surgeon, medical researcher*
Jung, Timothy Tae Kun *otolaryngologist*

Linaweaver, Walter Ellsworth, Jr. *physician*

## Rolling Hills Estates
Bellis, Carroll Joseph *surgeon, educator*

## Sacramento
Bogren, Hugo Gunnar *radiology educator*
Chapman, Michael William *orthopedist, educator*
Cunningham, Mary Elizabeth (Mary Cunningham-Lusby) *physician*
Fung, Maxwell Alexander *medical educator*
Howell, Lydia Pleotis *pathologist, educator*
Jackson, Richard Joseph *epidemiologist, educator, pediatrician, preventive medicine physician*
Kon, Alexander A. *pediatrician, educator*
Kravitz, Richard L. *medical educator, director*
Leong, Albin B. *pediatric pulmonologist, educator, pediatric allergist*
Lewin, John Calvert *medical association administrator*
Lim, Alan Young *plastic surgeon*
Lippold, Roland Will *retired surgeon*
Lynch, Peter John *retired dermatologist*
Malkin, Harold Marshall *retired medical researcher*
Nagy, Stephen Mears, Jr. *physician, allergist*
Rab, George T. *pediatric orthopedic surgeon*
Robinson, Muriel Cox *psychiatrist*
Sharma, Arjun Dutta *cardiologist*
Stevenson, Thomas Ray *plastic surgeon*
Styne, Dennis Michael *physician, educator*
Tung, Prabhas *plastic surgeon*
Wolfman, Earl Frank, Jr. *surgeon, educator*
Wolkov, Harvey Brian *oncologist, researcher*

## Saint Helena
Sakopoulos, Andreas George *cardiac and vascular surgeon*

## San Bernardino
De Haas, David Dana *emergency physician*

## San Bruno
Bradley, Charles William *podiatrist, educator*

## San Diego
Altamar, Hernan Orlando *urologist, military officer*
Benirschke, Kurt *retired pathologist, educator*
Blanchard, Jennifer Neely *physician, educator*
Chambers, Henry George *orthopedic surgeon*
DeMaria, Anthony Nicholas *cardiologist, educator*
Feifel, David *neurologist, psychiatrist*
Friedman, Paul Jay *retired radiologist*
Gleason, Matthew C. *plastic surgeon*
Goltz, Robert William *dermatologist, educator*
Gomes, Stacy Lorraine *medical educator, academic administrator*
Jacoby, Irving *physician*
Jamieson, Stuart William *cardiothoracic surgeon, educator*
Kapelanski, David Peter *cardiothoracic surgeon, educator*
Kaplan, George Willard *urologist*
Kaushansky, Kenneth *medical educator*
Kellogg, Huston Glenn *medical educator*
Krous, Henry Franklin *pathologist, educator*
Langenberg, Bret James *surgeon*
Levy, Jerome *dermatologist, retired military officer*
Naughton, Gail K. *biomedical researcher, academic administrator*
Ozerdem, Ugur *medical researcher, educator*
Pan, Henry Yue-Ming *clinical pharmacologist, cardiologist*
Parthemore, Jacqueline Gail *internist, educator, hospital administrator*
Pitt, William Alexander *cardiologist*
Pollack, Larry *plastic surgeon*
Ray, Albert *physician, educator*
Resnik, Robert *medical educator*
Ross, John, Jr. *cardiologist, educator*
Schmidt, Joseph David *urologist*
Talbot, Blake Strothers *retired urologist*
Wallace, Mark Raymond *physician*
Wasserman, Stephen Ira *allergist, immunologist, educator*
Whittington, Anne Elizabeth *diabetes educator*
Widder, Kenneth Jon *pathologist, educator*

## San Francisco
Amend, William John Conrad, Jr. *physician, educator*
Anooshian, Robert Vahan *plastic surgeon*
Bachman, David Christian *orthopedic surgeon*
Bainton, Dorothy Ford *pathologist, educator*
Barondes, Samuel Herbert *psychiatrist, educator*
Basbaum, Allan I. *medical educator, researcher*
Bass, Nathan M. *medical educator, researcher*
Bastian, Boris C. *dermatologist, medical educator*
Behrens, M. Kathleen *medical researcher*
Benet, Leslie Zachary *pharmacologist, educator*
Bikle, Daniel David *research physician*
Bluestone, Jeffrey Allen *immunology educator, researcher*
Boles, Roger *otolaryngologist*
Botvinick, Elias H. *nuclear medicine physician, researcher, medical educator*
Bourne, Henry R. *medicine, cellular and molecular pharmacology educator*
Bradford, David S. *surgeon*
Brotman, Martin *gastroenterologist*
Brown, Eric Joel *biomedical researcher*
Browner, Warren Seth *internist, educator, academic administrator*
Callaham, Michael L. *emergency physician, educator*
Capaldini, Lisa Claire *physician, educator*
Chi, John H. *neurosurgeon*
Ciccarone, Daniel *medical educator, researcher, physician*
Clever, Linda Hawes *physician*
Cobbs, Price Mashaw *social psychiatrist*
Cooper, Allen David *medical researcher, educator*
Crawford, J. Brooks *ophthalmologist, educator*
Crawford, Michael Howard *cardiologist, educator, researcher*
Cree, Bruce *neurologist*
Croughan, Mary *medical educator*
David, George *psychiatrist, economic theory lecturer*
Dawson, Chandler Robert *ophthalmologist, educator*

Deicken, Raymond Friedrich *psychiatrist, neuroscientist*
Deviren, Vedat *orthopedist, educator*
Engleman, Ephraim Philip *rheumatologist*
Epstein, Charles Joseph *pediatrician, geneticist, biochemist, educator*
Epstein, John Howard *dermatologist*
Erskine, John Morse *surgeon*
Ferriero, Donna M. *pediatric neurologist*
Fessel, Walford Jeffrey *rheumatologist*
Finberg, Laurence *pediatrician, educator, dean*
Fitzgerald, Paul A. *endocrinologist, educator*
Frick, Oscar Lionel *pediatrician, educator*
Ganem, Donald E. *immunologist*
Gellin, Gerald Alan *dermatologist*
Gibbs, Patricia Hellman *physician*
Glantz, Stanton A. *medical researcher*
Gooding, Charles Arthur *radiologist, physician, educator*
Gooding, Gretchen Ann Wagner *physician, educator*
Greene, Warner Craig *medical educator, medical association administrator*
Greenspan, Francis S. *physician*
Greenspan, John S. *dental and medical educator, researcher, academic administrator*
Gregoratos, Gabriel *medical educator*
Grossman, William *medical researcher, educator*
Grumbach, Melvin Malcolm *pediatrician, educator*
Havel, Richard Joseph *physician, educator*
Henderson, Isaac Craig *oncologist, researcher*
Higashida, Randall Takeo *radiologist, neurosurgeon, medical educator*
Hinman, Frank, Jr. *urologist, educator*
Hoffman, William Yanes *plastic surgeon*
Hsu, Chi-yuan *nephrologist, researcher*
Ikeda, Clyde Junichi *plastic and reconstructive surgeon*
Jonsen, Albert R(upert) *retired medical ethics educator*
Kan, Yuet Wai *hematologist, educator*
Katzung, Bertram George *pharmacologist*
Kenyon, Cynthia J. *medical researcher*
Kimmich, Robert André *psychiatrist*
Koltzova-Rang, Yulia K. *internist*
Koo, John Ying Ming *psychiatrist, dermatologist*
Krames, Elliot Stephan *anesthesiologist*
Kunwar, Sandeep *neurosurgeon*
Levy, Jay A. *medical educator*
Lo, Bernard *medical educator*
Low, Randall *internist, cardiologist*
Lucia, Marilyn Reed *physician*
Maas, Corey *plastic surgeon*
Mason, Dean Towle *cardiologist*
Mathes, Stephen John *plastic and reconstructive surgeon, educator*
McAninch, Jack Weldon *urological surgeon, educator*
McCulley, Timothy J. *ophthalmologist, surgeon, educator*
McCune, Joseph Mike *epidemiologist, educator, researcher*
Miller, Ronald D. *medical educator, researcher*
Miller, Walter Luther *pediatrician, educator*
Mustacchi, Piero *preventive medicine physician, educator*
Norris, Philip John *medical educator, researcher*
O'Connor, G(eorge) Richard *ophthalmologist*
Ousterhout, Douglas Kenneth *plastic surgeon*
Petrakis, Nicholas Louis *epidemiologist, medical researcher, educator*
Phillips, Theodore Locke *radiologist, educator*
Ristow, Brunno *plastic surgeon*
Roe, Benson Bertheau *surgeon, educator*
Romano, James John *plastic surgeon*
Rosinski, Edwin Francis *medical educator*
Rudolph, Abraham Morris *pediatrician, educator*
Rutherford, George Williams III *preventive medicine physician*
Schmidt, Robert Milton *preventive medicine physician, educator, medical association administrator*
Schrock, Theodore R. *surgeon*
Schroeder, Steven Alfred *medical educator*
Seebach, Lydia Marie *physician*
Shaw, Richard Eugene *cardiovascular researcher*
Sherr, Elliott Harold *neurologist, researcher*
Shinefield, Henry Robert *pediatrician*
Shinohara, Katsuto *medical educator*
Sickles, Edward *radiologist*
Smith, David Elvin *physician*
Smith, Lloyd Hollingsworth *physician*
Spivey, Bruce E. *ophthalmologist, educator, health facility administrator*
Stamper, Robert Lewis *ophthalmologist, educator*
Van Dyke, Craig *psychiatrist, director*
Volpe, Peter Anthony *surgeon*
Way, E(dward) Leong *pharmacologist, toxicologist, educator*
Wintroub, Bruce Urich *dermatologist, educator, researcher*
Yao, John Sen *physician*
Zippin, Calvin *epidemiologist, educator*

## San Gabriel
Chen, John Calvin *psychiatrist, educator*

## San Jose
Avakoff, Joseph Carnegie *medical consultant, law consultant*
Johnson, Allen Halbert *surgeon*
Lippe, Philipp Maria *neurosurgeon, educator, academic administrator*
Nelson, Lionel M. *otolaryngologist*
Press, Barry Harris Jay *plastic surgeon*
Stevens, David Alec *medical educator*

## San Juan Capistrano
Fisher, Delbert Arthur *pediatric endocrinologist, educator, health facility administrator*
Hawkins, Brandon James *podiatrist, surgeon*
Zalta, Edward *otolaryngologist, physician*

## San Luis Obispo
Hosn, Wally *plastic surgeon*
Pinkel, Donald Paul *pediatrician*

## San Marino
Terry, Roger *retired pathologist, consultant*

## San Mateo
Chabra, Anand *public health physician, epidemiologist*
Johnson, Leland Henry, Jr. *orthopedic surgeon*
Sutherland, Vanna Rae *psychiatrist*
Van Kirk, John Ellsworth *retired cardiologist*
Wong, Otto *epidemiologist*

## San Pablo
Woodruff, Kay Herrin *pathologist, educator*

## San Pedro
Kline, Frank Menefee *psychiatrist*

## San Ramon
Litman, Robert Barry *physician, writer, television and radio commentator*

## Santa Ana
Afifi, Alaa Youssef *cardiothoracic surgeon*
Myers, Marilyn Gladys *pediatric hematologist, oncologist*
Sporty, Lawrence Douglas *psychiatrist*

## Santa Barbara
Bischel, Margaret DeMeritt *physician, consultant*
Ellis, Eugene Joseph *cardiologist*
Fisher, Steven Kay *neurobiology educator*
Jovanovic, Lois *medical researcher*
Kohn, Roger Alan *surgeon*
Liebhaber, Myron I. *allergist*
Mathews, Barbara Edith *gynecologist*
Ray, Charles Dean *neurosurgeon, spine surgeon, bioengineer, inventor*
Riemenschneider, Paul Arthur *retired physician, retired radiologist*
Shackman, Daniel Robert *psychiatrist*

## Santa Clara
Chin, Albert Kae *research physician*

## Santa Cruz
Pletsch, Marie Eleanor *plastic surgeon*
Shorenstein, Rosalind Greenberg *internist*

## Santa Monica
Carr, Ruth Margaret *plastic surgeon*
Hoefflin, Steven M. *plastic surgeon*
Katz, Roger *pediatrician, educator, allergist, immunologist*
Kawamoto, Henry K. *plastic surgeon*
Lincoln, Thomas L. *pathologist, educator*
McGuire, Michael Francis *plastic surgeon*
Rand, Robert Wheeler *neurosurgeon, educator*
Resnick, Jeffrey I. *plastic surgeon*
Schultz, Victor M. *physician*
Shamban, Ava T. *dermatologist*
Shim, Elisabeth K. *dermatologist*
Singer, Frederick Raphael *medical researcher*
Stern, Walter Eugene *neurosurgeon, educator*
Thompson, Dennis Peters *plastic surgeon*
Tompkins, Ronald K. *retired surgeon, educator*
Wang, Jeffrey C. *surgeon*
Zarem, Harvey Alan *plastic surgeon*

## Santa Paula
Edwards, Samuel Roger *internist*
Tushla, Richard James *physician*

## Santa Rosa
Bozdech, Marek Jiri *physician, educator*
Cohn, Joseph David *surgeon*
Flanagan, Michael Brendan *obstetrician, gynecologist*
Leuty, Gerald Johnston *osteopathic physician, surgeon*
Smith, Thomas Kent *retired radiologist*
Trucker, Albert *retired plastic surgeon*

## Sausalito
Jampolsky, Gerald G. (Jerry Jampolsky) *psychiatrist*
Orbison, James Archer, Jr. *cardiologist, surgeon*
Ornish, Dean *medical association administrator, medical educator*

## Sepulveda
Yano, Elizabeth Martin *epidemiologist, researcher*

## Sierra Madre
Nation, Earl F. *retired urologist, educator*

## Sonoma
Emery, John Edward *plastic surgeon, vintner*
Gelpi, Armand Philippe *internist*

## South Pasadena
Whang, Sukoo Jack *pathologist, microbiologist*

## South San Francisco
Caro, Ivor *dermatologist*
Humphrey, Patrick Paul *pharmacologist*
Tessier-Lavigne, Marc Trevor *neurobiologist, researcher*

## Stanford
Abrams, Herbert LeRoy *radiologist, educator*
Arber, Daniel Alan *hematologist, pathologist*
Bauer, Eugene Andrew *dermatologist, educator*
Blau, Helen Margaret *pharmacology educator*
Brown, J. Martin *oncologist, educator*
Chase, Robert Arthur *surgeon, educator*
Cohen, Harvey Joel *pediatric hematology and oncology educator*
Dahan, Michael Haim *obstetrician, gynecologist, researcher*
Donaldson, Sarah Susan *radiologist*
Egbert, Peter Roy *ophthalmologist, educator*
Farquhar, John William *physician, educator*
Fee, Willard Edward, Jr. *otolaryngologist*
Fire, Andrew Z. *pathologist, educator, geneticist*
Friedman, Gary David *epidemiologist*
Fuller, Margaret Tatnall *biomedical researcher*
Garber, Alan Michael *internist, educator, economist*
Henderson, Victor Warren *behavioral and geriatric neurologist, epidemiologist, researcher, educator*
Hlatky, Mark Andrew *cardiologist, medical researcher*

Jacobs, Charlotte De Croes *medical educator, oncologist*
Jardetzky, Oleg *medical educator, researcher*
Koza, John R. *medical educator, writer*
Kraemer, Helena Antoinette Chmura *psychiatry educator*
Krensky, Alan Michael *pediatrician, educator*
Leibel, Steven Arnold *radiologist*
Levy, Ronald *medical educator, researcher*
Luo, Liqun *medical educator*
Malenka, Robert C. *psychiatrist, educator*
Mansour, Tag Eldin *pharmacologist, educator*
Mark, James B. D. *surgeon, educator*
Marmor, Michael Franklin *ophthalmologist, educator*
McDevitt, Hugh O'Neill *immunologist, educator*
McDougall, Iain Ross *nuclear medicine educator*
Mignot, Emmanuel *medical researcher*
Mitchell, Beverly Shriver *hematologist, oncologist, educator*
Oberhelman, Harry Alvin, Jr. *surgeon, educator*
Olcott, Cornelius, IV, *surgeon*
Owens, Douglas K. *physician, researcher*
Polan, Mary Lake *obstetrics and gynecology educator*
Reddy, Vadiyala Mohan *cardiothoracic surgeon*
Reitz, Bruce Arnold *cardiac surgeon, educator*
Robbins, Robert Clayton *surgeon*
Rosenberg, Saul Allen *oncologist, educator*
Rubenstein, Edward *physician, educator*
Schatzberg, Alan Frederic *psychiatrist, researcher*
So, Yuen T. *neurologist, educator*
Stamey, Thomas Alexander *urologist, educator*
Stefanick, Marcia Lynn *medical educator, researcher*
Umetsu, Dale T. *pediatrics educator, physician*
Weissman, Irving L. *medical researcher*
Zarins, Christopher Kristaps *surgeon, educator*

## Stockton
Nakanishi, Alan *ophthalmologist, state representative*

## Sunnyvale
Castellino, Ronald Augustus Dietrich *radiologist, educator*
White, Christine A. *internist, oncologist, pharmaceutical executive*

## Sylmar
Corry, Dalila Boudjellal *internist, educator*
Kamangar, Nader *pulmonologist, educator*
Liu, Paul Ishen *pathologist, educator*
Tully, Susan Balsley *pediatrician, educator*

## Tarzana
Handelsman, Yehuda *endocrinologist, preventive medicine physician*
Steinberg, Jeffrey Mark *obstetrician, gynecologist, medical researcher*

## Templeton
Abernathy, Shields B. *allergist, immunologist, internist*

## Thousand Oaks
Eisenberg, Paul Richard *cardiologist, consultant, educator*
Pakula, Anita Susan *dermatologist*

## Torrance
Brasel, Jo Anne *pediatrician, educator*
Brass, Eric Paul *internal medicine and pharmacology educator, academic administrator*
Budoff, Matthew Jay *cardiologist*
Emmanouilides, George Christos *physician, educator*
Hammer, Terence Michael *physician*
Hansen, James Edward *medical educator, researcher*
Ho, Mat Hoang *gynecologist, researcher, medical educator*
Howell, Irvin Wendell, Jr. *physician, consultant*
Mehringer, Charles Mark *medical educator*
Myrke, Byron Arnold *pathologist, educator*
Oudiz, Ronald *cardiologist*
Shitabata, Paul Kent *pathologist*
Stabile, Bruce Edward *surgeon*
Sun, Nora Chi-Jun *pathologist*
Swerdloff, Ronald S. *medical educator, physician, researcher*
Tanaka, Kouichi Robert *hematologist, educator*

## Tustin
Braunstein, Herbert *pathologist, educator*
Herdeg, Howard Brian *retired physician*

## Ukiah
McClintock, Richard Polson *dermatologist*

## Vallejo
Towne, Sarah Patton *physician*

## Ventura
Abul-Haj, Suleiman Kahil *pathologist*
Villaveces, James Walter *allergist, immunologist, consultant*

## Visalia
Hsu, Shu-Dean *hematologist, oncologist*
Riegel, Byron William *ophthalmologist*

## Walnut Creek
Cannon, Grace Bert *retired immunologist*
Carson, Jay Wilmer *pathologist, educator*
Man, Pang Ling *retired psychiatrist*

## West Hills
Monosson, Ira Howard *physician*

## Westminster
Luong, Khanh Vinh Quoc *nephrologist, researcher*
Nguyen, Lan Thi Hoang *physician, educator*

## Whittier
Arenowitz, Albert Harold *psychiatrist*
Prickett, David Clinton *physician*

## Woodland Hills
Fox, James Michael *orthopedic surgeon*

## COLORADO

**Aspen**
Oden, Robert Rudolph *surgeon*

**Aurora**
Alvero, Ruben J. *medical educator*
Battaglia, Frederick Camillo *physician*
Bunn, Paul A., Jr. *oncologist, educator*
Churchill, Mair Elisa Annabelle *medical educator*
Haas, Robert Lance *surgeon, consultant*
La Rosa, Francisco Guillermo *pathologist, researcher, educator*
Mellette, Julian Ramsey, Jr. *dermatologist, dermatologic surgeon*
Nora, Audrey Hart *physician*
Rust, Stephen Thomas *geriatrician*
Shore, James H(enry) *psychiatrist*

**Basalt**
Weill, Hans *medical educator*

**Boulder**
McFarland, Robert Bruce *physician*

**Colorado City**
Stelle, Robert E. *physician, retired educator*

**Colorado Springs**
Anderson, Paul Nathaniel *oncologist, educator*
Barber, Michael J. *cardiologist, educator*
Gifford, Marilyn Joyce *emergency physician, consultant*

**Denver**
Adler, Charles Spencer *psychiatrist*
Agostini, Juan C. *surgeon*
Atkins, Dale Morrell *retired physician*
Brantigan, Charles Otto *surgeon*
Brega, Kerry Elizabeth *physician, researcher*
Douglas, Ivor Samuel *medical educator, director*
Eickhoff, Theodore Carl *epidemiologist*
Eilert, Robert Ellis *orthopedist, surgeon, educator*
Fennessey, Paul Vincent *pediatrics and pharmacology educator, researcher*
Fletcher, Courtney Vance *pharmacologist, educator*
Gabow, Patricia Anne *internist, health facility executive*
Golitz, Loren Eugene *dermatologist, medical association administrator, pathologist*
Gravlee, Glenn P(age) *anesthesiologist, educator, director*
Greyson, Clifford Russell *internist*
Guber, Myles Stewart *surgeon*
Hoffman, Murray Stanley *internist, educator, cardiologist*
Hopfer, Christian Jean *psychiatrist, educator*
Huang, Linda Chen *plastic surgeon*
Iseman, Michael Dee *medical educator*
Jafek, Bruce William *otolaryngologist, educator*
Johnson, Candice Elaine Brown *pediatrician, educator*
Johnston, Richard Boles, Jr. *pediatrician, educator, biomedical researcher*
Jones, M. Douglas, Jr. *pediatrician, educator*
Kassan, Stuart S. *rheumatologist*
Kindt, Glenn W. *neurosurgeon, educator*
Koul, Hari Krishen *surgery professor, scientist*
Krikos, George Alexander *pathologist, educator*
Krugman, Richard David *pediatrician, academic administrator, educator*
Langsley, Pauline Royal *psychiatrist*
Larsen, Gary Loy *physician, researcher*
Lewis, Evan Larson *urologist*
Lillehei, Kevin Owen *neurosurgeon, educator*
Lubeck, Marvin Jay *ophthalmologist*
Lynch, David A. *radiologist, educator*
Marrack, Philippa Charlotte *immunologist, researcher*
Martin, Richard Jay *medical educator*
McCarter, Martin D. *surgeon, researcher*
Meyers, Arlen *physician*
Moore, Ernest Eugene, Jr. *surgeon, educator*
Mueller, Kathryn Lucile *medical educator*
Petty, Thomas Lee *internist, educator*
Pomerantz, Marvin *thoracic surgeon*
Porreco, Richard Patrick *physician*
Price, David W *physician, educator, reseachrer*
Rainer, William Gerald *cardiac surgeon*
Repine, John Edward *internist, educator*
Robertson, Lawrence Marshall, Jr. *neurosurgeon*
Schiff, Donald Wilfred *pediatrician, educator*
Schrier, Robert William *physician, educator*
Shapiro, Leland *epidemiologist, educator*
Sokol, Ronald Jay *pediatric gastroenterologist, researcher*
Stamm, Carol Ann *obstetrician, gynecologist*
Stern, Jacqueline *physician*
Studevant, Laura *medical association administrator*
Sujansky, Eva Borska *pediatrician, geneticist, educator*
Szefler, Stanley James *pediatrics and pharmacology educator*
Takeda, Yasuhiko *pathologist*
Taylor, Edward Stewart *obstetrician, educator*

**Durango**
Wigton, Chester Mahlon *physician*

**Englewood**
Knize, David Maurice *plastic surgeon*
McCrary, Brian Fountain *physician*
Woodward, John Simpson, Jr. *orthopedic surgeon*

**Fort Collins**
Phemister, Robert David *veterinary medical educator*
Rennick, John H. *psychiatrist, director*

**Glenwood Springs**
Jaffrey, Ira *oncologist, educator*

**Granby**
Holzworth, Robert Haviland *retired physician*

**Grand Junction**
Janson, Richard Anthony *plastic surgeon*
Michels, Ruth Yvonne *retired cytologist*

**Greeley**
Jaouen, Richard Matthie *plastic surgeon*

**Greenwood Village**
Grainger, John R. *medical association administrator*

**Highlands Ranch**
Bublitz, Deborah Keirstead *pediatrician*

**La Jara**
Portnoy, Darin Arthur *medical association administrator*

**Lafayette**
Mehl, Albert L. *pediatrician, poet, composer*
Thornbury, John Rousseau *radiologist, physician*

**Littleton**
Forstot, Stephan Lance *ophthalmologist*

**Lone Tree**
Washington, Reginald Louis *pediatric cardiologist*

**Loveland**
King, Joan Caluda *medical educator, neuroscientist*

**Montrose**
Boice, Judith Lynette *physician, writer, educator*

**Vail**
Bevan, William Arnold, Jr. *emergency physician*

**Wheat Ridge**
Fleischaker, Gordon Henry, Jr. *pediatrician*
Ogsbury, James Stanley III *neurosurgeon, educator*

**Wolcott**
Flacke, Joan Wareham *physician, anesthesiologist, educator*

## CONNECTICUT

**Avon**
Freymann, John Gordon *physician, educator*
Hinz, Carl Frederick, Jr. *immunologist, educator*
Wu, George Yung-hsing *medical educator, gastroenterologist*

**Bethany**
Niederman, James Corson *retired internist, educator*

**Branford**
Charlot, Joseph Leonce, Jr. *preventive medicine physician*
Tchernev, Velizar Tzvetanov *physician, research scientist*

**Bridgeport**
Lobdell, David Hill *pathologist*
Mcpherson, Craig A. *cardiologist, educator*
Nijensohn, Daniel Edgardo *neurosurgeon*

**Danbury**
Belsky, Joseph L. *endocrinologist*
Johns, William David *nuclear medicine physician, internist*
Leebens, Patricia Kay *psychiatrist*

**Derby**
Katz, David Lawrence *preventive medicine physician, researcher*

**Fairfield**
Burd, Robert Meyer *hematologist, oncologist, educator*

**Farmington**
Donaldson, James Oswell III *neurologist, educator*
Liebowitz, Neil Robert *psychiatrist*
Owens, Guy *retired neurosurgeon*
Rothfield, Naomi Fox *physician*
Runowicz, Carolyn Dilworth *physician*
Schenkman, John Boris *pharmacologist, educator*
Walker, James Elliot Cabot *physician*
Wand, Martin *ophthalmologist, educator*

**Glastonbury**
Singer, Paul Richard *ophthalmologist*

**Greenwich**
Blumberg, Joel Myron *cardiologist*
Ghogawala, Zoher *neurosurgeon*
Grant, Ronald Alfred *psychiatrist, pastoral counselor, psychoanalyst*

**Groton**
Umlauf, Jon *physician, director*

**Guilford**
Springgate, Clark Franklin *physician, researcher*

**Hamden**
Nuland, Sherwin *surgeon, writer*
Reiser, Morton Francis *psychiatrist, educator*

**Hartford**
Cole, Solon Robert *pathologist, educator*
Dworkin, Paul Howard *pediatrician*
Gillam, Linda Dawn *cardiologist, researcher*
Gould, Bruce Elliott *physician, medical educator, academic administrator*
Jahiel, Rene Ino *physician*
Jung, Betty Chin *epidemiologist, educator, nurse*
Kirton, Orlando Cecilio *surgeon, educator*
Lyons, Robert William *medical educator, epidemiologist, consultant*
Pachter, Lee M. *pediatrician*
Ramanan, Sundaram V. *internist, hematologist, oncologist*

**Killingworth**
Buchanan, J(ohn) Robert *physician, educator*

**Madison**
Snell, Richard Saxon *anatomist*

**Meriden**
Horton, Paul Chester *psychiatrist*
Perricone, Nicholas V. *dermatologist*

**Middlebury**
Arnold, William Parsons, Jr. *retired internist*

**Milford**
Lee, Sin Hang *pathologist, educator*

**Mystic**
Burrow, Gerard Noel *internist, educator*

**New Canaan**
Ackerman, Sigurd Howard *psychiatrist*
Coughlin, Francis Raymond, Jr. *surgeon, educator, lawyer*

**New Haven**
Aghajanian, George Kevork *medical educator*
Askenase, Philip William *medicine and pathology educator*
Baltimore, Robert Samuel *pediatrician, epidemiologist*
Barash, Paul George *anesthesiologist, educator*
Behrman, Harold Richard *endocrinologist, physiologist, educator*
Berland, Gretchen K. *medical educator, filmmaker*
Bloomgarden, Gary Michael *neurosurgeon*
Blumenfeld, Hal *neurologist, educator*
Boyer, James Lorenzen *internist, educator*
Braverman, Irwin Merton *dermatologist, educator*
Carling, Tobias John Eric *surgeon, research scientist*
Cheng, Yung-Chi Tommy *medical educator*
Cleary, Paul David *sociomedical educator*
Cohen, Lawrence Sorel *internist, educator*
Collins, William F., Jr. *neurosurgery educator*
Comer, James Pierpont *psychiatrist, educator*
Cooper, Jack Ross *pharmacology educator, researcher*
Cullen, Mark Richard *medical educator*
Davey, Lycurgus Michael *neurosurgeon*
Edelson, Richard L. *dermatology educator, director*
Ehrenkranz, Richard Allan *pediatrician*
Ferholt, J. Deborah Lott *pediatrician*
Fikrig, Erol *rheumatologist, medical educator*
Foster, Roger Sherman, Jr. *surgeon, educator, health facility administrator*
Genel, Myron *pediatrician, educator*
Gonzalez, Caleb *ophthalmologist, educator*
Goodrich, Isaac *neurosurgeon, educator*
Gross, Ian *academic pediatrician, neonatologist*
Horwich, Arthur L. *medical educator*
Horwitz, Sarah McCue *educator*
Hostetter, Margaret K. *pediatrician, medical educator*
Jatlow, Peter I. *pathologist, medical educator, researcher*
Kalyanpur, Arjun *radiologist*
Kashgarian, Michael *pathologist, educator*
King, Robert Alan *psychiatrist, educator*
Kushlan, Samuel Daniel *internist, educator, hospital administrator*
Leckman, James Frederick *psychiatry and pediatrics educator*
Leffell, David Joel *dermatologist, surgeon, writer, photographer, medical school administrator, educator*
Levine, Robert John *internist, educator*
Lewis, Melvin *psychiatrist, pediatrician, psychotherapist*
Lopez, Javier *psychiatrist*
Lytton, Bernard *urology educator*
Malawista, Stephen E. *medical educator*
McClain, Brenda C. *pain management physician*
Miller, I. George *physician, educator, researcher*
Mukherjee, Sandip Kumar *cardiologist*
Musto, David Franklin *medical researcher, educator, historian, consultant*
Persing, John Arthur *surgeon*
Powsner, Seth *psychiatrist, educator, medical researcher*
Powsner, Seth M. *psychiatrist, educator*
Proctor, Deborah Denise *gastroenterologist, educator*
Ritchie, J. Murdoch *pharmacologist, educator*
Rose, Aron D. *ophthalmologist, educator*
Ruchkin, Vladislav *psychiatrist*
Sartorelli, Alan Clayton *pharmacologist, educator*
Sasaki, Clarence Takashi *surgeon, educator*
Schlessinger, Joseph *pharmacology educator*
Schottenfeld, Richard Steven *psychiatrist*
Seashore, Margretta Reed *physician, educator*
Shapiro, Eugene David *pediatrician, epidemiologist, educator*
Shaywitz, Bennett Arthur *medical educator*
Shulman, Gerald I. *physician, scientist, endocrinologist, educator*
Sico, Jason Jonathon *neurologist, internist, consultant*
Smith, Brian Richard *hematologist, oncologist, pathologist*
Spencer, Dennis Dee *medical educator, director*
Stahl, Richard Sheldon *surgeon*
Stern, Robert *psychiatrist*
Swain, James Edward *psychiatrist, researcher*
Tsai, James C. *ophthalmologist, researcher*
Volkmar, Fred Robert *psychiatrist, educator, director*
Waxman, Stephen George *neurologist, neuroscientist*
Weiss, Robert M. *urologist, educator*
Wessel, Morris Arthur *retired pediatrician*
Zaret, Barry Lewis *cardiologist, medical educator*
Zhang, Xiang Yang *psychiatrist, researcher*
Zhang, Yawei *epidemiologist*

**New London**
Schoenberger, Steven Harris *physician, research consultant*
Urbanetti, John Sutherland *internist, consultant*

**Niantic**
Douglas, Robert Gordon, Jr. *physician*

**Norfolk**
Mermann, Alan Cameron *retired pediatric educator, chaplain*

**Norwalk**
Carius, Michael Lee *emergency medicine physician*
Falsone, Jack Joseph *physician*

**Old Greenwich**
Lorefice, Laurence Santo *psychiatrist*

**Putnam**
Day, John Anthony, Jr. *pulmonologist*

**Ridgefield**
Egan, Kenneth J. *dermatologist*

**Southington**
Byeff, Peter David *hematologist, oncologist*

**Stamford**
Cook, Colin Burford *psychiatrist*
Erichson, Robert B. *hematologist, oncologist*
Goodhue, Peter Ames *obstetrician, gynecologist, educator*
Hecht, Harvey Leon *radiologist*
Klein, Neil Charles *physician*
Masino, Frank A. *radiation oncologist*
Walsh, Thomas Joseph *ophthalmologist*

**Stratford**
Feinberg, Dennis Lowell *dermatologist*
Mahoney, Maurice Jeremiah *medical educator*

**Torrington**
Handelman, William Alan *physician*

**Vernon Rockville**
Marmer, Ellen Lucille *pediatrician, cardiologist*

**Wallingford**
Lelas, Snjezana *pharmacologist, researcher*
Tyczynski, Jerzy Edward *epidemiologist*

**Waterbury**
Dudrick, Stanley John *surgeon, research scientist, educator*
Fischbein, Charles Alan *pediatrician*
Garsten, Joel Jay *gastroenterologist*
Koliani, Leonardi *physician*

**Waterford**
London, David Bruce *psychiatrist*
Pierson, Anne Bingham *physician*

**West Hartford**
Silver, Herbert *physician*

**Westport**
Clausman, Gilbert Joseph *retired medical librarian*
Goodman, Stanley Erwin *surgeon*
Sacks, Herbert Simeon *psychiatrist, educator, consultant*

## DELAWARE

**Dover**
Wilson, Samuel Mayhew *surgeon*

**Lewes**
Saliba, Anis Khalil *surgeon*

**Milton**
Provost, Thomas Taylor *dermatology educator, researcher*

**Newark**
DePietropaolo, Daniel L. *physician, educator*
Lemole, Gerald Michael *surgeon*

**Rockland**
Levinson, John Milton *obstetrician, gynecologist*

**Wilmington**
Abdel-Misih, Raafat Z. *surgeon, educator*
Barthold, Julia Spencer *urologist, researcher*
Benes, Solomon *biomedical scientist, physician*
Casas-Melley, Adela Teresa *pediatrician, surgeon*
Cornelison, Floyd Shovington, Jr. *retired psychiatrist*
Frelick, Robert Westcott *physician, consultant*
Goldberg, Morton Edward *pharmacologist*
Harley, Robison Dooling *ophthalmologist, educator*
Klein, Gershon A. *pediatrician*
O'Brien, Christopher D. *medical researcher, educator*
Pell, Sidney *epidemiologist*
Walsh, Louisa Marcy *medical researcher, researcher*

## DISTRICT OF COLUMBIA

**Washington**
Ahmed, Atif Ali *pathologist*
Allen, Beverly E. *medical librarian*
Anthony, Virginia Quinn Bausch *medical association executive*
Appareddy, Vijaya L. *psychiatrist*
Avery, Gordon Bennett *medical educator, neonatologist*
Barnet, Robert Joseph *cardiologist, philosopher*
Batshaw, Mark Levitt *pediatrician*
Beers, Nathaniel Brittingham Savio *pediatrician*
Benjamin, Georges Curtis *emergency physician, consultant*
Benoit, Marilyn B. *psychiatrist, consultant*
Blumenthal, Susan Jane *psychiatrist, educator*
Borenstein, David Gilbert *internist, writer, rheumatologist*
Bourne, Peter Geoffrey *physician, educator, writer*
Bridges, Robert Russell III *obstetrician, gynecologist*
Burris, Boyd Lee *psychiatrist, psychoanalyst, physician, educator*
Callaway, Clifford Wayne *physician*

Callender, Clive Orville *surgeon*
Catoe, Bette Lorrina *pediatrician, educator*
Chase, Thomas Newell *neurologist, researcher, educator*
Cheng, Tsung O. *cardiologist, educator*
Chester, Alexander Campbell III *physician*
Cooper, Byron Stanley *internist, educator*
Curfman, David Ralph *neurosurgeon, educator, civic leader, musician*
Davidson, Richard J. *medical association administrator*
Davis, David Oliver *radiologist, educator*
Dennis, Gary C. *neurosurgeon, educator*
Deutsch, Stanley *retired anesthesiologist, educator*
Dey, Radheshyam Chandra *cytologist*
Dimberg, Lennart Axel *medical researcher, physician*
Dublin, Thomas David *retired preventive medicine physician*
Earll, Jerry Miller *internist, educator, endocrinologist*
Ein, Daniel *allergist*
Engler, Renata Johanna Martha *allergist, immunologist, internist, educator*
Epps, Roselyn Elizabeth Payne *pediatrician, educator*
Erdtmann, Frederick J. *physician, retired military officer*
Escolar, Diana M. *neurologist, researcher*
Faden, Alan Ira *neurology educator*
Fairbanks, David Nathaniel Fox *otolaryngologist, surgeon, educator*
Finkelstein, James David *physician, educator*
Gadson, Sandra L. *nephrologist, medical association administrator*
Gajewski, Donald Andrew *orthopedist, surgeon*
Gardner, William Albert, Jr. *pathologist, medical products executive*
Gehrig, Leo Joseph *retired surgeon*
Gelmann, Edward Paul *oncologist, educator*
Georgieva, Rennie T. *medical librarian*
Gordon, James Samuel *psychiatrist*
Gray, Sheila Hafter *psychiatrist, researcher*
Grealy, Mary R. *medical association administrator*
Hamburg, Margaret Ann (Peggy Hamburg) *public health administrator*
Harter, Donald Harry *neurologist, medical educator*
Hartman, Gary E. *pediatric surgeon*
Hong, Mun Kyung *internist*
Hsia, Judith Ann *physician*
Hussain, Syed Taseer *biomedical researcher, educator*
Jonas, Richard Andrew *medical educator*
Jose, Pedro A. *physician*
Kahn, Charles N., III, (Chip Kahn) *medical association administrator*
Kennedy, Richard Odell *physician*
Kirch, Darrell Gene *medical association administrator, former academic administrator, former dean*
Korn, David *pathologist, educator*
Kupersmith, Joel *internist, medical school dean*
Landau, Emanuel *epidemiologist*
Latham, Patricia S. *physician*
Lessin, Lawrence Stephen *hematologist, oncologist, educator*
Little, John William *plastic surgeon, educator*
Longnecker, David Eugene *anesthesiologist, educator*
Mandel, Harold George *pharmacologist, educator*
Maniscalco-Theberge, Mary Elizabeth *surgeon, medical educator*
Mann, Marion *pathologist, educator*
Mann, Oscar *retired physician, internist, educator*
Mattsson, Ake *psychiatrist, physician*
Maxey, Randall W. *medical researcher, health science association administrator*
McGinnis, James Michael *physician*
McLeod, David G. *urologist, educator*
Miller, Richard N. *former medical association administrator*
Murray, Robert Fulton, Jr. *physician*
Neviaser, Robert Jon *orthopaedic surgeon, educator*
Novitch, Mark *physician, retired pharmaceutical executive*
Oertel, Yolanda Castillo *pathologist, educator*
Paulson, Jerome Avrom *pediatrician*
Payne, Fred J. *epidemiologist, educator*
Pearse, Warren Harland *obstetrician, gynecologist, medical association administrator*
Pellegrino, Edmund Daniel *internist, educator, retired academic administrator*
Pincus, Stephanie Hoyer *dermatologist*
Potter, John Francis *oncologist, surgeon*
Puchalski, Christina M. *physician, medical educator*
Rankin, Edward Anthony *orthopedist, surgeon*
Rao, Mahadev *pharmacologist, researcher, molecular biologist*
Rayner, Victoria Leigh *medical educator, consultant*
Reaman, Gregory Harold *pediatric hematologist, oncologist*
Redman, Robert Shelton *pathologist, dentist*
Reich, Walter *psychiatrist, museum director, educator*
Ruckman, Roger Norris *pediatric cardiologist*
Ruehle, Charles Joseph *pathologist, military officer*
Ruetter, Gunter H *surgeon*
Sabshin, Melvin *psychiatrist, educator, health science association administrator*
Schuelein, Marianne Ida *neurologist, educator*
Shanahan, Sheila Ann *pediatrician, educator*
Simon, Gary Leonard *internist, educator*
Sly, Ridge Michael *pediatrician, educator, allergist, immunologist*
Smith, Lee Elton *surgery educator, retired military officer*
Spagnolo, Samuel Vincent *internist, educator, pulmonary specialist*
Spies, James B. *radiologist, educator*
Valachovic, Richard W. *medical association administrator*
Vezina, Gilbert *pediatric neuroradiologist*
Wartman, Steven A. *medical association administrator*
Werkman, Sidney Lee *psychiatrist, educator*
Wiesel, Sam W. *medical educator, academic administrator*

Winnie, Glenna Barbara *pediatric pulmonologist*
Wolfe, Sidney Manuel *physician*

## FLORIDA

### Amelia Island
Schiebler, Gerold Ludwig *pediatrician, educator*

### Atlantic Beach
Walker, Richard Harold *pathologist, educator*

### Bartow
Etheredge, Edward Ezekiel *retired surgeon*

### Bay Pines
Law, David Hillis *physician*
Stewart, Jonathan Taylor *psychiatrist, educator*

### Belleair
Dexter, Helen Louise *dermatologist, consultant*

### Boca Raton
Feinberg, Marc H. *neurologist*
Friedland, Michael Lawrence *medical educator*
Friend, Harold Charles *neurologist*
Goldman, Stuart Miles *podiatrist*
Johr, Robert Henry *dermatologist*
Kramer, Cecile Edith *retired medical librarian*
Lemanski, Larry Fredrick *medical educator, academic administrator*
Man, Daniel *plastic surgeon*
Norris, Charles Richard, Jr. *physician, psychiatrist*
Pasternack, Stefan Alan *psychiatrist, psychoanalyst*
Rubinson, Howard Alan *physician*
Sperry, Len Thomas *psychiatrist and preventive medicine educator*
Weiner, Howard Marc *physician*

### Bonita Springs
Dougherty, James *retired orthopedist*

### Boynton Beach
Glickman, Franklin Sheldon *dermatologist, educator*
Lisan, Philip *medical educator*
Pataky, Paul Eric *ophthalmologist*
Wick, Mitchell A. *physician*
Winters, Darcy LaFountain *medical association administrator*

### Bradenton
Vereb, Teresa B. *psychiatrist*

### Brandon
Mack, Arthur Neal *emergency medicine and family practice physician*

### Cape Coral
(Harrison) Flint, Nancy Elizabeth *retired medical association administrator*
Martin, Benjamin Gaufman *ophthalmologist*

### Clearwater
Bailey, Robin Keith *medical educator*
Blumencranz, Peter William *surgeon*

### Clearwater Beach
Whedon, George Donald *medical association administrator, researcher*

### Coral Gables
Balkany, Thomas Jay *otolaryngologist*
Brandt, Frederic Sheldon *dermatologist*
Musgrave, Franklyn Garfield *obstetrician, gynecologist*
Perez, Josephine *psychiatrist, educator*
Quillian, Warren Wilson, II, *pediatrician, educator*
Wolf, Aizik Loft *neurosurgeon*
Zvijac, John E. *orthopedist, surgeon*

### Coral Springs
Wechsler, Arnold *obstetrician, gynecologist*

### Dade City
Bala, Sam G. *surgeon*

### Daytona Beach
Duma, Richard Joseph *epidemiologist, microbiologist, educator, pathologist, researcher, physician*

### Deland
Blais, Michael Roland *retired urologist*
Goldberg, Paul Bernard *gastroenterologist, clinical researcher*

### Delray Beach
Rosenfeld, Steven Ira *ophthalmologist*
Sherwood, Louis Maier *endocrinologist, pharmaceutical executive*

### Deltona
Drewry, Marcia Ann *physician*

### Destin
Burden, William R. *plastic surgeon*

### Duck Key
Prout, George Russell, Jr. *medical educator, urologist*

### Englewood
Sanders, W(illiam) Eugene, Jr. *retired internist*

### Fernandina Beach
Barlow, Anne Louise *pediatrician, medical researcher*

### Fort Lauderdale
Bass, Harold Michael *plastic surgeon*
Chernow, Bart *critical care physician*
Cox, Linda Susan *allergist, immunologist*
Droege, Marcus *medical educator, researcher*
Glick, Richard Stephen *internist, rheumatologist*
Haugen, Christine *plastic surgeon*
Lodwick, Gwilym Savage *radiologist, educator*
Parker, Sasha Smilka *medical educator, nurse, consultant*

Revis, Don Ray, Jr. *plastic surgeon*
Tristano, Antonio Gino *medical researcher*
Velez, Ines *oral pathologist, educator*
Whitmore, Douglas Michael *physician*
Zfaz, Martin *medical director, treatment professional, consultant*

### Fort Myers
Arnall, Robert Esric *physician, health facility administrator*
Benbenisty, Keith Mitchell *dermatologist*
Meng, Gunter Richard *surgeon*
Schwartz, Robert *epidemiologist*
Steier, Michael Edward *cardiac surgeon*

### Fort Pierce
Partenheimer, Robert Chapin *emergency physician*
Starner, Don Edward *radiologist, educator*

### Gainesville
Baz, Maher Afif *internist, educator, medical director lung transplant program*
Behnke, Marylou *pediatrician, educator*
Berns, Kenneth Ira *physician*
Burns, Theodore Weber *gastroenterologist*
Cance, William George *surgery educator*
Carter, Christopher Scott *medical association administrator*
Copeland, Edward Meadors III *surgeon, educator*
Drummond, Willa Hendricks *neonatologist, educator, information technology executive*
Dunn, Ben Monroe *medical educator*
Flotte, Terence Robin *pediatrician, pulmonologist*
Garin, Eduardo H. *nephrologist*
Gonzalez-Peralta, Regino P. *pediatrician*
Greer, Melvin *medical educator*
Hardt, Nancy Sisson *pathology and laboratory medicine educator*
LeVeen, Robert Frederick *radiologist*
Limacher, Marian Cecile *cardiologist*
Mazzaferri, Ernest Louis *endocrinologist, educator*
Meakin, Faith Anne *medical library diector*
Mendenhall, Nancy Price *radiologist, educator*
Modell, Jerome Herbert *anesthesiologist, educator*
Neims, Allen Howard *pediatrician, educator, dean, researcher*
Pfaff, William Wallace *medical educator*
Rhoton, Albert Loren, Jr. *neurosurgeon, educator*
Rubin, Melvin Lynne *ophthalmologist, educator*
Small, Parker Adams, Jr. *pediatrician, educator*
Suzuki, Howard Kazuro *retired anatomist, educator*
Taylor, William Jape *physician*
Tisher, Charles Craig *nephrologist, educator, dean*
Toskes, Phillip Paul *gastroenterologist, educator, researcher*
Weiner, I. David *nephrologist*
Wingard, John Reid *medical educator*
Winter, William Ernest *physician, educator*

### Hialeah
Sosa, Jorge Luis *surgeon*

### Hollywood
Constantinescu, Alex R. *pediatrician, nephrologist*
Duffner, Lee R. *ophthalmologist*

### Inverness
Esquibel, Edward V. *psychiatrist, health facility administrator*

### Jacksonville
Aldana, Philipp Roque *neurosurgeon*
Atteberry, Linda Rose *surgeon, retired military officer*
Bartley, George B. *ophthalmologist, surgeon*
Bosworth, William Posey *physician, physical education educator*
Boylan, Kevin Bernard *neurologist*
Chang, Hernan Robert *infectious disease consultant*
De Soto, Hernando *pediatric anesthesiologist*
Enders, Lawrence John *preventive medicine physician, educator*
Goodwin, Jane Ayers *pediatric anesthesiologist*
Johnson, Douglas William *radiologist*
Mass, M. F. *allergist, immunologist*
Mizrahi, Edward Alan *allergist*
Mordecai, Monica Myers *anesthesiologist*
Muehrcke, Derek David *thoracic and cardiovascular surgeon*
Perdikis, Galen *plastic surgeon*
Radisky, Derek Charles *biomedical researcher, educator*
Raynor, Eileen Margolies *otolaryngologist, educator*
Supanich, Barbara Ann *physician*
Thorsteinsson, Gudni *physiatrist*
Van Cleve, Robert Baldwin *cardiologist*
Zenni, Elisa Alter *pediatrician*

### Jupiter
Ernst, Calvin Bradley *retired vascular surgery educator*
Sykes, Robin Alexis *plastic surgeon*
Zelnick, Ronald Stuart *surgeon*

### Key Biscayne
Palmer, Roger Farley *pharmacology educator*

### Key West
Wisniewski, P. Michelle *retired obstetrician, gynecologist*

### Kissimmee
Rajyaguru, Vrajlal Laljibhai *anesthesiologist*

### Lakeland
Jakub, James Ward *physician, surgical oncologist*
Roth, William Joseph *dermatologist*

### Largo
Grove, Jeffrey Scott *family practice physician*
Krolick, Merrill A. *cardiologist*
Wheat, Myron William, Jr. *cardiothoracic surgeon*

### Leesburg
Moore, Wistar *cardiovascular surgeon*

### Longboat Key
Frankel, Jack *pediatrician, allergist*

Herzog, Godofredo Max *physician*
McCollough, Newton Clark III *orthopaedic surgeon*
Schneiderman, Julius *retired orthopedic surgeon*

### Lutz
Cualing, Hernani Del Mundo *physician, researcher*

### Maitland
Cicilioni, Orlando Joseph *plastic surgeon*

### Marco Island
Krause, Charles Joseph *otolaryngologist*
Zecchino, Vincent *retired surgeon*

### Marianna
Brunner, William F. *surgeon*

### Melbourne
Greenblatt, Hellen Chaya *immunologist, microbiologist*
Grenevicki, Lance Francis *surgeon*
Magee, Thomas Henry *radiologist, educator*
Pocoski, David John *cardiologist*

### Miami
Anderson, Douglas Richard *ophthalmologist, educator, researcher*
Bandstra, Emmalee S. *physician, pediatrician, researcher, educator*
Beck, Morris *allergist*
Benjamin, Latanya T. *dermatologist*
Bird, Vincent G. *urologist, researcher*
Blechman, Wilbur Jordan *medical educator*
Block, Norman Louis *oncologist, educator*
Bolooki, Hooshang *cardiac surgeon*
Burke, Redmond Paul *pediatric cardiologist, surgeon*
Cardenas, Rene F. *nuclear medicine physician, oncologist*
Ciancio, Gaetano *transplant surgeon, urologist*
Davis, Janet *physician*
Davis, Richard Edmund *plastic surgeon*
Duchesne, Carlos A. *epidemiologist, military officer*
Eftekhari, Nasser *physiatrist*
Eisdorfer, Carl *psychiatrist, health facility administrator*
Elsas, Louis Jacob, II, *medical educator*
Eshraghi, Adrien A. *head and neck surgeon, medical educator, researcher*
Freshwater, Michael Felix *hand surgeon, educator*
Furst, Alex Julian *thoracic and cardiovascular surgeon*
Gelband, Henry *pediatric cardiologist*
Ginsberg, Myron David *neurologist*
Glatzer, Richard L. *orthopedist, surgeon*
Goldberg, Lee Dresden *endocrinologist, educator*
Goldstein, Burton Jack *psychiatrist*
Goodwin, W. Jarrard *otolaryngologist, educator*
Gutgsell, Nancy Snowden *medical researcher*
Heros, Roberto Cosme C. *neurosurgeon*
Herz, Marvin Ira *psychiatrist, researcher*
Howell, Ralph Rodney *pediatrician, geneticist, educator*
Krishan, Awtar *educator*
Lasseter, Kenneth Carlyle *pharmacologist*
Lemberg, Louis *cardiologist, educator*
Llorente, Maria D. *psychiatrist, geriatrician, educator*
Malinin, Theodore *medical educator, researcher*
Mendez, Luis Eduardo *medical educator, researcher*
Mintz, Daniel Harvey *endocrinologist, educator, academic administrator*
Morrison, Glenn *neurosurgeon*
Page, Larry Keith *neurosurgeon, educator*
Panthaki, Zubin Jal *medical educator, plastic surgeon*
Pham, Si Mai *cardiothoracic surgeon*
Pochi, Subbarayan Ramalingam *biomedical researcher*
Porter, Wayne Randolph *dermatologist*
Puliafito, Carmen Anthony *ophthalmologist, healthcare executive*
Regev, Arie *gastroenterologist, researcher, hepatologist*
Ricordi, Camillo *surgeon, medical researcher*
Rubell, Donald *gynecologist, hotel executive, art collector*
Rusconi, Paolo *pediatric cardiologist*
Schally, Andrew Victor *endocrine oncologist, researcher*
Schild, A. Frederick *surgeon*
Scully, Sean Patrick *orthopaedic surgeon, educator*
Skyler, Jay S. *medical educator, consultant*
Sussmane, Jeffrey Brett *pediatrician*
Swaminathan, Sethuraman *pediatrician, cardiologist*
Tejada, Francisco *physician, educator*
Thaller, Seth Ray *plastic surgeon*
Troen, Bruce Robert *medical educator*
Tzakis, Andreas Gerasimos *surgeon, educator, research scientist*
Wheeler, Steve Dereal *neurologist*
Wolff, Grace Susan *pediatric cardiologist*
Wolfson, Aaron Howard *radiation oncologist, educator*
Zaydon, Thomas John, Jr. *plastic surgeon*
Zwerling, Leonard Joseph *physician, educator*

### Miami Beach
Agatston, Arthur Stephen *cardiologist*
Martz, Willard Harry *physician*
Nash, Seymour Cy *surgeon, urologist*
Rogers, Mark Charles *physician, entrepreneur, anesthesiologist, pediatrician, educator*

### Naples
Brooks, Joae Graham *psychiatrist*
Crandall, Blane Mitchell *obstetrician, gynecologist*
Gehring, David Austin *cardiologist, physician, health facility administrator*
Greene, David *surgeon, researcher*
Randall, Neil Warren *gastroenterologist*
Schwartz, Stephen Gregory *ophthalmologist*
Temple, Donald *retired allergist, dermatologist*
Thomas, John Melvin *retired surgeon*

**Niceville**
Clark, Steven Jay *plastic surgeon, consultant*

**North Palm Beach**
Stein, Mark Rodger *allergist*

**Ocala**
Altenburger, Karl Marion *allergist*

**Oldsmar**
Gambone, Victor, Jr. *internist, geriatrician*

**Orange Park**
Fetchero, John Anthony, Jr. *otolaryngologist*

**Orlando**
Dafoe, William Alfred *surgeon*
DeCampli, William Michael *surgeon, researcher*
Dixit, Naznin *endocrinologist, director*
Hornick, Richard Bernard *physician*
Kolattukudy, Pappachan Ettoop *medical center executive, biochemist, educator*
Layish, Daniel T. *internist*
Marsh, Ella Jean *pediatrician*
Naser, Saleh A. *medical researcher, educator*
Okun, Neil Jeffrey *vitreoretinal surgeon*
Pollack, Robert William *psychiatrist, corporate financial executive*
Schott, John William *psychiatrist, investment advisor*
Shub, Harvey Allen *surgeon*
Taitt, Earl Paul *psychiatrist, military officer*

**Osprey**
Gross, James Dehnert *pathologist*

**Palm Beach**
Simon, Harold *radiologist*
Stambaugh, Reginald Jack *ophthalmologist*

**Palm Beach Gardens**
Small, Melvin D. *physician, educator*

**Palm Springs**
Abou-Sayed, Hatem *plastic surgeon*

**Panama City Beach**
Reading, Anthony John *retired psychiatrist, educator*

**Pensacola**
Bradshaw, Bascom Kyle *surgeon, science educator*
Canady, Alexa Irene *pediatric neurosurgeon, educator*
Gill, Becky Lorette *retired psychiatrist*
Redmond, Michael R. *ophthalmologist*
Sharma, Venkatanarayanan *surgeon, consultant, medical educator*
Vuksta, Michael Joseph *surgeon*

**Placida**
Prabhudesai, Mukund M. *pathology educator, health facility administrator, researcher, academic administrator*

**Plantation**
Stein, Alvin *surgeon*

**Pompano Beach**
Cherla, Gautam V. *physician, nephrologist, researcher*

**Ponte Vedra Beach**
ReMine, William Hervey, Jr. *retired surgeon*

**Port Charlotte**
Asperilla, Marianito O. (Mark Asperilla) *epidemiologist*

**Punta Gorda**
Hollinshead, Ariel Cahill *oncologist, educator, researcher*

**Royal Palm Beach**
Delgado, Rizal Reyes *psychiatrist, retired internist*

**Saint Petersburg**
Bercu, Barry Bernard *pediatric endocrinologist*
Betzer, Susan Elizabeth Beers *physician, geriatrician*
Buckspan, Randy Jay *plastic surgeon*
Collins, Paul Steven *vascular surgeon*
Gilbert, Gordon Joel *neurologist, electroencelographer*
Hamilton, John McFarland *plastic surgeon, real estate developer*
Iyer, Mohan N. *surgeon*
Lanza, Donald Charles *otolaryngologist, rhinologist*
Linhart, Joseph Wayland *retired cardiologist, educational administrator*
Pflum, William John *physician*
Root, Allen William *pediatrician, educator*
Rosenblum, Martin Jerome *ophthalmologist*
Simpson, Lisa Ann *physician, educator*
Thomas, Patrick Robert Maxwell *oncologist, educator, academic administrator*

**Sanford**
Oostwouder, Peter Henry *physician*

**Sarasota**
Apfelbach, George Leonard, Jr. *urologist*
Aull, Susan *physician*
Bennett, William F. *orthopedist, surgeon*
Bowers, Charles Richard *surgeon*
Cavanagh, Denis *gynecologist, obstetrician, educator, gynecological oncologist*
Cummings, Martin Marc *medical educator, physician, academic administrator*
El Shahawy, Mahfouz *internist, educator, cardiologist*
Iverson, Robert Louis, Jr. *internist, physician*
Jelks, Mary Larson *retired pediatrician*
Levy, Gerhard *pharmacologist*
Magenheim, Mark Joseph *physician, epidemiologist, educator*
Marks, Charles *surgeon, educator*
O'Malley, Thomas Anthony *gastroenterologist, internist*

Tuch, Howard Stanley *long-term care administrator, geriatrics services professional*
Umanoff, Dan F. *medical association administrator*
Welch, John Dana *retired urologist*
Zavon, Mitchell Ralph *occupational medicine physician*

**Stuart**
Stark, Richard Boies *surgeon, artist*

**Sun City Center**
Crow, Harold Eugene *physician, educator*

**Sunrise**
Singer, Richard P. *neurologist, researcher, director*

**Tallahassee**
Hernandez, Jose Yolando Balagtas *surgeon*
Hernandez, Minerva Cuadrante *physician, consultant*
Maguire, Charlotte Edwards *retired pediatrician*
Shamsham, Fadi Michel *cardiologist*

**Tampa**
Afield, Walter Edward *psychiatrist, educator, health facility administrator*
Agazzi, Siviero *neurosurgeon*
Barness, Lewis Abraham *physician*
Branch, William Terrell *urologist, educator*
Bunker-Soler, Antonio Luis *physician*
Cancio, Margarita R. *infectious disease physician*
Dalton, William Steven *oncologist, educator*
Eichberg, Rodolfo David *physiatrist, educator*
Gilbert-Barness, Enid F. *pathologist, educator*
Greenfield, George B. *radiologist*
Jacobs, Timothy Andrew *epidemiologist, consultant*
Jacobson, Howard Newman *obstetrics and gynecology educator, researcher*
Knox, Michael Dennis *medical educator, research center administrator*
Lockey, Richard Funk *allergist, immunologist, educator*
Malone, John I. *pediatrics educator, biomedical researcher*
McIlwain, Harris H. *physician, researcher*
Muroff, Lawrence Ross *nuclear medicine physician, educator*
Norman, Robert Andrew *dermatologist, educator*
Older, Jay Justin *ophthalmic plastic surgeon*
Olson, Robert Eugene *physician, biochemist, educator*
Pfeiffer, Eric Armin *psychiatrist, gerontologist, writer*
Pollara, Bernard *pediatrician, educator, immunologist*
Powers, Pauline Smith *psychiatrist, educator, researcher*
Pribor, Hugo Casimer *physician*
Rifkin, Stephen *nephrologist*
Rowlands, David Thomas *pathology educator*
Sanberg, Paul Ronald *medical educator*
Shenefelt, Philip David *dermatologist*
Shephard, Bruce Dennis *obstetrician, educator, medical writer*
Siegel, Richard Lawrence *immunologist, allergist*
Silbiger, Martin L. *radiologist, educator, dean*
Sinnott, John Thomas *internist, educator*
Smith, David John, Jr. *plastic surgeon*
Spellacy, William Nelson *obstetrician, gynecologist, educator*
Sullebarger, John Thompson *internist, educator, cardiologist*
Tebbi, Cameron K *hematologist, oncologist*
Torres-Roca, Javier Francisco *medical educator*
Watkins, Joan Marie *osteopath, physician*

**Titusville**
Duffy, John Charles *psychiatrist, educator, consultant*

**Venice**
Hrachovina, Frederick Vincent *retired osteopathic physician*

**Vero Beach**
Christopher, Robert Paul *retired physical medicine physician*
Enhorning, Goran *obstetrician, gynecologist*
Hilker, Robert Reuben John *medical educator, researcher, administrator, consultant*
Schwarz, Berthold Eric *psychiatrist*

**Weeki Wachee**
Finney, Roy Pelham, Jr. *urologist, surgeon, inventor*

**West Palm Beach**
Brumback, Clarence Landen *physician*
Coloso, Victor Francisco *pediatrician*
Kapnick, S. Jason *oncologist*
Levin, Ronald Mitchell *geriatrician*
Most-Levin, Carol Lynn *physician, geriatrician*
Newmark, Emanuel *ophthalmologist*
Pinsky, Mark A. *plastic surgeon*
Pottash, A. Carter *psychiatrist, hospital executive*
Whitfield, Graham Frank *orthopedic surgeon*
Wisnicki, Jeffrey Leonard *plastic surgeon*

**Weston**
Faierman, Tamy M. *plastic surgeon*
Malave, Andres *pharmacologist, educator*
Messa, Charles Angelo III *plastic surgeon*
Nogueras, Juan Jose *surgeon*
Samson, Michel Charles *plastic surgeon*

**Wimauma**
Palmer, Louis Thomas *pathologist*

**Winter Haven**
Susac, John Obren *neurologist, consultant*

**Winter Park**
Baker, James L., Jr. *plastic surgeon*
Pineless, Hal Steven *neurologist*

**GEORGIA**

**Acworth**
Oloni, Anthony Olushegun *medical association administrator, director*

**Albany**
Peach, Paul E. *physician, health facility administrator*

**Alpharetta**
Harris, James Herman *pathologist, neuropathologist, consultant, educator*

**Athens**
Bowen, John Metcalf *pharmacologist, toxicologist, educator*

**Atlanta**
Berkelhamer, Jay Ellis *pediatrician*
Bernardino, Carlo Roberto *ophthalmologist, educator*
Bostwick, John III *plastic surgeon, department chairman, medical educator*
Brandenburg, David Saul *gastroenterologist, educator*
Bremner, James Douglas *psychiatrist, researcher, education educator*
Burstein, Fernando David *plastic surgeon*
Cates, Christopher Upton *cardiologist*
Cooper, Gerald Rice *clinical pathologist*
Cooper-Ruspoli, Annie Nataf *psychiatrist, director*
Curran, James W. *epidemiologist, educator, dean*
Cwiak, Carrie Ann *obstetrician, gynecologist*
Davis, Lawrence William *radiation oncologist*
Davis, Michael *medical educator*
De Rosa, Christopher Thomas *biomedical researcher*
Dietz, William Harry *pediatrician*
D'Orsi, Carl Joseph *medical educator, radiologist, researcher*
Dutt, Kamla *medical educator*
Falk, Henry *pediatrician, epidemiologist, researcher*
Fermanis, Ernest George *urological surgeon*
Fortenberry, James Donald *pediatrician*
Frank, Erica *preventive medicine physician*
Frias, Jaime Luis *retired geneticist, educator*
Fry-Johnson, Yvonne Wilkins *pediatrician*
Galambos, John Thomas *internist, medical educator*
Ganaway, George Kenneth *psychiatrist, psychoanalyst, educator, researcher*
Gayle, Helene D. *pediatrician, public health service officer*
Gayles, Joseph Nathan, Jr. *medical association administrator, not-for-profit fundraiser, chemist*
Goldman, John Abner *rheumatologist, immunologist, educator*
Gordon, Frank Jeffrey *medical educator*
Hall, Wilbur Dallas, Jr. *medical educator*
Hardman, John B. *psychiatrist, director*
Hatcher, Charles Ross, Jr. *surgeon, health facility administrator*
Higginbotham, Eve Juliet *ophthalmologist, educator, dean*
Holtzheimer, Paul E. III *medical educator*
Horsburgh, Charles Robert *allergist*
Hudgins, Roger J. *pediatric neurosurgeon*
Hug, Carl Casimir, Jr. *pharmacology and anesthesiology educator, medical ethics educator*
Hughes, James Mitchell *epidemiologist, educator*
Igho-Pemu, Priscilla Eyikojoka *physician, educator, medical researcher*
Israili, Zafar Hasan *pharmacologist, educator*
Jackson, Fleda Mask *medical educator*
Johns, Michael Marieb Edward *otolaryngologist, academic administrator*
Jurkiewicz, Maurice John *surgeon, educator*
Kamb, Mary Louise *medical epidemiologist*
Karp, Herbert Rubin *neurologist, educator*
Kaul, Pushkar Nath *pharmacologist, educator*
Kellermann, Arthur L. *medical educator*
Khaitan, Leena *surgeon*
Klippel, John H. *physician, medical association administrator*
Letton, Alva Hamblin *surgeon, educator*
Lubin, Michael Frederick *physician, educator*
Mansour, Kamal A. *cardiothoracic surgeon*
Mantella, Tino J. *former medical association administrator*
Minneman, Kenneth Paul *pharmacology educator*
Nahai, Foad *plastic surgeon, educator*
Oakley, Godfrey Porter, Jr. *medical educator*
Olansky, Sidney *retired dermatologist*
Oyesiku, Nelson Mobolanle *neurosurgeon, neuroscientist*
Peacock, Lamar Batts *retired physician*
Rohr-Kirchgraber, Theresa M.B. *adolescent medicine*
Sands, Jeff Michael *medical educator*
Sexson, William Robert *pediatrician, educator*
Sherman, Roger Talbot *surgeon, educator*
Singh, Narendra *cardiologist, researcher, medical educator*
Smith, Robert Boulware III *vascular surgeon, educator*
Sola, Augusto *pediatrician, educator*
Spangler, Dennis Lee *physician*
Steinhaus, John Edward *retired anesthesiologist, educator*
Stillwagon, Gary Bouldin *radiation oncologist*
Taylor, Andrew T., Jr. *radiologist, educator*
Taylor, Robert N. *medical researcher, department chairman*
Thacker, Stephen Brady *medical association administrator, epidemiologist*
Udoff, Eric Joel *diagnostic radiologist*
Waring, George Oral III *ophthalmologist, surgeon*
Wenger, Nanette Kass *cardiologist, researcher, educator*
Westney, Gloria Elaine *medical educator*
Weyand, Cornelia M. *medical educator*
Willis, Isaac *dermatologist, educator*
Wineski, Lawrence E. *medical educator, biomedical researcher*
Yancey, Asa Greenwood, Sr. *physician, educator*
Yates, Jerome William *medical association administrator*

**Auburn**
Hutchinson, Leslie Julian *preventive medicine physician*

**Augusta**
Bollag, Wendy Bollinger *medical educator*
Carroll, James Edwin *child neurologist, researcher*
Dolen, William Kennedy *allergist, immunologist, pediatrician, educator*
Ellison, Lois Taylor *internist, educator, medical association administrator*
Fincher, Ruth Marie Edla *medical educator, dean*
Gambrell, Richard Donald, Jr. *endocrinologist, educator*
Given, Kenna Sidney *surgeon, educator*
Hooks, Vendie Hudson III *surgeon*
Horuzsko, Anatolij *medical researcher*
House, Fredrick Crisler *allergist*
Hsu, Stephen De *medical educator*
Johnson, William Michael *physician*
Lee, Gregory Price *neuropsychology educator*
Luxenberg, Malcolm Neuwahl *ophthalmologist, educator*
Mansberger, Arlie Roland, Jr. *surgeon*
Ownby, Dennis Randall *pediatrician, educator, allergist, researcher*
Parrish, Robert Alton *retired pediatric surgeon, educator*
Ryan, James Walter *physician, medical researcher*
Wray, Betty Beasley *allergist, immunologist, pediatrician*

**Brunswick**
Perniciaro, Charles Vincent *dermatologist, educator, entrepreneur*

**Buford**
Byrd, Larry Donald *behavioral pharmacologist*

**Columbus**
Chan, Philip *retired dermatologist, retired military officer*

**Dahlonega**
Nourbakhsh, M. Reza *medical educator*

**Decatur**
Bain, James Arthur *pharmacologist, educator*
Brown, William Virgil *internal medicine educator*
Harris, Maurice Daniel *internist*
Henderson, Ralph Hale *physician*

**Dublin**
Giannini, A. James *psychiatrist, educator, researcher, author*

**Duluth**
Derro, Robert Arthur *retired physician*
Evans, Paul *osteopath*

**Fort Stewart**
Warner, Christopher Hugh *psychiatrist*

**Kennesaw**
Barnett, Benjamin Lewis, Jr. *retired physician, educator*

**Lagrange**
Copeland, Robert Bodine *internist, cardiologist*
West, John Thomas *retired surgeon*

**Lawrenceville**
Fetner, Robert Henry *radiobiologist*

**Macon**
Brin, Foster Blake *psychiatrist*
Mayes, Alva Louie *physician, pediatrician*
Quiroga, Alicia Espinosa *physiatrist*
Robinson, Joe Sam *neurosurgeon, educator*
Schnell, Frederick Mark *oncologist, hematologist*
Young, Henry E. *tissue engineering medical educator*

**Marietta**
Gibb, Ginari Rene *psychiatrist*
Hagood, Murl Felton *surgeon*
Henderson, Cynthia *medical librarian*
Levere, Richard David *internist, educator*
Ranu, Harcharan Singh *biomedical scientist, administrator, orthopedic biomechanics educator*
Reed, James Whitfield *internist, educator, endocrinologist*

**Martinez**
Colborn, Gene Louis *anatomy educator, researcher*

**Reidsville**
Saad, Fathy Zaki *medical association administrator, physician*

**Roswell**
McCloud, Melody Theresa *obstetrician-gynecologist, surgeon*

**Savannah**
Everhard, Martin E. *surgeon*
Fishburne, John Ingram, Jr. *retired obstetrician/gynecologist, educator*
Hoskins, William John *obstetrician, educator, gynecologist*
Krahl, Enzo *retired surgeon*
Lindley, James Gunn, Jr. *neurosurgeon*
Skelton, William Douglas *physician*
Wirth, Fremont Philip, Jr. *neurosurgeon, educator*
Zoller, Michael *otolaryngologist, head and neck surgeon, educator*

**Smyrna**
Kell, Michael Jon *physician, researcher*

**Stockbridge**
Friedman, Robert Barry *neurosurgeon*

**Stone Mountain**
Gotlieb, Jaquelin Smith *pediatrician*

**Tifton**
Dorminey, Henry Clayton, Jr. *allergist*

**Valdosta**
Beal, John M. *surgeon, medical educator*
Morgan, Joe Leland *physician, psychiatrist*

**Warner Robins**
Gayton, Johnny Lee *ophthalmologist, educator, recreational facility executive*

## HAWAII

**Honolulu**
Ahmed, Iqbal *psychiatrist, consultant*
Brady, Stephen R.P.K. *physician*
Chesne, Edward Leonard *physician*
Curb, Jess David *medical educator, researcher*
Edwards, John Wesley, Jr. *urologist*
Fong, Bernard W.D. *physician, educator*
Goldstein, Sir Norman *dermatologist*
Goodhue, William Walter, Jr. *pathologist, military officer, educator*
Guerrero, Reuben Castro *oncologist, internist*
Hammar, Sherrel Leyton *medical educator*
Ho, Reginald Chi Shing *medical educator*
Kane, Thomas Jay III *surgeon, educator*
Kim, S. Peter *psychiatrist, educator, health facility administrator, researcher*
Lau, H. Lorrin *obstetrician, gynecologist*
Lee, Yeu-Tsu Margaret *surgeon, educator*
Maddock, Jay E. *medical educator*
Moreno-Cabral, Carlos Eduardo *cardiac surgeon*
O'Shughnessy, Edward Joseph *urologist, retired medical educator*
Parsa, Fereydoun Don *plastic surgeon*
Schatz, Irwin Jacob *cardiologist, educator*
Silva, Jana Kaida *obstetrician, maternal/fetal medicine specialist*
Sugiki, Shigemi *ophthalmologist, educator*

**Kailua**
Buratynski, Theresa Joan *physician*

**Kamuela**
Mc Dermott, John Francis *psychiatrist, physician*
Morgan, Andrew Lane *urologist, educator*

**Koloa**
Donohugh, Donald Lee *physician*

**Lahaina**
Percy, Helen Sylvia *physician*

**Lihue**
Culliney, John James *radiologist, educator*

**Mililani**
Gardner, Sheryl Paige *gynecologist*
Okita, George Torao *retired pharmacologist*

**Waikoloa**
Copman, Louis *radiologist*

## IDAHO

**Boise**
Redshaw, James Douglas *neurologist*

**Coeur D' Alene**
Gumprecht, Jane Caroline Doering *retired physician*

**Idaho Falls**
Lee, Glenn Richard *medical association administrator, educator*

**Post Falls**
Riggs, Jack Timothy *emergency physician, retired lieutenant governor*

## ILLINOIS

**Arlington Heights**
Jensen, Lynn Edward *retired medical association administrator, economist*
Ruder, John Regan *physician*

**Barrington**
Young, Michael Phillip *orthopedist, surgeon*

**Belleville**
Kappel, Stephen R. *retired orthopedist*

**Bloomington**
Trefzger, Richard Charles *surgeon*

**Bolingbrook**
Malicay, Manuel Alaban *physician*

**Champaign**
Freedman, Philip *internist, educator*
Gold, Paul Ernest *psychology and behavioral neuroscience educator*

**Chicago**
Abcarian, Herand *surgeon, educator*
Abelson, Herbert Traub *pediatrician, educator*
Adomavicius, Jonas *gastroenterologist, writer*
Aifantis, Ioannis *medical educator*
Albrecht, Ronald Frank *anesthesiologist*
Andersen, Burton Robert *immunologist, educator, medical historian*
Arnold, Damon Theodore *physician*
Arruda, Jose *nephrologist*
Artz, Andrew *hematologist, researcher*
Bakay, Roy Arpad Earle *neurosurgeon, educator*
Bakris, George L. *nephrologist, educator, clinical researcher*
Baldwin, DeWitt Clair, Jr. *pediatrician, educator*
Balk, Robert A. *medical educator*
Balsam, Theodore *physician*
Barker, Walter Lee *thoracic surgeon*
Baron, Joseph Mandel *hematologist*

Barton, John Joseph *obstetrician, gynecologist, educator, health facility administrator, researcher*
Beck, Robert N. *nuclear medicine educator*
Becker, Michael Allen *internist, rheumatologist, educator*
Bell, Carl Compton *psychiatrist, researcher*
Benson, Al Bowen III *oncologist, educator*
Black, Henry Richard *physician*
Boggs, Joseph Dodridge *pediatric pathologist, educator*
Bogolub, David Louis *physician*
Bonow, Robert Ogden *medical educator*
Bowman, James Edward *pathologist, educator*
Brasher, Aimee Elizabeth *surgeon*
Brendler, Charles Burgess *urologist, educator*
Briones, Teresita Landicho *medical researcher, educator*
Buchh, Basharat *pediatrician*
Burck, Joseph Russell *medical educator, consultant, minister*
Cameron, Kenzie Alynn *medical researcher, educator*
Caro, William Allan *dermatologist, educator, pathologist*
Celesia, Gastone Guglielmo *neurologist*
Chambers, Donald Arthur *biochemistry and molecular medicine educator*
Champagne, Ronald Oscar *medical association administrator*
Chan, Lawrence Siu-Yung *dermatologist, educator*
Charles, Allan G. *obstetrician, educator*
Charrow, Joel *pediatrician, educator, geneticist, director*
Chatterton, Robert Treat, Jr. *reproductive endocrinology educator*
Chiu, Brian Chih-Hung *epidemiologist*
Chmell, Samuel Jay *orthopedic surgeon*
Christoffel, Katherine Kaufer *pediatrician, epidemiologist, educator*
Chunprapaph, Boonmee *physician, educator*
Coe, Fredric L. *internist, educator, medical researcher*
Cohen, Melvin R. *physician, educator*
Colley, Karen J. *medical educator, researcher*
Conroe, Henry Gerald *psychiatrist*
Conway, James Joseph *radiologist, educator*
Curry, Raymond Howard *physician*
Davidson, Michael H. *cardiologist, researcher*
Davison, Richard *internist, educator*
Dayal, Vijay Shanker *medical educator, physician*
Diamond, Seymour *physician*
Dowlatshahi, Kambiz *surgeon, educator*
Dunaif, Andrea Elizabeth *endocrinologist*
Dunea, George *nephrologist, educator*
Edward, Deepak Paul *ophthalmologist, researcher*
Elias, Sherman *obstetrician, gynecologist, educator, clinical geneticist*
Evans, Thelma Jean Mathis *internist*
Feingold, Daniel Leon *anesthesiologist, consultant*
Feldman, Ted *cardiologist*
Ferguson, Mark Kendric *surgeon, educator*
Flaherty, Timothy Thomas *radiologist*
Freitag, Frederick Gerald *osteopathic physician*
Friedman, Michael *surgeon*
Galante, Jorge Osvaldo *orthopedic surgeon, educator*
Galatzer-Levy, Robert Milton *psychiatrist*
Geha, Alexander Salim *cardiothoracic surgeon, educator*
Gerbie, Albert Bernard *obstetrician, gynecologist, educator*
Gewurz, Anita Tartell *physician, medical educator*
Givone, Donna Marie *pharmacologist*
Glass, Ronald Bernhard Jacob *radiologist*
Golomb, Harvey Morris *hematologist, oncologist, educator*
Gorbien, Martin John *medical educator, geriatrician*
Gordon, Leo I. *hematologist, oncologist, educator*
Grayhack, John Thomas *urologist, educator*
Greenberger, Paul Allen *allergist, immunologist, educator, medical researcher*
Gregory, Stephanie Ann *hematologist, educator*
Griem, Katherine Leslie *radiation oncologist*
Hambrick, Ernestine *retired colon and rectal surgeon*
Harris, Gerald David *surgeon*
Hasnain, Memoona *medical educator, researcher*
Head, Louis Rollin, II, *surgeon*
Hellman, Samuel *radiologist, educator*
Herbst, Arthur Lee *obstetrician, gynecologist*
Hibbard, Judith Usher *obstetrician*
Hill, Carlotta H. *physician*
Honig, George Raymond *pediatrician*
Hsueh, Wei *pathologist, educator*
Huckman, Michael Saul *neuroradiologist, educator*
Hughes, John Russell *neurologist, educator*
Hussey, Michael Jude *obstetrician, educator*
Inan, Zabrin *psychiatrist*
Ivankovich, Anthony D. *anesthesiologist, educator*
Iyer, Kishore *transplant surgeon*
Jameson, James Larry *medical educator, endocrinologist, internist*
Jensen, Harold Leroy *medical liability insurance administrator, physician*
Jilhewar, Ashok *gastroenterologist*
Johnson, Timothy Patrick *health and social researcher*
Kahrilas, Peter James *medical educator, researcher*
Katz, Adrian Izhack *medical educator*
Kirschner, Barbara Starrels *gastroenterologist*
Kirsner, Joseph Barnett *physician, educator*
Kittle, Charles Frederick *surgeon*
Kloss, Linda L. *medical association administrator*
Kuiken, Todd Alan *medical researcher, rehabilitation services professional, educator*
Larsen, Erik *retired surgeon*
Lavani, Romeen M. *physician*
Lee, Raphael Carl *plastic surgeon, biomedical engineer*
Leff, Alan Richard *medical educator, researcher*
Leventhal, Bennett Lee *psychiatry and pediatrics educator, academic administrator*
Lindquist, Lee A. *geriatrician, educator*
Lopes, Demetrius Klee *neurosurgeon*
Lopez, Carolyn Catherine *physician*
Luchins, Daniel Jonathan *psychiatrist*
Lurain, John Robert III *gynecologist*

Mahaffey, John Christopher *medical association executive*
Malkinson, Frederick David *dermatologist, educator*
Martin, Gary Joseph *medical educator*
McKinney, William T. *psychiatrist, educator*
McLawhon, Ronald William *pathology educator, biochemist*
Meltzer, David Owen *internist, educator, economist*
Metz, Charles Edgar *radiology educator*
Millichap, Joseph Gordon *neurologist, educator*
Mirkin, Bernard Leo *pharmacologist, pediatrician*
Moawad, Atef *obstetrician, gynecologist, educator*
Morgan, Elaine R. *hematologist, oncologist, medical educator*
Naclerio, Robert Michael *otolaryngologist, educator*
Nahrwold, David Lange *surgeon, educator*
Narahashi, Toshio *pharmacology educator*
Nyhus, Lloyd Milton *retired surgeon, retired educator*
Olson, Jack Conrad, Jr. *geriatrician*
Page, Ernest *retired medical educator*
Pappas, George Demetrios *anatomist, cell biologist, educator*
Pasche, Boris Claude Roger *physician*
Poznanski, Andrew Karol *pediatric radiologist*
Prinz, Richard Allen *surgeon*
Pugh, Carla M. *surgeon, educator*
Rafeyan, Roueen *psychiatrist, educator*
Ramsey-Goldman, Rosalind *physician*
Replogle, Robert Lee *cardiovascular surgeon, thoracic surgeon*
Ridenour, Joey *medical association administrator, operations research specialist*
Robertson, William Wright, Jr. *orthopedist, educator*
Robinson, June Kerswell *dermatologist, educator*
Rogers, Eugene Jack *retired medical educator*
Roizen, Nancy J. *physician, educator*
Rosen, Steven Terry *oncologist, hematologist*
Ross, Lainie Friedman *pediatrician*
Rowley, Janet Davison *physician*
Saclarides, Theodore John *colon and rectal surgeon, educator*
Sandler, Richard H. *pediatric gastroenterologist*
Sandlow, Leslie Jordan *gastroenterologist, educator*
Schafer, Michael Frederick *orthopedic surgeon*
Schenck, Robert Roy *hand surgeon*
Schilsky, Richard Lewis *oncologist, researcher*
Sciarra, John J. *obstetrician, gynecologist, educator*
Scommegna, Antonio *obstetrician, gynecologist, educator*
Seeler, Ruth Andrea *pediatrician, educator*
Serota, Scott *medical association administrator*
Shields, Thomas William *surgeon, educator*
Short, Marion Priscilla *neurogenetics educator*
Siegler, Mark *internist, educator*
Smalheiser, Neil Raymond *neurobiologist*
Smith, Earl Charles *nephrologist, educator*
Smith, Lewis J. *medical educator, researcher*
Socol, Michael Lee *obstetrician, gynecologist, educator*
Song, David *plastic surgeon, medical educator*
Sparberg, Marshall Stuart *gastroenterologist, educator*
Steinhorn, Robin H. *neonatologist, educator*
Strassner, Howard Taft, Jr. *obstetrician, educator*
Stulberg, Samuel David *surgeon, physician*
Tallman, Martin Stuart *hematologist, oncologist*
Tanna, Angelo Peter *ophthalmologist, educator*
Telfer, Margaret Clare *internist, hematologist, oncologist*
Tomar, Russell Herman *pathologist, educator, researcher*
Valyi-Nagy, Tibor G. *neuropathologist, virologist*
Volgman, Annabelle Santos *cardiologist, educator*
Walker, Matthew *radiologist*
Walton, Robert Lee, Jr. *plastic surgeon*
Waxler, Beverly Jean *anesthesiologist, physician*
Webster, James Randolph, Jr. *physician*
Whitington, Peter Frank *pediatrics educator, pediatric hepatologist*
Wied, George Ludwig *physician*
Williams, Philip Copelain *obstetrician, gynecologist*
Williamson, Wayne C. *internist, geriatrician*
Willoughby, William Franklin, II, *retired physician, researcher*
Winjum, Stephen J. *medical association administrator*
Wissler, Robert William *pathologist*
Yaghmai, Dina *dermatologist, educator*
Yao, Mike *otolaryngologist*
Yao, Tito Go *pediatrician*
Yudkowsky, Rachel *medical educator*
Zee, Phyllis C. *physician, educator, researcher*
Zeine, Rana Ramsey *neuropathologist, research professor*
Zhang, John X *medical educator*

**Chicago Heights**
Yalavarthi, Ramaraja *physician*

**Darien**
Gardner, Howard Garry *pediatrician, educator*
Kulkarni, Bidy *reproductive endocrinologist, biomedical researcher, consultant*

**Deerfield**
Sanner, John Harper *retired pharmacologist*

**Des Plaines**
Adatto, Irving Jack *physician*
Quintanilla, Antonio Paulet *retired physician, educator*

**Dixon**
Polascik, Mary Ann *ophthalmologist*

**Elgin**
Yarkony, Gary Michael *physician, researcher*

**Elmhurst**
Blain, Charlotte Marie *internist, educator*

**Evanston**
Bloomer, William David *radiologist, oncologist, educator*

Crawford, James Weldon *psychiatrist, educator, administrator*
Gaiha, Vishnu Das *cardiologist*
Khandekar, Janardan Dinkar *oncologist, educator*
Miller, Stephen Herschel *surgeon, educator*
Mustoe, Thomas Anthony *physician, plastic surgeon*
Nelson, Richard Lawrence, Jr. *surgeon, educator*
Peterson, Lance Robert *physician*
Rosengart, Todd Kenneth *cardiothoracic surgeon, researcher, neurosurgeon, consultant*
Salafsky, Ira S. *pediatrician, educator*
Schwartz, Neena Betty *endocrinologist, educator*
Sener MD, Stephen Francis *oncologist, surgeon*
Sprang, Milton LeRoy *obstetrician, gynecologist, educator*
Stumpf, David Allen *pediatric neurologist*
Traisman, Howard Sevin *retired pediatrician*
Vick, Nicholas A. *neurologist*

**Fairfield**
Thomason, Nola Faye *emergency physician*

**Galena**
Bezkorovainy, Anatoly *medical educator, retired biochemist*

**Galesburg**
Tourlentes, Thomas Theodore *retired psychiatrist*

**Glen Ellyn**
Dieter, Raymond Andrew, Jr. *physician, thoracic and vascular surgeon*

**Glencoe**
Milloy, Frank Joseph, Jr. *surgeon*

**Glenview**
Casas, Laurie Ann *plastic surgeon*
Graff, Jeffrey G. *emergency physician*
Haebich, Arthur T. *retired surgeon, retired thoracic surgeon*

**Godfrey**
King, Ordie Herbert, Jr. *oral pathologist*

**Greenville**
Hall, Tracy Lynn *physician*

**Harvey**
Heilicser, Bernard Jay *emergency physician*

**Herrin**
Gauto, Nelson Fernando *plastic surgeon, consumer products company executive*

**Highland Park**
Roy, Hemant Kumar *gastroenterologist, researcher*
Saltzberg, Eugene Ernest *emergency physician, educator*

**Hillsboro**
Mulch, Robert F., Jr. *physician*

**Hines**
Best, William Robert *internist, educator, dean*

**Hinsdale**
Allen, James Edward *preventive medicine physician*
Brueschke, Erich Edward *physician, researcher, educator*
Dillon, Jane Elizabeth *otolaryngologist*
Gruft, James Harris *physiatrist, educator*
Lonchyna, Vassyl A. *thoracic surgeon*

**Joliet**
Layman, Dale Pierre *medical educator, researcher, writer*
Ring, Alvin Manuel *pathologist, educator*

**Lake Barrington**
Morris, Ralph William *chronopharmacologist*

**Lake Bluff**
Kyncl, John Jaroslav *pharmacologist*

**Lake Forest**
Callan, Clair Marie *physician, consultant*
Jones, Philip Newton *internist, educator*
Kelly, Daniel John *physician*
Levy, Nelson Louis *immunologist, educator, surgeon*
Pawl, Ronald Phillip *neurosurgery educator*
Salter, Edwin Carroll *retired pediatrician*
Weinberg, Milton, Jr. *retired cardiovascular and thoracic surgeon*
Wilbur, Richard Sloan *medical association administrator, physician*

**Lisle**
Colbert, Marvin Jay *retired internist, educator*

**Lombard**
Bachop, William Earl, Jr. *retired anatomist, zoologist*
Henkin, Robert Elliott *nuclear medicine physician*

**Long Grove**
Ausman, Robert K. *surgeon, research and development company executive*

**Macomb**
Dexter, Donald Harvey *surgeon, educator*

**Marion**
Schaede, Richard Edwin *retired family practice physician*

**Maywood**
Albain, Kathy S. *oncologist*
Aranha, Gerard V. *surgeon*
Biller, Jose *neurologist, educator*
Dado, Diane Valentina *plastic and reconstructive surgeon*
Gamelli, Richard Louis *surgeon, educator*
Gaynor, Ellen Rose *hematologist*
Gianopoulos, John George *obstetrician*
Hanin, Israel *pharmacologist, educator*
Light, Terry Richard *orthopedic hand surgeon*

Miele, Lucio *physician, medical researcher, pharmacologist*
Moran, John Francis *cardiologist*
Nand, Sucha *medical educator*
Newman, Barry Marc *pediatric surgeon*
Picken, Maria M. (Maria M. Mrozowicz-Picken) *pathologist*
Stankiewicz, James A. *otolaryngologist*
Ward, Kathleen Anne *radiologist*
Warpeha, Raymond Leonard *surgeon, educator*
Wheeler, John S., Jr. *urologist*

**Mc Gaw Park**
Bernardo, Angelito Alday *nephrologist, medical products executive*

**Melrose Park**
Klein, Lloyd William *cardiologist, researcher*

**Moline**
Arnell, Richard Anthony *radiologist*

**Naperville**
Bufalino, Vincent John *cardiologist, medical administrator*
Folk, Frank Anton *surgeon, educator*
Miller, Charles E. *gynecologist*
Pollak, Raymond *general and transplant surgeon*
Zinger, Michael *reproductive endocrinologist*

**Normal**
Cooley, William Emory, Jr. *radiologist*

**North Chicago**
Barsano, Charles Paul *medical educator, dean*
Bush, Eugene Nyle *pharmacologist, researcher*
Chedid, Antonio *pathologist, educator, researcher*
Gall, Eric Papineau *internist, educator*
Hawkins, Richard Albert *medical educator, administrator*
Kim, Yoon Berm *immunologist, educator*
Nair, Velayudhan *pharmacologist, educator, academic administrator*
Rudy, David Robert *physician, educator*
Sierles, Frederick Stephen *psychiatrist, educator*

**Northbrook**
Cucco, Ulisse P. *retired obstetrician, gynecologist*
Hindo, Walid Afram *radiology educator, researcher*
Rosenfeld, Robert Lee *psychiatrist*

**Oak Brook**
Christian, Joseph Ralph *physician*
Ding, Jianchi *embryologist, researcher*

**Oak Park**
Matsuda, Takayoshi *surgeon, educator, biomedical researcher*

**Oakbrook Terrace**
Becker, Robert Jerome *allergist, consultant*

**Orland Park**
Drugas, Theodore George *retired surgeon*

**Park Ridge**
Bitran, Jacob David *internist*
Pielet, Bruce William *obstetrician*
White, John Vincent *surgeon, consultant*

**Peoria**
Estes, Norman C. *surgeon, educator*
Lanzino, Giuseppe *physician*
Meriden, Terry *physician*

**Pinckneyville**
Cawvey, Clarence Eugene *retired physician*

**Quincy**
Daniels, James M. *medical educator*

**River Forest**
Moore, Vernon John, Jr. *pediatrician, consultant, lawyer*
Tiesenga, Marvin Francis *surgeon*

**Rockford**
Heerens, Robert Edward *physician*

**Saint Francisville**
Harezi, Ilonka Jo *medical technology research executive*

**Schaumburg**
Cabay, Robert John *physician, dentist*

**Skokie**
Levy, Mark Hirsch *internist, researcher, medical educator*

**Springfield**
Elble, Rodger Jacob *neurologist, researcher*
Frank, Stuart *cardiologist*
Godwin, John E. *hematologist*
Holland, John Madison *retired family practice physician*
Mikell, Frank Leonard *cardiologist*
Myers, Phillip Ward *otolaryngologist*
Rabinovich, Sergio *physician, educator*
Sumner, David Spurgeon *surgeon, educator*
Woodson, Gayle Ellen *otolaryngologist*
Yaffe, Stuart Allen *physician*
Zaricznyj, Basilius *orthopedic surgeon*

**Sterling**
Tóth, Peter Paul *physician, researcher*

**Sugar Grove**
Debartolo, Hansel Marion, Jr. *otolaryngologist, plastic surgeon*

**Urbana**
Kaufman, Jerome Benzion *retired neurosurgeon*
Krock, Curtis Josselyn *pulmonologist*
Nelson, Ralph Alfred *physician*
Oliphant, Uretz John *physician, surgeon*
O'Morchoe, Charles Christopher Creagh *anatomist, surgeon, educator*

**Washington**
Stine, Robert Howard *retired pediatrician, allergist*

**West Chicago**
Paulissen, James Peter *retired pediatrician, county official*

**Westchester**
Calder, Robert Austin *preventive medicine physician, administrator*

**Western Springs**
Thomas, Paul Augustus, Jr. *retired thoracic surgeon*

**Wheaton**
Ali, Fatima Z. *physician*
Bogdonoff, Maurice Lambert *physician*
McCartney, Charles Price *retired obstetrician, retired gynecologist*

**Wheeling**
Levitin, Yelena *surgeon*

**Wilmette**
Hier, Daniel Barnet *neurologist*

**Winnetka**
Rossi, Ennio C. *internist, educator*
Rubnitz, Myron Ethan *pathologist, educator*

**INDIANA**

**Alexandria**
Irwin, Gerald Port *physician*

**Anderson**
King, Charles Ross *physician*

**Bedford**
Hunter, Harlen Charles *orthopedic surgeon*

**Beech Grove**
Hughes, Charles E. III *plastic surgeon*

**Bloomington**
Bishop, Michael D. *emergency physician*
Moore, Ward Wilfred *medical educator*
O'Loughlin, Valerie Dean *medical educator*
Rink, Lawrence Donald *cardiologist*

**Bluffton**
Pitts, Neal Chase *rheumatologist*

**Carmel**
Cleary, Robert Emmet *gynecologist, infertility specialist*
Cohen, Marlene Lois *pharmacologist*

**Crown Point**
Mc Farland, James Joseph *cardiothoracic surgeon*

**Decatur**
Fitzgerald, Robert Hannon, Jr. *orthopedic surgeon*

**Dune Acres**
Martino, Robert Salvatore *orthopedic surgeon*

**Fishers**
Thomas, John Arlen *pharmacologist, educator, science administrator*

**Fort Wayne**
Brandt, William Edward *retired surgeon, retired consultant*
Lee, Shuishih Sage *pathologist*
Pauly, Evelyn May Rockwell *physician, educator, dermatology*
Richardson, Joseph Hill *physician, medical educator*
Salam, Gohar Azam *physician, director*
Sarkisian, Edward *dermatologist*

**Greenwood**
Atkins, Clayton H. *family physician, epidemiologist, educator*

**Hammond**
Ashbach, David Laurence *internist, nephrologist*

**Highland**
Steen, Lowell Harrison *retired physician*

**Indianapolis**
Allen, Stephen D. (Stephen Dean Allen) *pathologist, microbiologist*
Aprison, Morris Herman *experimental and theoretical neurobiology educator*
Bergstein, Jerry Michael *nephrologist*
Brandt, Ira Kive *pediatrician, geneticist*
Brickley, Richard Agar *retired surgeon*
Brown, Edwin Wilson, Jr. *preventive medicine physician, educator*
Broxmeyer, Hal Edward *medical educator*
Capello, William Naldo *surgeon*
Cheng, Liang *pathologist*
Coleman, John Joseph III *surgery educator*
Croffie, Joseph M. *gastroenterologist, educator*
Dalsing, Michael Cletus *surgeon, educator*
Daly, Walter Joseph *medical educator*
Dyken, Mark Lewis, Jr. *neurologist, educator*
Eigen, Howard *pediatrician, educator*
Einhorn, Lawrence Henry *oncologist, medical educator*
Feng, Gen-sheng *medical educator, researcher*
Foley, Brian Scott *physiatrist, medical educator*
Gardner, Thomas Allen *urologist, educator*
Ghetti, Bernardino Francesco *pathologist, educator, neuroscientist*
Green, Morris *pediatrician, educator*
Grosfeld, Jay Lazar *surgeon, educator*
Hale, Douglass Stuart *urogynecologist, director*
Hansell, Richard Stanley *obstetrician, gynecologist, educator*
Holden, Robert Watson *radiologist, educator, dean*
Hubbard, Jesse Donald *retired pathology educator*
Inui, Thomas Spencer *physician, educator*

Irwin, Glenn Ward, Jr. *medical educator, physician, academic administrator*
Jackson, Valerie Pascuzzi *radiologist, educator*
Johnston, Cyrus Conrad, Jr. *medical educator*
Kamendulis, Lisa M. *medical educator*
Kaye, Gordon Israel *pathologist, anatomist, educator*
Knoebel, Suzanne Buckner *cardiologist, educator*
Kunkler, Arnold William *retired surgeon, educator*
Ladd, Alan Preston *pediatrician, pediatric surgeon*
Lehman, Glen A. *gastroenterologist*
Lemberger, Louis *pharmacologist*
Lumeng, Lawrence *physician, educator*
MacDougall, John Duncan *thoracic surgeon*
Madura, James Anthony *surgeon, educator*
Manders, Karl Lee *neurosurgeon*
McKeag, Douglas Bruce *physician, educator*
Mehta, Rakesh Peter *medical educator*
Miyamoto, Richard Takashi *otolaryngologist*
Molitoris, Bruce Albert *nephrologist, educator*
Norins, Arthur Leonard *dermatologist, educator*
Nurnberger, John I., Jr. *psychiatrist, educator*
Pitt, Henry Anthony *surgeon, researcher, medical educator*
Richter, Judith Anne *pharmacologist, educator*
Robinson, Rebecca Lynne *medical researcher*
Rogers, Robert Ernest *medical educator*
Roth, Lawrence Max *pathologist, educator*
Sawada, Stephen George *cardiologist, researcher*
Schmetzer, Alan David *psychiatrist*
Sherman, Stuart *internist, gastroenterologist*
Siderys, Harry *surgeon, educator*
Smith, James Warren *pathologist, educator, microbiologist, parasitologist*
Stehman, Frederick Bates *obstetrician, gynecologist, educator*
Sutton, Gregory Paul *obstetrician, gynecologist*
Ware, J(oe) Anthony *cardiologist*
Watanabe, August Masaru *physician, educator, retired science association director*
Weber, George *oncology and pharmacology educator, researcher*
Weinberger, Myron Hilmar *medical educator*
Wilson, Fred M., II, *ophthalmologist, educator*
Woolling, Kenneth Rau *vascular internist*
Yao, Yongxue *immunologist*
Yee, Robert Donald *ophthalmologist*
Zipes, Douglas Peter *cardiologist, researcher*

**Lafayette**
Hamdi, Hamid S. *neurologist, neurorehabilitation specialist, consultant, researcher*
Maickel, Roger Philip *pharmacologist, educator*

**Logansport**
Brewer, Robert Allen *physician*

**Marion**
Fisher, Pierre James, Jr. *physician*

**Merrillville**
Doumanian, Heratch Ohannes *radiologist*
Wang, Josephine L. Fen *physician*

**Michigan City**
Mothkur, Sridhar Rao *radiologist*

**Mishawaka**
Sobol, Zbigniew W. *orthopedist, surgeon*

**Muncie**
Nanko, Raymond S. *physician*
Roch, Lewis Marshall, II, *ophthalmic surgeon, medical entrepreneur*

**Munster**
Singh, Manmohan *orthopedic surgeon, educator*

**New Albany**
Chowhan, Naveed Mahfooz *oncologist*

**Notre Dame**
Vakulenko, Sergei Borisovich *medical researcher, educator*

**Scottsburg**
Kho, Eusebio *surgeon*

**South Bend**
Anderson, Kenneth Paul *nephrologist, administrator*
Davis, Glen Anthony *pediatrician*

**Sullivan**
Chavez, Mary Ann *osteopathic family physician*

**Valparaiso**
Canganelli, Vincent Guglielmo *retired psychiatrist*
Kobak, Alfred Julian, Jr. *obstetrician, gynecologist*

**Walton**
Chu, Johnson Chin Sheng *retired physician*

**West Lafayette**
Borowitz, Joseph Leo *pharmacologist, educator*
Cramer, William Anthony *biochemistry and biophysics researcher, educator*
Frey, Harley Harrison, Jr. *retired anesthesiologist*
Poulos, James Thomas *endocrinologist, educator*
Rutledge, Charles Ozwin *pharmacologist, educator*
Stob, Martin *retired physiology educator*
Tacker, Willis Arnold, Jr. *medical educator, researcher*

**IOWA**

**Ames**
Fleming, Jon Lee *gastroenterologist*

**Cedar Rapids**
Maikon, Marc Steven *podiatrist*
Norris, Albert Stanley *psychiatrist, educator*

**Clinton**
Woodman, Grey Musgrave *psychiatrist*

**Clive**
Neis, Arthur Veral *healthcare and development company executive*

**Coralville**
Aly, Al S. *plastic surgeon*

**Davenport**
Shammas, Nicolas Wahib *internist, cardiologist*

**Des Moines**
Habib, Shahid *medical association administrator*
Olds, John Ward *internist*
Song, Joseph *pathologist, educator*
Wattleworth, Roberta Ann *physician*

**Iowa City**
Abboud, Francois Mitry *physician, educator*
Adams, Brian David *orthopaedic surgeon, educator*
Afifi, Adel Kassim *physician*
Andreasen, Nancy Coover *psychiatrist, educator, neuroscientist*
Beaver, Hilary A. *medical educator, ophthalmologist*
Bedell, George Noble *internist, educator*
Berg, Mary Jaylene *pharmacy educator, researcher*
Buckwalter, Joseph Addison *orthopedic surgeon, educator*
Burns, C(harles) Patrick *hematologist, oncologist*
Clifton, James Albert *physician, educator*
Cooper, Reginald Rudyard *orthopedic surgeon, educator*
Eckstein, John William *internist, educator, retired dean*
Fellows, Robert Ellis *medical educator, researcher*
Field, Robert W. *epidemiologist, health physicist, educator*
Galask, Rudolph Peter *obstetrician, gynecologist*
Gantz, Bruce Jay *otolaryngologist, educator*
Grose, Charles Frederick *pediatrician, epidemiologist*
Hammond, Harold Logan *oral and maxillofacial pathologist, educator*
Hartz, Arthur J. *medical researcher*
Heistad, Donald Dean *cardiologist*
Iannettoni, Mark David *thoracic surgeon, department chairman*
Kennedy, Colleen M. *medical educator*
Kerber, Richard E. *cardiologist*
Kisker, Carl Thomas *pediatrician, educator*
Konety, Badrinath R. *surgeon, researcher*
Lamping, Kathryn G. *medical educator, medical researcher*
Lauer, Ronald Martin *pediatric cardiologist, researcher*
Loening-Baucke, Vera *pediatrician, educator*
Long, John Paul *pharmacologist, educator*
Mason, Edward Eaton *surgeon*
Medh, Jheem D. *medical educator, biochemist, researcher*
Morriss, Frank Howard, Jr. *pediatrics educator*
Mullan, Brian *medical educator*
Murray, Jeffrey C. *medical educator, pediatrician*
Nelson, Herbert Leroy *psychiatrist*
Niebyl, Jennifer Robinson *obstetrician, gynecologist, educator*
Olshansky, Brian *internal medicine and cardiology educator, researcher, physician*
Peloso, Paul Michael *medical educator*
Ponseti, Ignacio Vives *orthopaedic surgery educator*
Richerson, Hal Bates *internist, allergist, immunologist, educator*
Sheffield, Val C. *medical geneticist*
Snyder, Peter M. *medical educator, medical researcher*
Strauss, John Steinert *dermatologist, educator*
Tsalikian, Eva *physician, educator*
Van Gilder, John Corley *neurosurgeon, educator*
Weinberger, Miles M. *pediatrician, educator*
Weintraub, Neal L. *medical educator, cardiologist*
Welsh, Michael James *medical educator, biophysicist, educator*
Williams, Richard Dwayne *physician, educator, urologist*
Ziegler, Ekhard Erich *pediatrics educator*

**Marshalltown**
Cassidy, Eugene Patrick *pathologist*
Thomas, David Llewellyn *physician*

**Sioux City**
Ayi, Bertha Serwa *infectious disease specialist, internist*
Kelly, Mary Elizabeth Wiese *medical educator*

**West Des Moines**
Alberts, Marion Edward *retired physician*

**KANSAS**

**Basehor**
Hart, Paul Vincent, Jr. *emergency and acute care physician, inventor*

**Coffeyville**
Hawley, Raymond Glen *pathologist*

**Concordia**
Fowler, Wayne Lewis, Sr. *internist*

**Fort Leavenworth**
Wilhelm, Gary Bretz *physician*

**Hutchinson**
Crater, Timothy Andrews *internist*

**Kansas City**
Aljitawi, Omar Salah *hematologist, oncologist*
Anderson, Harrison Clarke *pathologist, educator, biomedical researcher*
Arakawa, Kasumi *physician, educator*
Damjanov, Ivan *pathologist, educator*
Dunn, Marvin Irvin *physician*
Gattone, Vincent Henry, II, *medical researcher, anatomist*
Grantham, Jared James *nephrologist, educator*

Hudson, Robert Paul *medical educator*
Huet, Raul *psychiatrist*
Johnson, Joy Ann *diagnostic radiologist*
Krantz, Kermit Edward *obstetrician, department chairman*
Kriet, J. David *medical educator*
Lawrence, Walter Thomas *plastic surgeon*
Lee, Kyo Rak *radiologist, educator*
McCallum, Richard Warwick *medical researcher, clinician, educator*
Mohn, Melvin Paul *anatomist, educator*
Rawitch, Allen Barry *medical educator, academic administrator*
Schloerb, Paul Richard *surgeon, educator*
Sciolaro, Charles Michael *cardiothoracic and vascular surgeon*
Suzuki, Tsuneo *molecular immunologist*
Vacek, James *cardiologist*
Voogt, James Leonard *educator*
Ziegler, Dewey Kiper *neurologist, educator*

**Lawrence**
Buck, Henry William, Jr. *obstetrician, gynecologist*
Miller, Don Robert *surgeon, educator*

**Leawood**
Hartzler, Geoffrey Oliver *retired cardiologist*

**Manhattan**
Durkee, William Robert *retired internist*
Oehme, Frederick Wolfgang *medical researcher, educator*

**Olathe**
Monzon, Carlos Manuel *physician*

**Overland Park**
Landry, Mark Edward *podiatrist, researcher*

**Pittsburg**
Morgan, Lyle Warner, II, *medical educator*
Sullivan, William John *osteopath*

**Prairie Village**
Fairchild, Robert Charles *pediatrician*

**Salina**
Bell, Mark Gerald *physician, surgeon*

**Shawnee Mission**
Bell, Deloris Wiley *physician*
Fleming, Michael O. *physician*
Henley, Douglas E. *medical association administrator*
Price, James Gordon *physician, educator*
Thomas, Christopher Yancey III *surgeon, educator*

**Topeka**
Johns, William Howard *psychiatrist, neurologist*
Menninger, William Walter *psychiatrist*

**Wichita**
Burket, George Edward, Jr. *retired family physician*
Ferris, Bruce G. *plastic surgeon, educator*
Guthrie, Richard Alan *physician*
Rieger, James A. *plastic surgeon*

**KENTUCKY**

**Berea**
Lamb, Irene Hendricks *medical researcher*

**Bowling Green**
Cofoid, Paul Brian *physician*

**Danville**
Nickens, Harry Carl *medical association administrator*

**Elizabethtown**
Rahman, Rafiq Ur *oncologist, educator*

**Elkton**
Manthey, Frank Anthony *physician, director*

**Highland Heights**
Luse, Kimberly Ann *radiologist, educator*

**Lexington**
Anderson, James Wingo *physician*
Baumann, Robert Jay *child neurology educator*
Belin, Bruce *surgeon*
Bricker, John Timothy *pediatric cardiologist*
Chance, Kenneth Bernard, Sr. *endodontist educator, academic administrator*
Clawson, David Kay *orthopedic surgeon*
Davey, Diane Davis *pathologist, educator*
Hagen, Michael Dale *family physician educator*
Hayes, Don, Jr. *physician, researcher*
Holsinger, James Wilson, Jr. *physician*
Kaplan, Martin P. *allergist, immunologist, pediatrician*
Kibler, William Benjamin *orthopedist, surgeon*
Kwolek, Christopher John *surgeon, educator*
McRoberts, J. Williams *urologist, surgeon, researcher*
Means, Robert Taylor, Jr. *hematologist, educator*
Mukherjee, Debabrata *cardiologist, researcher*
Puffer, James C. *sports medicine physician, educator, medical association administrator*
Tollison, Joseph W. *family practice physician*
Walton, William W., Jr.
Weitzel, William David *psychiatrist*
Whayne, Thomas French, Jr. *cardiologist, educator*
Young, Paul Ray *medical association administrator, physician*

**Louisville**
Amin, Mohammad *urology educator*
Andrews, Billy Franklin *pediatrician, educator*
Aronoff, George Rodger *medicine and pharmacology educator*
Ballew, Laurie K. *psychiatrist*
Callen, Jeffrey Phillip *dermatologist, educator*
Chien, Sufan *surgeon, educator*

Cook, Larry Norman *pediatrician, neonatologist, educator*
Danzl, Daniel Frank *emergency physician*
Elin, Ronald John *pathologist, educator*
Farman, Allan George *radiologist, pathologist, educator*
Foulks, Gary Neal *ophthalmologist, educator*
Galandiuk, Susan *colon and rectal surgeon, educator*
Gall, Stanley Adolph *immunologist, researcher*
Garretson, Henry David *neurosurgeon*
Haynes, Douglas Martin *obstetrician, gynecologist, educator*
Holt, Homer Anthony, Jr. *urologist, educator*
Kaplan, Henry Jerrold *ophthalmologist, educator*
Lockwood, William Byron *physician*
Lord, Jonathan T. (Jack Lord) *medical association administrator*
McMasters, Kelly Marc *surgeon, educator*
Parker, Joseph Corbin, Jr. *pathologist, educator, department chairman*
Pasic, Resad *medical educator*
Pence, Hobert Lee *physician*
Polk, Hiram Carey, Jr. *surgeon, educator*
Richardson, James David *surgeon*
Schwab, John Joseph *psychiatrist, educator*
Scott, Ralph Mason *retired radiologist, educator*
Syed, Ibrahim Bijli *medical educator, physicist*
Thongboonkerd, Visith *nephrologist, researcher*
Waddell, William Joseph *pharmacologist, toxicologist*
Weeter, John Montgomery *plastic surgeon*
Weisskopf, Bernard *pediatrician, child behavior, development and genetics specialist, educator*
Wright, Jesse Hartzell *psychiatrist, educator*

**Newport**
Giuliani, Michael J. *medical educator*

**Owensboro**
Adams, Robert Douglas *cardiothoracic surgeon*

**Russellville**
Rogers, Gina Insco *medical association administrator*

**Waco**
Hackman, Vicki Lou *physician*

**LOUISIANA**

**Alexandria**
Hanley, Henry Gorman *cardiologist*
Norem, Richard Frederick *surgeon*
Webb, Watts Rankin *surgeon*

**Baton Rouge**
Bray, George August *internist, researcher, educator*
Cherry, William Ashley *surgeon, state health official, educator*
Gettys, Thomas Wigington *medical researcher*
Ishler, Harold LeRoy, Jr. *family medicine physician*
Kastin, Abba Jeremiah *endocrinologist, researcher*
Kidd, James Marion III *allergist, immunologist, educator*
Puyau, Francis Albert *retired radiology educator, physician*
Spell, Derrick W. *oncologist, educator*

**Belle Chasse**
Arimura, Akira *biomedical researcher, educator*

**Doyline**
Willis, Gladden Williams *pathologist, scientific photographer, tree farmer*

**Gonzales**
Adams, Jason D. *obstetrician, gynecologist*

**Kenner**
Farber, George Allan *dermatologist, educator*

**Lafayette**
Culotta, Frank Jay, Jr. *preventive medicine physician*
Meza, Luis Alberto *internist, researcher*

**Lake Charles**
Clement, Richard Joseph *retired obstetrician, gynecologist*
Drez, David Jacob, Jr. *orthopedic surgeon, educator*
Gunderson, Clark Alan *orthopedic surgeon*
Lacoste, Alan Daniel *physician, educator, medical company executive*

**Madisonville**
Young, Lucy Cleaver *retired physician*

**Mandeville**
Childress, Joel M. *medical educator*
Lamid, Sofjan *physician, educator*

**Many**
Behari, Vishnu N. *physician, health facility administrator*

**Marrero**
Kushner, Frederick Gary *cardiologist, medical educator*

**Metairie**
Edisen, Clayton Byron *physician*
Jacobs, Benjamin Franklin *cardiologist*
Lake, Wesley Wayne, Jr. *internist, allergist, medical educator*

**Minden**
Kemmerly, James Robert *obstetrician, gynecologist*

**Monroe**
Cooksey, John Charles *ophthalmologist, retired congressman*

**New Orleans**
Agrawal, Krishna Chandra *pharmacology educator*
Beck, David Edward *surgeon*
Berenson, Gerald Sanders *physician*
Cargille, Charles M. *internist, pain management physician, educator*
Cohn, Isidore, Jr. *surgeon, educator*
Domer, Floyd Ray *pharmacologist, educator*
Duncan, Margaret Caroline *physician*
Easson, William McAlpine *psychiatrist, educator*
Espinoza, Luis Rolan *rheumatologist, researcher*
Ewin, Dabney Minor *physician*
Fisher, James William *pharmacologist, medical educator*
Frohlich, Edward David *medical educator*
Fuselier, Harold Anthony, Jr. *urologist, director, educator*
Gould, Harry J. III *neurology educator*
Griffin, Jeffrey Farrow *surgeon*
Hollier, Larry Harold *vascular surgeon, hospital administrator, dean*
Hyman, Albert Lewis *cardiologist, educator*
Hyslop, Newton Everett, Jr. *infectious disease specialist*
Incaprera, Frank Philip *internist*
Kewalramani, Laxman Sunderdas *surgeon, consultant*
Kolinsky, Michael Allen *emergency physician*
Lewy, John Edwin *pediatric nephrologist*
Locke, William *retired endocrinologist*
Lopez, Manuel *immunology and allergy educator*
Martin, David Hubert *internist, epidemiologist, educator*
McFadden, P. Michael *physician, surgeon*
McSwain, Norman Ellsworth, Jr. *surgeon, educator*
Millikan, Larry Edward *dermatologist*
Navar, Luis Gabriel *physiology educator, researcher, director*
Nicholl, Jeffrey Scott *neurologist, educator*
Nichols, Ronald Lee *surgeon, educator*
Ochsner, John Lockwood *thoracic-cardiovascular surgeon*
O'Quinn, April Gale *obstetrician, gynecologist, educator*
Pankey, George Atkinson *internist, educator, researcher*
Puschett, Jules B. *nephrology educator, researcher*
Reza, Ali Hajmohammad *cardiologist*
Riddick, Frank Adams, Jr. *physician, healthcare administrator*
Rock, John Aubrey *gynecologist, obstetrician, educator, healthcare administrator, retired chancellor*
Stewart, Gregory Wallace *physician*
Straumanis, John Janis, Jr. *psychiatrist, educator*
Threefoot, Sam Abraham *physician, educator*
Timmcke, Alan Edward *colon and rectal surgeon*
Usdin, Gene Leonard *psychiatrist*
Waring, William Winburn *pediatric pulmonologist, educator*
Witherspoon, Lynn Ralph *physician*

**Opelousas**
Lafleur, Kenneth Charles *ophthalmologist*
Pinac, André Louis III *obstetrician, gynecologist*

**Shreveport**
Blondin, Joan *nephrologist educator*
Brannon, Guy Emilio *psychiatrist*
Conrad, Steven Allen *critical care and emergency physician, biomedical engineer, educator*
Fort, Arthur Tomlinson III *obstetrician, educator*
Griffith, Robert Charles *allergist, educator*
Heldmann, Maureen Gail *physician, radiologist*
Jawahar, Ajay *neurosurgeon, educator*
Jones, Kenneth B., Jr. *surgeon*
Jose, Bisquerra *psychiatrist*
Knight, Adina Kay *allergist, immunologist*
London, Steve Norman *obstetrician, gynecologist, educator*
McDonald, John Clifton *surgeon*
Misra, Raghunath Prasad *physician, educator*
Rigby, Perry Gardner *medical association administrator, internist, medical educator*
Ryder, Randall Taylor *nuclear medicine technologist, director*
Shelby, James Stanford *surgeon, researcher*
Tandon, Neeraj *cardiologist, educator*
Wolf, Robert Edward *physician, educator*

**Slidell**
McBurney, Elizabeth Innes *dermatologist, physician, educator*
Muller, Robert Joseph *gynecologist*

**Sulphur**
Toniette, Sallye Jean *physician*

**MAINE**

**Auburn**
Matthews, Margaret Ellen *physician*

**Augusta**
Hussey, John Francis *physician, geriatrician*

**Bangor**
Palmer, Thomas Howard, Jr. *retired surgeon*
Rosen, Clifford James *internist*

**Bar Harbor**
Gould, Douglas Bradley *biomedical researcher*
Nass, Meryl J. *physician, writer, research scientist*

**Belfast**
DeSilvey, Dennis Lee *cardiologist, educator, academic administrator*

**Biddeford**
Ford, Charles Willard *medical educator*

**Brunswick**
Aranson, Robert *physician, director*

**Deer Isle**
Smith, Gardner Watkins *physician*

**Lubec**
Hayes, Ernest M. *podiatrist*

**Orono**
Weiss, Robert Jerome *psychiatrist, educator*

**Portland**
Clark, Gordon Hostetter, Jr. *physician*
Montegut, Alain J. *physician, consultant*
Rockefeller, Richard Gilder *medical association administrator*

**South Portland**
Wheeler, Hewitt Brownell *surgeon, educator*

**Southport**
Gibson, Edgar Thomas *retired surgeon, educator*

**Topsham**
Arnold, Charles Burle, Jr. *psychiatrist, writer*

**Yarmouth**
Northrup, Christiane *obstetrician, gynecologist*

**MARYLAND**

**Aberdeen**
Cassady, Shawn Lawrence *psychiatrist*

**Aberdeen Proving Ground**
Craig, Stephen C. *osteopathic physician, army officer*
Willens, Scott *pharmacologist, military officer*

**Annapolis**
Green, David Charles *retired surgeon*
Halpern, Joseph Alan *physician*
Kushner, Jack *retired physician*
Welch, Robert Bond *ophthalmologist, educator*

**Arnold**
Harris, Roger Clark *psychiatrist, consultant*

**Baltimore**
Alves, Donald W. *emergency physician, educator*
Anderson, Jean R. *women's health physician*
Aurelian, Laure *medical sciences educator*
Bahrami, Hossein *epidemiologist, physician*
Baker, R. Robinson *surgeon*
Baker, Timothy Danforth *physician, educator*
Baumgartner, William Anthony *cardiac surgeon*
Belzberg, Allan Joel *neurosurgery educator*
Bigelow, George E. *psychology and pharmacology scientist*
Blakemore, Karin Jane *obstetrician, geneticist*
Blattner, William Albert *physician, epidemiology researcher*
Bochner, Bruce Scott *immunologist, educator*
Brem, Henry *neurosurgeon, educator, researcher*
Brieger, Gert Henry *medical educator*
Brodie, Angela M. *biomedical researcher, educator*
Brody, Eugene Bloor *psychiatrist, educator, editor*
Busuttil, Steven James *surgeon*
Cameron, Duke Edward *cardiac surgeon, educator*
Cao, Dengfeng *pathologist*
Carrier, France *medical educator*
Carson, Benjamin Solomon *neurosurgeon*
Chen, Yu *acupuncturist, Chinese herbologist*
Clements, Mary Lou *epidemiologist, educator*
Cohen, Steven Paul *anesthesiologist, researcher*
Colgan, Richard *medical educator*
Colomer, Veronica *medical educator, researcher*
Conway de Macario, Everly *immunologist, molecular biologist*
Cornwell, Edward E. III *surgeon*
Cummings, Charles William *otolaryngologist, educator*
Dang, Chi Van *hematology and oncology educator*
Dannenberg, Arthur Milton, Jr. *experimental pathologist, immunologist, educator*
DeAngelis, Catherine D. *pediatrics educator*
DeLateur, Barbara Jane *medical educator*
DePaulo, J. Raymond, Jr. *psychiatrist, researcher*
DeWeese, Theodore L. *radiation oncologist*
Diaz-Montes, Teresa P. *oncologist, obstetrician, gynecologist*
Dobs, Adrian Sandra *endocrinologist, educator*
Drachman, Daniel Bruce *neurologist, educator*
Eisenberg, Howard Michael *neurosurgeon*
Erozan, Yener Sahir *pathologist, educator*
Faden, Ruth R. *medical educator, ethicist, researcher*
Farber, Donna Lynn *medical researcher, educator*
Ferencz, Charlotte *pediatrician, epidemiologist, preventive medicine physician, educator*
Ferentz, Kevin Scott *physician*
Fox, Harold Edward *obstetrician, researcher, gynecologist, educator*
Freischlag, Julie Ann *surgeon*
Gimenez, Luis Fernando *physician, educator*
Godenne, Ghislaine Dudley *physician, psychotherapist, educator*
Goldberg, Morton Falk *ophthalmologist, educator*
Goldman, Lynn Rose *medical educator*
Gordis, Leon *physician*
Greenough, William Bates III *medical educator*
Griffin, John W. *neurologist, medical educator*
Griffith, Lawrence Stacey Cameron *cardiologist, educator*
Gustafson, Thomas *medical association administrator*
Haan, James Mathew *surgeon, researcher*
Harris, James Carol Overton, Jr. *psychiatrist, pediatrician*
Hellmann, David Bruce *medical educator*
Hofkin, Gerald Alan *gastroenterologist*
Holder, Lawrence Edward *radiologist, educator*
Hungerford, David Samuel *orthopedic surgeon, educator*
Jaar, Bernard Georges *nephrologist, researcher*
Johns, Richard James *medical educator*
Johnson, Kenneth Peter *neurologist, researcher*
Johnson, Richard Tidball *microbiology and neuroscience educator, virologist, researcher*
Joyce, David Lyle *surgeon*
Karpa, Jay Norman *surgeon*
Kastor, John Alfred *cardiologist, educator*
Katarzyna, Macura J. *radiologist, researcher*

Kelen, Gabor David *emergency physician*
Kelly, Deanna Lynn *pharmacologist, educator*
Kerr, Douglas Anthony *neurologist, researcher*
Kessler, Irving Isar *epidemiologist, consultant*
Knapp, David Allan *pharmaceutical educator, researcher, dean*
Kwon, Chul Soo *psychiatrist*
Lawrence, Robert Swan *physician, educator*
Lazarus, Gerald Sylvan *dermatologist, educator, dean*
Levien, David Harold *surgeon*
Lewison, Edward Frederick *surgeon*
Lichtenstein, Lawrence Mark *immunologist, allergist, educator*
Litrenta, Frances Marie *psychiatrist*
Long, Donlin Martin *surgeon, educator*
Longo, Dan Louis *internist, researcher, oncologist*
Macario, Alberto Juan Lorenzo *physician*
Mackowiak, Philp Arthur *medical educator, epidemiologist*
Manson, Paul Nellis *plastic surgeon*
Margolis, Simeon *physician, educator*
Matheson, Nina W. *medical researcher*
Matjasko, M. Jane *anesthesiologist, educator*
McHugh, Paul R. *psychiatrist, neurologist, educator*
McMillan, Julia A. *pediatrician*
Miller, Edward Doring *anesthesiologist, hospital administrator, dean*
Miller, Michael *physician, educator*
Moser, Hugo Wolfgang *physician*
Myslinski, Norbert Raymond *medical educator*
Nelkin, Barry David *oncology researcher and educator*
Nichols, David Gregory *anesthesiologist, pediatrician, educator*
Norman, Philip Sidney *physician*
Nyquist, Paul Alan *neurologist, researcher*
O'Toole, Tara Jeanne *medical educator, former federal agency administrator*
Perler, Bruce Alan *surgeon*
Powe, Neil Richard *physician, educator, epidemiologist, public health service officer*
Rayson, Glendon Ennes *internist, preventive medicine specialist, writer*
Roberts, Rosalinda Cusido *medical researcher, educator*
Rose, Noel Richard *immunologist, microbiologist, educator*
Rumbaugh, Jeffrey Arlin *neurologist, neuroscientist*
Samet, Jonathan Michael *epidemiologist, educator*
Saudek, Christopher D. *medical educator*
Schoenrich, Edyth Hull *internist, preventive medicine physician*
Schuster, Marvin Meier *retired physician, educator*
Silbergeld, Ellen Kovner *epidemiologist, researcher, toxicologist*
Siliciano, Robert F. *immunologist, medical educator*
Silverberg, Steven George *pathologist, educator*
Smith, Stephen Ross *endocrinologist*
Snyder, Solomon Halbert *psychiatrist, pharmacologist*
Sommer, Alfred *ophthalmologist, medical educator, researcher*
Song, Danny *radiation oncologist*
Sroka, Karen Jean *clinical director*
Starfield, Barbara Helen *pediatrician, educator*
Stephens, Joseph *psychiatrist, researcher*
Talalay, Paul *pharmacologist, educator*
Vogelstein, Bert *oncology educator*
Walsh, Patrick Craig *urologist*
Waterbury, Larry *physician, educator*
Weisfeldt, Myron Lee *cardiologist, educator*
Weiss, James Lloyd *cardiology educator*
Welker, James Anthony *physician*
Wilson, Donald Edward *internist, educator, dean*
Wu, Albert W. *medical educator*
Yang, Stephen C. *thoracic surgeon*
Young, Barbara *psychiatrist, psychotherapist, educator, photographer*

**Bethesda**
Akhondi, Hossein *internist, researcher*
Alter, Harvey J. *hematologist, educator*
Anderson, George Kenneth *physician, retired military officer, foundation administrator*
Apud, Jose Antonio *psychiatrist, educator*
Arons, Bernard S. *psychiatrist, educator, health services administrator*
Ashwell, Jonathan D. *medical researcher*
Berzofsky, Jay A. *medical researcher*
Brinton, Louise A. *cancer epidemiologist*
Brown, Dudley Earl, Jr. *psychiatrist, educator, health science association administrator, federal agency administrator, retired military officer*
Brown, Elizabeth E. *epidemiologist*
Bukh, Jens *medical researcher*
Bulas Kurzrok, Dorothy Isabella *pediatrician*
Cai, Tao *biomedical researcher*
Cairo, Armon Anthony *physician*
Candotti, Fabio *pediatrician*
Cao, Jie Jane *cardiologist, researcher*
Catherino, William Henry *endocrinologist*
Chanock, Robert Merritt *pediatrician*
Chen, Kevin Gang *oncologist, researcher, molecular pharmacologist*
Choyke, Peter L. *radiologist, researcher*
Christopher, Austin *neurologist, researcher*
Cohen, Robert Abraham *retired physician*
Cohen, Sheldon Gilbert *physician, historian, immunologist*
Compton, Wilson Martindale *psychiatrist, researcher*
Crout, J(ohn) Richard *pharmacologist, researcher*
Danforth, David Newton, Jr. *surgeon, oncologist*
De Cherney, Alan Hersh *obstetrics and gynecology educator*
Dietrich, Robert Anthony *pathologist, consultant, medical association administrator*
Emanuel, Ezekiel J. *oncologist, bioethicist*
Fine, Howard A. *medical researcher*
Fleisher, Thomas Arthur *physician*
Gabelnick, Henry Lewis *medical research administrator*
Gallin, John I. *medical researcher*
Gastwirth, Glenn Barry *medical association administrator*
Gershengorn, Marvin Carl *internist, researcher, educator*
Giedd, Jay Norman *psychiatrist*

Goldstein, Murray *medical research administrator*
Gonzalez, Frank J. *medical researcher*
Goodwin, Frederick King *psychiatrist*
Gottesman, Michael Marc *biomedical researcher*
Greenwald, Peter *epidemiologist, researcher*
Gress, Ronald E. *oncologist*
Guttman, Helene Nathan *biomedical researcher, consultant, transpersonal counselor*
Hallett, Mark *neurologist, educator, medical researcher, director*
Hanson, Glen R. *pharmacologist, educator*
Harlan, Linda Carol *epidemiologist*
Harris, Curtis Craig *medical researcher*
Haseltine, Florence Pat *obstetrician, gynecologist, medical association administrator*
Helman, Lee J. *medical researcher*
Herman, Mary Margaret *neuropathologist*
Hingson, Ralph W. *medical educator*
Hutton, John Evans, Jr. *surgeon, educator, retired military officer*
Ito, Yoichiro *pathologist, researcher*
Jaffe, Elaine Sarkin *pathologist*
Javitt, Jonathan C. *ophthalmologist*
Johann, Donald Joseph *biomedical researcher*
Joy, Robert John Thomas *medical educator*
Kapikian, Albert Zaven *physician, epidemiologist*
Keiser, Harry Robert *retired physician*
Kelly, Kathleen *medical researcher*
Kirschstein, Ruth Lillian *physician*
Klee, Claude Blenc *medical researcher*
Knable, Michael *medical researcher*
Kramer, Barnett Sheldon *oncologist*
Krause, Richard Michael *medical scientist, government official, educator, senior researcher*
Kuehl, W. Michael *medical researcher*
Kunos, George *pharmacologist*
Lane, H. Clifford *internist*
Larionov, Vladimir L. *medical researcher*
Li, Qingdi Quentin *physician, research scientist, medical educator*
Linehan, William Marston Marston *urologic surgeon, cancer researcher*
Lo, Cecilia Wen-Ya *biomedical researcher*
Longfellow, David *administrator*
Lowy, Douglas Ronald *oncologist, researcher*
Mackall, Crystal L. *medical researcher*
Marini, Ann Marie *medical researcher, educator*
Mattison, Donald Roger *gynecologist, toxicologist, educator, medical association administrator, public health service officer*
McCurdy, Harry Ward *otolaryngologist*
Melenhorst, Jan Joseph *immunologist*
Merlino, Glenn T. *medical researcher*
Metcalfe, Dean Darrel *medical research physician*
Mitchell, James B. *medical researcher*
Mullan, Fitzhugh *public health physician*
Muraro, Paolo A. *immunologist, neurologist*
Nabel, Elizabeth G. *cardiologist, researcher*
Neumann, Ronald Daniel *nuclear medicine physician, educator*
North, A. Frederick *physician*
Nyirjesy, Istvan *obstetrician, gynecologist*
Ognibene, Frederick Peter *internist*
Oldfield, Edward Hudson *neurosurgeon, researcher*
Oldham, Roger Jay *plastic surgeon*
Ommaya, Ayub Khan *neurosurgeon, educator*
Pastan, Ira Harry *medical researcher*
Paul, William Erwin *immunologist, researcher*
Perlin, Seymour *psychiatrist, educator*
Peterson, Charles Marquis *medical educator*
Poggi, Matthew Michael *radiation oncologist, researcher*
Pollard, Harvey B. *medical educator, neuroscientist*
Pommier, Yves Georges *medical researcher*
Quinnan, Gerald Vincent, Jr. *medical educator*
Quon, Michael James *medical researcher, internist*
Rall, Joseph Edward *physician*
Rapoport, Judith *psychiatrist*
Rennert, Owen Murray *pediatrician, geneticist, educator*
Reynolds, Herbert Young *internist*
Rhim, Johng Sik *physician, medical researcher*
Rice, Charles Lane *surgeon, educator*
Rider, Lisa G *pediatric rheumatologist, researcher*
Robbins, John Bennett *medical researcher*
Rosenberg, Steven A. *surgeon, researcher*
Rossouw, Jacques E. *preventive medicine physician, researcher*
Saffiotti, Umberto *pathologist*
Samelson, Lawrence Elliot *medical researcher*
Scarpa, Antonio *medical educator, researcher, director, physiologist*
Schrump, David Stuart *medical association administrator, researcher*
Shamburek, Robert Dean *gastroenterologist*
Shapeero, Lorraine G. *physician, researcher, educator*
Shulman, Lawrence Edward *biomedical researcher, rheumatologist*
Singer, Alfred *immunologist, researcher*
Smoller, Bruce Melvyn *psychiatrist*
Stetler-Stevenson, William George *pathologist*
Sturtz, Donald Lee *surgeon, educator, military officer*
Thorgeirsson, Snorri Sveinn *medical researcher*
Udey, Mark C. *dermatologist, researcher*
Ursano, Robert Joseph *psychiatrist*
Vaitukaitis, Judith Louise *medical researcher*
Volkow, Nora Dolores *medical researcher, director*
Vonderhaar, Barbara K. *medical researcher*
Waldmann, Thomas Alexander *medical researcher, physician*
Webster, Thomas Glenn *psychiatrist, educator*
Weinberger, Daniel R. *psychiatrist, neurologist*
Western, Karl August *physician, epidemiologist*
Work, Henry Harcus *psychiatrist, educator*
Wright, Pamela Ann *surgeon*
Wu, Carl *medical researcher*
Yuspa, Stuart Howard *oncologist*

**Bowie**
Dawodu, Segun Toyin *sports medicine physician, physiatrist*

**Chevy Chase**
Alpert, Seymour *anesthesiologist, educator*
Feldman, Bruce Allen *otolaryngologist*
Harlan, William Robert, Jr. *internist, educator, researcher*
Khairalla, Eric William *plastic surgeon*

Lynn, D. Joanne *physician, researcher*
Nelson, John Marshall *medical information services company executive*
Pilkerton, Arthur Raymond, Jr. *surgeon, educator*
Pogue, John Marshall *physician*
Resnik, Harvey Lewis Paul *psychiatrist*
Rose, John Charles *internist, educator*
Shannon, Stephen Curtis *medical association administrator, occupational health physician*
Williams, Charles Laval, Jr. *retired preventive medicine physician*

**Clinton**
Cruz, Wilhelmina Mangahas *critical care physician, educator*
Davis, Mark Cameron *radiologist*

**College Park**
Katz, Ronald Alan *dermatologist*
Sacks, Charles Bernard *psychiatrist, educator*

**Columbia**
Campbell-Alston, Deirdre Adina *anatomist, physiologist, researcher*
Hyman, Lawrence Robert *psychiatrist*
Strahlman, Richard Scott *pediatrician*

**Darnestown**
Cohen, Sanford Irwin *physician, educator*
Gottlieb, Julius Judah *podiatrist*

**Easton**
Rever, George Wright *psychiatrist, health facility administrator*

**Frederick**
Anderson, Arthur Osmund *pathologist, immunologist, military officer*
Blumenthal, Robert P. *medical researcher*
Byrd, R. Andrew *medical researcher*
Colburn, Nancy Hall *medical researcher*
Copeland, Neal G. *medical researcher*
Hanna, Michael George, Jr. *immunologist, pharmaceutical executive*
Keefer, Larry Kay *medical researcher*
Le Grice, Stuart F.J. *medical researcher*
Malin, Howard Gerald *podiatrist*
Marquez, Victor E. *medical researcher*
McMahon, James Brislin *medical researcher*
Oppenheim, Joost J. *allergist, immunologist, researcher*
Ortaldo, John R. *immunologist, researcher*
Sharifi, Nima *oncologist, researcher*
Strathern, Jeffrey N. *medical researcher*
Weissman, Allan M. *medical researcher*
Wlodawer, Alexander *medical researcher*

**Gaithersburg**
Brodine, Charles Edward *physician*
Dermody, William Christian *biomedical consultant*
Fratantoni, Joseph Charles *medical researcher, biotechnologist, hematologist*
Lenfant, Claude Jean-Marie *physician, director*
Schwartzberg, Allan Zelig *psychiatrist, educator*

**Greenbelt**
Obamogie, Mercy A. *physician*
Weltz, Martin David *hematologist*

**Kensington**
Mirkin, Gabe Baron *physician, medical educator, writer, radio personality*
Szára, Stephen István *pharmacologist, consultant*

**Linthicum**
Billig, Donal Michael *surgeon*

**Lutherville**
Baramki, Theodore Atallah *gynecologist, reproductive endocrinologist*

**Lutherville Timonium**
Meyer, Jon Keith *psychiatrist, psychoanalyst, educator*
Park, Lee Crandall *psychiatrist*
Sternberger, Ludwig Amadeus *neurologist, educator*

**Montgomery Village**
Durning, Steven James *internist, educator*

**North Bethesda**
Flax, Herman Jacob *physiatrist*
Richards, Mark E. *plastic surgeon, educator*

**Oakland**
Zakaluzny, Ihor Andrew *surgeon*

**Olney**
Uscinski, Ronald Henry *medical educator*

**Owings Mills**
Heck, Albert Frank *retired neurologist*

**Potomac**
Harvey, John Collins *internist, educator*
Korengold, George Matthew *physician*
Waugaman, Richard Merle *psychiatrist, educator*

**Reisterstown**
Gloth, F. Michael III *geriatrician*

**Rockville**
Barr, Solomon Efrem *allergist, educator*
Birns, Mark Theodore *physician*
Chretien, Paul Bernard *oncologist, medical researcher*
Clancy, Carolyn M. *internist, federal agency administrator*
DuPont, Robert Louis *psychiatrist, physician*
Gonzalez-Licea, Augustin *pathologist, public health service officer*
Goodman, Jesse *physician, director, public health facility administrator, research scientist*
Graham, Robert *medical association executive*
Herrera, Hector H. *urologist*
Hisada, Michie *physician, epidemiologist*
Kowarski, Allen Avinoam *endocrinologist, educator*
Leach, Berton Joe *medical educator*

Leventhal, Carl M. *neurologist, consultant, retired government agency administrator*
Lloyd, Douglas Seward *physician, public health administrator*
Malik, Waheed Ahmad *cardiologist*
McMurry, James Finley, Jr. *endocrinologist, researcher*
Moritsugu, Kenneth Paul *internist, federal official*
Steinberg, William Mark *physician*
Sundlof, Stephen Frederick *veterinary administrator*
Temple, Robert *physician, federal agency administrator*
Vorosmarti, James *physician*

**Silver Spring**
Adams, Diane Loretta *physician*
Beard, Lillian B. McLean *pediatrician, consultant*
Berger, Allan Sidney *psychiatrist, educator*
Bergmann-Leitner, Elke S. *immunologist, researcher*
Gaydos, Joel Carl *physician*
Gilbert, Charles Richard Alsop *obstetrician, gynecologist, surgeon, educator*
Heppner, Donald Gray, Jr. *immunology research physician, army officer*
Misbin, Robert *medical executive*
Mosholder, Andrew Donald *psychiatrist*
Taubman, Claudia *gynecologist*
Waldrop, Francis Neil *physician*
Walsh, Douglas Shawn *medical association administrator, dermatologist, director, military officer*

**Stevenson**
Hendler, Nelson Howard *physician, health facility administrator, director*

**Timonium**
Forrester, Alfred Whitfield *psychiatrist, educator*

**Towson**
Adams, Joseph Andrew *internist, health facility administrator, educator*
Meny, Robert George *former medical research administrator, physician*
Sell, Jeffrey Edward *heart surgeon*
Spodak, Michael Kenneth *forensic psychiatrist*
Wilkinson, Charles P. *ophthalmologist*

**Upper Marlboro**
Jones-Lukács, Elizabeth Lucille *physician*

**Waldorf**
Wiggins, Stephen Edward *physician*

**Wheaton**
White, Martha Vetter *allergist, immunologist*

**Woodbine**
Mc Indoe, Darrell Winfred *retired nuclear medicine physician*

## MASSACHUSETTS

**Acton**
Benz, Edward John, Sr. *clinical pathologist*

**Amesbury**
Heyman, Joseph Martin *obstetrician, gynecologist*

**Amherst**
Fleischman, Paul Robert *psychiatrist, writer*
Palmer, John Derry *physiology educator*

**Belmont**
Cohen, Bruce Michael *psychiatrist, educator, scientist, health facility administrator*
Coyle, Joseph Thomas *psychiatrist*
de Marneffe, Francis *psychiatrist, hospital administrator*
Frazier, Shervert Hughes, Jr. *psychiatrist, educator*
Grant, Marni Joy *psychiatrist*
Onesti, Silvio Joseph *psychiatrist*
Pope, Harrison Graham, Jr. *psychiatrist, educator*
Sifneos, Peter Emanuel *psychiatrist, educator*
Zhang, Kehong *pharmacologist, educator*

**Boston**
Abrahm, Janet Lee *hematologist, oncologist, education palliative care specialist*
Adelstein, S(tanley) James *radiologist, educator*
Akins, Cary Willard *surgeon, educator*
Albert, Martin Lawrence *behavioral neurologist, writer, educator, biomedical researcher*
Albright, Eric D. *medical librarian, director*
Alexander, Michael Paxson *neurologist*
Al-Mallah, Mouaz *cardiologist*
Alpert, Joel Jacobs *medical educator, pediatrician*
Alt, Frederick W. *geneticist, pediatrician*
Anderson, Kenneth Carl *physician, educator*
Angell, Marcia *pathologist, editor-in-chief*
Angelo, E. Joanne *child, adolescent and adult psychiatrist*
Antman, Karen H. *oncologist, educator, dean*
Apovian, Caroline M. *medical educator, director*
Archip, Neculai *medical educator, researcher*
Ausiello, Dennis Arthur *nephrologist*
Austen, K(arl) Frank *internist, educator*
Austen, W(illiam) Gerald *surgeon, educator*
Avery, Mary Ellen *pediatrician, educator*
Axelrod, Lloyd *endocrinologist, educator*
Baldwin, John Charles *surgeon, researcher*
Banks, Henry H. *orthopedist, educator, dean*
Barnett, Guy Octo *physician, educator*
Barouch, Dan Hung *physician, scientist, educator*
Bates, David Westfall *internist, educator, medical researcher*
Baughman, Kenneth Lee *cardiologist, educator*
Becker, James Murdoch *surgeon, educator*
Benacerraf, Baruj *pathologist, educator*
Benoist, Christophe O. *immunologist, educator*
Benz, Edward John, Jr. *internist, researcher, geneticist, educator, health facility administrator*
Bernhard, William Francis *thoracic surgeon, cardiovascular surgeon*
Berson, Eliot Lawrence *ophthalmologist, medical educator*
Bieber, Frederick Robert *medical geneticist*

Bigby, JudyAnn *medical educator*
Bistrian, Bruce Ryan *internist, educator*
Blacklow, Robert Stanley *internist, educator*
Bloch, Kurt Julius *physician*
Borus, Jonathan Frederick *psychiatrist, educator*
Brain, Joseph David *biomedical researcher, educator, ecologist, department chairman*
Braunwald, Eugene *physician, educator*
Brazelton, Thomas Berry *pediatrician, educator*
Brenner, Barry Morton *physician*
Briggs, Susan Miller *surgeon*
Burstein, Harold John *oncologist*
Busse, Paul Martin *oncologist, researcher*
Buxbaum, Robert C. (Robert Courtney Buxbaum) *internist*
Cahalane, Michael John *surgeon, medical educator*
Callow, Allan Dana *surgeon*
Canellos, George Peter *hematologist, educator, oncologist*
Cao, Xinhua *medical researcher*
Caplan, Louis Robert *neurologist, educator*
Carr, Daniel Barry *anesthesiologist, endocrinologist, medical researcher*
Chapman, Paul H. *pediatric neurosurgeon*
Chobanian, Aram *medical educator, cardiologist, former academic administrator*
Chui, David H. K. *hematologist, educator*
Ciraulo, Domenic Anthony *psychiatrist, educator*
Coffin, John Miller *medical researcher, biology professor*
Coffman, Jay Denton *internist, educator*
Cohen, Alan Seymour *internist*
Cohn, Lawrence H. *cardiothoracic surgeon*
Collier, R(obert) John *biomedical researcher, dean*
Corcoran, Paul John *physician*
Crowley, William Francis, Jr. *endocrinologist, educator*
Crum, Christopher Paul *pathologist, educator*
Daley, George Quentin *hematologist, biomedial research scientist*
Daly, Benedict Dudley Thomas, Jr. *cardiothoracic surgeon, educator*
D'Amico, Anthony Victor *radiation oncologist*
Delbanco, Thomas Lewis *medical educator, researcher*
DeMaso, David Ray *psychiatrist*
DeSanctis, Roman William *cardiologist, educator*
Devaiah, Anand K. *otolaryngologist*
DiNardo, James Anthony *anesthesiologist*
Dluhy, Robert George *physician*
Dolin, Raphael *medical educator*
Drazen, Jeffrey Mark *medical educator*
Duxbury, Mark *surgeon*
Dvorak, Harold Fisher *pathologist, educator*
Edelin, Kenneth Carlton *physician*
Egdahl, Richard Harrison *surgeon, educator, health science association administrator*
Eisenberg, Leon *psychiatrist, educator*
Ellis, Franklin Henry, Jr. *surgeon, educator*
Elshamy, Wael M. *medical educator*
Epler, Gary Robert *physician, author, educator*
Epstein, Arnold M. *medical educator*
Epstein, Franklin Harold *internist, educator*
Federman, Daniel David *medical educator, academic administrator, endocrinologist*
Fifer, Michael A. *cardiologist, educator*
Flier, Jeffrey S. *endocrinologist*
Folkman, Moses Judah *surgeon, educator*
Forse, Robert Armour *surgeon*
Frank, Samuel Arthur *neurologist*
Freedberg, A. Stone *physician*
Frei, Emil III *physician, educator, researcher*
Frigoletto, Fredric David, Jr. *physician*
Garber, Jeffrey Richard *endocrinologist*
Gawande, Atul A. *surgeon, writer*
Gelfand, Jeffrey Alan *physician, educator*
Gelman, Simon *anesthesiologist, educator*
Gilchrest, Barbara Ann *dermatologist*
Gipson, Ilene Kay *ophthalmologist, educator*
Glassroth, Jeffrey *internist, educator*
Glimcher, Melvin Jacob *orthopedic surgeon*
Goldberg, Irving Hyman *molecular pharmacology and biochemistry educator*
Goldie, Sue J. *health service researcher*
Gottlieb, Alice B. *dermatologist*
Gottlieb, Leonard Solomon *pathology educator*
Greenblatt, David J. *pharmacologist*
Greenes, Robert A. *medical educator*
Gregory, Shawn Alen *physician, researcher*
Grillo, Hermes Conrad *surgeon*
Grillone, Gregory Angelo *otolaryngologist*
Groopman, Jerome *medical educator*
Grundfast, Kenneth Martin *otolaryngologist*
Habener, Joel Francis *medical educator, researcher*
Hadlock, Theresa Anne *surgeon, otolaryngologist*
Halamka, John D. *emergency physician, information technology executive*
Hamrah, Pedram *ophthalmologist, researcher*
Harper, Marvin Bruce *pediatrics educator, hospital administrator*
Hayter, Robert Glenn *physician*
Healy, Gerald Burke *otolaryngologist*
Hedley-Whyte, John *anesthesiologist, educator*
Herndon, James Henry *orthopedic surgeon, educator*
Herzog, David Brandeis *psychiatrist*
Hettmer, Simone *hematologist, oncologist*
Hiatt, Howard H. *internist, educator*
Hickey, Paul Robert *anesthesiologist, educator*
Hilgenberg, Alan D. *surgeon, educator*
Hill, Nicholas S. *physician, researcher*
Hirsch, Erwin F. *surgeon, educator*
Howley, Peter Maxwell *pathology educator*
Hurwitz, Mark David *oncologist*
Ingwall, Joanne S. *medical educator, department chairman*
Irimia, Daniel *biomedical researcher*
Jaff, Michael Ritt *osteopath, internist*
Jones, Daniel Bougere *surgeon*
Joyce-Brady, Martin Francis *medical educator*
Kahn, Barbara B. *endocrinologist*
Kang, Jing X. *medical researcher, educator*
Kantoff, Philip W. *oncologist*
Kaplan, Marshall Myles *medical educator, researcher, gastroenterologist*
Karnovsky, Morris John *pathologist, biologist*
Kassirer, Jerome Paul *medical educator*
Kazemi, Homayoun *internist, educator*
Keating, Mark Taylor *physician, medical educator*

Kesari, Santosh *neurologist, oncologist, neuroscientist*
Khalsa, Sat Bir Singh *biomedical researcher*
Kiang, Nelson Yuan-sheng *medical educator*
Kieff, Elliott Dan *medical educator*
Kim, Ducksoo *radiologist, inventor, educator*
Kircher, Moritz Florian *radiologist, researcher*
Kitz, Richard John *anesthesiologist, educator*
Kleinman, Ronald Ellis *pediatrician*
Kocher, Mininder Singh *pediatric orthopaedic surgeon, epidemiologist*
Komaroff, Anthony Leader *physician*
Kopans, Daniel B. *radiologist, educator*
Krane, Stephen Martin *rheumatologist, educator*
Kressel, Herbert Yehude *medical educator*
Kuo, Winston Patrick *biomedical researcher*
Lamont, John Thomas *gastroenterologist, educator*
Laufer, Marc R. *obstetrician*
Lazar, Harold Lee *cardiothoracic surgeon*
Lee, Charles *cytologist*
Lee, Thomas Henry *internist, cardiologist, healthcare executive*
Ling, Pei-Ra *medical educator*
Little, John Bertram *radiologist, educator, researcher*
Livingston, David Morse *internist, biomedical researcher*
Lo Gerfo, Frank William *surgeon*
Loscalzo, Joseph *cardiologist, biochemist*
Ludwig, David S. *endocrinologist*
Mankin, Henry Jay *orthopedist, educator, health facility administrator*
Mannick, John Anthony *surgeon*
Manson, JoAnn Elisabeth *endocrinologist*
Marshansky, Vladimir Nikolaevich *medical educator, biochemist, cell biologist*
Mathisen, Douglas J. *thoracic surgeon*
McCormick, Marie Clare *pediatrician, educator*
McDougal, William Scott *urology educator*
McNeil, Barbara Joyce *radiologist, educator*
Meiri, Karina F. *medical educator*
Merk, Frederick Bannister *biomedical educator, researcher*
Meyer, Jack Edward *radiologist, educator*
Mihm, Martin Charles, Jr. *pathologist, educator*
Moellering, Robert Charles, Jr. *internist, educator*
Moorman, Donald Wayne *surgeon, healthcare administrator*
Morgan, James Philip *pharmacology and cardiology educator*
Nadelson, Carol Cooperman *psychiatrist, educator*
Nathan, David Gordon *pediatrician, educator*
Neufeld, Ellis Jacob *pediatrician, hematologist, researcher*
Nour, Nawal M. *obstetrician, gynecologist, health facility administrator*
O'Brien, J(ohn) Patrick *psychiatrist, educator*
Odze, Robert D. *pathologist*
Pallotta, Johanna Antonia (Johanna Stephen) *endocrinologist, educator*
Parad, Richard Barry *pediatrician, researcher*
Paul, Oglesby *cardiologist, educator*
Pearce, Elizabeth Niewoehner *endocrinologist, researcher*
Petersen, Robert Allen *pediatric ophthalmologist*
Pochi, Peter Ernest *physician*
Poser, Charles Marcel *neurology educator*
Poussaint, Alvin Francis *psychiatrist, educator*
Prout, Curtis *internist, educator*
Rabkin, Mitchell Thornton *physician, educator, hospital administrator*
Rao, Anjana *immunologist, educator*
Relman, Arnold Seymour *physician, educator, editor*
Reppert, Steven Marion *pediatrician, research scientist, educator*
Richie, Jerome Paul *surgeon, educator*
Ridker, Paul M. *cardiologist, educator*
Rocco, Angelo Gregory *anesthesiologist*
Rockoff, Mark Alan *pediatric anesthesiologist*
Rohrer, Richard Jeffrey *surgeon, educator*
Rosenblatt, Michael *internist, researcher, academic administrator, educator*
Rosenbloom, David Lee *medical educator, director*
Roth, Sanford Irwin *pathologist, educator*
Russell, Paul Snowden *surgeon, educator*
Rutkove, Seward Brian *neurologist, educator, neuroscientist*
Ryan, Thomas John *cardiologist*
Sachs, David Howard *surgeon, immunologist, educator*
Sadeghi-Nejad, Abdollah *pediatrician, educator*
Sahani, Dushyant V. *radiologist, educator*
Sallan, Stephen E. *pediatrician*
Saper, Clifford Baird *neurology educator*
Satchi-Fainaro, Ronit *medical educator*
Saxe, Glenn N. *child psychiatrist, researcher*
Schaller, Jane Green *pediatrician*
Schlossman, Stuart Franklin *physician, educator, researcher*
Schouten, Ronald *psychiatrist, educator*
Seddon, Johanna Margaret *ophthalmologist, epidemiologist*
Seidman, Christine E. *medical educator*
Selkoe, Dennis Jesse *neurologist, researcher, educator*
Sellke, Frank William *cardiothoracic surgeon, researcher*
Shields, Lawrence Thornton *orthopaedic surgeon, educator*
Shklar, Gerald *pathologist, periodontist, educator*
Shore, Miles Frederick *psychiatrist, educator*
Slack, Warner Vincent *medical educator, researcher*
Snydman, David Richard *infectious diseases specialist, educator*
Sodroski, Joseph G. *medical educator*
Sordo, Margarita *medical researcher*
Sparrow, Joshua D. *child psychiatrist*
Speizer, Frank E. *physician, researcher*
Spellman, Mitchell Wright *surgeon, academic administrator, educator*
Spiegel, Joan Elizabeth *anesthesiologist, educator*
Springer, Timothy Alan *health researcher, immunology educator*
Stair, Thomas Osborne *physician, educator*
Stampfer, Meir Jonathan *epidemiologist, nutritionist, educator*
Steere, Allen Caruthers, Jr. *physician, educator*

Stossel, Thomas Peter *medical educator, researcher, director*
Suh, Wonsuk Warren *radiation oncologist*
Suit, Herman Day *radiation oncologist, medical educator*
Surman, Owen Stanley *psychiatrist*
Swartz, Morton Norman *medical educator*
Taubman, Martin Arnold *immunologist, educator*
Thibault, George Edwin *medical educator, non-profit healthcare organization administrator*
Tilly, Jonathan L. *obstetrician, gynecologist, reproductive biologist*
Tompkins, Ronald Gary *surgeon, educator, biomedical investigator*
Toppelberg, Claudio O. *psychiatrist, researcher*
Trevos, S. Ted *nuclear medicine physician, educator, hospital administrator*
Trier, Jerry Steven *gastroenterologist, educator*
Tsao, Hensin *dermatologist, researcher*
Vacanti, Joseph Philip *pediatric and transplant surgeon*
Volpe, Joseph John *pediatrician, neurologist, educator*
Waldinger, Robert Jon *psychiatrist*
Wang, Zhi *biomedical researcher*
Warner, John J.P. *orthopedist, surgeon*
Warshaw, Andrew Louis *surgeon, researcher*
Weiss, Earle Burton *physician*
Werchniak, Andrew Eugene *dermatologist, educator*
Whittemore, Anthony Dunster *vascular surgeon, chief medical officer*
Willett, Walter Churchill *epidemiologist, educator*
Willock, Marcelle Monica *retired medical educator*
Wyszynski, Diego Federico *epidemiologist, educator*
Yoon, Young-sup *medical educator*
Young, Anne B. *neurologist, educator*
Yuan, Junying *medical educator, researcher*
Zervas, Nicholas Themistocles *neurosurgeon*
Zinner, Michael Jeffrey *surgeon, educator*
Zon, Leonard I. *pediatrics educator, researcher*

### Boylston
Hanshaw, James Barry *pediatrician, educator*

### Brockton
Carlson, Desiree Anice *pathologist*
Rothschild, William Baron *psychiatrist, educator*

### Brookline
Alarcon, Rogelio Alfonso *retired internist, retired researcher*
Burns, Padraic *physician, psychiatrist, psychoanalyst, educator*
Dow, Elias Charles *endocrinologist*
Goldsmith, Gary Norman *psychiatrist, psychoanalyst*
Jakab, Irene *psychiatrist*
Schwartz, Bernard *physician*
Tyler, H. Richard *physician*

### Burlington
Berkoben, John Perri *physician*
Choi, In-Sup *radiologist*
Clerkin, Eugene Patrick *physician, educator*
Cosgrove, Garth Rees *neurosurgeon*
Freidberg, Stephen Roy *neurosurgeon*
Gawoski, John Michael *physician*
Hurd, Joseph Kindall, Jr. *obstetrician, gynecologist*
Moschella, Samuel L. *dermatology educator*
Oberfield, Richard Alan *oncologist*
Schoetz, David John, Jr. *colon and rectal surgeon, educator*

### Cambridge
Barrett, J. Carl *medical researcher, molecular biologist, researcher*
Berwick, Donald Mark *medical institute administrator*
Brusch, John Lynch *physician, educator, hospital administrator*
Burr, Winthrop Ames *psychiatrist*
Chen, Lincoln Chin-ho *medical educator*
Cheng, Susan *medical researcher*
Eisen, Herman Nathaniel *immunology researcher, medical educator*
Eisenberg, Carola *psychiatrist, educator*
Ette, Ene Ikpong *clinical pharmacologist*
Ewing, Scott Edwin *physiatrist, educator*
Fishman, Mark Charles *biomedical researcher*
Friedman, Jeffrey Robert *psychiatrist, educator*
Havens, Leston Laycock *psychiatrist, educator*
Himmelstein, David U. *medical educator*
Hirsch, Martin Stanley *internist, epidemiologist, researcher*
Liau, Gene *medical educator*
London, Irving Myer *physician, educator*
Mathews, Joan Helene *pediatrician*
McCunney, Robert Joseph *physician*
Mootha, Vamsi Krishna *biomedical researcher, educator*
Nathanson, Larry *medical educator*
O'Shea, Erin K. *biomedical researcher*
Valenstein, Arthur F. *psychiatrist, educator*
Wacker, Warren Ernest Clyde *internist, educator*
Young, Laurence R. *biomedical researcher, biomedical engineer, aeronautical engineer, aerospace engineer*

### Charlestown
Ackerman, Jerome Leonard *biomedical researcher*
Faustman, Denise L. *immunologist*
Isselbacher, Kurt Julius *internist, educator*
Leaf, Alexander *preventive medicine physician, epidemiologist*
Potts, John Thomas, Jr. *physician, educator*
Zamecnik, Paul Charles *oncologist, medical researcher*

### Chelmsford
Menitoff, Paul Alan *psychiatrist*

### Chestnut Hill
Cohen, David Joel *medical educator*
Flax, Martin Howard *pathologist, retired educator*
Gottlieb, Marise Suss *epidemiologist*
Kosasky, Harold Jack *fertility researcher*
Salib, Philip I. *orthopedic surgeon*

### Clinton
Lanza, Robert Paul *medical scientist*

### Concord
Andrews, Joseph Lyon, Jr. *internist, pulmonologist, medical educator, writer*
Coles, Robert *child psychiatrist, educator, writer*

### Dover
Buyse, Marylou *pediatrician, geneticist, medical association administrator*

### East Boston
Patinkin, Terry Allan *physician*

### Falmouth
Sato, Kazuyoshi *pathologist*

### Fitchburg
Wellman, Robert Jonathan *medical educator*

### Framingham
Klapholz, Henry *obstetrician, gynecologist, educator*
Lavin, Philip Todd *medical researcher*
Ramachandran, Vasan Srini *medical educator*
Zamvil, Linda Susan *psychiatrist, educator*

### Gardner
Du Buske, Lawrence Michael *immunologist, rheumatologist*

### Gloucester
White, Harold Jack *pathologist*

### Harvard
Monath, Thomas Patrick *physician*

### Jamaica Plain
Pierce, Chester Middlebrook *retired psychiatrist, educator*

### Lexington
Li, Tongchuan *pharmacologist, researcher*
Paul, Norman Leo *psychiatrist, educator*
Waksman, Byron Halsted *immunologist, educator, medical association administrator*

### Lincoln
Brandt, John Henry *physician*

### Lowell
Dubner, Daniel William *pediatrician*

### Malden
Madhappan-Kempuraj, Bhuvaneshwari *medical researcher*

### Mattapoisett
Mazer, Mike *cardiologist, retired nephrologist, artist*

### Melrose
Desforges, Jane Fay *retired internist, hematologist, educator*

### Milford
Kashyap, Nitu *internist*
Lopez, Alvaro Benito *psychiatrist, director*

### Natick
Gottlieb, Michael Norman *internist, educator, health facility administrator*

### Needham
Osser, David Neal *psychiatrist, educator*

### New Bedford
Spongberg, Andrew K. *otolaryngologist, law educator*

### Newton
Bassuk, Ellen Linda *psychiatrist*
Bernier, George Matthew, Jr. *oncologist, educator, dean*
Jellinek, Michael Steven *psychiatrist, pediatrician*
May, Harold Louis *retired surgeon, not-for-profit developer*
Sasahara, Arthur Asao *cardiologist, educator, researcher*

### Newton Center
Eichler, Marc *neurosurgeon*

### North Dighton
Cserr, Robert *psychiatrist, physician, hospital administrator*

### Northborough
Fulmer, Hugh Scott *physician, educator*

### Norwood
Berliner, Allen Irwin *dermatologist*
Pence, Robert Dudley *biomedical researcher, consultant, hospital administrator*

### Orleans
Day, Emerson *physician*

### Oxford
Schur, Walter Robert *physician*

### Peabody
Lipman, Richard Paul *pediatrician*

### Petersham
Chivian, Eric Seth *psychiatrist, environmental scientist, educator*

### Pittsfield
Malkani, Prakash *neuroradiology educator*

**Reading**
Hambartsoumian, Edouard *obstetrician, researcher, embryologist*

**Rockland**
Blethen, Sandra Lee *pediatric endocrinologist*

**Shrewsbury**
Baguisi, Alexander *embryologist*

**South Wellfleet**
Blau, Monte *retired radiology educator*

**South Weymouth**
Young, Michael Chung-En *allergist, immunologist, pediatrician*

**Springfield**
Farkas, Paul Stephen *gastroenterologist*
Friedmann, Paul *surgeon, educator, research and development company executive*
Ganai, Sabha *surgeon, researcher*
Kottamasu, Mohan Rao (K.V.R. Mohan Rao) *physician, health facility administrator*
Liptzin, Benjamin *psychiatrist*
Lynn, Morton Daniel *orthopedist*
Maissel, Gerda Sharon *physician*
Martorell, Claudia *infectious diseases physician*
McGee, William Tobin *surgeon*
Petrone, William Francis *pediatrician, microbiologist, corporate executive*
Wenner, Steven Marc *orthopedist, surgeon*

**Stockbridge**
Shapiro, Edward Robert *psychiatrist, educator, health facility administrator, psychotherapist*

**Stoughton**
Joseph, Anthony Barnett *psychiatrist*

**Sudbury**
Lamont-Havers, Ronald William *retired physician, retired medical association administrator*

**Vineyard Haven**
Jacobs, Gretchen Huntley *psychiatrist*

**Waban**
Rogoff, Jerome Howard *psychiatrist, psychoanalyst, forensic expert*

**Waltham**
Hayes, Ailish Maire *pediatrician*
Lackner, James Robert *aerospace medicine educator*
Landaw, Stephen Arthur *physician, educator*
Leach, Robert Ellis *orthopedist, surgeon, educator*

**Watertown**
Moskowitz, Richard *physician*

**Wayland**
Edelman, Stuart Edward *psychiatrist*
Moncure, Ashby Carter *surgeon, educator*

**Wellesley**
Murray, Joseph Edward *retired plastic surgeon*
Sexton, John Joseph *oral and maxillofacial surgeon, educator*

**Wellesley Hills**
Spierings, Egilius Leonardus Hendricus *pharmacologist, neurologist, headache specialist*

**West Falmouth**
Bass, Norman Herbert *neurologist, educator, research scientist, hospital administrator, academic administrator*

**West Roxbury**
Frisbie, James Howard *retired internist*

**West Springfield**
Desai, Veena Balvantrai *obstetrician, gynecologist, educator*

**Weston**
Jayasankar, Subramanyan *orthopaedic surgeon*

**Westwood**
Bloomingdale, Lewis Morgan *retired psychiatrist*
Plimpton, Calvin Hastings *retired internist, university president*

**Williamstown**
Stuebner, Erwin August, Jr. *internist*
Wilkins, Earle Wayne, Jr. *retired surgery educator*

**Woods Hole**
Laster, Leonard *internist, gastroenterologist, academic administrator, educator, writer, biomedical researcher*

**Worcester**
Angelescu, Amanda Goseco *pediatrician, endocrinologist*
Bernhard, Jeffrey David *dermatologist, educator, editor*
Chandok, Dinesh *cardiologist, consultant*
Chen, Chun-Jen *immunologist, researcher*
Drachman, David Alexander *neurologist*
Geller, Jeffrey L. *psychiatrist, educator*
Hunter, Richard Edward *retired physician*
Kaufman, Paul D. *biomedical researcher, educator*
Madison, John Mark *pulmonologist, educator*
Marik, Paul Ellis *physician*
Mello, Craig C. *molecular medicine educator, researcher*
Menon, Mani *urological surgeon, educator*
Morse, Abraham Nicholas *obstetrician, gynecologist, educator*
Morse, Leonard J. *epidemiologist, public health service officer*
Selin, Lisa K. *physician*
Thompson, Michael David *physician*
Tonkonogy, Joseph Moses *physician, neuropsychiatrist, researcher*
Townes, Philip Leonard *pediatrician, educator*
Vickstrom, Kristina Rose *medical researcher*

Young, Stephen Bernard *urogynecologist, surgeon*
Zurier, Robert Burton *rheumatology educator*

**Yarmouth Port**
Gordon, Benjamin Dichter *pediatrician, educator, health facility administrator*

## MICHIGAN

**Ann Arbor**
Abrams, Gerald David *pathologist, educator*
Ansbacher, Rudi *physician*
Bacon, George Edgar *pediatrician*
Barsan, William George *emergency physician*
Bartlett, Robert Hawes *surgeon*
Bloom, Jane Maginnis *emergency physician*
Bowdler, Anthony John *internist, educator*
Boxer, Laurence Alan *physician, research educator*
Burdi, Alphonse Rocco *anatomist*
Burke, Robert Harry *surgeon, educator*
Cai, Hongliang *medical researcher*
Carlson, Bruce Martin *anatomist*
Casey, Kenneth Lyman *neurologist*
Cerny, Joseph Charles *urologist, educator*
Chey, William D *physician, researcher*
Coran, Arnold Gerald *pediatrician, surgeon*
Del Monte, Monte Anthony *medical educator*
Donabedian, Avedis *physician, educator*
Fajans, Stefan Stanislaus *retired internist*
Farmer, Cheryl Christine *internist, industrial hygienist*
Fullen, Douglas Randall *pathologist, educator*
Gadegbeku, Crystal Anne *medical educator*
Galea, Sandro *epidemiologist*
Gelehrter, Thomas David *medical educator, geneticist*
Gikas, Paul William *medical educator*
Gilman, Sid *neurologist*
Greden, John Francis *psychiatrist, educator*
Green, Carmen R. *anesthesiologist, pain medicine physician*
Greenfield, Lazar John *surgeon, educator*
Han, Yong Yun *medical educator*
Hoff, Julian Theodore *neurosurgeon, educator*
Hollenberg, Paul Frederick *pharmacology educator*
Horowitz, Samuel Boris *biomedical researcher, educational consultant*
Humes, Harvey David *nephrologist, educator*
Kaddoumi, Amal Farid *pharmacologist, researcher*
Konnak, John William *surgery educator*
Kuhl, David Edmund *nuclear medicine physician, educator*
Li, Jie Jack *pharmacologist*
Lichter, Allen S. *oncologist, educator, dean*
Lichter, Paul Richard *ophthalmology educator*
Lozoff, Betsy *pediatrician, educator*
Malek, Sami Nimer *oncologist, researcher, hematologist*
Mancuso, Peter *medical educator*
Margolis, Philip Marcus *psychiatrist, educator*
Markel, Howard *physician, educator*
Miller, Josef M. *otolaryngologist, educator*
Minter, Rebecca Manget *surgeon*
Modell, Stephen Mark *medical researcher, educator*
Monto, Arnold Simon *epidemiology educator*
Oliver, William John *pediatrician, educator*
Orringer, Jeffrey S. *dermatologist, educator*
Owyang, Chung *gastroenterologist, researcher*
Pipe, Steven W. *pediatrician, educator*
Pitt, Bertram *cardiologist, educator, consultant*
Powsner, Edward Raphael *physician*
Reddy, Venkat Narsimha *ophthalmologist, researcher*
Reynolds, R. Kevin *gynecologic oncologist*
Rosenthal, Amnon *pediatric cardiologist*
Sandler, Howard *medical educator*
Schottenfeld, David *retired epidemiologist, retired educator*
Schteingart, David Eduardo *internist*
Seibold, James Richard *physician, educator*
Silk, Kenneth R. *psychiatrist, medical educator*
Sloan, Herbert Elias *physician, surgeon*
Smith, Donald Cameron *retired preventive medicine physician*
Strang, Ruth Hancock *pediatrician, educator, cardiologist, priest*
Stross, Jeoffrey Knight *internist, educator*
Thompson, Norman Winslow *surgeon, educator*
Todd, Robert Franklin III *oncologist, educator*
Tsien, Christina *radiologist, oncologist*
Ward, Peter Allan *pathologist, educator*
Wechsler, Daniel Steven *medical educator*
Weg, John Gerard *physician*
Wicha, Max S. *oncologist, educator*

**Au Gres**
Dhawan, Vikas *plastic surgeon*

**Beverly Hills**
Castle, Maurice Emmett *orthopedist, surgeon*

**Bingham Farms**
Giles, Conrad Leslie *ophthalmic surgeon*

**Birmingham**
Edwards, Michael Gerard *physician*
Lerner, Martin A. *infectious disease physician*

**Bloomfield Hills**
Ball, Patricia Ann *physician*
Brent, Robert Lewis *urologist*
Coburn, Ronald Murray *ophthalmologist, surgeon*
Gagliardi, Raymond Alfred *physician*
Mathog, Robert Henry *otolaryngologist, educator*
Prasad, Niru *physician, television personality*
Stunz, John Henry, Jr. *retired physician, consultant*
Tolia, Vasundhara K. *pediatric gastroenterologist, educator*

**Chelsea**
Yarows, Steven Allen *internist*

**Clarkston**
Wydra, Frank Thomas *healthcare executive*

**Dearborn**
Fordyce, James George *physician*

**Detroit**
Abramson, Hanley Norman *pharmacy educator*
Afonso, Luis C. *cardiologist*
Ansari, Mohammed Rafiullah *surgeon*
Bock, Brooks Frederick *emergency physician*
Cohen, Sanford Ned *pediatrician, educator, academic administrator*
Dane, Jefic *internist, cardiologist*
Dombrowski, Mitchell Paul *obstetrician, researcher*
Gardin, Julius Markus *cardiologist, educator*
Hashimoto, Ken *dermatologist, educator*
Jefic, Dijana *nephrologist*
Jenkins-Anderson, Barbara Jeanne *pathologist, educator*
Kahkonen, Dorothy M. *endocrinologist*
Kaplan, Joseph *pediatrician*
Kelley, Mark Albert *physician, educator, health products executive*
Kim, Do Gyoon *biomedical researcher*
Lim, Henry Wan-Peng *dermatologist*
Lisak, Robert Philip *neurologist, researcher, educator*
Lupulescu, Aurel Peter *medical educator, researcher, physician*
Lusher, Jeanne Marie *pediatric hematologist, educator*
Maiese, Kenneth *neurologist, neuroscientist*
Mani, Nandita S. *medical librarian*
Mari, Giancarlo *obstetrician, gynecologist, educator*
Marunick, Mark Timothy *medical educator, dental educator*
Mclorie, Gordon Arthur *urologist, educator*
Miller, Orlando Jack *obstetrician, gynecologist, educator, geneticist*
Mubarak, Kamal K. *pulmonologist*
Nathanson, Saul David *oncologist, surgeon, educator*
Newton, Kenneth Kurt *physician, educator, administrator*
Nunn, Andre' Ronald *surgeon, health facility administrator*
O'Connell, John Bernard, Jr. *medical educator, department chairman*
Peres, Edward M. *preventive medicine physician, educator*
Prasad, Ananda Shiva *medical educator*
Reddy, Daniel Joseph *vascular surgeon*
Rivers, Emanuel P. *emergency physician, medical educator*
Rosman, Howard S. *cardiologist, educator*
Shields, Anthony Frank *oncologist, hematologist*
Silverman, Norman Alan *cardiac surgeon*
Smith, Wilbur Lazar *radiologist, educator*
Sokol, Robert James *obstetrician, gynecologist, educator*
Tyburski, James Gerard *surgeon*
Whitehouse, Fred Waite *endocrinologist, researcher*
Wiener, Joseph *pathologist, educator*
Yoo, George H. *otolaryngologist, medical educator*
Zak, Imad *radiologist, educator*
Zemlicka, Jiri *medical educator, researcher*

**East Lansing**
Beckmeyer, Henry Ernest *anesthesiologist, pain management specialist, medical educator*
Brody, Theodore Meyer *pharmacologist, educator*
Gottschalk, Alexander *radiologist, educator*
Magen, Jed Gary *child psychiatrist*
Pathak, Dorothy Rybaczyk *epidemiologist, researcher*
Pysh, Joseph John *neurologist*
Ristow, George Edward *neurologist, educator*
Rosenman, Kenneth D. *medical educator*
Watson, Ralph Edward *internist, educator*

**Farmington Hills**
Gordon, Craig Jeffrey *oncologist, educator*
Luby, Elliot Donald *psychiatrist, educator*

**Fife Lake**
Knecht, Richard Arden *family practitioner*

**Frankenmuth**
Shetlar, James Francis *physician*

**Grand Rapids**
Daniels, Joseph *neuropsychiatrist*
Verdier, David D'Ooge *ophthalmologist, educator*
Watkins, James Kelley *retired urologist*
Wendt, Vernon Earl *internist, cardiologist*
Wilt, Jeffrey Lynn *pulmonary and critical care physician, educator*

**Grosse Pointe**
Sphire, Raymond Daniel *anesthesiologist, educator*

**Grosse Pointe Woods**
Sul, Yi Chul *neurologist*

**Holland**
Zuidema, George Dale *surgeon, educator*

**Jackson**
Carrera, Jose *psychiatrist, child psychiatrist, psychoanalyst*

**Kalamazoo**
Bricker, Lee Alan *medical educator*
Saber, Alan A. *surgeon*
Toledo-Pereyra, Luis Horacio *transplant surgeon, researcher, historian educator*

**Lake Angelus**
Kresge, Bruce Anderson *retired physician*

**Lansing**
Kepros, John Paul *trauma surgeon*
Vincent, Frederick Michael, Sr. *neurologist, educator*

**Livonia**
Baskin, Victoria *child and adolescent psychiatrist*

**Mancelona**
Whelan, Joseph L. *neurologist*

**Marine City**
Brown, Ronald Delano *endocrinologist*

**Marquette**
Lincke, Eric Theodore *retired surgeon*
Mahmood, Tallat *oncologist, hematologist*

**Milford**
Oliveri, Eugene Alfred *gastroenterologist*

**Niles**
Gibbs, Denis Laurel *radiologist*

**Northport**
Schultz, Richard Carlton *plastic surgeon*

**Okemos**
Monson, Carol Lynn *osteopath, psychotherapist*

**Petoskey**
Meengs, William Lloyd *cardiologist*

**Richland**
Atkinson, Arthur John, Jr. *pharmacologist, educator, consultant*

**Rochester**
Fazzalari, Frank *cardiothoracic surgeon*

**Rochester Hills**
Badalament, Robert Anthony *urologist, oncologist*

**Roseville**
Pires, Luis A. *cardiologist, researcher*

**Royal Oak**
Britt, Stephen Thomas *medical educator*
Dworkin, Howard Jerry *nuclear medicine physician, educator*
Ernstoff, Raina Marcia *neurologist*
LaBan, Myron Miles *physician, hospital administrator*
O'Neill, William Walter *physician, educator*
Proctor, Conrad Arnold *physician*

**Saginaw**
Ferlinz, Jack *cardiologist, educator*
Hammel, Iriana Simona *geriatrician*
Manning, John Warren III *retired surgeon, medical educator*

**Saint Clair Shores**
Rodriguez, Daniela M. *plastic surgeon*

**Saint Joseph**
Wood, Dirk Gregory *surgeon, physician, forensic consultant*

**Southfield**
O'Hara, John Paul III *orthopedic surgeon*
Perez-Cruet, Mick (Miguelangelo) Jorge *neurosurgeon, educator*
Sobel, Robert A. *retired orthopedic surgeon*
Zubroff, Leonard Saul *surgeon*

**Taylor**
Lavery, Ian C. *colon and rectal surgeon, medical association administrator*

**Trenton**
Go, Benedict Anthony *internist*

**Troy**
Barton, Stanley L. *ophthalmologist, consultant*
Golusin, Millard R. *obstetrician, gynecologist*
Meerschaert, Joseph Richard *physician*
Schafer, Sharon Marie *anesthesiologist*

**West Bloomfield**
Jones, Lewis Arnold, Jr. *physician, radiologist, consultant*
Sarwer-Foner, Gerald Jacob *psychiatrist, educator*
Sawyer, Howard Jerome *physician*

## MINNESOTA

**Alexandria**
Weigel, Dennis Philip *orthopedic surgeon*

**Austin**
Rioux, Pierre August *psychiatrist*

**Burnsville**
Lakin, James Dennis *allergist, immunologist, director*

**Duluth**
Aufderheide, Arthur Carl *pathologist*
McKee, David Charles *neurologist*
Trachte, George Joseph *pharmacology educator*

**Eden Prairie**
Hardman, Harold Francis *pharmacology educator*

**Edina**
Rucker, Richard Douglas, Jr. *emergency physician*
Sandy, Lewis Gordon *physician, healthcare executive*
Tagatz, George Elmo *retired obstetrician, gynecologist, educator*
Van Beek, Allen Lester *plastic surgeon*

**Excelsior**
Bilka, Paul Joseph *retired physician*
Martinson, Elmer James *retired surgeon*

**Hastings**
Orr, Jennie Marie (Jennie Thomas) *family physician*

**Lauderdale**
Resch, Joseph Anthony *neurologist*

**Minneapolis**
Aamoth, Gordon M. *medical association administrator*
Arendt, Elizabeth Ann *orthopedist, educator*
Bache, Robert James *physician, medical educator*

Beilman, Greg J. *medical educator, researcher*
Blackburn, Henry Webster, Jr. *retired epidemiologist*
Blaes, Anne Hudson *internist*
Buchwald, Henry *surgeon, educator, researcher*
Burchell, Howard Bertram *retired internist*
Chavers, Blanche Marie *pediatrician, educator, researcher*
Craig, James Lynn *physician, health services administrator*
Cunningham, Bruce Langdon *plastic and reconstructive surgeon, educator*
Domino, Constance Mae *genetics researcher*
Dykstra, Dennis Dale *physiatrist*
Fisch, Robert Otto *medical educator*
Freese, Andrew *neurosurgeon, educator*
Gerberich, Susan Goodwin *epidemiologist, educator, medical researcher*
Haines, Stephen John *neurosurgeon*
Hanson, Arthur Stuart *physician, consultant*
Hanson, Daniel R. *psychiatrist, educator*
Hays, Thomas S. *medical educator, medical researcher*
Hom, David Brian *surgeon*
Ingbar, David H. *physician, researcher*
Joseph, Marilyn Susan *gynecologist*
Judson, Patricia Lynn *obstetrician, gynecologist, oncologist*
Keane, William Francis *nephrology educator, research foundation executive*
Kim, Suck-Won *psychiatrist, educator*
Koscheyev, Victor S. *emergency physician, researcher*
Leon, Arthur Sol *research cardiologist, exercise physiologist*
Leppik, Ilo E. *neurologist, educator*
Lin, Jizhen *otolaryngologist, researcher*
Loh, Horace H. *pharmacology educator*
Luepker, Russell Vincent *epidemiology educator*
Malmquist, Carl Phillip *psychiatrist*
Mandel, Sheldon Lloyd *dermatologist, educator*
McQuarrie, Donald Gray *surgeon, educator*
McSorley, Stephen J. *medical educator*
Miles, Steven Haverstock *geriatric medicine educator*
Miner, James Ross *emergency physician, educator*
Molina, J. Ernesto *thoracic surgeon, educator*
Moller, James Herman *pediatrician, educator*
Najarian, John Sarkis *surgeon, edueator*
Phibbs, Clifford Matthew *surgeon, educator*
Powell, Deborah Elizabeth *pathologist, dean*
Pyles, Lee Allan *cardiologist, biomedical researcher*
Quie, Paul Gerhardt *pediatrician, educator*
Schuman, Leonard M. *medical educator, academic administrator*
Slocum, Rosemarie *physician services consultant, recruiter*
Stenwick, Michael William *retired internist, geriatrician, consultant*
Thompson, Roby Calvin, Jr. *orthopedic surgeon, educator, department chairman*
Thompson, Theodore Robert *pediatric educator*
Toscano, James Vincent *medical foundation administrator*
Ulstrom, Robert A. *retired pediatrician*
Verby, John Edward, Jr. *physician, educator*
Wang, Yang *cardiologist, educator, medical researcher*
Wild, John Julian *surgeon, researcher, medical educator*
Zaleske, David Joseph *surgeon, research scientist, health facility administrator*

**Minnetonka**
Bahl, Tracy L. *healthcare executive*

**Olivia**
Cosgriff, James Arthur *physician*

**Rochester**
Aksamit, Allen J. *neurologist*
Archibald, Reginald Mac Gregor *pediatrician, endocrinologist, chemist, educator*
Bartholomew, Lloyd Gibson *physician*
Boeve, Bradley F. *neurologist*
Bowie, E(dward) J(ohn) Walter *hematologist, researcher*
Brown, Arnold Lanehart, Jr. *pathologist, educator, dean*
Cofield, Robert Hahn *orthopedic surgeon, educator*
Cooper, Leslie Trumbull *cardiologist, educator*
Cross, Shelley Ann *neurologist, neuro-ophthalmologist*
Currier, Bradford Leonard *spine and orthopedic surgeon*
Danielson, Gordon Kenneth, Jr. *cardiovascular surgeon, educator*
DeRemee, Richard Arthur *internist, educator, researcher*
Dilger, John Anthony *anesthesiologist, consultant*
Douglass, Bruce E. *physician*
Elkin, Peter Lewis *medical educator*
Engel, Andrew George *neurologist*
Fervenza, Fernando C. *nephrologist, educator*
Forstrom, Lee Arthur *physician*
Fye, W. Bruce III *cardiologist*
Geda, Yonas Endale *psychiatrist, researcher*
Gorman, Colum Alphonsus *retired endocrinologist*
Gracey, Douglas Robert *internist, educator, physiologist*
Haddy, Francis John *internist, educator*
Hodgson, Jane Elizabeth *obstetrician, gynecologist, consultant*
Hunder, Gene Gerald *rheumatologist, educator*
Kantarci, Kejal *radiologist, researcher*
Knopman, David S. *neurologist*
Kyle, Robert Arthur *medical educator, oncologist*
LaRusso, Nicholas F. *gastroenterologist, educator, scientist*
Lee, Hon-Chi *medical educator*
Lee, Kendall Han *neurosurgeon*
Lindor, Keith D. *gastroenterologist, researcher, hepatologist, dean*
Lucas, Alexander Ralph *child psychiatrist, educator, writer*
Mackenzie, Ronald Alexander *anesthesiologist*
Malkasian, George Durand, Jr. *obstetrician, educator*
McAlpine, Donald Eugene *physician*

Moir, Christopher Robert *surgeon*
Mrazek, David Allen *psychiatrist*
Neel, Harry Bryan III *surgeon, scientist, educator*
Nelson, Audrey May *physician*
Pairolero, Peter Charles *surgeon, educator*
Perry, Harold Otto *dermatologist*
Phillips, Sidney Frederick *gastroenterologist, educator*
Piepgras, David G. *neurosurgeon, educator*
Pittelkow, Mark Robert *physician, dermatologist, educator, medical researcher*
Platt, Jeffrey Louis *surgeon, director, immunologist, educator, pediatric nephrologist*
Pulido, Jose S. *physician*
Raffel, Corey *neurosurgeon, pediatrician*
Reitemeier, Richard Joseph *physician*
Rogers, Roy Steele III *dermatologist, educator, dean*
Rosenow, Edward Carl III *medical educator*
Sanchez-Sotelo, Joaquin *surgery consultant*
Schnelldorfer, Thomas *surgeon*
Siekert, Robert George *retired neurologist, retired educator*
Sim, Franklin H. *orthopedic surgery educator*
Smith, Hugh Cadham *cardiovascular diseases physician*
Steckelberg, James *epidemiologist, educator*
Stegall, Mark D. *surgeon, medical educator*
Stickler, Gunnar Brynolf *pediatrician*
Talley, Nicholas Joseph *medical educator, research scientist, physician*
Ward, Louis Emmerson *retired physician*
Weinshilboum, Richard M. *pharmacologist, educator, biomedical researcher*
Wells, Lloyd Allan *psychiatrist, educator*
Whisnant, Jack Page *neurologist*
Wiebers, David Owen *physician*
Wood, Douglas Lynn *medical educator*
Woods, John Elmer *plastic surgeon*

**Saint Cloud**
Olson, Barbara Ford *physician*

**Saint Louis Park**
Beecher, Lee Hewitt *psychiatrist*
Carpel, Emmett Franklin *ophthalmologist, consultant*

**Saint Paul**
Arora, Puneet Singh *endocrinologist, consultant, educator*
Broccard, Alain F. *pulmonologist*
Burton, Charles Victor *neurosurgeon*
Cavert, Henry Mead *retired physician, retired medical educator*
Edwards, Jesse Efrem *pathologist, educator*
Holter, Arlen Rolf *cardiothoracic surgeon*
Kalliainen, Loree K. *surgeon, educator*
Michael, Alfred Frederick, Jr. *physician, medical educator*
Roberts, William O. *sports medicine physician*
Swaiman, Kenneth Fred *pediatric neurologist, educator*
Westermeyer, Joseph John *psychiatrist*
Wilson, Leonard Gilchrist *medical educator*

**Stillwater**
Asch, Susan McClellan *pediatrician*
Lane, Stephen S. *ophthalmologist*

**Virginia**
Knabe, George William, Jr. *pathologist, educator*

**Wayzata**
Muschenheim, Frederick *retired pathologist*

**MISSISSIPPI**

**Flora**
Das, Suman Kumar *plastic surgeon, researcher*

**Gulfport**
Conrad, Harold Theodore *psychiatrist*

**Iuka**
Segars, Kelly Scott, Sr. *physician, banker*

**Jackson**
Barrett, Gene Richard *orthopedist*
Bloom, Sherman *retired pathology educator, photographer*
Chung, Sung Jang *pathologist*
Cowan, Bryan D. *medical educator, department chairman*
Cruse, Julius Major, Jr. *pathologist, educator*
de-Shazo, Richard Denson *medical educator, academic administrator*
Freeland, Alan Edward *orthopedic surgery educator, educator*
Hall, John E. *medical educator*
Herndon, Robert McCulloch *neurologist, researcher*
Houston, Gerry Ann *oncologist*
Hughson, Michael Donald *pathologist, researcher, medical educator*
Islam, Saleem *pediatric surgeon, researcher*
Izevbigie, Ernest B. *biomedical researcher*
Kyle, Patrick B. *biomedical researcher, educator*
Marshall, Gailen Daugherty, Jr. *allergist, educator*
Minocha, Anil *physician, educator, researcher*
Moll, George William *pediatrician, educator*
Munera, Pedro Antonio *child and adolescent psychiatrist*
Phillips, Joshua Phillips *pediatrician*
Roy, Sitesh Ranen *pediatrician, allergist, immunologist, educator*
Thigpen, James Tate *oncologist, educator*

**Laurel**
Lacey, Peeler Grayson *diagnostic radiologist*
Lindstrom, Eric Everett *ophthalmologist*

**Ocean Springs**
Austin, Claude Lidell *retired surgeon*

**Tutwiler**
Brooks, Sister Anne *osteopath*

**Whitfield**
Montgomery, John Harold *psychiatrist*

**MISSOURI**

**Belton**
Blim, Richard Don *retired pediatrician, health facility administrator*

**Chesterfield**
Qazi, Mujtaba A. *ophthalmologist*
Salem, Bakr Ibramim *cardiologist*

**Clayton**
Post, Stephen Lightner *retired psychoanalyst, educator*

**Columbia**
Anderson, Ralph Robert *endocrinologist, educator*
Colwill, Jack Marshall *physician, educator*
Cunningham, Milamari Antoinella *retired anesthesiologist*
Eggers, George William Nordholtz, Jr. *anesthesiologist, educator*
Govindarajan, Gurushankar *cardiologist, researcher*
Hardin, Christopher Demarest *medical educator*
James, Elizabeth Joan Plogsted *pediatrician, educator*
König, Peter *pediatrician, educator*
LeMaster, Joseph William *physician, epidemiologist*
Lewis, Michael Robert *medical researcher, educator*
Perry, Michael Clinton *internist, educator, academic administrator*
Potts, Jeffrey Thomas *biomedical researcher*
Puckett, Charles Linwood *plastic surgeon, educator*
Smith, Charles Jeffrey *radiologist, educator, research scientist*
Stephenson, Hugh Edward, Jr. *retired surgeon*
Sun, Albert Yung-Kwang *pharmacologist, educator*
Tarnove, Lorraine *medical association executive*
Tobias, Joseph Drew *pediatric anesthesiologist*
Witten, David Melvin *retired radiology educator*

**Florissant**
Tanphaichitr, Kongsak *rheumatologist, allergist, immunologist, internist*

**Fulton**
Garcia, Alfred Gerard *emergency physician, director*

**Joplin**
Habermann, James Herbert *retired pathologist*

**Kansas City**
Abuissa, Hussam *cardiologist*
Amoury, Raymond Anthony *retired surgeon, educator*
Angoff, Gerald Harvey *cardiologist*
Butler, Merlin Gene *physician, medical geneticist, educator*
Dimond, Edmunds Grey *medical educator*
Dinakar, Chitra *immunologist, allergist*
Fiorella, Russell Michael *pathologist*
Friedlander, Edward Robert *pathologist*
Hagan, John Charles III *ophthalmologist*
Heymach, George John III *physician, educator, health facility administrator, consultant*
Lofland, Gary Kenneth *cardiac surgeon*
Long, Edwin Tutt *surgeon*
McGregor, Douglas Hugh *pathologist, educator*
McKinsey, David Stephen *infectious diseases specialist*
McPhee, Mark Steven *gastroenterologist, educator*
Molteni, Agostino *pathology educator*
Piepho, Robert Walter *pharmacy educator, researcher*
Poston, Walker Seward, II, *medical educator, researcher*
Rada, David Charles *dermatologist*
Rymer, Marilyn Mollman *neurologist, researcher*
Truog, William Edward III *pediatrician, educator, researcher*

**Kirksville**
Evans, Maria Louise *medical educator*
French, Michael Francis *medical educator*

**Maryland Heights**
Miller, Steven *medical administrator*
Motchan, Dennis Glenn *physician*

**Oak Grove**
Davis, Jo *naturopathic physician*

**Rolla**
Yang, Jinbo *biomedical researcher*

**Saint Louis**
Acharya, Jayant Narahari *neurologist, educator*
Acharya, Vinita J *neurologist, researcher, educator*
Agarwal, Banke *gastroenterologist, educator*
Alpers, David Hershel *internist, educator*
Bach, Richard Gordon *internist, cardiologist, educator*
Bacon, Bruce Raymond *physician*
Ballinger, Walter Francis *surgeon, educator*
Berg, Leonard *retired neurologist, educator, researcher*
Berland, David I. *psychiatrist, educator*
Bjerregaard, Preben *cardiologist, educator*
Blumenthal, Herman Theodore *retired pathologist*
Burke, William *neurologist*
Cahill, Richard Anderson *medical educator*
Case-Schmidt, Mary E. *pathologist, educator*
Chaitman, Bernard Raymond *internist*
Chaplin, David Dunbar *medical research specialist, educator*
Chaplin, Hugh, Jr. *preventive medicine physician, educator*
Chole, Richard Arthur *otolaryngologist, department chairman*
Cloninger, Claude Robert *psychiatrist, researcher, epidemiologist, educator*

Constantino, John Nicholas *medical educator, researcher*
Correa-Perez, Juan Ramon *embryologist, science educator, director, lab administrator*
Cross, Anne Haney *neurologist, medical researcher*
Cryer, Philip Eugene *endocrinologist*
Dewald, Paul Adolph *psychiatrist, educator*
Dodge, Philip Rogers *neurologist, educator*
Donati, Robert Mario *physician, educational administrator*
Dorsett, Dale *medical educator*
Dougherty, Charles Hamilton *pediatrician*
Dykewicz, Mark Steven *physician*
Evens, Ronald Gene *radiologist, educator, health facility administrator*
Evers, Alex Steven *anesthesiologist, internist, educator*
Farria, Dione Marie *radiologist, educator*
Fitch, Coy Dean *internist, educator*
Fleshman, James W. *medical association administrator*
Flye, M. Wayne *surgeon, immunologist, educator, writer*
Fontana, Luigi *internist, researcher*
Gay, William Arthur, Jr. *thoracic surgeon*
Gelberman, Richard H. *orthopedist, surgeon*
Goldberg, Anne Carol *physician, educator*
Gordon, J. Eric *orthopedist, surgeon*
Gordon, Jeffrey Ivan *gastroenterologist, educator, molecular biologist, researcher*
Grossberg, George Thomas *psychiatrist, educator*
Grubb, Robert L., Jr. *neurosurgeon*
Hammerman, Marc Randall *nephrologist, educator*
Hanley, Thomas Patrick *obstetrician, gynecologist*
Heiken, Jay Paul *physician*
Hmiel, Stanley Paul *pediatrician, nephrologist, educator*
Holmes, Nancy Elizabeth *pediatrician*
Holtzman, David Michael *neurologist*
Hsueh, Eddy C. *surgeon, oncologist*
Hyers, Thomas Morgan *internist, biomedical researcher*
Jacobsohn MD, Eric *anesthesiologist*
Johnson, Robert Graham *surgeon, educator, researcher*
Kamel, Hosam Kamal *medical educator, researcher, geriatrician*
Kaminski, Donald Leon *surgeon, gastroenterologist, educator*
Kass, Michael Allen *ophthalmologist, educator*
Kipnis, David Morris *physician, educator*
Knutson, Alan Paul *pediatrician, immunologist, allergist*
Kolker, Allan Erwin *ophthalmologist*
Kornfeld, Stuart A. *hematology educator*
Kouchoukos, Nicholas Thomas *surgeon*
Krem, Maxwell Masters *internist*
Kroll, Kristen L. *medical educator*
Lewis, Robert David *ophthalmologist, educator*
Ludmerer, Kenneth Marc *medical educator*
Majerus, Philip Warren *physician*
Mantovani, John F. *pediatric neurologist*
Martin, Kevin John *nephrologist, educator*
McMahon, Robert M. *physician, lawyer*
Mendelsohn, Roy M. *psychiatrist*
Middelkamp, John Neal *pediatrician, educator*
Moon, Marc R. *cardiac surgeon*
Mooradian, Arshag Dertad *internist, educator*
Morley, John Edward *physician*
Myerson, Robert J. *radiologist, educator*
Neely, John Gail *otolaryngologist*
Neidorff, Michael F. *health care executive*
Newcomer, John Whitney *psychiatrist, researcher, educator*
Owens, William Don *anesthesiology educator*
Peck, William Arno *internist, educator, dean, academic administrator*
Prakash, Chandra *gastroenterologist, researcher*
Prensky, Arthur Lawrence *pediatric neurologist, educator*
Purkerson, Mabel Louise *physician, educator, physiologist*
Rao, Dabeeru C. (D.C. Rao) *epidemiologist, educator*
Rednam, Krishna Rao Venkata *ophthalmologist*
Rich, Michael W *physician, researcher*
Riew, K. Daniel *cervical spine surgeon*
Robins, Lee Nelken *medical educator*
Rosenbaum, Herbert Edwin *neurology educator*
Rosenblum, Barry Norton *physician*
Rothman, Steven Mark *pediatric neurologist, neuroscientist*
Royal, Henry Duval *nuclear medicine physician, educator, director*
Ryall, Jo-Ellyn M. *psychiatrist*
Saltman, Robert Jon *physician, medical educator*
Schonfeld, Gustav *medical educator, researcher, administrator*
Schwartz, Alan Leigh *pediatrician, educator*
Shapiro, Larry J. *pediatrician, educator, scientist, dean*
Siegel, Barry Alan *radiologist*
Singh, Inderjit *internist, nephrologist, medical educator*
Sita, Michael John *pharmacy educator*
Slavin, Raymond Granam *allergist, immunologist*
Smith, Morton Edward *ophthalmology educator, dean*
Spector, Gershon Jerry *otolaryngologist, educator, researcher*
Stack, Brendan Curran, Jr. *head and neck surgeon, researcher, educator*
Strunk, Robert Charles *physician*
Tao, Donghua *health sciences librarian*
Teitelbaum, Steven Lazarus *pathology educator*
Ternberg, Jessie Lamoin *pediatric surgeon, educator*
Thach, William Thomas, Jr. *neurologist, educator*
Thomas, Florian Patrick *physician, researcher*
Tiefenbrunn, Alan James *medical educator*
Ulett, George Andrew *psychiatrist*
Varvarer, Mark A. *otolaryngology professor*
Vij, Ravi *oncologist, researcher*
Walsh, David Joseph *pediatric neurologist, researcher*
Wedner, H. James *physician, researcher*
Weilbaecher, Katherine *oncologist*
Whyte, Michael P. *genetics educator, researcher, director*

Wilson, Margaret Mary Georgiana *geriatrician, researcher, physician*
Yarasheski, Kevin Edward *medical educator*
Yi, Xiaobin *anesthesiologist, pain management specialist*
Young, Leroy *plastic surgeon*
Young, Paul Andrew *anatomist*
Ziskind, Andrew A. *cardiologist, medical educator, health facility administrator*

**Saint Peters**
Boschert, Mark Thomas *plastic surgeon*
Wang, William Weiqi *physician*

**Sedalia**
Chaar, Bassem T. *hematologist, oncologist*

**Springfield**
Geter, Rodney Keith *plastic surgeon*
Hackett, Earl Randolph *neurologist*

**Town And Country**
Levin, Marvin Edgar *physician*

## MONTANA

**Big Sky**
Strickler, Jeffrey Harold *pediatrician*

**Billings**
Glenn, Guy Charles *pathologist*
Habein, Harold Clinton *retired surgeon*

**Great Falls**
Santin, Antonio *plastic surgeon*

**Missoula**
Fawcett, Don Wayne *retired anatomist*
Gillespie, Donald N. *immunologist, pediatrician*
Willstein, Gary Jay *orthopedist, surgeon*

**Whitefish**
Miller, Ronald Alfred *family physician*

## NEBRASKA

**Atkinson**
Sutherland, John Campbell *pathologist, educator*

**Bennington**
Burgher, Louis William *physician, educator, academic administrator*

**Elkhorn**
Walk, Louis Bernard *physician*

**Fort Calhoun**
Ware, Frederick *internist, educator, nephrologist*

**Hastings**
Dungan, John Russell, Jr., (12th Viscount Dungan of Clane, Hereditary Prince of Fermoy and Arra) *anesthesiologist, health facility administrator*

**Lincoln**
Koger, Michael Pigott *physician, writer*
Koszewski, Bohdan Julius *retired internist, medical educator*
Michels, Dale E. *physician*
Nafach, Jalal *endocrinologist*
Noren, Jerry Jay *medical educator*
Wilson, Charles Stephen *cardiologist, educator*

**Omaha**
Armitage, James O. *medical educator*
Balaji, K.C. *urologist, researcher*
Baltaro, Richard J. *pathologist, medical educator*
Benson, John Alexander, Jr. *internist, educator*
Casale, Thomas Bruce *medical educator*
Casey, Murray Joseph *physician, educator*
Desmangles, Jean-Claude *medical educator*
Fusaro, Ramon Michael *dermatologist, preventive medicine physician, researcher*
Hodgson, Paul Edmund *surgeon, department chairman*
Huurman, Walter William *pediatric orthopaedic surgeon, educator*
Imray, Thomas John *radiologist, educator*
Khoynezhad, Ali *cardiothoracic surgeon, researcher*
Kobayashi, Roger Hideo *allergy and immunology educator, microbiologist, educator*
Korbitz, Bernard Carl *hematologist, consultant*
Mardis, Hal Kennedy *urological surgeon, educator, researcher*
Maurer, Harold Maurice *pediatrician*
Mohiuddin, Syed Maqdoom *cardiologist, educator*
Nairn, Roderick *immunologist, educator, biochemist*
O'Brien, Richard L(ee) *physician, educator, academic administrator*
Plotkin, Horacio *pediatric endocrinologist, orthopedic surgeon, educator*
Potter, Jane Frances *physician*
Rendell, Marc S. *physician, researcher*
Rich, Eugene Carroll *internist*
Rogan, Eleanor Groeniger *oncologist, educator*
Skoog, Donald Paul *retired pathologist, educator*
Sooriyaarachchi, Gamini Sarathchandra *oncologist, hematologist, educator*
Swindells, Susan *HIV specialist*
Tinker, John Heath *anesthesiologist, educator*
Tomich, Paul George *obstetrician, director, gynecologist, educator*
Ward, Vernon Graves *retired internist*

**Papillion**
Dvorak, Allen Dale *radiologist*

**Scottsbluff**
Kabalin, John Nicholas *urologist*

## NEVADA

**Henderson**
Wax, Arnold *physician*

**Las Vegas**
Bandt, Paul Douglas *radiologist*
Buzard, Kurt Andre *ophthalmologist*
Goodenberger, Daniel Marvin *medical educator*
Gremse, David Albert *pediatrician, educator*
Hoepfner, Mark Thomas *surgeon*
Kurlinski, John Parker *physician*
Merkin, Albert Charles *pediatrician, allergist*
Moritz, Timothy Bovie *psychiatrist*
Noback, Richardson Kilbourne *medical educator*
Shires, George Thomas *surgeon, educator*
Speck, Eugene Lewis *internist*
Teng, Francis W. *surgeon*
Triglano, Lucien Lewis *physician*

**Reno**
Crognale, Michael Anthony *medical educator, neuroscientist, consultant*
Guneyi, Umit Ahmet *physician, consultant*
MacKintosh, Frederick Roy *oncologist*
Mashour, Steve *pulmonologist*
Small, Elisabeth Chan *psychiatrist, educator*
Zager, Bernard Solomon *physician, consultant*

## NEW HAMPSHIRE

**Alstead**
Moore, Michele Claire *physician*

**Bow**
Emery, Paul Emile *psychiatrist*

**Campton**
Scrimshaw, Nevin Stewart *physician, nutritionist, educator*

**Concord**
Bagan, Merwyn *neurological surgeon*
Vidaver, Robert Maxwell *medical educator*

**Grantham**
Figley, Melvin Morgan *radiologist, physician, educator*

**Hanover**
Chapman, Robert James *psychiatrist, educator*
Dmitrovsky, Ethan *oncologist, medical educator, researcher*
Petitto, Laura-Ann *cognitive neuroscience educator*
Rolett, Ellis Lawrence *cardiologist, educator*
Zubkoff, Michael *medical educator*

**Laconia**
Brody, Spencer John *pediatrician*
Dhillon, Samjot Singh *pulmonologist*

**Lebanon**
Bernat, James Lawrence *neurologist, educator*
Cohen, Jeffrey Allen *neurologist, educator*
Collins, E. Dale *surgeon, educator*
Cronenwett, Jack LeMoyne *vascular surgeon educator*
Darnall, Robert Allen *pediatrician, physiologist, educator*
Fanger, Michael W. *medical educator*
Ferrell, Richard Bradley *neuropsychiatrist*
Fillinger, Mark F. *vascular surgeon, researcher*
Glass, Donald David *anesthesiologist*
Gosselin, Benoit Jean *otolaryngologist, facial plastic surgeon, head and neck reconstructive surgeon*
Kelley, Maurice Leslie, Jr. *gastroenterologist, educator*
McCollum, Robert Wayne *epidemiologist, educator*
Oxman, Thomas Elliot *psychiatrist*
Silberfarb, Peter Michael *psychiatrist, educator*
Waugh, Theodore Rogers *orthopedic surgeon*
Whitley, Rob *medical educator, sociologist, researcher*

**Lee**
Young, James Morningstar *internist, military officer*

**Littleton**
Kelly, Dorothy Helen *pediatrician, educator*

**Lyme**
Cornwell, Gibbons Gray III *retired internist, educator*
McIntyre, Oswald Ross *physician*

**Manchester**
Danby, F. William *dermatologist, educator*

**Mirror Lake**
Culleton, James Frederick *neurologist*

**Nashua**
Hermansen, Marcus C. *pediatrics professor, director*
Knights, Edwin Munroe *pathologist*
Siroty, William Charles *physician*

**Portsmouth**
Lauter, M. David *physician*

**Rye**
Wilson, Ralph Sloan *retinal surgeon*

**Stoddard**
Cahill, George Francis, Jr. *physician, educator*

**Windham**
Levin, Murray Newman *retired surgeon*

## NEW JERSEY

**Basking Ridge**
Evdukimow, David Z. *plastic surgeon*
Panzarino, Saverio Joseph *physician*

**Belle Mead**
Goodnick, Paul Joel *psychiatrist*

**Bergenfield**
Dello Russo, Joseph *ophthalmologist*

**Berkeley Heights**
Momeni, Reza *plastic surgeon*

**Bernardsville**
Dixon, Rosina Berry *physician, pharmaceutical executive, consultant*

**Bridgewater**
Bernson, Marcella S. *psychiatrist*
Faruqi, Abdul Rab *physician, consultant, researcher*
Hirsch, Paul J. *orthopedist, surgeon, health facility administrator, medical educator*
Scully, John Thomas *obstetrician, gynecologist, educator*
Taylor, Duncan Paul *pharmacologist, researcher*

**Browns Mills**
Cha, Se Do *internist*
Moore, Roger Addison *pediatrician, anesthesiologist*

**Camden**
Ances, I. G. (I. George Ances) *obstetrician, gynecologist*
Hollenberg, Steven Michael *physician, researcher*
Parra, Raul O. *urologist, educator*
Parrillo, Joseph Edison, Jr. *allergist, immunologist, cardiologist*
Rajaram, Sri-Sujanthy *internist, medical educator*
Whalen, Thomas Vincent *pediatric surgeon*

**Cape May Court House**
Altman, Brian David *pediatric ophthalmologist*

**Cherry Hill**
Goldberg, Jack *hematologist*
Kahn, Marc Leslie *orthopedic surgeon*
Margolis, Gerald Joseph *psychiatrist, psychoanalyst*
Olearchyk, Andrew *cardiothoracic surgeon, educator*
Swibinski, Edward Thomas *internist, endocrinologist, educator*
Werbitt, Warren *gastroenterologist, educator*

**Cranford**
Mendelson, Joel Stuart *allergist, immunologist*

**Demarest**
Dornfest, Burton Saul *anatomy educator*

**Denville**
Husar, Walter Gene *neurologist, neuroscientist, educator*

**East Hanover**
Nemecek, Georgina Marie *molecular pharmacologist*
Purkayastha, Das D. *biostatistics director*

**East Orange**
Brundage, Gertrude Barnes *pediatrician*

**Edison**
Brisman, Jonathan *neurosurgeon*
Gizzi, Martin Sherman *neurologist, neurophysiologist*
Grewal, Raji Paul *neurologist, educator, medical researcher*
Walters, Arthur Scott *neurologist, educator, clinical research scientist*

**Elizabeth**
Berger, Harold Richard *physician*
Rosenstein, Neil *surgeon, genealogist, researcher*
Sananman, Michael Lawrence *neurologist*

**Englewood**
Bloomenstein, Richard B. *plastic surgeon*
Chiorazzi, Mary Lorraine *psychiatrist*
Cohen, Wendy E. *neurologist*
Dardik, Herbert *vascular surgeon, general surgeon*
Elias, Steven *surgeon*
Frieden, Faith Joy *obstetrician*
Goldweit, Richard Scott *cardiologist*
Harish, Ziv *allergist, immunologist*
Schlossman, Howard Harvey *psychoanalysis educator*
Tobias, Geoffrey *otolaryngologist, plastic surgeon*
Wuhl, Charles Michael *psychiatrist*

**Englewood Cliffs**
Yu, Fei *internist*

**Fair Lawn**
Namerow, David Mark *pediatrician*

**Flemington**
Rubin, Arkady *biostatistics and data management researcher, executive*
Rushton, Alan R. *physician, medical researcher, historian*

**Florham Park**
Weisberg, Lynne Willing *psychiatrist, consultant*

**Forked River**
Novak, Dennis E. *physician*

**Fort Lee**
Chessler, Richard Kenneth *gastroenterologist, endocrinologist*
Goldfarb, Joel Peter *internist, gastroenterologist*
Li, Tien-Shun *obstetrician, gynecologist, educator*

**Franklin Lakes**
Ginsberg, Barry Howard *endocrinologist, educator*

**Glen Ridge**
Rubin, Roberta Gail *retired pathologist*
Zbar, Lloyd Irwin Stanley *otolaryngologist, educator*

**Green Brook**
Hertzberg, Henry *retired radiologist*

**Guttenberg**
Wright, Jane Cooke *oncologist, educator, consultant*

**Hackensack**
Agress, Harry, Jr. *radiologist, nuclear medicine physician*
Basile, Anthony Stephen *pharmacologist, researcher*
De Groote, Robert David *general and vascular surgeon*
Gross, Peter Alan *epidemiologist, researcher*
Haines, Kathleen Ann *pediatrician, educator*
Masullo, Alfredo Salvatore *dermatologist*
Pecora, Andrew Louis *hematologist, oncologist*
Smith, Daniel *oncologist, gynecologist*

**Hackettstown**
Singh, Harjit *medical educator, artist*

**Haddonfield**
Capelli, John Placido *nephrologist, educator*
Fisher, George Ross III *physician, educator*
Gatti, Eugene Anthony *immunologist, pediatrician*
Jensh, Ronald Paul *retired anatomist*

**Hamilton**
Sipski, Mary Leonide *physiatrist, health facility administrator*
Sporn, Aaron Adolph *physician, educator*

**Hasbrouck Heights**
Colon, José Mariano *obstetrician, gynecologist, endocrinologist, educator*

**Hazlet**
Marcus, Abir A. *psychiatrist*
Wilson, Elizabeth Sawin *psychiatrist*

**Hillsborough**
Herman, David J. *infectious diseases physician*

**Hillsdale**
Copeland, Lois Jacqueline *physician*

**Jersey City**
Al-Bashir, Mohamed Fahmi *surgeon*
Demos, Nicholas John *physician, surgeon, researcher*

**Kendall Park**
Kesarwala, Hemant *pediatrician, educator*

**Lawrenceville**
Pouleur, Hubert Gustave *cardiologist, consultant*
Rosenthal, Albert Lester *dermatologist, educator*
Witte, Arnold Stewart *neurologist*

**Linden**
Bukosky, Richard J. *allergist*

**Livingston**
Rickert, Robert Richard *pathologist, educator*
Samojlik, Eugeniusz *medical educator, health facility administrator*

**Long Branch**
Luria, Martin Jay *endocrinologist*

**Lumberton**
Campagnolo, Mary Frances *physician*

**Maple Shade**
Abidi, S. Manzoor *neurologist*

**Maplewood**
Haggerty, Mary Ann *medical educator*
Shuttleworth, Anne Margaret *psychiatrist*

**Margate City**
Videll, Jared Steven *cardiologist*

**Marlton**
Kahn, Sigmund Benham *retired internist, dean*

**Medford**
Lawson-Ndu, Ovunda A. *emergency physician, surgeon*

**Monmouth Beach**
Danikas, Dimitrios *plastic surgeon*

**Monmouth Junction**
Brolin, Robert Edward *physician, surgeon*

**Monroe Township**
Spierer, Robert *family practice physician*

**Montclair**
Green, Amy *psychiatrist*
Holmes, Nathaniel J. *surgeon*
Rosen, Allen David *plastic surgeon*

**Morris Plains**
Fielding, Stuart *psychopharmacologist*
Goldenberg, David Milton *experimental pathologist, oncologist*

**Morristown**
Adler, Kenneth R. *oncologist*
Fiel, Stanley Bruce *internist, pulmonologist, educator, researcher*
Finkel, Marion Judith *internist, pharmaceutical administrator*
Parr, Grant Van Siclen *surgeon*
Scott, Richard Thomas, Jr. *reproductive endocrinologist*
Wong, James Robert *oncologist, educator*
Zaubler, Thomas Scot *psychiatrist, educator*

**Neptune**
Hanna, Niveen *surgeon*
Laraya-Cuasay, Lourdes Redublo *pediatrician, pulmonologist, educator*
Rice, Stephen Gary *medical educator, pediatrician, sports medicine physician*

**New Brunswick**
August, David Allen *surgeon*

Bachmann, Gloria Ann *obstetrician, gynecologist, educator*
Bertino, Joseph Rocco *physician, educator*
Borah, Gregory *surgeon, educator*
Boyarsky, Andrew Harold *surgeon, educator*
Carson, Jeffrey L. *internist*
Chandler, James John *surgeon, educator*
Corbett, Siobhan Aiden *surgeon*
Day-Salvatore, Debra Lynn *medical geneticist*
Drachtman, Richard Allan *pediatrician, educator*
Ettinger, Lawrence Jay *pediatric hematologist, oncologist, educator*
Golbe, Lawrence Ingram *neurologist*
Goldberg, Michael Ira *obstetrician, gynecologist*
Greenwald, Alfred Emanuel *retired cosmetic surgeon*
Kamen, Barton A. *pediatrician, educator*
Kaufman, Kenneth Roland *psychiatrist, educator*
Khachadurian, Avedis *physician*
Kostis, John Basil *cardiologist*
Lacy, Clifton R. *internist, commissioner*
Lambert, George H. *physician, director*
Lepore, Frederick Everett *neurologist, educator*
Leventhal, Elaine A. *internist*
Mann, Richard Alan *physician, educator*
Moreyra, Abel E. *medical educator*
Nissenblatt, Michael Jeffrey *medical oncologist*
Notterman, Daniel A. *educator, educator*
Olson, Robert Martin *plastic surgeon*
Pitchumoni, Capecomorin Sankar *gastroenterologist, educator*
Price, Mitchell R. *pediatric surgeon*
Raska, Karel Frantisek Julian, Jr. *pathologist, virologist, educator*
Saidi, Parvin *hematologist, medical educator*
Salas, Max *pediatrician, educator*
Schneider, Stephen Harley *medical educator*
Scholz, Peter M. *surgeon, director*
Snyder, Barbara K. *pediatrician, educator*
Spotnitz, Alan Jeffrey *cardiothoracic surgeon*
Todd, Mary Beth *oncologist, researcher*
Trooskin, Stanley Z. *surgeon*
Vintzileos, Anthony Mark *obstetrician, gynecologist*
Weiss, Lynne S. *pediatrician, educator*
Weiss, Robert Edward *urologist, educator*

**Newark**
Baker, Herman *medical educator, writer*
Baker, Stephen R. *physician*
Bethel, Colin Anthony Ivan *pediatric surgeon, educator*
Bielory, Leonard *allergist, immunologist, medical school administrator*
Camacho, Margarita Ticzon *cardiothoracic surgeon, educator*
Carmel, Peter W. *neurosurgeon*
Cherniack, Neil Stanley *pulmonologist, educator*
Cohen, Stanley *pathologist, educator*
Cook, Stuart Donald *neurologist, educator*
Correia, Joaquim Jose *physician*
Datiashvili, Ramazi O. *plastic surgeon*
Depre, Christophe *medical educator*
Ellner, Jerrold Jay *infectious diseases specialist*
Evans, Hugh E. *pediatrician, educator*
Granick, Mark S. *medical educator*
Haycock, Christine Elizabeth *retired medical educator*
Iffy, Leslie *medical educator*
Little, Alan Brian *gynecologist, educator*
Louria, Donald Bruce *medical educator*
Reichman, Lee Brodersohn *physician*
Ryan, Lisa Kathleen *environmental and medical science educator*
Schleifer, Steven J. *psychiatrist, educator*
Weiss, Gerson *endocrinologist, educator*

**Newton**
Colizza, Wayne Anthony *orthopaedic surgeon*
Scales, James Leonard, Jr. *orthopedic surgeon*

**North Brunswick**
Jones, Frank A., Jr. *psychiatrist, educator*

**Northfield**
Margolis, Thomas Ira *vitreoretinal ophthalmologist*

**Nutley**
Bridge, Thomas Peter *psychiatrist, researcher*
Mostillo, Ralph *medical association administrator*

**Ocean Grove**
Davis, John Mihran *surgeon, educator*

**Oradell**
Rosen, Jay Samuel *urologist, surgeon*

**Orange**
Agarwal, Shashi Kant *cardiologist*

**Paramus**
Liva, Edward Louis *eye surgeon*

**Paterson**
Fink, David Leonard *surgeon*
Salcedo, Jose Rodolfo *nephrologist*

**Peapack**
Eddey, Gary Erwin *physician, administrator, educator*

**Phillipsburg**
Drago, Joseph Rosario *urologist, educator*

**Piscataway**
Demissie, Kitaw *epidemiologist, educator*
Escobar, Javier Ignacio *psychiatrist*
Li, Mei-Ling *medical educator*
Menza, Matthew A. *psychiatrist*
Rhoads, George Grant *medical epidemiologist*
Sahota, Amrik *medical researcher, educator, lab administrator*
Swee, David Ethan *physician*
Trelstad, Robert Laurence *pathology educator, cell biologist*
Upton, Arthur Canfield *experimental pathologist, educator*

**Plainsboro**
Lansing, Martha Hempel *physician*

**Princeton**
Carr, Marcus Eugene, Jr. *internist*
Carver, David Harold *retired pediatrician*
German, Elaine *physician*
Girgis, Suzette *clinical pharmacologist, researcher*
Lavizzo-Mourey, Risa Juanita *medical foundation administrator, academic administrator*
Manyak, Michael John *urologist, educator, researcher*
Meade, Dale Michael *experimental physicist*
Mehlman, Myron A. *medical educator, toxicologist*
Mueller, Peter Sterling *psychiatrist, educator*
Sierocki, John Stanley *oncologist*
Sigal, Leonard H. *physician*
Sugerman, Abraham Arthur *psychiatrist, educator*
Troyanskaya, Olga *biomedical researcher, computer scientist*
von der Schmidt, Edward III *neurosurgeon, veterinarian*

**Princeton Junction**
Amenta, Peter Sebastian *pathologist*

**Red Bank**
Braddom, Randall Lee *physiatrist, educator*
Clever, Marcia Sue *psychiatrist*

**Ridgewood**
Baddoura, Rashid Joseph *emergency physician*
Bronstein, Eric H. *surgeon*

**River Edge**
Mueller, Richard L.P. *physician*

**Roseland**
Clemente, Celestino *physician, surgeon*
Panagides, John *pharmacologist*

**Saddle River**
Goodman, Jerome David *psychiatrist*
Weissmann, Heidi Seitelblum *radiologist, educator*

**Sewell**
Mandracchia, Vincent Joseph *podiatrist*

**Short Hills**
Chaiken, Bernard Henry *internist, gastroenterologist*
Duberstein, Joel Lawrence *internist, pulmonologist, educator*

**Somerset**
De Salva, Salvatore Joseph *retired pharmacologist, toxicologist*
Sofia, R. D. *pharmacologist*

**South Hackensack**
Jacobs, George Braun *neurosurgeon*

**South Plainfield**
Kwon, Ik Hyun *internist*

**South River**
Kirshner, Jacob *physician*

**Spring Lake**
Harrigan, John Thomas, Jr. *physician, obstetrician, gynecologist*

**Springfield**
Kerner, Michael Bernard *gastroenterologist*
Kwartler, Jed Aryeh *otolaryngologist*
Wosnitzer, Morey *urologist*

**Stratford**
Levitas, Andrew Stephen *child psychiatrist, educator*

**Summit**
Carniol, Paul J. *plastic and reconstructive surgeon, otolaryngologist*
Gaudino, Mario *physician, pharmaceutical company executive, scientist*
Greenberg, Rosalie *child psychiatrist*
Halperin, John Jacob *neurology educator, researcher*
Hodosh, Richard M. *neurosurgeon*
Hyans, Peter *plastic surgeon*
Sachs, Richard Gregory *cardiologist*

**Teaneck**
Halper, June *medical center director*
Ladenheim, Jules Calvin *neurosurgeon*
Rundback, John H. *radiologist, interventional radiology director*

**Tenafly**
Gerst, Paul Howard *physician*
Golomb, Frederick Martin *surgeon, educator*

**Tinton Falls**
Macdonald, Donald Arthur, Jr. *physician, surgeon*

**Toms River**
Marchese, Michael James, Jr. *radiation oncology*

**Trenton**
Gervasoni, James E., Jr. *medical researcher, oncologist*
Gomez, William *orthopedist*
Gupta, Rajendra Prasad *physician*
Thatsneyakul, Yaovares *pediatrician, consultant*
Zanna, Martin Thomas *physician*

**Turnersville**
DePace, Nicholas Louis *physician*

**Verona**
Malanga, Gerard Anthony *sports medicine physician, director*

**Vineland**
Clinton, Lawrence Paul *psychiatrist*

**Voorhees**
Glasofer, Eric David *allergist, immunologist, pediatrician, educator*

**Wall**
Monaco, Robert Anthony *radiologist*
Motley, John Paul *psychiatrist, consultant*
O'Neill, James Paul *psychiatrist*

**Wayne**
Gollance, Robert Barnett *ophthalmologist*
Jacobs-Carey, Sheila L. *retired immunologist*
Oriji, Gibson K. *medical educator, medical researcher*

**West Orange**
Brodkin, Roger Harrison *dermatologist, educator*
Casella, Anthony John *cardiologist*
Dispaltro, Franklin L. *plastic surgeon*
Filippone, Dennis R. *surgeon, consultant*
Gans, Bruce Merrill *physiatrist, educator, health facility administrator*
Gehl, Raymond Harold *psychiatrist, educator*
Ghali, Anwar Youssef *psychiatrist, educator*
Hill, George James *physician, educator*
Langsner, Alan Michael *pediatric cardiologist*
Linsenmeyer, Todd Alan *medical educator, physician*
Martin, Boston Faust *neurosurgeon*
Rogal, Gary Jeffrey *cardiologist*

**Westfield**
Vijayakumar, Asha *ophthalmologist*

**Westwood**
Landzberg, Joel Serge *cardiologist*

**Whitehouse Station**
Mahmoud, Adel A. *medical educator, pharmaceutical executive*

**Woodbury**
Stambaugh, John Edgar *oncologist, hematologist, educator, pharmacologist*

**Wyckoff**
Gartner, Joseph John, II, *obstetrician, gynecologist*
Marcus, Linda Susan *dermatologist*
Stahl, Alice Slater *retired psychiatrist*

## NEW MEXICO

**Alamogordo**
Ashdown, Franklin Donald *physician, composer*

**Albuquerque**
Bankhurst, Arthur Dale *medical educator, researcher*
Berman, Stanley Zissman *allergist, immunologist, educator, internist, department chairman*
Brown, Lee Kelvin *pulmonary, critical care and sleep medicine physician, researcher*
Chang, Barbara Karen *medical educator*
Cobb, John Candler *medical educator*
Eldredge, Jonathan DeForest *medical librarian, educator, social informaticist*
Fry, Donald Edmund *surgeon*
Heffron, Warren A. *physician, educator*
Keep, Marcus Floyd *neurosurgeon*
King, Lowell Restell *pediatric urologist*
Knospe, William Herbert *medical educator*
Mapel, Douglas Wayne *epidemiologist, educator, pulmonologist, critical care specialist*
Mason, William vanHorn *dermatologist*
Omer, George Elbert, Jr. *orthopaedic surgeon, educator*
Reichard, Robert Ross *pathologist*
Rivero, Dennis P. *orthopedist*
Ronel, Daniel Noel *plastic surgeon*
Rosenberg, Gary A. *neurologist*
Stevenson, James Richard *radiologist, educator, lawyer*
Strasburger, Victor C. *pediatrician*
Summers, William Koopmans *psychiatrist, internist, researcher*
Uhlenhuth, Eberhard Henry *psychiatrist, educator*

**Farmington**
Neidhart, James Allen *oncologist, educator*
Williams, Todd Edward *plastic surgeon*

**Los Alamos**
Smith, Fredrica Emrich *rheumatologist, internist*

**Portales**
Goodwin, Martin Brune *retired radiologist*

**Rodeo**
Scholes, Robert Thornton *allergist, researcher, science administrator*

**Roswell**
Choudhary, Adil Mushtaq *gastroenterologist*
Tabrez, Shams S.M. *gastroenterologist*

**Santa Fe**
Alfidi, Ralph Joseph *retired radiologist, educator, researcher*
Ballard, David Eugene *anesthesiologist*
Hoffmann, Louis Gerhard *immunologist, educator*
Kingsmore, Stephen Francis *physician, research scientist*
Kotin, Paul *pathologist*
Schiller, William Richard *surgeon*
Schwartz, George R. *physician, researcher*
Williams, Ralph Chester, Jr. *physician, educator*

**Shiprock**
Heusinkveld, John Michael *obstetrician, gynecologist*

## NEW YORK

**Akron**
Hoover, Eddie Lee *cardiothoracic surgeon, educator*

**Albany**
Arseneau, James Charles *physician*
Barron, Kevin Delgado *physician, educator*
Carl, Allen Laurence *surgery educator*

Catalano, Robert Anthony *ophthalmologist, hospital administrator, writer*
Cavaliere, Rossella *neurologist*
Davis, Paul Joseph *endocrinologist*
Greene, Jerry George *physician*
Hoffmeister, Jana Marie *cardiologist*
Howard, Lyn Jennifer *medical educator*
Klopott, Zvi Simcha *psychiatrist*
Lepow, Martha Lipson *pediatric educator, consultant*
Molho, Eric Steven *neurologist, researcher*
Smith, Terry Jay *endocrinology educator*
Snitkoff, Gail Goodman *immunologist, educator*
Swartz, Donald Percy *physician*
Tepper, Clifford *allergist, immunologist, educator*
Veille, Jean-Claude *obstetrician, educator*
Zimmerman, Earl Abram *neurologist, educator*

**Alfred Station**
Knowlton, Sylvia Kelley *physician*

**Amherst**
Roehmholdt, John Michael *urologist, educator*

**Amityville**
Upadhyay, Yogendra Nath *physician, educator*

**Ardsley**
Swift, Michael Ronald *internist, educator*

**Armonk**
Mellors, Robert Charles *physician, scientist, educator*

**Babylon**
Schwartz, Benjamin Michael *gynecologist, oncologist*

**Bay Shore**
Kirsch, Scott Douglas *family practice physician*

**Bedford**
Tischler, Gary Lowell *psychiatrist, educator*

**Bellerose**
Miller, Paul J. *orthopedist, surgeon*

**Briarcliff Manor**
Erkamp, Ramon Quido *medical researcher, consultant*
Pousada, Lidia *physician*

**Bronx**
Alderman, Elizabeth *pediatrician, educator*
Bark, Nigel Martyn *psychiatrist*
Bella, Jonathan N. *cardiologist*
Bigal, Marcelo E *physician, researcher*
Blaufox, Morton Donald *hypertension specialist, educator, nuclear medicine physician*
Brandt, Lawrence Jay *internist, gastroenterologist, educator*
Burgio, Michael *medical researcher*
Cimino, Christopher *medical educator, dean*
Cohen, Herbert Jesse *pediatrician, educator*
Correa, Nereida *women's health physician*
Coupey, Susan McGuire *pediatrician, educator*
Das, Ashoke Kumar *internist, consultant*
Demb, Howard Bertram *psychiatrist, educator, pediatrician, educator*
Drepaul, Loris Omesh *internist, infectious diseases physician*
Dutcher, Janice Jean Phillips *oncologist*
Fleischer, Norman Samuel *endocrinology administrator, medical educator*
Foreman, Spencer *pulmonologist, hospital administrator, director*
Frater, Robert William Mayo *surgeon, educator*
Freeman, Leonard Murray *radiologist, nuclear medicine physician, educator*
Fremman, Leonard Murray *medical educator*
Gallagher, Robert E. *medical educator, researcher*
Gibbs, Karen E. *physician, surgeon*
Greenstein, Stuart Mark *surgical educator*
Hait, Gershon *pediatric cardiologist*
Heagarty, Margaret Caroline *retired pediatrician*
Hilaris, Basil S. *radiation oncologist, educator*
Hirano, Asao *neuropathologist, educator*
Hodgson, W(alter) John (Barry Hodgson) *surgeon*
Horwitz, Susan Band *pharmacologist*
Jaffé, Ernst Richard *medical educator, dean*
Kahn, Thomas *medical educator*
Kalnicki, Shalom *radiologist, educator*
Karkanias, George B. *neurologist, educator*
Klein, Robert S. *medical educator*
Koss, Leopold G. *pathologist, educator*
Lieber, Charles Saul *internist, educator*
Maitra, Umadas *biomedical researcher, educator*
Margolin, Leon *physician*
Mendez, Hermann Armando *pediatrician, educator*
Nitowsky, Harold Martin *physician, educator*
Oertel, Michael *researcher, medical educator*
Olson, Todd Rowland *anatomist, medical educator, consultant*
Powers, Kenneth *urogynecologist*
Putterman, Chaim *rheumatologist, researcher*
Radel, Eva *pediatrician, hematologist*
Rajapaksa, Trikante N. *medical educator*
Rapin, Isabelle *physician*
Reichgott, Michael Joel *medical educator, dean, physician*
Romney, Seymour Leonard *obstetrician, educator*
Rosenstreich, David Leon *medical educator, immunologist, allergist*
Ruben, Robert Joel *pediatric otorhinolaryngologist, educator*
Sable, Robert Allen *gastroenterologist*
Safyer, Steven Michael *medical association administrator, physician*
Satir, Birgit H. *medical educator, researcher*
Scharff, Matthew Daniel *immunologist, cell biologist, educator*
Schaumburg, Herbert Howard *neurology educator*
Shafritz, David Andrew *physician, research scientist*
Shapiro, Nella Irene *surgeon, educator*
Solomon, Seymour *neurologist, consultant*
Sonnenblick, Edmund Hiram *medical educator, cardiologist*
Spitzer, Adrian *pediatrician, educator*
Stanley, E. Richard *biomedical researcher*

Stein, Ruth Elizabeth Klein *physician*
Veith, Frank J. *vascular surgeon, researcher, educator*
Walsh, Christine Ann *cardiologist*
Wiernik, Peter Harris *oncologist, educator*
Wolkoff, Allan Wayne *gastroenterologist, medical educator*

**Bronxville**
Bertles, John Francis *physician, educator*
DeMartino, Anthony Gabriel *cardiologist, internist*

**Brooklyn**
Ackerman, Jacob Lewis *ophthalmologist*
Alfonso, Antonio Escolar *surgeon*
Anziska, Brian Jeffrey *neurologist, educator*
Asarian, Armand Paul *surgeon*
Avram, Morrell M. *nephrologist, educator, consultant*
Bandler, Martin *physician*
Bernstein, Larry Howard *clinical pathologist*
Bhattacharya, Bhaswati *preventive medicine physician*
Biro, Laszlo *dermatologist*
Clark, Luther Theopolis *physician, educator, researcher*
Collins, Ronald Leslie Leopold *neurosurgeon*
Cottrell, James E. *anesthesiologist, medical educator*
Erber, William Franklin *gastroenterologist*
Friedman, Eli A. *nephrologist, educator*
Furchgott, Robert Francis *pharmacologist, educator*
Gheewala, Anup Rameshchandra *plastic surgeon, consultant*
Gotta, Alexander Walter *anesthesiologist, educator*
Hamarman, Stephanie *psychiatrist, educator*
Haratz, Natan *obstetrician, gynecologist*
Hollander, Gerald Martin *physician*
Inwood, David Gerald *psychiatrist*
Jacobowitz, Israel Jacob *cardiothoracic surgeon*
Kirshenbaum, Richard Irving *retired public health physician*
Kumar, Swati *epidemiologist, researcher*
Levy, Norman B. *psychiatrist, educator*
Li, John K.H. *pathologist, department chairman*
Lichstein, Edgar *cardiologist*
Lichter, Stephen Marc *oncologist*
Lowery, Robert Chesley *thoracic surgeon, educator*
Mark, Richard Kushakow *internist*
Mayer, Ira Edward *gastroenterologist*
Merlin, Lisa Ruth *neurologist, researcher*
Mirra, Suzanne Samuels *pathologist*
Moosazadeh, Kioomars *orthopedist, educator, physiatrist, researcher*
Norstrand, Iris Fletcher *psychiatrist, neurologist, educator*
Orugunta, Raveendra Babu *pediatrician*
Pertschuk, Louis Philip *pathologist, consultant*
Plotz, Charles Mindell *physician, educator*
Ponnambalam, Ananthasekar *pediatrician, gastroenterologist*
Price, Ely *dermatologist*
Purvin, Jack Mitchell *physician*
Rezkalla, Laurence *internist*
Rose, Arthur Louis *neurologist, educator*
Sacchi, Terrence J. *cardiologist*
Savits, Barry Sorrel *surgeon*
Schwarz, Richard Howard *obstetrician, gynecologist, educator*
Shalita, Alan Remi *dermatologist*
Shelov, Steven Patrick *pediatrician, educator*
Shulman, Abraham *otolaryngology educator, hospital administrator*
Tunuguntla, Hari Siva Gurunadha Rao *urologist*
Umpaichitra, Vatcharapan *pediatrician, endocrinologist*
Viswanathan, Ramaswamy *physician, educator*
Wolintz, Arthur Harry *neurologist, ophthalmologist*
Yogeswaran, Pararajasingam *physician*
Zamdborg, Yury *internist*

**Buffalo**
Ambrus, Clara Maria *physician*
Ambrus, Julian L. *physician, medical educator*
Ballow, Mark *immunologist, educator*
Barrios, George G. *colon and rectal surgeon*
Batt, Ronald Elmer *gynecologist, historian, biomedical research scientist*
Brody, Harold *neuroanatomist, educator, gerontologist*
Chu, Tsann Ming *immunochemist, educator*
Creaven, Patrick Joseph *pharmacologist*
Fine, Edward Jay *neurologist, educator*
Genco, Robert Joseph *immunologist, periodontist, educator, scientist*
Halbreich, Uriel Morav *psychiatrist, educator*
Hohn, David *physician*
Kurlan, Marvin Zeft *retired surgeon*
Lele, Amol Shashikant *obstetrician, gynecologist*
Leo, Raphael Jerome *psychiatrist, director, education educator, consultant*
Mahl, Thomas Christopher *physician, educator*
Milgrom, Felix *immunologist, educator*
Mindell, Eugene Robert *surgeon, educator*
Mutton, Holly Beth *psychiatrist*
Naughton, Bruce James *geriatrician, consultant*
Naughton, John Patrick *cardiologist, educator*
Piver, M. Steven *gynecologic oncologist*
Seller, Robert Herman *cardiologist, physician*
Shedd, Donald Pomroy *surgeon*
Sherris, David Allan *surgeon, researcher, educator*
Stoll, Howard Lester, Jr. *dermatologist*
Trevisan, Maurizio *epidemiologist*
Vladutiu, Adrian O. *physician, educator*
Wright, John Robert *pathologist, educator*

**Canaan**
Rothenberg, Albert *psychiatrist, educator*

**Canandaigua**
Beal, Myron Clarence *osteopath*
Wormer, Thomas Andrew *surgeon*

**Carthage**
Ebbels, Bruce Jeffery *retired physician, health facility administrator*

**Cedarhurst**
Cohen, Harris L. *diagnostic radiologist, consultant*

**Chester**
Amelar, Richard Daniel *urologist*

**Chestnut Ridge**
Day, Stacey Biswas *physician, medical educator*

**Cooperstown**
Bordley, James, IV, *surgeon*
Franck, Walter Alfred *rheumatologist, medical educator, health facility administrator*
Veenema, Ralph James *retired urologist*

**Cutchogue**
Reiley, Jorge Alberto *neurologist*

**Dobbs Ferry**
Kravath, Richard Elliot *retired pediatrician, educator*

**East Aurora**
Carfagna, Vincent O. *physician*

**East Hills**
Cervia, Joseph Steven *medical educator*

**East Setauket**
Malbon, Craig Curtis *pharmacology educator, dean*

**East Syracuse**
Nivarthi, Raju Naga *anesthesiology educator*

**Elmhurst**
Masci, Joseph Richard *medical educator*

**Elmira**
Graham, David Richard *orthopedic surgeon*
Nast, Edward Paul *cardiac surgeon*

**Elmsford**
Demopoulos, Harry Byron *retired pathologist, pharmaceutical researcher*
Panitz, Lawrence *physician*

**Fayetteville**
Cady, Robert Brown *pediatric orthopedic surgeon*
Chevli, Renate Naren *gynecologist, obstetrician*
Pirodsky, Donald Max *psychiatrist, educator*
Stewart, William A. *medical educator, neurosurgeon*

**Fishers Island**
Baue, Arthur Edward *surgeon, educator, retired health facility administrator*

**Fishkill**
Brocks, Eric *ophthalmologist, surgeon*

**Flushing**
Baik-Han, Won H. *pediatrician, educator, consultant*
Hon, John Wingsun *physician*
Nussbaum, Michel Ernest *physician*
Person, Philip *biomedical consultant, biochemist, dentist*

**Forest Hills**
Eden, Alvin Noam *pediatrician, writer*
Seldes, Richard M. *orthopedist, consultant*
Tvildiani, Dimitry *cardiologist*

**Fresh Meadows**
Godfrey, Philip M. *plastic surgeon*
Kaplan, Barry Hubert *physician*
Westrich, Geoffrey Howard *orthopaedic surgery*

**Garden City**
Brewer, Bruce William *plastic surgeon*
Deane, Leland Marc *plastic surgeon, director*
Douglas, Barry K. *plastic surgeon*
Findlay, Lorraine Anne *medical educator*
Good, Larry Irwin *gastroenterologist, educator*

**Garnerville**
Zugibe, Frederick Thomas *retired pathologist, forensic specialist*

**Garrison**
Callahan, Daniel John *biomedical researcher*

**Geneva**
Lieberg, Olaf U. *orthopaedic surgeon*

**Great Neck**
Breidbart, Rory Steven *endocrinologist*
Dines, David Michael *surgeon, educator*
Gold, Alan H. *plastic surgeon*
Goldman, Ira Steven *gastroenterologist*
Kechijian, Paul *dermatologist, educator*
Lieber, Constance E. *medical association administrator*
Rosenberg, Richard F. *physician, radiologist*
Samuel, Paul *retired cardiologist*
Scherr, Lawrence *internist, educator*
Schlesinger, Irwin D. *neurologist*
Shons, Alan Rance *plastic surgeon, surgical oncologist, educator*
Wolff, Edward *physician*

**Great River**
Hayman, Martin Arthur *psychiatrist, educator*

**Hamburg**
Calkins, Evan *physician, educator*

**Hartsdale**
Chait, Maxwell Mani *physician*

**Hastings On Hudson**
Rosch, Paul John *internist, educator*

**Hawthorne**
Nandedkar, Sanjeev Dattatraya *medical researcher, educator*

**Hewlett**
Cohen, David Leon *physician*
Steinfeld, Philip Sheldon *pediatrician*

**Huntington**
Alsop, Reese Fell *medical educator*
Engstrand, Beatrice C. *neurologist, educator*

**Ilion**
Gay, Douglas MacKenzie *pharmacologist*

**Ithaca**
Dietert, Rodney Reynolds *immunology and toxicology educator*
Foote, Robert Hutchinson *medical educator*
Kallfelz, Francis A. *veterinary medicine educator*
Nikitin, Alexander Yu. *pathologist*
Rivas, Ariel L. *biomedical researcher, educator*
Whitaker, Susanne Kanis *veterinary medical librarian*

**Jamaica**
Garner, Steven C. *radiologist, emergency physician*
Kemeny, M. Margaret *oncologist, surgeon, educator, hospital administrator*

**Jamestown**
DJang, Arthur H.K. *pathologist, preventive medicine physician*

**Jericho**
Schell, Norman Barnett *preventive medicine physician, consultant*

**Johnson City**
Goddard, Bryan Lance *physician, director*

**Katonah**
Bauman, Jonathan Hugh *psychiatrist*

**Kenmore**
Elibol, Tarik *gastroenterologist, educator*

**Kingston**
Johnson, Marie-Louise Tully *dermatologist, educator*

**La Fayette**
Cady, Duane Maynard *surgeon*

**Larchmont**
Rockland, Lawrence Howard *psychiatrist, educator*
Sklarew, Robert Jay *biomedical research educator, consultant*
Stahl, William Martin *retired surgeon*

**Lloyd Harbor**
Sheard, Charles III *dermatologist*

**Lockport**
Carr, Edward Albert, Jr. *pharmacologist, educator, physician*

**Mamaroneck**
Coleman, Marshall Donald *psychiatrist, psychoanalyst*
Halpern, Abraham Leon *psychiatrist*
McLarnon, Mary Frances *neurologist*

**Manhasset**
Bosworth, Jay L. *radiation oncologist*
Budman, Cathy Linda *psychiatrist, physician*
D'Olimpio, James Thomas *oncologist*
Esposito, Rick Anthony *physician, thoracic surgeon*
Milhorat, Thomas Herrick *neurosurgeon*
Pogo, Gustave Javier *cardiothoracic surgeon*
Rochelson, Burton L. *obstetrician*

**Manlius**
Prior, John Thompson *pathology educator*

**Maspeth**
Khashu, Bushan *urologist*

**Massapequa**
Zwanger, Jerome *physician*

**Melville**
Copperman, Stuart Morton *pediatrician, educator*

**Merrick**
Gutnik, Zhanna *gastroenterologist, consultant*

**Middletown**
Chevalier, Stefan Gary *plastic surgeon*

**Mineola**
Greenberg, Abby J. *physician*
Kokotos, William J. *cardiothoracic surgeon*
Niederman, Michael Steven *physician, educator*

**Mount Kisco**
Hayworth, Scott David *physician*
Kutty, Malik Anisjervan *plastic surgeon*
Perez, Louis Anthony *radiologist*
Powell, Jeffrey Scott *endocrinologist*
Schneider, Robert Jay *oncologist*

**Mount Sinai**
Feinberg, Sheldon Norman *pediatrician, educator*

**Mount Vernon**
Elkind, Arthur H. *physician*

**New City**
Esser, Aristide Henri *psychiatrist*
O'Dowd, Charles Edwyn *physician*

**New Hyde Park**
Badlani, Gopal *medical educator*
Bonagura, Vincent R. *pediatrician, educator, researcher*
Gecelter, Gary Raymond *gastrointestinal surgeon, researcher*
Goldberg, Itzhak D. *radiation oncologist*
Jacobson, Marc Stephen *pediatrician, educator*
Lanzkowsky, Philip *physician*
Love, Charito *nuclear medicine physician, researcher*
Mealie, Carl A. *emergency physician, educator*

Medarov, Boris I. *pulmonologist, researcher, critical care physician*
Myssiorek, David *surgeon*
Palestro, Christopher J. *physician*
Rini, Josephine Nancy *nuclear medicine physician*
Seltzer, Vicki Lynn *obstetrician, gynecologist*
Shenker, Ira Ronald *physician*
Smith, Robin Errol *pediatrician, neurologist, educator*

**New Rochelle**
Fauci, Peter Anthony, Jr. *surgeon*
Gitler, Bernard *cardiologist, critical care specialist*
Lin, Joseph Pen-Tze *retired radiologist*
Perry-Böttinger, Lynne Valencia *interventional cardiologist*
Rovinsky, Joseph Judah *obstetrician, gynecologist*
Schaffner, Adam David *plastic surgeon*

**New Windsor**
Mandel, Joel Emanuel *orthopedist*

**New York**
Abdel Dayem, Hussein Mahmoud *nuclear medicine physician, radiology educator*
Abraham, Nader G. *biomedical scientist*
Adlersberg, Jay Ben *internist*
Akerele, Evaristo Olanrewaju *psychiatrist, educator*
Alderson, Philip Otis *radiologist, educator*
Alikhani, Zoubin *internist, molecular biologist, researcher*
Alizadeh, Kaveh *plastic surgeon, educator*
Altman, Lawrence Kimball *physician, journalist*
Altman, Roy Peter *pediatric surgeon*
Ames, Richard Pollard *physician, educator, lecturer*
Antell, Darrick Eugene *plastic surgeon, educator*
Appelbaum, Paul Stuart *psychiatrist, medical educator, department chairman*
Armenakas, Noel Anthony *medical educator*
Aron, Alan Milford *pediatric neurology educator*
Ascherman, Jeffrey Alan *plastic and reconstructive surgeon*
Aston, Sherrell Jerone *plastic surgeon, educator*
Aufses, Arthur Harold, Jr. *surgeon, medical educator*
Austin, John H.M. *radiologist*
Axel, Richard *pathology and biochemistry educator*
Baden, Michael M. *pathologist, educator*
Balamaceda, Casilda *neurologist, oncologist*
Baldwin, David Shepard *physician*
Barakat, Richard *oncologist, gynecological surgeon*
Barchas, Jack D. *psychiatrist, medical researcher, educator, behavioral molecular neurobiologist*
Barker, Barbara Ann *ophthalmologist*
Barlow, Barbara Ann *surgeon*
Barondess, Jeremiah Abraham *physician*
Bartholomew, Lincoln Edwin *physician*
Bauer, Joel J. *surgeon, educator*
Belgorod, Barry Miles *surgeon, educator*
Ben-Avi, Simon Stephen *biomedical researcher, educator*
Beraka, George Joseph *plastic surgeon*
Berger, Frank Milan *biomedical researcher, research scientist, retired pharmaceutical executive*
Berger, Marvin *medical educator*
Bergman, Donald Arthur *endocrinologist, educator*
Berk, Paul David *internist, research scientist, educator*
Berkowitz, Richard Lee *obstetrician, gynecologist, director*
Berman, Carol Wendy *psychiatrist*
Berman, Russell Scott *oncologist, educator*
Bernstein, Robert M. *dermatologic surgeon*
Berry, Gail W. *psychiatrist, educator*
Berson, Anthony M. *oncologist*
Bessey, Palmer Quintard *surgeon*
Beverley, Cordia Luvonne *gastroenterologist*
Bhargava, Peeyush *nuclear medicine physician*
Bholat, Omar *surgeon*
Bickers, David Rinsey *dermatologist, educator, department chairman, health facility administrator*
Biel, Leonard, Jr. *urologist*
Bilsky, Mark Harvey *neurologist*
Bird, Hector Ramón *child psychiatrist, psychoanalyst, educator*
Blaser, Martin Jack *medical educator, researcher*
Blitzer, Andrew *otolaryngologist, educator, research scientist, writer*
Bochner, Bernard H. *urologic surgical oncologist*
Bogdonoff, Morton David *internist, educator*
Borer, Jeffrey Stephen *cardiologist*
Bosl, George Joseph *physician, oncologist*
Brauner, Gary Jules *dermatologist, cosmetic laser surgeon*
Breinin, Goodwin M. *physician*
Brennan, Murray Frederick *surgeon, oncologist*
Brodman, Michael Lewis *gynecologist, educator*
Brook, David William *psychiatrist, researcher*
Brown, Arthur Edward *physician*
Brown, Jason Walter *neurologist, educator, researcher*
Brust, John Calvin Morrison *neurologist, educator*
Buchbinder, Ellen Maud *allergist*
Buschke, Herman *neurologist*
Butler, Vincent Paul, Jr. *internist, educator*
Butts, Hugh Florenz *physician, psychiatrist, psychoanalyst*
Buxton, Douglas Francisco *ophthalmologist, educator*
Bystryn, Jean-Claude *dermatologist, educator*
Cammarata, Angelo *surgical oncologist*
Cammisa, Frank P., Jr. *surgeon, educator*
Cancro, Robert *psychiatrist, educator*
Cantor, Richard Ira *physician, corporate health executive*
Carr, Ronald Edward *ophthalmologist, educator*
Carucci, John A. *physician*
Case, David Bartlett *internist, educator*
Case, Robert Brown *physician*
Chahinian, A(ram) Philippe *oncologist*
Chandler, Michael Jonathan *allergist, physician*
Chandrasekhar, Sujana S. *otologist, educator, neurotologist*
Chang, Stanley *ophthalmologist*
Chapman, Paul B. *oncologist*

Charash, Bruce D. *cardiologist, educator*
Charon, Rita *medical educator*
Cherry, Sabrina *psychiatrist*
Chiu, David Tak Wai *surgeon*
Chutorian, Abe M. *pediatrician, educator*
Clark, Sheryl Diane *physician*
Close, Lanny Garth *otolaryngologist, educator*
Cohen, Carmel *oncologist*
Cohen, Howard A. *cardiologist*
Cohen, Noel Lee *otolaryngologist, educator*
Cohen, Seymour Martin *oncologist, hematologist, educator*
Cohen, Sidney Maximilian *neurologist*
Coleman, Donald Jackson *ophthalmologist, educator*
Coleman, Morton *oncologist, educator, hematologist*
Colen, Helen Sass *plastic surgeon*
Colen, Stephen R. *plastic and reconstructive surgeon*
Colten, Harvey Radin *pediatrician, educator*
Compte, Maria Emilia *physician, educator, administrator*
Constantinides, Minas Spiros *otolaryngologist, plastic surgeon*
Copeland, Michelle *plastic surgeon*
Cucin, Robert Louis *plastic surgeon, lawyer*
Cunningham-Rundles, Charlotte *physician, medical educator*
Davis, Kenneth Leon *psychiatrist, pharmacologist, medical educator*
Davis, Owen Kidder *physician, endocrinologist*
Defendi, Vittorio *medical association administrator, pathologist*
Desloge, Rosemary Byrne *otolaryngologist, educator*
De Vivo, Darryl Claude *pediatrician, neurologist*
Diaz, Angela *pediatrician, educator*
DiResta, Gene Robert *biomedical researcher, director*
Divon, Michael Y. *obstetrican and gynecologist*
Dohrenwend, Bruce Philip *epidemiologist, social sciences educator*
Dorfman, Howard David *pathologist, educator*
Downey, John Alexander *physician, educator*
Doyle, Eugenie Fleri *pediatrician, cardiologist, educator*
Dubois, Michel *anesthesiologist*
Du Mont, Nicolas *psychiatrist, educator*
Dupont, Jakob *oncologist, researcher*
Dworetzky, Murray *retired physician, educator*
Edelstein, Barbara A. *radiologist*
Elgert, Paul A. *cytotechnologist*
Erlenmeyer-Kimling, L. *psychiatrist, researcher*
Estabrook, Alison *surgeon, educator*
Evans, Mark Ira *obstetrician, geneticist*
Faedda, Gianni L. *psychiatrist, researcher*
Fahn, Stanley *neurologist, educator*
Farber, Saul Joseph *physician, educator*
Farris, Robert Linsy *ophthalmologist, director*
Feldman, Bernard Robert *physician*
Field, Steven Philip *medical educator*
Fins, Joseph Jack *internist*
First, Michael Bruce *psychiatrist, educator*
Fisher, Laura Lani *physician, medical educator*
Flach, Frederic Francis *psychiatrist*
Flax, Herschel *surgeon*
Formenti, Silvia C. *radiation oncologist*
Forrest, David Vickers *psychiatrist, educator*
Fortner, Joseph Gerald *surgeon, educator*
Foster, Craig Allen *plastic surgeon*
Fox, Arthur Charles *cardiologist, educator*
Frances, Richard Joseph *psychiatrist*
Frantz, Andrew Gibson *endocrinologist, educator, dean*
Freedman, Aaron David *medicine and biochemistry education, retired dean*
Freedman, Alfred Mordecai *psychiatrist, educator*
Freedman, Michael Leonard *geriatrician, educator*
Friedman, Alan Herbert *ophthalmologist*
Friedman, Ira Hugh *surgeon*
Friedman, Jeffrey M. *medical researcher, educator*
Fuster, Valentin *cardiologist, educator*
Gabrilove, Jacques Lester *physician*
Gaddipati, Sreedhar *obstetrician*
Galanter, Marc *psychiatrist, educator*
Gebbie, Kristine Moore *medical educator*
Gellhorn, Alfred *physician, educator*
Gendler, Ellen *dermatologist*
Gersony, Welton Mark *pediatrician, cardiologist, educator*
Gertler, Menard M. *physician, educator*
Giardina, Elsa Grace Vonna *cardiologist, educator*
Ginsberg, Henry *medical educator, researcher*
Girardi, Federico Pablo *surgeon, educator*
Glasberg, H(erbert) Mark *psychiatrist, educator*
Glasberg, Scot Bradley *plastic surgeon*
Glassman, Alexander Howard *psychiatrist, researcher*
Glesby, Marshall Jay *physician, educator*
Gliklich, Jerry *physician, educator*
Gold, Arnold P. *neurologist*
Goldberg, Nieca *cardiologist, educator*
Goldfarb, David S. *nephrologist, researcher*
Goldfrank, Lewis Robert *physician*
Goldsmith, Michael Allen *oncologist, educator*
Goldsmith, Stanley Joseph *nuclear medicine physician, educator*
Goldstein, Marc *surgeon, urologist, educator, health facility administrator*
Goldstein, Martin S. *obstetrician, gynecologist, educator*
Gollub, Marc Jeffrey *radiologist*
Gondolesi, Gabriel Eduardo *transplant surgeon*
González-Rodríguez, Salvador *dermatologist, educator*
Gordon, Alan Lee *psychiatrist*
Gordon, Marsha L. *dermatologist*
Gotschlich, Emil Claus *physician*
Gotto, Antonio Marion, Jr. *internist, educator*
Grafstein, Bernice *physiology and neuroscience educator, researcher*
Graham, Philip Lamar *epidemiologist, physician*
Green, George Edward *retired surgeon*
Green, Jack Peter *pharmacologist, educator*
Green, Maurice Richard *neuropsychiatrist*
Green, Wayne Hugo *psychiatrist, psychoanalyst*
Greene, Douglas A. *internist, educator*
Greenspun, David Todd *plastic and reconstructive surgeon*
Griffiths, Sylvia Preston *physician, educator*

Grossman, Melanie *dermatologist*
Guida, Robert Anthony *otolaryngologist, plastic surgeon*
Guthrie, Randolph Hobson, Jr. *plastic surgeon, consultant*
Haddad, Heskel Marshall *ophthalmologist, educator*
Haddad, Jamil Raouf *retired physician*
Hadden, John Winthrop *immunopharmacology educator*
Haight, David Hulen *ophthalmologist*
Hambrick, George Walter, Jr. *dermatologist, educator*
Hamburg, David A. *psychiatrist, foundation administrator*
Hammer, Scott M. *medical researcher, educator*
Hann, Lucy E. *radiologist, educator*
Harris, Henry William *physician*
Härtl, Roger *physician, researcher*
Hawkins, Katherine Ann *hematologist, educator, lawyer*
Hayes, Joseph G. *cardiologist, educator*
Henschke, Claudia Ingrid *physician, radiologist*
Hernández, Victor René Christian *medical researcher, consultant*
Herr, Harry Wallace *medical researcher, educator, surgeon, urologist*
Hertzig, Margaret E. *psychiatrist*
Hidalgo, David Arthur *plastic surgeon*
Hirsch, Harvey Stuart *psychiatrist*
Hirsch, Jules *physician, researcher*
Hirschhorn, Kurt *pediatrics educator*
Ho, David D. (Da-i Ho) *research physician, virologist, scientific organization director*
Hochlerin, Diane *pediatrician, educator*
Hoffman, Lloyd Alan *plastic surgeon*
Holland, Jimmie C. *psychiatrist, educator*
Holodny, Andrei Igor *radiologist*
Holt, Peter Rolf *gastroenterologist, educator*
Holzman, Robert Stephen *physician*
Hoskins, Donald W. *retired medical association administrator*
Hosseini, Khaled *internist, writer*
Hsu, Daphne T. *pediatrician, educator*
Hugo, Norman Eliot *retired plastic surgeon, retired educator*
Hyman, Bruce Malcolm *ophthalmologist*
Imber, Gerald *plastic surgeon*
Imperato, Joseph Edward *otolaryngologist*
Isaacson, Steven Robert *surgeon*
Jacobson, Julius H., II, *vascular surgeon, writer*
Jan, Dominique Michel *surgeon, educator*
Januzzi, James Louis *physician, internist, gastroenterologist*
Jarecki, Henry George *physician, financial planner*
Javitt, Norman B. *medical educator, researcher*
Jelks, Glenn William *plastic surgeon*
Jessell, Thomas M. *medical educator*
Johnson, Horton Anton *pathologist*
Johnson, Warren Douglas *infectious diseases physician, researcher*
Jonas, Saran *neurologist, educator*
Josephson, Jordan Stuart *otolaryngologist*
Jurka, Edith Mila *psychiatrist, researcher*
Kadar, Avraham *immunologist*
Kalsner, Stanley *pharmacologist, physiologist, educator*
Kanick, Virginia *retired radiologist*
Kanof, Norman B. *dermatologist*
Kapelman, Barbara Ann *internist, hepatologist, gastroenterologist, educator*
Kappas, Attallah *physician*
Karasu, T(oksoz) Byram *psychiatrist, educator, writer*
Karp, Nolan S. *plastic surgeon*
Kassimir, Joel Jack *dermatologist*
Katz, Bruce Elliot *dermatologist*
Katz, Jose *cardiologist, theoretical physicist, educator*
Katz, Lois Anne *internist, nephrologist*
Kaufman, David Marc *pediatric neurologist*
Kelly, Patrick Joseph *neurosurgeon, educator*
Killip, Thomas *cardiologist*
Kinne, David Weir *retired surgeon*
Kipshidze, Nicholas N. *medical association administrator, researcher*
Kizer, Jorge Ruben *cardiologist, epidemiologist*
Kleber, Herbert David *psychiatrist, educator*
Klein, Harvey *medical educator*
Klimstra, David S. *pathologist*
Knapp, Albert Bruce *gastroenterologist*
Knapp, Robert Charles *retired obstetrics and gynecology educator*
Kohn, Brenda *pediatrician, endocrinologist, consultant*
Kolker, Adam Ross *plastic surgeon, educator*
Kolodny, Edwin Hillel *neurologist, geneticist, director*
Komisar, Arnold *otolaryngologist, educator*
Koopman, Barbara Goldenberg *psychiatrist*
Kopenhaver, Patricia Ellsworth *podiatrist*
Koplewicz, Harold Samuel *child and adolescent psychiatrist*
Kourides, Ione Anne *endocrinologist, researcher, educator*
Kreek, Mary Jeanne *physician*
Kurli, Madhavi *ophthalmologist*
Labovitz, Daniel Lockett *neurologist*
Lachmann, Elisabeth Amanda *physician*
Lalwani, Anil Kumar *otolaryngologist*
Landrigan, Philip John *epidemiologist*
Langan, Marie-Noelle Suzanne *cardiologist, educator*
LaQuaglia, Michael Patrick *pediatric surgeon, neuroblastoma researcher*
Laragh, John Henry *cardiologist, surgeon, educator*
Larson, Steven Mark *physician*
Laskin, Richard Sheldon *orthopedic surgeon*
Lattimer, John Kingsley *physician, educator*
Laufman, Harold *surgeon, consultant*
Laurence, Jeffrey Conrad *immunologist, educator*
Lawson, William *otolaryngologist, educator*
Ledger, William Joe *obstetrician, educator*
Lee, Nancy *radiologist, oncologist*
Leeds, Norman E. *medical educator, radiologist*
Lefkovits, Albert Meyer *dermatologist*
Legato, Marianne *internist, medical educator*
Leifer, Edgar *physician, retired medical educator*
Lessnau, Klaus-Dieter Karl *pulmonologist, director, medical educator*

Levin, Frances R. *psychiatrist, educator*
Levounis, Petros *psychiatrist*
Levy, Albert *physician*
Lewis, Jonathan Joseph *surgical oncologist, molecular biologist, educator, entrepreneur*
Lewy, Robert Max *physician*
Libby, Daniel M. *pulmonologist*
Lieberman, James Sanford *physiatrist, neurologist*
Lindenmayer, Jean-Pierre *psychiatrist*
Lipkin, Martin *medical educator, researcher*
Lipton, Lester *ophthalmologist, entrepreneur*
Liu, Kai-Lih *epidemiologist*
Liu, Si-kwang *veterinary pathologist*
Lobo, Rogerio Arnaldo *obstetrician, gynecologist*
Lockshin, Michael Dan *rheumatologist*
Lodge, Henry Sears *physician*
Loeb, John Nichols *physician, educator*
Loo, Marcus Hsieu-Hong *urologist, physician, educator*
Lopez, Ralph Ivan *pediatrics educator*
Lorenc, Z. Paul (Paul Lorenc) *plastic surgeon*
Lyden, David Charles *oncologist, cell biologist*
Macdonald, John Stephen *oncologist, educator*
Macken, Daniel Loos *cardiologist, educator*
MacKinnon, Roger Alan *psychiatrist, educator*
Magro, Cynthia Maria *pathologist*
Maki, Robert G. *physician, oncologist*
Malkin, Stanley Lee *neurologist*
Manger, William Muir *internist, educator, writer, research scientist*
Mangla, Sundeep *radiologist, research scientist*
Marcus, Eric Robert *psychiatrist*
Margulis, Alexander Rafailo *physician, educator*
Marin, Deborah B. *psychiatrist, educator*
Marin, Michael L. *vascular surgeon*
Markowitz, Martin H. *biomedical researcher*
Marks, Paul Alan *oncologist, cell biologist, educator*
Marmor, Michael *epidemiologist, educator*
Masterson, James Francis *psychiatrist*
Matarasso, Alan *plastic and reconstructive surgeon*
Mayo-Johnston, Julia A. *psychiatry professor, psychotherapist*
McCabe, John Cordell *surgeon*
McClelland, Shearwood Junior *orthopaedic surgeon*
Mc Crory, Wallace Willard *pediatrician, educator*
McDowell, David Michael *psychiatrist, educator, researcher*
Mellins, Robert B. *pediatrician, educator*
Mesnikoff, Alvin Murray *psychiatrist, educator*
Michelis, Michael Frank *nephrologist*
Michels, Robert *psychiatrist, educator*
Michelsen, Christopher Bruce Hermann *surgeon*
Mildvan, Donna *infectious diseases physician*
Miller, Theodore T. *radiologist*
Milman, Doris Hope *retired pediatrician, psychiatrist, educator*
Mohr, Jay Preston *neurologist, educator*
Moore, Anne *physician*
Moses, Jeffrey Warren *cardiologist, educator*
Moss-Salentijn, Letty (Aleida Moss-Salentijn) *anatomist, educator*
Murphy, Ramon Jeremiah Castroviejo *physician, pediatrician*
Naftolin, Frederick *gynecologist, educator*
Naidich, Thomas Paul *neuroradiologist, educator*
Naka, Yoshifumi *surgeon, researcher*
Nass, Ruth *pediatric neurologist*
Nehal, Kishwer Sultana *dermatologist*
Neuberg, Hans W. *internist, educator*
Neuwirth, Robert Samuel *obstetrician, gynecologist, educator*
New, Maria Iandolo *pediatrician, educator*
Newhouse, Jeffrey H. *radiologist, educator*
Newman, Robert Gabriel *physician*
Newsome, Frederick V. *medical educator*
Nicholas, Stephen J. *orthopedic surgeon, sports medicine physician*
Nimkarn, Saroj *endocrinologist, researcher*
Novick, Nelson Lee *dermatologist, internist, consultant, surgeon, writer*
Novick, Stephen Alan *cardiologist*
Oberfield, Sharon Elefant *pediatric endocrinologist*
Ochoa, Manuel, Jr. *oncologist*
Oettgen, Herbert Friedrich *physician*
Ofri, Danielle *internist*
Oktem, Ozgur *medical researcher*
Olsson, Carl Alfred *urologist, department chairman*
Ordorica, Steven Anthony *obstetrician, gynecologist, educator*
O'Reilly, Richard John *pediatrician*
Orkin, Louis Richard *physician, educator*
Osborn, June Elaine *pediatrician, microbiologist, educator, foundation administrator*
Oz, Mehmet Cengiz *cardiac surgeon, writer*
Pacheco-Fowler, Victor *medical educator*
Panicek, David *radiologist*
Pappagallo, Marco *neurologist, pain medicine specialist*
Pastores, Gregory McCarthy *pediatrician, medical geneticist, researcher*
Pastores, Stephen M. *internist*
Pearlman, Steven Jay *otolaryngologist, educator, surgeon*
Pedley, Timothy Asbury, IV, *neurologist, educator, researcher*
Perin, Noel I. *neurosurgeon*
Pfeifer, Tracy M. *plastic surgeon*
Phillips, Gerald Baer *internal medicine scientist, educator*
Pierson, Richard Norris, Jr. *medical educator*
Pitman, Gerald H. *plastic surgeon*
Pitt, Jane *medical educator*
Plum, Fred *neurologist*
Podrug, Dinko *psychiatrist, educator*
Pogue, Velvie Anne *nephrologist, educator*
Polenz, Joanna Magda *psychiatrist*
Polydorides, Alexandros Demetrios *pathologist*
Pomp, Alfons *surgeon*
Posner, Jerome Beebe *neurologist, educator*
Potter, Hollis Gromisch *radiologist*
Prince, Alice Sara *pediatrician, educator*
Purcell, Karen Barlar *naturopathic physician, nutritionist, opera singer, writer*
Quackenbush, Margery Clouser *psychoanalyst, researcher*

Rabinowitz, Jack Grant *radiologist, educator*
Rainess, Alan Edward *psychiatrist, neurologist, educator*
Ramsay, David Leslie *physician, dermatologist, medical educator*
Rausen, Aaron Reuben *pediatric hematologist, oncologist*
Rayfield, Elliot James *medical educator*
Raynor, Richard Benjamin *neurosurgeon, educator*
Redo, S(averio) Frank *retired surgeon*
Reidenberg, Marcus Milton *physician, educator*
Reisberg, Barry *geriatric psychiatrist, neuropsychopharmacologist*
Rhodes, Rosamond *medical educator, philosophy educator*
Richert, John Rolin *neuroimmunologist, educator*
Rifkind, Arleen B. *pharmacologist, researcher, educator*
Ristich, Miodrag *psychiatrist*
Ritch, Robert Harry *ophthalmologist, educator*
Rivlin, Richard Saul *internist*
Romano, John Francis *dermatologist*
Romas, Nicholas Achilles *urologist, educator*
Romita, Mauro Charles *plastic surgeon*
Rose, Donald Joseph *orthopedist, surgeon*
Rosenberg, Harold Nmi *preventive medicine physician, consultant*
Rosenblum, Jay Alan *neurologist*
Rosenfeld, Isadore *cardiologist, educator*
Rosenfeld, Nachman *plastic surgeon*
Rosenfield, Allan *medical educator, dean, obstetrician, gynecologist*
Roshan, Daniel *obstetrician, gynecologist*
Rovit, Richard Lee *neurosurgeon*
Rowland, Lewis Phillip *neurology educator, editor, clinical investigator*
Rozbruch, S. Robert *orthopedist, researcher*
Rubin, Albert Louis *internist, nephrologist, educator*
Rubin, Gabriel Kevi *psychiatrist*
Rubin, Theodore Isaac *psychiatrist, writer*
Rudloff, Udo *surgeon, researcher*
Rusch, Valerie Williams *thoracic surgeon*
Sabbatini, Paul *gynecologist, educator*
Sachar, David Bernard *gastroenterologist, educator*
Sacks, Oliver Wolf *neurologist, writer*
Sadick, Neil Scott *dermatologist*
Sadock, Benjamin James *psychiatrist, educator*
Salans, Lester Barry *physician, research scientist, educator*
Salgo, Peter Lloyd *internist, writer, anesthesiologist, journalist, commentator*
Salky, Barry A. *surgeon*
Sampson, Hugh Albert, Jr. *medical educator*
Samstein, Benjamin *transplant surgeon*
Sandhu, Harvinder Singh *spinal surgeon, educator*
Saphir, Richard Louis *pediatrician*
Saxena, Brij B. *endocrinologist, biochemist, educator*
Sceusa, Nicholas A. *pharmacologist*
Schaffner, Bertram Henry *psychiatrist*
Schechter, Daniel Scott *child and adolescent psychiatrist, researcher*
Scher, Howard S. *oncologist*
Schiff, Howard Irwin *urologist*
Schlegel, Peter Niles *urologist, educator*
Schley, William Shain *otolaryngologist*
Schneck, Jerome M. *psychiatrist, historian, medical educator*
Schuster, Carlotta Lief *psychiatrist*
Schwartz, Irving Leon *internist, educator, research scientist*
Schwartz, Theodore H. *neurosurgeon*
Sclafani, Anthony Paul *plastic surgeon, author, biomedical researcher*
Scott, Susan Craig *plastic surgeon*
Sculco, Thomas Peter *surgeon*
Sedlin, Elias David *orthopedist, educator*
Seele, Pernessa C. *immunologist, health science association administrator*
Seely, Robert Daniel *cardiologist, medical association administrator*
Selby, Ronald M. *orthopedic surgeon*
Sessions, Roy Brumby *otolaryngologist, educator*
Shah, Jatin Premanand *head and neck surgeon, educator*
Shapiro, Theodore *psychiatrist, educator*
Shepherd, Gillian Mary *physician*
Sherman, John Eric *plastic surgeon*
Sherman, Spencer E. *ophthalmologist*
Shortliffe, Edward Hance *internist, medical educator, computer scientist*
Silver, Richard Tobias *oncologist, educator*
Sitarz, Anneliese Lotte *pediatrician, educator, physician*
Skolnik, Richard Alan *plastic surgeon*
Smith, Craig Richey *thoracic surgeon*
Snyderman, Nancy *surgeon, medical journalist*
Soave, Rosemary *internist*
Sobel, Howard D. *dermatologist*
Solomon, Gail Ellen *physician*
Sonett, Joshua Robert *medical educator, surgeon*
Spencer, Frank Cole *medical educator*
Speyer, James L. *oncologist*
Spiegel, Herbert *psychiatrist, educator*
Starren, Justin Bruce *medical educator*
Stein, Marvin *psychiatrist, historian*
Stein, Zena A. *retired epidemiologist, retired educator*
Steinberg, Jonathan S. *cardiologist, educator*
Stelzer, Paul *cardiac surgeon, educator*
Stewart, Michael Glenn *otolaryngologist, educator*
Stimmel, Barry *cardiologist, educator, internist, dean*
Stone, Michael Howard *psychiatry educator*
Stooler, Mark Benjamin *physician*
Stover, Diane Elizabeth *internist*
Stübgen, Joerg-Patrick *neurologist*
Sullivan, Alison Elizabeth *pediatrician, child psychiatrist*
Sultan, Mark R. *plastic surgeon*
Supino, Phyllis Gail *medical researcher, educator*
Swift, Ronnie Gorman *psychiatrist, educator*
Swistel, Daniel George *surgeon*
Tabbal, Nicolas G. *plastic surgeon*
Taha, Assad M. *surgeon*
Temple, Donald Edward *medical association administrator*
Tenenbaum, Joseph *cardiologist*
Thattassery, Emil George *internist*

Thomas, Stephen Jay *anesthesiologist*
Thomson, Gerald Edmund *physician, educator*
Tilson, M(artin) David III *surgeon, scientist, educator*
Tolchin, Joan Gubin *psychiatrist, educator*
Tomasulo, Patricia A. *medical librarian, plant pathologist, researcher*
Tortolani, Anthony John *surgeon, educator*
Tourlitsas, John Constantine *radiologist*
Trupp, Michael Saron *psychiatrist*
Turino, Gerard Michael *internist, educator*
Turtil, Lawrence Charles *psychiatrist*
Tzimas, Nicholas Achilles *orthopedic surgeon, educator*
Ulin, Richard Irwin *pediatric orthopedist, educator*
Van Bosse, Harold J.P. *orthopedic surgeon*
Vaughan, Edwin Darracott, Jr. *urologist, surgeon*
Veronneau-Troutman, Suzanne *retired ophthalmologist*
Vilcek, Jan Tomas *immunologist, medical educator*
Vlahov, David *epidemiologist*
Walden, Jennifer Lee *plastic surgeon*
Wallack, Joel Jeffrey *psychiatrist*
Wang, Frederick Mark *pediatrician, ophthalmologist, educator*
Wang, Lu Hai *medical educator, biochemist*
Warren, Russell Frederick *orthopedist*
Weiland, Andrew J. *orthopaedic surgeon*
Weinrauch, Harry *physician*
Weinstein, I. Bernard *oncologist, director, geneticist, educator*
Weiss, Carol Juliet *psychiatrist*
Weiss, Paul Richard *plastic surgeon*
Weissman, Myrna M. *epidemiologist, researcher, medical educator*
Weissmann, Gerald *internist, researcher, educator, editor, writer*
Welch, Martha Grace *physician, researcher*
Werman, David Sanford *psychiatrist, psychoanalyst*
Wexler, Leonard Howard *pediatric oncologist*
Wexler, Patricia Susan *dermatologist, surgeon*
Wharton, Ralph Nathaniel *psychiatrist, educator*
Whitehead, Edgar Douglas *urology educator*
Winawer, Sidney J. *physician, educator*
Winick, Myron *nutrition professor, physician*
Winn, H. Richard *surgeon*
Winston, Arnold *psychiatrist, educator*
Wittes, Robert E. *physician, science foundation director*
Wolden, Suzanne Leesa *pediatric radiation oncologist*
Wolfe, Scott W. *orthopedic hand surgeon*
Wolff, William I. *surgeon, educator*
Worman, Howard Jay *internist, educator*
Youm, Thomas *orthopedist, surgeon*
Young, Bruce Kenneth *obstetrician, gynecologist, educator*
Young, Estelle Irene *dermatologist, educator*
Yu, Yi-Hao *endocrinologist, educator, physician, research scientist*
Yurt, Roger William *surgeon, educator*
Zimmerman, Sol Shea *pediatrician*
Zinn, Keith Marshall *ophthalmologist, educator*
Zitrin, Arthur *physician*
Zucker-Franklin, Dorothea *internist, educator*

**Niagara Falls**
DeFelice, Eugene Anthony *internist, educator, magician*

**North Babylon**
Zitt, Myron J. *allergist, immunologist*

**North Tonawanda**
Megahed, Mohamed Salah *neurologist, educator*

**Northport**
Graber, Mark L. *internist*
Yeh, Shing-shing *geriatrician, researcher, internist*

**Orangeburg**
Greenberg, William Michael *psychiatrist*
Levine, Jerome *psychiatrist, educator*
Nixon, Ralph Angus *psychiatrist, educator, research neuroscientist*

**Orchard Park**
Lee, Richard Vaille *internist, educator*

**Pawling**
Caplan, Ronald Mervyn *obstetrician, gynecologist*

**Pearl River**
Boghaert, Erwin R. *oncology researcher*

**Pittsford**
Faloon, William Wassell *physician, educator*

**Port Jefferson**
Ahmad, Arif *surgeon*
Dranitzke, Richard J. *surgeon*

**Port Jervis**
DeCastro, Alfredo P. *physician, consultant*

**Poughkeepsie**
Carino, Aurora Lao *psychiatrist, health facility administrator*
Hansraj, Kenneth Karamchand *surgeon, research scientist*
Wolfersteig, Jean Lois *medical association administrator, educator*

**Purchase**
Frost, Elizabeth Ann McArthur *physician*

**Rego Park**
Winter, Darius Gerjon *internist*

**Rhinebeck**
Crum, Albert Byrd *psychiatrist, consultant*

**Richmond Hill**
Gintautas, Jonas *physician, scientist, administrator*

**Ridgewood**
Monroe, Leonora *surgeon*

**Rochester**
Akiyama, Toshio *cardiologist, educator, researcher*
Anderson, Porter Warren, Jr. *retired pediatrics educator*
Baum, John *physician*
Berg, Robert Lewis *physician, educator*
Bidlack, Jean Marie *pharmacologist, educator, medical researcher*
Blumberg, Neil *hematologist, educator*
Bonfiglio, Thomas Albert *pathologist, educator*
Brody, Bernard B. *internist, educator*
Brooks, Walter S. *dermatologist*
Burton, Richard Irving *orthopedist, educator*
Chess, Patricia R. *pediatrician, medical educator, researcher*
Chey, William Yoon *physician*
Cohen, Nicholas *immunologist, educator*
Davies, Mark G *vascular surgeon, vascular biologist*
DeWeese, James Arville *surgeon, educator*
Dreyfuss, Eric Martin *allergist*
Farmer, Richard Gilbert *academic physician, foundation administrator*
Galaria, Noreen Ahmad *physician, medical researcher, consultant*
Golden, Reynold Stephen *geriatrician, educator*
Goldstein, Marvin Norman *physician*
Griggs, Robert Charles *physician*
Guillet, Ronnie *pediatrician, educator*
Khorana, Alok Anand *oncologist, medical researcher*
Kurlan, Roger *neurologist, educator*
Lichtman, Marshall Albert *hematologist, educator, researcher*
Lyman, Gary Herbert *epidemiologist, cancer researcher, educator*
Lyness, Jeffrey Marc *psychiatrist, educator*
Maquat, Lynne E. *biomedical researcher*
McAnarney, Elizabeth R. *pediatrician, educator*
McDonald, Joseph Valentine *neurosurgeon*
McMeekin, Thomas Owen *dermatologist*
Mink, Jonathan W. *medical educator, researcher*
Moss, Arthur Jay *physician*
Nazarian, Lawrence Fred *pediatrician*
Patrick, Paul *emergency physician*
Pearson, Thomas Arthur *epidemiologist, educator*
Powers, James Matthew *neuropathologist*
Ravina, Bernard Mayer *neurologist*
Rowley, Peter Templeton *pediatrician, educator*
Smith, Julia Ladd *oncologist, physician*
Sparks, Charles Edward *pathologist, educator*
Sparks, Janet Lindsay Dehoff *pathologist, educator*
White, Ann Marie *medical educator*
Wiley, Jason LaRue, Jr. *neurosurgeon*
Williams, Thomas Franklin *physician, educator*
Wynne, Lyman Carroll *psychiatrist*

**Rockville Centre**
Teyan, Frederick Gene *pediatrician*

**Rome**
Min, Balshik *pathologist*

**Roslyn**
Druz, Regina Shmukler *cardiologist, researcher*
Greenberg, Steven M. *physician*
Gulotta, Stephen J. *cardiologist*
Mazlen, Roger Geoffrey *ophthalmologist, pharmacologist*

**Roslyn Heights**
Rogatz, Peter *retired physician*

**Rye**
Barker, Harold Grant *surgeon, educator*
Curtin, Brian Joseph *retired ophthalmologist*
Waltz, Joseph McKendree *neurosurgeon, educator*

**Rye Brook**
Lo Russo, Diane *radiologist*

**Sands Point**
Lear, Erwin *anesthesiologist, educator*

**Scarsdale**
Dulit, Everett Paul *psychiatrist, educator*
Edis, Gloria Toby *pediatrician*
Lipman, Marvin Matthew *medical educator*
Mercando, Anthony Dominic *cardiologist*
Moser, Marvin *physician, educator, author*
Solow, Robert Lawrence *plastic surgeon*

**Schenectady**
Depan, Harry John *cardiothoracic surgeon*
Schenck, John Frederic *physician*

**Scotia**
de la Rocha, Carlos A. *retired physician*

**Sleepy Hollow**
Chia, David Thien-Shing *internist, gastroenterologist*

**Slingerlands**
Ipsen, Carol Anne *psychiatrist, educator*

**Somers**
Reznick, Steven Michael *orthopedic surgeon, educator*
Rubin, Samuel Harold *internist, consultant*

**Staten Island**
Bruckstein, Alex Harry *internist, gastroenterologist, geriatrician*
Ferzli, George Salem *surgeon*
Maiman, Mitchell *oncologist, gynecologist*
Popler, Kenneth *behavioral health services administrator, psychologist*
Stathopoulos, Peter *internist*

**Stony Brook**
Andriola, Mary Repole *neurologist, pediatrician*
Baker, David A. *obstetrician, gynecologist, educator*
Corman, Marvin Leonard *surgeon, educator*
Dosik, Michael *breast cancer physician, hospital administrator, consultant*
Dugam, Alexander B. *plastic surgeon*
Fine, Richard Nisan *pediatrician, educator, dean*

Fritts, Harry Washington, Jr. *internist, educator*
Hurst, Lawrence *orthopedic surgeon*
Jonas, Steven *preventive medicine physician, author*
Kuchner, Eugene Frederick *neurosurgeon, educator, neuroscientist*
Lane, Dorothy Spiegel *preventive medicine physician*
Larson, Susan G. *anatomist, educator*
Leske, M. Cristina *medical researcher, educator*
Liang, Jerome Zhengrong *radiology educator*
Meyers, Morton Allen *radiologist, educator*
Mirza, Humair *cardiologist, educator*
Monheit, Alan Goodman *obstetrician, gynecologist*
Moore, William Henry *radiologist*
Priebe, Cedric Joseph, Jr. *pediatric surgeon*
Seifert, Frank C. *thoracic surgeon*
Steigbigel, Roy Theodore *epidemiologist, educator, research scientist*
Vlay, Stephen Charles *cardiologist, electrophysiologist*
Weisbrot, Deborah Marcia *psychiatrist*

**Suffern**
Codispoti, Andre John *allergist, immunologist*

**Syosset**
Rehm, Carolyn Agnes *pediatrician, educator*

**Syracuse**
Baker, Bruce Edward *orthopedic surgeon, consultant*
Becker, Lorne Arthur *family physician*
Caldicott, Catherine V. *medical educator, researcher*
Callahan, James Michael *physician, educator*
Fortune, John B. *medical educator*
Fredrickson, Bruce E. *orthopedist*
Gold, Joseph *medical researcher*
Grant, William Davis *family medicine educator, dean*
Horst, Pamela Sue *medical educator, physician*
Kaplan, Eugene Alken *psychiatry professor, department chairman*
Numann, Patricia Joy *surgeon, educator*
Rabuzzi, Daniel D. *medical association administrator*
Rogers, Sherry Anne *physician*
Streeten, Barbara Wiard *ophthalmologist, medical educator*
Szasz, Thomas Stephen *psychiatrist, educator, writer*
Williams, William Joseph *hematologist, educator*
Wolff, L. Thomas *physician, educator*

**Tarrytown**
Cocchiarella, Antonio *physician, educator*
Field, Barry Elliot *internist, gastroenterologist*
Mc Murtry, James Gilmer III *neurosurgeon*

**Tuxedo Park**
Regan, Ellen Frances (Mrs. Walston Shepard Brown) *ophthalmologist, educator*

**Upton**
Carsten, Arland Leon *radiobiologist, researcher, educator, consultant*
Hamilton, Leonard Derwent *physician, molecular biologist*

**Valhalla**
Aronow, Wilbert Solomon *physician, educator*
Brand, Donald Albert *medical researcher, educator*
Cimino, Joseph Anthony *preventive medicine physician, educator*
Cohen, Martin Bruce *physician*
Del Guercio, Louis Richard Maurice *surgeon, educator*
Frishman, William Howard *cardiologist, educator, department chairman, cardiovascular pharmacologist, gerontologist*
Goodman, Alvin Irwin *internist, nephrologist, educator*
Inchiosa, Mario Anthony, Jr. *pharmacologist*
Kline, Susan Anderson *medical educator, internist*
Madden, Robert Michael *surgeon, educator*
Marks, Stephen J. *neurologist, educator*
Niguidula, Faustino Nazario *surgeon, educator*
Peterson, Stephen Joseph *internist*
Slim, Michel S. *surgeon, educator, health facility administrator*
Spielvogel, David *thoracic surgeon*
Stringel, Gustavo *pediatric surgeon*
Stuhlmiller, David Fe *emergency physician*
Weinberg, Hubert *plastic surgeon*
Williams, Gary Murray *pathologist, educator*

**Vestal**
Grinberg, Raul *internist*

**Water Mill**
Chalif, Ronnie *medical association administrator, artist*
Hagstrom, Jack Walter Carl Kling *retired pathology educator*

**West Islip**
Cokinos, Stephan George *cardiologist*
Henesch, Stephen *pediatrician, radiologist*
Rifkin, Matthew D. *radiologist*

**White Plains**
Bernard, Robert William *plastic surgeon*
Biers, Martin Henry *physician*
Blass, John Paul *physician, biochemist*
Katz, Michael *pediatrician, educator*
Kutscher, Martin L. *pediatrician, neurologist*
Liebert, Peter Selig *pediatric surgeon, consultant*
Marano, Anthony Joseph *cardiologist*
Pfeffer, Cynthia Roberta *psychiatrist, educator*
Straus, Marc Joshua *internist, poet*
Volpe, Bruce Thomas *neurologist*
Weisburger, John Hans *medical researcher*

**Williamsville**
Ashton, Adam Keller *psychiatrist, educator*
Canfield, Cheryl Lucas *epidemiologist*
Neiman, Joseph Bruce *dermatologist, educator*
Ogra, Pearay L. *pediatrician, educator*
Reisman, Robert E. *allergist, educator*

**Yonkers**
Chumaceiro, Rolando Jose Mendez *family practice physician*
Daman, Harlan Richard *allergist, educator*
Spagnuolo, Mario *physician*

**Yorktown Heights**
Berk, George Ellis *cardiologist*
Mayer, Gerard J. *physician*

**Youngstown**
Gordon, Wilfred Edward Lawrence *retired obstetrician-gynecologist*

## NORTH CAROLINA

**Advance**
Guth, Caryl Joy *retired anesthesiologist*

**Asheville**
Eglinton, Daniel Thomas *orthopedist*
Hazlehurst, John Livingston *surgeon*
Turcot, Marguerite Hogan *medical researcher*
White, Terry Edward *physician*

**Banner Elk**
Hutcheson, James Sterling *retired physician, allergist*

**Brevard**
Finnerty, Frances Martin *medical administrator*

**Burlington**
Malinda, Paul F. *emergency physician*
Wilson, William Preston *psychiatrist, educator*

**Chapel Hill**
Adkins, Willis G. *medical association administrator, consultant*
Andreoni, Kenneth A. *surgeon*
Azar, Henry Amin *retired medical educator*
Bernard, Stephen Alan *oncologist*
Bondurant, Stuart *physician, educational association administrator*
Boucher, Richard C. *medical educator, researcher*
Bowman, Frederick Oscar, Jr. *retired cardiothoracic surgeon*
Callahan, Leigh Fleming *medical educator, researcher*
Carson, Culley Clyde III *urologist, educator*
Cefalo, Robert Charles *obstetrician, gynecologist*
Clemmons, David Robert *internist, educator*
Coeytaux, Remy Rene *physician, researcher*
Coles, William Henry *ophthalmologist, educator*
Collier, Albert M. *pediatrician, educator, director*
Crews, Fulton Timm *pharmacology educator*
Cromartie, William James *medical educator, researcher*
De Friese, Gordon H. *health services researcher*
De Rosa, Guy Paul *orthopedic surgery educator*
Dirschl, Douglas Ray *surgeon, educator*
Erdem, Nurum Filiz *geriatrician*
Finkel, Alan Glen *neurologist, educator*
Fletcher, Suzanne Wright *epidemiologist, medical educator, editor*
Fowler, Wesley Caswell, Jr. *obstetrician, gynecologist*
Gilman, Andrew Lee *pediatrician*
Goldsmith, Lowell Alan *medical educator*
Goyer, Robert Andrew *pathology educator*
Greganti, Mac Andrew *physician, medical educator*
Hawkins, David Rollo, Sr. *psychiatrist, educator*
Henson, O'Dell Williams, Jr. *retired anatomy educator*
Houpt, Jeffrey Lyle *psychiatrist, educator, former dean*
Hulka, Jaroslav Fabian *obstetrician, gynecologist*
James, Alton Everette, Jr. *radiologist*
Lachiewicz, Paul Francis *orthopedist, surgeon, educator*
Lavelle, John Paul *urologist*
Lohr, Jacob Andrew *pediatrician, educator*
Martikainen, A(une) Helen *retired health specialist educator*
McMillan, Campbell White *pediatrician, educator, hematologist*
Miller, C. Arden *physician, educator*
Pagano, Joseph Stephen *internist, researcher, educator*
Palmer, Jeffress Gary *hematologist, educator*
Peacock, Erle Ewart, Jr. *surgeon, lawyer, educator*
Pillsbury, Harold Crockett III *otolaryngologist*
Prather, Donna Lynn *psychiatrist*
Sheldon, George Frank *medical educator*
Simmons, Michael Anthony *pediatrician*
Spencer, Roger Felix *psychiatrist, educator*
Stockman, James Anthony III *pediatrician*
Taft, Timothy Ned *orthopedist, surgeon, sports medicine physician*
Tolley, Aubrey Granville *psychiatrist, health facility administrator*
Trejo, JoAnn *medical researcher*
Wilcox, Benson Reid *cardiothoracic surgeon, educator*
Wilfert, Catherine M. *medical association administrator, pediatrician, epidemiologist, educator*
Winfield, John Buckner *rheumatologist, educator*

**Charlotte**
Hall, James Bryan *gynecologist, oncologist*
Hanley, Edward Nathaniel *surgeon*
Huynh, Toan T. *surgeon, researcher*
Jacobs, Gordon Waldemar *surgeon, educator*
Kneisl, Jeffrey S. *oncologist, orthopedist*
Lapp, Charles Warren *internist, pediatrician*
Schafermeyer, Robert William *emergency physician, educator, health policy consultant*
Thompson, John Albert, Jr. *dermatologist*

**Clemmons**
Maloney, Sean Robert *physician, biomedical engineer*

**Durham**
Agre, Peter Courtland *medical educator*
Albala, David Mois *urologist, educator*

Anderson, William Banks, Jr. *ophthalmology educator*
Anlyan, William George *surgeon, educator, academic administrator*
Armstrong, Brenda Estelle *pediatrician, cardiologist*
Bennett, Peter Brian *medical researcher, educator*
Berger, Jeffrey S. *cardiologist*
Beyer, John Leslie *psychiatrist*
Blazer, Dan German, II, *psychiatrist, epidemiologist*
Blazing, Michael August *internist*
Bollinger, Ralph Randal *surgeon, researcher*
Borges-Neto, Salvador *radiologist, cardiologist, educator*
Bradford, William Dalton *pathologist, educator*
Brodie, Harlow Keith Hammond *psychiatrist, educator*
Buckley, Rebecca Hatcher *allergist, immunologist, pediatrician, educator*
Burks, A. Wesley *pediatrics educator*
Cai, Xinjiang *cardiologist, researcher*
Carter, James Harvey *psychiatrist, researcher*
Cohen, Harvey Jay *geriatrician, hematologist, oncologist, educator*
Cohen, Seth Morris *otolaryngologist, educator*
Colvin, O. Michael *medical association administrator, medical educator*
Cook-Deegan, Robert Mullan *physician, educator*
Coppridge, Alton James *urological surgeon*
Crawford, Jeffrey *oncologist, educator*
Dzau, Victor Joseph *cardiologist, director, researcher*
Edwards, Christopher Levon *medical association administrator*
Falletta, John Matthew *pediatrician, educator*
Foreman, John William *pediatrician, educator*
Frank, Michael M. *physician*
Freemark, Michael Scott *pediatric endocrinologist, educator*
Frothingham, Thomas Eliot *physician*
Gainetdinov, Raul Radkovich *pharmacologist, researcher*
Giannopoulos, Athina *physician, surgeon*
Goforth, Harold W. *physician, psychiatrist*
Greenfield, Joseph Cholmondeley, Jr. *physician, educator*
Hammond, Charles Bessellieu *obstetrician, gynecologist, educator*
James, Sherman Athonia *epidemiologist, educator*
Jennings, Robert Burgess *experimental pathologist, medical educator*
Jirtle, Randy *medical educator, geneticist*
Katz, Samuel Lawrence *pediatrician, researcher*
Kimmick, Gretchen *oncologist*
Kishnani, Priya Sunil *medical geneticist*
Klitzman, Bruce *physiologist, plastic surgery educator, researcher*
Koepke, John Arthur *hematologist, clinical pathologist*
Kurtzberg, Joanne *pediatrician, educator*
Lack, Leon *pharmacology and biochemistry educator*
Lefkowitz, Robert Joseph *physician, educator*
Leppert, Phyllis Carolyn *obstetrician, gynecologist*
Levin, Lawrence Scott *plastic surgeon*
Mackensen, Georg Burkhard *anesthesiologist, educator*
Mark, Daniel Benjamin *cardiologist*
Markert, Mary Louise *pediatrics educator*
Masand, Prakash S. *psychiatrist, researcher*
Matchar, David B. *physician, researcher*
McNamara, James O. *physician, scientist*
Means, Anthony Ross *pharmacology educator*
Mehta, Rajendra H. *cardiologist, researcher*
Michener, James Lloyd *medical educator*
Miller, David Edmond *physician*
Ohman, E. Magnus *cardiologist, educator*
Olsen, Elise *dermatologist, researcher*
Olufolabi, Adeyemi John *anesthesiologist*
Ostbye, Truls *medical researcher, educator*
Patel, Keyur *medical educator*
Pinnell, Sheldon Richard *dermatologist, researcher, retired educator*
Pizzo, Salvatore Vincent *pathologist*
Rabinovich, Egla Consuelo *pediatrician, rheumatologist*
Robboy, Stanley J. *pathologist, educator*
Ruch, David S. *orthopedist, surgeon*
Sabiston, David Coston, Jr. *surgeon, educator*
Sanders, Donald Benjamin *neurologist, educator*
Seewaldt, Victoria L. *medical educator, researcher*
Shelburne, John Daniel *pathologist*
Stafford, Mark Smith *anesthesiologist, researcher, education educator*
Tedder, Thomas Fletcher *immunology educator, researcher*
Thompson, William Moreau *radiologist, educator*
Weiner, Richard David *psychiatrist, researcher*
Wells, Samuel Alonzo, Jr. *surgeon, educator*
Wilcox, Allen James *epidemiologist*
Wilkins, Robert Henry *neurosurgeon, educator, editor*
Williams, Redford Brown *medical educator*
Young, Christopher C. *anesthesiologist*
Young, Terri L. *ophthalmologist*

**Fayetteville**
Fietsam, Robert, Jr. *physician*
Lowe, James Edward, Jr. *plastic and reconstructive surgeon*

**Four Oaks**
Jordan, Lyndon Kirkman *physician*

**Greensboro**
Houston, Frank Matt *dermatologist*
Stevens, Elliott Walker, Jr. *allergist, cardiologist, pulmonologist*

**Greenville**
Allison, Ron *oncologist, researcher*
Babb, Joseph Dolby *physician*
Cummings, James *pediatrician, educator*
James, James Franklin *psychiatrist, educator, academic administrator*
Johnson, Cynda Ann *physician, educator*
Lee, Kenneth Stuart *neurosurgeon, educator*
Pories, Walter Julius *surgeon, educator*
Schenarts, Paul Joseph *surgeon, educator*
Shiber, Joseph R. *emergency physician*

Tingelstad, Jon Bunde *retired pediatrician, educator*
Waugh, William Howard *physician, research scientist*

**Henderson**
Serafin, Donald *plastic surgeon, educator*

**Hendersonville**
Reinhart, John Belvin *retired child and adolescent psychiatrist, educator*
Roberts, James Allen *retired urologist, educator*

**Hickory**
Lefler, Wade Hampton, Jr. *ophthalmologist*

**High Point**
Bardelas, Jose Antonio *allergist*
Draelos, Zoe Diana *dermatologist, consultant*
Kandt, Raymond S. *neurologist*

**Hillsborough**
Johnston, William Webb *pathologist, educator*
Wallace, Andrew Grover *internist, educator, dean*

**Huntersville**
Atrak, Taisser M. *pediatrician, director*

**Mebane**
Langley, Ricky Lee *occupational medicine physician*

**Monroe**
Taylor, Jimmy Lynn *retired family practice physician, administrator*

**Pine Knoll Shores**
Graham, Gloria Flippin *dermatologist*

**Pisgah Forest**
Kempe, Ludwig George *neurosurgeon*

**Pittsboro**
Brownlee, Robert Calvin *pediatrician, educator*

**Raleigh**
Barish, Charles Franklin *internist, gastroenterologist, researcher*
Bateman, Angela Anderson *anesthetist*
Gordon, Morris Aaron *medical mycologist*
Hughes, Francis P. *medical association administrator*
Parsons, William Jonathan *cardiologist*
Riviere, Jim Edmond, Jr. *pharmacologist, educator, toxicologist*
Speer, Kevin Paul *surgeon*

**Research Triangle Park**
Roses, Allen David *neurologist, educator*

**Roanoke Rapids**
Adiga, Giridhar U. *geriatrician, pharmacologist, researcher, internist*

**Salisbury**
Kishev, Stephen Vasilev *urologist*

**Southern Pines**
Warren, Donald William *medical and dental educator*

**Spencer**
Kiser, Glenn Augustus *retired pediatrician, entrepreneur*

**Thomasville**
Sprinkle, Robert Lee, Jr. *podiatrist*

**Tryon**
Mellberg, James Richard *retired dental research chemist*

**Waxhaw**
Edwards, Irene Elizabeth (Libby Edwards) *dermatologist, educator, medical researcher*

**Waynesville**
McKinney, Alexander Stuart *retired neurologist*

**Wilmington**
Boyle, Joseph Hugh *psychiatrist*
De Maria, Alfred Anthony *neurologist*

**Wilson**
Kushner, Michael James *neurologist, consultant, educator*
Ladwig, Harold Allen *neurologist*

**Winston Salem**
Atala, Anthony John *surgeon*
Donofrio, Peter Daniel *neurology educator*
Dyer, Raymond B. *diagnostic radiology physician*
Eldridge, J. Charles *endocrinologist, researcher, medical educator*
Fleischer, Alan Bernard, Jr. *dermatologist, educator*
Greven, Kathryn McConnell *radiologist, oncologist*
Hammon, John William, Jr. *medical educator, thoracic surgeon*
Harle, Thomas Stanley *radiologist*
Henrichs, W(alter) Dean *dermatologist*
Hite, Robert Duncan *medical educator*
Howell, Charles Maitland *dermatologist*
Ibdah, Jamal A. *medical educator*
James, Francis Marshall III *anesthesiologist*
Kaur, Mandeep *dermatologist, educator*
Kohut, Robert Irwin *otolaryngologist, educator*
Maynard, Charles Douglas *radiologist*
Meis, Paul Jean *obstetrics and gynecology educator*
Moody, Dixon McGuire *radiologist*
O'Donovan, Cormac A. *neurologist, educator*
O'Steen, Wendall Keith *anatomist, neurologist, educator*
Podgorny, George *emergency physician*
Simon, Jimmy Louis *pediatrician, educator*
Sink, Kaycee M. *geriatrician, medical educator*
Stein, Barry Edward *medical educator*
Toole, James Francis *medical educator*

Torti, Frank Michael *internist, health facility administrator*
Weller, Robert Stephen *anesthesiologist*

**NORTH DAKOTA**

**Bismarck**
Kaushik, Prashant *rheumatologist, educator*
Schwartz, Judy Ellen *thoracic surgeon*

**Fargo**
Mitchell, James Edward *physician, educator*

**Grand Forks**
Crow, Judson Lewis *plastic surgeon*
Jackson, Jon *medical educator, consultant*
Lerma, Edgar Villanueva *nephrologist*
Sharma, Sushil K. *medical educator*
Sobus, Kerstin MaryLouise *physician, physical therapist*

**Williston**
Adducci, Joseph Edward *obstetrician, gynecologist*

**OHIO**

**Akron**
Allen, Marc Kevin *emergency physician, educator*
Emmett, John Colin *retired inventor, consultant*
Evans, Douglas McCullough *surgeon, educator*
Litman, George Irving *physician, educator*
Loud, Keith John *pediatrician*
Milsted, Amy *biomedical educator*

**Beachwood**
Moskowitz, Roland Wallace *internist*
Varner, Arthur E. *allergist, researcher*

**Bexley**
Yashon, David *neurosurgeon, educator*

**Bratenahl**
Jones, Trevor Owen *biomedical industry executive, management consultant*

**Brecksville**
Ventenilla, Aurora Curamen *psychiatrist*

**Brunswick**
Kuchynski, Marie *physician*

**Bryan**
Carrico, Virgil Norman *physician*

**Canton**
Howland, Willard J. *radiologist, educator*
Nadas, John Adalbert *psychiatrist, educator*

**Chagrin Falls**
Lingl, Friedrich Albert *psychiatrist*

**Chardon**
Dobyns, Brown McIlvaine *retired surgeon, educator*

**Cincinnati**
Alexander, James Wesley *surgeon, educator*
Balistreri, William Francis *pediatric gastroenterologist*
Bellet, Paul Sanders *pediatrician, educator*
Bezerra, Jorge Abdon *pediatrics educator, health facility administrator*
Biro, Frank M. *pediatrics educator*
Boat, Thomas Frederick *pediatrician, researcher, pulmonologist, educator*
Buncher, Charles Ralph *epidemiologist, educator, biostatistician*
Ching, Ho *surgeon*
De Courten-Myers, Gabrielle Marguerite *neuropathologist*
Diwan, Abhinav *medical educator, researcher*
Dunsker, Stewart B. *neurosurgeon*
Elluru, Ravindra G. *pediatric otolaryngologist*
Etges, Frank Joseph *parasitology educator*
Heaton, Charles Lloyd *dermatologist, educator*
Heimlich, Henry J. *physician, surgeon, educator*
Hess, Evelyn Victorine *medical educator*
Hillard, James Randolph *psychiatry educator*
Joffe, Stephen Neal *surgeon, medical educator*
Kereiakes, Dean James *cardiologist*
Kersten, Robert C. *ophthalmic plastic surgeon*
Kircher, Christopher *neurologist, consultant*
Kissela, Brett M. *neurologist*
Kukielka, Gilbert Leon *physician*
Kuntz, Charles, IV, *neurosurgeon*
Lehmann, Corinne E. *medical educator*
Levinson, Joseph E. *retired internist, rheumatologist, educator*
Loggie, Jennifer Mary Hildreth *retired physician, educator*
Lower, Elyse E. *physician, educator*
Maeder, Michael C. *endocrinologist*
Maltz, Robert *surgeon*
Mehta, Parinda Apurva *pediatrician, medical educator, hematologist, oncologist*
Nakata, Akinori *epidemiologist, researcher*
Nussbaum, Michael Scot *physician, medical educator*
Pathak, Sanjeev *psychiatrist, researcher*
Pomerantz, Wendy Jane *pediatrician, educator*
Pyne-Geithman, Gail Jean *medical educator, researcher*
Schreiner, Albert William *internist, educator*
Sundberg, Ruth Dorothy *hematologist, educator*
Vilter, Richard William, Sr. *retired internist, educator*
Visscher, Marty Orrico *biomedical researcher*
West, Clark Darwin *pediatric nephrologist, educator*
Whitsett, Jeffrey Allen *pediatric educator*
Wiot, Jerome Francis *radiologist*
Wood, Robert Emerson *pediatrics educator*
Zuccarello, Mario *neurosurgeon, researcher*

**Cleveland**
Abughali, Nazha *pediatrician, consultant*
Agani, Faton Hilmi *anatomist, educator*

Anderson, James M. *pathologist*
Awais, George Musa *obstetrician, gynecologist*
Baker, Saul Phillip *geriatrician, cardiologist, internist*
Barnett, Gene Henry *neurosurgeon*
Berger, Melvin *allergist, immunologist*
Bodner, Donald Roger *urologist, medical educator*
Bowerfind, Edgar Sihler, Jr. *internist, educator, retired medical association administrator*
Boyd, Arthur Bernette, Jr. *surgeon, clergyman, beverage company executive*
Brody, Robert *dermatologist, educator*
Bruner, William Evans, II, *ophthalmologist, educator, researcher*
Castele, Theodore John *radiologist*
Chak, Amitabh *gastroenterologist, researcher*
Chung, Benjamin John *urologist*
Cola, Philip Andrew *research administrator*
Connors, Alfred Francis *internist, researcher*
Cooper, Gregory Scott *epidemiologist, gastroenterologist, educator*
Cowan, Dale Harvey *internist, lawyer*
Daroff, Robert Barry *neurologist, educator*
Davis, Pamela Bowes *pediatric pulmonologist*
Denko, Joanne D. *psychiatrist, writer*
Dweik, Raed A. *physician, researcher, educator*
Eiben, Robert Michael *pediatric neurologist, educator*
Ellis, Lloyd H., Jr. *emergency physician, art historian*
Elston, Robert C. *medical educator*
Falcone, Tommaso *reproductive endocrinologist*
Fazio, Victor Warren *physician, colon and rectal surgeon*
Fung, John Julian *transplant surgeon, immunologist*
Gambetti, Perluigi *pathologist*
Garcia, Mario Jorge *cardiologist*
Hajj-Ali, Rula Adel *rheumatologist, researcher*
Hermann, Robert Ewald *retired surgeon*
Holzbach, Raymond Thomas *gastroenterologist, educator, writer*
Horwitz, Ralph Irving *internist, epidemiologist, educator, dean*
Iannotti, Joseph Patrick *orthopedic surgeon*
Kalmadi, Sujith Rao *oncologist, hematologist*
Kaouk, Jihad *urologist*
Kass, Lawrence *hematologist, oncologist, educator*
King, Joseph Thomas, Jr. *neurosurgeon*
Kinsella, Timothy J. *radiation oncologist*
Kraay, Matthew Joseph *orthopedist, educator*
Lamm, Michael Emanuel *pathologist, immunologist, educator*
Lefferts, William Geoffrey *internist, educator*
Lenkoski, Leo Douglas *retired psychiatrist, educator*
Lowe, John Burton *medical association administrator, molecular biologist, educator, pathologist*
Ma, Patrick C. *oncologist, researcher*
Macklis, Roger Milton *physician, educator, researcher*
Malangoni, Mark Alan *surgeon, educator*
Mazzone, Peter *physician*
McCrae, Keith R. *medical educator, researcher*
McHenry, Martin Christopher *physician, educator*
McQuarrie, Irvine Gray *neurosurgeon, educator*
Mhanna, Maroun Jean *pediatrician*
Miller, Holly Dara *physician, director, healthcare educator, researcher*
Minai, Omar Ahmad *physician*
Montague, Drogo K. *urologist*
Neuhauser, Duncan vonBriesen *medical educator*
Novick, Andrew Carl *urologist*
Olness, Karen Norma *medical educator*
Ornt, Daniel B. *physician*
Pujana, Maria Jose *neurologist*
Raaf, John Hart *surgeon, educator, health facility administrator*
Raghavan, Derek *oncologist, medical researcher and educator*
Rakita, Louis *retired cardiologist*
Ransohoff, Richard Milton *neurologist, researcher*
Rehm, Susan *physician*
Resnick, Martin I. *urologist, educator*
Rome, Ellen S. *physician*
Ruff, Robert Louis *neurologist, physiologist, researcher*
Segota, Ena *hematologist*
Shatila, Ahmad Hussain *surgeon, oncologist*
Shuck, Jerry Mark *surgeon, educator*
Sola, Srikanth *cardiologist*
Stanton-Hicks, Michael D'Arcy *anesthesiologist, pain medicine specialist*
Stavitsky, Abram Benjamin *immunologist, educator*
Stern, Robert C. *pediatrician, medical educator*
Taylor, Harris C. *endocrinologist, consultant*
Tetzlaff, John Edwin *physician*
Tubbs, Raymond Roy *pathologist*
Ubogu, Eroboghene Ekamereno *physician*
Walters, Mark Douglas *obstetrician, gynecologist*
Webster, Leslie Tillotson, Jr. *pharmacologist, educator*
Wish, Jay Barry *nephrologist, specialist*
Wolfman, Alan *medical educator, researcher*
Wolinsky, Emanuel *internist, educator*
Yetman, Randall John *plastic surgeon*
Young, Jess Ray *retired internist*

**Cleveland Heights**
Netzer, Nikolaus C. *physician, medical researcher, publishing executive*

**Columbus**
Balcerzak, Stanley Paul *hematologist, oncologist, director, retired medical educator*
Baliga, Ragavendra Ramakrishna *cardiologist, researcher*
Barth, Rolf Frederick *pathologist, educator*
Berntson, Gary Glen *psychiatry, psychology and pediatrics educator*
Beversdorf, David Quentin *neurologist, researcher*
Billings, Charles Edgar *physician*
Bloomfield, Clara Derber *oncologist, educator, medical institute administrator*
Blum, William George *hematologist, clinical researcher educator*
Boué, Daniel Robert *pediatric pathologist, neuropathologist, educator*
Brogan, Michael Dale *gastroenterologist, educator*
Bullock, Joseph Daniel *pediatrician, educator*

Capen, Charles Chabert *veterinary pathology educator*
Christoforidis, A. John *radiologist, educator*
Comstock, R. Dawn *epidemiologist, researcher*
Copelan, Edward A. *medical educator*
Doolittle, Kenneth Herbert *retired urologist*
Ellison, Edwin Christopher *surgeon, educator*
Feldman, David *cardiologist, director*
Galantowicz, Mark Edward *cardiothoracic surgeon*
Haque, Malika Hakim *pediatrician*
Huheey, Marilyn Jane *ophthalmologist, educator*
Khairy, Kaed Nabil *geriatrician*
Lander, Ruth A. *medical group and association administrator*
Leier, Carl Victor *internist, cardiologist*
Lewis, Richard Phelps *cardiologist, educator*
Long, Sarah Elizabeth Brackney *physician*
Lucey, Catherine Reinis *medical educator, department chairman*
Marsh, Clay Braden *pulmonologist, researcher*
McClung, Hugo Juhling *pediatrician, educator*
Moore, James Layne *neurologist, educator*
Morrison, Ashton Byrom *retired pathologist, medical school official*
Mueller, Charles Frederick *radiologist, educator*
Muscarella, Peter *physician*
Nappi, James Francis *hand surgeon, educator*
Needham, Glen Ray *entomology and acarology educator, researcher*
Newton, Herbert Bruce *oncologist*
Newton, William Allen, Jr. *pediatrician, pathologist*
Ruberg, Robert Lionel *surgery educator*
Rund, Douglas Andrew *emergency physician*
Sayers, Martin Peter *pediatric neurosurgeon*
Stoner, Gary David *cancer researcher*
Vogel, Thomas Timothy *surgeon, educator, lay worker*
Yu, Chack Yung *pediatrics educator, molecular biologist*
Zhao, Fang Li *medical researcher*

**Dayton**
Ambalavanan, Siva *nephrologist, educator*
Chin, Hong Woo *oncologist, educator, researcher*
Gillig, Paulette Marie *psychiatry educator, researcher*
Mohler, Stanley Ross *preventive medicine physician, educator*
Monk, Susan Marie *pediatrician, educator*
Mosier, William Arthur *psychiatrist, psychotherapist, director, medical educator, researcher*
Nanagas, Maria Teresita Cruz *pediatrician, educator*
Reiling, Walter Anthony, Jr. *surgeon*
Ruegsegger, Donald Ray, Jr. *radiological physicist, educator*
Simman, Richard *plastic surgeon, researcher*
Weinberg, Sylvan Lee *cardiologist, educator, editor, writer*
Wilson, William Campbell McFarland *gastroenterologist*

**Edgerton**
Wu, Lawrence Mg Hla Myin *physician*

**Fairfield**
Chin, Nee Oo Wong *reproductive endocrinologist*
Wilson, James Miller, IV, *cardiovascular surgeon, educator*

**Galena**
Berggren, Ronald Bernard *surgeon, retired educator*

**Grove City**
Kilman, James William *surgeon, educator*

**Jackson**
Dallura, Sal Anthony *physician*

**Kettering**
Cline, Allen Lee *endocrinologist, medical educator*

**Madison**
Stafford, Arthur Charles *medical association administrator*

**Mansfield**
Fulginiti, John III *surgeon*
Houston, William Robert Montgomery *ophthalmologist, surgeon*

**Mason**
Beary, John Francis III *rheumatologist, pharmaceutical executive, medical researcher*

**Mentor**
Combs, Steven Paul *orthopedic surgeon*

**Middletown**
Barrord, John Francis *otolaryngologist*

**North Canton**
Di Simone, Robert Nicholas *radiologist, educator*

**Norwalk**
Gutowicz, Matthew Francis, Jr. *radiologist*

**Norwood**
Wright, Creighton Bolter *cardiovascular surgeon, educator*

**Oregon**
Chablani, Lachman V. *pathologist*

**Painesville**
Malchesky, Paul S. *medical association administrator*

**Port Clinton**
Woodson, Riley Donald *thoracic and cardiovascular surgeon, lawyer*

**Portsmouth**
Akhtar, Muhammad I. *neurologist, researcher*

**Rootstown**
Nora, Lois Margaret *neurologist, educator, academic administrator, dean*

**Shaker Heights**
Smith, Jonathan David *medical educator*

**South Point**
Parikh, Jeannine Lubold *physician*

**Sylvania**
Burkhart, Craig Garrett *dermatologist, researcher*

**Toledo**
Bahhur, Nael Osama *physician*
Barrett, Michael John *anesthesiologist*
Cardwell, Michael Steven *obstetrician, educator*
Comerota, Anthony James *vascular surgeon, biomedical researcher*
Elmer, Lawrence William *neurologist, researcher*
Jacobs, Lloyd A. *vascular surgeon*
Martin, John Thomas *physician, author, educator*
Mulrow, Patrick Joseph *medical educator*
Rejent, Marian Magdalen *retired pediatrician*
Shaikh, Bahu Sultan *physician, educator*
Shelley, Walter Brown *dermatologist, educator*
Talmage, Lance Allen *obstetrician, gynecologist, military officer*

**Uniontown**
Krabill, Robert Elmer *osteopathic physician*

**Westerville**
Dawdy, W. David *pediatrician*
St. Pierre, Ronald Leslie *public health and medical educator, academic administrator*

**Willoughby**
Carter, John Robert *retired physician*

**Worthington**
Winter, Chester Caldwell *surgeon, educator, historian, writer*

**Wright Patterson Afb**
Reston, Rocky Russell *anesthesiologist, engineer, educator*

**Yellow Springs**
Von Gierke, Henning Edgar *biomedical science educator, former government official, researcher*

**Zanesville**
Kopf, George Michael *retired ophthalmologist*
Ray, John Walker *otolaryngologist, educator, broadcast commentator*

# OKLAHOMA

**Claremore**
Sneed, Guy Wayne *surgeon*
Whinery, Michael Albert *physician*
Wittenberg, Henry Taylor, Jr. *physician, surgeon*

**Guymon**
Lim, Jeffrey James *internist*

**Kingfisher**
Buswell, Arthur Wilcox *physician, surgeon*

**Lawton**
Webb, Orville Lynn *retired physician, pharmacologist, educator*

**Muskogee**
Kent, Bartis Milton *retired physician*

**Norman**
Cochran, Gloria Grimes *retired pediatrician*
Dille, John Robert *retired physician*

**Oklahoma City**
Andrews, Mitchell Dewayne *internist, educator, dean*
Bahr, Carman Bloedow *internist*
Bailey, David Michael *physician, internist*
Bogardus, Carl Robert, Jr. *radiologist, educator*
Bozalis, John Russell *physician*
Brandt, Edward Newman, Jr. *physician, educator*
Claflin, James Robert *pediatrician, allergist*
Collins, William Edward *aeromedical administrator, researcher, psychologist*
Comp, Philip Cinnamon *medical researcher*
Crawford, Steven Alan *physician, department chairman*
Culkin, Daniel Joseph *urologist, educator, department chairman*
Everett, Mark Allen *dermatologist, educator*
Farag, Noha Hassan *medical researcher*
Filley, Warren Vernon *allergist*
Foerster, David William *plastic surgeon*
Halverstadt, Donald Bruce *urologist, educator*
Hampton, James Wilburn *hematologist, oncologist*
Harolds, Jay Alan *radiologist, nuclear medicine physician*
Krempl, Greg *otolaryngologist*
Metcalf, Jordan Patrick *medical educator*
Parke, David Wilkin, II, *ophthalmologist, educator, health facility administrator*
Perez-Cruet, Jorge *psychiatrist*
Rahhal, Donald K. *obstetrician, gynecologist*
Raj, Tilak D. *anesthesiologist, educator*
Ross, Elliott Daniel *neurologist, researcher*
Rossavik, Ivar Kristian *obstetrician, gynecologist*
Schwartz, Jonathan Royal Lee *medical educator, researcher*
Thadani, Udho *physician, cardiologist*
Trotter, Timothy Howard *thoracic and cardiovascular surgeon, medical educator*
Wisdom, Peggy Jean *neurologist*
Wolraich, Mark Lee *pediatrician, educator*
Zuhdi, Nazih *retired surgeon, hospital administrator*

**Owasso**
Reed, Walter George, Jr. *retired osteopath*

**Shawnee**
Wilson, Robert Godfrey *radiologist*

**Stillwater**
Confer, Anthony Wayne *veterinary pathologist, educator*
Cooper, Donald Lee *physician*
Ewing, Sidney Alton *veterinary medical educator, parasitologist*
Zhang, Guolong *immunologist, educator*

**Tulsa**
Kalbfleisch, John McDowell *cardiologist, educator*
LaButti, Ronald S. *orthopedist*
McCullough, Robert Dale, II, *osteopath*
Nettles, John Barnwell *obstetrics and gynecology educator*
Plunket, Daniel Clark *pediatrician, educator*
Say, Burhan *retired physician*
Werlla, Vanessa Lynn *psychiatrist*

**Vinita**
Neer, Charles Sumner, II, *orthopedic surgeon, educator*

**Weatherford**
Wolgamott, Gary Dean *medical educator*

# OREGON

**Bend**
Dederer, Alexander *retired surgeon*

**Corvallis**
Baird, William McKenzie *chemical carcinogenesis researcher, biochemistry professor*
Steele, Robert Edwin *orthopedic surgeon*

**Eugene**
Gamet, Douglas *pediatrician*
Jewell, Mark Laurence *plastic surgeon*
Kimball, Reid Roberts *psychiatrist*
Loescher, Richard Alvin *retired gastroenterologist*
Roe, Thomas Leroy Willis *retired pediatrician*

**Gresham**
Zook, John Edwin *surgeon*

**Lake Oswego**
Hutchens, Tyra Thornton *pathologist, educator*
Julien, Robert Michael *anesthesiologist, writer*

**Medford**
Shekhar, Stephen S. *obstetrician, gynecologist*

**Milwaukie**
Sklovsky, Robert Joel *naturopathic physician, pharmacist, educator*

**North Plains**
Wood, James Anderson *cardiac surgeon*

**Oregon City**
Burke, William Romney *urologist*

**Portland**
Baker, Diane R.H. *dermatologist*
Barry, John Maynard *urologist*
Bennett, William Michael *internist, educator, nephrologist*
Blank, Eugene *pediatrician, radiologist, educator*
Bloom, Joseph D. *psychiatrist, medical educator*
Butler, John Lowe, IV, *psychiatrist, educator*
Campbell, John Richard *pediatric surgeon*
Casey, Daniel E. *psychiatrist, educator*
Crawshaw, Ralph *psychiatrist*
Darnall, Beth Denise *medical educator*
Druker, Brian Jay *medical educator, researcher*
Francis, Peter James *physician, ophthalmologist*
Fraunfelder, Frederick Theodore *ophthalmologist, educator*
Goodman, Richard H. *biomedical researcher*
Greer, Monte Arnold *endocrinologist, educator*
Hedges, Jerris *medical educator, health services researcher*
Jacob, Stanley Wallace *surgeon, educator*
Kendall, John Walker, Jr. *internist, researcher, dean*
Mazur, Dennis John *internal medicine physician, educator, features editor*
Ng, John Daniel *ophthalmologist, educator*
Patterson, James Randolph *physician*
Prendergast, William John *ophthalmologist*
Raitt, Merritt *cardiologist*
Ravichandran, Pasala Sankaran *cardiologist, thoracic surgeon, educator*
Rayhill, Stephen Corrigan *surgeon*
Robertson, Joseph E., Jr. *ophthalmologist, educator, dean*
Schmidt, Waldemar Adrian *pathologist, educator*
Scott, John D. *pharmacologist*
Shangraw, Robert Edward *medical educator, researcher*
Smith, Dennis B. *neurologist, educator*
Sutherland, Donald Wood *cardiologist*
Swan, Kenneth Carl *surgeon*
Taylor, Robert Brown *physician, educator, writer*
Weleber, Richard Gordon *ophthalmologist, geneticist, medical educator, researcher*
Wilson, William Harwell *psychiatrist, educator*
Zerbe, Kathryn Jane *psychiatrist*

**Roseburg**
Oliphant, Charles Romig *retired physician*

**Wilsonville**
Johnson, Martin Clifton *physician*

# PENNSYLVANIA

**Abington**
Redmond, John *oncologist*

**Allentown**
Barraco, Robert Don *surgeon*
Chang, Chris C.N. *pediatric surgeon*
Gaylor, Donald Hughes *surgeon, educator*

Hess, Leonard Wayne *obstetrician gynecologist, perinatologist*
Maffeo, Alphonse A. *anesthesiologist*
Palumbo, Robert Craig *sports medicine physician, director, not-for-profit developer*
Talsania, Jay S. *orthopedist, surgeon*

**Allison Park**
Dodani, Sunita *physician, educator*
Hollerman, Charles Edward *retired pediatrician*

**Bakerstown**
Beachley, Michael Charles *radiologist*

**Bala Cynwyd**
Kirschner, Ronald Allen *osteopathic plastic surgeon, ophthalmologist, educator*
Masket, Samuel *medical association administrator*
Shore, Eric Eugene *internist, consultant, lawyer*

**Bethlehem**
Bolash, Robert Benjamin *biomedical researcher*
Cole, Jack Eli *physician*

**Blue Bell**
Gorby-Schmidt, Martha Louise *pharmacologist, researcher*

**Bryn Mawr**
Brunt, Manly Yates, Jr. *psychiatrist*
Huth, Edward Janavel *internist, educator, editor*
Levitt, Robert E. *gastroenterologist*
Liu, Hans Hamilton *infectious disease physician, educator*
Noone, R. Barrett *plastic surgeon*
Price, Trevor Robert Pryce *psychiatrist, educator*

**Camp Hill**
Swamidoss, Stephenson *pathologist, health facility administrator*
Tokuhata, George K. *retired medical educator, epidemiologist, consultant*
Yates, James Arthur *plastic surgeon*

**Center Valley**
Risher, William Henry *cardiothoracic surgeon, educator*

**Coatesville**
Ainslie, George William *psychiatrist*
Bell, Robert Lloyd *retired neurosurgeon*
Makous, Norman *retired internist, cardiologist, educator*

**Collegeville**
Shen, Hua-Qiong (Joan) *clinical research director*
Stiles, Gary Lester *cardiologist, molecular pharmacologist, educator*

**Danville**
Bakri, Younes Noaman *surgeon, oncologist, gynecologist*
Blankenship, James Colegrove *cardiologist*
Pierce, James Clarence *surgeon, educator*
Ramdas, Jagadeesh *physician*

**Darby**
Eiser, Arnold Robert *physician executive, bioethicist, nephrologist, internist*

**Devon**
Earley, Laurence Elliott *retired medical educator*

**Dillsburg**
Jackson, George Lyman *retired nuclear medicine physician*

**Dunmore**
Sebastianelli, Mario Joseph *internist, nephrologist, health facility administrator*

**Easton**
Grunberg, Robert Leon Willy *nephrologist, educator*
Reese, Evan Charles, Jr. *orthopedist*

**Elkins Park**
Yun, Daniel Duwhan *physician, foundation administrator*

**Erie**
Brown, Gordon Earl *surgeon, consultant*
Mason, Gregg Claude *orthopedic surgeon, researcher*
Michaelides, Doros Nikita *internist, medical educator*
Parihar, Pradeep Singh *sports medicine physician*

**Etters**
Garloff, Samuel John *psychiatrist*

**Fountainville**
Brown, Madeline Morgan *internist*

**Gaines**
Beller, Martin Leonard *retired orthopaedic surgeon*

**Gibsonia**
Krause, Helen Fox *retired otolaryngologist*

**Gladwyne**
Katz, Julian *gastroenterologist, educator*
Kaye, Donald *internist, educator*
Morrison, Gail *internist, nephrologist, educator*
Pendergrass, Henry Pancoast *radiologist, nuclear medicine physician*
Webber, John Bentley *orthopedic surgeon*

**Glenshaw**
Dombrovski, Alexandre Y. *psychiatrist, researcher*

**Glenside**
Reiss, George Russell, Jr. *physician*

**Harrisburg**
Logue, James Nicholas *epidemiologist*
Rudy, Frank R. *pathologist*

**Haverford**
Aronson, Carl Edward *pharmacology and toxicology educator*
Goppelt, John Walter *physician, psychiatrist*

**Hershey**
Caputo, Gregory Michael *internist, educator*
Cherry, Robert A. *surgeon*
Davis, Dwight *cardiologist, educator*
Eyster, Mary Elaine *hematologist, educator*
Kauffman, Gordon Lee, Jr. *surgeon, educator*
Leaman, David Martin *cardiologist, educator*
Mackay, Donald Roy *plastic surgeon, educator*
Marks, James Garfield, Jr. *dermatologist*
Naeye, Richard L. *pathologist, educator*
Pierce, William Schuler *cardiac surgeon*
Severs, Walter Bruce *pharmacology educator, researcher*
Tan, Tjiauw-Ling *psychiatrist, educator*
Uhde, Thomas Whitley *medical educator*
Vesell, Elliot Saul *pharmacologist, educator*
Waldhausen, John Anton *retired surgeon, retired editor*
Wassner, Steven Joel *pediatric nephrologist, educator*
Zelis, Robert Felix *cardiologist, educator*

**Hollidaysburg**
Cottle, Harold Ranson *pathologist, laboratory executive*
Mariano, Ana Virginia *retired pathologist*

**Jenkintown**
Greenspan-Margolis, June E. *psychiatrist*
Sadoff, Robert Leslie *psychiatrist, educator*

**Kennett Square**
Richardson, Dean Wheeler *equine surgeon, veterinary educator*

**Lancaster**
Brod, Roy David *ophthalmologist, educator*
Burlingame, Mark Wayne *cardiothoracic surgeon*
Kendall, Leigh Wakefield *retired surgeon*

**Lemoyne**
Klein, Michael Elihu *physician*

**Lower Gwynedd**
Pendleton, Robert Grubb *pharmacologist*

**Malvern**
Rucker, Donald W. *emergency physician, educator, consultant*

**Media**
Li, Weiye *ophthalmologist, educator, biochemist*

**Middletown**
Walters, Marian R. *research administrator*

**Monongahela**
Yovanof, Silvana *physician*

**Mount Gretna**
Okamoto, Jeffrey Akira *psychiatrist*

**Narberth**
Strom, Brian Leslie *internist, educator*

**New Hope**
Ecker, Sidney Wolf *urologist, consultant*
Raabe, Gerhard Karl *epidemiologist*

**New Tripoli**
Hess, Darla Bakersmith *cardiologist, educator*

**Newtown**
Somers, Anne Ramsay *retired medical educator*

**Newtown Square**
Cordes, Eugene Harold *retired pharmacy and chemistry educator*
de Rivas, Carmela Foderaro *retired psychiatrist, retired health facility administrator*

**Paoli**
Burget, Dean Edwin, Jr. *plastic surgeon*

**Pennsburg**
Shuhler, Phyllis Marie *physician*

**Philadelphia**
Adetunji, Babatunde Abayomi *forensic psychiatrist*
Allevi, Angela *pediatrician*
Ances, Beau M. *neurologist*
Arce, A. Anthony *psychiatrist, educator*
Asbury, Arthur Knight *neurologist, educator*
Austrian, Robert *internist, medical educator, department chairman*
Baltuch, Gordon Hirsh *neurosurgeon*
Barchi, Robert Lawrence *clinical neurologist, neuroscientist, educator*
Barker, Clyde Frederick *surgeon, educator*
Baserga, Renato Luigi *pathology educator*
Baum, Stanley *radiologist, educator*
Baxt, William Gordon *medical educator*
Beck, Aaron Temkin *psychiatrist, educator*
Beck, John Robert *pathologist, information scientist*
Bibbo, Marluce *physician, educator*
Bilaniuk, Larissa Tetiana *neuroradiologist, educator*
Black, Perry *neurological surgeon, educator*
Blumberg, Baruch Samuel *medical researcher, educator*
Boden, Guenther *endocrinologist*
Bove, Alfred Anthony *medical educator*
Bowman, Marjorie Ann *physician, educator*
Brady, Luther W., Jr. *radiologist, educator*
Brunk, Samuel Frederick *oncologist*
Canning, Douglas Arthur *pediatrician, urologist*
Cassel, Christine Karen *physician*
Cawley, Michael J. *medical educator, pharmacist*
Chen, Lan X. *physician, educator*
Chisum, Melvin J. *retired internist*
Clearfield, Harris Reynold *physician*
Colman, Robert Wolf *hematologist, educator*
Conn, Rex Boland, Jr. *pathologist, educator*

Cooper, Edward Sawyer *cardiologist, internist, educator*
Cooper, Richard Alan *hematologist*
Cotsarelis, George *dermatologist, educator*
Coutifaris, Christos *gynecologist, research scientist*
Criner, Gerard Joseph *pulmonologist, director*
Dalinka, Murray Kenneth *radiologist, educator*
Daly, John M. *surgeon, educator*
d'Amato, Thomas Andrew *thoracic surgeon*
D'Angio, Giulio John *radiologist, educator*
Dasgupta, Indranil *physician, educator*
Davis, Glenn Craig *psychiatrist*
Dichter, Marc Allen *physician*
Dinoso, Vicente Pescador, Jr. *physician, educator*
DiPalma, Joseph Rupert *pharmacology educator, dean*
Djerassi, Isaac *medical researcher*
Douglas, Steven Daniel *immunologist, educator, director*
Dunn, Linda Kay *physician*
Ehrlich, George Edward *rheumatologist, consultant*
Eisen, Howard Joel *internist, researcher*
Feldman, Arthur M. *cardiologist*
Fisher, Robert *gastroenterologist, health facility administrator*
Fishman, Alfred Paul *physician*
FitzGerald, Garret Adare *medical educator*
Frank, Barbara Balis *gastroenterologist, educator*
Friedman, Harvey Michael *infectious diseases educator*
Gaiser, Robert Raymond *obstetric anesthesiologist, educator*
Gandy, Sam *neurologist, neuroscientist, educator*
Gardner, Timothy Joseph *surgeon, educator*
Gartland, John Joseph *physician, writer*
Gavrin, Jonathan Robert *medical educator, internist*
Gerner, Edward William *medical educator*
Glick, Jane Mills *biomedical researcher, educator*
Glick, John H. *oncologist, medical educator*
Goldhamer, David J. *medical educator, researcher*
Gonzalez-Scarano, Francisco Antonio *neurologist, virologist*
Greenstein, Jeffrey Ian *neurologist*
Gueson, Emerita Torres *obstetrician, gynecologist*
Hadjiliadis, Denis *physician*
Hansen-Flaschen, John Hyman *medical educator, researcher*
Horwitz, Eric M. *radiation oncologist*
Hosalkar, Harish Sadanand *pediatrician, orthopedist, surgeon, consultant*
Ischiropoulos, Harry *medical researcher, educator*
Jaffe, Richard Louis *psychiatrist*
Jessup, Mariell *physician, director*
Jiang, Hao *pharmacologist*
Jimenez, Sergio A. *internist, educator, rheumatologist*
Johnson, Joseph Eggleston III *physician, educator*
Jordan, V. Craig *endocrine pharmacologist, educator*
Kaiser, Larry Robert *thoracic surgeon*
Kang, Ju-Seop *medical educator, consultant, medical researcher*
Kauffman, Leon A. *internist, educator*
Kaufman, Russel Eugene *hematologist, oncologist*
Kaye, Edward Michael *physician, neurogeneticist*
Kazazian, Haig Hagop, Jr. *pediatrician, researcher, educator*
Kefalides, Nicholas Alexander *physician, educator*
Kelley, William Nimmons *physician, educator, science administrator, dean*
Kennedy, David William *otolaryngologist, medical educator, medical administrator*
Knudson, Alfred George, Jr. *medical geneticist*
Kresh, J. Yasha *cardiovascular researcher, educator*
Kurian, Kizhake C. *cardiologist, researcher*
Kurtz, Alfred Bernard *radiologist*
Lee, Virginia M. -Y. *medical educator, health science association administrator*
Leventhal, Lawrence Jay *rheumatologist, educator*
Levinson, Arnold Irving *allergist, immunologist*
Levitt, Jerry David *medical educator*
Lewis, Frank Russell, Jr. *surgeon*
Limoges, Richard Frederick *psychiatrist*
Lippa, Carol Frances *neurologist*
Lipshutz, Laurel Sprung *psychiatrist*
Loevner, Laurie Ann *physician, researcher*
Long, Sarah Sundborg *pediatrician, educator*
Lu, Jing *ophthalmologist, researcher*
Lubiniecki, Gregory Michael *physician*
Luo, Jin Jun *neurologist*
Madow, Leo *psychiatrist, educator*
Malkowicz, Stanley Bruce *urologist*
Mancall, Elliott Lee *neurologist, educator*
Marcotte, Paul John *neurosurgeon, educator*
Margo, Katherine Lane *family physician, educator*
Marino, Ignazio Roberto *transplant surgeon, educator, researcher*
Mastroianni, Luigi, Jr. *physician, educator*
Matsumoto, Teruo *surgeon, educator*
Maurer, Alan Harvey *nuclear medicine physician*
Meropol, Neal J. *oncologist, researcher*
Ming, Si-Chun *pathologist, educator*
Morrow, Monica *medical educator*
Nadkarni, Vinay *pediatrician, researcher*
Nash, David Bret *physician*
Naylor, Mary D. *medical professor, director*
Nimoityn, Philip *cardiologist*
Nowell, Peter Carey *pathologist, educator*
O'Malley, Bert William, Jr. *head and neck surgeon, educator, researcher*
Orange, Jordan Scott *immunologist, educator, researcher*
Ozols, Robert F. *oncologist*
Pien, Grace *medical educator*
Pines, Jesse M. *emergency physician, researcher*
Pinto-Martin, Jennifer Anne *epidemiologist, educator*
Platsoucas, Chris Dimitrios *immunologist*
Potsic, William Paul *otolaryngologist, educator*
Reivich, Martin *neurologist, neuroscientist*
Rickels, Karl *psychiatrist, educator*
Ritchie, Wallace Parks, Jr. *retired surgeon, educator*
Rogers, Fred Baker *medical educator*
Rorke-Adams, Lucy Balian *pathologist, educator*
Rosen, Arye *microwave, optoelectronics and medical researcher*

Rubin, Stephen Curtis *gynecologic oncologist, educator*
Russo, Irma Haydee Alvarez de *pathologist*
Saulino, Michael Francis *physiatrist*
Savage, Michael Paul *medicine educator, interventional cardiologist*
Schotland, Donald Lewis *retired medical educator, neurologist*
Schumacher, H(arry) Ralph *internist, rheumatologist, medical educator, researcher*
Schuster, Stephen John *hematologist, oncologist*
Schwartz, Gordon Francis *surgeon, educator*
Schwartz, Marshall Zane *pediatric surgeon*
Segal, Bernard Louis *cardiologist, educator*
Shields, Jerry Allen *ophthalmologist, educator*
Shuman, Charles R. *medical educator, internist*
Silberberg, Donald H. *neurologist*
Smith, David Stuart *anesthesiology educator, physician*
Sox, Harold Carleton, Jr. *physician, educator, editor*
Spaeth, George Link *ophthalmologist, educator, writer*
Spergel, Jonathan Michael *pediatrician, researcher, allergist, immunologist, researcher*
Stallings, Virginia A. *pediatric gastroenterologist*
Stuart, Marie Jean *physician, hematologist, researcher*
Stunkard, Albert James *psychiatrist, educator*
Sudak, Howard Stanley *psychiatrist, educator*
Suh, Byungse *medical educator*
Suzuki, Jon Byron *medical educator, periodontist, microbiologist*
Tannen, Richard Laurence *nephrology educator*
Tasman, William Samuel *ophthalmologist, educator*
Thompson, Craig B. *physician*
Tooker, John Phillip *internist, educator, medical association administrator*
Torg, Joseph Steven *orthopaedic surgeon, educator*
Tourtellotte, Charles Dee *internist, rheumatologist, educator*
Trojanowski, John Q. *medical educator, health facility administrator*
Tüzün, Erdem *neurologist, consultant*
Van Arsdalen, Keith Norman *urologist*
vanBemmelen, Paul S. *surgeon, educator*
Velazquez, Omaida Caridad *vascular surgeon, research scientist*
Vetter, Victoria L. *pediatric cardiologist, educator*
Volgin, Denys V. *medical researcher*
Wein, Alan Jerome *urologist, educator, researcher*
Weiner, Mark Gordon *medical educator*
Weitz, Howard Hy *cardiologist, educator*
Weller, Elizabeth Boghossian *child and adolescent psychiatrist*
Whitaker, Linton Andin *plastic surgeon*
Willi, Steven Matthew *physician, educator, researcher*
Wivel, Nelson Auburn *physician, medical researcher, educator*
Wolfe, John Hall *medical researcher, educator, consultant*
Wu, Hong *pathologist*
Yanoff, Myron *ophthalmologist*
Young, Donald Stirling *clinical pathology educator*
Young, Robert Crabill *medical researcher, science administrator, internist*
Zderic, Stephen Anthony *urologist, surgeon*
Zweiman, Burton *allergist, immunologist, educator*

**Pittsburgh**
Allen, Thomas E. *obstetrician, gynecologist*
Atwood, Charles W., Jr. *pulmonologist, researcher*
Bhatt, Bankim Ashok *endocrinologist, educator*
Brent, David A. *psychiatrist, medical educator*
Busquets, Miguel Antonio *ophthalmologist*
Chang, Thomas S. *radiologist*
Das, Phani Bhushan *thoracic surgeon*
Debski, Richard E. *medical educator*
DeGroat, William Chesney *pharmacology educator*
DeKosky, Steven Trent *neurologist*
Detre, Thomas *psychiatrist, educator*
Dixit, Balwant Narayan *pharmacology and toxicology educator*
Doft, Bernard Harvey *ophthalmologist*
Duquesnoy, Rene J. *medical educator, consultant*
Einhorn, Jerzy *internist, endocrinologist, consultant*
Fernstrom, John Dickson *psychiatry educator, researcher*
Fireman, Philip *pediatrician, allergist, immunologist*
Fisher, Bernard *surgeon, educator*
Fisher, Edwin R. *pathologist*
Fontes, Paulo A. *surgeon, educator*
Friday, Gilbert Anthony, Jr. *pediatrician*
Gennaula, Charles Paul *family practice physician*
Hardesty, Robert Lynch *surgeon, educator*
Heckler, Frederick Roger *plastic surgeon*
Herberman, Ronald Bruce *medical association administrator, immunologist*
Jannetta, Peter Joseph *neurosurgeon, educator*
Jeyabalan, Arundhathi *obstetrician, gynecologist*
Joyner, Claude Reuben, Jr. *cardiologist, educator*
Kane-Gill, Sandra Lucille *medical educator*
Kochanek, Patrick Michael *pediatrician, educator*
Levine, Arthur Samuel *pediatric hematologist, dean, educator, oncologist, researcher*
Levine, Macy Irving *physician*
Levine, T. Barry *cardiologist, educator*
Lowery, John Mason *obstetrician, gynecologist*
Luketich, James D. *thoracic surgeon, educator*
Lunsford, Lawrence Dade *medical educator, department chairman*
Lyjak Chorazy, Anna Julia *pediatrician, educator, retired health facility administrator*
MacLeod, Gordon Kenneth *internist, educator*
Mada, Sripal Reddy *pharmacologist, researcher*
Magovern, James Anthony *thoracic surgeon*
McCafferty, Leo Raymond *plastic surgeon*
McCormick, James Thomas *surgeon, researcher*
Mello-Thoms, Claudia *medical educator, researcher*
Mokotoff, Michael *pharmaceutical sciences educator*
Mosesso, Vincent Nicholas, Jr. *emergency physician, health facility administrator*

Mulsant, Benoit Henri *psychiatrist, educator, medical researcher*
Myers, Eugene Nicholas *otolaryngologist, educator*
Needleman, Herbert Leroy *psychiatrist, pediatrician*
Ness, Roberta *medical educator, researcher, dean*
O'Keefe, Denise Susan *biomedical researcher*
Palevsky, Paul Marc *nephrologist, educator*
Paterson, David Leslie *epidemiologist*
Pollack, Ian Fredric *physician, researcher*
Rogers, Robert Mark *physician*
Roth, Loren H. *psychiatrist*
Sanfilippo, Joseph Salvatore *gynecologic endocrinologist, educator*
Scott, C. Paul *physician, educator*
Sherman, Frederick Scott *pediatric cardiologist*
Siker, Ephraim S. *anesthesiologist*
Simmons, Richard L. *surgeon*
Soffronoff, Pierce *physician*
Squires, Robert H. *pediatrician, educator*
Srivastava, Sanjay K. *medical researcher*
Strick, Peter Leonard *psychiatrist, neurologist, educator*
Vogel, Victor Gerald *medical educator, researcher*
Wald, Niel *public health educator*
Watters, Edmond Clair *ophthalmologist, educator*
Winter, Peter Michael *anesthesiologist, educator*
Wu, Xianren *anesthesiologist, researcher*
Yellon, Robert Forrest *surgeon, medical educator*

**Plymouth Meeting**
Nobel, Joel J. *biomedical researcher*

**Reading**
Lusch, Charles Jack *oncologist*
Pumariega, Andres Julio *medical educator, researcher*

**Rydal**
Johnson, Waine Cecil *dermatologist, educator*

**Sayre**
Moody, Robert Adams *neurosurgeon*

**Somerset**
Nair, Velupillai Krishnan *cardiologist*

**Southampton**
Goldstein, Scott M. *ophthalmologist, surgeon*

**Springfield**
Mirman, Merrill Jay *physician, surgeon*

**State College**
Wilson, Keith B. *rehabilitation educator*

**Strasburg**
Morton, D. Holmes *physician*

**Sugarloaf**
Waldron, Theodore Charles *physician*

**Susquehanna**
Purkayastha, Arindam *surgeon*

**Swarthmore**
Carey, William Bacon *pediatrician, educator*

**Temple**
Denaro, Anthony Thomas *psychiatrist*

**Thorndale**
Hodess, Arthur Bart *cardiologist*

**University Park**
Stern, Robert Morris *gastroenterologist, psychologist, researcher*

**Upper Saint Clair**
Raymond, Bruce Allen *medical association administrator*

**Wayne**
Lief, Harold Isaiah *psychiatrist*

**Waynesboro**
Cryer, Theodore Hudson *ophthalmologist, educator*

**West Conshohocken**
Templeton, John Marks, Jr. *retired pediatric surgeon, foundation administrator*

**West Grove**
Snow, James Byron, Jr. *otolaryngologist, research administrator, educator*

**Wilkes Barre**
Casale, Alfred Stanley *thoracic and cardiovascular surgeon*

**Williamsport**
Martin, Thomas John *pediatrician, sports medicine physician*

**Wyndmoor**
Brown, Gary Christian *ophthalmologist, director*

**Wynnewood**
Alter, Milton *retired neurologist*
Dunton, Charles Joseph *gynecologist, oncologist*
Frankl, William Stewart *cardiologist, educator*
Kenton, Edgar Jackson III *neurologist*
Kowey, Peter R. *medical educator*
Marks, Gerald *surgeon, educator*
Rosefsky, Jonathan Benensohn *pediatrician*
Samuels, Louis Edward *cardiothoracic surgeon*

**Wyomissing**
Hildreth, Eugene A. *physician, educator*

**Yardley**
Fraser, David William *epidemiologist*
Newsom, John Harlan *physician*

**York**
Rhoads, Jonathan Evans, Jr. *surgeon, medical educator*

## RHODE ISLAND

### Barrington
Carpenter, Charles Colcock Jones *internist, educator*

### Little Compton
Small, Wilfred Thomas *surgeon, educator*

### Newport
Rous, Stephen Norman *urologist, educator*

### North Kingstown
Jarvis, William David *pharmacologist, researcher*

### Pawtucket
Bertini, Richard G. *orthopedist*
Chopra, Pradeep *physician, educator*
Glicksman, Arvin S(igmund) *radiation oncologist*

### Providence
Amaral, Joseph Ferreira *surgeon*
Aronson, Stanley Maynard *physician, educator*
Besdine, Richard William *medical educator, researcher*
Biron, Christine Anne *medical science educator, researcher*
Blazar, Andrew S. *reproductive endocrinologist*
Block, Stanley Hoyt *pediatrician, allergist*
Degroot, Leslie Jacob *medical educator*
Dill, Sara Worthing *dermatologist*
Donahue, John Edward *physician*
Easton, J(ohn) Donald *neurologist, educator*
Estrup, Faiza Fawaz *physician, educator*
Francis, Warren William *retired surgeon, educator*
Gilchrist, James Manning *neurologist, researcher, educator*
Gilmore, Judith Marie *physician*
Guggenheim, Frederick Gibson *psychiatrist, educator*
Jenny, Carole *physician, researcher*
Kane, Agnes Brezak *pathologist, educator*
Knopf, Paul Mark *immunologist*
Kramer, Peter David *psychiatrist, psychology professor*
LaFrance, William Curt Phillip, Jr. *neuropsychiatrist, educator, medical researcher*
Lewis, David Carleton *medical educator, academic administrator*
Mc Donald, Charles J. *dermatologist, educator*
Oh, William *physician*
Pueschel, Siegfried M. *pediatrician, educator*
Rhodes, Ramona Lagiers *medical educator, researcher*
Tucci, Joseph Ralph *endocrinologist, educator*
Vezeridis, Michael Panagiotis *surgeon, educator*
Wanebo, Harold J. *surgeon, educator*
Weitberg, Alan Barry *physician, researcher*
Wells, Alan Hilary *biomedical researcher*
Withey, Gary David *biomedical researcher*

### Riverside
Lekas, Mary Despina *retired otolaryngologist*

## SOUTH CAROLINA

### Aiken
Bransome, Edwin Dagobert, Jr. *internal medicine educator*

### Anderson
Chipman, Dennis Clarence, Jr. *forensic psychiatrist, consultant*

### Charleston
Austin, Linda S. *psychiatrist*
Bell, Norman Howard *endocrinologist, educator*
Bowman, C. Michael *physician*
Chiaramida, Salvatore *cardiologist, educator, health facility administrator*
Crawford, Fred Allen, Jr. *cardiothoracic surgeon, educator*
Daniell, Herman Burch *pharmacologist*
Diaz, Vanessa Astrud *medical educator*
Dobson, Richard Lawrence *dermatologist, educator*
Finn, Albert Frank, Jr. *physician*
Garr, David Ross *physician, educator*
Glassman, Armand Barry *physician, educator, pathologist*
Hoffman, Brenda Joyce *gastroenterology educator*
Jaffa, Ayad A. *medical educator, medical researcher*
Jaffe, Murray Sherwood *retired surgeon*
Khan, Mushfiquddin *neuropharmacologist, researcher*
Kraveka, Jacqueline Maria *pediatrician, oncologist*
Lazarchick, John *hematologist, educator*
Margolius, Harry Stephen *pharmacologist, physician*
Maria, Bernard L. *pediatric neurologist*
McCurdy, Layton *medical educator*
Mohr, Lawrence Charles *physician*
Oldham, John Michael *physician, psychiatrist, educator*
Osguthorpe, John David *otolaryngologist, educator*
Othersen, Henry Biemann, Jr. *surgeon, physician, educator*
Reves, Joseph Gerald (Jerry Reves) *anesthesiology educator, dean*
Rustin, Rudolph Byrd III *surgeon, educator*
Schoepf, U. Joseph *radiologist*
Simpson, William M., Jr. *family medicine educator*
Stuart, Robert Kenneth *internist, hematologist, oncologist, educator*
Underwood, Paul Benjamin *gynecologist, oncologist, educator*
Waller, John Louis *anesthesiologist, educator*
Wilson, Frederick Allen *gastroenterologist, educator, health facility administrator, medical educator*

### Columbia
Almond, Carl Herman *surgeon, physician, educator*
Barrett, O'Neill, Jr. *medical educator*
Brannon, William Lester, Jr. *neurologist, educator*
Brooker, Jeff Zeigler *cardiologist*

Dantzler, Malcolm Ulrich *retired physician*
da Silva, Ercio Mario *physician*
Derrick, C. Warren, Jr. *medical educator*
Donald, Alexander Grant *psychiatrist, educator*
Flanagan, Clyde Harvey, Jr. *psychiatrist, psychoanalyst, educator*
Gaffney, Thomas Edward *physician*
Horger, Edgar Olin III *retired obstetrics and gynecology educator*
Humphries, John O'Neal *cardiologist, dean*
Lounsbury, Dave Edmond *retired medical educator, retired military officer*
Sheppe, Joseph Andrew *surgeon*
Shmunes, Edward *dermatologist*
Still, Charles Neal *retired neurologist, medical educator, consultant*
Tripathi, Ramesh Chandra *ophthalmologist, researcher, educator*
Wright, Harry Hercules *psychiatrist*

### Conway
Delia, Claude William *retired physician, pathologist*
McMillan, Michael Reid *retired orthopedic surgeon*

### Daniel Island
McConnell, III, Bright *orthopaedic surgeon*

### Florence
Agnew, Samuel Gerard *orthopaedic traumatologist*
DeMichele, Domenic John *neurologist, neuroradiologist*
Imbeau, Stephen Alan *allergist*

### Greenville
Bonner, Jack Wilbur III *psychiatrist, educator, administrator*
Kilgore, Donald Gibson, Jr. *pathologist*

### Hilton Head Island
Birk, Robert Eugene *retired internist*
Brennan, John Thomas *surgeon*
Duvall, Charles Patton *internist, retired oncologist*
Engelman, Karl *physician*
Field, James Bernard *internist, educator*
Hewes, Robert Charles *radiologist*
Jarvis, William Robert *epidemiologist, educator*
Lattimer, Gary Lee *physician*
Roehrig, C(harles) Burns *internist, consultant*

### Inman
Fogarty, Charles Michael *pulmonologist, researcher*

### Isle Of Palms
Elliott, Larry Paul *radiologist, educator*
Wohltmann, Hulda Justine *pediatrician, endocrinologist*

### Mount Pleasant
Maize, John Christopher *dermatologist, educator*

### Myrtle Beach
Schwartz, Steve Wendelin *physician*

### Orangeburg
Smoak, Randolph Duncan, Jr. *surgeon*

### Rembert
Wangensteen, Stephen Lightner *surgery educator*

### Seneca
Uden, David Elliott *cardiologist, educator*

### Spartanburg
Hodge, Gameel Byron *retired surgeon*
Parmley, Richard Turner *pediatric hematologist, oncologist*

### Sullivans Island
Selby, John Bayne, Sr. *retired radiologist, medical educator*

### Surfside Beach
Favaro, Mary Kaye Asperheim *pediatrician, writer*

### West Columbia
Klutzow, Friedrich Wilhelm *neuropathologist*
Phillips, Karen Diane *surgeon*

## SOUTH DAKOTA

### Aberdeen
Gruca, Pawel Piotr *neuroradiologist*

### Sioux Falls
Fenton, Lawrence Jules *medical educator*
Gregg, John Bailey *surgery educator, researcher*
Jaqua, Richard Allen *pathologist*
Richards, George Alvarez *psychiatrist, educator*
Zawada, Edward Thaddeus, Jr. *physician, educator*

## TENNESSEE

### Chattanooga
Campbell, William O'Neal *retired physician*
Enriquez, Manuel Hipolito *physician*
Marshall, Willis Henry *psychiatrist*
Shuck, Edwin Haywood III *surgeon*

### Cookeville
Smolenski, Lisabeth Ann *physician*

### Fayetteville
Ralston, Joseph Frederick, Jr. *internist*

### Franklin
Moessner, Harold Frederick *allergist*

### Germantown
Lieberman, Phillip Louis *allergist, educator*
Mowry, Robert Wilbur *pathologist, educator*

### Gray
Combs, Stephen Paul *pediatrician, health facility administrator*

### Hendersonville
Burt, Alvin Miller III *anatomist, educator, cell biologist, writer*

### Hermitage
Rosdeutscher, John David *plastic surgeon*

### Hixson
Segler, Christopher Paige *surgeon, researcher*

### Jackson
Kamso-Pratt, Jimmy Michael *physician, administrator*
Swaim, Mark Wendell *physician, molecular biologist, gastroenterologist, photographer*

### Jefferson City
Muncy, Estle Pershing *physician*

### Johnson City
Coogan, Philip Shields *pathologist*
Giorgadze, Tamar Alfred *pathologist, physician*
Hamdy, Ronald Charles *geriatrician*
Kao, Race Li-Chan *medical educator*
Olsen, Martin E. *obstetrician, educator*

### Knoxville
Dudrick, Paul Stanley *oncologist, surgeon, educator*
Filston, Howard Church *pediatric surgeon*
Graber, Glenn C. *medical educator, educational consultant*
Kliefoth, A. Bernhard III *neurosurgeon*

### Maryville
Howard, Cecil Byron *pediatrician*

### Memphis
Allen, David Mark *psychiatrist, educator, director*
Amonette, Rex. A. *physician*
Anghelescu, Doralina Lucia *anesthesiologist*
Bhattacharya, Syamal Kanti *biomedical scientist, educator*
Carratù, Pierluigi *pulmonologist, researcher*
Chesney, Russell Wallace *pediatrician*
Cox, Clair Edward, II, *urologist, medical educator*
Currey, Thomas Arthur *ophthalmologist*
Dickerson, Roland Nelson *pharmacy educator*
Frey, William Rayburn *healthcare educator, consultant*
Gerald, Barry *retired radiology educator, neuroscientist*
Heimberg, Murray *pharmacologist, biochemist, physician*
Helton, Kathleen Jacobson *neuroradiologist*
Herrod, Henry Grady III *pediatrics professor, allergist, immunologist*
Hughes, Walter Thompson *pediatrician, educator*
Hunt, James Calvin *physician, academic administrator*
Kitabchi, Abbas Eqbal *medical educator*
Korones, Sheldon Bernarr *pediatrician, educator*
Lazar, Rande Harris *otolaryngologist*
Lipscomb, Gary Heston *obstetrician, gynecologist, academic administrator*
Luce, Edward Andrew *plastic surgeon*
Mansbach, Charles *gastroenterologist, researcher*
Mauer, Alvin Marx *pediatrician, educator*
Morreim, E. Haavi *medical ethics educator*
Nienhuis, Arthur Wesley *physician, researcher*
Razzouk, Bassem Ibrahim *hematologist, oncologist*
Riely, Caroline Armistead *gastroenterologist, educator*
Robertson, James Thomas *neurosurgeon*
Shochat, Stephen Jay *pediatrician, surgeon*
Stidham, Gregory L. *pediatrician, educator*
Van Middlesworth, Lester *physiology, biophysics and medicine educator, internist*
Waller, Robert Rex *ophthalmologist, educator, foundation administrator*
Wheless, James Warren *neurologist*
Wilcox, Harry Hammond *retired anatomist*

### Murfreesboro
Coleman, Jack Andrew, Jr. *otolaryngologist*

### Nashville
Allen, George Sewell *neurosurgery educator*
Allison, Fred, Jr. *internist, retired medical educator*
Arteaga, Carlos L. *medical researcher, director*
Baldwin, Harold Scott *pediatrician, educator*
Bates, George William *obstetrician, gynecologist, educator*
Bernard, Louis Joseph *surgeon, educator*
Brill, Aaron Bertrand *nuclear medicine educator*
Brown, Wendy Weinstock *nephrologist, educator*
Burnett, Lonnie Sheldon *obstetrics and gynecology educator*
Carroll, Frank Edward, Jr. *radiologist, medical researcher*
Chang, Sam S. *urologist, surgeon, educator*
Chari, Ravi S. *surgeon*
Davis, Stephen N. *endocrinologist*
DeHart, Roy Lynch *physician, educator*
Dimitri, Elia Charles *retired medical educator*
Dmochowski, Roger *urologist, educator*
DuBois, Raymond N. *medical educator, researcher*
Epps, Anna Cherrie *immunologist, educator, dean*
Etherington, Carol A. *medical association administrator*
Fazio, Sergio *medical educator, researcher*
Fields, James Perry *dermatologist, dermatopathologist, allergist, pharmacologist, pharmacist*
Fleischer, Arthur C. *medical educator, radiologist*
Gallagher, Martin Joseph *neurologist, neuroscientist*
Gorden, David Lee *surgeon, educator*
Griffin, Patti Elaine *medical educator, consultant*
Hays, Stephen Robert *pediatrician*
Ikizler, Talat Alp *medical educator*
Jarquin Valdivia, Adrian Alberto *neurologist, researcher*
Jennings, Henry Smith III *cardiologist*
Johnson, David *medical association administrator*

### Kallianpur, Asha R. *epidemiologist*
Kizilisik, Aydin Tarik *surgeon, researcher*
Lawton, Alexander Robert *immunologist, educator*
Lee, Donald Han *surgeon, orthopedist*
Lynch, John Brown *plastic surgeon, educator*
Marney, Samuel Rowe, Jr. *allergist, immunologist, educator*
Martin, Peter Robert *psychiatrist, pharmacologist*
Masys, Daniel Richard *medical educator, department chairman*
Mawn, Louise Ann *ophthalmologist, educator*
May, James M. *medical educator, researcher*
Morrow, Jason Drew *pharmacologist, educator*
Moses, Harold L. *oncologist*
Neilson, Eric Grant *physician, educator, health facility administrator*
Oates, John Alexander III *medical educator*
O'Neill, James Anthony, Jr. *pediatric surgeon, educator*
Ossoff, Robert Henry *otolaryngologist, surgeon*
Partain, Clarence Leon *radiologist, nuclear medicine physician, educator, health facility administrator*
Petrie, William Marshall *psychiatrist*
Pinson, Charles Wright *surgeon, educator, academic administrator*
Polk, David Brent *pediatrician, educator*
Ramsey, Lloyd Hamilton *medical educator*
Robertson, David *neurologist, educator*
Ross, Joseph Comer *pulmonologist, educator, academic administrator*
Rothman, Russell L. *medical educator*
Shack, R. Bruce *plastic surgeon*
Smith, Bradley E. *anesthesiologist*
Spengler, Dan Michael *orthopedic surgery educator, surgeon*
Stahlman, Mildred Thornton *pediatrician, pathologist, educator, medical researcher*
Stead, William Wallace *medical educator, researcher, department chairman*
Sternberg, Paul *ophthalmologist, researcher*
Thornton, Spencer P. *ophthalmologist, educator*
Torquati, Alfonso *surgeon, educator*
Wasserman, David H. *medical educator, researcher*
Yang, Edmund Yi-Bin *biomedical researcher, pediatric surgeon*

### Oak Ridge
Spray, Paul Ellsworth *retired surgeon*

### Ooltewah
Birch, Lorna May *geriatrician*

### Signal Mountain
Swann, Nat Henderson, Jr. *physician*

### Springfield
Kroser, Jonathan Mark *surgeon*

### Williamsport
Dysinger, Paul William *preventive medicine physician, educator*

### Winchester
Miller, Monte Baldwin *retired internist*

## TEXAS

### Abilene
Morgan, Clyde Nathaniel *dermatologist*

### Amarillo
Laur, William Edward *retired dermatologist*
Marupudi, Sambasiva Rao *surgeon, educator*
Parker, Gerald M. *osteopath, researcher*
Parker, Lynda Michele *psychiatrist*
Pratt, Donald George *physician*
Saadeh, Constantine Khalil *internist, medical educator, health facility administrator*
Siddiqui, Afzal A. *medical educator*

### Arlington
Adams, Quentin Mark *neurologist*
Tingley, Floyd Warren *retired internist*

### Austin
Bernstein, Robert *retired physician, federal official, retired military officer*
Buell, Walter F. *neurologist*
Elequin, Cleto, Jr. *retired physician*
Ersek, Robert Allen *plastic surgeon*
Fleeger, David Clark *colon and rectal surgeon*
George, Timothy Merrill *neurosurgeon, educator*
Ivy, John L. *medical educator, researcher*
Martin, Frederick Noel *audiology educator*
Neavel, Celia Beth *medical association administrator*
Painter, Theophilus Shickel, Jr. *internist, allergist*
Sawyer, William Dale *internist, educator, dean, foundation administrator*
Schleuse, William *retired psychiatrist, psychoanalyst*
Sutton, Beverly Jewell *psychiatrist*

### Baytown
Williams, Drew Davis *surgeon*

### Beaumont
Lozano, Jose *nephrologist*
Sooudi, Matthew M. *retired surgeon*

### Bellaire
Haywood, Theodore Joseph *physician, educator*
Pokorny, Alex Daniel *psychiatrist*

### Boerne
Wittmer, James Frederick *preventive medicine physician, educator*

### Brownsville
Imperial, Henry L. *internist*
Walss, Rodolfo J. *obstetrician, gynecologist, artist*

### Bryan
Anderson, Frank Gist, Jr. *ophthalmologist, educator*
Dirks, Kenneth Ray *medical educator, army officer*

## Canyon Lake
Williams, Thomas Eugene *pediatric hematologist, pediatric oncologist, pharmaceutical executive*

## Carrollton
Kelly, Ralph Whitley *emergency physician, health facility administrator*

## College Station
Carlton, Paul Kendall, Jr. *physician*
Kier, Ann B. Burnette *pathology educator*
Wenger, Scott Andrew *orthopedist, surgeon*

## Corpus Christi
Blankenship, Billy Jim *surgeon*
Cook, Kenneth Ray *radiologist*
Cox, William Andrew *cardiovascular thoracic surgeon*
Gentile, Hervé F. *plastic surgeon*
Kylstra, Johannes Arnold *physician*
Lim, Alexander Rufasta *neurologist, clinical investigator, clinical neurophysiologist, educator, writer*
Rutherford, Robert Barry *vascular surgeon*
Sisley, Nina Mae *physician, public health service officer*

## Dallas
Allen, Terry Devereux *retired urologist*
Azam, Anwar *cardiologist*
Beard, Bruce H. *retired psychiatrist*
Bergstresser, Paul Richard *dermatologist, educator*
Berry, Phil Hunter, Jr. *orthopedic surgeon*
Bick, Rodger Lee *hematologist, researcher, oncologist, educator*
Bonte, Frederick James *radiologist, educator, physician*
Boswell, George Marion, Jr. *orthopedist, health facility administrator*
Bowers, Daniel Charles *oncologist*
Brilakis, Emmanouil S. *cardiologist, educator*
Burns, Alton Jay *plastic surgeon*
Byrd, Henry Stephenson (Steve) *plastic surgeon, educator*
Caetano, Raul *psychiatrist, educator*
Cavanagh, Harrison Dwight *ophthalmologist, educator*
Choy, Hak *oncologist*
Cloud, Robert Royce *surgeon*
Cox, Rody P(owell) *internist, educator*
Eichenwald, Heinz Felix *physician*
Einspruch, Burton Cyril *psychiatrist*
Flatt, Adrian Ede *surgeon*
Fordtran, John Satterfield *physician*
Foster, Daniel Willett *medical educator*
Frenkel, Eugene Phillip *physician*
Fyfe, Alistair Ian *cardiologist, scientist, educator*
Gant, Norman Ferrell, Jr. *obstetrician, gynecologist, educator*
Gibby, Diane Louise *physician, plastic surgeon*
Gilman, Alfred Goodman *pharmacologist, educator*
Glick, Gina Phillips Moran *retired physician*
Grammer, John Colquitte *cardiologist*
Griffeth, Landis King *nuclear medicine physician*
Gross, Gary Neil *allergist, physician*
Gupta, Sachin *medical educator, physician*
Hamas, Robert Steven *plastic surgeon*
Hobbs, Helen Haskell *medical geneticist*
Holman, James *allergist*
Hurd, Eric Ray *rheumatologist, internist, educator*
Johnson, Robert Lee, Jr. *physician, educator, researcher*
Kaiser, Fran Elizabeth *endocrinologist, gerontologist*
Lewis, Jerry M. *psychiatrist, educator*
Lichliter, Warren Eugene *surgeon, educator*
Lister, George *pediatrician*
Maddrey, Willis Crocker *medical educator, internist, academic administrator, consultant, researcher*
Margolin, Solomon Begelfor *pharmacologist, consultant*
Marks, James Frederic *pediatric endocrinologist, educator*
Martin, Jack *physician*
Mayer, Tom G. *orthopedist, researcher*
Mc Clelland, Robert Nelson *surgeon, educator*
McCulley, James Parker *ophthalmologist, educator*
Mitchell, Teddy Lee *physician*
Mohl, Paul Cecil *psychiatrist, educator*
Mullins, Charles Brown *physician, academic administrator*
Nemunaitis, John J. *oncologist, medical association administrator*
Nestler, Eric J. *psychiatrist, researcher*
Nikaidoh, Hisashi *pediatric cardiac surgeon, professor*
North, Richard Ralph *neurologist*
Odom, Floyd Clark *surgeon*
Pownell, Patrick H. *plastic surgeon*
Roberts, William Clifford *medical association administrator*
Robertson, Rose Marie *cardiologist, educator*
Rohrich, Rodney James (Rod) *plastic surgeon, educator*
Rosenberg, Roger Newman *neurologist, educator, department chair*
Rush, Augustus John *psychiatrist, educator*
Saadeh, Sherif Nabil *gastroenterologist, hepatologist, researcher*
Sacco, David J. *neurosurgeon*
Salyer, Kenneth E. *surgeon*
Shapiro, Kenneth N. *neurosurgeon*
Sklar, Frederick H. *neurosurgeon*
Smith, Barry Samuel *physiatrist*
Stone, Marvin Jules *hematologist, oncologist, educator*
Suter, Robert Eduard *emergency physician, educator*
Swift, Dale Matthew *neurosurgeon*
Thiele, Dwain Louis *medical educator, department chairman*
Thompson, James Nicholas *medical association administrator*
Thompson, Jesse Eldon *vascular surgeon*
Uhr, Jonathan William *immunologist, educator, researcher*
Valentine, Rawson James *surgeon, educator*
Vernino, Steven *neurologist, researcher*
Waddell, Douglas Howard *family physician*

Wasserman, Richard Lawrence *pediatrician, educator*
Weprin, Bradley *neurosurgeon*
Wildenthal, C(laud) Kern *physician, educator*
Wilson, Jean Donald *endocrinologist, educator*
Wolfe, Gil I. *neurologist*

## El Paso
Hanbali, Fadi *neurosurgeon, educator*
Harlass, Frederick E. *obstetrician, gynecologist*
Magana, Jorge Carlos *pediatrician*
Morton, David Richard Dunlap *physician*
Taber, David O. *urological surgeon*
Williams, Darryl Marlowe *medical educator*
Zaloznik, Arlene Joyce *retired oncologist, retired military officer*

## Fort Sam Houston
Adams, Bruce Douglas *physician, researcher*
Hewitson, William Craig *physician, career officer*
Kragh, John Frederick, Jr. *orthopedist, educator*

## Fort Worth
Bailey, Susan Rudd *physician*
Black, Timothy Lee *physician*
Cottner, Donald *pathologist*
Cox, James Sidney *physician*
Gillette, Paul Crawford *pediatric cardiologist*
Hahn, Marc B. *physician, dean*
Hernandez, Angel W. *pediatric neurologist, epileptologist*
Lamensdorf, Hugh *urologist, educator*
Schussler, Irwin *psychiatrist, educator*
Tobey, Martin Alan *cardiologist*
Willard, Ralph Lawrence *surgeon, educator, physician, retired academic administrator*
Yanni, John Michael *pharmacologist*

## Frisco
Gajraj, Noor *anesthesiologist, educator*

## Galveston
Amador, Luis F. *medical educator*
Brown, Paul Sherman, Jr. *surgeon*
Burns, Chester Ray *retired medical educator*
Camacho, Maria E. *geriatrician, educator*
Dawson, Earl Bliss *medical educator*
Ernst, Randy *radiologist*
Essex, Francis Xavier *physician, educator*
Ferrando, Arny Anthony *medical researcher*
Gold, Daniel Howard *ophthalmologist, educator*
Goodwin, Jean McClung *psychiatrist*
Gwak, Young Seob *biomedical researcher*
Hawkins, Hal K(enneth) *pathologist*
James, Thomas Naum *cardiologist, educator*
Keeney, Susan E. *pediatrician, educator*
Klein, Gordon Leslie *pediatrician, educator*
Lin, Qing *medical educator*
Neugebauer, Volker Egdar *biomedical scientist, neuroscientist*
Nguyen-Oghalai, Tracy Uyentrang *medical educator, researcher*
Sandstead, Harold Hilton *physician, researcher, educator, director*
Smith, David English *pathologist, educator*
Tesh, Robert Bradfield *epidemiologist, educator*
Townsend, Courtney M. *surgeon*
Tyson, Kenneth Robert Thomas *surgeon, educator*
Vedernikov, Yuri P. *pharmacologist, educator*
White, Robert Brown *medical educator*
Yngve, David A. *orthopedist, surgeon*

## Garland
Haynsworth, Robert Francis, Jr. *anesthesiologist*

## Georgetown
Manning, Robert Thomas *internist, educator*
Schofield, James Roy *medical consultant, educator*

## Harlingen
Klein, Garner Franklin *cardiologist, internist*

## Houston
Agris, Joseph *plastic surgeon*
Alexanian, Raymond *hematologist*
Alford, Bobby Ray *otolaryngologist, educator, academic administrator*
Allen, Steven Jeffrey *anesthesiologist, educator*
Anderson, Peter Meade *pediatrician, oncologist*
Appel, Stanley Hersh *neurologist, educator*
Ayus, Juan Carlos *nephrologist*
Azizzadeh, Ali *surgeon, educator*
Babiera, Gildy V. *surgical oncologist, educator*
Bailey, Harold Randolph *surgeon, educator*
Ballo, Matthew T. *radiation oncologist, educator*
Barcenas, Camilo Gustavo *physician*
Barrett, Bernard Morris, Jr. *plastic and reconstructive surgeon*
Bast, Robert Clinton, Jr. *medical researcher*
Batsakis, John George *pathology educator*
Baumgartner, James Edumnd *pediatric neurosurgeon*
Beaudet, Arthur L. *medical genetics researcher*
Bethea, Louise Huffman *allergist*
Bodey, Gerald Paul *retired medical educator*
Boutros, Sean *plastic surgeon*
Brody, Baruch Alter *medical educator, academic administrator*
Buja, L. Maximilian *pathologist, academic administrator, educator*
Bungo, Michael William *cardiologist, educator, science administrator*
Burzynski, Stanislaw Rajmund *internist*
Buster, John Edmond *obstetrician, medical researcher*
Cacayorin, Edwin D. *medical association administrator, neurologist*
Cash, Camille Geneva *physician*
Catlin, Francis Irving *physician*
Chang, Chung-Che *hematopathologist, medical researcher, medical educator*
Chen, Hua *medical educator, researcher*
Cherek, Don R. *psychiatrist, educator*
Cheung, Min Rex *medical educator*
Chevray, Pierre M. *medical educator*
Chiou-Tan, Faye *physician*
Clifton, Guy L. *neurosurgeon, educator*
Cooley, Denton Arthur *surgeon, educator*
Couch, Robert Barnard *physician, medical researcher, educator, microbiologist, immunologist*

Coverdale, John Howard *psychiatrist*
Cox, James D. *radiologist*
Demmler, Gail Josephine *medical educator*
Deter, Russell Lee, II, *obstetrical ultrasonographer*
Diaz, Eduardo Manuel, Jr. *surgeon, educator*
Dodd, Gerald Dewey, Jr. *radiologist, educator*
Doubleday, Charles William *dermatologist, educator*
Drutz, Jan Edwin *pediatrics educator*
DuPont, Herbert Lancashire *medical educator, researcher*
Eisner, Diana *pediatrician*
Eng, Cathy *oncologist, educator*
Engelhardt, Hugo Tristram, Jr. *physician, educator*
Ertan, Atilla *medical educator, physician, researcher, health facility administrator*
Estey, Elihu Harris *medical educator*
Evans, Harry Launius *pathology educator*
Feigon, Judith Tova *ophthalmologist, educator, surgeon*
Fischer, Craig Leland *physician*
Fishman, Marvin Allen *pediatric neurologist, educator*
Fornage, Bruno Denis *radiologist, educator*
Freireich, Emil J. *hematologist, educator*
Friedman, Paul M. *dermatologist*
Frumovitz, Michael *oncologist*
Fu, Siqing *medical educator*
Gabbard, Glen Owens *psychiatrist, psychotherapist*
Gardezi, Syed A. *medical researcher*
Gigli, Irma *dermatologist, educator, academic administrator*
Gilbert, Mark R. *medical educator*
Giles, Francis J. *medical educator*
Goldman, Stanford Milton *medical educator*
Gorry, G. Anthony *medical educator*
Gould, Kenneth Lance *cardiologist, researcher, educator*
Graham, David Yates *gastroenterologist*
Graves, Daniel Edward *medical association administrator, researcher*
Grigore, Alina M. *anesthesiologist*
Grossman, Herbert Barton *urologist, researcher*
Grossman, Robert George *neurosurgeon, department chairman*
Gunn, Albert Edward, Jr. *internist, educator, health facility administrator, lawyer*
Gupta, Monesha *pediatrician, educator*
Guynn, Robert William *psychiatrist, educator*
Hall, Robert Joseph *internist, educator*
Hamill, Marshall Bowes *medical educator*
Hamilton, Carlos Robert, Jr. *endocrinologist, consultant, academic administrator*
Haynie, Thomas Powell III *physician*
Hong, Waun Ki *oncologist, researcher*
Hsu, Sylvia *dermatologist, educator*
Hunter, Robert Paul *pharmacologist*
Jankovic, Joseph *neurologist, educator*
Jemison, Mae Carol *physician, engineer, entrepreneur, philanthropist, former astronaut*
Jhingran, Anuja *oncologist, educator*
Johnson, Marilyn *retired obstetrician, retired gynecologist*
Jones, Edith Irby *internist*
Jordan, Paul Howard, Jr. *surgeon, educator*
Jordon, Robert Earl *physician*
Kahan, Barry Donald *surgeon, educator*
Kaufman, Raymond Henry *retired physician, retired educator*
Kearns, Richard J. *surgeon, educator*
Key, James Everett *ophthalmologist*
Kimyai-Asadi, Arash *surgeon*
Klein, Nora J. *pediatrician*
Kline, Mark Wendel *pediatric medicine educator*
Komaki Cox, Ritsuko U. *medical educator*
Kosten, Thomas R. *psychiatrist, educator*
Kraft, Irvin Alan *psychiatrist*
Lanza, Frank Leo *gastroenterologist, researcher*
Levin, Bernard *physician*
Levin, Victor A. *neurologist, oncologist, educator*
Lin, Peter H. *surgeon, researcher*
Liu, Jing *pathologist, educator*
Liu, Jinsong *pathologist*
Max, Ernest *surgeon*
Mayor, Heather Donald *molecular biology educator*
McPherson, Alice Ruth *ophthalmologist, educator*
Mendelsohn, John *oncologist, hematologist, educator, health facility executive*
Mentz, Henry A. III *plastic surgeon*
Milam, John Daniel *pathologist, educator*
Miller, Gary Evan *psychiatrist, mental health services professional*
Miller, Robert Harold *otolaryngologist, educator*
Mintz-Hittner, Helen Ann *physician, researcher*
Moody, Frank G. *surgeon*
Murad, Ferid *physician*
Murphy, William Alexander, Jr. *diagnostic radiologist, educator*
Nosé, Yukihiko *surgeon, educator*
Oh, Yun *oncologist*
Orengo-Nania, Silvia *ophthalmologist*
Ostrosky-Zeichner, Luis *epidemiologist, educator, physician*
Phung, Nguyen Dinh *medical educator*
Powers, William Edward *emergency physician, medical educator, surgeon*
Quiros-Tejeira, Ruben Eloy *pediatrician, educator*
Raijman, Isaac *gastroenterologist, educator*
Rakel, Robert Edwin *physician, educator*
Rapini, Ronald Peter *dermatology educator*
Rappaport, Norman Harvey *plastic surgeon*
Rassidakis, George Z. *pathologist, researcher*
Reece, Gregory Paul *plastic surgeon, educator*
Ribble, John Charles *medical educator*
Riley, William John *neurologist*
Risin, Semyon Aaron *pathologist, medical educator*
Robb, Geoffrey Lawrence *plastic surgeon*
Ross, Patti Jayne *obstetrics and gynecology educator*
Rudolph, Andrew Henry *dermatologist, educator*
Ruiz, Pedro *psychiatrist*
Saathoff, Myra Kathleen *orthoptist*
Sanderson, Mary Louise *medical association administrator*
Sargent, John *psychiatrist*
Sazama, Kathleen *pathologist, lawyer*

Scharold, Mary Louise *psychoanalyst, psychiatrist, educator*
Schoolar, Joseph Clayton *psychiatrist, pharmacologist, educator*
Shan, Kesavan *cardiologist, researcher*
Shearer, William Thomas *pediatrician, educator*
Shulman, Robert Jay *pediatrician, educator, nutritionist, gastroenterologist*
Simpson, Joe L. *medical educator*
Simpson, Joe Leigh *obstetrics and gynecology educator*
Smythe, Cheves McCord *internist, geriatrician, educator, dean*
Sostman, Dirk *medical educator*
Spira, Melvin *plastic surgeon*
Spitz, Margaret R. *epidemiologist, researcher*
Steely, Robert Lee *plastic surgeon*
Stewart, David James *oncologist, educator*
Sutton, Jeffrey Paul *physician, scientist*
Swick, Todd J. *medical association administrator*
Swisher, Stephen G. *thoracic surgeon*
Tanous, Helene Mary *radiologist, educator*
Thomas, Orville C. *retired allergist*
Torre-Amione, Guillermo *cardiologist, researcher*
Tsimberidou, Apostolia Maria *medical educator*
Tweardy, David John *physician, educator*
Vallbona, Carlos *physician*
Vanderploeg, James M. *preventive medicine physician*
Vaporciyan, Ara Asadur *thoracic surgeon, educator*
Varma, Datla G.K. *radiologist, researcher*
Vatta, Matteo *medical educator, researcher*
Walker, William Easton *surgeon, educator, lawyer*
White, Ronald Joseph *biomedical researcher, physiologist, educator*
Willerson, James Thornton *internist, educator*
Worthing, Louie Fabian III *plastic surgeon*
Yamaoka, Yoshio *gastroenterologist, researcher*
Yeoman, Lynn Chalmers *medical educator*
Young, David *anesthesiologist, educator*
Yung, Wai Kwan Alfred *neurology and neuro-oncology educator*
Zacharias, Nikolaos Marios *obstetrician, gynecologist*
Zhong, Miao *pharmacologist, researcher*
Zhou, Wei *surgeon*
Zoghbi, Huda Y. *neurologist, geneticist, educator*

## Humble
Trowbridge, John Parks *physician*

## Huntsville
Conwell, Halford Roger *physician*
Garner, Randall *medical educator*

## Irving
Ali, Ashraf *psychiatrist*

## Kerrville
Zuber, Randolph Clark *retired urologist*

## Killeen
Day, Charles R. *plastic surgeon*
Khwaja, Shamsuddin *neurologist, consultant*

## Kingsville
Sethi, Rajat *cardiologist, educator, research scientist*

## Lackland Afb
Fadare, Oluwole *pathologist, researcher, director*
Perry, William Brian *colorectal surgeon*

## Lubbock
Beck, George Preston *anesthesiologist, educator*
Frezza, Eldo E. *surgeon, educator*
Gill, Brian *orthopedist, surgeon*
Gill, Gurdev S. *orthopaedic surgeon*
Illner-Canizaro, Hana *physician, researcher, oral surgeon*
May, Donald Robert Lee *ophthalmologist, educator, academic administrator, farmer*
Sabatini, Sandra *physician*
Warren, Donald John *retired surgeon, educator*
Woolam, Gerald Lynn *surgeon*

## Magnolia
Girard, Louis Joseph *retired ophthalmologist, educator*

## Marshall
Sudhivoraseth, Niphon *pediatrician, immunologist, allergist*

## Mcallen
Casso, Ramiro Raul *physician, academic administrator*
Ramirez, Mario Efrain *physician*

## Meadowlakes
Nussbaum, Paul Stowell *retired urologist*

## Mineral Wells
Braun, Gustav Milan *otolaryngologist, surgeon*

## North Richland Hills
Wallace, William Edward *thoracic surgeon*

## Pasadena
Mullins, Jack Allen *cardiologist, educator*
Shapiro, Edward Muray *dermatologist*

## Pearland
McFarlin, Brian Keith *medical educator, researcher*
Visnegarwala, Fehmida *internist, educator*

## Plano
Friedman, Ronald M. *plastic surgeon*
Little, Joseph Hugh *plastic surgeon*

## Rockwall
Kotas, Robert Vincent *pediatrician, educator*

## San Angelo
Charlesworth, Ernest Neal *allergist, immunologist, dermatologist, educator*
Fischer, Duncan Kinnear *neurosurgeon*

**San Antonio**
Aust, Joe Bradley *surgeon, educator*
Baker, Floyd Wilmer *surgeon, retired military officer*
Becker, Quinn Henderson *orthopedic surgeon, military officer*
Beckmann, Charles Henry *cardiologist, educator*
Campbell, Robert Murray, Jr. *surgeon, researcher*
Corrigan, Helen González *retired cytologist*
Croft, Harry Allen *psychiatrist*
Cura, Marco Antonio *interventional radiologist, educator*
Danney, Mark Maxwell *pediatrician*
Dodd, Gerald D. III *radiologist*
Dumitru, Daniel *physiatrist*
Guerra, Fernando A. *pediatrician, health facility administrator*
Hare, Henry Phillip, Jr. *psychiatrist*
Jimenez, David Fernando *medical educator, department chairman*
Kamada-Cole, Mika M. *allergist, immunologist, medical educator*
Kasinath, Balakuntalam S. *medical researcher*
Katerndahl, David Arthur *medical educator*
Kaye, Celia Ilene *pediatrics educator*
Koneru, Suresh *plastic surgeon*
Kreisberg, Jeffrey I. *medical educator, researcher*
Lefeber, Edward James, Jr. *internist, educator*
LeMaistre, Charles Aubrey *retired internist, epidemiologist, educator*
Leon, Robert Leonard *psychiatrist, educator*
Martin, James Charles *physician*
McFee, Arthur Storer *physician*
McGill, Henry Coleman, Jr. *pathologist, educator, researcher*
Ognibene, Andre John *internist, educator, retired military officer*
O'Rourke, Robert A. *cardiologist, educator*
Palmaz, Julio C. *radiologist*
Paque, Ronald Edward *molecular immunologist*
Patterson, Jan Evans *epidemiologist, educator*
Pavuk, Marian *epidemiologist, researcher*
Persellin, Robert Harold *physician*
Pestana, Carlos *surgeon, retired dean, educator*
Pietz, Clint A. *pediatrician, educator*
Pruitt, Basil Arthur, Jr. *surgeon, retired military officer*
Restrepo, Ruben Dario *physician, educator*
Reuter, Stewart Ralston *retired radiologist*
Schenker, Steven *internist, educator*
Schnitzler, Robert Neil *cardiologist*
Shanklin, Kenneth Dale *plastic surgeon*
Smith, Reginald Brian Furness *retired anesthesiologist, educator*
Stallworth, Terresa Louise *psychiatrist, educator*
Verghese, Abraham Cheeran *internist, educator, writer*
Zilveti, Carlos Benjamin *preventive medicine physician, pediatrician*

**Seabrook**
Patten, Bernard Michael *neurologist, writer, educator*

**Temple**
Dehmer, Gregory Joseph *cardiologist*
Hayward, Ronald Hamilton *surgeon*
Holleman, Vernon Daughty *internist, educator*
Kuo, Lih *medical educator*
Lynch, Dennis James *plastic surgeon*
Sulak, Patricia Jane *gynecologist, educator*
Weber, Robert A. *surgeon*

**The Woodlands**
Desjardins, Raoul *medical association administrator, financial consultant*
Shannon, Thomas O. *plastic surgeon*

**Trophy Club**
Floyd, Judy Louise Casburn *anesthesiologist, political scientist*

**Tyler**
Kronenberg, Richard Samuel *physician, educator*
Neuenschwander, Pierre Fernand *medical educator*
Wrenn, Christopher Jay *physician*

**Waco**
Richie, Rodney Charles *critical care and pulmonary medicine physician*

**Webster**
Tarnam, Jafar *allergist, immunologist, pediatrician*

**Willis**
Rappaport, Martin Paul *internist, nephrologist, educator*

**UTAH**

**Bountiful**
Ross, Gerald Harvey *family practice and environmental medicine physician*

**Logan**
Roberts, Donald Wilson *pathologist, consultant*

**Mapleton**
Hillyard, Ira William *retired pharmacologist, retired educator*

**Provo**
Bott, Jay Cordell *oncologist, hematologist*
Peterson, Samuel Ray *dermatologist, department chairman*

**Salt Lake City**
Bauer, A. Robert, Jr. (August Robert Bauer Jr.) *surgeon*
Betz, A. Lorris *pediatrician, educator*
Burke, John Patrick *internist, educator*
Capecchi, Mario Renato *genetics educator*
Carey, John Clayton *pediatrician, educator, medical geneticist*
Dietlein, John R. *physician, health facility administrator*
Fujinami, Robert Shin *neurology educator*
Gray, Douglas D. *child and adolescent psychiatrist*
Grosser, Bernard Irving *psychiatrist, educator*

Hofmann, Aaron A. *orthopedist, surgeon, researcher*
Jaskowski, Troy D. *immunologist, researcher*
Kanner, Richard Elliot *physician, medical educator, consultant*
Layfield, Lester James *pathologist, educator*
McGann, Christopher John *cardiologist, educator*
McLeskey, Charles Hamilton *anesthesiologist, educator, pharmaceutical executive*
Meyers, Rebecka Louise *pediatric general surgeon*
Middleton, Anthony Wayne, Jr. *urologist, educator*
Moser, Royce, Jr. *preventive medicine physician, educator*
Nelson, John C. *obstetrician, gynecologist*
Nelson, Russell Marion *surgeon, educator*
Parkin, James Lamar *retired otolaryngologist, educator*
Sorensen, John B. *surgeon*
Tani, Lloyd Yasuo *pediatrician, educator*
Thomas, David Snow *plastic surgeon*
Wolf, Harold Herbert *pharmacy educator*

**VERMONT**

**Brattleboro**
Agallianos, Dennis Dionysios *psychiatrist*

**Burlington**
Cooper, Sheldon Mark *medical educator, immunologist, researcher, rheumatologist*
Davis, John Herschel *retired surgeon, educator*
Durfee, Herbert Ashley, Jr. *medical educator*
Gennari, F(rank) John *medical educator*
Grunberg, Steven Marc *medical educator*
Lucey, Jerold Francis *pediatrician*
Naylor, Magdalena Raczkowska *psychiatrist, educator*
Riddick, Daniel Howison *obstetrician, gynecologist, priest*
Sobel, Burton Elias *internist, educator*
Tampas, John P. *radiologist*
Vane, Dennis *physician*
Zhao, Feng-Qi *endocrinologist, educator*

**Dorset**
Bamford, Joseph Charles, Jr. *gynecologist, obstetrician, educator, medical missionary, author*

**Jacksonville**
Dell, Ralph Bishop *retired pediatrician, researcher*
Hein, Karen Kramer *pediatrician, epidemiologist*

**Norwich**
Katz, Arnold Martin *medical educator*

**Randolph Center**
Sax, Daniel Saul *neurologist, educator*

**South Burlington**
Shinozaki, Tamotsu *retired physician, retired anesthesiologist*

**Underhill**
Danforth, Elliot, Jr. *medical educator*

**West Danville**
Pollack, Irwin William *psychiatrist, educator*

**White River Junction**
Berman, Stephen Alan *neurologist*
Myers, Warren Powers Laird *internist, educator*

**Woodstock**
Killian, Edward James *retired pediatrician*

**VIRGINIA**

**Alexandria**
Balch, Charles M. *surgeon, educator*
Fisher, Donald Wayne *medical association administrator*
Hallman, Linda D. *medical association administrator*
Hurtado, Rodrigo Claudio *allergist*
Nicholas, Lynn B. *medical association administrator*
Rayman, Russell Barry *physician*
Wilhide, Stephen D. *medical association administrator*
Wilson, Tyler J. *medical association administrator*

**Annandale**
Gorsen, Robert Marc *neurosurgeon*
Shamburek, Roland Howard *physician*

**Arlington**
Adams, Hunter (Patch Adams) *internist, health facility administrator*
Nguyen-Dinh, Thanh *internist, geriatrician, acupuncturist*
Nirschl, Robert Phillip *orthopedic surgeon*
Runkle, Beatriz Pamela *medical educator, pediatrician*
Sanz, Luis E. *gynecologist, educator*
Thompson, Geraldine Kelleher Richter *retired orthopedist*
Yates, Allison A. *medical association administrator*

**Charlottesville**
Arlet, Vincent *orthopedist, surgeon*
Balogun, Rasheed Abiodun *medical educator*
Barrett, Eugene Joseph *physician, educator, researcher*
Beller, George A. *cardiologist, educator*
Cantrell, Robert Wendell *otolaryngologist, head and neck surgeon, educator*
Carey, Robert Munson *medical educator, physician*
Crosby, Ivan Keith *cardiac surgeon, educator*
Epstein, Robert Marvin *anesthesiologist, educator*
Flickinger, Charles Jann *anatomist, educator*
Guerrant, Richard Littleton *medical educator*
Hunt, William B. *pulmonologist*
Jevtovic-Todorovic, Vesna *physician, researcher*
Jones, Rayford Scott *surgeon, educator*
Kassell, Neal Frederic *neurosurgery educator*

Kattwinkel, John *pediatrician, educator*
Keats, Theodore Eliot *radiologist, educator*
Kelly, Thaddeus Elliott *medical geneticist*
Lin, Kant *plastic surgeon, educator*
Mandell, Gerald Lee *internist, educator*
Marshall, John Crook *internal medicine educator, researcher*
Mirmira, Raghavendra G. *endocrinologist, researcher, educator*
Morgan, Raymond F. *plastic surgeon*
Muller, William Henry, Jr. *surgeon, educator*
Nolan, Stanton Peelle *surgeon, educator*
Owen, John Atkinson, Jr. *internist, educator*
Peterson, Kent Wright *physician*
Phillips, Lawrence H., II, *neurologist, educator*
Platts-Mills, Thomas Alexander E. *immunologist, educator, researcher*
Powers, Robert David *physician*
Rehm, Patrice Koch *radiologist, educator*
Reynolds, Robert Edgar *academic administrator*
Rowlingson, John Clyde *anesthesiologist, physician, educator*
Sarembock, Ian Joseph *internist, cardiologist*
Scheld, William Michael *internist, educator*
Schneider, Edward Martin *retired internist, medical educator*
Stevenson, Ian *psychiatrist, educator*
Thorner, Michael Oliver *medical educator*
Tillack, Thomas Warner *pathologist, educator*
Weary, Peyton Edwin *retired medical educator*

**Chesapeake**
Jackson, Cynthia Ann *medical association administrator, health consultant*
Kovalcik, Paul Jerome *surgeon*
Raymond, Patricia *gastroenterologist, medical educator*

**Chester**
Walton, G. Clifford *physician*

**Christiansburg**
Hawley, Rollin James *neurologist*

**Fairfax**
Baghi, Heibatollah *medical educator*
Schulman, Joseph Daniel *physician, health facility administrator, medical geneticist, educator*
Snyder, Roger Alan *physician, neurologist*
Stage, Thomas Benton *psychiatrist*
Suh, Yongsook Victoria *plastic surgeon*

**Falls Church**
Elliott, Virginia F. Harrison *retired anatomist, publisher, educator, investment advisor, kinesiologist, philanthropist*
Kurtzke, John Francis, Sr. *neurologist, epidemiologist*
Lefrak, Edward Arthur *cardiovascular and thoracic surgeon*
Malek, M. Mike *medical association administrator*
Scott, Hugh Patrick *former surgeon, military officer, medical advisor*

**Gainesville**
Lee, Won Jay *radiologist*
Lukowsky, Gerhard Hans *internist*

**Keswick**
Rowe, William Joseph *internist*

**Langley Afb**
Vista, Jeff Peter *emergency medicine physician*

**Leesburg**
Mitchell, Russell Harry *dermatologist*

**Locust Grove**
Gulya, Aina Julianna *retired medical association administrator*

**Manquin**
Osgood, Nancy Jean *medical educator, writer*

**Marion**
Armbrister, Douglas Kenley *surgeon*

**Mc Lean**
Filerman, Gary Lewis *medical educator*
Laning, Robert Comegys *retired physician, retired military officer*
Wallace, Robert Bruce *retired surgeon*
Wright, William Evan *physician, consultant*

**Midlothian**
Friedel, Robert Oliver *physician*
O'Shanick, Gregory John *physician, medical association administrator*

**Monterey**
Tabatznik, Bernard *retired cardiologist*

**Newport News**
Behlmar, Cindy Lee *medical association administrator, management consultant*
Wargo, Lovetta Lynn *medical educator, physical therapist, writer*

**Norfolk**
Abuhamad, Alfred Z. *obstetrician, gynecologist, educator*
Fabrizio, Michael Dean *urologist*
Farmer, Evan R. *dermatologist, researcher*
Faulconer, Robert Jamieson *pathologist, educator*
Hood, Antoinette Foote *dermatologist*
Kreger, David Lawrence *gastroenterologist*
Lester, Richard Garrison *radiologist, educator*
Magee, William Preston, Jr. *plastic surgeon*
McCune, Thomas Robert *nephrologist, medical educator*
Oehninger, Sergio C. *endocrinologist, obstetrician, gynecologist*
Panneton, Jean M. *vascular surgeon*
Rohn, Reuben David *medical educator, director*
Sinacori, John Todd *surgeon, educator*
Stallings, Valerie A. *physician, state agency administrator*
Wadsworth, J. Trad *otolaryngologist, medical researcher*

Wolcott, Hugh Dixon *obstetrics and gynecology educator*

**North Garden**
Moses, Hamilton III *hospital administrator, neurologist*

**Oakton**
Travis, Tracy Leigh *emergency physician*

**Portsmouth**
Wolf, Jeffrey Stephen *physician*

**Reston**
Bornmann, Robert Clare *physician, medical consultant*
Harrison, William Henry *retired medical educator*

**Richmond**
Atkinson, Richard Lee, Jr. *internal medicine educator*
Ayres, Stephen McClintock *physician, educator*
Blumberg, Michael Zangwill *allergist*
Dunn, Leo James *obstetrician, gynecologist, educator*
Dutz-Kohout, Elfriede *physician, educator*
Fierro, Marcella Farinelli *forensic pathologist, educator*
Fowler, Alpha Alsbury III *physician, researcher*
Gehr, Lynne Connolly *anesthesiologist*
Ginder, Gordon Dean *internist, educator*
Hagan, Michael Philip *radiation oncologist*
Hardy, Richard Earl *rehabilitation counseling educator*
Hettema, John Michael *psychiatrist, researcher*
Kendler, Kenneth S. *medical educator*
Lawrence, Walter, Jr. *surgeon, educator*
Manjili, Masoud H. *immunologist, educator*
McClenahan, John Lorimer *retired radiologist*
Merrell, Ronald Clifton *surgeon, educator*
Mollen, Edward Leigh *pediatrician, allergist, clinical immunologist*
Mullinax, Perry Franklin *rheumatologist, immunologist, allergist*
Nestler, John Edwin *endocrinology educator*
Owen, Duncan Shaw, Jr. *internist, retired educator*
Richardson, David Walthall *cardiologist, educator, consultant*
Robinson, Susan Estes *pharmacology educator*
Schieken, Richard Merrill *physician*
Shipman, Jean Pugh *medical librarian*
Sirica, Alphonse Eugene *pathology educator*
Strauss, Jerome Frank III *reproductive endocrinologist, educator*
Torres Filho, Ivo *medical educator*
Turner, Elaine S. *allergist, immunologist*
Vijayaraman, Pugazhendhi *medical educator*
Wilkinson, David Stanley *pathologist, consultant, researcher, educator*
Xi, Lei *medical educator*

**Roanoke**
Hutcheson, Jack Robert *hematologist, medical oncologist*
Kennedy, Byron S. *medical researcher*

**Roseland**
Stemmler, Edward Joseph *physician, retired health facility administrator, dean*

**Spotsylvania**
Singleton, Tanya *nursing educator*

**Springfield**
Khalid, Humayun *neurosurgeon, educator*

**Suffolk**
Carroll, George Joseph *pathologist, educator*

**Vienna**
Schwartz, Richard Harvey *pediatrician*

**Virginia Beach**
Carlston, John A. *allergist*
Gregory, Roger Thorpe *surgeon, consultant*
McDaniel, David Henry *physician*
Schreiber, Mark Traudt *psychiatrist*

**Ware Neck**
Tabb, Waller Crockett *retired allergist, retired immunologist*

**White Stone**
Duer, Ellen Ann Dagon *anesthesiologist, general practitioner*

**Williamsburg**
Connell, Alastair McCrae *physician*
Davis, Richard Bradley *pathologist, educator, internist*
Jacoby, William Jerome, Jr. *internist, retired military officer*
Maloney, Milford Charles *retired internal medicine educator*
Steinsmith, William *internist, research scientist*

**Winchester**
Bechamps, Gerald Joseph *surgeon*
Helentjaris, Diane *physician*

**WASHINGTON**

**Auburn**
Nazaire, Michel Harry *physician*

**Bellevue**
Hackett, Carol Ann Hedden *physician*
Hackett, John Peter *dermatologist*
Marosan, George *plastic surgeon*
Phillips, Zaiga Alksnis *pediatrician*
Shifrin, Donald Lee *pediatrician*

**Bellingham**
Howe, Warren Billings *physician*
Zech, Edward R. *cardiothoracic surgeon*

**Burien**
Risse, Guenter Bernhard *physician, historian, educator*

**Centralia**
Miller, James McCalmont *pediatrician*

**Clyde Hill**
Condon, Robert Edward *surgeon, educator, consultant*

**Coupeville**
Mayhew, Eric George *medical researcher, educator, consultant*

**Edmonds**
Yoon, Jay Myoung *oncologist, hematologist, internist*

**Everett**
Smith, Thomas J. *surgeon, educator*
Valentine, Mark Conrad *dermatologist*

**Friday Harbor**
Geyman, John Payne *physician, educator*

**Issaquah**
Barchet, Stephen *obstetrician, gynecologist, retired military officer*

**Kirkland**
Aikawa, Jerry Kazuo *internist, educator*
Barto, Deborah Ann *physician*
Dunn, Jeffrey Edward *neurologist*

**Lynden**
Hibbs, Clair M. *retired pathologist*

**Mcchord Afb**
Heim, Lori Joan *physician*

**Mercer Island**
Dunner, David Louis *medical educator*
Elgee, Neil Johnson *retired internist, endocrinologist, educator*
Levenson, Robert Montie *retired physician*

**Mukilteo**
White, Lowell Elmond, Jr. *retired medical educator*

**Olympia**
Fisher, Nancy Louise *pediatrician, geneticist, retired nurse*

**Port Orchard**
Thoman, Mark Edward *pediatrician*

**Richland**
Bair, William J. *retired radiobiologist*

**Seattle**
Ansell, Julian S. *urologist, educator*
Appelbaum, Frederick Ray *oncologist*
Blake-Inada, Louis Michael *cardiologist, researcher*
Bornstein, Paul *medical educator, biochemist*
Bowden, Douglas McHose *neuropsychiatric scientist, science foundation director*
Bremner, William John *physician*
Buck, Linda B. *medical educator*
Catterall, William A. *pharmacology, neurobiology educator*
Chatard, Peter Ralph Noel, Jr. *aesthetic plastic surgeon*
Collette Breuner, Cora *pediatrician*
Dale, David C. *physician, educator*
Dawson, Patricia Lucille *surgeon*
Day, Robert Winsor *preventive medicine physician, researcher*
Ellis, Georgiana Kehr *internist, oncologist*
Eschbach, Joseph Wetherill *nephrology educator*
Fihn, Stephan D. *internist, educator*
Fine, James Stephen *physician*
Giblett, Eloise Rosalie *retired hematologist*
Goodkin, Robert *neurosurgeon, educator*
Groudine, Mark Terry *oncologist*
Guntheroth, Warren Gaden *pediatrician, educator*
Hazzard, William Russell *geriatrician, educator*
Heimfeld, Shelly *hematologist, immunologist, researcher*
Hellström, Ingegerd *medical researcher*
Henderson, Maureen McGrath *medical educator*
Holmes, King Kennard *medical educator*
Hornbein, Thomas Frederic *anesthesiologist*
Kahn, Steven Emanuel *medical educator*
Kalina, Robert Edward *ophthalmologist, educator*
Katon, Wayne J. *psychiatrist, researcher*
Kaufman, Joel Daniel *medical educator, medical researcher*
Khorasani, Leila *neurosurgeon*
Kimball, Harry Raymond *medical association administrator, medical educator*
Klebanoff, Seymour Joseph *medical educator*
Kraft, George Howard *physician, educator*
Krohn, Kenneth Albert *radiologist, educator*
Larrabee, Wayne Fox, Jr. *facial plastic surgeon*
Larson, Anne M. *internist*
Larson, Eric B. *medical educator, director*
Lemire, Ronald John *pediatrician, educator*
Maier, Ronald Vitt *surgeon, educator*
Mankoff, David Abraham *nuclear medicine physician*
Martin, George Monroe *pathologist, gerontologist, educator*
Matsen, Frederick Albert III *orthopedic educator*
Migita, Russell *pediatrician, emergency physician*
Moore, Daniel Charles *retired anesthesiologist*
Motulsky, Arno Gunther *internist, geneticist, educator*
Mulroy, Michael Francis, II, *anesthesiologist*
Nelson, James Alonzo *radiologist, educator*
O'Brien, Kevin D. *medical educator*
Pagon, Roberta Anderson *pediatrician, educator*
Papayannopoulou, Thalia *hematologist, oncologist, educator*
Parikh, Jay R. *radiologist*
Perrin, Edward Burton *biomedical researcher, public health educator*
Phillips, William Robert *physician*
Pierson, David John *medical educator*
Plorde, James Joseph *physician, educator*
Ravenholt, Reimert Thorolf *epidemiologist, researcher*

Rivara, Frederick Peter *pediatrician, educator*
Robertson, William Osborne *physician*
Rose, Eric *physician, consultant*
Sale, George Edgar *pathologist*
Saneto, Russell Patrick *pediatric neurologist, epileptologist, neurobiologist*
Sidbury, Robert *pediatrician*
Stamatoyannopoulos, George *internal medicine educator*
Steinberg, Kenneth Paul *medical educator*
Steiner, Robert Alan *neuroendocrinologist, educator*
Stenchever, Morton Albert *obstetrician, gynecologist*
Stolov, Walter Charles *medicine physiatrist, educator*
Thirlby, Richard Coller *surgeon*
Thomas, Edward Donnall *internist, hematologist, retired medical educator*
Todaro, George Joseph *pathologist, researcher*
Vallières, Eric *thoracic surgeon*
Vater, Youri L. *medical educator*
Vedder, Nicholas Blair *surgeon, researcher*
Walker, William O., Jr. *pediatrician*
Waterston, Robert Hugh *medical educator, researcher, medical geneticist, department chairman*
Weaver, Lois Jean *physician, educator*
Welk, Richard Andrew *plastic surgeon*
White, Emily *epidemiologist, researcher*
Yarington, Charles Thomas, Jr. *surgeon, educator, health facility administrator*
Yashruti, Salah Hadi *retired surgeon*
Yue, Agnes Kau-Wah *otolaryngologist*
Zager, Richard A. *medical educator, researcher*

**Shoreline**
Merendino, K. Alvin *surgeon, educator*

**Snoqualmie**
Coldwell, Douglas M. *radiologist*

**Spokane**
Cohen, Arnold Norman *gastroenterologist*
Garrison, Mark W. *medical educator*
Holbrook, Ryan F. *oncologist*
Lee, Hi Young *physician, acupuncturist*
Mielke, Clarence Harold, Jr. *hematologist*

**Tacoma**
Flemming, Stanley Lalit Kumar *physician, mayor, state legislator*
Larhs, Anthony Emil *nuclear medicine physician*

**University Place**
Pliskow, Vita Sari *anesthesiologist*

**Walla Walla**
Chaidarun, Sushela Songtanin *endocrinologist, researcher*
McIlvaine, Patricia Morrow *physician*

**Wenatchee**
Gotthold, William Eugene *emergency physician*
Knecht, Ben Harrold *surgeon*
Primm, Richard Kirby *physician*

**Woodinville**
Couser, William Griffith *medical educator, academic administrator, nephrologist*
Ericson, William B. *orthopedic hand surgeon*

## WEST VIRGINIA

**Clarksburg**
de la Pena, Cordell Amado *pathologist*
Lapuz-De La Pena, Erlinda Laron *pathology professor*

**Fairmont**
Wang, Shen K. *orthopedist, surgeon*

**Fayetteville**
Cook, Lewis Anderson *physician, anthropologist*

**Frankford**
Mazzio-Moore, Joan L. *retired radiology educator, physician*

**Huntington**
Cocke, William Marvin, Jr. *plastic surgeon, educator*
Miller, Stephen Blaine *plastic surgeon*
Molina, Rafael Evencio *retired urologist*
Mufson, Maurice Albert *infectious diseases physician, educator*
Nerhood, Robert Clarke *obstetrician, gynecologist*

**Kingwood**
Moyers, Sylvia Dean *retired medical librarian*

**Lewisburg**
Hamra, Mary M. *medical educator, researcher*

**Morgantown**
Albrink, Margaret Joralemon *medical educator*
Bryner, Randy *medical educator*
Chisholm, Lionel Donald John *ophthalmologist*
Ducatman, Alan Marc *physician*
Fleming, William Wright, Jr. *pharmacology educator, department chairman*
Glover, Douglas Dennis *obstetrics, gynecology and pharmacology educator*
Hill, Ronald Charles *surgeon, educator*
Jabbour, Nabil Milad *ophthalmologist*
Martin, James Douglas *neurologist*
Murray, Gordon Franklin *medical educator*
Petsonk, Edward Lee *pulmonologist, researcher*
Pinheiro, Germania Araujo *physician, researcher*
Wang, Desheng *cardiologist, physiologist, researcher*

**Ronceverte**
Hooper, Anne Dodge *pathologist, educator*

**South Charleston**
Klimek, Deborah Lynn *ophthalmologist*

**Wheeling**
Heceta, Estherbelle Aguilar *retired anesthesiologist*

## WISCONSIN

**Appleton**
Boren, Clark Henry, Jr. *general and vascular surgeon*
Luther, Thomas William *retired dermatologist*

**Baileys Harbor**
Schultz, Richard Otto *ophthalmologist, educator*

**Brookfield**
Olson, David Carl *physician*
Sood, Manu Raj *pediatrician, consultant*

**Brown Deer**
Simon, Jeffrey S. *psychiatrist*

**Eagle River**
Agre, James Courtland *physiatrist*

**Eau Claire**
Immerman, Steven Curtis *surgeon, oncologist*
Manz, Carl Walton *surgeon, educator*
Weber, Donald Frank *obstetrician, gynecologist*

**Fond Du Lac**
Treffert, Darold Allen *psychiatrist, writer, hospital administrator*

**Green Bay**
Milson, Bertram Irving *surgeon*

**Hales Corners**
Kuwayama, S. Paul *physician, immunologist, allergist*

**Hartland**
Atlee, John Light *retired physician, consultant*

**La Crosse**
Smith, Martin Jay *physician, biomedical research scientist*
Webster, Stephen Burtis *dermatologist, educator*

**Madison**
Albert, Daniel Myron *ophthalmologist, educator*
Burgess, Richard Ray *oncologist, educator, molecular biologist, researcher, biotechnologist, consultant*
Connors, Kenneth Antonio *retired pharmacy educator*
Cripps, Derek J. *dermatologist, educator*
Crow, James Franklin *retired genetics educator*
DeMets, David L. *medical educator, biomedical researcher*
Dempsey, Robert J. *neurologist*
Edwards, Niloo Mario *surgeon*
Fahien, Leonard August *physician, educator*
Farrell, Philip M. *physician, educator, dean, medical researcher*
Fleming, Michael F. *medical educator*
Ford, Charles Nathaniel *otolaryngologist, educator*
Graziano, Frank Michael *medical educator, researcher*
Greer, Frank Roland *pediatrician, neonatologist*
Haq, Cynthia *physician, educator*
Hinshaw, Molly A. *dermatologist*
Javid, Manucher J. *retired neurosurgery educator*
Jefferson, James Walter *psychiatrist, educator*
Johnson, Maryl Rae *cardiologist*
Karofsky, Peter Stuart *pediatrician, medical educator*
Krahn, Dean Dennis *psychiatrist, educator*
Laessig, Ronald Harold *preventive medicine and pathology educator, state official*
Lemanske, Robert F., Jr. *allergist, immunologist*
Linzer, Mark *medical educator, internist*
Lucey, Michael Ronan *gastroenterologist*
Lund, Dennis Paul *surgeon*
MacKinney, Archie Allen *physician*
Maki, Dennis G. *epidemiology educator*
Malter, James Samuel *pathologist, educator*
McBride, Patrick Edward *medical educator, dean*
Mehta, Minesh P. *oncologist, educator*
Noonan, Kenneth J. *pediatrician, surgeon, educator*
Nordby, Eugene Jorgen *orthopedic surgeon*
Peters, Henry Augustus *neurologist*
Pitot, Henry Clement III *pathologist, educator*
Reynolds, Ernest West *retired internist, educator*
Rikkers, Layton Frederick *surgeon*
Roberts, Leigh Milton *psychiatrist*
Rowley, Howard A. *neurologist, radiologist, educator*
Schutta, Henry Szczesny *neurologist, educator*
Smith, Catherine Arnott *medical informatics educator, researcher*
Sobkowicz, Hanna Maria *neurologist, researcher*
Sondel, Paul Mark *pediatric oncologist, educator*
Stein, James Howard *medical educator, researcher*
Trubetskoy, Olga V. *medical researcher, educator*
Walker, Duard Lee *medical educator*
Westman, Jack Conrad *child psychiatrist, educator*
Whiffen, James Douglass *surgeon, educator*
Wood, Gary Stewart *dermatologist, researcher*

**Manitowoc**
Trader, Joseph Edgar *orthopedic surgeon*

**Marshfield**
Kuehner, Marvin Ernest *surgeon*
Vidaillet, Humberto J., Jr. *physician, administrator, researcher*

**Mequon**
Braun, Michael Andrew *radiologist*
Terry, Leon Cass *neurologist, educator*

**Milton**
Enlow, Donald Hugh *retired anatomist, dean*

**Milwaukee**
Chan, Carlyle Hung-lun *psychiatrist, educator*
Fink, Jordan Norman *allergist, educator*
Foldy, Seth Leonard *physician, educator*

Gershan, William M. *pediatrician, educator*
Hur, Su-Ryong *physician, anesthesiologist*
Jordan, Ruth Ann *retired physician*
Kochar, Mahendr Singh *physician, educator, health facility administrator, writer, research scientist, consultant*
Krausen, Anthony Sharnik *plastic surgeon*
Kroft, Steven Howard *hematopathologist, medical educator*
Larson, David Lee *surgeon*
Levy, Stuart Arthur *pulmonologist, consultant*
Merati, Albert L. *otolaryngologist*
Namdari, Bahram *surgeon*
Pagel, Paul Stanley *anesthesiologist*
Schellhase, Kenneth George *medical educator, researcher*
Shaker, Joseph Louis *internist, educator*
Shetty, Kaup Rajmohan *endocrinologist, educator*
Simpson, Deborah *medical educator*
Soergel, Konrad Hermann *physician*
Stokes, Kathleen Sarah *dermatologist, educator*
Towne, Jonathan Baker *vascular surgeon*
Yancey, Kim Bruce *dermatology researcher*
Youker, James Edward *radiologist*

**Neenah**
Janitch, Michael Allen *plastic surgeon*

**Onalaska**
Waite, Lawrence Wesley *osteopathic physician, educator*

**Oshkosh**
Cooper, Janelle Lunette *neurologist, educator*

**Plover**
Loteyro, Corazon Bigata *physician*

**Racine**
Stewart, Richard Donald *internist, educator, writer*

**Thorp**
Alisky, Joseph Martin *physician, medical researcher*

**Wausau**
Gruling, Kay Ann *physician*

**Wauwatosa**
Hollister, Winston Ned *pathologist*
Kalogjera, Ikar Jaksa *psychiatrist, educator*

**West Allis**
Roth, Terence Vincent *surgeon*

## WYOMING

**Casper**
Bennion, Scott Desmond *physician*

**Laramie**
Kelley, Robert Otis *medical educator, anatomist*
Steiner, Joseph Francis *pharmacy educator*

## TERRITORIES OF THE UNITED STATES

### GUAM

**Hagatna**
Espaldon, Ernesto Mercader *plastic surgeon, former senator*

**Tamuning**
Rahmani, Kia M. *surgeon*

### PUERTO RICO

**Bayamon**
Cabrera-Otero, Sylvia *physician*

**Humacao**
MacDonald, Gordon Rhodes *retired urologist, military officer*

**Mayaguez**
Sahai, Hardeo *medical statistics educator*

**Mercedita**
Perez-Nieves, Roberto *plastic surgeon, educator*

**Ponce**
Ortiz-Cruz, Bethzaida *physician, educator*

**San German**
Ramirez-Lluch, Norman Felipe *orthopedic surgeon*

**San Juan**
Cordero, Jose Fernando *pediatrician, dean*
Cruz-Correa, Marcia R. *gastroenterologist, researcher*

## MILITARY ADDRESSES OF THE UNITED STATES

### EUROPE

**APO**
Leibrecht, Murl Edwin *preventive medicine physician, consultant, retired military officer*

### CANADA

### ALBERTA

**Calgary**
Lederis, Karolis Paul (Karl Lederis) *pharmacologist, educator, researcher*

Smith, Eldon *cardiologist, physiologist, educator*

## BRITISH COLUMBIA

**Parksville**
Weir, Bryce Keith Alexander *neurosurgeon, neurologist, educator*

**Vancouver**
Baird, Patricia Ann *physician, educator*
Doyle, Patrick John *otolaryngologist, department chairman*
Eaves, Allen Charles Edward *hematologist, health facility administrator*
Friedman, Sydney M. *anatomist, educator, medical researcher*
Hardwick, David Francis *pathologist*
Ling, Victor *oncologist, educator*
McGeer, Edith Graef *retired neurological science educator*
Mizgala, Henry F. *physician, consultant, retired medical educator*
Riedel, Bernard Edward *retired pharmaceutical sciences educator*
Sorensen, Poul Henrik Bredahl *physician, research scientist, pathologist*

## MANITOBA

**Winnipeg**
Haworth, James Chilton *pediatrics educator*
Schacter, Brent Allan *oncologist, health facility administrator*

## NOVA SCOTIA

**Halifax**
Casson, Alan Graham *thoracic surgeon, researcher*
Chowdhury, Dhiman *physician, consultant*
Langley, George Ross *medical educator*
Tonks, Robert Stanley *pharmacologist, educator, retired dean*

**Mahone Bay**
Collins, John Alfred *retired obstetrician, gynecologist, educator*

## ONTARIO

**Hamilton**
Bienenstock, John *pathologist, educator, health facility administrator*
Roland, Charles Gordon *physician, medical educator, historian*

**Kingston**
Kaufman, Nathan *retired pathologist, educator*
Low, James A. *physician*

**London**
Marotta, Joseph Thomas *medical educator*
Weijer, Charles *medical educator, researcher*

**Manotick**
Osmond, Dennis Gordon *anatomist, researcher, medical educator*

**Ottawa**
de Bold, Adolfo J. *pathologist, educator, physiologist, researcher*
Hagen, Paul Beo *pharmacologist*
Hurteau, Gilles David *retired obstetrician, gynecologist, educator, dean*
Lavoie, Lionel A. *physician, health science association administrator*
Vassilyadi, Michael *pediatric neurosurgeon*

**Toronto**
Angel, Aubie *endocrinologist, academic administrator*
Farkas, Leslie Gabriel *plastic surgeon*
Langer, Bernard *medical association administrator*
Lindsay, William Kerr *surgeon*
Mc Culloch, Ernest Armstrong *internist, educator*
Mulligan, Peter C. *plastic surgeon*
Nguyen, San Duy *psychiatrist, educator*
Ogilvie, Richard Ian *clinical pharmacologist*
Sole, Michael Joseph *cardiologist*
Till, James Edgar *medical educator, researcher*
Turner, Robert Edward *psychiatrist, educator*
Volpé, Robert *endocrinologist, researcher, educator*

**Windsor**
Ferguson, John Duncan *medical research educator*

## QUEBEC

**Montpellier**
Poirier, Louis Joseph *neurology educator*

**Montreal**
Burgess, John Herbert *cardiologist, educator*
Clermont, Yves Wilfrid *anatomy educator, researcher*
Cruess, Richard Leigh *orthopedic surgeon, dean*
Freeman, Carolyn Ruth *oncologist*
Genest, Jacques *nephrologist, clinical scientist, science administrator*
Gold, Phil *immunologist, educator, researcher*
Goldbloom, Victor Charles *pediatrician*
Goltzman, David *endocrinologist, educator, researcher*
Jones, Barbara Ellen *neurologist, educator*
Kramer, Michael Stuart *pediatric epidemiologist*
Mac Lean, Lloyd Douglas *surgeon*
Mulder, David S. *cardiovascular surgeon*
Nattel, Stanley *cardiologist, research scientist*
Scriver, Charles Robert *medical researcher, human geneticist, retired medical educator*
Snell, Linda S. *internist, educator*

**Verdun**
Gauthier, Serge Gaston *neurologist*

## SASKATCHEWAN

**Saskatoon**
Houston, C(larence) Stuart *radiologist, educator*

**Toronto**
Pollock, Bruce Godfrey *psychiatrist, educator*
Urbach, David Robert *surgeon, educator*

## ARGENTINA

**Buenos Aires**
Montes, Leopoldo Feliciano *dermatologist, educator*

## ASCENSION

**Claton**
Tonge, Bruce John *psychiatrist*

## AUSTRALIA

**Clayton**
Broadbear, Jillian Helen *medical researcher*

**Nedlands**
Marshall, Barry James *gastroenterologist*
Oxnard, Charles Ernest *anatomist, anthropologist, biologist, educator*

**Parkville**
Azer, Samy Aziz *gastroenterologist, medical educator*
Denton, Derek Ashworth *medical researcher, foundation administrator*
Metcalf, Donald *biomedical researcher*

**Queensland**
Ho, Yik Hong *colon and rectal surgeon*

## AUSTRIA

**Grossgmain**
Mueller, Christa *radiologist*

## BANGLADESH

**Dhaka**
Brooks, W. Abdullah *pediatrician, researcher*

## CAMEROON

**Mutengene**
Raghunathan, Pratima Lalita *epidemiologist*

## CHINA

**Shanghai**
Mao, Aiwu *physician, radiologist*

## CZECH REPUBLIC

**Prague**
Bubeník, Jan *cancer researcher, biology professor*
Tuma, Stanislav Josef *radiologist*

## ENGLAND

**Hinxton Cambridge**
Stratton, Michael Rudolf *medical educator, researcher*

**London**
Gardner, Jason P. *immunologist, biologist*
Muir-Taylor, Douglas James *ophthalmologist*
Rutter, Michael Llewellyn *child psychology educator*

**Redhill**
Donaldson, David *pathologist*

## FINLAND

**Helsinki**
Liewendahl, Bo Kristian *retired pathologist, nuclear medicine physician*

## FRANCE

**Paris**
Gontier, Jean Roger *medicine and physiology educator*

## GERMANY

**Bremen**
Fahle, Manfred *ophthalmology researcher*

**Furth**
Rau, Magda *ophthalmologist*

**Halle**
Schmoll, Hans Joachim *hematology and oncology educator*

**Mannheim**
Solz, Hermann *plastic surgeon*

**Regensburg**
Eisenmann-Klein, Marita *plastic surgeon*
Fichtner-Feigl, Stefan *surgeon, immunologist*

**Seeheim-Jugenheim**
Halama, Niels *physician, researcher*

**Tübingen**
Nüsslein-Volhard, Christiane *medical researcher*

**Wuppertal**
Schubert, Guenther Erich *pathologist*

## GREECE

**Athens**
Boudoulas, Harisios *cardiologist, researcher, medical educator*
Brilakis, Harry Stylianos (Harilaos Stylianos Brilakis) *ophthalmologist*

**Larisa**
Zacharoulis, Dimitris *surgeon, researcher*

## GUATEMALA

**Guatemala City**
Herrera-Llerandi, Rodolfo Eduardo *surgeon, educator*
Mishaan, Emilio *transplant surgeon, educator*

## INDIA

**Hyderabad**
Das, Undurti Narasimha *endocrinologist, rheumatologist*

**Lucknow**
Kumar, Raj *medical educator*

**New Delhi**
Azad, Raj Vardhan *ophthalmologist, educator, surgeon, consultant*

**Varanasi**
Kumar, Vikas *neuropharmacologist, researcher*

## ITALY

**Palermo**
Fiumara, Ettore *neurosurgeon*

## JAPAN

**Gunma**
Okada, Ryozo *medical educator, researcher*

**Hamamatsu**
Kaneko, Masao *radiology educator, researcher, specialist*

**Hirakata**
Shigemitsu, Toshiro *ophthalmologist, researcher*

**Kushimoto**
Akura, Junsuke *ophthalmologist, researcher*

**Ohsu Shiga**
Matsuda, Wakoto *neurosurgeon, researcher*

**Okayama**
Morooka, Hiroshi *neurosurgeon*
Okuda, Shigeru *medical educator*

**Saitama**
Hozumi, Motoo *medical educator, researcher*

**Sapporo**
Nakagawa, Koji *endocrinologist, educator*
Sakai, Yu *pathologist*

**Tochigi**
Honma, Koichi *pathologist, researcher*
Hyodo, Haruo *radiologist, educator*

**Tokorozawa**
Nakamura, Hiroshi *urology educator*

**Tokyo**
Fujimoto, Junichiro *pathologist*
Sakuta, Manabu *neurologist, educator*

**Toyama**
Sumiyoshi, Tomiki *psychiatrist, researcher*

## KENYA

**Mombasa**
Harrell, Jerry DeWitt *ophthalmologist, director*

## LEBANON

**Beirut**
Khatib, Rustom Atfat *gynecologist, researcher, endocrinologist, consultant, economist*
Moucharafieh, Ramzi Charif *orthopedist, surgeon*

## MOROCCO

**Rabat**
Rafi, Mostafa *ophthalmologist*

## NETHERLANDS

**Maastricht**
Van Praag, Herman Meir *psychiatrist, educator, researcher*

**Vlaardingen**
Smith, Arlan Robert *plastic and reconstructive surgeon*

## NIGERIA

**Enugu**
Ozumba, Benjamin Chukwuma *obstetrician, gynecologist, educator*

## PERU

**Trujillo**
Ungaro, Mario *pathologist, educator*

## POLAND

**Warsaw**
Pluta, Ryszard *neuropathologist, educator*

## REPUBLIC OF KOREA

**Daegu**
Yim, Man Bin *neurosurgeon, educator*

**Gwangju**
Kim, Kwang Seog *medical educator*

**Pusan**
Lee, Young Woo *neurosurgery educator*

**Seoul**
Chi, Je Geun *retired pathologist*
Jee, Won-Hee *radiologist, educator*

## RUSSIA

**Moscow**
Davydov, Dmitry M. *psychiatrist, researcher*
Zubritsky, Alexander Nickolaevich *pathologist*

## SAUDI ARABIA

**Riyadh**
Al Wathban, Jehad Abdullah *neuroradiologist*

## SINGAPORE

**Singapore**
Kuznetsov, Vladimir A. *biomedical researcher, computational biologist*

## SLOVENIA

**Maribor**
Strojnik, Tadej *neurosurgeon, researcher*

## SOUTH AFRICA

**Bloemfontein**
Stulting, Andries Andriessen *ophthalmologist*

## SPAIN

**Pamplona**
Masdeu, Jose Cruz *neurologist, health facility administrator*

## SWEDEN

**Göteborg**
Norrby, Klas Carl Vilhelm *pathology educator*

**Stockholm**
Ekman, Peter Erik *urologist, educator*

## SWITZERLAND

**Aargau**
Bodis, Stephan B. *radiologist, oncologist, educator*

**Basel**
Eriksen, Erik Fink *endocrinologist, internist, researcher*
Nidecker, Andreas Cornelis *radiologist, educator*

**Versoix**
Mahler, Halfdan Theodor *physician, health organization executive*

**Zurich**
Domingue, Gerald James *medical researcher, microbiologist, immunologist, educator, clinical bacteriologist*
Zinkernagel, Rolf Martin *immunology educator*

## TAIWAN

**Kaohsiung**
Chien, Yie W. *pharmaceutical science educator, academic administrator*
Wang, Gwo Jaw *orthopedic surgery educator*

**Taichung**
Ou, Yen-Chuan *urologist*

## TANZANIA

**Moshi**
Pomfret, David B. *medical educator, internist*

## TURKEY

**Adana**
Diler, Rasim Somer *psychiatrist, researcher*

**Ankara**
Kostakoglu, Lale *nuclear medicine educator, researcher*

**Istanbul**
Baksu, Alparslan *obstetrician, gynecologist, researcher*

## ADDRESS UNPUBLISHED

Abbas Borhan, Richat *medical association administrator*
Ablow, Keith Russell *writer*
Aboufakher, Rabeea *cardiologist*
Abrams, Arthur Jay *retired physician*
Achauer, Bruce Michael *plastic surgeon*
Achord, James Lee *retired gastroenterologist*
Adams, James Thomas *surgeon*
Aduen, Javier Francisco *physician, researcher*
Adzick, Nick Scott *surgeon, educator*
Aelony, Yossef *retired physician*
Aguilar-Bryan, Lydia *medical educator, researcher*
Aldrich, Franklin Dalton *medical researcher, consultant*
Alexander, Jessie Aronow *anesthesiologist*
Alexiades-Armenakas, Macrene Renee *dermatologist, scientist, researcher, educator, consultant*
Altekruse, Joan Morrissey *retired preventive medicine physician*
Altshuler, Kenneth Z. *psychiatrist, educator*
Amacher, Arthur Loren *neurosurgeon*
Amis, Edward Stephen, Jr. *radiologist, retired military officer*
Andela, Valentine Bisangena *medical researcher*
Anderson, Geraldine Louise *medical researcher*
Anderson, Richard McLemore *internist*
Andreoli, Thomas Eugene *physician*
Andrews, William Cooke *physician*
Andrus, Jennifer Gail *otolaryngologist, surgeon, medical educator, educational consultant*
Anis, Ather *physician*
Antoun, Mikhail *medicinal chemistry and pharmacognosy educator*
Anversa, Piero *medical educator*
Appenzeller, Otto *neurologist, researcher*
Applebaum, Edward Leon *otolaryngologist, educator*
Arenberg, Irving Kaufman Karchmer *otolaryngologist*
Argiris, Athanassios *oncologist, researcher*
Arnot, Bob (Robert Burns Arnot) *physician, medical correspondent, writer*
Atkinson, Holly Gail *physician, journalist, educator, human rights activist, writer*
Avant, Robert Frank *retired physician*
Badani, Ketan Kishore *surgeon*
Badgley, Theodore McBride *retired psychiatrist, neurologist*
Baerg, Richard Henry *podiatrist, surgeon*
Bagian, James P *physician, engineer*
Bailin, Michael Traherne *physician*
Baird, William David *retired anesthesiologist*
Bajad, Sunil *pharmacologist, researcher*
Bajaj, Mandeep *medical researcher, educator*
Baker, Richard *physician, consultant*
Bales, Gertrude A. *retired otolaryngologist*
Baliga, Radhakrishna *pediatrician, educator, nephrologist, director*
Ball, Carroll Raybourne *anatomist, researcher, medical educator*
Ball, Russell Allen *pathologist*
Baney, Richard Neil *physician, internist*
Banks, Marcus A. *medical librarian*
Bar, Robert S. *endocrinologist, educator*
Barasch, Eddy *physician*
Barbo, Dorothy Marie *obstetrician, gynecologist, educator*
Bardin, Clyde Wayne *biomedical researcher*
Barnes, Deborah Elaine *epidemiologist, educator*
Baron, Jeffrey *retired pharmacologist*
Basil, Biju *psychiatrist, researcher*
Basmajian, John Varoujan *medical researcher, educator*
Batalden, Paul Bennett *pediatrician, educator*
Baum, Jules Leonard *ophthalmologist, educator*
Baxter, John Darling *internist, endocrinologist, educator, health facility administrator*
Bayes, Beverley Joan *retired pediatrician*
Beattie, George Chapin *retired orthopedist, surgeon*
Becher, Julie Robin *medical researcher, educator*
Beck, Livia Grünwald *physician, psychiatrist*
Beckett, Victoria Ling *physician*
Beckson, Mace *psychiatrist*
Bellows, Charles Frederick III *surgeon, educator*
Benfield, John Richard *surgeon, educator*

Bennett, Edward Virdell, Jr. *surgeon*
Berglund, Robin G. *psychiatrist, management consultant*
Berlin, Fred Saul *psychiatrist, educator*
Bernanke, Harold *retired physician*
Bhargava, Pramod *nephrologist, educator, consultant*
Biebuyck, Julien Francois *medical educator, medical administrator*
Billion, John Joseph *surgeon, retired state representative*
Bin, Joo Won *physician*
Binder, Manuel Robert *surgeon*
Biro, Jan Charles *physician, research scientist*
Black, Keith Lanier *neurosurgeon, educator*
Blankfein, Robert Jerome *retired neurologist*
Blazina, Janice Fay *pathologist*
Bleicher, Sheldon Joseph *endocrinologist, medical educator*
Bloom, Eugene Charles *gastroenterologist, educator*
Blount, Benroe Wayne *physician*
Bonn, Ethel May *psychiatrist, educator*
Boone, Charles W. *physician, pathologist*
Boone, Stephen Christopher *retired neurosurgeon*
Botsford, Mary Henrich *retired ophthalmologist*
Boudreau, Robert James *nuclear medicine physician, researcher*
Bougas, James Andrew *physician, educator, surgeon*
Boulware, David R. *epidemiologist, researcher*
Boynes, Sean G. *dental anesthesiologist, researcher*
Braasch, John William *retired surgeon, consultant*
Brant, William *surgeon, urologist*
Braude, Robert Michael *retired medical librarian*
Brent, Robert Leonard *radiology and pediatrics educator*
Brewer, Timothy Francis III *retired cardiologist*
Bristow, William Harvey, Jr. *psychiatrist*
Brizio-Molteni, Loredana *surgeon, educator*
Bronfine, Boris Isaakovich *surgeon*
Broome, Claire Veronica *epidemiologist, researcher*
Broth, Richard *perinatologist*
Brott, Walter Howard *retired cardiac surgeon, educator, retired military officer*
Brown, James W. *gastroenterologist*
Broxmeyer, Lawrence *internist, researcher*
Bruce, David Lionel *retired anesthesiologist, educator*
Bruns, David Eugene *medical educator, researcher*
Brunt, Harry Herman, Jr. *psychiatrist*
Bubrick, Melvin Phillip *surgeon*
Bucove, Arnold David *psychiatrist*
Budenz, Donald L. *ophthalmologist, educator*
Buhain, Wilfrido Javier *medical educator*
Buist, Neil Robertson MacKenzie *pediatric educator, medical association administrator*
Buncke, Harry J. *retired plastic surgeon, retired educator*
Burk, Raymond Franklin, Jr. *internist, educator, medical researcher*
Burket, John McVey *retired dermatologist*
Bursten, Stuart Lowell *physician, biochemist*
Bustreo, Flavia *epidemiologist*
Butchko, Harriett Hays *physician*
Butler, Douglas John *physician*
Bynes, Frank Howard, Jr. *physician*
Cain, Russell M. *psychiatrist, educator, administrator*
Calvert, William Preston *radiologist*
Campbell, Andrew William *immunotoxicology physician*
Caplice, Noel M. *cardiologist, researcher*
Caplin, Olga Yeryomina *psychiatrist*
Carson, Dennis A. *immunologist, researcher, cancer biologist*
Carswell, Jane Triplett *retired family physician*
Casanova, Bruno *physician, researcher*
Casarella, William Joseph *physician*
Cassell, Eric Jonathan *physician*
Cassidy, Suzanne Bletterman *medical educator*
Caston, J(esse) Douglas *retired medical educator*
Castro, Maria Graciela *medical educator, geneticist, researcher*
Catalano, Louis William, Jr. *neurologist*
Caushaj, Philip Fillor *surgeon, educator*
Censullo, Michael *radiologist*
Cha, Charles *surgical oncologist*
Chafkin, Rita M. *retired dermatologist*
Chambliss, Linda R. *obstetrician, consultant*
Chang, Ellen T. *epidemiologist*
Chang, Victor Tsu-Shih *oncologist, researcher, educator*
Chang, Yuan *neuropathologist, researcher, educator*
Chapman, Daniel P. *epidemiologist*
Chassin, Jameson Lewis *retired surgeon*
Chaves-Carballo, Enrique *neuropediatrician*
Chiang, Michael Fred *physician*
Chilton, Lance Alix *pediatrician*
Chin, Peter S. *neurologist, researcher*
Chiu, Dorothy *retired pediatrician*
Chodosh, Hyman Louis *neurologist*
Chong, Kaman *osteopath*
Chorpenning, Frank Winslow *retired immunology educator, researcher*
Chretien, Jane Henkel *internist*
Christy, Nicholas Pierson *physician*
Cinti, Sandro K. *internist, educator*
Clausen, Jerry Lee *psychiatrist*
Cleaver, James Edward *radiologist, educator*
Clemendor, Anthony Arnold *obstetrician, gynecologist, educator*
Clemetson, Charles Alan Blake *physician*
Coble, Yank David, Jr. *internist, endocrinologist*
Coe, Rodney Michael *medical educator*
Coffey, Barbara Jane *psychiatrist*
Cohen, Burton A. *radiologist*
Cohen, Jordan Jay *former medical association executive*
Cohen, Sidney Mace *urologist*
Cohen, William Nathan *radiologist*
Colonnier, Marc Leopold *retired anatomist*
Conomy, John Paul *neurologist, educator, lawyer*
Conrad-England, Roberta Lee *pathologist*
Corker, Frank Thomas *physician, retired military officer*
Correa-de-Araujo, Rosaly Lia *medical researcher, medical educator*

Cowart, Griggsby Thomas *retired urologist*
Craighead, John Edward *pathology educator*
Cramer, Marvin Edward *internist, cardiologist*
Crino, Marjanne Helen *anesthesiologist*
Cronce, Paul Calvin *retired dermatologist*
Crowell, David Harrison *retired biomedical researcher*
Cruciani, Ricardo Alberto *physician*
Cua, Clifford L. *pediatrician, educator*
Culligan, Patrick John *obstetrician, urogynecologist, surgeon, researcher*
Curl, Leigh Ann *orthopedist, surgeon*
Dailey, Thomas Hammond *retired surgeon*
Daly, Miriam Shamer *retired family physician*
Danse, Ilene Homnick Raisfeld *physician, educator, toxicologist*
Date, Elaine Satomi *physiatrist, educator*
Davidson, Mayer B. *medical educator, endocrinologist, researcher*
Davie, Joseph Myrten *pathologist, immunologist, educator, science administrator*
Davis, Mary Helen *psychiatrist, educator*
Dawson, Geraldine *medical educator, social worker*
DeBakey, Michael Ellis *surgeon, educator*
DeBuono, Barbara Ann *physician, state official*
DelBello, Melissa P. *medical educator*
Delgado, Roger Rodriguez *surgeon, educator*
Delgado Guay, Marvin Omar *internist, geriatrician*
Deliman, Robert Michael *surgeon*
de Lorimier, Alfred Alexandre *retired pediatric surgeon*
Del Priore, Lucian V. *ophthalmologist, educator*
de Medeiros, Ricardo Brilhante *immunologist, educator*
DeMille, Dale Esther *clinical educator*
Deogaonkar, Milind S. *neurosurgeon, neuroscientist*
DePalma, Ralph George *surgeon, educator*
Dessureault, Sophie *oncologist, surgeon, educator*
Detweiler, David Kenneth *veterinary physiologist, educator*
Dews, P(eter) B(ooth) *retired pharmacology educator, physician*
Diamond, Gill *medical educator*
Diaz, Fernando Gustavo *neurosurgeon*
Dickson, James Francis III *surgeon*
Diehl, Louis F. *hematologist*
Diener, Erwin *immunologist*
Ding, Jinwen *biomedical researcher*
Diskin, Charles J. *internist, researcher*
Djang, David S.W. *physician*
Dodge, R(alph) Edward, Jr. *physician*
Doherty, Peter Charles *immunologist*
Dolev, Jacqueline *physician, researcher*
Dominiak, Barbara Jadwiga *pathologist, researcher*
Donley, Deedra Ann *medical educator*
Dosanjh, Amrita *medical educator*
Dow, David Sontag *retired ophthalmologist*
Drance, Stephen Michael *ophthalmologist, educator*
Draper, Edgar *psychiatrist*
Dreskin, Stephen Charles *immunologist, allergist*
Dryman, Amy *epidemiologist*
Dube, Shanta Rishi *epidemiologist, public health researcher, information technology manager*
Dubin, Howard Victor *dermatologist*
Dugan, Charles Clark *retired physician, retired surgeon*
Dumont, Allan Eliot *retired physician, educator*
Dunn, Jack Newton *urologist*
Durairaj, Vikram David *plastic surgeon*
Durant, John Ridgeway *retired oncologist, health facility administrator, consultant*
Durell, Jack *psychiatrist*
Dyar, Kathryn Wilkin *pediatrician*
Dyck, Walter Peter *gastroenterologist, educator, academic administrator*
Dziewanowska, Zofia Elizabeth *pharmaceutical executive*
Eachempati, Soumitra R. *surgeon*
Ecker, Robert Doniger *neurosurgeon*
Edwards, Charles Henry, Jr. *retired surgeon*
Edwards, Larry David *internist, educator, dean*
Ehlers, Kathryn Hawes (Mrs. James D. Gabler) *physician*
Eisenstat, Theodore Ellis *colon and rectal surgeon, educator*
Elgart, Mervyn L. *retired dermatologist, educator*
Elledge, Stephen Joseph *medical educator*
Ellis, Lawrence Dobson *internist, educator*
Engle, Howard A. *retired pediatrician*
Engle, Mary Allen English *retired physician*
Epps, Charles Harry, Jr. *retired orthopaedic surgery educator, dean*
Erbay, Nazli *radiologist*
Erkonen, William Edward *radiologist, medical educator*
Ernst-Fonberg, Mary Lou *biomedical researcher, educator*
Espinosa-Heidmann, Diego G. *ophthalmologist*
Esser, James Mark *cardiovascular and interventional radiologist*
Esterly, Nancy Burton *retired physician*
Etzel, Ruth Ann *pediatrician, epidemiologist, educator*
Evans, Wayne *obstetrician, perinatologist*
Evarts, Charles McCollister *orthopaedic surgeon*
Eviatar, Lydia *neurologist*
Fabunan, Ruben G. *physician, research scientist, inventor*
Fanos, Kathleen Hilaire *osteopathic physician, podiatrist*
Faris, James Vannoy *cardiologist, educator, health facility administrator*
Fariss, Bruce Lindsay *endocrinologist, consultant*
Farr, Barry Miller *physician, epidemiologist*
Faucett, Ralph E. *physician, surgeon*
Fawcett, H. Daniel *nuclear medicine radiologist*
Febbo, Phillip George *oncologist, researcher*
Feigin, Ralph David *medical association administrator, pediatrician, educator*
Feinstein, Robert P. *dermatologist*
Feldman, Eva Lucille *neurology educator*
Feldman, Marc David *psychiatrist*
Felgar, Raymond Eugene *pathologist, educator*
Ferguson, Earl Wilson *cardiologist, medical executive, telemedicine consultant*
Ferguson, Emmet Fewell, Jr. *surgeon*

Festekjian, Jaco H. *plastic surgeon, educator*
Filardo, Thomas Wesley *physician*
Filley, Christopher Mark *neurologist, researcher*
Fink, Mitchell Phillip *surgeon, researcher*
Fink, Raymond *medical educator*
Finkelstein, Daniel *ophthalmologist*
Fisher, Robert Darryl *cardiovascular and thoracic surgeon, lawyer*
Fitch, Frank Wesley *pathologist, educator, immunologist, dean*
Fleishman, Philip Robert *internist*
Flick, Arnold L. *retired physician, political organization worker*
Fluth, John Adam *medical educator*
Fogel, Esther Marian (Esther Marian Roseig) *veterinary researcher*
Fomon, Samuel Joseph *pediatrician, educator*
Forciea, Mary Ann *geriatrician*
Fornari, Victor Masliah *psychiatrist*
Fortmann, Stephen Paul *medical educator, researcher, epidemiologist*
Fountain, Karen Schueler *retired physician*
Fralinger, Jack Bruce *surgeon*
Franks, John Julian *anesthesiologist, educator*
Freeman, Theodore Monroe *physician*
Freudenberger, Ronald Steve *cardiologist, director*
Frey, Charles Frederick *surgeon, educator*
Fromm, Hans *gastroenterologist, educator, medical researcher*
Fu, Jianhua *medical researcher, educator*
Fukuda, Keiji *epidemiologist*
Furnas, David William *plastic surgeon, educator*
Gahagan, Thomas Gail *obstetrician, gynecologist*
Gajl-Peczalska, Kazimiera J. *retired surgeon, pathologist, educator*
Galbraith, William Bruce *internist, educator*
Gale, Stanley William *psychiatrist*
Galvin, Matthew Reppert *psychiatry educator*
Ganley, James Powell *retired ophthalmologist*
Garcia, Eduardo *neurologist, consultant*
Garrett, Marshall Lee *anesthesiologist, educator*
Gartner, Lawrence Mitchell *pediatrician, medical educator*
Gathright, John Byron, Jr. *colon and rectal surgeon, educator*
Gaylin, Willard *physician, educator*
Gelberg, Lillian *family medicine physician, educator*
Gencheva, Eugenia Svetoslavova *medical researcher*
Genieser, Nancy Branom *radiologist*
Genkins, Gabriel *physician*
George, Alfred L., Jr. *medical educator, researcher*
Georgitis, John *allergist, educator*
Gerald, Michael Charles *pharmacy educator, dean*
Gewitz, Michael Harold *pediatric cardiologist*
Gherardi, Gherardo Joseph *pathologist*
Gibbs, Ronald Steven *obstetrician, gynecologist, educator*
Gibson, Milton Eugene *cardiologist*
Gilchrist, Gerald Seymour *pediatric hematologist, oncologist, educator*
Gill, Thomas James III *pathologist, educator*
Gillespie, Gary Don *physician*
Ginsburg, Iona Horowitz *psychiatrist*
Glaser, Robert Joy *retired internist, foundation administrator*
Glass, Dorothea Daniels *physiatrist, educator*
Glassheim, Jeffrey Wayne *allergist, immunologist, pediatrician*
Godfrey, Norman V. *plastic surgeon*
Goffman, Thomas Edward *radiobiologist, oncologist*
Gold, Judith Hammerling *psychiatrist*
Goldberg, Mark Arthur *neurologist*
Goldberg, Martin *internist, educator*
Goldberg, Michael Ellis *neurologist, neuroscientist*
Golden, Gerald Samuel *retired national medical board executive*
Goldmann, Morton Aaron *cardiologist, educator*
Goldstein, Avram *pharmacology educator*
Goldstein, Dora Benedict *pharmacologist, educator*
Gonnering, Russell Stephen *ophthalmic plastic surgeon*
Gonzalez-Alegre, Pedro *neurologist, researcher*
Goodfellow, Robin Irene *surgeon*
Goodreau, Robert Charles *surgeon*
Goodwin, Alyson *psychiatrist*
Goodwin, Andrew Wirt, II *radiologist*
Gorin, Michael Bruce *ophthalmic molecular geneticist, educator*
Gottfried, Eugene Leslie *physician, educator*
Gourley, Greta Ann Kimbrough *pharmaceutical sciences educator*
Grabstald, Harry *urologist, oncologist*
Graham, David G. *preventive medicine physician, psychiatrist*
Graham, James Herbert *retired dermatologist*
Gray, Mary Jane *retired obstetrician, gynecologist*
Graziani, Leonard Joseph *pediatric neurologist, researcher*
Green, David *hematologist*
Green, Louis Harry *retired surgeon*
Green, Michael Jay *medical educator*
Greenberg, Carolyn Phyllis *retired anesthesiologist*
Greene, Donald Richard *dermatologist, educator*
Greenfield, Jason Michael *urologist*
Greenfield, Val Shea *ophthalmologist*
Greer, Kenneth E. *dermatologist*
Greer, Robert Bruce III *orthopedist, educator*
Grendell, James Henry *medical educator*
Griffen, Ward O., Jr. *surgeon, educator*
Griffith, B. Herold (Bezaleel Herold Griffith) *retired plastic surgeon, retired educator*
Grillo-López, Antonio J. *physician*
Griner, Paul Francis *physician*
Grossman, Jerome Harvey *medical educator, medical association administrator*
Grossman, Joyce Renee *pediatrician, internist*
Grunt, Jerome Alvin *retired pediatric endocrinologist*
Guarente, Leonard P. *medical geneticist, educator*
Guiterrez, Hector P. *surgeon*
Gulbrandsen, Patricia Hughes *physician*
Gunderson, Carl Harmon *neurologist, educator*
Guyer, Bernard *maternal and child health educator*
Haddy, Theresa Brey *pediatrician, educator, hematologist, oncologist*
Haft, Gail Klein *pediatrician*

Haggerty, Robert Johns *pediatrician, educator*
Hah, Mina *psychiatrist*
Haithcock, William Dana, Jr. *physician*
Hall, John Robert *psychiatrist*
Haller, Jordan Daniel *cardiovascular surgeon*
Halliday, William Ross *retired physician, speleologist, writer*
Hammond, Graeme Lord *surgeon, educator*
Hand, Roger *physician, educator*
Handford, H. Allen *retired psychiatrist, medical educator*
Hanna, Duke Ellsworth *retired neurological surgeon*
Hansell, John Royer *retired pathologist*
Hardaway, Robert Morris III *retired surgeon*
Harford, Robert R. *dermatologist*
Harmel, Merel Hilber *anesthesiologist, educator*
Harrigan, Rosanne Carol *medical educator*
Harrington, John Tolan *medical educator, internist, nephrologist, retired dean*
Harrington, John Walter *pediatrician, medical researcher*
Harris, Elaine K. *medical consultant*
Harrison, Lynn Henry, Jr. *cardiovascular surgeon, educator, director*
Harrop, Daniel Smith III *psychiatrist*
Hart, Cecil William Joseph *otolaryngologist, surgeon*
Harvey, Birt *retired pediatrician, educator*
Hasselmeyer, Eileen Grace *medical researcher*
Hawthorne, Douglas D. *medical association administrator*
H'Doubler, Francis Todd, Jr. *surgeon*
Healy, Bernadine P. *physician, educator, former federal official*
Heckadon, Robert Gordon *plastic surgeon*
Hedley-Whyte, Elizabeth Tessa *neuropathologist*
Heidelberger, Kathleen Patricia *physician*
Helfand, Arthur Erwin *podiatrist*
Hellerstein, David Joel *psychiatrist, researcher, writer*
Henderson, Melford J. *epidemiologist, molecular biologist, chemist*
Hendry, Jean Sharon *psychopharmacologist*
Henney, Christopher Scot *immunologist*
Henninger, Nils *neurologist, researcher*
Henry, John Bernard *pathologist, educator, academic administrator*
Heptinstall, Robert Hodgson *physician*
Herzberg, Laura Jill *pediatrician*
Heywang-Koebrunner, Sylvia H. *radiologist, educator*
Higginbotham, Edith Arleane *radiologist, researcher*
Hill, John Sylvester *allergist*
Hillard, Paula A *medical educator, physician*
Himes, John Harter *medical researcher, educator*
Hinterbuchner, Catherine N. *physician, medical educator*
Hinton, Pamela Sue *nutrition and sports medicine educator*
Hinz, William Max *retired pediatrician, military officer*
Hirose, Teruo Terry *surgeon, educator*
Hirsch, Lawrence Leonard *physician, retired educator*
Ho, Ralph Tinghan *radiologist*
Hochster, Howard S. *oncologist*
Hofsess, Donald William *retired physician*
Hogg, Judith E. *neurologist, educator*
Hogness, John Rusten *internist, educator, academic administrator*
Holifield-Kennedy, Linda R. *physician*
Holland, Robert Campbell *anatomist, educator*
Holmes, Frederick Franklin *retired medical educator, physician, researcher*
Holt, Cheryl L. *medical educator*
Holtzman, Robert Neil Nehemiah *neurosurgeon, neurologist*
Holz, George G., IV, *medical educator, research scientist*
Hood, William Boyd, Jr. *cardiologist, educator*
Horswill, C. Weir *retired obstetrician-gynecologist, photographer*
Hoskins, John Howard *retired urologist, educator*
Howard, Terry Thomas *obstetrician, gynecologist*
Howards, Stuart S. *urologist, educator*
Howell, Joel DuBose *internist, educator*
Howell, Julius Ammons *retired plastic surgeon*
Hricak, Hedvig *radiologist*
Huchton, Paul Joseph, Jr. *retired pediatrician*
Humayun, Mark S. *ophthalmologist, educator*
Hunstad, Joseph Paul *plastic surgeon, educator*
Hunzicker, Warren John *retired cardiologist, medical educator, consultant, health facility administrator*
Hutcheon, Duncan Elliot *physician educator*
Hutter, Adolph Matthew, Jr. *cardiologist, educator*
Huvos, Andrew *internist, cardiologist, educator*
Hyde, M. Deborah *neurosurgeon*
Iannuzzi Sucich, Michele F. *physician*
Irish, Thomas Sudan *retired plastic surgeon*
Iserson, Kenneth Victor *bioethicist, writer, medical educator*
Izenstark, Joseph Louis *retired radiologist, physician, educator*
Jackson, David Huntsman *retired cardiologist*
Jacobson, Eugene Donald *medical educator, academic administrator, researcher*
Jaffe, Bernard Michael *surgeon*
Jaffe, Charles J. *allergist*
Jalba, Mihai Sergiu *epidemiologist, pulmonologist, physician, researcher*
Janicak, Philip Gregory *psychiatrist, educator*
Jaquith, George Oakes *ophthalmologist*
Javitt, Daniel C. *psychiatrist, researcher*
Jayawardena, Vidya *surgeon, medical educator*
Johnson, Frank Edward *surgeon educator*
Johnson, Leonard Morris *retired pediatric surgeon*
Johnson, Pam Clarene *radiographer, bone densitometrist, consultant*
Johnson, Spencer *physician, writer*
Johnson, William G. *neurologist, educator*
Johnston, Frank Marion *retired general practice physician*
Johnston, Marilyn Frances-Meyers *physician, educator*
Jolly, Meenakshi *rheumatologist*
Jones, Amelia Susan *retired anesthesiologist*
Jones, Billy Ernest *retired dermatology educator*

Jorapur, Vinod *physician, researcher*
Joseph, Ramon Rafael *internist, educator*
Judge, Nancy Elizabeth *obstetrician, gynecologist*
Judge, Rajinder *psychiatrist*
Kaakaji, Wayel *neurosurgeon, educator*
Kable, Kelvin *physician*
Kamalakannan, Desikan *cardiologist*
Kantor, Harvey Sherwin *medical educator*
Kaplan, Gabriela Diana *radiologist*
Kaplan, Selna L. *medical educator*
Kaplowitz, Neil *gastroenterologist, educator*
Kapur, Vishesh *medical educator, epidemiologist*
Kaufman, Stephen Lawrence *radiologist, educator*
Ke, Yong *medical educator, researcher*
Keill, Stuart Langdon *psychiatrist*
Keller, Roberta Lynn *physician, researcher*
Kelley, Patrick Alan *neurologist, educator*
Kent, Donald Charles *retired physician*
Kent, Georgia L. *obstetrician, gynecologist, healthcare executive, educator*
Kerstann, Kimberly Fowler *epidemiologist, researcher*
Kettelkamp, Donald Benjamin *retired orthopedist*
Khachemoune, Amor *physician*
Khan, Arfa *radiologist, educator*
Khan, Navaid *pediatrician, researcher*
Khatib, Riad *infectious diseases physician, department head*
Khisti, Rahul Tryambak *neuropharmacologist, researcher*
Khuri, Fadlo Raja *oncologist, educator*
Kiechle, Frederick Leonard *pathologist*
Kiefer, Renata Gertrud *epidemiologist, pediatrician, economist, management consultant*
Kim-Farley, Robert James *epidemiologist, educator*
Kincaid, Marilyn Coburn *medical educator*
Kindberg, Shirley Jane *pediatrician*
King, Jason Eric *medical educator, researcher*
Kinzie, Jeannie Jones *radiation oncologist, nuclear medicine physician*
Kirchner, Peter Thomas *nuclear medicine physician, educator, consultant*
Kirkland, Rebecca Trent *endocrinologist*
Kirkpatrick, Charles Harvey *immunologist, researcher*
Kirkpatrick, Garland Penn *retired pediatrician*
Kirkwood, John *medical association administrator*
Kitt, Walter *psychiatrist*
Knapp, Howard Raymond *internist, clinical pharmacologist*
Knobloch, Ferdinand J. *psychiatrist, educator*
Kohrman, Arthur Fisher *pediatrics educator*
Kolff, Willem Johan *retired internist, medical educator*
Koller, Loren D. *veterinary medicine educator*
Korc, Murray *endocrinologist*
Koreman, Dorothy Goldstein *physician, dermatologist*
Krabbenhoft, Kenneth Lester *radiologist, educator*
Kramer, Richard Jay *gastroenterologist, educator*
Krathwohl, Mitchell *physician, researcher*
Kreider, Clement Horst, Jr. *neurosurgeon*
Krim, Mathilde *medical educator*
Kumar, Sanjaya *epidemiologist, biostatistician*
Kundel, Harold Louis *radiologist, educator*
Kunz, Alexandra Cavitt *physician, anthropologist, researcher*
Kurnick, Nathaniel Bertrand *retired oncologist, hematologist*
Kwik, Christine Irene *physician, retired military officer, retired foreign service officer*
La Bagnara, James, Jr. *otolaryngologist, educator*
Lake, Carol Lee *anesthesiologist, physician, educator*
Lakshmi-Narayanan, Salvadeeswaran *physician, consultant*
Lane, Richard Allan *preventive medicine physician, educator*
Lanham, Richard J. *oncologist, educator*
Larkin, John Edward, Jr. *orthopedic surgeon*
Larson, Richard Smith *pathologist, researcher*
Larson, Roger Keith *physician, writer*
Lauderdale, Vance, Jr. *anesthesiologist*
Lauterbach, Edward Charles *psychiatric educator*
Lauterstein, Joseph *cardiologist*
Lawless, Michael Rhodes *pediatrics educator*
Lawrence, David Long *radiologist*
Lawson, William Bradford *psychiatrist*
Layton, Robert Glenn *radiologist*
Leazer, William *retired biomedical consultant*
Ledford, Frank Finley, Jr. *retired surgeon, military officer*
Lester, Mark Charles *neurosurgeon*
Levin, Alan Scott *pathologist, allergist, immunologist, lawyer*
Levin, Jack *physician, educator, biomedical investigator*
Levitt, Seymour Herbert *radiologist, educator*
Li, Min *oncologist, educator*
Liebowitz, Daniel S.F. *retired medical educator*
Limbrick, David D., Jr. *neurosurgeon, researcher*
Lincicome, David Richard *biomedical scientist, animal scientist*
Lindsey, James Harvey *surgeon*
Linz, Anthony James *osteopathic physician, consultant, educator*
Liotta, Lance Allen *pathologist*
Lipkin, David Lawrence *physician*
Lipton, Glenn E. *orthopaedic surgeon*
Littlejohn, Lanny Franklin *emergency physician, military officer*
Litvan, Irene *neurologist*
Liu, Xiao *ophthalmologist, neurobiologist*
Loddenkemper, Tobias *neurologist*
Loder, Elizabeth Wentz *neurologist, educator, editor*
Lohmann, Christoph Hubertus *orthopaedic surgeon, researcher*
Lohmann, George Young, Jr. *neurosurgeon, health facility administrator, artist*
Lollis, David Scott *neurosurgeon*
Long, William Alexander, Jr. *retired pediatrician, retired medical educator*
Loomis, Salora Dale *psychiatrist*
Looney, Gerald Lee *medical educator, administrator*
Lopera, Gustavo Adolfo *cardiologist, electrophysiologist*
Loschen, Earl Lee *psychiatrist, educator*
Lowen, Robert Marshall *plastic surgeon*

Lu, Yen-Chiao Angel *medical researcher*
Luckett, Peter M. *pediatrician, educator*
Ludwig, Stephen *pediatrics and emergency medicine educator*
Luedeman, Gerald Warren *radiologist*
Lukes, Andrea S. *gynecologist, hematologist, researcher*
Macleod, Angus *retired internist*
Mage, Rose Goldman *immunologist, educator*
Magnes, Harry Alan *physician*
Magnuson, Jeffery Scott *surgeon*
Maguire, James Harvey *physician*
Mahmood, Nafeesa F. *physician, consultant*
Maioriello, Richard Patrick *retired otolaryngologist*
Mala, Theodore Anthony *physician, consultant*
Malach, Monte *physician*
Malone, Robert Wallace *surgeon*
Mamula, Petar *gastroenterologist, director*
Mangelsdorf, Thomas Kelly *psychiatrist, consultant*
Manyam, Bala Venkatesha *medical researcher, neurology educator*
Maranchie, Jodi Kathleen *urologist, oncologist, researcher*
Marcdante, Karen Jean *medical educator*
Marco, Cura A. *medical educator*
Marin, Mona *epidemiologist*
Marino, Giovanni *surgeon*
Markham, Charles Henry *neurologist*
Marko, Marlene *psychiatrist*
Markus, Ramsey *dermatologist*
Marneros, Alexander Georg *physician, researcher*
Marrin, Charles Ainsworth Staveley *cardiovascular and thoracic surgeon, educator*
Martin, Clyde Verne *psychiatrist*
Martin, Daniel C. *surgeon, gynecologist, educator*
Massad, Susan Moore *internist*
Massey, Robert Unruh *internist, educator, dean*
Matarasso, Seth L. *dermatologic surgeon*
Materson, Richard Stephen *physician, educator*
Mates, Susan Onthank *physician, educator, musician, writer*
Mathewson, Hugh Spalding *anesthesiologist, educator*
Matzke, Jay *internist*
Maves, Michael Donald *medical association executive*
Mayuga, Kenneth A. *cardiologist, researcher*
Mazza, David S. *pediatrician*
McCarthy-Allen, Mary Frances *medical foundation administrator, not-for-profit fundraiser, consultant*
McClure, Jack B. *retired thoracic surgeon*
McConnell, Michael V. *medical educator, researcher*
McCoy, Frederick John *retired plastic surgeon*
McCullough, David Legarde *urologist*
McDowell, Charles Lindsay *orthopedist, surgeon*
McGlashan, Thomas Hamel *psychiatrist, educator*
McGrath, Mary Helena *plastic surgeon, educator*
McLendon, Roger Edwin *pathologist*
Meadows, Gwendolyn Joann *retired behavioral disorders educator*
Meghani, Sheni *geriatrician*
Meilman, Edward *physician*
Mellins, Harry Zachary *radiologist, educator*
Mendels, Joseph *psychiatrist, educator*
Mengel, Charles Edmund *internist, educator*
Messerle, Judith Rose *retired medical librarian, retired public relations executive*
Michelson, Gary Karlin *orthopedic surgeon, inventor*
Millar, John Donald *physician, environmental services administrator, essayist, consultant, musician*
Miller, Anthony Bernard *physician, researcher*
Miller, Geoffrey *child neurologist*
Miller, Jack David R. *radiologist, physician, educator*
Miller, Ross Hays *retired neurosurgeon*
Miller, Tracy Lynn *medical office administrator*
Millikan, Clark Harold *physician*
Milnor, William Robert *physician*
Mitch, William Evans *nephrologist*
Modesto, Victor L. *surgeon*
Mohaideen, A. Hassan *surgeon, consultant, health products executive*
Molmenti, Ernesto P. *surgeon*
Monos, Dimitrios *medical educator, researcher*
Montanaro, Anthony *medical educator*
Montgomery, Hubert Theron, Jr. *physician, health care administration*
Montgomery, John Richard *pediatrician, educator*
Moore, Patrick S. *epidemiologist, researcher, educator*
Moossy, John *neurologist, consultant, pathologist*
Morgenstern, Kenneth E. *plastic surgeon*
Moser, Robert Lawrence *pathologist, health facility administrator*
Motto, Jerome Arthur *psychiatrist, educator*
Mountain, Clifton Fletcher *surgeon, educator*
Mulcahy, Gabriel M. *pathologist*
Murat, Yusef J. *plastic surgeon*
Murphey, Sheila Ann *infectious diseases physician, educator, researcher*
Murray, Raymond Harold *physician*
Mushlin, Alvin I. *medical educator, researcher*
Myerowitz, P(aul) David *cardiac surgeon, educator, writer*
Myers, Allen Richard *rheumatologist*
Myers, William Osgood *thoracic and cardiovascular surgeon*
Myers, Woodrow Augustus, Jr. *physician, health care management director*
Nadler, Sigmond Harold *surgeon*
Nair, Ganesh Kumar Venugopalan *endocrinologist, internist, educator*
Nardell, Edward Anthony *pulmonologist, researcher*
Nasr, Samih H. *pathologist, educator*
Navaneethan, Sankar Dass *physician*
Neiberger, Richard Eugene *pediatrician, nephrologist, educator*
Nelp, Wil B. *physician, medical educator*
Nelson, Christopher Grant *dermatologist*
Nelson, John Woolard *neurology educator, physician*
Nelson, Nancy Eleanor *physician, educator*
Nepomuceno, Cecil Santos *physician*
Nguyen, Khanh Gia *medical educator*

Nguyen, D.O., Tuan H. *plastic surgeon*
Nicholls, Richard Aurelius *retired obstetrician, gynecologist*
Nicholson, Henry Hale, Jr. *surgeon*
Nieto, Juan Manuel *emergency medicine physician*
Nixon, Daniel Walker *oncologist, researcher*
Noji, Eric K. *epidemiologist*
Nonas, Constantine James *retired general surgeon*
Noonan, Jacqueline Anne *pediatrician, educator*
Nora, James Jackson *physician, writer, educator*
Norbeck, George *psychiatrist, consultant*
Norrid, Henry Gail *osteopathic physician and surgeon, researcher, educator, healthcare facility administrator*
Novack, Alvin John *physician*
Nowak, Judith Ann *psychiatrist*
Olds, Jacqueline *psychiatrist, educator*
O'Leary, Dennis Sophian *accrediting body executive*
O'Leary, Sharon *obstetrician, gynecologist, researcher*
Omalu, Bennet Ifeakandu *physician, consultant*
Onuigbo, Macaulay Amechi *nephrologist, internist*
Oral, Elif Arioglu *endocrinologist, researcher*
Orlando, Lori Ann *medical researcher*
Orth, David Nelson *endocrinologist, educator, sculptor, potter*
Ory, Steven Jay *physician, educator*
Pacifico, Albert Dominick *cardiovascular surgeon*
Packard, John Mallory *physician, researcher*
Padian, Nancy *medical educator, epidemiologist*
Paino, Javier E. *physician*
Painter, Robert Lowell *surgeon, educator*
Pan, Vivien L. *obstetrician, gynecologist*
Papadonikolakis, Anastasios *orthopedist, surgeon*
Park, Myung Kun *medical educator*
Parker, Brent Mershon *retired medical educator, internist, cardiologist*
Parker, Gerald William *internist, health facility administrator, retired military officer*
Patchin, Rebecca J. *anesthesiologist, educator, administrator*
Patel, Uptal Dinesh *nephrologist, researcher*
Patki, Kiran C. *pharmacologist, researcher*
Patterson, Hubert Clifton *physician*
Patwardhan, Meenal B. *pathologist, researcher*
Pauly, John Edward *retired anatomist*
Pederson, William Christopher *plastic surgeon*
Pedini, Egle Damijonaitis *radiologist*
Pedini, Kenneth *radiologist*
Peixoto Neto, Jose Ulysses *internist, researcher*
Pellegrino, Peter *surgeon*
Pelletier, Louis Conrad *surgeon, educator, health facility administrator*
Pennardt, Andre M. *emergency physician*
Pereira, Fred A(lfred) *medical researcher*
Perl, Harold *neonatologist, pediatrician*
Perlmutter, David H. *physician, educator*
Pesola, Gene Raymond *physician*
Peszke, Michael Alfred *psychiatrist, writer*
Peters, William P. *oncologist, educator, science administrator, dean*
Peterson, Andrew James *physician, military officer*
Peterson, Ann Sullivan *physician, consultant*
Petz, Thomas Joseph *internist*
Pflum, Barbara Ann *retired allergist*
Phillips, John P(aul) *retired neurosurgeon*
Pierangeli, Silvia Susana *medical educator, consultant*
Pierce, Donald Shelton *retired orthopedic surgeon, educator*
Pierce, Michael Norman *internist*
Pindyck, Frank *surgeon*
Pinter, Gabriel George *retired physiology educator*
Pirko, Istvan *medical educator, neurologist, researcher, immunologist*
Pirro, Alfred Anthony, Jr. *emergency physician*
Pisters, Katherine M.W. *internist, medical educator*
Pittman, Roy Clinton, Jr. *neurosurgeon, theologian, lawyer, philosopher*
Podichetty, Vinod Kumar *medical researcher*
Poehling, Katherine *pediatrician*
Pohl, Hans George *pediatrician, urologist*
Poppers, Paul Jules *anesthesiologist, educator*
Porayko, Michael *physician, educator*
Prange, Hilmar Walter *neurology educator*
Prasad, Navin *ophthalmologist*
Prince, George Edward *retired pediatrician*
Prohovnik, Isak *medical educator*
Propst, Michael Truman *pathologist*
Prusiner, Stanley Ben *neurologist, biochemist, virologist, educator*
Pust, Ronald E. *physician, educator*
Quattlebaum, Robert Baskin *urologist*
Quattrone, Richard Douglas *physician, military officer*
Qutub, Amina Ann *biomedical researcher, entrepreneur*
Race, George Justice *pathology educator*
Radi, Zaher *pathologist*
Ragheb, Samia *immunologist, educator*
Raichle, Marcus Edward *radiology, neurology educator*
Raines, Jeff *biomedical scientist, medical research director*
Rajput, Farzan *cardiologist*
Rako, Susan *psychiatrist, writer*
Ram, Chitta Venkata *physician*
Ramirez-Rivera, Jose *physician*
Randall, Peter *retired plastic surgeon*
Randolph, Judson Graves *pediatric surgeon*
Ranney, Helen Margaret *retired internist, hematologist, educator*
Rausher, David Benjamin *internist, gastroenterologist*
Rawnsley, Howard Melody *pathologist, educator*
Reader, George G. *retired internal-public health medicine educator*
Rebhun, Joseph *allergist, immunologist, medical educator*
Redbord, Kelley Pagliai *dermatologist*
Reddy, Neelima G. *gastroenterologist, researcher*
Reddy, Ranga Vallela *anesthesiologist*
Regan, Peter Francis III *physician, medical educator*
Reid, Orien *former medical association administrator*
Reimschuessel, Renate *pathologist*
Reiss, Robert Francis *physician*
Ren, Xing Jian *physician*

Rewcastle, Neill Barry *neuropathologist*
Rhodes, Linda Jane *psychiatrist*
Richards, Larry Leonard *child and adolescent psychiatrist*
Richmond, Julius Benjamin *retired pediatrician, former Surgeon General of the United States, health policy educator*
Rigg, Charles Andrew *pediatrician*
Rizza, Frank Alfonso *retired surgeon, educator*
Roberts, Alan Silverman *orthopedic surgeon*
Roberts, Albert Dee *internist*
Roberts, Melville Parker *retired neurosurgeon*
Roberts, Stanley Dwayne *physician, educator, academic administrator*
Robinson, Bernard Pahl *retired thoracic surgeon, educator*
Robinson, Nathaniel David, Jr. *physician, consultant*
Robson, Martin Cecil *surgery educator, plastic surgeon*
Rodgers, Lawrence Rodney *internist, educator*
Rodriguez, Anne O'Meara *medical educator*
Rodriguez, William Julio *physician*
Roizen, Michael F. *anesthesiologist, medical educator*
Roman, Stanford Augustus, Jr. *medical educator, dean*
Romero, Javier Antonio *surgeon*
Roncal, Rogelio *psychiatrist*
Rosati, Diane Claire *epidemiologist, educator, artist*
Rosenblum, Mindy Fleischer *pediatrician*
Ross, Edward *cardiologist*
Ross, Leonard Lester *anatomist, educator*
Rotunda, Adam Michael *dermatologist*
Rubin, Robert Joseph *internist, consultant, nephrologist*
Rudley, Lloyd Dave *psychiatrist*
Russo, Jose *pathologist*
Russo, Vincent Joseph *surgeon*
Ryan, John Joseph *physician*
Sabin, Jorge A. *emergency physician, consultant*
Sacha, Robert Frank *osteopath, educator*
Sachs, Sharona *internist, researcher*
Salis, Ari *radiologist*
Samartzis, Dino *medical researcher, writer*
Sanchez, Rafael Camilo *internist, educator*
Sanfelippo, Peter Michael *thoracic surgeon*
San Jose, Angel Molina *surgeon*
Santos, Arthur Magno *thoracic cardiovascular surgeon*
Saravolatz, Louis Donald *epidemiologist, medical educator*
Sargent, William Winston *retired anesthesiologist*
Sawczuk, Ihor S. *urologist*
Scardino, Peter T. *urologic oncologic surgeon*
Schauf, Victoria *pediatrician, educator*
Scheiber, Stephen Carl *psychiatrist, director*
Schenker, Marc Benet *preventive medicine physician, medical educator, department chairman*
Schetky, Diane Heiskell *psychiatrist*
Schiaffino, S(ilvio) Stephen *retired medical association administrator*
Schiff, Martin *physician, surgeon*
Schneck, Stuart Austin *retired neurologist, educator*
Schneider, Calvin *physician*
Schneider, Jan *retired obstetrics and gynecology educator*
Schulman, Harold *obstetrician, gynecologist*
Schulman, Sidney *neurologist, educator*
Schultz, Robert Jordan *orthopaedic surgeon, educator*
Schwarz, M. Roy *physician, administrator*
Seiberling, Kristin Ann *otolaryngologist*
Seli, Emre Utku *reproductive endocrinology and infertility specialist, physician researcher*
Seltser, Raymond *epidemiologist, educator*
Sengupta, Shomik *internist*
Sever, John Louis *medical researcher, educator*
Sevrukov, Alexander Biron *radiologist, researcher*
Shabot, Myron Michael *critical care educator*
Shader, Richard Irwin *psychiatrist, pharmacologist, educator*
Shah, Nandlal Chimanlal *retired physiatrist*
Shane, John Marder *endocrinologist*
Sharp, Dan Steven *epidemiologist*
Shaw, Ronald Ahrend *physician, educator*
Sheldon, Stephen *pediatric sleep medicine educator, researcher*
Shelton, Richard Charles *psychiatrist, educator*
Shepard, Richard Blount *surgeon, educator*
Sheppard, Vanessa B. *medical educator*
Sher, Leo *psychiatrist*
Sherman, John Foord *biomedical consultant*
Sherman, Joseph Owen *pediatric surgeon*
Shetty, Mulki Radhakrishna *retired oncologist*
Shi, Jiaqi *medical educator*
Shield, Paul Harold *psychiatrist, educator*
Shih, Margaret *epidemiologist*
Shihab, Fuad Said *medical educator, researcher*
Shils, Maurice Edward *physician, educator, research scientist*
Shohet, Stephen Byron *medical educator*
Shoul, Melvin I. *retired surgeon*
Shrank, William H. *physician, researcher*
Shumacker, Harris B., Jr. *retired surgeon, educator, author*
Shuster, Frederick *retired internist, gastroenterologist*
Siddiqi, Javed *neurosurgeon*
Siffert, Robert Spencer *orthopedic surgeon*
Sigell, Leonard Trittack *pharmacologist, educator*
Sigmon, J. Lewis, Jr. *medical educator*
Silver, Malcolm David *pathologist, educator*
Simmons, Geoffrey Stuart *physician, educator, writer*
Simonian, Simon John *surgeon, scientist, educator, health science association administrator*
Simons, John Nelson *surgeon, consultant*
Singer-Chang, Gail Leslie *medical educator, consultant, social sciences educator*
Singh, Krishna Binod *obstetrician, gynecologist*
Sinning, Mark Alan *thoracic and vascular surgeon*
Skolnick, Lawrence *neonatal physician, medical association administrator*
Slachta, Gregory Andrew *urologist*
Slavit, David Hal *otolaryngologist*
Sloan, Michael Allan *neurologist*
Slotkin, Marvin Bernard *surgeon*

Smith, Debra A. *osteopath*
Smith, Martin Henry *retired pediatrician*
Smith, Stuart Lyon *psychiatrist, corporate financial executive*
Smith Fawzi, Mary C. *epidemiologist*
Smith-Singares, Eduardo *trauma surgeon, researcher*
Smits, Helen Lida *medical association administrator, educator*
Smyth, Nicholas Patrick Dillon *surgeon*
Snider, Gordon Lloyd *physician*
Snyderman, Ralph *medical educator, physician*
Sofair, Andre *epidemiologist, researcher*
Sohn, Rayna Mayer *medical researcher, legal association administrator*
Soltero-Harrington, Luis Rubén *retired surgeon, educator*
Son, Gwi-Ryung *medical educator*
Sontag, James Mitchell *oncologist, researcher*
Spackman, Thomas James *radiologist*
Speicher, Carl Eugene *pathologist*
Speir, William Arthur, Jr. *critical care physician*
Steckel, Richard J. *retired radiologist, educator, academic administrator*
Stein, Paul David *cardiologist*
Stein, Robert Benjamin *biomedical researcher, physician*
Steinbach, Lynne Susan *radiologist, educator*
Stemerman, David H. *radiologist*
Stollerman, Gene Howard *internist, educator*
Stolley, Paul David *medical educator, researcher*
Stone, James Robert *surgeon*
Stonnington, Henry Herbert *physician, educator, medical association administrator*
Strain, James Ellsworth *pediatrician, educator, retired medical association administrator*
Strongin, Jonathan David *physician*
Stuzin, James M. *plastic surgeon*
Sud, Pamela Rani *pulmonary and critical care physician, consultant*
Summerlin, William Talley *allergist, immunologist, dermatologist*
Summers, David Stewart *neurologist, consultant*
Sunde, Douglas *plastic surgeon*
Suprun, Harry Zvi *pathologist*
Sutnick, Alton Ivan *medical educator, consultant, dean, internist, researcher*
Sutton, Albert Philip *urologist*
Suzuki, Kunihiko *biomedical educator, researcher*
Swerdlow, Martin Abraham *pathologist, educator*
Swiecicki, Martin *retired neurosurgeon*
Taboada, Javier Gustavo *neurologist*
Tagiuri, Consuelo Keller *child psychiatrist, educator*
Talamo, Jonathan Haskell *ophthalmologist, educator*
Tamborlane, William V., Jr. *pediatrician, educator*
Tandon, Rajiv *psychiatrist, educator*
Taranta, Angelo (Visca Taranta) *physician, educator*
Taren, James Arthur *neurosurgeon, educator*
Taylor, Peyton Troy, Jr. *oncologist, educator*
Taylor, William Colton *physician, educator*
Tepper, Lloyd Barton *preventive medicine physician, educator*
Terr, Lenore Cagen *psychiatrist, writer*
Terris, Susan *physician, cardiologist, researcher*
Terry, Robert Davis *neuropathologist, educator*
Thomas, Claudia Lynn *orthopedic surgeon*
Thomas, William Scott *physician*
Thornton, Yvonne Shirley *obstetrician, writer, musician*
Thorsen, Marie Kristin *radiologist, educator*
Tidswell, Mark *medical educator*
Tomy, Kalapparambath Paul *radiologist*
Tooms, Robert Edwin *retired surgeon*
Tran, Henry An Tien *internist*
Tranquada, Robert Ernest *retired internist, educator*
Troost, Bradley Todd *neurologist, educator*
Tropez-Sims, Susanne *pediatrician, educator*
Tsoukas, Maria Magdalene *dermatologist, educator*
Tucker, Gary Jay *psychiatrist, educator*
Tulaimat, Aiman *physician*
Turk, Richard Errington *retired psychiatrist*
Turkiewicz, Anthony Michael *rheumatologist*
Turndorf, Herman *anesthesiologist, educator*
Turner, Harry Spencer *preventive medicine physician, educator*
Turner, John Sidney, Jr. *retired otolaryngologist, educator*
Uhl, Henry Stephen Magraw *internist, educator*
Unger, Roger Harold *physician, research scientist*
Vachher, Prehlad Singh *psychiatrist*
Vail, Thomas Parker *orthopaedic surgeon*
Vakili, Bahman Fakhimi *urologist*
Valentine, William Newton *retired physician, educator*
Van Brunt, Edmund Ewing *physician*
Van Heertum, Ronald Lanny *physician*
van Nagell, John Rensselaer *oncologist, gynecologist*
Van Stone, William Webb *psychiatrist*
Vapiwala, Neha *radiation oncologist*
Varnholt, Heike *pathologist*
Vasudev, Brahm Sarup *nephrologist*
Vest, Gayle Southworth *obstetrician, gynecologist*
Viamontes, George I. *psychiatrist, director*
Vittetoe, Marie Clare *retired clinical laboratory science educator*
Voetsch, Barbara *neurologist, researcher*
Volkman, Alvin *retired physician, research scientist, educator*
Vorel, Stanislav R. *psychiatrist, neuroscientist*
Vydareny, Kay Herzog *radiologist, medical educator*
Wahlheim, Paul Steven *emergency physician*
Walker, Daniel Reuben *surgeon*
Walker, Lorenzo Giles *surgeon, educator*
Wall, Matthew J., Jr. *surgeon, research scientist*
Wallace, Joyce Irene Malakoff *internist*
Wallerstein, Ralph Oliver *physician*
Wang, Nancy *pathologist, educator*
Ward, Chester Lawrence *physician, consultant*
Wasmuth, Carl Erwin *retired physician, lawyer*
Watanabe, Kyoichi A(loysius) *pharmacology educator, chemist*
Waterhouse, Keith *urologist, educator, retired surgeon*

Waters, William Carter III *retired internist, educator*
Watne, Alvin L. *retired surgeon, educator*
Watson, Donald Charles, Jr. *cardiothoracic surgeon, educator*
Way, Barbara Haight *retired dermatologist*
Wayburn, Edgar *internist, environmentalist*
Weinshenker, Naomi Joyce *clinical psychiatrist, educator, researcher*
Weiss, Lyn Denise *physician*
Weiss, Steven Gary *physician*
Weller, Thomas Huckle *physician, retired medical educator*
West, Gregory Alan *physician*
White, Augustus Aaron III *orthopaedic surgeon*
White, Gilbert Case, II, *internist, hematologist*
White, Kerr Lachlan *retired physician, foundation administrator*
White, Richard Thomas *radiologist*
Whitehorn, Clark Allan *retired urologist*
Whitman, Gregory Theodore *neurologist*
Whitsell, John Crawford, II, *general surgeon*
Wieland, Gilbert Darryl *medical researcher, anthropologist, gerontologist*
Wiggs, Eugene Overbey *ophthalmologist, educator*
Wilhelm, Morton *retired surgeon*
Wilk, Ronald *physician*
Wilkins, Fred Clayton *physician, educator, engineer*
Williams, James Buchanan *retired surgeon*
Williams, Robert Leon *retired psychiatrist, neurologist, educator*
Williams, Steven D. *plastic surgeon*
Wilmore, Douglas Wayne *surgeon, educator*
Wilson, Mary Elizabeth *epidemiologist, physician, educator*
Wilson, Myron Robert, Jr. *retired psychiatrist*
Wingate, Robert Lee, Jr. *internist*
Winslow, Walter William *psychiatrist, educator*
Wishnick, Marcia Margolis *pediatrician, educator, geneticist*
Woldman, Sherman *pediatrician*
Woo, Kenneth Roger *urologist*
Wood, Maurice *medical educator*
Woolston-Catlin, Marian *psychiatrist*
Worner, Theresa Marie *internist, educator*
Worrell, Richard Vernon *orthopedic surgeon, dean*
Wyngaarden, James Barnes *retired physician*
Xia, Guohua *scientist, physician, psychologist*
Yaffe, Sumner Jason *pediatrician, educator, science administrator*
Yalam, Arnold Robert *allergist, immunologist, consultant*
Yarchoan, Robert *clinical immunologist, researcher*
Yielding, K. Lemone *physician*
Yodaiken, Ralph E. *pathologist, occupational health physician, educator*
Yollick, Bernard Lawrence *otolaryngologist, surgeon*
Yood, Harold Stanley *retired internist*
Youmans, Julian Ray *neurosurgeon, educator*
Youngstrom, Paul Clarence *anesthesiologist*
Yuan, Zhaoxu *ophthalmologist, researcher*
Zambrano, Eduardo Vicente *pathologist, researcher*
Zangwill, Steven *pediatrician, cardiologist*
Zarins, Bertram *orthopedic surgeon*
Zawacki, Bruce Edwin *surgeon, educator, ethicist*
Zitrin, Charlotte Marker *psychiatrist, educator, researcher*
Zizic, Thomas Michael *physician, educator*
Zografi, George *pharmacologist, educator*
Zumwalt, Ross Eugene *forensic pathologist, educator*

# HUMANITIES: LIBERAL STUDIES

## UNITED STATES

### ALABAMA

**Auburn**
Amacher, Richard Earl *retired literature educator*
Lewis, Walter David *historian, educator*
Littleton, Taylor Dowe *humanities educator*

**Bessemer**
Stewart, Mary Frances *English professor*

**Birmingham**
Allen, Lee Norcross *historian, educator*
Burden, Cedric Jerome, Sr. *language professor*
Morton, Marilyn Miller *retired genealogy educator, researcher, retired history professor, travel company executive*
Turón, Mercedes *emeritus language professor*

**Daphne**
Hamilton, Virginia Van der Veer *historian, educator*

**Dothan**
Glanton, Jeraline Cain *retired language educator*

**Huntsville**
Lang, Sharon *historian*

**Jacksonville**
Spector, Daniel Earl *historian, educator*

**Jasper**
Lloyd, Karen D. *French language educator*

**Lillian**
Burnette, Ollen Lawrence, Jr. *historian*

**Loachapoka**
Schafer, Elizabeth Diane *historian, writer*

**Marion**
Bauer, David Woodfin *history professor*

**Mobile**
Gandy, Maurice Edward *language educator, writer*
Kargleder, Charles Leonard *language educator*
Steadman, John Marcellus III *retired language educator*

**Montgomery**
Cornett, Lloyd Harvey, Jr. *retired historian*
Daniell, Steven J. *language educator, department chairman*
Napier, Cameron Mayson Freeman *historic preservationist*
Wells, Wyatt Clinton *historian*
Westhauser, Karl E. *historian*

**Normal**
Kearns, Nancy J. *language educator*

**Ramer**
Napier, John Hawkins III *historian*

**Troy**
Blum, Elizabeth Dian *history professor*
McPherson, Milton Monroe *retired history professor*

**Tuscaloosa**
Brewer, Kathryn A. *English educator, researcher*
Crowley, John William *literature and language professor*
de Souza, Ismenia Sales *language educator*
Freyer, Tony Allan *historian, educator*
Hendrix, Mary Elizabeth *language educator, researcher*
Hocutt, Max Oliver *retired philosophy educator*
Janiga-Perkins, Constance Gabrielle *language educator*
Pass, Charlotte Louise *literature educator, consultant*

**Tuskegee Institute**
Gamble, Vanessa Northington *historian, healthcare educator, bioethicist*

### ALASKA

**Anchorage**
Kim, Taesoo *language educator*
Norris, Frank B. *historian*

**Fairbanks**
Schuldiner, Michael Joseph *language educator, writer*

**Juneau**
Ruotsala, James Alfred *historian, writer*

### ARIZONA

**Apache Junction**
Bracken, Harry McFarland *philosophy educator*
Maher, John *literature educator, writer*

**Casa Grande**
Landers, Patricia Glover *language educator*

**Davis Monthan Afb**
Miller, Charles Wallace *historian, environmental geologist, educator*

**Glendale**
Wise, John Macgregor *speech educator*

**Green Valley**
Brewington, Arthur William *retired English language educator*

**Parker**
Cravath, Jay Lewis *cultural educator*

**Phoenix**
Drnjevic, Jonathan Mark *language educator*
Rister, Gene Arnold *humanities educator*

**Prescott**
Roberts, Deborah Marie *historian, consultant*

**Safford**
Kaliher, Michael Dennis *historian, librarian*

**Scottsdale**
Gwinn, Mary Dolores *liberal studies organization administrator, writer*
Land, George A. *philosopher, consultant, writer*

**Sun City**
Oppenheimer, Max, Jr. *foreign language educator, consultant*

**Surprise**
Clark, Lloyd *historian, writer, educator*

**Tempe**
Adelson, Roger Dean *history professor, historian, editor*
Brack, O. M., Jr. *language educator*
Green, Monica H. *history professor*
Iverson, Peter James *historian, educator*
MacKinnon, Stephen R. *Asian studies administrator, educator*
Wetsel, William David *literature educator*
Wong, Timothy C. *language and literature educator*

**Tucson**
Adjarian, Maude Madeleine *literature educator, researcher*
Birkinbine, John, II, *philatelist*
Boyle, Christopher George *language educator, counseling administrator*
Dinnerstein, Leonard *historian, educator*
Gelfand, Howard Michael *history professor*
Herrnstadt, Richard Lawrence *American literature educator*
Jurkowitz, Lisa Amy *language educator*

Neff-Encinas, Julie Gay *bilingual education specialist, consultant*
Schulz, Renate Adele *German studies and second language acquisition educator*
Zepeda, Ofelia *linguist, educator*

## ARKANSAS

### Arkadelphia
Graves, John William *historian*
Trofimova, Irina (Irene) Alexeevna *literature and language professor*

### Conway
Stiritz, Marette McCauley *English language educator, consultant*
Ziegler, John Alan *historian, political scientist, educator*

### Fayetteville
Aiello, Thomas *historian, educator*
Levine, Daniel Blank *classical studies educator*
Sutherland, Daniel Ellyson *historian*

### Fort Smith
Colbert, Alice Taylor *history professor*

### Jonesboro
Elkins, Francis Clark *historian, educator, director*

### Little Rock
Vinikas, Vincent *historian, educator*

### Malvern
Schultz, Marvin E. *historian, educator*

### Mena
Eddleman, Floyd Eugene *retired language educator*

### Monticello
Babin, Claude Hunter *history professor*

### Pine Bluff
Hudspeth, Harvey Gresham *history professor*

### State University
Milner, Clyde A., II, *historian*

### West Fork
Higgins, Sarah Jean *literature and language professor*

### Wickes
Riley, Faith Lynch *retired historian, writer*

## CALIFORNIA

### Aliso Viejo
La Marca, Jeffry Peter *language educator, consultant*

### Arcadia
Yen, Wen-Hsiung *language and music professional, educator*

### Atherton
Bales, Royal Eugene *philosophy educator*

### Azusa
Esselstrom, David Dwight *literature educator, writer*

### Bakersfield
Flachmann, Michael Charles *English language educator*
Kegley, Jacquelyn Ann *philosophy educator*
Meyers, Christopher *humanities educator, consultant*
Peterson, Pamela Carmelle *language educator*

### Berkeley
Alter, Robert Bernard *literature educator, critic*
Anderson, William Scovil *classics educator*
Campbell, John *philosopher, educator*
Chihara, Charles Seiyo *philosophy educator*
Chytry, Josef V. *humanities educator*
Costa, Gustavo *Italian studies scholar*
Crews, Frederick Campbell *humanities educator, writer*
Donghi, Tulio Halperin *history professor*
Fitelson, Branden Eric *philosopher, educator*
Gallagher, M. Catherine *English literature educator*
Haber, Samuel *retired history professor*
Herr, Richard *history professor*
Karlinsky, Simon *language educator, writer*
Lichterman, Martin *history professor*
Litwack, Leon Frank *historian, educator*
Long, Anthony Arthur *classics educator*
Mavroudi, Maria *philologist, educator*
Middlekauff, Robert Lawrence *historian, educator, academic administrator*
Muscatine, Charles *language educator, writer*
Partridge, Loren Wayne *art historian, educator*
Rauch, Irmengard *linguist, educator*
Scheffler, Samuel *philosophy educator*
Selz, Peter Howard *art historian, educator*
Shannon, Thomas Frederic *German language educator*
Slezkine, Yuri *history professor*
Sloane, Thomas O. *speech educator*
Taruskin, Richard Filler *musicologist, educator*
Wakeman, Frederic Evans, Jr. *historian, educator*
Zwerdling, Alex *language educator*

### Cambria
Salaverria, Helena Clara *retired language educator*

### Carmel
Chung, Kyung Cho *Korean history specialist, educator, writer*
Wright, Constance Storey *retired humanities educator*

### Claremont
Ackerman, Gerald Martin *art historian, consultant*

Atlas, Jay David *philosopher, consultant, linguist, educator*
Barron, Hal S. *historian, history professor*
Burns, Richard Dean *historian, educator, writer*
Davis, Nathaniel *humanities educator*
Deese, E(thel) Helen *retired literature and language professor*
Kucheman, Clark Arthur *philosophy educator, religious studies educator*
Lofgren, Charles Augustin *historian, educator*
McKirahan, Richard Duncan *classics and philosophy educator*
Moss, Myra Ellen (Myra Moss Rolle) *philosophy educator*
Pinney, Thomas Clive *retired English language educator*
Shimkhada, Deepak *art historian*
Sontag, Frederick Earl *philosophy educator*
Wheeler, Geraldine Hartshorn *historian, writer*
Woodress, James Leslie, Jr. *language educator*

### Compton
Maradiaga Kieffer-Aanonsen, Nora Ludmila *language educator*

### Davis
Altisent, Marta *language educator*
Basile, Marie Elisabeth *historian, researcher*
Druzhnikov, Yuri Ilya *literature educator, writer*
Hayden, John Olin *English literature educator, writer*
Hoffman, Michael Jerome *humanities educator*
Irwin, Robert McKee *Spanish educator*
Waddington, Raymond Bruce, Jr. *language educator*
Williamson, Alan Bacher *literature educator, poet, writer*
Willis, Frank Roy *historian, educator*

### Dinuba
Surabian, Carol Anne *language educator, consultant*

### Fountain Valley
Le, Vinh Tu *retired language educator, translator*

### Fresno
Bundy-DeSoto, Teresa Mari *language educator, vocalist*
Kouymjian, Dickran *art historian, educator*

### Fullerton
Carrithers, Joseph Edward *English composition and literature educator*

### Glendale
de Grassi, Leonard *art historian, educator*

### Hacienda Heights
Dodson, Arleen Cecilia *language educator*

### Hayward
Hammond, Marian Corleene *retired literature educator*

### Hemet
Culverwell, Albert Henry *historian*

### Huntington Beach
Winterowd, Walter Ross *language educator*

### Irvine
Boyd, Carolyn Patricia *history professor*
Hine, Robert Van Norden, Jr. *historian, educator*
Iser, Wolfgang *retired literature educator, writer*
Lillyman, William John *language educator, academic administrator*
Pomeranz, Kenneth L. *history professor*
Seed, Patricia *historian, educator*
Wehmeier, Kai Frederick *philosopher, educator*

### Kagel Canyon
Paull, Katharine Everhart *language educator*

### La Jolla
Langacker, Ronald Wayne *linguistics educator*
McDonald, Marianne *classicist*
Miyoshi, Masao *literature educator, writer*
Olafson, Frederick Arlan *philosophy educator*
Oreskes, Naomi *science historian*
Thompson, Emily *historian*
Wesling, Donald Truman *English literature educator*
Wright, Andrew *English literature educator*

### La Verne
O'Brien, James D. *language educator, communications executive*

### Lakewood
Welch, Lynne G. *language and music educator*

### Livermore
Hiskes, Dolores G. *language educator*

### Long Beach
Alkana, Linda Kelly *history professor*
Beebe, Sandra E. *retired language educator, artist, writer*
Kusaba, Clifford Noboru *historian, educator*
Locklin, Gerald *language educator, poet, writer*
Nguyen, Huong Tran *former elementary and secondary language educator, former district office administrator*
Tang, Paul Chi Lung *philosophy educator*

### Los Altos
Nivison, David Shepherd *language educator, philosopher*

### Los Angeles
Alkon, Paul Kent *language educator*
Allen, Michael John Bridgman *language educator*
Alpers, Edward Alter *history professor*
Bahr, Ehrhard *Germanic languages and literature educator*
Boime, Albert Isaac *art historian, educator*
Bradshaw, Murray Charles *musicologist, educator*
Caram, Eve La Salle *language educator, writer*
Cohen, S(tephen) Marshall *philosophy educator*

Davidson, Herbert Alan *Near Eastern languages and cultures educator*
Dumitrescu, Domnita *Spanish language educator, researcher*
Frank, Peter Solomon *art historian, curator, art critic*
Hines, Thomas Spight *historian, educator, architecture critic*
Hundley, Norris Cecil, Jr. *historian, educator*
Kelley, Robin Davis Gibran *history professor, writer*
Kelly, Henry Ansgar *language educator*
Kolve, V. A. *English literature educator*
Laird, David *humanities educator emeritus*
Levine, Philip *classics educator*
Mellor, Ronald John *history professor*
Minkova, Donka *language educator*
Nakell, Martin R. *literature educator, writer*
Rouse, Richard Hunter *historian, educator*
Schaefer, William David *language educator*
See, Carolyn *English language educator, writer, book critic*
Smith, Bruce R. *language educator*
Stockwell, Robert Paul *linguist, educator*
Trenton, Patricia Jean *art historian*
Tritle, Lawrence Alan *history professor*
Troy, Nancy J. *art history educator*
Weber, Eugen *historian, educator, writer*
Wortham, Thomas Richard *literature and language professor*

### Malibu
Larson, Edward John *historian, educator, law educator*
Marshall, Donald Glenn *English language and literature educator*

### Marina
Madsen, Roy I., Jr. *language educator*

### Marina Del Rey
Rimer, John Thomas *language educator, academic administrator, writer*

### Merced
Hallman, Max O. *humanities professor, philosophy professor, director*

### Modesto
Nicholson, Coy Lee *English educator, writer*

### Monterey
Peet, Phyllis Irene *women's studies educator*

### Newport Beach
Brown, Giles Tyler *history professor, lecturer*
Mc Culloch, Samuel Clyde *history professor*

### Northridge
Omatsu, Glenn *Asian American studies professor*
Orenstein, Michael (Ian Orenstein) *philatelic dealer, columnist*

### Norwalk
Ernest, Roger Craig *language educator*

### Oakland
Berry, Kathleen A. *English language educator*

### Orange
Williams, Danna Beth *reading specialist*

### Oxnard
Hill, Alice Lorraine *historian, researcher, genealogist*

### Pacific Grove
Penney, Beth *language educator, editor, writer*

### Pacific Palisades
Perloff, Marjorie Gabrielle *literature educator*

### Palo Alto
Cherno, Melvin *humanities educator*
Knoles, George Harmon *history educator*
Mommsen, Katharina *retired literature and language professor, foundation administrator*
Ober, Josiah *history educator*

### Pasadena
Gregory, Timothy Peter *historian, consultant*
Kousser, J(oseph) Morgan *historian, educator*
Parr, James Allan *literature professor*
Williams, Bradley Bennett *historian*

### Pebble Beach
Dallmann, William Charles *speech educator, writer*
Hotelling, Neal Barry *historian, director*

### Piedmont
Putter, Irving *retired French language educator*

### Placerville
Nesbitt, Paul Edward *historian, author, educator*

### Pomona
Cranston, John Welch *historian, educator*

### Portola Valley
Carnochan, Walter Bliss *retired humanities educator*

### Rancho Cucamonga
Clarke, Orville Oliver, Jr. *art history educator*
Quinn, Dennis Michael *history professor*

### Rancho Santa Fe
Ruiz, Ramón Eduardo *history professor*

### Rialto
Hunley, John Dillard *retired historian, ombudsman*

### Riverside
Barkin, Kenneth David *history professor*
Elliott, Emory Bernard *language educator, school system administrator*

Jackson, Marguerite Faye Thurston *rhetoric and intercultural communications and language educator*
Salzman, Michele Renee *historian, educator*
Snyder, Henry Leonard *historian, educator, writer*
Yount, Gwendolyn Audrey *humanities educator*

### Rocklin
Blank, Lenore Kim *literature and language professor, consultant*

### Rohnert Park
Halavais, Mary Hoyt *history professor, researcher*

### Sacramento
Carr, Gerald Francis *language educator*
Heningburg, Keith Rudolph Valenteno *history professor, director*
Meindl, Robert James *language educator, poet*

### San Bernardino
Andersen, Jennifer Lotte *literature and language professor*

### San Diego
Amstadt, Nancy Hollis *retired language educator*
Brandes, Raymond Stewart *historian, educator, dean*
Dunlop, Marianne *retired language educator*
Peterson, Richard Hermann *retired history professor*
Swank, William George *historian, writer*
Vanderbilt, Kermit *language educator*
Wawrytko, Sandra Ann *humanities educator*
Withee, Diana Keeran *art historian, art dealer, educator*

### San Francisco
Bardsley, Kay *historian, archivist, dance professional*
Birnbaum, Lucia Chiavola *historian, educator*
Cherny, Robert Wallace *historian, educator*
Costa-Zalessow, Natalia *foreign language educator*
Dennehy, Raymond Leo *philosopher, educator*
Felstiner, Mary Lowenthal *history professor*
Hansen, Carol Louise *literature and language professor*
Kelley, Michael Garhart Roosevelt *historian, educator, writer*
McGuire, William Albert *humanities educator*
Needleman, Jacob *philosophy educator, writer*
Satin, Joseph *language educator, retired dean*
Stump, David James *philosopher, educator*

### San Juan Capistrano
Carlson, Lawrence Arvid *retired English language educator, real estate agent*

### San Luis Obispo
Ayral-Clause, Odile *language educator, writer*
Lynch, Joseph James *philosophy educator*

### San Marcos
Johnson, Christopher Stephen *history professor*
Watts, Jill Marie *history educator*

### San Marino
Rolle, Andrew *historian, writer*
Travis, Albert Hartman *retired ancient language educator*
Zall, Paul Maxwell *language educator, consultant*

### Santa Barbara
Abbott, Horace Porter *English literature educator*
Chafe, Wallace LeSeur *linguist, educator*
Collins, Robert Oakley *history professor*
Crawford, Donald Wesley *philosophy educator, university official*
Del Chiaro, Mario Aldo *art historian, archaeologist, etruscologist, educator*
Fingarette, Herbert *philosopher, educator*
Göllner, Marie Louise *musicologist, retired educator*
Gunn, Giles Buckingham *language educator, religious studies educator, global and international studies educator*
Helgerson, Richard *English literature educator*
Mahlendorf, Ursula Renate *literature educator*
McGee, James Sears *historian, educator*
Rose, Mark Allen *humanities educator*
Russell, Jeffrey Burton *historian, educator*
Wilkins, Burleigh Taylor *philosophy educator*

### Santa Cruz
Berger, Harry *literature and art history professor emeritus*
Stevens, Stanley David *historian, researcher, retired librarian, archivist*
Suckiel, Ellen Kappy *philosophy educator*

### Santa Paula
Lattimore, Steven *classicist, educator*

### Santa Rosa
Aman, Reinhold Albert *philologist, writer*

### Santee
Peters, Raymond Eugene *historian, writer*

### Seal Beach
Reynales, Barbara Wallace *literature educator*

### Sherman Oaks
Howe, Daniel Walker *historian, educator*

### Stanford
Baker, Keith Michael *history professor*
Bresnan, Joan W. *literature and language professor*
Dekker, George Gilbert *literature educator, writer*
Duus, Peter *retired historian*
Eitner, Lorenz Edwin Alfred *art historian, educator*
Felstiner, John *literature educator, translator*
Fredrickson, George Marsh *history professor*
Gelpi, Albert Joseph *language educator, department chairman, critic*
Jurafsky, Daniel *linguist*
Kennedy, David Michael *historian, educator*

Loftis, John, Jr., (John Clyde Loftis Jr.) *language educator*
Martin, Richard Peter *classics educator, consultant*
Moretti, Franco *professor of comparative literature*
Predmore, Michael Pennock *Spanish language and literature educator*
Robinson, Paul Arnold *historian, educator, writer*
Sheehan, James John *historian, educator*
Stansky, Peter David Lyman *historian, writer, retired history professor*
Traugott, Elizabeth Closs *linguist, educator, researcher*

**Stockton**
Limbaugh, Ronald Hadley *retired historian, cultural organization administrator*

**Thousand Oaks**
Reaves, Michaela Crawford *history professor*

**Torrance**
Imbarus, Aura *language educator, consultant*

**Vallejo**
Brown, Earl Kent *historian, minister*

**Van Nuys**
Ewing, Guin Porter *historian, art collector*
Zucker, Alfred John *English and history educator, academic administrator, historian*

**Venice**
Padilla, Mario René *literature educator, writer*

**Vista**
Nolte, Linda Marie *language educator*

**Whittier**
Reid, Ivonne Figueroa *language educator*

## COLORADO

**Aurora**
Taraborelli, Janice Conti *humanities educator, academic administrator*

**Basalt**
Moya, Sharon Staggs *language educator*

**Boulder**
Barchilon, Jacques *foreign language educator, researcher, writer*
Engel, Barbara Alpern *history professor*
Gonzalez-del-Valle, Luis Tomas *Spanish language educator*
Limerick, Patricia Nelson *history professor*
Rood, David S. *linguistics educator*

**Cherry Hills Village**
Conroy, Mary Elizabeth *history professor*

**Colorado Springs**
Cramer, Owen Carver *classics educator, department chairman*
Dassanowsky, Robert von *language educator, film producer, educator, writer*
Stavig, Mark Luther *language educator*
Sturdevant, Katherine Scott *historian, educator*
Tucker, Frank Hammond *history professor*
Yaney, George *retired history professor*

**Denver**
Frederick, Robert Allen *history professor*
Storey, Brit Allan *historian*

**Fort Collins**
McComb, David Glendinning *history professor*
Thiem, Jon Edgar *literature educator*
Tremblay, William Andrew *language educator, writer*

**Golden**
Dickinson, Carol Rittgers *art historian, writer*
Eckley, Wilton Earl, Jr. *humanities educator*
Pegis, Anton George *retired language educator*

**Greeley**
Downey, Matthew T. *history professor, writer*
Wilson, Sharon Rose *literature educator, researcher*
Worley, Lloyd Douglas *language educator*
Yagami, Kazuo *historian*

**Greenwood Village**
Chico, Beverly Ann *history professor, humanities educator*

**Lakewood**
Woodruff, Kathryn Elaine *literature and language professor*

**Palisade**
Fay, Abbott Eastman *history professor*

## CONNECTICUT

**Branford**
Whitaker, Thomas Russell *English literature educator*

**Colebrook**
McNeill, William Hardy *retired historian, writer*

**East Granby**
Scanlon, Lawrence Eugene *language educator*

**Essex**
Hieatt, Allen Kent *retired language educator*
Hieatt, Constance Bartlett *English language educator*

**Fairfield**
Levitt, Jesse *retired foreign language educator*
Miller, Frederick Edwin, Jr. *history professor, government agency administrator*
Newton, Lisa Haenlein *philosopher, educator*

**Farmington**
Reeves, John Drummond *retired English language professional, writer*

**Greenwich**
Wiener, Malcolm Hewitt *historian, writer*

**Guilford**
Colish, Marcia Lillian *history professor*
Hare, Peter Hewitt *philosophy educator*

**Hamden**
Kagan, Donald *historian, educator*
McClellan, Edwin *literature educator*

**Hartford**
Riggio, Milla C. *language educator, researcher*

**Ivoryton**
Osborne, John Walter *historian, educator, author*

**Meriden**
Chiarenza, Frank John *language educator*

**Middletown**
Buel, Richard Van Wyck, Jr. *retired history professor, editor, writer*
Crites, Stephen Decatur *philosopher, educator*
Gillmor, Charles Stewart *historian, researcher, educator*
Heimann-Hast, Sybil Dorothea *literature and language professor*
Meyer, Priscilla Ann *literature and language professor*
Pomper, Philip *historian, educator*
Reed, Joseph Wayne *American studies educator, artist*
Schwarcz, Vera *historian, educator, poet*
Shapiro, Norman Richard *literature and language professor*
Slotkin, Richard Sidney *literature educator*
Turco, Alfred, Jr. *language educator*
Wensinger, Arthur Stevens *literature and language professor, writer, translator*

**Milford**
Foster, Patrick R. *historian, writer*

**Naugatuck**
Scheithe, Jeanne Marie *language educator, mathematician, educator*

**New Britain**
Emeagwali, Gloria Thomas *humanities educator*
Heitner, John A. (Jack Heitner) *literature and language professor, writer*
Leeds, Barry Howard *literature and language professor*

**New Haven**
Abramson, Arthur Seymour *linguistics educator, researcher*
Bloom, Harold *humanities educator, writer*
Blum, John Morton *historian, educator*
Borroff, Marie *English language educator*
Brisman, Leslie *English literature educator*
Bynum, Terrell Ward *humanities educator, consultant*
Followay, Jonathan Scott *history professor*
Frank, Roberta *literature educator*
Gilbert, Creighton Eddy *art historian*
Goffart, Walter André *history professor*
Hallo, William Wolfgang *literature and language professor, writer*
Harries, Karsten *philosophy educator, researcher*
Hersey, George Leonard *retired art historian*
Hollander, John *humanities educator, poet*
Holquist, James Michael *literature educator, department chairman*
Hyman, Paula E(llen) *history professor*
Insler, Stanley *philologist, educator*
Kevles, Daniel Jerome *historian, educator*
Marcus, Ruth Barcan *philosopher, educator, writer, lecturer*
Mazzotta, Giuseppe Francesco *literature and language professor*
Peterson, Linda H. *English language educator*
Pollitt, Jerome Jordan *art historian, educator*
Prochaska, Alice *historian, librarian*
Prown, Jules David *art historian, educator*
Rawson, Claude Julien *literature and language professor*
Robinson, Fred Colson *language educator*
Scully, Vincent Joseph, Jr. *architectural historian, educator, writer*
Smith, John Edwin *philosophy educator*
Snyder, Timothy David *history professor, writer*
Spence, Jonathan Dermot *historian, educator*
Stewart, Paul James, Jr. *history educator*
Turner, Frank Miller *historian, educator*
Underdown, David Edward *historian, educator*
Wandycz, Piotr Stefan *historian, educator*
Winroth, Anders *historian, educator*
Wolterstorff, Nicholas Paul *philosophical theology educator*
Yeazell, Ruth Bernard *English language educator*

**New London**
Dudden, Alexis *history professor*

**North Haven**
Bennett, Harry Louis *history professor*
Katsaros, Thomas *historian, educator*

**Norwalk**
Nelson, Paula Morrison Bronson *reading specialist*
O'Connell, William Egan *English professor*

**Orange**
Davis, David Brion *historian, educator*

**Pleasant Valley**
Decker, Robert Owen *history professor, clergyman*

**Salisbury**
Kilner, Ursula Blanche *genealogist, educator, writer*

**Storrs Mansfield**
Cazel, Fred A., Jr. *history professor*

Charters, Ann *literature educator*
Coons, Ronald Edward *historian, educator*
Franklin, Wayne S. *literature and language professor, writer*
Gross, Robert Alan *history professor*
Overmyer-Velazquez, Mark *history professor*

**Trumbull**
Allen, Richard Stanley (Dick Allen) *literature and language professor, writer*

**Washington**
Leab, Daniel Joseph *history professor*

**West Hartford**
Collins, Alma Jones *language educator, writer*

**Windsor**
Auten, Arthur Herbert *history professor*

**Woodbridge**
Cone, Virginia Williams *retired historian*
Conte, Alberta *language educator*
Dupré, Louis *retired philosopher, educator*
Kleiner, Diana Elizabeth Edelman *art historian, educator, academic administrator*

## DELAWARE

**Hockessin**
Valbuena-Briones, Angel Julian *retired language educator, author*

**Newark**
Boylan, Anne Mary *historian*
Dawson, Carl *English literature educator*
Day, Robert Androus *literature and language professor, retired library director, editor, publisher*
Gibson, Ann Eden *art historian, educator*
Lathrop, Thomas Albert *language educator*
Semmel, Stuart *history professor*
Steiner, Roger Jacob *linguistics educator, writer, researcher*
Weintraub, Stanley *arts and humanities educator, writer*
Wolters, Raymond *historian, educator*

**Wilmington**
Kneavel, Ann Callanan *humanities educator, communications consultant*
Tolles, Bryant Franklin, Jr. *historian, educator*

## DISTRICT OF COLUMBIA

**Fort Mcnair**
Raines, Edgar Frank, Jr. *historian*

**Washington**
Ágoston, Gábor *history professor*
Albrecht, Kathe Hicks *art historian, visual resources manager*
Bader, William Banks *historian, former corporate executive, foundation executive*
Bedini, Silvio A. *historian, author*
Billington, James Hadley *historian, librarian*
Broun, Elizabeth *art historian, curator*
Brown, Carolyn Anne *literature and language professor, consultant*
Cheney, Lynne Vincent *humanities educator, writer*
Cua, Antonio S. *philosopher, educator*
Dallek, Robert *history professor, historian, writer*
Dougherty, Jude Patrick *philosopher, educator, dean*
Faith, Thomas Iain *historian, educator*
Farr, Judith Banzer *retired literature educator, writer*
Ferretti, Maddalena Funiciello *humanities educator*
Foss, Clive Frank Wilson *history professor*
French, Valerie *history professor*
Graves-Roman, Patricia Ann *language educator, writer*
Hammond, William Michael *historian, educator*
Hawke, Paul Henry *historian*
Heelan, Patrick Aidan *philosophy educator*
Horton, James Oliver *history educator*
Kalb, Marvin *public policy and government educator*
Kass, Leon Richard *humanities educator*
Kazin, Michael *historian, writer*
Kelley, David Christopher *philosopher*
Kennedy, Dane Keith *history professor*
Kennedy, Robert Emmet, Jr. *historian, educator*
Kreidler, Charles W(illiam) *linguist, educator*
Kreinheder, Hazel Fuller *genealogist, historian*
Latham, Ernest Hargreaves, Jr. *historian, educator*
Levinger, Matthew B. *historian*
Lightman, Marjorie *historian*
Livingston, Robert Gerald *historian, journalist*
Marr, Phebe Ann *retired historian, educator*
Miller, Jeanne-Marie Anderson (Mrs. Nathan J. Miller) *language educator, academic administrator*
Mori, Yoshiko *language educator*
Mujica, Barbara Louise *language educator, writer*
Neiditch, H. Michael *historian*
Poos, Lawrence Raymond *history educator*
Redd, Teresa M. *English language professor*
Robb, James Willis *romance languages educator*
Roberts, Jeanne Addison *retired literature educator*
Roberts, John W. *historian, federal agency official*
Rosenblatt, Jason Philip *literature and language professor*
Roshwald, Aviel Isaiah *history professor*
Sachar, Howard Morley *history professor*
Salamon, Linda Bradley *English literature educator*
Scott, Gary Thomas *historian*
Severino, Roberto *language educator, academic administration executive*
Shih, J. Chung-wen *Chinese language educator*
Simko, Jan *English, foreign language and literature educator*
Svoboda, Patricia Helen *art historian*
Taylor, Estelle Wormley *language educator, dean*

Taylor, Henry Splawn *retired literature educator, poet*
Trisco, Robert Frederick *church historian, educator*
Veatch, Robert Marlin *philosopher, researcher*
Voll, John Obert *history professor*
Wilkes, Donna Natalie *historian*
Witek, John W. *history professor*

## FLORIDA

**Belleair Bluffs**
Alexander, Christina Anamaria *translator, performing company executive*

**Big Pine Key**
Fleischer, Roland Edward *art history professor*

**Boca Raton**
Collins, Robert Arnold *literature and language professor*
Frank, Andrew K. *history professor*

**Bradenton**
Stewart, Priscilla Ann Mabie *art historian, educator*

**Cooper City**
Maugere, Dennis Paul *historian, educator*

**Coral Gables**
Sabat-Rivers, Georgina *Latin American literature educator*

**Daytona Beach**
Carmona, José Antonio *Spanish language educator, English language educator*
Kruse, Marylin Lynn *retired language educator*
Zenkovsky, Betty Jean *modern languages educator*

**Fort Lauderdale**
Austin, John Norman *classics educator*
Levy, Michael *philosopher, writer*

**Fort Myers**
Curtin, Constance O'Hara *language educator, writer*

**Fort Pierce**
Bateman, John Jay *classics educator*

**Fort Walton Beach**
Register, Annette Rowan *literature educator*

**Gainesville**
Davis, Richard Hunt, Jr. *historian*
Hartigan, Karelisa Voelker *classics educator*
Kushner, David Zakeri *musicologist*
Link, William Allen *history educator*
Pleasants, Julian McIver *history educator, summer school director*
Schmeling, Gareth *classics educator*

**Hillsboro Beach**
O'Connell, Richard (James) *English literature educator, poet*

**Jacksonville**
Carpenter, JoAnn Deakin *history professor*
Eschen, James L. *historian, educator*
Stanton, Robert John, Jr. *language educator*

**Key Biscayne**
Ross, Marilyn J. *language educator, communications educator*

**Lake Worth**
Wilson, William J. *language educator*

**Leesburg**
Duffy, John Lewis *retired Latin, English and reading educator*

**Lutz**
Currey, Cecil Barr *retired history professor*

**Marathon**
Wiecha, Joseph Augustine *language educator*

**Melbourne**
Jones, Elaine Hancock *humanities educator*

**Miami**
Camner, Howard *writing educator, writer, poet*
Falco-Leshin, JoAnna M. *literature and language professor*
King, John Allan, Jr. *history professor*
Leeder, Ellen Lismore *literature and language professor, literary critic*
Neu, Charles Eric *historian, educator*
Parks, Arva Moore *historian*
Schwartz, Kessel *modern language educator*
Welch, Judy Ann *language educator*
Zayas-Bazan, Eduardo *foreign language educator*

**Miami Shores**
Gonzalez, Pedro Blas *philosopher, educator*

**Miramar**
Huang, Guiyou *English studies educator, writer*

**Mulberry**
Bowman, Hazel Lois *retired English language educator*

**Naples**
Kinder, Suzanne Fonay Wemple *retired historian, retired educator*

**Oldsmar**
Thompson, Mack Eugene *historian, educator*

**Orlando**
Caldero-Figueroa, Ana Jhanilca *language educator*
Murphrey, Elizabeth Hobgood *history professor, librarian*
Pauley, Bruce Frederick *history professor*

**Palm Beach**
Gaudieri, Alexander V.J. *art historian, consultant, museum director*

**Panama City**
McWhorter, Susan Carol *English language educator*

**Pensacola**
Brown, Susan Louise *philosopher, educator*
Maddock, Lawrence Hill *retired language educator, writer*

**Port Charlotte**
Winters, Stanley B. *history professor, consultant, writer*

**Port Richey**
Long, Michael Eldon *government and history educator*

**Saint Augustine**
Oliver, Elizabeth Kimball *historian, writer*

**Sarasota**
Benowitz, June Melby *historian, educator*
Dungy, Kathryn R. *humanities educator*
Platt, Franklin Dewitt *retired history professor*
Taplin, Winn Lowell *historian, retired federal agency administrator*

**Tallahassee**
Bartlett, Richard Adams *retired history professor*
Golden, Leon *classicist, educator*
Halpern, Paul G. *history professor*
Hunt, Mary Alice *retired humanities educator*
Kaelin, Eugene Francis *retired philosophy educator*
Knetsch, Joe *historian*
Laird, Doris Anne Marley *retired humanities educator, musician*
Mamatey, Victor Samuel *historian, educator*
Mele, Alfred R. *philosophy educator*
Rogers, William Warren *historian, educator, publishing executive, writer*

**Tampa**
Anton, John Peter *philosopher, educator*
Frisch, Stefan A. *language educator*
Kasum, Michael *humanities educator, writer*
Mitchell, Mozella Gordon *language educator, minister*
Natarelli, Larissa Ivanovna *language educator, researcher*
Perry, James Frederic *philosophy educator, writer*

**Temple Terrace**
Crispell, Brian Lewis *history professor*

**Umatilla**
Balandran, Stella Varona *interpreter, lyricist, composer, writer*

**Winter Park**
Benedict, Dorothy Jones *genealogist, researcher*
Mason, Aimee Hunnicutt Romberger *retired philosophy and humanities educator*
Seymour, Thaddeus *language educator*
Wilson, Robley Conant, Jr. *language educator, editor, writer*

**GEORGIA**

**Alpharetta**
Whitley, Lena Frances *French educator*

**Americus**
Isaacs, Harold *history professor*

**Andersonville**
Boyles, Frederick Holdren *historian*

**Athens**
Freer, Coburn *language educator*
Kretzschmar, William Addison, Jr. *language educator*
Miller, Ronald Baxter *language educator, writer*
Ziemke, Earl Frederick *history professor, researcher*

**Atlanta**
Austin, Jeannette Holland *genealogist, writer*
Benario, Herbert William *classicist, educator*
Brown, Lorene B(yron) *retired library educator*
Burns, Thomas Samuel *history professor*
Chafee, Ingrid Roberta Hoover Coleman *retired language educator*
Fox-Genovese, Elizabeth Ann Teresa *humanities educator*
Gold, Hazel *Spanish language educator*
Hallen, Barry *philosopher, educator*
Hartle, Robert Wyman *retired literature and language professor*
Kuntz, Marion Lucile Leathers *classicist, educator, historian*
Lu, Hanchao *humanities educator, writer*
Luce, Willard Ray *historian, director*
McPhee, Sarah Collyer *art historian, educator*
Miller, Judith Ann *historian, educator*
Pindle, Arthur Jackson, Jr. *philosopher, researcher*
Stewart, Michael McFadden *speech professional*

**Augusta**
Dyer, James Harold, Jr. *language educator*
Klacsmann, Karen Towers *art historian, writer*
Mixon, Kenneth Wayne *history professor, department chairman*

**Cairo**
Oliver-Warren, Mary Elizabeth *retired library science educator, library and information scientist*

**Carrollton**
Steely, Melvin T. *language educator*

**Cochran**
Ricks, John Addison III *history professor*

**Decatur**
Dillingham, William Byron *literature educator, author*
Manley, Frank *language educator, writer*

**Douglas**
Seward, Lori A. *speech educator*

**Dunwoody**
Duvall, Marjorie L. *English and foreign language educator*

**Epworth**
Burgess, Lesa L. *language educator*

**Gainesville**
Nichols, Dana *language educator*

**Jackson**
Beasley, Anita Claire *reading specialist, consultant*

**Macon**
Fontenot, Chester J. *humanities educator, minister*
Huffman, Joan Brewer *history professor*

**Madison**
Aldridge, John Watson *language educator, writer*

**Morrow**
Gooden, Randall Scott *historian, archivist*

**Mount Vernon**
Toll, Larry Allen *history professor*

**Saint Simons Island**
Schneider, Duane Bernard *English literature educator*
Spivey, Ted Ray *language educator*

**Statesboro**
Woods, James M. *history professor*

**Valdosta**
Cronin, Kevin Stewart *historian, educator*

**Vidalia**
Melton, Thomas Ronald *history professor*

**Villa Rica**
Blevins, Ernest Everett *genealogist, researcher, historian*

**HAWAII**

**Honolulu**
Bender, Byron Wilbur *linguistics educator*
Dyen, Isidore *linguistic scientist, educator*
Farris, William Wayne *history professor*
Fujita, James Hiroshi *history educator*
Jordan, Amos Azariah, Jr. *foreign affairs educator, retired military officer*
Overstreet, Maryann Elizabeth *literature and language professor*
Rehg, Kenneth Lee *linguistics educator*
Seidensticker, Edward George *Japanese language and literature educator*
Stephan, John Jason *historian, educator*
Varley, Herbert Paul *Japanese language and cultural history educator*

**IDAHO**

**Boise**
Neil, J. Meredith *historian*

**Jerome**
Akers, Sharron Loella *language educator*

**Moscow**
Harris, Robert Dalton *history professor, researcher, writer*

**Pocatello**
Baergen, Ralph Neil *humanities educator*

**Rexburg**
Hartvigsen, M. Kip *literature and language professor*
Ivers, John Joseph *language educator, dean*

**ILLINOIS**

**Barrington**
Graham, Berta *humanities educator, researcher*

**Bloomington**
Bridges, Roger Dean *historian*

**Carbondale**
Ammon, Harry *history professor*
Gilbert, Glenn Gordon *retired linguistics educator*
Hahn, Robert Alan *philosophy educator*
Herstein, Gary L. *philosophy professor, researcher*
Lanigan, Richard Leo, Jr. *humanities educator, writer, editor*
Weeks, Theodore R. *history professor*
Werlich, David Patrick *history professor*

**Champaign**
Douglas, George Halsey *language educator, writer*
McGlathery, James Melville *retired foreign language educator*
Smith, Ralph Alexander *cultural and educational policy educator*
Watts, Emily Stipes *retired English language educator*

**Chicago**
Berk, Harlan Joseph *numismatist, writer*
Bevington, David Martin *English literature educator*
Biggs, Robert Dale *Near Eastern studies educator*
Boyer, John William *history professor, dean*
Brinkman, John Anthony *historian, educator*
Chakrabarty, Dipesh *history professor*

Chang, Peter M.J. *musicologist, educator*
Cohen, Charles Emil *art historian, educator*
Cohen, Ted *philosopher, educator*
Crone, Anna Lisa *Russian literature educator*
Cullen, Charles Thomas *historian, librarian*
De Armas, Frederick Alfred *foreign language educator*
Debus, Allen George *historian, educator*
Dembowski, Peter Florian *foreign language educator*
D'Emilio, John *humanities educator, writer*
Eze, Emmanuel Chukwudi *philosophy professor*
Frantzen, Allen John *English language educator*
Geyer, Michael *history professor*
Gossett, Philip *musicologist*
Grant, Robert McQueen *humanities educator*
Gray, Hanna Holborn *historian, educator*
Haley, George *Romance languages educator*
Harris, Neil *historian, educator*
Hast, Adele *historian, editor, writer*
Hellie, Richard *historian, educator*
Holli, Melvin George *history professor*
Johnson, Janet Helen *literature educator*
Kaegi, Walter Emil *history professor*
Karanikas, Alexander *language educator*
Katz, Friedrich *history educator*
Keenan, James George *classics educator*
Knight, Cranston S. *history professor*
Lawler, James Ronald *French language educator*
Liebenow, Franklin Eastburn, Jr. *English literature educator*
Manning, Sylvia *language educator*
Martinez, David Grey *classicist, educator*
McCloskey, Deirdre Nansen *economics and history educator*
Michaels, Walter Benn *English professor, writer*
Murrin, Michael J. *literature educator, writer*
Najita, Tetsuo *history professor*
Nashat, Guity *historian, education educator, researcher*
Nussbaum, Martha Craven *philosophy and classics educator*
Opitz, Donald L. *science historian*
Perone, Anthony Thomas III *language educator*
Podsiadlik, Edward *reading educator*
Remini, Robert Vincent *historian*
Roy, David Tod *literature educator*
Saller, Richard Paul *classics educator*
Sewell, William Hamilton, Jr. *historian*
Shanahan, Timothy Edward *urban education educator, researcher*
Shaughnessy, Edward Louis *language educator*
Sljivic-Simsic, Biljana B. *Slavic and Baltic languages educator*
Sochen, June *history professor*
Stanley, Amy Dru *history professor*
Stover, Leon (Eugene Stover) *retired anthropology professor, critic, writer*
Thaden, Edward Carl *history professor*
Van Patten, Bill *foreign language educator*
Weiner, Lynn Yvette *history professor, academic administrator*

**Edwardsville**
Liu, Yuliang *linguist, educator*
Petry, Alice Hall *scholar, educator, writer*

**Elmhurst**
Scurlock, Jo Ann *history professor, researcher*
Stanger, John Goodman *literature and language professor, archivist*

**Evanston**
Belting, Hans *art historian, educator, writer*
Hunwick, John Owen *history professor, language educator*
Kraut, Richard *humanities educator*
Pierrehumbert, Janet Breckenridge *language educator*
Reiss, Lenore Ann *language educator, retired secondary school educator*
Sheridan, James Edward *history professor*
Van Zanten, David Theodore *humanities educator*
Ver Steeg, Clarence Lester *historian, educator*
Weil, Irwin *literature and language professor*
Well, Irwin *language educator*
Wills, Garry *historian*
Wright, John *classics educator*

**Freeport**
Fiorenza, Samuel Thomas, Jr. *English educator*
Giaimo, Paul Sebastian *English and philosophy educator*

**Galesburg**
Hellenga, Robert Riner *language educator, writer*

**Gillespie**
Schwab, Sharon Kay *language arts educator, drama educator*

**Glen Ellyn**
Whisenhunt, William Benton *history professor*

**Glenview**
Epstein, Barbara Myrna Robbin *retired language educator*

**Highland Park**
Hoy, Suellen *historian*

**Hoffman Estates**
Kahn, Elizabeth *language educator, department chairman*

**Homewood**
Schillings, Denny Lynn *retired history professor, educational and grants consultant*

**Joliet**
Tijani, Hakeem Ibikunle *history professor, researcher*

**Lake Forest**
Park, David William *humanities educator*

**Lisle**
Gaddis, Vincent Ray *history professor*

**Mount Vernon**
Hall, Sharon Gay *retired language educator, artist*

**Normal**
Olsen, Patrice Elizabeth *history professor, photographer*
Shields, John Charles *literature educator*
Trouille, Mary Seidman *foreign language educator*

**Palatine**
Keres, Karen Lynne *literature and language professor*

**Robinson**
Chapman, Roger Eugene *historian, educator*

**Rock Island**
Skahill, Nathan B. *historian, educator*
Symons, Van Jay *humanities educator*

**Rockford**
Hicks, Stephen Ronald Craig *philosopher, educator*
Hoshaw, Lloyd *retired historian, educator*

**Seymour**
Carringer, Robert *language educator*

**Springfield**
Davis, George Cullom *historian*
Jackson, Jacqueline Dougan *literature educator, writer*
Temple, Wayne Calhoun *historian, writer*

**Urbana**
Antonsen, Elmer Harold *Germanic languages and linguistics educator*
Arnstein, Walter Leonard *retired historian*
Baron, Dennis E. *English language educator*
Brover-Lubovsky, Bella *musicologist*
Haile, H. G. *German language and literature educator*
Hendrick, George *retired English language educator*
Hoxie, Frederick Eugene *history professor*
Kaufmann, Urlin Milo *English literature educator*
Kim, Chin-Woo *linguist, educator*
Koenker, Diane P. *history professor*
Love, Joseph LeRoy *history professor, former cultural studies center administrator*
McColley, Robert McNair *historian, educator*
McKay, John Patrick *history professor*
Middeljans, April Lynn *literature educator*
Nelson, Cary Robert *language educator*
Nichols, John Alden *retired history professor*
Solberg, Winton Udell *historian, educator*
Talbot, Emile Joseph *French language educator*

**Westchester**
Masterson, John Patrick *retired language educator*

**Wheaton**
Noll, Mark A. *historian*

**Wilmette**
Monter, E. William *retired history professor*

**INDIANA**

**Bloomington**
Anderson, Judith Helena *English language educator*
Assensoh, Akwasi Bretuo *historian, educator*
Bernhardt-Kabisch, Ernest Karl-Heinz *English and comparative literature educator*
Choksy, Jamsheed Kairshasp *historian, religious scholar, humanities educator, language educator*
Dunn, Jon Michael *logician, dean*
Engber, Cheryl Ann *retired language educator, linguist*
Gremillion, Helen Claudia *humanities educator, director*
Gros Louis, Kenneth Richard Russell *humanities educator*
Hanson, Karen *philosopher, educator*
Henn, Barbara Jeanne *academic librarian*
Johnson, Owen Verne *historian, educator*
Juergens, George Ivar *history professor*
Lebano, Edoardo Antonio *foreign language educator*
Mickel, Emanuel John *foreign language educator*
Nordloh, David Joseph *literature and language professor, dean*
Peterson, M. Jeanne *historian, educator*
Ransel, David Lorimer *history professor*
Rosenberg, Samuel Nathan *French and Italian language educator*
Senchuk, Dennis M. *philosopher, educator*
Sinor, Denis *history professor, linguist*
Stoeltje, Beverly June *liberal studies educator*
Wilson, George Macklin *history educator, cultural studies center administrator*

**Carmel**
Sukapdjo, Wilma Irene *language educator*

**Cedar Lake**
Bocock, Scott Gregory *historian*

**Crawfordsville**
Barnes, James John *historian, educator*

**Culver**
Holaday, Allan Gibson *language educator*

**Evansville**
Baker, Ann Long *language educator*
Beavers, Anthony Francis *philosopher, educator*
Bigham, Darrel E. *history educator*

**Fort Wayne**
Caseldine-Bracht, Jennifer P. *philosopher, educator*
Miller, Dawn L. *composition literature educator*
Scheetz, Sister Mary JoEllen *English language educator*

**Greencastle**
Dittmer, John Avery *history professor*
Johnson, Cleveland Thomas *music historian, church musician*
Liu, Jinyu *history professor*

Spicer, Harold Otis *retired English language educator, communications educator*
Weiss, Robert Orr *speech educator*
Woodall, Susan Kay *language educator, librarian*

**Greenfield**
Bettler, Janet Louise Bell *foreign language educator*

**Hope**
Grimes, Todd R. *humanities educator*

**Indianapolis**
Baetzhold, Howard George *language educator*
Bodenhamer, David Jackson *historian, educator*
Boling, Joseph Edward *numismatist, retired military officer*
Connor, Ulla M. *linguistics educator*
Davis, Kenneth Wayne *language educator, business communication consultant*
Fuller, A. James *history professor*
Houser, Nathan *philosopher, educator*
Krasean, Thomas Karl *historian*
Mason, Thomas Alexander *historian, educator, author*
Nnaemeka, Obioma Grace *French language and women's studies educator, consultant, researcher*
Odell, James Calvin *history professor, theology studies educator*
Plater, William Marmaduke *literature and language professor, educator, academic administrator*

**Muncie**
Glass, James Arthur *historian, educator*
Hayashi, Tetsumaro *retired literature educator, writer, editor*
Zhuk, Sergei Ivanovich *history professor, researcher*

**Nashville**
Wills, Katherine V. Tsiopos *language educator*

**New Albany**
Beeby, James Matthew *history professor*
Thackeray, Frank W. *history professor*

**Notre Dame**
Appleby, R(obert) Scott *history educator*
Green, Catherine Gertrude *retired speech educator, retired secondary school educator*
Jemielity, Thomas John *language educator*
Lanzinger, Klaus *language educator*
Marsden, George M. *history professor, writer*
Matthias, John Edward *English literature educator*
McInerny, Ralph Matthew *philosopher, educator, writer*
O'Rourke, William Andrew *literature and language professor, writer*
Raymer, John David *literature and language professor*

**South Bend**
Cook, Pamela Margaret *French educator*
van Inwagen, Peter Jan *philosophy educator*

**Terre Haute**
Baker, Ronald Lee *folklore educator*
Carmony, Marvin Dale *retired linguist, educator*
De Marr, Mary Jean *English language educator*
Gennaro, Rocco Joseph *philosopher, educator*
Mehrens, Christopher Emile *musicologist, music librarian*

**Valparaiso**
Peters, Howard Nevin *foreign language educator*
Startt, James Dill *history educator*
Zhou, Yiqun *humanities educator*

**West Lafayette**
Bertolet, Rodney Jay *philosophy educator*
Blickenstaff, Channing Blount *retired language educator*
Broden, Thomas Francis III *French language educator*
Contreni, John Joseph, Jr. *humanities educator*
Mc Bride, William Leon *philosopher, educator*
Mork, Gordon Robert *historian, educator*
Woodman, Harold David *historian, educator*

**Winona Lake**
Norris, Mark Marston *historian, educator*

## IOWA

**Alton**
LeTendre, Beth Ann *language educator*

**Ames**
Avalos, Hector Ignacio *language educator*
Courteau, Joanna *foreign language educator*
Maxwell Dial, Eleanore *foreign language educator*
Nostwich, Theodore Daniel *literature educator, researcher*
Solensten, John Martin *retired English and American studies educator, writer*

**Cedar Falls**
Broadie, Richard R. *history professor*
Olivares-Cuhat, Gabriela Antonia *literature and language professor*
Olsen-Dunbar, Jessica Ida *sign language educator*
Schnucker, Robert Victor *historian, educator*

**Cedar Rapids**
Fitzpatrick, John Charles *humanities educator, curator*

**Centerville**
Moritz, Dana Dee *language educator*

**Decorah**
Kath, Ruth Robert *foreign language educator*

**Des Moines**
Archer, Julian Pratt Waterman *history professor*

Webb, Mary Christine *reading recovery educator, in-class reading specialist*

**Fairfield**
Rogers, Benjamin Franklin *retired history professor*

**Forest City**
Biggs, Douglas Lee *historian, educator*

**Grinnell**
Kaiser, Daniel Hugh *historian, educator*
Kintner, Philip L. *history professor*
Michaels, Jennifer Tonks *foreign language educator*

**Iowa City**
Addis, Laird Clark, Jr. *philosopher, educator, musician*
Aspel, Paulene Violette *retired language educator*
Duerlinger, James Peter *philosopher, educator*
Ertl, Wolfgang *German language and literature educator*
Folsom, Lowell Edwin *language educator*
Gelfand, Lawrence Emerson *historian, educator*
Green, Peter Morris *classics educator, writer, translator*
Hawley, Ellis Wayne *historian, educator*
Kerber, Linda Kaufman *historian, educator*
Mills, Margaret H. *linguist*
Porter, Horace Anthony *literature educator, writer*
Raeburn, John Hay *language educator*
Solbrig, Ingeborg Hildegard *literature educator, writer*

**Mount Pleasant**
Brereton, Todd Richard *history professor*

**Oskaloosa**
Porter, David Lindsey *history and political science professor, writer*

**Pella**
Den Adel, Raymond Lee *classics educator*

## KANSAS

**Atchison**
Jackson, Dan Adrian *language educator*
Lane, Elizabeth Ann *genealogist, researcher*

**Chanute**
Dillard, Dean Innes *English language educator, academic administrator*

**Dighton**
Stanley, Ellen May *historian, consultant*

**Emporia**
Lovett, Christopher C. *history professor, consultant*

**Fort Leavenworth**
King, Curtis Steeble *history professor*

**Hillsboro**
Kyle, Richard Granville *history professor, religion educator*

**Lawrence**
Alexander, John Thorndike *historian, educator*
Boyd, Beverly *English literature educator*
Cienciala, Anna Maria *history professor*
Eldredge, Charles Child III *art history educator*
Gunn, James Edwin *language educator*
Johnson, Wallace Stephen, Jr. *Asian languages educator*
Karcz, Andrzej *literature educator*
Li, Chu-Tsing *art historian, educator*
Saul, Norman Eugene *historian, educator*
Schoeck, Richard J. *English and humanities scholar, poet*
Tuttle, William McCullough, Jr. *history professor*
Woelfel, James Warren *philosophy and humanities educator*
Worth, George John *retired English literature educator*

**Leawood**
Ivey, Donald James *historian, archivist*

**Manhattan**
Higham, Robin *historian, editor, publisher*
Krysko, Michael Alexander *history professor*

**Mcpherson**
Kilgus, Ocie Arlene *language educator*

**North Newton**
Sprunger, Keith L. *historian, educator*

**Onaga**
Dillinger, Susan Alice *reading specialist*

**Topeka**
Bearman, Alan *historian*

**Wichita**
Bovee, David Steven *historian, educator*
Waters, Mary A. *literature and language professor*

## KENTUCKY

**Bowling Green**
Jackson, Carlton L. *history professor, writer*
Minton, John Dean *historian, educator*

**Georgetown**
Klotter, James C. *historian, educator*

**Highland Heights**
Ramage, James Alfred *history professor*

**Lexington**
Bodenbender, Michael Thomas *historian*
Campbell, Tracy *history professor*

Coffman, Edward McKenzie *retired history professor*
Thelin, John Robert *historian, educator, researcher*
Warth, Robert Douglas *history professor*

**Louisville**
Ford, Gordon Buell, Jr. *literature educator, writer*
Potter, Harold Claude *philosopher*

**Murray**
Whisenhunt, Donald Wayne *historian, educator, dean*

**Owensboro**
Lee, Anthony Wayne *literature and language professor*
West, William Robert *history professor*

**Richmond**
Coleman, David William *history professor*
Huch, Ronald Kind *historian, educator*
Nguyen, A. Minh Thong *philosopher, educator*

**Southgate**
Glenn, Jerry Hosmer, Jr. *retired language educator*

## LOUISIANA

**Baton Rouge**
Arceneaux, William *historian, educator, educational association administrator*
Cooper, William James, Jr. *history professor*
Culbert, David Holbrook *historian, educator, editor, writer*
Doty, Gresdna Ann *theatre historian, educator*
Hardy, John Edward *language educator, writer*
Hoffman, Paul Everett *history professor*
Lott, Bret *literature and language professor, writer*
Ricapito, Joseph Virgil (Giuseppe Ricapito) *literature educator*
Wheeler, Otis Bullard *retired language educator, retired director*

**Bogalusa**
Villarrubia, Glenda Boone *reading specialist, reading coordinator, educational consultant, educator*

**Lafayette**
Brasseaux, Carl Anthony *historian, educator, academic administrator, curator*
Carstens, Jane Ellen *retired library science educator*
Raffel, Burton Nathan *literature educator, poet, translator*

**Monroe**
Galle, Jeffrey Wayne *literature and language professor, department chairman*

**Natchitoches**
LeBreton, Marietta M. *history professor*
Wells, Carol McConnell *genealogist, retired archivist*

**New Orleans**
Brinkley, Douglas *historian, writer, educator*
Brumfield, William Craft *Slavic studies educator, photographer, writer*
Hasselbach, Karlheinz *literature educator*
Luza, Radomir Vaclav *historian, educator*
Michney, Todd Michael *history professor*
Paolini, Gilberto *literature educator*
Poesch, Jessie Jean *art historian*
Reck, Andrew Joseph *philosopher*
Schalow, Frank Hickey *philosopher, educator*
Vella, Christina *history professor*

**Ruston**
Dodge Robbins, Dorothy Ellin *language educator*
Halliburton, Lloyd *Romance philology educator*
Hankins, Jeffery Robin *history professor*

**Shreveport**
Plummer, Marguerite Reynolds *historian, educator*

## MAINE

**Bar Harbor**
Carpenter, William Morton *language educator, writer*

**Brunswick**
Hodge, James Lee *German language educator*
Levine, Daniel *historian, educator*

**Bucksport**
Ives, Edward Dawson *folklore educator*

**Castine**
Berleant, Arnold *philosopher*

**Dresden**
Turco, Lewis Putnam *language educator*

**Gorham**
Carey, David R., Jr. *history professor*

**Portland**
Schwanauer, Francis *philosopher, educator*

**Rockport**
Goodwin, Doris Helen Kearns *historian, writer*

**Sanford**
Allan, Jonathan David *autograph dealer, pop culture historian*

**Scarborough**
Sadik, Marvin Sherwood *art historian, consultant, retired museum director*

**Waterville**
Bassett, Charles Walker *literature and language professor*
Simon, David L. *art historian*

**West Boothbay Harbor**
Marshall, Howard Lowen *musicologist, retired music educator*

## MARYLAND

**Annapolis**
Brann, Eva Toni Helene *philosophy educator*
Symonds, Craig *historian, writer*

**Baltimore**
Achinstein, Peter Jacob *philosopher, educator*
Baldwin, John Wesley *history professor*
Celenza, Christopher S. *language educator*
Chapelle, Suzanne Ellery Greene *history professor*
Cohen, Warren I. *history professor*
Cooper, Jerrold Stephen *historian, educator*
Crockett, Bryan Lane *language educator, consultant*
Del Rosso, Jeana Marie *literature educator*
Ditz, Toby Lee *history professor*
Greene, Jack Phillip *historian, educator*
Irwin, John Thomas *humanities educator*
Johnson, Michael Paul *historian, educator*
Judson, Horace Freeland *history professor, writer*
Kessler, Herbert Leon *art historian, educator, academic administrator*
Knight, Franklin W. *historian, educator*
Kurth, Lieselotte *foreign language educator*
Lidtke, Vernon LeRoy *history professor*
McCarthy, Patricia Anne *reading educator*
Nichols, Stephen George *Romance languages educator*
Paulson, Ronald Howard *language educator, humanities educator*
Ranum, Orest Allen *historian, educator*
Smith, David Jeddie *American literature educator*
Ziff, Larzer *literature and language professor*

**Bel Air**
Lu, David John *historian, writer*

**Bethesda**
Achin, Milos Kosta *historian, writer*
Child-Olmsted, Gisèle Alexandra *retired language educator*
Fee, Elizabeth *medical historian, administrator*
Highfill, Philip Henry, Jr. *retired language educator*
van der Linden, Frank Morris *historian*

**Betterton**
Kohl, Benjamin Gibbs *historian, educator*

**Bowie**
LeCounte, Lola Houston *literature and language professor, educational consultant*
Sterling, Richard Leroy *English and foreign language educator*

**Chevy Chase**
Cline, Ruth Eleanor Harwood *translator*
Fern, Alan Maxwell *art historian, retired museum director*

**College Park**
Berlin, Ira *historian, educator*
Brush, Stephen George *historian, educator*
Collins, Merle *English and comparative literature educator*
Esh, Christian Rusell *history professor*
Haggh-Huglo, Barbara Helen *musicologist, educator*
Hallett, Judith Peller *classical studies educator*
Huglo, Michel Victor *musicologist*
Olson, Keith Waldemar *historian, educator*
Oster, Rose Marie Gunhild *foreign language professional, educator*
Panichas, George Andrew *language educator, critic, editor*
Pasch, Alan *philosopher, educator*
Weart, Spencer Richard *historian*

**Crofton**
Jamieson, Perry David *historian*

**Ellicott City**
Loerke, William Carl *art historian, educator*

**Glen Burnie**
Sanchez-Barnett, Susan Lynn *historian, educator*

**Hagerstown**
Nickerson, Rosemary Grzesik *humanities educator*
Potash, Martin H. *English educator*

**Harwood**
Dudley, William Sheldon *historian*

**Hyattsville**
Golden, Marita *English language educator, foundation executive*
Rodgers, Mary Columbro *literature educator, writer, academic administrator*

**Largo**
Seon, Yvonne *cultural educator, minister*

**Lusby**
Eshelman, Ralph Ellsworth *historian, consultant, paleontologist*

**Mitchellville**
Embree, Ainslie Thomas *history professor*
Heald, Morrell *humanities educator*

**Ocean Pines**
Fullerton, Jean Leah *retired language educator, researcher, census researcher*

**Pasadena**
De Pauw, Linda Grant *historian, educator, writer*

**Poolesville**
Kapsch, Robert James *engineering and architectural historian*

## Rockville
Cantelon, Philip Louis *historian*
Clarke, Nina Honemond *historian, writer, retired principal*
Hewlett, Richard Greening *historian*
Lide, James H. *historian*
Ware, Theresa *reading specialist, educator*

## Salisbury
Jones, Elizabeth Carol *language educator*

## Severna Park
Schick, Edgar Brehob *language educator*

## Silver Spring
Borkovec, Vera Z. *literature and language professor*
Calinger, Ronald Steve *historian*
Cole, Wayne Stanley *historian, educator*
Doherty, William Thomas, Jr. *historian, retired educator*
Johnson, Richard August *literature and language professor*
Papas, Irene Kalandros *English language educator, poet, writer*
Rothberg, Morey David *historian, editor*
Soderberg, Susan Cooke *historian, writer*

## Sparks
Suarez-Murias, Marguerite C. *retired language educator, retired literature educator*

## Towson
Ali, Omar H. *history professor*
Baker, Jean Harvey *history professor*
Propst, M. Teresa Carson *historian*

## Upper Marlboro
Brown, Mary Louvinia *literature and language professor, lawyer*

## Westminster
Gribben, Michele Ann *humanities educator*

# MASSACHUSETTS

## Amherst
Baker, Lynne Rudder *philosophy educator*
Benson, Lucy Wilson *historian, consultant*
Broadbridge, Anne Falby *history professor*
Brooks, A. Taeko *historian*
Gibson, Walker *retired language educator, poet, writer*
Kinney, Arthur Frederick *humanities educator, writer*
Minear, Richard Hoffman *history professor*
Oates, Stephen Baery *retired historian*
Pritchard, William H. *literature educator, writer*
Roeper, Thomas Walter *linguist, educator*
Rosbottom, Ronald Carlisle *language educator, humanities professor*
Rubin, Emanuel Leo *musicologist, composer*
Taubman, Jane Andelman *literature and language professor*
Wolff, Robert Paul *philosophy educator*
Wyman, David Sword *retired historian, educator*

## Andover
Dalton, Kathleen *history professor*

## Auburndale
Lindgren, Charlotte Holt *language educator*

## Belmont
Cavarnos, Constantine Peter *philosopher, writer*
Dohanian, Diran Kavork *art historian, educator*

## Beverly
Pierard, Richard Victor *history educator*

## Boston
Bai, Qianshen *art historian, educator*
Blakely, Allison *history professor*
Cardona, Rodolfo *Spanish language and literature educator*
Daniels, Norman *philosopher, educator*
Fong, Cynthia Ann *language educator*
Freeman, Joseph *automotive historian*
Hedges, Inez Kathleen *comparative literature educator*
Henry, DeWitt Pawling, II, *literature educator, art association administrator, writer*
Hintikka, Jaakko *philosopher, educator*
Jin, Xuefei (Ha Jin) *literature educator, writer*
Kleiner, Fred Scott *art historian, archaeologist, educator, editor*
Lyons, David Barry *philosophy and law educator*
Mc Carthy, Joseph Michael *historian, educator*
Mustafa, Shakir *English and Arabic language educator*
Price, Emmett George III *musicologist, educator, music minister*
Properzio, Paul J. *classicist, educator*
Rosen, Stanley Howard *humanities educator*
Tick, Judith *music historian, educator*
Wermuth, Paul Charles *retired language educator*

## Bridgewater
Karavites, Peter *retired historian*

## Brighton
Leistyna, Pepi *linguistics educator*

## Brookline
Michopoulos, Aristotle V. *humanities educator, researcher*
Moon, John Ellis van Courtland *retired historian*

## Byfield
deGrasse, Olga I. *language educator*

## Cambridge
Asani, Ali S. *foreign language and religious studies educator*
Bailyn, Bernard *historian, educator*
Bhabha, Homi K. *humanities educator, writer*
Blair, Ann *historian*
Bolster, Arthur Stanley, Jr. *history professor*

Brustein, Robert Sanford *literature and language professor, theater director, writer*
Buell, Lawrence Ingalls *language educator*
Capozzola, Christopher *historian*
Chomsky, (Avram) Noam *linguistics and philosophy educator*
Clausen, Wendell Vernon *retired classics educator*
Conley, Tom Clark *literature educator*
Craig, Albert M. *history professor, researcher*
Elkins, Caroline M. *history professor, writer*
Engell, James Theodore *language educator, department chairman*
Fanger, Donald Lee *Slavic language and literature educator*
Faust, Drew Gilpin *historian, educator*
Ferguson, Niall Campbell *history professor, writer*
Fisher, Philip J. *English language educator, literature educator*
Flier, Michael Stephen *Slavic languages educator*
Ford, Patrick Kildea *Celtic studies educator*
Gates, Henry Louis, Jr. *literature and language professor, historian*
Graham, Loren Raymond *historian, educator*
Greenblatt, Stephen Jay *literature and language professor, writer*
Guthke, Karl Siegfried *language educator*
Hamner, Suzanne Leath *retired history educator*
Hanan, Patrick Dewes *foreign language professional, educator*
Holmstrom, Bengt R. *philosopher, educator*
Iriye, Akira *historian, educator*
Jones, Christopher Prestige *classicist, educator, historian, consultant*
Kelly, Sean Dorrance *philosophy educator*
Keyser, Samuel Jay *linguist, educator*
Koester, Helmut Heinrich *history professor*
Laiou, Angeliki Evangelos *history professor*
MacMaster, Robert Ellsworth *historian, educator*
Maier, Charles Steven *history professor*
Maier, Pauline *historian, educator*
Malmstad, John Earl *literature and language professor*
Mazlish, Bruce *historian, educator*
McDonald, Christie Anne *literature and language professor, writer*
Menand, Louis *literature educator, writer*
Nykrog, Per *French literature educator*
O'Neil, Wayne *linguist, educator*
Owen, Edward Roger John (E. Roger Owen) *Middle Eastern studies professor, writer*
Reyes-Cubides, William *language educator, researcher, writer, actor*
Ritvo, Harriet *historian*
Rosenberg, Charles Ernest *historian, educator*
Rosenkrantz, Barbara Gutmann *science and medicine historian*
Rotberg, Robert Irwin *historian, political scientist, educator, academic administrator*
Sevcenko, Ihor *history professor, literature professor*
Simon, Eckehard (Peter) *foreign language educator*
Smail, Daniel Lord *history professor*
Smith, Merritt Roe *history professor*
Stauffer, John William *cultural historian*
Tarrant, Richard J(ohn) *classicist, educator*
Thernstrom, Stephan *historian, educator*
Thorburn, David *literature educator*
Trumpbour, John *historian, researcher, director*
Ulrich, Laurel Thatcher *historian, educator*
Vanger, Milton Isadore *historian, educator*
Vendler, Helen Hennessy *literature educator, poetry critic*
Ware, Susan W. *historian*
Weitzman, Arthur Joshua *language educator*
Ziolkowski, Jan Michael *medievalist educator*

## Canton
Parker, Virginia Marie *language educator*

## Chelmsford
DiPillo, Patricia Anne *language educator, researcher*

## Chestnut Hill
Blanchette, Oliva *philosophy educator*
Hachey, Thomas Eugene *British and Irish history educator*
O'Toole, James Michael *history educator*
Reed, James Eldin *historian, consultant, educator*
Valette, Rebecca Marianne *Romance languages educator*

## Danvers
Fox, John Joseph, Jr. *historian, educator*

## Dudley
Bickford, Crystal *literature and language professor, director*

## Fall River
Tinberg, Howard *language educator*

## Falmouth
Lamont, Rosette Clementine *language educator, journalist, translator*

## Framingham
Casper, Leonard Ralph *American literature educator*

## Granby
Ingham, Norman William *literature educator, genealogist*

## Great Barrington
Rodgers, Bernard Francis, Jr. *literature and language professor*

## Hingham
Richie, Margaret Bye *architectural historian*

## Lenox
Biron, Margaret M. *historian, educator*

## Leverett
Margolis, Nadia *language educator, translator, medievalist*

## Lexington
Kaledin, Eugenia Oster *American studies educator*

## Lowell
Aste, Mario Andrea *foreign language educator*
Carlsmith, Christopher *history professor*
McAfee, Noelle Claire *philosopher, educator*

## Medford
Bedau, Hugo Adam *philosophy educator*
Fyler, John Morgan *language educator*
Jackendoff, Ray Saul *linguistics educator*
Sherwin, Martin J. *history professor*
Ueda, Reed Takashi *historian, educator*

## Milton
Frazier, Marie Dunn *speech professional, public relations executive, personnel director*

## Needham
Kenslea, Timothy Joseph *historian, educator*

## Newton
Marshall, Robert Lewis *musicologist, educator*

## North Dartmouth
Peters, Morgan James *language educator, social studies educator, actor, writer, film director*
Yoken, Mel B(arton) *language educator, writer, radio personality*

## North Easton
Varella, Hazel L. *historian, educator*

## Northampton
Doss-Quinby, Eglal *language professional, educator*
Elkins, Stanley Maurice *historian, educator*
Ellis, Frank Hale *retired English literature educator*
Smith, Malcolm Barry Estes *philosopher, educator, lawyer*
von Klemperer, Klemens *historian, educator*

## Norton
Taylor, Robert Sundling *language educator, critic*

## Randolph
Morrissey, Edmond Joseph *philologist*

## Revere
Paananen, Victor Niles *language educator*

## Sheffield
Baritz, Loren *history professor*

## Sherborn
Cushing, Steven *linguist, educator, writer, researcher, consultant*

## Shutesbury
Creed, Robert Payson, Sr. *retired literature educator*

## South Deerfield
Kazar, John Dryden, Jr. *retired history professor*

## South Hadley
Berek, Peter *literature and language professor*
Brownlow, Frank Walsh *literature and language professor*
Farnham, Anthony Edward *language educator, department chairman*
Horsnell, Margaret Eileen *retired historian*
Mazzocco, Angelo *language educator, historian, linguist*
Straw, Carole Ellen *history professor*

## Springfield
Beagle, Jonathan McClellan *history professor*
Garabedian-Urbanowski, Martha Ann *foreign language educator*
Habermehl, Lawrence LeRoy *philosophy educator*
Miller, Leroy Paul, Jr. *language educator*

## Stoneham
Aastrrup, Rondi S. *English educator, principal*

## Waltham
Fischer, David Hackett *historian, educator*
Goodheart, Eugene *language educator*
Scheffler, Israel *philosopher, educator*
Schrecker, John *historian, educator*
Staves, Susan *humanities educator*

## Wellesley
Bidart, Frank *English educator, poet*
Martin, Tony *humanities educator*
Mistacco, Vicki E. *foreign language educator*

## Wellfleet
Mc Feely, William Shield *historian, writer*

## Weston
Higgins, Sister Therese *literature educator, former college president*
Jarzavek, John Brian *English and art history educator*
Oates, Mary Josephine *historian, educator*

## Weymouth
Gillespie, Barbara Joan *language educator*

## Williamstown
Bell, Robert *literature educator*
Dalzell, Robert Fenton, Jr. *historian, educator*
Dew, Charles Burgess *historian, educator*
Fuqua, Charles John *classicist, educator*
Graver, Lawrence Stanley *language educator*
Graver, Suzanne Levy *English literature educator*
Norton, Glyn Peter *literature educator*
Oakley, Francis Christopher *historian, educator*
Pistorius, George *language educator, educator*
Rudolph, Frederick *history professor*
Stamelman, Richard Howard *French and humanities educator*

## Worcester
Billias, George Athan *historian, educator*
Roorbach, Bill Forsyth *English language educator, writer*
Vaughan, Alden True *history professor*

Zeugner, John Finn *historian, educator, writer*

## Yarmouth Port
Weiner, Charles *historian, educator*

# MICHIGAN

## Ann Arbor
Blouin, Francis Xavier, Jr. *history professor*
Bornstein, George Jay *literary educator*
Chang, Chun-Shu *historian, educator, writer*
Chang, Hsueh-lun Shelley *historian, researcher, writer*
Cowen, Roy Chadwell, Jr. *language educator*
Crichton, Mary Christina *foreign language educator*
Curley, Edwin Munson *philosophy educator*
Delbanco, Nicholas Franklin *language educator, writer*
Dunnigan, Brian Leigh *historian, curator*
Eisenstein, Elizabeth Lewisohn *historian, educator*
Ferrell, Robert Hugh *historian, educator*
Feuerwerker, Albert *historian, educator*
Forsyth, Ilene Haering *art historian*
Garbaty, Thomas Jay *retired English language educator*
Hackett, Roger Fleming *historian, educator*
Izzo, Herbert John *language and linguistics educator, researcher*
Janko, Richard Charles Murray *humanities educator*
Knott, John Ray, Jr. *language educator*
McCarus, Ernest Nasseph *retired language educator*
Mizruchi, Mark Sheldon *sociology professor, business administration professor*
Munro, Donald Jacques *philosopher, educator*
Nelson, Roy Jay *retired French educator*
Perkins, Bradford *historian, educator*
Pernick, Martin Steven *history professor*
Pulgram, Ernst *language educator*
Railton, Peter Albert *philosophy educator*
Stein, Howard *humanities educator, economics professor*
Stolz, Benjamin Armond *foreign language educator*
Trautmann, Thomas Roger *history professor, anthropology educator*
Turits, Richard Lee *history professor*

## Berrien Springs
Homan, Michele Annette *language educator*

## Beulah
Tanner, Helen Hornbeck *historian, consultant*

## Brimley
Elder, Richard Wayne *history professor*

## Brownstown
Slingerland, Mary Jo *writing educator*

## Cadillac
DeVito, Karen Smith *French educator*

## Dearborn
Little, Daniel Eastman *philosopher, educator, director*
Papazian, Dennis Richard *historian, educator, commentator*

## Delton
Waring, Walter Weyler *literature and language professor*

## Detroit
Boykin, Peter Jeffrey *humanities educator*
Brill, Lesley *literature and film studies educator*
Brunk, Thomas Walter *art historian*
Covensky, Edith *language educator, poet*
Schwartz, Matthew Barahal *historian*
Small, Melvin *historian, educator*

## East Lansing
Anderson, David Daniel *retired humanities educator, writer, editor*
Bresnahan, Roger Jiang *humanities educator, researcher*
Bruno, Maria Frances *writing and cultural educator*
Fisher, Alan Washburn *historian, educator*
Harrison, Ann Tukey *foreign language educator*
Hine, Darlene Clark *history educator, administrator*
Mansour, George P. *Spanish language and literature educator*
Natoli, Joseph *language educator*
Schoenl, William James *history professor*
Seaton, James *humanities educator*
Tzitsikas, Helene *retired literature educator*

## Escanaba
Wood, D. Ann *language and music educator*

## Farmington
Ellens, J(ay) Harold *philosopher, educator, psychotherapist, minister*

## Grand Rapids
Carpenter, Joel Allan *historian*
Luttikhuizen, Henry M. *art historian, curator*
Schmidt, Gary David *language educator*

## Hillsdale
Stewart, David *history professor, researcher*

## Howell
Rohrabacher, Janet Hammond *genealogist, archivist*

## Jerome
Dillon, Merton Lynn *historian, educator*

## Kalamazoo
Breisach, Ernst A. *historian, educator*
Coss, Barbara Sue *humanities educator*
Dybek, Stuart *language educator, writer*
Julien, Catherine *history professor*

**Livonia**
Holtzman, Roberta Lee *French and Spanish language educator*

**Marquette**
Nicholson, Howard Lee *history professor*

**Monroe**
DeVries, James E. *historian, educator*

**Mount Pleasant**
Primeau, Ronald *literature educator, writer*

**New Era**
Grubb, Daniel Studd *literature and language professor, priest*

**Rochester**
Estes, Todd A. *historian*

**Roscommon**
Thiel, John Robert *history professor*

**Saginaw**
Houshiar, Bobbie Kay *language arts educator*

**West Bloomfield**
Williamson, Marilyn Lammert *literature educator, academic administrator*

**Ypsilanti**
Cere, Ronald Carl *languages educator, consultant, researcher*

## MINNESOTA

**Bemidji**
Weaver, Will(iam Weller) *language educator, writer*

**Duluth**
Schroeder, Fred Erich Harald *humanities educator*
Tezla, Albert *language educator*

**Forest Lake**
Marchese, Ronald Thomas *ancient history and archaeology educator*

**Mankato**
Janc, John J. *language educator*
Preska, Margaret Louise Robinson *historian, educational association administrator*

**Marshall**
Pichaske, David Richard *language educator*

**Minneapolis**
Bales, Kent Roslyn *language educator*
Cohen, Andrew David *language educator, applied linguist*
Erickson, Gerald Meyer *classical studies educator*
Farah, Caesar Elie *language educator*
Fergus, Patricia Marguerita *language educator, writer, editor*
Firchow, Evelyn Scherabon *German language and literature educator, writer*
Firchow, Peter Edgerly *language professional, educator, writer*
Garner, Shirley Nelson *language educator*
Karras, Ruth Mazo *history professor*
Kohlstedt, Sally Gregory *historian, educator*
Meyers, Miriam Watkins *retired language educator*
Pazandak, Carol Hendrickson *liberal arts educator*
Redhead, Ruth Willard *foreign language educator*
Ross, Donald, Jr. *language educator, academic administrator*
Seidel, Robert Wayne *science historian, educator*
Slade, George Gilbert *art historian*
Tracy, James Donald *historian, educator*
Weiss, Gerhard Hans *German language educator*

**Moorhead**
Buckley, Joan N. *retired literature and language professor*
Shoptaugh, Terry Lee *historian, archivist*

**Northfield**
Clark, Clifford Edward, Jr. *history professor*
Iseminger, Gary Hudson *philosophy educator*
Paas, John Roger *language educator*
Soule, George Alan *literature educator*
Yandell, Cathy Marleen *language educator*

**Saint Cloud**
Hofsommer, Donovan Lowell *history professor*

**Saint Paul**
Fitzharris, Joseph Charles *history educator*
Huzar, Eleanor Goltz *historian, educator*
Mather, Richard Burroughs *retired Chinese language and literature educator*
Monson, Dianne Lynn *literacy educator*
Weiner, Carl Dorian *historian*

**Vadnais Heights**
Polakiewicz, Leonard Anthony *foreign language and literature educator*

**Waseca**
Strand, Melvin LeRoy *English educator*

## MISSISSIPPI

**Cleveland**
Boschert, Thomas Neville *historian, educator*

**Clinton**
Bigelow, Martha Mitchell *retired historian*

**Gulfport**
Swetman, Glenn Robert *literature and language professor, poet*

**Hattiesburg**
Chambers, Douglas Brent *history professor*

Scarborough, William Kauffman *historian, educator*

**Magnolia**
Coney, Elaine Marie *language educator*

**Mayhew**
Marsh, Patricia Guyton *humanities educator*

**Mississippi State**
Lowery, Charles Douglas *historian, educator, dean*

**Oxford**
Landon, Michael de Laval *retired history professor*

**Senatobia**
Banham, Sandra Rodgers *language educator*

**University**
Jordan, Winthrop Donaldson *historian, educator*
Kiger, Joseph Charles *history professor*
O'Sullivan, Daniel E. *language educator*

## MISSOURI

**Canton**
Galloway, Robert Edward *literature and language professor, retired municipal official*

**Columbia**
Bien, Joseph Julius *philosophy educator*
Fulweiler, Howard Wells *language professional*
Horner, Winifred Bryan *humanities educator, researcher, consultant, writer*
Kvanvig, Jonathan Lee *philosophy educator*
Looser, Devoney Kay *English literature educator*
Mullen, Edward John, Jr. *Spanish language educator*
Overby, Osmund Rudolf *art historian, educator*
Schwartz, Richard Brenton *English language educator, dean, writer*
Strickland, Arvarh Eunice *history professor*
Timberlake, Charles Edward *historian, educator*

**Fayette**
Woodward, Ralph Lee, Jr. *historian, educator*

**Florissant**
Ashhurst, Anna Wayne *foreign language educator*
Jones, Brian Keith *speech educator*

**Fulton**
Pierson, Katricia Guyn *language educator*

**Gainesville**
Sayles, Wayne Gerald *numismatist, writer*

**Kansas City**
Burger, Delores Theresa *historian, writer*
Hodges Morgan, Anne *historian*
Hoffmann, Donald *architectural historian*

**Kirksville**
Ling, Huping *history professor*
Maldonado-Class, Joaquin *language educator*

**Kirkwood**
Collins, Steven G. *history professor*

**Liberty**
Crigger, Nancy J. *humanities educator, nursing educator*

**Marshall**
Zank, Virginia *literature and language professor*

**Maryville**
Brandon-Falcone, Janice Ilene *history educator*

**Morrisville**
Dunn, Traci *speech educator, theater educator*

**Point Lookout**
Kneeshaw, Stephen John *history professor, editor*

**Poplar Bluff**
Samuell, Tiechera Dawn *language educator*

**Saint Louis**
Barmann, Lawrence Francis *historian, educator*
Herbert, Kevin Barry John *classics educator*
Ruland, Richard Eugene *literature educator, critic, historian*
Sale, Merritt *classicist, educator, comparatist*
Schwarz, Egon *language educator, writer, critic*
van den Berg, Sara Jane *language educator*
Weixlmann, Joseph Norman, Jr. *language educator, academic administrator*
Wellman, Carl Pierce *philosophy educator*

**Salem**
Wood, Thomas Wesley *humanities educator, editor*

**Springfield**
Bartee, Wayne C. *humanities educator, department chairman*
Burgess, Ruth Lenora Vassar *speech and language educator*
Easley, June Ellen Price *genealogist*
Wolbrink, Shelley Amiste *history professor*

**Warrensburg**
Karen, Kathleen Foster *language educator*

**Washington**
Gregory, Ralph J. *historian, curator*

**Windyville**
Condron, Barbara O'Guinn *philosopher, educator, academic administrator, writer*

## MONTANA

**Bozeman**
Hufstetler, Mark Allan *historian*

Warrick, Kimberley Kaye *language educator, social studies educator*

**Missoula**
Kittredge, William Alfred *humanities educator*
Pavilack, Joann Clements *history professor*

## NEBRASKA

**Kearney**
Gonzalez, Eduardo *language educator, interpreter, translator*
Rohrer, James Russell *history professor*

**Lincoln**
Leinieks, Valdis *classicist, educator*
Mach, Jan Ellen Walkenhorst *literature educator, editor*
Price, Kenneth Marsden *humanities educator*
Sawyer, Robert McLaran *historian, educator*
Stover, John Ford *railroad historian, educator*

**Neligh**
Wright, Tammy Sue (Marshall) *language educator, comedian*

**North Platte**
Wohler, Ruth *humanities educator*

**Omaha**
Brayman, Jeannie Sue *language educator*
Brock, Stephen L. *language educator, consultant*
Kuhlman, Thomas Ashford *retired American studies educator, writer*
Okhamafe, Imafedia *philosophy and English educator*

## NEVADA

**Las Vegas**
Adams, Charles Lynford *English language educator*
Donaghy, Henry James *literature educator, academic administrator*
Gafford, Mary May Grimes *retired humanities educator*

**North Las Vegas**
Miller, Eleanor *English language and literature educator*

## NEW HAMPSHIRE

**Derry**
Holmes, Richard Dale *history consultant*
Sanborn, George Freeman, Jr. *genealogist*

**Durham**
Allen, Michael Austin *language educator*
Gold, Janet Nowakowski *Spanish language educator*
Hapgood, Robert Derry *language educator*
Harris, John William *historian, educator*
McCann, Francis (Frank) Daniel (Frank McCann) *historian, educator*
Simic, Charles *language educator, poet*

**Hanover**
Bien, Peter Adolph *language educator, writer*
Cook, William Wilbert *literature and language professor, department chairman*
Daniell, Jere Rogers, II, *retired historian*
Fuechtner, Veronika *language educator*
Garthwaite, Gene Ralph *historian, educator*
Gert, Bernard *philosopher, educator*
Heffernan, James Anthony Walsh *language and literature educator*
Kritzman, Lawrence David *humanities educator*
Luxon, Thomas Hyatt *language educator, director*
Mansell, Darrel Lee, Jr. *language educator*
Oxenhandler, Neal *literature educator, writer*
Russell, Robert Hilton *Romance languages and literature educator*
Scher, Steven Paul *literature educator*
Scherr, Barry Paul *foreign language educator*
Shewmaker, Kenneth Earl *history professor*

**Keene**
Crocker, Matthew Hallowell *historian, writer, researcher*
Higgins, Roland Louis *history professor*

**Kingston**
Walen, Harry Leonard *historian, lecturer, author*

**Meredith**
Heald, Bruce Day *English educator, historian, music educator*

**Nashua**
Phelps, Bonnie Noreen *language educator, secondary school educator*

**Portsmouth**
Harter, Hugh Anthony *foreign language educator*

**Rindge**
Burns, Gerald Thomas *literature and language professor*

## NEW JERSEY

**Atlantic Highlands**
Levine, George Lewis *literature and language professor, literary critic*

**Avon By The Sea**
Potter, Emma Josephine Hill *language educator*

**Belle Mead**
Brown, Elizabeth Schmeck *fashion historian*

**Bradley Beach**
Unger, Irwin *historian, educator*

**Cape May**
Savage, Maureen Walls *retired history professor*
Turner, Almon Richard *retired art historian, educator*

**Chester**
Lynch, Beverly Love *language educator*

**Cranford**
Russell, John Joseph *English educator*

**Dover**
Seadler, Stephen Edward *philosopher, writer*

**Dumont**
Sadock, Geoffrey J. *English professor*

**Ewing**
Liu, Xinru *history professor, researcher*

**Galloway**
Carson, Keith Elmer *history professor*

**Hamilton**
Cosentino, Andrew J. *retired art historian, curator*

**Hewitt**
Mollenkott, Virginia Ramey *English literature and language educator, writer, guest lecturer*

**Hightstown**
Schorske, Carl Emil *historian, educator*

**Jersey City**
Coreil, Raymond Clyde *language educator*
Jennings, Sister Vivien *literature and language professor*

**Lincroft**
Zigo, Paul Edward *historian, educator*

**Lodi**
McParland, Robert Patrick *literature educator, writer*

**Madison**
Rosales Herrera, Raúl Joaquin *language educator*
Skaggs, Merrill Maguire *humanities educator*

**Metuchen**
Kushinsky, Jeanne Alice *humanities educator*

**Montclair**
Adarkar, Aditya *humanities educator*
Nielsen, Wendy Christine *literature educator*
Stertz, Stephen Allen *historian, educator*

**Montville**
Lucibello, Alan Joseph *history professor*

**Morristown**
Fredericks, Robert Joseph *language company executive*

**New Brunswick**
Gillette, William *historian, educator*
Grob, Gerald N. *historian, educator*
Hartman, Mary Susan *historian, educator*
Jenkins, Reese V. *historian, educator*
Kelley, Donald Reed *historian*
O'Neill, William Lawrence *retired history professor*
Reed, James Wesley *social historian, educator*
Stich, Stephen Peter *philosophy educator*
Townsend, Carmilla D. *history professor, researcher*
Tu, Ching-I *humanities educator, researcher*

**Newark**
Lurie, Jonathan *history professor*
Schweizer, Karl Wolfgang *historian, educator, author*
Varzegar, Minoo *literature educator, reading specialist*

**Orange**
Thomas, Lois Baskerville *retired language educator*

**Paramus**
Mahoney, Joseph Francis *historian, educator*
Wasmer, Carmenia Ann *language educator*

**Princeton**
Aarsleff, Hans *linguistics educator*
Bowersock, Glen Warren *retired historian, educator*
Brombert, Victor Henri *literature educator, author*
Brown, Leon Carl *historian, educator*
Cooper, John Madison *philosophy educator*
Corngold, Stanley Alan *language educator, writer*
Darnton, Robert Choate *historian, educator*
Ermolaev, Herman Sergei *Slavic languages educator*
Frankfurt, Harry Gordon *philosophy professor*
Frey, Julia Bloch *language educator, art historian, educator*
Goheen, Robert Francis *classicist, educator, former ambassador*
Grafton, Anthony Thomas *history professor*
Habicht, Christian Herbert *history professor*
Harman, Gilbert Helms *philosophy educator*
Hartog, Hendrik *historian*
Hollander, Robert B., Jr. *romance languages educator*
Howarth, William (Louis Howarth) *literature and language professor, writer*
Howell, David Luke *history professor*
Hynes, Samuel *language educator, writer*
Jordan, William Chester *historian, educator*
Keeley, Edmund LeRoy *literature educator, writer, translator*
Knoepflmacher, Ulrich Camillus *literature educator*
Mc Pherson, James Munro *history professor*
Moote, A. Lloyd *history professor*
Moynahan, Julian Lane *retired literature educator, writer*
Nehamas, Alexander *philosophy educator*

Painter, Nell Irvin *historian, educator, writer*
Paret, Peter *historian*
Rabb, Theodore K. *historian, educator*
Rodgers, Daniel Tracy *historian, educator*
Rubin, Dorothy Molly *language educator, writer*
Schofield, Robert E(dwin) *historian, educator, academic administrator*
Scott, Joan Wallach *historian, educator*
Shimizu, Yoshiaki *art historian, department chairman*
Showalter, Elaine *humanities educator*
Walter, Hugo Günther *humanities educator, poet*
West, Cornel Ronald *humanities educator, writer*
White, Morton Gabriel *philosopher, writer, historian, retired educator*
Wilentz, Sean *historian, educator, writer*
Wilmerding, John *art historian, educator, curator*
Ziolkowski, Theodore Joseph *literature educator*

**Stewartsville**
Busch, Beverly Gail *English language educator, literature educator, instructional resource center administrator*

**Teaneck**
Fjordbotten, Alf Lee *language educator*
Gordon, Lois G. *language educator*
Wiener, Joel Howard *historian, educator*

**Toms River**
Bosley, Karen Lee *language educator, communications educator*
Chopyk, Dan Bohdan *language educator, poet*

**Trenton**
George, Emery Edward *foreign language and studies educator, writer*

**Wall**
Mudd, Mary Cordelia *historian*

**Wayne**
Rogoff, Paula Drimmer *English and foreign language educator*

**NEW MEXICO**

**Albuquerque**
Davies, Thomas Mockett, Jr. *history professor*
Davis, Jon L. *logistics consultant*
Fuller, Anne Elizabeth Havens *English language and literature educator, consultant*
Hutton, Paul Andrew *historian, educator, writer*
Lange, Dale Lowell *language educator, researcher*
Nocentelli, Carmen *literature educator*
Peña, Juan José *interpreter*
Richter, Harvena *retired literature educator, poet*
Sanabria, Enrique A. *history professor*
Thomson, Iain Donald *philosopher, educator*
Weixelman, Joseph Owen *history professor*

**Carlsbad**
Sandford, Mary Ann *Spanish language educator*

**Las Cruces**
Bloom, John Porter *historian, editor, administrator, archivist*

**Las Vegas**
Simpson, Dorothy Audrey *retired speech educator*

**Santa Fe**
Lehmberg, Stanford Eugene *historian, educator*
Maehl, William Henry *historian, academic administrator, consultant*

**Taos**
Bolls, Imogene Lamb *English language educator, poet*

**NEW YORK**

**Albany**
Applebee, Arthur Noble *English education researcher*
Donovan, Robert Alan *language educator*
Langer, Judith Ann *language educator*
Reese, William Lewis *philosophy educator*

**Amherst**
Kurtz, Paul *philosopher, educator, writer, publisher*
Shook, John Robert *philosopher*

**Annandale On Hudson**
Ashbery, John Lawrence *language educator, poet, playwright, art critic*

**Aurora**
Purdy, Laura *philosopher, educator*

**Binghamton**
Bix, Herbert Philip *historian, educator*
Brinker-Gabler, Gisela *literature educator*
Gaddis Rose, Marilyn *literature educator, translator*
Pavlovskis-Petit, Zoja *literature and language professor*
Sklar, Kathryn Kish *historian, educator*
Stein, George Henry *historian, educator, administrator*

**Brockport**
Blake, Robert William *retired literature and language professor, writer*
Dabbagh, Mahmoud *language educator, researcher*
Leslie, William Bruce *history professor*
White, Christopher Todd *language educator, anthropologist*

**Bronx**
Bullaro, Grace Russo *literature, film and foreign language educator, critic*
Dean, Nancy *literature educator, retired playwright*
Hallett, Charles Arthur, Jr. *language educator, humanities educator*

Himmelberg, Robert Franklin *historian, educator*
Spatt, Hartley Steven *humanities educator*
Ultan, Lloyd *historian, educator*
Valgemae, Mardi *language educator*

**Bronxville**
Peters, Sarah Whitaker *art historian, writer*
Pollin, Burton Ralph *language educator*

**Brooklyn**
Barran, Thomas Paul *language educator*
Blasi, Alberto *Romance languages educator, writer*
Buttaro, Lucia *language educator, consultant*
Curtis-Tweed, Phyllis Marie *humanities educator*
Flam, Jack Donald *art historian, educator*
Forsberg, Suzanne *humanities educator*
Jaffe, Louise *literature and language professor, writer*
King, Margaret Leah *history professor*
Lobron, Barbara L. *speech educator, editor, photographer, writer*
Lopate, Phillip *language educator, writer*
Pucci, Gabrielle Jennine *historian, educator*
Sanchez Korrol, Virginia *historian, educator*
Spector, Robert Donald *language educator*

**Buffalo**
Grant, Nathan L. *literary and cultural studies educator*
Iggers, Georg Gerson *history professor*
Merini, Rafika *humanities educator, writer, language educator*
Milligan, John Drane *historian, educator*
Payne, Frances Anne *literature educator, researcher*
Peradotto, John Joseph *retired classics educator, editor*
Ross, Gary Earl *writing educator*
Siedlecki, Peter Anthony *English language and literature educator*
Twagilimana, Aimable *language educator, writer*
Williams, Lillian Serece *historian, social studies educator*

**Canton**
Goldberg, Rita Maria *foreign language educator*

**Charlton**
Kekes, John *philosopher, educator*

**Churchville**
Clarke, Stephan Paul *retired language educator, writer*

**Clifton Park**
St. Clair, Helaine Denise *language educator*

**Cobleskill**
Rivera, Salvador, Jr. *history and sociology educator, researcher*

**Cooperstown**
Jones, Clyde Ray *historian, consultant*

**Coram**
Mohanty, Christine Ann *retired language educator, actress*

**Cortland**
Anderson, Donna Kay *musicologist, educator*

**Dobbs Ferry**
Poian, Edward Licio *historian*

**East Hampton**
Bromley, Bruce Ditmas *language educator, writer*
Swerdlow, Amy *historian, educator, writer*

**Elmira**
Leveen, Pauline *retired history professor, government professor*
Pucci, Anthony J. *English language educator*
Reddick, Bryan DeWitt *language educator, academic administrator*

**Fairport**
Graham, Susette Ryan *retired English educator*

**Flushing**
Bird, Thomas Edward *foreign language and literature educator*
Haller, Hermann W. *romance language educator*
Rabassa, Gregory *language educator, translator, poet*
Ranald, Margaret Loftus *English literature educator, author*
Tytell, John *literature educator, writer*

**Forest Hills**
Kra, Pauline Skornicki *French language educator*

**Fredonia**
Goetz, Thomas Henry Paul *literature educator*

**Fresh Meadows**
Duckett, Lila Wheeler *retired language educator, writer*

**Garden City**
Bouchard, Wendy Ann Borstel *language educator*
Hamblet, Wendy C. *philosopher, educator*
Jenkins, Kenneth Vincent *literature educator, writer*

**Gardiner**
Mabee, Carleton *historian, educator*

**Geneseo**
Gouvernet, Gerard Raoul *language educator*

**Getzville**
Saveth, Edward Norman *historian, educator*

**Greenvale**
Dinan, Susan Eileen *history educator*
Schor, Adam Matthew *history professor*

**Hamilton**
Pinchin, Jane *literature educator*

Rotter, Andrew Jon *history educator*
Soderberg, Dale LeRoy *language educator, drama director, producer*
Staley, Lynn *literature educator*

**Hancock**
Senia, Grace Melanie *language and music educator*

**Hempstead**
Jarvis, Scott E. *language educator*

**Hicksville**
Mund, Lorraine G. *English studies educator, writer*

**Hillsdale**
Parmet, Herbert Samuel *historian, writer*

**Houghton**
Howard, David Allyn *history professor*

**Ithaca**
Abrams, Meyer Howard *language educator*
Brazell, Karen Woodard *literature educator*
Colby Hall, Alice Mary *language educator*
Culler, Jonathan Dwight *English language educator*
Eddy, Donald Davis *language educator*
Fontaine, Michael Till (Michael Scott) *humanities educator*
Groos, Arthur Bernhard, Jr. *German studies educator, music educator*
Hohendahl, Peter Uwe *German language and literature educator*
Koschmann, J. Victor *history professor, academic program director*
LaCapra, Dominick Charles *historian, educator*
LaFeber, Walter Frederick *historian, educator, writer*
McDougal, Stuart Yeatman *comparative literature educator, author*
Porte, Joel Miles *language educator*
Radzinowicz, Mary Ann *language educator*
Rawlings, Hunter Ripley III *classicist, former academic administrator*
Sakai, Naoki *literature and language professor*
Silbey, Joel Henry *history professor*
Sosna, Morton Philip *historian, academic administrator*
Steinberg, Michael Philip *history professor*

**Jamaica**
Coppa, Frank John *historian, educator*
Harmond, Richard Peter *historian, educator*
Parmet, Robert David *historian, educator*

**Jamestown**
Langworthy, Traci I. *history professor*

**Jericho**
Astuto, Philip Louis *retired language educator*

**Keuka Park**
Armstrong, James Francis III *language educator, writer*

**Kings Park**
Fay, Thomas A. *philosopher, educator*

**Larchmont**
Folter, Roland *historian, rare book dealer, writer*

**Long Island City**
Coogan, Timothy Christopher, II, *history professor, researcher*
Russo, Lorraine *humanities educator*

**Mamaroneck**
Pritts, Gloria Piccia *historian*

**Mecklenburg**
Baptist, Edward E. *history professor*

**Middle Village**
Walter, John Frederick *historical researcher, genealogist*

**Middletown**
Henderson, Thomas Emmett *retired language educator, rare book dealer*

**Monsey**
Erickson, Barbara Martha *historian, writer*

**Mount Kisco**
Dore, Anita Wilkes *language educator*

**New Hyde Park**
Low, Frederick Emerson *language educator*

**New Paltz**
Brown, Peter David Gilson *German language educator*

**New Rochelle**
Fitch, Nancy Elizabeth *historian, educator*

**New York**
Apter, Emily *language educator*
Bagnall, Roger Shaler *history professor*
Baker, Paul Raymond *historian, educator*
Belknap, Robert Lamont *literature educator*
Bender, Thomas *historian, educator*
Berghahn, Volker Rolf *history professor*
Berlin, Heather Ayn *philosopher, educator*
Birns, Nicholas Boe *literature educator, editor*
Block, Ned *philosopher, educator*
Blumberg, Barbara Marilyn *history professor, writer*
Bonfante, Larissa *classics educator*
Brilliant, Richard *art historian, educator*
Brooks, Jerome Bernard *English and Afro-American literature educator*
Brown, Jonathan *art historian, art educator*
Bulliet, Richard Williams *historian, educator, writer*
Burbank, Jane Richardson *historian, educator*
Cahn, Steven Mark *philosopher, educator*
Caro, Robert Allan *historian, writer*

Cavallo, Jo Ann *language educator*
Caws, Mary Ann *literature and language professor*
Compagnon, Antoine Marcel *French language educator*
Cook, Blanche Wiesen *historian, educator, journalist*
de Menil, Lois Pattison *historian, philanthropist*
Donoghue, Denis *language professional, educator*
Dray, Philip *history professor, writer*
Driver, Martha Westcott *literature educator, researcher, writer*
Elderfield, John *art historian, museum curator*
Engel, David *historian*
Ferrante, Joan Marguerite *language educator, literature educator, writer*
Fine, Kit *philosophy educator*
Foner, Eric *historian, educator*
Gasman, Daniel E. *retired history professor, writer*
Gay, Peter *historian, educator, writer*
Ginter, Valerian Alexius *urban historian, educator*
Gluck, Carol *history professor*
Gordon, Linda *history educator*
Gottlieb, Beatrice *historian*
Gromada, Thaddeus V. *historian, academic administrator*
Harris, Frederick John *foreign language and literature educator*
Harris, Katherine Safford *speech and hearing educator*
Harris, William Vernon *history professor*
Hartman, Joan Edna *retired literature educator, provost*
Heffner, Richard Douglas *historian, educator, communications consultant, television producer*
Hendin, Josephine Gattuso *language educator, writer*
Herzog, John E. *numismatist*
Hirsch, Edward Mark *language educator, poet*
Hirschhorn, Bernard *educator, historian, researcher, writer*
Hoeflin, Ronald Kent *philosopher, writer*
Hovde, Carl Frederick *language professional, educator*
Howe, Florence *literature educator, writer, publisher*
Hu, Danian *history professor*
Hulsebosch, Daniel Joseph *historian, educator*
Jackson, Kenneth Terry *historian, academic administrator*
Jurkevich, Gayana *Spanish language educator, consultant*
Kaiser, Walter *language educator*
Karsen, Sonja Petra *retired literature educator*
Kastan, David Scott *literature educator, writer*
Katz, Esther *historian, educator*
Kaur, Harminder *language educator*
Kerz, Louise *historian*
Klass, Sheila Solomon *English language educator, writer*
Krinsky, Carol Herselle *art historian, educator*
Kroeber, Karl *language educator*
Kruger, Steven F. *literature educator*
Leibowitz, Herbert Akiba *literature and language professor, writer*
Lewyn, Ann Salfeld *retired English as a second language educator*
Linton, Donna Joan *foreign language educator, dean*
Lippman, Sharon Rochelle *art historian, filmmaker, art therapist*
London, Herbert Ira *humanities educator, academic administrator*
Low, Anthony *language educator*
Lyons, Bridget Gellert *language educator*
Malefakis, Edward E. *history professor*
Malin, Irving *language educator, critic*
Markowitz, Gerald E. *historian, educator*
May, Gita *literature educator*
Mayerson, Philip *classics educator*
Maynard, John Rogers *language educator*
Maysilles, Elizabeth *speech communication professional, educator*
Mehta, Linn Cary *literature educator*
Mendelson, Edward James *English literature educator*
Middendorf, John Harlan *English literature educator*
Middlebrook, Diane Wood *English language educator, writer*
Miller, Nancy K. *literature educator*
Miller, Peter N. *historian, educator*
Mintz, Samuel Isaiah *language educator, writer*
Mitterand, Henri C. *literature educator, writer*
Moreno, Barry *historian, writer*
Myers, Gerald E. *humanities educator*
Nafisi, Azar *humanities educator*
Nochlin, Linda *art history educator*
Odenweller, Robert Paul *philatelist, trade association administrator, retired pilot*
Oppenheimer, Paul *literature educator, poet*
Papalia, Diane Ellen *humanities educator*
Paxton, Robert Owen *historian, educator*
Perna, Michael Lewis *language educator*
Plottel, Jeanine Parisier *foreign language educator*
Quiñones Keber, Eloise *art historian, educator*
Randall, Francis Ballard *retired historian, educator, writer*
Ravitch, Diane Silvers *historian, educator, writer, government official*
Raymond, Dorothy Sarnoff *communications consultant, former actress, former singer*
Reynolds, David Spencer *humanities educator, writer*
Rheins, Carl Jeffrey *historian, director*
Richtman, Jack *French language educator*
Rosand, David *art historian, educator*
Rosenberg, John David *language educator, critic*
Rosenblum, Robert H. *art historian, educator*
Rosengarten, Frank *retired language educator, retired literature educator, writer*
Rothman, David J. *historian, educator*
Rowen, Ruth Halle *musicologist, educator*
Salvesen, Magda Abercromby *art and garden historian*
Saxton, Martha *history educator, writer*
Schama, Simon *historian, educator, author*
Scheindlin, Raymond Paul *literature educator, religious organization administrator*
Scribner, Charles III *art historian, writer*
Seigel, Jerrold Edward *historian, writer*

Selig, Karl-Ludwig *literature and language professor*
Shapiro, James Stephen *English professor*
Shneidman, J. Lee *historian, educator*
Solomon, Maynard Elliott *musicologist, retired recording industry executive*
Sourian, Eve Pocquet *French educator*
Spector, Johanna Lichtenberg *ethnomusicologist, former educator*
Stade, George Gustav *humanities educator*
Steiger, Randi Janine *English educator*
Steinberg, Leo *art historian, educator*
Stern, Fritz Richard *historian, educator*
Stevens, Rosemary A. *medicine and public health historian, artist*
Stimpson, Catharine Rosalind *literature educator, writer*
Tanner, Estelle Newman *oral historian*
Tanselle, George Thomas *language educator, foundation administrator*
Taran, Leonardo *classicist, educator*
Tusiani, Joseph *foreign language educator, author*
Unger, Peter Kenneth *philosophy educator*
Walker, Robert Harris *historian, writer, editor*
Warren, Arete Bernice *art historian*
Wasser, Henry *retired American literature and sociology educator*
Weil-Garris Brandt, Kathleen (Kathleen Brandt) *art historian*
Weinberg, H. Barbara *art historian, educator, curator*
Wixom, William David *art historian, museum administrator, educator*
Wolff, Larry *history professor*
Wortman, Marlene Stein *historian*
Wortman, Richard S. *historian, educator*
Wyschogrod, Edith *philosophy educator*
Yerushalmi, Yosef Hayim *historian, educator*
Yurchenco, Henrietta Weiss *musicologist, writer*
Zhang, Xudong *literature and language professor, department chairman*

**Newark**
Biddle, Jane Lammert *retired English educator*

**Newburgh**
Adams, Barbara *language educator, poet, writer*

**North Collins**
Bowman, Georgianne *historian, reporter*

**Oakland Gardens**
Polak, Emil Joseph *history professor, researcher*

**Oswego**
Smiley, Marilynn Jean *musicologist*

**Pittsford**
French, Henry Pierson, Jr. *retired historian, educator*

**Plattsburgh**
Tracy, Ann Blaisdell *retired language educator*

**Pleasantville**
Meisel, Martin *English and comparative literature educator*

**Port Washington**
Williams, George Leo *historian, retired secondary school educator, landmark director*

**Potsdam**
Harder, Kelsie Brown *retired language educator*
Lunt, Lora G. *language educator, director*

**Poughkeepsie**
Bartlett, Lynn Conant *English literature educator*
Daniels, Elizabeth Adams *English language educator*
Griffen, Clyde Chesterman *retired historian*
Hathaway, Richard Dean *retired language educator*
Hytier, Adrienne Doris *French language educator*
Peck, H. Daniel *literature educator*
Sharp, Ronald Alan *language educator, writer, dean*

**Purchase**
Waller, Gary Fredric *language educator, poet*

**Queens**
Beliavsky, Ninah *linguistics professor*

**Ravena**
Muth, Sharon A. *language educator*

**Rochester**
Chiarenza, Carl *art historian, critic, artist, educator*
Eaves, Morris Emery *English language educator*
Fausold, Martin Luther *history professor*
Gordon, Dane Rex *philosophy educator, minister*
Hauser, William Barry *historian, educator*
Herminghouse, Patricia Anne *foreign language educator*
Hollis, Susan Tower *history professor*
Johnson, Bruce Marvin *language educator*
Lansky, Lewis *history professor*
Meconi, Honey *musicologist, writer*
Thym, Jürgen *musicologist*
Young, Mary Elizabeth *history professor*
Zagorin, Perez *historian, educator*

**Rockville Centre**
Fitzgerald, Janet Anne *philosophy educator, academic administrator*

**Saint Bonaventure**
Mazon, Margaret Fausold *language educator*

**Saratoga Springs**
Boyers, Robert *literature and language professor*
Caruso, Adrienne Iorio *retired language educator*

**Scarsdale**
Graff, Henry Franklin *historian, educator*

**Schenectady**
Morris, John Selwyn *philosopher, educator, retired academic administrator*

**Selden**
Howard, Douglas L. *literature and language professor*

**Slingerlands**
Zacek, Joseph Frederick *historian, educator*

**Snyder**
Levine, George Richard *language educator*

**Southampton**
Brophy, James David, Jr. *humanities educator*

**Staten Island**
Holder, Calvin Beresford *history professor*
Nicholaou, Mary C(onstantine) *literature and language professor, publishing executive*
Omagu, Donald *history professor*
Taranto, Deborah Jean *literature and language professor, writer*

**Stony Brook**
Goldberg, Homer Beryl *language educator*
Grim, Patrick Neal *philosopher, logician*
Harris, Alice *linguist, educator*
Ihde, Don *philosopher, educator, dean*
Kuspit, Donald Burton *art historian, critic, educator*
Levin, Richard Louis *retired language educator*
Mignone, Mario B. *language educator*
Semmel, Bernard *historian, educator*
Simpson, Louis Aston Marantz *language educator, writer*

**Syracuse**
Alston, William Payne *philosophy educator*
Powell, James Matthew *history professor*
Sternlicht, Sanford *literature educator, writer*
Tatham, David Frederic *art historian, educator*
Waddy, Patricia A. *historian, architecture educator*

**Troy**
Ahlers, Rolf Willi *philosopher, theologian*

**Utica**
Wagner, Frederick Reese *retired language educator*

**Valhalla**
Leone, Stephen Joseph *language educator, computer technician, consultant*
Sclafani, Charles Carlo *language educator, department chairman*

**Vestal**
Quataert, Donald *historian, educator*

**Wantagh**
Galvan, Max *humanities educator*
Smits, Edward John *historian, consultant*

**Williamsville**
Brown, Stephen Ira *philosophy professor*
Drew, Fraser Bragg Robert *language educator*

## NORTH CAROLINA

**Andrews**
Fonda, Ronald Alan *epistemologist*

**Asheville**
Voigt, Ellen *literature educator*

**Boiling Springs**
Vanderburg, Timothy Warren *history professor*

**Boone**
Kitunda, Jeremiah Mutio *history professor, researcher*

**Buies Creek**
Stanke, Jaclyn *history professor*

**Cary**
Mata, Elizabeth Adams *language educator, land investor*

**Chapel Hill**
Baron, Samuel Haskell *historian*
Browning, Christopher R. *historian, educator*
Davis, Sarah Irwin *retired language educator*
Debreczeny, Paul *retired language educator, writer*
Feinberg, Lawrence Edward *language educator, researcher*
Filene, Peter Gabriel *history professor*
Flora, Joseph M(artin) *language educator*
Grendler, Paul Frederick *historian, educator*
Gura, Philip Francis *English and American literature educator*
Heninger, Simeon Kahn, Jr. *language educator*
Illiano, Antonio *language educator, researcher*
Kohn, Richard H. *historian, educator*
Ludington, Townsend *English and American studies educator*
Nelson, Philip Francis *musicologist, consultant, conductor*
Pease, William Henry *history professor*
Rabil, Albert, Jr. *humanities educator*
Schier, Donald Stephen *language educator*
Sices, David *language educator, translator*
Smith, Sidney Rufus, Jr. *linguist, educator*
Stephens, Laurence David, Jr. *linguist, investor, oil industry executive*
Strauss, Albrecht Benno *retired language educator, editor*
Tindall, George Brown *retired historian, educator*
Williamson, Joel Rudolph *humanities educator, writer*

**Charlotte**
Castro, Mary McDermott *language educator*
Myers, Robert Manson *language educator, writer*
Phillips, Harry Robert *language educator*

**Creedmoor**
Husketh, Alma Ormond *retired language educator*

**Davidson**
Cole, Richard Cargill *language educator*

**Durham**
Budd, Louis John *language educator*
Butters, Ronald Richard *language educator*
Chafe, William Henry *history professor*
Colton, Joel *historian, educator*
Davis, Calvin De Armond *historian, educator*
Hodgdon, Timothy John *historian, educator*
Kuwahara, Kuldip Kaur *literature and language professor*
Lerner, Warren *historian, educator*
Preston, Richard Arthur *historian*
Smith, Grover C(leveland) *language educator*
Thompson, James Howard *historian, librarian*
Whitlow, Stacey Mataxis *language educator*
Williams, George Walton *language educator*

**Efland**
Weinberg, Gerhard Ludwig *history professor*

**Elizabeth City**
Brown, Flora Bryant *history professor*

**Fearrington Village**
Cell, Gillian Townsend *retired historian, educator*

**Franklin**
Johnson, Herbert Alan *historian, lawyer*

**Graham**
Stanberry, D(osi) Elaine *English literature educator, writer*

**Greensboro**
Cushman, Keith *English professor*
Graham, Anthony *language educator*
Penninger, Frieda Elaine *retired literature educator*

**Greenville**
Beers, Burton Floyd *historian, educator*

**Hendersonville**
Harris, James Braxton *retired humanities educator, freelance/self-employed writer*

**Hickory**
Eller, Richard E. *history professor, writer*

**Jacksonville**
Fischer, Violeta Pèrez Cubillas *Spanish literature and linguistics educator*
Kimball, Lynn Jerome *historian*

**Jamestown**
Kinard, Jeff Sowers *historian, educator*

**Maggie Valley**
Pickard, John Benedict *language educator*

**Mount Olive**
Marbais, Peter Christian *language educator*

**New Bern**
White, James Edward III *historian, educator*

**Pembroke**
Vela, Richard Raul *literature educator*

**Pittsboro**
Boyce, Emily Stewart *retired library and information science educator, retired library and information scientist*
Rubin, Louis Decimus, Jr. *retired language educator, writer, publishing executive*

**Raleigh**
Hoch, Paul Frederick, Jr. *history professor*
Rhodes, Donald Robert *musicologist, educator, retired electrical engineer*
Surh, Gerald *history professor*

**Vilas**
Stolberg, Mary Margaret *historian*

**Wilmington**
Toplin, Robert Brent *history professor, television producer*

**Winston Salem**
Barnett, Richard Chambers *historian, educator*
Borwick, Susan Harden *musicologist, educator*
Hendricks, J(ames) Edwin *historian, educator, consultant, author*
Margitić, Milorad R. *language educator, researcher*
Schabacker, Elizabeth M. *literature educator*
Shapere, Dudley *philosophy educator*

## NORTH DAKOTA

**Bismarck**
Newborg, Gerald Gordon *state archives administrator*
Rettig, Pam *literature educator*

**Dunseith**
Ferris, Kade Michael *historian, anthropologist*

**Mayville**
Brunsdale, Mitzi Louisa, (Mallarian) *language educator, critic*
McMahon, Dalton Edward *history professor, social sciences educator, department chairman*

**Wahpeton**
Reubish, Gary Richard *English language educator*

## OHIO

**Akron**
Clinefelter, Ruth Elizabeth Wright *historian, educator*
Knepper, George W. *historian, educator*

Williams, William Proctor *literature educator*

**Athens**
Borchert, Donald Marvin *philosopher, educator*
Matthews, Jack (John Harold Matthews) *language educator, writer*
Torres, Daniel *literature educator*
Whealey, Lois Deimel *humanities scholar*

**Austintown**
Kope, Joseph B. *retired humanities educator*

**Berea**
Kennelly, Laura Ballard *literature educator, writer*

**Bowling Green**
Browne, Ray Broadus *popular culture educator*
Buffington, Robert Marshall *history professor*

**Brecksville**
Pappas, Effie Vamis *language educator, finance educator, writer, poet, artist*

**Cincinnati**
Alexander, John Kurt *history professor*
Bleznick, Donald William *Romance languages educator*
Ciani, Alfred Joseph *dean*
Harmon, Patrick *historian, retired editor, retired commentator*
Kalven, Janet *humanities educator, writer, consultant*
Samis, Charles Maurice *language educator, mathematics educator*
Schrier, Arnold *historian, educator*
Yeazell, Carol D. *language educator*

**Cleveland**
Baskind, Samantha *art historian*
Curnow, Kathy *art historian, educator*
Czuma, Stanislaw J. *historian*
Dancyger, Ruth *art historian*
Friedman, Barton Robert *language educator*
Greppin, John Aird Coutts *philologist, editor, educator*
Miller, Genevieve *retired medical historian*
Nelson, Sue Grodsky *humanities educator, consultant*
Salomon, Roger Blaine *retired language educator*
Taylor, Margaret Wischmeyer *retired language educator*

**Columbus**
Anderson, Donald Kennedy, Jr. *language educator*
Babcock, Charles Luther *classics educator*
Battersby, James Lyons, Jr. *language educator*
Beja, Morris *English literature educator*
Boyle, Kevin Gerard *historian, educator, writer*
Brooke, John L. *history professor*
Burnham, John Chynoweth *historian, educator*
Chu, Samuel C. *history professor, writer*
Findley, Carter Vaughn *historian, educator*
Fullerton, Mark David *historian, educator, dean*
Hare, Robert Yates *musicologist, educator*
Jarvis, Gilbert Andrew *humanities educator, writer*
Jebsen, Harry Alfred Arthur, Jr. *history professor*
Joseph, Brian Daniel *language educator*
Kasulis, Thomas Patrick *humanities educator*
Kuhn, Albert Joseph *language educator*
Peterson, Gale Eugene *historian*
Scanlan, James Patrick *philosophy and Slavic studies educator*
Stephan, Alexander Friedrich *German language and literature educator*
Williams, Susan Shidal *language educator*

**Concord**
Ulsenheimer, Dean *language educator*

**Cuyahoga Falls**
Walker, Suzannah Wolf *language educator*

**Dayton**
Bednarek, Janet Rose *history professor*
Freeland, Charles Harrell *literature educator*
Gabbert, Janice Jean *history, literature and language educator*
Harden, Oleta Elizabeth *literature educator, academic administrator*
McWhorter, Stanley Bruce *retired language educator*
Vice, Roy Lee *history professor*
Winkler, Jonathan Reed *historian, educator*

**Gambier**
Rutkoff, Peter M. *humanities educator*

**Granville**
Knobel, Dale Thomas *historian, educator, university president*
Lisska, Anthony Joseph *humanities educator, philosopher*
Santoni, Ronald Ernest *philosophy educator*

**Huron**
Ruble, Ronald Merlin *humanities and theater communications educator*

**Kent**
Beer, Barrett Lynn *historian*
Hassler, Donald Mackey, II, *English language educator, writer*
Marovitz, Sanford Earl *English language and literature educator*
Reid, S.W. *language educator*

**Kirtland**
Asnien, Phyllis Arline *humanities educator, writer*

**Mansfield**
Joyce, Steven James *German and comparative studies educator*
Phelps, Christopher *history professor*

**Marietta**
Kessler, Mark (Mickey) Milo *humanities educator, department chairman, playwright*
Neu, Irene Dorothy *historian, educator*
Wilbanks, Jan Joseph *retired philosopher*

**North Canton**
Heaphy, Leslie Anne *history professor*
Vazzano, Frank Paul *historian, educator*

**Oberlin**
Collins, Martha *English language educator, writer*
Ganzel, Dewey Alvin *English language educator*
Soucy, Robert Joseph *historian, educator*

**Oxford**
Pratt, William Crouch, Jr. *literature and language professor, writer*

**Painesville**
McQuaid, Kim *historian, educator, writer*

**Solon**
Gallo, Donald Robert *retired literature educator*

**Toledo**
Campbell, James *philosopher, educator*
Glaab, Charles Nelson *historian, educator*
Smith, Robert Freeman *history professor*

**Urbana**
Phillips, Julieanne Appleson *history professor*

**West Farmington**
Smith, Agnes Monroe *history professor*

**Westerville**
Chaney, Norman Richard *English studies educator*

**Wilberforce**
Onwudiwe, Ebere *humanities educator, writer*

**Yellow Springs**
Fogarty, Robert Stephen *historian, educator, editor*

**Youngstown**
Bowers, Bege Kaye *literature educator, communications educator, academic administrator*

**OKLAHOMA**

**Ada**
Daniel, Arlie V. *speech education educator*

**Enid**
Moore, Linda Lea LaCroix *literature educator, art educator*

**Lawton**
Hodgson, John *literature educator, editor*

**Norman**
Fears, Jesse Rufus *historian, educator, academic dean*
Lowitt, Richard *history professor*
Savage, William Woodrow, Jr. *historian, consultant, social sciences educator*

**Oklahoma City**
Holt, Karen Anita Young *language educator*
Musselman, Lloyd K. *history professor*
Todd, Joe Lee *historian*

**Stillwater**
Fischer, LeRoy Henry *historian, educator*
Luebke, Neil Robert *philosophy educator*
Max, Elizabeth *retired language educator*

**Tulsa**
Buckley, Thomas Hugh *historian, educator*
Faingold, Eduardo Daniel *language and linguistics educator, researcher*
Randle, Rodger A. *human relations professor, political science professor*

**OREGON**

**Corvallis**
Peterson, Barbara Ann Bennett *history professor, television personality*
Yu, Shiao-ling S. *humanities educator*

**Eugene**
Pascal, C(ecil) Bennett *classics educator*
Wickes, George *English literature educator, writer*

**Madras**
Ramsey, Jarold William *literature and language professor, writer*

**Mcminnville**
Yates, Willard Ross *retired humanities educator*

**Medford**
Frost, Orcutt William *historian, educator*

**Monmouth**
Balke, Frank H. *language educator, director*

**Port Orford**
Drinnon, Richard *retired historian*

**Portland**
Burke, Bernard Vincent *retired history professor*
Eifler, Mark Anthony *historian, educator*
Englert, Walter George *classics and humanities educator*
Horowitz, David A. *history professor, writer*
Knapp, Robert Stanley *English language educator*
Orloff, Chet *historian*
Schmidt, Stanley Eugene *retired speech educator*
Steinman, Lisa Malinowski *English literature educator, writer*
Vaughan, Thomas James Gregory *historian, writer*

**Redmond**
Blue, Frederick Judd *retired history professor, writer*

**Salem**
Dmytryshyn, Basil *historian, educator*

Kuhn, Gary D. *speech educator*

**Spray**
Fussner, F. Smith *history professor, retired rancher*

**Sutherlin**
Rose, Sarah Elizabeth *genealogist, writer, counselor, web site designer*

**PENNSYLVANIA**

**Ambler**
Hilty, James Walter *historian, educator, media consultant*

**Annville**
Foley, Brian Joseph *philosophy educator*
Tezanos-Pinto, Rosa *Hispanic American literature educator*

**Bala Cynwyd**
Dorwart, Bonnie Brice *historian, retired rheumatologist*
Murphey, Murray Griffin *history professor*

**Bethlehem**
Beidler, Peter Grant *language educator*
Parmet, Harriet Abbey L. *literature educator*
Saeger, James Schofield *history professor, writer*
Smolansky, Oles M. *retired humanities educator*

**Blakeslee**
Albano, Patrick Marino *historian, educator, archivist*

**Boyertown**
Fortes, Brenda Joyce *language educator*

**Bryn Mawr**
Dudden, Arthur Power *historian, educator*
Gaisser, Julia Haig *classics educator*
Krausz, Michael *philosopher, educator*
Lane, Barbara Miller (Barbara Miller-Lane) *humanities educator*
Lang, Mabel Louise *classics educator*
McCabe, Louise Beachboard *language educator*
Trout, Charles Hathaway *historian, educator*

**Canonsburg**
Southern, David *history professor*

**Carlisle**
Fox, Arturo Angel *Spanish language educator*
Shrader, Charles Reginald *historian*

**Chambersburg**
O'Connor, John Morris III *retired humanities educator*

**Chester**
Buck, Lawrence Paul *history professor, former academic administrator*

**Clarks Summit**
Cagley, Susan A. *history professor*

**Coatesville**
Stenz, Lisa Ann *reading specialist*

**Doylestown**
Donnelly, Michael William *language educator*

**East Petersburg**
Pedrow, Brenda M. *language educator*

**Easton**
Lamb-Faffelberger, Margarete Barbara *foreign language educator*
Schlueter, June Mayer *literature educator, writer*

**Elizabethtown**
Bartoli, Jill Sunday *reading and language arts educator*
Kenley, David Lynn *history professor*

**Elkins Park**
Davidson, Abraham Aba *art historian, educator, photographer*

**Fairfield**
Freund, John Richard *former English educator*

**Freeport**
Smits, Ronald Francis *language educator, poet*

**Gwynedd Valley**
McGarry, Lisa Coughlin *language educator*

**Harrisburg**
Dinniman, Andrew Eric *international studies and history professor, state senator*
Khanzhina, Helen P. *language and literature educator, translator*
Smith, Eric Ledell *historian*

**Haverford**
Brand, Charles Macy *history professor*
Gutwirth, Marcel Marc *literature educator*
Jorden, Eleanor Harz *linguist, educator*

**Hazleton**
Kemmerer, Kathleen Mary *language educator*

**Hershey**
Dellasega, Cheryl *humanities educator*

**Hummelstown**
Clouse, Jerry Allan *architectural historian*

**Kennett Square**
Curtin, Philip De Armond *history educator*

**La Plume**
Elliott, David Lindsey *literature educator*

**Lancaster**
Binkley, Luther John *philosophy educator*
Steiner, Robert Lisle *retired language educator*

**Lansdowne**
Purcell, Mary Hamilton *speech educator*

**Leesport**
Jackson, Eric Allen *philatelist*

**Lewisburg**
Payne, Michael David *English language educator*

**Lock Haven**
Story, Julie Ann *language educator*

**Loretto**
Jareb, Jerome *history professor, researcher*

**Lykens**
Sultzbaugh, John Stephan *historian, educator*

**Mc Keesport**
Preuss, Mary Herge *Spanish educator*

**Media**
Kessler, Carol Farley *English language educator*

**Merion Station**
Littell, Marcia Sachs *Holocaust and genocide studies professor*

**Millersville**
Miller, Steven Max *humanities educator*

**Nazareth**
Haynes, Thomas Morris *philosophy educator*

**New Castle**
Sands, Christine Louise *retired English educator*

**New Freedom**
Sedlak, Valerie Frances *retired English language educator, retired academic administrator*

**Paoli**
Boehlke, Frederick John *history professor*

**Philadelphia**
Beeman, Richard Roy *historian, educator*
Berry, Mary Frances *history professor, former federal agency administrator*
Daemmrich, Horst Sigmund *German language and literature educator*
Davis, Allen Freeman *history professor, writer*
de Paulo, Craig J. N. *philosopher, educator*
Fusco, Richard *English literature educator*
Gelles, Richard James *sociology professor, psychology professor, academic administrator*
Hahn, Steven *history professor, writer*
Knauer, Georg Nicolaus *philologist*
Logan, Marie-Rose van Stynvoort *literature educator, publishing executive, writer*
Lucid, Robert Francis *language educator*
Matus-Mendoza, Mariadelaluz *language educator, sociologist*
McDiarmid, Lucy *literature educator, writer*
Morello, Celeste Anne *historian, criminologist*
Moss, Roger William *historian, writer, administrator*
Perry, Constance Karin *philosopher, educator*
Peters, Edward Murray *history professor*
Regan, Robert Charles *English language educator*
Ridley, Harrison, Jr. *history professor*
Sachs, Katherine Stein *art historian*
Schiffman, Harold Fosdick *Asian language educator*
Sebold, Russell Perry III *Romance languages educator, writer*
Strehlke, Carl Brandon *art historian, curator*
Struck, Peter T. *classicist, educator*
Sugrue, Thomas J. *history professor, social sciences educator*
Welch, Charles Edgar, Jr. *retired English language educator, writer*
Winkler, Gail Caskey *historian, writer*
Woodside, Lisa Nicole *humanities educator*

**Phoenixville**
Lukacs, John Adalbert *historian, retired educator*

**Pittsburgh**
Anthony, Edward Mason *linguistics educator*
Balas, Edith *art historian, educator*
Clack, Jerry *classics educator*
Drescher, Seymour *historian, educator, writer*
Gale, Robert Lee *retired literature educator, critic*
Goldstein, Donald Maurice *historian, educator*
Gupta, Anil K. *philosophy professor*
Harris, Ann Birgitta Sutherland *art historian*
Hartner, John George *language educator*
Hearn, Fil *architectural history professor emeritus*
Hicks, Wendell *history professor, political scientist, publishing executive*
McClendon, Michele Rosalind *literature educator*
McDuffie, Keith A. *literature educator*
McNeil, Malcolm Ray *speech educator, researcher*
Miller, David William *historian, educator*
Paulston, Christina Bratt *linguistics educator*
Rawski, Evelyn Sakakida *history professor*
Rescher, Nicholas *philosopher, author, educator*
Sheon, Aaron *art historian, educator*
Tarr, Joel Arthur *historian, educator*
Trotter, Joe William, Jr. *history professor, writer*
Udler, Rubin Yakovlevich *linguist*
Weingartner, Rudolph Herbert *philosophy educator*
Zboray, Mary Saracino *historian*

**Pottsville**
Bodenberg, Lynn Alan *language educator*

**Rosemont**
Conwell, Marilyn Jane *language educator, consultant*

**Scranton**
Lawhon, Patricia Patton *literature and language professor, writer educator*
Shaffern, Robert William *history professor*
Zaydon, Jemille Ann *language educator, communications educator*

**Shippensburg**
Reber, Vera Blinn *history professor*

**State College**
Brault, Gerard Joseph *French language educator*
Goldschmidt, Arthur Eduard, Jr. *historian, educator, writer*
Redford, Donald Bruce *historian, archaeologist*
Robinett, Betty Wallace *educator*
Schmalstieg, William Riegel *retired Slavic languages educator*

**Sugarloaf**
Goldman-Price, Irene Carolyn *language educator*

**Swarthmore**
Morgan, Kathryn Lawson *retired historian, educator*
North, Helen Florence *classicist, educator*
Ostwald, Martin *retired classicist*

**Tamaqua**
Featro, Susan Mary *language educator, music educator*

**University Park**
Ebitz, David MacKinnon *art historian, educator, museum director*
Geiger, Roger Lewis *historian, educator*
Halsey, Martha Taliaferro *Spanish language educator*
Hogan, J. Michael *humanities educator*
Kadir, Djelal *literature educator*
Lima, Robert *language educator*
Naydan, Michael M. *foreign language educator*

**Villanova**
Bergquist, James Manning *history professor*
Helmetag, Charles Hugh *foreign language educator*
Hunt, John Mortimer, Jr. *classical studies educator*

**West Chester**
Gougher, Ronald Lee *language educator*
Heston, Thomas J. *historian, educator*
Hipple, Walter John *language educator*
Kletzien, Sharon Benge *language educator, department chairman*

**West Lawn**
Kovary, Loraine Theresa *language educator*

**Wilkes Barre**
Hepp, John Henry, IV, *historian, lawyer*

**Yardley**
Stanley, Gerard Francis *language educator*

**RHODE ISLAND**

**Jamestown**
Wright, Harrison Morris *historian, educator*

**Kingston**
Kim, Yong Choon *philosopher, theologian, educator*

**Middletown**
Carroll, Rosemary Frances *historian, educator, lawyer*

**Newport**
Haas, William Paul *humanities educator, retired academic administrator*

**North Kingstown**
Mellor, Kathy *National Teacher of the Year 2004, ESL educator*

**Providence**
Ackerman, Felicia Nimue *philosophy educator, writer*
Bensmaia, Reda *French studies educator, researcher*
Blasing, Mutlu Konuk *English language educator*
Donovan, Bruce Elliot *literature educator, dean*
Enteman, Willard Finley *retired philosopher*
Fornara, Charles William *historian, classicist, educator*
Gleason, Abbott *history professor*
Green, Angel Yvonne *literature educator*
Harleman, Ann *literature educator, writer*
Kim, Jaegwon *philosophy educator*
Konstan, David *classics and comparative literature professor, researcher*
Lesko, Leonard Henry *historian, educator, writer*
Lubar, Steven David *history professor, curator*
Monteiro, George *language educator, writer*
Putnam, Michael Courtney Jenkins *classics educator*
Raaflaub, Kurt Arnold *classics educator*
Ribbans, Geoffrey Wilfrid *language educator*
Robbins, Mark Walter *historian*
Rohr, Donald Gerard *history professor*
Saint-Amand, Pierre Nemours *humanities educator*
Schulz, Juergen *art historian, educator*
Sosa, Ernest *philosopher, educator*
Tagliabue, John Anthony *retired literature educator, poet*
Terras, Victor *literature and language professor*
Wideman, John Edgar *English literature educator, novelist*
Wood, Gordon Stewart *historian, educator, writer*
Wright, Carolyn D. (C.D. Wright) *language educator, poet*

**Saunderstown**
Waters, Chris Harold *literature and language professor, poet*

**Smithfield**
Litoff, Judy Barrett *history professor*

**SOUTH CAROLINA**

**Aiken**
Sykes, Richard Nesbit *retired history professor, department chairman*

**Beaufort**
Villena-Alvarez, Juanita I. *language educator, consultant*

**Blacksburg**
Dunkerly, Robert Matthew *historian*

**Bluffton**
Gilbert, Barbara Marie *literacy coach*

**Charleston**
Barrett, Michael Baker *historian, educator*

**Clemson**
Bailey, Beatrice Naff *language educator, researcher*
Lander, Ernest McPherson, Jr. *history and economics professor*
Riley, Helene Maria Kastinger *Germanist*

**Columbia**
Briggs, Ward Wright *classics educator*
Edgar, Walter Bellingrath *historian, educator*
Geckle, George Leo III *language educator*
Long, Eugene Thomas III *philosophy educator, academic administrator*
Sproat, John Gerald *historian, educator*
Stroup, Rodger Emerson *historian*
Synnott, Marcia Graham *history professor*
Vazsonyi, Nicholas *foreign languages educator*

**Denmark**
Lebby, Gloria C. *history professor*

**Due West**
Carlock, John Bruce, Jr. *language educator*

**Greenwood**
Cushing, Sara Elizabeth *language educator, writer*

**Nesmith**
Pressley, Deloris N. *literacy educator*

**North Myrtle Beach**
Damerst, William *language educator, humanities educator*

**Orangeburg**
McIver, Barbara Basore *language educator*

**Roebuck**
Revan, David R. *language educator*

**Spartanburg**
Deku, Afrikadzata *Afrikan scholar, writer, lecturer, educator*

**Tigerville**
Cook, Jeffery Blane *history professor, consultant*

**Winnsboro**
Meyer, Jack Allen *historian, consultant*

## SOUTH DAKOTA

**Brookings**
Evans, David Allan *language educator*
Funchion, Michael F. *historian, educator*

**Sioux Falls**
Carlson Aronson, Marilyn A. *language educator*
Huseboe, Arthur Robert *American literature educator*
Staggers, Kermit LeMoyne, II, *history professor, political science professor, state legislator, municipal official*

**Vermillion**
Basile, Joseph Lawrence *humanities educator*

## TENNESSEE

**Athens**
Dunn, Durwood *historian, educator*

**Big Sandy**
Chastain, Kenneth Duane *retired foreign language educator, writer*

**Chattanooga**
Gartman, Max Dillon *language educator*
Resnick, Irven Michael *philosophy educator*

**Clarksville**
Uffelman, Minoa D. *history professor*

**Collegedale**
Pettibone, Dennis Lynn *history professor*

**Dayton**
Cornelius, Richard Meredith *literature and language professor*
Ketchersid, William Lester *history professor*

**Gallatin**
Durham, Walter Thomas *historian, researcher*

**Jefferson City**
Baumgardner, James Lewis *history professor*

**Kingsport**
Wolfe, Margaret Ripley *historian, educator, consultant*

**Knoxville**
Brady, Patrick *language educator, writer*
Cutler, Everette Wayne *history professor*
Davis, John Kerr *philosopher, educator, lawyer*
Fisher, John Hurt *retired English language educator*

**Lewisburg**
Villines, Benita Curtis *language educator*

**Memphis**
Gudmestad, Robert H. *history professor*

Jolly, William Thomas *language educator*
Sherman, Janann Margaret *history professor, writer*
Stagg, Louis Charles *English language and literature educator*

**Morristown**
Conry, Ruth P *language educator*

**Murfreesboro**
Corlew, Robert Ewing *history professor, academic administrator*
Phillips, Philip Edward *English professor*

**Nashville**
Beach, Margaret Smith *retired language educator*
Boorman, Howard Lyon *history professor*
Compton, John Joseph *philosophy educator*
Conkin, Paul Keith *history professor*
Cook, Ann Jennalie *literature educator, cultural organization administrator*
Dachowski, Elizabeth Eileen *history professor*
Dickerson, Dennis Clark, Sr. *historian, educator*
Girgus, Sam B. *English literature educator*
Halperin, John William *English literature educator*
Hassel, Rudolph Christopher *language educator*
Jarman, Mark Foster *language educator*
Lancaster, John Stevens *historian, museum administrator*
Lee, Douglas A. *musicologist*
Medina, Jose *philosopher, educator*
Risko, Victoria J. *language educator*
Sevin, Dieter Hermann *literature and language professor*
Voegeli, Victor Jacque *historian, educator, dean*

**Sewanee**
Williamson, Samuel Ruthven, Jr. *historian, educator*
Winton, Calhoun *literature educator*

**Shiloh**
Allen, Stacy Dale *historian, parks director*

## TEXAS

**Arlington**
Herring, Susan Catherine *linguistics educator*
Hoefer, Richard A. *social work educator, non-profit management consultant*
Jernigan, Gray Marshall *historian, educator*
Porter, Laurin R. *literature and language professor*

**Austin**
Alofsin, Anthony *art historian, writer, educator, architect*
Asher, Nicholas Michael *philosophy professor, linguistics professor, research director*
Baltzer, Rebecca A. *musicologist, researcher, consultant*
Brown, Norman Donald *history professor*
Causey, Robert Louis *philosopher, educator, consultant*
Dechene, Arthur C., Jr. *philosopher, religious studies educator*
Dulles, John Watson Foster *history professor*
Escoto, Luz *language educator*
Farrell, Edmund James *retired English language educator, writer*
Freeman, Robert Schofield *musicologist, educator*
Friedman, Alan Warren *humanities educator*
Galinsky, Gotthard Karl *classicist, educator*
Gould, Lewis Ludlow *historian, educator*
Graham, Don Ballew *literature educator, writer*
Harms, Robert Thomas *linguist, educator*
Hinojosa-Smith, Roland *language educator, writer*
Jackson, William Vernon *Latin American studies and library science educator*
Kibler, William Westcott *French language and literature educator*
Lindstrom, Naomi Eva *language educator*
Lockett, Landon Johnson *retired linguist*
Louis, William Roger *historian*
MacKay, Carol Hanbery *literature educator*
Middleton, Christopher *Germanic languages and literature educator*
Moag, Rodney Frank *language educator, country and bluegrass singer, musician, record producer*
Moragné e Silva, Michèle Lowe *language educator*
Oshinsky, David M *history professor, writer*
Rich, John Martin *humanities educator, researcher*
Salinas, Celena Iris *reading specialist*
Seung, Thomas Kaehao *philosophy educator*
Staley, Thomas Fabian *language professional, academic administrator*
Sutherland, William Owen Sheppard *retired language educator, consultant ,*
Whitbread, Thomas Bacon *language educator, writer*

**Beaumont**
Bradley, Jerry Wayne *language educator, department chairman*
Needham, Keith Alan *language educator*

**Bertram**
Albert, Susan Wittig *writer*

**Bryan**
Bryant, Keith Lynn, Jr. *history professor*

**Canyon**
Stuntz, Jean Allison *history professor*

**College Station**
Buenger, Walter Louis *history professor, academic administrator*
Cannon, Garland *linguist, educator*
Dethloff, Henry Clay *historian, educator*
Ezell, Margaret M. *language educator*
Harner, James Lowell *historian, educator*
Monroe, Haskell Moorman, Jr. *retired history professor, retired dean, chancellor emeritus*
Unterberger, Betty Miller *history professor, writer*

**Commerce**
Linck, Charles Edward, Jr. *English language educator*

**Corinth**
Lowry, Sharon Kathleen *history professor*

**Corpus Christi**
Snouffer, Nancy Kendall *literature and language educator*
Wooster, Robert *history professor*

**Dallas**
Chavez, John Richard *historian, educator*
Chawner, Lucia Martha *language educator*
Comini, Alessandra *art historian, educator*
Countryman, Edward Francis *historian, educator*
Crain, John Walter *historian, educator*
Fagin, Stephen Andrew *historian*
Grissom, Mary Anne *speech educator*
Hunter, Robert Grams *retired language educator*
Johnson, Benjamin H. *history professor*
Terry, Marshall Northway, Jr. *language educator, writer*

**Denton**
Brannon-Wranosky, Jessica Sutton *history professor, researcher*
Hurley, Alfred Francis *historian, academic administrator emeritus, retired air force officer*
Kesterson, David Bert *language educator, dean*
Lawhon, Tommie Collins Montgomery *humanities educator*
Nik, Ninfa *literature and language professor*
Preston, Thomas Ronald *language educator, researcher*
Snapp, Harry Franklin *historian, educator*

**Devine**
Passty, Jeanette Nyda *literature and language professor, writer*

**El Paso**
Dailey, Maceo Crenshaw, Jr. *humanities educator*
Leyva, Yolanda Chavez *historian, educator, writer*
Lujan, Rosa Emma *bilingual specialist, trainer, consultant, assistant principal*
Müller, Gene Alan *historian, consultant*

**Fort Worth**
Bernard, Robert William *language educator, theology studies educator, humanities educator*
DeLotto, Jeffrey Daniel *language educator, writer*
Gilderhus, Mark Theodore *historian, educator*
Lott, R(obert) Allen *musicologist*
Patoski, Margaret Nancy *historian, educator*
Reuter, Frank Theodore *historian, educator*
Robin, Clara Nell (Claire Robin) *English language educator*
Shehan, Geraldean Harrison *ESL educator*
Woodworth, Steven Edward *history professor, writer*

**Galveston**
Bloomfield, Maxwell Herron III *retired history professor, retired law professor*

**Grapevine**
Stack, George Joseph *philosopher, writer*

**Greenville**
Grimshaw, James Albert, Jr. *retired language educator*

**Harlingen**
Martin, Leland Morris (Pappy Martin) *historian, educator*

**Houston**
Achenbaum, W(ilbert) Andrew *history professor, social sciences educator*
Belk, Joan Pardue *language and literature educator*
Castañeda, James Agustín *language educator, golf coach*
Chance, Jane *English literature educator*
Drew, Katherine Fischer *history professor*
Ehrmann, Susanna *language educator, photographer, writer*
Espree, Mildred Michelle *language educator, writer*
Huston, John Dennis *language educator*
Kanellos, Nicolás *language educator, liberal studies educator*
Lamb, Sydney MacDonald *language educator*
Leguillon, Rolande Lucienne *French educator*
Lowry, Montecue Judson *military historian*
Martin, James Kirby *historian, educator*
Mc Fadden, Joseph Michael *historian, educator*
Minter, David Lee *English literature educator*
Mintz, Steven H. *history professor*
Patten, Robert Lowry *language educator*
Pospisil, JoAnn *historian, archivist*
Pryor, William Daniel Lee *humanities educator*
Schnoebelen, Anne Mary *musicologist, educator*
Sher, George Allen *philosophy educator*
Starz, Mary Helen *language educator*
Thompson, Ewa M. *foreign language educator*
Vallbona, Rima-Gretel Rothe *retired foreign language educator, writer*
Weller, Cecil Eddie, Jr. *history educator*

**Huntsville**
Raymond, Kay E. (Kay Engelmann Raymond) *Spanish language educator, consultant*

**Irving**
Means, Richard Nathaniel Griffith *historian*
Sommerfeldt, John Robert *historian, educator*

**Kingsville**
Hunter, Leslie Gene *history educator*

**Longview**
Williams, Willie Alvin *retired literature educator*

**Lubbock**
Aoyama, Katsura *psycholinguist*
Bullock, James Jefferson, II, *literature and language professor, director*
Ketner, Kenneth Laine *philosopher, educator*

**Mesquite**
Dean, Sherry Lynn *language educator, speech professional*

**Missouri City**
de Kanter, Ellen Ann *retired English and foreign language educator*

**Montgomery**
Kelsey, Clyde Eastman, Jr. *philosophy educator, psychology professor*

**Mount Pleasant**
Vaughn, William Preston *retired historian, retired educator*

**Odessa**
Toruño-Haensly, Rhina M. *literature educator, researcher, writer*

**Paris**
Proctor, Richard Owen *historian, health facility administrator, military officer*

**Richardson**
Redman, Timothy Paul *language educator, writer*

**Round Top**
Lentz, Edwin Lamar *art historian*

**Rusk**
McMinn, J. B. *retired philosophy educator, composer*

**San Antonio**
Aguirre, Javier Ramos *historian, educator*
Cordova, Ruben Charles *art historian, educator, curator, photographer*
Dunn, James David *language educator*
Flores, Belinda Bustos *bilingual educator, administrator*
Leighton, Albert Chester *history professor*
Mendoza, Louis G. *literature educator, researcher*
Myers, Ellen Howell *historian, educator*
Rollin, Michael Fredrick *history professor*
Salvucci, Linda *history professor*
Smith, Rebecca Lynn *language educator*
Voigt, Joan (Joan McGuire Voigt) *retired literature and language professor*
von Raffler-Engel, Walburga (Walburga Engel) *retired language educator*

**San Marcos**
Ronan, Clifford John *literature and language professor*

**Stephenville**
Baker, Thomas Lindsay *history professor, museum director, consultant*
Schmelzer, Janet L. *history professor, researcher*
Zelman, Patricia Grace *history educator*

**Waco**
Hunt, Maurice Arthur *language educator, researcher*
Jeffrey, David Lyle *literature and language professor, writer*
Murray, Kathleen Sarah-Jane *literature and language professor*
Yang, Michael Vincent *literature and language professor, researcher*

**Wichita Falls**
Bourland, D(elphus) David, Jr. *linguist, educator*

## UTAH

**Cedar City**
Mills, James *language educator*

**Logan**
Culver, Milton Lawrence *historian, educator*

**Orem**
Clark, Bruce Budge *humanities educator*

**Provo**
Forster, Merlin Henry *foreign languages educator, writer, researcher*
Harreld, Donald James *history professor*
Lyon, James Karl *German language educator*
Murphy, John Joseph *literature educator, critic, editor*
Nokes, Jeffery D. *history professor*
Peer, Larry Howard *literature educator*
Young, Bruce Wilson *language educator*

**Salt Lake City**
Madsen, Brigham Dwaine *history professor*

**South Jordan**
Rowley, Maxine Lewis *retired home economics and consumer educator, retired department chairman*

**Tremonton**
Eakle, Arlene Haslam *genealogist*

## VERMONT

**Bennington**
Wang, Shunzhu *humanities educator, researcher, translator*

**Burlington**
Daniels, Robert Vincent *history professor, former state senator*
Hall, Robert William *philosophy educator, religious studies educator*

**Castleton**
Meloy, Judith Marie *humanities educator*

**Middlebury**
Albers, Jan Maria *historian, museum director*
Jacobs, Travis Beal *historian, educator*
Katz, Michael Ray *Slavic languages educator*
Vail, Van Horn *German language educator*

## CANADA

### BRITISH COLUMBIA

**Burnaby**
Kitchen, John Martin *historian, educator*

**North Saanich**
Saddlemyer, Ann (Eleanor Saddlemyer) *humanities educator, critic, theater historian*

**Richmond**
Durrant, Geoffrey Hugh *retired language educator*

**Vancouver**
Batts, Michael Stanley *retired language educator*
Bentley, Thomas Roy *retired language educator, writer*
Conway, John S. *history professor*
Nosco, Peter Erling *humanities educator, consultant*
Overmyer, Daniel Lee *humanities educator*
Pacheco-Ransanz, Arsenio *language educator, historian, educator*
Unger, Richard Watson *history professor*

### NEW BRUNSWICK

**Saint John**
Condon, Thomas Joseph *university historian*

### NOVA SCOTIA

**Halifax**
Gray, James *English literature educator*
Murray, Thomas John (Jock Murray) *medical humanities educator, physician, neurologist*

### ONTARIO

**Brampton**
Paikeday, Thomas M. *lexicographer, linguistic consultant*

**Flamborough**
Lee, Alvin A. *literary educator, scholar, author*

**Hamilton**
McKay, Alexander Gordon *classics educator*

**Kingston**
Akenson, Donald Harman *historian, educator*

**London**
Gerber, Douglas Earl *classics educator*

**Nepean**
Kallmann, Helmut Max *musicologist, retired librarian*

**North York**
Adelman, Howard *philosophy educator*
Thomas, Clara McCandless *retired literature educator*

**Ottawa**
Dray, William Herbert *philosophy educator*
Labarge, Margaret Wade *medieval history professor, historian, writer*
Squire, Anne Marguerite *retired humanities educator*
Staines, David McKenzie *language educator*

**Saint Catharines**
Sivell, John Norman *language educator*

**Toronto**
Blewett, David Lambert *English literature educator*
Granatstein, Jack Lawrence *historian*
Johnson, Robert Eugene *historian, academic administrator*
Millgate, Michael (Michael Henry Millgate) *retired literature educator*
Morey, Carl Reginald *musicologist*
Rapoport, Anatol *humanities educator, biophysicist*
Skvorecky, Josef Vaclav *literature educator, writer*
Wevers, John William *retired Semitic languages educator*

**Waterloo**
Haworth, Lawrence Lindley *philosophy educator*
Suits, Bernard Herbert *philosophy educator*

### PRINCE EDWARD ISLAND

**Montague**
Cregier, Don Mesick *historian, educator, researcher, consultant*

### QUEBEC

**Montreal**
Beugnot, Bernard Andre Henri *literature educator*
Kinsley, William Benton *literature educator*

**North Hatley**
Jones, Douglas Gordon *retired literature educator*

## MEXICO

**Mexico City**
Leon-Portilla, Miguel *historian, educator*

## AUSTRIA

**Graz**
Weisstein, Ulrich Werner *English literature educator*

## BRAZIL

**Canoas**
Sluberski, Thomas Richard *international educator, journalist, theologian*

## DENMARK

**Farum**
Larsen, Poul Steen *retired library educator*

## EL SALVADOR

**Santa Tecla**
Acosta, Barbara Dole *language educator*

## ENGLAND

**Cambridge**
Garrow, David Jeffries *historian, author*

**Lane End Bucks**
Blackton, Charles S(tuart) *history educator*

**London**
Abu-Deeb, Kamal Mikha'il *humanities educator*
Douglas, Mary Tew *anthropology and humanities educator*
Elson, Sarah Lee *art historian, consultant*
Graubard, Stephen Richards *historian, educator, editor*
Lowenthal, David *historian, geographer*
Rubin, Patricia Lee *art historian*

**Oxford**
Carey, John *language educator, critic*
Raz, Joseph *philosophy educator, law educator*

**Stoke-on-Trent**
Burwood, Stephen Meredith *historian, educator*

## FRANCE

**Paris**
Barrows, Leland Conley *historian, educator, editor*

**Vence**
Polk, William Roe *historian*

**Villeneuve d'Ascq**
Allain, Louis *literature educator*

## GERMANY

**Berlin**
Piper, Adrian Margaret Smith *philosopher, artist, educator*

**Münster**
Spevack, Marvin *language educator*

**Nuremberg**
Doerries, Reinhard René *historian, educator*

## HONG KONG

**Pokfulam**
McNaughton, William Frank *translator, educator*

## HUNGARY

**Budapest**
Fenyo, Jean-Pierre Ady *philosopher*

## ITALY

**Bologna**
Eco, Umberto *semiotics educator, author*

**Padua**
Shea, William Rene *historian, history and philosophy professor*

**Verona**
Pozzo, Riccardo *philosophy educator*

## JAPAN

**Kanagawa**
Fukatsu, Tanefusa *retired classicist, educator*

**Kashiwara**
Hori, Keiko *English literature educator*

**Mitaka**
Kazama, Toshio *humanities educator*

**Osaka**
Akase, Masako *humanities educator*

## KENYA

**Nairobi**
Wamutiso, Kineene *humanities educator*

## NETHERLANDS

**Amsterdam**
Kolko, Gabriel *historian, educator*

## SCOTLAND

**Cellardyke Fife**
Roff, William Robert *historian, educator, writer*

**Stirling**
Lenman, Bruce Philip *historian, educator*

## SPAIN

**Madrid**
Abellan, José Luis *humanities educator*

## SWEDEN

**Lerum**
Borei, Sven Hans Emil *translator*

## TAIWAN

**Taichung**
Lu, Shih-Peng *history professor*

**Taipei**
Dilley, Whitney Crothers *literature and language professor*

## ADDRESS UNPUBLISHED

Abbott, Rebecca Phillips *art historian, consultant, photographer, director*
Adams, David Parrish *historian, epidemiologist, educator*
Adamson, Lynda G. *literature educator, writer*
Adler, Raphael *retired humanities educator, speech pathology/audiology services professional*
Agnew, Kathleen Dianne Crosbie *language educator*
Aleinikov, Andrei Grigoryevich *linguist, educator*
Almeida, José Agustín *romance languages educator*
Amussen, Susan Dwyer *history professor*
Anderson, Dorothy S. *literature educator*
Anderson, Jeffrey Elton *history professor*
Anderson, Jerry Maynard *retired speech educator*
Angell, Richard Bradshaw *philosophy educator*
Ansbro, John Joseph *philosopher, educator*
Araujo, Ilka Vasconcelos *musicologist, educator*
Attebery, Louie Wayne *language educator, educator*
Avalle-Arce, Juan Bautista *Spanish language educator*
Azadpur, Mohammad *philosopher, educator*
Bailey, Charles-James Nice *linguistics educator*
Bailey, Scott Christopher *historian, educator*
Baker, Ronald James *language educator, academic administrator*
Bannister, Robert Corwin, Jr. *historian, educator*
Bartelt, William E. *historian, educator*
Basnett, Margaret G. *reading and language arts educator, consultant*
Baxter, Stephen Bartow *retired historian*
Baym, Nina (Nina Baym Stillinger) *literature educator, researcher*
Bean, Cathy Bao *humanities educator, writer*
Belk, Leotis S. *language educator*
Beman, Donald K. *writing and rhetoric educator, author*
Benivegna, Vito Nicholas *language educator*
Benseler, David P. *foreign language educator*
Bercovitch, Sacvan *English language professional, educator*
Berdahl, Robert Max *history professor, former academic administrator*
Beschloss, Michael *historian, writer, commentator*
Betz, Margaret Alison *women's studies educator, philosophy educator*
Biesenbach-Lucas, Sigrun *language educator, consultant*
Biles, Gloria C. *historian, educator*
Binns, Jane Camille *humanities educator*
Blackbourn, David Gordon *history professor*
Blackmun, Barbara Winston *art historian, educator, academic administrator*
Blake, King Charles *humanities educator, writer*
Blissett, William Frank *English literature educator*
Bloedel, Jeanne Helen *sign language educator, artist*
Blumin, Stuart M. *history professor*
Bok, Sissela *philosopher, writer*
Bolin, James Duane *history professor, writer*
Bolsterli, Margaret Jones *English professor, farmer*
Boly, Lillian Byronell *retired language educator*
Bordelon, Suzanne Mackie *writing and rhetoric educator*
Bosmajian, Haig Aram *speech communication educator*
Boyle, Richard John *art historian, author*
Bremer, Ronald Allan *genealogist, editor*
Brettell, Richard Robson *art historian, museum consultant, educator*
Brewer, Wanda Eastwood *retired literature educator*
Brewster, Elizabeth Winifred *literature educator, poet, writer*
Bridges, Leonard Hal *retired history educator, writer*
Brunner, Kathleen Marie *humanities educator*
Bunce, Christine A. *language educator*
Burchell, Kenneth Wayne *historian, appraiser*

Burns, William Earl *historian*
Bush, Sarah Lillian *historian*
Cachia, Pierre Jacques *Middle East languages and culture educator, researcher*
Caldwell, Louise Phinney *historical researcher, community volunteer*
Calleo, David Patrick *history professor, political scientist*
Cardenas, Brenda Eileen *literature and language professor, poet*
Carls, Alice Catherine *history professor*
Cawley, Joseph Douglas *retired reading professor*
Chambers, Audley C. *music historian, educator, researcher*
Chambers, Marjorie Bell *historian*
Chan, Sucheng *retired history professor, academic administrator, consultant*
Chandler, Alfred Dupont, Jr. *historian, educator*
Chappell, Fred Davis *language educator, poet*
Charles, Lola *interpreter*
Chase, Dawn Eileen *language educator*
Chesson, Michael Bedout *history professor, writer*
Ciabattari, Mark *historian, writer*
Ciraolo, Debra *sign language interpreter, consultant*
Clark, Eve Vivienne *linguist, educator*
Clogan, Paul Maurice *English language and literature educator*
Collins, Jean Katherine *language educator*
Collmer, Robert George *retired language educator*
Corrigan, Brian Jay *literature educator, writer*
Courtenay, William James *historian, educator*
Courtés, Joseph Jean-Marie *humanities educator, writer*
Courtney, Edward *retired classics educator*
Craver, Earlene *historian, educator*
Cunningham, William Francis, Jr. *literature and language professor, academic administrator*
Davis, Natalie Zemon *retired history professor*
Davis, Vivian *English language educator*
Delaty, Simone *retired language educator*
De Lorenzo, William E. *retired foreign language educator*
Demenchonok, Edward Vasilevich *philosopher, linguist, researcher, educator*
Demyanovich, Karen Lee *language educator*
Der-Houssikian, Haig *linguist, educator*
Descalzo de Blas, Alberto *humanities professor*
Dickstein, Morris *language educator, writer*
Djordjevic, Dimitrije *historian, educator*
Doebler, Bettie Anne *language educator, researcher, poet*
Dollinger, Marc Lindsey *historian*
Downes, Stephen Matthew *philosophy educator*
Downs, Dorothy Rieder *art historian, consultant, writer*
Duhl, Olga Anna *literature educator, researcher*
Dunbar, Maurice Victor *language educator*
Duquette, Jean-Pierre *retired French language and literature educator*
Durek, Dorothy Mary *retired language educator*
Dutton, Christine Frances *Spanish language educator*
Eadie, John William *historian, educator*
Ebert, Robert Peter *German language professor*
Eckstein, Jerome *philosopher, retired educator*
Edens, Betty Joyce *reading recovery educator*
Edwards, Annmarie Monica *language educator, career coach, entrepreneur*
Eire, Carlos *historian, educator, writer*
Eisner, Sigmund *retired English language educator*
Ellis, John Hubert *retired history professor*
Ellis, Joseph John Michael III *historian, history professor*
Emmett, Rita *professional speaker*
Erickson, Carol Jean *literature and language professor*
Espenlaub, Margo Linn *women's studies educator, writer, artist*
Essary, Andrew Charles *philosopher, educator, financial analyst*
Fahmy, Khaled *historian, educator*
Fatemi, Faramarz Saifpour *history professor, political science professor, consultant*
Feal, Gisele Catherine *foreign language educator*
Feeney, Matthew Edward *linguist, educator*
Fisher, Anita Jeanne (Kit Fisher) *retired language educator*
Flinner, Beatrice Jeffreys Allayaud *retired library and media sciences educator*
Flint, John E. *retired historian*
Fouraker, Lawrence *history professor*
Franklin, John Hope *historian, educator, author*
Froberg, Brent Malcolm *classics educator*
Gaddis, John Lewis *history professor*
Gaston, Paul Morton *retired history professor*
Gatewood, Willard Badgett, Jr. *retired historian, writer*
Gaustad, Edwin Scott *historian, educator*
Gerlach, Jeanne Elaine *English language educator*
Gettleman, Marvin E. *retired history professor*
Giesey, Ralph Edwin *retired historian*
Gillespie, Gerald Ernest Paul *comparative literature educator, writer*
Gillett, Mary Caperton *military historian*
Giordanengo, Sam Peter *history professor*
Glick, Ruth Burtnick *literature educator, writer*
Gofferje, Hadwig *retired language educator*
Goldman, Alvin Ira *philosopher, educator*
Gordon, Leonard H(erman) D(avid) *history educator*
Gorea, Lucia-Iosefina *language educator, poet*
Graham, Lanier *art historian, curator*
Grant, Linda Hess *language educator*
Greason, Walter David *history professor*
Greene, John Colton *retired historian*
Grilley, Beryl H. *retired speech educator*
Grinnell, Helen Dunn *musicologist, arts administrator*
Gritter, Elizabeth *historian, researcher*
Gruber, Ira Dempsey *historian, educator*
Gurspan, Susan Judith *language educator*
Hadda, Janet Ruth *language educator, lay psychoanalyst*
Hamblin, Terry Robert, Jr. *historian, educator*
Hamelin, Marcel *historian, educator*
Handy, Rollo Leroy *philosopher, researcher*
Hansen-Thomas, Holly Harbour *language educator*
Hardin, James Neal *language educator, writer*

Haring, Ellen Stone (Mrs. E. S. Haring) *philosophy educator*
Hart, Arthur Alvin *historian, author*
Hartwell, Carol L. *Spanish language educator, technical recruiter*
Hecht, Robert Anthony *history professor, writer*
Herbst, Jurgen *historian, educator*
Hoffman, Daniel (Gerard) *literature educator, poet*
Holloway, Ernest Robert III *historian, researcher*
Hong, Ran-E *literature educator*
Hood, Carra Leah *literature educator*
Howard, Michael Eliot *historian, educator*
Huegel, Donna Marie *historian, writer, artist, archivist*
Hughes, Thomas Parke *history professor*
Hunter, J(ames) Paul *literature and language professor, literary critic*
Hutcheon, Linda Ann *English language educator*
Iglesias, Maria Estrella *language educator, writer*
Isaac, Susan Victoria *literature and language professor, department chairman*
Iskander, Sylvia Wiese *English literature educator*
Ivry, Alfred Lyon *philosophy educator, historian*
Jacobson, Matthew Frye *historian, educator*
Jenness, Muriel Whitlock *reading specialist*
Johnson, Christopher Howard *historian*
Johnson, Janet Hovey *English language educator*
Johnson, John Prescott *retired philosophy educator*
Johnson, Phillip James *historian, educator, writer*
Jones, Peter d'Alroy *literature, writer, retired educator*
Kadonsky, Christine Elaine *historian, educator*
Kalbacken, Joan Muriel *foreign language educator, author*
Kaminsky, Alice Richkin *retired literature educator*
Kaplan, Robert B. *linguistics educator, consultant, researcher*
Kari, Daven Michael *English professor, religious studies educator*
Kastor, Frank Sullivan *language educator*
Kay, Aman B. *language educator, translator*
Kealey, Erin *philosopher*
Keeter, Lynn Carpenter *language educator*
Kenesson, Frank Girault *history educator, writer*
Kennett, Lee Boone, Jr. *historian, educator*
Kerney, Yolonda V. *music historian*
Khiterer, Victoria M. *historian*
Killebrew, Betty Rackley *language educator*
Kim, Marianne Weiss *humanities educator*
Kinney, Jeanne Kawelolani *English studies educator, writer*
Kleespies, Gavin W. *historian*
Klinghoffer, Judith Apter *historian, consultant*
Kolb, Harold Hutchinson, Jr. *language educator*
Koszarski, Richard *art historian, curator*
Kramer, Dale Vernon *retired language educator*
Kravitz, Ellen King *musicologist, educator*
Kryvko, Barbara *language educator, systems analyst*
Kucera, Henry *linguistics educator*
Kultermann, Udo *architectural and art historian, educator, writer*
Ladjevardi, Habib *historian*
LaFantasie, Glenn W. *historian, writer*
LaHood, Marvin John *retired language educator*
Laqueur, Walter *history professor, writer*
Larmon Peterson, Janine *history professor, consultant*
Laurent, Pierre-Henri *history professor*
Lawlor, LynnAnn Jennifer *reading educator*
Lawson, Carolina Donadio *language educator, translator*
Lee, Corinne Adams *retired English teacher*
Leon Rivera, Aida I. *language educator*
Levinsky, Frieda Libby *language educator*
Lewis, Douglas *retired art historian*
Lewis, Emanuel Raymond *historian, psychologist, retired librarian*
Lisio, Donald John *historian, educator*
Longsworth, Robert Morrow *language educator*
Loughran, James Newman *philosopher, educator, academic administrator*
Lowenthal, Constance *art historian, consultant*
Lyons, John David *literature and language professor*
MacDonald, Priscilla Ann *history professor*
MacDonald, Robert Alan *language educator*
Maehl, William Harvey *retired historian*
Mahoney, John L. *English literature educator*
Mahoney, Michael Robert Taylor *art historian, educator*
Maienschein, Jane Ann *historian, philosopher, educator*
Manuelian, Lucy Der *art historian, architecture educator*
Mapp, Edward Charles *speech educator*
Marcopoulos, George John *history professor*
Marée, Kathleen Nancy *retired language educator*
Marion, Marjorie Anne *English language educator, educational consultant*
Martin, Trisa *education and human development educator*
Marx, Michael William *language educator, writer*
Maryks, Robert A. *history professor*
Mathews, E. Anne Jones *retired library educator, academic administrator*
Mauskopf, Seymour Harold *history professor*
McCardell, John Malcolm, Jr. *history professor, academic administrator*
McCormick, John Owen *retired comparative literature educator*
McDermott, Agnes Charlene Senape *philosophy educator*
McDonald, Mary Frances *language educator*
McDonough, Richard Michael *philosophy educator*
McGann, Lisa B. Napoli *language educator*
McGill, Carla Ann *language educator*
McLemore-Wheeler, Linda M. *literature educator*
McMaster, Juliet Sylvia *English language educator*
Miller, Walter James *retired literature educator, writer*
Mindlin, Paula Rosalie *retired reading educator*
Miscella, Maria Diana *humanities educator*
Moller, Patricia Lynn *language educator*
Molloy, Sylvia *language educator*
Monaco, Chris *historian, writer, documentary filmmaker*

Morales, Marcia Paulette Merry *language educator, archaeologist*
Morgan, Edmund Sears *retired history professor*
Morrill, Penny Chittim *art historian*
Muegge, Uwe *terminology professor*
Murnion, William Edward *philosopher*
Murphy, Francis *language educator*
Murphy, Robert James *language educator, consultant, pianist, pipe organ performer*
Nagel, Thomas *philosopher, lawyer, educator*
Naumer, Carola *art historian, educator*
Nephew, Julia Anne *language educator*
Newman, Paul Douglas *history professor*
Newmark, Leonard Daniel *linguistics educator*
Nicholas, Lynn Holman *historian, researcher, writer*
Nitzarim, Yoel David *language educator*
Nochman, Lois Wood Kivi (Mrs. Marvin Nochman) *retired literature educator*
Noor, Ronny *language educator, writer*
Norberg, Arthur Lawrence, Jr. *historian, physicist, educator*
Nordman, Katie *reading specialist*
Nugent, Helen Jean *history professor*
Nugent, Walter Terry King *historian*
Odenigbo, Innocent Chukwunwike *linguist, writer, consultant*
Ogden, Benjamin *language educator*
Palmer, Marilyn Joan *English composition educator*
Palmieri, Dora Ann *retired language educator*
Palter, Robert Monroe *humanities educator*
Panzer, Mary Caroline *historian, museum curator*
Parkison, Aimee Dawn *language educator, writer*
Parsont, Mina Rainès-Lambé *retired literature educator*
Paschoud, François *classicist, educator*
Péladeau, Marius Beaudoin *art historian, historian, consultant, retired museum director*
Peña, Mary Anne *language educator*
Perdigó, Luisa Marina *foreign language and literature educator*
Perlingieri, Ilya Sandra *art history scholar, writer*
Petree, Sandra Ailey *language educator*
Pflanze, Otto Paul *history professor*
Pickrel, Paul *language educator*
Ping-Robbins, Nancy Regan *musicologist, educator*
Polzonetti, Pierpaolo *musicologist, music educator*
Post, Gaines, Jr. *retired history professor, dean, academic administrator*
Preston, Linda Carol Knight *retired English educator*
Proctor, Robert Neel *history educator*
Pulitzer, Emily Rauh (Mrs. Joseph Pulitzer Jr.) *art historian, consultant*
Pursell, Carroll Wirth *history educator*
Rakove, Jack Norman *history professor*
Rann, Robert Kennedy *humanities educator*
Rebay, Luciano *language educator, literary critic*
Recchiuti, John Louis *history professor*
Reed, Betty Jamerson *historian, educator*
Reeves, Kathleen Walker *English language educator*
Refai, Shahid *history professor*
Reh, Sheila Natkins *humanities educator*
Reid, Debra Ann *history professor*
Reiman, Donald Henry *language educator*
Resnick, Kirsten Fay Markuson *history professor*
Reynolds, Donald Martin *art historian, foundation administrator, educator*
Reznikov, Vladimir Lvovich *historian, playwright*
Riasanovsky, Nicholas Valentine *retired historian, educator*
Richards, David Gleyre *German language educator*
Richardson, Lawrence, Jr. *classicist, archaeologist*
Richardson, Robert Dale, Jr. *language educator*
Rickard, Ruth David *retired history professor, retired political science professor*
Ricks, Thomas Miller *historian, academic administrator*
Ritchie, Gisela Fuhrmann *foreign language educator*
Rizkallah, Morris Z. *translator*
Roalofs, Linda A. *language educator*
Roberts, Philip John *history professor, editor*
Robinson, Harlow Loomis *language educator, historian, writer*
Robinson, J(ohn) E(ric) *history professor, travel company executive*
Robinson, Mary Elizabeth Goff *retired historian, researcher*
Roche, Jeff *history professor*
Rodriguez, Timothy Allen *language educator*
Rogers, Katharine Munzer *English literature educator*
Rollins, Alfred Brooks, Jr. *historian, educator*
Rosenberg, David Alan *military historian, educator*
Rouman, John Christ *classics educator*
Ruffin, Herbert George, II, *history professor*
Ruoff, A. LaVonne Brown *language educator*
Russell, Andrew Benjamin *historian, educator*
Ryan, Marleigh Grayer *language educator*
Sage, C. J. *literature and language professor, editor, writer*
Saint-Jacques, Bernard *linguistics educator*
Salgado, Susana *musicologist, researcher, consultant*
Samuels, Maurice Anthony *French literature educator*
Sawai, Dahleen Emi *language educator*
Sayre, Robert Freeman *language educator*
Schadow, Karen E. *public speaking trainer, educator*
Schlagel, Richard H. *retired philosophy educator*
Schmidt, Albert John *retired history professor*
Schmitz, Dennis Mathew *retired language educator*
Schneider, Valerie Lois *retired speech educator*
Schor, Laura Strumingher *historian*
Schroeder, Brian S. *philosopher, educator*
Schwantes, Carlos Arnaldo *history professor, consultant*
Schwartz, Brian Michael *philosopher, think-tank executive*
Schwartz, Leon *foreign language educator*
Scott, Anne Byrd Firor *history professor*
Seniors, Paula Marie *history professor, researcher*
Sferrazza, Anthony Carl *historian, writer*

Shaeffer, John Nees *historian, educator*
Shannon, Catherine Barbara *history professor*
Sheffey, Ruthe T. *language educator*
Sheldon, Kathleen Eddy *historian*
Shepard, Suzanne V. *language educator*
Shillingsburg, Miriam Jones *literature educator, academic administrator*
Sieg, Kent G. *historian*
Silverman, Kenneth Eugene *language educator, writer*
Simons, Thomas W., Jr. *history professor*
Skinner, Daniel Thomas *language educator*
Smither, Howard Elbert *musicologist, educator*
Smock, Raymond William *historian*
Solomon, Robert Charles *philosopher, educator*
Spiegel, Jennifer *language educator*
Stendahl, Brita Kristina *humanities educator, social studies educator*
Stiebing, William Henry, Jr. *retired history professor*
Stoesen, Alexander Rudolph *retired history educator*
Stolarik, M. Mark *history professor*
Street, John Charles *linguistics educator*
Sullivan, Mary Rose *retired English language educator*
Sundstrom, Aileen Lois *speech educator*
Sutton, Julia *musicologist, dance educator*
Tall, Sonia Terry *humanities educator, researcher*
Tayler, Irene *English literature educator*
Taylor-Anderson, Jill *reading specialist*
Tedesco, Paul Herbert *humanities educator*
Teuscher, Simon Hans *history professor, researcher*
Thackray, Arnold Wilfrid *historian, educator, foundation administrator*
Thompson, Annie Laura (Laura Anne Thompson) *foreign language educator*
Thompson, John Herd *history professor*
Thomson, Virginia Winbourn *humanities educator, writer*
Thorson, Connie Capers *library educator*
Tice, Bradley Scott *humanities educator*
Tise, Larry Edward *historian, cultural organization administrator*
Titcomb, Caldwell *music and theatre historian*
Toller, Paige W. *philosopher, educator*
Tollison, Courtney L. *history professor*
Tong, Rosemarie *humanities educator, philosopher*
Toulmin, Stephen Edelston *humanities educator*
Trejos, Charlotte Marie *humanities educator, consultant*
Trelease, Allen William *historian, educator*
Tyrrell, Joseph Morten *retired history professor*
Valencia, Margarita *Spanish language educator*
van der Marck, Jan *art historian*
Vera Negron, Sandra *literature educator, translator*
Verhoff, Glen Charles *reading educator, choir director*
Walker, Beatriz Alem *language educator*
Walsh, Michael Thomas *historian, musician*
Washington, Garrett Lloyd *language educator*
Weber, Bruce Edward *art historian*
Weddle, Laura Mildred Thomas *retired language educator*
Werner, Donna *philosopher, educator*
Wetzel, Heinz *foreign language educator*
Wheeler, Burton M. *language educator, dean*
Whitburn, Merrill Duane *English literature educator*
White, Charles Sidney John *retired humanities educator*
Wiebenson, Dora Louise *architectural historian, editor, writer*
Wiener, Jon *history professor*
Williams, Robert Chadwell *history professor*
Wills, John Elliot, Jr. *retired historian, writer*
Wilson, Jerry Clark *language educator*
Winter, Marsha Terry *French language educator*
Wiswall, Dorothy Roller *language educator*
Wizda, Christine Anne *history professor*
Wolar, Glynn G. *history professor, lawyer*
Wood, Jerilyn Ruth *literature and language professor, secondary school educator, interior designer*
Woodbridge, John Dunning *history professor*
Wooton, Joel *history professor, basketball coach*
Worster, Ann Martin *historian*
Wright, Josephine Rosa Beatrice *musicologist, educator*
Wynne, Benjamin Ray *history professor*
Wyrsch, Carolyn Irwin *historian, educator*
Yannella, Donald *literature and language professor*
Zaferson, William S. *philosophy educator, publisher*
Zakim, Tom Edward *history professor*
Zimmermann, Thomas Callander Price *retired historian, educator*
Zukowski, Karen Ann *art historian, educator, writer, curator*

# HUMANITIES: LIBRARIES

## UNITED STATES

### ALABAMA

**Athens**
Kemp, Ann *retired librarian*

**Auburn University**
MacEwan, Bonnie *librarian, dean*

**Birmingham**
Beard, Craig Wyeth *librarian*
Murrell, Susan DeBrecht *librarian*
Spence, Paul Herbert *librarian*
Stephens, Jerry Wayne *librarian, director*

**Gardendale**
McKay, Marie Conyers *librarian, writer*

**Jacksonville**
Hubbard, William James *library director*
McAbee, Sonja Louise *library administrator*
Merrill, Martha *library and information scientist*

**Montgomery**
Shepard, Judith Bethea *librarian*

**Spanish Fort**
Economos, Cora Matheny *librarian*

**Tuscaloosa**
Mathews, Jennifer Kathleen *librarian, editor*

### ALASKA

**Anchorage**
Braund-Allen, Julianna Elise *librarian*
Frederiksen, Patience Ann *librarian*
Rollins, Alden Milton *archivist*

**Juneau**
Schorr, Alan Edward *librarian, publishing executive*
Shelton, Kathryn H. *librarian*

### ARIZONA

**Peoria**
Bailey, Claudia Jean *retired librarian, artist*

**Phoenix**
Anderson, Vicki *retired librarian*
Hanley, Fred William *librarian, educator*
Roof, Sally Jean-Marie *library and information scientist, educator*
Wells, GladysAnn *library director*
Willocks, Robert Max *retired librarian*

**Prescott Valley**
Beck, Doris Olson *retired library media director*

**Sun City**
Crisman, Mary Frances Borden *librarian*
Williams, William Harrison *retired librarian*

**Tempe**
Maynard, Michael *librarian*
Schmidt, Sherrie *library director, dean*

**Tucson**
Baker, Robert Kerry *college administrator, author, editor*
Pintozzi, Chestalene *librarian*
White, Herbert Spencer *library and information scientist, educator, dean*
Wolfe, William Jerome *librarian, language educator*

### ARKANSAS

**Batesville**
Bennett, Linda Lou *library director*

**Bella Vista**
Medin, Alice Louise *librarian*

**Fayetteville**
Cantrell, Andrea E. *library administrator*
Jones, Phillip John *librarian*

**Greers Ferry**
Martindale, Carla Joy *retired librarian*

**Little Rock**
Alsobrook, David Ernest *library director, archivist, historian*
Baker, Russell Pierce *archivist*
Mulkey, Jack Clarendon *retired library director*

**Lonoke**
Ross, Philip Rowland *retired library director*

**Monticello**
Guenter, Helen Marie Giessen *librarian*

**Russellville**
Zimmer, Connie Whitlow *librarian*

### CALIFORNIA

**Altadena**
Dutton, Pauline Mae *fine arts and reference librarian*

**Aptos**
Heron, David Winston *librarian*

**Auburn**
Sanborn, Dorothy Chappell *retired librarian*

**Bakersfield**
Duquette, Diane Rhea *library director*
Rump, Marjorie *library director*

**Berkeley**
Buckland, Michael Keeble *librarian, educator*
Harlan, Robert Dale *library and information scientist, educator, academic administrator*
Minudri, Regina Ursula *librarian, consultant*

**Beverly Hills**
Ramser, Wanda Tene *librarian, educator*

**Carson**
Anuakan, Robyn Iset *archivist, educator, film producer*

**Coalinga**
Russell, Beverly Ann *librarian, writer*

**Cupertino**
Fletcher, Homer Lee *librarian*

**Davis**
Sharrow, Marilyn Jane *library administrator*

**Downey**
Todd, Margaret Donnellan *librarian, director*

**El Cerrito**
Alldredge, Noreen S. *librarian*
Kao, Yasuko Watanabe *retired library director*

**Fremont**
Bray, Richard Daniel *librarian*
Lin, Sharon Shiang Chien *librarian*
Wood, Linda May *librarian*

**Fresno**
Gorman, Michael Joseph *library director, educator*

**Fullerton**
Ayala, John L. *retired librarian, dean*
Johnson, Carolyn Elizabeth *librarian*

**Glendale**
Michelson, Lillian *librarian, researcher*
Woolls, Esther Blanche *library science educator*

**Gustine**
Ramirez, Nola Marie *librarian*

**Irvine**
Gylseth, Doris Hanson (Doris Lillian Gylseth)
*retired librarian*

**Laguna Beach**
Anderson, Elizabeth Carmal (Bette Anderson)
*librarian, writer*

**Loma Linda**
Cimpoeru, Petre *archivist, educator*

**Long Beach**
Proust, Joycelyn Ann *retired librarian*

**Los Angeles**
Bates, Marcia Jeanne *information scientist educator*
Bergman, Emily Anne *librarian*
Chang, Henry C. *library administrator*
Cheng, Hong *library and information scientist*
Ciccone, Amy Navratil *art librarian*
Crampon, Jean Elaine *librarian*
Cuadra, Carlos Albert *library and information scientist, consultant*
Grassian, Esther Stampfer *librarian, educator*
Holmes, Fontayne *city librarian*
McGarry, Dorothy *librarian*
Patron, Susan Hall *librarian, writer*
Richardson, John Vinson, Jr. *library and information science professor*
Roby, Thomas Carter *conservator*
Shank, Russell *librarian, educator*
Shoaf, R. Wayne *librarian*
Song, Yongyi *librarian*
Strong, Gary Eugene *librarian*
Wooler, John William *multi-media specialist*

**Menlo Park**
White, Cecil Ray *librarian, consultant*

**Monterey**
Reneker, Maxine Hohman *librarian*

**Monterey Park**
Wilson, Linda *librarian*

**Mountain View**
Di Muccio, Mary-Jo *retired librarian*

**Northridge**
Duran, Karin Jeanine *librarian*

**Oakland**
Green, David Edward *retired librarian, priest, translator*
Lee, Ella Louise *librarian, educator*
Rubin, Rhea Joyce *library consultant*
Woodbury, Marda Liggett *librarian, writer*

**Oceanside**
Lange, Clifford Elmer *retired librarian*

**Pollock Pines**
Rickard, Margaret Lynn *library director, consultant*

**Pomona**
Jackson, Mary Ellen *librarian, consultant*

**Redlands**
Burgess, Larry Eugene *library director, historian, educator*

**Roseville**
Arnold, Barbara Cook *librarian*

**Sacramento**
Gray, Walter P. III *historian, archivist, consultant*
Killian, Richard M. *library director*
Starr, Kevin *librarian, educator*

**San Bernardino**
Burgess, Michael *librarian, writer*

**San Diego**
Brown, Barbara Sproul *retired librarian, consultant, writer*
Sauer, David Andrew *librarian, writer*
Tatár, Anna *library director*

**San Francisco**
Aldrich, Michael Ray *library curator, health educator*
Bocobo-Balunsat, Dalisay *librarian, journalist*
Brechka, Frank Tilson *retired librarian, historian*
Thacker-Estrada, Elizabeth Lorelei *librarian, historian*

**San Jacinto**
Smith, Diane Jans *librarian, educator*

**San Jose**
Light, Jane Ellen *librarian*
Schmidt, Cyril James *librarian*
Yiotis, Kristin *librarian, educator*

**San Juan Capistrano**
Peterson, Fred McCrae *retired librarian*

**Santa Ana**
Adams, John M. *library director*

**Santa Barbara**
Gartrell, David Christian *archivist*
Larsgaard, Mary Lynette *librarian, writer*

**Santa Clara**
Hopkinson, Shirley Lois *library and information scientist, educator*
Ostwald, Venice Eloise Varner *librarian, educator, minister, writer*

**Santa Cruz**
Ripma, Mary *librarian*

**Santa Rosa**
Pearson, Roger Lee *library director*
Rosaschi, Jim *librarian*

**Saratoga**
Chisholm, Margaret Elizabeth *retired library director*

**Sebastopol**
Sabsay, David *library director, consultant*

**Simi Valley**
Blackwood, Duke (R. Duke Blackwood) *library director*

**Stanford**
Danielson, Elena Schafer *retired archivist*
Derksen, Charlotte Ruth Meynink *librarian*
Keller, Michael Alan *librarian, musicologist*

**Thousand Oaks**
Brogden, Stephen Richard *library director*

**Visalia**
Anderson, Maureen Anne *retired librarian*

**Whittier**
Weismiller, Eleanor Kovacs *library director*

**Woodland Hills**
Zeitlin, Eugenia Pawlik *librarian, educator, writer*

**Yorba Linda**
Naftali, Timothy J. *library director, historian, educator, writer*

## COLORADO

**Boulder**
O'Brien, Elmer John *librarian, educator*
Wertheimer, Marilyn Lou *librarian, educator*

**Canon City**
Cochran, Susan Mills *research librarian*

**Colorado Springs**
Budington, William Stone *retired librarian*

**Denver**
Ashton, Rick James *retired librarian*
Dudden, Rosalind F. *librarian*
Garcia, June Marie *librarian*
Phillips, Dorothy Reid *retired medical library technician*
Smith, Sallye Wrye *librarian*
White, Joyce Louise *librarian*

**Edwards**
Chambers, Joan Louise *retired librarian, retired dean*

**Fort Collins**
Mc Clellan, William Monson *retired library director*

**Grand Junction**
Bragdon, Lynn Lyon *library administrator*

**Lakewood**
Knott, William Alan *library director*

**Lamar**
Green, Eric Roger *librarian*

**Louisville**
Maddock, Jerome Torrence *library and information scientist*

**Montrose**
Fritze, Sheila Kay *librarian*

**Pueblo**
Puls, Elaine Allison *retired librarian*

## CONNECTICUT

**Cheshire**
Walter, Kenneth Gaines *library director*

**Chester**
Harwood, Eleanor Cash *retired librarian*

**Coventry**
Aho, Sandra Christine *conservator*

**Fairfield**
Bryan, Barbara Day *retired librarian*

**Hamden**
Lucas, Doina C. *librarian*

**Hartford**
Kaimowitz, Jeffrey Hugh *librarian*
Wiggin, Kendall French *state librarian*

**Mystic**
Rogers, Brian Deane *librarian*

**New Britain**
Chasse, Emily Schuder *librarian, educator*

**New Haven**
Clarie, Thomas Cashin, II, *librarian*
Sease, Catherine *conservator, consultant*
Stahl, Nanette *librarian, biblicist*
Stuehrenberg, Paul Frederick *librarian*

**Niantic**
Deakyne, William John *library director, musician*
Morrill, Billie Alberta *librarian*

**North Canton**
Swibold, Gretchen Ann *librarian, writer*

**Orange**
Conant, Sally Lorensen *textile conservator, art historian*

**Simsbury**
Berberich, Patricia Louise *librarian*
Roberts, Celia Ann *librarian*

**Southbury**
Rorick, William Calvin *librarian, educator, portrait artist*

**Storrs Mansfield**
Franklin, Brinley *library director*
Kline, Nancy Mattoon *librarian*

**Wilton**
Poundstone, Sally Hill *library director*

**Woodbridge**
Westerberg, Kermit Berndt *librarian*

## DELAWARE

**New Castle**
Newell, Katherine Claiborne *librarian*

**Wilmington**
Williams, Richmond Dean *library consultant and appraiser*

## DISTRICT OF COLUMBIA

**Washington**
Bainbridge, Erika Ohara *librarian*
Baum, Ingeborg Ruth *librarian*
Beall, Julianne *librarian*
Bromley, Marilyn Modlin *librarian*
Carlson, Melinda Suzanne *librarian*
Chin, Cecilia Hui-Hsin *librarian*
Chute, Mary L. *library director*
Cooper, Ginnie *library director*
Cylke, Frank Kurt *librarian*
Dewey, Catherine Camille *conservator*
Dixson, Diane Elizabeth *acquisitions librarian, tax preparation business owner*
Dorn, Georgette Magassy *library official*
Doumato, Lamia *librarian, historian*
Galloway, Hoyt Wilson *library director*
Haley, Roger Kendall *librarian*
Harlem, Susan Lynn *librarian*
Hedges, Kamla King *library director*
Heiss, Harry Glen *archivist*
Holt, Helen *librarian, consultant, former government official*
Kalfatovic, Martin Robert *librarian, writer*
Lee, Hwa-Wei *librarian, educator, consultant*
Mann, Thomas *reference librarian*
Marcum, Deanna Bowling *library administrator*
Martin, Kathleen Suzanne *librarian*
Missar, Charles Donald *retired librarian*
Player, Thelma B. *librarian*
Rovelstad, Mathilde V(erner) *retired library and information scientist, educator*
Smith, George Vinal *librarian*
Thomas, Mary Augusta *library administrator*
Turtle, Neal Timothy *librarian*
Vogelsong, Diana Louise *librarian*
Wand, Patricia Ann *librarian*
Wattenmaker, Richard Joel *archivist, director*
Watts, Doris Earlene *retired librarian*
Wertz, Virginia Loryma *retired librarian*

## FLORIDA

**Clearwater**
Glymph, Dianne Tyler *librarian*

**Cocoa**
Rickling, Iraida Badillo *librarian*

**Daytona Beach**
Sigerson, Marjorie Lorraine *librarian*

**Deland**
Bradford, Jane Turner *librarian*
Caccamise, Genevra Louise Ball (Mrs. Alfred E. Caccamise) *retired librarian*
Ryan, Susan Magness *librarian, educator*

**Destin**
Burns, Jurate *library director*
Deel, Frances Quinn *retired librarian*

**Englewood**
McCall, Gene William *conservator, sculptor, artist, furniture designer*

**Fort Lauderdale**
Beach, Cecil Prentice *librarian*
Cannon, Robert Eugene *library director*
Hershenson, Miriam Hannah Ratner *librarian*

Riggs, Donald Eugene *librarian, academic administrator*

**Fort Walton Beach**
Hill, Carol Koelling *library director*

**Gainesville**
Canelas, Dale Brunelle *library director*

**Gulfport**
Bourke, Thomas Anthony *librarian, writer*

**Haines City**
Kirk, Sherwood *retired librarian*

**Hernando**
Park, Chung Il *retired librarian*

**Hialeah**
Medvinsky, Nathalia *library director*

**Jacksonville**
Gubbin, Barbara Ashley Brendon *library director*

**Lakeland**
Reich, David Lee *library director*

**Lighthouse Point**
Gauthier, Doreen Ann *librarian*

**Madison**
Hiss, Sheila Mary *librarian*

**Melbourne**
Helmstetter, Wendy Lee *librarian*

**Miami**
Comras, Rema *retired library director*
Santiago, Raymond *library director, educator*
Treyz, Joseph Henry *librarian*
Zaleski-Vegazo, Ilene *librarian*

**Naples**
Hall, Beverly Barton *librarian*

**Oakland Park**
Kilpatrick, Clifton Wayne *book dealer*

**Ocala**
Frow, Richard G. *retired librarian*
Tesmer, Nancy Ann Stutler *retired librarian*

**Orlando**
Allison, Anne Marie *retired librarian*
Hoeppner, Athena *librarian*
Hudson, Phyllis Janecke *librarian*

**Ormond Beach**
von Fettweis, Yvonne Caché *archivist, historian*

**Port Charlotte**
Donovan, William Alan *retired librarian*

**Saint Petersburg**
Kent, Allen *library and information sciences professor*

**Sanibel**
Allen, Patricia J. *library director*

**Sarasota**
Brandhorst, Wesley Theodore *retired library and information scientist*
De Gennaro, Richard *retired library director*
Hummel, Dana D. Mallett *librarian*
Retzer, Mary Elizabeth Helm *retired librarian*
Straight, Elsie Hosking *retired librarian, sculptor*

**Tallahassee**
Fiore, Carole Diane *library consultant*
Goldstein, Julia Sonia *librarian*
Thompson, Jean Tanner *retired librarian*
Washington, Karen *librarian, educator*
Zachert, Martha Jane *retired librarian*

**Tampa**
Harkness, Mary Lou *librarian*
McCook, Kathleen de la Peña *librarian, educator*

**University Park**
Compain, Rita *librarian*

**Venice**
Asp, William George *librarian*

**West Palm Beach**
Terwillegar, Jane Cusack *librarian, educator*

**Winter Park**
Bloodworth, Velda Jean *librarian, educator*
Rogers, Rutherford David *librarian*
Zhang, Wenxian *librarian*

## GEORGIA

**Athens**
Donovan, James M. *librarian, anthropologist*
McAlister, Sheila Anne *archivist*
Potter, William Gray, Jr. *library director*
Shoemaker, Rene Denise *librarian, artist*

**Atlanta**
Flagg Davis, Vivian Annette *librarian, researcher, public information officer*
Hakes, Jay Edward *library director, former federal agency administrator*
McCannon, Tricia Ann *multi-media specialist, writer, photographer, educator*
McDavid, Sara June *librarian*
Nosakhere, Akilah Shukura Montsho *librarian, consultant, editor, writer*
Roberts, Edward Graham *librarian*
Robison, Carolyn Love *retired librarian*
Wallace, Gladys Baldwin *librarian*
Yates, Ella Gaines *librarian, consultant*

**Cleveland**
Edwards, John Carver *retired archivist*

**Douglasville**
Hébert, Rebecca Lapczynski *archivist*

**Fayetteville**
Neal, Joan Burkes *librarian*

**Lithia Springs**
Moore, Lindy A. *librarian*

**Macon**
Preuit, Theresa *librarian*

**Marietta**
Kendall, Susan Gardes *librarian*

**Rome**
Doyle, James Donald, Jr. *librarian*
Mosley, Mary Mac *retired librarian*

**Tifton**
McClusky, Duncan Kemp *librarian*

**Warner Robins**
Merk, P. Evelyn *librarian*

## HAWAII

**Honolulu**
Flynn, David A. *librarian*
Perushek, Diane *university librarian*
Preble, Sarah Hamilton *art librarian, author, writer*
Schindler, Jo Ann *librarian, director*
Stigall, Phyllis Graham *retired librarian*
Wertheimer, Andrew B. *library and information scientist, educator*

**Kahului**
Tolliver, Dorothy *librarian*

**Kailua**
Wright, John Cotton *archivist, consultant*

**Lihue**
Stevens, Robert David *librarian, educator*

## IDAHO

**Moscow**
Force, Ronald Wayne *librarian*

**Nampa**
Rambo, Helen Marie *librarian*

## ILLINOIS

**Bloomington**
Olson, Rue Eileen *retired librarian*
Stroyan, Susan Elizabeth *librarian, administrator*

**Calumet City**
Muñoz, Romeo Solano *audio visual curator*

**Carbondale**
Bauner, Ruth Elizabeth *library director*
Carlson, David H. *dean*

**Champaign**
McDonough, Jerome Patrick *librarian*
Rayward, Warden Boyd *librarian, educator*
Ruan, Lian Jin *library director*

**Chicago**
Brown, Richard Holbrook *library director, historian, researcher*
Choldin, Marianna Tax *librarian, educator*
Davis, Mary Ellen K. *library director*
Funk, Carla Jean *library association director*
Gerdes, Neil Wayne *library director, educator*
Hanrath, Linda Carol *librarian, archivist*
Howse Binnington, Rachel Marie *archivist, consultant*
Miletich, Ivo *library and information scientist, bibliographer, educator, linguist, literature research specialist*
Nicoll, Jane Ellen *archivist, librarian*
Parr, Virginia Helen *retired librarian*
Rishworth, Susan Knoke *archivist, researcher*
Sullivan, Peggy *librarian, consultant*
Szydlowski, Joseph Edward *music librarian*
Wagner, Rose Mary *retired librarian*

**Chicago Heights**
Croarkin, Donald J. *librarian*
Stanko, Susan G. *librarian*

**Danville**
Lindemann, Ruth Burridge *librarian*

**Dekalb**
Hamilton, David Arnold *retired librarian*

**Des Plaines**
Miesse, James Everett *librarian*
Orme, Marianne Linette *librarian*

**Edwardsville**
Johnson, Charlotte Lee *librarian*

**Evanston**
Beatty, Virginia Lewis *librarian, archivist, consultant*
Bethel, Kathleen Evonne *librarian*
Bishop, David Fulton *library administrator*
Cates, Jo Ann *library director*
Crawford, Susan *library director, educator, editor, writer*
Pritchard, Sarah Margaret *library director*
Zipperer, Lorri Ann *librarian, consultant*

**Freeport**
Vogt, Lorna Corrine *retired librarian, small business owner*

**Greenview**
Full, Susan Gayle *librarian, educator*

**Indian Head Park**
Bamberger, Mary Ann *archivist, consultant*

**Jacksonville**
Gallas, Martin Hans *librarian*

**Joliet**
Johnston, James Robert *library director*

**Lake Forest**
Miller, Arthur Hawks, Jr. *librarian, archivist*

**Lincolnwood**
Beck, Cynthia Marie *archivist, researcher*

**Naperville**
Holba Puacz, Jeanne *librarian, educator*

**Quincy**
Tyer, Travis Earl *librarian, consultant*

**Richton Park**
Nevins, Patrick Fredrick *librarian*

**Riverside**
Van Cura, Joyce Bennett *librarian*

**Schaumburg**
Adrianopoli, Barbara Catherine *librarian*

**Skokie**
Anthony, Carolyn Additon *librarian*
Bush, Gail *librarian, educator, director, writer*

**South Holland**
Connolly, Carla Marie *librarian*

**Springfield**
Schroeder-Lein, Glenna Ruth *librarian, historian*

**Urbana**
Bennett, Scott Boyce *retired librarian, consultant*
Brichford, Maynard Jay *archivist*
Kaufman, Paula T. *librarian*
O'Brien, Nancy Patricia *librarian, educator*
Watson, Paula D. *retired librarian*

**West Chicago**
Kramer, Pamela Kostenko *librarian*

**Wheaton**
Thompson, Bert Allen *retired librarian*
Tucker, Beverly Sowers *library and information scientist*

**Wheeling**
Long, Sarah Ann *librarian*
Meehan, Tamiye Marcia *library director*

**Wilmette**
Hansen, Andrew Marius *retired library director*
Kenamore, Jane Allen *archivist*

## INDIANA

**Bloomington**
Legler, April Arington *librarian, educator*
Meho, Lokman I. *library and information scientist, educator*
Rudolph, Lavere Christian *library director*
Studwell, William Emmett *librarian, writer*

**Bluffton**
Elliott, Barbara Jean *librarian*

**Evansville**
Scheer, John C. *librarian*

**Fort Wayne**
Krull, Jeffrey Robert *library director*
McCaffery, Laura Belle *retired librarian*

**Hammond**
Carpenter, Kathryn Hammell *library director, educator*

**Hobart**
Mellon, Mary Regina *librarian*

**Indianapolis**
Gnat, Raymond Earl *librarian*
Terry, Linda Faye *librarian*
Young, Philip Howard *library director*

**Lafayette**
McKowen, Dorothy Keeton *librarian, educator*
Mobley, Emily Ruth *library director, educator, dean*

**Lake Village**
Emmrich, Mary Kaylene *librarian*

**Liberty**
Sowers, Marilyn Rae *librarian*

**Muncie**
Dolak, Fritz *librarian, information administrator*
Kroehler, Beth Ann *librarian*
Schaefer, Patricia *retired librarian*
Turner, Nancy K. *archivist, librarian*
Yeamans, George Thomas *librarian, educator*

**Notre Dame**
Hayes, Stephen Matthew *librarian*

**Richmond**
Farber, Evan Ira *librarian*
Kirk, Thomas Garrett, Jr. *librarian*

**South Bend**
Stankrauff, Alison Harper *archivist*

**Terre Haute**
Hardin, Steve *librarian*

**West Lafayette**
Andrews, Theodora Anne *retired librarian, educator*
Markee, Katherine Madigan *librarian, educator*
Nixon, Judith May *librarian*

**Whiting**
Downen, Madeline Elizabeth *retired hospital librarian*

## IOWA

**Cedar Rapids**
Renter, Lois Irene Hutson *retired librarian*

**Davenport**
Runge, Kay Kretschmar *library director*
Wiese, Glenda Coppersmith *librarian, archivist*

**Decorah**
Kemp, H. Jane *librarian*

**Grinnell**
Fyffe, Richard Coleman *librarian*
McKee, Christopher Fulton *librarian, historian, educator*

**Iowa City**
Baker, Nancy L. *university librarian, educator*
Bentz, Dale Monroe *university librarian*
Huttner, Sidney Frederick *librarian*
McCartney, David Farnham *archivist, educator*
Miller, Dwight Merrick *archivist, historian*
Pierce, Jennifer Burek *library and information scientist*

**Newton**
Padilla, Sue Ann *librarian*

**North Liberty**
Crowner, Dee Kay *library administrator*

**West Bend**
Wuebker, Colleen Marie *retired librarian*

**West Branch**
Mather, Mildred Eunice *retired archivist*
Walch, Timothy George *library director*

## KANSAS

**Abilene**
Holt, Dan *library director*

**Burr Oak**
Underwood, Deanna Kay *librarian*

**Enterprise**
Wickman, John Edward *librarian, historian*

**Lawrence**
Crowe, William Joseph *librarian*
Haricombe, Lorraine *library director, dean*
Williams, Sheryl Katheryn *archivist, librarian*

**Linwood**
Coatney, Sharon Ann *librarian, educator, editor*

**Olathe**
Morrison, Ray Leon *library director, education educator*

**Overland Park**
Kempf, Andrea Caron *librarian, educator*

**Pittsburg**
Lee, Earl Wayne *library science educator*

**Topeka**
Knecht, Robert Lee *archivist*

**Wichita**
Johnson, Ellen Schultz *retired music librarian, researcher*

## KENTUCKY

**Bowling Green**
Rabold, Charlene Franklin *librarian*
Smith, Charles Hyde *librarian, historian*

**Campbellsville**
Burch, John Russell, Jr. *library director*

**Cold Spring**
May, Debra Hardyman *librarian*

**Danville**
Pappas, Marjorie L. *library studies educator*

**Frankfort**
Gibbons, Judith A. *librarian*

**Highland Heights**
Kennedy, Colleen Jo Ann *librarian, educator*

**La Grange**
Morgan, Mary Dan *librarian*

**Lexington**
Birchfield, Martha *librarian*
Diedrichs, Carol Pitts *librarian, dean*
Mason, Ellsworth Goodwin *retired librarian*
Sineath, Timothy Wayne *librarian, educator, dean*
Steensland, Ronald Paul *librarian*
Young, Sandra Cooper *retired librarian*

**Louisville**
Bell, Mary Margaret *archivist*
Deering, Ronald Franklin *librarian, minister*
Keisling, Bruce Lowell *librarian*
Shobe, David Soren *librarian, director*

**Marion**
Henley, Darl Heathcott *librarian, educator*

**Morehead**
Besant, Larry Xon *retired librarian, administrator, consultant*
Nutter, Carol Angell *academic librarian*
Pritchard, Elsie Tomlinson *librarian*

**Somerset**
Huntsman, Mary Taylor *librarian, history professor*

**Wilmore**
Pohl, Gunther Erich *retired library administrator*

## LOUISIANA

**Baton Rouge**
Cargill, Jennifer S. *librarian, dean, educator*
Hayward, Olga Loretta Hines (Mrs. Samuel Ellsworth Hayward) *retired librarian*
Kinnison, Phyllis Marie *archivist*
Lusk, Glenna Rae Knight (Mrs. Edwin Bruce Lusk) *librarian*
McKnight, Michelynn *librarian*
Patterson, Charles Darold *librarian, educator*

**Covington**
Stahr, Beth A. *librarian*

**Metairie**
Dickerson, Lon Richard *library administrator*

**Monroe**
Smith, Donald Raymond *librarian*

**New Orleans**
Khaton, Sabrina Roslyn *librarian, accountant*
Skinner, Robert Earle *librarian, writer*

**Ponchatoula**
Kuechmann, Christopher Robert *library director*

**Schriever**
Shaffer, Margaret Minor *retired library director*

**Shreveport**
Brazile, Orella Ramsey *library director*
McLemore, Laura Lyons *archivist, history educator*
Pelton, James Rodger *librarian*
Wood, Julienne Louise *librarian, historian*

## MAINE

**Bangor**
Rea, Ann W. *librarian*

**Camden**
Moran, Elizabeth Ames *library director*

**Orono**
Risberg, Erica Lynn *archivist, film producer*

**Waterville**
Muehlner, Suanne Wilson *library director*

## MARYLAND

**Annapolis**
Papenfuse, Edward Carl, Jr. *archivist, state official*
Werking, Richard Hume *librarian, historian, academic administrator*

**Baltimore**
Allen, Norma Ann *librarian, educator*
Bradley, Wanda Louise *librarian*
Harris, Reginald Mervyn, Jr. *librarian, writer*
Hayden, Carla Diane *library director, educator*
Leonard, Angela Michele *librarian, educator*
Magnuson, Nancy *librarian*
Massey-Burzio, Virginia *librarian, writer*
McAdam, Paul Edward *retired library administrator*
Nasr, Nadia *librarian*
Tabb, Winston *librarian*

**Bethesda**
Humphreys, Betsy L. *librarian*
Knachel, Philip Atherton *librarian*
Lindberg, Donald Allan Bror *library director, pathologist, educator*
Yang, Key Paik *librarian, archivist*

**Boonsboro**
Butler, Naomi Witmer *librarian, educator*

**Bowie**
Mondale, S. Janiece *librarian*
Wardrip, Elizabeth Jane *retired librarian*

**Chestertown**
Rather, Lucia Porcher Johnson *library administrator*

**Chevy Chase**
Basa, Enikö Molnár *retired librarian*

**College Park**
Kurtz, Michael Joseph *archivist, educator*
Loiselle, Andrea Pugsley *archivist*
Lowell, Howard Parsons *archivist, federal agency administrator*
Lowry, Charles Bryan *librarian, dean*
Wasserman, Paul *library and information science professor*
Weinstein, Allen *archivist*

**Columbia**
Gruhl, Andrea Morris *librarian*
Klein, Sami Weiner *librarian*

**Crofton**
Williams, J. Linda *librarian*

**Funkstown**
Mallery, Mary Silcox *librarian, director*

**Germantown**
Lewis, Robert John Cornelius Koons *retired library director*

**Glen Burnie**
Mc Cabe, Gerard Benedict *retired library administrator*

**Greenbelt**
Hogensen, Margaret Hiner *retired librarian, consultant*
Moore, Virginia Bradley *librarian*

**Laurel**
Pikas, Christina Kirk *librarian, researcher*

**Potomac**
Broderick, John Caruthers *retired librarian*
Johnson, Sue O'Neill *retired library and information scientist*

**Rockville**
Hamilton, Parker *library director*
Lavoie, Daniel Joseph, II, *archivist, historian*
Renninger, Mary Karen *retired librarian*

**Saint Leonard**
Seifert, Betty L. *conservator, consultant*

**Salisbury**
Wolter, John Amadeus *librarian, federal official*

**Silver Spring**
Null, Elisabeth Higgins *librarian, editor*

**Springdale**
Keith, Patricia *multi-media specialist*

**Takoma Park**
von Hake, Margaret Joan *librarian*

**Towson**
Tull, Willis Clayton, Jr. *retired librarian*

**MASSACHUSETTS**

**Amherst**
Bridegam, Willis Edward, Jr. *retired librarian*
Schafer, Gerald Lewis (Jay Schafer) *library director*

**Andover**
Hatcher, Rebecca E. *field services representative, library archives consultant*

**Boston**
Armstrong, Rodney *librarian*
Christopher, Irene *librarian, consultant*
Desnoyers, Megan Floyd *archivist, educator*
Hebard, Barbara Adams *conservator*
Leff, Deborah *library director*
Margolis, Bernard Allen *library administrator*
Matz, Jenni *archivist, filmmaker*
Mifflin, Jeffrey Allen *archivist, consultant, historian, researcher*
Roth, James Michael *archivist*
Trinkaus-Randall, Gregor *librarian, archivist, preservation administrator*
Wendorf, Richard Harold *library director, educator*

**Cambridge**
Cole, Heather Ellen *librarian*
Copenhagen, Edward Blake *archivist, librarian*
Davis-Millis, Nina *librarian*
Flannery, Susan Marie *library administrator*
Koepp, Donna Pauline Petersen *librarian*
Mancusi-Ungaro, Carol *conservator, educator*
Stoddard, Roger Eliot *scholar*
Wolpert, Ann J. *library director*

**Canton**
Kelley, Irene W. *retired librarian, musician, artist*

**Carver**
Neubauer, Richard A. *library science educator, consultant*

**Chestnut Hill**
Yavarkovsky, Jerome Harold *library director*

**Dorchester**
James, Elaine McLean *retired librarian*

**East Orleans**
Natale, Barbara Gustafson *retired librarian*

**Lexington**
Freitag, Wolfgang Martin *retired librarian, educator*

**Lincoln**
Bracken, (Myra) Jeanne Munn *librarian, writer*

**Lowell**
Karr, Ronald Dale *librarian, historian*

**Marstons Mills**
Martin, Susan Katherine *librarian*

**Medford**
Belovari, Susanne *archivist, historian*
Kerr, Barbara E. *librarian, writer*
Michalak, Jo-Ann *library director*

**Mill River**
Jaffe, Katharine Weisman *retired librarian*

**Natick**
Rendell, Kenneth William *rare and historical documents dealer, consultant*

**Newton**
Glick-Weil, Kathy *library director*

**North Easton**
Bundy, Annalee Marshall *library director*

**Northampton**
Piccinino, Rocco Michael *librarian*

**Oak Bluffs**
Ball, Diane Altman *librarian*

**South Hadley**
Scanlon, Gail Gretchen *librarian, nurse*

**Springfield**
Stack, May Elizabeth *retired library director*
Utley, F. Knowlton *library director, educator*

**Weymouth**
Lamothe, Joanne Lewis *library director, consultant*

**Woburn**
Doyle, Thomas R. *archivist, consultant*
Preve, Roberta Jean *librarian, researcher*

**Woods Hole**
Gifford, Prosser *retired library administrator*

**Worcester**
Barr, Dorothy *librarian*
Dunlap, Ellen S. *library administrator*
Kuklinski, Joan Lindsey *librarian*
McCorison, Marcus Allen *librarian, cultural organization administrator*

**MICHIGAN**

**Adrian**
Fosbender, Jule Joann *retired librarian*
Geyer, Richard Douglas *librarian, poet*

**Allendale**
Murray, Diane Elizabeth *librarian*

**Ann Arbor**
Beaubien, Anne Kathleen *librarian*
Daub, Peggy Ellen *library administrator*
Didier, Elaine K. *library director, educator*
Dougherty, Richard Martin *library and information science professor*
Dunlap, Connie *librarian*
Gordon, Anitra *librarian*
Johnson, Brenda L. *university librarian*
Wilkins, John P. *university librarian*

**Battle Creek**
Lincoln, Margaret *library media specialist*

**Bloomfield Hills**
Papai, Beverly Daffern *retired library director*

**Cedar Lake**
Berlin, Gregory Alan *library director*

**Detroit**
Field, Judith Judy *librarian*
Godzak, Roman Paul *archivist*
Mika, Joseph John *library director, educator*
Powell, Ronald Rowe *library science educator*
Skowronski, Nancy *library director*
Spyers-Duran, Peter *librarian, educator*
Yee, Sandra Gayle Brown *librarian*

**East Lansing**
Chapin, Richard Earl *retired librarian*
Haka, Clifford Hughey *library director*

**Garden City**
Elmouchi, Joan Leslie *library director*

**Grosse Pointe**
Casey, Genevieve M(ary) *librarian, educator*

**Harsens Island**
Woodford, Arthur MacKinnon *retired library director, historian*

**Holt**
Smith, Betty W. *librarian*

**Kalamazoo**
Grotzinger, Laurel Ann *librarian, educator*

**Lansing**
Johnson, Veronica Ann Wilkerson *library director*

**Marquette**
Clumpner, Krista Ellis *library science educator*

**Midland**
Potts, Sandra *library director*

**Mount Pleasant**
Messick, Frederic Morton *librarian*

**Owosso**
Uptigrove, Kenneth R. *library administrator*

**Plymouth**
Berry, Charlene Helen *librarian, musician*
deBear, Richard Stephen *library director, consultant*

**Port Huron**
Wu, Harry Pao-Tung *retired librarian*

**Redford**
Karpinski, Huberta *library trustee*

**Saint Clair Shores**
Kaminski, Margaret *retired librarian*

**Southfield**
Naber, Faith *retired librarian, educator*

**Sterling Heights**
Stephens, Karen Lorene *librarian*

**MINNESOTA**

**Blue Earth**
Siem, Pauline M. *library director*

**Chisago City**
Miller, Robert Carl *retired library director*

**Duluth**
Pearce, Donald Joslin *retired librarian*

**Minneapolis**
Johnson, Donald Clay *librarian, curator*
Johnson, Margaret Ann (Peggy) *library administrator*
Kukla, Edward Richard *rare books & special collections librarian*
Lougee, Wendy Pradt *library director, educator*
Ostrem, Walter Martin *librarian, educator, consultant*
Selander, Lucy Mae *librarian*
Shaughnessy, Thomas William *retired librarian*

**Rochester**
Key, Jack Dayton *librarian*
Lange, Elizabeth Ann *retired librarian*
Nienow, Beth Marie *librarian*

**Roseville**
Miller, Suzanne Marie *library director, educator*

**Saint Cloud**
Inkster, Christine Davis *librarian, educator*

**Saint Paul**
Granger, Steven Tandvig *archivist, consultant*
Wagner, Mary Margaret *library and information scientist, educator*

**Saint Peter**
Haeuser, Michael John *library administrator*

**Zumbrota**
Post, Diana Constance *retired librarian*

**MISSISSIPPI**

**Alcorn State**
Yu, May Huang *librarian, educator*

**Columbus**
Tousley, Rebecca Perkins *retired librarian*
Wheeley, Nancy Janine *librarian*

**Jackson**
Smith, Sharman Bridges *state librarian*

**Mississippi State**
Delgado, Marica LaDonne *librarian, educator*

**Natchez**
McLemore, Joan Meadows *librarian, consultant*

**MISSOURI**

**Chesterfield**
Landram, Christina Louella *librarian*

**Columbia**
Almony, Robert Allen, Jr. *librarian*
Cogswell, Jim *library director*
Pinkerton, Marjorie Jean *librarian, educator*

**Greenwood**
Zeller, Marilynn Kay *retired librarian*

**Hermann**
Wilson, C. Daniel, Jr. *library director*

**Independence**
Devine, Michael J. *library director, educator*
Wilding, Richard *library director*

**Jefferson City**
Parker, Sara Ann *librarian, consultant*

**Kansas City**
Nelson, Freda Nell Hein *librarian*
Thomas, Marcia Markowitz *library director, educator*
Weidman, Jeffrey *librarian*

**Lake Lotawana**
Zobrist, Benedict Karl *library director, historian*

**Parkville**
Schultis, Gail Ann *library director*

**Saint Charles**
Bock, Angela Marie *retired librarian*

**Saint Louis**
Guenther, Charles John *librarian, writer*
Lauenstein, Ann Gail *librarian*
McGuire, Walter F. *library director*
Moloney, Christopher Xavier *multi-media specialist, marketing executive*

**Springfield**
Busch, Annie *library director*
Horny, Karen Louise *library administrator*

**Warrensburg**
Jurkowski, Odin Lech *librarian, educator*

**West Plains**
Vetter, Evelyn M. *librarian*

**MONTANA**

**Billings**
Cochran, William Michael *librarian*

**Forsyth**
Heser, Cheryl J. *library director*

**Helena**
Fitzpatrick, Lois Ann *library administrator*

**NEBRASKA**

**Beatrice**
Riedesel, Laureen Falk *library director*

**Kearney**
Hardesty, Larry Lynn *librarian*

**Lincoln**
Bicknell- Holmes, Tracy *librarian*
Giesecke, Joan Ruth *librarian, dean*
Montag, John Joseph, II *librarian*
Wagner, Rod *library director*

**York**
Gunselman, Kenneth David *library director*

**NEVADA**

**Carson City**
Jones, Sara Sue Fisher *librarian*
Rocha, Guy Louis *archivist, consultant, historian*

**Hawthorne**
Pierce, Mildred Louise *librarian*

**Henderson**
Taglienti, Paolina *librarian*

**Las Vegas**
Honsa, Vlasta *retired librarian*
McNeal, Betty Jean *librarian, writer*
Ramsey, Inez Linn *librarian, educator*
Reed, Ellen Beth *librarian*

**Reno**
Ross, Robert Donald *library director*

**NEW HAMPSHIRE**

**Berlin**
Doherty, Katherine Mann *librarian, writer*

**Durham**
Young, Arthur Price *librarian, educator*

**Exeter**
Thomas, Jacquelyn May *librarian*

**Goffstown**
Wajenberg, Arnold Sherman *retired librarian, educator*

**Hanover**
Horrell, Jeffrey Lanier *library administrator*

**Milton**
Edelman, Hendrik *library and information science professor*

**Newmarket**
Getchell, Sylvia Fitts *librarian*

**Plymouth**
Berona, David A. *library director, educator*

**NEW JERSEY**

**Camden**
Beck, Susan J. *academic librarian*

**Cliffside Park**
Chelariu, Ana Radu *library director*

**Edgewater**
Berliner, Barbara *retired librarian, consultant*

**Edison**
Riley, Barbara Polk *retired librarian*
Vellucci, Margaret Mary *librarian*

**Flanders**
Hilbert, Rita L. *librarian*

**Fort Lee**
Altomara, Rita Ecke *library director, writer*

**Glassboro**
Wright, William Cook *archivist, director*

**Glen Rock**
Savoie, Brietta Dolores *retired librarian*

**Haledon**
Dougherty, June Eileen *librarian*

**Hasbrouck Heights**
Reutty, Michele Marie *library director*

**Hoboken**
Widdicombe, Richard Palmer *librarian*

**Hopewell**
Baeckler, Virginia Van Wynen *librarian*
Woodward, Daniel Holt *librarian, researcher*

**Jersey City**
Bulaong, Grace F. *library director*
Jeng, Judy Horng *librarian*

**Lambertville**
Cusworth, Christyl J. *conservator, artist*

**Laurel Springs**
Cleveland, Susan Elizabeth *library administrator, researcher*

**Linden**
Purves, Dennis Patrick *library director*

**Livingston**
Sikora, Barbara Jean *library director*

**Lodi**
Karetzky, Joanne Louise *librarian*
Karetzky, Stephen *library director, educator, researcher*

**Long Branch**
Pachman, Frederic Charles *library director*

**Madison**
Beland, Matthew Robert *library assistant*
Rubinstein, Ernest *librarian, educator*

**Monmouth Junction**
Lawton, Deborah Simmons *librarian*

**Montclair**
McConnell, Lorelei Catherine *retired library director*

**New Brunswick**
Gaunt, Marianne I. *university librarian*
Puniello, Françoise Sara *librarian*
Sewell, Robert George *librarian*
Turock, Betty Jane *library and information science professor*

**Piscataway**
Etter, Zana Claire *library director*
Ranzan, David Aldrich *archivist*

**Point Pleasant**
Greene, Ellin *library service educator*

**Princeton**
Fox, Mary Ann Williams *librarian*
Trainer, Karin A. *librarian*

**Princeton Junction**
Butorac, Frank George *librarian, educator*

**Rockaway**
Kelsey, Ann Lee *library administrator*

**South Orange**
Bao, Xue-Ming *librarian, educator*

**Succasunna**
Romance, Mary C. *library director*

**Teaneck**
Weiss, Mitchell Joseph *librarian*

**Toms River**
Matteo, Christine E. *librarian*

**Trenton**
Russell, Joyce Anne Rogers *retired librarian*

**Union**
Darden, Barbara S. *library director*

**Vineland**
Schmid, Patti A. *library director*

**Voorhees**
Brahms, William Bernard *librarian, writer*

**Wayne**
Pardo, Janette M. *archivist, librarian*

**West Milford**
Hannon, Patricia Ann *library director*

**Whiting**
Randall, Lynn Ellen *librarian*

**Woodbridge**
Hurley, John *library director*

**NEW MEXICO**

**Albuquerque**
Fletcher, Marilyn Pendleton *retired librarian*
Freeman, Patricia Elizabeth *multi-media specialist, educational consultant*
Lewis, Linda Kathryn *librarian*
Neilly, Bruce David *librarian*
Snell, Patricia Poldervaart *librarian, consultant*
Wilkinson, Frances Catherine *librarian, educator*

**Carlsbad**
Regan Gossage, Muriel *librarian*

**Deming**
Becker-Klicker, Margaret Chan *library director*

**Gallup**
Sarath, Carol Ann *library and media coordinator*

**Los Alamos**
Ramsey, Margie *librarian*

**Santa Fe**
Myers, R. David *library director, dean*

**NEW YORK**

**Albany**
Aceto, Vincent John *librarian, educator*
Beverley, Barbara Sally *librarian, educator*
Cellery McCall, Patti *librarian*
Knee, Michael J. *science librarian, consultant*
Merbler, Candace Anne *librarian*
Paulson, Peter John *librarian, publishing executive*
Shubert, Joseph Francis *librarian*
Wilber, Roger Alan *library supervisor, writer*

**Alfred**
Johnson, Carla Conrad *library dean*

**Amherst**
Bobinski, Mary Form *library director*

**Astoria**
Dutikow, Irene Vladimirovna *librarian*

**Bayside**
Ausubel, Hillel *librarian*

**Beechhurst**
Wingate, Constance Blandy *retired librarian*

**Bellmore**
Andrews, Charles Rolland *library administrator*

**Brightwaters**
Kavanagh, Eileen J. *librarian*

**Brooklyn**
Hill, Victoria Ruth *librarian*
Mack-Harvin, Dionne *library director*
Schneider, Adele Goldberg *librarian, educator*
Sharify, Nasser *librarian, educator, writer*
Thomas, Lucille Cole *librarian*

**Buffalo**
Bobinski, George Sylvan *librarian, educator*
Camhi, Rebecca Ann *librarian, writer*
Finnegan, Marchand Marie (Shonnie Finnegan) *archivist, consultant*
Mahaney, Michael C. *library director*
Roberts, Stephen M. *library director*
Stoss, Frederick Warren *librarian, educator*

**Canaan**
Lewis, Marjorie *librarian*

**Corona**
Jackson, Andrew Preston *library director*

**Dansville**
Dearing, Teresa Allison *librarian*

**Dryden**
Slocum, Robert Bigney *retired librarian*

**Edmeston**
Blackman, Dorothy J. *library director*

**Endicott**
Dunscombe, Edward Andrew *library director*

**Goshen**
Watson, Georgianna *retired librarian*

**Greenport**
Velleman, Ruth Ann *retired librarian, educator*

**Hempstead**
Glassman, Paul *library administrator, architecture educator*

**Hyde Park**
Koch, Cynthia M. *library director*

**Ithaca**
Perry, Margaret *librarian, writer*
Thomas, Sarah E. *librarian*

**Jamaica**
Benson, James Allen *library science educator, academic administrator*
Galante, Thomas W. *library director*

**Kinderhook**
McCreight, JoAnn Oakley *retired librarian*

**Liverpool**
Wightman, Sharon Leilani *librarian*

**Marlboro**
Parker, Marion Hawkins *retired librarian*

**Mineola**
Hammer, Deborah Marie *librarian, paralegal*

**Nassau**
Benamati, Dennis Charles *librarian, editor, consultant*

**New Hartford**
Anthony, Donald Charles *librarian, educator*

**New Paltz**
Nyquist, Corinne Elaine *librarian*

**New York**
Alpi, Kristine Markovich *librarian, educator*
Belliveau, Gerard Joseph, Jr. *librarian*
Berger, Pearl *library director*
Berner, Andrew Jay *library director, writer*
Boziwick, George E. *music librarian, composer, curator*
Brewer, Karen *librarian*
Browar, Lisa Muriel *librarian*
Cohen, Selma *librarian, researcher*
Fedunok, Suzanne *retired librarian*
Finder, Lisa *librarian, researcher*
Fletcher, Harry George III *library director*
Hewitt, Vivian Ann Davidson (Mrs. John Hamilton Hewitt Jr.) *retired librarian*
Kagan, Ilse Echt *librarian, researcher, historian*
Kent, Susan *library director, consultant*
Khalil, Mounir A. *librarian, educator*
LeClerc, Paul *library director*
Little, Robert David *library science professor*
LoSchiavo, Linda Bosco *library director*
Lubetski, Edith Esther *librarian*
Lundquist, John Milton *librarian, Egyptologist, author, travel writer, photographer*
Mackey, Patricia Elaine *university librarian*
Mandel, Carol *librarian*
Margalith, Helen Margaret *retired librarian*
Mattson, Francis Oscar *retired librarian, rare book dealer, curator*
McGlamery, Barbara Ellen *librarian*
McKeever, Kent *library director, law librarian*
Meyerhoff, Erich *librarian, director*
Miller, Barbara Kenton *retired librarian*
Miller, Philip Efrem *librarian*
Neal, James G. *librarian*
Palmer, Robert Baylis *librarian*

Pierce, Charles Eliot, Jr. *library director, educator*
Rachow, Louis A(ugust) *librarian*
Record, William John *librarian*
Roff, Sandra *library and information scientist, educator, archivist*
Root, Nina J. *librarian, writer*
Roumani-Denn, Vivienne Rachel *library and information scientist, consultant*
Slawsky, Donna Susan *librarian, singer*
Stern, Madeleine Bettina *rare book dealer, writer*
Swan, Philip George *librarian, educator, director, artist*
Sweetman, Kimberly Burke *librarian, consultant*
Thomas, Dorothy *indexing consultant, writer*
Vilchez, Ricardo S. *library director*
Whittingham, Charles Arthur *library director, publishing executive*
Younger, Kirsten Jeanne *painting restoration specialist*

**Oneonta**
Johnson, Richard David *retired librarian*

**Piermont**
Brechtel, Unda Jurka *library director*

**Poughkeepsie**
Van Zanten, Frank Veldhuyzen *library director*

**Rexford**
Nitecki, Joseph Zbigniew *librarian*

**Rochester**
Buff, Iva Moore *librarian, musicologist*
Cohen, Ann Ellen *librarian*
Cunningham, Robert Del *librarian*
Dow, Ronald F. *librarian*
Swanton, Susan Irene *retired library director*

**Roslyn**
Siahpoosh, Farideh Tamaddon *librarian*

**Rye**
Harrington, Diane *librarian, writer*

**Saratoga Springs**
Anderson, Pauline Harriet *library consultant*

**Schenectady**
Huth, Geoffrey Anthony *archivist, artist*

**Staten Island**
Auh, Yang John *librarian, educational administrator*
Black, Lawrence *librarian*

**Stony Brook**
Cook, Jeannine Salvo *librarian, consultant*

**Syracuse**
Nicholson, Scott Richard *library scientist, researcher, educator*
Stam, David Harry *librarian*
Verheyen, Peter David *librarian, conservator*

**Tonawanda**
Loos, William H(enry) *librarian, consultant*

**White Plains**
Manville, Stewart Roebling *archivist*
Scott-Williams, Wendy Lee *library and information scientist*

**Williamsville**
Cloudsley, Donald Hugh *retired library administrator*

**Woodside**
Sfiroudis, Gloria Tides *library and information scientist, educator*

**NORTH CAROLINA**

**Chapel Hill**
Jones, Houston Gwynne *archivist, history professor*
Moran, Barbara Burns *librarian, educator*
Pruett, James Worrell *librarian, educator, musicologist*
Strauss, Diane Carol Wheeler *librarian, educator, writer*

**Charlotte**
Sintz, Edward Francis *librarian*

**Columbus**
Wetherby, Ivor Lois *librarian*

**Cove City**
Hawkins, Elinor Dixon (Mrs. Carroll Woodard Hawkins) *retired librarian*

**Davidson**
Park, Leland Madison *librarian*

**Durham**
Canada, Mary Whitfield *retired librarian*
Carrington, Bessie Meek *librarian*
Hensen, Steven Lee *archivist, librarian*

**Gastonia**
Burns, Judith O'Dell *library assistant, educator*

**Morganton**
Dorman, Lewis Robert, IV, *librarian, archivist*

**Murfreesboro**
Muller, William Albert III *retired library director*

**New Bern**
Jones, Victor Thomas, Jr. *librarian*
White, Rhea Amelia *library and information scientist*

**Raleigh**
Littleton, Isaac Thomas III *retired library director*
Nutter, Susan K. *librarian, academic administrator*

**Winston Salem**
Sutton, Lynn Sorensen *librarian*

**Winton**
Williams, Sue Darden *library director*

**NORTH DAKOTA**

**Bismarck**
Ott, Doris Ann *librarian*

**Mayville**
Karaim, Betty June *retired librarian*

**Wahpeton**
Dohman, Gloria Ann *librarian*

**OHIO**

**Akron**
Plummer, Karen Anne *librarian, educator*
Rebenack, John Henry *retired librarian*

**Alliance**
Clem, Harriet Frances *library director*

**Bellaire**
Kniesner, John Thomas *librarian*

**Bluffton**
Dudley, Durand Stowell *retired librarian*

**Bowling Green**
Singer, Carol Ann *librarian, researcher*

**Cadiz**
Thompson, Sandra Lee *library administrator*

**Cincinnati**
Abate, Anne Katherine *librarian, consultant, educator*
Bellingham, Roger Gerry *librarian, researcher, consultant*
Bestehorn, Ute Wiltrud *retired librarian*
Everson, Jean Watkins Dolores *librarian, media consultant, educator*
Fender, Kimber L. *library director*
Heran, Maggie *librarian*
Montavon, Victoria A. *university librarian, dean*
Proffitt, Kevin *archivist*
Reynolds, Marianne Geralyn *librarian*

**Cleveland**
Brhel, Richard Dennis *library director*
Downey, Kay *librarian*
Gardner, Richard Kent *retired librarian, educator, editor*
Thornton, Glenda Ann *librarian*
Venable, Andrew A., Jr. *library director*

**Columbus**
Branin, Joseph J. *library director*
Brown, Rowland Chauncey Widrig *library and information scientist, consultant*
Donovan, Maureen Hildegarde *librarian, educator*
El-Sherbini, Magda A. *librarian, educator*
Gilmore, Joanne R. *librarian*
Hengst, Linda Ruth *library director*
Losinski, Patrick A. *library director*
Olson, Carol Ann *retired librarian*
Olson, Ray Alan *librarian*
Sawyers, Elizabeth Joan *librarian, director*
Studer, William Joseph *library director*
Swarlis, Linda *library and information scientist*

**Dayton**
Klinck, Cynthia Anne *library director*
Wyllie, Stanley Clarke *retired librarian*

**Delaware**
Schlichting, Catherine Fletcher Nicholson *librarian, educator*

**Dublin**
Meyer, Betty Jane *former librarian*

**East Cleveland**
Linderman, Eric Graham *librarian*

**East Palestine**
Rohrbaugh, Lisa Anne *librarian*

**Elida**
Dicke, Candice Edwards *librarian, educator*

**Findlay**
Legg, Harolyn Lee *librarian*

**Hubbard**
Trucksis, Theresa A. *retired library director*

**Independence**
Dial, David Emory *librarian*

**Kent**
Maurer, Margaret Beecher *librarian, educator*
Weber, Mark W. *librarian, dean*

**Middleburg Heights**
Maciuszko, Kathleen Lynn *librarian, educator*

**Middletown**
Schaefer, Patricia Ann *retired librarian*

**Mount Healthy**
Scheffel, Kenneth Paul *retired archivist*

**North Ridgeville**
Cobbledick, Susie Diane *librarian*

**Northfield**
Stavole, Janet M. *librarian, library director*

**Oberlin**
English, Ray *library administrator*
Greenberg, Eva Mueller *retired librarian*

Moore, Jane Ross *librarian, educator*

## Oregon
Poad, Flora Virginia *retired librarian, retired elementary school educator*

## Parma
Feldman, Sari *library director*

## Pemberville
King, Laura Jane *librarian, genealogist*

## South Euclid
Zoller, Karen Ann *library director, art gallery director*

## Tiffin
Hillmer, Margaret Patricia *library director*

## Toledo
Scoles, Clyde Sheldon *library director*

## Wickliffe
Fisher, Nancy DeButts *library director*

## Wooster
Hickey, Damon Douglas *library director*

## Xenia
Vaughan, Doris Celestine Walker *retired librarian, educator*

# OKLAHOMA

## Ada
Greenstreet, Jennifer Kennis *librarian*

## Hodgen
Brower, Janice Kathleen *library and information scientist*

## Lawton
Bonnell-Mihalis, Pamela Gay Scoggins *library director*
Kroll, Connie Rae *librarian, information services consultant*

## Norman
Herstand, Jo Ellen *librarian*
Lee, Sul Hi *library administrator, dean*
Lester, June *library and information scientist, educator*
Sherman, Mary Angus *public library administrator*
Wallace, Danny P. *library and information scientist, educator*
Yi, Myongho *library and information scientist*

## Tulsa
Clement, Evelyn Geer *librarian, educator*

# OREGON

## Albany
White, Diane O'Donnell *retired librarian*

## Ashland
Billeter, Anne Margaret *librarian*
Gaulke, Mary Florence *retired library administrator*

## Astoria
Foster, Michael William *librarian*

## Beaverton
Pond, Patricia Brown *library and information scientist, educator*

## Eugene
Briston, Heather Irene *archivist*
Edwards, Ralph M. *librarian*
South, Ruth Eades *reference librarian*

## Portland
Browne, Joseph Peter *retired librarian*
Morgan, James Earl *librarian, administrator*

## Wilsonville
Humphrey, Lois Ellen *librarian*

# PENNSYLVANIA

## Allentown
Flautz, Nancy A. *librarian*
Sacks, Patricia Ann *librarian, consultant*

## Altoona
Kinney, Janis Marie *librarian, consultant*

## Annville
Paustian, Paul Robert *library director*

## Audubon
Tanis, James Robert *library director, history professor, clergyman*

## Beaver Falls
Miller, Albert Jay *retired library director*

## Bethlehem
Humphry, James III *retired librarian, publishing executive, educator*
Taggart, Bruce M. *library administrator*

## Bryn Mawr
Fletcher, Marjorie Amos *librarian*

## Coatesville
Sauer, James Leslie *librarian, educator*

## Coplay
Norbeck, Jack Carl *library exhibitor*

## Corsica
Elza, Betty Ann *retired librarian*

## Cranberry Township
Lorenz, John George *librarian, consultant*

## Du Bois
Emmer, Barbara Louise *retired librarian*

## Edinboro
Obringer, David C. *archivist, educator*

## Greensburg
Duck, Patricia Mary *librarian*

## Huntingdon
Stiffler, Stuart Alden *retired library director*

## Johnstown
Brice, Heather Weidenhofer *consulting librarian*

## Kingsley
McNabb, Corrine Radtke *librarian*

## Lancaster
Zeager, Lloyd *librarian*

## Lansdale
Nolan, Joan Parmeter *librarian*

## Mansfield
Donahue, Martha *retired librarian*

## Mc Murray
Celento, Florence M. *librarian*

## New Holland
Fanus, Pauline Rife *librarian*

## New Wilmington
Bolger, Dorita Yvonne Ferguson *librarian*

## Oxford
Hostert, Leona Teressa *librarian, researcher*

## Philadelphia
Alford, Larry P. *university librarian*
Arnold, Lee *library director, archivist*
Azzolina, David Sean *librarian*
Diaz, Magna M. *librarian*
Lane, Laura Alice *librarian*
Mancall, Jacqueline Cooper *library and information scientist, educator*
Mizumura, Megumi *conservator*
Schaeffer-Young, Judith *library director*
Shelkrot, Elliot L. *library director*
Wright, Barbara Clare *business librarian*

## Pittsburgh
Balazs, Kevin *conservator*
Dabrishus, Michael John *librarian*
Jenkins, Georgann Klaus *librarian*
Josey, E(lonnie) J(Unius) *librarian, retired state agency administrator*
Miller, Rush Glenn, Jr. *dean*
Minnigh, Joel Douglas *library director*
St. Clair, Gloriana Strange *librarian, dean*
Willard, Louis Charles *librarian*
Wohleber, Lynne Farr *archivist, librarian*

## Punxsutawney
Dinsmore, Roberta Joan Maier *library director*

## Reading
Mack, Sara Rohrbach *librarian, educator*
Wentzel, Judith Ann *retired librarian*

## Riegelsville
Banko, Ruth Caroline *retired library director*

## Scranton
Brandreth, Elizabeth Anne *library director*

## Somerset
Kline, Eva Jane *library services administrator, educator*

## Strasburg
Bell, Kurt Robert *archivist*

## University Park
Brockman, William S. *librarian*
Eaton, Nancy Ruth Linton *librarian, dean*
Hamburger, Susan *librarian*
Joyce, William Leonard *librarian*
Snavely, Loanne *library director*
Stout, Leon James *archivist, librarian*

## Villanova
Foight, Michael Patrick *librarian, archivist*

## Wayne
Garrison, Guy Grady *librarian, educator*

## Wilkes Barre
Mech, Terrence Francis *library director*

## Wyomissing
Doherty, Edmond John *retired librarian*

## Yardley
Soultoukis, Donna Zoccola *library director*

## York
Lloyd, June Burk *retired librarian, archivist*

# RHODE ISLAND

## Bristol
McMullen, Susan Taylor *librarian*

## Coventry
Schweinsburg, Jane Duberg *librarian*

## Kingston
Caldwell, Naomi Rachel *library and information scientist, educator, writer*
Keefe, Margaret Johnson *librarian*

## Providence
Hamerly, Michael T. *librarian, historian*
Hemmasi, Harriette Ann *university librarian*
Kramer, Ilse Elisabeth *rare book bibliographer, consultant*

## Wakefield
Alexander, Jacqueline Peterson *retired librarian*

## Warwick
Charette, Sharon Juliette *library administrator*

# SOUTH CAROLINA

## Aiken
Isaacs-Bright, Susan Virginia Kirkpatrick *librarian, consultant, advocate*

## Bluffton
Cann, Sharon Lee *retired health science librarian*

## Charleston
Basler, Thomas G. *librarian, educator*
Greene, Harlan *archivist, writer*

## Clinton
Meeks, Mary Janice *librarian*

## Columbia
Helsley, Alexia Jones *archivist*
Rawlinson, Helen Ann *librarian*
Toombs, Kenneth Eldridge *librarian*
Warren, Charles David *library administrator*
Willis, Paul Allen *librarian, dean*
Zimmerman, Nancy Picciano *library and information scientist, educator*

## Georgetown
Bazemore, Trudy McConnell *librarian*

## Greenville
Belk, F. Norman *librarian*

## North Augusta
Rowland, Arthur Ray *librarian*

## North Charleston
Mardikian, Paul *conservator*

## Orangeburg
Byers, Keith Thomas *librarian, educator*

# SOUTH DAKOTA

## Madison
Smith, Rise Louise *librarian*

## Sioux Falls
Thompson, Ronelle Kay Hildebrandt *library director*

# TENNESSEE

## Englewood
Brown, Helen Dodson *retired librarian*

## Germantown
Loper, Linda Sue *library director*

## Greeneville
Smith, Myron John, Jr. *librarian, author*

## Hermitage
Lyle, Virginia Reavis *retired archivist, genealogist*

## Jackson
Hoyle, Shetina Yevette *librarian*

## Johnson City
Norris, Carol Brooks *retired librarian*

## Kingsport
McDavid, Jo Collins *library manager*
Smith, JoAnn Carroll *library and information scientist*

## Knoxville
Behrend, Linda *librarian, writer*
Cottrell, Jeannette Elizabeth *retired librarian*
Dewey, Barbara I. *librarian, dean*
Felder-Hoehne, Felicia Harris *librarian, researcher*
Lowe, Alan Conner *library director*
Purcell, Aaron D. *archivist, historian*

## Lawrenceburg
Pope, Dorothy Mae *librarian*

## Lebanon
Burns, George Franklin *archivist, retired English language educator*

## Maryville
Tabor, Curtis Harold, Jr. *retired librarian, minister*

## Memphis
Drescher, Judith Altman *library director*
Park, Elizabeth Haskell *librarian, educator*
Pourciau, Lester John, Jr. *retired librarian*
Wallis, Carlton Lamar *librarian*

## Nashville
Radcliff, Joyce B. *librarian*
Stewart, David Marshall *librarian*

## Oak Ridge
Ball, Jacqueline Snyder *librarian, educator*
McNeilly, Kathy Eden *librarian, library director*

## Sewanee
Camp, Thomas Edward *retired librarian*
Watson, Gail H. *retired librarian*

## Sparta
Young, Olivia Knowles *retired librarian*

# TEXAS

## Abilene
Tucker, John Mark *librarian, educator*

## Aledo
Rowe, Sheryl Ann *librarian*

## Austin
Billings, Harold Wayne *library director, editor*
Emery, Jill *librarian*
Flowers, Betty Sue *library director, educator*
Gracy, David Bergen, II *archivist, information science educator, writer*
Heath, Fred Milton *library director, educator*
Larson, Jeanette Carolyn *librarian*
Lincoln, Timothy Dwight *library director*
Morrow, Sandra Kay *librarian*
Oram, Robert W. *library administrator*
Payne, John Ross *archivist, educator, library and information scientist, educator*
Rascoe, Paul Stephen *librarian, researcher*

## Brownsville
Ferrier, Douglas M. *librarian*

## Brownwood
Weeks, Patsy Ann Landry *librarian, educator*

## Canyon Lake
Bowden, Virginia Massey *librarian*

## Cedar Hill
Hickman, Traphene Parramore *retired library director, consultant*

## Cedar Park
Lam, Pauline Poha *library director*

## Coldspring
Bunch, Robert Craig *librarian*

## College Station
Cook, C. Colleen *librarian, dean*
Finch, Warren L., Jr. *library director, archivist*
Piscitelli, Felicia Ann *librarian, musician, musicologist*
Schultz, Charles Roy *archivist*

## Corpus Christi
Whitton, Lynda Jean *librarian, foundation administrator*

## Dallas
Bockstruck, Lloyd DeWitt *librarian*
Evans, Laurie *library director*
Ibach, Robert Daniel, Jr. *library director*
Thompson, B. Lolana *archivist*

## Denton
Nichols, Margaret Irby *librarian, educator, library and information scientist*
Poole, Eva Duraine *librarian*
Simpson, Carol Mann *librarian, educator, editor*
Snapp, Elizabeth *librarian, educator*
Swigger, Keith *library and information scientist, educator*

## El Paso
Gardner, Kerry Ann *librarian*

## Fort Worth
Ard, Harold Jacob *library administrator*
de Tonnancour, Paul Roger Godefroy *library administrator*
Li, Richard T. *retired library director, secondary school educator*

## Galena Park
Fierro, Robert, Jr. *librarian*

## Houston
Henington, David Mead *retired library director*
Henry, Charles Jay *library director*
James, Dean *librarian, writer*
Lawson, Rhea Brown *library director*
Miller, Sabrina Wares *librarian*
Radoff, Leonard Irving *librarian, consultant*
Russell, John Francis *retired librarian*
Witmer, John Richard *librarian*

## Huntsville
Hoffman, Frank William *library science educator, writer*

## Irving
Whisennand, Cynthia Simmons *librarian*

## Laredo
Weber, Janice Ann *library director, grant writer*

## Littlefield
Massengill, Ellen Webb *librarian*

## Lubbock
Wood, Richard Courtney *library director, educator*

## Marshall
Magrill, Rose Mary *library director*

## Mcallen
Kadhim, Estelle Beverly *librarian, educator*
McGee, William Howard John *library director*

## Midland
Dawkins, Diantha Dee *librarian*

## Montgomery
Smith, John Brewster *library administrator*

## Palestine
Williams, Franklin Cadmus, Jr. *bibliographer*

## Pharr
Liu, David T. *retired librarian*

## Richardson
Sall, Larry David *library director*

## ISRAEL

**Jerusalem**
Rozett, Robert Bernard *library director, historian*

## JAPAN

**Osaka**
Horii, Reiichi *library director, educator*

**Tokyo**
Tanabe, Noriaki *library director*

## KAZAKHSTAN

**Almaty**
Sadykova, Vera Philippovna *librarian, educator*

## LATVIA

**Riga**
Buholte, Agnese *library director*

## MALDIVES

**Male**
Habeeb, Habeeba Hussain *librarian*

## NORWAY

**Oslo**
Jakobsson, Arne P. *library director*

## SCOTLAND

**Edinburgh**
Matheson, Ann *librarian, writer*

## SWEDEN

**Stockholm**
Lidman, Tomas Erik *national archivist*

## SWITZERLAND

**Geneva**
Jacquesson, Alain L. *librarian*

## ADDRESS UNPUBLISHED

Abbott, George Lindell *retired librarian*
Abid, Ann B. *art librarian*
Adams, Mignon Strickland *library director*
Adkins, Thomas Samuel *library director*
Alexander, Rebecca *library director, artist*
Anderson, David Charles *librarian, writer*
Anderson, Herschel Vincent *retired librarian*
Anderson, Rachael Keller (Rachael Keller) *retired library director*
Ariens, Karla Rae *library director*
Baker, Carolyn Simmons *library director, consultant, researcher*
Baker, Zachary Moshe *librarian*
Bartelli, Alice Hill *librarian, secondary education educator*
Battin, Patricia Meyer *librarian*
Baumgart, Jessica K. *librarian*
Beatty, Judy Iola Spencer *library director*
Berkley, Erma Van Meter *retired librarian*
Berman, Miriam Naomi *librarian*
Biggs-Williams, Evelyn Ann *librarian*
Bino, Marial Desolyn *librarian, educator*
Blackburn, Joy Martin *retired librarian*
Bogie, Lana Cecil *librarian*
Bowen, Jean *retired librarian, consultant*
Brady, Jean Stein *retired librarian*
Bromwell, Jean Allen *librarian, writer*
Brooks Shoemaker, Virginia Lee *librarian*
Brown, Carol Ann *librarian, director*
Brown, Elizabeth Eleanor *retired librarian*
Bruch, Virginia Irene Sullivan *librarian, writer*
Bulow, Jack Faye *retired library director*
Burson, Betsy Lee *librarian*
Byrd, Joan Eda *librarian*
Campbell, Henry Cummings *librarian*
Cannon, Patricia Althen *librarian, writer*
Carpenter, Janella Ann *retired librarian*
Carter, Yvonne Breaux *retired librarian*
Cassell, Kay Ann *librarian*
Chabot, Joyce Jenkins *librarian*
Chirico-Elkins, Ursula *retired librarian*
Chow, Judy *library and information scientist, educator*
Chu, Ellin Resnick *librarian, consultant*
Clement, Hope Elizabeth Anna *retired librarian*
Clement, Yvonne Madeline *librarian*
Cochran, Carolyn *library director*
Cochran, Radeen M. *librarian*
Conaway, Margaret Grimes (Peggy Conaway) *library administrator*
Cooper, Jacquelyn Barber *librarian*
Costa, Kathy *retired librarian*
Crahan, Elizabeth Schmidt *librarian*
Crawford, Sheila Jane *librarian, reading specialist*
Curley, Elmer Frank *librarian*
Daffron, MaryEllen *retired librarian*
Dickinson, Donald Charles *library science professor*
Dickinson, Gail Krepps *library science educator*
Dintrone, Charles Vincent *retired librarian*
Domzella, Janet *retired library director*
Drake, Miriam Anna *retired librarian, educator, writer, consultant*

Duffy, Michael James, IV, *librarian*
Dunham, Elizabeth Grace *librarian*
Dykstra Lynch, Mary Elizabeth *library and information scientist, educator*
Dyson, Allan Judge *retired librarian*
Eaton, Katherine Girton *retired library educator*
Edmonds, Anne Carey *librarian*
Ellington, Mildred L. *librarian*
Elliott, Clark Albert *archivist, librarian, historian*
Else, Carolyn Joan *retired library director*
Elwood-Akers, Virginia Edythe *librarian, retired archivist*
Erickson, Alan Eric *librarian*
Erwin, Linda McIntosh *retired librarian*
Estes, Elaine Rose Graham *retired librarian*
Euster, Joanne Reed *retired librarian*
Fackler, Naomi Paula *retired librarian*
Fasick, Adele Mongan *library and information scientist, educator*
Fawcett, John Thomas *archivist*
Felsted, Carla Martindell *librarian, writer, editor*
Ferguson, Paul-Thomas *archivist, writer*
Focer-Richards, Linda Jean *library director*
Ford, Barbara Jean *librarian, educator*
Forester, Jean Martha Brouillette *retired librarian, educator, innkeeper*
Fox, Carol Jean *librarian*
Frank, Lawrence James *library director*
Frankel, Mary Ann (Kate Frankel) *librarian, educator*
Frantz, Ray William, Jr. *retired librarian*
Frederking, Kathy Hahn *elementary school librarian*
Funk, Vicki Jane *librarian*
Gabel, Emma Margaret *retired librarian*
Gainey, Lilah Leigh *librarian*
Gallant, Stephen Laurie *librarian*
Garypie, Rudolph Renwick *library director*
Gatch, Milton McCormick, Jr. *library director, clergyman, educator*
Giebel, Miriam Catherine *librarian, genealogist*
Gold, Leonard Singer *librarian, translator, curator*
Goodwyn, Betty Ruth *librarian*
Gould, Martha Bernice *retired librarian*
Gray, Gloria Meador *librarian*
Greenberg, Hinda Feige *library director*
Gregor, Dorothy Deborah *retired librarian*
Gudmundsson, Finnbogi *library administrator*
Gundersheimer, Werner Leonard *library director*
Hahn, Karla Lynn *librarian*
Haman, Sarah Armstrong *librarian*
Hangen, Terra *writer*
Hayton, Bernard Quentin, Jr. *library media specialist*
Hazekamp, Phyllis Wanda Alberts *retired library director*
Heanue, Anne Allen *retired librarian*
Henri, Janine Jacqueline *librarian*
Herold, Jeffrey Roy Martin *retired library director*
Hewitt, Ruth Price *librarian, educator*
Hoch, Ivo *former library director*
Hoke, Sheila Wilder *retired librarian*
Howard, Joseph Harvey *retired librarian*
Huff, Michael *librarian*
Hughes, Sue Margaret *retired librarian*
Hutchins, Mary Louise *retired library director*
Irwin, Mildred Lorine Warrick *library consultant, volunteer*
Jenkins, Darrell Lee *librarian*
Johnson, Clifton Herman *archivist, retired professional society administrator*
Johnson, Wayne Harold *librarian, retired municipal official*
Jones, Wanda Faye (Faye Williams Jones) *retired librarian, media specialist*
Kalana, David Sterling *director of information systems*
Kallenberg, John Kenneth *retired librarian*
Kaser, David *retired librarian, educator, consultant*
Kendall, Charles Terry *librarian*
Kesseler, Matthew John *librarian*
Ketchum, Irene Frances *library supporter*
Kirkland, Starr Melanie *librarian, writer*
Kiser, Nagiko Sato *retired librarian*
Klein, Susan Elaine *librarian*
Kleiner, Janellyn Pickering *librarian*
Knechtmann, James Allen *archivist, researcher*
Korenic, Lynette Marie *librarian*
Kreitzburg, Marilyn June *academic librarian*
Landry, Abbie Vestal *librarian*
LaPolt, Margaret *librarian*
Larson, Larry *retired librarian*
Lee, Harrison Hon *librarian, consultant*
Lee, Pali Jae (Polly Jae Stead Lee) *retired librarian, writer*
Lehner-Quam, Alison Lynn *library administrator*
Leonhardt, Thomas Wilburn *librarian, library director*
Lesiak, Karen Ann *librarian*
Levenback, Karen L. *librarian, archivist, educator, writer, editor*
Lindgren, William Dale *librarian*
Lovelace, Julianne *former library director*
Lowell, Virginia Lee *retired librarian*
Lucker, Jay K. *library consultant*
MacDonald, Alan Hugh *academic administrator*
Mackey, Margaret Emmie *library media specialist*
Mahood, Ramona Madson *library science educator, financial consultant*
Maltby, Florence Helen *library science educator*
Margoshes, Miriam Kagan *information specialist*
Marquis, Kathleen *librarian, archivist*
Massey, Stephen Charles *rare book dealer, consultant*
McBurney, Margot B. *retired librarian*
McCormick, Kathleen *archivist, educator*
McGlothlen, John M. *librarian*
McKinzie, James S. *librarian*
Meany, Philip Augustus *retired library director*
Metz, T(heodore) John *librarian, educator*
Meyer-Roux, Karen J. *archivist, art historian*
Miller, Alan Jay *rare book dealer, author*
Miller, Beverly A(nn) *reference librarian*
Miller, Jacqueline Winslow *library director*
Miller, Marilyn Lea *library and information scientist, educator*
Moody, Marilyn Dallas *retired librarian*
Moore, Julie L. *bibliographer, librarian*
Morgan, Jane Hale *retired library director*
Morton, Donald John *librarian*

Moulaison, Heather Lea *librarian, educator*
Moulder, Retha Ray *retired librarian, retired media specialist, freelance/self-employed educational consultant*
Musiker, Reuben *library director*
Naulty, Susan Louise *archivist*
Newlin, Lyman Wilbur *bookseller, consultant*
Noah, Julia Jeanine *retired librarian*
Ortego, Gilda Baeza *library director, educator*
Pakala, James Cotton *library director, minister*
Peters, Connie Jane *librarian, media specialist*
Pitman, LaVern Frank *librarian*
Pruter, Robert Douglas *librarian*
Reed, Jean T. *retired archivist*
Renfro, Patricia Elise *library director, academic administrator*
Repinski, Sara *library director*
Repp, Joan Mercedes *retired librarian*
Rhoads, James Berton *archivist, consultant, federal official, educator*
Ricketts, Sondra Lou *librarian*
Roark, Barbara Ann *librarian*
Roberts, Judith Marie *librarian, educator*
Robinson, Verna Cotten *retired librarian, real estate manager*
Rosenthal, Susan Barbara *retired librarian*
Rouse, Roscoe, Jr. *retired librarian, educator*
Runkle, Martin Davey *library director*
Sacchetti, Susanne Louise *librarian*
Sager, Donald Jack *librarian, consultant, retired publishing executive*
Savela, Judith Gheldof *librarian*
Scheiberg, Susan L. *librarian*
Schewe, Donald Bruce *archivist, library director*
Schlesinger, Deborah Lee *retired librarian*
Schlosser, Anne Griffin *librarian*
Scott, Carol Seeley *retired librarian, researcher*
Scott, Catherine Dorothy *librarian, library and information scientist, consultant*
Settles, Jeanne Dobson *retired librarian*
Shedlock, James *library director, consultant*
Shickley, Margaret S. *librarian*
Siefert-Kazanjian, Donna *corporate librarian*
Slavens, Thomas Paul *library science professor*
Smith, Barbara Jeanne *retired librarian*
Smith, Ruby Lucille *retired librarian*
Sokolowsky, Brian William *archivist, historian*
Solivan, Neida M. *librarian, educator, school system administrator*
Sparks, William Sheral *retired librarian*
Spelbring, Aaron Paul *archivist*
Sprince, Leila Joy *retired librarian*
Stavely, Keith Williams Fitzgerald *librarian*
Stewart, Dorothy K. *librarian*
Stone, Glenda Lee *librarian, genealogist*
Strait, Viola Edwina Washington *librarian*
Strober, Francine Lee *librarian, archivist*
Stubbs, Kendon Lee *retired librarian*
Summers, Lorraine Dey Schaeffer *retired librarian*
Suput, Ray Radoslav *librarian*
Sweetland, Loraine Fern *librarian, educator*
Taraki, Shirlee *librarian*
Tavella, Elise Shannon *librarian*
Thiele, Gloria Day *librarian, small business owner*
Trezza, Alphonse Fiore *librarian, educator*
Triipan, Maive *library director*
Tu, Susan *retired librarian*
Turner, Marguerite Rose Cowles *retired library director*
UmBayemake, Linda *library director*
VanMeter, Vandelia L. *retired library director*
Van Orden, Phyllis Jeanne *librarian, educator*
Varner, Joyce Ehrhardt *retired librarian*
Wang, Chen-ku *retired library director*
Wartluft, David Jonathan *retired librarian, minister*
Weaver, Barbara Frances *librarian, consultant*
Wegner, Lucy Siefert *information specialist*
Weingand, Darlene Erna *librarian, educator*
Weliver, Evelyn Ruth *academic librarian*
Wertsman, Vladimir Filip *librarian, writer, library and information scientist, translator*
Whitmore, Menandra M. *librarian*
Wilkins, Barratt (George Wilkins) *librarian*
Wilson, Patricia Potter *librarian*
Wingate, Bettye Faye *librarian, educator*
Winn, Carolyn Pautke *librarian, consultant*
Wong, Suzanne Crawbuck *librarian*
Woodrum, Patricia Ann *librarian*
Woods, Phyllis Michalik *librarian*
Wright, Jan Carol *indexer*
Wulff, Lois Yvonne *retired librarian*
Wynar, Bohdan Stephen *retired librarian, writer, editor*
Yiotis, Gayle *archivist, researcher, anthropologist, writer*
Young, Amy Y. *librarian*
Zack, Daniel Gerard *library consultant*

# HUMANITIES: MUSEUMS

## UNITED STATES

### ALABAMA

**Huntsville**
Baldaia, Peter *curator*

**Mc Calla**
Kes, Vicki *museum director*

**Mobile**
Richelson, Paul William *curator*

**Montgomery**
Johnson, Mark Matthew *museum administrator*

**Semmes**
McCann, Clarence David, Jr. *curator, artist*

### ARIZONA

**Fort Huachuca**
Jackson II, Ralph G. *curator*

**Green Valley**
Lusk, Harlan Gilbert *national park superintendent, business executive*

**Phoenix**
Ballinger, James K. *art museum executive*
Grinell, Sheila *museum director*

**Portal**
Zweifel, Richard George *curator*

**Scottsdale**
Krane, Susan *museum director, curator*

**Tempe**
Zeitlin, Marilyn Audrey *museum director*

**Tucson**
Dolan, Susan Mae *museum staff member*
King, James Edward *retired museum director, consultant*

### CALIFORNIA

**Arcata**
Bailey, Stephen Fairchild *retired museum director, ornithologist*

**Avalon**
Pedersen, Jeannine Lynn *curator*

**Bakersfield**
Enriquez, Carola Rupert *museum director*

**Berkeley**
Benedict, Burton *retired museum director, anthropologist*
Consey, Kevin Edward *museum administrator*
Day, Lucille Lang *museum administrator, educator, writer*
Grossman, Bonnie *art gallery director*

**Bodega Bay**
Cohen, Daniel Morris *museum administrator, marine biologist, researcher*

**Carlsbad**
Misiorowski, Elise Besson *museum director*

**Carmel Valley**
Wolfe, Maurice Raymond *retired museum director, educator*

**Carson**
Zimmerer, Kathy Louise *museum director*

**Claremont**
Comba, Steve Scott *museum director, artist*

**Culver City**
Coolidge, Matthew *curator*

**Irvine**
Stern, Jean *museum director*

**La Jolla**
Beebe, Mary Livingstone *curator*
Davies, Hugh Marlais *museum director*

**Long Beach**
Glenn, Constance White *art museum director, educator, consultant*
Luke, Gregorio *museum administrator*
Nelson, Harold Bernhard *museum director*

**Los Angeles**
Barron, Stephanie *curator*
Brand, Michael *museum director*
Byrnes, James Bernard *museum director, consultant*
Govan, Michael *museum director*
Greenfield, Mark Steven *art gallery director, artist*
Hirano, Irene Ann Yasutake *museum director*
Hopkins, Henry Tyler *museum director, art educator*
Komaroff, Linda *curator*
Philbin, Ann *art facility director*
Rich, Andrea Louise *museum administrator*
Strick, Jeremy *curator*
Talley, Vernon Andrew *museum administrator*
Zelevansky, Lynn *curator*

**Markleeville**
Edwards, Richard Charles *museum director*

**Oroville**
Dewey, David John *curator*

**Pasadena**
Bosley, Edward Richmond *historical site administrator*

**Rancho Palos Verdes**
Yassin, Robert Alan *museum director, curator*

**Redlands**
Griesemer, Allan David *retired museum director*

**Riverside**
Warren, Katherine Virginia *art gallery director*

**Sacramento**
Jones, Lial A. *museum director*

**San Carlos**
Schumacher, Henry Jerold *museum director, retired military officer*

**San Diego**
Cartwright, Derrick *museum director*
Hager, Michael W. *museum director*
Longenecker, Martha W. *museum director*

Petersen, Martin Eugene *curator*

**San Francisco**
Benezra, Neal *museum director, curator*
Buchanan, John Edward, Jr. *museum director*
Leviton, Alan Edward *curator*
O'Neill, Brian *national recreation area administrator*
Rinder, Lawrence R. *curator*
Rugoff, Ralph *curator*
Sano, Emily Joy *museum director*
Shank, J. William *art conservator*

**San Jose**
Hernandez, Jo Farb *museum director, consultant*
Keegan, Daniel T. *museum director*

**San Marino**
Murdoch, John *museum director*

**Santa Barbara**
Karpeles, David *museum director*

**Santa Clara**
Rivera, George *museum director*

**Stanford**
Siekierski, Maciej M. *curator*

**The Sea Ranch**
Baas, Jacquelynn *museum director, art historian*

**Yosemite National Park**
Forgang, David M. *curator*

## COLORADO

**Alma**
Swanson, Erik Christian *museum director*

**Colorado Springs**
LeMieux, Linda Dailey *museum director*
Randall, Jessy *curator, writer*

**Denver**
Payton, Cydney *museum director, curator*
Sharp, Lewis Inman *museum director, curator*
Teitz, Richard Stuart *museum director, educator*
Wilson, Steve *museum director*

**Erie**
Plehaty, Phyllis Juliette *retired curator*

## CONNECTICUT

**Hartford**
Holmes, Willard *museum director*
Sellers, Kate M. *art museum director*

**New Haven**
Hickey, Leo Joseph *museum curator, educator*
Meyers, Amy *museum director*
Sorkin, Jenni *curator, critic*
Storr, Robert *curator, art educator, painter*

**Old Lyme**
Stula, Nancy *museum director, curator*

**West Hartford**
Faude, Wilson Hinsdale *museum director, consultant*

**Weston**
Daniel, James *curator, writer*
Oliver, Sandra *art dealer, painter*

## DELAWARE

**Lewes**
Rudmann, Brent L. *museum director, educator*

**Wilmington**
Blankenship, Roy *conservator, artist, writer*
Bruni, Stephen Thomas *museum director*

## DISTRICT OF COLUMBIA

**Washington**
Bertin, Margaret A.H *museum administrator*
Blair, Thomas Delano *museum administrator*
Bloomfield, Sara J. *museum director*
Bretzfelder, Deborah May *retired museum staff member*
Buhler, Leslie Lynn *museum director*
Carr, Carolyn Kinder *art gallery director*
Dwyer Southern, Kathy *museum administrator*
Greenhalgh, Paul *museum director*
Hand, John Oliver *museum curator*
Harvey, Eleanor Jones *museum curator*
Ketchum, James Roe *curator*
Kornicker, Louis Sampson *museum curator*
Kurin, Richard *museum program director*
Larson, Judy L. *museum director, curator*
Legro, Patrice *museum director*
McKinney, David Duane *museum director, architectural historian*
Neufeld, Michael John *curator, historian*
Noe, Adrianne *museum administrator*
Ohlke, Amanda Anne *museum administrator, educator*
Pachter, Marc *museum director*
Patton, Sharon F. *museum director*
Perry, James Michael *museum administrator, historian*
Raby, Julian *art gallery director*
Radice, Anne-Imelda Marino *museum director, former federal agency administrator*
Rifkin, Ned *museum director*
Sant, Victoria P. *museum administrator*
Small, Lawrence M. *museum executive*
Solinger, Janet W. *museum executive*
Stevenson, Frances Kellogg *museum program director*
Stevenson, Nancy Nelson *museum director*

Viso, Olga *museum director*
Walker, Daniel *museum director*
West, W. Richard *museum director*
Withuhn, William Lawrence *curator, financial consultant*
Wolanin, Barbara Ann Boese *curator, art historian*

## FLORIDA

**Daytona Beach**
Libby, Gary Russell *museum director emeritus, writer*

**Fort Lauderdale**
Cavendish, Kim L. Maher *museum administrator*

**Gainesville**
Dickinson, Joshua Clifton, Jr. *museum director, educator*
Nagy, Rebecca Martin *museum director*
Willumson, Glenn Gardner *curator, art historian*

**Jacksonville**
Dundon, Margo Elaine *museum director*

**Key West**
Pennington, Claudia *museum director*
Wolz, Robert Joseph *museum director*

**Miami**
Delehanty, Suzanne *museum director*
Morgan, Dahlia *museum director, art educator*
Riley, Terence *curator, architect*
Selin, Nina Evvie *museum director, electric power industry executive, volunteer*

**Miami Beach**
Camber, Diane Woolfe *museum director*

**Naples**
Hathcock, William Parker III *studio director, publicist, curator*

**Niceville**
Valdés, Karen W. *art gallery director, educator*

**Orlando**
Beatty, Robert L. *education curator*
Morrisey, Marena Grant *art museum administrator*

**Palm Harbor**
Schlageter, Robert William *museum administrator*

**Pensacola**
Furlong, George Morgan, Jr. *museum program director, retired military officer*

**Saint Petersburg**
Connelly, David O'Brien *museum administrator, journalist*

**Sarasota**
Wetenhall, John *museum director*
Zahn, Carl Frederick *museum program director, photographer, graphics designer*

**Tallahassee**
Palladino-Craig, Allys *museum director, educator*

**Vero Beach**
Gedeon, Lucinda Heyel *museum director*

**West Palm Beach**
Orr-Cahall, Anona Christina *museum director, art historian*

## GEORGIA

**Atlanta**
Bibb, Daniel Roland *art restorer*
King, Linda Orr *museum director, consultant*
Nick, Lloyd *museum director, art educator*
Shapiro, Michael Edward *museum director*
Vigtel, Gudmund *retired museum director*

**Augusta**
Glaser, Nancy Jane *museum director*

**Cartersville**
Hopkins, Seth M. *museum director*

**Marietta**
Barksdale, Daryl *historic preservationist*

**Milledgeville**
Davis, Matthew Scott *curator, history professor*

**Savannah**
Lesko, Diane *museum director, curator*

## HAWAII

**Honolulu**
Klobe, Tom *art gallery director*

**Kaneohe**
Lagoria, Georgianna Marie *curator, writer, editor, visual art consultant*

**Mililani**
Magee, Donald Edward *retired national park service administrator*

## IDAHO

**Boise**
Close, Timothy *museum director*

**Coeur D' Alene**
Dahlgren, Dorothy *museum director*

**Inkom**
Jackson, Allen Keith *retired museum administrator*

**Pocatello**
Stucki, Margaret Elizabeth *art gallery director, writer, painter*

## ILLINOIS

**Carbondale**
Whitlock, John Joseph *museum director*

**Carterville**
Barkley Giffin, Adrienne F. *museum administrator, academic administrator*

**Chicago**
Alexander, Karen *museum staff member*
Balzekas, Stanley, Jr. *museum director*
Cuno, James *museum director*
Dittmer, Frances R. *curator*
Dohner, Markos *museum staff member, artist*
Fitzpatrick, Robert John *museum director*
Knappenberger, Paul Henry, Jr. *science museum director*
Mc Carter, John Wilbur, Jr. *museum executive*
Mosena, David R. *museum administrator*
Nordland, Gerald *museum administrator, historian, consultant*
Slemmons, Rod *museum director, art educator, curator*
Smith, Elizabeth Angele Taft *curator*
Teller, Alan *museum program director, photographer, educator*
Terrassa, Jacqueline *museum director*
Wood, James Nowell *museum director and executive*

**Evanston**
Danilov, Victor Joseph *museum administrator, educator, writer*
Robertson, David Alan *museum director, educator*

**Flossmoor**
MacMaster, Daniel Miller *retired museum official*

**Galena**
Narkiewicz-Laine, Christian K. *museum director, painter, poet*

**Oak Park**
Bachand, Cheryl Ann *curator, art history educator*

**Princeton**
Collins, N. Dana *art gallery owner, consultant, retired art educator*

**Rock Island**
Leinicke, Kris Gayman *museum director, educator*

**Springfield**
Hallmark, Donald Parker *museum director, educator*
Mc Millan, R(obert) Bruce *retired museum director, anthropologist*

## INDIANA

**Bloomington**
Calinescu, Adriana Gabriela *curator, art historian*

**Evansville**
Streetman, John William III *museum director*

**Indianapolis**
Anderson, Maxwell L. *museum director*
Noffze, Jennifer Noel *museum administrator*
Organ, Rita C. *museum administrator, consultant*

**Marion**
Felton, Wanda June *curator*

**Muncie**
Blume, Peter Frederick *museum director*

**Notre Dame**
Loving, Charles Roy *museum director, curator*

**Terre Haute**
Vollmer, David *museum director*

## IOWA

**Ames**
Pohlman, Lynette *museum director, curator*

**Cedar Falls**
Taylor, Darrell Richard *art gallery director, artist*

**Des Moines**
Thompson, Jerome Lafayette *curator*

## KANSAS

**Lawrence**
Hardy, Saralyn Reece *museum director*

**Pleasanton**
Earnest, Ola May *curator*

**Pratt**
Shrack, Christopher George *curator, educator*

**Wichita**
Jones, Schuyler *museum director, anthropologist*
Steiner, Charles K. *museum director, painter*

## KENTUCKY

**Lexington**
Walsh-Piper, Kathleen A. *museum director*

**Louisville**
Becker, Gail Roselyn *museum director*
Morrin, Peter Patrick *museum director*

**Novick, Aileen Mary** *historic site director, educator*

## LOUISIANA

**Deridder**
Mallory, Patricia Jody *museum curator*

**Lafayette**
Henderson, Mary Stanley *museum director, writer*

**New Orleans**
Bullard, Edgar John III *museum director*
Casellas, Joachim *art gallery executive*
Fagaly, William Arthur *curator*
Schehr, Kevin John *art gallery owner*

## MAINE

**Brunswick**
Kline, Katy *museum director*

**Hancock Point**
Silvestro, Clement Mario *museum director, historian*

**Lamoine**
Schmidt, Christine Alice *art gallery owner*

**Lewiston**
Bessire, Mark H.C. *museum director*

**Portland**
O'Leary, Dan *museum director*

**Rockland**
Crosman, Christopher Byron *museum director*

## MARYLAND

**Aberdeen Proving Ground**
Davis, Randolph Joseph *museum administrator, consultant*

**Annapolis**
Mason-Chaney, Lisa *curator*

**Baltimore**
Bolger, Doreen *museum director*
Lee, Steven Xavier *museum director, artist and environmentalist*
Rea, Evan Andrew *curator*
Vikan, Gary Kent *museum director*

**Bethesda**
Fraser, Catriona Trafford *art gallery director, photographer*

**Clinton**
Whittington, Ralph Edward *curator, librarian*

**College Park**
Quick, Edward Raymond *museum director, educator, curator*

**Friendship**
Clagett, Diana Wharton Sinkler *museum docent*

**Hyattsville**
Shestack, Alan *museum administrator*

**Landover**
Grasselli, Margaret Morgan *curator*
Powell, Earl Alexander III *art museum director*

**Mitchellville**
Marsh, Caryl Amsterdam *retired curator, retired psychologist*

**New Market**
Schuettinger, Bruce Michael *conservator*

**Severna Park**
Lively, Carter Cunningham *museum director*

**Silver Spring**
Woolard, Connie Ward *retired art gallery manager, art director*

**Suitland**
Johnson, Jessica Susan *conservator*

## MASSACHUSETTS

**Boston**
Cronin, Bonnie Kathryn Lamb *museum director*
Curran, Emily Katherine *museum director*
Emerson, Anne Devereux *museum administrator*
Hawley, Anne *museum director*
Hills, Patricia Gorton Schulze *curator, art historian*
Nold, Carl Richard *museum administrator*
Parmal, Pamela Ann *curator*
Price, Michael Witwer *art gallery owner, lawyer*
Rogers, Malcolm Austin *museum director, art historian*
Vermeule, Cornelius Clarkson III *museum curator*
Wu, Tung *curator, artist, art historian, educator*
Zannieri, Nina *museum director*

**Cambridge**
Farver, Jane *museum director*
Gaskell, Ivan George Alexander De Wend *art museum curator*
Kennedy, Roger George *museum program director, parks director*
Lentz, Thomas W. *museum director, curator*
Saywell, Edward *curator*
Sigel, Anthony B. *art conservator*
Slive, Seymour *museum director, art educator*
Tucker, Louis Leonard *retired historical society administrator*
Watson, Rubie S. *museum director*

**Charlestown**
Kiihne, Robert Spencer *exhibit director*

**Chestnut Hill**
Netzer, Nancy *museum director, art historian, educator*

**Fitchburg**
Jareckie, Stephen Barlow *museum curator*

**Lexington**
Ott, John Harlow *museum administrator*

**Marblehead**
Peterson, Pam M. *museum director*

**Milton**
Randall, Lilian Maria Charlotte *museum curator*

**Northampton**
Fabing, Suzannah *museum director*
Holbert, Kelly McKay *exhibition coordinator, art historian*

**Southfield**
Melvin, Ronald McKnight *retired museum director*

**Springfield**
Muhlberger, Richard Charles *museum director, writer, educator*

**Waltham**
Arena, Albert A. *museum director*

**Wellesley**
Mickenberg, David *museum director, art director, historian*

**West Brookfield**
Higgins, Brian Alton *art gallery owner, artist*

**Williamstown**
Conforti, Michael Peter *museum director, art historian*
Corrin, Lisa G. *museum director*

**Winchester**
Fitch, Blake *museum director, photographer, curator*

**Worcester**
Welu, James A. *art museum director*

## MICHIGAN

**Ann Arbor**
Bailey, Reeve Maclaren *museum curator*
Steward, James *museum director, art history educator*

**Charlevoix**
Miles, David Loren *museum director*

**Detroit**
Beal, Graham William John *museum director*
Darr, Alan Phipps *curator, historian*
Parrish, Maurice Drue *museum executive*
Peck, William Henry *curator, archaeologist, educator, art historian, writer*

**East Lansing**
Bandes, Susan Jane *museum director, educator*
Dewhurst, Charles Kurt *museum director, curator, language educator*

**Flint**
Henry, John Bailey *museum director*

**Orchard Lake**
Majewski, Karen Marie *curator*

## MINNESOTA

**Chaska**
Braun, Mary Edna *museum director*

**Minneapolis**
Griswold, William M. *museum director, curator*
Halbreich, Kathy *museum director*
King, Lyndel Irene Saunders *museum director*

**Saint Paul**
Archabal, Nina M(archetti) *historic site director*

**Saint Peter**
Myers, Donald James *museum director, art historian, educator*

## MISSISSIPPI

**Jackson**
Bradley, Betsy *museum director*

**Poplarville**
Hague, Ronn *museum director*

**Washington**
Branyan, Cheryl Munyer *museum administrator*

## MISSOURI

**Cape Girardeau**
Grand, Stanley I. *museum director, educator*

**Columbia**
Goodrich, James William *retired historian executive*

**Fredericktown**
Sudmeyer, Alice Jean *art gallery owner*

**Independence**
Potts, Barbara Joyce *retired historic site director*

**Kansas City**
Cozad, Rachael Blackburn *museum director*
McKenna, George LaVerne *art museum curator*
Scott, Deborah Emont *curator*
Wilson, Marc Fraser *art museum director*

**Saint Joseph**
Chilcote, Gary M. *museum director, reporter*
Oldman, Terry L. *museum director*

**Saint Louis**
Eyerman, Charlotte *curator, art historian*

## MONTANA

**Billings**
Peterson, Robyn Gayle *museum director*

**Missoula**
Brown, Robert Munro *museum director*
Millin, Laura Jeanne *museum director*

## NEBRASKA

**Beatrice**
Clawson, Rita Louise *curator*

**Boys Town**
Lynch, Thomas Joseph *museum director*

**Holdrege**
Cooper, Angela Dawn *historic site director*

**Lincoln**
Geske, Norman Albert *museum director*

**Omaha**
Precella, Jane Westbrook *museum shop director*

## NEVADA

**Las Vegas**
Herridge, Elizabeth *museum director*
Le Blanc, Suzanne *museum director*

## NEW HAMPSHIRE

**Newmarket**
Ellis, David Wertz *retired museum director*

**Portsmouth**
Nylander, Jane Louise *museum director, educator, writer*

## NEW JERSEY

**Gladstone**
Ocello, Claudia Barbara *museum program director*

**Holmdel**
Smith, Sibley Judson, Jr. *historic site administrator, educator*

**Montclair**
Sims, Patterson *curator*

**Morristown**
Miller, Steven H. *museum director*

**New Brunswick**
Perry, Gregory J. *museum director*

**Newark**
Price, Mary Sue Sweeney *museum director*
Reynolds, Valrae *museum curator*

**Princeton**
Livstone, Michael S. *database curator*
Taylor, Susan M. *museum director*

**Ramsey**
Libin, Laurence Elliot *retired curator*

## NEW MEXICO

**Albuquerque**
Baker, Laura Kay *art gallery owner, writer*

**Las Cruces**
Reynolds, Terry Ray *curator, anthropologist, educator*

**Placitas**
Smith, Richard Bowen *retired national park superintendent*

**Santa Fe**
Enyeart, James L. *museum director*
King, George G. *museum director*

**Silver City**
Bettison, Cynthia Ann *museum director, archaeologist*

**Taos**
Witt, David L. *curator, writer*

## NEW YORK

**Albany**
Miles, Christine Marie *museum director*

**Blue Mountain Lake**
Welsh, Caroline Mastin *curator, art historian*

**Bronx**
Block, Holly *museum director*

**Brooklyn**
Desmarais, Charles Joseph *museum director, writer*
Enseki, Carol *museum director*
Lehman, Arnold Lester *museum official, art historian*

**Buffalo**
Bayles, Jennifer Lucene *museum program director, educator*

**Carthage**
Desrosiers, Michele L. *curator*

**Cooperstown**
Kirkpatrick, Megan Leigh *museum administrator*

**Corning**
Spillman, Jane Shadel *curator, writer, researcher*
Whitehouse, David Bryn *museum director*

**Corona**
Finkelpearl, Tom *museum director*
Smith, Valerie *curator*

**Glens Falls**
Suffolk, Randall *museum director, curator*

**Hamilton**
Moynihan, William J. *museum executive*

**Hyde Park**
Hunt, Mark Alan *museum director*

**Katonah**
Simpson, William Kelly *curator, Egyptologist, educator*

**New York**
Adler, Tracy L. *curator*
Bailey, Colin Barry *curator*
Baragwanath, Albert Kingsmill *curator, writer*
Barlow, Anne Julia *curator*
Barnet, Peter *curator*
Barnett, Vivian Endicott *curator*
Basquin, Mary Smyth (Kit Basquin) *museum administrator*
Beck, Martha Ann *curator, director*
Bothmer, Dietrich Felix von *curator, archaeologist*
Brumley, Tom *museum director, artist*
Bull, David *fine art conservator*
Carboni, Stefano *curator*
Carneiro, Robert Leonard *curator, anthropologist*
Christiansen, Keith *curator*
Christoffers, Lynn Beryl *curator, artist*
Codding, Mitchell Allan *museum director, cultural organization administrator*
Cohan, James *art gallery director*
Cohen, Mildred Thaler *art gallery director*
de Montebello, Philippe Lannes *museum director*
Desai, Vishakha N. *museum director, professional society administrator*
Draper, James David *art museum curator*
Ferber, Linda S. *museum director*
Flood, Richard Sidney *curator*
Flynn, John J. *museum curator*
Foster, Carter *curator*
Freed, Stanley Arthur *retired museum curator*
Futter, Ellen Victoria *museum administrator*
Glimcher, Arnold B. *art gallery executive*
Golden, Thelma *curator*
Goss, Jared *curator*
Gumpert, Lynn *gallery director*
Gund, Agnes *retired museum administrator*
Haskell, Barbara *curator*
Henry, Sarah M. *museum staff member, historian*
Hoffman, Nancy *art gallery director*
Hotchner, Holly *museum director, curator, conservator*
Hoving, Thomas *museum director, consultant, writer*
Howat, John Keith *retired museum executive*
Ilse-Neuman, Ursula *curator*
Johnson, J. Stewart *curator, art consultant*
Kallir, Jane Katherine *art gallery director, author*
Kardon, Janet *museum director*
Kind, Phyllis *art gallery owner*
Kleeblatt, Norman L. *museum curator*
Kramer, Linda Konheim *curator, art historian*
Kuchta, Ronald Andrew *museum director, editor, curator*
Kujawski, Elizabeth Szancer *art curator, consultant*
Lerner, Martin *museum curator*
Levai, Pierre Alexandre *art gallery executive*
Levine, Louis D. *museum director, archaeologist*
Lowry, Glenn David *art museum director*
Lynch, Florence *art gallery director*
Martin, Mary-Anne *art gallery owner*
Mertens, Joan R. *museum curator, art historian*
Meyerhoff, Karen *museum director*
Mitchell, Patricia Edenfield *broadcast museum administrator*
Murdock, Robert Mead *curator*
Norris, Michael Byron *museum staff member*
Novacek, Michael John *curator, paleontologist*
O'Brien, Catherine Louise *museum administrator*
Pesner, Carole Manishin *art gallery owner*
Platnick, Norman I. *curator, entomologist*
Poulet, Anne Litle *museum director, art historian*
Rafferty, Emily Kernan *museum administrator*
Rosenbaum, Joan Hannah *museum director*
Rosevear, Cora *curator*
Sachs, Samuel, II, *museum director*
Simon, Ronald Charles *curator*
Sims, Lowery Stokes *museum curator, museum administrator, writer, educator,*
Subotnick, Ali *curator, writer*
Sutton, Karen E. *museum director*
Szarkowski, T(haddeus) John *museum administrator*
Tisch Sussman, Laurie *art gallery director*
Tobach, Ethel *retired curator*
Toll, Barbara Elizabeth *art gallery director*
Wardropper, Ian Bruce *museum curator, educator*
Weinberg, Adam D. *museum director*
Wheeler, Ward Christopher *curator*
Willis, Carol *museum director*
Zugazagoitia, Julian *museum director*

**Orient**
McNaught, William P. *museum director*

**Oyster Bay**
Kuehhas, Thomas Alan *museum director*

**Raquette Lake**
Bridger, Beverly Maria *historic site director*

**Rochester**
Bannon, Anthony Leo *museum director*
Keeler, William Conrad III *curator, librarian, archivist*
Maples, Philip G. *museum director*

**Sands Point**
Olian, JoAnne Constance *curator, art historian*

**Southampton**
Lerner, Abram *museum director, artist*
Martine, David Bunn *curator, artist*

**Stuyvesant**
Tripp, Susan Gerwe *museum director*

**Syracuse**
Pascucci, Marisa Jonell *curator, art historian*
Trop, Sandra *museum director*

**Treadwell**
Norris, Linda Beth *museum administrator*

**Tupper Lake**
Welsh, Peter Corbett *museum director, historian*

**Utica**
Schweizer, Paul Douglas *museum director*

**Waterford**
Gold, James Paul *museum director*

**Willsboro**
Gillilland, Thomas *art gallery director*

## NORTH CAROLINA

**Chapel Hill**
Bolas, Gerald Douglas *museum director, art historian, educator*
Riggs, Timothy Allan *museum curator*

**Durham**
Rorschach, Kimberly *museum director*

**Gastonia**
Duran, Carrie *museum staff member*

**Pinehurst**
Broadhurst, Judith Buck *art gallery owner*

**Raleigh**
Coffey, John William *museum curator*
Kuhler, Renaldo Gillet *retired museum director, medical illustrator*

**Wilmington**
Seapker, Janet Kay *museum administrator, historic site director, consultant*

**Wilson**
McKinnon, Karl Luther *museum director*

**Winston Salem**
Locklair, Paula Welshimer *museum administrator, curator*
Rauschenberg, Bradford Lee *museum program director*
Whittington, Stephen Lunn *museum director*

## NORTH DAKOTA

**Devils Lake**
Schiele, James Leo *museum director*

**Fargo**
Pauley, Edward E. *museum administrator*

## OHIO

**Akron**
Friedman, Richard Everett *curator, art appraiser*
Kahan, Mitchell Douglas *museum director*

**Athens**
Ahrens, Kent *museum director, art historian*

**Canton**
Perry, Stephen A. *museum administrator, former federal agency administrator*

**Cincinnati**
Betsky, Aaron *art museum director*
Brown, Daniel *curator, executive secretary*
Crew, Spencer *museum administrator*
DeWitt, Katharine Cramer *museum administrator*
Long, Phillip Clifford *museum director*
Shearer, Linda *museum director*

**Cleveland**
Rub, Timothy F. *museum director*
Thurmer, Robert *art gallery director*

**Columbus**
Caswell, Lucy Shelton *curator, educator*

**Dayton**
Meister, Mark Jay *museum director, professional society administrator*

**Groveport**
Motts, Warren Earl *museum director*

**Kirtland**
Johnston, Stanley Howard, Jr. *curator, rare book dealer*

**Toledo**
Bacigalupi, Don *museum director*

**University Heights**
Cook, Alexander Burns *curator, artist, educator*

**Youngstown**
Sturgill, James Aaron *museum administrator*

### OKLAHOMA

**Idabel**
Moy, Henry *museum director*

**Norman**
Lee, Eric McCauley *museum director, art historian*

**Ripley**
Chlouber, Dale Edward *curator*

**Tulsa**
Ferriso, Brian J. *museum director*

### OREGON

**Milwaukie**
Eichenger, Marilynne Katzen *museum administrator*

**Portland**
Taylor, J. Mary (Jocelyn Mary Taylor) *museum director, educator, zoologist*

### PENNSYLVANIA

**Altoona**
Moffitt, Charles William *art gallery director*

**Chadds Ford**
Duff, James Henry *museum director, environmental services administrator*
O'Hara, Virginia Anne *curator*

**Erie**
Vanco, John L. *art museum director*

**Fayetteville**
Etchison, Bruce *retired museum director, conservator*

**Grantham**
Mark, Kenneth Dean *museum director, educator*

**Harrisburg**
Mahey, John Andrew *retired museum director*

**Merion Station**
Gillman, Derek A. *museum director, academic administrator*

**Philadelphia**
Bantel, Linda Mae *former museum curator, consultant*
Burke, Brother Daniel *museum director, educator*
d'Harnoncourt, Anne *museum director, museum administrator*
Gould, Claudia *museum director*
Gregory, Joseph F. *art gallery director, art educator*
King, Barry M. *museum program director, artist*
McNamara, Kevin John *museum administrator*
Shoemaker, Innis Howe *art museum curator*
Sitarski, Stephen *historic site administrator*
van Rhyn, Jacqueline J. *curator*
Wint, Dennis Michael *museum director*

**Pittsburgh**
Armstrong, Richard *museum director, curator*
Black, Samuel Wade *curator*
Bodine, William Beekman, Jr. *museum director*
Dawson, Mary Ruth *curator, educator*
DeWalt, Bill *museum director*
Hillenbrand, David M. *museum administrator*
King, Elaine A. *curator, art historian, critic*

**Reading**
DeEsch, Vasti F. *museum registrar*
Dietrich, Bruce Leinbach *museum administrator, astronomer, educator*

**South Williamsport**
Ogurcak, Janice L. *museum director, educator*

**Strasburg**
Lindsay, George Carroll *former museum director*

**University Park**
Muhlert, Jan Keene *art museum director*

**Wynnewood**
Camp, Kimberly N. *museum administrator, artist*

### RHODE ISLAND

**Bristol**
Connell, James Burke *museum director*

**Kingston**
Tolnick Champa, Judith Ellen *art gallery director, curator*

**Newport**
Tinney, Harle Hope Hanson *museum administrator*

**Providence**
Fishman, Bernard Philip *museum director*

---

**Saunderstown**
Leavitt, Thomas Whittlesey *retired museum director, educator*

### SOUTH CAROLINA

**Columbia**
Brosius, Karen *museum director*
Inman, Beth Trammell *curator*

**Greenville**
Davis, Joan Carroll *retired museum director*

**Mount Pleasant**
Macdonald, Robert Rigg, Jr. *retired museum director*

**Pawleys Island**
Matelic, Candace Tangorra *museum director, educator*
Noble, Joseph Veach *retired museum director*

**Walterboro**
Drain, Danny *museum director*

**West Columbia**
Harmon, Horace Elmer, Jr. *museum director, consultant*

### TENNESSEE

**Crossville**
Elam, Leslie Albert *retired museum director*

**Greeneville**
Corey, Mark *historic site director*

**Jonesborough**
Gerhardt, E. Alvin, Jr. *retired museum director*

**Knoxville**
Smith, Todd D. *museum director*

**Memphis**
Czestochowski, Joseph Stephen *museum administrator*
Feldman, Kaywin *museum director, curator*

### TEXAS

**Austin**
Friis-Hansen, Dana *museum director*
Theriot, Edward C. *museum director*

**Canyon**
Frederickson, Mary Christine *conservator*

**Dallas**
Hoffman, Marguerite Steed *former art gallery director*
Lane, John Rodger *museum director*

**El Paso**
Sipiora, Leonard Paul *retired museum director, art appraiser*

**Fort Sam Houston**
Manguso, John A. *museum director*

**Fort Worth**
Auping, Michael G. *curator*
Breuer, Bradford R. *former museum director*
Fortson, Kay Kimbell Carter *museum administrator*
Potts, Timothy F. *museum director*
Price, Marla *museum director, curator*
Tyler, Ronnie Curtis *museum director, art historian*

**Fredericksburg**
Manhart, Marcia Y(ockey) *art museum director*

**Houston**
Bowron, Edgar Peters *art museum curator, administrator*
Helfenstein, Josef *museum director*
Latimer, Roy Truett *museum executive*
Lee, Janie C. *curator*
Marzio, Peter Cort *museum director*
Mayo, Marti *museum director, curator*
Ramirez, Mari Carmen *curator*
Severance, Diana Lynn *curator*
Tucker, Anne Wilkes *curator, historian, photographer, critic*

**Plano**
Godbold, Christopher Bourke *curator*

**Post**
Neff, Marie Taylor *museum director, artist*

**San Antonio**
Chiego, William J. *museum director*

### UTAH

**Hill AFB**
Hill, Mary Frances *curator, researcher*

**Provo**
Gray, Campbell *museum director*

**Salt Lake City**
George, Sarah B. *museum director*
Heuman, Joshua I. *curator*

### VERMONT

**Bennington**
Williams, Robert Joseph *retired museum director, educator*

---

**Manchester**
Kouwenhoven, Gerrit Wolphertsen *retired museum director*

**Middlebury**
Saunders, Richard Henry III *museum director*

**Montpelier**
Dumville, John P. *historic site director*

### VIRGINIA

**Alexandria**
Lundeberg, Philip Karl Boraas *curator, historian*

**Arlington**
Demetrion, James Thomas *retired museum director, consultant*

**Charlottesville**
Linden, Peppy G. *museum director*

**Keswick**
Nosanow, Barbara Shissler *museum program director, curator*

**Lynchburg**
Elson, James Martin *retired landmark director*

**Mc Lean**
Forman, Lee Lavinthal *museum administrator*

**Mount Vernon**
Rees, James Conway, IV, *historic site administrator*

**Onancock**
Verrill, John Howard *museum director*

**Richmond**
Nyerges, Alexander Lee *museum director*
Ravenal, John B. *curator*

**Roanoke**
Fitzgerald, Mary Eileen *museum program director*

**Sterling**
Friedheim, Jerry Warden *museum consultant*

**Tazewell**
Weeks, Ross Leonard, Jr. *museum executive*

**Williamsburg**
Christison, Muriel Branham *retired museum director, education educator*

### WASHINGTON

**Bellevue**
Warren, James Ronald *retired museum director, journalist*

**Bellingham**
Clark-Langager, Sarah Ann *curator, academic administrator*
Livesay, Thomas Andrew *museum director, educator*

**Redmond**
Sobey, Edwin J. C. *museum director, consultant, oceanographer*

**Seattle**
Andrews, Richard Otis *museum director*
Bufano, Ralph A. *retired museum executive*
Gates, Mimi Gardner *museum director*
Shirley, Donna *museum director, former aerospace engineer*

**Tacoma**
Callan, Josi Irene *museum director*

**Wenatchee**
Williams, Keith Roy *museum director*

### WEST VIRGINIA

**Huntington**
Culligan, Jenine Elizabeth *curator*

### WISCONSIN

**Cottage Grove**
Seltzner, Rachel *museum administrator, science educator*

**Madison**
Garver, Thomas Haskell *curator, consultant, writer*

**Milwaukee**
Carter, Curtis Lloyd *museum director*
Gordon, David *museum director*
Ketner, Joseph Dale *museum director, art historian*
Peltz, Cissie Jean *art gallery director, cartoonist*

**Racine**
Taragin, Davira Spiro *curator*

### WYOMING

**Cheyenne**
Wilson-McKee, Marie *museum director*

**Cody**
Donoghue, Ann Marie *museum administrator, consultant*

**Jackson**
Harris, Adam Duncan *curator*

**Laramie**
Guerin, Charles Allan *museum director, artist*

---

Moldenhauer, Susan *museum director, curator*

## CANADA

### ALBERTA

**Canmore**
Janes, Robert Roy *museum director, archaeologist, editor*

### BRITISH COLUMBIA

**Victoria**
Finlay, James Campbell *retired museum director*

### NEW BRUNSWICK

**Fredericton**
Lumsden, Ian Gordon *art gallery director*

### ONTARIO

**London**
Poole, Nancy Geddes *art gallery curator, writer*

**Ottawa**
McAvity, John Gillis *museum director, association executive, museologist*

### ADDRESS UNPUBLISHED

Adams, Margaret Bernice *retired museum official*
Anderson, Dean William *museum consultant*
Armenian, Gassia *curator, consultant*
Baker, D. James *museum administrator, environmental scientist*
Bell, Michael Steven *art curator*
Bergmann, Jeanette B. *exhibit designer*
Bishop, Budd Harris *retired museum director*
Carter, John Swain *retired museum director, consultant*
Castile, Rand (Jesse Randolph III) *retired museum director*
Chasin, Martin *art gallery director, consultant, educator*
Cikovsky, Nicolai, Jr. *retired curator, art historian, educator*
Cilella, Salvatore George, Jr. *museum director*
Collischan, Judy Kay *art gallery director, museum director, critic, artist*
Decatur, Raylene *former museum director*
Deutsch, James I. *curator*
Deutschman, Louise Tolliver *curator*
de Zegher, Catherine *museum director, curator*
Douglas, Diane Miriam *museum director*
Doyle, Christine Ellen *museum researcher, educator*
DuBois, Alan Beekman *retired art museum curator*
Ebie, William D. *retired museum director*
Faunce, Sarah Cushing *retired curator*
Feisthammel, Audrey Marie *museum director, educator*
Fri, Robert Wheeler *retired museum director*
Fromm, Annette Bacola *museum staff member*
Fuller, Glenn R. *park ranger*
Gabriel, Jeanette Hanisee *curator, art historian*
Grattan, Patricia Elizabeth *retired art gallery director*
Greenwald, Alice Marian *museum director*
Gribbon, Deborah *museum director*
Grossman, Cissy *curator, art historian*
Hasse, John Edward *music curator*
Hayes, Charles Franklin III *retired museum director*
Heidelberg, Michael *paintings conservator*
Hellmers, Norman Donald *retired historic site director*
Hodson, Sara Suzanne *manuscripts curator*
Ives, Colta Feller *museum curator, educator*
Jacobowitz, Ellen Sue *curator, museum administrator*
Kahn, James Steven *retired museum director*
Kelm, Bonnie G. *art museum director, educator, art appraiser, consultant*
Knowles, Elizabeth Pringle *museum director*
Krens, Thomas *museum director*
Lapp, Douglas Martin *museum director*
Lutts, Ralph Herbert *scholar, educator, museum administrator*
Martin, Robert Sidney *former museum director*
Maurer, Evan Maclyn *museum director*
McGarvie-Munn, Iain Lachlan *curator, writer, agent*
Mercuri, Joan B. *museum administrator*
Metcalf, William Edwards *museum curator, educator*
Millard, Charles Warren III *museum director, writer*
Naeve, Milo Merle *curator, director*
Nasgaard, Roald *museum curator*
Newman, Bruce Murray *retired art gallery owner*
Nickles, Shelley Kaplan *curator, educator*
Olea, Hector *curator*
Olin, David Lind *conservator*
Pal, Pratapaditya *curator*
Perrot, Paul Norman *museum director*
Peterson, James Lincoln *museum executive*
Phillips, Laughlin *retired museum director, retired editor*
Porter, Daniel Reed III *museum director*
Prakapas, Eugene Joseph *art gallery director*
Reid, Katherine Lee *retired museum director, curator*
Reuther, Ronald Theodore *museum director*
Rigaud, Edwin Joseph *museum administrator*
Robertson, Charles James *museum director emeritus*
Rouse, Terrie Suzitte *museum director*
Ryskamp, Charles Andrew *museum director, educator*

Sadinsky, Rachael *curator, art appraiser*
Schneider, Janet M. *museum administrator, painter, curator*
Segger, Martin Joseph *museum director, educator, art historian*
Shimoda, Jerry Yasutaka *retired national historic park manager*
Skramstad, Harold Kenneth, Jr. *museum consultant*
Sobel, Dean *museum director, curator, artist*
Spicer, Shirlene *history curator*
Steadman, David Wilton *retired museum director, deacon*
Stearns, Robert Leland *curator*
Stuart, Joseph Martin *museum administrator*
Summerfield, John *textile curator*
Trutor, Genevieve Williamson *museum director*
Walker, Roslyn Adele *retired museum director*
Way, Jacob Edson III *museum director*
Wieser, Siegfried *planetarium executive director*
Williams, Crissa Mary Van Vleck *museum administrator*
Williams, Elizabeth Ann *museum program director*
Wilson, Karen Lee *museum staff member, researcher*
Yates, Steven A. *curator, artist*

## INDUSTRY: MANUFACTURING
*See also* **FINANCE: FINANCIAL SERVICES**

## UNITED STATES

### ALABAMA

**Albertville**
Rice, Fuhrman D. (Runt Rice) *retired paper company executive*

**Birmingham**
Bennett, Joe Claude *pharmaceutical executive*
Cohen-DeMarco, Gale Maureen *pharmaceutical executive*
Gorrie, Miller *construction executive*
Hall, Robert Alan *construction company executive*
Harbert, Bill Lebold *retired construction corporation executive*
Holton, J(erry) Thomas *concrete company executive*
James, Donald M. *construction materials executive*
Khan, Ejaz A. *chemicals executive, controller*
Neal, Phil Hudson, Jr. *retired manufacturing executive*
Sklenar, Herbert Anthony *industrial products manufacturing company executive*
Styslinger, Lee Joseph, Jr. *manufacturing executive*
Tomkins, Mark E. *manufacturing executive*

**Montgomery**
Taylor, Watson Robbins *construction company executive*

**Opelika**
Jenkins, Richard Lee *manufacturing executive*

**Tuscaloosa**
Warner, Jack *paper company executive*

**Valley**
Ogle, D. Clark *textiles executive*

### ALASKA

**Haines**
Kaufman, David Graham *construction executive*

### ARIZONA

**Carefree**
Wearly, William Levi *retired manufacturing executive*

**Chandler**
Kim, James Joo-Jin *electronics company executive*
Owen, Robert H. *electronics executive*

**Mesa**
DeRosa, Francis Dominic *chemical company executive*
Stroble-Thompson, Colette Mary Houle *construction executive*

**Peoria**
Cook, Mary Margaret *steamfitter, educator*

**Phoenix**
Carter, Ronald Martin, Sr. *pharmaceutical executive*
Dewane, John Richard *retired manufacturing executive, small business owner*
Gallagher, Philip *electronics executive*
Giedt, Bruce Alan *paper company executive*
Jenkins, Maynard L., Jr. *automotive executive*
Klepinger, John William *trailer manufacturing company executive*
Martensen, Barbara *electronics executive*
Motsenbocker, Rex Alan *construction company executive*
Stegmayer, Joseph Henry *housing industry executive*
Tsang, Raymond *electronics executive*
Vallee, Roy A. *electronics executive*
White, Edward Allen *electronics executive*

**Prescott**
Parkhurst, Charles Lloyd *electronics executive*

**Scottsdale**
Farley, James Newton *retired manufacturing executive, electrical engineer*

Freedman, Stanley Marvin *manufacturing executive*
Gans, Eugene Howard *cosmetic and pharmaceutical company executive, consultant*
Grenell, James Henry *retired manufacturing company executive*
Howard, William Gates, Jr. *electronics company executive*
Jesky, T. J. *pharmaceutical products executive*
Lloyd, Eugene Walter *retired construction company executive*
Rethore, Bernard Gabriel *retired manufacturing and mining company executive*
Smith, Patrick W. (Rick Smith) *manufacturing executive*
Smith, Thomas P. *manufacturing executive*
Van Brunt, Gary T. *tire dealer company executive*
Walsh, Edward Joseph *food products executive, cosmetics executive*

**Surprise**
Lazar, Max Seymour *retired pharmaceutical company executive*

**Tempe**
Fulton, Ira *construction executive*
Ryaby, James Thomas *pharmaceutical executive, cellular biologist*

**Tucson**
Acker, Loren Calvin *medical products executive*
Leonard, Michael A. *retired automotive executive*

### ARKANSAS

**Fort Smith**
Flanders, Donald Hargis *manufacturing executive*

**Little Rock**
Bell, Richard Eugene *agricultural products executive, state official*
Givens, John Kenneth *automotive executive*
McCoy, Stuart Sherman *manufacturing executive*
Shell, Robert J. *construction executive*

**Springdale**
Beach, Jean Mrha *food products executive*
Bond, Richard L. *food products executive*
Dunn, Jeri R. *food products executive*
Leatherby, Dennis *food products executive*
Lee, Greg W. *food company executive*
Schaffer, Archie III *food products executive*
Tyson, John H. *food products executive*

**Tontitown**
McMennamy, Roger Neal *automotive executive*

### CALIFORNIA

**Alameda**
Caldwell, William Mackay, IV, *cloning and stem cell research company executive*
Williamson, Robert F. *pharmaceutical executive*

**Alamo**
Liggett, Lawrence Melvin *vacuum equipment manufacturing company executive*

**Anaheim**
Baumgartner, Anton Edward *automotive sales professional*
Halligan, Joseph William *snack food industry executive*
Kallay, Michael Frank, II, *medical products executive*

**Atherton**
Goodman, Sam Richard *electronics executive*
Hogan, Clarence Lester *retired electronics executive*

**Bakersfield**
Thomason, Scott *automobile executive*

**Belmont**
Endriz, John Guiry *retired electronics executive*

**Berkeley**
Janney, Daniel S. *health products executive*
Mettinger, Karl Lennart *pharmaceutical executive*

**Beverly Hills**
Winthrop, John *wines and spirits company executive*

**Bishop**
Naso, Valerie Joan *automotive dealership executive, travel company executive*

**Brisbane**
Mashouf, Manny *apparel executive*

**Burbank**
Joseff, Joan Castle *manufacturing executive*
Raulinaitis, Pranas Algis *electronics executive, consultant*

**Burlingame**
Azarnoff, Daniel Lester *pharmaceutical executive, consultant*

**Calabasas**
Dreier, R. Chad *construction and mortgage company executive*
Milne, Gordon A. *construction executive, mortgage company executive*

**Camarillo**
Cleary, Thomas Charles *technology company executive*
Weiss, Carl *aerospace company executive*

**Carlsbad**
Crooke, Stanley Thomas *pharmaceutical executive*

**Carmel Valley**
Kasson, James Matthews *electronics executive*

**Carson**
Bensussen, Gale K. *health products company executive*
Berenato, Joseph C. *manufacturing executive*
Heiser, James S. *manufacturing executive*

**Chatsworth**
Bhartia, Prakash *defense research management executive, researcher, educator*

**Chino**
Goodman, Lindsey Alan *furniture manufacturing executive, architect*

**City Of Industry**
Fernandez, Manuel G. *food products executive*
Perry, William Joseph *food processing company executive*

**Claremont**
Forti, William Bell *manufacturing executive*

**Colusa**
Carter, Jane Foster *agricultural industry executive*

**Corona**
Chao, Allen Y. *pharmaceutical executive*

**Coronado**
Sack, Edgar Albert *electronics company executive*

**Costa Mesa**
Mohajer, Dineh *cosmetics company executive*

**Cowan Heights**
Ruttencutter, Brian Boyle *manufacturing company executive*

**Crestline**
Merrill, Steven William *research and development company executive*

**Culver City**
Leve, Alan Donald *electronics executive*

**Cupertino**
Mathias, Leslie Michael *electronic manufacturing company executive*
Sobrato, John A. *construction executive*

**Cypress**
Garrett, Sharon *health services company executive*

**Dublin**
Whetten, John D. *food products executive*

**El Segundo**
Thiry, Kent J. *health products executive*

**Emeryville**
Chiasson, William B. *electronic games exeutive*
Goldstein, Jack *biopharmaceutical executive, microbiologist*
Kalinske, Thomas J. *education, video game and toy company executive*
Katz, Jeffrey G. *electronic games executive*
Pien, Howard *pharmaceutical executive*
Renton, Hollings C. *health products executive*

**Escalon**
Barton, Gerald Lee *food products executive*

**Fair Oaks**
Chernev, Melvin *retired beverage company executive*

**Foster City**
Bischofberger, Norbert W. *medical products company executive*
Denny, James M. *pharmaceutical executive, former retail executive*
Martin, John C. *pharmaceutical company executive*

**Fountain Valley**
Hoffman, Richard W. *automotive executive*

**Fremont**
Bagley, James W. *semiconductor equipment company executive*
Huang, Robert *electronics executive*
Korn, Laurence *health products executive*
Newberry, Stephen G. *semiconductor equipment company executive*
Rusch, Thomas William *manufacturing executive*
Zimmer, George A. *men's apparel executive*

**Fullerton**
Garrett, Scott T. *medical products executive*
McNamee, Lawrence Ross, Jr. *manufacturing executive*
Miller, Arnold *electronics executive*
Wareham, John P. *medical products executive*

**Hillsborough**
Keller, John Francis *retired food products executive, mayor*

**Hollywood**
Parks, Robert Myers *appliance manufacturing company executive*

**Huntington Beach**
McKnight, Robert B., Jr. *sporting goods manufacturing executive*

**Indio**
York, Douglas Arthur *manufacturing and construction company executive*

**Irvine**
Alspach, Philip Halliday *manufacturing executive*
Cortney, Michael C. *construction executive, civil engineer*
McGregor, Scott A. *electronics company executive*
Pyott, David Edmund Ian *pharmaceutical executive*
Scarborough, Stephen J. *construction executive*

Wetterau, Mark S. *food products/distributor executive*

**La Jolla**
Elander, Richard Paul *microbiologist, consultant*
Geckler, Richard Delph *retired metal products executive*
Snyder, Evan *cloning and stem cell company administrator, educator, neuroscientist*

**La Puente**
Hitchcock, Frederick E., Jr., (Fritz Hitchcock) *automotive company executive*

**La Quinta**
Sylk, Robert F. *casino marketing executive*

**Lake Forest**
Higby, Lawrence M. *medical products executive*
McCurley, Thomas W. *manufacturing executive*

**Lompoc**
Bongiorno, James William *electronics executive*

**Los Altos**
Beer, Clara Louise Johnson *retired electronics executive*

**Los Angeles**
Adler, Fred Peter *retired electronics company executive*
Bennett, Joel Herbert *construction executive*
Birren, James Emmett *research and development company executive*
Brodie, Simon *genetic cloning company executive*
Bush, Wes *defense, technology contracting executive*
Campion, Robert Thomas *manufacturing executive*
Davidson, Robert C., Jr. *manufacturing executive*
dePaolis, Potito Umberto *food company executive*
Emanuele, R.M. *pharmaceutical executive*
Hannah, David H. *metal products executive*
Hutchins, Joan Morthland *manufacturing executive, farmer*
Karatz, Bruce E. *construction executive*
Marciano, Maurice *apparel executive*
Perkins, William Clinton *manufacturing executive*
Resnick, Stewart Allen *diversified company executive*
Tamkin, S. Jerome *manufacturing executive, consultant*

**Lynwood**
Nelson, Maurice Sandy, Jr. *metal products company executive*

**Mckinleyville**
Thueson, David Orel *pharmaceutical executive, researcher, writer, educator*

**Menlo Park**
Bremser, George, Jr. *electronics executive*
Carlson, Curtis R. *electronics research industry executive*
Halperin, Robert Milton *retired electrical machinery company executive*
Jackson, Jeanne Pellegren *apparel executive*
Kamin, William Stephen *food products executive, photographer*
Litvack, Frank *medical products executive*
Marks, Michael E. *electronics executive*
Moos, Walter Hamilton *pharmaceutical company executive*
Saifer, Mark Gary Pierce *pharmaceutical executive*
Westcott, Brian John *manufacturing executive*

**Milpitas**
Cannon, Michael R. *electronics executive*
Hasler, William Albert *electronics executive*
Lin Chien, Chester *electronics executive*
London, Craig *electronics executive*
Moore, George W. *electronics executive*
O'Connor, Kevin *electronics executive*
Patel, Kiran *manufacturing executive*
Wang, Susan S. *manufacturing executive*

**Mission Viejo**
Faley, Robert Lawrence *retired instruments company executive*

**Modesto**
Long, David R. *food products executive*

**Montecito**
Meghreblian, Robert Vartan *manufacturing executive, physicist*
Purl, O. Thomas *retired electronics company executive*

**Monterey**
Hanlon, James Allison *confectionery company executive*
Nesheim, Robert Olaf *retired food products executive*

**Newport Beach**
Bennett, Bruce W. *retired construction executive, civil engineer*
Johnson, William Stanley *metal distribution company executive*
Lyon, William, Sr. *construction executive*
Rogers, Robert Reed *manufacturing executive*

**North Hills**
Iacocca, Lee (Lido Anthony Iacocca) *retired automotive manufacturing executive, venture capitalist*

**Oakland**
Batarse, Anthony Abraham, Jr. *automotive executive*
Heinrich, Daniel J. *chemicals executive*

**Oakville**
Mondavi, Robert Gerald *winery executive*

**Oxnard**
Kavli, Fred *retired manufacturing executive, retired engineering executive*

**Palm Desert**
Epstein, Marvin Morris *retired construction company executive*

**Palm Springs**
Brain, Jesse *manufacturing executive*

**Palo Alto**
Balzhiser, Richard Earl *research and development company executive*
Staprans, Armand *electronics executive*
Sullivan, William P. *electronics executive*
Wick, Michael M. *biotechnology executive*

**Palos Verdes Estates**
Mackenbach, Frederick W. *welding products manufacturing company executive*

**Palos Verdes Peninsula**
Grant, Robert Ulysses *retired manufacturing executive*
Leone, William Charles *retired manufacturing executive*
Thomas, Hayward *manufacturing executive*
Wilson, Theodore Henry *retired electronics executive, aerospace engineer*

**Pasadena**
Bishop, Robert Calvin *pharmaceutical company executive*
Hunter, Milton *construction company executive, retired career military officer*
Marlen, James S. *chemical, plastics and building materials manufacturing company executive*
McNulty, James F. *construction company executive*
O'Bryant, Daniel R. *manufacturing executive*
Smith, Howard Russell *manufacturing executive, director*
Tollenaere, Lawrence Robert *retired industrial products company executive*
Wadden, Christopher David *food products executive*
Watson, Noel G. *construction executive*

**Placerville**
Magelitz, Larry L. *construction company executive*
Sundgren, Donald E. *construction executive*

**Playa Del Rey**
Mishelevich, David Jacob *medical products executive*

**Pleasanton**
Gordon, Robert A. *food products executive, lawyer*
White, James D. *food products executive*

**Pomona**
Arriaga, Jesus V. *automotive parts company executive*

**Portola Valley**
Graham, William James *packaging company executive*

**Prather**
Coren, Lance Scott *automotive executive, consultant*

**Rancho Dominguez**
Janura, Jan Arol *apparel manufacturing executive*

**Rancho Murieta**
Irelan, Robert Withers *retired metal products executive*

**Rancho Santa Fe**
Derbes, Daniel William *manufacturing executive*
Jordan, Charles Morrell *retired automotive designer*
Step, Eugene Lee *retired pharmaceutical executive*

**Redding**
Emmerson, Archie Aldis (Red Emmerson, A.A. Emmerson) *sawmill owner*

**Redondo Beach**
Kagiwada, Reynold Shigeru *electronics executive*

**Redwood City**
Nosler, Peter Cole *construction company executive*
Wang, Chen Chi *electronics executive, real estate company executive, diversified financial services company executive*

**Rescue**
Ackerly, Wendy Saunders *construction company executive*

**Richmond**
Biddle, Michael *plastics company executive*

**Riverside**
Chamberlain, Willard Thomas *retired metal products executive*
Plowman, Boyd R. *automotive executive*
Smith, Elden Leroy *recreational vehicle and manufactured housing company executive*

**Rocklin**
Tal, Jacob *electronics executive*

**Sacramento**
Aldrich, Thomas Albert *former brewing executive, consultant*
Baccigaluppi, Roger John *agricultural products executive*

**San Anselmo**
Chiaverini, John Edward *construction company executive*

**San Carlos**
Gutow, Bernard Sidney *packaging manufacturing company executive*
Love, Ted W. *biotechnology company executive*

**San Clemente**
Clark, Earnest Hubert, Jr. *tool company executive*

Lopez, George A. *medical products executive*
Steinberg, Howard *chemical company executive, consultant*

**San Diego**
Devine, Brian Kiernan *pet food and supplies company executive*
Duddles, Charles Weller *food company executive*
Graham, Ginger L. *pharmaceutical executive*
Iversen, Leslie Lars *pharmaceutical executive*
Knuth, Dean Leslie *research and development company executive, golf consultant, writer*
Lewis, Alan James *pharmaceutical executive, pharmacologist*
Lundy-Slade, Bettie B. *retired electronics executive*
Ray, Gene Wells *industrial executive*
Rice, Clare I. *electronics company executive*
Rohn, William R. *biotechnology company executive*
Samant, Vijay B. *biotechnology company executive*
Shawver, Laura K. *biotechnology company executive*
Spanos, Alexander Gus *construction executive, professional sports team executive*
Theuer, Charles P. *pharmaceutical executive, researcher*
Thomas, Robert McGuffey *automotive executive, educator*

**San Francisco**
Anderson, R. John *apparel executive*
Campbell, Jeffrey C. *pharmaceutical executive*
Colman, Shoshana S. *pharmaceutical executive, researcher*
Haas, Robert Douglas *apparel executive*
Hammergren, John H. *pharmaceutical executive*
Hawkins, Trip *electronics executive*
Jewett, George Frederick, Jr. *forest products company executive*
Julian, Paul C. *health products executive*
Lyon, David William *research executive*
Marineau, Philip Albert *apparel executive*
McCauley, Matthew K. *apparel executive*
Mellor, Robert E. *building materials company executive, lawyer*
Ming, Jenny J. *retail apparel company executive*
Moreno, Albert F. *apparel executive, lawyer*
Morris-Tyndall, Lucy *construction executive*
Owen, Marc *health products executive*
Ross, Ivy *apparel executive, artist*
Seeger, Laureen E. *health products executive*
Seelenfreund, Alan *retired pharmaceutical company executive*
Shackley, Douglas John *fire alarm company executive*
Slipsager, Henrik C. *building services company executive*
Spratt, Randall N. *health products executive*
Tully, Herbert Bullard *chemical manufacturing executive*
Wolford, Richard G. *food products executive*
Zellerbach, William Joseph *retired paper company executive*

**San Jose**
Bell, W. Donald *electronics executive*
Fry, John C. *electronics executive*
Furr, Randy W. *electronics manufacturing executive*
Hill, Richard S. *manufacturing executive*
Maekawa, Koji Ogura *technology company administrator*
Perlegos, George *electronics executive*
Quadros, Paul D. *health products executive*
Russo, Paul M. *electronics executive*
Schroeder, Kenneth L. *electronics executive*
Sola, Jure *electronics executive*
White, David L. *electronics executive*
Zafiropoulo, Arthur *electronics executive*
Zaro, Brad A. *research and development company executive, biologist*

**San Mateo**
Kennedy, W(ilbert) Keith, Jr. *retired electronics executive, transportation executive*
Rabbat, Guy *electronics executive, consultant*

**Santa Barbara**
Coffin, Dwight Clay *retired grain company executive*
Levine, Joshua H. *medical products executive*
Mikhailovsky, Alexander *research and development company executive*
Potter, David Samuel *former automotive company executive*
Prindle, William Roscoe *retired glass company executive*

**Santa Clara**
Barrett, Craig R. *electronics company executive*
Barrett, Ronald W. *biopharmaceutical executive*
Dorchak, Glenda *electronics company executive*
Elkus, Richard J., Jr. *electronics company executive*
Faggin, Federico *electronics executive*
Grove, Andrew Steven *electronics executive*
Gutierrez, Si *electronics executive*
Halla, Brian L. *electronics executive*
Huang, Jen-Hsun *electronics executive*
Moore, Gordon E. *electronics executive, researcher*
Morgan, James C. *manufacturing executive*
Murray, Patricia *electronics company executive*
Otellini, Paul S. *electronics company executive*
Splinter, Michael R. *manufacturing executive*

**Santa Rosa**
Jackson, Jess S. *vintner*

**Santee**
Cantor, Thomas *research and development company executive*

**Saratoga**
Houston, Joseph Brantley, Jr. *optical instrument company executive*
Rollo, F. David *healthcare company executive, cardiologist*

**Sausalito**
Hawthorne, Lou *genetic cloning research company executive, researcher*
Polejaeva, Irina *genetic cloning company executive, researcher*

**Sherman Oaks**
Reiner, Thomas Karl *manufacturing executive, engineering scientist*

**Simi Valley**
Lewis, Richard B. *manufacturing and logistics executive*

**South San Francisco**
Brewer, Richard B. *biotechnology company executive*
Desmond-Hellmann, Susan *medical products manufacturing executive*
Gower, James M. *biotechnology company executive*
Lipsky, Ian David *manufacturing executive, science administrator, director*
Potter, Myrtle S. *research and development company executive*

**Stanford**
Elliott, David Duncan III *science company executive*
Miller, William Frederick *research and development company executive, educator, financial consultant*

**Sunnyvale**
Brachman, Ron *research and development company executive*
Burkett, Marvin D. *electronics executive*
McCollam, Craig A. *manufacturing executive*

**Thousand Oaks**
Dahl, Richard J. *food products executive*
Nanula, Richard *health products executive*
Sharer, Kevin W. *medical products company executive*

**Torrance**
Amemiya, Koichi *motor vehicle company executive*
Pfund, Edward Theodore, Jr. *electronics company executive*

**Tustin**
Hester, Norman Eric *chemical company technical executive, chemist*

**Ukiah**
Newell, Barbara Ann *coatings company executive*

**Upland**
Goodman, John M. *construction executive*

**Valencia**
Mann, Alfred *pharmaceutical executive*

**Vallejo**
Womack, Thomas Houston *manufacturing executive*

**Ventura**
Barber, Jerry Randel *medical device company executive*
Chouinard, Yvon *sportswear outfitter executive*

**Vernon**
Gavina, Pedro *coffee company executive*

**Villa Park**
Hawe, David Lee *manufacturing consultant, venture capitalist*

**Walnut**
Johnson, Keith Liddell *retired chemicals executive*

**Watsonville**
Dorey, William G. *construction executive*
Watts, David H. *construction company executive*

**West Hollywood**
Estevez, Luis de Galvez *designer, manufacturer*

**Westlake Village**
Colburn, Keith W. *electronics executive*
Murdock, David H. *food products executive*
Nichols, Steven *apparel executive*

**Wilmington**
Hamai, James Yutaka *manufacturing executive*

**Woodland Hills**
Gellert, Jay M. *health and medical products executive*
Morishita, Akihiko *manufacturing executive*

**Woodside**
Gates, Milo Sedgwick *retired construction company executive*

## COLORADO

**Arvada**
Holden, George Fredric *food products executive, consultant, public information officer, writer*

**Boulder**
Clark, Melvin Eugene *chemical company executive*
Mancino, John Gregory *software company executive*

**Breckenridge**
Ehrhorn, Richard William *electronics executive*

**Broomfield**
Hoover, R. David *packaging company executive*

**Denver**
Alvarado, Linda G. *construction executive*
Barry, Henry Ford *chemicals executive*

Boyer, William Joseph *food products executive*
Ferguson, Bruce A. *construction executive, contractor*
Hohner, Kenneth Dwayne *retired fodder company executive*
Leprino, James G. *food products executive*
Livingston, Johnston Redmond *manufacturing executive*
Mizel, Larry A. *housing construction company executive*
Oakes, Terry Louis *apparel executive*
Shaffer, Oren George *former manufacturing company executive*
Shaw, Michael Joseph *automotive executive*
Wolf, Timothy Van de Wint *food products executive*

**Durango**
Crail, Franklin E. *food products executive*

**Englewood**
Chavez, L.G., Jr., (Lloyd G. Chavez Jr.) *automotive executive*
Chavez, Lloyd G. *automotive executive*
Gertz, David Lee *homebuilding company executive*
Malone, James Richard *manufacturing executive*
Rheney, Susan O. *paper company executive*

**Golden**
Coors, Jeffrey H. *technology manufacturing executive*
Coors, Peter Hanson *brewery company executive*
Kiely, W. Leo III *brewery company executive*

**Greeley**
Carrico, Stephen J. *construction company executive*
Cordell, Larry Kenneth (L. Kenny) *agricultural products executive*
James, Philip J. *agricultural products executive*
Morgensen, Jerry Lynn *construction company executive*

**Greenwood Village**
Appel, Joel *household cleaner manufacturing executive*

**Jefferson**
Maatsch, Deborah Joan *manufacturing executive*

**Lakewood**
Heath, Gary Brian *manufacturing executive, engineer*

**Littleton**
Battilega, John A. *research and development company executive*

**Longmont**
Breuer, Werner Alfred *retired plastics company executive*
Zable, Barbara A. *manufacturing executive*

**Monument**
Karasa, Norman Lukas *home builder, developer, geologist*

**Wellington**
Grant, Lewis O. *agricultural products executive, meteorology educator*

**Westminster**
Michael, Hart E. *pharmaceutical executive*

## CONNECTICUT

**Bloomfield**
Coburn, Richard Joseph *electronics executive, electrical engineer*

**Branford**
Chapman, Roger Stevens, Jr. *construction company executive*

**Bridgeport**
Semple, Cecil Snowdon *retired manufacturing executive*

**Bristol**
Barnes, Carlyle Fuller *manufacturing executive*
Barnes, Wallace *manufacturing executive*

**Broad Brook**
Kement, Isabella Viniconis *retired construction company executive*

**Cheshire**
Keiser, David Wharton *pharmaceutical executive*

**Danbury**
Angel, Stephen F. *chemicals executive*
Martens, Juergen A. *pharmaceutical executive*
Reilley, Dennis H. *chemicals executive*
Sawyer, James S. *manufacturing executive*

**Darien**
Dordelman, William Forsyth *food company executive*
Sprole, Frank Arnott *retired pharmaceutical executive, lawyer*

**Dayville**
Funk, Michael S. *food products executive*
Townsend, Steven H. *food products executive*

**East Granby**
Kozlowski, Michael *automotive equipment executive*

**East Hartford**
Cassidy, John Francis, Jr. *industrial technology executive*

**Fairfield**
Beccalli, Ferdinando *manufacturing executive*
Daley, Pamela *diversified services, technology and manufacturing company executive*
Henson, Daniel S. *manufacturing executive*

Sherin, Keith S. *electrical manufacturing company executive*

**Greenwich**
Cameron, Dort *electronics executive*
Dettmer, Robert Gerhart *retired beverage company executive*
Farbish, Alfred B. *waterproofing materials executive*
Mango, Wilfred Gilbert, Jr. *construction executive, real estate company executive*
Van Dijk, Frits *food products executive*

**Hartford**
Chênevert, Louis *manufacturing executive*
David, George Alfred Lawrence *manufacturing executive*
Hermann, Robert Jay *former manufacturing executive, consultant*

**Lyme**
Bloom, Barry Malcolm *research and development company executive, consultant*

**Madison**
Golembeski, Jerome John *manufacturing executive*

**Middlebury**
Fickenscher, Gerald H. *chemicals company executive*
Wood, R. L. (Bob Wood) *chemicals executive*

**Milford**
Palazzi, Joseph Lazarro *manufacturing executive*

**Naugatuck**
Flannery, Joseph Patrick *manufacturing executive, director*

**New Canaan**
Burns, Ivan Alfred *grocery products and industrial company executive*
Sachs, John Peter *carbon company executive*

**New Haven**
Jacob, Deirdre Ann Bradbury *manufacturing executive, finance educator, consultant*

**North Branford**
Ingram, George *manufacturing executive*
Mead, Lawrence Myers, Jr. *retired manufacturing executive*

**Norwalk**
Guzzi, Anthony J. *construction executive*
Harris, Holton Edwin *plastics machinery manufacturing executive*
MacInnis, Frank T. *construction executive, securities trader, holding company executive*
White, Tony L. *health and medical products executive*

**Plainville**
Glassman, Gerald Seymour *metal products executive*

**Ridgefield**
Levine, Paul Michael *paper company executive, consultant*

**Riverside**
Deering, Allan Brooks *retired soft drink company executive*

**Somers**
Blake, Stewart Prestley *retired ice cream company executive*

**South Kent**
Samartini, James Rogers *retired appliance company executive*

**Southport**
Wheeler, Wilmot Fitch, Jr. *diversified manufacturing company executive*

**Stamford**
Balduino, Michael J. *paper company executive*
Buzzard, James A. *paper, packaging and chemical company executive*
Caldwell, Philip *retired automobile manufacturing company executive, retired finance company executive*
Evans, Robert Sheldon *manufacturing executive, director*
Faraci, John Vincent, Jr. *paper company executive*
Fast, Eric Carson *manufacturing executive*
Friedman, Michael *pharmaceutical executive*
Gladstone, Herbert Jack *manufacturing executive*
Harper, Arthur H. *manufacturing executive*
Horrigan, D. Gregory *packaging products executive*
Lesko, Newland A. *paper company executive*
Levitan, Gutman *research and development company executive, communications engineer*
Luke, John Anderson, Jr. *paper, packaging and chemical company executive*
Martin, Murray D. *manufacturing executive*
Motroni, Hector John *manufacturing executive*
Munera, Gerard Emmanuel *manufacturing executive*
Nevans, Roy Norman *food products executive, producer*
Parrs, Marianne M. *paper and lumber company executive*
Sackler, Mortimer D.A. *pharmaceutical executive*
Silver, R. Philip *packaging products executive*
Smith, J. Gordon *automotive executive*
Thomas, Dennis *retired paper company executive, retired federal official*
Udell, Howard R. *pharmaceutical executive*

**Thomaston**
Mühlanger, Erich *ski manufacturing company executive*

**Wallingford**
Cohen, Gordon S. *health products executive*
Jia, Weitao *dental products executive, researcher*
Loeffler, Martin H. *electronics executive*

**Waterbury**
Luedke, Frederick Lee *manufacturing executive*
Wood, Robert L. *chemicals executive*

**West Hartford**
Clear, Albert F., Jr. *retired hardware manufacturing company executive*
Raffay, Stephen Joseph *manufacturing executive, director*

**Westport**
Baker, Leonard Morton *manufacturing executive*
Breitbarth, S. Robert *manufacturing executive*
Defeo, Ronald M. *machinery manufacturing executive*
Hedge, Arthur Joseph, Jr. *manufacturing executive*
Widman, Phillip C. *machinery manufacturing executive*

## DELAWARE

**Dagsboro**
Mortenson, Thomas Theodore *health products executive, management consultant*

**Greenville**
Walker, Sally Barbara *retired glass company executive*

**Newark**
Gantzer, Mary Lou *medical products executive*

**Rockland**
Rubin, Alan A. *pharmaceutical and biotechnology consultant*

**Wilmington**
Borel, James Calvin *chemical company executive*
Donnelly, Edward J., Jr. *pharmaceutical executive*
Frywald, J. Erik *agricultural products executive*
Hodgson, John C. *manufacturing executive*
Holliday, Chad (Charles O. Holliday Jr.) *chemicals executive*
Johnson, W. Donald *research and development company executive*
Krol, John A. *retired diversified chemicals executive*
Kullman, Ellen Jamison *chemicals executive*
Lassen, John Kai *development company executive*
McLeer, Laureen Dorothy *drug development and pharmaceutical professional*
Pfeiffer, Gary M. *chemicals executive*
Rogerson, Craig Allan *manufacturing executive*
Rose, Selwyn H. *chemicals executive*
Sager, Philip Travis *pharmaceutical executive, cardiologist, researcher*
Uffner, Michael S. *automotive executive*
Vaddi, Krishna *pharmaceutical executive*

## DISTRICT OF COLUMBIA

**Washington**
Brown, Lester Russell *research and development company executive*
Buto, Kathleen A. *health products executive*
Choudhury, Raj Deo *automotive executive*
Clark, Jeffrey Raphiel *research and development company executive*
Cole, Kenneth W. *automotive executive*
Culp, H. Lawrence *manufacturing executive*
Girod, Bernard A. *electronics executive*
Giuliano, Louis J. *former industrial manufacturing company executive*
Griffin, Robert Thomas *automotive company executive*
Halperin, Jerome Arthur *retired pharmaceutical executive*
Harman, Sidney *audio and video company executive*
Herrett, Richard Allison *agricultural research institute administrator*
Kelly, Marguerite Stehli *fashion executive, consultant*
Mathews, Jessica Tuchman *research executive, federal official, newswriter*
Moore, Robert Madison *food products executive, lawyer*
Persinger, Del Louis *pharmaceutical company executive*
Principi, Anthony Joseph *pharmaceutical company executive, former secretary of veterans affairs*
Rales, Mitchell P. *automotive parts company executive*
Rales, Steven M. *automotive parts company executive*
Schorsch, Louis L. *metal products executive*
Shepherd, Alan J. *construction executive, management consultant*

## FLORIDA

**Amelia Island**
Adelman, Robert Paul *retired construction executive, lawyer*

**Anna Maria**
Kaiser, Albert Farr *manufacturing executive*

**Bartow**
Kincart, Robert Owen *technological executive*

**Boca Raton**
Feld, Joseph *construction executive*
Oussani, James John *manufacturing executive*
Wyatt, James Luther *drapery hardware company executive*

**Bonita Springs**
Costley, Gary Edward *food company executive*

**Boynton Beach**
Honeycutt, Kevin *construction executive, consultant*
Jensen, Reuben Rolland *former automotive company executive*

**Bradenton**
Bailey, Higgins D. *health products executive*
Carnes, James Edward *retired electronics executive*
Dudley, Perry, Jr. *retired electronics executive*
Howe, Carroll Victor *construction equipment company executive*
Price, Edgar Hilleary, Jr. *manufacturing executive, consultant*

**Cape Coral**
Stuart, Robert *container manufacturing executive*

**Clearwater**
Brady, Sheila Ann *manufacturing executive*
Brosious, Matthew James *manufacturing executive*
Chisholm, William DeWayne *retired construction contractor*
Kiehl, E. Robert *manufacturing executive, consultant*
Smith, Marion Pafford *retired avionics company executive*

**Coral Gables**
Burini, Sonia Montes de Oca *apparel manufacturing executive, public relations executive*

**Daytona Beach**
Scott, John Brooks *retired research and development company executive*

**Deerfield Beach**
Brown, Colin *automotive executive*

**Delray Beach**
Goldenberg, George *retired pharmaceutical executive*
Jacobson, Herbert Leonard *electronics executive*

**Fernandina Beach**
Ash, Frederick Melvin *retired manufacturing executive*

**Fort Lauderdale**
Craib, Kenneth Bryden *research and development company executive, physicist, economist*
Jackson, Michael J. *automotive retail company executive*
Levy, Michael *electronic manufacturing company executive*
Monaghan, Craig Thomas *automotive executive*
Peltzer, Douglas Lea *manufacturing executive*
Rojas, Jesus Jon *health products executive, researcher*

**Fort Myers**
Haug, Warren R. *research and development consultant*
Wendeborn, Richard Donald *retired manufacturing executive*

**Green Cove Springs**
Slade, Tom *manufacturing executive, political organization worker*

**Heathrow**
Darbelnet, Robert Louis *automobile association executive*

**Hialeah**
Engler, Eva Kay *dental and veterinary products company executive*
Fernandez, Jose L. *construction executive*

**Highland Beach**
Frager, Albert S. *retired food products executive*

**Hobe Sound**
Casey, Edward Paul *manufacturing executive*

**Hollywood**
Isenberg, Abraham Charles *shoe manufacturing company executive*
Spencer, Richard Thomas III *health products executive*

**Indian River Shores**
Wiegner, Edward Alex *manufacturing executive*

**Islamorada**
Gates, Richard Daniel *retired manufacturing executive*

**Jacksonville**
Jackson, Julian Ellis *food company executive*
Jones, Herman Otto, Jr. *agricultural products executive*
Kanders, Warren Beatty *manufacturing executive, investment banker*
Smith, David A. *medical services executive*
Welch, Philip Burland *electronics and office products company executive*

**Jupiter**
Feinberg, Herbert *apparel executive, real estate company executive*
Garfinkel, Harmon Mark *retired specialty chemicals company executive*

**Key Largo**
Davidson, Thomas Noel *metal products executive*

**Lady Lake**
Akins, Zane Vernon *agricultural products executive*

**Lake Mary**
Bindley, William Edward *pharmaceutical executive*

**Lakeland**
Hatten, William Seward *manufacturing executive, consultant*
Mutz, Oscar Ulysses *manufacturing and distribution executive*

**Largo**
MacDonald, Joseph Lester *retired metal products executive*

**Longwood**
Palmer, R. Scott *food products executive, educator*
Zahn, Richard Gregory *construction executive*

**Marco Island**
Guerrant, David Edward *retired food company executive*

**Medley**
Quirch, Guillermo, Jr., (Bill Quirch) *food distribution executive*

**Melbourne**
Buchanan, Richard Kent *electronics company executive*

**Melbourne Beach**
Glaubinger, Lawrence David *retired manufacturing company executive*

**Merritt Island**
Roub, Bryan R(oger) *electronics executive*

**Miami**
Borkan, William Noah *electronics executive, biomedical engineer, entrepreneur, venture capitalist, real estate developer*
Braman, Norman *automotive executive, former sports team executive*
Casares, Raul *manufacturing executive*
de Cespedes, Carlos M. *pharmaceutical executive*
de Cespedes, Jorge L. *pharmaceutical executive*
Diaz Oliver, Remedios *manufacturing executive*
Feldenkreis, George *apparel executive*
Frigo, James Peter Paul *industrial hardware company executive*
Frost, Phillip *pharmaceutical executive, dermatologist*
Nahmad, Albert H. *manufacturing executive*
Planas, Carlos *automotive executive*
Risi, Louis James, Jr. *manufacturing executive*

**Miami Beach**
Lanzkron, Rolf Wolfgang *manufacturing executive*

**Miramar**
Rissmann, William John *medical products executive*

**Naples**
Askins, Wallace Boyd *manufacturing executive*
Baldwin, Ralph Belknap *retired manufacturing executive, astronomer*
Butler, Frederick George *retired drug company executive*
Gade, Marvin Francis *retired paper company executive*
LaRusso, Anthony Carl *company executive, educator*
Salentine, Thomas James *pharmaceutical executive*
Sampson, John Eugene *food products executive, consultant*
Sekowski, Cynthia Jean *health products executive, medical consultant, contact lens specialist*
Vanderslice, Thomas Aquinas *electronics executive*
von Arx, Dolph William *food products executive*

**New Port Richey**
Lake, Victor Hugo *former manufacturing company executive*
Vajk, Hugo *manufacturing executive*

**North Palm Beach**
Freidheim, Cyrus F., Jr. *food products executive*
Hood, Edward Exum, Jr. *retired electronics executive*

**Orlando**
Brownlee, Thomas Marshall *manufacturing executive*
Cawthon, Frank H. *retired construction company executive*
Hughes, David Henry *manufacturing executive*
Morgan, Thomas I. *manufacturing executive*
Smyth, Joseph Vincent *manufacturing executive*
Wallace, Derrick Donnell *construction executive, accountant*

**Ormond Beach**
Connors, Michele Perrott *wholesale beverage company executive*

**Palm Beach**
Karman, James Anthony *manufacturing executive*

**Palm Beach Gardens**
Fleisher, Seymour *manufacturing executive*
Jaffe, Jeff Hugh *retired food products executive*
Staub, W. Arthur *health care products executive*

**Palm City**
Conklin, George Melville *retired food products executive*
Wishart, Ronald Sinclair *retired chemical company executive*

**Palm Coast**
Lewis, William Headley, Jr. *manufacturing executive*

**Palm Harbor**
Bennett, John Joseph *electronics executive*
Grace, John Eugene *business forms company executive*

**Pensacola**
Jones, Harry Gordon *electronics executive*

**Reddick**
Corwin, Joyce Elizabeth Stedman *construction company executive*

**Saint Petersburg**
Dimas, Marilyn J. *health products executive*
Lewis, Chris A. *manufacturing executive*
Main, Timothy L. *electronics company executive*
Mills, William Harold, Jr. *construction executive*
Mondello, Mark T. *manufacturing executive*
Morean, William D. *manufacturing executive*

**Franklin Park**
Simpson, Michael *retired metals service center executive*

**Glen Ellyn**
Cvengros, Joseph Michael *manufacturing company executive*

**Glenview**
Blase, Anthony Idomeneus *retired electronics executive, writer, poet*
Bruns, Nicolaus, Jr. *retired agricultural products executive, lawyer, educator*
Gillis, Marvin Bob *retired chemical executive, consultant*
Hickey, John Thomas *retired electronics company executive*
Kinney, Jon C. *metal products executive*
Mc Nitt, Willard Charles *food products executive*
Smith, Harold B. *manufacturing executive*

**Highland Park**
Hulseman, Robert L. *manufacturing executive*
Korzenski, Robert M. *manufacturing executive*
Rudo, Milton *retired manufacturing executive*

**Hoffman Estates**
Nicholas, Arthur Soterios *manufacturing executive*

**Itasca**
Fellowes, James *manufacturing executive*
Garratt, Reginald George *electronics executive*

**Lake Forest**
Begley, Christopher B. *pharmaceutical executive*
Campbell, Andrew *manufacturing executive*
Carroll, Barry Joseph *manufacturing and real estate executive*
Clark, Wesley M. *manufacturing executive*
Damico, Joseph F. *medical products executive*
Donovan, Timothy R. *automotive executive, lawyer*
Dreimann, Leonhard *manufacturing executive*
Hamilton, Peter Bannerman *manufacturing executive, lawyer*
Hammar, Lester Everett *retired manufacturing executive*
Haser, William H. *automotive executive*
Keyser, Richard Lee *distribution company executive*
Larson, Peter N. *manufacturing executive*
Leemputte, Peter G. *manufacturing executive*
McCoy, Dustan Elwood *manufacturing executive, lawyer*
Romans, Donald Bishop *manufacturing executive*
Trammell, Kenneth R. *automotive executive*

**Lanark**
Abbott, David Henry *manufacturing executive*

**Lincolnshire**
Anderson, David J. *manufacturing executive*
Carbonari, Bruce A. *metal products executive*
Lemonis, Marcus *automotive executive*
Simes, Stephen Mark *pharmaceutical executive*
Wesley, Norman H. *metal products executive*

**Lisle**
Krehbiel, Frederick August, II, *electronics executive*
Krehbiel, John H., Jr. *retired electronics company executive*
Slark, Martin P. *electronics executive*

**Mc Gaw Park**
Kesman, Anthony K. *medical products executive*

**Melrose Park**
Bernick, Howard Barry *manufacturing executive*
Lavin, Bernice E. *cosmetics executive*
Wechter, Clari Ann *manufacturing executive*

**Moline**
Jones, Nathan Jerome *farm machinery manufacturing company executive*
Lane, Robert W. *farm equipment manufacturing executive*
Milberg, Joachim *retired automotive executive*

**Mount Sterling**
Tracy, Patrick F. *food products executive*

**Mundelein**
Raviv, Gabriel *medical products executive*

**Muscatine**
Housh, E. William *manufacturing executive*

**Naperville**
Katai, Andrew Andras *chemical company executive*
Smetana, Mark *food products executive*
Wake, Richard W. *food products executive*
Wake, Thomas G. *food products executive*

**Niles**
Herb, Marvin J. *food products executive*

**Northbrook**
Green, David *manufacturing executive*

**Northfield**
Carlin, Donald Walter *retired food products executive, consultant*
Hadley, Stanton Thomas *manufacturing executive, director, lawyer*
Knight, James Atwood *manufacturing executive*
Lynch, Kirsten *food products executive*
Pratt, Murray Lester *manufacturing executive*
Rosenfeld, Irene B. *food products company executive*
Smeds, Edward William *retired food company executive*
Sneed, Paula Ann *food products executive*
Stepan, Frank Quinn *chemicals executive*
Stepan, Frank Quinn, Jr. (F. Quinn Stepan Jr.) *chemical company executive*

**Oak Brook**
Alvarez, Ralph *food products executive*

**Armario**, Jose *restaurant executive*
Onstead, R. Randall, Jr. *food products executive*
Skinner, James A. (James A. Skinner) *food products executive*
Thompson, Don *food products executive*

**Orland Park**
Gittelman, Marc Jeffrey *manufacturing and financial executive*

**Palatine**
Matsushima, Akira Paul *manufacturing executive*

**Palos Park**
Nelson, Lawrence Evan *manufacturing executive, consultant*

**Peoria**
Owens, James W. *manufacturing executive*

**Prospect Heights**
Byrne, Michael Joseph *manufacturing executive*

**River Forest**
Douglas, Kenneth Jay *food products executive*

**Rockford**
Bippus, David Paul *manufacturing executive*
O'Donnell, William David *retired construction firm executive*

**Rosemont**
Meinert, John Raymond *apparel executive, investment banker*
Reyes, J. Christopher *food products distribution executive*

**Schaumburg**
Delaney, Eugene A. *electronics executive*
Desai, Samir T. *electronics executive*
Galvin, Robert W. *electronics executive*
Soderberg, Leif G. *electronics company executive*
Soon-Shiong, Patrick *pharmaceutical executive*

**Trenton**
Barnett, Thomas Glen *manufacturing executive*

**Union**
Perlick, Richard Allan *steel company executive*

**Vernon Hills**
Kaplan, Edward L. *electronics executive*

**Warrenville**
Horne, John R. *farm equipment company executive*
Lannert, Robert Cornelius *manufacturing executive*

**Westchester**
Faison, Ralph E. *communications equipment manufacturing executive*
Scott, Samuel C. *food products executive*

**Wheeling**
Keats, Glenn Arthur *manufacturing executive*

**Wilmette**
Coughlan, Gary Patrick *pharmaceutical executive*
Pearlman, Jerry Kent *electronics company executive*

**Winnetka**
Markey, Maurice *food products executive*
Puth, John Wells *manufacturing executive, consultant*
Weldon, Theodore Tefft, Jr. *manufacturing executive*

**Wood Dale**
Storch, David *manufacturing executive*

**Woodridge**
Stall, Alan David *packaging company executive*

## INDIANA

**Anderson**
Carrell, Terry Eugene *manufacturing executive*

**Batesville**
Classon, Rolf Allan *pharmaceutical company executive*
Soderberg, Peter H. *health products executive*
Sorenson, Scott K. *manufacturing executive*

**Bloomington**
Cook, William Alfred *medical products executive*

**Brownstown**
Robertson, Joseph Edmond *grain processing company executive*

**Carmel**
Robertson, Stephen William *corporate compliance officer, government relations executive*
Shoup, Charles Samuel, Jr. *chemicals and materials executive*

**Columbus**
Boll, Charles Raymond *engine company executive*
Loughrey, R. Joseph *manufacturing executive*
Solso, Theodore M. *manufacturing executive*

**Elkhart**
Kloska, Ronald Frank *manufacturing executive*
Martin, Rex *manufacturing executive*
Mathias, Margaret Grossman *manufacturing company executive, leasing company executive*
Mischke, Frederick Charles *retired manufacturing executive*
Shuey, John Henry *manufacturing executive*

**Evansville**
Koch, Robert Louis, II, *manufacturing company executive, mechanical engineer*
Muehlbauer, James Herman *manufacturing and distribution executive*

**Fort Wayne**
Busse, Keith *manufacturing executive*

**Goshen**
Davis, Cole (Coleman Davis III) *recreational vehicle manufacturing executive*

**Indianapolis**
Brauer, Keith E. *medical products executive*
Dunayevich, Eduardo *pharmaceutical executive*
Hunt, Robert G. *construction company executive*
Kirkham, James Alvin *manufacturing executive*
Lacy, Andre Balz *industrial executive*
Lechleiter, John C. *pharmaceutical executive*
Lorell, Beverly H. *medical products executive*
Lugar, Thomas R. *manufacturing executive*
Mays, William G. *chemical company executive*
McConnell, William F., Jr. *medical products executive*
Mc Farland, H. Richard *food products executive*
Peribere, Jerome A. *agricultural products executive*
Ralston, Ronald Lee *manufacturing tradesman*
Rice, Derica *pharmaceutical company executive*
SerVaas, Beurt Richard *manufacturing executive*
Smith, K. Clay *machinery transport company executive*
Stewart, Paul Arthur *pharmaceutical company executive*
Taurel, Sidney *pharmaceutical executive*

**Lafayette**
Meyer, Brud Richard *retired pharmaceutical executive*

**Middlebury**
Corson, Thomas Harold *retired manufacturing executive*
Guequierre, John Phillip *manufacturing executive*

**Mishawaka**
Rubenstein, Pamela Silver *manufacturing executive*
Silver, Neil Marvin *manufacturing executive*

**Muncie**
Fisher, John Wesley *manufacturing executive, director*

**Munster**
Corsiglia, Robert Joseph *retired electrical construction company executive*

**Plainfield**
Laikin, Robert J. *electronics executive*

**Portage**
Popp, Joseph Bruce *manufacturing executive*

**Warsaw**
Elliott, J. Raymond *medical products executive*
Hann, Daniel P. *medical products executive, lawyer*
Noblitt, Niles L. *medical products executive*

**Washington**
Graham, David Bolden *food products executive*

## IOWA

**Ames**
Abbott, David L. *agricultural products executive*

**Cedar Rapids**
Erickson, Lawrence A. (Larry Erickson) *electronics executive*
Jones, Clayton M. *computer and electronics company executive*
Nyquist, John Davis *retired radio manufacturing company executive*

**Davenport**
Juckem, Wilfred Philip *manufacturing executive*

**Dubuque**
Crahan, Jack Bertsch *retired manufacturing executive*
Tully, Thomas Alois *building materials executive, consultant, educator*

**Humboldt**
Dodgen, John N. *manufacturing executive*

**Muscatine**
Askren, Stan A. *manufacturing executive*

**Newton**
Moore, George C. *manufacturing executive*

**Okoboji**
Pearson, Gerald Leon *food products executive*

**Pella**
Dout, Anne Jacqueline *manufacturing and sales company executive*

**Red Oak**
Stoner, Leonard D. *automotive parts company executive*

**Sioux City**
Bennett, Michael L. *agricultural products executive*

**Toddville**
Hazeltine, Gerald Lester *food products executive*

**West Des Moines**
Pomerantz, Marvin Alvin *manufacturing executive*

## KANSAS

**Abilene**
Britt, Ronald Leroy *retired manufacturing company executive*

**Hutchinson**
Dick, Harold Latham *manufacturing executive*

**Leawood**
Terry, Robert Brooks *food products executive, lawyer*

**Lenexa**
Ascher, James John *pharmaceutical executive*

**Mission**
Bresky, H. Harry *agricultural products executive*
Bresky, Steven J. *agricultural products executive*

**Olathe**
Burrell, Gary *retired manufacturing executive*
Kao, Min H. *manufacturing executive*

**Overland Park**
Linville, Randal L. *agricultural company executive*

**Paola**
Krum, Jack Kern *food products executive*

**Shawnee Mission**
Barger, Donald Gordon, Jr. *automotive products company executive*
Gamet, Donald Max *appliance company executive*

**Wichita**
Koch, David Hamilton *chemical company executive*

## KENTUCKY

**Bellevue**
Carpenter, Woodrow Wilson *manufacturing executive, ceramics engineer*

**Bowling Green**
Ahmed, S. Basheer *research and development company executive, educator*
Holland, John Ben *clothing manufacturing company executive*

**Covington**
Gemunder, Joel Frank *healthcare company executive*
O'Brien, James J. *manufacturing executive*

**Erlanger**
Cuneo, Dennis Clifford *automotive company executive*

**Fort Mitchell**
Drees, David G. *construction executive*
Drees, Ralph *construction executive*

**Highland Heights**
Kenny, Gregory B. *industrial equipment executive*

**Lexington**
Chowdhury, Dipak K. *pharmaceutical executive, researcher*
Gornik, Kathy *electronics executive*
Holland, Robert, Jr. *food products executive*

**Louisville**
Diaz, Paul J. *health products executive*
Goodman, Bruce *health products executive*
Heiden, Charles Kenneth *metal products executive, consultant, retired military officer*
Lechleiter, Richard A. *medical products executive*
Margulis, Heidi *health products executive*
Moya, Steve *health products executive*
Shield, Gene *health products executive*
Street, William May *beverage company executive*
Varga, Paul C. *beverage products executive*
Vogel, Werner Paul *retired machine company executive*
Wood, Phoebe A. *food products executive*

**Newport**
Castellini, Robert H. (Bob Castellini) *food products executive, professional sports team executive*

**Rineyville**
Jackson, Charles Wayne *food products executive, former telecommunications industry executive*

## LOUISIANA

**Baton Rouge**
Barfield, Tim *manufacturing executive*
Gill, Richard F. *construction engineering executive*

**Denham Springs**
May, Kenneth Nathaniel *retired food industry consultant*

**New Orleans**
Cospolich, James Donald *electronics executive, consultant*
Lundy, Larry *food franchise company executive*

**Ruston**
Deasy, William John *construction, engineering, and mining company executive*

**Slidell**
Stroud, Robert Arlen *medical equipment company executive*

## MAINE

**Andover**
Kaltsos, Angelo John *electronics executive, educator, photographer*

**Ellsworth**
Whedon, Ralph Gibbs *manufacturing executive*

### Grand Rapids
Baker, Hollis MacLure *furniture manufacturing company executive*
Currie, William G. *forest products executive*
Glenn, Michael B. *forest products executive*
Hackett, James P. *manufacturing executive*
Keane, James P. *manufacturing executive*
Murray, Mark Andrew *food products executive, former academic administrator, economist*
Sadler, David G(ary) *manufacturing executive*
Secchia, Peter F. *forest products executive, former United States ambassador to Italy*
Woodrick, Robert *food products executive*

### Grosse Pointe
Manetta, Richard L. *chemicals executive, lawyer*
Wilkinson, Warren Scripps *manufacturing executive*

### Grosse Pointe Farms
Obolensky, Marilyn Wall (Mrs. Serge Obolensky) *metals company executive*

### Holland
Haworth, Gerrard Wendell *office furniture manufacturing company executive*
Haworth, Richard G. (Dick Haworth) *office furniture manufacturer*

### Houghton
Utt, Glenn S., Jr. *retired medical products executive*

### Howell
Tupper, Leon F. *manufacturing executive*

### Jackson
Kelly, Robert Vincent, Jr. *metal products executive*

### Kalamazoo
Bergy, Dean H. *health products executive*
Hudson, Roy Davage *retired pharmaceutical executive*
MacMillan, Stephen P. *health products executive*

### Lansing
Stowers, Mark David *chemicals executive*

### Livonia
Cantie, Joseph S. *automotive executive*
Drouin, Joe *automotive executive*
Plant, John Charles *automotive equipment company executive*

### Madison Heights
Kafarski, Mitchell I. *chemical processing company executive*

### Mason
Dart, Kenneth B. *food container manufacturing executive*

### Midland
Allemang, Arnold A. *chemicals executive*
Burns, Stephanie A. *chemicals executive*
Carbone, Anthony J. *chemicals executive*
Cook, Phillip H. *chemicals executive*
Gambrell, Michael R. *chemicals executive*
Gross, Richard M. *chemicals executive*
Hampton, Leroy *retired chemical company executive*
Holder, Julie Fasone *chemicals executive*
Kepler, David E., II, *chemicals executive*
Kreinberg, Romeo *chemicals executive*
Liveris, Andrew N. *chemical company executive*
Reinhard, Joao Pedro *chemicals company executive*
Schmidt, William C. *retired chemicals executive*
Veurink, Gary R. *chemicals executive*
Walthie, Theo H. *chemicals executive*

### Milford
Bennur, Mallikarjuna *automotive executive*

### Monroe
Darrow, Kurt L. *manufacturing executive*

### Northville
Clawson, Curtis J. *manufacturing executive*
Clemens, Michael Terrence *furniture manufacturing representative*
Yost, James A. *manufacturing executive*

### Novi
Jeffe, Sidney David *automotive executive, engineer*
Johnson, Anthony *automotive executive*
Ligocki, Kathleen A. *auto parts company executive*
Mallak, James A. *auto parts company executive*

### Owosso
Acton, David L(awrence) *automobile company executive*

### Plymouth
Leuliette, Timothy D. *automotive executive*
Vlcek, Donald Joseph, Jr. *food products executive, wholesale distribution company, writer*

### Portage
Brown, John Wilford *health products executive*

### Rochester Hills
Denton, Lawrence A. *automotive executive*

### Romeo
Stryker, James William *retired automotive executive, former military officer*

### Roseville
Diez, Gerald F. *manufacturing executive, advertising executive*

### Royal Oak
Cook, Noel Robert *manufacturing executive*

### Saint Joseph
King, George Raleigh *retired manufacturing*

### Southfield
Alapont, José Maria *automotive executive*
DelGrosso, Douglas G. *manufacturing executive*
Gouldey, Glenn Charles *manufacturing executive*
Lynch, George Michael *auto parts manufacturing executive*
Maibach, Ben C. III *construction company executive*
Rossiter, Robert E. *interior auto parts manufacturing executive*

### Taylor
Manoogian, Richard Alexander *manufacturing executive*
Rosowski, Robert Bernard *manufacturing executive*

### Tecumseh
Herrick, Todd W. *manufacturing executive*

### Traverse City
Clous, James M. *electrical equipment company executive, engineer*
Parsons, John Thoren *manufacturing executive*

### Troy
Battenberg, J. T. III *automotive company executive*
Blahnik, John G. *electronics executive*
Buschmann, Siegfried *retired manufacturing executive*
Butler, Kevin M. *electronics executive*
Healy, Karen *automotive executive*
Lobo, Carlos *automotive executive*
Macher, Frank E. *automotive executive*
Mahone, Barbara Jean *automotive executive*
McClure, Charles G. *automotive executive*
Miller, Robert Stevens, Jr. *automotive executive*
O'Neal, Rodney *automotive company executive*
Pasricha, Atul *automotive executive*
Sharf, Stephan *automotive executive*
Sloan, Hugh Walter, Jr. *automotive executive*
Walker, Bette *automotive executive*

### Whitehall
Squier, David Louis *manufacturing executive*

### Wixom
Sugiyama, Toru Tom *automotive executive*

### Zeeland
Volkema, Michael A. *office furniture manufacturer*
Walker, Brian C. *manufacturing executive*

## MINNESOTA

### Austin
Ettinger, Jeffrey M. *food products executive, lawyer*
Johnson, Joel W. *food products executive*

### Bayport
Garofalo, Donald R. *window manufacturing executive*
Humphrey, James E. *manufacturing executive*

### Eagan
Clemens, T. Pat *manufacturing executive*

### Eden Prairie
Henningsen, Peter, Jr. *manufacturing executive*

### Edina
Brown, Charles Eugene *retired electronics company executive*
Kunin, Myron *hair care company executive*

### Golden Valley
Hogan, Randall J. *manufacturing executive, electronics executive*

### Hamel
Tiller, Thomas C. *manufacturing executive*

### Inver Grove Heights
Johnson, John D. *grain company executive*
Schmitz, John *grain company executive*

### La Crescent
Gelatt, Charles Daniel *manufacturing executive*

### Lindstrom
Messin, Marlene Ann *plastics company executive*

### Marshall
Beadle, John M. *food products executive*
Burr, Tracy L. *food products executive*
Pippin, M. Lenny *food products executive*
Schwan, Alfred *food products executive*

### Mendota Heights
Frechette, Peter Loren *dental products executive*

### Minneapolis
Bader, Kathleen M. *chemicals executive*
Buhrmaster, Robert C. *manufacturing executive*
Collins, Arthur D., Jr. *medical products executive*
Cook, William M. *manufacturing executive*
Corrigan, Frederic W. *agricultural products executive*
Curler, Jeffrey H. *packaging manufacturing executive*
Dallas, H. James *medical products executive*
Dimond, Robert B. *food products executive*
Durkin, G. Michael *food products executive*
Ferrari, Giannantonio *electronics executive*
George, William Wallace *former manufacturing executive*
Gockel, John Raymond *construction executive*
Graham, Allister P. *food products executive*
Hale, Roger Loucks *manufacturing executive, director*
Hawkins, William A. *medical products executive*
Hoffman, Michael J. *manufacturing executive*
Jacobs, Irwin Lawrence *diversified corporate executive*
Keiser, Kenneth E. *food products executive*
Lawrence, James A. *food products executive*
Lumpkins, Robert L. *food products executive*

### Mansfield, William L. *manufacturing executive*
Melrose, Kendrick Bascom *manufacturing executive*
Murphy, Daniel J., Jr. *aerospace and defense manufacturing company executive, military officer*
Oesterle, Stephen N. *medical products executive, cardiologist, medical educator*
Pletcher, Carol H. *chemicals executive*
Reyelts, Paul C. *chemical company executive*
Roe, John H. *manufacturing executive*
Rompala, Richard M. *chemical company executive*
Spoor, William Howard *food products executive*
Van Dyke, William Grant *manufacturing executive*
Wurtele, Christopher Angus *paint and coatings company executive*

### Minnetonka
Erlandson, Patrick J. *health products executive*

### Plymouth
Friswold, Fred Ravndal *manufacturing executive*
Kahler, Herbert Frederick *manufacturing executive*

### Rochester
Wood, Michael B. *medical products executive*

### Saint Paul
Buckley, George W. *manufacturing executive*
Campbell, Patrick D. *manufacturing executive*
Donaghy, James Edison *retired manufacturing executive, engineering educator*
Farrell, W. James *metal products manufacturing company executive*
Knudson, Mark Bradley *health products executive, venture capitalist*
Policinski, Chris *food products executive*
Schram, Lee J. *manufacturing executive*
Schuman, Allan L. *chemicals executive*
Starks, Daniel J. *medical technology and services executive*
Stroucken, Albert P. L. *chemical company executive*
Wiltz, James W. *medical products executive*

### Wayzata
Blodgett, Frank Caleb *retired food company executive*
Johnson, Sankey Anton *manufacturing executive*
Luthringshauser, Daniel Rene *manufacturing executive*
Staley, Warren R. *agricultural products and diversified services company executive*
Sullivan, Austin Padraic, Jr. *retired diversified food company executive*
Swanson, Donald Frederick *retired food company executive*

### Winona
Oberton, Willard D. *industrial supply company executive*

## MISSISSIPPI

### Hattiesburg
Chain, Bobby Lee *electrical contractor, former mayor*

### Jackson
Julian, Michael *grocery company executive*

### Pascagoula
Rideout, Jan G. *ship manufacturing company executive*

## MISSOURI

### Carthage
Flanigan, Matthew C. *manufacturing executive*
Haffner, David S. *manufacturing executive*
Jett, Ernest Carroll, Jr. *paper company executive, lawyer*
Wright, Felix E. *manufacturing executive*

### Centralia
Everhart, James Gray *retired manufacturing executive*

### Chesterfield
Bunch, Bob *manufacturing executive*
Carpenter, Will Dockery *chemicals executive*
Winter, William Earl *retired beverage company executive*

### Clayton
Lamoureux, Gerard William *container manufacturing company executive*
Rupp, Joseph D. *metal products executive*

### Fulton
Backer, William Earnest *food products executive*

### Grain Valley
Olsson, Björn Eskil *railroad supply company executive*

### Kansas City
Bass, Lee Marshall *food products company executive*
Berkley, Eugene Bertram (Bert Berkley) *envelope company executive*
Dees, Stephen Phillip *agricultural products executive, lawyer*
Dunn, Terrence P. *manufacturing executive*
Hebenstreit, James Bryant *agricultural products executive, venture capitalist*
Johnson, Richard Dean *pharmaceutical consultant, educator*

### Lees Summit
Henley, Joseph Oliver *manufacturing executive*

### Maryland Heights
Paz, George *health products executive*
Steward, David L. *technology company executive*
Tenholder, Edward J. *pharmaceutical executive*
Toan, Barrett A. *health products executive*

### Saint Charles
Pundmann, Ed John, Jr. *automotive company executive*

### Saint Louis
Armstrong, J. Hord III *pharmaceutical company executive*
Baker, W. Randolph *brewery executive*
Browde, Anatole *electronics company executive, consultant*
Brown, JoBeth Goode *food products executive, lawyer*
Busch, August A., IV, *food products executive*
Busch, August Adolphus III *brewery executive*
Clausen, Robert A. *chemicals executive*
Concibido, Vergel C. *research and development company executive, writer, inventor*
Edison, Bernard Alan *retired apparel executive*
Farr, David N. *electronics executive*
Fromm, Ronald A. *apparel executive*
Galvin, Walter J. *electrical equipment manufacturing executive*
Gupta, Surendra Kumar *chemicals executive*
Harvey, David R. *chemical company executive*
Hirsch, Raymond Robert *chemicals executive, lawyer*
Holliman, W. G. (Mickey), Jr. *furniture manufacturing executive*
Hunt, Kevin J. *food products executive*
Hunter, John C. III *chemicals executive*
Keyes, Marion Alvah, IV, *manufacturing executive*
Lambright, Stephen Kirk *brewing company executive, lawyer*
McGinnis, W. Patrick *diversified company executive*
Monroe, Thomas Edward *business and financial executive*
Nagarkatti, Jai Prakash *chemical company executive*
Quinn, Jeffry N. *chemicals executive, lawyer*
Reynolds, Robert A., Jr. *electric distributor executive*
Shanahan, Michael Francis *retired manufacturing executive, former hockey team executive*
Skarie, David P. *food products executive*
Stearley, Robert Jay *retired packaging company executive*
Stokes, Patrick T. *brewery company executive*
Swain, David O. *manufacturing executive*
Weldon, Virginia V. *retired food products executive, retired pediatrician*
Wilson, Martin D. *pharmaceutical executive*
Zwikelmaier, Kurt E. *pharmaceutical executive*

### Springfield
Henslee, Gregory L. *automotive executive*
O'Reilly, David E. *auto parts company executive*
O'Reilly, Lawrence P. *auto parts company executive*
Wooten, Rosalie (Rosalie O'Reilly Wooten) *automotive company executive*

### Webster Groves
Conerly, Richard Pugh *retired manufacturing executive*

### Wentzville
Cowger, Gary L. *automotive executive*

## MONTANA

### Big Sky
Ryan, Raymond D. *retired steel company executive, insurance company executive*

## NEBRASKA

### Lincoln
Fisher, Calvin David *food products executive*

### Lindsay
Parker, Gary Dean *manufacturing executive*

### Omaha
Faith, Marshall E. *grain company executive*
Goslee, Dwight J. *agricultural products executive*
Grewcock, Bruce E. *construction executive, mining executive*
Rodkin, Gary M. *food products executive*
Sharpe, Robert Francis, Jr. *food products company executive*
Stinson, Kenneth E. *construction and mining company executive*

## NEVADA

### Boulder City
Fisher, Paul Cary *writing supplies company executive*

### Carson City
Burns, Dan W. *manufacturing executive*
Noland, Robert LeRoy *retired manufacturing company executive*

### Genoa
Goode, John Martin *manufacturing executive*

### Henderson
Moon, David A. *manufacturing executive*

### Incline Village
Strack, Harold Arthur *retired electronics executive, military officer, financial consultant, writer*
Tedford, Jack Nowlan III *construction executive, small business owner*
Yount, George Stuart *paper company executive*

### Las Vegas
Jakopec, Carl Thomas *pharmaceutical executive*
Jones, Fletcher, Jr. *automotive company executive*
Root, Alan Charles *diversified manufacturing company executive*
Shuster, Carl *food products executive*
Trivelpiece, Craig Evan *computer electronics executive*

**Reno**
Jacobson, Raymond Earl *electronics executive*

## NEW HAMPSHIRE

**Bedford**
Cronin, Timothy Cornelius III *computer manufacturing executive*

**Bennington**
Verney, Richard Greville *paper company executive*

**Durham**
White, Ralph Paul *automotive executive, consultant*

**East Andover**
Gould, Donald Everett *retired chemical company executive, consultant*

**Hampton**
Clark, Kevin P. *medical products executive*
Della Penta, David T. *medical products executive*
Meister, Paul M. *medical products executive*
Montrone, Paul Michael *scientific instruments company executive*

**Keene**
Cohen, Richard B. *grocery company executive*
Miller, Rita *die-casting company executive, personnel consultant*

**Milton**
Shean, Timothy Joseph *manufacturing executive*

**Nashua**
Egan, John Frederick *retired electronics executive*
Seidel, Carl William *pharmaceutical company consultant*

**New Castle**
Baker, Robert I. *manufacturing executive*

**New London**
Condict, Edgar Rhodes *manufacturing executive, minister*

**North Hampton**
Taylor, Donald *retired manufacturing executive*

**Portsmouth**
Breen, Edward Deveaux *manufacturing executive*

**Stratham**
Swartz, Jeffrey B. *apparel executive*

**Winchester**
MacKay, Neil Duncan *plastics company executive, consultant*

## NEW JERSEY

**Barnegat**
Bronkowski, Mark John *textiles executive, real estate agent*

**Basking Ridge**
Conklin, Donald Ransford *retired pharmaceutical executive*

**Beach Haven**
Van Buren, William Benjamin III *retired pharmaceutical executive*

**Bridgeton**
Howell, James Burt III *retired agricultural products company sales consultant*

**Bridgewater**
Kennedy, James Andrew *chemical company executive*
Maynard, Kenneth Irwin *pharmaceutical executive, medical educator, researcher*

**Camden**
Conant, Douglas R. *food products executive*
Golub, Harvey *food products executive, former financial services company executive*
Reardon, Nancy Anne *food products executive*

**Carteret**
Vitrano, Frank G. *supermarket executive*
Volla, Steven L. *food products executive*

**Colts Neck**
Schmalz, Elizabeth Moody *cosmetics company executive*

**Cranbury**
Jaharis, Michael *pharmaceutical executive*

**Cranford**
Mazur, Leonard L. *pharmaceutical company executive*

**Denville**
Minter, Jerry Burnett *electronics executive*

**East Hanover**
Bess, Alan L. *pharmaceutical executive, physician*
Dodsworth, Roy W. *pharmaceutical company executive*
Harshman, Richard R. *manufacturing executive*

**East Rutherford**
Kutzer, Jamie *construction materials company executive*

**Edison**
Alexander, John Charles *pharmaceutical executive, preventive medicine physician*
Samek, Edward Lasker *medical transcription executive*

**Englewood Cliffs**
Neis, Arnold Hayward *pharmaceutical company executive*

**Fair Haven**
McKissock, David Lee *retired manufacturing company executive*

**Fairfield**
Stein, Robert Alan *electronics executive*

**Farmingdale**
Schluter, Peter Mueller *electronics executive*

**Fort Monmouth**
Schwering, Felix Karl *electronics executive, researcher*
Thornton, Clarence Gould *electronics executive, civilian military employee*

**Franklin Lakes**
Considine, John *pharmaceutical company executive*
Friedman, Martin Burton *retired chemicals executive*
Ludwig, Edward J. *medical technology executive*
Snow, David B. *pharmaceutical executive*

**Hainesport**
Sylk, Leonard Allen *manufacturing executive, real estate developer*

**Highlands**
Hansen, Christian Andreas, Jr. *plastics and chemical company executive*

**Hillsborough**
Kenyhercz, Thomas Michael *pharmaceutical company executive*

**Holmdel**
Kogelnik, Herwig Werner *electronics company executive*

**Hopatcong**
Reese, Harry Edwin, Jr. *electronics executive*

**Hope**
McDonald, John Joseph *electronics executive*

**Iselin**
Perry, Barry W. *manufacturing executive*
Smith, Orin Robert *chemical company executive*

**Jersey City**
O'Dea, William Patrick *research and development company executive*
Perhach, James Lawrence *pharmaceutical executive*
Pietrini, Andrew Gabriel *automotive aftermarket executive*

**Kendall Park**
Hershenov, Bernard Zion *research and development company executive*

**Kenilworth**
Bertolini, Robert J. *pharmaceutical executive*
Cox, Carrie *pharmaceutical executive*
Hassan, Fred *pharmaceutical executive*
Pickett, Cecil B. *pharmaceutical executive*

**Linden**
Covino, Charles Peter *chemicals executive*

**Little Silver**
Brennan, William Joseph *manufacturing executive*

**Livingston**
Candido, A. Michael *contracting company executive, real estate manager*

**Madison**
Essner, Robert Alan *pharmaceutical executive*
Mahady, Joseph M. *former pharmacy products company executive*
Martin, Kenneth J. *pharmaceutical executive*
Poussot, Bernard Jean *pharmaceutical executive*

**Mahwah**
Gerstein, David Brown *manufacturing executive, professional sports team executive*

**Marlboro**
Miller, Duane King *health and beauty care company executive*

**Medford**
Springer, Douglas Hyde *retired food products executive, lawyer*

**Metuchen**
Rhodes, Linda *pharmaceutical executive*

**Montvale**
Henkel, Herbert Ludwig *manufacturing executive*
Scullion, Tony *pharmaceutical executive*
Unterbeck, Axel Joachim *pharmaceutical executive, director*

**Morristown**
Cameron, Nicholas Allen *manufacturing executive*
Cote, David M. *diversified technology and manufacturing company executive*
Gilligan, Kevin *manufacturing executive*
Kirby, Fred Morgan, II, *manufacturing executive*
Williams, Joseph Dalton *pharmaceutical executive*

**Mount Holly**
Wille, John Jacob, Jr. *medical products executive, biologist*

**New Brunswick**
Darretta, Robert J. *pharmaceutical executive*
Deyo, Russell C. *health products executive*
Dormer, Michael J. *health products executive*
Fine, Roger Seth *pharmaceutical executive, lawyer*
Foster-Cheek, Kaye I. *health products executive*
Goggins, Colleen A. *health products executive*

**Haines**, William Joseph *retired pharmaceutical executive*
Larsen, Ralph S(tanley) *retired pharmaceutical executive*
Lenehan, James T. *pharmaceutical executive*
Liao, Mei-June *pharmaceutical executive, researcher*
Peterson, Per A. *health products executive*
Poon, Christine A. *pharmaceutical company executive*
Scodari, Joseph C. *health products executive*
Sosa, Joseph F. *pharmaceutical executive*
Valeriani, Nicholas J. *health products executive*
Weldon, William C. *pharmaceutical executive*

**New Providence**
Chatterji, Debajyoti *retired manufacturing executive*
McCaffrey, Robert Henry, Jr. *retired manufacturing company executive*

**Newark**
Emery, Charles Christian, Jr. *health care and information systems executive*

**North Brunswick**
Ghosh, Alok *pharmaceutical executive*

**Northvale**
Di Mino, André Anthony *manufacturing executive, consultant*

**Nutley**
English, Robert Joseph *electronics executive*

**Oakland**
Manheimer, Heidi *cosmetics company executive*

**Ocean City**
Juliana, James Nicholas *manufacturing executive*

**Paramus**
Forman, Beth Rosalyne *specialty food trade executive*
Maclin, Ernest *medical products executive*

**Park Ridge**
Frissora, Mark P. *automobile rental and leasing company executive*
Koch, Craig R. *automobile rental and leasing company executive*

**Peapack**
Rost, Peter *pharmaceutical company executive*

**Pennsauken**
Honickman, Harold *food manufacturing company executive*

**Pompton Plains**
Shrem, Charles Joseph *metals corporation executive*

**Princeton**
Bergman, Richard Isaac *health information executive*
Campbell, Robert Emmett *retired health products executive*
Cavanaugh, James Henry *health products executive, retired federal official*
Ghasemi, Seifi *chemicals executive*
Goldblatt, Barry Lance *manufacturing executive*
Kuebler, Christopher Allen *pharmaceutical executive*
Mollica, Joseph A. *pharmaceutical executive*
Olsen, Gregory H. *fiber optic manufacturing executive, researcher*
Wildnauer, Richard Harry *pharmaceutical executive*
Winn, Paul T. *electronics executive*

**Red Bank**
Sorsby, James Larry *home building company executive*

**Ridgefield**
Riggs, Rory B. *pharmaceutical executive*

**Ridgewood**
Healey, Frank Henry *retired chemicals executive*

**Riverton**
O'Brien, James Jerome *construction management consultant*

**Rochelle Park**
Schapiro, Jerome Bentley *chemicals executive*

**Saddle Brook**
Hickey, William V. *manufacturing executive*
Kelsey, David *manufacturing executive*

**Secaucus**
Dabah, Ezra *apparel executive*
Liao, Paul Foo-Hung *electronics executive*
Unanue, Robert I. *food products executive*

**Somerset**
Aronson, Louis Vincent, II, *manufacturing executive*
Jones, Andrew William *pharmaceutical executive*
Mittleberg, Eric Michael *pharmaceutical executive*

**South Hackensack**
Cohen, Brett I. *health products executive*

**South Orange**
Schectman, Stephen Barry *pharmaceutical executive*

**Summit**
Jackson, John Wyant *biotechnology company executive*
Lindars, Laurence Edward *retired health care products executive*
Longfield, William Herman *health products executive*
Zachary, Louis George *chemical company consultant*

**Teaneck**
Feinberg, Robert S. *plastics company executive, marketing professional*

**Trenton**
Ulsh, Gordon A. *battery manufacturing company executive*
Viscomi, Frank Joseph *pharmaceutical executive*

**Vincentown**
Foster, David Ramsey *soap company executive*

**Wayne**
Heyman, Samuel J. *chemical manufacturing company executive*
Jeffrey, Robert George, Jr. *manufacturing executive*

**West Orange**
Eisenberg, R. Neal *restoration company executive*

**West Paterson**
Lilley, David *chemicals executive*

**Westfield**
McLean, Vincent Ronald *former manufacturing company financial executive*

**Whitehouse Station**
Anstice, David W. *pharmaceutical executive*
Avedon, Marcia J. *pharmaceutical executive*
Bossidy, Larry (Lawrence Arthur Bossidy) *pharmaceutical company executive, former industrial manufacturing executive*
Clark, Richard T. *pharmaceutical company executive*
Deese, Willie A. *pharmaceutical executive*
Frazier, Kenneth C. *pharmaceutical executive, lawyer*
Gilmartin, Raymond V. *pharmaceutical company executive*
Lewent, Judy Carol *pharmaceutical executive*
Loescher, Peter Hans *pharmaceutical executive*
Martelet, Francois R. *pharmaceutical executive*
McGlynn, Margaret G. *pharmaceutical executive*
McGuire, John Lawrence *pharmaceutical executive*
Scalet, J. Chris (James Christopher Scalet) *pharmaceutical executive*
Wold-Olsen, Per *pharmaceutical executive*
Yarno, Wendy *pharmaceutical executive*

**Wyckoff**
Brown, James Joseph *manufacturing executive*

## NEW MEXICO

**Albuquerque**
Barker, Lynn M. *manufacturing executive*
Espat, Robert Eduardo, Sr. *industrialist*
Friberg, George Joseph *electronics company executive, entrepreneur*
Korman, Nathaniel Irving *research and development company executive*
Roberts, Dennis William *construction executive*

**Los Alamos**
Gregg, Charles Thornton *research and development company executive, researcher, molecular biologist*

**Placitas**
Golleher, George *food company executive*

**Sandia Park**
Wilczynski, Janusz S. *manufacturing executive, retired physicist*

## NEW YORK

**Albany**
D'Ambra, Thomas E. *pharmaceutical executive*
Heshmat, Hooshang *manufacturing executive*
Kuhla, Donald E. *chemicals executive*
Schulman, Ruth Meryl Aronson *research and development company executive*

**Amityville**
Soloway, Richard Lewis *electronics executive*

**Bohemia**
Rudolph, Scott *pharmaceutical executive*

**Briarcliff Manor**
Bingham, J. Peter *electronics research executive*

**Brooklyn**
Hood, Ernest Alva, Sr. *pharmaceutical company executive*
Zisser, Martin Shepherd *fur apparel manufacturer, investor, securities trader*

**Buffalo**
Rich, Robert E., Jr. *frozen foods company executive*
Starks, Fred William *chemicals executive*

**Cazenovia**
Carlson, William Clifford *defense industry executive, director, retired military officer*

**Clifton Park**
Scher, Robert Sander *instrument design company executive*

**Conklin**
Blouch, Timothy Craig *food company executive*

**Cooperstown**
Tilton, Webster, Jr. *contractor*

**Corning**
Behm, Forrest Edwin *glass manufacturing company executive*
Eggers, William D. *manufacturing executive, lawyer*

Houghton, James Richardson *manufacturing executive*
Miller, Joseph A. *chemicals executive*

**Cross River**
Lang, Robert Mays, Jr. *manufacturing executive*

**Derby**
Goodell, Joseph Edward *manufacturing executive*

**East Amherst**
Watson, Stewart Charles *construction executive*

**East Hampton**
Karp, Harvey Lawrence *metal products executive*

**East Northport**
Kehoe, Thomas J. *food products executive*

**Fairport**
Sands, Richard E. *food products executive*
Sands, Robert *food products executive*
Summer, Thomas S. *food products executive*

**Fayetteville**
Pachter, Irwin Jacob *pharmaceutical consultant*

**Flushing**
Henshel, Harry Bulova *watch manufacturer*
Hsu, Charles Jui-cheng *manufacturing company executive, advertising agent*

**Glen Cove**
Burnham, Harold Arthur *pharmaceutical executive, physician*

**Great Neck**
Arams, Frank Robert *electronics executive*

**Greenvale**
Krasnoff, Eric *health products executive*

**Hartsdale**
Martin, Daniel Richard *pharmaceutical executive*

**Hauppauge**
Hausman, Howard *electronics executive*

**Hicksville**
Tucci, Gerald Frank *manufacturing executive*

**Hoosick Falls**
Dodge, Cleveland Earl, Jr. *retired manufacturing executive, director*

**Hopewell Junction**
Novak, Robert Dennis *contractor, real estate developer*

**Islandia**
Artzt, Russell M. *electronics executive*

**Ithaca**
Cottrell, G. Walton *manufacturing executive*

**Jamestown**
Wellman, Barclay Ormes *furniture company executive*

**Lakewood**
Anderson, Raymond Quintus *diversified company executive*

**Larchmont**
Cavanna, Dino Francesco *chemicals executive*
Hinerfeld, Norman Martin *manufacturing executive*

**Lockport**
Schultz, Gerald Alfred (Jerry Schultz) *retired chemicals executive*
Steinagle, Martin Gene *contractor, paralegal, poet, writer*

**Locust Valley**
Schor, Joseph Martin *pharmaceutical executive, biochemist*

**Long Island City**
DiGiovanni, Eleanor Elma *scaffold installation company executive*

**Mamaroneck**
Mizrahi, Abraham Mordechay *retired health products executive, pediatrician*

**Melville**
Bergman, Stanley M. *health products executive*
Breslawski, James P. *health products executive*
Kissinger, Walter Bernhard *retired automotive executive*
Kornberg, Fred *electronics executive*
Minicozzi, Rob *electronics executive*
Mitchell, William Edmund *electronics executive*
Waddell, John Comer *electronics distribution company executive*

**Monroe**
Dierna, Joseph Biagio *construction company executive, land development consultant*

**New Hyde Park**
Klein, George *manufacturing company executive, systems analyst, consultant*
Neal, Elaine Zirli *health products executive*
Vultaggio, Don J. (Dominick Vultaggio) *beverage company executive*

**New Rochelle**
Tassone, Gelsomina (Gessie Tassone) *metal products executive*

**New York**
Adjemian, Vart K. *agricultural products executive*
Alford, Katherine *food products executive*
Amen, Robert M. *manufacturing executive, retired paper company executive*
Andreotti, Lamberto *pharmaceutical executive*

Armen, Garo H. *research and development company executive*
Bagger, Richard Hartvig *pharmaceutical executive*
Barnes, Jhane Elizabeth *fashion design company executive, designer*
Barton, Lewis *food products executive, consultant*
Bear, Stephen E. *pharmaceutical executive*
Bernstein, Richard Allen *food products executive*
Bodnar, Andrew G. *pharmaceutical executive*
Bonfield, Andrew R.J. *pharmaceutical executive*
Brandeis, Barry *apparel executive*
Bresani, Federico Fernando *manufacturing executive*
Call, Neil Judson *manufacturing executive*
Camilleri, Louis C. *consumer goods company executive*
Campbell, Robert David *manufacturing executive, metal products executive*
Carvette, Anthony M. *construction executive*
Casey, Gerard William *retired food products executive, lawyer*
Charron, Paul Richard *apparel executive*
Chirico, Emanuel *apparel executive*
Clarke, Kenneth Kingsley *retired electronics executive*
Cole, Kenneth D. *footwear and accessories company executive*
Cornelius, James Milton *pharmaceutical company executive*
Corr, Peter B. *pharmaceutical executive*
Demsey, John *cosmetics executive*
Denmark, Bernhardt *manufacturing executive*
Donaghy, James K. *construction executive, contractor*
Earl, Christopher D. *health products executive*
Farber, John J. *chemical company executive*
Feczko, Joe *pharmaceutical executive*
Fischer, Joseph L. *pharmaceutical executive*
Fribourg, Paul J. *grain company executive*
Geckle, Robert Alan *manufacturing executive*
Goodale, Toni Krissel *research and development company executive*
Gould, Harry Edward, Jr. *paper company executive*
Greeff, Douglas Haven *cosmetics executive*
Gromek, Joseph R. *apparel executive*
Hardwick, Charles Leighton *pharmaceutical executive, former state legislator*
Hartman, Bruce L. *apparel executive*
Hayden, Donald J., Jr. *pharmaceutical executive*
Hoffman, Ronald L. *manufacturing executive*
Howson, Tamar D. *pharmaceutical executive*
Jackson, Yvonne *pharmaceutical executive*
Juliber, Lois D. *manufacturing executive*
Jung, Andrea *cosmetics company executive*
Kelson, Richard B. *metal products executive*
Kennedy, David L. *cosmetics company executive*
Kindler, Jeffrey B. *pharmaceutical company executive, lawyer*
Kleinfeld, Klaus *electronics executive*
Koplik, Michael R. *durable goods company executive*
Krill, Kay (Katherine Lawther Krill) *apparel executive*
Krominga, Lynn *cosmetics executive, lawyer*
Kropf, Susan J. *cosmetics company executive*
Kunes, Richard W. *cosmetics executive*
LaMattina, John L. *pharmaceutical executive*
Langhammer, Fred H. *cosmetics company executive*
Lauder, Aerin *cosmetics executive*
Lauder, Evelyn H. *cosmetics executive*
Lauder, Leonard Alan *cosmetic and fragrance company executive*
Lauder, William P. *cosmetics executive*
Levin, Alan G. *pharmaceutical company executive*
Levinson, Robert Alan *textiles executive*
Lewis, Loida Nicolas *food products holding company executive*
Lifton, Robert Kenneth *manufacturing executive*
Lord, Marvin *apparel executive*
May, Peter William *business executive*
May, William Frederick *manufacturing executive*
McFadden, Mary Josephine *fashion industry executive*
McKinnell, Hank (Henry A. McKinnell Jr.) *pharmaceutical executive*
McKinnon, Floyd Wingfield *textile executive*
Mc Namara, Robert A. *construction company executive*
Mina, Richard T. *apparel executive*
Montero, Sylvia *pharmaceutical executive*
Moore, Charles Hewes, Jr. *manufacturing executive*
Moran, Juliette M. *retired chemicals executive*
Mosbacher, Georgette Paulsin *cosmetics executive*
Munroe, George Barber *retired mining and manufacturing company executive*
Muscari, Joseph Charles *manufacturing executive*
Natori, Josie Cruz (Josefina Almeda Cruz Natori) *apparel executive*
Palmer, Jason Michael *research and development company executive*
Panagos, Steven Gregory *food products executive*
Peltz, Nelson *manufacturing executive*
Perrin, Charles R. *light manufacturing executive*
Pietruski, John Michael, Jr. *pharmaceutical executive*
Pollard, Veronica *automotive executive*
Press, James E. *automotive executive*
Puschel, Philip P. *textiles executive*
Read, Ian C. *pharmaceutical executive*
Reece, Thomas L. *manufacturing executive*
Reed, W. Allen *automotive executive*
Rennert, Ira Leon *manufacturing executive*
Rosenberg, Robert Charles *housing corporation executive*
Rossettos, Nicholas J. *research and development company executive*
Rubin, Joel Edward *manufacturing executive*
Sasaki, Jun *steel company researcher*
Scarpa, A. Michael *apparel executive, corporate financial executive*
Schulhof, Michael Peter *electronics company executive*
Shedlarz, David L. *pharmaceutical executive*
Shineman, Edward William, Jr. *retired pharmaceutical executive*
Skule, John L. *pharmaceutical company executive*
Solomon, Howard *pharmaceutical executive*

Steere, William Campbell, Jr. *pharmaceutical executive*
Steiner, Jeffrey Josef *manufacturing executive*
Stockton, Susan *food products executive*
Stringer, Sir Howard *electronics company executive, retired media executive*
Sullivan, Trudy F. *apparel executive*
Szymanczyk, Michael E. *tobacco products executive*
Tapella, Gary Louis *manufacturing executive*
Targoff, Michael Bart *space and communications company executive*
Tisch, Andrew Herbert *corporate executive*
Tse, Charles Yung Chang *pharmaceutical executive, lawyer*
von der Heyden, Karl Mueller *retired manufacturing executive*
Waxman, Allen *pharmaceutical executive*
Whiting, Susan Dickinson *media research company executive*
Woods, Emily *apparel executive*
Woolard, Edgar S., Jr. *retired chemical company executive*
Zotos, Frederic P. *research and development company executive*

**Oneonta**
Insinga, Richard Charles *manufacturing company executive, marketing educator*

**Pittsford**
Dobbs, Herbert Hotaling *automotive executive, consultant, research scientist, retired military officer*

**Poughkeepsie**
Sherman, Ethan *contractor, publisher*
Slade, Bernard Newton *electronics executive*

**Purchase**
Bridgman, Peter Alwyn *beverage company executive*
Bryant, Daniel James *food and beverage company executive, former federal agency administrator*
Finnerty, Louise Hoppe *food products executive*
Lucio, Antonio J. *food products executive*
Nooyi, Indra K. *food products executive*
Nowell, Lionel L. *food products executive*
Reinemund, Steven S. *food products executive*
Thompson, Peter M. *retired food products executive*
Wallach, Kenneth L. *paper company executive*
White, Michael Dennis *food products executive*

**Rhinecliff**
Conklin, John Roger *retired electronics company executive*

**Rochester**
Bouyoucos, John Vinton *research and development company executive*
Brust, Robert H. *film processing company executive*
Collins, Christopher Carl *manufacturing executive*
Gustin, Carl E., Jr. *manufacturing executive*
Morphy, John *manufacturing executive*
Sieg, Albert Louis *photographic company executive*
Zarrella, Ronald L. *pharmaceutical executive*

**Roslyn Heights**
Guthart, Leo A. *electronics executive*

**Rye Brook**
Kuntzman, Ronald *research and development company executive*
Masson, Robert Henry *paper company executive*

**Sands Point**
Wurzel, Leonard *retired candy manufacturing company executive*

**Scarsdale**
Blitman, Howard Norton *construction executive*
Byers, John Raoul III *food products executive, conservationist*
Gelb, Harold Seymour *manufacturing executive, consultant, entrepreneur*
Johnson, Boine Theodore *manufacturing executive, mayor*

**Schenectady**
Fell, Samuel Kennedy (Ken Fell) *infosystems executive*
Sternlicht, Beno *research and development company executive*

**Seaford**
Setzler, William Edward *retired chemicals executive*

**Sidney**
Werner, David A. *paper company executive*

**Somers**
Sora, Sebastian Antony *business machines manufacturing executive, educator*

**Suffern**
Garbarini, William Nicholas *pharmaceutical executive*

**Syracuse**
Steigerwald, Louis John III *corporate executive*

**Tarrytown**
Yancopoulos, George D. *pharmaceutical executive*

**Troy**
Mehta, Shreefal *pharmaceutical executive, educator*

**Turin**
Klossner, Windy *food products executive*

**Utica**
Antzelevitch, Charles *research and development company executive*

**Valhalla**
De Nicola, Peter Francis *photographic distributor*

**Wantagh**
Blum, Melvin *chemical company executive, researcher*

**Webster**
Curtis, Deana A. *electronics executive, small business owner*
Duke, Charles Bryan *electronics executive, physicist, educator*

**West Seneca**
Bidlack, Jerald Dean *manufacturing executive*

**Westbury**
Brooks, David H. *manufacturing executive*

**White Plains**
Abrams, Leigh Jeffrey *manufacturing executive*
Fisher, Jerome *apparel executive*
Fowler, James D., Jr. *leadership executive*
Greene, Leonard Michael *manufacturing executive, aerospace transportation executive*
Loranger, Steven R. *industrial manufacturing company executive*

**Whitestone**
Bikoff, J. Darius *beverage company executive*
Rahr, Stewart *health medical products executive*

**Woodbury**
Guttenplan, Harold Esau *retired food company executive*

**Yonkers**
Holtz, Gilbert Joseph *steel company executive*
Lukach, Arthur S., Jr. *manufacturing executive*

**Youngstown**
Alpert, Norman *chemical company executive*

## NORTH CAROLINA

**Asheville**
Coli, Guido John *chemical company executive*

**Beaufort**
Cullman, Hugh *retired tobacco company executive*

**Belmont**
Stowe, Robert Lee III *textile company executive*

**Blowing Rock**
Barnebey, Kenneth Alan *food products executive*

**Burlington**
Elingburg, Wesley R. *health products executive*
Flagg, Raymond Osbourn *retired medical products executive*

**Cary**
Bogdanovich, Alexander *manufacturing executive*

**Chapel Hill**
Cummings, Sandra Eileen *medical products executive*

**Charlotte**
Belk, Thomas Milburn, Jr., (Tim Belk) *apparel executive*
Browning, Peter Crane *packaging company executive*
Dickson, Thomas Walter *textile company executive*
DiMicco, Daniel R. *manufacturing executive*
Kearney, Christopher J. *manufacturing executive, lawyer*
Larsen, Marshall O. *manufacturing executive*
Lea, Scott Carter *retired packaging company executive*
McKinnish, Richmond D. *manufacturing executive*
Moore, James L., Jr. *beverage company executive*
Munn, Stephen P. *manufacturing executive*
Nelson, Thomas C. *manufacturing executive*
O'Leary, Patrick J. *manufacturing executive*
Peacock, A(lvin) Ward *textile company executive*
Perkins, Jim C. *automotive executive*
Rachor, Jeffrey C. *automotive executive*
Seidel, James P. *manufacturing executive*
Siegel, Samuel *metals company executive*
Smith, B. Scott *automotive executive*
Smith, O. Bruton *automotive company executive*
Spangler, Clemmie Dixon, Jr. *construction company executive*
Squires, James Ralph *development company executive*
Sulg, Madis *manufacturing executive, entrepreneur*

**Durham**
Gillings, Dennis B. *medical products executive*
Ladd, Marcia Lee *medical products executive*
Maar, Rosina *medical products executive*
Sharma, Anand *manufacturing executive*

**Fayetteville**
Richardson, Emilie White *manufacturing executive, investment company executive, educator*

**Gastonia**
Kimbrell, Willard Duke *textiles executive*
Lawson, William David III *retired cotton company executive*

**Greensboro**
McDonald, Mackey J. *apparel executive*
Wiseman, Eric C. *apparel executive*

**Hertford**
Johnson, Donald Lee *retired agricultural materials processing company executive*

**High Point**
Fenn, Ormon William, Jr. *furniture company executive*

**Kitty Hawk**
Sjoerdsma, Albert *research and development company executive*

**Madison**
Millner, Thomas *manufacturing and holding company executive*

**Morrisville**
Harker, Brian *tobacco company executive*

**Mount Airy**
Woltz, Howard Osler, Jr. *retired metal products executive*

**Mount Holly**
Dickson, Alan T. *mill and holding company executive*

**Pine Knoll Shores**
Benson, Kenneth Victor *manufacturing executive, lawyer*

**Pinehurst**
O'Neill, John Joseph, Jr. *retired chemicals executive*

**Raleigh**
Prior, William Allen *electronics company executive*
Risher, James A. *electronics executive*
Sloan, O. Temple, Jr. *automotive equipment executive*
Zelnak, Stephen P., Jr. *construction materials company executive*

**Research Triangle Park**
Bierman, James L. *contract research organization executive*
Framil, Armando Ramon *pharmaceutical executive*
Ingram, Robert A. *pharmaceutical executive*
Russell, John S. *contract research organization executive*

**Rocky Mount**
Stubbs, Will, Jr. *pharmaceutical company manager*

**Statesville**
Stelzner, Paul Burke *textile company executive*

**Weldon**
Barringer, Paul Brandon, II, *lumber company executive*
Dhasmana, Bindu *paper company executive, chemist, researcher*

**Wilmington**
Buckland, Wendy *medical products executive*

**Winston Salem**
Brewster, Daryl G. *food products executive*
Chaden, Lee A. *apparel executive, former food products executive*
Hanes, Ralph Philip, Jr. *retired textiles executive, horse breeder*
Maselli, John Anthony *food products executive*
McKnight, Gregory Richard *research and development director*
Noll, Richard A. *apparel executive*

**OHIO**

**Akron**
Haines, Terry L. *plastics company executive*
Kaufman, Donald Leroy *building products executive*
Keegan, Robert J. *manufacturing executive*
Snider, George Runyon, Jr. *franchising company executive*
Wells, Norman, Jr. *metal products executive*

**Avon Lake**
Newlin, Stephen Dore *chemicals executive*
Patient, William F. *chemicals executive*

**Beachwood**
Demetriou, Steven J. *metal products executive*

**Bellville**
Hooker, James Todd *manufacturing executive*

**Canton**
Ewing, David Charles *automobile dealership executive*
Griffith, James W. *manufacturing executive*
Swidarski, Thomas W. *manufacturing executive*
Timken, Ward J., Jr. *manufacturing executive*

**Chagrin Falls**
Brophy, Jere Hall *manufacturing executive*
Heckman, Henry Trevennen Shick *retired metal products executive*

**Cincinnati**
Aguirre, Fernando *food products executive*
Byrnes, Bruce L. *manufacturing executive*
Christensen, Paul Walter, Jr. *retired gear manufacturing company executive*
deKool, L.M. (Theo DeKool) *food products executive*
Farmer, Richard T. *uniform rental and sales executive*
Farmer, Scott D. *apparel executive*
Fulmer, Michael Clifford *food company administrator*
Heschel, Michael Shane *retail food products executive*
Hutton, Edward Luke *medical products executive*
Jones, Daniel W. *manufacturing executive*
Kendle, Candace *pharmaceutical executive*
Maier, Jack C. *food products executive*
McDonald, Robert Alan (Bob McDonald) *manufacturing executive*
Pichler, Joseph Anton *food products executive*
Ruthman, Thomas Robert *manufacturing executive*
Schlotman, J. Michael *food products executive*
Stern, Joseph Smith, Jr. *former footwear manufacturing company executive*

**Cleveland**
Collins, Duane E. *manufacturing executive*
Connor, Christopher M. *manufacturing executive*
Cutler, Alexander MacDonald *manufacturing executive*
Decker, John William *metal products executive*
Haeck, James F. *manufacturing executive*
Holmes, Arthur S. *manufacturing executive*
Ivy, Conway Gayle *paint company executive*
Jenson, Jon Eberdt *metal products executive*
Keithley, Joseph Faber *electronic engineering manufacturing company executive*
Luke, Randall Dan *retired manufacturing executive, lawyer*
Mandel, Jack N. *manufacturing executive*
Pugh, David L. *manufacturing executive*
Thomas, Richard Stephen *construction executive*
Vande Steeg, Nickolas W. *manufacturing executive*
Washkewicz, Donald E. *manufacturing executive*
Weiss, Morry *greeting card company executive*

**Columbus**
Carter, William H. *chemicals executive*
Cottingham, Richard Sumner *paper company executive*
Daah-Krzykowski, Andre *pharmaceutical and nutritional manufacturing company administrator*
Evans, Daniel E. *manufacturing executive, restaurant chain company executive*
Kidder, C. Robert *food products executive*
Knilans, Michael Jerome *food products executive*
Kohrt, Carl Fredrick *research and development company executive*
Lazar, Theodore Aaron *retired manufacturing executive, lawyer*
Margolis, Jay M. *clothing executive*
McConnell, John P. *metal products executive*
Milford, Frederick John *retired research and development company executive*
Morrison, Craig O. *chemicals executive*
Ricart, Fred *automotive company executive*
Spoerry, Robert F. *manufacturing executive*
Wexner, Abigail *apparel executive*
Wigington, Ronald Lee *retired chemical information services executive*
Yenkin, Bernard Kalman *coatings and resins company executive*

**Cuyahoga Falls**
Butcher, Jack Robert (Jack Risin) *manufacturing executive, film producer, actor, artist*

**Dayton**
Duval, Daniel Webster *manufacturing executive*
Harlan, Norman Ralph *construction executive*
Isaacson, Milton Stanley (Jim Isaacson) *research and development company executive, engineer*
Mathile, Clayton Lee *pet food company executive*
McIlroy, Alan F. *manufacturing executive*

**Delaware**
Eells, William Hastings *retired automobile company executive*
Huml, Donald Scott *manufacturing executive*

**Dublin**
Borror, Douglas G. *construction company executive*
Clark, R. Kerry (Kerry Clark) *health products executive*
Clement, Henry Joseph, Jr. *diversified building products executive*
D'Antoni, David J. *chemicals executive*
Dolch, Gary D. *pharmaceutical executive*
Hammond, David *pharmaceutical executive*
Lamp, Benson J. *tractor company executive*
Lynch, Mike *health products executive*
Papa, Joseph C. *pharmaceutical executive*
Parrish, Mark *health products executive*
Rishel, James Burton *manufacturing executive, director*
Schlotterbeck, David L. *medical products executive*
Slagle, Tom *medical products executive*
Walsh, Daniel J. *medical products executive*
Walter, Robert D. *health products executive*
Winstead, Dwight *medical products executive*

**Elyria**
Mixon, Aaron Malachi III *medical products executive*

**Findlay**
Pond, Byron O., Jr. *manufacturing executive*
Stephens, D. Richard *manufacturing executive*
Weaver, Philip G. *tire company executive*

**Garrettsville**
Diskin, Michael Edward *plastics company executive, food service executive*

**Gates Mills**
Veale, Tinkham, II, *retired chemicals executive, engineer*

**Greenville**
Buchy, Jim *food products executive*

**Hamilton**
Epp, Mary Elizabeth *retired technologies consultant*

**Holland**
D'Anniballe, Priscilla Lucille *contracting company executive*

**Jackson Center**
Thompson, Wade Francis Bruce *manufacturing executive*

**Mansfield**
Gorman, James Carvill *manufacturing executive*

**Mason**
Kohlhepp, Robert J. *apparel executive*
Wilson, Frederic Sandford *pharmaceutical company executive*

**Mayfield Heights**
Rankin, Alfred Marshall, Jr. *manufacturing executive*

**Medina**
Matejka, Robert *chemicals executive*
Smith, Richey *manufacturing executive*
Sullivan, Frank C. *manufacturing executive*
Sullivan, Thomas Christopher *coatings company executive*

**Mentor**
Callsen, Christian Edward *health products executive*

**Middletown**
Wainscott, James Lawrence *steel industry executive*

**Milan**
Henry, Joseph Patrick *chemicals executive*

**New Albany**
Jeffries, Michael S. (Mike Jeffries) *apparel executive*

**New Bremen**
Dicke, James Frederick, II, *manufacturing executive*

**New Straitsville**
Eaton, Michael Christopher *contractor*

**North Canton**
Lynham, C(harles) Richard *manufacturing executive*

**North Ridgeville**
Stewart, Arden Ruth *retired automotive executive*

**Orrville**
Smucker, Richard K. *food products executive*
Smucker, Timothy P. *food products executive*

**Perrysburg**
King, John Joseph *manufacturing executive*

**Randolph**
Pecano, Donald Carl *automotive manufacturing executive*

**Richfield**
Anthony, Leonard Morris *steel company administrator, consultant*

**Solon**
Rosica, Gabriel Adam *retired manufacturing executive, electrical engineer*

**Tipp City**
Tighe-Moore, Barbara Jeanne *electronics executive*

**Toledo**
Brown, David T. *manufacturing executive*
Burns, Michael J. *automotive executive*
DeBacker, Michael L. *automotive executive, lawyer*
Gibara, Samir G. *tire manufacturing executive*
McCracken, Steven R. *textiles executive*
Romanoff, Milford Martin *retired building contractor*
Thaman, Michael H. *building material systems executive*

**West Chester**
Mack, Mark Philip *chemical company executive*

**Wickliffe**
Cooley, Charles P. *chemicals executive*
Hambrick, James L. *chemicals executive*

**Winchester**
Koford, Stuart Keith *electronics executive*

**Youngstown**
Kessler, Ronald N. *plastics company executive*

**OKLAHOMA**

**Bristow**
Primeaux, Henry III *automotive executive, author, speaker*

**Oklahoma City**
Lopez, John C. *meat processing company executive*
Murray, James William III *manufacturing executive, lawyer*
Pilcher, Gregory F. *manufacturing executive, lawyer*
Turner, Eugene Andrew *manufacturing executive*

**Tulsa**
Marshall-Chapman, Paula *food products executive*
Thomas, Robert Eggleston *retired manufacturing executive*

**OREGON**

**Ashland**
Meese, Celia Edwards *pharmaceutical company executive*

**Beaverton**
Blair, Donald W. *shoe manufacturing company executive*
Carter, James C. *apparel executive, lawyer*
Clarke, Thomas E. *apparel executive*
Knight, Philip Hampson *apparel executive*

**Boring**
Price, Dana Kenneth *foreman, automotive executive*

**Eugene**
Woolley, Donna Pearl *lumber company executive*

**Hillsboro**
Barnes, Keith Lee *electronics executive*

**Klamath Falls**
Wendt, Richard L. *manufacturing executive*

**Medford**
De Boer, Sidney B. *automotive executive*
Heimann, M.L. (Dick Heimann) *auto dealership executive*

**Portland**
Boyle, Gertrude *sportswear company executive*
Donegan, Mark *metal products executive*
Drinkward, Cecil *construction company executive*
Larsson, William Dean *manufacturing executive*
Pamplin, Robert Boisseau, Sr. *retired textile manufacturing executive*
Pamplin, Robert Boisseau, Jr. *manufacturing company executive, minister, writer*
Russell, Marjorie Rose *manufacturing executive*

**Tualatin**
Yavorsky, William D. *semiconductor company executive*

**Woodburn**
Preece, Scott *food products executive*

**PENNSYLVANIA**

**Allentown**
Baker, Dexter Farrington *manufacturing executive, director*
Clemmer, Richard L. *electronics executive*
Jones, John P. III *chemicals executive*
Lovett, John Robert *retired chemical company executive*

**Allison Park**
Backus, John King *former chemical company research administrator*

**Avondale**
Friel, Daniel Denwood, Sr. *manufacturing executive*

**Belle Vernon**
Wapiennik, Carl Francis *manufacturing executive, planetarium and science institute administrator*

**Bensalem**
Bern, Dorrit J. *apparel executive*

**Berwyn**
Burch, John Walter *mining equipment company executive*

**Bethlehem**
Barnette, Curtis Handley *steel company executive, lawyer*
Hartmann, Robert Elliott *retired manufacturing executive*
Marsh, Robert Harry *chemicals executive*
St. John, Anthony Paul *retired manufacturing executive*

**Blue Bell**
McAdam, Will *electronics executive, consultant*

**Bradford**
Rice, Lester *electronics company executive*

**Bristol**
Boneparth, Peter *apparel executive*
Kimmel, Sidney *apparel company executive*

**Camp Hill**
Twomey, Kevin *pharmaceutical executive*

**Canonsburg**
Coury, Robert J. *pharmaceutical executive*
Piatt, Jack Boyd *manufacturing executive*
Puskar, Milan *pharmaceuticals executive*

**Chambersburg**
Rumler, Robert Hoke *agricultural products executive, consultant, retired trade association administrator*

**Chesterbrook**
Hilzinger, Kurt John *health products executive*

**Collegeville**
Ruffolo, Robert R. *research and development company executive*

**Columbia**
Smith, Thomas Clair *retired manufacturing company executive*

**Conshohocken**
Lotman, Herbert *food processing executive*
Naples, Ronald James *manufacturing executive*
Spaeth, Karl Henry *retired chemicals executive, lawyer*

**Cranberry Township**
Hogberg, Carl Gustav *retired metal products executive*

**Denver**
Milner, Charles Fremont, Jr. *manufacturing executive*

**Devon**
Porter, Roger John *research and development company executive, neurologist, pharmacologist*

**Easton**
Sun, Robert Zu Jei *manufacturing company executive, inventor, educator*

**Eighty Four**
Magerko, Margaret Hardy (Maggie Magerko) *lumber company executive*

**Emmaus**

Bowers, Klaus D(ieter) *electronics executive, researcher*

**Erie**

Renkis, Alan Ilmars *plastics formulating company executive*

**Exton**

Dorsey, Jeremiah Edmund *pharmaceutical company executive*

**Greentown**

Forcheskie, Carl S. *former apparel company executive*

**Hanover**

Kline, Donald *food company executive*

**Hershey**

Cerminara, Frank *food products executive*
Davis, George F. *food products executive*
Lenny, Richard Herbert *food products executive, marketing professional*
Thomas, Andrea B. *food products executive*

**Hollidaysburg**

Bloom, Lawrence Stephen *retired clothing company executive*

**Horsham**

Christian, Mildred Stoehr *health products executive*
Sachs, Keith L. *manufacturing executive*
Toll, Robert Irwin *home construction company executive*

**King Of Prussia**

Webb, Richard Stephen *manufacturing executive*

**Lancaster**

High, S. Dale *construction executive*
Liddell, W. Kirk *specialty contracting company executive*
Lockhart, Michael D. *manufacturing executive*

**Langhorne**

Cohen, Fredric J. *pharmaceutical executive, consultant*

**Latrobe**

Cardoso, Carlos M. *metal products executive*
Tambakeras, Markos I. *machine tool manufacturer*

**Levittown**

Henshaw, Jonathan Cook *retired manufacturing executive*

**Ligonier**

Pilz, Alfred Norman *manufacturing executive*

**Limerick**

Sickler, John J. *manufacturing executive*

**Lyon Station**

Breidegam, DeLight Edgar, Jr. *battery company executive*

**Malvern**

Espe, Matthew J. *manufacturing executive*
Forese, James John *business machine company executive*
Paul, Gerald D. *electronics executive*
Rice, David H. *medical products executive*
Stetson, John Batterson, IV *construction executive*
Zandman, Felix *electronics executive*

**Marion Center**

Purdy, David Lawrence *medical products executive*

**Mc Murray**

Langenberg, Frederick Charles *manufacturing executive*

**Mechanicsburg**

Ortenzio, Robert A. *health and medical products executive*

**Newtown**

Ross, Edwin William *rubber company executive*

**Newtown Square**

Benenson, James, Jr. *manufacturer*
Grubb, Gary S. *pharmaceutical executive*

**North Wales**

Kim, Peter Sungbai *pharmaceutical research executive, educator, research and development company executive*

**Paoli**

Hermance, Frank S. *electronics executive*

**Philadelphia**

Avery, William Joseph *packaging manufacturing company executive*
Conway, John W. *manufacturing executive*
Croisetiere, Jacques M. *chemicals executive*
Fitzpatrick, J. Michael *chemicals executive*
Garnier, Jean-Pierre *pharmaceutical executive*
Gupta, Rajiv Lochan *chemicals executive*
Katherine, Robert Andrew *chemicals executive*
Kiefer, J. Richard, Jr. *retired corporate executive*
Leonard, William *retired food services company executive*
Meyer Weisgerber, Martha Lindsey *medical products executive*
Neubauer, Joseph *food services company executive*
Payne, Deborah Anne *retired medical company officer*
Potamkin, Robert *automotive executive*
Sohn, Catherine Angell *pharmaceutical executive, pharmacist*
Sutherland, L(ewis) Frederick *food products executive*

**Pipersville**

McNutt, Richard Hunt *manufacturing executive*

**Pittsburgh**

Barkus, Bruce E. *health products executive*
Belda, Alain J. P. *metal products executive*
Berkman, Louis *steel company executive*
Bunch, Charles E. *manufacturing executive*
Frank, Alan I W *manufacturing executive*
Harrell, Edward Harding *wine festival executive*
Harrison, Eric Jay *construction executive, consultant, artist*
Harshman, Richard J. *metal products executive*
Hassey, L. Patrick *metal products executive*
Heilman, Marlin Stephen *medical products executive*
Huntington, James Cantine, Jr. *retired equipment manufacturing company executive*
Jimenez, Joseph *management executive*
Johnson, William R. *food products executive*
Lego, Paul Edward *retired manufacturing executive*
Paul, Robert Arthur *steel company executive*
Plut, Stephen C. *protective equipment company executive*
Stein, Laura *food products executive*
Surma, John P., Jr. *metal products executive*
Van Oss, Stephen A. *electronics executive*
Winkleback, Arthur *food products executive*

**Portland**

Hutton, William Michael *manufacturing executive*

**Reading**

Ehlerman, Paul Michael *motorcycle and recreational batteries manufacturing company executive*

**Royersford**

Black, Jeffrey P. *manufacturing executive*

**Rydal**

Reese, Francis Edward *retired chemical company executive, consultant*

**Saint Davids**

Smalley, Christopher Joseph *pharmaceutical company professional*

**Saint Marys**

Johnson, J. M. Hamlin *manufacturing executive*

**Sewickley**

Bouchard, James Paul *metal products executive*
Thorbecke, Willem Henry *manufacturing executive, consultant*

**Shippensburg**

Collier, Duaine Alden *manufacturing and distribution company executive*

**State College**

Byrom, Fletcher Lauman *chemical manufacturing company executive*
Huck, John Lloyd *pharmaceutical executive*

**Sunbury**

Mills, William R. *food products executive*

**Valley Forge**

Dachowski, Peter Richard *manufacturing executive*
Hilyard, James Emerson *manufacturing executive*

**Warminster**

Hull, Lewis Woodruff *manufacturing executive*

**Warrendale**

O'Donnell, James V. *apparel executive*

**Wayne**

DePiano, Richard John *medical products executive*
Emmens, Matthew *research and development company executive*
Salinas, Eliseo *research and development company executive, researcher, psychiatrist*
Wilson, James Lawrence *retired chemical company executive*
Yost, R. David (David Yost) *pharmaceutical executive*

**West Chester**

Gadsby, Robin Edward *chemicals executive*
Griffiths, Jeffrey W. *electronics executive*
Heaps, Marvin Dale *retired food services company executive*

**West Point**

Choi, Dennis W. *pharmaceutical executive, neurologist, educator*

**Willow Street**

Jones, Joseph Louis *retired manufacturing executive*

**York**

Kunkle, Gary K., Jr., (Gerald K. Kunkle) *dental products company executive*
Wise, Bret W. *chemical company executive*

**Zelienople**

Efaw, Cary Ross *manufacturing executive*

**RHODE ISLAND**

**North Kingstown**

Novich, Bruce Eric *chemicals executive*

**Pawtucket**

Bifulco, Frank *toy company executive*
Goldner, Brian *toy company executive*
Holt, Richard B. *toy company executive*
Huebner, Charles J. *toy manufacturing executive*
Romanzi, Kenneth *toy manufacturing executive*
Trueb, Martin R. *toy company executive*
Wilson, E. David *toy company executive*

**Providence**

Bready, Richard Lawrence *manufacturing executive*
Choquette, Paul Joseph, Jr. *construction company executive*

Gilbane, Thomas F., Jr. *building company executive*
Papitto, Ralph Raymond *manufacturing executive*

**West Kingston**

Dowdell, Rodger B., Jr. *electronics executive*

**Woonsocket**

Sgarro, Douglas A. *pharmaceutical executive, lawyer*

**SOUTH CAROLINA**

**Aiken**

Seabrook, John Martin *retired food products executive, chemical engineer*

**Camden**

Daniels, John Hancock *agricultural products company executive*

**Charleston**

Martin, Roblee Boettcher *retired cement manufacturing executive*

**Clinton**

Cornelson, George Henry, IV, *retired textile company executive*

**Fort Mill**

Bowles, Crandall Close *textiles executive*
Cooper, Marvin D. *paper company executive*
Kutcher, Kenneth E. *manufacturing executive*

**Greenville**

Bauknight, Clarence Brock *construction executive, consultant, retail executive*
Maffucci, David G. *paper company executive*
Nemirow, Arnold Myles *paper company executive*
Newman, R. Donald *paper company executive*
Paterson, David J. *paper company executive*
Varin, Roger Robert *textile executive*

**Hartsville**

DeLoach, Harris E(ugene), Jr. *manufacturing executive, lawyer*
Hupfer, Charles J. *manufacturing executive*

**Hilton Head Island**

Cunningham, William Henry *retired food products executive*
Harty, James D. *former manufacturing company executive*
Lewis, Gene Evans *retired medical equipment company executive*
Love, Richard Emerson *retired equipment manufacturing company executive*
Mersereau, Hiram Stipe *wood products company consultant*
Pritchard, Dalton Harold *retired electronics executive*
Rulis, Raymond Joseph *manufacturing executive, consultant*
Russell, Allen Stevenson *retired metal products executive*
Wright, Marshall *manufacturing executive, diplomat*

**Kiawah Island**

Korb, William Brown, Jr. *retired manufacturing executive*

**Murrells Inlet**

Kelly, Gerald Wayne *chemical coatings company executive*

**North Charleston**

Zucker, Jerry *chemical manufacturing executive*

**Spartanburg**

Allen, G. Ashley *chemicals executive*
Dent, Frederick Baily *retired textiles executive, retired ambassador*
Milliken, Roger *textile/chemical company executive*

**SOUTH DAKOTA**

**Dakota Dunes**

Leman, Eugene D. *meat industry executive*

**Rapid City**

Daughenbaugh, Randall Jay *retired chemical company executive, consultant*
Voyles, C. Robert *electronics executive*

**Sioux Falls**

Christensen, David Allen *retired manufacturing executive*
Rosenthal, Joel *manufacturing executive*

**TENNESSEE**

**Bartlett**

Huffman, Delton Cleon, Jr. *pharmacy association executive*

**Brentwood**

Cash, W. Larry *health products executive*
Scarlett, Joseph H., Jr. *agricultural products executive*
Wright, James F. *agricultural products executive*

**Bristol**

Markison, Brian A. *pharmaceutical executive*

**Collegedale**

McKee, Ellsworth R. *food products executive*

**Collierville**

Smith, Vickie M. *chemicals executive*

**Franklin**

Andrews, William Frederick *manufacturing executive*

Jowdy, Jeffrey William *research and development company executive*
Morton, James Carnes, Jr. *automotive executive*
White, David R. *healthcare company executive*

**Kingsport**

Coover, Harry Wesley *manufacturing executive*
Deavenport, Earnest W., Jr. *chemical executive*
Ferguson, J. Brian *chemicals executive*
Findley, Don Aaron *manufacturing executive*
Head, William Iverson, Sr. *retired chemical company executive*
Lee, Theresa K. *chemicals executive*
Lorraine, Richard *chemicals executive*

**Knoxville**

Faires, Ross Norbert *manufacturing executive*
Martin, James Robert *identification company executive*

**Lebanon**

Evins, Dan W. *food products executive*

**Memphis**

Brafford, H. Wayne *paper company executive*
Dunnigan, T. Kevin *electrical and electronics manufacturing company executive*
Gestrich, Thomas E. *paper company executive*
Greiner, Charles H. *paper company executive*
Herbert, Paul *paper company executive*
Mantey, Elmer Martin *food company executive*
O'Hagan, William D. *metal products manufacturing company executive*
Pileggi, Dominic J. *electronics executive*
Rhodes, William C. III *automotive executive*
Stevens, David D. *health products executive*

**Nashville**

Bracken, Richard M. *healthcare company executive*
Cook, E. Gary *manufacturing executive*
Fitzgerald, Edmund Bacon *electronics executive*
Frost, Richard W. *manufacturing executive*
Frost, Rick *manufacturing executive*
Harris, J(acob) George *health products executive*
Hofstead, James Warner *laundry machinery company executive, lawyer*
Juszkiewicz, Henry Edward *musical instrument company executive*
Martin, Charles Neil, Jr. *health care management company executive*
Wire, William Shidaker, II, *retired apparel and footwear manufacturing company executive*

**Oak Ridge**

Poutsma, Marvin L. *retired chemical research administrator*

**Union City**

Graham, R(ichard) Newell *soft drink bottling company executive*

**TEXAS**

**Addison**

Holl, David B. *cosmetics company executive*
Rogers, Richard Raymond *cosmetics company executive*
Thompson, Charles Kerry *company executive*

**Alamo**

Pritchett, Thomas Ronald *retired metal and chemical company executive*

**Angleton**

Fu, Cary T. *electronics executive*
Nigbor, Donald E. *electronics executive*

**Arlington**

Mc Keen, Chester M., Jr. *retired manufacturing executive*

**Austin**

Culp, Joe C(arl) *electronics executive*
Duke, Carol Michiels *health products executive*
Inman, Bobby Ray *retired electronics executive*
Lang, Roberta Lynn *food products company executive, lawyer*
Mackey, John P. *food products executive*
Sullivan, Jerry Stephen *electronics executive*
Thornton, Joseph Scott *research and development company executive, materials scientist*
Vykukal, Eugene Lawrence *pharmaceutical executive, director*

**Bellaire**

Chavez, Brenda G. *construction executive, real estate agent*

**Boerne**

Richmond, James Ellis *retired restaurant company executive*

**Carrollton**

Heath, Jinger L. *cosmetics executive*
Hulbert, Paul William, Jr. *paper, lumber company executive*
Illes, George Maximilian *retired food products executive*

**College Station**

Palen, Joseph William *chemical process research company executive*

**Conroe**

Steed, Theresa Jean *manufacturing executive*

**Coppell**

McCally, Charles Richard *construction company executive, consultant, mathematician, educator*

**Corpus Christi**

Kane, Sam *meat company executive*

**Crowley**

Kemp, Thomas Joseph *retired electronics executive*

**Tacoma**
Hudson, Edward Voyle *apparel executive*
Hutchings, George Henry *food company executive*

## WEST VIRGINIA

**Beverly**
Pritt, Jeffrey Douglas *contractor, protective services official*

**Wheeling**
Bradley, James G. *metals company executive*

## WISCONSIN

**Appleton**
Boldt, Oscar Charles *construction executive, director*
Grayson, David S. *paper company executive*
Seifert, Kathi P. *manufacturing executive*
Spiegelberg, Harry Lester *retired paper company executive*

**Beloit**
Knueppel, Henry W. *manufacturing executive*

**Cedarburg**
Schaefer, Gordon Emory *food products executive*

**Clintonville**
Simpson, Vinson Raleigh *manufacturing executive, director*

**Dodgeville**
Comer, Gary C. *apparel executive*

**Fort Atkinson**
Jones, Alan Porter, Jr. *food manufacturing executive*

**Germantown**
Dohmen, John F. *pharmaceutical executive*

**Green Bay**
Kress, William F. *manufacturing executive*
Marsh, Miles L. *paper company executive*

**Hartland**
Burrus, Daniel Allen *research and development company executive, consultant*

**Kohler**
Kohler, Herbert Vollrath, Jr. *diversified manufacturing company executive*
Wells, Richard A. *manufacturing executive*

**La Crosse**
Drazkowski, Mark *food products executive*

**Madison**
Macfarlane, Alastair Iain Robert *manufacturing executive*
Shain, Irving *retired chemicals executive, academic administrator*

**Manitowoc**
Growcock, Terry D. *agricultural products executive*

**Markesan**
Chamberlain, Robert Glenn *retired tool manfacturing executive*

**Milwaukee**
Adami, Norman J. *brewery executive*
Barth, John M. *manufacturing executive*
Beals, Vaughn Le Roy, Jr. *retired motorcycle manufacturing executive*
Bishop, Charles Joseph *manufacturing executive*
Bleustein, Jeffrey L. *motorcycle company executive*
Colbert, Virgis W. *food products executive*
Colbert, Virgis William *food products executive*
Davis, Don H., Jr. *multi-industry high-technology company executive*
Feitler, Robert *shoe company executive*
Grade, Jeffery T. *manufacturing executive*
Hanson, John Nils *industrial high technology manufacturing company executive*
Jones, Paul W. *manufacturing executive*
Keyes, James Henry *manufacturing executive*
Manning, Kenneth Paul *specialty chemical company executive*
Martin, Vincent Lionel *retired manufacturing executive*
Myers, C. David *manufacturing executive*
Nosbusch, Keith D. *multi-industry high-technology company executive*
O'Toole, Robert Joseph *retired manufacturing executive*
Roell, Stephen A. *manufacturing executive*
Shiely, John Stephen *manufacturing executive, lawyer*
Sterner, Frank Maurice *manufacturing executive*
Ziemer, James L. *motorcycle company executive*

**Oconomowoc**
Peebles, Allene Kay *manufactured housing company executive*

**Oshkosh**
Siepmann, James Patrick *research and development company executive, retired physician*

**Pleasant Prairie**
Cherry, Peter Ballard *electrical products corporation executive*
Michaels, Jack D. *manufacturing executive*
Morrone, Frank *electronics executive*

**Racine**
Campbell, Edward Joseph *retired machinery company executive*
Johnson, H(erbert) Fisk *manufacturing executive*
Konz, Gerald Keith *retired manufacturing executive*

Rayburn, David B. *manufacturing executive*
Rosso, Jean-Pierre *electronics executive*
Wambold, Richard Lawrence *manufacturing executive*

**South Milwaukee**
Kitzke, Eugene David *research and development company executive*

**Sturtevant**
Johnson, S. Curtis *chemicals executive*
Lonergan, Edward F. *manufacturing executive*

**Sussex**
Losee, John Frederick, Jr. *manufacturing executive*
Stromberg, Gregory *printing ink company executive*

**Waukesha**
Hogan, Joseph M. *health products executive*
Maas, Duane Harris *distilling company executive*
Ramirez, Agustin A (Gus Ramirez) *auto parts manufacturing company executive*

**West Bend**
Gehl, William D. *manufacturing executive*

**Wisconsin Rapids**
Engelhardt, LeRoy A. *retired paper company executive*

## WYOMING

**Jackson**
Furrer, John Rudolf *retired manufacturing executive*

**Wilson**
Gordon, Stephen Maurice *manufacturing company executive, rancher*
Harrell, Samuel Macy *agribusiness executive*

## TERRITORIES OF THE UNITED STATES

### PUERTO RICO

**Dorado**
Diaz, Heriberto *medical products executive*
Spector, Michael Joseph *agribusiness executive*

## CANADA

### ALBERTA

**Calgary**
Holman, J(ohn) Leonard *retired manufacturing corporation executive*

### BRITISH COLUMBIA

**Richmond**
Cordoba, Mike *food products executive*

**Victoria**
Fuller, James Chester Eedy *retired chemical company executive*

### MANITOBA

**Winnipeg**
MacKenzie, George Allan *medical products executive*

### NEW BRUNSWICK

**Fredericton**
Grotterod, Knut *retired paper company executive*

### NOVA SCOTIA

**Stellarton**
Sobey, David Frank *food company executive*

### ONTARIO

**Aurora**
Lanthier, Ronald Ross *retired manufacturing executive*

**Cambridge**
White, Joseph Charles *manufacturing and retailing company executive*

**Concord**
Deveson, Gregory S. *automotive executive*

**Greely**
Lister, Earle Edward *retired research executive*

**Hamilton**
Mott, Rodney B. *metal products executive*

**Mississauga**
Kennedy, John W. *health products executive*
Melnyk, Eugene N. *pharmaceutical company executive, professional sports team executive*

**Nepean**
Chudobiak, Walter James *electronics executive*

**Ottawa**
Beare-Rogers, Joyce Louise *retired research and development executive*

**Peterborough**
Burwick, David *beverage company executive*

**Toronto**
Connell, Philip Francis *food industry executive*
Stadelman, William Ralph *chemicals executive*
Wleugel, John Peter *manufacturing executive*

### QUEBEC

**Montreal**
Molson, Eric H. *brewery company executive*
O'Neill, Daniel J. *brewery company executive*
Redfern, John D. *manufacturing executive*
Rolland, Lucien Gilbert *paper company executive, director*

### SASKATCHEWAN

**Regina**
Phillips, Roger *retired steel company executive*

## MEXICO

**Garza Garcia**
Alva, Salvador *food products executive*

**Mexico City**
Aramburúzabála, Maria Asunción *food products executive*
Vargas Legaspi, Juan *manufacturing executive*

## AUSTRALIA

**Milsons Point**
Foster, Milo George *manufacturing executive*

**Sydney**
Selley, Michael L. *pharmaceutical company executive*

## THE BAHAMAS

**Nassau**
Dingman, Michael David *manufacturing executive, investor*

## BELGIUM

**Brussels**
Buysse, Paul Henri Maria *manufacturing executive*

## CAYMAN ISLANDS

**Grand Cayman**
Abu-Ghazaleh, Mohammad *food products executive*

## ENGLAND

**Beckenham**
Lader, Malcolm Harold *pharmaceutical consultant*

**Buckinghamshire**
Castell, Sir William Martin *health products executive*

**Cheshunt Hertfordshire**
Leahy, Sir Terry *food products executive, marketing professional*

**London**
Baird, Dugald Euan *automotive executive*
Barnevik, Percy Nils *electrical company executive*
Bravo, Rose Marie *apparel executive*
Brennan, David R. *pharmaceutical executive*
Walsh, Paul S. *food products executive*

**Milton Keynes**
Throdahl, Mark Crandall *medical products executive*

**Surrey**
Vere Hodge, Richard Anthony *pharmaceutical executive, consultant*
Ahrendts, Angela J. *apparel executive*

## FINLAND

**Tampere**
Andriano, Kirk Patrick *pharmaceutical executive*

## FRANCE

**Paris**
Burke, Michael *apparel executive*
Choay, Patrick Henri *pharmaceutical executive*
Collomb, Bertrand Pierre *cement company executive*
Payri, Joel *pharmaceutical marketing executive*

## GERMANY

**Bad Homburg**
Klatten, Susanne Quandt *pharmaceutical executive*

**Düsseldorf**
Schulz, Ekkehard *metal products executive*

**Munich**
Bangle, Christopher Edward (Chris Bangle) *automotive company car designer*

**Schleusingen-Gethles**
Frank, Dieter *retired chemicals executive*

**Stuttgart**
Zetsche, Dieter *automotive executive*

## GREECE

**Athens**
Larounis, George Philip *manufacturing executive, director*

## HONG KONG

**Cheung Sha Wan**
Dyer, David F. *apparel company executive*

## JAPAN

**Minato**
Glauner, Frank J. *electronics executive*

**Tokyo**
Baba, Isamu *construction company executive*
Ohga, Norio *retired electronics executive*
Saba, Shoichi *electronics executive, director*
Wakumoto, Yoshihiko *electronics company executive, grants executive*

**Toyota**
Toyoda, Shoichiro *automotive executive*

## SINGAPORE

**Singapore**
McNamara, Michael *electronics executive*

## SPAIN

**Madrid**
Feltenstein, Harry David, Jr. *chemicals executive*

## SWEDEN

**Stockholm**
Johnson, Antonia Axson *food products executive*
Stewart, S. Jay *automotive executive*
Westerberg, Lars *automotive safety systems company executive*

## TAIWAN

**Taipei**
Chuang, Yii-Der *retired manufacturing executive, diplomat*

## VENEZUELA

**Caracas**
Salas, Randall Nouel *automotive company executive*

## ADDRESS UNPUBLISHED

Acerra, Michele (Mike Acerra) *engineering and construction company executive*
Adkinson, Brian Lee *manufacturing executive*
Alden, Ingemar Bengt *pharmaceuticals executive*
Alexander, Judd Harris *retired paper company executive*
Alig, Frank Douglas Stalnaker *retired construction company executive*
Allaire, Paul Arthur *former office equipment company executive*
Alm, John Richard *beverage company executive*
Amstutz, Daniel Gordon *agricultural products executive, consultant, retired federal agency administrator, retired grain company executive*
Amundson, Joy A. *pharmaceutical and health products executive*
Anderegg, Karen Klok *business executive*
Anderer, Joseph Henry *textile company executive*
Anderson, Joseph Norman *retired food products executive, retired academic administrator*
Anderson, Scott A. *electronics executive*
Andersson, Bo I. *automotive executive*
Andersson, Craig Remington *retired chemical company executive*
Angel, Albert D. *research and development company executive*
Archibald, Nolan D. *household and industrial products company executive*
Aschauer, Charles Joseph, Jr. *retired health products executive*
Atchison, Joseph Edward *pulp and paper industry consultant*
Augustsson, Peter *former automotive executive*
Barca, George Gino *international winery executive, financial investor, consultant*
Barna, Peter *chemical company financial executive*
Barrow, Robert Earl *retired agricultural products executive*
Bassin, Gilbert Sheldon *manufacturing executive, engineer*
Batts, Warren Leighton *retired manufacturing executive*
Baumgartner, Vito H. *manufacturing executive*
Beck, Albert *manufacturing executive*

Novak, Alan Lee *retired pharmaceutical company executive*
Oatway, Francis Carlyle *corporate executive*
O'Brien, George Aloysius, Jr. *paper company executive*
O'Connor, James G. *auto company executive*
O'Dell, Walden Wesley *manufacturing executive*
O'Donnell, Kevin *retired metal products executive*
O'Neill, Harry William *retired research market and opinion company executive*
Ordal, Caspar Reuben *retired cosmetics executive*
Oster, Lewis Henry *manufacturing executive, industrial engineer, consultant*
Owens, Charles Vincent, Jr. *pharmaceutical executive, consultant*
Pace, George W. *food products company executive*
Pacheco, Susan *automotive executive*
Padilla, James Jerome (Jim Padilla) *retired automotive executive*
Page, Raymond *research and development company executive*
Parker, Michael D. *chemicals executive*
Pattillo, Gary A. *beverage distribution executive*
Peapples, George Alan *retired automotive executive*
Pearce, Paul Francis *retired electronics executive, aerospace engineer*
Peck, Arthur John, Jr. *retired manufacturing executive, lawyer*
Perkins, Cheryl A. *paper company executive*
Petersen-Frey, Roland *manufacturing executive*
Peterson, Carl Eric *metal products executive, banker*
Peterson, Robert Austin *retired manufacturing executive*
Potts, Gerald Neal *manufacturing executive*
Pouletty, Philippe *health products executive*
Powell, Thomas Edward III *biological supply company executive, physician*
Preston, Seymour Stotler III *chemicals executive*
Pruis, John J. *manufacturing executive*
Pyatt, Kedar Davis, Jr. *research and development company executive*
Pylipow, Stanley Ross *retired manufacturing company executive*
Qualls, Robert L. *manufacturing executive, bank executive, educator, retired state official*
Queen, James E. *automotive executive*
Raghavan, Asuri *construction executive*
Rajagopalan, Dilip *pharmaceutical executive*
Ramadan, Nabih M. *pharmaceutical company official, educator*
Rankin, Douglas Houston *finance executive*
Rao, Rama Krishna R. *pharmaceutical company executive*
Rassman, Joel H. *home construction company executive*
Ratliff, Robert J. *retired farm equipment manufacturing executive*
Ray, Amrit *pharmaceuticals strategist, company executive*
Ray, Jane Zimrode *retired machine shop executive*
Regan, Paul Jerome, Jr. *manufacturing company executive, consultant*
Regelbrugge, Roger Rafael *steel company executive*
Reiniche, Dominique *food products executive*
Renne, Paul F. *retired food products executive*
Reyes, M. Jude *food products distribution executive*
Rhodes, Peter Edward *label company executive*
Rice, Donald B. *biotechnology company executive*
Richard, Edward H. *manufacturing executive, retired municipal official*
Richardson, Thomas Andrew *business executive, educator*
Richman, Peter *electronics executive*
Richter, Robert C. *retired automotive executive*
Risdon, Michael Paul *manufacturing executive*
Rivera, Richard Edwin *former restaurant chain executive*
Robbins, Ray C. *retired manufacturing executive*
Roberts, Michael J. *former food products executive*
Roesner, Peter Lowell *manufacturing executive*
Rohde, Bruce C. *food company executive, lawyer*
Rooke, David Lee *retired chemical company executive*
Roorda, John Francis, Jr. *manufacturing executive, consultant*
Rosenberg, Rudy *chemical company executive*
Rothwell, Timothy *pharmaceutical executive*
Routson, Clell Dennis *manufacturing executive*
Rucci, Anthony Joseph *health care products and services executive*
Rudick, A. Joseph *research and development company executive*
Rudy, Raymond Bruce, Jr. *retired food company executive*
Rui, Yong *research and development company executive*
Rukeyser, Robert James *manufacturing executive*
Rutsky, Lester *retired textiles executive, writer*
Ryan, George William *manufacturing executive*
Ryan, Joan *food company executive*
Rymar, Julian W. *manufacturing executive, director*
Saliba, Jacob *manufacturing executive*
Sapoff, Meyer *retired electronics executive*
Savin, Ronald Richard *chemicals executive*
Schwartz, Bernard Leon *retired space and communications company executive*
Selick, Howard E. (Barry Selick) *biotechnology executive*
Sellers, Donald R. *biotechnology company executive*
Serenbetz, Robert *manufacturing executive, financial planner*
Shapira, David S. *food products and retail grocery executive*
Shapiro, Robert B. *former food products manufacturing company executive*
Sharkey, Leonard Arthur *automobile company executive*
Shea, Bernard Charles *retired pharmaceutical executive*
Shepherd, Mark, Jr. *retired electronics company executive*
Sherman, George M. *former food products executive*

Sherman, Patsy O'Connell *retired manufacturing executive, chemist*
Sherwin, Stephen A. *health products executive*
Shlapak, Fred *electronics executive*
Shuster, Robert G. *electronics executive, consultant*
Siegel, Jack Morton *retired pharmaceutical executive*
Silverman, Stanley Wayne *chemical company executive*
Simeral, William Goodrich *retired chemical company executive*
Simon, Nicholas J. III *medical products executive*
Sissel, George Allen *manufacturing executive, lawyer, engineer*
Sleeman, Donald George *construction executive, contractor*
Slusser, Eugene Alvin *electronics executive, consultant*
Smith, Frederick Coe *retired manufacturing executive*
Smith, Goff *industrial equipment manufacturing executive*
Smith, Robert Hugh *retired engineering construction company executive*
Sobol, Robert E. *medical company executive*
Somers, Louis Robert *retired food company executive*
Sopranos, Orpheus Javaras *manufacturing executive*
Southerland, S. Duane *manufacturing executive*
Staginnus, Ulf *pharmaceutical executive, health economist*
Starr, Leon *retired chemical research company executive*
Stavropoulos, William S. *retired chemical company executive*
Steffensen, Dwight A. *former medical products and data processing services executive*
Stephens, Thomas G. *automotive executive*
Stern, Arthur Paul *electronics executive*
Stevens, Anne L. *retired automotive executive*
Stewart, Joseph Turner, Jr. *retired pharmaceutical executive*
Stiritz, William P. *food products executive*
Stone, Alan John *manufacturing company executive, real estate company executive*
Stott, Don S. *precious metals products executive*
Stranghoener, Larry W. *manufacturing executive*
Stratton, Robert *retired electronics executive*
Sullivan, Eugene John Joseph *manufacturing executive, director*
Sullivan, G. Craig *household products executive*
Szlam, Aleksander *manufacturing executive*
Szydlowski, Ralph *retired metal products executive*
Tabron, Wendy *paper company executive*
Tallett, Elizabeth Edith *biopharmaceutical company executive*
Tane, Susan Jaffe *retired manufacturing company executive*
Tannenberg, Dieter E.A. *retired manufacturing executive*
Tarrance, Vernon Lance, Jr. *research and development company executive*
Taylor, Robert Morgan *electronics executive*
Teagle, David Bryan *manufacturing executive*
Templin, Kenneth Elwood *paper company executive*
Teplow, Theodore Herzl *retired valve company executive*
Thomas, Lee Muller *former paper company executive, former government offical*
Thomas, Tom *retired plastics company executive*
Thomas-Graham, Pamela *apparel executive*
Thompson, Ralph Newell *former chemical corporation executive*
Thompson, Richard Leon *pharmaceutical executive, lawyer*
Thorp, Benjamin A. III *retired paper company executive*
Tinstman, Robert Allen *former construction company executive*
Tombros, Peter George *pharmaceutical executive*
Tomita, Kazuo (Joe) *automotive executive*
Torbica, Zeljko Marko *construction executive, educator*
Toupin, Harold Ovid *retired chemical company executive*
Trice, William Henry *paper company executive*
Turner, Andrew L. *healthcare management company executive*
Tutor, Ronald N. *construction company executive*
Uffelman, Malcolm Rucj *electronics executive*
Unanue, Joseph A. *retired food products executive*
Vallner, Joseph J. *medical products executive*
Van Tassel, James Henry *retired electronics executive*
Verderber, Joseph Anthony *capital equipment company executive*
Vitt, David Aaron *health products executive*
Volkhardt, John Malcolm *food products executive*
Washington, Lawrence J., Jr. *chemicals executive*
Wasson, James Walter *aircraft electronics manufacturing company executive*
Watkins, Dean Allen *electronics executive, educator*
Wavle, James Edward, Jr. *pharmaceutical company executive, lawyer*
Weaver, William Charles *manufacturing executive*
Weber, Mark *clothing company executive*
Wechsler, Sergio *automotive executive, consultant*
Weisswasser, Stephen *electronics executive*
Welburn, Edward T. *automotive executive*
Welch, Oliver Wendell *retired pharmaceutical executive*
West, Kenneth Irwin *automotive executive*
wHines, Anthony Loring *automotive executive*
White, Bertram Milton *chemicals executive*
Wiesen, Donald Guy *retired diversified manufacturing company executive*
Wiley, Carl Ross *timber company executive*
Willauer, Whiting Russell *retired manufacturing executive, systems engineer*
Williams, Dorothy Standridge *retired food products manager, civic worker*
Williams, Kevin W. *automotive executive*
Winkler, Joseph Conrad *former recreational products manufacturing executive*
Witt, Hugh Ernest *manufacturing executive, consultant*

Wolff, Brian Richard *metal products executive*
Wollert, Gerald Dale *retired food products executive, securities trader*
Wright, David L. *food and beverage company executive*
Wyatt, Lance B. *pharmaceutical executive*
Yeager, Kurt Eric *research and development company executive*
Yeric, Greg *electronics executive*
Yontz, Kenneth Fredric *medical and chemical company executive*
Young, Jay Maitland *health products executive, consultant*
Zabriskie, John L. *healthcare and agricultural products manufacturing company executive*
Zajac, John *semiconductor equipment company executive*
Zeffren, Eugene *cosmetics executive*

---

## INDUSTRY: SERVICE

### UNITED STATES

#### ALABAMA

**Alabaster**
Harvey, James Mathews, Jr. *communications specialist*

**Athens**
Lafevor, Kimberly Ann *human resources specialist, educator*

**Birmingham**
Etterer, Sepp *industrial relations specialist, consultant, application developer*
Floyd, John Alex, Jr. *marketing professional, director, horticulturist*
Furnas, Howard Earl *recreational facility executive, retired federal official*
Gardner, Gary Van *equipment manufacturing company official*
Harris, Aaron *management consultant*
Luckie, Robert Ervin, Jr. *advertising executive*
Stitt, Frank *food service executive*

**Columbiana**
Armistead, William Cole, Jr. *marketing professional*

**Gadsden**
Grimm, James R. (Ronald Grimm) *management consultant*

**Huntsville**
McIntyre-Ivy, Joan Carol *data processing executive*

**Hurtsboro**
Bouilliant-Linet, Francis Jacques *global management consultant*

**Mobile**
Hart, Eric Mullins *consumer products company executive*
Rummel, Harold Edwin *travel company executive, retail executive*

**Montgomery**
Holifield, Leonard Cleve *security firm executive, educator*
Luna, Patricia Adele *marketing executive*
Murkett, Philip Tillotson *human resource executive*

#### ALASKA

**Anchorage**
Porcaro, Michael Francis *advertising executive*

**Fairbanks**
Thompson, Daniel Emerson *vending machine service company executive*

#### ARIZONA

**Chandler**
Brunello-McCay, Rosanne *sales executive*
Williams, James Eugene *management consultant*
Willis, Edward Oliver *management consultant, state agency administrator*

**Flagstaff**
Bolin, Richard Luddington *industrial development specialist, consultant*

**Fountain Hills**
Lacy, Herman Edgar *management consultant*

**Glendale**
Yazzie, Aaron Franklin *events laborer*

**Green Valley**
Ragan, James Thomas *communications executive*

**Mesa**
Gottry, Steven Roger *communications executive, scriptwriter*
Johnson, Doug *advertising executive, public relations executive*
Luth, William Clair *retired research manager*
Murphy, Edward Francis *sales executive*

**Payson**
Hegarty, Christopher Joseph *management and financial consultant*

**Peoria**
Gould, Dorothy Mae *executive secretary, soprano*

Schindler, William Stanley *retired public relations executive*

**Phoenix**
Armstrong, Nelson William, Jr. *gaming company executive*
Curcio, Christopher Frank *deputy director*
Drain, Albert Sterling *business management consultant*
Feldberg, Harley *marketing professional*
Genrich, Mark L. *corporate communications director*
Hamada, Richard *computer company executive*
Moulton Reger, Sara Jonene *global management executive*
Smith, George *marketing professional*
Wright, Margaret Taylor *marketing consultant, publisher*

**Rio Verde**
Scott, Louis Edward *advertising executive*

**Scottsdale**
Allen, A. William, III, (Bill Allen) *food service executive*
Blinder, Martin S. *management consultant, art dealer*
Doglione, Arthur George *data processing executive*
Grier, James Edward *hotel executive, lawyer*
Highet, Mac *travel company executive*
Kumar, Kv *management consultant*
L'Allier, James Joseph *training services executive, educator*
Lavenson, Susan Barker *hotel corporate executive, consultant*
Maggard, Woodrow Wilson, Jr. *management consultant*
Robb, Cameron *wireless communications company executive*
Slager, Donald W. *waste management executive*
Strock, James Martin *communications executive, writer, entrepreneur*
Thompson, Bradford *chef*
Travers, Paul *company executive*
Zillmer, John J. *waste management administrator*

**Sierra Vista**
Bowen, Harry Ernest *management consultant*

**Sun City West**
Berkenkamp, Fred Julius *management consultant*
Forti, Lenore Steimle *management consultant*
Stevens, George Richard *business consultant, public information officer*

**Tempe**
Cortright, Barbara Jean *public relations executive, writer*
Meehan, Robert Henry *human resources executive, business educator, electronics executive*

**Tucson**
Barton, Stanley Faulkner *retired management consultant*
Cooper, Corinne *communications consultant, lawyer*
Hasselmo, Ann Hayes Die *executive recruiter, consultant, psychologist, educator, retired academic administrator*
Jones, Frank Wyman *management consultant, director, mechanical engineer*
Lewis, Wilbur H. *educational management consultant*
Rose, Hugh *management consultant*
Walker, Ronald Hugh *retired management consultant*
Williams, Alan Keiser *management consultant*

#### ARKANSAS

**Berryville**
Sanders, Larry Dale *funeral director, coroner*

**Conway**
Hatcher, Joe Branch *management consultant*

**Hot Springs**
Smart, Catherine Anne *retired administrative assistant*

**Hot Springs Village**
Henning, Lloyd Craig *retired inventory executive*

**Jonesboro**
Tims, Robert Austin *data processing official, pilot*

**Little Rock**
Barr, Frederick Reichert, Jr. *marketing executive*
McCaleb, Annette Watts *executive secretary*

**Pine Bluff**
Long, Edward Arlo *management consultant, retired manufacturing executive*

**West Memphis**
Howell, Kathy Aileen *advertising executive*

#### CALIFORNIA

**Agoura Hills**
Gressak, Anthony Raymond, Jr. *sales executive*

**Alameda**
Janowitz, Jeffrey Mark *management consultant*
Potash, Jeremy Warner *public relations executive*
Potash, Stephen Jon *public relations executive*

**Alamo**
Whalen, John Sydney *management consultant*

**Aliso Viejo**
Blum, Scott Allen *Internet company executive*
Grover, Neel *Internet company executive*

**Altadena**
Dobbins, Maggie Sonne *real estate investment company executive*
Eisen, Glenn Philip *management consultant, educator*

**Alviso**
Ramsay, Michael *communications company executive*
Rogers, Thomas Sydney *communications company executive*
Sordello, Steve *communications executive*

**Anaheim**
Miller, Mark A. *information technology training executive*

**Aptos**
Trounstine, Philip John *communications consultant, academic administrator*

**Atherton**
Anderson, Harry W. (Hunk) *retired food service executive*

**Belmont**
Vieux, Alex Serge *computer company executive, educator, journalist, entrepreneur*

**Berkeley**
Freese, Rich *marketing executive*
Waters, Alice *executive chef, restaurant owner, writer*

**Beverly Hills**
Bollenbach, Stephen Frasier *hotel executive*
Cantor, Alan Bruce *management consultant, application developer*
Hardy, Sean *chef*
Hart, Matthew J. *hotel and recreation executive*
Hefter, Lee *chef*
Hilton, Barron (William Barron Hilton) *hotel executive*
La Forgia, Robert M. *hotel executive*
McKenzie-Swarts, Molly *human resources specialist, hotel executive*
Riess, Gordon Sanderson *management consultant*
Zarem, Abe Mordecai *management consulting executive*

**Burbank**
Caouette, David Paul *public relations executive*

**Calabasas**
Stark, Martin J. *management consultant*

**Camarillo**
Cobb, Shirley Ann Dodson *public relations consultant, journalist*

**Cambria**
Morse, Richard Jay *human resources specialist, consultant*

**Carlsbad**
Conway, Daniel Edward *management consultant*
Heckmann, Richard J. *sporting goods company executive*
Wilson, Donald Grey *management consultant*

**Carmel**
Pippi, Mikel Eugene *food service executive*
Skidmore, Howard Franklyn *public relations counsel*
Smith, Gordon Paul *management consultant*

**Carpinteria**
Adizes, Ichak *management consultant, writer*
Puzder, Andrew F. *food service executive, lawyer*

**Chatsworth**
Weisbrod, Ken (Joseph Louis Weisbrod) *marketing professional*

**Chino Hills**
Nash, Sylvia Dotseth *management consultant*

**Claremont**
Hawkins, Gregory J. *consumer products company executive*

**Concord**
Travers, Judith Lynnette *human resources executive*

**Corona**
White, Joy Mieko *retired communications executive*

**Corona Del Mar**
O'Brien, John William, Jr. *management consultant*

**Corte Madera**
Tate, John William *consumer products company executive, former food products executive*

**Culver City**
Boonshaft, Hope Judith *public relations executive*

**Cupertino**
Jobs, Steven Paul *computer company executive*
Johnson, Allison *corporate communications specialist, marketing executive*
Oppenheimer, Peter *computer company executive*

**Daly City**
Hargrave, Sarah Quesenberry *consulting company executive, public relations executive*

**Dublin**
Chen, John S. *computer company executive*

**El Segundo**
Eckert, Robert A. *consumer products company executive*
Honeycutt, Van B. *computer company executive*
Kilpatrick, Frank Stanton *marketing executive*
Laphen, Michael W. *computer company executive*

McCarty, Shirley Carolyn *consumer products company executive*
McQuillin, Richard Ross *management consultant*
Tucker, Paul Thomas *computer company executive*
Vollrath, Frederick E. *human resources specialist, career officer*

**Encino**
Greenberg, Allan *advertising and marketing research consultant*

**Eureka**
Hannaford, Peter Dor *public relations executive, writer*

**Foster City**
Liu, Leonard *software services company executive*
Lutvak, Mark Allen *computer company executive*
Miller, Jon Philip *marketing professional, pharmaceutical executive*
Yan, Martin *celebrity chef*

**Fountain Valley**
Berman, Steven Richard *computer company executive*

**Fremont**
Lankford, James E. *food service executive*
Parikh, Mihir *consumer products company executive*
Pipkin, Robert Donald *quality assurance professional, cardiologist*
Tantra, Muljadi *corporate marketing professional*

**Fresno**
Ganulin, Judy *public relations professional*

**Fullerton**
Sowder, Kathleen Adams *marketing executive*

**Glendale**
Belk, Jennifer Elizabeth *human resources specialist*
Hughes, Bradley Wayne *storage company executive*
Misa, Kenneth Franklin *management consultant*
Stewart, Julia A. *food service executive*

**Granite Bay**
Holtz, Sara *marketing consultant*

**Half Moon Bay**
Fennell, Diane Marie *marketing professional, process engineer*

**Healdsburg**
Keane, Douglas *chef*

**Hemet**
Holley, Robert William *sales executive, minister*

**Hillsborough**
Westerfield, Putney *management consulting executive*

**Indian Wells**
Jennings, Richard Milburn *resort developer*
Kelley, John Paul *communications consultant*

**Indio**
Garra, Raymond Hamilton, II, *marketing executive*

**Irvine**
Baab, Carlton *advertising executive*
Coleman, J. Edward *computer company executive*
Karlovic, Martin Stephen *marketing executive, electrical engineer*
Phillips, Steve *computer company executive*
Pocock, J. Michael *communications executive*
Seller, Gregory Erol *marketing executive, consultant, writer*
Sherwood, Rod(erick) III *computer company executive*
Snyder, Rick (Richard D. Snyder) *computer company executive*

**Joshua Tree**
Hope, Harry Joe (Joeseph) *retired corporate communications specialist, writer*

**Kentfield**
Edgar, James Macmillan, Jr. *management consultant*

**La Habra**
Chase, Cochrane *advertising agency executive*

**La Jolla**
Bardwick, Judith Marcia *management consultant*
Kent, Paula *public relations, marketing and management consultant, lecturer*

**La Quinta**
Eversole, Barbara Louise *administrative assistant*
Henry, Nancy Louise *hospitality executive, mayor*

**La Verne**
Jalbert, Janelle Jennifer *executive recruiter, secondary school educator*

**Laguna Niguel**
Greenberg, Lenore *public relations professional*

**Larkspur**
Dellar, Michael D. *restaurant owner, hospitality industry consultant*

**Livermore**
Tripodes, James G. *nuclear safety and environmental regulatory affairs professional*

**Long Beach**
Brown, Roxanne (Jerene Roxanne Brown) *sales executive*
Halili, Antonio Marquez *facilities maintenance mechanic*
Sosoka, John Richard *consulting firm executive, engineer*

**Los Angeles**
Belkind, Elizabeth *chef*
Beltramo, Michael Norman *management consultant*
Bender, Dean *public relations executive*
Bianchi, Carisa *advertising company executive*
Bloch, Paul *public relations executive*
Bohle, Sue *public relations executive*
Bremond, Duane Benjamin *marketing professional*
Cecere, Domenico *homebuilding company executive*
Chang, Edward H. *computer company executive*
Chernin, Peter F. *multimedia company executive*
Clow, Lee *advertising agency executive*
Cora, Cat *chef*
Cotsen, Lloyd E. *retired consumer products company executive*
Crosby, Peter Alan *management consultant*
Dayton, Sky *telecommunications company executive*
Demeter, Dan A. *executive recruiting company executive*
Doll, Lynne Marie *public relations agency executive*
Faber, George Donald *retired communications executive*
Ferry, Richard Michael *retired executive recruiter*
Gale, Jeffrey *management consultant, business educator*
Giffin, Margaret Ethel (Peggy Giffin) *management consultant*
Gottfried, Ira Sidney *management consulting executive*
Gross, Lee *chef*
Hansen, Alexander E. *advertising agency executive*
Hansen, B(obby) J. *management consultant, real estate investor and developer*
Hartsough, Gayla Anne Kraetsch *management consultant*
Hatamiya, Lon Shoso *consultant, former state official*
Hateley, J. Michael *human resources executive*
Hill, Bonnie Guiton *consulting company executive*
Islam, Mohammad *chef*
Jensen, David Gram *management consultant*
Kalis, Murray *advertising agency executive, writer*
Kline, Richard Stephen *public relations executive*
Kozberg, Joanne Corday *public affairs consultant*
Krieger, Ellie *chef, dietitian, TV personality*
Lagasse, Emeril *chef, restaurant owner, television show host, writer*
LeFevre, David *chef*
Lentz, David *chef*
Levine, Michael *public relations executive, author, television and radio personality*
Mamer, John William *business educator*
Mathias, Alice Irene *business management consultant*
Mendoza, Ron *chef*
Murray, Alice Pearl *data processing company executive*
Nadler, Gerald *management consultant, educator*
Palevsky, Max *industrialist, director*
Peel, Mark *chef, restaurant owner*
Pondel, Roger S. *public relations executive*
Rice, Regina Kelly *marketing executive*
Richardson, James *chef*
Spindler, Paul *communications executive, consultant*
Splichal, Joachim *chef, restaurant owner*
Stern, James Coper *sales executive*
Stern, Susan Toy *human resources specialist*
Tabatabai, Jay (Magid) *travel company executive*
Tardio, Thomas A. *public relations executive*
Torres, Cynthia Ann *marketing professional*

**Malibu**
Dankanyin, Robert John *management consultant*
Tellem, Susan Mary *public relations executive*

**Manhattan Beach**
Deutsch, Barry Joseph *consulting and management development company executive*

**Marina Del Rey**
Gold, Carol Sapin *international management consultant, speaker, writer*
Jeffrey, John Orval *Internet company executive, lawyer*

**Menlo Park**
Kvamme, Mark D. *marketing professional*
Middleton, Teresa Muir *Internet company executive, researcher*
Waddell, M. Keith *human resources specialist*

**Milpitas**
Colligan, Ed *computer company executive, communications executive*
Corrigan, Wilfred J. *computer company executive*
Levy, Kenneth *computer company executive*
Talwalkar, Abhi Y. (Abhijit Y. Talwalkar) *computer company executive*
Tufano, Paul J. *computer company executive*

**Modesto**
Fedorchak, Timothy Hill *facility planning and program consulting executive*

**Monrovia**
Jemelian, John Nazar *management consultant*

**Montecito**
Hanley, Kevin Lance *maintenance company executive*

**Moreno Valley**
Calley, Tranquil Hudson *travel consultant, educator*
Guerrero, Donna Marie *sales executive*

**Moss Beach**
Glauthier, T. J. *management consultant*

**Mountain View**
Bennett, Stephen M. *computer company executive*
Bishop, Robert R. *computer company executive*
Campbell, William V. *computer company executive*

Cook, Scott David *computer software company executive*
East, John *computer company executive*
Kwon, Taek *Internet company executive*
Qureishi, A. Salam *computer company executive*

**Napa**
Chiarello, Michael *chef*
Eissmann, Walter James *consulting company executive*

**Newport Beach**
Di Massa, Ernani Vincenzo, Jr. *communications executive, television producer, writer*
McCue, Dennis Michael *management consultant*
Shonk, Albert Davenport, Jr. *advertising executive*
Wade, Michael Robert Alexander *marketing specialist*

**Newport Coast**
Evanoff, George C. *retired consumer products company executive*
Rollans, James O. *service company executive*

**Oak View**
Tennant, John Randall *management consultant*

**Oakland**
Brandford, Napoleon *security firm executive*
Kane, Jacqueline *human resources specialist*
Knauss, Donald R. *consumer products company executive*
Langenbach, Randolph *management analyst*
Lanzone, Jim *Internet company executive*
Lebda, Douglas R. *Internet company executive*
Parker, Melissa Bernice *advertising executive*
Stetler, Russell Dearnley, Jr. *investigator*
Williams, Carol H. *advertising executive*

**Oceanside**
Peckham, Donald *computer company executive*

**Orange**
Huber, H. Ronald *management consultant, educator*
Kelley, Robert Paul, Jr. *management consultation executive*

**Orinda**
Moose, Sandra Ohrn *management consultant*

**Palm Desert**
Miller, Donald Ross *management consultant*

**Palm Springs**
Arnold, Stanley Norman *management consultant, educator*
Scott, Walter, Jr. *business consultant*

**Palo Alto**
Bouchard, Gilles *computer company executive*
Bradley, R. Todd (Todd Bradley) *computer company executive, communications executive*
Dunn, Debra L. *computer company executive*
Estrin, Judith *computer company executive*
Flaxman, Jon E. *computer company executive*
Fruchterman, James Robert, Jr. *computer company executive, not-for-profit executive*
Halloran, Jean M. *human resources specialist*
Hurd, Mark V. *computer company executive*
Joshi, Vyomesh I. *computer company executive*
Lampman, Richard H. (Dick Lampman) *computer company executive*
Lyons, Cathy *computer company executive*
Mott, Randall D. (Randy Mott) *computer company executive*
Perez de Alonso, Marcela *human resources specialist, information technology executive*
Rehman, Saifur *web site design company executive*
Renfro, John M. *human resources specialist*
Robison, Shane V. *computer company executive*
Seethaler, William Charles *international business executive, consultant*
Ticknor, Carolyn M. *computer company executive*
Waller, Peter William *public relations executive*
Wayman, Robert Paul *computer company executive*
Winkler, Michael *computer company executive*
Zuckerberg, Mark (Mark Elliot Zuckerberg) *Internet company executive, entrepreneur, programmer*

**Paradise**
Bernstein, Elizabeth Ann *retired executive secretary*

**Pasadena**
Caine, Stephen Howard *data processing executive*
Kaplan, Gary *executive recruiter*
Stevens, Roy W. *sales and marketing executive*
Villanueva, Daniel D. *former communications executive, investment company executive*
Watkins, John Francis *management consultant*

**Paso Robles**
Boxer, Jerome Harvey *data processing executive, consultant, accountant, management consultant, vintager*

**Petaluma**
Purcell, Steven Richard *international management consultant, engineer, economist*

**Pleasanton**
Burd, Steven A. *food service executive*

**Potrero**
Reider, Shirley Ann *travel company executive*

**Rancho Palos Verdes**
Douglass, Craig Bruce *computer technology executive*

**Rancho Santa Fe**
Best, Jacob Hilmer, Jr. *retired hotel chain executive*
Matthews, Leonard Sarver *advertising and marketing executive*

Schirra, Walter Marty, Jr., (Wally Schirra) *business consultant, retired astronaut*

**Rancho Santa Margarita**
Parth, Frank R. *consulting company executive, educator*

**Redlands**
Rankin, Alex C. *management executive*

**Redwood City**
Cooperman, Daniel *computer software company executive, lawyer*
Henley, Jeffrey O. *computer software company executive*
Phillips, Charles E., Jr. *computer company executive*
Probst, Lawrence F. III *game systems company executive*
Sharpnack, Rayona *management consultant*
Stone, Herbert Allen *management consultant*
Wookey, John *computer software company executive*

**Riverside**
Valadez, Rudolph Antonio *security firm executive, consultant, writer, artist*

**Rutherford**
Staglin, Garen Kent *computer company executive, venture capitalist*

**Sacramento**
Franz, Jennifer Danton *public opinion and marketing researcher*
Swatt, Stephen Benton *communications executive, consultant*
Tract, Larry Scott *construction management consultant*

**Saint Helena**
Sone, Hiro *chef, restaurant owner, writer*

**Salinas**
Jeffries, Russell Morden *communications company official*

**San Andreas**
Maris, Anthony, Jr. *environmental services administrator*

**San Bernardino**
Martinez, Benjamin Ray *security officer, retired military non-commissioned officer*
Roberts, Katharine Adair *retired bookkeeper*

**San Carlos**
Eby, Michael John *marketing research and technology consultant*

**San Diego**
Adams, Loretta *marketing executive*
Bryan, John Rodney *management consultant*
Canales, Viola *management consulting executive, writer*
Cline, Stephanie E. *food service executive*
DiRuscio, Lawrence William *advertising executive*
Hoffner, John F. *food service executive*
Jacobs, Irwin Mark *communications executive*
Jacobs, Paul E. *communications company executive*
Jagoda, Barry Lionel *communications executive, writer*
Kameir, Christian *marketing executive*
Keitel, William E. *communications executive*
Lang, Linda A. *food service executive*
Larson, Mark Devin *communications executive*
Mosteller, James Wilbur III *data processing executive*
Myers, James M. *pet products executive*
Nelson, Craig Alan *management consultant*
Neumann, Linda Kay *marketing professional*
North, Robert L. *computer software executive*
Nugent, Robert J., Jr. *fast food company executive*
Padovani, Roberto *communications executive*
Payack, Paul J.J. *marketing professional, writer*
Rautenstrauch, Gary M. *marketing executive*
Robertson, Michael *Internet company executive*
Robins, Mitchell James *management consultant*
Warner, John Hilliard, Jr. *technical services company executive*
Wertheim, Robert Halley *national security consultant*

**San Francisco**
Bacas, Andrew R. *data processing executive*
Bancel, Marilyn *fund raising management consultant*
Benioff, Marc *Internet company executive*
Bernstein, Gerald William *management consultant, researcher*
Blanc, Maureen *public relations executive*
Bonnie, Shelby W. *computer company executive*
Broadway, Nancy Ruth *landscape company executive, consultant, model, actress*
Butenhoff, Susan Grace *public relations executive*
Coan, Eugene Victor *environmental services administrator*
Colton, Roy Charles *management consultant*
Conway, Craig A. *retired computer company executive*
Danko, Gary J. *chef*
Des Jardins, Traci *chef, restaurant owner*
Eddington, Thomas L. *human resources specialist, consultant*
Fake, Caterina *Internet company executive*
Falkner, Elizabeth *chef*
Gordon, Judith *communications consultant, writer*
Gudmundsson, Dadi *computer company executive*
Hara, George *computer company executive*
Jones, J. Gilbert *private investigator*
Jones, Stanton William *management consultant*
Kertzman, Mitchell E. *former software company executive, venture capitalist*
Kielarowski, Henry Edward *marketing executive*
Klammer, Joseph Francis *retired management consultant*
Kunz, Heidi *healthcare company executive*
LeFurgy, Rich *advertising executive*
Masio, Richard Frank *sales executive, director*

Molland, Maria U. *Internet company executive*
Moore, Kristen L. *marketing professional*
Murphy, Kathleen Anne Foley *communications executive*
Oakes, Nancy *chef, restaurant owner*
Parker, Diana Lynne *restaurant manager, special events director*
Plaisance, Melissa C. *consumer products company executive*
Pollack, Jeffrey Lee *restaurateur*
Pritzker, John A. *leisure services executive*
Saeger, Rebecca *advertising executive*
Solomon, Neal Edward *management consultant, executive recruiter, social theorist, entrepreneur, author*
Steppe, Stephen *management consultant*
Willner, Jay R. *consulting company executive*
Winkler, Agnieszka M. *marketing executive*

**San Gabriel**
Wong, Ronald W. *communications executive*

**San Jose**
Bannick, Matthew *Internet company executive*
Barnholt, Edward W. *former computer company executive*
Bostrom, Susan L. *marketing executive*
Bunn, Charles Nixon *management consultant*
Chizen, Bruce R. *computer company executive*
Cobb, William C. *Internet company executive*
Connors, Mary Jean *communications executive*
Dutta, Rajiv *Internet company executive*
Fister, Michael J. *computer company executive*
Jordan, Jeff *Internet company executive*
Justice, Richard *computer company executive*
Narayen, Shantanu *computer software company executive*
Omidyar, Pierre M. *Internet company executive*
Richardson, James *computer company executive*
Roelandts, Willem P. *data processing executive*
Schaller, Anthony Josef *technology management executive*
Scott, Edward William, Jr. *computer company executive*
Volpi, Mike *computer company executive*
Wallace, Richard P. *computer company executive*
Warnock, John Edward *computer company executive*
Whitman, Margaret C. (Meg Whitman) *Internet company executive*
Zwern, Arthur Louis *computer company executive*

**San Luis Obispo**
DuFresne, Armand Frederick *management consultant, engineering consultant*

**San Marcos**
Barnes, Howard G. *communications executive, film producer*

**San Mateo**
Chen, Steve *Internet company executive*
Gordon, William Bingham (Bing Gordon) *software marketing executive*
Helfert, Erich Anton *management consultant, writer, educator*
Hurley, Chad M. *Internet company executive*
Krikorian, Jason *consumer electronics company specialist*
Land, Karl-Heinz *corporate communications specialist*
Shah, Bhupen *consumer electronics company executive*

**San Rafael**
Bartz, Carol A. *computer software company executive*
Bass, Carl *computer software company executive*
Finkelstein, James Arthur *management consultant*
Wilson, Ian Holroyde *management consultant, futurist*

**San Ramon**
Cronin, Patricia Romero *computer company executive*

**San Ysidro**
Ortiz, Antonio Ignacio *public relations executive*

**Santa Ana**
Carter, Curtis William *communications executive*
Humes, William D. *computer company executive*
Tanaka, Richard I. *computer company executive*
Torrez, Caroline Herminia *human resources specialist, director, actress, musician, singer, dancer*

**Santa Barbara**
Emmons, Robert John *corporate executive, poet*
Morgan, Alfred Vance *management consulting company executive*
Scheinfeld, James David *retired travel company executive*
Schultz, Arthur Warren *retired communications executive*

**Santa Clara**
Bechtolsheim, Andy (Andreas Bechtolsheim) *software executive*
Bray, Tim (Timothy William Bray) *computer company executive, software developer*
Bryant, Andy D. *computer company executive*
Claflin, Bruce L. *software company executive*
Culbertson, Leslie S. *computer company executive*
Gelsinger, Patrick P. *computer company executive*
Hutcheson, Jerry Dee *manufacturing company executive*
Maloney, Sean M. *computer company executive*
Morris, Sandra K. *computer company executive*
Papadopoulos, Gregory Michael *computer company executive*
Pollace, Pamela L. *public relations executive*
Shavers, Cheryl L. *technology and business consultant*
Sodhani, Arvind *computer company executive*

**Santa Monica**
Auriana, Angelo *chef*
Bachrach, Charles Lewis *advertising agency executive*

Davie, Jill *chef*
Feniger, Susan *chef, television personality, writer*
Griffith, Huw *advertising executive*
Lempert, Philip *advertising executive, writer, news correspondent*
Milliken, Mary Sue *chef, television personality, writer*
Ovitz, Michael S. *communications executive*
Patel, Chandra Kumar Naranbhai *communications executive, educator, entrepreneur, researcher*
Postaer, Larry *advertising executive*
Rubin, Gerrold Robert *advertising executive*
Ryan, Jane Frances *corporate communications executive*
Straus, Matthew *wine director*
Wangard, Gregg *chef*

**Santa Rosa**
Ash, John *chef*

**Saratoga**
Syvertson, Clarence Alfred *management consultant, engineer*

**Scotts Valley**
Crandell, Kenneth James *management consultant, entrepreneur*
Luczo, Stephen J. *computer equipment company executive*
Park, Chong S. *computer company executive*
Pope, Charles C. *computer hardware company executive*
Watkins, William D. *computer hardware company executive*
Wingert, Michael J. *computer company executive*

**Seal Beach**
Burge, Willard, Jr. *software company executive*

**Sebastopol**
McCarthy, Thomas Edward *retired telecommunications executive*

**Sherman Oaks**
Cook, Paul Maxwell *technology company executive*
Dawson, David Smith *television executive*
Ross, Jeff *communications executive*
Winkler, Lee B. *business consultant*
Yasnyi, Allan David *communications company executive*

**Simi Valley**
Ritacco, Patsy Richard *sales executive*

**Soquel**
Tomash, Erwin *retired computer company executive*

**South Lake Tahoe**
Nason, Rochelle *conservation organization administrator*

**South San Francisco**
Lewis, Jason Alvert, Jr. *communications executive*

**Stockton**
Dornbush, Vicky Jean *medical billing systems executive*
Hackley, Carol Ann *public relations educator, consultant*
Jacobs, Marian *advertising executive*
Viscovich, Sir Andrew John *educational management consultant*

**Studio City**
Chambers, Clytia Montllor *retired public relations consultant*
Laba, Marvin *management consultant*
Mc Donald, Meg *public relations executive*
Moseley, Chris Rosser *marketing executive*
Richman, Anthony E. *textile rental industry association executive*
Silverman, Bruce Gary *advertising executive, consultant*

**Sun Valley**
Miller, Flemon Marshall *public works manager*

**Sunnyvale**
Braun, Lloyd *Internet company executive*
Butterfield, Stewart *Internet company executive*
Decker, Sue (Susan L. Decker) *Internet company executive*
Dunaway, Cammie *marketing executive*
Filo, David *Internet company executive*
Gifford, John F. *computer company executive*
Harari, Eli *computer company executive*
Koogle, Timothy K. *communications executive*
Lin, Frank C. *computer company executive*
Parnafes, Itzik *Internet company executive*
Raghavan, Prabhakar *Internet company executive*
Ratchev, Boris A *management consultant*
Rosensweig, Daniel L. *Internet company executive*
Sanders, Walter Jeremiah *computer company executive*
Sartain, Libby *human resources specialist*
Schneider, Hilary A. *Internet company executive*
Semel, Terry S. *Internet company executive*
Yang, Jerry *Internet company executive*

**Sutter Creek**
Sanders, Elizabeth Anne Weaver (Betsy Sanders) *management consultant, writer*

**Tehachapi**
Smith-Thompson, Patricia Ann *public relations consultant, educator*

**Torrance**
Signorovitch, Dennis J. *communications executive*

**Tracy**
Kiggins, Mildred L. *marketing professional*

**Turlock**
Harris, Randall Duane *management consultant, educator*

**Twentynine Palms**
Fultz, Philip Nathaniel *management analyst*

**Universal City**
Press, Terry *marketing executive*

**Upland**
Suh, Jung Sook Ky *personnel consultant*

**Vacaville**
Longoria, Steve *security firm executive, consultant*

**Valencia**
Pocrass, Richard Dale *management consultant*

**Vallejo**
Davis, William Albert *parks director*

**Van Nuys**
Greenberg, Daniel *electronics rental company executive*

**Venice**
Choo, Kristy *chef*
Mankin, Donald Aaron *management consultant, writer*

**Ventura**
Orfalea, Paul *printing, copying company founder, investment company executive*

**Villa Park**
Britton, Thomas Warren, Jr. *retired management consultant*

**Vista**
Mitchell, Thomas Edward, Jr. *communications cabling executive*

**Walnut Creek**
Henshaw, Guy Runals *management consultant*

**West Covina**
Musich, Robert Lorin *motivational speaker*

**West Hills**
Shirk, Jack Andrew *executive recruiter*

**West Hollywood**
Antin, Jonathan *hairstylist, entrepreneur*
DeWolfe, Chris T. *Internet company executive*
Einstein, Clifford Jay *advertising executive*
Feidelson, Marc *advertising executive*
Goin, Suzanne *chef*
Hodal, Melanie *public relations executive*
Lefebvre, Ludovic *chef*
Morris, Brian *advertising executive*
Suissa, David *advertising executive*

**Westlake Village**
Power, J.D., III, (James David Power III) *marketing executive*
Troxell, Lucy Davis *management consultant*

**Windsor**
Fieri, Guy *chef*

**Woodland Hills**
Ennis, Thomas Michael *management consultant*
Mulligan, David Keith *consulting company executive, securities arbitrator*
Stahlecker, Barbara Jean *marketing professional, consultant*

**Woodside**
Arthur, Greer Martin *leasing firm executive*

**Yountville**
Keller, Thomas A. *chef*
Lee, Corey *chef*

**COLORADO**

**Aspen**
Schendler, Auden *recreational facility executive*

**Aurora**
Reitan, Harold Theodore *management consultant*

**Black Hawk**
Jones, Linda May *tour guide, writer*

**Boulder**
Burns, Daniel Hobart *management consultant*
Collins, Jim *management researcher, author*
Hibbs, John David *computer company executive, electrical engineer, small business owner*

**Broomfield**
Crowe, James Quell (Jim Crowe) *communications executive*

**Castle Rock**
Sjostrom, Joan Sevier *retired travel company executive*

**Centennial**
Chandramouli, Srinivasan (Chandra Chandramouli) *management and systems consultant*

**Colorado Springs**
Bondurant, David William *marketing professional*
Yanney, Patrick Steven *human resources specialist*

**Denver**
Barr, Lois Faye *public relations executive, freelance/self-employed writer*
Blatter, Frank Edward *travel company executive*
Case, Paul Watson, Jr. *communications executive*
Dunham, Joan Roberts *administrative assistant*
Johnston, Gwinavere Adams *public relations consultant*
Karsh, Philip Howard *advertising executive*
Lazarus, Steven S. *management consultant, marketing consultant*
Lenk, Edward C. (Toby) *Internet company executive*

Murdock, Pamela Ervilla *travel and advertising company executive*
Myhren, Trygve Edward *communications company executive*
Neu, Carl Herbert, Jr. *management consultant*
Walker, Joan H. *marketing and communications executive*

**Durango**
Foster, James Henry *advertising executive, public relations executive*
Morris, Ronald Lew *management consultant, oil and gas industry executive, petroleum engineer*

**Englewood**
Campbell, Michael L. *recreational facility executive*
Fries, Michael T. *communications executive*
Han, Bernard L. *communications executive*
Maffei, Gregory B. *media company executive, former computer software company executive*
Malone, John C. *media company executive*
Miles, Amy E. *recreational facility executive*
Vogel, Carl E. *communications executive*

**Evergreen**
Evans, David Lynn *management consultant*

**Fort Collins**
Neil, Stuart *management consultant, real estate broker*

**Frederick**
Emlen, Warren Metz *retired computer company executive*

**Golden**
Olson, Marian Katherine *management consultant*

**Greeley**
Miller, Diane Wilmarth *retired human resources director*

**Greenwood Village**
Benson, Robert Craig III *business consultant*
Gold, Christina A. *data processing company executive*
Whealy, Michael Thomas *data processing executive, lawyer*
Wittman, Vanessa Ames *communications executive*

**Lakewood**
Martinen, John A. *travel company executive*

**Littleton**
Clark, Julie *consumer products company executive*
Dugan, Michael T. *communications executive*
Ergen, Charles W. *communications professional*
Hopping, William Russell *hospitality industry consultant, appraiser*
Kullas, Albert John *management consultant, systems engineer*
McDonnell, Michael R. *communications executive*

**Lone Tree**
Spisak, John Francis *management consultant executive*

**Longmont**
Newman, Dean Gordon *business consultant*

**Louisville**
Adams, Eula L. *data storage executive*

**Monument**
De Francesco, John Blaze, Jr. *public relations consultant, writer*

**Niwot**
Farrington, Helen Agnes *personnel director*

**Pueblo**
Maio, Heather Allen *environmental services administrator*

**Sedalia**
Cooley, Andrew Lyman *computer company executive*

**Snowmass Village**
Strand, Curt Robert *hotel executive*

**Winter Park**
Groswold, Gerald F. *retired resort executive, lawyer*

**CONNECTICUT**

**Beacon Falls**
Vignola, Andrew Michael, Sr. *computer company executive*

**Bridgeport**
Wasmer, Pedro E. *technology leasing company executive*

**Colebrook**
Burrows, John Edward *communications company executive*

**Cos Cob**
Murphy, Robert Blair *management consulting company executive*

**Cromwell**
Izzo, Lucille Anne *sales representative*

**Danbury**
Mann, Richard O. *public relations consulting company executive*

**Darien**
Cronk, Leonard *management consultant*
Kobak, James Benedict *management consultant*
McKim, Paul Arthur *management consultant, retired gas industry executive*
Morano, Gerard John *marketing executive*

**East Haddam**
Clarke, Cordelia Kay Knight Mazuy *management consultant, artist*
Clarke, Logan, Jr. *management consultant*

**Fairfield**
Johnsen, Walter Craig *security firm executive*
Luther, David Byron *management consultant*

**Farmington**
Trani, John M. *former consumer products company executive*

**Greenwich**
Ball, John Fleming *advertising executive, film company executive*
Bara, Jean Marc *finance and communications executive, artist*
Carmichael, William Daniel *management consultant, educator*
Donley, James Walton *management consultant*
Gierer, Vincent A., Jr. *tobacco and wine holding company executive*
Goergen, Robert B. *consumer products company executive*
Jacobs, Bradley S. *rental company executive*
Paulson, Paul Joseph *advertising executive*
Perless, Ellen *advertising executive*
Schlafly, Hubert Joseph, Jr. *communications executive*
Scott, John Constante *marketing company executive*
Scott, Mariette A. *marketing executive*
Srere, Benson M(ortimer) *communications executive, consultant*
Whitmore, George Merle, Jr. *management consulting company executive*
Wyman, Ralph Mark *security firm executive, healthcare company executive*

**Hartford**
Bucknall, William L., Jr. *human resources professional*
Harmon, Clara Chokenea *public relations/marketing executive*
McMahon, John E. *marketing analyst, director*

**Kent**
Friedman, Frances *public relations executive*

**Lakeville**
Levy, Ira Howard *marketing professional, real estate developer*

**Madison**
Britt, David Van Buren *retired educational communications executive*

**Milford**
DeLuca, Fred *food service executive*

**New Britain**
Loree, James M. *consumer products company executive*
Lundgren, John F. *consumer products company executive*

**New Canaan**
Axelson, Linda Rae *business director, event planning specialist*
Crossman, William Whittard *retired wire cable and communications executive*
Means, David Hammond *retired advertising executive*
Ward, Richard Vance, Jr. *management consultant*

**New Haven**
Huwiler, Joan P. *public relations executive, consultant*

**Newtown**
Cole, Richard John *marketing executive*
Goodwick, David Lee *advertising executive*

**Norwalk**
Czajkowski-Barrett, Karen Angela *human resources specialist*
Gold, Richard N. *management consultant*
Nightingale, William Joslyn *management consultant*
Stella, George *chef*
Yeosock, Michael Michael *funeral director, civil engineer*

**Old Saybrook**
Norcia, Stephen William *advertising executive*
Phillips, William E. *advertising agency executive*

**Redding**
McClure, Grover Benjamin *management consultant*
Welsh, John Francis *retired advertising executive*

**Ridgefield**
Lodewick, Philip Hughes *equipment leasing company executive*
Swartout, Torin Sherwin Roberts *logistics executive, transportation consultant*

**Riverside**
Geismar, Richard Lee *communications executive*
McSpadden, Peter Ford *retired advertising agency executive*
Schur, Jeffrey *advertising executive*

**Salisbury**
Block, Zenas *retired management consultant, educator*

**South Windsor**
Famiglietti, Nancy Zima *computer company executive*

**Southbury**
Caravatt, Paul Joseph, Jr. *communications executive*
Welton, Sharon Marie *food service executive*

**Southport**
Ambrosino, Ralph Thomas, Jr. *retired telecommunications executive*

**Stamford**
Burns, Ursula M. *printing company executive*
Burston, Richard Mervin *marketing executive*
Burton, Robert Gene *printing company executive*
Carter, Jerome N. *human resources specialist, paper company executive*
Dell, Warren Frank, II, *management consultant*
Elizondo, Patricia *sales executive*
Graf, Rudy J. *communications company executive*
Gross, Ronald Martin *consumer products company consultant*
Hicks, Wayland R. *rental company executive*
Hood, Todd Anthony *computer company executive, director*
Kucic, Joseph *management consultant, industrial engineer, network engineer, information security specialist*
Miller, Wilbur Hobart *retired management consultant*
Mulcahy, Anne Marie *printing company executive*
Nazemetz, Patricia *human resources specialist*
Pappas, Alceste Thetis *consulting company executive, educator*
Shassian, Donald R. *telecommunications company executive*
Silver, Charles Morton *communications company executive*
Steenburgh, Frank D. *consumer products company executive*
Vandebroek, Sophie Verdonckt *printing company executive*
Zimmerman, Lawrence A. *printing company executive*

**Storrs Mansfield**
Deotte, Michael J. *marketing professional*

**Waterford**
Walsh, Peter Joseph *marketing professional*

**West Hartford**
Glasser, Joseph *management consultant, educator*
Karotkin, Rose A. *marketing professional*

**Weston**
Falber, Harold Julius *marketing professional*
Murray, Thomas J. *advertising executive*

**Westport**
Aasen, Lawrence Obert *public relations executive*
Blau, Barry *marketing professional, financial consultant*
Kurz, Mitchell Howard *marketing communications executive*
Levien, Roger Eli *strategy and innovation executive*
Lewis, Margaret Mary *marketing professional*
Schriever, Fred Martin *management consultant, financial investor*

**Wilton**
Bishop, William Wade *advertising executive*
Farley, James Parker *retired advertising agency executive*
Mitchell, Richard Boyle *security firm executive*
Nickel, Albert George *advertising agency executive*
Weiland, Juliette Marie *public relations executive, freelance photographer, writer*

**Winsted**
Stawicki, Joseph John, Jr. *marketing executive*

**Woodbridge**
Alvine, Robert *industrialist, entrepreneur, world business leader, philanthropist, business owner*

**DELAWARE**

**Camden Wyoming**
Bailey, Kay Wood *management consultant*

**Greenville**
DeWees, Donald Charles *security firm executive*

**Milford**
Bergmann, William J. *personnel director*

**Wilmington**
Bloom, David Andrew *communications operations director*
Peterson, Russell Wilbur *environmental services administrator, retired governor*
Shipley, Samuel Lynn *advertising executive, public relations executive*

**DISTRICT OF COLUMBIA**

**Washington**
Aikens, Martha Brunette *park service administrator*
Andres, Jose *chef*
Augustine, Hilton H., Jr. *computer company executive*
Bartlett, John Wesley *consulting firm executive*
Berman, Ellen Sue *energy and telecommunications executive, theatre producer*
Brown, Warren *chef*
Browner, Carol M. *management consultant, former federal agency administrator*
Buben, Jeffrey Alan *restaurant owner, chef*
Cafritz, Peggy Cooper *communications executive*
Cashion, Ann *food service executive*
Chasen, Michael L. *Internet company executive*
Clifton, James K. *market research company executive*
Cohen, William Sebastian *consultant, former Secretary of Defense*
Comerford, Cristeta *chef*
Cook, Frances D. *management consultant*
Cope, Jeannette Naylor *executive search consultant*

Corso, John Anthony *management consultant, educator*
Dach, Leslie Alan *public relations company executive*
Davis, Rex Darwin *business consultant*
Dawson, Mimi Weyforth *public policy consultant*
Deaver, Michael Keith *public relations consultant*
Denysyk, Bohdan *marketing professional, consultant*
Dezenhall, Eric B. *management consultant, writer*
Duberstein, Kenneth Marc *management consultant, former White House chief of staff*
Fields, Stuart Howard *labor relations specialist*
Fishel, Andrew S. *managing director*
Ford, Carl W., Jr. *consulting firm executive, former federal agency administrator*
Fuller, Edwin Daniel *hotel executive*
Garvey, Jane *public relations executive*
Gest, Kathryn Waters *public relations executive*
Glantz, Gina *political consultant*
Grant, Carl N. *communications executive, sales executive*
Griffin, Kelly Ann *public relations executive, consultant*
Grigsby, Sharlyn Ann *human resources specialist*
Guzda, Henry Peter *industrial relations specialist*
Hagen, Wendy W. *public relations executive*
Hager, Susan Kulka *public relations executive*
Harrington, Kathleen M. *public relations company executive, former federal agency administrator*
Hatch, Cary Collins *advertising executive*
Havlicek, Franklin J. *communications executive*
Higgins, James Henry III *marketing executive*
Hightower, Dennis Fowler *retired entertainment company executive, educator*
Howard, Jack *industrial relations specialist, consultant*
Howe, Fisher *management consultant, retired government agency administrator*
Huberman, Benjamin *technology consultant*
Huggins, James Bernard *communications executive*
Jones, A. Elizabeth *corporate communications specialist, former federal agency administrator*
Kaludis, George *management consultant, publishing executive, educator*
Kingsley, Mary Lee *marketing professional*
Kotler, Milton *marketing company executive*
Kraus, Margery *management consultant, communications company executive*
Lasko, Joel *marketing executive*
Lindemann, Adam *communications executive*
Lisboa-Farrow, Elizabeth Oliver *public and government relations consultant*
Lovelace, Gail T. *human resources specialist*
Lubic, Benita Joan Alk *travel company executive*
Luchok, Joseph Alan *communications executive, consultant*
Mansfield, Edward Patrick, Jr. *advertising executive*
Marriott, John W. III *hotel executive*
Marriott, John Willard, Jr. *lodging and senior living executive*
McBride, Jonathan Evans *management consultant, director*
McQuillan, Laurence Joseph *communications consultant, educator*
Mederos, Carolina Luisa *public policy consultant*
Melnick, Howard A. *hotel executive*
Melton, Carol A. *communications executive*
Miller, Mary Jeannette *retired management consultant*
Moore, Bob Stahly *communications executive*
Morgan, Bruce Ray *management consultant*
Palumbo, Benjamin Lewis *public relations executive, consultant*
Patterson, Sally Jane *communications executive, consultant*
Pines, Wayne Lloyd *public relations executive*
Pouillon, Nora Emanuela *food service executive, chef*
Pucie, Charles R., Jr. *public affairs executive*
Pyle, Robert Noble *public relations executive*
Rainey, Jean Osgood *public relations executive*
Reed, Travis Dean *public relations consultant*
Rice, Lois Dickson *retired computer company executive*
Roberts, Carter S. *environmental services administrator*
Rosebush, James Scott *management consulting executive, former government official*
Rotunda, Donald Theodore *public relations consultant*
Roundtree, Jacqueline Washington *public relations executive, federal agency administrator*
Sasso, John *advertising and public strategies executive*
Seats, Peggy Chisolm *public affairs executive*
Shaw, William J. *hotel facility executive*
Shear, Natalie Pickus *conference and event management executive*
Skol, Michael *counter-money laundering consultant*
Skolfield, Melissa T. *public relations executive, government official*
Smith, Dean *communications advisor, arbitrator*
Smith, Nancy Lee *communications official*
Sorenson, Arne M. *hotel executive*
Stauffer, Thomas George *retired hotel executive*
Steventon, Robert Wesley *marketing executive*
Swain, Susan Marie *communications executive*
Tate, Sheila Burke *public relations executive*
Vickery, Raymond Ezekiel, Jr. *international business consultant, lawyer*
Villarreal, June Patricia *retired sales executive*
Vose, Kathryn Kahler *marketing executive, communications executive*
Walcott, John L. *communications executive*
Whittlesey, Judith Holloway *public relations executive*
Witt, James Lee *management consultant, former federal agency administrator*
Yulish, Charles Barry *retired public relations executive*

**FLORIDA**

**Arcadia**
White, Will Walter III *public relations consultant, writer*

**Bascom**
Hart, James Whitfield, Jr. *retired public relations executive, lawyer*

**Boca Grande**
Stolley, Alexander *advertising executive*

**Boca Raton**
Dorfman, Allen Bernard *international management consultant*
Dunhill, Robert *advertising executive*
Fowler, Gary Allen *management consultant*
Langbort, Polly *retired advertising executive*
Lazar, Charna L. *private investigator, security consultant, retired CIA officer*
Miller, Tonya Alicia *training and development specialist*
Monroe, William Lewis *human resources executive*
Ponzi Kay, Marylou *human resources specialist*
Schechterman, Lawrence *chef, business consultant*
Turner, Lisa Phillips *human resources executive*
Yoder, Patricia Doherty *public relations executive*

**Bonita Springs**
Hauserman, Jacquita Knight *management consultant*

**Boynton Beach**
Sondak, Arthur *retired management consultant*

**Bradenton**
Green, Raymond Ferguson St. John *marketing and advertising executive*
Houston, Stanley Dunsmore *retired public relations executive*
Robinson, Hugh R. *retired marketing executive*

**Cape Coral**
Milaski, John Joseph *management consultant*
Nightingale, Suzanne M. *management consultant*

**Casselberry**
Pantuso, Vincent Joseph *food service consultant*

**Celebration**
Renard, Meredith Anne *marketing and advertising professional*

**Clearwater**
Bazzone, Theresa (Terry) A. *sales executive*
Dutkowsky, Robert M. *computer company executive*
Grala, Jane M. *security firm executive*
Howells, Jeffrey P. *computer company executive*
Raymund, Steven A. *computer company executive*
Scarne, John *game company executive*

**Coconut Grove**
Softness, John *public relations executive*

**Coral Gables**
Buchsbaum, Karen Fuson *public relations executive, consultant*
Cole, Todd Godwin *management consultant, transportation*
Gould, Taffy *Internet company executive, real estate executive*
Hertz, Arthur Herman *communications executive*
Lomonosoff, James Marc *marketing professional*

**Daytona Beach**
Bivens, Carolyn Vesper *former advertising executive, golf association commissioner-elect*

**Deerfield Beach**
Moran, James M. *automotive sales executive*

**Deland**
Hodges, Brian W. *consumer products company executive*

**Delray Beach**
Charyk, Joseph Vincent *retired satellite telecommunications executive*
Ehrlich, Geraldine Elizabeth *management consultant*
Hardiman, Joseph Raymond *security firm executive*
Odland, Steve *consumer products company executive*

**Dunedin**
Metcalf, Robert John Elmer *industrial consultant*
Ruff, Kenneth *management consultant, information technology manager*

**Estero**
Steele, Richard J. *management consultant*

**Eustis**
King, Robert Howard *marketing professional*

**Fort Lauderdale**
Ambrose, Judith Ann *wedding planner*
Cantwell, John Walsh *advertising executive*
Castillo, Carmen *staffing company executive*
Cordesman, Michael J. *waste management administrator*
Fine, Howard Alan *management consultant*
Gerbino, John *advertising executive*
Jotcham, Thomas Denis *marketing communications executive*
Kjellmark, Eric William, Jr. *management consultant, performing company executive*
Koch, Katherine Rose *communications executive*
Krause, Roy G. *office staffing firm executive*
O'Connor, James E. *waste management executive*
Smith, Mark W. *management consultant*
Wojcik, Cass *decorative supply company executive, retired municipal official*
Zimmerman, Jordan *advertising executive, marketing professional*

**Fort Myers**
Antonic, James Paul *international marketing consultant*
Fox, Beverly *marketing professional*
Fulker, Edmund Norman *management consultant*

Goyak, Elizabeth Fairbairn *retired public relations executive*
Scott, George Alfred *advertising executive, writer*

**Fort Pierce**
Thoma, Richard William *chemical safety and waste management consultant*

**Grand Island**
Johnson, Tesla Francis *data processing executive, educator*

**Hallandale Beach**
Duffy, Earl Gavin *hotel executive*

**Havana**
Beare, Muriel Anita Nikki *public relations executive, author*

**Highland Beach**
Upbin, Hal J. *consumer products company executive*

**Hollywood**
Angstrom, Wayne Raymond *communications executive*
Sundel, Martin *management consultant, psychologist, educator*

**Jacksonville**
Fahner, Harold Thomas *marketing executive*
Matta, Mark W. *human resources specialist, manufacturing executive*
Maxwell, W(ilbur) Richard *retired management consultant*
Motsett, Charles Bourke *sales, marketing and leadership executive*
Nussbaum, Bennett *printing/copying company executive*
Prussin, Jeffrey A. *management consultant*
Schramm, Bernard Charles, Jr. *retired advertising agency executive*
Sederbaum, William *marketing professional*

**Jacksonville Beach**
Saltzman, Irene Cameron *consumer products company executive*

**Jupiter**
Baum, Herbert Merrill *consumer products company executive*
Gerson, Irwin Conrad *advertising executive*

**Key Biscayne**
Cardozo, Richard Nunez *marketing professional, educator, entrepreneur*
Evans, Peter Kenneth *advertising executive*

**Key Largo**
Chevins, Anthony Charles *retired advertising agency executive*

**Lake Buena Vista**
Rasulo, James A. *theme park executive*

**Lake Placid**
Adams, Herbert Ryan *management consultant, retired minister, mediator*

**Lake Wales**
Robinson, Richard Allen, II, *security firm executive, director*

**Lake Worth**
Saffir, Leonard *public relations executive*

**Lakeland**
Hrabusa, John T. *human resources specialist, food products executive*
Jenkins, Howard M. *supermarket executive*
Meads, Walter Frederick *communications executive, consultant, writer*
Phillips, David P. *grocery company executive*
Siedle, Robert Douglas *management consultant*
Waugaman, Richard William *sales executive*

**Longwood**
Bernabei, Raymond *management consultant*
Faller, Donald E. *marketing and operations executive*

**Lutz**
Miller, Bonnie Sewell *marketing professional, writer*

**Marco Island**
Kelly, Robert Donald *management consultant*

**Melbourne**
Farmer, Phillip W. *communications executive*
Koenig, Harold Paul *management consultant, ecologist, evangelist, writer*
Lance, Howard L. *communications executive, industrial engineer*
O'Neal, Kathleen Len *communications executive, writer, management speaker, financial consultant*

**Miami**
Amos, Betty Giles *food service executive, accountant*
Arison, Micky *cruise line company executive, professional sports team executive*
Bogusky, Alex *advertising executive*
Burgher, Cedric W. *food service executive*
Chidsey, John W. *food service executive*
Chwat, John *food service executive*
Cubas, Jose M(anuel) *advertising agency executive*
Dasburg, John Harold *restaurant executive*
Dye, H. Michael *marketing professional*
Ehrlich, Morton *marketing executive, management consultant*
Fromkin, Ava Lynda *management consultant, healthcare risk management services*
Henderson, Gene M. *marketing professional*
Nadeau, Joseph Eugene *health care management consultant, information systems consultant*
Pogede, Alexander *consulting company executive*
Salazar, Luis *management consultant, lawyer*

Schwartz, Gerald *public relations and fundraising agency executive*
Sherman, Beatrice Ettinger *hotel executive*
Van Aken, Norman *chef*
Warren, Mark Edward *cruise line executive, lawyer*
Weiser, Sherwood Manuel *hotel and corporation executive, lawyer*

**Miami Beach**
Sharlach, Jeffrey *public relations executive*

**Naples**
Ayres, John E., Jr. *hotel executive*
Berman, Robert S. *marketing consultant*
Bileydi, Sumer *advertising agency executive*
Cremer, Richard Eldon *marketing professional*
Kozitka, Richard Eugene *retired consumer products company executive*
Marshall, Charles *communications company executive*
Mehaffey, John Allen *marketing executive, publishing executive*
Moore, Mechlin Dongan *communications executive, management consultant*
Synnott, William Raymond *retired management consultant*
Weeks, Lee *hotel executive*

**New Port Richey**
Rhodes, Eric Foster *employee relations consultant, writer*

**North Fort Myers**
Bayuk, Thomas M., Sr. *restaurant owner, writer*
Gray, Carlos Gibson *restaurant manager, agricultural products supplier, entertainer, television producer*

**North Palm Beach**
Jaffe, Melvin *security firm executive*

**Ocala**
Sostilio, Robert Francis *office equipment marketing consultant*

**Ocoee**
Smith, Stephen F. *food service executive*

**Oldsmar**
Brunner, George Matthew *management consultant, retired manufacturing executive*

**Orlando**
Dawson, Leslie Naryne *quality assurance professional*
Madsen, Andrew H. *food service executive*
Mahoney, Mary *hotel executive*
Otis, Clarence, Jr. *restaurant executive*
Smetheram, Herbert Edwin *management consultant*
Yesawich, Peter Charles *advertising executive*

**Osprey**
Dyche, David Bennett, Jr. *management consultant*

**Palm Beach**
Fisher, Fenimore *business development consultant*
Flanagan, Joseph Patrick *advertising executive*
Karp, Richard M. *advertising executive, communications executive*
Moloney, Thomas Walter *management consultant*
Rumbough, Stanley Maddox, Jr. *industrialist*
Tiefel, William Reginald *hotel company executive*

**Palm Beach Gardens**
Mendelson, Richard Donald *former communications company executive*
Van Allen, Veronica Elaine *marketing and public relations professional*

**Palm Harbor**
Auld, Roberta Pemberton *retired human resources specialist*

**Plantation**
Schink, Robert Kelly *sales executive*

**Pompano Beach**
Calevas, Harry Powell *management consultant*
Hinson, Robert William *advertising executive, consultant*

**Ponte Vedra Beach**
Gold, Keith Dean *advertising and design executive*
Leek, Jay Wilbur *management consultant*
Linnen, Thomas Francis *international strategic management consulting executive*

**Port Charlotte**
Reynolds, Helen Elizabeth *management consultant*

**Safety Harbor**
Olbrick, Valerie Lyn *management consultant, information technologist*

**Saint Augustine**
Preysz, Louis Richter Fonss III *management consultant, educator*

**Saint Cloud**
Ortiz, Anthony *hotel executive*

**Saint Petersburg**
Kubiet, Leo Lawrence *advertising executive, consultant, marketing executive*
Mallory, Jeannine Marek *public relations and marketing professional*
Silver, Lawrence Alan *retired marketing professional*
Wales, Jimmy Donal (Jimmy Donal "Jimbo" Wales) *Internet company executive*

**Saint Petersburg Beach**
Bradshaw, John Robert Covington III *Internet company executive*

**Sanibel**
Brodbeck, William Jan *marketing professional*

**Santa Rosa Beach**
Rees, Lane Charles *industrial relations consultant*

**Sarasota**
Beck, Robert Alfred *hotel executive, educator*
Fendrick, Alan Burton *retired advertising executive*
Gittelson, Bernard *public relations consultant, author, lecturer*
Holcomb, Constance L. *sales and marketing management executive*
Landis, Edgar David *business consultant*
Lee, Nancy Ranck *management consultant*
Markin, Sheila Ruben *community relations executive*
Mattran, Donald Albert *management consultant, educator*
Poppel, Harvey Lee *management consultant, investment banker*
Schlegel, John Frederick *management consultant, personal trainer*
Shulman, Arthur *communications executive*
Slocum, Donald Hillman *consumer products company executive*

**Seffner**
Seaman, Jeffrey *consumer products company executive*

**Seminole**
Evans, Thomas Passmore *management consultant*

**Singer Island**
Dixson, J. B. *communications executive*

**Sunny Isles Beach**
Edelcup, Norman Scott *management and financial consultant*

**Sunrise**
Sorensen, Allan Chresten *service company executive*

**Tallahassee**
Morgante, John-Paul *human resources specialist*
Nasser, Joseph Yousef *public safety administrator, consultant*

**Tampa**
Barrow, Lionel Ceon, Jr. *communications consultant, marketing consultant*
Jones, Vaughn Paul *construction marketing executive*
Moltzon, Richard Francis *data processing executive*
Ortinau, David Joseph *marketing specialist, educator*
Studer, William Allen *security consultant, retired military officer*

**Tarpon Springs**
Crismond, Linda Fry *public relations executive*

**Titusville**
Stewart, David Witherington *business consultant*

**Venice**
Bluhm, Barbara Jean *communications agency executive*

**Vero Beach**
Fisher, Andrew *management consultant*
Grimes, Howard Ray *management consultant*
Kamman, Alan Bertram *communications consulting company executive*
Leonsis, Ted *media executive, professional sports team executive*
McNamara, John J(oseph) *advertising executive, writer*
Nichols, Carl Wheeler *retired advertising agency executive*
Spivak, Alvin A. *retired public relations executive*

**West Palm Beach**
Burgess, R. Brandon (Roy Brandon Burgess) *communications executive*
Darter, Jeffrey Allen *data processing professional*
Ronan, William John *management consultant*
Stauderman, Bruce Ford *advertising executive, writer*

**Weston**
Barnes, William Douglas *advertising executive*

**Winter Park**
Halladay, Laurie Ann *public relations consultant, food products executive*
Powers, Ronald George *management consultant*

**GEORGIA**

**Albany**
Robinson, J. Mack *communications executive*

**Alpharetta**
Braxton, Jerry W. *communications executive*

**Athens**
Cunningham, Tess *marketing professional*

**Atlanta**
Anderson, Al H., Jr. *communications executive*
Antunes, Joël *chef*
Arani, Ardy A. *marketing professional, sports association administrator*
Barnard, Patricia A. *human resources specialist*
Barros, Paulino R. *communications executive*
Betty, Charles Garry (Garry Betty) *Internet company executive*
Bradshaw, Rod Eric *personnel consultant*
Brown-Olmstead, Amanda *public relations executive*
Buoch, William Thomas *corporate executive*
Burge, William Lee *retired credit manager*
Capper, Natasha Lee *pastry chef*
Chartier, Kirk Lee Freund *business services executive*

Harris, Thomas L. *public relations executive*

**Hinsdale**
Whitney, William Elliot, Jr. *advertising agency executive*

**Hoffman Estates**
Dunn, Christopher Joseph *public affairs consultant*
Lee, Gregory A. *human resources specialist*
Rooney, John Edward *communications company executive*
Winckler, Alicia Jean *human resources director*

**Joliet**
Anderson, Carol Lee *communications executive*

**Kenilworth**
Steingraber, Frederick George *management consultant*

**La Grange**
Reggio, Vito Anthony *retired management consultant*

**Lake Bluff**
Fryburger, Vernon Ray, Jr. *advertising executive, finance educator*
Griem, John Michael *management consultant*
Scott, Karen Bondurant *consumer catalog company executive*

**Lake Forest**
Bramhall, Robert Richard *management consultant*
Carter, Donald Patton *retired advertising executive*
Chieger, Kathryn Jean *recreational facility executive*
Crawford, Robert W., Jr. *furniture rental company executive*
Johnson, Richard Darrell *management consultant*
Miller, Mark C. *waste management administrator*
Mohr, Roger John *retired advertising agency executive*
Rand, Kathy Sue *public relations consultant, public relations executive*
Stecko, Paul T. *packaging company executive*

**Libertyville**
Maczulski, Margaret Louise *event marketing professional, meeting manager*
Tullman, Glen *management consultant*

**Lincolnshire**
Roche, Mark A. *consumer products company executive, lawyer*

**Lincolnwood**
Lebedow, Aaron Louis *consulting company executive*

**Lisle**
Harris, Gregory Todd *customer service administrator*

**Litchfield**
Talley, Hayward Leroy *communications executive*

**Marengo**
Meredith, Owen Nichols *public relations executive*

**Melrose Park**
Bernick, Carol Lavin *consumer products company executive*
Cernugel, William John *consumer products company executive, distributor*

**Moline**
Schwiebert, Deborah Johnson *marketing executive*

**Morton Grove**
Smolyansky, Julie *consumer products company executive*

**Mount Prospect**
Sayers, Gale *computer company executive, retired professional football player*

**Naperville**
Bell, Bradley J. *water treatment company executive*
Fritz, Roger Jay *management consultant*
Modery, Richard Gillman *marketing executive, sales executive*

**Nashville**
Barber, Donald Gene, Jr. *purchasing agent*

**Niles**
Beton, John Allen *communications company executive*

**Normal**
Brehm, Joan M. *training services executive*
Devinatz, Victor Gary *industrial relations specialist, educator*

**Northbrook**
Clarey, John Robert *executive recruiter, consultant*
Crockett, Joan M. *human resources executive*
Pulsifer, Edgar Darling *retired leasing and sales company executive*
Ross, Debra Benita *marketing executive, jewelry designer*
Sprieser, Judith A. *former software company executive*
Sudbrink, Jane Marie *sales and marketing executive*
Wajer, Ronald Edward *management consultant*

**Northfield**
Vilim, Nancy Catherine *advertising executive*

**Oak Brook**
Crump-Caine, Lynn *food service executive*
DeLorey, John Alfred *printing company executive*
Fenton, Tim *food service executive*
Fields, Janice L. *food service executive*
Floersch, Richard *human resources specialist*
Glenn, J. Thomas *consumer products company executive*

Nelson, Robert Eddinger *retired management consultant*
Paull, Matthew H. *food service executive*
Stoelting, Curtis W. *consumer products company executive*
Turner, Fred L. *retired fast food company executive*

**Oak Park**
Cannon, Patrick Francis *public relations executive*
Devereux, Timothy Edward *advertising executive*

**Oakbrook Terrace**
Hegenderfer, Jonita Susan *public relations executive*
Pauldine, David J. *marketing executive, educator*

**Palatine**
Medin, Lowell Ansgard *management executive*

**Park Ridge**
Matthews, Roy S. *management consultant*
Williams, Sandra Lynn *ethics consultant*

**Peoria**
Banwart, Sidney C. *human resources specialist*

**Prospect Heights**
Lynch, William Thomas, Jr. *advertising executive*

**Riverside**
Dengler, Robert Anthony *management consultant*

**Rockford**
Albert, Janyce Louise *human resources specialist, retired business educator, banker, consultant*

**Rosemont**
Le Menager, Lois M. *incentive merchandise and travel company executive*

**Saint Charles**
O'Shea, Lynne Edeen *management consultant, educator*

**Schaumburg**
Brown, Gregory Q. *communications executive*
Fattori, Ruth A. *human resources specialist, electronics executive*
Hill, Raymond Joseph *packaging company executive*
Roman, Ray *communications executive*
Warrior, Padmasree *communications executive*
Zander, Edward J. *communications executive*

**Skokie**
Brennan, William P. (Bill Brennan) *computer company executive*
Karp, Gary *marketing and public relations executive*
Sperzel, George E., Jr. *former personal care industry executive*

**Springfield**
Stroh, Raymond Eugene *retired personnel executive*

**Vernon Hills**
Claassen, W(alter) Marshall *employment company executive*
Edwardson, John Albert *security firm executive*
Powers, Anthony Richard, Jr. *educational sales professional*

**Wauconda**
Meehan, Jean Marie Ross *human resources, occupational health and safety management consultant*

**Westchester**
Faulkner, Robert Lloyd *advertising executive, graphics designer*

**Wheaton**
Long, Charles Franklin *retired corporate communications executive*

**Willowbrook**
Foley, Joseph Lawrence *sales executive*

**Wilmette**
Chiaro, A. William *retired management consultant*

**Winnetka**
Cole, Kathleen Ann *advertising executive, social worker*
Thomas, John Thieme *management consultant*

**Woodridge**
O'Connor, William Michael *search company executive*

**INDIANA**

**Bloomington**
Spiro, Rosann Lee *marketing professional, educator*

**Carmel**
Rati, Robert Dean *retired data processing executive*

**Clinton**
Hess, Douglas Edwin *marketing executive*

**Corydon**
Walker, James Harper *retired security firm executive, writer*

**Crown Point**
Hendricks, Stanley Marshall, II, *executive recruiter, consultant*

**Evansville**
Zion, Roger Herschel *retired management consultant, retired congressman*

**Indianapolis**
Ayars, Patti *human resources specialist, health products executive*
Brown, Randy *human resources specialist*
Buranello, Raymond Terrence *quality assurance executive, chemist*
Gilman, Alan B. *restaurant company executive*
Kirkpatrick, Robert Hugh *communications executive*
Marsh, Don Ermal *supermarket executive*
Ruben, Gary A. *marketing and communications consultant*
Schenk, William Earl III *senior special agent, criminal investigator*
Spanogle, Robert William *marketing and advertising company executive, association administrator*

**Liberty**
Pringle, Lewis Gordon *marketing professional, educator*

**Monroeville**
Ray, Annette D. *executive secretary*

**Muncie**
Barber, Earl Eugene *management consultant*
Norris, Tracy Hopkins *retired public relations executive*

**Munster**
Neff, Bonita Dostal *communication development facilitator*

**Santa Claus**
Edwards, James Dallas III *management consultant*

**Valparaiso**
Blaschke, Lawrence Raymond *electronic security services professional*

**Wabash**
Scales, Richard Lewis *retired sales representative*

**West Lafayette**
Schendel, Dan Eldon *management consultant, finance educator*

**IOWA**

**Ames**
Davis, Wayne Pitman *public relations executive*

**Atlantic**
Johnson, Joan (Jan) Hope Voss *communications executive, photojournalist, public relations executive*

**Cedar Rapids**
Stolte, Larry Gene *marketing executive, retired computer and publishing company executive*
Wiese, Daniel Edward *marketing and communications researcher*

**Council Bluffs**
Davids, Roger Alex *food service executive*

**Milford**
Fontaine, Sue (Jeane Fontaine) *public relations professional*

**West Des Moines**
Marshall, Russell Frank *consulting company executive*

**KANSAS**

**Colby**
Baldwin, Irene S. *hotel executive, real estate developer*

**Junction City**
Werts, Merrill Harmon *retired management consultant*

**Lawrence**
McGowan, Rodger Alan *administrative assistant*

**Leawood**
King, Barbara Sackheim *travel company executive*

**Olathe**
Graham, James C. *food service executive*

**Overland Park**
Fuller, Michael B. *communications executive*
Gerke, Thomas A. *communications executive, lawyer*
Hill, Lloyd Lester *food service executive*

**Shawnee Mission**
Ingenthron, Mary Kay *marketing executive, museum consultant*
Mealman, Glenn *corporate marketing executive*
Mooney, Justin David *motel executive, consultant*
Putman, Dale Cornelius *management consultant, lawyer*

**Stilwell**
Keith, Dale Martin *management consultant*

**Topeka**
Sipes, Karen Kay *communications executive*

**Wichita**
Herr, Peter Helmut Friederich *sales executive*
Johnson, Steven M. *food service executive*
Koch, Charles de Ganahl *industrial company executive*
Lerman, Kenneth Barry *marketing professional, consultant*
Menefee, Frederick Lewis *advertising executive*

**KENTUCKY**

**Albany**
Smith, Eugenia Sewell *funeral home executive*

**Benton**
Glass, Mary Jean *management executive*

**Bowling Green**
Garrison, Geneva *retired administrative assistant*

**Covington**
Surber, David Francis *public relations executive, consultant, television producer, journalist*

**Crestwood**
Snow, Edwin Fawcett *management consultant*

**Hopkinsville**
Neville, Thomas Lee *food service company executive*

**Lexington**
Millard, James Kemper *marketing executive*

**Louisville**
Beck, Peter *marketing executive, minister*
Brown, Owsley, II, *diversified consumer products company executive*
Byerlein, Anne P. *human resources specialist, food products executive*
French, Michael Bruce *marketing executive*
Novak, David C. *restaurant company executive*
Power, David M. *advertising executive*
Power, Michael L. *advertising executive*
Shah, Atique R. *gaming activities executive*
Travis, Nigel *food service executive*
Wagner, James Miller *funeral director*
Watson, Gary Alan *management consultant*

**Paducah**
Justice, Phillip Howard *marketing professional*

**Versailles**
Troutt, Kenny *communications executive*

**LOUISIANA**

**Baton Rouge**
Greer, Jennifer *records analyst*

**Hammond**
Richardson, Thaddeus Maurice *funeral director*

**Lafayette**
Sides, Larry Eugene *advertising executive*

**Many**
Dutton, Frank Elroy *data processing executive, writer*

**Metairie**
Feran, Russell G. *sales executive*
Grimm, John Lloyd *marketing professional*
Nix, Linda Anne Bean *public relations executive*

**New Orleans**
Allerton, William III *public relations executive*
Bacot, Marie *management consultant, researcher*
Creppel, Claire Binet *hotel owner*
Johnson, Arnold Ray *public relations executive*
Matthews, Brenda J. *human resources specialist*
Tahir, Mary Elizabeth (Liz Tahir) *marketing professional, consultant, writer*

**Ruston**
Hudnall, Jarrett, Jr. *management consultant, educator, marketing professional*

**Shreveport**
Sandifer, Kevin Wayne *archival services executive*

**MAINE**

**Augusta**
Jacobson, James Lamma, Jr. *data processing company executive*

**Brooklin**
Schmidt, Klaus Dieter *marketing professional, management consultant, educator*

**Cape Neddick**
Ksypka, Helen *organizational consultant*

**Falmouth**
Kendrick, Peter Murray *communications executive, investor*
Winton, Linda *international trainer and consultant*

**Moody**
Wagstaff, Barbara Jane *marketing executive*

**Portland**
James, Tillian *ergonomist*
Keith, Robert Gordon *data processing executive, historian, researcher*

**South Portland**
Fetteroll, Eugene Carl, Jr. *human resources professional*

**Sumner**
Rudd, David William *management consultant, chemical engineer, consultant*

**Westbrook**
Bride, John W. *communications executive, entrepreneur*

**Whitefield**
Marden, Kenneth Allen *advertising executive*

**York**
Freeman, Neal Blackwell *communications corporation executive*

**York Beach**
MacRury, King *management consultant*

## MARYLAND

**Annapolis**
Branand, Claire Diane *advertising executive, writer*
Crosby, Ralph Wolf *communications executive*
Devanny, Louise Bell *public relations executive*
Jefferson, Ralph Harvey *international affairs consultant*
Martino, Peter Dominic *financial software company executive, real estate developer, real estate broker, federal agency administrator, consultant, management consultant*
Tosé, Maurice B. *communications executive*

**Baltimore**
Brotman, Phyllis Block *advertising executive, public relations executive*
Clarizio, Lynda M. *advertising executive, lawyer*
Dickinson, Jane W. *retired executive secretary, volunteer*
Dodge, Calvert Renaul *education and training executive, author, educator*
Durbin, Dean D. *marketing executive*
Friedman, Maria Andre *public relations executive*
Howes, James Guerdon *communications executive*
Kim, Lillian G. Lee *retired administrative assistant*
Moloney, Herbert W. III *advertising executive*
Talbot, Donald Roy *management consultant*
Williams, Roy L. *public relations executive, advocate*

**Beltsville**
Miller, Ted Robert *management consultant*
Quirk, Frank Joseph *management consulting company executive*
Ritz, David M. *photographic retail company executive*

**Bethesda**
Allnutt, Robert Frederick *management consultant, lawyer*
Ashkin, Ronald Evan *international executive*
Cody, Thomas Gerald *management consultant, writer*
Cutting, Mary Dorothea *audio and audio-visual communications company executive*
Durek, Thomas Andrew *computer company executive*
Johnson, Eugene Clare *data processing company executive*
Levy, Richard C. *television production executive, author, producer, inventor*
Marriott, Richard Edwin *hotel and contract services executive*
McClure, Brooks *management consultant*
Mc Gurn, Barrett *communications executive, writer*
Morrison, Nancy Anne *public affairs consultant*
Nassetta, Christopher J. *hotel facility executive*
Neill, Denis Michael *management consultant*
Terragno, Paul James *information industry executive*
Vanderryn, Jack *environmental services administrator*
Walter, W. Edward *hotel executive, corporate financial executive*

**Bozman**
Wyatt, Wilson Watkins, Jr. *communications executive, public affairs executive, writer*

**Cambridge**
Spahr, Elizabeth *environmental research administrator*

**Chestertown**
Docksteader, Karen Kemp *marketing professional*

**Chevy Chase**
Baruch, Jordan Jay *retired management consultant*
Michaelis, Michael *management and technical consultant*

**Cockeysville Hunt Valley**
Whitehurst, William Wilfred, Jr. *management consultant*

**Davidsonville**
Montague, Brian John *consulting company executive*

**Dayton**
Ferrera, Arthur Rocco *food distribution company executive*

**Easton**
U'Ren, Marie Rita *retired travel company executive, pre-school educator*

**Fort Washington**
Satterthwaite, George, II, *security firm executive*

**Gaithersburg**
Carey, John Edward *communications executive*
Landel, Michel *food service and management company executive*
Saunders, George Wendell *management consultant, retired government official*

**Gibson Island**
Forster, William Hull *management consultant*

**Glen Arm**
Lotz, George Michael *retired computer company executive, graphics designer, photographer*

**Greenbelt**
Fontaine, Kathleen Sturey *policy analyst*

**Hagerstown**
Higgins, M. Eileen *management consultant, educator*
Shaper, Christopher Thorne *sales executive*

**Hanover**
Bisciotti, Stephen J. *staffing company executive, professional sports team executive*

**Kensington**
Hum, Vance York *technology consulting executive*

**Lanham Seabrook**
Liggins, Alfred C. III *broadcasting company executive*

**Lutherville Timonium**
Brustein, Abram Isaac *sales executive, insurance company executive*

**Owings Mills**
McNiesh, Celeste Angela *sales executive*

**Potomac**
Foley, Joseph Patrick *public relations executive*
Medin, A. Louis *computer company executive*
Shirvinski, Adam John *management consultant*

**Riverdale**
Bernard, Cathy S. *management corporation executive*

**Rockville**
Valenti, Elizabeth Jeanne *environmental services administrator*

**Salisbury**
Wilmer, Ann *public relations executive*

**Severna Park**
Humphreys Troy, Patricia *communications executive*

**Silver Spring**
Altschul, B. J. *public relations counselor*
Burke, Margaret Ann *computer company executive, communications executive*
Carter-Johnson, Jean Evelyn *management consultant*
Hubbell, Katherine Jean *retired marketing professional*
Ledsinger, Charles A. *hotel executive*
Moreno, Donna Marie *communications executive*
Shih-Carducci, Joan Chia-mo *food service executive, educator, medical technologist, writer, biochemist*

**Solomons**
Harrington, John Vincent *retired communications executive, engineer, educator*

**Sparks**
Rallo, James Gilbert *management company executive*

**Stevensville**
Barrett, John Anthony *publishing and printing company financial executive*

**Towson**
Chase, Jacquelyn Veronica *marketing professional*
Passano, E. Magruder, Jr. *management consultant*

## MASSACHUSETTS

**Bedford**
Daltas, Arthur John *management consultant, software services manager*

**Belchertown**
Burstein, Michael Clifford *enterprise integration consultant*

**Belmont**
Bingham, George Walter Chandler *retired sales executive*
Klein, Martin Samuel *management consulting executive*

**Beverly**
Barger, Richard Wilson *hotel executive*

**Boston**
Berger, Jerome Morris *communications executive*
Bertino, Fred *advertising executive*
Billings, Rick *chef*
Buchin, Stanley Ira *management consultant, finance educator*
Burnham, David Henderson *management consultant*
Charns, Martin Paul *management research administrator, educator*
Connors, Jack, Jr. *advertising executive*
Coville, Andrea *public relations executive*
Cutter, Curtis Carly *consulting company executive*
DeWinter, Alex *wine director*
Dowd, Peter Jerome *public relations executive*
Eskandarian, Edward *advertising executive*
Farrar, Constance Mosher *marketing executive*
Finucane, Anne M. *communications executive, marketing executive*
FitzGerald, Maura *public relations executive*
Gardner, Geoff *chef*
German, Katherine L. *international consultant*
Gertsen, John *bar chef*
Hayes, Andrew Wallace, II, *consumer products company executive*
Hunter, Durant Adams *executive search company executive*
Hurd, J. Nicholas *executive recruiting consultant, former banker*
husbands, andy *chef*
Kelly, Francis J. III *global marketing company president and COO*
Lawner, Ron *advertising executive*
Leahy, John L. *software development company executive*
Levy, Stephen Raymond *retired data processing executive*
Luongo, C. Paul *public relations executive*
Lynch, Barbara *chef, restaurant owner*
Maffeo, Pino *chef*

**McGovern**, Lore Harp *communications executive, philanthropist*
McGovern, Patrick J. *communications executive*
Merrill, John *chef*
Moulton, Lynn *chef*
Porter, Michael E. *competitive strategy educator*
Pytka, Stephen Milton *office equipment executive*
Reese, C. Richard *data processing executive*
Reynoso, David *chef*
Rimpel, Auguste Eugene, Jr. *management and technical consulting executive*
Saunders, Donald Leslie *hotel executive, real estate developer*
Schlow, Michael *food service executive*
Shapiro, Eli *business consultant, educator, economist*
Trafidlo, James Francis *marketing communications executive, commercial photographer*
Tyszkowski, Robert *investigating services executive*
Wu, Guofa Felix *computer company executive*

**Brookline Village**
Frankenthaler, Stan *food service executive*

**Cambridge**
Adams, Jody *chef, restaurant owner*
Bianchi, Claudine *marketing executive*
Bremer, Gabriel *chef*
Clark, Maynard Stephen *vegetarian resource center administrator*
de Monteiro, Nadsa *chef*
Knickrehm, Glenn Allen *management executive*
Little, John Dutton Conant *management scientist, educator*
Lydon, Amanda *chef*
Maws, Tony *chef*
McBride, Robert Albert *training services executive*
Rowley, Geoffrey Herbert *management consultant*
Sapienza, Tony *public relations executive*
Shaw, Anthony Raymond, Jr. *research executive*
Sortun, Ana *food service executive*
Thomas, Edward LaBelle *company executive*
Zollar, Alfred *computer company executive*

**Canton**
Daley, Charles Mike *consumer products company executive*
Judson, Arnold Sidney *management consultant*
Luther, Jon *food service executive*

**Centerville**
Shapiro, Harvey *sales executive, journalist, writer, lyricist*

**Charlestown**
Wetherell, David S. *communications executive*

**Chatham**
Escalante, Judson Robert *business consultant*

**Chelmsford**
Fulks, Robert Grady *computer company executive*

**Chelsea**
Jenkins, Alexander III *consumer products company executive, consultant*

**Chestnut Hill**
O'Block, Robert Paul *management consultant*
Rosensaft, Lester Jay *management consultant, lawyer*

**Concord**
Davies, Michael A. M. *management consultant*
Eberle, William Denman *international management consultant*
Emerson, Richard B. *marketing company executive*

**Danvers**
Southwick, Paul *retired public relations executive*

**Dartmouth**
Washburn, Stewart Putnam *management consultant*

**Dedham**
Redstone, Shari E. *amusement company executive*

**Dover**
Bouh, Laszlo Joseph *marketing executive, mechanical engineer, chemist*
Mehta, Narinder Kumar *marketing executive*

**Duxbury**
Erickson, Phyllis Traver *marketing executive*
Keleher, Chantal Stone *marketing professional*

**Framingham**
DeWerth, Gordon Henry *management consultant*
Margolis, Bruce Lewis *human resources executive*
Meador, Charles Lawrence *management and systems consultant, educator*

**Gloucester**
Hausman, William Ray *fund raising and management consultant*
Littlefield, Paul Damon *retired management consultant*

**Hingham**
Macchia, David Alan *management consultant*

**Hopkinton**
Tucci, Joseph M. *computer software and services executive*

**Lakeville**
Kolva, Matthew *marketing professional*

**Lexington**
Cohen, Judah Levi *environmental services administrator*
Dougherty, Richard Hamlen *management consultant, healthcare consultant*

**Marlborough**
Murray, R. Scott *computer software company executive*

**Maynard**
Taylor, Jeff *Internet company executive*

**Medford**
Antonelli, Pattie Ellen *public relations executive*

**Nantucket**
Frasca, Gabriel *chef*

**Needham**
Bronner, Michael *advertising executive, education assistance company executive*
Grasso, James Anthony *public relations executive, educator*
Stein, Martin Matthew *management consultant*

**Newton**
Benner, Mary Wright *freelance/self-employed conference director*

**Newton Center**
Copithorne, David A. *public relations executive*

**North Chatham**
Rhinesmith, Stephen Headley *management consultant*

**Norton**
Holden, William *food service executive*

**Norwell**
Case, David Knowlton *management consultant*

**Norwood**
Fishman, Jerald G. *semiconductor executive*

**Osterville**
Sommers, William Paul *management consultant, research and development company executive*

**Palmer**
Dupuis, Robert Simeon *sales executive*

**Peabody**
Finch, Rogers Burton *association management consultant*
Gordon, Bernard M. *computer company executive*

**Pittsfield**
Hochfelder, Scott Z. *toy company executive, lawyer*

**Quincy**
Hall, John Raymond, Jr. *fire protection executive*

**Randolph**
Huntington, Robert Howard *business management executive*

**Rockport**
Wiberg, Lars-Erik *occupational compatibility consultant*

**Sherborn**
Hancock, William Frank, Jr. *management consultant*

**Spencer**
George, Patrick Joseph *entertainment company executive*

**Springfield**
Vincensi, Avis A. *sales executive, medical educator*

**Waban**
Rossolimo, Alexander Nicholas *management consultant*

**Waltham**
Buchholz, William James *communications executive, educator*
Schwartz, Steven Mark *marketing executive*

**Wellesley**
Heisler, Elwood Douglas *hotel executive*
Tsai, Ming *chef*

**Wellesley Hills**
Doorley, Thomas Lawrence III *management consultant*

**Westborough**
Schrager, Mindy Rae *software company professional*

**Westport**
Norcross, Alvin Watt *retired personnel administrator, consultant*

**Williamstown**
Robinson, Hobart Krum *management consulting company executive*
Sprague, John Louis *management consultant*

**Winchester**
Taggart, Ganson Powers *management consultant*

## MICHIGAN

**Ada**
DeVos, Richard Marvin, Sr. *former network marketing company executive*
Lyall, Lynn *consumer products company executive*
Van Andel, Steve Alan *consumer products company executive*
Weiss, Joseph Joel *consulting company executive*

**Ann Arbor**
Agno, John G. *management consultant*
Belcher, Louis David *marketing professional, retired mayor*
Brandon, David A. *food service executive*
Foley, Daniel Ronald *personnel director, lawyer*
Lindsay, June Campbell McKee *communications executive*
Martin, Claude Raymond, Jr. *marketing consultant, educator*

Nikoui, Hossein Reza *quality assurance professional*

**Auburn Hills**
MacDonald, John *marketing executive*
Rae, Nancy A. *human resources specialist, automotive executive*

**Benton Harbor**
Binkley, David A. *human resources specialist*

**Beulah**
Auch, Walter Edward *security firm executive*

**Birmingham**
Carter, Marsha Jean *public relations executive, poet*
Wagner, Bruce Stanley *marketing professional*

**Bloomfield Hills**
Adams, Charles Francis *advertising executive, real estate company executive*
Berline, James H. *advertising executive, public relations executive*
Bokhari, Raza Ali Babar *former marketing strategist*
Guarascio, Philip *advertising executive*
Sandy, William Haskell *training and communication systems executive*

**Brighton**
Schroeder, Stephanie Lynn *human resources specialist, director*

**Canton**
Wickus, James D. *food service executive*

**Dearborn**
Laymon, Joe W. *human resources specialist, automotive executive*

**Detroit**
Bassett, Tina *communications executive*
Brake, Willie Edward *computer company executive, educator*
Demos, Dave *marketing executive*
Middlebrook, John G. *marketing executive, advertising executive*
Novak, Raymond Francis *environmental services administrator, pharmacology educator*
Reece, Terry Allen *travel company executive, Internet company executive*
Schweitzer, Peter *advertising agency executive*

**East Lansing**
La Ferle, Carrie *advertising executive, educator*

**Farmington**
Werba, Gabriel *public relations consultant*

**Farmington Hills**
Yagahashi, Takashi *chef*

**Grand Rapids**
Dykstra, William Dwight *management executive, consultant*
Gordon, Dan A. *food service executive*
Messner, James W. *advertising executive*
Purchase-Owens, Francena *marketing professional, consultant, educator*
Spaulding, Dan *public relations executive*
Williams, Janice H. *business executive*

**Grosse Pointe**
Caldwell, John Thomas, Jr. *communications executive*

**Grosse Pointe Park**
Krebs, William Hoyt *industrial hygienist, health science association administrator*

**Hastings**
Jones, Kensinger *advertising executive, educator*

**Holland**
Garlough, William Glenn *marketing executive*

**Kalamazoo**
Lawrence, William Joseph, Jr. *retired corporate executive*

**Keego Harbor**
Gee, Sharon Lynn *funeral director, educator*

**Livonia**
Chowdhury, Subir *management consultant*
Maibach, Ben C., Jr. *consumer products company executive*

**Marquette**
Pesola, William Ernest *restaurant management executive*

**Mount Clemens**
Robinson, Earl, Jr. *marketing executive, transportation executive, educator, retired air force officer*

**Novi**
Kinsey, Charles John *industrial auctioneer, consultant, farmer, cattle breeder*

**Portage**
Seely, Robert Eugene *management consultant*

**Rockford**
Loux, Jonathan Dale *business development consultant, director*

**Royal Oak**
Stanalajczo, Greg Charles *computer company executive*

**Shelby Township**
Chalil, Joseph Mathew *sales executive, consultant*

**Southfield**
Barnett, Marilyn *advertising executive*

Caponigro, Jeffrey Ralph *public relations counselor*
Jackson, Roger A. *human resources specialist, automotive executive*
Kalter, Alan *advertising agency executive*

**Taylor**
Barry, Alan H. *consumer products company executive*
Wadhams, Timothy *consumer products company executive*

**Troy**
Adderley, Terence Edward *human resources executive*
Camden, Carl T. *human resources company executive*
Meyers, Christine Laine *marketing and media executive, consultant*

**Walled Lake**
Gillespie, J. Martin *sales and distribution company executive*

**Warren**
Hopp, Anthony James *advertising agency executive*
Zoubareff, Kathy Olga *administrative assistant*

**West Bloomfield**
Smith, Nancy Hohendorf *sales executive, marketing professional*

## MINNESOTA

**Austin**
Budd, Jim *communications manager*

**Bloomington**
Knotek, Robert Frank *retired management consultant, educator*

**Eden Prairie**
Cervilla, Constance Marlene *marketing consultant*
Verdoorn, D.R. (Sid) *food service executive*

**Farmington**
Wurdeman, Lew Edward *Internet company executive, consultant*

**Hastings**
Avent, Sharon L. Hoffman *manufacturing company executive*

**Hopkins**
Dunlap, William DeWayne, Jr. *advertising agency executive*

**Lake Crystal**
Pawlitschek, Donald Paul *management consultant*

**Mahtomedi**
Brainerd, Richard Charles *human resources executive, consultant, educator*

**Mankato**
Schreier, Bradley *management executive*
Taylor, Glen A. *direct mail and technology executive, professional sports team executive*

**Minneapolis**
Agyenkwah, Kennedy Seth *communications executive*
Blackwell, Todd V. *human resources specialist*
Bonneville, Katherine Ann *human resources specialist, consultant*
deBruin Sample, Anne *human resources specialist*
Diemand, Kim Eugene *human resources executive*
Fallon, Patrick R. *advertising executive*
Finkelstein, Paul D. *personal care industry executive*
Forsythe, Thomas M. *communications executive*
Gage, Edwin C., III, (Skip Gage) *travel and marketing services executive*
Johnson, Lola Norine *retired advertising and public relations executive, educator*
Kelly, Charles Harold *advertising executive*
Koutsky, Dean Roger *advertising executive*
McClanahan, Harry Allen III *management consultant*
Mouser, Les (Lyman Mouser) *advertising executive*
Pohlad, Robert C. *consumer products company executive*
Powell, Kendall J. *consumer products company executive*
Roth, Thomas *marketing executive*
Sanger, Stephen W. *consumer products company executive*
Scoville, James Griffin *industrial relations professor*
Tandon, Rajiv *training company executive*
Turner, Ronald L. *information services executive*
Veblen, Thomas Clayton *management consultant*
Viault, Raymond G. *food company executive*
Wickesberg, Albert Klumb *retired management consultant*
Wikman, Michael Raymond *advertising executive*
Woodman, Stewart *chef*
Yourzak, Robert Joseph *management consultant, educator, engineer*
Zimmermann, Robert Laurence *marketing professional*

**Minnetonka**
Bissell, Brent John *advertising and direct marketing executive*
Gillies, Donald Richard *marketing and advertising consultant, educator*
Nelson, Marilyn Carlson *hotel executive, travel company executive*
Porter, Jim *human resources specialist*
Schmidt, Russel Alan, II, *sales executive*

**Ottertail**
Blaha, Verle Dennis *consumer products company executive, electrical engineer*

**Pequot Lakes**
Gray, Allen (Ernest Bungaard) *communications executive*

**Rochester**
Hiniker, LuAnn *management consultant, educator, researcher, grants consultant*

**Saint Cloud**
Gangopadhyay, Partha *management consultant*

**Saint Paul**
Axelrod, Leonard *management consultant*
Baker, Douglas M., Jr. *service industry executive*
Brooks, Phillip *advertising executive*
Courtney, Eugene Whitmal *computer company executive*
Fitzgerald, Janice S. *public relations executive, academic administrator*
Fritze, Steven L. *service industry executive*

**Wayzata**
Schoen, Charles Judd *service executive*
Waldera, Wayne Eugene *crisis management executive*

## MISSISSIPPI

**Biloxi**
Love, James Sanford III *communications executive*

**Columbus**
Holt, Robert Ezel *data processing executive*
Labensky, Sarah Ross *culinary educator*

**Hattiesburg**
St. John, Robert *chef, writer*

**Ocean Springs**
Culberson, Gary Michael *hotel manager*

**Ridgeland**
Lewis, Larry Lisle *human resources specialist company executive*

## MISSOURI

**Blue Springs**
Page, Leslie Andrew *retired consumer products company executive*

**Branson**
Lanning, James Wilford *sales executive, retired music educator*

**Cape Girardeau**
Smallwood, Glenn Walter, Jr. *utility marketing management executive*

**Chesterfield**
Stork, Donald Arthur *advertising executive*
Welshans, Merle Talmadge *management consultant*

**Clayton**
Vecchiotti, Robert Anthony *management and organizational consultant*

**Columbia**
Helvey, William Charles, Jr. *communications specialist*

**Dover**
Jobe, Angela Francine *postmaster, writer*

**Fenton**
Kienker, James W. *marketing executive*
Lipovsky, Robert P. *marketing executive*
Maritz, W. Stephen *marketing professional, service executive*

**Independence**
Burnett, Crystal Blythe *marketing professional*
Evans, Margaret Ann *human resources administrator, business owner*

**Kansas City**
Baker, Ronald Phillip *service company executive*
Benner, Richard Edward, Jr. *marketing consultant, volunteer, investor*
Brown, Peter C. *movie theater company executive*
Courson, Marna B.P. *public relations executive*
Dillingham, John Allen *marketing professional*
Dwyer, William Michael *health care company marketing executive*
Hall, Donald Joyce, Sr. *greeting card company executive*
Hall, Donald Joyce, Jr. *consumer products company executive*
Hoffman, Gloria Levy *communications executive*
Robertson, Leon H. *management consultant, educator*
Solberg, Elizabeth Transou *public relations executive*
Warakomski, Alphonse Walter Joseph, Jr. *sales executive, marketing professional*

**Lake Saint Louis**
Dommermuth, William Peter *marketing consultant, educator*

**O Fallon**
Ractliffe, Robert Edward George *management executive*

**Raymore**
Mehl, Donald Edward *retired marketing professional*

**Richmond Heights**
Shaich, Ronald M. *food service executive*

**Saint Louis**
Bachmann, John William *security firm executive*
Bellville, Margaret (Maggie Bellville) *communications executive*

Bradley, Marilynne Gail *advertising executive, educator*
Burgess, Robert Ronald *human resources executive*
Curran, Michael Walter *management consultant*
Davis, Irvin *advertising executive, public relations executive, broadcast executive*
Drury, Charles Louis, Jr. *hotel executive*
Dugan, Jean Brodshaug *public relations executive*
Ferguson, Gary Warren *retired public relations executive*
Kennedy, Craig *rental company executive*
Khoury, George Gilbert *printing company executive, sports association executive*
Klein, Ward M. *consumer products company executive*
Kornblet, Donald Ross *retired communications company executive*
Lents, Peggy Iglauer *marketing professional*
Newman, Andrew Edison *restaurant manager*
Rosen, Fred *travel company executive*
Sibbald, John Ristow *management consultant*
Siemer, Paul Jennings *public relations executive*
Taylor, Andrew C. *rental and leasing company executive*
Taylor, Jack C. *rental and leasing company executive*
Tyler, William Howard, Jr. *advertising executive, educator*

**Warrenton**
Dapron, Elmer Joseph, Jr. *communications executive*

## MONTANA

**Helena**
Scheet, Ethel Louise *rental company executive, consultant*

## NEBRASKA

**Lincoln**
Hawley, Kimra *computer company executive*

**Omaha**
Caggiano, Joseph *advertising executive*
Eggers, James Wesley *executive search consultant*
Mew, Calvin Marshall *advertising executive*
Roskens, Ronald William *management consultant, retired academic administrator*
Ryan, Shelli Ann *public relations executive*

**Oneill**
Hedren, Paul Leslie *parks director, historian*

## NEVADA

**Carson City**
Welch, Richard LeRoy *personal improvement company executive*
Whaley, John A. *management consultant*

**Henderson**
Bruno, Cathy Eileen *management consultant, former state official, social sciences educator*
Cohan, George Sheldon *advertising executive, public relations executive*
Goldstein, Morris *retired consumer products company executive*

**Incline Village**
Mitton, Michael Anthony *environmental technology company executive*

**Las Vegas**
Adelson, Sheldon Gary *hotel executive*
Arce, Phillip William *hotel and casino executive*
Atwood, Charles L. *recreational facility executive*
Boyd, William S. *hotel and entertainment facility executive*
Brock, Holly Melinda *marketing professional*
Ensign, Michael S. *resort company executive*
Goodwin, Nancy Lee *computer company executive*
Griesche, Robert Price *hospital purchasing executive*
Hardie, George Graham *casino executive*
Huston, Joyce A. *web site design company executive*
Jacobs, Gary N. *hotel executive, lawyer*
Landau, Ellis *hotel executive*
Lanni, Terry (Joseph Terrence Lanni) *hotel corporation executive*
Loveman, Gary W. *gaming company executive*
MacPherson, Grant *chef*
Mataseje, Veronica Julia *sales executive*
Murren, James Joseph *recreational facility executive, hotel executive*
Neilsen, Craig H. *hotel executive*
Robins, David *chef*
Safford, Florence Viray Sunga *travel agent, consultant*
Satre, Philip Glen *casino entertainment executive, lawyer*
Schaeffer, Glenn William *casino corporate financial executive*
Shively, Judith Carolyn (Judy Shively) *administrative assistant*
Sillerman, Robert F. X. *communications executive, banker*
Sorrell, Michael E. *consulting company executive, hospitality executive*
Welter, William Michael *marketing and advertising executive*
Wilmott, Timothy J. *recreational facility executive*
Wynn, Stephen A. *hotel and entertainment facility executive*

**Reno**
Adams, Kenneth Robert *gaming analyst, writer, consultant, historian*
Ford, Victoria *retired public relations executive, writer, oral historian*
Frank, Lillian Gorman *human resources executive, management consultant*

Howard, Christopher Philip *management consultant, investor*

## NEW HAMPSHIRE

**Bedford**
Hall, Pamela S. *environmental services administrator*

**Center Harbor**
Shaw, Robert William, Jr. *management consultant, venture capitalist*

**Concord**
Roberts, George Bernard, Jr. *management and government relations consultant, former state legislator*

**Deering**
Spitzer, Morton Edward *management consultant*

**Enfield**
Gamache, Richard Donald *retired business development executive*

**Exeter**
Harmon, Richard Wingate *management consultant*

**Fitzwilliam**
Schott, John Robert *international consultant, educator*

**Grantham**
Hansen, Herbert W. *management consultant*

**Hampstead**
Hargreaves, David William *retired communications company executive*

**Hanover**
Burnham, Patricia White *consultant, advocate, writer, business executive*

**Litchfield**
Darlington, David William *management consultant*

**Londonderry**
Osen, Gregory Alan *water conditioning company executive*

**Merrimack**
Gallup, Patricia *computer company executive*

**Portsmouth**
Dumont, Mary *chef*

**Somersworth**
Gow, Linda Yvonne Carignan Cherwin *travel executive*

**Waterville Valley**
Saenger, Bruce Walter *consulting firm executive*

**West Lebanon**
Lawton, Jacqueline Agnes *retired communications executive, management consultant*

**Wilmot**
Zuehlke, Richard William *communications executive, consultant, writer*

## NEW JERSEY

**Allendale**
Bisanzo, Mark Thomas *sales executive*
DeFeo, Neil P. *consumer products company executive*
Petersen, Martin Ross *public affairs executive*

**Atlantic City**
Perry, James Benn *casino and hotel executive*

**Basking Ridge**
Buist, Richardson *retired corporate executive, retired banker*
McGuire, Garry K., Sr. *communications executive*
Moden, Joleen *communications executive*

**Bedminster**
Eslambolchi, Hossein *communications executive*
Gardner, David John *communications executive, sound recording engineer*
Graddick-Weir, Mirian *human resources specialist*
Hart, Terry Jonathan *communications executive*
Laroia, Rajiv *communications executive*
Weaver, Constance *communications executive*

**Bernardsville**
Dixon, Richard Wayne *retired communications company executive*
Teiger, David *management consultant*

**Bloomfield**
Marcus, Phillip Ronald *management consultant*

**Boonton**
Bona, Frederick Emil *public relations executive*
Ward, Solveig Maria *marketing professional*

**Brick**
Roache, Patrick Michael, Jr. *management consultant*
Shortess, Edwin Steevin *marketing consultant*

**Bridgewater**
Sethi, Shyam Sunder *management consultant*
Skidmore, James Albert, Jr. *management, computer technology and engineering services company executive*

**Butler**
Ward, Robert Allen, Jr. *advertising executive*

**Carteret**
Neff, Richard B. (Richie Neff) *consumer products company executive*

**Cedar Grove**
Carlozzi, Catherine L. *corporate communications consultant, writer*

**Cherry Hill**
Collins, Erica Harriet *communications executive, media consultant*

**Clifton**
Bronkesh, Annette Cylia *public relations executive*
DiNicola, Robert J. *consumer products company executive*

**Cranford**
Halleck, George Thomas *marketing professional*

**Cream Ridge**
Tomson, Jon Scott *management consultant*

**East Hanover**
Nelson, Barbara Kasztan *marketing professional*

**East Rutherford**
Kempner, Michael W. *public relations executive*
Kluge, John Werner *broadcasting and advertising executive*

**Edison**
Currie, Robert *communications executive*

**Englewood**
Fay, Toni Georgette *communications executive*

**Fair Haven**
Wyndrum, Ralph William, Jr. *communications consultant*

**Far Hills**
Alexandre, Kristin Kuhns *public relations executive, writer*

**Florham Park**
Fischer, Pamela Shadel *public relations executive*
Naimark, George Modell *marketing and management consultant*
Negi, Devendra S. *communications services company administrator*

**Fort Lee**
Seitel, Fraser Paul *public relations executive*

**Franklin Lakes**
Williams, Edward David *information technology management consultant*

**Gladstone**
Close, Donald Pembroke *management consultant*
Kenny, Jane M. *management consulting executive*

**Glen Ridge**
Agnew, Peter Tomlin *employee benefit consultant*

**Green Brook**
Bohanan, David John *management consultant*

**Green Village**
Swift, John Francis *retired health care advertising company executive*

**Hackettstown**
Van Campen, Stephen Bernard *executive recruiter, consultant*

**Haddonfield**
Baltake, Susan *marketing professional*
Bauer, Raymond Gale *sales professional*

**Hampton**
Yates, Michael Francis *management consultant*

**Hoboken**
Bostwick, Randell Armour *retired food service executive*
Fassoulis, Satiris Galahad *communications company executive*

**Holmdel**
Meyer, Robert Alan *management consultant*

**Jackson**
Woodman, G. Roger *management consultant*

**Kenilworth**
Johnson Velazco, Nancy Ruth *marketing professional*

**Kinnelon**
Klaas, Nicholas Paul *management consultant*

**Lawrenceville**
Adams, Christine Hanson *advertising executive*
Coleman, Wade Hampton III *management consultant, mechanical engineer, retired banker*
Cox, Teri Polack *public relations executive*
Weaver, Charles Lyndell, Jr. *marketing executive, educational consultant*

**Liberty Corner**
Ganz, Felix *marketing professional*

**Livingston**
Brody, Martin *hotel executive*

**Madison**
Byrd, Stephen Fred *human resource consultant*
O'Brien, Mary Devon *communications executive, consultant*

**Mahwah**
Gibbons, Robert Philip *management consultant, director*
Hilpert, Dale W. *retail shoe company executive*

**Maplewood**
Safian, Gail Robyn *public relations executive*

**Marlton**
Farwell, Nancy Larraine *public relations executive*
Klein, Gerhart Leopold *public relations executive*

**Matawan**
Amato, Vincent Vito *marketing and business consultant*

**Mendham**
Hambleton, George Blow Elliott *retired management consultant*

**Monmouth Junction**
Lancaster, Barbara Mae *management consulting company executive*

**Monroe Township**
Cushman, Helen Merle Baker *retired management consultant*
Meshowski, Frank Robert *business consultant*

**Montclair**
Greenwald, Robert *public relations executive*

**Moorestown**
Bennington, William Jay *management consultant*
Carson, William Charles *sales and marketing executive*
Schwerin, Horace S. *marketing research executive*

**Morristown**
Haselmann, John Philip *management consultant*
McConnell, John Howard *personnel management consultant, writer*
Weidenkopf, Thomas W. *human resources specialist*

**Mountainside**
Bertsch, Patricia Ann *nature center director*
Lipton, Bronna Jane *marketing communications executive*

**New Brunswick**
Bradley, Dondeena G. *consumer products company executive*

**New Providence**
D'Amelio, Frank Anthony *communications executive*
Del Tiempo, Sandra Kay *sales executive*
Doescher, William Frederick *communications executive*
Netravali, Arun N. *communications executive*

**Newark**
Courter, James A. (Jim Courter) *communications executive, retired congressman*
Jonas, Howard *communications executive*
Passantino, Benjamin Arthur *marketing executive*

**North Brunswick**
Bern, Ronald Lawrence *management consultant, writer*

**North Plainfield**
Dunbar, Holly Jean *communications executive, public relations executive*

**Oak Ridge**
Kieren, Thomas Henry *management consultant*

**Paramus**
Grinberg, Efraim *watch manufacturing company executive*
Grinberg, Gedalio *watch manufacturing company executive*

**Park Ridge**
Kennedy, Brian James *marketing executive*

**Parlin**
Mogensen, Charles Ray, Jr. *retired food service executive*

**Parsippany**
Bablin, Mark Edward *security administrator, mortgage consultant*
Belmonte, Steven Joseph *hotel chain executive*
Ferguson, Thomas George *retired healthcare advertising agency executive*
Weller, Robert N(orman) *hotel executive*

**Pilesgrove**
Midulcki, Richard Gintel *marketing professional*

**Piscataway**
Colcord, Herbert Nathaniel, III, (Skip Colcord) *corporate communications executive*

**Plainsboro**
Devine, Hugh James, Jr. *marketing executive*
Khan, Sajid A. *management consultant, entrepreneur*
Spiegel, Phyllis *public relations consultant, journalist*

**Princeton**
Bishop, James Francis *personnel director, consultant*
Cox, Douglas Lynn *management consultant, researcher*
Craigie, James R. *consumer products company executive, former sports equipment apparel company executive*
Davies, Robert Abel III *consumer products company executive*
Evslin, Tom *internet telephone service executive*
Makadok, Stanley *management consultant*
Morris, Mac Glenn *advertising executive*
Pfister, Marc *consumer products company executive, medical researcher*
Siegel, Laurie *human resources specialist*

**Princeton Junction**
Hirschman, Barry H. *human resources specialist*

**Randolph**
Chen, Kevin S. *management executive, consultant, educator*

**Ridgewood**
Warner, John Edward *advertising executive*

**Ringoes**
Tema-Lyn, Laurie *management consultant*

**Roseland**
Butler, Gary C. *computer company executive*
Weinbach, Arthur Frederic *computer company executive*

**Saddle River**
Roes, Nicholas A. *communications consultant, writer*

**Scotch Plains**
Johnsen, Karen Kennedy *marketing professional*
Margiotta, Joseph M. *printing company executive*

**Secaucus**
Marcus, Alan C. *public relations consultant*

**Short Hills**
Harwood, Jerry *market research executive*
Schaefer, Charles James III *advertising executive, consultant*

**Shrewsbury**
Baker, Gerald David *marketing executive, consultant*

**Somerset**
Brophy, Joseph Thomas *computer company executive*
Karas, James *public relations executive, engineering executive*
King, David T. *communications company financial executive*
Wallfesh, Henry Maurice *communications executive, writer*

**Somerville**
Dobrinsky, Susan Elizabeth *human resources director*
Grey, Ruthann E. *corporate communications specialist, director*

**Summit**
Fuess, Billings Sibley, Jr. *advertising executive*
Pace, Leonard *retired management consultant*
Weinstein, Stephen Brant *communications executive, researcher, writer*

**Teaneck**
Connola, Donald Pascal, Jr. *management consultant*
Lafer, Fred Seymour *data processing executive*

**Three Bridges**
Lawrence, Gerald Graham *management consultant*

**Toms River**
Kanarkowski, Edward Joseph *data processing company executive*

**Trenton**
Barclay, Warren M. *human resources specialist, researcher*
Holt, Jonathan Turner *public relations executive*

**Upper Montclair**
Tintle, Carmel Joseph *public relations executive*

**Ventnor City**
Bolton, Kenneth Albert *management consultant*

**Verona**
Poor, Suzanne Donaldson *advertising and public relations executive*

**Warren**
Blass, Walter Paul *management consultant, educator*
DiPietro, Ralph Anthony *management consultant, educator, marketing consultant*
Kozberg, Ronald Paul *health and human services administrator*

**Weehawken**
Kelleher, Kathleen *marketing professional*

**West Caldwell**
Dixon, Jo-Ann Conte *management consultant*
Page, Frederick West *business consultant*

**West Orange**
Kyle, Corinne Silverman *management consultant*

**Westfield**
Davoren, Steven Michael *marketing professional, psychologist*

**Westwood**
Radakovich, Daniel I. *communications executive, consultant*

**Whitehouse**
Shelton, Craig *food service executive*

**Wyckoff**
Lavery, Daniel P. *management consultant*

## NEW MEXICO

**Albuquerque**
Eichenberg, Peter Thompson *retired criminal investigator*
Gardner, Lenann McGookey *management consultant*
Horner, Harry Charles, Jr. *sales executive*
Martinez, J. Leonard *aerospace executive*
O'Toole, Robert John, II, *telemarketing consultant*
Royce, Stanton *motivational speaker, consultant, marketing professional, sales executive*
Westwood, Albert Ronald Clifton *management consultant, researcher*

**Clovis**
Simon, Trevor *management consultant, educator, human resources specialist*

**Los Alamos**
Kloepper, David Alan *retired management consultant*

**Moriarty**
Haver, Jurgen F. *marketing consultant*

**Sandia Park**
Greenwell, Ronald Everett *communications executive*

**Santa Fe**
Brandt, Richard Paul *communications and entertainment company executive*
Mercer, James Lee *management consultant*
Merrin, Seymour *computer company executive*
Miller, Dwight Richard *professional hair care industry executive, cosmetologist, consultant*
Welch, Jasper Arthur, Jr. *security company executive, consultant*

**NEW YORK**

**Albany**
Menges, Susan Debra Favreau *management consultant, retired protective services official*
Schalit, Robert Edward *advertising executive*

**Albion**
Minier, Lee N. *funeral director*

**Amherst**
Nickell, Joe *paranormal expert*

**Annandale On Hudson**
Darrow, Emily M. *public relations executive, writer*

**Armonk**
Bolduc, Ernest Joseph *management consultant, not-for-profit developer*
Kohnstamm, Abby E. *marketing executive*
Loughridge, Mark *computer company executive*
Sanchez, Adalio T. *data processing executive*

**Baldwin**
Chopra, Parveen Chander *management consultant, educator, researcher, community activist*

**Beacon**
Metz, Ferdinand *chef, educator, academic administrator*

**Bedford**
Husted, William Armstrong *sales executive*

**Bedford Corners**
Greene, Jesse J., Jr. *former computer company executive*

**Berlin**
Pelz, Caroline Duncombe *retired educational administrator*

**Bethpage**
Dolan, James L *communications executive*
Janczak, Andrew Anthony *marketing professional*
Mahony, Sheila Anne *retired communications executive*

**Brewster**
Shepard, Lance Hastings *marketing professional, consultant, newscaster*

**Bridgehampton**
Rattiner, Daniel Steven *communications executive*

**Bronx**
Hudson, Frederick Bernard *management consultant*
Samuels, Leslie Eugene *marketing consultant, management consultant*

**Bronxville**
Ellinghaus, William Maurice *communications executive*
Parsons, Andrew John *management consultant*

**Brooklyn**
Allison, Mary Ann *consulting company executive, writer, speaker*
Bolton, Saul *chef, food service executive*
Carswell, Lois Malakoff *botanical garden executive, consultant*
Chandan, Jit S. *management consultant, educator*
Galatianos, Gus A. *computer company executive, consultant, real estate developer, educator*
Greenwood, Monique *innkeeper, writer, restaurant owner*
Reichel, Walter Emil *advertising executive*
Reisler, Helen Barbara *public relations executive*
Smith, John W(esley), Jr. *data processing executive, consultant*

**Buffalo**
Daley, Ruth Margaret *advertising agency administrator*
Fryer, Appleton *sales executive, diplomat*
Goralski, Donald John *public relations executive, counselor*
Moran, Charles, Jr. *consumer products company executive*
Pegels, C. Carl *management consultant, educator*

**Canaan**
Hooper, Ian (John Derek Glass) *retired marketing communications executive*

**Cheektowaga**
Mruk, Eugene Robert *retired marketing professional, urban planner*

**Chester**
Mackerodt, Fred *public relations specialist*

**Claverack**
Barrett, William Gary *advertising and marketing executive*

**Croton On Hudson**
Plotch, Walter *management consultant, fund raising counselor*

**Delmar**
Button, Rena Pritsker *public relations executive*

**Dobbs Ferry**
Kalvin-Stiefel, Judy *public relations executive*

**East Hampton**
Garten, Ina *chef*
Mencher, Stuart Alan *sales and marketing executive*

**East Meadow**
Fuchs, Jerome Herbert *management consultant*

**Elmont**
Butera, Ann Michele *consulting company executive*

**Far Rockaway**
Epstein, Samuel Abraham *sales executive*

**Findley Lake**
Gundersen, Allison Maureen *management consultant*

**Floral Park**
Dudek, Henry Thomas *management consultant*

**Forest Hills**
Spiegel, Andrea *marketing executive*

**Garden City**
Conlon, Thomas James *marketing executive*
Doucette, Mary-Alyce *computer company executive*

**Glen Head**
Conway, David Antony *marketing professional*

**Great Neck**
Goldberg, Melvin Arthur *communications executive*

**Hancock**
DeLuca, Ronald *former advertising agency executive, consultant*

**Harrison**
Wilson, William James *marketing professional*

**Hartsdale**
Greenawalt, Peggy Freed Tomarkin *advertising executive*
Pell, Arthur Robert *human resources specialist, consultant, writer*

**Hastings On Hudson**
Del Colle, Paul Lawrence *communications administrator, educator*

**Haverstraw**
Alpert, Revell Judith *retired data processing executive*

**Hawthorne**
Wen, Sheree *computer company executive*

**Hempstead**
Connolly, Melissa Kane *public relations executive*

**Honeoye Falls**
Hillabrandt, Larry Lee *service industry executive*

**Huntington Station**
Cannistraci, Diane Frances *sales executive*

**Hurley**
Smith, Lewis Motter, Jr. *retired advertising and direct marketing executive*

**Hyde Park**
Ryan, L. Timothy *chef, educator, academic administrator*

**Ilion**
Nemyier, Margaret Gertrude *sales executive*

**Islandia**
Cooper, Nancy E. *computer software company executive*
Gupta, Yogesh *software company executive*
Robinson, Douglas *computer company executive*
Swainson, John *software company executive*

**Ithaca**
Merle, H. Etienne *restaurateur*
Park, Roy Hampton, Jr. *advertising executive*

**Jamaica**
Jawin, Ann Juliano *human resource specialist*

**Jericho**
Edson, Andrew Stephen *public relations executive*
Rosen, Robert Arnold *management consultant, real estate owner, manager, developer, investor, farmer*

**Lake Luzerne**
Goldstein, Manfred *retired management consultant*

**Lake Success**
Uchida, Kinya *consumer products company executive*

**Lancaster**
Neumaier, Gerhard John *environmental services administrator, consultant*

**Larchmont**
Greenwald, Carol Schiro *professional services marketing research executive*
Plumez, Jean Paul *advertising executive, consultant*

**Latham**
Schwartz, Robert William *management consultant*
Wilkes, Brent Ames *management consultant*

**Locust Valley**
Fletcher, Mary Lee *retired marketing professional*

**Loudonville**
Burstein, Sharon Ann *corporate communications specialist, apparel designer*

**Manlius**
Zlomek, Elizabeth A. *customer service/business processes specialist*

**Middle Island**
Andrews, Gaylen *public relations executive*
Linick, Andrew S. *direct marketing expert*

**Mount Kisco**
Novak, Gregory *marketing professional*

**New York**
Abernathy, James Logan *public relations executive*
Achenbaum, Alvin Allen *marketing and management consultant*
Agisim, Philip *advertising executive, marketing executive*
Aguiar, Yuri B. *advertising company executive*
Ahrens, Thomas H. *communications executive*
Aiello, Stephen *public relations executive*
Alexander, Roy *public relations executive, writer*
Allen, Alice *communications and marketing executive*
Alschuler, Steven *public relations executive, writer, consultant*
Andelbradt, Mark *chef*
Anderson, Arthur Allan *management consultant*
Andolsen, Alan Anthony *management consultant*
Andree, Tim *advertising executive*
Antonuccio, Joseph Albert *management consultant*
Appel, Marsha Ceil *advertising executive*
Applebaum, Stuart S. *public relations executive*
Aronson, Donald Eric *management consultant, tax consultant*
Axelrod, Norman N. (Norman Nathan Axelrod) *optical technical planning and application consultant*
Axthelm, Nancy *advertising executive*
Bachrach, Nancy *retired advertising executive*
Baglivo, Mary L. *advertising executive*
Baird, Lisa P. *marketing executive*
Baird, Richard *human resources specialist*
Barksdale, James Love *communications executive*
Barton, Richard N. *computer company executive*
Barton, Thomas Heisler *management consultant*
Bartow, Diane Grace *marketing professional, sales executive*
Baruch, Ralph M. *communications executive*
Bastianich, Lidia Matticchio *chef, food service executive*
Batali, Mario Francis *chef*
Baumgarten, Barbara *human resources specialist*
Becker, Franklin *chef*
Becker, Susan Kaplan *management and marketing communication consultant, educator*
Beecher, William Manuel *management consultant*
Beinecke, William Sperry *retired consumer products company executive*
Bell, David Arthur *advertising agency executive*
Benno, Jonathan *chef*
Berlin, Andrew Mark *advertising agency executive*
Bernard, David George *retired management consultant*
Bernbach, John Lincoln *marketing professional*
Biederman, Barron Zachary (Barry Biederman) *advertising agency executive*
Blamer, Steven W. *advertising executive*
Bleifer, Robert *chef*
Bloomgarden, Kathy Finn *public relations executive*
Boice, Craig Kendall *management consultant*
Bouley, David *chef*
Boulud, Daniel *chef, restaurant owner*
Bowman, Robert A. *Internet company executive*
Bradstock, John *advertising executive*
Brady, Adelaide Burks *public relations agency executive, giftware catalog executive*
Brainin, Gregory *chef*
Braverman, Robert Jay *management consultant, educator*
Brennan, Terrance *chef*
Brisman, Jennifer *event planning executive*
Brooke, Linda Hundley *human resources specialist*
Brymer, Charles Edward (Chuck Brymer) *advertising executive*
Burke, David *corporate and executive chef*
Burns, Kevin J. *computer software services executive*
Burson, Harold *public relations executive, director*
Burstell, Ed *personal care industry executive*
Burton, Peggy *advertising and marketing executive*
Busquet, Anne M. *Internet company executive*
Byrd, Eva Wilson *communications executive*
Calabrese, Rosalie Sue *management consultant, writer*
Capozzi, Lou *public relations executive*
Carmellini, Andrew *chef*
Cavior, Warren Joseph *communications executive*
Chajet, Clive *brand and corporate image consultant*
Chang, David *chef*
Cheney, Richard Eugene *public relations executive, psychoanalyst*
Chess, William *public relations executive*
Chicco, Gianfranco *healthcare communications executive*
Clarke, Frank William *communications executive*
Cogman, Don V. *public relations executive*
Cohn, Derek *marketing executive*
Colicchio, Tom *chef, food service executive*
Comstock, Beth (Elizabeth J. Comstock) *marketing executive*
Conley, Terence P. *human resources specialist*
Cook, Ian M. *consumer products company executive*
Cooper, Stephen F. *management consultant, corporate recovery executive*
Corbin, Herbert Leonard *public relations executive, director*

Cortese, Edward *marketing executive, public relations executive*
Cox, L. Kevin *human resources specialist*
Craig, Elizabeth Coyne *marketing executive*
Cramb, Charles W. *consumer products company executive*
Cruz, Juan-Carlos *chef*
Daly, Cheryl *communications executive, broadcast executive*
Danielides, Joannie C. *public relations executive*
Davidson, Donald William *advertising executive*
Dayson, Diane Harris *parks director, cultural organization administrator*
DeBow, Jay Howard Camden *public relations executive*
DeBow, Thomas Joseph, Jr. *advertising executive*
DeChellis, Josh *chef*
Delano, Lester Almy, Jr. *advertising executive*
DePrez, Gene Edward *management consultant*
Deutsch, Donny *advertising executive*
DeVard, Jerri *marketing professional*
Devitre, Dinyar S. *consumer products company executive, corporate financial executive*
de Vries, Madeline *public relations executive*
Devulder, Arnaud *sommelier*
Dhondt, Steven Thomas *development officer*
Diamond, Heidi Janice *marketing professional*
Dimling, John Arthur *marketing executive*
Doerfler, Ronald John *communications company executive*
Dolan, Michael *entertainment company executive, former advertising agency executive*
Dolan, Regina A. *security firm executive*
Donaldson, John Cecil, Jr. *consumer products company executive*
Dooner, John Joseph, Jr. *advertising executive*
Dru, Jean-Marie Paul *advertising executive*
Ducasse, Alain *chef*
Duff, Gill *advertising executive*
Dufresne, Wylie *chef, food service executive*
Dunne, Diane C. *marketing professional*
Dunst, Laurence David *advertising executive*
Duran, George *chef*
Edling, Lynn M. *knowledge management analyst*
Edlow, Kenneth Lewis *security firm executive*
Eisler, Susan Krawetz *advertising executive*
Elkes, Terrence Allen *communications executive*
Emanuel, Myron *corporate communications specialist, consultant*
Emerson, Andi (Mrs. Andi Emerson Weeks) *sales and advertising executive*
Ernst, John Louis *management consultant*
Esnault, Tony *chef*
Evans, Alfred Lee, Jr. *advertising executive*
Fajors, Nique *marketing executive*
Falai, Tacopo *chef*
Falk, Edgar Alan *public relations consulting executive, writer*
Farinelli, Jean L. *management consultant*
Faris, George N. *management consultant*
Feintuch, Henry Philip *public relations executive*
Feldman, Allan Roy *corporate development and marketing executive*
Feldman, Robert C. *public relations executive*
Fertitta, George A. *marketing executive*
Feskoe, Gaffney Jon *management consultant*
Fili-Krushel, Patricia *media company executive*
Fine, Deborah *Internet company executive, former apparel executive*
Fine, Jo Renée *management consultant*
Finley, Skip *communications executive*
Finn, Peter *public relations executive*
Flaherty, Tina Santi *corporate communications specialist, writer*
Flaum, Sander Allen *advertising and marketing executive*
Flay, Bobby *chef, restaurateur*
Fleischman, Barbara Greenberg *public relations consultant*
Florence, Tyler *chef*
Fluhr, Howard *consulting firm executive*
Folta, Carl D. *communications executive*
Forman, Leonard P. *media company executive*
Frank, William Fielding *computer company executive, consultant*
Frankfort, Lew *consumer products company executive*
Fudge, Ann Marie *advertising executive*
Furman, Anthony Michael *public relations executive*
Gallagher, Cornelius *chef*
Garfinkel, Lee *advertising agency executive*
Garron, Miriam *chef*
Garvin, Andrew Paul *computer company executive, writer*
Gatfield, Stephen J. *advertising executive*
Geier, Philip Henry, Jr. *advertising executive*
Geller, Robert James *advertising executive*
Genachowski, Julius *communications executive*
Gerard-Sharp, Monica Fleur *communications executive*
Gerberg, Judith Levine *management consultant*
Gianinno, Susan McManama *advertising executive*
Giblin, Jennifer *chef*
Gill, Linda A. *advertising executive*
Ginsburg, Sigmund G. *management and executive search consultant*
Glatt, Mitchell Steven *consumer products company executive*
Gold, Mari S. *public relations executive*
Goldfarb, Will *chef*
Goldschmidt, Charles *advertising agency executive*
Goldsmith, Clifford Henry *graphic design company executive*
Goldstein, Gary Sanford *executive recruiter*
Goldstone, Steven F. *former consumer products company executive*
Gomez, Francis Dean *consumer products company executive, former foreign service official*
Gottlieb, Jerrold Howard *advertising executive*
Grecich, Daryl George *marketing communications executive, editor-in-chief*
Green, William D. *management consulting firm executive*
Greenberg, David I. *consumer products company executive*
Greenland, Leo *advertising executive*
Griffy, Timothy T. *human resources specialist, finance company executive*
Grossman, Lawrence Kugelmass *former communications executive, advertising executive*

Gumbinner, Paul S. *advertising and executive recruitment agency executive*
Guskov, Sergey *security firm executive*
Gutenbrunner, Kurt *chef, food service executive*
Hammond, Lou Rena Charlotte *public relations executive*
Hanson, Stephen *food service executive*
Hatheway, John Harris *advertising agency executive*
Heekin, James Robson III *advertising executive*
Heinzerling, Larry Edward *communications executive*
Helmsley, Leona Mindy *hotel executive*
Herbert, Marilynne *public relations executive, freelance photographer*
Hertz, Suki *chef*
Hicks, Weston Milliken *security firm executive, securities analyst*
Hochhauser, Richard Michael *marketing professional*
Holzer, Harold *museum and marketing executive, historian, writer*
Hudes, Nana Brenda *marketing professional*
Hurst, Robert Jay *security firm executive*
Hynes, Aedhmar *public relations executive*
Ilson, Bernard *public relations executive*
Isogai, Masaharu *international corporate strategist, retired apparel executive*
Iuzzini, Johnny *chef*
Jacoby, Robert Harold *management consulting executive*
James, Robert Leo *advertising executive, director*
Jean-Baptiste, Tricia *public relations executive*
Jeffrey, Robert *advertising executive*
Johnnes, Daniel *chef*
Johnson, Harold Earl *human resources specialist*
Johnson, John William, Jr. *executive recruiter*
Johnson, Verdia E. *marketing professional*
Jonas, Gilbert *public relations and fund raising executive*
Jones, David *advertising executive*
Josell, Jessica (Jessica Wechsler) *public relations executive*
Just, Gemma Rivoli *retired advertising executive*
Karalekas, George Steven *advertising agency executive, political consultant*
Karp, Martin Everett *management consultant*
Kassel, Terry *human resources specialist*
Kavner, Robert M. *communications executive*
Kearney, Lynn *Culinary Manager*
Keenan, Michael Edgar *marketing professional*
Kekst, Gershon *public relations consultant*
Kelly, Peter *communications executive*
Kelmenson, Leo-Arthur *advertising executive*
Kinsolving, Charles McIlvaine, Jr. *marketing executive*
Konney, Paul Edward *consumer products company executive, lawyer*
Kotuk, Andrea Mikotajuk *public relations executive, writer*
Kraus, Norma Jean *human resources executive*
Kraushar, Jonathan Pollack *communications and media consultant*
Kreisberg, Neil Ivan *advertising executive*
Kreston, Martin Howard *advertising, marketing, public relations, and publishing executive*
Kreuther, Gabriel *chef*
Krinsky, Robert Daniel *consulting firm executive*
Krukowski, Jan *communications executive*
Kuperman, Robert Ian *retired advertising agency executive*
Kyriakou, Linda Grace *communications executive*
Laiskonis, Michael *chef*
Lang, George *restaurateur*
Langton, Cleve Swanson *advertising executive*
Lannamann, Richard Stuart *executive search consultant*
Larrick, Pamela Maphis *marketing executive*
Laumont, Philippe Emile *communications executive*
Lazarus, Shelly (Rochelle Braff Lazarus) *advertising executive*
Lee, Sandra *food service executive, product designer*
Leslie, Seymour Marvin *communications executive, director*
Leubert, Alfred Otto Paul *management consultant*
Levins, Ilyssa *public relations executive*
Lewis, Leland M. *hotel executive*
Lieberman, Dave *chef*
Lipman, Ira Ackerman *security service company executive*
Lipton, Charles *public relations executive*
Lipton, Joan Elaine *advertising executive*
Liu, Tony *chef*
Lo, Anita *chef*
Loeb, Larry Morris *communications company executive*
Loo, Santos *chef*
Lorber, Barbara Heyman *communications executive, event producer*
Lubars, David *advertising executive*
Lucht, John Charles *management consultant, writer*
Makovsky, Kenneth Dale *public relations executive*
Malgieri, Nick *food service executive, educator, chef, writer*
Mallozzi, Cos M. *public relations executive*
Malouf, Waldy *food service executive*
Manoff, Richard Kalman *advertising executive, writer, public health service officer, consultant*
Mansi, Joseph Anneillo *public relations company executive*
Marcosson, Thomas I. *management consultant, advertising executive*
Mark, Reuben *consumer products company executive*
Martin, John F. *management consultant*
Martinez, Arthur C. *consumer products company executive, former retail company executive*
Martínez-López, Carmen Leonor *management consultant, educator*
Masi, Jane Virginia *marketing and sales consultant*
Masters, Jon Joseph *corporate governance specialist, management consultant*
McAveney, Mary Susan *marketing executive*
McCabe, Mary F. *marketing professional*
McCaslin, Teresa Eve *human resources specialist*
McKelvey, Andrew J. *advertising executive*

McKenna, William Michael *advertising executive*
McLennan, Hamish *advertising executive*
Meigher, S. Christopher III *communications and media executive, publisher*
Merino, Junior *mixologist*
Merritt, Jean *consulting firm executive, psychotherapist*
Messner, Thomas G. *advertising executive, copywriter*
Meyer, Edward Henry *advertising agency executive*
Meyer, Scott *communications executive*
Miller, Ernest Charles *management consultant*
Miller, Neil Stuart *advertising executive*
Miller, Robert *advertising executive*
Moore, David J. *media company executive*
Morris, Stephen Burritt *marketing information company executive*
Moulton, Sara *chef, magazine editor*
Moyer, David S. *executive search consultant*
Murdoch, Rupert (Keith Rupert Murdoch) *multimedia company executive*
Murphy, James Edward *public relations and marketing executive*
Murphy, Kenneth F. *human resources specialist*
Murphy, Mark Joseph *enterprise sales executive*
Musham, Bettye Martin *consumer products executive*
Nadler-Hurvich, Hedda Carol *public relations executive*
Nash, Edward L. *advertising executive*
Neff, Thomas Joseph *search firm executive*
Nelson, Dean B. *media company executive*
Nelson, Merlin Edward *retired management consultant, lawyer*
Nelson, Ronald L. *travel services company executive, former film company executive*
Newman, Geraldine Anne *advertising executive*
Nieporent, Drew *restaurant group executive*
Nisenholtz, Martin Abram *telecommunications executive, educator*
Nish, Wayne Paul *chef, restaurant owner*
O'Brien, Dermot J. *human resources specialist*
Ogden, Peggy A. *retired personnel director*
Okuwa, Makoto *chef*
Olafsson, Olaf *communications executive*
Olinger, Carla D(ragan) *medical advertising executive*
Oppenheim, Robert *beauty industry executive*
O'Sullivan, Eugene Henry *retired advertising executive, management consultant*
Pace, Wayne H. *communications executive*
Palmer, Charlie *chef, restaurant manager*
Parrish, Steven C. *consumer products company executive*
Parsons, Richard Dean *communications executive*
Pasierb, Stephen John *advertising executive, marketing professional*
Paster, Howard G. *public relations and public affairs company executive*
Pasternack, David *chef*
Patrick, Stephen C. *consumer products company executive*
Payard, Francois *food service executive*
Pearlstine, Norman *communications consultant, former editor*
Pelaccio, Zakary *chef*
Perelman, Ronald Owen *consumer products company executive*
Perlgut, Mark Ralph *public relations executive*
Phillips, Graham Holmes *retired advertising executive*
Piliguian, Tro *advertising executive*
Planitzer, Russell E. *computer company executive*
Poe, Randall Ellsworth *public relations executive, author*
Polansky, Andy *public relations executive*
Pollock-O'Brien, Louise Mary *public relations executive*
Pompadur, I. Martin *communications executive*
Portale, Alfred *chef, restaurant owner*
Price, Robert *media and communications executive, investment banker, lawyer*
Primi, Don Alexis *advertising executive, public relations executive, rail transportation executive*
Quinlan, Mary Lou *former advertising executive, consultant*
Quintero, Ronald Gary *management consultant*
Radice, Frank J. *communications executive*
Raghavan, Sudheer *hotel executive*
Rauch, Arthur Irving *management consultant*
Reals Ellig, Janice *marketing professional, human resources consultant*
Reda, James Francis *business consultant*
Reed, Marc C. *human resources specialist, communications executive*
Reges, Marianna Alice *marketing executive*
Reilly, Edward T., Jr. *advertising executive*
Reinhard, Keith Leon *advertising executive*
Renauld, Cyril *chef*
Renna, Cathy *communications executive, activist*
Ressler, Peter D. *executive recruiter*
Reynolds, James *management consultant*
Richardson, Grace Elizabeth *consumer products company executive*
Ritchie, Richard Lee *media company executive*
Robbins, John Clapp *management consultant*
Roberts, Francis Stone *advertising executive*
Roberts, Kevin *advertising executive*
Robertson, Andrew *advertising executive*
Robinson, Peter M. *business association executive*
Roche, Gerard Raymond *management consultant*
Roche, Joyce M. *marketing executive*
Rose, Joanne W. *rating service executive*
Rosenshine, Allen Gilbert *advertising agency executive*
Roskin, William A. *communications executive*
Ross, Jo Ann *media buyer*
Roth, Michael I. *communications executive, lawyer*
Rothenberg, Robert Philip *public relations counselor*
Rubenstein, Howard Joseph *public relations executive*
Ruder, William *public relations executive*
Russo, Anthony Joseph *public relations professional*
Ryan, J. Brendan *advertising executive*
Samuelsson, Marcus (Kasshun Tsegie) *food service executive*

Sarbin, Hershel Benjamin *management consultant, lawyer, publishing executive*
Sawyer, Linda *advertising executive*
Saxton, Catherine Patricia *public relations executive*
Sayre, Linda Damaris *human resources professional*
Scarpelli, Bob *advertising executive*
Schaffer, Kenneth B. *communications executive, mechanical engineer, consultant*
Schatz, Gary Stewart *marketing professional*
Schrager, Ian *hotel executive*
Schupak, Leslie Allen *public relations company executive*
Schuster, Reid S. *advertising executive*
Schwab, Frank, Jr. *management consultant*
Schwartz, Alan Victor *advertising executive*
Seaman, Alfred Jarvis *retired advertising agency executive*
Secunda, Eugene *marketing professional, educator*
Seiden, Henry (Hank Seiden) *advertising executive*
Seiden, Steven Arnold *executive search consultant*
Serra, Matthew D. *consumer products company executive*
Shanahan, William Stephen *consumer products company executive*
Shapiro, Marvin Lincoln *communications company executive*
Shea, Martin M. *communications executive*
Sheehan, Mike *advertising executive*
Shepard, Thomas Rockwell III *advertising executive*
Sherman, Eugene Jay *retired marketing professional, retired economist*
Sherman, Norman Mark *advertising agency executive*
Siegel, Herbert Jay *communications executive, director*
Siegel, Lucy Boswell *public relations executive*
Silverman, Dan *chef*
Silverman, Henry Richard *travel services company executive*
Sinclair, Daisy *communications executive*
Smith, Barbara *food service executive, model*
Smith, Martin Jay *advertising executive, marketing executive*
Softness, Donald Gabriel *marketing professional, manufacturing executive*
Sorell, Kitty Julia *public relations executive*
Soter, George Nicholas *advertising executive*
Speros, James Demitrios *advertising executive*
Spiegel, Elwyn *advertising executive, art director*
Sprague, Peter Julian *software company executive, lecturer*
Stanton, Amy *marketing executive*
Stautberg, Susan Schiffer *communications executive*
Steves, Gale C. *marketing professional, writer, editor-in-chief, publishing executive*
Stratigos, William Narge *computer company executive*
Strear, Joseph D. *public relations executive*
Stroock, Mark Edwin, II, *public relations company executive*
Stuart, Lori Ames *public relations executive*
Sussman, Jeffrey Bruce *public relations and marketing executive*
Swid, Stephen Claar *communications executive, director*
Sykes, John *communications company executive*
Tanaka, Patrice Aiko *public relations executive*
Tarter, Fred Barry *advertising executive*
Taylor, Barbara Alden *public relations executive*
Thaler, Linda Kaplan *advertising executive*
Thomas, Mory *chef*
Tilson, Dorothy Ruth *word processing executive*
Tisch, Jonathan Mark *hotel company executive*
Torrenzano, Richard *public relations executive*
Tortorello, Nicholas John *public opinion and market research company executive*
Tourondel, Laurent *chef*
Upson, Stuart Barnard *advertising agency executive*
Ureña, Alex *chef*
Vermeer, Maureen Dorothy *sales executive*
Vick, Edward Hoge, Jr. *advertising executive*
Volk, Kristin *advertising agency executive*
von Baillou, Astrid *executive search consultant*
Vongerichten, Jean-Georges *food service executive*
Waltuck, David *chef, restaurant owner*
Wanell, William Charles *public relations executive*
Wasow, Omar *Internet company executive*
Waters, Donald Joseph *data processing executive*
Weiss, Myrna Grace *management consultant*
Wells, Peter Scoville *retired marketing professional*
Wenig, Devin Norse *communications executive*
Werfelman, William Herman, Jr. *public relations executive*
Whaley, Charles Henry, IV, *communications company executive*
Whited, Mary Elizabeth *marketing professional*
Wijnberg, Sandra S. *professional services company executive*
Willett, Roslyn Leonore *public relations executive, food service consultant, writer, editor*
Wolff, Richard Joseph *public relations executive, consultant, historian*
Worsham, Hal Glenn *marketing professional*
Wren, John D. *advertising executive*
Wright, Jason Howard Sebastian *communications executive*
Wright, Tony *advertising executive*
Zamarra, Galen *chef*

**Newark**
Hemmings, Madeleine Blanchet *management consultant, not-for-profit administrator, media consultant*

**Northport**
Donenfeld, Kenneth Jay *management consultant*

**Nyack**
Karp, Peter Simon *marketing executive*
Keil, John Mullan *advertising executive, artist*

**Oceanside**
Kyler, Arlene *advertising executive*

**Ossining**
Dolmatch, Theodore Bieley *management consultant*

**Ozone Park**
Singh, Seopaul *security firm executive*

**Palisades**
Lenton, Roberto Leonardo *environmental services administrator*
Schmetterer, Robert Allen *advertising executive*

**Pearl River**
Wang, John Xiaowu *computer company executive*

**Pelham**
Hearle, Douglas Geoffrey *public relations consultant*

**Penfield**
Weerasinghe, Renu M. *quality assurance professional*

**Pleasantville**
Eschweiler, Peter Quintus *planning consultant*

**Port Chester**
Ailloni-Charas, Dan *marketing executive*

**Port Washington**
Hackett, John Byron *advertising executive, lawyer*
Johnson, Tod Stuart *market research company executive*
Leeds, Richard *computer marketing executive*

**Poughkeepsie**
VanBuren, Denise Doring *corporate communications executive*

**Pound Ridge**
Rubino, John Anthony *management and human resources consultant*

**Purchase**
Amelio, Bill (William J. Amelio) *computer company executive*
Hudson, Dawn Emily *food service company executive*
Moore, Margaret D. *human resources specialist*
Nicholson, Cie (Cynthia Nicholson) *marketing executive, beverage company executive*
O'Sullivan, Frances K. *computer company executive*
Ward, Stephen M., Jr. *computer company executive*

**Quogue**
Burkhardt, Ronald Robert *advertising executive, writer, artist, filmmaker*

**Rensselaer**
Hull, Raymond Whitford *public relations executive*

**Rochester**
Berman, Robert L. *human resources specialist*
Goldberg-Schaible, Jocelyn Hope Schnier *market research professional*
Harris, Diane Carol *merger and acquisition consulting firm executive*
Harvey, Douglass Coate *retired photographic company executive*
Perez, Antonio M. *imaging company executive*
Ramirez, Stevan G. *consumer products company executive*
Vojt, Christine M. *quality assurance professional, microbiologist*
Wegman, Colleen *food service executive*
Wegman, Daniel R. *food service executive*

**Rockville Centre**
Beyer, Suzanne *advertising agency executive*
Pompan, Jack Maurice *management consultant*

**Roslyn**
Ulanoff, Stanley M. *communications executive*

**Rye**
Franklin, Martin E. *consumer products company executive*
Kaulakis, Arnold Francis *management consultant*
Pearson, Nathan Williams *communications executive, investment executive*

**Rye Brook**
Mariam, Thomas Fred *public relations executive, radio producer*

**Salisbury Mills**
Tersine, Brenda L. *funeral director*

**Saratoga Springs**
Masie, Elliott *training executive*

**Scarsdale**
Clark, Merrell Mays *management consultant*
Kaufman, Robert Jules *communications consultant, lawyer*
Laufer, Leonard Justin *management consultant*
Schultz, Harley *consulting company executive*

**Schenectady**
Golub, Lewis *supermarket company executive*
Golub, Neil M. *supermarket chain executive*

**Seaford**
Spencer, Jean *retired business executive*

**Setauket**
Robinson, Richard M. *communications executive*

**Skaneateles**
Huxford, J. David *retired sales executive*

**Sleepy Hollow**
Marshall, Michael Borden *marketing executive*
Schmidt, Klaus Franz *advertising executive*

**Somers**
Berisford, John L. *human resources specialist*
Cahill, John T. *consumer products company executive*
Drewes, Alfred H. *consumer products company executive*
Foss, Eric J. *consumer products company executive*
Wladawsky-Berger, Irving *communications executive*

**Staatsburg**
Wentworth, Dennis Ladd *historic sites and parks administrator*

**Staten Island**
Fafian, Joseph, Jr. *management consultant*
Khan, Tariq *marketing professional*

**Stony Brook**
Ohannessian, Harry Haroutune *travel agency executive*

**Syosset**
Cordaro, Joanne *human resources specialist, director*

**Syracuse**
Cooper, John Ambrose *management consultant, marketing professional*

**Tappan**
Fox, Muriel *retired public relations executive*

**Thornwood**
Bassett, Lawrence C *management consultant*

**Tuckahoe**
Brecher, Bernd *management consultant*

**Uniondale**
Redder, Thomas *consumer products company executive*

**Westbury**
McCann, Jim (James F. McCann) *consumer products company executive*

**Westhampton Beach**
Maas, Jane Brown *advertising executive*

**White Plains**
Adkins, Rodney *computer company executive*
Allen, Ralph Dean *diversified company corporate executive*
Brown, Ronald C. *hotel executive*
Colwell, Howard Otis *advertising executive*
Cotter, Robert F. *hotel executive*
David, Miles *marketing executive*
Heyer, Steven J. *hotel executive, former beverage company executive*
Lukaszewski, James Edmund *communications executive*
Sternlicht, Barry Stuart *hotel executive*
Sussberg, Milton Joel *marketing professional*
Vernon, Lillian *mail order company executive*

**Woodhaven**
Bolster, Jacqueline Neben (Mrs. John A. Bolster) *communications consultant*

**Yonkers**
Capodilupo, Elizabeth Jeanne Hatton *public relations executive*
Colabella, George Michael *management consultant, not-for-profit fundraiser*
Ortega, Maria A. *security firm executive, educator*

**Yorktown Heights**
Rosenblatt, Stephen Paul *marketing and sales promotion company executive*

**Youngstown**
Askins, Nancy Ellen Paulsen *training services executive*

**NORTH CAROLINA**

**Arden**
Baker, Kerry Allen *management consultant*

**Asheville**
Mundt, Barry Maynard *management consultant*

**Canton**
Dixon, Shirley Juanita *retired restaurant owner*

**Cary**
Ashley, James MacGregor *management consultant*
Craig, Harold Kent *mechanical contracting executive, systems analyst*
Wait, George William *sales executive*

**Chapel Hill**
Lochridge, Julie Deane *retired communications executive*

**Charlotte**
Bass-Hollis, Cynthia Gibson *environmental services administrator*
Carroll, David M. *communications professional*
Eppes, Thomas Evans *advertising executive, public relations executive*
Ignozzi, Bryan K. *management consultant*
Lisenby, Terry S. *waste management executive*
Lucas, Charles Craft III *executive recruiter*
Lyerly, Elaine Myrick *advertising executive*
Osteen, Louis *chef*
Van Alstyne, Vance Brownell *management consultant*
Wood, Donald Craig *retired marketing professional*

**Clayton**
Silberman, H. Lee *public relations executive, consultant*

**Denver**
McIntosh, Anita Jane *retired administrative assistant*

**Durham**
Barker, Karen *restaurant owner, chef*
Gunter, Emily Diane *communications executive, marketing professional, educator, real estate developer, writer*
Otterbourg, Robert Kenneth *public relations consultant, writer*
Taylor, James Francis *marketing professional*

**Elon**
Powell, William Council, Sr. *service company executive*

**Flat Rock**
Childress, Richard Thomas *international business consultant*

**Greensboro**
Formo, Brenda Terrell *travel company executive*
Sanders, William Eugene *marketing executive*
Staab, Thomas Robert *consumer product company financial executive*
Stone, Theresa M. *communications executive*

**Hampstead**
Walters, Sherwood George *management consultant, educator*

**Hertford**
McClung, Kenneth Austin, Jr. *training executive, performance consultant*

**Hickory**
George, Boyd Lee *consumer products company executive*

**Indian Trail**
Johnson, Frank William *marketing professional*

**Mooresville**
Johnston, James Wesley *retired consumer products company executive*
Niblock, Robert A. *consumer home products company executive*

**New Bern**
Naumann, William Carl *consumer products company executive*

**North Wilkesboro**
Parsons, Irene Adelaide *management consultant*

**Pinehurst**
Rees, Clifford Harcourt, Jr., (Ted Rees) *consulting company executive, retired trade association administrator, retired military officer*

**Pittsboro**
Griffith, Katherine Scott *retired communications executive, retired librarian*
Squire, Alexander *management consultant*

**Raleigh**
Doherty, Robert Cunningham *retired advertising executive*
Eberly, Harry Landis *retired communications company executive*
Karmanos, Peter, Jr. *computer company executive, professional sports team executive*
Leak, Robert Edwards *economic development consultant*
Mitchell, Memory Farmer *retired communications executive*

**Research Triangle Park**
Advani, Deepak *computer company executive*
Bandrowczak, Steven J. *computer company executive*
Bronstein, Lois Helene *marketing professional*

**Roxboro**
Hollingsworth, Brenda Jackson *employment consultant*

**Sanford**
Sodini, Peter J. *food service executive*

**Southern Pines**
Owings, Malcolm William *retired management consultant*

**Trinity**
McIlquham, David J. *consumer products company executive*

**Vass**
Glassman, Edward *public relations executive, educator, journalist*

**Wake Forest**
Gamble, Michael F. *human resources generalist*

**Waxhaw**
Ahern, John James *software company executive*

**Weaverville**
Parsons, Vinson Adair *retired computer company executive*

**Wilson**
Atkinson, Ann Lennette *funeral director*

**Winston Salem**
Griswold, George *marketing, advertising and public relations executive*
Gunzenhauser, Gerard Ralph, Jr. *management consultant, investor*
Ivey, Susan M. *tobacco company executive*
Marino, Nancy A. *marketing professional*
Shipko, Renee *marketing executive*

**NORTH DAKOTA**

**Fargo**
Tharaldson, Gary Dean *hotel developer, owner*

**OHIO**

**Akron**
Crawford, Robert John *credit company executive*
Geier, Kathleen T. *human resources specialist*
Sonnecken, Edwin Herbert *management consultant*

**Avon Lake**
Morton, David Ray *sales and marketing executive*

**Bowling Green**
Darrow, Arthur Lloyd *management consultant, educator*

**Cincinnati**
Antoine, Richard L. *human resources specialist, consumer products company executive*
Arnold, Susan E. *consumer products company executive*
Bateman, Sharon Louise *public relations executive*
Brown, Dale Patrick *retired advertising executive*
Campbell, Audrey Leigh *communications professional*
Daley, Clayton Carl, Jr. *consumer products company executive*
deCavel, Jean-Robert *chef*
Dillon, David Brian *retail grocery executive*
Dougherty, David Francis *business process outsourcing executive*
Goodman, Phyllis L. *public relations executive*
Hawkins, Lawrence Charles *management consultant, educator*
Henretta, Deborah A. *consumer products company executive*
Howe, John Kingman *manufacturing, sales and marketing executive*
Joffe, Craig P.R. *personal care industry executive*
Kernan, Jerome Bernard *retired marketing educator, researcher*
Kotchka, Claudia B. *consumer products company executive, accountant*
Lafley, Alan G. *consumer products company executive*
Morris, Margaret Elizabeth *marketing professional, small business owner*
Orr, James Francis *marketing executive, information technology executive*
Pepper, John Ennis, Jr. *former consumer products company executive, historical museum executive*
Puglise, J. Michael *management consultant*
Shanks, Earl *marketing professional*
Shipley, Tony L(ee) *software company executive*
Wall, Della *human resources specialist, manufacturing executive*
Zaring, Allen G. *homebuilding company executive*

**Cleveland**
Alazhar, Gail Grace *recreational facility executive, director*
Danco, Léon Antoine *management consultant, educator*
DeGroote, Michael G. *management consulting company executive*
Dunbar, Mary Asmundson *communications executive, public information officer, consultant, investor*
Fountain, Ronald Glenn *management consultant, corporate financial executive, entrepreneur, educator*
Gallagher, Patrick Francis Xavier *public relations executive*
Henry, Edward Frank *data processing executive*
Johnson, John Frank *professional recruitment executive*
Perkovic, Robert Branko *retired international management consultant*
Roop, James John *public relations executive*
Simmons, Clinton Craig *human resources executive*
Taw, Dudley Joseph *sales executive, director*
Woods, Jacqueline F. *public relations executive*

**Columbus**
Alban, Roger Charles *small business consultant*
Burke, Kenneth Andrew *advertising executive*
Davis, Steven A. *restaurant company executive*
Iammartino, Nicholas R. *corporate communications executive*
Kerner, Joseph Frank, Jr. *management consultant, educator*
Ledingham, John Allen *public relations specialist, educator, consultant*
McClain, Thomas Emerson *retired communications executive*
Ress, Charles William *management consultant*
Tipton, Clyde Raymond, Jr. *communications and resources development consultant*

**Dayton**
Daoud, George Jamil *hotel and motel consultant*
Geswein, Gregory T. *software company executive*
Nuti, William R. *computer services company executive*
Riley, David Richard *management consultant, retired military officer*
Ringler, James M. (James M. Ringler) *computer services company executive*
Tatar, Jerome F. *business products executive*

**Delaware**
Sparks, William B., Jr. *consumer products company executive*

**Dublin**
Anderson, Kerrii B. *food service executive*
Bird, Shelley *communications executive*
Kinman, Gary W. *landscape company executive*
Pickett, Lamar J. *food service executive*
Smith, K(ermit) Wayne *computer company executive*
Watkins, Carole S. *human resources specialist, medical products executive*
Wilkins, Jeffrey M. *computer company executive*

**Elyria**
Patton, Thomas James *marketing executive, sales executive*

**Galion**
Cobey, Ralph *industrialist*

**Gates Mills**
Abbott, James Samuel III *marketing executive*
Reitman, Robert Stanley *management consultant, not-for-profit advisor*

**Hudson**
Roemer, James Paul *data processing executive, writer*

**Jackson**
Benson, Steven Clark *management and engineering executive*

**Kent**
Bissler, Richard Thomas *mortician*

**Lake Milton**
Glomski, Edward Earl *sales executive*

**Lancaster**
Katlic, John Edward *management consultant*
Phillips, Edward John *consulting firm executive*

**Loveland**
Peters, Thomas J *management consultant, writer*

**Mansfield**
Pesec, David John *data systems executive*

**Marysville**
Hagedorn, James *landscape company executive*

**Maumee**
Konopinski, Virgil James *industrial hygienist, consultant*

**Mayfield Heights**
Newman, Joseph Herzl *advertising executive, consultant*
Rhein, Arthur *computer company executive*

**New Albany**
Duggan, Thomas Patrick *management consultant*

**Oberlin**
Cartier, Brian Evans *consumer products company executive*

**Olmsted Falls**
Faller, Dorothy Anderson *training services executive, consultant*

**Perrysburg**
Kovacik, Neal Stephen *hotel and restaurant executive*

**Powell**
Lee, Robert J. Y. *marketing professional*

**Rocky River**
Hosek, John Jude *planning organization executive*

**Salem**
Fehr, Kenneth Manbeck *retired computer company executive*

**Solon**
Benhoff, Edward Spreng *marketing professional*
Dutile, Robert Arthur *executive management consultant*

**Sylvania**
Ring, Herbert Everett *management executive*

**Toledo**
Block, Allan James *communications executive*
Paquette, Jack Kenneth *management consultant, writer, historian*

**West Chester**
End, William Thomas *marketing executive*

**Westerville**
Bainbridge, William L. *research firm executive, consultant*

**Westlake**
Doane, Tim *travel company executive*
Kuhn, Edwin P. *travel company executive*

**Wooster**
Schmitt, Wolf Rudolf *consumer products executive*

**Worthington**
Proctor, Allen Joseph *management consultant, economist*

**Xenia**
Nutter, Zoe Dell Lantis *retired public relations executive*

**Youngstown**
Estrin, Melvyn J. *computer products company executive*

**OKLAHOMA**

**Cleveland**
Henry, Kathleen Marie *marketing executive*

**Enid**
Taveggia, Thomas Charles *management consultant*

**Monkey Island**
Vanatta, Chester B. *management consultant, educator*

**Mustang**
Laurent, Jerry Suzanna *communications executive*

**Oklahoma City**
Ackerman, Raymond Basil *advertising executive*
Blackwell, John Adrian, Jr. *computer company executive*
Carballo, Bernard A. *computer company executive*
Greiner, Kenneth Donald, Jr. *retired management consultant, health facility administrator*

Grupe, Robert Charles *corporate communications specialist*
Houpt, Jeff *Internet company executive, executive secretary*
LaMotte, Janet Allison *retired management consultant*

**Tulsa**
Abbott, William Thomas *private investigator*
Gentry, Bern Leon, Sr. *management consultant*
Paxton, Gary L. *Auto rental company executive*

## OREGON

**Beaverton**
Anthony, Wilma Tylinda *customer service administrator*

**Bend**
Denton, Jody *chef*

**Eugene**
Bennett, Robert Royce *engineering and management consultant*
Cawood, Elizabeth Jean *public relations executive*

**Forest Grove**
Carson, William Morris *manpower planning and development advisor*

**Gleneden Beach**
Parker, Edwin Burke *communications executive*

**Jacksonville**
Hennion, Reeve Lawrence *communications executive*

**Lake Oswego**
Parrick, Gerald Hathaway *communications and marketing executive*
Zorkin, Melissa Waggener *public relations executive*

**Medford**
Entorf, Richard Carl *retired management consultant*

**Portland**
Barbeau, Monique Andrée *chef*
Boulot, Philippe *chef*
Conkling, Roger Linton *management consultant, business administration educator, retired utilities executive*
Hinckley, Gregory Keith *software industry executive*
Kirk, Jill *management consultant*
Linstone, Harold Adrian *management consultant, educator*
Paley, Vitaly *chef, food service executive*
Stanton, John W. *communications executive*
Stevens, Curtis *consumer products company executive*
Suwyn, Mark A. *building products executive*
Urbanowski, John Richard *lighting systems company official*
Wieden, Dan G. *advertising executive*

**Salem**
Benson, Steven Donald *marketing professional, mechanical engineer, writer*

**Tualatin**
Alley, Allen H. *semiconductor company executive*
Bouchard, Jeffrey B. *semiconductor company executive*
Fleischmann, Marc W. *semiconductor company executive*
Greenberg, Robert Y. *semiconductor company executive*
Hick, Kenneth William *marketing executive*
Olsen, Hans H. *semiconductor company executive*

**Wilsonville**
Press, Ron *marketing professional*

## PENNSYLVANIA

**Beach Lake**
Chatlos, William Edward *management consultant*

**Bethel Park**
Willard, John Gerard *communications executive, consultant, writer, educator*

**Blue Bell**
Carrow, John C. *computer company executive*
McGrath, Joseph W. *computer services company executive*

**Bryn Mawr**
Peters, Douglas Scott *health care executive*
Wheeler, Grace R. *retired market researcher*

**Camp Hill**
Crist, Christine Myers *consulting executive*

**Chambersburg**
Furr, Quint Eugene *marketing executive*
Neilson, Winthrop Cunningham III *communications executive, financial consultant, photographer*

**Conshohocken**
Thompson, Pamela Padwick *public relations executive*

**Cranberry Township**
Patten, Charles Anthony *management consultant, retired manufacturing company executive, writer, publisher*

**Doylestown**
McCafferty, Barbara Jean (BJ McCafferty) *sales executive*

**Gettysburg**
Hallberg, Budd Jaye *management consulting firm executive*

**Harrisburg**
Moritz, Milton Edward *security consultant*

**Huntingdon Valley**
Vollum, Robert Boone *management consultant*

**Ivyland**
Thorne, John Watson III *advertising and marketing executive*

**Kennett Square**
Hennes, Robert Taft *former management consultant, investment executive*

**King Of Prussia**
Clauson, Sharyn Ferne *consulting company executive, educator*

**Lafayette Hill**
Edwards, JoAnn Louise *human resources executive*

**Lancaster**
Benoit, Philip Grosvenor *communications executive, educator, writer*
Kelly, Robert Lynn *advertising executive*
Taylor, Ann *human resources specialist, educator*
Veitch, Boyer Lewis *printing company executive*

**Lebanon**
Deysher, Paul Evans *retired management consultant*
Moss, Richard Spencer *communications executive*

**Lewisburg**
Rote, Nelle Fairchild Hefty *management consultant*

**Manns Choice**
Braendel, Douglas Arthur *hotel executive*

**Media**
Barnett, Samuel Treutlen *consultant*
Garvin, Florence Ward *management consultant*

**Montgomeryville**
Schmidt, William Max *management consultant, marketing executive*

**Mountainhome**
Buttz, Charles William *outdoor advertising executive*

**Nottingham**
White, Richard Edmund *marketing executive*

**Oaks**
Marland, Alkis Joseph *leasing company executive, computer scientist, educator, financial planner*

**Palmyra**
Moseley, Marc Robards *sales executive*

**Penn Valley**
Newhall, John Harrison *retired business executive, management consultant*

**Philadelphia**
Armstrong, C. Michael *retired communications executive*
Backstrom, C. Stephen *communications executive*
Block, Arthur R. *communications executive, lawyer*
Breslow, Tina *public relations executive*
Burke, Stephen B. (Steve Burke) *communications company executive*
Dougherty Buchholz, Karen *communications executive*
Feninger, Claude *food service executive*
Finney, Graham Stanley *management consultant*
Foo, Susanna *chef*
Gans, Samuel Myer *temporary employment service executive*
Gatti, Leonard J. *communications executive*
Greene, Hans *warehouse manager*
Hemphill, John Lindsay III *administrative assistant*
Lee, Christopher *chef*
Logue-Kinder, Joan *public relations consultant*
McKee, Lynn B. *human resources specialist*
Mitchell, Brenda King *training services executive*
Morimoto, Masaharu *chef, television personality*
Pernot, Guillermo *chef, restaurant owner*
Roberts, Brian L. *communications executive*
Scott-Williams, Mildred P. *food service specialist*
Smith, Lawrence S. *communications executive*
Starr, Stephen *restaurant owner*
Tuan, Kailin *management consultant, educator*
Vetri, Marc *chef*
Walter, William G. *consumer products company executive*

**Phoenixville**
Brundage, Russell Archibald *retired data processing executive*

**Pittsburgh**
Bender, Charles Christian *retail home center executive*
Burger, Herbert Francis *retired advertising agency executive*
Dempsey, Jerry Edward *retired service company executive*
Fine, Milton *hotel company executive, lawyer*
Giel, James Arthur, Jr. *employee benefits consultant*
Hewitt, Thomas Francis *hotel executive*
Kilkeary, Kevin P. *hospitality executive*
Neel, John Dodd *cemetery executive*
Peterman, Donna Cole *communications executive*
Rangos, Alexander W. *waste management environmental services administrator*
Rathke, Sheila Wells *marketing professional, consultant*
Reichblum, Audrey Rosenthal *public relations executive, publishing executive*

**Richardson, J.** William *hotel executive*
Thomas, Paul D. *human resources specialist, metal products executive*

**Plymouth Meeting**
Kadel, Paula Ruth Ritchie *public relations executive*
Siegal, Jacob J. *management and financial consultant*

**Radnor**
Paier, Adolf Arthur *computer company executive, director*

**Reading**
Carlino, Peter M. *gaming company executive*
Dersh, Rhoda E. *management consultant, business executive*
Kraras, Gust C. *hotel executive*

**Ridley Park**
Walls, William Walton, Jr. *management consultant*

**Royersford**
Rhoads, Michael Dennis *sales executive*

**Rydal**
Boreen, Henry Isaac *computer company executive*

**Sadsburyville**
Gellman, Gloria Gae Seeburger Schick *marketing professional*

**Southeastern**
Rassbach, Herbert David *marketing executive*

**State College**
McKibbin, William Jeffrey *management consultant*
Subler, Edward Pierre *advertising executive*

**Steelton**
Zimmerman, Connie Ann *public administrator*

**Sunbury**
Rich, Norman S. *food service executive*
Weis, Robert Freeman *supermarket company executive*

**Swarthmore**
Krizek, Edwin John *marketing professional*

**Temple**
Stump, Richard Carl *environmental services administrator, consultant*

**University Park**
Grewal, Rajdeep *marketing professional, educator*

**Upper Darby**
Fearnley, C. J. *computer company executive*

**Valley Forge**
LaBoon, Lawrence Joseph *human resources specialist, consultant*

**Wallingford**
Adamiec, Jean Kraus *retired advertising executive*

**Washington Crossing**
Clevenger, Roy Edward *credit and collections manager*

**Wayne**
Carroll, Robert W. *retired management consultant*
Conde, Cristobal I. *computer company executive*
Mann, James L. *computer company executive*

**West Chester**
Czako, Alan H. *human resources specialist, benefits compensation analyst*
Dunlop, Edward Arthur *computer company executive*
Hanna, Colin Arthur *management consultant, political organization worker, consultant*
Meystel, Michael A. *Internet company executive*
Murray, Lawrence *management consultant*

**West Conshohocken**
Mullen, Eileen Anne *human resources executive*

**Williamsport**
Trometter, Mary Gloria *chef, educator*

**Willow Grove**
Asplundh, Christopher B. *tree service company executive*
Schiffman, Louis F. *management consultant*

**Willow Street**
Blevins, William Edward *management consultant*

**Wyncote**
Koppel, Ross *private investigator, sociology professor*

**Wynnewood**
Belinger, Harry Robert *retired food service executive*

**Yardley**
Huret, Barry S. *marketing professional, consultant*
Minter, Philip Clayton *retired communications company executive*
Newsom, Carolyn Cardall *management consultant*
Weaver, William Clair, Jr., (Mike Weaver) *human resources development executive*

**York**
Livingston, Pamela A. *corporate image and marketing management consultant*

## RHODE ISLAND

**Jamestown**
DiStefano, Gregory John *marketing professional*

**Middletown**
Leighton, Charles Milton *retired specialty consumer products executive*

**Narragansett**
Stark, Dennis Edwin *private investigator, retired bank executive*

**North Kingstown**
Kullberg, Gary Walter *advertising agency executive*

**Pawtucket**
Charness, Wayne Samuel *public relations executive*
Hargreaves, David R. *toy company executive*
Hassenfeld, Alan Geoffrey *consumer products company executive*
Verrecchia, Alfred Joseph *toy company executive*

**Providence**
Allio, Robert John *management consultant, educator*
D'Andrea, Vincent Charles *postal clerk*
Whiting, Brian Christopher *hospitality consultant*

**Wakefield**
Doody, Agnes G. *communications educator, management and communication consultant*

**Woonsocket**
Frappier, Pearl Peters *retired bookkeeper*

## SOUTH CAROLINA

**Aiken**
Coble, Paul Ishler *advertising agency executive*

**Beech Island**
Bartley, Jacqueline Prior *public relations executive, journalist*

**Bluffton**
Reuben, Alvin Bernard *communications and entertainment executive*

**Charleston**
Ballard, Mary Melinda *corporate communications specialist, consumer products company executive*
Barickman, Donald *chef*
Chardon, Marc d'Estournelles *software company executive*
De Wolff, Louis *management consultant*
Simmons, Susan Annette *management consultant, statistician, educator*
Waggoner, Robert *chef*
Winter-Switz, Cheryl Donna *travel company executive*

**Columbia**
Barnum, Mary Ann Mook *information management manager*
Barnum, William Douglas *retired communications executive*
Mahoney, Kimberly Lynne *event and facility executive*
Silver, Rick *marketing professional*

**Graniteville**
Learnard, James Michael *retired collections and bad debt manager, secondary school educator*

**Greenville**
Fitzgerald, Eugene Francis *management consultant*
Townes, Bobby Joe *travel agency executive*

**Greer**
Sundstrom, Harold Walter *public relations executive*

**Hartsville**
Cecil, Allan *corporate communications executive*

**Hilton Head Island**
Conn, Margaret Elbow *human resources specialist*
McKeldin, William Evans *management consultant*
Patton, Joseph Donald, Jr. *management consultant*
Woodrum, Robert Lee *executive search consultant*

**Ladson**
Jackson, Jonathan Michael *computer company executive, writer*

**Lake Wylie**
Buggie, Frederick Denman *management consultant*
Sanford, James Kenneth *public relations executive*

**Mauldin**
Looper-Wilson, Leah Marie *human resources specialist, controller, interior designer*
Wood, Myra Linden Frank *consultant*

**Pawleys Island**
Grubb, William Francis Xavier *consumer products company executive, marketing professional*

**Prosperity**
Jennings, Wirt Holman, Jr. *retired marketing executive*

**Seneca**
Strong-Tidman, Virginia Adele *marketing professional*

**Spartanburg**
Smithart-Oglesby, Debra Lynn *food service executive*

**Sullivans Island**
Norton, Fran *recreation director*

**Summerville**
Brooks, Jeffrey Martin *marketing and sales executive*

## TENNESSEE

**Chattanooga**
Pollard, C. William *environmental services executive*

**Gallatin**
Bradley, Nolen Eugene, Jr. *retired personnel executive, educator*

**Gatlinburg**
Cave, Kent R. *parks director*

**Germantown**
Arendall, Charles Steven *management consultant, educator*

**Jackson**
Harper, Ernest Lee, Jr. *sales executive*

**Knoxville**
Drennen, Jean Cobble *retired public relations executive, linguist*
Mayfield, T. Brient, IV, *media and computer executive*
Sansom, William B. *consumer products executive*

**La Vergne**
Ingram, David B. *entertainment company executive*

**Lebanon**
Woodhouse, Michael A. *restaurant holdings company executive*

**Lenoir City**
Edwards, C. Karen *consultant company executive*

**Memphis**
Abston, Dunbar, Jr. *management consultant*
Brown, R. Larry *human resources specialist, transportation executive*
Edwards, Doris Porter *computer specialist*
Hyde, Joseph R. III *retail auto parts executive*
Krieger, Robert Lee, Jr. *human resource/management consultant, educator, writer, travel/meeting planner, political analyst, internet marketing consultant*
Smith, J.E. Guido *marketing professional*

**Nashville**
Allbritton, Cliff *personal and organizational consultant*
Brett, John Brendan, Jr. *corporate advertising and public relations executive*
Brown, Tony Ersic *record company executive*
Hartley, Michael J. *travel company executive*
Hillenmeyer, Henry Reiling, Jr. *restaurant company executive*
Moore, William Grover, Jr. *management consultant, retired military officer*
Reynolds, Doris Elizabeth *management consultant, poet*
Steele, John M. *human resources specialist*
Van Mol, Louis John, Jr. *public relations executive*
Wright, Randy S. *management consultant*

**Oak Ridge**
Poling, Sheila R. *management consultant*

## TEXAS

**Addison**
Grote, Dick (Richard Charles Grote) *management consultant, educator, writer, radio commentator*

**Alpine**
Orr, Joseph Newton *recreational guide, outdoor educator*

**Amarillo**
Stubben, Dolus Jane (D. J. Stubben) *advertising executive*
Turks, Hildegard Maria (Hildegard Maria Chronis) *retired security investigator, writer*

**Arlington**
Beckham, Patrick Henry *retired corporate communications specialist*
English, Marlene Cabral *management consultant*
Sawyer, Dolores *motel chain executive*

**Austin**
Barrientos, Gonzalo *advertising executive, public relations executive, state legislator*
Bush, Neil *management executive*
Curle, Robin Lea *computer company executive*
Decaro, Angelo Anthony, Jr. *data processing executive*
Green, Shirley Moore *retired communications executive, public information officer*
Mathias, Reuben Victor (Vic Mathias) *organization executive, real estate investor*
Mathis, Marsha Debra *customer service administrator*
Mayer, Michel *computer company executive*
Mulconrey, Brian George *management consultant, futurist*
Pearson, Jim Berry, Jr. *human resources specialist*
Spence, Roy Milam, Jr. *advertising executive*
Winegar, Albert Lee *computer company executive*
York, Candace A. *marketing professional, writer*

**Bedford**
Horvat, Vashti *online marketing consultant*

**Canton**
Leibowitz, Vincent Paul *communications executive, media consultant*

**College Station**
Gunn, Clare Alward *travel consultant, writer, retired educator*
Hise, Richard Todd *marketing professional, educator, consultant*
Solymosy, Edmond Sigmond Albert *marketing professional, retired military officer*
Sosa, Lionel *advertising executive*

**Coppell**
Owen, Cynthia Carol *sales executive*

**Copperas Cove**
Stephens, Billie Lowell *quality assurance professional, writer*

**Dallas**
Bondy, Joanne *chef*
Bosch, Joseph A. *human resources specialist*
Brinker, Norman E. *restaurant company executive*
Brooks, Douglas H. *food service executive*
Bryant, L. Gerald *management consultant*
Campbell, Raymond III *publication director*
Carl, Robert E. *retired marketing company executive*
Collins, Philip A. *management consultant*
Crusemann, F. Ross (Frederick Ross Crusemann) *advertising agency official*
Dalton, Harry Jirou, Jr., (Jerry Dalton) *public relations executive*
Dawson, Edward Joseph *merger and acquisition executive*
Dieste, Tony *marketing professional*
Dinkins, Jane Poling *management consultant, application developer*
Dozier, David Charles, Jr. *advertising executive, public relations executive*
Edwards, Barry L. *leasing company executive*
Edwards, Warren D. *computer company executive*
England, Julie Spicer *computer company executive*
Fabre, Raul *management consultant*
Fairbairn, Ursula Farrell *human resources executive*
Gray, James Larry *international business executive*
Grimes, David Lynn *communications executive*
Harmel, Warren *marketing professional*
Hopson, Mary Louise Carstens *marketing consultant*
Horchow, S(amuel) Roger *marketing consultant*
King, Mark A. *computer company executive*
Koeppel, Peter Stafford *advertising executive*
Lane, Alvin Huey, Jr. *management consultant*
Leven, Stephen H. *human resources professional*
Levenson, Stanley Richard *public relations and advertising executive*
Lilyhorn, Gregory Dean *security firm executive*
Liskow, Frederic Cullen (Ric) *printing company executive*
May, Kenneth Austin *consumer products company executive*
Pace, Carolina Jolliff *communications executive, investor*
Palmer, Tony *marketing executive*
Parks, J. Michael *data processing executive*
Pearson, Robert Lawrence *executive recruiter*
Richards, Stanford Harvey *advertising agency executive, design studio executive*
Sonsteby, Charles M. *food service executive*
Spiegel, Lawrence Howard *advertising executive*
Stern, Andrew Milton *public relations executive*
Wagner, Todd *Internet company executive*
Weinkauf, William Carl *communications executive*
Weiss, Anthony A. *computer company executive*
Zeitlin, Laurie *printing company executive, information technology executive*

**Del Rio**
Prather, Gerald Luther *management consultant, retired judge, retired military officer*

**Denton**
Ryan, Melbagene T. *retired food service and nutrition director*

**El Paso**
Roberts, Ernst Edward *marketing consultant*

**Flower Mound**
Ross, Lesa Moore *quality assurance professional*
Salick, Anne *sales executive*

**Fort Worth**
Appel, Bernard Sidney *marketing professional, consultant, retired electronics executive*
Bradshaw, James Edward (Jim Bradshaw) *consultant*
Brundage, Jeffrey J. *human resources specialist, air transportation executive*
Johnson, J. Mitchell *communications executive*

**Fredericksburg**
Arnold, George Lawrence *retired advertising company executive*

**Frisco**
Hawk, Phillip Michael *service corporation executive*
Kern, Ronald Paul *computer company executive, dean, consultant*
Migdol, Marvin Jacob *public relations and marketing executive, consultant*

**Grapevine**
Fontaine, R. Richard *computer game company executive*

**Highland Village**
Richardson, K. Scott *sales executive*

**Houston**
Accardi, Larry J. *food service executive*
Adams, C. Lee *marketing executive*
Anderson, William, Jr., (William Albion Anderson Jr.) *management consultant*
Bradley, Melvin LeRoy *communications executive*
Coutermarsh, Eva Marina *personnel executive*
Cupp, B. Garland *computer company executive*
Curtiss, Jeff *consumer products company executive, lawyer*
Ellis, Raymond Clinton, Jr. *hotel executive, educator*
Flato, William Roeder, Jr. *software development company executive*
Gilbert, Jill Barson *management consultant*
Keating, Tim *chef*
Kors, R. Paul *search company executive*
Mampre, Virginia Elizabeth *communications executive*
Marshall, Gregory K. *food service executive*

Mays, Randall T. *communications company executive*
McCollam, Marion Andrus *consulting firm executive, educator*
Murdy, William F. *diversified services executive*
Myers, A. Maurice *waste management executive*
Myers, James Clark *advertising executive, public relations executive*
O'Donnell, Lawrence III *waste management executive*
Roberts, Paul *chef*
Ryan, Thomas L. *funeral company executive*
Saizan, Paula Theresa *management consultant*
Saunders, William Arthur *management consultant*
Smith, Claire *chef*
Springer, Wayne Gilbert *computer company executive*
Steiner, David P. *waste management executive*
Stephens, Sidney Dee *human resources specialist, retired chemical manufacturing company executive*

**Huntsville**
Stowe, Charles Robinson Beecher *management consultant, educator, lawyer*

**Hurst**
Bishara, Amin Tawadros *management and consulting firm executive*

**Irving**
Duffy, Dan *computer company executive*
Nugent, John Hilliard *communications executive*
Potter, Robert Joseph *technical and business executive*
Wicks, William Withington *retired public relations executive*

**Jacksboro**
Patterson, Ronald R(oy) *management consultant*

**Junction**
Evans, Jo Burt *communications executive, rancher*

**Kingsville**
Stanford, (Frances) Jane Herring *management consultant, educator, writer*

**Lubbock**
Dennison, Daniel Thomas *environmental compliance administrator, lab administrator*
Fontenot, Andrea Dean *communications executive*
Jugenheimer, Donald Wayne *advertising executive, communications educator, academic administrator*

**New Caney**
Hayes, Ann Carson *computer company executive*

**Ovalo**
Mooney, Allan W. *management consultant, foundation administrator*

**Plano**
Davis, Robert D. *rental company executive*
Dillon, Donald Ward *management consultant*
Dougherty, F(rancis) Kelly *data processing executive*
Fadel, Mitchell E. *rental company executive*
Fuller, Tony F. *rental company executive*
Heller, Jeffrey M. *data processing executive*
Montiel, Alfonso *data processing executive*
Scott, Terry Lee *communications executive*
Sivinski, Tina M. *human resources specialist*
Speese, Mark E. *rental company executive*
Theilmann, Michael T. *human resources specialist*

**Port Arthur**
Munoz, Andrea Lee *human resources specialist*

**Richardson**
Sperrin, Graham Frederick *marketing professional*

**Round Rock**
Dell, Michael S. *computer company executive*
Goodman, Kim *marketing professional, computer company executive*
Hudson, Michel Colette *management consultant*
Parra, Rosendo G. *computer company executive*
Rollins, Kevin B. *computer company executive*
Schneider, James M. *computer company executive*
Sheskey, Susan E. *computer company executive*
Wahl, William Bryan *marketing professional, real estate company officer*

**San Antonio**
(Foote) Boyd, Barbara Jo Ann *quality assurance professional*
Butt, Charles Clarence *food service executive*
Carr, Cassandra Colvin *communications company executive*
Garcia, Henry Frank *supply management and project management consultant*
Gray, Suzy *recreation director, educator*
Jennings, Karen *human resources specialist, telecommunications industry executive*
Marbut, Robert Gordon *communications executive, electronic security and broadcast executive, investor*
Mays, Mark Pitman *communication company executive*
Moya, Francisco Saez *consumer products company executive*
Nava, Carmen P. *communications executive*
Navarro, Max *supply chain management company executive*
Whitesell, Stephen Ernest *parks director*

**San Marcos**
Moore, Patsy Sites *food service consultant*
Wilson, Vicki Lynn *executive secretary, administrative assistant*

**Southlake**
Gilliland, Michael S. (Sam Gilliland) *travel company executive*
Peluso, Michelle *Internet company executive*
Sorge, Karen Lee *printing company executive, consultant*

**Spring**
Ciancimino, Joseph Andrew *data processing executive*

**Spring Branch**
Barban, Arnold Melvin *advertising executive, educator, writer*
Fasano, Anthony John *marketing consultant*

**Texas City**
Hodges, Richard Dean *instrument and electrical technician*

**The Woodlands**
Brenneman, Gregory D. *former food service executive*
Glenn, Gerald Marvin *marketing executive, engineering executive, construction executive*
Morrison, Scott David *management consultant, small business owner*

**Trophy Club**
Caffee, Virginia Maureen *executive assistant*
Holley, Cyrus Helmer *management consulting service executive*

**Waco**
Iglehart, Patricia Ann *business development and communications executive*
Voight, Carolyn Jean *administrative assistant*

**Wellington**
Sims, Lennie Coleman *part-time public relations consultant*

**Willis**
Snider, Robert Larry *management consultant*

## UTAH

**Midway**
Zenger, John Hancock *training company executive*

**Orem**
Morey, Robert Hardy *communications executive*
Sawyer, Thomas Edgar *management consultant*

**Park City**
Milner, Harold William *hotel executive*

**Salt Lake City**
Covey, Stephen Merrill Richards *business consultant, speaker, author*
Davis, Gene *public relations executive, state legislator*
Davis, Loyd Evan *defense industry marketing professional*
Howell, Scott Newell *computer company executive, state legislator*
Johnson, Jon L. *advertising executive*
Lee, Blaine Nelson *personnel director*

## VERMONT

**Burlington**
Post, Peter L. *marketing executive, writer*

**Colchester**
Jackson, Voleen *perfumer*

**East Dummerston**
Bertone, Thomas Lee *management consultant*

**Norwich**
Stevenson, Josiah, IV, *management consultant*

**Vergennes**
Hiscock, Richard Carson *marine safety investigator*

**Waitsfield**
Esty, David Cameron *marketing and communications executive*
Parrish, Thomas Kirkpatrick III *marketing consultant*

**Wilmington**
Little, Thomas M. *public relations executive*

**Winooski**
Racz, Irene *public relations executive*

**Woodstock**
Hoyt, Coleman Williams *postal consultant*
Matlins, Stuart M. *management consultant, publisher*

## VIRGINIA

**Abingdon**
Ramos-Cano, Hazel Balatero *caterer, chef, innkeeper, restaurateur, entrepreneur*

**Alexandria**
Anderson, Maynard Carlyle *security firm executive*
Armstrong, Cathal *chef*
Bozell, Brent (L. Brent Bozell III) *communications executive*
Coons, Barbara Lynn *public relations executive, librarian*
Devantier, Paul W. *communications executive, broadcast executive*
Fosdick, Cora Prifold (Cora Prifold Beebe) *management consultant*
Foster, Robert Francis *communications executive*
Frommer, Lawrence Julian *retired travel company executive*
Gallagher, Anne Porter *communications executive*
Geary, Patrick Joseph *security and emergency planning administrator, writer*
Harris, David Ford *management consultant, retired federal official*
Hilferty, Bryan Carey *public relations specialist*
Jackson, Gary Lee *security consultant*

Lantz, Phillip Edward *security firm executive, consultant*
Laurent, Lawrence Bell *communications executive, retired journalist*
Lightner, Candy (Candace Lynne Lightner) *non-profit management consultant, advocate*
McMillan, Charles William *consulting company executive*
Meisinger, Susan *human resources specialist*
Nelson, David Leonard *data processing executive*
Newton, Hugh C. *public relations executive*
Paulson, Gwen O. Gampel *government relations consultant, life and leadership coach*
Pitzer, Jack Todd *purchasing agent, consultant, educator*
Rogers, Paul A'Court *management consulting executive*
Sepp, Peter John *communications executive, writer*
Simmons, Richard De Lacey *mass media executive*
Stone, Ann Elizabeth *marketing agency executive, consultant, entrepreneur, volunteer*
Verburg, Edwin Arnold *management consultant*
Walker, Edward Keith, Jr. *retired management consultant, retired military officer*

**Annandale**
Bayou, Jean D. *administrative assistant*
Greinke, Everett Donald *management consultant*
Jarvis, Elbert, II, (Jay Jarvis) *employee benefits specialist*

**Arlington**
Alcalde, Hector *public relations executive*
Bennett, Christopher Lawrence *hotel executive, lawyer*
Claussen, Eileen Barbara *environmental services administrator, former federal agency administrator*
Cofoni, Paul M. *computer company executive*
DeFeo, Charles Joesph *Internet company executive*
Erwin, Frank William *human resources consultant*
Fay, Kevin J. *public relations executive*
Harrison, Emmett Bruce, Jr. *public relations counselor*
McCaslin, David E. *hotel executive*
McFarland, Walter Gerard *management consultant*
Newburger, Beth Weinstein *communications executive*
Rabaut, Thomas W. *defense industry executive*
Samburg, A. Gene *security company executive*
Warshawsky, Mark Joel *human resources specialist, former federal agency administrator*
Whetsell, Paul W. *hotel executive*
Zorthian, Barry *communications executive*

**Burgess**
Burch, Michael Ira *public relations executive, retired federal agency administrator*

**Burke**
Becraft, Carolyn Howland *communications executive*

**Chantilly**
Welles, Judith *public affairs executive*

**Charlottesville**
Brown, Holmes *public relations executive*

**Chesapeake**
Cox, Mark Stanley *public relations professional*

**Cobbs Creek**
Crum, John Kistler *management consultant*

**Dulles**
Cheney, Mary Claire *Internet company executive*
Miller, Jonathan F. *Internet company executive*

**Dumfries**
Locigno, Paul Robert *public relations executive*

**Fairfax**
Baker, Daniel Richard *computer company executive*
Hale, Thomas Morgan *professional services executive*
Witek, James Eugene *retired public relations executive*

**Falls Church**
Courtney, William Harrison *marketing professional*
Dao, Thuy Dinh *personal care industry executive*
Jones, Linda R. Wolf *consulting company executive*
Oliver, Walter M. *human resources specialist*
Shipko, Janet M. *human resources manager*
Walker, William Woodard, Jr. *management consultant, telecommunications technology executive*

**Fredericksburg**
Harrod, Audrey Hunter *retired executive secretary*

**Glasgow**
Riegel, Kurt Wetherhold *environmental protection executive*

**Great Falls**
Bachner, John Philip *business consultant*

**Herndon**
Huntoon, Nancy *security manager*
Parker, Kevin T. *computer software company executive*

**Keswick**
Woods, Reginald Foster *management consulting executive*

**Lake Ridge**
Ingrassia, Anthony Frank *human resource specialist*

**Leesburg**
Lobanov-Rostovsky, Oleg *management consultant*

**Manassas**
Foley, Michael Patrick *marketing professional educator*

**Mc Lean**
Estren, Mark James *communications executive, television producer, writer*
Frostic, Frederick Lee *strategic planning and defense policy consultant*
Jayne, Edward Randolph, II, *executive search consultant*
Klaassen, Paul J. *personal care industry executive*
Norman, William Stanley *travel and tourism executive*
O'Brien, Morgan Edward *communications executive, lawyer*
Olson, Walter Justus, Jr. *management consultant*
Orkand, Donald Saul *management consultant*
Paschall, Lee McQuerter *retired communications executive*
Rose, Susan Porter *management and governmental affairs consultant*
Shrader, Ralph W. *management consultant*
Smith, Esther Thomas *communications executive*
Verhalen, Robert Donald *consumer safety executive*
Watson, Jerry Carroll *advertising executive*
Webber, Diana L. *management consultant executive, engineering educator*
Wilton, Elisabeth Starr *management consultant*
You, Harry I. *consulting company executive, former computer software company executive*

**Middleburg**
McNichols, Gerald Robert *consulting company executive*

**Midlothian**
Wadsworth, Robert David *advertising executive*

**Norfolk**
Blount, Robert Haddock *management consultant, retired military officer*

**Oak Hill**
Okay, John Louis *management consultant*

**Oakton**
Terzian, Grace Paine *communications executive*

**Reston**
Easton, Glenn Hanson, Jr. *management consultant, federal official, military officer*
Ewell, Dena Lynette *administrative management executive*
Fernandez, Raul J. *data processing executive*
Kramer, Kevin M. *human resources specialist, consultant*
Maher, David Willard *Internet company executive*
Miller, Lynne Marie *environmental services administrator*
Montoni, Richard A. *management consultant*
Posey, Ada Louise *human resources specialist*
Sarreals, Sonia *data processing executive, consultant*
Schick, Michael William *public relations executive*
Stone, Lawrence D. *software company executive*

**Richmond**
Bohannon, Sarah Virginia *personnel professional*
Dan, Michael T. *security firm executive*
Fox, Sandra Gail *insurance marketing executive*
Hughes, Mike *advertising executive*
Jacobs, Harry Milburn, Jr. *advertising executive*
Joynes, Barbara Cole *marketing executive*
King, Allen B. *tobacco company executive*
Trott, Sabert Scott, II, *marketing professional, consultant*

**Seaford**
Jenkins, Margaret Bunting *human resources executive*

**Springfield**
Bruen, John Dermot *management consultant*
Edwards-LeBoeuf, Renee Camille *public relations executive, protective services official*

**Sterling**
Schrader, William L. *communications executive*
Wellisch, David *Internet company executive*

**Suffolk**
Hall, Wayne Michael *management consultant*

**Upperville**
Ross, John Emerson *public relations executive, writer*

**Vienna**
Cook, Jane Hampton *communications consultant*
Monroe, Robert Rawson *national security consultant*
Sheinbaum, Gilbert Harold *international management consultant*

**Virginia Beach**
Alexander, William Powell *business advisor*
Hilgers, John Jack William *management and transportation consultant*
Kennedy, David W. *marketing professional*
Wick, Robert Thomas *retired food service executive*

**Williamsburg**
Ackerman, Lennis Campbell *retired management consultant*
Hoving, John Hannes Forester *consulting firm executive*
Morris, Robert Louis *management consultant*

**Winchester**
Bonometti, Robert John *technology management and strategy executive*
Engelage, James Roland *management consultant*
Gaither, George Manney *marketing consultant*
Holman, Karen Marie Anderson *purchasing agent*

**WASHINGTON**

**Anacortes**
Hoffmann, Manfred Walter *consulting company executive*

**Bellevue**
Connors, John G. *former computer software company executive*
Hall, Eleanor Williams *public relations executive*
Myhrvold, Nathan P. *technology executive*
Pool, David *software executive*

**Bothell**
Hawthorne, Nan Louise *Internet company executive, consultant, web site designer, writer*

**Federal Way**
Dooley, James H. *product company executive*
Muzyka-McGuire, Amy *marketing professional, nutritionist, consultant*
Rogel, Edward P. *corporate human resources executive*

**Gig Harbor**
Stover, Miles Ronald *management consultant*

**Hunts Point**
Ebsworth, Barney A. *retired travel company executive*

**Issaquah**
Matthews, John *human resources specialist, wholesale distribution executive*

**Kennewick**
Brewton, Wesley Hopkins (Wes Brewton) *retired chef, retired real estate manager*

**Kirkland**
McCaw, Craig O. *communications executive*

**Lacey**
Breytspraak, John, Jr. *management consultant*

**Medina**
Dagnon, James Bernard *human resources executive*

**Mercer Island**
Dykstra, David Charles *management executive, consultant, accountant, author, educator*

**Parkland**
Johnson, LuAn K. *disaster management consultant*

**Port Ludlow**
Krugman, Stanley Lee *international management consultant*

**Redmond**
Ballmer, Steven Anthony *computer software company executive*
Bradford, Joanne K. *computer software company executive*
Driftmier, David King *data processing executive*
Flake, Gary William *computer software company executive*
Gates, Bill (William Henry Gates III) *computer software company executive*
Herzog, Eric Allen *marketing professional*
Johnson, Kevin *computer software company executive*
Leblond, Antoine *computer company executive*
Liddell, Christopher P. *computer software company executive*
Martinez, Maria *computer software company executive*
Mathews, Mich *computer company executive*
Mundie, Craig James *computers software company executive*
Ozzie, Ray (Raymond E. Ozzie) *computer software company executive*
Shirley, Jon Anthony *software company executive*

**Seattle**
Allen, Paul Gardner *computer company executive, professional sports team executive*
Bates, Charles Walter *human resources executive, lawyer*
Bezos, Jeffrey Preston *multimedia company executive*
Brown, Michael W. *former communications company executive*
Burns, Michael Joseph *operations and sales-marketing executive*
Carsberg, Scott *chef*
Davis, Stephen B. *Internet company executive, lawyer*
Donald, James L. *food service executive*
Duryee, David Anthony *management consultant*
Eastham, John D. *marketing executive*
Elgin, Ron Alan *advertising executive*
Eller, Marlin *security firm executive*
Gerwick-Brodeur, Madeline Carol *marketing and timing professional*
Glaser, Robert *communications executive*
Halvarsson, Misha *business development strategist*
McConnell, J. Daniel *marketing and public relations professional*
Miyata, Keijiro *culinary arts educator*
Pace, David A. *human resources specialist, retail executive*
Patton, Jody *management company executive*
Sasenick, Joseph Anthony *consumer products company executive*
Schultz, Howard *beverage service executive, professional basketball team owner*
Wilson, Jason *chef*

**Shoreline**
Hutton, Winfield Travis *management consultant, educator*

**Spokane**
Hilst, Glenn Rudolph *environmental sciences administrator, researcher*
Moe, Orville Leroy *racetrack executive*
Stirpe, Josh A. *sales executive*
Tsutakawa, Edward Masao *management consultant*

**Tacoma**
Bartlett, Norma Thyra *retired administrative assistant*
Taylor, Peter van Voorhees *advertising and public relations consultant*

**Vancouver**
Kodis, Mary Caroline *marketing consultant*
Ogden, Valeria Munson *management consultant, state representative*
Regan, Elizabeth Anne *bail bond agent*
Warner, Matthew Douglas *executive recruiter*

**Walla Walla**
Potts, Charles Aaron *management executive, writer, publishing executive*

**Woodinville**
Love, Keith Sinclair *communications executive*

**WEST VIRGINIA**

**Charleston**
Mc Gee, John Frampton *communications company executive*

**Huntington**
Reynolds, Marshall Truman *printing company executive*

**Morgantown**
Blakeman, Robyn L. *advertising executive, educator*

**Triadelphia**
McCullough, John Phillip *management consultant, educator*

**White Sulphur Springs**
Kleisner, Ted J. *hotel executive*

**WISCONSIN**

**Algoma**
Golomski, William Arthur Joseph *consulting company executive*

**Appleton**
Geller, Scott A. *management consultant*

**Brookfield**
Dillon, Donald F. *data processing executive*
Jensen, Kenneth R. *data processing executive*
Nickerson, Greg *public relations executive*
Yabuki, Jeffrey W. *data processing company executive, former accounting company executive*

**Darien**
Miller, Malcolm Henry *manufacturing sales executive, real estate developer*

**Eau Claire**
Leary, Robin Janell *executive secretary, municipal official*

**Janesville**
Butters, John Patrick *travel company executive, educator*
Roth, Sarah Eve *occupational safety professional*

**Kohler**
Kohler, Laura E. *human resources executive*

**Lake Geneva**
Weed, Edward Reilly *marketing executive*

**Madison**
Hempe, A. Henry *labor relations specialist, labor arbitrator, lawyer*
Henderson, Arvis Burl *data processing executive, biochemist*
Kuzuhara, Loren Wyatt *management consultant, educator*
Nell, Herman *consumer products company executive*
Piper, Odessa *chef*
Smith, Gary W.H. *retired sales executive*

**Menasha**
Streeter, Stephanie Anne *printing company executive*

**Menomonee Falls**
Jeffries, Telvin *human resources specialist, retail executive*

**Mequon**
Elias, Paul S. *retired marketing executive*

**Middleton**
Lee, Leslie Warren *marketing executive, educator*

**Milwaukee**
Arbit, Bruce *direct marketing executive, consultant*
Davidson, Rick *staffing company executive*
Davis, Susan F. *human resources specialist*
Hagerman, Douglas M. *consumer products company executive, lawyer*
Hunter, Victor Lee *marketing executive, consultant*
Jacobs, Bruce Edward *management consultant*
Joerres, Jeffrey A. *staffing company executive*
Joseph, Jules K. *retired public relations executive*
Laughlin, Steven L. *advertising executive*
Long, Tom *marketing executive*
Mahler, Stephanie Irene *retired administrative manager*
Randall, William Seymour *leasing company executive*
Rivera-Velazquez, Maria *marketing professional*
Saam, Robert Harry *human resources specialist, consultant*
Van Handel, Michael J. *staffing company executive*

**Plymouth**
Gentine, Lee Michael *marketing professional*

**Racine**
Johnson-Leipold, Helen P. *outdoor recreation company executive*
Johnson-Marquart, Winnie *consumer products company executive*

**Klein**, Gabriella Sonja *retired communications executive*

**Rice Lake**
Kostka, Ronald Wayne *marketing consultant*

**Sheboygan**
Biró, Marcel *chef*

**Sturtevant**
Lawton, Gregory E. *sales and marketing executive*

**Waterford**
Karraker, Louis Rendleman *retired corporate executive*

**Wausau**
Wadzinski, Mary Beth *administrative assistant*

**WYOMING**

**Jackson**
Herrick, Gregory Evans *computer company executive*

## TERRITORIES OF THE UNITED STATES

### GUAM

**Hagatna**
Sablan, David J. *marketing professional, political organization worker*

### PUERTO RICO

**Manati**
Martinez, Heriberto *human resources manager*

**San Juan**
Ramos, Victor Jose *computer company executive, educator*

### VIRGIN ISLANDS

**St Thomas**
O'Bryan, James A. *communications specialist, political organization administrator*

## CANADA

### ALBERTA

**Edmonton**
McKenna, Patrick James *management consultant*

### BRITISH COLUMBIA

**Vancouver**
Campbell, Bruce Alan *corporate coach*
Saywell, William George Gabriel *business development and management consultant*

**Victoria**
Nuttall, Richard Norris *management consultant, physician*

### NOVA SCOTIA

**Halifax**
Gratwick, John *management consulting executive, writer, consultant*

### ONTARIO

**Chatham**
McKeough, William Darcy *supply company executive*

**Freelton**
Sonnenberg, Hardy *data processing executive, researcher, electrical engineer*

**Niagara-on-the-Lake**
Nielsen-Jones, Ian Richard *lottery and gaming executive, consultant*

**Ottawa**
Courtois, Bernard Andre *communications executive*
Griller, David *management consultant*
McLure, John Douglas *management consultant, former Canadian government official*
Silverman, Ozzie *consulting strategist*

**Saint Catharines**
Bergevin, V. Réal *customer relationship management executive*

**Toronto**
Ames, Steven *management consultant*
Bandeen, Robert Angus *management consultant*
Bloomberg, Lawrence S. *security firm executive, art appraiser*
Carder, Paul Charles *retired advertising executive*
Curlook, Walter *management consultant*
Dooher, Donna *chef*
Fatt, William Robert *hotel executive*
Fierheller, George Alfred *communications executive*
Gregor, Tibor Philip *retired management consultant*
Pinto, Maxwell Salustiano *management consultant*

Rogers, Edward Samuel *communications company executive*
Seiersen, Nicholas Steen *management consultant*

### QUEBEC

**Leclercville**
Morin, Pierre Jean *retired management consultant, social services administrator*

**Montreal**
Beauregard, Luc *public relations executive*
Neveu, Jean *printing company executive*
Sirois, Charles *communications executive*

**Rosemere**
Hopper, Carol *incentive program administrator, trade association administrator*

**Whistler**
Rae, Barbara Joyce *employee placement company executive*

## MEXICO

**Mexico City**
Nicholas, Ronald Wayde *business consultant*

## AUSTRALIA

**Brighton**
Bellin, Howard *management consultant*

**North Sydney**
Scott, Brian Walter *management consultant*

## CHINA

**Beijing**
Ma, Mary (Mary Ma Xuezheng) *computer company executive*

## EGYPT

**Cairo**
Fahmy, Ibrahim Mounir *hotel executive*

## ENGLAND

**Berkshire**
Everitt-Newton, Katherine Evelyn *international management consultant*

**Canterbury**
Holwell, Peter *management consultant*

**Chiswick London**
Dyson, Tim *public relations executive*

**Dorset**
Randle, Peter *communications company executive*

**London**
Friis, Janus *Internet company executive, entrepreneur*
Hallissey, Michael *retired management consultant*
Leaf, Robert Stephen *public relations executive*
Nelson, Walter Henry *communications consultant, author*
Oliver, Jamie *chef, television personality*
Verwaayen, Ben J.M. *communications company executive*
Zennström, Niklas *Internet company executive, entrepreneur*

**Stroud**
Robinson, John Beckwith *development management consultant*

**Surrey**
Weston, Sir John (Sir Philip John Weston) *company non-executive director, retired diplomat*

## FRANCE

**Antibes**
Fouillade, Jean-Paul Eric *management consultant*

**Issy les Moulineaux**
de Pouzilhac, Alain Duplessis *advertising executive*

**Marseille**
Boutterin, Emmanuel *public relations executive*

**Paris**
Courtaud, Bernard Jean-Jacques *human resource consulting executive*
Marcus, Claude *advertising executive*

## GERMANY

**Dresden**
Gluch, Steffen *company executive*

**Fulda**
Beckman, James Wallace Bim *management consultant, educator*

**Munich**
Stoek, Thomas *management professional, sales professional*

**Neu Isenburg**
Hoare-Temple, Piers Howard *building maintenance executive*

## GIBRALTAR

**Irishtown**
De Leon, Russ *Internet company executive*

## GREECE

**Marousi**
Joannou, Dakis *hotel executive*

## HONG KONG

**Kowloon**
Fung, Victor K. (Victor Fung Kwok King) *consumer products trading company executive*

## IRELAND

**Dublin**
McCauley, Kristina Akemi *project coordinator*

## JAPAN

**Kanagawa**
Hoshino, Yoshiro *industrial relations specialist, educator*

**Mito**
Kobayashi, Susumu *retired computer company executive*

**Tokyo**
Chiba, Machiko *cooking advisor*

## SCOTLAND

**Edinburgh**
Biegel, Kimberly Ann *communications executive, public relations officer*

## SOUTH AFRICA

**Lesotho**
Davis, Sarah Frances *management consultant, bishop*

**Pretoria**
Stocks, Rundell Kingsley *management, construction, education and general consultant*

## SWEDEN

**Saltsjö-Duvnäs**
Gyll, John Sören *marketing executive*

**Solna**
Fleisher, Frederic Elliott *communications executive*

## ADDRESS UNPUBLISHED

Abdel-Monsef, Hani Ahmed *marketing professional*
Abrams, Jonathan *Internet company executive*
Adler, Larry *marketing professional*
Adrean, Lee *communications executive*
Agee, Claudia *executive secretary, tax specialist*
Alderfer, Clayton Paul *organizational consultant, writer*
Alexander, Faith Dorothy *retired training services executive*
Allen, Bennie Carnel *employee relations specialist*
Allen, Louis Alexander *management consultant*
Allen, Richard Vincent *international business consultant, former national security advisor*
Allmon, Michael W, Sr. *sales executive*
Amatangelo, Nicholas S. *retired printing company executive, document management executive, finance, marketing, and management educator*
Amparado, Keith D. *communications company executive*
Anand, Sanjay *training services executive, consultant, entrepreneur, educator*
Anderson, Herbert W. *consumer products company executive*
Anderson, Mark Robert *data processing executive, biochemist*
Anderson, Paul Irving *management executive*
Anderson, Tom *Internet company executive*
Ando, Kunitake *consumer products company executive*
Annunziata, Robert *fiber optics company executive*
Anschutz, Philip F. *communications executive, professional sports team executive*
Appelbaum, Yonatan Asher *administrative assistant, city manager*
Appell, Louise Sophia *retired consulting company executive*
Ardai, Charles E. *online services executive*
Armstrong Squall, Paula Estelle *executive secretary*
Asensi, Gustavo *advertising executive, cinematographer*
Aubriot, Eric *chef*
Ayers, Charlie *chef*
Bachelder, Cheryl Anne *marketing professional*
Baczko, Joseph R. *consumer products executive*
Balick, Kenneth D. *international business development consultant*

Bamberger, Gerald Francis *plastics marketing consultant*
Bang, Jens *communications company executive*
Barca, Kathleen *marketing executive*
Bario, Patricia Yaroch *retired public relations executive*
Barnett, Elizabeth Hale *organizational consultant*
Barrett, Beverly Frances *public relations specialist*
Bartlett, David *management consultant*
Bauer, Barbara Ann *marketing consultant*
Bazelides, Diane *public relations executive*
Beasley, Barbara Starin *sales executive, marketing professional*
Becker, Ray Everett *management consultant*
Becker, Robert A. *advertising executive*
Beider, Marlys Anna *hotel executive, writer*
Bell, George F. *computer company executive*
Bellanger, Florian *food service executive, educator*
Bennett, Saul *public relations agency executive*
Benney, Douglas Mabley *direct marketing executive, consultant*
Berger, Frank Stanley *management consultant*
Bergeson, James *advertising executive*
Berman, Cheryl R. *advertising company executive*
Berman, Sandra Rita *retired personnel director*
Binder, Amy Finn *public relations company executive*
Biondi, Frank J., Jr. *entertainment company executive*
Birk, John Richard *management consultant*
Bisconti, Ann Stouffer *public opinion research company executive*
Blaine, Davis Robert *valuation consultant, investment banker*
Blanchard, Townsend Eugene *retired service companies executive*
Blatz, Linda Jeanne *sales manager*
Bloom, Gary L. *data processing executive*
Bloomberg, Mary Beth *public affairs executive*
Blum, Bradley D. *former food service executive*
Boatwright, Charlotte Jeanne *marketing professional, public relations executive*
Boehlke, William Fredrick *public relations executive, consultant*
Boehnen, David Leo *food service executive, lawyer*
Boles, Eric Paul *staffing company executive*
Booth, Margaret A(nn) *communications company executive*
Borges, William III *management consultant*
Botkin, Monty Lane *computer company executive*
Boudreaux, John *marketing and public relations executive*
Bourdain, Anthony *chef, writer*
Bow, Stephen Tyler, Jr. *business executive*
Bowes, Henry Edward *retired communications executive*
Boyda, Debora *advertising executive*
Boysen, Jonea Gene *marketing executive*
Braddock, Richard S. *internet company executive*
Bradford, Susan Anne *management consultant, writer*
Brady, Andrea Rassin *marketing executive*
Brady, Donna Elizabeth *sales executive, marketing executive, performing company executive*
Breakstone, Kay Louise *public relations executive*
Brennan, Donna Lesley *public relations company executive*
Brennen, Stephen Alfred *management consultant*
Brenner, David H. *marketing executive*
Bridges-Kemp, Leslie LaVerne *administrative assistant*
Britt, Rebecca Fae *communications executive*
Broderson, Thelma Sylvia *retired marketing professional*
Brooks, Gary *crisis management and family business consultant*
Brotman, Stuart Neil *management consultant, law educator, former museum administrator*
Brown, Jeanette L. *environmental protection administrator*
Brown, Susan L. *internet and marketing services professional*
Brumfield, Jack *communications executive*
Buck, Earl Wayne *private investigator, motel owner*
Bultas, William Fitzgerald *Internet company executive*
Burgdoerfer, Jerry J. *marketing and distribution executive*
Burge, John Wesley, Jr. *management consultant*
Burkle, Ronald W. *former food service executive, business investor*
Burnett, Iris Jacobson *corporate communications specialist*
Burnham, J. V. *retired sales executive*
Burtnett, Jane S. *public relations consultant*
Butler, Robert Leonard *retired sales executive*
Butler, Robert Thomas *retired advertising executive*
Butts, Carol Henderson *human resources specialist, consultant*
Cage, Jack Hays *executive search consultant*
Callan, John Garling *business strategy consultant*
Carlson, Kenneth George *data processing executive*
Carp, Daniel A. *former consumer products company executive*
Carter, Dennis Lee *marketing professional*
Carter, Jaine M(arie) *human resources specialist, director*
Cartwright, Talula Elizabeth *management consultant*
Casadesus, Penelope Ann *advertising executive, film producer*
Cecil, Alex Thomson *travel executive*
Cervantes, Michelle *marketing professional*
Chakrin, Lewis M. *consumer products company executive*
Chamberlain, William Edwin, Jr. *management consultant*
Chandler, Robert Leslie *public relations executive*
Charles, Elizabeth C. *administrative assistant*
Chaseman, Joel *communications consultant*
Chen, Kenichi *chef*
Childs, John David *retired computer company executive*
Choueifati, Antoine (Tony Choueifati) *computer company executive*
Christian, Lori Coffelt *marketing professional*

Mallo-Garrido, Josephine Ann *advertising executive*
Malone, Claudine Berkeley *management consultant*
Malphurs, Roger Edward *biomedical marketing executive*
Maneker, Roberta S(ue) *public relations executive*
Manley, John Hugo *computer company executive, educator*
Mansfield, James E. *marketing professional, consultant*
Manzi, Jim P. *computer software company executive*
Markey, Randolph David *marketing professional*
Marlowe, Kathleen Scott *employment analyst*
Marshall, Robert Charles *computer company executive*
Martin, Charles Fontaine *management consultant*
Martin, Edwin Wilson *corporate director, columnist, educational consultant*
Martin, James Kay *management consultant*
Martin, Renee Cohen *forensic document examiner, author, expert witness*
Masaki, Takahisa *translation company executive, educator*
Mascheroni, Eleanor Earle *marketing communications executive*
Massey, William Walter, Jr. *sales executive*
Massoudi, Bahram Barry *management consultant*
Matschullat, Robert W. *former consumer products company executive*
Matthew, Lyn *sales executive, consultant, marketing professional*
Mattoli, Agostino Marron *management consultant*
Maxfield, Louisa Fonda Gribble *executive secretary*
Mayer, Allan *communications consultant, writer*
Mazzola, Mario *computer company executive*
McBride, Thomas Dwayne *management consultant*
McCandless, Carolyn Keller *retired human resources specialist*
McCarthy, Daniel William *management consultant*
McCloskey, J(ohn) Michael *retired environmental services administrator*
McCormick, Cori *marketing executive, vocalist, community leader*
McCoy, Debra Marlene Black *sales executive*
McDade, James Russell *management consultant*
McDonald, Peter D *airline executive*
McElwreath, Sally Chin *corporate communications executive*
McGee, Patrick Edgar *postal service clerk*
McGowan, Michele Patrice *advertising executive*
McGuire, John W., Sr. *advertising executive, marketing professional, writer*
McHenry, Julie *communications executive*
McKeown, Lorraine Laredo *travel company executive, writer*
Mc Kinney, David E(wing) *retired information processing products company executive, museum administrator*
McNair, Robert C. *communications executive*
McNamara, Tom *scientific consulting corporation executive*
McPherson, Donald Scott *labor and employment arbitrator/mediator*
McVeigh-Pettigrew, Sharon Christine *communications consultant*
Meads, Donald Edward *management services company executive*
Mechlowicz, David *purchasing agent*
Mendlin, Ronald C. *employment specialist, writer*
Menutis, Jamie *training services executive, writer*
Merrill, Frank Harrison *data processing executive, consultant*
Merriman, Chrisann *marketing professional*
Merullo-Boaz, Lisa Helen *marketing and fundraising executive*
Mikiewicz, Anna Daniella *marketing and international business export manager*
Miles, Laveda Ann *advertising executive*
Miles, Michael Arnold *consumer products executive*
Miller, Bernard Joseph, Jr. *advertising executive*
Miller, Ellen S. *marketing executive*
Miller, Robin *chef, nutritionist, editor*
Mitchell, Gregory Alan *management consultant*
Mitchell, John Charles *marketing professional*
Mitelman, Bonnie Cossman *editor, writer*
Moffat, MaryBeth *consulting company executive*
Moody, Kathryn Currier *communications executive, educator*
Moore, Thomas Andrew *former medical communications company executive*
Moradi, Ahmad F. *software company executive*
Moran, Charles A. *security firm executive, educator*
Morden, John Reid *security-business intelligence consultant*
Morgan, James Durward *retired computer company executive*
Mracky, Ronald Sydney *marketing executive, tourism consultant, media specialist*
Muczynski, Paul Frank *human resources specialist*
Mulcahy, Robert Edward *management consultant*
Mulchahey, Terry S. *human resources executive, management consultant*
Munson, Lawrence Shipley *management consultant*
Murgatroyd, Eric Neal *data processing executive*
Murphy-Daniels, Karen Ilene *environmental services administrator, safety engineer*
Mustard, Lewis Williams *management consultant, educator*
Nagler, Leon Gregory *retired management consultant*
Nason, Dolores Irene *computer company executive, social welfare administrator, minister*
Naumovska, Biljana *control assurance consultant*
Neel, Judy Murphy *management consultant*
Nelson, Bruce (Murray Bruce Nelson) *former consumer products company executive*
Nelson, Kimberly Terese *computer software company executive, former federal agency administrator*
Neuman, Michael A. *former communications company executive*
Nevares, Lane Gordon *travel company executive, writer, photographer*
Nevin, Robert Charles *information systems executive*

Niles, Thomas Michael Tolliver *former business association executive*
Noel, Jeanne Kay *biotechnology company executive*
Noonan, Susan Abert *public relations executive*
Norton, Nathaniel Goodwin *marketing executive*
O'Brien, David Peter *corporate director*
O'Brien, Robert John, Jr. *public relations executive, former government official, air force officer*
O'Connor, Betty Lou *retired hotel executive, food service executive*
Odom, Judy *software company executive*
Olins, Robert Abbot *communications research executive*
Olson, Dale C. *public relations executive*
Olson, Harold Roy *computer company executive*
Oppedahl, Phillip Edward *computer company executive*
O'Shea, Catherine Large *marketing and public relations consultant*
O'Shields, Charlie *marketing professional*
Ostberg, Henry Dean *marketing executive*
Ostrow, Joseph W. *advertising executive*
O'Sullivan, Paul Kevin *management and instructional systems consultant*
Palmerlee, April Wahlstedt *management consultant*
Palumbo, Matthew Aloysius *marketing executive*
Parke, Robert Leon *retired communications executive*
Patterson, Dennis Joseph *management consultant*
Peden, Keith J. *human resources specialist*
Penny, Roger Pratt *retired management consultant*
Penrod, Marian Penuel *personnel consultant, retired school librarian*
Pépin, Jacques G. *chef*
Peppel, Michael E. *computer company executive*
Perdunn, Richard Francis *management consultant*
Perlmutter, Barbara S. *retired advertising executive*
Perlmutter, Diane F. *marketing executive*
Perry, Chris Nicholas *retired advertising executive*
Perry, Sir Michael (Sir Michael Sydney Perry) *industrialist*
Peters, LeRoy Richard *materials management consulting company executive*
Pleasants, John *Internet company executive*
Plottel, Gloria Susanne Stone *marketing professional*
Polen-Dorn, Linda Frances *communications executive*
Porteous, Skipp *private investigator, writer*
Portway, Patrick Stephen *telecommunications consulting company executive, educator*
Post, Richard Bennett *retired human resources executive*
Potter, James Earl *retired international hotel management company executive*
Poza, Ernesto *management consultant, educator*
Price, David B., Jr. *management consultant*
Pride, Benjamin David *sales executive*
Proctor, Barbara Gardner *advertising agency executive, writer*
Prokopis, Emmanuel Charles *computer company executive*
Pruett-Lawson, Jo Ann *marketing professional, special events coordinator*
Pryor, Tommi Thornbury *marketing professional*
Puck, Wolfgang *chef*
Puetz, Pamela Ann *human resources executive*
Quinn, Mary M. *communications executive, marketing director*
Railsback, Sherrie Lee *management consultant, educator*
Rairdin, Craig Allen *software company executive, software developer*
Ransom, Margaret Palmquist *public relations executive*
Ray, Rachael *chef, television personality*
Read, Tony John *management consultant*
Reed, Anne F. Thomson *management consultant*
Reilly, Charles Edmund, Jr. *communications executive*
Reisman, Judith Ann Gelernter *media communications executive, educator*
Rescoe, Michael E. *computer company executive*
Rhea, Jerry Dwaine *consumer lending director*
Rich, Jeffrey A. *computer company executive*
Richards, Carmeleete A. *computer company executive, network administrator, consultant*
Rinaldi, Tina *travel company executive, writer*
Ripert, Eric *food service executive*
Robbins, James O. *former communications executive*
Robins, Norman Alan *management consultant, retired metal products executive*
Robinson, Hugh Granville *consulting management company executive*
Robinson, Linda Gosden *communications executive*
Rogers, Elyse MacFadyen *communications and foundation executive*
Roland, Donald Edward *advertising executive*
Rondum, Kai Damien *marketing executive*
Rook, Vicki Lynn *safety specialist*
Roseman, Jack *computer services company executive*
Rosen, Arthur Marvin *advertising executive*
Rosenberg, Robert Michael *retired restaurant franchise company executive*
Rosenfield, James Harold, Sr. *communications executive*
Rowe, Richard R. *on-line information and management services company executive*
Rowland, Pleasant T. *toy company executive, publisher*
Rowny, Michael J. *communications executive*
Rubin, Martin N. *meeting planner, consultant*
Ruggles, Rudy Lamont, Jr. *international security advisor*
Russ, Edmond Vincent, Jr. *marketing professional*
Russell, Carol Ann *personnel service company executive*
Russell, Charles William III *communications executive, writer*
Ryan, William *executive*
Rydholm, Ralph Williams *advertising executive*
Sacks, Temi J. *public relations executive*
Safian, Shelley Carole *advertising executive*
Saligman, Harvey *retired consumer products and services company executive*

Sanchez, Fausto H. *advertising executive*
Sandage-Mussey, Elizabeth Anthea *retired market research executive*
Sandler, Norman *communications executive*
Sassa, Scott M. *former internet company executive*
Sauerhaft, Stan *retired public relations executive, retired consultant*
Schadt, James Phillip *investment and software executive*
Scheer, Teva Scheer *human resources specialist*
Schlensker, Gary Chris *landscape company executive*
Schneider, Donald (Charles Schneider) *communications executive*
Schocket, Sandra Klamkin *career management consultant, writer*
Schonberg, Alan Robert *personnel director*
Schreckinger, Sy Edward *advertising executive, consultant*
Schrock, Donald E. *communications executive*
Schubert, Helen Celia *public relations executive*
Schuessler, John T. (Jack Schuessler) *retired food service executive*
Schulz, Raymond Alexander *medical marketing professional, consultant*
Searl, Hanford Williams, Jr. *communications executive, journalist, actor*
Sease, Gene Elwood *communications executive*
Seelig, Gerard Leo *management consultant*
Seidman, Glenn Elliott *sales executive, marketing professional, consultant*
Selkowitz, Arthur *retired advertising executive*
Shaftman, Fredrick Krisch *telephone communications executive, lawyer*
Shain, Kenneth Stephen *management consultant, writer*
Shaker, William Haygood *marketing professional, public policy reformer*
Shapiro, Sumner *consulting firm executive, retired naval officer*
Sharick, Merle Dayton, Jr. *sales executive*
Sharples, Ruth Lissak *communications executive*
Shaw, Jack Allen *communications company executive*
Sheehan, Robert James, II, *management and market research consultant*
Shevitz, Mark H. *sales promotion and marketing executive*
Shikuma, Eugene Yujin *travel company executive*
Shultz, Delray Franklin (Lucky Shultz) *business coach, consultant*
Sibilla, Suzanne Rose *training and organizational development consultant*
Sidebottom, William George *communications executive*
Siegel, George Henry *management consultant*
Siegel, Herbert Bernard *management consultant*
Silva, Luis M. *marketing professional*
Simecka, Betty Jean *marketing executive*
Simon, Marc *communications executive*
Simpson, Andrea Lynn *communications executive*
Sincoff, Michael Z. *human resources and marketing executive*
Singer, David Michael *marketing executive, public relations executive*
Singleton-Wood, Allan James *communications executive*
Skala, Gary Dennis *management consultant*
Skulski, Tia *human resources specialist*
Slosberg, Mike *advertising executive*
Sollender, Joel David *management consultant, financial executive, accountant*
Sorstokke, Ellen Kathleen *marketing executive, educator*
Speakes, Larry Melvin *public relations executive, writer*
Speer, Richard John *security consultant*
Spellman, Douglas Toby *advertising executive*
Spivak, Joan Carol *communications executive*
Stanzione, Daniel C. *communications company executive*
Stark, Diana *public relations executive*
Starkweather, Frederick Thomas *retired data processing executive*
Stengel, Ronald Francis *management consultant*
Stenitzer, George Ignatius *corporate communications specialist*
Stepanski, Anthony Francis, Jr. *computer company executive*
Stevens, Art *public relations executive*
Stevens, Berton Louis, Jr. *data processing executive*
Stewart, Arthur Irving, III, (Art Stewart) *management consultant*
Stiles, Virginia Ford *data processing executive, poet*
Stone, Curtis *celebrity chef*
Stone, James Howard *management consultant*
Stone, Linda *former computer company executive, consultant, speaker, writer*
Stover, Kenneth Alan *sales executive*
Strasser, Gabor *management consultant*
Stuart, Spencer Raymond *management consultant*
Stubbs, Katrina Childs *management consultant, educator*
Stults, Walter Black *management consultant, trade association administrator*
Sudarsky, Jerry M. *industrialist*
Sueltz, Patricia C. *computer company executive*
Sykes, Kathryn Rosemarie *human resources specialist, consultant*
Taber, Geoffrey Alexander *quality assurance professional*
Taplett, Lloyd Melvin *human resources specialist, consultant*
Tarbutton, Lloyd T. *hotel executive, consultant*
Tarr, Curtis W. *management consultant, educator*
Tegge, Patricia Ann *retired administrative assistant*
Temerlin, Liener *advertising executive*
Tenney, Frank Putnam *marketing executive*
Terry, Elizabeth Hudson *personal care industry executive, realtor*
Tesarek, Dennis George *retired business consultant, writer, educator*
Thomas, Joe Carroll *retired human resources director*
Thompson, Craig Snover *corporate communications executive*
Thompson, Dean M., II, *marketing executive*

Thompson, Richard Stephen *management consultant*
Tian, Li *computer company executive, educator*
Tilney, Elizabeth A. *marketing executive*
Timmerman, Anne N. *retired public relations executive*
Tocci, Neil Michael *marketing executive, educator, corporate communications executive*
Toevs, Alden Louis *management consultant, researcher*
Travi, Jason *chef*
Tremain, Alan *hotel executive*
Tribus, Myron *management consultant, educator*
Triplett, Arlene Ann *management consultant*
Tripp, Marian Barlow Loofe *retired public relations executive*
Trivisonno, Nicholas Louis *communications company executive, accountant*
Troop, Paul Melvin *public relations executive, journalist*
Tuft, Mary Ann *executive search firm executive*
Turkel, Stanley *hotel executive, management consultant*
Turner, William Cochrane *international management consultant*
Unwin, Stephen Forman *advertising executive, educator*
Uvena, Frank John *retired printing company executive, lawyer*
Vallerand, Philippe Georges *sales executive*
Van der Horst, Brian Christopher *communications consultant, author, educator*
Van Dine, Alan Charles *advertising agency executive, writer*
VanNatta-Gail, Mary Louise *public relations executive*
Viner, Peter *communications executive*
Vosloo, Paul *public relations executive*
Wade, Daniel M. *recreational facility executive, hotel executive*
Wadley, M. Richard *consumer products executive*
Walke, David Michael *business advisory, consulting and research executive*
Walker, Gloria Lee *training services executive*
Walker, Ronald Tracy *retired personnel director*
Wallington, Patricia McDevitt *computer company executive*
Walmsley, Priscilla Helen *computer company executive*
Walsh, William Albert *management consultant, retired military officer*
Walter, Carmel Monica *security firm executive, writer*
Walter, J. Jackson *management consultant, foundation administrator*
Walters, Matthew Paul *recreational facility executive, consultant*
Ward, Jonathan P. *former service company executive*
Wardlow, Benjamin Franklin III *sales executive*
Weathersby, George Byron *management company executive*
Webb, Maynard G., Jr. *retired Internet company executive*
Webb, William Timothy *mobile communications professional*
Weber, Kenneth J. *hotel executive*
Wegman, Harold Hugh *management consultant*
Weil, Lynne Amy *communications executive, writer*
Weiner, Richard *public relations executive*
Weinstein, Marta *packaging services company executive*
Weismantel, Gregory Nelson *management consultant, computer company executive*
Weiss, Jerry Kenneth *sales executive, consultant, marketing professional*
Weissman, Morris *printing company executive*
Wendlinger, Robert Matthew *communications and memory consultant*
Werner, Stuart Lloyd *computer services company executive*
Weston, Saundra Olivia (Saundra Laidlaw) *quality assurance professional, minister*
Wheaton, M. Gene *investigator, consultant*
Wicks, David O., Jr. *communications executive*
Williams, John Charles, II, *data processing executive*
Williams, Louis Clair, Jr. *public relations executive*
Williams, Terrie Michelle *public relations executive*
Willig, Karl Victor *computer company executive*
Wimpress, Gordon Duncan, Jr. *management consultant, foundation administrator*
Winnick, Gary *communications executive*
Wise, Richard Reynolds *management consultant*
Wittenberg, Alexander *museum publicist*
Woldridge, Scott *outsourced human resources company executive*
Wolf, Linda S. *retired advertising executive*
Wolf, Stephen M. *consumer products company executive, former airline executive*
Wolf, William Martin *computer company executive, consultant*
Wood, Dennis *communications executive*
Wood, Frances Diane *medical secretary, artist*
Worboys, Roger Dick *retired communications executive*
Worley, Donald Lee *quality assurance professional*
Worth, Gary James *communications executive*
Wyse, Lois *advertising executive, writer*
Yang, Chau-Jye (Jay) *management consultant*
Yansouni, Cyril J. *computer company executive*
Yocam, Delbert Wayne *retired software products company executive*
Yopconka, Natalie Ann Catherine *secretary, computer specialist, educator, entrepreneur, small business owner*
Youst, David Bennett *career development educator*
Zeglis, John D. *communications executive, lawyer*
Zeller, Joseph Paul *advertising executive*
Zelnick, Strauss *entertainment company executive*
Zhang, Ming *business and management consultant*
Ziegler, James L. *marketing executive*

Zinnen, Robert Oliver *management consultant, consultant*

## INDUSTRY: TRADE

### UNITED STATES

#### ALABAMA

**Birmingham**
George, Frank Wade *small business owner, antiquarian book dealer*
Martin, R. Brad *retail executive*
Pizitz, Richard Alan *retail executive, real estate company officer*

**Dothan**
Malugen, J.T. (Joe Thomas) *retail executive*

**Mobile**
Jones, Joseph Seymour *small business owner, poet*

**Talladega**
Weaver, Robert Cooper *small business owner, volunteer*

**Tuscaloosa**
Blackburn, John Leslie *small business owner*

#### ALASKA

**Anchorage**
Schnell, Roger Thomas *small business owner, retired state official*

**Wrangell**
Smith, Kimmie Christine *small business owner*

#### ARIZONA

**Carefree**
Howell, William Robert *retail company executive*

**Chandler**
Basha, Edward N., Jr. *grocery chain owner*

**Peoria**
Black, Melissa J. *small business owner*

**Phoenix**
Francis, Philip L. *retail executive*

**Scottsdale**
Williams-De Silva, Lisa Annette *small business owner, adult nurse practitioner*

**Sedona**
Connor, Nancy L. *small business owner*

**Tucson**
Fay, Mary Anne *retail executive*

#### ARKANSAS

**Bentonville**
Castro-Wright, Eduardo *retail executive*
Chambers, Susan (M. Susan Chambers) *retail executive*
Degn, Douglas J. *retail executive*
Dillman, Linda M. *retail executive*
Dobbs, Johnnie *retail executive*
Duke, Michael T. *retail executive*
Fleming, John *retail executive*
Ford, Rollin *retail executive*
Glass, David D. *retail executive, professional sports team executive*
Herkert, Craig R. *retail executive*
Jackson, Lawrence V. *retail executive*
McMillion, Doug *retail executive*
Menzer, John Bruce *retail executive*
Mora, Alberto J. *retail executive, lawyer*
Schoewe, Thomas M. *retail executive*
Scott, H. Lee, Jr., (Harold Lee Scott Jr.) *retail executive*
Simon, William *retail executive*
Walton, Rob (Samuel Robson Walton) *discount department store chain executive*
Watts, Claire A. *retail executive*
Zorn, Eric Stuart *retail executive*

**Little Rock**
Dillard, Mike *retail executive*
Dillard, William, II, *department store chain executive*

#### CALIFORNIA

**Bodega Bay**
Freeman, Donna Cook *small business owner*

**Camarillo**
Van House, Robert Arthur *small business owner, contractor*

**Carmel**
Aurner, Robert Ray, II, *retail development executive*

**Cathedral City**
Jackman, Robert Alan *retail executive*

**City Of Commerce**
Martin, Richard J. *food wholesale executive*
Plamann, Alfred A. *wholesale distribution executive*

**Colton**
Brown, Jack H. *supermarket company executive*

**Corona Del Mar**
Freeman, Richard Dean *new business start-up service company executive*

**Fortuna**
Johnson, Louanna B. *retired small business owner*

**Fremont**
Liang, Christine *import company executive*

**Fresno**
Winslow, Norman Eldon *small business owner*

**Irvine**
Nelson, Courtney Ann *small business owner*

**La Puente**
Rojo De Santos, Anita *shop owner, writer*

**Laguna Beach**
Pelton, Virginia Lue *small business owner*

**Lake Forest**
Milligan, Steve *retail executive*
Shakeel, Arif *retail executive*

**Los Altos**
Orr, Susan Packard *small business owner, foundation administrator*

**Los Angeles**
Ganz, Julian, Jr. *retail executive*
Hawley, Philip Metschan *retired retail executive, management consultant*
Roeder, Richard Kenneth *business owner, lawyer*
Sinay, Joseph *retail executive*

**Menlo Park**
VanHook, Tracie Lynnette *small business owner*

**Modesto**
Piccinini, Robert M. (Bob Piccinini) *grocery store chain executive*

**Newport Coast**
Pavony, William H. *retail executive, consultant*

**Orange**
Busby, Nita June *small business owner*

**Orinda**
Somerset, Harold Richard *retired retail executive*

**Pacific Palisades**
Diehl, Richard Kurth *retail executive, consultant*

**Palm Springs**
Wiesner, John Joseph *retail chain store executive*

**Palos Verdes Peninsula**
Slayden, James Bragdon *retired retail executive*

**Petaluma**
Gervais, Cherie Nadine *small business owner*

**Pleasant Hill**
Abraham-Helman, Cheryl Goodrich *small business owner*

**Pleasanton**
Balmuth, Michael A. *retail executive*
Ferber, Norman Alan *retail executive*
Peters, James C. *retail executive*
Renda, Larree M. *retail executive*

**Redding**
Streiff, Arlyne Bastunas *business owner, educator*

**Riverside**
White, Clara Jo *small business owner, consultant*

**San Diego**
Saito, Frank Kiyoji *import and export firm executive*

**San Francisco**
Fisher, Donald G. *retail executive*
Fisher, Doris *retail executive*
Fisher, Robert J. *retail executive*
Folkman, David H. *retail, wholesale and consumer products consultant*
Harriss, Cynthia Therese (Cynthia Therese Clarke) *retail executive*
Lester, W. Howard *retail executive*
McCollam, Sharon L. *retail executive*
Pollitt, Byron H., Jr. *retail executive*
Pressler, Paul S. *retail executive*
Sage-Gavin, Eva Marie *retail executive*
Tasooji, Michael B. *retail executive*
Ullman, Myron Edward, III, (Mike Ullman) *retail executive*

**San Jose**
Davido, Scott *retail executive*

**Santa Rosa**
Monk, Diana Charla *small business owner*

**Stockton**
Blodgett, Elsie Grace *small business owner, property manager*

**Valencia**
Joy, Alexa *small business owner, artist, educator*

**Walnut Creek**
Bryant, Warren F. *retail executive*
Laddon, Michael M *retail executive*

**West Sacramento**
Coyne, William J. *retail executive, former member house representatives*
Teel, Joyce Raley *retail executive*

**Westminster**
Nguyen, Duoc Tan *small business owner*

**Yountville**
Bedell, Jay Dee *small business owner, writer*

#### COLORADO

**Aurora**
Onyeuku, Alfred Eme *small business owner, consultant*

**Boulder**
Blacker, Helen Virginia *business manager, aeronautical engineer*

**Colorado Springs**
Noyes, Richard Hall *bookseller*

**Denver**
Cashman, Michael Richard *small business owner*
Cheris, Elaine Gayle Ingram *business owner*
Clinch, Nicholas Bayard III *small business owner*
Schwartz, Jeffrey H. *distribution facilities executive*

**Englewood**
Morton, John Douglas *retail executive*

**Loveland**
Rodman, Sue A. *wholesale company executive, artist, writer*

#### CONNECTICUT

**Avon**
Kling, Phradie (Phradie Kling Gold) *small business owner, educator*

**Enfield**
Squires, William Allen *distribution company executive*

**Essex**
Thompson, George Lee *retail executive, consultant*

**Fairfield**
Wexler, Herbert Ira *retail company executive*

**Greenwich**
Rudy, Kathleen Vermeulen *small business owner*

**Mansfield Center**
Petrus, Robert Thomas *internet business owner, investor*

**New London**
Johnson, Diana Atwood *business owner, innkeeper*

**Norwalk**
Bennett, Carl *retired discount department store executive*

**Stamford**
Gilman, Kenneth B. *retail executive*
Hollinger, Morton *small business owner, artist*

**Westport**
Kovatch, Carol Wilhelm *small business owner*

#### DELAWARE

**Rehoboth Beach**
Walker, Bonnie Lee *small business owner*

#### DISTRICT OF COLUMBIA

**Washington**
Chalkley, Jacqueline Ann *retail company executive*
Donna, Roberto *restaurateur, chef*
Smith, Jack Carl *import/export company executive*
Stern, Paula *international trade consultant*

#### FLORIDA

**Boca Grande**
Winterer, Victoria Thompson *small business owner*

**Boca Raton**
Ricciardi, Salvatore *wholesale distribution executive*

**Bradenton**
Beall, Robert Matthews, II, *retail executive*
Rutstein, Stanley Harold *apparel retailing company executive*

**Casselberry**
Renee, Lisabeth Mary *small business owner, art designer*

**Clearwater**
Henderson, Janet Lynn *small business owner*
Maxwell, Richard Anthony *retail executive*
Turley, Stewart *retired retail company executive*

**Delray Beach**
Brown, Charles E. *retail executive*
Carter-Miller, Jocelyn *retail executive*
Holifield, Mark *retail executive*
Luechtefeld, Monica *retail executive*
van Kaldekerken, Rolf *retail executive*

**Fort Lauderdale**
Chung, Chia Mou (Charles Chung) *former Oriental art business owner*
Dwors, Robert F. *retail executive*
Ferrando, Jonathan P. *retail executive*
Maroone, Michael E. *car and truck sales executive*

**Gainesville**
McClellan, Richard Augustus *retired small business owner*
Silas, Nancy *small business owner*

**Hialeah**
Herran, Agustin (Tino Herran) *supermarket executive, real estate company executive*
Herran, Manuel A. *supermarket chain executive*

**Jacksonville**
Fisher, Michael D. *retail executive*
Lynch, Peter L. *retail executive*
McCook, Richard Paul *grocery chain financial executive*
Skelton, H. Jay *retail executive, investment company executive*
Stein, Jay *retail executive*

**Key Biscayne**
de la Cruz, Carlos *wholesale distribution executive*

**Lakeland**
Barnett, Hoyt R. (Barney Barnett) *supermarket company executive*

**Merritt Island**
Smith, David Edward *small business owner, aerospace engineer, aerospace scientist*

**Miami**
Chaplin, Harvey *wine and liquor wholesale executive*
Ferrari, Leonardo *small business owner*
Navarro, Jose F., Jr. *retail executive*
Nunez Ojeda, Elpidio *food distribution executive*
Rawl, Arthur Julian (Lord of Cursons) *retail executive, consultant, accountant, writer*
Richards-Vital, Claudia *small business owner, recreational facility executive*

**Miami Lakes**
Perez de la Mesa, Manuel Jose *swimming pool company executive*

**Miramar**
Catalano, Carl Philip *small business owner*

**Naples**
Ludwig, Richard Joseph *small business owner*

**Opa Locka**
Capo, Luis E. *furniture company executive*

**Orlando**
Arlt, Devon Taylor *small business owner*
Smetanka, Sally S. *small business owner*

**Palm Beach**
Radner, Sidney Hollis *retired retail executive*

**Palm Beach Gardens**
Day, Lawrence C. *auto parts executive*
Runge, Donald Edward *food wholesale company executive*

**Pembroke Pines**
Schaefer, Bonnie (E. Bonnie Schaefer) *retail executive*
Schaefer, Marla L. *retail executive*

**Saint Augustine**
Bishop, Claire DeArment *small business owner, retired librarian*

**Saint Petersburg**
Erman, Aila *small business owner*

**San Antonio**
Beverland, Jack Edwin *retired retail executive, folk artist*

**Sarasota**
Meyer, B. Fred *small business executive, home designer and builder, product designer*

**Tampa**
Davis, Blondell Gilliam *business manager, evangelist, artist, author, poet*
Eddy, Colette Ann *aerial photography studio owner, photographer*
Keller, Shari Ann *small business owner*

**Titusville**
Atwood, Frelda Garland *small business owner, computer scientist, consultant*

**University Park**
Walker, Jane Stewart *small business owner, publishing executive, educator*

**Winter Park**
Alfond, Theodore B. *retired shoe company executive*
Kindlund, Newton Carlton *retail executive*

#### GEORGIA

**Alpharetta**
Greene, Melinda Jean *retail maintenance analyst*

**Atlanta**
Blake, Francis Stanton *retail executive, lawyer*
Dayhoff, Diane *retail executive*
DeAngelo, Joe *retail executive*
Judd, George R. *wholesale distribution executive*
Kalafut, George Wendell *retired distribution company executive, retired naval officer*
Liebert, Carl C. III *retail executive*
Macadam, Stephen E. *wholesale distribution executive*
Malcolm, Gloria J. *small business owner*
Marcus, Bernard *retired retail executive*
Ridley, Clarence Haverty *retail executive*
Seegers, Harvey *retail executive*

**Decatur**
Solomon, Hilda Pearl *wholesale executive*

**Dunwoody**
Maddox, Jerry Aven *retail executive*

**Macon**
Davis, Anita Yvonne *small business owner, writer*

**Marietta**
Short-Mayfield, Patricia Ahlene *business owner*

**Norcross**
Galfas, Timothy, II, *wholesale distribution executive*

**Social Circle**
Penland, John Thomas *retired import/export and development company executive*

**Valdosta**
Halter, Henry James, Jr., (Diamond Jim Halter) *retail executive*

**IDAHO**

**Boise**
Herbert, Kathy J. *retail executive*
Long, William D. *grocery store executive*

**White Bird**
Lathrop, Lawrence Erwin, Jr. *retired small business owner, retired forester*

**ILLINOIS**

**Charleston**
Ball-Saret, Jayne Adams *small business owner*

**Chicago**
Cesario, Robert Charles *retail executive, consultant*
Deli, Anne Tynion *retail executive*
Field, Marshall *retail executive*
Heidemann, Lyle G. *retail executive*
Robins, Joel *import/export company executive*
Tomaino, Joseph Carmine *former retail executive, former postal inspector*
Vrablik, Edward Robert *import/export company executive*

**Deerfield**
Bernauer, David W. *retail executive*
Rein, Jeffrey A. *retail executive*
Rudolphsen, William M. *retail executive*
Taylor, Trent E. *retail executive*

**Des Plaines**
Gochnauer, Richard Wallis *wholesale distribution executive*

**Glen Ellyn**
Baloun, John Charles *retired wholesale distribution executive*

**Glencoe**
Nebenzahl, Kenneth *rare book and map dealer, author*

**Hoffman Estates**
Crowley, William C. *retail executive*
Good, Mark *retail executive*
Kelly, Gerald F, Jr. *retail executive*
Lewis, Aylwin B. *retail executive, former food service company executive*
Meads, Mindy *merchandising and design executive*
O'Leary, Robert J. *retail executive*
White, William III *retail executive*

**Hoopeston**
Hicks, Carol Ann *small business owner, educator*

**Itasca**
Duncan, Sam K. *retail executive*

**Jacksonville**
Ware, Jon Dean *retail executive*

**Lake Bluff**
Ochsner, Othon Henry, II, *importer, restaurant critic*

**Lake Forest**
Ysasi-Diaz, Gloria *wholesale distribution executive*

**Lincolnshire**
Knopik, Robert *retail executive, consultant*

**Lombard**
Barnholt, Brandon K. *retail executive*

**Melrose Park**
Kloster, Carol Good *wholesale distribution executive*

**Morton Grove**
McKenna, Andrew James *wholesale distribution executive, printing company executive, sports association executive*

**Oak Brook**
Hodnik, David F. *retail company executive*

**River Grove**
Litzsinger, Richard Mark *retail executive*
Stanton, Kathryn *retail executive*

**Rock Island**
Kirklin-Darif, Dianna Lynn *small business owner*

**Saint Charles**
LaHood, Julie Ann *small business owner*

**Schaumburg**
Richter, Glenn *retail executive*

**Wheeling**
Schulman, Alan Michael *small business owner*

**INDIANA**

**Columbus**
Jorgensen, Virginia Dyer *antique dealer, museum consultant*

**Elkhart**
Drexler, Rudy Matthew, Jr. *professional law enforcement dog trainer*

**Fort Wayne**
Cast, Anita Hursh *small business owner*
Curtis, Douglas Homer *small business owner*

**Indianapolis**
Cohen, Alan H. *retail executive*

**Jasper**
Newman, Leonard Jay *retail jewel merchant, gemologist*

**Valparaiso**
Mosco, Scott Morris *small business owner*

**IOWA**

**Ankeny**
Lamb, Ronald M. *convenience stores executive*

**Davenport**
Sievert, Mary Elizabeth *small business owner, retired secondary school educator*

**West Des Moines**
Pearson, Ronald Dale *retail food stores corporation executive*

**KANSAS**

**Kansas City**
Baska, James Louis *wholesale grocery company executive*

**Neodesha**
James, Charles (Chuck) Edward *small business owner, writer*

**Shawnee Mission**
Moeller, Laura Lee *retired retail executive, library and information consultant*

**Topeka**
Cantrell, Duane L. *retail executive*
Porzig, Ullrich E. *retail executive*
Rubel, Matthew Evan *retail executive*

**KENTUCKY**

**Bowling Green**
Gipson, Jim *wholesale distribution executive*

**Eubank**
Karriker, Danny Allen *small business owner, protective services official*

**Louisville**
Smith, Donald Ray *magazine dealer*

**Winchester**
Book, John Kenneth (Kenny Book) *retail store owner*

**LOUISIANA**

**Coushatta**
Wiggins, Mary Ann Wise *small business owner, educator*

**Houma**
Walters, Steven Anthony *small business owner, consultant*

**MAINE**

**Kennebunk**
Escalet, Frank Diaz *small business owner*

**Portland**
Stanley, Eliot Hungerford *small business owner, writer, lawyer*

**Sedgwick**
Donnell, William Ray *small business owner, communications executive*

**MARYLAND**

**Baltimore**
Cain, Marcena Jean Beesley *retail executive*
Carper, Gertrude Esther *small business owner, real estate developer*
Hug, Richard Ernest *small business owner*
Schilling, Franklin Charles, Jr. *retail management professional*

**Brandywine**
Johnson, Madge Richards *business owner, fundraiser, consultant*

**Catonsville**
Toomey, Sister Stephana *small business owner*

**Forest Hill**
Klein, Shirley Snyderman *retail executive*

**Kensington**
Fasusi, Jimmy Adebayo *small business owner*

**Pikesville**
Stein, Bernard Alvin *retail executive, consultant*

**Potomac**
Carper, Fern Gayle *small business owner, writer*
Shapiro, Richard Gerald *retail executive, consultant*

**Silver Spring**
Miller, Kendra Danette *art services business owner, consultant*

**MASSACHUSETTS**

**Auburn**
Baker, David Arthur *retired small business owner, manufacturing executive*

**Canton**
Bentas, Lily Haseotes *retail executive*
Brenner, Harry J. *retail executive*
Reichman, Joel H. *retail executive*

**Framingham**
Cammarata, Ben (Bernard Cammarata) *retail executive*
Feldberg, Sumner Lee *retired retail executive*
Mahoney, John J. *office supply company executive*
Meyrowitz, Carol *retail executive*
Miles, Michael A., Jr. *retail executive*
Naylor, Jeffrey Gordon *retail executive*
Sargent, Ronald L. *retail office and business products executive*
Vassalluzzo, Joseph S. *retail company executive*

**Lawrence**
Barbagallo, Joseph C. *small business owner*

**Medfield**
McQuillen, Jeremiah Joseph *distribution executive*

**Natick**
Wedge, Michael T. *wholesale distribution executive*
Zarkin, Herbert J. *retail executive*

**Pittsfield**
Staley, Greg *retail executive*

**Quincy**
Conley, Olga L. *retail executive*

**Worcester**
Candib, Murray A. *retail executive, consultant*

**MICHIGAN**

**Ann Arbor**
Jones, George L. *retail executive*
Pollock, Lawrence I. *retail executive, investment company executive*

**Bad Axe**
Sullivan, James Gerald *small business owner*

**Bingham Farms**
Krevsky, Margery Brown *talent agency executive*

**Bloomfield Hills**
Robinson, Jack Albert *retail executive*

**Grand Rapids**
DeLapa, Judith Anne *business owner*
Meijer, Hank *retail company executive*
Sturken, Craig C. *retail executive*
Zigerelli, Lawrence *retail products company executive*

**Harbor Beach**
Falkenberg, Mary Elaine *small business owner*

**Houghton Lake**
Manley, Janet Zeegers *retired small business owner*

**Muskegon**
McKitrick, James Thomas *retired retail executive*

**Naubinway**
Beaudoin, Robert Lawrence *small business owner*

**Reed City**
Rautiola, Norman A. *small business owner, manufacturing executive*

**Saginaw**
Marsh, Doris Elaine *retired ballet school owner*

**Southfield**
Primo, Joan Erwina *retail and real estate consulting business owner*

**Troy**
Austin, Karen *retail executive*
Elder, Irma *retail executive*
Lueken, Harold W. *retail executive*
Strome, Stephen *distribution company executive*

**MINNESOTA**

**Eden Prairie**
Jackson, Darren Richard *retail executive*
Jackson, Michael L. *wholesale distribution executive*
Knous, Pamela K. *wholesale distribution executive*
Noddle, Jeffrey *retail and food distribution executive*

**Edina**
Finkelstein, Phil *retail executive*
Froemming, Herbert Dean *retired retail executive*

**Minneapolis**
Ahlers, Linda L. *retail executive*
Dunn, Brian J. *retail executive*
Francis, Michael R. *retail executive*
Gralnek, Minda *retail executive*
Hale, James Thomas *retail executive, lawyer*

Marshall, Ron *retail executive*
Paulu, Frances Brown *retired international center administrator*
Schulze, Richard M. *retail executive*
Scovanner, Douglas *retail executive*
Steinhafel, Gregg W *retail executive*
Stephenson, Vivian M. *former retail executive*
Trestman, Frank D. *distribution company executive, director*
Ulrich, Robert J. *retail executive*
Walden, John *retail executive*

**Richfield**
Anderson, Bradbury H. *retail executive*

**Saint Paul**
Nash, Nicholas David *retail executive*

**Walker**
Collins, Thomas William *caterer, consultant*

**MISSOURI**

**Charleston**
Cassell, Lucille Richardson *small business owner*

**Chesterfield**
Kleffner, Gregory William *retail executive, accountant*
Ross, E. Earl *small business owner*

**Cuba**
Work, Bruce Van Syoc *small business owner, consultant*

**Independence**
Francis, Mary Frances Van Dyke *small business owner, real estate company executive, retired editor*

**Kansas City**
Baker, Sharlynn Ruth *livery and limousine service owner*

**Kingsville**
Stimac, John Anthony *small business owner, poet, cartoonist, inventor*

**Lebanon**
Louderback, Kevin Wayne *business owner*

**O Fallon**
Wood, Leslie Ann *retail administrator*

**Overland**
Clark, Maxine *retail executive*

**Saint Louis**
Berger, Wayne C. *retail executive*
Bridgewater, Bernard Adolphus, Jr. *retired retail executive*
Capps, W. Lee III *retail executive*
Fingleton, Thomas D. *retail executive*
McNamara, William P. *retail executive*
Schnuck, Craig D. *grocery store company executive*
Skinner, Robert C., Jr. *retail executive*

**NEBRASKA**

**Omaha**
Cappellano, Rosemarie Zaccone *small business owner*

**Sidney**
Cabela, Richard N. *retail executive*
Highby, Dennis *retail executive*

**NEVADA**

**Henderson**
Fehr, Gregory Paris *marketing and distribution company executive*
Marcovitz, Leonard Edward *retail executive*

**NEW HAMPSHIRE**

**Campton**
Benton, Geraldine Ann *preschool owner, director*

**Keene**
Harris, Reuben *wholesale distribution executive*
Lichtenstein, Sally (Ali) Tucker *small business owner, writer, English and women's studies educator*

**New Castle**
Friese, George Ralph *retail executive*

**Rochester**
Coviello, Robert Frank *retail executive*

**NEW JERSEY**

**Carteret**
Standley, John T. *food market executive*

**Clifton**
Giles, William (Bill) T. *retail executive*

**Colts Neck**
Mauro, Anthony Peter *small business owner*

**Elizabeth**
Gellert, George Geza *food importing company executive*

**Freehold**
Foster, Eric Harold, Jr. *retail executive*

**Hoboken**
Schultz, Kenneth Carl *antiques dealer*

**Linden**
Suliga, Joseph *small business owner*

**Little Falls**
Birnberg, Jeffrey *small business owner*

**Monroe Township**
Zelin, Jerome *retired retail executive*

**New Milford**
Walsh, Joseph Michael *magazine distribution executive*

**North Bergen**
Slatner, Thomas Allen *bookseller*

**North Brunswick**
Shaw, Roslyn Lee *small business owner, retired elementary school educator*

**Park Ridge**
Ciannella, Joeen Moore *small business owner*

**Paterson**
Papageorgis, Jack *small business owner*

**Pennington**
Donnelly, Gerard Kevin *marketing and retail executive*

**Princeton**
Bergman, Victoria Besterman *small business owner, consultant*
Campbell, Mildred Corum *business owner, nurse*
Hochschwender, Karl Albert *international trade and government relations consultant*

**Union**
Eisenberg, Warren *retail executive*
Feinstein, Leonard *retail executive*
Temares, Steven H. *retail executive*

**Wayne**
Arthur, Ray *retail executive*
Arthur, Raymond L. *retail toy and game company executive*
Barbour, John *retail executive*
Brockett, Francesca L. *retail executive*
Derby, Deborah *retail executive*
Kay, Christopher K. *retail executive, lawyer*
Markee, Richard L. *retail executive*
Storch, Gerald L. *retail executive*

**Wilkesboro**
Jennings, Perry G. *retail executive*

## NEW MEXICO

**Chimayo**
Vigil, Rose Ann *business owner, weaver*

## NEW YORK

**Albany**
Higgins, Robert J. *retail entertainment executive*

**Appleton**
Singer, Thomas Kenyon *international business consultant, fruit grower*

**Bellport**
Regalmuto, Nancy Marie *small business owner, consultant*

**Bronx**
Lyons, Maxine Evadney *small business owner, poet*

**Brooklyn**
Moehring, Fred Adolf *wholesale distribution executive*

**Katonah**
Levine, Pamela Gail *business owner*

**New York**
Archbold, Michael G. *retail executive*
Blum, Paul *retail executive*
Bolton, Alon *retail executive*
Brown, Andreas Le *retail executive, art gallery owner*
Bryan, Scott *business owner, chef*
Castagna, Vanessa J. *retail executive*
Catsimatidis, John Andreas *retail executive*
Chaney, Gerald M. *retail executive*
Dreiling, Richard *retail executive*
Drexler, Millard S. (Mickey Drexler) *retail executive*
Fernandez, James *retail products executive*
Frasch, Ron L. *retail executive*
Friedman, Rachelle *music retail executive*
Karp, Roberta Schuhalter *retail executive, lawyer*
Kowalski, Michael J. *retail products executive*
Laurie, Nancy Walton *retail executive*
Lazarus, Adrienne *retail executive*
Lombardi, Joseph J. *retail executive*
Lundgren, Terry J. *retail company executive*
Mello, Dawn *retail executive*
Michelson, Gertrude Geraldine *retired retail executive*
Mondlin, Marvin *retail executive, rare book dealer*
Noce, Donna *retail executive*
Quinn, James E. *retail executive*
Quint, Ira *retail executive*
Riggio, Leonard *book store company executive*
Riggio, Stephen *book store company executive*
Riley, William *wholesale distribution executive, writer, conservationist*
Sadove, Stephen Irving *retail executive*
Safro, Millicent *small business owner, decorative arts scholar, writer*
Schiller, Justin Galland *antiquarian bookseller, researcher, editor*
Schmults, Edward *retail executive*
Sherman, Jeffrey Barry *retail executive*
Snyder, Todd *retail executive*
Spector, Anita Frohmann *buyer*

Stanton, Ronald P. *export company executive*
Toulantis, Marie J. *retail executive*
Washburn, Joan Thomas *small business owner*

**Riverhead**
Carpenter, Angie M. *small business owner, editor, county legislator*

## NORTH CAROLINA

**Black Mountain**
Ingle, Robert P. *retail executive*
Lanning, James W. *retail executive*

**Charlotte**
Alexander, R. David *retail executive*
Belk, John Montgomery *retired retail executive, former mayor*
Belk, John R. *retail executive*
Gambrell, Sarah Belk *retail executive*
Kelly, R. James *retail executive*
Levine, Howard R. *retail executive*

**Durham**
Lieberman, Rochelle Phyllis *small business owner*

**Fayetteville**
Shaffer, Denny Richard *small business owner*

**Greensboro**
Goulder, Gerald Polster *retail executive, management consultant, lawyer*
Orlowsky, Martin L. *executive manager*

**Highlands**
Shaffner, Randolph Preston *shop owner, educator, writer, publisher*

**Mooresville**
Black, Kenneth W., Jr. *retail executive*

**North Wilkesboro**
Whiddon, Thomas E. *retail executive*

**Rocky Mount**
Wordsworth, Jerry L. *wholesale distribution executive*

**Salisbury**
Candler, Faxon David *small business owner*

**Sanford**
Kelly, Daniel J. *retail executive*

**Wilkesboro**
Hull, Robert F., Jr., (Bob Hull) *retail executive*

**Winston Salem**
Strickland, Robert Louis *retired retail executive*

## NORTH DAKOTA

**Fargo**
McWilliams, Carey Scott *small business owner, writer*

## OHIO

**Avon Lake**
Parke, M(argaret) Jean *retired business owner, editor*

**Chesterland**
Aster, Ruth Marie Rhydderch *business owner*
Wood, Kenneth Anderson *small business owner, display designer*

**Cincinnati**
Hodge, Robert Joseph *retail executive*
Hoguet, Karen M. *retail executive*
McGeorge, Don W. *retail executive*
Zimmerman, James M. *retail company executive*

**Cleveland**
Crosby, Fred McClellan *retail executive*
Hennessy, Sean P. *retail executive*

**Columbus**
Fishman, Steven S. *retail executive*
Holtz, Diane *retail executive*
Potter, Michael J. *retail stores executive*
Redgrave, Martyn Robert *retail executive*
Schlesinger, Leonard Arthur *retail executive*
Schottenstein, Jay L. *retail executive*
Stevens, Kenneth T. *retail executive*
Thompson, David W. *retail executive*
Turney, Sharon Jester *retail executive*
Wexner, Leslie Herbert *retail executive*
Wilansky, Heywood *retail executive*

**Dayton**
Jenefsky, Jack *wholesale company executive*
Petrick, Joseph Anthony *small business owner, management consultant, educator*

**Grove City**
Rudy, Monica Elaine *small business owner, music educator*

**Hudson**
Webb, Darrell *retail executive*

**Newark**
Black, Boyd Carson *small business owner*

**Pickerington**
Callander, Kay Eileen Paisley *business owner, retired education educator, writer*

**Reynoldsburg**
Fiske, Neil S. *retail executive*

**Shaker Heights**
Killeen, Michael F. *retail executive*

**Toledo**
Grundish, Lee Anne *small business owner, writer*

**Youngstown**
Catoline-Ackerman, Pauline Dessie *small business owner*

## OKLAHOMA

**Oklahoma City**
Davis, Emery Stephen *wholesale food company executive*
Peace, H. W., II, *small business owner, retired oil industry executive*

## OREGON

**Beaverton**
Parker, Mark G. *retail executive*

**Portland**
Thoen, Doris Rae *retired small business owner*

**Salem**
Winters, Jackie F. *small business owner, foundation administrator*

**Tualatin**
Peters, Robert Wayne *small business owner*

## PENNSYLVANIA

**Altoona**
Sheetz, Stanton R. *grocery retail executive*

**Berwyn**
Fry, Clarence Herbert *retired retail executive*

**Camp Hill**
Hall, Christopher S. *retail executive*
Lovett, Keith W. *retail executive*
Miller, Robert G. *drug store chain company executive*
Sammons, Mary F. *retail executive*
Shirtliff, Bryan *retail executive*

**Eighty Four**
Hardy, Joseph A., Sr. *wholesale distribution executive*

**Erie**
Hagen, Thomas Bailey *business owner, former state official, retired insurance company executive*

**Haverford**
Laird, Shirley Eder *small business owner, communications executive*

**Johnstown**
Borkow, Mary P. *small business owner*

**Mercer**
DaCosta, Caroline Lee *small business owner*

**Pipersville**
Sigety, Cornelius Edward *small business owner*

**Pittsburgh**
Stack, Edward W. *retail executive*

**Shiremanstown**
Nesbit, William Terry *small business owner, consultant*

**Washington**
Erdner, Jon W. *small business owner, securities trader*

**Williamsport**
Largen, Joseph *retail executive, purchasing agent*

**Wormleysburg**
Grass, Alexander *retail executive*

**York**
Grumbacher, Tim *retail executive*

## RHODE ISLAND

**Woonsocket**
Bodine, Chris W. *retail executive*
Ferdinandi, V. Michael *retail executive*
Merlo, Larry J. *retail executive*
Rickard, David B. *retail executive*
Ryan, Thomas M. *drug store chain executive*

## SOUTH CAROLINA

**Bluffton**
Orenstein, Fran M. *small business owner, writer*

**Hilton Head Island**
Davis, Mary Martha (Marty Davis) *small business owner, consultant*

**Lexington**
Kennedy, Sandra Elaine *small business owner*

**Yemassee**
Olendorf, William Carr, Jr. *small business owner*

## TENNESSEE

**Gallatin**
Ellis, Joseph Newlin *retired wholesale distribution executive*

**Hermitage**
Reid, Donna Joyce *small business owner*

**Knoxville**
Walker, W. Jack *retired small business owner*

**Mc Minnville**
Harris, Charles Edgar *retired wholesale distribution company executive*

**Memphis**
Hayes, Michael J. *retail executive*
Wright Carrier, J. T. *business owner*

**Nashville**
Zibart, Michael Alan *wholesale book company executive*

## TEXAS

**Athens**
Geddie, Thomas Edwin *retired small business owner*

**Austin**
Girling, Robert George William III *business owner*
Wilson, Margaret Scarbrough *retail executive*

**Bastrop**
Reaves, Melvin Junior *retired small business owner*

**Beaumont**
Alter, Nelson Tobias *retail executive, wholesale distribution executive*

**Corpus Christi**
Finley, George Alvin III *wholesale executive, oil industry executive*

**Dallas**
Augur, Marilyn Hussman *distribution executive*
Bracken, Frank D. *retail executive*
Haggar, J. M. III *retail executive*
Hegi, Frederick B., Jr. *wholesale distribution executive*
Moneypenny, Edward William *retail executive*
Tansky, Burton M. *department store executive*
Wyly, Charles Joseph, Jr. *retail executive*

**El Paso**
Korth, Charlotte Williams *retail executive*
Miller, Deane Guynes *salon and cosmetic studio owner*

**Fort Worth**
Day, Julian C. *retail executive*
Girouard, Marvin J. *retail executive*
Michero, William Henderson *retired retail executive*
Roach, John Vinson, II, *retail company executive*
West, Sylvia Wandell *small business owner, director, educator, researcher*

**Gainesville**
Brooks, Jerry Robert *small business owner*

**Horseshoe Bay**
Simpson, H. Richard (Dick Simpson) *retail buyer*

**Houston**
Castillo, Josephine *small business owner, educator*
Gaucher, Jane Montgomery *retail executive*
Levit, Max *wholesale distribution executive, food service executive*
Spitler, Kenneth F. *wholesale distribution executive*
Texas, Sam Fayad *small business owner, political activist*
Woodhouse, John Frederick *food distribution company executive*

**Humble**
Hatch, Richard Clawson *small business owner, magician*

**Irving**
Burton, Betsey (Mary Elizabeth Burton) *retail executive*
Buthman, Mark A. *retail executive*
Rouleau, R. Michael *retail executive*
Wyly, Samuel E. *retail executive*

**Longview**
McKinley, Jimmie Joe *small business owner*

**Plano**
Cavanaugh, Robert B. *department store executive*
Harris, Wayne *retail executive*
Neppl, Walter Joseph *retired retail executive*
Questrom, Allen I. *retail executive*
Raish, Stephen E *retail executive*
West, Catherine G. *retail executive*

**Powell**
Emerson, Harriett Anne *small business owner*

**San Antonio**
Williams, Docia Schultz *small business owner*

**Seabrook**
Spears, James Grady *small business owner*

**Snyder**
Gray, Donna Lea *small business owner*

**Tyler**
Brookshire, Bruce G. *retail grocery store executive*
Edwards, D. M. *retail executive, wholesale distribution executive, real estate company executive*

**Vernon**
Mikkelsen, Barbara Berry *retired retail executive, rancher*

**Waxahachie**
Johnson, Ronald Kay *retail company executive*

**Wimberley**
Ellis, John *small business owner*

## UTAH

**Salt Lake City**
Fields, Debbi (Debra Fields Rose) *cookie franchise executive*

## VERMONT

**Colchester**
Lawton, Lorilee Ann *small business owner, accountant*

**Danby**
Peel, Harris *retired small business owner*

**Vergennes**
Grant, Edwin Randolph *retail executive, manufacturing executive*

## VIRGINIA

**Bristow**
Schrock, Simon *retail executive*

**Charlottesville**
Crutchfield, William Gayle, Jr. *retail executive*

**Chesapeake**
Brock, Macon F., Sr. *retail company executive*
Brock, Macon F., Jr. *retail company executive*
Coble, Frederick Charles *retail executive*
Sasser, Bob *retail company executive*
Sasser, Robert *retail executive*

**Fairfax**
Pugh, Arthur James (Jay Pugh) *retired retail executive*

**Mc Lean**
Vandemark, Robert Goodyear *retired retail executive*

**Midlothian**
MacAvery, Tristan Alexander (Tristan Black Wolf) *small business owner, writer, actor*

**Occoquan**
Nemecek, Albert Duncan, Jr. *retail executive, investment banker, management consultant*

**Purcellville**
Sharples, Winston Singleton *automobile importer and distributor*

**Reston**
Lee, Jong Rim *strategic sourcing executive*

**Richmond**
Casini, Jane Sloan *wholesale distribution executive*
Dias, Fiona P. *retail executive*
Schoonover, Philip J. *retail executive*
Sharp, Richard L. *retail company executive*

**Salem**
Brand, Edward Cabell *retail executive*

**Upperville**
Powell Gebhard, Joy Lee (Bok Sin Lee) *small business owner*

**Vienna**
Edwards, Phillip Milton *retired import/export company executive*

**Williamsburg**
Cauthen, Charles Edward, Jr. *retired retail executive, management consultant*

## WASHINGTON

**Everett**
Olsen-Estie, Jeanne Lindell *golf course owner*

**Issaquah**
Brotman, Jeffrey H. *wholesale distribution executive*
DiCerchio, Richard D. *wholesale distribution executive*
Galanti, Richard A. *wholesale business executive*
Sinegal, James D. *wholesale distribution executive*

**Redmond**
Brakken, William *home improvement retail executive*

**Seattle**
Bridge, Herbert Marvin *retail executive*
Leale, Olivia Mason *small business owner, import marketing executive*
Moya, Cynthia Ann *small business owner, librarian*
Nordstrom, Blake W. *retail executive*
Nordstrom, Bruce A. *department store executive*

**Silverdale**
Balcomb, Mary Nelson *small business owner*

**Spokane**
Chamberlain, Barbara Kaye *small business owner, communications executive*
Leighton, Jack Richard *small business owner, former educator*
Sines, Randy Dwain *retail executive*

**Tacoma**
Frantz, Dale Nelson *automobile import processing company executive*

**Vancouver**
Scott, Gary LeRoy *small business owner, photographer*

**Yakima**
Newland, Ruth Laura *small business owner*

## WEST VIRGINIA

**Martinsburg**
Ayers, Anne Louise *small business owner, consultant, counselor*

## WISCONSIN

**Beloit**
Hendricks, Kenneth *wholesale distribution executive*

**Bowler**
Bartholomaus, Brett William *small business owner*

**Eau Claire**
Helland, Mark Duane *small business owner*
Menard, John R., Jr. *home improvement retail executive*

**Green Bay**
Eugster, Jack Wilson *retail executive*

**Madison**
Fahien, Rose Marian *small business owner*

**Menomonee Falls**
Mansell, Kevin B. *retail executive*
Marshall, Jeffery M. *retail executive*
McDonald, Wesley S. *retail executive*
Montgomery, R. Lawrence *retail executive*

**Milwaukee**
Mariano, Robert A. *retail executive*

## WYOMING

**Jackson**
Law, Clarene Alta *small business owner, retired state legislator*

# CANADA

## ALBERTA

**Calgary**
Slater, Cody *retail executive*

## MANITOBA

**Winnipeg**
Cohen, Albert Diamond *retail executive*

## ONTARIO

**Toronto**
Verschuren, Annette *retail executive*

# CHINA

**Shanghai**
Chueh, Chun Fei *import/export company executive*

# ENGLAND

**London**
Habgood, Anthony John *wholesale distribution executive*

# SWEDEN

**Stockholm**
van den Bosch, Margareta *apparel company executive*

# ADDRESS UNPUBLISHED

Adamson, James B. *retail executive*
Babrowski, Claire Harbeck *retail executive*
Baker, Edward Kevin *retail executive*
Barlow, John Leon *retired retail executive*
Barnes, Sandra Kay *small business owner*
Barth, David Keck *wholesale distribution executive, consultant*
Bell, Sharon Kaye *small business owner*
Bernstein, Ellen *business owner*
Blackwell, Vickie Jan *small business owner*
Blagden, Susan Lowndes *retired small business owner*
Blum, Gerald Henry *retired retail executive*
Boire, Ron *retail executive*
Boyer, Jeffrey N. *former retail executive*
Busch, Joyce Ida *small business owner*
Carlson-Rukavina, Patricia Ann *small business owner*
Castro, Teresa Jacira *small business owner*
Chevalier, Paul Edward *retired retail executive, lawyer*
Conaway, Charles C. *former retail company executive*
Connolly, Violette M. *small business owner*
Cope, Kenneth Wayne *retail executive*
Cosby, Mark S. *retail executive*
Cox, Joy Dean *small business owner*
Criancamilli, Andrew A. *retail executive*
DeVivo, Ange *retired small business owner*
Dodds-Metts, Rebecca *wholesale company executive*
Donley, Russell Lee III *small business owner, former state legislator*
Dowling, Doris Anderson *business owner, educator, consultant*
Drury, John R. *retail executive*
Dufour, Jack Edward *small business owner, retired special education educator*
Dunham, John L. *retail company executive*
Dusenbury, Ruth Ellen Cole *business owner*
Edwards, Patrick Ross *retail executive, lawyer, management consultant*
Edwards, Priscilla Ann *small business owner*
Ettore, Joseph R. *retired discount department store chain executive*
Evans, James D., Jr. *retail executive*
Evans, Robert George, Jr. *retail and mail order executive*
Eyler, John H., Jr. *retail toy and game company executive*
Farr, Ivanne Estelle *small business owner, consultant, artist, sculptor*
Feuer, Marshall Zev *import/export company executive*
Fields, Douglas Philip *building supply wholesale company executive*
Finnigan, Robert Emmet *retired small business owner*
Follit, Evelyn V. *retail executive*
Gamroth, Arthur Paul *small business owner*
Goldner, Sheldon Herbert *retired import/export company executive*
Goldstein, Michael *retail executive*
Goldstein, Norman Ray *international trading company executive, consultant*
Gorey, Thomas C. *retail executive*
Gozon, Richard C. *retired paper distribution executive*
Gust, Anne Baldwin *former retail apparel company executive*
Guzman, Carole L. *small business owner*
Hambrecht, Patricia G. *retail executive*
Hirsch, Larry Joseph *retired retail executive, lawyer*
Holzkamp, Jane Strauss *business owner*
Jenkins, Charles H., Jr. *retail company executive*
Johnson, Dolores Estelle *retired small business owner*
Jourdan, Toni Christina *small business owner, actress, writer*
Kipper, Barbara Levy *wholesale distribution executive*
Kirby, Odell *retired small business owner, newswriter, writer*
Kogut, John Anthony *wholesale distribution executive*
Kwasnick, Paul Jack *retail executive*
Lacy, Alan Jasper *retired retail executive*
Lang, William Charles *retail executive*
LaPorta, Sara *retail executive*
Larrimore, Randall Walter *retired wholesale company executive*
Lazaran, Frank *former retail executive*
Lifson, Kalman Alan *retired retail executive, bank executive, portfolio manager*
Lipsey, Joseph, Jr. *wholesale distribution executive*
Livingston, James Bristol *educational services owner, writer, retired secondary school educator*
London, Michael *retail executive*
Lopez, M. Edward *small business owner*
Marcus, Lee Evan *small business owner, consultant, educator*
Masten, Jacqueline Gwendolyn *small business owner*
Matthews, Norman Stuart *retail executive*
McClendon, Irvin Lee, Sr. *small business owner, editor*
McConnell, Jack Baylor *retired corporate executive, physician*
McDougall, Ronald Alexander *restaurant executive*
McGraw, Lavinia Morgan *retired retail executive*
Medaglia, Elizabeth Ellen *small business owner*
Meek, Forrest Burns *retired trading company executive*
Mench, John William *retail executive, electrical engineer*
Metz, Steven William *small business owner*
Milstein, Monroe Gary *retail executive*
Mortenson, Janice Gayle Mills *business owner, accountant*
Nemiroff, Maxine Celia *small business owner, art historian*
Newman, Richard Lancaster *aviation consultant, educator*
Nicolas, Kenneth Lee *import/export company executive*
Nishimura, Joseph Yo *retired retail executive, accountant*
Orem, Cassandra Elizabeth (Sandra Orem) *small business owner, educator, holistic health consultant and practitioner*
Oxnam, Philip Linton *small business owner*
Paterson, Robert E. *retail executive*
Peach, Robert Westly *retired small business owner, engineer*
Perez, William D. *retail executive*
Peterson, Gary J *retail executive*
Pham, Lara Bach-Vien *small business owner*
Phillips, Kathleen Gay *small business owner*
Post, Jerry T *retail executive*
Pride, Dena Beth *small business owner*
Ransome, Ernest Leslie III *retail executive*
Raskin, Michael A. *retail executive, director*
Raymond, Ural Wayne *retired retail executive*
Reece, Karyn Lynn *small business owner, consultant*
Ritchey, Samuel Donley, Jr. *retired retail executive*
Roberts, Patricia Lee *small business owner, consultant*
Rodbell, Clyde Armand *retired distribution executive*
Rogaczewski, Sherrie Reece *small business owner, singer*
Rohner, Bonnie-Jean *small business owner, computer scientist, consultant*
Rowland, Allen R. *former retail executive*
Ruland, Mildred Ardelia *retail executive, retail buyer*
Samson, Alvin *former distributing company executive, consultant*
Scott, Sylvia Jane *small business owner*
Segal, Robert S. *retail executive*
Shannon, Patrick S. *retail executive*
Spitzer, Matthew Lawrence *retired retail store executive*
Stettner, Jerald Walter *retired retail executive*
Stronach, Belinda *former retail executive*
Swanson, Kurt *small business owner, artist*
Szczublewski, Wendy Sue *small business owner, musician, freelance/self-employed writer*
Terry, Carole Cosgrove *small business owner, historian, researcher*
Thompson, Mary Koleta *small business owner, not-for-profit developer*
Tudor, Brenda S. *retail company executive*
Turner, Natalie A. *retired consultant*
Van Gelder, Marc Christiaan *retail executive*
Vernon, Carl Atlee, Jr. *retired wholesale food distributor executive*
Wagner, Cheri J. *business owner*
Wallpher, Luis Antonio *small business owner, painter, writer*
Weiss, Michael Allen *retail executive*
Wessling, Gregory Jay *retail executive*
Willingham, Mary Maxine *fashion retailer*
Wolf, Charles A. *retail camera and photographic supplies executive*
Woodrow, Kenneth B. *retired retail company executive*
Zimmers, Vivian Eleanor *small business owner, consultant*

# INDUSTRY: TRANSPORTATION

## UNITED STATES

### ALABAMA

**Abbeville**
Anderson, Ruth T. *retired air traffic controller*

**Birmingham**
Campbell, Charles Alton *transportation executive*
Haworth, Michael Elliott, Jr. *aerospace company executive*

**Gulf Shores**
Wallace, John Loys *retired aviation services executive*

### ALASKA

**Anchorage**
Shively, John Terry *cruise line executive*
Sullivan, George Murray *transportation executive, consultant, retired mayor*
Williams, Eleanor Joyce *retired government air traffic control specialist*

### ARIZONA

**Goodyear**
Borton, George Robert *retired airline captain*

**Grand Canyon**
Bryant, Leland Marshal *business and nonprofit executive*

**Phoenix**
Cunningham, Robert W. *trucking executive*
Enzor, Gary R. *trucking executive*
Gillette, Robert J. *aerospace transportation executive*
Johnson, Robert D. *aerospace transportation executive*
Moyes, Jerry C. *transportation executive*

**Prescott**
Waldock, William David *aerospace transportation executive*

**Tempe**
Crellin, Alan W. *air transportation executive*
Kerr, Derek J. *transportation executive*
Parker, W. Douglas (Doug Parker) *air transportation executive*

**Tucson**
Mercker, Mary Alice *aviation school administrator*

### ARKANSAS

**Bella Vista**
Pogue, William Reid *retired astronaut, foundation administrator, aerospace scientist, consultant*

**Fort Smith**
Davidson, Robert A. *trucking executive*
Young, Robert A. III *freight systems executive*

**Huntsville**
Carr, Gerald Paul *retired astronaut, retired engineer, retired marketing professional, retired military officer*

**Lowell**
Garrison, Wayne *transportation executive*
Hunt, J. B. (Johnnie Bryan Hunt) *retired transportation executive*
Thompson, Kirk *transportation executive*

### CALIFORNIA

**Beverly Hills**
Willson, James Douglas *aerospace transportation executive*

**Concord**
Orris, Donald C. *freight transporation executive*

**Dana Point**
Wolf, Karl Everett *aerospace transportation executive, communications executive*

**Edwards**
Brand, Vance Devoe *astronaut, director*

**El Segundo**
Freeland, Pete *aerospace transportation executive, consultant*
Musk, Elon *aerospace transportation executive*

**Fremont**
Smith, Bernald Stephen *retired pilot*

**Hermosa Beach**
Kokalj, James Edward *retired aerospace administrator*

**Huntington Beach**
Burson, Thomas Daniel *retired aerospace executive*

**Irvine**
Crowley, Daniel Francis, Jr. *transportation and logistics executive*

**La Jolla**
Drake, Hudson Billings *aerospace executive, electronics executive*

**La Mesa**
Hansen, Grant Lewis *retired air transportation executive*

**La Palma**
Knowles, Marie L. *transportation executive*

**Long Beach**
Myers, John Wescott *air transportation executive*

**Los Angeles**
Bruce, William A. *airport executive*
Gasich, Welko Elton *retired aerospace transportation executive, management consultant*
Ingram, Theodore Francis *transportation executive*
Mager, Artur *retired aerospace executive*
Mall, William John, Jr. *aerospace transportation executive, retired military officer*
Myers, Albert F. *aerospace executive*
Park, Sam-Koo *transportation executive*

**Malibu**
Ensign, Richard Papworth *transportation executive*

**Marina Del Rey**
Gregg, Lucius Perry, Jr. *aerospace transportation executive*

**Mojave**
Binnie, Brian *pilot, transportation executive*
Melvill, Michael W. *aircraft company executive, experimental test pilot*

**Newbury Park**
Lindsey, Joanne M. *flight attendant, poet*

**Oakland**
Andrasick, James Stephen *transportation executive*
Haskell, Arthur Jacob *retired water transportation executive*

**Oceanside**
Miller, Donald Eugene *retired air traffic controller*

**Palo Alto**
O'Brien, Raymond Francis *transportation executive*

**Palos Verdes Estates**
Smith, Stephen Randolph *aerospace executive*

**Palos Verdes Peninsula**
Slusser, Robert Wyman *aerospace transportation executive*

**Pasadena**
Kennard, Lydia H. *airport terminal executive*

**Pleasanton**
Wu, Jia Hao *transportation executive, researcher, consultant*

**Ramona**
Hoffman, Wayne Melvin *retired airline official*

**Redlands**
Skomal, Edward Nelson *retired aerospace transportation executive, electromagnetic environments consultant*

**Richmond**
Shladover, Steven Elliot *transportation research professional*

**Sacramento**
Acree, G. Hardy *airport executive*

**San Diego**
Mc Kinnon, Clinton Dan *aerospace transportation executive*
Reading, James Edward *transportation executive*

**San Francisco**
Foret, Mickey Phillip *retired air transportation executive*
Martin, John L. *airport executive*
Royer, Kathleen Rose *pilot*

**San Jose**
Stapleton, Beverly Cooper *aerospace executive*

**San Luis Obispo**
Williams, David Alexander *retired chief pilot*

**San Mateo**
Pileggi, Jennifer Wendy *transportation services executive*
Stotlar, Douglas W. *transportation executive*
Trabitz, Eugene Leonard *aerospace company executive*

**Santa Monica**
Roney, Robert Kenneth *retired aerospace transportation executive*

**Saratoga**
Reagan, Joseph Bernard *retired aerospace executive, management consultant*

**Simi Valley**
Eberhard-Neveaux, Christine *aviation executive, dispute resolution executive*

**Stockton**
Biddle, Donald Ray *aerospace transportation executive*

**Torrance**
Brown, Adriane M. *aerospace transportation executive*
Esmond, Donald V. *transportation executive*
Yamamoto, Akimasa *transportation executive*

**Ventura**
Downs, Floella McIntyre *retired ferry pilot, instructor, flight examiner*

**COLORADO**

**Denver**
McMorris, Jerry *transportation company executive, sports team executive*

**Littleton**
Kleinknecht, Kenneth Samuel *retired air transportation executive*

**CONNECTICUT**

**Hartford**
Page, Stephen Franklin *aerospace transportation executive*

**Noank**
Leeds, Robin Leigh *transportation executive*

**Stamford**
Barker, James Rex *water transportation executive, director*
Tregurtha, Paul Richard *water transportation executive*

**DELAWARE**

**Lewes**
Poulterer, William Taylor III *river pilot*

**DISTRICT OF COLUMBIA**

**Washington**
Altschul, Alfred Samuel *airline executive*
Carmody, Carol Jones *transportation executive, former federal agency administrator*
Chapman, Thomas B. *air transportation executive*
Donovan, George Joseph *transportation executive, consultant*
Downs, Thomas Michael (Tom Downs) *transportation executive*
Kummant, Alexander K. *rail transportation executive*
Willis, Kevin *airport administrator*

**FLORIDA**

**Boca Raton**
Garelick, Martin *retired transportation executive*
Iacobucci, Edward E. *air transportation executive, former software company executive*

**Fort Lauderdale**
Donaway, Carl D. *messenger service executive*

**Jacksonville**
Crowe, Jeffrey C. *transportation executive*
Gerkens, Henry H. *trucking executive*
Kneller, Michael *transportation services executive*
Ward, Michael J. *rail transportation executive*

**Medley**
Leinbach, Tracy A. *transportation executive*

**Miami**
Bald, Gary M. *cruise line executive, former federal agency administrator*
Cento, Juan N. *delivery service executive*
Centro, Juan N. *air transportation executive*
Fain, Richard David *cruise line executive*
Swienton, Gregory T. *transportation company executive*
Williams, Eric Joseph *transportation executive*

**Naples**
Myers, Robert Jay *retired air transportation executive*

**Orlando**
Kennedy, James W. *aerospace transportation executive*
Leonard, Joseph B. *airline company executive*
Pearlman, Louis Jay *aviation executive, entertainment company executive*

**Plantation**
Fellows, John *delivery service executive*
Smartt, Bill *air courier company executive*
Waller, Stephen *air transportation executive*

**Ponte Vedra Beach**
Hamilton, William Berry, Jr. *retired transportation executive*

**Sanibel**
Hasselman, Richard B. *retired rail transportation executive*

**Satellite Beach**
Loney, Mary Rose *former airport administrator, aviation industry consultant*

**Thonotosassa**
Jordan, Frederick Leroy *trucking executive*

**Vero Beach**
Ingwersen, Martin Lewis *water transportation executive*

**Weeki Wachee**
Luffsey, Walter Stith *air transportation executive, consultant*

**GEORGIA**

**Alpharetta**
Chatlen, Stanley Lee *transportation executive*
McCullough, Ross A., Jr. *delivery service executive*

**Atlanta**
Barnes, David A. *delivery service executive*
Bastian, Edward H. *air transportation executive*
Beystehner, John J. *transportation executive*
Bridges, Shirley Walton *air transportation executive*
Darden, Calvin *delivery service executive*
DeCosta, Benjamin R. *airport executive*
Eskew, Michael L. *package distribution company executive*
Grinstein, Gerald *air transportation executive*
Hill, Allen Edward *transportation services executive*
Loewy, Robert Gustav *aerospace executive, engineering educator*
McDevitt, John *delivery service executive*
Robb, Curtis *air transportation executive*
Stent, Terry *pilot, art collector*

**Decatur**
Duffy, Thomas M. *transportation services executive, lawyer*

**Marietta**
Clarkson, Lawrence William *air transportation executive*

**Newnan**
McBroom, Thomas William, Sr. *aviation consultant*

**Roswell**
Dolan, Dennis Joseph *pilot, lawyer*

**HAWAII**

**Honolulu**
Doane, W. Allen *water transportation executive*

**IDAHO**

**Boise**
Ilett, Frank, Jr. *trucking executive, educator*

**Idaho Falls**
Thorsen, James Hugh *retired aviation director, retired airport manager*

**ILLINOIS**

**Arlington Heights**
Hudson, Ronald Morgan *aviation planner*

**Chicago**
Andolino, Rosemarie *airport terminal executive*
Apelbaum, Phyllis L. *delivery messenger service executive*
Bell, James A. *aerospace transportation executive*
Burkhardt, Edward Arnold *rail transportation executive*
Fischbach, Charles Peter *rail transportation executive, consultant, lawyer, arbitrator, mediator*
Gibson, Roger *air transportation executive*
Hill, Shepard W. *air transportation executive*
Lower, Joseph *air transportation executive*
Luttig, J. Michael (John Michael Luttig) *aerospace transportation executive, former federal judge*
McNerney, James, Jr., (W. James McNerney) *aerospace transportation executive, former manufacturing executive*
Nord, Henry J. *transportation executive*
Tilton, Glenn F. *air transportation executive*

**Downers Grove**
Yeager, David P. *transportation executive*

**Elk Grove Village**
Brace, Frederic F. (Jake Brace) *air transportation executive*

**Lake Forest**
Krasnewich, Kathryn *water transportation executive*

**Marion**
Crane, Hugh Wingate *railroad executive*

**Naperville**
Benson, Kevin E. *transportation executive*
Stangl, Peter E. *transportation executive*

**Oak Brook**
Duerinck, Louis T. *retired rail transportation executive, lawyer*
Veno, Ronald James, Jr. *travel industry executive*

**Park Ridge**
Carr, Gilbert Randle *retired railroad executive*

**Warrenville**
Ustian, Daniel C. *trucking executive*

**Westmont**
Kelley, Brian P. *transportation executive*

**Wood Dale**
Goodwin, James E. *retired air transportation executive*

**INDIANA**

**Fort Wayne**
Sperone, Kenneth J. *transportation executive*

**Griffith**
Luetschwager, Mary Susan *transportation executive*

**Indianapolis**
Mikelsons, J. George *air transportation executive*
Wensits, David L. *aerospace transportation executive*

**Noblesville**
Morrison, Joseph Young *transportation executive, consultant*

**Princeton**
Okamoto, Seizo *transportation executive*

**IOWA**

**Des Moines**
Kandris, Michael *trucking executive*

**KANSAS**

**Overland Park**
Zollars, William D. *freight company executive*

**Wichita**
Meyer, Russell William, Jr. *air transportation executive*

**KENTUCKY**

**Franklin**
Clark, James Benton *retired rail transportation executive*

**Louisville**
Carranza, Jovita *delivery service executive*
Hayes, William Meredith *pilot, retired military officer*

**LOUISIANA**

**New Orleans**
Chetta, Holly Ann *transportation executive*
Johnson, Peter Forbes *transportation executive, business owner*

**MARYLAND**

**Baltimore**
Glassman, Jon David *aerospace executive*
McDaniel, Wayne Allen *transportation executive, consultant*

**Bethesda**
Kubasik, Christopher E. *aerospace transportation executive*
Smith, Albert E. *areonautics company professional*
Tourino, Ralph Gene *aerospace transportation executive*

**Gaithersburg**
Owen, Thomas Barron *aerospace transportation executive, retired military officer*

**Owings Mills**
Colussy, Dan Alfred *aviation executive*

**Patuxent River**
Vitatoe, Lee Anne *aerospace medicine executive, aerospace physiologist*

**Potomac**
Fthenakis, Emanuel John *air transportation executive*

**MASSACHUSETTS**

**Belmont**
Baddour, Anne Bridge *pilot*

**Boston**
Klotz, Charles Rodger *water transportation executive, investment company executive*

**Brookline**
Frankel, Ernst Gabriel *shipping and aviation business executive, educator*

**Cambridge**
John, Richard Rodda *transportation executive*

**Chatham**
Bohman, Raynard Frederick, Jr. *transportation executive, consultant, professional society administrator*

**Concord**
Smith, Eric Parkman *retired railroad executive*

**Cotuit**
Ballou, Kenneth Walter *retired business executive, retired dean*

**East Boston**
Coy, Craig P. *airport terminal executive*

**Falmouth**
McInnes, Donald Gordon *rail transportation executive*

**Gloucester**
Oder, Frederic Carl Emil *retired aerospace transportation executive*

**North Billerica**
Mellon, Timothy *transportation executive*

**Waltham**
Caine, Franklyn A. *aerospace transportation executive*
Neumann, Ed *human resource executive*

## MICHIGAN

**Ann Arbor**
Bagian, James Philip *former astronaut, public health service officer, medical educator*
Drake, John Warren *aviation consultant*
Yamashina, Tadashi (George) *transportation executive*

**Detroit**
Ali, Murad Cajetan *transportation executive, writer*

**Grand Rapids**
Auwers, Stanley John *motor carrier executive*

**Waterford**
Randall, Karl W. *air transportation executive, lawyer*

## MINNESOTA

**Eagan**
Steenland, Douglas M. *air transportation executive*

**Eden Prairie**
Lindbloom, Chad M. *transportation executive*
Radunz, Paul A. *transportation executive*
Wiehoff, John P. *trucking executive*

**Minneapolis**
Harper, Donald Victor *retired transportation and logistics educator, consultant*
Nyrop, Donald William *air transportation executive*
Olson, James Richard *retired transportation executive*

**North Oaks**
Engle, Donald Edward *retired rail transportation executive, lawyer*

**Saint Paul**
Cohen, Neal S. *former air transportation executive*
Wilson, Gary Lee *airline company executive*

**Warba**
Currie, Earl James *transportation executive*

## MISSISSIPPI

**Pass Christian**
Clark, John Walter, Jr. *water transportation executive*

## MISSOURI

**Fenton**
Huber, Scott *transportation services executive*
McClure, Richard H. *transportation executive*
Stadler, Gerald P. *transportation executive*

**Kansas City**
Baisden, Eleanor Marguerite *retired airline compensation executive, consultant*

**Saint Louis**
Albaugh, James F. *aerospace transportation executive*
Graff, George Stephen *aerospace transportation executive*
Griggs, Leonard LeRoy, Jr. *air transportation executive, consultant*
McDonnell, Sanford Noyes *air transportation executive*
Ross, Donald *transportation executive*

**Springfield**
Moss, Elizabeth Lucille (Betty Moss) *retired transportation executive*

**Tecumseh**
Davis, Michael Chase *retired aerospace engineering executive, retired military officer*

## NEBRASKA

**Omaha**
Davidson, Richard K. *railroad company executive*
Knight, Robert M., Jr. *rail transportation executive*
Smithey, Donald Leon *airport authority director*
Werner, Clarence L. *transportation executive*
Young, James R. *railroad transportation executive*

## NEVADA

**Las Vegas**
Walker, Randall H. *air transportation executive*

**Nellis Afb**
Malachowski, Nicole *pilot*

**Reno**
Shoen, Edward Joseph *transportation and insurance companies executive*

**Stateline**
Sprague, Billy Michael *aerospace transportation executive*

**Yerington**
Burrowes, Robert Arthur *transportation consultant, travel-tour operator*

## NEW JERSEY

**Cherry Hill**
Resor, Randolph Richardson *transportation consultant*

**Flemington**
Kettler, Carl Frederick *airline executive*

**Martinsville**
Weiss, Allan Joseph *transport company executive, lawyer*

**Moonachie**
Ueltschi, Albert Lee *air transportation executive*

**Morristown**
Olcott, John Whiting *air transportation executive*

**Mount Laurel**
Batory, Ronald Louis *rail transportation executive*

**Mullica Hill**
Rose, Carol Ann *retired air transportation executive*

**Newark**
Baer, Susan M. *airport executive*
Warrington, George D. *rail transportation executive*

**North Bergen**
Pohan, Armand *transportation executive, professional hockey club executive, lawyer*

**Pennington**
Kelly, Quentin Thorn *water and power company executive, writer*

**Roseland**
Sugahara, Byron Masahiko *transportation executive*

**Union**
White, Robert Leslie Gordon, Jr. *aerospace transportation executive*

**Wharton**
Krosser, Howard S. *aerospace transportation executive*

**Woodbridge**
Santulli, Richard T. *air transportation executive*

## NEW MEXICO

**Albuquerque**
Figueroa, Francisco Armando *aerospace transportation executive, accountant*
Masefield, Oliver Leslie Peter *aerospace transportation executive, aerospace engineer*
Weh, Allen Edward *aviation executive*

## NEW YORK

**Albany**
Joyce, William George, Jr. *transportation executive*

**Babylon**
Collis, Charles *air transportation executive*

**Bethpage**
Baglio, Vincent Paul *aerospace transportation executive*

**Carmel**
Shen, Chia Theng *retired water transportation executive, religious organization administrator*

**Centerport**
Trotta, Ric Charles *aerospace transportation executive, consultant*

**Cooperstown**
Rich, Walter George *railroad transportation executive*

**Flushing**
Kroeppel, Warren *airport terminal executive*

**Forest Hills**
Neeleman, David *air transportation executive*

**Garden City**
Campbell, James R. *transportation executive*

**Greenport**
Jackson, Richard Montgomery *air transportation executive*

**Jamestown**
Walker, Timothy Craig *transportation executive*

**Kingston**
McGuire, Thomas Peter *water transportation executive, secondary school educator*

**New York**
Apostolakis, James John *shipping company executive, pharmaceutical executive*
Armstrong, Neil A. *former astronaut*
Chao, James Si-Cheng *maritime executive*
Evans, James Hurlburt *retired transportation and natural resources executive*
Fugazy, William Denis *transportation company executive*
Moss, Sara E. *delivery service executive, lawyer*
Salerno, F. Robert *car rental company executive*
Schiano, Charles *transportation executive*
Sinagra, Jack G. *air transportation executive*
Spinetta, Jean-Cyril *airline executive*
Thayer, Russell III *air transportation executive*
Treitel, David Henry *aviation executive*
Weinstein, Martin *aerospace transportation executive, manufacturing executive, materials scientist*

**Northport**
Reinertsen, Norman *retired air transportation executive*

**Peekskill**
Harte, Andrew Dennis *transportation company executive, travel agent*

## NORTH CAROLINA

**Chapel Hill**
Moellering, John Henry *aviation maintenance company executive*

**Charlotte**
Handy, John W. *shipping company executive, retired military officer*

**Cherryville**
Mayhew, Kenneth Edwin, Jr. *retired transportation executive*

**Kannapolis**
Thigpen, Alton Hill *transportation executive*

**Spindale**
Howard, Elizabeth Ann Blanton *transportation executive*

## OHIO

**Akron**
Moriarty, John Timothy *transportation consultant, writer*

**Cleveland**
Dannemiller, John C. *transportation company executive*

**Columbus**
Mason, Raymond E., Jr. *distributing company executive*

**Pottersburg**
Bilderback, George Garrison III *transportation and logistics professional*

**Rocky River**
Shively, Daniel Jerome *retired transportation executive*

**Wilmington**
Hete, Joseph C. *air transportation executive*

**Xenia**
Bigelow, Daniel James *aerospace executive*

## OKLAHOMA

**Grove**
Trippensee, Gary Alan *retired aerospace executive*

## OREGON

**Eugene**
Toolson, Kay *transportation executive*

**Medford**
Rogers, Gardner Spencer *railroad company executive*

**Portland**
Guillen, Jerome *trucking executive*

## PENNSYLVANIA

**Allentown**
Doughty, George Franklin *airport administrator*

**Bristol**
Shenefelt, Arthur B. *transportation executive, consultant*

**Clarion**
Canaday, Doris Charlene *retired traffic representative*

**Philadelphia**
Terry, John Joseph *transportation investor*

**Radnor**
Cunningham, James Gerald, Jr. *transportation company executive*

**Red Lion**
Hartman, Charles Henry *transportation executive, educator, not-for-profit executive*

**Washington**
Kastelic, Robert Frank *aerospace transportation executive*

**Wilkes Barre**
Holtzman, Marc Lawrence *catalog chain executive*

**York**
Grossman, Robert Allen *transportation executive*

## RHODE ISLAND

**Providence**
Campbell, Lewis B. *aerospace technology executive*

## SOUTH CAROLINA

**Columbia**
Conrad, Paul Ernest *transportation consultant*

**Greer**
Jackson, J. Garrett (Gary Jackson) *airport terminal executive*

**Hilton Head Island**
Hoppin, Thomas Edward *retired transportation executive*

## TENNESSEE

**Chattanooga**
Harlin, Ray M. *trucking executive*
Pate, Lisa M. *transportation services executive, lawyer*
Quinn, Patrick *transportation executive*

**Memphis**
Aaholm, Sherry A. *delivery service executive*
Carter, Robert B. *delivery service executive*
Glenn, T. Michael *delivery/messenger service executive*
Graf, Alan B., Jr. *transportation executive*
Harris, Terrell Lee (Terry Harris) *delivery services company executive, former prosecutor*
Reid, Karen Denise *aerospace transportation executive, writer*
Richards, Christine P. *transportation services executive*
Smith, Frederick Wallace *delivery service executive*

**Morristown**
Johnson, Evelyn Bryan *airport terminal executive*

**Nashville**
Ingram, Orrin Henry, II, *transportation executive*

## TEXAS

**Arlington**
Joyner, Henry Curtis *airline executive*

**Dallas**
Adams, John Lewis *transportation executive*
Arpey, Gerard J. *air transportation executive*
Barrett, Colleen Crotty *air transportation executive*
Fegan, Jeffrey P. *airport executive*
Kelleher, Herbert David *air transportation executive, lawyer*
Kelly, Gary C. *air transportation executive*
Laney, David M. *railroad industry executive, lawyer*
Wright, Laura L. *air transportation executive*

**Denton**
Alatzas, George *delivery service company executive*

**Fort Worth**
Bowler, Peter M. *air transportation executive*
Brennan, Edward A. *air transportation executive, former retail executive*
Endres, Arthur P. (Skip Endres) *rail transportation executive*
Hoferer, Paul R. *rail transportation executive, lawyer*
Horton, Thomas W. *air transportation executive, former telecommunications company executive*
Hund, Thomas N. *rail transportation executive*
Kennedy, Gary F. *air transportation executive, lawyer*
Krebs, Robert Duncan *rail transportation company executive*
Rose, Matthew K. *rail transportation executive*

**Fredericksburg**
Scannell, William Edward *aerospace transportation executive, consultant, psychologist*

**Houston**
Ashby, Jeffrey S. *astronaut*
Baker, Ellen Shulman *astronaut, physician*
Barry, Allan Ronald *ship pilot, corporate executive*
Brandenstein, Daniel Charles *astronaut, retired military officer*
Burbank, Daniel C. *astronaut*
Cabana, Robert D. *aerospace transportation executive, astronaut*
Cagle, Yvonne Darlene *astronaut*
Camarda, Charles J. *astronaut*
Chiao, Leroy *astronaut*
Cockrell, Kenneth Dale *astronaut*
Coleman, Catherine G. *astronaut*
Crane, James R. *delivery service executive*
Currie, Nancy Jane *astronaut*
Ferguson, Christopher J. *astronaut*
Fincke, Edward Michael (Mike) *astronaut*
Foreman, Michael J. *astronaut*
Fossum, Michael E. *astronaut*
Higginbotham, Joan E. *astronaut*

Howell, Jefferson Davis, Jr. *aerospace transportation executive, retired military officer*
Jett, Brent W., Jr. *astronaut, military officer*
Kelly, James M. *astronaut, military officer*
Kelly, Mark E. *astronaut*
Kilrain, Susan *astronaut*
Kregel, Kevin R. *astronaut*
Lawrence, Wendy B. *astronaut*
Leonard, Charles H. (Chuck Leonard) *air transportation executive*
Lindsey, Steven W. *astronaut, military officer*
Lu, Edward Tsang *astronaut*
MacLean, Steve(n) G. *astronaut*
McArthur, William Surles, Jr. *astronaut, retired military officer*
Melroy, Pamela Ann *astronaut*
Misner, Jeffrey J. *air transportation executive*
Nespoli, Paolo Angelo *astronaut*
Noguchi, Soichi *astronaut*
Nowak, Lisa M. *astronaut, military officer*
Ochoa, Ellen *astronaut*
Parazynski, Scott E. *astronaut*
Pettit, Donald R. *astronaut, flight engineer, researcher*
Ream, James B. (Jim Ream) *air transportation executive*
Ross, Jerry L. *astronaut*
Runco, Mario, Jr. *astronaut, Earth scientist, meteorologist, spacecraft window engineer, information technology manager*
Sellers, Piers J. *astronaut*
Shapirov, Salizhan Shakirovich *cosmonaut*
Sharipov, Salizhan Shakirovich *cosmonaut*
Smisek, Jeffery A. *airline company executive*
Stefanyshyn-Piper, Heidemarie M. *astronaut*
Stone, Robert G., Jr. *water transportation executive*
Tanner, Joseph Richard *astronaut*
Thirsk, Robert Brent *astronaut*
Thomas, Andrew S.W. *astronaut*
Vittori, Roberto *astronaut*
Vladimirovich, Vinogradov Pavel *cosmonaut*
Walker, Charles D. *astronaut*
Wheelock, Douglas H. *astronaut, military officer*
Williams, Sunita L. *astronaut*
Wilson, Stephanie D. *astronaut*
Yuen, Benson Bolden *air transportation executive, consultant, software executive*
Zamka, George D. *astronaut*

**Irving**
Plaskett, Thomas George *transportation executive, director*

**Lindale**
Carter, Thomas Smith, Jr. *retired rail transportation executive*

**San Antonio**
Rush, W. Marvin *trucking executive*

**Zavalla**
Devlin, Cynthia M. *air transportation executive, consultant*

## UTAH

**North Salt Lake**
Bouley, Joseph Richard *pilot*

**Orem**
Snow, Marlon O. *trucking executive, state agency administrator*

**Saint George**
Atkin, Jerry C. *air transportation executive*

**Salt Lake City**
Courtney-Wilds, Noreen *air transportation executive*

## VERMONT

**Middlebury**
Bergesen, Robert Nelson *transportation consultant*

## VIRGINIA

**Alexandria**
Stempler, Jack Leon *aerospace executive*

**Arlington**
Baldanza, B. Ben *transportation executive*
Beier, Anita P. *air transportation executive*
Chiames, Christopher L. *air transportation executive*
Davis, David M. *air transportation executive*
de St. Aubin, Philip *aerospace transportation executive*
Gault, Jeffrey Wayne *air transportation executive*
Gifford, Jonathan Lewis *transportation policy researcher, educator*
Glass, Jerrold A. *air transportation executive*
Harrington, George Fred *retired air transportation executive*
Hullin, Tod Robert *aerospace transportation executive*
Lakefield, Bruce R. *air transportation executive*
Mainwaring, Thomas Lloyd *transportation executive, director*
Prestifilippo, John *air transportation executive*
Serck-Hanssen, Eilif *air transportation executive*
Stokes, B. R. *transportation executive, consultant*
Wahlquist, Andrew Folkman *government affairs executive*

**Catlett**
Broderick, Anthony James *air transportation executive*

**Chesterfield**
Congdon, John Rhodes *transportation executive*

**Dulles**
Elias, Antonio L. *aerospace transportation executive*

**Falls Church**
Poza, Hugo Bernardo *aerospace company executive*

**Gainesville**
Levell, Edward, Jr. *retired airport director, aviation consultant*

**Mc Lean**
Checchi, Alfred A. *air transportation executive, financial consultant*

**Newport News**
Schievelbein, Thomas Clayton *shipyard executive, sales executive*

**Norfolk**
Goode, David Ronald *transportation company executive*
McKinnon, Arnold Borden *retired transportation company executive*
Moorman, Charles W. *transportation executive*
Tobias, Stephen C. *rail transportation executive*

**Poquoson**
Holloway, Paul Fayette *retired aerospace transportation executive*

**Reston**
Harris, Paul Lynwood *retired aerospace transportation executive*
Kreyling, Edward George, Jr. *retired railroad executive*
Studeman, Bill (William Oliver Studeman) *aerospace transportation executive, former federal agency administrator, retired naval officer*

**Richmond**
Goodwin, Mark B. *transportation services executive, lawyer*
Kaczka, Jeff *trucking and relocation services executive*
Suggs, Leo H. *transportation executive*
Watkins, Hays Thomas *retired railroad executive*

**Sterling**
Thompson, David Walker *astronautics company executive*

**Vienna**
Anderson, Eric C. *aerospace transportation executive*
Beyer, Barbara Lynn *transportation executive, consultant*
Rogers, Raymond Jesse *retired federal railroad associate administrator*

**Williamsburg**
Barausky, Kenneth P. *aerospace company executive*
Spitzer, Cary Redford *avionics consultant, electrical engineer*
Starry, Donn Albert *retired aerospace corporate executive, retired military officer*

## WASHINGTON

**Belfair**
Hager, Robert Worth *retired aerospace transportation executive*

**Ellensburg**
Hoover, Amy Lynn *pilot, educator*

**Seattle**
Ayer, William S. *air transportation executive*
Beighle, Douglas Paul *aerospace transportation executive*
Carson, Scott E. *aerospace transportation executive*
Cline, Robert Stanley *retired air freight company executive*
Hirschmann, Franz Gottfried *aerospace executive*
Rankin, William Lee *air transportation scientist*
Rose, Peter J. *delivery service executive*
Taylor, Michael J. *shipbuilding company executive*
Tilden, Bradley D. *air transportation executive*

**Spanaway**
Loete, Steven Donald *pilot*

**Vancouver**
Robertson, Joel Thomas *railroad executive*

## WISCONSIN

**Appleton**
Petinga, Charles Michael *transportation executive*

**Green Bay**
Gannon, Thomas A. *trucking executive*
Lofgren, Christopher B. *trucking executive*
Schneider, Donald J. *trucking company executive*

**Oshkosh**
Bohn, Robert G. *transportation company executive*

## WYOMING

**Worland**
Woods, Lawrence Milton *airline company executive*

## CANADA

## NOVA SCOTIA

**Halifax**
Renouf, Harold Augustus *retired transportation executive*

## ONTARIO

**Brampton**
Savoie, Leonard Norman *transportation company executive*

## QUEBEC

**Montreal**
Rochette, Louis *water transportation executive*

**Saint-Sauveur**
Hanigan, Lawrence *retired rail transportation executive*

## AUSTRALIA

**Springfield**
Spalvins, Janis Gunars *steamship company executive*

## DENMARK

**Thisted**
Nordqvist, Erik Askbo *transportation executive*

## ENGLAND

**London**
Kallakis, Achilleas Michalis S. *transportation executive, real estate company executive*
van Hoften, James Dougal Adrianus *former astronaut, transportation executive*

## JAPAN

**Tokyo**
Kaneko, Isao *air transportation executive*
Matsuda, Masatake *rail transportation executive*

## RUSSIA

**Moscow**
Padalka, Gennady Ivanovich *cosmonaut*

## SWITZERLAND

**Geneva**
Aaronson, Robert Jay *air transportation executive*
Ballin, William Christopher *international shipping advisor, investment advisor*

## ADDRESS UNPUBLISHED

Adolph, Kathryn Ann *passenger service employee*
Aldrin, Buzz *retired astronaut*
Ames, Donald Paul *retired air transportation executive*
Bain, Douglas G. *retired aerospace transportation executive, lawyer*
Bergrun, Norman Riley *aerospace executive*
Birstein, Seymour Joseph *aerospace transportation executive*
Brazier, Don Roland *retired railroad executive*
Brown, Donald Douglas *transportation executive, consultant, retired military officer*
Brown, Robert E. *transportation executive*
Carty, Donald J. *airline company executive*
Collins, Eileen Marie *astronaut*
Compton, William F. *retired air transportation executive*
Cook, Richard Kelsey *aerospace transportation executive*
Cook, Stephen Champlin *retired shipping company executive*
Crowder, Richard Morgan *pilot*
Dansby, Ronnie *transportation executive*
Dely, Steven *retired aerospace company executive*
Dewar, James McEwen *marketing, aerospace and defense executive, developing nations consultant*
Dressler, David Charles *retired aerospace transportation executive*
Duelfer, Charles Alfred *aerospace transportation executive, weapons inspector, director*
Felix, Cheryl A. *air transportation executive*
Fish, Howard Math *aerospace transportation executive*
Garriott, Owen Kay *astronaut, scientist*
Gitner, Gerald L. *air transportation executive, investment banker*
Goldstein, Bernard *transportation executive, hotel executive*
Graebner, James Herbert *transportation executive*
Graser, Alfred J. *airport terminal executive, director*
Gray, Richard Arden *retired transportation executive*
Gulcher, Robert Harry *air transportation executive*
Hahn, Virginia Lynn *reservations agent*
Heckel, John Louis (Jack Heckel) *aerospace management executive*
Heitz, Edward Fred *freight traffic consultant*
Higginbottom, Samuel Logan *retired air transportation executive*
Huybrechts, Steven Marc *space system technologist*
Johnson, Robert *airport terminal executive*
Judd, Christopher J. *transportation executive*
Keenan, Anthony Lee *trucking executive*
Kellner, Lawrence W. (Larry Kellner) *air and aerospace transportation company executive*
King, Edward William *retired transportation executive*
Knutsen, Gregg Evan *transportation executive*

Koch, John Howard *retired air transportation executive, transportation engineer, consultant*
Kondas, Nicholas Frank *retired shipping company executive*
Lesko, Harry Joseph *transportation executive*
Lewis, Andrew Lindsay, Jr., (Drew Lewis) *former transportation and natural resources executive*
Lewis, Arthur Dee *aerospace transportation executive*
Lewis, Martin Edward *transportation executive, oil trader, foreign government concessionary*
Logan, Henry Vincent *transportation executive, consultant*
Malishenko, Timothy Peter *aerospace company executive*
Marshall, Charles Noble *rail transportation executive*
Masiello, Rocco Joseph *air transportation executive, consultant*
McCaig, Jeffrey James *transportation company executive*
McCarthy, Paul Fenton *aerospace transportation executive, retired military officer*
McDonough, Gerald Clyde *transportation leasing company executive, manufacturing executive*
Merrick, George Boesch *aerospace transportation executive*
Miller, Paul David *aerospace transportation executive, retired admiral*
Miller, Sanford *car rental company executive*
Mullin, Leo Francis *airline executive*
Palumbo, Michael J. *air transportation executive*
Parker, James Francis *former air transportation executive, lawyer*
Pickering, Thomas Reeve *former aerospace transportation executive, former diplomat*
Pope, John Charles *former airline company executive*
Precourt, Charles J. *astronaut, retired military officer*
Raskin, Fred Charles *retired transportation and utility holding company executive, educator*
Ratnathicam, Chutta *transportation executive*
Reed, John Shedd *former railway executive*
Ruegg, Donald George *retired rail transportation executive*
Saleh, Brian Behrooz *aerospace transportation executive*
Savitz, Maxine Lazarus *aerospace transportation executive*
Schaefer, C. Barry *rail transportation executive, investment company executive*
Schaupp, Joan Pomprowitz *trucking executive, writer*
Seliga, Charles G. *airport administrator*
Shargin, Yuri Georguevich *flight engineer, cosmonaut*
Shockley, Edward Julian *retired air transportation executive*
Smith, Edwin E. *aerospace transportation executive*
Smith, Michael L. *transportation company executive*
Smith, Russell Francis *transportation executive*
Snowden, Lawrence Fontaine *retired air transportation executive, retired military officer*
Stevens, Robert J. *aerospace transportation executive*
Stromquist, Kenneth James, Jr. *pilot, retired military officer*
Swalm, Thomas Sterling *aerospace transportation executive, retired military officer*
Swinburn, Charles *rail transportation executive*
Tague, John P. *air transportation executive*
Tyurin, Mikhail *cosmonaut*
Wallace, F. Blake *retired aerospace transportation executive, retired mechanical engineer*
Warner, Emily Hanrahan Howell *retired pilot, writer*
Washburn, Donald Arthur *retired transportation executive, investor*
Werkema, Mark Andrew *pilot, writer*
Yeager, Jeana *aviator*
Yeager, Phillip Charles *transportation company executive*
Young, John Watts *retired astronaut*
Zell, Samuel *transportation leasing company executive*

---

## INDUSTRY: UTILITIES, ENERGY, RESOURCES

## UNITED STATES

## ALABAMA

**Foley**
St. John, Henry Sewell, Jr. *utility company executive*

## ALASKA

**Fairbanks**
Beistline, Earl Hoover *mining consultant*
Kokjer, Kenneth Jordan *telecommunication systems planner*

## ARIZONA

**Phoenix**
Brown, Denny L. *utilities executive*
Corella, John C., Jr. *telecommunications industry executive*
Post, William Joseph *utility executive*
Snider, Timothy R. *mining executive*
Whisler, James Steven *mining executive, lawyer, rancher*

**Scottsdale**
Birkelbach, Albert Ottmar *retired oil industry executive*

Holliger, Frederic Lee *oil industry executive*
Trimble, Thomas James *retired utilities executive, lawyer*

**Sedona**
Dansby, John Walter *retired oil industry executive*

**Show Low**
Pershing, Robert George *retired telecommunications industry executive*

**Tempe**
Hickson, Robin Julian *mining company executive*

**Tucson**
Heller, Frederick *retired mining executive*
Jamison, Harrison Clyde *retired oil company executive*
Maxon, Don Carlton *mining executive, construction executive, consultant*
Peeler, Stuart Thorne *gas industry executive, consultant*
Peters, Charles William *nuclear energy industry executive*

**Youngtown**
Black, Robert Frederick *retired gas industry executive*

## ARKANSAS

**El Dorado**
Deming, Claiborne Payne *oil industry executive*
Nolan, William C., Jr. *energy executive*
Watkins, Jerry West *retired oil company executive, lawyer*

**Fayetteville**
Scharlau, Charles Edward III *natural gas company executive*

**Little Rock**
Bemis, Michael B. *utility company executive*
Ford, Joe Thomas *telephone company executive, former state senator*
Ford, Scott T. *telecommunications industry executive*
Frantz, Francis X. *telecommunications industry executive, lawyer*
Orsini, Tom *retired telecommunications company executive*

**Russellville**
Cooper, Robert Michael *consultant, retired nuclear energy industry specialist*

## CALIFORNIA

**Alameda**
Lu, Hong Liang *telecommunications industry executive*

**Alamo**
Shiffer, James David *retired utilities executive*

**Berkeley**
Baack, Lawrence James *energy executive, education educator*

**Camarillo**
MacAlister, Robert Stuart *retired oil industry executive*

**Carmel**
Hamilton, Lyman Critchfield, Jr. *telecommunications industry executive*

**Elk Grove**
Romano, Sheila June *telecommunications industry professional, writer, artist*

**Folsom**
Regan, William Joseph, Jr. *energy company executive*

**Goleta**
Jerphagnon, Olivier L. *telecommunications industry executive*

**Irvine**
Shirilau, Mark Steven *utilities executive*

**La Jolla**
Rinaker, Samuel Mayo, Jr. *retired utilities executive*

**La Palma**
Thelander, Beverly *oil company executive*

**Los Angeles**
Chazen, Stephen I. *oil industry executive*
Irani, Ray R. *oil, gas and chemical company executive*
Mandles, Martinn Heroe *facility services company executive*
Nelson, Larry Dean *telecommunications and computer systems company executive, consultant*
Pryor, Richard Walter *telecommunications executive, retired air force officer*

**Martinez**
Meyer, Jarold Alan *oil company research executive*

**Mill Valley**
Premo, Paul Mark *oil industry executive*

**Newport Coast**
Swan, Peer Alden *public utility executive*

**Pacific Palisades**
Klein, Joseph Mark *retired mining executive*
Mulryan, Henry Trist *mining executive, consultant*

**Palo Alto**
Cohen, Karl Paley *nuclear energy consultant*

Cullen, James G. *telecommunications industry executive*
Loewenstein, Walter Bernard *nuclear energy industry executive*

**Palos Verdes Peninsula**
Christie, Hans Frederick *retired utilities executive*

**Pasadena**
Gross, Bill *energy executive*
White-Thomson, Ian leonard *retired mining executive*

**Petaluma**
Frederickson, Arman Frederick *mining executive, petroleum engineer*

**Rosemead**
Bryson, John E. *utilities executive*
Collins, Jodi M. *utilities executive*
Fohrer, Alan J. *utilities company executive*
McDaniel, Thomas R. *utilities executive*
Pizarro, Pedro *electric power industry executive*
Rosenblum, Richard Mark *utilities executive*
Smith, Anthony L. *utilities executive*

**San Diego**
Altman, Steven R. *telecommunications executive*
Felsinger, Donald E. *utilities corporation executive*
Sarkar, Sandip *telecommunications industry executive, researcher*
Schmale, Neal E. *utilites company executive*

**San Francisco**
Darbee, Peter A. *electric power company executive*
Dickinson, Wade *oil industry executive, educator*
Flittie, Clifford Gilliland *retired petroleum company executive*
Glynn, Robert D., Jr. *electric power and gas industry executive*
Goldstein, David Baird *energy executive, physicist*
Sproul, John Allan *retired utilities executive*

**San Jose**
Bodensteiner, Lisa M. *utilities executive, lawyer*
Capellas, Michael D. *telecommunications industry executive*
Curtis, Ann B. *utilities executive*
Derr, Kenneth T. *energy executive*
Macias, E. James *utilities executive*
Malis, Andrew Gary *telecommunications company executive*
Mason, Thomas R. *utilities executive*
May, Robert P. *energy executive*
Prasad, Neil A. *telecommunications industry executive, computer company executive*
Tabbut, Loreen M. *power industry executive*

**San Mateo**
Ginn, Sam L. *telephone company executive*

**San Ramon**
Bethancourt, John E. *oil industry executive*
Gass, John D. *oil industry executive*
Laidlaw, William Samuel Hugh *oil company executive*
O'Reilly, David J. *oil industry executive*
Robertson, Peter James *oil company executive*
Watson, John S. *oil company executive*
Wirth, Michael K. (Mike Wirth) *oil company executive*
Zygocki, Rhonda I. *oil industry executive*

**Santa Barbara**
Mc Duffie, Malcolm *oil industry executive*

**Santa Clara**
Burke, Conrad *energy executive*
Koomen, Cornelis Jan *telecommunications and electronics executive*

**Santa Rosa**
Wagner, Harold A. *retired gas industry executive*

**South Pasadena**
Finnell, Michael Hartman *mining executive*

**Stanford**
Brinegar, Claude Stout *retired oil industry executive*

**Sunnyvale**
Olson, James (Jim Olson) *telecommunications industry executive*

## COLORADO

**Boulder**
Hill, Melvin James *retired oil industry executive*

**Broomfield**
Patel, Sunit *telecommunications industry executive*

**Centennial**
Owens, Marvin Franklin, Jr. *oil industry executive, director*

**Denver**
Anderson, Donald H. *energy executive*
Danos, Robert McClure *retired oil company executive*
Dea, Peter Allen *gas industry executive, geologist*
Dyer, Edward James *public utilities commissioner*
Goeringer, Steven John *telecommunications industry executive*
Hall, Larry Dean *utilities executive, lawyer*
Hansen, Bruce D. *mining executive*
Kruger, Paula *telecommunications industry executive*
Krysiak, William J. *gas industry executive*
Larson, Randall J. *energy executive*
Lassonde, Pierre *mining executive*
Macey, William Blackmore *oil industry executive*
Mayer, Frederick Rickard *oil industry executive*
Murdy, Wayne William *mining company executive, financial officer*
Norman, John Edward *petroleum landman*

Notebaert, Richard C. *telecommunications industry executive*
Senty, James A. *energy executive*
Thompson, Lohren Matthew *oil company executive*
Trueblood, Harry Albert, Jr. *oil industry executive*

**Englewood**
Schleyer, William T. *cable company executive*

**Golden**
Matthews, Thomas Michael *former energy company executive*
von Roedern, Bolko Graf *energy executive, researcher*

**Littleton**
Fryt, Monte Stanislaus *petroleum company executive, speaker, advisor*

**Loveland**
Bierbaum, J. Armin *petroleum company executive, consultant*

## CONNECTICUT

**Darien**
Smith, Elwin Earl *mining and oil company executive*

**Fairfield**
Cassidy, Katherine *energy executive*
Conaty, William J. *electric power industry executive*
Trotter, Lloyd G. *electric power industry executive*

**Glastonbury**
Dixon, Robert F. *telecommunications executive*

**Greenwich**
Alonzo, Martin Vincent *mining and aluminum company executive, investor, financial consultant*
Davidson, Thomas Maxwell *oil industry executive*
DeCrane, Alfred Charles, Jr. *petroleum company executive*

**Guilford**
Morgan, Leon Alford *retired utilities executive*

**Hartford**
Butler, Gregory B. *utilities executive, lawyer*
Shivery, Charles W. *utilities executive*

**New Canaan**
McIvor, Donald Kenneth *retired petroleum company executive*

**Old Greenwich**
Allen, Jefferson F. *oil industry executive*

**Orange**
Powers, Timothy H. *electric power industry executive*

**Ridgefield**
Habashy, Tarek *oil industry executive, director*

**Southport**
Damson, Barrie Morton *oil and gas exploration company executive*

**Stamford**
Bijur, Peter I. *retired petroleum company executive*
Mc Kinley, John Key *retired oil company executive*
Neal, A. Michael *utilities executive*
Nissen, David R. *utilities executive*

## DELAWARE

**Wilmington**
Cosgrove, Howard Edward, Jr. *utilities executive*

## DISTRICT OF COLUMBIA

**Washington**
Bradshaw, Richard Eugene *science and technology government relations consultant*
Buchan, Douglas Charles *gas industry executive, government agency administrator*
Davidson, Peter *telecommunications industry executive*
DeGraffenreidt, James H., Jr. *gas company executive*
Fraulino, Philip Samuel *telecommunications industry executive*
Friedman, Gregory H. *energy administrator*
King, Gwendolyn S. *retired utility company executive, retired federal official*
McCollam, William, Jr. *utilities executive*
McGee, Robert Merrill *oil industry executive*
McSlarrow, Kyle E. *telecommunications association executive, former federal agency administrator*
Sant, Roger W. *retired energy executive*
Williams, Andrew W. *energy executive*
Wraase, Dennis Richard *utilities executive, accountant*

## FLORIDA

**Belleair Beach**
Ayers, Richard Wayne *electric power industry executive, writer, journalist*

**Boca Raton**
Gralla, Eugene *natural gas company executive*

**Bradenton**
Watkins, William, Jr. *electric power industry executive*

**Deerfield Beach**
Laser, Charles, Jr. *oil company executive*

**Fort Lauderdale**
Borras, Jaime *telecommunications industry executive*

**Gainesville**
Milbrath, Robert Henry *retired petroleum industry executive*

**Jacksonville**
Francis, James Delbert *oil industry executive*

**Key West**
Evans, John Derby *telecommunications industry executive*

**Largo**
Dolan, John E. *retired utilities executive, consultant*

**Longwood**
Cirello, John *utility and engineering company executive*

**Miami**
Claure, R. Marcelo *telecommunications industry executive*
Kasbar, Michael J. *energy executive*
Stebbins, Paul H. *energy executive*
Weiser, Ralph Raphael *oil industry executive*

**Naples**
Marino, William Francis *telecommunications industry executive, consultant*

**North Palm Beach**
Hay, Lewis III *utilities company executive*

**Palm Beach Gardens**
Harnett, Joseph Durham *oil industry executive*
Ziglar, James W. *telecommunications industry executive, federal administrator, investment banker, lawyer, educator*

**Ponte Vedra Beach**
Green, Norman Kenneth *retired oil industry executive, former naval officer*
Wood, Quentin Eugene *oil industry executive*

**Rosemary Beach**
Rose, Michael Elvin *oil and gas exploration company executive*

**Saint Petersburg**
Fleming, William Sloan *energy executive, computer company executive*

**Saint Petersburg Beach**
Garnett, Stanley Iredale, II, *utilities executive, lawyer*

**Sarasota**
Torrey, Richard Frank *utilities executive*

**Stuart**
Riordan, James Quentin *retired oil industry executive, lawyer*

**Tallahassee**
Laughlin, William Eugene *retired electric power industry executive*

**Tampa**
Brown, Troy Anderson, Jr. *retired electric power industry executive*
Hudson, Sherrill W. *energy executive*

**Vero Beach**
Bennett, Jack Franklin *oil industry executive*
Fitzgeorge, Harold James *former oil and gas company executive*

**West Palm Beach**
Kiely, Dan Ray *telecommunications industry executive, bank executive, consultant*
Koch, William I. *energy company executive*

## GEORGIA

**Alpharetta**
Heyman, John H. *energy executive*
Mulhauser, Craig H. *energy executive*

**Atlanta**
Arroyo, F. Thaddeus *telecommunications industry executive*
Bolch, Carl Edward, Jr. *petroleum company executive, lawyer*
Carbonell, Joaquin R. III *telecommunications industry executive, lawyer*
Carter, Stephen M. *telecommunications manufacturing industry executive*
Clift, W.E. *telecommunications industry executive*
Cowan, Keith O. *telecommunications industry executive*
de la Vega, Ralph *wireless telecommunications industry executive*
Dykes, Ronald Mitchell *retired telecommunications industry executive*
Feidler, Mark L. *telecommunications industry executive*
Fuller, S(heri) Marce *energy executive*
Muller, Edward Robert *energy executive, lawyer*
Palmer, Ben M. *gas industry executive*
Ramsey, Ira Clayton *retired petroleum industry executive*
Ratcliffe, David M. *utilities executive*
Reynolds, Edgar L. *telecommunications industry executive*
Reynolds, Paula Rosput *energy executive*
Sibbernsen, Richard *telecommunications industry executive*
Sigman, Stanley T. *telecommunications industry executive*
Smith, Elmer *telecommunications industry executive*

Smith, William L. *telecommunications industry executive*
Somerhalder, John W., II, *energy executive*

**Duluth**
McCracken, William Henry *retired mining executive*

**Gainesville**
Leet, Richard Hale *oil industry executive*

## HAWAII

**Honolulu**
Lau, Constance H. (Connnie Lau) *electric power industry executive*

**Waikoloa**
Calvert, Delbert William *retired energy executive*

## ILLINOIS

**Argonne**
Ban, Stephen Dennis *gas industry executive*

**Aurora**
Fisher, Thomas Lee *gas industry executive*

**Barrington**
Perry, I. Chet *petroleum company executive*

**Chicago**
Brooker, Thomas Kimball *oil industry executive*
Carlson, LeRoy Theodore, Jr. *telecommunications industry executive*
Clark, Frank M. *utilities executive*
Morrow, Richard Martin *retired oil company executive*
Patrick, Thomas M. *gas utility company executive*
Rowe, John William *utilities executive*
Strobel, Pamela B. *energy executive*

**Deerfield**
Zywicki, Robert Albert *retired electric power industry executive*

**Flossmoor**
Pierce, Shelby Crawford *oil industry executive, consultant*

**Joliet**
Easton, Kenneth Glenn *retired utilities executive*

**Naperville**
Birck, Michael John *telecommunications industry executive*
Hawley, Richard L. *utilities executive*
Prabhu, Krish Anant *telecommunications industry executive, educator*
Strobel, Russ M. *gas industry executive, lawyer*

**River Forest**
Batlivala, Robert Bomi D. *oil industry executive, economics professor*

**Schaumburg**
O'Connor, James, Jr., (Jim O'Connor) *telecommunications industry executive*

**Warrenville**
Darukhanavala, Phiroz P. (Daru Darukhanavala) *energy executive*

## INDIANA

**Columbus**
Able, Warren Walter *natural resource company executive, physician*

**Evansville**
Ellerbrook, Niel Cochran *gas industry executive*

**Frankfort**
Stonehill, Lloyd Herschel *gas industry executive, mechanical engineer*

**Lawrenceburg**
Dautel, Charles Shreve *retired mining company executive*

**Merrillville**
Neale, Gary Lee *utilities executive*
Skaggs, Robert C., Jr. *utilities executive, lawyer*

## IOWA

**Des Moines**
Abel, Gregory E. *utility company executive*
Sokol, David L. *energy services provider company executive*

## KANSAS

**Eskridge**
Taylor, Russell Benton *mining executive*

**Overland Park**
Betts, Gene M. *telecommunications industry executive*
Ferrell, James Edwin *nuclear energy industry executive*
Horen, Jeffrey Harry *telecommunications executive*
Kuppuswamy, Carthy *telecommunications industry executive*
Strandjord, M. Jeannine *telecommunications industry executive*

**Pittsburg**
Nettels, George Edward, Jr. *retired mining executive*

**Shawnee Mission**
Pressman, Ronald R. *utilities executive*

**Topeka**
Chandler, Charles Q., IV, *energy executive*
Haines, James S., Jr. *energy executive*
Spencer, William Edwin *retired telecommunications industry executive, engineer*

**Wichita**
Cadman, Wilson Kennedy *retired utilities executive*
Feilmeier, Steve *energy executive*

## KENTUCKY

**Ashland**
Hatfield, Bennett K. *mining executive*
Weaver, Carlton Davis *retired oil industry executive*
Yancey, Robert Earl, Jr. *retired oil industry executive*

**Crescent Springs**
Chellgren, Paul Wilbur *energy industry executive*

**Lexington**
Boyd, James Robert *energy executive*

**Louisville**
Hale, Roger W. *utilities company executive*
Ronald, Peter *utilities executive*
Staffieri, Victor A. *energy executive*

## LOUISIANA

**Monroe**
Ewing, R. Stewart *telecommunications company executive*
Fouts, James Fremont *mining company executive*
Post, Glen Fleming III *telecommunications industry executive*

**New Orleans**
Adkerson, Richard C. *mining executive*
Lind, Thomas Otto *barge transportation company executive*
Moffett, James Robert *energy executive*
Taylor, Phyllis Miller *energy executive*
Williams, Ronald David *telecommunications industry executive*

## MAINE

**Casco**
Brown, Ronald Osborne *telecommunications and computer systems consultant*

**New Gloucester**
Jasinski, Kenneth M. *energy executive*

**Portland**
von Schack, Wesley W. *utilities executive*

**Yarmouth**
Haynes, Peter Lancaster *utilities executive*

## MARYLAND

**Annapolis**
Marienthal, George *telecommunications industry executive*

**Baltimore**
Chagnoni, Kathleen *energy executive*
Ihrie, Robert *oil, gas and real estate company executive*
Owsley, Thomas L. *oil industry executive*
Rosenberg, Frank Blaustein *petroleum company executive*
Rosenberg, Henry A., Jr. *petroleum company executive*
Shattuck, Mayo Adams III *utilities executive*

**Bethesda**
Chebaane, Mohamed *water management specialist, consultant*
Cope, Laurence Brian *utilities executive, economist, consultant*
McMurphy, Michael Allen *energy company executive, lawyer*
Olmsted, Jerauld Lockwood *telephone company executive*
Starkey, Russell Bruce, Jr. *energy executive*
Welch, John Kirtland *nuclear energy industry executive*

**Burtonsville**
Kettell, II, Ralph Wallis *mining executive, mining engineer*

**Gaithersburg**
Delgado, Dwighd D(ubied) *electric power industry executive*

**Lutherville Timonium**
Bevis, Robert E. *retired oil industry executive*

**Rockville**
Griffith, Jerry Dice *energy executive, management consultant*

**Silver Spring**
Cunningham, Keith Allen *nuclear energy industry executive, accountant, lawyer, engineer*
Jacobs, George *broadcast engineering consulting company executive*

## MASSACHUSETTS

**Boston**
Kennedy, Joseph Patrick, II, *utilities executive, former congressman*

May, Thomas J. *electric company executive*
Stobaugh, Robert Blair *oil industry executive*

**Centerville**
Anderson, Gerald Edwin *retired utilities executive*
Scherer, Harold Nicholas, Jr. *electric power industry executive*

**Chelsea**
Kaneb, John A. *oil industry executive*
Petrowski, Joe *oil industry executive*

**Harwich Port**
Staszesky, Francis Myron *electric power industry executive, consultant*

**Needham**
Cogswell, John Heyland *retired telecommunications industry executive, financial consultant*
Rafferty, James Paul *telecommunications executive*

**Westborough**
Bok, Joan Toland *utilities executive*

**Weston**
Goldstein, Arthur Louis *retired utilities executive*

## MICHIGAN

**Detroit**
Anderson, Gerard M. *energy executive*
Earley, Anthony Francis, Jr. *utilities company executive, lawyer*
Ellyn, Lynne *energy executive*
Ewing, Stephen E. *natural gas company executive*

**Jackson**
Joos, David W. *energy executive*
Webb, Thomas J. *utilities executive*
Whipple, Kenneth *utilities executive*

**Shelby Township**
Fillbrook, Thomas George *telephone company executive*

**Troy**
Opie, John D. *retired electric power industry executive*

## MINNESOTA

**Burnsville**
O'Brien, Gerald James *utilities executive*

**Eden Prairie**
Switz, Robert E. *telecommunications executive*

**Minneapolis**
Fowke, Benjamin G.S. III *energy executive*
Gogel, Raymond E. *energy executive*
Kelly, Richard C. *energy executive*

**Pequot Lakes**
Lane, Kathleen Margaret *refrigeration company official*

## MISSISSIPPI

**Jackson**
Lampton, Leslie B., Sr. *oil industry executive*
Waites, Robert Guinn *utilities executive*

## MISSOURI

**Chesterfield**
Bunch, C. Robert *oil industry executive, lawyer*

**Clayton**
Novelly, Paul Anthony *petrochemical and refining company executive*

**Kansas City**
Baker, John Russell *utilities executive*
Chesser, Michael J. *gas and electric power industry executive*
Dobson, Rick *energy executive*
Mackenzie, Nanci *gas company executive*
Potter, George William, Jr. *mining executive*
Riggins, William G. *electric power industry executive*
Stamm, Keith G. *energy executive*

**Lebanon**
Beavers, Roy Lackey *retired utilities executive, volunteer, writer*

**Saint Louis**
Baxter, Warner L. *energy executive*
Boyce, Gregory H. *energy executive*
Brown, Bobby R. *retired coal company executive*
Engelhardt, Irl F. *coal company executive*
Leer, Steven F. *mining executive*
Rainwater, Gary L. *electric power industry executive*
Smit, Neil *telecommunications industry executive*
Yaeger, Douglas Harrison *gas industry executive*

**Springfield**
Jura, James J. *electric utility executive*

## MONTANA

**Billings**
Nance, Robert Lewis *oil industry executive*

**Missoula**
Brumit, Lawrence Edward III *oil industry executive*

## NEBRASKA

**Lincoln**
Schorr, Paul C. III *electrical contracting executive*

**Omaha**
Crouse, Jerry K. *energy company executive*
Hawks, Howard L. *energy executive*
Scott, Walter, Jr. *telecommunications industry executive*

## NEVADA

**Las Vegas**
Laub, William Murray, Sr. *retired utilities executive*
Shaw, Jeffrey William *gas industry executive*

**Reno**
Brennan, Susan Mallick *utilities executive*
Gundersen, Wayne Campbell *energy executive, consultant*
Higgins, Walter M. III *electric power industry executive*

**Winnemucca**
Hesse, Martha O. *gas industry executive*

## NEW HAMPSHIRE

**Portsmouth**
Powers, Henry Martin, Jr. *oil industry executive*

## NEW JERSEY

**Basking Ridge**
Collis, Sidney Robert *retired telephone company executive*
D'Ambrosio, Louis J. *telecommunications industry executive*
Matthews, Craig Gerard *retired energy executive*
Peterson, Donald Kent *telecommunications industry executive*

**Bedminster**
Flaherty, Kathleen Ruth *telecommunications industry executive*
Hannigan, William J. *telecommunications industry executive*
Strigl, Dennis F. *telecommunications industry executive*

**Belmar**
Downes, Laurence M. *gas industry executive*

**Chatham**
Sundberg, Carl-Erik Wilhelm *telecommunications executive, researcher*

**Eatontown**
Sullivan, Timothy Patrick *telecommunications company executive*

**Holmdel**
Snyder, Michael F. *telecommunications industry executive*

**Kirkwood Voorhees**
Barr, J. James *company executive*

**Maplewood**
Joel, Amos Edward, Jr. *telecommunications consultant*

**Morristown**
Hafer, Frederick Douglass *utilities executive*
Martine, Cathy *telecommunications industry executive*

**Mount Laurel**
Rabbe, David Ellsworth *oil industry executive*

**Murray Hill**
Brewington, James *telecommunications industry executive*
Christy, Cindy *telecommunications industry executive*
Davidson, Janet G. *telecommunications industry executive*

**New Providence**
Carapezzi, William R., Jr. *telecommunications industry executive, lawyer*
Kritzmacher, John A. *telecommunications industry executive*
Mejia, Jose A. *telecommunications industry executive*
O'Shea, William (Bill) T. *telecommunications industry executive*
Russo, Patricia F. *telecommunications company executive*

**Newark**
Ferland, E. James *electric power industry executive*

**Nutley**
Mallard, Stephen Anthony *retired utilities executive*

**Peapack**
Walsh, Philip Cornelius *retired mining executive*

**Piscataway**
Talpade, Rajesh *telecommunications industry executive*

**Princeton**
Crane, David W. *energy executive*
McCullough, John Price *retired oil company executive*

**South Plainfield**
Lewandowski, Andrew Anthony *utilities executive, consultant*

## Summit
Chynoweth, Alan Gerald *retired telecommunications industry executive*

## Voorhees
Correll, Donald L. *water services company executive*

## Watchung
Cohen, Melvin Irwin *retired communications systems and technology executive*

## Whippany
Alexander, Mark A. *energy executive*

# NEW MEXICO

## Albuquerque
Long, Robert Leroy *retired utilities executive, consultant*
Ofte, Donald *nuclear energy industry executive, consultant*
Robinson, Charles Paul *nuclear energy industry executive, diplomat*
Sterba, Jeffry E. *energy executive*

## Farmington
Macaluso, Frank Augustus *oil industry executive, bank executive*

## High Rolls Mountain Park
Ellison, Luther Frederick *oil industry executive*

## Hobbs
Garey, Donald Lee *oil industry executive*

## Roswell
Anderson, Donald Bernard *oil industry executive*
Robinson, Mark Leighton *gas industry executive, petroleum engineer, farmer*

## Santa Fe
Duhaime, Nina Lee *energy executive, research and development company executive*

# NEW YORK

## Bronxville
Gelfand, Neal *oil industry executive*

## Brooklyn
Bishar, John Joseph, Jr. *utilities executive, lawyer*
Catell, Robert Barry *gas industry executive*
Fani, Robert J. *gas industry executive*

## Greenvale
Cordaro, Matthew Charles *energy and utility executive, educator*

## Irvington
Carey, Edward John *utilities executive*

## New York
Alpert, Warren *oil industry executive, foundation administrator*
Babbio, Lawrence T. *telecommunications industry executive*
Bardin, Mary Beth *telecommunications company executive*
Bartlett, Thomas A. *telecommunications industry executive*
Brown, Edward James, Sr. *utilities executive*
Burch, Stephen A. *telecommunications industry executive*
Burke, Kevin *utilities executive*
Casey, Thomas Jefferson *clean energy executive and entrepreneur, environmental activist*
D'Alessio, Frederick D. *telecommunications company executive*
Denson, Terry *telecommunications industry executive*
Diercksen, John W. *telecommunications industry executive*
Freilich, Joan Sherman *utilities executive*
Gould, Andrew *oil industry executive*
Hess, John B. *oil industry executive*
Kelly, Anastasia D. (Stasia Kelly) *telecommunications industry executive, lawyer*
Killian, John F. *telecommunications industry executive*
Lataille, Ronald H. *telecommunications industry executive*
Luce, Charles Franklin *retired utilities executive, lawyer*
Lyons, John Matthew *telecommunications industry executive, broadcast executive*
McGrath, Eugene R. *utility company executive*
Morse, Edward Lewis *petroleum industry executive*
Mossavar-Rahmani, Bijan *oil and gas company executive*
Noam, Eli Michael *telecommunications industry executive, educator*
Noski, Charles H. *telecommunications executive*
Osborne, Richard de Jongh *mining and metals company executive*
Ruesterholz, Virginia P. *telecommunications industry executive*
Seidenberg, Ivan G. *telecommunications industry executive*
Tauke, Thomas Joseph *telecommunications company executive, former congressman*
Toben, Doreen A. *telecommunications industry executive*
Webster, Catherine T. *telecommunications industry executive*
Wrobel, Bruce J. *energy and utilities company executive*

## Niskayuna
Mangan, John Leo *retired electric power industry executive, international trade specialist*

## Rochester
VanderLinden, Camilla Denice Dunn *telecommunications industry executive*

## Rye
Lawi, David Steven *utilities executive, merchant banker*

## Syracuse
Kerr, Darlene Dixon *electric power company executive*

## Wappingers Falls
Nolan, John Thomas, Jr. *retired oil industry administrator*

## White Plains
Underweiser, Irwin Philip *mining executive, lawyer*

## Williamsville
Ackerman, Philip Charles *utilities executive, lawyer*
Kennedy, Bernard Joseph *retired utilities executive*

# NORTH CAROLINA

## Asheville
Haynes, John Mabin *retired utilities executive*

## Charlotte
Anderson, Paul Milton *energy executive*
Fowler, Fred J. *energy executive*
Hauser, David L. *electric power industry executive*
Mogg, Jimmy W. *gas industry executive*
Rogers, James Eugene *electric and gas utility executive*
Shaw, Ruth G. *energy company executive*
Skains, Thomas E. *gas industry executive*

## Raleigh
Clapp, Allen Linville *electric supply and communications utility consultant, mediator/arbitrator*
Johnson, William Dean *power company executive*
McArthur, John R. *utilities executive, lawyer*
McGehee, Robert B. *energy executive*
Smith, Sherwood Hubbard, Jr. *retired electric utilities executive*

## Southern Shores
Kegel, William George *mining company executive*

## Statesville
Grogan, David R. *work saver company executive*

# NORTH DAKOTA

## Bismarck
Hildestad, Terry D. *energy executive*
Robinson, Warren Lowe *utilities executive*

# OHIO

## Akron
Alexander, Anthony J. *electric power industry executive*
Marsh, Richard H. *utilities company executive*
Smart, George M. *energy executive, former packaging company executive*
Vespoli, Leila L. *energy executive, lawyer*

## Chagrin Falls
Miller, John Robert *oil industry executive*

## Cincinnati
Bryant, John *utilities executive*
Ehrnschwender, Arthur Robert *former utility company executive*
Esamann, Douglas F. *utilities executive*
Ficke, Gregory C. *utilities executive*
Foley, Cheryl M. *electric power industry executive*
Gaines, Bennett L. *utilities executive*
Janson, Julia S. *utilities executive*
Murphy, Theodore R., II, *utilities executive*
Newton, Frederick J. III *utilities executive*
Turner, James Lee *utilities executive, lawyer*

## Cleveland
Brinzo, John S. *mining executive*
Kuehn, Richard Arthur *telecommunications consultant*
Stropki, John M., Jr. *electric power industry executive*

## Columbus
Koeppel, Holly Keller *electric power industry executive*
Morris, Michael G. *utilities executive*
Tomasky, Susan *electric power industry executive*
Vassell, Gregory S. *electric utility consultant*

## Findlay
Yammine, Riad Nassif *retired oil industry executive*

## Lima
Pranses, Anthony Louis *retired electric power industry executive*

## Perrysburg
Williamson, John Pritchard *retired utilities executive*

## South Charleston
Weatherby, Donald Alan *telecommunications industry executive, writer*

# OKLAHOMA

## Bartlesville
Mulva, James Joseph *oil industry executive*
Price, Joe D. *pipeline developer*
Silas, Cecil Jesse *retired petroleum company executive*

## Enid
Ward, Llewellyn Orcutt III *oil industry executive*

## Jennings
Nixon, Arlie James *gas and oil company executive*

## Oklahoma City
Campbell, David Gwynne *petroleum executive, geologist*
Harlan, Ross Edgar *retired utility company executive, writer, lecturer, consultant*
Hefner, William Johnson, Jr., (W. John Hefner Jr.) *oil and gas industry executive*
Kirkpatrick, John Elson *retired oil industry executive, retired naval reserve officer*
McClendon, Aubrey K. *energy executive*
Moore, Steven E. *energy executive*
Nichols, J. Larry *energy executive, lawyer*
Richels, John *energy executive, lawyer*
Ward, Tom L. *energy executive*
Wohleber, Robert Michael *oil industry executive*

## Tulsa
Bender, James J. *oil industry executive, lawyer*
Berlin, Steven Ritt *oil industry executive*
Braumiller, Allen Spooner *gas industry executive, geologist*
Cadieux, Chester *gas industry executive*
Chappel, Donald R. *petroleum pipeline company executive*
Dotson, George Stephen *oil industry executive*
Horkey, William Richard *retired oil industry executive*
Ingram, Charles Clark, Jr. *energy executive*
Kneale, James C. *gas company executive*
Kronfeld, Edwin *natural gas company executive*
Kyle, David L. *gas industry executive*
Malcolm, Steven J. *petroleum pipeline company executive*
Nedom, H. Arthur *petroleum consultant*

# OREGON

## Lincoln City
Morrow, James Thomas *energy executive*

## Portland
Bacon, Vicky Lee *lighting services executive*

## Tualatin
West, Michael G. *electric power industry executive*

# PENNSYLVANIA

## Allentown
Biggar, John R. *utilities energy executive*
Grey, Robert J. *energy executive, lawyer*
Hecht, William F. *electric power industry executive*
Miller, James H. *electric power industry executive*

## Allison Park
Sullivan, Neil Maxwell *oil and gas company executive*

## Bryn Mawr
Braha, Thomas I. *oil industry executive*

## Camp Hill
Fazzolari, Salvatore D. *mining products executive*
Hathaway, Derek C. *mining products executive*

## Coraopolis
Koepfinger, Joseph Leo *retired utilities executive*

## Gladwyne
Patten, Lanny Ray *gas industry executive*

## Greensburg
Evanson, Paul John *utilities executive*
Goulding, Philip L. *energy executive*

## King Of Prussia
Bissell, Eugene V.N. *gas industry executive*
Greenberg, Leon Richard *energy executive, lawyer*
Mendicino, Anthony J. *gas company executive*
Walsh, John L. *energy executive*

## Philadelphia
Adawi, Nadia Sharon *energy executive*
Albertini, William Oliver *retired telecommunications industry executive*
Calman, Robert Frederick *mining executive*
Delaney, Terence (Terry) P. *gas industry executive*
Drosdick, John Girard *oil company executive*
Fischer, Bruce G. *gas industry executive*
Fretz, Deborah McDermott *oil industry executive*
Hofmann, Thomas W. *petroleum company executive*
Krott, Joseph P. *gas industry executive, comptroller*
Kuritzkes, Michael S. *gas industry executive, lawyer*
McNeill, Corbin Asahel, Jr. *utilities executive*
Mulé, Ann C. *oil industry executive*
Mulholland, Paul A. *gas industry executive*
Naku, Rolf D. *gas industry executive*
Owens, Robert W. *gas industry executive*
Roberts, Ralph Joel *telecommunications industry executive, cable broadcast executive*

## Pittsburgh
Bartley, Burnett Graham, Jr. *oil industry executive*
Gerber, Murry S. *gas, oil and utilities executive*
Harvey, J. Brett *energy executive*
Stirewalt, John Newman *coal company executive*
Wagner, Florence Zeleznik *retired telecommunications industry executive*

## Presto
Moeller, Audrey Carolyn *retired energy company executive, retired corporate secretary*

## Wayne
Lefevre, Thomas Vernon *retired utilities executive*

## Wilkes Barre
Lindemann, George L. *gas industry executive*

# SOUTH CAROLINA

## Columbia
Marsh, Kevin B. *energy executive*
Timmerman, William B. *utilities executive, accountant*

## Hilton Head Island
Simpson, John Wistar *utilities executive, consultant*

## Murrells Inlet
Justice, Franklin Pierce, Jr. *oil industry executive*

## Myrtle Beach
Atkinson, Harold Witherspoon *utilities executive, consultant, real estate broker*

## Sheldon
Lowrie, William G. *former oil company executive*

# TENNESSEE

## Knoxville
McCullough, Glenn L., Jr. *electric power industry executive*
Moore, Richard Wayne *electric power industry executive, former prosecutor*

## Nashville
Adams, Kenneth Stanley, Jr., (Bud Adams) *energy executive, professional sports team executive*

# TEXAS

## Austin
Anderson, Lynn D. *telecommunications industry executive*
Brigham, Ben M. *oil industry executive*
Day, Robert Michael *oil company executive*
Deisler, Paul Frederick, Jr. *retired oil company executive*
Galloway, Gale Lee *oil and gas executive, rancher*
Gibson, Jerry Leigh *oil industry executive*
Groten, Barnet *energy executive*
Haas, Joseph Marshall *retired petroleum consultant*

## Carrollton
Brown, Kevin *telecommunications industry executive*
Johnson, James L. *telecommunications industry executive*
Parker, Terry S. *telecommunications industry executive*

## Channelview
Nyberg, Donald Arvid *oil industry executive*

## Corpus Christi
Benner, Richard Walter *oil industry executive, petroleum engineer, geologist*
Haas, Paul Raymond *petroleum company executive*
Norman, Wyatt Thomas III *landman, consultant*
Paulson, Bernard Arthur *oil industry executive, consultant*

## Dallas
Best, Robert Wayne *gas transmission company executive, lawyer*
Biegler, David W. *energy executive*
Blessing, Edward Warfield *petroleum company executive*
Campbell, Kevin P. *oil industry executive*
Clifton, Matthew P. *petroleum refining company executive*
Davis, Barry E. *energy executive*
Davis, Ray C. *energy executive*
Farell, Dan *utilities executive*
Fielder, Charles Robert *retired oil industry executive*
Gratton, Patrick John Francis *oil industry executive*
Harless, Katherine J. *telecommunications industry executive*
Hunt, Ray L. *petroleum company executive*
Jennings, James Burnett *oil industry executive*
Jones, Everett Riley, Jr. *oil industry executive*
Middleton, James Arthur *oil and gas company executive*
Nevins, William J. *oil and gas brokerage executive, consultant*
Norsworthy, Lamar *petroleum company executive*
Nye, Erle Allen *electric power industry executive, lawyer*
Perry, George Wilson *oil and gas company executive*
Pickens, Boone (Thomas Boone Pickens Jr.) *oil industry executive*
Rees-Jones, Trevor D. *oil industry executive*
Sizer, Phillip Spelman *gas industry executive, retired oil industry executive*
Slawter, John David, Jr. *oil industry executive*
Thorne, Carl F. *gas industry executive*
Warren, Kelcy L. *energy executive*
Wilder, C. John (John Wilder) *energy executive*
Wilson, Richard A. *oil and gas industry support services executive*

## El Paso
Foster, Paul L. *oil industry executive*

## Fort Worth
Boschetti, Philip J. *oil industry executive*
Brumley, Ira Jon *gas industry executive*
Brumley, Jon S. *oil industry executive*
Fortson, Ben J. *oil industry executive*
Hudson, Edward Randall, Jr. *gas and oil industry executive*
Hyde, Clarence Brodie, II, *oil industry executive*
Moncrief, Richard W. *oil industry executive*
Moncrief, William Alvin, Jr. *oil and gas producer*
Simpson, Bob R. *energy executive*

## Frisco
Mackenzie, John *retired oil industry executive*

**Gainesville**
McCormack, Lowell Ray *oil industry executive, corporate financial executive, consultant*

**Horseshoe Bay**
Jorden, James Roy *oil industry executive, consultant*

**Houston**
Armstrong, Greg L. *oil industry executive*
Barracano, Henry Ralph *retired oil company executive, management consultant*
Blanton, Jack Sawtelle *oil industry executive*
Bonneville, Richard Briggs *retired gas industry executive*
Bookout, John Frank, Jr. *oil industry executive*
Bowen, William Jackson *retired gas industry executive*
Bryan, J(ames) P(erry), Jr. *energy executive*
Campbell, Eileen M. *oil industry executive*
Carriere, Margaret E. *energy executive*
Carrig, John A. *oil industry executive*
Carroll, Milton *oil industry executive*
Caruso, Nick J. *energy executive*
Cazalot, Clarence P., Jr. *oil industry executive*
Chalmers, David B. *petroleum executive*
Clark, James R. *oil industry executive*
Colson, John R. *electric power industry executive*
Comer, Clarence C. *gas industry executive*
Cox, Frank D. (Buddy Cox) *oil industry executive*
Creel, Michael Allen *energy executive*
Dasari, Ganeswara R. *oil industry executive*
Davidson, Charles D. *energy executive*
Davis, Leon *oil industry executive*
Deaton, Chad C. *oil and gas industry executive*
DeVault, John Lee *oil industry executive, geophysicist*
Dice, Bruce Burton *gas industry executive*
Dreyer, Alec Gilbert *electric power industry executive*
Drury, Leonard Leroy *retired oil company executive*
Duncan, Dan L. *gas company executive*
Dunham, Archie Wallace *petroleum company executive, chemicals executive*
Erikson, Sheldon R. *oil industry executive*
Farris, G. Steven *oil and gas production company executive*
Foshee, Douglas *gas industry executive*
Frederickson, Philip L. *oil industry executive*
Frost, John Elliott *minerals company executive*
Fulwiler, Robert Neal *oil industry executive*
Furbacher, Stephen A. *energy executive*
Gallogly, James Lawrence *oil industry executive, lawyer*
Gaut, C. Christopher *gas industry executive*
Gibbs, James R. *oil industry executive*
Goldman, Robert W. *retired gas and oil industry executive*
Goodman, Herbert Irwin *petroleum company executive*
Goodman, Joe Read *utilities executive*
He, Hui *energy executive*
Hemminghaus, Roger Roy *energy company executive, chemical engineer*
Hildebrand, Jeffrey D. *oil industry executive*
Irwin, John Robert *oil and gas industry executive*
Jacobs, Mark M. *energy executive, corporate financial executive*
Jines, Michael L. *utilities executive*
Johnson, Wayne D. *gas industry executive*
Keiser, Robert Lee *retired gas and oil industry executive*
Kerr, Baine Perkins *oil industry executive*
Kinder, Richard Dan *natural gas pipeline, oil and gas company executive*
Kirkland, John David *oil and gas company executive, lawyer*
Knickel, Carin S. *oil industry executive*
Kramer, Phillip D. *oil industry executive*
krohn, Tracy W. *oil industry executive, gas industry executive*
Kuehn, Ronald L., Jr. *natural resources company executive*
Kuntz, Hal Goggan *petroleum exploration company executive, rancher*
Lesar, David J. *oil industry executive*
Limbacher, Randy L. *energy executive*
Lowe, John E. *oil industry executive, accountant*
Matheny, Kenneth L. *oil industry executive*
Mathis, James Forrest *retired petroleum company executive*
McClanahan, David M. *energy executive*
McGill, Stuart R. *oil industry executive*
Miller, Merrill Anthony, Jr. *oil industry executive*
Mire, Weldon J. *oil industry executive, human resources specialist*
Papa, Mark Gary *oil and gas industry executive*
Pefanis, Harry N. *oil industry executive*
Plank, Raymond *energy executive*
Ragauss, Peter A. *oil industry executive*
Raspino, Louis A. *energy executive*
Roberts, David E., Jr. *oil industry executive*
Roff, J(ohn) Hugh, Jr. *energy executive*
Shackouls, Bobby S. *oil and gas industry executive*
Shaper, C. Park *energy executive*
Shapiro, Steven J. *energy executive*
Smith, Dan F. *oil industry executive*
Smith, David Kingman *retired oil company executive, consultant*
Snyder, C. Byron *electric power industry executive*
Staff, Joel V. *energy executive*
Stewart, J.W. *energy executive, lawyer*
Swanson, Douglas E. *oil industry executive*
Szescila, Andrew J. *oil industry executive*
Thompson, Jerry E. *oil industry executive*
Thompson, Jon L. *retired oil industry executive*
Trice, David A. *oil industry executive*
Trogus, Frank J. *oil industry executive*
Van Dyke, Gene *oil industry executive*
Van Wagenen, Paul G. *gas industry executive*
Wiley, Michael E. *oil industry executive*
Williams, Robert Henry *oil industry executive*
Williamson, Bruce A. *gas industry executive*
Wilson, Edward Converse, Jr. *oil and natural gas production company executive*
Wilson, Floyd C. *oil industry executive*
Wyatt, Oscar Sherman, Jr. *energy company executive*

**Irving**
Cavanaugh, Lucille J. *oil industry executive*
Cohen, Kenneth P. *oil industry executive, lawyer*
Dahan, Rene *oil industry executive*
Dingle, Philip *oil industry executive*
Humphreys, Donald D. *oil industry executive*
Longwell, Harry J. *retired oil industry executive*
Matthews, Charles W., Jr. *oil industry executive*
Mulva, Patrick T. *oil industry executive*
Sheffield, Scott D. *oil industry executive*
Tillerson, Rex W. *oil company executive*

**Mc Kinney**
Dickinson, Richard Raymond *retired oil company executive*

**Midland**
Grover, Rosalind Redfern *oil and gas company executive*

**Missouri City**
Tchamengo, Mathias Ngoufi *energy executive, mathematician*

**Plano**
Chopra, Anil *oil industry executive*
Satz, Jeffrey S. *telecommunications industry executive, consultant*
Schuh, Frank Joseph *oil industry executive, consultant*

**Pottsboro**
Hanning, Gary William *utilities executive, consultant, water transportation executive*

**Richardson**
Cox, David Leon *telecommunications industry executive*

**Salado**
Parks, Lloyd Lee *oil industry executive*

**San Antonio**
Arthur, Gary L., Jr. *energy executive*
Blank, Steven A. *energy executive*
Booke, Keith D. *energy executive*
Brown, Mary Rose *energy executive*
Browning, Jay D. *energy executive*
Callaway, James W. *telecommunications industry executive*
Ciskowski, Michael S. *energy executive*
Crownover, Mike *energy executive*
Dorman, David W. *telecommunications industry executive*
Edwards, Gene *energy executive*
Ellis, James D. *telecommunications industry executive, lawyer*
Gorder, Joe *energy executive*
Greehey, William Eugene (Bill Greehey) *energy company executive*
Kahan, James S. *telecommunications industry executive*
Killinger, Clayton *energy executive*
King, Gregory C. *petroleum company executive*
Klaerner, Curtis Maurice *gas industry executive*
Klesse, William R. (Bill Klesse) *energy executive*
Lindner, Richard G. *telecommunications industry executive*
Marcogliese, Richard J. *energy executive*
Miller, Forrest E. *telecommunications industry executive*
Renfro, Norm *energy executive*
Smith, Bruce Alfred *oil industry executive*
Stephenson, Randall L. *telecommunications industry executive*
Upton, Wade *energy executive*
Whitacre, Edward E., Jr. *telecommunications company executive*
Wilkins, Rayford, Jr. *telecommunications industry executive*
Wiskocil, Angiolina *telecommunications industry executive*
Wright, Gregory A. *energy executive*
Zesch, Hal *energy executive*

**Snyder**
Castellano, Dawnmarie *oil industry executive, consultant*
Siegel, Mark S. *energy executive*

**Spring**
Corbett, Luke R. *former energy company executive*

**The Woodlands**
Allison, Robert James, Jr. *retired oil and gas company executive*
Hackett, James T. *oil industry executive*
Larson, James R. *retired oil industry executive*
Manson, Lewis Auman *energy executive*
Mitchell, George Phydias *gas and petroleum company executive*
Sharman, Richard Lee *telecommunications executive, consultant*
Wilcox, Raymond I. *oil industry executive*

**Tyler**
Hughes, Arthur Hyde *accountant, energy industry executive, accountant*

**Whitewright**
Burg, John Parker *electric power industry executive*

**UTAH**

**Ogden**
Adams, J. Phillip *oil industry executive*

**Park City**
Edwards, Howard Lee *retired oil and gas industry executive, lawyer*

**Salt Lake City**
Cash, Roy Don *retired gas and petroleum company executive*
Holding, R. Earl (Robert Earl Holding) *oil company executive*

Rattie, Keith O. *gas industry executive*

**VERMONT**

**Barnard**
Larson, John Hyde *retired utilities executive*

**Dorset**
Hittle, Richard Howard *gas industry executive, oil industry executive, consultant*

**North Clarendon**
Freed, Walter Everett *petroleum company executive, state representative*

**VIRGINIA**

**Abingdon**
Quillen, Michael J. *energy executive*

**Alexandria**
Copulos, Milton Russell *energy executive*
Hirsch, Robert Louis *energy analyst, consultant*
Smith, Jeffrey Greenwood *gas industry executive, retired military officer*

**Arlington**
Bakke, Dennis W. *energy company executive*
Hanrahan, Paul Thaddeus *utilities executive*
Harker, Victoria D. *electric power industry executive*
Luraschi, William R. *utilities executive, lawyer*

**Chesterfield**
Love, Dana Francis Ignatius *telecommunications industry executive*

**Fairfax**
Cramer, H. R. (Hal Cramer) *oil industry executive*
Simon, J. Stephen *oil industry executive*

**Herndon**
Gilbert, Douglas Brainerd *telecommunications industry executive*

**Lynchburg**
Womack, Edgar Allen, Jr. *energy executive, consultant, nuclear technology consultant*

**Mc Lean**
Mandl, Alex J(ohann) *telecommunications company executive*
Singh, K. Paul *telecommunications industry executive*

**Reston**
Conway, William E., Jr. *telecommunications industry executive, venture capitalist*
Donahue, Timothy M. *telecommunications industry executive*
Forsee, Gary D. *telecommunications industry executive*
Grivner, Carl J. *telecommunications industry executive*
Kelly, Thomas N., Jr. *telecommunications industry executive*
Kennedy, Leonard Jervey *telecommunications industry executive, lawyer*
Saleh, Paul N. *telecommunications industry executive*
Shindler, Steven *telecommunications industry executive*
West, Barry J. *telecommunications industry executive*

**Richmond**
Alewine, Betty *retired telecommunications industry executive*
Blankenship, Don L. *energy executive*
Capps, Thomas Edward *utilities company executive, lawyer*
Capps, Thos E. *energy executive*
Chewning, Thomas N. *energy executive*
Farrell, Thomas Francis *energy executive*

**Sterling**
Oller, William Maxwell *retired energy executive, retired military officer*

**WASHINGTON**

**Bellevue**
Reynolds, Stephen Philip *utility company executive*
Valdman, Bertrand A. *utilities executive*
Williamson, Charles R. *retired energy company executive*

**Kirkland**
Chapple, John H. *telecommunications industry executive, former professional sports team executive*

**Olympia**
Oberbillig, Molly Castleman *utilities executive*

**Sequim**
Beaton, Roy Howard *retired nuclear energy industry executive*

**Spokane**
Eliassen, Jon Eric *retired utilities executive, corporate financial executive*
Ely, Gary G. *utilities company executive*

**WEST VIRGINIA**

**Bluefield**
Reid, William James *mining executive*

**WISCONSIN**

**Green Bay**
Weyers, Larry Lee *energy executive*

**La Crosse**
Rude, Brian David *utilities company executive*

**Madison**
Barr, James III *telecommunications company executive*
Bisbee, Joyce Evelyn *retired utility company executive*
Harvey, William D. *utilities executive, lawyer*
Protsch, Eliot G. *utilities executive, corporate financial executive*

**Milwaukee**
Klappa, Gale E. *energy executive*
Leverett, Allen L. *energy executive*

**WYOMING**

**Casper**
Stroock, Thomas Frank *oil and gas company executive*

**Riverton**
Bebout, Eli Daniel *oil industry executive*

## TERRITORIES OF THE UNITED STATES

**VIRGIN ISLANDS**

**St Thomas**
Prior, Cornelius Bernard, Jr. *utilities executive, financial consultant*

## CANADA

**ALBERTA**

**Calgary**
Anderson, J.C. *oil industry executive, gas industry executive, rancher*
Arledge, David A. *energy executive*
Daniel, Patrick D. *energy executive*
Haskayne, Richard Francis *retired petroleum company executive*
Horton, William Russell *retired utilities executive*
McKinnon, F(rancis) A(rthur) Richard *utilities executive*
Morgan, Gwyn *oil and gas executive*
Pourbaix, Alexander *energy executive*
Seaman, Daryl Kenneth *oil industry executive*
Southern, Nancy C. *utilities executive*
Swartout, Hank B. *oil and gas industry executive*

**Red Deer**
Donald, Jack C. *gas industry executive*

**BRITISH COLUMBIA**

**Vancouver**
Friedland, Robert M. *mining executive*
Keevil, Norman B. *mining executive*
Lyons, Terrence Allan *mining executive*

**NOVA SCOTIA**

**Halifax**
Mann, David *energy and services company executive*

**ONTARIO**

**Brockville**
Spalding, James Stuart *retired telecommunications industry executive*

**North York**
Blundell, William Richard Charles *retired electric company executive*

**Toronto**
Clark, Maura J. *oil and gas industry executive*
Kerr, David Wylie *utilities executive*
Martin, Robert William *retired utilities executive*
Munk, Peter *mining executive*
Osler, Gordon Peter *retired utilities executive*
Wilson, Lynton Ronald *retired telecommunications industry executive*

**QUEBEC**

**Montreal**
Cyr, J. V. Raymond *telecommunications industry executive*

**Calgary**
Maier, Gerald James *gas industry executive*

**Niagara Falls**
Watson, George W. *energy executive*

## CHINA

**Beijing**
Wu, Ying *telecommunications industry executive*

## ECUADOR

**Quito**
Almeida, Francisco *telecommunications industry executive*

## ENGLAND

### Aberdeen
Hill, Gregory Paul *oil industry executive*

### London
Duffy, Simon P. *telecommunications industry executive*
Greener, Sir Anthony *telecommunications industry executive*
Mooney, James F. *telecommunications industry executive*
Polk, George Washington *telecommunications executive, entrepreneur*

## JAPAN

### Yokohama
Ito, Noboru *electric power industry executive*

## NETHERLANDS

### Rotterdam
van Wachem, Lodewijk Christiaan *petroleum company executive*

### The Hague
Cook, Linda Z. *utilities executive*

## PANAMA

### Panama
Bowling, Woodrow Wilson *telecommunications industry executive, insurance company executive*

## ADDRESS UNPUBLISHED

Ackerman, F. Duane (Duane Ackerman) *telecommunication industry executive*
Adams, Valencia I. *telecommunications industry executive*
Anderson, Richard A. *telecommunications industry executive*
Anderson, Robert Orville *oil and gas company executive*
Arlidge, John Walter *retired utilities executive*
Arthur, John Morrison *retired utilities executive*
Auchinleck, Richard H. *exploration company executive*
Bachmann, Richard Arthur *oil company executive*
Bailey, Keith E. *petroleum pipeline company executive*
Barham, Charles Dewey, Jr. *electric power industry executive, lawyer*
Barnes, Wesley Edward *energy and environmental executive*
Barrow, Thomas Davies *retired oil and mining company executive, consultant*
Baumgartner, John H. *gas industry executive*
Bennett, Robert R. *telecommunications company executive*
Berry, William Willis *retired utilities executive*
Boniface, Barry *telecommunications industry executive*
Brewer, Lynn *energy executive*
Brothers, John Alfred *retired oil company executive, chemicals executive*
Brown, Stephen S. *telecommunications industry executive*
Browne, (Edmund) John Phillip (Lord Browne of Madingley) *oil industry executive*
Bruce, James Edmund *retired utilities executive*
Burns, Richard *telecommunications industry executive*
Burrow, Harold *retired gas industry executive*
Butler, Jack Fairchild *electric power industry executive*
Caillé, André *public service company executive*
Campbell, James P. *utilities executive*
Chelle, Robert Frederick *electric power industry executive, educator*
Childers, Charles Eugene *mining company executive*
Clark, Philip Raymond *nuclear utility executive, engineer*
Coffin, Bertha Louise *retired telecommunications industry executive*
Conger, Harry Milton *mining company executive*
Curtis, Edward Joseph, Jr. *gas industry executive, management consultant*
Dallas, Terry G. *gas industry executive*
Dickey, Joseph William *utilities executive, engineer*
Dietler, Cortlandt S. *oil industry executive*
Di Giovanni, Anthony *retired coal mining company executive*
Dragoumis, Paul *electric utility company executive*
Draper, E(rnest) Linn, Jr. *retired electric utility executive*
Droege, Mark E. *telecommunications industry executive*
Dunn, Rebecca M. *telecommunications industry executive*
English, Floyd Leroy *telecommunications industry executive*
Erskine, Rodney D. *oil industry executive*
Esrey, William Todd *telecommunications company executive*
Fagin, David Kyle *gas industry executive*
Finger, Harold Ben *nuclear energy industry executive, consultant, government agency administrator*
Ford, Judith Ann Tudor *retired natural gas distribution company executive*
Frieson, Ronald E. *telecommunications industry executive*
Frisbee, Don Calvin *retired utilities executive*
Fuller, Sandra Vivian *oil and gas industry executive*
Funderburg, Jan *telecommunications industry executive*
Gabel, Ronald Glen *telecommunications executive*

Gardiner, Hobart Clive *petroleum company executive*
Gerard, Roy Dupuy *retired oil company executive*
Gottschalk, Charles M. *international energy consultant*
Gratz, Jay M. *steel company executive*
Green, Richard Calvin, Jr. *electric power and gas industry executive*
Greene, Margaret H. *telecommunications industry executive*
Greer, Carl Crawford *petroleum company executive*
Gurian, Mal *telecommunications executive*
Hall, Milton Reese *retired oil company executive, accountant, controller*
Hallacy, Don *telecommunications industry executive*
Harris, Isiah, Jr. *telecommunications industry executive*
Heiney, John Weitzel *former utilities executive*
Helton, Sandra Lynn *telecommunications industry executive*
Herron, Edwin Hunter, Jr. *energy consultant*
Hines, Andrew Hampton, Jr. *utilities executive*
Howard, James Joseph III *utility company executive*
Huffman, James Thomas William *oil industry executive*
Hurst, Leland Lyle *natural gas company executive*
Hyland, Geoffrey Fyfe *retired energy executive*
Jackson, Robert William *retired utilities executive*
Johnson, Curtis Lildon *retired oil industry executive*
Johnson, Mark J. *mining executive*
Kaculi, Xhemal T. *oil industry analysis/design engineer*
Kaiser, Robert A. *telecommunications industry executive*
Kelly, Robert D *energy executive*
Kertz, Hubert Leonard *telephone company executive*
Kettel, Edward Joseph *retired oil industry executive*
King, William Collins *retired oil industry executive*
Kirkby, Maurice Anthony *oil industry executive*
Lambert, Christina *telecommunications executive*
Lauer, Len J. *former telecommunications executive*
Lee, Donna A. *telecommunications industry executive*
Leonard, J. Wayne *energy executive*
Lewis, Floyd Wallace *former electric utility executive*
Lilly, Edward Guerrant, Jr. *retired utilities executive*
Long, Alfred B. *retired oil industry executive*
Loveland, Eugene Franklin *retired gas industry executive*
Luft, Robert v.d. *energy executive*
Lutz, Matthew Charles *oil industry executive, geologist*
Lynch, Thomas J. *telecommunications industry executive*
MacFarlane, John Charles *utilities executive*
Maddox, Lyndell E. *utilities company executive*
Martinez, Placido *energy executive*
Mauch, Robert Carl *energy and financial services executive*
McCabe, Joseph, Jr. *telecommunications industry executive*
Mc Carthy, Walter John, Jr. *retired utilities executive*
McCormick, William Thomas, Jr. *electric and gas company executive*
McCready, Kenneth Frank *former electric utility executive*
McGinn, Richard A. *telecommunications company executive*
McSweeny, William Francis *petroleum company executive, author*
Montgomery, Roy Delbert *retired gas industry executive*
Morrell, Gene Paul *gas industry executive, consultant*
Munsey, Virdell Everard, Jr. *retired utilities executive*
Nicholson, Leland Ross *retired utilities executive, energy consultant*
Noto, Lucio A. *gas and oil industry executive*
Nurenberg, David *retired oil company executive*
O'Connor, James John *retired utility company executive*
Odom, Rod D., Jr. *telecommunications industry executive*
O'Hare, James Raymond *energy executive*
Olson, Robert Edward *coal mining executive*
O'Malley, Thomas D. *petroleum industry executive*
Ormasa, John *retired utilities executive*
Osterhoff, James Marvin *retired telecommunications company executive*
Outlaw, Lanny F. *gas company executive*
Owens, William Arthur (Bill Owens) *telecommunications industry executive, retired military officer*
Pate, William *telecommunications industry executive*
Peon, Roberto *telecommunications industry executive*
Perry, Kenneth Walter *retired integrated oil company executive*
Phillips, Robert Glenn *energy executive*
Pierce, Lisa Margaret *telecommunications industry executive, marketing professional, educator*
Portal, Gilbert Marcel Adrien *oil industry executive*
Priory, Richard Baldwin *former electric power industry executive*
Quillen, Lloyd Douglas *oil and gas executive*
Quirk, Kathleen L. *mining executive*
Ramjee, Ramachandran *telecommunications industry executive, computer scientist*
Rawson, Richard J. *telecommunications industry executive, lawyer*
Raymond, Lee R. *retired oil company executive*
Rendu, Jean-Michel Marie *mining executive*
Richman, Paul *semiconductor industry executive, educator*
Roberts, Lawrence Gilman *telecommunications industry executive*
Roe, Thomas Coombe *former utility company executive*

Rogers, Justin Towner, Jr. *retired utility company executive*
St. Clair, Thomas McBryar *mining and manufacturing company executive*
Salerno, Frederic V. *retired telecommunications company executive*
Sanchez, Antonio Rodolfo, Jr. *oil industry executive*
Sanders, Charles Franklin *energy executive, consultant*
Schenck, Jack Lee *retired electric utility executive*
Schenker, Leo *retired utilities executive*
Scobey, David W., Jr. *telecommunications industry executive*
Scott, Isadore Meyer *retired energy executive*
Serkes, Jeffrey D. *former energy executive*
Shannon, W. Patrick *telecommunications industry executive*
Sloan, Robert D. *energy executive, lawyer*
Smith, Gordon Ray *utilities executive*
Smith, Paul Vergon, Jr. *retired gas industry executive*
Spagnolo, Mark F. *telecommunications industry executive*
Sprow, Frank Barker *oil company executive*
Sullivan, Kathryn Meara *telecommunications industry executive*
Terry, Richard Edward *public utility holding company executive*
Thomas, Kenneth Glyndwr *mining executive*
Thompson, Jack Edward *mining company executive*
Thorn, Terence Hastings *energy executive, consultant, writer*
Tillinghast, John Avery *utilities executive*
Todd, Zane Grey *retired utilities executive*
Townsend, Thomas Perkins *former mining company executive*
Travis, Vance Kenneth *petroleum business executive*
Trutter, John Thomas *telecommunications industry executive, educator, writer*
Tucker, H. Richard *oil industry executive*
Turner, Thomas Marshall *telecommunications executive, consultant*
Vermylen, Paul Anthony, Jr. *oil industry executive*
Voss, William Charles *retired oil company executive*
Wannier, Mario Marc-Antoine *oil industry executive, multi-media specialist, director*
Weaver, William Schildecker *retired electric power industry executive*
Weeks, William Rawle, Jr. *oil industry executive*
Wentworth, Lynn A. *telecommunications industry executive*
Wickstrom, Jon Alan *telecommunications executive, consultant*
Wilkerson, Matha Ann *retired oil company executive*
Williams, Neville *solar power corporation executive*
Wilson, Walter Clinton *retired gas industry executive*
Wood, Willis Bunn, Jr. *retired utilities executive*
Woodburn, William A. *utilities executive*
Wright, Randolph Earle *retired petroleum company executive*
Yackira, Michael William *electric power industry executive*

## INFORMATION TECHNOLOGY
*See also* SCIENCE: MATHEMATICS AND COMPUTER SCIENCE

## UNITED STATES

### ALABAMA

**Auburn University**
Adrian, Anne Mims *computer technician*

**Florence**
Foote, Avon Edward *web developer/producer, communications educator*

**Mobile**
McCleery, Winston Theodore *information technology executive*

### ARIZONA

**Phoenix**
Kamins, Edward *information technology executive*

**Scottsdale**
Faig, Harold *information technology executive*
Stott, Brian *software company executive, consultant*

**Tempe**
Crown, Eric J. *information systems executive*
Crown, Timothy A. *computer technology company executive*
Fennessy, Richard A. *information technology executive*
Laybourne, Stanley *computer technology company executive*
Smith, Branson M. *computer technology company executive*

**Tucson**
Donoghue, John Charles *application developer, consultant*
Fredericksen, Dick Hartman *retired computer programmer*

### CALIFORNIA

**Antelope**
Nenov, Ivo P. *mathematical and software researcher*

**Arcadia**
Ingram, C. Kendal (Ken Ingram) *information technology executive, non-profit organization administrator*

**Berkeley**
Karp, Richard Manning *computer science educator*
Séquin, Carlo H. *computer science educator*
Wieczorek, John Richard *application developer, systems analyst*

**Calabasas**
Jones, Richard K. *information technology executive*

**Chatsworth**
Komm, Kermit Matthew *software engineer*

**Claremont**
Vallabhajosyula, Ravishankar Rao *application developer*

**Costa Mesa**
Berman, Stuart B. *information technology executive*

**Cupertino**
Bregman, Mark *information technology executive*
Clyde, Robert Allan *computer software engineer*
Ive, Jonathan *information technology executive, product designer*
Johnson, Ron *information technology executive*
Krauss, Kirk J. *application developer, writer*
Nielsen, Tod *information technology executive*
Schiller, Philip W. *information technology executive*
Serlet, Bertrand *information technology executive*
Tamaddon, Sina *information technology executive*
Thompson, John W. *information technology executive*

**Cypress**
Romero, Tony *information technology executive*

**Danville**
Bergsten, James Robert *computer technology architect*

**Del Mar**
Fricke, Martin Paul *science company executive*

**Emeryville**
Smith, Christopher Allen *information technology executive, financial executive*

**Folsom**
Bahbah, Amr G. *application developer, consultant*
Haga, Enoch John *computer educator, writer*
Krishnaswamy, Dilip *computer architect*

**Fremont**
Tang, John *network technician, information scientist, educator*

**Fresno**
Edwards, Lynne Marie *information technology consultant*

**Glen Ellen**
Hurlbert, Roger William *information technology executive*

**Irvine**
Pardo, Robert *game designer, video game software company executive*

**La Jolla**
Wang, Xudong *network architect, researcher*

**Lafayette**
Lewis, Sheldon Noah *technology consultant*

**Lake Forest**
Massengill, Matthew H. *data storage company executive*

**Los Alamitos**
Weinberger, Frank *information management consultant*

**Los Angeles**
Boehm, Barry William *computer science educator*
Harrison, Blair *information technology executive*
Jones, Gerald Paul *information technology educator*

**Martinez**
Tong, Siu Wing *computer programmer*

**Menlo Park**
Cassidy, Mike *online game company executive*
Hewlett, Walter B. *application developer*
Mangiola, Mark *information technology executive*
Murphy, Matt *information technology executive*
Scoble, Robert *podcast network company executive, blog writer*
Zdeblick, Mark James *information technology executive*

**Milpitas**
Treichel, Helmuth W.A. *technology executive*

**Modesto**
Kushar, Kent *information technology executive*

**Monterey Park**
Tsao, Gus *information technology executive*

**Mountain View**
Armstrong, Tim *information technology executive*
Baker, Mitchell *computer software development foundation administrator*

Bosworth, Adam *software engineer*
Brin, Sergey Mihailovich *information technology executive*
Brown, Shona *information technology executive*
Burton, Jeremy *information technology executive*
Cassidy, Sukhinder Singh *information technology executive*
Cerf, Vinton Gray *information technology executive*
Coughran, William M., Jr. *information technology executive, researcher*
Drummond, David C. *information technology executive, lawyer*
Eustace, Alan *information technology executive*
Gillis, Edwin *information technology executive*
Hagerman, Kristof *information technology executive*
Huber, Jeff *information technology executive*
Hughes, Gregory *information technology executive*
Kamangar, Salar *information technology executive*
Kordestani, Omid *information technology executive*
Matin, Arthur *information technology executive*
Mayer, Marissa Ann *information technology executive*
Page, Larry (Lawrence E. Page) *information technology executive*
Reyes, George *information technology executive*
Rivera, Miriam *information technology executive, lawyer*
Rosenberg, Jonathan *information technology executive*
Rosing, Wayne *information technology executive*
Sandberg, Sheryl *information technology executive*
Schmidt, Eric Emerson *information technology executive*
Schneier, Bruce *information technology executive*
Schrage, Elliot *information technology executive*
Sclavos, Stratton *information technology executive*
Singh, Sangita *information technology and marketing executive*

**Palo Alto**
Bernstein, Mark *information technology executive*
Denzel, Nora *information technology executive*
Greene, Diane *information technology executive*
Lal, Dhananjay *information technology executive, researcher*
Mayo, Robert N. *computer science researcher*
Montgomery, Kevin *information technology executive*
Payton, Paul Max *application developer*

**Pleasanton**
Bergquist, Rick *software company executive*
Dubois, Guy *software company executive*
Gregoire, Michael P. *software company executive*
Gupta, Ram *software company executive*

**Redondo Beach**
Sloan, Michael Dana *information systems specialist, management consultant*

**Redwood City**
Burkhardt, Roger *information technology executive*
Catz, Safra *computer software company executive*
Davidson, Mary Ann *information technology executive*
Ellison, Larry (Lawrence Joseph Ellison) *computer software company executive*
Hagart-Alexander, Claud *software engineer*
Lee, V. Paul *entertainment software company executive*
Rohde, James Vincent *software systems company executive*
Smith, Nancy L. *information technology executive*

**Sacramento**
Hummel, John *information technology executive*

**San Bernardino**
Baek, Eun-Ok *instructional technology educator*

**San Diego**
Gilleland, John Rogers *technology company executive*
Goldstein, Mark Kingston Levin *information technology executive, researcher*
Rastetter, Wiliam H. *biotechnology company executive*
Short, Jay Milton *biotechnology company executive*
Simpson, William *information technology manager, consultant*
Suycott, Mark Leland *program manager, retired military officer*
Tom, Lawrence *technology executive*

**San Francisco**
Buckmaster, Jim *online community bulletin board company executive*
Fanning, Shawn *information technology executive*
Kapor, Mitchell David *application developer, foundation administrator*
Pure, Pamela J. *information technology executive*
Rosedale, Philip *computer software company executive*
Salmi, Mika *information technology executive*
Trott, Mena *application developer*

**San Jose**
Ashburn, Thomas *information technology executive*
Belluzzo, Rick E. (Richard E. Belluzzo) *information technology executive, former computer software company executive*
Boston, Brad *information technology executive*
Chambers, John Thomas *computer systems network executive*
Chen, Deanford Frederick *software engineer*
Chuang, Alfred S. *information technology executive*
Coleman, William T. *information technology executive*
Farnham, Timothy *information technology executive*
Fishback, Dennis *information technology executive*
Helleboid, Olivier *information technology executive*
Hoffman, Charles E. *information technology executive*

Ill, Charles III *information technology executive*
Karandikar, Yogesh Dinkar *software engineer*
Klein, William M. (Bill Klein) *information technology executive*
Loiacono, John P. *information technology executive*
Meltzer, Cliff *information technology executive*
Morgridge, John P. *computer systems network executive*
Patryshev, Vlad *application developer*
Powell, Dennis D. *computer systems network executive*
Sauvageau, Yvon *application developer*
Scheinman, A. Daniel *computer system networks executive*
Swan, Robert H. *information technology executive*

**San Mateo**
Farmer, Dan *computer security researcher, computer programmer*
Shaheen, George T. *software company executive*
Siebel, Thomas M. *software company executive*

**San Ramon**
Moore, Justin Edward *information technology executive*
Schofield, James Roy *computer programmer*

**Santa Ana**
Abramo, Guy P. *information technology executive*
Flastrup, Asger *information technology executive*
Foster, Kent B. *information technology executive*
Koppen, Hans T. *information technology executive*
Murai, Kevin *information technology executive*
Salem, Karen E. *information technology executive*
Spierkel, Gregory M. *information technology executive*
Veasey, Byron Keith *information systems consultant*

**Santa Barbara**
Boehm, Eric Hartzell *information technology executive*

**Santa Clara**
Beveridge, Crawford *information technology executive*
Canepa, Mark A. *information technology executive*
Dai, Weili *information technology executive*
Howe, Bill *information technology executive*
Lehman, Michael Evans *information technology executive*
McNealy, Scott Glenn *information technology executive*
Peterson, Marissa *information technology executive*
Samenuk, George *software security company executive*
Schwartz, Jonathan Ian *information technology executive*
Sutardja, Sehat *information technology executive*

**Scotts Valley**
Janssen, James Robert *consulting software engineer*

**South Pasadena**
Hsieh, Ming *information technology executive*

**South San Francisco**
Cittadini, Pete *reporting applications platform company executive*
Letts, Nathan P. *biotechnology executive, lawyer*
Nierenberg, Nico *software developer company executive*
Ryan, Tom *reporting applications platform company executive*

**Stanford**
Feigenbaum, Edward Albert *retired computer science educator*

**Sunnyvale**
Andreessen, Marc *software company executive, internet innovator*
Bazzi, Samer *application developer, consultant*
Benhamou, Eric A. *information technology company executive*
Calderoni, Robert M. *software company executive*
Cambou, Bertrand *information technology executive*
Edwards, William T. (Billy Edwards) *information technology executive*
Hawkins, Jeff *information technology company executive*
Kriens, Scott G. *information technology executive*
McCoy, Thomas *information technology executive*
McVeigh, Patrick (Pat) *software developer company executive*
Meyer, Derrick R. *information technology executive*
Morris, Iain *information technology executive*
Nagel, David *software developer company executive*
Nazem, Farzad *information technology executive*
Perdikou, Kim *information technology executive*
Ruiz, Hector de Jesus *information technology executive*
Sindu, Pradeep *information technology executive*
Xie, Ken *software company executive*

**Tracy**
Johnson, Ronald Leonard *information technology executive, small business owner*

**Tustin**
Kim, Dong Wook *information technology executive*

**West Sacramento**
Wilson, Eric F.G. *information technology executive*

**Woodland Hills**
Stratton, Gregory Alexander *application developer, director, mayor*

## COLORADO

**Boulder**
Kenney, Belinda Jill Forseman *information technology executive*
Rodriguez, Juan Alfonso *information technology executive*

**Broomfield**
O'Hara, Kevin J. *information technology executive*

**Colorado Springs**
Gibson, John Robert *software engineer*

**Denver**
Thompson, Joseph Paul *retired systems administrator*
Walker, Radford *web architect*

**Englewood**
Fote, Charles T. *information technology company executive*

**Greenwood Village**
Duques, Ric (Henry C. Duques) *information technology company executive*

**Littleton**
Marion, John Martin *instructional technology educator*

**Louisville**
Kocol, Robert S. *information technology executive*
Martin, Patrick J. *technology company executive*

## CONNECTICUT

**Danbury**
Collar, Emilio, Jr. *information systems consultant*
Williamson, Brian David *information systems executive, consultant*

**East Granby**
Carter, Adrian Lindsey Gould *information technology manager*

**Fairfield**
Carlucci, David R. *information technology executive*
Fash, Victoria R. *business executive*
Immelt, Jeffrey R. *diversified technology and services company executive*
Reiner, Gary M. *diversified technology and services company executive*
Rice, John G. *diversified technology and services executive*

**Mashantucket**
Yale, John Paul *computer systems developer*

**New Britain**
Margiotta, Mary-Lou Ann *application developer*

**New London**
Carpenter, Bruce William *information technology manager, director*

**Newtown**
Coates, John Peter *technical executive*

**Norwich**
Pudlo, Steven Edward *computer technician*

**Stamford**
Dammerman, Dennis Dean *diversified technology and services company executive*
Freeborn, Philip *information technology executive*
Wilderotter, Maggie (Mary Agnes Wilderotter) *software company executive, former cable television executive*
Wilens, Michael Engber *information technology executive, biologist, microscopist*

**Westport**
Frese, Edward Scheer, Jr., (Ted Frese) *information technology executive, consultant*

## DELAWARE

**Newark**
Godwin, Ralph Edward *retired computer operator*

## DISTRICT OF COLUMBIA

**Washington**
Belak, Michael James *information technology executive*
Booth, R. Corey *information technology executive*
Day, Melvin Sherman *information and telecommunications company executive*
Golden, James Leslie *information technology executive, retired military officer*
Greer, Mark Francis *information technology executive*
Gross, Patrick Walter *information technology executive*
Hungate, Joseph Irvin III *information technology executive*
Leslie, Donald S. *information technology manager*
McConnell, Bruce William *information technology executive*
Meyer, Paul *information technology executive*
Otto, Robert L. *information technology executive*
Rose, George Andrew *application developer, information systems specialist*
Shields, Christopher Andrew *website director*
Wertheim, Mitzi Mallina *information technology executive*
Wilson, Carl *information technology executive*

## FLORIDA

**Boca Raton**
Breakstone, Robert Albert *information technology executive, consumer products company executive, consultant*

**Celebration**
Johnson, Derrick M. *information technology executive*

**Clearwater**
Duerst, Andreas *information technology executive*
Martino, Richard *application developer, mathematician, educator*

**Deerfield Beach**
Yerves, Ken *information technology executive*

**Fort Pierce**
Hurley, William Joseph *retired information technology executive*

**Hollywood**
Barish, Randall David *application developer*

**Jacksonville**
Chambers, Jack Allen *application developer, educator*
Payne, Timothy D. *information technology executive*
Portell, Keith S *application developer, consultant*

**Melbourne Beach**
Cooper, Roger Merlin *information technology executive, school system administrator, federal agency administrator*

**Miami**
Clark, James H. *former software company executive, real estate company executive*
Watson, Doug *information technology executive*

**Naples**
Thomas, Gary Lynn *information technology executive*

**Newberry**
Thornton, J. Ronald *technology consultant*

**Orlando**
Young, Gilbert John, Jr. *systems administrator*

**Ormond Beach**
Burke, Marguerite Jodi Larcombe *application developer, consultant*

**Palm Coast**
Bentley, Douglas Leo, Sr. *retired information technology manager*

**Punta Gorda**
Ott, Walter Richard *information technology executive*

**Saint Petersburg**
Frazier, A. D., Jr. *information technology executive, lawyer*

**Sanibel**
Trevor, Alexander Bruen *information technology manager, consultant*

**Spring Hill**
Timmins, Allan S. *information technology manager, educator*

**Tallahassee**
Ladner, Kysandra Marie *information technology manager*

**Tampa**
Bedgood, Alvin J. *information technology manager*
Mangiapane, Joseph Arthur *information technology executive*

**Venice**
Kleinlein, Kathy Lynn *training and development executive*

**Winter Park**
Steward, Sherry Ann *information technology executive, educator*

## GEORGIA

**Alpharetta**
Lademacher, Hartmut *computer software and services company executive*
McCormick, James K. *application developer*
Travers, James M. *application developer*

**Atlanta**
Fleury, Marc *application developer*
Flynn, Owen V. *information technology executive*
Lim, Sung Kyu *information technology educator*
Miller, Sue *information technology executive*

**Canton**
Wilson, Brian Andrew *computing performance consultant, educator, writer, editor*

**Lithonia**
Greene, John Edward, Jr. *network technician*

**Norcross**
Beck, Joshua James *information technology executive*

**Savannah**
Phillips, Robert L., Jr. *application developer, consultant*

**Swainsboro**
Watt, Dwight, Jr., (Arthur Dwight Watt Jr.) *computer programming and microcomputer specialist*

## IDAHO

### Boise
Kirklin, Vance Lane *software company executive*
Mahoney, James E. *information technology executive*

## ILLINOIS

### Burr Ridge
Rosenberg, Robert Brinkmann *information technology executive*

### Chicago
Bergstein, Melvyn *information technology executive*
Buckley, Joseph Paul III *computer technician*
Costin, Joseph Laurence, Jr. *information services executive*
Dwyer, Dennis D. *information technology executive*
Garzolini, Judith A. *information technology manager*
Glazer, Hilary *information technology manager, writer*
Jao, Chiang *information technology educator*
Larson, Nancy Celeste *information technology manager*
Noonan, Jack *application developer*
Reisman, Andrew Louis *information technology executive, lawyer*
Sviokla, John Julius *technology consultant*
Zucker, David F. *information technology executive*

### Crystal Lake
Halperin, Richard George *information technology executive*

### Effingham
Franklin, William Price *computer programmer*

### Libertyville
Shen, Xiaohui *application developer, researcher*

### O Fallon
Bjerkaas, Carlton Lee *information technology executive*

### Savoy
McConnell, William Stewart *application developer*

### Schaumburg
Morrison, Patricia B. *information technology executive*

### Vernon Hills
Klein, Barbara A. *information technology executive*
Leahy, Christine A. *information technology executive*

### Villa Park
Camp, Jeffery Mark *web site designer, military officer*

### Warrenville
Data, Art J. *information technology executive*

### Winnetka
Sick, William Norman, Jr. *technology company executive*

### Woodridge
Puthenpurakal, Joseph Mathew *information technology executive*

## INDIANA

### Beech Grove
Byrkett, Gary Lee *information technology manager*

### Bloomington
Dunning, Jeremy David *application developer, dean, educator*
Henson, Jane Elizabeth *information management professional, adult education educator*
Smith, Janet Sue *systems specialist*

### Carmel
Bostick, Russell M. *information technology executive*

### Indianapolis
Lowe, Mary Katherine *technology company executive, writer*
Niederberger, Jane *information technology executive*

### Spencer
Young, Frederic Higson *information systems executive, data processing consultant*

### Terre Haute
Frey, Susan M. *information specialist*

## IOWA

### Clear Lake
Siska, Robert John *software engineer*

### Council Bluffs
Bragg, MaryAnn *technical facilitator*

### Des Moines
Ellis, Mary Louise Helgeson *information technology company executive*

### Waverly
Brunkhorst, Robert John *computer programmer, analyst*

## KANSAS

### Andover
Whiteside, Mel L. *information technology manager, educator, small business owner*

### Kansas City
Olofson, Tom William *technology company executive*

### Manhattan
Streeter, John Willis *information systems manager*

### Overland Park
Leonard, Markus Dayle *software systems engineer*
Lucas, James Raymond *project manager*

## KENTUCKY

### Lexington
Curlander, Paul Joseph *technology executive*

### Louisville
Hultgren, John Robert *information systems professional, flight paramedic*
Martin, David Allen *application developer, computer scientist*

### Owensboro
Whear, J. Kevin *information technology executive*

### Prospect
Kehlbeck, Joseph H. *software developer, consultant*

## MAINE

### Yarmouth
Grover, Mark Donald *application developer, computer scientist*

## MARYLAND

### Baltimore
Park, Mary Woodfill *information consultant, librarian, writer*
Strull, Gene *technology consultant, retired manufacturing executive*

### College Park
Hendler, James Alexander *computer science educator, consultant*
Miller, Raymond Edward *computer science educator*

### Frederick
Merrill, Daniel A. *program manager*

### Hyattsville
Asongu, Januarius Jingwa *information technology*

### Rockville
Gibson, William M. *technology company executive*
Haber, Margaret Wilson *informatics specialist, director*
MacArthur, Diana Taylor *advanced technology executive*
Mehan, Ashok *information technology executive*
Proffitt, John Richard *information technology executive, educator, public official*

### Silver Spring
Rice, Rick Blackburn *application developer, systems analyst*

### Suitland
Basinger, William Daniel *computer programmer*

### Westminster
Wheatley, Charles Henry III *information technology executive*

## MASSACHUSETTS

### Allston
Kneece, Richard C. *information technology executive*

### Bedford
Wilson, John Atkins, II, *application developer*

### Beverly
Smith, Derek Armand *information technology executive*

### Boston
Ascenzo, Carl *information technology executive*
Grammer, Jeffrey *wireless semiconductor company executive*
Kumar, Vikram Sheel *information technology executive*
Lane, Kathy S. *information technology executive, consumer products company executive*
Poor, Robert *wireless semiconductor company executive*
Stallman, Richard Matthew *software developer*

### Cambridge
Brooks, Rodney Allen *information technology executive, educator*
Gagliardi, Ugo Oscar *systems software architect, educator*
Greenberg, Jerry A. *information technology executive*
Mandl, Robert *application developer*
Moore, J. Stuart *information technology executive*
Mullen, James C. *biotechnology company executive*
Roberts, Edward Baer *technology management educator*
Teevan, Jaime *application developer, researcher*

### Duxbury
Zachmann, William Francis *computer and communications industry market research company executive*

### Foxboro
Martin, Peter Gerard *computer technician, consultant, secondary school educator*

### Framingham
Feldman, Susan Eleanor *technology analyst*

### Lynn
D'Entremont, Edward Joseph *application developer, educator*

### Mashpee
Kilmartin, Joseph Francis, Jr. *information technology executive*

### Newton
Bagalay, John Earl *information technology executive, consultant*

### Newton Highlands
Bricklin, Daniel *software designer, consultant*

### North Reading
Eracar, Yonet *information technology manager*

### Salem
McKenzie, Walter L. *information technology executive, consultant*

### Sudbury
McCree, Paul William, Jr. *systems design and engineering company executive*

### Wakefield
Singleton, Shirley *software development executive*

### Waltham
Bleicher, Paul Alan *information technology executive, physician*
Hovsepian, Ronald W. *network management software company executive*
Messman, Jack L. *network management software company executive*
Russell, Dana C. *information technology executive, accountant*

### Woburn
Mehra, Raman Kumar *aerospace and defense technology executive, automotion and control engineering researcher*

## MICHIGAN

### Belleville
Ibrahim, Faroog Abdel-Kareem *information technology executive*

### Bloomfield Hills
Weil, John William *technology management consultant*

### Dearborn
McKeage, Alice Jane *computer programmer*

### Midland
Duncan, Christopher *information technology executive*

### Troy
Walker, Bette M. *information technology executive*

### West Bloomfield
Cox, Clifford Ernest *information systems consulting executive, former academic administrator*

### Ypsilanti
Boone, Morell Douglas *information technology educator*

## MINNESOTA

### Eagan
Gouin, Warner Peter *information technology consultant*

### Eden Prairie
Borlik, Robert W. *information technology executive*

### Lino Lakes
Jezierski, Scott *wireless monitoring, security, and surveillance company executive*

### Minneapolis
Perlman, Lawrence *retired information technology executive*

### Minnetonka
Moon, James Russell *technology education educator*

## MISSISSIPPI

### Jackson
Krause, Denise D. *information technology manager, educator*

## MISSOURI

### Fenton
Hoffman, Gilbert L. *information technology executive*

### Hazelwood
Burleski, Joseph Anthony, Jr. *information technology executive*

### Kansas City
Amigoni, Michael *information technology executive*
McDonnell, Thomas A. *information technology executive*
Patterson, Neal L. *information systems company executive*
Thompson, Mary Elizabeth *application developer*
West, Marc *information technology executive*

### Saint Louis
Elliott, Susan Spoehrer *information technology executive*
Hassell, Stephen C. *information technology executive*
Pollack, Seymour Victor *computer science educator*

## NEBRASKA

### Columbus
Cunningham, Paris Lynn *systems administrator, consultant*

### Omaha
Barker, Thomas B. *information technology executive*

## NEVADA

### Incline Village
Duffield, David A. *application developer, former computer software company executive*

### Las Vegas
Moore, Michael James *information technology executive*
Stanley, Tim *information technology executive*

### North Las Vegas
Folden, Norman C. (Skip Folden) *information systems executive, consultant*

### Reno
Matthews, Thomas J. *game company executive*
Ragavan, Anpalaki Jeyabalasinkham *software developer, researcher*

## NEW HAMPSHIRE

### Franconia
Schaffer, David Edwin *retired systems administrator*

### Nashua
Smith, Thomas Raymond III *software engineer*

### Weare
White, Karen Ruth Jones *information systems executive*

## NEW JERSEY

### Bedminster
Ripp, Joseph Allen *information technology executive*

### Cherry Hill
Schelm, Roger Leonard *information systems specialist*

### Cliffwood
Jaros, Robert James *information technology executive*

### Hackensack
Mavrovic, Paul J. *information technology executive*

### Harrison
Winkleblech, Eileen *computer technology educator, career planning administrator*

### Landing
Taylor, Alexander A. *information technology analyst, freelance/self-employed musician*

### Madison
Shelby, Bryan Rohrer *information systems management consultant*

### Manalapan
Chatterjee, Subhajit *information technology executive*

### Morristown
Musa, John Davis *information technology executive, writer*

### Murray Hill
Bruch, Ruth E. *information technology executive*

### New Brunswick
Griffin, Gary Arthur *technological products executive*

### Newark
Edwards, Samuel Lawrence, II, *information technology executive, writer*
Nash, Alicia *application developer, physicist*

### Piscataway
Kenney, Mary R. *software engineer*

### Pompton Plains
Guida, Pat *information broker, literature chemist*

### Princeton
Hillier, James *retired technology management executive, researcher*
Slabaugh, Gregory Gibran *application developer*

**Roseland**
Graham, Patricia *information technology executive*

**South Orange**
Hoffert, Eric Michael *application developer, information technology executive*

**Sparta**
Bhattacharyya, Dev *information technology executive, consultant*

**Union City**
Portes, Fernando A. *project manager*

## NEW MEXICO

**Albuquerque**
Alexis, Tracy L. *project manager, project specialist, information technology manager, small business owner*
Orona, Joseph Ryan *information technology executive*
Wellborn, Charles Ivey *information technology consultant*

**Las Cruces**
Kilmer, Neal Harold *application developer*

## NEW YORK

**Albany**
Fogelman, Martin Lee *information technology manager, educator*

**Armonk**
Donofrio, Nicholas M. *information technology executive*
Gerstner, Louis Vincent, Jr. *retired information technology executive*
Harreld, James Bruce *information technology executive*
Horn, Paul M. *information technology executive, crystallographer*
Kelly, John E. III *information technology executive*

**Brooklyn**
Doucette, David Robert *information technology executive*
Gilmore, Jennifer A.W. *computer specialist, educator*

**Corning**
Flaws, James B. *technology executive*

**East Setauket**
Simons, James Harris *technology company executive*

**Endicott**
Markovich, Voya R. *information technology executive*

**Glen Wild**
Kaszas, William Joseph *technology educator*

**Greenwich**
Edsforth, Maureen McGill *instructional technology specialist*

**Hawthorne**
Yoffa, Ellen J. *information technology executive*

**Hemlock**
Hodgeman, Michelle A. *technology educator*

**Hicksville**
Notaro, Anthony *application developer*
Yen, Henry Chin-Yuan *computer systems programmer, software engineer, consulting company executive*

**Holtsville**
Iannuzzi, Salvatore *information technology executive*

**Islandia**
Cini, Kenneth D. *information technology executive*

**Ithaca**
Elber, Ron *computer science educator*

**Jamaica**
Chropufka, Mark A. *information technology executive, poet*

**Larchmont**
Wit, David Edmund *software company executive*

**Maspeth**
Heppa, Douglas Van *computer specialist*

**Melville**
Settle, Mark *information technology executive*
Webber, Pamela D. *information technology executive*

**Mount Vernon**
Chagula, Paul Machiya *information technology executive, consultant*

**New York**
Baron, Andrew Michael *blog website producer, educator, composer*
Bonnell, Bruno *information technology executive*
Caponnetto, Marianne *information technology executive*
Chang, Mona Mei-Hsuan *computer programmer, analyst*
Groberg, James Jay *information technology executive*
Haddock, Robert Lynn *information services entrepreneur, writer*
Iqbal, Syma U. *information technology executive*

Kavalerchik, Boris Yakovlevich *application developer, researcher*
Kheradpir, Shaygan *information technology executive*
King, George A. *technology executive, lawyer*
Kozik, Susan S. *information technology executive*
Lowe, Ida Brandwayn *information technology manager*
McGraw, Harold W., III, (Terry McGraw) *information technology company executive*
Mehlman, Lon Douglas *information technology specialist, investment banker, venture capitalist*
Obernauer, Marne, Jr. *technology industry executive*
O'Connor, Kevin *computer programing executive*
Padmanabhan, Anand *information technology executive*
Parkinson, John S. *information technology executive*
Pierce, David *information technology executive*
Ramachandra, Goutham K. *software architect, software developer*
Rubin, Harry Meyer *software industry executive*
Shaw, Steven A. *information technology executive*
Steber, John H. *information technology executive*
Stein, Ellen Gail *information technology manager*
Taylor, Humphrey John Fuusitt *information technology executive*
Widlund, Olof Bertil *computer science educator, mathematician*
Woods, Dan *information technology manager, consultant*

**Niskayuna**
Huening, Walter Carl, Jr. *retired consulting application engineer*

**Pittsford**
Herge, Henry Curtis, Jr. *information technology executive, consultant*

**Poughkeepsie**
Bari, Paola *application developer*

**Saugerties**
Levine, Phillip Paul *application developer, poet, actor*

**Scarsdale**
Huff, Mona L. *information technology executive*

**Somers**
Sanford, Linda S. *information technology executive*

**Syracuse**
Coskun, Erman *information systems educator*
Gartner, Joseph Charles *business systems administrator*

**Tarrytown**
Kenney, Dion Patrick *information technology executive, entrepreneur*

**Troy**
Demertzoglou, Pindaro Epaminonda *systems administrator, education educator*

**Webster**
Cusick, Patricia A. *information technology executive*

**White Plains**
MacDonald, J. Randall *information technology executive, human resources specialist*
Mills, Steven A. *information technology executive*
Palmisano, Samuel J. *information technology executive*
Rometty, Ginny (Virginia M. Rometty) *information technology executive*
Williams, Edward W. *information technology executive*

**Yorktown Heights**
Joshi, Rajiv V. *information technology manager, researcher*
Winterton, Joseph Henry *computer software executive*

## NORTH CAROLINA

**Cary**
Buckler, Sheldon A. *technology company executive*
Goodnight, James H. *software company executive*
Sall, John *information technology executive*

**Chapel Hill**
Edmunds, Douglas B. *information technology executive, consultant*

**Charlotte**
Johnson, Charles E., II, *technology company executive*

**Raleigh**
Szulik, Matthew J. *information technology executive*
Wadhwa, Vivek *information technology executive*

**Research Triangle Park**
Gentzsch, Wolfgang *grid computing and networking service company executive*

## NORTH DAKOTA

**Bismarck**
McDowell, Jefferey Thomas *information technology educator*

**Dickinson**
Mattheis, Theresa Judith *webmaster, educator*

## OHIO

**Cincinnati**
Cloyd, G. Gil *information technology executive*
Guard, Roger *information technology executive*

Laney, Sandra Eileen *information technology executive*

**Columbus**
Taylor, Celianna Isley *information systems specialist*

**Dayton**
Jones, Peter Hayward *design strategist, researcher*
Pasupuleti, Venumadhav *information technology executive*
Pincetic, Jose E. *information technology executive*

**Dublin**
Davids, Jody R. *information technology executive*

**Miamisburg**
McLaughlin, Allan D. *information technology executive*

**Troy**
Platfoot, Christopher W. *systems administrator, information technology executive*

**Upper Sandusky**
Baker, Harrison Scott *application developer, consultant*

**Westlake**
Whitehouse, John Harlan, Jr. *systems software consultant, diagnostician*

## OKLAHOMA

**Ada**
Baker, Judith Ann *retired computer technician*

**Edmond**
Smock, Donald Joe *information technology manager, political scientist*

## OREGON

**Beaverton**
Cohen, Stuart F. *software development company executive*
Torvalds, Linus Benedict *application developer*

**Hillsboro**
Daim, Tugrul Unsal *technology management specialist, educator*
Grawrock, David W. *security architect*

**Portland**
Cunningham, Ward (Howard G. Cunningham) *open source technology executive*
Vanderslice, Ellen *information technology manager, composer*
Wright, Adam *information technology executive*

**Wilsonville**
Harker, John V. *information technology executive*

## PENNSYLVANIA

**Allentown**
Beck, Glenn E. *information technology executive*
Dickson, John T. *information technology executive*

**Bristol**
Lanham, Paul C. *information technology executive*

**Carlisle**
Wyn-Jones, Alun (William Wyn-Jones) *software developer, mathematician*

**Coatesville**
Burton, Mary Louise Himes *information technology executive*

**Cranberry Township**
Pfeiffer, Gary R. *information technology manager*

**Dallas**
Broskoske, Stephen L. *information technology educator*

**Horsham**
Nanda, Vivek (Vic Nanda) *software quality executive*

**Johnstown**
Sheehan, Edward James *retired night vision and electro-optics specialist*

**Levittown**
Lombardi, Michael *application developer*
Zhu, Aiming *application developer*

**Philadelphia**
Gaillard, Theodore Lee, Jr. *information technology manager, English educator*
Manas, Gerald Bennett *information technology manager*
Morris, Richard L. *information technology executive*
Woods, Deirdre *information technology executive*

**Pittsburgh**
Carlson, Brent *information technology executive*
Drawbaugh, Daniel *information technology executive, biomedical engineer*
Humphrey, Watts Sherman *information technology executive, writer*
Shack, Timothy G. *information technology executive*
Vrabel, Mark *information resources specialist*
Woods, Allan P. *information technology executive*

**Reading**
Hart, LeRoy Banks *systems administrator, director*
Shin, Dong Hee *technology educator*

**Spring House**
Payn, Clyde Francis *technology company executive*

**State College**
Lane, Jill Lyza *instructional systems educator, researcher*

**Swarthmore**
Kaufman, Antoinette Dolores *information technology manager*

## RHODE ISLAND

**Providence**
Authelet, Keith A. *information technology executive*
Erikson, G(eorge) E(mil) (Erik Erikson) *information specialist, anatomist, archivist, science historian*
Savage, John Edmund *computer science educator, researcher*

**West Greenwich**
Caffrey, Thomas J. *gaming technology and services company executive*
Duggan, John David, Jr. *computer technician*

## SOUTH CAROLINA

**Columbia**
Duggan, Kevin *information technology professional*
Hudson, Carolyn Brauer *application developer, educator*

**Greenville**
Baur, Michael L. *information technology executive*

**North Charleston**
Jarrett, Stephen McAllister *information technology executive*

**Orangeburg**
James, Rodney Arthur *systems administrator, application developer, minister*

## SOUTH DAKOTA

**Dakota Dunes**
Peyer, Joan *information technology executive*

**Sioux Falls**
Quam, Ryan *application developer*

## TENNESSEE

**Brentwood**
Lee, Robert Erich *information technology consultant*

**Kingsport**
Hale, Jerry B. *information technology executive*

**Memphis**
Griffin, Clement M. *information technology executive*

**Nashville**
Williams, Noel Brown *information technology executive*

**Oakland**
Terry, Theo B. III *technology executive*

**Sparta**
Lentini, Joseph Charles *webmaster, systems analyst*

## TEXAS

**Arlington**
Touse, David Jesse *web application developer*
Muntz, David S. *information technology executive*

**Austin**
Craparo, John S. *information technology executive*
Lam, Simon Shin-Sing *computer science educator*
Vita-More, Natasha *information technology executive*

**Bandera**
Bartley, Dee Gray *information technology executive*

**Conroe**
Johnson, Raymond K. *information technology manager*

**Dallas**
Banzhof, Carl E. *information technology executive*
Beer, James A. *information technology executive, former air transportation executive*
Cave, Ellis *information technology executive*
Deason, Darwin *information technology executive*
Kruse, Ann Gray *computer programmer*
Pickton, Robert (Bob) J. *information technology executive*

**Denton**
Alemneh, Daniel Gelaw *information technology manager, educator*
Garcia, Oscar Nicolas *computer science educator*
Sutcliffe, Tami *web page designer*

**El Paso**
Olisa, Nzedegwu Robert III *information technology executive, manufacturing executive*

**Flower Mound**
Flake, Wayne *information technology executive*

**Hempstead**
Propst, Catherine Lamb *biotechnology company executive, pharmaceutical company executive*

**Houston**
Beauchamp, Robert E. *information technology executive*
Ellis, Randall Spencer *technological services company executive*
Kramm, Deborah Ann *information technology executive*
Liles, Clifton Roy *application developer*

**Keene**
Miller, Rebecca Lynn *software engineer*

**Laredo**
Lakshmana, Viswanath *information technology executive*

**Plano**
Ansari, Amir *digital home and multimedia management technology company executive*
Ansari, Anousheh *digital home and multimedia management technology company executive, first female civilian space traveler*
Ansari, Hamid *digital home and multimedia management technology company executive*
Fahle, William August, Jr. *application developer*
Feld, Charles S. *information technology executive*
Gordon, Storrow Moss *information technology executive, lawyer*
James, Michael Thames *information technology executive, consultant*
Marmol, Guillermo G. (Gil Marmol) *information technology executive*
McClaskey, Michael Keith *information technology executive*
Ryu, Manho *application developer*
Schuckenbrock, Stephen *information technology executive*
Vargo, Ronald Paul *information technology applications executive*
Wyman, Richard Thomas *information technology manager, researcher*

**Richardson**
Dian, Jianwei *application developer*
Safka, Jim *information technology executive*
Udeshi, Tushar Jairaj *application developer, consultant*

**San Antonio**
Gardner, Raymond Alan *webmaster, writer*

**Southlake**
Jackson, Jeffery M. *information technology executive*

**Waco**
Edgington, Theresa *information technology executive, educator*
Lowe, John David *information technology educator, educational consultant*

**UTAH**

**Bluffdale**
Harr, Joshua *information technology executive*

**Draper**
Jacobsen, Laren *retired programmer*

**Lindon**
McBride, Darl *information technology executive*

**Provo**
Moon, David C. *information technology executive*

**Salt Lake City**
Mendenhall, Robert W. *information technology executive*

**VIRGINIA**

**Alexandria**
Callaghan, John William, Jr. *information technology manager, retired military officer*
Davis, Ruth Margaret (Mrs. Benjamin Franklin Lohr) *information technology executive*
Nodeen, Janey Price *information technology executive*
Sheffield, Greg *liberal media blogger*
Sheffield, Matthew *liberal media blogger*

**Annandale**
Khim, Jay Wook *information technology executive*
Luftglass, Maribeth *information technology manager*
Samuelson, Douglas Alan *information technology executive*

**Arlington**
Jacoby, Lowell Edwin (Jake Jacoby) *information technology executive, retired military officer*
London, J. Phillip *information technology executive*
Niccolls, Wesley Oliver, Sr. *retired electronics technician*
Woods, Willie E. *information specialist*

**Dulles**
McKinley, John *information technology executive*
Payne, Jeffery E. *software quality management company executive*

**Fairfax**
Golden, John Joseph, Jr. *information technology executive*

**Falls Church**
Gosnell, Nanci Little *information technology executive, nurse*
McCue, David J. *information systems specialist, entrepreneur*

**Glen Allen**
Shelby, Ronald Van Dorn *information technology executive, consultant*

**Herndon**
Hermansen, John Christian *application developer, linguist, consultant*

**Mc Lean**
Balakrishnan, Kashyap *information technology manager, consultant*
Barker, Joshua *information technology executive*

**Norfolk**
Maly, Kurt John *computer science educator*

**Portsmouth**
Moody, Barbara Keller *systems administrator*

**Reston**
Kirkland, Rodney F. *information technology executive, consultant*
Salisbury, Alan Blanchard *information technology officer*

**Richmond**
Amado, Joseph S. *information technology executive*
Guzmàn, David R. *information technology executive*
McDermid, Margaret E. *information technology executive, engineer*

**Springfield**
Quick, Danny Richard *computer systems engineer*

**WASHINGTON**

**Bellevue**
Cohen, Bram *web programmer*
Simonyi, Charles *software engineer*
Tian, Hongqi *application developer, researcher*

**Federal Way**
Mersereau, Susan *information systems company executive, data processing executive*

**Oak Harbor**
Meaux, Alan Douglas *retired computer technician, artist*

**Redmond**
Ayala, Orlando *information technology executive*
Bach, Robert J. (Robbie Bach) *information technology executive*
DelBene, Kurt *information technology executive*
DeVaan, Jon S. *information technology executive*
Fathi, Ben *information technology executive*
Flessner, Paul *information technology executive*
Guday, Shai *program director*
Lee, Bryan *information technology executive*
Markezich, Ron *information technology executive*
Muglia, Robert L. *information technology executive*
Nadella, Satya *information technology executive*
Smith, Bradford Lee *information technology executive, lawyer*
Turner, Kevin (B. Kevin Turner) *information technology executive*
Valentine, Brian *information technology executive*
Vaskevitch, David *information technology executive*

**Seatac**
Wells, Roger Stanley *software engineer*

**Seattle**
Bandrowski, Paul *information technology executive*
Crenshaw, Edward Lee, Sr. *aviation electronics technician*
Dalzell, Rick *information technology executive*
Desouza, Kevin Clyde *application developer*
Lazowska, Edward Delano *computer science educator*
McConney, Mary E. *information technology executive*

**Tacoma**
Archangelsky, Dmitry A. *application developer, researcher*

**WEST VIRGINIA**

**Charleston**
Gardner, Edward Tytus III *information technology executive*

**Martinsburg**
Day, Michael Gordon *information technology executive, educator*

**WISCONSIN**

**Brookfield**
Nickolett, Chip *information technology executive, consultant*

**Green Bay**
Lynch, Matthew J. *information technology executive, retail executive*

**Mequon**
Bayne, Jay Stewart *information technology executive, consultant*

**Middleton**
Piefer, Gregory Richard *information technology executive*

**WYOMING**

**Casper**
Davis, Lois Ann *computer specialist, educator*

**CANADA**

**ALBERTA**

**Edmonton**
Davis, Wayne Alton *computer science educator*

**NOVA SCOTIA**

**Halifax**
LeValliant, Debbie *information technology executive*

**ONTARIO**

**Waterloo**
Balsillie, Jim *information technology executive*
Lazaridis, Mike *information technology executive, entrepreneur*

**AUSTRALIA**

**Altona**
Daniel-Dreyfus, Susan B. Russe *information technology executive*

**ENGLAND**

**London**
Assousa, George Elias *information technology executive, physicist, corporate executive*

**FRANCE**

**Paris**
Courtois, Jean-Philippe *information technology executive*

**GERMANY**

**Walldorf**
Agassi, Shai *application developer, director*
Williams, Richard Charles *computer programmer, consultant*

**ITALY**

**Rome**
Stigliano, Jose Maria *information technology executive, computer scientist*

**JAPAN**

**Tokyo**
Harada, Norio *software engineer, researcher, educator*

**NETHERLANDS**

**Haarlem**
Calhoun, David L. *information and media company executive*

**NEW ZEALAND**
Gould, Wayne *application developer, retired judge*

**SWEDEN**

**Göteborg**
Kmiecik, Andy *application developer*

**ADDRESS UNPUBLISHED**
Abu-Mostafa, Ayman Said *application developer, consultant*
Africa, Colby Tait *information technology executive, poet*
Alexander, Nancy A. *information technology manager, consultant*
Ali, Mohammed Zamshed *information technology executive, researcher*
Alvey, Brian *blogger*
Anania, Andrea *information technology executive*
Anderson, Christine Marlene *software engineer*
Anderson, Jacqueline Annette *information technology specialist*
Arrington, Michael *blogger, former corporate lawyer*
Arsic, Antoinette *information specialist*
Baer, Ralph Henry *video game developer, engineering consultant*
Bass, Steven Craig *computer science educator*
Bennett, Robert LeRoy *computer software development company executive*
Berners-Lee, Sir Timothy John *inventor of world wide web, research scientist, writer*
Berry, Richard Lewis *information technology manager, writer, magazine editor, lecturer, programmer*
Bluitt, Karen *information technology executive*
Boyd, Kenneth R. *web programmer, mathematician*
Bramhall, Debra A. *information technology manager, consultant*
Briggs, Thomas Henry *computer science educator*

Brown, Richard Harris *former information technology executive*
Caparro, James *information technology executive, former record company executive*
Castle, James Cameron *information technology executive*
Cherin, Stephen J. *application developer, management consultant*
Clementz, David M. *information technology executive*
Cole, David W. *information technology executive*
Cosell, Bernard *retired computer systems architect*
Costandi, Wisam Emile *application developer, biomedical researcher, consultant*
Coullard, Chad *information systems specialist*
Creswell, Dorothy Anne *computer consultant*
Dajnowicz, Jan *software and hardware designer, researcher*
Davis, Suzanne Spiegel *retired information specialist*
DiFilippo, Armand *information technology executive*
Dobis, Charles, Jr. *systems administrator*
Donohue, Susan K. *information technology executive, researcher*
Doud, Wallace C. *retired information technology executive*
Easter, Mark Wayne *information technology director*
Egan, Richard John *retired information technology executive, former ambassador*
Etheridge, Diana Carol *internet business executive*
Fairobent, Douglas Kevin *computer programmer*
Frei, Brent R. *computer software executive*
Fuller, Cassandra Miller *applications specialist*
Fuller, Sara V. *technology trainer*
Gareau, Jean L. *application technology executive*
Gattu, Balaji *information technology executive*
Goggin, John R. *software engineer*
Goldberger, Arthur Earl, Jr. *information technology executive*
Grant, Daniel Gordon *information technology executive*
Guo, Dongbai *application developer*
Gurspan, Mitchell Scott *technology architect, writer*
Ha, Chong Wan *information technology executive*
Hantman, Barry G. *software engineer*
Hariton, Lorraine Jill *information technology executive*
Hayes, Jonathan *information technology executive, hardware and product designer*
Heck, Debra Upchurch *information technology, procurement professional*
Hemann, Raymond Glenn *research company executive*
Henkins, Robert S. *information systems professional*
Hill, Patricia Francine *information technology executive, educator*
Holt, George, Jr. *information technology executive*
Hornby, Kenneth Peter *information technology manager*
Horner, Grace Ann *application developer*
Howard, H. William *information technology executive*
Hu, Weigang *software engineer*
Hurttgam, Mark Howard *information technology manager*
Jaw, Andrew Chung-Shiang *software analyst*
Johansson, Nils A. *information services executive*
Jones, Carleton Shaw *information technology executive, lawyer*
Jones, Gwenyth Ellen *information technology executive*
Jordan, Michael Hugh *information technology executive*
Kadel, Lee A. *information technology manager, systems analyst*
Klauberg, William Joseph *information technology executive*
Krishnaswamy, Mukunda *information technology executive, entrepreneur*
Kull, Bryan Paul *information technology executive*
La Blanc, Robert Edmund *information technology executive*
Larson, Janice Talley *application developer*
Lau, Joanna T. *information technology executive*
Lawrie, J. Michael *former software company executive*
Leven, Linda *application developer, writer, actress, model, artist*
Levinson, Marina *information technology executive*
Levy, Leslie Ann *application developer*
Li, Mike Peng *information technology executive*
Libutti, Frank *information technology company executive, former federal agency administrator, retired military officer*
Lyles, Mark Bradley *advanced technology company executive*
Maclean, Rhonda *information technology executive*
Maruoka, Jo Ann Elizabeth *retired information systems manager*
Masagutov, Vakhid Erkinjonovich *application developer*
Mattrick, Donald A. *interactive entertainment software company executive*
McCaffrey, Cindy *information technology executive*
McCausland, Peter *technology company executive*
Menon, Jai M. *information technology manager*
Minshall, Greg *computer programmer*
Morgan, M. Jane *computer systems consultant*
Morrissey, Edward T., II, *conservative political blogger, nationally-syndicated radio co-host, columnist*
Mueller, Gary Alfred *software engineer*
Nelson, Sandra E. *information technology executive*
Nicols, Angela C. *software engineer, consultant*
O'Connor, John Joseph *information technology manager*
Omer, Margaret Vaughan (Peggy Omer) *retired computer technician, artist*
Papathomas, Georgia Nikolakopoulou *technology executive*
Paris, Steven Mark *application developer*
Paul, Vivek *information technology executive*

Pelton, Walter Eugene *information technology executive, mathematician, physicist*
Persad, Chadee *information technology manager*
Podkul, Theodore B., Jr. *systems support specialist*
Polese, Kim *software company executive*
Reay, Stefanie *application developer, educator*
Riccitiello, John S. *former interactive software/gaming executive, venture capitalist*
Rose, Paul Edward *systems administrator, educator*
Schatz, Wayne Ardale *district technology coordinator, educator*
Schirmer, Andrew L. *application developer*
Schneider, Sharon M. *systems administrator, information technologist*
Schwartz, Stephen Blair *retired information technology executive*
Sedighi, Artin *application developer, researcher*
Slater, Lori Annette *project manager*
Smith, Theodore Glenn *webmaster*
Snow, Claude Henry, Jr. *information services executive, consultant*
Stevens, Gregory Scott *information technology manager*
Still, Homer I. *information technology executive*
Tevanian, Avadis, Jr. *information technology executive*
Thompson, Kenneth *software engineer*
Unrau, Jack *application developer*
Vaidyanathan, Ganesh *information technology executive, educator*
Visocki, Nancy Gayle *information services consultant*
Wang, Youcheng *information technology educator*
Weigle, Peggy *information technology executive*
White, Jan Tuttle *information technology executive*
Wilhelmi, Cynthia Joy *information technology manager, information scientist, consultant*
Willingham, Deborah N. *information technology executive*
Witkins, James P. *information technology executive*
Wolfram, David Anthony *information technology manager*
Wurth, Monty *information technology manager*
Youngjohns, Robert H. *information technology executive*
Zehring, Karen *information executive*
Zelek, Charles Andrew *program specialist, director*
Zimmerman, Myron *information technology executive*

---

## INTERNET *See* INFORMATION TECHNOLOGY

---

## LAW: JUDICIAL ADMINISTRATION

---

## UNITED STATES

### ALABAMA

**Ashland**
Ingram, Kenneth Frank *retired state supreme court justice*

**Birmingham**
Bennett, Thomas B. *federal judge*
Houston, James Gorman, Jr. *retired state supreme court justice*
Pointer, Sam Clyde, Jr. *retired federal judge, lawyer*
Pryor, William Holcombe, Jr. *federal judge, former state attorney general*

**Mobile**
Butler, Charles Randolph, Jr. *federal judge*
Cox, Emmett Ripley *federal judge*
Graddick, Charles Allen *judge*
Granade, Callie Virginia Smith *federal judge*
Howard, Alex T., Jr. *federal judge*
Johnstone, Douglas Inge *retired state supreme court justice, lawyer*
Milling, Bert William, Jr. *judge*
Pittman, Virgil *federal judge*

**Montgomery**
Black, Robert Coleman *judge, lawyer*
Bolin, Michael F. *state supreme court justice*
Brown, Jean Williams *former state supreme court justice*
Carnes, Edward E. *federal judge*
Dubina, Joel Fredrick *federal judge*
Godbold, John Cooper *federal judge*
Harwood, Robert Bernard, Jr. *state supreme court justice*
Hobbs, Truman McGill *federal judge*
Maddox, Alva Hugh *retired state supreme court justice*
McPherson, Vanzetta Penn *magistrate judge*
Nabers, Drayton, Jr. *state supreme court chief justice, retired insurance company executive*
Parker, Tom *state supreme court justice, lawyer*
See, Harold Frend *state supreme court justice*
Smith, Patricia M. (Patti Smith) *state supreme court justice*
Steele, Rodney Redfearn *judge*
Stuart, Jacquelyn L. *state supreme court justice*
Woodall, Thomas A. *state supreme court justice*

### ALASKA

**Anchorage**
Bryner, Alexander O. *state supreme court chief justice*
Burgess, Timothy M. *federal judge, former prosecutor*

Eastaugh, Robert L. *state supreme court justice*
Fabe, Dana Anderson *state supreme court justice*
Matthews, Warren Wayne *state supreme court justice*
Singleton, James Keith *federal judge*
von der Heydt, James Arnold *federal judge*

**Fairbanks**
Kleinfeld, Andrew J. *federal judge*

**Juneau**
Carpeneti, Walter L. *state supreme court justice*

### ARIZONA

**Phoenix**
Anderson, Lawrence Ohaco *United States magistrate judge, lawyer*
Bales, W. Scott *state supreme court justice*
Berch, Rebecca White *state supreme court justice, lawyer*
Broomfield, Robert Cameron *federal judge*
Canby, William Cameron, Jr. *federal judge*
Carroll, Earl Hamblin *federal judge*
Gaines, Francis Pendleton III *judge*
Hawkins, Michael Daly *federal judge*
Hurwitz, Andrew D. *state supreme court justice*
Jones, Charles E. *retired state supreme court chief justice*
Martone, Frederick J. *judge*
McGregor, Ruth Van Roekel *state supreme court justice*
McNamee, Stephen M. *federal judge*
Myers, Robert David *judge*
Ryan, Michael D. *state supreme court justice*
Schroeder, Mary Murphy *federal judge*
Silver, Roslyn Olson *federal judge*
Silverman, Barry G. *federal judge*
Strand, Roger Gordon *federal judge*
Weisenburger, Theodore Maurice *retired judge, poet, educator*
Winthrop, Lawrence Fredrick *judge*

**Tucson**
Brammer, J. William, Jr. *judge, lawyer*
Lacagnina, Michael Anthony *judge*
Marquez, Alfredo C. *federal judge*
Roll, John McCarthy *judge*

### ARKANSAS

**Batesville**
Harkey, John Norman *judge*

**El Dorado**
Barnes, Harry Francis *federal judge*

**Fayetteville**
Hendren, Jimm Larry *federal judge*
Smith, Lavenski R. (Vence Smith) *federal judge*

**Little Rock**
Arnold, Morris Sheppard *federal judge*
Bird, Samuel N. *judge*
Corbin, Donald L. *state supreme court justice*
Dickey, Betty C. *state supreme court justice*
Glaze, Thomas A. *state supreme court justice*
Gunter, James Houston, Jr. *state supreme court justice*
Hannah, James *state supreme court justice*
Imber, Annabelle Clinton *state supreme court justice*
Roaf, Andree Layton *judge*
Wilson, William R., Jr. *federal judge*
Wright, Susan Webber *federal judge*

**Texarkana**
Stroud, John Fred, Jr. *judge*

### CALIFORNIA

**Alameda**
Bartalini, C. Richard *judge*

**Fresno**
Coyle, Robert Everett *federal judge*
Ishii, Anthony W. *judge*

**Los Angeles**
Alarcón, Arthur Lawrence *federal judge*
Bufford, Samuel Lawrence *federal judge*
Chavez, Victor Edwin *judge*
Collins, Audrey B. *judge*
Fleming, Macklin *retired judge*
Johnson, Earl, Jr. *judge, author*
Kelleher, Robert Joseph *judge*
Manella, Nora Margaret *judge*
Marshall, Consuelo Bland *federal judge*
Mosk, Richard Mitchell *judge*
Rafeedie, Edward *federal judge*
Tevrizian, Dickran M., Jr. *judge*
Timlin, Robert J. *judge*
Yager, Thomas C. *retired judge*
Zelon, Laurie Dee *judge*

**Mendocino**
Masterson, William A. *retired judge*

**Oakland**
Jensen, D. Lowell *judge, lawyer, federal official*
Newsome, Randall Jackson *judge*
Tchaikovsky, Leslie J. *federal judge*

**Pasadena**
Boochever, Robert *judge*
Fernandez, Ferdinand Francis *federal judge*
Fisher, Raymond Corley *federal judge*
Goodwin, Alfred Theodore *federal judge*
Hall, Cynthia Holcomb *federal judge*
Johnson, Barbara Jean *retired judge, lawyer*
Kozinski, Alex *federal judge*
Nelson, Dorothy Wright (Mrs. James F. Nelson) *federal judge*
Paez, Richard A. *federal judge*
Rymer, Pamela Ann *federal judge*
Smith, Milan Dale, Jr. *federal judge*

Tashima, Atsushi Wallace *federal judge*
Wardlaw, Kim A. McLane *federal judge*

**Pauma Valley**
Lewis, Gerald Jorgensen *judge*

**Riverside**
Holmes, Dallas Scott *judge, educator*

**Sacramento**
Callahan, Consuelo Maria *federal judge*
Karlton, Lawrence K. *federal judge*
Levi, David F. *federal judge*
Moulds, John F. *judge*
Van Camp, Brian Ralph *judge*

**San Diego**
Bowie, Peter Wentworth *judge, educator*
Brewster, Rudi Milton *judge*
Gonzalez, Irma Elsa *federal judge*
Harutunian, Albert T(heodore) III *judge*
McKeown, Mary Margaret *federal judge*
Porter, Louisa S. *federal judge*
Thompson, David Renwick *federal judge*
Thompson, Gordon, Jr. *federal judge*
Turrentine, Howard Boyd *federal judge*
Wallace, J. Clifford *federal judge*

**San Francisco**
Baxter, Marvin Ray *state supreme court justice*
Bea, Carlos Tiburcio *federal judge*
Berzon, Marsha S. *federal judge*
Browning, James Robert *federal judge*
Chin, Ming W. *state supreme court justice*
Corrigan, Carol A. *state supreme court justice*
Fletcher, William A. *federal judge, law educator*
George, Ronald M. *state supreme court chief justice*
Haerle, Paul Raymond *judge*
Henderson, Thelton Eugene *federal judge*
Ikuta, Sandra Segal *federal judge*
Illston, Susan Y. *federal judge*
Jarvis, Donald Bertram *judge*
Kennard, Joyce L. *state supreme court justice*
Kolkey, Daniel Miles *former judge, lawyer*
Moreno, Carlos R. *state supreme court justice*
Noonan, John T., Jr. *federal judge, law educator*
Patel, Marilyn Hall *judge*
Robertson, Armand James, II, *judge*
Schwarzer, William W. *federal judge*
Sneed, Joseph Tyree III *federal judge*
Walker, Vaughn R. *federal judge*
Werdegar, Kathryn Mickle *state supreme court justice*
Zimmerman, Bernard *judge*

**San Jose**
Whyte, Ronald M. *judge*

**San Marino**
Mortimer, Wendell Reed, Jr. *judge*

**Santa Ana**
Barr, James Norman *retired federal judge*
Ferguson, Warren John *federal judge*
Stotler, Alicemarie Huber *federal judge*

**Santa Barbara**
Aldisert, Ruggero John *federal judge*

**South San Francisco**
Grandsaert, John Leo *judge*

**Studio City**
Gold, Arnold Henry *judge*

**Woodland Hills**
Mund, Geraldine *judge*
Pregerson, Harry *federal judge*

### COLORADO

**Broomfield**
Scott, Gregory Kellam *former state supreme court justice, lawyer*

**Denver**
Bender, Michael Lee *state supreme court justice*
Coan, Patricia A. *judge*
Coats, Nathan B. *state supreme court justice*
Ebel, David M. *federal judge*
Eid, Allison *state supreme court justice*
Figa, Phillip S. *judge*
Gorsuch, Neil McGill *federal judge, lawyer*
Hobbs, Gregory James, Jr. *state supreme court justice*
Kane, John Lawrence, Jr. *judge*
Keithley, Roger Lee *judge*
Kirshbaum, Howard M. *retired judge*
Krieger, Marcia Smith *federal judge*
Lucero, Carlos *federal judge*
Martinez, Alex J. *state supreme court justice*
McWilliams, Robert Hugh *federal judge*
Miller, Walker David *judge*
Mullarkey, Mary J. *state supreme court chief justice*
Nottingham, Edward Willis, Jr. *federal judge*
Rice, Nancy E. *state supreme court justice*
Rovira, Luis Dario *state supreme court justice*
Satter, Raymond Nathan *judge*
Tymkovich, Timothy Michael *federal judge*

**Englewood**
Erickson, William Hurt *retired state supreme court justice*

**Fort Collins**
Gandy, H. Conway *retired judge, state official*

**Golden**
Rodgers, Frederic Barker *judge*

**Leadville**
Watson, Jack Crozier *retired state supreme court justice*

**Loveland**
Porfilio, John Carbone *federal judge*

### CONNECTICUT

**Bridgeport**
Eginton, Warren William *federal judge*

**Hartford**
Bieluch, William Charles *judge*
Borden, David M. *state supreme court justice*
Chatigny, Robert Neil *federal judge*
Droney, Christopher F. *judge*
Katz, Joette *state supreme court justice*
Martinez, Donna F. *federal judge*
Newman, Jon O. *federal judge*
Norcott, Flemming L., Jr. *state supreme court justice*
Palmer, Richard N. *state supreme court justice*
Peters, Ellen Ash *retired judge*
Schaller, Barry R. *judge*
Squatrito, Dominic J. *judge*
Sullivan, William J. *state supreme court justice*
Vertefeuille, Christine Siegrist *state supreme court justice*
Wright, Douglass Brownell *retired judge, lawyer*
Zarella, Peter T. *state supreme court justice*

**New Britain**
Meskill, Thomas J. *federal judge*

**New Haven**
Arterton, Janet Bond *federal judge*
Berdon, Robert Irwin *judge*
Cabranes, José Alberto *judge*
Calabresi, Guido *federal judge, law educator*
Dorsey, Peter Collins *federal judge*
Walker, John Mercer, Jr. *federal judge*
Winter, Ralph Karl, Jr. *federal judge*

**Oxford**
Marano, Richard Michael *judge*

**Vernon Rockville**
Purnell, Oliver James III *judge*

**Waterbury**
McDonald, Francis Michael *judge trial referee, retired state supreme court justice*
Upson, Thomas Fisher *judge, retired state senator, lawyer*

### DELAWARE

**Dover**
Ridgely, Henry duPont *state supreme court justice*

**Georgetown**
Holland, Randy James *state supreme court justice*

**Wilmington**
Ambro, Thomas L. *federal judge*
Berger, Carolyn *state supreme court justice*
Jacobs, Jack Bernard *state supreme court justice*
Parrish, Karl Joseph *judge, lawyer*
Parsons, Donald Francis *judge*
Robinson, Sue L(ewis) *federal judge*
Roth, Jane Richards *federal judge*
Stapleton, Walter King *federal judge*
Steele, Myron Thomas *state supreme court chief justice*

### DISTRICT OF COLUMBIA

**Washington**
Alito, Samuel Anthony, Jr. *US Supreme Court Justice*
Allegra, Francis M. *federal judge, retired federal official*
Archer, Glenn LeRoy, Jr. *federal judge*
Armen, Robert N. *federal judge*
Bacon, Sylvia *judge, law educator*
Baker, James Edgar *federal judge, law educator*
Bartnoff, Judith *judge*
Baskir, Lawrence M. *federal judge*
Bates, John D. *federal judge*
Bayly, John Henry, Jr. *judge*
Beghe, Renato *federal judge*
Belson, James Anthony *judge*
Blackburne-Rigsby, Anna *judge*
Block, Lawrence J. *federal judge*
Breyer, Stephen Gerald *United States Supreme Court Justice*
Brown, Janice Rogers *federal judge, former state supreme court justice*
Bryson, William Curtis *federal judge*
Burnett, Arthur Louis, Sr. *judge*
Carey, David P. *judge, career military officer*
Carluzzo, Lewis R. *federal judge*
Chabot, Herbert L. *federal judge*
Chiechi, Carolyn Phyllis *federal judge*
Clevenger, Raymond Charles III *federal judge*
Cohen, Mary Ann *federal judge*
Couvillion, David Irvin *federal judge*
Crawford, Susan Jean *federal judge*
Dawson, Howard Athalone, Jr. *federal judge*
Dean, John F. *federal judge*
de Puget, Albert Borg Olivier *magistrate judge*
Dyk, Timothy Belcher *federal judge*
Edwards, Harry Thomas *federal judge*
Effron, Andrew S. *federal judge*
Erdmann, Charles Edgar *federal judge, former state supreme court justice*
Farrell, Michael W. *judge*
Ferren, John Maxwell *judge*
Fisher, John R. *judge*
Foley, Maurice Brian *federal judge*
Friedman, Daniel Mortimer *federal judge*
Gajarsa, Arthur J. *judge*
Gale, Joseph H. *federal judge*
Garland, Merrick Brian *federal judge*
Gerber, Joel *federal judge*
Gibson, Reginald Walker *federal judge*
Ginsburg, Douglas Howard *federal judge*
Ginsburg, Ruth Bader (Joan Ruth Bader Ginsburg) *United States Supreme Court Justice*
Glickman, Stephen H. *judge*
Green, Joyce Hens *federal judge*
Greene, William P., Jr. *federal judge*
Griffith, Thomas Beall *federal judge*

Hagel, Lawrence B. *federal judge*
Haines, Harry Allen *federal judge*
Halpern, James S. *federal judge*
Henderson, Karen LeCraft *federal judge*
Hewitt, Emily Clark *federal judge, minister*
Holmes, Mark V. *judge*
Horn, Marian Blank *federal judge*
Jacobs, Julian I. *federal judge*
Kavanaugh, Brett Michael *federal judge*
Kennedy, Anthony McLeod *United States Supreme Court Justice*
Kessler, Gladys *federal judge*
King, Warren R. *judge*
Kollar-Kotelly, Colleen *federal judge*
Kramer, Noël Anketell *judge*
Lance, Alan George *federal judge, former state attorney general*
Laro, David *federal judge*
Leon, Richard J. *federal judge*
Lettow, Charles Frederick *federal judge*
Lourie, Alan David *federal judge*
Mack, Julia Cooper *retired judge*
Marchand, Michael J. *judge, career military officer*
Margolis, Lawrence Stanley *federal judge*
Marvel, L. Paige *federal judge*
Mayer, Haldane Robert *federal judge*
McPherson, James E. *judge*
Mencher, Bruce Stephan *judge*
Merow, James F. *federal judge*
Michel, Paul Redmond *federal judge*
Miller, Christine Odell Cook *federal judge*
Miller, George W. *federal judge, lawyer*
Moore, Kimberly Ann *federal judge, law educator*
Moorman, William A. *federal judge, retired career military officer*
Newman, Pauline *federal judge*
Panuthos, Peter J. *federal judge*
Parr, Carolyn Miller *federal judge*
Plager, S. Jay *federal judge*
Prost, Sharon *federal judge*
Rader, Randall Ray *federal judge*
Randolph, A. Raymond (Arthur Raymond Randolph) *federal judge*
Rives, Jack L. *judge, career military officer*
Roberts, John Glover, Jr. *United States Supreme Court Chief Justice*
Robertson, James *federal judge*
Rogers, Judith Ann Wilson *federal judge*
Romig, Thomas J. *judge, career military officer*
Rothstein, Barbara Jacobs *federal judge*
Ruiz, Vanessa *judge*
Ruwe, Robert Paul *federal judge*
Scalia, Antonin *United States Supreme Court Justice*
Schall, Alvin Anthony *federal judge*
Schoelen, Mary Jeanette *federal judge*
Schwelb, Frank Ernest *judge*
Sentelle, David Bryan *federal judge*
Smith, Loren Allan *federal judge*
Smith, Roy Philip *judge*
Souter, David Hackett *United States Supreme Court Justice*
Steadman, John Montague *judge*
Stevens, John Paul *United States Supreme Court Justice*
Sullivan, Emmet G. *judge*
Sweeney, Margaret Mary *federal judge*
Swift, Stephen Jensen *federal judge*
Tatel, David Stephen *federal judge*
Terry, John Alfred *judge*
Thomas, Clarence *United States Supreme Court Justice*
Thompson, Phyllis D. *judge, lawyer*
Thornton, Michael B. *federal judge*
Turner, James Thomas *judge*
Vasquez, Juan Flores *federal judge*
Wagner, Annice McBryde *judge*
Wagner, Curtis Lee, Jr. *judge*
Wald, Patricia McGowan *retired federal judge*
Walton, Reggie Barnett *judge*
Washington, Eric T. *judge*
Wells, Thomas B. *federal judge*
Wheeler, Thomas Craig *federal judge*
Wherry, Robert Allen, Jr. *federal judge, lawyer*
Williams, Mary Ellen Coster *federal judge*
Williams, Stephen Fain *federal judge*
Wolski, Victor J. *federal judge, lawyer*
Wright, Daniel V. *judge, carrer military officer*
Yoder, Ronnie A. *judge*

## FLORIDA

### Belleair
Blackmar, Charles Blakey *state supreme court justice*

### Boynton Beach
Bernstein, Edwin S. *judge*

### Clearwater
Greer, George W. *judge*

### Destin
Robinson, Wilkes Coleman *retired federal judge*

### Fort Lauderdale
Beach, Marcia Ellen *judge*
Gonzalez, Jose Alejandro, Jr. *federal judge*
Ray, Raymond B. *federal judge*
Seltzer, Barry S. *federal judge*
Zloch, William J. *federal judge*

### Fort Myers
Schoonover, Jack Ronald *senior judge*
Shafer, Robert Tinsley, Jr. *judge*

### Jacksonville
Boyer, Tyrie William *judge, law educator*
Hill, James Clinkscales *federal judge*
Melton, Howell Webster, Sr. *federal judge*
Schlesinger, Harvey Erwin *judge*
Tjoflat, Gerald Bard *federal judge*

### Longboat Key
Morse, Marvin Henry *retired judge*

### Merritt Island
Johnson, Clarence Traylor, Jr. *state judge*

### Miami
Barkett, Rosemary *federal judge*
Cristol, A. Jay *federal judge*
Davis, Edward Bertrand *retired federal judge, lawyer*
Graham, Donald Lynn *federal judge*
Highsmith, Shelby *federal judge*
King, James Lawrence *federal judge*
Marcus, Stanley *federal judge*
Miller, Udell, Bronwyn *judge*
Seitz, Patricia Ann *judge*
Siegel, Paul *judge*
Ungaro-Benages, Ursula Mancusi *federal judge*
Wilson, Thomas Strong, Jr., (Tam Wilson) *judge*

### Naples
Gindin, William Howard *retired judge*

### Ocala
Hodges, William Terrell *federal judge*

### Orlando
Fawsett, Patricia Combs *federal judge*
Thorpe, Janet Claire *judge*
Young, George Cressler *federal judge*

### Safety Harbor
Dail, Joseph Garner, Jr. *retired judge*

### Saint Petersburg
Grube, Karl Bertram *judge*
Roney, Paul Hitch *federal judge*

### Tallahassee
Anstead, Harry Lee *state supreme court justice*
Bell, Kenneth B. *State Supreme Court Justice*
Cantero, Raoul G. III *state supreme court justice*
Grimes, Stephen Henry *retired state supreme court justice*
Harding, Major Best *former state supreme court chief justice*
Lewis, R. Fred *state supreme court justice*
McCord, Guyte Pierce, Jr. *retired judge*
Pariente, Barbara J *state supreme court justice*
Quince, Peggy A. *judge*
Strickland, Delphene Coverston *judge*
Webster, Peter David *judge*
Wells, Charles Talley *state supreme court justice*

### Tampa
Jenkins, Elizabeth Ann *federal judge*
Kovachevich, Elizabeth Anne *judge*
Wilson, Charles Reginald *federal judge*

### West Palm Beach
Paine, James Carriger *federal judge*

## GEORGIA

### Atlanta
Benham, Robert *state supreme court justice*
Bihary, Joyce *federal judge*
Birch, Stanley Francis, Jr. *federal judge*
Carley, George H. *state supreme court justice*
Carnes, Julie Elizabeth *judge*
Deane, Richard Hunter, Jr. *former federal judge, lawyer*
Duffey, William Simon, Jr. *federal judge, former prosecutor*
Edmondson, J.L. (James Larry Edmondson) *federal judge*
Evans, Orinda D. *federal judge*
Feldman, Joel Martin *magistrate judge*
Hines, Preston Harris *state supreme court justice*
Hull, Frank Mays *federal judge*
Hunstein, Carol *state supreme court justice*
Kravitch, Phyllis A. *federal judge*
Melton, Harold D. *state supreme court justice*
Murphy, Margaret Hackett *US bankruptcy judge*
O'Kelley, William Clark *federal judge*
Sears, Leah Ward *state supreme court chief justice*
Thompson, Hugh P. *state supreme court justice*
Ward, Horace Taliaferro *federal judge*

### Augusta
Bowen, Dudley Hollingsworth, Jr. *federal judge*

### Columbus
Laney, John Thomas III *federal judge*

### Macon
Anderson, Robert Lanier III *federal judge*
Brown, Stephen Phillip *judge*
Hershner, Robert Franklin, Jr. *judge*
Owens, Wilbur Dawson, Jr. *federal judge*

### Marietta
Smith, George Thornewell *retired state supreme court justice*

### Newnan
Drake, W. Homer, Jr. *federal judge*

### Rome
Murphy, Harold Loyd *federal judge*

### Savannah
Edenfield, Berry Avant *federal judge*
Moore, William Theodore, Jr. *federal judge*

## HAWAII

### Honolulu
Acoba, Simeon Rivera, Jr. *state supreme court justice, educator*
Clifton, Richard Randall *federal judge*
Duffy, James Earl, Jr. *state supreme court justice*
Gillmor, Helen *federal judge*
Levinson, Steven Henry *state supreme court justice*
Moon, Ronald T.Y. *state supreme court chief justice*
Nakayama, Paula Aiko *state supreme court justice*
Watanabe, Corinne Kaoru Amemiya *judge, state official*

## IDAHO

### Boise
Burdick, Roger S. *state supreme court justice*
Eismann, Daniel T. *state supreme court justice*
Jones, James Thomas *state supreme court justice, former state attorney general*
McDevitt, Charles Francis *retired judge, lawyer*
Nelson, Thomas G. *federal judge*
Trott, Stephen Spangler *federal judge*
Trout, Linda Copple *state supreme court justice*
Winmill, B. Lynn *federal judge*

### Idaho Falls
Shindurling, Jon J. *judge*

### Twin Falls
Hohnhorst, John Charles *judge*

## ILLINOIS

### Barrington
Wynn, Thomas Joseph *judge, educator*

### Benton
Foreman, James Louis *retired judge*
Gilbert, J. Phil *federal judge*

### Chicago
Bauer, William Joseph *federal judge*
Bower, Glen Landis *judge, lawyer*
Bucklo, Elaine Edwards *United States district court judge*
Burke, Anne M. *state supreme court justice*
Castillo, Ruben *federal judge*
Conlon, Suzanne B. *federal judge*
Cudahy, Richard D. *federal judge*
Easterbrook, Frank Hoover *federal judge*
Fairchild, Thomas Edward *federal judge, former state supreme court justice*
Fitzgerald, Thomas Robert *state supreme court justice*
Flaum, Joel Martin *federal judge*
Funderburk, Raymond *judge*
Garman, Rita B. *state supreme court justice*
Gottschall, Joan B. *judge*
Hart, William Thomas *federal judge*
Hyman, Michael Bruce *judge*
Johnson, Glenn Thompson *retired judge*
Kilbride, Thomas L. *state supreme court justice*
Lefkow, Joan Humphrey *federal judge*
Leighton, George Neves *retired judge*
Leinenweber, Harry D. *federal judge*
Miller, Benjamin K. *retired state supreme court justice*
Moran, James Byron *federal judge*
Nordberg, John Albert *federal judge*
Norgle, Charles Ronald, Sr. *federal judge*
Pallmeyer, Rebecca Ruth *judge*
Posner, Richard Allen *federal judge*
Rovner, Ilana Kara Diamond *federal judge*
Shadur, Milton Irving *judge*
Sonderby, Susan Pierson *federal judge*
Thomas, Robert R. *state supreme court justice*
Williams, Ann Claire *federal judge*
Wood, Diane Pamela *federal judge*
Zagel, James Block *federal judge*

### Downers Grove
McGarr, Frank James *retired federal judge, consultant*

### Maple Park
Nickels, John L. *retired state supreme court justice*

### Nashville
Karmeier, Lloyd A. *state supreme court justice*

### Peoria
Heiple, James Dee *retired state supreme court justice*
Mihm, Michael Martin *federal judge*

### Petersburg
Wood, Harlington, Jr. *federal judge*

### Rockford
Reinhard, Philip G. *federal judge*

### Rolling Meadows
Roti, Thomas David *judge*

### Springfield
Evans, Charles H. *federal judge*
Mills, Richard Henry *federal judge*

### Wheaton
Leston, Patrick John *judge*

## INDIANA

### Evansville
Capshaw, Tommie Dean *judge*

### Fort Wayne
Lee, William Charles *judge*

### Indianapolis
Barker, Sarah Evans *judge*
Boehm, Theodore Reed *state supreme court justice*
Dickson, Brent E. *state supreme court justice*
Foster, Kennard P. *magistrate judge*
Givan, Richard Martin *retired judge*
Hamilton, David F. *judge*
McKinney, Larry J. *federal judge*
Rucker, Robert D. *state supreme court justice*
Shepard, Randall Terry *state supreme court chief justice*
Sullivan, Frank, Jr. *state supreme court justice*

### Kokomo
Stein, Eleanor Bankoff *retired judge*

### Lafayette
Kanne, Michael Stephen *federal judge*

## IOWA

### Cedar Rapids
Hansen, David Rasmussen *federal judge*
Mc Manus, Edward Joseph *federal judge*
Melloy, Michael J. *federal judge*

### Chariton
Stuart, William Corwin *judge*

### Council Bluffs
Peterson, Richard William *retired judge, retired lawyer*

### Des Moines
Bremer, Celeste F. *judge*
Cady, Mark S. *state supreme court justice*
Carter, James Harvey *state supreme court justice*
Colloton, Steven M. *federal judge*
Fagg, George Gardner *federal judge*
Harris, K. David *senior state supreme court justice*
Hecht, Daryl L. *state supreme court justice*
Larson, Jerry Leroy *state supreme court justice*
McGiverin, Arthur A. *former state supreme court chief justice*
Streit, Michael J. *state supreme court justice*
Ternus, Marsha K. *state supreme court chief justice*
Vietor, Harold Duane *federal judge*
Walters, Ross A. *federal judge*
Wiggins, David Stewart *state supreme court justice*
Wolle, Charles Robert *judge*

### Ida Grove
Snell, Bruce M., Jr. *retired judge*

### Osceola
Reynoldson, Walter Ward *retired judge, lawyer*

### Sioux City
O'Brien, Donald Eugene *federal judge*

## KANSAS

### Kansas City
Lungstrum, John W. *federal judge*
Vratil, Kathryn Hoefer *federal judge*
Waxse, David John *judge*

### Lawrence
Briscoe, Mary Beck *federal judge*
Tacha, Deanell Reece *federal judge*

### Topeka
Allegrucci, Donald Lee *state supreme court justice*
Beier, Carol Ann *state supreme court justice*
Crow, Sam Alfred *judge*
Davis, Robert Edward *state supreme court justice*
Larson, Edward *retired state supreme court justice*
Luckert, Marla Jo *state supreme court justice*
Marquardt, Christel Elisabeth *judge*
McFarland, Kay Eleanor *state supreme court chief justice*
Nuss, Lawton R. *state supreme court justice*
Robinson, Julie Ann *judge*
Rogers, Richard Dean *federal judge*
Rosen, Eric S. *state supreme court justice*

### Wichita
Brown, Wesley Ernest *federal judge*

## KENTUCKY

### Bowling Green
Huddleston, Joseph Russell *judge*
Minton, John D., Jr. *state supreme court justice*

### Fort Thomas
Wehr, William James *judge*

### Frankfort
Lambert, Joseph Earl *state supreme court chief justice*
Scott, Will T. *state supreme court justice*
Wintersheimer, Donald Carl *state supreme court justice*

### Lexington
Coffman, Jennifer Burcham *judge*
Keller, James *retired state supreme court justice*
Roach, John C. *state supreme court justice*
Varellas, Sandra Motte *judge*

### London
Siler, Eugene Edward, Jr. *federal judge*

### Louisville
Boggs, Danny Julian *federal judge*
Heyburn, John Gilpin, II, *federal judge*
Martin, Boyce Ficklen, Jr. *federal judge*
McAnulty, William E., Jr. *state supreme court justice*
Simpson, Charles R. III *judge*

### Madisonville
Spain, Thomas B. *retired state supreme court justice*

### Murray
Buckingham, David Cowan *judge*

### Paducah
Graves, John William *state supreme court justice*
King, W. David *judge*

### Lagrange
Brown, George E. *judge, educator*

### South Bend
Manion, Daniel Anthony *federal judge*
Ripple, Kenneth Francis *federal judge*
Sharp, Allen *federal judge*

**Pikeville**
Van Tatenhove, Gregory F. *federal judge, former prosecutor*

**Richmond**
Chenault, James Stouffer *judge*

## LOUISIANA

**Baton Rouge**
Cole, Luther Francis *former state supreme court associate justice*
Noland, Christine A. *judge*
Parker, John Victor *judge*
Polozola, Frank Joseph *federal judge*
Riedlinger, Stephen C. *federal judge*

**Lafayette**
Davis, William Eugene *federal judge*
Duhe, John Malcolm, Jr. *federal judge*

**New Orleans**
Beer, Peter Hill *federal judge*
Berrigan, Helen Ginger *federal judge*
Brown, Jerry A. *federal bankruptcy judge*
Calogero, Pascal Frank, Jr. *state supreme court justice*
Clement, Edith Brown *federal judge*
Dennis, James Leon *federal judge*
Duplantier, Adrian Guy *federal judge*
Duval, Stanwood Richardson, Jr. *judge*
Johnson, Bernette Joshua *state supreme court justice*
Kimball, Catherine D. *state supreme court justice*
Knoll, Jeannette Theriot *state supreme court justice*
Livaudais, Marcel, Jr. *federal judge*
Mentz, Henry Alvan, Jr. *retired federal judge*
Ortique, Revius Oliver, Jr. *retired judge*
Porteous, G. Thomas, Jr. *judge*
Traylor, Chet D. *state supreme court justice*
Victory, Jeffrey Paul *state supreme court justice*
Weimer, John L. *state supreme court justice*
Wiener, Jacques Loeb, Jr. *federal judge*

**Ponchatoula**
Kuhn, James Edward *judge*

**Shreveport**
Shemwell, Robert H. *federal judge*
Stagg, Tom *federal judge*
Stewart, Carl E. *federal judge*

## MAINE

**Auburn**
Clifford, Robert William *state supreme court justice*

**Bangor**
Silver, Warren M. *state supreme court justice*

**Portland**
Alexander, Donald G. *state supreme court justice*
Bradford, Carl O. *judge*
Calkins, Susan W. *state supreme court justice*
Carter, Gene *judge*
Coffin, Frank Morey *federal judge*
Dana, Howard H., Jr. *state supreme court justice*
Glassman, Caroline Duby *state supreme court justice*
Hornby, David Brock *federal judge*
Levy, Jon D. *state supreme court justice*
Lipez, Kermit V. *federal judge, former state supreme court justice*
McKusick, Vincent Lee *retired judge, arbitrator, lawyer, mediator*
Saufley, Leigh Ingalls *state supreme court chief justice*

**Rockland**
Collins, Samuel W., Jr. *judge*

## MARYLAND

**Accokeek**
Beddow, Richard Harold *retired judge*

**Annapolis**
Battaglia, Lynne Ann *judge*
Greene, Clayton, Jr. *judge*

**Baltimore**
Bell, Robert M. *judge*
Blake, Catherine C. *judge*
Bredar, James Kelleher *judge*
Derby, Ernest Stephen *federal judge*
Garbis, Marvin Joseph *judge*
Gauvey, Susan Kathryn *judge*
Harvey, Alexander, II, *retired federal judge*
Legg, Benson Everett *federal judge*
Motz, Diana Gribbon *federal judge*
Motz, John Frederick *federal judge*
Niemeyer, Paul Victor *judge*
Rodowsky, Lawrence Francis *retired state judge*

**Bethesda**
Harris, Stanley S. *retired judge, arbitrator, mediator*
Nejelski, Paul Arthur *retired judge, freelance writer*

**Greenbelt**
Chasanow, Howard Stuart *retired judge, mediator*
Messitte, Peter Jo *judge*
Titus, Roger Warren *judge*

**Rockville**
Megan, Thomas Ignatius *retired judge*
Raker, Irma S. *judge*

**Salisbury**
Cathell, Dale Roberts *judge*

**Towson**
Wilner, Alan M. *judge*

**Upper Marlboro**
Harrell, Glenn T., Jr. *judge*

## MASSACHUSETTS

**Boston**
Boudin, Michael *federal judge*
Bowler, Marianne Bianca *federal judge*
Campbell, Levin Hicks *federal judge*
Collings, Robert Biddlecombe *judge*
Connolly, Thomas Edward *judge*
Cordy, Robert J. *state supreme court justice*
Cowin, Judith Arnold *state supreme court judge*
Dreben, Raya Spiegel *judge*
Feeney, Joan N. *judge*
Gorton, Nathaniel M. *federal judge*
Greaney, John M. *state supreme court justice*
Ireland, Roderick L. *state supreme court justice*
Katzmann, Gary Stephen *judge*
Keeton, Robert Ernest *federal judge*
Lasker, Morris E. *judge*
Lindsay, Reginald Carl *judge*
Lynch, Sandra Lea *federal judge*
Marshall, Margaret Hilary *state supreme court chief justice*
O'Connor, Francis Patrick *former state supreme court justice*
Sosman, Martha B. *state supreme court justice*
Spina, Francis X. *state supreme court justice*
Stahl, Norman H. *judge*
Stearns, Richard Gaylore *judge*
Tauro, Joseph Louis *federal judge*
Torruella, Juan R. *federal judge*
Young, William Glover *federal judge*
Zobel, Rya Weickert *federal judge*

**Cambridge**
Dilday, Judith Nelson *judge*
Kaplan, Benjamin *judge*

**Harwich Port**
Smith, Ralph Wesley, Jr. *retired federal judge*

**Longmeadow**
Keady, George Cregan, Jr. *judge*

**Springfield**
Neiman, Kenneth Paul *judge*

**Worcester**
Boroff, Henry Jack *federal judge, educator*

## MICHIGAN

**Ann Arbor**
Guy, Ralph B., Jr. *federal judge*
O'Meara, John Corbett *federal judge*

**Detroit**
Callahan, J(ohn) William (Bill Callahan) *judge*
Corrigan, Maura Denise *state supreme court justice*
Edmunds, Nancy Garlock *federal judge*
Feikens, John *federal judge*
Friedman, Bernard Alvin *federal judge*
Keith, Damon Jerome *federal judge*
Kelly, Marilyn *state supreme court justice*
Kennedy, Cornelia Groefsema *federal judge*
Levin, Charles Leonard *state supreme court justice*
Mallett, Conrad LeRoy, Jr. *former state supreme court chief justice, hospital administrator*
Morgan, Virginia Mattison *judge*
Rosen, Gerald Ellis *federal judge*
Ryan, James Leo *federal judge*
Taylor, Anna Diggs *federal judge*

**Grand Rapids**
Bell, Robert Holmes *federal judge*
Brenneman, Hugh Warren, Jr. *judge*
Miles, Wendell A. *federal judge*
Quist, Gordon Jay *federal judge*

**Kalamazoo**
Enslen, Richard Alan *federal judge*

**Lansing**
Cavanagh, Michael Francis *state supreme court justice*
Markman, Stephen J. *state supreme court justice*
McKeague, David William *judge*
Suhrheinrich, Richard Fred *federal judge*
Taylor, Clifford Woodworth *state supreme court justice*
Young, Robert P., Jr. *state supreme court justice*

**Saint Clair Shores**
Hausner, John Herman *retired judge*
Ryan, Harold Martin *judge*

**Southfield**
Graves, Ray Reynolds *retired judge*

**Traverse City**
Weaver, Elizabeth A. *state supreme court justice*

## MINNESOTA

**Eden Prairie**
Arthur, Lindsay Grier *retired judge, editor, writer*

**Lake Elmo**
Tomljanovich, Esther M. *retired judge*

**Minneapolis**
Alton, Ann Leslie *judge, lawyer, educator*
Davis, Michael J. *judge*
Doty, David Singleton *federal judge*
Lebedoff, Jonathan Galanter *retired judge, mediator*
Loken, James Burton *federal judge*
Montgomery, Ann D. *federal judge, educator*
Murphy, Diana E. *federal judge*

**Noel**, Franklin Linwood *judge*
Rosenbaum, James Michael *federal judge*

**Minnetonka**
Rogers, James Devitt *judge*

**Richfield**
Amdahl, Douglas Kenneth *retired state supreme court justice*

**Saint Paul**
Alsop, Donald Douglas *federal judge*
Anderson, G. Barry *state supreme court justice*
Anderson, Paul Holden *state supreme court justice*
Anderson, Russell A. *state supreme court chief justice*
Hanson, Samuel Lee *state supreme court justice*
Kyle, Richard House *federal judge*
Lancaster, Joan Ericksen *judge*
Lay, Donald Pomeroy *federal judge*
Meyer, Helen M. *state supreme court justice*
Page, Alan C. *state supreme court justice*
Willis, Bruce Donald *judge*

## MISSISSIPPI

**Aberdeen**
Davidson, Glen Harris *federal judge*

**Batesville**
Carlson, George Clarence, Jr. *state supreme court justice*

**Decatur**
Gordon, Marcus *judge*

**Greenville**
Orlansky, Julian David *judge*

**Gulfport**
Senter, Lyonel Thomas, Jr. *federal judge*

**Jackson**
Banks, Fred Lee, Jr. *former state supreme court presiding justice, lawyer*
Barksdale, Rhesa Hawkins *federal judge*
Cobb, Kay Beevers *state supreme court justice, retired state senator*
Diaz, Oliver E., Jr. *state supreme court justice*
Dickinson, Jess H. *state supreme court justice*
Easley, Charles D., Jr. *state supreme court justice*
Graves, James E. *state supreme court justice, educator*
Jolly, E. Grady *federal judge*
Lee, Tom Stewart *judge*
Randolph, Michael K. *state supreme court justice*
Smith, James W., Jr. *state supreme court justice*
Sugg, Robert Perkins *retired judge*
Waller, William Lowe, Jr. *state supreme court justice*

**Natchez**
Bramlette, David C. III *federal judge*

**Oxford**
Mills, Michael Paul *judge*

## MISSOURI

**Cape Girardeau**
Blanton, Lewis M. *federal judge*

**High Ridge**
Karll, Jo Ann *retired judge, lawyer*

**Jefferson City**
Knox, William Arthur *judge*
Limbaugh, Stephen Nathaniel, Jr. *state supreme court judge*
Price, William Ray, Jr. *state supreme court justice*
Russell, Mary Rhodes *state supreme court justice*
Stith, Laura Denvir *state supreme court justice*
Teitelman, Richard B. *state supreme court justice*
White, Ronnie L. *state supreme court justice*
Wolff, Michael A. *state supreme court judge*

**Kansas City**
Benton, William Duane *federal judge*
Bowman, Pasco Middleton, II, *judge*
Gibson, John Robert *federal judge*
Laughrey, Nanette Kay *federal judge*
Whipple, Dean *federal judge*
Wright, Scott Olin *federal judge*

**Marshfield**
Knust, Daniel Max *judge*

**Saint Louis**
Filippine, Edward Louis *federal judge*
Gruender, Raymond W. *federal judge, former prosecutor*
Hamilton, Jean Constance *judge*
Heaney, Gerald William *federal judge*
Jackson, Carol E. *federal judge*
Limbaugh, Stephen Nathaniel *federal judge*
Medler, Mary Ann L. *federal judge*
Noce, David D. *federal judge*
Rendlen, Charles Earnest, III, (Sketch Rendlen) *federal judge, lawyer*
Shaw, Charles Alexander *judge*
Stohr, Donald J. *federal judge*

**Springfield**
Parrish, John Edward *state appellate judge*

## MONTANA

**Billings**
Fagg, Russell *judge, lawyer*
Thomas, Sidney R. *federal judge*

**Glendive**
McDonough, Russell Charles *retired state supreme court justice*

**Helena**
Cotter, Patricia O'Brien *state supreme court justice*
Gray, Karla Marie *state supreme court justice*
Harrison, John Conway *retired state supreme court justice*
Leaphart, W. William *state supreme court justice*
Morris, Brian *state supreme court justice*
Nelson, James C *state supreme court justice*
Regnier, James *retired state supreme court justice*
Rice, Jim *state supreme court justice*
Warner, John Arnan *state supreme court justice*

**Missoula**
Molloy, Donald William *federal judge, lawyer*

**Polson**
Turnage, Jean Allen *retired state supreme court chief justice*

## NEBRASKA

**Lincoln**
Beam, Clarence Arlen *federal judge*
Connolly, William M. *state supreme court justice*
Gerrard, John M. *state supreme court justice*
Hastings, William Charles *retired state supreme court chief justice*
Hendry, John V. *state supreme court justice*
Kopf, Richard G. *federal judge*
McCormack, Michael *state supreme court justice*
Miller-Lerman, Lindsey *state supreme court justice*
Piester, David L(ee) *magistrate judge*
Stephan, Kenneth C. *state supreme court justice*
Urbom, Warren Keith *federal judge*
Wright, John F. *state supreme court justice*

**Omaha**
Riley, William Jay *federal judge*
Ross, Donald Roe *federal judge*
Shanahan, Thomas M. *judge*
Strom, Lyle Elmer *judge*

## NEVADA

**Carson City**
Agosti, Deborah Ann *retired senior justice*
Gibbons, Mark *state supreme court justice*
Hardesty, James *state supreme court justice*
Maupin, A. William *state supreme court justice*
Parraguirre, Ronald David *state supreme court justice*
Rose, Robert Edgar *state supreme court justice*

**Las Vegas**
Becker, Nancy Anne *state supreme court justice*
Bybee, Jay Scott *federal judge, former federal agency administrator*
Douglas, Michael Lawrence *state supreme court justice*
Mahan, James Cameron *judge*
Pro, Philip Martin *judge*
Rawlinson, Johnnie Blakeney *federal judge*

**Reno**
Brunetti, Melvin T. *federal judge*
Hug, Procter Ralph, Jr. *federal judge*
McKibben, Howard D. *federal judge*
Reed, Edward Cornelius, Jr. *federal judge*
Sandoval, Brian Edward *federal judge, former state attorney general*

## NEW HAMPSHIRE

**Concord**
Barbadoro, Paul James *federal judge*
Broderick, John T., Jr. *state supreme court chief justice*
Dalianis, Linda Stewart *state supreme court justice*
DiClerico, Joseph Anthony, Jr. *federal judge*
Duggan, James E., Jr. *state supreme court justice*
Galway, Richard E., Jr. *state supreme court justice*
Hicks, Gary Ellis *state supreme court justice*
Howard, Jeffrey R. *federal judge*
McAuliffe, Steven James *federal judge*
Mulrhead, James Russell *federal judge*

## NEW JERSEY

**Atlantic City**
Knight, Edward R. *judge, psychologist, law educator*

**Camden**
Brotman, Stanley Seymour *federal judge*
Irenas, Joseph Eron *judge*
Laskin, Lee B. *judge, state senator*
Simandle, Jerome B. *federal judge*

**Egg Harbor Township**
Lashman, Shelley Bortin *retired judge*

**Flemington**
Buchsbaum, Peter A. *judge*

**Hackensack**
Kestin, Howard H. *judge*
Stein, Gary S. *retired judge, lawyer*

**Millburn**
Kuttner, Bernard A. *retired judge, lawyer*

**Newark**
Barry, Maryanne Trump *federal judge*
Debevoise, Dickinson Richards *federal judge*
Fuentes, Julio M. *federal judge*
Garth, Leonard I. *judge*
Greenaway, Joseph Anthony, Jr. *judge*
Hochberg, Faith S. *US district court judge*

**Somerville**
Albin, Barry Todd *state supreme court justice*

## Trenton

Cooper, Mary Little *judge*
Cowen, Robert E. *federal judge*
Greenberg, Morton Ira *federal judge*
LaVecchia, Jaynee *state supreme court justice*
Long, Virginia *state supreme court justice*
Poritz, Deborah T. *state supreme court justice, retired state attorney general*
Rivera-Soto, Roberto A. *state supreme court justice*
Wallace, John E. *state supreme court justice*
Zazzali, James R. *state supreme court justice*

## NEW MEXICO

### Albuquerque

Black, Bruce D. *judge*
Conway, John E. *federal judge*
Hansen, Curtis LeRoy *federal judge*
Hartz, Harris L *federal judge*
Parker, James Aubrey *federal judge*

### Roswell

Baldock, Bobby Ray *federal judge*

### Santa Fe

Chavez, Edward L. *state supreme court justice*
Kelly, Paul Joseph, Jr. *federal judge*
Maes, Petra Jimenez *state supreme court justice*
Minzner, Pamela Burgy *state supreme court justice*
Serna, Patricio *state supreme court justice*
Vázquez, Martha Alicia *federal judge*
Yalman, Ann *judge, lawyer*

### Silver City

Hodges, Norman *retired district judge*

## NEW YORK

### Albany

Graffeo, Victoria A. *state appeals court judge*
Kaye, Judith Smith *state appeals court judge*
Levine, Howard Arnold *judge*
Meader, John Daniel *judge*
Miner, Roger Jeffrey *federal judge*
Read, Susan Phillips *state appeals court judge*

### Binghamton

Peckham, Eugene Eliot *judge, lawyer*

### Brooklyn

Amon, Carol Bagley *federal judge*
Bramwell, Henry *federal judge*
Dearie, Raymond Joseph *federal judge*
Garaufis, Nicholas G. *district court judge*
Gershon, Nina *federal judge*
Glasser, Israel Leo *federal judge*
Gleeson, John *judge, educator*
Irizarry, Dora L. *federal judge*
Johnson, Sterling, Jr. *federal judge*
Korman, Edward R. *federal judge*
Mann, Roanne L. *federal judge*
Orenstein, James *federal judge*
Pollak, Cheryl L. *federal judge*
Raggi, Reena *federal judge*
Reichbach, Gustin Lewis *state supreme court justice*
Ross, Allyne R. *federal judge*
Ryan, Leonard Eames *judge*
Sifton, Charles Proctor *federal judge*
Townes, Sandra L. *federal judge*
Trager, David G. *federal judge*
Weinstein, Jack Bertrand *federal judge*

### Buffalo

Bucki, Carl Leo *judge*
Elfvin, John Thomas *federal judge*
Skretny, William Marion *federal judge*

### Central Islip

Bernstein, Stan *federal bankruptcy judge*
Boyle, E. Thomas *federal magistrate judge*
Cyganowski, Melanie L. *bankruptcy judge*
Eisenberg, Dorothy *federal judge*
Feuerstein, Sandra Jeanne *judge*
Hurley, Denis R. *federal judge*
Platt, Thomas Collier, Jr. *federal judge*
Seybert, Joanna *federal judge*
Spatt, Arthur Donald *federal judge*
Wall, William D. *federal judge*

### Garden City

Harwood, Stanley *retired judge, lawyer, arbitrator, mediator*

### New York

Andrias, Richard T. *judge*
Aquilino, Thomas Joseph, Jr. *federal judge, law educator*
Batts, Deborah A. *federal judge*
Berman, Richard Miles *judge*
Blinder, Albert Allan *judge*
Carman, Gregory Wright *federal judge*
Casey, Richard Conway *federal judge*
Castel, P. Kevin *federal judge*
Cedarbaum, Miriam Goldman *federal judge*
Chin, Denny *federal judge*
Ciparick, Carmen Beauchamp *state appeals court judge*
Cote, Denise Louise *federal judge*
Daniels, George Benjamin *federal judge*
Duffy, Kevin Thomas *federal judge*
Eastman, Elrich Allan *retired judge*
Eaton, Richard Kenyon *federal judge*
Feinberg, Wilfred *federal judge*
Francis, James Clark, IV, *federal judge*
Freedman, Helen E. *judge*
Gerber, Robert Evan *judge*
Gordon, Leo Maury *federal judge*
Griesa, Thomas Poole *federal judge*
Gropper, Allan Louis *bankruptcy judge*
Haight, Charles Sherman, Jr. *federal judge*
Hall, Peter W. *federal judge, former prosecutor*
Holwell, Richard J. *federal judge*
Jacobs, Dennis *federal judge*
Jones, Barbara S. *federal judge*

Kaplan, Lewis A. *federal judge*
Karas, Kenneth M. *federal judge*
Katzmann, Robert Allen *federal judge*
Kearse, Amalya Lyle *federal judge*
Keenan, John Fontaine *federal judge*
Koeltl, John George *federal judge*
Kram, Shirley Wohl *federal judge*
Leisure, Peter Keeton *federal judge*
Leval, Pierre Nelson *federal judge*
Lynch, Gerard E. *federal judge*
Marrero, Victor *federal judge, lawyer*
McLaughlin, Joseph Michael *federal judge, law educator*
Meron, Theodor *judge, law educator, researcher*
Musgrave, R. Kenton *federal judge*
Owen, Richard *federal judge*
Patterson, Robert Porter, Jr. *federal judge*
Peck, Andrew Jay *federal judge*
Pogue, Donald Carl *federal judge*
Preska, Loretta A. *federal judge*
Rakoff, Jed Saul *federal judge, author*
Restani, Jane A. *federal judge*
Ridgway, Delissa Anne *federal judge*
Sack, Robert David *federal judge, law educator*
Sand, Leonard B. *federal judge*
Smith, George Bundy *state appeals court judge*
Smith, Robert Sherlock *state appeals court judge*
Sotomayor, Sonia *federal judge*
Sprizzo, John Emilio *federal judge*
Stanceu, Timothy Charles *federal judge*
Straub, Chester John *federal judge*
Swain, Laura Taylor *federal judge*
Sweet, Robert Workman *federal judge*
Tsoucalas, Nicholas *federal judge*
Wesley, Richard C. *federal judge*
Wood, Kimba M. *federal judge*

### Poughkeepsie

Dolan, Thomas Joseph *judge*
Rosenblatt, Albert Martin *state appeals court judge*

### Rochester

Kehoe, L. Paul *state judge*
Siragusa, Charles J. *judge*
Witmer, G. Robert *retired state supreme court justice*

### Sag Harbor

Pierce, Lawrence Warren *retired federal judge*

### Smallwood

Golden, Elliott *judge*

### Syracuse

McCurn, Neal Peters *federal judge*
Munson, Howard G. *federal judge*
Pooler, Rosemary S. *federal judge*
Scullin, Frederick James, Jr. *federal judge*

### Utica

Cardamone, Richard J. *federal judge*

### West Seneca

Siegel, Carolyn Augusta *judge, lawyer, social worker*

### White Plains

Brieant, Charles La Monte *federal judge*
Carey, John *judge*
Conner, William Curtis *federal judge*
Hardin, Adlai Stevenson, Jr. *judge*
Nastasi, Aldo A. *judge*
Parker, Barrington D., Jr. *federal judge, lawyer*

## NORTH CAROLINA

### Asheville

Thornburg, Lacy Herman *federal judge*

### Charlotte

Horn, Carl III *federal judge*
Mullen, Graham C. *judge*
Voorhees, Richard Lesley *federal judge*
Whitney, Frank DeArmon *federal judge, former prosecutor*

### Elizabeth City

Boyle, Terrence W. *federal judge*

### Greensboro

Frye, Henry E. *retired state supreme court chief justice*
Osteen, William L. *federal judge*
Stocks, William L. *federal judge*
Tilley, Norwood Carlton, Jr. *federal judge*

### Hendersonville

Franks, Stephen Field *retired judge*

### Raleigh

Brady, Edward Thomas *state supreme court justice*
Duncan, Allyson K. *federal judge*
Eagles, Sidney Smith, Jr. *judge*
Edmunds, Robert Holt, Jr. *state supreme court justice*
Martin, Mark D. *State Supreme Court Justice*
McGee, Linda Mace *judge, lawyer*
Parker, Sarah Elizabeth *state supreme court chief justice*
Timmons-Goodson, Patricia *state supreme court justice*
Wainwright, George L., Jr. *state supreme court justice*

### Randleman

Jordan, Lillian B. *judge*

### Wilmington

Fox, James Carroll *federal judge*

### Winston Salem

Beaty, James Arthur, Jr. *federal judge*
Eliason, Russell Allen *judge*

## NORTH DAKOTA

### Bismarck

Crothers, Daniel J. *State Supreme Court Justice*
Kapsner, Carol Ronning *state supreme court justice*
Maring, Mary Muehlen *state supreme court justice*
Neumann, William Allen *retired state supreme court justice*
Sandstrom, Dale Vernon *state supreme court justice*
VandeWalle, Gerald Wayne *state supreme court chief justice*

### Fargo

Bright, Myron H. *federal judge*
Bye, Kermit Edward *federal judge, lawyer*
Magill, Frank John *federal judge*

### Minot

Kerian, Jon Robert *retired judge*

## OHIO

### Akron

Bell, Samuel H. *federal judge, educator*
Shea-Stonum, Marilyn *federal bankruptcy judge*

### Bowling Green

Baird, James Abington *retired judge*

### Cincinnati

Beckwith, Sandra Shank *federal judge*
Black, Robert L., Jr. *retired judge*
Clay, Eric L. *federal judge*
Cook, Deborah L. *federal judge, former state supreme court justice*
Dlott, Susan Judy *judge, lawyer*
Griffin, Richard Allen *federal judge*
Hopkins, Jeffrey P. *federal judge*
Painter, Mark Philip *judge*
Perlman, Burton *judge*
Rogers, John Marshall *judge, law educator*
Sutton, Jeffrey S. *federal judge*
Weber, Herman Jacob *district judge*

### Cleveland

Aldrich, Ann *judge*
Boyko, Christopher Allan *federal judge*
Burke, Lillian Walker *retired judge*
Markus, Richard M. *judge, arbitrator*
Matia, Paul Ramon *retired judge*
Moore, Karen Nelson *judge*
Oliver, Solomon, Jr. *judge*
O'Malley, Kathleen M. *federal judge*
Rhew, Perry James *federal judge*
Wells, Lesley *federal judge*

### Columbus

Caldwell, Charles M. *federal judge*
Cole, Ransey Guy, Jr. *federal judge*
Frye, Richard Arthur *judge*
Holschuh, John David *federal judge*
Lanzinger, Judith Ann *state supreme court justice*
Mc Cormac, John Waverly *judge*
Moyer, Thomas J. *state supreme court chief justice*
Norris, Alan Eugene *federal judge*
O'Connor, Maureen *state supreme court justice*
O'Donnell, Terrence *state supreme court justice*
Pfeifer, Paul E. *state supreme court justice*
Resnick, Alice Robie *state supreme court justice*
Sellers, Barbara Jackson *federal judge*
Smith, George Curtis *judge*
Stratton, Evelyn Lundberg *state supreme court justice*

### Dayton

Clark, William Alfred *federal judge*
Knapp, James Ian Keith *judge*

### Kettering

Porter, Walter Arthur *retired judge*

### Lucasville

Reno, Ottie Wayne *former judge*

### Toledo

Carr, James Gray *federal judge*

### Warren

Nader, Robert Alexander *judge, lawyer*

## OKLAHOMA

### Langley

Rogers, Chris Ellen *judge*

### Lawton

Moore, Roy Dean *retired judge*

### Norman

Trimble, Preston Albert *retired judge*

### Oklahoma City

Cauthron, Robin J. *federal judge*
Colbert, Thomas *state supreme court justice*
Edmondson, James E. *state supreme court justice*
Hargrave, Rudolph *state supreme court justice*
Henry, Robert Harlan *federal judge, former attorney general*
Holloway, William Judson, Jr. *federal judge*
Kauger, Yvonne *state supreme court justice*
Lavender, Robert Eugene *state supreme court justice*
Leonard, Timothy Dwight *judge*
Opala, Marian Peter *state supreme court justice*
Russell, David L. *federal judge*
Taylor, Steven W. *state supreme court justice*
Thompson, Ralph Gordon *federal judge*
Watt, Joseph Michael *state supreme court justice*
West, Lee Roy *federal judge*
Winchester, James R. *state supreme court justice*

### Tulsa

Gabbard, Douglas, II, (James Gabbard) *judge*
Goodman, Jerry L(ynn) *judge*

## OREGON

### Portland

Beatty, John Cabeen, Jr. *judge*
Dunn, Randall Lawson *judge*
Graber, Susan P. *federal judge*
Jones, Robert Edward *federal judge*
Leavy, Edward *federal judge*
Mosman, Michael W. *federal judge, former prosecutor*
O'Scannlain, Diarmuid Fionntain *federal judge*
Panner, Owen M. *federal judge*
Redden, James Anthony *federal judge*
Skopil, Otto Richard, Jr. *federal judge*
Van Hoomissen, George Albert *state supreme court justice*

### Salem

Balmer, Thomas Ancil *state supreme court justice*
Carson, Wallace Preston, Jr. *state supreme court justice*
De Muniz, Paul J. *state supreme court chief justice*
Durham, Robert Donald, Jr. *state supreme court justice*
Gillette, W. Michael *state supreme court justice*
Kistler, Rives *state supreme court justice*
Linde, Hans Arthur *state supreme court justice*
Peterson, Edwin J. *retired judge, mediator, law educator*
Riggs, R. William *state supreme court justice*

### Troutdale

Unis, Richard L. *judge*

## PENNSYLVANIA

### Allentown

Platt, William Henry *judge*

### Duncansville

Smith, D. Brooks *federal judge*

### Easton

Van Antwerpen, Franklin Stuart *federal judge*

### Erie

Mencer, Glenn Everell *federal judge*

### Harrisburg

Rambo, Sylvia H. *federal judge*
Saylor, Thomas G. *state supreme court justice*

### Mechanicsburg

Eakin, J. Michael *state supreme court justice*

### Philadelphia

Angell, Mary Faith *federal magistrate judge*
Baldwin, Cynthia Ackron *state supreme court justice*
Buckwalter, Ronald Lawrence *federal judge*
Castille, Ronald D. *state supreme court justice*
Chagares, Michael Arthur *federal judge*
Coleman, Gerald Charles *judge, law educator*
Diamond, Paul Steven *federal judge, lawyer, educator*
Fullam, John P. *federal judge*
Joyner, J(ames) Curtis *judge*
Kelly, Robert F. *federal judge*
Ludwig, Edmund Vincent *federal judge*
McKee, Theodore A. *federal judge*
Nygaard, Richard Lowell *federal judge*
O'Neill, Thomas Newman, Jr. *federal judge*
Pollak, Louis Heilprin *judge, educator*
Reed, Lowell A., Jr. *federal judge*
Rendell, Marjorie O. *federal judge*
Robreno, Eduardo C. *federal judge*
Scirica, Anthony Joseph *federal judge*
Shapiro, Norma Sondra Levy *federal judge*
Sigmund, Diane Weiss *judge*
Sloviter, Dolores Korman *federal judge*
Welsh, Diane M. *federal judge*
Yohn, William H(endricks), Jr. *federal judge*

### Pittsburgh

Ambrose, Donetta W. *federal judge*
Baer, Max *state supreme court justice*
Brosky, John G. *retired judge*
Cappy, Ralph Joseph *state supreme court chief justice*
Cohill, Maurice Blanchard, Jr. *federal judge*
Conti, Joy Flowers *judge*
Diamond, Gustave *federal judge*
Fisher, D. Michael *federal judge*
Fitzgerald, Judith Klaswick *federal judge*
Flaherty, John Paul, Jr. *chief justice emeritus*
McCullough, M. Bruce *judge*
Ross, Eunice Latshaw *retired judge*
Sensenich, Ila Jeanne *judge*
Standish, William Lloyd *judge*
Weis, Joseph Francis, Jr. *federal judge*
Zappala, Stephen A. *state supreme court justice*
Ziegler, Donald Emil *retired federal judge*

### Scranton

Blewitt, Thomas Michael *chief federal magistrate judge*
Conaboy, Richard Paul *federal judge*
Kosik, Edwin Michael *federal judge*
Nealon, William Joseph, Jr. *federal judge*
O'Malley, Carlon Martin *judge*
Vanaskie, Thomas Ignatius *federal judge*

### Washington

Mc Cune, Barron Patterson *retired federal judge*

### West Chester

Griffith, Edward *judge*

### West Conshohocken

Newman, Sandra Schultz *state supreme court justice*

### OKLAHOMA (cont.)

Holmes, Jerome A *federal judge*
Holmes, Sven Erik *federal judge, educator*
Kern, Terry C. *judge*
Seymour, Stephanie Kulp *federal judge*

## TERRITORIES OF THE UNITED STATES

### AMERICAN SAMOA

**Pago Pago**
Kruse, F. Michael *judge*
Richmond, Lyle L. *judge*

### GUAM

**Hagatna**
Carbullido, F. Philip *judge*
Manibusan, Joaquin V.E., Jr. *magistrate judge*
Maraman, Katherine Ann *judge*
Torres, Robert J., Jr. *judge*
Tydingco-Gatewood, Frances Marie *judge*
Unpingco, John Walter Sablan *chief federal judge*
Weeks, Janet Healy *retired supreme court justice*

### NORTHERN MARIANA ISLANDS

**Saipan**
Castro, Alexandro C. *commonwealth supreme court justice*
Demapan, Miguel S. *commonwealth supreme court justice*
Manglona, John A. *commonwealth supreme court justice*
Munson, Alex Robert *judge*

### PUERTO RICO

**Hato Rey**
Cerezo, Carmen Consuelo *judge*

**San Juan**
Acosta, Raymond Luis *federal judge*
Dominguez, Daniel R. *judge*
Fiol Matta, Liana *judge*
Fusté, José Antonio *federal judge*
Fuster, Jaime B. *judge*
Hernandez-Denton, Federico *judge*
Rebollo-Lopez, Francisco *judge*
Rivera Perez, Efrain E. *judge*
Rodriguez, Annabelle *judge, former attorney general*

**Viejo San Juan**
Casellas, Salvador E. *judge*

### VIRGIN ISLANDS

**Charlotte Amalie**
Barnard, Geoffrey W. *magistrate judge*

**Christiansted**
Finch, Raymond Lawrence *federal judge*

**St Croix**
Cannon, George W., Jr. *magistrate judge*

**St Thomas**
Gomez, Curtis V. *district judge*

## CANADA

### ALBERTA

**Calgary**
Major, John Charles *judge*

**Edmonton**
Fraser, Catherine Anne *Canadian chief justice*
Stevenson, William Alexander *retired justice of Supreme Court of Canada*

### NEW BRUNSWICK

**Fredericton**
Strange, Henry Hazen *judge*

### NOVA SCOTIA

**Halifax**
Glube, Constance Rachelle *retired judge*

### ONTARIO

**Bracebridge**
Evans, John David Daniel *judge*

**Ottawa**
MacKay, William Andrew *judge*
Margeson, Theodore Earl *judge*
McLachlin, Beverley *Canadian supreme court chief justice*
Strayer, Barry Lee *retired judge*

**Toronto**
Boland, Janet Lang *judge*
McMurtry, R. Roy *federal judge*

### QUEBEC

**Montreal**
Gonthier, Charles Doherty *retired judge*

**Westmount**
Rothman, Melvin L. *retired judge*

### SASKATCHEWAN

**Regina**
Bayda, Edward Dmytro *retired chief justice*

## BELIZE

**Belize City**
Brown, Sir George Noel *judge*

## EGYPT

**Cairo**
Elaraby, Nabil A. *judge, former diplomat*

## GERMANY

**Göttingen**
Starck, Christian Walter *judge, retired law educator*

## NETHERLANDS

**The Hague**
Aldrich, George Hoover *judge, arbitrator*
Allison, Richard Clark *judge*
Buergenthal, Thomas *judge*
Higgins, Dame Rosalyn *judge*
Jiuyong, Shi *judge*
Kooijmans, Pieter Hendrik *judge*
Koroma, Abdul G. *judge*
Owada, Hisashi *judge*
Parra-Aranguren, Gonzalo *judge*
Rezek, Francisco *judge, former supreme court justice*

## ADDRESS UNPUBLISHED

Aboussie, Marilyn *retired judge*
Albritton, William Harold III *federal judge*
Anthony, Joan Caton *administrative judge*
Askey, William Hartman *United States magistrate judge, lawyer*
Austin, John DeLong *retired judge*
Baca, Joseph Francis *retired judge*
Baer, Harold, Jr. *senior federal judge*
Batchelder, Alice M. *federal judge*
Baynes, Thomas Edward, Jr. *retired judge, lawyer, educator, mediator*
Bedsworth, William W. *judge*
Bert, Ellis Lawrence *retired judge*
Bertelsman, William Odis *federal judge*
Bissell, John W. *retired judge*
Black, Susan Harrell *federal judge*
Blatz, Kathleen Anne *former state supreme court justice*
Blume, Herbert *judge*
Bosson, Richard Campbell *state supreme court justice*
Bowman, John J. *judge*
Brackett, Colquitt Prater, Jr. *judge, lawyer*
Brady, M. Jane (Muriel Jane Brady) *judge, former state attorney general*
Brett, Thomas Rutherford *federal judge*
Brown, Robert Laidlaw *state supreme court justice*
Buchanan, Theresa Carroll *judge*
Buchwald, Naomi Reice *federal judge*
Bush, Lynn Jeanne *federal judge*
Callow, William Grant *retired judge*
Castagna, William John *federal judge*
Chapman, Robert Foster *federal judge*
Coffey, John Louis *federal judge*
Cohn, Avern Levin *district judge*
Colaianni, Joseph Vincent *judge*
Compton, Allen T. *retired state supreme court justice*
Cooper, William S. *retired state supreme court justice*
Cyr, Conrad Keefe *federal judge*
Daugherty, Frederick Alvin *federal judge*
Day, Roland Bernard *retired judge*
Dela Cruz, Jose Santos *retired commonwealth supreme court justice*
Ditter, J. William, Jr. *federal judge*
Dixon, John Morris, Jr. *retired judge, lawyer*
Dunn, Melvin Edward *retired judge*
Eaton, Joe Oscar *federal judge*
Enoch, Craig Trively *retired judge*
Epstein, Judith Ann *judge*
Fay, Peter Thorp *federal judge*
Fein, Roger Gary *judge*
Firestone, Nancy B. *federal judge*
Fiscus, Thomas J. *former judge, career military officer*
Fletcher, Norman S. *state supreme court justice*
Freeman, Charles E. *state supreme court justice*
Gebelein, Richard Stephen *judge, former state attorney general*
Glennon, Charles Edward *retired judge, lawyer*
Gorence, Patricia Josetta *judge*
Grant, Isabella Horton *retired judge*
Hamblen, Lapsley Walker, Jr. *retired judge*
Harris, Dale Hutter *retired judge*
Hightower, Jack English *retired judge, congressman*
Hodge, Verne Antonio *judge*
Hogan, Thomas Francis *federal judge*
Holdaway, Ronald M. *retired federal judge*
Howard, George, Jr. *federal judge*
Hunt, William E., Sr. *retired state supreme court justice*
Ingram, George Conley *judge*
Jackson, Thomas Penfield *federal judge*
Jenkins, Michael Grady *judge*
Johnstone, Martin E. *retired state supreme court justice*
Jones, Phyllis Gene *judge*
Jordan, Michelle Denise *judge*
Karr, Stephen William *retired judge*
Kenworthy, William Eugene *judge*
Kline, Norman Douglas *retired judge*

Kramer, Kenneth Bentley *retired federal judge, former congressman*
Krupansky, Blanche Ethel *retired judge*
Kunkle, William Joseph *judge, lawyer*
Lake, I. Beverly, Jr. *retired state supreme court justice*
Lavorato, Louis A. *retired state supreme court justice*
Lee, Dan M. *retired state supreme court chief justice*
Legge, Charles Alexander *federal judge*
Linn, Richard *federal judge*
Lively, Pierce *retired federal judge*
Low, Harry William *judge*
Lyons, Champ, Jr. *state supreme court justice*
Manglona, Ramona V. *judge, former attorney general*
McCown, Hale *retired judge*
McKee, Harry W. *retired federal judge*
McKee, Roger Curtis *retired federal judge*
McMorrow, Mary Ann Grohwin *retired state supreme court justice*
McRae, Charles R. (Chuck McCrae) *former state supreme court justice*
Metzner, Charles Miller *federal judge*
Moore, Daniel Alton, Jr. *retired state supreme court justice*
Moore, Roy S. *former state supreme court chief justice*
Nadeau, Joseph P. *retired state supreme court justice*
Nangle, John Francis *federal judge*
Nelson, David Aldrich *judge*
Nelson, Frederick Dickson *judge*
Neuman, Linda Kinney *retired state supreme court justice, lawyer*
Newbern, William David *retired state supreme court justice*
Nigro, Russell M. *former state supreme court justice*
O'Connor, Sandra Day *retired United States Supreme Court Justice*
Papadakos, Nicholas Peter *retired state supreme court justice*
Payne, Mary Libby *retired judge*
Phillips, James Dickson, Jr. *retired federal judge*
Pokras, Sheila Frances *retired judge*
Potter, Robert Daniel *federal judge*
Prado, Edward Charles *federal judge*
Prather, Lenore Loving *former state supreme court chief justice*
Quillen, William Tatem *retired judge, lawyer, educator*
Reinhardt, Stephen Roy *federal judge*
Rice, Walter Herbert *federal judge*
Robart, James Louis *federal judge, lawyer*
Roper, John Marlin, Sr. *federal magistrate judge*
Roszkowski, Stanley Julian *retired federal judge*
Schroeder, Gerald Frank *state supreme court chief justice*
Schultz, Louis William *retired judge*
Senechal, Alice R. *federal magistrate judge, lawyer*
Shearing, Miriam *retired state supreme court chief justice*
Sheedy, Patrick Thomas *judge*
Shepherd, Bobby E. *federal judge*
Shubb, William Barnet *judge*
Silberman, Larry (Laurence Hirsch Silberman) *federal judge*
Smith, Fern M. *judge*
Spector, Rose *former state supreme court justice*
Squires, John Henry *judge*
Stacy, Frances H. *federal judge*
Stafford, William Henry, Jr. *federal judge*
Staker, Robert Jackson *retired judge*
Stanton, Louis Lee *federal judge*
Stewart, Annette *judge*
Sullivan, Eugene Raymond *judge*
Sypolt, Diane Gilbert *retired judge*
Thornton, Ray *retired state supreme court justice, former congressman*
Thurmond, George Murat *judge*
van Gestel, Allan *judge*
White, Helene Nita *federal judge*
Wicker, Thomas Carey, Jr. *retired judge*
Wittig, Don *judge*
Young, C. Clifton *former state supreme court justice*

## LAW: LAW PRACTICE AND ADMINISTRATION

## UNITED STATES

### ALABAMA

**Andalusia**
Fuller, William Sidney *lawyer*

**Anniston**
Klinefelter, James Louis *lawyer*

**Arab**
Beuoy, David Lee *lawyer*

**Birmingham**
Alexander, James Patrick *lawyer, educator*
Baker, David Remember *lawyer*
Balch, Samuel Eason *lawyer*
Blan, Ollie Lionel, Jr. *retired lawyer*
Brown, Ephraim Taylor, Jr. *lawyer*
Carmody, Richard Patrick *lawyer*
Carruthers, Thomas Neely *lawyer*
Chapman, Lavonya Kelley *lawyer, director*
Christian, Thomas William *lawyer*
Clark, William Northington *lawyer, retired military officer*
Coleman, Brittin Turner *lawyer*
Coleman, John James III *lawyer, educator*
Cooper, N. Lee *lawyer*
Corliss, Deane Kenworthy *lawyer*
Deer, Richard Alan (Alan Deer) *lawyer*
Denson, William Frank III *lawyer*

Farley, Joseph McConnell *lawyer*
Friend, Edward Malcolm III *lawyer, educator*
Gale, Fournier Joseph III *lawyer*
Garner, Robert Edward Lee *lawyer*
Givhan, Robert Marcus *lawyer*
Goggans, Dana *paralegal, private investigator*
Hansen, Charles James *lawyer*
Haskell, Wyatt Rushton *lawyer*
Hinton, James Forrest, Jr. *lawyer*
Howell, William Ashley III *lawyer*
Hughey, James Fletcher, Jr. *lawyer*
Kracke, Robert Russell *lawyer*
Lacy, Alexander Shelton *retired lawyer*
Langum, David John *law educator, historian*
Long, Deborah Joyce *lawyer*
Long, Thad Gladden *lawyer*
Mc Millan, George Duncan Hastie, Jr. *lawyer, former state official*
McWhorter, Hobart Amory, Jr. *lawyer*
Mills, William Hayes *lawyer*
Molen, John Klauminzer *lawyer*
Palmer, Robert Leslie *lawyer*
Powell, Charles Arthur III *lawyer*
Powell, Jerry W. *lawyer*
Redden, Lawrence Drew *lawyer*
Rogers, Ernest Mabry *lawyer*
Rotch, James E. *lawyer*
Rountree, Asa *lawyer*
Selfe, Edward Milton *lawyer*
Small, Clarence Merilton, Jr. *lawyer*
Spransy, Joseph William *corporate lawyer*
Stabler, Lewis Vastine, Jr. *lawyer*
Thompson, Tracy Michelle *lawyer*
Trimmier, Charles Stephen, Jr. *lawyer*
Vinson, Laurence Duncan, Jr. *lawyer*
Weeks, Arthur Andrew *lawyer, educator*
Wells, Huey Thomas, Jr. *lawyer*
Whatley, Joe Ramon, Jr. *lawyer*
Wilson, James Charles, Jr. *lawyer*
Wrinkle, John Newton *lawyer*
Yoder, Stephen Alan *lawyer*

**Demopolis**
Lloyd, Hugh Adams *lawyer*

**Huntsville**
Huckaby, Gary Carlton *lawyer*
Ryan, L. Thomas, Jr. *lawyer*
Watson, S.A. *lawyer, retired judge*

**Jacksonville**
Wang, Hanrong *law librarian, educator, library and information scientist*

**Kinston**
Sumblin, Anne Stone *lawyer*

**Mobile**
Armbrecht, William Henry III *retired lawyer*
Braswell, Louis Erskine *lawyer*
Harris, Benjamin Harte, Jr. *lawyer*
Helmsing, Frederick George *lawyer*
Holland, Lyman Faith, Jr. *lawyer*
Holmes, Broox Garrett *lawyer*
Murchison, David Roderick *lawyer*
Peebles, E(mory) B(ush) III *lawyer*
Rhodes, Deborah J. *prosecutor*
Roedder, William Chapman, Jr. *lawyer*
York, David P. *prosecutor*

**Montgomery**
Byars, Walter Ryland, Jr. *lawyer*
Campbell, Maria Bouchelle *lawyer, consultant*
Canary, Leura Garrett *prosecutor*
Dees, Morris Seligman, Jr. *lawyer*
Ely, Robert Eugene *lawyer, author, educator*
Hamner, Reginald Turner *lawyer*
Hester, Douglas Benjamin *lawyer*
Kloess, Lawrence Herman, Jr. *retired lawyer*
Langford, Charles Douglas *lawyer*
Laurie, Robin Garrett *lawyer*
Lawson, Thomas Seay, Jr. *lawyer, actor*
Leslie, Henry Arthur *lawyer, retired bank executive*
Lewis, Joseph Brady (Jay Lewis) *lawyer*
McElvy, James Douglas *lawyer*
McFadden, Frank Hampton *lawyer, former judge*
Methvin, Thomas James *lawyer*
Salmon, Joseph Thaddeus *lawyer*
Segall, Robert D. *lawyer*
Stevenson, Bryan Allen *lawyer*
Volz, Charles Harvie, Jr. *lawyer*

**Mountain Brook**
Southerland, Henry DeLeon, Jr. *retired lawyer, civil engineer*

**Opelika**
Samford, Yetta Glenn, Jr. *lawyer, director*

**Sheffield**
Hamby, Gene Malcolm, Jr. *lawyer*

**Tuscaloosa**
Cook, Camille Wright *retired law educator*
Ryan, Jenny Rebeka *lawyer*
Smith, Ralph Harrison *lawyer*

**Tuskegee**
Gray, Fred David *lawyer*

### ALASKA

**Anchorage**
Butler, Rex Lamont *lawyer*
Cantor, James Elliot *lawyer*
Cohen, Nelson P. *prosecutor*
Cooke, Christopher Robert *lawyer, retired judge*
De Lisio, Stephen Scott *lawyer, director, pastor*
Ealy, Jonathan Bruce *lawyer*
Grahame, Heather H. *lawyer*
Hughes, Mary Katherine *lawyer*
Katcher, Jonathon A. *lawyer*
Langworthy, Robert H. *law educator*
McClintock, Donald William III *lawyer*
Oesting, David W. *lawyer*
Ostrovsky, Lawrence Zelig *lawyer*
Pradell, Steven *lawyer*
Reeves, James N. *lawyer*

Roberts, John Derham *lawyer*
Serdahely, Douglas J. *lawyer, former state judge*
Walther, Dale Jay *lawyer*

**Fairbanks**
Bodwell, Lori *lawyer*

**Juneau**
Cole, Charles Edward *lawyer, state attorney general*
Rozell, William Barclay *lawyer*

**Kodiak**
Jamin, Matthew Daniel *lawyer, judge*

**Nondalton**
Gay, Sarah Elizabeth *lawyer*

**Salcha**
Rice, Julian Casavant *lawyer*

**ARIZONA**

**Carefree**
Putney, Mark William *lawyer, utilities executive*

**Eloy**
O'Leary, Thomas Michael *lawyer*

**Flagstaff**
Aspey, Frederick Morris (Fritz Aspey) *lawyer*

**Marana**
Augello, William Joseph *lawyer*

**Mesa**
Hudkins, John W. *lawyer*

**Paradise Valley**
Tubman, William Charles *lawyer*

**Phoenix**
Allen, Robert Eugene Barton *lawyer*
Alsentzer, William James, Jr. *lawyer*
Bain, C. Randall *lawyer*
Baker, William Dunlap *lawyer*
Bakker, Thomas Gordon *lawyer*
Beabeau, Olivier Andre *prosecutor*
Beams, Christian C. *lawyer*
Begam, Robert George *lawyer*
Birk, David R. *lawyer*
Blanchard, Charles Alan *lawyer, retired state senator*
Bouma, John Jacob *lawyer*
Burke, Timothy John *lawyer*
Chanen, Steven Robert *lawyer*
Charlton, Paul K. *prosecutor, lawyer*
Chen, George *lawyer*
Cole, George Thomas *lawyer*
Colton, Sterling David (David Colton) *lawyer*
Comus, Louis Francis, Jr. *lawyer*
Condo, James Robert *lawyer*
Cooledge, Richard Calvin *lawyer*
Coppersmith, Sam *lawyer*
Crozier, Scott A. *lawyer*
Davies, David George *lawyer, educator*
Dawson, John Joseph *lawyer*
DeBerry, Dennis Charles *lawyer*
Derdenger, Patrick *lawyer*
Derouin, James Gilbert *lawyer*
Dunipace, Ian Douglas *lawyer*
Ehmann, Anthony Valentine *lawyer*
Everett, James Joseph *lawyer*
Everroad, John David *lawyer*
Feinstein, Allen Lewis *lawyer*
Fenzl, Terry Earle *lawyer*
Fine, Charles Leon *lawyer*
Gaffney, Donald Lee *lawyer*
Gallagher, Michael L. *lawyer*
Gilbert, Donald Roy *lawyer*
Goldstein, Stuart Wolf *lawyer*
Gomez, David Frederick *lawyer*
Grant, Merwin Darwin *lawyer*
Griller, Gordon Moore *legal association administrator, consultant*
Grimwood, Helen Perry *lawyer*
Haga, David L. *lawyer*
Halpern, Barry David *lawyer*
Hammond, Larry Austin *lawyer*
Harrison, Mark Isaac *lawyer*
Hayden, William Robert *lawyer*
Hicks, William Albert III *lawyer*
Hochuli, Edward G. *lawyer*
Hoecker, Thomas Ralph *lawyer*
Holden, Michael John *lawyer*
Howard, William Matthew *arbitrator, writer, lawyer*
Hoxie, Joel P. *lawyer*
Huntwork, James Roden *lawyer*
Jakubczyk, John Joseph *lawyer*
James, Charles E., Jr. *lawyer*
Jirauch, Charles W. *lawyer*
Johnson, Christopher D. *lawyer*
Kant, Robert S. *lawyer*
Klahr, Gary Peter *retired lawyer*
Klausner, Jack Daniel *lawyer*
Klein, R. Kent *lawyer*
Knoller, Guy David *lawyer*
Kurn, Neal *lawyer*
Levetown, Robert Alexander *lawyer*
Lubin, Stanley *lawyer*
Magyar, Kim S. *lawyer*
Martori, Joseph Peter *lawyer*
May, Bruce Barnett *lawyer*
McKee, Roger A. *lawyer*
McRae, Hamilton Eugene III *lawyer*
Merritt, Nancy-Jo *lawyer*
Miller, Robert J. *lawyer*
Olsen, Alfred Jon *lawyer*
Pietzsch, Michael Edward *lawyer*
Placenti, Frank Michael *lawyer*
Platt, Warren E. *lawyer*
Refo, Patricia Lee *lawyer*
Rivera, Jose de Jesus *lawyer*
Rose, Scott A. *lawyer*
Rosenfeld, Lawrence J. (Larry) *lawyer*
Ross, Richard Frederick *lawyer*
Rudolph, Gilbert Lawrence *lawyer*
Sanders, Barry R. *lawyer*

Schneider, Elizabeth Kelley *law librarian*
Sherk, Kenneth John *lawyer*
Silverman, Alan Henry *lawyer*
Smock, Timothy Robert *lawyer*
Storey, Norman C. *lawyer*
Tennen, Leslie Irwin *lawyer, consultant*
Thompson, Terence William *lawyer*
Thumma, Samuel Anderson *lawyer*
Ulrich, Paul Graham *lawyer, writer, editor*
Verbin, Jeffrey Harold *lawyer*
Walker, Richard K. *lawyer*
Williams, Quinn Patrick *lawyer*
Wirken, Charles William *lawyer*
Wolf, G. Van Velsor, Jr. *lawyer*
Yarnell, Michael Allan *lawyer*

**Prescott**
Madden, Paul Robert *lawyer, director*

**Scottsdale**
Bullerdick, Kim H. *lawyer, petroleum executive*
Buri, Charles Edward *lawyer*
Calise, Nicholas James *lawyer*
Crawford, Robert F. *lawyer*
Helm, Steven M *lawyer*
Hermann, Robert John *lawyer*
Hutchison, Stanley Philip *retired lawyer*
Krupp, Clarence William *lawyer, health facility administrator*
Lindgren, D. Kenneth, Jr., (Derbin Kenneth Lindgren Jr.) *retired lawyer*
Lowry, Edward Francis, Jr. *lawyer*
Marks, Merton Eleazer *lawyer, international arbitrator, mediator, consultant*
Nielsen, Greg Ross *lawyer*
Overgaard, Cordell Jersild *lawyer, rancher, director*
Smith, David Burnell *lawyer, state legislator*

**Sun City**
Keesling, Karen Ruth *lawyer*
Treece, James Lyle *retired lawyer*

**Surprise**
Fennelly, Jane Corey *lawyer*

**Tempe**
Dhillon, Janet L. *lawyer*
Marchant, Gary Elvin *lawyer*
Matheson, Alan Adams *law educator*
Sims, Michael Louis *lawyer*
Spritzer, Ralph Simon *lawyer, educator*

**Tucson**
Amhowitz, Harris J. *lawyer, educator*
Betteridge, Frances Carpenter *retired lawyer, mediator*
Blackman, Jeffrey William *lawyer*
Daum, Bryan Edwin *lawyer*
Dobbs, Dan Byron *lawyer, educator*
Esposito, Joseph Louis *lawyer*
Feldman, Stanley George *lawyer*
Froman, Sandra Sue *lawyer*
Gantz, David Alfred *lawyer, academic administrator*
Goldman, Gloria A. *lawyer*
Gonzales, Richard Joseph *lawyer*
Grand, Richard D. *lawyer*
Jurkowitz, Daniel S. *lawyer, prosecutor, judge*
Kimble, William Earle *lawyer*
Kozolchyk, Boris *law educator, consultant*
Kuklin, Susan Beverly *law librarian, lawyer*
Kuykendall, Gregory John *lawyer*
Mc Donald, John Richard *lawyer*
Meehan, Michael Joseph *lawyer*
Miller, Michael Douglas *lawyer*
Morrow, James Franklin *lawyer*
Pace, Thomas M. *lawyer*
Piccarreta, Carl Alan *lawyer*
Rose, Carol Marguerite *law educator*
Samet, Dee-Dee *lawyer*
Schorr, S. L. *lawyer*
Simmons, Sarah R. *lawyer*
Spaeth, Jan Mills *jury consultant*
Staubitz, Arthur Frederick *retired lawyer, retired health products executive*
Strong, John William *lawyer, educator*
Tindall, Robert Emmett *lawyer, educator*
Treadwell-Rubin, Pamela A. *lawyer*
Zlaket, Thomas Andrew *lawyer, former state supreme court chief justice*

**Yuma**
Hossler, David Joseph *lawyer, law educator*
Hunt, Gerald Wallace *lawyer*

**ARKANSAS**

**Ashdown**
Finley, John Cyrus III *lawyer, judge*

**Benton**
Krueger, Marlo Bush *retired lawyer*

**Bentonville**
Gean, Thomas C. *lawyer, former prosecutor*
Hyde, Thomas D. *lawyer*

**Cherokee Village**
Burke, Richard Kitchens *lawyer, educator*

**Conway**
Johnson, James Douglas (Jim Johnson) *lawyer*

**Crossett**
Hubbell, Billy James *lawyer*

**El Dorado**
Cossé, Steven A. *lawyer*

**Fayetteville**
Bassett, Woodson William, Jr. *lawyer*
Epley, Lewis Everett, Jr. *retired lawyer*
Kester, Charles Melvin *lawyer*
Nance, Cynthia Eleanor *law educator*
Pearson, Charles Thomas, Jr. *lawyer, director*
Roberts, Michael T. *law educator, lawyer*

**Fort Smith**
Babb, Douglas J. *lawyer*
Balfe, Robert Cramer III *prosecutor*
Cooper, Richard F. *lawyer*
Daily, Thomas A. *lawyer*
Meadors, C. Brian *lawyer*

**Helena**
Roscopf, Charles Buford *lawyer*

**Jonesboro**
Deacon, John C. *lawyer*
Perkins, George Brant *lawyer*

**Little Rock**
Allen, H. William *lawyer*
Anderson, Philip Sidney *lawyer*
Boe, Myron Timothy *lawyer*
Cherry, Sandra Wilson *lawyer*
Cross, J. Bruce *lawyer*
Cummins, Bud *prosecutor*
Fitzhugh, Kathryn Corrothers *law librarian*
Gunter, Russell Allen *lawyer*
Hall, John Wesley, Jr. *lawyer*
Hargis, David Michael *lawyer*
Haught, William Dixon *lawyer, writer*
Hope, Ronald Arthur *lawyer*
James, William Owen, Jr. *lawyer*
Lemke, Judith A. *lawyer*
May, Ronald Alan *lawyer*
Murphey, Arthur Gage, Jr. *law educator*
Nelson, Edward Sheffield *lawyer, retired utilities executive*
Schroeder, Paul J., Jr. *lawyer*
Sherman, William Farrar *lawyer, former state legislator*
Stewart, Amy Lee *lawyer*
Stockburger, Jean Dawson *lawyer*
Ursery, Frederick Stanley *lawyer*
Witherspoon, Carolyn Brack *lawyer*

**Monticello**
Ball, William Kenneth *lawyer*

**North Little Rock**
Patty, Claibourne Watkins, Jr. *lawyer*
Welch, Morgan E. *lawyer*

**Pine Bluff**
Jones, John Harris *retired lawyer*
Sims, David Lloyd *lawyer*
Strode, Joseph Arlin *lawyer*

**Prescott**
Vasser, Albert Glenn *lawyer*

**Springdale**
Gonzalez-Pita, J. Alberto *lawyer*
Hudson, R. Read *lawyer, food products executive*

**Warren**
Claycomb, Hugh Murray *lawyer, writer*

**West Memphis**
Fogleman, Julian Barton *lawyer*

**CALIFORNIA**

**Alameda**
Boltwood, Russell Lewis *lawyer, telecommunications industry executive*

**Alamo**
Madden, Palmer Brown *lawyer*

**Aliso Viejo**
Fisher, Lawrence N. *lawyer, engineering company executive*

**Alta Loma**
Klein, Henry *lawyer*

**Atherton**
Ferris, Robert Albert *lawyer, venture capitalist*

**Auburn**
Lyon, Bruce Arnold *lawyer, educator*

**Bakersfield**
Tornstrom, Robert Ernest *lawyer, oil industry executive*

**Belvedere Tiburon**
Allan, Walter Robert *lawyer*
Stotter, Lawrence Henry *lawyer*

**Berkeley**
Arguedas, Cristina Claypoole *lawyer*
Barnes, Thomas G. *law educator*
Berring, Robert Charles, Jr. *law educator, law librarian, legal association administrator*
Blackburn, Robert Parker *lawyer*
Buxbaum, Richard M. *lawyer, educator*
Choper, Jesse Herbert *law educator, dean*
De Goff, Victoria Joan *lawyer*
Eisenberg, Melvin A. *law educator*
Feeley, Malcolm McCollum *law educator, political scientist*
Halbach, Edward Christian, Jr. *law educator*
Haley, George Patrick *lawyer*
Kadish, Sanford Harold *law educator*
Kagan, Robert Allen *law educator*
Kay, Herma Hill *law educator*
McNulty, John Kent *lawyer, educator*
Meador, Ross DeShong *lawyer*
Menell, Peter Seth *law educator*
Meyer, Roberta *mediator, communication consultant*
Mishkin, Paul J. *lawyer, educator*
Moran, Rachel *law educator*
Pope, Alexander H. *retired lawyer*
Scheiber, Harry N. *law educator*
Seligman, Brad *lawyer*
Shapiro, Martin *law educator*
Wolfram, Charles William *law educator*
Woodhouse, Thomas Edwin *lawyer, trust company administrator*

**Yoo**, John Choon *law educator, former federal agency administrator*
Zimring, Franklin E. *lawyer, educator*

**Beverly Hills**
Anderson, Kenneth Allen *lawyer, hotel executive*
Bortman, David *lawyer*
Brockovich-Ellis, Erin *legal researcher*
Burns, Marvin Gerald *lawyer*
Factor, Max III *arbitrator, mediator*
Fagel, Bruce G. *lawyer, former emergency physician*
Fine, Richard Isaac *lawyer*
Hogan, Steven L. *lawyer*
Horwin, Leonard *retired lawyer*
Isaacman, Alan L. *lawyer*
Jaffe, F. Filmore *lawyer, retired judge*
Karlin, Michael Jonathan Abraham *lawyer*
Kleiner, Madeleine A. *lawyer*
Phillips, Stacy D. *lawyer*
Ramer, Bruce M. *lawyer*
Rosky, Burton Seymour *lawyer*
Rowles, Michael G. *lawyer*
Russell, Irwin Emanuel *lawyer*
Schiff, Gunther Hans *lawyer*
Sobelle, Richard E. *lawyer*
Thompson, Richard Dickson *lawyer*

**Bodega Bay**
Sorensen, Linda *lawyer*

**Bonita**
Kline, Paul Conley *lawyer*

**Burbank**
Brandis, Bernardine *lawyer*
Braverman, Alan N. *lawyer*

**Burlingame**
Cotchett, Joseph Winters *lawyer, writer*

**Calabasas**
Geckle, Timothy J. *lawyer*
Grimwade, Richard Llewellyn *lawyer*

**Carlsbad**
Hanscom, Eric Alan *lawyer*
McCracken, Steven Carl *lawyer*
Moore, David Robert *lawyer*

**Carmel**
Bengert, W. Raymond *lawyer, chemical engineer*

**Century City**
Clark, Shaun C. *lawyer*
Mak, Kitty *lawyer*

**Chino**
Determan, John David *lawyer*

**Claremont**
Ansell, Edward Orin *lawyer*
Ferguson, Cleve Robert *lawyer, educator*

**Coalinga**
Frame, Ted Ronald *lawyer*

**Copperopolis**
Wooster, Kelly C. *lawyer*

**Corona**
Buchen, David A. *lawyer*
Everett Nollkamper, Pamela Irene *legal association administrator, educator*

**Corona Del Mar**
Allen, Russell G. *lawyer*
Holley, Colin C. *prosecutor*

**Coronado**
Herring, Charles David *lawyer, educator*
Raushenbush, Walter Brandeis *retired law educator*

**Costa Mesa**
Barbarosh, Craig A. *lawyer*
Caldwell, Courtney Lynn *lawyer, real estate consultant*
Daniels, James Walter *lawyer*
Frieden, Clifford E. *lawyer*
Gay, William Tolin *lawyer*
Grogan, Virginia S. *lawyer*
Guilford, Andrew John *lawyer*
Hay, Howard Clinton *lawyer*
Jones, H(arold) Gilbert, Jr. *lawyer*
Marshall, Ellen Ruth *lawyer*
Mooradian, George T. *lawyer*
Morrow, Donald L. *lawyer*
Rose, I. Nelson *lawyer, educator*
Ruben, Richard S. *lawyer*
Schaaf, Douglas Allan *lawyer*
Scheuneman, Christine A. *lawyer*
Tennyson, Peter Joseph *lawyer*

**Culver City**
Nicholas, Frederick M. *lawyer*

**Cupertino**
Courville, Arthur F. *lawyer*
Svalya, Phillip Gordon *lawyer*

**Cypress**
Konowiecki, Joseph Samuel *lawyer, health facility administrator*
Olschwang, Alan Paul *lawyer, crossword puzzle author*

**Danville**
Candland, D. Stuart *lawyer*
Jones, Orlo Dow *retired lawyer, retired pharmaceutical executive*

**Darwin**
Palazzo, Robert Paul *lawyer, accountant*

**Davis**
Bartosic, Florian *lawyer, educator*
Bruch, Carol Sophie *law educator*
Imwinkelried, Edward John *law educator*
Poulos, Joan Graham *lawyer*

Wolk, Bruce Alan *law educator*
Wydick, Richard Crews *lawyer, educator*

**Del Mar**
Seitman, John Michael *arbitrator, mediator, lawyer*

**Diablo**
Burnison, Boyd Edward *lawyer*

**East Palo Alto**
Bates, William III *lawyer*
Lesser, Henry *lawyer*
Rinsky, Arthur C. *lawyer*

**El Cajon**
Silverberg, Lewis Henry *lawyer, consultant*

**El Segundo**
Fisk, Hayward Dan *lawyer, computer company executive*
Hunter, Larry Dean *lawyer*
Muhlbach, Robert Arthur *lawyer*
Willis, Judy Ann *lawyer*

**Emeryville**
Bartels, Ursula Brennan *lawyer*
Howe, Drayton Ford, Jr. *lawyer*

**Encino**
Genga, John Michael *lawyer*
Smith, Selma Moidel *lawyer, composer*
Sungaila, Mary-Christine (M.C. Sungaila) *lawyer*

**Escondido**
Guinn, Stanley Willis *lawyer*

**Eureka**
Robinson, Michael Kevin *lawyer*

**Fairfield**
Haas, Richard *lawyer*

**Fallbrook**
Sorbello, Joseph Charles *retired lawyer*

**Felton**
Kulzick, Ken Stafford *retired lawyer, writer*

**Foster City**
Lonnquist, George Eric *lawyer*

**Fountain Valley**
Broderick, Daniel P. *lawyer*

**Fremont**
Chien-Hale, Elizabeth *lawyer*

**Fresno**
Ewell, A. Ben, Jr. *lawyer, small business owner*
Jenkins, David Ray *lawyer*
Lambe, James Patrick *lawyer*
Little, Kevin Gerard *lawyer*
Palmer, Samuel Copeland III *lawyer*

**Fullerton**
Ackerman, Richard Charles *lawyer, state legislator*
Bush, William Merritt *lawyer*
Goldstein, Edward David *lawyer, former glass company executive*
May, William Hathaway *lawyer*
Moerbeek, Stanley Leonard *lawyer*
Roberts, Mark Scott *lawyer*
Steinmeyer, Robert Jay *retired lawyer*

**Glendale**
Ebersole, Todd Michael *lawyer*
Hoffman, Donald M. *lawyer*
Kazanjian, Phillip Carl *lawyer, educator*
Kendrick, Katherine *lawyer*
King, Keith B.W. *lawyer*
MacDonald, Kirk Stewart *lawyer*
Martinetti, Ronald Anthony *lawyer*
Ross, Bruce Shields *lawyer*
Scott, A. Timothy *lawyer*
Stack, Kevin J. *lawyer*

**Gold River**
Andrew, John Henry *lawyer, writer*

**Greenbrae**
Bonapart, Alan David *lawyer*
Perry, E. Lynn *lawyer*

**Half Moon Bay**
Lambert, Frederick William *lawyer, educator*

**Hayward**
Beck, Edward William *lawyer*
Smith, John Kerwin *lawyer*
Thorpe, John Milton *lawyer*

**Healdsburg**
Kemp, Alson Remington, Jr.

**Hercules**
Richards, Gerald Thomas *lawyer, educator, writer*

**Huntington Beach**
Baroni, Michael L. *lawyer*
Garrels, Sherry Ann *lawyer*
Nikas, Richard John *lawyer*

**Imperial Beach**
Merkin, William Leslie *retired lawyer*

**Indian Wells**
FitzGerald, John Edward III *lawyer*
McDermott, Thomas John, Jr. *lawyer*

**Indio**
De Salva, Christopher Joseph *lawyer, consultant*

**Inverness**
Ciani, Judith Elaine *retired lawyer*

**Irvine**
Basombrio, Juan C. *lawyer*
Bastiaanse, Gerard C. *lawyer*

Beard, Ronald Stratton *lawyer*
Claster, William D. *lawyer*
DuBose, Guy Steven *lawyer*
Dull, David A. *lawyer*
Grabowski, Richard J. *lawyer*
Halvorsen, Clay A. *lawyer, construction executive*
Huang, Wendy Wan-Juoh *lawyer*
Ingram, Douglas Stephen *lawyer*
Keller, Jennifer L. *lawyer*
Knobbe, Louis Joseph *lawyer, educator*
Lowe, Kathlene Winn *lawyer*
Mattson, Robert Marvin, Jr. *lawyer*
Merken, Leo *lawyer*
Morisseau, Fay Edwin *lawyer*
Narayan, Ash *lawyer*
Pianko, Theodore A. *lawyer*
Pitcher, Thomas B. *lawyer*
Rooklidge, William Charles *lawyer*
Specter, Richard Bruce *lawyer*
Sunshine, Steven H. *lawyer*
Tachner, Leonard *lawyer*
Thomas, Jeffrey T. *lawyer*
Tyler, Michael Robert *lawyer*
Umberg, Thomas John *lawyer*
Wintrode, Ralph Charles *lawyer*

**King City**
Anderson, Peter David *lawyer*

**La Canada Flintridge**
Costello, Francis William *lawyer*

**La Jolla**
Buchholz, Debby *lawyer*
Karlen, Peter Hurd *lawyer, writer*
Kirchheimer, Arthur E(dward) *lawyer, stock exchange executive*
Mayer, James Hock *lawyer, mediator*
Wilkins, Floyd, Jr. *lawyer, educator*
Wilson, Bonnie Jean *lawyer, educator, investor*

**La Verne**
Barrett, Robert Matthew *lawyer, educator*

**Lafayette**
Davies, Paul Lewis, Jr. *retired lawyer*

**Laguna Hills**
Reinglass, Michelle Annette *lawyer*

**Larkspur**
Greenberg, Myron Silver *lawyer*
Ratner, David Louis *retired law educator*
Willson, Prentiss, Jr. *retired lawyer*

**Long Beach**
Bursley, Kathleen A. *lawyer*
Calhoun, John R. *lawyer*
Deukmejian, George *lawyer, retired governor*
Haile, Lawrence Barclay *lawyer*
Helwick, Christine *lawyer*
Sinclitico, Dennis J. *lawyer*
Wise, George Edward *lawyer*

**Los Altos**
Justice-Moore, Kathleen E. *lawyer*
Yang, Roxana Hwu *lawyer, investor*

**Los Angeles**
Aaron, Benjamin *law educator, arbitrator*
Abell, Nancy L. *lawyer*
Adamek, Charles Andrew *lawyer*
Adams, Thomas Merritt *lawyer*
Adell, Hirsch *lawyer*
Adler, Erwin Ellery *lawyer*
Adler, Michael I. *lawyer*
Adler, Sara *arbitrator, mediator*
Ahrens, Mary Elizabeth *lawyer*
Alden, John W. *lawyer*
Allen, David C. *lawyer*
Allred, Gloria Rachel *lawyer*
Altman, Scott *law educator, dean*
Aminian Baghai, Arash *lawyer*
Anderson, Charles David *lawyer*
Angel, Arthur Ronald *lawyer, consultant*
Antin, Michael *lawyer*
Apfel, Gary *lawyer*
Arbisser, Aton *lawyer*
Arenella, Peter Lee *law educator*
Arnold, Dennis B. *lawyer*
Aronoff, Vera *law librarian*
Aronson, Seth *lawyer*
Aronzon, Paul S. *lawyer*
Asperger, James *lawyer*
Austen, Karl Ramsdell *lawyer*
Azad, Susan Stott *lawyer*
Bakaly, Charles George, Jr. *lawyer, mediator*
Baker, Donald P. *lawyer*
Barrett, Jane Hayes *lawyer*
Barsky, Wayne Mitchell *lawyer*
Barth Menzies, Karen Ann *lawyer*
Barton, Alan Joel *lawyer*
Barza, Harold A. *lawyer*
Baum, Michael Lin *lawyer*
Bauman, Stephen Adrian *lawyer*
Baumann, Richard Gordon *lawyer*
Baumgarten, Ronald Neal *lawyer*
Bender, Charles William *lawyer*
Bendix, Helen Irene *lawyer*
Bernacchi, Richard Lloyd *lawyer*
Bertero, Karen E. *lawyer*
Bibicoff, Hillary Sue *lawyer*
Bitting, William M. *lawyer*
Blencowe, Paul Sherwood *lawyer, private investor*
Blendell, Elizabeth A. *lawyer*
Bloomberg, Coe Arthur *lawyer*
Blumberg, Grace Ganz *lawyer, educator*
Bobbitt, Leroy *lawyer*
Bodkin, Henry Grattan, Jr. *lawyer*
Boehmer, Richard Arthur *lawyer*
Bogen, Andrew E. *lawyer*
Bonesteel, Michael John *lawyer*
Bonner, Robert Cleve *lawyer*
Boras, Kim *lawyer*
Bordy, Michael Jeffrey *lawyer*
Boxer, Lester *lawyer*
Boyce, David S. *lawyer*
Boyle, Kevin Richard *lawyer*
Bradley, Lawrence D., Jr. *lawyer*
Branca, John Gregory *lawyer, consultant*

Brandler, Jonathan M. *lawyer*
Braun, David A(dlai) *lawyer*
Bressan, Paul Louis *lawyer*
Brian, Brad D. *lawyer*
Brill, Laura W. *lawyer*
Brittenham, Skip *lawyer*
Brown, Michael K. *lawyer*
Bryan, Greyson *lawyer*
Bryan, Karen Smith *lawyer*
Burch, Robert Dale *lawyer*
Burke, Yvonne Watson Brathwaite (Mrs. William A. Burke) *lawyer*
Byrd, Christine Waterman Swent *lawyer*
Calabrese, Joseph A. *lawyer*
Carey, Stevens Anthony *lawyer*
Carlson, Robert Edwin *lawyer*
Carr, Willard Zeller, Jr. *retired lawyer*
Casamassima, Christopher T. *lawyer*
Castro, Leonard Edward *lawyer*
Cate, Jan Harris *lawyer*
Cermak, John Frank, Jr. *lawyer*
Chapman Holley, Shawn Snider *lawyer*
Chiate, Kenneth Reed *lawyer*
Christ, Roxanne E. *lawyer*
Christol, Carl Quimby *lawyer, political science professor*
Christopher, Warren Minor *lawyer, former secretary of state*
Chu, Morgan *lawyer*
Chung, Tong Soo *lawyer*
Clair, John J., Jr. *lawyer*
Clark, R(ufus) Bradbury *lawyer, director*
Cleary, William Joseph, Jr. *lawyer*
Cochran, Steve *lawyer*
Cohen, Cynthia Marylyn *lawyer*
Cole, William L. *lawyer*
Coleman, Rexford Lee *lawyer, educator*
Collier, Charles Arthur, Jr. *lawyer*
Conley, Mark A. *lawyer*
Cook, Melanie K. *lawyer*
Cooley, Steve *prosecutor*
Cooper, Robert E. *lawyer*
Copeland, Trent Brehon *lawyer*
Costello, Kenneth R. *lawyer*
Coupe, James Warnick *lawyer*
Court, Michelle Williams *lawyer, director*
Curtiss, Thomas, Jr. *lawyer*
Dana, Lauren Elizabeth *lawyer*
D'Angelo Melby, Donna Marie *lawyer*
Daniels, John Peter *lawyer*
Darby, G(eorge) Harrison *lawyer*
Darden, Christopher Allen *lawyer, actor, writer*
Dastin, Barry L. *lawyer*
Daum, John F. *lawyer*
Davidson, Jeffrey S. *lawyer*
Davis, Gray (Joseph Graham Davis) *lawyer, former governor*
De Brier, Donald Paul *lawyer*
de Castro, Hugo Daniel *lawyer*
Decker, Richard Jeffrey *lawyer*
Delgadillo, Rockard J. (Rocky Delgadillo) *lawyer*
Denham, Robert Edwin *lawyer, investment company executive*
Diamond, Stanley Jay *lawyer*
DiMeglio, David J. *lawyer*
Dinel, Richard Henry *lawyer*
Dodd, Jan Eve *lawyer*
Donovan, John Arthur *lawyer*
Dudziak, Mary Louise *law educator*
Dunham, Scott H. *lawyer*
Easton, Mark *lawyer*
Eatman, Louis Perkins *lawyer*
Emanuel, William Joseph *lawyer*
English, Stephen Raymond *lawyer*
Eskenazi, Bonnie Elise *lawyer*
Evans, Gregory Lawrence *lawyer*
Fairbank, Robert Harold *lawyer*
Farmer, Robert Lindsay *lawyer*
Farrar, Stanley F. *lawyer*
Feigen, Brenda S. *lawyer, film producer, writer*
Fein, Ronald Lawrence *lawyer*
Feldman, Lewis G. *lawyer*
Fenning, Lisa Hill *lawyer, mediator, retired judge*
Fields, Bertram Harris *lawyer*
Fields, Henry Michael *lawyer*
Finkel, Evan *lawyer*
Finnegan, Michael J. *lawyer*
Fisher, Richard N. *lawyer*
Flagel, Mark Alan *lawyer*
Fleer, Keith George *lawyer, retired film company executive*
Follick, Edwin Duane *law educator, dean, chiropractor*
Foss, Robert Fletcher *lawyer*
Frackman, Russell Jay *lawyer*
Fragner, Matthew Charles *lawyer*
Freier, Elliot G. *lawyer*
Frimmer, Paul Norman *lawyer*
Futami, Norman *lawyer*
Gallo, Jon Joseph *lawyer*
Galton, Stephen Harold *lawyer*
Garbacz, Gregory A. *lawyer*
Garrett, Elizabeth *law educator, academic administrator*
Gasparetti, Lorenzo E. *lawyer*
Geragos, Mark John *lawyer*
Gest, Howard David *lawyer*
Gilbertson, John T. *lawyer*
Girard, Robert David *lawyer*
Girardi, Thomas Vincent *lawyer*
Glazer, Michael *lawyer*
Glover, Stephen I. *lawyer*
Goldman, Allan Bailey *lawyer*
Goldman, Benjamin Edward *lawyer*
Goldman, Donald Aaron *lawyer*
Goldman, Stanley A. *law educator*
Goodman, Max A. *lawyer, educator*
Gorman, Joseph Gregory, Jr. *lawyer*
Gould, David *lawyer*
Grady, Mark F. *law educator, former dean*
Graves, Anna Marie *lawyer*
Gray, Jan Charles *lawyer, business owner*
Gray, Jeremy J.F. *lawyer*
Green, William Porter *lawyer*
Greenberg, Gordon Alan *lawyer*
Grobe, Charles Stephen *lawyer, accountant*
Grode, Susan A. *lawyer*
Gross, Allen Jeffrey *lawyer*
Grossman, Steven L. *lawyer*
Gurfein, Peter J. *lawyer*
Hahn, Elliott Julius *lawyer*

Halberstadter, David *lawyer*
Halkett, Alan Neilson *lawyer*
Handler, Carole Enid *lawyer, city planner*
Handler, Joel F. *law educator*
Handzlik, Jan Lawrence *lawyer*
Hansell, Dean *lawyer*
Hanson, John J. *retired lawyer*
Harkness, Nancy P. *lawyer*
Harris, D. Alan *lawyer*
Hartigan, John Francis *lawyer*
Havel, Richard W. *lawyer*
Haviland, Peter L. *lawyer*
Hayutin, David Lionel *lawyer*
Hebert, William N. *lawyer*
Heinke, Rex S. *lawyer*
Heller, Philip *lawyer*
Hemminger, Pamela Lynn *lawyer*
Henry, Carl Nolan *lawyer*
Herron, Vincent H. *lawyer*
Heyck, Theodore Daly *lawyer*
Heyler, Grover Ross *retired lawyer*
Hieronymus, Edward Whittlesey *retired lawyer*
Hight, B. Boyd *retired lawyer*
Holliday, Thomas Edgar *lawyer*
Holscher, Mark Charles *lawyer*
Holtzman, Robert Arthur *lawyer*
Hoye, Maria Pilar *lawyer*
Hudson, Jeffrey Reid *lawyer*
Huebner, David *lawyer*
Hufstedler, Seth Martin *lawyer*
Hufstedler, Shirley Mount (Mrs. Seth M. Hufstedler) *lawyer, former federal judge*
Husar, Linda S. *lawyer*
Hyman, Jonathan *lawyer*
Hyman, Milton Bernard *lawyer*
Hyman, Ursula H. *lawyer*
Iredale, Nancy Louise *lawyer*
Irving, Paul Howard *lawyer*
Irwin, Philip Donnan *lawyer*
Jeffrey, Sheri *lawyer*
Johnson, Jonathan Edwin, II, *lawyer*
Jordan, Martha B. *lawyer*
Jordan, Robert Leon *lawyer, educator*
Kamine, Bernard S. *lawyer*
Kanoff, Mary Ellen *lawyer*
Kanter, Sandra May *lawyer*
Karst, Kenneth Leslie *law educator*
Katz, Jason Lawrence *lawyer, insurance company executive*
Katzenstein, Andrew M. *lawyer*
Keville, Terri Donna *lawyer*
Kieffer, George David *lawyer*
Kindel, James Horace, Jr. *lawyer*
Kirwan, Betty-Jane *lawyer*
Kirwan, R. DeWitt (Kyle) *lawyer*
Kitchens, Dean J. *lawyer*
Klein, Eric A. *lawyer*
Klinger, Marilyn Sydney *lawyer*
Kollar, Linda Randlett *lawyer*
Kranwinkle, Conrad Douglas *lawyer, broadcast executive*
Krupka, Robert George *lawyer*
Kuechle, John Merrill *lawyer*
Kunowski, Herbert Peter *lawyer*
Kupietzky, Moshe Joseph *lawyer*
Kveton, Kyle *lawyer*
Kwoh, Stewart *lawyer, cultural organization administrator*
Langan, Kenneth J. *lawyer*
Langberg, Barry Benson *lawyer*
Lappen, Chester I. *lawyer*
Lauchengco, Jose Yujuico, Jr. *lawyer*
Lavin, Laurence Michael *lawyer*
Lawler, Jean Marie *lawyer*
Layne, Jonathan K. *lawyer*
Leanse, Thomas J. *lawyer*
Leibow, Ronald Louis *lawyer*
Lemkin, Jeffrey W. *lawyer*
Lesser, Joan L. *lawyer*
Letwin, Leon *law educator*
Leung, Frankie Fook-Lun *lawyer*
Levenson, Laurie L. *law educator*
Levine, Jerome L. *lawyer*
Levine, Meldon Edises *lawyer, retired congressman*
Levine, Thomas Jeffrey Pello *lawyer*
Lewis, Marjorie Ehrich *lawyer*
Lindholm, Dwight Henry *lawyer*
Lipsig, Ethan *lawyer*
Logan, Ben H. III *lawyer*
Long, Gregory Alan *lawyer*
Lui, Elwood *lawyer*
Lund, James Louis *lawyer*
Lynch, Patrick *lawyer*
MacIntosh, Jay W. *lawyer, realtor, actress*
MacLaughlin, Francis Joseph *lawyer*
Mancino, Douglas Michael *lawyer*
Marder, John Adam *lawyer*
Margo, Rod David *lawyer*
Marmorstein, Victoria E. *lawyer*
Marshall-Daniels, Meryl *mediator, executive coach*
Mayorkas, Alejandro *lawyer, former prosecutor*
McAniff, Edward John *lawyer*
McKinzie, Carl Wayne *lawyer*
McKnight, Frederick L. *lawyer*
McLane, Frederick Berg *lawyer*
McNevin, Christopher J. *lawyer*
Meer, Jon Douglas *lawyer*
Meisinger, Louis M. *lawyer*
Melby, Donna D. *lawyer*
Mersel, Marjorie Kathryn Pedersen *lawyer*
Mesereau, Thomas Arthur, Jr. *lawyer*
Meshki, Hamed *lawyer*
Metzger, Robert Streicher *lawyer*
Meyer, Bruce D. *lawyer*
Meyer, Catherine Dieffenbach *lawyer*
Meyer, Michael Edwin *lawyer*
Michaelson, Jon *lawyer*
Millard, Neal Steven *lawyer, educator*
Miller, Milton Allen *lawyer*
Mintz, Marshall Gary *lawyer*
Modabber, Zia F. *lawyer*
Montgomery, Robert K. *lawyer*
Morgenthaler-Lever, Alisa *lawyer*
Morrissey, J. Richard *lawyer*
Mort, Peter J. *lawyer*
Moskowitz, Joel Steven *lawyer*
Munger, Molly *lawyer*
Murray, Anthony *lawyer*
Neely, Sally Schultz *lawyer*
Neiter, Gerald Irving *lawyer*

Nelson, Grant Steel *law educator*
Newman, Michael Rodney *lawyer*
Nicholas, William Richard *lawyer*
Niles, John Gilbert *lawyer*
Nobumoto, Karen S. *prosecutor*
Nochimson, David *lawyer*
Norris, William Albert *lawyer, mediator, retired judge*
Nugent, Gary W. *lawyer*
Ochoa, Arthur J. *lawyer, hospital administrator*
O'Connell, Kevin *lawyer*
O'Donnell, Pierce Henry *lawyer*
Oh, Angela E. *lawyer*
Ohlgren, Joel R. *lawyer*
O'Leary, Prentice Lee *retired lawyer*
Oliver, Dale Hugh *lawyer*
Olsen, Frances Elisabeth *law educator, theorist*
Olson, Ronald Leroy *lawyer*
Oppenheim, Charles B. *lawyer*
Oppenheimer, Randy (Mark Randall Oppenheimer) *lawyer*
Ordin, Andrea Sheridan *lawyer*
Ostroff, Peter I. *lawyer*
Owen, Michael Lee *lawyer*
Pachino, Barton P. *lawyer*
Palmer, Pamela S. *lawyer*
Palmieri, Victor Henry *lawyer, director, investment advisor*
Parsky, Gerald Lawrence *lawyer*
Pasich, Kirk Alan *lawyer*
Perez, Edith R. *lawyer*
Perlis, Michael Fredrick *lawyer*
Perron, Edward Adrian *lawyer*
Perry, Ralph Barton III *lawyer*
Pesta, Ben W., II *lawyer, writer*
Peterson, Kurt C. *lawyer*
Peterson, Linda S. *lawyer*
Petrocelli, Daniel M. *lawyer*
Petroff, Laura R. *lawyer*
Pircher, Leo Joseph *lawyer, director*
Piuze, Michael Joseph *lawyer*
Poindexter, William Mersereau *lawyer*
Pollock, John Phleger *lawyer*
Porter, John E. *lawyer*
Power, John Bruce *lawyer*
Preonas, George Elias *lawyer*
Presant, Sanford Calvin *lawyer, educator, writer, tax specialist*
Price, William Charlie *lawyer*
Pruetz, Adrian Mary *lawyer*
Quicksilver, William Todd *lawyer*
Quinn, John B. *lawyer*
Quinn, John J. *lawyer*
Rabinovitz, Joel *lawyer, educator*
Racine, Scott H. *lawyer*
Rae, Matthew Sanderson, Jr. *lawyer*
Raeder, Myrna Sharon *lawyer, educator*
Rakow, Jay *lawyer, film company executive*
Rappeport, Ira J. *lawyer*
Rath, Howard Grant, Jr. *lawyer*
Ray, Gilbert T. *lawyer*
Reddick, C.N. (Frank)lin III *lawyer*
Reeves, Barbara Ann *lawyer*
Reid, E. Lewis *lawyer*
Reisman, Ellen Kelly *lawyer*
Renwick, Edward S. *lawyer*
Reuben, Don Harold *lawyer*
Reyes Robbins, Ann Marie *lawyer, researcher, educator, former magistrate judge*
Rice, Constance LaMay *lawyer*
Richards, Eric Albert Stephan *lawyer*
Richland, Kent Lewis *lawyer*
Richter, Stuart M. *lawyer*
Riff, Lawrence P. *lawyer*
Rishwain, James Michael, Jr. *lawyer*
Rising, Kevin D. *lawyer*
Rogers, David Booth *lawyer*
Rosen, Kevin S. *lawyer*
Rosenthal, Sol *lawyer*
Rosett, Arthur Irwin *lawyer, educator*
Rotell, Cynthia A. *lawyer*
Rothenberg, Alan I. *lawyer, professional sports association executive*
Ruhl, Mary B. *lawyer*
Rust, Neil W. *lawyer*
Ruthberg, Miles N. *lawyer*
Rutter, Marshall Anthony *lawyer*
Sacks, Robert A. *lawyer*
Salvaty, Benjamin Benedict *lawyer*
Samet, Jack I. *lawyer*
Samuels, Mark A. *lawyer*
Sanders, Kathryn A. *lawyer*
Saxe, Deborah Crandall *lawyer*
Schmidt, Karl A. *lawyer*
Schuchard, Robert L. *lawyer*
Schwartz, Robert M. *lawyer*
Scott, Michael Dennis *lawyer*
Scoular, Robert Frank *lawyer*
Seto, Theodore Paul *lawyer, educator*
Shanks, Patricia L. *lawyer*
Shapiro, Robert *lawyer*
Sheehan, Lawrence James *lawyer*
Sheller, John Willard *lawyer*
Sherrell, John Bradford *lawyer*
Sherwood, Allen Joseph *retired lawyer*
Shields, Patrick M. *lawyer*
Shortz, Richard Alan *lawyer*
Shultz, John David *lawyer*
Siegel, Robert (Bob) A. *lawyer*
Silbergeld, Arthur F. *lawyer*
Simmons, Richard J. *lawyer*
Snider, Darryl *lawyer*
Sohaili, Hushmand *lawyer*
Solish, Jonathan Craig *lawyer*
Stamm, Alan *lawyer*
Starrett, Lucinda *lawyer*
Stein, Laurence Jay *lawyer*
Stein, Sheryl E. *lawyer*
Stephens, George Edward, Jr. *lawyer*
Stier, Byron G. *law educator*
Stinehart, William, Jr. *retired lawyer*
Stone, Gregory Paul *lawyer*
Stone, Lawrence Maurice *lawyer, educator*
Strickland, Julia B. *lawyer*
Strong, George Gordon, Jr. *lawyer, management consultant*
Sweeney, Paul W., Jr. *lawyer*
Tarr, Ralph William *lawyer, former federal government official*
Taylor, Minna *lawyer*
Tepper, R(obert) Bruce, Jr. *lawyer*

Terry, Timothy P. *lawyer*
Terry, W. Burks *lawyer*
Thomas, Geoffrey L. *lawyer*
Thorpe, Geogory B. *lawyer*
Title, Gail Migdal *lawyer*
Tobisman, Stuart Paul *lawyer*
Treister, George Marvin *lawyer*
Trost, Glenn W. *lawyer*
Trygstad, Lawrence Benson *lawyer*
Tsircou, Kyriacos Stavrou *lawyer*
Ukropina, James R. *lawyer*
Van de Kamp, John Kalar *lawyer*
Vanyo, Bruce Gordon *lawyer*
Varat, Jonathan D. *law educator, dean*
Varner, Carlton A. *lawyer*
Vaughn, William Weaver *retired lawyer*
Volpert, Richard Sidney *lawyer*
von Kalinowski, Julian Onesime *lawyer*
Walker, Paul R. *lawyer*
Warren, Robert Stephen *lawyer*
Wasser, Dennis Matthew *lawyer*
Wasser, Laura Allison *lawyer*
Wasserman, William Phillip *lawyer*
Wayte, Alan (Paul Wayte) *lawyer*
Weatherup, Roy Garfield *lawyer*
Weiner, Perrie M. *lawyer*
Weinstock, Harold *lawyer*
Weiss, Walter Stanley *lawyer*
Weissman, Barry Leigh *lawyer*
Westreich, Benzion Joseph *lawyer*
White, Robert Joel *lawyer*
Willett, Robert E. *lawyer*
Williams, Bart H. *lawyer*
Williams, Harold Marvin *lawyer, retired foundation administrator, retired academic administrator, retired federal agency administrator*
Williams, Richard Thomas *lawyer*
Williams, Robert E. *lawyer*
Wine, Mark Philip *lawyer*
Winterman, Craig L. *lawyer*
Wolfen, Werner F. *lawyer*
Wong, Stova *law firm executive*
Wood, Willard Mark *lawyer*
Woodland, Irwin Francis *lawyer*
Woods, Daniel James *lawyer*
Woodsome, Edwin Valentine, Jr. *lawyer*
Wright, Kenneth Brooks *lawyer*
Yang, Debra Wong *prosecutor*
York, Gary Alan *lawyer*
Ziegler, Peter F. *lawyer*
Ziffren, Kenneth *lawyer*

**Los Gatos**
Allan, Lionel Manning *lawyer*

**Lynwood**
Sterling, Arthur James *retired legal assistant*

**Malibu**
Holmes, Henry W. *lawyer*
Naegele, Timothy Duncan *lawyer*

**Marina Del Rey**
Donzis, Paul Bennett *lawyer, finance educator, ophthalmologist, educator*
Schulman, Robert S. *lawyer*

**Martinez**
Couch, Georgia Kaye Wisner *lawyer, musician, educator*
Williams, Charles Judson *lawyer, writer*

**Menlo Park**
Brest, Paul A. *law educator, foundation administrator*
Chao, Howard H. *lawyer*
Charlson, Michael Lloyd *lawyer*
Clarkson, Robert T. *lawyer*
Edwards, John Wesley, II, *lawyer*
Fisher, Ora T. *lawyer*
Haslam, Robert Thomas III *lawyer*
Hearst, William Randolph III *lawyer, former newspaper publisher*
Karel, Steven *lawyer*
Kaufman, Christopher Lee *lawyer*
Kelly, Daniel Grady, Jr. *lawyer*
Kennelly, Dennis L. *lawyer*
Kerman, Peter F. *lawyer*
Kirk, Cassius Lamb, Jr. *retired lawyer, investor*
Krinsky, David A. *lawyer*
Madison, James Raymond *lawyer*
Medearis, Mark A. *lawyer*
Mendelson, Alan Charles *lawyer*
Mummery, Daniel R. *lawyer*
Yang, Joseph *lawyer*

**Mill Valley**
Cole, Richard Charles *lawyer*
Nemir, Donald Philip *lawyer*
Schwartzbach, M. Gerald *lawyer*
Selvig, Jettie Pierce *lawyer*

**Milpitas**
Pursel, David G. *lawyer*
Stevens, Glenn H. *lawyer*

**Mission Viejo**
Ruben, Robert Joseph *lawyer*
Tuohey, Conrad Gravier *lawyer*

**Modesto**
Truong, D. Hiep *lawyer*

**Monterey**
Bomberger, Russell Branson *lawyer, writer*
Gaver, Frances Rouse *lawyer*
Haddad, Louis Nicholas *paralegal*
Soskin, William H. *lawyer, accountant*

**Morgan Hill**
Foster, John Robert *lawyer*

**Mountain View**
Nash, Horace Lyons *lawyer*
Pasahow, Lynn Harold *lawyer*

**Napa**
Snow, Tower Charles, Jr. *lawyer*

**Newport Beach**
Baskin, Scott David *lawyer*
Cano, Kristin Maria *lawyer*
Carmichael, David Richard *lawyer*
Clark, Thomas P., Jr. *lawyer*
Currie, Robert Emil *retired lawyer*
Fehner, Michael Richard *lawyer*
Goldstein, Michael Gerald *lawyer, director*
Herron, J. Jay *lawyer*
Klink, Fredric J. *lawyer*
Mallory, Frank Linus *lawyer*
Mandel, Maurice, II, *lawyer, educator, mediator*
Millar, Richard William, Jr. *lawyer*
Quinlan, Francis E. *lawyer*
Schiff, Laurie *lawyer*
Schnapp, Roger Herbert *lawyer, consultant*
Schwarzstein, Richard Joseph *lawyer*
Singer, Gary James *lawyer*
Thompson, Jennifer Lee *lawyer*
Tracy, James Jared, Jr. *retired legal association administrator*
Weissbard, Samuel Held *lawyer*
Wentworth, Theodore Sumner *lawyer*

**North Hollywood**
Davis, Edmond Ray *lawyer*

**Northridge**
Avsharian, Roupen *prosecutor, academic administrator*
Runquist, Lisa A. *lawyer*
Walcher, Alan Ernest *lawyer*

**Oak Park**
Vinson, William Theodore *lawyer*

**Oakland**
Allen, Jeffrey Michael *lawyer*
Banke, Kathy M. *lawyer*
Bryant, Arthur H. *lawyer*
Davies, Colleen T. *lawyer*
Deming, Willis Riley *lawyer*
Drexel, Baron Jerome *lawyer*
Foust, Lawrence L. *lawyer*
Jackson, Mark Edward *lawyer, real estate broker*
Johnson, Kenneth F. *lawyer*
Kazan, Steven *lawyer*
Kohn, Steven M. *lawyer*
Linzner, Joel *lawyer*
Quinby, William Albert *lawyer, arbitrator, mediator*
Reese, Charles Woodrow, Jr. *lawyer*
Roster, Michael *lawyer*
Shapiro, David W. *prosecutor*
Wallis, Eric G. *lawyer*
Wood, James Michael *lawyer*

**Occidental**
Archer, Richard Joseph *lawyer*

**Oceanside**
Sullivan, Patrick James *lawyer*

**Ontario**
Dunn, Donald Jack *law librarian, educator, dean, lawyer*

**Orange**
Batchelor, James Kent *lawyer*
Duncan, John Alexander *lawyer*

**Orinda**
Hetland, John Robert *law educator*
Walsh, Joseph Richard *lawyer*

**Pacific Palisades**
Cale, Charles Griffin *lawyer, real estate company executive, corporate financial executive*
Flattery, Thomas Long *lawyer, legal administrator*
Sevilla, Stanley *lawyer*
Verrone, Patric Miller *lawyer, writer*

**Palm Desert**
Bernhard, Herbert Ashley *lawyer*
La Rocca, Phillip R. *lawyer, educator*
Reinhardt, Benjamin Max *lawyer, arbitrator, mediator*

**Palm Springs**
Diodosio, Charles Joseph *lawyer*
Kimberling, John Farrell *retired lawyer*

**Palo Alto**
Abrams, William F. *lawyer*
Baskins, Ann O. *lawyer, computer company executive*
Baum, Brandon *lawyer, law educator*
Beatus, Brian J. *lawyer*
Benton, Lee F. *lawyer*
Bradley, Donald Edward *lawyer*
Chang, Carmen *lawyer*
Chinnis, C. Cabell, Jr. *lawyer*
Climan, Richard Elliot *lawyer*
Coyle, Edward Leo *lawyer, retired banker*
Davidson, Gordon Kirby *lawyer*
de Alcuaz, Anthony *lawyer*
del Calvo, Jorge A. *lawyer*
Fairman, Marc P. *lawyer*
Feldman, Boris *lawyer*
Flaum, Keith Avery *lawyer*
Fordis, Jean Burke *lawyer*
Frankle, Diane Holt *lawyer*
Fromm, Jeffery Bernard *lawyer*
Gaither, James C. *lawyer*
Greco, Joseph A. *lawyer*
Halluin, Albert Price *lawyer*
Hiscox, Frank S. *lawyer*
Ivey, Thomas J. *lawyer*
Jackson, Cynthia L. *lawyer*
King, Kenton J. *lawyer*
Korman, Martin *lawyer*
Lynch, Timothy Jeremiah-Mahoney *lawyer, educator, theologian, realtor, writer*
Masur, Joshua Michael *lawyer*
McCall, Jennifer Jordan *lawyer*
Miller, Michael Patiky *lawyer*
Miller, Scott D. *lawyer*
Monroy, Gladys H. *lawyer*
Neal, Stephen Cassidy *lawyer*
Nopar, Alan Scott *lawyer*

Nordlund, Donald Craig *lawyer*
Nuchi, Lior O. *lawyer*
O'Rourke, C. Larry *lawyer*
Park, Marina H. *lawyer*
Patten, Valerie Lynn *lawyer*
Patterson, Robert Edward *lawyer*
Petkanics, Donna M. *lawyer*
Phair, Joseph Baschon *lawyer*
Pitchford, Mark A. *lawyer*
Radcliffe, Mark Flohn *lawyer*
Robinson, Walter J. III *lawyer*
Roos, John Victor *lawyer*
Salmon, Denis R. *lawyer*
Saper, Jeffrey D. *lawyer*
Shi, Qin *lawyer, technologist*
Shulman, Ron E. *lawyer*
Smith, Gregory C. *lawyer*
Sonsini, Larry W. *lawyer*
Sullivan, Dennis C. *lawyer*
Sundheim, George (Duf) *lawyer, political organization worker*
Tiffany, Joseph Raymond, II, *lawyer*
Unkovic, Nicholas C. *lawyer*
Van Atta, David Murray *lawyer*
Vaughn, Issac J. *lawyer*
Voight, Jerry D. *lawyer*
Walker, Ann Yvonne *lawyer*
Waltzer, Garrett J. *lawyer*
Wheeler, Raymond Louis *lawyer*
White, Rick *lawyer, former congressman*

**Palos Verdes Estates**
Blackman, Lee L. *lawyer*
DeLuce, Richard David *lawyer*

**Paramount**
Hall, Howard Harry *lawyer*

**Pasadena**
Call, Merlin Wendell *lawyer*
Calleton, Theodore Edward *lawyer, educator*
D'Angelo, Robert William *lawyer*
Haight, James Theron *lawyer*
Hickman, Rose *lawyer*
Hunt, Gordon *lawyer*
Koelzer, George Joseph *lawyer*
Leeson, Peter *lawyer*
Logan, Francis Dummer *retired lawyer*
Markley, William C. *lawyer*
Mosher, Sally Ekenberg *lawyer, musician*
Mueth, Joseph Edward *lawyer*
Myers, R(alph) Chandler *lawyer*
Solis, Carlos *lawyer*
Tanner, Dee Boshard *retired lawyer*
van Schoonenberg, Robert G. *lawyer*
Wyatt, Joseph Lucian, Jr. *lawyer, writer*
Yohalem, Harry Morton *lawyer*

**Pittsburg**
Williscroft-Barcus, Beverly Ruth *retired lawyer*

**Pleasanton**
Askanas, Mark S. *lawyer*
Opperwall, Stephen Gabriel *lawyer*

**Point Richmond**
Edginton, John Arthur *lawyer*

**Portola Valley**
Nycum, Susan Hubbell *lawyer*
Olson, Walter Gilbert *lawyer*

**Rancho Cordova**
Harrell, Gary Paul *lawyer*

**Rancho Mirage**
Leydorf, Frederick Leroy *lawyer*
Pierno, Anthony Robert *lawyer*

**Rancho Santa Fe**
Legro, Stanley Wayne *environmental lawyer*
Mezzullo, Louis Albert *lawyer*
Peterson, Nad A. *retired lawyer*
Woolley, Roger Swire *lawyer*

**Rancho Santa Margarita**
Curtis, John Joseph *lawyer, writer*

**Redwood City**
Bell, Frank Ouray, Jr. *lawyer*
Fitzpatrick, Will *lawyer*
Millard, Richard Steven *lawyer*
Powers, Matthew Douglas *lawyer*
Sullivan, Kathleen Marie *lawyer, educator, former dean*
Wilhelm, Robert Oscar *lawyer, civil engineer*

**Richmond**
Dolberg, David Spencer *lawyer*
Jenkins, Everett Wilbur, Jr. *lawyer, writer, historian*

**Riverside**
Carney, Jane W. *lawyer*
Darling, Scott Edward *lawyer*
Heiting, James Otto *lawyer*
Marlatt, Michael James *lawyer*
McGill, Leonard John *lawyer*

**Rolling Hills**
Rumbaugh, Charles Earl *arbitrator, mediator, educator, lawyer*

**Rosemead**
Danner, Bryant Craig *lawyer*

**Sacramento**
Bell, Wayne S. *lawyer, state agency official*
Blake, D. Steven *lawyer*
Bowen, Debra Lynn *lawyer, state legislator*
Caso, Anthony T. *lawyer*
Day, James McAdam, Jr. *lawyer*
Fait, Glenn A. *lawyer, educator*
Faust, Mara Leah *prosecutor*
Friedman, Morton Lee *lawyer*
Houpt, James Edward *lawyer*
Keiner, Christian Mark *lawyer*
Malloy, Michael Patrick *law educator, consultant*
Robbins, Stephen J. M. *lawyer*
Scott, McGregor W. *prosecutor, lawyer*

Taylor, Joseph Evans *law educator*

**Saint Helena**
Seavey, William Arthur *lawyer, vintner*

**Salinas**
Etienne, Myron E., Jr. *lawyer*

**San Anselmo**
Murphy, Barry Ames *lawyer*
Truett, Harold Joseph, III, (Tim Truett) *lawyer*

**San Carlos**
Lee, John Jin *lawyer*

**San Diego**
Allen, P. Blake *lawyer*
Armstong, Robert G. *lawyer*
Bell, Robert Jeffrey *lawyer*
Bleiler, Charles Arthur *lawyer*
Brierton, Cheryl Lynn *lawyer*
Brooks, John White *lawyer*
Brooks, Juanita Rose *lawyer*
Brown, LaMar Bevan *lawyer*
Brownlie, Robert William *lawyer*
Celentino, Christopher *lawyer*
Chatroo, Arthur Jay *lawyer*
Chaudhri, Javade *lawyer*
Cohn, Marjorie F. *law educator, legal association administrator*
Copeland, Robert Glenn *lawyer*
Corbett, Luke Robinson *lawyer*
Daucher, Donald A. *lawyer*
Dollarhide, Mary C. *lawyer*
Dorne, David J. *lawyer*
Dostart, Paul Joseph *lawyer, investor, director, entrepreneur*
Dyer, Charles Richard *law librarian, law educator*
Eigner, William Whitling *lawyer*
Fauchier, Dan Ray *arbitrator, mediator, law educator, construction executive*
Fisch, Sanford Michael *lawyer*
Forbes, Brian L. *lawyer*
Gerber, Robert Scott *lawyer*
Haile, Lisa A. *lawyer*
Heaton, Roger Laurence *lawyer*
Heidrich, Robert Wesley *lawyer*
Hofflund, Paul *lawyer*
Insogna, Anthony M. *lawyer*
Kinsbruner Bush, Jennifer *lawyer*
Klinedinst, John David *lawyer*
Lam, Carol C. *prosecutor, lawyer*
Lathrop, Mitchell Lee *lawyer*
Law, David Stephen *law educator, political science professor*
Lerach, William S. *lawyer*
Lupin, Louis Martin *lawyer*
Manbeck, Alexandra T. *lawyer*
McClellan, Craig Rene *lawyer*
McGinnis, Robert Earl *lawyer*
McMahon, Gerald Lawrence *lawyer*
Mebane, Julie S. *lawyer*
Mittermiller, James Joseph *lawyer*
Morris, Grant Harold *law educator*
Mullen, James Joseph III *lawyer*
O'Malley, James Terence (Terry) *lawyer*
Philipp, Adam Lief Kakimoto *lawyer*
Pray, Ralph Marble III *lawyer*
Pugh, Richard Crawford *lawyer, educator*
Rains, Cameron Jay *lawyer*
Rehmus, Charles Martin *arbitrator*
Roberts, William S. *lawyer*
Root, George Lincoln, Jr. *lawyer*
Roseman, Charles Sanford *lawyer*
Ross, Terry D. *lawyer*
Santee, Dale William *lawyer, air force officer*
Schoville, Dennis A(rnold) *lawyer*
Schulman, Alan *lawyer*
Scott, Douglas Edward *lawyer*
Shepherd, Bruce P. *lawyer*
Shippey, Sandra Lee *lawyer*
Smith, Steven Ray *law educator*
Snyder, David Richard *lawyer*
Swinton, Stephen P. *lawyer*
Thorn, Robert Charles *lawyer*
Vitek, Reginald A. (Reg) *lawyer*
Wagner, Sandra M. *lawyer*
Weaver, Michael James *lawyer*

**San Francisco**
Abbott, Barry Alexander *lawyer*
Alderman, William Fields *lawyer*
Alexis, Geraldine M. *lawyer*
Alioto, Angela Mia *lawyer*
Allecta, Julie *lawyer*
Allen, Jose R. *lawyer*
Anderson, Edward Virgil *lawyer*
Arbuthnot, Robert Murray *lawyer*
Atkinson, Gordon C. *lawyer*
Bailey-Wells, Deborah *lawyer*
Baker, James P. *lawyer*
Bancroft, James Ramsey *lawyer*
Barbagelata, Robert Dominic *lawyer*
Bauer, Steven M. *lawyer*
Baxter, Ralph H., Jr. *lawyer*
Baysinger, Kara *lawyer*
Belaga, Debra S. *lawyer*
Bennett, Paul Frederick *lawyer*
Benvenutti, Peter J. *lawyer*
Bleich, Jeffrey Laurence *lawyer, educator*
Blum, Robert M. *lawyer*
Bomse, Stephen V. *lawyer*
Bondoc, Rommel *lawyer*
Borowsky, Philip *lawyer*
Bostwick, James Stephen *lawyer*
Boven, Douglas George *lawyer*
Brandel, Roland Eric *lawyer*
Brosnahan, James (Jerome) *lawyer*
Brothers, Lynda Lee *lawyer*
Brown, Donald Wesley *lawyer*
Brown, Walter Francis, Jr. *lawyer*
Broyles, Deborah J. *lawyer*
Bruen, James A. *lawyer*
Burden, James Ewers *lawyer*
Burns, Brian Patrick *lawyer*
Burt, Richard *lawyer*
Bushnell, Roderick Paul *lawyer*
Cabraser, Elizabeth Joan *lawyer*
Camahort, Steve L. *lawyer*
Campbell, Scott Robert *lawyer, former food products executive*

Canady, Richard Warren *lawyer*
Carrow, Robert Duane *lawyer, barrister*
Cartmell, Nathaniel Madison III *lawyer*
Chao, Cedric C. *lawyer*
Clowes, John Howard *lawyer*
Coleman, Kathryn Anne *lawyer*
Coleman, Thomas Young *lawyer*
Collins, Mary Ann *lawyer*
Cominos, Dion Nicholas *lawyer*
Coombe, George William, Jr. *lawyer, retired bank executive*
Corash, Michèle B. *lawyer*
Cranston, Mary Bailey *lawyer*
Crawford, Roy Edgington III *lawyer*
Curran, Mary *lawyer*
Czachor, Bruce Lawrence, *consultant*
Danoff, Eric Michael *lawyer*
Davis, Roger Lewis *lawyer*
Dell, Robert Michael *lawyer*
DeMuro, Paul Robert *lawyer*
Diekmann, Gilmore Frederick, Jr. *lawyer*
Dolinko, Robert A. *lawyer*
Donnelly, Thomas M. *lawyer*
Donner, Michael F. *lawyer*
Dryden, Robert Eugene *lawyer*
Dryovage, Mary Margaret *lawyer*
Duffy, Jan *lawyer*
Dunne, Kevin Joseph *lawyer*
Dwyer, Carrie Elizabeth *lawyer*
Edwards, Robin Morse *lawyer*
Eigner, Richard Martin *lawyer*
Epsen, Robert A. *lawyer*
Ericson, Bruce Alan *lawyer*
Eth, Jordan David *lawyer*
Falk, Jerome B., Jr. *lawyer*
Fergus, Gary Scott *lawyer*
Finberg, James Michael *lawyer*
Finck, Kevin William *lawyer*
Fink, Scott Alan *lawyer*
Fogel, Paul David *lawyer*
Folberg, Harold Jay *lawyer, educator, dean*
Fong, Kevin Murray *lawyer*
Foster, David Scott *lawyer*
Freud, Nicholas S. *lawyer*
Friedman, Barbara Lorie *lawyer*
Friedman, K. Bruce *lawyer*
Friese, Robert Charles *lawyer*
Furth, Frederick Paul *lawyer*
Garvey, Joanne Marie *lawyer*
Getto, Ernest John *lawyer*
Gillette, Patricia K. *lawyer*
Glazer, Jack Henry *lawyer*
Goodwin, David B. *lawyer*
Greene, Richard Lawrence *lawyer*
Gresham, Zane Oliver *lawyer*
Guggenhime, Richard Johnson *lawyer*
Haas, Raymond P. *lawyer*
Haber, Scott R. *lawyer*
Halloran, Michael James *lawyer*
Haratani, Joan Mei *lawyer*
Harris, Kamala D. *prosecutor*
Harvey, D. Peter *lawyer, educator*
Hasson, Kirke Michael *lawyer*
Hecker, Peter S. *lawyer*
Heilbron, David Michael *lawyer, arbitrator, mediator*
Hendrick, James T. *lawyer*
Heng, Donald James, Jr. *lawyer*
Henson, Ray David *law educator, consultant*
Hernandez, Gary A. *lawyer*
Herrera, Dennis J. *lawyer*
Higgins, Daniel B. *lawyer*
Hilton, Stanley Goumas *lawyer, educator, writer*
Hinman, Harvey DeForest *lawyer*
Hirsch, (William) Reece *lawyer*
Hisert, George Arthur *lawyer*
Hofmann, John Richard, Jr. *retired lawyer*
Holden, Frederick Douglass, Jr. *lawyer*
Hosie, Spencer *lawyer*
Howard, Carl *retired lawyer*
Hubbell, Robert B. *lawyer*
Hudner, Philip *lawyer, rancher*
Hui, Helen Yuen Hing *lawyer*
Hunt, James L. *lawyer*
Hunter, William Dennis *lawyer*
Jaffe, Seth Roth *lawyer, retail executive*
James, David Lee *lawyer, writer, international advisor*
Johnson, Michelle L. *lawyer*
Johnson, Stephen Patrick Howard *lawyer*
Jones, Frances Mary *law librarian*
Joseph, Allan Jay *lawyer*
Juster, Kenneth Ian *lawyer*
Kasanin, Mark Owen *lawyer*
Kee, Terry Michael *lawyer*
Keker, John Watkins *lawyer*
Kelly, J. Michael *lawyer*
Kennedy, Raoul Dion *lawyer*
Kern, Brad D. *lawyer*
Kern, John McDougall *lawyer*
Kimport, David Lloyd *lawyer*
Knapp, Charles Lincoln *law educator*
Knebel, Jack Gillen *lawyer*
Knutzen, Martha Lorraine *lawyer*
Koeppel, John A. *lawyer*
Kozloff, Theodore J. *lawyer*
Krane, Hilary K. *lawyer*
Krevans, Rachel *lawyer*
Kuhl, Paul Beach *lawyer*
Lacovara, Michael *lawyer*
Lane, Nathan III *lawyer*
Larrabee, Matthew L. *lawyer*
Larson, John William *lawyer*
Lee, Richard Diebold *lawyer, educator*
Leshy, John David *lawyer, educator, solicitor*
Levie, Mark Robert *lawyer*
Levin, Barry Steven *lawyer*
Lieff, Robert Lawrence *lawyer*
Lindstrom, Gregory P. *lawyer*
Livermore, Samuel Morgan *lawyer*
Livsey, Robert Callister *lawyer*
Londen, Jack W. *lawyer*
Lopes, James Louis *lawyer*
Lowell, Frederick K. *lawyer*
Lowenthal, Steven R. *lawyer*
Lyons, James Elliott *lawyer*
Maier, Peter Klaus *lawyer*
Malkin, Joseph M. *lawyer*
Maly, Michael Kip *lawyer*
Mann, Bruce Alan *lawyer, bank executive, investment banker*

Manning, Jerome Alan *retired lawyer*
Marchant, David Judson *lawyer*
Marshall, Patrick C. *lawyer*
Marshall, Raymond Charles *lawyer*
Martel, John Sheldon *lawyer, writer*
Mattes, Martin Anthony *lawyer*
McDiarmid, Bruce W. *lawyer*
McElhinny, Harold John *lawyer*
McGinnis, James Landon *lawyer*
McGuckin, John Hugh, Jr. *lawyer*
McKenzie, John F. *lawyer*
McKeon, Jami Wintz *lawyer*
McNally, Thomas Charles III *lawyer*
Meyerson, Ivan D. *lawyer, corporate financial executive*
Michels, David A. *lawyer*
Miles, Donald F. *lawyer*
Miller, Ann G. *lawyer*
Miller, William Napier Cripps *lawyer*
Miller, William Napier Cripps *lawyer*
Minnick, Malcolm David *lawyer*
Mitchell, Bruce Tyson *lawyer*
Morrissey, John Carroll, Sr. *lawyer*
Murray, Kathleen Anne *lawyer*
Musfelt, Duane Clark *lawyer*
Odgers, Richard William *lawyer*
Offer, Stuart Jay *lawyer*
Okeke, Christian Nwachukwu *law educator*
Olson, Karl *lawyer*
Olson, Robert Howard *lawyer*
O'Neal, Stephen V. *lawyer*
Palmer, Venrice Romito *lawyer, educator*
Pape, Glenn Michael *lawyer, financial planner*
Park, Roger Cook *law educator*
Paterson, Eva *legal association director, educator*
Paxton, Jay Lee *lawyer*
Penskar, Mark Howard *lawyer*
Petty, George Oliver *lawyer*
Pickett, Donn Philip *lawyer*
Platto, Jamie Scott *lawyer*
Plishner, Michael Jon *lawyer*
Pope, Marcia L. *lawyer*
Popofsky, Melvin Laurence *lawyer*
Preuss, Charles Frederick *lawyer*
Pringle, Paul C. *lawyer*
Radlo, Edward John *lawyer, mathematician*
Ragan, Charles Ransom *lawyer*
Reding, John Anthony, Jr. *lawyer*
Reese, John Robert *lawyer*
Renfrew, Charles Byron *lawyer*
Renne, Paul A. *lawyer*
Rice, Denis Timlin *lawyer*
Richards, Norman Blanchard *lawyer*
Richey, Mary Ellen *lawyer*
Robinson, Ralph W. *lawyer*
Roethe, James Norton *lawyer*
Rogan, Richard A. *lawyer*
Roger, Kent M. *lawyer*
Rosen, Joshua Nathan *lawyer*
Rosen, Sanford Jay *lawyer*
Rosenfeld, Robert A. *lawyer*
Ross, Jeffrey S. *lawyer*
Rubenstein, Donald P. *lawyer*
Rubin, Michael *lawyer*
Russoniello, Joseph Pascal *lawyer, dean*
Ryan, Kevin V. *prosecutor, lawyer*
Sanders, Joel Steven *lawyer*
Savage, Mark Randall *lawyer*
Sax, Paul J. *lawyer*
Seabolt, Richard L. *lawyer*
Seegal, John Franklin *lawyer*
Seff, James M. *lawyer*
Seneker, Carl James, II, (Kim Seneker) *lawyer*
Shenk, George H. *lawyer*
Shiffman, Michael A. *lawyer*
Silk, Thomas *lawyer*
Singer, Allen Morris *lawyer*
Siniscalco, Gary Richard *lawyer*
Smegal, Thomas Frank, Jr. *lawyer*
Smith, Brian D. *lawyer*
Smith, Kerry Clark *lawyer*
Snyder, Darin W. *lawyer*
Soberon, Presentacion Zablan *state bar administrator*
Sommers, Stephen Anthony *lawyer*
Sparks, Thomas E., Jr. *lawyer*
Spustek, Maria S. *lawyer*
Staring, Graydon Shaw *lawyer*
Steel, Michael J. *lawyer*
Steer, Reginald David *lawyer*
Stephens, Shand Scott *lawyer*
Stinnett, Terrance LLoyd *lawyer*
Story, Joan H. *lawyer*
Street, Paul Shipley *lawyer*
Stromberg, Ross Ernest *lawyer*
Strother, James M. *lawyer*
Studley, Jamienne Shayne *lawyer, educator*
Sugarman, Myron George *lawyer*
Sullivan, Robert Edward *lawyer*
Sutton, John Paul *lawyer*
Taylor, William James (Zak Taylor) *lawyer*
Thomas, William Scott *lawyer*
Thompson, Patrick S. *lawyer*
Thompson, Robert Charles *lawyer*
Thornton, Charles Victor *lawyer*
Tobin, James Michael *lawyer*
Traynor, John Michael *lawyer*
Uilkema, John K. *lawyer*
Van Buskirk, Ronald E. *lawyer*
Vazquez-Azpiri, A. James *lawyer*
Veaco, Kristina *lawyer*
Venning, Robert Stanley *lawyer*
Vesely, Jeffrey M. *lawyer*
Wald, Peter Allen *lawyer*
Wang, William Kai-Sheng *law educator*
Weber, Arnold I. *lawyer*
Weber, Paula M. *lawyer*
Weir, Robert H. *lawyer*
Weitzel, Mark P. *lawyer*
Welborn, Caryl Bartelman *lawyer*
Whelan, John William *law educator*
Whitehead, David Barry *lawyer*
Wild, Nelson Hopkins *lawyer*
Williams, Linda C. *lawyer*
Wilson, John D. *lawyer*
Wilson, John Pasley *law educator*
Wingate, C. Keith *law educator*
Wirum, Andrea A. *lawyer*
Wolfe, Cameron Withgot, Jr. *lawyer*
Wong, Stanton D. *lawyer*
Wood, Robert Warren *lawyer*

Woods, James Robert *lawyer*
Worthington, Bruce R. *lawyer*
wwGiacomini, Gary T. *lawyer*
Wyle, Frederick S. *lawyer*
Yost, Nicholas Churchill *lawyer*
Young, Bryant Llewellyn *lawyer*
Young, Douglas Rea *lawyer*
Zeldin, Kim S. *lawyer*
Ziegler, R. W., Jr. *lawyer, consultant*
Ziering, William Mark *lawyer*
Zilber, Norman Albert *lawyer*
Zischke, Michael Herman *lawyer*

**San Jose**
Cottle, Karen Olson *lawyer*
Denver, Thomas H.R. *lawyer*
Gallo, Joan Rosenberg *lawyer*
Hernández, Fernando Vargas *lawyer*
Jacobson, Michael R. *lawyer, Internet company executive*
Katzman, Richard Alan *lawyer, arbitrator*
Kraw, George Martin *lawyer, writer*
McKeithen, R.L. Smith (Smith McKeithen) *lawyer*
McManis, James *lawyer*
Mitchell, David Walker *lawyer*
Nissly, Kenneth L. *lawyer*
Robinson, Archie Stirling *lawyer*
Sauers, William Dale *lawyer, playwright*
Silver, Melvyn David *lawyer, arbitrator*
Stein, John C. *lawyer*
Stutzman, Thomas Chase, Sr. *lawyer*
Towery, James E. *lawyer*

**San Juan Capistrano**
Suzuki, Yasuhiko *retired law educator*

**San Marino**
Cranston, Howard Stephen *lawyer, management consultant*
Galbraith, James Marshall *lawyer, corporate financial executive*
Tomich, Lillian *lawyer*

**San Mateo**
Anderlini, P. Terry *lawyer*
Grill, Lawrence J. *lawyer, accountant, bank executive*
Kenney, William Fitzgerald *lawyer*
Monaco, Daniel Joseph *lawyer*
O'Reilly, Terence John *lawyer*
Simpson, Murray L. *lawyer*
Slabach, Stephen Hall *lawyer*

**San Rafael**
Chilvers, Robert Merritt *lawyer*
Drexler, Kenneth *lawyer*
Ingram, Robert Bruce *lawyer*
Roth, Hadden Wing *lawyer, mediator, arbitrator*
Sterling, Marcia Kemp *lawyer*

**San Ramon**
James, Charles Albert *lawyer*

**Santa Ana**
Aitken, Wylie A. *lawyer*
Borges, Fredrick Mario *lawyer*
Cahill, Richard Frederick *lawyer*
Callahan, Daniel J. *lawyer*
Capizzi, Michael Robert *prosecutor*
Digorgio, Kenneth *lawyer*
Dillard, John Martin *lawyer, pilot*
Harley, Robison Dooling, Jr. *lawyer, educator*
Hueston, John Charles *prosecutor*
Mei, Tom Y. K. *lawyer*
Storer, Maryruth *law librarian*
Wagner, John Leo *lawyer, retired judge*

**Santa Barbara**
Cappello, A. Barry *lawyer*
Elliott, Warren G. *lawyer*
Herman, James Edward *lawyer*
Sanger, Robert Marshall *lawyer*
Shames, Henry Joseph *lawyer*
Sneddon, Thomas William, Jr. *prosecutor*

**Santa Clara**
Alexander, George Jonathon *lawyer, educator*
Clark, John M. III *lawyer*
Dillon, Michael A. *lawyer*
Dunlap, F. Thomas, Jr. *lawyer, retired electronics executive*
Glancy, Dorothy Jean *lawyer, educator*
Hsieh, Marina Cing *lawyer, educator*
Shannon, David M. *lawyer*
Simon, James Lowell *lawyer*
Sunwolf, *law educator, writer*

**Santa Clarita**
Kotler, Richard Lee *lawyer*

**Santa Monica**
Cooper, Jay Leslie *lawyer*
Cron, Steven Michael *lawyer*
Dienes, Louis Robert *lawyer*
Geiser, Thomas Christopher *lawyer, insurance company executive*
Greifinger, David Ross *lawyer*
Grossman, Marshall Bruce *lawyer*
Hinerfeld, Robert Elliot *lawyer*
Jones, William Allen *lawyer*
Kinney, James Howard *lawyer, real estate company executive*
Kirkland, John C. *lawyer*
Lawton, Eric *lawyer, artist, photographer, writer*
Levin, Marvin Eugene *lawyer*
McMillan, M. Sean *lawyer*
Modisett, Jeffrey A. *lawyer, former state attorney general*
Morgan, Kermit Johnson *lawyer*
Preble, Laurence George *lawyer*
Risman, Michael *lawyer, real estate developer, broker*
Sherman, Victor *lawyer*
Wilson, Hugh Steven *lawyer*

**Santa Rosa**
Clement, Clayton Emerson *lawyer*
Courteau, Girard Robert *retired prosecutor*
O'Connor, Paul Daniel *lawyer*

**Sausalito**
Albert, Ronald Peter *lawyer*
Berkman, William Roger *lawyer, army reserve officer*
Gordon, Robert Eugene *lawyer*

**Sebastopol**
Rappaport, Stuart Ramon *lawyer*

**Sherman Oaks**
Ardalan, Pezhman Christopher *lawyer*
Crump, Gerald Franklin *retired lawyer*
Feldman, Phillip *lawyer*
Levin, Evanne Lynn *lawyer, educator*
Medearis, Miller *lawyer*

**Sierra Madre**
Browder, William Bayard *lawyer*

**Sonoma**
Obninsky, Victor Peter *lawyer*

**Stanford**
Alexander, Janet Cooper *law educator*
Bankman, Joseph *law educator*
Banks, R. Richard *law educator*
Cohen, William *law educator*
Cole, G. Marcus *law educator*
Craswell, Richard *law educator*
Daines, Robert M. *law educator*
Ehrlich, Thomas *law educator*
Fisher, George *law educator*
Ford, Richard Thompson *law educator*
Franklin, Marc Adam *law educator*
Fried, Barbara H. *law educator*
Friedman, Lawrence M. *law educator*
Gilson, Ronald Jay *law educator*
Goldstein, Paul *lawyer, educator*
Gould, William Benjamin, IV, *lawyer, educator, federal agency administrator*
Greely, Henry T. (Hank Greely) *law educator*
Grey, Thomas C. *law educator*
Grundfest, Joseph Alexander *law and business educator*
Heller, Thomas Charles *law educator*
Hensler, Deborah Rosenfield *law educator*
Karlan, Pamela Susan *law educator*
Klausner, Michael David *law educator*
Lemley, Mark Alan *law educator*
Lessig, L. Lawrence III *lawyer, law educator, writer*
Mann, J. Keith *retired law educator, arbitrator*
Marshall, Lawrence C. *law educator*
Martinez, Jenny S. *lawyer*
Méndez, Miguel Angel *law educator*
Polinsky, A. Mitchell *law and economics educator*
Rabin, Robert L. *law educator*
Radin, Margaret Jane *law educator*
Rhode, Deborah Lynn *law educator*
Scott, Kenneth Eugene *lawyer, educator*
Sofaer, Abraham David *lawyer, educator, judge, consultant*
Spaulding, Norman W. III *law educator*
Strnad, Jeff (James Frank Strnad II) *law educator*
Thompson, Buzz (Barton H. Thompson Jr.) *law educator*
Weiner, Allen S. *law educator*
Weisberg, Robert *law educator*
Williams, Howard Russell *law educator*

**Stockton**
Knapp, Christian Jakob *lawyer*
Parish, William Henry *lawyer*

**Studio City**
Miller, Charles Maurice *lawyer*

**Sunnyvale**
Brigden, John *lawyer*
Callahan, Michael John *lawyer*

**Thousand Oaks**
Gentile, Joseph F. *lawyer, educator*
Scott, David J. *lawyer*

**Tiburon**
Cohn, Nathan *retired lawyer*
Widman, Gary Lee *lawyer*

**Torrance**
Bryan, Sharon Ann *lawyer*
Carlson, Terrance L. *lawyer, aerospace transportation executive*
Kohan, Betsy Burns *lawyer*
Moore, Christopher M. *lawyer*
Petillon, Lee Ritchey *lawyer*

**Tustin**
Kraft, Henry Robert *lawyer*

**Universal City**
Golper, John Bruce *lawyer*

**Valencia**
King, Wayne T. *lawyer*

**Van Nuys**
Arabian, Armand *arbitrator, mediator, lawyer*

**Visalia**
Crowe, John T. *lawyer*

**Walnut**
McKee, Catherine Lynch *lawyer, educator*

**Walnut Creek**
Curtin, Daniel Joseph, Jr. *lawyer*
Gill, Margaret Gaskins *lawyer*
Ginsburg, Gerald J. *lawyer, management consultant*
Hanschen, Peter Walter *lawyer*
Nord, Paul Elliott *lawyer, accountant*
Pagter, Carl Richard *lawyer*
Rainey, William Joel *lawyer*
Skaggs, Sanford Merle *lawyer*

**West Covina**
Ebiner, Robert Maurice *lawyer*
Galen, Albert John *retired lawyer*
McHale, Edward Robertson *retired lawyer*

**West Hollywood**
Margolin, Bruce M. *lawyer*

**Westlake Village**
Carter, C. Michael *lawyer*
Strote, Joel Richard *lawyer*

**Woodland Hills**
Even, Randolph M. *lawyer*
Glick, Earl A. *lawyer*
Kaufman, Albert I. *lawyer*
Preston, John Elwood *lawyer*
Schor, Suzi *lawyer, psychologist*
Westen, Brodie Curtis, Jr., (Curt Westen) *lawyer*

## COLORADO

**Alamosa**
Garcia, Castelar Medardo *lawyer*

**Arvada**
Robey, Mark Douglas *lawyer*

**Aurora**
Katz, Michael Jeffery *lawyer*
Khanna, Kishanlal K. *lawyer, educator*
Stauffer, Scott William *lawyer, accountant*

**Boulder**
Bintliff, Barbara Ann *law educator, library director*
Bruff, Harold Hastings *law educator, former dean*
Deaktor, Darryl Barnett *lawyer*
Echohawk, John Ernest *lawyer*
Fenster, Herbert Lawrence *lawyer*
Fiflis, Ted James *lawyer, educator*
Flowers, William Harold, Jr. *lawyer*
Gray, William R. *lawyer*
Lacy, Mary T. (Mary Keenan) *prosecutor*
Lenzen, Glenn Howard, Jr. *lawyer*
Nehls, Richard Charles *lawyer*
Peterson, Courtland Harry *law educator*
Porzak, Glenn E. *lawyer*
Steuben, Norton Leslie *lawyer, educator*
Underwood, Anthony Paul *lawyer*
Wittemyer, John *lawyer*
Yee, Sienho *law educator*

**Broomfield**
Baker, Charles E. *lawyer*
Stortz, Thomas C. *lawyer, communications executive*

**Centennial**
Miller, Cheryl Lynn *former paralegal, artist, art educator*

**Colorado Springs**
Adams, Deborah Rowland *lawyer*
Greene, Edith Leslie *legal consultant, psychology educator*
Kubida, William Joseph *lawyer*
McCready, Guy Michael *lawyer*
Payne, Billy (William Porter Payne) *real estate lawyer, sports association executive*
Sargent, Walter Harriman, II, *lawyer*
Swanson, Victoria Clare Heldman *lawyer*

**Denver**
Aro, Edwin Packard *lawyer*
Austin, H(arry) Gregory *lawyer*
Bader, Gerald Louis, Jr. *lawyer*
Baer, Richard N. (Rich Baer) *lawyer*
Bain, Donald Knight *lawyer*
Banks, Britt D. *lawyer*
Belitz, Paul Edward *lawyer*
Bell, Stephen D. *lawyer*
Benson, Robert Eugene *lawyer*
Benton, Auburn Edgar *lawyer*
Berry, Robert Worth *lawyer, retired law educator, retired military officer*
Bess, Charles Wayne *lawyer*
Blair, Andrew Lane, Jr. *lawyer, educator*
Blitz, Stephen M. *lawyer*
Blum, Gary Bernard *lawyer*
Breeskin, Michael Wayne *lawyer*
Brega, Charles Franklin *lawyer, director*
Briggs, Steve Clement *lawyer*
Butler, David *lawyer*
Bye, James Edward *lawyer*
Cain, Douglas Mylchreest *lawyer*
Campbell, Leonard M. *lawyer*
Campbell, William J. *lawyer*
Carlson, Erik B. *lawyer*
Carrigan, Jim R. *arbitrator, mediator, retired judge*
Cheroutes, Michael Louis *lawyer*
Cooper, Billy J. *lawyer*
Cooper, Paul Douglas *lawyer*
Cope, Thomas Field *lawyer*
Copeland, Eugene Leroy *lawyer, writer*
Cortez, Miles Cogley, Jr. *lawyer*
Cox, William Vaughan *lawyer, arbitrator*
Dauer, Edward Arnold *law educator*
Davis, R. Steven *lawyer*
Dean, James Benwell *lawyer*
Deutsch, Harvey Elliot *lawyer*
Dowdle, Patrick Dennis *lawyer*
Driver, Michael J. *lawyer*
Duffy, William J. *lawyer*
Dunham, Stephen Sampson *lawyer*
DuVivier, Katharine Keyes *lawyer, educator*
Eid, Troy A. *prosecutor*
Elliff, J(ohn) Eric *lawyer*
Featherstone, Bruce Alan *lawyer*
Gehres, James *retired lawyer*
Grant, Patrick Alexander *lawyer*
Grissom, Garth Clyde *lawyer, director*
Haddon, Harold Alan *lawyer*
Hammerman, Susan Frances Weissfeld *lawyer*
Hanna, Juliet Marie *lawyer*
Harris, Dale Ray *lawyer, arbitrator, mediator*
Hartley, James Edward *lawyer*
Heiserman, Robert Gifford *lawyer*
Hendrix, Lynn Parker *lawyer*
Hensen, Stephen Jerome *lawyer*
Hoagland, Donald Wright *lawyer*
Hodges, Joseph Gilluly Jr. *lawyer*
Holme, Richard Phillips *lawyer*
Hopfenbeck, George Martin, Jr. *lawyer*

Houtsma, Peter C. *lawyer*
Imig, William Graff *lawyer, lobbyist*
Irwin, R. Robert *lawyer*
Jacobs, Paul Alan *lawyer*
Jones, Kendor Pentecost *lawyer*
Jones, Richard Michael *lawyer*
Jonsen, Eric Richard *lawyer*
Judd, Joel Stanton *lawyer*
Kahn, Edwin Sam *lawyer*
Keller, Glen Elven, Jr. *lawyer*
King, James M. *lawyer*
Kintzele, John Alfred *lawyer*
Krendl, Cathy Stricklin *lawyer*
Larson, Heather Coulter *lawyer*
Levy, Mark Ray *lawyer*
Low, Andrew M. *lawyer*
Low, John Wayland *lawyer*
Lutz, John Shafroth *lawyer*
Lyons, James M. *lawyer*
Mackey, Pamela Robillard *lawyer*
Maldonado, Kirk Francis *lawyer*
Marquess, Lawrence Wade *lawyer*
Martz, Clyde Ollen *lawyer, educator*
Mathis, Karen J. *lawyer, legal association administrator*
Mauro, Richard Frank *retired lawyer, investment company executive*
McCabe, John L. *lawyer*
McCarthy, Michael S. *lawyer*
McConnell, Michael Theodore *lawyer*
McInnis, Scott Steve *lawyer, former congressman*
McIntosh, Carolyn Leigh *lawyer*
McMichael, Donald Earl *lawyer*
Merker, Steven Joseph *lawyer*
Miller, Gale Timothy *lawyer*
Miller, Robert Nolen *lawyer*
Mitchem, Allen P. *lawyer*
Montgomery, C. Michael *lawyer*
Murane, William Edward *lawyer*
Newcom, Jennings Jay *lawyer, director*
O'Conner, Loretta Rae *lawyer*
Olsen, M. Kent *lawyer, educator*
Osman, Lee R. *lawyer*
Palmer, David Gilbert *lawyer*
Petros, Raymond Louis, Jr. *lawyer*
Quiat, Gerald M. *lawyer*
Quiat, Marshall *lawyer*
Rich, Robert Stephen *lawyer*
Roesler, John Bruce *lawyer*
Ruppert, John Lawrence *lawyer*
Samuels, Donald L. *lawyer*
Sayre, John Marshall *lawyer, former government official*
Seawell, Donald Ray *lawyer, performing company executive*
Shaheen, Anthony Joseph *lawyer*
Shea, Kevin Michael *lawyer*
Shepherd, John Frederic *lawyer*
Smiley, John Clinton *lawyer*
Steefel, David Simon *lawyer*
Talley, Steven K. *lawyer*
Thomasch, Roger Paul *lawyer*
Tisdale, Douglas Michael *lawyer*
Truhlar, Robert J. *lawyer*
Ulrich, Theodore Albert *lawyer*
Villano, Stephen Paul *lawyer*
Weber, Matthew George *lawyer*
Wheeler, Malcolm Edward *lawyer, educator*
Williams, Michael Anthony *lawyer*
Wohlgenant, Richard Glen *lawyer, director*
Woodward, Lester Ray *lawyer*
Wunnicke, Brooke *lawyer*
Yegge, Robert Bernard *law educator, retired dean*

**Durango**
Burnham, Bryson Paine *retired lawyer*

**Englewood**
DeMuth, Alan Cornelius *lawyer*
DeMuth, Laurence Wheeler, Jr. *lawyer, utilities executive*
Karstaedt, Arthur R. III *lawyer*
Lidstone, Herrick Kenley, Jr. *lawyer*
Moskowitz, David K. *lawyer*
Orsini, Rosemary *lawyer*
Smith, Mark Christopher *lawyer*
Spencer, Margaret Gilliam *lawyer*
Steinhauser, John William *retired lawyer*
Tanabe, Charles Y. *lawyer*
Touff, Michael *lawyer*
Zoeller, Mark L. *lawyer, printing company executive*

**Fort Collins**
Carlson, Alan Douglas *lawyer*
Johnson, Donald Edward, Jr. *lawyer*
Murphy, Dennis Joseph *lawyer*
Rogers, Garth Winfield *lawyer*
Schwartz, Allen R. *lawyer*

**Frisco**
Helmer, David Alan *lawyer*

**Golden**
Eiberger, Carl Frederick *lawyer*
Kopel, David Benjamin *lawyer*
Phillipson, Donald E. *lawyer*

**Greenwood Village**
Aspinwall, David Charles *lawyer, insurance company executive*
Dewald, Bruce Wayne *lawyer*
Dymond, Lewis Wandell *lawyer, educator*
Poe, Robert Alan *lawyer*
Ramsey, John Arthur *lawyer*
Rothrock, Lindsey Nichole *lawyer*

**Highlands Ranch**
Judson, Philip Livingston *retired lawyer, consultant*

**Howard**
Hopkins, Donald J. *retired lawyer*

**Lakewood**
Guyton, Samuel Percy *retired lawyer*
Humphrey, Charles Edward, Jr. *lawyer*
McElwee, Dennis John *lawyer, former pharmaceutical company executive*

**Littleton**
Meyer, Milton Edward, Jr. *retired lawyer, artist*

Michaels Hollander, Erica *law educator*

**Lone Tree**
Spelts, Richard John *lawyer*

**Louisville**
Roellig, Mark D. *lawyer*

**Loveland**
Clark, Roger Earl *lawyer*
DiFalco, John Patrick *lawyer, arbitrator*
Kaufman, William George *lawyer*

**Morrison**
Bowen, Peter Geoffrey *arbitrator, finance educator*

**Norwood**
Reagan, Harry Edwin III *lawyer*

**Pagosa Springs**
Kelly, Reid Browne *lawyer*

**Parker**
Greenberg, Morton Paul *lawyer, consultant, life settlement broker*

**Pueblo**
Farley, Thomas T. *lawyer*
O'Callaghan, R.J. Patrick *lawyer*

**Pueblo West**
Kogovsek, Daniel Charles *lawyer*

**Rocky Ford**
Mendenhall, Harry Barton *lawyer*

**Windsor**
Downey, Arthur Harold, Jr. *lawyer, mediator*

## CONNECTICUT

**Bloomfield**
Messemer, Glenn Matthew *lawyer*

**Bridgeport**
Bowen, Patrick Harvey *lawyer, consultant*
Laccavole, Dennis Mark *lawyer*

**Danbury**
Yamin, Robert Joseph *lawyer*

**Darien**
Prince, Kenneth Stephen *lawyer*

**Derby**
McEvoy, Sharlene Ann *law educator*

**East Hartford**
Dubin, Joseph William *federal mediator*
Teller, Adam J. *lawyer*

**Fairfield**
Caruso, Daniel F. *lawyer, judge, former state legislator*
Denniston, Brackett Badger III *lawyer*
Ury, Frederic Stephen *lawyer*
Wales, Gwynne Huntington *retired lawyer*

**Farmington**
Wiechmann, Eric Watt *lawyer*

**Greenwich**
Atkins, Ronald Raymond *lawyer*
Brandrup, Douglas Warren *lawyer*
Coleman, Joel Clifford *lawyer*
Gelfman, Robert William *retired lawyer*
Kreiger, Bruce D. *lawyer*
Lanning, Christopher Glenn *lawyer*
Lynch, William Redington *lawyer*
More, Douglas McLochlan *lawyer*
Nimetz, Matthew *lawyer, investment company executive*
Pascarella, Henry William *lawyer*
Paul, Roland Arthur *lawyer*
Schoonmaker, Samuel Vail III *lawyer*
Selby, Leland Clay *lawyer*
Sexton, David Farrington *lawyer, bank executive*
Storms, Clifford Beekman *lawyer*
Verney, Richard H. *lawyer*
Welt, Philip Stanley *lawyer, consultant*

**Hamden**
Margulies, Martin B. *lawyer, educator*
Peterson, George Emanuel, Jr. *retired lawyer*

**Hartford**
Alfano, Charles Thomas, Sr. *lawyer*
Anthony, Julian Danford, Jr. *lawyer*
Berall, Frank Stewart *lawyer*
Bergenn, James Walter *lawyer*
Blumberg, Phillip Irvin *law educator*
Bonee, John Leon III *lawyer*
Buck, Gurdon Hall *lawyer, urban planner, mediator*
Cain, George Harvey *lawyer, legal association administrator*
Corey, Paul J. *lawyer*
Coyle, Michael Lee *lawyer*
Del Negro, John Thomas *lawyer*
Dempsey, Edward Joseph *lawyer*
Godfrey, Robert Douglas *lawyer*
Harkin, Ruth R. *lawyer*
Harrison, Thomas Flatley *lawyer*
Johnson, Dwight Alan *lawyer*
Kennedy, Jack Stanners *lawyer*
Klippel, Charles H *lawyer, insurance company executive*
Leonhardt, Clifton Andrew *lawyer, public information officer*
Lloyd, Alex *lawyer*
Lotstein, James Irving *lawyer*
Louden, William Bruce *lawyer*
Lyon, James Burroughs *lawyer*
Merriam, Dwight Haines *lawyer, land use planner*
Miller, Jeffrey Clark *lawyer*
Nolan, John Blanchard *lawyer*
Oakes, Dennis *lawyer, insurance company executive*

Richter, Donald Paul *lawyer*
Ryan, David Thomas *lawyer*
Schroth, Peter William *lawyer, management and law educator*
See, Edmund M. *lawyer*
Sheils, Paul T. *lawyer*
Space, Theodore Maxwell *lawyer*
Strohmenger, Thomas C *lawyer*
Tancredi, James J. *lawyer*
Taylor, Allan Bert *lawyer*
Thompson, James Alexander, Jr. *lawyer*
Trachsel, William Henry *corporate lawyer*
Vacchelli, Robert Francis *lawyer*
Valentine, Debra A. *lawyer*
Voigt, Richard *lawyer*
Wolin, Neal Steven *lawyer*
Wolman, Martin *lawyer*

**Lakeville**
Jones, Ronald David *retired lawyer*

**Litchfield**
Fiederowicz, Walter Michael *lawyer*
Fishman, Mitchell Steven *lawyer*

**Madison**
Brennan, Daniel Edward, Jr. *former state judge*
Clendenen, William Herbert, Jr. *lawyer*

**Milford**
Berchem, Robert Lee, Sr. *lawyer*
Hogan, John W., Jr. *lawyer*

**New Britain**
Tedford, Deborah J. *lawyer*

**New Canaan**
Resor, Stanley Rogers *retired lawyer*
Steinmetz, Richard Bird, Jr. *lawyer*
Troy, Richard Hershey *lawyer*
Wolff, Sanford Irving *lawyer*

**New Haven**
Ackerman, Bruce Arnold *law educator*
Ayres, Ian *law educator, economist*
Balkin, Jack M. *law educator*
Benkler, Yochai *law educator*
Brilmayer, R. Lea *lawyer, educator*
Burt, Robert Amsterdam *lawyer, educator*
Carter, Stephen Lisle *law educator*
Chua, Amy *law educator*
Cole, Elsa Kircher *lawyer*
Coleman, Jules L. *law educator*
Dalton, Harlon L. *law educator*
Damaska, Mirjan Radovan *law educator*
Danaher, John Anthony III *prosecutor*
Days, Drew S. III *lawyer, educator*
Donohue, John Joseph *law educator*
Duke, Steven Barry *law educator*
Ellickson, Robert Chester *law educator*
Eskridge, William Nichol, Jr. *law educator*
Esty, Daniel Cushing *law educator, lawyer*
Fiss, Owen M. *law educator*
Freed, Daniel Josef *law educator*
Gastwirth, Donald Edward *lawyer, literary agent*
Geisler, Thomas Milton, Jr. *lawyer*
Gewirtz, Paul D. *lawyer, educator*
Gildea, Brian Michael *lawyer*
Graetz, Michael J. *law educator*
Greenfield, James Robert *lawyer*
Hansmann, Henry Baethke *law educator*
Johnstone, Quintin *law educator*
Kahan, Dan M. *law educator*
Kahn, Paul W. *law educator*
Klevorick, Alvin K. *law and economics educator*
Langbein, John Harriss *lawyer, educator*
Macey, Jonathan R. *law educator*
Marcus, Edward Leonard *lawyer, political organization worker*
O'Connor, Kevin James *prosecutor, lawyer*
Peters, Jean Koh *law educator*
Post, Robert Charles *law educator*
Priest, George L. *law educator*
Reisman, William Michael *lawyer, educator*
Resnik, Judith *law educator*
Rose-Ackerman, Susan *law and political economy educator*
Rubenfeld, Jed *law educator*
Schloss, Irving Steven *lawyer*
Schneider, David Walter *lawyer*
Schuck, Peter Horner *lawyer, educator*
Schwartz, Alan *law educator*
Siegel, Reva *law educator*
Silk, James J. *law educator*
Smith, Henry E. *law educator*
Solomon, Robert A. *law educator*
Stapleton, James Francis *lawyer*
Stith-Cabranes, Kate *law educator*
Sullivan, Shaun Stuart *lawyer*
Sweet, Alec Stone *law educator*
Wagoner, Walter Dray, Jr. *lawyer*
Zimmermann, Jeremy Gray *lawyer*

**New London**
Asselin-Connolly, John Thomas *lawyer*
Reardon, Robert Ignatius, Jr. *lawyer*

**Norfolk**
Jessup, Philip Caryl, Jr. *retired lawyer*

**North Stonington**
Svengalis, Kendall Frayne *law librarian, educator, publishing executive*

**Norwalk**
Burton, David K. *lawyer*
Cammaker, Sheldon Ira *lawyer*
Jacobs, Mark Randolph *lawyer*
Knopp, Alex *lawyer, mayor*
Raikes, Charles FitzGerald *retired lawyer*
Sawch, William B. *lawyer*

**Old Greenwich**
Gayda, Michael D. *lawyer*

**Orange**
Davies, Richard Warren *lawyer*

**Redding**
Gooch, Anthony Cushing *retired lawyer*

Quinn, Andrew Peter, Jr. *lawyer, retired insurance company executive*

**Ridgefield**
Wiegley, Roger Douglas *lawyer*

**Roxbury**
Friedman, John Maxwell, Jr. *lawyer*

**Shelton**
Vine, Leo *lawyer*
Williamson, Keith Harvey *lawyer*

**Simsbury**
Houlihan, Charles Daniel, Jr. *lawyer*

**Southbury**
Auerbach, Ernest Sigmund *lawyer, insurance company executive, writer*
Russell, Allan David *lawyer*

**Stamford**
Bainton, J(ohn) Joseph *lawyer*
Barreca, Christopher Anthony *lawyer*
Birenbaum, Jonathan *lawyer*
Critelli, Michael J. *lawyer, manufacturing executive*
duPont, Augustus Irénée *lawyer*
Fisher, Richard S. *lawyer*
Frenkel, Steven I. *lawyer*
Gold, Steven Michael *lawyer*
Griffith, Forrest Lee III *lawyer*
Hawkins, John Donald, Jr. *lawyer*
Hogan, Frank W. III *lawyer, manufacturing executive*
Hubschman, Henry A. *lawyer*
Mayes, Michele Coleman *lawyer*
McGeeney, John Stephen *lawyer*
McGrath, Richard *lawyer*
Merritt, William Alfred, Jr. *retired lawyer, real estate company executive*
Miller, Gregory James *lawyer*
Mitten, Russ *lawyer, telecommunications industry executive*
Nichols, Ralph Arthur *lawyer*
Perle, Eugene Gabriel *lawyer*
Rose, Richard Loomis *lawyer*
Shanman, James Alan *lawyer*
Skidd, Thomas Patrick, Jr. *lawyer*
Snediker, David E. *lawyer*
Staab, Diane D. *lawyer*
Teitell, Conrad Laurence *lawyer, writer*
Weitzel, William Conrad, Jr. *lawyer*
Willkie, Wendell Lewis, II, *lawyer*

**Stonington**
Brown, Meredith M. *lawyer*
Cole, Richard A. *retired lawyer*

**Storrs Mansfield**
Tucker, Edwin Wallace *law educator*

**Stratford**
O'Rourke, James Louis *lawyer*

**Trumbull**
Williams, Ronald Doherty *lawyer*

**Waterbury**
Dost, Mark W. *lawyer*
Wolfe, Harriet Munrett *lawyer*

**West Mystic**
Liberty, Frank J. *lawyer*

**Weston**
Aibel, Howard James *arbitrator, mediator*
Cohen, Fred Howard *lawyer, investment company executive*
Murray, Stephen James *lawyer*

**Westport**
Barberi, Robert Obed *lawyer*
Carr, Cynthia *lawyer*
Cohen, Eric I. *lawyer*
Daw, Harold John *lawyer, director*
Heyman, Ronnie Feuerstein *lawyer*
Margolis, Emanuel *lawyer, educator*
Razzano, Pasquale Angelo *lawyer*
Sheiman, Ronald Lee *lawyer*

**Wilton**
Adams, Thomas Tilley *lawyer*
Duke, Robert Dominick *lawyer*
Fricke, Richard John *lawyer*
Healy, James Casey *lawyer*
Slater, Ralph Evan *lawyer*

**DELAWARE**

**Bear**
McCann, Richard Stephen *lawyer*

**Dover**
Ennis, Bruce Clifford *retired lawyer*
Young, Robert Bond *lawyer*

**Greenville**
Long, Linda Ann *lawyer*

**Milton**
Carrow, Milton Michael *law educator*

**Newark**
Elson, Charles Myer *law educator*
Mangone, Gerard J. *maritime law educator*

**Wilmington**
Bader, John Merwin *retired lawyer*
Baumann, Julian Henry, Jr. *lawyer*
Carpenter, Edmund Nelson, II, *retired lawyer*
Connolly, Colm F. *prosecutor*
Cousins, Scott David *lawyer*
Devine, Donn *lawyer, genealogist, municipal official*
DiLiberto, Richard Anthony, Jr. *lawyer*
Du Pont, Pierre Samuel, IV, *lawyer, former governor of Delaware*

Finkelstein, Jesse Adam *lawyer*
Floyd, Israel J. *lawyer, chemicals executive*
Freeh, Louis Joseph *lawyer, retired federal agency administrator*
Green, James Samuel *lawyer*
Hannigan, Patricia C. *prosecutor*
Herdeg, John Andrew *lawyer*
Holzman, James L(ouis) *lawyer*
Johnston, William David *lawyer*
Jolles, Janet K. Pilling *lawyer*
Kirk, Richard Dillon *lawyer*
Kirkpatrick, Andrew Booth, Jr. *lawyer*
Klayman, Barry Martin *lawyer*
Krahmer, Johannes Robert *lawyer*
Kristol, Daniel Marvin *retired lawyer*
Magee, Thomas Hugh *lawyer*
McDowell, Charles S. *lawyer*
Mekler, Arlen B. *lawyer, chemist*
Mobley, Stacey J. *lawyer, consumer products company executive*
Nolen, Samuel Augustus *lawyer*
Paschetto, John J. *lawyer*
Rodgers, Stephen John *lawyer, physician, consultant*
Salinger, Frank Max *lawyer*
Schnee, Carl *lawyer, former prosecutor*
Semple, James William *lawyer*
Stargatt, Bruce M. *lawyer*
Sullivan, Lawrence Matthew *lawyer*
Tumas, Michael B. *lawyer*
Ward, Rodman, Jr. *lawyer, director*
Welch, Edward P. *lawyer*
Wier, Richard Royal, Jr. *lawyer*
Winslow, Helen Littell *lawyer*

**DISTRICT OF COLUMBIA**

**Washington**
Aaronson, David Ernest *lawyer, educator*
Abbott, Alden Francis *lawyer, federal official*
Abeles, Charles Calvert *retired lawyer*
Abernathy, Kathleen Quinn *lawyer, former commissioner*
Acheson, David Campion *retired lawyer, policy analyst, writer*
Adams, David G. *lawyer*
Adams, Frances Grant, II, *lawyer*
Adams, John Jillson *lawyer*
Adams, Roger C. *lawyer*
Adamson, Terrence Burdett *lawyer*
Adducci, Steven A. *lawyer*
Adler, Howard Bruce *lawyer*
Adler, Robert Martin *lawyer*
Agarwal, Pavan K. *lawyer*
Agrast, Mark David *lawyer*
Aitken, Andrew C. *lawyer*
Alberg, James L. *lawyer*
Albertson, Terry L. *lawyer*
Albrecht, Ralph P. *lawyer*
Aldock, John Douglas *lawyer*
Aldonas, Grant D. *lawyer, former federal agency administrator*
Alexander, Clifford Joseph *lawyer*
Alexander, Donald Crichton *lawyer*
Alvarez, Scott G. *lawyer*
Ambrose, Myles Joseph *lawyer*
Ames, Robert G. *lawyer*
Amron, Cory M. *lawyer*
Anderson, Frederick Randolph, Jr. *lawyer, educator*
Anderson, James E. *lawyer*
Anderson, Stanton Dean *lawyer*
Andrew, Giaccia A. *lawyer*
Andrew, Joseph Jerald *lawyer*
Andrews, Mark Joseph *lawyer*
Andril, David T. *lawyer*
Anthony, Stephen Pierce *lawyer*
Apatoff, David B. *lawyer*
Apple, James Glenn *lawyer, educator*
Armen, Margaret Meis *lawyer*
Assaf, Eugene F. *lawyer*
Attridge, Daniel F. *lawyer*
Atwood, James R. *lawyer*
Auberger, Marcia A. *lawyer*
Avil, Richard Daniel, Jr. *lawyer*
Axelrod, Jonathan Gans *lawyer*
Ayer, Donald Belton *lawyer*
Ayres, Kenneth James *lawyer*
Babayi, Robert S. *lawyer*
Babby, Lon S. *lawyer*
Bader, W(illiam) Reece *lawyer*
Badillo, Alejandro *lawyer*
Baer, William J. *lawyer*
Baim, Eric M. *lawyer*
Bain, Scott E. *lawyer*
Baker, Howard Henry, Jr. *lawyer, former ambassador, former senator*
Baker, P. Jean *lawyer, mediator*
Baldridge, J. Douglas *lawyer*
Ball, Markham (Robert Ball) *lawyer, arbitrator, educator*
Balmford, Kathryn Elizabeth *lawyer*
Banoun, Raymond *lawyer*
Banzhaf, John F. III *legal association administrator, law educator*
Baran, Jan Witold *lawyer, educator*
Barbash, Barry P. *lawyer*
Barcella, Ernest Lawrence, Jr. *lawyer*
Barclay, George N. *lawyer*
Bardin, David Jonas *lawyer*
Barnes, Donald Michael *lawyer*
Barnes, Mark James *lawyer*
Barnett, Helaine M. *lawyer*
Barnett, Robert Bruce (Bob Barnett) *lawyer*
Barrie, John Paul *lawyer, educator*
Barron, Myra Hymovich *lawyer*
Barry, Dennis M. *lawyer*
Barshefsky, Charlene *lawyer, former diplomat*
Bartlett, John Laurence *lawyer*
Barusch, Ronald Charles *lawyer*
Baskin, Maurice *lawyer*
Basseches, Robert Treinis *lawyer*
Batla, Raymond John, Jr. *lawyer*
Battocchi, Ronald Silvio *lawyer*
Bauer, Richard P. *lawyer*
Bauer, Robert F. *lawyer*
Baumann, Linda Adriene *lawyer*
Baumbusch, Peter L. *lawyer*
Baumgarten, Jon A. *lawyer*
Baum-Villavicencio, Lynne Miriam *lawyer*

Bayh, Birch Evans, Jr. *lawyer, former senator*
Bear, Dinah *lawyer*
Becker, Brandon *lawyer*
Becker, Stephan E. *lawyer*
Beckwith, Edward Jay *lawyer*
Bedell, Dennis Peters *lawyer, educator*
Behan, Kathleen A. (Kitty Behan) *lawyer*
Beisner, John Herbert *lawyer*
Bell, Joseph Charles *lawyer*
Bell, Stephen Robert *lawyer*
Beller, Herbert N. *lawyer*
Bellinger, John B. III *lawyer, consultant, federal official*
Bello, Judith Hippler *lawyer, trade association administrator*
Benitez, Brigida *lawyer*
Benner, C. Jonathan *lawyer*
Bennett, Alan R. *lawyer*
Bennett, Alexander Elliot *lawyer*
Bennett, Robert Stephen *lawyer*
Ben-Veniste, Richard *lawyer*
Beresford, Douglas Lincoln *lawyer*
Bergner, Jane Cohen *lawyer*
Berl, Joseph M. *lawyer*
Berlack, Evan Raden *lawyer*
Berlin, Kenneth *lawyer*
Berman, Joshua G. *lawyer*
Berman, Paul Justin *lawyer*
Bernabei, Lynne Ann *lawyer*
Bernard, Lawrence B. *lawyer*
Berner, Frederic George, Jr. *lawyer*
Bernhard, Berl *lawyer*
Bernstein, Mitchell Harris *lawyer*
Bernthal, Eric L. *lawyer*
Berrington, Craig Anthony *lawyer*
Berthelsen, Richard A. *lawyer*
Berz, David Richard *lawyer*
Best, Judah *lawyer*
Bieber, Sander M. *lawyer*
Bierman, James Norman *lawyer*
Billauer, Barbara Pfeffer *lawyer, educator*
Bintz, Edward E. *lawyer*
Birnkrant, Henry Joseph *lawyer*
Bishop, James Dodson *lawyer, mediator*
Black, Stephen Franklin *lawyer, playwright*
Blair, Robert Allen *lawyer*
Blake, Jonathan Dewey *lawyer*
Blazek-White, Doris *lawyer*
Bleakley, Peter Kimberley *lawyer*
Bloch, Susan Low *law educator*
Block, Joseph G. *lawyer*
Bloom, David I. *lawyer*
Bodner, John, Jr. *lawyer*
Boehm, Steven Bruce *lawyer*
Bogard, Lawrence Joseph *lawyer*
Boggs, George Trenholm *lawyer*
Boggs, Thomas Hale, Jr. *lawyer, director*
Boisture, Robert A. *lawyer*
Boland, Christopher Thomas, II, *lawyer*
Bolger, Robert J., Jr. *lawyer*
Bondareff, Joan M. *lawyer, retired government agency administrator*
Bonvillian, William Boone *lawyer*
Bookoff, Leslie *lawyer*
Born, Brooksley Elizabeth *retired lawyer*
Borsari, George Robert, Jr. *lawyer, commentator*
Bosch, Michele C. *lawyer*
Bosco, Mary Beth *lawyer*
Boskey, Bennett *lawyer*
Boyd, Benjamin S. *lawyer*
Boyd, Thomas Marshall *lawyer*
Braga, Stephen Louis *lawyer*
Braker, Gregory S. *lawyer*
Brame, Joseph Robert III *lawyer*
Braswell, Mark K. *lawyer*
Breaux, John Berlinger *lawyer, communications professor, former senator*
Brecher, Mitchell Fredrick *lawyer*
Bregman, Arthur Randolph *lawyer, educator*
Brenner, Janet Maybin Walker *lawyer*
Briggs, Alan Leonard *lawyer*
Brockway, David Hunt *lawyer*
Brody, Peter Martin *lawyer*
Brogan, Stephen (Steve) J. *lawyer*
Bromwich, Michael Ray *lawyer*
Bronstein, Alvin J. *lawyer*
Brower, Charles Nelson *lawyer, judge*
Brown, Barbara Berish *lawyer*
Brown, David Nelson *lawyer*
Brown, Donald Arthur *lawyer*
Brown, Preston *lawyer*
Brown, Richard L. *lawyer*
Brown, Thomas Philip III *lawyer*
Browne, Richard Cullen *lawyer*
Brownell, F. William *lawyer*
Bruce, Carol Elder *lawyer*
Bruce, Estel Edward *lawyer*
Bruemmer, Russell John *lawyer*
Bruno, Philippe M. *lawyer*
Brunsvold, Brian Garrett *lawyer, educator*
Buc, Nancy Lillian *lawyer*
Buckley, Jeremiah Stephen *lawyer*
Bucklin, Donald Thomas *lawyer*
Buechner, Jack W(illiam) *lawyer, consultant, educational association administrator*
Buffon, Charles Edward *lawyer*
Buffone, Samuel J. *lawyer*
Bulleit, Thomas Nelson, Jr. *lawyer*
Burchfield, Bobby Roy *lawyer*
Burdett, James R. *lawyer*
Burdick, Rick L. *lawyer*
Burka, Robert Alan *lawyer*
Burke, Edmund W. *lawyer*
Burnley, James Horace, IV, *lawyer*
Burns, Stephen Gilbert *lawyer*
Burt, Jeffrey Amsterdam *lawyer*
Busby, David *lawyer*
Buscemi, Peter *lawyer*
Bush, Karen Lee *lawyer*
Butcher, Karen A. *lawyer*
Butler, Mary K. *prosecutor*
Butler, Michael Francis *lawyer*
Calamaro, Raymond Stuart *lawyer*
Callery, T. Grant *lawyer*
Calvani, Terry *lawyer*
Cameron, Donald B., Jr. *lawyer*
Campbell, Nancy Duff *lawyer*
Cantor, Herbert I. *lawyer*
Caplin, Mortimer Maxwell *lawyer, educator*
Caproni, Valerie E. *lawyer, federal agency administrator*

Carey, Sarah Collins *lawyer*
Carlisle, Linda Elizabeth *lawyer*
Carneal, George Upshur *lawyer*
Carney, Robert Thomas *lawyer*
Carpenter, Russell H., Jr. *lawyer*
Carpenter, Sheila Jane *lawyer*
Carr, Lawrence Edward, Jr. *lawyer*
Carter, Barry Edward *law educator*
Carter, William Joseph *lawyer*
Casserly, James Lund *lawyer*
Cassidy, Robert Charles, Jr. *lawyer*
Cavalier, Gina M. *lawyer*
Cavanaugh, James Michael *lawyer*
Chabot, Elliot Charles *lawyer*
Chandler, James Phillip *law educator*
Chanin, Michael Henry *lawyer*
Charytan, Lynn R. *lawyer*
Chatilovicz, Peter *lawyer*
Chavous, Kevin P. *lawyer*
Chopko, Mark E. *lawyer*
Choukas-Bradley, James Richard *lawyer*
Christaldi, Brian *lawyer*
Christian, Betty Jo *lawyer*
Chused, Richard Harris *law educator*
Ciatto, Frank A. *lawyer*
Cirulnick, Arthur E. *lawyer*
Clagett, Brice McAdoo *lawyer, writer, genealogist*
Clark, LeRoy D. *law educator*
Clayton, Carol A. *lawyer*
CLayton, Michael F. *lawyer*
Coan, Carl A.S., Jr. *lawyer*
Coats, Daniel Ray *lawyer, former ambassador, former senator*
Cobb, Calvin Hayes, Jr. *lawyer*
Cobb, Ty *lawyer*
Cobbs, Nicholas Hamner *lawyer*
Coffield, Shirley Ann *lawyer, educator*
Cohen, Benedict S. *lawyer*
Cohen, David Blair *lawyer*
Cohen, Louis Richard *lawyer*
Cohen, Nelson Craig *lawyer*
Cohen, Sheldon Stanley *lawyer*
Cohen, Wayne R. *lawyer*
Cohn, Sherman Louis *lawyer, educator*
Colaizzi, Roger A. *lawyer*
Cole, John Pope, Jr. *lawyer*
Cole, Robert Theodore *lawyer*
Coleman, Lynn R. *lawyer*
Collins, Daniel Francis *lawyer*
Collinson, Dale Stanley *lawyer*
Colson, Earl Morton *lawyer, educator*
Comstock, Robert Francis *lawyer*
Condrell, William Kenneth *lawyer*
Connelly, Warren E. *lawyer*
Conner, Frank M. (Rusty) III *lawyer*
Conron, Michael William *lawyer*
Cook, Harry Clayton, Jr. *lawyer*
Cook, Michael Harry *lawyer*
Cook, William E., Jr. *lawyer*
Cooke, Edmund *lawyer*
Cooney, John Fontana *lawyer*
Cooper, Alan Samuel *lawyer, educator*
Cooper, J. Michael *lawyer*
Cooper, Richard Melvyn *lawyer*
Cooper, Ronald Stephen *lawyer*
Cooper, Thomas J. *lawyer*
Cope, John R(obert) *lawyer*
Cople, William James III *lawyer*
Corn-Revere, Robert *lawyer*
Cortese, Alfred William, Jr. *lawyer, consultant*
Coston, William Dean *lawyer*
Coulter, William Kirk *lawyer*
Covucci, George E. *lawyer*
Cowan, Eric Ward *lawyer*
Cowan, Joyce A. *lawyer*
Cox, Kenneth Allen *lawyer, consultant, communications executive*
Cox, M. Carolyn *lawyer*
Coyne, Patrick Joseph *lawyer*
Craft, Robert Homan, Jr. *lawyer*
Craig, Gregory Bestor *lawyer*
Craven, Donald B. *lawyer*
Crawford, Brett A. *lawyer*
Crisman, C. Benjamin, Jr. *lawyer*
Crocker, Thomas Edward *lawyer*
Crosby, William Duncan, Jr. *lawyer*
Cross, Meredith B. *lawyer*
Crowley, Juanita V. *lawyer*
Crown, Michele Fleurette *lawyer*
Cruden, John Charles *lawyer*
Crump, John *lawyer*
Cullen, Thomas Francis, Jr. *lawyer*
Culvahouse, Arthur Boggess, Jr *lawyer*
Cummings, Frank *lawyer*
Curtin, Peter J. *lawyer*
Cushing, Mark L. *lawyer*
Cutler, Stephen M. *lawyer, former federal agency administrator*
Cymrot, Mark Alan *lawyer*
Cys, Richard L. *lawyer*
Daley, Henry J. *lawyer*
Dalley, George Albert *lawyer, consultant*
Dane, Stephen Mark *lawyer*
Daniels, Diana M. *lawyer, publishing executive*
Dark, Okianer Christian *law educator*
Davidow, Charles E. *lawyer*
Davidson, Daniel Ira *lawyer*
Davidson, Daniel Morton *lawyer*
Davidson, Tom William *lawyer*
Davies, Charles R. *lawyer*
Davis, William E. *lawyer*
Davison, Calvin *retired lawyer*
Deal, Jill B. *lawyer*
Dean, Paul Regis *retired law educator*
Dean, Richard N. *lawyer*
Debevoise, Eli Whitney, II, *lawyer*
Debolt, Paul A. *lawyer*
Dees, C. Stanley *lawyer*
Deese, Pamela McCarthy *lawyer*
deKieffer, Donald Eulette *lawyer*
de Leon, Sylvia A. *lawyer*
De Martino, Ralph Victor *lawyer*
Dembling, Paul Gerald *lawyer, former government official*
Denger, Michael Louis *lawyer*
Denison, Mary Boney *lawyer*
Dewey, Elizabeth R. *lawyer*
Dicello, Francis P. *lawyer*
Dickstein, Sidney *lawyer*
Dienelt, John F. *lawyer*
Diercks, Walter Elmer *lawyer*

diGenova, Joseph E. *lawyer*
Diner, Bryan C. *lawyer*
Dinh, Viet D. *law educator*
Disheroon, Fred Russell *lawyer*
Doebbler, Curtis F.J. *lawyer*
Dolan, Edward Charles *lawyer*
Dolan, Michael William *lawyer*
Dole, Bob (Robert Joseph Dole) *lawyer, retired senator*
Dolin, Mitchell F. *lawyer*
Donegan, Charles Edward *lawyer, educator*
Doolittle, Jesse William, Jr. *lawyer*
Doria, Marilyn L. *lawyer*
Dorsen, David M(ilton) *lawyer*
Dotson, Donald L. *lawyer*
Dowd, John Maguire *lawyer*
Doyle, A. Patrick *lawyer*
Drinan, Robert Frederick *law educator*
Drysdale, Douglas D. *lawyer*
Duff, James C. *lawyer*
Duffy, John Fitzgerald *lawyer, educator*
Duncan, Robert Michael *lawyer, political organization administrator*
Dunn, H. Stewart, Jr. *lawyer*
Dunner, Donald Robert *lawyer*
Durney, Michael Cavalier *lawyer*
Dwyer, Maureen Ellen *lawyer*
Dye, Stuart Selley *lawyer*
Eastment, Thomas James *lawyer*
Easton, John Jay, Jr. *lawyer*
Eckland, William S *lawyer*
Economon, Paul David *lawyer, management consultant*
Edelman, Peter Benjamin *lawyer, educator*
Edge, Joe D. *lawyer*
Edlavitch, Susan T. *lawyer*
Edson, Charles Louis *lawyer*
Efros, Ellen Ann *lawyer*
Ehrenhaft, Peter David *lawyer*
Ehrlich, Alan Marshall *lawyer, educator*
Eichen, Jeffrey L. *lawyer*
Eisenberg, Meyer *lawyer*
Eisenstat, David H. *lawyer*
Eisenstein, Laurence Jay *lawyer*
Eizenstat, Stuart Elliot *lawyer, former federal agency administrator*
Elcano, Mary S. *lawyer*
El-Fishawy, Saad Samuel *lawyer*
Ellett, Ted (E. Tazewell Ellett) *lawyer*
Ellicott, John LeMoyne *lawyer*
Elliott, Edwin Donald, Jr. *lawyer, educator, federal agency administrator*
Ellis, Courtenay *lawyer*
Elmer, Brian Christian *lawyer*
Elrod, Eugene Richard *lawyer*
Emden, Craig A. *lawyer*
Engel, John *lawyer*
Epstein, Ellen Chubin *prosecutor*
Epstein, Gary Marvin *lawyer*
Epstein, Lionel Charles *lawyer*
Epstien, Jay Alan *lawyer*
Evans, David C. *lawyer*
Evans, Robert David *legal association executive*
Everett, Ralph Bernard *lawyer*
Ewing, Ky Pepper, Jr. *lawyer*
Fahmy Hudome, Randa *lawyer*
Fairbanks, Richard Monroe III *lawyer, retired ambassador*
Fales, Lisa Jose *lawyer*
Farabow, Ford Franklin, Jr. *lawyer*
Faust, Emanuel, Jr. *lawyer*
Fedders, John Michael *lawyer*
Feffer, Gerald Alan *lawyer*
Feinberg, Kenneth Roy *lawyer, law educator*
Feldhaus, Stephen Martin *lawyer*
Feldman, Clarice Rochelle *lawyer*
Feldman, Mark B. *lawyer*
Feldman, Roger David *lawyer*
Fels, Nicholas Wolff *lawyer*
Fendrich, Roger Paul *lawyer*
Fennell, Stephen A. *lawyer*
Ferrand, Louis George *lawyer*
Ferrara, Ralph C. *lawyer*
Ferrell, Elizabeth Ann *lawyer*
Ferrell, Michael J. *lawyer*
Ferris, Charles Daniel *lawyer, former government official*
Fiedler, Marc *lawyer, advocate*
Field, Andrea Bear *lawyer*
Fielding, Fred Fisher *lawyer*
Finkel, Eugene Jay *lawyer*
Firestone, Charles Morton *lawyer, educator*
Fieldhouse, Benjamin Postell III *lawyer*
Fisher, Bart Steven *lawyer, educator, investment banker*
Fishman, Ira *lawyer*
Fitton, Tom J. *lawyer*
Fitzgerald, Kevin C. *lawyer*
Fitzpatrick, James Franklin *lawyer*
Flagg, Ronald Simon *lawyer*
Flannery, Ellen Joanne *lawyer*
Fleischaker, Marc L. *lawyer*
Fleischman, Aaron I. *lawyer*
Flowe, Carol Connor *lawyer*
Flyer, Michael R. *lawyer*
Ford, Ann K. *lawyer*
Forester, John Gordon, Jr. *lawyer*
Forrest, Herbert Emerson *lawyer*
Fortuno, Victor M. *lawyer*
Foscarinis, Maria *lawyer*
Foster, C(harles) Allen *lawyer*
Foster, Hope S. *lawyer*
Fox, Hamilton Phillips, III, (Phil Fox) *lawyer*
Fox, Thomas C. *lawyer*
Frank, Richard Asher *lawyer, health products executive*
Frank, Robert J. *lawyer*
Frank, Theodore David *lawyer*
Freed, Joel M. *lawyer*
Freedman, Jay Weil *lawyer*
Fried, Bruce Merlin *lawyer*
Frisby, Herbert Russell *lawyer*
Frost, Edmund Bowen *lawyer*
Frost, Martin, III, (Jonas Martin Frost III) *lawyer, former congressman*
Furey, Roger P. *lawyer*
Gable, Edward Brennan, Jr. *lawyer*
Gallagher, Michael David *lawyer, former federal agency administrator*
Gallas, Philip S. *lawyer*
Gardiner, Kent A. *lawyer*

Garland, Gloria Jean *lawyer, consultant*
Garr, Sally D. *lawyer*
Garrett, Theodore Louis *lawyer*
Garrish, Theodore John *lawyer*
Gaskell, Judith Ann *law librarian*
Gaynor, Kevin Allen *lawyer*
Geller, Kenneth Steven *lawyer*
Geltman, Edward Alan *lawyer*
Genetski, Christian S. *lawyer*
Geniesse, Robert John *lawyer*
Gephardt, Dick (Richard Andrew Gephardt) *lawyer, former congressman*
Gerber, Melanie K. *lawyer*
Gerson, Stuart Michael *lawyer*
Gesner, Lawrence H. *lawyer*
Gibbs, Lawrence Blair *lawyer*
Gideon, Kenneth Wayne *lawyer*
Gilfoyle, Nathalie Floyd Preston *lawyer*
Gillan, Kayla J. *lawyer*
Gillon, Peter M. *lawyer*
Ginsburg, Charles David *lawyer*
Ginsburg, Gilbert J. *lawyer, educator*
Ginsburg, Martin David *lawyer, educator*
Gittleman, Richard M. *lawyer*
Glancz, Ronald Robert *lawyer*
Glasgow, Norman Milton *lawyer*
Gleklen, Jonathan Ian *lawyer*
Glick, Leslie Alan *lawyer*
Glover, Jere Walton *lawyer*
Glynn, Edward F., Jr. *lawyer*
Goelzer, Daniel Lee *lawyer*
Goewey, David W. *lawyer*
Gold, Peter Frederick *lawyer*
Goldberg, Fred T., Jr. *lawyer*
Goldberg, Jolande Elisabeth *law librarian, lawyer*
Goldberg, Seth A. *lawyer*
Goldblatt, Steven Harris *law educator*
Golden, Cornelius Joseph, Jr. *lawyer*
Goldman, Steven Mark *lawyer*
Goldsmith, Barry Richard *lawyer, former federal agency administrator*
Goldsmith, Willis Jay *lawyer*
Goldstein, Frank Robert *lawyer*
Goldstein, Michael B. *lawyer*
Goldstein, Thomas C. *lawyer*
Gollin, Michael A. *lawyer*
Gorelick, Jamie Shona *lawyer*
Gorman, Joyce J(ohanna) *lawyer*
Gorrell, J. Warren, Jr. *lawyer*
Goshorn, Richard Henley *lawyer*
Gostin, Lawrence O. *lawyer, educator*
Gottfried, Keith Evan *lawyer*
Gottlieb, Robert Gene *lawyer*
Graham, Thomas, Jr. *lawyer*
Graham, Thomas Richard *lawyer*
Grainger, Amanda R. *lawyer*
Green, Donald Hugh *lawyer*
Green, Douglas G. *lawyer*
Green, Richard C. *lawyer*
Green, Thomas Charles *lawyer*
Greenberger, I. Michael *lawyer*
Greenwald, John Doyle *lawyer*
Grenier, Edward Joseph, Jr. *lawyer*
Griffis, Kirby T. *lawyer*
Griner, G. Christopher *lawyer*
Gross, Kenneth Andrew *lawyer*
Grunberg, Nancy R. *lawyer*
Gulland, Eugene D. *lawyer*
Gurdak, Michael P. *lawyer*
Gutierrez, Jay Matthew *lawyer*
Guttman, Egon *law educator*
Haber, Jonathan H. *lawyer*
Hagner, John D. *lawyer*
Hailey, Gary D. *lawyer*
Haines, Martha Mahan *lawyer*
Halvorson, Newman Thorbus, Jr. *lawyer*
Hampton, Philip G., II, *lawyer*
Hand, Lloyd N. *lawyer*
Hanlon, Stephen F. *lawyer*
Hanlon, William R. *lawyer*
Hansen, Kenneth *lawyer*
Hanzlik, Rayburn DeMara *lawyer*
Harman, William Boys, Jr. *lawyer*
Harrington, Anthony Stephen *lawyer, diplomat, business executive*
Harrington, Clifford M. *lawyer*
Harris, Don Victor, Jr. *lawyer*
Harris, Jeffrey *lawyer*
Harris, Scott Blake *lawyer*
Harrison, Earl David *lawyer, real estate company officer*
Harrison, Marion Edwyn *lawyer*
Harrison, Mark B. *lawyer*
Harrison, Todd A. *lawyer*
Hart, Christopher Alvin *lawyer*
Harvey, Sheila McCafferty *lawyer*
Harwood, John H., II, *lawyer*
Hassett, Joseph Mark *lawyer*
Hastings, Douglas Alfred *lawyer*
Hauptman, Gregory B. *lawyer*
Hauser, Richard Alan *lawyer, foundation administrator*
Hausfeld, Michael D. *lawyer*
Hayes, David John *lawyer*
Hayes, John C., Jr. *lawyer*
Haynes, R. Michael *lawyer*
Haynes, William James, II, *lawyer*
Haythe, Winston McDonald *lawyer, educator, real estate investor*
Hebert, Jay Howell *lawyer*
Heckman, Jerome Harold *lawyer*
Heenan, Michael Terence *lawyer*
Heffernan, James Vincent *lawyer*
Hefferon, Thomas Michael *lawyer*
Hefter, Laurence Roy *lawyer*
Heideman, Richard D. *lawyer*
Heimberg, Scott M. *lawyer*
Heintz, John Edward *lawyer*
Heller, Jack Isaac *lawyer*
Heller, John Roderick III *lawyer, corporate financial executive*
Heller, Mark A. *lawyer*
Henderson, Douglas Boyd *lawyer*
Henderson, Frances J. *lawyer*
Henke, Michael John *lawyer, educator*
Hennessy, Ellen Anne *lawyer, financial analyst, educator*
Henry, Ronald Kenneth *lawyer*
Hensler, David J. *lawyer*
Herlihy, Scott C. *lawyer*
Herrling, Christopher J. *lawyer*

Herzstein, Robert Erwin *lawyer*
Hewitt, Paul Buck *lawyer*
Heymsfeld, David Alan *lawyer*
Heyward, Peter E. *lawyer*
Hiatt, Jonathan Paul *lawyer, labor union administrator*
Higgins, Claudia R. *lawyer*
Higuchi, Shirley A. *lawyer*
Hills, Carla Anderson *lawyer, former secretary of housing and urban development*
Hills, Roderick M. *lawyer, former government official*
Hirschhorn, Eric Leonard *lawyer*
Hittner, George J. *lawyer*
Hobbs, Ann S. *lawyer*
Hobbs, Caswell O. III *lawyer*
Hoffinger, Adam Steven *lawyer*
Hoffman, E. Leslie *lawyer*
Hoffman, Joel Elihu *lawyer*
Hoffman, Kenneth R. *lawyer*
Holder, Eric H. *lawyer, former federal agency administrator*
Hollingsworth, Joe Gregory *lawyer*
Hollis, Sheila Slocum *lawyer*
Hopson, Mark D. *lawyer*
Horahan, Edward Bernard III *lawyer*
Horn, Charles M. *lawyer*
Horn, Donald Herbert *lawyer*
Horne, Michael Stewart *lawyer*
Hornyak, Joseph P. *lawyer*
Horowitz, Philip Martin *lawyer*
Horton, Philip W. *lawyer*
House, W(illiam) Michael *lawyer*
Howard, Jeffrey Hjalmar *lawyer*
Howard, Roscoe Conklin, Jr. *lawyer, former prosecutor*
Hubbard, Richard L. *lawyer*
Huberman, Richard Lee *lawyer*
Hudgins, Willie L., Jr. *lawyer*
Huge, Harry *lawyer*
Hughes, Elizabeth R. (Beth) *lawyer*
Hughes, Marija Matich *law librarian*
Hulkower, Mark J. *lawyer*
Hunnicutt, Charles Alvin *lawyer*
Hut, A. Stephen *lawyer*
Hutchinson, Asa (W. Asa Hutchinson) *lawyer, former federal agency administrator*
Hutchinson, James S. (Jamie) *lawyer*
Hutt, Peter Barton *lawyer*
Huttler, Stephen B. *lawyer*
Hyatt, Thomas Karl *lawyer*
Hyman, Lester Samuel *lawyer*
Ireland, Oliver *lawyer*
Irving, Thomas L. *lawyer*
Isbell, David Bradford *lawyer, educator*
Jackson, John Howard *lawyer, educator*
Jacobsen, Raymond Alfred, Jr. *lawyer*
Jacobson, David Edward *lawyer*
Jacobson, Richard Lee *lawyer, educator*
Jakes, J. Michael *lawyer*
Jamar, Steven Dwight *law educator*
Jankowsky, Joel *lawyer*
Janney, Christopher G. *lawyer*
Jatras, James George *lawyer*
Jeffress, William Horace, Jr. *lawyer*
Jenkins, Thomas H. *lawyer*
Jennings, Deborah E. *lawyer*
Jensen, Mark A. *lawyer*
Jensen, Thomas C. *lawyer*
Jochum, James J. *lawyer, former federal agency administrator*
Johnson, David Raymond *lawyer*
Johnson, Philip McBride *lawyer*
Johnson, Richard A. *lawyer*
Jolly, Bruce O. *lawyer*
Jonas, John Francis *lawyer*
Jones, Aidan Drexel *lawyer*
Jones, George Washington, Jr. *lawyer*
Jones, Kelsey A. *lawyer, educator*
Jones, Michael D. *lawyer*
Jordan, Robert Elijah III *lawyer*
Journey, Drexel Dahlke *lawyer*
Joyce, Frederick Mark (Rick) *lawyer*
Kabel, Robert James *lawyer*
Kafka, Gerald Andrew *lawyer*
Kahan, Jonathan Seth *lawyer*
Kahn, Edwin Leonard *lawyer*
Kail, Floyd Michael *lawyer*
Kaplan, Gilbert B. *lawyer*
Kaplan, Paul A. *lawyer*
Kaplan, Steven *lawyer*
Kaplun, Paul I. *lawyer*
Kapp, Robert Harris *lawyer*
Kappler, Ann M. *lawyer, finance company executive*
Kass, Benny Lee *lawyer*
Kassinger, Theodore William (Ted R. Kassinger) *lawyer, former federal agency administrator*
Katyal, Neal K. *law educator*
Katz, John W. *lawyer, state official*
Katz, Sherman E. *lawyer*
Katzen, Sally *lawyer, educator*
Kaufman, Joshua Jacob *lawyer*
Kaufman, Thomas Frederick *lawyer, educator*
Keeney, John Christopher *lawyer*
Keeney, John Christopher, Jr. *lawyer*
Keiner, R(obert) Bruce, Jr. *lawyer*
Keitelman, Jeffrey Robert *lawyer*
Kelly, David M. *lawyer*
Kelly, Thomas J., Jr. *lawyer*
Kelly, William Charles, Jr. *retired lawyer*
Kendall, David E. *lawyer*
Kennard, Mary Elizabeth *lawyer*
Kenney, Robert James, Jr. *lawyer*
Kerr, Stuart H. *lawyer, think-tank executive*
Kessler, Judd Lewis *lawyer*
Kies, Kenneth J. *lawyer*
Kiko, Colleen Duffy *lawyer*
Kiko, Philip George *lawyer*
Kilberg, William Jeffrey *lawyer, director*
Killefer, Campbell *lawyer*
Kim, Sukhan *lawyer*
Kinberg, Robert *lawyer*
King, Patricia Ann *law educator*
Kingham, Richard Frank *lawyer*
Kirk, Dennis Dean *lawyer*
Kirsch, Laurence Stephen *lawyer*
Kiser, Chérie R. *lawyer*
Kissel, Peter Charles *lawyer*
Kittrell, Steven Dan *lawyer*
Kittrie, Nicholas *international lawyer, writer*

Klain, Ronald Alan *lawyer*
Klarfeld, Peter James *lawyer*
Klawiter, Donald Casimir *lawyer*
Klee, Ann Renee *lawyer*
Klein, Michael Roger *lawyer, foundation administrator*
Kline, Thomas R. *lawyer*
Knapp, Rosalind Ann *lawyer*
Knauer, Leon Thomas *lawyer*
Knowles, Jeffrey D. *lawyer*
Koch, George William *lawyer*
Koch, Kathleen Day *lawyer*
Kolasky, William Joseph, Jr. *lawyer*
Korth, Fritz-Alan *lawyer*
Kovacic-Fleischer, Candace Saari *law educator*
Kracov, Daniel A. *lawyer*
Kramer, Andrew Michael *lawyer*
Kramer, William David *lawyer*
Krasnow, Erwin Gilbert *lawyer*
Kriesberg, Simeon M. *lawyer*
Kroener, William Frederick III *lawyer, lawyer*
Krump, Gary Joseph *lawyer, judge*
Kurz, Raymond A. *lawyer*
Kurzweil, Jeffrey *lawyer*
Kushner, Gary Jay *lawyer*
Kutler, Alison L. *lawyer*
Kutz, Alexandra Ellen *prosecutor*
Lackey, Michael E., Jr. *lawyer, educator*
Lake, William Truman *lawyer*
Lambert, Jeremiah Daniel *lawyer, educator*
Lambert, Steven Charles *lawyer*
Lamm, Carolyn Beth *lawyer*
Landry, Brock R. *lawyer*
Lane, Bruce Stuart *lawyer*
Lane, John Dennis *lawyer*
Langdon, James Calhoun, Jr. *lawyer*
Laporte, Gerald Joseph Sylvestre *lawyer*
Lardent, Esther Ferster *lawyer, consultant*
Larroca, Raymond G. *lawyer*
Larson, Philip C. *lawyer*
Latham, Patricia Horan *lawyer*
Latham, Peter Samuel *lawyer*
Latham, Weldon Hurd *lawyer*
Latimer, Allie B. *retired lawyer*
Latimer, Katharine Ruth *lawyer*
Laughlin, Felix B. *lawyer*
Laughlin, Gregory H. (Greg Laughlin) *lawyer, former congressman*
Laughlin, James Harold, Jr. *lawyer*
Lavelle, Joseph P. *lawyer*
Lavine, Henry Wolfe *lawyer*
Lawler, William E. III *lawyer*
Lazarus, Arthur, Jr. *lawyer*
Lazarus, Kenneth Anthony *lawyer*
Lee, Edward *lawyer*
Lee, Ronald Derek *lawyer*
Leeds, Henry West *lawyer*
Leibold, Arthur William, Jr. *lawyer*
Leipold, James G. *lawyer*
Lemov, Michael R. *lawyer*
Leo, Leonard A. *legal association administrator, lawyer*
Lessenco, Gilbert Barry *lawyer*
Lever, Jack Q., Jr. *lawyer*
Levin, Edward M. *lawyer*
Levin, Edward Ross *lawyer*
Levine, Henry David *lawyer*
Levinson, Lawrence Edward *lawyer*
Levinstein, Mark Steven *lawyer, educator*
Levy, Gregg H. *lawyer*
Levy, Mark Irving *lawyer*
Lewis, Daniel Martin *lawyer*
Lewis, David John *lawyer*
Lewis, Eleanor Roberts *lawyer*
Lewis, Guy A. *prosecutor*
Lewis, Mark K. *lawyer*
Lewis, William Henry, Jr. *lawyer*
Lewris, Basil J. *lawyer*
Lichtenbaum, Peter *lawyer, former federal agency administrator*
Lichtenstein, Elissa Charlene *legal association executive*
Liebeskind, Richard *lawyer*
Liebman, Ronald Stanley *lawyer*
Lifschitz, Judah *lawyer*
Lightfoot, William P., Jr. *lawyer*
Lighthizer, Robert E. *lawyer*
Lindsey, Seth Mark *lawyer*
Liss, Jeffrey Fred *lawyer, educator*
Litt, Robert S. *lawyer*
Livingston, Bob (Robert Linlithgow Livingston Jr.) *lawyer, retired congressman*
Livingston, Donald Ray *lawyer*
Locklear, Arlinda Faye *lawyer*
Loeb, G. Hamilton *lawyer*
Loepere, Carol Colborn *lawyer*
Loots, James Mason *lawyer*
Lopatin, Alan G. *lawyer*
Lowe, Randall B. *lawyer*
Lowell, Abbe David *lawyer*
Lowther, Frederick M. *lawyer*
Lubic, Robert Bennett *law educator*
Lupo, Raphael V. *lawyer*
Luque, Nancy *lawyer*
Lurensky, Marcia Adele *lawyer*
Luskin, Robert David *lawyer*
Lybecker, Martin Earl *lawyer*
Lyons, Dennis Gerald *lawyer*
Lyons, Francis Xavier *lawyer*
Lyons, Mona *lawyer*
MacBeth, Angus *lawyer*
Macdonald, David Robert *lawyer, pension fund administrator*
Macleod, John Amend *lawyer*
Madden, Murdaugh Stuart *lawyer*
Madden, Thomas James *lawyer, educator*
Magielnicki, Robert L. *lawyer*
Mahinka, Stephen Paul *lawyer*
Majev, Howard Rudolph *lawyer*
Malinowski, Matthew J. *lawyer*
Mallory, Charles King III *lawyer*
Manatt, Charles Taylor *lawyer*
Mandel, Michael S. *lawyer*
Manning, Michael J. *lawyer*
Manson, Joseph Lloyd III *lawyer*
Marchant, Byron *lawyer*
Marcuss, Stanley Joseph *lawyer*
Margeton, Stephen George *law librarian*
Marinaccio, Charles Lindbergh *lawyer, consultant*
Markoski, Joseph Peter *lawyer*
Marks, Herbert Edward *lawyer*

Marks, Richard Daniel *lawyer*
Martin, David Briton Hadden, Jr. *lawyer*
Martin, Guy *lawyer*
Martin, John Charles *lawyer*
Martin, Kate Abbott *lawyer*
Martin, Keith *lawyer*
Martin, Thomas Stephen *lawyer*
Marvin, Charles Rodney, Jr. *lawyer*
Mathis, John Prentiss *lawyer*
May, Timothy James *lawyer*
Mayers, Daniel Kriegsman *lawyer*
Mayo, George Washington, Jr. *lawyer*
Mays, Janice Ann *lawyer*
Mazo, Mark Elliott *lawyer*
McBride, Michael Flynn *lawyer*
McCabe, Edward Aeneas *lawyer*
McCann, Clifton Everett *lawyer*
McClure, Frederick Donald *lawyer*
McClure, William Pendleton *lawyer*
McConnell, Nicholas Stillwell *lawyer*
McCormack, Douglas P. *lawyer*
McDaniels, William E. *lawyer*
McDavid, Janet Louise *lawyer*
McDiarmid, Robert Campbell *lawyer*
McDowell, Heather L. *lawyer*
McElveen, Junius Carlisle, Jr. *lawyer*
McGovern, Michael *lawyer*
McGrath, Kathryn Bradley *lawyer*
McGuan, Kathleen H. *lawyer*
McGuirl, Marlene Dana Callis *law librarian, educator*
McHugh, James Lenahan, Jr. *lawyer*
McIsaac, Christopher C. *lawyer*
McKeever, Joseph Francis III *lawyer*
McLean, R. Bruce *lawyer*
McLucas, William Robert *lawyer, former federal agency administrator*
McMahon, Joseph Einar *lawyer, consultant*
McNamara, Michael T. *lawyer*
Mc Phee, Henry Roemer *lawyer*
Mc Pherson, Harry Cummings, Jr. *lawyer*
Mead, Christopher *lawyer*
Mead, Kenneth Minor *lawyer, former federal agency administrator*
Means, Thomas Cornell *lawyer*
Meese, Edwin III *law and public policy educator, former United States attorney general*
Melamed, Arthur Douglas *lawyer*
Meloy, Sybil Piskur *retired lawyer*
Memmott, Scott A. *lawyer*
Menaker, Frank H., Jr. *lawyer*
Mendelsohn, Bruce S. *lawyer*
Mendoza, Julie C. *lawyer*
Menkel-Meadow, Carrie Joan *law educator*
Meshulam, Deborah R. *lawyer*
Meyer, Dennis Irwin *lawyer*
Meyer, Katherine Anne *lawyer*
Meyer, Lindsay Beardsworth *lawyer*
Michaelson, Martin *lawyer*
Mickey, Paul F(ogle), Jr. *lawyer*
Migdal, Nelson *lawyer*
Milch, Thomas H. *lawyer*
Miles, David Michael *lawyer*
Miles, John Jeffries *lawyer*
Miller, Andrew Pickens *lawyer*
Miller, H. Todd *lawyer*
Miller, James Forrest *lawyer*
Miller, John T., Jr. *lawyer, educator*
Miller, Marshall Lee *lawyer*
Miller, R. Charles *lawyer*
Millian, John C. *lawyer*
Mills, Thomas L. *lawyer*
Milstein, Elliott Steven *lawyer, educator, academic administrator*
Minardi, Ann Segura *lawyer, musician*
Mirengoff, Paul E. *lawyer, political blogger*
Mirkow, Frank J. *lawyer*
Mirvahabi, Farin *lawyer*
Mishkin, Barbara Friedman *lawyer*
Moates, G. Paul (Paul Moates) *lawyer*
Moe, Richard Palmer *lawyer*
Moffitt, William Benjamin *lawyer*
Mogel, William Allen *lawyer*
Moler, Elizabeth Anne *lawyer*
Montedonico, Joseph *lawyer*
Mooney, Marilyn *lawyer*
Moore, Amy Norwood *lawyer*
Moore, Jerry A. III *lawyer*
Moorehead, Donald V. *lawyer*
Moran, Anne E. *lawyer*
Morgan, Daniel Louis *lawyer, educator*
Moring, John Frederick *lawyer*
Morse, M. Howard *lawyer*
Moses, Alfred Henry *lawyer, writer, diplomat*
Mostoff, Allan Samuel *lawyer, consultant*
Moyer, Homer Edward, Jr. *lawyer*
Muckenfuss, Cantwell Faulkner III *lawyer*
Muir, J. Dapray *lawyer*
Muleta, John B. *lawyer*
Mulloy, Patrick Aloysius *lawyer*
Murphy, Betty Southard (Mrs. Cornelius F. Murphy) *lawyer*
Murphy, J. Andrew *lawyer*
Murphy, Joseph Albert, Jr. *lawyer*
Murry, Harold David, Jr. *lawyer*
Mwenda, Kenneth Kaoma *legal association administrator, consultant*
Nace, Barry John *lawyer*
Naeve, Clifford Mike *lawyer*
Nagel, Trevor W. *lawyer*
Nager, Glen D. *lawyer*
Namrow, Eric S. *lawyer*
Navarro, Bruce Charles *lawyer*
Nemeroff, Michael Alan *lawyer*
Nesbitt, La Fonte *lawyer*
Ness, Andrew David *lawyer*
Nethercutt, George Rector, Jr. *lawyer, consultant, former congressman*
Newberry, Edward J. *lawyer*
Newell, Mark E. *lawyer*
Newstead, Jennifer G. *lawyer*
Nickel, Henry V. *lawyer*
Niehuss, John Marvin *lawyer*
Nirenberg, Darryl D. *lawyer*
Nolan, John Edward *lawyer*
Nordhaus, Robert Riggs *lawyer*
Norton, Floyd Ligon, IV, *lawyer*
Norwood, Deborah Anne *law librarian*
Novick, Robert T. *lawyer*
Nuland, Anthony C. J. *lawyer*
Oakley, Robert Louis *law librarian, educator*

Oberdorfer, John L. *lawyer*
O'Brien, Steven D. *lawyer*
Odle, Robert Charles, Jr. *lawyer*
O'Donnell, Patrick Emmett *lawyer*
O'Donnell, Terrence *lawyer*
Olchyk, Samuel *lawyer*
Olender, Jack Harvey *lawyer*
Olmstead, Cecil Jay *lawyer*
Olson, Pamela Faith *lawyer, former federal agency administrator*
Olson, Theodore Bevry *lawyer, former federal agency administrator*
Oman, Ralph *lawyer*
O'Neil, Thomas Francis III *lawyer*
O'Neill, Brian Dennis *lawyer*
O'Neill, John H., Jr. *lawyer*
O'Neill, William Patrick *lawyer*
Onel, Suzan *lawyer*
Oosterhuis, Paul William *lawyer*
Oppenheimer, Franz Martin *lawyer*
Oshinsky, Jerold *lawyer*
Osnos, David Marvin *lawyer, director*
O'Toole, Francis J. *lawyer*
Overman, Dean Lee *lawyer, investor, writer*
Owen, Roberts Bishop *lawyer, arbitrator*
Owen, Stephen Lee *lawyer*
Oyler, Gregory Kenneth *lawyer*
Padgett, Nancy Weeks *law librarian, consultant, lawyer*
Page, Rodney Fred *lawyer*
Painter, William Hall *law educator*
Palmer, Christopher E. *lawyer*
Pantaleo, Peter S. *lawyer*
Pape, Stuart M. *lawyer*
Paper, Lewis J. *lawyer, educator*
Park, Jin-Suk *lawyer*
Parker, Rich *lawyer*
Passaic, Joseph G. *lawyer*
Pate, Michael Lynn *lawyer*
Patton, Thomas Earl *lawyer*
Paul, John Charles *lawyer*
Paul, William McCann *lawyer*
Pavlick, John J., Jr. *lawyer*
Payton, John *lawyer*
Pearlman, Ronald Alan *lawyer, educator*
Pearson, Rebecca E. *lawyer*
Peck, Robert Stephen *lawyer, educator*
Pedersen, William Francis *lawyer*
Pell, Terence J. *legal association administrator*
Pemberton, Alan A. *lawyer*
Pensabene, Judith K. *lawyer*
Perkins, Nancy Leeds *lawyer*
Perlman, Matthew Saul *lawyer*
Perlstein, William James *lawyer*
Peters, Frederick Whitten *lawyer*
Peterson, Charles Hayes *lawyer*
Petrash, Jeffrey Michael *lawyer*
Petruzzelli, Julie A. *lawyer*
Pfeiffer, Margaret Kolodny *lawyer*
Pfeiffer, Steven Bernard *lawyer*
Phillips, Carter Glasgow *lawyer*
Phillips, John R. *lawyer*
Pickens, Scott E. *lawyer*
Pierson, Stuart F. *lawyer*
Piorkowski, Joseph D., Jr. *lawyer, physician, educator, military officer*
Pittman, Lisa *lawyer*
Pitts, James T. *lawyer*
Plaine, Daniel J. *lawyer*
Plaine, Lloyd Leva *lawyer*
Plave, Lee Jonathan *lawyer*
Plotkin, Mark Elliott *lawyer*
Podberesky, Samuel *lawyer*
Podesta, John David *law educator, former White House chief of staff*
Poe, David Russell *lawyer*
Polon, Ira H. *lawyer*
Poneman, Daniel Bruce *lawyer*
Popofsky, Mark S. *lawyer*
Portnoy, Elliott Ivan *lawyer*
Postol, Lawrence Philip *lawyer*
Potenza, Joseph Michael *lawyer*
Potter, Caryl A. III *lawyer*
Potts, Stephen Deaderick *lawyer*
Povich, David *lawyer*
Powers, Mary Ellen *lawyer*
Powers, Richard Edward, Jr. *lawyer*
Pozen, Sharis Arnold *lawyer*
Preston, Richard McKim *lawyer*
Preston, Stephen W. *lawyer*
Prettyman, Elijah Barrett, Jr. *lawyer*
Prezioso, Giovanni P. *lawyer*
Price, Daniel Martin *lawyer*
Price, Griffith Baley, Jr. *lawyer*
Price, Joseph Hubbard *lawyer*
Pritchard, Therese D. *lawyer*
Proger, Phillip A. *lawyer*
Przypyszny, John R. *lawyer*
Pupkin, Barry A. *lawyer*
Pusey, William Anderson *lawyer*
Quale, John Carter *lawyer*
Quarterman, Cynthia Louise *lawyer*
Quigley, Michael *lawyer*
Quigley, Thomas J. *lawyer, director*
Quinn, Kenneth Phillip *lawyer*
Quinn, Thomas H. *lawyer*
Quint, Arnold Harris *lawyer*
Rabinovitz, Bruce H. *lawyer*
Racine, Karl A. *lawyer*
Racine, Richard B. *lawyer*
Raher, Patrick Michael *lawyer*
Raim, David Matthew *lawyer*
Raimi, Burton Louis *lawyer*
Raimo, Bernard (Bernie Raimo) *lawyer*
Ramey, Carl Robert *lawyer*
Ramirez, Ted L. *lawyer*
Rauh, Carl Stephen *lawyer*
Raul, Alan Charles *lawyer*
Reade, Claire Elizabeth *lawyer*
Reeder, Joe Robert *lawyer, former federal official*
Rehnquist, Janet *lawyer, former federal agency administrator*
Reichertz, Peter Stuart *lawyer*
Reichs, Kerry E. *lawyer*
Reid, Inez Smith *lawyer, educator, judge*
Rein, Bert Walter *lawyer*
Reynolds, Nicholas S. *lawyer*
Rice, Paul Jackson *lawyer, educator*
Rich, John Townsend *lawyer*
Richards, Femi Soyinka *lawyer*
Richards, Suzanne V. *lawyer*

Richmond, David Walker *retired lawyer*
Richmond, Marilyn Susan *lawyer*
Rickard, Lisa Ann *lawyer*
Rickert, Anthony H. *lawyer*
Rill, James Franklin *lawyer*
Ring, Carlyle C. *lawyer*
Rissetto, Harry A. *lawyer*
Rizzi, Robert A. *lawyer*
Robbins, Robert B. *lawyer*
Roberts, James Harold III *lawyer*
Roberts, Michael G. *lawyer*
Roberts, Michele A. *lawyer*
Rochon, Mark *lawyer*
Rockefeller, Edwin Shaffer *lawyer*
Rocque, Vincent Joseph *lawyer*
Rodemeyer, Michael Leonard, Jr. *lawyer*
Rogan, Michael P. *lawyer*
Rogers, William Dill *lawyer*
Rogovin, John A. *lawyer*
Rohner, Ralph John *lawyer, educator, dean*
Rohrbach, Peter Alpaugh *lawyer*
Roll, David Lee *lawyer*
Romanow, Josh *lawyer*
Romeo, Peter John *lawyer*
Rose, Jonathan Chapman *lawyer*
Rosen, Jeffrey Adam *lawyer, federal agency administrator*
Rosenblatt, Peter Ronald *lawyer, former ambassador*
Rosenbloom, David Harry *political science and law educator*
Rosenbloom, H(arry) David *lawyer*
Rosenhauer, James Joseph (Jim Rosenhauer) *lawyer*
Rosenkrantz, Steven Jay *lawyer*
Rosenthal, Douglas Eurico *lawyer*
Rosenthal, Steven Siegmund *lawyer*
Rosman, Michael E. *lawyer*
Ross, Douglas *lawyer*
Ross, Stanford G. *lawyer, government official*
Ross, Terence P. *lawyer*
Rossides, Eugene Telemachus *lawyer, writer*
Rothenberg, Pamela V. *lawyer*
Rothstein, Paul Frederick *lawyer, educator*
Rouvelas, Emanuel Larry *lawyer*
Rowden, Marcus Aubrey *lawyer, retired government agency administrator*
Rowe, Richard Holmes *lawyer*
Roycroft, Howard Francis *lawyer*
Rubel, Eric A. *lawyer*
Rubin, Kenneth Allen *lawyer*
Ruddy, Frank *lawyer, retired ambassador*
Rule, Charles Frederick (Rick Rule) *lawyer*
Russell, Michael James *lawyer*
Russin, Jonathan *lawyer, consultant*
Ruthenberg, Kirk R. *lawyer*
Rutstein, David W. *lawyer, food products executive*
Ruttenberg, Charles Byron *lawyer*
Ruttinger, George David *lawyer*
Ryerson, Paul Sommer *lawyer*
Sacher, Steven Jay *lawyer*
Salem, George Richard *lawyer*
Salsbury, Michael H. *lawyer*
Saltzburg, Stephen Allan *law educator, consultant*
Samuelson, Kenneth Lee *lawyer*
Sandman, James Joseph *lawyer*
Sanford, Bruce William *lawyer*
Santos, Leonard Ernest *lawyer*
Sartori, Michael A. *lawyer*
Satterthwaite, Janet F. *lawyer*
Saunders, Mary Jane *lawyer*
Sayler, Robert Nelson *lawyer, educator*
Scanlon, Kerry Alan *lawyer*
Schiff, Janis Boyarsky *lawyer*
Schiffer, Lois Jane *lawyer*
Schill, Charles F. *lawyer*
Schiller, Jonathan David *lawyer*
Schmeltzer, Edward *lawyer*
Schmidt, William Arthur, Jr. *lawyer*
Schneider, Lawrence Alan *lawyer*
Schneider, Matthew Roger *lawyer*
Scheller, Marina Velentgas *lawyer*
Schnitzer, Steven C. *lawyer*
Schwaab, Richard Lewis *lawyer*
Schwalb, Brian L. *lawyer*
Schwartz, Daniel C. *lawyer*
Schwartz, Victor Elliot *lawyer, educator*
Schwartzman, Andrew Jay *lawyer*
Schwebel, Stephen Myron *arbitrator, mediator, legal advisor*
Schwinger, David *lawyer*
Scott, Thomas Jefferson, Jr. *lawyer, electrical engineer*
Scully, Thomas A. *lawyer, former federal agency administrator*
Seale, Ronald Armbrust *lawyer*
Sears, John Patrick *lawyer*
Sears, Mary Helen *lawyer*
Sega, A. Christopher *lawyer*
Segal, Theodore D. *lawyer*
Segall, Wynn H. *lawyer*
Senger, Jeffrey M. *lawyer*
Sessions, William Steele *lawyer, former FBI director*
Shaffer, David James *lawyer*
Shapiro, Howard M *lawyer, former prosecutor*
Sharma, Tina *lawyer*
Shay, Albert W. *lawyer*
Shelley, Herbert Carl *lawyer*
Sherer, Samuel Ayers *lawyer, urban planner, consultant*
Sherman, Gerald Howard *lawyer, educator*
Sherman, Jonathan Henry *lawyer*
Sherzer, Harvey Gerald *lawyer*
Shrinsky, Jason Lee *lawyer*
Shull, Joe A. *lawyer*
Shulman, Stephen Neal *lawyer*
Shumaker, Gregory M. *lawyer*
Siegel, David B. *lawyer*
Siegel, Richard David *lawyer, former government official*
Siekman, Thomas Clement *lawyer*
Sikora, Clifford S. *lawyer*
Silberg, Jay Eliot *lawyer*
Silbert, Earl J. *lawyer*
Silver, Harry R. *lawyer*
Silverman, William A. *lawyer*
Silverstein, Martin J. *lawyer, former ambassador*
Simon, Gregory *lawyer*
Simon, Karla W. *law educator*
Simon, Kenneth Mark *lawyer*

Simons, Lawrence Brook *lawyer*
Simpson, John M. *lawyer*
Sims, Joe *lawyer*
Sinel, Norman Mark *lawyer*
Singer, Daniel Morris *lawyer*
Singer, Richard M. *lawyer*
Singleton, Harry Michael *lawyer*
Sinick, Marshall S. *lawyer*
Sjoblom, Thomas V. *lawyer*
Skall, Gregg P. *lawyer*
Skancke, Nancy J. *lawyer*
Slater, Rodney E. *lawyer, emergency management executive, former secretary of transportation*
Slater, Valerie A. *lawyer*
Slaughter, Kenneth S. *lawyer*
Slocombe, Walter Becker *lawyer, former federal agency administrator*
Smith, Brian William *lawyer, former government official*
Smith, Christopher (Kit Smith) *lawyer*
Smith, Daniel Clifford *lawyer*
Smith, Dwight Chichester III *lawyer*
Smith, Herbert G., II, *lawyer*
Smith, Jack David *lawyer*
Smith, Jeffrey Hartman *lawyer*
Smith, Michael (Carl Michael Smith) *lawyer, former federal agency administrator*
Smith, Russell Louis *lawyer*
Smith, Tefft Weldon *lawyer*
Smith, Turner Taliaferro, Jr. *lawyer*
Smyth, Paul Burton *lawyer*
Snyder, Allen Roger *lawyer*
Sohn, Michael N *lawyer*
Sokal, Allen Marcel *lawyer*
Sokler, Bruce Douglas *lawyer*
Solano, Henry L. *lawyer*
Sollers, Joseph Sedwick III *lawyer*
Solodky, Howard N. *lawyer*
Solomons, Mark Elliott *lawyer, art dealer, entrepreneur*
Sommers, Mark *lawyer*
Sonde, Theodore Irwin *lawyer*
Sophir, Eric L. *lawyer*
Sorokowski, Andrew Dennis *lawyer, researcher*
Spaeder, Roger Campbell *lawyer*
Spears, James M(it) *lawyer*
Spector, Phillip Louis *lawyer*
Spencer, George Henry *lawyer*
Spiegel, Daniel Leonard *lawyer*
Spiliotes, Nicholas James *lawyer*
Spivak, Mark R. *lawyer*
Spiwak, Lawrence J. *legal association administrator*
Sprague, Mary Gabrielle *lawyer*
Stack, Robert B. *lawyer*
Stanfield, Jeffrey L. *lawyer*
Starr, Judson Wilmarth *lawyer*
Stayin, Randolph John *lawyer*
Steer, John Richard *lawyer*
Stein, Daniel Alan *lawyer*
Steinberg, Andrew B. *lawyer*
Steinwurtzel, Richard A. *lawyer*
Stephens, Theodore Reed *lawyer*
Stern, Elizabeth Espin *lawyer*
Stern, Gerald Mann *lawyer*
Stern, Samuel Alan *lawyer*
Sterrett, Samuel Black *lawyer, former judge*
Stevens, Herbert Francis *lawyer, educator*
Stevens, Paul Schott *lawyer*
Stewart, David Pentland *lawyer, educator*
Stock, Stuart Chase *lawyer*
Stoll, Richard Giles *lawyer*
Stouck, Jerry *lawyer*
Strand, Margaret N. *lawyer*
Strauss, Robert Schwarz *lawyer, retired ambassador*
Strauss, Stanley Robert *lawyer*
Stromberg, Clifford Douglas *lawyer*
Stromberg, Jean Wilbur Gleason *lawyer*
Stroup, Richard L. *lawyer*
Stucky, Scott Wallace *lawyer*
Stumpf, Mark Howard *lawyer*
Sullivan, Brendan V., Jr. *lawyer*
Sullivan, John J. *lawyer*
Sullivan, Mary Anne *lawyer, government agency administrator*
Sullivan, Timothy *lawyer*
Sundermeyer, Michael S. *lawyer*
Sussman, Monica Hilton *lawyer*
Sutherland, Daniel W. *lawyer*
Swankin, David Arnold *lawyer, consumer products company executive*
Swendiman, Alan Robert *lawyer*
Taft, William Howard, IV, *lawyer*
Tallent, Stephen Edison *lawyer*
Tannenwald, Peter *lawyer*
Tannon, Jay Middleton *lawyer*
Taronji, Jaime, Jr. *lawyer*
Tauber, Mark J. *lawyer*
Taurman, John David *lawyer*
Taylor, James, Jr. *lawyer*
Taylor, Nancy Elizabeth *lawyer*
Taylor, Ralph Arthur, Jr. *lawyer*
Taylor, William Woodruff III *lawyer*
Teague, Randal Cornell, Sr. *lawyer*
Teal, Gilbert Earle, II, *lawyer, coast guard officer*
Teichler, Stephen Lin *lawyer*
Temko, Stanley Leonard *lawyer*
Tendler, Paul Marc *lawyer*
Tenenbaum, Jeffrey S. *lawyer*
Thomas, Ritchie Tucker *lawyer*
Thomas, Scott E. *lawyer, former commissioner*
Thompson, Tommy (Thomas George Thompson) *lawyer, former secretary of health and human services*
Thornburgh, Dick (Richard L. Thornburgh) *lawyer, former United States attorney general*
Thornton, D. McCarty (Mac Thornton) *lawyer*
Tiedemann, Charles Welch (Chad Tiedemann) *lawyer*
Tigar, Michael Edward *law educator*
Tillman, Eugene *lawyer*
Todaro, Peter M. *lawyer*
Tompkins, Joseph Buford, Jr. *lawyer*
Topelius, Kathleen Ellis *lawyer*
Torgerson, William T. *lawyer, electric power industry executive*
Townsend, Brian Douglas *paralegal*
Townsend, John Michael *lawyer*
Trager, Michael David *lawyer*
Trooboff, Peter Dennis *lawyer*

Troyer, Thomas Alfred *lawyer*
Tsacoumis, Stephanie *lawyer*
Tuohey, Mark Henry III *lawyer*
Turner, Jim (James W. Turner) *lawyer, former congressman*
Tyle, Craig S. *lawyer, investment company executive*
Tyler, Peggy Lynne Bailey *lawyer*
Tyner, Lee Reichelderfer *lawyer*
Uehlein, Edward Carl, Jr. *lawyer*
Unger, Laura Simone *lawyer, commissioner*
Urwitz, Jay P. *lawyer*
Vacketta, Carl Lee *lawyer, educator*
Vakerics, Thomas Vincent *lawyer*
Valentine, Steven Richards *lawyer*
Vanderver, Timothy Arthur, Jr. *lawyer*
Van Horn, Charles E. *lawyer*
Van Tine, Kirk Kelso *lawyer, former federal agency administrator*
Verner, James Melton *lawyer*
Verrill, Charles Owen, Jr. *lawyer*
Verveer, Philip L. *lawyer*
Vickery, Ann Morgan *lawyer*
Victory, Nancy J. *lawyer, former federal agency administrator*
Villa, John Kazar *lawyer*
Villacorta, Ybet *lawyer*
Vince, Clinton Andrew *lawyer*
Vodra, William Wilson *lawyer*
Volner, Ian D. *lawyer*
Voorhees, Theodore, Jr. *lawyer*
Wagner, Martha Jo *lawyer*
Waite, Barbara L. (Pixie) *lawyer*
Wald, Douglas L. *lawyer*
Wald, Robert Lewis *lawyer*
Waldman, Daniel *lawyer*
Waldron, Gerard J. *lawyer*
Walgren, Doug (James R. Walpole) *lawyer, former congressman*
Walker, Mary L. *lawyer*
Wall, Christopher Read *lawyer*
Wallace, Don, Jr. *law educator*
Walpole, Jim (James R. Walpole) *lawyer*
Walsh, Alexandra M. *lawyer*
Walsh, Michael J. *lawyer*
Walter, Sheryl Lynn *lawyer*
Ward, Alan S. *lawyer*
Ward, Erica Anne *lawyer, educator*
Warin, Roger E. *lawyer*
Warren Ellison, Tasheaya L. *tax attorney*
Waters, Jennifer Nash *lawyer*
Watkin, Virginia Guild *retired lawyer*
Waxman, Seth Paul *lawyer*
Webber, Richard John *lawyer*
Webster, William Hedgcock *lawyer, former CIA director*
Wedgwood, Ruth *law educator, international affairs expert*
Wegener, Mark Douglas *lawyer*
Weidenfeld, Edward Lee *lawyer*
Weigel, Kenneth George *lawyer*
Weiner, Kenneth Brian *lawyer*
Weiner, Robert Neil *lawyer*
Weingarten, Reid H. *lawyer*
Weinman, Howard Mark *lawyer*
Weinmann, Eric *retired lawyer*
Weinreich, Gadi *lawyer*
Weinstein, Harris *lawyer*
Weisgall, Jonathan Michael *lawyer*
Weiss, Arnold Hans *lawyer*
Weiss, Mark Anschel *lawyer*
Weiss, Stephen J. *lawyer*
Weissman, William R. *lawyer*
Wellen, Robert Howard *lawyer*
Wenner, Charles Roderick *lawyer*
West, Gail Berry *lawyer*
West, Joseph D. *lawyer*
West, Togo Dennis, Jr. *lawyer, retired cabinet member*
Westbrook, Reeves C. *lawyer*
White, Robert I. *lawyer*
Whiting, Richard Albert *lawyer*
Wiacek, Raymond J. *lawyer*
Wieder, Bruce Terrill *lawyer, electrical engineer*
Wilchins, Howard Martin *lawyer*
Wilder, Roland Percival, Jr. *lawyer*
Wiley, Richard Emerson *lawyer*
Wilkins, Robert L. *lawyer*
Williams, E. Faye *lawyer, political organization executive, health products executive*
Williams, Karen Hastie *lawyer*
Williamson, Edwin Dargan *lawyer, former federal official*
Wilner, Thomas Bernard *lawyer*
Wilson, D. Edward, Jr. *lawyer*
Wilson, Gary Dean *lawyer*
Wilson, Michael Moureau *lawyer, physician*
Wine, L. Mark *lawyer*
Winland, Thomas W. *lawyer*
Winston, Judith Ann *lawyer*
Winter, Douglas E. *lawyer, writer*
Wintrol, John Patrick *lawyer*
Wise, Joan S. *lawyer*
Wiseman, Alan M(itchell) *lawyer*
Wiseman, Thomas G. *lawyer*
Wiss, Marcia A. *lawyer*
Wixon, Henry N. *lawyer*
Wolf, William B., Jr. *lawyer*
Wolff, Alan William *lawyer*
Wolff, Elroy Harris *lawyer*
Wolff, Paul Martin *lawyer, sculptor*
Woodall, Samuel Roy, Jr. *lawyer*
Woodworth, Ramsey Lloyd *lawyer*
Work, Charles Robert *lawyer*
Worsley, James Randolph, Jr. *lawyer*
Worthy, K(enneth) Martin *retired lawyer*
Worthy, Patricia Morris *lawyer, educator*
Wrathall, James R. *lawyer*
Wray, Christopher Asher *lawyer, former federal agency administrator*
Wray, Robert *lawyer*
Wright, James Ralph *lawyer*
Wyatt, Richard L., Jr. *lawyer*
Wyss, John Benedict *lawyer*
Yablon, Jeffery Lee *lawyer*
Yambrusic, Edward Slavko *lawyer, consultant*
Yannucci, Thomas David *lawyer*
Yoches, Edward Robert *lawyer*
Young, Howard J. *lawyer*
Zagaris, Bruce *lawyer*
Zane, Phillip Craig *lawyer*
Zaucha, Jerome J. *lawyer*

Zax, Leonard A. *lawyer*
Zeidman, Philip Fisher *lawyer*
Zentay, John H. *lawyer*
Ziegler, Janice H. *lawyer*
Zimmer, Richard Alan *lawyer, retired congressman*
Zimmerman, Edwin Morton *lawyer*
Zipp, Joel Frederick *lawyer*
Zolandz, Michael E., Jr. *lawyer*
Zotter, Bruce C. *lawyer*
Zuckman, Harvey Lyle *law educator*
Zwillinger, Marc J. *lawyer*

## FLORIDA

### Alachua
Gaines, Weaver Henderson *lawyer*

### Altamonte Springs
Heindl, Phares Matthews *lawyer*
Nanton, Nicholas David *lawyer*

### Anna Maria
Hoffmann, Carl Konrad *lawyer*

### Aventura
McKenna, Peter Dennis *lawyer*

### Bascom
Brooten, Kenneth Edward, Jr. *lawyer, writer, researcher*

### Boca Raton
Anise, Nader *lawyer*
Arent, Albert Ezra *retired lawyer*
Beber, Robert H. *lawyer, diversified financial services company executive*
Buckstein, Mark Aaron *lawyer, educator, mediator*
Cowen, Edward S. *lawyer, consultant*
Fier, Elihu *lawyer, educator*
Godofsky, Stanley *lawyer*
Gracin, Hank *lawyer*
Hermann, Philip J. *lawyer*
Kassner, Herbert Seymore *lawyer*
Kitzes, William Fredric *lawyer, advocate, researcher*
Koch, Robert Charles *lawyer, community activist*
Martin, James Russell *lawyer*
McNair, Russell Arthur, Jr. *lawyer*
Reinstein, Joel *lawyer*
Roselli, Richard Joseph *lawyer*
Wallach, Steven Ernst *lawyer, pilot*
Yaffa, Andrew Bryan *lawyer*

### Bonita Springs
Dignan, Thomas Gregory, Jr. *lawyer*
Hastings, Vivien N. *lawyer*
Nevin, Hugh Williamson, Jr. *lawyer*

### Boynton Beach
Solkoff, Scott M. *lawyer*

### Bradenton
Brenner, Frank *lawyer*
Padgett, Gail Blanchard *lawyer*

### Brandon
Curry, Clifton Conrad, Jr. *lawyer*

### Brooksville
Brown, James Milton *law educator*
Cario, Jeffrey Peter *lawyer*

### Cape Coral
Parrett, Sherman O. *lawyer*

### Celebration
Schroeder, James White *retired lawyer*

### Clearwater
Coleman, Jeffrey Peters *lawyer*
Dougall-Sides, Leslie K. *lawyer*
Hogan, Elwood *lawyer*
Johnson, Timothy Augustin, Jr. *lawyer*
Pope, Fred Wallace, Jr. *lawyer*
Sandefer, G(eorge) Larry *lawyer*
Tragos, George Euripedes *lawyer*
Vetter, David R. *lawyer*
Zschau, Julius James *lawyer*

### Cocoa
Pound, Frank R., Jr. *lawyer*

### Coral Gables
Anthony, Andrew John *lawyer*
Buell, Rodd Russell *lawyer*
Dady, Robert Edward *lawyer*
Hall, Miles Lewis, Jr. *lawyer*
Hirschhorn, Joel *lawyer*
Hoffman, Carl H. *lawyer*
Matthews, Joseph Michael *lawyer*
McGrane, Miles A. III *lawyer*
Moss, Ambler Holmes, Jr. *lawyer, educator, former ambassador*
Sacher, Charles Philip *lawyer*
Touby, Kathleen Anita *lawyer*

### Dade City
Brennan, Thomas Emmett *lawyer*

### Daytona Beach
Harris, Christy Franklin *lawyer*
Neitzke, Eric Karl *lawyer*

### Delray Beach
Fannin, David Cecil *lawyer*
Larry, R. Heath *lawyer, director*
Silberman, Charlotte Schatzberg *retired lawyer, artist*

### Englewood
Clark, Bret Shawn *lawyer*

### Fort Lauderdale
Adams, S. C(hase) *lawyer, writer, radio and television commentator, financial consultant*
Arneson, Margaret Susan *lawyer*
Bogenschutz, J. David *lawyer*
Brogan, Francis B., Jr. *lawyer*

Bronstein, Dina B. *lawyer*
Bunnell, George Eli *lawyer, director*
Bustamante, Nestor *lawyer*
Coleman, Phyllis *law educator*
Dressler, Robert A. *lawyer*
Haliczer, James Solomon *lawyer*
Hargrove, John Russell *lawyer*
Hess, George Franklin, II, *lawyer*
Hester, Julia A. *lawyer*
Hirsch, Jeffrey Allan *lawyer*
Jarvis, Robert Mark *law educator*
Kelly, John Patrick *lawyer*
Kubler, Frank Lawrence *lawyer*
Lataif, Lawrence P. *lawyer*
Leighton, James H. *law educator, department chairman*
Lyons, Bruce M. *lawyer*
Meeks, William Herman III *lawyer*
Morris, Gerald Michael *lawyer, educator*
Moss, Stephen Bruce *lawyer*
Neimark, Cort Alan *lawyer*
Nyce, John Daniel *lawyer*
O'Brien, Patrick T. *lawyer*
Oltman, John Harold *patent lawyer*
Richmond, Gail Levin *law educator*
Rodriguez, Carlos Augusto *lawyer*
Russell, Terrence Joseph *lawyer*
Sanders, Dale R. *lawyer*
Schreiber, Alan Hickman *lawyer*
Sherman, Richard Allen, Sr. *lawyer*
Sullivan, Edward Delano *lawyer, investor*
Tacher, Robert Frederick *lawyer*
Turner, Hugh Joseph, Jr. *lawyer*
Udolf, Bruce Lee *lawyer*

### Fort Myers
Colasurd, Richard Michael *lawyer*
Medvecky, Robert Stephen *lawyer*

### Fort Pierce
Conklin, Howard Lawrence *lawyer*

### Gainesville
Boyes, Patrice Flinchbaugh *lawyer*
Criser, Marshall M. *lawyer, retired academic administrator*
Gordon, Michael Wallace *law educator*
Hiers, Richard Hyde *lawyer, educator, writer*
Israel, Jerold Harvey *law educator*
Maurer, Virginia Gallaher *law educator*
Smith, David Thornton *lawyer, educator*
Van Alstyne, W. Scott, Jr. *lawyer, educator*
Weyrauch, Walter Otto *law educator*

### Haines City
Mc Dougall, Dugald Stewart *retired lawyer*

### Hallandale Beach
Engel, Tala *lawyer*

### Hobe Sound
Markoe, Frank, Jr. *lawyer, health facility administrator*

### Hollywood
Korthals, Candace Durbin *lawyer*
Rogovin, Lawrence H. *lawyer*

### Homestead
Ireland, Patricia *lawyer*

### Jacksonville
Ansbacher, Barry Barnett *lawyer*
Appel, Laurence Bruce *lawyer, retail executive*
Beytagh, Francis X. *law educator*
Boyer, Tyrie Alvis *lawyer*
Bradford, Dana Gibson, II, *lawyer*
Bullock, Bruce Stanley *lawyer*
Callender, John Francis *lawyer*
Cannon, L. Kinder III *lawyer*
Cavendish, Michael Robert *lawyer*
Commander, Charles Edward *lawyer, real estate consultant*
Farmer, Guy Otto, II, *lawyer*
Fawbush, Andrew Jackson *lawyer*
Ferguson, Thomas Crooks *lawyer*
Gabel, George DeSaussure, Jr. *lawyer*
Getman, Willard Etheridge *lawyer, arbitrator, mediator*
Hardesty, W. Marc *lawyer, educator*
Hill, Debra S. *lawyer*
Israel, Kimberly Held *lawyer*
Kelso, Linda Yayoi *lawyer*
Kent, John Bradford *lawyer*
Killea, Michael F. *lawyer*
Lee, Lewis Swift *lawyer*
Legler, Mitchell Wooten *lawyer*
Main, James L. *lawyer*
McBurney, Charles Walker, Jr. *lawyer*
McWilliams, John Lawrence III *lawyer*
Milton, Joseph Payne *lawyer*
Moseley, James Francis *lawyer*
Owen, Dennis P. *lawyer*
Rinaman, James Curtis, Jr. *lawyer*
Schupp, Robert Warren *law educator*
Sheppard, William J. *lawyer*
Skinner, Halcyon E. *lawyer*
Thomas, Archibald Johns III *lawyer*
Weaver, Dianne Jay *lawyer*
White, Edward Alfred *lawyer*

### Jacksonville Beach
Mahorner, James M. *lawyer*

### Jasper
McCormick, John Hoyle *lawyer*

### Juno Beach
Knapp, George M. *lawyer*

### Jupiter
Click, David Forrest *lawyer, investment advisor*

### Key Largo
Mattson, James Stewart *lawyer, environmental scientist, educator*

### Key West
MacDougall, Peter *retired lawyer*

**Lake Mary**
Shanahan, Rebecca M. *lawyer*

**Lake Placid**
Roberts, William B. *lawyer*

**Lake Worth**
Feuer, Bradley Scott *lawyer, physician*

**Lakeland**
Attaway, John A., Jr. *lawyer*
Cooper, James Russell *retired law educator*
Kittleson, Henry Marshall *lawyer*
Koren, Edward Franz *lawyer*
Wendel, John Fredric *lawyer, consultant*

**Lauderdale By The Sea**
Yonkman, Fredrick Albers *lawyer, management consultant*

**Leesburg**
Fechtel, Vincent John *legal administrator*

**Longboat Key**
Freeman, Richard Merrell *retired lawyer*

**Longwood**
Tomasulo, Virginia Merrills *retired lawyer*

**Marco Island**
Kaner, Harvey Sheldon *lawyer*
Kerstetter, Wayne Arthur *law educator*

**Medley**
O'Meara, Vicki A. *lawyer*

**Melbourne**
Ballantyne, Richard Lee *lawyer*
Brown, Seymour R. *lawyer*
Cacciatore, S. Sammy *lawyer*

**Miami**
Acosta, Alex (Rene Alexander Acosta) *prosecutor, former federal agency administrator*
Alvarez, Cesar L. *lawyer*
Anderson, Terence James *law educator*
Aronovitz, Tod *lawyer*
Arsht, Adrienne *lawyer, broadcast executive, bank executive*
Astigarraga, Jose I(gnacio) *lawyer*
Backman, Gerald Stephen *retired lawyer*
Baker, Thomas Eugene *law educator*
Bass, Hilarie *lawyer*
Baumberger, Charles Henry *lawyer*
Berg, Martin David *lawyer*
Berman, Bruce Judson *lawyer*
Black, Roy *lawyer*
Bloom, Mark David *lawyer*
Blumberg, Edward Robert *lawyer*
Brochin, Robert M. *lawyer*
Brown, Lewis Nathan *lawyer*
Brown, Robert Donald *lawyer*
Buell, Edward Rick, II, *lawyer*
Burnett, Henry *lawyer*
Burr, Scott Allen *lawyer*
Campos-Orrego, Nora Patricia *lawyer, consultant*
Casey, Daniel Arthur *lawyer*
Cohen, Jeffrey Michael *lawyer*
Connor, Terence Gregory *lawyer*
Cosgrove, John Francis *lawyer, mayor*
Critchlow, Richard H. *lawyer*
Dienstag, Cynthia Jill *lawyer*
Dunn, Richard M. *lawyer*
England, Arthur Jay, Jr. *lawyer, former state justice*
Epstein, Gary M. *lawyer*
Fatovic, Robert Dean *lawyer, transportation executive*
Ferrell, Milton Morgan, Jr. *lawyer*
Fleit, Martin *lawyer*
Fornaris, Carl A. *lawyer*
Gang, Robert C. *lawyer*
Garrett, Richard G. *lawyer*
Giusto, Richard J. *lawyer*
Golden, John Dennis *lawyer*
Gong, Edmond Joseph *lawyer*
Gorson, Matthew B. *lawyer*
Gragg, Karl Lawrence *lawyer*
Greer, Alan Graham *lawyer*
Gross, Leslie Jay *lawyer, real estate broker, mortgage company executive*
Grossman, Robert Louis *lawyer*
Hall, Adam Stuart *lawyer*
Hall, Andrew Clifford *lawyer*
Halsey, Douglas Martin *lawyer*
Hartz, Steven Edward Marshall *lawyer, educator*
Hector, Louis Julius *lawyer*
Hoffman, Kenneth Cary *lawyer*
Hoffman, Larry J. *lawyer*
Holifield, Marilyn J. *lawyer*
Houlihan, Gerald John *lawyer*
Hrinak, Donna Jean *lawyer, former ambassador*
Hudson, Robert Franklin, Jr. *lawyer*
Imperato, Joseph John *lawyer, composer*
Jacobson, Bernard *lawyer*
Jhabvala, Farrokh *lawyer*
Johnston, Philip Connelly *lawyer*
Katz, Lawrence Sheldon *lawyer*
Klock, Joseph Peter, Jr. *lawyer*
Korchin, Judith Miriam *lawyer*
Kreitzer, Michael N. *lawyer*
Lampen, Richard Jay *lawyer, investment banker*
Landy, Burton Aaron *lawyer*
Leibowitz, Mark Alan *lawyer*
Levin, Oscar *lawyer*
Levine, Robert Jeffrey *lawyer*
Long, Maxine Master *lawyer*
Louis, Paul Adolph *lawyer*
Loumiet, Juan P. *lawyer*
Martinez-Fraga, Pedro J. *lawyer*
McCain, David B. *lawyer*
Mehta, Eileen Rose *lawyer*
Mena, Daniel *lawyer, arbitrator*
Mencio, George, Jr. *lawyer*
Menendez Cambo, Patricia *lawyer*
Miller, James M. *lawyer*
Milstein, Richard Craig *lawyer*
Morrison, Richard A. *lawyer*
Murphy, Timothy James *lawyer*
Nachwalter, Michael *lawyer*

Nuernberg, William Richard *lawyer*
O'Connor, Kathleen Mary *lawyer*
Osman, Edith Gabriella *lawyer*
Papy, Charles C. III *lawyer*
Pena, Guillermo Enrique *lawyer*
Pratt, John Patrick *lawyer*
Quentel, Albert Drew *lawyer*
Reilly, Kenneth James *lawyer*
Reiter, Luis *lawyer*
Rubin, Steven D. *lawyer*
Ruiz, Olga *lawyer, educator*
Samole, Myron Michael *lawyer, management consultant*
Schuette, Charles A. *lawyer*
Schulman, Clifford A. *lawyer*
Simmons, Sherwin Palmer *lawyer*
Sirvén, José E. *lawyer*
Skolnick, Holly R. *lawyer*
Skolnick, S. Harold *lawyer*
Smith, Richard C. (Dick) *lawyer*
Sonberg, Steven *lawyer*
Stanley, Sherry A. *lawyer*
Stansell, Leland Edwin, Jr. *lawyer, mediator, educator*
Steinberg, Marty *lawyer*
Stokes, Paul Mason *lawyer*
Stotts, Dennis Martin *lawyer*
Strafer, G. Richard *lawyer*
Stratos, Kimarie Rose *lawyer, sports association executive*
Thornburg, Frederick Fletcher *lawyer*
Todd, Karyn L. *lawyer*
Traurig, Robert Henry *lawyer*
Vento, M. Thérèse *lawyer*
Walton, Rodney Earl *lawyer*
Weems, Lori K. *lawyer*
Weiner, Lawrence *lawyer*
Weinger, Steven Murray *lawyer*
Weinstein, Andrew H. *lawyer*
Wing, James David *lawyer*
Wiseheart, Malcolm Boyd, Jr. *lawyer*
Zack, Stephen Neal *lawyer*

**Miami Beach**
Arbuz, Joseph Robert *lawyer*

**Miami Gardens**
Ersek, Gregory Joseph Mark *lawyer*
Light, Alfred Robert *law educator*

**Naples**
Anderson, John Thomas *lawyer*
Blumenthal, Ronnie *lawyer*
Bruce, Jackson Martin, Jr. *lawyer*
Crehan, Joseph Edward *lawyer*
Doub, William Offutt *lawyer*
Ericson, Roger Delwin *lawyer, forest resource company executive*
Faison, William Franklin, II, *lawyer, retired manufacturing corporation executive*
Lowery, William Herbert *lawyer*
Mancuso, John Henry *retired lawyer, bank executive*
McCaffrey, Judith Elizabeth *lawyer*
McMackin, F. Joseph III *lawyer*
McSwiney, Charles Ronald *lawyer*
Norton, Elizabeth Wychgel *lawyer*
Parry, Timothy R. *lawyer*
Petersen, David L. *lawyer*
Smith, Numa Lamar, Jr. *lawyer*
Snyder, Marion Gene *lawyer, retired congressman*
Stevens, William Kenneth *lawyer*
Westman, Carl Edward *lawyer*

**New Port Richey**
Focht, Theodore Harold *lawyer, educator*
Mills, Edward Warren *lawyer*

**New Smyrna Beach**
Dunagan, Walter Benton *lawyer, educator*

**Niceville**
Havens, Jason Edward *lawyer*

**North Fort Myers**
Miller, William Charles *lawyer*

**North Palm Beach**
Tancer, Edward F. *lawyer, utilities executive*

**Orlando**
Abbott, Charles Warren *lawyer*
Ahlers, Glen-Peter, Sr. *law library director, educator, consultant*
Butterfield, Benjamin Parrish *lawyer*
Christiansen, Patrick T. *lawyer*
Conti, Louis Thomas Moore *lawyer*
Doppelt, Ava K. *lawyer*
Eagan, William Leon *lawyer*
Fleming Brown, Julie A. *legal association administrator*
Frey, Louis, Jr. *lawyer, federal official*
Gray, J. Charles *lawyer, cattle rancher*
Handley, Leon Hunter *lawyer*
Hoctor, James Joseph *lawyer*
Jespersen, Robert Randolph *lawyer*
Kelaher, James Peirce *lawyer*
Lefkowitz, Ivan Martin *lawyer*
Leonhardt, Frederick Wayne *lawyer*
Lowndes, John Foy *lawyer*
Mock, Frank Mackenzie *lawyer*
Moskowitz, Deborah Lynn *lawyer*
Motes, Carl Dalton *lawyer*
Murrell, Robert George *lawyer*
Nadeau, Robert Bertrand, Jr. *lawyer*
Pare, John Z. *lawyer*
Pierce, John Gerald (Jerry Pierce) *lawyer*
Ragland, Robert Allen *lawyer*
Reed, John Kalen *lawyer*
Rounsaville, Keith Eugene *lawyer*
Sheaffer, William Jay *lawyer*
Shives, Paula J. *lawyer*
Sims, Roger W. *lawyer*
Skambis, Christopher Charles, Jr. *lawyer*
Subin, Eli Harold *lawyer*
Weiss, Christopher John *lawyer*
Yates, Leighton Delevan, Jr. *lawyer*

**Palatka**
Baldwin, Allen Adail *lawyer, writer*

**Palm Beach**
Adler, Frederick Richard *lawyer, corporate financial executive*
Canary, Nancy Halliday *lawyer*
Crawford, Sandra Kay *lawyer*
Parker, Ellis Jackson III *lawyer, broadcaster*

**Palm Beach Gardens**
Auerbach, Paul Ira *lawyer*
Freedman, Warren *lawyer, educator, judge*
Newman, Stephen Michael *lawyer*
O'Brien, Thomas George III *lawyer*

**Palm Coast**
Patz, Edward Frank *retired lawyer*

**Palm Harbor**
Rezanka, Thomas W. *lawyer*

**Patrick Afb**
McAlwee, Martin Frederick *lawyer*

**Pensacola**
Bookman, Alan B. *lawyer*
Bozeman, Frank Carmack *lawyer*
Ferguson, Michael Lambert *lawyer, educator*
Geeker, Nicholas Peter *lawyer, judge*
Levin, Fredric Gerson *lawyer*
Soloway, Daniel Mark *lawyer*
Windham, John Franklin *lawyer, educator*

**Plant City**
Buchman, Kenneth William *lawyer*
Sparkman, Steven Leonard *lawyer*

**Polk City**
Closen, Michael Lee *retired law educator*

**Pompano Beach**
Fauss, David H. *legal consultant*
Gude, Nancy Carlson *lawyer*

**Ponte Vedra Beach**
Davis, Wendell, Jr. *lawyer*
Kuhn, Bowie K. *lawyer, former professional baseball commissioner, consultant*

**Port Saint Lucie**
Lambert, George Robert *lawyer, realtor*

**Royal Palm Beach**
Gardner, Elizabeth Michelle *lawyer*

**Saint Augustine**
Brady, James Joseph *labor arbitrator*

**Saint Petersburg**
Bairstow, Frances Kanevsky *arbitrator, mediator, educator*
Battaglia, Anthony Sylvester *lawyer*
Biasotti, Robert E. *lawyer*
Carnesoltas, Ana-Maria *lawyer*
Escarraz, Enrique III *lawyer*
Georges, Richard Martin *lawyer, educator*
Glass, Roy Leonard *lawyer*
Jacob, Bruce Robert *law educator*
Janney, Oliver James *lawyer*
Keane, Michael J. *lawyer*
Kiefner, John Robert, Jr. *lawyer, educator*
Lang, Joseph Hagedorn *lawyer*
Mann, Sam Henry, Jr. *retired lawyer*
Matecki, Paul L. *lawyer*
Paver, Robert L. *lawyer*
Ross, Howard Philip *lawyer*

**Sanford**
Capps, James Leigh, II, *lawyer, military officer*
Mamele, Richard Louis *lawyer*

**Sanibel**
Rothschild, Donald Phillip *retired lawyer, arbitrator*

**Sarasota**
Christopher, William Garth *lawyer*
Ehrlich, Bernard Herbert *lawyer, trade association administrator*
Garland, Richard Roger *lawyer*
Greenfield, Robert Kauffman *retired lawyer*
Heitler, George *lawyer*
Hull, J(ames) Richard *retired lawyer*
Keltner, Robert Earl *lawyer, researcher, hotel executive*
Knickerbocker, Robert Platt, Jr. *retired lawyer*
Oelbaum, Harold *lawyer*
Tachna, Ruth C. *retired lawyer*

**Sebring**
McCollum, James Fountain *lawyer*

**Seminole**
Carrere, Charles Scott *law educator, judge*

**South Miami**
Keedy, Christian David *lawyer*

**Stuart**
Gary, Willie E. *lawyer*
Moreno, Christine Margaret *lawyer*

**Tallahassee**
Aurell, John Karl *lawyer*
Baggett, Fred W. *lawyer*
Barnett, Martha Walters *lawyer*
Bielby, Lorence Jon *lawyer*
Buck, Thomas Randolph *retired lawyer, retired diversified financial services company executive*
Burnaman, Ross Stafford *lawyer*
Cherniga, Michael J. *lawyer*
Cummings, Frederic Alan *lawyer*
Curtin, Lawrence N. *lawyer*
Dariotis, Terrence Theodore *lawyer*
DeFoor, J. Allison, II, *lawyer*
Ervin, Robert Marvin *lawyer*
France, Belinda Takach *lawyer, business owner*
Glover, Erica D. *lawyer*
Harper, Robert Augustus *lawyer*
Holcomb, Lyle Donald, Jr. *retired lawyer*
Johnson, Kelly Overstreet *lawyer*
Kerns, David Vincent *lawyer*

**Levine, A. Kenneth *lawyer***
Levine, A. Kenneth *lawyer*
Miller, Gregory R. *prosecutor*
Miller, Morris Henry *lawyer*
Mindlin, Steven Todd *lawyer*
Minnick, Bruce Alexander *lawyer*
Phipps, Benjamin Kimball, II, *lawyer*
Reid, Sue Titus *law educator*
Terry, Anne Curtis *lawyer, writer*
Teson, Fernando Roberto *law educator, consultant*
Waas, George Lee *lawyer*
Walker, Karen D. *lawyer*
Weinberger, Steven *lawyer, educator*
Zaiser, Kent Ames *lawyer*

**Tampa**
Albritton, Arthur Dallas *lawyer*
Barkin, Marvin E. *lawyer*
Barton, Bernard Alan, Jr. *lawyer*
Black, Caroline Kapusta *lawyer*
Blacklidge, Raymond Mark *lawyer*
Campbell, Richard Bruce *lawyer*
Christian, Terry Clifton *lawyer*
Clendinen, Craig P. *lawyer*
Corcoran, Clement Timothy III *lawyer, retired judge*
Cunningham, Anthony Willard *lawyer*
Davidson, Charles Thomas *lawyer*
Davis, Richard Earl *lawyer*
Diehr, Beverly Hunt *lawyer*
Doliner, Nathaniel Lee *lawyer*
Ellwanger, Thomas John *lawyer*
Gilbert, Leonard Harold *lawyer*
Gonzalez, Joe Manuel *lawyer*
Grammig, Robert (Bob) James *lawyer*
Hamilton, William F. *lawyer*
Holliday, Ronald Sturgis *lawyer*
Huneycutt, Alice Ruth *lawyer*
Jamieson, Michael Lawrence *lawyer*
Jones, John Arthur *lawyer*
Kelly, Thomas Paine, Jr. *retired lawyer*
Lane, Robin *lawyer*
LaRussa, Rudy G. *lawyer*
Levine, Jack Anton *lawyer*
MacDonald, Thomas Cook, Jr. *lawyer, mediator*
Martin, Gary Wayne *lawyer*
McAdams, John Pope *lawyer*
McBride, William Howard, Jr. *lawyer*
McDevitt, Sheila Marie *lawyer, energy executive*
O'Neill, Albert Clarence, Jr. *lawyer*
Pellett, Jon Michael *lawyer*
Perez, Paul Ignatius *prosecutor, lawyer*
Roberson, Bruce Heerdt *lawyer*
Robinson, John William, IV, *lawyer*
Sasso, Gary L. *lawyer*
Schwenke, Roger Dean *lawyer*
Smith, William Reece, Jr. *lawyer*
Somers, Clifford Louis *lawyer*
Stallings, Norman (Charles Norman Stallings) *lawyer*
Stalnaker, Lance Kuebler *lawyer*
Stiles, Mary Ann *lawyer, writer, lobbyist*
Thomas, Gregg Darrow *lawyer*
Thomas, Wayne Lee *lawyer*
Vogt, Martha Diane *lawyer*
Wagner, Frederick William (Bill Wagner) *lawyer*
Waller, Edward Martin, Jr. *lawyer*
Yang, Grace H. *lawyer*
Yerrid, C. Steven *lawyer*
Young, Gwynne A. *lawyer*

**Venice**
Clarke, Edward Owen, Jr. *lawyer*
Miller, Allan John *lawyer*

**Vero Beach**
Ahrensfeld, Thomas Frederick *retired lawyer*
Case, Douglas Manning *lawyer*
Havens, Charles William III *retired lawyer*
Higgs, John H. *lawyer*

**Village Of Golf**
Sutter, William Paul *lawyer*

**West Palm Beach**
Ackerman, David P. *lawyer*
Barre, Steven Craig *lawyer*
Beall, Kenneth Sutter, Jr. *lawyer*
Beasley, James W., Jr. *lawyer*
Bregman, Howard *lawyer*
Chopin, L. Frank *lawyer*
Chopin, Susan Gardiner *lawyer*
Clark, David William Layne *lawyer, councilman*
Conrad, Bette Anne Kester *lawyer, writer, minister*
Cooper, Margaret Leslie *lawyer*
Coyle, Dennis Patrick *lawyer, retired utilities executive*
Damsel, Charles H., Jr. *lawyer*
Gildan, Phillip Clarke *lawyer*
Henry, Thornton Montagu *lawyer*
Hill, Thomas William, Jr. *lawyer, educator*
Kamen, Michael Andrew *lawyer*
Lamb, Kevin Thomas *lawyer*
Link, Scott J. *lawyer*
Loring, Arthur *lawyer, diversified financial services company executive*
Marker, Shaun James *lawyer*
Miller, Richard Jackson (Rick Miller) *lawyer*
Montgomery, Robert Morel, Jr. *lawyer*
Moore, George Crawford Jackson *lawyer*
Mrachek, Lorin Louis *lawyer*
Orlovsky, Donald Albert *lawyer*
Raab, Ira Jerry *lawyer, judge*
Rosen, Marvin Shelby *lawyer*
Royce, Raymond Watson *lawyer, rancher, citrus grower, investor*
Terry, Karen Elizabeth *lawyer*
Vilchez, Victoria Anne *lawyer*
Zeller, Ronald John *lawyer*

**Windermere**
McGuire, Edward David, Jr. *lawyer*

**Winter Park**
Dempsey, Bernard Hayden, Jr. *lawyer*
Hadley, Ralph Vincent III *lawyer*
Heinle, Richard Alan *lawyer*
Jontz, Jeffry Robert *lawyer*
Ladha-Karmali, Shainoor *lawyer*
Morgan, Mary Ann *lawyer*
Troutman, Holmes Russell *lawyer*

## GEORGIA

### Alpharetta
Hatcher, Barbara A. *lawyer*

### Athens
Beaird, James Ralph *lawyer, educator, dean*
Carlson, Ronald Lee *law educator*
Chaffin, Verner Franklin *lawyer, educator*
Ellington, Charles Ronald *lawyer, educator*
Hellerstein, Walter *lawyer*
Houser, Ronald Edward *lawyer, arbitrator, mediator*
Huszagh, Fredrick Wickett *lawyer, educator, information technology executive*
Kurtz, Paul Michael *law educator*
Puckett, Elizabeth Ann *law librarian, educator*
Shipley, David Elliott *lawyer, educator*
Tolley, Edward Donald *lawyer*

### Atlanta
Abbott, Herschel Lee, Jr. *lawyer*
Abernathy, Thomas Edwards, IV, *lawyer*
Abrams, Harold Eugene *lawyer*
Addison, James W. *lawyer*
Albert, Ross Alan *lawyer*
Aldridge, John *lawyer*
Alexander, Kent B. *lawyer*
Alexander, Miles Jordan *lawyer*
Allen, Pinney L. *lawyer*
Allen, Randall L. *lawyer*
Altman, Robert *lawyer*
Anderson, Peter Joseph *lawyer*
Asbill, Richard M. *lawyer*
Attridge, Richard Byron *lawyer*
Austin, Jesse Hinnant III *lawyer*
Baker, Thomas William *lawyer*
Barkoff, Rupert Mitchell *lawyer*
Barnett, Preston B. *lawyer, communications executive*
Barr, Robert Laurence, Jr. *lawyer*
Barwick, William D. *lawyer*
Bassett, Peter Q. *lawyer*
Batson, Richard Neal *lawyer*
Beckham, Walter Hull III *lawyer*
Bell, Griffin Boyette *lawyer, former United States attorney general*
Bennett, Jay D. *lawyer*
Bergeson, Donna Pottis *lawyer*
Billington, Barry E. *lawyer*
Bird, Francis Marion, Jr. *lawyer*
Bird, Wendell Raleigh *lawyer*
Blackburn, William Stanley *lawyer*
Blackstock, Jerry B. *lawyer*
Blank, A(ndrew) Russell *lawyer*
Bloodworth, Albert William Franklin *lawyer*
Boisseau, Richard Robert *lawyer*
Bonds, John Wilfred, Jr. *lawyer*
Bondurant, Emmet Jopling, II, *lawyer*
Boone, J. William *lawyer*
Boone, John Temple *lawyer*
Booth, Gordon Dean, Jr. *lawyer*
Bowden, Henry Lumpkin, Jr. *lawyer*
Bowling, Daniel S. III *lawyer*
Branch, Thomas Broughton III *lawyer*
Bratton, James Henry, Jr. *lawyer*
Brecher, Armin George *lawyer*
Brewster, William Howard *lawyer*
Brown, Janine *lawyer*
Buffenstein, Daryl R. *lawyer*
Butterworth, S. Kendall *lawyer*
Byrne, Granville Bland III *lawyer*
Cadenhead, Alfred Paul *lawyer*
Calhoun, David *lawyer*
Carpenter, David Allan *lawyer*
Carson, Christopher Leonard *lawyer*
Cavin, Kristine Smith *lawyer*
Chilivis, Nickolas Peter *retired lawyer*
Chisholm, Tommy *lawyer, utilities executive*
Clarke, Thomas Hal *lawyer*
Cobb, Charles Kenche, Jr. *lawyer, real estate broker*
Cohen, Ezra Harry *lawyer*
Cohen, George Leon *lawyer*
Cohen, Lori G. *lawyer*
Cohen, N. Jerold *lawyer*
Collins, Steven M. *lawyer*
Conboy, Kevin *lawyer*
Connell, Paul J. *lawyer*
Cook, Don Lloyd *lawyer, consultant, marketing educator*
Cook, Philip Carter *lawyer*
Crews, William Edwin *lawyer*
Croft, Terrence Lee *lawyer, mediator, arbitrator*
Culhane, John Joseph *lawyer*
Curtis, J. Vaughan *lawyer*
Cutshaw, Kenneth Andrew *lawyer*
Dalton, John Joseph *lawyer*
David, Todd R. *lawyer*
Davis, Benjamin Alando *lawyer*
Davis, Frank Tradewell, Jr. *lawyer*
Deming, N. Karen *lawyer*
Denny, Richard Alden, Jr. *retired lawyer*
DeSimone, Samuel Richard *lawyer*
Despriet, John G. *lawyer*
Domby, Arthur H. *lawyer*
Douglas, John Lewis *lawyer*
Draper, Stephen Elliot *lawyer, engineer*
Driver, Walter W., Jr. *lawyer*
Duffie, L. Traywick *lawyer*
Dunlevie, Steven S. *lawyer*
Durrett, James Frazer, Jr. *retired lawyer*
Eckl, William Wray *lawyer*
Edwards, Stephen Allen *lawyer*
Egan, Michael Joseph *retired lawyer, state legislator*
Elgison, Martin J. *lawyer*
Elliott, Mark Lee *lawyer*
Etheridge, Jack Paul *arbitrator, mediator, retired judge*
Fancher, Kristen L. *lawyer*
Farnham, Clayton Henson *lawyer*
Felton, Jule Wimberly, Jr. *lawyer*
Fernandez, Frank L. *lawyer, retail executive*
Fleming, Julian Denver, Jr. *lawyer*
Forbes, Theodore McCoy, Jr. *arbitrator, mediator, retired lawyer*
Forry, Robert H. *lawyer*
Fortin, Raymond D. *lawyer*
Frederick, Paula J. *lawyer*
Gambrell, David Henry *lawyer*

Gary, Marc *lawyer*
Genberg, Ira *lawyer*
Gerakitis, Richard *lawyer*
Gignilliat, R. Read *lawyer*
Girth, Marjorie Louisa *lawyer, educator*
Goizueta Rawls, Olga Maria *lawyer*
Goldstein, Elliott *lawyer, director*
Grady, Kevin E. *lawyer*
Gramlich, Larry E. *lawyer*
Graves, Judson *lawyer*
Greene, Kevin C. *lawyer*
Greer, Bernard Lewis (Ben), Jr. *lawyer*
Grice, Richard W. *lawyer*
Groton, James Purnell *lawyer, arbitrator*
Grout, Robert W. *lawyer*
Hackett, Stanley Hailey *lawyer*
Harkey, Robert Shelton *retired lawyer*
Harris, Harold Stephen, Jr. *lawyer*
Harvey, James A. *lawyer*
Hasson, James Keith, Jr. *lawyer, educator*
Hatcher, James A. *lawyer*
Hawks, Barrett Kingsbury *lawyer*
Hay, Peter Heinrich *law educator*
Hays, Richard R. *lawyer*
Heberton, George H. *lawyer*
Herman, John C. *lawyer*
Hinchey, John William *lawyer*
Hinson, H. Douglas *lawyer*
Hoff, Gerhardt Michael *lawyer, insurance company executive*
Hopkins, John David *lawyer*
Howard, Harry Clay *lawyer*
Hunter, Forrest Walker *lawyer*
Hutchins, John P. *lawyer*
Ide, Roy William III *lawyer*
Izard, John *lawyer*
Janney, Donald Wayne *lawyer*
Jenkins, Albert Felton, Jr. *lawyer*
Johnson, Charles S. III *lawyer*
Johnson, John H. *lawyer*
Johnson, Weyman Thompson, Jr. *lawyer*
Jones, Glower Whitehead *lawyer*
Jordak, John A., Jr. *lawyer*
Jordan, Katherine D. (Kate Jordan) *lawyer*
Katz, Joel Abraham *lawyer*
Kaufman, Mark David *lawyer*
Kaywood, Sam K., Jr. *lawyer*
Kelly, James Patrick *lawyer*
Kessler, Richard Paul, Jr. *lawyer*
Kilgore, Cada T. III *lawyer*
Killorin, Robert Ware *lawyer*
Kitchens, William H. *lawyer*
Kneisel, Edmund M. *lawyer*
Knowles, Marjorie Fine *law educator, dean*
Kontio, Peter *lawyer*
Kraus, Hans Michael *lawyer*
Lackland, Theodore Howard *lawyer*
Lamberth, James A. *lawyer*
Lamon, Harry Vincent, Jr. *lawyer*
Landau, Michael B. *law educator*
Landon, James Henry *lawyer*
Latham, John L. *lawyer*
Leonard, David Morse *lawyer*
Lester, Charles Turner, Jr. *lawyer*
Lewis, Stephen E. *lawyer*
Linkous, William Joseph, Jr. *lawyer*
Lipshutz, Robert Jerome *lawyer, former government official*
Lowe, Jonathan Wayne *lawyer*
Lower, Robert Cassel *lawyer, educator*
Manning, George Taylor *lawyer*
Marshall, Dante *lawyer*
Marshall, John Treutlen *lawyer, educator*
Marvin, Charles Arthur *law educator*
Mason, Karol V. *lawyer*
Mast, Kent E. *lawyer*
McAlpin, Kirk Martin *lawyer*
McClure, Teri Plummer *lawyer*
McNeill, Thomas Ray *lawyer*
Mercer, John T.W. *lawyer*
Miele, Stefano M. *lawyer*
Miller, Douglas Linn *lawyer*
Mize, Gerald L., Jr. *lawyer*
Mobley, John Homer, II, *lawyer*
Moeling, Walter Goos, IV, *lawyer*
Morgan, Elizabeth Ann *lawyer*
Mowrey, Robert D. *lawyer*
Mull, Gale W. *lawyer*
Murphy, Kenyon W. *lawyer*
Myers, Johnnie Dumas *law educator*
Nahmias, David E. *prosecutor*
Newman, Stuart *lawyer*
Newton, Floyd Childs III *lawyer*
Noe, Elizabeth Hardy *lawyer*
Norman, Albert George, Jr. *lawyer*
Nurkin, Sidney J. *lawyer*
Oakley, Mary Ann Bryant *lawyer*
Orr, A. Summey III *lawyer*
Owens, Laura Lewis *lawyer*
Palmer, Charles F. *lawyer*
Pelypenko, Elizabeth *lawyer*
Persons, W. Ray *lawyer, educator*
Petrik, Michael Thomas *lawyer*
Piassick, Joel Bernard *lawyer*
Pike, Larry Samuel *lawyer*
Poe, H. Sadler *lawyer*
Pottle, Steven L. *lawyer*
Price, Elizabeth Anne *lawyer*
Prince, David Cannon *lawyer*
Quillian, J. Kirk *lawyer*
Quittmeyer, Peter Charles *lawyer*
Rafuse, Nancy E. *lawyer, director*
Ragland, William McKenzie, Jr. *lawyer, real estate developer*
Reed, Glen Alfred *lawyer*
Reinhardt, Daniel Sargent *lawyer*
Remar, Robert Boyle *lawyer*
Rhodes, Thomas Willard *lawyer*
Richter, Carolyn Peterson *lawyer*
Riddell, Stephen W. *lawyer*
Riggs, Gregory Lynn *lawyer*
Riordan, Robert P. *lawyer*
Rochelle, Dudley Cecile *lawyer*
Rogers, DeWitt Ralph *lawyer*
Roseborough, Teresa Wynn *lawyer*
Rusche, Mark C. *lawyer*
Sanders, Carl E. *lawyer, former governor*
Savell, Edward Lupo *lawyer*
Schroder, Jack Spalding, Jr. *lawyer*
Schulte, Jeffrey Lewis *lawyer*
Shapiro, George Howard *retired lawyer*

Sibley, James Malcolm *retired lawyer*
Silverstein, Leonard A. *lawyer*
Slaughter, Nathaniel G. III *lawyer*
Smith, Alexander Wyly, Jr. *lawyer*
Smith, Edward Kendrick *lawyer*
Smith, Frank G. III *lawyer*
Smith, Jeffrey Michael *lawyer*
Smith, Scott C. *lawyer, legal association administrator*
Smith, Sidney Oslin, Jr. *lawyer*
Spangler, John I. III *lawyer*
Stein, Grant T. *lawyer*
Stephenson, Mason Williams *lawyer*
Stockton, David A. *lawyer*
Sweeney, Neal James *lawyer*
Swift, Frank Meador *lawyer*
Tanenbaum, Allan Jay *lawyer*
Tanner, W(alter) Rhett *lawyer*
Taylor, George Kimbrough, Jr. *lawyer*
Tennant, Thomas Michael *lawyer*
Thomas, Lizanne *lawyer*
Thorpe, Jane Fugate *lawyer*
Thrower, Randolph William *lawyer*
Travis, Robert M. *lawyer*
Varner, Chilton Davis *lawyer*
Vaughn, Michael S. *law educator*
Wade, Nicole Jennings *lawyer*
Wakefield, Stephen Alan *lawyer*
Walsh, W. Terence *lawyer*
Webb, Robert W., Jr. *lawyer*
Wellon, Robert G. *lawyer*
White, Benjamin Taylor *lawyer*
Wigmore, Steven P. *lawyer*
Williams, David Howard *lawyer*
Williams, Neil A. *lawyer*
Williams, Robert P., II, *lawyer*
Williamson, R. Mark *lawyer*
Wilson, Brent Lawrence *lawyer, mediator*
Wilson, James Hargrove, Jr. *lawyer*
Withrow, William N., Jr. *lawyer*
Wofford, Milton Russell, Jr. *lawyer*
Wood, L. Lin, Jr. *lawyer*
Wright, Frederick Lewis, II, *lawyer*
Wright, Peter Meldrim *lawyer*

### Augusta
Knox, Wyckliffe Austin, Jr. *lawyer*
Miller, Alfred Montague *lawyer*

### Braselton
Romer, Denise Patrice *lawyer*

### Calhoun
Perillo, Salvatore J. *lawyer*

### College Park
Patterson, P(ickens) Andrew *lawyer*

### Columbus
Brinkley, Jack Thomas *lawyer, retired congressman*
McGlamry, Max Reginald *retired lawyer*
Page, William Marion *lawyer*
Patrick, James Duvall, Jr. *lawyer*
Poydasheff, Robert Stephen *lawyer*
Sprouse, James Edward *lawyer*
Wooten, Joel Orba, Jr. *lawyer*

### Decatur
Williams, Rita Tucker *lawyer*

### Douglas
Hayes, Dewey *lawyer*

### Dublin
Greene, Jule Blounte *lawyer*

### Duluth
Lupton, Stephen D. *lawyer*
Sloan, Donnie Robert, Jr. *lawyer*

### Dunwoody
Callison, James W. *retired lawyer, air transportation executive*

### Gainesville
Schuder, Raymond Francis *lawyer*

### Hamilton
Byrd, Gary Ellis *lawyer*

### Jasper
Marger, Edwin *lawyer*

### Lawrenceville
Veysey, Michael Charles *lawyer*

### Lithia Springs
Longobardo, Guy Alfred *lawyer*

### Macon
Ennis, Edgar William, Jr. *lawyer*
Jones, Frank Cater *retired lawyer*
Robinson, W. Lee *lawyer*
Wiggins, James L. *lawyer*
Wood, Frank Maxwell *prosecutor, lawyer*

### Madison
DuBose, Charles Wilson *lawyer*

### Marietta
Bentley, Fred Douglas, Sr. *lawyer*
Clay, Charles Commander (Chuck Clay) *lawyer, former state senator*
Hellrung, Stephen Andrew *lawyer*
Ingram, Robert D. *lawyer*
Nowland, James Ferrell *lawyer*
Volentine, Richard J., Jr. *lawyer*

### Metter
Doremus, Ogden *lawyer*

### Moultrie
Collum, Rick Daniel *lawyer*

### Newnan
Franklin, Bruce Walter *lawyer*

### Norcross
McIntosh, Robert B. *lawyer*

Xie, Jeff Zhengquan *lawyer*

### Perry
Geiger, James Norman *lawyer*

### Roswell
Baker, Anita Diane *lawyer*
Birmingham, Richard Gregory *lawyer*
Bruckner, William J. *lawyer*
Nilsen, Arthur Christian *lawyer*
Roland, Raymond William *lawyer, mediator*

### Saint Marys
Smith, Charles Courtland, Jr. *lawyer, state legislator*

### Saint Simons Island
Taylor, Philip Raymond *lawyer*
Thau, William Albert *lawyer*

### Sandy Springs
Owen, Robert Hubert *lawyer, real estate broker*

### Savannah
Berry, Jack K. *lawyer*
Bowman, Catherine McKenzie *lawyer*
Dickey, David Herschel *lawyer, accountant*
Dixon, Harry D., Jr., (Donnie Dixon) *lawyer, former prosecutor*
Forbes, Morton Gerald *lawyer*
Lee, Ernest William, II, *lawyer*
Searcy, William Nelson *lawyer, director*
Stillwell, Walter Brooks III *lawyer*
Thompson, Richard S. *lawyer, former prosecutor*
Wood, Lisa Godbey *prosecutor*

### Sea Island
Revoile, Charles Patrick *lawyer*

### Sky Valley
Wilkinson, Albert Mims, Jr. *lawyer*

### Smyrna
Seigler, Michael Edward *lawyer, librarian*

### Statesboro
Franklin, James Burke *lawyer*
Wilson, LeVon Edward *lawyer, educator*

### Tifton
Reinhardt, George Robert *lawyer*

### Tucker
Taylor, George B., Jr. *lawyer*

### Valdosta
Dodd, Roger J. *lawyer*
Edwards, Edith Martha *lawyer*

### Watkinsville
Wright, Robert Joseph *lawyer*

### West Point
Humphries, M. Clayton, Jr. *lawyer*

## HAWAII

### Honolulu
Adams, Jo-Ann Marie *lawyer*
Akiba, Lorraine Hiroko *lawyer*
Akinaka, Asa Masayoshi *lawyer*
Bloede, Victor Carl *lawyer, consultant, director*
Boas, Frank *retired lawyer*
Callies, David Lee *lawyer, educator*
Case, James Hebard *lawyer*
Char, Vernon Fook Leong *lawyer*
Cowan, Stuart Marshall *lawyer*
Dang, Marvin S.C. *lawyer*
Deaver, Phillip Lester *lawyer*
Devens, Paul *retired lawyer*
Dupont, Ralph Paul *lawyer, educator*
Edmunds, John Sanford *lawyer*
Fukumoto, Leslie Satsuki *lawyer*
Gay, E(mil) Laurence *lawyer*
Gelber, Don Jeffrey *lawyer*
Godbey, Robert Carson *lawyer*
Greeley, Burnham H. *lawyer*
Hart, Brook *lawyer*
Hazlett, Mark A. *lawyer*
Heller, Ronald Ian *lawyer*
Imanaka, Mitchell Akio *lawyer*
Katayama, Robert Nobuichi *retired lawyer*
Lacy, John Robert *lawyer*
Lee, Dale W. *lawyer*
Lilly, Michael Alexander *lawyer, writer*
Loo, Wilson M.N. *lawyer, judge*
Louie, David Mark *lawyer*
Marks, Michael J. *lawyer*
Mau-Shimizu, Patricia Ann *lawyer*
Miller, Richard Sherwin *law educator*
Miyasaki, Shuichi *lawyer*
Nakata, Gary Kenji *lawyer*
Nasky, H. Gregory (Harold Gregory Nasky) *lawyer*
Okinaga, Lawrence Shoji *lawyer*
Portnoy, Jeffrey Steven *lawyer*
Reber, David James *lawyer*
Sakamoto, Ronald Rikio *lawyer, construction executive*
Sato, Glenn Kenji *lawyer*
Starshak, James L. *lawyer*
Turbin, Richard *lawyer*

### Kihei
Burns, Richard Gordon *retired lawyer, writer, consultant*

### Kula
Maloney, Michael Patrick *lawyer, mediator, arbitrator*
Richardson, Robert Allen *retired lawyer, educator*
Rohlfing, Frederick William *lawyer, retired judge, political scientist*

## IDAHO

### Boise
Geston, Mark Symington *lawyer*
Leroy, David Henry *lawyer*

McGown, John, Jr. *lawyer*
Meyer, Christopher Hawkins *lawyer*
Minnich, Diane Kay *legal association administrator*
Moss, Thomas E. *prosecutor*
Myers, William Gerry III *lawyer*
Park, William Anthony (Tony Park) *lawyer*
Richardson, Betty H. *lawyer, former prosecutor*
Rubocki, Melanie Goedeker *lawyer*
Shurtliff, Marvin Karl *lawyer*
Silak, Cathy R. *lawyer, former state supreme court justice*
Sims, John R. *lawyer*
Uranga, Jean R. *lawyer*
VanHole, William Remi *lawyer*

**Caldwell**
Kerrick, David Ellsworth *lawyer*

**Hailey**
Youngblood, Deborah Sue *lawyer, speech pathology/audiology services professional*

**Kamiah**
Mills, Lawrence *lawyer, business and transportation consultant*

**Ketchum**
Holland, Robert James *retired lawyer*

**Lewiston**
Tait, John Reid *lawyer*

**Moscow**
Greene, Timothy Geddes *lawyer*
Vincenti, Sheldon Arnold *law educator, lawyer*

## ILLINOIS

**Arlington Heights**
Tucker, Bowen Hayward *lawyer*

**Barrington**
Lee, William Marshall *lawyer*
Wyatt, James Frank, Jr. *lawyer*

**Belleville**
Bauman, John Duane *lawyer*
Hess, Frederick J. *lawyer*
Miller, Jan Paul *lawyer, former prosecutor*
Ripplinger, George Raymond, Jr. *lawyer*

**Bloomington**
Bragg, Michael Ellis *lawyer, insurance company executive*
Sullivan, Laura Patricia *lawyer, insurance company executive*

**Burr Ridge**
Brennan, James Joseph *lawyer, bank executive*
Decker, Richard Knore *lawyer*

**Calumet City**
Scullion, Annette Murphy *lawyer, educator*

**Carbondale**
Clemons, John Robert *lawyer*
Duggan, James Edgar *law librarian*
Lee, Mark Richard *lawyer, educator*

**Carrollton**
Strickland, Hugh Alfred *lawyer*

**Carthage**
Glidden, John Redmond *lawyer*

**Cary**
Narusis, Regina Gyté Firant *lawyer*

**Champaign**
Joy, Richard Marks *lawyer*
Kindt, John Warren *lawyer, educator*
Krause, Harry Dieter *law educator*
Maggs, Peter Blount *lawyer, educator*
Mamer, Stuart Mies *lawyer*
Mc Cord, John Harrison *lawyer, educator*
Miller, Harold Arthur *lawyer*
Nowak, John E. *law educator*

**Chicago**
Abrams, Lee Norman *lawyer*
Acker, Ann E. *lawyer*
Acker, Frederick George *lawyer*
Adelman, Stanley Joseph *lawyer*
Adelman, Steven Herbert *lawyer*
Alberts, Barry S. *lawyer*
Allen, Henry Sermones, Jr. *lawyer*
Allen, Ronald Jay *law educator*
Allen, Thomas Draper *lawyer*
Anderson, David Boyd *lawyer, metal products executive*
Anderson, J. Trent *lawyer*
Anderson, Kimball Richard *lawyer*
Anderson, William Cornelius III *lawyer*
Angst, Gerald L. *lawyer*
Anthony, Michael Francis *lawyer*
Antonio, Douglas John *lawyer*
Anvaripour, M. A. *lawyer*
Appel, Nina Schick *law educator, dean, academic administrator*
Archer, James G. *retired lawyer*
Armstrong, Edwin Richard *lawyer*
Aronson, Virginia L. *lawyer*
Athas, Gus James *lawyer*
Auerbach, Marshall Jay *lawyer*
Avery, Robert Dean *lawyer*
Axley, Frederick William *lawyer*
Badel, Julie *lawyer*
Baer, John Richard Frederick *lawyer*
Bailey, Robert Short *lawyer*
Baird, Douglas Gordon *law educator, dean*
Baird, James *lawyer*
Baker, Bruce Jay *lawyer*
Baker, Pamela *lawyer*
Baldwin, Shaun McParland *lawyer*
Banoff, Sheldon Irwin *lawyer*
Barden, Larry A. *lawyer*
Barker, William Thomas *lawyer*

Barnes, James Garland, Jr. *lawyer*
Barr, John Robert *retired lawyer*
Barron, Harold Sheldon *lawyer*
Barron, Howard Robert *lawyer*
Bart, Susan Therese *lawyer*
Bartlit, Fred Holcomb, Jr. *lawyer*
Bashwiner, Steven Lacelle *lawyer*
Baugher, Peter V. *lawyer*
Baumgartner, William Hans, Jr. *lawyer*
Bayles, Deborah Lynn *lawyer*
Beck, Philip S. *lawyer*
Becker, Scott *lawyer*
Beem, Jack Darrel *retired lawyer*
Bellows, Laurel Gordon *business lawyer*
Bennett, Robert William *law educator*
Bennington, Thomas Francis *lawyer, county official*
Berens, Mark Harry *lawyer*
Berenzweig, Jack Charles *lawyer*
Berger, Robert Michael *lawyer*
Berkoff, Adam T. *lawyer*
Berkowitz, Sean M. *prosecutor*
Berman, Debbie *lawyer*
Berner, Robert Lee, Jr. *lawyer*
Bernstein, Charles Bernard *lawyer*
Bernstein, H. Bruce *lawyer*
Bernstein, Lisa E. *law educator*
Berolzheimer, Karl *lawyer*
Biebel, Paul Philip, Jr. *lawyer*
Bitner, John Howard *lawyer*
Bixby, Frank Lyman *retired lawyer*
Bleiweiss, Shell J. *lawyer*
Block, Neal Jay *lawyer*
Blount, Michael Eugene *lawyer*
Boberg, Wayne D. *lawyer*
Bodenstein, Ira *lawyer*
Boehnen, Daniel A. *lawyer*
Bogaard, Jonathan Harvey *lawyer*
Boggs, Catherine J. *lawyer*
Boies, Wilber H. *lawyer*
Bosselman, Fred Paul *law educator*
Bouma, Robert Edwin *lawyer*
Bowe, William J(ohn) *lawyer*
Bowen, Stephen Stewart *lawyer*
Bowman, Cynthia Grant *law educator*
Boykins, Michael L. *lawyer*
Boyle, John Francis *lawyer*
Bramnik, Robert Paul *lawyer*
Brice, Roger Thomas *lawyer*
Bridgman, Thomas Francis *retired lawyer*
Brizzolara, Charles Anthony *lawyer, director*
Bro, Ruth Hill *lawyer*
Brogan, Lisa S. *lawyer*
Bromley, Richard *lawyer*
Brown, Alan Crawford *lawyer*
Brown, Donald James, Jr. *lawyer*
Brown, Gregory K. *lawyer*
Brown, Matthew S. *lawyer*
Bryant, David J. *lawyer*
Bulger, Brian Wegg *lawyer*
Burke, John Michael *lawyer*
Burke, Thomas Joseph, Jr. *lawyer*
Burns, Robert Patrick *law educator*
Burns, Terrence Michael *lawyer*
Busey, Roxane C. *lawyer*
Buss, Emily *law educator*
Butler, John William, Jr. *lawyer*
Calabresi, Steven G. *law educator*
Callahan, Michael R. *lawyer*
Campbell, William J., Jr. *lawyer*
Canty, Dawn M. *lawyer*
Carlin, Dennis J. *lawyer*
Carlson, Walter Carl *lawyer*
Carpenter, David William *lawyer*
Carr, Jeffrey W. *lawyer, manufacturing executive*
Carr, Walter Stanley *lawyer*
Carren, Jeffrey P. *lawyer*
Carroll, James J. *lawyer*
Carroll, William Kenneth *lawyer, educator, psychologist, theologian*
Case, Mary Anne *law educator*
Ceko, Theresa C. *law educator, lawyer*
Chafetz, Barry Richard *lawyer*
Chandler, Kent, Jr. *lawyer*
Chapman, John Stuart *lawyer*
Cheely, Daniel Joseph *lawyer*
Chemers, Robert Marc *lawyer*
Cherry, Daniel Ronald *lawyer*
Chiles, Stephen Michael *lawyer*
Clark, James Allen *lawyer, educator*
Clark, James E. *lawyer*
Clemens, Richard Glenn *lawyer*
Cloutier, Kevin M. *lawyer*
Cohen, Melanie Rovner *lawyer*
Cole, Thomas Amor *lawyer*
Collen, John *lawyer, educator*
Comella, Phillip L. *lawyer*
Congalton, Christopher William *lawyer*
Conklin, Thomas William *lawyer*
Conlon, William F. *lawyer*
Conway, Michael Maurice *lawyer*
Copeland, Edward Jerome *lawyer*
Costello, John William *lawyer*
Crane, Charlotte *law educator*
Crane, Mark *lawyer*
Craven, George W. *lawyer*
Crawford, Dewey Byers *lawyer*
Crisham, Thomas Michael *lawyer*
Crosby, John Bartlett *lawyer, health science association administrator*
Crossan, John Robert *lawyer*
Crull, Jan, Jr. *lawyer*
Cummings, Andrea J. *lawyer*
Cunningham, Robert James *lawyer*
Currie, David Park *law educator*
Cusack, John Thomas *lawyer*
Custer, Charles Francis *lawyer*
Daley, Michael Joseph *lawyer*
Daley, Susan Jean *lawyer*
Dam, Kenneth W. *law educator, former federal agency administrator*
Dandridge, LeNor *paralegal*
Dasso, James Daniel *lawyer*
Davis, Michael W. *lawyer*
Davis, Muller *lawyer*
Davis, Scott Jonathan *lawyer*
Dechene, James Charles *lawyer*
Dees, Richard Lee *lawyer*
de Hoyos, Debora M. *lawyer*
Deitrick, William Edgar *lawyer*
de Lasa, José M. *lawyer*

Delp, Wilbur Charles, Jr. *lawyer*
Denvir, Robert F. *lawyer*
Desideri, Lawrence R. *lawyer*
D'Esposito, Julian C., Jr. *lawyer*
Despres, Leon Mathis *lawyer, former city official*
Devine, Richard A. (Dick DeVine) *lawyer*
DeVries, James Howard *lawyer*
DeWolfe, John Chauncey, Jr. *lawyer*
DeYoe, David P. *lawyer*
Diamond, Shari Seidman *law professor, psychology professor*
Dixon, Stewart Strawn *lawyer, consultant*
Dockterman, Michael *lawyer*
Dolan, Michael F. *lawyer*
Dondanville, Patricia *lawyer*
Donlevy, John Dearden *lawyer*
Douglas, Charles W. *lawyer*
Downs, Robert K. *lawyer*
Doyle, John Robert *lawyer*
Drake, Francis LeBaron *law librarian*
Drizin, Steven A. *law educator, lawyer*
Dube, Monte I. *lawyer*
DuCanto, Joseph Nunzio *lawyer, educator*
Duhl, Michael Foster *lawyer*
Duncan, John Patrick Cavanaugh *lawyer*
Dunlop, Karen Owen *lawyer*
Dunn, Edwin Rydell *lawyer*
Dunning, Jeffrey Patrick *lawyer*
Durchslag, Stephen P. *lawyer*
Durkin, Kevin P. *lawyer*
Dykstra, Paul Hopkins *lawyer*
Eaton, Maja Campbell *lawyer*
Edwards, Charles Lloyd *lawyer*
Edwards, Christine Annette *lawyer*
Egan, Kevin James *lawyer*
Eggert, Russell Raymond *lawyer*
Eimer, Nathan Philip *lawyer*
Ekdahl, Jon Nels *lawyer*
Elden, Gary Michael *lawyer*
Ellis, Stuart L. *lawyer*
Elrod, Steven M. *lawyer*
Elson, Alex *lawyer, educator, arbitrator*
Elson, John S. *legal educator*
Emerson, Carter Whitney *lawyer*
English, John Dwight *lawyer*
Eovaldi, Thomas L. *law educator*
Epstein, Richard A. *law educator*
Erens, Jay Allan *lawyer*
Esrick, Jerald Paul *lawyer*
Evanich, Kevin Reese *lawyer*
Even, Francis Alphonse *lawyer*
Fahner, Tyrone C. *lawyer, former state attorney general*
Farber, Bernard John *lawyer*
Fayhee, Michael R. *lawyer*
Fazio, Peter Victor, Jr. *lawyer*
Feinstein, Fred Ira *lawyer*
Feldman, Mark I. *lawyer*
Fellows, Jerry Kenneth *lawyer*
Felsenthal, Steven Altus *lawyer*
Ferber, Leonard *lawyer*
Ferguson, Stanley Lewis *lawyer*
Ferrini, James Thomas *lawyer*
Field, Robert Edward *lawyer*
Fields, Barry E. *lawyer*
Filpi, Robert Alan *lawyer*
Fina, Paul Joseph *lawyer*
Findlay, Donald Cameron *lawyer, former federal agency administrator*
Finke, Robert Forge *lawyer*
Fischel, Daniel R. *law educator*
Fitzgerald, Patrick J. *prosecutor*
Fort, Jeffrey C. *lawyer*
Foudree, Bruce William *lawyer*
Fowler, Don Wall *lawyer*
Fox, Paul T. *lawyer*
Franch, Richard Thomas *lawyer*
Francis, Clinton William *law educator*
Franklin, Richard Mark *lawyer*
Frederick, Thomas James *lawyer*
Freed, Mayer Goodman *law educator*
Freeman, Lee Allen, Jr. *lawyer*
Freeman, Louis S. *lawyer*
Friedli, Helen Russell *lawyer*
Friedman, Lawrence Milton *lawyer*
Friedman, Roselyn L. *lawyer, mediator*
Fross, Roger Raymond *lawyer*
Fuller, Perry Lucian *lawyer*
Furlane, Mark Elliott *lawyer*
Gaggini, John Edmund *lawyer*
Galainena, M. David *lawyer*
Gallopoulos, Gregory Stratis *lawyer*
Gangemi, Columbus Rudolph, Jr. *lawyer, educator*
Garber, Samuel B. *lawyer, retail executive*
Garcia, Paul R. *lawyer*
Gavin, John Neal *lawyer*
Gavin, Steven J. *lawyer*
Gearen, John Joseph *lawyer*
Gecker, James M. *lawyer*
Geiman, J. Robert *lawyer*
Gelman, Andrew Richard *lawyer*
George, John Martin, Jr. *lawyer*
Geraghty, Diane C. *law educator*
Geraldson, Raymond I., Jr. *lawyer*
Gerber, Dean N. *lawyer*
Gerlits, Francis Joseph *lawyer*
Gerstein, Mark Douglas *lawyer*
Gibbons, William John *lawyer*
Gilbert, Howard N(orman) *lawyer, director*
Gilford, Steven Ross *lawyer*
Gilson, Jerome *lawyer, writer*
Ginsburg, Allen J. *lawyer*
Gladden, James Walter, Jr. *lawyer*
Glieberman, Herbert Allen *lawyer*
Godfrey, Richard Cartier *lawyer*
Golan, Stephen Leonard *lawyer*
Goldblatt, Stanford Jay *lawyer*
Good, Steven Loren *real estate consultant*
Gordon, James S. *lawyer, director*
Gordon, Phillip *lawyer*
Gottlieb, Gidon Alain Guy *law educator*
Graham, David F. *lawyer*
Grant, Robert Nathan *lawyer*
Graves, Robert J. *lawyer*
Greenbaum, Lewis *lawyer*
Greenberg, Richard T. *lawyer*
Grimm, Terry M. *lawyer*
Grossman, Robert Mayer *lawyer*
Guthman, Jack *lawyer*
Gutstein, Solomon *lawyer*
Hagy, James C. *lawyer*

Hahn, Arthur W. *lawyer*
Hahn, Frederic Louis *lawyer*
Hall, Jeffrey A. *lawyer*
Halperin, Errol R. *lawyer*
Hamburger, Philip Andrew *law educator*
Hammes, Jeffrey C. *lawyer*
Hannah, Wayne Robertson, Jr. *lawyer*
Hannay, William Mouat III *lawyer*
Hanson, Ronald William *lawyer*
Harcourt, Bernard E. *law educator*
Hardgrove, James Alan *lawyer*
Harmon, Teresa Wilton *lawyer*
Harrington, Carol A. *lawyer*
Harrington, James Timothy *lawyer*
Harris, Susan V. *lawyer*
Harrison, Holly A. *lawyer*
Harrold, Bernard *lawyer*
Hartz, Michael O. *lawyer*
Haskins, Charles Gregory, Jr. *lawyer*
Hayes, David John Arthur, Jr. *legal association executive*
Hayward, Robert M. *lawyer*
Hayward, Thomas Zander, Jr. *lawyer*
Heatwole, Mark M. *lawyer, director*
Heinz, John Peter *lawyer, educator*
Heinz, William Denby *lawyer*
Heisler, Quentin George, Jr. *lawyer*
Helman, Robert Alan *lawyer*
Helmholz, R(ichard) H(enry) *law educator*
Henderson, Janet E. E. *lawyer*
Hendrickson, John P. *lawyer*
Henning, Joel Frank *lawyer, writer*
Henry, Frederick Edward *lawyer*
Hensel, Paul H. *lawyer*
Herald, J. Patrick *lawyer*
Herbert, William Carlisle *lawyer*
Herman, Sidney N. *lawyer*
Hess, Sidney J., Jr. *lawyer*
Hetz, Joseph F. *lawyer*
Hickman, Frederic W. *retired lawyer*
Hilliard, David Craig *lawyer, educator*
Hilliker, Donald Beckstett *lawyer*
Hirshman, Harold Carl *lawyer*
Hodes, Scott *lawyer*
Hofer, Roy Ellis *lawyer*
Hoff, John Scott *lawyer*
Hoffman, Richard Bruce *lawyer*
Hoffman, Valerie Jane *lawyer*
Homburger, Thomas Charles *lawyer*
Horwich, Allan *lawyer*
Hoskins, Richard Jerold *lawyer*
Howe, Jonathan Thomas *lawyer*
Howell, R(obert) Thomas, Jr. *lawyer, former food company executive*
Hummel, Gregory William *lawyer*
Hunt, Lawrence Halley, Jr. *lawyer*
Hynes, Brian *lawyer, lobbyist*
Irukera, Babatunde Ayokunle *lawyer*
Isaacson, Samuel B. *lawyer*
Jachino, Daneen L. *legal administrator*
Jacobs, Caryn Leslie *lawyer, former prosecutor*
Jacobson, Marian Slutz *lawyer*
Jacobson, Richard Joseph *lawyer*
Jacoby, John Patrick *lawyer*
Jacover, Jerold Alan *lawyer*
Jager, Melvin Francis *lawyer*
Joern, Charles Edward, Jr. *lawyer*
John, Peter C. *lawyer*
Johnson, Elmer William *lawyer*
Johnson, Garrett Bruce *lawyer*
Johnson, Richard Fred *lawyer*
Jones, Sandra Yvonne *lawyer*
Joseph, Robert Thomas *lawyer*
Joslin, Rodney Dean *lawyer*
Junewicz, James J. *lawyer*
Kallick, David A. *lawyer*
Kaminski, David P. *lawyer*
Kantrow, Josh Mark *lawyer*
Kaplan, Jared *lawyer*
Kaplan, Joel H. *lawyer*
Karlin, Edward J. *lawyer*
Katz, Avrum Sidney *lawyer*
Katz, Stuart Charles *lawyer, musician*
Kauffman, Peter H. *lawyer, energy executive*
Kaufman, Andrew Michael *lawyer*
Kellman, Sandra Y. *lawyer*
Kelly, Charles Arthur *lawyer*
Kenney, Colleen M. *lawyer*
Kenney, Crane H. *lawyer*
Kenney, Frank Deming *lawyer*
Kikoler, Stephen Philip *lawyer*
Kim, Michael Charles *lawyer*
King, Sharon Louise *lawyer*
Kins, Juris *lawyer*
Kissel, Richard John *lawyer*
Kistenbroker, David H. *lawyer*
Kitch, Paul R. *lawyer*
Kite, Steven B. *lawyer*
Klenk, James Andrew *lawyer*
Klenk, Timothy Carver *lawyer*
Knight, Christopher Nichols *lawyer*
Knox, James Marshall *lawyer*
Koch, Steven *lawyer, investment banker, finance company executive*
Kohn, Shalom L. *lawyer*
Kolek, Robert Edward *lawyer*
Kopelman, Ian Stuart *lawyer*
Koppelman, Andrew Martin Mayer *law educator*
Kozak, John W. *lawyer*
Kramer, Andrea S. *lawyer*
Krasny, Paula J. *lawyer*
Kravitt, Jason Harris Paperno *lawyer*
Kresse, William Joseph *lawyer, educator, accountant*
Kriss, Robert J. *lawyer*
Krivicich, John Augustine *lawyer*
Kroll, Barry Lewis *retired lawyer*
Kroot, Jason M. *lawyer*
Ladd, Jeffrey Raymond *lawyer*
Laidlaw, Andrew R. *lawyer*
Landes, William M. *law educator*
Landow-Esser, Janine Marise *lawyer*
Laner, Richard Warren *lawyer*
Lang, Gordon, Jr. *retired lawyer*
Lanznar, Howard S. *lawyer*
Lassar, Scott R. *lawyer, former prosecutor*
Latimer, Kenneth Alan *lawyer*
Lefco, Kathy Nan *law librarian*
Lemein, Gregg D. *lawyer*
Leonard, Laura L. *lawyer*
LeRoy, Spencer III *lawyer*

Levenfeld, Milton Arthur *lawyer*
Levi, John G. *lawyer*
Levin, Charles Edward *lawyer*
Levin, Jack S. *lawyer*
Levin, Lawrence Daniel *lawyer*
Levine, Laurence Harvey *lawyer*
Levy, Peter A. *lawyer*
Leyhane, Francis John III *lawyer*
Libowsky, Stephen David *lawyer*
Lien, John Donovan *lawyer*
Liggio, Carl Donald *lawyer*
Lindgren, James *law educator*
Linklater, William Joseph *lawyer*
Lipton, Lois Jean *lawyer*
Litwin, Burton Howard *lawyer*
Livingston, Bradford Lee *lawyer*
Lochbihler, Frederick Vincent *lawyer*
Lockwood, Gary Lee *lawyer*
Lona, Marie A. *lawyer*
Looman, James R. *lawyer*
Lorch, Kenneth F. *lawyer*
Lowinger, Frederick Charles *lawyer*
Lubet, Steven *law educator*
Lubin, Donald G. *lawyer*
Luning, Thomas P. *lawyer*
Luscombe, George A., II, *lawyer*
Lutter, Paul Allen *lawyer*
Lyerla, Bradford Peter *lawyer*
Lynch, John Peter *lawyer*
Macaulay, Susan Jane *lawyer, law educator*
MacCarthy, John L. *lawyer*
MacCarthy, Terence Francis *lawyer*
MacKinnon, Kevin Scott *lawyer*
Malinowski, Arthur Anthony *lawyer, arbitrator*
Malkin, Cary Jay *lawyer*
Malovany, Howard *lawyer*
Mancoff, Neal Alan *lawyer*
Mandell, Floyd A. *lawyer*
Mansfield, Karen Lee *lawyer*
Manzo, Edward David *lawyer*
Martin, Arthur Mead *lawyer*
Martin, Laura Keidan *lawyer*
Marwedel, Warren John *lawyer*
Mason, Richard J. *lawyer*
Matis, Nina B. *lawyer*
Matsakis, Elias N. *lawyer*
McCaleb, Malcolm, Jr. *lawyer*
McChesney, Fred S. *law educator*
McCloy, Elizabeth K. *lawyer*
McClure, James Julius, Jr. *lawyer, former city official*
McCormick, Steven D. *lawyer*
McCracken, Thomas James, Jr. *lawyer*
McCue, Judith W. *lawyer*
McDermott, John Henry *lawyer*
McDonald, Sally J. *lawyer*
McDonald, Thomas Alexander *lawyer*
McDonough, John Michael *lawyer*
McGaan, Andrew Raymond *lawyer*
McGovern, Peter John *law educator*
McGowan, Michael Jeremy *lawyer*
McGrath, William Joseph *lawyer*
McLaren, Richard Wellington, Jr. *lawyer*
McLaughlin, T. Mark *lawyer*
McMenamin, John Robert *lawyer*
McVisk, William Kilburn *lawyer*
Mehlman, Mark Franklin *lawyer*
Mehrberg, Randall Eric *lawyer*
Melbinger, Michael S. *lawyer*
Melton, David Reuben *lawyer*
Meltzer, Bernard David *law educator*
Michaels, Richard Edward *lawyer*
Michalak, Edward Francis *lawyer*
Mihelic, Tracey L. *lawyer*
Mikva, Abner Joseph *lawyer, retired judge*
Miller, Kenneth W. *lawyer*
Miller, Lee I. *lawyer*
Miller, Paul J. *lawyer*
Miller, Peter C. *lawyer*
Miller, Stephen Ralph *lawyer*
Millien, Raymond *lawyer*
Mims, Joyce Elaine *lawyer*
Minichello, Dennis *lawyer*
Minow, Newton Norman *lawyer, educator*
Montgomery, Charles Barry *lawyer*
Montgomery, William Adam *lawyer*
Morency, Paula J. *lawyer*
Morgan, Betsy Stelle *lawyer*
Morgan, Donna Evensen *lawyer*
Morof, Jeffrey W. *lawyer*
Morrison, Portia Owen *lawyer*
Morrow, John E. *lawyer*
Morsch, Thomas Harvey *law educator, lawyer*
Motherway, Nicholas J. *lawyer*
Mullen, J. Thomas *lawyer*
Mullen, Michael T. *lawyer*
Murdock, Charles William *lawyer, educator*
Murphy, Kathleen M. *lawyer*
Murray, Daniel Richard *lawyer*
Murtaugh, Christopher David *lawyer*
Myers, Lonn William *lawyer*
Napolitano, Steven V. *lawyer*
Neely, Ellen J. *lawyer*
Neff, David M. *lawyer*
Neis, James Michael *lawyer*
Neumeier, Matthew Michael *lawyer, educator*
Newman, Terry E. *lawyer*
Nicklin, Emily *lawyer*
Nicolaides, Mary *lawyer*
Niehaus, Mary C. *lawyer*
Nijman, Jennifer T. *lawyer*
Niro, Cheryl *lawyer*
Nitikman, Franklin W. *lawyer*
Nord, Robert Eamor *lawyer*
Notz, John Kranz, Jr. *arbitrator, mediator, retired lawyer*
Novak, Mark *lawyer*
Novak, Theodore J. *lawyer*
Novotny, David Joseph *lawyer*
Nowacki, James Nelson *lawyer*
Nussbaum, Bernard J. *lawyer*
Nyhan, Lawrence J. (Larry) *lawyer*
O'Brien, James Phillip *lawyer*
Odorizzi, Michele L. *lawyer*
Oesterle, Eric Adam *lawyer*
O'Hagan, James Joseph *lawyer*
O'Leary, Daniel Vincent, Jr. *lawyer*
Olian, Robert Martin *lawyer*
Olson, Steven R. *lawyer*
O'Malley, John Daniel *lawyer, educator, banker*
O'Neil, Michael C. *lawyer*

O'Neill, Bridget R. *lawyer*
Ostfeld, Gregory Edward *lawyer*
Pallasch, B. Michael *lawyer, director*
Palmer, John Bernard III *lawyer*
Palmer, Robert Towne *lawyer, bank executive*
Palmore, Rick (Roderick A. Palmore) *lawyer*
Panich, Danuta Bembenista *lawyer*
Parkhurst, Beverly Susler *lawyer, administrative law judge*
Parkhurst, Todd Sheldon *lawyer*
Partridge, Mark Van Buren *lawyer, educator, mediator, writer*
Parzen, Stanley Julius *lawyer*
Pascal, Roger *lawyer*
Pavalon, Eugene Irving *lawyer*
Pedersen, Peer *lawyer*
Pelton, Russell Meredith *lawyer*
Pengra, R. Rene *lawyer*
Perzek, Philip John *lawyer*
Pesch, Ellen P. *lawyer*
Peters, Charles H.R. *lawyer*
Petersen, Donald Sondergaard *lawyer*
Peterson, Kenneth Allen, Jr. *lawyer*
Peterson, Randall Theodore *law educator, law librarian*
Peterson, Ronald Roger *lawyer*
Picker, Randal C. *law educator*
Piekarski, Victor J. *lawyer*
Pinsky, Michael S. *lawyer*
Pirok, Edward Warren *lawyer, consultant*
Pitt, George *lawyer, investment banker*
Pollock, Earl Edward *lawyer*
Posner, Eric A. *law educator*
Power, Joseph Aloysius, Jr. *lawyer*
Presser, Stephen Bruce *lawyer, educator*
Prior, Gary L. *lawyer*
Pritikin, David T. *lawyer*
Prochnow, Douglas Lee *lawyer*
Qasim, Imad Isa *lawyer*
Quaini, Duane C. *lawyer*
Rankin, James Winton *lawyer*
Ranney, George A., Jr. *lawyer*
Rapoport, David E. *lawyer*
Rappaport, Richard J. *lawyer*
Ratner, Gerald *lawyer*
Rea, Anne E. *lawyer*
Reategui, Lisa J. *lawyer*
Redish, Martin Harris *legal educator*
Redman, Clarence Owen *lawyer*
Reich, Allan J. *lawyer*
Reicin, Ronald Ian *lawyer*
Reidy, Daniel Edward *lawyer*
Reis, Leslie Ann *law educator, lawyer*
Reiter, Michael A. *lawyer, educator*
Relias, John Alexis *lawyer*
Remien, Natalie A. *lawyer*
Resnick, Donald Ira *lawyer*
Reum, James Michael *lawyer*
Reyes, Victor H. *lawyer*
Reynolds, Thomas A. III *lawyer*
Rhind, James Thomas *lawyer*
Rich, Nancy Jean *lawyer*
Richard, Howard M. *lawyer*
Richards, Brian F. *lawyer*
Richardson-Lowry, Mary *lawyer*
Richman, Joan M. *lawyer*
Richman, John Marshall *lawyer, food products executive*
Richmond, James Glidden *lawyer*
Rieger, Mitchell Sheridan *lawyer*
Riley, James B., Jr. *lawyer*
Ritchie, P. Scott *lawyer*
Ritchie, William Paul *lawyer*
Rizzo, Ronald Stephen *lawyer*
Robbins, Ellen Sue *lawyer, educator*
Roberts, Dorothy E. *law educator*
Roberts, John Charles *law educator*
Roin, Julie *law educator*
Rollo, Sherry Lee *lawyer*
Rooney, Matthew A. *lawyer*
Roper, Harry Joseph *lawyer*
Ropski, Gary Melchior *lawyer*
Rosen, Barry S. *lawyer*
Rosenbloom, Lewis Stanley *lawyer*
Rosenblum, Judith A. *law educator*
Rosenfield, Andrew M. *lawyer, educator*
Rotner, Philip R. *lawyer*
Rubin, E(rwin) Leonard *lawyer*
Rudnick, Lewis G. *lawyer*
Rudnick, Paul David *lawyer*
Rudoy, Herbert L. *lawyer*
Rudstein, David Stewart *law educator*
Rundio, Louis Michael, Jr. *lawyer*
Rupert, Donald William *lawyer*
Russell, Paul Frederick *lawyer*
Rutkoff, Alan Stuart *lawyer*
Ruxin, Paul Theodore *lawyer*
Ryan, Edward F. *lawyer*
Ryan, Thomas F. *lawyer*
Sabl, John J. *lawyer*
Sacoff, Robert W. *lawyer*
Salpeter, Alan N. *lawyer*
Sanchez, Vincent A. *lawyer*
Sandberg, Craig M. *lawyer*
Sanders, Richard Henry *lawyer*
Saunders, George Lawton, Jr. *lawyer*
Sawyier, Michael Tod *lawyer, director*
Schaffer, Henry M. *lawyer*
Schaffner, Howard Sheldon *lawyer*
Scharf, Stephanie A. *lawyer*
Schiller, Donald Charles *lawyer*
Schink, James Harvey *lawyer*
Schmidt, John R. *lawyer*
Schneider, Dan W. *lawyer, consultant*
Schneider, Robert Jerome *lawyer*
Schoonhoven, Ray James *retired lawyer*
Schopf, William Grant *lawyer*
Schoumacher, Bruce Herbert *lawyer*
Schreck, Robert A., Jr. *lawyer*
Schriver, John T. III *lawyer*
Schultz, Kurt Lee *lawyer*
Schulz, Keith Donald *corporate lawyer, writer*
Schwartz, Donald Lee *lawyer*
Scogland, William Lee *lawyer*
Selman, Russell Bertram *lawyer*
Sennet, Charles Joseph *lawyer*
Sennett, Michael *lawyer*
Sergi, Vincent A.F. *lawyer*
Serritella, William David *lawyer*
Serwer, Alan Michael *lawyer*
Sessions, Barbara C. *lawyer*

Sfikas, Peter Michael *lawyer, educator*
Shank, Suzanne Adams *lawyer*
Shapiro, Keith J. *lawyer*
Shapiro, Stephen Michael *lawyer*
Shapiro, Steven A. *lawyer*
Shapo, Helene S. *law educator*
Shapo, Marshall Schambelan *lawyer, educator*
Sheffield, Jeffrey T. *lawyer*
Shepard, Michael J. *prosecutor*
Sherman, Ian Matthew *lawyer*
Sherman, Jeremy P. *lawyer*
Shields, Thomas Charles *lawyer*
Shindler, Donald A. *lawyer*
Shulruff, Stuart P. *lawyer*
Siegel, Howard Jerome *lawyer*
Silberman, Alan Harvey *lawyer*
Silets, Harvey Marvin *lawyer*
Silverman, Gary R. *lawyer*
Silverman, Ross O. *lawyer*
Simon, George T. *lawyer*
Simon, John Bern *lawyer*
Simon, Seymour *lawyer, former state supreme court justice*
Skilling, Raymond Inwood *lawyer*
Skinner, Mary Jacobs *lawyer*
Sklarsky, Charles B. *lawyer*
Smart, Allen Rich, II, *retired lawyer*
Smedinghoff, Thomas J. *lawyer*
Smith, Arthur B., Jr. *lawyer*
Smith, Todd A. *lawyer*
Smolen, Lee M. *lawyer*
Solow, Michael Barry *lawyer*
Spain, Richard Colby *lawyer*
Spector, David M. *lawyer*
Spellmire, George W. *lawyer*
Spindler, George S. *lawyer, retired oil industry executive*
Sproger, Charles Edmund *retired lawyer*
Sprowl, Charles Riggs *lawyer*
Stack, Paul Francis *lawyer*
Stallworth, Stanley B *lawyer*
Stanhaus, James Steven *lawyer*
Starkman, Gary Lee *lawyer*
Stassen, John Henry *lawyer*
Steinberg, Morton M. *lawyer*
Sternstein, Allan J. *lawyer*
Stetler, David J. *lawyer*
Stevens, Stanley M. *lawyer*
Stevenson, Adlai Ewing III *lawyer, retired senator*
Stiegel, Michael Allen *lawyer*
Stillman, Nina Gidden *lawyer*
Stoll, John Robert *lawyer, educator*
Stone, Geoffrey Richard *lawyer, educator*
Stone, Susan A. *lawyer*
Strauss, David A. *law educator*
Streff, William Albert, Jr. *lawyer*
Strohm, Bruce C. *lawyer, real estate company executive*
Sullivan, Barry *lawyer*
Sullivan, Marcia Waite *lawyer*
Sullivan, Thomas Patrick *lawyer*
Sunstein, Cass Robert *law educator*
Sweeney, James Raymond *retired lawyer*
Swibel, Howard Jay *lawyer*
Swibel, Steven Warren *lawyer*
Swiecicki, Peter *lawyer*
Swiger, Elinor Porter *lawyer*
Tabin, Julius *lawyer, physicist*
Tarun, Robert Walter *lawyer*
Tetzlaff, Theodore R. *lawyer*
Theobald, Edward Robert *lawyer*
Thies, Richard Brian *lawyer*
Thomas, Frederick Bradley *lawyer*
Thomas, Stephen Paul *lawyer*
Thompson, James Robert, Jr. *lawyer, former governor*
Thompson, Michael *lawyer*
Tiller, Emerson H. *law educator*
Tobin, Craig Daniel *lawyer*
Toohey, James Kevin *lawyer*
Toth, Bruce A. *lawyer*
Treston, Sherry S. *lawyer*
Trost, Eileen Bannon *lawyer*
Truskowski, John Budd *lawyer*
Tryban, Esther Elizabeth *lawyer*
Ungaretti, Richard Anthony *lawyer*
Valukas, Anton Ronald *lawyer, former prosecutor*
Vermeule, Adrian *law educator*
Vezeau, Timothy J. *lawyer*
Vishneski, John Stanley III *lawyer*
Vishny, Paul Harvey *lawyer*
Vojvodich, Sava Alexander *lawyer*
Vree, Roger Allen *lawyer*
Wakschlag, Milton Samuel *lawyer*
Walker, Debra Bess *lawyer*
Walsh, Michael S. *lawyer*
Wander, Herbert Stanton *lawyer*
Wanke, Ronald Lee *lawyer*
Weaver, Timothy Allan *lawyer*
Webb, Dan K. *lawyer*
Weber, Susan A. *lawyer*
Weinberg, Walter S. *lawyer*
Weinkopf, Friedrich J. *lawyer*
Weinsheimer, William Cyrus *lawyer*
Weisbach, David A *law educator*
Weiss, John Robert *lawyer*
Weissman, Michael Lewis *lawyer*
Welsh, Kelly Raymond *lawyer, investment company executive*
Whalen, Wayne W. *lawyer*
White, Henry F., Jr. *legal association administrator, retired military officer*
White, Linda Diane *lawyer*
Wieczorek, Dennis E. *lawyer*
Wildman, Max Edward *lawyer, director*
Wine-Banks, Jill Susan *lawyer*
Wise, William Jerrard *lawyer*
Witcoff, Sheldon William *lawyer*
Wolf, Charles Benno *lawyer*
Wolfe, David Louis *lawyer*
Wood, Mark D. *lawyer*
Woodford, Peter C. *lawyer*
Wright, Judith Margaret *law librarian, educator, dean*
Yuracko, Kimberly *law educator*
Zabel, Sheldon Alter *lawyer, law educator*
Zagel, Margaret Maxwell *lawyer*
Zemm, Sandra Phyllis *lawyer*
Zenner, Sheldon Toby *lawyer*
Zhao, Jia *lawyer*
Zolno, Mark S. *lawyer*

## Chicago Heights
Cifelli, John Louis *lawyer*

## Cicero
Paprocki, Thomas John *lawyer, priest*

## Crystal Lake
Shank, William O. *lawyer*
Wade, Edwin Lee *lawyer, writer*

## Danville
Anderson, Claudia Smith *lawyer*

## Decatur
Dunn, John Francis *lawyer, state representative*
Reising, Richard P. *lawyer*
Smith, David James *corporate lawyer*

## Deerfield
Birmingham, William Joseph *retired lawyer*
Green, Dana I. *lawyer, human resources specialist*
Pearson, Louise S. *lawyer*
Persky, Marla Susan *lawyer*
Sabatino, Thomas Joseph, Jr. *lawyer*
Scott, Theodore R. *retired lawyer*
Vollen, Robert Jay *lawyer*

## Des Plaines
Gold, Deidra D. *lawyer*

## Downers Grove
Kaput, Jim L. *lawyer*
Siedlecki, Nancy Therese *lawyer, funeral director*

## Elgin
Golden, Loren S. *lawyer*

## Elk Grove Village
Lovejoy, Paul Robert *lawyer*

## Elmwood Park
Spina, Anthony Ferdinand *lawyer*

## Evanston
Creamer, Robert Allan *lawyer*
Dana, David *law educator*
Morrison, John Horton *lawyer*
Nechin, Herbert Benjamin *lawyer*
Salem, Richard Allen *mediator*
Schulte, Bruce John *lawyer*
Witwer, Samuel Weiler, Jr. *lawyer*

## Fairview Heights
Tenpas, Ronald J. *prosecutor, lawyer*

## Flossmoor
Garrison, Ray Harlan *lawyer*

## Galva
Everett, Reynolds Melville, Jr. *lawyer*
Massie, Michael Earl *lawyer*

## Geneva
Tyler, Lloyd John *retired lawyer*
Weiler, Rory Thomas *lawyer*

## Genoa
Cromley, Jon Lowell *lawyer*

## Glen Ellyn
Hudson, Dennis Lee *lawyer, retired arbitrator, federal official*
O'Connell, Daniel James *lawyer*
Sandrok, Richard William *lawyer*
Ulrich, Werner *patent lawyer*

## Glencoe
Perlberg, Jules Martin *lawyer*

## Glenview
Berkman, Michael G. *lawyer*
Dawson, Suzanne Stockus *lawyer*
Knox, James Edwin *lawyer*

## Granite City
Rarick, Philip Joseph *lawyer, retired state supreme court justice*

## Hanover
Bleveans, John *lawyer*

## Hickory Hills
Lustig, Margaret Gallagher *lawyer*

## Highland Park
Gash, Lauren Beth *lawyer, state legislator*
Karol, Nathaniel H. *lawyer, consultant*
Nelson, Richard David *lawyer*
Schindel, Donald Marvin *retired lawyer*

## Hoffman Estates
Zopp, Andrea Lynne *lawyer, retail executive*

## Itasca
Broad, Matthew *lawyer*
Rosengren, John Charles *lawyer*

## Jacksonville
Kuster, Larry Donald *lawyer*

## Joliet
Lenard, George Dean *lawyer*
Teas, Richard Harper *lawyer*

## Kankakee
Deck, Gregory A. *lawyer*

## Kenilworth
Feng, Paul Yen-Hsiung *lawyer, chemist*
McKittrick, William Wood *lawyer*
Weaver, Clifford Lee *retired lawyer, winery owner*

## La Grange
Kerr, Alexander Duncan, Jr. *lawyer*

## Lafox
Seils, William George *lawyer*

**Lake Forest**
Covington, George Morse *retired lawyer*
Emerson, William Harry *retired lawyer*
Faulkner, James Vincent, Jr. *lawyer*
Francois, William Armand *lawyer*
Howard, John Lawrence *federal agency lawyer*
Palmer, Ann Therese Darin *lawyer*
Parker, Dean E. *lawyer*
Prochnow, Herbert Victor, Jr. *retired lawyer*
Sikorovsky, Eugene Frank *retired lawyer*
Smith, Marschall Imboden *lawyer*

**Lake Zurich**
Scott, John Joseph *lawyer*

**Lincolnshire**
Michalik, John James *legal association administrator*
Para, Gerard Albert *lawyer, real estate broker, consultant*

**Lincolnwood**
Carroll, Howard William *state legislator*
Zaremski, Miles Jay *lawyer*

**Litchfield**
Floreth, Frederick Dennis *lawyer*

**Long Grove**
Conway, John K. *lawyer*
Davis, Britton Anthony *retired lawyer*
Obert, Paul Richard *lawyer, manufacturing executive*

**Marengo**
Franks, Herbert Hoover *lawyer*

**Melrose Park**
Schmidt, Gary P. *lawyer, personal care industry executive*

**Mokena**
Sangmeister, George Edward *lawyer, consultant, congressman*

**Moline**
Jenkins, James Robert *lawyer, chemicals executive*
Nowinski, Frank Lawrence *lawyer*

**Mount Vernon**
Harvey, Morris Lane *lawyer*

**Naperville**
Corvino, Beth Byster *lawyer*
Gracey, Paul C., Jr. *lawyer, utilities executive*
Larson, Mark Edward, Jr. *lawyer, educator, financial planner*
Tibble, Douglas Clair *lawyer*

**Northbrook**
Abbey, G(eorge) Marshall *lawyer, retired health facility administrator*
Bohlender, Hugh Darrow *lawyer*
Lapin, Harvey I. *lawyer*
Rosemarin, Carey Stephen *lawyer*
Rotchford, Patricia Kathleen *lawyer, mediator*
Sernett, Richard Patrick *lawyer*
Stewart, Charles Leslie *lawyer*
Wallace, Harry Leland *lawyer*

**Oak Brook**
Barnes, Karen Kay *lawyer*
Bennett, Margaret Airola *lawyer*
Congalton, Susan Tichenor *lawyer*
Hollins, Mitchell Leslie *lawyer*
Marinaccio, Lee Anthony *lawyer*
Santona, Gloria *lawyer*
Sherman, Jennifer L. *lawyer*

**Oak Park**
Schubert, Blake H. *lawyer*
Sengpiehl, Paul Marvin *lawyer, retired state official*

**Olympia Fields**
Nuding, Doris Leona *law librarian, researcher*

**Oswego**
May, Frank Brendan, Jr. *lawyer*

**Palatine**
Victor, Michael Gary *lawyer, physician*
Zamarin, Ronald George *lawyer*

**Park Forest**
Goodrich, John Bernard *lawyer, consultant*

**Park Ridge**
LaRue, Paul Hubert *retired lawyer*

**Peoria**
Allen, Lyle Wallace *lawyer*
Bertschy, Timothy L. *lawyer*
Buda, James B. *lawyer, manufacturing executive*
Parsons, Richard Hugo *lawyer*
Woods, Michael Lee *lawyer*

**Prospect Heights**
Leopold, Mark F. *lawyer*

**Rockford**
Johnson, Thomas Stuart *lawyer*
Reno, Roger *lawyer*
Tuite, Gerald Francis *lawyer, commercial real estate manager*

**Rolling Meadows**
Breakstone, Donald S. *lawyer*

**Rosemont**
Nichols, Robert Hastings *lawyer*

**Schaumburg**
Lawson, A. Peter *lawyer*
Marshall, John David *lawyer*
Nehs, William Scott (Scott Nehs) *lawyer*

**Shorewood**
Heaphy, John Merrill *lawyer*

**Springfield**
Darby, Karen Sue *legal association administrator*
Dodge, James William *lawyer, educator*
Kerr, Gary Enrico *lawyer, educator*
LeBlang, Theodore Raymond *law educator, lawyer*
Londrigan, Thomas Foster *lawyer*
Malany, Le Grand Lynn *lawyer, engineer, bank executive*
Mathewson, Mark Stuart *lawyer, editor*
Stuart, Robert Allan, Jr. *lawyer*
Van Meter, Abram DeBois *lawyer, retired banker*

**Sterling**
Pace, Ole Bly III *lawyer*

**Sycamore**
Tucker, Watson Billopp *lawyer*

**Taylorville**
Austin, Daniel William *lawyer*

**Tinley Park**
Kenny, Mary Alice *lawyer*

**Toledo**
Prather, William C. III *lawyer, writer*

**Urbana**
Balbach, Stanley Byron *lawyer*
Endres, Arthur Bryan *law educator*
Fitz-Gerald, Roger Miller *lawyer*
Frederick, Robert George *lawyer*
Grossman, Margaret Rosso *law educator*
Rich, Robert F. *law educator, political science professor*
Webber, Carl Maddra *lawyer*

**Warrenville**
Boardman, Robert A. *retired lawyer*
Covey, Steven K. *lawyer*
Johnson, Douglas Wells *lawyer*

**Waukegan**
Henrick, Michael Francis *lawyer*

**Western Springs**
Hanson, Heidi Elizabeth *lawyer*

**Westmont**
Ford, Ralph A. *lawyer, moving and relocation company executive*

**Wheaton**
Kincaid, John Bruce *lawyer*
Stein, Lawrence A. *lawyer*

**Willowbrook**
Walton, Stanley Anthony III *lawyer*

**Wilmette**
Atkinson, Jeff John Frederick *lawyer, educator, writer*
Baisley, James Mahoney *retired lawyer*
Bunge, Jonathan Gunn *lawyer*

**Winnetka**
Crowe, Robert William *lawyer, mediator*
Ellwood, Scott *lawyer*
Greenblatt, Ray Harris *lawyer*
Hales, Daniel B. *lawyer*
McWhirter, Bruce J. *retired lawyer*
Webster, David Macpherson *lawyer*

**Woodridge**
Farrug, Eugene Joseph, Sr. *retired lawyer*

**Woodstock**
Ackley, Robert O. *lawyer*

**INDIANA**

**Batesville**
de Maynadier, Patrick D. *lawyer*

**Bloomington**
Aman, Alfred Charles, Jr. *law educator*
Baude, Patrick Louis *law educator*
Nunn, Ken *lawyer*
Shreve, Gene Russell *law educator*

**Carmel**
Burkett, Robert E., Jr. *lawyer, insurance company executive*

**Columbus**
Harrison, Patrick Woods *lawyer*
Rose, Marya Mernitz *lawyer*

**Danville**
Baldwin, Jeffrey Kenton *lawyer, educator*
Baldwin, Patricia Ann *lawyer*

**Elkhart**
Gassere, Eugene Arthur *lawyer, investment company executive*
Treckelo, Richard M. *lawyer*

**Evansville**
Clouse, John Daniel *lawyer*
Harrison, Joseph Heavrin *lawyer*
Hayes, Philip Harold *lawyer*
Heidorn, Robert E. *lawyer*
Miller, Daniel Raymond *prosecutor*
Reed, Helen Skuggedal *law librarian, musician*

**Fort Wayne**
Cain, Tim J. *lawyer*
Colvin, Sherrill William *lawyer*
Helmke, Paul (Walter Paul Helmke Jr.) *lawyer, former mayor*
Pope, Mark Andrew *lawyer, academic administrator*
Shoaff, Thomas Mitchell *lawyer*
Tourkow, Joshua Isaac *lawyer*

**Franklin**
Hamner, Lance Dalton *prosecutor*

**Gary**
Hall, John Henry *lawyer, historian, educator*
Michelstetter, Stanley Hubert *lawyer*

**Greenwood**
Van Valer, Joe Ned *lawyer, real estate developer*

**Hammond**
Capp, David A. *former prosecutor*
DeGuilio, Jon E. *lawyer*
Diamond, Eugene Christopher *lawyer, health facility administrator*
Van Bokkelen, Joseph Scott *prosecutor*

**Highland**
Gladish, David Stephen *lawyer*

**Indianapolis**
Albright, Terrill D. *lawyer*
Allen, David James *lawyer*
Armitage, Robert Allen *lawyer*
Avery, Melissa J. *lawyer*
Badger, David Harry *lawyer*
Beckwith, Lewis Daniel *lawyer*
Boldt, Michael Herbert *lawyer*
Born, Samuel Roydon, II *retired lawyer, mediator*
Bowman, Frank O. *law educator*
Braly, Angela F. *lawyer, insurance company executive*
Brooks, Susan W. *prosecutor*
Butt, P. Lawrence *lawyer*
Carmichael, Daniel P. *lawyer*
Carney, Joseph Buckingham *lawyer*
Choplin, John M., II, *lawyer*
Crews, Kenneth Donald *law educator, legal consultant, dean*
Daniels, Deborah Jean *lawyer, former federal agency administrator*
Downs, Thomas K. *lawyer*
Drentlicher, David *lawyer, educator, physician*
Dutton, Stephen James *lawyer*
Elberger, Ronald Edward *lawyer*
Ewbank, Thomas Peters *lawyer, retired banker*
Fels, James Alexander *lawyer*
Fisher, James R. *lawyer*
FitzGibbon, Daniel Harvey *lawyer*
Fruehwald, Kristin Gail *lawyer*
Funk, David Albert *retired law educator*
Gilliland, John Campbell, II, *lawyer*
Hollingsworth, Martha Schmidt *lawyer*
Hovde, F. Boyd *lawyer*
Jegen, Lawrence A. III *law educator*
Johnstone, Robert Philip *retired lawyer*
Kahlenbeck, Howard, Jr. *retired lawyer*
Kappes, Philip Spangler *lawyer*
Kashani, Hamid Reza *lawyer, computer consultant*
Kemper, James Dee *lawyer*
Kerr, William Andrew *lawyer, educator*
Kirk, Carol *lawyer*
Klaper, Martin Jay *lawyer*
Knebel, Donald Earl *lawyer*
Koeller, Robert Marion *lawyer, director*
Kury, Bernard Edward *lawyer*
Lamkin, Martha Dampf *lawyer, foundation administrator*
Lee, Stephen W. *lawyer*
Lisher, Mary Katherine *lawyer*
Lobley, Alan Haigh *retired lawyer*
Lofton, Thomas Milton *lawyer*
Lowe, Louis Robert, Jr. *lawyer*
Maine, Daniel Roland *lawyer*
McCrory, Michael Keith *lawyer*
Merrill, William H., Jr. *lawyer, corporate financial executive*
Miller, David W. *lawyer*
Mills, Jeffrey D. *prosecutor*
Neff, Robert Matthew *lawyer, finance company executive*
Newman, Norman Richard *lawyer*
Nolan, Alan Tucker *lawyer, writer, arbitrator*
Osborn, Kathy *lawyer*
Padgett, Gregory Lee *lawyer*
Paul, Stephen Howard *lawyer*
Pence, Linda Lee *lawyer*
Pennamped, Bruce Michael *lawyer*
Petersen, James L. *lawyer*
Pilgrim, Jill *lawyer, consultant*
Polak, Jonathan G. *lawyer*
Reynolds, Robert Hugh *lawyer*
Roberts, William Everett *lawyer*
Russell, David Williams *lawyer*
Rusthoven, Peter James *lawyer*
Ryder, Henry Clay *lawyer*
Scaletta, Phillip Ralph III *lawyer*
Schlegel, Fred Eugene *lawyer*
Scism, Daniel Reed *lawyer*
Shula, Robert Joseph *lawyer*
Sommer, James Koch *lawyer*
Stayton, Thomas George *lawyer*
Strain, James Arthur *lawyer*
Tabler, Bryan G. *lawyer*
Tabler, Norman Gardner, Jr. *lawyer*
Tabler, Susan Beidler *lawyer*
Townsend, Earl C., Jr. *lawyer, writer*
Whale, Arthur Richard *retired lawyer*
White, James Patrick *law educator*
Wishard, Gordon Davis *lawyer*
Wood, William Jerome *lawyer*
Zoeller, David Louis *lawyer*

**Jeffersonville**
Hoehn, Elmer Louis *lawyer, educator, state agency administrator, consultant, federal agency administrator*

**Kokomo**
Maugans, John Conrad *lawyer*

**La Porte**
Kaminski, Leon R. *lawyer*

**Lafayette**
Hart, Russell Holiday *retired lawyer*
Laszynski, Robert Steven *lawyer*
McCully, Thomas Richardson *lawyer*

**Merrillville**
Brenman, Stephen Morris *lawyer*
Compton, Clyde D. *lawyer*
Gioia, Daniel August *lawyer*

Miller, Richard Allen *lawyer*

**Muncie**
Dennis, Ralph Emerson, Jr. *lawyer*
Kelly, Eric Damian *lawyer, educator*

**Munster**
Amber, Douglas George *lawyer*

**New Albany**
Bourne, James E. *lawyer*

**Notre Dame**
Blakey, G. Robert (George Robert Blakey) *law educator*
Gunn, Alan *retired law educator*
Robinson, John Hayes *law educator*

**Plainfield**
Fivel, Steven Edward *lawyer*

**Shelbyville**
Lisher, James Richard *lawyer*
McNeely, James Lee *lawyer*

**South Bend**
Carey, John Leo *lawyer*
Reinke, William John *lawyer*
Seall, Stephen Albert *lawyer*
Shaffer, Thomas Lindsay *lawyer, educator*
Vogel, Nelson J., Jr. *lawyer*

**Terre Haute**
Bopp, James, Jr. *lawyer*

**Valparaiso**
Gaffney, Edward McGlynn *law educator, dean*

**Vincennes**
Emison, Ewing Rabb, Jr. *lawyer*

**IOWA**

**Ankeny**
Wirtz, Eli J. *lawyer, retail executive*

**Burlington**
Hoth, Steven Sergey *lawyer, educator*

**Cedar Rapids**
Chadick, Gary Robert *lawyer*
Collins, Kevin Heath *lawyer*
Larson, Charles W. *prosecutor*
Nazette, Richard Follett *lawyer*
Pundt, Richard Arthur *lawyer*
Riley, Tom Joseph *lawyer*
Wilson, Robert Foster *lawyer*

**Charles City**
Mc Cartney, Ralph Farnham *lawyer*

**Clear Lake**
Enabnit, Ted *retired lawyer*

**Clinton**
Smith, Lauren Ashley *lawyer, clergyman, physicist, journalist*

**Coralville**
Coulter, Charles Roy *lawyer*

**Davenport**
Dettmann, David Allen *lawyer*
Hood, James Michael *lawyer*
Skora, Susan Sundman *lawyer*

**Des Moines**
Begleiter, Martin David *law educator, consultant*
Begleiter, Ronni Frankel *lawyer*
Carroll, Frank James *lawyer, educator*
Clark, William Robert, Jr. *lawyer*
Claypool, David L. *lawyer*
Conlin, Roxanne Barton *lawyer*
Critelli, Nicholas (Nick) *lawyer, barrister*
Crook, Charles Samuel III *lawyer*
Fisher, Thomas George *lawyer, media specialist*
Fisher, Thomas George, Jr. *lawyer*
Foxhoven, Jerry Ray *lawyer*
Haggerty, Joseph K. *lawyer, insurance company executive*
Hansell, Edgar Frank *lawyer*
Harris, Charles Elmer *retired lawyer*
Hill, Luther Lyons, Jr. *lawyer*
Jensen, Dick Leroy *lawyer*
Koehn, William James *lawyer*
Landwehr, Amy Marie *lawyer*
Malm, Richard Allan *lawyer*
Nickerson, Don C. *lawyer, retired prosecutor, judge*
Norris, Glenn L. *lawyer*
Peddicord, Roland Dale *lawyer*
Power, Joseph Edward *lawyer*
Shaff, Karen E. *lawyer, insurance company executive*
Shors, John Dennis *lawyer*
Simpson, Lyle Lee *lawyer*
Wharton, John Michael *lawyer*
Whitaker, Matthew George *prosecutor*

**Dubuque**
Hammer, David Lindley *lawyer, writer*

**Grundy Center**
Kliebenstein, Don *retired lawyer*

**Harlan**
Salvo, J. C. *lawyer*

**Iowa City**
Bonfield, Arthur Earl *lawyer, educator*
Downer, Robert Nelson *lawyer*
Gittler, Josephine *law educator*
Hines, Norman William *law educator, retired dean*
Holland, James Joseph *lawyer*
Kurtz, Sheldon Francis *lawyer, educator*
Tomkovicz, James Joseph *law educator*
Wing, Adrien Katherine *law educator*

**Jefferson**
Pauley, James Leroy, Jr. *retired lawyer*

**Keokuk**
Hoffman, James Paul *lawyer*

**Le Mars**
Murphy, Patrick Neil *lawyer*

**Marshalltown**
Brennecke, Allen Eugene *lawyer*

**Muscatine**
Johnson, James I. *lawyer*
Nepple, James Anthony *lawyer*

**Nevada**
Countryman, Dayton Wendell *lawyer*

**Newton**
Scholten, Roger Keith *lawyer*

**Ottumwa**
Krafka, Mary Baird *lawyer*

**Sioux City**
Fredregill, Alan *lawyer*
Mayne, Wiley Edward *lawyer*
Peterson, Delaine Charles *lawyer, bank executive*

**West Des Moines**
Cortese, Joseph Samuel, II, *lawyer*
Hockenberg, Harlan David *lawyer*
McEnroe, Michael Louis *lawyer*
Tully, Robert Gerard *lawyer*

## KANSAS

**Bucyrus**
Hoffman, John Raymond *lawyer*

**Garden City**
Loyd, Ward Eugene *lawyer, state legislator*

**Halstead**
Bender, Jack Sinclair III *retired lawyer*

**Hutchinson**
Hayes, John Francis *lawyer*
Swearer, William Brooks *lawyer*

**Kansas City**
Benien, Ruth Marie *lawyer*

**Lawrence**
Casad, Robert Clair *legal educator*
Hoeflich, Michael Harlan *law educator, department chairman*
Turnbull, H. Rutherford III *lawyer, educator*
Winter, Winton Allen, Jr. *lawyer, state legislator*

**Leavenworth**
Crow, Martha Ellen *lawyer*
Crow, Michael P. *lawyer*

**Leawood**
Devlin, James Richard *lawyer*

**Lincoln**
Crangle, Robert D. *lawyer, management consultant, entrepreneur*

**Overland Park**
Balloun, Joseph Eugene *lawyer*
Callahan, Michael Thomas *arbitrator, consultant, construction executive, writer*
Gaar, Norman Edward *lawyer, former state senator*
Griswold, Thomas L. *lawyer*
Keplinger, Bruce (Donald Keplinger) *lawyer*
Klamann, John Michael *lawyer*
Murray, Thomas Veatch *lawyer*
Stanton, Roger D. *lawyer*
Woods, Richard Dale *lawyer*

**Salina**
Owens, William Dean *lawyer*

**Shawnee Mission**
Badgerow, John Nicholas *lawyer*
Bond, Richard Lee *lawyer, state senator*
Johntz, John Hoffman, Jr. *lawyer*
Nulton, William Clements *retired lawyer*
Snyder, Willard Breidenthal *lawyer*
Sparks, Billy Schley *lawyer*
Starrett, Frederick Kent *lawyer*
Vandever, William Dirk *lawyer*

**Topeka**
Concannon, James M. *lawyer, educator, dean*
Elrod, Linda Diane Henry *lawyer, educator*
Griffin, Ronald Charles *law educator*
Hayse, Richard Franklin *lawyer*
Hecht, Robert D. *lawyer*
Hejtmanek, Danton Charles *lawyer*
Irick, Larry D. *lawyer, energy executive*
Keefer, J(ames) Michael *lawyer*
Schroer, Gene Eldon *lawyer*
Snyder, Brock Robert *lawyer*

**Wichita**
Arnel, Kevin J. *lawyer*
Ayres, Ted Dean *lawyer*
Badger, Ronald Kay *lawyer*
Docking, Thomas Robert *lawyer, former state lieutenant governor*
Johnson, Kevin Blaine *lawyer, educator*
Melgren, Eric Franklin *prosecutor, lawyer*
Sevart, Daniel Joseph *lawyer*
Stephenson, Richard Ismert *lawyer*
Thompson, Lee (Morris Thompson) *lawyer*

## KENTUCKY

**Bowling Green**
Rudloff, William Joseph *lawyer*
Wilcher, Larry K. *lawyer*

**Bromley**
Sloan, David B. *lawyer*

**Covington**
Hausrath, David L. *lawyer*
Kerr, Thomas Robert *lawyer*
Mehling, Christopher John *lawyer*
Robinson, William T.(Bill) III *lawyer*
Stepner, Donald Leon *lawyer*

**Crestwood**
Ray, Ronald Dudley *lawyer*

**Frankfort**
Bowling, Charles Bryan *legal association administrator*
Breeding, Carl Wayne *lawyer*
Carroll, Julian Morton *lawyer, retired governor, state senator*
Hatchett, Edward Bryan, Jr. *lawyer*
Palmore, John Stanley, Jr. *retired lawyer*

**Glasgow**
Baker, Walter Arnold *lawyer*

**Harrods Creek**
Keeney, Steven Harris *lawyer*

**Henderson**
Gold, Steven Douglas *lawyer*
Sullivan, William Litsey *lawyer*

**Lexington**
Barr, Philip Douglas *lawyer*
Beshear, Steven Lynn *lawyer*
Cole, Vincent J. *lawyer*
Curtz, Chauncey S.R. *lawyer, real estate company executive*
Fryman, Virgil Thomas, Jr. *lawyer*
Garmer, William Robert *lawyer*
Goldman, Alvin Lee *lawyer, educator, arbitrator*
Hiestand, Sheila Patricia *lawyer*
Miller, Daniel Harlan *lawyer*
O'Brien, Stephen Mazyck III *lawyer*
Piper, George Chilton *lawyer*
Thapar, Amul R. *prosecutor*

**London**
Keller, John Warren *lawyer*

**Louisville**
Ardery, Philip Pendleton *lawyer*
Barr, James Houston III *lawyer*
Buckaway, William Allen, Jr. *lawyer*
Campbell, Christian Larsen L. *lawyer*
Casi, Paul Aldo, II, *lawyer*
Conner, Stewart Edmund *lawyer*
Cowan, Frederic Joseph *lawyer*
Crutcher, Michael Bayard *lawyer, consumer products company executive*
Davidson, Gordon Byron *lawyer*
Dilger, Craig *lawyer*
Dudley, George Ellsworth *lawyer*
Duffy, Martin Patrick *lawyer*
Ethridge, Larry Clayton *lawyer*
Faller, Rhoda *lawyer*
Fuchs, Olivia Anne Morris *lawyer*
Gilman, Sheldon Glenn *lawyer*
Hipwell, Arthur P. *lawyer, managed health care company executive*
Hopson, Edwin Sharp *lawyer*
Huber, David L. *prosecutor*
Hunter, William Jay, Jr. *lawyer*
Juber, David L. *prosecutor*
Klotter, John Charles *retired law educator*
Lay, Norvie Lee *law educator*
Luber, Thomas J(ulian) *lawyer*
Lyndrup, Peggy B. *lawyer*
McCall, John Richard *lawyer*
Mellen, Francis Joseph, Jr. *lawyer*
Northern, Richard *lawyer*
Osborn, John Simcoe, Jr. *lawyer*
Palmer, Larry Isaac *lawyer, educator*
Pedley, Lawrence Lindsay *lawyer*
Pelfrey, D. Patton *lawyer*
Riedman, Mary Suzanne *lawyer*
Rose, Charles Alexander *lawyer*
Runyon, Keith Leslie *lawyer, editor*
Silverthorn, Robert Sterner, Jr. *lawyer*
Skees, William Leonard, Jr. *lawyer*
Talbott, Ben Johnson, Jr. *lawyer*
Vish, Donald H. *lawyer, writer, photographer*
Welsh, Sir Alfred John *lawyer, investment advisor*
Westberry, Robert Kent *lawyer*

**Prospect**
Aberson, Leslie Donald *lawyer*
Willenbrink, Rose Ann *retired lawyer*

## LOUISIANA

**Alexandria**
Gist, Howard Battle, Jr. *lawyer*

**Baton Rouge**
Blackman, John Calhoun, IV, *lawyer*
Calabrese, Michael Raphael *lawyer, consultant*
Combe, John Clifford, Jr. *lawyer*
Dugas, David Roy *prosecutor, lawyer*
Graphia, Gary P. *lawyer*
Green, Stuart Paul *law educator*
Hymel, L(ezin) J(oseph) *lawyer, former prosecutor*
Litvinoff, Saul *law educator, lawyer*
McKay, Michael Wendell *lawyer*
Pugh, George Willard *law educator*
Richards, Marta Alison *lawyer*
Riddick, Winston Wade, Sr. *lawyer*
Rubin, Michael Harry *lawyer, educator*
Stapp, Dan Ernest *retired lawyer, utilities executive*
Taylor, John McKowen *lawyer*
Unglesby, Lewis O. *lawyer*

**Covington**
Rice, Winston Edward *lawyer*
Snyder, Charles Aubrey *lawyer*

**Destrehan**
Ates, J. Robert *lawyer*

**Griffith**, Steven Franklin, Sr. *lawyer, insurance agent*

**Hammond**
Pittman, Iddo, Jr. *retired lawyer*

**Kaplan**
LeMoine, Frank Eugene *lawyer, judge*

**La Place**
Cicet, Donald James *lawyer*

**Lafayette**
Angers, Winston Thomas *lawyer, publishing executive*
Davidson, James Joseph III *lawyer*
Goforth, William H. *lawyer*
Judice, Marc Wayne *lawyer*
Neuner, Frank X., Jr. *lawyer*
Saloom, Kaliste Joseph, Jr. *lawyer, retired judge*
Skinner, Michael David *lawyer, lobbyist, consultant*

**Lake Charles**
Veron, J. Michael *lawyer, writer*

**Mandeville**
Christian, John Catlett, Jr. *lawyer*
Deano, Edward Joseph, Jr. *lawyer, retired state legislator*
Ewen, Pamela Binnings *retired lawyer*

**Marksville**
Riddle, Charles Addison III *district attorney, former state legislator*

**Metairie**
Album, Jerald Lewis *lawyer*
Fantaci, James Michael *lawyer*
Nehrbass, Seth Martin *lawyer*
Rosen, Charles, II, *retired lawyer*

**Monroe**
Sartor, Daniel Ryan, Jr. *lawyer*

**New Iberia**
Hamilton, Roger Paul, Jr. *lawyer*

**New Orleans**
Abaunza, Donald Richard *lawyer*
Abbott, Hirschel Theron, Jr. *lawyer*
Acomb, Robert Bailey, Jr. *lawyer, educator*
Alsobrook, Henry Bernis, Jr. *lawyer*
Barry, Francis Julian, Jr. *lawyer*
Benjamin, Adelaide Wisdom *retired lawyer, retired community volunteer and activist*
Benjamin, Edward Bernard, Jr. *lawyer*
Bieck, Robert Barton, Jr. *lawyer*
Cheatwood, Roy Clifton *lawyer*
Childress, Steven Alan *law educator*
Christovich, Alvin Richard, Jr. *lawyer*
Claverie, Philip deVilliers *lawyer*
Coleman, James Julian *lawyer*
Coleman, James Julian, Jr. *lawyer, industrialist, real estate company executive*
Crusto, Mitchell Ferdinand *lawyer, educator*
Didriksen, Caleb H. III *lawyer*
Falgoust, Dean Thomas *lawyer, accountant*
Force, Robert *law educator*
Garcia, Patricia A. *lawyer*
Gay, Esmond Phelps *lawyer*
Goins, Richard Anthony *lawyer, educator*
Healy, George William III *lawyer, mediator*
Herman, Russ Michel *lawyer*
Hoffman, Donald Alfred *lawyer*
Hurley, Grady Schell *lawyer*
Jones, Philip Kirkpatrick, Jr. *lawyer*
Judell, Harold Benn *lawyer*
Lemann, Thomas Berthelot *lawyer*
Letten, James B. *prosecutor*
Longwell, Kelly (A. Kelton Longwell) *lawyer*
Looney, Joseph W. *lawyer*
Lovett, William Anthony *law and economics educator*
Lowe, Robert Charles *lawyer*
Marcus, Bernard *lawyer, arbitrator, mediator*
McGlone, Michael Anthony *lawyer*
McMillan, Lee Richards, II, *lawyer*
Miller, Pierre Valcour, II, *lawyer*
Mintz, Albert *lawyer*
Molony, Michael Janneson, Jr. *lawyer, arbitrator, mediator*
Norwood, Colvin Gamble, Jr. *lawyer*
Nuzum, Robert Weston *lawyer*
Osakwe, Christopher *lawyer, educator*
Pearce, John Y. *lawyer*
Perlis, Sharon A. *lawyer*
Redmann, John William *lawyer, consultant, school system administrator*
Roberts, Gary Raymond *lawyer, educator*
Rodriguez, Antonio Jose *lawyer*
Rosen, William Warren *lawyer*
Simon, H(uey) Paul *lawyer*
Singreen, Shirley Ann Basile (Mrs. Harry Voss Singreen) *lawyer, consultant*
Smith, Juanita Bérard *lawyer, artist*
Thomas, Joseph Winand *lawyer*
Vance, Robert Patrick *lawyer*
Vaudry, J. William, Jr. *lawyer*
Wolfe, Richard Peel *lawyer*
Worley, Robert Bruce, Jr. *lawyer*

**Shreveport**
Achee, Roland Joseph *lawyer*
Bryant, J(ames) Bruce *lawyer*
Carmody, Arthur Roderick, Jr. *lawyer, director*
Chastain, Merritt Banning, Jr. *lawyer*
Cox, John Thomas, Jr. *lawyer*
Feldman, Larry, Jr. *lawyer*
Goodman, Robert Uhle *lawyer*
Hetherwick, Gilbert Lewis *lawyer*
Nelson, Ralph Stanley *lawyer*
Payne, Roy Steven *lawyer*
Perlman, Jerald Lee *lawyer*
Ramey, Cecil Edward, Jr. *lawyer*
Shea, Joseph Lawrence, Jr. *lawyer*
Washington, Donald W. *prosecutor*

**Slidell**
Singletary, Alvin D. *lawyer*

## MAINE

**Augusta**
Cragin, Charles Langmaid *lawyer*
Donahue, Joseph Gerald *lawyer*
Johnson, Phillip Edward *lawyer*
Wilkinson, Lester F., Jr. *lawyer*

**Bangor**
Bickford, Meris J. *lawyer, bank executive*
Rudman, Paul Lewis *lawyer, former state supreme court justice*

**Brunswick**
Owen, H. Martyn *retired lawyer*

**Castine**
Wiswall, Frank Lawrence, Jr. *lawyer, educator*

**Georgetown**
Chapin, Richard *arbitrator, director*

**Hebron**
Marchetti-Ponte, Karin *lawyer, land conservation consultant*

**Orrs Island**
Nelson, Robert Louis *lawyer*

**Portland**
Duff, John A. *law educator*
Graffam, Ward Irving *lawyer*
Harvey, Charles Albert, Jr. *lawyer*
Hunt, David Evans *lawyer*
Lancaster, Ralph Ivan, Jr. *lawyer*
LeBlanc, Richard Philip *lawyer*
Mitchell, Carol L. *lawyer*
Nelson, Michael Allan *lawyer*
O'Brien, Murrough Hall *lawyer*
Opperman, John R. *lawyer*
Rundlett, Ellsworth Turner III *lawyer*
Silsby, Paula D. *prosecutor*
Stauffer, Eric P. *lawyer*
Thompson, Peter L. *lawyer*
White, Jeffrey Munroe *lawyer*
Zarr, Melvyn *lawyer, educator*

**Raymond**
Coughlan, Patrick Campbell *lawyer, mediator*

**Saco**
Prescott, Dana E. *lawyer*

**South Portland**
Delva, Paul D. *lawyer*

**Tenants Harbor**
Bates, John Cecil, Jr. *lawyer*

**Wells**
Carleton, Joseph George, Jr. *lawyer, state legislator*

## MARYLAND

**Abingdon**
Wolf, Martin Eugene *lawyer, educator*

**Annapolis**
Levitan, Laurence *lawyer, retired state senator*
Lillard, John Franklin III *lawyer*
Nolan, James P. *lawyer*
Perkins, Roger Allan *lawyer*
Poe, Luke Harvey, Jr. *lawyer*

**Ashton**
Whelan, Roger Michael *lawyer, educator*

**Baltimore**
Baker, Constance H. *lawyer*
Bartlett, James Wilson III *lawyer*
Berlage, Jan Ingham *lawyer*
Berns, Peter Vernon *lawyer*
Blanton, Edward Lee, Jr. *lawyer*
Brockmeyer, Michael F. *lawyer*
Burch, Francis Boucher, Jr. *lawyer*
Calvert, Walter Randolph *lawyer*
Capute, Courtney G. *lawyer*
Carbine, James Edmond *lawyer*
Carlin, Paul Victor *legal association executive*
Cason, Alan C. *lawyer*
Chalk, David *lawyer*
Chaplin, Peggy Louie *lawyer*
Chiu, Hungdah *law educator*
Ciccolo, Angela *lawyer*
Civiletti, Benjamin Richard *lawyer, former United States attorney general*
Cole, Emried Dargan, Jr. *lawyer*
Cook, Bryson Leitch *lawyer*
Coons, Thomas Wayne *lawyer*
Coppel, Lawrence David *lawyer*
Crowe, Thomas Leonard *lawyer*
Curran, Robert Bruce *lawyer*
Deeley, C. Carey, Jr. *lawyer*
Devan, Deborah Hunt *lawyer*
Dewey, Joel Allen *lawyer*
DiBiagio, Thomas Michael *lawyer, former prosecutor*
Dougherty, John C. *lawyer*
Dunn, Jeffrey A. *lawyer*
Eisner, Jonathan David *lawyer*
Ellin, Marvin *lawyer*
Evans, Nolly Seymour *lawyer*
Eveleth, Janet Stidman *law association administrator*
Fergenson, Arthur Friend *lawyer*
Fisher, Morton Poe, Jr. *lawyer*
Frenkil, Steven David *lawyer*
Frerichs, Herbert Donald, Jr. *lawyer*
Friedman, Louis Frank *lawyer*
Gaither, John Francis, Jr. *lawyer, health products executive*
Gately, Mark Donohue *lawyer*
Gendron, Andrew *lawyer*
Gillece, James Patrick, Jr. *lawyer*
Goldman, Brian Arthur *lawyer, accountant*
Gonya, Jeffrey Keenan *lawyer*
Gray, Frank Truan *lawyer*

Gray, Oscar Shalom *lawyer*
Guben, Jan K. *lawyer*
Hafets, Richard Jay *lawyer*
Hanks, James Judge, Jr. *lawyer*
Hecht, Donald D. *lawyer*
Hirsh, Theodore William *lawyer*
Honemann, Daniel Henry *lawyer*
Howard, John Vincent, Jr. *lawyer*
Howell, Harley Thomas *lawyer*
Immelt, Stephen J. *lawyer*
Johnson, Harry Sterling *lawyer*
Johnston, Edward Allan *lawyer*
Johnston, George W. *lawyer*
Jones, John Martin, Jr. *lawyer*
Kandel, Nelson Robert *lawyer*
Kenney, Brigid E. *lawyer*
Kolkin, Mitchell *lawyer*
Kremen, Richard M. *lawyer*
Levin, Edward Jesse *lawyer*
Levine, Richard E. *lawyer*
Liebmann, George W(illiam) *lawyer*
Loucks, Allen Frazier *prosecutor, lawyer*
Lundy, Audie Lee, Jr. *lawyer*
MacWilliams, Michael Broughton *lawyer*
Mathias, James D. *lawyer*
Mathias, Robert Joseph *lawyer*
McClung, A(lexander) Keith, Jr. *retired lawyer*
McPherson, Donald Paxton III *lawyer*
McWilliams, John Michael *lawyer*
Meagher, Anthony L. *lawyer*
Miller, Decatur Howard *lawyer*
Moser, M(artin) Peter *lawyer*
Ohly, D. Christopher *lawyer*
Orman, Leonard Arnold *lawyer*
Parvis, Peter P. *lawyer*
Perschetz, Arthur Driban *lawyer*
Plant, Albin MacDonough *lawyer*
Pokempner, Joseph Kres *lawyer*
Pollak, Joanne Elizabeth *lawyer*
Pollak, Mark *lawyer*
Provorny, Frederick Alan *lawyer, educator*
Radding, Andrew *lawyer*
Ravenell, Kenneth W. *lawyer*
Redden, Roger Duffey *lawyer*
Reno, Russell Ronald, Jr. *lawyer*
Reynolds, William Leroy *lawyer, educator*
Robinson, Zelig *lawyer*
Rosenstein, Rod J. *prosecutor*
Rosenthal, William J. *lawyer*
Schlaff, Barbara E. *lawyer*
Schochor, Jonathan *lawyer, educator*
Schwartz, Howard S. *lawyer*
Scriggins, Larry Palmer *lawyer, director*
Sfekas, Stephen James *lawyer, educator*
Shapiro, Harry Dean *lawyer*
Shea, James L. *lawyer*
Shelton, Robert Arthur *lawyer*
Shepherd, Kevin L. *lawyer*
Short, Alexander Campbell *lawyer*
Silver, Michael Joel *lawyer*
Sirota, Wilbert H. *lawyer*
Smith, Robert G. *lawyer*
Smith, Robert W., Jr., (Jay Smith) *lawyer*
Somer-Greif, Penny Lynn *lawyer*
Suggs, Kenneth *lawyer*
Summers, Thomas Carey *lawyer*
Sykes, Melvin Julius *lawyer*
Thompson, Otho M. *lawyer, former solicitor*
Tiburzi, Paul A. *lawyer*
Tilghman, Richard Carmichael, Jr. *lawyer*
Walker, Irving Edward *lawyer*
Walter, Harold Mark *lawyer*
Warren, Melissa Allison *lawyer*
Wasserman, Richard Leo *lawyer*
Watkins, John B. *lawyer*
White, Pamela Janice *lawyer*
Whitman, Marland Hamilton, Jr. *lawyer*
Wilson, Thomas Matthew III *lawyer*
Winn, James Julius, Jr. *lawyer*
Wright, James Dorsey *lawyer*
Yoskowitz, Irving Benjamin *lawyer, merchant banker*
Zinkham, W. Robert *lawyer*

**Bel Air**
Helfrich, Cornelius David *lawyer*

**Bethesda**
Abdoo, Elizabeth A. *lawyer*
Aisenberg, Irwin Morton *retired lawyer*
Baird, Bruce Allen *lawyer*
Bauersfeld, Carl Frederick *lawyer*
Berman, Marshall Fox *lawyer*
Chapman, Gerald Frederick *lawyer, banker*
Comey, James B., Jr. *lawyer, aerospace company executive, former federal agency administrator*
Daniels, Michael Paul *lawyer*
Deckelbaum, Nelson *lawyer*
DiPietro, Ralph John *lawyer*
Downey, Arthur Thomas III *lawyer*
English, William deShay *lawyer, director*
Eule, Norman Louis *lawyer*
Feuerstein, Donald Martin *lawyer*
Frosh, Brian Esten *lawyer, state senator*
Hewes, Laurence Ilsley III *lawyer, management consultant*
Marks, Jonathan Bowles *mediator, arbitrator*
Nelson, William Eugene *lawyer*
Pasternak, N. Alfred *lawyer, accountant*
Pipkin, James Harold, Jr. *lawyer*
Rosenberg, Mark Louis *lawyer*
Ross, William Warfield *lawyer*
Ryan, Joseph *lawyer*
Schifter, Richard *lawyer*
Schoettler, James Anthony, Jr. *lawyer*
Silver, David *lawyer*
Weinberger, Alan David *lawyer, business executive*
Zielinski, Thomas C. *lawyer*

**Catonsville**
Hubbard, Herbert Hendrix *lawyer*
Zumbrun, Alvin John Thomas *law and criminology educator*

**Chevy Chase**
Bruder, George Frederick *lawyer*
Coerper, Milo George *lawyer, priest*
Curzan, Myron Paul *lawyer*
Gildenhorn, Joseph Bernard *lawyer, real estate company executive, retired diplomat*
Groner, Beverly Anne *retired lawyer*

Mackall, Laidler Bowie *retired lawyer*
Murphy, John Condron, Jr. *lawyer*
Nichols, Henry Eliot *lawyer, director, savings and loan association executive*
Pollard, Michael Ross *lawyer, health science association administrator*
Toy, Charles David *lawyer*

**College Park**
Meagher, Joseph Patrick *law educator, consultant*

**Columbia**
Bennett, P. Tyson *lawyer*
Closson, Walter Franklin *child support prosecutor*
Maseritz, Guy B. *lawyer*
Shaw, Donald Hardy *lawyer*

**Crownsville**
Irish, Leon Eugene *lawyer, educator, non-profit organization executive*

**Derwood**
Mylonakis, Stamatios Gregory *lawyer, consultant*

**Easton**
Ikenberry, Henry Cephas, Jr. *lawyer*
Maffitt, James Strawbridge *lawyer*

**Fort Washington**
Alexander, Gary R. *lawyer, state legislator, lobbyist*
Vaughan, James Joseph Michael *lawyer*

**Gaithersburg**
Jestrab, Frank F. *retired lawyer*
McDowell, Donna Schultz *lawyer, educator*

**Germantown**
Chawla, Tejpal Singh *lawyer*

**Glyndon**
Renbaum, Barry Jeffrey *lawyer*

**Greenbelt**
Billingsley, Lance W. *lawyer*
Fax, Charles Samuel *lawyer*
Greenwald, Andrew Eric *lawyer*

**Hagerstown**
Berkson, Jacob Benjamin *lawyer, writer*
Poole, D. Bruce *lawyer*

**Hunt Valley**
Carmean, C. William *lawyer*
Carney, Stephen Patrick *lawyer, retired insurance company executive*

**Hyattsville**
Levy, David Lawrence *retired lawyer, legal association administrator*

**Kensington**
Dauster, William Gary *lawyer, economist*

**Lutherville Timonium**
Brown, Ellyn L. *lawyer, consultant*

**North Potomac**
Lehman, Leonard *retired lawyer, consultant*

**Oxford**
Bellinger, Edgar Thomson *lawyer*

**Patuxent River**
Fitzhugh, David Michael *lawyer*

**Pikesville**
Putzel, Constance Kellner *lawyer*

**Potomac**
Feldman, Myer *lawyer*
Hall, William Darlington *lawyer*
Meyer, Lawrence George *lawyer*
Peter, Phillips Smith *lawyer*
Reback, Richard Neal *lawyer*
Redding, Robert Ellsworth *lawyer*
Sherwood, Arthur Lawrence *lawyer*
Troffkin, Howard Julian *lawyer*

**Randallstown**
Holt, John J. *mediator, retired human resources specialist, arbitrator*

**Reisterstown**
Frank, Robert Louis *lawyer*

**Rockville**
Barkley, Brian Evan *lawyer, political organization worker, consultant*
Berryman, Richard Byron *lawyer*
Boetticher, Helene *retired lawyer*
Cheston, Sheila Carol *lawyer*
Clancy, Patrick L. *lawyer*
Conroy, J. Michael *lawyer, judge*
Davis, James H. *lawyer*
De Jong, David Samuel *lawyer, educator*
Donnally, Robert Andrew *lawyer*
Frye, Roland Mushat, Jr. *lawyer*
Grozbean, Stuart Harvey *lawyer*
Kadish, Richard L. *lawyer*
Karp, Ronald Alvin *lawyer*
Karson, Emile *lawyer*
Kerxton, Alan Smith *lawyer*
Knight, Edward S. *lawyer, federal official*
Pehrson, Gordon Oscar, Jr. *lawyer, venture capitalist*
Rothenberg, Alan David *lawyer*
Thompson, James Lee *lawyer*
Tomar, Richard Thomas *lawyer*
Van Grack, Steven *lawyer*

**Saint Michaels**
Brown, Omer Forrest, II, *lawyer*

**Salisbury**
Clarke, William A. Lee III *lawyer*

**Silver Spring**
Bernard, Hugh Yancey, Jr. *law educator, retired law librarian*
Calvert, Gordon Lee *retired legal association executive*
Craig, Paul Max, Jr. *retired lawyer*
Lipstein, Robert A. *lawyer*
Neuhauser, Frank Louis *retired lawyer*
Pacuska, Alison Brandi *paralegal*
Rachanow, Gerald Marvin *lawyer, pharmacist*

**Towson**
Ayres, Jeffrey Peabody *lawyer*
Bowen, Lowell Reed *lawyer*
Brennan, Michael J. *lawyer*
Carney, Bradford George Yost *lawyer, educator*
China, Daniel William *lawyer*
Lutz, Randall Matthew *lawyer*
Proctor, Kenneth Donald *lawyer*
Vettori, Paul Marion *lawyer*
Zink, John H. III *lawyer*

**Trappe**
Paul, James Caverly Newlin *law educator, retired dean*

**Upper Marlboro**
Morrison, Anne Deinlein *law librarian*

**West Bethesda**
Scully, Roger Tehan, II, *lawyer*

**Westminster**
Dulany, William Bevard *lawyer*
Preston, Charles Michael *lawyer*

**MASSACHUSETTS**

**Amherst**
Howland, Richard Moulton *retired lawyer*

**Arlington**
Simpson, Russell Avington *retired lawyer*

**Barnstable**
Paquin, Thomas Christopher *lawyer*

**Belmont**
Greer, Gordon Bruce *retired lawyer, writer*
Zito, Frank R. *lawyer, accountant*

**Boston**
Abbott, William Saunders *lawyer*
Abrams, Roger Ian *lawyer, educator*
Allen, Rosemary M. *lawyer*
Apjohn, Nelson George *lawyer*
Aresty, Jeffrey M. *lawyer*
Armistead, (Ivor) Cary III *lawyer*
Aronson, Neil H. *lawyer*
Atkins, William Paul *lawyer*
Auerbach, Joseph *former lawyer, law educator*
Bachman, Katharine Elizabeth *lawyer*
Baddour, Steven A. *lawyer, state legislator*
Bae, Frank S.H. *law librarian, educator*
Baker, Hollie L. *lawyer*
Balliro, Joseph James, Sr. *lawyer*
Baram, Michael S. *lawyer, law educator*
Barker, Christopher B. *lawyer*
Barnard, Deborah E. *lawyer*
Barshak, Edward Joel *lawyer*
Becker, Fred Ronald *lawyer*
Benjamin, William Chase *lawyer*
Bennett, Richard Edward *lawyer*
Bernhard, Alexander Alfred *lawyer*
Berube, Brian A. *lawyer*
Bines, Harvey Ernest *lawyer, educator, writer*
Black, Edward G. *lawyer*
Bloch, Donald Martin *lawyer*
Bodner, Randall Wayne *lawyer*
Bohnen, Michael J. *lawyer*
Bok, John Fairfield *retired lawyer*
Bonifaz, John Cristopher *lawyer*
Borden, Mark G. *lawyer*
Bornheimer, Allen Millard *lawyer*
Braceras, Roberto M. *lawyer*
Bragg, Lawrence D. III *lawyer*
Breakstone, Marc L. *lawyer*
Brodley, Joseph F. *lawyer, consultant, dean*
Brody, Richard Eric *lawyer*
Brown, Michael Robert *lawyer*
Buchanan, Robert McLeod *lawyer*
Burke, Matthew M. *lawyer*
Burleigh, Lewis Albert *lawyer*
Burling, James C. *lawyer*
Burnett, Elizabeth B. *lawyer*
Burns, Thomas David *lawyer*
Burnstein, Daniel *lawyer*
Burstein, Harvey *lawyer, educator*
Burt, Frank Davies *lawyer, real estate company executive*
Burton, Thomas Russell *lawyer*
Cahill, Lawrence R. *lawyer*
Caporizzo, A. William *lawyer*
Carney, J. W., Jr. *lawyer*
Carroll, James Edward *lawyer*
Casner, Truman Snell *lawyer*
Cesari, Robert A. *lawyer*
Chang, Hemmie *lawyer*
Cleary, John Joseph (Jack) *lawyer*
Codinha, J. William *lawyer*
Coffey, James Francis *lawyer*
Cogan, John Francis, Jr. *lawyer*
Cohn, Andrew Howard *lawyer*
Coleman, Dennis M. *lawyer*
Crawford, Ian *lawyer*
Cronin, Philip Mark *lawyer*
Cubell, Howard Alan *lawyer*
Curtin, John Joseph, Jr. *lawyer*
Cutrell, Charles C. III *lawyer*
Daley, Paul Patrick *lawyer*
DeBevoise, Charles Henry *lawyer*
Delaney, John White *lawyer*
Dennis, Kevin M. *lawyer*
de Rham, Casimir, Jr. *lawyer*
Devlin, Peter J. *lawyer*
Di Cola, Joan Barbara *lawyer*
Dillon, James Joseph *lawyer*
Dineen, John K. *lawyer*
Donahue, Charlotte Mary *lawyer*

Dougherty, Thomas James *lawyer*
Draper, Thomas B. *lawyer*
Drechsler, Thomas *lawyer*
Duffy, James Francis III *lawyer*
Dynner, Alan Roy *lawyer*
Ebb, Peter L. *lawyer*
Egbert, Richard Michael *lawyer*
Ehrlich, M. Gordon *lawyer*
Elefante, Michael Barrett *lawyer*
Elrifi, Ivor R. *lawyer*
Engel, David Lewis *lawyer*
Englander, John C. *lawyer*
Eurich, Richard Rex *lawyer*
Fay, Michael Leo *lawyer*
Feeherry, Anthony M. *lawyer*
Felter, John Kenneth *lawyer*
Fine, David A. *lawyer*
Finn, Terrence M. *lawyer*
Fischer, Eric Robert *lawyer, educator*
Fischer, Mark Alan *lawyer*
Fitzgerald, Warren Franklin *lawyer*
Floor, Richard Earl *lawyer*
Fortier, Albert Mark, Jr. *lawyer*
Fox, Francis Haney *lawyer*
Fraser, Robert Burchmore *lawyer*
Freedman, Joel F. *lawyer*
Freishtat, Harvey W. *lawyer*
Gaff, Brian Michael *lawyer*
Galvani, Paul B. *lawyer*
Garvin, Michele M. *lawyer*
Gaudreau, Russell A., Jr. *lawyer, educator*
Gault, Robert Mellor *lawyer*
Gauron, Paul R. *lawyer*
Gelb, Richard Mark *lawyer*
Gilbert, David A. *lawyer*
Gill, Robert Tucker *lawyer*
Giner, A. Silvana *lawyer*
Giso, Frank III *lawyer*
Gleason, Daniel J. *lawyer*
Glosband, Daniel Martin *lawyer*
Goldstein, Jane D. *lawyer*
Gonson, S. Donald *lawyer*
Goodman, Louis Allan *lawyer*
Gossels, Claus Peter Rolf *lawyer*
Greco, Michael S. *lawyer*
Green, Karen F. *lawyer*
Greer, Allen Curtis, II, *lawyer, investment management executive*
Haddad, Ernest Mudarri *lawyer*
Haddad, Mark E. *lawyer*
Haley, Paul Richard *lawyer, state legislator*
Hall, David *law educator, dean, department chairman*
Hall, Henry Lyon, Jr. *lawyer*
Halston, Daniel William *lawyer*
Halström, Frederic Norman *lawyer*
Handly, Kevin John *lawyer, educator*
Hanlon, Francis X. *lawyer*
Harrington, John Michael, Jr. *lawyer*
Harvey, Christopher P. *lawyer*
Hawkey, G. Michael *lawyer, real estate developer*
Hayes, Robert Francis *lawyer*
Healy, Martin Russell *lawyer*
Hieken, Charles *lawyer*
Hoort, Steven Thomas *lawyer*
Howe, Janice W. *lawyer*
Hrones, Stephen Baylis *lawyer, educator*
Huston, Julia *lawyer*
Janos, Ellen L. *lawyer*
Johnston, Richard Alan *lawyer*
Johnston, Susan A. *lawyer*
Jones, Jeffrey Foster *lawyer*
Jones, Sheldon Atwell *retired lawyer*
Jordan, Alexander Joseph, Jr. *lawyer*
Kalkstein, Joshua Adam *lawyer*
Kanin, Dennis Roy *lawyer*
Kearns, Ellen Cecelia *lawyer*
Keating, Michael Burns *lawyer, educator*
Kehoe, William Francis *lawyer*
Keller, Stanley *lawyer*
Kerry, Cameron F. *lawyer*
Kidder, George Howell *lawyer*
Kirchick, William Dean *lawyer*
Kirsch, Robert L. *lawyer*
Klem, Christopher A. *lawyer*
Klieman, Rikki Jo *lawyer, legal analyst*
Knag, Paul Everett *lawyer*
Kociubes, Joseph Leib *lawyer*
Kopelman, Leonard *lawyer*
Lampert, James B. *lawyer*
Last, Michael P. *lawyer*
Lazarow, Robin S. *lawyer*
LeBlanc, Marianne Camille *lawyer*
Lee, William F. *lawyer*
Leibowitz, Hal J. *lawyer*
Lepore, Ralph Thomas III *lawyer*
Lettieri, Richard J. (Richard Joseph Lettieri) *lawyer*
Levine, William Michael *lawyer*
Licata, Arthur Frank *lawyer*
Lieberman, Michael J. *lawyer*
Litwin, Paul Jeffrey *lawyer*
Loder, John Mark *lawyer*
Loeser, Hans Ferdinand *lawyer*
Looney, William Francis, Jr. *lawyer*
Loria, Martin A. *lawyer*
Lyons, Paul Vincent *lawyer*
Macdonald, Peter J. *lawyer*
MacLeish, Roderick, Jr. *lawyer*
Malt, Ronald Bradford *lawyer*
Mansfield, Christopher Charles *lawyer*
Markey, John K. *lawyer*
Martin, Stanley Allen *lawyer*
Matuschak, Mark G. *lawyer*
Mayer, William P. *lawyer*
McAuliffe, Rosemary *lawyer*
McKenzie, Elizabeth McDaniel *law librarian*
McPhee, Joan *lawyer*
Meal, Douglas H. *lawyer*
Menna, Gilbert G. *lawyer*
Menoyo, Eric Felix *lawyer*
Mercer, Richard James *lawyer*
Merrill, Stephen *lawyer, consultant, retired governor*
Meserve, William George *lawyer*
Messing, Ellen Jean *lawyer*
Meyer, Andrew C. C., Jr. *lawyer*
Mikels, Richard Eliot *lawyer*
Miller, Michelle D. *lawyer*
Miller, Peter M. *lawyer*
Milstein, Richard Sherman *lawyer*

Mirabito, Anthony Jason *law educator, lawyer*
Moncreiff, Robert P. *lawyer*
Mone, Michael Edward *lawyer*
Montgomery, John T. *lawyer*
Montgomery, Susan Barbieri *lawyer*
Mooney, Michael Edward *lawyer*
Moore, Gregory E. *lawyer*
Moriarty, George Marshall *lawyer*
Muldoon, Robert Joseph, Jr. *lawyer*
Murley, Susan W. *lawyer*
Nagle, James W. *lawyer*
Nelson, Patricia L. *lawyer*
Novack, Kenneth Joseph *lawyer*
Nunnally, Allen C. *lawyer*
Nutt, Robert L. *lawyer, educator*
O'Connell, Mary-Kathleen *lawyer*
O'Donnell, Thomas Lawrence Patrick *lawyer*
O'Leary, Joseph Evans *lawyer*
Olsen, Hans Peter *lawyer*
O'Neill, Philip Daniel, Jr. *lawyer, educator*
O'Reilly, William R., Jr. *lawyer*
Orsmond, Gareth Iain *lawyer, musician*
Paine, William H. *lawyer*
Pappalardo, A. John *former prosecutor, lawyer*
Park, William Wynnewood *law educator*
Partan, Daniel Gordon *retired lawyer*
Patterson, John de la Roche, Jr. *lawyer*
Peckham, Thomas Elwood *lawyer*
Perera, Lawrence Thacher *lawyer*
Perkins, John Allen *lawyer*
Pham, Chinh H. *lawyer*
Pierce, Rudolph F. *lawyer*
Polebaum, Mark Neal *lawyer*
Pomeroy, Robert Corttis *lawyer*
Popeo, R. Robert *lawyer*
Porcelli, Frank Paul *lawyer*
Porter, Jeffrey R. *lawyer*
Poss, Stephen Daniel *lawyer*
Preston, Jerome, Jr. *retired lawyer*
Price, Robert F. *lawyer*
Quayle, Dwight W. *lawyer*
Raish, David Langdon *lawyer*
Reardon, Frank Emond *lawyer*
Renehan, Richard William *lawyer*
Reppert, Sibley Putnam *lawyer*
Richmond, Alice Elenor *lawyer*
Rines, Robert Harvey *lawyer, educator, physicist, composer*
Ritt, Roger Merrill *lawyer*
Robinson, Andrea J. *lawyer*
Rondeau, Patrick John *lawyer*
Ropple, Lisa M. *lawyer*
Rose, Alfred O. *lawyer*
Rosenberg, Peter N. *lawyer*
Rosenfeld, Jonathan D. *lawyer*
Ross, Nelson G. *lawyer*
Rudavsky, Dahlia C. *lawyer*
Rudman, Jeffrey B. *lawyer*
Ryan, Allan Andrew, Jr. *lawyer, director, educator, writer*
Sargeant, Ernest James *lawyer, educator*
Sartory, Thomas J. *lawyer*
Sawyer, William C. *lawyer*
Scherkenbach, Frank Everett *lawyer*
Sears, John Winthrop *lawyer*
Shapiro, Robert N. *lawyer*
Shapiro, Sandra *lawyer*
Sheehan, Gregory D. *lawyer*
Sherman, Robert Alan *lawyer*
Shilepsky, Nancy Sue *lawyer*
Shulkin, Martin B. *lawyer*
Sigel, John D. *lawyer*
Singer, Steven D. *lawyer*
Sirkin, Joel H. *lawyer*
Sloan, David Scott *lawyer*
Smith, Craig R. *lawyer*
Smith, Edwin Eric *lawyer*
Smith, Philip Jones *lawyer*
Soden, Richard Allan *lawyer*
Solet, Maxwell David *lawyer*
Southard, William G. *lawyer*
Southgate, Richard W. *lawyer, director*
Speer, Brownlow Main *lawyer*
Steinberg, Donald R. *lawyer*
Steinberg, Laura *lawyer*
Stern, Donald Kenneth *lawyer*
Stillwell, R. Newcomb *lawyer*
Stokes, James Christopher *lawyer*
Storey, James Moorfield *lawyer*
Sugarman, Paul Ronald *lawyer, educator, academic administrator*
Sullivan, Michael J. *prosecutor*
Sunstein, Bruce David *lawyer*
Surkin, Elliot Mark *lawyer*
Swaim, C. Hall *lawyer*
Swope, Jeffrey Peyton *lawyer*
Tarantino, Louis Gerald *lawyer, management consultant*
Taylor, Patrick Lawrence *lawyer, educator*
Taylor, Thomas William *lawyer*
Touster, Saul *law educator*
Troupe, William Harold *lawyer*
Tse, Marian A. *lawyer*
Tuchmann, Robert *lawyer*
Vance, Verne Widney, Jr. *retired lawyer*
Vaughan, Herbert Wiley *retired lawyer*
Walek, David B. *lawyer*
Ware, Paul F., Jr. *lawyer*
Weiner, Stephen Mark *lawyer*
Weitzel, John Patterson *lawyer*
Wellington, Carol Strong *law librarian*
Weltman, David Lee *lawyer*
Westcott, John McMahon, Jr. *lawyer*
Westra, James R. *lawyer*
White, Barry Bennett *lawyer*
Whitley, L. Tracee *lawyer*
Whitlock, John L. *lawyer*
Whitters, James Payton III *lawyer, educator*
Wilcox, Steven Alan *lawyer*
Williams, John Taylor *lawyer*
Woodburn, Ralph Robert, Jr. *lawyer*
Young, Raymond Henry *lawyer*
Zack, Arnold Marshall *lawyer, mediator, arbitrator, judge*

**Brighton**
Garber, Paul William *lawyer*

**Burlington**
Cerveny, David John *lawyer*

**Cambridge**
Alford, William P. *law educator*
Andrews, William Dorey *law educator*
Barron, David Jeremiah *law educator*
Bartholet, Elizabeth *law educator*
Bebchuk, Lucian Arye *law educator, finance educator*
Bok, Derek Curtis *law educator, former university president*
Brewer, Scott *law educator*
Clark, Robert Charles *law educator, former dean*
Coates, John C., IV, *law educator*
Dershowitz, Alan Morton *law educator*
Desan, Christine *law educator*
Donahue, Charles, Jr. *law educator*
Downey, Richard Ralph *lawyer, consultant, accountant, management consultant*
Elhauge, Einer Richard *law educator*
Fallon, Richard H., Jr. *law educator*
Ferrell, Allen F. *law educator*
Field, Martha Amanda *law educator*
Fisher, Roger Dummer *negotiation expert, law educator*
Fisher, William W. III *law educator*
Frug, Gerald E. *law educator*
Glendon, Mary Ann *law educator*
Halley, Janet E. *law educator*
Halperin, Daniel I. *law educator*
Hanson, Jon D. *law educator*
Hay, Bruce L. *law educator*
Heineman, Benjamin Walter, Jr. *lawyer*
Horwitz, Morton J. *law educator*
Jackson, Howell E. *law educator*
Jolls, Christine Margaret *law educator*
Kaplow, Louis *law educator*
Kaufman, Andrew Lee *law educator*
Kennedy, David William *law educator*
Kennedy, Duncan McLean *law educator*
King, William Bruce *retired lawyer*
Kraakman, Reinier Herman *law educator*
Lau, Vincent W. *lawyer*
Manning, John F. *law educator*
Mansfield, John H. *law educator*
Martin, Harry Stratton III *law educator, law librarian*
McGurk, Michael R. *lawyer*
Meltzer, Daniel J. *law educator*
Michelman, Frank I. *law educator*
Miller, Arthur Raphael *law educator*
Miller, Steven E. *professor of international affairs*
Minow, Martha Louise *law educator*
Mnookin, Robert Harris *law educator*
Moore, Mark Harrison *criminal justice and public policy educator*
Nesson, Charles R. *law educator*
Ogletree, Charles J., Jr. *law educator*
Parker, Richard Davies *law educator*
Patton, Bruce M. *law educator, management consultant*
Ramseyer, J. Mark *law educator*
Riley, Lynne F. *lawyer*
Sander, Frank Ernest Arnold *law educator*
Sapers, Carl Martin *lawyer, educator*
Sargentich, Lewis D. *law educator*
Schauer, Frederick Franklin *law educator*
Scott, Hal S. *law educator*
Shapiro, David Louis *law educator*
Shavell, Steven M. *law educator*
Simmons, Kenneth Joseph *lawyer*
Singer, Joseph William *law educator*
Steiker, Carol S. *law educator*
Steiner, Henry Jacob *law and human rights educator*
Stuntz, William John *law educator*
Subramanian, Guhan *law educator*
Tribe, Laurence Henry *law educator*
Vagts, Detlev Frederick *law educator*
Warren, Alvin Clifford, Jr. *law educator*
Warren, Elizabeth A. *law educator*
Weinreb, Lloyd Lobell *law educator*
Westfall, David *lawyer, educator*
White, Lucie E. *law educator*
Wilkins, David Brian *law educator*
Wirth, Peter *lawyer*
Wolfman, Bernard *lawyer, educator*
Zhang, Cynthia Hongbing *lawyer*
Zittrain, Jonathan L. *law educator*

**Canton**
Pace, David A. *lawyer*

**Chatham**
Popkin, Alice Daniels *lawyer*

**Concord**
Bander, Edward Julius *law librarian emeritus, lawyer*
Delehant, Joseph Henry *lawyer*

**Danvers**
Haber, Frederic *lawyer*

**Dennis Port**
Singer, Myer R(ichard) *lawyer*

**Dover**
Craver, James Bernard *lawyer*
Edwards, Carl Norman *lawyer*

**East Boston**
Crawford, Linda Sibery *lawyer, educator*

**Edgartown**
Gatting, Carlene J. *lawyer*

**Fitchburg**
Bartsch, Noel R. *lawyer*

**Florence**
Platt, Rutherford Hayes *law educator, geographer, consultant*

**Framingham**
VanWoerkom, Jack A. *lawyer, retail executive*
Vrabel, Joseph P. *lawyer*

**Gloucester**
Birchfield, John Kermit, Jr. *lawyer*
Nicholls, Bruce Gilbert *lawyer*

**Hanover**
Barreira, Brian Ernest *lawyer*

**Holyoke**
Resnic, Burton S. *lawyer*

**Hyannis**
Segersten, Robert Hagy *lawyer, investment banker*

**Ipswich**
Getchell, Charles Willard, Jr. *lawyer, publisher, foundation executive*

**Lexington**
Hines, Edward Francis, Jr. *lawyer*
Kent, Robert Brydon *law educator*

**Lincoln**
Gnichtel, William Van Orden *lawyer*

**Lowell**
Curtis, James Theodore *lawyer*
Martin, William Francis, Jr. *lawyer*
O'Donnell, Kathleen Marie *lawyer*

**Lynnfield**
McGivney, John Joseph *lawyer*

**Marblehead**
Page, George Alfred, Jr. *lawyer*

**Marion**
Worley, Robert William, Jr. *retired lawyer*

**Medford**
Berman, David *lawyer, poet*
Bishop, Richard Woodrow *lawyer, writer*
Salacuse, Jeswald William *lawyer, educator*

**Natick**
Grassia, Thomas Charles *lawyer, writer*
Oulton, Donald Paul *lawyer*
Sandman, Paul William *lawyer*
Walker, Kellye L. *lawyer*

**New Bedford**
Benoit, Richard Armand *lawyer, retired police chief*

**Newburyport**
Connolly, James Thomas *lawyer*

**Newton**
Baron, Charles Hillel *lawyer, educator*
Coquillette, Daniel Robert *lawyer, educator*
Frankenheim, Samuel *retired lawyer*
Glazer, Donald Wayne *lawyer, corporate financial executive, educator*
Huber, Richard Gregory *lawyer, educator*
Metzer, Patricia Ann *lawyer*
Rivlin, Rachel *lawyer*

**Newton Center**
Snyder, John Gorvers *lawyer*

**North Andover**
Grady, Kenneth Alan *lawyer*

**Northampton**
Hastings, Wilmot Reed *lawyer, writer*
Miles, Harry Lehman *lawyer, educator*

**Plymouth**
Della-Giustina, Jo-Ann Subotin *lawyer*

**Prides Crossing**
Garcia, Adolfo Ramon *lawyer*

**Quincy**
Hayes, Mary Dianne Wixted *lawyer*

**Randolph**
Johnson, Laurence Michael *lawyer*

**Salem**
Moran, Philip David *lawyer*
Rabchenuk, Paul Thomas *lawyer*

**Sandwich**
Troy, Robert Sweeney, Sr. *lawyer*

**Sherborn**
Borgeson, Earl Charles *law librarian, educator*
Goglia, Charles A., Jr. *lawyer*

**Siasconset**
Rauch, George Washington *lawyer, director*

**Southborough**
Kriegsman, Edward Michael *lawyer*

**Springfield**
Dibble, Francis Daniel, Jr. *lawyer*
Liguori, Robert *lawyer, insurance company executive*
Nicolai, Paul Peter *lawyer*
Oldershaw, Louis Frederick *retired lawyer*
Parke, David Alan *lawyer*
Santopietro, Albert Robert *lawyer*
Susse, Sandra Slone *lawyer*
Weiss, Ronald Phillip *lawyer*

**Stoughton**
Gabovitch, Steven Alan *lawyer, accountant*
George, Arthur Charles *lawyer*

**Truro**
Friedman, Edward David *lawyer, arbitrator*

**Wakefield**
Courtenay, Lisa A. *paralegal, foundation administrator*

**Waltham**
Chory, John H. *lawyer*
Dickie, Robert Benjamin *lawyer, educator*
Dulchinos, Peter *lawyer*
Stephens, Jay B. *lawyer, manufacturing executive*

**Watertown**
Smith, Debra L. *lawyer*

**Wellesley**
Carlson, Christopher Tapley *lawyer*
Pike, Judith Robyn *lawyer*
Silberman, Robert A. S. *lawyer*
Wong, Bella Toy Funnd *lawyer*

**West Chatham**
Rowley, Glenn Harry *lawyer*

**West Falmouth**
Carlson, David Bret *retired lawyer*

**West Tisbury**
Schwartz, Edward Arthur *lawyer*

**Weston**
Lashman, L. Edward *arbitrator, mediator, consultant*
Thomas, Roger Meriwether *lawyer*

**Winchester**
Bigelow, Robert P. *lawyer, arbitrator, mediator, journalist*

**Windsor**
Leaf, Martin Norman *lawyer*

**Winthrop**
Brown, Patricia Irene *retired law librarian, lawyer*

**Worcester**
Baldiga, Joseph Hilding *lawyer*
Chernin, Russell Scott *lawyer*
Cowan, Fairman Chaffee *lawyer*
Donnelly, James Corcoran, Jr. *lawyer*
Huber, J. Kendall *lawyer*
Lougee, David Louis *lawyer*
Mirick, John O. *lawyer*
Van Nostrand, Richard Charles *lawyer*

## MICHIGAN

**Ada**
McCallum, Charles Edward *lawyer*

**Ann Arbor**
Allen, Layman Edward *law educator, research scientist*
Ben-Shahar, Omri *law and economics educator*
Buesser, Anthony Carpenter *lawyer*
Carney, Thomas Daly *lawyer*
Clark, Sherman J. *law educator*
Cooper, Edward Hayes *lawyer, educator*
Croley, Steven P. *law educator*
Damschroder, Timothy Robert *lawyer*
Darlow, Julia Donovan *lawyer*
DeVine, Edmond Francis *lawyer*
Dobranski, Bernard *law educator*
Duquette, Donald Norman *law educator*
Eisenberg, Rebecca S. *law educator*
Ellmann, Douglas Stanley *lawyer*
Frier, Bruce Woodward *law educator*
Garcia, Elisa Dolores *lawyer*
Garris, Michael Jack *lawyer*
Gray, Whitmore *lawyer, educator*
Green, Thomas Andrew *law and history educator, lawyer*
Gross, Samuel R. *law educator*
Halberstam, Daniel *law educator*
Hathaway, James C. *law educator*
Herzog, Don *law educator, political science professor*
Howse, Robert Lloyd *law educator, consultant*
Joscelyn, Kent Buckley *lawyer*
Kahn, Douglas Allen *legal educator*
Kamisar, Yale *lawyer, educator*
Katz, Ellen D. *law educator*
Khanna, Vikramaditya *law educator*
Krier, James Edward *law educator, writer*
Krislov, Marvin *lawyer, educator*
Kuehn, George E. *lawyer*
Laycock, Harold Douglas *law educator, writer*
Leary, Margaret A. *law librarian, library director*
Lempert, Richard Owen *lawyer, educator*
Logue, Kyle D. *law educator*
MacKinnon, Catharine Alice *lawyer, educator, writer*
Mendelson, Nina *law educator*
Miller, William Ian *legal educator*
Parson, Edward A. *law educator*
Payton, Sallyanne *law educator*
Reed, John Wesley *lawyer, educator*
Regan, Donald H. *law educator*
Reimann, Mathias W. *law educator*
Reingold, Paul D. *law educator, lawyer*
Ryan, Marianne Elizabeth *lawyer*
St. Antoine, Theodore Joseph *retired law educator, arbitrator*
Sandalow, Terrance *law educator*
Schneider, Carl Edward *law educator*
Scott, Rebecca J. *law educator*
Simpson, A.W. Brian *law educator*
Soper, Philip *law educator*
Stein, Eric *retired law educator*
Sullivan, Teresa Ann *law and sociology educator, academic administrator*
Vining, Joseph (George Joseph Vining) *law educator*
Waggoner, Lawrence William *law educator*
Walsh, James Joseph *lawyer*
West, Mark D. *law educator*
White, James Boyd *law educator*
Whitman, Christina Brooks *law educator*

**Auburn Hills**
Horiszny, Laurene Helen *lawyer*
O'Brien, William J. III *lawyer*

**Battle Creek**
Markey, James Kevin *lawyer*

**Bay City**
Greve, Guy Robert *lawyer*

**Beverly Hills**
Hertzberg, David Gordon *retired lawyer*

### Bingham Farms
Baumkel, Mark S. *lawyer*
Goren, Steven Eliot *lawyer*

### Birmingham
Elsman, James Leonard, Jr. *lawyer*
Kienbaum, Thomas Gerd *lawyer*
Sweeney, Thomas Frederick *lawyer*
Wells, Steven Wayne *lawyer*

### Bloomfield Hills
Banas, C(hristine) Leslie *lawyer*
Burstein, Richard Joel *lawyer*
Charla, Leonard Francis *lawyer, publishing executive*
Clippert, Charles Frederick *lawyer*
Dawson, Stephen Everette *lawyer*
Devaney, Dennis Martin *lawyer, educator*
Gold, Edward David *lawyer*
Googasian, George Ara *lawyer*
Kasischke, Louis Walter *lawyer*
Kirk, John MacGregor *lawyer*
Ledwidge, Patrick Joseph *lawyer*
LoPrete, James Hugh *lawyer*
Martin, J(oseph) Patrick *lawyer, judge*
McCuen, John Francis, Jr. *lawyer*
McDonald, Patrick Allen *lawyer, educator, arbitrator*
Meyer, George Herbert *lawyer*
Nern, Christopher Carl *lawyer*
Norris, John Hart *lawyer, director*
Rader, Ralph Terrance *lawyer*
Simon, Evelyn *lawyer*
Smith, H(arold) Lawrence *lawyer*
Snyder, George Edward *lawyer*
Solomon, Mark Raymond *lawyer, educator*
Sommerfeld, David William *lawyer, educator*
Stewart, Michael B. *lawyer, mechanical and aerospace engineer*
Stoller, John R. *lawyer*
Williams, J. Bryan *lawyer*
Williams, Walter Joseph *lawyer*
Wise, John Augustus *lawyer, director*

### Dearborn
Fox, Stacy L. *lawyer*
Kahn, Mark Leo *arbitrator, educator*
Taub, Robert Allan *lawyer*

### Detroit
Amsden, Ted Thomas *lawyer*
Archer, Dennis Wayne *lawyer, former mayor*
Bilstrom, Jon Wayne *lawyer*
Boocock, Stephen William *lawyer*
Brand, George Edward, Jr. *retired lawyer*
Brustad, Orin Daniel *lawyer*
Calkins, Stephen *lawyer, educator*
Candler, James Nall, Jr. *lawyer*
Charfoos, Lawrence Selig *lawyer*
Cohan, Leon Sumner *lawyer, retired electric company executive*
Cohen, Norton Jacob *lawyer*
Collier, James Warren *retired lawyer*
Collins, Jeffrey G. *lawyer, former prosecutor*
Connor, Laurence Davis *lawyer, director*
Cothorn, John Arthur *lawyer*
Cranmer, Thomas William *lawyer*
Deason, Herold McClure *lawyer*
Diehl, Nancy J. *lawyer*
Drutchas, Gregory G. *lawyer*
Dudley, John Henry, Jr. *lawyer*
Dunn, William Bradley *lawyer*
Gamache, Kathleen Anne *law librarian*
Gershel, Alan M. *prosecutor*
Gross, James George *lawyer*
Gushee, Richard Bordley *lawyer*
Hall, Elliott Sawyer *lawyer*
Hampton, Verne Churchill, II, *lawyer*
Herstein, Carl William *lawyer*
Kamins, John Mark *lawyer*
Kessler, Philip Joel *lawyer*
Krsul, John Aloysius, Jr. *lawyer*
Lamborn, LeRoy Leslie *law educator*
Lawrence, John Kidder *lawyer*
Lewis, David Baker *lawyer*
Lockman, Stuart M. *lawyer*
Mamat, Frank Trustick *lawyer*
Maurer, David Leo *lawyer*
McIntyre, Michael John *lawyer, educator*
McKim, Samuel John III *lawyer*
Miller, George DeWitt, Jr. *lawyer*
Mitseff, Carl *lawyer*
Morford, Craig S. *prosecutor*
Murphy, Stephen Joseph III *prosecutor*
Myers, Rodman Nathaniel *lawyer*
Peters, John Douglas *lawyer, artist*
Peterson, Bruce D. *lawyer*
Rassel, Richard Edward *lawyer*
Raymond, Richard Gerard, Jr. *lawyer*
Rogers, Hon Paulletto *researcher, writer*
Rozof, Phyllis Claire *lawyer*
Saxton, William Marvin *lawyer*
Schwartz, Alan E. *lawyer, director*
Scott, John Edward Smith *lawyer*
Sedler, Robert Allen *law educator*
Shannon, Margaret Anne *lawyer*
Smith, James Albert *lawyer*
Sparrow, Herbert George III *lawyer, educator*
Tarnacki, Duane L. *lawyer*
Thelen, Bruce Cyril *lawyer*
Thurber, Peter Palms *lawyer*
Timm, Roger K. *lawyer*
Turner, Reginald Maurice, Jr. *lawyer*
Valade, Alan Michael *lawyer*
Volz, William Harry *lawyer, educator*
White, Katherine E. *law educator*
Whiteman, Richard Mark *lawyer*
Wittlinger, Timothy David *lawyer*
Wu, Frank H. *law educator, journalist*
Wyrick, Jermaine Albert *lawyer*

### East Lansing
Essa, Daniel F. *lawyer*
Johnson, Clark Cumings *lawyer, educator, dean*
Lashbrooke, Elvin Carroll, Jr. *law educator, consultant*
Revelos, Constantine Nicholas *law educator, writer*
Wilkinson, William Sherwood *lawyer*

### Farmington Hills
Brodhead, William McNulty *lawyer, retired congressman*
Fenton, Robert Leonard *lawyer, writer, film producer*
Meyer, Philip Gilbert *lawyer*
Seifman, Barry A. *lawyer*
Shaevsky, Mark *lawyer*

### Frankfort
Gerberding, Miles Carston *lawyer*

### Franklin
Pappas, Edward Harvey *lawyer*

### Grand Rapids
Barnes, Thomas John *lawyer*
Botsford, Jon Douglas *lawyer*
Bradshaw, Conrad Allan *retired lawyer*
Brinkmeyer, Scott S. *lawyer*
Bursch, John Joseph *lawyer*
Chiara, Margaret M. *prosecutor, lawyer*
Curtin, Timothy John *lawyer*
Davis, Henry Barnard, Jr. *lawyer*
Harris, Richard W. *law educator, lawyer, accountant*
McGarry, John Everett *lawyer*
Mears, Patrick Edward *lawyer*
Sytsma, Fredric A. *lawyer*
Walters, George O. *lawyer*

### Grosse Pointe
Goss, James William *lawyer*

### Grosse Pointe Park
Centner, Charles William *lawyer, educator*
Mogk, John Edward *law educator, association executive, consultant*

### Harbor Springs
Smith, Wayne Richard *lawyer*

### Hickory Corners
Bristol, Norman *lawyer, arbitrator, retired food products executive*

### Highland
Bullard, Willis Clare, Jr. *lawyer*

### Inkster
Bullock, Steven Carl *lawyer*

### Jackson
Marcoux, William Joseph *lawyer*
Smith, S. Kinnie, Jr. *lawyer*
Smith, Stanton Kinnie, Jr. *lawyer*

### Kalamazoo
Bus, Roger Jay *lawyer*
Enslen, Pamela Chapman *lawyer*
Gordon, Edgar George *retired lawyer*
Hall, Curtis E. *lawyer*

### Lake Orion
Robinson, Marietta S. *lawyer*

### Lansing
Baker, Frederick Milton, Jr. *lawyer*
Brewer, Mark Courtland *lawyer*
Cawthorne, Dennis Otto *lawyer*
Demlow, Daniel J. *lawyer*
Ewert, Quentin Albert *lawyer, consultant*
Fink, Joseph Allen *lawyer*
Foster, Joe C., Jr. *lawyer, lawyer*
Kelley, Frank Joseph *lawyer, former state attorney general*
Kulick, Peter J. *lawyer*
Marvin, David Edward Shreve *lawyer*
Stockmeyer, Norman Otto *law educator, consultant*
Weiner, William P. *law educator*

### Livonia
Hoffman, Barry Paul *lawyer*

### Midland
Kalil, Charles James *lawyer, chemicals executive*

### Monroe
Cohn, Morton Ray *lawyer*
Graham, W. Thomas *lawyer*
Lipford, Rocque Edward *lawyer*

### Mount Pleasant
Lynch, John Joseph *lawyer*

### Muskegon
McKendry, John H., Jr. *lawyer*
Nehra, Gerald Peter *lawyer*

### Northville
Cauley, Patrick C. *lawyer*

### Novi
Nanian, Marjorie Kay *lawyer, photographer, educator*

### Pinckney
Britton, Clarold Lawrence *lawyer, consultant*

### Plymouth
Haynes, Richard Terry *lawyer*
Longhofer, Ronald Stephen *lawyer*
Martina, Carlo Jack *lawyer*
Robinson, Logan Gilmore *lawyer*

### Rapid City
Ring, Ronald Herman *lawyer*

### Saginaw
Zanot, Craig Allen *lawyer*

### Saline
Anderson, Austin Gothard *lawyer, consultant, academic administrator*

### Sault Sainte Marie
Miller, Jennifer Jean *lawyer, law educator*
Morello, Steven John *lawyer*

### Southfield
Andreoff, Christopher Andon *lawyer*
Bassey, Ronald D. *tax attorney*
Brooks, Ernie L. *lawyer*
Darling, Robert Howard *lawyer*
Dawson, Dennis Ray *lawyer, manufacturing executive*
Fieger, Geoffrey Nels *lawyer*
Hotelling, Harold *law and economics educator*
Leuchtman, Stephen Nathan *lawyer*
Morganroth, Mayer *lawyer*
Ninivaggi, Daniel A. *lawyer*
Ponitz, John Allan *lawyer*
Porter, Thomas W.B. *lawyer*
Ritchie, Alexander Buchan *lawyer*
Rochkind, Louis Philipp *lawyer*
Sherbin, David M. *lawyer*
Sullivan, Robert Emmet, Jr. *lawyer*
Toll, Sheldon Samuel *lawyer*
Winzenreid, James Ernest *lawyer, entrepreneur*

### Sterling Heights
Novak, Joseph Anthony *law librarian*

### Sylvan Lake
Derdarian, Christine Anne *lawyer*

### Taylor
Hirsch, David L. *lawyer*
Leekley, John Robert *lawyer*

### Traverse City
Quandt, Joseph Edward *lawyer, educator*

### Troy
Alterman, Irwin Michael *lawyer*
Arbuckle, Brad B. *lawyer*
Baker, Vernon G., II, *lawyer*
Cunningham, Gary H. *lawyer*
Gelder, John William *lawyer*
Haron, David Lawrence *lawyer*
Hilton, Michael E. *lawyer*
Kruse, John Alphonse *lawyer*
May, Alan Alfred *lawyer*
Moore, Daniel Michael *lawyer*
Pearce, Harry Jonathan *lawyer, manufacturing executive*
Thoms, David Moore *lawyer*
Webster, Robert Byron *lawyer*

### Waterford
Hall, Terrence Lyon *lawyer*

### Wyandotte
Pentiuk, Randall Alan *lawyer*

### Ypsilanti
Eggertsen, John Hale *lawyer*

## MINNESOTA

### Austin
Cavanaugh, James W. *lawyer*

### Bemidji
Kief, Paul Allan *lawyer*

### Bloomington
Broeker, John Milton *lawyer*
Grinnell, Joseph Fox *lawyer*
Mooty, John William *lawyer*

### Chatfield
Opat, Matthew John *lawyer*

### Detroit Lakes
Stowman, David L. *lawyer*

### Duluth
Amberg, Deborah Ann *lawyer*
Burns, Richard Ramsey *lawyer*

### Eagan
Johnson, Jaren Lee *lawyer*
Simon, Barry Philip *lawyer, air transportation executive*
Todd, John Joseph *lawyer*

### Eden Prairie
Feuss, Linda Anne Upsall *lawyer*
Gilbert, James A. *lawyer, former state supreme court justice*
Nilles, John Michael *lawyer*

### Edina
Bakken, Eric Allen *lawyer*
Burk, Robert S. *lawyer*
Neff, Fred Leonard *lawyer*

### Golden Valley
Ainsworth, Louis Lynde *lawyer, manufacturing executive*
Schlichting, William Henry *lawyer, writer*

### Grand Marais
Hennessy, William Joseph *prosecutor*

### Hallock
Malm, Roger Charles *lawyer*

### Inver Grove Heights
Kastelic, David Allen *lawyer*

### Maple Grove
Boyd, Kelly A. *lawyer, law educator*

### Marshall
Paskach, David M. *lawyer, food products executive*

### Medford
Paschke, Jerry Bryan *lawyer*

### Medina
McConnell, Mary Patricia *lawyer*

### Minneapolis
Ahern, Michael James *lawyer*
Anderson, Eric Scott *lawyer*

Anderson, Leslie J. *lawyer*
Baillie, James Leonard *lawyer*
Berens, William Joseph *lawyer*
Berg, Thomas Kenneth *lawyer*
Bergerson, David Raymond *lawyer*
Borger, John Philip *lawyer*
Brand, Steve Aaron *lawyer*
Branson, Timothy E. *lawyer*
Breimayer, Joseph Frederick *patent lawyer*
Bress, Michael E. *retired lawyer*
Brink, David Ryrie *lawyer*
Bruner, Philip Lane *lawyer*
Buckingham, Elizabeth C. *lawyer*
Buratti, Dennis P. *lawyer*
Busdicker, Gordon Gene *retired lawyer*
Caplan, Allan Hart *lawyer*
Cattanach, Robert Edward, Jr. *lawyer*
Champlin, Steven Kirk *lawyer*
Christiansen, Jay David *lawyer*
Ciresi, Michael Vincent *lawyer*
Clary, Bradley G. *lawyer, educator*
Cole, Phillip Allen *lawyer*
Conn, Gordon Brainard, Jr. *lawyer*
Constantine, Katherine A. *lawyer*
Diviney, Craig David *lawyer*
Dorenkamp, Theodore III *lawyer*
Durocher, Vernle C. (Skip), Jr. *lawyer*
Eck, George Gregory *lawyer*
Eng, Holly S.A. *lawyer*
Engh, N. Rolf *lawyer*
Erstad, Leon Robert *lawyer*
Faricy, John Hartnett, Jr. *lawyer*
Flom, Gerald Trossen *lawyer*
Forneris, Jeanne M. *lawyer*
Frase, Richard Stockwell *law educator*
French, John Dwyer *retired lawyer*
Gagnon, Craig William *lawyer*
Garon, Philip Stephen *lawyer*
Garton, Thomas William *lawyer*
Genereux, L. Joseph *lawyer*
Gill, Richard Lawrence *lawyer*
Gordon, Corey Lee *lawyer*
Gottschalk, Stephen Elmer *lawyer*
Greener, Ralph Bertram *lawyer*
Grussing, Bruce Douglass *lawyer*
Hagglund, Clarance Edward *lawyer, publishing executive*
Hamel, Mark Edwin *lawyer*
Hansen, Robyn L. *lawyer*
Hanson, Kent Bryan *lawyer*
Hart, Buster Clarence *lawyer*
Haynsworth, Harry Jay, IV, *law educator*
Hayward, Edward Joseph *lawyer*
Heiberg, Robert Alan *lawyer*
Hendrixson, Peter S. *lawyer*
Henson, Robert Frank *lawyer*
Herr, David Fulton *lawyer, educator*
Hinderaker, John Hadley *lawyer, political blogger*
Hippee, William H., Jr. *lawyer*
Hobbins, Robert Leo *lawyer*
Holden, Susan M. *lawyer*
Howland, Joan Sidney *law librarian, educator*
Hunt, Kay Nord *lawyer*
Jackson, J. David *lawyer*
Jarboe, Mark Alan *lawyer*
Johannsen, Marc Alan *lawyer*
Johnson, Gary M. *lawyer*
Johnson, Larry Walter *lawyer*
Jonason, William A. *lawyer*
Joyce, Joseph M. *lawyer*
Kaplan, Sheldon *lawyer, director*
Kelly, A. David *lawyer*
Keppel, William James *lawyer, educator, writer*
Keyes, Jeffrey J. *lawyer*
Kirtley, Jane Elizabeth *law educator*
Klaas, Paul Barry *lawyer*
Knopf, Matthew J. *lawyer*
Koneck, John Michael *lawyer*
Lancaster, Peter McCreery *lawyer*
Landry, Paul Leonard *lawyer*
Lavik, Bricker L. *lawyer*
Lazar, Raymond Michael *lawyer, educator*
Lebedoff, David Miller *lawyer, writer*
Lillehaug, David Lee *lawyer*
Lindsay, Michael Anthony *lawyer*
Lucke, Stephen P. *lawyer*
Lueck, Martin R. *lawyer*
Magid, Creighton (Chip) Reid *lawyer*
Magnuson, Roger James *lawyer*
Manthey, Thomas Richard *lawyer*
Marshall, Siri Swenson *lawyer*
Martin, Judith Moran *lawyer*
Martin, Phillip Hammond *lawyer*
Martinson, Bradley James *lawyer*
Matthews, James Shadley *lawyer*
McDermott, Kathleen E. *lawyer*
McDonald, John J., Jr. *lawyer*
McGunnigle, George Francis *lawyer, judge*
McIntyre, John Lawrence *lawyer*
McLaughlin, Patrick J. *lawyer*
Mellum, Gale Robert *lawyer*
Meshbesher, Ronald I. *lawyer*
Morrison, Fred LaMont *law educator, dean*
Nelson, Gary Michael *lawyer*
Nelson, Richard Arthur *lawyer*
Novak, Leslie Howard *lawyer*
Oh, Allen James *lawyer*
O'Neill, Brian Boru *lawyer*
Palmer, Brian Eugene *lawyer*
Paulose, Rachel *prosecutor*
Peterson, Neal N. *lawyer*
Peterson, William George *lawyer*
Pfau, James Michael *lawyer*
Platt, Nina *law librarian*
Pratte, Robert John *lawyer*
Price, Joseph Michael *lawyer*
Radmer, Michael John *lawyer, educator*
Raskind, Leo Joseph *law educator*
Rasmussen, Teresa J. *lawyer, insurance company executive*
Ratchye, Boyd Havens *lawyer*
Reinhart, Robert Rountree, Jr. *lawyer*
Reister, Raymond Alex *retired lawyer*
Remele, Lewis Albert, Jr. *lawyer*
Rockenstein, Walter Harrison, II, *lawyer*
Rockwell, Winthrop Adams *lawyer*
Roe, Roger Rolland, Jr. *lawyer*
Rothenberg, Elliot Calvin *lawyer, writer*
Saeks, Allen Irving *lawyer*
Safley, James Robert *lawyer*
Sawicki, Zbigniew Peter *lawyer*

Sawyer, Charles F. *lawyer*
Schneider, Elaine Carol *lawyer, researcher, writer*
Schnell, Robert Lee, Jr. *lawyer*
Schnobrich, Roger William *lawyer*
Shaheen, Christopher T. *lawyer*
Shnider, Bruce Jay *lawyer*
Short, Marianne Dolores *lawyer*
Silver, Alan Irving *lawyer*
Simonson, James S. *lawyer*
Sipkins, Peter W. *lawyer*
Sippel, William Leroy *lawyer*
Sisk, Gregory Charles *lawyer, educator*
Skare, Robert Martin *lawyer, director*
Soland, Norman R. *corporate lawyer*
Sortland, Paul Allan *lawyer*
Stageberg, Roger V. *lawyer*
Stern, Leo G. *lawyer*
Stoeri, William R. *lawyer*
Struthers, Margo S. *lawyer*
Struyk, Robert John *lawyer*
Sullivan, E. Thomas *law educator*
Swanson, David P. *lawyer*
Thorson, Steven Greg *lawyer*
Tinkham, Thomas W. *lawyer*
Trucano, Michael *lawyer*
Vander Molen, Thomas Dale *lawyer*
Waloske, Michael James *lawyer*
Wegerson, Edward J. *lawyer*
Whelpley, Dennis Porter *lawyer*
Wicks, John R. *lawyer*
Windhorst, John William, Jr. *lawyer*
Yost, Gerald B. *lawyer*
Younger, Judith Tess *law educator*
Zalk, Robert H. *retired lawyer*

**Minnetonka**
Freeman, Gerald Russell *lawyer*
Heckt, Melvin Dean *lawyer*
Lubben, David J. *lawyer*
Van Brunt, William A. *lawyer*

**North Oaks**
Woods, Robert Edward *lawyer*

**North Saint Paul**
O'Brien, Daniel William *lawyer, lumber company executive*

**Northfield**
Lundergan, Barbara Keough *lawyer*

**Owatonna**
Birk, Peg J. *lawyer*

**Pipestone**
Scott, William Paul *lawyer*

**Plymouth**
Saville, Derric James *lawyer*

**Rochester**
Dittrich, Steven Michael *lawyer*

**Saint Paul**
Allison, John Robert *lawyer*
Bell, Lawrence T. *lawyer*
Daly, Joseph Leo *law educator*
Deretich, George *lawyer*
Galvin, Michael John, Jr. *lawyer*
Gehan, Mark William *lawyer*
Geis, Jerome Arthur *lawyer, law educator*
Janzen, Peter S. *lawyer*
Johnson, Paul Oren *lawyer*
Jones, C. Paul *lawyer, educator*
Jones, Patricia L. *lawyer*
Kirsch, Steven Jay *lawyer*
Kirwin, Kenneth Francis *law educator*
Larson, David Allen *law educator*
Lebedoff, Randy Miller *lawyer*
Leighton, Robert Joseph *lawyer*
Seymour, McNeil Vernam *lawyer*
Spence, Kenneth F. III *lawyer*
Zibell, Donald Fredrick *lawyer*
Ziegler, Richard Ferdinand *lawyer*

**Shakopee**
McCloud, Samuel Alfred *lawyer*

**South Saint Paul**
Atkins, Joseph Eugene *lawyer, state representative*
Pugh, Thomas Wilfred *lawyer*

**Waseca**
Deike, Keith Lawrence *lawyer*

**Wayzata**
Alton, Howard Robert, Jr. *lawyer, food company executive, real estate executive*
Reutiman, Robert William, Jr. *lawyer*

**Winona**
Brosnahan, Roger Paul *retired lawyer*

## MISSISSIPPI

**Bay Saint Louis**
Bernstein, Joseph *lawyer*

**Biloxi**
Dornan, Donald C., Jr. *lawyer*
Farrior, James L. III *lawyer*

**Carthage**
Moran, Mitch *lawyer*

**Eupora**
Meek, Walter Buchanan *retired lawyer, director*

**Flowood**
Barnes, Harris H., III, (Trip Barnes) *tax lawyer*
Wilson, William Roberts, Jr., (Bob Wilson) *lawyer, apparel executive*

**Greenville**
Martin, Andrew Ayers *lawyer, physician, educator*

**Greenwood**
Swayze, Charles J., Jr. *lawyer*

**Gulfport**
Owen, Joe Sam *lawyer*
Phillips, Joy Lambert *lawyer, banker*

**Hattiesburg**
Adelman, Michael Schwartz *lawyer*
King, Ernest Wade *law educator*

**Hernando**
Brown, William A. *lawyer, mediator, arbitrator*

**Jackson**
Adams, Charles P., Jr. *lawyer*
Burch, Donald Victor *lawyer*
Chatham, Lloyd Reeve *lawyer*
Clark, David Wright *lawyer*
Corlew, John Gordon *lawyer*
Ellingburg, C. Michael *lawyer*
England, John F. *lawyer*
Franks, James R. (Jamie), Jr. *lawyer, state legislator*
Fuselier, Louis Alfred *lawyer*
Hafter, Jerome Charles *lawyer*
Henegan, John C(lark) *lawyer*
Hosemann, C. Delbert, Jr. *lawyer*
Howell, Joel Walter III *lawyer*
Hughes, Byron William *oil industry executive*
Hutchison, Mark Stevenson *lawyer*
Lampton, Dunn O. *prosecutor*
McDavid, John Sanford *lawyer*
McIntyre, James G. *lawyer*
Moize, Jerry Dee *lawyer, federal official*
O'Mara, James Wright *lawyer*
Purdy, William Richard *lawyer*
Roberts, Richard Charlton III *lawyer*
Scanlon, Pat H. *lawyer*
Sweet, Dennis C. III *lawyer*
Thames, Lee Davis *lawyer*
Welch, W(alter) Scott III *lawyer*

**Ocean Springs**
Luckey, Alwyn Hall *lawyer*

**Oxford**
Greenlee, Jim Ming *prosecutor*
Hoffheimer, Michael Harry *law educator*
Howorth, David Bishop *lawyer*

**Philadelphia**
Duncan, Mark *district attorney*

**Ridgeland**
Pemberton, William Bertram, II, *lawyer*

**Southaven**
Taylor, Ronald Louis *lawyer*

**Tupelo**
Clayton, Claude F., Jr. *lawyer*

## MISSOURI

**Cape Girardeau**
Limbaugh, David *lawyer*
McManaman, Kenneth Charles *lawyer*

**Chesterfield**
Denneen, John Paul *lawyer*
Gerard, Jules Bernard *law educator*
Hier, Marshall David *lawyer*
Pollihan, Thomas Henry *lawyer*

**Clayton**
Mohrman, Henry Joe, Jr. *lawyer, investment manager*
Pain, George H. *lawyer*
Tremayne, Eric Flory *lawyer*

**Columbia**
Bunn, Ronald Freeze *lawyer, academic administrator*
Easton, Stephen Douglas *law educator, lawyer*
Fisch, William Bales *law educator*
Harter, Philip J. *lawyer, educator*
Mays, William Gay, II, *lawyer, real estate developer*
Phillips, Walter Ray *law educator*
Welliver, Warren Dee *lawyer, retired judge*
Westbrook, James Edwin *law educator*
Whitman, Dale Alan *lawyer, educator*
Zylstra, Alexandria *lawyer*

**Earth City**
Wallace, Bob (Robert Eugene Wallace Jr.) *lawyer*

**Hillsboro**
Howald, John William *lawyer*

**Hollister**
Lowther, Gerald Halbert *lawyer*

**Independence**
Albano, Michael Santo John *lawyer*
Cady, Elwyn Loomis, Jr. *medicolegal consultant*
Jackson, James Bruce *lawyer*
Terry, Jack Chatterson *lawyer*

**Jefferson City**
Baker, Wade Franklin *retired state bar executive*
Barrett, David F. *lawyer*
Bartlett, Alex *lawyer*
Deutsch, James Bernard *lawyer*
Tettlebaum, Harvey M. *lawyer*

**Joplin**
Scott, Robert Haywood, Jr. *lawyer*

**Kansas City**
Anderson, Christopher James *lawyer*
Atkinson, David Neal *law educator*
Ayers, Jeffrey David *lawyer*
Bates, William Hubert *lawyer*
Beck, William Q. *lawyer*
Beckett, Theodore Charles *lawyer*
Beihl, Frederick *retired lawyer*
Belzer, Irvin V. *lawyer*
Berkowitz, Lawrence M. *lawyer*
Bevan, Robert Lewis *lawyer*

Blanton, W. C. *lawyer*
Bradshaw, Jean Paul, II, *lawyer*
Brake, Timothy L. *lawyer*
Brandt, William Perry *lawyer*
Brous, Thomas Richard *lawyer*
Clarke, Milton Charles *lawyer*
Clegg, Karen Kohler *lawyer*
Connor, Kevin M. *lawyer*
Cross, William Dennis *lawyer*
Deacy, Thomas Edward, Jr. *lawyer*
Dicus, Stephen Howard *lawyer*
Dietrich, William Gale *lawyer, real estate developer, consultant*
Egan, Charles Joseph, Jr. *lawyer, consumer products company executive*
Eldridge, Truman Kermit, Jr. *lawyer*
Foster, Mark Stephen *lawyer*
Frantze, David Wayne *lawyer*
Freeman, Frederick Roe *lawyer*
Gardner, Brian E. *lawyer*
Geroe, Michael R. *lawyer*
Gorman, Gerald Warner *lawyer*
Heeter, James A. *lawyer*
Hindman, Larrie C. *lawyer*
Johnson, Mark Eugene *lawyer*
Johnson, Mark P. *lawyer*
Johnston, John Steven *lawyer*
Kaplan, Harvey L. *lawyer*
Kilroy, John Muir *lawyer*
Kilroy, William Terrence *lawyer*
King, Richard Allen *lawyer*
Langworthy, Robert Burton *lawyer*
Lashley, Curtis Dale *lawyer*
Levings, Theresa Lawrence *lawyer*
Lindsey, David Hosford *lawyer*
Litan, Robert Eli *lawyer, economist*
Magariel, Dale L. *law librarian*
Magill, Kent B. *lawyer*
Martucci, William Christopher *lawyer*
Matheny, Edward Taylor, Jr. *lawyer*
McKinney, Janet Kay *law librarian*
McLarney, Charles Patrick *lawyer*
McManus, James William *lawyer*
Mick, Howard Harold *lawyer*
Milton, Chad Earl *lawyer*
Moore, Stephen James *lawyer*
Mordy, James Calvin *lawyer*
Murphy, John F. *lawyer*
Newsom, James Thomas *lawyer*
Northrip, Robert Earl *lawyer*
O'Dear, Craig Steven *lawyer*
Palmer, Dennis Dale *lawyer*
Pelofsky, Joel *lawyer*
Pemberton, Bradley Powell *lawyer*
Plax, Karen Ann *lawyer*
Popper, Robert *lawyer, retired dean*
Price, James Tucker *lawyer*
Prugh, William Byron *lawyer*
Redfearn, Paul L. III *lawyer*
Respeliers, Patrick J. *lawyer*
Robb, Gary Charles *lawyer*
Sampson, William Roth *lawyer*
Schelling, Donald Lawrence *lawyer*
Schlozman, Bradley J *prosecutor*
Schult, Thomas P. *lawyer*
Setzler, Edward Allan *lawyer*
Sexton, J. Stan *lawyer*
Shaw, John W. *lawyer*
Shughart, Donald Louis *retired lawyer*
Spaeth, Nicholas John *lawyer, former state attorney general*
Spalty, Edward Robert *lawyer*
Spencer, Richard Henry *lawyer*
Tanner, Eric Benson *lawyer*
Toll, Perry Mark *lawyer, educator*
Tyler, John Edward III *lawyer*
Van Dyke, Thomas Wesley *lawyer*
Vering, John Albert *lawyer*
Versfeld, Leon *lawyer*
Viani, James Laurence *lawyer*
Ward, R. Lawrence *lawyer*
Whisler, Joe B. *lawyer*
Whittaker, Judith Ann Cameron *lawyer*
Wirken, James Charles *lawyer*
Wolf, Jerome Thomas *lawyer*
Woody, Teresa Ann *lawyer*
Woolley, Brian N. *lawyer*
Wyrsch, James Robert *lawyer, educator, writer*

**Lake Saint Louis**
Callahan, Robert John, Jr. *lawyer, arbitrator*

**Louisiana**
Smith, Philip G. *lawyer*

**Manchester**
Forsman, Alpheus Edwin *retired lawyer*

**Maryland Heights**
Boudreau, Thomas M. *lawyer*

**Moberly**
Tatlow, Gary Arthur *lawyer*

**O Fallon**
Nieters, Gerard Anthony *lawyer*

**Osage Beach**
Peth, Howard Allen *law educator*
Troutwine, Gayle Leone *lawyer*

**Saint Charles**
Weber, William Randolph *lawyer*

**Saint Joseph**
Kranitz, Theodore Mitchell *lawyer*

**Saint Louis**
Alber, John I. *lawyer*
Appleton, R. O., Jr. *lawyer*
Arnold, Fred English *lawyer*
Arnold, John Fox *lawyer*
Atwood, Hollye Stolz *lawyer*
Aylward, Ronald Lee *lawyer*
Babler, Wayne E. *lawyer, retired utilities executive*
Baldwin, Edwin Steedman *lawyer*
Ball, Dan H. *lawyer*
Banks, Eric Kendall *lawyer*
Barnickol, Karl R. *lawyer*

Baum, Gordon Lee *lawyer, non-profit organization administrator*
Becker, David Mandel *law educator, author, consultant*
Bobak, Mark T. *lawyer*
Bonacorsi, Mary Catherine *lawyer*
Breece, Robert William, Jr. *lawyer*
Brickey, Kathleen Fitzgerald *law educator*
Brickler, John Weise *lawyer*
Brickson, Richard Alan *lawyer*
Brody, Lawrence Andrew *lawyer*
Brownlee, Robert Hammel *lawyer*
Bryan, Henry C(lark), Jr. *retired lawyer*
Buckley, Kevin William *lawyer*
Burroughs, Harold R. *lawyer*
Carp, Larry *lawyer*
Carr, Gary Thomas *lawyer*
Charlson, Alan Edward *lawyer, retail executive*
Clear, John Michael *lawyer*
Conner, Patrick T. *lawyer*
Conran, Joseph Palmer *lawyer*
Copeland, Douglas Allen *lawyer*
Cornfeld, Dave Louis *lawyer*
Cornfeld, Richard Steven *lawyer*
Corrigan, William M. *lawyer*
Cousins, Steven *lawyer*
Covington, Ann K. *lawyer, former state supreme court justice*
Cullen, James D. *lawyer*
Cupples, Stephen Elliot *lawyer*
Danforth, John Claggett *lawyer, former ambassador, former senator*
Dorwart, Donald Bruce *lawyer*
Dowd, Edward L., Jr. *lawyer, former prosecutor*
Dowd, Thomas F. *lawyer*
Downey, Michael Patrick *lawyer*
Duesenberg, Richard William *lawyer*
Eagleton, Thomas Francis *lawyer, former senator*
Ebert, Robert T. *lawyer*
Elliott, Howard, Jr. *lawyer, gas industry executive*
Ellis, Dorsey Daniel, Jr. *lawyer, educator*
Epstein, Robert Harry *lawyer*
Evans, Lawrence E. *lawyer, educator*
Fahrenkrog, Eugene Henry, Jr. *lawyer*
Falk, William James *lawyer*
Fessenden, Ann T. *law librarian*
Fournie, Raymond Richard *lawyer*
Gillis, John Lamb, Jr. *lawyer*
Godiner, Donald Leonard *lawyer*
Goebel, John J. *lawyer*
Goldstein, Steven *lawyer*
Goran, Mark H. *lawyer*
Gray, Charles Elmer *lawyer, rancher, investor*
Greaney, Thomas L. *law educator, lawyer*
Green, Dennis Joseph *lawyer*
Greenley, Beverly Jane *lawyer, educator*
Guarigila, Dale A. *lawyer*
Guerri, William Grant *lawyer*
Hackmann, Frank H. *lawyer*
Hanaway, Catherine Lucille *prosecutor*
Hansen, Charles *lawyer*
Harris, Whitney Robson *lawyer, educator, military officer, volunteer*
Hayman, Randy E. *lawyer*
Hellmuth, Theodore Henning *lawyer*
Hiles, Bradley Stephen *lawyer*
Inkley, John James *lawyer*
Jaudes, Richard Edward *lawyer*
Jayne, Thomas R. *lawyer*
Johnson, E. Perry *lawyer*
Johnson, Sandra Hanneken *law educator*
Joley, Lisa Annette *lawyer*
Jones, Robert Gerard *lawyer*
Keller, Juan Dane *retired lawyer*
Klobasa, John Anthony *lawyer*
Kuhlmann, Fred Mark *lawyer*
Lane, Frank Joseph, Jr. *lawyer*
Lause, Michael Francis *lawyer*
Lebowitz, Albert *lawyer, writer*
Lents, Don Glaude *lawyer*
Lieberman, Edward Jay *lawyer*
Lohman, Janette Massie *lawyer, educator*
Lonsberg, John V. *lawyer*
Lowenhaupt, Charles Abraham *lawyer*
Lowther, Thomas Edward *lawyer*
Ludwig, Fredrick J. *lawyer*
Lynch, Robert Martin *lawyer, consultant*
Mandelstamm, Jerome Robert *lawyer*
Martin, Lisa Demet *lawyer*
Massey, Raymond Lee *lawyer*
McCarter, Charlton Chase *lawyer*
McDaniel, James Edwin *lawyer*
McKinnis, Michael B. *lawyer*
Meisel, George Vincent *lawyer*
Merrill, Charles Eugene *lawyer*
Metcalfe, Walter Lee, Jr. *lawyer*
Michenfelder, Albert A. *lawyer*
Mohan, John J. *lawyer*
Moore, McPherson Dorsett *lawyer*
Mulligan, Michael Dennis *lawyer*
Murray, George E. *lawyer*
Neville, James Morton *retired lawyer, consumer products company executive*
Newman, Charles Andrew *lawyer*
Noel, Edwin Lawrence *lawyer*
O'Keefe, Michael Daniel *lawyer*
Olson, Robert Grant *lawyer*
O'Malley, Kevin Francis *lawyer, writer, educator*
Palans, Lloyd Alex *lawyer*
Peper, Christian Baird *lawyer*
Perotti, Rose Norma *lawyer*
Phoenix, G. Keith *lawyer*
Pickle, Robert Douglas *lawyer, apparel executive*
Riddle, Veryl Lee *lawyer*
Ritterskamp, Douglas Dolvin *lawyer*
Roodman, David A. *lawyer*
Rose, Albert Schoenburg *lawyer, educator*
Rothert, Anthony Edward *lawyer, director*
Rubenstein, Jerome Max *lawyer*
Sachs, Alan Arthur *lawyer*
Sale, Llewellyn III *lawyer*
Schwartz, Steven H. *lawyer*
Seabaugh, William F. *lawyer*
Sestric, Anthony James *lawyer*
Sherby, Kathleen Reilly *lawyer*
Smith, Arthur Lee *lawyer*
Sneeringer, Stephen Geddes *lawyer*
Stoneman, Mark L. *lawyer*
Sullivan, Steven R. *lawyer*
Talen, Bruce L. *lawyer*
Teasdale, Kenneth Fulbright *lawyer*

Terry, Nicholas P. *law educator*
Tishler, Richard Norman *lawyer*
Turley, Michael Roy *lawyer*
Vandiver, Thomas K. *lawyer*
Van Fleet, Lisa A. *lawyer*
Virtel, James John *lawyer*
Wack, Thomas E. *lawyer*
Wagner, Raymond Thomas, Jr. *lawyer, legal association administrator*
Walker Tucker, Dana *lawyer*
Walsh, Thomas Charles *lawyer*
Watters, Richard Donald *lawyer*
Weiss, Charles Andrew *lawyer*
Welch, David William *lawyer*
Willard, Gregory Dale *lawyer*
Wilson, Margaret Bush *lawyer*
Wilson, Michael E. *lawyer*
Withers, W. Wayne *lawyer*
Wolff, Frank Pierce, Jr. *lawyer*
Wright, Philip B. *lawyer*
Yawitz, Richard A. *lawyer*
Young, Marvin Oscar *lawyer*

**Sedalia**
Rice, James Briggs, Jr. *lawyer*

**Springfield**
McDonald, William Henry *lawyer*
Schnake, Richard Lane *lawyer*

**Stockton**
Hammons, Brian Kent *lawyer*

**Town And Country**
Fagerberg, Roger Richard *lawyer*

## MONTANA

**Billings**
Cromley, Brent Reed *lawyer, state senator*
Haughey, James McCrea *lawyer, artist*
Mercer, William W. *prosecutor*
Thompson, James William *lawyer*
Towe, Thomas Edward *lawyer*

**Bozeman**
Nelson, Steven Dwayne *lawyer*
Wylie, Paul Richter, Jr. *lawyer*

**Columbia Falls**
Chisholm, Dean D. *lawyer*

**Dillon**
Suenram, Andy *lawyer*

**Great Falls**
Doherty, Steve *lawyer, state legislator*
Hartelius, Channing Julius *lawyer*
Manning, John Willard *lawyer*

**Havre**
Maristuen, Keith A. *lawyer*

**Helena**
Franz, Holly Jo *lawyer*
Meadows, Judith Adams *law librarian, educator*

**Missoula**
Bowman, Jean Louise *lawyer, civic worker*
George, Alexander Andrew *lawyer*
Sullivan, Robert John *lawyer*
Willey, Charles Wayne *lawyer*

**Whitehall**
Bernard, Donald Ray *retired law educator*

## NEBRASKA

**Broken Bow**
Sennett, John O. *lawyer*

**Columbus**
Schumacher, Paul Maynard *lawyer*

**Lincoln**
Binning, John Harlan *lawyer*
Guthery, John M. *lawyer*
Hewitt, James Watt *retired lawyer*
Leiter, Richard Allen *law librarian, educator*
Lichty, Warren Dewey, Jr. *lawyer*
Ogle, Robbin Sue *criminal justice educator*
Rembolt, James Earl *lawyer*
Ridenour, Brian Kent *lawyer*
Robak, Kim M. *lawyer*
Rowe, David Winfield *lawyer*

**Omaha**
Achelpohl, Steven Edward *lawyer*
Barrett, Frank Joseph *lawyer, insurance company executive*
Brownrigg, John Clinton *lawyer*
Caporale, D. Nick *lawyer*
Creigh, James Carey *lawyer*
Dahlk, Thomas Harlan *lawyer*
Dittrick, William G. *lawyer*
Fairbanks, Charles F. *law educator*
Fitzgerald, James Patrick *lawyer*
Gleason, James Mullaney *lawyer, insurance company executive*
Grant, John P. *lawyer*
Heavican, Michael G. *prosecutor*
Hemmer, J. Michael *lawyer*
Hupp, Michael M. *lawyer*
Jansen, James Steven *lawyer*
Jenkins, Melvin Lemuel *lawyer*
Jensen, Sam *lawyer*
Krutter, Forrest Nathan *lawyer*
McCusker, Thomas J. *lawyer, insurance company executive*
Rock, Harold L. *lawyer*
Schropp, Tobin *lawyer*
Stenberg, Donald B. *lawyer*
von Bernuth, Carl W. *lawyer, diversified financial services company executive*
Wells, Roger W. *lawyer*

## NEVADA

**Carson City**
McCarthy, Ann Price *lawyer*
Taggart, Paul Gordon *lawyer*

**Elko**
Puccinelli, Andrew James *lawyer*

**Las Vegas**
Arum, Robert *lawyer, sports events promoter*
Bersi, Ann *lawyer*
Bogden, Daniel G. *prosecutor*
Brammell, Stephen Harrison *lawyer*
Bridges, B. Ried *lawyer*
Brown, Joseph Wentling *lawyer*
Bryan, Richard H. *lawyer, educator, former senator*
Christensen, John William *lawyer*
Collins, Frank Edwin *lawyer*
Consul, Vincent A. *lawyer*
DeLury, Bernard Edward, Jr. *lawyer*
Faiss, Robert Dean *lawyer*
Gentile, Dominic P. *lawyer*
Gostin, Irwin *retired lawyer*
Hilbrecht, Norman Ty *lawyer*
James, Mark A. *lawyer, former state legislator*
Leleu, Jonathan Paul *lawyer*
Lovell, Carl Erwin, Jr. *lawyer*
Lukens, John Patrick *lawyer*
McNulty, James Francis, Jr. *lawyer, consultant*
Moss, Gary Curtis *lawyer*
Norville, Craig Hubert *lawyer*
Rosen, Leon *lawyer*
Sheets, Thomas R. *lawyer, gas industry executive*
Sklar, Alan Curtis *lawyer*
Solomon, Jack Avrum, Jr. *lawyer, automotive executive, art dealer*
Sturman, Glorida J. *lawyer*
Wilson, Joseph Morris III *lawyer*

**Reno**
Bell, Robert Cecil *lawyer*
Clontz, Donna *lawyer, writer, consultant*
East, Ernest Earl *lawyer, electric power industry executive*
Fletcher, Douglas Charles *lawyer*
Hafter, Jacob Louis *lawyer, paramedic*
Hibbs, Loyal Robert *lawyer*
Johnson, David D. *lawyer, game company executive*
Klinefelter, Gary V. *lawyer*
Pagni, Albert Frank *lawyer*
Robison, Kent Richard *lawyer*
Santos, Herbert Joseph, Jr. *lawyer*
White, John, Jr. *lawyer*

## NEW HAMPSHIRE

**Concord**
Baldwin, Carolyn Whitmore *lawyer*
Colantuono, Thomas Paul *prosecutor, former state legislator*
Gartrell, Donald Everett *lawyer*
Heard, Charles Wolfe *lawyer, consultant*
Hesse, Richard A. *law educator*
Hilliard, Russell F. *lawyer*
Potter, Fred Leon *lawyer, retired insurance company executive*
Rath, Thomas David *lawyer, retired prosecutor*
Uchida, Richard Y. *lawyer*
Young, Sherilyn Burnett *lawyer*

**Dover**
Catalfo, Alfred, Jr., (Alfio Catalfo) *lawyer*

**Hampton**
DuChene, Todd Michael *lawyer*

**Hanover**
Gardner, Peter Jaglom *lawyer, publishing executive*
Lundquist, Weyman Ivan *lawyer*

**Henniker**
Gleason, James D. *lawyer*

**Keene**
Bell, Ernest Lorne III *retired lawyer*
Gross, Mark *lawyer, food products executive*

**Littleton**
Gallagher, James C. *lawyer*
Merritt, Thomas Butler *lawyer*

**Lyme**
Carmichael, Donald Scott *retired lawyer, retired corporate financial executive*

**Manchester**
Haffer, Edward Anthony *lawyer*
Holmes, Ralph F. *lawyer*
Hutchins, Peter Edward *lawyer*
Middleton, Jack Baer *lawyer*
Monson, John Rudolph *lawyer*
Sklar, Daniel William *lawyer*
Wells, Robert Alfred *lawyer*
Wright, Mark A. *lawyer*

**Nashua**
Grasso, Kristina Marie *lawyer*
Hanson, Arnold Philip *retired lawyer*
Lumbard, Eliot Howland *lawyer, educator*

**Newport**
Stamatakis, Carol Marie *lawyer, former state legislator*

**Orford**
Martin, Allen *retired lawyer*

**Peterborough**
Bass, Perkins *retired lawyer, congressman*

**Plainfield**
Brown, Judith Olans *retired lawyer, educator*

**Portsmouth**
Doleac, Charles Bartholomew *lawyer*

Lytton, William Bryan *lawyer*
Tober, Stephen Lloyd *lawyer*
Volk, Kenneth Hohne *lawyer*

**Warner**
Coolidge, Daniel Scott *lawyer*

## NEW JERSEY

**Asbury Park**
Rosenbloom, Norma Frisch *lawyer*

**Barnegat Light**
Gibbs, Frederick Winfield *lawyer, communications executive*

**Basking Ridge**
Craven, Pamela F. *lawyer*

**Bloomfield**
Lordi, Katherine Mary *lawyer*
Weisert, Kent Albert Frederick *lawyer*

**Bridgewater**
Dahling, Gerald Vernon *lawyer*
Steinhart, Jessica *lawyer*

**Budd Lake**
Webb, John Gibbon III *lawyer*

**Burlington**
Tang, Paul C. *lawyer*

**Caldwell**
Castano, Gregory Joseph *lawyer*

**Camden**
Kaden, Ellen Oran *lawyer, consumer products company executive*
Pomorski, Stanislaw *lawyer, educator*

**Carteret**
Strassler, Marc A. *corporate lawyer*

**Chatham**
Finestein, Russell Mark *lawyer*
Jacobs, Andrew Robert *lawyer*
Zegas, Alan Lee *lawyer*

**Cherry Hill**
Garrigle, William Aloysius *lawyer*
Kole, Janet Stephanie *lawyer, writer*
Myers, Daniel William, II, *lawyer*
Rose, Joel Alan *legal consultant*
Van Syoc, Clifford Lee *lawyer*
Weinstein, Steven D. *lawyer*

**Clifton**
Feinstein, Miles Roger *lawyer*

**Cranford**
Bergen, Bruce Harry *lawyer*
McCreedy, Edwin James *lawyer*

**East Brunswick**
Applebaum, Charles *lawyer*

**Edison**
Behr, Omri M. *lawyer*
Traub, Richard Kenneth *lawyer*
Vercammen, Kenneth Albert *lawyer, prosecutor*

**Elmwood Park**
Mangano, Louis *lawyer*

**Fairfield**
Connell, William Terrence *lawyer, judge*

**Flemington**
Miller, Louis H. *lawyer*

**Florham Park**
Altieri, James M. *lawyer*
Chase, Eric Lewis *lawyer*
Hardin, William Downer *retired lawyer*
Hull, Gerald W., Jr. *lawyer*
Kandravy, John *lawyer*
Laulicht, Murray Jack *lawyer*
Lavey, Stewart Evan *lawyer*
Long, Stephen R. *lawyer*
Malone, Robert K. *lawyer*
Nittoly, Paul Gerard *lawyer*
O'Connell, Daniel Francis *lawyer*
Pantel, Glenn Steven *lawyer*
Reid, Charles Adams III *lawyer*
Ridley, John A. *lawyer*
Rosenthal, Jeffrey M. *lawyer*
Smith, Theodore S. *lawyer*
Stryker, David Michael *lawyer*

**Fort Lee**
Goldberg, Harry Finck *lawyer, consultant*

**Franklin Lakes**
Healy, Bridget M. *lawyer*
Machlowitz, David Steven *lawyer*

**Freehold**
Anderson, James Francis *lawyer*

**Garfield**
Herpst, Robert Dix *lawyer, optical materials company executive*

**Greenwich**
Lane, Mark *lawyer, educator, writer*

**Hackensack**
Abut, Charles C. *lawyer*
Caminiti, Donald Angelo *lawyer*
Corcoran, Robert Thomas *lawyer*
Greenberg, Steven Morey *lawyer*
Horowitz, Donald *lawyer*
Latimer, Stephen Mark *lawyer*
Mullin, Patrick Allen *lawyer*
Pollinger, William Joshua *lawyer*
Rich, Tara Schillari *lawyer*
Vort, Robert A. *lawyer*

**Hackettstown**
Mulligan, Elinor Patterson *lawyer*

**Haddonfield**
Ewan, David E. *lawyer*
Iavicoli, Mario Anthony *lawyer*

**Hamilton**
Ebert, Lawrence Burton *lawyer*

**Ho Ho Kus**
Bryan, Thomas Lynn *lawyer, educator*

**Hoboken**
Sommers, George R. *lawyer*

**Hopewell**
Lester, Pamela Robin *lawyer*

**Iselin**
Dornbusch, Arthur A., II, *lawyer*

**Jersey City**
Ott, Gilbert Russell, Jr. *lawyer*
Yaworsky, Bohdan *law educator*

**Kenilworth**
Connors, Joseph Conlin *lawyer, pharmaceutical executive*
Hoffman, John Fletcher *lawyer*

**Keyport**
Colmant, Andrew Robert *lawyer*

**Lakewood**
Bielory, Abraham Melvin *lawyer, finance company executive*

**Laurel Springs**
Wood, Leonard James *lawyer*

**Liberty Corner**
Apruzzese, Vincent John *lawyer*

**Little Falls**
Oliver, Raymond A. *lawyer*

**Little Silver**
Schmidt, Daniel Edward, IV, *lawyer, arbitrator*

**Livingston**
Ingato, Robert Joseph *lawyer*
Klein, Peter Martin *lawyer, retired transportation executive*
Rinsky, Joel Charles *lawyer*

**Madison**
O'Connor, Charles P. *lawyer*
Stein, Lawrence V. *lawyer*

**Mahwah**
Bear, Larry Alan *retired lawyer, educator*

**Manalapan**
Altruda, Paul F. *lawyer*
Stone, Fred Michael *lawyer*

**Maplewood**
Joseph, Susan B. *lawyer*

**Marlboro**
Bass, David Steven *law educator, arbitrator, mediator*

**Medford**
Kondracki, Edward Anthony *lawyer*

**Millburn**
Diamond, Richard S. *lawyer*

**Milltown**
Haws, Robert John *lawyer*

**Montvale**
Nachtigal, Patricia *lawyer*

**Moorestown**
Buckman, William H. *lawyer*

**Morristown**
Aspero, Benedict Vincent *lawyer*
Bromberg, Myron James *lawyer*
Coleman, James H., Jr. *lawyer, former state supreme court justice*
Detrizio, Charles Santo *lawyer*
Gillen, James Robert *lawyer, insurance company executive*
Herzberg, Peter Jay *lawyer*
Humick, Thomas Charles Campbell *lawyer*
Hyland, William Francis *lawyer*
Korf, Gene Robert *lawyer*
Kreindler, Peter Michael *lawyer*
Nagle, Ronald T. *lawyer*
Newman, John Merle *lawyer*
Nolan, J. Michael, Jr. *retired lawyer*
O'Grady, Dennis Joseph *lawyer*
Parker, Mary Lou *lawyer*
Pollock, Stewart Glasson *lawyer, state supreme court justice*
Rose, Robert Gordon *lawyer*
Sherman, Sandra Brown *lawyer*
Stanton, Patrick Michael *lawyer*

**Mountain Lakes**
Daniel, Royal Thomas III *lawyer, mechanical engineer, accountant*

**Mountainside**
Helander, Robert Charles *lawyer, arbitrator*

**New Brunswick**
Biribauer, Richard Frank *lawyer*
Miller, Lynn Fieldman *lawyer*
Polanco, Katiusca *lawyer*
Yorke, Marianne *lawyer, real estate executive*

**New Providence**
McCarthy, G. Daniel *lawyer*
Reinsdorf, Judith A. *lawyer*

**New Vernon**
Kushen, Allan Stanford *retired lawyer*

**Newark**
Amalfe, Christine A. *lawyer*
Askin, Frank *law educator*
Berry, Andrew T. *lawyer*
Bizub, Johanna Catherine *law librarian*
Blumrosen, Alfred William *law educator*
Brescher, John B., Jr. *lawyer*
Cahn, Jeffrey Barton *lawyer*
Christie, Christopher James *prosecutor, lawyer*
Christie, Scott S. *lawyer*
Corbin Walker, Karol *lawyer*
Cummis, Clive Sanford *lawyer*
Cunningham, LeeAnn *assistant prosecutor*
Day, Edward Francis, Jr. *lawyer*
Dee, Francis X. *lawyer*
Defeis, Elizabeth Frances *law educator, lawyer*
Eittreim, Richard MacNutt *lawyer*
English, Nicholas Conover *lawyer*
Farmer, John Joseph *lawyer, former state attorney general*
Garde, John Charles *lawyer*
Gauster, Stephen Wilhelm *lawyer, corporate financial executive*
Gibbons, John Joseph *lawyer, retired federal judge*
Goldstein, Bruce I. *lawyer*
Goldstein, Marvin Mark *lawyer*
Haring, Eugene Miller *lawyer*
Heller, William J. *lawyer*
Karp, Donald Mathew *lawyer, banker*
Kott, David Russell *lawyer*
Krovatin, Gerald *lawyer*
La Rocco, Anthony P. *lawyer*
Levin, Simon *lawyer*
Levine, Benjamin *lawyer*
Lorell, Jeffrey W. *lawyer*
Maran, David *lawyer*
McGuire, William B(enedict) *lawyer*
McLean, David J. *lawyer*
Milita, Martin Joseph *lawyer*
Neuer, Philip David *lawyer, real estate consultant*
Reilly, William Thomas *lawyer*
Robertson, William Withers *lawyer*
Rothschild, Gita F. *lawyer*
Schillinger, Randi *lawyer*
Selover, R. Edwin *lawyer*
Siegal, Joel Davis *lawyer*
Simmons, Peter *lawyer, urban planner, educator*
Stewart, Michael T. *lawyer*
Timoni, Stephen Anthony *lawyer, accountant*
Tischman, Michael Bernard *lawyer*
Van Deusen, Lois M. *lawyer*
Ward, Roger Coursen *lawyer*
Yamner, Morris *lawyer*
Zuckerman, Herbert Lawrence *lawyer*

**Newton**
Cox, William Martin *lawyer, educator*

**Ocean City**
Kyriazis, Arthur John (Athanasios Ioannis Kyriazis) *lawyer, biotechnologist*

**Oradell**
Blakeslee, Edward Eaton *lawyer, insurance company executive*
Mavroudis, John M. *lawyer*
Parish, J. Michael *lawyer, mutual fund executive, writer*

**Paramus**
Levy, Joseph *lawyer*

**Parsippany**
Cox, Melvin Monroe *lawyer*
Ray, Robert William *lawyer*

**Paterson**
Mussano, Theodore Anthony *retired court services supervisor*

**Piscataway**
Gustafsson, Mary Beth *lawyer*
Lee, Barbara Anne *law educator, dean*
Smith, Bob *lawyer, educator, state senator*

**Pitman**
Cloues, Edward Blanchard, II, *lawyer*

**Plainfield**
Ellington II, Michael L. *lawyer*

**Princeton**
Ackourey, Peter Paul *lawyer*
Anderson, Ellis Bernard *retired lawyer, pharmaceutical executive*
Beidler, Marsha Wolf *lawyer*
Bergman, Edward Jonathan *lawyer, educator*
Burgess, Robert Kyle *lawyer*
Connor, Geoffrey Michael *lawyer*
Donohue, Andrew John *lawyer, securities executive*
Durst, Robert Joseph, II, *lawyer*
Frantz, Robert Wesley *lawyer*
Frenier, Diane M. *lawyer*
Greenman, Jane Friedlieb *lawyer, human resources executive*
Hall, Robert Turnbull III *lawyer*
Hill, James Scott *lawyer*
Kaplowitz, Karen (Jill) *lawyer, consultant*
Katz, Stanley Nider *law history educator*
Kenny, Robert *lawyer*
Law, Stuart A., Jr. *lawyer*
Luchak, Frank Alexander *lawyer*
Picco, Steven Joseph *lawyer*
Sullivan, Diane P. *lawyer*
Szwalbenest, Benedykt Jan *lawyer*
Theroux, William Gerard *lawyer*
Ufford, Charles Wilbur, Jr. *lawyer*
Vinicombe, Charles James *lawyer*
Warren, William L. *lawyer*

**Randolph**
Zelante, Thomas Andrew *lawyer*

**Red Bank**
Reinhart, Peter Sargent *lawyer*

**Ridgewood**
Harris, Micalyn Shafer *lawyer, educator, arbitrator, consultant, mediator*

**Rivervale**
Falcon, Raymond Jesus, Jr. *lawyer*

**Roseland**
Benson, James Bracken *lawyer*
Eakeley, Douglas Scott *lawyer*
Hayden, Joseph A., Jr. *lawyer*
Kohl, Benedict M. *lawyer*
Leit, David Edward *lawyer*
Lowenstein, Alan Victor *lawyer*
Lubit, Beverly Weiss *lawyer, science educator*
McMahon, Edward Richard *lawyer*
Positan, Wayne John *lawyer*
Stern, Herbert Jay *lawyer*
Tarino, Gary Edward *lawyer*
Vanderbilt, Arthur T., II, *lawyer*
Wovsaniker, Alan *lawyer, educator*

**Rumson**
Mardinly, George John *lawyer*

**Saddle Brook**
Cohn, Albert Linn *lawyer*
Pearlman, Peter Steven *lawyer*
White, H. Katherine *lawyer*

**Scotch Plains**
Klock, John Henry *lawyer*
Shaw, Alan *lawyer*

**Sewell**
Crouse, Farrell R. *lawyer*

**Ship Bottom**
Shackleton, Richard James *lawyer, director*

**Short Hills**
Cooper, Russell John III *lawyer*
Fast, Kenneth H. *lawyer*
Hazlehurst, Robert Purviance, Jr. *lawyer*
Marshall, John Patrick *lawyer*
Novack, Robert *lawyer*
Schirmeister, Charles F. *retired lawyer*
Siegfried, David Charles *retired lawyer*

**Shrewsbury**
Michaelson, Peter Lee *lawyer*

**Somerville**
Fleischman, Joseph Jacob *lawyer*
Hutcheon, Peter David *lawyer*
Robinson, William Richard *lawyer*
Sponzilli, Edward George *lawyer*

**South Orange**
Delo, Ellen Sanderson *retired lawyer*

**South Plainfield**
Santoro, Frank Anthony *lawyer*

**Sparta**
McMeen, Sheila Taenzler *retired lawyer*

**Springfield**
Goldsmith, Jeffrey H. *lawyer*
Kraemer, Waldron *lawyer*
Mytelka, Arnold Krieger *lawyer*

**Summit**
English, Jerry Fitzgerald *lawyer, educator*
Kenyon, Edward Tipton *lawyer*
Mehner, Roger *lawyer*
Pfaltz, Hugo Menzel, Jr. *lawyer*
Woller, James Alan *lawyer*

**Trenton**
Bigham, William J. *lawyer*
Caldwell, Wesley Stuart III *lawyer, lobbyist*
Deltuvia, John Joseph, Jr. *systems and procedural analyst*
Hubbs, Julie Christine *lawyer*
Mojer-Torres, Lisa Nan *lawyer*
Sterns, Joel Henry *lawyer*

**Turnersville**
Rabil, Mitchell Joseph *lawyer*

**Union**
Bottitta, Joseph Anthony *lawyer*

**Ventnor City**
Campbell, Thomas Douglas *legal association administrator*

**Voorhees**
Suflas, Steven William *lawyer*

**Wall**
Nucciarone, A. Patrick *lawyer*

**Warren**
DiFrancesco, Donald T. *lawyer*
Jacobson, Gary Steven *lawyer*
O'Neill, Michael J., Jr. *lawyer, insurance company executive*

**Wayne**
Gelman, Jon Leonard *lawyer*
Schwartz, David Jay *lawyer*
Tumolo, Michael L. *corporate lawyer*

**West Orange**
McKinney, John Adams, Jr. *lawyer*
Samson, David *lawyer*
Sweeney, Gerald Bingham *lawyer*

**West Paterson**
Smith, Roy *lawyer*

**Westfield**
Bobis, Daniel Harold *lawyer*

**Woodbridge**
Barcan, Stephen Emanuel *lawyer*
Brown, Morris *lawyer*

Wood, J. Warren, III, (Joshua Warren Wood III) *lawyer*

**NEW MEXICO**

**Albuquerque**
Bardacke, Paul Gregory *lawyer, retired federal official*
Beach, Arthur O'Neal *lawyer*
Bova, Vincent Arthur, Jr. *lawyer, consultant, photographer*
Cargo, David Francis *lawyer, former governor*
Chavez, Martin Joseph *lawyer, mayor*
DeCandia, Donald Alan *lawyer*
Eaves, John M. *lawyer*
Ellis, James W. *law educator*
Farmer, Terry D(wayne) *lawyer*
Franse, R. Nelson *lawyer*
Goldberg, Catherine T. *lawyer*
Hart, Frederick Michael *law educator*
Iglesias, David Claudio *prosecutor*
Keleher, Michael Lawrence *lawyer*
Lasater, W(illiam) Robert, Jr. *lawyer*
Long, Stephen Carrel Mike *lawyer*
Moore, Charles Loyd *lawyer*
Nathanson, Paul S. *lawyer, educator*
O'Brien, Daniel J. *lawyer*
Ortiz, Patrick T. *lawyer*
Ricco, Edward Robert *lawyer*
Roehl, Jerrald J. *lawyer*
Salazar, John Paul *lawyer*
Schuler, Alison Kay *lawyer*
Sisk, Daniel Arthur *lawyer*
Slade, Lynn *lawyer*
Thornton, J. Duke *lawyer*
Throckmorton, Rex Denton *lawyer*
Vigil, Charles J. *lawyer*

**Bayard**
Foy, Thomas Paul *lawyer, retired state legislator, retired bank executive*

**Carlsbad**
Byers, Matthew T(odd) *lawyer, educator*

**Corrales**
Arkin, Michael Barry *lawyer, arbitrator, writer*

**Farmington**
Titus, Victor Allen *lawyer*

**Roswell**
Kraft, Richard Lee *lawyer*
Olson, Richard Earl *lawyer, state legislator*

**Santa Fe**
Aarons, Stephen D. *lawyer*
Abeles, Richard Alan *lawyer*
Adams, Mark Kildee *lawyer*
Brannen, Jeffrey Richard *lawyer*
Burton, John Paul (Jack Burton) *lawyer*
Carpenter, Richard Norris *retired lawyer, energy consultant*
Casey, Patrick Anthony *lawyer*
Dodds, Robert James III *lawyer*
Johnson, Reverdy *lawyer*
Justice, Jack Burton *retired lawyer, writer*
Moll, Deborah Adelaide *lawyer*
Pound, John Bennett *lawyer*
Schwarz, Michael *lawyer*
Stevens, Ron A. *lawyer, advocate, surveyor*

**Santa Rosa**
Alcott, Colin C. *prosecutor*

**Seneca**
Monroe, Kendyl Kurth *retired lawyer*

**Taos**
Boles, David LaVelle *lawyer*

**NEW YORK**

**Albany**
Bagyi, John Martin *lawyer*
Bonventre, Vincent Martin *lawyer, educator*
Cogen, Richard M. *lawyer*
Everett, James W., Jr. *lawyer*
Kelly, Raymond Aloysius, Jr. *lawyer, educator*
Koff, Howard Michael *lawyer*
Powers, John Kieran *lawyer*
Rostow, Charles Nicholas *lawyer, educator*
Sandhaas, Jill T. *lawyer*
Scott, William Proctor III *lawyer*
Sheehan, Deborah Hardick *lawyer*
West, Thomas S. *lawyer*
Yanas, John James *lawyer, director*

**Albertson**
Berlin, Mark A. *lawyer*

**Amagansett**
Zychick, Joel David *lawyer*

**Amherst**
Pajak, David Joseph *lawyer, consultant*

**Ardsley On Hudson**
Stein, Milton Michael *retired lawyer*

**Armonk**
Boies, David *lawyer*
Lineen, Edward M. *lawyer, information technology executive*
Quinn, James W. *lawyer*
Rosenberg, Michael *lawyer*
Wertheim, Ram D. *lawyer*

**Baldwin**
Onyido, John Chike *lawyer*

**Ballston Spa**
Brown, Ifigenia Theodore *lawyer*

**Bellerose**
Dornagon, Mandy M. *lawyer*

**Bethpage**
Schwartz, Jonathan D. *lawyer*

**Binghamton**
Anderson, Warren Mattice *lawyer*
Gates, Gregory Ansel *lawyer*
Gerhart, Eugene Clifton *lawyer*
Gouldin, David Millen *lawyer*

**Bohemia**
Fisher, Irene B. *lawyer*

**Briarcliff Manor**
Bernstein, Nadia Jacqueline *lawyer*
Bower, Thomas Michael *lawyer*

**Bronx**
Balka, Sigmund Ronell *lawyer*
Cornfield, Melvin *lawyer, director*
McKeown, William B. *lawyer*
Richman, Murray *lawyer*

**Bronxville**
Cutler, Kenneth Burnett *lawyer, investment company executive*
Falvey, Patrick Joseph *lawyer*
Fuller, David Otis, Jr. *lawyer*
Garber, Robert Edward *lawyer, insurance company executive*
Hagendorn, William Hull *lawyer*

**Brooklyn**
Barabash, Claire *lawyer, special education services professional, psychologist*
Bloomfield, David Charles *lawyer, educator, not-for-profit public executive*
Elliot, Cameron Robert *lawyer*
Fairstein, Linda A. *prosecutor, writer*
Golanski, Alani *lawyer*
Josephson, William Howard *retired lawyer*
Kamins, Barry Michael *lawyer*
Karmel, Roberta Segal *lawyer, educator*
Maslow, Aaron D. *lawyer*
Mauskopf, Roslynn R. *prosecutor*
Murphy, Kathleen Mary *former law firm executive, alternative healing professional*
Pearsall, Otis Pratt *retired lawyer*
Poser, Norman Stanley *law educator*
Roth, Robert *lawyer, journalist*
Taylor, Shannon *lawyer, not-for-profit developer*

**Buffalo**
Barber, Janice Ann *lawyer*
Bean, Edwin Temple, Jr. *lawyer*
Brydges, Thomas Eugene *lawyer*
Day, Donald Sheldon *lawyer*
Dubber, Markus Dirk *law educator*
Flynn, Terrance Patrick *prosecutor, lawyer*
Gardner, Arnold Burton *lawyer*
Glanville, Robert Edward *lawyer*
Goldberg, Neil Alan *lawyer*
Goldblatt, Samuel *lawyer*
Grasser, George Robert *lawyer, real estate developer, consultant*
Greene, Robert Michael *lawyer*
Halpern, Ralph Lawrence *lawyer*
Hayes, J. Michael *lawyer*
Headrick, Thomas Edward *lawyer, educator*
Heilman, Pamela Davis *lawyer*
Jasen, Matthew Joseph *lawyer, retired judge*
Kristoff, Karl W. *lawyer*
Lippes, Gerald Sanford *lawyer*
Manning, Kenneth Alan *lawyer*
Mather, Lynn *law educator, political science professor*
Merriman, Kevin Thomas *lawyer*
Monahan, John Michael *lawyer*
Mucci, Gary Louis *lawyer*
O'Donnell, Denise Ellen *lawyer, former prosecutor*
Odza, Randall M. *lawyer*
O'Loughlin, Sandra S. *lawyer*
Pearson, Paul David *lawyer, arbitrator, mediator*
Rachlin, Lauren David *lawyer*
Ruppar, Peter Geoffrey *lawyer*
Sahlem, James Robert *law librarian*
Salisbury, Eugene W. *lawyer, judge*
Segalla, Thomas Francis *lawyer*
Viney, Christopher Robert *health lawyer*
Wisbaum, Wayne David *lawyer*
Tunkman, Mark William *lawyer*

**Camillus**
Armani, Frank Henry *retired lawyer*

**Canaan**
Pennell, William Brooke *lawyer*

**Carle Place**
Collins, Richard David *lawyer, writer*

**Carmel**
Laporte, Cloyd, Jr. *retired lawyer, retired manufacturing executive*

**Cazenovia**
Shattuck, George Clement *retired lawyer*

**Cedarhurst**
Taubenfeld, Harry S. *lawyer*

**Chappaqua**
Romney, Richard Bruce *lawyer*

**Chautauqua**
Schmidt, Edward Craig *lawyer*

**Cold Spring Harbor**
Wallin, James Peter *lawyer*

**Commack**
Steindler, Walter G. *retired lawyer*

**Corning**
Hatton, Vincent Paul *lawyer*
Ughetta, William Casper *lawyer, manufacturing executive, director*

**Cortland**
Taylor, Leland Baridon *lawyer*

**Croton On Hudson**
Hoffman, Paul Shafer *lawyer*

**Delhi**
Hartmann, James M. *lawyer*

**Dobbs Ferry**
Juettner, Diana D'Amico *lawyer, educator*

**Dunkirk**
Woodbury, Robert Charles *lawyer*

**East Greenbush**
McConville, Edward Patrick *lawyer*

**East Hampton**
Ehren, Charles Alexander, Jr. *lawyer, educator*
Twomey, Thomas A., Jr. *lawyer, educator*

**East Meadow**
Adler, Ira Jay *lawyer*

**East Northport**
Juliano, John Louis *lawyer*

**East Norwich**
Busner, Philip H. *retired lawyer, judge*

**East Syracuse**
Atlas, Craig Mitchell *lawyer*

**Elmira**
Winner, George Henry *lawyer*

**Fairport**
Bartlett, Cody Blake *retired lawyer*

**Far Rockaway**
Helfgott, Samson *lawyer*

**Floral Park**
Chatoff, Michael Alan *lawyer*
Corbett, William John *lawyer, public relations executive, consultant*

**Flushing**
Schwartz, Estar Alma *lawyer*

**Forest Hills**
Addabbo, Dominic Lucian *lawyer*
Kourides, Peter Theologos *lawyer*

**Forestville**
Adams, Lee Towne *lawyer*

**Franklin Square**
Vanora, Jerome Patrick *lawyer*

**Fredonia**
Sullivan, Michael Joseph *lawyer*

**Freeport**
Berg, Alan *lawyer, arbitrator*

**Fresh Meadows**
Greenberg, Robert Jay *law educator*

**Garden City**
Calamari, Joseph August *law librarian*
Cook, George Valentine *lawyer, consultant*
DaSilva, Willard H. *lawyer, educator*
DiMascio, John Philip *lawyer*
Fishberg, Gerard *lawyer*
Freedman, Monroe Henry *law educator*
Ingber, Larry H. *lawyer*
Jones, Lawrence Tunnicliffe *lawyer*
Kaplan, Joel Stuart *lawyer*
Klein, Arnold Spencer *lawyer*
Mastaglio, Peter James *lawyer*
Meng, M. Kathryn *lawyer*
Minicucci, Richard Francis *lawyer, former hospital administrator*
Persons, John Wade *lawyer*
Schwarz, Carl A., Jr. *lawyer*
Tamigi, Peter F. *lawyer*

**Geneva**
Brind, David Hutchison *lawyer, judge*

**Glen Cove**
Mills, Charles Gardner *lawyer*

**Glens Falls**
Bartlett, Richard James *lawyer*
McMillen, Robert Stewart *lawyer*
Pontiff, Paul E. *lawyer*

**Gouverneur**
Leader, Robert John *lawyer*

**Greenvale**
Halper, Emanuel B(arry) *lawyer, real estate developer, consultant, writer*
Manzari, Laura Lynn *law educator*

**Harrison**
Kramer, Alan Sharfsin *lawyer*

**Hartsdale**
Kroll, Arthur Herbert *lawyer, educator, writer*

**Hastings On Hudson**
Edelman, Paul Sterling *lawyer*

**Hempstead**
Mahon, Malachy Thomas, Sr. *lawyer, educator*

**Hicksville**
Giuffré, John Joseph *lawyer*
Lieberman, Douglas Mark *lawyer*

**Hillsdale**
Lunde, Asbjorn Rudolph *lawyer*

**Hollis**
Jairam, Khelanand Vishvaykanand *lawyer*

**Holtsville**
Lieb, Peter *lawyer*

**Hudson**
Agata, Burton C. *lawyer, educator*

**Huntington**
Brettschneider, Rita Roberta Fischman *lawyer*
German, June Resnick *lawyer*
Hochberg, Ronald Mark *lawyer*
Klein, Richard Daniel *law educator*
Morris, Jeffrey Brandon *law educator*
Munson, Nancy K. *lawyer*
Selkirk, Alexander MacDonald, Jr. *lawyer*
Tucker, William P. *lawyer, writer*

**Irvington**
Jackson, Thomas Gene *lawyer*

**Islandia**
Handal, Kenneth V. *lawyer*
Pruzansky, Joshua Murdock *lawyer*

**Ithaca**
Alexander, Gregory Stewart *law educator*
Barcelo, John James III *law educator*
Clermont, Kevin Michael *law educator*
Cramton, Roger Conant *lawyer, educator*
Eisenberg, Theodore *law educator*
Germain, Claire Madeleine *law librarian, educator, lawyer*
Gold, Michael Evan *law educator*
Hay, George Alan *law and economics educator*
Hillman, Robert Andrew *lawyer, educator, retired dean*
Martin, Peter William *lawyer, educator*
Roberts, E. F. *law educator*
Schneiderman, Anne Mercedes *lawyer, neurobiologist*
Summers, Robert Samuel *lawyer, author, educator*
Thoron, Gray *lawyer, educator*

**Jamaica**
Angione, Howard Francis *lawyer, retired editor*
Brown, Kenneth Lloyd *lawyer*
Castro-Blanco, James *law educator*

**Jamestown**
Idzik, Martin Francis *lawyer*

**Jamesville**
DeCrow, Karen *lawyer, educator, writer*

**Jericho**
Blau, Harvey Ronald *lawyer*

**Kew Gardens**
Adler, David Neil *lawyer*

**Lake Success**
Lee, Brian Edward *lawyer*

**Larchmont**
Berridge, George Bradford *retired lawyer*
Bloom, Lee Hurley *lawyer, consultant, retired consumer products company executive*
Burkett, Bradford Charles *lawyer*
McSherry, William John, Jr. *lawyer, consultant*
Pelton, Russell Gilbert *retired lawyer*
White, Thomas Edward *lawyer*

**Latham**
Catalano, Jane Donna *lawyer*
Conway, Robert George, Jr. *lawyer*

**Livingston Manor**
Root, Stuart Dowling *lawyer, retired government agency administrator, retired banker*

**Lockport**
Penney, Charles Rand *lawyer, civic worker*

**Malverne**
Benigno, Thomas Daniel *lawyer*

**Manhasset**
Black, Robert *lawyer*
Kaminsky, Arthur Charles *lawyer*
Wachtler, Sol *lawyer, educator*

**Massapequa**
Van Gorder, John Frederic *lawyer*

**Melville**
Ettinger, Michael Saul *lawyer*
Komaroff, Stanley *lawyer*
Lane, Arthur Alan *lawyer*

**Middletown**
Kossar, Ronald Steven *lawyer*

**Millbrook**
Grant, Stephen Allen *lawyer*

**Mineola**
Bartlett, Clifford Adams, Jr. *lawyer*
Halloran, Daniel James *lawyer*
Lynn, Robert Patrick, Sr. *lawyer*
Paterson, Basil Alexander *lawyer*
Schaffer, David Irving *lawyer*
Tankoos, Sandra Maxine *court reporting services executive*

**Montauk**
Kahn, Richard Dreyfus *lawyer*

**Mount Kisco**
Kilbourn, Joseph A. *lawyer*

**Mount Vernon**
Weisman, Richard Scott *lawyer*

**Nassau**
Moldoff, William Morris *retired lawyer*

**Neponsit**
Re, Edward Domenic *law educator, retired judge*

**New Hartford**
Chapin, Mary Q. *arbitrator, director, mediator, writer*

**New Hyde Park**
Jaffe, Richard S. *lawyer*
Offner, Eric Delmonte *lawyer*
Pegalis, Steven E. *lawyer*

**New Rochelle**
Blotner, Norman David *lawyer, real estate broker, corporate financial executive*
Ferencz, Benjamin Berell *lawyer*
Gunning, Francis Patrick *lawyer, insurance company executive*
Hasson, Adam Isaac *lawyer*

**New York**
Aaron, Roger S. *lawyer*
Aaron, Stewart D. *lawyer*
Abatemarco, Tracy J. *lawyer*
Abrahams, Robert M. *lawyer*
Abramowitz, Elkan *lawyer*
Abrams, Floyd *lawyer, educator*
Abrams, Robert *lawyer, state attorney general*
Abuhoff, Daniel Mark *lawyer*
Adair, Wendell Hinton, Jr. *lawyer*
Adams, Daniel Nelson *lawyer*
Adams, George Bell *lawyer*
Adams, John Hamilton *lawyer*
Adams, Robert Brereton *lawyer*
Adler, Amy M. *law educator*
Adler, Barry E. *law educator, academic administrator*
Aidinoff, M(erton) Bernard *retired lawyer*
Ainbinder, Bruce *lawyer*
Albert, Garett J. *lawyer*
Alcott, Mark Howard *lawyer*
Alden, Steven Michael *lawyer*
Alessandroni, Venan Joseph *lawyer*
Alfieri, Vincent *lawyer*
Allen, Leon Arthur, Jr. *lawyer*
Allen, William Thomas *law educator*
Allerhand, Joseph S. *lawyer*
Almon, Lorie *lawyer*
Alperin, Stuart N. *lawyer*
Alter, Eleanor Breitel *lawyer*
Alter, Paul R. *lawyer*
Altman, Steven Lawrence *lawyer*
Amdur, Martin Bennett *lawyer*
Amsterdam, Anthony Guy *law educator*
Amsterdam, Mark Lemle *lawyer*
Anders, David Brian *prosecutor*
Andresen, Malcolm *lawyer*
Andrews, Gordon Clark *lawyer*
Andriola, Rocco F. *lawyer, diversified financial services company executive*
Andrus, Roger Douglas *lawyer*
Anesh, Mark K. *lawyer*
Angland, Joseph *lawyer*
Angus, Patricia Marie *lawyer*
Anthoine, Robert *lawyer, educator*
Appel, Albert M. *lawyer*
Appelbaum, Ann Harriet *lawyer*
Aquila, Francis Joseph *lawyer*
Arabatzis, Constance Elaine *lawyer*
Arditi, Ralph *lawyer*
Arenson, Gregory K. *lawyer*
Arkin, Stanley S. *lawyer*
Arlen, Jennifer Hall *law educator*
Armbrust, Joseph W., Jr. *lawyer*
Aronson, Clifford Hank *lawyer*
Arouh, Jeffrey Alan *lawyer*
Arquit, Kevin James *lawyer*
Arrow, Allen H. *lawyer*
Ash, Karen Artz *lawyer*
Atkins, Peter Allan *lawyer*
Auslander, Mitchell J. *lawyer*
Axelrod, Charles Paul *lawyer*
Axinn, Stephen Mark *lawyer*
Ayoub, Elsa *lawyer*
Bach, Thomas Handford *lawyer, investor*
Bachelder, Joseph Elmer III *lawyer*
Badertscher, David Glen *law librarian, consultant*
Bahlke, Conrad George *lawyer*
Baio, Joseph T. *lawyer*
Baity, John Cooley *lawyer*
Baker, Mark M. *lawyer, law educator*
Baker, Stuart David *lawyer*
Bamberger, Michael Albert *lawyer*
Bancroft, Margaret Armstrong *lawyer*
Banks, Michael C. *lawyer*
Bankston, Archie Moore *lawyer*
Bannigan, Eugene F. *lawyer*
Bansal, Preeta D. *lawyer*
Barandes, Robert *lawyer*
Barasch, Clarence Sylvan *lawyer*
Barasch, Mal Livingston *lawyer*
Barbur, Peter T. *lawyer*
Barckhaus, Rachel *paralegal*
Barenberg, Mark *law educator*
Barist, Jeffrey *lawyer*
Barnard, Kevin Francis *lawyer*
Barnard, Robert N. *lawyer*
Baron, Mitchell Neal *lawyer*
Baron, Robert Howard *lawyer*
Barr, Thomas D. *lawyer*
Barr, William Pelham *lawyer, former United States attorney general*
Barrett, David A. *lawyer*
Barry, Desmond Thomas, Jr. *lawyer*
Barshay, Scott A. *lawyer*
Bartfeld, Daniel D. *lawyer*
Bartlett, Joseph Warren *lawyer*
Bason, George R., Jr. *lawyer*
Bass, Franklin F. *lawyer*
Bassen, Ned Henry *lawyer*
Bateman, Maureen Scannell *lawyer*
Bauer, Douglas F. *retired lawyer*
Baumgardner, John Ellwood, Jr. *lawyer*
Baumgarten, Sidney *lawyer*
Baumrin, Bernard Stefan Herbert *lawyer, educator*
Beattie, Richard Irwin *lawyer*
Beck, Andrew James *lawyer*
Becker, Steven H. *lawyer*
Beckman, Michael *lawyer*
Beeken, Timothy K. *lawyer*
Beekman, William Bedloe *lawyer*
Been, Vicki Lynn *law educator*
Beeney, Garrard Russ *lawyer*
Beerbower, Cynthia Gibson *lawyer*
Beerbower, John Edwin *lawyer*
Beeson, Ann *lawyer*
Beinecke, Candace Krugman *lawyer*
Bell, Jonathan Robert *lawyer*

Beller, Gary A. *lawyer, finance company executive, insurance company executive*
Bellows, Carl D. *lawyer*
Ben-Ami, Leora *lawyer*
Bender, John Charles *lawyer*
Benenson, Mark Keith *lawyer*
Benjamin, Jeff *lawyer, pharmaceutical executive*
Benkard, James W. B. *lawyer*
Bennett, Robert Scott *lawyer*
Bennett, Scott Lawrence *lawyer*
Berg, Madelaine R. *lawyer*
Bergan, Edmund Paul, Jr. *lawyer*
Berger, George *lawyer*
Berger, Max W. *lawyer*
Bergman, Arlene *lawyer*
Bergmann, Peter George *lawyer*
Bergtraum, Howard Michael *lawyer*
Berkery, Rosemary T. *lawyer, investment company executive*
Berkley, Peter Lee *lawyer*
Berman, Keith *solicitor, lawyer*
Bermann, George Alan *law educator*
Bern, Marc Jay *lawyer*
Bernard, Richard Phillip *lawyer*
Bernick, David M. *lawyer*
Bernstein, Daniel Lewis *lawyer*
Bernstein, David William *lawyer*
Bernstein, Donald Scott *lawyer*
Bernstein, Robert Jay *lawyer*
Bernstein, Warren J. *lawyer*
Berry, Dean C. *lawyer*
Beshar, Christine *lawyer*
Beshar, Peter Justus *lawyer, insurance company executive*
Beshar, Robert Peter *lawyer*
Beslow, William S. *lawyer*
Bevilacqua, Louis J. *lawyer*
Bezanson, Thomas Edward *lawyer*
Bezozo, Kenneth K. *lawyer*
Bialkin, Kenneth Jules *lawyer, director*
Bialo, Kenneth Marc *lawyer*
Bicks, Peter Andrews *lawyer*
Bienenstock, Martin J. *lawyer*
Bird, Paul S. *lawyer*
Birnbaum, Edward Lester *lawyer*
Birnbaum, Sheila L. *lawyer, educator*
Black, Barbara Aronstein *legal history educator*
Black, James Isaac (Jib) III *lawyer*
Black, Jerry Bernard *lawyer*
Black, Louis Engleman *lawyer*
Blackman, Kenneth Robert *lawyer*
Blair, Michael Walter *lawyer*
Blair, William McCormick, Jr. *lawyer*
Blanc, Roger David *lawyer*
Blanchard, Kimberly Staggers *lawyer, educator*
Blasi, Vincent A. *law educator*
Blassberg, Franci J. *lawyer*
Blatt, Gregory R. *lawyer*
Blattmachr, Jonathan George *lawyer*
Bleich, J. David *law educator, rabbi*
Blivaiss, David Harvey *lawyer, accountant*
Bliwise, Lester Martin *lawyer*
Block, Dennis Jeffrey *lawyer*
Block, William Kenneth *lawyer*
Bloom, Lisa Read *lawyer*
Blume, Lawrence Dayton *lawyer*
Blumkin, Linda Ruth *lawyer*
Boast, Molly Shryer *lawyer*
Bobrow, Richard S. *lawyer, former diversified financial services executive*
Bockstein, Herbert *lawyer*
Bogatin, Marc *lawyer*
Bogdanos, Matthew F. *lawyer, reserve military officer*
Bohm, Richard D. *lawyer*
Booth, Mitchell B. *lawyer*
Borchard, William Marshall *lawyer*
Borisoff, Richard Stuart *lawyer*
Bornstein, Gary A. *lawyer*
Bosses, Stevan J. *mediator, arbitrator*
Bottari, Paul J. *lawyer*
Boulhosa, Michael L. *lawyer*
Bowden, William P., Jr. *lawyer, bank executive*
Bowers, William Charles *lawyer*
Boxer, Leonard *lawyer*
Boyle, Edward J. *lawyer*
Brach, Richard S. *lawyer*
Bradley, E. Michael *lawyer*
Brady, Bruce Morgan *lawyer*
Brafman, Benjamin *lawyer*
Braid, Frederick Donald *lawyer*
Braun, Jeffrey Louis *lawyer*
Breglio, John F. *lawyer*
Brennan, Patrick J. *lawyer*
Breslow, Stephanie R. *lawyer*
Brett, Barry J. *lawyer*
Brett, Harry P. *lawyer*
Briffault, Richard *law educator*
Bring, Murray H. *retired lawyer*
Broadwater, Douglas Dwight *lawyer*
Brock, Charles Lawrence *lawyer, diversified financial services company executive, investment banker*
Broder, Douglas Fisher *lawyer*
Brodsky, David Michael *lawyer*
Brodsky, Samuel *lawyer*
Bromberger, Allen Richard *lawyer*
Brome, Thomas Reed *lawyer*
Brooks, Daniel Townley *lawyer*
Brooks, Roger G. *lawyer*
Broude, Richard Frederick *lawyer, educator*
Browdy, Joseph Eugene *lawyer*
Brown, Paul M. *lawyer*
Brown, Ralph Sawyer, Jr. *retired lawyer*
Brownstein, Andrew Richard *lawyer*
Brownwood, David Owen *lawyer*
Brumm, James Earl *lawyer, import/export company executive*
Brundige, Robert William, Jr. *lawyer*
Bruner, Jerome S. *law educator*
Bryan, Barry Richard *lawyer*
Buchman, M. Abraham *lawyer*
Buckholz, Robert E., Jr. *lawyer*
Buckley, Susan *lawyer*
Buckman, James Edward *lawyer*
Burak, H(oward) Paul *lawyer*
Burdette, Brooks R. *lawyer*
Burgess, Lynne A *lawyer*
Burgman, Dierdre Ann *lawyer*
Burgweger, Francis Joseph Dewes, Jr. *lawyer*
Burns, Arnold Irwin *lawyer*

Burns, Sarah Ellen *law educator*
Burns, Stephen L. *lawyer*
Burrows, Kenneth David *lawyer*
Burrows, Michael Donald *lawyer*
Bursky, Herman Aaron *lawyer*
Burstein, Judd *lawyer*
Bushnell, George Edward III *lawyer*
Butler, Samuel Coles *lawyer*
Butler, William Joseph *lawyer, educator*
Buttenwieser, Lawrence Benjamin *lawyer*
Butterman, Jay Ronald *lawyer*
Caginalp, Aydin S. *lawyer*
Cagney, Lawrence K. *lawyer*
Caiazzo, Nicholas R. *lawyer*
Calder, James J. *lawyer*
Caldwell, Leslie Ragon *lawyer, former prosecutor*
Callagy, John M. *lawyer*
Cambria, Christopher C. *lawyer*
Camera, Nicholas J. *lawyer*
Cameron, Timothy G. *lawyer*
Cami, Russell *lawyer*
Canellos, Peter Constantine *lawyer*
Cannell, John Redferne *lawyer*
Canoni, John David *lawyer*
Cantor, Melvyn Leon *retired lawyer*
Cappuccio, Paul T. *lawyer, communications executive*
Cardozo, Benjamin Mordecai *lawyer*
Cardozo, Michael A. *lawyer*
Carlin, David H. *lawyer*
Carmon, Haggai *lawyer*
Carnell, Richard Scott *law educator*
Carter, James Hal, Jr. *lawyer*
Carter, Zachary W. *lawyer*
Cashman, Gideon *lawyer*
Caulfield, Jerome Joseph *lawyer*
Cavanagh, William G. *lawyer*
Caytas, Ivo George *lawyer*
Cendali, Dale Margaret *lawyer*
Cesare, Christine B. *lawyer*
Chaitman, Helen Davis *lawyer*
Champion, Sara Stewart *lawyer*
Chapman, Craig E. *lawyer*
Chapnick, David B. *lawyer*
Chappell, John Charles *lawyer*
Chase, Oscar Gottfried *law educator*
Chatzinoff, Howard *lawyer*
Chavkin, Jeffrey S. *lawyer*
Chazen, Hartley James *lawyer*
Chazen, Leonard *lawyer*
Chell, Beverly C. *lawyer*
Chen, Wesley *lawyer*
Chepiga, Michael Joseph *lawyer*
Chesler, Evan Robert *lawyer*
Chevigny, Paul Graves *law educator*
Chiang, Yung Frank *law educator*
Chiarchiaro, Frank John *lawyer*
Chida, Junaid Hasan *lawyer*
Chilstrom, Robert Meade *lawyer*
Chin, Sylvia Fung *lawyer*
Chinn, Adam *lawyer*
Chirls, Richard *lawyer*
Christensen, Henry III *lawyer*
Christy, Arthur Hill *lawyer*
Chromow, Sheri P. *lawyer*
Chun, Eunu *lawyer*
Church, Pamela T. *lawyer*
Cipolla, Mark *lawyer*
Clark, Bruce E. *lawyer*
Clark, Carolyn Cochran *lawyer*
Clark, James Joseph *lawyer*
Clark, Jonathan Montgomery *lawyer*
Clark, Merrell Edward, Jr. *lawyer*
Clark, Ramsey *lawyer, former United States attorney general*
Clary, Richard Wayland *lawyer*
Cliff, Walter Conway *lawyer*
Coffee, John Collins, Jr. *legal educator*
Coffey, John P. (Sean) *lawyer*
Cohen, Edmund Stephen *lawyer*
Cohen, Henry Rodgin *lawyer*
Cohen, Jeffrey E. *lawyer*
Cohen, Joshua Robert *lawyer*
Cohen, Robert Stephan *lawyer*
Cohn, David Stephen *lawyer*
Cole, Charles Dewey, Jr. *lawyer*
Cole, Lewis George *lawyer*
Coleman, Charles Payson, Jr., (Payson Coleman) *lawyer*
Coleman, Stuart H. *lawyer*
Colihan, James Charles *lawyer*
Coll, John Peter, Jr. *lawyer*
Collazo, Ernest J. *lawyer*
Collins, Elwood F. *lawyer*
Collins, J. Barclay, II, *lawyer, oil industry executive*
Collins, John F. *lawyer*
Collins, Kevin T. *lawyer*
Collins, Wayne Dale *lawyer*
Conboy, Kenneth *lawyer, retired federal judge*
Connery, Michael M. *lawyer*
Connolly, Kevin Jude *lawyer*
Connors, Peter J. *lawyer*
Conrad, Winthrop Brown, Jr. *lawyer*
Constantine, Jan Friedman *lawyer*
Conston, Henry Siegismund *lawyer*
Cook, Michael Lewis *lawyer*
Cook, Robert S., Jr. *lawyer*
Cooper, James D. *lawyer*
Cooper, Michael Anthony *lawyer*
Cooper, Stephen Herbert *retired lawyer*
Corbin, Sol Neil *lawyer*
Cornell, Henry *lawyer*
Cornell, John Robert *lawyer*
Costikyan, Edward N. *lawyer*
Cowan, Wallace Edgar *retired lawyer*
Craft, Randal Robert, Jr. *lawyer*
Cramer, Edward Morton *lawyer, music company executive*
Crames, Michael J. *lawyer*
Crane, Benjamin Field *lawyer*
Crane, Roger Ryan, Jr. *lawyer*
Crary, Miner Dunham, Jr. *lawyer*
Crean, Peter Thomas *lawyer*
Creel, Thomas Leonard *lawyer*
Creenan, Katherine Heras *lawyer*
Crichlow, David A. *lawyer*
Critchlow, Charles Howard *lawyer*
Crowell, Kenneth E. *lawyer, chemical engineer*
Cubitto, Robert John *lawyer*
Cuiffo, Frank Wayne *lawyer*

Cundiff, Victoria Anne *lawyer*
Cuneo, Donald Lane *lawyer, educator*
Cunha, Mark Geoffrey *lawyer*
Cunningham, Noël B. *law educator*
Cunningham, Robert L., Jr. *lawyer*
Cuomo, Mario Matthew *lawyer, former governor*
Curtis, Frank R. *lawyer*
Curtis, Susan M. *lawyer*
Cusack, John T. *lawyer*
Czarniak, Julia A. *lawyer*
Czepiel, Lori Anne *lawyer*
Dabney, H. Slayton, Jr. *lawyer*
Daitz, Ronald Frederick *lawyer*
D'Amato, Alfonse M. *lawyer, senator*
Damrosch, Lori Fisler *law educator*
Danilow, Greg A. *lawyer*
Dannhauser, Stephen J. *lawyer*
Dansky, Ira M. *lawyer*
Darrell, Norris, Jr. *lawyer*
Darrow, Jill E(llen) *lawyer*
Davenport, Kirk Addison *lawyer*
Davenport, Margaret Andrews *lawyer*
David, Reuben *lawyer*
Davidson, Douglas E. *lawyer*
Davidson, George Allan *lawyer*
Davidson, Robert Bruce *retired lawyer*
Davidson, Sheila Kearney *lawyer, insurance company executive*
Davis, Evan Anderson *lawyer*
Davis, Florence Ann *lawyer*
Davis, Gordon J. *lawyer*
Davis, Kevin E. *law educator*
Davis, Lisa E. *lawyer*
Davis, Martha Frances *lawyer*
Davis, Michael Steven *lawyer*
Davis, Richard Ralph *lawyer*
Davis, Trayton M. *lawyer*
Deaver, James T.H. *lawyer*
Debo, Vincent Joseph *lawyer, director, manufacturing executive*
Delaney, Jeffrey J. *lawyer*
Delikat, Michael *lawyer*
Della Rocca, Steven *lawyer*
Del Tufo, Robert J. *lawyer, former state attorney general*
DeMasi, Karin A. *lawyer*
De Natale, Andrew Peter *lawyer*
DeNiro, Mary Lyn S. *lawyer*
Dennis, Willie E. *lawyer*
DeOrchis, Vincent Moore *lawyer*
Derzaw, Richard Lawrence *lawyer*
De Sear, Edward Marshall *lawyer*
Desmarais, John M. *lawyer*
Despins, Luc *lawyer*
Detjen, David Wheeler *lawyer*
Devine, Donald F. (Don) *lawyer*
Diamond, Bernard Robin *lawyer*
Diamond, Brian *lawyer*
Diamond, David Howard *lawyer*
Di Angelo, Christopher J. *lawyer*
Diaz-Cruz, Mario III *lawyer*
DiBlasi, Gandolfo Vincent *lawyer*
Dichter, Barry Joel *lawyer*
Dine, Jeffrey Malcolm *lawyer*
DiSalvatore, William P. *lawyer*
DiSciullo, Alan Michael *lawyer*
Diskant, Gregory L. *lawyer*
Dlugoff, Marc Alan *lawyer*
Dobbins, David Foster *lawyer*
Donald, Norman Henderson III *lawyer*
Donovan, Richard Edward *lawyer*
Doody, John *lawyer*
Dopf, Glenn William *lawyer*
Dorf, Michael C. *law educator*
Dorkey, Charles E. III *lawyer*
Dorsen, Norman *lawyer, educator*
Douglas, James McCrystal *lawyer*
Doyle, Joseph Anthony *retired lawyer*
Doyle, Paul Francis *lawyer*
Drebsky, Dennis Jay *lawyer*
Drechsler, Beatrice Krain *lawyer*
Dreyfuss, Rochelle Cooper *law educator*
Drucker, Richard Allen *lawyer*
Dubin, James Michael *lawyer*
Dubin, Morton Donald, II, *lawyer*
Duffy, Edmund Charles *lawyer*
Duffy, W. Leslie *lawyer*
Duncan, Patricia *lawyer, broadcast executive*
Dunham, Christopher Cooper *lawyer*
Dunham, Wolcott Balestier, Jr. *lawyer*
Dunn, M(orris) Douglas *lawyer*
Dunn, Thomas E. *lawyer*
Dunn, Vincent *lawyer*
Dworkin, Ronald Myles *law educator*
Dwyer, Gary Joseph *lawyer*
Eakins, William Shannon *lawyer*
Earle, Victor Montagne III *lawyer*
Edelman, Scott A. *lawyer*
Edelson, Gilbert Seymour *lawyer*
Edelstein, Mark S. *lawyer*
Edgar, Harold Simmons Hull *legal educator*
Edgerton, Malcom James *retired lawyer*
Edlin, Richard A. *lawyer*
Edwards, Steven Mark *lawyer*
Ehrenbard, Robert *lawyer*
Ehrenkranz, Joel S. *lawyer*
Einhorn, David Allen *lawyer*
Einstein, Steven Henry *lawyer, investment banker*
Eisen, LizabethAnn R. *lawyer*
Eisen, Robert L. *lawyer*
Eisenberg, Barbara Anne K. *lawyer*
Eisert, Edward Gaver *lawyer*
Elkin, Judith *lawyer*
Elkin, Steven Robert *lawyer*
Elmore, Leonard Joseph *lawyer*
Elsen, Sheldon Howard *lawyer*
Emmerich, Adam Oliver *lawyer*
Engel, Ralph Manuel *lawyer*
English, Thomas Francis *lawyer*
Entwistle, Andrew John *lawyer, consultant*
Epling, Richard Louis *lawyer*
Epstein, Jeremy G. *lawyer*
Epstein, Melvin Gerard *lawyer*
Epstein, Michael Alan *lawyer*
Ercklentz, Enno Wilhelm, Jr. *lawyer*
Ericson, Robert Walter *lawyer*
Estlund, Cynthia *law educator*
Estreicher, Samuel *lawyer, educator*
Ettinger, John Riche *lawyer*
Evans, John Thomas *lawyer*
Evans, Martin Frederic *lawyer*

Evarts, William Maxwell, Jr. *lawyer*
Eyre, Paul P. *lawyer*
Faber, Peter Lewis *lawyer*
Fabricant, Robert Edmund *lawyer*
Fader, Bruce E. *lawyer*
Fagan, Jeffrey A. *law educator*
Fagen, Leslie Gordon *lawyer*
Fagin, Allen Ian *lawyer*
Fales, Haliburton, II, *lawyer*
Farber, Seth C. *lawyer*
Fasman, Zachary Dean *lawyer*
Fass, Peter Michael *lawyer, educator*
Faulkner, Walter Thomas *lawyer, director*
Fazio, Vic (Victor Herbert Fazio Jr.) *lawyer, former congressman*
Feder, Arthur A. *lawyer, legal association administrator*
Feder, Saul E. *lawyer*
Feiler, William S. *lawyer*
Feiman, Ronald Mark *lawyer*
Feit, Glenn Martin *lawyer*
Feldberg, Michael Svetkey *lawyer*
Felder, Raoul Lionel *lawyer*
Feldman, Franklin *retired lawyer, printmaker*
Fenn, Patrick B. *lawyer*
Fenster, Albert M. *lawyer*
Fensterstock, Blair Courtney *lawyer*
Ferguson, Milton Carr, Jr. *lawyer*
Ferguson, Robert A. *law educator*
Fernandez, Jose Walfredo *lawyer, department chairman*
Fessel, Robin D. *lawyer*
Fey, Albert Eugene *lawyer*
Field, David Anthony *lawyer*
Filler, Ronald Howard *lawyer*
Finch, Edward Ridley, Jr. *lawyer, educator, retired diplomat, ambassador*
Fine, Drew S. *lawyer*
Fineman, Steven E. *lawyer*
Fink, Robert Steven *lawyer, writer, educator*
Finkelson, Allen *lawyer*
Finkelstein, Allen Lewis *lawyer*
Finkelstein, Bernard *lawyer*
Finkelstein, David S. *lawyer*
Finkelstein, Stuart M. *lawyer*
Finley, John G. *lawyer*
Finley, Steven R. *lawyer*
Finnerty, Joseph Gregory, Jr. *lawyer*
Finnerty, Joseph Gregory III *lawyer*
First, Harry *law educator*
Fischer, Mark David *lawyer*
Fishbein, Peter Melvin *lawyer*
Fisher, Ann Bailen *lawyer*
Fisher, Robert I. *lawyer*
Fishman, Ellen Beth *lawyer*
Fishman, Fred Norman *lawyer*
Fiske, Robert Bishop, Jr. *lawyer*
Fitts, Nelson Orus *lawyer*
FitzPatrick, James A., Jr. *lawyer*
Fleder, Robert Charles *lawyer*
Fleischer, Arthur, Jr. *lawyer*
Fleischman, Edward Hirsh *lawyer, consultant*
Fleischmann, Dennis C. *lawyer*
Fleming, Peter Emmet, Jr. *lawyer*
Fleming, Ronald A. *lawyer*
Flesher, Gail A. *lawyer*
Fletcher, Anthony Lee *lawyer*
Fletcher, George P. *law educator*
Flint, George Squire *lawyer*
Flom, Joseph Harold *lawyer*
Florescue, Leonard George *lawyer*
Flumenbaum, Martin *lawyer*
Fodor, Susanna Serena *lawyer*
Fogelnest, Robert *lawyer*
Fogg, Blaine Viles *lawyer*
Fogg, William V. *lawyer*
Ford, Paul B. *lawyer*
Forrest, Katherine B. *lawyer*
Forrest, Kenneth B. *lawyer*
Forstadt, Joseph Lawrence *lawyer*
Forster, Arnold *lawyer, author*
Fox, Donald Thomas *lawyer*
Fraidin, Stephen *lawyer*
Franck, Thomas Martin *law educator*
Frank, Lloyd *lawyer, director, retired chemicals executive*
Frank, William P. *lawyer*
Franke, Katherine M. *law educator*
Franklin, Blake Timothy *lawyer*
Frazza, George S. *lawyer*
Fredericks, Wesley Charles, Jr. *lawyer*
Fredericks, William Curtin *lawyer*
Freedman, Gerald M. *lawyer*
Freeman, David John *lawyer*
Freeman, Scott M. *lawyer*
Freilicher, Morton *lawyer, educator*
French, John III *lawyer, director*
Freund, Fred A. *retired lawyer*
Frey, Andrew Lewis *lawyer*
Freyer, Dana Hartman *lawyer*
Freyre, Angela Mariana *lawyer*
Fricklas, Michael David *lawyer, broadcast executive*
Fried, Burton Theodore *lawyer*
Fried, Donald David *lawyer*
Fried, Richard L. *lawyer*
Friedman, Alan Roy *lawyer*
Friedman, Barry *law educator*
Friedman, Bart *lawyer*
Friedman, Dennis J. *lawyer*
Friedman, George *lawyer*
Friedman, Jeffrey J. *lawyer*
Friedman, Max *lawyer*
Friedman, Samuel Selig *lawyer*
Friedman, Wilbur Harvey *lawyer*
Frischling, Carl *lawyer*
Frommer, William S. *lawyer*
Frumkin, Joseph B. *lawyer*
Fry, Elizabeth H. W. *lawyer*
Fry, Morton Harrison, II, *lawyer*
Fuchs, Nancy E. *lawyer*
Fuerth, Glenn J. *lawyer*
Fuzesi, Stephen, Jr. *lawyer, communications executive*
Gabay, Donald *lawyer*
Gaffney, John T. *lawyer*
Gallagher, Brian John *lawyer*
Galluzzo, Jay A. *lawyer*
Gambro, Michael S. *lawyer*
Ganz, David L. *lawyer*
Ganz, Howard Laurence *lawyer*

Garbus, Martin Solomon *lawyer*
Garcia, Angela G. *lawyer*
Garcia, Michael J. *prosecutor, former federal agency administrator*
Gardner, Gary A. *lawyer*
Garfinkel, Barry Herbert *lawyer*
Garland, David William *law educator, sociology educator*
Garland, Sylvia Dillof *lawyer*
Garment, Leonard Israel, *lawyer, author*
Garner, Melvin C. *lawyer*
Garson, Gary Wayne *lawyer*
Gartner, Murray *lawyer*
Gartner, Steven J. *lawyer*
Garvey, Richard Anthony *retired lawyer*
Gastwirth, Seth Allen *lawyer*
Gaughan, Eugene Francis *lawyer, retired accountant*
Gay, Darrell S. *lawyer*
Geelan, John *lawyer*
Geistfeld, Mark *law educator*
Gelb, Judith Anne *lawyer*
Gelfand, David R. *lawyer*
Gelston, Philip A. *lawyer*
Geltzer, Robert Lawrence *lawyer, arbitrator, mediator, retired retail executive*
Genova, Diane Melisano *lawyer*
Genova, Joseph Steven *lawyer*
Genty, Philip *law educator*
Geoghegan, Patricia *lawyer*
Geraghty, Patrick D. *lawyer*
Gerard, Whitney Ian *lawyer*
Gerspach, Thomas Joseph *lawyer*
Getnick, Neil Victor *lawyer*
Gewirtz, Elliot *lawyer*
Ghani, Cyrus *lawyer*
Giaccio, Anthony *lawyer*
Giannetti, Thomas Leonard *lawyer*
Gibbons, Robert John *lawyer*
Giegerich, Thomas William *lawyer*
Gifford, William C. *lawyer, educator*
Gill, E. Ann *lawyer*
Gillers, Stephen *lawyer, educator, academic administrator*
Gillespie, George Joseph III *lawyer*
Gillespie, Michael J. *lawyer*
Gillette, Clayton P. *law educator, academic administrator*
Gillispie, Robert J. *lawyer*
Girden, Eugene Lawrence *lawyer*
Gitter, Max *lawyer*
Gittes, Franklin M. *lawyer*
Giuliani, Rudy (Rudolph William Louis Giuliani III) *consultant, lawyer, former mayor*
Glasser, Stephen C. *lawyer*
Glassman, Steven J. *lawyer*
Glekel, Jeffrey Ives *lawyer*
Gliatta, Stephen *lawyer*
Glickstein, Steven *lawyer*
Goetz, Maurice Harold *lawyer*
Gold, Martin Elliot *lawyer, educator*
Gold, Richard L. *lawyer*
Gold, Simeon *lawyer*
Gold, Stuart Walter *lawyer*
Goldbard, Laura E. *lawyer*
Goldberg, Jay *lawyer*
Goldberg, Victor Paul *law educator*
Golden, Arthur F. *lawyer*
Golden, Daniel H. *lawyer*
Goldfein, Shepard *lawyer*
Goldman, Charles Norton *retired corporate lawyer*
Goldman, Lawrence Saul *lawyer*
Goldman, Louis B. *lawyer*
Goldman, Michael S. *lawyer*
Goldschmid, Harvey Jerome *law educator, commissioner*
Goldsmith, Lee Selig *lawyer, physician*
Goldstein, Alvin *lawyer*
Goldstein, Charles Arthur *lawyer*
Goldstein, Howard Warren *lawyer*
Goldstein, Jonathan *lawyer*
Goldstein, Marcia Landweber *lawyer*
Goldstein, Sandra Cara *lawyer*
Golick, Toby *law educator, legal services administrator*
Golove, David M. *law educator*
Goodale, James Campbell *lawyer, educator, television producer, media columnist*
Goodfriend, Herbert Jay *lawyer*
Goodhartz, Gerald *law librarian*
Goodman, Gary A. *lawyer*
Goodridge, Allan D. *lawyer*
Goott, Alan F(ranklin) *lawyer*
Gordon, David A. *lawyer*
Gordon, Jeffrey Neil *law educator*
Gordon, Michael Mackin *lawyer*
Gordon, Robert Jay *lawyer, educator*
Gordon, Stephen Louis *lawyer*
Gordon, Stuart A. *lawyer*
Gormley, Kenneth *lawyer*
Goshen, Zohar *law educator*
Gotthoffer, Lance *lawyer*
Gottlieb, Robert W. *lawyer*
Gotts, Ilene Knable *lawyer*
Grad, Frank Paul *lawyer, educator*
Graff, George Leonard *lawyer*
Granito, Frank H. III *lawyer*
Granoff, Gary Charles *lawyer, investment company executive*
Grassi, Joseph F. *lawyer, mediator, arbitrator*
Gray, Stacey M. *lawyer*
Grayer, Elizabeth L. *lawyer*
Greaney, Michael E. *lawyer*
Green, Alvin *lawyer, consultant*
Greenawalt, Robert Kent *lawyer, educator*
Greenbaum, Maurice Coleman *lawyer*
Greenberg, Daniel Lawrence *lawyer*
Greenberg, Gary Howard *lawyer*
Greenberg, Ira George *lawyer*
Greenberg, Jack *lawyer, educator*
Greenberg, Joel I. *lawyer*
Greenberger, Howard Leroy *lawyer, educator*
Greene, Bernard Harold *lawyer*
Greene, Ira S. *lawyer*
Greene, Mark I. *lawyer*
Greene, Norman L. *lawyer*
Greenman, Frederick F., Jr. *lawyer*
Greenman, Paula S. *lawyer*
Greenspon, Robert Alan *lawyer*
Greenwald, David *lawyer*

Greenzang, Katherine *lawyer, insurance company executive*
Gregory, Robin N. *lawyer*
Grehan, Kevin J. *lawyer*
Greilsheimer, James Gans *lawyer*
Greiner, Stephen W. *lawyer*
Griffin, Michael F. *lawyer*
Griffith, William R. *lawyer*
Gross, John H. *lawyer*
Gross, Karen Charal *lawyer*
Gross, Steven Ross *lawyer*
Grossman, Dan Steven *lawyer*
Grossmann, Edward A. *lawyer*
Grubin, Sharon Ellen *lawyer, former federal judge*
Grubman, Allen J. *lawyer*
Gruenberger, Peter *lawyer*
Grushkin, Jay D. *lawyer*
Guedry, James Walter *lawyer, retired manufacturing executive*
Guggenheim, Martin Franklin *lawyer, educator*
Gupta, Paul R. *lawyer*
Gustafson, Albert Katsuaki *lawyer, engineer*
Gwathmey, Gaines *lawyer*
Haffner, F. Kinsey *lawyer*
Hahn, Arlene Arin *lawyer*
Haig, Robert Leighton *lawyer*
Haimes, Burton Kenneth *lawyer*
Haims, Bruce David *lawyer*
Halberstam, Malvina *law educator, lawyer*
Haley, James F., Jr. *lawyer*
Hall, John Herbert *lawyer*
Hall, Richard *lawyer*
Hall, Thomas J. *lawyer*
Hallake, Marcello *lawyer*
Halliday, Joseph William *lawyer*
Halperin, Richard E. *lawyer, finance company executive*
Hamburg, Charles Bruce *lawyer*
Hamm, David Bernard *lawyer*
Handelsman, Lawrence Marc *lawyer*
Handler, Arthur M. *lawyer*
Handley, Siobhan A. *lawyer*
Hansen, Kristopher M. *lawyer*
Hanson, Jean Elizabeth *lawyer*
Haracz, Stephen M. *lawyer*
Harbison, James Wesley, Jr. *lawyer*
Harkrider, John David *lawyer*
Harms, David B. *lawyer*
Harper, Emery Walter *lawyer*
Harper, Gerard Edward *lawyer*
Harris, Adam C. *lawyer*
Harris, Arlene *lawyer*
Harris, Joel B. (Joel Bruce Harris) *lawyer*
Harris, Theresa *lawyer*
Harrison, S. David *lawyer*
Hart, Arnold Zackery *lawyer*
Hart, Joseph Thomas Campbell *lawyer*
Hart, Mary T. *lawyer*
Hart, Robert M. *lawyer*
Hartnett, William M. *lawyer*
Hartnick, Alan Jay *lawyer, educator*
Hartzell, Andrew Cornelius, Jr. *retired lawyer*
Harvey, Peter C. *lawyer, former state attorney general*
Hasday, Robert Joel *lawyer*
Hass, Lawrence Joel *lawyer*
Hathaway, Gerald Thomas *lawyer*
Hauser, Rita Eleanore Abrams *lawyer*
Hawke, Roger Jewett *lawyer*
Hayden, Raymond Paul *lawyer*
Hayes, Eddie (Edward W. Hayes) *lawyer*
Hayes, Gerald Joseph *lawyer*
Hazan, Scott L. *lawyer*
Headley, Mark J. *lawyer*
Healy, Harold Harris, Jr. *lawyer*
Healy, J. Kevin *lawyer*
Healy, Nicholas Joseph *retired lawyer*
Hearn, George Henry *lawyer, water transportation executive*
Hedden, Andrew S. *lawyer*
Hefter, Michael C *lawyer*
Heftler, Thomas E. *lawyer*
Heinzelman, Kris F. *lawyer*
Heisler, Stanley Dean *lawyer*
Heitner, Kenneth Howard *lawyer*
Hellenbrand, Samuel Henry *lawyer*
Heller, Robert Martin *lawyer*
Hellerer, Mark R. *lawyer*
Henderson, Donald Bernard, Jr. *lawyer*
Henderson, Kenneth Lee *lawyer*
Henryson, Herbert, II, *lawyer*
Henze, William F., II, *lawyer*
Herbst, Todd L. *lawyer*
Herlihy, Edward D. *lawyer*
Herman, Kenneth Beaumont *lawyer*
Herman, Peter Windley *lawyer*
Herschlein, James D. *lawyer*
Hershcopf, Gerald Thea *retired lawyer*
Hershkoff, Helen *law educator*
Hertz, Michael K. *lawyer*
Herz, Andrew Lee *lawyer*
Herzeca, Lois Friedman *lawyer*
Hess, Michael David *lawyer*
Hewitt, John R. *lawyer*
Hiden, Robert Battaile, Jr. *lawyer*
Hill, Alfred *law educator*
Hillman, Peter N. *lawyer*
Hirsch, Barry *lawyer*
Hirsch, Irving B. *lawyer*
Hirsch, Jerome S. *lawyer*
Hirschfeld, Michael *lawyer*
Hirshfield, Stuart *lawyer*
Hirshon, Sheldon Ira *lawyer*
Hirshowitz, Melvin Stephen *lawyer*
Hoblin, Philip J., Jr. *securities lawyer*
Hoch, Benjamin *lawyer*
Hodes, Robert Bernard *lawyer*
Hoff, Jonathan M. (Jonathan Morind Hoff) *lawyer*
Hoffman, Mathew *lawyer*
Holley, Steven Lyon *lawyer*
Holman, Bud George *lawyer*
Holmbo, Todd A. *lawyer*
Holmes, Stephen T. *law educator*
Holsenbeck, George Penn *lawyer*
Holtzman, Elizabeth *lawyer*
Holtzmann, Howard Marshall *lawyer, judge*
Honig, Jonathan David *lawyer*
Hooker, Wade Stuart *lawyer*
Horowitz, Steven Gary *lawyer*
Houck, Rudolph S.(Rob) *lawyer*
Howe, Richard Rives *lawyer*

Howitt, John P. *lawyer*
Hritz, George F. *lawyer*
Hruska, Alan J. *lawyer*
Huck, L. Francis *lawyer*
Hudspeth, Stephen Mason *lawyer*
Huhs, John I. *lawyer*
Hulbert, Richard Woodward *lawyer*
Hull, Philip Glasgow *lawyer*
Hummel, Keith R. *lawyer*
Hunt, Franklin Griggs *lawyer*
Hupper, John Roscoe *retired lawyer*
Hurlock, James Bickford *retired lawyer*
Huttner, Constance S. *lawyer*
Hyde, David Rowley *lawyer*
Hyman, Alan Barry *lawyer*
Hyman, Jerome Elliot *lawyer*
Hynes, Patricia Mary *lawyer*
Ichel, David W. *lawyer*
Immergut, Mel M. *lawyer*
Ingram, Samuel William, Jr. *lawyer*
Insel, Michael S. *lawyer*
Intriligator, Marc Steven *lawyer*
Isaacson, Allen Ira *lawyer*
Isquith, Fred Taylor *lawyer*
Issacharoff, Samuel *law educator*
Issler, Harry *lawyer*
Ivanhoe, Robert J. *lawyer*
Ivanick, Carol W. Trencher *lawyer*
Jackson, Jack P. *lawyer*
Jacob, Edwin J. *lawyer*
Jacob, Marvin Eugene *lawyer*
Jacobs, Albert Lionel, Jr. *lawyer*
Jacobs, Arnold Stephen *lawyer*
Jacobs, Paul *lawyer*
Jacobs, Robert Alan *lawyer*
Jacobson, Gilbert H. *lawyer, director*
Jacobson, Jerold Dennis *lawyer*
Jaffe, Alan Steven *lawyer*
Jaffe, Helene D. *lawyer*
Jaffe, Mark M. *lawyer*
Janklow, Morton Lloyd *lawyer, literary agent*
Janowitz, James Arnold *lawyer*
Jassy, Everett Lewis *lawyer*
Jebejian, Sarkis *lawyer*
Jerome, John James *lawyer*
Jeydel, Richard K. *lawyer*
Jock, Paul F., II *lawyer*
Joffe, Robert David *lawyer*
Johnson, David J., Jr. *lawyer*
Johnson, James D. *lawyer*
Johnson, Jeh Charles *lawyer*
Johnson, Peter James, Jr. *lawyer, legal analyst*
Johnson, W. Clayton *lawyer*
Jones, James A. III *lawyer*
Jordan, Nora Margaret *lawyer*
Jordan, Vernon Eulion, Jr. *lawyer*
Joseph, Gregory Paul *lawyer*
Joseph, Leonard *lawyer*
Juceam, Robert E. *lawyer*
Kaden, Lewis B. *lawyer, educator*
Kafin, Robert Joseph *lawyer*
Kahan, Marcel *law educator*
Kahn, Alan Edwin *lawyer*
Kahn, Anthony F. *lawyer*
Kailas, Leo George *lawyer*
Kalik, Mildred *lawyer*
Kalish, Arthur *lawyer*
Kalish, Myron *lawyer*
Kambour, Annaliese Spofford *lawyer, media company executive*
Kamin, Sherwin *lawyer*
Kaminsky, Alan *lawyer*
Kamm, Linda Heller *lawyer*
Kandel, William Lloyd *lawyer, arbitrator, educator, mediator, writer*
Kane, Richard Joseph *lawyer*
Kanner, Frederick W. *lawyer*
Kanter, Carl Irwin *retired lawyer*
Kanter, Stacy J. *lawyer*
Kanzer, Alan *lawyer*
Kaplan, Carl Eliot *lawyer*
Kaplan, Cathy M. *lawyer*
Kaplan, Joseph Solte *retired lawyer*
Kaplan, Mark Norman *lawyer*
Kaplan, Paul Michael *lawyer, educator*
Kaplan, Susan *lawyer*
Karatz, William Warren *lawyer*
Karls, John Spencer *lawyer, accountant*
Karp, Brad S. *lawyer*
Karp, David C. *lawyer*
Kartiganer, Joseph *retired lawyer*
Kasowitz, Marc Elliot *lawyer*
Kassebaum, John Philip *lawyer*
Katcher, Richard David *lawyer*
Katsh, Salem Michael *lawyer*
Katz, Avery W. *law educator*
Katz, Avi *lawyer*
Katz, David A. *lawyer*
Katz, Jerome Charles *lawyer*
Katz, Robert James *lawyer*
Katz, Ronald Scott *lawyer*
Katz, Stuart Z. *lawyer*
Katzberg, Robert F. *lawyer*
Kaufman, Robert Max *lawyer, director*
Kaufman, Stephen Edward *lawyer*
Kavaler, Thomas J. *lawyer*
Kavoukjian, Michael Edward *lawyer*
Kaye, Stephen Rackow *lawyer*
Kayle, Bruce E. *lawyer*
Kayser, Leo III *lawyer*
Kazanjian, John Harold *lawyer*
Kean, Hamilton Fish *lawyer*
Keany, Sutton *lawyer*
Keene, Lonnie *lawyer*
Keller, Bruce P. *lawyer*
Kelley, David N. *lawyer, former prosecutor*
Kelly, Christopher M. *lawyer*
Kelly, Thomas Michael *lawyer*
Kelman, Edward Michael *lawyer*
Keltner, Thomas Nethery, Jr. *lawyer*
Kende, Christopher Burgess *lawyer, educator*
Keneally, Kathryn Marie *lawyer*
Kennedy, John B. *lawyer*
Kennedy, Michael John *lawyer*
Kennedy, Robert Francis, Jr. *lawyer, environmentalist*
Kenney, John Joseph *lawyer*
Kensington, Costa Nicholas *lawyer*
Kent, Steven *lawyer*
Keogh, Kevin *lawyer*
Kepke, Matthew Aaron *lawyer*

Kern, George Calvin, Jr. *lawyer*
Kernochan, John Marshall *lawyer, educator*
Kessel, Mark *lawyer*
Kessler, Jeffrey L. *lawyer*
Kezsbom, Allen *lawyer*
Kheel, Robert J. *lawyer*
Kiekhofer, William Henry *lawyer*
Kiernan, John S. *lawyer*
Kies, David M. *lawyer*
Kiessling, B. Robbins *lawyer*
Kilpatrick, Donald G. *lawyer*
Kimball, John Devereux *lawyer*
King, Henry Lawrence *lawyer*
King, Stephen C. *lawyer, commissioner, educator*
Kingsbury, Benedict *law educator*
Kinney, Stephen Hoyt, Jr. *lawyer*
Kinzler, Thomas Benjamin *lawyer*
Kirby, John Joseph, Jr. *lawyer*
Kirkham, D. Collier *lawyer*
Kirschbaum, Myron *lawyer*
Klapper, Molly *lawyer, educator*
Klapper, Richard H. *lawyer*
Kleckner, Robert George, Jr. *retired lawyer*
Klein, Eleazer *lawyer*
Klein, Martin I. *lawyer*
Klein, Richard S. *lawyer*
Kleinbard, Edward D. *lawyer*
Kleinberg, Norman Charles *lawyer*
Klemann, Gilbert Lacy, II, *lawyer*
Kline, Eugene Monroe *lawyer*
Klinger, Alan Mark *lawyer*
Klingsberg, David *lawyer*
Klipstein, Robert Alan *lawyer*
Klotz, Martin B. *lawyer*
Knight, Robert Huntington *lawyer, bank executive*
Kobak, James Benedict, Jr. *lawyer, educator*
Kobrin, Lawrence Alan *lawyer*
Koch, Edward Irving *lawyer, former mayor*
Koegel, William Fisher *lawyer*
Koen, Robert G. *lawyer*
Koepff, Paul R. *lawyer*
Kohl, Robert L. *lawyer*
Kohlmann, Susan J. *lawyer*
Kohn, Immanuel *lawyer*
Kolbe, Karl William, Jr. *lawyer*
Kolker, Lawrence Paul *lawyer*
Koob, Charles Edward *lawyer*
Koopersmith, Kim *lawyer*
Koral, Alan Max *lawyer*
Kornberg, Alan William *lawyer*
Kornfeld, Neil S. *lawyer*
Kornhauser, Lewis *law educator*
Kornreich, Edward Scott *lawyer*
Korotkin, Michael Paul *lawyer*
Koslow, Jonathan L. *lawyer*
Kraemer, Lillian Elizabeth *lawyer*
Kraines, Merrill M. *lawyer*
Kramer, George P. *lawyer*
Krane, Steven Charles *lawyer*
Krasner, Daniel Walter *lawyer*
Krasnow, Richard P. *lawyer*
Kraus, Douglas M. *lawyer*
Kreidman, Perry L. *lawyer*
Kreitzman, Ralph J. *lawyer*
Krieger, Sanford *lawyer*
Krouse, George Raymond, Jr. *lawyer*
Krupman, William Allan *lawyer*
Krupp, Fred D. *lawyer, environmental services administrator*
Kubek, Gary W. *lawyer*
Kuby, Ronald Lawrence *lawyer*
Kuck, Lea Haber *lawyer*
Kuh, Richard Henry *lawyer*
Kuhbach, Robert Gerdes *lawyer*
Kuntz, Lee Allan *lawyer*
Kuntz, William Francis, II *lawyer, educator*
Kurtz, Jerome *retired lawyer, educator*
Kurz, William Charles Frederick *lawyer*
Kurzweil, Harvey *lawyer*
LaBarre, Dennis W. *lawyer*
Lack, Robert Joel *lawyer*
Lacovara, Philip Allen *lawyer*
Lacy, Robinson Burrell *lawyer*
Lamia, Thomas Roger *lawyer*
Lanchner, Bertrand Martin *lawyer, advertising executive*
Landau, David H. *lawyer*
Langan, Richard F., Jr. *lawyer*
Lansner, Ruth L. *lawyer*
Larose, Lawrence Alfred *lawyer*
Lascher, Alan Alfred *lawyer*
Latza, William D. *lawyer*
Lauer, Eliot *lawyer*
Lavin, Howard S. *lawyer*
Law, Sylvia A. *law educator*
Lebow, Mark Denis *lawyer*
Lederman, Lawrence *lawyer, writer, educator*
Lee, In-Young *lawyer*
Lee, Jerome G. *lawyer*
Lee, Paul Lawrence *lawyer*
Lefcourt, Gerald B. *lawyer*
LeFevre, David E. *lawyer, professional sports team executive*
Lefkowitz, David S. *lawyer*
Lefkowitz, Howard N. *lawyer*
Lehman, Mark E. *lawyer*
Leibert, Burton M. *lawyer*
Leichtling, Michael Alfred *lawyer*
Leland, Richard G(uy) *lawyer*
Lenobel, Jeffrey A. *lawyer*
Leonard, Edwin Deane *lawyer*
Lerner, Eric M. *lawyer*
Lerner, Jonathan J. *lawyer*
Lerner, Richard E. *lawyer*
Lesch, Michael Oscar *lawyer*
Lesk, Ann Berger *lawyer*
Levander, Andrew Joshua *lawyer*
Levie, Joseph Henry *lawyer, banker*
Levin, Michael Joseph *lawyer*
Levin, Peter S.W. *lawyer*
Levine, Robert Jay *lawyer*
Levine, Ronald Jay *lawyer*
Levinson, Daryl J. *law educator*
Levitan, David M(aurice) *lawyer, educator*
Levy, Stanley Herbert *lawyer*
Lewin, Robert *lawyer*
Lewyn, Thomas Mark *lawyer*
Li, Tze-chung *lawyer, educator*
Liberman, Enrique Eduardo *lawyer*
Liddle, Jeffrey L. *lawyer*
Liebenson, Jeffrey M. *lawyer*

Lieberman, Nancy Ann *lawyer*
Liebman, Lance Malcolm *law educator*
Liebmann, Jeff S. *lawyer*
Liftin, John M. *lawyer*
Liman, Lewis Jeffrey *lawyer*
Lindauer, Erik D. *lawyer*
Lindblom, Marjorie Press *lawyer*
Lindo, Stephen T. *lawyer*
Lindsay, George Peter *lawyer*
Link, Robert O., Jr. *lawyer*
Linker, Arthur S. *lawyer*
Linsenmeyer, John Michael *lawyer*
Lippert, Nels T. *lawyer*
Lipscomb, James Louis *lawyer, insurance company executive*
Lipsky, Burton G. *lawyer*
Liptak, Adam *lawyer, reporter*
Lipton, Martin *lawyer*
Liss, Norman *lawyer*
Littenberg, Michael Richard *lawyer*
Litvack, Sanford Martin *lawyer*
Litwin, Ethan *lawyer*
Lloyd, William Frederick *lawyer*
Loacker, Lynn J. *lawyer*
Lobenfeld, Eric Jay *lawyer*
Lobl, Herbert Max *lawyer, writer*
Loengard, Richard Otto, Jr. *lawyer*
Logan, Kenneth Richard *lawyer*
London, Martin *lawyer*
Longstreth, Bevis *lawyer*
Lopez, Gerald P. *law educator*
Loss, Margaret Ruth *lawyer*
Lotwin, Stanford Gerald *lawyer*
Loughran, Peter J. *lawyer*
Lowenfeld, Andreas Frank *law educator*
Lowenfels, Fred M. *lawyer*
Lowenfels, Lewis David *lawyer*
Lowenstein, Louis *law educator*
Lowy, George Theodore *lawyer*
Lum, Larry *lawyer*
Lund, Daniel Peter *lawyer*
Lunding, Christopher Hanna *lawyer*
Lupert, Leslie Allan *lawyer*
Luria, Mary Mercer *lawyer*
Lutzker, Joel E. *lawyer*
Luxenberg, Arthur Martin *lawyer*
Lynch, Loretta E. *lawyer, former prosecutor*
Lynch, Luke Daniel, Jr. *lawyer*
Lynn, Theodore Stanley *lawyer*
Lyon, Carl Francis, Jr. *lawyer*
Macan, William Alexander, IV, *lawyer*
MacCrate, Robert *lawyer*
Mack, Dennis Wayne *lawyer*
MacRae, Cameron Farquhar III *lawyer*
Macris, Michael *lawyer*
Madden, John J. *lawyer*
Madison, George W. *lawyer*
Mahon, Arthur Joseph *lawyer*
Maidman, Richard Harvey Mortimer *lawyer*
Maitland, Guy Edison Clay *lawyer*
Malamud, Deborah C. *law educator*
Malfa, Frances *lawyer*
Malina, Michael *lawyer*
Malkin, Peter Laurence *lawyer, investor*
Mallin, Joel *lawyer*
Mallow, Matthew J. *lawyer*
Malman, Laurie L. *law educator*
Maloney, Sean Patrick *lawyer, former federal official*
Mandelstam, Charles Lawrence *lawyer*
Maneker, Morton M. *lawyer*
Maney, Michael Mason *lawyer*
Mantle, Raymond Allan *lawyer*
Marcus, Eric Peter *lawyer*
Marcus, Maria Lenhoff *lawyer, educator*
Marcusa, Fred Haye *lawyer*
Margulis, Howard Lee *lawyer*
Mariani, Michael Matthew *lawyer*
Mark, Jonathan I. *lawyer*
Markard, Marlene Maria *lawyer*
Markel, Gregory Arthur *lawyer*
Marks, Ramon Paul *lawyer*
Maroney, Thomas Joseph *lawyer*
Marooney, Richard T. *lawyer*
Marriott, David R. *lawyer*
Marshall, Sheila Hermes *lawyer*
Martin, George J., Jr. *lawyer*
Martin, Malcolm Elliot *lawyer*
Martin, Renwick D. *lawyer*
Martone, Patricia Ann *lawyer*
Marx, Owen Cox *lawyer*
Marzulli, John Anthony, Jr. *lawyer*
Masin, Michael Terry *lawyer*
Maslow, Will *lawyer, legal association administrator*
Mason, Christopher May *lawyer*
Massad, Timothy G. *lawyer*
Materna, Joseph Anthony *lawyer*
Mathers, William Harris *lawyer*
Mattei, Ivan E. *lawyer*
Matteson, William Bleecker *lawyer*
Matthews, Edwin Spencer, Jr. *lawyer*
Matus, Wayne Charles *lawyer*
Mavroidis, Petros *law educator*
Maxfield, Guy Budd *lawyer, educator*
Mayer, Carl Joseph *prosecutor, lawyer*
Mayer, Christopher *lawyer*
Mayer, Theodore V.H. *lawyer*
Mayerson, Sandra Elaine *lawyer*
McAtee, Darin P. *lawyer*
McCabe, David J. *lawyer*
McCaffrey, Carlyn Sundberg *lawyer*
McCaw, Robert Bruce *lawyer*
McClimon, Timothy John *lawyer*
McCormack, William F. *lawyer*
McCulloch, Kenneth John *lawyer*
McDavid, William Henry *lawyer*
McGanney, Thomas *lawyer*
McGeady, Paul Joseph *lawyer*
McGinn, Timothy J. *lawyer*
McGoldrick, John Lewis *lawyer*
McGowen, Lorraine S. *lawyer*
McGrath, Thomas John *retired lawyer, writer, film producer*
McHenry, Barnabas *lawyer*
McLaughlin, Joseph Thomas *lawyer*
McNamara, J. Donald (John Donald McNamara) *retired lawyer, business executive*
Mehler, Gordon *lawyer*
Meili, Barbara *lawyer*
Melton, Howell W., Jr. *lawyer*

Sorell Stehr, Deborah K. *lawyer*
Sorgi, Leonard *lawyer*
Sorkin, David James *lawyer*
Sorkin, Ira Lee *lawyer*
Sorkin, Laurence Truman *lawyer*
Sorter, George Hans *accounting and law educator, consultant*
Soussloff, Andrew D. *lawyer*
Sovern, Michael Ira *law educator*
Soyster, Margaret Blair *lawyer*
Spanbock, Maurice Samuel *lawyer*
Spatt, Robert Edward *lawyer*
Spear, Harvey M. *lawyer*
Spelfogel, Evan J. *lawyer, educator*
Spellman Sweet, Julia T. *lawyer*
Sperling, Allan George *lawyer*
Spillane, Dennis Kevin *lawyer*
Spinak, Jane M. *law educator*
Spivak, Leonard A. *lawyer*
Squire, Walter Charles *lawyer*
Srulowitz, Marvin *lawyer*
Standard, Kenneth G. *lawyer*
Stapleton, Benjamin F. III *lawyer*
Starer, Brian Douglas *lawyer*
Stathis, Nicholas John *lawyer*
Stein, Jane Wallison *lawyer*
Stein, Ronald J. *lawyer*
Stein, Stephen William *lawyer*
Steinberg, Arthur Jay *lawyer*
Steinberg, Howard Eli *lawyer, diversified financial services company executive*
Steines, John P., Jr. *law educator*
Stephenson, Alan Clements *lawyer*
Stern, Donald Allan *lawyer*
Sternman, Joel W. *lawyer*
Steuer, Richard Marc *lawyer*
Stevens, Michael N. *lawyer*
Stever, Donald Winfred *lawyer*
Stewart, Richard Burleson *law educator*
Stillman, Charles Allen *lawyer*
Stimpson, Scott David *lawyer*
Stoll, Neal Richard *lawyer*
Stone, David Philip *lawyer*
Stone, Merrill Brent *lawyer*
Stopnik, Scott H. *lawyer*
Stratton, Walter Love *lawyer*
Strauss, Peter L(ester) *law educator*
Strickon, Harvey Alan *lawyer*
Strock, Marcus *lawyer*
Strom, Milton Gary *lawyer*
Strossen, Nadine *legal association administrator, law educator*
Strum, Jay Gerson *lawyer*
Struve, Guy Miller *lawyer*
Stuart, Alice Melissa *lawyer*
Stuart, Walter Bynum, IV, *lawyer*
Sturm, Susan P. *law educator*
Sturman, Deborah Muscha *lawyer, columnist*
Sugarman, Irwin J. *lawyer*
Sulds, Jonathan L. *lawyer*
Sullivan, John W. *lawyer*
Summit, Stuart A. *lawyer*
Sussman, Alexander Ralph *lawyer*
Sutin, Alan N. *lawyer*
Suydam, John J. *lawyer*
Sweeney, John Francis *lawyer*
Sweeney, Thomas Joseph, Jr. *lawyer*
Synnott, Aidan John *lawyer*
Taber, Kenneth W. *lawyer*
Tahbaz, Christopher K. *lawyer*
Tancredi, Laurence Richard *law educator, psychologist*
Tanenbaum, Edward *lawyer*
Tanenbaum, Jeffrey L. *lawyer*
Tanenbaum, William Alan *lawyer*
Tanner, Douglas Alan *lawyer*
Tarnoff, Jerome *lawyer*
Taylor, Edward A. *lawyer*
Taylor, Errol Bancroft *lawyer*
Taylor, John Chestnut III *lawyer*
Taylor, Willard B. *lawyer*
Teich, Howard Bernard *lawyer, volunteer, public information officer*
Teiman, Richard Barry *lawyer*
Tenney, Dudley Bradstreet *retired lawyer*
Terrell, J. Anthony *lawyer*
Terry, Frederick Arthur, Jr. *lawyer*
Terry, James Joseph, Jr. *lawyer*
Testa, Michael Harold *lawyer*
Thackeray, Jonathan E. *lawyer*
Thal, Steven Henry *lawyer, consultant*
Thalacker, Arbie Robert *lawyer, director*
Thomas, Jeremiah Lindsay III *lawyer*
Thomas, Roger Warren *lawyer*
Thoyer, Judith Reinhardt *lawyer*
Thurm, David Aaron *lawyer, publishing executive*
Thurston, Sally A. *lawyer*
Tiano, Linda V. *lawyer*
Tierney, James Edward *law educator, former state attorney general*
Tilewick, Robert *lawyer*
Tillinghast, David Rollhaus *lawyer*
Tillinghast, Edward Hudson III *lawyer*
Tirana, Bardyl Rifat *lawyer*
Todd, Ronald Gary *lawyer*
Tolley, B. Cary III *lawyer*
Toumey, Donald Joseph *lawyer*
Townsend, Robert I. III *lawyer*
Tracey, Dennis Henry III *lawyer*
Tract, Marc Mitchell *lawyer*
Treadway, James Crispin Curran Corbett *lawyer, brokerage house executive, investor, federal official*
Trepper, Myron *lawyer*
Tuchmann, Eric P. *lawyer*
Tulchin, David Bruce *lawyer*
Tung, Ko-Yung *lawyer*
Turitzin, John N. *lawyer*
Turner, E. Deane *lawyer*
Turner, Roger D. *lawyer*
Tween, Douglas M. *lawyer, former prosecutor*
Udell, Richard *lawyer*
Underberg, Mark Alan *lawyer*
Unger, Sydney Elliott *lawyer*
Upham, Frank K. *law educator*
Uram, Gerald Robert *lawyer*
Urowsky, Richard J. *lawyer*
Valente, Peter Charles *lawyer*
Vardell, James C. III *lawyer*
Varet, Michael A. *lawyer*
Vassallo, Edward E. *lawyer*

Vassil, John Charles *lawyer*
Vega, Matias Alfonso *lawyer*
Verde, Michael I. *lawyer*
Vernon, Darryl Mitchell *lawyer*
Versfelt, David Scott *lawyer*
Victor, A. Paul *lawyer*
Viener, John D. *lawyer*
Vig, Vernon Edward *lawyer*
Vine, Stephen M. *lawyer*
Vinegrad, Alan *prosecutor*
Vingoe, D. Grant *lawyer*
Vining, Barbara *lawyer*
Vitale, Thomas M. *lawyer*
Vittor, Kenneth Mark *lawyer*
Vladeck, Judith Pomarlen *lawyer*
Vollweiler, Cheryl P. *lawyer*
von Mehren, Robert Brandt *retired lawyer*
Vyskocil, Mary Kay *lawyer*
Wachsberger, Chaim *lawyer*
Wachtel, Norman Jay *lawyer*
Wachtell, Herbert M. *lawyer*
Waddell, Mark E. *lawyer*
Wailand, George *lawyer*
Waks, Jay Warren *lawyer*
Wald, Bernard Joseph *lawyer*
Wald, Wayne A. *lawyer*
Waldenberg, Alan S. *lawyer*
Waldman, Seymour Morton *lawyer*
Waldron, Jeremy James *law educator*
Walker, John Lockwood *lawyer*
Walker, Kim A. *lawyer*
Wall, Charles R. *lawyer*
Wallace, Edward Corbett *lawyer*
Wallace, Nora Ann *lawyer*
Wallace, Walter C. *lawyer, government official*
Wallach, Eric Jean *lawyer*
Walpin, Gerald *lawyer*
Wang, Albert Huai-En *lawyer*
Wang, Xinshing *lawyer*
Warden, John Lehman *lawyer*
Warnke, Gordon E. *lawyer*
Warren, Irwin Howard *lawyer*
Warren, James I. *lawyer*
Warren, William Bradford *lawyer*
Washburn, David Thacher *lawyer*
Watson, Solomon Brown, IV, *lawyer, publishing executive*
Waxenberg, Jay David *lawyer*
Webster, Susan *lawyer*
Ween, Martin M. *lawyer*
Weiksner, Sandra S. *lawyer*
Weinberg, Herschel Mayer *lawyer*
Weinberg, Jeffrey J. *lawyer*
Weinberger, Harold Paul *lawyer*
Weiner, Andrew Jay *lawyer*
Weiner, Earl David *lawyer*
Weiner, Stephen Arthur *lawyer*
Weingarten, Marc *lawyer*
Weinroth, Lois L. *lawyer*
Weinschel, Alan Jay *lawyer*
Weinstock, Leonard *lawyer*
Weisbrod, Carl *lawyer, public official*
Weiss, Jonathan Arthur *lawyer*
Weiss, Lawrence N. *lawyer*
Weiss, Lisa Ann *lawyer*
Weiss, Melvyn I. *lawyer*
Weissman, David L. *lawyer*
Weissmann, Andrew *lawyer, former prosecutor*
Weithorn, Stanley Stephen *lawyer*
Weld, Jonathan Minot *lawyer*
Wellington, Harry Hillel *lawyer, educator*
Wells, Christopher M. *lawyer*
Wells, Theodore V., Jr. *lawyer*
Welshimer, Mark J. *lawyer*
Weltman, Edward S. *lawyer*
Wender, Ira Tensard *lawyer*
Wenig, Cindy L. *lawyer*
Werder, Richard I., Jr. *lawyer*
Werner, Robert L. *lawyer, consultant*
Wesely, Edwin Joseph *lawyer*
Wesely, Marissa Celeste *lawyer*
West, Stephen Kingsbury *lawyer, director*
Westreich, Neil P. *lawyer*
Wetmore, Keith Chidester *lawyer*
Wexelbaum, Michael *lawyer*
Whelan, William J. III *lawyer*
Whitaker, G(eorge) Warren *lawyer*
White, Fred B. III *lawyer*
White, Harry Edward, Jr. *lawyer*
White, John Patrick *lawyer*
White, Mary Jo *lawyer, former prosecutor*
White, W. Christopher *lawyer*
Whitmer, Frederick Lee *lawyer*
Whitney, Jonathan B. *lawyer*
Whitson, Jerry E. *lawyer*
Whoriskey, Robert Donald *lawyer*
Wilcox, John Caven *lawyer, financial executive*
Wildermuth, Bruce R. *lawyer*
Wiles, Michael E. *lawyer*
Wilkinson, John Hart *lawyer*
Willett, John A. *lawyer*
Williams, Anthony *lawyer*
Williams, Patricia J. *law educator*
Williams, Vaughn Charles *lawyer*
Williams, William John, Jr. *lawyer*
Williamson, Douglas Franklin, Jr. *lawyer*
Willig, Kenneth C. H. *lawyer*
Willis, William Ervin *lawyer*
Willner, Barry A. *lawyer*
Wilson, Paul Holliday, Jr. *lawyer*
Wilson, Peter Scott *lawyer*
Wilson, Rowan D. *lawyer*
Windels, James H.R. *lawyer*
Windels, Paul, Jr. *lawyer*
Winfield, Richard Neill *lawyer*
Wing, John Russell *lawyer*
Winterer, Philip Steele *lawyer*
Wintner, Mark S. *lawyer*
Wise, Aaron Noah *lawyer*
Wiseman, Michael Martin *lawyer*
Witkin, Eric Douglas *lawyer*
Witmeyer, John Jacob III *lawyer*
Witten, Roger Michael *lawyer*
Witzel, Steven M. *lawyer*
Wohl, Frank Harold *lawyer*
Wolf, Barry M. *lawyer*
Wolfe, James Ronald *retired lawyer*
Wolff, Jesse David *lawyer*
Wolkoff, Eugene Arnold *lawyer*
Wollman, Eric *lawyer*
Woolery, James C. *lawyer*

Wray, Cecil, Jr. *lawyer*
Wynne, William Francis *lawyer*
Yablon, Heather D. *lawyer*
Yamin, Michael Geoffrey *lawyer*
Yankwitt, George B(ruce) *lawyer*
Yelenick, Mary Therese *lawyer*
Yerman, Fredric Warren *lawyer*
Yodowitz, Edward Jay *lawyer*
Young, Alice *lawyer*
Young, John Edward *lawyer*
Young, Jonathan *lawyer*
Young, Nancy *lawyer*
Youngwood, Alfred Donald *lawyer*
Zabel, William David *lawyer*
Zagorin, Janet Susan *legal firm administrator, marketing professional*
Zaitzeff, Roger Michael *lawyer*
Zammit, Joseph Paul *lawyer*
Zauderer, Mark Carl *lawyer*
Zedrosser, Joseph John *lawyer*
Zelinsky, Edward Alan *law educator*
Zerin, Steven David *lawyer*
Ziegler, Henry Steinway *lawyer*
Ziegler, John Augustus, Jr. *lawyer*
Zifchak, William C. *lawyer*
Zimand, Harvey Folks *lawyer*
Zimmerman, Diane Leenheer *law educator*
Zimmett, Mark Paul *lawyer, educator*
Zirinsky, Bruce R. *lawyer*
Zito, Robert John Amadeus *lawyer*
Zivin, Norman H. *lawyer*
Zochowski, T. Robert, Jr. *lawyer*
Zoogman, Nicholas Jay *lawyer*
Zornow, David Merrill *lawyer*
Zubkoff, Daniel J. *lawyer*
Zuckerman, Paul Herbert *lawyer*
Zukerman, Michael *lawyer*
Zulack, Mary Marsh *law educator*
Zweibel, Joel Burton *retired lawyer*

**Newark**
Reid, James Edward *lawyer*

**Old Chatham**
Severs, Charles A. III *lawyer*

**Oneida**
Matthews, William Doty *lawyer, director, consumer products company executive*

**Orchard Park**
Sullivan, Mortimer Allen, Jr. *lawyer*

**Oswego**
Greene, Stephen Craig *lawyer*

**Oyster Bay**
Coates, Winslow Shelby, Jr. *lawyer*
Wachsman, Harvey Frederick *lawyer, neurosurgeon*

**Patchogue**
Esteve, Edward V. *lawyer*

**Pawling**
Berlandi, Brian Lawrence *lawyer*

**Pearl River**
Meyer, Irwin Stephan *lawyer, accountant*

**Pelham**
Gaffney, Mark William *lawyer*

**Pittsford**
Braunsdorf, Paul Raymond *lawyer*
Hampson, Thomas Meredith *lawyer*
Hartman, James Matthew *lawyer*
Stonehill, Eric *lawyer*
Turri, Joseph A. *lawyer*
Willett, Thomas Edward *lawyer*

**Plainview**
Maune, James J. *lawyer*

**Pleasantville**
Brizel, Michael Alan *lawyer*

**Port Washington**
Lingelbach, Albert Lane *lawyer*
Rush, Curt Stefan *lawyer*
Ullman, Leo Solomon *lawyer*

**Poughkeepsie**
Ostertag, Robert Louis *lawyer*
Taphorn, Joseph Bernard *lawyer*
Teal, Arabella W. *lawyer, former state attorney general*

**Purchase**
Dostart, Thomas J. *lawyer*
Hanft, Noah Jonathan *lawyer*
Kelly, Edmund Joseph *lawyer, bank executive, investment banker*
Thompson, Larry Dean *lawyer, former federal agency administrator*
Wallach, Ira David *lawyer, corporate financial executive*

**Rensselaerville**
Fletcher, Raymond Russwald, Jr. *lawyer*

**Riverhead**
Maggipinto, V. Anthony *lawyer*

**Rochester**
Adair, Donald Robert *lawyer*
Blyth, John E. *lawyer, educator*
Buckley, Michael Francis *lawyer*
Buzard, A. Vincent *lawyer*
Clifford, Eugene Thomas *lawyer*
Dolin, Lonny H. *lawyer*
Doyle, Justin P. *lawyer*
Fitzgerald, John T., Jr. *lawyer*
Geiger, Alexander *lawyer*
Goldman, Joel J. *retired lawyer*
Gootnick, Margery Fischbein *lawyer*
Harris, Wayne Manley *lawyer*
Harter, Ralph Millard Peter *lawyer, educator*
Kelley, Stephen Michael *lawyer*
Kunkel, Barbara J. *law firm executive*

Kurland, Harold Arthur *lawyer*
LaBarge, Jeffrey Howard *lawyer*
Law, Michael R. *lawyer*
Lundback, Staffan Bengt Gunnar *lawyer*
McCrory, John Brooks *retired lawyer*
Moore, James Conklin *lawyer*
Morris, James E. *lawyer, judge, educator*
Morrison, Patrice Burgert *lawyer*
Nusbaum, Beryl *lawyer*
Palermo, Anthony Robert *lawyer*
Paley, Gerald Larry *lawyer*
Payment, Kenneth Arnold *lawyer*
Price, Richard Edward *lawyer*
Robfogel, Susan Salitan *lawyer*
Rosenhouse, Michael Allan *lawyer, editor, consultant, columnist*
Schumacher, Jon Lee *lawyer*
Stewart, Sue S. *lawyer*
Trueheart, Harry Parker III *lawyer*
Turner, Scott MacNeely *lawyer*
Vigdor, Justin Leonard *lawyer*
Waite, Stephen Holden *lawyer*
Wild, Robert Warren *lawyer*
Witmer, George Robert, Jr. *lawyer*

**Rome**
Simons, Richard Duncan *lawyer, retired judge*

**Rye**
Goldstein, Peter Dobkin *lawyer*

**Sands Point**
Hoynes, Louis LeNoir, Jr. *lawyer*

**Saratoga Springs**
Coreno, Mary Elizabeth *lawyer*

**Scarsdale**
Angel, Dennis *lawyer*
Belasco, Steven Ronald *lawyer*
Benedict, James Nelson *lawyer*
Beuchert, Edward William *lawyer*
Clapman, Peter Carlyle *lawyer, finance company and corporate governance consultant*
Gerber, Roger Alan *lawyer, consultant*
Hoffman, Richard M. *lawyer*
Van Gundy, Gregory Frank *retired lawyer*

**Schoharie**
Duncombe, Raynor Bailey *lawyer*

**Scottsville**
Williams, Henry Ward, Jr. *lawyer, writer*

**Smithtown**
Dowis, Lenore *lawyer*
Goodman, Richard Shalem *lawyer, orthopedic surgeon*

**Somers**
Rothman, Bernard *lawyer*

**South Richmond Hill**
Scheich, John F. *lawyer*

**South Salem**
Cowles, Frederick Oliver *lawyer*

**Southampton**
Lopez, David *lawyer*
Platt, Jonathan James *lawyer*

**Staten Island**
Humphries, Edward Francis *lawyer*

**Syosset**
Bermas, Stephen *lawyer*

**Syracuse**
Baldwin, Robert Frederick, Jr. *lawyer*
Bodow, Wayne R. *defender*
Cherundolo, John Charles *lawyer*
Crane, David Michael *prosecutor, former judge advocate, educator*
Engel, Richard Lee *lawyer, educator*
Fiske, Jordan Jay *lawyer, retired prosecutor*
Fitzpatrick, James David *lawyer*
Ford, Steven J. *lawyer, manufacturing executive*
Gaal, John *lawyer*
Givas, Thomas Peter *lawyer*
Hayes, David Michael *lawyer*
Herzog, Peter Emilius *retired legal educator*
Hole, Richard Douglas *lawyer*
Lee, David Ames *lawyer, banker, editor, writer*
Luchsinger, John Francis, Jr. *lawyer*
Mukerji, Indranil *lawyer*
O'Connor, Michael E. *lawyer*
Richardson, M. Catherine *lawyer*
Rivette, Francis Robert *lawyer*
Suddaby, Glenn T. *prosecutor, lawyer*
Traylor, Robert Arthur *lawyer*

**Tonawanda**
Brett, Jay Elliot *lawyer*

**Troy**
Finkel, Sanford Norman *lawyer*
Frost, Jerome Kenneth *lawyer*
Jones, E. Stewart, Jr. *lawyer*

**Uniondale**
Berzow, Harold Steven *lawyer*
Duffy, James Raymond *lawyer*
Kotula, Michael Anthony *lawyer*
Lemle, Robert Spencer *lawyer*
Levy, Robert S. *lawyer*
Pratt, George Cheney *law educator, retired judge*

**Valatie**
Dorsey, Richard J. *lawyer*

**Wappingers Falls**
Maissel, Raina Eve *lawyer*

**Warwick**
McManus, Robert Francis *lawyer*

**Waterford**
Glavin, James Henry III *lawyer*

Hardy, William Robinson *lawyer*
Harris, Irving *lawyer*
Hawkins, William H., II, *lawyer*
Heldman, James Gardner *lawyer*
Heldman, Paul W. *lawyer, food service executive*
Hermanies, John Hans *retired lawyer*
Hoefle, H. Frederick *lawyer*
Hoffheimer, Daniel Joseph *lawyer*
Holschuh, John David, Jr. *lawyer*
Johnson, James J. *lawyer*
Katz, Reuven J. *lawyer*
Kelley, John Joseph, Jr. *lawyer*
Kiel, Frederick Orin *lawyer*
Kordons, Uldis *lawyer*
Lawrence, James Kaufman Lebensburger *lawyer*
Lawson, Kenneth L. *lawyer*
Lesick, John Richard *retired lawyer, consultant*
Lindberg, Charles David *lawyer*
Lloyd, David Livingstone, Jr. *lawyer*
Lockwood, Bert Berkley, Jr. *law educator*
Longenecker, Mark Hershey, Jr. *lawyer*
Mahon, Stephen C. *lawyer*
Manley, Robert Edward *lawyer, economist*
Manly, Marc Edward *lawyer*
Mann, David Scott *lawyer*
Maxwell, Robert Wallace, II, *lawyer*
McClain, William Andrew *lawyer*
McGavran, Frederick Jaeger *lawyer*
Mc Henry, Powell *lawyer*
Metz, Jerome Joseph, Jr. *lawyer*
Meyers, Karen Diane *lawyer, educator*
Meyers, Pamela Sue *lawyer*
Nechemias, Stephen Murray *lawyer*
Oberhaus, Geoffrey Luther *lawyer*
Olson, Robert Wyrick *lawyer*
O'Reilly, James Thomas *lawyer, educator, writer*
Parker, R. Joseph *lawyer*
Petrie, Bruce Inglis *lawyer*
Reichert, David *lawyer*
Reynolds, Paul L *lawyer*
Rich, Robert Edward *lawyer*
Rose, Donald McGregor *retired lawyer*
Rubin, Robert Samuel *lawyer*
Ryan, James Joseph *retired lawyer*
Schuck, Thomas Robert *lawyer, farmer*
Shore, Thomas Spencer, Jr. *retired lawyer*
Silbersack, Barbara Wyspianska *law librarian*
Silbersack, Mark Louis *lawyer*
Swigert, James Mack *lawyer*
Thompson, James E. *lawyer*
Tobias, Paul Henry *lawyer*
Tomain, Joseph Patrick *law educator, retired dean*
Townsend, Robert J. *lawyer*
Trauth, Joseph Louis, Jr. *lawyer*
Vander Laan, Mark Alan *lawyer*
Vogel, Cedric Wakelee *lawyer*
Wales, Ross Elliot *lawyer*
Weeks, Steven Wiley *lawyer*
Wilson, Christopher J. *lawyer*
Woodside, Frank C. III *lawyer, educator, physician*
Zavatsky, Michael Joseph *lawyer*
Zealey, Sharon Janine *lawyer*

## Cleveland

Adamo, Kenneth Roberts *lawyer*
Adams, Albert T. *lawyer*
Andorka, Frank Henry *lawyer*
Andrews, Oakley V. *lawyer*
Ashmus, Keith Allen *lawyer*
Austin, Arthur Donald, II, *lawyer, educator*
Bacon, Brett Kermit *lawyer*
Bauer, Fred D. *lawyer*
Bays, James C. *lawyer*
Berick, James Herschel *lawyer*
Binford, Gregory Glenn *lawyer*
Braverman, Herbert Leslie *lawyer*
Bravo, Kenneth Allan *lawyer*
Brennan, Maureen *lawyer*
Brucken, Robert Matthew *lawyer*
Burge, David Alan *lawyer, writer*
Burke, Kathleen B. *lawyer*
Cairns, James Donald *lawyer*
Calkins, Benjamin *lawyer*
Callahan, Thomas James *lawyer*
Carrick, Kathleen Michele *law librarian*
Carson, Van *lawyer*
Clarke, Charles Fenton *lawyer*
Coleman, Deborah Ann *lawyer*
Collin, Thomas James *lawyer*
Conner, William Herbert *lawyer*
Coquillette, William Hollis *lawyer*
Crist, Paul Grant *lawyer*
Cudak, Gail Linda *lawyer*
Currivan, John Daniel *lawyer*
DeMetz, Kathleen Susan *lawyer*
Demitrack, Thomas *lawyer*
DiVenere, Anthony Joseph *lawyer*
Doris, Alan S(anford) *lawyer*
Dorrell, John S. *lawyer, insurance company executive*
Drinko, John Deaver *lawyer*
Dugan, Patrick J. *lawyer*
Duncan, Ed Eugene *lawyer*
Duvin, Robert Phillip *lawyer*
Emrick, Charles Robert, Jr. *lawyer*
Fabens, Andrew Lawrie III *lawyer*
Falsgraf, William Wendell *retired lawyer*
Fay, Regan Joseph *lawyer*
Feinberg, Paul H. *lawyer*
Fischer, Michelle K. *lawyer*
Fletcher, Robert *retired lawyer*
Friedman, Harold Edward *lawyer*
Friedman, James Moss *lawyer*
Ganske, Lyle G. *lawyer*
Glaser, Robert Edward *lawyer*
Goins, Frances Floriano *lawyer*
Gold, Gerald Seymour *lawyer*
Goldfarb, Bernard Sanford *lawyer*
Goler, Michael David *lawyer*
Goodman, David S. *lawyer*
Grossman, Theodore Martin *lawyer*
Hagen, Daniel C. *lawyer*
Haiman, Irwin Sanford *lawyer*
Harris, Paul N *lawyer*
Hastings, Susan C. *lawyer*
Heiman, David Gilbert *lawyer*
Henes, Samuel Ernst *lawyer*
Hochman, Kenneth George *lawyer*
Hoerner, Robert Jack *lawyer*
Hogg, James Stuart *lawyer*
Hollington, Richard Rings, Jr. *lawyer*
Horst, J. Robert *lawyer*

Horvitz, Michael John *lawyer*
Jacobs, Leslie William *lawyer*
Janke, Ronald Robert *lawyer*
Jenks, Carl M. *lawyer*
Jorgenson, Mary Ann *lawyer*
Kahrl, Robert Conley *lawyer*
Karp, Marvin Louis *lawyer*
Katcher, Richard *lawyer*
Katz, Lewis Robert *law educator*
Kelly, Dennis Michael *lawyer*
Kestner, Robert Steven *lawyer*
Kilbane, Catherine M. *lawyer*
Kilbane, Thomas Stanton *lawyer*
Knerly, Stephen John, Jr. *lawyer*
Kohn, William Irwin *lawyer*
Korngold, Gerald *law educator, former dean*
Kramer, Edward George *lawyer*
Kramer, Eugene Leo *lawyer*
Kurit, Neil *lawyer*
Lawniczak, James Michael *lawyer*
Lease, Robert K. *lawyer*
Leavitt, Jeffrey Stuart *lawyer*
Leddy, Patrick John *lawyer*
Leiken, Earl Murray *lawyer*
Lennox, Heather *lawyer*
Lewis, John Bruce *lawyer*
Lewis, John Francis *lawyer*
Lowe, James Allison *lawyer, educator*
Lowenkamp, Cynthia Dellis *lawyer*
Maloney, Mary D. *lawyer*
Marting, Michael G. *lawyer*
Mason, Thomas Albert *retired lawyer*
Mast, Bernadette Mihalic *lawyer*
Mc Cartan, Patrick Francis *lawyer*
McCarthy, Mark Francis *lawyer*
McKee, Thomas Frederick *lawyer*
McLaughlin, Patrick Michael *lawyer*
Mehlman, Maxwell Jonathan *law educator*
Messinger, Donald Hathaway *lawyer*
Meyer, G. Christopher *lawyer*
Millisor, Kenneth Ray *lawyer*
Millstone, David Jeffrey *lawyer*
Moore, Kenneth Cameron *lawyer*
Newman, John M., Jr. *lawyer*
Nicols, Howard J.C. *lawyer*
O'Keefe, Francis Ronald *lawyer*
Ollinger, W. James *lawyer*
Owendoff, Stephen Peter *lawyer*
Pace, Stanley Dan *lawyer*
Pallam, John James *lawyer*
Parobek, Drew Thomas *lawyer*
Pearlman, Samuel Segel *lawyer, educator*
Perris, Terrence George *lawyer*
Perry, George Williamson *lawyer*
Piraino, Thomas Anthony, Jr. *lawyer*
Podboy, Alvin Michael, Jr. *law librarian, director*
Pogue, Richard Welch *lawyer*
Pollock, R. Jeffrey *lawyer*
Putka, Andrew Charles *lawyer*
Rains, M. Neal *lawyer*
Rapp, Robert Neil *lawyer*
Rawson, Rachel L. *lawyer*
Rawson, Robert H., Jr. *lawyer*
Reminger, Richard Thomas *lawyer, artist*
Reppert, Richard Levi *lawyer*
Rickert, Jeanne Martin M. *lawyer*
Roberts-Mamone, Lisa A. *lawyer*
Rosenbaum, Jacob I. *retired lawyer*
Ruben, Alan Miles *law educator*
Sawyer, Raymond Terry *lawyer, consultant, theater producer*
Schaefer, David Arnold *lawyer*
Shapiro, Fred David *lawyer*
Sicherman, Marvin Allen *lawyer*
Slinger, Michael Jeffery *law librarian, director*
Sogg, Wilton Sherman *lawyer*
Solomon, Randall Lee *lawyer*
Stanley, Hugh Monroe, Jr. *lawyer*
Stanton, R. Thomas *lawyer*
Steindler, Howard Allen *lawyer*
Stellato, Louis Eugene *lawyer*
Stevens, Thomas Charles *lawyer*
Stokes, Louis *lawyer, former congressman*
Storey, Robert Davis *lawyer*
Strauch, John L. *lawyer*
Striefsky, Linda A(nn) *lawyer*
Strimbu, Victor, Jr. *lawyer*
Stuhan, Richard George *lawyer*
Summers, William Lawrence *lawyer*
Swartzbaugh, Marc L. *lawyer*
Szaller, James Francis *lawyer*
Thimmig, Diana M. *lawyer*
Thomas, Dynda A. *lawyer*
Toohey, Brian Frederick *lawyer*
Toomajian, William Martin *lawyer*
von Mehren, George M. *lawyer*
Waldeck, John Walter, Jr. *lawyer*
Wallach, Mark Irwin *lawyer*
Watson, Richard Thomas *lawyer*
Weaver, Robin Geoffrey *lawyer, educator*
Weber, Robert Carl *lawyer*
Weiler, Jeffry Louis *lawyer*
White, Gregory A. *prosecutor*
Whitney, Richard Buckner *lawyer*
Withers, Carl Raymond *lawyer*
Wong, Margaret Wai *lawyer*
Young, James Edward *lawyer*
Zambie, Allan John *lawyer*

## Cleveland Heights

Chilcote, Lee A. *lawyer*

## Columbus

Adams, John Marshall *lawyer*
Anderson, Jon Mac *lawyer, educator*
Bailey, Daniel Allen *lawyer*
Barnes, Wallace Ray *retired lawyer*
Bennett, Robert Thomas *lawyer, professional athletics manager*
Berndt, Ellen German *lawyer*
Bridgman, G(eorge) Ross *lawyer*
Brooks, Richard Dickinson *lawyer*
Brown, Herbert Russell *lawyer, writer*
Brown, Philip Albert *lawyer*
Brubaker, Robert Loring *lawyer*
Buchenroth, Stephen Richard *lawyer*
Carnahan, John Anderson *retired lawyer*
Carpenter, Michael H. *lawyer*
Chester, John Jonas *lawyer, educator*
Cross, Jeffrey D. *lawyer, electric power industry executive*
Crowder, Marjorie Briggs *lawyer*

Cvetanovich, Dan L. *lawyer*
DeRousie, Charles Stuart *lawyer*
Di Lorenzo, John Florio, Jr. *retired lawyer*
Dixon, Matthew Richard *lawyer*
Fahey, Richard Paul *lawyer*
Fay, Terrence Michael *lawyer*
Fisher, Lloyd Edison, Jr. *lawyer*
Fried, Samuel P. *lawyer*
Gall, John Ryan *lawyer*
Gibson, Rick J. *lawyer*
Grauer, David W. *lawyer*
Greek, Darold I. *lawyer*
Gross, James Howard *lawyer*
Hairston, George W. *lawyer*
Hardymon, David Wayne *lawyer*
Harwood, Sandra Stabile *lawyer, state representative*
Hatler, Patricia Ruth *lawyer*
Haubiel, Charles W., II, *lawyer*
Hill, Kathleen Blickenstaff *lawyer, nursing educator, mental health nurse*
Hollenbaugh, H(enry) Ritchey *lawyer*
Huffman, Fordham E. *lawyer*
Hutson, Jeffrey Woodward *lawyer*
Johnson, Mark Alan *lawyer*
Keane, John B. *lawyer*
Ketcham, Richard Scott *lawyer*
Kuehnle, Kenton Lee *lawyer*
Kurtz, Charles Jewett III *lawyer*
La Cour, Louis Bernard *retired lawyer*
Liston, Jefferson Edward *lawyer*
Long, Thomas Leslie *lawyer*
Mann, William Craig *lawyer*
Markus, Kent Richard *lawyer*
McConnaughey, George Carlton, Jr. *retired lawyer*
McCutchan, Gordon Eugene *retired lawyer, insurance company executive*
McDermott, Kevin R. *lawyer*
McKenna, Alvin James *lawyer*
Miller, Terry Morrow *lawyer*
Minor, Robert Allen *lawyer*
Mirman, Joel Harvey *lawyer*
Moloney, Thomas E. *lawyer*
Morgan, Dennis Richard *lawyer*
Moul, William Charles *lawyer*
Nissl, Colleen Kaye *lawyer*
Oman, Richard Heer *retired lawyer*
O'Shaughnessy, Christopher T. *lawyer*
Petricoff, M. Howard *lawyer, educator*
Phillips, James Edgar *lawyer*
Pigman, Jack Richard *lawyer*
Pressley, Fred G., Jr. *lawyer*
Quigley, John Bernard *law educator*
Radnor, Alan T. *lawyer*
Ramey, Denny L. *bar association executive director*
Ray, Frank Allen *lawyer*
Reasoner, Willis Irl III *lawyer*
Rector, Susan Darnell *lawyer*
Ridgley, Thomas Brennan *lawyer*
Robinson, Barry R. *lawyer*
Robol, Richard Thomas *lawyer*
Rose, Michael Dean *retired lawyer, educator*
Ryan, Joseph W., Jr. *lawyer*
Saad, Michael D. *lawyer*
Saxbe, William Bart *lawyer, former United States attorney general*
Schrag, Edward A., Jr. *lawyer*
Shane, Peter Milo *law educator*
Sheward, Richard S. *lawyer*
Shumate, Alex *lawyer*
Sidman, Robert John *lawyer*
Sites, Richard Loren *lawyer, educator*
Sowald, Heather Gay *lawyer*
Stein, Arland Thomas *lawyer*
Stern, Geoffrey *lawyer*
Stinehart, Roger Ray *lawyer*
Taggart, Thomas Michael *lawyer*
Tait, Robert E. *lawyer*
Tarpy, Thomas Michael *lawyer*
Thomas, Duke Winston *lawyer*
Todd, William Michael *lawyer*
Tripp, Thomas Neal *lawyer, political scientist*
Turano, David A. *lawyer*
Tyack, Thomas Michael *lawyer*
Walker, Charles Henri *lawyer*
Warner, Charles Collins *lawyer*
Whipps, Edward Franklin *lawyer*
Wightman, Alec *lawyer*
Winkler, John Frederick *lawyer, educator*

## Cuyahoga Falls

Jones, John Frank *retired lawyer*

## Dayton

Burick, Lawrence T. *lawyer*
Carbone, Carrie Elizabeth *lawyer*
Chernesky, Richard John *lawyer*
Farquhar, Robert Nichols *lawyer*
Faruki, Charles Joseph *lawyer*
Hadley, Robert James *lawyer*
Heyman, Ralph Edmond *lawyer*
Hoak, Jonathan S., Sr. *lawyer*
Jenks, Thomas Edward *lawyer*
Johnson, C. Terry *lawyer*
Kinlin, Donald James *lawyer*
Lockhart, Gregory Gordon *prosecutor*
Macklin, Crofford Johnson, Jr. *lawyer*
Rion, John Hayes *lawyer*
Rogers, Richard Hunter *lawyer*
Saul, Irving Isaac *lawyer*
Vaughn, Noel Wyandt *lawyer*
Wasylyna, Victor J. *lawyer*
Wilberding, Merle Francis *lawyer*

## Dublin

Fong, Ivan Kenneth *lawyer*
Maloon, Jerry L. *lawyer, director*
McCorkle, Leon Marshall, Jr. *lawyer, educator*
Tenuta, Luigia *lawyer*
Williams, Paul Stratton *lawyer*

## Eaton

Thomas, James William *lawyer*

## Fairfield

Crane, Debra K. *lawyer*

## Findlay

Kline, James Edward *lawyer*

## Fremont

Magoon, Maggie E. *law educator, director*

## Gambier

Leech, Charles Russell, Jr. *lawyer*

## Howard

Lee, William Johnson *lawyer*

## Hudson

Gentile Sachs, Valerie Ann *lawyer*
Merwin, John David *lawyer, former governor*

## Independence

Kola, Arthur Anthony *lawyer*

## Ironton

Allen, Craig Adams *lawyer, director*

## Jackson

Lewis, Richard M. *lawyer*

## Kettering

Eubank, David Lynn *lawyer, consultant*

## Lakewood

McAndrews, James Patrick *lawyer*

## Lancaster

Libert, Donald Joseph *lawyer*

## Lima

Robenalt, John Alton *lawyer*

## Marietta

Fields, William Albert *lawyer*

## Marysville

Aronowitz, David M. *lawyer, chemicals executive*

## Massillon

Netzly, Dwight H. *lawyer*

## Maumee

Burchinow, Naran U. *lawyer*
Fallat, Dale William *lawyer*
Marsh, Benjamin Franklin *lawyer*
Tuschman, James Marshall *lawyer*
Witherell, Dennis Patrick *lawyer*

## Miamisburg

Byrd, James Everett *lawyer*

## Middletown

Horn, David C. *lawyer*
Rathman, William Ernest *retired lawyer, minister*

## Moreland Hills

Groetzinger, Jon, Jr. *lawyer, pharmaceutical executive*

## Mount Vernon

Ressing, Thomas Garrett *lawyer*

## Newark

Mantonya, John Butcher *lawyer*
Mencer, Jetta *lawyer*
Meyer, Christopher Richard *lawyer*

## North Canton

Dettinger, Warren Walter *lawyer*

## Oregon

Bryce, Robert W. *lawyer*

## Orrville

Harlan, M. Ann *lawyer*

## Painesville

Orosz, Richard Thomas *lawyer*

## Pepper Pike

Schnell, Carlton Bryce *lawyer*

## Saint Marys

Kemp, Barrett George *lawyer*

## Salem

Goll, Geoffrey Steven *lawyer*

## Seaman

Young, Vernon Lewis *retired lawyer*

## Shaker Heights

Bates, Walter Alan *retired lawyer*
Ekelman, Daniel Louis *lawyer*

## Springfield

Harkins, Daniel Conger *lawyer*
Lagos, James Harry *lawyer*

## Terrace Park

Naylor, Paul Donald *retired lawyer*

## Toledo

Anspach, Robert Michael *lawyer*
Baehren, James W. *lawyer*
Baker, Richard Southworth *lawyer*
Dalrymple, Thomas Lawrence *retired lawyer*
Jackson, Reginald Sherman, Jr. *lawyer, educator*
Krull, Stephen Keith *lawyer*
La Rue, Carl Forman *lawyer*
O'Connell, Maurice Daniel *lawyer*
Pletz, Thomas Gregory *lawyer*
St. Clair, Donald David *lawyer*
Skiver, Stephen Allen *lawyer, physician*
Spitzer, John Brumback *lawyer*
Webb, Thomas Irwin, Jr. *lawyer, director*
Wicklund, David Wayne *lawyer*

## Warren

Rossi, Anthony Gerald *lawyer*

## Westerville

Helvey, Edward Douglas *lawyer*
Young, Sheldon Mike *lawyer, author*

## Westlake

Donahue, Charles Bertrand, II, *lawyer*

Skulina, Thomas Raymond *lawyer*

**Wickliffe**
Kidder, Fred Dockstater *retired lawyer*

**Willoughby**
Driggs, Charles Mulford *lawyer*

**Wooster**
Kennedy, Charles Allen *lawyer*

**Worthington**
Albert, Robert Hamilton *lawyer*
Brinkman, Dale Thomas *lawyer*

**Xenia**
Chappars, Timothy Stephen *lawyer*

**Youngstown**
Roth, Daniel Benjamin *lawyer, engineering company executive*
Rupeka, Robert W. *court administrator*

**Zanesville**
Micheli, Frank James *lawyer*

## OKLAHOMA

**Altus**
Oden, Waldo Talmage, Jr. *lawyer*

**Bartlesville**
Connor, James William *lawyer*

**Broken Arrow**
Stewart, Murray Baker *retired lawyer*

**Chandler**
Swanson, Robert Lee *lawyer*

**Cherokee**
Stein, Sam Lee *lawyer*

**Claremore**
Steidley, Juan Dwayne *lawyer, judge*

**Edmond**
Lester, Andrew William *lawyer*
Loving, Susan Brimer *lawyer, former state official*

**Enid**
Jones, Stephen *lawyer*

**Frederick**
Evans, Michael D. *lawyer*

**Guthrie**
Davis, Frank Wayne *lawyer*

**Guymon**
Wood, Donald Euriah *retired lawyer*

**Mcalester**
Cornish, Richard Pool *lawyer*

**Muskogee**
Sperling, Sheldon J. *prosecutor*

**Noble**
Winchell, Michael George *lawyer*

**Norman**
Fairbanks, Robert Alvin *lawyer*
Petersen, Catherine Holland *lawyer*

**Oklahoma City**
Askins, Jari *lawyer, department chairman, state representative*
Bailey, Burck *lawyer*
Balkman, Thad *lawyer, state representative*
Boaz, Stephen Scott *lawyer*
Brophy, Alfred Laurence III *law educator*
Calvey, Kevin *lawyer, state representative*
Cargill, Lance *lawyer, state representative*
Court, Leonard *lawyer, educator*
Cunningham, Stanley Lloyd *lawyer*
Derrick, Gary Wayne *lawyer*
Fenton, Elliott Clayton *lawyer*
Garbrecht, Robert I. *lawyer*
Hanna, Terry Ross *lawyer, small business owner*
Hood, Henry J. *lawyer, energy executive*
Johnson, Robert Max *lawyer*
Kenney, John Arthur *lawyer*
Kline, David Adam *lawyer, educator, writer*
Legg, William Jefferson *lawyer*
Ligon, Duke R. *lawyer*
MacDougall, Vicki Lawrence *law educator, writer*
Manchester, Susan Jean *lawyer, artist*
Mather, Stephanie June *lawyer*
McCampbell, Robert Garner *lawyer, former prosecutor*
Moler, Edward Harold *retired lawyer*
Morgan, Fred *lawyer, state representative*
Nelon, Robert Dale *lawyer*
Nesbitt, Charles Rudolph *lawyer, energy executive, consultant*
Neville, Jack L. (Drew), Jr. *lawyer*
Ogle, James David (David Ogle) *lawyer*
Pain, Betsy M. *lawyer*
Paul, William George *lawyer*
Richter, John Charles *prosecutor*
Rockett, D. Joe *lawyer, director*
Ross, William Jarboe *lawyer*
Ryan, Patrick M. *lawyer*
Shinn, Ronald Theodore *lawyer*
Steinhorn, Irwin Harry *lawyer, educator, corporate financial executive*
Stong, Roger Alan *lawyer*
Stringer, L. E. (Dean Stringer) *retired lawyer*
Tompkins, Raymond Edgar *lawyer*
Towery, Curtis Kent *lawyer*
Tuepker, Max C. *lawyer*
Turpen, Michael Craig *lawyer*
Venters, Harley Eugene *lawyer*
Walsh, Lawrence Edward *lawyer*
Woods, Harry Arthur, Jr. *lawyer*
Yuill, Barbara Krebs *lawyer*

**Ponca City**
Northcutt, Clarence Dewey *lawyer*
Raley, John Wesley, Jr. *lawyer*

**Poteau**
Sanders, Douglas Warner, Jr. *lawyer, judge*

**Pryor**
Stinson, Marion Dennis *lawyer, land use planner, judge*

**Sapulpa**
Gardner, Dale Ray *lawyer*

**Sayre**
Brooks, David Eugene *lawyer*

**Stillwater**
Clark, Gary Carl *lawyer*
DeLacerda, Melissa Griner *lawyer*
Fischer, Richard Samuel *lawyer*

**Tinker Afb**
Livingston, Douglas Mark *lawyer*

**Tulsa**
Affeldt, Thomas Michael *lawyer*
Arrington, John Leslie, Jr. *lawyer*
Balman, Steven K. *lawyer*
Barker, John Roy *lawyer*
Belsky, Martin Henry *law educator, dean*
Biolchini, Robert Fredrick *lawyer*
Boudreau, Daniel J. *law educator, retired state supreme court justice*
Bryant, Hubert Hale *lawyer*
Cooper, Richard Casey *lawyer*
Crawford, B. *lawyer*
Davenport, Gerald Bruce *lawyer*
Eagleton, Edward John *lawyer*
Eldridge, Richard Mark *lawyer*
Engel, David Wayne *lawyer, federal official*
Farrell, John L., Jr. *lawyer, consultant, corporate financial executive*
Frey, Martin Alan *lawyer, educator*
Gaberino, John Anthony, Jr. *lawyer*
Hatfield, Jack Kenton *lawyer, accountant*
Hooper, George Getman *lawyer*
Howard, Gene Claude *lawyer, retired state senator*
Huckin, William Price, Jr. *prosecutor*
Huffman, Robert Allen, Jr. *lawyer*
Imel, John Michael *lawyer*
Johnson, Cornelius Raymond *prosecutor*
Kihle, Donald Arthur *lawyer*
Langenkamp, R. Dobie *law educator, lawyer*
Luthey, Graydon Dean, Jr. *lawyer, educator*
O'Meilia, David E. *prosecutor, lawyer*
Plumb, Charles Sumner III *lawyer*
Schuller, Stephen Arthur *lawyer*
Slicker, Frederick Kent *lawyer*
Steltzlen, Janelle Hicks *lawyer*
Strecker, David Eugene *lawyer*
Sturdivant, James M. *lawyer*
Sutton, Jonathan Mark *lawyer*
Walker, Floyd Lee *lawyer*
Williamson, Walter Bland *lawyer*

**Vinita**
Johnston, Oscar Black III *lawyer*

**Yukon**
Hixson, Wendell Mark *lawyer*

## OREGON

**Beaverton**
Vardavas, Stephanie J. *lawyer*

**Brookings**
Maxwell, William Stirling *retired lawyer*

**Central Point**
Ingraham, Laura *lawyer, political commentator*
Richardson, Dennis Michael *lawyer, educator*

**Corvallis**
Achterman, Gail Louise *lawyer*
Frohnmayer, John Edward *lawyer, writer*

**Dayton**
Anderson, Herbert Hatfield *lawyer, farmer*

**Eugene**
Aldave, Barbara Bader *lawyer, educator*
DuPriest, Douglas Millhollen *lawyer*
Hildreth, Richard G. *law educator, lawyer*
Jacobson, Jon L. *law educator*
Lowry, Robert Dudley *lawyer*
Scoles, Eugene Francis *lawyer, educator*

**Jacksonville**
O'Connor, Karl William (Goodyear Johnson) *retired lawyer*

**Lake Oswego**
Hill, Gary D. *lawyer*
Kuntz, Joel Dubois *lawyer*

**Lincoln City**
Arant, Eugene Wesley *lawyer*

**Mcminnville**
Thompson, Robert Samuel *retired lawyer*

**Medford**
Carter, William G. *lawyer*
Deatherage, William Vernon *lawyer*

**Oregon City**
Lounsbury, Steven Richard *lawyer*

**Portland**
Abravanel, Allan Ray *lawyer*
Arthur, Michael Elbert *lawyer, investment advisor*
Backlar, Byron *lawyer*
Bauman, Frank Anthony *retired lawyer*
Bernstine, Daniel O'Neal *law educator, academic administrator*
Brenneman, Delbert Jay *lawyer*

Cable, John Franklin *lawyer*
Canaday, Richard A. *lawyer*
Chevis, Cheryl Ann *lawyer*
Clark, Jennie L. *lawyer, webmaster*
Cook, Nena *lawyer*
Crowell, John B., Jr. *lawyer, former government official*
Dailey, Dianne K. *lawyer*
Dubanevich, Keith Scott *lawyer*
Eakin, Margaretta Morgan *lawyer*
English, Stephen Francis *lawyer*
Epstein, Edward Louis *lawyer*
Ernst, David A. *lawyer*
Fell, James Frederick *lawyer*
Feuerstein, Howard M. *lawyer*
Foley, Ridgway Knight, Jr. *lawyer, writer*
Franzke, Richard Albert *lawyer*
Glasgow, William Jacob *lawyer, venture capitalist, business executive*
Greene, Herbert Bruce *lawyer, investor, entrepreneur*
Grossmann, Ronald Stanyer *lawyer*
Hanlon, Michael Gregory *lawyer*
Harnden, Edwin A. *lawyer*
Helmer, M(artha) Christie *lawyer*
Hinkle, Charles Frederick *lawyer, educator*
Hinshaw, Robert Edward *lawyer*
Houser, Douglas Guy *lawyer*
Immergut, Karin J. *prosecutor*
Jarvis, Peter R. *lawyer*
Johnson, Mark Andrew *lawyer*
Jolles, Bernard *lawyer*
Josephson, Richard Carl *lawyer*
Kanter, Stephen *lawyer, educator, dean*
Kennedy, Jack Leland *lawyer*
Kester, Randall Blair *lawyer*
Knoll, James Lewis *lawyer*
Larpenteur, James Albert, Jr. *retired lawyer*
Livingston, Louis Bayer *lawyer*
Love, William Edward *lawyer*
Lowry, David Burton *lawyer*
Maloney, Robert E., Jr. *lawyer*
Margolin, Phillip Michael *lawyer*
Matarazzo, Harris Starr *lawyer*
McKelvey, Connie Elkins *lawyer*
Miller, William Richey, Jr. *lawyer*
Mowe, Gregory Robert *lawyer*
Noonan, William Donald *lawyer, physician*
Nunn, Robert Warne *lawyer*
Purcell, John F. *lawyer*
Richardson, Campbell *retired lawyer*
Richter, Peter Christian *lawyer*
Rosen, Steven O. *lawyer*
Ryan, John Duncan *lawyer*
Sand, Thomas Charles *lawyer*
Schuster, Philip Frederick, II, *lawyer, writer, educator*
Simpson, Robert Glenn *lawyer*
Snyder, Joan Paula *lawyer*
Stewart, Milton Roy *lawyer*
Stone, Richard James *lawyer*
Sullivan, Edward Joseph *lawyer*
Tongue, Thomas Healy *lawyer*
Tucker, Roy W. *lawyer*
Van Valkenburg, Edgar Walter *lawyer*
Waggoner, James Clyde *lawyer*
Westwood, James Nicholson *lawyer*
Whinston, Arthur Lewis *lawyer*
White, Douglas James, Jr. *lawyer*
Williamson, Charles Ready III *lawyer*
Wilson, Owen Meredith, Jr. *lawyer, mediator, arbitrator*
Wood, Marcus Andrew *lawyer*
Zalutsky, Morton Herman *lawyer*

**Salem**
Abrams, Marc *lawyer, political organization worker*
Breen, Richard F., Jr. *law librarian, lawyer, educator*
Haselton, Rick Thomas *lawyer*
Mannix, Kevin Leese *lawyer, political organization executive*
Nafziger, James Albert Richmond *law educator*
Swaim, Michael E. *lawyer, former mayor*

**Sandy**
Rieke, Forrest Neill *lawyer*

**Wilsonville**
Ekman, Donald J. *lawyer, retail executive*

## PENNSYLVANIA

**Abington**
Bildersee, Robert Alan *lawyer*

**Allentown**
Altemose, Mark Kenneth *lawyer*
Brown, Robert Wayne *lawyer*
Brown, W(illiam) Douglas *lawyer*
Holt, Leon Conrad, Jr. *lawyer, chemicals executive*
McGinley, Paul Anthony, Jr. *lawyer*
Noonan, Charles Thomas *lawyer*

**Allison Park**
Ewalt, Henry Ward *lawyer*
Herrington, John David III *retired lawyer, director*
Ries, William Campbell *lawyer*
Rulis, Christopher C. *lawyer*

**Ardmore**
Heinzen, Bernard George *lawyer*

**Bala Cynwyd**
Garrity, Vincent Francis, Jr. *lawyer*
Lundy, Joseph E. *lawyer*
Schwartz, Jeffrey Byron *lawyer*
Shiekman, Philip Miner *lawyer*
Wiener, Thomas Eli *lawyer*

**Bensalem**
Stern, Colin D. *lawyer, retail executive*

**Berwyn**
Seidel, Arthur Harris *lawyer*
Watters, Edward McLain III *lawyer*
Wood, Thomas E. *lawyer*

**Bethlehem**
Leeson, Joseph Francis, Jr. *lawyer*
Spry, Donald Francis, II, *lawyer*

**Blue Bell**
Elliott, John Michael *lawyer*
Rounick, Jack A. *lawyer, clothing retail executive*
Sundheim, Nancy Straus *lawyer*
Swansen, Samuel Theodore *lawyer*

**Brookville**
Achille, John G. *lawyer*

**Bryn Mawr**
Carbine, Sharon *lawyer*
Frick, Benjamin Charles *lawyer*
Mezvinsky, Edward M. *lawyer*
Narin, Stephen B. *lawyer*

**Camp Hill**
Mackin, Charles Philip, Jr. *lawyer*
Sari, Robert B. *lawyer, retail executive*

**Canonsburg**
Williams, Stuart Alan *lawyer, educator*

**Carlisle**
Butler, William Elliott *lawyer, educator*

**Chadds Ford**
Cohen, Felix Asher *lawyer*
Gordon, William Edmund, Jr. *lawyer*
Whitney, Douglas Edgar, Sr. *retired lawyer*

**Clarion**
Pope, Kent Smith *lawyer*

**Clarks Summit**
Beemer, John Barry *lawyer*

**Conshohocken**
Bramson, Robert Sherman *lawyer*

**Danville**
Gubbiotti, Christine M. *lawyer*

**Downingtown**
Wusinich, Joseph F. III *lawyer, educator*

**Doylestown**
Elliott, Richard Howard *lawyer*

**Easton**
Brown, Robert Carroll, Jr. *lawyer*
Scheer, Joel Martin *lawyer*

**Edinboro**
Travis, Grant Carner *lawyer*

**Elkins Park**
Myers, Kenneth Raymond *lawyer*

**Erie**
Thelin, Stephen Russell *lawyer*
Van Gorder, Jan Reid *lawyer, insurance company executive*
Yochim, Joseph Adolph *lawyer*

**Etters**
Steps, Barbara Jill *lawyer*

**Exton**
Hedges, Donald Walton *lawyer*

**Fayetteville**
Molitor, Graham Thomas Tate *lawyer*

**Fogelsville**
Hauck, Jeffrey Peter Artorius Martel *lawyer, protective services official*

**Frazer**
Osborn, John Edward *lawyer, pharmaceutical industry executive, former government official*

**Frenchville**
Hicks, James Thomas *lawyer, physician*

**Gettysburg**
Benfield, Ann Kolb *lawyer*

**Gladwyne**
Acton, David *lawyer*
Booth, Harold Waverly *lawyer, finance company executive*

**Glassport**
Lippard, Thomas Eugene *lawyer*

**Grove City**
McBride, Milford Lawrence, Jr. *lawyer*

**Harleysville**
Browne, Michael Leon *lawyer*
Kauffman, Robert A. *lawyer*

**Harrisburg**
Adams, Barbara *lawyer*
Angino, Richard Carmen *lawyer*
Barasch, David M. *lawyer, former prosecutor*
Brenner, Thomas Edward *lawyer*
Cline, Andrew Haley *lawyer*
Dejoie, Louis Armand *lawyer, management consultant*
Diehm, James Warren *lawyer, educator*
Fine, David R. *lawyer*
Golden, Thomas M. *lawyer*
Hanson, Robert DeLolle *retired lawyer*
Kane, Yvette *lawyer, judge*
Kelly, Robert Edward, Jr. *lawyer*
Klein, Michael D. *lawyer*
Kope, Shane Brien *lawyer*
Kraus, David Robert *lawyer*
Lappas, Spero Thomas *lawyer*
Meilton, Sandra L. *lawyer*
Miller, Leslie Anne *lawyer*
Scaringi, Melanie Walz *lawyer*
Sheldon, J. Michael *lawyer, educator*
Strouss, Carleton O. *lawyer*

Sullivan, John Cornelius, Jr. *lawyer*
Warshaw, Allen Charles *lawyer*
West, James Joseph *lawyer*
Zavacky, Susan Kline *law librarian*

**Haverford**
Mathews, Timothy Newlyn *lawyer*
Palmer, Richard Ware *retired lawyer*
Stiller, Jennifer Anne *lawyer*
Stroud, James Stanley *retired lawyer*

**Havertown**
Bala, Gary Ganesh *lawyer, financial planner*
Siegel, Daniel Joel *lawyer*

**Hershey**
Snyder, Burton Harold *lawyer*

**Horsham**
Best, Franklin Luther, Jr. *lawyer*

**Huntingdon Valley**
Krzyzanowski, Richard L. *lawyer*

**Jenkintown**
Bales, John Foster III *retired lawyer*
Dickstein, Joan Borteck *arbitrator, consultant*
Kaiser, Tracy Misson *paralegal, educator*

**Jones Mills**
Fish, Paul Waring *lawyer*

**Kennett Square**
Conard, Alfred Fletcher *legal educator*
Partnoy, Ronald Allen *lawyer*

**King Of Prussia**
Gilbert, Bruce Rits *lawyer*
Schneider, Pam Horvitz *lawyer*

**Kingston**
Meyer, Martin Jay *lawyer*

**Lake Harmony**
Polansky, Larry Paul *legal association administrator*

**Lancaster**
Babic, Michael Walter *lawyer*
Burkholder, Michele Stawinski *lawyer*
Nast, Dianne Martha *lawyer*
Rigas, John Nicholas *lawyer*
Zimmerman, Donald Patrick *lawyer*

**Latrobe**
Greenfield, David W. *lawyer*

**Lawrenceville**
Castagnera, James Ottavio *lawyer, journalist*

**Lewisburg**
Fernsler, John Paul *lawyer*

**Malvern**
Cameron, John Clifford *lawyer, health science association administrator*
Liu, Don H. *lawyer*

**Mc Murray**
Brzustowicz, John Cinq-Mars *lawyer*
Sherry, John Sebastian *lawyer*

**Media**
Blake, David Gordon *lawyer*
Durham, James W. *lawyer*
Emerson, Sterling Jonathan *lawyer*
Ewing, Robert Clark *lawyer*
Garrison, Susan Kay *lawyer*
Heller, Richard Martin *lawyer, educator*

**Mendenhall**
Reinert, Norbert Frederick *lawyer, retired chemicals executive*
Stone, F. L. Peter *lawyer*

**Moon Township**
Alstadt, Lynn Jeffery *lawyer*

**Murrysville**
Ferri, Karen Lynn *lawyer*

**New Buffalo**
Cramer, John McNaight *lawyer*

**New Kensington**
Wallace, Henry Jared, Jr. *lawyer*

**Newtown**
Kardos, Mel D. *lawyer, educator*
Zicherman, David L. *lawyer, educator, financial consultant*

**Newtown Square**
Kendall, Robert Louis, Jr. *lawyer*

**Norristown**
Aman, George Matthias III *lawyer*
Britt, Earl Thomas *lawyer*
Devine, James I. *lawyer*
Rees, Thomas Dynevor *lawyer*

**Philadelphia**
Aaron, Kenneth Ellyot *lawyer*
Abramowitz, Robert Leslie *lawyer*
Adamany, David Walter *law and political science educator, former academic administrator*
Adler, Matthew *law educator*
Allen-Castellitto, Anita LaFrance *law educator*
Ammon, Gary D. *lawyer*
Anders, Jerrold P. *lawyer*
Angel, Marina *law educator*
Arem, Lawrence Jay *lawyer*
Austin, Regina *law educator*
Auten, David Charles *lawyer*
Auten, Donald R. *lawyer*
Awad, George John *lawyer*
Bachman, Arthur *lawyer*
Baker, Stephen C. *lawyer*
Barnett, Bonnie Allyn *lawyer*

Barrett, John J., Jr., (John James Barrett Jr.) *lawyer*
Barton, Thomas J. *lawyer*
Battipaglia, Joseph Anthony *lawyer*
Beck, Phyllis Whitman *lawyer, retired judge*
Berger, David *lawyer*
Berger, Harold *lawyer, electrical engineer*
Berger, Lawrence Howard *lawyer*
Berkley, Emily Carolan *lawyer*
Berkman, Richard Lyle *lawyer*
Bernard, John Marley *lawyer, educator*
Bernheim, Daniel S. *lawyer*
Bershad, Jack R. *retired lawyer*
Beyer, Aaron Jay *lawyer*
Binder, David Franklin *lawyer, writer*
Black, Allen Decatur *lawyer*
Black, Creed C., Jr. *lawyer*
Blume, Fred *lawyer*
Boggia, Eugene Stephen *lawyer*
Bogutz, Jerome Edwin *lawyer, educator*
Bonovitz, Sheldon M. *lawyer*
Boss, Amelia Helen *lawyer, educator*
Bovaird, Brendan Peter *lawyer*
Brandt, Jennifer Anne *lawyer*
Bressler, Barry E. *lawyer*
Brier, Bonnie Susan *lawyer*
Briscoe, Jack Clayton *lawyer*
Brookman, Marc D. *lawyer*
Brooman, David J. *lawyer*
Brown, Stephen D. *lawyer*
Brown, William Hill III *lawyer*
Browne, Stanhope Stryker *lawyer*
Bryans, Henry S. *lawyer*
Buchholz, Carl M. *lawyer*
Burbank, Stephen Bradner *law educator*
Burde, Howard Alan *lawyer*
Burdumy, Stephen T. *lawyer*
Cades, Stewart Russell *lawyer, communications executive*
Calvert, Jay H., Jr. *lawyer*
Cannon, John III *lawyer*
Carroll, Mark Thomas *lawyer*
Casper, Charles B. *lawyer*
Chang, Howard Fenghau *law educator, consultant*
Chanin, Bernard *lawyer*
Cherken, Harry Sarkis, Jr. *lawyer*
Child, John Sowden, Jr. *lawyer*
Chimples, George *lawyer*
Christenbury, T. Daniel *lawyer*
Clark, Peter S., II, *lawyer*
Clark, William H., Jr. *lawyer*
Clauss, Peter Otto *lawyer*
Clothier, Robert Clarkson *lawyer*
Coleman, Robert J. *lawyer*
Colli, Bart Joseph *lawyer*
Collings, Robert L. *lawyer*
Comisky, Hope A. *lawyer*
Congdon, Charles B. *lawyer*
Connor, Joseph Patrick III *lawyer*
Cooney, J(ohn) Gordon, Jr. *lawyer*
Cooper, Frank G. *lawyer*
Cox, Roger Frazier *lawyer*
Coyne, Charles Cole *lawyer*
Cozen, Stephen Allen *lawyer*
Cramer, Harold *lawyer*
Crawford, James Douglas *lawyer*
Damsgaard, Kell Marsh *lawyer*
D'Angelo, Christopher Scott *lawyer*
Davis, Alan Jay *lawyer*
Delacato, Carl Henry *lawyer*
deLisle, Jacques *law educator*
Del Raso, Joseph Vincent *lawyer*
Dennis, Andre L. *lawyer*
Devlin, John Gerard *lawyer, writer*
Diaz, Nelson A. *lawyer*
Dichter, Mark S. *lawyer*
Donohue, James J. *lawyer*
Donohue, John Patrick *lawyer*
Dorfman, John Charles *lawyer*
Drake, William Frank, Jr. *lawyer*
Dubin, Leonard *lawyer*
Duffy, Seamus C. *lawyer*
Dworetzky, Joseph Anthony *lawyer, city manager*
Efstratiades, Anastasius *lawyer*
Esser, Carl Eric *lawyer*
Ewald, William Bragg III *law educator, philosopher*
Ey, Robert M. *law librarian*
Faberman, Austin S. *lawyer*
Fader, Henry Conrad *lawyer*
Fala, Herman C. *lawyer*
Feirson, Steven B. *lawyer*
Feldman, Eric Adam *law educator, academic administrator*
Fickler, Arlene *lawyer*
Fiebach, H. Robert *lawyer*
Finkelstein, Claire *law educator*
Finkelstein, Joseph Simon *lawyer*
Flanagan, Joseph Patrick, Jr. *retired lawyer*
Floyd, Michael O'S. *lawyer*
Fodera, Leonard V. *lawyer*
Frank, George Andrew *lawyer*
Frank, Harvey *lawyer, writer*
Fritton, Karl Andrew *lawyer*
Gadon, Steven Franklin *lawyer*
Garcia, Rudolph *lawyer*
Genkin, Barry Howard *lawyer*
Girard-diCarlo, David Franklin *lawyer*
Goldberg, Joseph *lawyer*
Goldstein, William Marks *lawyer*
Goodman, Stephen Murry *lawyer*
Goodrich, Herbert Funk, Jr. *lawyer*
Gorberg, David J. *lawyer*
Gordon, Sarah Barringer *law educator*
Grant, M. Duncan *lawyer*
Grant, Richard W. *lawyer*
Grove, David Lavan *lawyer*
Haimm, Neil Keith *lawyer*
Haines, Clifford E. *lawyer*
Haley, Vincent Peter *retired lawyer*
Hamilton, Stephen David Derwent *lawyer*
Hangley, William Thomas *lawyer*
Harkins, John Graham, Jr. *lawyer*
Harris, Judith E. *lawyer*
Harvey, Gregory Merrill *lawyer*
Haviland, Bancroft Dawley *lawyer*
Henrich, William Joseph, Jr. *lawyer*
Hickok, D. Alicia *lawyer*
Hoelscher, Robert James *lawyer*
Hoffman, Alan Jay *lawyer*
Howard, David Miles *lawyer*

Hunter, James Austen, Jr. *lawyer*
Johnston, Jason Scott *law educator*
Jones, Robert Jeffries *lawyer*
Kahn, James Robert *lawyer*
Kaier, Edward John *lawyer*
Kaplinsky, Alan S. *lawyer*
Kassner, Andrew Charles *lawyer*
Katz, Leo *law educator*
Kessler, Alan Craig *lawyer*
Kiernan, Edward Philip *lawyer*
Kiniry, William F., Jr. *lawyer*
Klasko, Herbert Ronald *lawyer, educator, writer*
Klein, Howard Bruce *lawyer, law educator*
Kline, Thomas Richard *lawyer*
Knoll, Michael Steven *law educator*
Koc, Lorraine K(iessling) *lawyer*
Kopp, Charles Gilbert *lawyer*
Kraeutler, Eric *lawyer*
Kreimer, Seth F. *law educator, lawyer*
Krekstein, Michael Harry *lawyer*
Kûbler, Friedrich Karl *law educator*
Laguzzi, Carina *lawyer*
Lasher, Lori L. *lawyer*
Lavorgna, Gregory Joseph *lawyer*
Ledwith, John Francis *lawyer*
Leech, Noyes Elwood *lawyer, educator*
Lefton, Ira S. *lawyer*
Lehr, Michael L. *lawyer*
Leonard, Thomas *lawyer*
Levensten, Scott David *lawyer*
Levering, Kathryn H. *lawyer*
Levin, A. Leo *law educator, retired government official*
Levin, Murray Simon *lawyer*
Lewis, John Hardy, Jr. *lawyer*
Libonati, Michael Ernest *law educator, writer*
Lichtenstein, Robert Jay *lawyer*
Lipman, Frederick D. *lawyer, writer, law educator*
Lombard, John James, Jr. *lawyer, writer*
Lonergan, Robert A. *lawyer*
Love, William Allan *lawyer, educator*
Loveless, George Group *retired lawyer*
MacGregor, David Bruce *lawyer*
Madva, Stephen Alan *lawyer*
Magaree, W(illiam) Scott III *lawyer*
Magaziner, Fred Thomas *lawyer*
Malloy, Michael P. *lawyer*
Mann, Bruce H. *law educator, historian*
Mann, Theodore R. *lawyer*
Mannino, Edward Francis *lawyer, educator*
Mattoon, Peter Mills *lawyer*
McCausland, Margaret A. *lawyer, educator*
McConnel, W. Bruce *lawyer*
McGarrigle, Thomas J. *lawyer*
McHugh, James Joseph *lawyer*
McKeever, John Eugene *lawyer*
McKenzie, James W., Jr. *lawyer*
McMenamin, Richard F. *lawyer*
McQuiston, Robert Earl *lawyer*
Meehan, Patrick Leo *prosecutor*
Meigs, John Forsyth *lawyer*
Melinson, Gregg R. *lawyer*
Meyers, Howard L. *lawyer*
Michel, H. John, Jr. *lawyer*
Milbourne, Walter Robertson *lawyer*
Miller, Henry Franklin *lawyer*
Milone, Francis Michael *lawyer*
Mirabello, Francis Joseph *lawyer*
Molitor, Steven John *lawyer*
Mooney, Charles William, Jr. *law educator*
Morris, Thomas Bateman, Jr. *lawyer*
Morse, Stephen J. *law educator*
Moss, Arthur Henshey *lawyer*
Nicholas, Robert A. *lawyer*
O'Connor, Joseph A., Jr. *lawyer*
Ominsky, Alan Jay *lawyer, medical educator*
Ominsky, Harris *lawyer*
O'Reilly, Timothy Patrick *lawyer*
Pagliaro, James Domenic *lawyer*
Panitch, Ronald Louis *lawyer*
Pappert, Jerry (Gerald J. Pappert) *lawyer, former state attorney general*
Parchomovsky, Gideon *law educator*
Parry, William DeWitt *lawyer*
Pollack, Michael *lawyer*
Pollack, William Bruce *lawyer*
Price, Robert Stanley *lawyer*
Promislo, Daniel *lawyer, small business owner*
Putnam, Alfred W., Jr. *lawyer*
Rabinowitz, Mark I. *lawyer*
Rachofsky, David J. *lawyer*
Rackow, Julian Paul *lawyer*
Ramsey, Natalie D. *lawyer*
Reed, Michael Haywood *lawyer*
Reich, Abraham Charles *lawyer*
Reiss, John Barlow *lawyer*
Reitz, Curtis Randall *lawyer, educator*
Rhodes, Alice Graham *lawyer, not-for-profit developer, consultant*
Roberts, Carl Geoffrey *lawyer*
Robinson, Paul Harper *lawyer, educator*
Rock, Edward Baron *law educator*
Romano, Carmen J. *lawyer*
Roosevelt, Kermit *law educator*
Rosenberg, Howell K. *lawyer*
Rosenbloom, Morey Stephen *lawyer*
Ross, Daniel R. *lawyer*
Ross, Murray Louis *lawyer*
Saint-Antoine, Paul Hewitt *lawyer*
Samuel, Ralph David *lawyer*
Sanchirico, Chris William *law educator*
Satinsky, Barnett *lawyer*
Schachtman, Nathan A. *lawyer*
Scheppele, Kim Lane *law educator*
Scher, Howard Dennis *lawyer*
Schneider, Carl William *lawyer*
Schneider, Richard Graham *lawyer*
Schoff, Dennis L. *lawyer*
Schorling, William Harrison *lawyer*
Scott, Donald Allison *retired lawyer*
Segal, Robert Martin *lawyer*
Sharbaugh, Thomas J. *lawyer*
Shay, Kathleen M. *lawyer*
Sheils, Denis Francis *lawyer*
Shestack, Jerome Joseph *lawyer*
Shiekman, Lawrence Zeid *lawyer*
Shropshire, Kenneth L. *law educator*
Shuldiner, Reed *law educator*
Siegel, Bernard Louis *lawyer*
Sigmond, Richard Brian *lawyer*
Simkanich, John Joseph *lawyer, engineer*

Skeel, David Arthur *law educator*
Smith, John Francis III *lawyer*
Solano, Carl Anthony *lawyer*
Spaeth, Edmund Benjamin, Jr. *retired lawyer, retired law educator, former judge*
Spector, Martin Wolf *lawyer*
Spolan, Harmon Samuel *lawyer*
Sprague, Richard A. *lawyer*
Steinberg, Robert Philip *lawyer*
Stern, Eric L. *lawyer*
Stern, Joan Naomi *lawyer*
Strasbaugh, Wayne Ralph *lawyer*
Strickler, Matthew M. *lawyer*
Stuart, Glen R(aymond) *lawyer*
Stuntebeck, Clinton A. *lawyer*
Summers, Clyde Wilson *law educator*
Suplee, Dennis Raymond *lawyer*
Swain, Clifford H. *lawyer*
Sweet, James M. *lawyer*
Szautner, Christian Andreas *lawyer*
Taney, Francis Xavier, Jr. *lawyer*
Temin, Michael Lehman *lawyer*
Tepper, H. Marc *lawyer*
Tiger, Ira Paul *retired lawyer*
Vaira, Peter Francis *lawyer*
Wachter, Michael L. *law and finance educator*
Wajert, Sean Peter *lawyer*
Walters, Christopher Kent *lawyer*
Wax, Amy Laura *law educator*
Webb, William Yerick *lawyer*
Weil, Jeffrey George *lawyer*
Weinstein, David *lawyer, educator*
Weisberg, Morris L. *retired lawyer*
Wellington, Ralph Glenn *lawyer*
Whiteside, William Anthony, Jr. *retired lawyer*
Wiener, Ronald Martin *lawyer*
Wild, Richard P. *lawyer*
Wittels, Barnaby Caesar *lawyer, writer*
Wolff, Deborah H(orowitz) *lawyer*
Wright, Minturn Tatum III *retired lawyer*
Wrobleski, Jeanne Pauline *lawyer*
Yaruss, Howard Seth *lawyer*
Zuckerman, Brian David *lawyer*

**Pittsburgh**
Abbott, Kevin Charles *lawyer*
Allen, Rachel Lorey *lawyer*
Aronson, Mark Berne *retired lawyer, advocate*
Artz, John Curtis *lawyer*
Basinski, Anthony Joseph *lawyer*
Beck, Paul A. *lawyer*
Bissoon, Cathy *lawyer*
Bleier, Michael E. *lawyer, director*
Blenko, Walter John, Jr. *lawyer*
Blum, Eva Tansky *lawyer*
Booker, Daniel I. *lawyer*
Boswell, William Paret *lawyer*
Brendel, John S. *lawyer*
Brown, David Ronald *lawyer*
Brownlee, David A. *lawyer*
Buchanan, Mary Beth *prosecutor*
Burkoff, John Michael *law educator*
Cahouet, Ann P. *lawyer*
Cameron, Douglas E. *lawyer*
Candris, Laura A. *lawyer*
Caroselli, William R. *lawyer*
Cheever, George Martin *lawyer*
Colen, Frederick Haas *lawyer*
Coney, Aims C., Jr. *lawyer, labor-management negotiator*
Connors, Eugene Kenneth *lawyer, educator*
Cooper, Thomas Louis *lawyer*
Cowan, Barton Zalman *lawyer*
Damico, David A. *lawyer*
Daniel, Robert Michael *lawyer*
Davis, Lewis U., Jr. *lawyer*
DeForest, Walter Pattison III *lawyer*
Delano, Jonathan William *lawyer, journalist*
Demmler, John Henry *retired lawyer*
DeNinno, David L. *lawyer*
Donnelly, Thomas Joseph *lawyer, director*
Doty, Robert Walter *lawyer*
Dugan, John F. *lawyer*
Dunlop, Scott Graham *lawyer*
Ehrenwerth, David Harry *lawyer*
Ellsworth, Laura E. *lawyer*
Evans, Bruce Dwight *lawyer*
Fawcett, David B. III *lawyer*
Flechtner, Harry Marshal *law educator*
Flinn, Michael James *lawyer*
Frank, Ronald William *lawyer*
Frolik, Lawrence Anton *law educator, lawyer, consultant*
Geeseman, Robert George *lawyer*
Goldberg, Mark Joel *lawyer*
Guadagnino, Frank T. *lawyer*
Hackett, Mary J. *lawyer*
Halpern, Richard I. *lawyer*
Hartman, Ronald G. *lawyer*
Harty, James Quinn *lawyer*
Hellman, Arthur David *law educator, consultant*
Hershey, Dale *lawyer, educator*
Hershey, Nathan *lawyer, educator*
Hill, John Howard *retired lawyer*
Hitt, Leo N. *lawyer, educator*
Hollinshead, Earl Darnell, Jr. *lawyer*
Holsinger, Candice Doreen *lawyer, accountant*
Hull, John Daniel, IV, *lawyer*
Hurnyak, Christina Kaiser *lawyer*
Johnson, Robert Alan *lawyer*
Jones, Craig Ward *retired lawyer*
Jones, James M. *lawyer*
Jordan, Gregory B. *lawyer*
Kalis, Peter John *lawyer*
Kenrick, Charles William *lawyer*
Ketter, David Lee *lawyer*
King, Robert Alan *lawyer*
Klett, Edwin L. *lawyer*
Knox, Charles Graham *lawyer*
Leech, Frederick C. *lawyer*
Leibowitz, Marvin *lawyer*
Lerman, Terry Allen *lawyer*
Litman, Roslyn Margolis *lawyer*
London, Alan E. *lawyer*
Lovett, Robert G. *lawyer*
Lyncheski, John E. *lawyer*
Mahone, Glenn R. *lawyer*
McCartney, Robert Charles *retired lawyer*
McDevitt, Jerry S. *lawyer*
McGough, Walter Thomas, Jr. *lawyer*
McLaughlin, John Sherman *lawyer*
Meisel, Alan *law educator*

Messner, Robert Thomas *lawyer, bank executive*
Miller, James Robert *lawyer*
Mulvihill, Keithley D. *lawyer*
Murdoch, David Armor *lawyer*
Murrin, Regis Doubet *lawyer*
Mutterperl, William Charles *lawyer, corporate financial executive*
Naugle, Louis A. *lawyer*
Newlin, William Rankin *lawyer*
Nogay, Arlie R. *lawyer*
Norris, James Harold *lawyer*
Ober, Russell John, Jr. *lawyer*
O'Connor, Edward Gearing *lawyer*
Olson, Stephen M(ichael) *lawyer*
Orsatti, Ernest Benjamin *lawyer*
Phillips, Larry Edward *lawyer*
Picadio, Anthony Peter *lawyer*
Plowman, Jack Wesley *lawyer*
Pohl, Paul Michael *lawyer*
Powderly, William H. III *lawyer*
Pudlin, Helen Pomerantz *lawyer*
Pugliese, Robert Francis *lawyer, manufacturing executive*
Pusateri, David P. *lawyer*
Randolph, Robert DeWitt *lawyer*
Raynovich, George, Jr. *retired lawyer*
Reed, W. Franklin *lawyer*
Restivo, James John, Jr. *lawyer*
Rosenberger, Bryan David *lawyer*
Scheinholtz, Leonard Louis *lawyer*
Schwab, Arthur James *lawyer*
Schwendeman, Paul William *lawyer*
Shuman, Joseph Duff *lawyer*
Silverman, Arnold Barry *lawyer*
Singer, Paul Meyer *lawyer*
Sokulski, Gary A. *law firm executive*
Strader, James David *lawyer*
Stroyd, Arthur Heister, Jr. *lawyer*
Sweeney, Clayton Anthony *lawyer, business executive*
Symons, Edward Leonard, Jr. *lawyer, educator, investment advisor*
Tarasi, Louis Michael, Jr. *lawyer*
Thompson, Thomas Martin *lawyer*
Thurman, Andrew Edward *lawyer*
Turner, Harry Woodruff *lawyer*
Ubinger, John Walter, Jr. *lawyer*
Ummer, James Walter *lawyer*
Unkovic, John Clark *lawyer*
Van Kirk, Thomas L. *lawyer*
Vater, Charles J. *lawyer*
Veeder, Peter Greig *lawyer*
Vogrin, Joseph Edward III *lawyer*
Walton, Jon David *lawyer*
Weiss, Marcia J. *lawyer, educator*
Williams, Stephen Edward *lawyer*
Wycoff, William Mortimer *lawyer*
Yorsz, Stanley *lawyer*

**Radnor**
Bertolino, Dean A. *lawyer*
Simon, David Frederick *lawyer*

**Reading**
LePage, Clifford Bennett, Jr. *lawyer*
Linton, Jack Arthur *lawyer*
Rothermel, Daniel Krott *lawyer, bank executive*

**Reynoldsville**
Wheeler, Mark Andrew, Sr. *lawyer*

**Scranton**
Burke, Henry Patrick *lawyer*
Haggerty, James Joseph *lawyer*
Marino, Thomas A. *prosecutor, lawyer*

**Solebury**
Cross, Robert William *lawyer, venture capitalist*
Valentine, H. Jeffrey *legal association executive*

**Spring City**
Mayerson, Hy *lawyer*

**Spring House**
Rosoff, William A. *lawyer*

**Springfield**
Maclay, Donald Merle *retired lawyer*

**Swarthmore**
Elman, Gerry Jay *lawyer*

**Trevose**
Totaro, Samuel C., Jr. *lawyer*

**Uniontown**
Coldren, Ira Burdette, Jr. *lawyer*

**Valley Forge**
Mesher, John R. *lawyer*
Sprague, William Douglas *lawyer*

**Villanova**
Bersoff, Donald Neil *lawyer, educator, psychologist*
Maule, James Edward *law educator*
Murphy, John Francis *law educator, consultant*
Scheffler, Stuart Jay *lawyer*
Zearfoss, Herbert Keyser *retired lawyer*

**Washington**
Lerner, William C. *lawyer*
Posner, David S. *lawyer*
Richman, Stephen I. *lawyer*

**Wayne**
Gross, Lawrence Alan *lawyer*
Wilson, Bruce Brighton *lawyer, retired transportation executive*

**West Chester**
Babcock, Charles Witten, Jr. *lawyer*
Ewing, Joseph Neff, Jr. *retired lawyer*
Kaufman, Daniel J. *lawyer*
Lamb, William H. *lawyer, former state supreme court justice*
Teti, Louis Nicholas *lawyer*

**West Conshohocken**
Odell, Herbert *lawyer*

Teillon, Louis Pierre, Jr. *lawyer*

**Wilkes Barre**
O'Donnell, Catherine Rose *lawyer*

**Williamsport**
Carlucci, William Philip *lawyer*

**York**
Addison, Brian Michael *lawyer*
Davis, Jane G. *lawyer*
Hoffmeyer, William Frederick *lawyer, educator*

## RHODE ISLAND

**Barrington**
Soutter, Thomas Douglas *retired lawyer*

**Bristol**
Flanders, Robert G., Jr. *lawyer, educator, legal association administrator*

**Cranston**
Alston, Jametta O. *lawyer*
Tammelleo, A. David *lawyer, editor, publisher*

**East Greenwich**
Dence, Edward William, Jr. *lawyer, bank executive*

**Hope Valley**
Walker, Howard Ernest *lawyer*

**Newport**
McConnell, David Kelso *lawyer*
Scheck, Frank Foetisch *retired lawyer*

**Pawtucket**
Belliveau, Kathrin Pagonis *lawyer*
Nagler, Barry *lawyer*

**Portsmouth**
Levie, Howard S. (Howard Sidney Levie) *lawyer, educator*

**Providence**
Berkelhammer, Robert Bruce *lawyer*
Bulman, John *lawyer*
Carlotti, Stephen Jon *lawyer*
Conley, Patrick T. *lawyer, writer, historian, educator, real estate developer*
Corrente, Robert Clark *prosecutor*
Curran, Joseph Patrick *lawyer*
Donnelly, Kevin William *lawyer*
Edwards, James King *retired lawyer*
Farrell, Margaret Dawson *lawyer*
Ferruolo, Stephen Carl *lawyer, historian*
Fogarty, Edward Michael *lawyer*
Gamboli, Michael A. *lawyer*
Gasbarro, Pasco, Jr. *lawyer*
Johnson, Vahe Duncan *lawyer*
Jones, Lauren Evans *lawyer*
Kean, John Vaughan *retired lawyer*
Kraemer, Michael Frederick *lawyer*
Licht, Richard A. *lawyer*
Lipsey, Howard Irwin *lawyer, educator*
Lynch, William Joseph *lawyer*
McAndrew, Thomas Joseph *lawyer*
McCann, Gail Elizabeth *lawyer*
McElroy, Michael Robert *lawyer*
McIntyre, Jerry L. *lawyer*
Mittleman, Richard Samuel *lawyer*
Nails, Kenneth H. *lawyer*
Roney, John M. *lawyer*
Salter, Lester Herbert *lawyer*
Sherman, Deming Eliot *lawyer*
Staples, Richard Farnsworth *lawyer*
Weinstein, Philip Merrill *lawyer*

**Scituate**
Gorham, Bradford *lawyer*

**Warwick**
Knowles, Charles Timothy *lawyer, state legislator, military officer, educator*
St. Pierre, Michael A. *lawyer*

**Westport**
Grodd, Leslie Eric *lawyer*

**Woonsocket**
Lankowsky, Zenon P. *lawyer, retail executive*
Roszkowski, Joseph John *lawyer*

## SOUTH CAROLINA

**Aiken**
Amabile, John Louis *lawyer*
Pearce, Richard Lee *lawyer*
Rudnick, Irene Krugman *lawyer, educator, former state legislator*

**Beaufort**
Harvey, William Brantley, Jr. *lawyer, retired lieutenant governor*

**Bluffton**
Edgett, William Maloy *lawyer, arbitrator*

**Charleston**
Bell, James L. *lawyer*
Branham, C. Michael *lawyer*
Cox, Walter Thompson III *lawyer, law educator, retired federal judge*
Dominick, Paul Allen *lawyer*
Donnem, Roland William *retired lawyer, real estate developer, health facility administrator*
Farr, Charles Sims *lawyer*
Fenno, Edward Thorndike *lawyer*
Freer, Robert Elliott, Jr. *lawyer*
Grant, J. Kirkland *lawyer, educator*
Kahn, Ellis Irvin *lawyer*
McCullough, Ralph Clayton, II, *law educator*
Musheff, Todd M. *lawyer*
Patrick, Charles William, Jr. *lawyer*
Robinson, Neil Cibley, Jr. *lawyer*
Rosen, Richard S. *lawyer*

**Clemson**
Cox, Headley Morris, Jr. *lawyer, educator*

**Columbia**
Anderson, Charles Hill *lawyer*
Arthur, Hugh Thomas (H. Thomas Arthur II) *lawyer*
Arvay, Nancy Joan *lawyer*
Bernstein, Barry Joel *lawyer*
Blanton, Hoover Clarence *lawyer*
Cotty, William Frank (Bill Cotty) *lawyer, state legislator*
deHolczer, Paul *lawyer*
Finkel, Gerald Michael *lawyer*
Gibbes, William Holman *lawyer*
Gray, Elizabeth Van Doren *lawyer*
Handel, Richard Craig *lawyer*
Harvey, Jonathan Matthew *lawyer*
Huggins, Laura H. *lawyer*
Land, John Calhoun III *lawyer, state legislator*
Lloyd, Reginald Ivan *prosecutor*
Matthews, Steve Allen *lawyer*
McCutchen, Thomas English, Jr. *lawyer*
McLeod, Walton James *lawyer, state legislator*
Mood, Francis P., Jr. *lawyer, utilities executive*
Morrison, Stephen George *lawyer*
Nexsen, Julian Jacobs *lawyer*
Sowell, Thornwell F. (Biff) *lawyer*
Swerling, Jack Bruce *lawyer*
Tate, Harold Simmons, Jr. *lawyer*
Yarborough, Clinton Joseph *lawyer*

**Conway**
Martin, Gregory Keith *lawyer, mayor*

**Graniteville**
Bell, Robert Morrall *lawyer*

**Greenville**
Edwards, Harry LaFoy *lawyer*
Estridge, Larry D. *lawyer*
Ferguson, Donald Littlefield *retired lawyer*
Grubbs, R(obert) Howard *lawyer*
Horton, James Wright *retired lawyer*
Hutson, Melvin Robert *lawyer*
Massey, Raymond David *lawyer*
Mauldin, John Inglis *public defender*
McKinney, Ronald W. *lawyer*
Oxner, George Dewey, Jr. *lawyer*
Phillips, Joseph Brantley, Jr. *lawyer*
Riley, Richard Wilson *lawyer, former federal official*
Smoak, Lewis Tyson *lawyer*
Todd, John Dickerson, Jr. *retired lawyer*
Walters, Johnnie McKeiver *lawyer*
Wyche, Cyril Thomas *lawyer*
Wyche, Madison Baker III *lawyer*

**Greenwood**
Nexsen, Julian Jacobs, Jr. *lawyer*

**Hilton Head Island**
Becker, Karl Martin *lawyer*
Esposito, John Vincent *lawyer*
Hagoort, Thomas Henry *lawyer*

**Irmo**
Brown, Leonard Ashleigh (Smokey), Jr. *lawyer*

**Johns Island**
Carter, Mary Andrews *paralegal*

**Lexington**
Lide, Vinton DeVane *lawyer*

**Mount Pleasant**
Glenn, Edward Vernon Ferrell *lawyer, consultant*

**Myrtle Beach**
Breen, David Hart *lawyer*

**Newberry**
Partridge, William Franklin, Jr. *lawyer*
Partridge, III, W. F. *lawyer, defender*

**Rock Hill**
Hardin, James Carlisle III *lawyer, educator*

**Spartanburg**
Dineen, Joseph Lawrence *legal association administrator, consultant*
Smith, William Douglas *lawyer*

**Walterboro**
Cone, George Wallis *lawyer*

## SOUTH DAKOTA

**Aberdeen**
Richards, Carlyle Edward *lawyer*

**Britton**
Farrar, Frank Leroy *lawyer, former governor*

**Ipswich**
Beck, Vaughn Peter *lawyer*

**Pierre**
Gerdes, David Alan *lawyer*
Johnson, Julie Marie *lawyer, lobbyist, judge*
Riter, Robert C., Jr. *lawyer*
Thompson, Charles Murray *lawyer*

**Plankinton**
Bucher, Steven John *lawyer*

**Rapid City**
Foye, Thomas Harold *lawyer*
Goodsell, G. Verne *lawyer*
Helmers, Steven J. *lawyer, energy executive*

**Sioux Falls**
Hayes, Robert E. *lawyer*
Jackley, Martin J. (Marty Jackley) *prosecutor*
Knapp, Thomas Joseph *lawyer*
Marshall, Mark F. *lawyer*
Tapken, Michelle G. *prosecutor*
Welk, Thomas John *lawyer*

## TENNESSEE

**Brentwood**
Blackstock, James Fielding *lawyer*
Mc Creary, James Franklin *lawyer, mediator*
Provine, John Calhoun *retired lawyer*

**Bristol**
Bellamy, John A.A. *lawyer*

**Chattanooga**
Bahner, Thomas Maxfield *lawyer*
Campbell, Paul III *lawyer*
Peck, Douglas Edward *lawyer*
Summers, Gerald Howard (Jerry Summers) *lawyer*

**Collierville**
Springfield, James Francis *retired lawyer, banker*

**Covington**
Gordon, J. Houston *lawyer, political organization worker*

**Fayetteville**
Dickey, John Harwell *lawyer*

**Franklin**
Sutter, Lawrence A. *lawyer, educator*

**Goodlettsville**
Lanigan, Susan S. *lawyer*

**Humboldt**
Boyte, George Griffin *lawyer*

**Johnson City**
Epps, James Haws III *lawyer*

**Jonesborough**
Jenkins, Ronald Wayne *lawyer, engineer, mediator*

**Knoxville**
Coleman, Shannon DeShae *lawyer, educator*
Congleton, Joseph Patrick *lawyer, preservationist*
Dedrick, James R. *prosecutor*
Dillard, W. Thomas *lawyer*
Galligan, Thomas C., Jr. *law educator*
Hebbeler, Regis J. *lawyer*
Lucas, John Allen *lawyer*
Rayson, Edwin Hope *lawyer*
Reynolds, Glenn Harlan *law educator*
Ritchie, Albert *lawyer*
Wheeler, John Watson *lawyer*
Worthington, Carole Yard Lynch *lawyer*
Worthington, Robert Fletcher *lawyer*

**Mc Ewen**
Williams, John Lee *lawyer*

**Memphis**
Allen, Newton Perkins *lawyer*
Bobango, John Allen *lawyer*
Broadhurst, Jerome Anthony *lawyer*
Buckner, Thomas Randolph *lawyer*
Carr, Oscar Clark III *lawyer*
Clark, Ross Bert, II, *lawyer*
Clippard, Richard F. *prosecutor*
Cody, Walter James Michael *lawyer, retired state attorney general*
Cook, August Joseph *lawyer, accountant*
Doggrell, Henry Patton *lawyer*
Goldsmith, Harry Louis *lawyer*
Haltom, William H. *lawyer*
Harvey, Albert C. *lawyer*
Heiter, Matthew Stephen *lawyer*
Jackson, Thomas Francis III *lawyer*
Johnson, Harry A. III *lawyer, finance company executive*
Kustoff, David F. *prosecutor*
Ledbetter, Paul Mark *lawyer, writer*
Masterson, Kenneth Rhodes *lawyer*
Matthews, Paul Aaron *lawyer*
McClusky, Lorna S. *lawyer*
Morgan, Colby Shannon, Jr. *lawyer*
Noel, Randall Deane *lawyer*
Norris, Charles Head *lawyer, manufacturing executive*
Pope, Thaddeus Mason *law educator*
Rutledge, Roger Keith *lawyer*
Schuler, Walter T. *lawyer*
Scroggs, Larry Kenneth *lawyer, state legislator*
Smith, Maura Abeln *lawyer, paper company executive*
Steinhauer, Gillian *lawyer*
Tate, Stonewall Shepherd *lawyer*
Trammell, Bradley Ellis *lawyer*
White, Nicholas L. *law educator*
Winchester, Richard Lee, Jr. *lawyer*

**Nashville**
Barfield, Henry Lee, II, *lawyer*
Baskette, Roger DuVal, Sr. *lawyer*
Bass, James Orin, Sr. *lawyer*
Belton, Robert *law educator*
Bloch, Frank Samuel *law educator*
Blumstein, James Franklin *law educator, lawyer, consultant*
Bostick, Charles Dent *retired lawyer*
Cantrell, Luther E., Jr. *lawyer*
Cheek, James H. III *lawyer, educator*
Cobb, Stephen A. *lawyer*
Cohen, Stephen Ira *lawyer, state legislator*
Cohen, William Mark *lawyer*
Covington, Robert Newman *law educator*
Cowart, Richard G. *lawyer*
Day, John Arthur *lawyer*
Dennen, Keith Cameron *lawyer*
Edge, Kathryn Reed *lawyer*
Edwards, Mark E. *lawyer*
Gannon, John Sexton *lawyer, management consultant, arbitrator, mediator*
Gillmor, John Edward *lawyer*
Griffith, James Leigh *lawyer*
Grimes, R. Dale *lawyer*
Hardin, Edward Lester, Jr. *lawyer*
Hart, Richard Banner *lawyer*
Jacobs, Sharon O. *lawyer*
King, David A. *lawyer*
Ledyard, Robins Heard *lawyer*
Lodge, J. Richard *lawyer*

Lyon, Philip Kirkland *lawyer*
Madu, Leonard Ekwugha *lawyer, human rights advocate, columnist*
Maier, Harold Geistweit *lawyer, educator*
Martin, Henry Alan *public defender*
May, Joseph Leserman (Jack May) *retired lawyer*
Mayden, Barbara Mendel *lawyer*
Norris, Thomas Bryant *lawyer*
Norwood, E(dward) Andrew *lawyer*
Pinkley, Thomas Harold *lawyer*
Quinlan, J(oseph) Michael *lawyer*
Ramsaur, Allan Fields *legal association administrator, lobbyist*
Rubin, Edward *law educator, dean*
Schirg, Brandon Michael *lawyer*
Schreiber, Kurt Gilbert *lawyer*
Sims, Wilson *lawyer*
Stuart, Donald Bruce *lawyer*
Tarpley, John R. *lawyer*
Thomas, Randall Stuart *lawyer, educator*
Thomas, Robert Paige *lawyer*
Thompson, Jennifer Lynn *lawyer*
Tuke, Robert Dudley *lawyer, educator*
Vines, James K. *prosecutor, lawyer*
Viscusi, W(illiam) G. Kip *law and economics educator*
Waterman, Robert A. *lawyer*
Yuspeh, Alan Ralph *lawyer, health company executive*

**Pigeon Forge**
Catron, Stephen Barnard *lawyer, real estate developer, director*

**Powell**
Hyman, Roger David *lawyer*

**Sevierville**
Waters, John B. *lawyer*

**Soddy Daisy**
Leitner, Paul Revere *lawyer*

**Trenton**
Smith, Jeffrey A. *lawyer*

**Union City**
Graham, Hardy Moore *lawyer*

**Waverly**
Peeler, William James *lawyer*


**TEXAS**

**Abilene**
Boone, Billy Warren *lawyer, retired judge*
Hacker, Gary Lee *lawyer*
Sartain, James Edward *lawyer*

**Addison**
Beck, Charles Wesley, II, *lawyer*

**Amarillo**
Madden, Wales Hendrix, Jr. *lawyer*

**Arlington**
Goodman, Toby Ray *lawyer*

**Austin**
Allday, Martin Lewis, Jr. *lawyer*
Anderson, David Arnold *law educator*
Anton, Richard Henry *lawyer*
Baker, Mark Bruce *lawyer, educator*
Bass, Robert Clifford, Jr. *lawyer*
Blunck, Tedde *lawyer, engineer, engineering company executive*
Bobbitt, Philip Chase *law educator, writer*
Boehm, John C., Jr. *lawyer*
Botsford, David L. *lawyer*
Brown, Frank Beverly, IV, *lawyer*
Buell, Samuel W. *law educator, lawyer*
Cannon, James Washington, Jr. *lawyer*
Cantú, Norma V. *law educator, former federal official*
Churgin, Michael Jay *law educator*
Clark, Pat English *lawyer*
Cook, J(ohn) Rowland *lawyer*
Cook, Michael L. *lawyer*
Cruz, Ted *lawyer*
Cunningham, Judy Marie *lawyer*
Davis, Robert Larry *lawyer*
Demond, Walter Eugene *lawyer*
De Rose, Peter Louis *lawyer*
Dougherty, John Chrysostom III *retired lawyer*
Dyer, Cromwell Adair, Jr. *lawyer, legal association administrator*
Ewell, Gary L. *lawyer*
Feazell, Vic *lawyer*
Fernandes, Edward F. *lawyer*
Gallerano, Andrew John *lawyer*
Gangstad, John Erik *lawyer*
Gary, James M. *lawyer*
Gibbins, Bob *lawyer*
Giblin, Pamela M. *lawyer*
Goldstein, E. Ernest *lawyer, consultant*
Golemon, Ronald Kinnan *lawyer*
Graglia, Lino Anthony *lawyer, educator*
Graham, Seldon Bain, Jr. *lawyer, engineer*
Greene, John Joseph *lawyer*
Greig, Brian Strother *lawyer*
Hale, Louis Dewitt *lawyer*
Hamilton, Dagmar Strandberg *lawyer, educator*
Hamilton, Robert Woodruff *retired legal association administrator, retired law educator*
Harris, Catherine Kirk *law librarian*
Harrison, Richard Wayne *lawyer*
Helman, Stephen Jody *lawyer*
Henderson, George Ervin *lawyer*
Ikard, Frank Neville, Jr. *lawyer*
Janes, Brandon Chaison *lawyer*
Jentz, Gaylord Adair *law educator*
Killough, David E. *lawyer*
Kirk, Terrence *lawyer*
Knepp, Christopher A. *lawyer*
Lochridge, Lloyd Pampell, Jr. *lawyer*
Lochridge, Patton G. *lawyer*
Marshall, Richard Paul, Jr. *lawyer*
McCullough, Frank Witcher III *lawyer*

McDaniel, Myra Atwell *lawyer, former state official*
McKetta, John J. III *lawyer*
Mersky, Roy Martin *law educator, legal association administrator*
Morton, R. Steven *lawyer*
Moss, Bill Ralph *lawyer*
Moss, Logan Vansen *lawyer*
Mullenix, Linda Susan *law educator*
Osborne, Duncan Elliott *lawyer*
Otto, Byron Leonard *lawyer, state agency administrator*
Parrish, William M. *lawyer*
Pena, Richard *lawyer*
Phillips, Thomas Royal *lawyer, former state supreme court chief justice*
Pirkey, Louis Thomas *lawyer*
Prather, Laura Lee *lawyer, educator*
Probus, Michael Maurice, Jr. *lawyer*
Ritchey, Brent Dylan *lawyer*
Roan, Forrest Calvin, Jr. *lawyer*
Sampson, John J. *law educator*
Schuurman, Willem Gerhard *lawyer*
Schwartz, Aaron Robert *lawyer, former state legislator*
Sherman, Max Ray *lawyer, dean, former state senator*
Strauser, Robert Wayne *lawyer*
Sturley, Michael F. *law educator*
Sutton, John F., Jr. *lawyer, educator, dean*
Temple, Larry Eugene *lawyer*
Tottenham, Terry Oliver *lawyer*
Volk, William R. *lawyer*
Voyles, Robb Lawrence *lawyer*
Watkins, Joe Bill *lawyer*
Weddington, Sarah Ragle *lawyer, educator*
Weinberg, Louise *law educator, writer*
Weinman, Daryl Gail *lawyer*
Weintraub, Russell Jay *lawyer, educator*
Wentworth, Earl Jeffrey *lawyer, realtor, state legislator*
West, Royce *lawyer, state legislator*
Westbrook, Jay Lawrence *law educator*
Winters, Sam *lawyer*
Wood, Donald F. *lawyer*

**Beaumont**
Black, Robert Allen *lawyer*
Dowell, James Dale *lawyer*
Dryden, Woodson E. *lawyer*
Johnson, Leanne *lawyer*
Orwig, Matthew Dane *prosecutor, lawyer*
Payne, James Erick *lawyer*
Scofield, Louis M., Jr. *lawyer*

**Bellaire**
Jacobus, Charles Joseph *lawyer, title company executive, writer*
Kramer, Adam Miles *lawyer*
Lilienstern, O. Clayton *lawyer, educator*

**Brenham**
Moorman, Richard Hal, IV, *lawyer*

**Brownfield**
Hammons, Allen James, Jr. *lawyer*

**Bryan**
Miller, Thomas Eugene *lawyer, writer*

**Bullard**
Mote, Clyde A *lawyer*

**Carrollton**
Abney, Sherrie R. *lawyer, mediator, arbitrator*
Riggs, Arthur Jordy *retired lawyer*

**Cleburne**
MacLean, John Ronald *lawyer*

**College Station**
Godfrey, Cullen Michael *lawyer, academic administrator*

**Colleyville**
Whittenberg, Ira Orville *lawyer*

**Conroe**
Bowersox, Thomas H. *lawyer*

**Corpus Christi**
Branscomb, Harvie, Jr. *lawyer*
Potter, Allan L. *lawyer*
Watts, Mikal C. *lawyer*

**Dallas**
Acker, Rodney *lawyer*
Ackerman, Deborah *lawyer*
Adams, Richard Lloyd *lawyer*
Aldous, Charla G. *lawyer*
Anderson, Barbara McComas *lawyer*
Anderson, E. Karl *lawyer*
Anglin, Michael Williams *lawyer*
Babcock, Charles Lynde, IV, *lawyer*
Baggett, W. Mike *lawyer*
Bangs, Nelson A. (Tony Bangs) *lawyer*
Barbour, David A. *lawyer*
Baron, Frederick M. *lawyer*
Becker, Jeffrey M. *lawyer*
Beuttenmuller, Rudolf William *lawyer*
Bickel, John W., II, *lawyer*
Birkeland, Bryan Collier *lawyer*
Bliss, Robert Harms *lawyer*
Boone, Michael Mauldin *lawyer*
Brainin, Stacy L. *lawyer*
Bramblett, George, Jr. *lawyer*
Brin, Royal Henry, Jr. *lawyer*
Bromberg, Alan Robert *law educator, lawyer*
Brooks, Ben A. *lawyer*
Bumpas, Stuart Maryman *lawyer*
Burke, William Temple, Jr. *lawyer*
Cain, David H. *lawyer, former state legislator*
Cantrill, Thomas H. *lawyer*
Carpenter, Gordon Russell *retired lawyer, banker*
Case, Thomas Louis *lawyer*
Chase, J. Scott *lawyer*
Clark, Robert Murel, Jr. *lawyer*
Cloutman, Edward Bradbury III *lawyer*
Coggins, Paul Edward, Jr. *lawyer*
Coleman, James Edwin, Jr. *lawyer*

Coleman, Robert Winston *lawyer*
Collins, Bruce W. *lawyer*
Colson, Randall Elwin *lawyer*
Conner, Terry W. *lawyer*
Copley, Edward Alvin *lawyer*
Cowart, T(homas) David *lawyer*
Cowles, Jim E. *lawyer*
Cox, John Michael *lawyer*
Crain, Russell Jon *lawyer*
Creel, Luther Edward III *lawyer*
Crichton, Thomas, IV, *lawyer*
Crotty, Robert Bell *lawyer*
Crowley, James Worthington *retired lawyer, investor, financial consultant*
Daly, Gail M. *law librarian, educator*
Davis, Clarice McDonald *lawyer*
Davis, Joe A. *lawyer*
Dawson, William B. *lawyer*
Deckelman, William L., Jr. *lawyer*
Demarest, Sylvia M. *lawyer*
Doke, Marshall J., Jr. *lawyer*
Drapkin, Dennis B. *lawyer*
Dutton, Diana Cheryl *lawyer*
Dyess, Bobby Dale *lawyer*
Eaton, Michael William *lawyer, educator*
Egan, Byron F. *lawyer*
Eichman, John C. *lawyer*
Ellis, Alfred Wright (Al Ellis) *lawyer*
Emery, Herschell Gene *lawyer*
Estep, Robert Lloyd *lawyer*
Everbach, Otto George *lawyer*
Fanning, Barry Hedges *lawyer*
Farquhar, Robert Michael *lawyer*
Feld, Alan David *lawyer*
Fenner, Suzan Ellen *lawyer*
Fifield, William O. *lawyer*
Figari, Ernest Emil, Jr. *lawyer, educator*
Fijolek, Richard M. *lawyer*
Fillmore, Robert M. *lawyer*
Finkelstein, William Berndt *lawyer*
Flanagan, Christie Stephen *lawyer*
Flegle, Jim L. *lawyer*
Forshey, Michael S. *lawyer*
Fortado, Michael George *lawyer*
Franze, Laura Marie *lawyer*
Freling, Richard Alan *lawyer*
French, Joseph Jordan, Jr. *lawyer*
Freytag, Sharon Nelson *lawyer*
Frisbie, Curtis Lynn, Jr. *lawyer*
Galvin, Charles O'Neill *law educator*
Gardner, Stephen Henry *lawyer*
Garner, Bryan Andrew *law educator, consultant, writer*
Garner, Daniel C. *lawyer*
Gilchrist, Henry *lawyer*
Glancy, Walter John *lawyer*
Glendenning, Don Mark *lawyer*
Godwin, Donald Everett *lawyer*
Gompf, Henry L. (Hank) *lawyer*
Goodstein, Barnett Maurice *lawyer*
Goolsby, Michelle *lawyer, food products executive*
Gores, Christopher Merrel *lawyer*
Greef, Charles E. (Stormy Greef) *lawyer*
Grzych, Kari Shelton *lawyer*
Hammond, Herbert J. *lawyer, arbitrator, mediator*
Hartnett, Will Ford *lawyer*
Hartt, Grover III *lawyer*
Hennessy, Daniel Kraft *lawyer*
Henry, Vic Houston *lawyer*
Hensley, Noel M. B. *lawyer*
Hernandez, Frank Patrick *lawyer, judge*
Hicks, Marion Lawrence, Jr., (Larry Hicks) *lawyer*
Hinshaw, Chester John *lawyer*
Hirschman, Karen L. *lawyer*
Hollingsworth, John Mark *lawyer*
Holmes, James Hill III *lawyer*
Hubach, Francis P. (Frank), Jr. *lawyer*
Huffman, Gregory Scott Combest *lawyer*
Hughes, Vester Thomas, Jr. *lawyer*
Humble, Monty Garfield *lawyer*
Hurwitz, Ann *lawyer*
Hutchison, Ray Ray (E. Ray Hutchison) *lawyer*
Israeloff, Sim *lawyer, mayor*
Jayson, Melinda Gayle *lawyer*
Jessup, Clifton R., Jr. *lawyer*
Jordan, William Davis *lawyer*
Keithley, Bradford Gene *lawyer*
Kennedy, Marc J. *lawyer*
Kent, David Charles *lawyer*
Kerr, Guy Hardie *lawyer*
Kinnebrew, Jackson Metcalfe *lawyer*
Kinzie, Jack L. *lawyer*
Kitner, David N. *lawyer*
Kneipper, Richard Keith *lawyer*
Kobdish, George Charles *lawyer*
Kober, John A. *lawyer*
Kroney, Robert Harper *lawyer*
Kuhn, Willis Evan, II, *lawyer, mediator*
Lacy, John Ford *retired lawyer*
Ladik, Steven M. *lawyer*
Lan, Donald Paul, Jr. *lawyer*
Lastelick, Jerry *lawyer*
Leatherbury, Thomas Shawn *lawyer*
Lee, Carl B. *lawyer*
Lee, George Terry, Jr. *lawyer*
Lindley, Hamilton P. *lawyer*
Lowe, John Stanley *law educator*
Lowenberg, Michael *lawyer*
Lowery, David J. *lawyer*
Makel, Larry A. *lawyer*
Mankoff, Ronald Morton *retired lawyer*
Manteuffel, Robert Lee *lawyer*
Mareiniss, Darren Peter *lawyer, physician*
Maris, Stephen S. *lawyer, educator*
Martin, Boe Willis *lawyer*
Massman, Richard Allan *lawyer*
Mayo, Thomas William *law educator*
McAtee, David Ray *lawyer*
McCombs, David Louis *lawyer*
McCurley, Mary Johanna *lawyer*
McDole, Sydney Bosworth *lawyer*
Mc Elhaney, John Hess *lawyer*
McGowan, Patrick Francis *lawyer*
McKnight, Joseph Webb *lawyer, educator, historian*
McNamara, Lawrence John *lawyer*
McNamara, Martin Burr *lawyer, former gas industry executive*
McNeil, Barry *lawyer*
McWilliams, Mike C. *lawyer*
Menges, John Kenneth, Jr. *lawyer*

Micciche, Daniel John *lawyer*
Mighell, Kenneth John *lawyer*
Miller, Charles P. *lawyer*
Miller, R. Terry *lawyer*
Mills, Jerry Woodrow *lawyer*
Mitchell, Patrick E. *lawyer*
Montgomery, Will S. *lawyer*
Moore, Cheryl Jerome (Cheryl Milkes Jerome) *lawyer*
Moore, Edward Warren *lawyer*
Moore, Nathan P. *lawyer*
Moore, Weldon Leslie *lawyer*
Mueller, Mark Christopher *lawyer*
Nelson, Elaine Edwards *lawyer*
Nichols, Henry Louis *lawyer*
Nolan, John Michael *lawyer*
Pennington, Karen Harder *lawyer*
Peterson, Edward Adrian *lawyer*
Pew, John Glenn, Jr. *lawyer*
Phelan, Robin Eric *lawyer*
Pingree, Bruce Douglas *lawyer*
Pleasant, James Scott *lawyer*
Poole, David P. *lawyer*
Portman, Glenn Arthur *lawyer*
Powers, Timothy Eugene *lawyer*
Preston, Shawn *lawyer*
Price, John Aley *lawyer*
Purnell, Charles Giles *lawyer*
Purnell, Maurice Eugene, Jr. *lawyer*
Reid, Rust Endicott *lawyer*
Rice, John S. *lawyer*
Riddle, Michael Lee *lawyer*
Ringle, Brett Adelbert *lawyer, oil industry executive, gas industry executive*
Roberts, Harry Morris, Jr. *lawyer*
Rodgers, John Hunter *lawyer*
Roper, Richard B. III *prosecutor*
Ryan, Dennis Neil *lawyer*
Samuel, Greg R. *lawyer*
Schaeffler, Georg *lawyer, manufacturing executive*
Schartz, Elizabeth A. *lawyer*
Schpok, Terry M. *lawyer*
Schreiber, Howard E. *lawyer*
Schreiber, Sally Ann *lawyer*
Scow, Aaron Arney *lawyer*
See, Robert Fleming, Jr. *lawyer*
Sharry, Janice Vyn *lawyer*
Sheeder, Robert Elwood *lawyer*
Shepherd, Jon Glen *lawyer*
Sims, William D., Jr. *lawyer*
Sinak, David Louis *lawyer*
Sloman, Marvin Sherk *lawyer*
Spears, Robert Fields *lawyer*
Stalcup, Joe Alan *lawyer, dean*
Steinberg, Lawrence Edward *lawyer*
Stewart, Daniel Clark *lawyer*
Stewart, Kenneth L. *lawyer*
Stockard, James Alfred *lawyer*
Storey, Charles Porter *lawyer*
Strock, William C. *lawyer*
Szuwalski, Andre Michael *lawyer*
Templin, Donald C. *lawyer*
Thomson, Basil Henry, Jr. *lawyer*
Thomson, Roger F. *lawyer*
Tompkins, Alan W. *lawyer*
True, Roy Joe *lawyer*
Tubb, James Clarence *lawyer*
Urbanowicz, E. Peter (Eugene Peter Urbanowicz Jr.) *lawyer*
Veach, Robert Raymond, Jr. *lawyer*
Villareal, Patricia J. *lawyer*
Walkowiak, Vincent Steven *lawyer*
Wallace, Anderson, Jr. *lawyer, educator*
Walters, Robert C. *lawyer*
Warman, Lynnette R. *lawyer*
Watler, Paul C. *lawyer*
Wehrmann, Paul Alan *lawyer*
Welch, Gerald Thomas *lawyer, electrical engineer*
West, Glenn D. *lawyer*
Westfall, Constance Courtney *lawyer*
Whitaker, Elizabeth D. *lawyer*
White, James Richard *lawyer*
Willingham, Clark Suttles *lawyer*
Wilson, Claude Raymond, Jr. *lawyer*
Wilson, Jonathan C. *lawyer*
Wilson, Robert E. *lawyer*
Wilson, Taylor *lawyer*
Wolin, Robert Everett *lawyer*
Woram, Brian J. *lawyer*
Wortley, Micahel D. *lawyer*
Wright, Alan *lawyer*
Wu, Kathleen J. *lawyer*
Young, Barney Thornton *lawyer*
Young, William D. *lawyer*
Zahn, Donald Jack *lawyer*
Zisman, Barry Stuart *lawyer*

**Denton**
Lawhon, John III *lawyer, retired county official*
Lewis, Mark *lawyer*
Loveless, Darcy E. *lawyer*
Waage, Mervin Bernard *lawyer*

**Desoto**
Boyanton, Janet Shafer *lawyer*

**El Paso**
Feuille, Richard Harlan *lawyer, director*
Gibson, Sidney Kay *retired lawyer*
Marshall, Richard Treeger *lawyer*
Smith, Tad Randolph *lawyer*

**Ennis**
Swanson, Wallace Martin *lawyer*

**Euless**
Paran, Mark Lloyd *retired lawyer*

**Farmers Branch**
Blachly, Jack Lee *lawyer*

**Flower Mound**
Hunt, David Ford *lawyer*

**Fort Worth**
Broiles, David *lawyer*
Brown, C. Harold *lawyer*
Brown, Richard Lee *lawyer*
Chalk, John Allen, Sr. *lawyer*
Dean, Beale *lawyer*
Dent, Edward Dwain *lawyer*

Elliott, Frank Wallace *lawyer, educator*
Friedman, Walker C. *lawyer*
Hall, Randy Jarvis *lawyer*
Harbour, Ted Ira *lawyer*
Harcrow, E. Earl *lawyer*
Hart, John Clifton *lawyer*
Hayes, Larry B. *lawyer*
Ingram, Denny Ouzts, Jr. *lawyer, law educator*
Kelly, Dee J. *lawyer*
Kelly, Raymond Boone III *lawyer*
Law, Thomas Hart *lawyer*
Lawrence, J. Rodney *retired lawyer*
McConnell, Michael Arthur *lawyer*
Miller, Kleber C. *lawyer*
Minton, Jerry Davis *lawyer, consultant, retired banker*
Munn, Cecil Edwin *lawyer*
Quinn, Francis Xavier *arbitrator, consultant, mediator, writer, law educator*
Sharpe, James Shelby *lawyer*
Tillman, Karen Sue *lawyer*
Tillman, Massie Monroe *mediator, arbitrator, art gallery owner, retired judge*
Wallace, R. H., Jr. *lawyer*
Watson, Robert Francis *lawyer*
Weekley, Frederick Clay, Jr. *lawyer*
West, Robert Grady *lawyer*

## Galveston
Caldwell, Garnett Ernest *lawyer*
Neves, Kerry Lane *lawyer*
O'Toole, Austin Martin *lawyer, mediator*
Salch, Steven Charles *lawyer, mediator, arbitrator*

## Georgetown
Bryce, William Delf *lawyer*

## Grapevine
Franks, Jon Michael *lawyer, mediator*

## Heath
Kolodey, Fred James *lawyer*

## Houston
Addison, Linda Leuchter *lawyer, writer, commentator, columnist*
Adrogué, Sofia *lawyer*
Aiyer, Jay Kumar *lawyer*
Allen, Denise *legal association administrator*
Allen, Frank Clinton, Jr. *lawyer, chemical engineer*
Allender, John Roland *lawyer*
Anani, Tariq *lawyer*
Anderson, Eric Severin *lawyer*
Andrews, Sally S. *lawyer*
Asmus, David F. *lawyer*
Atlas, Scott J. *lawyer*
Ayers, Howard T. *lawyer*
Bachmann, Richard H. *lawyer*
Backus, Marcia Ellen *lawyer*
Baker, C. Mark *lawyer*
Baker, Robert W. *lawyer*
Barbour, Larry Gregory *lawyer*
Bargfrede, James Allen *lawyer*
Barnett, Edward William *lawyer*
Bates, Shawn M. *lawyer*
Bech, Douglas York *retired lawyer, resort executive*
Beckworth, John B. *lawyer*
Beirne, Martin Douglas *lawyer*
Bell, Jerry Arch, Jr. *lawyer*
Bellatti, Lawrence Lee *lawyer*
Berg, David Howard *lawyer*
Berry, Nandita V. *lawyer*
Biery, Evelyn Hudson *lawyer*
Bilger, Bruce R. *lawyer*
Blackshear, A. T., Jr. *lawyer*
Bland, John Lloyd *lawyer*
Botley, Calvin *lawyer, judge*
Boulware, Margaret A. *lawyer*
Boyce, Maria Wyckoff *lawyer*
Brann, Richard Roland *lawyer*
Bridges, David Manning *lawyer*
Brinson, Gay Creswell, Jr. *retired lawyer*
Brodsky, Donald W. *lawyer*
Brunson, John Soles *lawyer, investor*
Buckingham, Edwin John III *lawyer*
Buckley, Vincent H. *lawyer*
Burch, Voris Reagan *mediator, arbitrator, retired lawyer*
Burgert, David Lee *lawyer*
Burton, Charles William *lawyer*
Burton, Joseph Randolph *lawyer*
Bux, William John *lawyer*
Caddy, Michael Douglas *lawyer*
Caldwell, Richard H. *lawyer*
Cameron, Jeffrey M. *lawyer*
Carmody, James Albert *lawyer*
Carr, Edward A. *lawyer*
Carstarphen, Edward Morgan III *lawyer*
Carter, John Francis, II, *lawyer*
Carter, John Loyd *lawyer*
Casarez, Rueben Charles *lawyer*
Caudill, William Howard *lawyer*
Chapman, Cynthia B. *lawyer*
Chavez, J. Anthony *lawyer*
Cheavens, Joseph D. *lawyer*
Clarke, Douglas E. *lawyer*
Clarke, Robert Logan *lawyer*
Clore, Lawrence Hubert *lawyer*
Cochran, Fielding B. III *lawyer*
Coghlan, Kelly Jack *lawyer*
Colbert, Kevin LeRoy *lawyer*
Coleman, Francis J., Jr. *lawyer*
Coley, Randolph C. *lawyer*
Conlon, Michael William *lawyer*
Cook, B. Thomas *lawyer*
Corken, Heather Marie *lawyer*
Cornelison, Albert Otto, Jr., (Bert Cornelison) *lawyer*
Cox, James Talley *lawyer*
Crocker, Charles Allan *lawyer*
Cunningham, Tom Alan *lawyer*
Dameris, Thad Thano *lawyer*
Day, Jonathan S. *lawyer*
Degabrielle, Donald J., Jr. *prosecutor*
DeGuerin, Dick *lawyer*
Del Valle, Teresa Jones *lawyer*
DeMent, James Alderson, Jr. *lawyer*
Devlin, Francis James *lawyer*
Dilg, Joseph Carl *lawyer*
Dillard, Michael E. *lawyer*

Dillard, Stephen C. *lawyer*
Dinkins, Carol Eggert *lawyer*
Dodd, Jeff C. *lawyer*
Donley, Billy Martin *lawyer*
Donnelly, Rosemarie *lawyer*
Douglas, James Matthew *law educator, dean*
Douglass, John Jay *lawyer, educator*
Dunlop, Fred Hurston *lawyer*
Dykes, Osborne Jefferson III *lawyer*
Eckhardt, William Rudolf III *lawyer*
Eiland, Gary Wayne *lawyer*
Engerrand, Kenneth G. *lawyer, educator*
Essmyer, Michael Martin *lawyer*
Eubank, J. Thomas *lawyer*
Fabugais, Trisha *law librarian*
Farenthold, Frances Tarlton *lawyer*
Farnsworth, T. Brooke *lawyer*
Ford, Thomas W., Jr. *lawyer*
Foster, Charles Crawford *lawyer, educator*
Fullenweider, Donn Charles *lawyer*
Gagnon, Stewart Walter *lawyer*
Galvin, Kerry A. *lawyer*
Garza, Erik David *lawyer*
Gates, Stephen Frye *lawyer, oil industry executive*
Gerachis, George Matthew *lawyer*
Gibson, Rex Hilton *lawyer*
Gilpin, Patrick J. *lawyer, educator*
Gissel, L. Henry, Jr. *lawyer*
Goode, Coralyn *lawyer*
Goodman, Barry Michael *lawyer*
Gorman, Sean *lawyer*
Gover, Alan Shore *lawyer*
Graebner, Carol F. *lawyer*
Gray, Robert F., Jr. *lawyer*
Grossberg, Marc Elias *lawyer*
Guest, Floyd Emory, Jr. *lawyer*
Gunter, Joseph Clifford III *lawyer*
Gutheinz, Joseph Richard, Jr. *lawyer, writer, retired military officer*
Hall, Anthony W., Jr. *lawyer*
Hall, Charles Washington *lawyer*
Hamel, Douglas E. *lawyer*
Handlin, Danita L. *lawyer*
Hanower, Lee David *lawyer*
Harper, A(lfred) J(ohn), II, *lawyer*
Harrington, Bruce Michael *lawyer, investor*
Harris, Warren Wayne *lawyer*
Hartrick, Janice Kay *lawyer*
Harvin, David Tarleton *lawyer*
Hawes, Clay Erik *lawyer*
Haynes, Richard *lawyer*
Heeg, Peggy A. *lawyer, former gas industry executive*
Heinrich, Randall Wayne *lawyer*
Hewitt, Lester L. *lawyer*
Higgins, Pauline Edwards *lawyer*
Hinton, Paula Weems *lawyer*
Hlavinka, Paul Thomas *lawyer*
Hoeg, Matthew *lawyer*
Holloway, Gordon Arthur *lawyer*
Hollyfield, John Scoggins *lawyer*
Holstead, John Burnham *retired lawyer*
Horton, Donald J. *lawyer*
Hoyt, Mont Powell *lawyer*
Hudson, Franklin *lawyer, real estate developer*
Hudspeth, Chalmers Mac *lawyer, educator*
Hull, Robert Joe *lawyer*
Hunsaker, Barry, Jr. *lawyer*
Hurley, R. Bruce *lawyer*
Irvin, Michael P. *lawyer*
Ivey, Jack Todd *lawyer*
Jamail, Joseph Dahr, Jr. *lawyer*
Jansen, Donald Orville *retired lawyer*
Jewell, Robert V. *lawyer*
Johnson, Alisa B. *lawyer, energy company executive*
Jones, Frank Griffith *lawyer*
Jordan, W. Carl *lawyer*
Kaplan, Lee Landa *lawyer*
Kay, Joel Phillip *lawyer*
Keith, Susan S. *lawyer*
Kelly, Hugh Rice *lawyer, retired energy executive*
Kelly, T. Mark *lawyer*
Kelly, William Franklin, Jr. *lawyer*
Kennedy, John Edward *lawyer*
Ketchand, Robert Lee *lawyer*
Knobloch, Charles Saron *lawyer, geophysicist*
Koenig, Rodney Curtis *lawyer, rancher*
Kratochvil, L(ouis) Glen *lawyer*
Krebs, Arno William, Jr. *lawyer*
Kruse, Layne E. *lawyer*
LaBoon, Robert Bruce *lawyer*
Lacy, Terri *lawyer*
LaFuze, William L. *lawyer*
Lake, Kathleen Cooper *lawyer*
Lanier, Mark (W. Mark Lanier) *lawyer*
Lannie, Paul Anthony *lawyer*
Larkin, Lee Roy *retired lawyer*
Lassetter, Scott D. *lawyer*
Lemmer, William C. *lawyer*
Lewis, Chip *lawyer*
Lewis, Edward Clark *lawyer*
Lewis, Kevin Paul *lawyer*
Liberato, Lynne *lawyer*
Listengart, Joseph *lawyer*
Locke, Gene L. *lawyer*
Looser, William Gregory *lawyer*
Lopez, David Tiburcio *lawyer, educator, arbitrator, mediator*
Lott, Marley *lawyer*
Lynch, John F. *lawyer*
Marston, Edgar Jean III *lawyer*
Martin, J. Clark *lawyer*
Martin, Jay Griffith *lawyer*
Martin, Paul Edward *lawyer*
Mason, Dwayne L. *lawyer*
Massad, Stephen Albert *lawyer*
Mattox, Sharon M. *lawyer*
McCarter, Louis Eugene *lawyer*
McClure, Daniel M. *lawyer*
McClure, Jeffrey B. *lawyer*
McCreary, Frank E. III *lawyer*
McDaniel, Jarrel Dave *lawyer*
McFall, Donald Beury *lawyer*
McLeod, Chanse L. *lawyer*
McMahon, Catherine Driscoll *lawyer*
McQuarrie, Claude Monroe III *lawyer*
Melton, Stephen Reid *lawyer*
Miller, Barry Rixmann *lawyer*
Miller, Gary C. *lawyer*
Minor, Sterling Arthur *lawyer*

Moehlman, Michael Scott *lawyer*
Moncure, John Lewis *lawyer*
Moore, Tim *lawyer*
Murphy, Ewell Edward, Jr. *lawyer*
Nacol, Mae *lawyer*
Nathan, Arthur M. *lawyer*
Nations, Howard Lynn *lawyer*
Neslage, John Edward *lawyer*
Niebruegge, Michael E. *lawyer*
Nolen, Roy Lemuel *retired lawyer*
O'Brien, Eva Fromm *lawyer*
Oldham, Darius Dudley *lawyer*
Oldham, J. Thomas *lawyer, educator*
O'Quinn, John M. *lawyer*
Ostendorf, Lance Stephen *lawyer, educator, financial consultant*
Osterberg, Edward Charles, Jr. *lawyer*
Oxford, Patrick C. *lawyer*
Pearson, Michael P. *lawyer*
Perez, Jose Rafael, Jr. *lawyer*
Perich, Thomas J. *lawyer*
Pierce, Frank Powell *lawyer, judge*
Plaeger, Frederick Joseph, II, *lawyer*
Poitevent, Edward Butts, II, *lawyer*
Porter, Thomas William III *lawyer*
Pravel, Bernarr Roe *lawyer*
Pugh, William Whitmell Hill III *lawyer*
Pursley, Jack Stephen *lawyer, consultant*
Raley, John Wesley III *lawyer*
Ramsey, Michael W. *lawyer*
Rapoport, Nancy B. *law educator*
Ray, Hugh Massey, Jr. *lawyer*
Ray, Hugh Massey III *lawyer*
Reasoner, Harry Max *lawyer*
Roach, Robert Michael, Jr., (Randy Roach) *lawyer*
Robertson, James Woolsey *lawyer*
Robin, Alan Jay *lawyer*
Rogers, Arthur Hamilton III *lawyer*
Rommel, A. Ross, Jr. *lawyer*
Rowland, Robert Alexander III *lawyer*
Rozzell, Scott Ellis *lawyer*
Runnels, David G. *lawyer*
Ryan, Jason Michael *lawyer*
Ryan, Stephen M. *lawyer*
Ryan, Vince *lawyer*
Sales, James Bohus *lawyer*
Sapp, Walter William *lawyer, gas industry executive*
Saunders, Charles Albert *lawyer*
Schaffer, Stuart F. *lawyer*
Schechter, Arthur Louis *lawyer*
Schick, Robert Michael *lawyer*
Schwartz, Charles Walter *lawyer*
Schwartzel, Charles Boone *lawyer*
Schwind, William F., Jr. *lawyer, oil industry executive*
Seale, Robert Arthur, Jr. *lawyer*
Secrest, George McCall, Jr. *lawyer*
Segal, Steven E. *retired lawyer*
Shaddock, Carroll Sidney *lawyer*
Shely, John B. *lawyer*
Sheppard, Ben H., Jr. *lawyer*
Shurn, Peter Joseph III *lawyer*
Siegler, Kelly R. *lawyer*
Silva, Eugene Joseph *lawyer*
Sing, William Bender *lawyer*
Smith, Alison Leigh *lawyer*
Smith, Martha Lee *lawyer*
Smith, Walter John *lawyer*
Smith, William Ashley *lawyer, investment banker, energy executive*
Sonfield, Robert Leon, Jr. *lawyer*
Spalding, Andrew Freeman *lawyer*
Stewart, Pamela L. *lawyer*
Still, Charles Henry, Sr. *lawyer*
Stradley, William Jackson *lawyer*
Streng, William Paul *lawyer, educator*
Stryker, Steven Charles *retired lawyer*
Sullivan, Charles, Jr. *retired lawyer*
Sullivan, John F. III *lawyer*
Susman, Stephen Daily *lawyer*
Sutton, Neal S. *lawyer*
Swan, Michael K. *lawyer*
Swift, Robert J. *lawyer*
Sydow, Michael David *lawyer*
Szalkowski, Charles C. *lawyer*
Taheri, Marshall M. *lawyer, educator*
Tartt, Blake *lawyer*
Thompson, Sandra Guerra *lawyer, educator*
Touchy, Deborah K.P. *lawyer, accountant*
Tripp, Karen Bryant *lawyer*
Trull, Thomas G. *lawyer*
Van Fleet, George Allan *lawyer*
Van Winkle, Danny L. *lawyer*
Varner, David Eugene *lawyer*
Vaughan, Jack M. *lawyer*
Vickery, Edward Downtain *lawyer*
Vogel, Jennifer *lawyer*
Wagner, Leslie *lawyer*
Wallace, Barron F. *lawyer*
Walls, Robert Hamilton, Jr. *lawyer*
Walton, Dan Gibson *lawyer*
Watson, John Allen *lawyer*
Webb, Jack M. *lawyer*
Weber, Fredric Alan *lawyer*
Weiner, Sanford Alan *lawyer*
Weller, Philip Douglas *lawyer*
Welsh, H. Ronald *lawyer*
Westby, Timothy Scott *lawyer, researcher*
Wheelan, R(ichelieu) E(dward) *lawyer*
Whilden, Robert Harral, Jr. *lawyer*
Whiting, Hugh Richard *lawyer*
Whittenburg, Justin M. *lawyer*
Wilde, Carlton D. *lawyer, director*
Williams, Lowell Craig *lawyer, employee relations executive*
Williams, O'Banion III *lawyer*
Williamson, Peter David *lawyer*
Wittenbraker, Rick L. *lawyer*
Wood, Michael W *lawyer*
Woods, Ronald G. *lawyer, former prosecutor*
Worthington, William Albert III *lawyer*
Wray, Thomas Jefferson *lawyer*
Wynne, John Carlton *lawyer*
Wyrsch, Martha B. *lawyer, energy executive*
Yeates, Marie R. *lawyer*
Yetter, R Paul *lawyer*
Yokubaitis, Roger T. *lawyer*

## Humble
Pickle, George Edward *lawyer*

## Hunt
Gambrell, James Bruton III *lawyer, educator*

## Irving
Beach, Charles Addison *lawyer*
Beasley, Mark V. *lawyer*
Gabriel, Eberhard John *lawyer, bank executive*
McCray, Ronald David *lawyer*
Molay, Hilary S. *lawyer*
Robinson, Lawrence Dewitt *lawyer*
Shuff, Ronald F. *lawyer*
Sudbury, David Marshall *lawyer*
Sullivan, Paul E. *lawyer, oil industry executive*

## Kilgore
Rorschach, Richard Gordon *lawyer*

## La Marque
Disher, David Alan *lawyer, consultant*

## Lamesa
Saleh, John *lawyer*

## Longview
Harrison, Guy Newell *lawyer*
Welge, Jack Herman, Jr. *lawyer*

## Lubbock
Beyer, Gerry Wayne *lawyer, educator*
Kelley, John Timothy *lawyer, animal breeder*
Phelan, Marilyn Elizabeth *law educator*
Purdom, Thomas James *lawyer*

## Mc Kinney
Albano, Christine Grace *lawyer*

## Mcallen
Connors, Joseph Aloysius III *lawyer*

## Midland
Estes, Andrew Harper *lawyer*
MacDonald, Leland Lloyd *lawyer*
Martin, C. D. *lawyer*
Taylor, Nicholas C. *lawyer, state agency administrator, energy executive*

## Missouri City
Hodges, Jot Holiver, Jr. *retired lawyer, corporate financial executive*

## New Braunfels
Benfield, Marion Wilson, Jr. *law educator*

## North Richland Hills
Reed, Glenn W. *lawyer*

## Plano
Altabef, Peter Anthony *lawyer*
Bober, Joanne L. *lawyer*
Bonet, Frank Joseph *retired lawyer*
Fay, Donald P. *lawyer*
Hemingway, Richard William *law educator*
Korst, Christopher A. *lawyer, rental company executive*
Levine, Harold *lawyer*
Mondul, Donald David *patent lawyer*
Rodolph, Grant *lawyer*

## Pottsboro
Thomas, Ann Van Wynen *retired law educator*

## Richardson
Conkel, Robert Dale *lawyer, consultant*
Martin, Richard Kelley *lawyer*
Olson, Dennis Oliver *lawyer*
Sowers, Wesley Hoyt *lawyer, management consultant*
Stoll, William Frederick, Jr. *lawyer*

## Rockwall
White, Todd William *lawyer, educator*

## San Angelo
Sutton, John Ewing *lawyer*

## San Antonio
Bennett, Steven Alan *lawyer*
Bettac, Robert Edward *lawyer*
Bowers, Kim *lawyer, energy executive*
Chasnoff, Barry A. *lawyer*
Cicconi, James William *lawyer, telecommunications industry executive*
Collins, Kevin Lloyd *lawyer*
Emery, Nancy Beth *lawyer*
Golden, Stephen L. *lawyer*
Guenther, Jack Egon *lawyer*
Hardy, Harvey Louchard *retired lawyer*
Henry, Peter York *lawyer, mediator*
Hilley, Van Galen *lawyer*
Labenz-Hough, Marlene *mediator*
Maloney, Marynell *lawyer*
Moynihan, John Bignell *retired lawyer*
Parrish, Charles *lawyer*
Pearl, James Hildred *lawyer*
Perry, Robert Michael *lawyer, consultant, rancher*
Pfeiffer, Philip John *lawyer*
Reams, Bernard Dinsmore, Jr. *law educator*
Ruttenberg, Frank Z. *lawyer*
Schenker, Cecil *lawyer*
Schlueter, David Arnold *law educator*
Schmutz, John Francis *lawyer*
Schoenbaum, Alan *lawyer*
Spears, Sally *lawyer*
Steen, John Thomas, Jr. *lawyer*
Sutton, Johnny Keane *prosecutor, lawyer*
Vazquez, Gilbert Falcon *lawyer*
Wallis, Ben Alton, Jr. *lawyer*
Weir, W. Thomas *lawyer*
Wells, Tullos *lawyer*
Wheatley, Seagal V. *lawyer, legal association administrator*
Wyker, Kenneth E. *lawyer*
Yates, Norris William, Jr. *lawyer*

## Southlake
Brunig, Robert Arthur *lawyer*
Schwarte, David A. *lawyer, travel company executive*

## Spring
Farley, Andrew Newell *lawyer, consultant*
Hendricks, Randal Arlan *lawyer*

## Sugar Land
Hitchcock, Bion Earl *lawyer*
Le, Chi-Dinh *law educator, writer*

## Temple
Pickle, Jerry Richard *lawyer*

## The Woodlands
Bohannon, Paul M. *lawyer*
Hagerman, John David *lawyer, investment advisor*
Ripley, Charlene A. *lawyer*
Schlacks, Stephen Mark *lawyer*
Stahl, Craig L. *lawyer*

## Trinidad
Conant, Allah B., Jr. *lawyer*

## Tyler
Ellis, Donald Lee *lawyer*

## Waco
Mc Swain, Angus Stewart, Jr. *retired law educator*
Morrison, Michael Dean *lawyer, law educator*
Smith, Cullen *lawyer*
Vander Woude, Richard John *lawyer*

## Weatherford
King, Douglas Michael *lawyer, accountant*

## Wimberley
Brinsmade, Lyon Louis *retired lawyer*

## Yoakum
Kvinta, Charles J. *lawyer*
Williams, Walter Waylon *lawyer, agricultural products supplier*

# UTAH

## Coalville
Thomas, David Lindsey *lawyer, state senator*

## Logan
Daines, N. George *lawyer*
West, Stephen Allan *lawyer*

## Manti
Petersen, Benton Lauritz *paralegal*

## Midvale
Dahl, Everett E. *lawyer*

## North Salt Lake
Barden, Robert Christopher *lawyer, writer, psychologist, educator*

## Ogden
Mecham, Glenn Jefferson *lawyer, mayor*

## Orem
Michell, Auriel Ibn *lawyer, writer*

## Provo
Abbott, Charles Favour *lawyer*
Averett, Steven Elmo *law librarian*
Brown, Joseph William *retired lawyer*
Hansen, H. Reese *law educator, former dean*
Hill, Richard Lee *lawyer*
Thomas, David Albert *law educator, director*
Williams, Gerald R. *law educator*

## Saint George
Terry, Gary A. *lawyer, director, former trade association executive*

## Salt Lake City
Adams, John A. *lawyer*
Adams, Joseph Keith *lawyer*
Baldwin, John *legal association administrator, lawyer*
Barusch, Lawrence Roos *lawyer*
Baucom, Sidney George *lawyer*
Bendinger, Gary Frederick *lawyer*
Berman, Daniel Lewis *lawyer*
Bird, David R. *lawyer*
Blackburn, Michael Dale *lawyer, educator*
Christensen, Ray Richards *lawyer*
Clayton, Richard D. *lawyer*
Conard, Jane Reister *lawyer*
Cornaby, Kay Sterling *lawyer, retired state senator*
Dewsnup, Ralph L. *lawyer*
Gardiner, Lester Raymond, Jr. *retired lawyer*
Greenwood, David A. *lawyer*
Hanni, Glenn Charles *lawyer*
Holtkamp, James Arnold *lawyer, educator*
Jensen, Dallin W. *lawyer*
Kirkham, John Spencer *lawyer, director*
Matsumori, Douglas *lawyer*
Moore, Debra *lawyer*
Moore, James R. *lawyer*
Nydegger, Rick D. *lawyer*
Ockey, Ronald J. *lawyer*
Prince, William B. *lawyer*
Rasmussen, Thomas Val, Jr. *lawyer, small business owner*
Reeder, F. Robert *lawyer*
Scofield, David Willson *lawyer*
Smith, Janet Hugie *lawyer*
Sorenson, Stephen Jay *prosecutor*
Spurgeon, Edward Dutcher *lawyer, educator, foundation administrator*
Thompson, Neil Daniel *retired lawyer*
Threedy, Debora Lynn *law educator*
Tolman, Brett L. *prosecutor*
Verhaaren, Harold Carl *lawyer*
Wangsgard, Chris Prince *lawyer*
Zimmer, Markus Bernhard *legal association administrator*
Zimmerman, Michael David *lawyer*

## South Jordan
Larson, Bryan Alan *lawyer*

## Springville
Ashworth, Brent Ferrin *lawyer*

## Vernal
Judd, Dennis L. *lawyer*

# VERMONT

## Barre
Koch, Thomas Frederick *lawyer*

## Brattleboro
Reid, David G. *lawyer*

## Burlington
Anderson, Thomas D. *prosecutor*
Dinse, John Merrell *lawyer*
Kirby, David V. *prosecutor*
Montroll, Andrew H. *lawyer, councilman*
Rendall, Donald James, Jr. *lawyer*

## Castleton
Stafford, Robert Theodore *lawyer, retired senator*

## Essex Junction
Sweetser, Susan W. *lawyer, advocate, retired state legislator*

## Montpelier
Diamond, M. Jerome *lawyer, retired state attorney general*
Errecart, Joyce *lawyer*
Guild, Alden *retired lawyer*
Saxman, Anna Esther *lawyer*
Valerio, Matthew F. *lawyer*

## Morrisville
Simonds, Marshall *retired lawyer*

## Newport
Pepyne, Edward Walter *lawyer, educator, psychologist*

## Rutland
Crowley, Arthur Edward, Jr. *lawyer*

## Saint Johnsbury
Marshall, John Henry *lawyer*

## Shelburne
Canfield, Andrew Trotter *lawyer, writer*

## South Royalton
Dycus, Stephen *law educator*
Wroth, L(awrence) Kinvin *law educator*

## Springfield
Lawrence, Wesley M. *lawyer*

## Stowe
Siegel, David Burton *lawyer*
Whiteman, Joseph David *retired lawyer, manufacturing company executive*

## Warren
Raphael, Albert Ash, Jr. *retired lawyer*

## White River Junction
Kainen, Michael Roland *lawyer, state representative*

## Woodstock
Zonay, Thomas A. *lawyer*

# VIRGINIA

## Abingdon
Moore, Suzan E. *lawyer*

## Alexandria
Blue, Catherine Anne *lawyer*
Burch, John Thomas, Jr. *lawyer*
Dennison, Donald Lee *lawyer*
DiMuro, Bernard Joseph *lawyer*
Drennan, Joseph Peter *lawyer*
Flater, Morris Eugene *lawyer*
Georges, Peter John *lawyer*
Goldfarb, Ronald Lawrence *lawyer, writer, literary agent*
Higgins, Mary Celeste *lawyer, researcher*
Hobson, James Richmond *lawyer*
Holcomb, Richard Dennis *lawyer*
Huckabee, Harlow Maxwell *lawyer, writer*
Hudgins, David Drake *lawyer*
Kelly, Nancy Frieda Wolicki *lawyer*
Kopp, Eugene Paul *lawyer*
Kotlarchuk, Ihor O. E. *lawyer*
Lapidus, Kevin S. *lawyer*
McDowell, Charles Eager *lawyer, retired military officer*
Mossinghoff, Gerald Joseph *lawyer, educator*
O'Hara, John Patrick *lawyer, consultant*
Palmer, Adam P. *lawyer*
Paturis, E(mmanuel) Michael *lawyer*
Pyle, Howard *lawyer, consultant*
Redway, Jonathan *lawyer*
Rosenberg, Chuck (Charles P. Rosenberg) *prosecutor*
Schultz, Franklin M. *retired law educator*
Straub, Peter Thornton *lawyer*
Sturtevant, Brereton *retired lawyer, retired federal official*
Swift, Stephen Christopher *lawyer*
Von Drehle, Ramon Arnold *lawyer*
Williams, John Edward *lawyer*

## Annandale
Jollie, Susan Barbara *lawyer*

## Arlington
Anthony, Robert Armstrong *lawyer, educator*
Berkowitz, Edward C. *lawyer*
Brenner, Edgar H. *legal association administrator*
Burgess, David *lawyer*
Cohen, Sheldon Irwin *lawyer*
Crouch, Richard Edelin *lawyer*
Doyle, Gerard Francis *lawyer*

Gainer, Ronald Lee *lawyer*
Green, Richard Alan *retired lawyer*
Johnson, Charles Owen *retired lawyer*
Kelly, John James *lawyer*
Korman, James William *lawyer*
Lanier, Elizabeth K. *lawyer*
Leslie, Gregg P. *lawyer*
Litman, Richard Curtis *lawyer*
Lohr, Michael F. *lawyer*
Malone, William Grady *retired lawyer*
Martin, Harry C. *lawyer*
McDermott, Francis Owen *retired lawyer*
Meisel, Michael J. *lawyer*
Mellor, Chip (William H. Mellor) *lawyer*
Nagin, Lawrence M. *lawyer*
O'Neill, Michael Edmund *law educator*
O'Sullivan, Lynda Troutman *lawyer*
Parker, Jeffrey Scott *law educator*
Pelton, Erik Michael *lawyer*
Petro, Lee George *lawyer*
Robb, Chuck (Charles Spittal Robb) *law educator, former senator*
Rotunda, Ronald Daniel *law educator, consultant*
Rousselot, Peter Frese *lawyer, consultant*
Schmidt, Paul Wickham *lawyer*
Thorne, John *lawyer*
Uncapher, Mark Elson *lawyer, trade association administrator*
Walker, Woodrow Wilson *retired lawyer, real estate investor, farmer*
Wilderotter, James Arthur *lawyer*
Williams, Paul Robert *lawyer, foreign policy analyst*

## Ashburn
Kelly, Anastasia Donovan *lawyer*

## Blacksburg
Jensen, Walter Edward *retired lawyer, educator*

## Blackstone
Allen, Jeffrey Rodgers *lawyer*

## Burke
Hipfel, Steven J. *lawyer*

## Centreville
Etters, Ronald Milton *retired lawyer, former government official*
Fells, Robert Marshall *lawyer*

## Chantilly
Becker, James Richard *lawyer*
DeLeon, Charles *lawyer*

## Charlottesville
Abraham, Kenneth Samuel *law educator*
Balnave, Richard D. *law educator*
Bonnie, Richard Jeffrey *law educator, lawyer, consultant*
Buck, D. Ruth *legal research and writing educator*
Cannon, Jonathan Z. *lawyer, educator*
Chandler, Lawrence Bradford, Jr. *lawyer*
Cohen, George Meredith *law educator*
Coughlin, Anne M. *law educator*
Cushman, Barry *law educator*
Dooley, Michael P. *law educator*
Dudley, Earl C., Jr. *law educator*
Fitchett, Taylor *law librarian*
Forde-Mazrui, Kim Abubakar Ali *law educator*
Fox, Charles Dunsmore, IV, *lawyer*
Gilliam, George Harrison *lawyer*
Goetz, Charles John *law and economics educator*
Groiss, Fred George *lawyer*
Harrison, John Collier *law educator*
Henderson, Stanley Dale *lawyer, educator, arbitrator*
Hochberg, Bayard Zabdial *retired lawyer*
Hodous, Robert Power *lawyer*
Howard, Arthur Ellsworth Dick *law educator*
Hurwitz, Deena R. *lawyer*
Kennedy, Cornelius Bryant *retired lawyer*
Kensington, Andrew Justus *litigation specialist*
Kitch, Edmund Wells *law educator*
Kordana, Kevin A. *law educator*
Kraus, Jody S. *law educator*
Landess, Fred Stone *retired lawyer*
Leslie, Douglas L. *law educator*
Lilly, Graham C. *law educator*
Magill, M(ary) Elizabeth *law educator*
Mahoney, Julia Delong *law educator*
Mahoney, Paul G. *law educator*
Martin, David Alan *law educator*
Meador, Daniel John *law educator*
Menefee, Samuel Pyeatt *lawyer, researcher*
Middleditch, Leigh Benjamin, Jr. *lawyer, educator*
Monahan, John T. *law educator, psychologist*
Moore, John Norton *lawyer, educator, diplomat*
Nelson, Caleb Edward *law educator*
O'Brien, David Michael *law educator*
O'Connell, Jeffrey *law educator*
Riley, Margaret Foster (Mimi Riley) *law educator*
Robinson, Mildred Wigfall *law educator*
Rutherglen, George A. *law educator*
Scott, Elizabeth S. *law educator*
Scott, Robert Edwin *law educator*
Setear, John K. *law educator*
Sinclair, Kent *law educator*
Slaughter, Edward Ratliff, Jr. *lawyer*
Stephan, Paul Brooke III *law educator*
Turner, Robert Foster *law educator, writer*
Verkerke, J. Hoult *law educator*
Wadlington, Walter James *law educator*
Walker, W. Laurens *law educator*
Walt, Steven David *law educator*
Wenger, Larry Bruce *law librarian, educator*
White, George Edward *law educator, lawyer*
Whitehead, John Wayne *lawyer, educator, writer*
Woolhandler, Ann *law educator*

## Chester
Gray, Charles Robert *lawyer*

## Danville
Abreu, Luis Alberto *lawyer*
Regan, Michael Patrick *lawyer*
Talbott, Frank III *lawyer*

## Fairfax
Anderson, David Lawrence *lawyer*

Arntson, Peter Andrew *lawyer*
Baird, Charles Bruce *lawyer, consultant*
Bobzien, David P. *lawyer*
Codding, Frederick Hayden *lawyer*
Downey, Richard Lawrence *lawyer*
Fagan, John Ernest *lawyer*
Folk, Thomas Robert *lawyer*
Gillespie, Samuel H. III *lawyer, oil industry executive*
Hopson, Everett George *retired lawyer*
Keith, John A(ugustine) C(hilton) *lawyer*
Mackall, Henry Clinton *lawyer*
Rieger, Michael Ira *lawyer*
Rust, John Howson, Jr. *lawyer, state legislator*
Sanderson, Douglas Jay *lawyer*
Simpson, Carter B. *lawyer*

## Fairfax Station
Carver, George Allen, Jr. *retired lawyer*

## Falls Church
Burroughs, Benton, Jr. *mergers and acquisitions lawyer*
Christman, Bruce Lee *lawyer*
Dewey-Balzhiser, Anne Elizabeth Marie *lawyer*
Diamond, Robert Michael *lawyer*
Golden, Wilson *lawyer*
Honigberg, Carol Crossman *lawyer*
Luchini, Joseph S. *lawyer*
Meserve, Richard Andrew *lawyer*
Perkins, Jack Edwin *lawyer*
Pischke, Vail W. *lawyer, judge*
Rooney, Kevin Davitt *lawyer*
Savner, David A. *lawyer*
Thomas, William Griffith *lawyer*
Van Cleve, Ruth Gill *retired lawyer*
Ward, Joe Henry, Jr. *retired lawyer*
Waxman, Bruce I. *lawyer*
Wood, John Martin *lawyer*

## Fort Belvoir
Harms, John Kevin *lawyer*
Kiechel, Walter, Jr. *lawyer*

## Franklin
Cobb, G. Elliott, Jr. *lawyer*

## Fredericksburg
Dahnk, Jean Patricia *lawyer*

## Front Royal
Bonzagni, Vincent Francis *lawyer*

## Glen Allen
Batzli, Terrence Raymond *lawyer*
den Hartog, Grace Robinson *lawyer*
Levit, Jay J(oseph) *lawyer*
Weaver, Mollie Little *lawyer*

## Gloucester
Hicks, C. Flippo *lawyer*

## Great Falls
Cass, Ronald Andrew *lawyer, former dean*
Mitchell, Roy Shaw *lawyer*
Neidich, George Arthur *lawyer*

## Grundy
Davis, W. Jeremy *lawyer, dean*
McGlothlin, Michael Gordon *lawyer*
Shinn, Clinton Wesley *lawyer*

## Hampton
Nelson, Wallace Jay *lawyer*

## Hayes
Casson, Richard Frederick *lawyer, hotel executive*
Phillips, Elizabeth Jason *lawyer, state agency administrator*

## Haymarket
Frank, Jacob *lawyer*

## Heathsville
McKerns, Charles Joseph *lawyer*

## Hot Springs
Deeds, Robert Creigh *lawyer, state legislator*

## Ivy
Wilcox, Harvey John *lawyer*

## Leesburg
Levin, Mark Reed *legal foundation administrator, lawyer*

## Lexington
Kirgis, Frederic Lee *law educator*
Wiant, Sarah Kirsten *law librarian, educator, director*

## Locust Grove
Huntsman, Lawrence Darrow *lawyer, director*

## Lovettsville
Flannery, John Philip *lawyer*

## Lynchburg
Healy, Joseph Francis, Jr. *lawyer, retired air transportation executive*
Packert, G(ayla) Beth *retired lawyer*

## Manakin Sabot
Bright, Craig Bartley *lawyer*

## Marion
Johnson, Douglas Blaikie *lawyer*

## Mc Lean
Alexander, Fred Calvin, Jr. *lawyer*
Appler, Thomas L. *lawyer*
Aucutt, Ronald David *lawyer*
Black, David Wayne *lawyer*
Brady, Phillip Donley *lawyer*
Brown, Margaret Ann *lawyer*
Brown, Thomas Cartmel, Jr. *lawyer*
Byrnes, William Joseph *lawyer*
Cawley, Thomas J. *lawyer*
Chapple, Thomas Leslie *lawyer*
Church, Randolph Warner, Jr. *lawyer*

Corson, J. Jay, IV, *lawyer*
Donovan, David P. *lawyer*
Duvall, Richard Osgood *lawyer*
Finneran, John G., Jr. *lawyer*
Gammon, James Alan *lawyer*
Giragosian, C. Christopher *lawyer*
Glassman, M. Melissa *lawyer*
Gotts, Lawrence J. *lawyer*
Herge, J. Curtis *lawyer*
Hess, Adam R. *lawyer*
Hoffmann, Martin Richard *lawyer*
Horan, Richard T., Jr. *legal association administrator, lawyer*
Ingersoll, William Boley *lawyer, real estate developer*
Jackson, William Paul, Jr. *lawyer*
Knebel, John Albert *lawyer, retired government agency administrator*
Koehler, Robert H. *lawyer*
LeSourd, Nancy Susan Oliver *lawyer, writer*
Lewis, James (Jim) M. *lawyer*
Main, David C. *lawyer*
Marino, Michael Frank III *lawyer*
Meltzer, Steven Lee *lawyer*
Miller, David L. *lawyer*
Miller, Donald Eugene *lawyer*
Molineaux, Charles Borromeo *lawyer, arbitrator, columnist, poet*
Morris, James Malachy *lawyer*
Murphy, Thomas Patrick *lawyer*
Porter, Philip Drew *lawyer*
Price, Ilene Rosenberg *lawyer*
Reiff, Laura Foote *lawyer*
Sirilla, George M. *lawyer*
Sparks, Robert Ronold, Jr. *lawyer*
Stump, John Sutton *retired lawyer*
Tansill, Frederick Joseph *lawyer*
Townsend, Christopher Gordon *lawyer*
Van Lare, Wendell John *lawyer, director*
Wall, Barbara Wartelle *lawyer*
Woolsey, R. James (Robert James Woolsey) *lawyer, former CIA director*
Zirkle, Warren E. *lawyer*

**Middlebrook**
Bernstein, Arthur D(onald) *lawyer, consultant*

**Middleburg**
Beddall, Thomas Henry *lawyer*
Boardman, Harold Frederick, Jr. *lawyer, retired corporate financial executive*

**Midlothian**
Hall, Franklin Perkins *lawyer, bank executive, state official*
Nuckols, Otis Wills *lawyer, educator*

**Norfolk**
Albert, Alan Dale *lawyer*
Baird, Edward Rouzie, Jr. *retired lawyer*
Bishop, Bruce Taylor *lawyer*
Corcoran, Andrew Patrick, Jr. *lawyer*
Cranford, Page Deronde *lawyer*
Davis, Terry Hunter, Jr. *lawyer*
Dimino, Joseph C. *lawyer*
Drescher, John Webb *lawyer*
Grierson, Kevin William *lawyer*
Holloway, John Early *lawyer*
James, Gus John, II, *lawyer*
Padgett, John David *lawyer*
Parker, Richard Wilson *lawyer, retired rail transportation executive*
Pearson, John Yeardley, Jr. *lawyer*
Poston, Anita Owings *lawyer*
Rephan, Jack *lawyer*
Russell, C. Edward, Jr. *lawyer*
Ryan, John Morgan *lawyer*
Shannon, John Sanford *lawyer, retired rail transportation executive*
Sims, Hunter W., Jr. *lawyer*
Stillman, Gregory N. *lawyer*

**Oakton**
Duesenberg, Robert H. *retired lawyer*

**Orange**
Thomas, Franklin A. III *lawyer*

**Petersburg**
Burns, Cassandra Stroud *prosecutor*
Everitt, Alice Lubin *labor arbitrator*
Spero, Morton Bertram *retired lawyer*

**Portsmouth**
Porter, J. Ridgely III *lawyer*

**Prince George**
Brown, Del M. Mauhrine *lawyer, educator*

**Prince William**
Foote, John Holland *lawyer*

**Pulaski**
McCarthy, Thomas James, Jr. *lawyer*

**Radford**
Turk, James Clinton, Jr. *lawyer*

**Reston**
Blakely, William D. *lawyer*
Bredehoft, Elaine Charlson *lawyer*
Burgujian, Richard V. *lawyer*
Foley, Christopher P. *lawyer*
Fowler, David Lucas *corporate lawyer*
Frankel, Kenneth M. *lawyer*
Hill, David Warren *lawyer*
Keler, Marianne Martha *lawyer*
Kirsch, Mark A. *lawyer*
Lipsey, Charles E. *lawyer*
McJunkin, John G. *lawyer*
Platt, Leslie A. *lawyer*
Rau, Lee Arthur *lawyer*
Ruxin, Robert H. *lawyer*
Scharff, Joseph Laurent *lawyer*
Spander, Deborah L. *lawyer*
Tifford, John Mark *lawyer*
Toole, John Harper *lawyer*
Westermeier, John Thomas, Jr. *lawyer, educator*

**Richmond**
Bagley, Philip Joseph III *lawyer*

Bagley, Terrence M. *lawyer*
Bates, John Wythe III *lawyer*
Beales, Randolph A. *lawyer, former state attorney general*
Belcher, Dennis Irl *lawyer*
Betts, James Edward *lawyer*
Booker, Lewis Thomas *lawyer*
Brasfield, Evans Booker *lawyer*
Brissette, Martha Blevins *lawyer*
Brockenbrough, Henry Watkins *lawyer*
Bryson, William Hamilton *law educator*
Burke, John K(irkland), Jr. *lawyer*
Burrus, Robert Lewis, Jr. *lawyer*
Cafritz, Diane L. *lawyer*
Carrell, Daniel Allan *lawyer*
Catlett, Richard H., Jr. *retired lawyer*
Clinard, Robert Noel *lawyer*
Cogbill, John Valentine III *lawyer*
Cutchins, Clifford Armstrong, IV, *lawyer*
Davenport, Bradfute Warwick, Jr. *lawyer*
Denny, Collins III *lawyer*
Derry, William R., Jr. *lawyer*
Dray, Mark Stanley *lawyer*
Eckstein, Maya M. *lawyer*
Edmonds, Thomas Andrew *legal association administrator*
Ellis, Andrew Jackson, Jr. *lawyer*
Fauls, Ted (Thomas E. duB. Fauls) *lawyer*
Fitzsimmons, Ellen Marie *lawyer*
Freeman, George Clemon, Jr. *lawyer*
Gary, Richard David *lawyer*
Gluck, Michelle H. *lawyer*
Goodpasture, Philip Henry *lawyer*
Goolsby, Allen Cunningham III *lawyer*
Grey, Robert J., Jr. *lawyer*
Hackney, Virginia Howitz *lawyer*
Hall, Stephen Charles *lawyer*
Heaton, Stuart Alan *lawyer*
Hettrick, George Harrison *lawyer*
Irwin, Donald Paulding *lawyer*
Janis, William R. *lawyer, state legislator*
Johnston, Francis Claiborne, Jr. *lawyer*
Kearfott, Joseph Conrad *lawyer*
Kilgore, Jerry W. *lawyer, former state attorney general*
King, William H., Jr. *lawyer*
Konvicka, Jason Wade *lawyer*
Landin, David Craig *lawyer*
Ledbetter, David Oscar *lawyer*
Lutz, Jacob A. (Jake) III *lawyer*
Mahoney, George LeFevre *lawyer*
Marshall, Gary S. *lawyer*
McClard, Jack Edward *lawyer*
McElligott, James Patrick, Jr. *lawyer*
McFarlane, Walter Alexander *lawyer, educator*
Meath, James V. *lawyer*
Minardi, Richard A. (Rick), Jr. *lawyer*
Moore, T. Justin III *lawyer*
Moore, Thurston Roach *lawyer*
Morris, James Watson III *lawyer*
O'Toole, Deborah Shea *lawyer*
Pinckney, Charles Cotesworth *lawyer*
Pollard, Overton Price *retired lawyer*
Pope, Robert Dean *lawyer*
Powell, Lewis Franklin III *lawyer*
Pulley, J. Waverly, III, (Waverly Pulley) *lawyer*
Rainey, Gordon Fryer, Jr. *lawyer*
Redmond, David Dudley *lawyer*
Reed, Austin F. *lawyer*
Rhoads, Mark B. *lawyer*
Richardson, David L. *lawyer*
Rick, Roseleen P. *lawyer*
Rigsby, Linda Flory *lawyer*
Rinaca, James M. *lawyer*
Robertson, Gregory B. *lawyer*
Rohman, Thomas P. *lawyer*
Rolfe, Robert Martin *lawyer*
Rowe, William L. S. *lawyer*
Ryland, Walter H. *lawyer*
Schwarzschild, Jane L. *lawyer*
Seabolt, Robert D. *lawyer*
Sharer, John Daniel *lawyer*
Shiembob, Mark S. *lawyer*
Slater, Thomas Glascock, Jr. *lawyer*
Slaughter, Alexander Hoke *lawyer*
Smith, Julious Perry, Jr. *lawyer*
Smith, R. Gordon *lawyer*
Somerville, George Arnold *lawyer*
Spahn, Gary Joseph *lawyer*
Starke, Harold Eugene, Jr. *lawyer*
Starr, Edward H., Jr. *lawyer*
Stone, Jacquelyn Flnis *lawyer*
Strickland, William Jesse *lawyer*
Stutts, James F. *lawyer*
Swartz, Charles Robert *lawyer*
Thomas, John Charles *lawyer*
Thompson, Paul Michael *lawyer*
Thro, William Eugene *lawyer*
Totten, Randolph Fowler *lawyer*
Troy, Anthony Francis *lawyer*
Vaughan, C. Porter III *lawyer*
Waddell, William Robert *lawyer*
Walsh, William Arthur, Jr. *lawyer*
Warthen, Harry Justice III *lawyer*
Watts, Stephen Hurt, II, *lawyer*
Wellford, Hill B., Jr. *lawyer*
Williams, Amy McDaniel *lawyer*
Witt, Walter Francis, Jr. *lawyer*
Wright, Wiley Reed, Jr. *lawyer, retired judge, mediator*

**Roanoke**
Anderson, Phillip V. *lawyer*
Bates, Harold Martin *lawyer*
Brownlee, John L. *prosecutor*
Butler, Manley Caldwell *retired lawyer*
Effel, Laura *lawyer*
Fishwick, John Palmer *retired lawyer, railroad executive*
Glenn, Robert Eastwood *lawyer*
Lemon, William Jacob *lawyer*
Magee, A. Carter *lawyer, educator*
Margolin, Eric Mitchell *lawyer*
Marshall, Heman Alexander III *lawyer*
Steele, Anita Martin (Margaret Anne Martin) *law librarian, law educator*
Thomson, Paul Rice, Jr. *lawyer*
Woodrum, Clifton A. III *lawyer, retired state legislator*

**Salem**
Griffith, H(oward) Morgan *lawyer*

Young, James Marion *lawyer*

**South Riding**
Murray, Michael Patrick *lawyer*

**Spotsylvania**
Manthei, Richard Dale *retired lawyer, health products executive*

**Springfield**
Chappell, Milton Leroy *lawyer*
Englert, Roy Theodore *lawyer*

**Sterling**
Clegg, Roger Burton *lawyer*

**Vienna**
Dolan, William D. III *lawyer*
Gary, Stuart Hunter *lawyer*
Gavin, Donald Glenn *lawyer, educator*
Mackesey, Daniel R. *lawyer*
Maguire, Margaret Louise *lawyer*
Maiwurm, James John *lawyer*
Peters, Geoffrey Wright *lawyer, fundraising executive*
Razzano, Frank Charles *lawyer*
Schwartz, Philip *lawyer*
Titus, Bruce Earl *lawyer*
Walsh, William L., Jr. *lawyer*
Whitaker, Thomas Patrick *lawyer*
Yurow, Michael Jay *lawyer*

**Virginia Beach**
Baldwin, Stanley F. *lawyer*
Barney, Michael E. *lawyer*
Christiansen, Margaret Louise *law librarian, lawyer*
Harrell, Charles Lydon, Jr. *lawyer*
Jones, Robert Griffith *law educator, mayor*
Pickett, Owen Bradford *lawyer, former congressman*
Sekulow, Jay Alan *lawyer*
Spitzli, Donald Hawkes, Jr. *lawyer*

**Ware Neck**
McVey, Henry Hanna III *retired lawyer*

**Williamsburg**
Church, Dale Walker *lawyer*
Clark, Morton Hutchinson *lawyer*
Graham, David Browning *lawyer*
Marcus, Paul *law educator*
Margolin, Robert Jeremy *lawyer*
Merritt, James Edward *lawyer*
Sullivan, Timothy Jackson *lawyer, educator, retired academic administrator*

**Woodstock**
Walton, Morgan Lauck III *lawyer*

## WASHINGTON

**Anacortes**
Cavanaugh, Michael Everett *lawyer, arbitrator, mediator*
Glein, Richard Jeriel, Sr. *lawyer*

**Bainbridge Island**
Fischer, Thomas Covell *law educator, consultant, writer*

**Bellevue**
Christianson, Jeffrey A. *lawyer*
Hannah, Lawrence Burlison *lawyer*
Kari, Donald G. *lawyer*
Morie, G. Glen *lawyer, manufacturing executive*
Sebris, Robert, Jr. *lawyer*
Sweeney, David Brian *lawyer*

**Bellingham**
Anderson, David Bowen *lawyer*
Packer, Mark Barry *lawyer, financial consultant, foundation official*
Raas, Daniel Alan *lawyer*

**Bothell**
Gustafson, Alice Fairleigh *lawyer*

**Bremerton**
Cunningham, Gary Allen *lawyer*

**Centralia**
Buzzard, Steven Ray *lawyer*

**Colfax**
Webster, Ronald B. *lawyer*

**Eastsound**
Hoagland, Karl King, Jr. *lawyer*

**Everett**
Ostergaard, Joni Hammersla *lawyer*

**Federal Way**
Dowdy, Robert Alan *lawyer, director*
Nance, John Joseph *lawyer, writer, air traffic controller, announcer, consultant*

**Gig Harbor**
Thompson, Ronald Edward *lawyer*

**Hoquiam**
Kessler, Keith Leon *lawyer*

**Issaquah**
Benoliel, Joel *lawyer*

**Kennewick**
Hames, William Lester *lawyer*

**Keyport**
Treacy, Gerald Bernard, Jr. *lawyer*

**Mercer Island**
Anderson, Peter MacArthur *retired lawyer*
Medved, Robert Allen *lawyer*

**Mount Vernon**
Moser, C. Thomas *lawyer*

**Newcastle**
Erxleben, William Charles *lawyer, data processing executive*

**Olympia**
Isaki, Lucy Power Slyngstad *lawyer*
Roe, Charles Barnett *lawyer*

**Port Angeles**
Taylor, S. Brooke *lawyer*

**Pullman**
Savage, David William *lawyer*

**Redmond**
Burt, Thomas William *lawyer*
Heynssens, Paul Brian *lawyer, electrical engineer*

**Seattle**
Alkire, John D. *lawyer, arbitrator, mediator*
Alsdorf, Robert Hermann *lawyer*
Andrews, J. David *lawyer*
Baruffi, Kumi Yamamoto *lawyer*
Berman, Steve William *lawyer, author*
Birmingham, Richard Joseph *lawyer*
Blair, M. Wayne *lawyer*
Blom, Daniel Charles *lawyer, investor, retired insurance company executive*
Blumenfeld, Charles Raban *lawyer*
Boeder, Thomas L. *lawyer*
Boggs, Paula Elaine *lawyer*
Boman, Marc Allen *lawyer*
Bridge, Jonathan Joseph *lawyer, retail executive*
Bringman, Joseph Edward *lawyer*
Brown, Michael Jay *lawyer*
Burke, William Thomas *lawyer, educator*
Chapman, Fay L. *lawyer*
Char, Patricia Helen *lawyer*
Claflin, Arthur Cary *lawyer*
Cross, Bruce Michael *lawyer*
Cullen, Jack Joseph *lawyer*
Cunningham, Janis Ann *lawyer*
Davis, John MacDougall *lawyer*
DeVore, Paul Cameron *lawyer*
Dillow, John David *lawyer*
Dolan, Andrew Kevin *lawyer*
Dong, Nelson G. *lawyer*
Donlan, Dan Joseph *lawyer*
Dotten, Michael Chester *lawyer*
Ellis, Stephen Charles *lawyer*
Emory, Meade *lawyer*
Fisher, Jeffrey L. *lawyer*
Frush, Curtis James *lawyer*
Gaffney, Joseph M. *lawyer*
Gerrard, Keith *lawyer*
Giles, Robert Edward, Jr. *lawyer*
Gittinger, D. Wayne *lawyer*
Glover, Karen Elaine *lawyer*
Gonzalez, Carmen Gracia *law professor*
Gores, Thomas C. *lawyer*
Gormèzano, Keith *arbitrator, writer, web site designer*
Gorton, Slade (Thomas Slade Gorton III) *lawyer, former senator*
Grace, Ryan Thomas *lawyer*
Gradel, James D. *lawyer*
Graham, Stephen Michael *lawyer*
Gray, Marvin Lee, Jr. *lawyer*
Green, William L. *lawyer*
Haman, Raymond William *retired lawyer*
Hansen, Wayne W. *lawyer*
Hazelton, Penny Ann *law librarian, educator*
Hermsen, James R. *lawyer*
Hill, G. Richard *lawyer*
Hilpert, Edward Theodore, Jr. *retired lawyer*
Hineline, Curt Roy *lawyer*
Hollinrake, John D., Jr. *lawyer*
Holtan, Ramer B., Jr. *lawyer*
Huston, John Charles *law educator*
Hutcheson, Mark Andrew *lawyer*
Israel, Allen D. *lawyer*
Jaffe, Robert Stanley *lawyer*
Johnson, Bruce Edward Humble *lawyer*
Jones, Randal R. *lawyer*
Judson, C(harles) James (Jim Judson) *lawyer*
Kane, Alan Henry *lawyer*
Kaplan, Robert David *lawyer*
Kargian, John B. *lawyer*
Klein, Otto George III *lawyer*
Koegen, Roy Jerome *lawyer*
Koehler, Reginald Stafford III *lawyer*
Koh, Steve Y. *lawyer*
Kraft, James Allen *lawyer*
Kuhrau, Edward W. *lawyer*
Landefeld, Stewart M. *lawyer*
Leitzell, Terry Lee *lawyer*
Lemly, Thomas Adger *lawyer*
Lisbakken, James Robert *lawyer*
Locke, Gary F. *lawyer, former governor*
Losey, Beverley Brown *lawyer*
Maleng, Norm *prosecutor*
Manning, J. Richard *lawyer*
Marchese, Lisa Marie *lawyer, educator*
McCann, Richard Eugene *lawyer*
McCune, Philip Spear *lawyer*
McKay, John *prosecutor, lawyer*
Mussehl, Robert Clarence *lawyer*
Neukom, William H. *lawyer*
Niemi, Janice *retired lawyer, retired state legislator*
Oehler, Richard William *lawyer*
Olsen, Harold Fremont *lawyer*
Paget, Joel Hathaway *lawyer*
Palmer, Douglas S., Jr. *lawyer*
Parks, Patricia Jean *lawyer*
Parris, Mark S. *lawyer, professional athletes consultant*
Paul, Thomas Frank *lawyer*
Pedersen, Jamie D. *lawyer*
Petrie, Gregory Steven *lawyer*
Prentke, Richard Ottesen *lawyer*
Price, John R. *lawyer, educator*
Pritchard, Llewelyn George *lawyer*
Pym, Bruce Michael *lawyer*
Rasmussen, Frederick Tatum *lawyer*
Redman, Eric *lawyer*
Reynvaan, Michael Thomas *lawyer*
Rieke, Paul Victor *lawyer*

Ritter, Daniel Benjamin *lawyer*
Robinson, Jeffrey P. *lawyer*
Rondeau, George Charles, Jr. *lawyer*
Rosen, Jon Howard *lawyer*
Ruddy, James W. *lawyer*
Russell, Robie George *lawyer*
Schneider, Harry H., Jr. *lawyer*
Schultheis, Patrick Joseph *lawyer*
Schwab, Evan Lynn *lawyer*
Smith, Scott A. *lawyer*
Soltys, John Joseph *lawyer*
Spitzer, Hugh D. *lawyer*
Squires, William Randolph III *lawyer*
Steichen, Randall R. *lawyer*
Stoebuck, William Brees *law educator*
Stokke, Diane Rees *lawyer*
Takenaka, Toshiko *lawyer, educator*
Treiger, Irwin Louis *lawyer*
Tune, James Fulcher *lawyer*
Vestal, Josephine Burnet *lawyer*
Vogel, David Seth *lawyer*
Vosk, Ted W. *lawyer*
Wagoner, David Everett *lawyer, arbitrator*
Ward, Ronald R. *lawyer*
Wechsler, Mary Heyrman *lawyer*
Williams, J. Vernon *retired lawyer*
Williams, Nancy *lawyer*
Wilson, L. Michelle *lawyer*
Wilson, Richard Randolph *lawyer*

**Spokane**
Clarke, Judy *lawyer*
Connolly, Kenneth Thomas *lawyer*
Eymann, Richard Charles *lawyer*
Harbaugh, Daniel Paul *lawyer*
Kovacevich, Robert Eugene *lawyer*
McDevitt, James A. *prosecutor, lawyer*

**Tacoma**
Carlisle, Dale L. *lawyer*
George, Nicholas *lawyer, entrepreneur*
Gordon, Joseph Harold *lawyer*
Holt, William E. *lawyer, department chairman*
Krueger, James A. *lawyer*
Miller, Judson Frederick *lawyer, retired military officer*
Waldo, James Chandler *lawyer*

**Tukwila**
Fitzpatrick, Thomas Mark *lawyer*

**Tumwater**
Edmondson, Frank Kelley, Jr. *lawyer, legal administrator*

**Walla Walla**
Hayner, Herman Henry *lawyer*

**Yakima**
Larson, Paul Martin *lawyer*

**WEST VIRGINIA**

**Beckley**
Rhoades, Marye Frances *paralegal*

**Charleston**
Betts, Rebecca A. *lawyer*
Brown, James Knight *lawyer*
Dissen, James Hardiman *lawyer*
Hurt, Charles Edward *lawyer*
Love, Charles Marion III *lawyer*
McCuskey, John F. *lawyer*
Miller, Charles T. *prosecutor*
Neely, Richard *lawyer*
Robinson, E. Glenn *lawyer*
Rowe, Larry Linwell *lawyer, former state senator*
Rowe, Richard Edwin *lawyer*
Stanton, George Patrick, Jr. *lawyer*
Taylor, Larry D. *lawyer*
Zak, Robert Joseph *lawyer*

**Clarksburg**
West, James C., Jr. *lawyer*

**Fairmont**
Aloi, Michael John *lawyer*

**Huntington**
Bagley, Charles Frank III *lawyer*
Underwood, Mark Forest *lawyer*

**Hurricane**
Hill, David Lawrence *lawyer, real estate agent*

**Lewisburg**
Ford, Richard Edmond *lawyer*

**Martinsburg**
Hill, Philip Bonner *lawyer*
Martin, Clarence Eugene III *lawyer*
Rice, Lacy I., Jr. *lawyer*

**Morgantown**
Fisher, John Welton, II, *lawyer, educator, academic administrator*
Fusco, Andrew G. *lawyer*
Morris, William Otis, Jr. *lawyer, educator*
Scudiere, Debra Hodges *lawyer*

**Oak Hill**
Hamilton, Pat Ray *retired lawyer, state representative*

**Princeton**
Prudich, Gregory S. *lawyer*

**Romney**
Saville, Royce Blair *lawyer*

**Wheeling**
Bailey, John P. *lawyer*
Hill, Barry Morton *lawyer*
Valdrini, Rita *prosecutor*

**WISCONSIN**

**Appleton**
Samson, Harvey Gilbert *lawyer*

**Black River Falls**
Lister, Thomas Edward *lawyer*

**Brookfield**
Winsten, Saul Nathan *lawyer*

**Deerfield**
Pappas, David Christopher *lawyer*

**Eau Claire**
Frank, John LeRoy *lawyer, educator, federal official*

**Elkhorn**
Sostarich, Mark Edward *lawyer*

**Germantown**
Ehlinger, Ralph Jerome *lawyer*

**Grafton**
Maynard, John Ralph *lawyer*

**Green Bay**
Burnett, Ralph George *lawyer*
Nixon, Timothy Francis *lawyer*

**Greendale**
Vinent-Cantoral, Aida R. *mediator*

**Hales Corners**
Case, Karen Ann *lawyer*

**Janesville**
Steil, George Kenneth, Sr. *lawyer*

**Kenosha**
Constant, Terry Lynn *lawyer*
Giza, David Alan *lawyer*
Marrinan, Susan Faye *lawyer*

**La Crosse**
Klos, Jerome John *lawyer, director*
Nix, Edmund Alfred *lawyer*
Sleik, Thomas Scott *lawyer*

**Lake Geneva**
Braden, Berwyn Bartow *lawyer*

**Madison**
Bablitch, William A. *lawyer, retired state supreme court justice*
Baldwin, Gordon Brewster *retired law educator*
Barnhill, Charles Joseph, Jr. *lawyer*
Barnick, Helen *retired judicial clerk*
Berson, Bennett Jay *lawyer*
Bochert, Linda H. *lawyer*
Boykoff, Thomas M. *retired lawyer*
Bremer, Howard Walter *lawyer, consultant*
Bugge, Lawrence John *lawyer, educator*
Charo, Robin Alta *law educator*
Curtis, Charles G., Jr. *lawyer*
Field, Henry Augustus, Jr. *lawyer*
Hanson, David James *lawyer*
Heymann, S. Richard *lawyer*
Hildebrand, Daniel Walter *lawyer*
Howell, Roberta F. *lawyer*
Langer, Richard J. *lawyer*
Latta, Richard Allen *lawyer*
Lavers, Richard Marshall *lawyer*
Linstroth, Tod Brian *lawyer*
McCallum, Laurie Riach *state government lawyer*
Melli, Marygold Shire *law educator*
Mohs, Frederic Edward *lawyer*
Mowris, Gerald William *lawyer*
Peterson, Erik Charles *prosecutor*
Prange, Roy Leonard, Jr. *lawyer*
Ragatz, Thomas George *lawyer*
Ranney, Joseph Austin *lawyer*
Schott, Donald Karl *lawyer*
Skilton, John Singleton *lawyer*
Spencer, Christopher S. *lawyer, insurance company executive*
Steingass, Susan R. *lawyer*
Sweeney, Timothy C. *lawyer*
Temkin, Harvey L. *lawyer*
Vaughan, Michael Richard *lawyer*
Walsh, David Graves *lawyer*
White, William Fredrick *lawyer*

**Manitowoc**
Jones, Maurice D. *lawyer*

**Mauston**
Curran, Paul Saether *lawyer*

**Menasha**
Kneezel, Ronald D. *lawyer*

**Menomonee Falls**
Schepp, Richard D. *lawyer, retail executive*

**Mequon**
Andritzky, Joseph George *law educator*
O'Shaughnessy, James Patrick *lawyer, consultant*
Whyte, George Kenneth, Jr. *lawyer*

**Middleton**
Berman, Ronald Charles *lawyer, accountant*
Nora, Wendy Alison *lawyer*

**Milwaukee**
Abraham, William John, Jr. *lawyer*
Alverson, William H. *lawyer*
Babler, Wayne E., Jr. *lawyer*
Bailey, Thomas Anthony *lawyer*
Ballman, Patricia Kling *lawyer*
Bannen, John Thomas *lawyer*
Barnes, Paul McClung *lawyer*
Berdan, Robert J. *lawyer*
Berkoff, Marshall Richard *lawyer*
Biehl, Michael Melvin *lawyer, writer*
Biller, Joel Wilson *lawyer, retired diplomat*
Biskupic, Steven M. *prosecutor, lawyer*
Boer, Ralf Reinhard *lawyer*

Bolger, T(homas) Michael *lawyer*
Braeger, Jessica Lynn *lawyer*
Branch, Joseph C. *lawyer*
Bremer, John M. *lawyer*
Bruce, Peter Wayne *lawyer, insurance company executive*
Busch, John Arthur *lawyer, educational association administrator*
Cannon, David Joseph *lawyer*
Casey, John Alexander *lawyer*
Casper, Richard Henry *lawyer*
Chokey, James A. *lawyer*
Christiansen, Keith Allan *lawyer*
Clark, James Richard *lawyer*
Connolly, Gerald Edward *lawyer*
Cutler, Richard W. *lawyer*
Daily, Frank J(erome) *lawyer*
Dionisopoulos, George Allan *lawyer*
Emanuel, John F. *lawyer*
Fellows, Gerald Lee *lawyer*
Florsheim, Richard Steven *lawyer*
Fraser, Alexander Paul *lawyer*
Frauen, Kurt Herman *lawyer*
Frautschi, Timothy Clark *lawyer*
Friebert, Robert Howard *lawyer*
Friedman, James Dennis *lawyer*
Gaines, Irving David *lawyer*
Galanis, John William *lawyer*
Gallagher, Richard Sidney *lawyer*
Gefke, Henry Jerome *lawyer*
Geilfuss, C. Frederick, II, *lawyer*
Gemignani, Joseph Adolph *lawyer*
Geske, Janine Patricia *law educator*
Ghiardi, James Domenic *lawyer, educator*
Goodkind, Conrad George *lawyer*
Graber, Richard William *lawyer, political organization worker*
Guerin, D. Michael *lawyer*
Haberman, F. William *lawyer*
Habush, Robert Lee *lawyer*
Harrington, John Timothy *retired lawyer*
Hase, David John *lawyer*
Hatch, Michael Ward *lawyer*
Hoffman, Nathaniel A. *lawyer*
Holz, Harry George *lawyer*
Iding, Allan Earl *lawyer*
Ireland, Emory *lawyer*
Jackson, Tamara Nicole *lawyer*
Jaspan, Stanley S. *lawyer*
Jost, Lawrence John *lawyer*
Kamps, Charles Q. *retired lawyer*
Karp, David Barry *lawyer*
Kennedy, John Patrick *lawyer, corporate financial executive*
Kircher, John Joseph *law educator*
Kringel, Jerome Howard *lawyer*
Krueger, Raymond Robert *lawyer*
Kubale, Bernard Stephen *lawyer*
Kurtz, Harvey A. *lawyer*
Kushner, Beth *lawyer*
LaBudde, Roy Christian *lawyer*
Lane, Jeffrey H. *lawyer*
Levit, William Harold, Jr. *lawyer*
Lione, Gail Ann *lawyer*
Lueders, Wayne Richard *lawyer*
Lynch, Michael *lawyer, staffing company executive*
Martin, Quinn William *lawyer*
McGaffey, Jere D. *retired lawyer*
McGinnity, Maureen Annell *lawyer*
McKeown, James T. *lawyer*
McSweeney, Maurice J. (Marc McSweeney) *lawyer*
Meldman, Robert Edward *lawyer*
Melin, Robert Arthur *lawyer*
Mitten, Matthew J. *law educator, lawyer*
Mulcahy, Robert William *lawyer*
Oldfather, Chad Michael *law educator*
Phillips, Thomas John *lawyer*
Pindyck, Bruce Eben *lawyer, corporate financial executive*
Richman, Stephen Erik *lawyer, consultant*
Romoser, W. David *lawyer*
Ryan, Patrick Michael *lawyer*
Santelle, James Lewis *prosecutor*
Schnur, Robert Arnold *lawyer*
Scrivner, Thomas William *lawyer*
Sennett, Nancy J. *lawyer*
Shapiro, Robyn Sue *lawyer, educator*
Shriner, Thomas L., Jr. *lawyer*
Sturm, William Charles *lawyer*
Surridge, Stephen Zehring *lawyer, writer*
Terschan, Frank Robert *lawyer*
Trecek, Timothy Scott *lawyer*
Tully, Catherine T. *lawyer*
Tyson, Joseph B., Jr. *lawyer*
Van Vugt, Eric J. *lawyer*
Wiley, Edwin Packard *retired lawyer*
Will, Trevor Jonathan *lawyer*
Williams, Allen W., Jr. *lawyer*
Williams, Clay Rule *lawyer*

**Monroe**
Kittelsen, Rodney Olin *lawyer*

**Oak Creek**
Giblin, Louis *lawyer*

**Oshkosh**
Blankfield, Bryan J. *lawyer, automotive executive, accountant*
Kelly, John Martin *lawyer*

**Pewaukee**
Ward, James A. *lawyer*

**Racine**
Coates, Glenn Richard *lawyer*

**Ripon**
Prissel, Barbara Ann *paralegal, law educator*

**Sheboygan**
Mohr, Jeffrey Thomas *lawyer*

**Union Grove**
Stern, Walter Wolf III *lawyer*

**Waukesha**
Cauley, James Robert *lawyer*
McCoy, John V. *lawyer*
Moran, Kevin Paul *lawyer*

Nettesheim, Timothy Alan *lawyer*

**Wausau**
Drengler, William Allan John *lawyer*
Etten, Stewart Louis *lawyer*
Orr, San Watterson, Jr. *lawyer*

**Wauwatosa**
Alexander, Robert Gardner *lawyer*
Heath, Robert F. *lawyer*
Savage, Thomas Ryan *lawyer*

**Williams Bay**
Tobin, Dennis Michael *lawyer*

**WYOMING**

**Buffalo**
Kirven, Timothy J. *lawyer*

**Casper**
Durham, Harry Blaine III *lawyer*
Lowe, Robert Stanley *lawyer*
Sullivan, Michael John *lawyer, former ambassador*

**Cheyenne**
Burke, E. James *lawyer, state supreme court justice*
Carlson, Kathleen Bussart *law librarian*
Freudenthal, Steven Franklin *lawyer, political organization worker*
Mead, Matthew Hansen *prosecutor*
Palma, Jack D. *lawyer*
Sansonetti, Thomas L. *lawyer, former federal agency administrator*

**Gillette**
Bailey, Daniel B. *lawyer, entrepreneur*
Lubnau, Thomas Edwin, II, *lawyer*
Michaels, Deborah Downey *lawyer*

**Jackson**
Schuster, Robert Parks *lawyer*
Spence, Gerry (Gerald Leonard Spence) *lawyer, writer*

**Laramie**
Kinney, Lisa Frances *lawyer*
Lauer, Warren *lawyer*

**Powell**
Dean, Patricea Louise *lawyer, law educator, small business owner*

**Riverton**
Girard, Nettabell *lawyer*

**Wheatland**
Hunkins, Raymond Breedlove *lawyer, rancher*

**TERRITORIES OF THE UNITED STATES**

**GUAM**

**Tamuning**
Aguigui, Ignacio Cruz *lawyer*

**NORTHERN MARIANA ISLANDS**

**Saipan**
Rapadas, Leonardo M. *prosecutor, lawyer*

**PUERTO RICO**

**Old San Juan**
Weinstein-Bacal, Stuart Allen *lawyer, educator*

**San Juan**
Casellas, Ricardo F. *lawyer*
Corrada del Rio, Baltasar *lawyer, retired former state supreme court justice*
Garcia, Humberto Sigifredo *former prosecutor, lawyer*
Gil, Guillermo *prosecutor*
Hoglund, Heath *lawyer*
Negron-Garcia, Antonio S. *law educator, former territory supreme court justice*
Pierluisi, Pedro R. *lawyer*
Rodriguez-Diaz, Juan E. *lawyer*

**VIRGIN ISLANDS**

**Charlotte Amalie**
Feuerzeig, Henry Louis *lawyer*

**Christiansted**
Bland, James Theodore, Jr. *lawyer*
Grey, Samuel T. *lawyer*

**St Thomas**
Carty, Amos W. *lawyer*
Jenkins, Anthony Jerome *prosecutor*

**MILITARY ADDRESSES OF THE UNITED STATES**

**EUROPE**

**APO**
Kammerer, Kelly Christian *lawyer*

## CANADA

### ALBERTA

**Calgary**
Lougheed, Peter *lawyer, former Canadian premier*
McEwen, Alexander Campbell *legal association administrator, consultant, cadastral studies educator, former Canadian government official, land use planner*

### BRITISH COLUMBIA

**Burnaby**
Switlo, Janice Georgina Alice E. *barrister, solicitor, mediator, consultant*
Wainwright, David Stanley *patent agent*

**Sooke**
Howard, John Lindsay *lawyer*

**Vancouver**
McEachern, Allan *lawyer*
Penikett, Tony *mediator, negotiator, writer, political organization worker*
Peterson, Leslie Raymond *barrister*

### MANITOBA

**Winnipeg**
Anderson, David Trevor *law educator*
Edwards, Clifford Henry Coad *law educator*
Schnoor, Jeffrey Arnold *lawyer*

### NEW BRUNSWICK

**Rothesay**
Fairweather, Robert Gordon Lee *retired lawyer*

### NOVA SCOTIA

**Halifax**
Dexter, Robert Paul *lawyer*

### NUNAVUT

**Kugaaruk**
Rodnunsky, Sidney *lawyer, educator*

### ONTARIO

**Markham**
Gulden, Simon *lawyer, management consultant, consultant*

**Ottawa**
d'Aquino, Thomas *lawyer, educator, entrepreneur*
Tassé, Roger *lawyer, former Canadian government official*
Urie, John James *retired lawyer, former Canadian federal judge*

**Thornhill**
Lublinski, Michael *lawyer*

**Toronto**
Arthurs, Harry William *lawyer, educator, academic administrator*
Chester, Robert Simon George *lawyer*
Davis, William Grenville *lawyer, former Canadian government official*
Dickens, Bernard Morris *law educator*
Dubin, Charles Leonard *lawyer*
Farquharson, Gordon MacKay *lawyer, director*
Iacobucci, Frank *lawyer, judge, academic administrator*
Kaufman, Donna S. *lawyer*
Peterson, David Robert *lawyer, former Canadian government official*

### QUEBEC

**Ile Perrot**
Lalonde, Marc *lawyer, former Canadian government official*

**Montreal**
Lacoste, Paul *law educator, academic administrator*
Popovici, Adrian *law educator*
Pound, Richard William Duncan *lawyer, accountant*
Robb, James Alexander *lawyer*

**Quebec City**
LeMay, Jacques *lawyer*
Morin, Louis *lawyer*
Verge, Pierre *legal educator*

**Sainte-Foy**
Normand, Robert *retired lawyer*

**Sillery**
Dinan, Robert Michael *lawyer*

**Westmount**
Fortier, L. Yves *barrister*

### SASKATCHEWAN

**Regina**
MacKay, Harold Hugh *lawyer*

**Saskatoon**
Ish, Daniel Russell *law educator, academic administrator*

**Toronto**
Stanley, Deirdre *lawyer*

## AUSTRALIA

**Melbourne**
Browne, Jeffrey Francis *lawyer*

## BANGLADESH

**Kushtia**
Latifur Rahaman, Rasul Boaksh *legal association administrator*

## BELGIUM

**Brussels**
Barnum, John Wallace *lawyer*
Bustin, George Leo *lawyer*
Horton, Linda Rae *lawyer*

## BERMUDA

**Hamilton**
McCormick, Hugh Thomas *lawyer*

## CHINA

**Beijing**
Christianson, Jon L. *lawyer*
Lehman, Edward E. *lawyer*
Thomas, Robert Morton, Jr. *lawyer*

**Hong Kong**
Halperin, David Richard *lawyer*
Nelson, Steven Craig *lawyer*

**Shanghai**
Lin, Maria C. H. *lawyer*

## DENMARK

**Copenhagen**
Elmer, Michael Bendik *legal administrator*

## ENGLAND

**Beverley**
Edles, Gary Joel *lawyer, law educator*

**London**
Fabricant, Arthur E. *lawyer, corporate financial executive*
Glazer, Barry David *lawyer*
Gottesman, A(rthur) Edward *lawyer*
Haubold, Samuel Allen *lawyer*
Hudson, Manley O., Jr. *lawyer*
Montgomery, John Warwick (Baron of Kiltartan and Lord of Morris, Comte de St. Germain de Montgommery) *law educator, theologian*
Morrison, William David *lawyer*
Phocas, George J. *lawyer*
Plapinger, William A. *lawyer*
Quillen, Cecil Dyer III *lawyer*
Rolle, Martha Collins (Martha Traudt Collins) *lawyer*
Smith, Robert Michael *lawyer, mediator, arbitrator*
Stevens, Robert Bocking *lawyer*
Stojkovic, Dusan *lawyer*
Stopford, Philip *lawyer*
Thomas, Allen Lloyd *lawyer, private investor*
Zonana, Victor *lawyer, educator*

**Middlesex**
Lynch, John Edward, Jr. *lawyer*

**Wiltshire**
Sherwin, James Terry *lawyer*
Aufhauser, David D. *lawyer, former federal agency administrator*

## FINLAND

**Helsinki**
Juhani, Erma *lawyer, former stock exchange executive*

## FRANCE

**Draguignan**
Frame, Nancy Davis *lawyer*

**Paris**
Baum, Axel Helmuth *lawyer*
Salans, Carl Fredric *lawyer*

## GERMANY

**Frankfurt**
Simitis, Spiros *legal educator*

## GUATEMALA

**Guatemala City**
Mayora-Alvarado, Eduardo Rene *lawyer, law educator*

## INDONESIA

**Jakarta**
Hsi, Edward Yang *lawyer, venture capitalist, industrialist*

## ISRAEL

**Be'er Sheva**
Frenkel, David Arie *law professor*

**Jerusalem**
Rosenne, Meir *lawyer, federal agency administrator*

**Tel Aviv**
Gross, Joseph H. *lawyer, educator*

## ITALY

**Rieti**
Truini Palomba, Maria Giuseppina *supreme court lawyer, judge*

**Rome**
McGurn, William Barrett III *lawyer*

## JAPAN

**Hachioji**
Kojima, Takeshi *law educator, arbitrator, writer*

**Tokyo**
Dixon, Bonnie Lynn *lawyer*
Shirai, Shun *law educator*

## LUXEMBOURG

**Kirchberg**
Leger, Philippe *legal administrator*

## NETHERLANDS

**The Hague**
Boed, Roman A. *legal administrator*

## NORWAY

**Oslo**
Fitzpatrick, Whitfield Westfeldt *lawyer*
Fleischer, Carl August *law educator, consultant*

## PHILIPPINES

**Manila**
Sumida, Gerald Aquinas *lawyer*

## POLAND

**Cracow**
Kasper, Horst Manfred *lawyer*

## REPUBLIC OF KOREA

**Seoul**
O'Brien, Timothy James *lawyer*

## SCOTLAND

**Edinburgh**
Macneil, Ian Roderick *lawyer, educator*

## SPAIN

**Madrid**
Herrero Rodriguez de Miñon, Miguel *lawyer, consultant, legislator*

## SWITZERLAND

**Chateau d'Oex**
Berman, Joshua Mordecai *lawyer, manufacturing executive*

**Geneva**
Capron, Alexander Morgan *lawyer, educator, bioethicist*
McDougall, Gay *lawyer*

**Zurich**
Hammesfahr, Robert Winter *lawyer*

## TAIWAN

**Tainan**
Chen, Chun-Jen *lawyer, educator*

## TANZANIA

**Arusha**
Rapp, Stephen John *international prosecutor*

## UNITED ARAB EMIRATES

**Abu Dhabi**
Taylor, Frederick William, Jr., (Fritz Taylor) *lawyer*

## UNITED STATES

**San Juan**
Rodriguez-Velez, Rosa *prosecutor*

## VENEZUELA

**Caracas**
Eljuri, Elisabeth *lawyer*

## VIETNAM

**Ho Chi Minh City**
Israel, Barry John *lawyer*

### ADDRESS UNPUBLISHED

Abbott, Kenneth Wayne *law educator*
Abbott, Lawrence E. *lawyer*
Adams, Arlin Marvin *lawyer, retired judge, arbitrator, mediator*
Adams, Daniel Fenton *law educator*
Adams, James Charles *lawyer*
Adams, Thomas Lynch, Jr. *lawyer*
Aikman, Albert Edward *lawyer*
Aksen, Gerald *arbitrator, lawyer, educator*
Alberger, William Relph *lawyer, retired government agency administrator*
Albin, Barry G. *lawyer, rabbi*
Alemu, Fitsum Achamyeleh *lawyer, researcher*
Alevizos, Susan Bamberger *lawyer, writer, musician*
Alfred, Stephen Jay *retired lawyer*
Allen, Toni K. *lawyer*
Allen, William Hayes *lawyer, educator*
Alpern, Andrew *lawyer, architect, historian*
Altman, Robert Alan *lawyer*
Amar, Akhil Reed *law educator*
Ames, Marc L. *retired lawyer*
Amestoy, Jeffrey Lee *law educator, former state supreme court chief justice*
Anderson, Thomas Dunaway *retired lawyer*
Andres, Greg D. *prosecutor, lawyer*
Andrews, David Ralph *lawyer*
Ansley, Shepard Bryan *lawyer*
Areen, Judith Carol *law educator, dean*
Arnold, Alanna S. Welling *lawyer*
Arnold, Jerome Gilbert *lawyer*
Arrowood, Catharine Biggs *lawyer*
Ashcroft, John David *law educator, former United States attorney general*
Ashton, Harris John *lawyer*
Askew, Kim Juanita *lawyer*
Atkinson, Nolan N., Jr. *lawyer*
Aune, Debra Bjurquist *lawyer*
Babb, Frank Edward *lawyer*
Babbin, Jed Lloyd *lawyer*
Bagan, Grant Alan *lawyer*
Bagley, William Thompson *lawyer*
Bailey, F. Lee (Francis Lee Bailey) *lawyer*
Bain, William Donald, Jr. *lawyer, chemicals executive*
Baird, Thomas Bryan, Jr. *retired lawyer*
Baker, Donald *lawyer, director*
Baker, William Thompson, Jr. *lawyer*
Bakkensen, John Reser *lawyer*
Ball, James Herington *retired lawyer*
Bamberger, Phylis Skloot *lawyer, educator, retired judge*
Barash, Anthony Harlan *lawyer*
Barlow, William Kyle *lawyer, state legislator*
Barnes, Susan Lewis *lawyer*
Barr, Charles F. *lawyer, insurance company executive*
Bartz, David John *lawyer*
Baruch, Hurd *retired lawyer*
Baughman, R(obert) Patrick *lawyer*
Baum, Stanley David *lawyer*
Bauman, Frederick Carl *lawyer*
Bean, Bruce Winfield *lawyer*
Beck, Stuart Edwin *lawyer*
Beldock, Myron *lawyer*
Bell, Albert Jerome *lawyer*
Bell, Haney Hardy III *lawyer*
Bell, John William *lawyer*
Belleville, Philip Frederick *lawyer*
Bencivengo, Cathy Ann *lawyer*
Bergan, William Luke *lawyer*
Berger, Robert Bertram *lawyer*
Berger, Sanford Jason *retired lawyer, retired securities dealer, retired real estate broker*
Bergstein, Daniel Gerard *lawyer*
Beringer, William Ernst *mediator, arbitrator, lawyer, retired manufacturing executive*
Berkley, Robert Clarkson *retired lawyer*
Berle, Peter Adolf Augustus *lawyer, media director*
Berman, Lori Beth *lawyer*
Bernstein, Merton Clay *law educator, arbitrator*
Berrey, Robert Forrest *lawyer*
Besing, Ray Gilbert *lawyer, educator*
Best, Laurence Edward *lawyer*
Bidwell, James Truman, Jr. *lawyer*
Bierig, Jack R. *lawyer, educator*
Birmingham, Thomas F. *lawyer, former state legislator*
Black, William Rea *lawyer*
Blackford, Robert Newton *lawyer, director*
Bleicher, Samuel Abram *lawyer, government agency administrator*
Bloch, Stuart Marshall *lawyer, banker*
Bloomer, Harold Franklin, Jr. *retired lawyer*
Blow, George *lawyer*
Boal, Ellis *lawyer*
Boho, Dan L. *lawyer*
Bondi, Harry Gene *lawyer*
Bonesio, Woodrow Michael *lawyer*

Booher, Alice Ann *lawyer*
Borenstein, Mark A. *lawyer*
Bork, Robert Heron *law educator, retired federal judge*
Borkowski, John Joseph *lawyer*
Borowitz, Albert Ira *lawyer, writer*
Bosl, Phillip L. *retired lawyer*
Bost, Thomas Glen *lawyer, educator*
Bouvier, Marshall Andre *lawyer*
Bower, Jean Ramsay *lawyer, writer*
Boyd, Joseph Arthur, Jr. *lawyer*
Boyd, William Sprott *lawyer*
Bradley, Amelia Jane *lawyer*
Brady, Edward Thomas, Jr. *lawyer, writer*
Brafford, William Charles *lawyer*
Branagan, James Joseph *lawyer*
Bransdorfer, Stephen Christie *retired lawyer*
Brantz, George Murray *retired lawyer*
Braun, Jerome Irwin *lawyer*
Bredehoft, John Michael *lawyer*
Brehl, James William *lawyer*
Brenneman, Russell Langdon *retired lawyer*
Brewer, Roy Edward *lawyer*
Briskman, Louis Jacob *lawyer*
Brister, Bill H. *lawyer, former bankruptcy judge*
Brodhead, David Crawmer *lawyer*
Brooke, Edward William *lawyer, retired senator*
Broughton, Phillip Charles *lawyer, director*
Brown, B. Andrew *lawyer*
Brown, Charles Dodgson *lawyer*
Brown, Geraldine Reed *lawyer, management consultant*
Brown, J. E. (Buster Brown) *lawyer, consultant*
Brown, Margaret deBeers *lawyer*
Brown, Peter Stewart *lawyer*
Brown Spitzmueller, Janiece Marie *lawyer*
Bruess, Charles Edward *lawyer*
Bryson, Nancy Southard *lawyer, former federal agency administrator*
Buchanan, William H., Jr. *retired lawyer, venture capitalist*
Buchmann, Alan Paul *lawyer*
Buckley, Frederick Jean *lawyer*
Buckley, Kristy Loraine *lawyer, accountant*
Buda, Thaddeus J., Jr. *retired lawyer*
Budd, Wayne A. *lawyer*
Bugliosi, Vincent T. *lawyer*
Burack, Michael Leonard *lawyer*
Burcham, David W. *law educator*
Burke, Linda Beerbower *lawyer, mining executive, metal products executive*
Burkey, Lee Melville *lawyer*
Burris, Steven Michael *lawyer*
Burton, Richard Jay *lawyer*
Busch, Arthur Allen *lawyer*
Buttrey, Donald Wayne *lawyer*
Cacciatore, Ronald Keith *lawyer*
Calderon, Ernest *lawyer*
Calise, William Joseph, Jr. *lawyer*
Cambrice, Robert Louis *lawyer*
Camilleri, Michael *lawyer, educator*
Campbell, Frederick Hollister *retired lawyer, historian*
Campbell, George Emerson *lawyer*
Campion, Thomas Francis *lawyer*
Cape, Billie Jean *lawyer*
Caraway, Stephanie Schankerman *prosecutor*
Cardinali, Albert John *lawyer*
Carey, Jana Howard *lawyer*
Carmack, Mildred Jean *retired lawyer*
Carnesi, Kenneth Brian *lawyer*
Carpenter, Susan Karen *defender*
Carpenter, Victoria J. *lawyer*
Carroll, Joseph J(ohn) *lawyer*
Carroll, Raoul Lord *lawyer, investment banker*
Carter, Jeanne Wilmot *lawyer, publishing executive*
Casey, Robert Reisch *lawyer*
Casselman, William E., II, *lawyer*
Cassidy, John Harold *lawyer*
Castel, Jean Gabriel *lawyer, educator, international arbitrator*
Castro, Raul Hector *lawyer, retired governor, retired ambassador*
Cazalas, Mary Rebecca Williams *lawyer, nurse*
Chaifetz, David Harvey *lawyer*
Chaleff, Gerald Lawrence *lawyer*
Chamberlin, Michael Meade *lawyer*
Chance, Steven Kent *lawyer*
Charles, Robert Bruce *lawyer, former federal agency administrator*
Chave, Carol *arbitrator, retired lawyer*
Cheatham, Robert William *retired lawyer*
Cheek, Michael Carroll *lawyer*
Chefitz, Joel Gerald *lawyer*
Cherovsky, Erwin Louis *lawyer, writer*
Christensen, Karen Kay *lawyer*
Citron, Diane *lawyer*
Clark, Beverly Ann *retired lawyer*
Clark, Beverly Jean *lawyer, mediator*
Clark, Donald Otis *lawyer*
Clark, Karen Heath *lawyer*
Cleesattle, Jodi Lynn *lawyer*
Clubb, Bruce Edwin *retired lawyer*
Cobb, Miles Alan *retired lawyer*
Cohen, Christopher B. *lawyer*
Cohen, Jeffrey *lawyer*
Cohen, Joel J. *lawyer, investment banker*
Coleman, John Michael *lawyer, consumer products company executive*
Coleman, Robert Lee *retired lawyer*
Coleman, William Thaddeus, Jr. *lawyer, former secretary of transportation*
Coletti, John Anthony *lawyer, retail executive, real estate company executive*
Collins, Theodore John *lawyer*
Colodny, Edwin Irving *lawyer, retired air transportation executive*
Colton, Sterling Don *retired lawyer, retired hotel executive*
Comisky, Ian Michael *lawyer*
Compton, Robert H. *lawyer*
Conley, Ned Leroy *lawyer*
Connell, William D. *lawyer*
Connelly, Sharon Rudolph *lawyer*
Conner, Lindsay Andrew *lawyer*
Conrad, David Williams *retired lawyer*
Conway, Thomas J. *retired lawyer*
Cooley, Seth van den Hoek *lawyer*
Cooper, George *lawyer, consultant, writer*
Cooper, Hal Dean *lawyer*
Corle, James Thomas *lawyer*

Coughlan, Kenneth L. *lawyer*
Cowperthwait, Lindley Murray *lawyer*
Cowser, Danny Lee *lawyer, mental health specialist*
Cox, Chapman Beecher *retired lawyer, retired charitable organization executive, retired aerospace executive*
Cox, Marshall *lawyer*
Coyle, Martin Adolphus, Jr. *lawyer, consultant*
Cranney, Marilyn Kanrek *retired lawyer*
Crawford, Carol Tallman *law educator*
Crawford, Muriel Laura *lawyer, educator, writer*
Cremins, James Smyth *lawyer*
Crocker, Saone Baron *lawyer*
Cronson, Robert Granville *lawyer*
Crowe, James Joseph *lawyer*
Cunningham, Alice Welt *law and mathematics educator*
Curtis, Susan Grace *lawyer*
Cutler, Laurence Jeffrey *lawyer*
Daniel, Marilyn S. *lawyer*
Daub, Hal (Harold John Daub Jr.) *lawyer*
Daughton, Donald *lawyer*
Davidson, Anne Stowell *lawyer*
Davis, C. VanLeer III *lawyer*
Davis, Clarence Clinton, Jr. *lawyer*
Davis, Roger Edwin *lawyer, retired retail executive*
Davis, William Allison, II, *retired lawyer*
Dawson, Mary E. *lawyer*
Day, Kahlil Amyn *mediator, lawyer*
Dean, Michael M. *lawyer*
DeLaTorre, Phillip Eugene *law educator*
Dellagloria, John Castle *lawyer, educator*
Dennis, Patricia Diaz *lawyer*
Deutsch, Peter R. *former congressman*
DeVore, Daun Aline *lawyer*
DeVylder, Edgar Paul, Jr. *lawyer*
Dewees, Jennifer T. *lawyer*
Diamond, Stuart *lawyer, educator, business executive*
Dickson, Constance Pierce *law librarian*
Dickstein, Michael Ethan *mediator, arbitrator, lawyer*
Diehl, Deborah Hilda *lawyer*
Di Massa, Rudolph J., Jr. *lawyer*
Dimitry, Theodore George *retired lawyer*
Dixon, Paul Edward *lawyer, metal products executive, manufacturing executive*
Dokurno, Anthony David *lawyer*
Dolan, Peter Brown *lawyer*
Dolph, Wilbert Emery *lawyer*
Donlon, William James *retired lawyer*
Donohoe, Jerome Francis *lawyer*
Dorkin, Frederic Eugene *lawyer*
Douglas, Daniel G. *lawyer*
Dowley, Joseph Kyran *lawyer, congressman*
Doyle, David C. *lawyer*
Drabkin, Murray *lawyer*
Draper, Gerald Linden *retired lawyer*
Dreher, Frederick W. *lawyer*
Driscoll, Kimberlee Marie *lawyer*
Drost, Marianne *lawyer*
Dryden, Mary Elizabeth *law librarian, writer, actress*
Dubin, David Meyer *lawyer, educator*
Dubin, Stephen Victor *lawyer*
Dubuc, Carroll Edward *lawyer*
DuFresne, Elizabeth Jamison *retired lawyer*
Dundas, Philip Blair, Jr. *lawyer*
Dune, Steve Charles *retired lawyer*
Dunfee, Thomas Wylie *law educator*
Dunn, Robert Lawrence *lawyer*
Durgin, Diane *arbitrator, lawyer, mediator*
Duringer, David Robert *lawyer*
Dutile, Fernand Neville *law educator*
Dvorson, Natalya *lawyer*
Dwyer, John P. *law educator*
Early, Bert Hylton *lawyer, consultant*
Eason, William Everette, Jr. *lawyer*
Eaton, Larry Ralph *lawyer*
Edwards, Richard Alan *retired lawyer*
Elderkin, E(dwin) Judge *retired lawyer*
Elicker, Gordon Leonard *retired lawyer*
Ellenberger, Jack Stuart *law librarian*
Embry, Stephen Creston *lawyer*
Emmett, James Robert *retired lawyer*
Engelhardt, John Hugo *lawyer, bank executive*
Eno, Woodrow E. *lawyer, retired insurance company executive*
Erlebacher, Arlene Cernik *retired lawyer*
Ernst, Daniel Pearson *lawyer*
Estes, Carl Lewis, II, *lawyer*
Etra, Lionel *lawyer*
Ettinger, Joseph Alan *lawyer*
Eustis, Albert Anthony *lawyer, diversified financial services company executive*
Evans, Eric Alan *retired lawyer*
Everdell, William *retired lawyer*
Faber, Michael Warren *lawyer*
Fanwick, Ernest *lawyer*
Farmakides, John Basil *lawyer*
Farmer, Cornelia Griffin *lawyer, consultant, county hearings official*
Feigenbaum, David Louis *lawyer*
Feldkamp, John Calvin *retired lawyer, educator*
Feldman, H. Larry *lawyer*
Feller, Lloyd Harris *lawyer*
Fellman, Gerry Louis *lawyer, arbitrator*
Fenech, Craig E. *lawyer*
Fenech, Joseph Charles *lawyer*
Ferguson, Bradford Lee *lawyer*
Field, Arthur Norman *lawyer*
Fine, Lawrence B. *lawyer*
Finelsen, Libbi June *lawyer*
Finizio-Bascombe, Jamie Julia *lawyer*
Fiorito, Edward Gerald *lawyer*
Fitzgerald, John Warner *law educator*
Flanagan, Norman Patrick *lawyer*
Flanary, Donald Herbert, Jr. *lawyer*
Flick, John Edmond *lawyer*
Flinn, Charles Gallagher *lawyer, priest*
Flower, David, Jr. *retired lawyer, retired tax specialist*
Ford, George Burt *retired lawyer*
Foreman, Edward Rawson *retired lawyer*
Forry, John Ingram *lawyer*
Fortenbaugh, Samuel Byrod III *lawyer*
Fortner, Hueston Gilmore *lawyer, writer, composer*
Foster, David Lee *lawyer*
Foster, Judith Christine *lawyer, writer*

Fowler, Flora Daun *retired lawyer*
Fox, Eleanor Mae Cohen *lawyer, educator, writer*
Fox, Lawrence J. *lawyer*
Frankel, James Burton *retired lawyer*
Franklin, Michael Harold *arbitrator, lawyer, consultant*
Frasier, Ralph Kennedy *lawyer, bank executive*
Freedman, Robert Louis *lawyer*
Freeman, Tom M. *lawyer*
Frick, David Rhoads *lawyer, retired insurance company executive*
Fried, Charles *law educator*
Friedman, Joel William *law educator*
Friedman, Paul Richard *lawyer*
Friedman, Richard Nathan *lawyer*
Frisch, Sidney, Jr. *lawyer, real estate developer*
Frue, William Calhoun *lawyer*
Fuller, Robert Ferrey *lawyer, investor*
Fuller, Samuel Ashby *retired lawyer, mining executive*
Furbush, David Malcolm *lawyer*
Furman, Howard *arbitrator, lawyer, mediator*
Gaberman, Harry *retired lawyer*
Gaines, Cherie Adelaide *lawyer*
Gamble, E. James *lawyer, accountant*
Garth, Bryant Geoffrey *lawyer, educator*
Gee, Robert Neil *law librarian*
Gelber, Robert Cary *law librarian*
Genser, Jared Matthew *lawyer*
Gentner, Joshua D. *lawyer*
George, Gay *lawyer*
George, Joey Russell *lawyer*
Getzendanner, Susan *lawyer*
Giampietro, Wayne Bruce *lawyer*
Gibb, Roberta Louise *lawyer, artist*
Gibson, William Willard, Jr. *law educator*
Gilbert, Ronald Rhea *lawyer*
Ginsberg, Ernest *lawyer, banker*
Gladden, Joseph Rhea, Jr. *lawyer*
Glaser, Patricia L. *lawyer*
Glasser, Ira Saul *former civil liberties organization administrator*
Glosser, Jeffrey Mark *lawyer*
Gobel, John Henry *lawyer*
Goering, Kevin W. *lawyer*
Gold, Harold Arthur *lawyer*
Goldberg, David Theo *law educator, writer*
Golden, Joseph Aaron *lawyer*
Goldschmidt, Lynn Harvey *lawyer*
Gomez, Melissa Mordell *trial consultant*
Goodenow, Robert W. *lawyer, former sports association administrator*
Goodman, Elizabeth Ann *retired lawyer*
Gordley, James Russell *law educator*
Gordon, George G. *lawyer*
Gorske, Robert H. *lawyer*
Gould, Lewis F., Jr. *lawyer*
Gourley, Sara J. *lawyer*
Gourvitz, Elliot Howard *lawyer*
Graham, William Henry *lawyer*
Graves, Todd Peterson *former prosecutor*
Gray, Justin Y. *lawyer*
Gray, William H. III *lawyer, former non profit association administrator, retired congressman*
Grayson, Edward Davis *lawyer, manufacturing executive*
Green, Carol H. *lawyer, educator*
Green, Carole L. *lawyer*
Greenberg, Ronald David *lawyer, educator*
Greene, Tracy A. *lawyer*
Greenebaum, Leonard Charles *retired lawyer*
Grieb, Elizabeth *lawyer*
Griffin, Campbell Arthur, Jr. *retired lawyer*
Grodsky, Jamie Anne *law educator*
Groetken, Troy Alan *lawyer, pharmacist*
Gross, Richard Benjamin *lawyer, film producer*
Grutman, Jewel Humphrey *lawyer, writer*
Gudenberg, Harry Richard *arbitrator, mediator*
Gurstel, Norman Keith *lawyer*
Gutman, Richard Edward *lawyer*
Hackel-Sims, Stella Bloomberg *lawyer, former government official*
Hackett, Robert John *lawyer*
Hackett, Wesley Phelps, Jr. *lawyer*
Hackney, Hugh Edward *lawyer*
Hajek, Robert J., Sr. *lawyer, real estate broker*
Haley, George Brock, Jr. *retired lawyer*
Hall, James Evan *lawyer*
Hall, Joan Torrens *lawyer*
Hall, John Hopkins *retired lawyer*
Hall, William N. *lawyer*
Halleck, Charles White *lawyer, photographer, former judge*
Halpern, James Bladen *lawyer*
Hamel, Rodolphe *retired lawyer, pharmaceutical executive*
Hammond, Glenn Barry, Sr. *lawyer, electrical engineer*
Hampton, Kevin Michael *lawyer, real estate agent*
Handler, Harold Robert *lawyer*
Handschu, Barbara Ellen *lawyer*
Hanes, Leigh B., Jr. *lawyer*
Hanket, Mark John *lawyer*
Hansen, Nick Dane *lawyer*
Hardie, James Hiller *retired lawyer*
Hardin, Hal D. *lawyer, judge, former US attorney*
Hardin, Paul III *law educator*
Harding, Marc Steven *lawyer*
Harff, Charles Henry *retired lawyer, retired manufacturing executive*
Harnack, Don Steger *retired lawyer*
Harper, Conrad Kenneth *lawyer*
Harriman, John Howland *retired lawyer*
Harris, Richard Eugene Vassau *lawyer*
Harrison, Charles Maurice *retired lawyer, retired communications executive*
Harvey, Marc S(an) *lawyer, historian, law educator*
Hasko, Judith Ann *lawyer*
Hassan, Ibne *lawyer, diplomat, political philosopher, international strategist*
Hattar, Jacqueline *lawyer*
Hauver, Constance Longshore *lawyer*
Hawthorne, Bruce N. *lawyer, former telecommunications industry executive*
Hayes, Byron Jackson, Jr. *retired lawyer*
Hazard, Geoffrey Cornell, Jr. *law educator*
Heath, Richard Eddy *lawyer*
Heckler, Gerard Vincent *lawyer*
Hedberg, Steven Michael *lawyer*

Heffelfinger, Thomas Backer *former prosecutor, lawyer*
Heffron, Howard A. *lawyer*
Heider, Jon Vinton *retired lawyer*
Heiligenstein, Christian Enric *lawyer*
Heineman, Andrew David *retired lawyer*
Heise, John Irvin, Jr. *lawyer*
Helfer, Michael Stevens *lawyer, corporate executive*
Henderson, Harold L. *retired lawyer*
Henderson, Thomas Henry, Jr. *lawyer, former legal association executive*
Hendrickson, D. John *lawyer*
Hendry, Andrew Delaney *lawyer, consumer products company executive*
Henkel, Kathryn Gundy *lawyer*
Hennessy, Dean McDonald *lawyer, director, municipal official*
Henry, Robert John *lawyer*
Hermann, Donald Harold James *law educator*
Hernandez, David N(icholas) *lawyer*
Herring, Jerone Carson *retired lawyer, bank executive*
Herringer, Maryellen Cattani *lawyer*
Hershatter, Richard Lawrence *lawyer, writer*
Hess, Glen E. *lawyer*
Hester, Thomas Patrick *lawyer*
Heymann, Philip Benjamin *law educator*
Heywood, Harriett *lawyer, consultant*
Higginbotham, John Taylor *lawyer*
Hiler, Bruce A. *lawyer*
Hill, Harold Nelson, Jr. *lawyer*
Hillman, Noel L. *former prosecutor*
Ho, Eric Caleb *lawyer*
Hofer, Stephen Robert *lawyer*
Hoffman, Alan Craig *lawyer, consultant*
Hoffman, S. David *lawyer, engineer, educator, artist, military officer*
Hoffmann, Christoph Ludwig *lawyer*
Holbrook, Connie C. *lawyer*
Holland, George Edison, Jr., (Ed Holland) *lawyer*
Holman, James J. *lawyer*
Holmes, Michael Gene *lawyer*
Holt, Marjorie Sewell *lawyer, retired congresswoman*
Holt, Thaddeus *lawyer*
Holtzschue, Karl Bressem *lawyer, author, educator*
Honeystein, Karl *lawyer, media specialist*
Honnold, John Otis *law educator*
Hopkins, George Mathews Marks *retired lawyer, engineering executive*
Horlick, Gary Norman *lawyer, educator*
Horstmann, John F. *lawyer*
Horwitz, Donald Paul *lawyer*
Hough, Thomas Henry Michael *retired lawyer, educator*
Howell, Donald Lee *lawyer*
Hoyt, Robert F. *lawyer*
Hsu, Emilie Tien-Jung *lawyer*
Humphreys, Robert Russell *lawyer, consultant, arbitrator*
Hunter, Jack Duval *retired lawyer*
Hunterton, C. Stanley *lawyer*
Hybl, William Joseph *lawyer, foundation administrator*
Hyde, Alan Litchfield *retired lawyer*
Iamele, Richard Thomas *retired law librarian*
Idzik, Daniel Ronald *retired lawyer*
Ieyoub, Richard Phillip *lawyer, former state attorney general*
Igoe, Thomas J., Jr. *lawyer*
Iklé, Richard Adolph *lawyer*
Irvine, John Alexander *lawyer*
Jack-Moore, Phyllis *strategist, educational consultant*
Jackson, Raymond Sidney, Jr. *lawyer*
Jackson, Susan Marie *paralegal*
Jacobowitz, Harold Saul *lawyer*
Jacobs, John Patrick *lawyer*
Jaffin, Charles Leonard *lawyer*
Jambor, Robert Vernon *lawyer*
Jameson, Paula Ann *retired lawyer*
Jamison, Daniel Oliver *lawyer*
Javits, Joshua Moses *lawyer*
Jennings, Thomas Parks *lawyer*
Jetton, C. Loring, Jr. *lawyer*
Jimenez, Marcos Daniel *former prosecutor*
Joelson, Mark René *lawyer*
Johnson, Barbara Elizabeth *lawyer*
Johnson, Craig W. *lawyer*
Johnson, E. Scott *lawyer*
Johnson, Eugene Laurence *lawyer*
Johnson, James Terence *lawyer, educator, minister*
Johnson, Karen A. *legal association administrator*
Johnson, Lael Frederic *lawyer*
Johnson, Richard Tenney *lawyer*
Johnson, Rufus Winfield *lawyer*
Johnson, Scott William *lawyer, bank executive, political blogger*
Johnston, James R. *lawyer*
Johnston, John Devereaux, Jr. *retired law educator*
Jones, Douglas Wiley *lawyer*
Jones, Elaine R. *former legal association administrator, civil rights advocate*
Jones, Keith Alden *lawyer*
Jones, Mary Gardiner *lawyer, educator, consumer products company executive*
Jones, William Rex *law educator*
Jordan, Jerry Dale *lawyer, gas industry executive*
Joyce, Joseph James *lawyer, food products executive*
Kane, Alice Theresa *lawyer*
Kantor, Mark Alan *lawyer, arbitrator*
Kantrowitz, Susan Lee *lawyer*
Kaplan, Barry Martin *lawyer*
Kaplan, Elaine D. *lawyer*
Kaplan, Helene Lois *lawyer*
Kapner, Lewis *lawyer*
Kapnick, Richard Bradshaw *lawyer*
Kaster, Laura A. *lawyer*
Katz, Sanford Noah *lawyer, educator*
Kauffman, David Lin *lawyer*
Kauffman, David Joseph *lawyer*
Kaumeyer, Linda Louise *lawyer, educator*
Kaye, Stuart Martin *lawyer*
Keatinge, Robert Reed *lawyer*
Keaty, Robert Burke *lawyer, business consultant*
Keeling, J(ohn) Michael *lawyer, trade association executive*
Keen, Victor F. *lawyer*
Keith, William Douglas *lawyer*

Kelley, James Francis *lawyer*
Kelly, Pamela B. *lawyer*
Kempf, Donald G., Jr. *retired lawyer*
Kennedy, Harold Edward *lawyer*
Kennedy, Thomas J. *lawyer*
Kenrich, John Lewis *retired lawyer*
Ketels, Gerhard H. *lawyer*
Khoury, Kenneth F. *lawyer*
Kienitz, LaDonna Trapp *lawyer, librarian, municipal official*
Kilbourn, William Douglas, Jr. *law educator*
Killeen, Michael John *lawyer*
Kimball, Richard Arthur, Jr. *retired lawyer*
King, David Roy *lawyer*
King, James Forrest, Jr. *lawyer*
King, Michael Howard *lawyer*
King, Rebecca J. *lawyer, consultant*
King, Robert Lucien *retired lawyer*
Kitagawa, Audrey Emiko *retired lawyer*
Klafter, Cary Ira *lawyer*
Klamon, Lawrence Paine *lawyer*
Klatell, Robert Edward *lawyer*
Klaus, Charles *retired lawyer*
Klayman, Larry Elliott *lawyer, legal association administrator*
Kleiman, Bernard *lawyer*
Klein, Eugene *lawyer*
Klein, Linda Ann *lawyer*
Klein, Paul E. *lawyer*
Klitenic, Jason *lawyer*
Klott, David Lee *lawyer*
Knecht, James Herbert *retired lawyer*
Knight, Gary *lawyer, educator, writer*
Kohlstedt, James August *lawyer*
Kohn, Adam M. *lawyer*
Kolbert, Kathryn *lawyer, educator*
Kolodny, Stephen Arthur *lawyer*
Korn, Peter A. *arbitrator, mediator, educator*
Kotcher, Shirley J.W. *lawyer*
Kotler, Lawrence Joel *lawyer*
Kozlowski, Ellen Rhoda *lawyer*
Kramer, Paul R. *lawyer*
Kranzow, Ronald Roy *lawyer*
Kratt, Peter George *lawyer*
Kreindler, Marla J. *lawyer*
Krivoshia, Eli, Jr. *lawyer*
Krohnke, Duane W. *retired lawyer*
Kubo, Edward Hachiro, Jr. *prosecutor*
Kumble, Steven Jay *lawyer*
Lacer, Alfred Antonio *lawyer, educator*
Lackland, John *lawyer, nurseryman*
Lanahan, Daniel Joseph *lawyer*
Lanam, Linda Lee *lawyer*
Landis, Gregory P. *lawyer*
Landreth, Kathryn E. *lawyer*
Landy, Lisa Anne *lawyer*
Lange, William Michael *lawyer*
Larzelere, Kathy Lynn Heckler *paralegal*
Lashley, Lenore Clarisse *lawyer*
Lasky, David *lawyer*
Lathrope, Daniel John *law educator*
Laudone, Anita Helene *lawyer*
Lavey, Warren G. *lawyer*
Lavin, Terrence J. *lawyer*
Lawless, Thomas William *lawyer*
Lawrence, Glenn Robert *arbitrator, mediator, lawyer*
Lea, Lorenzo Bates *lawyer*
Leary, Thomas Barrett *lawyer, former federal agency administrator*
Lederer, Peter David *lawyer*
Lee, Wayne J. *lawyer*
Leibowitt, Sol David *lawyer*
Leigh, Richard E., Jr. *lawyer*
Leone, William J. *former prosecutor, lawyer*
Levin, Roger Michael *lawyer*
Levine, Alan *lawyer*
Levinson, Kenneth S. *lawyer, corporate financial executive*
Levinson, Peter Joseph *retired lawyer*
Levy, David *retired lawyer, insurance company executive, consultant*
Libassi, Frank Peter *lawyer*
Licke, Wallace John *lawyer*
Lidsky, Ella *retired law librarian*
Liebeler, Susan Wittenberg *lawyer*
Lightstone, Ronald *lawyer*
Lilly, Thomas Gerald *retired lawyer*
Linde, Maxine Helen *lawyer, corporate financial executive, investor*
Linett, David *retired lawyer*
Link, George Hamilton *retired lawyer*
Lipsman, Richard Marc *lawyer, educator*
Lipton, Robert Steven *lawyer*
Litman, Harry Peter *lawyer, educator*
Loder, David E. *lawyer*
Logan, James Kenneth *lawyer, retired judge*
Logstrom, Bridget A. *lawyer*
Lombard, Richard Spencer *lawyer*
Long, Charles Thomas *lawyer, history professor*
Long, Clarence Dickinson III *lawyer*
Lorch, Ernest Henry *lawyer*
Lorne, Simon Michael Michael *lawyer*
Love, Michael Joseph *lawyer*
Lubick, Donald Cyril *lawyer*
Lucas, Paul David Mark *lawyer*
Lungulescu, Alicia M. *paralegal*
Lurie, Alvin David *lawyer*
Lutringer, Richard Emil *lawyer*
Lynch, Thomas Wimp *lawyer*
Mabey, Ralph R. *lawyer*
MacDonald, Donald Paul *lawyer*
MacKinnon, John Alexander *lawyer*
Maclin, Alan Hall *lawyer*
Madigan, Elizabeth M. *lawyer*
Madsen, H(enry) Stephen *retired lawyer*
Magurno, Richard Peter *lawyer*
Maher, Francesca Marciniak *lawyer, former air transportation executive*
Malkin, Michael M. *lawyer*
Malloy, John Richard *lawyer, chemicals executive*
Malloy, Timothy J. *lawyer*
Mann, Donegan *lawyer*
Manne, Henry Girard *lawyer, consultant, economist, educator, retired dean*
Manos, Christopher Lawrence *lawyer, mediator*
Margolis, Daniel Herbert *lawyer*
Marinis, Thomas Paul, Jr. *lawyer*
Marker, Marc Linthacum *lawyer, investor, entrepreneur*
Marshall, Kathryn Sue *lawyer*

Martin, Alice Howze *prosecutor*
Martin, John William, Jr. *retired lawyer, automotive executive*
Martin, William Edwin *lawyer*
Martineau, Robert John *retired law educator*
Matayoshi, Coralie Chun *lawyer, bar association executive*
Mathewson, George Atterbury *retired lawyer*
Matschullat, Dale Lewis *lawyer*
Mattson, Stephen Joseph *retired lawyer*
May, Henry Stratford, Jr. *lawyer*
Mayer, James Joseph *retired corporate lawyer*
Maynard, Robert Howell *retired lawyer*
McAllister, Singleton Beryl *lawyer*
McAmis, Edwin Earl *lawyer*
McAvoy, John Joseph *lawyer*
McCarrick, John F. *lawyer*
McCarthy, J. Thomas *lawyer, educator*
McCarthy, Vincent Paul *lawyer*
McClain, Tim S. *lawyer*
Mc Clendon, William Hutchinson III *retired lawyer*
McConnell, Edward Bosworth *legal association administrator, lawyer*
McConnell, John William, Jr. *lawyer*
Mc Cormack, Francis Xavier *lawyer, former oil company executive*
McCormick, David Arthur *lawyer*
McCoy, John Joseph *lawyer*
McCue, Howard McDowell III *lawyer, educator*
McCurley, Robert Lee, Jr. *lawyer, educator*
McDonald, Bradley G. *lawyer*
McDonnell, Barbara *lawyer*
McDougall, Roderick Gregory *lawyer*
McDowell, John Henry, Jr. *lawyer*
McFadden, Nancy Elizabeth *lawyer*
McGrath, J. Paul *lawyer*
McGuire, Timothy James *lawyer, editor, columnist*
McIntosh, Terrie Tuckett *lawyer*
McIntyre, Anita Grace Jordan *lawyer*
McKean, Robert Jackson, Jr. *retired lawyer*
McKeown, William P. *retired lawyer*
McLaughlin, Joseph *lawyer*
McLendon, Melburne Dekalb *lawyer, arbitrator*
McMahon, James E. *lawyer, former prosecutor*
McMahon, Thomas Michael *lawyer*
McManus, Richard Philip *lawyer, agricultural products executive*
McMillan, Robert Ralph *lawyer*
Mc Quade, Lawrence Carroll *lawyer, investment company executive*
McQuigg, John Dolph *retired lawyer*
Medalie, Richard James *lawyer*
Mehltretter, Kathleen M. *former prosecutor*
Meltzer, Jay H. *lawyer, retail executive*
Mendelson, Joan Rintel *lawyer*
Mercer, Edwin Wayne *lawyer*
Merring, Robert Alan *lawyer, arbitrator, mediator*
Merritt, Bruce Gordon *lawyer*
Messier, Pierre *lawyer, manufacturing executive*
Metcalfe, Robert Davis III *lawyer*
Metzger, Jeffrey Raul *lawyer*
Meyer, Max Earl *lawyer*
Meyerson, Stanley Phillip *lawyer*
Michael, Mark Dixwell *lawyer*
Mikesell, Richard Lyon *lawyer, financial counselor*
Miller, John Eddie *lawyer*
Miller, Robert Joseph *lawyer, former governor*
Miller, Thurmond Aubrey *lawyer*
Miller, Warren Lloyd *lawyer*
Millimet, Erwin *lawyer*
Milner, Irvin Myron *retired lawyer*
Milsten, Robert B. *lawyer*
Minahan, Daniel Francis *lawyer, retired manufacturing executive*
Mingle, James John *lawyer*
Mintz, M. J. *lawyer*
Miquelon, Miriam F. *former prosecutor, lawyer*
Mitau, Lee R. *lawyer, bank executive*
Mitchell, Briane Nelson *lawyer*
Mitchell, David Benjamin *lawyer, arbitrator, mediator*
Mitchell, William Graham Champion *lawyer, corporate officer*
Moford, Craig S. *prosecutor*
Moon, Barbara G. *lawyer*
Moore, Betty Jo *legal assistant*
Morgan, Charles Russell *lawyer*
Morgan, Dennis Keith *lawyer*
Morphy, James Calvin *lawyer*
Morrison, Donald William *lawyer*
Morrison, John James *lawyer*
Morse, Robert Harry *lawyer*
Mossawir, Harve H., Jr. *retired lawyer*
Mosteller, Robert P. *law educator*
Mow, Robert Henry, Jr. *lawyer*
Moya, Patrick Robert *lawyer*
Mudd, John O. *lawyer*
Muller, Peter *lawyer, film company executive, retail executive*
Muller, Scott William *lawyer*
Munsell, Elsie Louise *retired lawyer*
Murchison, David Claudius *lawyer*
Murphy, Daniel Ignatius *lawyer*
Murphy, Lewis Curtis *lawyer, former mayor*
Murphy, Sandra Robison *lawyer*
Myers, Jesse Jerome *lawyer*
Nagle, Robert Owen *lawyer*
Nanda, Ved Prakash *law educator, director, academic administrator*
Naples, Caesar Joseph *lawyer, educator*
Nash, Melvin Samuel *lawyer*
Natcher, Stephen Darlington *retired lawyer, electronics executive*
Nelson, Allyson Lyn *lawyer*
Nelson, Carl Roger *retired lawyer*
Neuhaus, Joseph Emanuel *lawyer*
Newman, Carol L. *lawyer*
Newman, Howard Neal *lawyer, educator*
Newman, Joan Meskiel *lawyer*
Nissman, David M. *lawyer, former prosecutor*
Noddings, Sarah Ellen *lawyer*
Nolen, William Giles *lawyer, accountant*
Ober, Richard Francis, Jr. *lawyer, director, banker*
O'Brien, Charles H. *retired lawyer, retired judge*
O'Brien, J. Willard *lawyer, educator*
O'Connell, Philip Raymond *retired lawyer, paper company executive*
O'Donnell, John Michael *lawyer*
O'Dowd, Sarah A. *lawyer*

Oettinger, Julian Alan *lawyer, pharmaceutical executive*
Ogg, Wilson Reid *lawyer, retired judge, poet, publishing executive, educator*
O'Keefe, Edward Franklin *lawyer*
Oliver, Samuel William, Jr. *retired lawyer*
Orlebeke, William Ronald *retired lawyer, writer*
Oshima, Michael W. *lawyer*
O'Sullivan, Judith Roberta *lawyer, writer, artist*
Otis, Lee (Sarah) Liberman *lawyer, educator*
Painter, Richard William *lawyer, educator*
Painton, Russell Elliott *retired lawyer, retired mechanical engineer*
Pal, Prabir Kumar (Sunny Pal) *lawyer*
Parker, Douglas Martin *retired lawyer, writer*
Parker, John Francis *retired lawyer*
Parode, Ann *lawyer*
Parr, Royse Milton *retired lawyer, writer*
Partida, Gilbert A. *lawyer*
Partridge, Bruce James *lawyer, educator, writer*
Pascale, Daniel Richard *lawyer*
Pasco, Hansell Merrill *retired lawyer*
Pastorek, Paul G. *lawyer*
Pate, R. Hewitt (Robert Hewitt Pate III) *lawyer, former federal agency administrator*
Patrick, Deval Laurdine *lawyer*
Patrick, Victor Phillip *lawyer*
Patton, James Richard, Jr. *lawyer*
Paul, Eve W. *retired lawyer*
Paul, Richard Wright *lawyer*
Pavarini, Peter Alfred *lawyer*
Pear, Charles E., Jr. *lawyer*
Peltz, Paulette Beatrice *corporate lawyer*
Pereyra-Suarez, Charles Albert *lawyer*
Perez - Gomez, Ada Iris *law educator*
Perkiel, Mitchel H. *lawyer*
Perretta, Michael A. *lawyer*
Perrin, Michael Warren *lawyer*
Perritt, Henry Hardy, Jr. *law educator*
Peshkin, Samuel David *lawyer*
Petrillo, Leonard Philip *lawyer, retired investment company executive*
Pfaffenroth, Peter Albert *lawyer*
Phillips, Dorothy Kay *lawyer*
Phillips, Leo Harold, Jr. *lawyer*
Piga, Stephen Mulry *retired lawyer*
Pitcher, Griffith Fontaine *lawyer*
Poliakoff, Gary A. *lawyer, educator*
Pollard, Henry *arbitrator, mediator*
Polsby, Allen Isaac *retired lawyer*
Poppler, Doris Swords *lawyer*
Porter, Michael Pell *lawyer*
Portnoy, Sara S. *lawyer*
Powers, Elizabeth Whitmel *lawyer*
Pratt, Robert Windsor *lawyer*
Prem, F. Herbert, Jr. *retired lawyer*
Prewoznik, Jerome Frank *retired lawyer*
Price, Alfred Lee *lawyer, mining executive*
Prince, Andrew Steven *lawyer, retired government agency administrator*
Propp, Steven H. *legal analyst*
Purtle, John Ingram *lawyer, former state supreme court justice*
Pytell, Robert Henry *retired lawyer, former judge*
Quarles, James Linwood III *lawyer*
Quay, Thomas Emery *lawyer*
Quigley, Leonard Vincent *lawyer*
Quillen, Cecil Dyer, Jr. *lawyer, consultant*
Radford, R. S. *lawyer, law educator*
Ragone, Tara Adams *lawyer*
Rappaport, James Wyant *lawyer, real estate developer*
Ratner, Michael D. *lawyer*
Rawls, Frank Macklin *lawyer*
Raymond, David Walker *lawyer*
Reardon, George Martin *lawyer*
Reath, George, Jr. *lawyer, mediator, arbitrator*
Reed, James C., Jr. *lawyer*
Reeder, James Arthur *lawyer*
Reeder, Robert Harry *retired lawyer*
Reese, Robert M. *retired lawyer*
Regenstreif, Herbert *lawyer*
Reich, Laurence *lawyer*
Reiche, Frank Perley *lawyer, former federal commissioner*
Reiser, Richard Scott *lawyer*
Reiss, Jerome *retired lawyer*
Reister, Ruth Alkema *lawyer, finance company executive*
Reiter, Glenn Mitchell *lawyer*
Reveal, Ernest Ira III *retired lawyer*
Rew, Lawrence Boyd *lawyer*
Reynolds, William Bradford *lawyer*
Rhyne, Sidney White *retired lawyer*
Ricciardi, Lawrence R. *lawyer*
Rice, Leonard S. *lawyer*
Richardson, John Carroll *lawyer, financial consultant*
Richardson, Margaret Milner *retired lawyer*
Ricks, Joycia Camilla *retired lawyer*
Ring, Renee Etheline *lawyer*
Rissman, Burton Richard *lawyer*
Robbins, Norman Nelson *lawyer*
Roberts, William H. *lawyer*
Robinson, Davis Rowland *lawyer, international arbitrator*
Rochlin, Paul R. *lawyer*
Rodenburg, Clifton Glenn *lawyer*
Roditti, Esther C(laire) *lawyer, writer*
Rodriguez, Carolyn *lawyer*
Roe, Mark J. *law educator*
Rohrbach, Heidi A. *lawyer*
Rosenberg, Sheli Zysman *lawyer, finance company executive*
Rosenfeld, Arthur Herbert *lawyer*
Rosenn, Harold *lawyer*
Ross, Michael Aaron *lawyer*
Ross, Michael Charles *lawyer*
Rossetti, Armand John, Jr. *lawyer*
Roth, Michael *lawyer*
Rothman, Howard Joel *lawyer*
Rowe, Audrey *paralegal*
Rozoff, Jonathan Mark *legal consultant*
Rubenfeld, Stanley Irwin *lawyer, director, mediator, arbitrator*
Rubin, Richard Allan *lawyer*
Rudolph, Wallace Morton *law educator*
Ruemmler, Kathryn H. *prosecutor*
Ruhm, Thomas Francis *retired lawyer*
Rushforth, Brent N. *lawyer*
Ryan, Cynthia Rhoades *lawyer*

Sack, Sylvan Hanan *lawyer*
Sadowski, Peter T. *lawyer*
St. Claire, Frank Arthur *lawyer*
Saliterman, Richard Arlen *lawyer*
Sampson, David Synnott *lawyer*
Santman, Leon Duane *lawyer, former federal government executive*
Sapp, John Raymond *lawyer*
Sattler, Bruce Weimer *lawyer*
Saunders, Lonna Jeanne *lawyer, newscaster*
Saunders, Terry Rose *lawyer*
Sax, Joseph Lawrence *lawyer, educator*
Saxon, John David *lawyer, educator, policy analyst, educator*
Schaefer, William Goerman *lawyer*
Scharf, Michael Paul *law educator*
Schlick, Austin C. *lawyer*
Schmults, Edward Charles *lawyer, think-tank executive*
Schoenwald, Maurice Louis *retired lawyer*
Schram, Ronald Byard *lawyer*
Schultz, Dennis Bernard *lawyer*
Schultz, Vicki L. *law educator*
Schwab, Eileen Caulfield *lawyer, educator*
Schwartz, Bernard Julian *lawyer*
Schwartz, Leonard Jay *retired lawyer*
Schwed, Roger E. *lawyer*
Schwerdtner, Frederick Howard *lawyer, retired police commander, real estate broker*
Sczudlo, Walter Joseph *lawyer*
Segal, Phyllis Nichamoff *mediator*
Seidman, Ellen Shapiro *lawyer, government official*
Seigel, Stuart Evan *lawyer*
Sells, Fawn Leigh *paralegal, writer*
Servodidio, Thomas Gerard *lawyer*
Sessums, T. Terrell *lawyer*
Shaffer, Richard James *lawyer, retired manufacturing executive*
Shambaugh, Stephen Ward *lawyer*
Shapiro, Edwin Stanley *lawyer, judge*
Shapiro, Marc S. *lawyer*
Shapiro, Sander Wolf *retired lawyer*
Sharkey, Robert Emmett *lawyer*
Sharkey, Vincent Joseph *lawyer*
Shattuck, Cathie Ann *lawyer, former government official*
Shaw, Curtis S *lawyer*
Shaw, L. Edward, Jr. *lawyer*
Shaw, Nina L. *lawyer*
Sheldon, Terry Edwin *lawyer, investment advisor*
Shere, Dennis *lawyer, writer, retired publishing executive*
Sheriff, Seymour *retired lawyer*
Sherling, Fred W. *lawyer*
Shook, Ann Jones *lawyer*
Shriver, Sargent (Robert Sargent Shriver Jr.) *lawyer*
Shuman, Samuel Irving *lawyer, educator*
Sides, Jack Davis, Jr. *lawyer*
Siebert, Thomas L. *lawyer, former ambassador*
Siemer, Deanne Clemence *lawyer*
Sigety, Charles Edward *lawyer, financial planner*
Silvestri, Gina *lawyer*
Simon, Robert G. *lawyer*
Sinnott, Stephen P. *prosecutor*
Sinor, Howard Earl, Jr. *lawyer*
Skigen, Patricia Sue *lawyer*
Skolnik, Barnet David *retired lawyer*
Slavitt, David Walton *retired lawyer*
Slonaker, Norman Dale *lawyer*
Smith, Carole Dianne *retired lawyer, editor, writer, product developer*
Smith, George Patrick, II, *lawyer, educator*
Smith, James A. *lawyer*
Smith, Walton Napier *lawyer*
Smith, William Charles *retired lawyer*
Smith, Yolanda Ippolito *law educator, researcher, writer*
Smoot, Oliver Reed, Jr. *lawyer, trade association administrator*
Smouse, H(ervey) Russell *lawyer*
Snyder, Jean Maclean *lawyer*
Snyder, Stephen Edward *lawyer, mediator*
Soble, Mark Richard *lawyer*
Sochynsky, Yaroslav *lawyer, arbitrator, mediator*
Sokol, Jan D. *lawyer*
Solkoff, Jerome Ira *lawyer, educator*
Solls, Mark A. *lawyer*
Soroko, John J. *lawyer*
Sowande, Beverly Folasade *lawyer, educator*
Spanninger, Beth Anne *lawyer*
Sparks, John Edward *lawyer*
Speers, Roland Root, II, *lawyer*
Spicer, S. Gary (Samuel Gary Spicer) *lawyer, writer, educator*
Spiegel, Jayson Leslie *lawyer, professional society administrator*
Spitzberg, Irving Joseph, Jr. *lawyer*
Springer, Paul David *lawyer, film company executive*
Staley, John Fredric *lawyer*
Stark, Robert J. *lawyer*
Statz, Olga *law educator*
Stedman, Richard Ralph *retired lawyer*
Steffey, Fred H. *lawyer*
Stein, Robert Allen *legal association administrator, law educator*
Stein, Stanley Richard *lawyer, food service executive*
Steptoe, Mary Lou *lawyer*
Stern, Joseph A. *lawyer*
Stiller, Shale David *lawyer, educator*
Stinnett, J. Daniel *lawyer*
Stoiber, Carlton Ray *nuclear law consultant, freelance/self-employed cartoonist*
Stone, Andrew Grover *lawyer*
Stone, Donald Raymond *lawyer*
Stone, Edward Herman *lawyer*
Stone, Marc J. *lawyer*
Strantz, Nancy Jean *law educator, consultant*
Strauchon-Verner, Kimberly *lawyer*
Streb, Paul Gerard *arbitrator*
Streicher, James Franklin *retired lawyer*
Sullivan, William Francis *lawyer*
Surles, Richard Hurlbut, Jr. *retired law librarian*
Susman, Morton Lee *lawyer*
Sussman, Howard Sivin *lawyer*
Sutter, Laurence Brener *lawyer*
Swacker, Frank Warren *lawyer*
Swann, Richard Rockwell *lawyer, banker*
Sweeney, Deidre Ann *lawyer*

Szymanski, Patrick Joseph *lawyer*
Taft, Sheldon Ashley *retired lawyer*
Tallman, Ann Marie *lawyer*
Tancer, Robert Stephen *prosecutor, educator*
Tancs, Linda Ann *lawyer*
Tanenbaum, Jay Harvey *lawyer*
Tavrow, Richard Lawrence *lawyer*
Taylor, Charles *law educator*
Taylor, Hubert G. *lawyer*
Taylor, Job III *lawyer*
Terp, Thomas Thomsen *lawyer*
Terrell, G. Irvin *lawyer*
Thiele, Howard Nellis, Jr. *lawyer*
Thomajan, Robert *lawyer, management consultant*
Thoman, Henry Nixon *lawyer*
Thomas, Frank M., Jr. *lawyer*
Thomas, Franklin Augustine *lawyer, consultant*
Thomas, Patricia Anne *retired law librarian*
Thompson, Holley Marker *lawyer, consultant, marketing professional*
Thompson, Philip C. *lawyer, investment advisor, educator*
Thurmond, J. Strom, Jr. *lawyer, former prosecutor*
Tierney, Kevin Joseph *lawyer, arbitrator, mediator, director*
Tikosh, Mark Axente *lawyer*
Tingle, James O'Malley *retired lawyer*
Tinkelman, Joan *lawyer*
Title, Peter Stephen *lawyer*
Titus, Christina Maria *lawyer*
Toedt, D(ell) C(harles) III *lawyer*
Toensing, Victoria *lawyer*
Tolins, Roger Alan *lawyer*
Tomlinson, John Randolph *lawyer*
Tondel, Lawrence Chapman *lawyer*
Toohey, Philip S. *retired lawyer*
Toomey, Richard Andrew, Jr. *lawyer*
Torgerson, Larry Keith *lawyer*
Torkildson, Raymond Maynard *lawyer*
Torre, Gary Jerome *retired lawyer*
Traeger, Charles Henry III *lawyer*
Trautman, William Ellsworth *lawyer*
Treacy, Vincent Edward *lawyer*
Trimble, Phillip Richard *law educator*
Trimble, Sandra Ellingson *lawyer*
Trimble, William Cattell, Jr. *retired lawyer*
Tu, Hoang Huy *lawyer*
Tucker, Laurey Dan *lawyer*
Turner, George Mason *lawyer*
Turpening, Patricia Eileen Keller *retired law librarian*
Twardy, Stanley Albert, Jr. *lawyer*
Tyson, David Richard *lawyer, political party official*
Vacco, Dennis C. *lawyer*
Van Bogaert, Cynthia A. *lawyer*
Van Graafeiland, Gary P. *lawyer*
Van Hollen, John Byron *former prosecutor, lawyer*
Van Vleet, William Benjamin *lawyer, retired insurance company executive*
Vila, Adis Maria *lawyer, business government executive*
von Sauers, Joseph F. *lawyer*
Wagner, Arthur Ward, Jr. *lawyer*
Walker, Craig Michael *lawyer*
Walker, Mark A. *lawyer*
Walker, Richard Henry *lawyer*
Wallack, Rina Evelyn *lawyer*
Wallison, Frieda K. *lawyer*
Walmer, Edwin Fitch *retired lawyer*
Walsh, Joseph Thomas *law educator, retired state supreme court justice*
Wanger, Eugene Gilkison *retired lawyer*
Warner, Karl K. *former prosecutor*
Warnock, William Reid *lawyer*
Waters, Timothy J. *lawyer*
Weaver, Delbert Allen *retired lawyer*
Webster, Robert Kenly *lawyer*
Weil, Peter Henry *lawyer*
Weiner, Peter H. *lawyer*
Weinman, Glenn Alan *lawyer*
Weisberg, David Charles *lawyer*
Weiss, Kenneth Andrew *lawyer, educator*
Weiss, Simona *retired paralegal*
Weldon, Jeffrey Alan *lawyer*
Welnak, Llowell A. *retired lawyer*
Welsh, John Beresford, Jr. *retired lawyer*
Wendel, Charles Allen *lawyer*
Werthan, Jeffrey Michael *lawyer*
Wessling, Robert Bruce *retired lawyer*
West, Natalie Elsa *lawyer*
Weston, Michael C. *retired lawyer*
Wetherill, Eikins *lawyer, investment company executive*
Wheeler, R(ichard) Kenneth *lawyer, educator*
Wheeler, Stephen Frederick *legal administrator*
Whelan, Stephen Thomas, Jr. *lawyer*
White, Jill Carolyn *lawyer*
White, John Joseph III *lawyer*
Whitley, Joe D. (Joseph Dally Whitley) *lawyer*
Whitmore, Bruce G. *lawyer*
Wiggins, Charles Henry, Jr. *lawyer*
Wilburn, Mary Nelson *lawyer, writer, poet, translator*
Wilcox, Mark Dean *lawyer*
Wildhack, William August, Jr. *lawyer*
Wiley, Richard Arthur *lawyer*
Willard, Richard Kennon *lawyer, former pharmaceutical company executive*
Williams, Wesley Samuel, Jr. *lawyer*
Willner, Kenneth M. *lawyer*
Wilson, Rhys Thaddeus *lawyer*
Wise, Sandra Casber *lawyer*
Wittig, Raymond Shaffer *lawyer, intellectual property technology manager*
Wolf, Maurice *retired lawyer*
Wolfson, Michael George *retired lawyer*
Wong-Diaz, Francisco Raimundo *lawyer, educator*
Wood, Robert Charles *lawyer, real estate developer*
Woodard, Joseph Lamar *law librarian, educator*
Woods, Gerald Wayne *lawyer*
Wooldridge, William Charles *lawyer*
Worenklein, Jacob Joshua *lawyer*
Wright, Robert Payton *lawyer*
Wruble, Bernhardt Karp *lawyer*
Wuebbling, Donald J. *lawyer, insurance company executive*
Wyatt, Robert Lee, IV, *lawyer*
Wyckoff, E. Lisk, Jr. *lawyer*
Yeager, Mark Leonard *lawyer*

Young, John Hardin *lawyer*
Young, Thomas Lee *lawyer*
Yurchuck, Roger Alexander *retired lawyer*
Zarro, Janice Anne *lawyer*
Ziegler, William Alexander *lawyer*
Zimmerman, Jean *lawyer*
Zoeller, Donald J. *lawyer*
Zohn, Martin Steven *lawyer*

---

## MEDICINE See HEALTHCARE: MEDICINE

---

## MILITARY

---

## UNITED STATES

### ALABAMA

**Alexander City**
Shuler, Ellie Givan, Jr. *retired military officer, museum administrator*

**Auburn**
Tolbert, Clinton Jame *army officer, machinist*

**Birmingham**
Davis, Gwendolyn Louise *military officer, educator, literature educator*

**Elberta**
Wilkinson, Edward Anderson, Jr. *retired military officer, manufacturing executive*

**Enterprise**
Garrett, Thomas W. *retired career officer*
Parker, Ellis D. *retired military officer*

**Huntsville**
Williamson, Donald Ray *retired career Army officer*

**Madison**
Parlier, Greg H. *military officer, engineer, research scientist*

**Montgomery**
Turley, Susan Lynn Welker *military officer*
Uzzell-Baggett, Karon Lynette *career officer*

### ARIZONA

**Davis Monthan Afb**
Woods, Sharhonda Michele *military officer*

**Green Valley**
Bennett, Bradley Frederick *retired military officer, science association director*

**Tucson**
Wickham, John Adams, Jr. *retired army officer*

**Yuma**
Hudson, John Irvin *retired career officer*

### ARKANSAS

**Blytheville**
Slowik, Richard Andrew *air force officer*

**Mountain Home**
Baker, Robert Leon *military officer*

### CALIFORNIA

**Arroyo Grande**
Oseguera, Palma Marie *retired career officer*

**Carlsbad**
Kauderer, Bernard Marvin *retired naval officer, consultant*

**Chula Vista**
Briggs, Franklin Henry *retired naval officer*
Worthington, George Rhodes *retired naval officer*

**Coronado**
Butcher, Bobby Gene *retired military officer*
Moore, Edward, Jr. *career officer*

**El Segundo**
Hamel, Michael A. *career officer*

**Escondido**
Briggs, Edward Samuel *naval officer*

**Folsom**
Jefferds, William John *military officer*

**Healdsburg**
Eade, George James *retired military officer, researcher*

**La Jolla**
Counts, Stanley Thomas *retired military officer, retired electronics executive*

**Lemoore**
Schwerdtfeger, Henry Douglas *military officer, physiologist*

**Long Beach**
Higginson, John *retired career officer*

**Monterey**
Hoivik, Thomas Harry *military educator, international consultant*
Matthews, David Fort *career officer*
Schrady, David Alan *civilian military employee, educator*

**Oxnard**
Kirschbaum, Alan Ira *air force officer, systems integration specialist*

**Palo Alto**
Parker, James Wesley *former naval officer, investment company executive*

**Pebble Beach**
Mauz, Henry Herrward, Jr. *retired naval officer*

**San Diego**
Covey, Dana Curtis *military officer, orthodontist, surgeon*
Darmstandler, Harry Max *retired military officer*
Koenig, Harold Martin *former United States Navy surgeon general*

**San Marcos**
Jones, William Henry *retired military officer*

**Santa Ana**
Steinken, William Theodore, Jr. *military officer, secondary school educator*

**Santa Barbara**
Conley, Philip James, Jr. *retired air force officer*

**Santa Maria**
Roadarmel, Stanley Bruce *civilian military employee*

**Seaside**
Gales, Samuel Joel *retired civilian military employee, counselor*

**Windsor**
Sparks, Bennett Sher *military officer*

### COLORADO

**Colorado Springs**
Bowen, Clotilde Marion Dent *retired military officer, psychiatrist*
Skora, Wayne Philip *retired air force officer*

**Denver**
Charlip, Ralph Blair *military officer, health facility administrator*

**Dillon**
Dugan, Michael Joseph *former career officer, health agency executive*

**Durango**
Fogleman, Ronald Robert *retired air force officer, consultant*

**Englewood**
Ahearn, Joseph August *military officer, civil engineer*

**Monument**
Breckner, William John, Jr. *retired military officer*

**Peterson Afb**
Keating, Timothy J. *career military officer*
Lord, Lance W. *career military officer*

**U S A F Academy**
Weida, Johnny A. *career military officer*
Westermann, Edward Burton *military officer, analyst, educator*

### CONNECTICUT

**Groton**
Stoddard, Patrick Clare *retired military systems consultant, computer engineer*

**New London**
Bald, Ronald James *military officer*
Van Sice, James *career military officer, academic administrator*

**Niantic**
Hunt, Francis Howard *retired navy laboratory official*

**Wallingford**
Wojtasik, Joseph T. *retired military officer, small business owner*

**Waterford**
Hinkle, Muriel Ruth Nelson *naval warfare analysis company executive*

### DISTRICT OF COLUMBIA

**Bolling Afb**
Dendinger, William J. *career officer, chaplain*

**Fort Mcnair**
Miller, David Allen *air force officer*

**Washington**
Allen, Thad William *career military officer*
Altenburg, John D., Jr. *career military officer, lawyer*
Anderson, William Carl *civilian military employee, lawyer*
Arthur, Donald C. *career military officer*
Aviles, Dionel Michael *civilian military employee, former federal agency administrator*
Bolden, Charles F., Jr. *astronaut, career officer*
Bowman, Frank Lee (Skip Bowman) *retired military officer*

Boyd, Charles Graham *retired military officer, national security consulting firm executive*
Bradley, John A. *career officer*
Buckenmaier, Chester III *military officer, anesthesiologist*
Campbell, James L. *military career officer*
Clark, Wesley Kanne *retired military officer, emergency management executive, educator*
Cody, Richard A. *career military officer*
Cofer, Jonathan H. *career officer*
Conway, James T. *career military officer*
Crawford, Hunt Dorn, Jr. *retired military officer, educator, diplomat*
Crea, Vivien S. *career military officer*
Cross, Terry M. *career military officer*
Crowe, William James, Jr. *former Chairman of the Joint Chiefs of Staff, international consultant*
DuBois, Raymond Francis, Jr. *civilian military employee, former marketing professional*
Dyke, Charles William *retired army officer*
Eastin, Keith E. *civilian military employee, lawyer*
Etter, Delores M. *civilian military employee*
Forsten, Robert Douglas *military officer, psychiatrist*
Fraser, William M. III *career military officer*
Froman, Veronica Zasadni *career officer*
Geren, Pete (Preston M. Geren III) *civilian military employee, former congressman*
Gerry, Dale Francis *military officer, legislative staff member*
Giambastiani, Edmund P., Jr. *career military officer*
Gibson, Emmitt E. *career officer*
Gill, Clair F. *military career officer*
Griffin, Robert H. *career military officer*
Hagee, Michael W. *career military officer*
Harvey, Francis J. *civilian military employee*
Harvey, John Collins, Jr. *military officer*
Helmly, James R. *career military officer*
Hemingway, Thomas L. *career military officer, lawyer*
Hobbins, William T. *career officer*
Huston, John Wilson *military officer, historian*
Kern, Paul John *retired military officer*
King, James C. *retired officer*
Leaf, Howard Westley *retired military officer*
Lewis, Mark J. *civilian military employee, aerospace engineer*
Lichte, Arthur J. *career military officer*
Lietzau, William Kendall *career officer, lawyer*
MacDonald, Bruce E. *career military officer, lawyer*
Maples, Michael D. *career military officer*
Mateczun, John Matthew *career military officer*
Moseley, T. Michael (Teed Michael Moseley) *career military officer*
Mullen, Michael G. *career military officer*
North, Gary L. *career military officer*
Odom, William Eldridge *career military officer*
Ohle, David H. *military career officer*
Pace, Peter *Chairman of the Joint Chiefs of Staff*
Paige, Kathleen K. *naval officer*
Payton, Sue C. *civilian military employee*
Potter, Lorraine K. *career military officer*
Ralston, Joseph W. *retired military officer*
Renuart, Victor E., Jr. *career military officer*
Retz, William Andrew *naval consultant, retired naval officer*
Robison, Victor James, Jr. *retired military officer*
Sams, Ronald E. *career military officer*
Sandkuhler, Kevin M. *military officer*
Schmitt, John K. *army officer*
Schoomaker, Peter J. *career military officer*
Schwartz, Norton A. *career military officer*
Sega, Ronald Michael *civilian military employee, former dean*
Sharp, Walter L. (Gary Sharp) *career military officer*
Sinn, Jerry L. *army officer*
Swift, Charles *career military officer, lawyer*
Weaver, Christopher E. *naval officer*
Wennergren, David M. *civilian military employee*
Wholley, Michael Christopher *retired military officer, lawyer*
Willard, Robert F. *career military officer*
Winter, Donald C. *civilian military employee, former science administrator*
Woodley, John Paul, Jr. *civilian military employee, lawyer*
Wynne, Michael Walter *civilian military employee*
Zinni, Anthony Charles *retired military officer*

### FLORIDA

**Altoona**
Westbrook, Clinton Howard *retired military petty officer, retired protective services official*

**Celebration**
Whelden, Craig B. *retired army officer*

**Cocoa Beach**
Adkisson, Hubert Keith *military officer*

**Eglin Afb**
Head, William Christopher *military officer, health care administrator*
Richardson, Douglas J. *career officer*

**Englewood**
Watts, Ronald Lester *retired military officer*

**Fort Lauderdale**
Schnoor, Jon Peter *military officer*

**Haines City**
Clement, Robert William *retired air force officer*

**Indian Harbor Beach**
Scanlon, Charles Francis *retired military officer, writer*

**Jacksonville**
Delaney, Kevin Francis *retired military officer, consultant*
Lestage, Daniel Barfield *retired military officer, physician*

**Lake Forest**
Ross, Jimmy Douglas *retired military officer*

**Longwood**
Smyth, Joseph Patrick *retired military officer, physician*

**Melbourne**
Laposata, Joseph Samuel *army officer*
Simokaitis, Frank Joseph *military officer, lawyer*

**Miami**
Clem, Ralph S. *career officer, educator*
Craddock, Bantz J. *career military officer*

**Miami Gardens**
Vangates, Dess *retired military officer*

**Naples**
Delano, Victor *retired naval officer*
Slaff, Allan Paul *military officer, academic administrator, educator, entrepreneur*

**New Port Richey**
Miller, Harvey William *retired military officer*

**Orlando**
Bigum, Randall K. *retired military officer*
Krise, Thomas Warren *retired military officer, literature educator*
Limpus, Charles Everett III *non-commissioned officer*

**Oviedo**
Parker, Harry Lee *retired army officer, academic administrator*

**Palm Beach Gardens**
Giordano, Andrew Anthony *retired naval officer*

**Panama City**
Moore, Derrick Lanier *military officer*

**Sarasota**
Cooper, William Ewing, Jr. *retired army officer*
Gauch, Eugene William, Jr. *retired air force officer*
Heiser, Rolland Valentine *former army officer, foundation administrator*

**Tallahassee**
Davis, Larry Michael *air force officer, healthcare manager, consultant*

**Tampa**
Abizaid, John Philip *career military officer*
Haggis, Arthur George, Jr. *retired military officer, educator, publisher*
Matheny, Charles Woodburn, Jr. *former army officer, civil engineer, city official*

**West Palm Beach**
Thomashow, Steven Roy *military officer, intelligence officer*

## GEORGIA

**Atlanta**
Donald, James Edward *retired career officer, government agency executive*

**Columbus**
Tipton, James D. *retired military officer, education educator*

**Forest Park**
Honoré, Russel L. *career military officer*

**Fort Benning**
Kotwal, Russ Steven *military officer, physician*

**Fort Mcpherson**
Emery, Carolyn Vera *civilian military employee, retired non-commissioned officer*
Piacentini, Nicholas A., Jr. *military officer*
Stultz, Jack C. *career military officer*

**Fort Stewart**
Webster, William G., Jr. *career military officer*

**Jonesboro**
Galvin, John Rogers *retired army officer, law educator*

**Louisville**
Hoover, John Elwood *former military officer, consultant, author, United States military history speaker*

**Stockbridge**
Collins, Oliver Jack *military officer, secondary school educator*

**Warner Robins**
Nugteren, Cornelius *air force officer*

**Woodbine**
Konetzni, Albert H., Jr. *career officer*

## HAWAII

**Camp H M Smith**
Fallon, William J. *career military officer*

**Honolulu**
Hays, Ronald Jackson *career officer*
Wellein, Marsha Diane Akau *military educator, director*

## ILLINOIS

**Batavia**
Brown, Gerald Curtis *retired military officer, retired engineering executive*

**Mattoon**
Phipps, John Randolph *retired army officer*

**O Fallon**
Voellger, Gary A. *business consulting executive, retired air force officer*

**Rockford**
Borling, John Lorin *military officer*

**Scott Air Force Base**
Hendricks, Ian P.B. *military officer, health facility administrator*

## INDIANA

**Indianapolis**
Poel, Robert Walter *military officer, physician*

## KANSAS

**Fort Leavenworth**
Anderson, David Allen *military officer, educator*
Berlin, Robert Harry *military studies educator*
Cupp, Orville Shawn *military officer*
Petraeus, David Howell *career military officer*

**Lenexa**
Capps, Jack Lee *military officer, educator*

**Manhattan**
Myers, Richard Bowman *former Chairman of the Joint Chiefs of Staff*

## KENTUCKY

**Saint Catharine**
Donathan, David Allen *retired military officer*

## LOUISIANA

**New Orleans**
Cotton, John G. *career military officer*

## MAINE

**Stockton Springs**
Snyder, Arnold Lee, Jr. *retired military officer, research director*

## MARYLAND

**Aberdeen Proving Ground**
Halstead, Rebecca S. *career military officer*

**Annapolis**
Grooms, Bruce Estes *career military officer*
Rempt, Rodney P. *career military officer, academic administrator*
Trost, Carlisle Albert Herman *retired naval officer*

**Arnold**
Williams, James Arthur *retired military officer, information technology executive*

**Bethesda**
Daniel, Charles Dwelle, Jr. *retired military officer*
Kem, Richard Samuel *retired army officer*
Less, Anthony Albert *retired naval officer*
Peck, Edward Lionel *retired foreign service officer, corporate executive*
Ricciardi, Richard *military officer*
Schmidt, Raymond Paul *military officer, historian, government agency administrator*

**Burtonsville**
Hudson, McKinley *retired military officer, retired zoological park administrator*

**Fort George G Meade**
Kera, Tiiu *career officer*

**Fort Washington**
Wooten, Ralph G. *career officer*

**Frederick**
Allwlight, Joseph William *civilian military employee*
Kelsey, Ronald Grant *retired military officer, environmental engineer*

**Hyattsville**
Chang, Jim C. I. *air force executive*

**Oxon Hill**
Demby, Byron Gerard *military officer*

**Silver Spring**
Brog, David *former air force officer, consultant*

**Solomons**
Dorsey, James Francis, Jr. *naval officer*

**Timonium**
Sagerholm, James Alvin *retired naval officer*

## MASSACHUSETTS

**Burlington**
Dyer, Joseph Wendell *retired naval officer*

**Hanscom Afb**
Harper, David Taylor *civilian military employee*
Johnson, Charles L., II, *military officer*

**Natick**
Miller, George David *retired military officer, not-for-profit executive*

**North Oxford**
Carney, Roger Francis Xavier *retired military officer*

**Osterville**
Schwarztrauber, Sayre Archie *former naval officer, maritime consultant*

**Springfield**
Ervin, Billy Maxwell *retired military officer*

## MICHIGAN

**Hastings**
Adrounie, V. Harry *retired military medical service officer, science educator, environmentalist*

## MINNESOTA

**Plymouth**
Shadley, Robert D. *retired army officer*

## MISSISSIPPI

**Keesler Afb**
Van Goor, Anthony Jay *military officer*

**Pass Christian**
McCardell, James Elton *retired naval officer*

**Stennis Space Center**
Lever, John A. *civilian military employee*

**Vicksburg**
Faith, Jonathan Mark *retired military officer*

## MISSOURI

**Chesterfield**
Willis, Frank Edward *retired air force officer*

**Florissant**
Reese, Alferd George *retired army civilian logistics specialist*

**Poplar Bluff**
Young, William Webb *military officer, aire warfare specialist, poet*

**Saint Louis**
Strevey, Tracy Elmer, Jr. *army officer, surgeon, health facility administrator*

## MONTANA

**Hamilton**
Henley, Jack Carson *retired military officer*

## NEBRASKA

**Offutt Afb**
Cartwright, James E. *career military officer*
Sumpter, Wayne *military officer, physician*

## NEVADA

**Las Vegas**
Tollman, Aaron Paul *military officer*

## NEW JERSEY

**Fort Dix**
Adams, Keith Robert *military officer*

**Princeton**
Unruh, Howard K., Jr. *military officer, university administrator*

**South Orange**
Collins, John W., Jr. *retired military officer, technologist, educator*

## NEW MEXICO

**Albuquerque**
Flournoy, John Charles, Sr. *retired civilian military employee, retired military officer*

**Las Cruces**
Arthur, Paul Keith *retired military officer*

**Santa Fe**
Peat, Randall Dean *military analyst, retired military officer*
Sumner, Gordon, Jr. *retired military officer*

**Taos**
Vickers, Robert Edwin *retired military officer, historian, writer*

## NEW YORK

**Fayetteville**
Meigs, Montgomery Cunningham, Jr. *retired military officer, educator*

**Forest Hills**
Sanchez, Victor Hugo *retired military non-commissioned officer*

**Fort Drum**
Youngs, Michael Theron, Jr. *non-commissioned officer*

**Hamburg**
Markulis, Henryk John *career military officer*

**Kings Point**
Stewart, Joseph D. *career military officer, academic administrator*

**Marcellus**
Taylor, Robert Wilson *military officer, publishing executive*

**New York**
Prueher, Joseph W. *retired military officer, former ambassador*

**Plattsburgh**
Davis, Harley Cleo *retired military officer, manufacturing executive*

**Rome**
Ferens, Daniel Vincent *civilian military employee*

**Watertown**
Francis, Danny Marvin *retired military officer*

**West Point**
Boettner, Daisie Dawson *military officer, mechanical engineering educator*
Bozeman, Laura Beth *military officer, educator*
Hagenbeck, Franklin Lee *career military officer*
Scaparrotti, Curtis M. *career military officer*

## NORTH CAROLINA

**Fort Bragg**
Anderson, Curtis Thorwald, II, *military officer*
Fishback, Ian *military officer*

**Pinehurst**
Carroll, Kent Jean *retired naval officer*

**Research Triangle Park**
Sculley, Patrick David *retired army officer, science honor society director*

**Spring Hope**
Hildreth, James Robert *retired air force officer*

## OHIO

**Cincinnati**
Randolph, Leonard McElroy, Jr. *career officer*
Smittle, Nelson Dean *military analyst, artist*

**Dayton**
Heil, Michael Lloyd *military officer, academic administrator*
Michels, Joseph B. *military officer, dean*

**Tiffin**
Einsel, David William, Jr. *retired army officer, consultant*

**Wright Patterson Afb**
Amend, Joseph H. III *military officer*
Cranston, Stewart E. *career officer*

## OKLAHOMA

**Edmond**
Hopwood, Howard Hoppy Perry *military officer*

**Oklahoma City**
Reimer, Dennis J. *retired career military officer*
Riggs, William Gerald *military officer, small business owner*

**Tinker Afb**
Goodman, Ernest Monroe *military officer*

## OREGON

**Lake Oswego**
McPeak, Merrill Anthony *retired military officer*

## PENNSYLVANIA

**Bensalem**
Long, Robert C. *retired military officer, management consultant*

**Bethlehem**
Rokke, Ervin Jerome *military officer, academic administrator*

**Clarks Green**
Kubic, Charles Richard *retired civil engineer*

**Evans City**
Pagonis, William Gus *retired army general*

**Gettysburg**
Coughenour, Kavin Luther *career officer, military historian*

**Glenshaw**
Wilkes, John Michael *military officer, auditor*

**Harrisburg**
Renner, William Scott *retired military officer*

**Johnstown**
Samples, Jerry Wayne *military officer, educator*

**King Of Prussia**
Gallis, John Nicholas *retired military officer, executive leadership training consultant*

**Mechanicsburg**
Derr, William James *retired non-commissioned officer*

**Philadelphia**
Dobbs, Stanley *military officer, information quality engineer*

Horton, Van H. *military officer, priest, writer*

## RHODE ISLAND

**Newport**
Carpenter, Stanley Dean MacDonald *military officer, educator*

**Portsmouth**
Bergstrom, Albion Andrew *retired military officer, educator*

## SOUTH CAROLINA

**Aiken**
Chelberg, Robert Douglas *military officer*

**Bluffton**
Brown, Dallas Coverdale, Jr. *retired military officer, historian, educator*
Pendley, William Tyler *military officer, educator*

**Charleston**
Grinalds, John Southy *military officer, retired academic administrator*
Watts, Claudius Elmer III *retired military officer*

**Clemson**
Clausen, Hugh Joseph *retired army officer*

**Fort Jackson**
Brinsfield, John Wesley *military officer, educator*

**Hilton Head Island**
Brown, Arthur Edmon, Jr. *retired army officer*

**Irmo**
Parks, Garry Lee *military officer*

**New Zion**
Gibbons, Robert Butler, Jr. *retired military officer*

**Newberry**
Lander, James Albert *retired military officer, controller*

**Sumter**
Kellum, Donald Arthur *military officer*
Olsen, Thomas Richard, Sr. *air force officer*

**Wedgefield**
McLaurin, Hugh McFaddin III *military officer, museum program director*

**York**
Blackwell, Paul Eugene, Sr. *military officer*

## TEXAS

**Austin**
Vande Hey, James Michael *retired air force officer*

**Belton**
Shoemaker, Robert Morin *retired military officer, commissioner*

**College Station**
Schunicht, Shannon Anthony *retired military officer, political scientist*

**Fort Bliss**
Dorritie, Mary *military officer, psychologist*

**Fort Hood**
Metz, Thomas Frederic *career military officer*
Odierno, Raymond T. *career military officer*

**Fort Sam Houston**
Coppola, Martin Nicholas *military officer, educator*

**Fort Worth**
Lichtman, David Michael *retired military officer, orthopedist, educator, health facility administrator*
Nicholas, Nicholas Constantine *retired military officer*

**Helotes**
Hale, James Michael *military officer*

**Houston**
Gutheinz, James O'Leary *military officer, law clerk*
Gutheinz, Michael John *military officer, law clerk*

**Lubbock**
Huffman, Walter B. *retired army officer, dean, law educator*

**Mission**
Eyre, Pamela Catherine *retired career officer*

**Randolph Afb**
Ellis, Edward R. *career officer*
Looney, William R. III *career military officer*

**Sachse**
Eichelberger, Charles Bell *retired career officer*

**San Antonio**
Kline, John William *retired military officer, management consultant*
Koziol, John Craig (Craig Koziol) *career military officer*
Lebras, Paul J. *retired career military officer*

**Sheppard Afb**
Cook, Sharla J. *career officer*

**The Woodlands**
Jones, Lincoln III *military officer*

## UTAH

**Dugway**
Davis, Vernon Thomas *military officer, researcher*

**Hill AFB**
Bergren, Scott C. *career officer*
Embry, Glenn Robert *military officer*

**Provo**
Baum, Kerry Robert *retired military officer, director*

**Saint George**
Riley, James Clifford *military career officer*

**Salt Lake City**
Anselmi, John Michael *military officer, educator*

## VIRGINIA

**Alexandria**
Adams, Ranald Trevor, Jr. *retired air force officer*
Blair, Dennis Cutler *career officer*
Bowman, Richard Carl *defense consultant, retired air force officer*
Brown, Frederic Joseph *military officer*
Burke, Kelly Howard *retired military officer, entrepreneur, philanthropist*
Curtin, Gary Lee *air force officer*
Dunn, Bernard Daniel *former naval officer, consultant*
Edmonds, Albert J. *career officer*
Fedorochko, William, Jr. *retired military officer, military analyst*
Kroesen, Frederick James *retired army officer, consultant*
Larson, Charles Robert *naval officer*
Loren, Donald Patrick *retired military officer*
Simmons, Edwin Howard *military officer, historian*
Wilson, Charles H. (Charles Harrison Wilson) *retired air force officer, financial planner, human resource development professional*
Wolfe, Thad Allison *air force officer*

**Arlington**
Blum, Steven (H. Steven Blum) *career military officer*
Coady, Philip James, Jr. *retired naval officer*
DeFilippi, George *retired air force officer*
Dodgen, Larry J. *career military officer*
Forrester, Eugene Priest *retired military officer*
Graves, Ernest, Jr. *retired army officer, consultant, engineer*
Griffin, Paul, Jr. *navy officer, engineer, educator*
Hokborg, Sven-Olof *military officer*
Kamgar-Parsi, Behzad *military officer, research scientist*
Krusa-Dossin, Mary Ann *military officer*
McCaffrey, Barry Richard *retired military officer*
McKinley, Craig R. *career military officer*
Miller, Kenneth Gregory *retired air force officer*
Putnam, George W., Jr. *retired army officer*
Rogers, Alan Victor *former career officer*
Schultz, Roger C. *career military officer*
Singstock, David John *military officer*
Sullivan, Gordon R. *retired career officer*
Vaughn, Clyde A. *career military officer*

**Burke**
Pfister, Cloyd Harry *former military officer, consultant*

**Chesapeake**
Powers, Robert Lawrence *retired civilian military employee*
Taylor-Hines, Regina Anita *civilian military employee*

**Dulles**
Glacel, Robert Allan *retired military career officer*

**Dumfries**
Avrit, Richard Calvin *defense consultant, career officer*

**Fairfax**
Johnson, Wallace *retired army officer*
Rosenkranz, Robert Bernard *military officer*

**Falls Church**
Gray, D'Wayne *retired marine corps officer*
Hill, Mack C. *career officer*
Rostker, Bernard *civilian military employee*
Underwood, Paula Kay *military officer*

**Fort Belvoir**
Anderson, Frank J., Jr. *retired career officer*
Clark, Trudy H. *career officer*
Crenshaw, Horace, Jr. *military officer*
St. John, Adrian, II, *retired army officer*

**Fort Myer**
Hart, Herbert Michael *military officer*

**Great Falls**
Cowhill, William Joseph *retired naval officer, consultant*

**Gum Spring**
Dilworth, Robert Lexow *career military officer, educator*

**Hampton**
Abner, Harold Loyd *military officer, consultant*
Crawford, Tommy F. *career officer*

**Haymarket**
Seely, James Michael *retired military officer, defense consultant, small business owner*

**Langley Afb**
Blalock, Thomas Sullivan, Jr. *military officer*
Keys, Ronald E. *career military officer*

**Leesburg**
Brown, James Robert *retired air force officer*

**Lexington**
Peay, J.H. Binford III *retired army officer*
Taylor, Wesley Bayard, Jr. *retired army officer*

**Lynchburg**
Snead, George Murrell, Jr. *military officer, research scientist, consultant*

**Mc Lean**
Layman, Lawrence *naval officer*
Yarborough, William Glenn, Jr. *military officer, forester*

**Merrifield**
Earner, William Anthony, Jr. *naval officer*

**Millboro**
Minetree, James Lawrence III *retired military officer, educator*

**Norfolk**
Kernan, William Frank *career officer*
Nathman, John B. *career military officer*
Quinlan, Kenneth J., Jr. *military officer*
Reason, J. Paul *naval officer*
Smith, Lance L. *career military officer*
Train, Harry Depue, II, *retired naval officer*

**Oakton**
Frost, S. David *retired naval officer*

**Occoquan**
Vercauteren, Richard Frank *career officer*

**Potomac Falls**
Trainor, Bernard Edmund *retired military officer*

**Quantico**
Dotto, Peter Attilius *retired marine corps officer, defense consultant*

**Reston**
Jumper, John Phillip *retired military officer*
Miller, John Edward *military officer, educational association administrator, information technology executive*
Naylon, Michael Edward *retired army officer*

**Rosslyn**
Seidel, Charles Kenneth *military officer*

**Round Hill**
Tice, Raphael Dean *military officer*

**Springfield**
Ginn, Richard Van Ness *retired military officer, health products executive*

**Suffolk**
Picotte, Leonard Francis *naval officer*

**Vienna**
Chandler, Hubert Thomas *former army officer*
Jenkins, Robert Gordon *retired military officer, federal official*
Webb, William Loyd, Jr. *retired military officer*

**Virginia Beach**
Apperson, Jack Alfonso *retired army officer, management executive*
Stansberry, James Wesley *air force officer*

**White Stone**
Wroth, James Melvin *retired military officer*

**Woodbridge**
Erickson, Robert W. *military officer, educator, consultant*
Grassilli, Leo Joseph *retired military officer, fuel consultant*
Hollingsworth, Bobby G. *career officer*
Messerschmidt, William Harclerode *retired non-commissioned officer, musician*

## WASHINGTON

**Anacortes**
Higgins, Robert (Robert Walter Higgins) *career officer, physician*

**Lynnwood**
Jenes, Theodore George, Jr. *retired military officer*

**Tacoma**
Baxter, Sheila R. *career military officer*

## MILITARY ADDRESSES OF THE UNITED STATES

### EUROPE

**APO**
Dempsey, Martin E. *career military officer*
Mason, Kevin George *military officer, military analyst*
Prendergast, Kenneth Lee Michael, Jr. *career officer*

### CANADA

**ONTARIO**

**Ottawa**
de Chastelain, A(lfred) John G(ardyne) D(rummond) *Canadian army officer, diplomat*
Tellier, Henri *retired Canadian military officer*

## BELGIUM

**Brussels**
Baptiste, Thomas L. *career military officer*
Jones, James L., Jr. *career military officer*

## ENGLAND

**Oxford**
Walker, Amber Michelle *military officer*

## GERMANY

**Heidelburg**
Yarvis, Jeffrey Scott *military officer, social worker*

## GHANA

**Accra**
Oppey, Mark Ofusy *career officer*

## SAUDI ARABIA

**Riyadh**
Faraidy, Abdulaziz Abdullah *retired military officer*

## ADDRESS UNPUBLISHED

Ackermann, Bret Thomas *military officer, emergency physician*
Adams, Patrick O. *career officer*
Aldridge, Donald O'Neal *military officer*
Ambrose, Michelle *military officer, psychologist*
Anderson, Edgar Ratcliffe, Jr. *career officer, physician, health facility administrator*
Anderson, William Robert *career naval officer*
Astriab, Steven Michael *military officer*
Austin, Robert Clarke *naval officer*
Bajek, Frank Michael *retired military officer, financial consultant*
Bankers, James *military officer*
Barber, James Alden *navy officer, educator*
Barno, David W. *career military officer*
Bartrem, Duane Harvey *retired military officer, residential designer, building consultant*
Begert, William J. *lieutenant general United States Air Force*
Bell, Burwell Baxter III *career military officer*
Block, Emil Nathaniel, Jr. *retired air force officer*
Bowen, James Thomas *career officer*
Brakebill, Jean Newton *military officer, nurse, educator*
Brown, Doug (Bryan Doug Brown) *career military officer*
Brownlee, Les (Romie Leslie Brownlee) *former civilian military employee*
Buker, Robert Hutchinson, Sr. *army officer, thoracic surgeon*
Carstens, David Henry *military officer*
Casey, George William, Jr. *career military officer*
Caudill, Tom Holden *military analyst*
Chiarelli, Peter W. *career military officer*
Clapper, James R., Jr. *retired military officer, former federal agency administrator*
Clark, Vernon E. *retired military officer*
Cooning, Craig R. *career officer*
Cooper, Charles Donald *military association executive, editor, retired military officer*
Cougill, Roscoe McDaniel *retired military officer*
Cullison, Thomas R. *career military officer*
Darby, Joseph M. *reservist*
Dawson, Howard W., Jr. *military officer*
Decker, Michael H. *civilian military employee*
DeLuca, Anthony J. *civilian military employee*
DiBattiste, Carol A. *military officer*
Dozier, James Lee *former army officer*
Dupre, Felix *career military officer*
Eaton, James David III *military officer*
Eberhart, Ralph E. *retired military officer*
Edwards, Warren Chappelle *military career officer*
Eikenberry, Karl W. *career military officer*
Elam, Fred Eldon *retired military officer*
Engel, Richard L. *career officer*
Fargo, Thomas Boulton *retired career military officer*
Farmer, Kenneth Lloyd, Jr. *career military officer*
Fisher, Stephen Todd *retired military officer, health science association administrator, consultant*
Fitz-Enz, David G. *retired military officer, television producer*
Floyd, Otis Henry *retired military officer, adult education educator*
Foote, Evelyn Patricia *retired military officer*
Franks, Tommy Ray *retired military officer*
Galloway, William Rodney *military officer*
Gardner, Emerson N., Jr. *military officer*
Garner, Jay Montgomery *retired military officer*
Gatanas, Harry D. *career officer*
George, Lynnane Ellis *military officer*
Geraci, Richard V. *military officer, government agency administrator*
Gerras, Stephen Joseph *military officer, psychologist*
Goetschius, James Brian *military officer, urban planner*
Goslin, Thomas B. *career officer*
Gray, David Lawrence *retired air force officer*
Greeley, Jennifer Ann *military officer, educator*
Green, Kevin Patrick *career officer*
Green, Stanley E. *military officer*
Gunhus, Gaylord T. *military career officer*
Guthrie, Wallace Nessler, Jr. *naval officer*
Haddock, Raymond Earl *retired career officer*
Haines, Dennis G. *military officer*
Harper, Henry H. *retired military officer*
Harris, Marcelite Jordan *retired career officer*
Hauck, Frederick Hamilton *retired military officer, retired astronaut, retired aerospace executive*
Hayes, Bernard M. *military officer, researcher*
Heckman, Gary Walter *military career officer*
Henry, Charles Howard *non-commissioned officer*

Herriford, Robert Levi, Sr. *military officer*
Hessert, Wilfred *retired military officer*
Hodgkins, William F. *career officer*
Holland, Charles R. *career military officer*
Holmes, Michael L. *career officer*
Howell, Deborah S. *army officer*
Jacquard, Michael David *civilian military employee*
Johnson, Hansford Tillman *former civilian military employee*
Johnson, Joyce *retired military officer*
Johnson, Silas R., Jr. *retired military officer*
Jones, Anthony Ray *military career officer*
Jones, David Charles *retired air force officer, former chairman Joint Chiefs of Staff*
Juskowiak, Terry Eugene *career military officer*
Kadish, Ronald T. *retired career military officer*
Keene-Burgess, Ruth Frances *military official*
Kelley, Joseph E. *career officer*
Kelley, Larry Dale *retired army officer*
Kellogg, Joseph K., Jr. *military career officer*
Kendrick, Kerry *military officer*
Kennedy, William F. *retired military officer*
Kerwin, Walter Thomas, Jr. *career officer, consultant*
Kiley, Kevin C. *career military officer*
Kuklok, Kevin B. *career officer*
Kutyna, Donald Joseph *air force officer*
Lamontagne, Donald A. *career officer*
LaPorte, Leon Joseph *retired military officer*
Lennox, William James, Jr. *retired military officer*
Lindquist, Michael Adrian *career military officer*
Long, Peter Avard Chipman *retired military officer*
Lynch, Jessica *military officer*
Lynch, William J. *career officer*
Lyons, John W(inship) *retired civilian military employee, chemist, consultant*
Manganaro, Francis Ferdinand *naval officer*
Mangual, Jesus A. *army officer*
Mann, Eric Louis *retired military officer, mathematics professor, researcher*
Marlow, Edward A. *former army officer*
Martin, Gregory S. *air force officer*
Martin, James Victor, Jr. *foreign service officer, writer*
Mc Fadden, George Linus *retired army officer*
McFarren, Freddy E. *military career officer*
McLean, Craig Elliott *retired non-commissioned officer*
McNeill, Dan K. *military career officer*
Metzger, James W. *career military officer*
Mize, David M. *marine corps officer*
Moloff, Alan Lawrence *retired military officer, physician*
Moore, William Leroy, Jr. *career officer, internist*
Moorhead, Glen W. (Wally) III *career officer*
Morgan, Thomas Rowland *retired marine corps officer*
Moulitsas Zúniga, Markos *former military officer, blog writer*
Mullen, William Joseph III *military analyst, retired army career officer*
Nabors, Robert L. *military officer*
Netto, Amba Cecile *military officer*
Nyland, William Lewis *retired military officer*
O'Berry, Carl Gerald *former military officer, electrical engineer*
Oberst, Richard B. *military officer, hospital administrator*
Olson, Phillip Roger *naval officer*
Orsini, Eric Andrew *military officer*
Palmer, Dave Richard *retired military officer, academic administrator*
Parent, Rodolphe Jean *retired Canadian air force officer, pilot*
Partridge, William J. *military officer, government agency administrator*
Penn, Buddie J. *civilian military employee*
Peterson, Joseph F. H. *military officer*
Pettit, Donald P. *retired career officer*
Pirie, Robert Burns, Jr. *defense analyst*
Price, Robert Ira *coast guard officer*
Radzik, Albin F. *military analyst, consultant*
Rees, Raymond F. *military officer*
Rein, Christopher M. *military officer*
Rhoades, M. Stephen *career officer*
Riddle, Wesley Allen *army officer, writer*
Rigdon, David Tedrick *military officer, geneticist, director*
Riggs, John M. *army officer*
Robinson, David Brooks *retired naval officer*
Robinson, Ronald Gene *military officer, political science professor*
Roche, James Gerard *former civilian military employee*
Rogers, Bernard William *military officer*
Roudebush, James Gordon *career military officer*
Rubenstein, David Aaron *military officer, healthcare administrator*
Ryder, Donald J. *military career officer*
Sanchez, Ricardo S. *career military officer*
Sanderson, James Richard *retired naval officer, financial consultant*
San Diego, Armando Gonda *retired military officer, pathologist, consultant*
Scholes, Edison Earl *military officer*
Shalikashvili, John Malchase *former Chairman of the Joint Chiefs of Staff*
Shaw, John Frederick *retired naval officer*
Shinseki, Eric Ken *retired military officer*
Shipway, John Francis *retired career officer*
Smith, Zannie O. *retired career officer*
Smoker, Roy Ellis *retired military officer*
Solomon, Billy K. *army officer*
Springer, Robert Dale *retired air force officer, consultant, lecturer*
Stierle, Linda J. *military officer*
Strock, Carl A. *career military officer*
Sullivan, Paul F. *career officer*
Sutton, Peter U. *military officer*
Tallent, Hamlin B. *career officer*
Tarantino, David A., Jr. *military officer, emergency physician*
Taylor, George Peach, Jr. *career military officer*
Teets, Peter B. *former civilian military employee*
Toedt, Michael Edgar *military officer, hospital administrator*
Truckenbrodt, Yolanda Bernabe *retired air force officer, consultant*
Tuttle, Jerry Owen *retired military officer, information technology executive*

Van Winkle, Hans A. *military officer*
Vessey, John William, Jr. *military officer*
Viñas, Richard Roculan *non-commissioned officer*
Vincent, Hal Wellman *military officer, investor*
Vines, John R. *career military officer*
von Kaenel, Howard J. *army officer*
Ward, William E. *career military officer*
Watts, Helena Roselle *military analyst*
Welser, William III *military officer*
West, Walter Matthew *military officer*
Weyman, Steven Aloysius *retired military officer*
Wheeler, Albin Gray *retired military officer, retail executive, educator*
Wilson, Frances C. *career military officer*
Yeosock, John John *military officer*
Yingling, John A. *military officer*
Yoon, E. Yul *retired career officer*
Zais, Mitchell M. *career military officer*
Zuick, Ernest Ronald, Jr. *career officer, advertising executive*

# REAL ESTATE

## UNITED STATES

### ALABAMA

**Arab**
Hammond, Ralph Charles *real estate executive*

**Birmingham**
Coleman, Stephen Beasley, Jr. *real estate broker, writer*
Copeland, Hunter Armstrong *retired real estate company executive*
Voncannon, Eric R. *real estate company executive*

**Dothan**
Dean, Bobby Frank *real estate agent*

**Mobile**
Clark, Hattie Giles *real estate broker, real estate appraiser*

**Montgomery**
Cassels, Martha Beasley *realtor, real estate developer*

**Tuscaloosa**
McFarland, James William *real estate company executive, consultant*
McFarland, James William, Jr. *real estate manager*

### ALASKA

**Girdwood**
Trautner, John James *real estate executive*

### ARIZONA

**Phoenix**
De Michele, O. Mark *real estate company executive*
Hanneman, LeRoy C., Jr. *real estate executive*
Lewis, Orme, Jr. *real estate company executive, land use adviser*
Sertich, Kelli Ann *land use planner*

**Prescott**
Masotti, Louis Henry *real estate educator, consultant*

**Scottsdale**
Behrens, Robert Chadwick *real estate company executive*
Dorrance, Bennett *real estate company executive*
Hadder, Donald Everett, Sr. *urban planner*

**Sedona**
Copeland, Suzanne Johnson *real estate company executive*

**Tempe**
Carlyle, Eric *real estate company executive*
Jungbluth, Kirk E. *real estate appraiser*
Kim, Joochul *urban planner, educator*

**Tucson**
Carman, Mary Ann *realtor, writer, retired medical/surgical nurse*
Longan, George Baker III *real estate company executive*
Tang, Esther Don *real estate developer, consultant, social worker*

### ARKANSAS

**Blytheville**
Baker, Carlene Poff *real estate agent, reporter*

**Magnolia**
Juniker, Anthony Michael *real estate developer, consultant*

**Rogers**
Cooper, John Alfred, Jr. *community development company executive*

### CALIFORNIA

**Apple Valley**
Yule, Caroll Jane *real estate broker*

**Aptos**
Nicholson, Joseph Bruce *real estate developer*

**Bakersfield**
Chidgey, Guy Clement *real estate company executive*

**Beverly Hills**
Bergman, Nancy Palm *real estate investment company executive*
Glazer, Guilford *real estate developer*
Shapell, Nathan *financial and real estate executive*
Tamkin, Curtis Sloane *real estate development company executive*
Victor, Robert Eugene *real estate company executive, lawyer*

**Brentwood**
Albers, Lucia Berta *land developer*

**Camino**
McCarthy, Brian Nelson *real estate developer*

**Chula Vista**
Heise, Steven Anthony *surveyor, consultant*

**City Of Industry**
Roski, Edward P., Jr. *real estate developer, professional sports team executive*

**Costa Mesa**
Cohen, Stanley *commercial real estate developer*

**El Segundo**
Kay, Kenneth Jeffrey *real estate company executive*

**Foster City**
Butcher, C. Preston *real estate company executive*

**Fountain Valley**
Smith, Marie Edmonds *real estate agent, property manager*

**Fresno**
Fortune, Larry M. *real estate broker*
Raven, Patricia Elaine (Penny Raven) *real estate broker, developer, columnist, gas industry executive*

**Glendale**
Gedjeyan, Hovannes John *real estate broker*
Khatchathurian, Hovik Malhami *real estate broker*

**Granite Bay**
Kemper, Dorla Dean Eaton (Dorla Dean Eaton) *real estate broker*

**Huntington Beach**
Duong, John Quoc *real estate developer*

**Irvine**
Chronley, James Andrew *real estate executive*
Stack, Geoffrey Lawrence *real estate developer*
Vandell, Kerry Dean *real estate consultant, educator, director, finance educator*
Windsor, Adrian Sharon *real estate broker, literature and language professor*

**La Jolla**
Anthony, Harry Antoniades *retired city planner, architect, educator*
Foley, L(ewis) Michael *real estate company officer*

**Laguna Beach**
Hanauer, Joe Franklin *real estate company officer*

**Laguna Niguel**
York, James Orison *real estate executive*

**Long Beach**
Davies, Grace Lucille *real estate educator*

**Los Angeles**
Cushman, John C. III *real estate company executive*
Linsk, Michael Stephen *real estate company executive*
Ross, Stan *real estate company executive*
Rouze, Jeffrey Alan *real estate executive*
Sterling, Donald T. *real estate mogul, professional basketball team executive*
Swartz, Roslyn Holt *real estate company executive*
Willie, Brett *real estate company executive*
Wirta, Raymond E. *real estate company executive*

**Napa**
Jeffords, Tracy H. *real estate company officer*

**Newport Beach**
Bren, Donald L. *real estate company executive*
Fawcett, John Scott *real estate developer*
Kenney, William John, Jr. *real estate developer*
Olenicoff, Igor *real estate company executive*

**Ontario**
Previtti, James P. *real estate executive*

**Palm Springs**
Coffey, Nancy *real estate broker*

**Palmdale**
Anderson, R(obert) Gregg *real estate company executive*

**Palo Alto**
Klein, Robert Nicholas, II, *real estate developer*
McIntyre, Robert Wheeler *retired conservation organization executive*
Moore, Cassandra Chrones *real estate broker*
Wong, Y(ing) Wood *real estate investment company executive, real estate development company executive, venture capital investment company executive*

**Pasadena**
Crowley, John Crane *real estate developer*

**Rancho Mirage**
Blixseth, Timothy *real estate developer*

**Rancho Santa Fe**
Dieffenbach, Otto Weaver III *real estate company executive*
O'Driscoll, Margaret Millar (Peggy O'Driscoll) *real estate broker*

**Redondo Beach**
Abernethy, Robert John *real estate developer*

**Riverside**
Pratt, John Jackson *property manager, retired utilities worker*

**Roseville**
Yarrigle, Charlene Sandra Shuey *realtor, investment advisor*

**Ross**
Nicholson, William Joseph *energy and environmental consultant*

**Sacramento**
Lukenbill, Gregg *real estate developer, sports promoter*

**San Diego**
Oldham, Maxine Jernigan *real estate broker*

**San Francisco**
Bracken, Thomas Robert James *real estate investment executive*
Freund, Fredric S. *real estate broker, real estate manager*
Shorenstein, Walter Herbert *commercial real estate development company executive*
Wang, An-Yi (Anne) Chou *real estate broker*

**San Jose**
Rothblatt, Donald Noah *urban and regional planner, educator*

**San Rafael**
Roulac, Stephen E. *real estate consultant*

**Santa Ana**
Hughes, Chrstopher *real estate company executive*

**Santa Clara**
Arrillaga, John *real estate company executive*
Berg, Carl E. *real estate developer*

**Santa Cruz**
Dilbeck, Charles Stevens, Jr. *real estate company executive*

**Santa Monica**
Wachs, Martin *urban planning educator, author, consultant*

**Sherman Oaks**
Jackson, Chris *real estate broker*

**Stockton**
Michailoff, Ian Robert *real estate broker, land use planner*

**Thousand Oaks**
Wolff, Stuart *online real estate executive*

**Tulare**
Hefflefinger, Clarice Thorpe *retired real estate broker*

**Twain Harte**
Kinsinger, Robert Earl *property company executive, educational consultant*

**Vista**
Cavanaugh, Kenneth Clinton *retired real estate consultant*

**Walnut Creek**
Ostrander, Willis Frederick *retired real estate appraiser*

**West Sacramento**
Kalachov, Ellada *realtor*

**Westlake Village**
Long, W. Michael *real estate company executive*

### COLORADO

**Boulder**
Stepanek, Joseph Edward *real estate developer, consultant*

**Colorado Springs**
Christensen, C. Lewis *real estate developer*

**Denver**
Considine, Terry *real estate company executive*
Mandarich, David D. *real estate corporation executive*

**Fort Collins**
Jensen, Margaret *real estate broker*

**Greenwood Village**
Liniger, Dave *real estate company executive*

**Littleton**
Grant, Newell M. *real estate investment manager*

**Louisville**
Schonbrun, Michael K. *senior housing developer and operator*

**Monument**
Boggs, Steven Eugene *real estate broker, lawyer*

**Vail**
Kelton, Arthur Marvin, Jr. *real estate developer*

**Woody Creek**
Jenkins, Robert Berryman *real estate developer*

## CONNECTICUT

### Bethel
Kurfehs, Harold Charles *real estate executive*

### Danbury
Anderson, Alan Reinold *real estate company executive, computer security firm executive, consultant*

### Greenwich
Badman, John III *real estate developer, architect*
Griggs, Nina M. *realtor*
Urstadt, Charles J. *real estate company officer*

### New Haven
Alexander, Bruce Donald *real estate executive, educator*
Harrison, Henry Starin *real estate appraiser, educator, entrepreneur*

### North Haven
Westerfield, Carolyn Elizabeth Hess *urban planner*

### Norwalk
Soper, Jeannine *real estate agent*

### Old Greenwich
Parris, Sally Nye *real estate agent*

### Redding
Addison, Jason Lawrence *multifamily community development executive*

### Stamford
Koproski, Alexander Robert *real estate company executive*

## DELAWARE

### Dover
Taylor, Suzonne Berry Stewart *real estate broker*

### Rehoboth Beach
Little, R. Donald *real estate entrepreneur*

### Wilmington
Maley, Patricia Ann *preservation planner*

## DISTRICT OF COLUMBIA

### Washington
Anlian, Steven James *urban planner, consultant*
Blackwelder, Brent Francis *environmentalist*
Brooks, Jane K. *real estate agent, educator*
Carr, Thomas A. *real estate company executive*
Gibbons, Petch *real estate company executive*
Hawkins, Philip Linton *real estate executive*
Janes, William Sargent *real estate company executive*
John, Frank Herbert, Jr. *real estate appraiser, investor, marketing executive*
Jones, Susan Dorfman *real estate broker, writer*
Stone, Roger David *environmentalist*
Train, Russell Errol *environmentalist*
Wallace Douglas, Jean *conservationist*
Wheeler, Douglas Paul *conservationist, state agency administrator, lawyer*

## FLORIDA

### Boca Raton
Goray, Gerald Allen *real estate company executive, lawyer*
Innes-Brown, Georgette Meyer *real estate broker, insurance broker*
O'Connell, Theresa Aurora *title company executive*

### Bonita Springs
Starkey, Jerry L. *real estate developer*

### Cedar Key
Starnes, Earl Maxwell *retired urban and regional planner, retired architect, retired educator*

### Coral Gables
Balzebre, Anthony Francis, Sr. *real estate developer, investor*
Milton, Jose *real estate development company executive*
Milton, Joseph *real estate development company executive*

### Fort Lauderdale
Markos, Chris *retired real estate company executive*
Parrish, Lori Nance *property appraiser*
Taylor, Ralph Orien, Jr. *real estate developer, investor*
Weiss, David I. *real estate company executive, lawyer, writer*

### Gainesville
York, Vermelle Cardwell *retired real estate broker and developer*

### Hutchinson Island
Welch, Martha Lynn *environmentalist, educator*

### Jacksonville
Aleschus, Justine Lawrence *retired real estate broker*
Bodkin, Ruby Pate *real estate broker, educator*
Clarkson, Charles Andrew *real estate investment executive*

### Key West
Taylor, Victoria *real estate rehabilitator, sculptor*

### Lake Suzy
Ogan, Russell Griffith *real estate broker*

### Longwood
Gasperoni, Emil, Sr. *realtor, real estate developer*

### Maitland
Vallee, Judith Delaney *environmentalist, writer, not-for-profit fundraiser*

### Miami
Codina, Armando M. *real estate developer*
Miller, Stuart A. *real estate executive, lawyer*
Nestor Castellano, Brenda Diana *real estate company executive*
Perez, Jorge M. *real estate developer*
Raffel, Leroy B. *real estate developer*
Salvaneschi, Luigi *real estate developer, management consultant, educator*
West, Macdonald *real estate executive*

### Naples
de Maleissye Melun, Countess Judith *realtor*
Dorio, Martin Matthew, Jr. *real estate company executive, investor*
Dykstra, David Allen *real estate company executive*
Keller, Theodore G., Jr. *investment property owner and manager*
Llewellyn, Leonard Frank *real estate broker, investment company executive*
Stastny, John Anton *real estate executive*

### Niceville
Rasmussen, Robert Dee *retired real estate appraiser*

### North Miami Beach
Sipzner, Howard M. *real estate executive*

### Ocala
Booth, Jane Schuele *real estate company officer, real estate broker*

### Ocean Ridge
Mueller, Gerard *realtor, investor, former Internet executive*

### Orlando
Gidel, Robert Hugh *real estate investor*

### Ormond Beach
Buonamano, Anthony F. *real estate agent, retired postal service worker*

### Palm Beach
Bagby, Martha L. Green *real estate holding company executive, writer, publishing executive*
Coudert, Dale Hokin *real estate executive, marketing consultant*
Dillard, Rodney Jefferson *real estate executive*
Klotsche, Charles Martin *real estate company executive, photographer, writer, financial columnist*

### Palm Beach Gardens
VanButsel, Michael R. *real estate broker, construction executive*

### Palm Coast
Barnes, Judith Ann *real estate company executive*

### Panama City
Navon, Robert *real estate investor, retired publisher*

### Ponte Vedra Beach
Berry, Clare Gebert *real estate broker*

### Port Charlotte
Wall, Edward Millard *environmental consulting executive*

### Safety Harbor
Crafton-Masterson, Adrienne *real estate company executive*

### Saint Petersburg
Hurley, John Kenneth *real estate company executive, merchant banking executive*
Kanstoroom, David Arnold *real estate developer, entrepreneur*

### Saint Petersburg Beach
Hurley, Frank Thomas, Jr. *realtor*

### Sarasota
Levitt, Jaren *real estate company officer*
Tourkantonis, Arthur Charles *real estate consultant, lawyer*

### Satellite Beach
Miller, Susan Laura *real estate company executive, retired special education educator*

### Sebring
Sherrick, Daniel Noah *real estate broker*

### Stuart
Johnson, Sailee *realtor*

### Sunrise
Maken, Sonny *real estate company executive, real estate developer*

### Tallahassee
Campbell, Frances Harvell *real estate developer*
Lisenby, Dorrece Edenfield *realtor*

### Tampa
Krone, Norman Bernard *real estate developer, lawyer*
Schild, Nancy Lois *realtor, music educator*

### Titusville
Morton, Craig Richard *real estate investor*

### Vero Beach
Freeman, Donald Wilford *real estate developer, horse breeder*

### West Palm Beach
Kramer, Eleanor *retired real estate broker, tax specialist, financial consultant*

## GEORGIA

### Alpharetta
Cline, Stewart M. *real estate executive*
Weitz, John Jerome, Jr. *city planner*

### Athens
Melton, Wayne Charles *real estate executive*

### Atlanta
Adams, David Porterfield III *business appraiser*
Comstock, Robert Donald, Jr. *real estate executive*
Gregory, Henry D., Jr. *real estate company executive*
Haralson, Michael *real estate agent*
Ossewaarde, Anne Winkler *real estate company executive*
Raines, Tim D. *real estate company executive*
Terwilliger, J. Ronald *real estate company executive*
Wieland, John *real estate executive*
Winchester, Jesse Gregory *commercial real estate company executive*

### Canton
Fitzgerald, Gregory Allan *real estate broker, entrepreneur*

### Clarkston
Charania, Barkat *real estate consultant*

### Folkston
Crumbley, Esther Helen Kendrick *retired real estate agent, retired secondary school educator, councilman*

### Forsyth
Coleman, Steven Andrew *surveyor*

### Marietta
Carnes, James Donald *real estate manager*
McAuley, Thomas H. *real estate executive*

### Newnan
Barron, Thomas Willis *real estate broker*

### Norcross
Cohen, Barry P. *real estate investment management company executive*

### Peachtree City
Clark, James Kermit, Jr. *real estate executive*

### Stone Mountain
Malone, Embry *property manager, advocate*

### Toccoa
Maypole, John Floyd *real estate company executive*

### Woodstock
Colgan, George Phillips *real estate developer, real estate appraiser*

## HAWAII

### Honolulu
Albano, Andres, Jr. *real estate developer, real estate broker*
Lighter, Eric Aaron *real estate developer, law enforcement software developer, consultant*

### Kailua
Wong, Wallace *real estate investor*

### Koloa
Cobb, Rowena Noelani Blake *real estate broker*

## IDAHO

### Donnelly
Ferensowicz, Michael Jay *real estate company executive*

### Idaho Falls
Thorsen, Nancy Dain *real estate broker*

### Troy
Hepler, Merlin Judson, Jr. *real estate broker*

## ILLINOIS

### Aurora
Stephens, Steve Arnold *real estate broker*

### Champaign
Guttenberg, Albert Ziskind *planning educator*

### Chicago
Beitler, J. Paul *real estate developer*
Berger, Miles Lee *land economist*
Bluhm, Neil Gary *real estate company executive*
Bohn, Charlotte Galitz *retired real estate executive*
Brennan, Michael *real estate company executive*
Bucksbaum, John *real estate company executive*
Bucksbaum, Matthew *real estate investment trust company executive*
Bynoe, Peter Charles Bernard *real estate developer, lawyer*
Callahan, Timothy T. *real estate company executive*
Campbell, Gavin Elliott *real estate investor and developer*
Crocker, Douglas, II, *real estate executive*
Daley, Vincent Raymond, Jr. *real estate company executive, consultant*
Daly, Patrick F. *real estate executive, architect*
Darchun, Lino Auksutis *real estate professional*
Duncan, Bruce W. *real estate company executive, hotel executive*
Durbin, Jack E. *real estate company executive*
Eubanks-Pope, Sharon G. *real estate company executive, entrepreneur*
Ezgur, Michael *real estate company executive*

### Field, Karen Ann (Karen Ann Schaffner) *real estate broker*
Fox, Leslie B. *real estate company executive*
Freibaum, Bernard *real estate development company executive*
Galowich, Ronald Howard *real estate company executive, venture capitalist, pilot*
Geleerd, James (Jake Geleerd) *property manager*
Geoga, Douglas Gerard *real estate developer, lawyer*
Heneghan, Thomas P. *real estate company executive*
Jarrett, Valerie Bowman *real estate company executive, stock exchange executive*
Julmy, Camille P. *real estate company executive*
Kincaid, Richard D. *real estate company executive*
Klebba, Raymond Allen *property manager*
Matanky, James E. *real estate developer*
Michaels, Robert A. *real estate development company executive*
Neithercut, David J. *real estate company officer*
Pacher, Nancy A. *real estate company executive*
Pappas, Philip James *real estate company executive*
Patterson, Jeffrey A. *real estate company executive*
Primo, Quintin E. III *real estate company executive*
Shidler, Jay H. *real estate company executive*
Walsh, Matthew M. *real estate developer*
Winslow, Robert A. *real estate company executive*
Wirtz, William Wadsworth *real estate company executive, professional sports team executive*

### Dundee
Ulakovich, Ronald Stephen *real estate developer*

### East Saint Louis
Thomas, Mary Lee *property manager*

### Highland Park
Stein, Paula Jean Anne Barton *hotel real estate company executive, real estate broker*

### Lake Zurich
Schultz, Carl Herbert *real estate developer*

### Northbrook
Levy, Arnold S(tuart) *real estate company executive*
Metz, Adam S. *real estate company executive*
Perelman, Jeffrey E. *real estate company executive*

### Westmont
Harten, Ann M. *relocation services executive*

## INDIANA

### Elkhart
Vite, Frank Anthony *realtor*

### Fort Wayne
Glick, Anna Margaret *real estate broker, consultant*

### Greenwood
Tomlin, Jeanne Brannon *real estate broker, small business owner*

### Indianapolis
Borns, Robert Aaron *real estate developer*
Cohoat, Matthew A. *real estate company executive*
Mullen, Thomas Edgar *real estate consultant*
Oklak, Dennis D. *real estate company executive*
Simon, David *real estate company officer*
Simon, Herbert *real estate developer, professional basketball team executive*
Simon, Melvin *real estate developer, professional sports team executive*
Simon, Melvon *real estate company officer*
Sokolov, Richard Saul *real estate company executive*
Sterrett, Steven E. *real estate company officer*

### Jeffersonville
Reisert, Charles Edward, Jr. *realtor*

### Newburgh
Tierney, Gordon Paul *real estate broker, genealogist*

## IOWA

### Cedar Rapids
Baermann, Donna Lee Roth *real estate property executive, retired insurance analyst*
Knepper, Eugene Arthur *realtor*

### Des Moines
Woehler, Joel Lee *real estate asset manager*

## KANSAS

### Leawood
Joslin, Janine Elizabeth *preservationist, consultant*

### Olathe
Harmon, Roger E. *environmentalist*
Hart, Michele *real estate agent*

## KENTUCKY

### Frankfort
Collins, Hubert *real estate broker, state representative*

### Franklin
Kelley, Brad M. *conservationist, real estate developer*

### Lexington
Gable, Robert Elledy *real estate investment company executive*

**Louisville**
Glogower, Michael Howard *real estate company executive, consultant*

**Middlesboro**
Daniel, Barbara Ann *realtor, advertising executive*

## LOUISIANA

**Baton Rouge**
Skillman, Ernest Edward, Jr. *real estate sales and management executive*

**Covington**
Gilman-Anderson, Susan Ellen *real estate company executive, consultant*
Maurin, James E. *real estate executive*

**Leesville**
Thompson, Darlene Bennett *realtor, musician*

**New Orleans**
Canizaro, Joseph *real estate developer*
Jones, Glenn Earle *property management executive*
Lupo, Robert Edward Smith *real estate developer and investor*

## MAINE

**Bangor**
Foster, Walter Herbert, Jr. *real estate company executive*

**Gardiner**
Gosline, Norman Abbot *real estate appraiser, consultant*

**Portland**
Sigfridson, Andrew Carl *real estate broker, investor*

## MARYLAND

**Baltimore**
DeVito, Mathias Joseph *retired real estate company executive*
Gabriel, Donald Albert *real estate company executive*
Millspaugh, Martin Laurence *real estate developer, consultant*

**Berlin**
Passwater, Barbara Gayhart *real estate broker*

**Bethesda**
Clark, A. James *real estate company executive*

**Chevy Chase**
Lee, Brenda Baker *real estate company executive*
Noonan, Patrick Francis *conservation executive*

**Columbia**
Deering, Anthony Wayne Marion *real estate developer*
McCuan, William Patrick *real estate company executive*
McGregor, Douglas A. *real estate company executive*

**Frederick**
Whelihan, Alan Stuart *real estate developer, automotive executive*

**North Bethesda**
Lerner, Theodore *real estate company executive*

**Phoenix**
Meyerhoff, Robert E. *real estate developer, philanthropist, art collector, horse breeder*

**Potomac**
Dickerman, Serafina Poerio *real estate broker, consultant*
Eaves, Maria Perry *realtor*

**Rockville**
Frazier, Walter Ronald *real estate investment company executive*

**Salisbury**
Nutter, David George *city planner*

**Silver Spring**
McCray, Lora *real estate developer*

**Takoma Park**
Urciolo, John Raphael, II, *real estate developer, real estate educator, finance educator*

**Westminster**
Erb, Betty Jane *retired real estate agent*

## MASSACHUSETTS

**Amherst**
Bentley, Richard Norcross *regional planner, writer, educator*
Larson, Joseph Stanley *environmentalist, educator*

**Andover**
Darling, Beverly Jones *retired real estate agent, artist*

**Boston**
Beal, Robert Lawrence *real estate executive*
Holland, James R. *real estate company officer*
Linde, Edward H. *real estate manager*
Lovejoy, George Montgomery, Jr. *real estate company executive*
Lundgren, Richard John *real estate executive, preservationist, city planner*
Radloff, Robert Albert *real estate company executive*

Wiggleworth, Margaret *property manager*

**Cambridge**
de Marneffe, Barbara Rowe *historic preservationist*
Fleming, Ronald Lee *urban planner, consultant*
Spunt, Shepard Armin *real estate company executive, management and financial consultant*
Susskind, Lawrence Elliott *urban planner, educator, mediator*
Vigier, François Claude Denis *city planning educator*
Wood, Richard Robinson *real estate company executive*

**Fairhaven**
Hotchkiss, Henry Washington *real estate broker, financial consultant*

**Fall River**
Brion, Norma M. *real estate broker*

**Falmouth**
Milkman, Marianne Friedenthal *retired city planner*

**Gloucester**
Sallah, Majeed (Jim Sallah) *retired real estate developer*

**Lexington**
Linkov, Igor *conservationist, consultant*

**Natick**
Strauss, Harlee Sue *environmentalist, consultant*

**Newton**
Karp, Stephen R. *real estate developer*
Nahigian, Robert John *real estate company executive, consultant*

**Shrewsbury**
Falter, Robert Gary *real estate broker, educator*

**Waltham**
Nelson, Arthur Hunt *real estate company executive*

**Wellesley**
Fineberg, Gerald *real estate company executive*
Roberts, Sandra Brown *real estate company executive*

**Winchester**
Blackham, Ann Rosemary (Mrs. J. W. Blackham) *realtor*

## MICHIGAN

**Ann Arbor**
Clark, Thomas B., Sr. *real estate broker*
Surovell, Edward David *real estate company executive*

**Bingham Farms**
Silverman, Gilbert B. *retired real estate developer, art collector*

**Bloomfield Hills**
Larson, Robert Craig *real estate company officer*
Taubman, Robert S. *real estate developer*

**East Lansing**
Anderton, James Franklin, IV, *real estate company executive*

**Flat Rock**
Cerasuolo, Jennifer Lyn *preservationist*

**Grosse Ile**
Smith, Veronica Latta *real estate company officer*

**Grosse Pointe Shores**
LaHood, Mary Anne *real estate investor*

**Haslett**
Hotaling, Robert Bachman *urban planner, educator*

**Niles**
Tenney, Jane Morris *real estate developer*

**Northville**
Green, Jody *real estate company executive, real estate broker*

**Saginaw**
Cline, Thomas William *real estate leasing company executive, management consultant*

**White Lake**
Clyburn, Luther Linn *real estate broker, real estate appraiser*

## MINNESOTA

**Aitkin**
Lane, Chuck J. *real estate developer*

**Duluth**
Bowman, Roger Manwaring *real estate company officer*

**Minneapolis**
Boelter, Philip Floyd *real estate company officer, construction executive*
Forsyth, Ann *urban planner, educator*
Kreiser, Frank David *real estate executive*
Stuebner, James Cloyd *real estate developer, contractor*

## MISSISSIPPI

**Meridian**
Church, George Millord *retired real estate company executive*

**Vicksburg**
Nichols, William Owen *conservationist*

## MISSOURI

**Ash Grove**
Johnson, Iver Christian *retired real estate appraiser*

**Chesterfield**
Morley, Harry Thomas, Jr. *real estate executive*

**Earth City**
Kroenke, E. Stanley *real estate developer, professional sports team executive*

**Gray Summit**
Desloge, Christopher Davis, Sr. *real estate company executive, merchant banking and consulting executive*

**Holden**
Martin, Laurabelle *property manager*

**Ironton**
Sebastian, Phylis Sue (Ingram) *real estate broker, antique appraiser, real estate appraiser*

**Kansas City**
Shutz, Byron Christopher *real estate company officer*

**Lake Saint Louis**
Lang, Danny Robert *planning consultant*
Royal, William Henry *retired real estate developer, architect*

**Saint Joseph**
Rachow, Sharon Dianne *realtor*

**Saint Louis**
Burkhart, Mark *real estate company executive*
Drey, Leo *environmentalist*
Koehler, Harry George *real estate executive*
Meissner, Edwin Benjamin, Jr. *retired real estate broker*
Sutter, Jane Elizabeth *conservationist, science educator*

**Springfield**
Aull, Elizabeth Berryman *real estate development executive*
Carlson, Thomas Joseph *real estate developer, lawyer*

**Stockton**
Jackson, Betty L. Deason *real estate developer*

## MONTANA

**Great Falls**
Stevens, George Alexander *real estate broker*

## NEBRASKA

**Lincoln**
Tadesse, Tsegaye *climatologist, researcher*
Tavlin, Michael John *real estate company executive, manufacturing executive*

## NEVADA

**Carson City**
Alexander, Jack Dudley III *natural resources consultant*

**Henderson**
Woodriff, Lee *company executive*

**Las Vegas**
Egidio, Martha L. *real estate broker and salesman*
Jabara, Michael Dean *real estate developer, former technology entrepreneur*
Lee, Theodore Bo *real estate developer*
Murray, Krystal A. *real estate broker*
Sullivan, Christopher David *real estate broker, real estate attorney*

## NEW HAMPSHIRE

**Portsmouth**
Cunningham, Valerie S. *historic preservationist, researcher*

## NEW JERSEY

**Atlantic Highlands**
Hawley, Joseph. B. *property management executive, educator*

**Bedminster**
Hudacsko, Dennis Wayne *urban planner*

**Cape May Point**
Chandler, Marguerite Nella *real estate company executive*

**Cherry Hill**
Copsetta, Norman George *real estate executive*

**Cranford**
Mack, William L. *real estate investment company executive*

**Englewood Cliffs**
Books, Roberta Paula *real estate finance executive*

**Flemington**
Salamon, Renay *real estate broker*

**Florham Park**
Gale, Stan *real estate company executive*
Yeager, Mark *real estate company executive*

**Haworth**
Strum, Brian J. *real estate company officer*

**Hightstown**
Finn, Gerald C. *real estate company executive*
Finn, Jeffrey M. *real estate company executive*

**Morristown**
Lieblich, Frederich *real estate consultant*

**Pine Brook**
Marlow, Ian Michael *real estate company executive*

**Red Bank**
Hovnanian, Ara K. *real estate developer*
Hovnanian, Kevork S. *real estate developer*

## NEW MEXICO

**Albuquerque**
Davis, Betty Bourbonia *real estate company executive*
Stahl, Jack Leland *real estate company executive*

**Las Cruces**
Parsley, Steven Dwayne *title company executive*

**Mora**
Hanks, Eugene Ralph *real estate developer, rancher, forester, retired military officer, investor*

## NEW YORK

**Astoria**
Kaufman, George S. *real estate company executive*

**Briarcliff Manor**
Kepcher, Carolyn *real estate company executive*

**Bronx**
Carter, Majora *urban planner*

**Brooklyn**
Stuckey, James P. *real estate developer*

**Canaan**
Belknap, Michael H. P. *real estate developer*

**Douglaston**
Balbi, Kenneth Emilio *environmental specialist, researcher*
Levine, Jeffrey E. *real estate developer*

**Dundee**
Miller, Ronald K. *real estate broker, educator*

**Elma**
Wirth, Sandra Lee *real estate company owner*

**Elmsford**
Raymond, George Marc *city planner, educator*

**Goshen**
Ward, William Francis, Jr. *real estate investment broker*

**Harrison**
Strone, Michael Jonathan *real estate consultant, lawyer*

**Larchmont**
Levi, James Harry *real estate executive, investment banker*

**Liverpool**
De Long, Jacob Edward *real estate broker*

**Melville**
Campofranco, Salvatore *real estate company executive*

**Mount Vernon**
Rossini, Joseph *contracting and development corporate executive*

**New Hyde Park**
Agin, Herbert *real estate company executive*
Flynn, Michael J. *real estate executive*
Henry, David B. *real estate company executive*
Pappagallo, Michael V. *realty company executive*

**New York**
Beinecke, Frances G. *environmentalist*
Clark, Ric *real estate company executive*
Close, Michael John *property manager, lawyer*
Consolo, Faith Hope *real estate broker*
Corcoran, Barbara *real estate company executive*
Esposito, Louis *real estate developer*
Farley, Katherine G. *real estate company executive*
Fox-Freund, Barbara Susan *real estate company executive*
Garfield, Leslie Jerome *real estate executive*
Gochberg, Thomas *real estate investor, investment banker*
Gosin, Barry M. *real estate company executive*
Grau, Marcy Beinish *real estate broker, former investment banker*
Gural, Jeffrey R. *real estate company executive*
Hackett, Kevin R. *real estate company executive, lawyer*
Hemmendinger, H. Dale *real estate executive*
Herman, Dorothy *real estate broker*
Hernstadt, Judith Filenbaum *city planner, real estate executive, broadcast executive*
Kalikow, Peter Stephen *real estate developer, former publishing executive*
Kogod, Robert P. *philanthropist, former real estate company executive*
Krasnow, Kenneth *real estate company executive*
Kuhn, James D. *real estate company executive*
Laurie, Craig *real estate company executive*

Levine, Judy Kendall *real estate broker, interior designer, writer*
Litwin, Leonard *real estate company executive*
Marshall, Alton Garwood *real estate agent, consultant*
Miles, John R. *real estate development company executive*
Milstein, Paul *real estate developer*
Mosler, Bruce E. *real estate company executive*
Nichols, Edie Diane *real estate developer*
Pearl, Mary Corliss *wildlife conservationist*
Petz, Edwin V. *real estate company executive, lawyer*
Phillips, Karen A. *urban planner*
Quinlan, Robert Conrad *real estate developer*
Rampe, Kevin M. *real estate developer*
Resnick, Scott N. *real estate company executive*
Rose, Daniel *real estate company executive, consultant*
Rose, Elihu *real estate executive*
Rosen, Aby J. *real estate developer*
Ross, George H. *real estate company executive, lawyer*
Ross, Stephen M. *real estate company executive*
Roth, Steven *real estate executive*
Ruben, Lawrence *real estate developer, real estate company executive, lawyer*
Rufrano, Glenn *real estate company executive*
Scott, Stanley DeForest *real estate company executive*
Siderow, Neil *real estate company executive*
Siegel, Stephen *real estate company executive*
Silverstein, Larry A. *real estate developer*
Smith, Andrew Alfred, Jr. *urban planner*
Speyer, Jerry I. *real estate company executive*
Stern, Leonard Norman *real estate developer, former pet supply manufacturing company executive*
Tighe, Mary Ann *real estate company executive*
Tishman, John L. *realty and construction company executive*
Weiss, Donald S. *real estate developer*
Wilson, Robert Frank *retired real estate broker, artist*

**Pawling**
Wood, Christopher L.J. *real estate executive*

**Rochester**
Pettinella, Edward *real estate company executive*

**Rye**
Feinberg, Norman Maurice *real estate company executive*

**Southampton**
Sheehy, Betty Jo *real estate company executive, investment advisor*
Thomas, Violeta de los Angeles *real estate broker*

**Stony Brook**
Koppelman, Lee Edward *regional planner, educator*

**Syracuse**
Peng, Feng *environmentalist*

## NORTH CAROLINA

**Ararat**
Marsh, Joseph Virgil *real estate broker, retired investment advisor*

**Boone**
Conrad, David Paul *business broker, real estate developer, retired food service executive*

**Chapel Hill**
Weiss, Shirley F. *retired urban and regional planner, economist, educator*

**Charlotte**
Cox, Linda Smoak *real estate broker*
Harris, John W. *real estate company executive*
Wiggins, Nancy Bowen *real estate broker, market research consultant*

**Durham**
Chapman, Robert Lee III *real estate developer*
Reckhow, Kenneth Howland *conservationist, educator*

**Fayetteville**
Kendrick, Mark Cleveland *real estate executive*

**Greensboro**
Russell, Anne Wrenn *property manager*

**Raleigh**
Deihl, Susan Galyen *preservationist*
Fritsch, Edward *real estate company executive*
Willer, Edward Herman *real estate broker*

**Statesville**
Redman, William Walter, Jr. *realtor*

## NORTH DAKOTA

**Bismarck**
Clairmont, William Edward *real estate developer*

## OHIO

**Beachwood**
Jacobstein, David M. *real estate company executive*

**Cincinnati**
Dunigan, Dennis Wayne *real estate executive*
Pitstick, Si A. *real estate agent*
Randman, Barry I. *real estate developer*
Ten Eyck, Dorothea Fariss *real estate agent*

**Cleveland**
Carney, Tana *real estate company executive*
Gould, Bonnie M. *realtor*

---

Jacobs, Richard E. *real estate company executive, sports team owner*
Ratner, James *real estate developer*
Swetland, David Wightman *real estate company executive, investment company executive*

**Columbus**
Pizzuti, Ronald A. *real estate developer*
Pyatt, Leo Anthony *retired real estate broker*
Schuler, Robert Leo *appraiser, consultant*

**Dayton**
Stout, Donald Everett *real estate developer, environmental services administrator*
Wertz, Kenneth Dean *real estate company officer*

**Hebron**
Slater, Wanda Marie Worth *property manager*

**Hudson**
Stec, John Zygmunt *retired real estate company officer*

**Salem**
Barcey, Harold Edward Dean (Hal Barcey) *real estate consultant*

**Shaker Heights**
Solganik, Marvin *real estate executive*

**Shelby**
Phelan, Martha Armstrong *realtor*

**Wilmington**
Evans, Elizabeth Ann West *retired real estate agent*

**Youngstown**
Camacci, Michael A. *real estate broker, real estate developer, consultant*
DeBartolo, Edward John, Jr. *real estate developer, former professional football team owner*

## OKLAHOMA

**Oklahoma City**
Bradford, Dennis Doyle *real estate broker, real estate developer*

**Tulsa**
Ball, Rex Martin *urban planner, architect*

## OREGON

**Gladstone**
Beals, Herbert Kyle *urban planner, historian, consultant*

**Lake Oswego**
Marietta, Elizabeth Ann *real estate broker*

**Portland**
Packard, Robert Goodale III *urban planner*
Standring, James Douglas *real estate developer*

**Springfield**
Davis, George Donald *executive land use policy consultant*

## PENNSYLVANIA

**Allentown**
Saab, Deanne Keltum *real estate broker, appraiser*

**Blue Bell**
Deschaine, Barbara Ralph *retired real estate broker*

**Bryn Mawr**
Pew, Robert Anderson *retired real estate and equipment leasing corporation officer*

**Erie**
Gottschalk, Frank Klaus *real estate company executive*

**Horsham**
Barzilay, Zvi *real estate developer*
Toll, Bruce Elliot *real estate developer*

**Indiana**
Masilela, Calvin Onias *land use planner, educator*

**Philadelphia**
Barnett, Jonathan *urban planner, educator, architect*
Cunningham, Jessie Jerome *real estate investor, import/export company executive, entrepreneur, small business owner*
Kaplan, Barbara Jane *retired city planner*
Mellman, Leonard *real estate developer, consultant*
Mendelow, Clive G. *real estate company executive*
Peck, Robert McCracken *naturalist, historian, writer*

**Southeastern**
Zlotolow-Stambler, Ernest *real estate executive, architectural executive*

**York**
Rebert, Jephrey Lee *urban planner, musician*

## RHODE ISLAND

**Foster**
Sawyer, Mildred Clementina *retired real estate agent*

## SOUTH CAROLINA

**Aiken**
Hallman, Cecilia Ann *real estate consultant*

---

**Charleston**
Limehouse, Harry Bancroft, Jr. *real estate developer, transportation consultant*

**Columbia**
Morgan, Constance Louise *real estate company executive*

**Greenville**
Crawford, William David *real estate broker, consultant*

**Hilton Head Island**
Gruchacz, Robert S. *real estate company officer*

## SOUTH DAKOTA

**Rapid City**
Hamilton, Douglas Warren *real estate executive*

**Sioux Falls**
Wilkes, Jeffrey Blaine *real estate appraiser*

## TENNESSEE

**Chattanooga**
Foy, John N. *real estate company executive*
Lebovitz, Stephen D. *property manager*

**Hendersonville**
Spain, Mary Ann *realtor, educator, historian, writer*

**Knoxville**
Beeler, Sandra Gillespie *realtor*

**Loudon**
Hicks, Betty Harris *real estate broker, real estate company executive*

**Memphis**
Edwards, Martin *real estate company executive*

**Nashville**
Beck, Robert Beryl *real estate executive*

## TEXAS

**Addison**
Cotter, Ka *real estate company executive*
Kimbler, Larry Bernard *real estate executive, accountant*
Ragusa, Elysia *real estate company executive*
Staubach, Roger Thomas *real estate executive, former professional football player*

**Argyle**
Stallings, Frank, Jr. *realtor, director*

**Austin**
Mazzetti, Robert F. *real estate manager, retired orthopedic surgeon*
Schoenemann, David Leroy *real estate broker, small business owner*
Stoll, William Hermann *real estate company executive*

**Boerne**
Daugherty, Linda Hagaman *real estate company executive*

**College Station**
Jackson, Thomas O. *real estate appraiser, urban planner*

**Dallas**
Cherry, William Speakman *real estate broker, consultant*
Crow, Trammell *real estate company executive*
Doran, Mark Richard *real estate financial executive*
Duvall, William (Bill) C. *real estate company executive*
Eller, Timothy R. (Tim Eller) *real estate company executive, construction executive*
Marlow, Patricia Bair Bond *realtor*
Nalley, Michael Douglas *real estate company executive*
Nasher, Raymond D. *real estate developer, art collector*
Solender, Robert Lawrence *retired real estate company executive, retired publishing executive*
Sulentic, Robert E. *real estate company executive*

**El Paso**
Lyle, James Arthur *real estate broker*

**Galveston**
McLeod, E. Douglas *real estate developer, lawyer*
Shelton, Kenneth R., Jr. *real estate company executive, artist*

**Garland**
McGrath, James Thomas *real estate investment company executive*

**Grand Prairie**
Mathis, Prudence Marchman *realtor*

**Hillsboro**
McClendon, Fred Vernon *real estate professional, consultant, equity and realty appraiser, financial consultant*

**Houston**
Barrere, Jamie Newton *real estate company executive*
Blackburn, Sadie Gwin Allen *conservation executive*
Campo, Richard J. *real estate company executive*
Debrovner, Martin *real estate company executive*
Duncan, Robert *real estate company executive*
Goldsmith, Billy Joe *real estate broker, rancher*
Gregory, William Roger *real estate company executive*

---

Harding, Steve *real estate company executive*
Heard, Larry *real estate company executive*
Karba, Gerhard W. *real estate company executive*
Kollaer, Jim C. *real estate executive, architect*
Lanier, Robert C. (Bob Lanier) *real estate owner, real estate developer, former mayor*
Morris, Malcolm Stewart *title company executive, lawyer*
Pearson, Lee O. *real estate investment trust executive*
Strudler, Robert Jacob *real estate development executive*
Waltrip, Robert L. *environmentalist, funeral company executive*

**Killeen**
Evans, Carl M. *business executive*

**Plano**
Ford, H. Ross III *real estate company executive*
Hilton, Steven J. *real estate developer*
Landon, John R. *real estate developer*
Perot, Ross (H. Ross Perot, Henry Ross Perot) *real estate company executive, investment company executive, data processing executive*
Perot, Ross, Jr. (Henry Ross Perot Jr.) *real estate developer, professional sports team executive*

**Port Aransas**
Turner, Elizabeth Adams Noble (Betty Turner) *real estate company executive*

**San Antonio**
Burke, Betty Jane *retired real estate manager*
Condos, Barbara Seale *real estate broker, real estate developer, investor*
Sinkin, Fay Marie *environmentalist*
Williamson, Fletcher Phillips *real estate broker*

**Southlake**
Wuetig, Joyce Linda *realtor*

**Waco**
Rusling, Barbara N(eubert) *real estate broker*

## UTAH

**Midvale**
Teerlink, J(oseph) Leland *real estate developer*

**Santa Clara**
Tolbert, Beth Willden *real estate company executive, real estate broker*

## VERMONT

**Randolph**
French, Patsy *property manager, state representative*

## VIRGINIA

**Alexandria**
Artemel, Agnes Palmer *land use planner, director*
Blair, Bryce *real estate company executive*
Michael, Ann Dozier Marino *real estate broker*

**Annandale**
Jung, Esther *real estate broker, realtor, real estate consultant, small business owner*

**Appomattox**
Beatson, LeGrande Guerry *environmental health specialist*

**Arlington**
Watkins, Birge Swift *real estate investment executive*

**Chesterfield**
Jacobson, Thomas Elton *urban planner, county official*

**Falls Church**
Cazan, Sylvia Marie Buday (Mrs. Matthew John Cazan) *retired real estate executive*

**Mc Lean**
Nobil, James Howard, Jr. *real estate investor, developer, broker, consultant*
Talbot, Martha Hayne *conservationist, biologist*

**Newport News**
Goldberg, Stanley Irwin *real estate company executive*

**Reston**
Ringo, Jerome *conservationist*

**Richmond**
Chandler, Theodore Lindy, Jr. *title insurance company executive, lawyer*
Foster, Charles H. *title insurance company executive*
Tuck, Grayson Edwin *real estate agent, gas industry executive*

## WASHINGTON

**Bellingham**
Bourm, Roger Michael *real estate broker, investor, property manager*

**Edmonds**
Bell, Nancy Lee Hoyt *real estate investor, middle school educator, volunteer*

**Federal Way**
Fulton, Daniel S. *corporate real estate executive*

**Olympia**
Gillispie, Mark A. *real estate broker*

**Seattle**
Dillard, Marilyn Dianne *property manager*
Sasaki, Tsutomu (Tom Sasaki) *real estate company executive, trade association administrator, consultant*
Sauter, Michael Joseph *real estate company executive*
True, William L. (Bill True) *retired real estate company executive*

**Sequim**
Jackson, Patrick Joseph *real estate company officer*

**Spanaway**
McKinnon, James Buckner *real estate sales executive, writer, researcher*

**Spokane**
Covey, Michael J. *forest products and real estate executive*

**Vancouver**
Gienger, Barbara J. *realtor, land developer*

## WISCONSIN

**Beaver Dam**
Butterbrodt, John Ervin *real estate company officer*
Manthe, Cora De Munck *real estate company executive*

**Belgium**
Sullivan, Patricia W. (Terry Sullivan) *real estate trainer*

**Lake Mills**
Lazaris, Pamela Adriane *community planning and development consultant*

**Madison**
Ring, Gerald J. *real estate developer, insurance company executive*

**Wauwatosa**
Franke, Brent Douglas *real estate/insurance executive*

## WYOMING

**Casper**
Elliott, Marian Kay *real estate manager*

## TERRITORIES OF THE UNITED STATES

### VIRGIN ISLANDS

**St Thomas**
de Jongh, John P., Jr. *real estate company executive*
Dudley, George H.T. *real estate company executive*
Meyers, Stuart Irwin *real estate developer*
Williams, Wesley S., Jr. *real estate company executive*

## CANADA

### NOVA SCOTIA

**Stellarton**
Sobey, Donald Creighton Rae *real estate developer*

### ONTARIO

**Etobicoke**
McIntyre, John George Wallace *real estate developer, management consultant*

**Ottawa**
Gordon, Steve *real estate company executive*

**Toronto**
Carrothers, Gerald Arthur Patrick *environmental and city planning educator*
Dimma, William Andrew *real estate executive*
Eagles, Stuart Ernest *real estate company officer*
Farley, Tom *real estate company executive*
Tanenbaum, Joey *real estate developer*

### MEXICO

**Garza Garcia**
Gustafson, Eric William *real estate investor, wildlife habitat conservationist*

### ENGLAND

**London**
Hall, Sir Peter Geoffrey *urban and regional planning educator*

### HONG KONG

**Hong Kong**
Lee, Shau Kee *real estate developer*

---

## KENYA

**Nairobi**
Maathai, Wangari *environmentalist, consultant*

## MONACO

**Monte Carlo**
Lovett, Laurence Dow *retired real estate and steamship executive*

## SPAIN

**Adeje**
Grindley, Bruce Alan *real estate agency executive*

## ADDRESS UNPUBLISHED

Argyros, George L. *real estate company executive, former ambassador*
Aulbach, George Louis *retired real estate company executive*
Austin, Grant William *real estate appraiser*
Banks, Robert Kaley *real estate executive, lawyer, food products executive*
Barney, Austin Dunham, II, *real estate developer*
Bartlett, Arthur Eugene *real estate company executive*
Bartolini, Bruce Anthony *real estate executive*
Beal, Merrill David *conservationist, museum director*
Bell, Christopher Douglas *commercial real estate broker, corporate counsel*
Bergau, Frank Conrad *real estate, commercial and investment properties executive*
Berliner, Ruth Shirley *real estate company executive*
Bernhardt, Arthur Dieter *urban planner, consultant*
Bonin, Paul Joseph *real estate company executive, bank executive*
Broek, Howard Windolph *real estate executive*
Brooks, Michael Paul *retired urban planning educator*
Broughton, James Walter *real estate development executive, consultant*
Casden, Alan I. *real estate company executive*
Chase, J. Vincent *property manager*
Chesler, Doris Adelle *real estate broker*
Compton, William Thomas *real estate investor*
Corey, Kenneth Edward *urban planning and geography educator, researcher*
Corkran, Virginia B. *retired real estate agent*
Corradini, Deedee *real estate company executive, former mayor*
Cross, Robert Louis *retired realtor, landscape architect, land use planner, writer, real estate appraiser*
Dasso, Jerome Joseph *real estate educator*
Davis, John Warren *real estate broker, consultant*
Davis, Mary Byrd *conservationist, researcher*
DeBock, Ronald Gene *real estate company executive*
DeYoung, Marilyn Brant-Chandler *retired urban planner, farmer*
Di Cecco, James *real estate company executive*
Dickey, Robert Marvin (Rick Dickey) *property manager*
Dodge, Adriana *real estate investor, educator*
Dysart, Benjamin Clay III *conservationist, consultant, engineer*
Ellett, Alan Sidney *real estate developer*
Ellis, William Ben *environmental educator, retired utility executive*
English, Bruce Vaughan *environmentalist, consultant*
Estrin, Richard William *real estate broker*
Fischer, Michael Ludwig *environmental executive*
Fischer, Zoe Ann *real estate company executive, property company executive, marketing company executive*
Frankel, Stuart *real estate company executive*
Furlotti, Alexander Amato *real estate company executive, investment company executive*
Gasper, Ruth Eileen *real estate executive*
Gilbert, Frederick E. *development planner, Africanist, consultant*
Glindeman, Henry Peter, Jr. *real estate developer*
Goddess, Lynn Barbara *real estate investor*
Godwin, Ralph Lee, Jr. *real estate executive*
Goldspiel, Arnold Nelson *real estate executive*
Grosfeld, James *real estate development company executive*
Hakala, Karen Louise *retired real estate specialist*
Hankowsky, William P. *real estate company executive*
Hatkoff, Craig Mitchell *real estate executive, educator*
Hedreen, Richard C *real estate developer*
Hedrich, Cleda Pollard *real estate broker, writer*
Hefner, Thomas L. *real estate company executive*
Hero, Aphrodite S. *retired real estate developer, retired personnel director*
Hietala, Valerie Grace *realtor, environmentalist, educator*
Holleb, Doris B. *urban planner, economist*
Horton, Finis Gene *real estate manager*
Howell, William Page *real estate company executive*
Ingberman, Sima *real estate company officer*
Jacobs, Luke Kennedy *environmentalist*
Jennison, Brian (Lester) *environmental specialist*
Johnson, Kay Durbahn *real estate manager, consultant*
Kremer, Honor Frances (Noreen Kremer) *real estate broker, small business owner*
Lachapelle, Cleo Edward *retired real estate broker*
Lamy, M. Rebecca (Mary Rebecca Lamy) *consultant, land developer, government official*
Lax, Philip *land developer, space planner*
Ledford, Janet Marie Smalley *real estate appraiser, consultant*
Lehman, Joan Alice *real estate company executive*
Louargand, Marc Andrew *real estate executive, financial consultant*
MacDonald, Scott *real estate company executive*

---

Maguire, Robert Francis III *real estate investor*
Mann, Clarence Charles *retired real estate company officer*
Mayro, Karl R. *realtor*
Mazzarelli, Debra Jean *real estate broker*
McMahan, John William *real estate investment advisor*
McNeil, Edward Warren *real estate company executive*
Mercurio, Renard Michael *real estate company executive*
Messenkopf, Eugene John *real estate developer, hotel executive*
Meyer, Daniel Kramer *real estate executive*
Michael, George T. *real estate manager, real estate developer*
Mohamed, Joseph, Sr. *real estate broker, real estate developer, farmer*
Moser, Jeffery Richard *real estate manager*
Oakes, Judy Dianne *real estate broker*
Page, Patricia (Patty) Newton *real estate broker, real estate company executive*
Passaro, Paul Charles *real estate company executive*
Payne, Daniel Harold (Harold Payne) *real estate developer, small business owner*
Pence, Jean Virginia (Jean Pence) *retired real estate broker*
Perkins, Charles Theodore *real estate developer, consultant*
Potter, J. Stewart *property manager*
Rau, David Edward *real estate consultant*
Reschke, Michael W. *real estate company officer*
Ridloff, Richard *real estate investment advisor, lawyer, consultant*
Riley, Joe *real estate executive*
Ross, Beverley Long *real estate broker*
Sanquist, Nancy Johnson *real estate consultant, educator*
Sassen, Saskia *urban planner, educator*
Schell, Melvin Frank, Jr. *real estate agent*
Shvo, Michael *real estate broker*
Simons, Ryan William *urban planner*
Smith, Robert J., Jr. *real estate executive*
Snook, Paul *real estate company executive*
Taubman, A. Alfred *real estate developer*
Toshach, Clarice Oversby *real estate developer, retired computer company executive*
Totlis, Gust John *retired title insurance company executive*
Trump, Donald John *real estate developer*
Vella, Ruth Ann *real estate executive*
Walker, Michael Charles, Sr. *retired services executive*
Weiss, Scott Alan *commercial real estate consultant*
Whaley, Ross Samuel *environmentalist, educator*
Williams, Phyllis Cutforth *retired realtor*
Woods, Sandra Kay *real estate executive*
Yeonas, George C. *real estate executive*
Young, James E. *real estate company executive, consultant, engineer*

---

## RELIGION

## UNITED STATES

## ALABAMA

**Andalusia**
Patterson, Edwin *minister*

**Bessemer**
Collins, Patricia Ann *pastor, pastoral counselor*

**Birmingham**
Hull, William Edward *theology studies educator*
Nash, Warren Leslie *minister*
Scales, William Clinton, Sr. *minister, small business owner*

**Greensboro**
Massey, James Earl *retired clergyman, retired educator*

**Hayden**
King, Vickie Ruth *minister, shop owner*

**Mobile**
Lipscomb, Oscar Hugh *archbishop*
Roby, Jasper *bishop*

## ALASKA

**Anchorage**
Schwietz, Roger L. *archbishop*

## ARIZONA

**Duncan**
Ouzts, Eugene Thomas *minister, secondary education educator*

**Flagstaff**
Lapsley, James Norvell, Jr. *minister, educator*

**Green Valley**
Pike, George Harold, Jr. *religious organization administrator, clergyman*

**Hereford**
Seeland, Arthur David *bishop*

**Phoenix**
Kuzma, George Martin *retired bishop*
Olmsted, Thomas James *archbishop*
Schenkel, Barbara Ann *minister, nurse, social worker*

**Scottsdale**
Coutts, Lawrence Robert *publisher*

---

**Sun City**
Cooper, Vivian M. *minister, writer*
Hamilton, Ronald Ray *minister*
Randall, Claire *retired religious organization administrator*

**Tempe**
Emerson, Charles LeRoy *religious studies educator*

**Tucson**
Davis, Rendell Ashton *minister, social worker*
Ingram, Charles Owen *priest, educator*
Perret, Gary William *priest, educator*

## ARKANSAS

**Conway**
Leffler, Jean Riise *religious organization administrator*
Reddin, George *religious organization administrator*

**El Dorado**
Lee, Vernon Roy *minister*

**Little Rock**
Boswell, Bill Reeser *religious organization executive*
Chappelle, Richard Allen, Sr. *bishop*

**Marion**
Hughes, Michael Randolph *evangelist*

## CALIFORNIA

**Altadena**
Willans, Jean Stone *bishop, religious organization administrator*

**Angwin**
Maxwell, Donald Malcolm *clergyman, theology studies educator*

**Atascadero**
Jones, Kathryn Cherie *pastor*

**Auburn**
Moore, Billie Jo *minister*

**Bakersfield**
Frazier, Jo Frances *religious organization administrator, writer*

**Berkeley**
Mudge, Lewis Seymour *theologian, educator, university dean*
Welch, Claude (Claude Raymond Welch) *theology studies educator*

**Bradbury**
Campbell, Robert Charles *minister, theology studies educator*

**Burbank**
Bower, Richard James *minister*

**Castro Valley**
Morrison, Glenn Leslie *minister*

**Claremont**
Genung, Dan Baldwin *minister, writer*
Sanders, James Alvin *retired minister, retired religious studies educator*

**Corona**
Wood, Brenda Jean *pastor, evangelist*

**Costa Mesa**
Ratcliff, Donald Earl *minister, educator*
Williams, William Corey *theology educator, consultant*

**Duarte**
Drinkill, James Lawrence *minister*

**Escondido**
Linzey, Verna May *minister, writer*

**Fountain Valley**
Einstein, Stephen Jan *rabbi*

**Fresno**
Steinbock, John Thomas *bishop*
Xiong, Tousu Saydangnmvang *minister, theology studies educator*

**Fullerton**
Levesque, Paul Joseph *religious studies educator*

**Garden Grove**
Schuller, Robert Harold *minister, writer*

**Happy Camp**
Black, Barbara Ann *publisher*

**Hollywood**
Schuster, Peggy Lindner (Pravrajika Brahmaprana) *sister, nun*

**La Jolla**
Freedman, David Noel *religious studies educator*
Waddy, Lawrence Heber *writer*

**La Mirada**
Edwards, John Kent *religious studies educator, minister*

**Laguna Woods**
Wheatley, Melvin Ernest, Jr. *retired bishop*

**Lakewood**
Carr, Firpo Wycoff *bible scholar, educator, writer*

**Long Beach**
Jeynes, William Hettich *religious studies educator, religious organization administrator, minister*

**Los Angeles**
Borvitz, Mark Jay *rabbi, counselor*
Boyd, Malcolm *minister, writer*
Breuer, Stephen Ernest *religious organization administrator*
Freehling, Allen Isaac *rabbi*
Knight, Henry L. *minister*
Mahony, Roger Michael *archbishop*
Miscavige, David *head of religious order*
Ogilvie, Lloyd John *clergyman*
Phillips, Keith Wendall *minister*
Williams, Ronald Dean *minister, religious organization administrator*

**Los Gatos**
Sawyer, Malcolm James, Jr. *religious studies educator*

**Midway City**
Allen, Frances Michael *publisher*

**Newport Beach**
Ortlund, Anne (Elizabeth Anne Ortlund) *writer, musician*

**Oakland**
Jakubowsky, Frank Raymond *religious writer*

**Orange**
Brown, Tod David *bishop*
Mc Farland, Norman Francis *bishop*

**Palm Desert**
Ponder, Catherine *clergywoman*
Stenhouse, Everett Ray *clergy administrator*

**Palm Springs**
Jones, Milton Wakefield *publisher*
Martin, Ann Bodenhamer *minister, writer*

**Palo Alto**
Forbes, Alfred Dean *religious studies researcher*

**Pasadena**
Bradley, James Edwin *religious studies educator*
Kincaid, Hazel Victoria *evangelist*
Shuster, Marguerite *minister, educator*

**Porterville**
Golden, Raymond Lee *retired theology studies educator, retired minister*

**Portola Valley**
Garsh, Thomas Burton *publisher*

**Redding**
Nicholas, David Robert *minister, college president*

**Redlands**
Huntley, William Barney *religious studies professor*

**Reedley**
Dick, Henry Henry *minister*

**Sacramento**
Cole, Glen David *minister*
Keddy, James *religious organization administrator*
Quinn, Francis A. *bishop*

**San Bernardino**
Del Riego, Rutilio J. *bishop*

**San Diego**
Brom, Robert H. *bishop*
Cabrera, Quincy Rodolfo *minister, educator*
Downing, David Charles *retired minister*
Fleischmann, Paul *religious organization administrator, minister*
Hunt, Barnabas John *priest, religious organization administrator*
Mathes, James R. *bishop*

**San Francisco**
Kelly, James Anthony *priest*
Rosen, Moishe *religious organization founder*

**San Jose**
Beizer, Lance Kurt *priest, lawyer*
Es-Haq, Fereidoun *minister, marriage and family therapist*
Zes, Tikey A. *music minister*

**San Juan Capistrano**
Warren, Rick Duane *minister, writer*

**Santa Barbara**
Smith, Bill *religious organization administrator*

**Santee**
Morris, Henry Madison III *minister, writer, speech professional, consultant*

**Sonora**
Chandler, Edwin Russell *clergyman, writer*

**Stockton**
Knight, Norman Gladstone *minister*
Null, Paul Bryan *minister*

**Studio City**
Meenan, Alan John *clergyman, theology studies educator*

**Thousand Oaks**
Everson, Joseph *theology studies educator*
Hudson, Barbara *writer, actor*

**Upland**
Jordan, Charles Wesley *retired bishop*

**Vallejo**
McGowan, Thomas Randolph *retired religious organization administrator*

**Visalia**
Levine, Suzin Nancy Leah *religious organization administrator*

**West Hollywood**
Perry, Troy D. *minister, religious organization administrator*

## COLORADO

**Aurora**
Nichols, Clyde Richard *minister, consumer products company executive*
Stifel, Frederick Benton *minister, biochemist, nutritionist*

**Centennial**
Buxton, Zane Kelly *pastor*

**Colorado Springs**
Johnson, Henry Fred *clergy*
Loux, Gordon Dale *philanthropic consultant*

**Denver**
Burrell, Calvin Archie *minister*
Chaput, Charles J. *archbishop*
Morgan, David Forbes *minister*
Sheeran, Michael John Leo *priest, academic administrator*
Wilke, LeRoy *retired church administrator*

**Dillon**
Follett, Robert John Richard *publisher*

**Fort Collins**
Chorpenning, H. R. III *minister*
Rolston, Holmes III *theology studies educator, philosopher*

**Greeley**
van Gorp, Gary Wayne *clergyman*

**Lafayette**
Short, Ray Everett *minister, sociologist, educator, writer*

**Lakewood**
Hickman, Ruth Virginia *Bible educator*

**Littleton**
Groothuis, Douglas Richard *minister, educator*

**Louisville**
Marsh, Donald Pete *chaplain*

**Wheat Ridge**
Wilcox, Mary Marks *retired Christian education consultant, educator*

## CONNECTICUT

**Bloomfield**
Cronin, Daniel Anthony *emeritus archbishop*

**Bridgeport**
Lori, William E. *bishop*

**Colchester**
Nikirk, Silva Susan *minister, writer, dancer*

**East Hartford**
Jackson, Joseph Essard *religious organization administrator*

**Fairfield**
Lakeland, Paul Francis *religious studies educator*

**Farmington**
Walker, George W. *bishop*

**Greenwich**
Johnson, Herbert Michael *publisher*
Moore, John Plunkett Dennis *publisher*

**Hamden**
Forman, Charles William *religious studies educator*
Malherbe, Abraham Johannes *retired religious studies educator, writer*
Weinstein, Stanley *Buddhist studies educator*

**Hartford**
Hamilton, Hugh Basil *minister*
Macaluso, Christie A. *bishop*
Mansell, Henry J. *archbishop*
Markham, Ian Stephen *theology studies educator, dean*
Silk, Mark Reuel *religious studies educator, writer*
Winter, Miriam Therese (Gloria Frances Winter) *nun, religious studies educator*

**Lyme**
Bessie, Simon Michael *publisher*

**Manchester**
Scholsky, Martin Joseph *retired priest*

**Middletown**
Rockwood, Irving E., Jr. *publisher*

**New Haven**
Meeks, Wayne A. *religious studies educator*

**New London**
Clarke, Florence Dorothy *minister, educator*

**Norwich**
Cote, Michael Richard *bishop*
Hart, Daniel Anthony *bishop*

**Redding**
Begell, William *publisher*

**Ridgefield**
Davie, Malcolm Henderson *minister, retired municipal official*

**Southport**
Twiname, John Dean *minister, human services administrator*

**Storrs Mansfield**
Baldwin, Carlita Rose *minister*

**Torrington**
Drobena, Thomas John *minister, educator*

**Wilton**
Davis, Joel *publisher*

**Woodstock Valley**
Allaby, Stanley Reynolds *clergyman*

## DELAWARE

**Middletown**
Cataldi-May, Lauren Michelle *head of religious order, music director*

**Wilmington**
Saltarelli, Michael A. *priest*

## DISTRICT OF COLUMBIA

**Washington**
Ahmed, Akbar S. *religious studies educator*
Allen, William Jere *minister*
Anderson, Vinton Randolph *bishop*
Baxter, Nathan Dwight *dean*
Burke, John *priest*
Di Lella, Alexander Anthony *biblical studies educator*
Dunn, James Milton *retired religious organization administrator*
Dunton, James Raynor *publisher*
Fitzmyer, Joseph Augustine *theology studies educator, priest*
Godsey, John Drew *retired minister, theology educator emeritus*
Jones, Coletta L. *senior pastor*
Knoll, Charles D. *priest, educator, musician*
Maldonado, F. César *priest, educator*
Marrett, Michael McFarlene *chaplain*
McCrabb, Donald Raymond *pastoral field educator*
O'Brien, Edwin Frederick *archbishop*
Outlaw, Wanda Cecelia *priest*
Ross, Robinette Davis *publisher*
Saperstein, Marc Eli *religious studies educator, rabbi*
Wallis, Jim *religious speaker, activist, writer*
Weigel, George Shillow, Jr. *theologian*
Zikmund, Barbara Brown *minister, religious organization administrator, educator*

## FLORIDA

**Bartow**
Meuser, Fredrick William *retired church administrator, historian*

**Boca Raton**
Agler, Richard Dean *rabbi*

**Coral Gables**
Fitzgerald, John Thomas, Jr. *religious studies educator*

**Crawfordville**
Brumby, James Remley, III, (Knox Brumby) *retired priest*

**Delray Beach**
Wells, Mary Elizabeth Thompson *deacon, director, chaplain, director*

**Fort Myers**
Drushal, Mary Ellen *parish administrator, education educator, former academic administrator*

**Fort Walton Beach**
Williams, Bethtina Qubré *minister*

**Jacksonville**
Holliday, Patricia Ruth McKenzie *evangelist*
Mueller, Cherone *religious organization administrator, writer, minister*
Taylor, Robert M. *minister*
Tyler Guidry, Carolyn E. *bishop*

**Lakeland**
Dusing, Michael Lee *theology educator*
Morris, Gregory K. *minister, consultant*

**Miami**
Noonan, John Gerard *bishop*
Weeks, Marta Joan *retired priest*

**Miami Shores**
Favalora, John Clement *archbishop*

**Milton**
Collins, Joda Lee *minister*

**Naples**
Weiss, Daniel Edwin *minister, educator*

**New Port Richey**
O'Farrell, Mark Theodore *religious organization administrator*

**Ocala**
Massa, Conrad Harry *retired religious studies educator*

**Orlando**
Forbes, Daniel Merrill *minister*
Moulton, Richard Way *minister*
Wenski, Thomas Gerard *bishop*

**Penney Farms**
Muilenburg, John Powell *minister*

**Pensacola**
Mountcastle, William Wallace, Jr. *philosophy and religion educator*
Ricard, John H. *bishop, educator*

**Plantation**
Harris, Eleanor Lynne K. (E. Lynn Harris) *religious studies educator, literature educator, minister, writer*

**Saint Augustine**
Couture, Sister Diane Rhea *sister, artist, educator*
McCarty, Doran Chester *religious organization administrator*

**Saint Petersburg**
Lemoi, Brian Andr *religious organization administrator, religious studies educator, writer*
Petty, M. S. Marty *publisher*

**Sarasota**
Jones, Tracey Kirk, Jr. *retired minister, educator*
Kerr, Donald Craig *retired minister*
McFarlin, Diane Hooten *publisher*

**Tampa**
de Chant, Dell *religious studies educator*
Lallance, Leroy Odom *music minister*

**Venice**
Nevins, John J. *bishop*

**Vero Beach**
Beran, Denis Carl *publisher*
Clokey, Rebecca Louise *minister*

**West Palm Beach**
Giuffrida, Tom A. *publisher*
Nolan, Richard Thomas *clergyman, educator*
Westman, Steven Ronald *rabbi*

**Winter Garden**
Reeher, James Irwin *minister*

**Winter Haven**
Boully, LaJuan Bonnie *minister, religious studies educator*

## GEORGIA

**Albany**
Revills, Isaiah *minister*

**Americus**
Reckford, Jonathan Thomas More *nonprofit organization administrator*

**Atlanta**
Brelsford, Theodore William, Jr. *theology studies educator*
Bryant, Gregory Alexander *bishop*
Gregory, Wilton D. *archbishop*
Keiller, James Bruce *clergyman, dean*
Patton, Laurie Louise *religious studies educator, writer*
Rosser, Essie *minister, counselor, marketing professional*
Waters, John W. *minister, educator*

**Augusta**
Davis, Minnie P. *minister*
MacLeod, James L. *minister, finance company executive, art gallery owner*

**Crawford**
Spears, Louise Elizabeth *minister, secondary school educator*

**Dacula**
Murphree, Harold T. *retired minister*

**Decatur**
Clarke, Erskine *religious history professor, writer*
Hale, Cynthia Lynette *religious organization administrator*

**Dublin**
Sapp, Peggy G. *pastor, editor, writer, speech professional*

**Lawrenceville**
Brannon, Ronald Roy *retired minister*
Gericke, Paul William *minister, educator*
Walker, Donald Murray *minister*

**Macon**
Franklin, Roosevelt *minister*
Staton, Cecil Pope, Jr. *writer, educator, broadcast executive*

**Mc Rae**
Allen, Annette *minister*

**Mcdonough**
Hall, Mark *youth pastor, christian rock artist*

**Metter**
Guido, Michael Anthony *evangelist*

**Norcross**
Granger, Philip Richard *minister*

**Peachtree City**
Dillard, George Stewart III *minister*

**Savannah**
Boland, John Kevin *bishop*

**Tifton**
Roberts, Curtis Creed *minister, writer*

**Vidalia**
Fountain, Edwin Byrd *minister, librarian, poet*

**Woodstock**
Collins, David Browning *religious institution administrator*

## HAWAII

**Honolulu**
Masters, Elaine *religious studies educator, writer*
Merrifield, Donald Paul *ministries coordinator*
Silva, Clarence *bishop*

**Kahului**
Domingo, Cora Maria Corazon Encarnacion *minister*

**Kapaa**
Veylanswami, Satguru Bodhinatha *head of religious order*

## IDAHO

**Nampa**
Bowers, Curtis Ray, Jr. *chaplain*

## ILLINOIS

**Batavia**
Yeary, Sheridan Todd *pastor, educator*

**Belleville**
Baricevic, Sister John LaLande *nun, mathematician, educator*
Braxton, Edward K. *bishop*
Studer, Louis *priest, religious organization administrator*
Wittenbrink, Boniface Leo *priest*

**Bloomington**
Skillrud, Harold Clayton *minister, retired bishop*

**Chicago**
Almen, Lowell Gordon *church official*
Barbour, Claude Marie *minister, educator*
Betz, Hans Dieter *theology studies educator*
Brummel, Mark Joseph *religious organization administrator*
Farrakhan, Louis *religious organization administrator*
Gadus, Peg *religious studies director*
George, Francis Eugene Cardinal *cardinal*
Hanson, Mark S. *bishop*
Jegen, Sister Carol Frances *religious studies educator*
Lathon, Sheraine *clergyman*
Mansueto, Joseph Daniel *publisher*
Marshall, Cody *bishop*
McDonald, Theresa Beatrice Pierce (Mrs. Ollie McDonald) *church official, minister*
Muhammad, Ava *minister and national spokesperson for the Nation of Islam*
Pintchman, Tracy *religious studies educator*
Pittelko, Roger Dean *clergyman, theology studies educator*
Sandmel, David Fox *rabbi, educator*
Senior, Donald Paul *religious organization administrator*
Shafer, Eric Christopher *minister*
Snyder, Graydon F. *religion educator*
Thistlethwaite, Susan Brooks *religious organization administrator*
Thurston, Stephen John *pastor*
Tipton, Margaret Ann *religious organization administrator, writer*
Wall, James McKendree *minister, editor*
Yu, Anthony C. *religion and literature educator*

**Evanston**
Kieckhefer, Richard *religion educator*
Sedgwick, Timothy Foster *religion educator*

**Flossmoor**
Cary, William Sterling *retired church executive*

**Galesburg**
Fitch, Martha Jean *minister*

**Galva**
Swatos, William Henry, Jr. *priest, sociologist*

**Itasca**
Constant, Anita Aurelia *publisher*

**Joliet**
Kaffer, Roger Louis *bishop*

**Lake Forest**
Feinberg, Jeffrey Enoch *religious studies educator, writer*

**Libertyville**
Schroeder, W(illiam) Widick *religion educator*

**Lincoln**
Wilson, Robert Allen *religion educator*

**Lisle**
Mallak, Augustine Kenneth *monk, music educator*

**Moline**
Johnson, Mary Lou *lay worker, educator*

**Naperville**
Raccah, Dominique Marcelle *publisher*

**Niles**
Grace, John Joseph *retired priest*

**Park City**
Aquino, Armando Co *minister, consultant*

**Peoria**
Parsons, Donald James *retired bishop*
Saxon, Randall Lee *pastor, author, educator*

**Prospect Heights**
Anderson, Hugh George *bishop*

**River Forest**
O'Meara, Thomas Franklin *priest, educator*

**Riverside**
Marty, Martin Emil *theology studies educator*

**Rockford**
Aniol, Scott Michael *pastor*
Doran, Thomas George *bishop*
McClelland, Patricia G. *minister*
Schlub, Teresa Rae *minister*

**Springfield**
Beckwith, Peter Hess *bishop*
Bell, John Perry *minister, religious organization administrator*

**Wauconda**
Gotthardt, Mary Jane *religious studies educator*

**Wheaton**
Pappas, Barbara Estelle *biblical studies educator, author*
Schwanda, Tom *religious studies educator*
Warner, William Kent, Jr. *religious organization administrator, consultant*

## INDIANA

**Anderson**
Conrad, Harold August *retired religious pension board executive*
Kufeldt, George *biblical educator*
Lambert, Lloyd Laverne *minister*

**Burlington**
Roussakis, Peter Ellwood *minister, publisher*

**Carmel**
Rund, Rex Benjamin *church administrator, music director*

**Evansville**
Hoy, George Philip *clergyman, county official, state legislator*
Jackson, Jill Ann Kremer *church administrator, musician*

**Fishers**
Christenson, Le Roy Howard *missions consultant*

**Fort Wayne**
Mann, David William *minister*

**Fortville**
Horner, Sylvia Ann *minister, real estate broker*

**Indianapolis**
Bates, Gerald Earl *retired bishop*
Buechlein, Daniel Mark *archbishop*
Crow, Paul Abernathy, Jr. *retired minister*
Dickinson, Richard Donald Nye *clergyman, theology studies educator*
Enright, William Gerald *religious institute administrator*
French, Tarence Wade, Sr. *minister*
Hamm, Richard L. *church administrator*
Page, Curtis Matthewson *minister*
Polston, Mark Franklin *minister*
Roger, Janice Lowenstein *cantor*
Smith, Donald Archie *religious business executive, consultant*
Thuesen, Peter Johannes *religious studies educator, writer*
Towne, Edgar Arthur *theologian, educator*
Watkins, Harold Robert *minister*
Waynick, Catherine Elizabeth Maples *bishop*
Woodring, DeWayne Stanley *religious organization administrator*

**Jasper**
Brenner, Raymond Anthony *priest*

**Lafayette**
Minor, Ronald Ray *minister*

**Marion**
Walker, Corran Jones *evangelist*

**Merrillville**
Marchina, Darlene B. *religious coordinator*

**Muncie**
Farr, Barbara F. *minister*
Greve, Todd Allen *minister*

**Munster**
Taylor, Gloria A. *minister, educator*

**Noblesville**
Wilson, Norman Glenn *church administrator, writer*

**Notre Dame**
Davis, Stacy Nicole *religious studies educator*
Ladewski, Roman Sebastian *priest, educator*
Williams, Oliver Franklin *priest, educator*

**Terre Haute**
Chambers, Curtis Allen *clergyman, church administrator*

**Winona Lake**
Davis, John James *religion educator*
Julien, Thomas Theodore *religious denomination administrator*

## IOWA

**Cedar Falls**
Lindberg, Duane R. *bishop, historian*

**Decorah**
Farwell, Elwin D. *minister, consultant*

**Des Moines**
Charron, Joseph L. *bishop*

**Dubuque**
Burkhart, John Ernest *minister, theology studies educator*
Hanus, Jerome George *archbishop*

**Fort Dodge**
Kitterman, Ralph Donald *retired member of clergy*

**Grinnell**
Mitchell, Orlan E. *clergyman, academic administrator*

**Iowa City**
Bozeman, Theodore D. *religion educator*
Cogan, Nancy Adams *chaplain, poet*

**Sioux City**
Mack, Thomas Russell *foundation administrator, management consultant*

**Sioux Rapids**
Jarvis, Steve Lee *religious studies educator, coach*

**Springville**
Beals, Karen Marie Downey *pastor*

**Waterloo**
Waters, Ronald W. *theology studies educator, church administrator, pastor*

**West Des Moines**
Stines, Fred, Jr. *publisher*

## KANSAS

**Baxter Springs**
Whiteley, Henry Howard *religious studies educator, minister*

**Clifton**
Compton, Doris Martha *lay worker*

**Copeland**
Birney, Walter Leroy *religious administrator*

**Kansas City**
Keleher, James P. *bishop*
Naumann, Joseph F. *archbishop*

**Manhattan**
Gillispie, Harold Leon *minister*

**Prairie Village**
Vogel, Arthur Anton *clergyman*

**Shawnee Mission**
Mandl, Herbert Jay *rabbi*

**Topeka**
Goetz, Roger Melvin *minister*
Hollomon, Frederick Shelton *retired minister*

**Westwood**
Brown, Gerald Eugene *minister*

**Wichita**
Jackels, Michael Owen *bishop*

## KENTUCKY

**Crestwood**
Roy, Elmon Harold *minister*

**Elizabethtown**
Phelps, Dennis Lane *minister, educator, author*

**Hopkinsville**
Soberal, Isabel M. *minister, music educator, social worker*

**Louisville**
Boykin, Gladys *retired religious organization administrator*
Dale, Judy Rien *religious organization administrator, consultant*
Gray, Joan S. *head of religious order*
Kelly, Thomas Cajetan *archbishop*
Rainer, Thomas Spratling *pastor*
Zimmerman, Gideon K. *minister*

**Owensboro**
McRaith, John Jeremiah *bishop*

**Paducah**
Fejes, Robert R. *minister*

**Paris**
Steffer, Robert Wesley *clergyman*

**Pineville**
Whittaker, Bill Douglas *minister*

**Richmond**
Ballard, Michael Ray (Mickey Ballard) *minister, music educator*
Wright, John Daniel *minister*

**Wilmore**
Kinlaw, Dennis Franklin *clergyman, religious organization administrator*

## LOUISIANA

**Baton Rouge**
Koehler, Robert Brien *priest*
Phillabaum, Leslie Ervin *publisher*
Witcher, Robert Campbell, Sr. *bishop*

**Columbia**
McGee, Bruce D. *evangelist*

**Crowley**
Foreman, Alfred G. *theologian, philosopher*

**Donaldsonville**
Watson, Stanley Ellis *clergyman, small business owner*

**Gilbert**
Bell, Wallace Edward *minister, insurance agent*

**New Orleans**
Carter, James Clarence *pastor, educator*
Hughes, Alfred Clifton *archbishop*
Schulte, Francis B. *retired archbishop*

**Ponchatoula**
Warden, Waldia Ann *archdiocese official, director*

**Shreveport**
Friend, William Benedict *bishop*
Webb, Donald Arthur *minister*

**Springhill**
Morgan, Larry Ronald *minister*

**Tioga**
Brandow, Stephen Jon *priest*

## MAINE

**Augusta**
Clark, Beth *retired minister*

**Brunswick**
Visser, Richard Edgar *minister*

**Kingfield**
Silver, Sally *minister*

**Portland**
Ives, Samuel Clifton *minister*
Knudsen, Chilton Abbie Richardson *bishop*

**South Bristol**
Lasher, Esther Lu *minister*

## MARYLAND

**Baltimore**
Byron, William James *minister, retired academic administrator, finance educator*
Hicks, Sherman Gregory *pastor*
Mocko, George Paul *minister*
Schumann, Jill *religious organization administrator*
Strickland, Marshall Hayward *bishop*

**Catonsville**
Wynn, John Charles *clergyman, retired theology studies educator*

**Chestertown**
Bish, Richard Hayes *missionary, educator*

**Columbia**
Davis, Benjamin George *theologian, educator*
Gillespie, Charles Kevin *priest, educator*
Ziegler, Gwendolyn Woods *minister, consultant*

**Elkridge**
Byrd, Alicia D. *minister, sociologist*

**Ellicott City**
McNaughton, Kenneth John *former publisher*

**Gaithersburg**
Hall, Arthur Raymond, Jr. *retired minister*
Rupert, Hoover (Lynn Hoover Rupert) *minister, writer*

**Hyattsville**
O'Connor, Kevin Thomas *religious organization administrator*
Wuerl, Donald William *archbishop*

**Kingsville**
Stanliford, Ronald Dawson *minister, educator*

**La Plata**
Mariya, Deborah Luethje *minister*

**Marydel**
LaBarge, Christopher W. *priest*

**Mitchellville**
Brubaker, Lauren Edgar *minister*

**Rock Hall**
Mariner, Linda Ketterman *minister*

**Silver Spring**
Beach, Bert Beverly *clergyman*
Chery, Reginald *minister*
Herbers, Tod Arthur *publisher*
O'Meara, Noel P. *priest, religious organization administrator*

## MASSACHUSETTS

**Amherst**
Wills, David Wood *minister, educator*

**Andover**
Simone, Joseph *clergyman, educator*

**Auburn**
Bachelder, Robert Stephen *minister*

**Auburndale**
Gulbrandsen, Natalie Webber *religious association administrator*

**Berlin**
Lohr, Harold Russell *retired bishop*

## Boston
Harris, Barbara Clementine *bishop*
Harris, Gayle Elizabeth *bishop*
Hehir, J. Bryan *priest, educator, social services administrator*
Kessler, Diane Cooksey *religious organization administrator, minister*
Mason, Herbert Warren, Jr. *religion and history educator, author*

## Braintree
Robertson, Michael Swing *minister*

## Brighton
O'Malley, Sean Patrick Cardinal *Archbishop of Boston, cardinal*

## Brockton
Lightford, Melvin *minister*

## Brookline
Skeete, Helen Watkins *minister, counselor*

## Cambridge
Fiorenza, Francis P. *religion educator*
Gomes, Peter John *clergyman, educator*
Graham, William Albert *religious studies educator, history educator*
Horn, Henry Eyster *retired minister*
Kaufman, Gordon Dester *theology studies educator*
Kujawa-Holbrook, Sheryl *theology studies educator, academic administrator*
Schuessler Fiorenza, Elisabeth *theology studies educator*

## Chestnut Hill
Goizueta, Roberto Segundo *theology studies educator*
Helmick, Raymond Glen *priest, educator*
Mc Innes, William Charles *priest, academic administrator*

## Jamaica Plain
White-Hammond, Gloria E. *pastor, pediatrician, human rights advocate*

## Lawrence
Weaver, Peter David *bishop, religious organization administrator*

## Marblehead
Tamaren, Michele Carol *spiritual director, writer, retired special education educator, personal coach, presenter*

## Medford
O'Leary, David *priest, theologian, educator*
Penick, Ann Clarisse *minister, counselor*

## Methuen
McNaughton, William John *retired bishop*

## North Andover
Norris, Rebecca Sachs *religious studies educator*
Wenzel, James Andrew *religious studies educator*

## Northampton
Derr, Thomas Sieger *religion educator*
Donfried, Karl Paul *theology studies educator, minister*

## Norton
Worthley, Harold Field *retired minister, educator*

## Shelburne Falls
Evelyn, Phyllis *minister*

## Springfield
McDonnell, Timothy Anthony *bishop*

## Vineyard Haven
Kimball, Julie Ellis *small press publisher, humorist, writer*

## Waltham
Brettler, Marc Zvi *religious studies educator*

## Weston
Barry, William Anthony *priest, writer*

## Westwood
Bier, Louis Henry Gustav *minister*

## Williamstown
Eusden, John Dykstra *theology studies educator, minister*

## Worcester
Parsons, Edwin Spencer *clergyman, educator*
Reilly, Daniel Patrick *retired bishop*

## MICHIGAN

## Albion
Raj, Selva J. *religious studies educator*

## Ann Arbor
Gomez, Luis Oscar *Asian and religious studies educator, clinical psychology educator*

## Bloomfield Hills
Mc Gehee, H(arry) Coleman, Jr. *retired bishop*
Syme, Daniel Bailey *rabbi, institution executive*

## Clarkston
Keough, James Gillman, Jr. *minister*

## Detroit
Hunke, David L. *publisher*
Maida, Adam Joseph Cardinal *cardinal*
Vigneron, Allen Henry *theology studies educator, rector, auxiliary bishop*

## Farmington
Penberthy, Stanley Josiah, Jr. *publisher*

## Farmington Hills
Plaut, Jonathan Victor *rabbi*

## Flint
Bonner, Darlene E. *minister, writer*

## Gaylord
Cooney, Patrick Ronald *bishop*

## Grand Rapids
Beals, Paul Archer *religious studies educator*
Beeke, Joel Robert *minister, educator, writer*
DeVries, Robert K. *retired publisher, consultant*
Hurley, Walter Allison *bishop*

## Holland
Cook, James Ivan *clergyman, educator*
Van Voorst, Robert E. *theology educator, minister*

## Jackson
Popp, Nathaniel *archbishop*

## Kalamazoo
Badra, Robert George *theology studies educator, humanities educator*

## Livonia
Haggard, Joan Claire *church musician, piano instructor, accompanist, adjudicator*

## Roscommon
Mainprize, Donald Charles *minister, writer*

## Saginaw
Carlson, Robert James *bishop*

## Southfield
Ibrahim, Ibrahim N. *bishop*
Willingham, Edward Bacon, Jr. *ecumenical minister, administrator*

## Spring Arbor
Thompson, Stanley B. *church administrator*

## Traverse City
Burton, Betty June *retired pastor*

## Ypsilanti
Stuppard-Byars, Doris J. *minister*

## MINNESOTA

## Austin
Alcorn, Wallace Arthur *minister, writer*

## Burnsville
Fischer, Michael W. *minister, musician*

## Collegeville
Sayles, Letory Bruno *retired priest, monk*

## Cottage Grove
Hudnut, Robert Kilborne *clergyman, writer*

## Crookston
Balke, Victor H. *bishop*

## Edina
Brown, Laurence David *retired bishop*
Putnam, Frederick Warren, Jr. *bishop*
Worthing, Carol Marie *retired minister*

## Excelsior
Fenske, Jerald Allan *minister*
Parker, Robert Chauncey Humphrey *clergyman, publishing executive*

## Grand Rapids
Merrill, Arthur Lewis *retired theologian*

## Inver Grove Heights
Koenig, Robert August *minister, educator*

## Lake Elmo
Schultz, Clarence John *minister*

## Mankato
Orvick, George Myron *religious organization administrator, minister*
Purscell, Keith William *minister*

## Minneapolis
Chemberlin, Peg *minister, religious organization administrator*
Hamel, William John *church administrator, minister*
Mason, Barbara Fountain *minister*
Miller, William Alvin *clergyman, author, lecturer*

## Nisswa
Meier, Christian Beach *pastor*

## Northfield
Swanson, Stephen Olney *minister, retired English educator*

## Rochester
Rinden, David Lee *clergyman*

## Rosemount
Aadland, Thomas Vernon *minister*

## Roseville
McMillan, Mary Bigelow *retired minister, volunteer*

## Saint Paul
Flynn, Harry Joseph *archbishop*
Habiger, James David *religious studies educator*
Hopper, David Henry *theologian, educator*
McNamee, Sister Catherine *theology studies educator*
Rogness, Michael *religious studies educator, minister*

## Saint Peter
Jodock, Darrell Harland *minister, educator*

## Savage
Soderquist, Ronald Bruce *minister, consultant, religious organization administrator*

## Woodbury
Woodruff, Ellen Louise *chaplain*

## MISSISSIPPI

## Clinton
Hensley, John Clark *religious organization administrator, minister*

## Ellisville
McNair, Emma Louise *minister*

## Indianola
Matthews, David *clergyman*

## Jackson
Gordon, Granville Hollis *church official*

## Mound Bayou
Kamphefner, Pius *minister*

## MISSOURI

## Ballwin
Ackerson, Charles Stanley *minister, educator, social worker*

## Bridgeton
Asma, Lawrence Francis *priest*
Hylla, Linda Kay *sister, social worker*

## Excelsior Springs
Mitchell, Earl Wesley *clergyman*

## Fayette
Keeling, Joe Keith *theology studies educator, retired dean*

## Florissant
Stormer, John Anthony *retired minister, writer, publisher*

## Hollister
Hopper, Ruby Lou *clergy member*

## Independence
Tyree, Alan Dean *clergyman*

## Kansas City
Cunningham, Paul George *minister*
Diehl, James Harvey *church administrator*
Finn, Robert W. *bishop*
Hebenstreit, Jean Estill Stark *religion educator, practitioner*
Knight, John Allan *clergyman, theology studies educator*
Petosa, Jason Joseph *publisher*
Volk, Timothy Alan *youth minister*

## Keytesville
McVeigh, Glenna Faye *minister*

## Lees Summit
Mosley, Glenn Richard *religious organization administrator, minister*

## Liberty
Morgans, Bob D. *minister*

## Ozark
Thornton, Andrew John *minister*

## Poplar Bluff
Black, Ronnie Delane *religious organization administrator, mayor*
Carr, Charles Louis *retired religious organization administrator*

## Raymore
Miller, William Lee, Jr. *minister*

## Rush Hill
Scheffler, Lewis Francis *pastor, educator, research scientist*

## Saint Louis
Baumer, Martha Ann *minister*
Brighton, Louis Andrew *religious studies educator*
Burke, Raymond Leo *archbishop*
DaCorte, Allan Francis *financial consultant*
Doggett, John Nelson, Jr. *clergyman*
Kieschnick, Gerald B. *religious organization administrator*
Mahsman, David Lawrence *writer*
Merrell, James Lee *writer, minister*
O'Donnell, Edward Joseph *bishop, retired editor*
Wiley, Gregory Robert *publisher*

## Springfield
Haltom, Michael Fred *religious studies educator, military officer*
Hornsby, Teresa J. *theology studies educator, writer*
Trask, Thomas Edward *religious organization administrator*

## Wentzville
Park, Young H. *dean*

## MONTANA

## Helena
Jones, Charles Irving *bishop*

## Kalispell
Vickers, Lee Louise *minister*

## NEBRASKA

## Lincoln
Bruskewitz, Fabian W. *bishop*
Wiersbe, Warren Wendell *clergyman, writer, lecturer*

## Omaha
Curtiss, Elden Francis *archbishop*
Ward, Vanessa Gayle *religious organization administrator, minister, consultant*

## Papillion
Zuerlein, Damian Joseph *priest*

## NEVADA

## Las Vegas
Bishop, Leo Kenneth *clergyman, educator*
Freeman, J. P. Ladyhawk *vicar, underwater exploration, security and transportation executive, educator, model*
Luckett, Byron Edward, Jr. *chaplain, retired military officer*

## Reno
Apassa, Cyril Omo-Osagie *clergyman, educator*
Chrystal, William George *minister*
Savoy, Douglas Eugene *bishop, writer, religious studies educator*
Walrath, Harry Rienzi *retired minister*

## NEW HAMPSHIRE

## Center Sandwich
Booty, John Everitt *retired theology studies educator*

## Concord
Robinson, V. Gene (The Right Reverend V. Gene Robinson) *bishop*

## Gilford
Wood Parrish, Victoria Ann *minister*

## Loudon
Moore, Beatrice *religious organization administrator*

## Manchester
Christian, Francis Joseph *bishop*

## West Chesterfield
Garinger, Louis Daniel *religion educator*

## NEW JERSEY

## Bloomfield
Glasser, Lynn Schreiber *publisher*

## Camden
Galante, Joseph A. *bishop*

## Cherry Hill
Bryan, Henry Collier *clergyman, retired secondary school educator*

## Denville
Tartaglia, Richard V. *priest*

## Eatontown
Priesand, Sally Jane *rabbi*

## Edison
Roskoski, John *religious studies educator, coach*

## Elizabeth
Bomrind, Mitchel J. *rabbi*

## Englewood
Saliba, Philip E. *archbishop*

## Freehold
Jawidzik, Edward Mark *priest*

## Hackensack
Burt, Gwynne Elayne *minister, theology studies educator*

## Hightstown
Hull, Gretchen Gaebelein *lay worker, writer, lecturer*

## Indian Mills
Schroeder, James Edward *minister, consultant*

## Jersey City
Katz, Colleen *publisher*

## Lakewood
Levovitz, Pesach Zechariah *rabbi*

## Mahwah
Padovano, Anthony Thomas *theologian, educator, literature educator*

## Marlton
Clemens, David Allen *minister*

## Metuchen
Demkovitz, Russell Bernard *deacon, cemetery director*

## Moorestown
Clark, Maryliz M. *retired minister*

## Morris Plains
Spong, John Shelby *retired bishop, writer, columnist*

## Morristown
Hastings, Mary Jane *minister*

**Neptune**
Manuel, Sandra Lorraine *minister*

**New Brunswick**
Bowden, Henry Warner *religion educator*

**Newark**
Darmento, Ralph Joseph *religious organization administrator, educator, school system administrator*
Howard, M(oses) William, Jr. *minister*
Myers, John Joseph *archbishop*
Stephens, B. Consuela *minister, consultant*

**Ocean City**
Hughes, Robert G. *minister, religious organization administrator*

**Point Pleasant**
Marjanczyk, Joseph Anicetus *priest*

**Pomona**
Constantelos, Demetrios John *priest, educator*

**Princeton**
Armstrong, Richard Stoll *minister, educator, poet*
Belshaw, George Phelps Mellick *bishop*
Dougherty, Peter Joseph *publisher*
Metzger, Bruce Manning *clergyman, educator*
Miller, Patrick Dwight, Jr. *religious studies educator, minister*
Stackhouse, Max Lynn *religious studies educator*
West, Charles Converse *retired theologian*

**Ridgewood**
Kiernan, Richard Francis *publisher*

**Rutherford**
Gerety, Peter Leo *archbishop*

**South River**
Jackiewicz, Frederick Waclaw *priest*

**Teaneck**
Holmes, Miriam H. *publisher*
Meno, John Peter *chorepiscopus*

**Toms River**
Donaldson, Marcia Jean *lay worker*

**Trenton**
Old, Hughes Oliphant *theologian, minister*

**Warren**
Wildrick, Kenyon Jones *minister*

**Watchung**
Miller, John Ronald *minister*

**West Milford**
Stelpstra, William John *minister*

**West Paterson**
Pataki, Andrew *bishop*

**West Windsor**
Yoseloff, Thomas *publisher*

**Willingboro**
Bass, Joseph Oscar *retired minister*

**Woodbury**
Doughty, A. Glenn *minister*

**NEW MEXICO**

**Albuquerque**
Sheehan, Michael Jarboe *archbishop*

**Moriarty**
Moonwalker, Tu *minister, counselor, artist*

**Portales**
Overton, Edwin Dean *retired campus minister, educator*

**NEW YORK**

**Adams Center**
Hood, Thomas Gregory *minister*

**Albany**
Bowen, Mary Lu *ecumenical administrator*
Hubbard, Howard James *bishop*
Kruegler, Catherine A. *sister, parochial school educator*

**Albion**
Allamon, Karen Henn *minister*

**Angola**
Green, Gerard Leo *priest, educator*

**Baldwin Place**
Kurian, George Thomas *publisher*

**Belmont**
Lasher, Sandra Lee *minister, artist*

**Brainard**
Isaksen, Robert L. *retired bishop*

**Bronx**
Dulles, Avery *cardinal, theologian*
Grassano, Thomas David *minister*
Hennessy, Thomas Christopher *priest, educator, retired dean*
Hunt, George William *priest, magazine editor*
Parker, Everett Carlton *clergyman*

**Brooklyn**
Al-Hafeez, Humza *minister, editor*
DiMarzio, Nicholas Anthony *bishop*
Jones, Rudolph *minister*

**Buffalo**
Kmiec, Edward Urban *bishop*
McKenzie, Denise *religious organization administrator, academic administrator*

**Cambridge**
Kriss, Gary W(ayne) *priest*

**Centerport**
McQueeney, Henry Martin, Sr. *publisher*
Stevens, Martin Brian *publisher*

**Coxsackie**
Moyna, John Lawrence *priest*

**Douglaston**
Valero, René Arnold *clergyman*

**Elmhurst**
Cush, John Patrick *priest, theology studies educator*

**Glen Head**
Huber, Don Lawrence *publisher*

**Hempstead**
Zagano, Phyllis *religious studies educator*

**Kingston**
Tsirpanlis, Constantine N. *theology, philosophy, classics and history educator*

**Larchmont**
Rainier, Robert Paul *publisher, consultant*

**Lockport**
Ludwig, Patricia Marie *pastor*

**Long Beach**
Cahill, Joan *nun, educator*

**Mechanicville**
Rhodes, Alan Charles *minister*

**Medford**
Kealey, Edward J. *priest, historian*

**Mexico**
Halse, Frank Adams, Jr. *retired minister*

**Middle Village**
Kolatch, Alfred Jacob *publisher*

**New York**
Ashley, Willard Walden C., Sr. *minister*
Balter, Bernice *religious organization administrator*
Caine, Edward Peter *religious organization administrator*
Church, Frank Forrester *minister, columnist*
Cone, James Hal *theologian, educator, author*
Conlon, Peggy Eileen *publisher*
Demetrios, (Demetrios Trakatellis) *archbishop*
Doherty, Thomas *publisher*
Driver, Tom Faw *theologian, writer, advocate*
Eisen, Arnold M. *theologian*
Fargis, Paul McKenna *publisher, publishing executive, consultant, book developer*
Forbes, Christopher (Kip Forbes) *publisher*
Friedman, Herbert A. *rabbi, educator, not-for-profit fundraiser*
Friedman, J. Roger *publisher*
Gage, Robert Clifford *minister*
Giniger, Kenneth Seeman *publisher*
Ginsberg, Hersh Meier *rabbi, religious organization administrator*
Griswold, Frank Tracy III *bishop*
Hirsch, Roseann Conte *publisher*
Hudson, Christopher John *publisher*
Kern, William Bliem, Jr. *minister*
Kitashirakawa, Michihisa *head of religious order*
Molho, Emanuel *publisher*
Ochs, Carol Rebecca *theologian, writer, theology studies educator, philosopher*
O'Keefe, Vincent Thomas *clergyman, educational association administrator*
Paro, Jeff *publisher*
Powell, Thomas Arthur *publisher*
Powers, Edward Alton *minister, educator*
Reidy, Carolyn Kroll *publisher*
Romanos, John, Jr. (Jack Romanos) *publisher*
Roskam, Catherine S. *bishop*
Ross, Norman Alan *publisher*
Roth, Sol *rabbi*
Rusch, William Graham *religious organization administrator*
Schori, Katharine Jefferts *bishop*
Schorsch, Ismar *theology studies educator, rabbi*
Shriver, Donald Woods, Jr. *theologian, educator*
Simpson, Mary Michael *priest, psychotherapist*
Stolper, Pinchas Aryeh *religious organization executive, rabbi*
Straub, Gregory S. *priest*
Talley, Truman Macdonald *publisher*
Tannenbaum, Bernice Salpeter *national religious organization executive*
Thurman, Robert A.F. *theology studies educator, philosopher*
Tucker, Alan David *publisher*
Weinreb, Tzvi Hersh *religious organization administrator, rabbi*
Welsh, Donald Emory *publisher*
Whiteman, Douglas E. *publisher*
Wiener, Marvin S. *rabbi, editor, executive*
Williams, Frederick Boyd *priest*
Wolnek, Stephen S. *religious organization administrator*
Yoffie, Erich H. *religious organization administrator*
Yu, Andrew *minister*
Zeldin, Richard Packer *publisher*

**Newport**
Wilson, Eldon Ray *minister*

**Niskayuna**
Nichols, Albert Myron *retired minister*

**Nyack**
Cozart, Helen Ray *church administrator, educator*

**Mann**, Kenneth Walker *retired minister, psychologist*

**Ogdensburg**
Cunningham, Robert Joseph *bishop*

**Ossining**
Scheffler, Eckart Arthur *publisher*

**Pine Plains**
Shafer, Michael Gales *priest*

**Poughkeepsie**
Glasse, John Howell *retired philosophy and theology educator*
Harmelink, Herman III *minister, writer, religious studies educator*

**Red Hook**
Pastrana, Ronald Ray *Biblical theology professor, psychotherapist, retired public school system administrator*

**Rochester**
Clark, Matthew Harvey *bishop*
Elliott, Ralph H *minister, educator*
Goodell, Gary Lloyd *minister, educator*
Gripe, Alan Gordon *minister*
Kelley, Lucille Knight *minister, retired neurology and special duty nurse*
Lacey, Dorothy Ellen *theology studies educator, religious organization administrator*
Middleton, J. Richard *religious studies educator*
Tobin, Barbara Kay *minister*
Webster, Gordon Visscher, Jr. *minister*

**Rockville Centre**
Salvato, Scott Vincent *minister*

**Saint James**
Batule, Robert John *priest, writer*

**Scarsdale**
Johnson, William Alexander *clergyman, philosophy educator, theology educator*
Rubenstein, Jacob Samuel *rabbi*

**Spring Valley**
Stedge-Fowler, Joyce *retired clergywoman*

**Staten Island**
Pasciuto, Joseph Doria *priest*

**Syosset**
Theodosius, *retired leader of the Orthodox Church in America*

**Syracuse**
Costello, Thomas Joseph *retired bishop*
Emery, Robert Allan *minister*
Jerge, Marie Charlotte *minister*
Lang, James Patrick *priest*
Mooney, Edward Fiske *religious studies educator*
Moynihan, James M. *bishop*

**Troy**
Phelan, Thomas *clergyman, academic administrator, educator*

**Uniondale**
Stewart, Cynthia Willis *minister*

**Unionville**
Kemnitz, Thomas Milton *publisher*

**Williamsville**
Jones, Robert Alfred *retired clergyman*

**Wolcott**
Searle, Robert Ferguson *minister*

**Yonkers**
Gunner, Murray *retired religious organization administrator*

**Youngstown**
Lamb, Charles F. *retired minister, retired educator*

**NORTH CAROLINA**

**Asheboro**
Clark, Lawrence James *minister*
Mac Kenzie, James Donald *clergyman*

**Brevard**
Flory, Margaret Martha *retired religious organization administrator*

**Cary**
Taylor, David Wyatt Aiken *retired clergyman*

**Chapel Hill**
Chang, Kuk Won *theology educator, researcher, pastor*

**Charlotte**
Brown, Harold Ogden Joseph *religious studies educator*
Freeman, Sidney Lee *minister*
Graham, Billy (William Franklin Graham) *evangelist*
Graham, Franklin (William Franklin Graham III) *evangelist, missionary*
Gregory, Jeannette T. *publisher, writer*
Grigg, Eddie Garman *minister, educator*
Hawker, James Francis *priest, school system administrator*
McKay-Wilkinson, Julie Ann *minister, marriage and family therapist*
Oliver, John William Posegate *minister*
Walker, Jewett Lynius *clergyman, church official*

**Dunn**
Wilson, Douglas Leonard *minister, educator*

**Durham**
Dorn, Louis Otto *retired minister*
Meyers, Eric Mark *religion educator*

**Smith**, Harmon Lee, Jr. *clergyman, theology studies educator*
Steinmetz, David Curtis *religious studies educator*
Westbrook, Don Arlen *minister*

**Greensboro**
Dziordz, Walter Michael *priest*

**Greenville**
Jackson, Bobby Rand *minister*

**Hendersonville**
Trexler, Edgar Ray *minister, editor*
Ward, Beverly Allen *church administrator, music educator*

**High Point**
Wood, Stephen Wray *minister, educator, legislator, singer, songwriter*

**Lake Junaluska**
Tullis, Edward Lewis *retired bishop*

**Lexington**
Cuthrell, Carl Edward *retired clergyman, lawyer, educator*
Rector, Phillip Alan *minister, musician*

**Lumberton**
Johnson, Judy Van *minister, educator*
Tolar, Anne Melton *minister, music educator*

**Monroe**
Kyle, John Emery *retired religious organization administrator*

**Pikeville**
Sauls, Don *clergyman*

**Raleigh**
Henderson, Shirley Elizabeth *minister*
Lolley, William Randall *minister*
Scoggin, Blainard Elmo *religious educator*

**Salisbury**
Bamberg-Revis, Ethel M. *minister, educator*

**Smithfield**
McClain, Gregory David *chaplain*

**Taylorsville**
Ross, David Edmond *church official*

**Trenton**
Dillahunty, George Robert *minister*

**Waynesville**
Hale, Joe (Joseph Rice) *church organization executive*
Stokes, Mack Boyd (Marion Boyd Stokes) *bishop*

**Windsor**
Mizelle, Alan Keith *minister*

**Winston Salem**
Capps, Richard Henry *retired minister*
Harrelson, Walter Joseph *minister, educator*
Hunt, Ellen *minister, evangelist*
Ludolf, Marilyn Marie Keaton *lay worker*
Mendez, John *minister*
Rights, Graham Henry *retired minister*
Spach, Jule Christian *church executive*
Winn, Albert Curry *clergyman*

**NORTH DAKOTA**

**Fargo**
Foss, Richard John *bishop*

**OHIO**

**Ashland**
Watson, JoAnn Ford *theology studies educator*

**Bowling Green**
Versteeg, Robert John *minister, actor, writer*

**Canton**
Mann, John Martin *minister*

**Chesterland**
Ruble, Bernard Roy *minister, educator, personnel director, labor relations consultant*

**Cincinnati**
Adams, Mendle Eugene *minister*
Anderson, Joan Balyeat *theology studies educator, minister*
Duffy, Virginia *minister*
Harrington, Jeremy Thomas *priest, publishing executive*
Pilarczyk, Daniel Edward *archbishop*
Sallquist, Gary Ardin *minister, non-profit executive*
Zola, Gary Phillip *rabbi, historian*

**Cleveland**
Buhrow, William Carl *religious organization administrator*
Pilla, Anthony Michael *bishop*
Sherry, Paul Henry *minister, religious organization administrator*
Wedge, Eric *archbishop*

**Columbus**
Darling, George Curtis *minister, administrator*
Walls, James Douglas *minister*

**Dayton**
Leigh, Gloria Lorraine *retired religious studies educator*
Stutzman, L. Lee *pastor*

**Euclid**
Obloy, Leonard Gerard *priest*

**Findlay**
Fry, Charles George *theologian, educator*

**Holland**
Matthews, Christian William, Jr. *minister*

**London**
Hughes, Clyde Matthew *religious denomination executive*

**Macedonia**
Battle, Hilary Howard *minister, educator*

**Milford**
Kelley, Donald Frank *retired minister, elementary school educator*

**Millersburg**
Trubee, R. Eldon *minister, writer*

**Sebring**
Doty, James Edward *minister, psychologist*

**Steubenville**
Scanlan, Michael *priest, academic administrator*
Sheldon, Gilbert Ignatius *clergyman*

**Tipp City**
Hartland, James Robert *retired minister*

**Wadsworth**
Wozniak, Judith T. *pastor*

**Washington Court House**
Dunlap, Jeffrey Lee *minister, educator*

**Wauseon**
Stutzman, Donna J. *minister*

**Westerville**
Schultz, Arthur LeRoy *clergyman, educator*

**Westlake**
Loehr, Marla *chaplain*

**Wickliffe**
Pevec, Anthony Edward *bishop*

**Xenia**
Drangsholt, James K. *brother, music educator*

**OKLAHOMA**

**Bartlesville**
Sweem, Billy Don *archbishop*

**Bethany**
Leggett, James Daniel *bishop*

**Lawton**
Ellenbrook, Carolyn Kay *religious organization administrator*

**Midwest City**
Smith, Stephen K. *minister*

**Oklahoma City**
Beltran, Eusebius Joseph *archbishop*
Crawford, James Leroy *minister, retired theology studies educator*
Hampton, Carol McDonald *priest, educator, historian*
Jemison, Major Lewis *pastor, religious organization administrator*
Ridley, Betty Ann *theology studies educator*
Sudbury, John Dean *religious organization administrator*
Taylor-White-Grigsby, Queen Delores *minister, consultant*

**Shawnee**
Farrand, James Clinton *minister, consultant*
Wilks, Thomas Milton *religious studies educator, minister*

**Tulsa**
Cox, William Jackson *retired bishop*
Gottschalk, Sister Mary Therese *nun, hospital administrator*
Osborn, La Donna Carol *clergywoman*
Roberts, Oral (Granville Oral Roberts) *clergyman*

**Vinita**
Wright, Jo Anne *priest*

**OREGON**

**Corvallis**
Dennis, John Davison *minister*

**Eugene**
Graziano, Margaret A. *chaplain, recreational therapist, educational consultant, volunteer*
Sanders, Jack Thomas *religious studies educator*

**Medford**
Hellemose, Aage *minister*

**Portland**
Beauchamp, E(dward) William *priest, lawyer, university administrator, management educator*

**Turner**
Ratzlaff, Ruben Menno *theology studies educator, minister*

**West Linn**
Richards, Herbert East *retired minister, commentator*

**Wilsonville**
Langrock, Karl Frederick *writer, retired academic administrator*

**PENNSYLVANIA**

**Akron**
Dickinson, Margery Elsie *missionary, clinical psychologist*

**Allentown**
Cullen, Edward Peter *bishop*
Revak, Francis Charles *priest, educator*

**Altoona**
Anthony, Bertha M. *minister*

**Bethlehem**
Steffen, Lloyd Howard *minister, religious studies educator*

**Beyer**
Cornell, William Harvey *clergyman*

**Bradford**
Cox, J. Arthur *minister*

**Bridgeville**
Irvine, Peter Bennington *clergyman*

**Camp Hill**
Johnston, Thomas McElree, Jr. *retired church administrator*

**Chambersburg**
Yeun, Paul Lorenzo *clergy member*

**Clarion**
Grejda, Gail Fulton *dean*

**Clinton**
Talbot, Mary Lee *minister*

**Cranberry Township**
Tiller, Olive Marie *retired church worker*

**Drexel Hill**
Thompson, William David *minister, educator*

**Dunmore**
Timlin, James Clifford *bishop*

**Elizabethtown**
Brown, Dale Weaver *clergyman, theology studies educator*

**Enola**
Trout, Gwenn Louise *minister*

**Erie**
Trautman, Donald W. *bishop*

**Farrell**
Patton-Newell, Janet Lavelle *minister*

**Fayetteville**
Daywalt, Lee Eric *minister, museum administrator*

**Grove City**
Schaefer, Paul Robert *religious studies educator*

**Gwynedd**
LeFevre, Perry Deyo *minister, theologian, educator*

**Haverford**
Kee, Howard Clark *religion educator*

**Havertown**
Koenig, Norma Evans *retired religious studies educator*
Koenig, Robert Emil *clergyman*

**James Creek**
Durnbaugh, Donald Floyd *church history educator, researcher*

**Jenkintown**
Black, Thomas Donald *retired religious organization administrator*

**Johnstown**
Miloro, Protopresbyter Frank *religious organization administrator, theology studies educator*
Nicholas, (Richard G. Smisko) *bishop*
Smisko, Nicholas Richard *bishop, educator*

**Lafayette Hill**
Miller, Nancy Lois *senior pastor*

**Lancaster**
Glick, Garland Wayne *retired theological seminary president*

**Lewisburg**
Jump, Chester Jackson, Jr. *clergyman, church official*

**Malvern**
Brighton, Ruth Louise *lay worker, educator*

**Philadelphia**
Bartlett, Allen Lyman, Jr. *retired bishop*
Burch, Francis Floyd *clergyman*
Carven, John Winslow *priest*
Dyson, Michael Eric *religious studies educator, writer*
Krych, Margaret A. *religious organization administrator, educator*
Maginnis, Robert P. *bishop*
Marple, Dorothy Jane *retired church executive*
Rigali, Justin Francis Cardinal *archbishop*
Shaw, William J. *religious organization administrator*
Shelton, Kenneth N. *bishop*
Sulyk, Stephen *retired archbishop*
Trulear, Harold Dean *minister, theological educator, social researcher*

**Pittsburgh**
Brauner, Ronald Allan *theology studies educator*
Koedel, Robert Craig *minister, historian, educator*

Mason-Hipkins, Patricia *minister*
McCoid, Donald James *bishop*
Mc Dowell, John B. *bishop*
Miller, William Charles *theological educator*
Schaub, Marilyn McNamara *theology studies educator*
Zeolla, Kim Anne *minister*

**Quarryville**
Harris, Robert Laird *minister, theology educator emeritus*

**Saint Peters**
Detterline, Milton E., Jr. *minister*

**Sayre**
Bentley, Dianne H. Glover *minister, consultant*

**Scranton**
De Celles, Charles Edouard *theologian, educator*

**Selinsgrove**
Thomforde, Christopher Meredith *minister*

**South Canaan**
Herman, *archbishop, head of Orthodox Church in America*

**Sunbury**
Ely, Donald J(ean) *retired clergyman, secondary school educator*

**Swarthmore**
Field, Dorothy Maslin *minister*
Frost, Jerry William *religious studies educator, history professor, retired library director, researcher*
Moreland, Robert Lyle *minister*

**Tylersport**
Raub, Donald Wilmer *minister, author*

**Upper Darby**
Samten, Losang *spiritual leader, artist*

**Valley Forge**
Medley, Alex Roy *executive minister*
Wright-Riggins, Aidsand F. III *religious organization executive*

**Villanova**
Donohue, Peter M. *priest, theater educator, director*

**Waynesboro**
Coles, Robert Nelson, Sr. *religious organization administrator*

**Wilkes Barre**
O'Hara, Thomas J. *priest, academic administrator, educator*

**Willow Street**
Yrigoyen, Charles, Jr. *retired church denomination executive*

**Wynnewood**
Sider, Ronald J. *theology educator, author*
Wachs, Saul Philip *religious studies educator*

**RHODE ISLAND**

**East Providence**
Spina, Douglas John *priest, educator*

**Lincoln**
Barlow, August Ralph, Jr. *minister*

**Middletown**
Demy, Timothy James *military chaplain*

**Providence**
Frerichs, Ernest Sunley *religious studies educator*
Spoolstra, Linda Carol *minister, educator, religious organization administrator*
Tobin, Thomas J. *bishop*
Wolf, Geralyn *bishop*

**Woonsocket**
Morris, Mary Elizabeth *pastor*

**SOUTH CAROLINA**

**Anderson**
Williford, Velma Jean *minister*

**Charleston**
Donehue, John Douglas *interdenominational ministries executive*
Salmon, Edward Lloyd, Jr. *bishop*

**Columbia**
Adams, John Hurst *bishop*

**Easley**
Sustar, T. David *religious organization administrator*

**Florence**
Baroody, Albert Joseph, Jr. *pastoral counselor*

**Irmo**
Branham, Mack Carison, Jr. *retired religious organization administrator, minister*

**Leesville**
Crumley, James Robert, Jr. *retired bishop*

**Sumter**
McFadden, Lee Vernon *religious organization administrator*

**Taylors**
Smith, Morton Howison *religious organization administrator, educator*

**White Rock**
Aull, James Stroud *retired bishop*

**SOUTH DAKOTA**

**Yankton**
Wentzlaff, Sister Maribeth Faye *nun, director*

**TENNESSEE**

**Antioch**
Worthington, Melvin Leroy *minister, writer*

**Brentwood**
Stephens, Shirley Lynne *writer, editor*

**Chattanooga**
Haden, Benjamin *minister, retired publishing executive, broadcast executive*
Hodge, Raymond Douglas *minister*
Ragon, Robert Ronald *clergyman*

**Clarksville**
Maynard, Terrell Dennis *minister*

**Cleveland**
Hughes, Ray Harrison *minister, religious organization administrator*
Taylor, William Al *church administrator*

**Cordova**
Vaughn, Cary Edward *minister, director*

**Germantown**
Allison, Beverly Gray *retired religious organization administrator, theology studies educator*

**La Follette**
Eads, Ora Wilbert *clergyman, church administrator*

**Loudon**
Hallstrand, Sarah Laymon *denomination executive*
Jones, Robert Gean *religion educator*

**Madison**
Collins, Joyce A.P. *minister, librarian, educator, realtor*

**Memphis**
Magrill, Joe Richard, Jr. *religious organization administrator, minister*
Patterson, Gilbert Earl *bishop*
Steib, James Terry *bishop*
Todd, Virgil Holcomb *clergyman, theology studies educator*
Walker, Randolph Meade *minister*

**Murfreesboro**
Locke, Gregory Duane *evangelist*

**Nashville**
Bigham, Wanda Durrett *religious organization administrator*
Chapman, Morris Hines *denominational executive*
Draper, James Thomas, Jr., (Jimmy Draper) *clergyman*
Forlines, Franklin Leroy *minister, educator*
Hall, Richard Clyde, Jr. *retired religious educational administrator*
Land, Richard Dale *minister, religious organization administrator*
Page, Frank S. *head of religious order*
TeSelle, Eugene Arthur, Jr. *religion educator*

**Sewanee**
Parsley, Henry Nutt, Jr. *bishop, academic administrator*

**TEXAS**

**Arlington**
Lingerfelt, B. Eugene, Jr. *minister*

**Austin**
Hitchcock, Joanna *publisher*
Wahlberg, Philip Lawrence *former bishop*

**Beaumont**
Denham, Michael Thomas *minister*

**Bertram**
O'Lynn, Robert G., II, *minister*

**Brownsville**
Fitzpatrick, John J. *bishop*
Pena, Raymundo Joseph *bishop*

**Cleburne**
Bushor, Mark Eldon *pastor, writer, consultant*

**Dallas**
Blue, John Ronald (J. Ronald Blue) *evangelical mission executive*
Carnes, Joseph Sydney *clergyman*
Curran, Charles Edward *theology studies educator, priest*
Daves, Don Michael *minister*
Gilmore, Marshall *bishop*
Grahmann, Charles V. *bishop*
Jakes, T.D. *bishop*
Pauley, Shirley Stewart *religious organization executive*
Pinson, William Meredith, Jr. *pastor, writer, administrator*
Turknett, James C. *minister*
Valentine, Foy Dan *clergyman*
Wiles, Charles Preston *minister*

**Duncanville**
Lang, James Devore, Jr. *ministry executive*

**El Campo**
Fisher, Robert Bruce *priest*

**Fort Worth**
Gilbert, James Cayce *minister*
Lawson, Carole Jean *religious educator, author, poet*
Patterson, Paige *church administrator, former seminary president*
Rogers, Charles Ray *minister, religious organization administrator*

**Greenville**
Welch, Louise Banner *retired minister*

**Houston**
DiNardo, Daniel N. *archbishop*
Fiorenza, Joseph A. *retired archbishop*
Foger, Frances Murchison *minister*
Joyce, James Daniel *clergyman*
Karff, Samuel Egal *rabbi*
Montgomery, Cleothus *minister*
Nielsen, Niels Christian, Jr. *theology studies educator*
Osteen, Joel *minister*

**Hurst**
Shapley, Gregory Paul *head of religious order, music director*

**Jacksonville**
Blaylock, James Carl *clergyman, librarian*

**Kerrville**
Jordan, Sam Latron *minister, mediator*

**Lubbock**
Blevins, Stanley Nance *minister, educator*

**Mcallen**
Sutton, William Blaylock *pastor*

**Mineola**
McCann, Evelyn Louise Johnson *retired minister, retired counselor*

**Nocona**
Frailey, S. Clark *minister*

**Palestine**
Sellers, Wayne Chadick *retired publisher, retired editor*

**Paris**
Proctor, June *retired religious organization administrator, writer*

**Richardson**
Lowe, J. Allen *minister*
Williams, James Francis, Jr. *religious organization administrator*

**Round Top**
Killion, Vida Frazier *minister, writer*

**San Antonio**
Evans, Betty Vaughn *minister*
Gomez, José H. *archbishop*
Mc Allister, Gerald Nicholas *retired bishop, minister*

**Schulenburg**
Clark, I. E. *publisher*

**Spring**
Hunt, T. W. (Thomas Webb Hunt) *retired religion educator*
Rex, Lonnie Royce *religious organization administrator*

**Temple**
Beyer, Richard J. *priest, writer*

**The Woodlands**
Machle, Edward Johnstone *religious studies educator, philosopher*

**Victoria**
Fellhauer, David E. *bishop*

**Waco**
Stratton, Margaret Anne *minister*
Talbert, Charles Harold *theologian, educator*

**UTAH**

**Ogden**
Harrington, Mary Evelina Paulson (Polly Harrington) *writer, educator*

**Salt Lake City**
Eyring, Henry Bennion *bishop*
Hinckley, Gordon B. *religious organization administrator*
Holland, Jeffrey R. *religious organization administrator*
Irish, Carolyn Tanner *bishop*
Monson, Thomas Spencer *religious organization administrator, retired publishing executive*
Niederauer, George H. *bishop*
Smith, Eldred Gee *church leader*

**VERMONT**

**Burlington**
Angell, Kenneth Anthony *bishop*

**Colchester**
Blacketor, Paul Garber *minister*

**Middlebury**
Ferm, Robert Livingston *religion educator*

**Northfield**
Wick, William Shinn *clergyman, chaplain, pastor*

**Pawlet**
Buechner, Carl Frederick *minister, author*

**Quechee**
Wood, R. Stewart, Jr. *retired bishop*

**White River Junction**
Rutter, Frances Tompson *retired publisher*

**Wolcott**
Fisher, Neal Floyd *religious organization administrator*

**VIRGINIA**

**Alexandria**
Moshier, David Irwin *church administrator*
Snyder, Larry *priest, social services administrator*

**Arlington**
Earl, Sister Patricia Helene *religious studies educator, director*

**Blacksburg**
Grover, Norman LaMotte *theologian, philosopher*

**Chantilly**
Chrzanowski, Laye Jeannette *publisher*

**Charlottesville**
Finley, Robert Van Eaton *minister*
Scott, Nathan Alexander, Jr. *minister, educator, critic*
Thompson, Augustine Craig *priest, historian*

**Charlottesvle**
Walker, Beverly Ann *minister, health facility administrator*

**Chatham**
Ruef, John Samuel *clergyman*

**Dinwiddie**
McCray, Doris Raines *minister*

**Falls Church**
Bankson, Marjory Zoet *former religious association administrator*
Benton, Nicholas Frederick *publisher*
Lotz, Denton *minister, church official*

**Front Royal**
Andes, Larry Dale *minister*

**Glen Allen**
Anderson, James Frederick *clergyman*

**Great Falls**
Drummond, Alexander R. *priest, church administrator*

**King George**
Agnew, Christopher Mack *minister, historian*

**Lawrenceville**
Williams, Harold Lee *religious studies educator, minister, coach, director*

**Lexington**
Beckley, Harlan R. *religious studies educator*

**Lynchburg**
Falwell, Jerry Lamon *minister*

**Lyndhurst**
Dieter, Melvin Easterday *retired minister, educator*

**Manassas**
Ferguson, Whitworth III *pastor*

**Martinsville**
Plonk, William McGuire *retired minister*

**Mechanicsville**
Gerrish, Brian Albert *theologian, educator, retired minister*

**Midlothian**
Hanes-Stevens, LaVerne E. *minister, social services administrator*

**Mineral**
Speer, Jack Atkeson *publisher*

**Norfolk**
Gallagher, Carol Joy *bishop*

**Radford**
McNeil, Ramsey English *religious studies educator*

**Richmond**
DiLorenzo, Francis X. *bishop*
Fuller, Reginald Horace *clergyman, biblical studies educator*
Ingram, Thomas Bryan *religious development consultant*
Lee, Peter James *bishop*
Leggett, Gloria Jean *minister*
Robertson, LaVerne *minister*

**Roanoke**
Schumm, Darla Yzonne *religious studies educator*

**Springfield**
Kalkwarf, Leonard V. *minister*

**Vienna**
Burr, Ronald Edwin *publisher*

**Virginia Beach**
Christy, Larry Todd *publisher*
Taylor, Lewis Jerome, Jr. *retired priest*
Williams, John Rodman *theologian, educator, clergyman*

**Williamsburg**
Holmes, David Lynn *religion educator*

**Winchester**
Behr, Ken *religious organization administrator*
Nelson, Paul D. *retired religious organization administrator*

**Yorktown**
Wood, James Edward, Jr. *religion educator, author*

**WASHINGTON**

**Bellevue**
Berkley, James Donald *clergyman*

**Bremerton**
Fernandes, Phil *religious organization administrator, religious studies educator, philosophy educator, pastor*

**Index**
Davis, Pierre C. (Peter Pathfinder Davis) *priest*

**Langley**
Le Roy, Robert Powell *retired minister, educator, writer*

**Marysville**
Kell, Lyle Nicholas *retired minister, retired real estate broker*

**Prosser**
Cooper, Lynn Dale *retired minister, retired navy chaplain*

**Seattle**
Bowes, Peter Joseph *priest, educator, director*
Brunett, Alexander J. *archbishop*
Burrows, Elizabeth MacDonald *religious organization executive, educator*
Fluke, Lyla Schram (Mrs. John M. (Lyla) Fluke Sr.) *publisher*
Palmer, Earl Frank *minister*
Rivera, Bavi Edna (Nedi Rivera) *bishop*
Robb, John Wesley *religion educator*

**Spokane**
Edwards, James Robert *minister, educator*
Inviolata, Maria *sister, educator*
Lee, Richard Francis James *evangelical clergyman, media consultant, lawyer*
Polley, Harvey Lee *retired missionary, math and science educator*
Skylstad, William S. *bishop*

**Sunnyside**
Capener, Regner Alvin *minister, electronics engineer, writer*

**Tacoma**
Wiegman, Eugene William *minister, academic administrator*

**Tukwila**
Robinson, Howard Arthur, Jr. *minister*

**University Place**
Seiber, Richard Allan *retired minister*

**Vancouver**
Congdon, Roger Douglass *theology studies educator, minister*
Crews, William Odell, Jr. *religious organization administrator*

**WEST VIRGINIA**

**Beckley**
Rehbein, Edward Andrew *minister, geologist, consultant*

**Charleston**
Scott, Olof Henderson, Jr. *priest*

**Morgantown**
Hudson, David M. *minister*

**Pennsboro**
Poling, Kermit William *minister*

**Wheeling**
Thurston, Bonnie Bowman *religious studies educator, minister, poet*

**WISCONSIN**

**Cottage Grove**
Baird, Robert Dahlen *retired theology studies educator*

**Green Bay**
Geisendorfer, James Vernon *religious writer, researcher*

**Iola**
Mishler, Clifford Leslie *publisher*

**Madison**
Deming, Joan *clergy*
Fitchen, Allen Nelson *publisher*
Fox, Michael Vass *theology studies educator*
Little, George Daniel *clergyman*

**Milwaukee**
Dolan, Timothy Michael *archbishop*
Melander, Rochelle *writer, life coach*
Stubbe, Ray William *minister, writer*
Weakland, Rembert G. *retired archbishop*

**Nashotah**
Munday, Robert Stevenson *priest, dean*

**Ogema**
Giese, Robert James *minister*

**Oshkosh**
Barwig, Regis Norbert James *priest*

**Sturgeon Bay**
Van Duyse, Francis Donald (Fritz Van) *publisher*

**West Bend**
Murdy, Jill Maria *liturgy director, music director, educator*

## TERRITORIES OF THE UNITED STATES

**AMERICAN SAMOA**

**Pago Pago**
Weitzel, John Quinn *bishop*

**FEDERATED STATES OF MICRONESIA**

**Chuuk**
Samo, Amando *bishop*

**PUERTO RICO**

**San Juan**
Aponte Martinez, Luis Cardinal *retired archbishop*
González Nieves, Roberto Octavio *archbishop*

## CANADA

**BRITISH COLUMBIA**

**Prince George**
Kerr, Nancy Karolyn *pastor, mental health services professional*

**Victoria**
Hollis, Reginald *archbishop*

**NEWFOUNDLAND AND LABRADOR**

**Corner Brook**
Payne, Sidney Stewart *retired archbishop*

**ONTARIO**

**Brampton**
Bastian, Donald Noel *retired bishop*

**Cambridge**
MacBain, William Halley *minister, theology studies educator, academic administrator*

**Kitchener**
Winger, Roger Elson *retired church administrator*

**Ottawa**
Macklem, Michael Kirkpatrick *publisher*
Ryan, William Francis *priest*

**Paris**
Hooper, Wayne Nelson *retired clergy member*

**Sault Sainte Marie**
Ferris, Ronald Curry *bishop*

**Thorold**
O'Mara, John Aloysius *retired bishop*

**Toronto**
Finlay, Terence Edward *retired archbishop*
Hutchison, Andrew Sandford *archbishop*
McWilliam, Joanne Elizabeth *retired theology studies educator*
Novak, David *theology studies educator, rabbi*

**Waterloo**
Van Seters, John *retired biblical literature educator*

**Willowdale**
Irwin, John Wesley *publisher*

**Windsor**
La Rocque, Eugene Philippe *retired bishop*

**QUEBEC**

**Beauharnois**
Lebel, Robert *retired bishop*

**Jonquière**
Couture, Jean Guy *bishop*

**Montreal**
Turcotte, Jean-Claude Cardinal *archbishop*

**Quebec City**
Stavert, Alexander Bruce *archbishop*

**Rimouski**
Blanchet, Bertrand *archbishop*

**Westmount**
Coolidge, Robert Tytus *deacon, historian, educator*

**North Hatley**
Salt, Alfred Lewis *priest*

## MEXICO

**Aguascalientes**
Godinez Flores, Ramon *bishop*

## THE BAHAMAS

**Nassau**
Harrison, Johnnie Sheppard *religious organization administrator*

## BELGIUM

**Brussels**
Jadot, Jean Lambert Octave *clergyman*

## ENGLAND

**London**
Hunsberger, Alice Chandler *religion educator, human rights activist, scholar*

**Tunbridge Wells**
Howden, Frank Newton *priest, humanities educator*

## ITALY

**Rome**
Benedict XVI, His Holiness Pope (Joseph Alois Ratzinger) *Pope of Roman Catholic Church, Bishop of Rome*
Kolvenbach, Peter Hans *priest, head of religious order*
Levada, William Joseph Cardinal *archbishop emeritus, cardinal*

**Vatican City**
Foley, John Patrick *archbishop*
Stafford, J. Francis Cardinal *archbishop*
Stafford, James Francis *cardinal*
Szoka, Edmund Casimir Cardinal *archbishop*

## SINGAPORE

**Singapore**
Berkram, Patricia Clarke *religious studies educator*

## SOUTH AFRICA

**Cape Town**
Tutu, Desmond Mpilo *retired archbishop*

## SWEDEN

**Malmö**
Liljefors Persson, Bodil *history of religions educator*

## ADDRESS UNPUBLISHED

AdamS, Sharon Butler *minister, philosopher, researcher*
Allison, Andrew Marvin *church administrator*
Alvis, Joel Lawrence, Jr. *minister*
Ambrozic, Aloysius Cardinal (His Eminence Aloysius Cardinal Ambrozic) *archbishop*
Anderson, Gregg W. *minister*
Anderson, John Firth *retired religious organization administrator, retired librarian*
Anjulis, Stanley Joseph *retired church administrator*
Apuron, Anthony Sablan *archbishop*
Armstrong, (Arthur) James *minister, educator, consultant, writer*
Aronson, Jason *publisher*
Baehr, Theodore *religious organization administrator, writer, communications executive*
Baldwin, Leah Zavin *minister, writer, interior designer, educator*
Ball, Jim *minister*
Banks, Deirdre Margaret *retired church organization administrator*
Baumhart, Raymond Charles *religious organization administrator*
Bayne, David Cowan *priest, educator, lawyer*
Bechtol, Larry Owen *pastor*
Beldon, Sanford T. *publisher*
Bender, Ross Thomas *minister*
Bernstein, Edward Charles *rabbi*
Be Vier, William A. *retired religious studies educator*
Bickford, Margaret Wyatt *minister*
Black, Hillel Moses *publisher*
Blevins, Kent *religious studies educator*
Bodey, Richard Allen *minister, educator*
Booth, John Nicholls *minister, writer, photographer*
Bosco, Anthony Gerard *bishop*
Bothwell, John Charles *retired archbishop*
Broadwater, James E. *publisher*
Brokke, Catherine Juliet *retired mission executive*
Brooks, Babert Vincent *publisher*
Brown, Deborah Eleanor *priest*
Bunkowske, Eugene Walter *religious studies educator*
Capon, Edwin Gould *retired religious organization administrator, minister*
Carlson, Natalie Traylor *publisher*
Castle, Howard Blaine *retired religious organization administrator*
Cates, Dennis Lynn *minister*
Cedar, Paul Arnold *church executive, minister*
Charles, George P. *religious studies educator*
Christopher, Sharon A. Brown *bishop*
Clement, John Edward Strausz *retired minister, retired religious organization administrator, minister*
Cobb, John Boswell, Jr. *clergyman, educator*
Colon-Hernandez, Jeffrey *minister*
Conway, Michael James *priest*
Cooper, George David *minister, writer*

Corbett, Gordon Leroy *minister*
Crabtree, Davida Foy *minister*
Cyford, Janet Irene *Spiritualist medium, meditation consultant*
Dames, Terren *religious studies educator*
Dipko, Thomas Earl *retired minister, retired religious organization administrator*
Dockstader, Deborah Ruth *minister*
Donoghue, John Francis *archbishop*
Donovan, Dennis Dale *priest*
Douglass, Jane Dempsey *retired theology educator*
Duty, David Jon *minister, music educator*
Egan, Edward Michael Cardinal *archbishop, cardinal*
English-Anderson, San Dei *minister*
Epp, Eldon Jay *religion educator*
Ewing, Elisabeth Anne Rooney *priest*
Ewing, James E. *priest*
Fager, Everett Dean *minister*
Fazio, Evelyn M. *publisher, writer, agent, editor*
Finnegan, Sara Anne (Sara F. Lycett) *publisher*
Fitchett, George A. *theologian, educator*
FitzGerald, Kyriaki Antonia *theologian, psychologist*
Flye, Carolyn Marie *minister*
Flynt, Larry Claxton, Jr. *publisher*
Forst, Marion Francis *bishop*
Fort, Robert Bradley *minister*
Frazier, Eloise M. *minister*
Fry, Hedy *Member of Parliament*
Fullard, Henrietta *minister*
Galyon, James William *minister*
Gemignani, Michael Caesar *clergyman, retired secondary school educator*
Gerstner, Jonathan Neil *religious studies educator*
Godfrey, Donal Charles *priest*
Grady, Sandra C. *minister, counselor*
Gralla, Milton *retired publisher*
Grant, Leonard Tydings *clergyman*
Griffin, James Anthony *bishop*
Hagelstein, Robert Philip *publisher*
Hambidge, Douglas Walter *archbishop*
Hamilton, David Eugene *minister, educator*
Harper, Marsha Wilson *retired religious organization administrator*
Harris, Nicholas George *publisher*
Harris, Rogers Sanders *bishop*
Harvey, Louis-Charles *minister, seminary president, religion educator*
Haryono, Ignatius Wibisono *writer*
Hawkes, Mary Newgeon *retired minister, educator*
Hawkins, Harold Stanley *pastor, school director, police chaplain*
Helm, Judith *retired clergywoman*
Hernandez, Ramon Robert *retired minister, school librarian*
Holle, Reginald Henry *retired bishop*
Holyfield-Vega, Doretta Joyce *religious studies educator*
Holz, Carl Wayne *retired theologian*
Hultstrand, Donald Maynard *bishop*
Hunter, Juanita Walters *minister*
Huras, William David *retired bishop*
Hurley, Francis T. *retired archbishop*
Huron, Roderick Eugene *minister, writer*
Ihenacho, David Asonye *campus chaplain*
Imesch, Joseph Leopold *bishop*
Jabs, Aura Lee *minister, educator*
Jaoudi, Maria M. *religious studies educator, humanities educator*
Jarrell, Charles Michael *bishop*
Jiler, William Laurence *publisher*
Johnson, Gordon Gilbert *theology studies educator, minister*
Jones, William Augustus, Jr. *retired bishop*
Keeler, William Henry Cardinal *cardinal*
Kelley, Edward Allen *publisher*
Krause, Edward Charles *priest, educator*
Kucera, Daniel William *retired bishop*
Landes, George Miller *biblical studies educator*
Landon, John William *retired minister, social worker, educator*
Lansdale, H. Parker *minister, historian, not-for-profit fundraiser*
LaVerdiere, Claudette Marie *nun, head of religious order*
Lazovsky, Lorna Deane *minister*
Leavy, Herbert Theodore *publisher*
Levy, Valery *publisher*
Lewis, Victor Wayne *minister*
Light, Arthur Heath *bishop*
Linzey, James Franklin *minister, military officer, vocalist*
Loew, Brenda *publisher*
Lohmuller, Martin Nicholas *retired bishop*
Long, Jennifer J. *minister*
Lopez, Patricia Nell *minister, educator*
Loppnow, Milo Alvin *clergyman, former church official*
Luetkehoelter, Gottlieb Werner (Lee Luetkehoelter) *retired bishop, clergyman*
Lugenbeel, Edward Elmer *publisher*
Mackey, Jeffrey Allen *priest*
Mali, Paul *publisher, retired management educator*
Martin, Helen Loene *minister*
McCann, Margaret Ann *sister, educator*
McCarrick, Theodore Cardinal *archbishop emeritus*
McClellan, Larry Allen *minister, educator*
McDonald, Vivian *minister*
McKee, Adele Dieckmann *retired church music director, educator*
McKinley, Ellen Bacon *priest*
McMaster, Belle Miller *religious organization administrator*
McQuilkin, John Robertson *theology studies educator, writer, academic administrator*
McSwain, Larry Lee *religious studies educator*
Meier, George Karl III *minister, lawyer*
Melczek, Dale J. *bishop*
Melvin, Billy Alfred *clergyman*
Metzger, Paul Louis *theologian, director*
Milligan, Sister Mary *theology studies educator, consultant*
Mischke, Carl Herbert *retired religious association executive*
Moore, Alma Donst *writer, lyricist*
Morgan, Peter Monroe *religious organization administrator, minister*
Morrow, Hubert W. *retired minister, retired theology studies educator, writer, educator*

Muckerman, Norman James *priest, writer*
Muhammad, Claudette Marie *religious organization administrator*
Mullan, Donald William *archbishop*
Mulvee, Robert Edward *bishop*
Mutti, Albert Frederick *retired minister*
Navasky, Victor Saul *publisher*
Nieva, Constantino S. *priest, researcher*
Norgren, William Andrew *retired religious denomination administrator*
Normann, Margaret Ella *deacon, educator*
Nottingham, William Jesse *retired religious organization administrator, retired minister*
Nunes, Winifred O. *minister, educator*
Nunn, Charles Burgess *retired religious organization administrator*
Nwokoye, Patrick Ikechukwu *priest, researcher*
Oden, William Bryant *bishop, educator*
Ogden, Maurice B. *retired minister, writer*
Ogdon, Michael William *minister, music educator*
Oh, Mark Edward *minister*
O'Hare, Joseph Aloysius *priest, editor-in-chief, former academic administrator*
Ortiz, Angel Vicente *church administrator*
Osborne, James Alfred *religious organization administrator*
Ostaszewski, Alyce Vitella *religion educator*
Osvath, Ludovic Lajos *minister*
Owen, Paul *religious studies educator*
Palms, Roger Curtis *writer, educator, minister*
Payton, Donna S. *minister*
Peck, Paul Lachlan *minister*
Perko, Francis Michael *church administrator, researcher*
Pittman, Gregory David *pastor, musician*
Place, Michael D. *priest, former health association administrator*
Plomp, Teunis (Tony Plomp) *minister*
Post, Avery Denison *retired church official*
Post, Stephen Garrard *theologian, philosopher, educator*
Pressman, Jacob *retired rabbi*
Preus, David Walter *bishop, minister*
Pryor, Eric Jon *minister, writer*
Purtle, Dorothy L. *religious studies educator*
Ramey, Eudora Malois *minister*
Reynolds, Lewis Dayton *pastor*
Righter, Walter Cameron *retired bishop*
Rosenbaum, Belle Sara *religious studies educator, religious organization administrator*
Samra, Nicholas James *bishop*
Scharlemann, Robert Paul *theology studies educator, minister*
Schlieker, Janice Elaine Jones *campus minister*
Schuelke, John Paul *religious organization administrator*
Seale, James Millard *retired religious organization administrator, minister*
Shaheen, Shaheen Azeez *minister, textiles executive*
Sharpton, Alfred Charles, Jr. *minister, political activist*
Shotwell, Malcolm Green *minister*
Sims, Bennett Jones *minister, educator*
Singletary, Patricia Ann *minister*
Sledge, Lela Bell *minister*
Sloyan, Gerard Stephen *theology studies educator, priest*
Smith, D(aisy) Mullett *publisher*
Solano, Julio Rafael *priest, educator*
Staggers, Mary E. *minister*
Stewart, Barbara Lynn *church administrator*
Storey, Gregory Dean *publisher, editor*
Sypher, Francis J. *retired theology studies educator*
Taylor, June Ruth *retired minister*
Thompson, Richard Lloyd *retired pastor*
Truehill, Marshall, Jr. *minister*
Unsworth, Richard Preston *minister, educator, director*
Vasko, Peter Theodore Frederick *priest*
Vest, R. Lamar *church administrator*
Villano, Mark Anthony *minister, educator*
Vlazny, John George *archbishop*
Waite, Douglas John *chaplain*
Wantland, William Charles *retired bishop, lawyer*
Weber, Gloria Richie *retired minister, retired state legislator*
Webster, John Crosby Brown *minister, educator*
Weinkauf, Mary Louise Stanley *retired clergywoman, educator*
Westerhoff, John Henry III *clergyman, theology studies educator*
Wilkin, Richard Edwin *clergyman, religious organization administrator*
Williams, Ervin Eugene *religious organization administrator*
Wills, Charles Francis *retired religious organization administrator*
Wilson, Lois M. *minister*
Wilson, Warren Samuel *clergyman*
Winslow, David Allen *chaplain, retired military officer*
Wisehart, Mary Ruth *retired religious organization administrator*
Wolf, Carrie Irene *religious organization administrator, musician*
Wolford, Kathryn Frances *religious organization administrator*
Woods, J. P. *religious organization administrator*
Wooten, Cecil Aaron *retired religious organization administrator*
Wooten, Joan Hedrich *minister*
Youngman, LuAnn L. *minister*

## SCIENCE: LIFE SCIENCE

## UNITED STATES

## ALABAMA

**Anniston**
Howell, Laura Clark *biologist, educator, small business owner*

**Auburn**
Ball, Donald Maury *agronomist, consultant*
Brewer, Jesse Wayne *entomologist, educator*
Guertal, Elizabeth Anderson *agronomist, educator*
Klesius, Phillip Harry *microbiologist, researcher*
Tian, Hanqin *ecologist, educator*

**Birmingham**
Bloomer, Joseph Robert *geneticist, educator*
Cao, Xu *science educator*
Finley, Sara Crews *medical geneticist, educator*
Korf, Bruce Richard *clinical geneticist, neurologist*
Ma, He-Ping *physiologist*
Schafer, James Arthur *physiologist*

**Bremen**
Blair, Stephanie Lynn *science educator*

**Huntsville**
Bearden, Thomas Eugene *research scientist, researcher*
Gillani, Noor Velshi *atmospheric scientist, researcher, educator*
Richardson-Weninegar, Loretta Lynne *biologist, educator*

**Jacksonville**
Blair, Benjie G. *biology professor*
Carter, Robert Eugene, Jr. *forester, educator*

**Mobile**
French, Elizabeth Irene *biology professor, musician*

**Montgomery**
Bibb, Kartz E. *biology professor*
Sass, Neil Leslie *toxicologist*

**Talladega**
Schwinghamer, Mary Denise *veterinarian*

**Tuscaloosa**
Caldwell, Guy Alexander *biology professor, biomedical researcher*
Darden, William Howard, Jr. *biology professor*

**Tuskegee Institute**
Stevens, Clauzell *plant pathologist*

## ALASKA

**Anchorage**
Nielsen, Jennifer Lee *molecular ecologist, researcher*
Parker, Walter Bruce *arctic research specialist, consultant*

**Fairbanks**
Chapin, F. Stuart III *ecologist*
Day, Robert Hugh *marine ecologist*
Geml, József *geneticist*
Kessel, Brina *ornithologist, educator, researcher*
Margraf, Francis Joseph, Jr. *marine biologist, educator*

**Juneau**
Goldstein, Michael I. *ecologist*
Shepard, Beatrice L. *retired microbiologist, historian*
Siddeek, Mohamed Shareef Mohamed *marine biologist, educator*

## ARIZONA

**Benson**
Duppstadt, William Homer *retired botanist, educator, lay worker*

**Flagstaff**
Abrams, Jesse B. *forester, researcher*
Cortner, Hanna Joan *retired research scientist, political scientist*
Hammond, Howard David *retired botanist, editor*
Sisk, Thomas Daniel *ecologist, educator*

**Glendale**
Gergus, Erik *biology professor*

**Maricopa**
Kimball, Bruce Arnold *soil scientist*

**Phoenix**
Logvin, Marshall Paul *biologist, educator*
Papp, Harry *science association administrator*

**Sacaton**
Stephenson, Larry Kirk *geography educator, financial planner*

**Scottsdale**
Northey, William Thomas *microbiologist, educator*

**Sun City**
Joyce, Jeffrey *research scientist, consultant*

**Surprise**
Veigel, Jon Michael *science administrator*

**Tempe**
Curtiss, Roy III *life sciences professor*
Hölldobler, Berthold Karl *zoologist*
Jacobs, Mark *biology professor, dean*
Lohr, Dennis E. *research scientist, education educator*
Page, Robert Eugene, Jr. *biology professor*
Poste, George Henry *biology professor, former pharmaceutical company executive*
Uttal, William R(eichenstein) *psychology and engineering educator, research scientist*
Younger, Jarred Wayne *research scientist*

**Tucson**
Acker, Robert Flint *retired microbiologist*
Brusca, Richard Charles *biologist, researcher, educator, science administrator*

Fritts, Harold Clark *botanist, educator*
Gerba, Charles Peter *microbiologist, educator*
Griffith, Caitlin Ann *science educator*
Hay, Richard Le Roy *geology educator*
Haynes, Caleb Vance, Jr. *geology and archaeology educator*
Hildebrand, John G(rant) *neuroscientist, educator*
Hubbard, William Bogel *planetary sciences educator*
Hughes, Malcolm Kenneth *dendrochronologist, educator, administrator*
Hull, Herbert Mitchell *botanist, researcher*
Jeter, Wayburn Stewart *retired microbiologist, educator*
Johnson, Paula D. *veterinarian*
Lai, LiWen *geneticist, educator*
McPherson, Guy Randall *ecology educator, researcher*
Moran, Nancy A. *ecologist, educator*
Snyder, Richard Gerald *research scientist, administrator, educator, consultant*
Titley, Spencer Rowe *geology educator*
Yocum, Harrison Gerald *horticulturist, botanist, educator, researcher*
Zegura, Stephen Luke *biologist, anthropologist, educator*
Zou, Changping *research scientist, educator*

**Wikieup**
Brattstrom, Bayard Holmes *biology professor*

## ARKANSAS

**Cherokee Village**
Hollingsworth, John Alexander *retired science and mathematics educator, writer*

**Conway**
Larroya Runge, Saroj Nilu *biologist, educator*

**Fayetteville**
Bell, Debbie McCulley *science educator*
Brown, Avert Hayden *animal scientist, educator*
Brown, Connell Jean *retired animal science educator*
Morris, Justin Roy *food scientist, consultant*
Musacchia, X(avier) J(oseph) *physiology and biophysics educator*
Musick, Gerald Joe *retired entomology educator*

**Jefferson**
Binienda, Zbigniew Karol *research scientist, consultant*
Schwetz, Bernard Anthony *toxicologist*

**Little Rock**
Casciano, Daniel Anthony *biologist, educator*
Gealt, Michael A. *environmental microbiologist, educator*
McSwain, Byrdie Engle *laboratory scientist, immunohemotologist*
Wight, Patricia Anne *neuroscience educator*

**State University**
Bouldin, Jennifer L. *research scientist*

**Stuttgart**
Counce, Paul Allen *physiologist, educator*

## CALIFORNIA

**Alameda**
Cho, Myeong-Je *plant biologist, researcher*
Schoeler, George Bernard *medical entomologist*

**Albany**
Schwimmer, Sigmund *food enzymologist*

**Atherton**
Coleman, Robert Griffin *geology educator*

**Bakersfield**
Kreber, Lisa Ann *neuroscientist, psychologist*

**Berkeley**
Baldwin, Bruce Gregg *botany educator, researcher*
Barrett, Reginald Haughton *wildlife management educator*
Botchan, Michael R. *molecular biologist, biochemist*
Brenner, Sydney *molecular biologist, researcher*
Casida, John Edward *toxicology and entomology professor*
Chapela, Ignacio H. *biologist, researcher*
Chen, Lu *neurobiologist, biology professor*
Cline, Thomas Warren *geneticist, educator*
Cooper, William Secord *information science educator*
Deacon, Terrence William *science educator*
Doudna, Jennifer A. *molecular biologist, educator*
Fleiszig, Suzanne Mariane Janete *optometry educator*
Hlusko, Leslea Jane *science educator*
King, Nicole *molecular biologist, educator*
Levine, Mark David *science administrator, director*
Lichtenberg, Allan Joseph *science educator*
Lidicker, William Zander, Jr. *zoologist, educator*
Manga, Michael *earth science educator, geophysicist*
Merenlender, Adina Maya *biologist*
Oster, George F. *molecular biologist, environmental biologist*
Rubin, Edward M. *geneticist, medical researcher*
Saraph, Prasad Vaman *research scientist, industrial engineer*
Schekman, Randy W. *molecular biology administrator, biochemist*
Scott, Eugenie Carol *science foundation director, anthropologist*
Seil, Fredrick John *retired neuroscientist*
Sime, Karen Rachel *entomologist*
Teeguarden, Dennis Earl *forest economist, educator*
Trauner, Dirk *science educator*
Wake, David Burton *biology professor*
Wake, Marvalee Hendricks *biology professor*

**Bodega Bay**
Clegg, James Standish *physiologist, biochemist, educator*
Hand, Cadet Hammond, Jr. *retired marine biologist*

**Brawley**
Kellogg, Nancy V. *science educator*

**Carlsbad**
Hale, David Fredrick *biotechnology executive*

**Carson**
Han, Jianchao *science educator*

**Chico**
Kistner, David Harold *biology professor*

**Claremont**
Phillips, Ian M. *physiologist, educator*
Raval, Alpan *computational biologist, mathematics professor*

**Costa Mesa**
Lattanzio, Stephen Paul *astronomy educator*

**Covina**
Li, Baoyan *science educator, researcher*

**Davis**
Ardans, Alexander Andrew *veterinarian, educator, lab administrator*
Ball, Barry Allen *veterinarian, researcher*
Barbour, Michael G(eorge) *botanist, educator, ecologist, consultant*
Baskin, Ronald Joseph *biophysicist educator, dean*
Colvin, Harry Walter, Jr. *physiology educator*
Day, Howard Wilman *geology educator*
Enders, Allen Coffin *anatomy educator*
Epstein, Emanuel *plant physiologist*
Gottlieb, Leslie *geneticist, educator*
Greenwood, M. R. C. *biologist, nutrition educator, former academic administrator*
Hess, Charles Edward *environmental horticulture educator*
Holyoak, Marcel *ecologist, educator*
Hope, Hakon *research scientist*
Horwitz, Barbara Ann *physiologist, educator, consultant*
Lauchli, Andre E. *science educator*
Meyer, Margaret Eleanor *retired microbiologist*
Moyle, Peter Briggs *marine biologist, educator*
Mukherjee, Amiya K. *metallurgy and materials science educator*
Murphy, Terence Martin *biology professor*
Patricelli, Gail Lisa *biology professor*
Qualset, Calvin O. *agronomist, educator*
Rappaport, Lawrence *plant physiology and horticulture educator*
Ronald, Pamela C. *plant pathologist, educator*
Rost, Thomas Lowell *retired botany educator*
Roth, John Roger *geneticist, biology educator*
Schoener, Thomas William *zoology educator, researcher*
Sillman, Arnold Joel *physiologist, educator*
Trimmer, Jim *neuroscientist, educator*
Turcotte, Donald Lawson *geophysical sciences educator*
Van Alfen, Neal K. *plant pathologist*
Watt, Kenneth Edmund Ferguson *zoology educator*

**Del Mar**
Farquhar, Marilyn Gist *cell biologist, pathologist, educator*

**Duarte**
Smith, Steven Sidney *molecular biologist*

**El Segundo**
Seymour, Scott *science administrator*

**Emeryville**
Choi, Doo-Sup *molecular biologist*
Houghton, Michael *geneticist*
White, Raymond Leslie *geneticist*

**Escondido**
Sloan, Anne Elizabeth *food scientist, writer*

**Fair Oaks**
Hoehn, Robert Guthrie *science educator*

**Fairfield**
Gelpke, Peter Hall *science educator, department chairman*

**Fresno**
Burnett, Lynn Barkley *health science educator*
McConnell, Charles Prescott *retired science educator*
Winter, Robert Frank *biologist, educator*

**Fullerton**
Woyski, Margaret Skillman *retired geology educator*

**Gilroy**
Barham, Warren Sandusky *horticulturist*

**Goleta**
Wu, Jingchun *research scientist*

**Healdsburg**
Vedros, Neylan Anthony *microbiologist, educator*

**Hermosa Beach**
Chi, Lois Wang *retired biology professor, research scientist*

**Hopland**
Jones, Milton Bennion *retired agronomist*

**Irvine**
Ayala, Francisco José *geneticist, educator*
Briscoe, Adriana Darielle *biology professor*
Demetrescu, Mihai Constantin *research scientist, educator, computer company executive*
Lenhoff, Howard Maer *biological sciences educator, academic administrator*

Riley, Sally Jean *science educator*
Stanbridge, Eric John *biology professor*
Steward, Oswald *neuroscience educator, researcher*
Thigpen, Stephen P. *horticulture products company executive*
Wallace, Douglas C. *geneticist, educator*

**Kelseyville**
Sandmeyer, E. E. *toxicologist, consultant*

**Kensington**
Stent, Gunther Siegmund *molecular biologist, educator*

**La Jolla**
Barshop, Bruce A. *science educator*
Brooks, Charles Lee III *computational biophysicist, educator*
Chrispeels, Maarten Jan *biology professor*
Elman, Jeffrey Locke *cognitive sciences educator*
Emr, Scott David *biology professor, consultant*
Evans, Ronald M. *microbiologist, educator*
Gaasterland, Terry *biotechnologist, educator*
Gilbert, James Freeman *geophysics educator*
Guillemin, Roger C.L. *physiologist*
Haxo, Francis Theodore *marine biologist*
Helinski, Donald Raymond *biologist, educator*
Jambon, Martin Rufus *research scientist*
Kassel, Daniel Brian *biotechnologist, researcher*
Lewin, Ralph Arnold *biologist*
Liu, Shumo *molecular biologist*
Macagno, Eduardo R. *biology professor, dean*
Rahman, Yueh-Erh *biologist*
Richman, Douglas Daniel *medical virologist, educator, internist*
Schroeder, Julian Ivan *biology professor*
Sherman, Irwin William *biological sciences educator, academic administrator*
Thomas, Charles Allen, Jr. *molecular biologist, educator*
Tyrberg, Björn *cell biologist*
West, John Burnard *physiologist, educator*
Wilkie, Donald Walter *retired biologist, aquarium administrator*

**Livermore**
Anastasio, Michael R. *science foundation director*
Raymond, Jason *geneticist, microbiologist*

**Loma Linda**
Longo, Lawrence Daniel *physiologist, educator, obstetrician, gynecologist*
Schwab, Ernest Roe III *physiology educator, researcher*
Taylor, Barry Llewellyn *microbiologist, educator*

**Long Beach**
Mills, Don Harper *pathology and psychiatry educator, lawyer*
Schubel, Jerry Robert *marine scientist educator, dean*

**Los Alamitos**
Aberman, Harold Mark *veterinarian*

**Los Altos**
Fraknoi, Andrew *astronomy educator, astronomical society executive*
King, Chi-Yu *research scientist*

**Los Angeles**
Agnew, John A. *science educator*
Baker, Robert Frank *molecular biologist, educator*
Banerjee, Utpal *biology professor, research scientist*
Boles, Richard Gregory *clinical geneticist, researcher*
Bottjer, David John *earth science and biology educator*
Butcher, Larry L. *neuroscientist, educator*
Connor-Dominguez, Billie Marie *science information professional*
Craft, Cheryl Mae *neurobiologist, anatomist, researcher*
Diamond, Jared Mason *biologist, writer*
Finegold, Sydney Martin *microbiology educator*
Fischer, Alfred George *geology educator*
Gasson, Judith C. *research scientist*
Ghez, Andrea Mia *astronomy educator, physics educator*
Gilman, John Joseph *research scientist*
Goldberg, Robert B. *molecular biologist, biology professor*
Gordon, David *research scientist*
Gordon, Malcolm Stephen *biology professor*
Greenberger, Martin *biotechnologist, information scientist, educator*
Grinnell, Alan Dale *neuroscientist, educator*
Guo, Wei *research scientist*
Khawli, Leslie Albert *research scientist, educator*
Lake, James *microbiologist, educator*
Lee, John Joon *research scientist, minister*
Ljubimov, Alexander V. *molecular biologist, cell biologist, researcher*
Lu, John Kuew-Hsiung *physiology educator, endocrinologist*
Lunt, Owen Raynal *biologist, educator*
Melnick, Michael *geneticist, educator*
Mohr, John Luther *biologist, environmental consultant*
Morrison, Sherie Leaver *microbiologist, educator*
Mullan, John H. *science administrator*
Orme, Antony Ronald *geography educator*
Rosenfeld, John Lang *geology educator*
Sachs, George *biology professor, physician*
Sanford, James L. *science administrator*
Schopf, James William *paleobiologist, researcher, educator*
Simmons, Donna Marie *neuroscientist, histotechnologist, neuroendocrinologist, researcher*
Sinenko, Sergey A. *biologist, geneticist, researcher*
Siniawski, Matthew *science educator*
Slamon, Dennis J. *research scientist*
Sonnenschein, Ralph Robert *physiologist*
Szego, Clara Marian *cell biologist, educator*
Taylor, Charles Ellett *biology educator*
Thompson, Paul Matthew *neuroscientist*
Tontonoz, Peter *molecular biologist, educator*

Villablanca, Jaime Rolando *neuroscientist, medical educator*
Winet, Howard *research scientist, medical educator*
Wright, Ernest Marshall *physiologist, consultant*
Wright, Sandra *science administrator*
Xie, Lai-Hua *physiologist*
Xue, Yongkang *science educator*

**Malibu**
Hunt, Valerie Virginia *electrophysiologist, educator*

**Marina Del Rey**
McGowen, Gerald Ellis *biologist*

**Martinez**
Kimbrell, Deborah Ann *geneticist, educator*

**Menlo Park**
Nilsson, Anders Robert *science educator, researcher*

**Mill Valley**
Lieberman, Morton A. *science educator*

**Modesto**
Moe, Andrew Irving *veterinarian*

**Moffett Field**
Freund, Friedemann T. *research scientist, educator*
Friedmann, E(merich) Imre *biologist, educator*
Harper, Lynn D. *biologist*
Kittel, Peter *research scientist*
Lissauer, Jack Jonathan *astronomy educator*
Morrison, David *science administrator, researcher*

**Monrovia**
Kimnach, Myron William *botanist, horticulturist*

**Monterey**
Boger, Dan Calvin *science professor, consultant*
Packard, Julie *aquarium administrator*
Packard Burnett, Nancy *biologist*
Widmer, Chad L. *marine biologist, researcher*

**Moss Landing**
Robison, Bruce H. *marine biologist*

**Mountain View**
Cabrol, Nathalie Agnes *research scientist*
Tarter, Jill Cornell *science foundation director, astronomer, researcher*

**Nevada City**
Whitsel, Richard Harry *retired biologist, entomologist*

**Norco**
Morrison, James V. *biology professor*

**Oakland**
Earle, Sylvia Alice *research biologist, oceanographer*
Krauss, Ronald Maxwell *research scientist, endocrinologist, educator*
Willson, Clyde D. *biologist, educator*

**Orange**
Wechsler, Steven L *virologist, researcher*

**Palm Desert**
Sausman, Karen *zoological park administrator*

**Palm Springs**
Petermann, Hans Jürgen *research scientist*

**Palo Alto**
Anderson, Charles Arthur *retired science administrator*
Briggs, Winslow Russell *plant biologist, educator*
Ernst, Wallace Gary *geology educator, dean*
Gerety, Robert John *microbiologist, researcher, pediatrician, pharmaceutical executive*
Johnson, Noble Marshall *research scientist*
Sanders, William John *research scientist*
Tsien, Richard Winyu *biology professor*

**Parlier**
Stapleton, James Jay *agricultural scientist, consultant*

**Pasadena**
Abelson, John Norman *biology professor*
Davidson, Eric Harris *molecular and developmental biologist, educator*
Dickinson, Michael *physiologist*
Goldreich, Peter Martin *astrophysics and planetary physics educator*
Huang, Alice Shih-hou *research scientist*
Konishi, Masakazu *neuroscientist, educator*
Lester, Henry Allen *biology professor*
Meyerowitz, Elliot Martin *biology professor, educator*
Revel, Jean-Paul *biology professor*
Scott, David Clinton *research scientist*
Steidel, Charles C. *astronomy educator*
Tirrell, David A. *research scientist, educator*
Varshavsky, Alexander Jacob *molecular biologist*
Wang, Jia *research scientist*
Wasserburg, Gerald Joseph *geology and geophysics educator*
Zewail, Ahmed Hassan *chemistry and physics educator, consultant, editor*

**Pebble Beach**
Neville, Roy Gerald *research scientist, chemical executive, consultant*

**Pomona**
Keating, Eugene Kneeland *animal scientist, educator*
Saviola, Beatrice Jeaneane *microbiologist*

**Porterville**
Syrdahl, Rickelle Lyn *biology professor*

**Richmond**
Desmond, Edward *microbiologist, consultant*
Janda, John Michael *microbiologist*

**Riverside**
Clegg, Michael Tran *genetics educator, researcher*
Green, Harry Western, II, *geology and geophysics educator*
Hall, Anthony Elmitt *agriculturist, physiologist*
Hyman, Bradley C. *biology professor, geneticist*
Kuzina, Ludmila V. *microbiologist, researcher*
Millar, Jocelyn G. *entomologist, educator*
Page, Albert Lee *soil science educator, researcher*
Van Gundy, Seymour Dean *plant pathologist, educator*

**Sacramento**
Carmona, Tamyra Rae *biology professor*
Dong, Michael Hon *toxicologist*
Rosenberg, Dan Yale *retired plant pathologist*
Winterton, Shaun Leslie *entomologist, educator*

**San Bernardino**
Fernandez-Miyakawa, Mariano Enrique *biologist, research scientist*

**San Carlos**
Wolff, Ronald Keith *toxicologist, researcher*

**San Clemente**
Riem, Michelle Johanna *science educator*

**San Diego**
Bartus, Raymond Thomas *neuroscientist, writer, pharmaceutical executive*
Bernstein, Sanford Irwin *biology professor*
Carretero, Ricardo *science educator*
Cotter, Philip David *molecular biologist, geneticist*
Crutchfield, Susan Ramsey *neurophysiologist*
Dulbecco, Renato *biologist, educator*
Eckhart, Walter *molecular biologist, educator*
Gage, Fred H. *neuroscientist, medical educator*
Getis, Arthur *geography educator*
Hayes, Claude Quinten Christopher *research scientist, inventor*
Kadous, Tamer Adel *research scientist*
Metzgar, David Lee *biologist*
Myers, Douglas George *zoological society administrator*
Panetta, Joseph Daniel *biotechnologist, director*
Sejnowski, Terrence Joseph *science educator*
Seth, Anil Kumar *neuroscientist, researcher*
Squire, Larry Ryan *neuroscientist, psychologist, educator*
Tozer, William Evans *entomologist, educator*
Vause, Edwin Hamilton *research foundation administrator*

**San Francisco**
Alberts, Bruce Michael *cell biologist, former foundation administrator*
Baxter-Lowe, Lee Ann *science educator*
Blackburn, Elizabeth Helen *molecular biologist*
Dallman, Mary F. *physiologist, science educator*
DeRisi, Joseph L. *science educator, biochemist*
Ganong, William F(rancis) *physiologist, educator*
Heyneman, Donald *parasitology and tropical medicine educator*
Kerlikowske, Karla *research scientist*
La Farge, Timothy *retired plant geneticist*
Likova, Mineva, Lora T. *research scientist*
Mandra, York T. *geology educator*
Márquez-Magaña, Leticia Maria *biology professor*
McCormick, Frank *research scientist*
Seago, Jean Ann *science educator*
Sillman, Amy *cell biologist*
Tlsty, Thea Dorothy *research scientist, educator*
Tricaro, Robert Collet *biologist, educator, editor, poet*
Vidwans, Smruti Jayant *microbiologist*
Werb, Zena *cell biologist, educator*
Wolff, Sheldon *radiobiology educator*
Wyse, Roger Earl *physiologist, department chairman*
Yamamoto, Keith Robert *molecular biologist, educator*

**San Jacinto**
Stange, Sharon (Sherri) *science educator*

**San Jose**
Brundage, Adrienne Leane *biologist, educator, entomologist*

**San Juan Capistrano**
White, Beverly Jane *cytogeneticist*

**San Marcos**
Fabry, Victoria Joan *biology professor*
Sheath, Robert Gordon *botanist, educator*

**San Marino**
Benzer, Seymour *neuroscience educator*

**Santa Barbara**
Badash, Lawrence *science history educator*
Christman, Arthur Castner, Jr. *science advisor, consultant*
Crowell, John C(hambers) *geology educator, researcher*
Dunne, Thomas *geology educator*
Kryter, Karl David *retired research scientist*
Schneider, Edward Lee *botanist, researcher*
Tucker, Shirley Lois Cotter *botanist, educator*

**Santa Clara**
Rong, Haisheng *research scientist*

**Santa Cruz**
Epps, Harland Warren *astronomy educator, optical design consultant*
Griggs, Gary Bruce *science administrator, oceanographer, geologist, educator*
Haussler, David H. *molecular biologist, educator*
Huskey, Harry Douglas *information and computer science educator*
Langenheim, Jean Harmon *biologist, educator*
Lay, Thorne *geosciences educator*
Osterbrock, Donald E(dward) *astronomy educator*

**Santa Monica**
Goldman, Charles A. *science administrator*
Orlando, Maria *behavioral scientist*

Salveson, Melvin Erwin *management sciences company executive, educator*

**Santa Rosa**
Schafer, John Francis *plant pathologist, researcher*

**Santee**
Hardy, Ben (Benson B. Hardy) *orchid nursery executive*

**Sausalito**
Gulland, Frances M. *veterinarian, researcher*

**Shafter**
Ulloa, Mauricio *geneticist, researcher*

**Sonora**
Tolhurst, Jeffrey Wayne *science educator, information systems educator*

**Soquel**
Stephens, Robert *horticulturist*

**South San Francisco**
Goodman, Corey Scott *neuroscientist, educator, biotechnologist*
Levinson, Arthur David *biotechnology research company executive*
Scheller, Richard H. *physiologist, science educator*

**Stanford**
Arvin, Ann Margaret *microbiology and immunology educator, researcher*
Baylor, Denis Aristide *neuroscientist, educator*
Blandford, Roger David *science educator*
Brown, Patrick O. *molecular biologist, educator*
Campbell, Allan McCulloch *bacteriology educator*
Cohen, Stanley Norman *geneticist, educator*
Cork, Linda Katherine *veterinary pathologist, educator*
Daily, Gretchen Cara *ecologist, environmental services administrator*
Davis, Mark M. *microbiologist, educator*
Davis, Ronald Wayne *genetics researcher, biochemistry educator*
Dirzo, Rodolfo *science educator, researcher, biologist*
Ehrlich, Paul Ralph *biology professor*
Francke, Uta *geneticist, educator*
Hanawalt, Philip Courtland *biology professor, researcher*
Lee, Peter Poon-Hang *biotechnologist, educator*
McConnell, Susan K. *neuroscientist*
Mooney, Harold Alfred *plant ecologist*
Ngo, Khiem Viet *research scientist*
Purevdorj-Gage, Laura Boloroo *research scientist*
Roughgarden, Joan E. *biology professor*
Shapiro, Lucy *molecular biology educator*
Shooter, Eric Manvers *retired neurobiology professor, consultant*
Somerville, Christopher Roland *botanist, educator*
Spudich, James A. *biology professor*
Stearns, Timothy P. *biology professor, geneticist*
Sturrock, Peter Andrew *space science and astrophysics educator*
Theriot, Julie *microbiologist, medical educator*
Yanofsky, Charles *retired biology professor*

**Stockton**
Magness, Rhonda Ann *retired microbiologist*

**Sunset Beach**
Pridham, Thomas Grenville *retired microbiologist*

**The Sea Ranch**
Hayflick, Leonard *microbiology educator, writer*

**Thermal**
Wallis, Judith Lynn *science educator*

**Thousand Oaks**
Malmuth, Norman David *research scientist*

**Tujunga**
Ancu, Edward Florin *veterinarian*

**Tulare**
Berge, Anna Catharina Björnsdotter *veterinarian, epidemiologist*

**Walnut Creek**
Seaborg, David Michael *evolutionary biologist*

**Westlake Village**
Kodigala, Subba Ramaiah *research scientist*

**Westminster**
Allen, Merrill James *marine biologist*

**Woodland**
Squires, Richard Felt *research scientist*

**Woodland Hills**
Fox, Stuart Ira *physiologist*

**COLORADO**

**Aurora**
Dooley, J. Gordon *food scientist*
Holmes, Randall Kent *microbiology educator, academic administrator, internist, epidemiologist*
Horwitz, Kathryn Bloch *molecular biologist, educator, breast cancer researcher*
Weedin, James Frank *biology professor, researcher*

**Boulder**
Adams, William Walter III *science educator*
Armstrong, David Michael *biology professor*
Byerly, Radford, Jr. *science administrator*
Clifford, Steven Francis *science administrator, director*
Demmig-Adams, Barbara *science educator*
Dubin, Mark William *neuroscientist, educator, academic administrator*
Floyd, Ted *ornithologist, writer*
Knoelker, Michael T.F. *science observatory director*

Leuliette, Eric W. *research scientist*
Meier, Mark Frederick *research scientist, educator, artist, small business owner*
Mitchell, Joan LaVerne *research scientist*
Pace, Norman R. *science educator, microbiologist*
Roble, Raymond Gerald *science administrator*
Serafin, Robert Joseph *science center administrator, electrical engineer*
Snow, Theodore Peck *astrophysics educator*
Southwick, Charles Henry *zoologist, educator*
Staehelin, Lucas Andrew *cell biology professor*
Tolbert, Margaret A. *geochemistry educator*
Wood, William Barry III *biologist, educator*

**Carbondale**
Cowgill, Ursula Moser *biologist, educator, environmental consultant*

**Colorado Springs**
Bramschreiber, Terry Lee *science educator*
Bybee, Rodger Wayne *science administrator*
Driscoll, Lori *neuroscientist, educator*
Herron, Sherry Shelton *biology professor*
West, Ralph Leland *veterinarian*

**Denver**
Bogdan, Gregory Michael *toxicologist, researcher*
Cohrs, Randall J. *microbiologist, virologist*
Ehret, Josephine Mary *microbiologist, researcher*
Freiheit, Clayton Fredric *zoo director*
Hail, Numsen, Jr. *biologist, researcher*
Richardson, Elizabeth Hall *retired ecologist*

**Fort Collins**
Bai, Ying *research scientist*
Follett, Ronald Francis *soil scientist*
Hobbs, N. Thompson *science administrator*
Johnson, Robert Britten *geology educator*
Keim, Wayne Franklin *retired agronomist, geneticist*
Lumb, William Valjean *veterinarian*
Mortvedt, John Jacob *soil scientist, researcher*
Peng, Junhua *molecular biologist*
Peterson, Gary Andrew *agronomics researcher*
Sankaran, Mahesh *ecologist*
Seidel, George Elias, Jr. *zoology educator*
Seward, Nathan William *biologist, researcher*
Simmons, Mark Pitkin *botanist, educator*
Terauds, Juris *retired science educator, research scientist*

**Glenwood Springs**
Kelley, Robert Daryl *biology professor, mathematics professor*

**Golden**
Bettinghaus, Erwin Paul *research scientist*
Weimer, Robert Jay *geology educator, energy consultant, civic leader*

**Littleton**
Hill, Thane Clayton *science educator*
Vail, Charles Daniel *veterinarian, consultant*

**Longmont**
Dierks, Richard Ernest *veterinarian, academic administrator*

**Northglenn**
Hemlock, Roberta Leigh *veterinary technician*

**Nucla**
Sandefur, Denice Lee *science educator*

**U S A F Academy**
Mertz, Bryan Paul *science educator*
Veverka, Donald Victor *science educator*

**Westminster**
Reynolds-Sakowski, Dana Renee *science educator*

**CONNECTICUT**

**East Glastonbury**
Smith, David Clark *research scientist*

**Farmington**
Bronner, Felix *physiologist and biophysicist, educator, painter*
Rothfield, Lawrence I. *microbiology educator*

**Hamden**
Adair, Eleanor Reed *environmental biologist*
Bigland-Ritchie, Brenda Rachel *physiologist, educator, neurophysiology researcher*
Smith, David Martyn *retired forestry educator*

**Madison**
Kilbourne, Edwin Dennis *virologist, educator*
Stevenson, Robert Edwin *microbiologist, consultant*

**Meriden**
Lee, Henry C. *forensic scientist*

**Middletown**
Zito, Christopher Richard *molecular biologist, biochemist*

**Mystic**
Ballard, Robert Duane *marine geologist*
Hutchison, Dorris Jeannette *retired microbiologist, educator*

**New Britain**
Shen, Xiaoping *science educator*

**New Canaan**
Grace, Julianne Alice *retired biotechnologist*

**New Haven**
Altman, Sidney *biology professor*
Anderson, John Fredric *science administrator, entomologist, researcher*
Aronson, Peter Samuel *physiologist, researcher*
Brown, Thomas Huntington *neuroscientist*
Chandler, William Knox *physiologist*

Cicchetti, Domenic Vincent *research scientist, educator*
Ciuparu, Dragos Mihael *research scientist, educator*
DuBois, Arthur Brooks *physiologist, educator*
Galston, Arthur William *biology professor*
Graedel, Thomas Eldon *industrial ecology educator, researcher*
Hong, Baoming *research scientist, engineer*
Novick, Peter J. *cell biologist, educator*
Pollard, Thomas Dean *cell biologist, educator*
Redmond, Donald Eugene, Jr. *neuroscientist, educator*
Shepherd, Gordon Murray *neuroscientist, educator*
Summers, William Cofield *science educator*
Waggoner, Paul Edward *agricultural scientist*

**New London**
Tassinari, Melissa Sherman *reproductive toxicologist*

**North Haven**
Glaser, Gilbert Herbert *retired neuroscientist, educator*

**Old Greenwich**
DeOrchis, Frankie Juanita *forester, writer*

**Putnam**
Craig, Robert James *ornithologist, educator*

**Storrs Mansfield**
Devereux, Owen Francis *retired metallurgy educator*
Gaxiola, Roberto Adrian *plant biologist, researcher*
Laufer, Hans *developmental biologist, educator*
Marcus, Philip Irving *virology educator, researcher*

**Wallingford**
Hartz, Richard Allen *research scientist*

**West Simsbury**
Morest, Donald Kent *neuroscientist, educator*

**DELAWARE**

**Dover**
Fondong, Vincent N. *virologist, educator*

**Greenville**
Schroeder, Herman Elbert *scientific consultant*

**Newark**
Campbell, Linzy Leon *molecular biology researcher, educator*
DeLorme, Michael *toxicologist, researcher*
Schaefer, Paul William *retired entomologist*

**Wilmington**
Darko, Denis F. *research scientist, educator, physician*
Hartzell, Charles R. *science foundation director, cell biologist, biochemist*
Santiago, Melissa *neuroscientist*
Sippel-Wetmore, Frances Marie *microbiologist, retired business owner*
Waritz, Richard Stefan *toxicologist, researcher*

**DISTRICT OF COLUMBIA**

**Washington**
Affronti, Lewis Francis, Sr. *microbiologist, educator*
Allan, Ronald Gage *academic research coordinator*
Ampy, Franklin Roosevelt *zoologist, educator*
Anand, Rajen S. *physiologist, educator*
Apple, Martin Allen *science executive, scientist, educator*
Banks, Richard Charles *ornithologist*
Berg, Patricia Elene *molecular biologist*
Bernthal, Frederick Michael *science foundation director*
Bryant, Cory Michael *food scientist, researcher*
Carhart, Homer Walter *retired research scientist*
Case, Larry D. *agricultural education specialist*
Challinor, David *retired biologist*
Chamot, Dennis *science policy executive*
Coleman, Bernell *physiologist, educator*
Colglazier, E. William *science academy administrator, physicist*
Corell, Robert Walden *science administrator, educator*
Creedon, Jeremiah F. *aeronautical research laboratory administrator*
Dantzler, Andrew Alan *science administrator*
Davis, Donald Ray *entomologist*
Davis, Randy Lee *soil scientist*
Deem, Sharon Lynn *veterinarian, epidemiologist*
Elias, Thomas Sam *botanist, author*
Falk, Diane M. *research information specialist, librarian, writer, editor, director*
Feldbaum, Carl *biotechnologist*
Feulner, Edwin J., Jr. *research foundation executive*
Hall, Jason Piers Wilton *biologist*
Hampden Thompson, Gillian M.H. *research scientist*
Harding, Fann *retired science administrator*
Hazen, Robert Miller *research scientist, writer*
Hope, William Duane *retired zoologist, curator*
Hotez, Peter Jay *research scientist, educator*
Huntress, Wesley Theodore, Jr. *research scientist*
Jackson, Margaret Elizabeth *science educator*
Kennedy, Eugene Richard *microbiologist, university dean*
Lappin, Debra R. *research scientist*
Leshner, Alan Irvin *science administrator*
Li, Li *research scientist*
Malcom, Shirley Mahaley *science association executive*
McClung, Gwendolyn *soil microbiologist*
Meyers, Wayne Marvin *microbiologist, physician*
Morse, Larry Eugene *botanist, conservationist*
Nabholz, Joseph Vincent *biologist, ecologist*

Neureiter, Norman P. *science association director*
Nicolson, Dan Henry *plant taxonomist*
Nightingale, Elena Ottolenghi *pediatric geneticist, academic administrator, educator*
Pilcher, Carl B. *astrobiologist*
Pyke, Thomas Nicholas, Jr. *science administrator*
Reischauer, Robert D. *research organization executive*
Ridenour, Amy Moritz *research center administrator*
Siegel, Frederic Richard *geology educator*
Spelman, Lucy H. *zoological park administrator*
Tidball, M. Elizabeth Peters *physiologist, educator*
Tingus, Steven James *physiologist, researcher*
Torrey, Barbara Boyle *research council administrator*
Ucko, David Alan *science foundation official*
Ullman, Michael Thomas *science educator*
Umelo, Anthony N. *science educator*
Wasshausen, Dieter Carl *botanist*
West, Robert MacLellan *science educator, consultant*

## FLORIDA

### Boca Raton
Furman, Mark Evan *neuroscientist*
Lee, Xiaoyang *scientist*
Samuels, William Mason *physiology association executive*

### Bradenton
Diana, John Nicholas *physiologist*

### Coral Gables
Kohen, Elli *science educator*
Lucà-Moretti, Maurizio *research scientist, medical researcher, nutritionist, researcher*

### Delray Beach
Chavin, Walter *biological sciences educator, researcher*

### Fort Myers
Beever, James William III *biologist*

### Fort Pierce
Rice, Mary Esther *biologist*
Widder, Edith Anne *biologist*

### Gainesville
Arbogast, Richard Terrence *entomologist, researcher*
Besch, Emerson Louis *physiologist, educator, retired dean*
Burridge, Michael John *veterinarian, educator, research director*
Buzgo, Matyas *biologist, botanist*
Cantliffe, Daniel James *horticulture educator*
Dilcher, David Leonard *paleobotany educator, researcher*
Drury, Kenneth Clayton *biologist*
Dunford, James Christopher *entomologist, educator*
Fletcher, Bradley Scott *molecular biologist, hematologist*
Green, Eleanor Myers *veterinarian, educator*
Gridley, Kelly Elizabeth *biotechnologist, researcher*
Grobman, Arnold Brams *retired biology educator, retired academic administrator*
Grobman, Hulda Gross (Mrs. Arnold B. Grobman) *health science educator*
Gunn, Rebekah Gray *veterinarian*
Gutekunst, Richard Ralph *microbiology professor*
Hall, David Walter *botanist, consultant*
Himes, James Albert *retired veterinary medicine educator*
Hoy, Marjorie Ann *entomology educator*
Jones, Richard Lamar *entomology educator*
Mead, Frank Waldrein *taxonomic entomologist*
Nguyen, Ru *entomologist*
Nicoletti, Paul Lee *retired veterinarian, educator*
Palmer, Todd Michael *ecologist, educator*
Popenoe, Hugh Llywelyn *soils educator*
Price, Donald Dennis *neuroscientist, psychologist*
Purcifull, Dan Elwood *retired plant virologist, retired educator*
Quesenberry, Kenneth Hays *agronomy educator*
Raghavan, Sivakumar *food scientist*
Schmidt-Nielsen, Bodil Mimi (Mrs. Roger G. Chagnon) *retired physiologist, retired educator*
Tsinеira, Anton Alvin *food engineer, educator, consultant*
Vierck, Charles John, Jr. *neuroscience educator*
Yamamoto, Janet Kazuko *science educator*
Yu, Simon Shyi-Jian *entomologist, educator*

### Gulf Breeze
Menzer, Robert Everett *retired toxicologist, educator*

### Hobe Sound
Hand, Peter James *neurobiologist, educator*

### Homestead
Dong, Quan *ecologist*
Roberts, Larry Spurgeon *biological science educator, zoologist*

### Jacksonville
Mandal, Prabir Kumar *biologist, educator*

### Jupiter
Weissmann, Charles *molecular biologist, educator*

### Key Largo
Frankovich, Thomas Anthony *biologist, researcher*

### Lake Alfred
Chung, Kuang-Ren *plant pathologist, educator*
Kender, Walter John *horticulturist, educator*

### Lake Worth
Franco, Don Alvado *veterinarian*

### Lakeland
Pospichal, Marcie W. *neuroscientist, psychologist, educator*

### Melbourne
Helmstetter, Charles Edward *microbiologist*
Shaikh, Muzaffar Abid *management sciences educator*
Storrs, Eleanor Emerett *science administrator, consultant*
Winkelmann, Kurt Joseph *science educator*

### Miami
Buchwald, Peter Sandor *science association director*
Lubs, Herbert Augustus *genetics educator, administrator*
Manzello, Derek Paul *marine biologist*
Muench, Karl Hugo *clinical geneticist*
Ostlund, H. Gote *marine biologist, educator*
Pettigrew, Grady Gil Landers *biology professor*
Rodriguez, Irmina Bestard *science educator*

### Miami Gardens
Bell, Taunjah Patrease *research scientist*

### New Port Richey
Adams, Jean Marie *biology professor*
Day, Peter Rodney *geneticist, educator*

### Orlando
Kincaid, John Peter *science educator*
Klemenz, Christine F. *science educator, researcher*
Sohn, Yongho *science educator*

### Palm City
Boss, Manley Leon *plant physiologist*

### Palm Coast
Bullard, Ervin Trowbridge *horticulturist*

### Palm Harbor
Calhoun, John Vincent *research scientist*

### Panama City
Cortes, Enric *marine biologist*

### Pensacola
Bennett, Wayne A. *marine biologist, educator*
Kaplan, Joyce Bridget *zoologist, educator*

### Port Saint Lucie
Austin, Philip *research scientist*

### Punta Gorda
O'Neal, Lyman Henry *biology educator*

### Ruskin
Briscoe, Anne M. *retired science educator*

### Saint Augustine
Okech, Bernard Achero *parasitologist, entomologist*
Xue, Rui-De *entomologist*

### Saint Petersburg
Byrd, Isaac Burlin *retired biologist*
D'Elia, Christopher Francis *marine biologist, educator, academic administrator*
Mueller, O. Thomas *molecular geneticist, pediatrics educator*

### Sarasota
Clark, Eugenie *zoologist, educator*
Mahadevan, Kumar *marine life administrator, researcher*

### Spring Hill
Rothenberg, Linda Ann *science educator*

### Stuart
Robinson, Michael Hill *retired zoological park director, biologist*

### Tallahassee
Herrick, Nathan *biologist*
Khalil, Mohammed K. *research scientist, medical educator*

### Tampa
Cress, William Douglas *biology professor, researcher*
Germroth, Peter *biologist, educator*
Hickman, Hugh V. *science educator, researcher*
Lim, Daniel Van *microbiology educator*
Thulton, Tatyana Anatoly *biologist, researcher*

### Tequesta
Larson, Edythe K. *science educator*

### Valrico
Jurch, George R., Jr. *retired science educator*

### Vero Beach
Darsie, Richard Floyd, Jr. *medical entomologist*

### West Palm Beach
Gottlieb, Andrew D. *aquatic ecologist*

### Winter Haven
Grierson, William *retired agriculturist*

## GEORGIA

### Adairsville
Dobson, Suzanne *science educator*

### Alpharetta
Balows, Albert *microbiologist, educator*
Johnston, William David *biotechnologist, director*

### Athens
Avise, John Charles *geneticist, educator*
Baile, Clifton A. *biologist, researcher*
Bennetzen, Jeffrey L. *molecular biologist*
Box, Elgene Owen *ecologist, educator*
Cederbaum, Sandra Bloomfield *biologist*
Shockley, Floyd Wayne *entomologist*
Tyler, David Earl *retired veterinary medical educator*
Wessler, Susan R. *biologist, educator*

### Atlanta
Abdul-Ghaffar, Aswad Jawhar *physiologist, consultant*
Circeo, Louis Joseph, Jr. *research scientist, civil engineer*
Compans, Richard W. *microbiology educator*
Cox, Nancy Jane *microbiologist*
de Waal, Frans B.M. *biologist, psychology professor*
Fowler, Bruce Andrew *toxicologist, researcher, public health service official*
Glass, Roger I. *virologist*
Jeffery, Geoffrey Marron *medical parasitologist*
Levin, Bruce R. *biology professor*
Lynn, David G. *biology professor, chemistry professor*
Shepherd, Iain Thomas *biologist, educator*
Spitznagel, John Keith *retired microbiologist, immunologist, physician*
Swanagan, Jeffery S. *aquarium administrator*
Thompson, Herbert Alden *microbiologist, public health scientist*
Wang, Yuhang *science educator*
Warren, Stephen Theodore *human geneticist, educator*

### Augusta
Baker, Carleton Harold *physiology educator*
Inscho, Edward William *physiology educator*

### Decatur
Cavallaro, Joseph John *retired microbiologist*

### Gainesville
Lowrey, Alex Andre *biology professor*
May, Sterling Randolph *biology professor, department chairman*

### Griffin
Doyle, Michael Patrick *microbiologist, educator, director*

### Lilburn
Hester, Felicia Campbell *science educator*

### Lithonia
Baxter, Gene Francis *chemical researcher, consultant*

### Martinez
Chaudhary, Shaukat Ali *ecologist, plant taxonomist*

### Newnan
Krach, Dale James *science educator, athletic trainer*

### Norcross
Dibb, David Walter *research association administrator*
Wagner, Robert Earl *retired agronomist*

### Peachtree City
Turner, Lynda E. *science educator*

### Savannah
Eaves, George Newton *science foundation director, educator*
Purnell, Elissa T. *biology professor*

### Suwanee
Decker, Michael John *neuroscientist*

### Swainsboro
Stracher, Glenn Blair *geology educator, research scientist*

### Young Harris
Arnold, Paul T. *biologist, educator*

## HAWAII

### Honolulu
Abbott, Isabella Aiona *retired biology educator*
Brill, Richard C. *physical science educator*
Fok, Agnes Kwan *retired cell biologist, educator*
Gubler, Duane J. *research scientist, educator, virologist*
Hue, Nguyen Van *soil scientist, chemist, educator*
Kamemoto, Fred Isamu *retired zoologist*
Mandel, Morton *molecular biologist*
Sagawa, Yoneo *horticulturist, educator*
Zamzow, Jill Patricia *biologist, consultant*

### Kailua
Shank, Charles Vernon *science administrator, educator, physicist*

### Waikoloa
Morris, Victor Franklin, Jr. *retired meteorology educator*

## IDAHO

### Blackfoot
Asmus, Elaine G. *science educator*

### Kimberly
Strausbaugh, Carl Alan *plant pathologist*
Tasumi, Masahiro *science educator*

### Moscow
Bohach, Carolyn Hovde *science educator, researcher*
Roberts, Lorin Watson *botanist, educator*

### Parma
Lee, Jungmin *food scientist, researcher*

## ILLINOIS

### Argonne
Schriesheim, Alan *science administrator*

### Aurora
Elgar, Sharon Kay *science educator*

---

Lundquist, Robert *science educator*

### Berwyn
Parker, Alan John *veterinary neurologist, educator, researcher*

### Brookfield
Rabb, George Bernard *zoologist, conservationist*
Rudnick, Jamie *geneticist, research scientist*

### Buffalo Grove
Schrader, Kara Jean *science educator*

### Carbondale
Burr, Brooks Milo *zoology educator*

### Carterville
Krapf, Keith Alan *science educator*

### Champaign
Abd-El-Khalick, Fouad Sami *science educator*
Batzli, George Oliver *ecology educator*
Dmitriev, Dmitry A. *entomologist, researcher*
Harroff, Natasha Karena *science educator, consultant*
Levin, Geoffrey Arthur *botanist*
Ridlen, Samuel Franklin *agriculture educator*

### Chicago
Albrecht-Buehler, Guenter Wilhelm Herbert *biologist*
Borisy, Gary G. *molecular biology professor*
Chakrabarty, Ananda Mohan *microbiologist*
Chauhan, Neelima B. *neuroscientist, researcher*
Davidson, Richard Laurence *geneticist, educator*
Desjardins, Claude *physiologist, dean*
Despa, Florin *research scientist*
Ernest, J. Terry *ocular physiologist, educator*
Fisher, Lester Emil *retired zoo administrator*
Frederick, John Eugene *science educator*
Fukui, Yoshio *biology professor*
Goodman, Steven Michael *conservation biologist*
Greenberg, Bernard *retired entomologist*
Houk, James Charles *physiologist, educator*
Kaput, Jim *science administrator, educator*
Khodarev, Nikolai Nikolaevich *biologist, researcher*
Lau, Lester F. *science educator, researcher*
Lerman, Zafra Margolin *science and public policy professor*
Li, Wen-Hsiung *geneticist*
Mateles, Richard Isaac *biotechnologist*
McClintock, Martha K. *biologist, educator*
Mugnaini, Enrico *neuroscience educator*
Olopade, Olufunmilayo Falusi (Funmi Olopade) *geneticist, educator, oncologist, hematologist*
Olshansky, Stuart Jay *science educator*
Park, Thomas Joseph *biology researcher, educator*
Roizman, Bernard *virologist, educator*
Sivananthan, Sivalingam *science educator*
Smith, Cynthia Janese *science educator*
Solaro, Ross John *physiologist, biophysicist*
Storb, Ursula Beate *molecular genetics and cell biology educator*
Yamada, Tohru *biologist, educator, researcher, director*

### Coal City
DiGiusto, Elaine Bessie *science educator*

### Downers Grove
Brekke, Stewart Ernest *retired chemistry and physics educator*

### Edwardsville
Brugam, Richard Blair *biology educator*

### Evanston
Dallos, Peter John *neurobiologist, educator*
Enroth-Cugell, Christina Alma Elisabeth *neurophysiologist, educator*
Hacek, Donna Marie *microbiologist, researcher*
Novales, Ronald Richards *zoologist, educator*
Weertman, Johannes *materials science educator*
Widom, Jonathan *biology professor*
Wu, Tai Te *biological sciences and engineering educator*

### Glen Ellyn
Grosser, William F. *science educator*
Poromackam, Margarita Ritllova *science educator, environmental scientist*

### Glenview
Kinigakis, Panagiotis *research scientist, researcher, engineer, writer*

### Havana
Sass, Gregory George *ecologist, researcher*

### Lebanon
Jewett, Thomas O. *science educator, writer*

### Lisle
Smith, Jared Russell William *research executive, research scientist, consultant, poet*
Ware, George Henry *botanist*

### Macomb
Barclay, Martha Jane *science educator, research scientist*

### Normal
Brown, Lauren Evans *zoologist, researcher, educator*

### North Chicago
Roberts, Barry Lester *biologist, educator*

### Northbrook
King, Robert Charles *biologist, educator*

### Oak Brook
Quist, Arjan *biotechnologist, director*

### Orland Park
Burfeind, Betty Ruth *science educator*

### Peoria
Kurtzman, Cletus Paul *microbiologist, researcher*

Tuggle, Marla L. *science educator*

**Princeton**
Webber, Adam Brooks *science educator*

**River Forest**
Saffold, Monroe *science educator, consultant*

**Rock Island**
Anderson, Richard Charles *geology educator*

**Savoy**
Sinclair, James Burton *retired plant pathology educator, consultant*

**Skokie**
Montague, Ann Hood *veterinarian*

**Springfield**
Masternak, Michal Mateusz *biotechnologist, educator, molecular biologist, researcher*
Munyer, Edward Arnold *zoologist*
Snyder, Darlene Nootens *science educator, mathematics educator*

**Sugar Grove**
DeLay, Larry Gene *science educator, photographer*

**Summit Argo**
Koutchma, Tatiana Nicolaevna *food scientist, educator*

**Urbana**
Berenbaum, May Roberta *entomology educator*
Bernard, Richard Lawson *retired geneticist, educator*
Buetow, Dennis Edward *physiologist, educator*
Chow, Poo *forester*
Crang, Richard Francis Earl *botanist, writer, research scientist*
Crofts, Antony Richard *biochemistry and biophysics educator*
Delcomyn, Fred *physiology educator, neurobiology educator*
Ehrlich, Gert *science educator, researcher*
Frazzetta, Thomas Henry *evolutionary biologist, educator*
Greenough, William Tallant *psychobiologist, educator*
Heichel, Gary Harold *agronomist, educator*
Holt, Donald A. *agronomist, consultant, researcher, retired academic administrator*
Kirkpatrick, R(obert) James *geology educator*
Kuhlenschmidt, Mark Stuart *microbiologist, researcher*
Kwasinski, Alexis *research scientist*
Larkin, Denis M. *geneticist, researcher*
Mc Glamery, Marshal Dean *agronomist, educator, weed scientist*
Meyer, Richard Charles *microbiologist, educator*
Misic, Mark M. *exercise physiologist, researcher*
Nanney, David Ledbetter *geneticist, educator*
Newmark, Phillip Allan *biology professor*
Ra, Hyungshim Yoo *biologist, researcher*
Ridgway, Marcella Davies *veterinarian*
Robinson, Gene Ezia *biologist, educator*
Seigler, David Stanley *botanist, educator, chemist*
Splittstoesser, Walter Emil *botanist, educator*
Whitt, Gregory Sidney *evolution educator*
Williams, Martha Ethelyn *information science educator*

**West Chicago**
Mott, Thomas Charles *science educator*

**Westchester**
Webb, Emily *retired plant morphologist*

**Woodstock**
Dorn, Diane M. *science educator*

**INDIANA**

**Bloomington**
Clevenger, Sarah *botanist, consultant*
Gest, Howard *microbiologist, educator*
Ketterson, Ellen D. *biologist, educator*
Nolan, Val, Jr. *retired biologist, lawyer*
Rieseberg, Loren *botanist, educator*
Ruesink, Albert William *biologist, plant sciences educator*
Weinberg, Eugene David *microbiologist, educator*
Zhu, Chen *science educator, consultant*

**Carmel**
Rott, Stephen Ross *biologist, educator*

**Delphi**
McCain, Daniel *retired agronomist*

**Evansville**
Segebarth, Marsha Lynn *biology professor*

**Gary**
Schoon, Kenneth James *science educator, writer*

**Indianapolis**
Babsky, Andriy M. *biologist, researcher*
Banya, Santonino Ku'Caya *science educator*
Burr, David Bentley *anatomy educator*
Ochs, Sidney *neurophysiology researcher, editor, writer*
Rhoades, Rodney Allen *physiologist, educator*
Thomas, Jerry Arthur *soil scientist*
Wu, Min *cell biologist, researcher, educator*

**Lafayette**
Nicholson, Ralph Lester *botanist, educator*

**Madison**
Grahn, Ann Wagoner *retired science administrator*

**Muncie**
Hendrix, Jon Richard *biology professor*
Henzlik, Raymond Eugene *zoophysiologist, educator*
Mertens, Thomas Robert *biology professor*

Wise, Charles Davidson *science educator*

**Notre Dame**
Burns, Peter C. *science educator, engineering educator*
Jensen, Richard Jorg *biologist, educator*
Kulpa, Charles F. *microbiology professor, department chairman*
Pollard, Morris *microbiologist, educator*
Shrader-Frechette, Kristin *science educator*

**Pittsboro**
Swango, Colleen Jill *science educator*

**Terre Haute**
Sparks, Dale W. *biologist, research scientist*

**Valparaiso**
Schlender, William Elmer *management sciences educator*

**West Lafayette**
Albright, Jack Lawrence *animal science and veterinary educator*
Amstutz, Harold Emerson *veterinarian, educator*
Hoxie, Robert Prynne *retired entomologist*
Hunt, Michael O'Leary *wood science educator, engineering educator*
Jabbari, Esmaiel *polymer scientist, researcher*
Jackson, Scott Allen *biology professor*
Janick, Jules *horticultural scientist, educator*
Le Master, Dennis Clyde *forester, educator, retired economist*
Mason, Sally Kay Frost *biology professor, academic administrator*
Nelson, Philip Edwin *food scientist, educator*
Ohm, Herbert Willis *agronomy educator, agriculturist*
Orvis, Kathryn S. *science educator*
Sherman, Louis Allen *biology professor, department chairman*

**IOWA**

**Ames**
Anderson, Lloyd Lee *physiologist, educator*
Beran, George Wesley *veterinary microbiology educator*
Greve, John Henry *veterinary parasitologist, educator*
Hallauer, Arnel Roy *geneticist*
Hatfield, Jerry Lee *plant pathologist, meteorologist*
Hendrich, Suzanne *toxicologist*
Johnson, Lawrence Alan *cereal technologist, educator, administrator*
Karlen, Douglas Lawrence *soil scientist, researcher*
Lee, Seong-Jae *research scientist*
Mengeling, William Lloyd *retired veterinarian, virologist*
Mertins, James Walter *entomologist*
Moore, Kenneth James *agronomist, educator*
Munkvold, Gary P. *plant pathologist, educator*
O'Berry, Phillip Aaron *retired veterinarian*
Ross, Richard Francis *veterinarian, educator, dean, microbiologist*
Seaton, Vaughn Allen *retired veterinary pathology educator*
Sebranek, Joseph G. *science educator*
Thompson, Louis Milton *agronomy educator, researcher*
Tylka, Gregory L. *plant pathologist, educator*
Willham, Richard Lewis *zoology educator*

**Coralville**
Behlke, Mark Aaron *biotechnologist, research scientist*

**Des Moines**
Mitchell, Stuart *medical entomologist, consulting physician*
Rosen, Matthew Stephen *botanist, consultant*

**Dubuque**
Beardsley, Shelley J. *science educator*

**Eldridge**
Downing, Paul R. *sports science educator*

**Grinnell**
Walker, Waldo Sylvester *biologist, educator, academic administrator*

**Iowa City**
Apicella, Michael Allen *microbiologist, educator*
Campbell, Kevin Peter *physiology and biophysics educator*
Hausler, William John, Jr. *microbiologist, educator, public health service officer*
Husted, Russell Forest *research scientist*
Kessel, Richard Glen *zoology educator*
Lim, Ramon (Khe-Siong Lim) *neuroscience educator, researcher*
Maxson, Linda Ellen *biologist, educator*
Miller, Jordan D. *physiologist*
Mullins, Robert F. *cell biologist*
Pessin, Jeffrey E. *physiology educator*
Stay, Barbara *zoologist, educator*
Wunder, Charles C(ooper) *physiologist, biophysicist, educator*

**Mapleton**
Stodola, Steven James *science educator*

**Pella**
Eastin, Matthew David *science educator*

**Storm Lake**
Lenzmeier, Brian A. *biology professor, researcher*

**West Burlington**
Sharp, Joan Diane *biology professor*

**KANSAS**

**Emporia**
Sundberg, Marshall David *biology professor*

**Hays**
Coyne, Patrick Ivan *physiological ecologist*

**Lansing**
Rawlings, Gregory Owen *science educator, consultant*

**Lawrence**
Angino, Ernest Edward *retired geology educator, retired engineering educator*
Armitage, Kenneth Barclay *retired biology professor*
Byers, George William *retired entomology educator*
Greenfield, Michael Dennis *biology educator, researcher*
Johnston, Richard Fourness *biologist, educator*
Lichtwardt, Robert William *mycologist*
Shankel, Delbert Merrill *microbiologist, biologist, educator*

**Manhattan**
Bhadriraju, Subramanyam Venkata *entomologist, consultant*
Erickson, Howard Hugh *veterinarian, physiology educator*
Kirkham, M. B. *plant physiologist, educator*
Olds, David Andrew *food scientist, educator*
Posler, Gerry Lynn *agronomist, educator*

**Neosho Falls**
Bader, Robert Smith *biology and zoology educator, researcher*

**Olathe**
Goodwin, Becky K. *educational technology resource educator*

**Overland Park**
Goetz, Kenneth Lee *cardiovascular physiologist, research consultant, writer*

**Parsons**
Lomas, Lyle Wayne *agricultural research administrator, educator*

**Wichita**
Dierks, Melinda Adair *science educator*
Liao, Haitao *science educator, researcher*
Park, Chan Hyung *cell biologist, physician*
Rogers, Michael E. *exercise physiology educator, researcher*

**KENTUCKY**

**Bowling Green**
Marcus, Jeffrey M. *science educator*

**Columbia**
Reliford, Judy Lynn Petty *science educator*

**Cynthiana**
Bandurski, Bruce Lord *retired ecologist, environmental scientist*

**Frankfort**
Frye, Wilbur Wayne *retired soil science educator, researcher, administrator*
Gomelsky, Boris *geneticist, educator*
Huebner, Ruth A. *science educator, researcher*

**Lexington**
Huffman, Gerald P. *science administrator, educator*
Humphries, Asa Alan, Jr. *biologist, educator, dean*
Kasperbauer, Michael John *plant physiology educator, researcher*
Mitchell, George Ernest, Jr. *zoology educator*
Robinson, Thomas Christopher *health science educator*
Sekulic, Dusan P. *science educator, engineering educator, researcher*
Straus, Robert *behavioral sciences educator*
Timoney, Peter Joseph *veterinarian, educator, virologist, consultant*

**Louisville**
Chaires, Jonathan Bradford *research scientist, educator*
Egilmez, Nejat K. *science educator*
Foster, William R. *zoological park administrator*
Muezzinoglu, Mehmet Kerem *research scientist*
Robinson, David Lowell *biology professor*

**Owensboro**
Caplan, Geralyn Marie *biology professor*

**Richmond**
Branson, Branley Allan *biology professor*

**LOUISIANA**

**Alexandria**
Robinson, Cathy D. *science educator*

**Baton Rouge**
Besch, Everett Dickman *veterinarian, dean emeritus, educator*
Burns, Paul Roger *forester, educator*
Chapman, Russell Leonard *botany educator*
Hansel, William *biology professor*
Head, Jonathan Frederick *cell biologist*
Laine, Roger A. *biology professor*
Lopez, Mandi J. *veterinarian, scientist*
Superneau, Duane William *geneticist, physician*
Tipton, Kenneth Warren *retired agricultural administrator, researcher*
Travagli, Renato Alberto *neuroscientist, researcher*
Tyagi, Mayank *research scientist*
Wong, Wai Hing *marine biologist, researcher*

**Chauvin**
Sammarco, Paul W. *marine science researcher and educator*
Sammarco, Paul William *ecologist, researcher*

**Cut Off**
Mestayer, Mary Frances *science educator*

**Natchitoches**
Whitehead, Malcolm T. *research scientist*

**New Orleans**
Allen, Gary Curtiss *geology educator*
Beard, Elizabeth Letitia *physiologist, educator*
Blackwell, James E. *retired science educator*
Ivens, Mary Sue *microbiologist, medical mycologist*
Mitchell, Kenneth David *physiologist, educator*
Rajan, Latha *microbiologist, educator*

**MAINE**

**Bar Harbor**
Coleman, Douglas *research scientist, educator*
Leiter, Edward Henry *cell biologist, researcher*

**Damariscotta**
Fuller, Melvin Stuart *botany educator*

**Farmington**
Mathews, Linnea Koons *science educator, librarian*

**Kennebunk**
Pozdeev-Freeman, Yuri *research scientist*

**Kittery Point**
Green, Edward Crocker *research scientist*

**Mount Desert**
Crawford, Richard Bradway *biologist, biochemist, educator*

**Old Town**
Ritz, George F. *forester, consultant*

**Portland**
Coburn, Andrew F. *research scientist educator*
Gainey, Louis F., Jr. *biology educator*
Maher, Christine R. *biologist, educator*

**Sangerville**
Harris, Norman Edwin *food scientist, consultant*

**MARYLAND**

**Aberdeen Proving Ground**
Stuebing, Edward Willis *research scientist*

**Baltimore**
Allen, Ronald John *astrophysics educator, researcher*
Bhardwaj, Anish *neuroscientist, medical educator*
Brady, Joseph Vincent *behavioral biologist, educator*
Broda-Hydorn, Susan *entomologist*
Brown, Donald David *biology professor*
Dawson, Valina L. *science educator*
DeTolla, Louis James *research scientist, veterinarian*
Dickfeld, Timm-Michael *electrophysiologist, cardiologist, educator*
Diop, Nafissatou *research scientist*
Gall, Joseph Grafton *biologist, researcher, educator*
Gallo, Robert Charles *research scientist*
Goldberg, Alan Marvin *toxicologist, educator*
Greider, Carol Widney *molecular biology professor*
Hansen, Barbara Caleen *physiologist, science educator*
Huganir, Richard Lewis *neuroscientist, educator, researcher*
Lee, Michael Kiwon *neuroscientist*
Littlefield, John Walley *geneticist, cell biologist, pediatrician*
Lorizzo, Robert P. *science administrator*
Massof, Robert William *neuroscientist, educator*
McKusick, Victor Almon *geneticist, educator, physician*
Mendell, Joshua T. *molecular biologist, geneticist, educator*
Mountcastle, Vernon Benjamin *retired neuroscientist*
Redfield, Robert R. *virologist, medical educator*
Sack, George Henry, Jr. *molecular geneticist*
Savonenko, Alena *neuroscientist, educator*
Sidransky, David *molecular biologist*
Stewart, Doris Mae *biology professor*
Suskind, Sigmund Richard *microbiology educator*
Taguchi, Katsuyuki *science educator*
Trpis, Milan *vector biologist, educator*
Trujillo, J. Roberto *virologist*
Wolman, M. Gordon *geography educator*
Zaveri, Dimple Jigish *microbiologist, medical technician*

**Beltsville**
Bae, Hanhong *molecular biologist, researcher*
Collins, Anita Marguerite *research geneticist*
Klun, Jerome Anthony *entomologist, researcher*
Luo, Yaguang *food scientist, researcher*
Nemes, Attila *soil scientist, researcher*
Palm, Mary Egdahl *mycologist*
Schneider, Edwin Kahn *research scientist*
Stolwijk, Jan Adrianus Jozef *physiologist, biophysicist*

**Bethesda**
Basavappa, Ravi *biophysical science educator*
Bennink, Jack Richard *microbiologist, researcher*
Brady, Roscoe Owen *neurogeneticist, educator*
Burns, Drusilla Lorene *microbiologist*
Di Paolo, Joseph Amedeo *geneticist*
Dorr, Ann Pierce *science educator*
Ehrenfeld, Ellie (Elvera Ehrenfeld) *biologist, researcher*
Francomano, Clair Ann *geneticist*
Frank, Martin *physiologist, educator, medical association administrator*
Greenberg, Judith Horovitz *geneticist*
Grisham, Joe Wheeler *cell biologist, educator*

**Rochester Hills**
Unakar, Nalin Jayantilal *biological sciences educator*

**Saline**
Cruden, Robert William *botany educator*

**Troy**
Sastry, Shivashankar Kudur *retired entomologist*

**West Bloomfield**
Barr, Martin *science educator, academic administrator*

## MINNESOTA

**Duluth**
Johnson, Arthur Gilbert *microbiology educator*

**Mankato**
Benner, Autumn Rae *science educator*

**Mapleton**
John, Hugo Herman *natural resources educator*

**Marcell**
Aldrich, Richard John *agronomist, educator*

**Minneapolis**
Adams, John Stephen *geography educator*
Banerjee, Subir Kumar *science educator*
Danielson, James Walter *retired research microbiologist*
Dworkin, Martin *microbiologist, educator*
Georgopoulos, Apostolos P. *neuroscientist, neurologist, educator*
Gorham, Eville *retired ecologist*
Haase, Ashley Thomson *microbiology professor, researcher*
Jemmerson, Ronald *science educator, researcher*
Johnson, Kenneth Harvey *veterinary pathologist*
Koyano-Nakagawa, Naoko *biologist, researcher*
Newman, Eric A. *neuroscientist*
Porter, Philip Wayland *geography educator*
Serstock, Doris Shay *retired microbiologist, civic worker, educator*
Sinha, Akhouri A. *cell and development biologist, researcher*
Warman, Eduardo Norberto *research scientist*
Watson, Dennis Wallace *microbiologist, educator*

**Morris**
Ordway, Ellen *biologist, educator, entomologist, researcher*

**Rochester**
Maher, L. James III *molecular biologist*
Ordog, Tamas *research scientist, educator*
Shepard, Laura Ann *microbiologist, researcher*
Van Dyke, Daniel L. *geneticist*

**Roseville**
Marten, Gordon Cornelius *agronomist, educator, federal agency administrator*

**Saint Joseph**
Kirick, Daniel John *agronomist*

**Saint Louis Park**
Frestedt, Joy Louise *research scientist, science administrator*

**Saint Paul**
Barker, Frederick Keith *biologist*
Barnwell, Franklin Hershel *zoology educator*
Busch, Robert Henry *geneticist, researcher*
Cheng, Hwei H(sien) *soil scientist, agronomic and environmental science educator*
Davis, Margaret Bryan *paleoecology researcher, educator*
Diesch, Stanley La Verne *veterinarian, educator*
Domnisoru, Cristian *science educator*
Ek, Alan Ryan *forester, educator*
Goyal, Sagar M. *virologist, educator*
Kommedahl, Thor *plant pathology educator*
Leonard, Kurt John *retired plant pathologist, director*
May, Georgiana *biologist, educator*
McKinnell, Robert Gilmore *retired zoologist, biology professor, geneticist*
Phillips, Ronald Lewis *plant geneticist, educator*
Roy, Robert Russell *toxicologist*
Sadowsky, Michael J. *microbiologist, educator*
Stadelmann, Eduard Joseph *retired plant physiologist, educator, researcher*

**Saint Peter**
Costello, Patricia Anne *neuroscientist, educator*

**Tracy**
Myhr, Gayle E. *consumer science educator*

## MISSISSIPPI

**Fulton**
Mastin, Lynn P. *biology professor*

**Gautier**
Egerton, Charles Pickford *anatomy and physiology educator*

**Jackson**
Cho, Hyun Jung *biology professor*
Lewis, Robert Edwin, Jr. *pathology and immunology educator, researcher*

**Mississippi State**
Reddy, Kambham Raja *botanist, educator*
Topsakal, Erdem *science educator*

**Ocean Springs**
Brown-Peterson, Nancy J. *biologist*

**Oxford**
Keiser, Edmund Davis, Jr. *biologist, educator*
Rego, Cesar *science educator, researcher*

**Saucier**
Finley, Emma Rosemary *science educator*

**Stoneville**
Morales-Ramos, Juan Alfredo *entomologist, researcher*
Ranney, Carleton David *retired plant pathologist*

**Tupelo**
Miles, Sharon Kathleen *microbiologist, educator*

**University**
Duke, Stephen Oscar *physiologist, research scientist, educator*

**Walls**
Tharnish, Rose Maries Lehman *veterinarian*

## MISSOURI

**Bolivar**
Huser, Carl Frank *retired biology professor*

**Chesterfield**
Williams, Luther Steward *research scientist*

**Columbia**
Blevins, Dale Glenn *agronomy educator*
Finkelstein, Richard Alan *retired microbiology educator, consultant*
LaCrue, Alexis Nichole *parasitologist*
Men, Hongsheng *biologist, researcher*
Mitchell, Roger Lowry *retired agronomy educator*
Morehouse, Lawrence Glen *veterinarian, educator, academic administrator*
Mustapha, Azlin *food scientist, educator*
Poehlmann, Carl John *agronomist, researcher*
Puttler, Benjamin *entomologist*
Roberts, R. Michael *animal scientist, biochemist, educator*
Schaeffer, Mary L. *geneticist*
Van Sambeek, Jerome William *physiologist, educator*
Vogt, Albert Ralph *forester, educator, program director*
Yanders, Armon Frederick *biological sciences educator, science administrator*

**Eureka**
Lindsey, Susan Lyndaker *zoologist*

**Kansas City**
Hawley, R. Scott *research scientist*
Krumlauf, Robert Eugene *neuroscientist, educator*
Neaves, William Barlow *cell biologist, educator*
Spigarelli, James L. *science administrator*
Suedmeyer, William Kirk *veterinarian*

**Marshall**
Mills, Mark S. *biology professor*

**Maryland Heights**
Gillette, Richard Gareth *neurophysiology educator, researcher*

**Park Hills**
Holmes, Jeanne Owen *horticulture educator*

**Rolla**
Reis, Signo Tadeu *research scientist, consultant*
Signo, Reis T. *science educator*

**Saint Louis**
Ackers, Gary Keith *biophysical chemistry educator, researcher*
Allen, Garland Edward *biology professor, biologist, writer*
Ding, Cody *science educator*
Elgin, Sarah Carlisle Roberts *biology professor, researcher*
Fraley, Robert T. *biotechnologist*
Grant, Hugh *biotechnology company executive*
Green, Maurice *molecular biologist, educator, virologist*
Hoessle, Charles Herman *zoological park administrator, director*
Howard, Michael Joseph *neuroscientist, researcher*
Kaul, Siddharth *neuroscientist, researcher*
Korotev, Randall L. *research scientist, editor*
Miller, James Gegan *research scientist*
Schaal, Barbara Anna *evolutionary biologist, educator*
Skornia, Stacy Lynn *research scientist*
Stein, Phyllis Kravet *research scientist*
Templeton, Alan Robert *biology professor*
Woolsey, Thomas Allen *neuroscientist, biologist*

**Springfield**
Fredrick, LaRita Denise *science educator*
McKnight, Mark L. *biology professor, researcher*

**Villa Ridge**
Laskowski, Leonard Francis, Jr. *microbiologist*

**West Plains**
Wilcoxson, Roy Dell *plant pathologist, researcher, educator*

## MONTANA

**Bozeman**
Patten, Duncan Theunissen *ecologist educator*

**Emigrant**
Logan, Jesse A. *ecologist, researcher*

**Great Falls**
Kumar, Rajeev *research scientist*

**Helena**
Johnson, John Philip *geneticist, researcher*

**Moccasin**
Chen, Chengci *science educator, research scientist*

## NEBRASKA

**Lincoln**
Francis, Charles Andrew *agronomy educator, consultant*
Genoways, Hugh Howard *systematic biologist, educator*
Hanway, Donald Grant *retired agronomist, educator*
Hoffmann, Richard John *biology professor, dean*
Massengale, Martin Andrew *agronomist, educator, university president*
Stoddard, Robert H. *geography educator*
Taylor, Stephen Lloyd *toxicologist, educator, food scientist*
Vidaver, Anne Marie *plant pathology educator*

**Omaha**
Badeer, Henry Sarkis *physiology educator*
Brenneman, Rick Alan *conservation geneticist*
Eckerson, Joan M. *exercise physiologist, researcher*
Jesteadt, Walt *research scientist, educator*
Simmons, Lee Guyton, Jr. *zoological park director*

**Papillion**
Snelling, James Anthony *biology professor, technologist*

## NEVADA

**Las Vegas**
Capanna, Albert Howard *neuroscientist, neurosurgeon, lawyer, banker*

**Pahrump**
Evans, Charles Wayne, II, *biologist, researcher*

**Reno**
Gifford, Gerald Frederic *retired science educator*

## NEW HAMPSHIRE

**Durham**
Aitkenhead-Peterson, Jacqueline Ann *soil scientist, educator*
Croce, Ronald Victor *neuroscientist, educator*
Pistole, Thomas Gordon *microbiology professor, researcher, department chairman*

**Hanover**
Gazzaniga, Michael S. *neuroscientist, psychologist*
Guerinot, Mary Lou *biology professor*
Langford, George Malcolm *cell biology educator*

**Lebanon**
Munck, Allan Ulf *physiologist, educator*

**Plymouth**
D'Aleo, Judith Anne *biotechnologist, consultant*

**Sanbornton**
Weiant, Elizabeth Abbott *retired biology professor*

## NEW JERSEY

**Basking Ridge**
Riesenberger, John Richard *science administrator*

**Branchburg**
Hulse, Robert Douglas *biotechnologist*

**Closter**
Ribary, Urs *neuroscientist, educator*

**Cranford**
Jenssen, Warren Donald *microbiologist, consultant*

**East Brunswick**
Dombrowski, Anne Wesseling *retired microbiologist*

**Highland Park**
Feuerwerker, Elie *biologist, educator*
Youm, Gunwoong *food scientist*

**Highlands**
Psuty, Norbert Phillip *marine sciences educator*

**Hoboken**
Abel, Robert Berger *science administrator*

**Hopatcong**
Oken, Robert *retired neuroscientist, consultant*

**Jersey City**
Klyatis, Lev Matusovich *test and reliability scientist*
Singer, Howard Jack *biology professor, researcher*

**Kenilworth**
Pickett, Cecil Bruce *cell biologist*

**Madison**
Demain, Arnold Lester *microbiologist, educator*

**Montclair**
Chinard, Francis Pierre *physiologist, educator, consultant physician*
Du, Chunguang Charles *biologist, educator*

**New Brunswick**
Ehrenfeld, David William *biology professor, writer*
Funk, Cyril Reed, Jr. *agronomist, educator*
Lachance, Paul Albert *food science educator, clergyman*
Maramorosch, Karl *virologist, educator*
Saracevic, Tefko *information science educator*
Smouse, Peter E. *ecologist, educator*
Tedrow, John Charles Fremont *soils educator*
Zachariah, Emmanuel Selvanayagam *science educator, researcher*

**New Providence**
Gupta, Piyush *research scientist*

**Newark**
Cheng, Mei-Fang *psychobiology educator, neuroscientist*
Gaussin, Vinciane *science educator*
Ledeen, Robert Wagner *neuroscientist, educator*
Vatner, Stephen F. *physiologist, researcher, research scientist*
Weis, Judith Shulman *biology professor*
Zaborszky, Laszlo *neuroscientist*

**Parsippany**
Bandi, Nagesh *research scientist*

**Piscataway**
Arnold, Edward (Eddy Arnold) *research scientist, educator*
Denhardt, David Tilton *molecular and cell biology educator*
Essien, Francine B. *biologist, educator*
Ferstandig Arnold, Gail *research scientist, educator*
McGhee, George Rufus *palebiologist, educator*

**Plainfield**
Frost, David *retired biology professor, medical editor, consultant*

**Port Norris**
Canzonier, Walter Jude *shellfish aquaculturist*

**Princeton**
Altmann, Jeanne *zoologist, educator*
Altmann, Stuart Allen *biologist, educator*
Ballou, Janice Donelon *research director*
Bassler, Bonnie L. *molecular biologist*
Botstein, David *geneticist, educator*
Dayanik, Savas *science educator*
Drakeman, Donald Lee *biotechnologist, pharmaceutical executive*
Drakeman, Lisa N. *biotechnologist*
Enquist, Lynn William *molecular biologist*
Gould, Elizabeth *neuroscientist, educator*
Gould, James L. *biology professor*
Grant, Peter Raymond *biologist, researcher, educator*
Jacobs, William Paul *botanist, educator*
Shenk, Thomas Eugene *molecular biology educator, academic administrator*
Shrivastava, Ajay *biologist, researcher*
Wieschaus, Eric F. *molecular biologist, educator*
Witkin, Evelyn Maisel *retired geneticist*

**Red Bank**
Fred, Rogers Murray III *veterinary oncologist*

**Shrewsbury**
Westerman, Liane Marie *research scientist executive*

**Skillman**
Sharma, Om Prakash *clinical research and development executive*

**Somerset**
Tsou, Yu-Min *science administrator, chemistry researcher*

**Summit**
Barer, Sol Joseph *biotechnology company executive*

**Tinton Falls**
Hoelzler, Michael Gebhard *veterinarian, surgeon*

**West Orange**
Hwang, Karen *research scientist*

## NEW MEXICO

**Albuquerque**
Cadavid, Luis Fernando *biologist*
Hager, Gordon Douglas *scientist, engineering educator*
Henderson, Rogene Faulkner *toxicologist, researcher*
Hsi, David Ching Heng *plant pathologist, geneticist, educator*
Mauderly, Joe Lloyd *pulmonary toxicologist*
Muggenburg, Bruce Al *retired veterinary physiologist*
Waide, Robert Bruce *ecologist, researcher*
Woodward, Joan B. *science association director*

**Flora Vista**
Kerr, Rebecca Spangler *science educator*

**Gila**
Woodward, Hope *soil scientist, biologist*

**Hondo**
Pawley, Ray L. *retired zoological park administrator, curator*

**Las Cruces**
Tonn, Robert James *retired entomologist*

**Santa Fe**
Harding, Marie *ecological executive, artist*
McDermott, Sandra *national park administrator*
Smith, Philip Meek *science administrator, consultant*

**Socorro**
Boston, Penelope J. *science educator, researcher*

## NEW YORK

**Albany**
Frank, Joachim *molecular biologist, educator, biophysicist*
Mannella, Carmen A. *research scientist*
Schneider, Allan Stanford *biophysics, neuroscience and pharmacology educator, biomedical research scientist*
Stewart, Margaret McBride *biology professor, researcher*

**Amherst**
Abbas, June M. *science educator*

**Binghamton**
Klir, George Jiri *systems science educator*
Naslund, Howard Richard *geological science educator*
Zhu, Weixing *ecologist, educator*

**Bronx**
Adinolfi, Marion Darlyne *research scientist*
Bennett, Michael Vander Laan *neuroscience educator*
Cabart, Pavel *molecular biologist*
Goodrich, James Tait *neuroscientist, neurosurgeon*
Moore, Donald Emerson III *zoological park administrator, curator, wildlife biologist*
Schaller, George Beals *zoologist*
Sullivan, Daniel Joseph *biology professor, priest*
Waelsch, Salome Gluecksohn *geneticist, educator*

**Brooklyn**
Altura, Bella T. *physiologist, educator*
Altura, Burton Myron *physiologist, educator*
Barriere, Isabelle Huguette *science educator, researcher*
Gabriel, Mordecai Lionel *biologist, educator*
Kutlin, Andrei *microbiologist, immunologist, researcher*
Lipson, Steven Mark *virologist, microbiologist, environmental scientist, educator*
Medbury, Scot Daniel *botanical garden executive*
Ranck, James Byrne, Jr. *neuroscience researcher, educator*
Roker, Christopher A. *microbiologist, photographer*
Scalia, Frank R. *neuroscientist*
Schiffman, Gerald *microbiologist, educator*
Vassalle, Mario *physiologist*

**Buffalo**
Duax, William Leo *biologist, researcher*
Ghadersohi, Ali *veterinarian, researcher*
Ma, Yingyu *research scientist*
Ridgley, Frank Nelson *veterinarian*
Zawicki, Joseph Leo *science educator*

**Burnt Hills**
DeVries, Robert Charles *research scientist*

**Cicero**
DeVault, Travis L *wildlife biologist, researcher*

**Cobleskill**
Ingels, Jack Edward *horticulture educator*

**Cold Spring Harbor**
Stillman, Bruce *molecular biologist*
Watson, James Dewey *molecular biologist, educator*

**Cooperstown**
Butts, William Lester *entomologist, researcher*
Harman, Willard Nelson *malacologist, educator*

**Cortlandt Manor**
Traille, Joy Myra *microbiologist, eldercare service provider*

**East Aurora**
Keem, Michael Dennis *veterinarian*
Sand, Seaward Alwyn *geneticist, researcher*

**Floral Park**
Isenberg, Henry David *microbiology educator*

**Flushing**
Commoner, Barry *biologist, educator*

**Fredonia**
Benton, Allen Haydon *biology professor*

**Garden City**
Podwall, Kathryn Stanley *biology professor*
Prabhakar, Kumkum *biology professor*
Prattis, Susan Marie *veterinarian, educator*

**Geneva**
Siebert, Karl Joseph *food science educator, consultant*

**Great Neck**
Puttlitz, Donald Herbert *microbiologist*

**Hamilton**
Frey, Frank Michael *biology professor*

**Homer**
Gustafson, John Alfred *biology professor*

**Ithaca**
Alexander, Martin *microbiologist, educator*
Davies, Peter John *plant physiology educator, researcher*
Dev, Chekitan *science educator*
Eisner, Thomas *biologist, educator*
Fick, Gary Warren *agronomist, educator*
Fitzpatrick, John Weaver *ornithologist, researcher*
Gillett, James Warren *ecotoxicology educator*
Greene, Harry W. *biology professor*
Hairston, Nelson George, Jr. *ecologist, educator*
Henry, Susan Armstrong *biology professor, dean*
Hoy, Ronald Raymond *neurobiology educator*
Jagendorf, André Tridon *physiologist*
Kennedy, Wilbert Keith, Sr. *agronomy educator, retired university official*
Kingsbury, John Merriam *botanist, educator*
Korf, Richard Paul *mycology educator*
Lengemann, Frederick William *retired physiology educator*
Leopold, A. Carl *plant physiologist*
Mai, William Frederick *plant nematologist, educator*
Mooney, Kailen Andrews *ecologist, educator*
Mortlock, Robert Paul *microbiologist, educator*
Nicholson, Sean *science educator*
Novak, Joseph Donald *science educator*
Pimentel, David *entomologist, educator*
Poppensiek, George Charles *retired veterinary scientist, retired educator*

Provine, William B. *biology professor*
Regenstein, Joe M. *food scientist, educator*
Schlafer, Donald Hughes *veterinary pathologist*
Temple, Elise *neuroscientist*
Trautmann, Nancy Morton *science educator, writer*
Viands, Donald Rex *plant breeder, educator*
Walcott, Charles *neurobiology and behavior educator*
Wasserman, Robert Harold *biology professor*
Welch, Ross Maynard *plant physiologist, educator*
Wootton, John Francis *physiology educator*

**La Fayette**
Amidon, David R. *science educator, coach*

**Millbrook**
Likens, Gene Elden *biology and ecology educator*

**Morrisonville**
Fuller, Katherine T. *science educator, department chairman*

**Mount Kisco**
Laster, Richard *biotechnologist, consultant*

**Mount Vernon**
Young, Paula Eva *animal shelter director*

**Neponsit**
Nicastri, Ann Gilbert *science educator*

**New York**
Abbott, Geoffrey Winston *physiologist, researcher*
Blobel, Günter *cell biologist, educator*
Bock, Walter Joseph *zoology educator*
Botkin, Daniel Benjamin *biologist, environmental scientist, writer*
Caesar, Godfrey Wrensford *biologist, educator*
Calame, Kathryn Lee *microbiologist, educator*
Carey, Kim *veterinarian*
Carlson, Marian Bille *geneticist, researcher, educator*
Catanzaro, Daniel Frank *molecular biologist, educator*
Chaganti, Raju S. *geneticist, educator, researcher*
Chalfie, Martin *biology professor*
Chan, Siu-Wai *materials science educator*
Chen, Elizabeth Shan Shan *research scientist*
Chen, Xi *research scientist*
Cohen, David Harris *neuroscientist, educator, academic administrator*
Cohen, Joel Ephraim *biologist, educator, demographer*
Dales, Samuel *microbiologist, virologist, educator*
Darnell, James Edwin, Jr. *molecular biologist, educator*
Davis, Jessica G. *geneticist*
de Lange, Titia *research scientist, educator*
Desnick, Robert John *human geneticist*
Dobrof, Rose Wiesman *gerontology educator*
Eckhardt, Laurel Ann *biologist, researcher, educator*
Edelman, Jack Robert *science educator*
Feldman, Samuel Mitchell *neuroscientist, educator*
Filardi, Christopher Edward *biologist, researcher*
Fiser, Andras *science educator*
Fuchs, Elaine V. *molecular biologist, educator*
Gardner, Esther P. *neuroscientist, physiologist, educator*
Giancotti, Filippo Giusto *molecular biologist, educator*
Godson, Godfrey Nigel *molecular geneticist, educator*
Greengard, Paul *neuroscientist, educator*
Hawkins, Robert Drake *science educator*
Heicklen, Alice *biologist*
Hirschhorn, Rochelle *genetics educator*
Jebara, Tony *science educator*
Kampmann, Martin *cell biologist*
Kelley, Darcy B. *biology professor*
Kelly, Thomas Jesse, Jr. *molecular biologist*
Kondo, Reena *science educator, artist*
Landry, Donald William *physician scientist*
Leaman, Leonard S., Jr. *science educator*
Lederberg, Joshua *geneticist, educator*
LeDoux, Joseph E. *neuroscientist, educator*
Lee, Lillian Vanessa *microbiologist*
Littman, Dan R. *microbiologist*
Llinás, Rodolfo Riascos *neuroscientist, researcher*
Maack, Thomas *physiology professor*
Maas, Werner Karl *microbiology educator*
MacKinnon, Roderick *neuroscientist, educator*
Manley, James L. *molecular biologist, educator*
McEwen, Bruce Sherman *neuroscientist, educator*
Moroz, Pavel Emanuel *retired research scientist*
Morrison, John Henry *neuroscientist, educator, lab administrator*
Morse, Stephen Scott *virologist, epidemiologist, immunologist, educator*
Moy, Richard L. *virologist*
Pikitch, Ellen Karen *science educator*
Pollack, Robert Elliot *biologist, educator, writer*
Prives, Carol *biologist, educator*
Ptashne, Mark Steven *molecular biology professor*
Quimby, Fred William *pathology educator, veterinarian*
Ravetch, Jeffrey Victor *molecular biologist, immunologist, educator*
Raz, Amir *neuroscientist, educator*
Revenkova, Ekaterina *biologist, researcher*
Rothman, James Edward *cell biologist, educator*
Rozen, Jerome George, Jr. *entomologist, researcher, curator*
Sadler Edepli, Kirsten *biologist, educator*
Saunders, Sylvia Christie *biologist, educator*
Segal, Sheldon Jerome *biologist, educator, foundation administrator*
Seyedi, Nahid *physiologist, researcher*
Shelanski, Michael L. *cell biologist, educator*
Silverstein, Samuel Charles *cellular biology and physiology professor, researcher*
Simon, Eric Jacob *neuroscientist, educator*
Stotzky, Guenther *microbiologist, educator*
Strickland, Sidney *neuroscientist; educator*
Theis, Martin *neuroscientist, researcher*
Troy, Carol Marie *neuroscientist*
Wharton, Danny Carroll *zoo biologist*
Whitt, Ward *science educator*
Wiesel, Torsten Nils *neurobiologist, educator*

Willner, Judith P. *clinical geneticist, pediatrician, educator*
Windhager, Erich Ernst *physiologist, educator*
Young, Michael Warren *geneticist, educator*
Yuferov, Vadim *research scientist*

**Orangeburg**
Yaragudri, Vinod K. *neuroscientist, researcher*

**Orchard Park**
Urbanski, Jane F. *retired microbiologist*

**Owego**
Kemp, Eugene Thomas *retired veterinarian*

**Palisades**
Richards, Paul Granston *geophysics educator, seismologist*

**Pearl River**
Zagursky, Robert *microbiologist, researcher*

**Pelham**
Hembury, Todd *science educator*

**Peru**
Dawson, James Clifford *environmental science educator, geologist*

**Pittsford**
Coleman, Paul David *neurobiology educator, researcher*

**Plattsburgh**
Mihuc, Timothy Brian *science foundation director*

**Pleasantville**
Tao, Lixin *computer science educator*

**Port Chester**
Brescia, Alicia *science educator, vice principal*

**Port Washington**
Kwak, Seung-Keon *research scientist*

**Potsdam**
Baymak, Melek Sirin *science educator, researcher*

**Purchase**
Ehrman, Lee *geneticist, educator*

**Rochester**
Alder, Donna Bordelon *biologist, educator*
Chen, Di *bone biologist*
Clarkson, Thomas William *toxicologist, educator*
Doty, Robert William *neuroscientist, physiologist, educator*
Frisina, Robert Dana *neuroscientist, educator*
Huxlin, Krystel Raluka *neuroscientist, educator*
Polevoda, Bogdan V. *research scientist*
Rodgers, Suzanne Hooker *physiologist, consultant*
Rose, Robert Charles *virologist, researcher*

**Rome**
Simonin, Howard A. *biologist*

**Saint Albans**
Norfleet, Leontine Sandra *retired biologist*

**Schenectady**
Fleischer, Robert Louis *geology professor*
Stevens, Roy W. *microbiologist, researcher, photographer*

**Stanfordville**
Tetor, David R. *agriculturist, consultant*

**Stony Brook**
Lennarz, William Joseph *research biologist, educator*
Rohlf, F. James *biologist, educator*
Sreebny, Leo M. *oral biology and pathology professor*
Vencl, Fredric Vincent *biologist, researcher*

**Syracuse**
Lawler, Mark Clyde *geology professor*
Meinig, Donald William *geography educator*
Stork, Christine Mary *toxicologist, pharmacist*
Verrillo, Ronald Thomas *neuroscience educator, researcher*

**Tivoli**
Keesing, Felicia *biology professor*
Sethi, Gautam *environmental professor*

**Troy**
Berg, Daniel *science and technology educator*
Ehrlich, Henry Lutz *biology professor*
Watson, E Bruce *science educator*
Zurbenko, Igor Georg *science educator*

**Upton**
Chaudhari, Praveen *science administrator, materials physicist*
Paul, Peter *science administrator*
Sutherland, Betsy Middleton *biologist*

**Valhalla**
Darzynkiewicz, Zbigniew D. *research scientist*

**Victor**
Morris, G. Michael *science educator*

**White Plains**
Smith, Gerard Peter *neuroscientist*

**Yaphank**
Narain, Ralph B. *biologist*

**Yorktown Heights**
d'Heurle, François Max *research scientist, engineering educator*
Wynne, James J. *research scientist*

## NORTH CAROLINA

**Asheboro**
Jones, David M. *zoological park administrator*

**Asheville**
Parresol, Bernard Ross *research scientist, statistician*
Puckett, Derek Lee *biologist, researcher*

**Beaufort**
Cox, Tara M. *marine biologist, researcher*
Ramus, Joseph S. *marine biologist*

**Boone**
Martin, Vicki Joan *biology professor*

**Buies Creek**
Guzman, Karen *science educator*

**Carrboro**
Baumhover, Alfred Henry *entomologist, researcher*

**Chapel Hill**
Feduccia, J. Alan *biologist, educator*
Judd, Burke Haycock *geneticist*
Mueller, Nancy Schneider *retired biology professor*
Richardson, Stephen Giles *biotechnologist, director*
Rogers, John James William *geology educator*
Salmon, Edward Dickinson *cell biologist, educator*
Smithies, Oliver *geneticist, educator*
Stumpf, Walter Erich *cell biology and pharmacology professor, researcher*
Zeng, Ming *molecular biologist, researcher*

**Charlotte**
Horowitz, Carol Y. *science educator*
Ruiz, Macedonio *entomologist*

**Clemmons**
Suber, Robert L., Sr. *toxicologist, researcher*

**Durham**
Blum, Jacob Joseph *physiologist, educator*
Gilbert, John Ray *geneticist, researcher*
Gillham, Nicholas Wright *geneticist, educator*
Hogan, Brigid L.M. *molecular biologist*
Jarvis, Erich David *neurobiologist, educator*
Keene, Jack Donald *molecular genetics and microbiology educator*
Kulminski, Aliaksandr M. *research scientist*
Mushak, Paul *toxicologist, consultant*
Nevins, Joseph Roy *geneticist, educator*
Pearsall, Samuel Haff III *ecologist, geographer, foundation administrator*
Pimm, Stuart L. *ecology educator*
Rouse, Doris Jane *physiologist, research scientist*
Schmidt-Nielsen, Knut *physiologist, educator*

**Elizabeth City**
Storie, Eric Duane *science administrator*

**Elon**
Touchette, Brant William *biologist, researcher*

**Fayetteville**
Dembosky, John A., Jr. *science educator*

**Greensboro**
Goktepe, Ipek *food scientist, educator*
Noble, Ralph C. *animal scientist, department chairman*

**Greenville**
Meggs, William Joel *toxicologist, allergist, emergency physician, educator*
Wiley, John Edwin *cytogeneticist*

**Hendersonville**
Brittain, James Edward *science and technology educator, researcher*

**Morrisville**
Bolognesi, Dani Paul *virologist, educator*

**Raleigh**
Annetta, Len *science educator*
Aronson, Arthur Lawrence *retired veterinarian, toxicologist, pharmacologist*
Barefoot, Aldos Cortez, Jr. *forester, educator*
Benson, D(avid) Michael *plant pathologist*
Brown, Robert Dale *wildlife science educator, dean*
Burkholder, Joann M *harmful algae educator*
Cook, Maurice Gayle *soil science educator, consultant*
Cooper, Arthur Wells *ecologist, educator*
Davey, Charles Bingham *soil scientist, educator*
Deitz, Lewis Levering *entomologist, educator, researcher*
Dunphy, Edward James *science educator, crop science extension specialist*
Edens, Frank Wesley *physiologist*
Goodman, Major Merlin *botanical sciences educator*
Hardin, James W. *botanist, educator, herbarium curator*
Havlin, John Leroy *soil scientist, educator*
Hodgson, Ernest *toxicologist, educator*
Mackay, Trudy Frances Charlene *genetics professor*
Moore, Jeannette Aileen *animal nutrition educator*
Moreland, Donald Edwin *physiologist*
Qu, Rongda *biologist, educator*
Sanders, Douglas Charles *horticulturist, researcher, educator*
See, Miles Todd *animal scientist, educator*
Stuber, Charles William *retired genetics educator, researcher*
Timothy, David Harry *retired biology professor*

**Research Triangle Park**
Bond, Enriqueta Carter *science administrator*
Fought, Lorianne *plant pathologist*
Haynes, Victoria F. *science administrator*
Mumford, Stephen Douglas *research scientist*

**Wilmington**
Kelley, Patricia Hagelin *geology educator*
Mintzes, Joel J. *biology professor, researcher*

**Wingate**
Dirks, Amie Jeanette *physiologist, educator*

**Winston Salem**
Hegde, Ashok *research scientist, educator*
Laxminarayana, Dama *geneticist, researcher, educator*
Porter-Kelley, Johanna Marie *microbiology educator, researcher*
Swords, William Edward *microbiologist, educator*

## NORTH DAKOTA

**Bisbee**
Keller, Michelle R. *science educator*

**Bismarck**
Nordlie, Margaret A. *biology professor, director*

**Fargo**
Schmidt, Claude Henri *retired science administrator*

**Grand Forks**
Carlson, Edward C. *anatomy educator, cell biologist, department chairman*
Seelan, Santhosh Kumar *science educator, department chairman*

## OHIO

**Akron**
Spencer, Jeff *biologist, educator*

**Archbold**
Henry, Dinah D. *science educator*

**Athens**
Cuddington, Kim Michelle *ecologist, educator*

**Bowling Green**
Clark, Eloise Elizabeth *biologist, educator*
Nagi, Lillian S. *biology professor*

**Cincinnati**
Biagini, Raymond E. *toxicologist, immunochemist scientist*
Chistyakov, Dmitry Alexandrovich *research scientist*
Farage, Miranda A. *research scientist*
McDaniels, Audrey Evelyn *microbiologist*
Meller, Jaroslaw *biotechnologist, information scientist, educator*
Miller, Brian Douglas *science educator*
Nebert, Daniel Walter *molecular geneticist, research administrator*
Saal, Howard Max *clinical geneticist, pediatrician, educator*
Schaefer, Frank William III *microbiologist, researcher*
Schiff, Gilbert Martin *virologist, microbiologist, medical educator*
Silberstein, Edward Bernard *nuclear medicine educator, oncologist, researcher*
Souter, Philip Frank *research scientist*
Ure, Colin *research scientist*
Zegers, Mirjam M. *cell biologist, researcher*

**Cleveland**
Blackwell, John *science educator*
Dell'Osso, Louis Frank *neuroscience educator*
Jacobs, Michael Roy *microbiologist, researcher*
Lando, Jerome Burton *macromolecular science educator*
Suri, Jasjit S. *research scientist*
Taylor, Steve Henry *zoologist*

**Columbus**
Ausich, William Irl *geology educator*
Blanco, Humberto *soil scientist, researcher*
Braig, Eugene C., IV, *biologist*
Cheesman, Kerry Lee *biology educator, researcher*
Corbato, Charles Edward *geology educator, academic administrator*
Croce, Carlo M. *research scientist*
Faure, Gunter *geology educator*
Floyd, Gary Leon *plant cell biologist*
Foland, Kenneth A. *geological sciences educator*
Fry, Donald Lewis *physiologist, educator*
Glaser, Ronald *microbiologist, educator*
Hinchcliff, Kenneth W. *veterinarian, educator*
Kapral, Frank Albert *microbiologist and immunology educator*
Moyer, Ryan P. *marine biologist*
Newsom, Gerald Higley *astronomy educator*
Ouyang, Anli *research scientist*
Peterle, Tony John *zoologist, educator*
Piggrem, Gary Wayne *science educator, writer*
Roth, Robert Earl *ecologist, educator*
Sostaric, Joe Zeljko *research scientist*
Triplehorn, Charles A. *entomologist, educator*
Viatchenko-Karpinski, Serge *biologist, researcher*
von Recum, Andreas F. *veterinarian, bioengineer*
Westman, Judith Ann *clinical geneticist, dean*
Wood, Jackie Dale *physiologist, educator, researcher*
Woodley, Frederick William *molecular biologist, geneticist, educator*
Zartman, David Lester *retired zoology educator, researcher*

**Dayton**
Gomez-Cambronero, Julian *cell biologist, biochemist, educator*
Hofmann, Marie-Claude *cell biologist, educator, research scientist*

**Delaware**
Bahrick, Harry Phillip *science educator, researcher*

**Elyria**
Foote, Nathan Maxted *retired physical science educator*

**Granville**
Haubrich, Robert Rice *biology professor*

**Hamilton**
Munson, Richard Howard *horticulturist*

**Oberlin**
Benzing, David Hill *biologist, educator*
Luck, Dennis Noel *biologist, educator, researcher*

**Oxford**
Eshbaugh, W(illiam) Hardy *botanist, educator*
Robinson, Michael Lee *biologist*

**Perrysburg**
Cranny, Theresa M. *veterinarian*

**Saint Clairsville**
Butler, Andrew Kimmins, Jr. *physiologist, educator*

**Springfield**
Ryu, Kyoo-Hai Lee *physiologist*

**Toledo**
Chakraborty, Joana *physiologist, educator, science administrator*
Cosentino, Mary Jane *retired science educator*
Lee, Soon Jin *geneticist, educator*
McGrady, Angele Vial *psychophysiologist*
Noormets, Asko *ecologist*

**Wooster**
Saif, Linda J. *veterinary scientist, virologist, immunologist*
Velleman, Sandra Gayle *molecular biology educator, researcher*

**Wyoming**
Cooley, William Edward *research scientist, consultant*

**Yellow Springs**
Webb, Paul *physiologist, educator, researcher, consultant*

**Youngstown**
Amin, Isam Eldin *science educator, researcher*

**Zanesville**
Kish, Steven Gene *science educator*

## OKLAHOMA

**Ada**
Wilson, John Thomas *microbiologist*

**Edmond**
Stone, Paul Alan *biologist, educator*

**Langston**
Mallik, Muhammad Abdul-Bari *soil microbiologist*

**Lawton**
Pazoureck, Rebecca Kieffer *food sciences professor*

**Norman**
Bluestein, Howard Bruce *meteorology educator*
Brown, Harley Procter, Jr. *zoology educator, entomologist, researcher*
Hutchison, Victor Hobbs *biologist, educator*
Kessler, Edwin *meteorology educator, consultant*
Sonleitner, Frank Joseph *zoology educator*
Taylor, Kenneth Lapham *science educator*

**Oklahoma City**
Branch, John Curtis *biology professor, lawyer*
Dubowski, Kurt Max *toxicologist, educator, consultant*
Lewis, Russell *toxicologist, researcher*

**Park Hill**
Yeager, Debra Lyn *science educator*

**Pawhuska**
Strahm, Samuel Edward *veterinarian*

**Ponca City**
Wann, Laymond Doyle *retired petroleum research scientist*

**Sand Springs**
Quinn, Art Jay *retired veterinarian, educator*

**Shawnee**
Way, Helen Sue *science educator*

**Stillwater**
Grischkowsky, Daniel Richard *research scientist, educator*
Royer, Tom A. *entomologist, educator*

**Tulsa**
Norvell, John Edmondson III *retired neuroscientist, educator*

**Weatherford**
Boggs, Lisa Lynn *biology professor*

## OREGON

**Albany**
Ares, Adrian *research scientist*

**Ashland**
Christianson, Roger Gordon *biology professor, department chairman*

**Beaverton**
Wall, Brian Raymond *forest economist, business consultant, researcher*
Wang, Baoliang (Bob Wang) *applications scientist, researcher*

**Clackamas**
Kostow, Kathryn E. *conservation biologist*

**Corvallis**
Chambers, Kenton Lee *botany educator*
Cho, Jang-Cheon *microbiologist, researcher*
Chung, Woon-Gye *toxicologist, researcher*

**Frakes**, Rodney Vance *plant geneticist, educator*
Loper, Joyce E. *plant pathologist, educator*
Morita, Richard Yukio *microbiology and oceanography educator*
Poinar, George Orlo, Jr. *entomologist, science educator*
Smith, Alvin Winfred *veterinarian, educator*
Trempy, Janine Elysia *microbiologist*
Westwood, Melvin Neil *horticulturist, pomologist*

**Eugene**
Matthews, Brian W. *molecular biology educator*

**Florence**
Marble, Duane Francis *geography educator, researcher*

**Pendleton**
Klepper, Elizabeth Lee *retired physiologist*

**Portland**
Balkowiec, Agnieszka Zofia *science educator, researcher*
Cady, Sherry L. *astrobiologist, educator*
Hagenstein, William David *forester, consultant*
Khalil, Mohammad Aslam Khan *environmental science educator, engineering educator, physics professor*

**Salem**
Erickson, Ray Charles *retired wildlife biologist*

**Talent**
MacMillen, Richard Edward *biological sciences educator, researcher*

**Wilsonville**
Gordon, John Charles *forestry educator*

**Yachats**
Gerdemann, James Wessel *plant pathologist, educator*

## PENNSYLVANIA

**Annville**
Kline, Donald E. *science educator*
Verhoek, Susan Elizabeth *botany educator*

**Bala Cynwyd**
Corliss, John Ozro *zoology educator*

**Bethlehem**
Kodama, Kenneth Philip *science educator, academic administrator*

**Bryn Mawr**
Crawford, Maria Luisa Buse *geology educator*
Hackman, Nadine Brokaw *veterinarian*

**Cheyney**
Wenyi, Bi *science educator*

**Collegeville**
Billiard, Julia *cell biologist, researcher*

**Danville**
Enman, John Aubrey *science educator*

**Doylestown**
Mishler, John Milton (Yochanan Menashsheh ben Shaul) *science educator, artist*

**Du Bois**
Forthun, Larry F. *science educator, consultant*

**Edinboro**
Miller, G(erson) H(arry) *science administrator, mathematician, computer scientist, chemist*

**Elkins Park**
Hutapea, Parsaoran *science educator, researcher*

**Exton**
Hidalgo, Ismael J. *pharmaceutical scientist*

**Gettysburg**
Hendrix, Sherman Samuel *biology professor, researcher*

**Glenside**
Kim, Kathryn Spitzer *geneticist, consultant, science educator*

**Hanover**
Mayer, Jody Lynn (Jody Lynn Noel) *exercise physiologist*

**Harrisburg**
Kilbride, Susan A. Richie *physiologist, researcher*

**Haverford**
DiBerardino, Marie Antoinette *developmental biologist, educator*

**Hershey**
Chinoy, Mala R. *biologist, educator*
Hopper, Anita Klein *molecular genetics educator*
Undar, Akif *research scientist, biomedical engineer, educator*
Zagon, Ian Stuart *neuroscience and anatomy educator, researcher, inventor*

**Horsham**
Ahmed, Elias *microbiologist*

**King Of Prussia**
Perlstein, Itay *research scientist*

**Latrobe**
Rhodes, Michael E. *biologist, educator*

**Lewisburg**
Shapiro, Arthur Gilman *science educator*
Sojka, Gary Allan *biologist, educator, academic administrator*

**Lock Haven**
Dondong, Jia *nanoscience educator, physics professor*

**Mansfield**
Sternick, John Lewis *biology professor*

**Media**
Brobeck, John Raymond *physiology educator*

**Mifflinville**
Farber, Phillip Andrew *retired biological and allied health sciences educator*

**Milton**
Kurtz, Dborah L. *science educator, department chairman*

**Muncy**
Temons, Mark Joseph *science educator*

**Narberth**
Nathanson, Neal *virologist, epidemiologist, educator*

**Philadelphia**
Armstrong, Clay *physiology educator*
Brinster, Ralph Lawrence *biologist, educator*
Cerundolo, Rosario *veterinarian, educator*
Dewan, Vikram H. *zoological park administrator*
Eisenstein, Toby K. *microbiology professor*
Fisher, Aron Baer *physiology educator*
Furth, John Jacob *molecular biologist, educator, pathologist*
Hammond, Benjamin Franklin *microbiologist, educator*
Hua, Xianxin *cell and cancer biology educator*
Jackson, Laird Gray *geneticist, internist, educator*
Kaji, Akira *microbiology scientist, educator*
Koprowski, Hilary *microbiologist, educator*
Lambertsen, Christian James *environmental physiologist, physician, educator*
Patrick, Ruth (Mrs. Ruth Hodge Van Dusen) *botany educator, curator*
Pepe, Frank A. *cell and developmental biology educator*
Pyeritz, Reed Edwin *geneticist, educator, medical researcher*
Robert, Kalb Gordon *neuroscientist, educator, neurologist*
Rubin, Benjamin Arnold *microbiologist, immunologist, medical educator, researcher*
Scandura, Joseph Michael *neuroscientist, application developer*
Schutsky, Keith Barry *neuroscientist, researcher*
Silvers, Willys Kent *geneticist*
Skalka, Anna Marie *molecular biologist*
Testa, Joseph R. *cytogeneticist*
Tucker, Anita Lynn *science educator*
Wang, Jiongjiong *neuroscientist, educator*
White, Howard D. *information science educator*

**Phoenixville**
Hanlon, Barbara Jean *family and consumer sciences educator*

**Pipersville**
Erickson, Edward Leonard *biotechnologist, consultant*

**Pitcairn**
Rose, Robert Didier *neurophysiologist*

**Pittsburgh**
Amara, Susan *neuroscientist*
Amemiya, Shigeru *science educator*
Berry, Guy Curtis *polymer science educator, researcher*
Cassidy, William Arthur *geology and planetary science educator*
Cruz, Robyn Flaum *research scientist*
Druzdzel, Marek Jozef *information systems educator, researcher*
Ehrlich, Garth David *molecular biologist*
Feingold, David Sidney *microbiology and biochemistry educator, researcher*
Gollin, Susanne Merle *cell biologist, researcher*
Harrold, Ronald Thomas *research scientist*
Hatfull, Graham F. *microbiologist, educator*
Jones, Elizabeth Winifred *biology professor*
Kanade, Takeo *science educator, director*
Kiger, Robert William *botanist, researcher, science historian, educator*
LaJohn, Lawrence Anthony *research scientist*
Lazo, John Stephen *science educator, director*
Lyons-Weiler, James *science educator, bioinformatics educator, composer, singer*
Marazita, Mary Louise *genetics researcher*
Marsh, Gary Martin *environmental biostatistician epidemiologist educator*
McPherson, Elizabeth Wright *clinical geneticist*
Moore, Robert Yates *neuroscience educator*
Partanen, Carl Richard *biology professor*
Plaskon, Juanita Eve *biotechnologist, educator*
Saaty, Thomas Lorie *science educator*
Schatten, Gerald Phillip *stem cell biologist, reproductive biologist, educator*
Seol, Dai-Wu *geneticist, educator*
Willke, Theodore Lawrence *research facility director*

**State College**
Madjid, A. Hamid *retired science educator*

**Swarthmore**
Gilbert, Scott Frederick *biologist, educator, author*
O'Connell, Virginia Adams *science educator*

**Titusville**
Tress, Nancy Barsic *biologist, educator*

**Union City**
Thomas, Paul Milton *retired science educator*

**University Park**
Barnes, Hubert Lloyd *geochemistry educator*
Brenchley, Jean Elnora *microbiologist, researcher, science administrator*
Buskirk, Elsworth Robert *physiologist, educator*

Coleman, Michael Murray *polymer science educator*
Fedoroff, Nina Vsevolod *research scientist, consultant, educator*
Fowler, H(oratio) Seymour *retired science educator*
Grenfell, Bryan Thomas *biology professor*
Hedges, Stephen Blair *biology professor, researcher*
Preston, Stephanie Danette *science educator, researcher*
Price, Mitch *biology professor*
Roy, Della Martin *materials science educator, researcher*
Stinson, Richard Floyd *retired horticulturist, educator*

**Valley Forge**
Erb, Robert Allan *physical scientist*

**Villanova**
Monck, Mary C. *science educator*

**Wayne**
Krutsick, Robert Stanley *retired science administrator*
Thelen, Edmund *research executive*

**West Point**
Schaffner, Carolyn Marie *research administrator, biologist*

**Wilkes Barre**
Hayes, Wilbur Frank *retired biology professor*

**Wynnewood**
Prendergast, George C. *cancer biologist, researcher*
Rubin, Leonard Sidney *physiologist, educator, researcher*

**York**
Buckel, Mark Andrew *biologist, educator*

## RHODE ISLAND

**Cranston**
Vavala, Domenic Anthony *research scientist, educator, retired military officer*

**Kingston**
Hufnagel, Linda Ann *biology professor, researcher*
Markin, Karen Mary *research scientist, journalist*

**Narragansett**
Goos, Roger Delmon *retired mycologist*

**Newport**
Chace, Jameson Fales *ecologist, educator*
Koch, Robert Michael *research scientist, consultant, educator*

**Providence**
Block, Bartley Cavanough *biologist, educator*
Donoghue, John Phillip *neuroscience educator, neurotechnology company executive*
Dowben, Robert Morris *physiologist, educator*
Schmitt, Johanna Marie *plant population biologist, educator*
Takao, Motoharu *physiologist*

## SOUTH CAROLINA

**Aiken**
Bertsch, Paul M. *ecologist, director*
Zhang, Chuanlun *microbiologist, researcher*

**Charleston**
Goodrich, James A. *veterinarian, researcher*
Ogretmen, Besim *science educator, molecular biologist, researcher*
Pandey, Janardan P. *agronomist, educator*
Simson, Jo Anne *retired anatomy and cell biology educator*
Yu, Shan Ping *neuroscientist, educator*

**Clemson**
Camper, Nyal Dwight *plant physiology educator*

**Columbia**
Aelion, C. Marjorie *science educator*
Koley, Goutam *science educator*
Raychoudhury, Samir *biology professor, researcher*
Watabe, Norimitsu *biologist, marine biologist, educator*
Wideman, Ida Devlin *science educator*

**Conway**
Dame, Richard Franklin *marine biology educator*

**Cordova**
Hill, Elizabeth Lee *science educator*

**Florence**
Rae, John Gibson III *biology professor*
West, Jesse Michael *pediatric neuropsychologist*

**Greenville**
Cureton, Claudette Hazel Chapman *biology professor*

**Hilton Head Island**
Adams, William Hensley *ecologist, educator*
Lefer, Allan Mark *physiologist*

**Little River**
Maloney, Terry *horticulturist, educator*

**Mount Pleasant**
Friedrich, Lawrence Vincent *research scientist*

**North Charleston**
Fiedorczyk, Daniel Paul *science educator*

**Pawleys Island**
Kay, Thomas Oliver *agricultural consultant*

**Pickens**
Lofink, Glenda Jean *science educator*

**Prosperity**
Long, William McMurray *physiology educator*

**Rock Hill**
Mitchell, Paula Levin *biology professor, editor*

**Simpsonville**
Pratt, Harry Davis *retired entomologist*

**Spartanburg**
Leonard, Walter Raymond *retired biology professor*

**Wadmalaw Island**
Henne, James Patrick *marine biologist*

## SOUTH DAKOTA

**Brookings**
Jenks, Jonathan Alden *biologist, educator*
Moldenhauer, William Calvin *soil scientist*

## TENNESSEE

**Clarksville**
Puhl, Jennifer Joyce *physiologist*

**Cookeville**
Airhart, Douglas L. *horticulturist, educator*

**Fayetteville**
Wolfhard, Hans Georg *retired research scientist*

**Franklin**
Hill, Jon Matthew *science educator, secondary school educator*
Thornsberry, Clyde *microbiologist*

**Kingsport**
Ogbonnaya, Chuks Alfred *entomologist, agronomist, environmentalist*

**Knoxville**
Anderson, Ilse Janell *clinical geneticist*
Bentley, Michael Lee *science educator*
Chen, James Pai-fun *biology professor, researcher*
Childers, Michael *science educator*
Gavrilets, Sergey Yurievich *biologist, educator*
Mazur, Peter *physiologist, cryobiologist*
McMahon, Susan Henderson *biology professor*
Simberloff, Daniel *biologist, educator*

**Loudon**
Stafford, William Franklin *veterinarian, educator*

**Memphis**
Curran, Thomas *molecular biologist, educator*
Freeman, Bob A. *retired microbiology educator, retired dean*
Gottlieb, Eric Inness *science educator*
Hofmann, Polly A. *physiologist, science educator*
Howe, Martha Morgan *microbiologist, educator*
Li, Wei *science educator, director*
Webster, Robert G. *virologist, educator*

**Nashville**
Catania, Kenneth C. *neuroscientist, educator*
Fanning, Ellen *biology professor, research scientist*
Granner, Daryl Kitley *physiology and medicine educator*
Orgebin-Crist, Marie-Claire *retired biology professor, department chairman*
Phillips, John A(tlas) III *geneticist, educator*
Tulsiani, Daulatram P. *biologist, researcher*
Zhou, Suping *biologist, research scientist, educator*

**Oak Ridge**
Aytug, Tolga *science educator*
Culiat, Cymbeline Tancongco *geneticist*

**Sewanee**
Yeatman, Harry Clay *biologist, educator*

## TEXAS

**Amarillo**
Cummins, Joseph M. *biotechnology company executive*

**Arlington**
Formanowicz, Daniel Robert *science educator, department chairman*
Smith, Charles Isaac *geology educator*

**Austin**
Biesele, John Julius *biologist, educator*
Drummond Borg, Lesley Margaret *geneticist*
Fryxell, Greta Albrecht *marine botany educator, oceanographer*
Grant, Verne Edwin *biology professor*
Holz, Robert Kenneth *retired geography educator*
Hubbs, Clark *zoologist, researcher*
Hussain, Muhammad Mustafa *research scientist*
Jacobson, Antone Gardner *retired zoology educator*
Meyers, Lauren Ancel *biologist*
Patterson, Donald Eugene *research scientist*
Qiu, Lili *science educator*
Simpson, Beryl Brintnall *botany educator*
Sutton, Harry Eldon *geneticist, educator*

**Bandera**
Bartley, William Call *science administrator*

**Beaumont**
Reay-Jones, Francis Peter Fortnum *entomologist, researcher*

**Bellaire**
Loonam, Anna McCredie *science educator*

**Bogata**
Marris, Roy O. *agriculturist, consultant*

**Brooks City-Base**
Miller, Carolyn Lyons *microbiologist, military officer*

**Bryan**
Julson, Amanda Palmer *science educator*
Milford, Murray Hudson *retired soil science educator*

**Bushland**
Li, Hong *soil scientist, researcher*

**Cedar Park**
Albin, Leslie Owens *biology professor*

**College Station**
Acuff, Gary R. *food scientist, educator*
Armstrong, Robert Beall *physiologist, educator*
Beaver, Bonnie Veryle *veterinarian, educator*
Borlaug, Norman Ernest *agricultural scientist*
Drees, Bastiaan Meijer *entomologist*
Gali, Hariprasad *research scientist*
Granger, Harris Joseph *physiologist, educator*
Hagel, Kris *research scientist*
Hall, Timothy Couzens *biology professor, consultant*
Kohel, Russell James *geneticist*
McCrady, James David *veterinarian, educator*
Neill, William Harold, Jr. *fisheries science professor, researcher*
Qian, Yongchang *molecular toxicologist*
Storey, J. Benton *horticulturist, educator*
Tai-Seale, Ming *science educator, consultant*
Wilding, Lawrence Paul *retired pedology educator, soil science consultant*

**Corsicana**
Carroll, Ray Dean, Sr. *veterinarian*

**Dallas**
Brown, Michael Stuart *geneticist, educator, science administrator*
Goldstein, Joseph Leonard *molecular biologist, educator*
McKnight, Steven Lanier *molecular biologist*
Parada, Luis Fernando *science educator*
Reinert, James A. *entomology educator*
Russell, David W. *molecular geneticist*
Sudhof, Thomas Christian *molecular genetics educator*
Vitetta, Ellen S. *microbiologist, educator, immunologist*

**Diboll**
Fisher, Richard Forrest *research scientist, editor-in-chief*

**El Paso**
Gill, Thomas Edward *science educator*
Moschopoulos, Panagis *science educator*
Salas, Guillermo *biologist, educator, medical technician*
Silva, Michael Anthony *biologist, educator*

**Fort Worth**
Gracy, Robert *science educator*
Kelly, Janet *science educator*

**Galveston**
Esenaliev, Rinat O. *science educator, lab administrator*
Frederickson, Christopher John *neuroscientist*
Makino, Shinji *virologist, educator*
Markides, Kyriakos Socrates *gerontology educator*
Murphy, Frederick Augustus *virologist, researcher*
Willis, William Darrell, Jr. *neuroscientist, educator*
Zimmerman, Roger Joseph *fishery biologist*

**Georgetown**
Deviney, Marvin Lee, Jr. *science administrator, director*

**Houston**
Baughn, Robert Elroy *microbiology educator*
De Bremaecker, Jean-Claude *geophysics educator*
Diagaradjane, Parmeswaran *research scientist*
Dikeocha, Ndu *biology professor*
Durham, Susan K. *research scientist*
Estes, Mary K. *virologist*
Jurtshuk, Peter, Jr. *microbiologist, educator*
Koo, Jaseok Peter *science educator*
Levy, Eugene Howard *planetary sciences educator, researcher*
Lin, Shiaw-Yih (Phoebus Lin) *cell biologist, researcher, medical educator*
Mao, Li *molecular biologist, educator*
Mendelson, Robert Allen *polymer scientist, rheologist*
Mgmeme, Festus N. *biology professor, pharmacist*
Nelson, David Loren *geneticist, educator*
Shetty, Gunapala *biologist, researcher, educator*
Steele, James Harlan *retired veterinarian*
Strong, Louise Connally *geneticist*
Wriggers, Willy Rudolf *science educator*

**Kingsville**
Henke, Scott E. *wildlife educator*

**Kingwood**
van Beem, Janny *geneticist, researcher*

**La Ward**
Lin, Ming T. *plant pathologist*

**Lubbock**
Chatterjee, Sankar *geology educator*
Hentges, David John *microbiology educator*
Jackson, Raymond Carl *cytogeneticist*
Skoog, Gerald Duane *science educator*
Wendt, Charles William *soil scientist, educator*

**Pearland**
Shurtleff, Malcolm C. *plant pathologist, consultant*
Würsig, Bernd Gerhard *marine biology educator*
Zhou, Juhua *molecular biologist*

**Plano**
MacAlpine, Michelle Lewis *neuroscientist*

**Port Aransas**
Schake, Lowell Martin *zoology educator, writer*

**Richardson**
Atzori, Marco *neuroscientist, educator*
Gray, Donald Melvin *molecular and cell biology educator*
McMechan, George *science educator*
Wood, Joseph George *neuroscientist, educator*

**Rockport**
Berkebile, Charles Alan *geology educator, hydrogeology researcher*

**Rockwall**
Villarino, Mario Alberto *veterinarian, researcher*

**Round Rock**
Schneider, Dennis Ray *microbiology educator and executive*

**San Angelo**
Lara, Cynthia Lynn *science educator*

**San Antonio**
Akella, Umasundari Srivenkata *research scientist*
Bai, Yidong *molecular biologist, educator*
Burch, James Leo *science research institute executive*
Göring, Harald Heinz Herbert *geneticist, researcher*
Irving, George Washington III *veterinarian, researcher, small business executive*
Lyons, Kelly Guadalupe *science educator, researcher*
Mamtani, Manju Rameshlal *geneticist, researcher*
McComas, David John *science administrator, space physicist*
McIntosh, Dennis Keith *veterinarian, consultant*
Mummidi, Srinivas *veterinarian, research scientist, educator*
Nedal, Arar Hamdi *research scientist*
Perry, George *neuroscientist, educator*
Wahl, Rosemarie *biologist, educator*
Wang, Yufeng *science educator*

**San Marcos**
Dharmasiri, Nihal *molecular biologist, educator*
McLean, Robert James Cameron *microbiologist, educator*

**Smithville**
Scofield, Virginia Lee *research scientist*

**Spring**
Griffin, Kelly Ann *science educator*

**Uvalde**
Ramsey, Frank Allen *veterinarian, retired army officer*

**Vernon**
Malinowski, Dariusz Piotr *horticulturist, educator*

**Waco**
Hillis, William Daniel *biology professor*
Lind, Owen Thomas *biology professor*

**Warda**
Kunze, George William *retired soil scientist*

## UTAH

**Brookside**
McMahon, James Patrick *ecologist, consultant*

**Cedar City**
Mayron, Lewis Walter *clinical ecology consultant*

**Logan**
Aust, Steven Douglas *biochemistry, biotechnology and toxicology educator*
McNeal, Lyle Glen *science educator, rancher, consultant*
Rasmussen, Harry Paul *horticulture and landscape educator*

**Providence**
Vest, Hyrum Grant, Jr. *retired horticultural sciences educator*

**Provo**
Blake, George Rowland *soil scientist, educator, environmental scientist, researcher*
Crookston, R. Kent *agronomy educator*
Gray, Howard Richard *science educator*
Hastriter, Michael Wayne *medical entomologist*
McArthur, Eldon Durant *geneticist, researcher*
Woodbury, Dixon John *physiologist, educator, research scientist*
Zhang, Libing *botanist*

**Salt Lake City**
Carlquist, John Frederick *microbiologist, immunologist*
Coley, Phyllis Dewing *biology professor*
Newmark, William D. *conservation biologist*
Salisbury, Frank Boyer *botanist, educator, writer*

## VERMONT

**Brattleboro**
Ames, Adelbert III *neuroscientist, educator*

**Burlington**
Gouli, Vladimir Vasilievich *entomologist*
Heinrich, Bernd *biologist, educator*
Keeton, William Scott *ecologist, educator*
Kindstedt, Paul Stephen *food science educator*

**Charlotte**
Hamilton, Lawrence Stanley *forest consultant*
Melby, Edward Carlos, Jr. *veterinarian*

**Greensboro**
Hill, Lewis Reuben *horticulturist, nursery owner, writer*

**Hinesburg**
Fay, Glenn Mills, Jr. *science educator*

**Morrisville**
Lechevalier, Hubert Arthur *microbiology educator*
Lechevalier, Mary Pfeil *retired microbiologist, educator*

**Waterbury**
Travis, Randall Howard *retired physiologist, retired endocrinologist*

## VIRGINIA

**Alexandria**
Borum, Olin Henry *retired government scientist*
Vosbeck, Elizabeth Just *retired geneticist*
Woolley, Mary Elizabeth *science administrator, advocate*

**Amissville**
Hunter, Beverly Claire *research scientist, educator*

**Arlington**
Abler, Ronald Francis *geography educator*
Bement, Arden Lee, Jr. *science foundation director*
Boesz, Christine C. *science foundation administrator*
Brown, Sandra *forest ecologist, researcher*
Cehelsky, Marta *scientific organization executive*
Crosby, Michael P. *science administrator*
Fuchs, Roland John *geography educator, academic administrator*
Glaser, Gerard R. *science administrator*
Harris, William James, Jr. *retired science administrator*
Held, Joe Roger *retired veterinarian*
Olsen, Kathie Lynn *science foundation director*
O'Neill, Brian *science administrator*
Ordway, Frederick Ira III *science educator, consultant, researcher, writer*
Vasquez, Jo Anne *retired science educator*

**Ashburn**
Bawa, Raj *biotechnology educator, nanotechnologist*
Rubin, Gerald Mayer *biochemistry educator*

**Blacksburg**
Burkhart, Harold Eugene *forester, educator*
Cowles, Joe Richard *biology professor*
De Datta, Surajit Kumar *soil scientist, agronomist, educator*
Gregoire, Timothy Gordon *forestry researcher*
Kelly, James Michael *plant and soil scientist*
McKenna, James Richard *agronomy educator*
Porter, Duncan MacNair *research scientist*

**Charlottesville**
Chevalier, Roger Alan *astronomy educator, consultant*
Garrett, Reginald Hooker *biology professor, researcher*
Hornberger, George Milton *environmental science educator*
Menaker, Michael *biology professor*
Molhoek, Kerrington Ramsey *research scientist*
Templeton, Dennis J. *research scientist, pathologist*
Tuttle, Jeremy Ballou *neuroscientist*

**Chester**
White, Jessica Bailey *biology professor*

**Dahlgren**
Rayms-Keller, Alfredo *molecular biologist*

**Fairfax**
Soyfer, Valery Nikolayevich *geneticist, biophysicist*
Sun, Donglian *meteorologist*

**Falls Church**
Bryan, Billie Marie (Mrs. James A. Mackey) *retired biologist*
Hart, C(harles) W(illard), Jr. *zoologist, curator*

**Farmville**
Palombella, Anthony Lewis *biology professor*

**Front Royal**
Douglas, J(ocelyn) Fielding *toxicologist, consultant*

**Galax**
Dunson, William Albert *biology professor, ecological consultant*

**Gloucester Point**
Bush, Elizabeth Olney *marine lab technician*

**Haymarket**
Katz, Alan Charles *toxicologist*

**Keswick**
Rafajko, Robert Richard *science administrator*

**Lansdowne**
Miller, Dorothy Anne Smith *retired cytogenetics educator*

**Lexington**
Hamilton, E. William *biology professor*
Spencer, Edgar Winston *geology educator*

**Manassas**
Isbister, Jenefir Diane Wilkinson *microbiologist, researcher, educator, consultant*
Jong, Shung-Chang *mycologist*

**Mc Lean**
DeGiovanni-Donnelly, Rosalie Frances *biologist, educator*
Talbot, Lee Merriam *ecologist, educator, director*

**Newport News**
Harris, Charles George *research scientist, consultant*

**Norfolk**
Haoudi, Abdelali *science educator*
Heck, Henry D'Arcy *retired toxicologist, consultant*
Jeng, Hueiwang Cook *environmental science professor*
Oelberg, David George *neonatologist educator, researcher*

**Reston**
Shank, Fred Ross *food scientist*

**Richmond**
Boadle-Biber, Margaret Clare *physiologist, educator*
Walsh, Scott Wesley *reproductive physiologist, researcher*

**Ridgeway**
Keen, Joe Louis *biology professor*

**Suffolk**
Phipps, Patrick Michael *plant pathology educator*
Williams, Nikkia Sekeena *science educator*

**Triangle**
Thomas, Lindsey Kay, Jr. *research ecology biologist, educator, consultant*

**Vienna**
Liu, Cejun *science educator, researcher, program analyst*

**Williamsburg**
Griffith, Melvin Eugene *entomologist, public health service officer*
Guastaferro, Angelo *space science administrator, consultant*
Novikova, Irina *science educator*

**Yorktown**
Elmahboub, Widad Ibrahim *science educator*

## WASHINGTON

**Anacortes**
Puglisi, Melany P. *marine chemical ecologist, researcher*

**Bainbridge Island**
Skotheim, Robert Allen *botanist, educator*

**Bellevue**
Thompson, Winston Mark Obed *entomologist, consultant, writer*
Whatmore, George Bernard *research scientist, writer, internist*

**Bellingham**
Ross, June Rosa Pitt *biologist, educator*

**Kennewick**
Cobb, William Thompson *environmental and agricultural consultant*

**Lopez Island**
Brownstein, Barbara Lavin *geneticist, educator, director*

**Olympia**
Heilenday, Frank Tod *science educator*

**Prosser**
Proebsting, Edward Louis, Jr. *retired horticulturist*

**Pullman**
Hosick, Howard Lawrence *cell biology professor, academic administrator*
Ibekwe, Abasiofiok Mark *soil scientist, educator*
Sprunger, Leslie Karen *physiology educator, educator*
Thomashow, Linda Suzanne *microbiologist*

**Richland**
Chou, Charissa J. *staff scientist*
Corrales, Louis Rene *research scientist, director*

**Seattle**
Bassingthwaighte, James Bucklin *physiologist, educator, medical researcher*
Beyers, William Bjorn *geography educator*
Boersma, P. Dee *marine biologist, educator*
Charlson, Robert Jay *atmospheric sciences educator*
Choi, Jee Woong *research scientist*
Creager, Joe Scott *geology and oceanography educator*
Daniel, Thomas L. *zoology educator*
Eisenman, Robert N. *research scientist*
Feigl, Eric Otto *physiology educator*
Fidel, Raya *information science educator*
Fournier, R. E. Keith *biologist*
Franklin, Jerry Forest *forest ecologist, educator*
Greenberg, E. Peter *microbiologist*
Gunderson, Donald Raymond *fisheries educator and researcher*
Hartwell, Leland Harrison (lee hartwell) *geneticist, educator*
Hellström, Karl Erik *science educator, researcher*
Hendrickson, Anita Elizabeth *biology professor*
Hille, Bertil *physiology educator*
Hood, Leroy Edward *molecular biologist, educator*
Hosken, Nancy Ann *research scientist*
Kaneko, Chris R.S. *research scientist*
Karr, James Richard *ecologist, educator, research director*
Kenny, George Edward *pathobiology educator*
King, Ivan Robert *astronomy educator*
King, Mary-Claire *geneticist, educator*
Kirby, Ronald Eugene *fish and wildlife research administrator*
Kirschner, Marc Alan *neuroscientist*
Klausner, Richard D. *cell biologist, researcher*
Kruckeberg, Arthur Rice *botanist, educator*

Kuhl, Patricia K. *science educator*
McDermott, Susanne Finckh *fisheries biologist*
Ning, Xue-Han (Hsueh-Han Ning) *physiologist, researcher*
Olstad, Roger Gale *science educator*
Riddiford, Lynn Moorhead *biologist, educator*
Rutherford, Suzanne L. *geneticist*
Scheuerell, Mark David *biologist, researcher*
Schiffrin, Milton Julius *physiologist*
Sims, John Ernest *biologist, researcher*
Smith, Orville Auverne *physiology educator*
Szkody, Paula *astronomy educator, researcher*
Woods, James Sterrett *toxicologist*
Wott, John Arthur *arboretum and botanical garden executive, horticulture educator*

**Snohomish**
Bond, William *science educator*

**Washougal**
Guillory, Richard John *retired science educator*

**Wenatchee**
Elfving, Don C. *horticulturist, educator*
Schrader, Lawrence Edwin *plant physiologist*

## WEST VIRGINIA

**Bruceton Mills**
Butcher, Fred R. *biochemistry professor, academic administrator*

**Clarksburg**
Walmsley, James Naylor *hydroponic farming executive*

**Huntington**
Lake, Esta Elizabeth *science educator*

**Institute**
Ruhnke, Timothy R. *zoologist, educator*

**Kearneysville**
Biggs, Alan Richard *plant pathologist, educator*

**Morgantown**
Attfield, Michael Deryck *research scientist*
Cochrane, Robert Lowe *biologist*
Gladfelter, Wilbert Eugene *physiology educator*
Nath, Joginder *genetics and biology educator, researcher*
Wenger, Sharon Louise *cytogeneticist, researcher, educator*

## WISCONSIN

**Appleton**
Maravolo, Nicholas C. *biology professor*

**Ashland**
Paruk, James David *biology professor*

**Baraboo**
Meine, Curt *biologist, writer*
Wittstruck, Thorne Michael *physiologist*

**Beaver Dam**
Mezei, Geoffrey D. *physiologist*

**Clintonville**
Primmer, Lillian Juanda *science educator*

**Cottage Grove**
Lund, Daryl Bert *food science educator*

**Janesville**
Klubertanz, Thomas H. *biology professor, entomologist*

**Madison**
Allen, Timothy Frank Herbert *botanist, educator*
Beyer-Mears, Annette *physiologist*
Boughman, Janette W. *evolutionary biologist, educator*
Brock, Thomas Dale *retired microbiology professor*
Carpenter, Stephen Russell *ecology educator*
Cassinelli, Joseph Patrick *astronomy educator*
De Foliart, Gene Ray *retired entomologist, researcher, educator*
Dierauf, Leslie Ann *wildlife veterinarian, conservation biologist, consultant*
Easterday, Bernard Carlyle *veterinary medicine educator*
Evert, Ray Franklin *botany educator*
Greaser, Marion Lewis *science educator*
Greenspan, Daniel S. *molecular biologist, educator*
Guillery, Rainer Walter *anatomy educator*
Handelsman, Jo *plant pathologist, educator*
Hopen, Herbert John *horticulture educator*
Iltis, Hugh Hellmut *botanist, educator, environmental advocate*
Ives, Anthony Ragnar *ecologist*
Jeanne, Robert Lawrence *entomologist, educator*
Kaesberg, Paul Joseph *virology researcher*
Kemnitz, Joseph William *physiologist, researcher*
Lepczyk, Christopher Andrew *ecologist, biologist, ornithologist, research scientist*
Marrett, Cora B. *science educator*
Miller, Paul Dean *breeding consultant, geneticist, educator*
Newcomb, Eldon Henry *retired botany educator*
Olson, Norman Fredrick *food science educator*
Pella, Milton Orville *science educator*
Rueckert, Roland Rudyard *retired virologist, educator*
Sharkey, Thomas David *botanist, educator*
Susman, Millard *geneticist, educator*
Szybalski, Waclaw *geneticist, educator*
Thomson, James Alexander *molecular biologist, educator*
Whitlon, Donna Sue *neuroscientist, researcher*

**Marshfield**
Hartwig, Randall Eugene *science educator*

**Menomonee Falls**
Janzen, Norine Madelyn Quinlan *clinical laboratory scientist*

**Milwaukee**
Cowley, Allen Wilson, Jr. *physiologist*
Kampine, John P. *anesthesiology and physiology educator*
Olivier, Michael *physiologist, educator*
Schumann, Gail L. *plant pathologist, educator*

**Shawano**
Heikes, Keith *science administrator*

**Sheboygan**
Strysick, Michael Otto *ecologist, physicist, microbiologist, researcher*

**Superior**
DuBois, Robert Bradford *natural resources research scientist*

## WYOMING

**Jackson**
Cox, Paul Alan *ethnobotanist, educator*

**Laramie**
Ren, Jun *science educator, research scientist*

## TERRITORIES OF THE UNITED STATES

### PUERTO RICO

**Aguadilla**
Gómez-Jiménez, Carlos *science educator, microbiologist, geneticist*

## CANADA

### ALBERTA

**Calgary**
Jones, Geoffrey Melvill *physiology research educator*
Walker, Roger Geoffrey *geology educator, consultant*

**Edmonton**
Christian, Ralph Gordon *agriculturist, researcher, animal health consultant, veterinarian*
Cossins, Edwin Albert *biology professor, academic administrator*
Gough, Denis Ian *geophysics educator*
Stelck, Charles Richard *geology educator*

### BRITISH COLUMBIA

**Sidney**
Bigelow, Margaret Elizabeth Barr (M.E. Barr) *retired botany educator*
Kendrick, William Bryce *biologist, consultant, editor*

**Vancouver**
Donaldson, Edward Mossop *research scientist, marine biologist, consultant*
Jones, David Robert *retired zoology educator*
Lindsey, Casimir Charles *zoologist, educator*
Mc Lean, Donald Millis *microbiologist, educator, pathologist, pediatrician*
McNeill, John Hugh *pharmaceutical sciences educator*
Newman, Murray Arthur *aquarium administrator*
Phillips, Anthony George *neurobiology researcher*
Phillips, John Edward *zoologist, educator*
Rennie, Paul Steven *research scientist, surgeon*
Shaw, Michael *biologist, educator*
Sinclair, Alastair James *geology educator*
Wellington, William George *entomologist, ecologist, educator*

**Victoria**
Turpin, David Howard *biologist, educator, academic administrator*

### MANITOBA

**Winnipeg**
Alfa, Michelle Josephine *microbiologist, educator*
Persaud, Trivedi Vidhya Nandan *anatomy educator, researcher, consultant*

### NEWFOUNDLAND AND LABRADOR

**Saint John's**
Rochester, Michael Grant *geophysics educator*

### NOVA SCOTIA

**Dartmouth**
Mann, Kenneth Henry *marine ecologist*

**Halifax**
Hall, Brian Keith *biology professor, writer*

### ONTARIO

**Bowmanville**
Evans, Essi H. *research scientist*

**Downsview**
Forer, Arthur H. *biology professor, researcher, editor*

**Guelph**
Beveridge, Terrance James *microbiology professor, researcher*
Bewley, John Derek *botany researcher, educator*
Kasha, Kenneth John *agriculturist, educator*

**Kingston**
Leggett, William C. *biology professor, academic administrator*
Wyatt, Gerard Robert *biology professor, researcher*

**London**
Lala, Peeyush Kanti *research scientist, educator*

**North York**
Davey, Kenneth George *biologist, educator, academic administrator*
Regan, David *neuroscientist*

**Ottawa**
Baum, Bernard Rene *research scientist*
Carty, Arthur John *science policy advisor, research administrator*
Hughes, Stanley John *retired mycologist*
Perry, Malcolm Blythe *biologist, researcher*
Storey, Kenneth Bruce *biology professor*
Veizer, Ján *geology educator*
Whitehead, J Rennie *science administrator, consultant*

**Peterborough**
Davis, Gordon Richard Fuerst *retired biologist, translator*
Hutchinson, Thomas Cuthbert *ecology and environmental educator*

**Scarborough**
White, Calvin John *zoo executive, zoological association executive, financial manager*

**Stittsville**
MacLeod, Robert Angus *microbiology educator, researcher*

**Toronto**
Carlen, Peter Louis *neuroscientist, educator, science administrator, researcher*
Chandra, Ranjit Kumar *research scientist, educator, physician*
Cook, Stephen Arthur *mathematics and computer science educator*
Dunlop, David John *geophysics educator, researcher*
Liversage, Richard Albert *cell biologist, educator*
MacLennan, David Herman *research scientist, educator*
Masui, Yoshio *zoology educator*
Tobe, Stephen Solomon *zoology educator*

**Waterloo**
Hynes, Hugh Bernard Noel *biologist, educator*
Warner, Barry Gregory *ecologist, educator*

**QUEBEC**

**Laval**
Talbot, Pierre Joseph *microbiologist, researcher*

**Montreal**
Aguayo, Alberto Juan *neuroscientist*
Carroll, Robert Lynn *biology professor, paleontologist, curator, museum director*
Chang, Thomas Ming Swi *research scientist, biotechnologist, educator*
Gibbs, Sarah Preble *biologist, educator*
Jolicoeur, Paul *molecular biologist*
Leblond, Charles Philippe *anatomy educator, researcher*
Milic-Emili, Joseph *physiologist, educator*
Mysak, Lawrence Alexander *oceanographer, climatologist and mathematics educator*

**Pointe-Claire**
Lapointe, Lucie *research management executive*

**Quebec City**
Potvin, Pierre *physiologist, educator*

**Saint Jean Sur Richelieu**
Trudel, Marc J. *botanist, educator*

**Sherbrooke**
Bourget, Edwin Robert *marine ecologist, educator*

**SASKATCHEWAN**

**Saskatoon**
Babiuk, Lorne Alan *virologist, immunologist, researcher*
Huang, Pan Ming *soil science educator*
Kartha, Kutty Krishnan *plant pathologist*
Sonntag, Bernard H. *agronomist, researcher, public information officer*

**Sainte Anne de Bellevue**
Grant, William Frederick *geneticist, educator*

**Toronto**
Josselyn, Sheena A. *research scientist, educator*

**AUSTRALIA**

**Randwick**
Hall, Peter Francis *physiologist*

**BELGIUM**

**Antwerp**
Snyders, Dirk Johan *electrophysiologist and biophysicist educator*

**CROATIA**

**Zagreb**
Štambuk, Nikola *research scientist*

**CZECH REPUBLIC**

**Prague**
Šebek, Michael *research scientist, entrepreneur*

**ENGLAND**

**Cambridge**
Huxley, Sir Andrew (Sir Andrew Fielding Huxley) *physiologist, educator*
Klug, Aaron *molecular biologist*
Rees, Martin John *astronomy educator*

**Durham**
Parman, Stephen Wayne *science educator*

**Kent Cranbrook**
Hattersley-Smith, Geoffrey Francis *retired government research scientist*

**Leeds**
Phillips, Oliver *tropical forest ecologist, researcher*

**London**
Morris, Desmond (John) *zoologist, writer, artist*

**Oxford**
Harvey, Paul H. *evolutionary biologist, researcher*

**FRANCE**

**Compiegne**
Dubuisson, Bernard Louis *science educator, administrator*

**Gif-sur-Yvette**
Duplessy, Jean Claude *research scientist*

**Noisy-le-Grand**
Le Quéré, Jean François Marie *scientific instrumentation researcher*

**Paris**
Jacob, François *biologist, educator*
Kourilsky, François Michel *research scientist*
Raharinaivo, André Léon *research scientist, educator*

**Saint Etienne**
Vergnaud, Jean-Maurice *science educator, researcher*

**Vandoeuvre-les-Nancy**
Blazy, Pierre François *science educator*

**GERMANY**

**Düsseldorf**
Stuhl, Oskar Paul *scientific and regulatory consultant*

**Stuttgart**
von Klitzing, Klaus *research facility administrator, physicist*

**INDIA**

**Bagalkot**
Chitme, Havagiray Revanappa *science educator*

**New Delhi**
Narain, Prem *agricultural scientist, educator, researcher*

**Warangal**
Puddubboina, Venkataiah *botanist, researcher*

**ISRAEL**

**Kiryat Shmone**
Gophen, Moshe *research scientist*

**Rehovot**
Sachs, Leo *geneticist, educator*

**ITALY**

**Naples**
Tarro, Giulio *virologist*

**Rome**
Levi-Montalcini, Rita *neurobiologist, researcher*

**JAPAN**

**Chiba**
Arai, Toshihiko *retired microbiology and immunology educator*
Hattori, Naozo *science educator*

**Sapporo**
Asari, Eikichi *information sciences educator, researcher*

**Tokyo**
Ishii, Akira *parasitologist, allergist, malariologist*

**KENYA**

**Nairobi**
Mignouna, Hodeba-Jacob Douwehan *geneticist, researcher*

**NEW ZEALAND**

**Palmerston North**
Krone, Cheryl A. *research scientist, consultant*

**NORWAY**

**Kjeller**
Maeland, Arnulf Julius *research scientist*

**PAKISTAN**

**Faisalabad Punjab**
Siddique, Muhammad *poultry pathobiologist*

**POLAND**

**Warsaw**
Koscielak, Jerzy *research scientist*

**REPUBLIC OF KOREA**

**Seoul**
Chun, Jang Ho *science educator, researcher*
Kim, Yong-Hak *microbiologist*

**ROMANIA**

**Bucharest**
Badic, Mihai *research scientist*

**SWITZERLAND**

**Basel**
Arber, Werner *microbiologist*
Gehring, Walter Jakob *biology professor, geneticist*

**Zurich**
Wüthrich, Kurt *molecular biologist, biophysicist, educator*

**ADDRESS UNPUBLISHED**

Abdullaev, Yalchin *neuroscientist, educator*
Able, Kenneth Paul *biology professor*
Adamson, Dan Klinglesmith *retired science association executive*
Aguirregabiria, Victor *science educator*
Ahearne, John Francis *science foundation director, researcher*
Ahrens, Franklin Alfred *veterinary pharmacology educator*
Alfano, Robert R. *science educator, engineering educator*
Altman, Lawrence Gene *biologist, educator*
Andrews, Richard Vincent *physiologist, educator*
Andrews, Sherri *science educator, consultant*
Antikas, Theodore G. *veterinarian*
Araiza, Roberto *research scientist*
Ares, Manuel, Jr. *biology professor, research scientist*
Arking, Robert *geneticist, gerontologist, educator*
Arnott, Howard Joseph *biology professor, dean*
Arroyo, Marino *science educator*
Arya, Vikram *research scientist*
Atkin, J Myron *science educator*
Aubrey, Douglas P *ecologist, researcher*
Auer, Matthew Robert *science educator*
Awadalla, Philip *geneticist, researcher*
Backus, Elaine Athene *entomologist, educator*
Bagby, Bethanye Branch *biology professor*
Bansil, Arun *research scientist*
Barlow, John Sutton *neuroscientist, lexicographer*
Barnard, Donald Roy *medical and veterinary entomologist*
Barnes, Robert F *agronomist*
Barnes-Kempton, Isabel Janet *retired microbiologist, dean*
Barnhart, Charles Elmer *zoology educator*
Beachy, Philip Arden *molecular biology educator*
Beggs, William H. *microbiologist, researcher*
Bell, Rosonald Renae *toxicologist*
Bentley, Charles Raymond *geophysics educator*
Beraldi, Hugo *microbiologist*
Berra, P. Bruce *computer science educator*
Bers, Donald Martin *physiology educator*
Bhat, Bal Krishen *geneticist, plant breeder*
Bick, Katherine Livingstone *neuroscientist, educator, medical researcher*
Bidwell, Roger Grafton Shelford *biologist, educator*
Bilbo, Thomas Earl *biology professor*
Bishop, William Peter *science administrator, management consultant, rancher, musician*
Block, Barbara Ann *biology professor*
Bodvarsson, Gudmunder *research scientist*
Bonner, John Tyler *biology professor*
Bottone, Edward Joseph *microbiologist, educator*
Boyle, Tatiana Gennadievna *research scientist*
Bremner, John McColl *agronomy and biochemistry educator*
Bridgewater, Albert Louis *retired science foundation administrator*
Brown, Jeannette Elizabeth *retired science educator*
Browne, Frederick Douglas *physiologist, educator*
Buchwald, Nathaniel Avrom *retired physiology professor*

Burkes, Lionel Seaton *science educator, writer, researcher*
Burton, Lawrence DeVere *agriculturist, educator*
Calambokidis, John *biologist*
Caldwell, Elwood Fleming *food scientist, educator*
Callan, Sandra Lee *biologist*
Cardoza, Yasmin Judith *agronomist, entomologist, researcher*
Carter, Bruce L.A. *biotechnologist, director*
Case, Ted Joseph *educator*
Cerchio, Salvatore *biologist*
Chang, Susan Marina *neuroscientist*
Chavan Patil, Mahesh *research scientist*
Cheng, Yue *molecular geneticist, pathologist*
Chitnis, Ashay *research scientist*
Choi, Hack Sun *molecular biologist, researcher*
Chun, Asaph Y. *research scientist*
Clayton, David A(lvin) *biology professor*
Cohen, Stanley *retired biochemistry educator*
Coker, Christine E.H. *horticulturist, researcher*
Colwell, Rita Rossi *microbiologist, former federal agency administrator, medical educator*
Connolly, Jeffrey James *biologist*
Conover, Lloyd Hillyard *retired research scientist*
Conway, William Gaylord *zoologist, zoo director, conservationist*
Cook, Clarence Edgar *science administrator, consultant*
Coughlin, Shaun R. *research scientist*
Couronne, Olivier *research scientist*
Cox, Robert Harold *physiology educator*
Cravats, Monroe *science educator*
Creech, John Lewis *botanist, consultant*
D'Alesandro, Philip Anthony *parasitologist, immunologist, retired medical educator*
Daves, Glenn Doyle, Jr. *science educator, chemist, researcher*
DeBakey, Lois *science administrator, educator*
Deckard, Steve Wayne *science educator, academic administrator*
Decker, Walter Johns *toxicologist*
Degryse, Bernard *cell biologist*
DelParigi, Angelo *research scientist*
Dennehy, John Joseph *evolutionary biologist*
Despommier, Dickson Donald *microbiology educator, parasitologist*
Deuel, Cassandra Lee *science educator*
Deutsch, Kathleen Pilarcik *aquarist*
Dey, Moul *molecular biologist, researcher*
Dirksen, Robert Thomas *science professor*
Doman, Elvira *retired science administrator*
Donfack, Joseph *microbiologist, geneticist*
Dugan, Patrick Raymond *microbiologist, educator, dean*
Durham Norman, Thena Monts *microbiologist, researcher, health facility administrator*
Edwards, Charles *neuroscientist, educator*
Elgamel, Mohamed *science educator, researcher*
Ellner, Paul Daniel *retired microbiologist*
Eno, Amos Stewart *natural resource foundation administrator*
Epel, David *biologist, educator*
Ericson, Jonathon Edward *environmental health science educator, researcher*
Erwin, Donald Carroll *plant pathology educator*
Eugster, Albrecht Konrad *veterinarian, laboratory director*
Evans, Christopher Lee *medical entomologist*
Fan, Yong *research scientist*
Farabaugh, Christopher Scott *toxicologist, researcher*
Farkas, Daniel Frederick *food science and technology educator*
Feir, Dorothy Jean *entomologist, educator, physiologist*
Fingerman, Milton *biologist, educator*
Fischer, Charlotte Froese *research scientist, educator*
Fisher, Dale Dunbar *animal scientist, dairy nutritionist*
Fiszer-Szafarz, Berta (Berta Safars) *research scientist, researcher*
Flemming, David Paul *biologist*
Fomenkov, Alexey Ivanovich *molecular biologist, educator*
Ford, Donna Michelle *biology professor*
Fox, Michael Wilson *veterinarian, animal scientist*
Foy, Charles Daley *retired soil scientist*
Freeman, Delma C., Jr. *science association director*
Fritzky, Edward V. *biotechnology company executive*
Gabor-Hotchkiss, Magda *research scientist, librarian*
Gage, Patrick (Leonard Patrick Gage) *biotechnologist, pharmaceutical consultant*
Ganguly, Swaroop *research scientist*
Garbers, Samantha *research scientist*
Gay, William Ingalls *veterinarian, retired health science association administrator*
Germundsson, Roger *research scientist*
Gerritsen, Mary Ellen *vascular and cell biologist*
Gift, James Joseph *aquatic toxicologist*
Gjerset, Ruth Anne *research scientist, educator*
Glysch, Randall Lee *research scientist*
Goldstein, Walter Elliott *biotechnology executive*
Gomez-Uchida, Daniel *marine biologist, geneticist*
Goodall, Jane *zoologist*
Goodwin, Richard Hale *biology professor*
Gowans, Sir James Learmonth *science administrator, immunologist*
Grunder, Hermann A. *science administrator, director, research scientist*
Gruneich, Jeffrey Alan *biotechnologist, director*
Guo, ZengKui *research scientist*
Habermann, Helen Margaret *botanist, educator*
Haegerich, Tamara *behavioral scientist*
Hale, Wesley Raymond *research scientist, chemical engineer*
Hall, Zach Winter *science administrator*
Harlin, Marilyn Miler *marine botany educator, researcher, consultant*
Harris, Richard E. *neuroscientist, acupuncturist*
Hauptmann, Randal Mark *biotechnologist*
Hayakawa, Kan-Ichi *retired food scientist*
Heinicke, Ralph Martin *science administrator, consultant*
Helgeson, John Paul *plant pathology and botany educator*
Hemmingsen, Barbara Bruff *retired microbiologist*
Herzog, Jennifer A. *biology professor*

Heyer, Stephanie *science educator*
Hildebrand, Verna Lee *human ecology educator*
Hilliard, Sam Bowers *geography educator*
Hillis, Llewellya W. *marine biology educator*
Hitchcock, Karen Ruth *biology professor, dean, academic administrator*
Honour, Lynda Charmaine *research scientist, psychotherapist, educator*
Hopkins, Robert Charles *chemistry and biophysics educator*
Hoskins, Alexander L. (Pete Hoskins) *retired zoological park administrator*
Howard-Peebles, Patricia Nell *clinical cytogeneticist*
Hoye, Robert Earl *systems science educator*
Huang, Hong *bioinformatics specialist*
Huie, Carol P. *information science educator*
Jagiello, Georgiana M. *geneticist, educator*
Jannesari Ladani, Leila *research scientist*
John, Edwin McPherson, Jr. *zoologist, educator, entomologist, researcher*
Jones, Kerri-Ann *director scientific organization*
Jones, Marvin Lamar *histologist*
Jung, Sangwook *neurobiologist*
Kamrin, Michael Arnold *toxicology educator*
Karp, Gerald Charles *biologist, educator, writer*
Kennedy, Charles *retired neuroscientist, retired medical educator*
Kharbanda, Kusum K. *biologist, educator*
Kim, Charles Wesley *microbiology educator*
Kim, Won Gyu *research scientist*
King, David Alan *ecologist*
Kirk, Mark D. *biologist, educator*
Kirsch, Thorsten *cell biologist, educator*
Kirsteuer, Ernst Karl Eberhart *biologist, curator*
Koenig, Maureen Catherine *science educator*
Kolb, James A. *science foundation director, writer*
Kornguth, Steven Edward *biologist*
Krylov, Dmitri *biologist*
Kulanthaivel, Palaniappan *research scientist*
Kulnane, Laura Shapiro *geneticist*
Kumako, Kuami Mawunyo *agricultural scientist*
Kung, Patrick Chung-Shu *biotechnologist*
Kushlan, James Anthony *science administrator, educator, conservationist, writer*
Kyesmu, Pius Michael *biology professor, researcher*
Lafever, Howard Nelson *botanist, educator, geneticist*
Langer, Glenn Arthur *cellular physiologist, educator*
Laughlin, Daniel Charles *ecologist*
LaVelle, Arthur *anatomy educator*
Layne, James Nathaniel *vertebrate biologist*
Leath, Kenneth Thomas *plant pathologist, educator, agriculturist, consultant*
Lee, Allen Michael *science educator*
Lemard, Glendene Anthea Nuala *research scientist*
Lenters, John Derick *geoscience educator*
Leventhal, Ruth *retired parasitology educator, university official*
Lewis, Brian Kreglow *retired physiologist, computer scientist*
Li, Jian-Yang *research scientist*
Lingle, Sarah Elizabeth *research scientist*
Lippincott, James Andrew *retired biochemistry and biological sciences educator*
Loehle, Craig *mathematical ecologist*
Lotsch, Alexander *scientist*
Low, Morton David *retired neuroscientist, healthcare educator*
Luan, Sheng *biology professor*
Lublinsky, Michael *research scientist*
Lustyk, Mary Kathleen *neuroscientist, educator*
Lynch, Harry James *retired biologist*
Lynch, John Thomas *retired science administrator, physicist*
Ma, Jun *environmental consultant*
Ma, Yewei *research scientist*
Mark, Hon Fong Louie *cytogeneticist*
Maroni, Donna Farolino *biologist, researcher*
Martin, Joseph Vinson *neuroscientist, educator*
Martino, Joseph Paul *research scientist, researcher*
Matlock, John Hudson *science administrator, materials engineer*
Matsko, Andrey B. *research scientist*
Mattox, Johnny Lynn *biologist, educator*
Maunder, Addison Bruce *agronomic research company executive*
Mays, George Walter, Jr. *educational technology educator*
McBride, Carol Bailey *science educator, consultant*
McCann, Peter Paul *biology researcher, educator*
McClellan, Roger Orville *toxicologist*
McDonald, Tracy Kathleen *science educator*
McDowell, Elizabeth Mary *retired pathology educator*
McGrath, Kevin Gary *library science educator*
McGraw, Donald Jesse *biologist, science historian, writer*
McShefferty, John *retired research scientist, personal care industry executive, consultant*
McVoy, Michael Arthur *virologist*
Meerow, Alan William *geneticist, horticulturist, botanist*
Menn, Julius Joel *retired research scientist, consultant*
Middlebrook, Geoffrey Cole *environmental educator*
Miekka, Jeanette Ann *retired science educator*
Miftahof, Roustem Narimanovich *science educator, researcher*
Miller, Louis Howard *biologist, researcher*
Miller, Patrick William *research scientist, educator*
Mitchell, John Laurin Amos *biological science educator*
Montgomery, Larry Dale *biologist*
Moore, Tirin *neuroscientist, educator*
Moritz, Chad Henry *research scientist*
Mosallaei, Hossein *science educator*
Moskovitz, Jackob *biology professor*
Moss, Thomas Henry *science foundation director, physicist*
Mudavanhu, Blessing *research scientist*
Murarka, Shyam Prasad *science and engineering educator, administrator*
Murray, Patrick Robert *microbiologist, educator*
Nadadur, Srikanth S *molecular biologist*
Nanos, George Peter, Jr. *science administrator, military officer, physicist*

Napoli, Joseph Stephen *horticulturist, conductor*
Nevitt, Gabrielle A. *zoologist, educator, ecologist*
Nikaido, Hiroshi *microbiologist*
Nyberg, Stanley Eric *research scientist*
Onufriev, Alexey *science educator*
Oshima, Junko *science educator, researcher*
Ostlind, Dan A. *retired parasitologist*
Paganelli, Charles Victor *physiologist, educator*
Palade, George Emil *research scientist, educator*
Parnell-Booth, Ruby Sheree *science educator*
Pedersen, Pedie *physiology educator*
Penwell, Rebecca Ann *science educator*
Persad, Anand Bhopraj *entomologist*
Perschbacher, Peter Wesley *environmental science educator, research scientist*
Peter, Richard Ector *zoology educator, dean*
Peterson, David Maurice *retired physiologist*
Petkovic, Lucia M. *research scientist*
Pettit, Ghery DeWitt *retired veterinary medicine educator*
Phan, K. Luan Dinh *neuroscientist, psychiatrist*
Phillis, John Whitfield *physiologist, educator*
Pirl, Joerg Norbert *toxicologist, consultant*
Plotkin, Stanley Alan *virologist*
Plummer, Gayther L. *retired climatologist*
Polley, Richard Donald *microbiologist, chemist*
Polston, Eva Kornberg *neuroscientist, educator*
Poutsma, John C. *science educator*
Powell, Bradford Scott *research scientist, educator*
Putnam, William Lowell *science association administrator*
Pyle, Donald Norris, II, *biologist*
Rabó, Jule Anthony *research scientist, consultant*
Randall, David John *physiologist, zoologist, educator*
Raviprakash, Kanakatte *molecular biologist*
Redmon, Larry Allen *agronomist, educator*
Register, Karen *microbiologist, researcher*
Regnery, Russell Lawrence *microbiologist*
Riggsby, Ernest Duward *science educator, educational consultant*
Roberts, Linda M. *science educator*
Rodecker, Stephen Bailey *science specialist, secondary school educator*
Roeller, Herbert Alfred *biology professor*
Rogan, Michael T. *neuroscientist*
Rogers, Jack David *plant pathologist, educator*
Rogers, Ruth Frances *retired microbiologist*
Romano, Gaetano *research scientist, educator*
Rose, Michael Robertson *evolutionary biology educator, consultant*
Russell, James Benjamin *microbiologist, educator, research scientist*
Rybak, Ilya A. *neuroscientist, biophysicist, educator*
Saalfeld, Fred Erich *science educator, researcher*
Sabatini, David Domingo *cell biologist, biochemist*
Sahelijo, Leonardo *geneticist, researcher*
Saldanha, John *biologist, director*
Salkind, Michael Jay *science administrator, metallurgical engineer*
Sanders, Aaron Perry *radiation biophysics educator*
Sanger, Frederick *retired molecular biologist*
Sattler, Rolf *retired plant morphologist, educator*
Schaechter, Moselio *microbiology educator*
Schnepf, Harry Ernest *microbiologist, consultant*
Schultz, Stanley George *physiologist, educator, dean*
Scott, T. Gordon *chemistry and math educator, writer*
Semyonov, Oleg G. *research scientist*
Setser, Carole Sue *food scientist, educator*
Shahied, Ishak I. *science educator*
Shaw, Helen Lester Anderson *nutrition educator, researcher, retired dean*
Shepard, Katherine *science educator, consultant*
Shi, Stone D. H. *research scientist*
Shrestha, Anil *ecologist*
Shrotriya, Vishal *research scientist*
Silverthorn, Dee Unglaub *physiologist, educator*
Simon, Melvin I. *molecular biologist, educator*
Simpson, Frederick James *retired science administrator*
Simpson, Michael Marcial *science specialist, consultant*
Sjostrand, Fritiof Stig *biologist, educator*
Slayman, Carolyn Walch *geneticist, educator*
Smaw, Shercoda Genee *research scientist*
Smeltzer, Debra Jean *botanist*
Smith, Catherine Marie *science educator*
Smith, Hamilton Othanel *molecular biologist, educator*
Snow, Joel Alan *research director*
Sokal, Robert Reuven *biology professor, writer*
Sperelakis, Nicholas, Sr. *physiology and biophysics educator, researcher*
Spiegel, Melvin *retired biology professor*
Sponsler, George Curtis III *science administrator, lawyer*
Stark, Nellie May *forester, ecologist, educator*
Steeves, John G. (Jack Steeves) *science educator, consultant*
Stickle, David Walter *microbiologist*
Stickney, Robert Roy *fisheries educator*
Sullivan, Nicholas G. *science educator*
Sze, Sing-Hoi *science educator, researcher*
Tadros, Fawzi M. *educator*
Talmage, David Wilson *retired microbiologist, retired educator, retired dean*
Tandler, Bernard *cell biology educator*
Tatavarthy, Aparna *biologist, researcher*
Taylor, Roy Lewis *botanist, educator*
Thomas, Adrian Wesley *research scientist, director, retired science educator*
Thomas, Teresa Ann *microbiologist, educator*
Thomson, Keith Stewart *biologist, author*
Thorne, Stephen H. *research scientist*
Todhunter, John Anthony *toxicologist, consultant*
Tosun, Ali Saman *science educator*
Touwaide, Alain Jacques André *science educator, researcher*
Tripathi, GN R *research scientist, educator*
Tsiros, Michael *science educator, researcher*
Tytler, Linda Jean *science administrator, retired state legislator*
Ullman, Edwin Fisher *biotechnologist, consultant*
Unger, Paul Walter *retired soil scientist*
VanMany, Seng Dao *microbiologist*
Vasilyev, Dmitry *research scientist*
Vaughn, James English, Jr. *neurobiologist*

Vella, Monica C. *science educator*
Villa-Komaroff, Lydia *molecular biologist, educator, academic administrator*
Vincent, James Louis *biotechnology company executive*
Vishniac, Ethan Tecumseh *astronomy educator*
Voss, Regis Dale *agronomist, educator*
Wan, Julia Chang *retired science educator*
Wang, Hong-Wei *biologist*
Wang, Ying *chemistry and physical science researcher*
Ward, Thomas *research scientist*
Weinstein, Michael P. *marine scientist, administrator*
Weinstein, Milton Charles *decision scientist, educator*
Weller, Milton Webster *wetland ecologist, educator*
Weydt, Patrick Roman Philipp *neuroscientist*
Williams, George Christopher *biologist, ecology and evolution educator*
Wilson, Kenneth Geddes *physics research administrator*
Witte, Owen Neil *microbiologist, molecular biologist, educator*
Wong, Deborah M. *science educator*
Wright, Kristopher *biology professor*
Wright, Theodore Robert Fairbank *biologist, educator*
Xi, Cecilia Q. *research scientist*
Yao, Jianan Johnny *research scientist, consultant*
Ye, Rick W. *microbiologist*
Yerrick, Randy Kregg *science educator*
Young, Judith Anne *animal conservationist*
Yu, Jun *biologist*
Yunis, Jorge Jose *anatomy, pathology, and microbiology educator*
Zaghloul, Norann Amir *geneticist, research scientist*
Zangen, Abraham *neuroscience researcher, consultant*
Zhang, Zhongjian *research scientist*
Zhao, Xueheng *research scientist*
Zhdanov, Boris *research scientist*
Zhu, Yong *research scientist*
Zuk, Judith *retired botanist, director*
Zuker, Charles S. *neuroscientist, biology professor*
Zwislocki, Jozef John *neuroscience educator, researcher*

## SCIENCE: MATHEMATICS AND COMPUTER SCIENCE *See also* INFORMATION TECHNOLOGY

## UNITED STATES

### ALABAMA

**Attalla**
Saffels, Anna Wayne Brothers *retired mathematician, educator*

**Auburn**
Diawara, Norou *mathematician, researcher*
Govil, Narendra Kumar *mathematics professor*

**Birmingham**
Afgan, Enis *computer scientist, researcher*
Peeples, William Dewey, Jr. *mathematics professor*
Reilly, Kevin Denis *computer scientist, educator*
Wheeler, Ruric E. *mathematics professor*
Whigham, Mark Anthony *computer scientist*
Woodbury, Max Atkin *mathematics professor*

**Florence**
Johnson, Johnny Ray *retired mathematics professor*

**Huntsville**
Freas, George Wilson, II, *computer scientist, consultant*
Pruitt, Alice Fay *mathematician, engineer*
Zutaut, Steven Eric *systems analyst, application developer*

**Marion**
Price, Ray Hampton *mathematics professor*

**Mobile**
Hain, Thomas Franz *computer scientist, educator*

**Montgomery**
Boncek, John James *mathematics professor*
Foguel, Tuval Shmuel *mathematician, department chairman*
Kim, Ki Hang *mathematician*

### ALASKA

**Anchorage**
Fitch, Mark *mathematics professor*

### ARIZONA

**Fountain Hills**
Israel, Robert Allan *statistician*

**Phoenix**
Doto, Irene Louise *statistician*
Pillamarri, Seshasayi *computer scientist and engineer, researcher*
Vaughn, Richard P. *mathematics professor*

**Prescott**
Semon, Warren Lloyd *information scientist, educator*

**Scottsdale**
Drake, Albert Estern *retired statistics educator, farming administrator*

**Sierra Vista**
Sizemore, Nicky Lee *computer scientist*

**Tempe**
Aist, Gregory S. *computer scientist, linguist*
Kambhampati, Subbarao *computer scientist, educator*
Roudenko, Svetlana *mathematics professor*
Smith, Harvey Alvin *mathematics professor, consultant*
Yau, Stephen Sik-sang *computer scientist, information scientist, educator*

**Tucson**
Ward, Robin A. *mathematics professor*
Willoughby, Stephen Schuyler *mathematics professor*

**Yuma**
Hodson, Roy Goode, Jr. *retired logistician*

### ARKANSAS

**Arkadelphia**
Buscher, Darin G. *mathematics professor*

**Batesville**
Carius, Robert Wilhelm *mathematics professor, retired military officer*
Williams, Darrick Shad *mathematician*

**Conway**
Duan, Qiang *computer scientist, educator*

**Fayetteville**
Venkatesh, Viswanath *information systems professional, educator, consultant*

**Jefferson**
Moon, Hojin *statistician*

**Little Rock**
Chiang, Chia-Chu *computer scientist, educator*

**Magnolia**
Avard, Joseph L. *mathematician, educator*

**Monticello**
Annulis, John Thomas *mathematics professor*

**Pine Bluff**
Lakew, Dejenie Alemayehu *mathematician*
Shannon-Gragg, Tenita Leanette *computer scientist, educator*

**Russellville**
Finan, Marcel Bassil *mathematics professor, researcher*

### CALIFORNIA

**Bakersfield**
Fiedler, Joseph Robert *mathematician, educator*

**Berkeley**
Agogino, Alice Merner *computer scientist, mechanical engineer, educator*
Aldous, David J. *statistics professor*
Arveson, William Barnes *mathematics professor*
Bergman, George Mark *mathematician, educator*
Berlekamp, Elwyn Ralph *mathematics professor*
Bickel, Peter John *statistician, educator*
Borcherds, Richard Ewen *mathematics professor, educator*
Chorin, Alexandre Joel *mathematician, educator*
Colella, Philip *mathematician*
Dunlop, Neil *computer scientist, department chairman*
Eisenbud, David *mathematics professor*
Gluss, Brian *mathematician, statistician, engineer, systems expert*
Goldberg, Evgueni *computer scientist*
Goldberg, Kenneth Yigael *computer engineering educator, artist*
Graham, Susan Lois *computer scientist, consultant*
Jones, Vaughan Frederick Randal *mathematician, educator*
Osserman, Robert *mathematician, educator, writer*
Patterson, David Andrew *computer scientist, educator, consultant*
Schoenfeld, Alan Henry *mathematician, researcher, educator, educator*
Simon, Horst D. *computer scientist*
Vojta, Paul Alan *mathematics professor*
Wagner, David *computer scientist, educator*
Wolf, Joseph Albert *mathematician, educator*
Xie, Ganquan *mathematician, computational geophysical scientist, educator*
Zelmanowitz, Julius Martin *mathematics professor, academic administrator*

**Brea**
Painchaud, Phillip Andre *metrologist*

**Carlsbad**
Halberg, Charles John August, Jr. *mathematics professor*

**Claremont**
Coleman, Courtney Stafford *mathematician, educator*
Grabiner, Judith Victor *mathematics professor*
Grabiner, Sandy *mathematics professor*
Henriksen, Melvin *mathematician, educator*
Myhre, Janet *mathematician, educator*
Pippenger, Nicholas John *mathematician, researcher, computer scientist, educator*

**Costa Mesa**
DeMille, Dianne Lynne *mathematics professor, academic administrator*

**Davis**
Fannjiang, Albert *mathematician, educator*
Su, Zhendong *computer scientist, educator*
Temple, John Blake *mathematics professor*
Tracy, Craig Arnold *mathematics educator*
Wegelin, Jacob Andreas *statistician*

**Elk Grove**
McDavid, Douglas Warren *executive research consultant*

**Fairfield**
Spake, Reuben Michael *mathematics professor, researcher*

**Foster City**
Scheer, Janet Kathy *mathematics professor*

**Gardena**
Bornino-Glusac, Anna Maria *retired mathematics professor*

**Gilroy**
McCarty, Robert Clarke *mathematician*

**Glendale**
Kay, Alan C. *computer scientist, nonprofit organization executive*

**Granada Hills**
Shoemaker, Harold Lloyd *information scientist*

**Hayward**
Duncan, Doris Gottschalk *information systems educator*

**Huntington Beach**
Sward, Andrea Jeanne *information and computer scientist, musician*

**Irvine**
Finkelstein, Mark *mathematician, educator*
Guidotti, Patrick *mathematician, educator*
Hoffman, Donald David *cognitive and computer science educator*
Kaneda, Masayoshi *mathematics professor, researcher*
Saari, Donald Gene *mathematician, department chairman, economist*
Shen, Ba-Zhong *mathematician, computer scientist*
Wan, Frederic Yui-Ming *mathematician, educator*
Yazdi, Ahmad *computer scientist, researcher*

**La Jolla**
Adams, Marc Anthony *medical statistician, researcher*
Burgin, George Hans *computer scientist, educator*
Deutsch, Alin Bernard *computer scientist, educator*
Halkin, Hubert *mathematics professor, research mathematician*
Kehler, Andrew S. *computer scientist, educator*
Martin, James John, Jr. *systems analyst, retired research and development company executive*
Rajasekar, Arcot *computer scientist*
Rosen, Judah Ben *computer scientist*
Wallach, Nolan R. *mathematician, consultant*
Wulbert, Daniel Eliot *mathematician, educator*

**Laguna Hills**
Green, Millie Ann *mathematician, educator*

**Los Angeles**
Adleman, Leonard M. *computer scientist, educator*
Bekey, George Albert *computer scientist, educator*
Brown, John S. *computer scientist*
Chen, Tony F. *mathematics professor, dean*
Dabrowska, Dorota Maria *statistician, educator*
Delaney, Matthew Sylvester *mathematics professor, academic administrator*
Golomb, Solomon Wolf *mathematician, educator, director, electrical engineer*
Gordon, Basil *retired mathematics professor*
Kleinrock, Leonard *computer scientist*
Martin, Donald A. *mathematics professor*
Moschovakis, Yiannis Nicholas *mathematics professor*
Pearl, Judea *computer scientist, educator*
Port, Sidney Charles *mathematician, educator*
Reinman, Glenn D. *computer scientist, educator*
Roberts, Paul Harry *mathematics professor*
Tao, Terence Chi-Shen *mathematics professor*
Vendlinski, Terry P. *computer scientist, educator*
Walter, Virginia Ann *information scientist, educator*
Waterman, Michael Spencer *mathematics professor, biology professor*
Zame, William R. *mathematician, educator*

**Marina Del Rey**
Neumann, Clifford *computer scientist, educator*

**Menlo Park**
Bourne, Charles Percy *information scientist, educator*
Luong, Quang-Tuan *computer scientist*
Neumann, Peter Gabriel *computer scientist*
Sutherland, Ivan E. *computer scientist*
Vincent, Regis *computer scientist*

**Moffett Field**
Srivastava, Ashok Narain *computer scientist, consultant*

**Monterey**
Denning, Peter James *computer scientist, engineer*
Luqi, *computer science professor*
Neta, Beny *mathematics educator, researcher*

**Moss Landing**
Lange, Lester Henry *mathematics professor*

**Palo Alto**
Farmer, David Wayne *mathematician*
Penn, Lee *information scientist, consultant, journalist*

**Pasadena**
Candes, Emmanuel Jean *mathematics professor*
Holzmann, Gerard Johan *computer science researcher*
Keller, Herbert Bishop *mathematics professor*
Knowles, James Kenyon *applied mathematician, educator*
Luxemburg, Wilhelmus Anthonius Josephus *mathematics professor*
Todd, John *mathematician, educator*

**Pearblossom**
Goldman, Gary Steven *computer scientist, consultant*

**Playa Vista**
Noh, Jun-yong *computer scientist, researcher*

**Pomona**
Agvanian, Youri *mathematician, educator, physicist*

**Portola Valley**
Kuo, Franklin F. *computer scientist, electrical engineer*

**Rancho Santa Margarita**
Berta, Melissa Rose *mathematics professor*

**Redondo Beach**
Casey, Michael Scott *mathematician*

**Redwood Valley**
Speed, Cynthia Agnes *retired mathematics professor*

**Riverside**
Mao, Changxuan *statistician*
Ratliff, Louis Jackson, Jr. *mathematics professor*
Shapiro, Victor Lenard *mathematics professor*

**Roseville**
Reichmann, Péter Iván *mathematics professor*

**Sacramento**
Crawford, Robert Lawrence *mathematics professor*
Gordon, Vahl Scott *computer scientist, educator*
Norman, Ben Eric *mathematician, educator*

**San Diego**
Hales, Alfred Washington *mathematics professor, consultant*
Kuniyuki, Ken Toshio *mathematics professor*
LeFevre, Jeff P. *computer scientist*
Palacios, Antonio *mathematics professor*
Tsybakov, Boris Solomon *information theory and communication networks researcher, educator*
Van Tassel, Lowell Thomas *mathematics professor*

**San Francisco**
Gray, James N. *computer scientist*
Kao, John Sterling *mathematician, educator*
Low, Arnold Kinman *systems executive*

**San Jose**
Goldston, Daniel A. *mathematics professor, researcher*
Ho, Yinhsin *retired mathematician, artist*
Matusow, Steven S. *mathematics professor*
Selinger, Patricia Griffiths *computer science professional*
Swope, William Clarence *computer scientist, researcher*
Togasaki, Shinobu *computer scientist*

**San Marino**
Lashley, Virginia Stephenson Hughes *retired computer science educator*

**San Rafael**
Barker, Celeste Arlette *computer scientist*

**Santa Ana**
Re Velle, Jack B(oyer) *statistician, consultant*

**Santa Barbara**
Johnsen, Eugene Carlyle *mathematician, educator*
Minc, Henryk *mathematics professor*
Simons, Stephen *mathematics professor, researcher*

**Santa Clara**
Smith, Stephen Allen *mathematician, educator*

**Santa Cruz**
Stormes, John Max *systems analyst*
Widom, Harold *mathematician, educator*

**Santa Monica**
Sun, Li *statistician*

**Stanford**
Batzoglou, Serafim *computer scientist, educator*
Cohen, Paul Joseph *mathematician*
Cottle, Richard Warren *retired operations research educator*
Efron, Bradley *statistician, educator*
Eliashberg, Yakov *mathematician, educator*
Karlin, Samuel *mathematics professor, researcher*
Keller, Joseph Bishop *mathematician, educator*
Knuth, Donald Ervin *computer sciences educator*
Koller, Daphne *computer scientist*
Lai, Tze Leung *mathematician, educator*
Lambers, James Vincent *mathematician, researcher, petroleum engineer*
McCarthy, John *computer scientist, educator*
Rhee, Soo-Yon *information scientist*
Rubin, Karl Cooper *mathematics educator*
Schoen, Richard Melvin *mathematics professor, researcher*
Ullman, Jeffrey David *computer scientist, educator*
Whittemore, Alice *biostatistician*

**Thousand Oaks**
El Fattah, Yousri M. *computer scientist*
Sladek, Lyle Virgil *mathematician, educator*

**Torrance**
Kerstiens, Gene J. *mathemagenician, consultant*

**Westlake Village**
Munson, John Backus *computer scientist, retired data processing executive*

**Westminster**
Le, Anh Quang *mathematics professor*

**Yucaipa**
Crise, Robert D., Jr. *mathematics professor*

## COLORADO

**Boulder**
Ellis, Homer Godsey *mathematics professor, physicist, researcher*
Glover, Fred William *information scientist, director, educator*
Mendez, Celestino Galo *mathematics professor*
Mycielski, Jan *retired mathematics professor*

**Colorado Springs**
Fagin, Barry Steven *computer science educator, writer*
Rangaswamy, Kulumani M. *mathematician, educator*
Simmons, George Finlay *retired mathematics professor*
Zhou, Xiaobo *computer scientist, educator*

**Denver**
Kuppireddi, Sireesh *computer scientist*
Payne, Stanley E. *mathematics professor*

**Fort Collins**
Mielke, Paul William, Jr. *statistician, consultant*

**Greeley**
Miller, Nathaniel Gregory *mathematics professor*

**Highlands Ranch**
Lampard, Greg Edward *computer scientist, educator*

**Silverthorne**
Riley, Mary Jane *computer scientist*

## CONNECTICUT

**Ansonia**
Kerpa, Gary J. *computer science consultant*

**Cheshire**
Tufte, Edward Rolf *statistician, educator*

**Fairfield**
Bennedum, Charles L. *computer scientist, educator, band director*
Eigel, Edwin George, Jr. *mathematics professor, retired university president*

**Middletown**
Comfort, William Wistar *mathematics professor*
Grothendieck, Alexandre *retired mathematician*
Linton, Fred Ernest Julius *mathematics professor, department chairman*

**New Britain**
Kjell, Bradley Pryor *computer scientist, educator*
O'Connell, Brian Michael *computer scientist, educator*

**New Haven**
Coifman, Ronald R. *mathematician, educator*
Feigenbaum, Joan *computer scientist, educator*
Fischer, Michael John *computer science educator*
Gueorguieva, Ralitza *biostatistician*
Margulis, Gregory A. *mathematics professor, researcher, science educator*
Massey, William S. *mathematician, educator*
Mostow, George Daniel *mathematics professor*

**Stamford**
Frank, Laura Jean *computer scientist*

**Storrs Mansfield**
Gui, Changfeng *mathematics professor*

**West Haven**
Kyriakides, Tassos Constantino *biostatistician*

**Wilton**
Brown, James Thompson, Jr. *operations research specialist, information scientist*

## DELAWARE

**Newark**
Berk, Dawn *mathematics professor*
Colton, David Lem *mathematician, educator*
Luke, David Russell *mathematician, educator*
Stark, Robert Martin *mathematician, civil engineer, educator*

## DISTRICT OF COLUMBIA

**Washington**
Bevan, William Charles *systems analyst*
Coles, Bertha Sharon Giles *information scientist*
Eftekhari, Abe *computer scientist, department chairman*
Eller, Matthias M. *mathematics professor*
Feil, Michael Bruce *statistician*
Gillman, Daniel W. *information scientist*
Gray, Mary Wheat *statistician, lawyer*
Hedges, Harry George *retired computer scientist*
Kotz, Samuel *statistician, educator, translator, editor*
Luo, Tao *mathematics professor*
Lutterodt, Clement H. *mathematician, educator*
MacDonald, Purificacion O. *statistician, researcher*
Martin, Donald Eugene Kemp *mathematics professor, statistician*
Omole, Duncan Wambogo *information scientist, corporate communications specialist*
Raphael, Louise Arakelian *mathematician, educator*
Redd, Kenneth Eric *statistician, researcher*
Ryan, David Alan *systems analyst*
Saworotnow, Parfeny Pavlovich *mathematician, educator*
Shaw, William Frederick *statistician*
Szekely, Zoltan *mathematics professor*

Viehe, Karl William *mathematics professor, lawyer, brokerage house executive*

## FLORIDA

**Bonita Springs**
Powell, Robert Ellis *mathematics professor, dean*

**Boynton Beach**
Warga, Jack *mathematician, educator*
Waterman, Daniel *mathematician, educator*

**Coral Gables**
Shyu, Mei-Ling *information scientist, educator*

**Daytona Beach**
Pagan Ortiz, Alex Omar *computer systems analyst, educator*
Seenith, Sivasundaram *mathematician, educator*

**Delray Beach**
Beckman, Frank Samuel *computer science educator, researcher*
Hegstrom, William Jean *retired mathematics professor*

**Dunedin**
Klingbiel, Paul Herman *retired information scientist*

**Fort Lauderdale**
Littman, Marlyn Kemper *information scientist, educator*
Sun, Junping *computer science professor*

**Fort Myers**
Faith, Ruth L. *retired mathematician*

**Gainesville**
Agresti, Alan *statistics educator*
Banerjee, Arunava *computer scientist, educator*
Bednarek, Alexander Robert *mathematician, educator*
Dinculeanu, Nicolae *mathematician, educator*
Weinrich, Brian Erwin *mathematician, computer scientist*

**Hollywood**
Isaacs, Godfrey Leonard *retired mathematician*

**Jacksonville**
Robinson, Christine Marie *mathematics professor*

**Key West**
Kalb, Chester H. *mathematics professor*

**Largo**
Camara, Vincent Antonin Reginald *mathematician, educator, statistician, researcher*

**Melbourne**
Lakshmikantham, Vangipuram *mathematics professor*
Menezes, Ronaldo P. *computer scientist, educator*

**Miami**
Chen, Shu-Ching *computer science educator*
Clarke, Peter John *computer scientist, educator, educational consultant*
Cosner, George Christopher *mathematics professor*
Dimitriou, Dolores Ennis *computer consultant*
Pan, Guoquan Victor *mathematics professor, computer science educator*

**Milton**
McKinney, George Harris, Jr. *training systems analyst*

**Orlando**
Balci, Murat *computer scientist, educator*
Berrios, Joseph Stephen *computer scientist, educator*
Deo, Narsingh *computer scientist, educator*
Lisetti, Christine Laetitia *computer scientist, educator*
Marinescu, Dan Cristian *computer sciences educator, consultant*
Nashed, M. Zuhair *mathematics professor, editor*
Su, Xiaogang *statistician, educator*
Varvak, Mark *mathematician, researcher*

**Palm Harbor**
Williams, Thomas Arthur *biomedical computing consultant, psychiatrist*

**Panama City**
Phelps, Daniel Christopher *information scientist, researcher*

**Patrick Afb**
Kohn, Paul Franklin *mathematician*

**Pensacola**
Ford, Kenneth M. *computer scientist, educator*

**Plant City**
Golden, Sonya A. *mathematics professor*

**Riviera Beach**
Berliner, Hans Jack *retired computer scientist*

**Saint Augustine**
Jurgens, Julie Graham *mathematics professor*

**Saint Petersburg**
Fishman, Mark Brian *computer scientist, educator*
Galperin, Boris *mathematician, physicist, oceanographer, educator*
White, June Miller *mathematics professor, educational consultant*

**Sarasota**
Jacobson, Melvin Joseph *mathematician, educator*

**Tallahassee**
Gilmer, Robert *mathematics professor*
Hunter, Christopher *retired mathematics professor*
Kercheval, Alec Norton *mathematician*

Navon, Ionel Michael *mathematics professor*
Nichols, Eugene Douglas *mathematics professor*

**Tampa**
El-Hadidy, Bahaa *information scientist, educator, consultant*
Kersaint, Gladis *mathematics professor, researcher*
Roop, Mitchell A. *information scientist*

**West Palm Beach**
Groves, Ann M. *mathematician, educator*

## GEORGIA

**Athens**
Bargmann, Rolf Erwin *computer scientist, educator*

**Atlanta**
Ames, William Francis *mathematician, educator*
Carroll, Blayne Earl *mathematics educator*
Ellison, Earl Otto *computer scientist*
Foley, James David *computer scientist, educator*
Huo, Xiaoming *mathematician, educator*
Macur, Patricia Alice *systems analyst, application developer*
Mitrophanov, Alexander Yuryevich *mathematician, researcher*
Morrison, Gregory Bernard *information scientist*
Oliker, Vladimir *mathematician, educator*
Pan, Yi *computer science educator*
Pu, Calton *computer scientist*
Rusodimos, Iason *mathematics professor*
Thompson, Shirley Williams *mathematics professor*
Wilding, Diane *computer scientist, consultant*
Wu, De Ting *mathematics professor, researcher, writer*
Zadeh, Javad Hamadani *mathematics professor*

**Augusta**
Craig, Cynthia Mae *mathematics professor*

**Columbus**
Lumbard, Trina Yvette *mathematician, educator*

**Decatur**
Selby, Gail Diana *computer scientist*

**Duluth**
Kimmich, Madeline P. *business operations consultant*

**Jonesboro**
Harris, Queen Wiggs *mathematician, educator*

**Kennesaw**
Xu, Chong-wei *computer scientist, educator*

**Lilburn**
Lynberg, Christopher A. *systems analyst, researcher*

**Lovejoy**
Onukwuli, Francis Osita *computer scientist, secondary school educator, mathematician*

**Macon**
Huthnance, Edward Dennis, Jr. *mathematics professor*

**Savannah**
Tessema, George *mathematician, educator*

**Statesboro**
Barjis, Joseph *computer scientist, educator*

**Valdosta**
Wares, Arsalan *mathematics professor*

## HAWAII

**Hilo**
Figueroa-Centeno, Ramón *mathematics professor*
Li, Shuguang *mathematics professor, researcher*

**Honolulu**
Chyba, Monique *mathematics professor*
Swanson, Richard William *retired statistician*

**Paia**
Loomis, James Cook *mathematician, cyberneticist, writer, educator, navigator*

## IDAHO

**Moscow**
Bobisud, Larry Eugene *mathematics professor*
Shafii, Bahman *statistician, educator, researcher*

## ILLINOIS

**Argonne**
Lindert, Eric Alton *operations research specialist, small business owner*

**Carbondale**
Asoh, Derek Ajesam *information scientist, educator*
Headrick, Todd Christopher *mathematical statistician, educator*
Neuman, Edward George *mathematician, educator*

**Champaign**
Roussos, Louis Ablen *statistician, psychology professor*
Turquette, Atwell Rufus *logician*

**Charleston**
McBride, Jonica Helene *mathematics professor*

**Chicago**
Angulo, David Sigfredo *computer scientist, educator*

Aschenbrenner, Matthias Josef *mathematician, educator*
Ash, J. Marshall *mathematician, educator*
Bona, Jerry Lloyd *mathematician, educator*
Dardai, Shahid Moinuddin *computer science educator*
Drinfeld, Vladimir Gershonovich *mathematician, educator*
Dupont, Todd F. *mathematics professor*
Erber, Thomas *mathematics professor, physics professor*
Foster, Ian Tremere *computer scientist*
Goharian, Nazli *computer scientist, educator*
Hanson, Floyd Bliss *mathematician*
Hwang, Yujong *information scientist, educator*
Kirkpatrick, Anne Saunders *systems analyst*
Krawczyk, Eva *information scientist, educator*
Kwembe, Tor Anthony *mathematics professor, researcher*
Morris, Ashley *information scientist, educator*
O'Hara, Paul P. *mathematics professor*
Ong, Michael King *mathematician, educator, bank executive*
Prakash, Jai *computer scientist, educator*
Stigler, Stephen Mack *statistician, educator*
Tangora, Martin Charles *mathematician, educator*
Thisted, Ronald Aaron *statistician, educator, consultant*
Tsai, Jingpha (Jeffrey Tsai) *computer scientist, educator*
Usiskin, Zalman Philip *mathematics educator*
Wirszup, Izaak *mathematician, educator*

**Decatur**
Gaffney, Sean *information scientist*

**Deerfield**
Bialek, Paul Richard *mathematics professor*

**Dekalb**
Ewell, John Albert III *mathematician, educator*

**Elmhurst**
MacInnes, Sally Ackerman *computer education educator*

**Evanston**
Davis, Stephen Howard *applied mathematics professor*
Devinatz, Allen *retired mathematician, educator*
Jerome, Joseph Walter *mathematics professor*
Manin, Yuri Ivanovich *mathematician*
Matkowsky, Bernard Judah *mathematician, educator*
Olmstead, William Edward *mathematics professor*
Tanner, Martin Abba *statistician, educator*
Zelinsky, Daniel *mathematics professor*

**Glen Ellyn**
Lenard, Anthony Edward *mathematics professor*
Nunamaker, Susan Sun *mathematics professor*
Rothmaler, Peter Antell *mathematician, educator*

**Jacksonville**
Calderhead, Kyle D. *mathematics professor*

**La Grange Park**
Butler, Margaret Kampschaefer *retired computer scientist*

**Lisle**
Meeker, Ralph D. *computer scientist, information scientist, educator*
Townsley, Lisa Gail *mathematics professor*

**Nauvoo**
Ivie, Evan Leon *computer science educator*

**Palatine**
Bokhari, Naila *mathematician, educational consultant*

**Plainfield**
Reichenbach, Linda Louise *mathematician, educator, language educator*

**Springfield**
Mims, Merrill Ted *computer scientist, department chairman*

**Sugar Grove**
Del Medico, Amy *mathematics professor*

**University Park**
Hakala, Reino William *mathematician, educator*

**Urbana**
Amir, Eyal *computer scientist, educator*
Burkholder, Donald Lyman *mathematician, educator*
Carroll, Robert Wayne *mathematics professor*
Gray, John Walker *mathematician, educator*
Henson, C. Ward *mathematician, educator*
Knight, Frank Bardsley *mathematics professor*
Liebman, Judith Rae Stenzel *retired operations research specialist*
Schupp, Paul Eugene *mathematician, educator*
Sreenivas, Ramavarapu S. *mathematics professor*
Tondeur, Philippe Maurice *mathematician, educator*
Yoon, Wonyong *computer scientist, researcher*

**Westchester**
Pavelka, Elaine Blanche *mathematics professor*

## INDIANA

**Bloomington**
Buente, Wayne Gerald *information scientist, researcher*
McRobbie, Michael Alexander *computer scientist, researcher, academic administrator*
Prosser, Franklin Pierce *computer scientist*
Purdom, Paul Walton, Jr. *computer scientist*
Puri, Madan Lal *mathematics professor*
Solomon, Bruce Michael *mathematician, educator*
Temam, Roger M. *mathematician, educator*

**Evansville**
Kimberling, Clark Hershall *mathematics professor, small business owner*

**Fort Wayne**
Beineke, Lowell Wayne *mathematics professor*
Romary, Thomas Gerald *mathematician, educator, writer*
Stoll, Wilhelm *mathematics professor*

**Gary**
Jacobs, Chandra J. *mathematician, educator*

**Greencastle**
Anderson, John Robert *retired mathematics professor*

**Hammond**
Ruan, Weihua *mathematician*

**Indianapolis**
Chen, Jake Yue *computer scientist, bioinformatician*
Cliff, Johnnie Marie *mathematics professor, chemistry professor*
Cravens, Gary Dean *information scientist, physician*
Reid, William Hill *mathematics professor*
Yovits, Marshall Clinton *information scientist, educator, dean*

**Kokomo**
Ramos, Jamie *information scientist*

**Lafayette**
Drazin, Michael Peter *mathematician, researcher*

**Muncie**
Ali, Mir Masoom *statistician, educator*
Cartwright, Susan Merrick *mathematician, educator*
East, David Harold *mathematics professor*
Shobe, Franklin Dale *mathematician, educator*

**Notre Dame**
Evens, Samuel Robert *mathematics professor*
Goetz, Abraham *retired mathematics professor*
Kogge, Peter Michael *computer scientist, educator*
Sommese, Andrew John *mathematics professor*

**Syracuse**
Metcalf, Philip Leslie *mathematics professor, career planning administrator*

**Terre Haute**
Bagert, Donald Joseph *computer scientist, educator*

**West Lafayette**
Abhyankar, Shreeram Shankar *mathematics professor*
Danielli-Garofalo, Donatella *mathematics professor*
Wood, Terry Lee *mathematics professor*

**Westville**
Serwatka, Judy Ann *computer and information systems educator*

## IOWA

**Ames**
Dahiya, Rajbir Singh *mathematics professor, researcher*
David, Herbert Aron *retired statistician, educator*
Fuller, Wayne Arthur *statistics educator*
Kang, Dae-Ki *computer scientist*

**Cedar Falls**
Haack, Joel K. *mathematics professor, academic administrator*

**Cedar Rapids**
Bahadur, Birendra *displays research specialist*

**Eagle Grove**
Sundberg, Gordon Neil *retired mathematics and computer sciences instructor*

**Grinnell**
Adelberg, Arnold Melvin *mathematics professor, researcher*

**Iowa City**
Bognar, Matthew *statistician, educator*
Broffitt, James Drake *statistician, educator*
Hogg, Robert Vincent, Jr. *mathematical statistician, educator*
Jorgensen, Palle E.T. *mathematician, educator*
Moore, Brian Edward *mathematics professor*
Robertson, Timothy Joel *statistician, educator*

## KANSAS

**Emporia**
Emerson, Marion Preston *mathematics professor*

**Hutchinson**
Gamber, Kenneth M. *mathematics professor, farmer*

**Lawrence**
Himmelberg, Charles John III *mathematics professor, researcher*
Lerner, David Evan *mathematician*
Pasik-Duncan, Bozenna Janina *mathematics professor, researcher*

**Overland Park**
Burger, Henry G. *vocabulary scientist, anthropologist, writer*
Carpenter, Nancy E. *mathematics professor*

**Pittsburg**
Harris, James Dean *computer scientist, educator*

**Shawnee Mission**
Flora, Jairus Dale, Jr. *statistician*

## KENTUCKY

**Frankfort**
Al-Hamdani, Wasim A. *computer science educator*

**Hazard**
Cory, Cynthia Strong *mathematics professor*
Stewart, Sharon Rose *mathematics professor*

**Lexington**
Charnigo, Richard John, Jr. *statistician, educator*
Mostert, Paul Stallings *retired mathematician*

**Louisville**
Datta, Somnath *statistician, educator*
Nasraoui, Olfa *computer scientist, educator, electrical engineer*
Rempala, Grzegorz A. *mathematician, statistician, educator*

**Somerset**
Armstrong, Anthony L. *mathematics professor*

## LOUISIANA

**Baton Rouge**
Meyinsse, Joseph Appolinaire *mathematics professor, researcher*
Quartararo, Philip, Jr. *mathematics professor*

**Eunice**
Joubert, Lorrie B. *mathematics professor*

**Lafayette**
Cain, Judith Sharp *mathematics professor, consultant*

**New Orleans**
Birtel, Frank Thomas *mathematician, philosopher, educator*
Hà, Tài Huy *mathematician*
Harvey, John Grover *mathematics professor, information scientist*
Yang, DaGang *mathematician, educator*

**Shreveport**
Brandl, Mary-Katherine *mathematics professor*

## MAINE

**Orono**
Dodge, Clayton Willard *mathematics professor*

**Palermo**
Anderson, Alfred Oliver *mathematician, consultant*

**West Bath**
Jorgensen, Jenny *mathematician, educator*

## MARYLAND

**Adamstown**
Tidball, Charles Stanley *computer scientist, educator*

**Adelphi**
Kirwan, William English, II, *mathematics professor, academic administrator*

**Annapolis**
Crawford, Carol Gloria *mathematician, educator*
Sheppard, John Wilbur *computer research scientist*

**Ashton**
Smith, Kent Ashton *information scientist, consultant*

**Baltimore**
Bausell, R. Barker, Jr. *research methodology educator*
Boardman, John Michael *mathematician, educator*
Choudhury, Dipa *mathematician, educator*
Lidtke, Doris Keefe *retired computer science educator*
Moulton, Lawrence Hale *statistician, educator*
N'guerekata, Gaston Mandata *mathematician, department chairman*
Rosenberg, Edwin Harold *systems analyst*
Rubin, Aviel David *computer science educator, writer*
Shiffman, Bernard *mathematician, educator*
Wierman, John Charles *mathematician, educator*
Woodson, Leon C. *mathematics professor*

**Bethesda**
Joo, Jungnam *statistician*
Kennevan, Walter James *computer science educator*
Moriyama, Iwao Milton *statistician, consultant*
Moshman, Jack *statistical consultant*
Park, Yonil *statistician*
Tilley, Carolyn Bittner *information scientist*
Weiss, George Herbert *mathematician, consultant*
Zheng, Gang *mathematician, statistician, researcher*

**Catonsville**
Clelland, Nelda Diane *mathematics professor*

**College Park**
Antman, Stuart Sheldon *mathematician, educator*
Basili, Victor Robert *computer science educator*
Lucas, Henry Cameron, Jr. *information scientist, educator, writer*
Minker, Jack *computer scientist, educator*
Warner, C(harles) Robert *mathematics professor*
Yorke, James Alan *mathematician, educator*

**Columbia**
Gregorie, Corazon Arzalem *operations research specialist*

**Jersey City**
Mastro, Victor John *mathematician, educator*
Metallo, Frances Rosebell *mathematics professor*

**Lakewood**
Houle, Joseph E. *mathematics professor*

**Mahwah**
Potocka, Katarzyna *mathematics professor*

**Matawan**
Campbell, Earl Duncan *computer consultant*
Rivera-Dominguez, Alberto *mathematician, educator, mechanical engineer*

**Middletown**
Rosenberg, Eric *mathematician*

**Mount Laurel**
Huttner, Louise Ann *mathematician, educator*

**Neptune City**
DeValue, John M. *retired computer science educator*

**Neshanic Station**
Muckenhoupt, Benjamin *retired mathematics professor*

**New Brunswick**
Kahn, Jeffry *mathematics professor*
Kruskal, Martin David *mathematical physicist, astrophysicist, educator*
Kulikowski, Casimir Alexander *computer scientist, engineer, educator*
Scanlon, Jane Cronin *mathematics professor*

**Newark**
Miura, Robert Mitsuru *mathematician, researcher, educator*
Muratov, Cyrill B. *mathematician, educator*
Verkhovsky, Boris *computer scientist, educator*

**Oradell**
Tong, Hing *mathematician, educator*

**Perth Amboy**
Washington, Marcel Maurice *statistician, researcher*

**Piscataway**
Chaovalitwongse, Wanpracha *mathematician, researcher*
Hammer, Peter L. *mathematics professor, researcher*
Iwaniec, Henryk *mathematics professor*
Li, Yanyan *mathematician, educator*
Reiley, T(homas) Phillip *systems analyst, consultant*

**Princeton**
Aizenman, Michael *mathematics professor, physics professor, researcher*
Bhargava, Manjul *mathematics professor, researcher*
Bombieri, Enrico *mathematician, educator*
Bourgain, Jean *mathematician*
Chang, Sun-Yung Alice *mathematics professor*
Chazelle, Bernard *computer science educator*
Deligne, Pierre René *mathematician*
Fefferman, Charles Louis *mathematics professor*
Felton, Edward William *computer scientist, educator*
Gunning, Robert Clifford *mathematician, educator*
Haberman, Shelby Joel *statistician, educator*
Katz, Nicholas M. *mathematician*
Khutoryansky, Naum M. *mathematician, educator*
Kobayashi, Hisashi *computer scientist, dean*
Kollár, János *mathematics professor*
Langlands, Robert Phelan *mathematician, educator*
Leader, Solomon *retired mathematics professor*
Levin, Simon Asher *mathematician, ecologist, educator*
Lu, Xiaoguang *computer scientist*
MacPherson, Robert Duncan *mathematician, educator*
Nash, John Forbes, Jr. *mathematician, researcher*
Okounkov, Andrei *mathematics professor*
Selberg, Atle *retired mathematician*
Sinai, Yakov G. *theoretical mathematician, educator*
Singer, Burton Herbert *statistics educator*
Stein, Elias M. *mathematician, educator*
Voevodsky, Vladimir *mathematician*
Wiles, Andrew J. *mathematician, educator*
Zhao, Wenyi *systems analyst*

**Princeton Junction**
Wu, Huan-ter *statistician*

**Randolph**
Sarmiento-Fernandez, Jorge *mathematics professor, consultant*

**Ridgefield Park**
Litwinowicz, Anthony *information scientist, researcher*

**Rivervale**
Posamentier, Alfred Steven *mathematics professor, dean*

**Roseland**
Zhu, Junhong *biostatistician*

**Short Hills**
Loren, Allan Z. *business information company executive*

**Somerset**
Becker, Phyllis *systems analyst*

**Teaneck**
Chen, Zong *computer scientist, educator*
Zwass, Vladimir *computer science and information systems educator*

**West Orange**
Ko, Chia-Wen *biostatistician, researcher*

**Willingboro**
Ingerman, Peter Zilahy *systems analyst, consultant*

**Woodbury**
Zimmer, Janie Louise *mathematics professor, academic administrator*

**Yardville**
Zweig, Steven Frederick *statistician*

## NEW MEXICO

**Albuquerque**
Bell, Stoughton *computer scientist, mathematician, educator*
Lee, Sang-Joon *statistical professor*
Stone, Alexander Paul *mathematics professor*

**Hobbs**
Roan, William C. *mathematics professor*

**Las Cruces**
Ahmed, Abdelali *computer scientist*
Muller, David Eugene *mathematics professor, computer scientist, educator*
Sweezy, Caroline *mathematician, educator*
Tran, Son Cao *computer science educator*

**Los Alamos**
Kao, Chih-Yue Jim *computer scientist, educator*
Lipnikov, Konstantin *mathematician*

**Santa Fe**
Gallegor, Mary Ellen *mathematics professor*
Kellner, Richard George *mathematician, computer scientist*

**Socorro**
Wang, Bixiang *mathematician*

## NEW YORK

**Albany**
Reinhold, Karin *mathematics professor*
Rosenkrantz, Daniel J. *computer science educator*

**Alfred**
Smith, Mark Arthur *information scientist, educator*

**Ardsley**
Grad, Arthur *mathematician, educator*

**Aurora**
Sievers, Sally Riedel *mathematics professor*

**Batavia**
Rigerman, Ruth Underhill *mathematics professor*

**Bayside**
Chugh, Om Parkash *mathematics professor, researcher, forensics specialist*
Fabricant, Mona *mathematics and computer science educator*

**Binghamton**
Arcones, Miguel A. *mathematics professor*
Hilton, Peter John *mathematician, educator*
Zacks, Shelemyahu *mathematical sciences educator*

**Bronx**
Koranyi, Adam *mathematics professor*
Lyons, Damian M. *computer scientist, director*
Rose, Israel Harold *mathematics professor*
Seltzer, William *statistician, social science administrator*

**Brooklyn**
Butler, Alice Gloria *mathematician, educator*
Freilich, Gerald *mathematics professor*
Lutwak, Erwin *mathematician, educator*
Menil, Violeta Cruz *mathematician, educator, consultant*
Pennisten, John William *computer scientist, actuary, linguist*
Sakhnovich, Lev Aronovich *mathematics educator, researcher*
Weill, Georges Gustave *mathematics professor*

**Buffalo**
Biondini, Gino *mathematics professor*
Coburn, Lewis Alan *mathematics professor*
Hauptman, Herbert Aaron *mathematician, educator, researcher*
Kelemen, Arpad *computer scientist, information scientist*
Penniman, W. David *information scientist, educator, management consultant*
Seitz, Mary Lee *mathematics professor*
Shapiro, Stuart Charles *computer scientist, educator*
Vishwanath, Arun *information scientist, educator*
Wiesenberg, Russel John *statistician*

**Canandaigua**
Howard, Jeffrey M. *computer science professor*

**Clinton**
Bailey, Mark W. *computer scientist, educator*

**Farmingdale**
Winn, John Arthur, Jr. *mathematics educator*

**Flushing**
Mendelson, Elliott *mathematician, educator*

**Garden City**
High, Robert V. *statistician, educator*

**Hamilton**
Tucker, Thomas William *mathematics professor*

**Hawthorne**
Dan, Asit *computer scientist, research scientist*
Gong, Leiguang *computer scientist, researcher*

Mihaila, George Andrei *computer scientist, researcher*
Ward, Christopher *computer scientist, researcher*

**Ithaca**
Billera, Louis J(oseph) *mathematics professor*
Bramble, James Henry *mathematician, educator*
Dynkin, Eugene B. *mathematics professor*
Earle, Clifford John, Jr. *mathematician*
Gross, Leonard *mathematics professor*
Hartmanis, Juris *computer scientist, educator*
Hopcroft, John Edward *computer scientist, educator*
Kleinberg, Jon M. *computer scientist, educator*
Morgenstern, Matthew *computer scientist*
Nerode, Anil *mathematician, educator*
Shore, Richard Arnold *mathematics professor*
Trotter, Leslie Earl *operations research specialist, educator*

**Jackson Heights**
Sohmer, Bernard *mathematics professor, administrator*

**Kenmore**
Kenny, John Edward *computer analyst*

**New York**
Agwu, Nkechi Madonna *mathematics professor*
Aschoff, Lawrence Michael (Mick Aschoff) *computer information scientist*
Barquero, Pedro B. *mathematician, researcher*
Bellovin, Steven M. *computer science educator*
Chichilnisky, Graciela *mathematician, educator, economist, writer*
Christ, Lily Esther Shih *mathematics professor*
Chu, C. K. *applied mathematician, educator*
Derman, Cyrus *mathematical statistician*
Edwards, Harold Mortimer *mathematics professor*
Frankel, Martin Richard *statistician, educator, consultant*
Gaifman, Haim *mathematician, philosopher, educator*
Garabedian, Paul Roesel *mathematics professor*
Goldstein, Avraham *mathematician, computer scientist*
Gomory, Ralph Edward *mathematician, foundation administrator*
Gross, Jonathan Light *computer scientist, mathematician, educator*
Gyles, Robert *mathematics professor*
Hershkop, Shlomo *computer scientist, educator*
Kurnow, Ernest *statistician, educator*
Lax, Peter David *mathematician, educator*
Lin, Fang-Hua *mathematics professor*
Morawetz, Cathleen Synge *mathematician*
Mowshowitz, Abbe *computer scientist*
Moyne, John Abel *computer scientist, linguist, educator*
Newman, Charles Michael *mathematician, physicist, educator*
Nirenberg, Louis *mathematician, educator*
Nogina, Elena Y. *mathematics professor, researcher*
Paik, Myunghee Cho *statistician, educator*
Pierre, Dwight Anthony *mathematician, educator*
Pnueli, Amir *computer science educator*
Rindskopf, David *statistician, educator*
Rizkin, Iosif *systems, circuits, and computer scientist, writer*
Schulzrinne, Henning G. *computer science educator*
Sellers, Peter Hoadley *mathematician, educator*
Sloujitel, Jacob Ben *mathematics professor, researcher*
Sullivan, Dennis P. *mathematics professor*
Taylor, Jean Ellen *mathematics professor, researcher*
Traub, J(oseph) F(rederick) *computer scientist, educator*
Weitzner, Harold *mathematics professor*

**Newburgh**
Fothergill, Lee James *mathematics professor*

**Old Westbury**
Altabet, Meryl Joyce *mathematics professor*
Gordon, Florence Shanfield *mathematics professor*

**Ozone Park**
Joanidhi, Zhani *mathematician, educator*

**Pittsford**
Hollingsworth, Jack Waring *mathematics professor*

**Port Washington**
Roy, Ranja *mathematician, educator*

**Poughkeepsie**
Steinhorn, Charles Ira *mathematician, educator*

**Rhinebeck**
Scherr, Allan Lee *computer scientist, software executive*

**Rochester**
Yuan, Bo *computer scientist, educator*

**Rome**
Bello, Paul F. *computer scientist*

**Schaghticoke**
O'Connor, Abigail Elizabeth *mathematician, educator, science educator*

**Schenectady**
Otto, Peter *information scientist, educator*

**Selden**
Cook, Lisa Marie *mathematics professor, mathematics learning center coordinator*

**Staten Island**
Ionescu, Adrian *information scientist, educator*

**Stony Brook**
Anderson, Michael Thomas *mathematics professor, researcher, director*
Glimm, James Gilbert *mathematician, educator*
Laspina, Peter Joseph *computer resource educator*

Lawson, H(erbert) Blaine, Jr. *mathematician, educator*
Milnor, John Willard *mathematician*
Tucker, Alan Curtiss *mathematics professor*

**Syracuse**
Graver, Jack Edward *mathematics professor*
Hansen, Per Brinch *computer scientist, researcher*
Hsu, Lifang *statistician, department chairman*
Malhotra, Yogesh *computer scientist, educator, computer engineer*
Pardee, Otway O'Meara *computer scientist, educator*
Shroyer-Keno, Joan Elane *information analyst*

**Tarrytown**
Maun, Mary Ellen *computer consultant*

**Troy**
Acar, Evrim *computer scientist*
Drew, Donald Allen *mathematical sciences educator*
Magdon-Ismail, Malik *computer science professor*
Szymanski, Boleslaw Karol *computer scientist, educator, entrepreneur*

**West Hempstead**
Guggenheimer, Heinrich Walter *mathematician, educator*

**Westbury**
Sandler, Gerald Howard *computer scientist, educator, information technology executive*

**Williamsville**
Berner, Robert Frank *managerial statistics educator, administrator*

**Yorktown Heights**
Choi, Changhwan *operations research specialist*
Hoffman, Alan Jerome *mathematician, educator*
Iyengar, Arun K. *computer scientist*
Lei, Hui *computer scientist*
Saon, George A. *computer scientist, researcher*
Winograd, Shmuel *mathematician*

## NORTH CAROLINA

**Archdale**
O'Hara, Karen Ann *mathematician, educator*

**Boone**
Schneberger, Scott L. *information systems educator*

**Cape Carteret**
Mullikin, Thomas Wilson *mathematics professor*

**Cary**
Fan, Wei *operations research specialist*

**Chapel Hill**
Brooks, Frederick Phillips, Jr. *computer scientist, educator*

**Charlotte**
Kawczak, Janusz *mathematician, educator*
Klibanov, Michael Victor *mathematics professor*
Wright, Wayne Kenneth *federal agency statistician*

**Cullowhee**
Willis, Ralph Houston *mathematics professor*

**Davidson**
Klein, Benjamin Garrett *mathematics professor, consultant*

**Durham**
Edelsbrunner, Herbert *computer scientist, educator, mathematician*
Pieper, Carl F. *statistician, educator*
Sowa, Artur *mathematician, researcher*

**Fayetteville**
Truong, Dothang *information scientist, educator*

**Greensboro**
Xu, Jinsheng *computer scientist, educator*

**Hendersonville**
Dalton, Robert Edgar *retired mathematician, computer scientist*

**Raleigh**
Bakalov, Bojko Nentchev *mathematician*
Chou, Wushow *retired computer scientist*
Chukwu, Ethelbert Nwakuche *mathematics professor*
Nguyen, Hoan Kim Huynh *mathematician*
Pao, Chia-Ven *mathematics professor*
Wetsch, John Robert *information scientist*
Windham, Donald Eric *bioinformatics analyst*

**Research Triangle Park**
Biemer, Paul Philip *statistician, educator*

**Rocky Mount**
Killoran, Thomas M. *mathematics professor, department chairman*

**West Jefferson**
Merrion, Arthur Benjamin *mathematics professor, tree farmer*

**Wilmington**
Herman, Russell Leland *mathematics professor, physics professor*

**Winston Salem**
Sawyer, John Wesley *retired mathematics and computer science educator, consultant*

## NORTH DAKOTA

**Mayville**
Champion, Kathleen Ann *mathematics professor*

**Fort Worth**
Doran, Robert Stuart *mathematician, educator*
Fan, Peng *mathematician*
Sullenberger, Ara Broocks *mathematics professor*

**Houston**
Gardner, Everette Shaw, Jr. *information sciences educator, consultant, author*
Glowinski, Roland *mathematics professor*
Golubitsky, Martin Aaron *mathematician, educator*
Hempel, John P. *mathematics professor*
Hodgess, Erin Marie *statistics educator*
Kakadiaris, Ioannis *computer science educator*
Kavraki, Lydia *computer scientist, educator*
Miller, Charles Rickie *systems analyst, engineering executive*
Scott, David Warren *statistics educator*
Sirisaengtaksin, Ongard *computer scientist, mathematician, educator*
Swartz, Michael D. *statistical geneticist*
Tapia, Richard Alfred *mathematics professor*
Tong, Louis Lik-Fu *information scientist*
Tucker, Susan *mathematics professor*
Veech, William Austin *mathematics professor*
Wang, Chao-Cheng *mathematician, engineer*
Wright, Clark Phillips *computer systems specialist*

**Irving**
Conger, Sue Ann *computer information systems educator*

**Kingsville**
Cecil, David Rolf *mathematician, educator*

**Laredo**
Cai, Gangshu *computer science professor*
Goonatilake, Rohitha *mathematician, educator*
Wu, Fuming *computer science educator*

**Lewisville**
Ferguson, R. Neil *computer scientist, consultant*

**Lubbock**
Seshaiyer, Padmanabhan *mathematician, educator*

**Marshall**
Capehart, Steven Russell *mathematics professor*

**Mesquite**
Sepulvado, Joseph Michael *computer information scientist*

**Odessa**
Bouquin, Samantha Erin *mathematics professor*

**Richardson**
Easttom, Chuck *computer scientist, educator*
Tate, William Fleming, IV, *mathematics educator*
Wiorkowski, John James *mathematics professor*

**Round Rock**
Khalid, Humayun *computer scientist, consultant*

**San Antonio**
Arciniega, Armando *mathematics professor*
Estep, Myrna Lynne *systems analyst, philosophy educator*
Fariabi, Said *mathematics professor*
Redfield, Carol Ann Luckhardt *computer scientist, educator*

**Sherman**
Joshi, Madhukar *statistician, consultant*

**Texas City**
Robertson, Paul Francis *mathematician, educator*

**Tyler**
Bailey, Nan Hutchins *mathematician, educator*

**Valley Mills**
Odell, Patrick Lowry *mathematics professor*

**Waco**
Sheng, Qin *mathematics professor*

**Whitehouse**
Cavanaugh, Charles Davis *computer scientist, educator*

**Wichita Falls**
Stringfellow, Catherine Veronique *computer scientist, educator*

**UTAH**

**Logan**
Symanzik, Juergen *statistician, educator*

**Orem**
Moore, Hal G. *mathematician, educator*

**Salt Lake City**
Chaara, Mohammed *statistician, consultant*
Cherkaev, Andrej Vsevolodovich *mathematician, educator*
Livne, Oren Eliezer *mathematician, educator*
Post, Gina *mathematics professor, researcher*

**VERMONT**

**North Bennington**
Adler, Irving *mathematician*

**Northfield**
Poodiack, Robert D. *mathematics professor*

**Norwich**
Snapper, Ernst *mathematics professor*

**VIRGINIA**

**Alexandria**
Chen, Fen *mathematician, educator, researcher*

Dowling, Dean Edward *information scientist, educator*
Shrier, Stefan *mathematician, educator*

**Arlington**
Perry, Walter Leo *information scientist, operations research specialist*

**Blacksburg**
Arnold, Jesse Charles *retired statistician*
Good, Irving John *statistician, educator, philosopher*
Hovakimyan, Naira *mathematician, educator*
Posey, Eldon Eugene *mathematician, educator*
Varadarajan, Srinidhi *computer scientist*

**Charlottesville**
Horgan, Cornelius Oliver *mathematics professor, engineering educator*
MacAskill, Lloyd Edwin *systems analyst, consultant*
Parshall, Karen Virginia Hunger *mathematician*
Thomas, Lawrence Eldon *mathematics professor*

**Chesapeake**
Locke, L. Muriel *mathematician, educator*

**Clifton**
Hoffman, Karla Leigh *mathematician, educator*

**Danville**
Tucker, Gary Allan *information scientist, educator, minister*

**Dulles**
McGraw, Gary *computer scientist, writer*

**Emory**
Jones, Jerry Lee *computer educator*

**Fairfax**
Harrison, Robert Allen *systems analyst*
Mulvaney, Mary Frederica *systems analyst*
Zhang, Xinwen *computer scientist, researcher*

**Fort Belvoir**
Clema, Joe Kotouc *computer scientist*
Miglio, Sheryl Ann *computer scientist*
Thompson, Carlynn Jean *information scientist*

**Fort Lee**
Corona, Joseph Anthony *operations research analyst, mathematician, educator*

**Fredericksburg**
Hajek, Otomar *mathematician, educator*

**Gainesville**
Bendig, Judith Joan *information systems specialist, computer company executive*

**Hampton**
Nazaryan, Hovakim *mathematician, researcher*
Verma, Arun K. *mathematician, educator*

**Heathsville**
Stubbs, Susan Conklin *retired statistician*

**Herndon**
Douglass, Robert Joseph, Jr. *computer scientist*
Draper, William David *systems administrator*
Hollis, Katherine Mary *information scientist, consultant*

**Leesburg**
Hetzel, Alice M. *statistician, researcher*

**Lexington**
Tierney, Michael John *mathematics professor*

**Lynchburg**
Terzic, Petar *mathematician, educator*

**Manakin Sabot**
Thompson, Walter David, Jr. *systems analyst*

**Manassas**
Bruno, Irene Evelyn *mathematician, educator*

**Mc Lean**
Lillard, Mark Hill III *computer scientist, consultant, retired military officer*

**Newport News**
Summerville, Richard M. *mathematician, academic administrator*

**Norfolk**
Earl, Archie William, Sr. *mathematician, educator*
Fang, Ming *mathematics professor*

**Richlands**
Thornhill, M. Jerry *mathematics professor*

**Richmond**
Charlesworth, Arthur Thomas *mathematics professor*
Choi, Hongsik *computer science professor*

**Roanoke**
Smith, Nora Nunnery *information scientist, educator*
Wallace, Linda Kay *mathematics professor*

**Sterling**
Martin, Roger John *computer scientist*

**Sweet Briar**
Wassell, Stephen Robert *mathematics professor, researcher*

**Vienna**
Gardenier, John Stark *statistician, philosopher, researcher, writer*
Gardenier, Turkan Kumbaraci *statistician, researcher*

**Virginia Beach**
Pugsley, Richard Dallas *mathematics professor*

**Williamsburg**
Fedorov, Andriy Yuri *computer scientist, researcher*
Rodman, Leiba *mathematician*

**WASHINGTON**

**Eastsound**
de Boor, Carl-Wilhelm R. *mathematician*

**Ellensburg**
Comstock, Dale Robert *mathematics professor*

**Everett**
Walbesser, Henry Herman *computer science educator*

**Federal Way**
Cunningham, John Randolph *project manager*

**Kelso**
McLain, Paul King *systems analyst*

**Kenmore**
Sobolewski, John Stephen *computer scientist, director, consultant*

**Kennewick**
Cochran, James Alan *mathematics professor, department chairman*

**Orcas**
Greever, John *retired mathematics professor*

**Pullman**
Kallaher, Michael Joseph *mathematics professor*
Medidi, Muralidhar *computer scientist, educator*

**Redmond**
Freedman, Michael Hartley *mathematician, educator*
Kimmich, Jon Bradford *computer science program executive*
Lomet, David Bruce *computer scientist*
Oliver, Nuria *computer scientist*

**Richland**
Petrini, Fabrizio *computer scientist, researcher*

**Seattle**
Breslow, Norman Edward *biostatistics educator, researcher*
Criminale, William Oliver, Jr. *applied mathematics professor*
Doran, Charles Francis, Jr. *mathematician, mathematics professor*
Gillispie, Steven Brian *systems analyst, researcher*
Kalet, Ira Joseph *medical computer scientist*
Klee, Victor La Rue *mathematician, educator*
Lee, John Marshall *mathematics professor*
Marshall, Donald E. *mathematics professor*
Mason, Robert McSpadden *information scientist, educator, dean*
Michael, Ernest Arthur *mathematics professor*
Segal, Jack *mathematics professor*

**Tacoma**
Stuart, Jeffrey L. *mathematics professor, consultant*

**Yakima**
Jongeward, George Ronald *retired systems analyst*

**WEST VIRGINIA**

**Montgomery**
Munasinghe, Ranjith Arachchige *mathematics professor, engineer*

**WISCONSIN**

**Beaver Dam**
Jimenez, Juan F. *mathematician, educator*

**Green Bay**
Conley, William Cleland *statistician, educator*

**Madison**
Askey, Richard Allen *mathematician, educator*
Beck, Anatole *mathematician, educator*
Draper, Norman Richard *statistician, educator*
Johnson, Millard Wallace, Jr. *mathematics professor, engineering educator*
Kurtz, Thomas Gordon *mathematics professor*
Malkus, David Starr *mathematician*
Mau, Bob *statistician*
Ney, Peter Ernest *mathematician, educator*
Robinson, Stephen Michael *mathematician, educator*

**Manitowoc**
McBride, Craig Patrick *mathematics professor*

**Menomonie**
Schmidt, Laura Jean *mathematics professor*

**Milwaukee**
Mao, En *information scientist, educator, research scientist*

**Oshkosh**
Price, Kenneth L. *mathematics professor*
Shahzad, M. Ahmad *computer scientist*

**Pleasant Prairie**
Biland, Alan Thomas *computer integrated manufacturing executive*

**Whitewater**
Baica, Malvina Florica *mathematician, educator, researcher*
Nam, Ki-Bong *mathematics professor*

**WYOMING**

**Casper**
Wildman, Peter Roberts *mathematics professor*

## TERRITORIES OF THE UNITED STATES

**PUERTO RICO**

**Mayaguez**
Collins, Dennis Glenn *mathematics professor*

**San Juan**
Keyantuo, Valentin *mathematician, educator*
Pasnicu, Cornel *mathematician, educator*
Teleman, Silviu *mathematician, educator*

## MILITARY ADDRESSES OF THE UNITED STATES

**EUROPE**

**APO**
Simpson, Sandra Kay *operations research specialist*

## CANADA

**BRITISH COLUMBIA**

**Vancouver**
Clark, Colin Whitcomb *mathematics professor*
Feldman, Joel Shalom *mathematician*
Granirer, Edmond Ernest *mathematician, educator*
Sion, Maurice *mathematics professor*

**Victoria**
Manning, Eric *computer scientist, educator, dean, researcher*
Meadow, Charles *information scientist, writer*

**NEW BRUNSWICK**

**Saint Andrews**
Anderson, John Murray *operations research specialist, consultant, retired academic administrator*

**NOVA SCOTIA**

**Halifax**
Fillmore, Peter Arthur *mathematician, educator*

**ONTARIO**

**Kingston**
Campbell, Louis Lorne *mathematics professor*

**London**
Bauer, Michael Anthony *computer scientist, educator*
Borwein, David *mathematics professor*

**Ottawa**
Csörgő, Miklós *mathematics and statistics educator*
Dlab, Vlastimil *mathematics professor, researcher*
Fellegi, Ivan Peter *statistician*

**Toronto**
Friedlander, John Benjamin *mathematician, educator*
Gotlieb, Calvin Carl *computer scientist, educator*
Rooney, Paul George *mathematics professor*

**Waterloo**
Aczél, János Dezső *mathematician*
Gladwell, Graham Maurice Leslie *mathematician, civil engineering educator*
Paldus, Josef *mathematics professor*

**QUEBEC**

**Montreal**
Moser, William Oscar Jules *mathematics professor*
Suen, Ching Yee *computer scientist, educator, researcher*

**Quebec City**
Theodorescu, Radu Amza Serban *mathematician, educator*

**SASKATCHEWAN**

**Regina**
Symes, Lawrence Richard *computer science educator, university dean*

## BULGARIA

**Blagoevgrad**
Stefanov, Stefan Minev *mathematics professor, researcher*

## CHINA

**Beijing**
Wei, Yuchuan *mathematician, electrical engineer, physicist, researcher*

**Shanghai**
Lu, Bao-Liang *computer scientist, educator*
Hsieh, Din-Yu *applied mathematics professor*

## CZECH REPUBLIC

**Brno**
Klapka, Jindřich Ludvík *mathematician, research scientist*

**Prague**
Holena, Martin *computer scientist*

## ENGLAND

**Leicester**
Harijan, Ram *technology transfer researcher*

**London**
Gelenbe, Sami Erol *computer scientist, engineering educator*
Ralston, Anthony *computer scientist, mathematician, educator*

## FRANCE

**Orvault**
Lorand, Cedric *information scientist, translator*

**Paris**
Serre, Jean-Pierre *mathematician, scholar*
Yuechiming, Roger Yue Yuen Shing *mathematics professor*

**Valbonne**
Junker, Ulrich *computer scientist, researcher*

## GERMANY

**Berlin**
Jochmann, Frank *mathematician*

**Braunschweig**
Diethelm, Kai *mathematician, researcher*
Leseberg, Dieter Wolfgang Michael *mathematician*

**Bremen**
Wells, Raymond O'Neil, Jr. *mathematics professor, researcher*

## HONG KONG

**South Horizons**
Chen, Concordia Chao *mathematician*

## INDIA

**Kolkata**
Mazumder, Bijoy Singha *mathematician, educator, researcher*

**Salem**
Thandapani, Ethiraj *mathematics professor*

## ITALY

**Turin**
Rossi, Guido A(ntonio) *mathematics professor, researcher*

## JAPAN

**Gifu**
Hatada, Kazuyuki *mathematician, educator*

**Gunma**
Hironaka, Heisuke *mathematics professor, academic administrator*

**Ibaraki**
Urabe, Tohsuke *mathematics professor, researcher*

**Kasugai**
Miyake, Yasuji *computer science educator*

**Tokyo**
Eto, Hajime *retired information scientist, educator*
Kato, Shuichi *information scientist, educator*
Yaku, Takeo T. *computer scientist, educator*

## PORTUGAL

**Lisbon**
Campos, Luís Manuel Braga da Costa *mathematics, physics, acoustics and aeronautics educator*

## REPUBLIC OF KOREA

**Kyungpuk**
Kim, Hyun-Sung *information scientist, educator*

---

**Seoul**
Keum, Jong-Hae *mathematician, educator*
Oh, Myoungho *computer scientist, educator*

## RUSSIA

**Moscow**
Novikov, Sergei Petrovitch *mathematician*
Romanovski, Mikhail Rem *mathematician*
Varlamov, Vladimir Valentinovich *mathematics educator*

## SCOTLAND

**Edinburgh**
Atiyah, Sir Michael Francis *mathematician*

## SWEDEN

**Orno**
Hallberg, Bengt O. *systems strategy director, fiber optic specialist*

**Västerås**
Xiong, Ning *computer scientist, researcher*

## TURKEY

**Kocaeli**
Sevilgen, Fatih Erdogan *computer scientist, educator*

## ADDRESS UNPUBLISHED

Adaikkalavan, Raman *computer scientist, educator*
Airoldi, Edoardo Maria *statistician, researcher, computer scientist, consultant*
Allore, Heather Gwynn *statistician*
Arden, Bruce Wesley *retired computer scientist, retired engineering educator*
Armstrong, Sonya M. *mathematics professor, researcher*
Arrigo, Danny *mathematics professor*
Bailar, Barbara Ann *retired statistician*
Barrett, Lida Kittrell *mathematics professor*
Bayram, Saziye *mathematics professor*
Bender, Virginia Best *computer scientist, educator*
Bentley, Donald Lyon *mathematics professor, statistics educator, minister*
Bhadra, Jayanta *computer scientist, electrical engineer*
Bhatnagar, Sudeept *computer scientist, researcher*
Birrer, Stefan *computer scientist, researcher*
Bleicher, Michael Nathaniel *mathematics professor*
Bloch, Anthony Michael *mathematician, educator*
Boardman, Elizabeth Drake *computer security professional*
Bobbitt, James Lyle *computer programmer, systems analyst*
Bollapragada, Ramesh *information scientist, educator*
Boschmans, Barbara *mathematics professor*
Brahnam, Sheryl *computer scientist, researcher*
Browder, Felix Earl *mathematician, educator*
Budur, Nero *mathematician*
Caldwell, Cindy Sue *mathematics professor*
Cameron, Kirk MacGregor Drummond *statistician*
Champine, George A. *computer scientist*
Chang, Samuel Henry *computer scientist, educator*
Chati, Mandar Kalidas *operations research specialist*
Cheeger, Jeff *mathematics educator*
Chen, Shuang *computer science professional*
Choi, Ji Young *mathematics professor*
Choi, Youngok *information science educator*
Chow, Timothy Yi-Chung *mathematician, systems engineer*
Christin, Nicolas *computer scientist, researcher*
Chung, Wingyan *computer scientist, information scientist, educator*
Clarke, Jay A. *mathematics professor*
Cohen, Michael Paul *retired statistician*
Conn, Richard Lee *computer scientist, educator*
Conrad, Myriam Sylvie *mathematics professor*
Corbett, Lenora Meade *mathematician, community college educator*
Coskunuzer, Baris *mathematician*
Craft, Hassell Henry III *mathematician, educator*
Dave, Karen *computer scientist, educator*
De Both, Tanya *statistician*
Deng, Li *computer scientist, researcher*
Desai, Mukund N. *mathematician, researcher*
Doty, Stephen Richard *mathematics professor*
Downey, Deborah Ann *systems specialist*
Dumitras, Adriana *computer scientist*
Easton, Roger L. *former operations research specialist, consultant*
Edwards, Stephen Anthony *computer scientist, educator*
Efird, Jimmy Thomas *statistician*
Elliott, David LeRoy *mathematician, educator, engineering educator*
Emerson, Jamie *statistician, educator*
Erovenko, Igor V. *mathematics professor*
Esunge, Julius Njome *mathematician, statistician*
Exner, Frank Kepler *information scientist, indexer*
Farid, Farid O. *mathematician, educator*
Fields-Harris, Deborah Carol *mathematician, educator*
Fossum, Robert Merle *mathematician, educator*
Frankston, Robert M. *computer software executive, developer*
Freedman, Daniel *computer scientist, educator*
Fursin, Leonid Grigorievich *computer scientist, researcher*
Ganesh, Bikshandi *computer scientist, researcher*
Gerson, Donald Jerome *computer scientist, consultant, photographer, small business owner*
Gessaman, Margaret Palmer *mathematician, educator, retired dean*

---

Gifford, Marjorie Fitting *mathematician, educator, consultant*
Goldberg, Samuel *retired mathematician, foundation administrator*
Goldstein, Jerome Arthur *mathematics professor*
González, Bárbara Patricia *mathematics professor*
Gopal, Kreshna *computer scientist, researcher*
Gosciewski, Robert Louis *logistician*
Grasserbauer, Doris *computer scientist, mathematician, educator*
Grechanik, Jeffrey *operations research specialist*
Greever, Margaret Quarles *retired mathematics educator*
Griffith, Rosita Denise *mathematics professor, chemistry professor*
Griffiths, Phillip A. *mathematician, retired academic administrator*
Guild, Jeffrey K. *mathematics professor*
Guo, Chao-Yu *statistician, educator*
Halberstam, Heini *mathematics professor*
Halitsky, Steve *data analyst, statistician, researcher*
Hamel, Louis Reginald *systems analysis consultant*
Hamlen, Kevin William *computer scientist, educator*
Hardie, Michael Howard *mathematician, educator*
Harnedy, Joan Catherine Holland *retired systems analyst*
Hayes, David Ryan *mathematics professor*
Heyborne, Susan Kay *mathematician, educator*
Holford, Theodore Richard *biostatistician, educator*
Holland, Michael James *computer services administrator*
Hoppensteadt, Frank Charles *mathematician, educator, dean*
House, Stephen Eugene *information systems consultant*
Howard, Steve *mathematician, educator*
Hu, Hongde *mathematics professor*
Jackson, Deborah Cheryl *mathematician*
Jiang, Tao *mathematician, educator*
Johnstone, Iain Murray *statistician, educator, consultant*
Jones, Anita Katherine *computer scientist, educator*
Kadota, Takashi Theodore *mathematician, electrical engineer*
Kamvar, Sepandar D. *mathematician, artist*
Kang, Sheon Young *mathematics professor*
Kang, Soon-Yi *mathematician, educator*
Karim, Mohammed Rezaul *mathematics professor*
Karnaugh, Maurice *computer scientist, educator*
Kasami, Tadao *information science educator*
Kessler, Keith *retired computer scientist*
Khasawneh, Shadi Turki *computer scientist*
Kilby, Sarah L. *mathematician, educator*
Kimbrough, Pamela Seed *mathematics and chemistry professor, finance educator*
Kirshbaum, Jon Alan *systems analyst, consultant, retired systems administrator*
Kleeman, Richard *mathematics professor*
Krantz, Steven George *mathematics professor, writer*
Kushner, Todd Roger *computer scientist, application developer*
LaCurts, Carvel L. *mathematics professor*
Lakaemper, Rolf *computer science educator*
Lampson, Butler Wright *computer scientist*
Lange, Frederick Edward, Jr. *computer information systems architect*
Lawrence, John Patrick *statistician*
Leavelle, Tommy Lee *mathematics professor*
Leppard, Stephanie Jean *systems analyst, artist*
Lerner, Vladimir Semion *computer scientist, educator*
Lewis, Suford *computer scientist, consultant*
Li, Xiaojie *statistician, researcher*
Libert, Cleo Patricia *computer scientist, consultant*
Liu, Yong *computer scientist, researcher*
Longstreet, John Charles *retired computer scientist*
Lotspiech, Jeffrey *computer scientist, consultant*
Lu, Wenbin *statistician, educator*
Luther, Norman Yeomans *retired mathematics professor*
Lynch, Robert Emmett *mathematics professor*
Manika, John Francis *computer systems educator, computer information systems analyst*
March, Michael E. *propulsion systems analyst, consultant*
Marchiori, Massimo *computer scientist*
Massad, Jordan Elias *mathematician*
Matoax, Luminita *mathematician, professor, consultant*
Meslinsky, Lynette C. *mathematics professor*
Mikhelson, Sergei *mathematician, educator*
Mills, Kevin Lee *computer scientist, researcher*
Mohanty, Saraju P. *computer scientist, educator*
Nation, David Arthur *retired computer scientist, sculptor*
Neusel, Mara Dicle *mathematician, educator*
Newbury, Kirsten Rae *computer scientist, educator*
Nguyen, Dong *computer scientist, researcher, application developer, educator*
Nicoara, Andreea Carina *mathematics professor*
Norton, Peter K. *retired computer utilities programmer, writer*
Ongley, Lauri *mathematics professor*
Orr, Richard Clayton *mathematician, retired securities trader*
Orszag, Steven Alan *applied mathematician, educator*
Pair, Jackson Jarrell *computer scientist, media consultant*
Perlis, Robert Vincent *mathematician, educator*
Pollock, Karen Anne *computer analyst*
Quoquoi, Gadema K. *computer consultant*
Racherla, Gopal *computer scientist, researcher*
Rajendran, Srividhya *computer scientist, researcher*
Ramos-Rinze, Jorge Rafael *computer scientist*
Reed, David Patrick *information scientist*
Reynolds, Devalyn L. *mathematician, educator*
Riffenburgh, Robert Harry *biostatistician, researcher*
Rine, Mark Bradigan *metrology specialist*
Ritter, Jack Charles *mathematician, computer graphics designer*
Rochette, Alexandre C. *computer scientist*
Roitman, Judith *mathematician, educator*

---

Romero, Pedro Rafael *information scientist, researcher*
Rorissa, Abebe *information scientist, educator*
Rozin, Boris *mathematician, researcher*
Rudolph, Heidi Anne Jantz *mathematician, educator*
Sa, Ping *statistician, educator*
Salinas, Tracie McLemore *mathematics professor*
Schneider, Edgar Rolf Gottfried *retired mathematician, application developer, writer*
Schupp, Russ *computer professor*
Sellmann, Meinolf *computer science educator*
Shearrow, Samuel Carl *mathematics professor*
Sherman, Jimmie Lee *mathematician, educator*
Shier, Gloria Bulan *mathematics professor*
Sills, Richard Reynolds *scientist, educator*
Sinha, Rakesh Kumar *computer scientist, researcher*
Sloane, Neil James Alexander *mathematician, researcher*
Slobodnik, Ricci *mathematician, educator*
Snygg, John *mathematician, educator*
So, Jungmin *computer scientist, researcher*
Spinrad, Robert Joseph *computer scientist*
Sridhara, Vinay *computer scientist*
Stager, John C. *information scientist, educator*
Štěpánek, Petr *computer science educator*
Sukumar, Sreenivas Rangan *operations research specialist, electrical engineer, computer engineer*
Suppes, Patrick *statistician, philosopher, psychologist, educator*
Tan, Alson *computer scientist*
Thorsen, Steven N. *mathematics professor, military officer*
Thurston, William Paul *mathematician*
Tobiassen, Barbara Sue *systems analyst, consultant, volunteer*
Tymoczko, Julianna Sophia *mathematics professor*
Tyrl, Paul *mathematics professor, researcher*
Urbanski, Joseph V. *mathematics educator*
Wan, Ming *computer scientist, researcher*
Watkins, Ann Esther *mathematics professor*
Weier, Carlton Timothy *retired mathematics professor*
Welna, Cecilia *retired mathematics professor, dean*
Wenger, John Childs *retired mathematics educator, labor union administrator*
West, Eric M. *mathematician, educator*
Whicker, Amy Marie *computer science professor*
White, Carol Simpson *mathematics professor*
Wilkins, J. Ernest, Jr. *mathematician, educator*
Williams, Ronald Oscar *mathematician*
Wimpffen, Otto Rudolph *mathematics professor*
Winder, Robert Owen *mathematician, computer engineer, geophysicist*
Wozniak, Stephen Gary *computer scientist, philanthropist*
Xia, Yuni *information scientist, educator*
Xie, Minge *statistician, educator*
Yackel, James William *mathematician, academic administrator*
Yershov, Andrei R. *computer scientist*
Young, Barry Harrison *retired mathematician, mechanical engineer*
Young, Lai-Sang *mathematician, educator*
Yuksel, Murat *computer scientist, researcher*
Zeilberger, Doron *mathematics professor, researcher*
Zelmanov, Efim Isaakovich *mathematician, educator*
Zhang, Shu *statistician*
Zierler, Neal *retired mathematician*
Zyroff, Ellen Slotoroff *information scientist, classicist, educator*

---

# SCIENCE: PHYSICAL SCIENCE

## UNITED STATES

### ALABAMA

**Auburn**
Neely, William Charles *chemistry professor, consultant, research scientist*

**Auburn University**
Bhattarai, Gandhi Raj *research scientist, educator*
Ortiz, Joseph Vincent *chemistry professor, department chairman*

**Birmingham**
Miyagawa, Ichiro *physicist*
Robinson, Edward Lee *retired physics professor, consultant*
Vyazovkin, Sergey *chemistry professor*

**Dothan**
Mocker, Hans Walter *physicist*

**Florence**
Cale, William Graham, Jr. *environmental sciences educator, university administrator, researcher*
Dolmatov, Valeriy Konstantinovich *physicist, researcher*

**Huntsville**
Allan, Barry David *research chemist, government official*
Brandon, Walter Wiley, Jr. *retired physicist, retired aerospace engineer*
Costes, Nicholas Constantine *aerospace scientist, educator, retired government agency administrator*
Dahm, Werner K. *aerodynamicist*
Dimmock, John Oliver *physicist, educator*
Norman, Ralph Louis *retired physicist, consultant*
Oluseyi, Hakeem Muata *astrophysicist, educator*
Paciesas, William Simon *astrophysicist, educator*
Parnell, Thomas Alfred *physicist*
Smith, Robert Earl *space scientist*
Stuhlinger, Ernst *physicist*
Vaughan, William Walton *atmospheric scientist*
Wright, John Collins *retired chemistry professor*

**Livingston**
Wymer, Douglas A. *environmental scientist, educator, ecologist*

**Normal**
Edwards, Matthew E. *physicist, educator*

**Tuscaloosa**
Dixon, David Adams *chemistry professor, researcher*
LaMoreaux, Philip Elmer *geologist, hydrologist, consultant*
Mancini, Ernest Anthony *geologist, educator, researcher*
Periaswamy, Padmini *materials scientist, researcher*
Vincent, John Bertram *chemist, educator*

**Tuskegee**
Powell, Nichole Larai *chemistry professor, researcher*

## ALASKA

**Anchorage**
Kreig, Raymond Arthur *terrain analysis consulting firm executive*
Nelson, Steven W. *geologist, educator*

**Fairbanks**
Cahill, Catherine Frances *environmental scientist, educator*
Duffy, Lawrence Kevin *biochemist, educator*
Fathauer, Theodore Frederick *meteorologist*
Kramm, Gerhard *meteorologist, researcher*
Lingle, Craig Stanley *glaciologist, educator*
Roederer, Juan Gualterio *retired physics professor*

**Saint Paul Island**
Lestenkof, Aquilina Debbie *environmental advocate*

## ARIZONA

**Amado**
Criswell, Stephen *astronomer*

**Chandler**
Meieran, Eugene Stuart *materials scientist*

**Flagstaff**
Herkenhoff, Kenneth Edward *geologist, researcher*
Millis, Robert Lowell *astronomer, science observatory director*
Shoemaker, Carolyn Spellman *planetary astronomer*
Wynne, J. Judson *research scientist, ecologist*

**Green Valley**
Ramette, Richard Wales *chemistry professor*

**Litchfield Park**
McKeighen, Ronald Eugene *physicist*

**Phoenix**
Everett, Paul Marvin *physicist*
Gilberg, Mark Richardson *environmental scientist, director*

**Rio Rico**
Lowell, J(ames) David *geological consultant, cattle rancher*

**Scottsdale**
Kinsinger, Jack Burl *chemist, educator*

**Sierra Vista**
Ponder, Herman *geologist*

**Tempe**
Goronkin, Herbert *physicist*
Johnson, Shane Richard *research scientist, consultant*
Juvet, Richard Spalding, Jr. *chemistry professor*
McKelvy, Michael John *chemist, research scientist*
Pettit, George Robert *chemist, educator, cancer researcher*
Seeling, Patrick *research scientist, educator*
Smith, David John *physicist, researcher*
Theodore, David *research scientist*

**Tucson**
Angel, James Roger Prior *astronomer*
Baker, Victor Richard *geologist, hydrologist, researcher, research scientist, educator*
Barrett, Bruce Richard *physics professor*
Bloembergen, Nicolaas *physicist, researcher*
Broadfoot, Albert Lyle *physicist*
Crawford, David L. *astronomer*
Davis, Stanley Nelson *hydrologist, educator*
De Young, David Spencer *astrophysicist, educator*
Dunn, Floyd *biophysics professor, biomedical engineering educator*
Falco, Charles Maurice *physicist, researcher*
Frieden, B. Roy *mathematical physicist*
Girardeau, Marvin Denham *physics professor*
Green, Richard Frederick *astronomer*
Gruhl, James *energy scientist, artist*
Gutsche, Carl David *chemistry professor*
Hall, Henry Kingston, Jr. *chemistry professor*
Hays, James Fred *geologist, educator*
Hill, Henry Allen *physicist, researcher*
Hunten, Donald Mount *planetary scientist, educator*
Jefferies, John Trevor *astrophysicist, director*
Karkoschka, Erich *planetary science researcher, writer*
Kennicutt, Robert Charles, Jr. *astronomer*
Kessler, John Otto *physicist, researcher*
Lamb, Willis Eugene, Jr. *physicist, researcher*
Lane, Melissa D. *planetary geologist, researcher*
Lucas, Pierre *materials scientist, educator*
Marcialis, Robert Louis *planetary astronomer*
McGrath, Dominic Vincent *chemistry professor*
Meijer, Arend *geochemist, consultant*
Morrison, Roger Barron *geologist*
Mould, Jeremy Richard *astronomer*

Neugebauer, Marcia *physicist, researcher*
Neuman, Shlomo P. *hydrologist, educator*
Pacholczyk, Andrzej Grzegorz *astrophysicist*
Prewitt, Charles Thompson *geochemist*
Roemer, Elizabeth *retired astronomer, retired educator*
Smith, Verne V. *astronomer*
Sprague, Ann Louise *aerospace scientist*
Strittmatter, Peter Albert *astronomer, educator*
Swalin, Richard Arthur *scientist, company executive*
Tifft, William Grant *retired physics professor, scientist*
Whitaker, Ewen Adair *retired astronomer*
Wolff, Sidney Carne *astronomer, science administrator*

## ARKANSAS

**Batesville**
Meinzer, Beverly Anne *chemist, educator*

**Bella Vista**
Johnson, A(lyn) William *chemistry professor, writer, researcher, consultant*

**Fayetteville**
Abu-Safe, Husam Hamza *physics professor*
King, Jerry Wayne *chemist, researcher, engineer*
Naumov, Ivan I. *physicist, educator*
Steele, Kenneth Franklin, Jr. *hydrologist*
Wilkins, Charles L. *chemist, educator*

**Little Rock**
Braithwaite, Wilfred John *physics professor*
Darsey, Jerome Anthony (Jerry Darsey) *chemistry professor, consultant*

**Pine Bluff**
Walker, Richard Brian *chemistry professor*

## CALIFORNIA

**Agoura Hills**
Currie, Malcolm Roderick *aerospace executive, automotive executive, research scientist*

**Alhambra**
Huang, Jia-Sheng Jack *optics scientist, researcher*
Im, Jaemo *research scientist*

**Atascadero**
Ogier, Walter Thomas *retired physics educator*

**Atherton**
Fried, John H. *chemist*
Gill, Stephen Paschall *retired physicist, mathematician*

**Auburn**
Ferber, Robert Rudolf *retired physics researcher, educator, science administrator*
Hess, Patrick Henry *chemist, researcher*

**Bayside**
Cocks, George Gosson *retired chemical microscopy professor*

**Berkeley**
Alivisatos, Armand Paul *chemist, educator*
Arkin, Adam *research scientist, educator*
Attwood, David Thomas *physicist, researcher*
Barnett, R(alph) Michael *theoretical physicist, educational agency administrator*
Bartlett, Neil *chemist, emeritus educator*
Bergman, Robert George *chemist, educator*
Bertozzi, Carolyn R. *chemistry professor*
Bousso, Raphael *physicist, educator*
Bragg, Robert Henry *physicist, researcher*
Calendar, Richard Lane *biochemistry educator*
Cerny, Joseph III *chemistry professor, retired dean, retired director*
Chamberlin, Michael John *retired biochemistry professor*
Chew, Geoffrey Foucar *physicist*
Chu, Steven *physics professor, director*
Clarke, John *physics professor*
Debonnel, Christophe *research scientist*
Diamond, Richard Martin *nuclear chemist*
Fowler, Thomas Kenneth *physicist*
Fréchet, Jean Marie Joseph *chemistry professor*
Freedman, Stuart Jay *nuclear science educator*
Gaillard, Mary Katharine *physicist, educator*
Glaser, Donald Arthur *physicist*
Goldhaber, Gerson *astrophysicist, researcher*
Hahn, Erwin Louis *physicist, educator*
Halpern, Martin Brent *physics professor*
Hang, Bo *biochemist*
Hearst, John Eugene *chemistry professor, consultant, research scientist*
Hoffman, Darleane Christian *chemistry professor*
Jackson, J(ohn) David *physicist, researcher*
Jacobs, Peter Martin *physicist*
Jeanloz, Raymond *geophysics educator*
Keasling, Jay D. *chemistry professor, research scientist*
Keiling, Andreas Detlef *physicist, researcher*
Kerth, Leroy T. *physics professor*
Kirz, Janos *physicist*
Klinman, Judith Pollock *biochemist, educator*
Koshland, Daniel Edward, Jr. *biochemist, educator*
Kurtzman, Ralph Harold, Jr. *biochemist, researcher, consultant*
Langridge, Robert *biophysicist, educator, computational biologist*
Lanzara, Alessandra *physics professor*
Leemans, Wim Pieter *physicist*
Lester, William Alexander, Jr. *chemist, educator*
Lin, Robert Peichung *physicist, educator, researcher*
Linn, Stuart Michael *biochemist, educator*
Lu, Adolph *physicist, researcher*
Ma, Chung-Pei Michelle *astronomer, educator*
Mandelstam, Stanley *physicist*
Marcy, Geoffrey W. *astronomer, physicist, educator*
Markowitz, Samuel Solomon *chemistry professor*

Marnay, Chris *research scientist*
McKee, Christopher Fulton *physicist, astronomer, educator*
Miller, Norman Leslie *meteorologist, hydrologist, researcher*
Miller, William Hughes *theoretical chemist, educator*
Novakov, Tihomir None *physicist, researcher*
Pavlath, Attila Endre *chemist, researcher*
Perlmutter, Saul *astrophysicist, educator*
Perry, Dale Lynn *chemist*
Pines, Alexander *chemistry educator, researcher, consultant*
Price, Paul Buford *physicist, researcher*
Quinn, Nigel William Trevelyan *research scientist*
Rasmussen, John Oscar *nuclear research scientist*
Raymond, Kenneth Norman *chemistry professor, researcher*
Ritchie, Robert Oliver *materials science educator, director*
Roy, Prabir Kumar *physicist*
Sessler, Andrew Marienhoff *physicist*
Shugart, Howard Alan *physicist, researcher*
Somorjai, Gabor Arpad *chemist, educator*
Steiner, Herbert Max *physics professor*
Strauss, Herbert Leopold *chemistry professor*
Streitwieser, Andrew, Jr. *chemistry professor*
Thompson, Anthony Wayne *metallurgist, educator, consultant*
Townes, Charles Hard *physics professor*
Valentine, James William *paleontologist, educator, writer*
Vega, Reinaldo *research scientist*
Yang, Peidong *material science researcher*

**Beverly Hills**
Shapiro, Isadore *materials scientist, consultant*

**Boron**
Fisher, Richard Paul *chemist*

**California City**
Paiva, Clifford Anthony *physicist, consultant*

**Canyon Lake**
Schilling, Frederick Augustus, Jr. *geologist, consultant*

**Carlsbad**
Lu, Taijin *physical chemist, researcher*
Smith, Warren James *optical scientist, consultant, lecturer, author*

**Carmel**
Vagnini, Livio Lee *chemist, consultant, forensic specialist*

**Castaic**
Holmes, Dale Arthur *optics scientist*

**Chico**
Mejia, Barbara Oviedo *retired chemistry professor*

**China Lake**
Bennett, Jean Louise McPherson *physicist, research scientist*

**Claremont**
Hansch, Corwin Herman *chemistry professor*
Helliwell, Thomas McCaffree *physicist, researcher*
Van Hecke, Gerald Raymond *chemist, educator*

**Concord**
Seshadri, Srivatsan *optics scientist*

**Corona Del Mar**
Britten, Roy John *biophysicist*

**Crescent City**
Carter, Neville Louis *geophysicist, educator*

**Cypress**
Cully, Joseph Andrew *hazard substance scientist*

**Davis**
Burri, Betty Jane *research chemist*
Cahill, Thomas Andrew *physicist, researcher*
Conn, Eric Edward *plant biochemist*
Jungerman, John Albert *physics professor*
Kaloper, Nemanja *physics professor, researcher*
Liu, Gang-Yu *chemist, educator*
Liu, Kai *physics professor*
Nash, Charles Presley *chemistry professor*
Ohara, Noriaki *hydrologist*
Shackelford, James Floyd *materials science educator, researcher*
Stumpf, Paul Karl *biochemistry professor emeritus*
Troy, Frederic Arthur, II, *medical biochemistry professor*
Volman, David Herschel *chemistry professor*

**Discovery Bay**
Mikalow, Alfred Alexander, II, *deep sea diver, marine surveyor, marine diving consultant*

**Duarte**
Yoshida, Akira *biochemist*

**Edwards**
Liu, Chi Tsieh *aerospace scientist, researcher*

**El Dorado Hills**
Bartlett, Robert Watkins *metallurgist, educator, consultant*

**El Granada**
Heere, Karen R. *astrophysicist*

**Emeryville**
Gombocz, Erich Alfred *biochemist*
Masri, Merle Sid *biochemist, consultant*

**Escondido**
Tomomatsu, Hideo *chemist*

**Foster City**
Hotz, Henry Palmer *retired physicist*
Zaidi, Iqbal Mehdi *biochemist, research scientist*

**Fountain Valley**
Armstrong, Jeffrey Lee *oceanographer*
Davis, Jeremy Matthew *chemist*

**Fresno**
Anglen, Brandy Lynn *geologist, educator*
Kauffman, George Bernard *chemistry professor*
Wample, Robert Lee *research scientist, director*

**Fullerton**
Childers, James Gregory *physicist, educator, research scientist*
Shapiro, Mark Howard *physicist, educator, dean*

**Glen Ellen**
Berkland, James Omer *geologist*

**Hayward**
Fury, Michael Andrew *materials scientist, research and development company executive*

**Hemet**
Berger, Lev Isaac *physicist, researcher*

**Hercules**
Subramanian, Mani N. *chemistry professor*

**Irvine**
Bander, Myron *physics professor, dean*
Benford, Gregory Albert *physicist, writer*
Clark, Bruce Robert *geologist, consultant*
Dzyaloshinskii, Igor Ekhielievich *physicist*
Finlayson-Pitts, Barbara Jean *chemistry professor*
Ge, Nien-Hui *chemist, educator*
Madou, Marc *materials scientist, educator*
Maradudin, Alexei A. *physics professor*
McLaughlin, Calvin Sturgis *biochemistry professor*
Nowick, Arthur Stanley *metallurgy and materials science educator*
Phalen, Robert Franklynn *environmental scientist*
Ritz, Thorsten *biophysics professor*
Rose, Irwin A. (Ernie Rose) *biochemist, educator*
Rowland, Frank Sherwood *chemistry professor*
Rynn, Nathan *physics professor, consultant*
Wallis, Richard Fisher *physicist, researcher*
White, Stephen Halley *biophysicist, educator*
Zhou, Wei *research scientist*

**Kensington**
Appelman, Evan Hugh *retired chemist*
Connick, Robert Elwell *retired chemistry professor*

**La Canada Flintridge**
Baines, Kevin Hays *astronomer, planetary scientist*

**La Jolla**
Andre, Michael Paul *physicist, educator*
Arnold, James Richard *chemist, educator*
Asmus, John Fredrich *physicist*
Backus, George Edward *theoretical geophysicist*
Berger, Wolfgang H. *oceanographer, educator, geologist, space director*
Boger, Dale L. *chemistry professor*
Bradner, Hugh *retired physics professor*
Branscomb, Lewis McAdory *physicist, researcher*
Burbidge, E. Margaret *astronomer, educator*
Burbidge, Geoffrey *astrophysicist, educator*
Continetti, Robert E. *chemistry professor*
Cox, Charles Shipley *oceanography researcher, educator*
Davis, Brian Keith *biophysicist, researcher*
Dennis, Edward Alan *chemistry and biochemistry professor*
Dixon, Jack Edward *biological chemistry professor, consultant*
Driscoll, Charles Frederick *physicist, educator*
Edelman, Gerald Maurice *biochemist, neuroscientist, educator*
Feher, George *biophysicist, educator*
Fogler, Michael *physicist*
Harilal, Sivanandan S. *physicist, researcher*
Heeb, Mary Jo *biochemist, researcher*
Hendrickson, David Norman *chemistry professor*
Hermann, Thomas C. *chemistry professor*
Itano, Harvey Akio *biochemistry educator*
Kabantsev, Andrey *physicist, educator*
Kadonaga, James Takuro *biochemist*
Kearns, David Richard *chemistry professor*
Kelly, Jeffrey W. *chemist, educator*
Kennel, Charles Frederick *physics professor, academic administrator, government official*
Kitada, Shinichi *biochemist*
Kolodner, Richard David *biochemist, educator, director*
Lal, Devendra *nuclear geophysics educator*
Lauer, James Lothar *physicist, researcher*
Low, Philip Steven *research scientist*
Lydon, Nicholas B. (Nick Lydon) *biochemist, pharmaceutical executive, researcher*
Maple, M. Brian *physics professor*
Marti, Kurt *chemistry professor*
McCammon, James Andrew *chemistry professor*
Miller, Stanley Lloyd *chemistry and biochemistry professor*
Molina, Mario Jose *physical chemist, educator*
Nicolaou, K. C. *chemistry professor*
O'Neil, Thomas Michael *physicist, researcher*
Patton, Stuart *biochemist, educator*
Ride, Sally Kristen *physics professor, research scientist, retired astronaut*
Rotenberg, Manuel *physics professor*
Schimmel, Paul Reinhard *biochemist, biophysicist, educator*
Schuller, Ivan Kohn *physicist*
Sham, Lu Jeu *physics professor, physicist*
Sharpless, K. Barry *chemist, educator*
Shor, George G., Jr. *geophysicist, oceanographic administrator, engineer*
Shuler, Kurt Egon *chemist, educator*
Siegel, Jay Steven *chemistry educator*
Sinha, Sunil Kumar *physicist*
Somerville, Richard Chapin James *atmospheric scientist, educator*
Taylor, Susan Serota *biochemist, researcher*
Thiemens, Mark H. *chemistry professor*
Tsien, Roger Yonchien *chemist, cell biologist*
Tsuji, Frederick Ichiro *biochemist, molecular biologist*
Van Lint, Victor Anton Jacobus *physicist*

Wang, Lei *biochemist*
Watson, Kenneth Marshall *physics professor*
Wolynes, Peter Guy *chemistry researcher, educator*
Zimmermann, Joerg *biophysicist*

**Laguna Hills**
Rossiter, Bryant William *chemistry consultant*

**Livermore**
Alder, Berni Julian *physicist, researcher*
Cowgill, Donald Franklin *physicist*
Glassley, William E. *geochemist, researcher*
Glenzer, Siegfried Heinz *physicist, educator, researcher*
Hooper, Edwin Bickford *physicist*
Kidder, Ray Edward *physicist, consultant*
Kirkwood, Robert Keith *applied physicist*
Lassila, David H. *materials scientist, researcher*
Leith, Cecil Eldon, Jr. *retired physicist*
Nuckolls, John Hopkins *physicist, researcher*
Sack, Seymour *nuclear scientist*
Santer, Benjamin David *atmospheric scientist*
Shotts, Wayne J. *nuclear scientist, federal agency administrator*
Spiller, Eberhard Adolf *physicist, researcher*
Tarter, Curtis Bruce *physicist, science administrator*
Weber, Stephen Vance *physics researcher*
Xie, Shaocheng *atmospheric scientist*

**Long Beach**
Bauer, Roger Duane *chemistry professor, consultant*
Hu, Chi Yu *retired physicist, educator*
McGaughey, Charles Gilbert *retired biochemist*

**Los Altos**
Vickers, Roger Spencer *physicist, researcher, environmental artist*

**Los Angeles**
Anderson, W. French *biochemist, physician, educator*
Batamack, Patrice Theodore Desire *chemistry professor, researcher*
Benson, Sidney William *chemistry researcher*
Bhaumik, Mani Lal *physicist*
Boyer, Paul D. *biochemist, educator*
Chu, Chi-Cheng *research scientist*
Clarke, Steven Gerard *chemistry professor*
Coleman, Paul Jerome, Jr. *physicist, researcher*
Cornwall, John Michael *physics professor, consultant*
Coroniti, Ferdinand Vincent *physics professor, astronomy educator*
Dows, David Alan *chemistry professor*
Dunn, Arnold Samuel *biochemistry educator*
Dunn, Bruce Sidney *materials scientist, educator*
Fuhrman, Jed Alan *biological oceanographer*
Fulco, Armand John *biochemist*
Ganas, Perry Spiros *researcher*
Ghil, Michael *atmospheric scientist, geophysicist*
Guo, Zhanhu *researcher*
Hellwarth, Robert Willis *physicist, researcher*
Horn, Cindy Harrell *environmental advocate*
Houk, Kendall Newcomb *chemistry professor*
Jacoby, Neil Herman, Jr. *astronautical scientist, engineer, consultant*
Kaplan, Isaac Raymond *chemistry professor*
Kassner, Michael Ernest *materials science educator, researcher*
Kedes, Laurence Herbert *biochemistry professor, physician, researcher*
Kivelson, Margaret Galland *physicist*
Koga, Rokutaro (Rocky Koga) *physicist*
Krupp, Edwin Charles *astronomer*
Kwon, Ohyun *chemist, educator*
Levine, Raphael David *chemistry professor*
Li, Yong-Gang Frank *research scientist, educator*
Lieber, Michael Randall *biochemist, educator*
Lopez-Arce Martinez, Paula *geologist, researcher*
Lyons, James Richard *research scientist*
Maki, Kazumi *physicist, researcher*
Markland, Francis Swaby, Jr. *biochemist, educator*
Mureika, Jonas R. *physics professor*
Neufeld, Elizabeth Fondal *biochemist, educator*
Nimni, Marcel Ephraim *biochemistry educator*
Olah, George Andrew *chemist, educator*
Paulson, Donald Robert *chemistry professor*
Pellegrini, Claudio *physicist, educator*
Reiss, Howard *chemistry professor*
Roberts, Sidney *biological chemist*
Scott, Robert Lane *chemist, educator*
Shapiro, Jerald Steven *chemist, bank executive*
Smith, Emil L. *biochemist, educator*
Stahl, Frieda Axelrod *physicist, researcher, physics professor*
Stanton, Robert James, Jr. *geologist, educator*
Stellwagen, Robert Harwood *biochemistry professor*
Stoddart, J. Fraser *chemistry professor*
Thorne, Richard Mansergh *physicist*
Trimble, Stanley Wayne *hydrologist*
Tsao, Jennie Ching-I *research scientist, educator*
Vidale, John Emilio *geologist*
Walker, Raymond John *physicist*
Whitten, Charles Alexander, Jr. *physics professor*
Wittry, David Beryle *physicist, researcher*
Woodruff, Fay *paleoceanographer, geological researcher*
Wudl, Fred *chemistry professor*

**Los Gatos**
Foy, Wade Hampton *retired research scientist*
Johnson, Philip Leigh *geologist*

**Malibu**
Liu, David Shiao-Kung *research scientist, consultant*
Pepper, David M. *physicist, educator, writer*
Phelps, Amanda C. *materials scientist, researcher*

**Marina**
Shane, William Whitney *astronomer*

**Mckinleyville**
Peithman, Roscoe Edward *physicist, educator*

**Menlo Park**
Allen, Matthew Arnold *physicist*

Andrews, Dudley Jo *geophysicist*
Bernstein, Lawrence R. *inorganic chemist, pharmaceutical chemist*
Bukry, John David *geologist*
Bynum, Gretchen Luepke *geologist*
Crosley, David Risdon *chemical physicist*
Dorfan, Jonathan Mannie *physicist, researcher*
Drell, Sidney David *physicist, researcher*
Hodgson, Keith O. *chemistry professor*
Kuwabara, James Shigeru *research hydrologist*
McGarr, Arthur Francis *geophysicist*
Michael, Andrew Jay *geophysicist*
Mill, Theodore *chemist, researcher*
Parsons, Tom *geophysicist, researcher*
Pejakovic, Dusan *physicist*
Penzias, Arno Allan *astrophysicist, research scientist, information scientist*
Pivi, Mauro *physicist*
Richter, Burton *physicist, educator*
Taylor, Richard Edward *physicist, researcher*
Teytelman, Dmitry *physicist*
Wang, Jian *materials scientist, researcher*

**Merced**
Winston, Roland *physicist, researcher*

**Mission Viejo**
Glasky, Alvin Jerald *retired medical research scientist*

**Moffett Field**
Berenji, Hamid Reza *research scientist, educator*
Makeev, Maxim A. *physicist*
Malkova, Natalia *physicist, mathematician, researcher*
Mattioda, Andrew Lige *research chemist, scientist*
Nemani, Ramakrishna Rao *research scientist*
Straume, Tore *biophysicist, researcher*
Vercoutere, Wenonah Annrea *research scientist*

**Monrovia**
Zolodz, Melissa D. *scientist*

**Montecito**
Wheelon, Albert Dewell *physicist*

**Monterey**
Jiang, Qingfang *research scientist*
Le, Ly Ngoc (Le Ngoc Ly) *environmental physicist, educator, research scientist*

**Moss Landing**
Brewer, Peter George *ocean geochemist*
Clague, David A. *geologist*

**Mountain View**
Shostak, G. Seth *astronomer, writer*
Showalter, Mark Robert *astronomer*
Summers, David Patrick *chemist, astrobiologist*
Yan, Qing *bioinformatics scientist*

**Murrieta**
Lake, Bruce Meno *physicist*

**Napa**
Shin, Ernest Eun-Ho *physicist, educator, researcher*

**Newbury Park**
Monteau, Norman Keith *gemologist*

**Newport Beach**
Kolyer, John McNaughton *materials scientist, retired chemist*

**North Hollywood**
Thomson, John Ansel Armstrong *biochemist*

**Northridge**
Smathers, James Burton *medical physicist, educator*
Stampke, Stuart Reh *physicist, researcher*

**Oakland**
Brust, David *physicist*
Carwell, Hattie Virginia *health physicist*
Chen, Shengzao *seismologist, consultant*
Linford, Rulon Kesler *physicist, electrical engineer*

**Oceanside**
Miyagawa, Hiroaki *materials scientist, researcher*

**Palo Alto**
Andersen, Torben Brondt *optical researcher, astronomer, software engineer*
Flory, Curt Alan *research physicist*
Frye, William Emerson *physicist, engineer*
Herring, Conyers (William Conyers Herring) *retired physicist, educator*
Huberman, Bernardo A. *physicist*
Kase, Kenneth R. *radiation physicist, consultant*
Martin, Robert Bruce *chemistry professor*
Moon, Ronald Leslie *materials scientist*
Perl, Martin Lewis *physicist, educator, chemical engineer*
Saxena, Arjun Nath *physicist*
Scher, Erik *physical chemist*
Schulz, Michael *physicist*
Shen, Bo *research scientist*
Skoog, Douglas Arvid *retired chemistry educator, writer*
Title, Alan M. *astrophysicist*
Van de Walle, Chris Gilbert *physicist*

**Palos Verdes Estates**
Paulikas, George Algis *retired physicist*

**Pasadena**
Albee, Arden Leroy *geologist, educator*
Ali, Ahmed Haider *geophysicist*
Allen, Clarence Roderic *geologist, educator*
Anderson, Don Lynn *geophysicist*
Barish, Barry C. *physics professor, researcher*
Barnes, Charles Andrew *physicist, researcher*
Beauchamp, Jesse Lee (Jack Beauchamp) *chemistry professor*
Beer, Reinhard *atmospheric scientist*
Boehm, Felix Hans *physicist, researcher*

Brown, Michael E. *astronomer, astronomy educator*
Byun, Sung Hun *research scientist*
Chahine, Moustafa Toufic *atmospheric scientist*
Chan, Sunney Ignatius *chemist, educator*
Chiang, Wen-Li *hydrologist*
Dervan, Peter Brendan *chemistry professor*
DeSalvo, Riccardo *research scientist*
Dressler, Alan Michael *astronomer*
Duxbury, Thomas Carl *planetary scientist*
Frautschi, Steven Clark *physicist, researcher*
Freedman, Wendy Laurel *astronomer, educator*
Fu, Lee-Lueng *oceanographer*
Golombek, Matthew Philip *research scientist, planetary geologist*
Goodstein, David Louis *physics professor*
Gray, Harry Barkus *chemistry professor*
Grubbs, Robert Howard *chemistry professor*
Gurnis, Michael Christopher *geological sciences educator*
Heindl, Clifford Joseph *physicist, researcher*
Hitlin, David George *physicist, researcher*
Jun, Insoo *nuclear scientist, researcher*
Kavanagh, Ralph William *physics professor*
Lange, Andrew E. *astrophysicist*
Litvine, Vladimir A. *research scientist, physicist*
Lopes, Rosaly Mutel Crocce *astronomer, planetary geologist*
Marcus, Rudolph Arthur *chemist, educator*
Mayo, Stephen L. *biochemist*
McGill, Thomas Conley *physics educator*
Mc Koy, Basil Vincent Charles *theoretical chemist, educator*
Munich, Mario Enrique *research scientist, electronics executive*
Oemler, Augustus, Jr. *astronomer, educator*
Politzer, Hugh David *physicist, educator*
Preskill, John Phillip *physics professor*
Quake, Stephen R. *physics professor, researcher*
Roberts, John D. *chemist, educator*
Sackmann, Inge-Juliana *astrophysicist*
Sandage, Allan Rex *astronomer*
Sargent, Anneila Isabel *astrophysicist*
Sargent, Wallace Leslie William *astronomer, educator*
Sekanina, Zdenek *astronomer*
Spilker, Linda Joyce *aerospace scientist*
Stone, Edward C. *physicist, researcher*
Thorne, Kip Stephen *physicist, researcher*
Tombrello, Thomas Anthony, Jr. *physics professor*
Vogt, Rochus Eugen *physicist, researcher*
Webster, Christopher R. *chemist, physicist, research scientist*
Wilcox, Jaroslava Zitkova *physicist*
Yeomans, Donald Keith *astronomer*

**Pilot Hill**
Freitas, Robert Archibald, Jr. *research scientist*

**Pleasanton**
Stallings, Charles Henry *retired physicist*

**Point Mugu**
Fisk, Charles John *meteorologist, researcher, consultant*

**Pomona**
Bidlack, Wayne Ross *nutritional biochemist, toxicologist, food scientist*

**Ramona**
Yoldas, Bulent Erturk *materials scientist, educator*

**Rancho Palos Verdes**
Smirnov, Alexei Vladimirovich *research scientist, consultant*

**Rancho Santa Fe**
Creutz, Edward Chester *physicist, museum director*

**Redlands**
Clopine, Gordon Alan *consulting geologist, educator*

**Redondo Beach**
Foster, John Stuart, Jr. *physicist, former defense industry executive*
Martin, Melissa Carol *radiological physicist*
Mulvey, Gerald John *meteorologist*

**Ridgecrest**
Bennett, Harold Earl *physicist, optics researcher*
St. Amand, Pierre *geophysicist*

**Riverside**
Pogorelov, Nikolai *physicist, researcher*
Rabenstein, Dallas Leroy *chemistry professor*
Wudka, Jose *physics professor*

**Rohnert Park**
Cominsky, Lynn Ruth *physics and astronomy educator*

**Rolling Hills Estates**
McCreight, Louis Ralph *retired materials scientist*

**Sacramento**
Gebers, Michael A. *research scientist*
Purdy, James Aaron *medical physics professor*
Rosenfeld, Arthur H. *physics professor, researcher*

**San Bernardino**
Evans, Hiram Kraig *forensic chemist*

**San Carlos**
Dafforn, Geoffrey Alan *biochemist*
Rathmann, George Blatz *genetic engineering company executive*

**San Clemente**
Wolfram, Thomas *physicist, educator*

**San Diego**
Cantor, Charles Robert *biochemistry professor*
Cobble, James Wikle *chemistry professor*
Georgakakos, Konstantine Peter *hydrologist, researcher*
Haener, Juan A. *physicist*

L'Annunziata, Michael Frank *chemist, consultant, nuclear scientist*
Lao, Lang Li *nuclear fusion research physicist*
Pincus, Howard J. *geologist, engineer, educator*
Schissel, David Paul *physicist, director*
Shneour, Elie Alexis *biophysicist, researcher, historian*
Steemers, Frank J. *research scientist*
Stetson, Robert Francis *retired metallurgist*
Timoshchuk, Victor Arkadyevich *research scientist*
Verma, Inder M. *biochemist*
Woods, Linda Lee *chemistry professor*

**San Francisco**
Archer, Cristina Lozej *meteorologist*
Batterman, Boris William *physicist, educator, academic administrator*
Burlingame, Alma Lyman *chemist, educator*
Cluff, Lloyd Sterling *earthquake geologist*
Dill, Kenneth Austin *pharmaceutical chemistry educator*
Grodsky, Gerold Morton *biochemistry professor*
Hale, Victoria G. *chemist, pharmaceutical executive*
James, Thomas Larry *chemistry professor*
Julius, David *biochemist*
Marshall, Grayson William, Jr. *materials scientist, biomedical engineer, health sciences educator, dentist*
Rutter, William J. *biochemist, educator*
Tyler, Christopher William *scientist, director*
Walter, Peter *biochemist*

**San Jose**
Bandic, Zvonimir Z. *physicist, researcher, electrical engineer*
Craford, M. George *physicist, research administrator*
Eigler, Donald Mark *physicist*
Madra, Satbir Singh *materials researcher, mechanical engineer*
Parkin, Stuart Stephen Papworth *materials scientist*
Winters, Harold Franklin *physicist*

**San Luis Obispo**
Grismore, Roger *physics professor, researcher*
Hafemeister, David Walter *physicist*

**San Rafael**
Pomerantz, Martin Arthur *astronomer, educator, physicist*

**San Ramon**
Salazar-Tio, Rafael *physicist, researcher*

**Santa Ana**
Kropp, William Rudolph *physicist*

**Santa Barbara**
Ahlers, Guenter *physicist, researcher*
Awschalom, David Daniel *physicist*
Bowers, Michael Thomas *chemistry professor*
Bruice, Thomas C. *chemist, educator*
Caldwell, David Orville *physics professor*
Dow, Brian Christopher *geologist, educator*
Evans, Anthony Glyn *materials scientist, educator*
Ford, Peter C. *chemistry professor*
Gossard, Arthur Charles *physicist, researcher*
Gross, David Jonathan *physicist*
Heeger, Alan Jay *physicist, educator*
Hubbard, Arthur Thornton *chemist, educator*
Kennedy, John Harvey *chemistry professor*
Kohn, Walter *physicist, retired educator*
Kozyrev, Andrei Nikolaevich *research scientist*
Langer, James Stephen *physicist, researcher*
Luyendyk, Bruce Peter *geophysicist, educator, academic administrator*
Macdonald, Ken Craig *geophysicist*
Meinel, Aden Baker *optics scientist*
Peale, Stanton Jerrold *physics educator*
Pilgeram, Laurence Oscar *biochemist*
Polchinski, Joseph G. *physicist, science educator*
White, Robert Stephen *retired physics professor*
Witherell, Michael S. *physicist, educator*
Young, Michael Kent *physics professor*

**Santa Clara**
Cutler, Leonard Samuel *physicist*
Dai, Guang-ming George *optics scientist*
Gozani, Tsahi *nuclear physicist*
Lau, John Hon Shing *electronics scientist*
Lee, Chun Wai *physicist, process engineer, educator*

**Santa Cruz**
Brown, George Stephen *physics professor*
Bunnett, Joseph Frederick *chemist, educator*
Faber, Sandra Moore *astronomer, educator*
Flatté, Stanley Martin *physicist, researcher*
Hill, Terrell Leslie *chemist, researcher, biophysicist*
Klein, Spencer Robert *physicist, researcher*
Kraft, Robert Paul *astronomer, educator*
Sands, Matthew Linzee *physicist, researcher*
Wipke, W. Todd *chemistry professor*

**Santa Monica**
Intriligator, Devrie Shapiro *physicist*
Park, Edward Cahill, Jr. *retired physicist*

**Santa Rosa**
Banks, Peter Morgan *physics professor*
Gentemann, Chelle Leigh *oceanographer*

**Scotts Valley**
Haisch, Bernard Michael *astronomer, researcher*

**Sherman Oaks**
Caren, Robert Poston *aerospace scientist*

**Solana Beach**
Agnew, Harold Melvin *physicist*

**South San Francisco**
Ruggles, Sandra Waugh *biophysicist*

**Stanford**
Baldwin, Robert Lesh *biochemist, educator*
Berg, Paul *biochemist, educator*

Bienenstock, Arthur Irwin *physicist, educator, federal official*
Brauman, John I. *chemist, educator*
Bube, Richard Howard *retired materials scientist, educator*
Collman, James Paddock *chemistry professor*
Dimopoulos, Savas *physics professor, theoretical physicist*
Fetter, Alexander Lees *theoretical physicist, educator*
Flinn, Paul Anthony *materials scientist*
Harbaugh, John Warvelle *geologist, educator*
Harbury, Pehr A.B. *biochemist, educator*
Harrison, Walter Ashley *physicist, researcher*
Kennedy, Donald *environmental scientist, educator, editor*
Keren, Kinneret *biophysicist*
Kool, Eric T. *chemist, educator*
Kornberg, Arthur *biochemist, educator*
Kornberg, Roger David *biochemist, structural biologist*
Kovach, Robert Louis *geophysics educator*
Lehman, I(srael) Robert *biochemist, educator*
Little, William Arthur *physicist, researcher*
Matson, Pamela Anne *environmental scientist, science educator*
Mueller, Holger *physicist*
Osheroff, Douglas Dean *physics professor, researcher*
Ross, John *physical chemist, educator*
Segall, Paul *geologist, educator*
Shenker, Stephen *physics professor*
Solomon, Edward Ira *chemistry professor, researcher*
Stryer, Lubert *biochemist, educator*
Susskind, Leonard *physicist, educator*
Thompson, George Albert *geophysicist, educator*
Trost, Barry Martin *chemist, educator*
Wagoner, Robert Vernon *astrophysicist, educator*
Walt, Martin *physicist, educator*
Wender, Paul Anthony *chemistry professor*
Wojcicki, Stanley George *physicist, researcher*
Zare, Richard Neil *chemistry professor*

**Stockton**
Gross, Paul Hans *retired chemistry professor*
Samoshin, Vyacheslav Vladimirovich *chemistry professor, science educator, researcher*
Whiteker, Roy Archie *retired chemistry professor*

**Sunnyvale**
Chang, William Zhi-Ming *research scientist*
Holmes, Richard Brooks *mathematical physicist*
Wu, Yider *research scientist*
Yang, Ming-Hsuan *research scientist*

**Temecula**
Chung, Hee M. *retired nuclear scientist*

**Thousand Oaks**
Benedek, Kálmán Pál *biochemist, consultant*
Remmele, Richard L., Jr. *research scientist*
Zhang, Zhongqi *chemist*

**Torrance**
Kim, Keehoon *cybernetic scientist*
Lieberman, Robert Arthur *physicist*
Rogers, Howard H. *retired chemist*

**Valencia**
Levy, Ezra Cesar *aerospace scientist, real estate agent*

**Van Nuys**
Ahern, Sean Christopher *aerospace scientist*

**Vista**
Rodriguez-Cruz, Sandra Enid *chemist, researcher*

**Walnut Creek**
Heftmann, Erich *biochemist*
Wu, Tse Cheng *chemist, researcher*

**Westminster**
Zeng, Eddy Yongping *chemist*

**Woodland Hills**
Sharma, Brahama D. *chemistry professor*

## COLORADO

**Arvada**
Mullineaux, Donal Ray *geologist*

**Boulder**
Araujo-Pradere, Eduardo A. *geophysicist, researcher*
Bartlett, David Farnham *physics professor*
Chappell, Charles Franklin *meteorologist, consultant*
Clark, Wallace Lee, Jr. *physicist*
Cornell, Eric Allin *physics professor*
DePuy, Charles Herbert *chemist, educator*
Dryer, Murray *physicist, educator*
Dudhia, Jimy *atmospheric scientist*
Eisele, Fred Louis *atmospheric chemist*
Esposito, Larry Wayne *planetary astronomer*
Faller, James Elliot *physicist, researcher*
Fleming, Rex James *meteorologist*
Garstang, Roy Henry *astrophysicist, educator*
Gosling, John Thomas *space plasma physicist, researcher*
Hall, John Lewis *physicist, researcher*
Hermann, Allen Max *physics professor*
Ho, Shu-Peng *research scientist*
Hogg, David Clarence *physicist*
Horikis, Theodoros *research scientist*
Jin, Deborah *physicist, educator*
Joselyn, Jo Ann *space scientist*
Kapteyn, Henry Cornelius *physics professor, engineering educator*
Kellogg, William Welch *meteorologist, researcher*
King, Edward Louis *retired chemistry professor*
Koch, Tad Harbison *chemistry professor, researcher*
LeMasurier, Wesley Ernest *geology educator, researcher*
LeMone, Margaret Anne *atmospheric scientist*
Linsky, Jeffrey L. *astrophysicist*

Low, Boon Chye *physicist*
Lu, Chungu *meteorologist, researcher, educator*
Mahlman, Jerry David *retired meteorologist*
Malde, Harold Edwin *retired federal government geologist*
Oh, Seongshik *physicist, researcher*
Pankove, Jacques Isaac *retired physicist, researcher*
Phelps, Arthur Van Rensselaer *physicist, consultant*
Randa, James Paul *physicist, electrical engineer*
Ravishankara, Akkihebal R. *chemist*
Roellig, Leonard Oscar *physics professor*
Rundle, John Belting *physicist, researcher*
Salby, Murry L *atmospheric and oceanic sciences professor*
Smythe, William Rodman *physicist, researcher*
Stern, Alan (S. Alan Stern, Sol Alan Stern) *astrophysicist, researcher*
Tatarskii, Valerian Il'Ich *physics researcher*
Tolbert, Bert Mills *biochemist, educator*
Trenberth, Kevin Edward *atmospheric scientist*
Washington, Warren Morton *meteorologist*
Westwater, Edgeworth Rupert *physicist*
Wieman, Carl E. *physics professor*

**Brighton**
Rinkenberger, Richard Krug *physical scientist, geologist, consultant*

**Colorado Springs**
Corry, Charles Elmo *geophysicist, not-for-profit developer*
Siddoway, Christine Helen Smith *geology educator*
Stahl, Philip Anthony *physicist, educator*

**Denver**
Babayev, Djangir Ali Ikram *physicist, researcher*
Bufe, Charles Glenn *geophysicist, researcher*
Caine, Jonathan Saul *geologist, researcher*
Cobban, William Aubrey *paleontologist*
Eaton, Gareth Richard *chemistry professor, dean*
Fails, Thomas Glenn *geologist*
Gries, Robbie Rice *geologist, gas and petroleum company executive*
Johnson, Walter Earl *geophysicist*
Kerwin, Michael William *environmental science educator*
Landon, Susan Melinda *petroleum geologist*
Morrison, Kendra Ann *environmental scientist*
Neumann, Herschel *retired physics professor*
Ormes, Jonathan Fairfield *astrophysicist, researcher, educator*
Smith, Dwight Morrell *chemistry professor, academic administrator*
Weihaupt, John George *geophysics educator, academic administrator*

**Dillon**
Roder, Hans Martin *retired physicist, consultant*

**Durango**
Cristol, Stanley Jerome *retired chemistry professor*

**Evergreen**
Haun, John Daniel *petroleum geologist, educator*
Heyl, Allen Van, Jr. *geologist*

**Fort Collins**
Bamburg, James Robert *biochemistry professor*
Bikos, Daniel Ernest *meteorologist*
Cheng, William Y. Y. *meteorologist, educator*
Fixman, Marshall *chemist, educator*
Guo, Yuanqing *research scientist*
Knaff, John Albert *research scientist*
Konor, Celal Sukru *meteorologist, researcher*
Lokupitiya, Ravindra Shanthakumar *research scientist*
Martin, Denise Ann *safety and environmental health manger*
Meyers, Albert Irving *chemistry professor*
Patton, Carl Elliott *physicist, educator*
She, Chiao-Yao *physics professor, researcher*

**Fraser**
Shaw, Roger Walz *physicist, educator*

**Golden**
DeSanto, John A. *physicist, educator, mathematics professor*
Hamilton, Warren Bell *geologist, researcher, geophysicist, educator*
Krauss, George *metallurgist*
Lee, SeHee *energy scientist*
Lufkin, John L. *geologist, educator, publishing executive*
Metzger, Wyatt K. *physicist*
Pollack, Gerald Leslie *physicist, researcher*
Taylor, P. Craig *physics professor*
Trefny, John Ulric *college president*
Wang, Dong *chemist, researcher*
Zhong, Dalong *materials scientist, consultant*

**Grand Junction**
Rutz, Richard Frederick *physicist, researcher*

**Greeley**
Szczyrba, Igor Nicholas *mathematical physicist, consultant*

**Highlands Ranch**
Brierley, James Alan *biohydrometallurgy consultant*

**Lakewood**
Hansen, Richard Olaf *geophysicist, educator, director*
Quinn, John Michael *physicist, geophysicist*
Samal, Abani Ranjan *geologist*

**Littleton**
Paull, Richard Allen *geologist, educator*

**Louisville**
Brault, James William *physicist*

**Ridgway**
Lathrop, Kaye Don *nuclear scientist, educator*

**Windsor**
Mayer, Victor James *geologist, educator*

## CONNECTICUT

**Bridgeport**
Chih, Chung-Ying *physicist, consultant*

**Clinton**
Panayotov, Christo Angelov *research scientist, consultant*

**East Lyme**
Mylari, Banavara L. *retired chemist*

**Farmington**
Goodson, Richard Carle, Jr. *chemist*
Osborn, Mary Jane Merten *biochemist, educator*
Spencer, Richard Paul *biochemist, educator, physician*

**Greenwich**
Davenport, Lee Losee *physicist*

**Groton**
Harwood, Harold James, Jr. *biochemist*
Swindell, Archie Calhoun, Jr. *research biochemist, statistician*
Wallach, Morton L. *scientist*

**Guilford**
Handschumacher, Robert Edmund *biochemistry professor*

**Ledyard**
Chiang, Albert Chinfa *polymer chemist*

**Manchester**
Galasso, Francis Salvatore *materials scientist*

**Middletown**
Ettre, Leslie Stephen *chemist*
Fry, Albert Joseph *chemistry professor*

**New Britain**
Baskerville, Charles Alexander *geologist, educator*

**New Haven**
Adair, Robert Kemp *physicist, educator*
Baltay, Charles *physicist, educator*
Behar, Kevin L. *research scientist*
Berson, Jerome Abraham *chemistry professor*
Braze, F. David *research scientist*
Casten, Richard Francis *physicist, educator*
Chupka, William Andrew *chemical physicist, educator*
Curran, Lisa M. *environmental scientist, educator*
Engelman, Donald Max *molecular biophysics and biochemistry educator*
Galantucci, Bruno *research scientist*
Girvin, Steven Mark *physicist, researcher*
Korchagin, Vladimir *astrophysicist*
Mac Dowell, Samuel Wallace *retired physics professor*
Marchesi, Vincent Thomas *biochemist, educator*
Mattina, MaryJane Incorvia *chemist*
Molaei, Goudarz *research scientist*
Parker, Peter D.M. *physicist, educator, researcher*
Poutrina, Ekaterina *optics scientist, researcher*
Ramirez, Ainissa *materials scientist*
Sandweiss, Jack *physicist, researcher*
Saunders, Martin *chemistry educator, researcher*
Schepartz, Alanna *biochemist, educator*
Shulman, Robert Gerson *biophysics professor*
Steitz, Joan Argetsinger *biochemistry professor*
Stone, Alfred Douglas *physicist, educator*
Tully, John Charles *research chemical physicist*
Wiberg, Kenneth Berle *chemist, educator*
Wolf, Werner Paul *physicist, researcher*
Zeller, Michael Edward *physicist, researcher*

**New London**
Zimmer, Marc *chemistry professor*

**New Milford**
Fabricand, Burton Paul *physicist, researcher*

**North Haven**
Herzenberg, Arvid *physicist, researcher*

**Norwalk**
Dvornek, Linda Smith *chemist*

**Rocky Hill**
Chu, Hsien-Kun *chemist, researcher*

**Stamford**
Chang, Ted T. *chemist*
Colthup, Norman Bertram *retired spectroscopist*

**Storrs Mansfield**
Bartram, Ralph Herbert *physicist*
Klemens, Paul Gustav *physicist, researcher*
Marcus, Harris Leon *materials science educator*
Reifsnider, Kenneth Leonard *metallurgist, educator*
Stwalley, William Calvin *physics professor, chemistry professor*

**Waterford**
Johnson, Gary William *environmental scientist, consultant*

**West Hartford**
Dubé, Cynthia Christine *physics educator, consultant, video producer*
Gould, Laurence Ira *physicist*

**West Haven**
Onton, Ann Louise Reuther *chemist*

**Westport**
Smith, Peter Wolfgang *physicist, artist*

**Woodbury**
Skinner, Brian John *geologist, educator*

## DELAWARE

**Middletown**
Hall, Peter Michael *physics professor, electronics engineer*

**Newark**
Appelbaum, Ian *research scientist, educator*
Burmeister, John Luther *chemistry professor, consultant*
Esrey, Elizabeth Gove Goodier *chemist, biologist*
Matsumoto, Roger Lee Ken *research scientist, artist*
Murray, Richard Bennett *retired physics professor*
Polenova, Tatyana *chemistry professor, researcher*
Rayle, Heather Lynnette *chemist*
Vassiliou, Eustathios *chemist, consultant*

**Wilmington**
Jaycox, Gary Delmar *research scientist*
Kaiser, Mary Agnes *chemist, chemical company executive*
Keating, Mimi Y. *chemist*
Kissa, Erik *retired chemist, consultant*
Kwolek, Stephanie Louise *chemist, researcher*
Meng, Hong *chemist*
Parshall, George William *chemist, researcher*
Petrucci-Samija, Maria *chemist*
Subramanian, Mas *research scientist*

## DISTRICT OF COLUMBIA

**Washington**
Alexander, Joseph Kunkle, Jr. *physicist*
Andreadis, Tim D. *physicist, researcher*
Barbara, Paola *physicist, educator*
Beall, James Howard *physicist, educator*
Berendzen, Richard *astronomer, educator, author*
Bierly, Eugene Wendell *meteorologist, science foundation director*
Boss, Alan Paul *astrophysicist*
Ciesla, Fred John *astrophysicist, meteoriticist, researcher*
Davidson, Eugene Abraham *biochemist, educator, academic administrator*
Dutro, John Thomas, Jr. *geologist, paleontologist*
Dutta, Biprodas *physics professor*
El Khadem, Hassan Saad *chemistry professor, researcher*
Esfandiary, Mary S. *physicial scientist, operations consultant*
Fogleman, Guy Carroll *physicist, mathematician, educator*
Girard, James Emery *chemistry professor*
Goldstein, Allan Leonard *biochemist, educator*
Hallgren, Richard Edwin *meteorologist*
Harwit, Martin Otto *astrophysicist, writer, educator, museum director*
Hirji, Rafik F. *water resources expert*
Jacobs, David Ernest *environmental health scientist*
Jacobs, Verne Louis *physicist, researcher*
Karle, Isabella L. *chemist*
Karle, Jerome *physicist, researcher*
Keyworth, George Albert *physicist, consulting company executive*
Knopman, Debra Sara *environmental scientist, director, hydrologist, policy analyst*
Komarov, Andrei M. *biophysicist, research scientist*
Ledley, Robert Steven *biophysicist*
Lehman, Donald Richard *physicist, educator, academic administrator*
Lehmberg, Robert Henry *research physicist*
Leventhal, Paul *nuclear scientist*
Lowy, Daniel A. *research scientist, educator, historian*
Lozansky, Edward Dmitry *physicist, consultant, writer*
Maran, Stephen Paul *astronomer*
Marlay, Robert Charles *physicist, engineer*
Meijer, Paul Herman Ernst *physicist, educator*
Montgomery, John A. *physicist*
Mough, Scott Thomas *chemist*
Pojeta, John, Jr. *geologist, researcher*
Press, Frank *geophysicist*
Rosenberg, Jerome David *physicist*
Ross, Malcolm *minerals consultant*
Sayre, Edward Vale *chemist*
Shanny, Ramy *physicist*
Shapero, Donald Campbell *physicist, government official*
Sheppard, Scott S. *astronomer*
Singer, Maxine Frank *retired biochemist, science association director*
Solomon, Sean Carl *geophysicist, lab administrator*
Spilhaus, Athelstan Frederick, Jr. *oceanographer, director*
Stanley, Jean-Daniel *geological oceanographer*
Stiber, Neil Alan *environmental scientist*
Tkachev, Sergey Nikolayevich *geophysicist*
Uberall, Herbert Michael Stefan *physicist, researcher*
White, John Arnold *physics professor, research scientist*
White, Robert Mayer *meteorologist*
Yochelson, Ellis L(eon) *paleontologist*
Youtcheff, John Sheldon *physicist*
Zacharias, Norbert *astronomer*

## FLORIDA

**Alachua**
Carlisle, Casey Allen *chemist, educator*
Schneider, Richard T. (Richard Theodore Schneider) *optics scientist, researcher, engineer*

**Boca Raton**
Louda, J. William *chemist, biochemist, educator*
Weissbach, Herbert *biochemist, researcher*

**Bonita Springs**
Brown, Theodore Lawrence *chemistry professor*

**Boynton Beach**
Osipow, Lloyd I. *chemist, consultant*

**Bradenton**
Brunk, William Edward *astronomer*
Compton, Charles Daniel *chemistry professor*

**Brooksville**
Flannery, Michael Sidney *environmental scientist*
McBride, Tamera Shawn Dew *geologist*

**Coral Gables**
Einspruch, Norman Gerald *physicist, engineering educator*
Glaser, Luis *biochemistry educator*
Hirschberg, Joseph Gustav *physicist, educator*
Leblanc, Roger Maurice *chemistry professor*
Van Vliet, Carolyn Marina *physicist, researcher*

**Dade City**
Burdick, Glenn Arthur *physicist, engineering educator*

**Dania Beach**
Spieler, Richard Earl *oceanographer, educator*

**Daytona Beach**
Bennett, Byron Lee *chemistry professor, researcher*
David, Valentina S. *physics professor*

**Delray Beach**
Zarwyn, Berthold *physicist, consultant*

**Dunedin**
Asefa, Tirusew *hydrologist*

**Fort Lauderdale**
Itkin, Ivan *nuclear scientist, mathematician*

**Fort Myers**
Curtin, David Yarrow *chemist, educator*
Horecker, Bernard Leonard *retired biochemistry professor*
Missimer, Thomas Michael *geologist*

**Gainesville**
Cousins, Robert John *nutritional biochemist, educator*
Hanrahan, Robert Joseph *chemist, educator*
Hummel, Rolf Erich *materials scientist, educator*
Jacobs, Alan Martin *physicist, researcher*
Katritzky, Alan Roy *chemistry professor*
Kumar, Pradeep *physics professor, researcher*
Micha, David Allan *chemistry professor, physics professor*
Mitselmakher, Guenakh *physics professor, researcher*
Mosier, Arvin Ray *chemist, researcher*
Ohrn, Nils Yngve *chemistry and physics educator*
Ramanathan, Ragulan *chemistry researcher*
Schultz, Gregory S. *biochemist*
Singley, John Edward, Jr. *retired environmental scientist, consultant*
Vala, Martin Thorvald *chemistry professor, researcher*

**Gonzalez**
Plischke, Le Moyne Wilfred *chemist, researcher*

**Jacksonville**
Beattie, Donald A. *aerospace scientist, consultant*
Dikici, Engin *research scientist*

**Jupiter**
Jacobson, Jerry Irving *biophysicist, theoretical physicist, medical researcher*

**Key West**
Trammell, Herbert Eugene *retired physicist*

**Lake Worth**
Bachrach, Howard L. *biochemist*

**Lakeland**
McFarlin, Richard Francis *retired industrial chemist, researcher*

**Lantana**
Balis, Moses Earl *biochemist, educator*

**Longboat Key**
Stapleton, Harvey James *physics professor*

**Lutz**
Koff, Fred William *retired research chemist*

**Marco Island**
Foster, Edward John *engineer physicist*

**Melbourne**
Nelson, Gordon Leigh *chemist, educator*
Trefry, John H. III *chemical oceanographer, educator*
Wiseman, Floyd Landis *chemist*

**Miami**
Aberson, Sim David *meteorologist, researcher*
Cobb, Hugh Dimmock III *meteorologist*
Donelan, Mark Anthony *physicist*
Fine, Rana Arnold *chemical and physical oceanographer*
Freire, Jose A. *physicist, writer*
Grewer, Christof Theodor *biophysicist*
Hansell, Dennis A. *oceanography educator*
Li, Qi *research scientist, consultant*
Majumdar, Sharanya Jyoti *meteorologist, educator*
Mayfield, Max *meteorologist*
Mooers, Christopher Northrup Kennard *physical oceanographer, educator*
Sanchez, Danmary *research scientist*
Sarkar, Malancha *research scientist, educator*

**Naples**
Leitner, Alfred *retired mathematical physicist, educator, educational film producer*
Marcuvitz, Nathan *physicist, educator*

**Orlando**
Baker, Peter Mitchell *laser scientist, educator*
Blue, Joseph Edward *physicist*
Flinchbaugh, David Edward *physicist*

---

Flitsiyan, Elena S. *physicist, physics educator*
Liboff, Richard Lawrence *physicist, researcher*
Llewellyn, Ralph Alvin *physics professor*
Norris, Charles Donald *chemistry professor*
Ting, Robert Yen-ying *physicist*

**Ormond Beach**
Kanfer, Julian Norman *biochemist, educator*

**Palm Beach Gardens**
Levitt, George *retired chemist*

**Palm Harbor**
Hardies, Mark Lee *physics professor, mathematics professor*

**Palmetto Bay**
Nakashima, Tadayoshi *retired biochemist, researcher*

**Pensacola**
Howell, Everette Irl *physicist, researcher*
Steinhoff, Raymond O(akley) *consulting geologist*

**Poinciana**
Williams, Donald John *physicist, researcher*

**Punta Gorda**
Fullman, Robert Louis *metallurgy consultant*

**Saint Petersburg**
Hsu, Tsong Han *chemist, researcher*

**Sanford**
Dickison, Alexander Kane *physical science educator*

**Sarasota**
Pierce, Richard Harry *oceanographer*

**Tallahassee**
Choppin, Gregory Robert *chemistry professor*
Elsner, James Brian *meteorologist, educator*
Gleeson, Thomas Alexander *retired meteorologist*
Herndon, Roy Clifford *physicist*
Kroto, Harold Walter *chemistry researcher, educator*
Loper, David Eric *geophysicist, mathematician*
Marshall, Alan George *chemistry and biochemistry educator*
Moulton, Grace Charbonnet *retired physicist*
Pfeffer, Richard Lawrence *meteorology and geophysics educator*
Robson, Donald *physics educator*
Schrieffer, John Robert *physics professor, science administrator*
von Molnár, Stephan *physics professor, director*
Zou, Xiaolei *meteorologist, educator*

**Tampa**
Johnson, Anthony O'Leary (Andy Johnson) *meteorologist, consultant*
Joseph, Babu *chemical educator*
Killinger, Dennis Karl *physicist, educator*
Seyfang, Andreas Georg *biochemist, educator*
Zhu, Yiliang *research scientist, educator*

**Tavares**
Reynolds, Bruce Grahlmann *physicist*

**Venice**
Feldmann, Edward George *pharmaceutical chemist, pharmacologist*

**West Palm Beach**
Gu, Binhe *environmental scientist*
Hagerthey, Scot Edward *environmental scientist*
Ogden, John Clifton III *environmental scientist, director*

**Winter Park**
Blossey, Erich Carl *chemistry professor*
Koltko-Rivera, Mark Edward *research scientist*

# GEORGIA

**Alpharetta**
Bridges, Alan Lynn *physicist, researcher, application developer, computer scientist*

**Athens**
Black, Clanton Candler, Jr. *biochemistry professor, researcher*
Black, Marsha C. *environmental scientist*
Chu, Chung Kwang *medicinal chemistry professor*
Darvill, Alan G. *biochemist, botanist, educator*
Delgado, Mark Crawford *chemist, educator*
Johnson, Michael Kenneth *chemistry professor*
Law, John Harold *biochemistry educator*
Oh, Yongseok *physicist*
Schaefer, Henry Frederick III *chemistry professor*
Yang, Charles Qi-Xiang *chemistry educator, researcher, consultant*
Yen, William Mao-Shung *physicist, consultant*

**Atlanta**
Allison, Stuart Anthony *chemistry professor, researcher*
Ashby, Eugene Christopher *chemistry professor*
Cramer, Howard Ross *geologist, environmental consultant*
Dickinson, Robert Earl *atmospheric scientist, educator, retired science administrator*
Finkelstein, David Ritz *physicist, educator, consultant*
Fox, Ronald Forrest *physicist, educator*
Gonzalez, Ruben Rene *biochemist, researcher*
Kahn, Bernd *radiochemist, educator*
Krishnamurthy, Ramesh Saligrama *environmental scientist, researcher*
Li, RongLin *research scientist*
Lin, Ming-Chang *physical chemistry professor, researcher*
Massey, Walter Eugene *physicist, academic administrator*
Perera, Unil A.G. *physics educator, researcher*
Polk, Malcolm *chemistry professor*

---

Snyder, Robert Lyman *materials scientist, educator*
Strekowski, Lucjan *chemistry professor*
Wiesenfeld, Kurt Arn *physicist, researcher*
Wong, Ching-Ping *chemist, materials engineer*
Zeng, Fanxing *chemist*

**Augusta**
Owen, Mary Anne *nuclear scientist, educator*
Sullivan, Jennifer Case *research scientist*
Yu, Robert Kuan-jen *biochemistry professor*

**Barnesville**
Gahr, Allan Arthur *chemistry professor*

**Brunswick**
Mihal, Sandra Powell *research scientist*

**Byron**
Bai, Cheng *biochemist, researcher*

**Carrollton**
Harris, Randa R. *research scientist, educator*

**Douglasville**
Adams Johnson, Arnita D. *chemist, educator*

**Kennesaw**
Kidonakis, Nikolaos *physicist*

**Oxford**
Patrick, Heather R. *chemistry professor*

**Peachtree City**
Roobol, Norman Richard *chemistry professor, consultant*

**Savannah**
Sanders, James Grady *biogeochemist*
Walter, Paul Hermann Lawrence *chemistry professor*
Windom, Herbert Lynn *oceanographer, environmental scientist*

**Stone Mountain**
Reichert, Leo Edmund, Jr. *biochemist, department chairman, endocrinologist*

# HAWAII

**Hawaii National Park**
Swanson, Donald Alan *geologist*

**Honolulu**
Aucan, Jerome Pierre *oceanographer*
Dousset, Benedicte *research scientist*
Hawke, Bernard Ray *planetary scientist, researcher*
Hey, Richard Noble *marine geophysicist*
Ihrig, Judson La Moure *chemist*
Keil, Klaus *geology educator, consultant*
Khan, Mohammad Asad *geophysics educator, retired minister, former senator of Pakistan*
Kong, Laura S. L. *geophysicist*
Kudritzki, Rolf-Peter *astronomer, educator*
Lebedev, Konstantin Vladimirovich *oceanographer, researcher*
Mader, Charles Lavern *chemist*
McMurtry, Gary Michael *geochemist, educator*
Pakvasa, Sandip *physicist*
Raleigh, Cecil Baring *geophysicist*
Seff, Karl *chemistry educator*

**Kailua**
Rosendal, Hans Erik *retired meteorologist*

**Kihei**
Borchers, Robert Reece *physicist, science administrator*

# IDAHO

**Boise**
Punnoose, Alex *physics professor*

**Emmett**
Bennett, Gary Lee *physicist, consultant*

**Idaho Falls**
Abbott, Michael Lehman *environmental scientist*

**Moscow**
Miller, Maynard Malcolm *geologist, educator, science administrator, former state legislator*
Renfrew, Malcolm MacKenzie *chemist, educator*
Shreeve, Jean'ne Marie *chemist, educator*

# ILLINOIS

**Abbott Park**
Kempf, Dale J. *chemist*

**Albion**
Curtis, Cyril Dean *retired physicist*

**Argonne**
Abrikosov, Alexei Alexeyevich *physicist*
Ahmad, Irshad *physicist, nuclear scientist*
Derrick, Malcolm *physicist*
Jorgensen, James Douglas *research physicist*
Kopasz, John Peter *chemist*
Kukhtin, Alexander V. *chemist*
Perlow, Gilbert Jerome *retired physicist, retired editor*
Peshkin, Murray *physicist*
Shpyrko, Oleg G. *physicist*
Srinivasan, Shankar Pattamadai *materials scientist, researcher*
Steindler, Martin Joseph *chemist*
Uprety, Krishna K. *physicist, materials scientist*

**Arlington Heights**
Smith, Norman Obed *retired physical chemist, educator*

---

**Batavia**
Balbekov, Valeri I. *physicist, researcher*
Chen, Mu-Chun *physicist, researcher*
Jonckheere, Alan Mathew *physicist*
Lach, Joseph Theodore *physicist*
Lykken, Joseph David *physicist*
Mokhov, Nikolai V. *physicist, researcher*
Oddone, Piermaria Jorge *experimental particle physicist*
Raja, Rajendran *physicist*
Rakhno, Igor *physicist*

**Bolingbrook**
Sabau, Carmen Sybile *retired chemist*

**Bourbonnais**
Armstrong, Douglas *organic chemist, educator*

**Carbondale**
Bekele, Elias Getahun *research scientist*
Oyana, Tonny J. *geoscientist, educator*
Patwardhan, Amit *research scientist*
Pinter, Nicholas *geologist*

**Champaign**
Balbach, Harold Edward *environmental scientist*
Buschbach, Thomas Charles *geologist, consultant*
Cartwright, Keros *hydrogeologist, researcher*
Gross, David Lee *geologist*
Krug, Edward Charles *environmental scientist*
Rebeiz, Constantin Anis *plant biochemist, educator, lab administrator, foundation administrator*
Slichter, Charles Pence *physicist, researcher*
Wolfram, Stephen *physicist, computer company executive*

**Chicago**
Blumberg, Avrom Aaron *physical chemistry professor*
Chandiwal, Amito *research scientist*
Chang, Yong *research scientist*
Clayton, Robert Norman *chemist, educator*
Cronin, James Watson *physicist, researcher*
Eastman, Dean Eric *physicist, researcher*
Freed, Karl Frederick *chemistry professor*
Ghani, Rayid *research scientist*
Giger, Maryellen Lissak *medical physicist, educator*
Gislason, Eric Arni *chemistry professor*
Gomer, Robert *chemistry professor*
Greaves, William Webster *chemist*
Grossman, Lawrence *geochemist*
Guggenheim, Stephen *geology educator*
Halpern, Jack *chemist, educator*
Harvey, Jeffrey A. *physics professor*
Harvey, Ronald Gilbert *research chemist*
Hast, Malcolm Howard *biomedical scientist, medical educator*
Herzenberg, Caroline Stuart Littlejohn *physicist*
Hildebrand, Roger Henry *astrophysicist, physicist*
Hopson, James Allen *paleontologist*
Iqbal, Zafar Mohd *biochemist, molecular biologist, toxicologist, consultant, cancer researcher, pharmacologist*
Kadanoff, Leo Philip *physicist, educator*
Kleppa, Ole J. *chemistry professor*
Kouvel, James Spyros *physicist, educator*
Krawetz, Arthur Altshuler *chemist, science administrator*
Lee, Bao-Shiang Bob *biochemist, researcher*
Liao, Shutsung *biochemist, molecular oncologist*
Makinen, Marvin William *biophysicist, educator*
Nagel, Sidney Robert *physics professor*
Nambu, Yoichiro *physics professor*
Newcomb, Martin Eugene, Jr. *chemistry professor*
Oehme, Reinhard *physicist, researcher*
Olsen, Edward John *geologist, educator, curator*
Palmer, Patrick Edward *radio astronomer, educator*
Pilcher, James Eric *physicist*
Rasinariu, Constantin *physics professor*
Reiffel, Leonard *physicist, consultant*
Richter, Frank M. *geophysicist, educator*
Rosner, Jonathan Lincoln *physicist, researcher*
Rosner, Robert *astrophysicist, educator*
Sager, William Fredrick *retired chemistry professor*
Srivastava, Anurag K. *research scientist*
Steiner, Donald Frederick *biochemist, physician, educator*
Turco, Michael Anthony *physicist, researcher*
Truran, James Wellington, Jr. *astrophysicist, educator*
Turner, Michael Stanley *astrophysics professor, researcher*
Wang, Yanbin *physicist, researcher*

**Dekalb**
Dyshkant, Alexander Sergeevich (Alexandre Sergeivich Dychkant) *physicist, researcher*
Hosmane, Narayan Sadashiv *chemistry professor*
Kimball, Clyde William *physicist, researcher*

**Des Plaines**
Pestova, Ekaterina *scientist*

**Downers Grove**
Green, David William *chemist, educator*
Hubbard, Lincoln Beals *medical physicist, consultant*

**Elk Grove Village**
Jan, Chwu-Ching Hwang *environmental chemistry consultant*

**Evanston**
Allred, Albert Louis *chemistry professor*
Basolo, Fred *chemistry professor*
Brown, Laurie Mark *physicist, researcher*
Chang, R. P. H. *materials science educator*
Godwin, Hilary A. *chemistry professor, research scientist*
Ibers, James Arthur *chemist, educator*
Jacobson, Andrew Darin *geochemist*
Jennings, Hamlin Manson *materials scientist, educator*
Lambert, Joseph Buckley *chemistry professor*
Margoliash, Emanuel *biochemist, educator*
Moore, C. Bradley *chemistry professor*

Oakes, Robert James *physics professor*
Odom, Teri Wang *chemist*
Sachtler, Wolfgang Max Hugo *chemistry professor, engineer, educator*
Seidman, David N(athaniel) *materials scientist, engineer, educator*
Silverman, Richard Bruce *chemist, educator, biochemist*
Ulmer, Melville Paul *physics and astronomy educator*
Van Duyne, Richard Palmer *analytical chemistry educator, chemical physics educator*
Walter, Robert Irving *retired chemistry professor*
Wessels, Bruce W. *materials scientist, educator, department chairman*

**Galesburg**
Schwartzman, Peter David *environmental scientist, educator*

**Glen Ellyn**
Mooring, F. Paul *physics editor*

**Glenview**
Rorig, Kurt Joachim *chemist, science association director, educator*

**Grayslake**
Barrington, Leonard Barry *chemist, educator, writer*

**Great Lakes**
Tiba, Amer *research scientist*

**Hinsdale**
Kaminsky, Manfred Stephan *physicist*

**Homewood**
Parker, Eugene Newman *retired physicist, retired educator*

**Lake Forest**
Weston, Arthur Walter *chemist, consultant, retired chemicals executive*

**Lemont**
Inokuti, Mitio *physicist, educator*
Williams, Jack Marvin *research chemist*

**Libertyville**
Grote, Jonathan *chemist, researcher*
Korenev, Sergey Alexandrovich *physicist*

**Lombard**
McCoy, Jeanie Shearer *analytical chemist, consultant*

**Maywood**
Bermes, Edward William, Jr. *biochemist, educator*

**Mount Carmel**
Fornoff, Frank J(unior) *retired chemistry educator, consultant*

**Naperville**
Arzoumanidis, Gregory G. *chemist*
Sellers, Gregory Jude *physicist*
Xiao, Yanan *physicist, researcher*

**North Chicago**
Loga, Sanda *physicist, researcher*
Olejniczak, Edward Thaddeus *research scientist*

**Northfield**
Shabica, Charles Wright *geologist, earth science educator*

**Park Ridge**
Hrejsa, Allen Francis *physicist, consultant*

**Peoria**
Chamberlain, Joseph Miles *retired astronomer, educator*
Nielsen, Harald Christian *retired chemist, researcher*

**Rockford**
Turner, Dallas G., Jr. *physics professor*

**Springfield**
Bandyopadhyay, Sucharita *research scientist*

**Urbana**
Beak, Peter Andrew *chemistry professor*
Charlevoix, Donna J. *meteorologist, educator*
Ginsberg, Donald Maurice *physicist, researcher*
Granato, Andrew Vincent *physics professor, researcher*
Greene, Joseph E. *material science researcher*
Gruebele, Martin *chemistry professor, biophysicist, educator*
Hou, Xiaoqiang *mineralogist, geochemist, spectroscopist*
Iben, Icko, Jr. *astrophysicist, educator*
Jackson, Edwin Atlee *retired physicist, retired educator*
Jeon, Won J. *research scientist*
Jonas, Jiri *chemist, educator*
Kieffer, Susan Werner *geologist, educator, media consultant*
Klein, Miles Vincent *physics professor*
Lauterbur, Paul Christian *chemistry professor*
Leggett, Anthony James *physics professor, researcher*
Lu, Yi *chemistry professor*
Martinez, Todd J. *chemistry professor*
Petrov, Ivan *physicist, materials scientist*
Rowland, Theodore Justin *physicist, researcher*
Salamon, Myron Ben *physicist, educator, dean*
Schweizer, Kenneth Steven *physics professor*
Sharif, Behzad *research scientist*
Snyder, Lewis Emil *astrophysicist, educator*
Suslick, Kenneth Sanders *chemistry professor*
Switzer, Robert Lee *biochemistry professor*
Watson, William Douglas *astrophysicist*
Woese, Carl R. *biophysicist, microbiology educator*
Zimmerman, Steven Charles *chemistry professor*

**Wadsworth**
Ahmad, Moghisuddin *chemist, researcher*

**Wilmette**
Rocek, Jan *chemist, educator*

**Woodridge**
Shen, Sin-Yan *physicist, acoustical engineer, musicologist*

## INDIANA

**Bloomington**
Basu, Abhijit *geologist, educator*
Cameron, John M. *nuclear scientist, educator, science administrator*
Clemmer, David E. *chemistry professor, researcher*
Easton, Susan Dawn *biochemist, educator*
Edmondson, Frank Kelley *retired astronomer*
Hanson, Gail G. *physicist, researcher*
Hattin, Donald Edward *geologist, educator*
Hites, Ronald Atlee *chemist, educator*
Huffman, John Curtis *chemist*
Kauffman, Erle Galen *geologist, paleontologist*
Letsinger, Robert Lewis *chemistry professor*
Macfarlane, Malcolm Harris *physicist, educator*
Oh, Sangyoon *research scientist*
Peters, Dennis Gail *chemist*
Pollock, Robert Elwood *nuclear scientist*
Smith, Ronald Thomas *environmental scientist*

**Brownsburg**
Conway, Dwight Colbur *retired chemistry professor*

**Chesterton**
Crewe, Albert Victor *physicist, researcher, artist*

**East Chicago**
Valia, Hardarshan S. *research scientist*

**Elkhart**
Free, Helen Murray *chemist, consultant*
Pugia, Michael J. *research scientist, educator*

**Indianapolis**
Fife, Wilmer Krafft *retired chemistry professor*
Lau, Pauline Young *chemist*
Mirsky, Arthur *retired geologist, educator*
Olson, Byron Louis *biochemist, educator*
Seevers, Robert H. *chemist*
Snare, Leroy Earl *physicist, physics educator*
Wong, David T. *biochemist, researcher*

**Lafayette**
Feuer, Henry *retired chemist*
Gartenhaus, Solomon *physicist, educator*
Loeffler, Frank Joseph *physicist, educator*
Porile, Norbert Thomas *chemistry professor*

**Madison**
Tatera, James Frank *chemist*

**Muncie**
Harris, Joseph McAllister *retired chemist*

**Notre Dame**
Bennett, David Paul *astrophysicist*
Huber, Paul William *biochemistry professor, researcher*
Maurice, Patricia Ann *geochemist, educator*
Meisel, Dan *chemist*
Trozzolo, Anthony Marion *chemistry professor*
Woehr, Andreas *physics professor*

**Terre Haute**
Guthrie, Frank Albert *chemistry professor*
Halpern, Arthur Merrill *chemistry professor*
Inlow, Jennifer Kay *chemistry professor, researcher*

**Valparaiso**
Cook, Addison Gilbert *chemistry professor*

**West Lafayette**
Adelman, Steven Allen *chemist, educator*
Ahmed, Shaikh Shahid *physicist, researcher*
Barnes, Virgil Everett, II, *physics professor*
Chang, Ching-jer *medicinal chemistry educator*
Cooks, R(obert) Graham *chemist, educator*
Diamond, Sidney *chemist, educator*
Judd, William Robert *engineering geologist, educator*
Kirchmaier, Ann *biochemist, researcher*
Lipschutz, Michael Elazar *chemistry professor, consultant, researcher*
McMillin, David Robert *chemistry professor*
Morrison, Harry *chemistry professor*
Negishi, Ei-ichi *chemistry professor*
Overhauser, Albert Warner *physicist*
Rossmann, Michael George *biochemist, educator*
Stahly, G. Patrick *chemist*

## IOWA

**Ames**
Armstrong, Daniel Wayne *chemist, educator*
Barnes, Richard George *physicist, researcher*
Barton, Thomas Jackson J. *chemistry professor, researcher*
Bytautas, Laimutis *chemist, educator*
Clem, John Richard *physicist, educator*
Fritz, James Sherwood *chemist, educator*
Hong, Mei *chemistry professor*
Horowitz, Jack *biochemistry educator*
Jacobson, Robert Andrew *chemistry professor*
Jenks, Cynthia J. *research scientist*
Lo, Chester C.H. *research scientist*
Schlagel, Deborah "Devo" Lynn *chemist, materials scientist*
Smith, John Francis *materials science educator*
Tabatabai, M. Ali *chemist, biochemist*
Yeung, Edward Szeshing *chemist*

**Cedar Falls**
Koob, Robert Duane *chemistry professor, academic administrator*

**Des Moines**
Bartschat, Klaus Richard Wilhelm *physics professor*

**Grinnell**
Swartz, James Edward *chemistry professor, educator, dean*

**Iowa City**
Baker, Richard Graves *geologist, educator, palynologist*
Burton, Donald Joseph *chemistry professor*
Conway, Thomas William *biochemist, educator*
Donelson, John Everett *biochemistry professor, molecular biologist*
Gurnett, Donald Alfred *physics professor*
Montgomery, Rex *biochemist, educator*
Prisinzano, Thomas Edward *chemistry professor, researcher*
Titze, Ingo Roland *physics professor*

**Le Mars**
Rebstock, Theodore Lynn *chemist, educator, retired research scientist*

**Panora**
Hartman, James Austin *retired geologist*

**Spencer**
Lemke, Alan James *environmental specialist*

**West Des Moines**
Lynch, David William *physicist, retired educator*

## KANSAS

**Kansas City**
Drake, Kenneth David *geologist*
Swint-Kruse, Liskin *biochemist, educator*

**Lawrence**
Ammar, Raymond George *physicist, researcher*
Dreschhoff, Gisela Auguste Marie *physicist, researcher*
Enos, Paul *geologist, educator*
Gerhard, Lee Clarence *geologist, educator*
Harmony, Marlin Dale *chemistry professor*
Kaesler, Roger L. *paleontologist, educator*
Landgrebe, John Allan *chemistry professor*
Merriam, Daniel F(rancis) *geologist*
Mitscher, Lester Allen *chemist, educator*
Ralston, John Peter *theoretical physicist, educator*
Stella, Valentino John *chemistry professor*

**Manhattan**
Hammaker, Robert Michael *chemist, educator*
Jiang, Hongxing *physics professor, researcher*
Klabunde, Kenneth J. *chemistry professor, researcher*
Le, Anh-Thu *physicist, researcher*

**Overland Park**
Ostby, Frederick Paul, Jr. *meteorologist, retired government official, science administrator*

**Topeka**
Randall, Anthony Shields *environmental scientist, military officer*

**Wichita**
Andrew, Kenneth L. *physicist, researcher, physics professor*

## KENTUCKY

**Berea**
Majumdar, Kingshuk *physics professor, researcher*

**Bowling Green**
Slocum, Donald Warren *chemist, researcher*

**Frankfort**
Zourarakis, Demetrio Periferachis *natural resource scientist*

**Hagerhill**
Blevins, Danny Keith *science educator, astronomer*

**Lexington**
Brock, Carolyn Pratt *chemist, educator*
Ehmann, William Donald *chemistry professor*
Elitzur, Moshe *physicist, researcher*
Ettensohn, Frank Robert *geologist, educator*
Hamilton-Kemp, Thomas Rogers *organic chemist, educator*
Hojahmat, Marhaba *research scientist*
Kern, Bernard Donald *retired physicist*

**Louisville**
Belanger, William Joseph *chemist, consultant*
Singh, Amar V. *research scientist*
Taylor, Kenneth Grant *chemistry professor*
Yazdanpanah, Mehdi Mohammad *physicist, researcher*

**Sturgis**
Thornsberry, Willis Lee, Jr. *chemist*

## LOUISIANA

**Baton Rouge**
Guzik, Theodore Gregory *astrophysicist, researcher*
Hamed, Shadpour *research assistant*
Mc Glynn, Sean Patrick *physical chemist, educator*
O'Connell, Robert Francis *physics professor*
Robinson, James William *chemistry professor*
Traynham, James Gibson *chemist, educator*
Warner, Isiah Manuel *chemistry professor*
Younathan, Ezzat Saad *retired biochemistry educator*
Young, David P. *physics professor*
Zhou, Liming *environmental scientist*

**Covington**
Vercellotti, John Raymond *chemist, researcher*

**Grambling**
Seetala, Naidu V. *physics professor, researcher*

**Metairie**
Arthur, Jett Clinton *retired chemist*

**New Orleans**
Perdew, John Paul *physics professor*
Prockop, Darwin Johnson *biochemist, medical educator*
Rosensteel, George Thomas *physics professor, nuclear physicist*
Tipler, Frank Jennings III *physicist*

**Pearl River**
Cantrell, Joseph Sires *chemistry professor*

**Pineville**
Nanna, Michael Edward *chemist, researcher*

**Walker**
Michel, Jacqueline *geochemist*

## MAINE

**Blue Hill**
Young, David Michael *biochemist, molecular biologist, internist, educator*

**Brunswick**
Broene, Richard Dale *chemistry professor*
Page, David Sanborn *biochemist, educator, environmental scientist, consultant*

**Freeport**
Panish, Morton B. *retired physical chemist*

**Kittery**
McNally, James Henry *physicist, defense consultant*

**Lewiston**
Semon, Mark David *physicist, researcher*

**Orono**
He, Zhongqi *chemist, researcher*

**Peaks Island**
Bohan, Thomas Lynch *physicist, lawyer*

**Saco**
Ames, Ted *environmental scientist*

**West Boothbay Harbor**
Goes, Joaquim Ignacio *oceanographer, researcher*

## MARYLAND

**Aberdeen Proving Ground**
Carrieri, Arthur Helmut *physicist, researcher*
Kalinowski, Caroline Marie *environmental scientist*
Mackay, Raymond Arthur *chemist*
Steger, Ralph James *chemist*

**Adelphi**
Agwu, Idika Ume *chemist, educator, reading specialist*
Brandt, Howard Edward *physicist*
Gaunaurd, Guillermo C. *physicist, researcher, engineer*

**Ammendale**
Goodpaster, John Vincent *chemist*

**Annapolis**
Bontoyan, Warren Roberts *chemist, lab administrator*
Clotworthy, John Harris *oceanographic consultant*
Hammer, Jacob Myer *physicist, consultant*
Pinkney, Alfred Eli *environmental scientist*
Schneider, Carl Stanley *physics professor, researcher*
Wolf, Alfred A. *physicist, educator*

**Baltimore**
Beer, Michael *biophysicist, educator, environmentalist*
Deutsch, Robert William *physicist*
Dicello, John Francis, Jr. *physicist, researcher*
Eichhorn, Gunther Louis *chemist, researcher*
Fulton, Thomas *theoretical physicist, educator*
Giacconi, Riccardo *astrophysicist, educator*
Green, Robert Edward, Jr. *physicist, researcher*
Haig, Frank Rawle *physics professor, priest*
Hauser, Michael George *astrophysicist*
Helm, Donald Cairney *geologist, engineer, educator*
Jones, Hendree Evelyn *research scientist, psychologist*
Judd, Brian Raymond *physicist*
Kaplan, Alexander Efimovich *physics educator, engineering educator*
Krolik, Julian Henry *astrophysicist, educator*
Lee, Yung-Keun *physicist, researcher*
Margon, Bruce Henry *astrophysicist, educator*
Marsh, Bruce David *geologist, educator*
Mixson, Archibald James *research scientist, internist, endocrinologist*
Moos, H. Warren *physicist, educator, astronomer, director*
Norman, Colin Arthur *astrophysics educator*
Pan, William Kuang-Yao *research scientist*
Posner, Gary Herbert *chemist, educator*
Puzia, Thomas H. *astronomer, educator*
Riess, Adam Guy *astronomer, educator*
Roseman, Saul *biochemist, educator*
Shamoo, Adil Elias *biochemist, educator*
Silverstone, Harris J. *chemistry professor*
Sinha, Neeti *biophysicist, researcher*
Stanley, Steven Mitchell *paleontologist, educator*
Steiner, Robert Frank *biochemist*
Townsend, Craig Arthur *chemistry educator*
Weaver, Kenneth Newcomer *geologist, state agency administrator*

**Gloucester**
Socolow, Arthur Abraham *geologist*

**Hanscom Afb**
Mailloux, Robert Joseph *physicist*
Mittleman, Steven David *physicist, researcher*

**Harwich**
Worrell, Francis Toussaint *retired physics professor*

**Haverhill**
DeSchuytner, Edward Alphonse *biochemist, educator*

**Ipswich**
Herrmann, Robert Lawrence *biochemist, educator*

**Leominster**
Kerns, Christian Randolph *chemist*

**Lexington**
Buchanan, John Machlin *biochemistry professor*
Dionne, Gerald Francis *research physicist, educator, consultant*
Ehrenfeld, John Roos *environmental policy educator*
Huang, Robin K. *research scientist*
Oliner, Arthur Aaron *physicist, researcher*
Silverman, Sam Mendel *physicist, lawyer*
Steiner, John William *retired biophysicist*
Wang, Chi Hua *chemist, education educator*
Williamson, Richard Cardinal *physicist*

**Lowell**
Kannenberg, Lloyd Chambers *physicist, researcher*
Karakashian, Aram Simon *physics professor*
Pullen, David John *physicist, researcher*

**Medford**
Cavallaro, Mary Caroline *retired physics professor*
Gunther, Leon *physicist, educator*
Kumar, Krishna *chemistry professor*
Mujat, Mircea *optics scientist*
Schneps, Jack *physics professor, department chairman*
Shultz, Mary Jane *chemist, educator*

**Needham**
Holt, Stephen S. *astrophysicist*

**Newburyport**
Robinson, Enders Anthony *geophysicist, educator, writer*

**Newton**
Aronow, Saul *radiological physicist, consultant*
Dunlap, William Crawford *physicist*
Jeanloz, Roger William *biochemist, educator*
Lichtin, Norman Nahum *chemistry professor*

**Newton Center**
Philippe, Paul *chemist*

**North Andover**
Swallow, Kathleen Clinedinst *chemistry professor*

**North Dartmouth**
Hsu, Jong-Ping *physicist, educator*

**Roxbury**
Simons, Elizabeth R(eiman) *biochemist, educator*

**Shrewsbury**
Nixon, Eugene Ray *chemist, educator*

**South Dartmouth**
Mellberg, Leonard Evert *physicist*

**South Hadley**
Bergen, Robert Ludlum, Jr. *retired materials scientist*
Williamson, Kenneth Lee *chemistry professor*

**Springfield**
Maniscalco, Ignatius Anthony *chemistry professor*

**Wakefield**
Trogolo, Jeffrey A. *research scientist*

**Waltham**
Abbott, Laurence Frederick *physics educator*
Deser, Stanley *physicist, researcher*
Epstein, Irving Robert *chemistry professor*
Foxman, Bruce Mayer *chemist, educator*
Lees, Marjorie Berman *biochemist, neuroscientist*
Snider, Barry B. *organic chemist*

**Watertown**
Lin, Juchui Ray (Ju-Chui Lin) *polymer scientist*

**Wayland**
Clark, Melville, Jr. *physicist, consultant, electrical engineer*
Wolff, Peter Adalbert *physicist, researcher*

**Wellesley**
Charpie, Robert Alan *physicist, researcher*
Kato, Walter Yoneo *physicist*
Snitzer, Elias *physicist*

**Westford**
Paine, Robert J. *environmental scientist, consultant*

**Weston**
Lin, Alice Lee Lan *physicist, researcher, educator*
Wang, Chia Ping *physicist, researcher*

**Williamstown**
Crampton, Stuart Jessup Bigelow *physicist, researcher*
Markgraf, J(ohn) Hodge *chemist, educator*
Park, David Allen *physicist, researcher*
Pasachoff, Jay Myron *astronomer, educator*
Wobus, Reinhard Arthur *geologist, educator*

**Winchester**
Milburn, Richard Henry *physics professor*

von Stackelberg, Katherine Ellen *environmental scientist, consultant*

**Woburn**
Popov, Oleg *physicist*

**Woods Hole**
Behn, Mark Dietrich *marine geophysicist, educator*
Berggren, William Alfred *geologist, research micropaleontologist*
Cohen, Seymour Stanley *biochemist, educator*
Evans, Rob L. *geophysicist, researcher*
Gagosian, Robert B. *chemist, educator*
Hart, Stanley Robert *geochemist, educator*
Steele, John Hyslop *marine scientist, oceanographic institute administrator*
Stephen, Ralph Archibald *geophysicist, researcher*
Uchupi, Elazar *geologist, researcher*

**Worcester**
Chaudhury, Sujoy Krishna *research scientist*
Gnanaraj, Joseph Sathiya *research scientist*

## MICHIGAN

**Allendale**
Ambrose, Bradley Scott *physics professor, researcher*

**Ann Arbor**
Agranoff, Bernard William *biochemist, educator*
Akerlof, Carl William *physics professor*
Annesley, Thomas Michael *clinical chemist, pathology educator*
Ashe, Arthur James III *chemistry professor*
Bartell, Lawrence Sims *chemist, educator*
Blinder, Seymour Michael *chemistry professor, physics professor, researcher*
Choe, Seungho *physicist, researcher*
Chupp, Timothy Edward *physicist, educator, academic administrator*
Clarke, Roy *physicist, researcher*
Dekker, Eugene Earl *biochemistry educator*
Filisko, Frank Edward *physicist, researcher*
Griffin, Henry Claude *chemistry professor*
Haddock, Fred(erick) T(heodore), Jr. *retired astronomer*
Hagel, William Carl *metallurgical consultant*
Jie, Lian *research scientist*
Jones, Lawrence William *retired physicist*
Kesler, Stephen Edward *geology educator*
Killeen, Timothy Laurence *aerospace scientist, science administrator*
Krimm, Samuel *physicist, researcher*
Krisch, Alan David *physics professor*
Lahann, Joerg *chemist*
Mazzeo, Anthony R. *chemist*
Morris, Michael David *chemistry professor*
Neal, Homer Alfred *physics professor, researcher, academic administrator*
Nordman, Christer Eric *chemistry professor*
Nriagu, Jerome Okon *environmental geochemist*
Oh, So-Ryeok *research scientist*
Parkinson, William Charles *physics professor, researcher*
Robertson, Richard Earl *physical chemist, educator*
Roe, Byron Paul *physics professor*
Saltiel, Alan Robert *biochemist*
Savit, Robert Steven *physics professor, consultant*
Van der Voo, Rob *geophysicist*
Veltman, Martinus J.G. *retired physics educator*

**Belleville**
Wilson, David James *chemistry researcher, educator*

**Birmingham**
Smith, George Wolfram *physicist, researcher*

**Chassell**
Spain, James Dorris, Jr. *biochemist, educator*

**Chelsea**
Crane, Horace Richard *physicist, researcher*
Weinreich, Gabriel *physicist, minister, educator*

**Dearborn**
Parker, Gordon Arthur *chemistry professor*

**Detroit**
Bowen, David R. *science and technology educator, consultant*
Drescher, Dennis George *biochemist, researcher*
Frade, Peter Daniel *chemist, educator, administrator*
Gupta, Suraj Narayan *physicist, researcher*
Kirschner, Stanley *chemist*
Krawetz, Stephen Andrew *molecular medicine and genetics scientist, educator*
Oliver, John Preston *chemistry professor*
Stewart, Melbourne George, Jr. *physicist, researcher*
Svoboda, Mary Beth *health physicist, environmental science educator*

**East Lansing**
Abolins, Maris Arvids *physicist, educator*
Austin, Sam M. *physicist, educator*
Blosser, Henry Gabriel *physicist*
Brown, Boyd Alex *physicist, researcher*
Case, Eldon Darrel *materials science educator*
D'Itri, Frank Michael *environmental research chemist*
Dye, James Louis *chemistry professor*
Gelbke, Claus-Konrad *nuclear physics educator*
Harrison, James Francis *chemistry professor, researcher*
Harrison, Michael Jay *physicist, educator*
Kanatzidis, Mercouri G. *chemist, educator*
Kaplan, Thomas Abraham *physicist, educator*
Preiss, Jack *biochemistry professor*

**Farmington Hills**
Chapman, Gilbert Bryant *physicist*
Theodore, Ares Nicholas *chemist, researcher*

**Grand Rapids**
Menninga, Clarence *retired geologist*

**Grosse Pointe Park**
Orton, Colin George *medical physicist*

**Highland**
Brown, Ray Kent *biochemist, physician, educator*

**Houghton**
Brown, Richard Edwin *chemistry professor, researcher*

**Interlochen**
Nadji, Taoufik *physics professor, mathematician*

**Ironwood**
Rondeau, Clement Robert *petroleum geologist*

**Kalamazoo**
Askew, Thomas Rendall *physics educator, researcher, consultant*
Greenfield, John Charles *biochemist*
Huffman, David Lee *chemistry professor, researcher*
Kim, Moonkoo *marine environmental chemist*

**Kentwood**
Yovich, Daniel John *chemist, educator*

**Leland**
Small, Hamish *chemist*

**Midland**
Chao, Marshall *chemist*
Dorman, Linneaus Cuthbert *retired chemist*
Dreyfuss, M(ax) Peter *research chemist, educator*
Klosin, Jerzy *research chemist*
Merrington, Adrian *researcher, educator, rheologist*
Nowak, Robert Michael *chemist*

**Mount Pleasant**
Dietrich, Richard Vincent *geologist, educator*
Peyrefitte, Ashton George, Jr. *meteorologist, educator*

**Northville**
Bohm, Henry Victor *physicist*

**Okemos**
Burnett, Jean B. (Mrs. James R. Burnett) *biochemist, educator*

**Rochester**
Elder, Ken R. *physicist, educator*

**Rochester Hills**
Fritzsche, Hellmut *physics professor*

**Three Rivers**
Boyer, Nicodemus Elijah *chemist, consultant*

**University Center**
Clarey, Timothy Lee *geologist, educator*

**Warren**
Herbst, Jan Francis *physicist, researcher*

**West Bloomfield**
Harwood, Julius J. *metallurgist, educator*

**Ypsilanti**
Barnes, James Milton *physics professor, astronomy professor*

## MINNESOTA

**Austin**
Holman, Ralph Theodore *retired biochemistry professor, nutritionist*

**Bloomington**
Bekrenev, Anatoliy *physicist*

**Ellsworth**
Shurr, George W. *geologist, consultant*

**Golden Valley**
Allen, Martin *chemistry educator, consultant*

**Mahtomedi**
Holmen, Reynold Algott Emanuel *chemist*

**Minneapolis**
Ackerman, Eugene *biophysics professor*
Carr, Peter William *chemistry professor*
Chakraborty, Sombuddha *research scientist*
Dalluge, Joseph James *chemist*
Goldman, Allen Marshall *physics professor*
Halley, James Woods *physics professor*
Kohlstedt, David Lee *geophysicist, educator*
Kuhi, Leonard Vello *astronomer, academic administrator*
Marshak, Marvin Lloyd *physicist, researcher*
Portoghese, Philip Salvatore *medicinal chemist, educator*
Shifman, Mikhail *physicist*
Truhlar, Donald Gene *chemist, educator*
Wright, Herbert E(dgar), Jr. *geologist*

**Moorhead**
Strong, Judith Ann *chemist, educator*

**Northfield**
Cederberg, James *retired physics professor*
Noer, Richard J. *physics professor, researcher*

**Oakdale**
Tran, Nang Tri *research scientist, electrical engineer*

**Rochester**
Greenleaf, James Fowler *biophysics educator*
Kao, Pai Chih *clinical chemist*

**Saint Cloud**
Krystyniak, Rebecca Ann *chemistry professor*

**Saint Paul**
Ferrey, Mark Laurence *environmental scientist, researcher*
Hobbie, Russell Klyver *physics professor*
Newmark, Richard Alan *chemist*
Ouderkirk, Andrew J. *corporate scientist*
Perry, James Alfred *environmental scientist, consultant, science educator, academic administrator*
Prager, Stephen *chemistry professor*
Rubens, Sidney Michel *physicist, consultant*
Van Pilsum, John Franklin *biochemist, educator*

## MISSISSIPPI

**Alcorn State**
Hunt, Clinton, Jr. *chemistry professor*

**Bay Saint Louis**
Hurlburt, Harley Ernest *ocean modeling and prediction scientist*
Lewando, Alfred Gerard, Jr. *oceanographer*

**Columbus**
Gingerich, Samuel Beryl *chemistry professor, academic administrator*

**Hattiesburg**
Miao, Wujian *chemistry professor*
Nanda, Ajaya Kumar *chemist, educator*

**Jackson**
Olendski, Oleg *physicist*
Smith, Edgar Eugene *biochemist, educator, academic administrator*

**Mississippi State**
Acar, Erdem *aerospace scientist, researcher*

**Ocean Springs**
Biber, Patrick D. *oceanographer*

**Starkville**
Huang, Junmin *chemist, researcher*

**Stennis Space Center**
Chin-Bing, Stanley Arthur *physicist, educator*

**University**
Aranchuk, Vyacheslav *research scientist*
Breazeale, Mack Alfred *research scientist, educator*

## MISSOURI

**Clinton**
Kelsay, David Roland *chemist*

**Columbia**
Bauman, John E., Jr. *chemistry professor*
Decker, Wayne Leroy *meteorologist, educator*
Gehrke, Charles William *biochemistry professor*
Hawthorne, Marion Frederick *chemistry professor*
Katti, Kattesh V. *biochemist, educator, research scientist*
Mashhoon, Bahram *physicist, researcher*
Randall, Douglas D. *biochemist, educator*
Randall, Linda Lea *biochemist, educator*
Weisman, Gary Andrew *biochemist*

**Creve Coeur**
Bockserman, Robert Julian *chemist*

**Ferguson**
Chubb, Charles Ray *physicist, researcher*

**Independence**
Lemon, Leslie Roy *radar meteorologist*

**Kansas City**
Cheng, Kuang Lu *chemist, educator*
Dias, Jerry Ray *chemistry professor, researcher*
Parizek, Eldon Joseph *geologist, educator, dean*
Rost, William Joseph *chemist*
Surguchov, Andrei P. *biochemist, ophthalmologist, researcher*
Wheeler, James Donlan *chemistry professor*
Wilkinson, Ralph Russell *retired biochemistry educator, toxicologist*

**Kirksville**
Festa, Roger Reginald *chemist, educator*

**Lees Summit**
Hubbard, Harold Mead *energy and environmental systems consultant, retired research executive*

**Liberty**
Philpot, John Lee *retired physics professor*

**Rolla**
Adawi, Ibrahim Hasan *physics professor*
Alexander, Ralph William, Jr. *physics professor*
Mc Farland, Robert Harold *retired physicist*

**Saint Charles**
Ayyagari, Rao L. *biochemistry professor*

**Saint Louis**
Agarwal, Ramesh Kumar *aeronautical scientist, researcher, educator*
Bender, Carl Martin *physics professor, consultant*
Burgess, James Harland *physics professor, researcher*
Clark, John Walter *physics professor*
Colletti, Ronald F. *chemist, researcher*
Cowsik, Ramanath *physics professor*
Fitzpatrick, Susan *biochemist, neurologist, foundation administrator*
Frieden, Carl *biochemist, educator*
Friedlander, Michael Wulf *physicist, researcher*
Gibbons, Patrick Chandler *physicist, researcher*
Gokel, George William *organic chemist, educator*

Gross, Michael Lawrence *chemistry professor*
Gustafson, David I *environmental scientist, researcher*
Handel, Peter H. *physics professor*
Hawkins, Pamela Leigh Huffman *biochemist*
Israel, Martin Henry *astrophysicist, educator, academic administrator*
Kusky, Timothy M. *geologist, educator*
Lin, Tien-Sung Tom *chemistry professor*
Macias, Edward S. *chemistry professor, dean, academic administrator*
Murray, Robert Wallace *chemistry professor*
Norberg, Richard Edwin *physicist, researcher*
Rath, Nigam P. *research scientist, educator*
Sly, William S. *biochemist, educator*
Will, Clifford Martin *physicist, researcher*
Zinner, Ernst K. *physics educator, earth and planetary science educator, researcher*

**Springfield**
Dong, Lifeng *materials scientist, physicist*
Sedaghat-Herati, Reza *chemistry professor*
Thompson, Clifton C. *retired chemistry professor, academic administrator*

## MONTANA

**Billings**
Carter, Gary Wayne *environmental health specialist*
Paul, Bessie Margrette *retired weaher forecaster*

**Bozeman**
Grieco, Paul Anthony *chemistry professor*
Han, Jiaping *research scientist*
Horner, John Robert *paleontologist, researcher, curator*
Jacobsen, Jeffrey Scott *environmental scientist*

**Columbia Falls**
Spade-Shenker, George Lawrence (George Shenker) *research scientist*

**Dayton**
von Volborth, Alexis *geochemist, geological engineering educator*

**Great Falls**
Knudson, Ruthann *environmental consultant, anthropologist, archaeologist*

**Missoula**
Jakobson, Mark John *retired physics professor*

**Monarch**
Baker, David Warren *earth scientist*

## NEBRASKA

**Crete**
Holmes, Andrea *chemistry professor, researcher*

**Lincoln**
Eckhardt, Craig Jon *chemistry professor*
Gaskell, C. Martin *astronomer, educator, composer*
Harwood, David M. *geologist, educator*
Jones, Lee Bennett *chemistry professor, academic administrator*
Sellmyer, David Julian *physicist, researcher*
Yoder, Bruce Alan *chemist*

**Omaha**
Bergt, Gregory Paul *chemist, consultant*
Rea, Roger Uhl *chemistry educator, consultant*
Stickle, Douglas Franklin *biochemist*
Zepf, Thomas Herman *retired physics professor*

## NEVADA

**Carson City**
Crawford, John Edward *geologist, consultant*

**Henderson**
Anspaugh, Lynn Richard *research biophysicist*
Holloway, Robert Wester *radiochemist*
Trivelpiece, Alvin William *physicist, educator, consultant*
Troitski, Igor *laser scientist, researcher*

**Las Vegas**
Broca, Laurent Antoine *aerospace scientist*
Hua, Fred Huizhong *materials scientist*
Mon, Kevin G. *research scientist*
Sadineni, Suresh Babu *research scientist*
Shannon, Samuel A. *chemist*

**North Las Vegas**
Benson, Allen B. *chemist, educator, consultant*

**Reno**
Mitchell, David Lancaster *research educator*
Price, Jonathan G. *geologist*
Sladek, Ronald John *physics professor*
Taranik, James Vladimir *geologist, educator*

**Sparks**
Bonham, Harold Florian *research geologist, consultant*

## NEW HAMPSHIRE

**Glen**
Zager, Ronald I. *chemist, consultant*

**Grantham**
Grimley, Robert Thomas *chemistry professor*

**Hanover**
Curphey, Thomas John *chemist, researcher*
Doyle, William Thomas *physicist, retired educator*
Fesen, Robert A. *astronomer, educator*
Hughes, Russell Profit *chemistry professor*
Kantrowitz, Arthur *physicist, researcher, educator*

Montgomery, David Campbell *retired physics professor*
Wegner, Gary Alan *astronomer*

**Jaffrey**
Walling, Cheves Thomson *chemistry professor*

**Litchfield**
Miller, Dawn Marie *retired meteorologist*

**Meredith**
Hatch, Frederick Tasker *research scientist, consultant*

**Plymouth**
McGuire, Keven James *hydrologist, educator*

**Salem**
Simmons, Marvin Gene *retired geophysics educator*

## NEW JERSEY

**Basking Ridge**
Morgan, Samuel P(ope) *physicist, applied mathematician*

**Belle Mead**
Shiv, Kumar *bioscientist*

**Berkeley Heights**
Geusic, Joseph Edward *physicist*
Mac Rae, Alfred Urquhart *physicist, electrical engineer*

**Bogota**
Condon, Francis Edward *retired chemistry professor*

**Bridgewater**
Albrethsen, Adrian Edysel *metallurgist, consultant*

**Demarest**
Ruderman, Warren *chemist*

**East Brunswick**
McDowell, Wilbur Benedict *retired chemist consultant*

**East Windsor**
Shoemaker, Frank Crawford *retired physicist*

**Edison**
Gilmore, Adam Matthew *biophysicist*

**Garfield**
Yakimovich, Vladimir *chemist, director*

**Glassboro**
Ramanujachary, Kandalam V. *chemistry professor, researcher*

**Highland Park**
Brudner, Harvey Jerome *physicist*

**Hoboken**
Bose, Ajay Kumar *chemistry professor*
Eide, Hans A. *physicist, educator*
Moon, Deok Hyun *research scientist*
Schmidt, George *physicist, educator*

**Iselin**
Ilinich, Oleg *chemist, researcher*
Liu, Xinsheng *chemist*

**Jackson**
Arminas, Scott Arnold *chemist, poet, writer*

**Jersey City**
Koster, Emlyn Howard *geologist, educator*

**Kenilworth**
Jia, Yanlin *research scientist*
Korfmacher, Walter Averill *chemist, researcher*

**Lafayette**
Muscalo, David *geologist, environmental consultant*

**Lakewood**
Karol, Frederick John *retired industrial chemist*

**Leonia**
Kurtz, Anthony David *physicist*

**Maplewood**
Johnson, Dewey, Jr. *retired biochemist*
Tatyrek, Alfred Frank *retired chemist, environmental engineer*

**Middletown**
Lundgren, Carl William, Jr. *physicist*

**Montclair**
Passchier, Sandra *geologist, educator*

**Mountainside**
Vice, Susan F. *medicinal chemist*

**Neptune**
Aguiar, Adam Martin *chemist, educator*

**New Brunswick**
Feigenson, Mark Daniel *geologist, educator*
Pandey, Ramesh Chandra *chemist, chemicals executive*
Previdi, Michael *meteorologist, research scientist*
Robock, Alan *meteorology professor*
Strauss, Ulrich Paul *chemist, educator*
Yu, Jurong *chemist*

**New Providence**
Chandross, Edwin Arthur *chemist*
Gasparyan, Arman *physicist*
Helfand, Eugene *chemist*
Sivco, Deborah Lee *materials scientist, researcher*

**Newark**
Asatryan, Rubik *chemistry professor, researcher*
Frenkel, Gerald *biochemist, educator*
Lanzerotti, Louis John *physicist*
Thompson, Hugh Walter *chemistry professor*

**Nutley**
Kong, Norman *chemist*

**Oldwick**
Sinfelt, John Henry *chemist*

**Picatinny Arsenal**
Owens, Frank James *physicist*

**Piscataway**
Al-Sharab, Jafar Farhan *materials scientist, researcher*
Cohen, Morrel Herman *physicist, biologist, educator*
Idol, James Daniel, Jr. *chemist, educator, inventor, consultant*
Jones, Roger Alan *chemistry professor, researcher, consultant*
Kotliar, B. Gabriel *physics professor*
Leath, Paul Larry *physicist, educator, former university official*
Lebowitz, Joel Louis *mathematical physicist, educator*
Lindenfeld, Peter *physics professor*
Manowitz, Paul *biochemist, researcher, educator*
Polefka, Thomas Gregory *biochemist*
Robbins, Allen Bishop *physics professor*
Rokhlenko, Alexander *research scientist, educator*
Toby, Sidney *retired chemistry professor*
Yacowitz, Harold *biochemist, nutritionist*
Zimmermann, Frank Martin *physicist, educator, research scientist*

**Pomona**
Sharon, Yitzhak Yaakov *physicist, researcher*

**Pompton Plains**
Gummel, Hermann Karl *retired physicist, lab administrator*

**Port Murray**
Kunzler, John Eugene *physicist*

**Princeton**
Adler, Stephen Louis *physicist*
Anderson, Philip W. *physicist*
Brinkman, William Frank *physicist, research and development company executive*
Bryan, Kirk, Jr. *meteorologist, oceanographer, researcher*
Carter, Emily Ann *physical chemist, researcher, educator*
Cava, Robert J. *chemistry professor*
Chaikin, Paul M. *physicist*
Chen, Thomas *mathematical physicist, researcher, educator*
Choueiri, Edgar Y. *research scientist, physics and engineering educator, director*
Christman, Edward Arthur *physicist*
Das, Jagabandhu *chemist, researcher*
Davidson, Ronald Crosby *physicist, researcher*
Dyson, Freeman John *retired physics professor*
Fisch, Nathaniel Joseph *physicist*
Fitch, Val Logsdon *physics professor*
Florey, Klaus Georg *chemist, pharmaceutical consultant*
Giordmaine, Joseph Anthony *physicist*
Goldston, Robert J. *research scientist*
Grisham, Larry Richard *physicist*
Groves, John Taylor III *chemist, educator*
Haldane, F. Duncan M. (Frederick Duncan Michael Haldane, Duncan Haldane) *physics educator*
Happer, William, Jr. *physicist, researcher*
Hoke, Molly Elizabeth *chemist, research scientist*
Hulse, Russell Alan *physicist*
Hut, Piet *astrophysics educator*
Jenkins, Edward Beynon *research astronomer*
Kammen, Daniel Merson *environmental physicist, researcher*
Kauzmann, Walter Joseph *chemistry professor*
Lieb, Elliott Hershel *physicist, educator, mathematician, educator*
Lin, Hai *physicist*
Long, Frank Wesley, Jr. *chemist*
Maldacena, Juan *physicist, researcher*
Manabe, Syukuro *meteorologist*
McClure, Donald Stuart *physical chemist, educator*
Morgan, William Jason *geophysics educator*
Nolet, Guust *geophysicist*
Ong, Nai-Phuan *physicist, researcher*
Oppenheimer, Michael *physicist*
Ostriker, Jeremiah Paul *astrophysicist, educator*
Page, Lyman Alexander, Jr. *physicist*
Ramaprasad, Kackadasam Raghavachar *physical chemist*
Royce, Barrie Saunders Hart *physicist, researcher*
Rutherford, Paul Harding *physicist*
Seiberg, Nathan *physics professor*
Shaohua Kevin, Zhou *research scientist*
Sheffield, Justin *hydrologist, researcher*
Smith, Arthur John Stewart *physicist, researcher*
Sterzer, Fred *research physicist*
Stier, Roger Edwin *chemist, researcher*
Taylor, Edward Curtis *chemistry professor*
Taylor, Joseph Hooton, Jr. *radio astronomer, physicist*
Torquato, Salvatore *materials scientist, chemistry professor*
Tremaine, Scott Duncan *astrophysicist*
Van Houten, Franklyn Bosworth *geologist, educator*
Vecchi, Gabriel Andrés *geophysicist*
Ward, Bess B. *oceanographer, educator*
Wheeler, John Archibald *physicist, educator*
Wightman, Arthur Strong *physicist, researcher*
Witten, Edward *mathematical physicist*

**Rahway**
Garcia, Maria Luisa *biochemist, researcher*
Kaczorowski, Gregory John *biochemist, researcher, science administrator*

**Skillman**
Diaz, Teresita Perez *chemist*

**South Orange**
Sahiner, Mehmet Alper *physics professor, researcher*

**Stewartsville**
Eckert, John Andrew *chemist, technical consultant*

**Stirling**
Walsh, Peter Joseph *physics professor*

**Summit**
Phillips, James Charles *physicist, researcher*
Vandenberg, Joka Maria *physicist, researcher*

**Teaneck**
Haas, Gerhard Julius *chemistry professor*

**Trenton**
Baron, Lisa Ann *environmental scientist*

**Union**
Zois, Constantine Nicholas Athanasios *meteorologist, educator*

**West Caldwell**
Surmatis, Joseph D. *retired chemist*

## NEW MEXICO

**Albuquerque**
Cardimona, David Anthony *physicist, researcher*
Cramer, James Dale *physicist, scientific company executive*
Emin, David *physicist*
Enke, Christie George *chemistry professor, consultant*
Gander, John Edward *biochemistry educator*
Guenther, Arthur Henry *research scientist, educator*
Leeper, Ramon Joe *physicist*
Loftfield, Robert Berner *biochemistry professor*
Muller, Richard Partain *chemist, researcher*
Paine, Robert Treat *chemistry educator*
Papyrin, Anatolii Nikiforovich *physicist, researcher*
Petsev, Dimiter Nikolov *chemistry professor*
Ruiz, Carlos Leon *nuclear scientist, physicist*
Van Devender, J. Pace *research scientist, science administrator*

**Hobbs**
Chang, Dahwei *physics professor*

**Las Cruces**
Gibbs, William Royal *physics professor, researcher*
Rayson, Gary Donn *chemistry educator*
Richardson, Albert Edward *chemistry professor, researcher*
Shukla, Manoj K. *soil physicist*

**Los Alamos**
Atcher, Robert Whitehill *chemist, educator*
Bauer, Eric Dietzgen *physicist*
Becker, Stephen A. *physicist*
Blagoev, Krastan Blagoev *physicist, biophysicist*
Brown, Lowell Severt *physicist, researcher*
Cowan, Robert Duane *physicist*
Cucchietti, Fernando Martin *physicist, researcher*
Engelhardt, Albert George *physicist*
Gibson, Benjamin Franklin *physicist*
Grilly, Edward Rogers *physicist*
Harlow, Francis Harvey *physicist, paleontologist, research scientist*
Hendricks, John Stanley *computational physicist*
Johnson, Mikkel Borlaug *physicist*
Judd, O'Dean P. *physicist*
Keepin, George Robert, Jr. *physicist*
Korber, Bette Tina Marie *chemist*
Kubas, Gregory Joseph *research chemist*
Louis, William Charles III *physicist*
Mead, William Charles *physicist*
Mihalas, Dimitri Manuel *astrophysicist, educator*
Mitchell, Terence Edward *materials scientist*
Mottola, Emil *physicist, researcher*
Nix, James Rayford *nuclear physicist, consultant*
Pack, Russell T. *theoretical chemist*
Picraux, Samuel Thomas *physicist, researcher*
Press, William Henry *physicist, computer scientist*
Rosen, Louis *physicist*
Selden, Robert Wentworth *physicist, consultant*
Sharp, David Howland *physicist*
Smith, James Lawrence *research physicist*
Swift, Gregory *physicist*
Taylor, Raymond Dean *physicist*
Terrell, James (Nelson James Terrell) *physicist*
Thompson, Joe D. *physicist*
Vitev, Ivan Mateev *physicist, researcher*
Weronski, Pawel *physicist, researcher*
West, Geoffrey B. *theoretical physicist, physics professor*
WoldeGabriel, Giday *research geologist*
Zhang, Dongxiao *research scientist*

**Los Lunas**
Seiler, Fritz Arnold *physicist*

**Mayhill**
Pastor, Stephen Daniel *chemistry professor, researcher, consultant*

**Placitas**
Long, Timothy Scott *chemist, consultant*

**Santa Fe**
Cheetham, Alan Herbert *paleontologist*
Cowan, George Arthur *chemist, bank executive, director*
Fisher, Robert Alan *laser physicist*
Gell-Mann, Murray *theoretical physicist, educator*
Giovanielli, Damon Vincent *physicist, consultant*
Hammer, Charles F. *chemistry professor*
Kronberg, Philipp Paul *physicist, educator*
Kropschot, Richard Henry *retired physicist, lab administrator*

Lee, David Mallin *physicist*
Leibowitz, Jack Richard *physicist, educator*
Lynn, John Eric *nuclear physicist, researcher, consultant*
Stalker, James Raghi *meteorologist, environmental services administrator*
White, David Hywel *physics professor, researcher*

**Socorro**
Schery, Stephen Dale *physicist*

**NEW YORK**

**Albany**
Corelli, John Charles *physicist, researcher*
Frisch, Harry Lloyd *chemist, educator*
Keyser, Daniel *atmospheric scientist, educator*
Kim, Jai Soo *retired physicist*
Rej, Robert *biochemist*
Schalk, Gerwin *research scientist, software engineer*

**Alfred**
Boehlert, Carl Joseph *materials scientist, educator*
Pye, Lenwood David *materials science educator, researcher, consultant*

**Amherst**
Ismail, Abu Zafar Mohamed *physics professor, researcher*

**Ballston Spa**
Westbrook, Jack Hall *metallurgist, consultant*

**Big Flats**
Keck, Donald Bruce *physicist*

**Binghamton**
Coates, Donald Robert *geologist, educator*
Whittingham, M(ichael) Stanley *chemist*

**Briarcliff Manor**
Bhargava, Rameshwar Nath *physicist*

**Bronx**
Hartil, Kirsten *research scientist*
Menthena, Anuradha *research scientist*
Yalow, Rosalyn Sussman *biophysicist*

**Brookhaven**
Kouts, Herbert John Cecil *retired physicist*

**Brooklyn**
Aizin, Gregory *physicist, educator, researcher*
Castleman, Louis Samuel *retired metallurgist, educator*
Charton, Marvin *chemist, educator*
Fleyshman, Bentsion *physicist, researcher, retired mathematician*
Franco, Victor *theoretical physics educator*
Kawatra, Mahendra P. *physics professor, mathematics professor*
Mook, Sarah *retired chemist*
Mourokh, Lev Grigorievich *physicist, researcher*
Shcherbakova, Estella *chemist, mathematician, educator*
Sheverev, Valery A. *physics professor, consultant*
Tamir, Theodor *electrophysics researcher, educator*
Wolf, Edward Lincoln *physicist, educator*
Zavitsas, Andreas Athanasios *chemistry professor, researcher*

**Buffalo**
Amborski, Leonard Edward *retired chemist*
Anbar, Michael *biophysics professor*
Baier, Robert Edward *chemist, educator*
Bright, Frank Vernon *chemistry professor*
Churchill, Melvyn Rowen *chemistry professor*
Dolnick, Bruce Jeffrey *research scientist, consultant*
Frerichs, Valerie *chemistry professor, researcher*
Jain, Piyare Lal *physics professor*
Patel, Mulchand Shambhubhai *biochemist, researcher*
Reitan, Paul Hartman *geologist, educator*
Treanor, Charles Edward *physicist, researcher*

**Canandaigua**
Lowther, Frank Eugene *research physicist*

**Chappaqua**
O'Neill, Robert Charles *inventor, consultant*

**Clinton**
Ring, James Walter *physics professor*

**Corning**
Fehlner, Francis Paul *chemist, consultant*
Miller, Roger Allen *physicist*

**Delmar**
Matuszek, John Michael, Jr. *environmental scientist, educator, consultant*

**East Hampton**
Garrett, Charles Geoffrey Blythe *physicist, consultant*

**Farmingdale**
Purandare, Yeshwant K. *chemistry educator, consultant*

**Flushing**
Engel, Robert Ralph *chemist, educator, dean*
Evans, Cherice M. *chemistry professor*
Goldman, Norman Lewis *chemistry professor*
Hu, Huping *biophysicist, lawyer*
Mirkin, Michael V. *chemistry professor*

**Freeport**
Pullman, Maynard Edward *biochemist*

**Geneva**
Roelofs, Wendell Lee *biochemistry professor, consultant*

**Hannacroix**
Schwebler, Stephen *retired chemist*

**Hawthorne**
Batstone, Joanna Louise *physicist*

**Hopewell Junction**
Nayfeh, Hasan Munir *research scientist*

**Ithaca**
Ashcroft, Neil William *physics professor, researcher*
Bassett, William Akers *retired geologist, educator*
Bauman, Dale Elton *nutritional biochemistry professor*
Berkelman, Karl *retired physics professor*
Bilderback, Donald Heywood *physicist, researcher*
Buhrman, Robert A. *physics professor, researcher*
Burns, Joseph Arthur *planetary science educator*
Cisne, John Luther *mineralogist, educator*
Craighead, Harold G. *physicist, educator*
Csaki, Csaba *physicist*
Fitchen, Douglas Beach *physicist, researcher*
Freed, Jack Herschel *chemist, educator*
Ginsparg, Paul *physicist*
Goldsmith, Paul Felix *physics professor, astronomy professor*
Gottfried, Kurt *physicist, researcher*
Greisen, Kenneth Ingvard *physicist, emeritus educator*
Hess, George Paul *biochemist, educator*
Hoffmann, Roald *chemist, educator*
Holcomb, Donald Frank *physicist, academic administrator*
Isakovic, Abdel *physicist, researcher*
Kinoshita, Toichiro *physicist*
Lee, David Morris *physics professor*
Lumley, John Leask *physicist, researcher*
McLafferty, Fred Warren *chemist, educator*
McMurry, John Edward *chemistry professor*
McQuade, Tyler *chemist*
Mikhailichenko, Alexander A. *physicist, researcher*
Oliver, Jack Ertle *geophysicist, educator*
Orlov, Yuri F. *nuclear physicist, human rights activist*
Pohl, Robert Otto *physics professor*
Reppy, John David, Jr. *physicist, educator*
Richardson, Robert Coleman *physics professor, researcher*
Salpeter, Edwin Ernest *physical sciences educator*
Scheraga, Harold Abraham *physical chemistry professor*
Squyres, Steven Weldon *astronomy educator, planetary geology researcher*
Thomas, J. Earl *retired physicist*
Widom, Benjamin *chemistry professor*
York, James Wesley, Jr. *theoretical physicist, educator*

**Jamaica**
Greenberg, Jacob *biochemist, educator, consultant*

**Latham**
Stallman, Donald Lee *environmental executive*

**Lewiston**
Dexter, Theodore Henry *chemist*

**Manhasset**
Dabideen, Darrin *research scientist*

**Manlius**
Martonosi, Anthony Nicholas *biochemistry professor, researcher*
O'Reilly, Mary *environmental scientist, educator*

**Melville**
Damadian, Raymond Vahan *biophysicist*

**New Paltz**
Lavallee, David Kenneth *chemistry professor, academic administrator*

**New Rochelle**
Margolin, Harold *metallurgical educator*

**New York**
Allison, Michael David *space scientist, educator*
Bederson, Benjamin *physicist, researcher*
Berne, Bruce J. *chemistry professor*
Beshers, Daniel Newson *retired materials scientist*
Birman, Joseph Leon *physics professor*
Borowitz, Sidney *retired physics professor*
Breslow, Esther May Greenberg *biochemistry professor, researcher*
Breslow, Ronald Charles *chemist, educator*
Brus, Louis Eugene *physical chemist*
Campbell, George, Jr. *physicist, university administrator*
Chakravarty, Suvobrata *research scientist, biophysicist*
Cheh, Huk Yuk *electrochemist*
Chen, Gang *research scientist, educator*
Cheng, Chuen Yan *biochemist, educator*
Chou, Ting-Chao *inventor, educator*
Cohen, Ezechiel Godert David *physicist, researcher*
Cross, George Alan Martin *biochemistry professor, researcher*
Cummins, Herman Zachary *physicist*
Danishefsky, Samuel J. *chemistry professor*
Erickson, Mitchell Drake *chemist, environmental scientist*
Erlanger, Bernard Ferdinand *biochemist, educator*
Fraenkel, George Kessler *chemistry professor*
Fusaro, Peter C. *environmental scientist, consultant*
Goulianos, Konstantin *physicist, educator*
Gutzwiller, Martin Charles *theoretical physicist, research scientist*
Haiman, Zoltan *astronomer, educator*
Haines, Thomas Henry *biochemist, educator, researcher*
Hansen, James E. *physicist, meteorologist, federal agency administrator*
Harris, Cyril Manton *physicist, educator, acoustical engineer, engineering and architecture author*
Hendrickson, Wayne A(rthur) *biochemist, educator*
Hoffert, Martin Irving *aerospace scientist, educator*
Hoffman, Linda M. *chemist, educator*
Huang, Limin *chemist, researcher*

**Kaku, Michio** *theoretical nuclear physicist, educator*
Khuri, Nicola Najib *physicist, researcher*
King, Edward Joseph *clinical chemist, laboratory administrator*
Krasna, Alvin Isaac *biochemist, educator*
Kuo, John Tsungfen *geophysicist, educator, researcher*
Lee, Tsung-Dao *physicist, researcher*
Levin, Janna *physicist, educator*
Lubell, Michael Stephen *physicist, educator*
Mac Low, Mordecai-Mark *astrophysicist*
Markiewicz, Leszek *research biochemist*
Marshall, Thomas Carlisle *applied physics professor*
McDermott, Ann Elizabeth *chemistry professor*
McKay, Kenneth Gardiner *retired physicist, retired electronics company executive*
Middleton, David *physicist, applied mathematician, educator*
Mueller, Alfred H. *physics professor, researcher*
Nickoloff, Edward Lee *radiology educator*
Norell, Mark Allen *paleontologist, curator*
Nye, Bill S. *research scientist, engineer, comedian, writer, inventor*
Oreskes, Irwin *biochemistry educator*
Pace, Antonietta *chemistry professor*
Pechukas, Philip *chemistry professor*
Percus, Jerome Kenneth *physicist, researcher*
Pinczuk, Aron *physicist*
Polvani, Lorenzo M. *physics professor*
Pope, Martin *chemist, educator*
Pucknat, John Godfrey *chemist, researcher*
Roeder, Robert Gayle *biochemist, molecular biologist, educator*
Rossow, William Brigance *physics professor*
Russell, Charlotte Sananes *biochemistry professor, researcher*
Sarachik, Myriam Paula Morgenstein *physics professor, condensed matter physicist*
Sidran, Miriam *retired physicist*
Silkov, Antonina *research scientist*
Stork, Gilbert *chemistry professor*
Störmer, Horst Ludwig *physicist*
Stroke, Hinko Henry *physicist, researcher*
Tu, Jiufeng J. *physics professor*
Turro, Nicholas John *chemistry professor*
Tyson, Neil DeGrasse *astrophysicist, museum director*
Upmacis, Rita Karina *chemist*
Vitkalov, Sergey A. *physicist, educator*
Werthamer, Nathan Richard *physicist*

**Niagara Falls**
Bharadwaj, Prem Datta *physics professor*
Knowles, Richard Norris *chemist*

**Niskayuna**
Eberhard, Jeffrey W. *physicist, researcher*
Edelheit, Lewis S. *research physicist*
Kambour, Roger Peabody *retired polymer physical chemist, researcher*
Rawson, James Rulon Young *chemist*
Varanasi, Kripa Kiran *research scientist*
Wan, Julin *materials scientist*
White, Frederick Andrew *retired physics professor, retired physicist*

**Oneonta**
Hickey, Francis Roger *physicist, researcher*
Horner, Carl Matthew *chemistry professor*

**Orangeburg**
Lajtha, Abel *biochemist*

**Palisades**
Broecker, Wallace S. *geophysics educator*
Kellogg, Herbert Humphrey *metallurgist, educator*
Kent, Dennis V. *paleomagnetist, educator, researcher*

**Patchogue**
Marr, Robert Bruce *physicist, researcher*

**Pearl River**
Barringer, William Charles *retired chemist*
Hamann, Philip Ross *chemist, researcher*
Matsuka, Yury V. *biochemist, research scientist*
Yuan, Yonghui *chemist, researcher*

**Pittsford**
Goldstein, David Arthur *biophysicist, educator*

**Potsdam**
ben-Avraham, Daniel *physics professor*
Fendler, Janos Hugo *chemistry professor*
Islam, Muhammad Azadul *physicist, educator, researcher*
Matijevic, Egon *chemistry professor*

**Poughkeepsie**
Lang, William Warner *physicist*

**Rensselaer**
Willis, John Patrick *chemist*

**Ridge**
Adams, Peter David *physicist, writer, editor*
Blume, Martin *physicist*

**Rochester**
Bigelow, Nicholas Pierre *physicist, researcher*
Blanton, Thomas N. *chemist, researcher*
Boeckman, Robert Kenneth, Jr. *chemistry professor, organic chemistry researcher*
Buff, Frank Paul *chemist, educator*
Cain, Burton Edward *retired chemistry professor*
Conwell, Esther Marly *physicist, researcher*
Duarte, Francisco Javier *physicist, researcher*
Eisenberg, Richard S. *chemistry professor*
Ertsgaard, Edwin Paul *physicist*
Ferbel, Thomas *physicist, educator*
Figer, Donald F. *astronomer, educator*
Houde-Walter, Susan *optics scientist, educator*
Jagannathan, Ramesh *research scientist*
Kampmeier, Jack August Carlos *chemist, educator*
Kende, Andrew Steven *chemist, educator*
Knauer, James Philip *physicist*
Knox, Robert Seiple *physicist, researcher*
Kwok, Wingchi Edmund *physicist*

Lavine, James Philip *physicist*
Lever, O. William, Jr. *chemist*
Li, James Chen Min *materials science educator*
Makous, Walter Leon *visual scientist, educator*
McKenty, Patrick *research scientist*
Melissinos, Adrian Constantin *physicist, researcher*
Meyerhofer, David D. *physicist, educator*
Moore, Duncan Thomas *optics scientist, educator*
Saunders, William Hundley, Jr. *retired chemist, educator*
Sharma, Gaurav *imaging scientist, electrical engineer*
Sherman, Fred *biochemist, educator*
Simon, Albert *retired physicist, retired engineer, retired educator*
Thorndike, Edward Harmon *physicist*
Yip, Kwok Leung *physicist, researcher*

**Rouses Point**
Weierstall, Richard Paul *retired pharmaceutical chemist*

**Scarborough**
Wittcoff, Harold Aaron *chemist*

**Scarsdale**
Porosoff, Harold *chemist, science administrator, research and development company executive*

**Schenectady**
Chen, Tao-Seng *medical physicist, consultant*
Finks, Robert Melvin *paleontologist, educator*
Frost, Robert Edwin *chemistry professor*
Katz, Samuel *retired geophysics educator*

**Scotia**
Webster, Harold Frank *physicist*

**Sherburne**
Dodd, Jack Gordon, Jr. *physicist, researcher*

**Shoreham**
Li, Zizhong *research scientist*

**Somers**
Hehenberger, Michael *chemist, researcher*

**South New Berlin**
Brennan, Brian William *industrial physicist*

**South Setauket**
Friedlander, Gerhart *nuclear chemist*

**Staten Island**
Yang, Song-Yu *biochemist*

**Stony Brook**
Alexander, John Macmillan, Jr. *chemistry professor*
Bokuniewicz, Henry Joseph *oceanography educator*
Bonner, Francis Truesdale *chemist, educator, dean*
Brown, Gerald Edward *physicist, researcher*
Chen, JiuHua *physicist, geophysicist, educator*
Gavrilov, Dmitri N. *research scientist*
Geller, Marvin Alan *meteorology educator, researcher*
Kahn, Peter B. *physics professor*
Ojima, Iwao *chemistry professor*
Swanson, Robert Lawrence *oceanographer, academic program administrator*

**Syracuse**
Baldwin, John Edwin *chemistry professor*
Call, David Andrew *meteorologist*
Honig, Arnold *physics professor, researcher*
Liu, Lizhong *physicist*
Prucha, John James *geologist, educator*
Schiff, Eric Allan *physics professor*
Smith, Kenneth Judson, Jr. *chemistry professor*
Vook, Richard Werner *retired physics professor*

**Troy**
Biyik, Emrah *research scientist*
Ferris, James Peter *chemist, educator*
Friedman, Gerald Manfred *geologist, educator*
Giaever, Ivar *physicist*
Krause, Sonja *chemistry professor*
Levinger, Joseph Solomon *physicist, researcher*
Linhardt, Robert John *chemistry professor*
Medicus, Heinrich Adolf *physicist, educator*
Persans, Peter David *physics educator, researcher*
Potts, Kevin T. *retired chemistry professor*
Shan, Yufeng *research scientist*
Sperber, Daniel *physicist*

**Upton**
Alamgir, Faisal M. *materials scientist*
Baltz, Anthony John *physicist*
Bond, Peter Danford *physicist*
Fowler, Joanna S. *chemist*
Goldhaber, Maurice *physicist, researcher*
Hendrie, Joseph Mallam *physicist, nuclear engineer*
Lindenbaum, S(eymour) J(oseph) *physicist*
Lowenstein, Derek Irving *physicist*
Meinhold, Charles Boyd *health physicist*
Rau, Ralph Ronald *retired physicist*
Samios, Nicholas Peter *physicist*
Setlow, Jane Kellock *biophysicist*
Setlow, Richard Burton *biophysicist, researcher*
Sutin, Norman *chemist, researcher*
Tannenbaum, Michael J(ay) *physicist*
Wei, Xiangdong *physicist, researcher*

**Wappingers Falls**
Maissel, Leon Israel *physicist, engineer*

**Webster**
Zhang, Shengliang *materials scientist, physicist*

**Wellsville**
Van Tyne, Arthur Morris *geologist*

**White Plains**
Surpris, Joseph W. *research scientist*

**Yorktown Heights**
Avouris, Phaedon *chemical physicist*

Keyes, Robert W. *physicist, researcher*
Koester, Steven John *research scientist*
Lang, Norton David *physicist*
Lanzerotti, Mary Yvonne *physicist, researcher*
Ning, Tak Hung *physicist, microelectronic technologist*
Tersoff, Jerry David *physicist*
Tutuc, Emanuel *research scientist*
Wu, Chai Wah *research scientist*

## NORTH CAROLINA

### Asheville
Haggard, William Henry *meteorologist*
Kessler, Donald Joe *research scientist, physicist, consultant*
Meyerson, Seymour *retired chemist*
Sun, Bomin *environmental scientist*
Zarnoch, Stanley Joseph *research scientist, statistician*

### Beaufort
Bonaventura, Celia Jean *biochemist, researcher*

### Cary
Kung, Pang-Jen *materials scientist, electrical engineer*

### Chapel Hill
Berkowitz, Max *physical chemist, researcher*
Brookhart, Maurice S. *chemist*
Bursey, Maurice M. *retired chemistry professor*
Desimone, Joseph M. *chemist, educator*
Dolan, Louise Ann *physicist*
Eliel, Ernest Ludwig *chemist, educator*
Forman, Donald T. *biochemist, educator*
Frampton, Paul Howard *physics researcher, educator*
Kim, Chong Soong *aerosol science and inhalation dosimetry researcher*
Klein, Martin Jesse *physicist, educator, science historian*
Lee, Kuo-Hsiung *medicinal chemistry professor*
Ligett, Waldo Buford *chemist*
Macdonald, James Ross *physicist, researcher*
Mersini - Houghton, Laura *physicist, educator*
Merzbacher, Eugen *retired physics professor*
Mitchell, Earl Nelson *physicist, researcher*
Parr, Robert Ghormley *chemistry professor*
Pedersen, Lee G. *chemistry professor*
Rial, José Antonio *geophysicist, educator*
Sancar, Aziz *research biochemist*

### Charlotte
Paviet-Hartmann, Patricia *chemist, researcher*
Rodite, Robert R.R. *research scientist, finance and computer consultant, educator*

### Durham
Fridovich, Irwin *biochemistry professor*
Hammes, Gordon G. *chemistry professor*
Han, Moo-Young *physicist, educator*
Hellinga, Homme Wytzes *biochemist, educator, researcher*
Hobbs, Marcus Edwin *retired chemistry professor*
Jaszczak, Ronald Jack *physicist, researcher, consultant*
Joklik, Wolfgang Karl *biochemist, virologist, educator*
Meyer, Horst *physics professor*
Mikhailov, Stepan Fedorovich *physicist, researcher*
Modrich, Paul L. *biochemistry professor*
Moss, Marcia Lynn *retired biochemist*
Pearsall, George Wilbur *materials scientist, educator, mechanical engineer, consultant*
Pirrung, Michael Craig *chemistry professor, consultant*
Quinn, Jarus William *physicist, former association executive*
Tselev, Alexander *physicist, researcher*

### Greensboro
Clark, Clifton Bob *physicist*
Zhong, Haizhen *research scientist, educator*

### Greenville
Morehead, Andrew Turner, Jr. *chemistry professor*
Toburen, Larry Howard *physicist, researcher*

### Hayesville
Galloway, David Craig *chemist*

### Hendersonville
Saby, John Sanford *physicist, consultant*

### Horse Shoe
Roskoski, Robert, Jr. *biochemist, educator, author*

### Morrisville
Roy, Biswadev *scientist*

### Mount Olive
Maqbool, Muhammad *physics professor*

### Pinehurst
Huizenga, John Robert *nuclear chemist, educator*
Swanson, Richard Everett *physics professor, dean*

### Raleigh
Aspnes, David Erik *physicist, researcher*
Bernholc, Jerzy *physicist, educator*
Gillette, Dale Alan *research scientist*
Hubbe, Martin A. *chemistry professor, consultant*
Jung, Kang *research scientist*
Mitchell, Gary Earl *physicist, researcher*
Osteryoung, Janet Gretchen *chemistry professor*
Ranjan, Vivek *research scientist*
Reynolds, C. Lewis, Jr. *materials scientist, educator*
Sheng, Quan *chemist*
Swaisgood, Harold Everett *biochemist, educator*
Whitten, Jerry Lynn *chemistry professor*

### Research Triangle Park
Fisher, Robert Perry *environmental scientist, researcher*
Selkirk, James Kirkwood *biochemist, researcher*
Tong, Quansong *environmental scientist*

Wani, Mansukhlal Chhaganlal *chemist*

### Spencer
Barnes, Melver Raymond *retired chemist*

### Stella
Quin, Louis DuBose *chemist, educator*

### Washington
Blackwell, F. Oris *environmental scientist, educator*

### Wilmington
Ao, Qi *nuclear scientist, educator*

### Winston Salem
Kerr, William C. *physics professor*
Mallett, T. Conn *biochemist, educator*
Mohammed, Abdul K. *chemist, educator*
Mokrasch, Lewis Carl *neurochemist, educator*
Rodgman, Alan *chemist, consultant*
Salsbury, Freddie R., Jr. *physics professor, educator*

## NORTH DAKOTA

### Fargo
Ihle, Thomas *physicist, education educator*
Jaseja, Mahesh *chemistry professor, researcher*
Tallman, Dennis Earl *chemistry professor, research scientist*
Wagner, Alexander Johannes *physicist, educator*

### Grand Forks
Hoffmann, Mark R. *physical chemist, educator*
Thomasson, Kathryn Ambler *chemistry educator, researcher*

## OHIO

### Akron
Gent, Alan Neville *physicist, researcher*
Kennedy, Joseph Paul *chemist, researcher*

### Athens
Nance, Richard Damian *geologist, consultant*

### Aurora
Su, Sunyu *physicist*

### Beachwood
Garber, Joseph Max *meteorologist*
Krieger, Irvin Mitchell *retired chemistry professor*

### Beavercreek
Gupta, Vijay Kumar *retired chemistry professor*

### Bluffton
Rich, Ronald Lee *chemistry professor*

### Bowling Green
Midden, William Robert *chemist, educator*

### Bratenahl
Dunn, Horton, Jr. *organic chemist*

### Cincinnati
Algeo, Thomas John *geologist, educator*
Ashley, Kevin Edward *research chemist*
Briskin, Madeleine *oceanographer, paleontologist*
Chester, Thomas Lee *chemist*
Federle, Thomas W. *environmental scientist, microbiologist*
Francis, Marion David *consulting chemist*
Goodman, Bernard *physics professor*
Jensen, Elwood Vernon *biochemist*
Kawahara, Fred Katsumi *research chemist*
Marcott, Curtis Allen *chemist, researcher*
Meal, Larie *chemistry professor, researcher, consultant*
Putnam, Frank William *biochemistry educator, immunologist, educator*
Relyea, Carl Miller *retired hydrologist*
Riehle, Barry Steven *physicist, researcher*
Soukup, Victor Gerald *chemist*
Sullivan, James F. *physicist, researcher*
Witten, Louis *physics professor*

### Cleveland
Ball, David Warren *chemistry professor*
Bidelman, William Pendry *astronomer, educator*
Carey, Paul Richard *biophysicist*
Chamis, Christos Constantinou *aerospace scientist, educator*
Dowell, Michael Brendan *chemist*
Jenkins, Thomas Llewellyn *physics professor*
Klopman, Gilles *chemistry professor*
Kowalski, Kenneth Lawrence *physicist, researcher*
Krauss, Lawrence Maxwell *physicist, astronomy educator, researcher, author*
Landau, Bernard Robert *biochemist, educator, internist*
Rogers, Charles Edwin *physical chemistry professor*
Schuele, Donald Edward *retired physics professor, dean*
Shashkin, Pavel Nikolayevich *biochemist*
Smith, Mark Anthony *biochemist, educator*
Stojkovic, Dejan B. *physicist, educator*
Terburg, Bart Paul *physicist, industrial engineer*
Tyson, Daniel S. *chemist, researcher*
Weaver, John Carl *chemist, educator*
Zhang, Nengli *research scientist*
Zhu, Dongming *materials scientist*

### Columbus
Adelson, Edward *physicist, educator, musician*
Behrman, Edward Joseph *biochemistry educator*
Chisholm, Malcolm Harold *chemistry professor*
Cornwell, David George *biochemist, educator*
Crespo-Hernández, Carlos E. *research scientist, educator*
Daehn, Glenn Steven *materials scientist*
Elliot, David Hawksley *geologist, educator*
Herbst, Eric *physicist, astronomer, chemist*
Heremans, Joseph Pierre *physicist*
Janpudgee, Panuwat *research scientist*

Ling, Ta-Yung *physicist*
Madia, William Juul *chemist*
Miller, Terry Alan *chemistry professor*
Min, David Byong *chemist, educator, research scientist*
Petrov, Alexander Alexandrov *research scientist, educator*
Preobrazhensky, Alexander Anatoliyevich *biochemist*
Reibel, Kurt *physicist, researcher*
St. Pierre, George Roland, Jr. *materials scientist, engineering executive, educator*
Soloway, Albert Herman *medicinal chemist*
Vishnu, Abhinav *research scientist*
Wali, Mohan Kishen *environmental scientist, forester, educator*
Wilkins, John Warren *physics professor*
Wojcicki, Andrew Adalbert *chemist, educator*

### Copley
Weil, Edward David *chemist, researcher, consultant, educator*

### Dayton
Battino, Rubin *retired chemistry professor*
Duangthip, Thammarat *research scientist*
Guan, Shan *materials scientist*
Look, David Charles *physicist, researcher*
Nielsen, Philip Edward *physicist, research manager*

### Kent
Baeseman, Jenny L. *environmental scientist, educator*
Dahl, Peter Steffen *geologist, educator*

### Marietta
Jache, Albert William *retired chemistry professor, academic administrator, research scientist*
Putnam, Robert Ervin *chemist, consultant*

### Middletown
Marine, Susan Sonchik *analytical chemist, educator*

### Mount Vernon
Miller, Joyce Catherine *chemistry professor, research scientist*

### New Albany
Williams, James Case *metallurgist*

### Norwalk
Germann, Richard P(aul) *pharmaceutical company chemist, chemicals executive*

### Norwood
Jones, Hobert W. *health physics and radiochemistry consultant*

### Oberlin
Carlton, Terry Scott *retired chemist, educator*
Weinstock, Robert *physics professor*

### Oxford
Cox, James Allan *chemistry professor*
Danielson, Neil David *chemistry educator*
Gordon, Gilbert *chemist, educator*
Macklin, Philip Alan *retired physics professor*
Rauckhorst, William Herman *physics professor, academic administrator*

### Rootstown
Chiang, John Young Ling *biochemistry professor, researcher*

### Sandusky
Fuller, Jonathan *retired geologist*

### Toledo
Averill, Bruce Alan *chemistry professor*

### Upper Arlington
Relle, Ferenc Matyas *chemist*

### Wadsworth
Furry, Benjamin K. *chemist*

### Walton Hills
Elliott, Stanley B. *chemist, researcher*

### Wickliffe
Krause, Marjorie N. *biochemist*

### Wright Patterson Afb
Burggraf, Larry W. *chemist*
Fernelius, Nils Conard *physicist*
Garscadden, Alan *physicist*

### Yellow Springs
Spokane, Robert Bruce *biophysical chemist*

## OKLAHOMA

### Ada
Stafford, Donald Gene *chemistry professor*
Wang, Mingyu *hydrologist, environmental scientist*

### Alva
Batalha da Conceicao, Jose Joao *chemistry professor, researcher*

### Bartlesville
Hogan, John Paul *chemistry researcher, consultant*

### Fort Towson
Pike, Thomas Harrison *plant chemist*

### Norman
Beasley, William H. *meteorology professor*
Doswell, Charles Arthur III *meteorologist*
Droegemeier, Kelvin K. *meteorologist, educator*
Dryhurst, Glenn *chemistry educator*
Wren, Jonathan Daniel *research scientist*

### Oklahoma City
Alaupovic, Petar *biochemist, educator*
Butnev, Viktor Yurievich *research scientist*

Zhu, Hua *biochemist, researcher*

### Seminole
Laule, Gerhard Helmut *chemistry professor, researcher*

### Skiatook
Harwell, Kenneth E. *chemist, researcher, consultant*

### Stillwater
Kotov, Nicholas Alexander *chemist, educator*

### Tulsa
Blais, Roger Nathaniel *physics professor, academic administrator*
Bregman, Martin Louis *geologist, geophysicist, educator*
Busch, Daniel Adolph *geologist, educator*

## OREGON

### Ashland
Abrahams, Sidney Cyril *physicist, crystallographer*
Grover, James Robb *chemist, editor*

### Corvallis
Dalrymple, Gary Brent *research geologist*
Drake, Charles Whitney *physicist*
Krueger, James Harry *chemistry educator*
Lee, Yun-Shik *physics professor*
Lubchenco, Jane *environmental scientist, marine ecologist, science association director*
Mathews, Christopher King *biochemist, educator*
Perlin, Alexandr *oceanographer*
Van Holde, Kensal Edward *biochemistry educator*
Yeats, Robert Sheppard *geologist, educator*

### Dallas
White, Donald Harvey *retired physics professor*

### Eugene
Crasemann, Bernd *physicist, researcher*
Csonka, Paul L. *theoretical physicist, educator*
Deshpande, Nilendra Ganesh *physics professor*
Donnelly, Russell James *physicist, educator*
Griffith, Osbie Hayes *retired chemistry professor*
Maurer, Robert Distler *retired industrial physicist*
Mazo, Robert Marc *retired chemistry professor*
Retallack, Gregory John *geologist, educator*
Richmond, Geraldine Lee *chemist, educator*
von Hippel, Peter Hans *chemistry professor, researcher*
Youngquist, Walter Lewellyn *geologist, consultant*

### Hillsboro
Fan, Chonglun *materials scientist, researcher, engineer*

### Portland
Claycomb, Cecil Keith *biochemist, educator*
Cohen, Norm *chemist*
Proctor, James David *environmental scientist, educator*
Weeks, Wilford Frank *retired geophysics educator, glaciologist*
Wetzel, Karl Joseph *physics professor, dean*

### Salem
Gillette, P. Roger *physicist, systems engineer*

## PENNSYLVANIA

### Abington
Schuster, Ingeborg Ida *chemistry professor*

### Alcoa Center
Ray, Siba Prasad *materials scientist, ceramics scientist*

### Allentown
Orphanides, Gus George *licensing executive*
Tamboli, Dnyanesh Chandrakant *research scientist*

### Altoona
Reed, Carey S. *chemistry professor*
Weiss, Brock Landon *physics professor*

### Berwyn
Devlin, Thomas McKeown *biochemist, educator*

### Bethlehem
Heindel, Ned Duane *chemistry professor*
Herman, Richard Gerald *research chemist, consultant, educator*
Lyman, Charles Edson *materials scientist, educator*
Smyth, Donald Morgan *chemistry professor, researcher*

### Carlisle
Laws, Kenneth L. *physics professor*
Long, Howard Charles *retired physics professor*

### Chadds Ford
Webster, Owen Wright *chemist*

### Chester
Kul, Ismail *chemistry professor*

### Clarion
Vega, Anthony Jude *meteorologist, researcher*

### Collegeville
Stein, Steven H. *pharmaceutical research scientist*

### Danville
Chan, Yiumo *biochemist*

### Derry
Goodman, Frederick Denis *environmental scientist, educator*

### Doylestown
Brink, Frank, Jr. *biophysicist, former educator*

**East Stroudsburg**
Bergo, Conrad Hunter *chemistry professor*

**Feasterville Trevose**
Dickstein, Jack *chemist*

**Harrisburg**
Stanley, Edward Alexander *geologist, researcher, retired director, forensic specialist*

**Haverford**
Roelofs, Lyle Dean *physicist, researcher*

**Hazleton**
Vice, Daniel Hoy *geologist, educator*

**Huntingdon Valley**
Godfrey, John Carl *medicinal chemist*
Leibholz, Stephen Wolfgang *physicist, information technology executive, entrepreneur*

**Indiana**
Bencloski, Joseph W. *geography educator*

**Kennett Square**
Wilson, Armin *retired chemist*

**Landenberg**
Ness, Norman Frederick *astrophysicist, educator, academic administrator*

**Latrobe**
Maize, Mohamed Anis *physics professor*

**Lincoln University**
Venerable, Grant Delbert, II, *chemist, educator, systems scientist*
Williams, Willie, Jr., *physicist, researcher*

**Mansfield**
Davis, Scott Alan *chemistry professor*

**Media**
Voltz, Sterling Ernest *physical chemist, researcher*

**Mount Joy**
Lodde, Gordon Maynard *health physics consultant*

**New Holland**
Papadakis, Emmanuel Philippos *physicist, consultant*

**New Wilmington**
Long, Kenneth Maynard *chemistry professor*

**Newtown Square**
Cooper, Charles Fisher *chemist, researcher*
Grey, Roger Allen *chemist, researcher*

**Orefield**
Armor, John N. *chemical company scientist, consultant, research manager*

**Philadelphia**
Ajzenberg-Selove, Fay *physicist, researcher*
Bortnick, Newman Mayer *research chemist*
Burlingame, Gary Alfred *environmental scientist*
Burstein, Elias *physicist, researcher*
Childress, Scott Julius *medicinal chemist*
Cohn, Mildred *retired biochemist, retired educator*
Dalton, David Robert *chemistry professor*
Englander, Sol Walter *biochemistry and biophysics educator, medical educator*
Fitts, Donald Dennis *chemist, educator*
Frankel, Sherman *physicist, educator*
Glusker, Jenny Pickworth *chemist*
Gogotsi, Yury *materials scientist, educator*
Hameka, Hendrik Frederik *chemist, educator*
Han, Yilong *physicist, researcher*
Hirschmann, Ralph Franz *chemist*
Intemann, Robert Louis *physics professor, researcher*
Klein, Michael Lawrence *research chemist, educator*
Kritchevsky, David *biochemist, educator*
Kurzweg, Timothy Paul *physicist, educator*
Langacker, Paul George *physics professor*
Larson, Donald Clayton *physics professor, consultant*
Ma, C-M (Charlie) *physicist, educator*
MacDiarmid, Alan Graham *metallurgist, educator*
Noordergraaf, Abraham *biophysics educator*
Panasyuk, George Yuryevich *physicist, researcher*
Shen, Benjamin Shih-Ping *astrophysicist, educator*
Smith, Amos Brittain III *chemist, educator*
Vitek, Vaclav *materials scientist*
Voet, Donald Herman *biochemist, educator, writer*
Wales, Walter D. *physicist, researcher*
Wickstrom, Eric *biophysical chemist, educator*
Winkler, Jeffrey D. *chemist*
Yang, Shu *materials scientist*

**Pittsburgh**
Anderson, Scott Richard *geologist, consultant*
Asher, Sanford Abraham *chemist, educator*
Biondi, Manfred Anthony *physicist*
Bothner-By, Aksel Arnold *chemist*
Carr, Walter James, Jr. *research physicist, consultant*
Choyke, Wolfgang Justus *physicist*
Cohen, Bernard Leonard *physicist, researcher*
Coltman, John Wesley *physicist*
DiMatteo, Tiziana *physics professor*
Emmerich, Werner Sigmund *physicist, educator*
Feller, Robert Livingston *chemist, art conservation scientist*
Gerjuoy, Edward *physicist*
Gomez, Roberto Onofre *physicist, consultant*
Janis, Allen Ira *retired physicist, educator*
Kim, Yongbok *physicist*
Laughlin, David Eugene *materials scientist, educator, metallurgist, consultant*
Lowe, Irving Jack *physics educator*
Maher, James Vincent, Jr. *physics professor, academic administrator*
Massalski, Thaddeus Bronislaw *materials scientist, educator*
Matyjaszewski, Krzysztof *chemist, educator*
Morningstar, Colin Jon *physicist, researcher*
Nagle, John Frederick *physicist*

Park, Chando *materials scientist, researcher*
Petoud, Stéphane *chemistry professor, researcher*
Pratt, David Wixon *chemistry professor*
Resnick, Robert *physicist, researcher*
Rosenberg, Jerome Laib *chemist, educator*
Sekerka, Robert Floyd *physics and mathematics professor*
Singh, Chandralekha *physics professor*
Trevits, Michael Anthony *geologist*
White, Robert Marshall *retired physicist, retired educator, retired government official, consultant*
Yates, John Thomas, Jr. *chemistry professor, research scientist*
Young, Hugh David *physics professor, writer*

**Pottstown**
Hergert, Herbert Lawrence *consultant*

**Scranton**
Marx, David Earl *chemistry professor, consultant*

**South Park**
Lotze, Barbara *retired physicist*

**Spring House**
Reitz, Allen Bernard *organic chemist*

**State College**
Garrett, Steven Lurie *physicist*
Ginoza, William *former biophysics educator*

**Swarthmore**
Bilaniuk, Oleksa Myron *physicist, researcher*
Pasternack, Robert Francis *chemistry professor*

**University Park**
Alexander, Stephon Haigh-Solomon *physics professor, musician*
Allcock, Harry R. *chemistry professor*
Badding, John Victor *chemistry professor*
Blackadar, Alfred Kimball *meteorologist, educator*
Cahir, John Joseph *meteorologist, educator, educational administrator*
Castleman, Albert Welford, Jr. *physical chemist, educator*
Chan, Moses Hung Wai *physicist, researcher*
Dutton, John Altnow *meteorologist, educator*
Garrison, Barbara Jane *chemistry professor*
Hosler, Charles Luther, Jr. *meteorologist, educator*
Howell, Benjamin Franklin, Jr. *geophysicist, educator*
Jackman, Lloyd Miles *chemistry professor*
Ma, Xiaoliang *research scientist*
Mahan, Gerald Dennis *physicist, researcher*
Mann, Michael E. *physicist, educator, climatologist*
Mor, Gopal Kumar *materials scientist, researcher*
Varghese, Oomman Kulathinthekkethil *materials scientist, researcher*
White, William Blaine *geochemist, researcher*
Winograd, Nicholas *chemist*

**Villanova**
Edwards, John Ralph *retired chemist, educator*
Ludwig, Oliver George *chemistry professor*
Papaefthymiou, Georgia C. *physicist, educator*
Phares, Alain Joseph *physicist, researcher*

**Wallingford**
Severdia, Anthony George *chemistry researcher*

**Warminster**
Gamarnik, Moisey Yankelevich *solid state physicist*

**Waynesburg**
Maguire, Mildred May *chemistry professor, researcher*

**West Point**
Farber, Leonid *materials scientist*
Trepakova, Elena S. *research scientist*
Yang, Zhi-Qiang *chemist*

**Wexford**
Bossart, Paul Nathaniel, Jr. *geologist, geophysicist, consultant*

**Wyndmoor**
Pfeffer, Philip Elliot *biophysicist*

**Wynnewood**
Cohen, Gordon M. *chemist, researcher*
Rosen, Gerald Harris *physicist, consultant, educator*

**RHODE ISLAND**

**East Greenwich**
Carlson, Shawn Eric *physicist, educator*

**Kingston**
Boving, Thomas B. *hydrologist, educator*
Fastovsky, David E. *geoscientist, educator*

**Narragansett**
Nixon, Scott West *oceanography science educator*
Pilson, Michael Edward Quinton *oceanography educator*
Pockalny, Robert *geophysicist, researcher*

**Providence**
Avery, Donald Hills *metallurgist, educator*
Briant, Clyde Leonard *metallurgist, educator*
Carpenter, Gene Blakely *crystallography and chemistry educator*
Cooper, Leon N *physicist, researcher*
Dahlberg, Albert Edward *biochemistry professor*
Elbaum, Charles *physicist, educator, researcher*
Estrup, Peder Jan *physics and chemistry professor*
Gerritsen, Hendrik Jurjen *physics professor, researcher*
Head, James William III *geological sciences educator*
Lanou, Robert Eugene, Jr. *physicist, researcher*
Levin, Frank S. *physicist, educator*
Stratt, Richard Mark *chemistry researcher, educator*

Tauc, Jan *retired physics professor*
Valles, James M., Jr. *physics professor*

**Wakefield**
Moore, George Emerson, Jr. *geologist, educator*

**SOUTH CAROLINA**

**Aiken**
Dewberry, Raymond Allen *research scientist, combat engineer*
Dickson, Paul Wesley, Jr. *physicist*

**Bluffton**
Croft, George T. *physicist*

**Charleston**
Fragile, Patrick Christopher *physics professor, astrophysicist, researcher*

**Clemson**
Abramovitch, Rudolph Abraham *chemistry educator*
Beyerlein, Adolph Louis *retired chemist, educator*
Daw, Murray S. *physics professor*
DesMarteau, Darryl Dwayne *chemistry professor, geology educator*
Doerr, Marvin LeRoy *chemist, researcher, educator*
Lewis, Barbara Sue *chemist*

**Columbia**
Edge, Ronald Dovaston *physics professor*
Kubodera, Kuniharu *physicist, educator*
Nagpal, Madan Lal *biochemist, educator, researcher*
Preedom, Barry Mason *physicist, researcher*
Samuel, May Linda *environmental scientist*
Shafer, John Milton *hydrologist, consultant, data processing executive*

**Johns Island**
Norton, Norman James *retired exploration geologist, educator*

**Mount Pleasant**
Thordarson, William *retired hydrogeologist*

**Rock Hill**
Sebhatu, Mesgun *physics professor*

**Spartanburg**
Jones, Gail Renee *chemistry professor, biology professor, chiropractor*

**SOUTH DAKOTA**

**Freeman**
Ries, Edward Richard *petroleum geologist, consultant*

**Rapid City**
Smith, Paul Letton, Jr. *geophysicist*

**Sioux Falls**
Gerdes, Anthony Martin *research scientist, health science association administrator*
Viste, Arlen Ellard *chemistry professor*

**Spearfish**
Erickson, Richard Ames *physicist, emeritus educator*

**Yankton**
Choony, Nandeo *chemistry professor, researcher*

**TENNESSEE**

**Brentwood**
Chappell, Charles Richard *space scientist*
Heiser, Arnold Melvin *astronomer*

**Clinton**
Hutchens, Gail R. *chemist*

**Cookeville**
Wells, John Calhoun *physics professor*

**Knoxville**
Contescu, Cristian Ion *chemist, researcher*
Gentry, Robert Vance *physicist, researcher, writer*
Hatcher, Robert Dean, Jr. *geologist, educator*
Joy, David Charles *research scientist, educator*
Liu, Yang *geologist, researcher*
Nayak, Subhadarshi *research scientist*
Plummer, E. Ward *physics professor*
Renshaw, Amanda Frances *retired physicist, nuclear engineer*
Schweitzer, George Keene *chemistry professor*
Wunderlich, Bernhard *physical chemistry professor*

**Maryville**
Weeks, Robert Andrew *materials science researcher, educator*

**Memphis**
Crane, Laura Jane *retired chemist*
Desiderio, Dominic Morse, Jr. *chemistry and neurochemistry professor*
Fain, John Nicholas *biochemistry educator*
Franceschetti, Donald Ralph *physicist, educator*
Harris, Delphia F. *chemistry professor, consultant*
Shaik, Jahangheer Shareef *research scientist*
Wildman, Gary Cecil *chemist, researcher*

**Murfreesboro**
Weller, Martha Riherd *physics and astronomy professor, consultant*

**Nashville**
Chytil, Frank *biochemist*
Dettbarn, Wolf-Dietrich *neurochemist, pharmacologist, educator*
Egli, Martin *crystallographer, educator*
Feldman, Leonard Cecil *physicist*

Fort, Tomlinson *chemist, chemical engineering educator*
Hamilton, Joseph Hants, Jr. *physicist, researcher*
Hercules, David Michael *chemistry professor, consultant*
Hess, B. Andes, Jr. *chemistry professor*
Hwang, Jae-Kwang *physicist, researcher*
Inagami, Tadashi *biochemistry professor*
Lukehart, Charles Martin *chemistry professor*
Roos, Charles Edwin *physicist*
Sen, Anjan Ananda *physicist, researcher*
Silberman, Enrique *physicist, director*
Surowiec, Andrew Julius *biophysicist, researcher*
Zavalin, Andrey I. *optics scientist, educator*

**Oak Ridge**
Bhuiyan, Md Shafiqur Rahman *materials scientist*
Boatner, Lynn Allen *research physicist*
Borie, Bernard Simon, Jr. *retired physicist, educator*
Carlsmith, Roger Snedden *chemistry and energy conservation researcher*
Fogle, Michael Roy, Jr. *physicist*
Goyal, Amit *research scientist*
Hartman, Frederick Cooper *retired biochemist*
Harvey, John Arthur *nuclear physicist*
Hu, Zhiyu *research scientist, educator*
Katoh, Yutai *materials scientist*
Krause, Manfred Otto *physicist*
Kronenberg, Andreas *nuclear chemist, radiochemist, nuclear technology consultant*
Larson, Bennett Charles *solid state physicist, researcher*
Lynch, Vickie Evette *research scientist*
Maienschein, Fred *retired physicist*
Messman, Jamie M. *polymer chemist*
Nephew, Edmund A. *physicist, retired mayor*
Pinnaduwage, Lal Ariyaratna *physicist, researcher*
Plasil, Franz *physicist*
Pouchard, Line Catherine *research scientist, educator*
Rucker, Thomas Lee *physicist*
Schwenterly, Stanley William *physicist, researcher*
Strickler, Dennis Johnson *research scientist*
Watson, Evelyn Egner *radiation scientist*
Zucker, Alexander *physicist, researcher*

**Signal Mountain**
Howe, Lyman Harold III *chemist, researcher*

**TEXAS**

**Amarillo**
Moridani, Majid Y. *research scientist, educational consultant*

**Arlington**
Dollar, David *chemistry professor*
Gelb, James Martin *physicist*
Krishnamurthy, Mahesh *research scientist*
Shanmugam, Ganapathy *geologist, researcher*
Willoughby, Sarah-Margaret C. *retired chemist, educator, chemical engineer, consultant*

**Austin**
Bash, Frank Ness *astronomer, educator*
Bengtson, Roger Dean *physicist, department chairman*
Boggs, James Ernest *chemistry professor*
DeWitt-Morette, Cécile *physicist*
Duncombe, Raynor Lockwood *astronomer*
Erskine, James Lorenzo *physics professor*
Fisher, William Lawrence *geologist, educator, dean*
Folk, Robert Louis *geologist, educator*
Fonken, Gerhard Joseph *retired chemistry professor, retired academic administrator*
Gavenda, J(ohn) David *physicist*
Gentle, Kenneth William *physicist*
Griffy, Thomas Alan *physics professor*
Groat, Charles George *geologist, former federal agency administrator*
Hackert, Marvin LeRoy *chemistry professor, biophysical researcher*
Hudec, Michael Robert *geologist, researcher*
Lagow, Richard James *chemistry professor*
Mano, Nicolas P. *research scientist*
Mark, Hans Michael *physicist, former federal agency administrator*
Martin, Stephen F. *chemist, educator, researcher*
McBride, Earle F. *geologist, educator*
Mear, Charles Eugene *geologist, consultant*
Milliken, Kitty Lou *research scientist*
Mooney, John Bradford, Jr. *oceanographer, consultant, engineer*
Phillips, Joseph Daniel *geophysicist, oceanographer*
Richmond, Marvin Elliot *astronomer, educator*
Rossky, Peter Jacob *chemistry professor, researcher*
Schwitters, Roy Frederick *physicist, researcher*
Sessler, Jonathan Lawrence *chemistry professor*
Stewart, Kent Kallam *analytical biochemistry educator*
Swinney, Harry Leonard *physics professor*
Wheeler, John Craig *astrophysicist, writer*
White, John Michael *chemistry professor*
Wilson, Clark R. *geophysicist, educator*
Zeng, Hongliu Henry *geophysicist, geologist*

**Beaumont**
Bahrim, Cristian *physicist, educator*
Nelson, Chris B. *physics professor*

**Bryan**
McIntyre, John Armin *physics professor*

**Calvert**
Alemán, Marthanne Payne *environmental scientist, consultant*

**College Station**
Arnowitt, Richard Lewis *retired physics professor*
Clearfield, Abraham *chemistry educator*
Cotton, Frank Albert *chemist, educator*
Darensbourg, Marcetta York *chemistry professor*
Dessler, Alexander Jack *astrophysicist, educator*
Duce, Robert Arthur *atmospheric chemist, oceanographer, educator*

Eaton, Gordon Pryor *geologist, consultant*
Fackler, John Paul, Jr. *chemistry professor*
Goodman, David Wayne *research chemist, educator*
Hardy, John Christopher *physicist, researcher, educator*
Laane, Jaan *chemistry professor*
McIntyre, Peter Mastin *physicist, researcher*
Nachman, Ronald James *chemist, researcher*
Nica, Ninel *physicist*
O'Connor, Rod *chemist, consultant, inventor*
Prescott, John Mack *biochemist, retired university administrator*
Scott, Alastair Ian *chemistry professor*
Wagner, Amy *oceanographer*
Wild, James Robert *biochemistry and genetics professor*

**Commerce**
West, Keith *physicist*

**Copper Canyon**
Nickon, Alex *chemist, educator*

**Dallas**
Baxter, Richard Henry *research scientist*
Brooks, James Elwood *geologist, educator*
Deisenhofer, Johann *biochemistry professor, researcher*
Gibbs, James Alanson *geologist, consultant*
Marshall, John Harris, Jr. *geologist, oil industry executive*
Ray, Bradley Stephen *petroleum geologist*
Senkayi, Abu Lwanga *environmental scientist*
Sharp, William Wheeler *geologist*
Wheeler, Edward Norwood *chemical consultant*

**Denton**
Anand, Aman *research scientist*
Kim, Hansoo *materials scientist, researcher*
Kobe, Donald Holm *physics professor*
Krokhin, Arkadii *physics professor*
McDaniel, Floyd Delbert, Sr. *physics professor, researcher*
Ryu, Dojin *chemist, educator*

**El Paso**
Hagedorn, Eric A. *physics professor*
Peralta-Videa, Jose R. *environmental scientist, researcher*

**Fort Worth**
Bailey, James Stephen *scientist*
Caldwell, Billy Ray *geologist*
Flynn, Patrick M. *research scientist, educator*
Quarles, Carroll Adair, Jr. *physicist, researcher*
Reinecke, Manfred G. *chemistry professor*
Webb, Theodore Stratton, Jr. *aerospace scientist, consultant*

**Freeport**
Stevens, James C. *chemist*

**Galveston**
Balaban, Alexandru T. *chemistry professor, researcher*
Crown, Eric Daniel *research scientist*
Gorenstein, David G. *chemistry and biochemistry professor*

**Houston**
Alauddin, Mian M. *chemist, educator*
Anderson, Richard Carl *geophysical exploration company executive*
Baker, Stephen Denio *physics professor*
Bakulin, Andrey *geophysicist*
Bally, Albert W. *retired geologist, geology educator*
Bogard, Donald Dale *planetary geochemist*
Bonner, Billy Edward *physics professor*
Brandt, I. Marvin *chemist, engineer*
Brotzen, Franz Richard *materials scientist, educator*
Burke, Kevin Charles Antony *geologist*
Chu, Paul Ching-Wu *physicist, director, academic administrator, educator*
Chu, Wei-Kan *physicist, researcher*
Corley, Larry Steven *chemist*
Cundin, Luisiana Xavier *physicist, educator*
Curl, Robert Floyd, Jr. *chemistry professor*
Forney, Jan Lynette *geophysicist*
Gibson, Everett Kay, Jr. *aerospace scientist, geochemist*
Goloby, George William, Jr. *environmental scientist, editor*
Gordon, Lawrence *geologist, consultant*
Hackerman, Norman *chemist, academic administrator*
Hoffman, Ronald Bruce *biophysicist, consultant, life scientist*
Hulet, Randall Gardner *physics professor*
Hussain, Moinuddin Syed *geologist, engineer, consultant*
Karner, Stephen Leslie *geophysicist*
Kevan, Larry *chemistry professor*
Kinsey, James Lloyd *chemist, educator*
Kit, Saul *retired biochemist, educator*
Kochi, Jay Kazuo *chemist, educator*
Kouri, Donald Jack *chemist, educator*
Lane, Neal Francis *physics professor, retired federal agency administrator*
Liang, Edison Parktak *astrophysicist, plasma physicist, educator, researcher*
Liu, Yuhong *geologist*
Lucid, Shannon W. *biochemist, astronaut*
Mackwell, Stephen Joseph *geophysicist, educator*
Peslier, Anne H. *geochemist*
Pinsky, Lawrence Steven *physics professor*
Reiff, Patricia Hofer *space physicist, educator*
Reso, Anthony *geologist, educator, earth resources economist*
Rong, Shu *materials scientist, researcher*
Scuseria, Gustavo Enrique *theoretical chemist*
Slaugh, Lynn H. *retired chemist*
Talwani, Manik *geophysicist, educator*
Viswanathan, Gopalakrishnan *metallurgist, researcher*
Wei, Ying *chemist*
Weinstein, Roy *physics professor*
Wilson, Thomas Leon *physicist, researcher*
Xue, Dong Cynthia *research scientist, consultant*

Zhang, Chunlong *environmental scientist, engineer*
Zhu, Jiang *materials scientist*
Zubarev, Eugene *chemistry professor*

**Irving**
Eaker, Charles William *chemistry professor*

**Kaufman**
Hausler, Rudolf Heinrich *research chemist*

**Kerrville**
Shaw, Alan Bosworth *geologist, retired paleontologist*
Sparks, Don Bertrand *retired geophysicist*

**Kingsville**
Bashir, Sajid *chemist, educator, research scientist*
Grassman, Lon Irvin, Jr. *research scientist*

**Lubbock**
Adamcik, Joe Alfred *retired chemistry professor, lawyer*
Eng, Sothy *research scientist*
Everse, Johannes *biochemist, researcher*

**Mc Kinney**
Frank, Steven Neil *chemist*

**Midland**
Berner, Leo De Witte, Jr. *retired oceanographer*

**Nacogdoches**
Bowen, Donald Edgar *physics professor, former academic administrator*

**Odessa**
Gutierrez, Kristopher James *physicist, researcher*
Robinson, J. Michael *chemistry professor, researcher*

**Prairie View**
Ciftja, Orion *physicist, researcher*

**Richardson**
Manton, William Inwood *geologist, educator*
Rutford, Robert Hoxie *geologist, educator*
Sprague, Charles Warren *geologist*

**San Antonio**
Allegrini, Frédéric *research scientist, educator*
Budalur, Thyagarajan Subbanarayan *chemistry professor*
Cragnolino, Gustavo Adolfo *research scientist*
Datta, Rupali *geochemist, educator*
Gruber, John Balsbaugh *physics professor*
Losiewicz, Michael David *biochemist, educator*
Lyle, Robert Edward *chemist*
Markwell, Dick R(obert) *retired chemist*
Masters, Bettie Sue Siler *biochemist, educator*
Negrete, George Raymond *chemistry professor, researcher*
Paul, Debajyoti *geologist, educator*
Pensado, Osvaldo *research scientist*
Sablik, Martin John *research physicist*
Synek, Miroslav *physicist, chemist, world affairs consultant*
Urbach, Adam Robert *chemistry professor*
Walmsley, Judith Abrams *chemistry professor*
Wei, Ronghua *research scientist*

**Southlake**
Herrmann, Debra McGuire *chemist, educator*

**Sugar Land**
Downs, Hartley H. III *chemist*
Goodwin, Anthony Robert Holmes *chemist, editor*
Huston, Daniel Cliff *geophysicist*

**Temple**
Asea, Alexzander *research scientist*

**Texas City**
Fuchs, Owen George *chemist*

**Uvalde**
Graham, Robert Albert *physicist, researcher, curator*

**Waco**
Pedrotti, Leno Stephano *physics professor*

**UTAH**

**Brigham City**
Hepworth, John Leonard *chemist, researcher*

**Draper**
Wright, Stuart I. *materials scientist, materials engineer*

**Dugway**
Phan, Richard Man *chemist*

**Holladay**
O'Halloran, Thomas Alphonsus, Jr. *retired physicist, retired researcher*

**Logan**
Edwards, William Farrell *physics professor, researcher*
Schunk, Robert Walter *space physics research administrator*

**North Logan**
Powers, Linda Sue *biophysicist, educator, biomedical engineer*

**Orem**
Benson, Alvin K. *physicist, geophysicist, consultant, educator*

**Provo**
Cheney, Brigham Vernon *physical chemist, consultant*
Deng, Shenglou *chemistry professor*
Henderson, Douglas James *physicist, educator, chemist, researcher*
Izatt, Reed M. *chemistry researcher*

Vanfleet, Howard Bay *physicist, educator*

**Salt Lake City**
Dick, Bertram Gale, Jr. *physics professor*
Foltz, Rodger Lowell *chemistry professor*
Gortatowski, Melvin Jerome *retired chemist*
Kim, Sung Wan *chemistry professor*
Lloyd, Ray Dix *health physicist*
Mattis, Daniel Charles *physicist, researcher*
Miller, Jan Dean *metallurgy educator*
Miller, Joel Steven *inorganic and organic materials chemist*
Olson, Ferron Allred *metallurgist, educator*
Parry, Robert Walter *chemistry professor*
Poulter, Charles Dale *chemist, educator, consultant*
Salomonson, Vincent Victor *meteorologist, educator*
Stang, Peter John *organic chemist*
Straight, Richard Coleman *photobiologist, natural philosopher*
Velick, Sidney Frederick *research biochemist, educator*
Zhdanov, Michael Semenovich *geophysicist, educator*
Zipser, Edward J. *meteorologist, educator*

**VERMONT**

**Arlington**
Pond, Thomas Alexander *physics professor, academic administrator*

**Burlington**
Nyborg, Wesley Lemars *physics professor*

**Colchester**
Butenas, Saulius *research scientist*

**Middlebury**
Winkler, Paul Frank, Jr. *astrophysicist, educator*

**Shelburne**
White, William North *retired chemistry professor*

**Thetford**
Hoagland, Mahlon *biochemist, educator*

**VIRGINIA**

**Alexandria**
Carter, William Harold, Sr. *physicist, researcher, electrical engineer*
Fainberg, Anthony *physicist*
Gutsch, William Anthony, Jr. *astronomer*
Lipnick, Robert Louis *chemist, toxicologist*
Masterson, Kleber Sanlin, Jr. *physicist*
Milling, Marcus Eugene, Sr. *geologist*
Muir, Warren Roger *chemist, educator*
Reiss, Richard *environmental consultant*
Romney, Carl F. *seismologist*
Toulmin, Priestley *retired geologist*

**Annandale**
Matuszko, Anthony Joseph *research chemist, administrator, educator*
Raab, Harry Frederick, Jr. *retired physicist*

**Arlington**
Berg, John Richard *chemist, former federal government executive*
Bigeleisen, Jacob *chemist, educator*
Chubb, Talbot Albert *physicist, consultant*
Ensminger, Luther Glenn *retired chemist*
Erb, Karl Albert *physicist, government official*
Gergely, Tomas *astronomer*
Keister, Bradley Dean *physicist, director*
Matthews, Allan Freeman *geologist*
Schwartz, Lyle Howard *materials scientist, science administrator*
Whitcomb, James Hall *geophysicist, foundation administrator*
Zirkind, Ralph *physicist, educator*

**Big Stone Gap**
Holbrook, Tracy Lonzie Lee *chemistry professor, small business owner*

**Blacksburg**
Asryan, Levon V. *physicist, electronics engineer, materials scientist*
Celik, Hayati *chemist*
Dzuuriu, Minodugun Fernand *physical chemist*
de Wolf, David Alter *physicist, educator*
Graybeal, Jack Daniel *chemist, educator*
Mo, Luke Wei *physicist, researcher*

**Charlottesville**
Bloomfield, Louis Aub *physicist, researcher*
Carter, William Walton *physicist, researcher*
Chordia, Mahendra Devichand *chemist, researcher*
Fraser, Cassandra Lynne *chemist, educator*
Fredrick, Laurence William *astronomer, educator*
Gaskin, Felicia *biochemist, educator*
Good, Richard Standish *geologist*
Grimes, Russell Newell *inorganic chemist, educator*
Hecht, Sidney Michael *chemistry professor*
Hobbs, Charles Roderick Bruce, Jr. *retired geologist*
Hunt, Donald Frederick *chemistry professor*
Lo, Kwok-Yung *astronomer, educator, researcher*
MacDonald, Timothy Lee *chemistry professor*
Sarazin, Craig Leigh *astronomer*
Seidelmann, Paul Kenneth *astronomer, educator*
Sundberg, Richard Jay *chemistry professor*
Vanden Bout, Paul Adrian *astronomer, physicist, educator*
Weber, Hans Jürgen *physics professor*

**Chesterfield**
Young, Kenneth Wayne *environmental health specialist*

**Clifton**
Brooks, Matthew Wayne *agrichemical regulatory chemist, consultant*

**Dahlgren**
Bressler, Barry Lee *physicist, systems analyst*

**Fairfax**
Ko, Jang Wan *research scientist, educator*
Morowitz, Harold Joseph *biophysicist, educator*
Steger, Edward Herman *retired chemist*
Xing, Guang-Qian *aerospace scientist*

**Falls Church**
Akkara, Joseph Augustine *chemist, educator*

**Hampden Sydney**
Porterfield, William Wendell *chemist, educator*

**Hampton**
Choi, Yonghoon *environmental scientist*
Fadika, Gibril Owereh *research scientist, educator*
Jin, Zhonghai *physicist*
Remsberg, Ellis Edward *meteorologist, researcher*
Tripathi, Ram Kishore *physicist, researcher*
Yamakov, Vesselin Ivanov *aerospace scientist, researcher*

**Harrisonburg**
Baker, George Harold III *physicist, educator*

**Hartfield**
Johnson, Carl Randolph *chemist, educator*

**Heathsville**
Winkel, Raymond Norman *aerospace scientist, consultant, retired military officer*

**Locust Grove**
Stein, Richard Louis *chemist, educator*

**Lynchburg**
McClenon, John Raymond *retired chemistry professor*
Morgan, Evan *retired chemist*

**Mc Lean**
Gifford, Franklin Andrew, Jr. *meteorologist, consultant*
Theon, John Speridon *meteorologist, researcher*

**Newport News**
Cardman, Lawrence Santo *physics professor, researcher*
Epelbaum, Evgeny *physicist*

**Norfolk**
Noginov, Mikhail A. *physicist, researcher, educator*

**Petersburg**
Brown, Jack D(elbert) *chemist, researcher*
Stronach, Carey Elliott *physicist, researcher*

**Radford**
Zweifel, Paul Frederick *retired physics professor*

**Reston**
Dickman, Robert S. *aerospace institute administrator, retired military officer*
Hirsch, Robert Maurice *hydrologist*
Kramish, Arnold *physicist, historian, writer*
Naeser, Nancy Dearien *geologist, researcher*
Wang, Jin *research scienti*

**Richmond**
Fenn, John Bennett *chemist, e...*
Reshchikov, Michael A. *physics professor, researcher*
Sun, Qiang *scientist, educator*
Teddai, William Andrew *biochemist, molecular oncologist*

**Roanoke**
Al-Zubaidi, Amer Aziz *physicist, researcher*

**Springfield**
Benson, William Edward (Barnes) *geologist*
Campbell, Francis James *retired chemist*

**Staunton**
Lossing, Wallace William *inventor, minister*

**Vienna**
Bhide, Manohar Gopal *nuclear scientist, educator*
Wiesnet, Donald Richard *retired hydrologist*

**Williamsburg**
Starnes, William Herbert, Jr. *chemist, educator*

**Winchester**
Ludwig, George Harry *retired physicist, electrical engineer*

**WASHINGTON**

**Bellingham**
Brakke, Myron Kendall *retired research chemist, educator*
Cox, David Jackson *biochemistry professor*
Morse, Joseph Grant *chemistry educator*
Nelson, George Driver *astronomer, educator, former astronaut*

**Bothell**
Kolker, Eugene *research scientist*

**Bremerton**
Abel, Bob *physics professor, researcher*

**Camano Island**
O'Connor, Thomas Edward *petroleum geologist, management consultant*

**Everett**
Brown, Frederick Calvin *retired physics professor*

**Federal Way**
Ma, Zhenkui *remote sensing applications scientist, consultant*

**Freeland**
Calio, Anthony John *research scientist, operations research specialist*

**Friday Harbor**
Agosta, William Carleton *chemist, educator*

**Lynnwood**
Olsen, Kenneth Harold *geophysicist, astrophysicist, historian*

**Manchester**
Fearon, Lee Charles *chemist*

**Mukilteo**
Liu, Hui (Robin Liu) *principal scientist, consultant, author*

**Olympia**
Bloomquist, Rodney Gordon *geologist*

**Pullman**
Banas, Emil Mike *physicist, researcher*
Hinman, George Wheeler *physics professor*
Ryan, Clarence Augustine, Jr. *biochemistry professor*

**Redmond**
Meshii, Masahiro *materials science educator*

**Richland**
Bevelacqua, Joseph John *physicist, researcher*
Elderkin, Charles Edwin *retired meteorologist*
Kathren, Ronald Laurence *health physicist*
Moore, Emmett Burris, Jr. *physical chemist, educator*
Murphy, Mark Kenneth *physicist, researcher*
Onishi, Yasuo *environmental researcher*
Peters, Leonard K. *environmental scientist*
Runkle, Robert Charles *physicist*
Shin, Yongsoon *research scientist*
Tsiklauri, Georgi Victor *physicist, researcher*

**Seattle**
Andersen, Niels Hjorth *chemistry professor, consultant, biophysicist, researcher*
Atwater, Brian F. *geologist*
Baum, William Alvin *astronomer, educator*
Bernard, Eddie Nolan *oceanographer*
Bichsel, Hans *physicist, consultant, researcher*
Bodansky, David *physicist, researcher*
Brodsky, Anatol M. *research scientist*
Brown, Robert Alan *physicist, educator*
Brownlee, Donald Eugene, II, *astronomer, educator*
Christian, Gary D. *chemistry professor*
Christiansen, Walter Henry *aerospace scientist, educator*
Davidson, Ernest Roy *chemist, educator*
Dehmelt, Hans Georg *physicist, educator*
Deming, Jody Wheeler *oceanography educator*
El-Moslimany, Ann Paxton *paleoecologist, educator, writer*
Engel, Thomas *chemistry professor*
Evans, Bernard William *geologist, educator*
Fischer, Edmond Henri *biochemistry educator*
Fischer, Fred Walter *physicist, engineer, educator*
Floss, Heinz G. *chemistry professor, researcher*
Gates, R. Jordan *meteorologist*
Gerhart, James Basil *physics professor*
Halver, John Emil *nutritional biochemist*
Heath, George Ross *oceanographer*
Henley, Ernest Mark *physics professor, retired dean*
Krebs, Edwin Gerhard *biochemistry educator*
Kwiram, Alvin L. *physical chemistry professor, university official*
Lubatti, Henry Joseph *physicist, researcher*
Malins, Donald Clive *biochemist, researcher*
Mukadam, Anjum Shagufta *astronomer*
Muy-Rivera, Martin *biochemist, researcher*
Olmstead, Marjorie Ann *physics professor*
Porter, Stephen Cummings *geologist, educator*
Rabinovitch, Benton Seymour *chemist, educator emeritus*
Reinhardt, William Parker *chemical physicist, educator*
Runte, Alfred *environmental historian, consultant*
Stern, Edward Abraham *physics professor*
Thouless, David James *retired physicist, educator*
Wilets, Lawrence *physicist, educator*
Wurster, Charles Frederick *environmental scientist, educator*
Yuan, Chun *physicist, educator*

**Silverdale**
Walske, M(ax) Carl, Jr. *physicist*

**Spokane**
Crosby, Glenn Arthur *chemistry professor*

**Tukwila**
Weidner, Mark *environment research executive*

**University Place**
Foster, Charles Carlton *physicist*

**Walla Walla**
Wade, Leroy Grover, Jr. *chemistry educator*

**WEST VIRGINIA**

**Fairmont**
Swiger, Elizabeth Davis *chemist, educator*

**Morgantown**
Beattie, Diana Scott *biochemistry professor*
Han, Runlin *biochemist, researcher*
Koepke, Mark *physics professor*
Park, Ju-Hyeong *environmental scientist, public health service officer*
Seehra, Mohindar Singh *physics professor, researcher*

**Parkersburg**
Sperati, Carleton Angelo *retired chemist*

**South Charleston**
Atkins, Kenneth Earl *retired chemist*

**WISCONSIN**

**Kenosha**
Arion, Douglas Norman *physicist, researcher*
Kolb, Vera M. *chemist, educator*

**Lake Geneva**
Dobray, Alan Michael *theoretical physicist, research scientist*

**Madison**
Anderson, Louis Wilmer, Jr. *physicist, researcher*
Barger, Vernon Duane *physicist, educator*
Botez, Dan *physicist*
Bruch, Ludwig W. *physicist, researcher*
Burris, Robert Harza *biochemist, educator*
Callen, James Donald *plasma physicist, nuclear engineer*
Carroll, Sean B. *research scientist, geneticist, biologist, educator*
Christensen, Nikolas Ivan *geophysicist, educator*
Churchwell, Edward Bruce *astronomer, educator*
Clay, Clarence Samuel *acoustical oceanographer*
Cleland, W(illiam) Wallace *biochemistry educator*
Coppersmith, Susan Nan *physicist*
Craddock, Campbell (John Campbell Craddock) *geologist, educator*
Crim, Forrest Fleming, Jr. *chemist, educator*
Curtiss, Charles Francis *chemist, educator*
Dahl, Lawrence Frederick *chemistry professor*
DeWerd, Larry Albert *medical physicist, educator*
Dott, Robert Henry, Jr. *geologist, educator*
Evenson, Merle Armin *chemist, educator*
Fang, Guang Yin *physicist*
Farrar, Thomas C. *chemist, educator*
Forest, Cary B. *physicist, educator*
Gellman, Samuel Helmer *chemist, educator*
Golovkin, Igor *physicist*
Greenler, Robert George *physics professor, researcher*
Griffin, Martin P.A. *research scientist*
Hokin, Lowell Edward *biochemist, educator*
Kanskar, Manoj *physicist, engineering executive*
Kiessling, Laura Lee *chemist, researcher*
Knox, James C. *geologist, educator*
Kutzbach, John E. *climate scientist*
Lagally, Max Gunter *physics professor*
Lardy, Henry A. (Henry Arnold Lardy) *biochemistry professor*
Lawler, James Edward *physics professor*
Lazarian, Alex *physics professor*
Li, Kai *chemist, research scientist*
Lin, Chun Chia *research physicist, educator*
Maher, Louis James, Jr. *geologist, educator*
Morton, Stephen Dana *chemist, consultant*
Mukerjee, Pasupati *chemistry professor*
Pondrom, Lee Girard *physicist, researcher*
Pray, Lloyd Charles *geologist, educator*
Rich, Daniel Hulbert *chemistry professor*
Scherer, Victor Richard *physicist, computer scientist, consultant, musician*
Skinner, James Lauriston *chemist, educator*
Tomé, Wolfgang Axel *physicist, researcher, educator*
Vaughan, Worth Edward *retired chemistry professor*
Workman, Jerome James, Jr. *chemist*
Yu, Hyuk *chemist, educator*
Zimmerman, Howard Elliot *chemist, educator*

**Milwaukee**
Allen, Bruce *physicist*
Bader, Alfred Robert *chemist*
Burch, Thaddeus Joseph, Jr. *physics professor, director*
Buss, Daniel Frank *environmental scientist*
Griffith, Owen Wendell *biochemistry professor*
Haworth, Daniel Thomas *chemistry professor*
Hendee, William Richard *medical physics educator, academic administrator, radiologist*
Hossain, M. Mahmun *chemistry professor, researcher*
Janda, Lubomir Miro *organic chemist*
Kaltchev, Matey *chemistry professor, department chairman*
Salsbury, Timothy Ian *research scientist*

**Washington Island**
Raup, David Malcolm *paleontology educator*

**Williams Bay**
Hobbs, Lewis Mankin *astronomer*

**WYOMING**

**Casper**
Ptasynski, Harry *geologist, oil industry executive*
Wold, John Schiller *geologist, former congressman*

**Kelly**
Knowles, William Standish *retired chemist*

**Laramie**
Grandy, Walter Thomas, Jr. *physicist, researcher*
Meyer, Edmond Gerald *energy scientist, retired chemistry professor, academic administrator, entrepreneur*
Roark, Terry Paul *astronomer, educator*

**TERRITORIES OF THE UNITED STATES**

**PUERTO RICO**

**Angeles**
Avila, Charlie A. *physics researcher, inventor*

**Humacao**
Tremblay, Raymond L. *ecology and biological conservation educator, researcher*

**Mayaguez**
Jia, Weiyi *physics professor, researcher*

**Vega Alta**
Matos, Cruz Alfonso *environmental consultant*

**CANADA**

**ALBERTA**

**Calgary**
Campbell, Finley Alexander *geologist, consultant*

**Edmonton**
Bindiganavile, Vivek Srinivasan *research scientist, educator*
Harris, Walter Edgar *chemistry professor*
Kay, Cyril Max *biochemist, educator*
Rutter, Nathaniel Westlund *geologist, educator*

**BRITISH COLUMBIA**

**Delta**
Russell, Richard Doncaster *geophysics educator, academic administrator*

**Lions Bay**
Bartholomew, Gilbert Alfred *retired physicist*

**Sidney**
van den Bergh, Sidney *astronomer*

**Vancouver**
Affleck, Ian Keith *physics educator*
Hardy, Walter Newbold *physics professor, researcher*
Vogt, Erich Wolfgang *physicist, academic administrator*

**Victoria**
Batten, Alan Henry *astronomer*
Best, Melvyn Edward *geophysicist*
Hutchings, John Barrie *astronomer, researcher*
Israel, Werner *physics educator*
Leffek, Kenneth Thomas *retired chemist, educator*
Morton, Donald Charles *astronomer*
Wiles, David McKeen *chemist*

**West Vancouver**
Wynne-Edwards, Hugh Robert *geologist, educator, entrepreneur*

**MANITOBA**

**Winnipeg**
Schaefer, Theodore Peter *retired chemistry professor*
Smith, Ian Cormack Palmer *biophysicist*

**NEWFOUNDLAND AND LABRADOR**

**Saint John's**
Gibbons, Rex Vincent *geologist*

**NOVA SCOTIA**

**Dartmouth**
Elliott, James A. *oceanographer, researcher*

**Halifax**
Dahn, Jeff Raymond *physics professor*
Hiltz, Arnold Aubrey *retired chemist*
Jones, William Ernest *chemistry professor*

**Tatamagouche**
Roach, Margot Ruth *retired biophysicist, educator*

**ONTARIO**

**Collingwood**
Morley, Lawrence Whitaker *geophysicist, consultant*

**Deep River**
Davies, John Arthur *retired physics professor, engineering educator, research scientist*
Milton, John Charles Douglas *nuclear physicist, researcher*

**Guelph**
Dickinson, William Trevor *hydrologist, educator*

**Hamilton**
Datars, William Ross *physicist, researcher*
Gillespie, Ronald James *chemistry professor, researcher, writer*
Spenser, Ian Daniel *chemistry professor*
Sprung, Donald Whitfield Loyal *physics professor*

**Kingston**
Ewan, George Thomson *physicist, researcher*
Stewart, Alec Thompson *physicist, educator*
Szarek, Walter Anthony *chemist, educator*

**London**
Bancroft, George Michael *chemical physicist, educator*
Dreimanis, Aleksis *emeritus geology educator*
Fyfe, William Sefton *geochemist, educator*
Stewart, Harold Brown *biochemist*

**Manotick**
Hobson, George Donald *retired geophysicist*

**Ottawa**
Alper, Howard *chemistry professor*
Halliday, Ian *astronomer*
Harington, Charles Richard *vertebrate paleontologist*

**Holmes**, John Leonard *chemistry professor*
Ingold, Keith Usherwood *chemist, educator*
Kates, Morris *biochemist, educator*
Ramsay, Donald Allan *physical chemist*
Schneider, William George *chemist, research consultant*
St-Onge, Denis Alderic *geologist, research scientist, educator*

**Richmond Hill**
Garrison, Robert Frederick *astronomer, educator*

**Toronto**
Bohme, Diethard Kurt *chemistry professor*
Brook, Adrian Gibbs *chemistry professor*
Goring, David Arthur Ingham *chemist, educator*
Hofmann, Theo *biochemist, educator*
Kresge, Alexander Jerry *chemistry professor*
Litherland, Albert Edward *physics professor*
Packham, Marian Aitchison *biochemistry professor*
Polanyi, John Charles *chemist, educator*
Pritchard, Huw Owen *chemist, educator*
Shepherd, Gordon Greeley *space physics educator, researcher*
Stoicheff, Boris Peter *physicist, researcher*

**Waterloo**
Morgan, Alan Vivian *geologist, educator*
Smolin, Lee *physicist, researcher, writer*
Wen, Geyi *applied physics professor*

**Willowdale**
Goldberg, David Meyer *retired biochemist*

**Windsor**
Thibert, Roger Joseph *clinical chemist, educator*

**QUEBEC**

**Laval**
Baroudy, Bahige Mourad *biochemist, researcher*

**Montreal**
Barrette, Jean *physicist, researcher*
Das Gupta, Subal *physics professor, researcher*
Eisenberg, Adi *chemist*
Johnstone, Rose Mamelak (Mrs. Douglas Johnstone) *biochemistry educator*
Leroy, Claude *physics professor, researcher*
Michaud, Georges Joseph *physics professor*
Perlin, Arthur Saul *chemistry professor*
Podgorsak, Ervin B. *medical physicist, educator, administrator*
Solomon, Samuel *biochemistry educator, administrator*
Sourkes, Theodore Lionel *biochemistry professor*
Taras, Paul *physicist, researcher*
Vinet, Luc *physicist, educator*
Whitehead, Michael Anthony *chemistry professor*

**Outremont**
Levesque, Rene Jules Albert *retired physicist*

**Pointe-Claire**
Bachynski, Morrel Paul *physicist*

**Sherbrooke**
Tremblay, André-Marie *physicist*

**SASKATCHEWAN**

**Saskatoon**
Hirose, Akira *physics professor, researcher*

**Halifax**
Matta, Chérif Farid *chemistry professor*

**Hamilton**
Ayers, Paul W. *chemistry professor*

**Ontario**
Armstrong, Robin Louis *physics professor, physicist*

**Saskatoon**
Giesy, John Paul, Jr. *environmental scientist, educator*

**Sherbrooke**
Deslongchamps, Pierre *chemistry professor*

**Vancouver**
Grant, Edward Robert *chemistry professor, science association executive*

**Waterloo**
Bernath, Peter *chemistry professor*

**MEXICO**

**Cuernavaca**
Bolivar Zapata, Francisco *biochemist*

**Saltillo**
Anderson, Brooks Doran, II, *geologist, consultant*

**AUSTRALIA**

**Canberra**
Taylor, Stuart Ross *geochemist, writer*

**Sydney**
Hora, Heinrich *physicist*

**AUSTRIA**

**Vienna**
Pohl, Adolf Leopold *clinical chemist, quality assurance consultant*

## BELGIUM

**Brussels**
de Duve, Christian René *chemist, educator*

**Liège**
Mosora-Stan, Florentina Ioana *physics professor*

## BRAZIL

**Sao Paulo**
Grellet-Tinner, Gerald *paleontologist*

**Sorocaba**
Martins, Nelson *physics professor*

## CHINA

**Beijing**
Yang, Chen Ning Franklin *physicist, educator*
Yang, Guangrong *physicist, researcher, educator*
Zhou, Bang Rong *physicist, researcher*

## COLOMBIA

**Bogota**
Botero, Alonso *physicist, educator*

## CZECH REPUBLIC

**Prague**
Čejka, Jiří *retired chemist, researcher*
Jungwirth, Tomas *physicist, researcher*
Kotrla, Miroslav *physicist*

## DENMARK

**Copenhagen**
Mottelson, Ben Roy *physicist*
Pethick, Christopher John *physicist*

## ENGLAND

**Bedfordshire**
Gelman, Leonid Moiseevich *research scientist, educator*

**Cambridge**
Buckingham, Amyand David *chemistry professor*
Edwards, Sir Samuel Frederick *physicist, researcher*
Hawking, Stephen William *astrophysicist, mathematician*

**Falmer**
Cornforth, Sir John Warcup *chemist*

**Leeds**
Slechta, Jiri *theoretical physicist*

**London**
Scott, Raymond Peter William *chemistry professor, writer*
Stelle, Kellogg Sheffield *physicist*

**Oxford**
Halasyamani, P. Shiv *inorganic chemist, researcher*

**Oxfordshire**
Gates, David Allen *physicist, researcher, educator*

**Reading**
Spencer, David Anthony *geologist, researcher, educator*

## FRANCE

**Besancon**
Boillat, Guy Maurice Georges *mathematical physicist*

**Chatenay-Malabry**
Evesque, Pierre Henri *physics researcher*

**Creteil**
Renoux, André *physicist, researcher*

**Le Vesinet**
Hillion, Pierre Théodore Marie *mathematical physicist*

**Orleans**
Price, David Cecil Long *physicist, researcher*

**Orsay**
Friedel, Jacques *retired physics professor*

**Paris**
Constantin, Emilia *physicist, researcher*
de Gennes, Pierre-Gilles *physicist, educator*
Lehn, Jean-Marie Pierre *chemistry professor*

**Villefranche-sur-Mer**
Legendre, Louis *oceanographer, educator, research scientist*

## GERMANY

**Aachen**
Pinchuk, Anatoliy Oleksijovych *physicist*

**Augsburg**
Kunes, Jan *physicist*

**Berlin**
Eichler, Hans Joachim *physics professor*
Mantsch, Henry Horst *chemistry professor*
Nölting, Bengt *physicist, researcher*

**Frankfurt**
Greiner, Walter Albin Erhard *physicist*
Michel, Hartmut *biochemist*

**Garching**
Genzel, Reinhard *astrophysicist, educator*

**Göttingen**
Sheldrick, George Michael *chemistry professor, crystallographer*
Toennies, Jan Peter *research chemical physicist*

**Munich**
Huber, Robert *biochemist, educator*

**Paderborn**
Thim, Frank *physicist, astronomer*

**Stutensee**
Barbian, Otto Alfred *physicist*

**Stuttgart**
Cardona, Manuel *physics professor*

## GREECE

**Athens**
Miliotis, Demitrios *physics professor*

**Mandra**
Panagopoulos, Panagiotis Nikos *physicist, researcher*

**Piraeus**
Papachristou, Costas John *physicist, researcher*

## HONG KONG

**Kowloon**
Hung, Edward *research scientist*

## HUNGARY

**Budapest**
Rakos, Balázs *physicist, researcher*
Szigeti, János *physicist*

**Debrecen**
Csikai, Gyula *physicist, researcher*

## INDIA

**Chennai**
Krishnani, Kishore Kumar *research scientist*

**Delhi**
Mitra, Asoke Nath *retired physicist, researcher*

**Kanpur**
Joglekar, Satish Dinkar *physicist, educator*

**New Delhi**
Yadav, Hari Om *research scientist*

## IRAN

**Tehran**
Jalali-Heravi, Mehdi *chemistry professor, researcher*

## ISRAEL

**Be'er Sheva**
Carmeli, Moshe *theoretical physicist*

**Netanya**
Tsitverblit, Naftali Anatol *physicist, fluid mechanics engineer, researcher*

**Ra'anana**
Hayon, Elie M. *chemist, educator*

**Tel Aviv**
Jortner, Joshua *physical chemist, educator*

## ITALY

**Como**
Casati, Giulio *theoretical physics professor*

**Padua**
Onofrio, Roberto *physicist, researcher*

**Rome**
Maraviglia, Bruno *physicist, researcher*

## JAPAN

**Gyoda**
Shibasaki, Yoshio *chemistry professor, researcher*

**Hiroshima**
Suzuki, Nobutaka *chemistry professor*

**Okayama**
Ubuka, Toshihiko *biochemist, educator, academic administrator*

**Osaka**
Ikeda, Kazuyosi *physicist, poet*
Ishii, Sakae *retired physicist*

**Shinjuku**
Shimada, Haruo *physical chemistry educator*

**Tokyo**
Esaki, Leo (Esaki Leona) *physicist, foundation executive, university president*
Fuketa, Toyojiro *physicist*
Fukuda, Atsuo *physicist, materials science researcher, educator*
Iida, Shuichi *physicist, educator*
Sakurada, Yutaka *retired chemist*
Suzuki, Akira *physics professor*

**Utsunomiya**
Yorikawa, Hiroharu *physicist, researcher*
Taketomi, Susamu *physicist, researcher*

## JORDAN

**Irbid**
El-Migdadi, Fayig *biochemist, educator, molecular biologist*

## MALAYSIA

**Petaling Jaya**
Wong, Kuok-Shoong Daniel *research scientist*

**Serdang**
Soetedjo, Hariyadi *materials scientist, researcher*

## NETHERLANDS

**Utrecht**
't Hooft, Gerardus (Gerard 't Hooft) *physicist, researcher*

## NORWAY

**Lilleström**
Gjessing, Dag Trygveson *physicist*

**Oslo**
Gjønnes, Jon Kjell *physics professor*

## POLAND

**Bydgoszcz**
Czajkowski, Gerard Zygfryd *physicist, researcher*

## REPUBLIC OF KOREA

**Ansan**
Yeh, Sang-Wook *research scientist*

**Seoul**
Kang, Byoung-Cheorl *research scientist*
Kim, Chul Sung *physicist, educator*

**Suwon**
Son, Seung Uk *chemistry professor, researcher*

**Wonju**
Jeon, Byong-Hun *chemistry professor, researcher*

## ROMANIA

**Bucharest**
Zamfir, Nicolae Victor *physicist, researcher*

**Sibiu**
Marutoiu, Constantin Constantin *chemistry professor, researcher*

## RUSSIA

**Biysk**
Efimov, Valerey Grigorijevich *physicist, researcher*

**Ivanovo**
Vladimirova, Tatyana Vladeriana *chemist, researcher*

**Kazan**
Yulmetyev, Renat Muzipovich *physicist, educator*

**Moscow**
Ginzburg, Vitaly Lazarevich *physicist*
Karasev, Vladimir *physicist, researcher*
Toshchakov, Vladimir Yurevich *biochemist*

**Pushchino**
Uversky, Vladimir Nikolaevich *biophysicist, researcher*

**Yurga**
Apasov, Alexander Mikhailovich *physicist, educator*

## SRI LANKA

**Kelaniya**
Punyasena, Munasinghe Arachchige *physicist, educator*

## SWEDEN

**Göteborg**
Svensson, Robert Charles Wilhelm *physicist, researcher*

**Örebro**
Persliden, Jan R. G. *physicist*

**Österskär**
Bolin, Bert Richard Johannes *atmospheric physicist, meteorologist, researcher*

## SWITZERLAND

**Geneva**
Charpak, Georges *physicist, nuclear scientist*
Peskov, Vladimir Dmitrievich *physicist, consultant, physics professor*
Steinberger, Jack *physicist, researcher*

**Yverdon-les-Bains**
Egolf, Peter William *physicist*

**Zurich**
Binnig, Gerd Karl *physicist, educator*
Ernst, Richard Robert *chemist, educator*
Eschenmoser, Albert *chemist*

## TAIWAN

**Taipei**
Lee, Yuan Tseh *chemistry professor*

## UNITED ARAB EMIRATES

**Abu Dhabi**
Sun, Yuefeng *research scientist, educator*

## WALES

**Swansea**
Evans, Myron Wyn *physicist, researcher*

## ADDRESS UNPUBLISHED

Ahmad, Ali *research scientist, consultant*
Alexander, Thomas G. *chemist, researcher*
Alpen, Edward Lewis *biophysicist, educator*
Alpher, Ralph Asher *physicist, educator*
Amy, Jonathan Weekes *chemist, educator*
Ancker-Johnson, Betsy *physicist, engineer, retired automotive executive*
Aprà, Edoardo *research scientist*
Atlas, David *meteorologist, research scientist*
Backus, Sterling *physicist*
Bajura, Rita A. *research scientist*
Baldwin, George Curriden *physicist, researcher*
Barr, John Baldwin *chemist, research scientist*
Bauer, Henry Hermann *chemistry and science educator*
Becchetti, Frederick Daniel, Jr. *physicist, researcher*
Beck, David Paul *biochemist*
Beckwith, Steven Van Walter *astronomy educator*
Behrendt, John Charles *geophysicist, researcher, writer*
Behrens, James William *physicist, administrator, author*
Bellini, Francesco *chemist*
BenDor, Todd K. *environmental scientist*
Benjamin, Arlin James *physicist*
Bennett, Charles Leonard *astrophysicist, educator*
Bennett, William Ralph, Jr. *physicist, researcher*
Berger, Valeriy *physicist, optical engineer*
Berlin, Kenneth Darrell *chemistry professor, consultant, researcher*
Bernstein, Elliot Roy *chemistry professor*
Bernstein, Robert H. *physicist*
Bersin, Richard Lewis *physicist*
Biederman, Edwin Williams, Jr. *retired geologist*
Bikales, Norbert M. *chemist, science administrator*
Bittman, Robert *chemistry professor, researcher*
Blander, Milton *chemist*
Blankenbecler, Richard *physicist, educator*
Bodanszky, Miklos *chemist, educator*
Boschmann, Erwin *chemistry professor*
Bostrom, Carl Otto *physicist, research facility administrator*
Boyer, Herbert Wayne *retired biochemist*
Bradbeer, Clive *biochemistry educator*
Bretthauer, Erich Walter *chemist, educator*
Browne, John Charles *physicist, researcher, lab administrator*
Bucknum, Michael John *crystallographer, educator*
Bunyan, Ellen Lackey Spotz *retired chemist*
Butler, James Newton *retired chemist*
Butler, Orton Carmichael *retired climatologist, retired educator*
Cai, Ming Zhi *chemist, researcher, film producer*
Calavia, Jose Emilio *physics professor*
Calvert, Jack George *atmospheric chemist, educator*
Campbell, Mary Stinecipher *retired chemist*
Capasso, Federico *physicist*
Cathou, Renata Egone *chemist, consultant*
Chadsey, Harold A. *astronomer, physicist*
Champion, Kenneth Stanley Warner *physicist*
Chang, Clarence Dayton *retired chemist*
Cheng, Lili *research scientist*
Cheng, Richard *chemist*
Cheong, Soonwuk *research scientist*
Christoffersen, Ralph Earl *chemist, researcher, director*
Church, Eugene Lent *physicist, consultant*
Cok, Ronald Steven *research scientist*
Colbern, Steven Garrett *chemist, researcher*
Compton, W. Dale *physicist, researcher, engineer*
Conrath, Barney Jay *astrophysicist*

Cooper, Austin Morris *chemist, consultant, chemical engineer, researcher*
Cotruvo, Joseph Alfred *environmental sciences administrator*
Cox, Robert Hames *chemist, consultant*
Crabtree, Robert Howard *chemistry professor, consultant*
Craven, Stephen M. *retired research chemist*
Critoph, Eugene *retired physicist, nuclear energy industry executive*
Cuatrecasas, Pedro Martin *research biochemist, pharmaceutical executive*
Curott, David Richard *physics professor*
Currie, Philip John *research paleontologist, educator, museum curator*
Cushing, Glen E *aerospace scientist, researcher*
Daniels, James Maurice *retired physicist*
Daniels, William Burton *retired physicist, educator*
Dash, Sanford Mark *aerospace scientist*
Day, Richard Allen *retired chemistry professor*
de Planque, E. Gail *physicist*
Deryuga, Vyacheslav O. *nuclear physicist*
Detert, Miriam Anne *chemical analyst*
Deutsch, John Ludwig *chemistry professor, researcher*
Diallo, Souleymane *research scientist, educator*
Dickens, Justin Kirk *nuclear physicist*
Dickey, Tommy D. *oceanographer, educator*
Dixon, Gordon Henry *biochemist, educator*
Dodin, Ilya *research scientist*
Dow, Garnett McCormick *geologist, consultant*
Drahos, Sandra P. *retired chemist*
Draper, David Stewart *aerospace scientist*
Dugan, Gerald F. *physicist, educator*
Dunn, Gordon Harold *physicist, researcher*
Eberly, Joseph Henry *physics professor, consultant, quantum optics scientist*
Eck, Robert Edwin *retired physicist*
Edwards, Helen Thom *physicist*
Eickhorst, Kristin Michele *research scientist*
Einhorn, Martin B. *physicist, educator*
Emery, Alan Roy *scientist, museum administrator, business executive*
Erdmann, Joachim Christian *retired physicist*
Esquivel, Agerico Liwag *retired research physicist*
Esteller, Rosana *research scientist*
Evans, Dennis Hyde *chemist, educator*
Evans, Susan A. *chemist*
Ewen, H. I. *physicist*
Ewen, John A. *chemist*
Fabiano, Nicola *physicist, researcher*
Falkowski, Paul Gordon *biological oceanographer*
Fan, Xuejun *research scientist*
Farmer, Crofton Bernard *atmospheric physicist*
Fennema, Owen Richard *food chemistry educator*
Fey, Willard *global environmental researcher, educator*
Finkenstadt, Victoria Lynne *chemist*
Finlayson, John Sylvester *retired biochemist*
Fitzgerald, Terry A. *research scientist*
Floyd, Edward Roach *retired physicist*
Fons, Eric Wallace *physics professor*
Ford, Kenneth William *physicist*
Forster, Harriet Herta *physicist, educator*
Forsyth, Richard J. *chemist*
Fowler, Alan Bicksler *retired physicist*
Fox, John David *physics professor, physicist*
Fradkin, David Milton *physicist, researcher*
Franks, Elizabeth Ann *environmental scientist*
Franz, John E. *bio-organic chemist, researcher*
Franz, Judy R. *physics professor*
French, Julia McAllister (Judy McAllister French) *environmental consultant*
Friedlander, Charles Douglas (Chuck Friedlander) *aerospace scientist, consultant*
Fruchtnicht, Erich Harold *health physicist, webmaster, consultant*
Fuhs, G. Wolfgang (Georg Wolfgang Fuhs) *environmental research manager*
Gabel, Connie *chemist, educator*
Gaffin, David Morris *meteorologist, researcher*
Galli, John Ronald *physicist, educator*
Galloway, Eilene Marie *space and astronautics consultant*
Gardner, Wilford Robert *physicist, researcher*
Garmany, Catharine Doremus *astronomer*
Garwin, Richard Lawrence *physicist*
Garzarella, Anthony *physicist, educator*
Gedevanishvili, Shalva *materials scientist, researcher*
Gelboin, Harry Victor *biochemistry educator, researcher*
Georgiev, Georgi Yordanov *physics professor*
German, Randall Michael *materials scientist, educator*
Geyer, Wayne Rockwell *oceanographer*
Ghosh, Kartik C. *physics professor, researcher*
Gilani, Tariq Hasan *physics professor, researcher*
Gilinsky, Victor *physicist*
Gilmore, Angelo Scotty *physicist, systems engineer*
Glashow, Sheldon Lee *physicist, researcher*
Gluckstern, Robert Leonard *physics professor*
Golden, David Edward *physicist*
Goldstein, Irving Solomon *chemistry professor, consultant*
Goodman, Charles David *physicist, researcher*
Goodwin, Michael Mark *research scientist, electrical engineer, computer science engineer*
Gorbaty, Martin Leo *chemist, researcher*
Gordon, William Edwin *educator, electrical engineer, academic administrator*
Gorski, Waldemar *chemist, educator*
Govindjee, *biophysics, biochemistry, and biology professor*
Grady, Lee Timothy *pharmaceutical chemist*
Grave de Peralta, Luis Ernesto *research scientist*
Griffiths, Robert Budington *physics professor*
Grimes, James Gordon *geologist*
Guha, Hillol *hydrologist, researcher*
Gunter, William Dayle, Jr. *physicist, consultant*
Halpern, Alvin Michael *retired physicist, educator, consultant*
Hamermesh, Bernard *physicist, researcher*
Hanks, Alan R. *chemistry professor*
Hanson, Harold Palmer *physicist, editor, academic administrator, government official*
Hardy, Ralph W. F. *biochemist*
Hart, Howard Roscoe, Jr. *retired physicist*
Haslett, Jared Wooddell *physicist, educator*
He, Jinghao *materials scientist*

Heeschen, David Sutphin *astronomer, educator*
Heller, Adam *chemist, researcher*
Hermann, Robert Bell *physical chemist, consultant*
Herzfeld, Charles Maria *physicist, educator*
Hibbs, Robert Andrews *analytical chemistry professor*
Higgs, Brandon Wayne *research scientist, educator*
Hodges, Robert Stanley *biochemist, educator, biotechnologist, researcher*
Hoeg, Donald Francis *chemist, consultant, research and development company executive*
Hoffleit, Ellen Dorrit *astronomer*
Holland, Patrick L. *chemistry professor*
Holman, David Hughes *research scientist*
Holt, William Henry *retired physicist, researcher*
Holub, Robert Frantisek *nuclear chemist, physicist*
Horton, Robert Carlton *geologist*
Howard, Robert Franklin *observatory administrator, astronomer*
Hoyt, Roger Franklin *physicist*
Hu, Esther Ming *astronomer, educator*
Huang, Chuanyong *materials scientist, researcher*
Huang, Wei-Cho *research scientist*
Hubbard, Gregory Scott *physicist*
Hulet, Ervin Kenneth *retired nuclear chemist*
Hunsucker, Robert Dudley *physicist, electrical engineer, educator, researcher*
Hunter, James Edward *chemist, consultant*
Huo, Jinshan *materials scientist*
Hwang, Cordelia Jong *retired chemist*
Ignatiev, Alex *physics researcher*
Ilas, Germina *research scientist*
Inlow, Rush Osborne *chemist*
Ishii, Yoshinori *environmental science educator, science writer*
Ivanov, Vladimir V. *chemistry professor, researcher*
Ivey, Elizabeth Spencer *retired physicist, educator*
Jackson, Kenneth Arthur *physicist, researcher*
Jivetin, Alexander *geophysicist, educator*
Johnson, Arthur William, Jr. *retired research scientist*
Johnson, Charles Leslie *aerospace physicist, consultant*
Johnson, Francis Severin *physicist*
Jones, Thornton Keith *chemist, researcher*
Jordan, Kenneth D. *chemistry professor*
Jordan, Robert Reed *retired geologist, educator*
Jordan, Thomas Fredrick *physics professor*
Kalman, Gabor Jeno *physicist, educator*
Kamanu, Uchemadu Chee *chemist*
Kanak, Katharine Marie *meteorologist, researcher*
Kaneyoshi, Takahito *physicist, educator*
Karplus, Paul Andrew *biochemistry educator*
Kasprzak, Lucian Alexander *physicist, researcher, materials scientist*
Kastner, Marc Aaron *physics professor*
King, Marva E. *environmental scientist*
Kirshenbaum, Kent *chemist, educator*
Kiss, István Z. *chemist, researcher*
Kistiakowsky, Vera *physical researcher, educator*
Kiziltas, Semiha *research scientist, engineer*
Klaehn, John A. *chemist, researcher*
Klein-Seetharaman, Judith *biochemist*
Klema, Ernest Donald *nuclear physicist, educator*
Kondratyuk, Sergiy *physics professor, researcher*
Korovyanko, Oleg J. *physicist*
Kraichnan, Robert Harry *physicist, consultant*
Kraus, Naomi *retired chemistry professor*
Kresa, Kent *retired aerospace executive*
Krueger, Arlin James *physicist*
Kuckuck, Robert *physicist, science administrator*
Kuhlmann-Wilsdorf, Doris *materials scientist, inventor, retired educator*
Kustin, Kenneth *chemist*
Langerak, Esley Oren *retired research chemist*
Laporte, Leo Frederic *geologist, educator, paleontologist*
Latham, Tamara Beryl *chemist, researcher*
Leachtenauer, Jon Clark *optical scientist*
LeBlond, Paul Henri *oceanographer, educator*
Lederman, Leon Max *physicist, researcher*
Lehmann, (A) Spencer *retired chemist, retired chemical engineer*
Lemke, James Underwood *physicist*
Lepping, Ronald P. *astrophysicist, researcher*
Leupold, Herbert August *physicist*
Levenson, Marc David *optics and lasers specialist, editor*
Levy, Gad *atmospheric scientist, educator, statistician*
Liang, Yanan *research scientist*
Lichten, William L. *retired physics professor*
Lightman, Alan Paige *physics professor, writer*
Lin, Ronghui *chemist, researcher*
Lomont, Chris *research scientist*
Los, Marinus *retired agrochemical researcher*
Lott, Kyle Franklin *chemist, educator*
Louie, Steven Gwon Sheng *physics professor, researcher*
Lovins, Amory Bloch *physicist, energy consultant*
Lucas, William Ray *aerospace scientist, consultant*
Lukacs, Michael Edward *electro-optics researcher*
Lurix, Paul Leslie, Jr. *chemist*
Luukanen, Arttu *research scientist*
Ma, Vu *chemist*
MacQueen, Robert Moffat *solar physicist*
Maddin, Robert *metallurgist, educator*
Magill, Joseph Henry *chemist, educator*
Maling, George Croswell, Jr. *physicist*
Marcuse, Dietrich *retired physicist*
Marinetti, Guido V. *biochemistry professor*
Mashnik, Stepan G. *physicist*
Matthews, Manyalibo Joseph *physicist, researcher*
McCormick, Donald Bruce *retired biochemist, educator*
McMillan, Robert Walker *physicist, consultant*
McNamara, Daniel Edward *geologist, seismologist*
McTague, John Paul *materials scientist, educator, chemist, researcher*
Melvin, Peter Joseph *astrophysicist, educator*
Mendelson, Sol *physical science educator, consultant*
Metz, Carsten *research scientist*
Meunier, Vincent *physicist*
Miller, Phillip Edward *environmental scientist*
Mills, Douglas L. *physics professor*
Mislow, Kurt Martin *chemist, educator*
Moeck, Peter *crystallographer, materials scientist*
Mohan, Ram S. *chemistry professor*

Mollenauer, Linn Frederick *retired physicist, writer*
Monroe, Frederick Fales *geologist, oceanographer*
Mosqueira, Ignacio *astronomer, writer*
Mudd, S. Harvey *retired biochemist*
Mukerjee, Shaibal *environmental scientist*
Mullis, Kary Banks *biochemist*
Nakamura, Toru *research scientist, educator*
Napoli, Joseph Leonard *biochemist*
Nemec, Josef *retired organic chemist, researcher*
Nevill, William Albert *chemistry professor*
Newkirk, John Burt *retired metallurgical research administrator*
Nirenberg, Marshall Warren *biochemist*
Nobles, Laurence Hewit *retired geology educator*
Noyes, Henry Pierre *physicist*
Ogliaruso, Michael Anthony *retired chemist, educator, actor*
Oka, Takeshi *physicist, physical chemist, astronomer, educator*
Okada, Kazunori *research scientist*
Olshan, Judd David *environmental scientist*
Onah, Ejembi John *chemist, researcher*
Oort, Abraham Hans *meteorologist, researcher, educator*
Orttung, William Herbert *chemistry professor*
O'Shea, Donald C. *physicist, educator, optical engineer*
Pan, Deming *chemistry professor*
Pan, Liang Ru *physicist, researcher*
Panofsky, Wolfgang Kurt Hermann *physicist, researcher*
Patankar, Ravindra *research scientist, educator*
Patchett, Arthur Allan *medicinal chemist, pharmaceutical executive*
Peiris, Suhithi Mahesica *chemist, researcher*
Pendyala, Ramarao *chemist, educator*
Petersen, Arne Joaquin *chemist*
Phelps, Michael Edward *biophysics professor*
Philander, Samuel George Harker *oceanographer*
Pirkle, Earl Charnell *retired geologist*
Plummer, Leonard Niel *geochemist*
Popa, Mihaela Alina *research scientist*
Portis, Alan Mark *physicist, researcher*
Pound, Robert Vivian *physics professor*
Pradzynski, Andrzej Henryk *chemist*
Price, Clifford Warren *retired metallurgist, researcher*
Proctor, Richard James *geologist, consultant*
Profeta, Salvatore, Jr. *chemist, educator*
Puccinelli, Daniele *research scientist*
Pursey, Derek Lindsay *retired physics professor*
Pytlinski, Jerzy Teodor *physicist, educator, research scientist*
Pytte, Agnar *physicist, retired academic administrator*
Qi, Zhigang *materials scientist, chemist*
Qiu, Hai *research scientist*
Quinn, Helen Rhoda Arnold *physicist*
Qutub, Musa Yacub *hydrogeologist, educator, consultant*
Radmilovic, Velimir *materials scientist, researcher*
Ragent, Boris *physicist*
Raouafi, Nour-Eddine *astrophysicist, researcher*
Raziano, Amanda *environmental scientist*
Read, Virginia Hall *retired biochemistry professor*
Redding, Rogers Walker *physics professor, academic administrator*
Reichmanis, Elsa *chemist*
Reynik, Robert John *materials scientist, consultant, science educator*
Reynolds, Peter James *physicist*
Rhee, Hongjoo *materials scientist*
Rhyne, James Jennings *condensed matter physicist*
Rice, Stuart Alan *chemist, educator*
Richards, Austin Ames *physicist, artist*
Richardson, Charles Clifton *biochemist, educator*
Riley, Monica *microbiologist, educator*
Rinebold, Alice June *environmental scientist*
Roberts, Thomas George *retired physicist*
Robertson, John Archibald Law *nuclear scientist*
Robertson, Robert Graham Hamish *physicist*
Rodin, Eugene *aerospace scientist, researcher, engineering educator*
Rogers, Elizabeth Parker *retired chemistry professor*
Rohr, Davis Charles *aerospace consultant, retired military officer*
Roman, Nancy Grace *astronomer, consultant*
Romanowski, Thomas Andrew *physicist, educator*
Roque-Malherbe, Rolando Marcos Antonio *research scientist, institute director*
Rose, Marian Henrietta *physics researcher*
Rosenberg, Eli Ira *physicist, educator*
Rosenkilde, Carl Edward *retired physicist*
Rosenstein, Robert Alan *scientific consultant*
Roychowdhury, Abhijit *chemist, entrepreneur*
Rubin, Vera Cooper *astronomer, researcher*
Ruedenberg, Klaus *theoretical chemist, educator*
Rybczyk, Joseph Anthony *physicist, researcher, writer, inventor*
Ryu, Jae *hydrologist*
Sabb, Annmarie Louise *retired chemist*
Sahrakorpi, Seppo *physicist, researcher*
Salamone, Joseph Charles *polymer chemistry professor*
Sarma, Pallav *research scientist*
Satinover, Jeffrey B. *physicist, psychiatrist, writer*
Sayre, David *physicist*
Schellman, John A. *chemistry professor*
Schock, Robert Norman *geophysicist*
Schonhorn, Harold *chemist, researcher*
Schreiber-Abshire, Wendy Ellen *meteorologist*
Schutz, Donald Frank *geochemist, environmental corporate executive*
Schwartz, Richard Dean *retired astronomer*
Schwartz, Shirley E. *retired chemist, researcher*
Scully, Marlan Orvil *physics professor*
Sengupta, Abhijit *molecular and optical physicist*
Shamatava, Irma *physicist, researcher*
Shao, Zhifeng *biophysics educator*
Sharp, Joshua S. *biochemist*
Shaw, Melvin Phillip *physicist, engineering educator, psychologist*
Sheinin, Rose *biochemist, educator*
Shetty, Umesha *chemist, researcher*
Shirley, David Arthur *chemistry professor, science administrator*
Sikorski, James Alan *research chemist*
Silver, Lynn Leslie *research scientist, consultant*
Simon, John Douglas *chemistry educator*

Simpson, Robert Homer *meteorologist, consultant*
Singer, S(iegfried) Fred *geophysicist, educator*
Sitnyakovsky, Roman Emmanuil *scientist, writer, inventor, translator*
Smith, Allan Laslett *research scientist, educator*
Smith, Charles Haddon *geologist, consultant, retired federal agency administrator*
Smith, Christopher T. *environmental health officer*
Smith, H. Morgan *environmental scientist, educator*
Solomon, Susan *chemist, scientist*
Solon, Leonard R(aymond) *retired physicist, educator, consultant*
Song, Jie *chemistry professor*
Song, Sun-Ju *materials scientist*
Souza, Valerie M. *research scientist*
Spejewski, Eugene Henry *physicist, consultant*
Squibb, Samuel Dexter *chemistry professor*
Srinivasan, Rangaswamy *chemical physicist*
Stavrev, Krassimir K. *chemist, researcher*
Steenbergen, Judith N. *research scientist*
Stellman, Keith M. *meteorologist, researcher*
Stern, Robin Lauri *medical physicist*
Stevenson, Paul Michael *physics professor, researcher*
Stever, Horton Guyford *aerospace scientist, educator, aerospace engineer, consultant*
Stief, Louis John *chemist*
Stockbauer, Roger Lewis *physicist, educator*
Straus, Leon Stephan *physicist*
Stringer, John *retired materials scientist*
Strouth, Baron Howard Steven *geologist, mining engineer*
Stubbs, Gerald *biochemist, educator*
Sukhatme, Jai *research scientist*
Sullivan, Kathryn D. *geologist, former astronaut, former science association executive*
Sunderman, Duane Neuman *chemist, research and development company executive*
Suttie, John Weston *biochemist*
Symchowicz, Samson *retired biochemist*
Tabazadeh, Azadeh *environmental scientist, researcher*
Tam, Sunny Wing Yee *physicist*
Tangherlini, Frank Robert *physics educator*
Taylor, Kathleen (Christine Taylor) *physical chemist, researcher*
Thomas, John Howard *astrophysicist, mechanical engineer, educator*
Thompson, Lorin Andrew III *chemist*
Thoppil, Prasad *oceanographer, researcher*
Thorhaug, Anitra L. *environmental scientist, educator*
Thornton, Kathryn C. *physicist, astronaut*
Thurnauer, Marion Charlotte *chemist*
Tressler, James F. *physicist, researcher*
Tsai, Victor Chen *geophysicist*
Tsigelny, Igor *research scientist*
Tsvankin, Ilya Daniel *geophysics educator*
Tu, Fang *research scientist*
Tuchman, Avraham (Avi) *physicist, researcher*
Tunick, Michael Howard *chemist*
Tuul, Johannes *physics professor, researcher*
Ufimtsev, Pyotr Yakovlevich *physicist, electrical engineer, educator*
Upgren, Arthur Reinhold, Jr. *astronomer, educator, writer*
Vallee-Rettke, Joan E. *chemistry educator, science education consultant*
Vanderwalker, Diane Mary *materials scientist*
Van Horn, Hugh M. *physicist, astronomer, educator*
Vanier, Jacques *physicist*
Velasquez-Garcia, Luis Fernando *research scientist, consultant*
Velden, Christopher Scott *meteorologist, researcher*
Velisavljevic, Nenad *physicist*
Veronis, George *geophysics educator*
Vishnoi, Nisheeth Kumar *research scientist*
Vook, Frederick Ludwig *physicist, consultant*
Wall, Frederick Theodore *retired chemistry professor*
Wallace, Jane House *retired geologist*
Wallace, Robert Earl *geologist*
Walters, Robert Ancil *physicist, mathematician*
Walther, Adriaan *retired physics professor*
Wang, Perry G. *chemist, researcher*
Wang, Yinmin *materials scientist, educator*
Warble, Charles Edward *materials scientist*
Warshawsky, Isidore *physicist, consultant*
Watkins, George Daniels *physics professor*
Weinberg, Steven *physics professor*
Weinreb, Michael Philip *physicist*
Weisburger, Elizabeth Kreiser *retired chemist*
Weisz, Paul B(urg) *physicist, researcher, chemical engineer*
Wellner, Marcel Nahum *research scientist, educator*
Westerhout, Gart *retired astronomer*
Whalin, Robert W. *physicist*
Wheeler, John Oliver *geologist*
White, Alice Elizabeth *physicist, researcher*
Wickman, Leslie *research scientist, science administrator*
Wilson, Peggy Mayfield *retired chemist*
Wilson, Robert Woodrow *radio astronomer*
Winant, Clinton D. *oceanographer, educator*
Winicov, Ilga Butelis *biochemist, educator*
Wolff, Manfred Ernst *medicinal chemist, pharmaceutical executive*
Wong, Ah-San *planetary scientist, composer, writer*
Woodruff, Truman O(wen) *physicist, emeritus educator*
Workman, John Mitchell *chemist*
Wyrtki, Klaus *oceanography educator*
Xu, Shaohua *biochemist, researcher*
Yates, David John C. *chemist, researcher*
Yau, Siu-Tung *physics professor*
York, Herbert Frank *physics professor*
Yu, Hengyong *research scientist*
Yu, Shaocai *research scientist*
Zakim, David *biochemist*
Zaleski, Jan Franciszek *biochemist*
Zhang, Jinsong *chemistry professor*
Zhang, Yanwen *research scientist*
Zhao, Tong *research scientist*
Zhao, Wei (Wayne) *materials scientist, researcher, transmission electron microscopist*

Zheng, Lingyi Albert *materials scientist, materials engineer, researcher*
Zhou, Dayong *research scientist*
Zhou, Shao Man *chemist, researcher*

# SOCIAL SCIENCE

## UNITED STATES

### ALABAMA

**Arab**
Black, Daniel Hugh *retired social studies educator*

**Auburn**
Correia, Christopher John *psychologist, educator*
Seroka, James Henry *social studies educator, academic administrator*

**Auburn University**
Beard, Thomas Randolph *economics professor*

**Birmingham**
Bradley, Laurence Alan *psychologist*
Cecil, Heather *psychologist, educator*
Freeman, Arthur Merrimon III *psychology professor, dean*
Nunn, Grady Harrison *retired political science professor*
Taub, Edward *psychology researcher*
Uswatte, Gitendra *psychology professor*

**Dothan**
Cotter, Melanie K. *psychologist, consultant*
Wright, Burton *sociologist*

**Duncanville**
Prescott, Perry Don *psychology professor, counselor*

**Florence**
Hansen, Vagn Keith *political science educator, college administrator*

**Hartselle**
Slate, Joe Hutson *psychologist, educator*

**Jacksonville**
Dunaway, Carolyn Bennett *retired sociology professor*

**Lillian**
Moyer, Kenneth Evan *psychologist, educator*

**Mobile**
Suess, James Francis *retired clinical psychologist*

**Montevallo**
Staik, Irene McVay *psychology professor*

**Montgomery**
Clark, Daniel Curtis *psychologist*
Wendzel, Robert Leroy *political science professor*

**Mount Vernon**
Ernst, Allen Christopher *psychologist, educator*

**Pell City**
Passey, George Edward *psychologist, educator*

**Troy**
Rinehart, James Forrest *international relations professor*

**Tuscaloosa**
Abdel-Ghany, Mohamed *economics professor*
Baklanoff, Eric Nicholas *economist, educator*
Cramer, Dale Lewis *retired economics professor*
Enders, Walter *economics professor*
Fish, Mary Martha *economics professor*
Marino, Carolyn *psychologist*

### ALASKA

**Anchorage**
Ippolito, Maria F. *psychologist, educator*
Obermeyer, Theresa Nangle *sociology educator*

**Fairbanks**
Irish, Joel David *anthropologist*

**Juneau**
Wessen, Douglas John *psychologist*

### ARIZONA

**Flagstaff**
McDonald, Craydon Dean *psychologist*
Pavlik, William Bruce *psychologist, educator*

**Fountain Hills**
Jan, George Pokung *political science professor*

**Gila Bend**
Barnes, William Wayne *geographer, writer*

**Gilbert**
Metcalf, Virgil Alonzo *economics professor*

**Mesa**
Ewing, Ann Tway *psychology professor*

**Phoenix**
Doss, Sylvia M. *psychologist, educator*
Huelster, Jeffery James *social studies educator*
LaPointe, Gregory Vincent *psychologist*
Masters, Jonathan Edward *clinical psychologist*
Newman, Donald Lynn *psychologist, consultant*
Peralta, Everett Figueroa *social sciences educator*

Roberts, Christopher Wayne *psychologist, educational consultant*
Thiel, Peter *social sciences educator*

**Scottsdale**
Baker, Edward Martin *engineering and industrial psychologist*
Levidow, Debra *psychologist*

**Sells**
Steere, Peter Lawson *archaeologist, historian*

**Tempe**
Gordon, Leonard *retired social sciences educator*
Hechter, Michael Norman *sociologist*
Johanson, Donald Carl *physical anthropologist*
Li, Wei *social sciences educator*
Myint, Soe Win *geographer, educator*
Pasqualetti, Martin J. *geography educator*
Prescott, Edward C. *economist, educator*
Rowley, Beverley Davies *sociologist*
Sackton, Frank Joseph *public affairs educator*
Simon, Sheldon Weiss *political science educator*
Weigend, Guido Gustav *geographer, educator*

**Tucson**
Allen, John Jeffrey Beck *psychology professor*
Axinn, George Harold *rural sociology educator*
Block, Michael Kent *economics professor, law educator, former government official*
Bootzin, Richard R. *psychology professor, researcher*
Breiger, Ronald Louis *social sciences educator*
Christie, Nancy Gail *psychology professor*
Clarke, James Weston *political science professor, writer*
Coan, Richard Welton *psychologist, educator*
Cota, Hortensia *social studies educator*
Larwood, Laurie *psychologist*
Reitan, Ralph Meldahl *clinical neuropsychologist, former educator*
Satten, Wayne Richard *psychologist*
Serido, Joyce *psychologist, researcher*
Smith, David Wayne *psychologist, educator*
Soren, David *archaeologist, educator, writer, filmmaker*
Stini, William Arthur *anthropologist, educator*
Thompson, Raymond Harris *retired anthropologist, educator*
Underwood, Jane Hainline Hammons *anthropologist, educator*

**Yuma**
Mendoza, San Juana Jane *school psychologist*
Norton, Dunbar Sutton *economic developer*

### ARKANSAS

**Conway**
Pearson, Brooks C. *geography educator, consultant*

**Fayetteville**
Andrew, Horowitz Warren *economics professor*
Costrell, Robert Michael *economist*
Mc Gimsey, Charles Robert III *anthropologist*
Mendez, Fabio *economist, researcher*

**Hot Springs**
Bailey, Robert E. *behaviorist, biologist, chemist, consultant*

**Huntsville**
Roach, Lonnie Calvin *social studies educator*

**Little Rock**
Briscoe, David Lloyd *academic sociologist, educator*
Clark, Shawn L. *psychologist, educator*
Kaza, Greg John *economist, educator*
Ledbetter, Calvin Reville, Jr., (Cal Ledbetter) *political science professor, legislator*

**North Little Rock**
Lierly, John A. *psychologist*

**Omaha**
Shaddox, Michael Scott *social studies educator*

**Pine Bluff**
Engle, Carole Ruth *aquaculture economics professor*
Hunt, Kami Mays *geography, educator*

**Powhatan**
Clark, Lloyd Wayne *social studies educator, minister*

### CALIFORNIA

**Alameda**
Troll, Lillian Ellman *psychologist, educator*

**Albany**
Marsh, Richard Charles *psychologist, educator, writer*

**Anaheim**
Gobar, Alfred Julian *retired economic consultant, educator*

**Arcata**
Bowker, Lee Harrington *sociologist, educator, writer*
Emenhiser, JeDon Allen *political science professor, dean*

**Azusa**
Miyake, Stephanie Ann *psychology professor, director, marriage and family therapist*

**Bakersfield**
Osterkamp, Dalene May *psychology educator, artist*

**Banning**
Gladden, Garnett Lee *psychologist, educator*

Saubel, Katherine Siva *Indian culture consultant, educator*

**Barstow**
Nyborg, Kenneth Wayne *retired social sciences educator, small business owner*

**Benicia**
Nelson, Elmer Kingsholm, Jr., (Kim Nelson) *political scientist, educator, writer, mediator, consultant*

**Berkeley**
Aggarwal, Vinod K. *political science professor*
Akerlof, George Arthur *economics professor*
Alhadeff, David Albert *economics professor*
Auerbach, Alan Jeffrey *economist, educator*
Auffhammer, Maximilian *economics professor*
Baumrind, Diana *research psychologist*
Bellah, Robert Neelly *sociologist, educator*
Brandes, Stanley Howard *anthropology educator, writer*
Cheit, Earl Frank *economist, educator*
Chetty, Raj *economics professor*
Collier, David *political science professor*
Deck, Richard Allen *political scientist, consultant, writer, volunteer*
Edelman, Lauren B. *sociologist, law educator*
Foster, George McClelland, Jr. *anthropologist, educator*
Hakansson, Nils Hemming *economist, educator*
Howell, Francis Clark *anthropologist, educator*
Jensen, Arthur Robert *psychologist, educator*
Joseph, Jay *psychologist, writer*
Joyce, Rosemary Alexandria *anthropology educator, department chairman*
Karabel, Jerome Bernard *sociologist, educator*
Keeler, Theodore Edwin *economics professor*
Kirch, Patrick Vinton *anthropology educator, archaeologist*
Lee, Ronald Demos *demographer, economist, educator*
Letiche, John Marion *economist, educator*
Luker, Kristin *sociology educator*
Maisel, Sherman Joseph *economist, educator*
Maslach, Christina *psychology professor*
McFadden, Daniel Little *economist, educator*
Muir, William Ker, Jr. *political science professor*
Nader, Laura *anthropologist, educator*
Norgaard, Richard Bruce *economist, educator, consultant*
Obstfeld, Maurice *economics professor, consultant*
Petiet, Carole Anne *psychologist*
Polsby, Nelson Woolf *political science professor*
Quigley, John Michael *economist, educator*
Rausser, Gordon C(lyde) *agricultural and resource economics educator*
Reich, Michael *economics professor*
Romer, Christina Duckworth *economist, educator*
Romer, David *economics professor*
Rosenzweig, Mark Richard *psychologist, neuroscientist, educator*
Scotchmer, Suzanne Andersen *economics professor*
Smolensky, Eugene *economics professor*
Sulloway, Frank Jones *social sciences educator, historian*
Varian, Hal Ronald *economics professor*
Wilensky, Harold L. *political science professor, sociologist, researcher*
Williamson, Oliver Eaton *economics professor, law professor*
Wolfinger, Raymond Edwin *retired political science professor*
Zysman, John Adler *political scientist, educator*

**Bradbury**
Clare, Kenneth Guilford *economist, consultant*

**Burlingame**
Schwantes, Robert Sidney *international relations executive*

**Carlsbad**
Fikes, Jay Courtney *anthropology educator, art dealer*

**Carmichael**
Hellmuth, William Frederick *economics professor*

**Carpinteria**
Schmidhauser, John Richard *political science professor*

**Carson**
Palmer, Beverly Blazey *psychologist, educator*

**Chico**
McNall, Scott Grant *sociologist, educator, academic administrator*
Smith, Valene Lucy *anthropology educator, educator*

**Chino Hills**
Fisher, Teresa Marie *psychologist, forensic specialist*

**Chula Vista**
Bauman, Noel James *psychologist*

**Claremont**
Borcherding, Thomas Earl *economist*
Burdekin, Richard Charles Keighley *economics professor*
Csikszentmihalyi, Mihaly *psychology professor*
Halpern, Diane F. *psychology educator, professional association executive*
Jaffa, Harry Victor *political philosophy educator emeritus*
Lasswell, Marcia Lee *psychologist, educator*
Leeb, Charles Samuel *psychologist*
Likens, James Dean *economics professor*
Lipman-Blumen, Jean *public policy and organizational behavior educator*
Morgan, Ann Marie *psychologist*
Rossum, Ralph Arthur *political science professor*

**Compton**
Drew, Sharon Lee *sociologist*
McKnight, Carl Phillip *psychologist*

**Concord**
Turnbull, Thomas Leigh *social studies educator, secondary school educator*

**Costa Mesa**
Escobar, Evelyn Ernestine *psychologist*

**Culver City**
Maltzman, Irving Myron *psychology professor*

**Danville**
Whalen, Thomas Earl *psychology professor*

**Davis**
Bower, John Richard Fenn *archaeologist, educator*
Bryant, Brenda K. *psychologist*
Cohen, Lawrence Edward *sociologist, educator, criminologist*
Eerkens, Jelmer W. *archaeologist, educator*
Flowers, Ross A. *psychologist*
Groth, Alexander Jacob *political science professor*
Knittel, Christopher Roland *economics professor, consultant*
Mason, William A(lvin) *psychologist, educator, researcher*
McHenry, Henry Malcolm *anthropologist, educator*
Musolf, Lloyd Daryl *political science professor, educational association administrator*
Owings, Donald Henry *psychologist, educator*
Quinzii, Martine *economics professor*
Rothchild, Donald Sylvester *political science professor*
Simonton, Dean Keith *psychology professor*
Skinner, G(eorge) William *anthropologist, educator*
Smith, Michael Peter *social sciences educator, researcher*
Sosnick, Stephen Howard *economics professor*
Spindler, George Dearborn *anthropologist, educator, writer*
Sumner, Daniel Alan *economist, educator*
Treguboff, William Jack *psychologist*
Wegge, Leon Louis François *retired economics educator*

**Del Mar**
Boynton, Robert Merrill *retired psychology professor*
Quinn, Katherine Sarah *psychologist*

**El Segundo**
Harwick, Wayne Thomas *economist*

**Escondido**
Damsbo, Ann Marie *psychologist*
Newsome, Melinda *anthropologist*

**Fairfax**
Kadoyama, Margaret *anthropology educator, management consultant*

**Fresno**
Battista, Matthew Antonio *psychologist, neuroscientist*
Dackawich, S. John *sociology educator, academic administrator*
Joseph, James William *political scientist, consultant, educator*
O'Connor, Kevin John *psychologist, educator*

**Fullerton**
Dolhinow, Rebecca *geographer, educator*
Kaisch, Kenneth Burton *psychologist, priest*
Parman, Susan Morrissett *anthropologist, writer*
Zettel, Laura A. *psychology professor, researcher*

**Garden Grove**
Greenslade, Cindy Louise *psychologist*

**Glendale**
Hadley, Paul Ervin *international relations educator*
Irwin, Dianne E. *psychology professor*
Shahshahani, Ahmad *economics professor*

**Granada Hills**
Aller, Wayne Kendall *psychologist, educator, computer company executive, property manager*

**Granite Bay**
Hartmann, Frederick Howard *retired political science professor*

**Hayward**
Keevy Manning, Gretchen Marie *psychologist, educator*
Staudohar, Paul David *economics professor, labor arbitrator*

**Hemet**
Levine, Elaine Prado *psychologist, music educator, artist, small business owner*

**Hermosa Beach**
Wickwire, Patricia Joanne Nellor *psychologist, educator*

**Highland**
Miller, R. Warburton *psychologist, farmer*

**Hollywood**
Fisher, Joel Marshall *political scientist, educator, wine consultant*

**Irvine**
Aigner, Dennis John *economics professor, consultant*
Burton, Michael Ladd *anthropology educator*
Danziger, James Norris *political science professor*
Feldman, Martha Sue *political scientist, educator*
Gallardo, Miguel E. *psychologist*
Haier, Richard J. *psychologist, researcher, psychology professor*
Hinderaker, Ivan *retired political science professor*
Huff, C(larence) Ronald *sociologist, criminologist, educator*
Lave, Charles Arthur *economics professor*
Lefebvre, Vladimir A. *psychologist, researcher*
Luce, R(obert) Duncan *psychology professor*

Margolis, Julius *economics professor*
Schonfeld, William Rost *political science professor*
Sperling, George *psychologist, educator*
White, Douglas Richie *anthropology educator*

**La Jolla**
Cain, William Stanley *experimental psychologist, educator, researcher*
Coburn, Marjorie Foster *psychologist, educator*
Cowhey, Peter Francis *international relations educator, consultant*
Farson, Richard Evans *psychologist*
Fowler, Raymond Dalton *psychologist, educator*
Granger, Clive William John (Sir Clive Granger) *retired economist*
Harris, Philip Robert *management and space psychologist*
Jacobson, Gary Charles *political science professor*
Kaplan, Robert Malcolm *health researcher, educator*
Lake, David A. *political science professor*
Machina, Mark Joseph *economist*
Mandler, George *psychologist, educator*
Mandler, Jean Matter *psychologist, educator*
Phelps, Jerry Scott *psychologist, educator*
Poole, Keith T. *political science professor*
Rauch, James E. *economics professor*
Schneider, Benjamin *psychology professor, consultant*
Scull, Andrew T. *sociologist, educator*
Starr, Ross Marc *economist, educator*

**Laguna Beach**
Bent, Alan Edward *political science professor*

**Lake Forest**
Smoot, Skipi Lundquist *psychologist*

**Lancaster**
Ellsworth, Richard German *psychologist*
Holley, Susan L. *psychologist*

**Larkspur**
Saxton, Lloyd *psychologist, writer*

**Loma Linda**
Vermeersch, David Adam *psychologist*

**Long Beach**
Baber, Walter Franklin *political science professor*
Hershberger, Scott Laurence *psychologist, educator, statistician, researcher*
Huyck, Charles Krishna *geographer, consultant*

**Los Angeles**
Aberbach, Joel David *political science professor, writer*
Allen, Walter Recharde *sociology educator*
Allen, William Richard *retired economist*
Álvarez, Rodolfo *sociology educator, consultant*
Anawalt, Patricia Rieff *anthropologist, researcher*
Aoki, Masanao *economics professor*
Bennett, Charles Franklin, Jr. *biogeographer, educator*
Brudnoy, ... Rogers *sociology educator*
Champagne, Duane Willard *sociology educator*
Clark, Burton Robert *sociologist, educator*
Darby, Michael Rucker *economist, educator*
Davis, Susie Francisca *psychologist*
Dekmejian, Richard Hrair *political science professor*
Demsetz, Harold *economist, educator*
Dr. Phil, (Phillip Calvin McGraw) *psychologist, television personality*
Eisenstein, Edward Milton *psychologist, physiologist, biophysicist, educator*
Ellickson, Bryan Carl *economics professor*
Emigh, Rebecca Jean *social sciences educator*
Fanselow, Michael Scott *psychology professor*
Forness, Steven Robert *educational psychologist*
Goldschmidt, Walter Rochs *anthropologist*
Goldstein, Michael Saul *sociologist*
Harberger, Arnold Carl *economist, educator*
Intriligator, Michael David *economist, educator*
Klein, Benjamin *economics professor, consultant*
La Force, James Clayburn, Jr. *economist, educator*
Lear, Lyn Davis *psychologist*
Levine, Robert Arthur *economist, educator, policy writer*
Malamuth, Neil Moshe *psychology and communication educator*
Mays, Vickie M. *psychology professor*
Montoya, Velma *economist, consultant*
Morgner, Aurelius *economist, educator*
Nelson, Howard Joseph *geographer, educator*
Nuechterlein, Keith H. *psychology professor*
O'Neil, Harold Francis *psychologist, educator*
Raven, Bertram H(erbert) *psychology professor*
Sears, David O'Keefe *psychology professor*
Shearer, Derek Nocross *political science professor, diplomat, academic administrator*
Shneidman, Edwin S. *psychologist, thanatologist*
Sklar, Richard Lawrence *political science professor*
Sood, Neeraj *economist, researcher*
Stanish, Charles *anthropologist, educator*
Strack, Stephen Naylor *psychologist*
Taylor, Shelley E. *psychology researcher, educator*
Telles, Cynthia Ann *psychologist*
Thompson, Earl Albert *economics professor*
Thompson, Richard Frederick *psychologist, educator, neuroscientist*
Totten, George Oakley III *political science professor*
Turner, Ralph Herbert *sociologist, educator*
Watson, Sharon Gitin *psychologist*
Wittrock, Merlin Carl *educational psychologist*
Wong, James Bok *economist, chemical engineer, technologist, consultant*
Wood, Nancy Elizabeth *psychologist, educator*
Zeitlin, Maurice *sociology educator*

**Los Gatos**
Ohanjanian, Ruzanna *clinical psychologist*

**Madera**
Glynn, James A. *sociology educator, writer*

**Malibu**
Moore, Stanley Wayne *political science professor*

**Menlo Park**
Clair, Theodore Nat *educational psychologist*
Sullivan, Nancy Elizabeth *pediatric neuropsychologist*
Vane, Sylvia Brakke *anthropologist, writer*

**Mill Valley**
Harner, Michael James *anthropologist, educator*

**Millbrae**
Thomlinson, Ralph *demographer, educator*

**Modesto**
Berry, John Charles *psychologist, academic administrator*

**Moffett Field**
Cohen, Malcolm Martin *psychologist, researcher*

**Montclair**
Duvall, Michele Denise *school psychologist, marriage and family therapist*

**Monterey**
Reese, William Albert III *clinical neuropsychologist*

**Monterey Park**
Amezcua, Charlie Anthony *social science counselor*

**Newport Beach**
Allison, M(arvin) Lawrence (Larry Allison) *psychologist*
Whittemore, Paul Baxter *psychologist*

**North Hollywood**
Totton, Carl Allen, II, *psychologist*

**Northridge**
Mitchell, Rie Rogers *psychologist, counselor, educator*

**Novato**
Criswell, Eleanor Camp *psychologist*

**Oakland**
De Vos, George Alphonse *psychologist, anthropologist*
Farrell, Kenneth Royden *economist*
Neeley, Beverly Evon *sociologist, consultant*
Theroux, David Jon *economist, educator, research and development company executive*

**Oceanside**
Hertweck, E. Romayne *psychology professor*
Powers, Sonia Nodle *psychologist, consultant*

**Orange**
Booth, Donald Richard *economist, educator*
Hunt, Janice Susan *psychologist*
Stevens, Cherita Wyman *social sciences educator, writer*

**Orinda**
Amoroso, Richard Louis *psychologist, educator*

**Pacific Palisades**
Griver, Jeanette A. *psychologist, consultant*
Hoffenberg, Marvin *retired political science professor*
Katz, George Gershon *psychologist*
Longaker, Richard Pancoast *retired political science professor*

**Palm Desert**
Bantz, Jody Lenore *psychologist*

**Palo Alto**
Beutler, Larry Edward *psychologist, educator*
Calvin, Allen David *psychologist, educator*
Flanagan, Robert Joseph *economics professor*
Hammett, Benjamin Cowles *psychologist*
Moos, Rudolf H. *psychologist, researcher*
Scitovsky, Anne Aickelin *economist, researcher*
Sherlock, Phyllis Krafft *psychologist*

**Palos Verdes Estates**
DiPaul, Christopher *psychologist*

**Pasadena**
Atkins, David Charles *psychology professor*
Horner, Althea Jane *psychologist*
Ledyard, John Odell *economics professor, consultant*
Munger, Edwin Stanton *political geography educator*
Scudder, Thayer *anthropologist, educator*

**Patton**
Ermshar, Annette Lorene *psychologist, educator*

**Pleasant Hill**
Richard, Robert Carter *psychologist*

**Pomona**
Garrity, Rodman Fox *psychologist, educator*

**Portola Valley**
March, James Gardner *social sciences educator*
Ward, Robert Edward *retired political science professor, academic administrator*

**Rancho Santa Fe**
Laidlaw, Pamela Nielsen *psychologist*

**Rancho Santa Margarita**
Lawson, Thomas Cheney *fraud examiner*

**Redding**
Skropanic, Jessica T. *sociologist, educator*

**Redlands**
Pedace, Roberto L. *economics professor*
Zeller, Anchard Frederic *retired psychologist*

**Redondo Beach**
McWilliams, Margaret Ann *home economist, educator, writer*

**Riverside**
Calfee, Robert Chilton *psychologist, educator*
Carpenter, Mark Warren *social sciences educator*
Gonzalez-Rivera, Gloria *economics professor*
Griffin, Keith Broadwell *retired economics professor*
Kordus, Marcella Natasha *psychologist*
Petrinovich, Lewis Franklin *psychologist, educator*
Rosenthal, Robert *psychology professor*
Turk, Austin Theodore *social studies educator*

**Rohnert Park**
Byrne, Noel Thomas *sociologist, educator*
Poe, William Clay *archaeologist, educator*
Steiner, John Michael *sociologist, educator*

**Roseville**
Larson, Kenneth Leroy, Jr. *psychologist, educator*

**Sacramento**
Behrman, Bruce Ward *social sciences educator*
Bruce, Thomas Edward *thanatologist, psychology professor*
Covin, David L. *retired political science professor*
Majesty, Melvin Sidney *psychologist, consultant*
Newland, Chester Albert *public administration educator*
Post, August Alan *retired economist, artist*
Sherwood, Robert Petersen *retired social sciences educator*
Yang, Yung Y. *economics professor, consultant*

**San Diego**
Clague, Christopher K(arran) *economics professor*
Edwards, Darrel *psychologist*
Emerick, Robert Earl *retired sociologist, educator*
Heer, David Macalpine *sociology educator*
Hoston, Germaine Annette *political science professor*
Lane, Sylvia *economist, educator*
Lewis, Shirley Jeane *retired psychologist*
Scott, Richard Malachi *psychologist*
Shedroff, Sharon D. *psychologist, researcher, anthropologist, consultant*
Sheldon-Morris, Tiffini Anne *clinical psychologist, consultative examiner*
Stoessinger, John George *political science professor*
Tsou, Ming-Hsiang *geographer, educator*
Twenge, Jean M. *psychology professor, writer*
Weeks, John Robert *geographer, social studies educator*

**San Francisco**
Chase, Alexandra Nin *psychologist, writer*
Cirese, Robert Charles *economist, real estate consultant*
de Vries, Brian *gerontologist, researcher*
Edelstein, Michael R. *psychologist, writer*
Estes, Carroll Lynn *sociologist, educator*
Folkman, Susan *research psychologist*
Fox, Patrick John *sociology educator*
Gamson, Joshua Paul *sociology educator, writer*
Hudson, Darril *political scientist, educator*
Jamison, Dean Tecumseh *economist*
Krippner, Stanley Curtis *psychologist*
Marston, Michael *economist, consultant*
Murphy, Sheigla Brighid *sociologist, researcher*
Ratum, Cecilia Bangloy *retired psychologist*
Rice, Dorothy Pechman (Mrs. John Donald Rice) *medical economist*
Rubin, Seth Isaiah *psychologist*
Samuelson, Kristin Weaver *clinical psychologist, educator*
Satre, Derek Davies *psychologist, researcher*
Sedway, Lynn Massel *real estate economist*
Soh, Chunghee Sarah *anthropology educator*
van den Daele, Leland Douglas *psychology professor, psychological measurement company executive*

**San Jose**
Braden, Jeffery P. *psychology educator*
Cedolini, Anthony John *psychologist*
DiGiacomo, Richard *social studies educator, writer*
McDowell, Jennifer *sociologist, composer, playwright*
Shao, Otis Hung-I *retired political science professor*
Voth, Alden H. *political science professor*

**San Luis Obispo**
Fairbanks, William Louis, II, *anthropologist, educator*
Fisher, Eric O'Neill *economist*

**San Marino**
Martin, Olivia Jean *social studies educator*

**San Mateo**
Watters, Ann Oliva *psychologist, educator*

**San Ramon**
Kalicki, Jan H. *economist, political scientist, energy executive*

**Santa Barbara**
Aswani, Shankar (Shankar Aswani-Canela) *anthropologist, educator*
Bohn, Henning *economist, educator*
Comanor, William S. *economist, educator*
Cotton, John Whealdon *psychology professor*
Davidson, Roger H(arry) *political science professor*
Erasmus, Charles John *anthropologist, educator*
Goodchild, Michael Frank *geographer, educator*
Jochim, Michael Allan *archaeologist*
Kendler, Howard H(arvard) *psychologist, educator*
Kuhn, Peter Joseph *economics professor, consultant*
Mack, Judith Cole Schrim *retired political scientist*
Mayer, Richard Edwin *psychology professor*
Sherman, Alan Robert *psychologist, educator*
Weidemann, Celia Jean *social sciences educator, management consultant, financial consultant*

**Santa Clara**
Field, Alexander James *economics professor, dean*

**Santa Clarita**
Walker, Robert F. *social studies educator*

**Santa Cruz**
Chemers, Martin M. *psychologist, educator*
Cheung, Yin-Wong *economics professor*
Child, Frank Clayton *economist, educator*
Eischen, Donald F. *psychologist, educator, writer*
Langhout, Regina D. *psychology professor*
Pettigrew, Thomas Fraser *social psychologist, educator*
Pratkanis, Anthony Richard *social psychologist, educator*
Resneck-Sannes, Helen *psychologist*
Roby, Pamela Ann *sociologist, educator*
Smith, M(ahlon) Brewster *retired psychologist, educator*

**Santa Monica**
Ellickson, Phyllis Lynn *political scientist*
Friedman, Monroe *psychologist, educator, consultant, editor, writer*
Gray, Laura B. *psychology professor, counselor*
Kurtzman, Joel Allan *economist*
Maglione, Margaret A. *public policy analyst, researcher*
Moskos, Charles C. *social studies educator*
Reville, Robert T. *economist*
Smith, James Patrick *economist*
Wolf, Charles, Jr. *economist, educator*

**Santa Rosa**
Jandrey, Becky Lee *psychologist*

**Seaside**
Mendoza, Ruben G. *anthropologist, educator, archaeologist*

**Somerset**
Carr, Les *psychologist, educator*

**Sonora**
Clarke, Paula Katherine *anthropologist, researcher, social studies educator*

**South Pasadena**
Martin, Richard D. *social studies educator*

**Stanford**
Anderson, Martin Carl *economist*
Arrow, Kenneth Joseph *economist, educator*
Bandura, Albert *psychologist, educator*
Bendor, Jonathan *economics professor, researcher*
Benkard, Charles Lanier *economics professor*
Bobo, Lawrence D. *sociologist*
Brody, Richard Alan *political science educator, researcher*
Bulow, Jeremy Israel *economist*
Bunzel, John Harvey *political science professor*
Damon, William Van Buren *developmental psychologist, educator, writer*
David, Paul Allan *economist, economic historian*
Diamond, Larry *political scientist*
Enthoven, Alain Charles *economist, educator*
Fetterman, David Mark *anthropologist, educator*
Friedman, Milton *retired economist*
Fuchs, Victor Robert *economist, educator*
Gage, Nathaniel Lees *retired psychologist, retired educator*
Greif, Avner *economics professor*
Hall, Robert Ernest *economics professor*
Hansen, Peter Reinhard *economics professor*
Hickman, Bert George, Jr. *economist, educator*
Howell, James Edwin *economist, educator*
Huntington, Hillard Griswold *economist*
Inkeles, Alex *sociology educator*
Krumboltz, John Dwight *psychologist, educator*
Kurz, Mordecai *economics professor*
Laitin, David Dennis *political science professor*
Lepper, Mark Roger *psychologist, educator*
Lewis, John Wilson *political science professor*
Maccoby, Eleanor Emmons *psychology professor*
Martin, Joanne *social sciences educator*
Mc Lure, Charles E., Jr. *economist, consultant*
Monin, Benoît *psychology professor*
Moore, Thomas Gale *economist, educator*
Noll, Roger Gordon *economist, educator*
Oyer, Paul *economist*
Pearson, Scott Roberts *retired economics professor*
Ricardo-Campbell, Rita *economist, educator*
Roberts, Donald John *economics professor, business professor, consultant*
Scott, W(illiam) Richard *sociology educator*
Shultz, George Pratt *economics professor, former secretary of state*
Sowell, Thomas *economist, syndicated columnist*
Van Horne, James Carter *economist, educator*
Wolak, Frank Anthony *economics professor*
Zimbardo, Philip George *psychologist, educator, writer*
Zitzewitz, Eric *economics professor*

**Stockton**
Roll, Renée F. *retired psychologist*

**Tiburon**
Barron-Druckrey, Eleanor *psychologist*

**Turlock**
Ahlem, Lloyd Harold *psychologist*

**Union City**
Feinberg, Richard Alan *psychologist*

**Valencia**
Jones, Christopher Charles *psychologist*

**Ventura**
Bradley, Jerry Alan *psychologist, consultant*
Naurath, David Allison *engineering psychologist, researcher*

**Walnut Creek**
Keith, Bruce Edgar *political scientist, genealogist*

**Watsonville**
West, Karrie L. *school psychologist*

**Whittier**
Hearn, Kathleen E. *psychologist*

## COLORADO

**Arvada**
Yamamoto, Kaoru *retired psychology professor*

**Aspen**
Manosevitz, Martin *psychologist*

**Aurora**
Hughes, Brad, Jr. *economist*
Olson, Allison W. *social studies educator*

**Bethune**
Williams, Donna M. *social studies educator*

**Boulder**
Adler, Patricia Ann *sociologist, educator*
Beer, Francis Anthony *political science professor*
Bourne, Lyle Eugene, Jr. *psychology professor*
Churchill, Ward L. *social sciences educator, advocate*
Greenberg, Edward Seymour *political science professor*
Irvine, Leslie *sociologist, educator*
Jessor, Richard *behavioral science educator, director, psychologist, educator*
Kintsch, Walter *retired psychology professor*
McDonald, Dorcas *psychologist, educator*
Menken, Jane Ava *demographer, educator*
Schneider, Vivian I. *psychologist, researcher*
Walker, Deward Edgar, Jr. *anthropologist, educator*
White, Gilbert F. (Gilbert Fowler White) *geographer, educator*

**Broomfield**
Potter, James Michael *archaeologist, consultant*

**Centennial**
Milliken, John Gordon *research economist*

**Colorado Springs**
Brooks, Glenn Ellis *political science professor, educational association administrator*
Farrer, Claire Anne Rafferty *anthropologist, educator*
Johnson, Daniel Kent Neil *economist, educator*
Saviano, Jeffrey D. *criminologist, consultant*
Standing Bear, Zugguelgeres Galafach *criminologist, educator, forensic specialist*
Vandeputte, Dixie Dianne *psychologist, educator*

**Denver**
Adelman, Jonathan Reuben *political science professor*
Axelrod, Evan M. *psychologist, educator*
Conger, John Janeway *psychologist, educator*
Curl, Layton Seth *psychologist, consultant, educator*
Hoffman, Elizabeth *economics professor*
Nelson, Sarah Milledge *archaeology educator*
Snyder, Charles Royce *sociologist, educator*
Winters, Richard Allen *mineral economist*
Zimet, Carl Norman *psychologist, educator*

**Dolores**
Kreyche, Gerald Francis *retired philosophy educator*

**Durango**
Jones, Janet Lee *psychologist, educator*
Zeller, Christopher Lee *preservation archaeologist*

**Fort Collins**
Bennett, Thomas LeRoy, Jr. *clinical neuropsychology educator*
Kang, Soo K. *social sciences educator*
Kogan, Lori R. *psychology professor, consultant*
Sedei Rodden, Pamela Jean *psychologist, director*
Suinn, Richard Michael *psychologist*
Thilmany, Dawn Denise *economist, educator*

**Fountain**
Hazlett, David Lawrence *social studies educator*

**Golden**
Petrick, Alfred, Jr. *economist, educator*

**Grand Junction**
Bacon, Phillip *geographer, author, consultant*
Morton, Louis George *retired social sciences educator*

**Greeley**
McDaniel, Bruce Alan *economist, educator*

**Highlands Ranch**
Hendrick, Hal Wilmans *human factors educator*

**Lakewood**
Kulkarni, Kishore Ganesh *economics professor, consultant*

**Limon**
Richards, Ann Adair *psychologist*

**Longmont**
Watkins, John Goodrich *psychologist, educator*

**Loveland**
Ahmann, John Stanley *retired psychologist*
Schilling, Arleen Marie *social studies educator*
Walker, Laurie Shannon *psychologist, counselor*

**Pine**
Jones, David Milton *economist, educator*

## CONNECTICUT

**Bridgeport**
Maloney, Maureen Murphy *social sciences educator*

**Brookfield**
Lock, Timothy G. *psychologist*
Stern, Michael Lawrence *psychologist, educator*

**Chester**
Hilsman, Roger *political scientist, educator*

**Cromwell**
Günther-Stirn, Dagmar Dorothea *retired social sciences educator*

**Danbury**
Tolor, Alexander *psychologist, educator*

**Fairfield**
Kleine, Herman *economist*
Loris, Michelle *psychologist, educator*
Morehouse, Sarah McCally *retired political science professor*

**Farmington**
Ledgerwood, David M. *psychologist, researcher*

**Glastonbury**
Bollinger, Lori *economist*

**Greenwich**
Fleming, Martin *economist, strategist*
Grossman, Sanford Jay *former economics professor, financial consultant*

**Guilford**
Chatt, Allen Barrett *psychologist, neuroscientist*
Shelton, Darlene *psychologist, consultant*

**Hartford**
Ancona, Cara B. *psychologist, educator*
Gastmann, Albert Lodewijk *retired political science professor, retired language professor, writer*
Gunderson, Gerald Axel *economics professor*

**Higganum**
de Brigard, Emilie *anthropologist, consultant*

**Lebanon**
Brodie, Kevin Stuart *social studies educator*

**Manchester**
Fitzgerald, Mary Irene *retired school psychologist*
Jimiena, Paul *futurist, writer*

**Meriden**
Losada-Zarate, Gloria *psychologist*

**Middlebury**
Phillips, Walter Mills III *psychologist, educator*

**Middletown**
Bonin, John Paul *economics professor*
Harris, Dale Benner *psychologist, educator*
Lovell, Michael C. *economics professor*
Miller, Richard Alan *economist, educator*
Scheibe, Karl Edward *psychology professor*
Wasch, William Karl *gerontologist, consultant*

**Milford**
Boyer, Carolyn Merwin *school psychologist*
Schwartz, Richard Edward Derecktor *retired sociologist, educator*

**Moosup**
Perkins- Banas, Melissa Veronica *psychologist*

**Naugatuck**
Suscovich, David J. *neuropsychologist, marriage and family therapist*

**New Haven**
Andrews, Donald Wilfrid Kao *economics professor*
Applewhite, Harriet Branson *political science educator*
Bell, Wendell *sociologist, educator, futurist*
Bergemann, Dirk Paul Hans *economics professor*
Blatt, Sidney Jules *psychology professor, psychoanalyst, investigator*
Bracken, Paul *political science professor*
Brownell, Kelly David *psychologist, educator*
Chevalier, Judith A. *economics professor, finance professor*
Coe, Michael Douglas *retired anthropologist*
Conklin, Harold Colyer *anthropologist, educator*
Crakes, Gary Michael *economics professor*
Ember, Carol R. *anthropology educator, writer*
Ember, Melvin Lawrence *anthropologist, educator*
Erikson, Kai *sociologist, educator*
Errington, James Joseph *anthropology educator*
Evenson, Robert Eugene *economist, educator*
Fair, Ray Clarence *economics professor*
Green, Donald Philip *political scientist, educator*
Heninger, George Robert *psychology professor, researcher*
Marks, Lawrence Edward *psychologist, educator*
Marmor, Theodore Richard *political science professor*
Mayhew, David Raymond *political science professor*
McGuire, William James *psychologist, educator*
Mostaghimi, Mehdi *economist, educator*
Phillips, Peter Charles Bonest *economist, educator, researcher*
Pospisil, Leopold Jaroslav *anthropologist, educator, law educator*
Ranis, Gustav *economist, educator*
Roemer, John E. *economics educator*
Russett, Bruce Martin *political science professor*
Schowalter, John Erwin *child and adolescent psychiatry educator*
Schultz, T. Paul *economics professor*
Shiller, Robert James *economist, educator*
Shubik, Martin *economics professor*
Skowronek, Stephen Lee *political scientist, educator*

Stevens, Joseph Charles *psychology professor*
Torgler, Benno *economist, researcher*
Wagner, Allan Ray *psychology professor*
Wynn, Karen *psychologist, educator, researcher*
Zigler, Edward Frank *psychologist, educator*

**New London**
Fainstein, Norman *sociology professor, former academic administrator*

**North Haven**
Dahl, Robert Alan *political science professor*
Mahl, George Franklin *retired psychologist, educator*

**Norwalk**
Brown, William Terrel *psychology professor, educational consultant*
Fischman, Eric D. *psychologist, special education educator*

**Old Lyme**
Johnson, James Myron *psychologist, educator*

**Old Saybrook**
Hoffman, Ellendale McCollam *psychologist, counselor*

**Sharon**
Mesniaeff, Gregory *economist, securities analyst*

**Southbury**
Atwood, Edward Charles *economist, educator*

**Stamford**
Robins, Robert Sidwar *political science professor, department chairman*
Teeters, Nancy Hays *economist, director*

**Storrs**
Kiene, Susan Maria *psychologist*

**Storrs Mansfield**
Katz, Leonard *psychology professor, researcher*

**Stratford**
LaDonna, Frank *psychologist*

**Voluntown**
Thevenet, Patricia Confrey *social studies educator*

**Wallingford**
Cline, John Carroll *psychologist*

**Waterford**
Hinkle, Janet *psychologist*

**West Hartford**
Gitterman, Alex *social work educator*

**Westport**
Manley, John Frederick *political scientist, educator*

**Willimantic**
Escoto, Carlos Aurelio *psychology professor, researcher*
Free, Rhona Campbell *economics professor*

## DELAWARE

**Greenville**
Reeder, Charles Benton *retired economic consultant*

**Lewes**
DeBastiani, Roberta *school psychologist*

**Newark**
Bilinsky, Yaroslav *political scientist*
Butkiewicz, James Leon *economics professor, researcher, consultant*
DiRenzo, Gordon James *sociologist, psychologist, educator*
Levia, Delphis F., Jr. *geography professor*
Pika, Joseph A. *political scientist, educator, educational association administrator*
Tannian, Francis Xavier *economist, educator*

**Wilmington**
Genetta, Ann H. *psychologist, neuropsychologist*
Kneavel, Thomas Charles, Jr. *psychologist, educator*

## DISTRICT OF COLUMBIA

**Washington**
Aaron, Henry J. *economist*
Aaron, Henry Jacob *economics professor*
Aguirre, Maria Sophia *economics professor*
Albanese, Jay Samuel *criminologist, educator*
Arend, Anthony Clark *social studies educator, academic administrator*
Aring, Monika Kosmahl *policy economist, consultant, researcher*
Åslund, Anders *economist*
Baer, Michael Alan *political scientist, educator*
Banzhaf, Henry Spencer *economist*
Bartlett, Bruce Reeves *economist, columnist*
Bayyan, Aquil F. *social studies educator, basketball coach*
Becker, Mary Louise *political scientist*
Bergmann, Barbara Rose *economics professor*
Besen, Stanley Martin *economist*
Biggs, Jeffrey Robert *political scientist*
Bolino, August Constantino *economics professor*
Bonato, Leo *economist*
Bramson, Leon *social scientist, educator*
Brimmer, Andrew Felton *economist, consultant*
Bruck, Nicholas *economist, educator*
Buckley, Jacquelyn Anastasia *educational psychologist, researcher*
Burk, Martha Gertrude *political psychologist*
Burtless, Gary Thomas *economist, consultant*
Cain, Bruce Edward *political science professor, consultant*

Calder, Kent Eyring *political science professor, federal agency administrator*
Carpenter, Ted Galen *political scientist*
Cavanagh, John Henry *political economist*
Cline, Eric H. *archaeologist, anthropologist, classicist, educator*
Cline, William Richard *economist, educator*
Craig, John Tucker *economist, consultant*
Crocker, William Henry *ethnologist, researcher*
Danziger, Raphael *political scientist, researcher*
David, Martin Heidenhain *economics professor*
Davison, Carole Sawyer *retired economist*
Day, Lincoln Hubert *demographer, educator*
Dickens, William Theodore *economic researcher*
Dillon, Wilton Sterling *anthropologist, foundation administrator*
Doran, Charles Francis *political scientist, consultant*
Downs, Anthony *economist, consultant, real estate consultant*
Eads, George Curtis *economic consultant*
Eduardo, Ley *economist*
English, Richard Allyn *sociologist, educator*
Epstein, Gerald Lewis *technology and security policy analyst*
Ershler, William Baldwin *biogerontologist, educator*
Etzioni, Amitai *sociologist, educator*
Feshbach, Murray *demographer, educator*
Friedman, Robert Sidney *political science professor*
Furchtgott-Roth, Harold Wilkes *economist, consultant*
Galston, William Arthur *political scientist, educator*
Gapen, Michael T. *economist*
Gillingham, Robert Fenton *economist, consultant*
Gordon, Lincoln *political economist*
Grapin, Jacqueline G. *economist*
Gross, Leon Jay *psychometrician*
Gubser, Peter Anton *political scientist, writer, educator*
Halperin, Morton H. *political scientist*
Halperin, Samuel *education and training policy analyst*
Helms, Robert Brake *economist, science administrator*
Hess, Stephen *political scientist, writer*
Hillsman, Sally T. *sociologist*
Hudnut, William Herbert III *political scientist*
Hudson, Michael Craig *political science professor*
Hufbauer, Gary Clyde *economist, lawyer, educator*
Hughes, Kent Higgon *economist*
Jacobson, Allen Howard *economist*
Jaspersen, Frederick Zarr *economist*
Joyner, Christopher Clayton *international relations educator*
Kaufman, Leonard H. *psychologist*
Kemp, Geoffrey Thomas Howard *political scientist, consultant*
Kendrick, John Whitefield *economist, educator, consultant*
Kirkpatrick, Jeane Duane Jordan *political scientist, federal official*
Kitchen, John Howard *economist*
Kravis, Marie-Josee Drouin *economist*
Krulfeld, Ruth Marilyn *anthropologist, educator*
Kuh, Charlotte Virginia *economist*
Kushmeider, Rose Marie *economist*
Kuzio, Taras *political scientist*
Kvint, Vladimir Lev *economist, mining engineer, finance educator*
Kybal, Elba Gómez del Rey *economist, not-for-profit developer*
Laden, Ben Ellis *economist, writer*
Lardy, Nicholas Richard *economist, educator*
LaRouche, Lyndon H., Jr. *economist*
Leahy, Arthur Stephen *economist, educator*
LeoGrande, William Mark *political science professor, writer*
Levinson, Nanette Segal *international relations educator*
Lieber, Robert James *political science professor*
Makalou, Oumar *economic advisor*
Manchester, Paul Brunson *economist*
Mann, Thomas Edward *political scientist*
Marcuss, Rosemary Daly *economist*
Martin, Linda Gaye *demographer, economist*
Martinez, Herminia S. *economist, banker*
McMillion, Charles Wayne *economist, educator, consultant*
Meggers, Betty Jane *anthropologist, researcher*
Mellor, John Williams *economist, consultant*
Millar, James Robert *economist, educator, university official*
Miller, James Clifford III *economist*
Miller, Margery *psychologist, educator, speech pathology/audiology services professional, mental health services professional*
Minarik, Joseph John *economist, researcher*
Mistral, Jacques *economist*
Murray, Charles Alan *social scientist*
Mussa, Michael L. *economist, educator*
Nagorski, Zygmunt *political scientist, writer*
Nash, John Davidson Jr. *economist*
Nelsen, Hart Michael *sociologist, educator*
Niskanen, William Arthur, Jr. *economist, think-tank executive*
Noland, Marcus *economist, educator*
Norquist, Grover Glenn *economist*
O'Connor, Karen *political science professor, researcher, writer*
Orszag, Jonathan Marc *economist, consultant*
Orszag, Peter Richard *economist*
Ortner, Donald J. *biological anthropologist, educator*
Osicka, Teresa D. *health economist, consultant*
Palomares, Ronald S. *psychologist*
Pasurka, Carl A., Jr. *economist*
Perito, Robert Michael *political scientist*
Perry, George Lewis *research economist, consultant*
Phillips, Karen Borlaug *economist, rail transportation executive*
Pickenpaugh, Thomas Edward *archaeologist, anthropologist*
Popkin, Joel *economist, consultant*
Prestowitz, Clyde Vincent, Jr. *economist, researcher*
Quintanilla-Villanueva, Rosalinda *economist*
Radner, Roy *economist, educator, researcher*

Randall, Robert L(ee) *ecological economist*
Raut, Lakshmi Kanta *economist, educator*
Reich, Bernard *political science professor*
Relyea, Harold Clarence *political scientist, writer*
Richardson, Paul Joseph *economist*
Rivlin, Alice Mitchell *economics professor, former federal official*
Roberts, Markley *economist, educator*
Rodriguez, Rita Maria *economist*
Rosenau, James Nathan *political scientist, educator, writer*
Rosenberg, Joel Barry *government economist*
Rupp, Kalman *economist*
Ryn, Claes Gösta *political science professor*
Sawhill, Isabel Van Devanter *economist*
Scheffman, David Theodore *economist, management educator, consultant*
Schley, Wayne Arthur *political scientist, consultant*
Schneider, Mark *political science professor*
Schorr, Lisbeth Bamberger *sociologist, researcher*
Scott, Charneta Claudetta *psychologist, educator*
Scrivner, Ellen M. *psychologist*
Seifert, Jeffrey W. *political scientist, researcher*
Shambaugh, David Leigh *political scientist, educator, writer*
Shivakumar, Sujai *political economist, policy advisor*
Snyder, Jed C. *foreign affairs specialist*
Solomon, Elinor Harris *economics professor*
Steinberg, David Isaac *social sciences educator, consultant*
Stelzer, Irwin Mark *economist*
Stent, Angela E. *political scientist, educator, director*
Stephenson, Sherry Madeline *trade economist*
Struelens, Michel Maurice Joseph Georges *political science professor, consultant*
Strum, Philippa *political science professor, researcher*
Sunley, Emil McKee *economist*
Tenet, George John *diplomacy professor, former CIA director*
Tharp, Roland George *psychology professor*
Tucker, Jonathan Brin *political scientist*
Turner, John Andrew *economist*
Vajda, Judith Parsons *psychology professor*
Vamvakidis, Athanasios *economist*
Vigfusson, Robert John *economist*
Vita, Michael *economist*
Weicher, John Charles *economist, research director*
Weinhold, Linda Lillian *psychologist, researcher*
Weintraub, Sidney *economist, educator*
Whitehurst, Grover Jay *psychologist, educator, federal official*
Wilensky, Gail Roggin *economist, researcher*
Willner, Ann Ruth *political scientist, educator*
Willner, Dorothy *anthropologist, educator*
Wunderlich, Gooloo S. *demographer, statistician, policy analyst*

## FLORIDA

**Boca Raton**
Broadfield, Douglas *biological anthropologist, researcher*
Hung, Chao-shun *economics professor, researcher*
Shalom, Galit *psychologist*

**Bradenton**
Castro, Valentino *psychologist, counseling administrator*

**Cape Coral**
Shuman, Carolyn Rae (Thorburn) *psychologist, columnist, writer, nurse*

**Clearwater**
Luginbuehl, Marsha L. *psychologist*
Peterson, James Robert *engineering psychologist*

**Coral Gables**
Frohock, Fred Manuel *political science professor*
Humphries, Joan Ropes *psychologist, educator*
Nijman, Jan *geographer, educator*

**Deerfield Beach**
Panitz, Daniel R. *psychologist, consultant*

**Deland**
Bailey, T. Wayne *political science professor*

**Delray Beach**
Dye, Thomas Roy *political science professor*
Levinson, Harry *psychologist, educator*
Make, Isabel Rose *multicultural studies educator, adult education educator, small business owner*

**Dunedin**
O'Dea, J. David *psychologist, educator*

**Dunnellon**
Dixon, W(illiam) Robert *retired psychologist*

**Estero**
Routh, Donald K. (Donald Kent Routh) *psychologist, educator*

**Fort Lauderdale**
Azrin, Nathan Harold *psychologist, educator*
Collins, Ronald William *psychologist, educator*
Gagnon Blodgett, Michelle Dawn *psychologist*
McCluskey, Neil Gerard *gerontologist, educator, literary agent*

**Fort Myers**
Sprinkel, Beryl Wayne *economist, consultant*

**Gainesville**
Albarracín, Dolores *psychologist, educator*
Brown, William Samuel, Jr. *communication sciences and disorders educator*
Cohen, Joel *social sciences educator, consultant*
Dewsbury, Donald Allen *psychologist*
Grove, David D. *anthropology professor*
Harrison, Faye Venetia *anthropologist, educator, writer*
Milanich, Jerald Thomas *archaeologist, curator*

Moore, John Hartwell *anthropology educator, consultant*
Moss, Charles Britt *economics educator*
Opdyke, Neil Donald *geology educator*
Shih, Chuan-kang *anthropologist*
Teitelbaum, Philip *psychologist*
von Mering, Otto Oswald *anthropology educator*
Wagner, Eric Armin *retired sociologist*
Wass, Hannelore Lina *educational psychology educator*

**Hollywood**
Foreman, Edwin Francis *economist, real estate broker*

**Homestead**
Armenteros, Eduardo Carlos *psychologist, educator*

**Jacksonville**
Godfrey, John Munro *economic consultant*
Montgomery, Suzanne Howard *psychologist*

**Key Biscayne**
Reynolds, Paul Davidson *social sciences educator*

**Lake Mary**
Bowden, Helen Frances *psychologist*

**Lakeland**
Masters, Sharon Kay *sociologist, educator*
Schultz, David Franklin *psychologist*

**Longboat Key**
Tata, Robert Joseph *retired geographer, educator*

**Longwood**
Calderón, Jaime A. *psychologist, educator*

**Lutz**
Ellis, Leslie Elaine *psychologist*

**Maitland**
Von Hilsheimer, George Edwin III *neuropsychologist*

**Miami**
Arango, Penelope Corey *psychologist, consultant*
Armstrong, F. Daniel *psychologist, educator*
Bravo, Irene Maria *psychologist, educator*
Burnett, Keitha Denise *social studies educator*
Diaz, Tania *psychology professor*
Field, Julia Allen *futurist, strategist, environmentalist*
Fine, Jeffrey Louis *psychologist, educator, writer*
Huysman, Arlene Weiss *psychologist, educator, writer*
Kanet, Roger Edward *political science professor*
Lechner, Suzanne Caryn *psychology professor*
Liddle, Howard A. *psychologist, researcher*
Mustelier, Margarita M. *psychologist, director*
Russell, Elbert Winslow *neuropsychologist*
Salazar-Carrillo, Jorge *economics professor*
Weagraff, Patrick James *psychology professor, writer*

**Miami Beach**
Kalsner-Silver, Lydia *psychologist*

**North Miami**
Jean, Rojeanne *psychologist, educator*

**Orlando**
Ashe, Diane Davis *psychology professor, sport psychology consultant*
Dickie, Mark T. *economics professor*
Jacques, Peter Jon *political science professor*

**Panama City**
Caiazzo, Tom A *political scientist, educator*
Roberts, Paul Craig III *economics professor, writer, columnist*

**Pensacola**
Arnold, Barry Raynor *philosophy educator, medical ethicist*
Davis, Wesley D. *psychologist, educator*
Killian, Lewis Martin *sociology educator*

**Plantation**
Costa, Paul Joseph *psychologist*
Jaegerman, Patricia *psychologist*

**Ponte Vedra Beach**
Wu, Hsiu Kwang *economist, educator*

**Port Charlotte**
Von Holden, Martin Harvey *psychologist*

**Port Saint Lucie**
Augelli, John Pat *geographer, educator, writer, consultant, rancher*

**Saint Augustine**
Henderson, Hazel *economist, writer*
Kelly, Yvan J. *economics professor, professional basketball scout*

**Saint Petersburg**
Chenneville, Tiffany Ann *psychologist, educator*
Lowery, Solomon J. *social studies educator*
Rosenblum, Zina Michelle Zarin *psychology professor, marketing professional, researcher*
Stokes, Melvin Kirklin *psychologist*

**Sanibel**
Crown, David Allan *criminologist, educator*

**Sarasota**
Gordon, Sanford Daniel *economics professor*
Lynch, Martin Francis *psychology professor*
Masters, John Christopher *psychologist, educator, writer*
Watson, Joyce Morrissa *forensic and clinical psychologist*

**South Miami**
Villacian, Vanessa Luisa *psychologist*

**Sparr**
Tovi, Murray *futurist, research scientist*

**Stuart**
Smithson, Charles Wayne *economist, consultant*

**Sun City Center**
Hall, John Fry *retired psychologist*
Leonard, William Norris *economist, educator*

**Tallahassee**
Calhoun, Joseph Patrick *economics professor, researcher*
Glueckauf, Robert Lewis *psychologist, educator*
Guy, Mary Ellen Johnston *political science professor*
Holcombe, Randall Gregory *economics professor*
Johnson, Benjamin F., VI, *economist, consultant*
Laird, William Everette, Jr. *economics professor*
Nam, Charles Benjamin *demographer, sociologist, educator, writer*
Thompson, Gregory Lee *social sciences educator*

**Tampa**
Coleman, Rodney Albert *political scientist, consultant*
Dsurney, John *psychologist*
Forsythe, Robert Elliott *economics professor*
Genshaft, Judy Lynn *psychologist, educator*
Gironda, Ronald James *psychologist*
Jacobsen, Paul *psychologist*
Karver, Marc Stuart *psychologist, educator*
Kimmel, Ellen Bishop *psychologist, educator*
Lynch, Michael Joseph *criminologist, educator*
MacManus, Susan Ann *political science professor, researcher*
Miliziano, John C. *social studies educator*
Piper, John Richard *political science professor*
Spielberger, Charles Donald *psychologist, educator*
Weiner, Irving Bernard *psychologist*

**Tequesta**
Swets, John Arthur *psychologist, researcher*

**Venice**
Gooding, Charles Thomas *psychologist, educator, retired academic administrator*

**West Palm Beach**
Gold, Bela *economist, educator*

**Weston**
Alexander, Cynthia Louise *psychologist, educator*
Gamarra, Alberto Neil *psychologist, educator*
Kortlander, Susan Elizabeth *psychologist*

## GEORGIA

**Acworth**
Hutchins, Robert William *social studies educator, military officer*

**Albany**
Stallworth, Charles Derotha, Jr. *psychologist*

**Alpharetta**
Marsella, Anthony Joseph *psychologist, educator*

**Athens**
Allsbrook, Ogden Olmstead, Jr. *retired economics professor*
Bertsch, Gary Kenneth *political science professor*
Bullock, Charles Spencer III *political science educator, author, consultant*
Clute, Robert Eugene *political science professor*
Dunn, Delmer Delano *political science professor*
Fincher, Cameron Lane *psychology professor*
Garbin, Albeno Patrick *sociology educator*
Kamerschen, David Roy *economist, educator*
Nichols, William Curtis *psychologist, educator, marriage and family therapist, consultant*
Pollack, Robert Harvey *psychology professor*

**Atlanta**
Bahl, Roy Winford *economist, educator, consultant*
Chiang, Tze I. *economist, researcher, consultant*
Garland, LaRetta Matthews *psychologist, nursing educator*
Gay, Robert Derril *behavioral health consultant*
Harvey, Adia M. *sociology professor*
Kelley, Linda Elaine Spadafora *school psychologist, educator*
Knapp, Charles Boynton *economist, educator, former university president*
Lilenfeld, Lisa Rachelle *psychology professor, psychologist*
Mialon, Hugo *economics professor*
Muth, Richard Ferris *economics professor*
Nemeroff, Charles Barnet *neurobiology and psychiatry educator*
Reese, Cynthia Dene *psychologist, educator, quality assurance professional, risk management consultant*
Rein, David B. *economist, researcher*
Snarey, John Robert *psychologist, educator*
Speckhart, Dawn Seidner *bone marrow transplant/leukemia psychologist*
Thomas, Peter Charles *psychologist, educator*
Thursby, Jerry Gilbert *economics professor, consultant, department chairman*
Wald, Michael Leonard *economist*
Williams, Sondra Beth *social studies educator, department chairman*

**Augusta**
Davis, Catherine Lucy *psychologist, diabetes researcher*

**Bainbridge**
Dixon, Lugenia *psychology educator*

**Blairsville**
Jones, Mary Emma B. *psychologist*

**Carrollton**
Cao, Li *social studies educator*
Clark, Janet Eileen *political science professor*

**Columbus**
McFarland, Samuel P., Jr. *psychologist*

**Dahlonega**
Newman, Thomas Daniel *archaeologist, school system administrator, minister*

**Decatur**
Lucius, Randall H. *psychologist*

**East Point**
Johnson, Hardwick Smith, Jr. *school psychologist*

**Evans**
Zachert, Virginia *retired psychologist*

**Fort Stewart**
Thompson, Frankie Mazie *school psychologist*

**Gainesville**
Battle, Julie Vicknair *psychology professor*
Frank, Mary Lou Bryant *psychologist, educator*

**Griffin**
Shockley, Carol Frances *psychologist, psychotherapist*

**Hapeville**
Meshack, Marques D. *social studies educator*

**Lilburn**
Neumann, Thomas William *archaeologist*

**Macon**
Beaulier, Scott Alex *economics professor*
Cook, Charlotte C. *psychologist*
Lewis, Sandra Combs *research psychologist, writer*

**Marietta**
Dudley, Gary Edward *psychologist*

**Milledgeville**
Barron, Sheree S. *psychology professor, consultant*
Oetter, Doug R. *geography professor*

**Norcross**
Conway, Hobart McKinley, Jr. *futurist*

**Oxford**
Cody, William Bermond *political science professor*

**Pembroke**
Woodward, Serena *school psychologist*

**Rome**
Harbin, Frank Rockwell *psychologist*
Johnson, Alberta Clark *psychology professor*

**Roswell**
Klein, John Jacob *retired economist*

**Savannah**
Cebula, Richard John *economist, educator*

**Statesboro**
Henry, Nicholas Llewellyn *public administration educator*
Lloyd, Margaret Ann *psychologist, educator*
Nettles, Saundra R. Murray *psychologist, writer, educator*

**Stone Mountain**
Farngalo, Rosemarie Merritt *school psychologist*
Moales, Yvonne Edwards *school psychologist*

**Suwanee**
Cox, Albert Harrington, Jr. *economist*

**Toccoa Falls**
Brock, Dorothy Dixon *psychologist, psychology professor*

## HAWAII

**Hilo**
Brown, Daniel Edward *social sciences educator*
Dixon, Paul William *psychologist, educator*

**Holualoa**
Scarr, Sandra Wood *retired psychology educator, researcher*

**Honolulu**
Bitterman, Morton Edward *psychologist, educator*
Cho, Lee-Jay *social scientist, demographer*
Finucane, Melissa Lucille *psychologist, researcher*
Fullmer, Daniel Warren *former psychologist, educator*
Hunt, Terry L. *archaeologist, educator*
Ishikawa-Fullmer, Janet Satomi *psychologist, educator*
Laney, Leroy Olan *economist, banker, educator*
Lee, Sang-Hyop *economist*
Levister, Raymond Lee *psychologist*
Mark, Shelley Muin *economist, educator*
Nordyke, Eleanor Cole *demographer, researcher, community health nurse*
O'Brien, Kendra Allen *psychologist, researcher*
Paige, Glenn Durland *political scientist, educator*
Pearsall, Paul *psychologist, educator*
Pedersen, Paul Bodholdt *psychologist, educator*
Pinckney, Neal T. *psychologist, retired educator*
Riggs, Fred Warren *political science professor*
Staats, Arthur W. *psychology professor*
Suh, Dae-Sook *political science professor*

**Kailua**
Stamper, Ewa Szumotalska *psychologist*
Tavares, Samantha *psychologist, educator*

**Kailua Kona**
Liepack, Scot Alan *psychologist*

**Kapaa**
Klontz, Bradley T. *psychologist, consultant*

## IDAHO

**Boise**
Overgaard, Willard Michele *retired political scientist*
Pfouts, Ralph William *economist, consultant*
Slaughter, Richard Arthur *political scientist, economist, educator*

**Meridian**
Rehder, Jon *social studies educator*

**Pocatello**
Piland, Neill Finnes *health services economist, researcher, educator*

**Sandpoint**
Glock, Charles Young *sociologist, writer*

**Sun Valley**
Stewart, John Todd *economist, consultant*

## ILLINOIS

**Arlington Heights**
Griffin, Jean Latz *political strategist, writer, publisher*
Tongue, William Walter *economics and business consultant, educator*

**Barrington**
Chung, Joseph Sang-hoon *economics professor*
Kunkel, Nancy Angela *psychologist*
Vertino, Anthony Dominic *psychologist*
Wood, Andrée Robitaille *archaeologist, researcher*

**Belvidere**
Mc Nelly, Frederick Wright, Jr. *psychologist*

**Bloomingdale**
Irgang, Lisa Beth *psychologist*

**Calumet City**
Swansey, Micah Kassio *psychologist*

**Carbondale**
Benford, Robert Dee *social studies educator, editor*
Clark, M. H. *quantitative psychologist*

**Champaign**
Arnould, Richard Julius *economist, educator, consultant, dean*
Davis, James Henry *retired psychology educator*
Drasgow, Fritz *psychology professor*
Dulany, Donelson Edwin, Jr. *psychology professor*
Eriksen, Charles Walter *psychologist, educator*
Roese, Neal J. *psychology professor, consultant*
Scott, Anna Marie Porter Wall *sociology educator*
Triandis, Harry Charalambos *psychologist, educator*

**Chicago**
Bajich, Milena Tatic *psychologist*
Baum, Bernard Helmut *sociologist, educator*
Becker, Gary Stanley *economist, educator*
Bertenthal, Bennett Ira *psychologist, educator*
Bidwell, Charles Edward *sociologist, educator*
Brookens, Carl *psychologist*
Bryant, Fred Boyd *psychology professor*
Coase, Ronald Harry *economist, educator*
Cohler, Bertram Joseph *social sciences educator, psychologist*
Cox, Charles C. *economist*
Cropsey, Joseph *retired political science professor*
Cruthird, Robert Lee *sociology educator*
Dawson, Michael C. *political science professor*
Elshtain, Jean Bethke *social sciences educator*
Epstein, Lee Joan *political science professor, law educator*
Fernandez, James *anthropology educator*
Fogel, Robert William *economist, educator, historian*
Freeman, Leslie Gordon *anthropologist, educator*
Freeman, Susan Tax *anthropologist, educator, culinary historian*
Friedrich, Paul *anthropologist, linguist, poet*
Gannon, Sister Ann Ida *retired philosophy educator*
Gibson, McGuire *archaeologist, educator*
Ginsburg, Norton Sydney *retired geographer*
Gould, John Philip *economist, educator*
Graber, Doris Appel *political scientist, writer, editor*
Harrow, Martin *psychologist, educator*
Hastie, Reid *psychology professor*
Heckman, James Joseph *economist, educator*
Hollis-Sawyer, Lisa Ann *psychologist, gerontologist, researcher*
Kaplan, Morton A. *political science professor*
Karlin, Sy N. *social studies educator*
Knutson, Kristen Lynn *anthropologist, sleep researcher*
Larson, Allan Louis *political scientist, educator, lay worker*
Laumann, Edward Otto *sociology educator*
Levitt, Steven D. *economics professor*
Liu, Ben-chieh *economist*
Lowe, Sandra Elveta *psychologist*
Lucas, Robert Emerson, Jr. *economist, educator*
McCloskey, Michael *social sciences educator*
McNeill, G. David *psychologist, educator*
Menchik, Daniel Aron *researcher*
Mikesell, Marvin Wray *geography educator*
Morewitz, Stephen John *behavioral scientist, consultant, sociologist, educator*
Murphy, Kevin M. *economics professor*
Myerson, Roger Bruce *economist, educator*
Nicholas, Ralph Wallace W. *anthropologist, educator*
Peltzman, Sam *economics professor*
Rosen, George *economist, educator*
Sanders, Jacquelyn Seevak *psychologist, educator*

Segerstrale, Ullica Christina *social sciences educator, researcher*
Simons, Helen *school psychologist, psychotherapist, educator*
Simpson, Dick Weldon *political science educator*
Smagner, John Patrick *applied behavior analyst, educator*
Smith, David Paul *psychologist, researcher*
Smith, Raymond Thomas *anthropology educator*
Smith, Stan Vladimir *economist, finance company executive*
Spring, Bonnie Joan *psychology professor*
Staller, John Edward *archaeologist, anthropologist, educator*
Taub, Richard Paul *social sciences educator*
Thompson, Richard *psychologist*
Townsend, Robert Morris *economics professor, researcher*
Upshaw, Harry Stephan *psychologist, educator*
Walberg, Herbert John *psychologist, educator, consultant*
Zellner, Arnold *economics, econometrics and statistics professor*
Ziliak, Stephen T. *economics professor*
Zoloth, Laurie Susan *bioethicist*
Zonis, Marvin *political scientist, educator*

**Chillicothe**
Tallon, Edward Joseph *social studies educator*

**Dekalb**
Molnar, Andrea Katalin *anthropology professor*
Shernoff, David Jordan *psychology professor*
Slotsve, George Aaron *economist, educator, consultant*
Valentiner, David Peter *psychologist, educator*

**Downers Grove**
Feeney, Don Joseph, Jr. *psychologist*

**East Saint Louis**
Jones, Laura M. *psychologist, consultant*

**Edwardsville**
Browne, Dallas *anthropologist, educator*
DeGarmo, Denise Kay *political scientist, educator*
Rehg, Jennifer *anthropology educator*

**Evanston**
Braeutigam, Ronald Ray *economics professor, educational association administrator*
Canes-Wrone, Brandice *political scientist, educator*
Gentner, Dedre *psychology professor*
Gordon, Robert James *economics professor*
Hurter, Arthur Patrick *economist, educator*
Irons, William George *anthropology educator*
Kalai, Ehud *economist, researcher, educator*
Mills, Edwin Smith *economics professor*
Mineka, Susan *psychology professor*
Olszewski, Wojciech *economist, mathematician*
Reiter, Stanley *economist, educator*
Richeson, Jennifer Anne *psychology professor, researcher*
Satterthwaite, Mark A. *economics professor*
Weisbrod, Burton Allen *economist, educator*

**Glen Ellyn**
Frateschi, Lawrence Jan *economist, statistician, educator*

**Glenview**
Farber, Isadore E. *psychologist, educator*
Geller, William Alan *criminologist, consultant, protective services official*

**Grayslake**
Lorence, Michael Franklin *social sciences educator*

**Hinsdale**
Dederick, Robert Gogan *economist*

**Huntley**
Saporta, Jack *psychologist, educator*

**Jacksonville**
Hardin, Susan Jean *social studies educator, department chairman*

**Joliet**
Holmgren, Myron Roger *social sciences educator*

**Lincolnwood**
Earnest, Craig Hopkins *psychologist, consultant*

**Lovington**
Duncan, Linda B. *social studies educator*

**Macomb**
Deng, Yongxin *geography educator, ecology educator*
Hetzel-Riggin, Melanie Dyan *psychology professor*
Walzer, Norman Charles *economics professor*

**Maryville**
Stark, Patricia Ann *psychologist*

**Moline**
Garvin-Hunthey, Lynn M. *psychologist*
Penn, J. B. *economist*

**Naperville**
Cowlishaw, Mary Lou *government educator*
McCallum, Gerald Christopher *clinical psychologist*
Navin-O'Meara, Cynthia L. *school psychologist*

**Normal**
Alferink, Larry Allen *psychology professor*

**Northbrook**
Di Spigno, Guy Joseph *industrial psychologist, international management consultant*
Gyoerkoe, Kevin L. *psychologist, director*

**Orland Park**
Antia, Kersey H. *industrial and clinical psychologist, consultant*
Osmanski, Adam E. *social studies educator*

**Palos Park**
Peckenpaugh, Donald Hugh *psychologist, consultant, writer*

**Peoria**
Huffcutt, Allen Ivan *psychology professor*

**Pontiac**
Schultz, Heidi Renee *psychologist*

**River Forest**
Froehle, Bryan Thomas *sociologist, director*

**River Grove**
Stein, Thomas Henry *social sciences educator*

**Rockford**
Clodius, Robert LeRoy *retired economist*

**Rockton**
Polaski, Thomas Brian *social studies educator, department chairman*

**Springfield**
Phillips, John Robert *political scientist, educator*
Wehrle, Leroy Snyder *economist, educator*

**Streamwood**
Ackert, Lynee L. *social studies educator*

**Urbana**
Althaus, Scott L. *political science professor*
Baer, Werner *economist, educator*
Basak, Chandramallika *psychologist, researcher*
Carmen, Ira Harris *political scientist, educator*
Gabriel, Michael *psychology professor*
Giles, Eugene *anthropology educator*
Gove, Samuel Kimball *retired political science professor*
Leuthold, Raymond Martin *agricultural economics professor*
Lüschen, Günther Rudolf Friedo *social sciences educator*
Nettl, Bruno *anthropologist, musicologist, educator*
Resek, Robert William *economist*
Schmidt, Stephen Christopher *agricultural economist, educator*
Soffer, Olga *archaeologist, educator*
Thompson, Robert Lee *agricultural economist, educator*
Wirt, Frederick Marshall *retired political scientist, educator*
Yu, George Tzuchiao *political science professor*

**Western Springs**
Harken, Bruce R. *social studies educator*
Zamora, Marjorie Dixon *retired political science professor*

**Wheaton**
Riley, Betty Anne *psychologist, educator*

**Wilmette**
Schloss, Nathan *retired economist*
Walker, Ronald Edward *psychologist, educator*

**Winnetka**
Krueger, Deborah A. Blake *school psychologist, consultant*

**Woodstock**
Wertheimer-Sexton, Willa Renee *clinical psychologist*

## INDIANA

**Bloomington**
Baye, Michael Roy *economics professor*
Becker, William Edward *economist, consultant*
Brehm, Sharon Stephens *psychology professor, former academic administrator*
Clark, Gracia Courtright *anthropologist*
Conrad, Geoffrey Wentworth *archaeologist, educator*
Estes, William Kaye *psychologist, educator*
Guth, Sherman Leon (S. Lee Guth) *psychologist, educator*
Kreft, Steven Francis *economics professor*
O'Meara, Patrick O. *political science professor*
Ostrom, Elinor *political science professor, researcher*
Ostrom, Vincent A(lfred) *political science professor*
Patrick, John Joseph *social sciences educator*
Peebles, Christopher Spalding *anthropologist, educator, dean, academic administrator*
Reingold, David Ami *sociologist, educator*
Risinger, C. Frederick *social studies educator*
Rugman, Alan Michael *international business educator*
St. John, Edward P. *social sciences educator*
Thorelli, Sarah V. *economist, researcher*
von Furstenberg, George Michael *economics professor, researcher*

**Carmel**
Rychlak, Joseph Frank *psychologist, educator*

**Columbus**
Lamborn, Richard Lee *psychologist*
Williams, Robert Joseph *behavioral health services executive, psychologist*

**Crothersville**
Scifres, Stephanie L. *psychologist*

**Evansville**
Bennett, Stephen Earl *retired political science professor*

**Fort Wayne**
Toole, James Gray *political science professor*

**Granger**
Craypo, Charles *labor economics professor*

**Greenwood**
Hagedorn, Alan Patrick *social studies educator*
Waldkoetter, Raymond Oliver *psychologist, consultant*

**Hanover**
Porter, Karen Ann *anthropologist, educator*

**Indianapolis**
Cardwell, Sue Webb *psychology professor*
Divita, James J. *retired social studies educator, writer, researcher*
Fastenau, Philip S. *neuropsychologist, educator*
Featherstonaugh, Henry Gordon *psychologist, health facility administrator*
Gregg, Stephen Thompson *political scientist, consultant*
Kessler, Marcia Lynn *school psychologist*
Mirola, William Andrew *sociologist, educator*
Swindle, Ralph Wilson, Jr. *research psychologist*
Tatom, John Anthony *economist*

**Kokomo**
Wysong, Earl Edward *sociologist, educator*

**Lafayette**
Hardin, Lowell Stewart *retired economics professor*
Schönemann, Peter Hans *psychologist, educator*
Schweickert, Richard Justus *psychologist, educator*

**Lebanon**
Goodwin, John Charles *social studies educator*

**Muncie**
Bogg, Richard Allan *sociologist, educator*
Cheng, Chu Yuan *economics professor*
Swartz, B(enjamin) K(insell), Jr. *archaeologist, educator*

**New Albany**
Crump, Claudia *geographer, educator*

**New Castle**
Chilton, Todd Longstreet *psychologist*

**Notre Dame**
Arnold, Peri Ethan *political scientist*
Bartell, Ernest *economist, educator, priest*
Cummings, Edward Mark *psychology professor, researcher*
Despres, Leo Arthur *sociologist, anthropologist, educator, academic administrator*
Goulet, Denis André *development ethicist*
Hallinan, Maureen Theresa *sociologist, educator*
Mirowski, Philip Edward *economics professor*
Swartz, Thomas R. *economist, educator*
Valenzuela, Julio Samuel *sociologist, educator*
Walshe, Aubrey Peter *political science professor*
Weigert, Andrew Joseph *sociology educator*
Welch, Michael R. *sociologist, educator*
Zuckert, Catherine Heldt *political science educator, writer, editor*

**South Bend**
Carrington, Michael Davis *criminal justice and security consultant*
Dowty, Alan Kent *political scientist, educator*

**Terre Haute**
Leigh, Janis *clinician*

**West Lafayette**
Cicirelli, Victor George *psychologist*
Connor, John Murray *economics professor*
Dumas, Jean E. *psychology professor*
Farris, Paul Leonard *agricultural economist*
Gruen, Gerald Elmer *psychologist, educator*
Horwich, George *economist, educator*
Perrucci, Robert *sociologist, educator*
Preckel, Paul Veitch *agricultural economics educator, researcher*
Shively, Gerald E. *economist, educator*
Swensen, Clifford Henrik, Jr. *psychologist, educator*
Tyner, Wallace Edward *agricultural economics educator*
Weidenaar, Dennis Jay *retired economics professor*
Weinstein, Michael Alan *political science professor*

## IOWA

**Ames**
Fox, Karl August *economist, educator, eco-behavioral scientist*
Harl, Neil Eugene *economist, educator, lawyer, writer*

**Cedar Falls**
Gilgen, Albert Rudolph *retired psychologist, retired educator*

**Clive**
Miller, Kenneth Edward *sociologist, educator*

**Davenport**
Achs, Jack Horst *social studies educator*

**Des Moines**
Demorest, Allan Frederick *retired psychologist*
Quirmbach, Herman Charles *economics professor*
Simmons, Suzan *psychologist*

**Fayette**
Barker, Richard Alexander *organizational psychologist*

**Iowa City**
Albrecht, William Price *economist, educator, government official*
Barkan, Joel David *political science professor*
Duff, Kevin *neuropsychologist, psychiatry professor*
Fethke, Gary C. *economics professor, academic administrator*
Fuller, John Williams *economics professor*
Geweke, John Frederick *economics professor*

Kim, Chong Lim *political science professor*
Loewenberg, Gerhard *political science professor*
Nathan, Peter E. *psychologist, educator*
Siebert, Calvin D. *economist, educator*
Simon, J. Richard (Jennings Richard Simon) *psychologist, educator*
Skinstad, Anne Helene *psychologist, researcher*
Wasserman, Edward Arnold *psychology professor*

**Newton**
Tisdale, Thomas J. *social studies educator*

**West Des Moines**
Bakari, Rosenna *educational psychology professor, consultant*
Thornton, John Edwin *social studies educator*

**KANSAS**

**Bern**
Dassel-Stuke, Donna Jane *psychologist, educator*

**Colby**
McVay, Micheal Ray *social sciences educator, department chairman*

**Derby**
Clark, Susan Matthews *psychologist*

**Emporia**
Mallein, Darla J. *social studies educator*

**Fort Leavenworth**
Mullis, Tony Randall *social studies educator*

**Garden City**
Thomas, Gregory Hall *psychology professor*

**Kansas City**
Penick, Elizabeth C. *psychologist*
Smarr, Tracy Jean *psychologist*

**Lawrence**
Barnett, William Arnold *economics professor*
Heller, Francis Howard *retired political science professor, retired law educator*
Stull, Donald David *anthropologist, educator*

**Manhattan**
Babcock, Michael Ward *economics professor*
Barkley, Andrew Paul *economics professor*
Benton, Stephen LeRoy *psychology professor, researcher*
Eyman, Susanne Kohn *clinical psychologist*
Murray, John Patrick *psychologist, educator, researcher*
Phares, E. Jerry *retired psychology professor*
Thomas, Lloyd Brewster *economics professor*

**Mulvane**
Kraft, William Earl *social studies educator*

**North Newton**
Eitzen, David Stanley *sociologist, educator*

**Saint John**
Robinson, Alexander Jacob *retired psychologist*

**Topeka**
Spohn, Herbert Emil *psychologist*

**Wichita**
Ericson, David Frank *political scientist, educator*
Farmer, Steven *psychology professor*
Moore, Leon, Jr. *social studies educator*

**KENTUCKY**

**Bowling Green**
Cangemi, Joseph Peter *psychologist, consultant, educator*

**Campbellsville**
Chowning, John E. *political scientist, educator, minister*

**Corbin**
Doby, John Thomas *social psychologist*

**Georgetown**
Bates, Clyde Thomas *retired economics professor*

**Highland Heights**
Donnelly, Sharlotte K. B. Neely *anthropology educator, writer*

**Independence**
Hopgood, James F. *anthropologist, educator*

**Lexington**
Beal, Donald Gordon *clinical psychology educator*
Gallagher, Eugene Bennett *sociologist, medical educator*
Hochstrasser, Donald Lee *cultural anthropologist, community health and public administrator*
Reed, Michael Robert *agricultural economist*
Stempel, John Dallas *international studies educator*
Wildasin, David E(arl) *economics professor*
Worell, Judith P. *psychologist, educator*

**Louisville**
Beggan, James K. *sociologist, educator*
Blandford, Jim, Jr. *social studies educator*
Goheen, Nan J. *psychologist*
Portes, Pedro René *psychology professor, department chairman*
Stanton, M(orris) Duncan *psychologist, researcher, dean*
Tanguay, Peter Eugene *child and adolescent psychiatry educator*
Tasman, Allan *psychiatry educator*

**Morehead**
Miller, Green Russell *economist, educator*
Reilley, Sean Patrick *psychology professor, consultant*

**Paintsville**
Hovee, Mark John *psychologist*

**Richmond**
Gershtenson, Joe *political science professor*

**Versailles**
Stober, William John, II, *economics professor*

**Villa Hills**
Giesbrecht, Martin Gerhard *retired economics professor, musician*

**LOUISIANA**

**Alexandria**
Thevenot, Maude Travis *retired home economist*

**Baton Rouge**
Cramer, Gail Latimer *economist*
Dumais, Susan A. *sociology professor*
Guedry, Leo J. *agricultural economics educator*
Riopelle, Arthur Jean *psychologist*
Sandoz, George Ellis, Jr. *political science educator*
Schechter, Lynn Renee *psychologist*
Sluyter, Andrew *geographer, educator*

**Bossier City**
Paris, Norma Jean *psychologist, educator*

**Denham Springs**
Grimmer, Cindy C. *social studies educator*

**Hammond**
Hill, Catherine Parham *school psychologist*
Levi, Danilo *sociologist, educator, director*

**Harahan**
O'Neal, Edgar Carl *psychology professor*

**Lake Charles**
Middleton, George, Jr. *clinical child psychologist*

**Metairie**
Falco, Maria Josephine *political scientist*
Wood, Jonathan Stuart *economist, educator*

**Monroe**
Bulot, James John *gerontologist, educator*
Smith, Pamela LaTrice *school psychologist*

**New Orleans**
Andrews, E. Wyllys *archaeologist, educator*
Balée, William L. *anthropology educator*
Boudreaux, Kenneth Justin *economist, educator*
Fleischer, Barbara Jane *organizational psychologist, consultant, researcher*
Langston, Thomas Samuel *political science professor*
Moely, Barbara E. *psychologist, educator*
Olson, Richard David *psychology professor*
Thompson, Martyn Philip *political and literary studies educator, translator*
Ukpolo, Victor *economics educator*
VanLandingham, Mark Jennings *sociologist, educator*

**Pineville**
Thrasher, Fay C. *clinical psychologist*

**Ruston**
Sale, Tom S. III *financial economist*

**Shreveport**
Dai, Yong *psychologist, educator*
Joiner, Gary Dillard *cartographer, writer, history professor*
Street, Jeanne *psychologist*

**MAINE**

**Augusta**
Bourque, Bruce Joseph *archaeologist, educator*
Nickerson, John Mitchell *political science professor*

**Bath**
Galleher, Gay *psychologist*
Stoudt, Howard Webster *biological anthropologist, consultant*

**Brunswick**
Fuchs, Alfred Herman *psychologist, educator*
Putnam, Samuel Patrick *psychologist*

**Falmouth**
Pierce, Philip Sargent *clinical psychologist*

**Farmington**
Melcher, James Patrick *political scientist, educator*

**Little Deer Isle**
Mills, David Harlow *psychologist, professional society administrator*

**Orono**
Cohn, Steven Frederick *sociology educator, consultant*
Dalton, Timothy John *economics professor*
Goldstone, Sanford *psychologist, educator*

**Portland**
Ryden, Kent C. *social studies educator*

**Readfield**
Gower, Shane *social studies educator*

**Surry**
Pickett, Betty Horenstein *psychologist*

**Waterville**
Gemery, Henry Albert *economics professor*
Gilkes, Cheryl Louise Townsend *sociologist, educator, minister*
Yeterian, Edward Harry *psychologist, educator, administrator*

**MARYLAND**

**Annapolis**
Connolly, Janet Elizabeth *retired sociologist, retired criminal justice educator*

**Baltimore**
Anderson, Gerard Fenton *economist, academic administrator*
Asuncion-Miller, Lana Martina *school psychologist*
Batten, Sonja Victoria *psychologist, educator*
Bellack, Alan Scott *clinical psychologist*
Bright, Margaret *sociologist*
Catania, A(nthony) Charles *psychologist, educator*
Cooper, Joseph *political scientist, educator*
Dickey, George Edward *economist, educator, water transportation executive*
Dietze, Gottfried *political science professor*
Freeland, Claire Ann Bennett *psychologist*
Gartner, John D. *clinical psychologist, educator*
Green, Bert Franklin, Jr. *retired psychology professor*
Grossman, Joel B(arry) *political science educator*
Henderson, Lenneal Joseph, Jr. *political science professor*
Howard, J. Woodford, Jr. *retired political science professor*
Karni, Edi *economics professor*
Kirkhart, Matthew Wayde *psychology professor*
Kumar, Martha Joynt *political science educator*
Maccini, Louis John *economist, educator*
Melick, Clifford Francis *sociologist, researcher*
Salamon, Lester Milton *political science professor*
Sentinek, Kelly Marie *social studies educator*
Sorkin, Alan Lowell *economist, educator*
Yantis, Steven George *psychology educator*

**Bethesda**
Banik, Sambhu Nath *psychologist*
Barton, Jean Marie *psychologist, educator*
Duncan, Constance Catharine *psychologist, educator, researcher*
Germain, Gale Inoff *research psychologist*
Heravi, Mehdi *economist*
Holland, Robert Carl *economist*
Krantz, David S. *psychology educator, researcher*
Lystad, Mary Hanemann (Mrs. Robert Lystad) *sociologist, writer*
Mishkin, Mortimer *neuropsychologist*
Orr, Larry L. *economist*
Raullerson, Calvin Henry *political scientist, consultant*
Reynolds, Robert Joel *economist, consultant*
Solomon, Robert *economist*
Taylor, William Jesse, Jr. *international security studies educator, research institute senior advisor*

**Bowie**
Bushnell, David Sherman *social psychologist, consultant*
Yager, Joseph Arthur, Jr. *economist, consultant*

**Chestertown**
Littlefield, Lauren Montenegro *psychologist, educator*
Wendel, Richard Frederick *economist, educator, consultant*

**Chevy Chase**
Alexander, Arthur Jacob *economist*
Hickman, R(obert) Harrison *political pollster, strategist*
Krupnick, Janice Lee *psychologist, psychotherapist, educator*
Norwood, Bernard *economist*
Norwood, Janet Lippe *economist*
Opper, Barbara Negri *financial economist*

**College Park**
Aruoba, S. Boragan *economics professor*
Destler, I. M(ac) *political scientist, foreign policy writer*
Dill, Bonnie Thornton *sociology educator*
Epstein, Norman B. *psychologist, marriage and family therapist, educator*
Gaylin, Ned L. *psychologist, educator*
Hall, William Sterling *psychology educator*
Hill, Clara Edith *psychologist, educator*
Just, Richard Eugene *economist, consultant, agriculturist, educator*
Kleidon, Axel *geographer, educator*
Lent, Robert William *psychologist*
Nerlove, Marc Leon *economics professor*
Olson, Charles Eric *economist*
Presser, Harriet Betty *social studies educator*
Presser, Stanley *social sciences educator, researcher*
Quester, George Herman *political science professor*
Rust, John Philip *economist, educator*
Schelling, Thomas Crombie *economist*
Sigall, Harold Fred *psychology professor*
Sorenson, Georgia Lynn Jones *political science professor*

**Cumberland**
Heckert, Paul Charles *sociologist, educator*

**Ellicott City**
Freeman, Lisa Marie Yacono *psychologist*
Webster, Sharon B. *economist*

**Gaithersburg**
Killgore, William Dale (Scott), Jr. *neuropsychologist*

**Hagerstown**
Cooper, G. David *psychologist*
Ward, Spring Tina *history and political science educator*

**Hampstead**
Dotterweich, Patrick Timothy *social studies educator*

**Laurel**
McMenamin, Terence Michael *economist*

**Lexington Park**
Donely, George Anthony Thomas III *retired economist*

**Lutherville**
Smith, Michelle Sun *psychologist*

**Lutherville Timonium**
Muuss, Rolf Eduard *retired psychologist, author*

**Mc Henry**
Kelly, Robert William *economist*

**Mitchellville**
Blasier, Cole *political scientist*
Henle, Peter *retired economist, arbitrator*

**North East**
Perry, Josie Lynn *social studies educator*

**Potomac**
Jones, Sidney Lewis *economist, researcher, educator*
Oh, John Kie-Chiang *political science professor, academic administrator*
Reichley, A. James *political scientist*
Rotberg, Iris Comens *social scientist*
Sammons, Morgan Taylor *psychologist*
Vadus, Gloria A. *scientific document examiner*
Walker, Charls Edward *economist, consultant*
Wonnacott, Paul *retired economics professor*

**Rockville**
Hoffman, Jeffrey David *school psychologist*
Mealy, J. Burke *clinical psychologist*
Niewiaroski, Trudi Osmers (Gertrude Niewiaroski) *social studies educator*
Stefano, Kenneth *psychologist, psychotherapist*

**Salisbury**
Losonczy-Marshall, Marta Elizabeth *psychologist, educator*

**Shady Side**
Devine, Donald J. *political science professor, consultant*

**Silver Spring**
Ahmad, Mirza Muzaffar *economic advisor*
Alexander, Herbert E. *political scientist*
Dalton, J. Joseph *psychologist, consultant*
Hsueh, Chun-tu *political scientist, educator, foundation administrator, historian*
Mohr, Christina *retired economist*
Moon, Marilyn Lee *economist*
Oswald, Rudolph A. *economist*
Rayburn, Carole Ann (Mary Aida) *psychologist, researcher, writer, consultant*
Sibley, Lynn M. *anthropologist, educator*
Striner, Herbert Edward *economics professor*

**Takoma Park**
Leitma, Grant *psychologist, educator*

**Temple Hills**
Smith, Irving *gerontologist*

**Towson**
Nelson, H. Wayne *gerontologist, advocate*
Zweback, Stanley *psychologist, educator*

**Westminster**
Saxton, Celeste Dawn *social studies educator, consultant*
Spencer, Kimberly Ann *psychologist*

**MASSACHUSETTS**

**Acton**
Evans, Robert, Jr. *economics professor*

**Agawam**
Sylvester, John Andrew *social studies educator*

**Amherst**
Averill, James Reed *psychology professor*
Berger, Seymour Maurice *social psychologist*
Daehler, Marvin William *psychology professor*
Folbre, Nancy *economics educator*
Keen, Rachel *psychology professor*
Klare, Michael Thomas *social sciences educator, director*
Rayner, Keith *psychology professor, researcher*
Strickland, Bonnie Ruth *psychologist, educator*
Taubman, William Chase *political science professor, writer*
Woodbury, Richard Benjamin *anthropologist, educator*

**Babson Park**
Genovese, Francis Charles (Frank Genovese) *economist, educator, editor-in-chief, writer*

**Barnstable**
Randolph, Robert Lee *economist, educator*

**Bedford**
Kalman, David *social sciences educator*

**Belmont**
Harper, David George *psychologist, educator*
Levendusky, Philip George *psychologist, academic administrator, educator*

**Berkley**
Murtagh, Michael Paul *psychologist*

**Boston**
Allinson, Deborah Louise *economist*
Appley, Mortimer Herbert *psychologist, retired academic administrator*
Canning, David *economist*
Dentler, Robert Arnold *sociologist, educator*
Ellis, Randall Poor *economist, educator*
Farmer, Paul Edward *medical anthropologist*
Gamst, Frederick Charles *social anthropologist*
Gleason, Jean Berko *psychology professor*
Grossman, Frances Kaplan *psychologist*

Hammond, Norman David Curle *archaeology educator, researcher*
Herzlinger, Regina *economist, educator, writer*
Horrigan, Brian Richard *economist*
Järbe, Torbjörn Ulf Christian *psychologist, educator*
Lawrence, Paul Roger *retired psychology professor*
Lundgren, Lena Margareta *social sciences educator, researcher*
Manning, Peter Kirby *criminal justice educator*
Markham, Jesse William *economist, educator*
Masi, Dale A. *social sciences educator, research and development company executive*
Merton, Robert C. *economist, educator*
Newhouse, Joseph Paul *economist, educator*
O'Hern, Jane Susan *psychologist, educator*
Palmer, David Scott *political scientist, educator*
Plotkin, Irving H. (Irving Herman Plotkin) *economist, consultant*
Ra'anan, Uri (Heinz Felix Frischwasser) *international politics educator*
Salinger, Michael Alvin *economist, educator*
Scorzelli, James Francis *counseling psychology educator*
Smith, Linda Santos *psychologist, medical educator*
Smith-Doerr, Laurel *sociologist*
White, Deborah O. *forensic psychologist*
Yeager, Peter Cleary *sociologist, educator*

**Brookline**
Cromwell, Adelaide M. *sociology educator*

**Cambridge**
Acemoglu, Daron (K. Daron Acemoglu) *economics professor*
Alesina, Alberto *economist, educator*
Alt, James Edward *political science professor*
Anderson, William Henry *psychobiology educator*
Angrist, Joshua D. *economics educator*
Bailyn, Lotte *psychologist, educator*
Banerjee, Abhijit Vinayak *economics professor*
Bator, Francis Michel *economist, educator*
Berndt, Ernst Rudolf *economist, educator*
Bishop, Robert Lyle *economist, educator*
Blackmer, Donald Laurence Morton *political scientist*
Borjas, George J(esus) *economics professor*
Calabrese, Joseph D. *psychologist, educator*
Caramazza, Alfonso *psychology professor*
Cestnick, Laurie L. *neuropsychologist, educator, scientist*
Cohen, Joshua *political science professor*
Cooper, Richard Newell *economist, educator*
Dominguez, Jorge Ignacio *political scientist, educator*
Eckaus, Richard Samuel *economist, educator*
Ellison, Peter Thorpe *anthropology professor*
Feldstein, Martin Stuart *economist, educator*
Flad, Rowan Kimon *social sciences educator*
Forbes, Kristin J. *economics professor, former federal official*
Friedman, Benjamin Morton *economics professor*
Frisch, Rose Epstein *population sciences researcher*
Gardner, Howard Earl *psychologist, educator, writer*
Gilbert, Daniel *psychology professor*
Glaeser, Edward Ludwig *research economist, educator*
Greenstone, Michael *economics professor, researcher*
Hart, Oliver D'Arcy *economics professor*
Hausman, Jerry Allen *economics professor, consultant*
Hausmann, Ricardo *economics professor, director*
Hoffmann, Inge Schneier *psychologist, educator*
Huntington, Samuel Phillips *political science educator*
Jacoby, Henry Donnan *economist, educator*
Jencks, Christopher Sandys *sociologist, educator*
Johnson, Willard Raymond *political science professor*
Jorgenson, Dale Weldeau *economist, educator*
Joskow, Paul Lewis *economist, educator*
Kagan, Jerome *psychologist, educator*
Kaysen, Carl *economics professor*
Keniston, Kenneth *psychologist, educator*
Kennedy, Stephen Dandridge *economist, researcher*
Keyfitz, Nathan *sociologist, educator, demographer*
Kleinman, Arthur Michael *medical anthropology and psychiatry educator*
Kremer, Michael *economist, educator*
Lamberg-Karlovsky, Clifford Charles *anthropologist, archaeologist*
Langer, Ellen Jane *psychologist, educator, writer, artist*
Lieberson, Stanley *sociologist, educator*
Linsky, Marty *public policy educator, consultant*
Maher, Brendan Arnold *retired psychology educator, editor*
Mankiw, Gregory (Nicholas Gregory Mankiw) *economics professor, former federal official*
Mansbridge, Jane Jebb *political scientist, educator*
McNally, Richard James *clinical psychologist, educator*
Meyer, John Robert *economist, educator*
Mitten, David Gordon *classical archaeologist*
Moore, Sally Falk *anthropology educator*
Nye, Joseph Samuel, Jr. *political science professor, former dean*
Perkins, Dwight Heald *economics professor*
Pinker, Steven A. *psychologist, educator*
Poterba, James Michael *economics professor*
Power, Samantha J. *public policy educator, writer*
Pye, Lucian Wilmot *political science educator*
Rightmire, George Philip *anthropology educator*
Rodrik, Dani *economics and international affairs educator*
Rogoff, Kenneth Saul *economics professor*
Rosenblum, Nancy Lipton *political science professor*
Rosovsky, Henry *economist, educator*
Sampson, Robert J. *sociologist, educator*
Samuelson, Paul Anthony *economist, educator*
Sapolsky, Harvey Morton *political scientist, educator*
Scherer, Frederic Michael *economics professor*
Sen, Amartya Kumar *economist, educator*

Siegel, Abraham J. *economics professor, academic administrator*
Skolnikoff, Eugene B. *political science professor*
Solow, Robert Merton *economist, educator*
Stager, Lawrence E. *archaeologist, educator*
Stock, James H. *economics professor*
Taymor, Betty *political science professor*
Thompson, Dennis Frank *political science professor, consultant*
Verba, Sidney *political science professor, academic administrator*
Vogel, Ezra F. *sociology educator*
Waters, Mary Catherine *sociology educator*
Willie, Charles Vert *social sciences educator*
Wilson, William Julius *sociology educator*
Yip, Winnie *health economics educator*
Zeidenstein, George *population educator*
Zinberg, Dorothy Shore *sociologist, educator*

**Chestnut Hill**
Carfora, John Michael *economics professor, academic administrator*

**Dartmouth**
Kahrl, Benjamin Richards *social studies educator, department chairman*

**Dorchester**
Medeiros, Jennifer Lynn *school psychologist, consultant*

**Gloucester**
McCarl, Henry Newton *economist, geologist, consultant, venture capitalist*

**Hopkinton**
Newbrander, William Carl *health economist, management consultant*

**Ipswich**
Jennings, Frederic Beach, Jr. *economist, saltwater flyfishing guide*

**Lexington**
Jordan, Judith Victoria *clinical psychologist, educator*
Nichols, Albert L. *economic consultant*
Papanek, Gustav Fritz *economist, educator*

**Lowell**
Dinh, Khanh Thi *psychology professor, consultant*

**Marblehead**
Speller, Kerstin G. Rinta *psychologist*

**Medford**
Ambady, Nalini *social psychologist, educator, researcher*
Conklin, John Evan *sociology educator*
DeBold, Joseph Francis *psychologist, educator*
Elkind, David *psychology professor*
McKay, Ryan Thomas *psychologist*
Miczek, Klaus Alexander *psychology professor*
Sommers, Samuel R *psychologist*
Spolaore, Enrico *economist*

**Melrose**
Henken, Bernard Samuel *clinical psychologist, speech pathologist*

**Nantucket**
Sangree, Walter Hinchman *social anthropologist, educator*

**Natick**
Sedo, Manuel Arturo *neuropsychologist, researcher*

**Needham**
Boulding, Elise Marie *sociologist, educator*
Lyons, Maureen P. *social studies educator*

**Newton**
Holbik, Karel *economics professor*
White, Burton Leonard *retired educational psychologist, writer, consultant*

**Newton Center**
Adams, F. Gerard *economist, educator*

**North Dartmouth**
Barrow, Clyde Wayne *social sciences educator*

**Northampton**
Rose, Peter Isaac *sociologist, writer*

**Quincy**
Spangler, Arthur Stephenson, Jr. *psychologist*

**Salem**
Goss, Laurence Edward, Jr. *geographer, educator*
Higgins, Gina O'Connell *psychologist, writer*

**Shrewsbury**
Lucas, Sandra J. *psychologist*

**Somerville**
Brams, Marvin Robert *economist, mental health counselor, interfaith minister, educator*

**South Hadley**
Tatum, Beverly Daniel *psychology and education educator*

**Sudbury**
Diette, Kelly A. *psychologist*

**Waltham**
Altman, Stuart Harold *economist, educator*
Domar, Alice Diane *psychologist, educator*
McCulloch, Rachel *economist, educator*
Quinn, Michael *economics educator*
Saxe, Leonard *social psychologist, educator*
Sekuler, Robert William *psychologist, educator*
Shepard, Donald Sloane *public policy research educator*

**Wellesley**
Eilts, Hermann Frederick *international relations educator, retired diplomat*
Giddon, Donald B(ernard) *psychologist, educator*
Miller, Linda B. *political scientist*
Morant, Ricardo Bernardino *psychology professor*
Stettner, Edward A. *political science professor*

**Westborough**
Antalek, Eileen Elizabeth *educational psychologist, consultant*
Staffier, Pamela Moorman *psychologist*

**Westfield**
Zayac, Linda Mary *sociologist, educator*

**Weston**
Kraft, Gerald *economist*

**Whitinsville**
Plaud, Joseph Julian *psychology educator*

**Williamstown**
Bolton, Roger Edwin *economist, educator*
Cramer, Phebe *psychologist*
Fuller, Renee Nuni *psychologist, educational publisher*
Kassin, Saul *psychology professor*
Sheahan, John Bernard *economist, educator*
Solomon, Paul Robert *neuropsychologist, educator*
Weiner, Bruce Barnet *psychologist*

**Worcester**
Dolgon, Corey *sociology educator, political activist*
Mathisen, Howard *psychologist, educator, minister*
Novarro, Neva K. *economics professor*
Ott, Attiat Farag *economist, educator*

## MICHIGAN

**Adrian**
Weathers, Milledge Wright *retired economics professor*

**Ann Arbor**
Apperson, Jean *psychologist*
Arlinghaus, Sandra Judith Lach *mathematical geographer, educator*
Behling, Charles Frederick *psychologist, educator*
Bishop, Elizabeth Shreve *psychologist*
Bornstein, Morris *economist, educator*
Brown, Donald Robert *psychology professor*
Cain, Albert Clifford *psychologist, educator*
Cohen, Malcolm Stuart *economist*
Converse, Philip Ernest *retired social sciences educator*
Courant, Paul Noah *economist, educator, academic administrator*
Crocker, Jennifer *psychology professor, researcher*
Deardorff, Alan Verne *economist, educator*
Dominguez, Kathryn Mary *economist, educator*
Ellsworth, Phoebe Clemencia *psychology professor*
Freedman, Ronald *sociology educator*
Frey, William H. *demographer, educator*
Fusfeld, Daniel Roland *economist*
Gramlich, Edward Martin *public policy educator, former bank executive*
Haefner, Don Paul *retired psychology educator*
Hagen, John William *psychology professor*
House, James Stephen *sociological social psychologist, educator*
Inglehart, Marita Rohr *psychologist, educator, researcher*
Irvine, Judith Temkin *anthropologist, educator*
Jackson, James Sidney *psychologist, educator*
Johnston, Lloyd Douglas *social sciences educator*
Kestenbaum, Lawrence *political science educator*
Kingdon, John Wells *political science professor*
Kmenta, Jan *retired economics professor*
Lord, Catherine *psychology professor, psychologist*
Manis, Melvin *psychologist, educator*
Markovits, Andrei Steven *political science professor*
Mc Cracken, Paul Winston *retired economist, business educator*
Mitchell, Edward John *economist, retired educator*
Moholy-Nagy, Hattula *archaeologist*
Nisbett, Richard Eugene *psychology professor*
Paige, Jeffery Mayland *sociologist, educator*
Parsons, Jeffry Redinson *anthropologist, educator*
Pedley, John Griffiths *archaeologist, educator*
Pienta, Amy Mehraban *sociologist, demographer*
Quintyn, Conrad Bezekiah *anthropologist, educator*
Schwarz, Norbert *psychology professor*
Shapiro, Matthew David *economist, educator*
Stafford, Frank Peter, Jr. *economics professor, consultant*
Tichy, Noel M. *psychology professor, academic administrator*
Waltz, Susan *political scientist, educator*
Whitman, Marina Von Neumann *economist, educator*
Williams, Melvin Donald *anthropologist, educator*
Woronoff, Israel *former psychology educator*
Zucker, Robert A(lpert) *psychologist*

**Auburn Hills**
Etefia, Florence Victoria *retired school psychologist*

**Baraga**
Hodges, Douglas Sargent *social studies educator*

**Birmingham**
Filter, Terrance Anderson *clinical psychologist*

**Bloomfield Hills**
Sugrue, Dennis Patrick *psychologist*

**Detroit**
Braid, Ralph M. *economics professor*
Cantoni, Louis Joseph *retired psychology professor, sculptor, poet*
Fleming, George Robert *psychologist*
Goodman, Allen Charles *economist, educator*
Greene, Harold H. *psychology professor*

Jendrzejewski, Roxanne Marie *social studies educator, language educator*
Martin, John E *psychologist, educator*
McCrae, Jocelyn Diane *psychologist, educator*
Pietrofesa, John Joseph *psychologist, educator*

**East Lansing**
Abeles, Norman *psychologist, educator*
Abramson, Paul Robert *political scientist, educator*
Baillie, Richard Thomas *economist, educator*
Ballbach, Philip Thornton *political consultant, investor*
Crewe, Nancy Moe *retired psychology educator*
Dow, Steven Benjamin *social studies educator*
Gass, Gertrude Zemon *psychologist, researcher*
Haider, Steven John *economics professor*
Iglesias, Emma Maria *economics professor*
Koo, Anthony Ying Chang *economist, educator*
Kreinin, Mordecha Eliahu *economics professor*
Ladenson, Mark Lawrence *economist, educator*
Manderscheid, Lester Vincent *agricultural economics educator*
Menchik, Paul Leonard *economist, educator*
Press, Charles *retired political science educator*
Schmitt, Neal *psychology professor, department chairman*
Winder, Clarence Leland *psychologist, educator*

**Farmington Hills**
Robinson, Amorie Alexia *psychologist, educator*
Toth, Brian M. *social studies educator*

**Grand Rapids**
Pisacreta, Richard *psychology professor*
Sherman, Gregory Albert *psychologist*
Shoemaker, Allen L. *psychology professor, consultant*
Tiemstra, John Peter *economics professor*

**Holland**
Holmes, Jack Edward *political science professor*

**Kalamazoo**
Mc Allister, Lester Belden *economics professor*

**Lansing**
Sweet, Margaret Ann *psychology educator*

**Midland**
Hoerneman, Calvin A., Jr. *economics professor*

**Mount Pleasant**
Beehr, Terry A. *psychology professor*
Jeon, Yongil *economics professor*

**Munising**
Hughes, Patti L. *social sciences educator*

**Muskegon**
Akker, Arlene F. *social sciences educator*
Crummett, Allan Warren *psychologist*

**Northport**
Thomas, Philip Stanley *economist, educator*

**Okemos**
Solo, Robert Alexander *economist, educator*

**Onaway**
Wregglesworth, Kymberli April *social studies educator*

**Perry**
Suehr, Cindy L. *social studies educator, language educator*

**Port Huron**
Moss, Carl Arthur *psychologist*

**Rochester**
Clark, Jon Brian *psychologist*

**Saugatuck**
Genetski, Robert James *economist*

**Southfield**
Gregory, Karl Dwight *economics professor, consultant*
Thimotheose, Kadakampallil George *psychologist*
Weiner, Karen Colby (Karen Lynn Colby) *psychologist, lawyer*

**Suttons Bay**
Periard, Douglas Dee *social studies educator*

**Troy**
DeSantis, Mike G. *social studies educator*

**University Center**
Hill, Alan Gordon *sociologist, educator*

**West Bloomfield**
Marx, Thomas George *economist*

**Ypsilanti**
Weinstein, Jay A. *social sciences educator, researcher*

## MINNESOTA

**Duluth**
Rapp, George Robert (Rip Rapp) *geology and archeology educator*

**Edina**
Fenwick, Sheridan Mellon *psychologist, director*
Gottesman, Irving I. *psychologist, educator*

**Grand Marais**
Hattery, Robert Wilber *political science educator*

**Mankato**
Friend, Donald Agar *geographer, educator*
Lopez, Jose Javier *geographer, educator*

**Maple Grove**
Ones, Deniz S. *psychologist, educator*

**Minneapolis**
Arbisi, Paul Anthony *psychologist, educator*
Bancroft, Ann E. *polar explorer*
Berscheid, Ellen S. *psychology professor, writer, researcher*
Bouchard, Thomas Joseph, Jr. *psychology professor, researcher*
Brown, Robert John *social sciences educator, consultant*
Burns, Matthew Kevin *psychology professor*
Chipman, John Somerset *economist, educator*
Erickson, W(alter) Bruce *business and economics educator, entrepreneur*
Hagedorn, Hildi *psychologist, researcher*
Hansen, Jo-Ida Charlotte *psychology professor, researcher*
Harris, Michael Lawrence *psychologist, consultant*
Holt, Robert Theodore *political science professor, educator, dean*
Hurwicz, Leonid *economist, educator*
Knoke, David Harmon *sociology educator*
Kudrle, Robert Thomas *economist, educator*
Lewis, Stephen Richmond, Jr. *economist, educator*
Nightingale, Edmund Joseph *clinical psychologist, educator, consultant*
Ostrom, Don *political science professor*
Overmier, J. Bruce *psychology professor*
Pick, Anne Danielson *psychology professor*
Reiss, Ira Leonard *retired sociology educator, writer*
Schreiner, John Christian *economics consultant, software publisher*
Shively, William Phillips *political scientist, educator*
Troup, Elliott V., Jr. *psychologist*
Ward, David Allen *sociology educator*
Weinberg, Richard Alan *psychologist, educator*
Ysseldyke, James Edward *psychology professor*

**Moorhead**
Halmrast, Lynn James *psychologist*
Noblitt, Harding Coolidge *political scientist, educator*
Stafford, Bonnie *social studies educator*
Trainor, John Felix *retired economics professor*

**Northfield**
Clark, William Hartley *political science professor*

**Rochester**
Hauri, Peter J. *psychology professor, researcher*

**Round Lake**
Holger, Jon C. *social studies educator*

**Saint Cloud**
Frank, Stephen Ira *political science professor, department chairman*

**Saint Paul**
Fulton, Robert Lester *sociology educator*
Jessup, Paul Frederick *financial economist, educator*
Johnson, Badri Nahvi *social studies educator, real estate company officer*
Rossmann, Jack Eugene *psychologist, educator*
Ruttan, Vernon Wesley *agricultural economist, educator*

**Saint Peter**
Hilbert, Richard Andrew *sociologist, educator*
Mc Rostie, Clair Neil *economics professor*

**Sauk Centre**
Ross, Jeffrey Alan *social studies educator*

**Winona**
Holm, Joy Alice *goldsmith, psychology professor, artist, art educator*

**Young America**
Luecke, Robert Kenneth *social studies educator, department chairman*

**MISSISSIPPI**

**Clinton**
Hutson, Martha Gillon *social studies educator, consultant*

**Hattiesburg**
Davis, Charles Raymond *political scientist, educator*
Sutton, Robert James *social studies educator, special education educator*
Zeigler-Hill, Virgil *psychology professor*

**Jackson**
Suess, James Francis *retired psychiatry educator*

**Mississippi State**
Clynch, Edward John *political science professor, public information officer*

**Morton**
Cox, Marlina R. *social studies educator*

**Saltillo**
Newell, Joyce R. *social studies educator*

**University**
Shughart, William Franklin, II, *economics professor, consultant*

**MISSOURI**

**Advance**
Lanpher, Ben Evert *psychologist, researcher*

**Bolivar**
Brown, Autry *psychology professor, clergyman*

**Chillicothe**
Stull, Kenneth Lee *social studies educator*

**Columbia**
Bank, Barbara J. *sociology educator*

Biddle, Bruce Jesse *social psychologist, educator*
Brekhus, Wayne Herbert *sociologist, educator*
Kausler, Donald Harvey *retired psychology professor*
LoPiccolo, Joseph *psychologist, educator, author*
Rowlett, Ralph Morgan *archaeologist, educator*
Speakman, Robert J. *archaeologist, chemist, researcher*

**Edwards**
Findley, Kathryn E.C. *psychologist*

**Kansas City**
Edmiston, Kelly Dane *economist, researcher*
Glaros, Alan G. *psychologist, researcher*
Nagle, Jean Susan Karabacz *retired sociologist, psychologist*
O'Neill, Paul John *retired psychology educator*
Roosa, Jan Bertorotta *psychologist, writer*

**Maryville**
Edwards, Carla E. *psychology professor*

**Mexico**
Eastman, Harold Dwight *retired social studies educator, journalist*

**Mount Vernon**
Martin, Thomas A. *psychologist*

**Saint Ann**
Thurman, Victoria L. *school psychologist*

**Saint Clair**
Pitman, Pamela Rae *psychologist*

**Saint Joseph**
Boor, Myron Vernon *psychologist, educator*

**Saint Louis**
Beck, Lois Grant *anthropologist, educator, author*
Blanton-Kuhl, Wendy Renee *social studies educator*
Browman, David L(udvig) *archaeologist*
Entessar, Tahmineh *political scientist, educator*
Goldman, Scott Barry *psychologist*
Greenbaum, Stuart I. *economist, educator*
Griffith, Thea R. L. *psychologist, researcher*
Kling, Merle *political scientist, university official*
Leguey-Feilleux, Jean-Robert *political scientist, educator*
Lenzen, Dana Diane *social studies educator*
Leven, Charles Louis *economics educator*
Le Vine, Victor Theodore *retired political science professor*
Loevinger, Jane *psychologist, educator*
Miller, Gary J. *political economist*
Niblack, Tracey *social studies educator*
North, Douglass Cecil *economist, educator*
O'Connell, Daniel Craig *psychologist, educator*
Olney, John William *psychiatry professor*
Ozawa, Martha Naoko *social work educator*
Salisbury, Robert Holt *political science professor*
Sharpe-Taylor, Linda *psychologist*
Shine, Katina Lynniece Wilbon *neuropsychologist, consultant*
Storandt, Martha *psychologist*
Trinkaus, Erik *paleoanthropologist, educator*
Weidenbaum, Murray Lew *economist, educator*
Williams, Mary Alice Baldwin *retired home economist, volunteer*
Witherspoon, William *investment economist*

**Springfield**
Buttacy, Anthony *social studies educator*
Gill, Angela Sue *clinical psychologist*
Wadsworth, Jacob Robert *social studies educator*

**Warrensburg**
Lundervold, Duane A. *psychology professor*

**MONTANA**

**Bozeman**
Duffié, Mary Katharine *anthropologist, educator*
Gray, Philip Howard *former psychologist, writer, educator*
Stroup, Richard Lyndell *economist, educator, writer*

**Colstrip**
Birk Shy, Dawn Marie *psychologist*

**Great Falls**
Anderson, Norman F. *social studies educator*

**Missoula**
Grieves, Forest Leslie *political science professor, department chairman*
Lopach, James Joseph *political science professor*
McKeown, Ashley *biological anthropologist, educator*
Wollersheim, Janet Puccinelli *psychology professor*

**NEBRASKA**

**Alliance**
Haefele, Edwin Theodore *political theorist, consultant*

**Chadron**
Carnot, Mary Jo *psychologist, educator*

**Lincoln**
Deegan, Mary Jo *sociology educator*
McCutcheon, Allan Lee *sociology educator*
Peterson, Wallace Carroll, Sr. *economics professor*

**Omaha**
Clark, Terry Dee *political scientist, educator*
Lindner, Jennifer Lynn *pediatric psychologist*
Louisa, Angelo Joseph *social studies educator, researcher*
Ross, Larry *sociologist, anthropologist, educator*
Wilson, Daniel Richard *anthropologist, physician*

Wunsch, James Stevenson *political science professor*

**Scottsbluff**
Wylie, Guy Stephen *psychologist, educator*

**NEVADA**

**Elko**
Hockett, Bryan Scott *archaeologist*

**Ely**
Alderman, Minnis Amelia *psychologist, educator, small business owner*

**Gardnerville**
Smith, Roderick Joel *behavioral consultant, researcher, educator*

**Incline Village**
Jones, Robert Alonzo *economist*

**Las Vegas**
Cole, Ann Harriet *psychologist, consultant*
Donohue, Bradley Christopher *psychology professor*
Goodall, Leonard Edwin *public administration educator*
Jelen, Ted G. *political scientist*
Shelton, Samantha *psychologist*
Silver, N. Clayton *psychology professor, consultant*
Weeks, Gerald *psychologist, educator*

**Reno**
Chapman, Samuel Greeley *political science professor, criminologist*
Crowley, Joseph Neil *political science professor, former academic administrator*
Cummings, Nicholas Andrew *psychologist*
Hayes, Steven Charles *psychologist, educator*
Haynes, Gary Anthony *archaeologist*
Kemmelmeier, Markus *sociologist, psychologist, educator*
Leland, Joy Hanson *retired anthropologist, researcher*
Weinberg, Leonard Burton *political scientist*

**Yerington**
Price, Judith Holm *educational psychologist*

**NEW HAMPSHIRE**

**Durham**
Palmer, Stuart Hunter *sociology educator*
Romoser, George Kenneth *political and social science educator*

**Francestown**
Foster, Margery Somers *economics professor*

**Hanover**
Bower, Richard Stuart *retired economist*
Demko, George Joseph *geographer*
Fischel, William Alan *economics professor*
Hall, Raymond *social studies educator*
Kleck, Robert Eldon *psychology professor*
Lyons, Gene Martin *political scientist, educator*
Masters, Roger Davis *political scientist, educator, toxicologist*
Riggs, Lorrin Andrews *psychologist, educator*
Rutter, Jeremy Bentham *archaeologist, educator*
Starzinger, Vincent Evans *political scientist, educator*
Welsch, Robert Louis *anthropologist, curator*

**Henniker**
Braiterman, Thea Gilda *economics professor, state legislator*

**Keene**
Baldwin, Peter Arthur *psychologist, educator, author, minister*
Hackett, John Thomas *retired economist*
Scioli, Anthony *psychologist, educator*

**Lebanon**
Emery, Virginia Olga Beattie *psychologist, researcher*
McDonald, Brenna Cathleen *psychologist*
Rosenberg, Stanley David *psychologist, educator*

**Manchester**
Carrier, Celine A. *psychologist*

**Portsmouth**
Wener, Brian D. *psychologist*

**NEW JERSEY**

**Allenwood**
Carbone, Diane M. *psychologist, consultant*

**Branchville**
MacMurren, Harold Henry, Jr. *psychologist, lawyer*
Thomas, William H. *anthropologist, director*

**Burlington**
Haws, Elizabeth Anne *psychologist, director*

**Camden**
Blyn, George *economics professor*
Harrison, Russell Sage *political science professor, consultant, social studies educator*
Worrall, John Dennis *economics professor, consultant, writer*
Yamada, Tetsuji *health economist, educator*

**Clifton**
Klein-Von Reiche, Samuelle *psychologist*

**Cranbury**
Hawver, Dennis A. *psychologist, consultant*

**East Brunswick**
Johnson, Edward Elemuel *psychologist, educator*

**East Orange**
Wolff, Derish Michael *economist, department chairman*

**Englewood Cliffs**
Farrell, Patricia Ann *psychologist, educator, writer*

**Florham Park**
Brodkin, Adele Ruth Meyer *psychologist*

**Fort Lee**
Kofman, Mikhail *economist, engineering executive*

**Hamilton**
Paul, William Gerald *educational psychologist*

**Hammonton**
Henshaw, Louise Ann *school psychologist*

**Hasbrouck Heights**
Perham, Roy Gates III *industrial psychologist*

**Jackson**
Leveson, Irving Frederick *economist*

**Jersey City**
Ohiwerei, Godwin Oiseozoje *sociologist, educator*
Urso, Ida *psychologist*

**Lakewood**
Levine, Stephen M. *psychologist, educator*

**Lawrenceville**
Oglesby, Jennifer Marie *clinical psychologist, neuropsychologist*
Stein, Sandra Lou *educational psychology professor*

**Little Ferry**
Briggs, Alice *clinical child psychologist*

**Livingston**
Friedman, Merton Hirsch *retired psychologist, educator*

**Lodi**
Guillory, Ann Verrett *psychologist, educator*

**Lyndhurst**
Bunda, Stephen Myron *political advisor, counselor, lawyer, classical philosopher*

**Madison**
Jennings, George Harold *psychology professor*
Kaboub, Fadhel *economics professor, consultant*

**Mahwah**
Perez-Strumolo, Lysandra Marie *psychologist, educator*

**Manasquan**
Boodey, Cecil Webster, Jr. *retired political science professor*

**Montclair**
Lang, Gerhard *psychology professor*

**Mount Laurel**
Giampetro, Kathleen A. *school psychologist*

**Mountain Lakes**
Loomis, Rebecca C. *psychologist*

**New Brunswick**
Alexander, Robert Jackson *economist, educator*
Clauss-Ehlers, Caroline S. *psychologist, educator, journalist*
Elias, Maurice Jesse *psychology educator*
Glasser, Paul Harold *sociologist, educator, social worker, university administrator*
Glickman, Norman Jay *economist, urban policy analyst*
Kubik, Jan *political science professor*
Leventhal, Howard *health psychology educator, researcher*
Mechanic, David *social sciences educator*
Reock, Ernest C., Jr. *retired social studies educator, director*
Rockoff, Hugh Touff *economist, educator*
Rosenberg, Seymour *psychologist, educator*
Sullivan, Margaret Wolan *research psychologist, educator*
Tiger, Lionel *social scientist, anthropology consultant*
Toby, Jackson *sociologist, educator*

**New Providence**
Roth, Robert Howard *psychologist*

**Newark**
Adler, Freda Schaffer (Mrs. G. O. W. Mueller) *criminologist, educator*
Carroll, John Douglas *mathematical and statistical psychologist, educator*
Ferguson, Yale Hicks *political scientist, educator*
Harber, Kent D. *psychology professor*
Hiltz, Starr Roxanne *sociologist, educator, writer, consultant, computer scientist*
Holzer, Marc *public administrator educator*
Pagán, Gilberto, Jr. *psychologist*

**North Brunswick**
Burge, Micah Benjamin *school psychologist*

**Oakland**
Guller, Irving Bernard *forensic, clinical psychologist, consultant, writer*

**Oldwick**
Haymaker, Douglas James *psychologist, researcher*

**Palisades Park**
Schmarge, Agapi Georgiou *social studies educator*

## Paramus
Hochberg, Lois J. *school psychologist*
Lieberman, Charles *economist*
Perkins-Munn, Tiffany Sabrena *psychologist, researcher*

## Parsippany
François, Andre J. *psychologist, educational association administrator*

## Paterson
Paulhus, Thomas A. *social studies educator*

## Piscataway
Chu, Brian Christopher *psychology professor*
Goss, Mary E. Weber *sociology educator*
Kormann, Russell Jay *psychologist, consultant*
McCrady, Barbara Sachs *psychologist, educator*
Monheit, Alan Craig *economist, educator*
Peterson, Donald Robert *psychologist, educator, academic administrator*
Schwebel, Milton *psychologist, educator*
West, Mark Otto *psychology professor*
Zerubavel, Eviatar *sociologist, educator*

## Princeton
Basáñez, Miguel Ebergenyi *political scientist, educator*
Denabou, Roland Jean-Marc *economist, educator*
Blackman, Sue Anne Batey *economics researcher*
Blinder, Alan Stuart *economist, educator*
Bogan, Elizabeth Chapin *economist, educator*
Chow, Gregory Chi-Chong *economist, educator*
Coffey, Joseph Irving *political scientist, educator*
Cook, Michael Allan *social sciences educator*
Cooper, Joel *psychologist, educator*
Doig, Jameson Wallace *political science professor*
Friedberg, Aaron Louis *political science professor*
Geertz, Clifford James *anthropology educator*
Girgus, Joan Stern *psychologist, educator, director*
Gordenker, Leon *political science professor*
Greenstein, Fred Irwin *political science professor*
Gross, Charles Gordon *psychology professor*
Hitz, Frederick Porter *public and international affairs educator*
Hoebel, Bartley Gore *psychologist, educator*
Kahneman, Daniel *psychology professor*
Kateb, George Anthony *political science professor*
Keller, Suzanne *sociologist, psychotherapist*
Kenen, Peter Bain *economist, educator*
Keohane, Robert Owen *political scientist, educator*
Krugman, Paul Robin *economics professor*
Lazarus, Arnold Allan *psychologist, educator*
Lewis, Bernard *retired social studies educator*
Lewis, John Prior *economist, educator*
Malkiel, Burton Gordon *economist, educator*
Maskin, Eric Stark *economics professor*
Miller, George Armitage *psychologist, educator*
Parry, Scott Brink *psychologist*
Quandt, Richard Emeric *economics professor*
Rosen, Harvey Sheldon *economics professor, former federal official*
Rothschild, Michael *economics professor*
Rozman, Gilbert Friedell *sociologist, educator*
Shapiro, Harold Tafler *economics professor, former academic administrator*
Shear, Theodore Leslie, Jr. *archaeologist, educator*
Sigmund, Paul Eugene *political science professor*
Small, Mario L. *sociologist, educator*
Starr, Paul Elliot *sociologist, educator, editor, writer*
Tienda, Marta *demographer, educator*
Trussell, James *economist, educator, dean*
Walzer, Michael *political science professor*
Westoff, Charles Francis *demographer, educator*
Willig, Robert Daniel *economics professor*
Willingham, Warren Willcox *psychologist*

## Red Bank
Dale, John Denny *economist, business executive*
McWhinney, Madeline H. (Mrs. John Denny Dale) *economist, director*

## Ridgefield Park
Magdosko, Paula *school psychologist*

## Saddle River
Lasser, Gail Maria *psychologist, educator*

## Scotch Plains
Hallard, Wayne Bruce *retired economist*

## Sewell
Gonnella, Renee *school psychologist*

## Somerset
Lichtig, Leo Kenneth *health economist*

## Springfield
Shilling, A. Gary *economist, consultant*

## Summit
Deming, Frederick Wilson *retired economist, banker*

## Teaneck
Brudner, Helen Gross *social sciences educator*
Cassimatis, Peter John *economics professor*

## Tenafly
Blank, Marion Sue *psychologist, educator*

## Titusville
Bhattacharjya, Ashoke Sanjoy *economist, researcher*

## Trenton
Lattanzi, Gregory Denis *archaeologist*

## Union
Kim, Youn-Suk Ernest *economist, educator*

## Verona
Aronow, Edward *psychologist, educator*

## Wall
De Santo, Donald James *psychologist, educational association administrator*

## Washington
Castner, Bret A. *social studies educator*

## Wayne
Salny, Abbie Feinstein *psychologist*

## Westfield
Simon, Martin Stanley *economist, consultant*

## Westwood
Fabrikant, Craig Steven *psychologist*

## Whitehouse Station
Hunsche, Elke Greta Irma *economist*

# NEW MEXICO

## Albuquerque
Calkins, Ralph Nelson *retired economics professor*
Condie, Carol Joy *anthropologist, science administrator*
Harris, Fred R. *political scientist, educator, retired senator*
Hester, Reid Kevin *psychologist, researcher*
Jung, Rex Eugene *psychologist, researcher*
May, Philip Alan *sociologist, educator*
Ralsh, Carol Brooks *anthropologist, archaeologist*
Schwerin, Karl Henry *anthropology educator, researcher*
Stuart, David Edward *anthropologist, writer, educator*

## Clovis
Collins, John Lester *psychologist*

## Corrales
Adams, James Frederick *psychologist, educator, academic administrator*

## El Prado
Young, Jon Nathan *archaeologist*

## Las Cruces
DeMers, Michael N. *geographer, researcher, educator, consultant*
Roscoe, Stanley Nelson *psychologist, aeronautical engineer*

## Las Vegas
Riley, Carroll Lavern *anthropology educator*

## Milan
Wilkins-Cordery, Renee Helene *psychologist*

## Santa Fe
Anderson, Darrell Edward *psychologist, educator*
Harmon, Judith S *anthropologist*
Perry, Nancy Estelle *psychologist*
Williams, Stephen *anthropologist, educator*

## Silver City
Gilbert, Kathie Simon *economist, educator*
Lopez, Linda Carol *social sciences educator*

# NEW YORK

## Albany
Capaldi, Elizabeth Ann Deutsch *psychological sciences professor*
Hartman, Brett Thomas *psychologist, writer*
Hawley, Ilissa Kotzin *social studies educator*
Ley, Ronald *psychologist, educator*
Nathan, Richard P(erle) *political science professor*
Pezzulo, Jacqueline *psychologist, researcher*
Polimeni, John Matthew *economics professor*
Teevan, Richard Collier *retired psychology professor*
Thompson, Frank Joseph *political science professor*
Ward, Russell Avery *sociologist, educator*
Zimmerman, Joseph Francis *political scientist, educator*

## Amherst
Brown, Murray *economist, educator*

## Annandale On Hudson
Papadimitriou, Dimitri Basil *economist, educator, academic administrator*
Zacharias, Ajit *economist*

## Auburn
Dello Stritto, Ellen M. *retired social studies educator*
Pelkey, Lawrence Michael *school psychologist*

## Averill Park
Haines, Walter Wells *retired economics professor*
Messia, Robert A. III *social studies educator*

## Bayside
Ohrenstein, Roman Abraham *economist, educator, rabbi*

## Bellmore
Dacek, Joanne Carole *psychologist*

## Binghamton
Isaacson, Robert Lee *psychologist, educator*
James, Gary Douglas *biological anthropologist, educator, researcher*
Levis, Donald James *psychologist, educator*
Mazrui, Ali Al'Amin *political science professor, researcher*
Stahl, Peter William *archaeologist, educator*

## Brentwood
Liebert, Lynn Langenbach *psychologist, educator*

## Bronx
Durglishvili, Nana Z. *psychologist, language educator*
Macklin, Ruth *bioethics educator*
Muller, Katherine Lynn *clinical psychologist*
Rappaport, Lisa N. *psychologist*
Rego, Simon Alexander *psychologist*

## Brooklyn
McCabe, Paul Christopher *psychologist, educator*
Miller, Daniel Weiss *psychologist*
Nye, William Roger *psychologist*
O'Doherty, Susan Ann *psychologist, writer*
Reinisch, June Machover *psychologist, educator*
Sesin, Maria Carmen *psychologist, researcher*

## Buffalo
Frone, Michael R. *psychologist, researcher*
Gort, Michael *economics professor*
Lamb, Charles Moody *political scientist, educator*
Levy, Kenneth Jay *psychology professor, academic administrator*
Li, Guofang *social sciences educator*
Reinhold, Sandra Lynne *psychologist*
Simms, Leonard Jay *psychology professor*
Tedlock, Barbara Helen *anthropologist, educator, academic administrator*

## Canton
Auster, Nancy Eileen Ross *economics professor*
Young, Jeffrey Thomas *economics professor*

## Castile
Krolikowski, Gary E. *social sciences educator*

## Chappaqua
Schwarz, Wolfgang *psychologist*

## Conesus
Dadrian, Vahakn Norair *retired sociology educator*

## Cortlandt Manor
Lupiani, Jennifer Lynne *school psychologist*

## Croton On Hudson
Reinhard, Kenneth Edward *psychologist*

## Delhi
Van Brunt, Arthur Hoffman (Peter) *economist, educator*

## Dobbs Ferry
Culhane, Hind Rassam *psychologist, educator, historian*
Kraetzer, Mary C. *sociologist, educator, consultant*

## East Elmhurst
Scott, Lionel Franklin *psychologist, educator*

## East Meadow
Albert, Gerald *clinical psychologist*
Jeziorski, Michael A. *social studies educator*

## Farmingdale
Goodstone, Michael S. *psychology professor, consultant*

## Flushing
Beveridge, Andrew Alan *sociologist, educator, consultant*
Pellitteri, John Steven *psychologist, psychotherapist, educator*
Smith, Charles William *social sciences educator*

## Fredonia
Hewitt, Holly E. *workforce development professional, reporter*

## Freeport
Ferentino, Sheila Connolly *psychologist, consultant*

## Garrison
Murray, Thomas Henry *bioethics educator, writer*

## Geneseo
Olczak, Paul Vincent *psychologist, educator*

## Glen Oaks
Lencz, Todd *psychologist, researcher*

## Great Neck
Christie, George Nicholas *economist, consultant*
Joskow, Jules *economic research company executive*
Minkoff, Jack *retired economics professor*

## Greenport
Watts, Harold Wesley *economist, educator*

## Greenvale
Kusukawa, Akira *demographer, educator*

## Groveland
Battersby, Harold Ronald *retired anthropologist, archaeologist, linguist*

## Hamilton
Haines, Michael Robert *economist, educator*
Simpson, Nicole B. *economics professor*

## Hartsdale
Butler, Kevin J. *social studies educator*

## Hempstead
Bose, Meena *political science professor*
Shafritz, Keith Michael *psychology professor*
Udolf, Roy *psychology professor, lawyer*
Wattel, Harold Louis *economics professor*

## Hopewell Junction
Lemy, Marie Edith *psychologist, educator*

## Ithaca
Ascher, Robert *anthropologist, educator, archaeologist, film producer*
Basu, Kaushik *economics professor*
Beneria, Lourdes *economist, educator*
Chapman, Lewis Duane *economist*
Darlington, Richard Benjamin *retired psychologist, retired educator, researcher*
Easley, David *economics professor*
Eells, Gregory Todd *psychologist, director*
Fireside, Harvey Francis *political scientist, educator*

## Wertz, Frederick
Wertz, Frederick *psychologist, educator*

## Heckathorn
Heckathorn, Douglas D. *sociologist, educator, epidemiologist*
Jarrow, Robert Alan *economist, educator*
Kahn, Alfred Edward *economist, educator, government official*
Kenkel, Donald Scott *economist*
Kennedy, Kenneth Adrian Raine *biological anthropologist, forensic anthropologist*
Lowi, Theodore Jay *political science professor*
Lyons, Thomas Patrick *economics professor*
Majumdar, Mukul Kumar *economist, educator*
Mueller, Betty Jeanne *social work educator*
Neisser, Ulric *psychology professor*
Pelto, Gretel H. *nutritional anthropologist, educator*
Pinstrup-Andersen, Per *economist, educator*
Rader, Nancy Louise de Villiers *psychology professor, consultant*
Smidt, Seymour *economics professor*
Smith, Robert John *anthropology educator*
Thorbecke, Erik *economics professor*
Tomek, William Goodrich *agricultural economist*
Vanek, Jaroslav *economist, educator*
Waldman, Michael *economist, educator*

## Jamaica
Chirico, Donna M, *psychologist, educator, researcher*
Lees, Francis *economics professor*

## Johnstown
DiNitto, Andrew Joseph *political scientist, educator*

## Katonah
Wenglowski, Gary Martin *economist*

## Lancaster
Walsh, Edward F. *social studies educator*

## Larchmont
Siegel, Nathaniel Harold *sociology educator*

## Lindenhurst
Kaufman, Susan Shiffman *psychologist*

## Little Neck
Weinblatt, Alan S. *psychologist*

## Loudonville
Booker, James *economics professor, consultant*

## Manhasset
Savage, Clare Leavy *school psychologist*
Tippy, Margaret O'Shea *psychologist*

## Melville
Grayson, Gerald Herbert *economist, educator, arbitrator, writer*

## Mexico
Sade, Donald Stone *anthropology educator*

## Millbrook
Flexner, Kurt Fisher *economist, educator*

## New Paltz
Schnell, George Adam *geographer, educator*

## New Rochelle
Berlage, Gai Ingham *sociologist, researcher*
Rutstein, Eleanor H. *psychologist*

## New York
Adrian, Tobias *economist*
Amihud, Yakov *economics professor*
Andreassi, John Lawrence *psychologist, educator*
Arther, Richard Oberlin *polygraphist, educator*
Ashman, Teresa Anne *neuropsychologist*
Bardach, Joan Lucile *clinical psychologist*
Beck, Nathaniel L. *political science professor*
Betts, Richard Kevin *political science professor*
Blechner, Mark Jacob *psychologist, educator*
Bond, Alma Halbert *psychoanalyst, author*
Bowers, Patricia Eleanor Fritz *economist*
Braham, Randolph Lewis *political science professor*
Brams, Steven John *political science professor*
Browne, Joy *psychologist, radio personality*
Buck, Louise Zierdt *psychologist*
Campano, Fred *economics professor, statistician consultant*
Caraley, Demetrios James *political science professor, writer, editor*
Carr, Arthur Charles *psychologist, educator*
Chamberlain, Neil Cornelius Wolverton *economist, emeritus educator*
Chan, Anthony *economist*
Chelstrom, Marilyn Ann *political science educator, consultant*
Clamar, Aphrodite J. *psychologist*
Cohen, Mitchell S. *political science professor*
Cohen, Stephen Frand *political scientist, writer, historian, educator, commentator*
Comitas, Lambros *anthropologist, educator*
Connelly, Joan Breton *archaeologist*
Dalton, Dennis Gilmore *political science professor*
DeGregorio, Carlo *social studies educator*
del Cerro, Gerardo *sociologist, researcher*
deMause, Lloyd *psychologist*
de Menil, Georges *economist, educator*
Demeny, Paul George *demographer, researcher*
Denmark, Florence Harriet Levin *psychology professor*
Dowling, Edward Thomas *economics professor*
Duke, Anthony Drexel *retired sociologist, educator, philanthropist*
Edwards, Franklin R. *economist, educator, consultant*
Elinson, Jack *social sciences educator*
Ellis, Albert *clinical psychologist, educator, author*
Engler, Robert *political science professor*
Epstein, Cynthia Fuchs *sociology educator, writer*
Feldman, Ronald Arthur *sociologist, educator*
Fischer, Herbert Steven *social studies educator*
Fishbein, William *psychologist, neuroscientist*
Fishman, Steven T. *psychologist*
Fosler, Gail D. *economist*
Fox, Richard Gabriel *anthropologist, educator*
Franklin, Julian Harold *political science professor*

Galanter, Eugene *psychologist, educator*
Gallagher, Maureen J. *psychologist*
Gans, Herbert J. *sociologist, educator*
Gilligan, Carol *psychologist, writer*
Glanzer, Murray *psychology professor*
Glass, David Carter *psychologist, educator*
Glickman, Michael Richard *social studies educator*
Goldman, George David *psychologist*
Gorenstein, Ethan Ezra *psychologist, educator*
Griffin, Anne *political scientist, educator*
Grody, Deborah *psychologist, director*
Gross, Feliks *sociologist, educator, writer*
Grossman, Michael *economics professor*
Gullo, Stephen Pernice *psychologist, corporate executive*
Gundle, Sarah Shoshana *psychologist*
Habachy, Suzan Salwa Saba *economist, not-for-profit developer*
Haber, Pierre-Claude *psychologist*
Halper, Thomas *political science professor*
Harkavy-Friedman, Jill Martine *psychologist*
Heeger, David J. *psychology professor*
Heilbrun, James *economist, educator*
Heyde, Martha Bennett *psychologist*
Higgins, Edward Tory *psychology professor, research scientist*
Hill, Marjorie Jean *psychologist, association executive*
Holloway, Ralph Leslie *anthropology educator*
Hormats, Robert David *economist, investment banker*
Hoxter, Curtis Joseph *international economic advisor, public relations executive*
Ivanovitch, Michael S. *economist*
Jacoby, Jacob *consumer psychology educator*
Jasso, Guillermina *sociologist, educator*
Jerolmack, Colin *sociologist*
Jervis, Robert *political science professor*
Kandel, Denise Bystryn *sociologist*
Kaplan, Lawrence Jay *economist, educator*
Kaplow, Julie B. *psychologist, educator*
Karl, Kurt Erskine *economist*
Kavesh, Robert A. *economist, educator*
Kazemi, Farhad *political scientist, educator*
Krauss, Herbert Harris *psychologist*
Kurzweil, Edith *social sciences educator, editor*
Laibman, David *economist, educator*
Lazarcik, Gregor *economist, educator, financial research company executive*
Leahey, Miles Cary *economist*
Leahy, Robert Louis *psychologist*
Legvold, Robert *political science professor*
Lehman, Edward William *social studies educator, researcher*
Levin, Henry Mordechai *economist, educator*
Lew, Jacob *public administration educator*
Lichtblau, John H. *economist*
Liff, Zanvel A. *psychologist*
Lipsey, Robert Edward *economist, educator*
Lothian, James Robert *economist, educator*
MacLeod, William Bentley *economics professor, law professor*
Maldonado-Bear, Rita Marinita *economist, educator*
Marable, Manning *social science educator, writer*
Marks, Lillian Shapiro *secretarial studies educator, retired, writer, editor*
Mason, Susan E. *social sciences educator, consultant*
Mc Cullough, J. Lee *industrial psychologist*
Meyer-Bahlburg, Heino F.L. *psychology professor*
Midlarsky, Elizabeth Ruth *psychology professor*
Miller, Ruby Sills *retired gerontologist*
Mischel, Walter *psychology professor*
Mroz, John Edwin *political scientist*
Mundell, Robert Alexander *economist, educator*
Murphy, Austin de la Salle *economist, educator, banker*
Nadiri, M. Ishaq *economics professor, researcher, consultant*
Nathan, Andrew James *political science educator*
Neria, Yuval Y. *psychologist, educator*
Netzer, Dick *economics professor*
Oh, Joong-Hwan *sociologist*
O'Neill, June Ellenoff *economist*
Park, Cynthia *sociology educator, consultant*
Patrick, Hugh Talbot *economist, educator*
Peck, Fred Neil *economist, educator*
Persell, Caroline Hodges *sociologist, educator, author, researcher, consultant*
Petchesky, Rosalind Pollack *political scientist, educator, social sciences educator*
Phelps, Edmund Strother *economics professor*
Piven, Frances Fox *political scientist, educator*
Psomiades, Harry John *political science professor*
Pye, Gordon Bruce *economist*
Rath, Joseph F. *psychologist, researcher, educator*
Richman, Sophia *psychologist*
Riss, Eric *psychologist*
Rivlin, Benjamin *political science professor*
Robock, Stefan Hyman *retired economics professor*
Rosaldo, Renato Ignacio, Jr. *cultural anthropology educator*
Rosenthal, Howard Lewis *political science professor*
Rothman, Barbara Katz *sociology educator*
Sachs, Jeffrey David *economist, educator*
Sands, Harry *psychologist, health administrator, researcher*
Sandy, Sandra V. *psychologist*
Scanlon, Rosemary *economist*
Scelsa, Joseph Vincent *sociologist, educator, dean*
Schotter, Andrew Roye *economics professor, consultant*
Schwab, George David *social sciences educator, writer*
Schwartz, Anna Jacobson *economist*
Sheldon, Eleanor Harriet Bernert *sociologist, writer*
Silver, Morris *economist, educator*
Simon, Jacqueline Albert *political scientist, writer*
Small, George LeRoy *geographer, educator*
Solecki, R. Stefan *anthropologist, educator*
Spencer, Charles S. *anthropologist*
Steele, Howard L. *psychology professor*
Stiglitz, Joseph Eugene *economics professor, former federal official*
Studer, Patricia S. *psychologist*

Suarez-Orozco, Carola Elisabeth *psychology professor*
Sundararajan, Arun *economist, educator*
Tallmer, Margot Sallop *psychologist, gerontologist, psychoanalyst*
Taylor, Lance Jerome *economics professor*
Tepper, Lynn Marsha *gerontologist, educator*
Terris, Lillian Dick *psychologist, health facility administrator*
Tester, Leonard Wayne *psychology professor*
Thurston, Thom Buster *economics professor, consultant*
Todaro, Michael Paul *economics professor, consultant*
Vora, Ashok *financial economist*
Wade, Estelle B. *psychologist, psychoanalyst*
Walter, Ingo *economics professor*
Weisberg-Samuels, Janet S. *psychologist*
Weiss, Samuel Abraham *psychologist, psychoanalyst*
White, Lawrence J. *economics professor*
Wolff, Edward Nathan *economist, educator*
Wolman, William *economist, journalist, broadcaster*
Zawistowski, Stephen Louis *psychologist, educator*
Zeichner, Harvey *psychologist*

**Niagara University**
Osberg, Timothy Michael *psychologist, educator, researcher*

**Niskayuna**
Wright, Theodore Paul, Jr. *political science professor*

**Old Westbury**
Ozelli, Tunch *economics professor*

**Oneonta**
Beitzel, Brian *educational psychologist*
Hill, Donald Raymond *anthropologist, educator*
Malhotra, Ashok Kumar *philosophy educator*
vom Saal, Walter *psychology professor*

**Oswego**
Delaney, Tim *sociologist, educator*
Gordon, Norman Botnick *psychologist, educator*
Malgieri, Lewis Joshua *psychologist, consultant*

**Oyster Bay**
Landrón, Ana *school psychologist*

**Palisades**
Balstad, Roberta *social scientist*

**Pittsford**
Steamer, Robert Julius *political science professor*
Sterns, Samantha *gerontologist, researcher*

**Plainview**
Wenderoff, Alan J. *psychologist, educator*

**Pleasant Valley**
Marshall, Natalie Junemann *economics professor*

**Port Chester**
Sotelo-Dynega, Marlene *psychologist*

**Port Washington**
Bartell, Susan Silver *psychologist, writer*

**Potsdam**
Stillwell, Arlene M. *psychologist, educator*
Wickman, Peter M. *sociologist, educator*

**Poughkeepsie**
Johnson, M. Glen (Maurice Glen Johnson) *political science professor*
Phipps, Peter A. *psychology professor*
Scileppi, John A. *psychologist, educator*

**Purchase**
Newton, Esther Mary *anthropologist, educator*
Ryan, Edward W. *economics professor*

**Queensbury**
Bower, Rose Janet *psychologist, educator*

**Rego Park**
Feldman, Rachel Beth *psychologist*

**Rochester**
Aslin, Richard N. *psychology professor, researcher*
Bluhm, William Theodore *political scientist, educator*
Deci, Edward Lewis *psychologist, educator*
Fenno, Richard Francis, Jr. *political scientist, educator*
Freeman, Leslie Jean *neuropsychologist, researcher*
Hopkins, Thomas Duvall *economics professor*
Laties, Victor Gregory *psychologist, educator*
Levy, Harold David *psycholinguist*
Long, John Broaddus, Jr. *economist, educator*
McDowell, David J. *psychology professor*
Mc Kenzie, Lionel Wilfred *economist, educator*
Newport, Elissa L. *psychology professor*
Niemi, Richard Gene *political science educator*
Peloquin, Lori Jeanne *clinical psychologist*
Phelps, Charles Elliott *economics professor, director*
Primo, David Martin *political science professor*
Regenstreif, S(amuel) Peter *political scientist, educator*
Vernarelli, Michael Joseph *economics professor, consultant, academic administrator*
Wagner, Aureen Pinto *psychologist, educator*
Zax, Melvin *psychologist, educator*

**Rockville Centre**
Lewittes, Don Jordan *psychologist*

**Rye Brook**
Aquino, Joseph Mario *clinical psychologist*

**Saratoga Springs**
Miller, Anita Diane *psychologist*

**Scarborough**
Parks, Robert Henry *consulting economist, educator*

**Scarsdale**
Cohen, Irwin *economist*

**Schenectady**
Board, Joseph Breckinridge, Jr. *political scientist, educator*
Huszar, Andrew Louis *school psychologist*

**Somers**
Trzasko, Joseph Anthony *psychologist, educator*

**South Richmond Hill**
Singh, Ronald *social sciences educator, researcher*

**Staten Island**
Arievitch, Igor *psychology professor*
Franzone, Eric Scott *psychologist*
Kuppersmith, Judith Carolyn *psychology professor*
Piedilato, Janet *psychologist*
Piegari, James A. *psychologist*
Stolz, Theodora *psychologist*

**Stony Brook**
Benitez-Silva, Hugo A. *economics professor*
Carr, Edward Gary *psychology professor*
Kramer, Karen Leslie *anthropologist, educator*
Stolzberg, Mark Elliott *psychologist*
Stone, Elizabeth Cecilia *anthropology educator*
Tanur, Judith Mark *sociologist, educator*
Travis, Martin Bice *retired political scientist, educator*

**Syracuse**
Birkhead, Guthrie Sweeney, Jr. *political scientist, dean*
Braungart, Richard Gottfried *social sciences educator, political scientist*
Kriesberg, Louis *sociologist, educator*
Leontieva, Luba *psychologist, researcher, psychiatrist*
Masters, Kevin S. *psychology professor*
McIntyre, Laura Lee *psychology professor, consultant*
Monmonier, Mark *geographer, writer*
Wilkinson, Louise Cherry *psychology professor, dean*

**Tarrytown**
Pontrelli, Laura Alison *psychologist*
Weiner, Max *psychology professor*

**Tonawanda**
Brunger, Eric Geoffrey *social studies educator, coach*

**Troy**
Brazil, Harold Edmund *political science professor*

**Valhalla**
Urban, Diane *psychologist, educator*

**Valley Stream**
Gonzalez, Jennifer *school psychologist*

**Warwick**
Kaminsky, Anatol *political science professor, writer*

**West Point**
Keith, Bruce Edward *sociologist*

**White Plains**
Kaushik, Surendra Kumar *economist*

**Woodbury**
Agresti, Miriam Monell *psychologist*

**Woodstock**
Lieberman, Josefa Nina *psychologist, educator, writer*

**Yonkers**
Lupiani, Donald Anthony *psychologist*
Monegro, Francisco *alternative medicine consultant, psychology professor*

**NORTH CAROLINA**

**Asheville**
Burgard, Jesse F. *psychologist*
Dickens, Charles Henderson *retired social sciences educator*

**Biltmore Forest**
Sgro, Joseph Anthony *retired psychologist, educator*

**Carrboro**
Barbarin, Oscar Anthony *psychologist*

**Cary**
Thayer, Paul William *psychology educator, consultant*

**Cashiers**
O'Connell, Edward James, Jr. *psychologist, educator, systems administrator, consultant*

**Chapel Hill**
Baroff, George Stanley *psychologist, educator*
Brown, Frank *social sciences educator*
Fieleke, Norman Siegfried *economist, educator*
Fox, Ronald Ernest *psychologist*
Girdler, Susan Scott *psychologist, educator, researcher*
Gottlieb, Gilbert *psychobiologist, educator*
Gray, Virginia Hickman *political science professor*
Hartlyn, Jonathan *political scientist, educator*
Jones, Lyle Vincent *psychologist, educator*
Latané, Bibb *social psychologist*
Lowman, Robert Paul *psychology professor, academic administrator*
Norton, Edward C. *economist, educator*

Prange, Arthur Jergen, Jr. *psychology professor, neuroscientist*
Rindfuss, Ronald Richard *social studies educator*
Schoultz, Lars *political scientist, educator*
Smith, James Finley *economist, educator*
Stenberg, Carl W. III *public administration educator, dean*
Steponaitis, Vincas Petras *archaeologist, anthropologist, educator*
Treml, Vladimir Guy *economist, educator*
Wasik, Barbara Hanna *psychologist, educator*
Weinstein, Sidney *neuropsychologist*
Wilson, Glenn *economist, educator*
Wright, Deil Spencer *political science professor*

**Charlotte**
Goolkasian, Paula A. *psychologist, educator*
Hicks-Ray, Denyse *psychologist, commentator*
Neel, Richard Eugene *economist, educator*
Pyle, Gerald Fredric *geographer, educator*
Vazquez Rivera, Ornela Amliv *psychologist*
Webster, Murray Alexander, Jr. *sociologist, educator*

**Cullowhee**
Mulligan, Robert Francis, Jr. *economist, civil engineer*

**Davidson**
Palmer, Edward L. *psychologist, educator, writer*
Ross, Clark Grant *economics professor*

**Durham**
Aldrich, John Herbert *political science professor*
Blackburn, John Oliver *economist, consultant*
Bunch, Michael Brannen *psychologist, educator*
Carson, James Wood *psychologist*
Clotfelter, Charles T. *economics professor*
Conklin, George Henry *sociologist, educator*
Cook, Philip Jackson *economist, educator*
Elliot, Jeffrey M. *political science professor, department chairman*
Holsti, Ole Rudolf *political scientist, educator*
Jordan, Kerry Elizabeth *psychologist, researcher*
Kelley, Allen Charles *economist, educator*
Land, Kenneth Carl *sociologist, educator, demographer*
Lockhead, Gregory Roger *psychology professor*
McClain, Paula Denice *political scientist, educator*
Rossi, Barbara *economics professor*
Simons, Elwyn LaVerne *physical anthropologist, primatologist, paleontologist, educator*
Sloan, Frank Allen *economist, educator*
Staddon, John Eric Rayner *psychology professor, neurobiology professor, zoology professor*
Surwit, Richard Samuel *psychology professor*
Talley, Joseph Eugene *psychologist*

**Elizabeth City**
Lee, Jennifer Jarman *social studies educator*

**Fayetteville**
McKnight, Kelly Marie *psychologist*

**Greensboro**
Chandler, Austin Grace *psychologist*
Goldman, Bert Arthur *psychologist, educator*
Helms-VanStone, Mary Wallace *anthropology educator*
Proffer, Andrew *psychologist*
Shelton, David Howard *economics professor*

**Greenville**
Aziz, Shahnaz *psychology professor*
Bjorkman, Sylvia Johnson *psychologist*

**High Point**
Corey, James William *political scientist, educator*
Fox, Gerald Trent *social sciences educator, consultant*

**Hillsborough**
Goodwin, Craufurd David *economics professor*
Piper, Don Courtney *political scientist, educator*

**Jacksonville**
Guyer, Charles Grayson, II, *psychologist*

**Lillington**
Evans, Warden Lee *social studies educator*

**Morganton**
Dickison, Julie Anne *psychologist, researcher*

**Newport**
Rettie, Dwight Fay *retired political science educator, writer*

**Pittsboro**
Richardson, Richard Judson *retired political science professor*

**Raleigh**
Allen, Steven Glen *economics professor, business professor*
Fantz, Janet Nelsen *school psychologist*
Imade, Lucky Osagie *political scientist, educator*
Newman, Slater Edmund *psychologist, educator*
Taddesse, Samuel *economist, consultant*

**Saluda**
Cutright, Phillips *sociologist, educator*

**Wilmington**
Schuhmann, Peter W. *economist, educator*

**Winston Salem**
Chen, Frederick H. *economist*
Heckelman, Jac C *economics professor*
Karnes, Lucia Rooney *psychologist*
King, Arthur Thomas *economics professor, retired air force officer*
Twiggs, Dennis Glenn *psychologist, writer*

**NORTH DAKOTA**

**Fargo**
Hektner, Joel Martin *psychology professor*

Riley, Thomas Joseph *anthropologist, educational association administrator*

**Grand Forks**
Bradley, April Rain *psychology professor*
Penland, James Granville *psychologist*
Russell, Sue Ann *clinical psychologist*
Tyler, John Duke *psychologist, educator*

**Minot**
Ellis, Lee *social sciences educator*

## OHIO

**Ada**
Durkin, Keith Francis *sociologist, researcher*

**Akron**
Kubick, Robert J., Jr. *school psychologist*
York, Jeffrey Michael *school psychologist*

**Ashland**
Ford, Lucille Garber *economist, educator*

**Athens**
McNamara, John Regis *psychology educator*
Stump, Earl Spencer *psychologist*
Ungar, Irwin Allan *botany educator*
Vedder, Richard Kent *economics professor*

**Bath**
Coyne, Thomas Joseph *economics professor, finance professor*

**Beachwood**
Mardell, Carol Dolores *psychology professor*

**Bellbrook**
Maier, Donna Marie *psychologist*

**Berea**
Kevin, Braaten S. *social studies educator*
Peart, Sandra Joan *economics professor, researcher*

**Bowling Green**
Berger, Bonnie G. *sport psychologist, educator*
Gilbert, Erin Leigh *social studies educator*
Guion, Robert Morgan *psychologist, educator*
Hakel, Milton Daniel, Jr. *psychologist, educator, writer, consultant*
McCaghy, Charles Henry *retired social sciences educator*

**Cambridge**
Reisner, Andrew Douglas *psychologist*

**Canton**
de Oliveira, Ebenézer Aguiar *psychology professor, researcher*

**Cedarville**
Firmin, Michael Wayne *psychology professor*

**Centerville**
Kauffold, Ruth Elizabeth *psychologist*

**Cincinnati**
Andritzky, Frank William *political science educator*
Ashley, Lynn *social sciences educator, consultant*
Bieliauskas, Vytautas Joseph *psychologist, educator*
Bishop, George Franklin *political scientist, educator*
Bluestein, Venus Weller *retired psychologist, educator*
Dember, William Norton *retired psychologist, educator*
Laffitte, Larry James *industrial organizational psychologist, consultant*
Macks, Ryan Jeffrey *psychologist*
Mai, Aimee Marie *social studies educator*
Scarborough, Vernon Lee *archaeologist, anthropologist*
Steiner, Benjamin M. *criminologist, researcher*
Tang, Mei *psychology professor*

**Cleveland**
Amkraut, Brian *social studies educator*
Bate, Brian R. *retired psychologist*
Beall, Cynthia *anthropologist, educator*
Binstock, Robert Henry *public policy educator, writer*
Carlsson, Bo Axel Vilhelm *economics professor*
Carrol, Edward Nicholas *psychologist*
Deal, William Thomas *school psychologist*
Detterman, Douglas Kenward *psychologist, researcher*
Hokenstad, Merl Clifford, Jr. *social work educator*
Kolb, David Allen *psychologist, educator*
Mayland, Kenneth Theodore *economist*
McHale, Vincent Edward *political science professor*
Myers, Eddie Earl *psychologist*
Salem, Dorothy Carlson *social sciences educator, history professor*
Sibley, Willis Elbridge *anthropology educator, consultant*

**Columbus**
Alger, Chadwick Fairfax *political scientist, educator*
Baird, Leonard Lynn *social scientist, educator, researcher, editor*
Brewer, Marilynn B. *psychology professor*
Carmichael, Jason Thomas *political science professor, researcher*
Cheng, Yungrang Laura *social sciences educator*
Ellingson, Jill Evelyn *psychologist, educator*
Gilliom, Morris Eugene *social studies and global educator*
Hillier, Ashleigh Jane *psychology professor*
Ingram, Mark Steven *psychologist, social services administrator*
Johnson, Neal Frederick *psychologist, educator*
Kessel, John Howard *political scientist, educator*
Kiecolt-Glaser, Janice Kay *psychologist*
Larsen, Clark Spencer *anthropology educator*

Millett, Stephen Malcolm *futurist, consultant, historian*
Mirzaie, Ida A. *economics professor*
Mueller, John Ernest *political science professor, dance critic*
Naylor, James Charles *psychologist, educator*
Peterson, Ruth D. *sociologist*
Reiss, Steven *psychology professor*
Sporleder, Thomas Lynn *economist, researcher*
Tilley, John Lewis *psychologist*
Tybout, Richard Alton *economics professor*
Viezer, Timothy Wayne *economist, investment company executive*
Weisberg, Herbert Frank *political science professor*

**Cuyahoga Falls**
Roth, Gregory Edward *social studies educator*

**Dayton**
McCloskey, Kathy Ann *psychologist*

**Findlay**
Peters, Milton Eugene *educational psychologist*

**Hudson**
Sorgi, Mercedes Prieto *psychologist*

**Kent**
Bianchi, Alison Jean *sociologist, educator*
Feinberg, Richard *anthropologist, educator*
House-Soremekun, Bessie *political science professor*
McKee, David Lannen *economics professor*
Williams, Donald R. *social sciences educator*
Williams, Harold Roger *economist, educator*

**Louisville**
Faigley, Joseph Raymond *social studies educator*
Hostetler, Andrew Leon *social studies educator*

**Mansfield**
Hussain, Nayyer *economics professor*

**Massillon**
Steele, Kathryn Ann *social studies educator, gifted and talented educator*

**Middletown**
Gilmore, June Ellen *psychologist*

**Moreland Hills**
Tolchinsky, Paul Dean *organization design psychologist*

**Oberlin**
Taylor, Richard Wirth *retired political science professor*

**Oxford**
Bergen, Doris *psychologist, educator*
Berry, Stephen D. *psychology educator, researcher*
Dawisha, Adeed *political science professor*
Miller, Norman Calvin *economist*
Rejai, Mostafa *political science professor*
Sheehan, James Joseph *social studies educator*

**Pataskala**
Ripley, Randall Butler *political scientist, educator*

**Pepper Pike**
Alexander-Haynes, Sandra *psychologist, educator*

**Ripley**
Curtis, Russell Glenn *social studies educator*

**Shaker Heights**
Ludwig, L(owell) Mark *social studies educator*

**Springfield**
Little, Stephanie Ann *psychology professor, researcher*

**Strongsville**
Blumer, Frederick Elwin *retired philosophy educator*

**Sugar Grove**
Dombrowski, Karen S. *social studies educator, education educator*

**Tiffin**
Donaldson, Leonard W. *political science professor*
Gridley, Mark Charles *psychologist*

**Toledo**
Davis, David Howard *political science professor*
Funk, Jeanne B. *psychology professor*
Heintz, Carolinea Cabaniss *retired home economist, retired educator*
Rokicki, Lori Ann *psychologist*

**University Heights**
Carrington, Gary *psychologist*
Eslinger, Kenneth Nelson *social sciences educator*

**Wilberforce**
Anyalewechi, Patrick Okechukwu *psychology professor*

**Wright Patterson Afb**
Boff, Kenneth Richard *engineering research psychologist*
Pinkus, Alan R. *engineering research psychologist*

**Yellow Springs**
Caldwell, John Alvis, Jr. *experimental psychologist*

**Youngstown**
Binning, William Charles *political science professor*
Mehra, Jagdish *economics professor*
Usip, Ebenge Etefia *economics professor*

## OKLAHOMA

**Achille**
Gorman, Randall Howard *social sciences educator, real estate appraiser*

**Bartlesville**
Jackson, Brian Kelly *economics professor*

**Claremore**
Woller, Kevin Marc Peter *psychology professor, researcher*

**Durant**
Kennedy, Elizabeth Carol *psychologist, educator*

**Edmond**
Necco, Edna Joanne *school psychologist*

**Goodwell**
Duren, Brad L. *social studies educator*

**Lawton**
Leveron, Bud *psychologist, educator*

**Noble**
Caddell, Lyndal R. *social studies educator*

**Norman**
Affleck, Marilyn *retired sociology educator*
Henderson, George *educational sociologist, educator*

**Oklahoma City**
Adams, Russell Lee *neuropsychologist*
Craig, George Dennis *economics professor, consultant*
Morgan, Catherine Marie *psychologist, writer*
Poole, Richard William *economist*
Rundell, Orvis Herman, Jr. *psychologist, educator*
Schroeder, David J. Dean *psychologist*

**Seminole**
Stewart, Jacquelin Maria Connelly *psychology professor, consultant*

**Stillwater**
Darcy, Robert Emmett *political science and statistics professor*
Steindl, Frank George *economist, educator*

**Tulsa**
Briggs, Robert LeRoy *geographer, educator, lawyer*
Brooker, Timothy Douglas *social studies educator*

**Woodward**
Fisher, Deena Kaye *social studies education administrator*

## OREGON

**Ashland**
Bornet, Vaughn Davis *social sciences educator, historian, researcher*
Fujitsubo, Lani Charlene *psychology professor*

**Corvallis**
Castle, Emery Neal *economist, educator*
Gillis, John Simon *retired psychologist, educator*
Harter, Lafayette George, Jr. *retired economics professor*
Ray, Edward John *economics professor, academic administrator*

**Dallas**
Nathan, Gerald Dale *retired psychologist, researcher, writer*

**Eugene**
Bichsel, Ruth J. *psychologist, educator*
Freyd, Jennifer Joy *psychology professor*
Khang, Chulsoon *economics professor*
Littman, Richard Anton *psychologist, educator*
Peterson, Donna Rae *gerontologist*
White, Patricia Marie *psychology professor, researcher*
York, Richard *sociologist, educator*
Zinbarg, Richard Evan *psychologist, educator*

**Forest Grove**
Gibby-Smith, Barbara *psychologist, nurse*

**Hillsboro**
Canakapalli, Sri K. *psychologist*

**La Grande**
Thompson, Joan (Jo) *anthropologist*

**Lake Oswego**
Rhinewine, Joseph P. *psychologist*

**Newberg**
Adams, Wayne Verdun *pediatric psychologist, educator*
Warford, Patricia *psychologist*

**Newport**
Quarles, Jeanne C. *psychology professor*

**Portland**
Anastasiou, Harry *international peace and conflict studies professor*
Davis, James Allan *gerontologist, educator*
Kristof, Ladis Kris Donabed *political scientist, writer*
Matarazzo, Joseph Dominic *psychologist, educator*
Matarazzo, Ruth Gadbois *psychologist, educator*
McNeil, Mona Margaret *clinical psychologist*
Sikora, Darryn Marie *pediatric psychologist*
Wiens, Arthur Nicholai *psychology professor*

**Salem**
Warnath, Maxine Ammer *psychologist, arbitrator*

**Tigard**
Yesilada, Birol Ali *political science professor*

## PENNSYLVANIA

**Abington**
Halnon, Karen Bettez *sociologist, educator*

**Allentown**
Brinson, Jennifer L. *social studies educator*

**Bethlehem**
Aronson, Jay Richard *economics professor, researcher, academic administrator*
Scheirer, William Kenneth *economist, consultant*
Schwartz, Eli *retired economics professor, writer*
Smolansky, Bettie Moretz *sociology educator*
Wittreich, Warren James *consultant*

**Bloomsburg**
Holloway, Sybil Lymorise *psychologist, writer*
Leitzel, Jeffrey Dale *psychology professor*

**Blue Bell**
Brew, Wayne William *geography educator*

**Bryn Mawr**
Anderson, Eric Edward *psychologist, consultant, health facility administrator, educator*
Porter, Judith Deborah Revitch *sociologist*

**Butler**
Miller, Patrick M. *social studies educator*

**Camp Hill**
Markley, Kenneth Alan *psychologist*

**Carlisle**
Jones, Oliver Hastings *consulting economist*

**Coopersburg**
Bednar, Charles Sokol *political science professor*

**Coraopolis**
Beaver, William R. *sociology professor*

**Coudersport**
Kysor, Daniel Francis *psychologist*

**Downingtown**
Sweeney, Sarina Marie *psychologist, consultant*

**Doylestown**
Bowers, Nell S. *psychologist*
Ginsberg, Barry Gavrille *psychologist, marriage and family therapist*

**Easton**
Kincaid, John *political science professor, editor*

**Erie**
Ayrault, Evelyn West *psychologist, writer*
Bennett, Charles Andrew *economics professor, department chairman*

**Exton**
Roth, William McKinley *psychologist*

**Fairless Hills**
Rosella, John Daniel *clinical psychologist, educator*
Swope, Megan Elizabeth *social studies educator*

**Friendsville**
Babb, Harold *psychologist, educator*

**Gettysburg**
Schein, Virginia Ellen *psychologist, editor*

**Glenside**
Jones, Elaine F. *psychologist, educator*

**Greensburg**
Ramm, Douglas Robert *psychologist*

**Grove City**
Ranker, Dennis W. *social studies educator*

**Hanover**
Shue, Robert A. *social studies educator*

**Haverford**
Northrup, Herbert Roof *economist*

**Hershey**
Butterfield, Andrea Christine *psychology educator, educational association administrator*

**Indiana**
Black, Lynanne *psychologist, educator*
Garvin, C(larence) Alexander, Jr. *economics professor*
Mc Cauley, R. Paul *criminologist, educator*
Reynolds, Virginia Edith *sociologist, anthropologist, educator, artist*
Stern, T. Noel *political science professor*

**Jacobus**
Secula, Jennifer Michele *psychologist*

**Kelton**
Gulick, Walter Lawrence *psychologist, educator, retired academic administrator*

**Kutztown**
Gupta, Venu Gopal *psychology professor*

**Langhorne**
Heuer, Frederick August III *social studies educator*

**Lebanon**
Seyfert, Paul *social studies educator*

**Lewisburg**
Candland, Douglas Keith *psychology professor*
Kinnaman, Thomas Christopher *economics professor, researcher*

**Lincoln University**
Nwachuku, Levi Akalazu *social sciences and behavioral studies educator*

**Lititz**
Wilczak, Paul Francis *psychologist*

**Lock Haven**
Forbes, Edward John III *retired developmental psychologist, educator*

**Mc Donald**
Chambon, Mary Virginia *social studies educator*

**Meadville**
Adams, Earl William, Jr. *retired economics professor*

**Mill Hall**
Klacik, Lora Anne *school psychologist*

**Nazareth**
Bast, Kimberly Ann *social studies educator*

**Orefield**
Langman, Peter Fabbri *psychologist, poet, playwright*

**Perkasie**
Dillingham, Lee *social studies educator*

**Philadelphia**
Behrman, Jere Richard *economics professor*
Blank, Michael Bernard *psychologist*
Cass, David *economist, educator*
Chrysikou, Evangelia G. *psychology professor*
Clark, John J. *economist, finance educator*
Coché, Judith *psychologist, educator*
Cunningham, Jacqueline Lemmé *psychologist, educator, researcher*
Danien, Elin C. *archaeologist, researcher*
Davey, Adam *gerontologist, researcher*
Diebold, Francis X. *economist, educator*
Eiberson, Jeffrey Lawrence *psychologist, consultant*
Erdmann, James Bernard *educational psychologist*
Evan, William Martin *sociologist, educator*
Fox, Renée Claire *sociology educator*
Frankel, Francine Ruth *political science professor*
Goodenough, Ward Hunt *anthropologist, educator*
Goyette, Kimberly Ann *sociology professor*
Guillen, Mauro Federico *sociology and management educator*
Harvey, John Adriance *psychologist, educator, pharmacologist, researcher*
Henisz, Witold Jerzy *social sciences educator*
Jordan, Will James *sociologist, educator*
Klausner, Samuel Zundel *sociologist, educator*
Klein, Lawrence Robert *economist, educator*
Madden, Janice Fanning *economics professor*
Marion, Linda Sheetz *psychology educator*
McGlone, Gerard J. *psychology professor*
Meredith, Lisa Ann Marie *social studies educator, consultant*
Meyer, Marshall Warner *sociology educator, finance educator*
Newcombe, Nora *psychology professor*
Orne, Emily Carota *psychologist, researcher*
Perlman, Barry Steven *sociologist, educator*
Postlewaite, Andrew William *economics professor, department chairman*
Raff, Daniel Martin Gorodetsky *economist, historian, educator*
Rescorla, Robert Arthur *psychology professor*
Rima, Ingrid Hahne *economics professor*
Rutkowski, Duane Joseph *social studies educator*
Sabloff, Jeremy Arac *archaeologist*
Seligman, Martin E.P. *psychologist, educator*
Sharer, Robert James *archaeologist*
Sherman, Lawrence William *criminologist*
Shure, Myrna Beth *psychologist, educator*
Smith, Rogers Mood *political scientist, educator*
Summers, Robert *economics professor*
Thomas, Janet Y. *political science professor, researcher*
Wadden, Thomas Anthony *psychologist, educator*
Wallace, Anthony Francis Clarke *anthropologist, educator*
Zuberi, Tukufu *sociologist, educator*
Zuckerman, Marvin *retired psychologist*

**Pittsburgh**
Barry, Herbert III *psychologist, educator*
Blumstein, Alfred *urban and public affairs educator*
Branstetter, Lee Gilbert *economics professor*
Brustein, William Irving *sociology educator*
Cagney, William Robert *psychologist*
Curry, Nancy Ellen *psychologist, psychoanalyst, educator*
Davis, Otto Anderson *economics professor*
Dawes, Robyn Mason *psychology professor*
Eaton, Joseph W. *sociology educator*
Fararo, Thomas John *sociologist, educator*
Fischhoff, Baruch *psychologist, educator*
Glaser, Robert *psychology professor*
Holzner, Burkart *retired sociologist, educator*
Klatzky, Roberta Lou *psychologist, educator*
Kydland, Finn E. *economics professor*
Lave, Judith Rice *economics professor*
McClelland, James Lloyd *psychologist, educator, cognitive neuroscientist*
Meltzer, Allan H. *economist, educator*
Ogul, Morris Samuel *political science professor, consultant*
Perel, James Maurice *pharmacology and psychiatry educator, researcher*
Perlman, Mark *economist, educator*
Perloff, Robert *psychologist, educator*
Schorr-Ribera, Hilda Keren *psychologist*
Strauss, Robert Philip *economics professor*
Sussna, Edward *economist, educator*
Work, Jane Allen *psychologist*

**Radnor**
Rosnow, Ralph Leon *psychologist, educator*
Sicoli, Mary Louise Corbin *psychologist, educator*

**Royersford**
Krell-Morris, Cheri Lee *psychologist*

**Rydal**
Heebner, Albert Gilbert *retired economist, retired educator, retired bank executive*

**Schuylkill Haven**
Couch, Stephen Robert *sociologist, educator*

**Scranton**
Parente, William Joseph *political science professor*
Yamanouchi, Midori *social sciences educator*

**Selinsgrove**
Rousu, Matthew C. *economics professor*

**Shippensburg**
France, Olin Kenneth, Jr. *psychologist*
Hale, Robert L. *psychologist, educator*
Kalist, David E. *economics professor*

**State College**
Isenberg, Ann Marie *psychologist*
Schaie, K. Warner (Klaus Warner Schaie) *human development and psychology educator*

**Stroudsburg**
Abbruzzese, John A., Jr. *psychologist, retired administrator, educator*

**Swarthmore**
Keith, Jennie *anthropology educator, academic administrator, writer*
Marecek, Jeanne *psychologist, educator*

**Titusville**
Altomare, Erica Von Scheven *psychologist*

**University Park**
De Jong, Gordon Frederick *demography professor, director*
Eckhardt, Robert Barry *biological anthropologist, geneticist, geneticist, educator*
Ford, Donald Herbert *psychologist, educator*
Humphrey, Craig Reed *social studies educator*
Klein, Philip Alexander *economist*
Newsome, Lee Ann *anthropologist, educator*
Peck, Andrew *psychologist, educator*
Ray, William Jackson *psychologist*
Roy, Rustum *citizen scientist*

**Villanova**
Johannes, John Roland *political science professor, dean*
Langran, Robert Williams *political scientist, educator*
Malik, Hafeez *political science professor*

**Washington**
Klitz, Timothy S. *psychologist, educator*

**Wayne**
Burton, Noelle M. *clinical psychologist, psychoanalyst*
Stayton, William Ralph *psychologist, educator*

**West Chester**
Zlotowski, Martin *psychologist*

**Westfield**
Walker, Bonnie Lou *social studies educator*

**RHODE ISLAND**

**Coventry**
Chait, Andrea Melinda *psychologist, behavior analyst*

**Kingston**
Newman, Barbara Miller *psychologist, educator*
Turnbaugh, William Arthur *archaeologist, educator*

**Newport**
Brown, David William *economist, educator, consultant*

**Portsmouth**
Willis, Christopher Scott *school psychologist, writer*

**Providence**
Anderson, James Alfred *cognitive science professor*
Borts, George Herbert *economist, educator*
Feldman, Allan Maurice *economist*
Goldscheider, Frances K. *sociologist, educator*
Goldstein, Sidney *sociologist, educator, demographer*
Heath, Dwight Braley *anthropologist, educator*
Hopmann, Philip Terrence *political science educator*
Houston, Stephen D. *anthropologist, educator*
Mancebo, Maria Celmira *psychologist*
Marcus, Bess H. *psychologist, medical educator, health facility administrator*
Marsh, Robert Mortimer *sociologist, educator*
Paolino, Ronald Mario *clinical psychologist, consultant, psychopharmacologist, pharmacist*
Putterman, Louis G. *economics professor*
Ryder, Harl Edgar *economist, educator*
Shapiro, Ronald Gary *psychologist*
Siqueland, Einar *psychologist, educator*
Stein, Jerome Leon *economist, educator*
Stultz, Newell Maynard *retired political science professor*
Wetle, Terrie Fox *gerontologist, educator, dean*

**Smithfield**
Joseph, Antoine L. *sociologist, educator*
Morahan-Martin, Janet May *psychologist, educator*

**Wakefield**
Newman, Philip Robert *psychologist*

**SOUTH CAROLINA**

**Abbeville**
Cellura, A(ngele) Raymond *psychologist*

**Belton**
Watson, Melinda S. *social studies educator*

**Boiling Springs**
Rucker, Margaret Rickenbacker *psychologist, special education educator*

**Chapin**
Freitag, Carol Wilma *political scientist*

**Charleston**
Bowman, Daniel Oliver *retired psychologist*
Carek, Donald J(ohn) *child psychiatry educator*
Gillespie, John David *political science educator*
Kimmel, Herbert David *psychologist, educator*
Rieder, Sherry L. *psychologist*
Ruggiero, Kenneth Joseph *psychologist*
Saldana, Lisa *psychology professor, consultant*
Sharpe, Kathryn Moye *retired psychologist*
Smedley, Charles Vincent *social studies educator*

**Clemson**
Melton, Gary Bentley *psychologist, educator*

**Clinton**
Lipford, Jody Woods *economics professor*

**Columbia**
Glad, Betty *political scientist, educator*
Kegley, Charles William, Jr. *political science professor*
Kiker, Billy Frazier *economics professor*
Leader, Jonathan M *archaeologist, researcher*
Martin, Robert William *econometrician*
Powell, Donald Ashmore *clinical research psychologist*
Wilder, Ronald Parker *economics professor*

**Greenville**
Trevillian, Wallace Dabney *retired economics professor, retired dean*
Westrope, Martha Randolph *psychologist, consultant*

**Greer**
McAbee, Thomas Allen *psychologist*

**Mount Pleasant**
Bilas, Richard A. *economist*

**Rock Hill**
Manetta, Ameda Avrill *social sciences educator*

**SOUTH DAKOTA**

**Aberdeen**
Hedges, Mark Stephen *clinical psychologist*

**Brookings**
Gilbert, Howard Alden *retired economics professor*

**Canton**
Perkinson, Robert Ronald *psychologist, consultant*

**Huron**
Strom, Debra Elaine *social studies educator*

**Lennox**
Brendtro, Larry Kay *psychologist*

**Sioux Falls**
Himler, Thomas Charles *psychologist*
Kuntz, Carol B. *psychologist, educator, marriage and family therapist*
Williams, W. Vail *psychologist*

**Vermillion**
Clem, Alan Leland *retired political scientist, educator*
Wang, X. T. (Xiaotian Wang) *psychologist, educator*

**TENNESSEE**

**Belvidere**
Dean, Raymond S. *psychology professor, director*

**Bolivar**
Boyle, Candyace *psychologist*

**Chattanooga**
Rabin, Alan A. *economics professor*
Wilson, Richard Lee *political science professor*

**Germantown**
Depperschmidt, Thomas Orlando *economist, consultant*

**Jackson**
Evans, Sean *political science professor*

**Johnson City**
Zimmern-Reed, Annette Wacks *psychologist*

**Knoxville**
Bass, William Marvin III *anthropology educator*
Harris, Diana Koffman *sociologist, educator*
Infante, Isa Maria *political scientist, educator, lawyer, writer*
Jones, Robert Emmet *sociologist, educator*
Moore, Wendy Leigh *anthropology professor*
Stephens, Otis Hammond, Jr. *political science professor, law educator*

**Memphis**
Adler, Amy Gullett *school psychologist*
Battle, Allen Overton, Jr. *psychologist, educator*
Berman, Jeffrey Scott *psychology professor*
Johnson, Johnny *research psychologist, consultant*
Truman, Bridget Mary *psychologist*

**Murfreesboro**
Breault, Kevin D. *social studies educator, researcher*
Klein, Christopher Carnahan *economist*
Schmidt, Stephen R. *psychology professor*

**Nashville**
Ascencao, Erlete Malveira *psychologist, educator*
Blair, Margaret Mendenhall *economist, consultant, law educator*
Blake, Randolph *psychology professor*

**Buckles, Stephen Gary** *economist, educator*
Carpenter, Laura M. *sociologist, educator*
Cornfield, Daniel Benjamin *sociology educator*
Guinsburg, Philip Fried *alcohol and substance abuse counselor*
Gwin, Dorothy Jean Bird *retired psychology professor, dean*
Hargrove, Erwin Charles, Jr. *political science professor*
Havens, Murray Clark *political scientist, educator*
Hinshaw, Carroll Elton *economics professor*
Hollon, Steven Dennis *psychology professor, psychologist*
Lazar, Irving *psychologist*
McCarty, Richard Charles *psychology professor, dean*
Morton-Young, Tommie *psychology professor, writer*
Ridley, Carolyn Fludd *retired social studies educator*
Schoggen, Phil H(oward) *psychologist, educator*
Singh, Surendra P. *agricultural economics professor, consultant*
Strupp, Hans Hermann *psychologist, educator*
Wen, Quan *economics professor, researcher*
Westfield, Fred Meinhard *economics professor*

**Oak Ridge**
Colston, Freddie Charles *political science professor*

**Winchester**
Eslick, Heather Bass *psychologist*

**TEXAS**

**Alpine**
Sechrest, Larry James *economist, educator*

**Alvin**
Raniseski, Jean *psychology professor*

**Amarillo**
Ayad, Joseph Magdy *retired psychologist*

**Arlington**
Brainerd, Charles J(on) *psychologist, mathematics professor*
Buckner, Joyce *psychologist, educator*
Cole, Richard Louis *political scientist, educator*
Koc, Cagatay *economics professor*
Ramsey, Charles Eugene *sociologist, educator*

**Austin**
Alissa, Sherry *psychologist, educator*
Blodgett, Warren Terrell *public affairs educator*
Buchanan, Bruce, II, *political science professor*
Burnham, Walter Dean *political science professor*
Cooper, William Wager *economics professor, accounting and finance professor, dean*
Drake, Stephen Douglas *psychologist, health facility administrator*
Dusansky, Richard *economist, educator*
Eaton, David *natural resource policy studies educator*
Firey, Walter Irving, Jr. *retired sociologist*
Glade, William Patton, Jr. *economics professor*
Glenn, Norval Dwight *sociologist, educator*
Guli, Laura Ann *psychologist, educator*
Hamermesh, Daniel Selim *economics professor*
Hardin, Dale Wayne *political science professor*
Hester, Thomas Roy *anthropologist, educator*
Holtzman, Wayne Harold *psychologist, educator*
Jones, Matthew Carl *researcher, educator*
Kendrick, David Andrew *economist, educator*
Kuchar Glynn, Tiffany Elizabeth *psychologist*
Loehlin, John Clinton *psychologist, educator*
Magee, Stephen Pat *economics professor, finance professor*
Markman, Arthur Brian *psychology professor*
McFadden, Dennis *psychologist, educator*
Meston, Cindy M(ay) *psychologist, educator*
Roach, James Robert *retired political science professor*
Rostow, Elspeth Davies *political science professor*
Schmitt, Karl Michael *retired political scientist*
Serafine, Mary Louise *psychologist, educator, lawyer*
Walter, Virginia Lee *psychologist, educator*
Williams III, Roberton Capell *economics professor*

**Bellaire**
Mayo, Clyde Calvin *psychologist, educator*

**Big Spring**
Willbanks, Jill Ann *home economist, educator*

**Brooks City-Base**
Villarreal, Roberto Escamilla *retired political science researcher, educator, administrator*

**Brownsville**
Soldan, Angelika *political science educator, philosopher*

**Canyon**
Thoman, Roy Edward *political scientist, educator*

**College Station**
Arnold, J(ames) Barto III *marine archaeologist*
Bass, George Fletcher *retired archaeology educator*
Furubotn, Eirik Grundtvig *economics professor*
Greenhut, Melvin Leonard *economist, educator*
MacOpiyo, Laban Adero *geographer, researcher, ecologist*
Meier, Kenneth John *political scientist*
Moroney, John Rodgers *economist, educator*
Steffy, John Richard *nautical archaeologist, educator*
Van Riper, Paul Pritchard *political science professor*

**Colleyville**
Lusby, Elizabeth Keene *psychologist*

**Corpus Christi**
Cutlip, Randall Brower *retired psychologist, university president emeritus*

REFERENCE BOOK
Use in Reference
Desk Only

**DENMARK**

**Copenhagen**
Kurrild-Klitgaard, Peter political science professor
Olgaard, Anders economics professor

**EGYPT**

**Cairo**
Hawass, Zahi archaeologist, educator, writer

**ENGLAND**

**Bath**
Zalewska, Anna economist, researcher

**Cambridge**
Mirrlees, Sir James Alexander economics

**London**
Renfrew, Andrew Colin (Lord Renfrew of Kaimsthorn) archaeologist, educator, director
Richard, Alison Fettes anthropology educator
Dahrendorf, Lord Ralf Gustav sociologist, educator
Junz, Helen B. economist
Kuper, Adam Jonathan anthropologist, educator, professor
Portes, Richard David economics professor

**Reading**
Dunning, John Harry economics educator

**ESTONIA**

**Tallinn**
Kõõma, Arno economist, educator

**FRANCE**

**Paris**
Cherkaoui, Mohamed sociologist
Fitoussi, Jean-Paul Samuel economist, educator
Kouyaté, Lansana economist, federal official, diplomat

**GEORGIA**

**Tbilisi**
Urushadze, Levan Z. political scientist, human rights activist

**GERMANY**

**Apo**
Adams, Julian Timothy psychologist

**Bonn**
Albach, Horst economist

**Göttingen**
Achtenberg, Frank economics professor

**Munich**
Whetten, Lawrence L. international relations educator

**GUATEMALA**

**Antigua**
Rosenthal, Gert economist

**HONG KONG**

**Kowloon**
Qiu, Larry Dongxiao economics professor

**INDONESIA**

**Jakarta**
Tilaar, Henry A.R. social sciences educator

**ISRAEL**

**Arad**
Hollander, Samuel economist, educator

**ITALY**

**Pietrasanta Lucca**
Bugliani, Ann C. international studies educator

**Pisa**
Settis, Salvatore archaeologist, art historian

**Rome**
Gros-Pietro, Gian Maria economics professor
Scognamiglio Pasini, Carlo economics and finance professor, senator
Wesley, John Richard economist

**JAPAN**

**Ibaraki**
Kawano, Toshiaki retired economics professor

**Kobe**
Inoue, Shun sociologist

**Machida**
Miyazaki, Koichi economics professor

**Mie**
Isshiki, Masayuki sociologist, educator, dean

**Nagoya**
Kajima, Motohisa sociology educator

**Tokyo**
Fukushima, Kiyohiko economist
Gyohten, Toyoo economist
Hirayama, Eiji psychologist, educator
Maki, Atsushi economics professor
Nishiyama, Chiaki economist, educator
Watanabe, Satoshi Patten economist, researcher

**Tsukuba**
Hanaki, Nobuyuki economics professor

**Yokohama**
Kuroda, Yasumasa political science professor, researcher

**NETHERLANDS**

**Haarlem**
Green, Zachary Gabriel psychologist

**Utrecht**
Tielman, Rob A.P. social sciences educator

**NEW ZEALAND**

**Wellington**
Wu, Lisa Maria psychologist

**NIGERIA**

**Ijebu Ode**
Adedeji, Adebayo economist, retired federal official, academic administrator

**NORWAY**

**Oslo**
Karlsen, Paul Johan psychologist, researcher, writer

**PHILIPPINES**

**Makati**
Thompson, Willard Scott (W. Scott Thompson) social sciences educator

**REPUBLIC OF KOREA**

**Kwangju**
Lee, Jung-Koo economist, educator

**Seoul**
Ahn, Choong Yong economics professor

**RUSSIA**

**Moscow**
Gregoriev, Sergei Aleksandrovich political scientist, researcher
Salykov, Boris Georgievich economist, politician

**SPAIN**

**Madrid**
Merino, Fernando economist, researcher, educator
Pérez-Diaz, Victor Miguel sociology educator

**SRI LANKA**

**Colombo**
Spain, James William political scientist, writer

**SWITZERLAND**

**Geneva**
Richter, Frank-Jürgen economist, consultant, educator
Sidjanski, Dusan economist, educator

**TAIWAN**

**Pingtung**
Fan, Tai-Sheng Allen social scientist in computer education and computing, educator

**Taipei**
Lo, Fu-chen economist, educator, ambassador

**THAILAND**

**Bangkok**
Komell, Ronald Frank economist

**TURKEY**

**Ankara**
Gürkaynak, Refet S. economist, consultant

**UKRAINE**

**Odessa**
Vasiliev, Alexander Valeryovich economist, metallurgical engineer

**ADDRESS UNPUBLISHED**

Abraham, Katharine Gail economics professor
Abdelnasser, Justine E. psychologist
Adams, Robert McCormick anthropologist, educator
Adler, Nancy Elinor psychologist, educator
Ahmed, Syed Z. anthropologist
Alberti-Chappell, Roxana Dearing psychologist
Alexander, Ascención (Cency) H. school consultant
Albert, Robert Z. economist, educator
Alker, Hayward Rose political scientist, educator
Allen, Bruce Templeton retired economics professor
Allen, William Sheridan retired social sciences professor
Alpher, Victor Seth clinical psychologist, consultant
Altman, Irwin psychologist, educator
Altuse, Joel Paul social sciences educator
Alvord, Scott Thomas forensic psychologist
Anling, Frederick economist, educator, investment advisor
Anderson, Bernard E. Economist
Anderson, James George sociologist, educator, communications educator
Anthony-Perez, Bobbie Cotton Murphy retired psychology professor
Aponte, Frances psychologist, educator
Arcale, Frank psychologist, writer
Aschheim, Joseph retired economics professor, educator
Auld, Frank psychologist, educator
Auli, Lara Kristin psychologist, educator
Avant, Gayle political scientist, educator
Averch, Harvey Allan economist, educator, retired academic administrator
Aviles, Alice Alers psychologist, educator
Avilrod, Stephen Harvey global economic consultant, economist
Azman, Rosiana Lynne psychologist, educator
Baba, Marietta Lynn anthropologist, academic administrator
Babcock-Lumish, Terry Lynne economic geographer
Baker, Lisa E. psychology professor
Baker, Marjane L. social studies educator
Baker, Paul Thornell anthropology educator
Bandyopadhyay, Subhayu economics professor
Barnes, Samuel Henry political science professor
Barrett, Minna Sara psychologist, educator
Bashi, Vilna Francine sociology professor
Bateson, Mary Catherine retired anthropology professor
Bathke, Douglas social studies educator
Bell, Margret E. psychologist
Bellah, Lisa Danielle psychologist, educator
Benoit, Jo psychologist, consultant
Bergsten, C. Fred economist
Bernsen, Harold John political scientist, educator, retired military officer
Bertha, Elizabeth social sciences educator, psychologist, minister
Biles, Lagen Asbury psychologist
Birdsall, Nancy economist
Blackwell, Calvin economics professor
Bloomfield, Lincoln Palmer political scientist, retired
Bluth, B. J. (Elizabeth Jean Catherine Bluth) sociologist, aerospace technologist
Bohanan, Paul James anthropologist, retired
Bohn, Marsha J. anthropologist, researcher
Bonnell, Victoria Eileen sociologist, educator
Bourguignon, Erika Eichhorn anthropologist, educator
Bredfeldt, John Creighton economist, financial analyst, retired military officer
Bricker, Harvey Miller retired anthropology educator
Bricker, Victoria Reifler anthropologist, educator
Briggs, Philip James political science professor
Brooks, Lynda Barbara psychologist, writer
Brown, Amira Khalila neuropsychologist, researcher
Buchin, Jean psychologist, educator
Bugenial, James Frederick Thomas retired researcher
Bullard, Judith Eve psychologist, systems engineer
Burns, Joseph M. economist
Burns, Marcelline retired psychologist, researcher
Butki, Brian David psychologist, educator
Butler, John Scott economist, educator
Cacioppo, John Terrance psychologist, educator
Cadigan, John social sciences educator
Cao, Yang sociologist, educator
Caplow, Theodore sociologist
Cartiner, Geoffrey Owen economist, director
Carlsen, Mary Baird clinical psychologist
Carlson, Roger David psychologist, educator
Caron, Lonnie Canning educational psychologist, minister
Cascela, Jennifer school psychologist, educator
Casper, Julie Ann geographer, writer
Chang, Won economist
Chao, Ruth psychologist, researcher
Christian, James Wayne economist
Clark, Caleb Morgan political scientist, educator
Clark, Jere Walton economics professor, researcher
Cochran, John P. economics professor
Collier, Heather Elisha psychometrist
Collier, William Gayle psychology professor
Collins, Harket retired economist, retired manufacturing executive, retired publishing executive
Cousineau, Tara M. psychologist, research scientist
Cullari, Salvatore Santino clinical psychologist, educator, writer
Dang, Hai geographer
Daniel, Coldwell III economist, educator, entrepreneur
Daniels, Arlene Kaplan sociology educator
Danielsen, Albert Leroy economics professor, energy and utilities consultant
Da Pena, Eileen psychologist
Davidheiser, Mark social sciences educator, researcher
Davidson, John Kenneth, Sr. sociologist, educator, researcher, writer, consultant
Dawkins, Marva Phyllis psychologist, educator
Dawood, Khytam psychologist
Day, Joyce Cerejo school psychologist, educator
Daza, Stephanie anthropologist, educator
Dean, Edwin Robinson economist, educator
Deka, John economist
Derevan, William Maxfield geographer, historical consultant
De Vans, Jeannette Mary psychologist, educator
Dewald, William Guenther economist
Dickerson, James Alan psychologist
Dickinson, Dwight psychologist
Diem, Richard A. social studies educator
Dilleto-Macaluso, Kristen Ann psychologist, consultant
DiPrima, Richard Joseph neuropsychologist
Dobransky, Lev Eugene economics professor, diplomat
Dobyns, Henry (Farmer) anthropology consultant, advisor
Dole, Arthur Alexander former chairman professor, department chairman educator
Doll, Chad A. social studies educator
Dore, Patricia Ann psychologist
Dowd, Morgan Daniel retired political science professor, retired dean
Downor, Robert Lynn international affairs analyst
Drummond, Dorothy Weitz geography education and political consultant, editor, writer
Duckworth, Angela Lee psychologist
Duffy, Ann retired social studies educator
Durell, Viviane G. anthropologist, educator, small business owner
Earle, Timothy Keese anthropology educator
East, Alison J. psychologist
Ebert, Viola Roth neuropsychologist, entrepreneur
Ecklund-Johnson, Eric Philip psychologist
Eggert, Robert John, Sr. economic consultant
Eisenmann, Russell psychology professor
Eley, Lynn W. political science professor, retired
Elickson, Donald Lien retired economist, county mayor
Engel, Bernard Theodore psychologist, educator, official
Engel, Charles economics professor, educator
Engel, Joan Marcia Lezar psychologist, applied animal behaviorist
Erickson, Stephanie Ann psychologist
Eriksson, Steven social studies educator
Eron, Leonard David psychology professor
Evans, Frederick John psychologist
Evans, Karen Ann social studies educator
Evans, Ruth Q. psychologist, educator
Farah, Martha psychology educator
Farmer, Christopher J. political scientist, writer
Feinberg, Lynn Friss gerontologist
Feldman, Shirley Clark retired psychologist
Fattig, Elissa school psychologist
Fels, Kendigs economist, educator
Filippelli Mirandola, Linda Patricia school professor
Finberg, Elaine Agnes psychologist, editor
Fisher, Seymour psychologist, educator
Fishman, Joshua Aaron sociolinguist, educator
Fondacaro, Mark Robert psychology professor
Fontes, Patricia J. psychologist
Franklin, Margery Bodansky psychology professor, researcher
French, Laurence Armand social sciences educator
Friedman, James Winstein economist, educator
Firesen, Ronald Lee economics professor
Fromkl, K. Hubert banking economist
Frost, Ellen Louise political economist
Funseki, Robert Lloyd Eric Martin international consultant, retired diplomat
Ganelli, Giovanni economist
Galluci-Breithaupt, Adrianne psychologist, social worker
Gaber, Robert psychologist
Garcia, Patricia child development psychologist, researcher
Gardner, Marvin Allen, Jr. pastoral and clinical psychologist
Garnuo, Ralph Michael biomedical anthropologist, biologist, educator
Garzarelli, Elaine Marie economist
Gay, David Edward Ryan economist
Geake, Raymond Robert psychologist
Genis, Alice Singer economist
Gershkuny, Beth Suzanne psychologist, educator
Gerson, Darrin William clinical psychologist, educator
Getch, Lynne social studies educator
Glendining, Terry Sky psychologist
Godeering, Joshua Ray social sciences educator
Goldstein, Stephen Eugene community consultant
Goleman, Daniel Jay psychologist, journalist
Golub, Sharon Bramson retired psychologist, educator
Graniel, Nira psychologist, researcher
Grant, Carmen Hill psychologist, psychotherapist
Graves, Joseph Scott economics and management consultant
Greely, Andrew Moran sociologist, writer
Greenberg, Ira Arthur psychologist
Greenwood, Janet Kae Daly psychologist, academic administrator, marketing professional

Greenberg, Martin Alan criminologist, educator
Hall, James Curtis business professor
Hulsey, Timothy Lee psychology professor,
   director, dean
Leary, David Edward psychologist, educator
Palen, J(oseph) John social sciences educator

**Springfield**
Chatelier, Paul Richard aviation psychologist
de Haan, Henry John research psychologist

**Sterling**
Blum, John Curtis agricultural economist
Cleveland, Harlan political scientist, public affairs
   executive

**Suffolk**
Langston, Suzanne Jordan social studies educator

**Sweet Briar**
Miller, Reuben George retired economics
   professor

**Vienna**
Allen, Jane Folger psychologist
Tyler, Robert R. psychologist, consultant

**Warrenton**
Malmgren, Harald Bernard economist
Otallah, John August school psychologist
Pribram, Karl Harry neuroscience and psychology
   educator, brain researcher

**Williamsburg**
Blakey, Michael Louis anthropologist, educator
Krakauer, Sarah Yael psychologist
Lange, Carl James retired psychology professor
Smith, Roger Winston retired political theory
   educator

**Winchester**
Zimmermann, Laura psychology professor,
   researcher

**Wise**
Michael, George Joseph political scientist

**Woodproof**
Orrock, Roger Dickson agricultural educator

**WASHINGTON**

**Bellevue**
Walsmith, Charles Rodger psychologist, educator

**Bellingham**
Burdge, Rabel James sociology educator

**Camano Island**
de Vries, Rimmer economist

**Colville**
Cauton, Sarah Alexander psychologist, educator

**Friday Harbor**
MacGinitie, Walter Harold psychologist, educator

**Hansville**
Blalock, Ann Bonar evaluation researcher

**Issaquah**
Drazdoff, Nola Gay psychologist

**La Conner**
Garcia, John psychologist, educator
Knopf, Kenyon Alfred economist, educator

**Lacey**
Ortmeyer, Carl Edward retired demographer

**Mercer Island**
Abi-Hashem, Naji psychologist, educator
Kessler, Gale Suzanne psychologist, educator

**Olympia**
Jun, Heesoon psychology professor

**Pullman**
Jenness, Valerie sociologist, educator
Johnson, Monica Kirkpatrick sociologist, educator
Kinzel, Julie A. sociologist, educator
Kohler, Timothy A. social sciences educator
McSweeney, Frances Kaye psychology professor
Warner, Dennis Allan psychology professor
Wright, John William psychology educator

**Richland**
Roop, Joseph McLeod economist

**Seattle**
Abbott, Robert Dean psychology professor
Borgatta, Edgar F. sociologist, educator
Brammer, Lawrence Martin psychologist, educator
Fiedler, Fred Edward retired organizational
   psychologist
George, Alexander Lawrence political scientist,
   psychology educator
Gross, Edward retired sociologist
Hansen, Richard Emory psychologist
Hirschman, Charles, sociologist, educator
Lindner, Karen Carr psychologist, consultant,
Olson, David John political science professor
Patrick, Donald Lee sociologist, educator
Plotnick, Robert David economic consultant,
   educator
Prinsley, Gordon D. psychologist, educator
Reskin, Barbara F. sociologist
Rosenbaum, Jeffrey Ira consulting psychologist
Sarason, Irwin G. psychology professor
Schwartz, Pepper Judith sociologist, educator
Turnovsky, Stephen John economics professor
Tuthill, Oliver W., Jr. psychologist, consultant
van den Berghe, Pierre Louis sociologist

---

Carter, Charlene Ann psychologist

**Milwaukee**
Shafer, Byron Edwin American government
   educator
Sack, Robert David geography professor
Rice, Joy Katharine psychologist, educator
Nichols, Donald Arthur economist, educator
Muelle, Willard Fritz economics professor
Hansen, W. Lee economics professor
Haller, Archibald Orben sociologist, educator
Greenfield, Norman Samuel psychologist, educator
Graf, Truman Frederick agricultural economist,
   professor, researcher
Goldberger, Arthur Stanley economist, educator
Davidson, Richard J. psychology and psychiatry
   professor
Culbertson, Frances Mitchell psychology professor
Chapman, Loren J. psychology professor
Brock, William Allen III economist, educator
Bennett, Kenneth Alan retired biological
   anthropologist
Ataway, Kevin C. social studies educator
Anderano, Ralph Louis economist, educator

**Madison**
Wilson, Van Voorhis, Carmen R. psychology
   professor

**La Crosse**
Cyr, Arthur J. political science professor,
   economics professor

**Kenosha**
Alesch, Daniel James social sciences educator,
   researcher

**Green Bay**
Brosio, Richard Anthony social studies educator

**Glendale**
Williams, Sally J. psychologist, educator

**Fond Du Lac**
Bhargava, Ashok retired economics professor

**Fitchburg**
Croft, Candace Ann psychology professor
Dick, Raymond Dale psychologist, educator
Meade, Andrew John social studies educator

**Fennimore**
Wilt, Tom economics researcher, educator

**Eau Claire**
Baumann, Carol Edler retired political scientist

**Cascade**
Zander, Gaillienne Glashow psychologist

**Brookfield**
Davis, Harry Rex political science professor

**Beloit**

**WISCONSIN**

Fearn, Noelle E. criminologist, educator

**Pullman**
Childers, Robert Joseph psychologist,
   consultant
Branch, Michael Lee social studies educator,

**Parkersburg**
Montgomery-Downs, Hawley Evelyn psychologist,
   researcher
Waller, Stacey psychologist,
   researcher
Kim, Hong Nack political science professor
D'Souza, Gerard Eugene economist, educator
Callejo, David Marcos social sciences educator,
   administrator
Bell, Lewis Clay economics professor, government
   researcher

**Morgantown**
Mitah, Mohammad Sulaiman economics professor,
   researcher

**Institute**
Fulda, Michael political scientist, educator, space
   policy researcher

**Fairmont**
DiPino, Raymond Kim psychologist

**Charleston**

**WEST VIRGINIA**

Cox, Catherine Nolan psychologist

**Woodinville**
Belay, Halelom economist, educator

**Walla Walla**
Craven, James Michael (OmahkohkiaayoʼiʼPoyi)
   economist, educator

**Vancouver**
Bourgaize, Robert G. economist

**University Place**
Finn, Jerry social sciences educator

**Tacoma**
May, Richard B. psychology professor

**Spokane**
Houseman, Gerald L. political science professor,
   writer

---

Copes, Parzival economist, researcher

**West Vancouver**
Shaw, Timothy Milton political science professor

**Victoria**
Walker, Michael Angus economist, director,
   researcher
Tees, Richard Chisholm psychology professor
Suedfeld, Peter psychologist, educator
Shearer, Ronald Alexander economics professor,
   policy analyst educator
Nemetz, Peter Newman economist, researcher,
   sociology educator, academic administrator
Marchak, Maureen Patricia anthropology and
   public policy researcher
Laponce, Jean A. political scientist, educator
Holsti, Kalevi Jacque political scientist,
   department chairman
Feaver, George Arthur political science professor,
   physiology professor, researcher
Cynader, Max Sigmund psychology professor,
   educator

**Vancouver**
Kimura, Doreen psychology professor, researcher
Braningham, Paul Jeffrey criminologist, educator

**Burnaby**

**BRITISH COLUMBIA**

Randhawa, Bikkar Singh retired psychologist,
   educator

**Saint Albert**
Freeman, Milton Malcolm Roland anthropology
   educator

**Edmonton**
Stebbins, Robert Alan sociology educator

**Calgary**

**ALBERTA**

**CANADA**

Folch-Serrano, Karen D. psychologist, consultant
Toro-Alfonso, Jose psychology professor,
   researcher

**San Juan**
Aguero, Joseph Edward psychology professor,
   psychologist, educator

**Mayaguez**

**PUERTO RICO**

**TERRITORIES OF THE UNITED STATES**

Breitenbach, Mary Louise McGraw psychologist,
   chemical dependency counselor

**Wilson**
Turner, Del L. social studies educator

**Lyman**
Gill, George Wilhelm anthropologist
Gray, Christine Ann Winistok sociologist
   consultant
Shogren, Jason Fredrick economics professor
Shaffer, Sherrill Lynn economist
Crocket, Thomas Dunstan economics professor
Chai, Winberg political science professor,
   foundation administrator
Allen, John Logan geographer, department
   chairman

**Laramie**
Newman, Steven David psychologist, consultant

**Cheyenne**

**WYOMING**

LaBianka, Gregory Allen social studies educator

**Wonewoc**
Hawkins, Brett William retired political science
   professor

**Whitefish Bay**
Franze, Robert Dennis social studies educator
Graham, George Andrew, Jr. psychologist,
   consultant

**Waukesha**
Berg, Patricia J. social studies educator

**Washburn**
Carroll, David William psychology professor

**Superior**
Cwierniak, Robert L. psychologist, psychology
   consultant

**Stevens Point**
Grubery, Martin political science professor

**Oshkosh**
Siecker, Kristine Ellen school psychologist,
   consultant

**Oconomowoc**
Quereshi, Mohammed Younis retired psychologist,
   professor
Paulson, Belden Henry political scientist, educator

---

Bannister, Judith demographer, educator

**Beijing**

**CHINA**

McLennan, Andrew M. economics professor
Blakely, Edward James economics professor

**Sydney**
Leigh, Andrew Keith economist, researcher

**Australian National University**
Neil, Sandra Eilleen Silverberg psychologist

**Armadale**

**AUSTRALIA**

Lopez-Murphy, Ricardo Hipolito economist

**Buenos Aires**

**ARGENTINA**

Katchanovski, Ivan G. political scientist,
   researcher

**Toronto**
Tremblay, Marc Adelard anthropologist, educator

**Sainte-Foy**
Belanger, Gerard economics professor

**Quebec City**
Dufour, Jean-Marie economist, statistician,
   educator

**Outremont**
Waller, Harold Myron political science professor,
   researcher
Vaillancourt, Jean-Guy sociology educator
Trigger, Bruce Graham anthropologist, educator
Szabo, Denis criminologist, educator
Stewart, Jane psychology professor
Raynauld, Andre economist, educator
Paul, T. V. social sciences educator,
   educator
Normandeau, Andre Gabriel criminologist,
Nayar, Baldev Raj political science professor
Marzumins, Kenneth N. economist
Melzack, Ronald psychology professor
Ikawa-Smith, Fumiko anthropologist, educator
Brecher, Michael political science professor
Brecher, Irving economics professor

**Montreal**

**QUEBEC**

Failding, Harold Joseph sociology educator

**Waterloo**
Rose, Jeffrey Raymond economist, educator,
   public servant, trade unionist
Prat, Robert Cranford political scientist, writer
Munro, John Henry Alexander economics
   professor, writer
Macdonald, Hugh Ian economics professor, public
   policy professor, retired academic administrator
Helleiner, Gerald Karl economics professor
Grayson, Albert Kirk social studies educator
Goldfarb, Martin sociologist, researcher
Ferguson, Kingsley George retired psychologist
Dobson, Wendy Kathleen economics professor
DeWitt, David B. political scientist, educator,
   political organization worker

**Toronto**
Stevenson, Garth social sciences educator

**Saint Catharines**
Brooks, David Barry resource economist

**Ottawa**
Flock, Howard psychology professor

**North York**
Olley, Robert Edward economist, educator

**Niagara-on-the-Lake**
Wonnacott, Ronald Johnston economics professor
Laidler, David Ernest William economics professor
Davenport, Paul economics professor

**London**
Meisel, John political scientist
MacKinnon, James Gordon economist, educator
Kaliski, Stephan Felix economics professor

**Kingston**
Ryan, Ellen Bouchard psychology professor,
   gerontologist
George, Peter James economist, educator

**Hamilton**

**ONTARIO**

Stairs, Denis Winfield political science professor,
   department chairman

**Halifax**
Parr-Johnston, Elizabeth economist, consultant

**Chester Basin**

**NOVA SCOTIA**

Kenyon, Gary Michael gerontologist, educator

**Fredericton**

**NEW BRUNSWICK**

**Dallas**
Betts, Dianne Conally economist, educator
Borynack, Zachary C. psychologist
Cochran, Mona Shainfeld retired economics professor
Free, Mary Moore biological and medical anthropologist
Friedel, David Alan archaeologist, anthropologist
Gibby, Mabel Emil Kunce psychologist, educator
Kemper, Robert Van anthropologist, educator, minister
Oualline, Viola Jackson psychologist, consultant
Saving, Jason economist
Walters, Scott Timothy psychologist, educator

**Denton**
Betfiglio, Valentine John political science professor
Quinn, James T. social studies educator
Ver Duin, D'Arlene X. sociologist, researcher
Yang, Philip Q. social sciences educator
Zottarelli, Lisa Katherine sociologist

**Edinburg**
Mollick, Andre Varella economics professor, researcher

**El Paso**
Cooper, Theodore Victor psychologist, educator
Fullerton, Thomas Mankin, Jr. economist
Penley, Julie Anne psychologist, educator

**Fort Hood**
Moore, Bret A. psychologist, military officer

**Fort Worth**
Colauca, Beth pediatric neuropsychologist
Dees, Sandra Kay Martin psychologist, research scientist
Jackson, Donald Wilson political science professor, lawyer
Mullendore, Walter Edward retired economist
Oropeza, Peter E. psychologist, consultant
Simpson, Dennis Dwayne psychologist, educator

**Galveston**
Auslander, Beth Ann psychologist

**Georgetown**
Loprato, Joseph evolutionary sociologist, writer
Muir-Braddus, Jacqueline Elizabeth psychology educator

**Grapevine**
Wilson, Darren Duane social studies educator, basketball coach

**Harlingen**
Bald, Thomas Robert social studies educator
Lytle, Michael Allen criminologist, consultant

**Houston**
Ayadi, Mary Olufemi health economist, educator
Brito, Dagobert Llanos economics professor
Bryant, John Bradbury economics professor, consultant
Carman, Carol A. psychologist, educator, consultant
Condit, Linda Faulkner retired economist
Cuthbertson, Gilbert Morris political science professor
Davidson, Chandler sociologist, educator
Foster, Dale Warren political scientist, educator, real estate agent, accountant, management consultant
Francis, James Stephen, Jr. economics professor, psychologist
Jenkins, Sheila Alnita psychologist
Lachar, Barbara Leeser psychologist, educator
Lehrer, Kenneth Eugene economic consulting
Lewis, Lisa psychologist, administrator, company executive
Manrique, Justo Rafael economist, educator
Martin, William C. social studies educator, writer
Miller, Janel Harding psychologist
Neuhaus, Graham Frank psychology professor
Paul, Gordon Lee behavioral scientist, psychologist
Rehm, Lynn Paul psychologist, educator
Sickles, Robin C. economics and statistics professor
von der Mehden, Fred R. political science professor
Whitaker, Gilbert Riley, Jr. economics professor, academic administrator, business economist
Yaisenko, Yuri Petrovich economics professor, mathematician

**Huntsville**
Miller, Rowland Spence psychologist, writer

**Hurst**
Mabry, Philip T. political scientist, consultant

**Keller**
Meixner, Cliff Dale social studies educator, literature and language professor

**Keller**
Riggs, William W. social sciences educator

**Laredo**
Meixner, Cliff Dale social studies educator, literature and language professor

**Levelland**
Skinner, Peggy June psychology professor, consultant

**Longview**
Winsted, Donald Eugene III psychologist, consultant

**Lubbock**
Edwards, Martin S. political scientist, educator

**Mansfield**
Rejesus, Roderick Moralio agricultural and applied economist
Reiwald, Christian Walter school psychologist, military officer

**Marshall**
O'Day, Patrick Michael sociologist, educator

**McAllen**
Galdeano, Daniel Rodriguez social studies educator
Rebula, Avelino Luis public administration educator
Trainor, Debora Jean school psychologist, consultant

**Mesquite**
Byrd, Kathryn Susan psychologist, educator

**Midland**
Sherpa, Fran Magruder geography educator

**New Braunfels**
Wilson, James Lee retired geology educator, consultant

**Odessa**
Worley, Robert Michael criminologist, educator

**Olney**
Timmons, Gordon David economics professor, farmer

**Plano**
Glenn, Marshall Andrew psychologist
Lombardo, Elizabeth Roessler psychologist, physical therapist

**Post**
Earl, Lewis Harold economist, consultant, lawyer

**Richardson**
Andrews, Melinda Wilson human development researcher
Berry, Brian Joe Lobley geographer, educator, researcher
Griffith, Daniel Alva geography educator
Holmes, Jennifer Smith political scientist, educator
Sandler, Todd Michael economist, political scientist educator

**San Antonio**
Anderson, Anita L. psychology professor
Austin, Lola Houston psychologist
Bellows, Thomas John political scientist, educator
Breit, William economist, educator, writer
Brooks, Franklin Ramon psychologist, military officer
Case, Elizabeth Joy psychology and educational assessment director
Fonseca, Joseph Mojica, Jr. political science professor
Furino, Antonio economist, educator
Gambita, Richard Anthony political science professor
Hannon, Brenda Ann Marie psychologist, educator, researcher
Mott, Peggy Laverne sociologist, educator
Ribble, Ronald George psychologist, educator, writer, behavioral consultant
Spiro, Herbert Zalmon political scientist, ambassador
Spregins, Johnnie David sociology and cultural studies educator

**San Marcos**
Trepagnier, Barbara A. sociology educator
Hofer, Martha K. political science professor

**Stafford**
Krenck, Mary Louise political scientist, researcher

**Sugar Land**
Harbhance, Sean Lalsingh parapsychologist

**Victoria**
Harrington, Rick psychology professor

**Waco**
Elkins, Gary R. psychologist, educator
Matlock-Hetzel, Susan psychologist, educator
Sharp, Ronald Arvell sociology educator

**UTAH**

**Boulder**
Gove, Walter R. sociology educator

**Bountiful**
Mangum, Garth Leroy retired economist

**Cedar City**
White, Lynn H. psychology professor, researcher

**North Logan**
Edmondson, Richard Shawn psychologist

**Provo**
Brown, Ralph Browning sociologist, educator
Creer, Thomas Laselle sociologist, educator, writer
Hill, Edward Jeffrey family life educator
Kunz, Phillip Ray sociologist, educator
Pedersen, Darhl Max psychology professor
Porter, Blaine Robert Milton sociology professor, psychology professor
Sawyer, Melvin Wayne psychologist
Worthen, Vaughn Eugene psychologist, educator

**Salt Lake City**
Benjamin, Lorna Smith psychologist
Bilginsoy, Cihan economics professor
Livne, Nava Levia psychologist, researcher
O'Connell, James F. anthropologist, educator
Rider, Richard Francis psychologist

**Sandy**
Durham, Lynn Ellen school psychologist
Smith, Willard Grant psychologist

**Washington**
De Vany, Arthur Stacy economics professor, criminologist, researcher

**VERMONT**

**Barre**
Black, Percy psychology professor

**Bennington**
Graham, Jamie L. psychologist

**Brandon**
Farnsworth, Frank Albert retired economics professor

**Brattleboro**
Kokov, Benjamin retired clinical psychologist

**Burlington**
Cutler, Stephen Joel sociologist, educator
Delay, Eugene Raymond psychologist, educator, researcher
Lawson, Robert Bernard psychology professor
Sampson, Samuel Franklin sociology educator

**Castleton**
Roper, Scott Christopher geographer, researcher

**Charlotte**
Naylor, Thomas Herbert economist, educator, consultant

**Greensboro**
Gilpin, Robert George, Jr. political science professor

**Middlebury**
Lamberti, Marjorie retired social studies educator

**Montgomery Center**
Okravec, Eileen M. anthropologist, artist

**Norwich**
Foster, Michael Kirk anthropologist, linguist

**Wallingford**
Gutmann, David Leo psychology professor

**White River Junction**
Kutter, Catherine Jane psychologist

**VIRGINIA**

**Alexandria**
Ahrari, Ehsan M. political science professor, dean
Bezold, Clement futurist
Carville, James, Jr. (Chester James Carville) political scientist, consultant
Eskew, Henry Lawrence, Jr. economist, consultant
Hinkle, Wade P. political scientist
Johnson, Edgar McCarthy psychologist
Krieger, Gerald Peter psychologist
Lindsey, Sara Ann sociologist, educator
Mann, Seymour Zalmon retired political scientist, professor, labor union administrator
Matalin, Mary Allen social studies educator
McConville, Judy Allen social studies educator
Reid, Harry Charles economist, researcher

**Annandale**
Bragg, Cheryl Fuller psychologist
Carvalho, Julie Ann psychologist

**Arlington**
Boorstein, Laurence economist, educator
Bradshaw, Norman M. behavioral science educator
Buckley, Francis H. economist, law educator
Clump, Michael Aden psychologist, educator, lawyer
Coats, Warren L., Jr. economist
Davis, Lynn Etheridge political scientist, educator
Durham, Mary Sherrill psychologist, writer
Gramm, Wendy Lee economics professor, retired government agency administrator
Gunn, Joseph Ridgeway III consulting economist
Howenstine, E. Jay housing economist
Jackson-Cherry, Lisa Rene psychologist, educator
Siddayao, Corazon Morales economist, educator
Sundquist, James Lloyd retired political scientist, consultant
Vitz, Paul Clayton psychologist, educator

**Blacksburg**
Bryant, Clifton Dow sociologist, educator
Jannuzi, F. Tomasson economics professor

**Bluemont**
Kobetz, Richard William criminologist, consultant

**Charlottesville**
Abraham, Henry Julian political science professor
Cornell, Dewey Gene psychologist
Elzinga, Kenneth Gerald economics professor
Handler, Jerome Sidney anthropology professor
Hanft, Ruth S. Samuels economist, consultant
Henry, Laurin Luther public affairs educator
Hess, Frederick social sciences educator, writer
Hetherington, Eileen Mavis psychologist, educator
Hymes, Dell Hathaway anthropologist, educator
Kiewra, Gustave Paul psychologist, educator
Moreno, Jonathan bioethicist
Olsen, Edgar Oliver economics professor
Pate, Robert Hewitt, Jr. counselor educator
Quandt, William Bauer political scientist
Reppucci, Nicholas Dickon psychologist, educator
Rhoads, Steven Eric political science professor
Sabato, Larry Joseph political science professor
Skinner, Jonathan Snowden economics educator, director
Sykes, Gresham M'Cready sociologist, educator, artist
Wagner, Roy anthropologist educator, researcher
Whitaker, John King psychology professor

**Danville**
Lea, Robert Lee III social sciences educator

**Eastville**
Williams, Ida Jones consumer and home economics educator, writer

**Emory**
Morris, Thomas Robbins political scientist, educator, academic administrator

**Fairfax**
Barth, Michael Carl economist
Bennett, James Thomas economics professor
Boneau, C. Alan psychology professor, researcher
Buchanan, James McGill economist, educator
Dennis, Rutledge M. sociologist, educator
Kash, Don Eldon political scientist
Pfiffner, James Price political science professor
Pruitt, Dean Garner psychologist, educator
Smith, Vernon Lomax economics professor, researcher
Steele, Howard Loucks economic development researcher
Tolchin, Susan Jane political science professor, writer
Travis, Toni-Michelle C. political scientist, educator
Wagner, Richard E. economist, educator
Williams, Thomas Rhys anthropologist, educator
Williams, Walter E. economics professor

**Falls Church**
Calkins, Susanah Eby retired economist
Clizbe, John Anthony psychologist, social services administrator
Colander, David Charles economist, educator
Fink, Charles Augustin behavioral systems scientist
Green, James Wyche sociologist, anthropologist, consultant, psychotherapist
Martin, Lisa Marie sociologist
Roussel, Lee Dennison economist
Weiss, Armand Brel economist, association management executive

**Farmville**
Dorrill, William Franklin political scientist, educator
Stein, David Bernard psychologist, educator

**Fort Belvoir**
O'Kane, Barbara Lynn research psychologist

**Fredericksburg**
Crippen, Timothy Alan sociology educator
Ramperad, Peggy A. Snellings sociologist, consultant
Sisk, Fred Dean retired cartographer

**Glen Allen**
Harter, John J. economic analyst

**Hampton**
Holmes, Leonard George psychologist, researcher

**Harrisonburg**
Rosser, John Barkley, Jr. economics professor

**Jamestown**
Kelso, William M. archaeologist

**Jeffersonton**
Armor, David J. sociologist

**Jonesville**
Geyer, Matthew Douglas psychologist, educator

**Leesburg**
Gunberg, Edwin Woodrow, Jr. counseling psychologist, consultant, researcher

**Lexington**
Chambers, Jay Lee clinical psychologist
Duncan, Floyd Harold social studies educator, department chairman, retired military officer
Elmes, David Gordon psychologist, educator
Jarard, Leonard Everett psychologist, educator
Winfrey, John Crawford educator

**Lynchburg**
Duff, Ernest Arthur political scientist, educator

**Mc Lean**
Auerbach, Anita L. psychologist, consultant
Hjort, Howard Warren economist, consultant
Johnson, Ormunde Evan George economist
Kohl, Maurice S. corporate executive
Nothaft, Frank Emile economist
Schneider, Peter Raymond political scientist
Sinilides, John government relations executive
Zakharin, Dov Solomon economist, government official

**Mechanicsville**
Trombley, Erik John social studies educator
Wells, Mary Julia psychologist

**Midlothian**
Stringham, Luther Winters retired economist, retired health facility administrator

**Norfolk**
Harper, William Thomas III psychologist, educator
Neumann, Serina Ann Louise psychologist, researcher

**Purcellville**
Crow, Robert Theodore economist, trade association executive

**Reston**
Mendis, Patrick economist, geographer, educator
Payne, Roger Lee geographer

**Richmond**
Benecke, John Patrick psychologist
Geary, David Patrick criminal justice educator, consultant, writer